Weiss Ratings' Investment Research Guide to Stock Mutual Funds

Weiss Ratings' Investment Research Guide to Stock Mutual Funds

Summer 2019

GREY HOUSE PUBLISHING

Weiss Ratings
4400 Northcorp Parkway
Palm Beach Gardens, FL 33410
561-627-3300

WeissRatings
Independent. Unbiased. Accurate. Trusted.

Published by Grey House Publishing, Inc., located at 4919 Route 22, Amenia, NY 12501; telephone 518-789-8700. Grey House Publishing neither guarantees the accuracy of the data contained herein nor assumes any responsibility for errors, omissions or discrepancies. Grey House Publishing accepts no payment for listing; inclusion in the publication of any organization, agency, institution, publication, service or individual does not imply endorsement of the publisher.

Grey House Publishing

Edition #9, Summer 2019

ISBN: 978-1-64265-197-3

Contents

Terms and Conditions

Date of Data Analyzed: June 30, 2019

Welcome to Weiss Ratings' Investment Research Guide to Stock Mutual Funds

With investing such a complex subject and the enormous popularity of mutual funds as a simple way to enter the markets it is no surprise that consumers need assistance. It is a complex subject and consumers want unbiased, independent guidance in helping them find a path to investing that is focused on their needs.

This is where Weiss Ratings comes in. We take all the data and process it, daily, to ensure that you receive not only the most up-to-date rating possible but also data that you may not easily find elsewhere. We publish this data in guides, and on our website so that you can feel empowered to make decisions about your investing future. Our focus is on balance and our ratings reflect this. No matter how strong a return has been if the level of risk taken is too high, in our opinion, then the overall rating will be reduced.

Weiss Ratings' Mission Statement

Weiss Ratings' mission is to empower consumers, professionals, and institutions with high quality advisory information for selecting or monitoring a financial services company or financial investment.

In doing so, Weiss Ratings will adhere to the highest ethical standards by maintaining our independent, unbiased outlook and approach for our customers.

Why rely on Weiss Ratings?

Weiss Ratings are fundamentally incomparable to nearly all other ratings available in America today. Here's why …

Complete Independence

We are America's only 100% independent rating agency covering stocks, ETFs, mutual funds, insurance companies, banks, and credit unions; and our independence is grounded in a very critical difference in the way we do business: Unlike most other rating agencies,

- we never accept compensation from any company for its rating;
- we never allow companies to influence our analysis or conclusions (although they are always free to provide us with supplemental data that's not publicly available);
- we reserve the right to publish our ratings based exclusively on publicly available data;
- we never suppress publication of our ratings at a company's request; and
- we are always dedicated to providing our analysis and opinions with complete objectivity.

Dedication to End Users -- Investors and Consumers

Other rating agencies derive most of their revenues from the very same companies that they cover.

In contrast, our primary source of revenues is the end user – investors seeking the best combination of risk and reward, plus consumers seeking the best deals with the most safety.

Unmatched Accuracy and Performance

Our independence and objectivity help explain why the U.S. Government Accountability Office (GAO) concluded that Weiss was first in warning consumers about future insurance company failures three times more often than our closest competitor (A.M. Best) and why, in comparison to S&P or Moody's, there was no contest.

It's the reason why The New York Times wrote "Weiss was the first to warn of dangers and say so unambiguously."

And it's also why The Wall Street Journal was able to report that the Weiss Stock Ratings outperformed all Wall Street investment banks, brokers and independent research organizations in a third-party study of stock ratings.

Broader Coverage

While other rating agencies focus mostly on larger companies that can afford to pay them large fees, Weiss Ratings covers all companies, large or small, as long as they report sufficient data for us to analyze. This allows us to provide far broader coverage, including nearly all U.S.-traded stocks, ETFs and mutual funds plus nearly all U.S. banks, credit unions and insurance companies.

Overall ...

Weiss Ratings gives you more accuracy, more choices, and better wealth-building potential – all with stronger risk protection and safety.

How to Use This Guide

The purpose of the *Weiss Ratings' Investment Research Guide to Stock Mutual Funds* is to provide investors with a reliable source of investment ratings and analyses on a timely basis. We realize that past performance is an important factor to consider when making the decision to purchase shares in a mutual fund. The ratings and analyses in this Guide can make that evaluation easier when you are considering stock mutual funds. The rating for a particular fund indicates our opinion regarding that fund's past risk-adjusted performance.

When evaluating a specific mutual fund, we recommend you follow these steps:

Step 1 Confirm the fund name and ticker symbol. To ensure you evaluate the correct mutual fund, verify the fund's exact name and ticker symbol as it was given to you in its prospectus or appears on your account statement. Many funds have similar names, so you want to make sure the fund you look up is really the one you are interested in evaluating.

Step 2 Check the fund's Investment Rating. Turn to Section I, the *Weiss Ratings' Investment Research Guide to Stock Mutual Funds*, and locate the fund you are evaluating. This section contains all stock mutual funds analyzed by Weiss Ratings, including those that did not receive an Investment Rating. All funds are listed in alphabetical order by the name of the fund with the ticker symbol following the name for additional verification. Once you have located your specific fund, the fourth column after the ticker symbol under the Ratings header shows its overall Investment Rating. Turn to *About Weiss Investment Ratings* for information about what this rating means.

Step 3 Analyze the supporting data. In addition to the Weiss Mutual Fund Rating are some of the various measures we have used in rating the fund. Refer to the Section I introduction to see what each of these factors measures. In most cases, lower rated funds will have a low reward rating and/or a low risk rating (i.e., high volatility). Bear in mind, however, that the Weiss Mutual Fund Rating is the result of a complex proprietary computer-generated analysis which cannot be reproduced using only the data provided here.

Step 4 When looking to identify a mutual fund that achieves your specific investing goals, we recommend the following:

- **Check the listing of the Largest funds.** If your priority is to stick with large funds because you believe that the size of the fund matters then these funds should be looked at. In this listing of the 100 largest funds you can also be assured that the Weiss Mutual Fund Rating is just as important as for the smallest fund.
- **Check the listing of the Best All-Around funds.** If your priority is to achieve a balanced return with the amount of risk being taken then check out this listing. We have selected funds with better returns, lower expense and with a maximum initial investment of $5,000 or less required.
- **Check the listing of the Consistent Return Buy rated funds.** If your priority is to achieve a consistent return over at least a five-year period, including the last three months then check out this listing. We have selected the highest rated funds with excellent five-year returns with a size of invested assets to give them a substantial

base. At the same time, we have looked for the smallest initial investment we could find.

- **Check the High Performance funds.** If your priority is to achieve the highest return, balanced with the amount of risk we have chosen the top mutual funds with the best financial performance. Not just "Buy" rated these funds have hit our demanding criteria of being in the top 25% of total returns for funds over a number of time-periods. Keep in mind that past performance alone is not always a guide to future performance.

- **Check the funds with Low Volatility.** On the other hand, if ultimate safety is your top priority, check out our list the top recommended mutual funds with the lowest volatility. These funds may have lower performance ratings than some other funds, but can provide a safe place for your savings.

- **Check out the Top-Rated Funds by Fund Type.** If you are looking to invest in a particular type of mutual fund turn to our listing of "Buy" rated Mutual Funds by Fund Type. There you will find the top mutual funds with the highest performance rating in each category.

Step 5 Refer back to Section I. Once you have identified a particular fund that interests you, refer back to Section I, the Index of Stock Mutual Funds, for a more thorough analysis.

If you are interested in contacting a provider, refer to the Index of Providers in the Appendix, where you will find the telephone number, address and website for all providers listed in this guide.

Step 6 Always remember:

- **Read our warnings and cautions.** In order to use Weiss Investment Ratings most effectively, we strongly recommend you consult the Important Warnings and Cautions. These are more than just "standard disclaimers." They are very important factors you should be aware of before using this guide.

- **Stay up to date.** Periodically review the latest Weiss Mutual Fund Ratings for the funds that you own to make sure they are still in line with your investment goals and level of risk tolerance. You can find more detailed information and receive automated updates on ratings through www.weissratings.com

Data Source: Weiss Ratings
Morningstar, Inc.

Date of data analyzed: June 30, 2019

About Weiss Investment Ratings

Weiss Investment Ratings of stocks, ETFs and mutual funds are in the same realm as "buy," "sell" and "hold" ratings. They are designed to help investors make more informed decisions with the goal of maximizing gains and minimizing risk. Safety is also an important consideration. The higher the rating, the more likely the investment will be profitable. But when using our investment ratings, you should always remember that, by definition, all investments involve some element of risk.

A	Strong Buy
B	Buy
C	Hold or Avoid
D	Sell
E	Strong Sell

Our **Overall Rating** is measured on a scale from A to E based on each fund's risk and performance. The funds are analyzed using the latest daily data available and the quarterly filings with the SEC. Weiss takes thousands of pieces of fund data and, based on its own model, balances reward against the amount of risk to assign a rating. The results provide a simple and understandable opinion as to whether we think the fund is a BUY, SELL, or HOLD.

Our **Reward Rating** is based on the total return over a period of up to five years, including net asset value and price growth. The total return figure is stated net of the expenses and fees charged by the fund. Based on proprietary modeling the individual components of the risk and reward ratings are calculated and weighted and the final rating is generated.

Our **Risk Rating** includes the risk ratings of component stocks where applicable and also includes the financial stability of the fund, turnover where applicable, together with the level of volatility as measured by the fund's daily returns over a period of up to five years. Funds with greater stability are considered less risky and receive a higher risk rating. Funds with greater volatility are considered riskier, and will receive a lower risk rating. In addition to considering the fund's volatility, the risk rating also considers an assessment of the valuation and quality of a fund's holdings.

In order to help guarantee our objectivity, we reserve the right to publish ratings expressing our opinion of an investment reward and risk based exclusively on publicly available data and our own proprietary standards for safety. But when using our investment ratings, you should always remember that, by definition, all investments involve some element of risk.

Current Weiss Ratings Distribution of Stock Mutual Funds

as of June 30, 2019

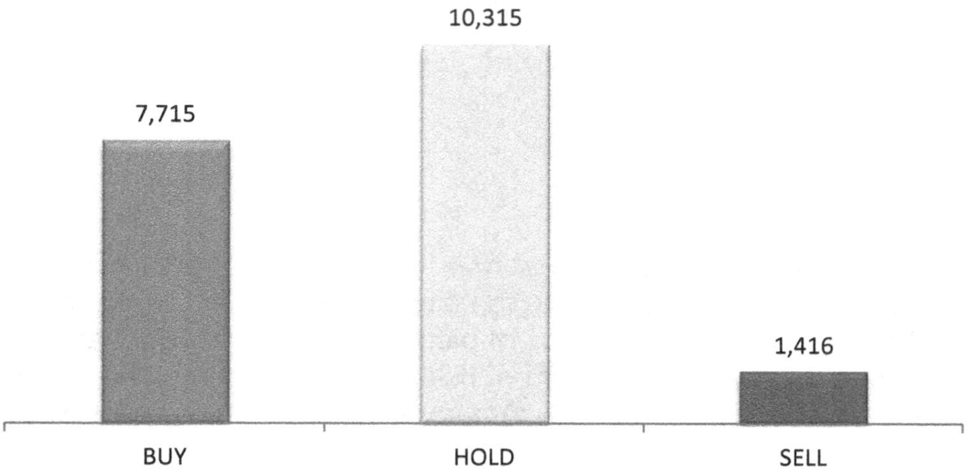

What Our Ratings Mean

Weiss Mutual Funds, Closed-End Funds, and Exchange Traded Funds Ratings represent a completely independent, unbiased opinion of funds—now, and in the future. The funds are analyzed using the latest daily data available and the quarterly filings with the SEC. Weiss takes thousands of pieces of fund data and, based on its own model, balances reward against the amount of risk to assign a rating. The results provide a simple and understandable opinion as to whether we think the fund is a BUY, SELL, or HOLD.

In order to help guarantee our objectivity, we reserve the right to publish ratings expressing our opinion of an investment reward and risk based exclusively on publicly available data and our own proprietary standards for safety. But when using our investment ratings, you should always remember that, by definition, all investments involve some element of risk.

Strong Buy

A **Excellent.** The fund has an excellent track record for maximizing performance while minimizing risk, thus delivering the best possible combination of total return on investment and reduced volatility. It has made the most of the recent economic environment to maximize risk-adjusted returns compared to other mutual funds. Although even the best funds can decline in a down market, our "A" rating can generally be considered the equivalent of a "Strong Buy".

Buy

B **Good.** The fund has a good track record for balancing performance with risk. Compared to other mutual funds, it has achieved above-average returns given the level of risk in its underlying investments. Although even good funds can decline in a down market, our "B" rating is considered the equivalent of a "Buy".

Hold or Avoid

C **Fair.** In the trade-off between performance and risk, the fund has a track record which is about average. It is neither significantly better nor significantly worse than most other funds. With some funds in this category, the total return may be better than average, but this can be misleading if the higher return was achieved with higher than average risk. With other funds, the risk may be lower than average, but the returns are also lower. Although funds can be driven higher or lower by general market trends, our "C" rating can generally be considered the equivalent of a "Hold" or "Avoid."

Sell

D **Weak.** The fund has underperformed the universe of other funds given the level of risk in its underlying investments, resulting in a weak risk-adjusted performance. Thus, its investment strategy and/or management has not been attuned to capitalize on the recent economic environment. Even weak funds can rise in an up market. However, our "D" rating can generally be considered equivalent to a "Sell."

Strong Sell

E **Very Weak.** The fund has significantly underperformed most other funds given the level of risk in its underlying investments, resulting in a very weak risk-adjusted performance. Thus, its investment strategy and/or management has done just the opposite of what was needed to maximize returns in the recent economic environment. Even some of the weakest funds can rise in certain market conditions. However, our "E" rating can generally be considered the equivalent of a "Strong Sell."

\+ The plus sign is an indication that the fund is in the upper third of the letter grade.

\- The minus sign is an indication that the fund is in the lower third of the letter grade.

U Unrated. The fund is unrated because it is too new to make a reliable assessment of its risk-adjusted performance. Typically, a fund must be established for at least one year before it is eligible to receive a Weiss Investment Rating.

Important Warnings & Cautions

1. A rating alone cannot tell the whole story. Please read the explanatory information contained here, in the section introductions and in the appendix. It is provided in order to give you an understanding of our rating methodology as well as to paint a more complete picture of a mutual fund's strengths and weaknesses.

2. Investment ratings shown in this directory were current as of the publication date. In the meantime, the rating may have been updated based on more recent data. Weiss Ratings offers a notification service for ratings changes on companies that you specify. For more information visit www.weissratings.com.

3. When deciding to invest in or sell holdings in a specific mutual fund, your decision must be based on a wide variety of factors in addition to the Weiss Mutual Fund Rating. These include any charges you may incur from switching funds, to what degree it meets your long-term planning needs, and what other choices are available to you. Weiss Ratings recommends that you should always consult an independent financial advisor over your investment decisions.

4. Weiss Mutual Fund Ratings represent our opinion of a mutual fund's past risk adjusted performance. As such, a high rating means we feel that the mutual fund has at least achieved above-average returns at the same time as it has balanced risk and returns. A high rating is not a guarantee that a fund will continue to perform well, nor is a low rating a prediction of continued weak performance. Any references to "Buy", "Hold", or "Sell" correlate with our opinion of a particular fund and Weiss Mutual Fund Ratings are not deemed to be a recommendation concerning the purchase or sale of any mutual fund.

5. All funds that have the same Weiss Investment Rating should be considered to be essentially equal from a risk/reward perspective. This is true regardless of any differences in the underlying numbers which might appear to indicate greater strengths.

6. Our rating standards are more consumer-oriented than those used by other rating agencies. We make more conservative assumptions about the amortization of loads and other fees as we attempt to identify those funds that have historically provided superior returns with only little or moderate risk.

7. We are an independent rating agency and do not depend on the cooperation of the managers operating the mutual funds we rate. Our data is obtained from a data aggregator. Data is input daily, as available, into our proprietary models where a complex series of algorithms provide us with ratings based on quantitative analysis. We do not grant mutual fund managers the right to stop or influence publication of the ratings. This policy stems from the fact that this Guide is designed for the information of the consumer.

Mutual Funds vs. Exchange-Traded Funds... Which is Right For You?

Both ETF's and Mutual Funds give you an inexpensive and easy way to diversify your investments and allow you to gain access to different asset classes with a single purchase. Ultimately, you'll need to consider a variety of factors including your tax strategy, the amount of money available to invest, and your overall investment strategy in order to determine which option is right for you.

Mutual Funds

Pros

- Mutual Funds are typically actively managed compared to ETF's which are typically tracking an index. Some of the better fund managers can regularly beat an index, although they will mostly have higher fees associated with them.
- Bigger Universe: There are over 28,000 Mutual Funds vs. less than 2,000 ETF's. You'll have more choices if you choose mutual funds, though the gap is narrowing every year.

Cons

- Mutual funds can only be purchased or sold at the end of the trading day after the market closes and their price is based on Net Asset Value (NAV), the value of fund assets minus liabilities divided by the number of shares.
- Mutual Fund holders can only see the holding of the Funds on a semi-annual basis.
- They are more tax prone- because the buying and selling within the fund by the Portfolio Manager creates more taxable events.
- Higher Minimum Investments

Stock Mutual Funds vs. Bond Mutual Funds

- Primarily, investors purchase stock mutual funds for appreciation or growth from within the companies inside the mutual fund itself. Conversely, bond mutual funds are primarily targeted for income reasons, since the entities inside a bond mutual fund give off income in the form of a coupon payment. Bonds and stocks frequently have an inverse relationship in market cycles, bonds will do well in down markets and stocks will do well in bull markets. For this reason, and for other diversification principles, it's important to have both bond and stock mutual funds in a long term retirement portfolio.
- It's important to note that there are exceptions to this rule, some stocks funds will give off an income in the form of dividend payments and many bond funds seek appreciation as well as income.
- There are risks associated with both bond and stock mutual funds. The risks in stock funds are primarily "market risk" meaning if the overall market is trending lower many stock funds will follow. The risks associated with bond funds are mostly associated with interest rates. In an environment with interest rates rising bond prices will follow and vice versa.

Exchange-Traded Funds (ETFs)

Pros

- ETFs offer much more flexibility. ETFs trade like stocks. They are priced on what Investors believe is Fair Market Value and you can buy and sell shares throughout the day.
- ETFs offer much more transparency, which means that investors can typically see the fund's holdings on a daily basis
- ETFs are more tax efficient than Mutual Funds. Because they are based off an index, there are fewer taxable events. Keep in mind, however, that capital gains and dividends are taxed the same as a Mutual Fund.
- ETFs have a lower expense ratio. In 2016, the average was .23 vs .82 of actively managed funds according to the Investment Company Institute.
- ETFs typically require lower minimum investments. Most of the time you can buy just a single share of the fund.
- You are typically paying a commission on buying and selling an exchange-traded fund. You'll pay a front or back end load when you purchase regular Mutual Funds.

Cons

- Some ETFs have limited choices in their asset class. Mutual Funds typically have more options.
- Given that an ETF trades like a stock, every purchase or sale requires paying a commission.

Section I:
Index of Stock Mutual Funds

Investment Ratings and analysis of all rated and unrated Open End and Closed End Stock Mutual Funds. Funds are listed in alphabetical order.

Section I: Contents

This section contains Weiss Investment Ratings, key rating factors, and summary financial data for 20,000 stock mutual funds. Funds are listed in alphabetical order.

Left Pages

Fund Name

Describes the fund's assets, regions of investments and investment strategies. Many funds have similar names, so you want to make sure the fund you look up is really the one you are interested in evaluating. In many cases, the Fund Name indicates the Class of the fund.

The most common Classes are:

Class A: This class of Mutual Fund typically has a front-end sales load and a loaded fee structure. Although the fees for Class A may typically be lower, because they normally charge front end fees, your initial amount invested will be lower and your overall return will be affected. An annual asset based fee may well be levied, although this is typically lower than other classes.

Class B: This class of shares, instead of a front-end or back-end sales load normally charges fees called a contingent deferred sales charge (CDSC). This fee is paid if you sell the shares within a certain period of time and may well decline after each year. An annual asset based fee is likely to be levied. Often a Class B share will convert to Class A within a couple of years of reaching the end of the CDSC expiry at which point Class A fees will be initiated.

Class C: A C-share is a class of mutual fund with a level load. They typically don't have front-end loads, but do sometimes have back-end loads. They are usually around 1% but are sometimes eliminated after the shares are held for over a year. Annual asset based fees are normal for this class of share.

Class I: This class is sold to institutional shareholders. Also called Y-Shares, these have different fees and do not charge traditional loads.

Class R: R share funds, Also known as K shares, are for retirement accounts, and the R share class mutual funds are only available through employer-sponsored retirement plans. R share mutual funds do not have any loads, but they do have annual asset based fees typically of around 0.25% to 0.50%.

MARKET

Ticker Symbol

An arrangement of characters (usually letters) representing a particular security listed on an exchange or otherwise traded publicly. When a company issues securities to the public marketplace, it selects an available ticker symbol for its securities which investors use to place trade orders. Every listed security has a unique ticker symbol, facilitating the vast array of trade orders that flow through the financial markets every day. If a ticker symbol is not assigned to a particular fund, the International Securities Identification Number (ISIN) is displayed.

Traded On (Exchange)

The stock exchange on which the fund is listed. The core function of a stock exchange is to ensure fair and orderly trading, as well as efficient dissemination of price information. Exchanges such as: NYSE (New York Stock Exchange), AMEX (American Stock Exchange), NNM (NASDAQ National Market), and NASQ (NASDAQ Small Cap) give companies, governments and other groups a platform to sell securities to the investing public. NASDAQ CM is abbreviated as NAS in this table.

FUND TYPE, CATEGORY & OBJECTIVE

Fund Type

Describes the fund's assets, regions of investments and investment strategies.

Open End Fund

A type of mutual fund that does not have restrictions on the amount of shares the fund will issue. If demand is high enough, the fund will continue to issue shares no matter how many investors there are. Open-end funds also buy back shares when investors wish to sell.

Closed End Fund

They are launched through an Initial Public Offering in order to raise money and then trade in the open market just like a stock or an ETF. They only issue a set amount of shares and, although their value is also based on the Net Asset Value, the actual price of the fund is affected by supply and demand, allowing it to trade at prices above or below its real value.

Category

Identifies funds according to their actual investment styles as measured by their portfolio holdings. This categorization allows investors to spread their money around in a mix of funds with a variety of risk and return characteristics.

Prospectus Objective

Gives a general idea of a fund’s overall investment approach and goals.

RATINGS

Overall Rating
The Weiss rating measured on a scale from A to E based on each fund's risk and performance. See the preceding section, "What Our Ratings Mean," for an explanation of each letter grade rating.

Reward Rating
This is based on the total return over a period of up to five years, including net asset value and price growth. The total return figure is stated net of the expenses and fees charged by the fund. Based on proprietary modeling the individual components of the risk and reward ratings are calculated and weighted and the final rating is generated.

Risk Rating
This is includes the risk ratings of component stocks where applicable and also includes the financial stability of the fund, turnover where applicable, together with the level of volatility as measured by the fund's daily returns over a period of up to five years. Funds with greater stability are considered less risky and receive a higher risk rating. Funds with greater volatility are considered riskier, and will receive a lower risk rating. In addition to considering the fund's volatility, the risk rating also considers an assessment of the valuation and quality of a fund's holdings.

Recent Upgrade/Downgrade
An "Up" or "Down" indicates that the Weiss Mutual Fund rating has changed since the publication of the last print edition. If a fund has had a rating change since March 31, 2019, the change is identified with an "Up" or "Down."

MINIMUMS

Open to New Investors
Indicates whether the fund accepts investments from those who are not existing investors. A "Y" in this column identifies that the fund accepts new investors. No data in this column indicates that the fund is closed to new investors. The fund may be closed to new investors because the fund's asset base is getting too large to effectively execute its investing style. Although, the fund may be closed, in most cases, existing investors are able to add to their holdings.

Minimum Initial Investment
The smallest investment amount a fund will accept to establish a new account. This amount could be $0 or any other number set by the fund.

Right Pages

MINIMUMS (continued)

Minimum Additional Investment
The smallest additional investment amount a fund will accept in an existing account.

TOTAL RETURNS

3-Month Total Return
The rate of return on an investment over three months that includes interest, capital gains, dividends and distributions realized.

6-Month Total Return
The rate of return on an investment over six months that includes interest, capital gains, dividends and distributions realized.

1-Year Total Return
The rate of return on an investment over one year that includes interest, capital gains, dividends and distributions realized.

3-Year Total Return
The rate of return on an investment over three years that includes interest, capital gains, dividends and distributions realized.

5-Year Total Return
The rate of return on an investment over five years that includes interest, capital gains, dividends and distributions realized.

PERFORMANCE

Dividend Yield (TTM)
Trailing twelve months dividends paid out relative to the share price. Expressed as a percentage and measures how much cash flow an investor is getting for each invested dollar. **Trailing Twelve Months (TTM)** is a representation of a fund's financial performance over the most recent 12 months. TTM uses the latest available financial data from a company's interim, quarterly or annual reports.

Expense Ratio
A measure of what it costs an investment company to operate a mutual fund. An expense ratio is determined through an annual calculation, where a fund's operating expenses are divided by the average dollar value of its assets under management. Operating expenses may include money spent on administration and management of the fund, advertising, etc. An expense ratio of 1 percent per annum means that each year 1 percent of the fund's total assets will be used to cover expenses.

3-Year Standard Deviation
A statistical measurement of dispersion about an average, which depicts how widely the returns varied over the past three years. Investors use the standard deviation of historical performance to try to predict the range of returns that are most likely for a given fund. When a fund has a high standard deviation, the predicted range of performance is wide, implying greater volatility. Standard deviation is most appropriate for measuring risk if it is for a fund that is an investor's only holding. The figure cannot be combined for more than one fund because the standard deviation for a portfolio of multiple funds is a function of not only the individual standard deviations, but also of the degree of correlation among the funds' returns. If a fund's returns follow a normal distribution, then approximately 68 percent of the time they will fall within

one standard deviation of the mean return for the fund, and 95 percent of the time within two standard deviations.

3-Year Beta

A three year measure of volatility, or systematic risk, of a security in comparison to the market as a whole. A beta of less than 1 means that the security will be less volatile than the market, a beta larger than 1 means more volatility. Beta value cannot be calculated if less than 24 months of pricing is available.

ASSETS

NAV (Net Asset Value)

A fund's price per share. The value is calculated by dividing the total value of all the securities in the portfolio, less any liabilities, by the number of fund shares outstanding.

Total Assets (MIL)

The total of all assets listed on the institution's balance sheet. This figure primarily consists of loans, investments, and fixed assets. Total Assets are displayed in millions.

ASSET ALLOCATION & TURNOVER

Asset Allocation

Indicates the percentage of assets in each category. Used as an investment strategy that attempts to balance risk versus reward by adjusting the percentage of each asset in an investment portfolio according to the investor's risk tolerance, goals and investment time frame. Allocation percentages may not add up to 100%. Negative values reflect short positions.

%Cash

The percentage of the fund's assets invested in short-term obligations, usually less than 90 days, that provide a return in the form of interest payments. This type of investment generally offers a low return compared to other investments but has a low risk level.

%Stocks

The percentage of the fund's assets invested in stock.

%Bonds

The percentage of the fund's assets invested in bonds. A bond is an unsecured debt security issued by companies, municipalities, states and sovereign governments to raise funds. When a company issues a bond it borrows money from the bondholder to boost the business, in exchange the bondholder receives the principal amount back plus the interest on the determined maturity date.

%Other

The percentage of the fund's assets invested in other financial instruments.

Turnover Ratio
The percentage of a mutual fund or other investment vehicle's holdings that have been replaced with other holdings in a given year. Generally, low turnover ratio is favorable, because high turnover equates to higher brokerage transaction fees, which reduce fund returns.

BULL & BEAR MARKETS

Last Bull Market Total Return
The fund's total return (the rate of return on an investment over a period of time that includes interest, capital gains, dividends and distributions realized) during the last market upswing. A **Bull Market** is a financial market condition in which prices are rising or are expected to rise. Bull markets are characterized by optimism, investor confidence and expectations that strong results will continue.

Last Bear Market Total Return
The fund's total return (the rate of return on an investment over a period of time that includes interest, capital gains, dividends and distributions realized) during the last market downturn. A **Bear Market** is a financial market condition in which the prices of securities are falling, investors anticipate losses, and selling of securities increases.

FEES

Front End Fee (%)
A commission or sales charge applied at the time of the initial purchase of an investment. The fee percentage is generally based on the amount of the investment. Larger investments, both initial and cumulative, generally receive percentage discounts based on the dollar value invested. Fees are displayed as a percent.

Back End Fee (%)
A fee that investors pay when withdrawing money from an investment within a specified number of years, usually five to 10 years. The back-end load is designed to discourage withdrawals and typically declines for each year that a shareholder remains in a fund. The fee is a percentage of the value of the share being sold. Fees are displayed as a percent.

Inception Date
The date on which the fund began its operations. The commencement date indicates when a fund began investing in the market. Many investors prefer funds with longer operating histories. Funds with longer histories have longer track records and can thereby provide investors with a more long-standing picture of their performance.

	MARKET		FUND TYPE, CATEGORY & OBJECTIVE		RATINGS				MINIMUMS	
Fund Name	Ticker Symbol	Traded On	Fund Type	Category and (Prospectus Objective)	Overall Rating	Reward Rating	Risk Rating	Recent Up/ Downgrade	Open to New Investors	Min Initial Investment
1290 Convertible Securities Fund Class A	TNFAX	NAS CM	Open End	Convertibles (Convertible Bond)	B-	C	B+	Down	Y	1,000
1290 Convertible Securities Fund Class I	TNFIX	NAS CM	Open End	Convertibles (Convertible Bond)	B-	C	B+	Down	Y	1,000,000
1290 Convertible Securities Fund Class R	TNFRX	NAS CM	Open End	Convertibles (Convertible Bond)	B-	C	B+		Y	0
1290 DoubleLine Dynamic Allocation Fund Class A	TNXAX	NAS CM	Open End	Cautious Alloc (Asset Alloc)	B	C	A-	Up	Y	1,000
1290 DoubleLine Dynamic Allocation Fund Class I	TNVDX	NAS CM	Open End	Cautious Alloc (Asset Alloc)	B	C+	A-	Up	Y	1,000,000
1290 DoubleLine Dynamic Allocation Fund Class R	TNYRX	NAS CM	Open End	Cautious Alloc (Asset Alloc)	B-	C	A-	Up	Y	0
1290 GAMCO Small/Mid Cap Value Fund Class A	TNVAX	NAS CM	Open End	US Equity Small Cap (Growth)	C	C-	B-		Y	1,000
1290 GAMCO Small/Mid Cap Value Fund Class I	TNVIX	NAS CM	Open End	US Equity Small Cap (Growth)	C	C-	B-		Y	1,000,000
1290 GAMCO Small/Mid Cap Value Fund Class R	TNVRX	NAS CM	Open End	US Equity Small Cap (Growth)	C	C-	B-		Y	0
1290 GAMCO Small/Mid Cap Value Fund Class T	TNVCX	NAS CM	Open End	US Equity Small Cap (Growth)	C	C-	B-		Y	1,000
1290 Global Talents Fund Class A	TNYAX	NAS CM	Open End	Global Equity Large Cap (Growth)	C	C	C+		Y	1,000
1290 Global Talents Fund Class I	TNYFX	NAS CM	Open End	Global Equity Large Cap (Growth)	C	C	C+		Y	1,000,000
1290 Global Talents Fund Class R	TNTRX	NAS CM	Open End	Global Equity Large Cap (Growth)	C	C	C+	Up	Y	0
1290 Low Volatility Global Equity Fund Class I	TNZIX	NAS CM	Open End	Global Equity Large Cap (Growth)	C	C	B		Y	1,000,000
1290 Multi-Alternative Strategies Fund Class A	TNMAX	NAS CM	Open End	Multialternative (Growth)	C	C-	B-		Y	1,000
1290 Multi-Alternative Strategies Fund Class I	TNMIX	NAS CM	Open End	Multialternative (Growth)	C	C	B		Y	1,000,000
1290 Multi-Alternative Strategies Fund Class R	TNMRX	NAS CM	Open End	Multialternative (Growth)	C	C-	B-		Y	0
1290 Retirement 2020 Fund Class I	TNIIX	NAS CM	Open End	Target Date (Asset Alloc)	C	C	B		Y	1,000,000
1290 Retirement 2025 Fund Class I	TNJIX	NAS CM	Open End	Target Date (Asset Alloc)	C	C	B		Y	1,000,000
1290 Retirement 2030 Fund Class I	TNKIX	NAS CM	Open End	Target Date (Asset Alloc)	C	C	B		Y	1,000,000
1290 Retirement 2035 Fund Class I	TNLIX	NAS CM	Open End	Target Date (Asset Alloc)	C	C	B		Y	1,000,000
1290 Retirement 2040 Fund Class I	TNNIX	NAS CM	Open End	Target Date (Asset Alloc)	C	C	B		Y	1,000,000
1290 Retirement 2045 Fund Class I	TNOIX	NAS CM	Open End	Target Date (Asset Alloc)	C	C	B		Y	1,000,000
1290 Retirement 2050 Fund Class I	TNWIX	NAS CM	Open End	Target Date (Asset Alloc)	C	C	B		Y	1,000,000
1290 Retirement 2055 Fund Class I	TNQIX	NAS CM	Open End	Target Date (Asset Alloc)	C	C	B		Y	1,000,000
1290 Retirement 2060 Fund Class I	TNXIX	NAS CM	Open End	Target Date (Asset Alloc)	C	C	B		Y	1,000,000
1290 SmartBeta Equity Fund Class A	TNBAX	NAS CM	Open End	Global Equity Large Cap (Growth)	B	C+	B+	Up	Y	1,000
1290 SmartBeta Equity Fund Class I	TNBIX	NAS CM	Open End	Global Equity Large Cap (Growth)	B	C+	B+	Up	Y	1,000,000
1290 SmartBeta Equity Fund Class R	TNBRX	NAS CM	Open End	Global Equity Large Cap (Growth)	B	C+	B+	Up	Y	0
1290 SmartBeta Equity Fund Class T	TNBCX	NAS CM	Open End	Global Equity Large Cap (Growth)	B	C+	B+	Up	Y	1,000
1290 VT Convertible Securities Portfolio Class IB			Open End	Convertibles (Convertible Bond)	C	C-	B	Down	Y	0
1290 VT Convertible Securities Portfolio Class K			Open End	Convertibles (Convertible Bond)	C	C-	B-	Down	Y	0
1290 VT DoubleLine Dynamic Allocation Portfolio Class IB			Open End	Moderate Alloc (Growth & Income)	C	C-	B-	Down	Y	0
1290 VT DoubleLine Dynamic Allocation Portfolio Class K			Open End	Moderate Alloc (Growth & Income)	C	C-	B-	Down	Y	0
1290 VT Energy Portfolio Class IB			Open End	Energy Sector Equity (Growth)	D+	D+	C-	Down	Y	0
1290 VT Energy Portfolio Class K			Open End	Energy Sector Equity (Growth)	C-	D+	C-		Y	0
1290 VT Equity Income Portfolio Class IA			Open End	US Equity Large Cap Value (Growth & Income)	C+	C-	B+		Y	0
1290 VT Equity Income Portfolio Class IB			Open End	US Equity Large Cap Value (Growth & Income)	C+	C-	B+		Y	0
1290 VT Equity Income Portfolio Class K			Open End	US Equity Large Cap Value (Growth & Income)	C+	C-	B+		Y	0
1290 VT GAMCO Mergers & Acquisitions Portfolio Class IA			Open End	Market Neutral (Growth)	C	C-	C+		Y	0
1290 VT GAMCO Mergers & Acquisitions Portfolio Class IB			Open End	Market Neutral (Growth)	C	C-	C+		Y	0
1290 VT GAMCO Mergers & Acquisitions Portfolio Class K			Open End	Market Neutral (Growth)	C	C-	B-	Down	Y	0
1290 VT GAMCO Small Company Value Portfolio Class IA			Open End	US Equity Small Cap (Small Company)	C	C-	B-		Y	0
1290 VT GAMCO Small Company Value Portfolio Class IB			Open End	US Equity Small Cap (Small Company)	C	C-	B-		Y	0
1290 VT GAMCO Small Company Value Portfolio Class K			Open End	US Equity Small Cap (Small Company)	C	C-	B-		Y	0
1290 VT Low Volatility Global Equity Portfolio Class IB			Open End	Global Equity Large Cap (Growth)	C+	C	B	Down	Y	0
1290 VT Low Volatility Global Equity Portfolio Class K			Open End	Global Equity Large Cap (Growth)	C+	C	B	Down	Y	0
1290 VT Micro Cap Portfolio Class IB			Open End	US Equity Small Cap (Growth)	C+	C-	B		Y	0
1290 VT Micro Cap Portfolio Class K			Open End	US Equity Small Cap (Growth)	C+	C-	B		Y	0
1290 VT Moderate Growth Allocation Portfolio Class IB			Open End	Moderate Alloc (Asset Alloc)	U	U	U		Y	0
1290 VT Moderate Growth Allocation Portfolio Class K			Open End	Moderate Alloc (Asset Alloc)	U	U	U		Y	0
1290 VT Multi-Alternative Strategies Portfolio Class IB			Open End	Multialternative (Growth)	D+	D	C	Up	Y	0

★ Expanded analysis of this fund is included in Section II.

Min Additional Investment	3-Month Total Return	6-Month Total Return	1-Year Total Return	3-Year Total Return	5-Year Total Return	Dividend Yield (TTM)	Expense Ratio	3-Yr Std Deviation	3-Year Beta	NAV	Total Assets (MIL)	%Cash	%Stocks	%Bonds	%Other	Turnover Ratio	Last Bull Market Total Return	Last Bear Market Total Return	Front End Fee (%)	Back End Fee (%)	Inception Date
	TOTAL RETURNS					PERFORMANCE				ASSETS		ASSET ALLOCATION & TURNOVER					BULL & BEAR		FEES		
50	3.56	17.77	7.04	35.83		2.03	1.25	10.24	1.18	11.12	24.8	3	2	1	0	45			4.50		Jul-15
	3.63	17.92	7.21	36.85		2.26	1	10.28	1.18	11.12	24.8	3	2	1	0	45					Jul-15
	3.61	17.66	6.79	34.99		1.81	1.5	10.23	1.18	11.12	24.8	3	2	1	0	45					Jul-15
50	3.48	12.61	7.65	21.88		1.49	1.2	6.26		10.98	60.6	5	27	66	2	79			5.50		Mar-16
	3.58	12.71	7.93	22.74		1.73	0.95	6.23		10.99	60.6	5	27	66	2	79					Mar-16
	3.49	12.51	7.38	21.03		1.26	1.45	6.22		10.97	60.6	5	27	66	2	79					Mar-16
50	0.31	15.65	-1.77	35.92		0.18	1.25	15.62	1	12.78	103.0	6	94	0	0	49			5.50		Nov-14
	0.47	15.83	-1.50	37.05		0.43	1	15.6	0.99	12.8	103.0	6	94	0	0	49					Nov-14
	0.31	15.54	-2.05	34.87		0	1.5	15.67	1	12.71	103.0	6	94	0	0	49					Nov-14
50	0.47	15.83	-1.50	37.03		0.43	1.25	15.66	1	12.8	103.0	6	94	0	0	49			2.50	1.00	Nov-14
50	2.21	17.88	-2.19	33.19		0	1.25	14.23	1.19	12.46	27.9	5	95	0	0	26			5.50		Apr-16
	2.36	18.07	-1.87	34.37		0.08	1	14.24	1.19	12.54	27.9	5	95	0	0	26					Apr-16
	2.14	17.71	-2.43	32.30		0	1.5	14.25	1.19	12.36	27.9	5	95	0	0	26					Apr-16
	3.45	14.17	9.87			2.3	0.65			11.68	3.4	1	99	0	0	4					Feb-17
50	0.09	4.51	0.46	4.16		0.43	1.65	3.91	19.92	10.18	18.6	40	29	14	5	5			5.50		Jul-15
	0.19	4.72	0.72	4.95		0.68	1.4	3.88	20.07	10.19	18.6	40	29	14	5	5					Jul-15
	0.00	4.42	0.21	3.45		0.19	1.9	3.94	20.33	10.14	18.6	40	29	14	5	5					Jul-15
	3.11	11.71	7.62			1.32	0.65			11.25	10.7	2	52	46	0	8					Feb-17
	3.42	12.88	8.10			1.24	0.65			11.48	17.7	2	62	36	0	4					Feb-17
	3.40	13.82	8.10			1.56	0.65			11.53	5.9	2	71	27	0	3					Feb-17
	3.46	14.09	8.20			1.33	0.65			11.66	7.4	2	76	22	0	2					Feb-17
	3.54	14.84	8.39			1.71	0.65			11.68	3.4	2	81	17	0	2					Feb-17
	3.59	15.34	8.30			1.54	0.65			11.8	5.0	2	86	13	0	2					Feb-17
	3.67	15.94	8.46			1.68	0.65			11.85	3.5	1	91	8	0	2					Feb-17
	3.74	16.52	8.42			1.75	0.65			11.92	3.3	1	96	3	0	2					Feb-17
	3.72	16.89	8.57			1.75	0.65			11.97	3.2	1	99	0	0	2					Feb-17
50	5.36	18.57	11.76	37.74		1.05	1.15	9.94	0.85	12.96	23.6	1	99	0	0	49			5.50		Nov-14
	5.44	18.75	12.03	38.68		1.27	0.9	9.91	0.84	12.98	23.6	1	99	0	0	49					Nov-14
	5.28	18.39	11.50	36.64		0.82	1.4	9.91	0.84	12.94	23.6	1	99	0	0	49					Nov-14
50	5.36	18.66	11.94	38.71		1.27	1.15	9.93	0.85	12.97	23.6	1	99	0	0	49			2.50	1.00	Nov-14
	-7.60	-5.22	-1.62	21.05	31.23	3.14	1.3	8.21	1.02		21.6	3	5	0	2	35					Oct-13
	-7.53	-5.05	-1.45	21.98	32.86	3.38	1.05	8.23	1.02		21.6	3	5	0	2	35					Oct-13
	-4.86	-1.29	-0.50	14.47	16.45	0.55	1.25	5.91			56.3	4	23	72	0	175					Aug-12
	-4.77	-1.12	-0.17	15.41	17.90	0.79	1	5.89			56.3	4	23	72	0	175					Aug-12
	-15.31	-14.63	-3.68	-3.58	-29.73	2.41	0.9	19.81	1.06		5.1	1	99	0	0	20					Oct-13
	-15.40	-14.61	-3.60	-3.00	-28.97	2.64	0.65	19.76	1.06		5.1	1	99	0	0	20					Oct-13
	-6.71	-2.20	0.70	23.98	37.77	1.65	1	9.74	1.01		577.5	2	98	0	0	41	23.93	-17.76			Dec-04
	-6.68	-2.19	0.70	24.08	37.65	1.65	1	9.73	1.01		577.5	2	98	0	0	41	24.05	-17.91			Dec-98
	-6.70	-2.03	0.95	24.93	39.36	1.89	0.75	9.79	1.01		577.5	2	98	0	0	41	23.93	-17.75			Aug-11
	-2.26	0.34	-0.04	12.09	18.44	0.17	1.34	5.51	0.47		221.1	15	84	0	0	138	5.85	-5.42			Jun-07
	-2.20	0.42	0.02	12.16	18.45	0.17	1.34	5.48	0.47		221.1	15	84	0	0	138	5.78	-5.53			May-03
	-2.16	0.49	0.20	12.97	19.91	0.41	1.09	5.49	0.47		221.1	15	84	0	0	138	6.02	-5.51			Aug-11
	-11.01	-7.10	-4.10	26.89	33.81	0.62	1.08	13.04	0.85		3,089	3	97	0	0	10	25.92	-23.09			Jul-07
	-11.00	-7.10	-4.10	26.88	33.82	0.62	1.08	13.04	0.85		3,089	3	97	0	0	10	25.86	-23.19			Aug-88
	-10.94	-6.98	-3.86	27.85	35.51	0.86	0.83	13.03	0.85		3,089	3	97	0	0	10	26.01	-23.16			Aug-11
	-3.34	0.10	1.89	27.53	40.08	2.55	0.9	7.58	0.95		9.9	1	99	0	0	34					Oct-13
	-3.25	0.27	2.14	28.59	41.94	2.8	0.65	7.55	0.94		9.9	1	99	0	0	34					Oct-13
	-15.02	-7.12	7.85	37.74		0	1.15	18.07	1.06		145.3	0	99	0	1	58					Apr-14
	-14.89	-6.94	8.15	38.75		0.21	0.9	18.12	1.07		145.3	0	99	0	1	58					Apr-14
	3.29						1.1			10.71	11.4	2	53	44	0						Jan-19
	3.28						0.85			10.72	11.4	2	53	44	0						Jan-19
	-2.55	-2.94	-1.92				1.65				4.9	32	28	21	11	0					Nov-17

	MARKET		FUND TYPE, CATEGORY & OBJECTIVE		RATINGS				MINIMUMS	
Fund Name	Ticker Symbol	Traded On	Fund Type	Category and (Prospectus Objective)	Overall Rating	Reward Rating	Risk Rating	Recent Up/ Downgrade	Open to New Investors	Min Initial Investment
1290 VT Multi-Alternative Strategies Portfolio Class K			Open End	Multialternative (Growth)	D+	D	C	Up	Y	0
1290 VT Natural Resources Portfolio Class IB			Open End	Natl Resources Sec Equity (Natl Res)	C-	D+	C	Down	Y	0
1290 VT Natural Resources Portfolio Class K			Open End	Natl Resources Sec Equity (Natl Res)	C-	D+	C	Down	Y	0
1290 VT Real Estate Portfolio Class IB			Open End	Real Estate Sector Equity (Real Estate)	C	C	C+		Y	0
1290 VT Real Estate Portfolio Class K			Open End	Real Estate Sector Equity (Real Estate)	C	C	C+		Y	0
1290 VT Small Cap Value Portfolio Class IB			Open End	US Equity Small Cap (Small Company)	C	C-	B	Down	Y	0
1290 VT Small Cap Value Portfolio Class K			Open End	US Equity Small Cap (Small Company)	C	C-	B	Down	Y	0
1290 VT SmartBeta Equity Portfolio Class IB			Open End	Global Equity Large Cap (Equity-Income)	C+	C-	B+		Y	0
1290 VT SmartBeta Equity Portfolio Class K			Open End	Global Equity Large Cap (Equity-Income)	C+	C-	B+		Y	0
1290 VT Socially Responsible Portfolio Class IA			Open End	US Equity Large Cap Growth (Growth)	C+	C-	B+	Down	Y	0
1290 VT Socially Responsible Portfolio Class IB			Open End	US Equity Large Cap Growth (Growth)	C+	C-	B+	Down	Y	0
13D Activist Fund Class A	DDDAX	NAS CM	Open End	US Equity Mid Cap (Growth)	C	C-	B-		Y	2,500
13D Activist Fund Class C	DDDCX	NAS CM	Open End	US Equity Mid Cap (Growth)	C	C-	C+		Y	2,500
13D Activist Fund Class I	DDDIX	NAS CM	Open End	US Equity Mid Cap (Growth)	C	C	B-		Y	1,000,000
1789 Growth and Income Fund Class Class C	PSECX	NAS CM	Open End	Aggressive Alloc (Growth & Income)	B-	C	B+		Y	2,000
1789 Growth and Income Fund Class P	PSEPX	NAS CM	Open End	Aggressive Alloc (Growth & Income)	B-	C	B+		Y	2,000
1919 Financial Services Fund Class A	SBFAX	NAS CM	Open End	Financials Sector Equity (Financial)	C	C	C+		Y	1,000
1919 Financial Services Fund Class C	SFSLX	NAS CM	Open End	Financials Sector Equity (Financial)	C	C	C+		Y	1,000
1919 Financial Services Fund Class I	LMRIX	NAS CM	Open End	Financials Sector Equity (Financial)	C	C	C+		Y	1,000,000
1919 Socially Responsive Balanced Fund Class A	SSIAX	NAS CM	Open End	Moderate Alloc (Balanced)	B	C+	B+		Y	1,000
1919 Socially Responsive Balanced Fund Class B	SESIX	NAS CM	Open End	Moderate Alloc (Balanced)	B	C+	B+			1,000
1919 Socially Responsive Balanced Fund Class C	SESLX	NAS CM	Open End	Moderate Alloc (Balanced)	B	C+	B+		Y	1,000
1919 Socially Responsive Balanced Fund Class I	LMRNX	NAS CM	Open End	Moderate Alloc (Balanced)	B	C+	B+		Y	1,000,000
361 Domestic Long/Short Equity Fund Class I	ADMZX	NAS CM	Open End	Long/Short Equity (Growth)	B-	C	B+	Up	Y	100,000
361 Domestic Long/Short Equity Fund Class Y	ADMWX	NAS CM	Open End	Long/Short Equity (Growth)	B-	C	B+	Up	Y	1,000,000
361 Domestic Long/Short Equity Fund Investor Class	ADMQX	NAS CM	Open End	Long/Short Equity (Growth)	C+	C	B+	Up	Y	2,500
361 Global Equity Absolute Return Fund Class I	AGRZX	NAS CM	Open End	Market Neutral (Growth & Income)	U	U	U		Y	2,500
361 Global Equity Absolute Return Fund Class Y	AGRWX	NAS CM	Open End	Market Neutral (Growth & Income)	U	U	U		Y	1,000,000
361 Global Equity Absolute Return Fund Investor Class	AGRQX	NAS CM	Open End	Market Neutral (Growth & Income)	U	U	U		Y	2,500
361 Global Long/Short Equity Fund Class I	AGAZX	NAS CM	Open End	Long/Short Equity (Growth)	C	C-	B		Y	2,500
361 Global Long/Short Equity Fund Class Y	AGAWX	NAS CM	Open End	Long/Short Equity (Growth)	C	C-	B		Y	1,000,000
361 Global Long/Short Equity Fund Investor Class	AGAQX	NAS CM	Open End	Long/Short Equity (Growth)	C	C-	B		Y	2,500
361 Global Managed Futures Strategy Fund Class I	AGFZX	NAS CM	Open End	Alternative Miscellaneous (Income)	C	C-	C		Y	100,000
361 Global Managed Futures Strategy Fund Investor Class	AGFQX	NAS CM	Open End	Alternative Miscellaneous (Income)	C	C-	C		Y	2,500
361 Macro Opportunity Fund Class I	AGMZX	NAS CM	Open End	Global Macro (Growth)	D+	D	C-	Down	Y	100,000
361 Macro Opportunity Fund Investor Class	AGMQX	NAS CM	Open End	Global Macro (Growth)	D+	D	C-	Down	Y	2,500
361 Managed Futures Strategy Fund Class I	AMFZX	NAS CM	Open End	Alternative Miscellaneous (Income)	C-	D+	C		Y	100,000
361 Managed Futures Strategy Fund Investor Class	AMFQX	NAS CM	Open End	Alternative Miscellaneous (Income)	C-	D+	C		Y	2,500
361 U.S. Small Cap Equity Fund Class I	ASFZX	NAS CM	Open End	US Equity Small Cap (Small Company)	C-	D+	C-		Y	100,000
361 U.S. Small Cap Equity Fund Class Y	ASFWX	NAS CM	Open End	US Equity Small Cap (Small Company)	C-	D+	C-		Y	1,000,000
361 U.S. Small Cap Equity Fund Investor Class	ASFQX	NAS CM	Open End	US Equity Small Cap (Small Company)	C-	D+	C-		Y	2,500
7Twelve Balanced Portfolio Class 3			Open End	Moderate Alloc (Balanced)	C+	C	B	Up	Y	0
7Twelve Balanced Portfolio Class 4			Open End	Moderate Alloc (Balanced)	C+	C	B	Up	Y	0
AAM/Bahl & Gaynor Income Growth Fund Class A	AFNAX	NAS CM	Open End	US Equity Large Cap Blend (Equity-Income)	B	B-	B+		Y	2,500
AAM/Bahl & Gaynor Income Growth Fund Class C	AFYCX	NAS CM	Open End	US Equity Large Cap Blend (Equity-Income)	B	C+	B+		Y	2,500
AAM/Bahl & Gaynor Income Growth Fund Class I	AFNIX	NAS CM	Open End	US Equity Large Cap Blend (Equity-Income)	B	B-	B+		Y	25,000
AAM/HIMCO Global Enhanced Dividend Fund Class A	HGDAX	NAS CM	Open End	Global Equity Large Cap (Equity-Income)	D+	D	C	Up	Y	2,500
AAM/HIMCO Global Enhanced Dividend Fund Class C	HGDCX	NAS CM	Open End	Global Equity Large Cap (Equity-Income)	D+	D	C	Up	Y	2,500
AAM/HIMCO Global Enhanced Dividend Fund Class I	HGDIX	NAS CM	Open End	Global Equity Large Cap (Equity-Income)	D+	D	C	Up	Y	25,000
AAM/Phocas Real Estate Fund Class A Shares	APRAX	NAS CM	Open End	Real Estate Sector Equity (Real Estate)	C+	C	B-	Down	Y	2,500
AAM/Phocas Real Estate Fund Class I Shares	APRIX	NAS CM	Open End	Real Estate Sector Equity (Real Estate)	C+	C	B-	Down	Y	25,000
AAMA Equity Fund	AMFEX	NAS CM	Open End	US Equity Large Cap Blend (Growth)	C	D+	B	Up	Y	10,000

★ Expanded analysis of this fund is included in Section II.

Min Additional Investment	TOTAL RETURNS 3-Month Total Return	6-Month Total Return	1-Year Total Return	3-Year Total Return	5-Year Total Return	PERFORMANCE Dividend Yield (TTM)	Expense Ratio	3-Yr Std Deviation	3-Year Beta	ASSETS NAV	Total Assets (MIL)	ASSET ALLOCATION & TURNOVER %Cash	%Stocks	%Bonds	%Other	Turnover Ratio	BULL & BEAR Last Bull Market Total Return	Last Bear Market Total Return	FEES Front End Fee (%)	Back End Fee (%)	Inception Date
	-2.45	-2.74	-1.58				1.4				4.9	32	28	21	11	0					Nov-17
	-10.44	-11.24	-2.34	23.49	-11.33	2.57	0.9	15.78	0.99		20.2	1	99	0	0	13					Feb-13
	-10.42	-11.12	-2.10	24.36	-10.20	2.8	0.65	15.77	0.99		20.2	1	99	0	0	13					Feb-13
	-2.75	1.01	0.44	13.74	29.80	3.31	0.91	10.3	0.99		27.0	0	99	0	1	30					Feb-13
	-2.65	1.10	0.69	14.46	31.38	3.55	0.66	10.3	0.99		27.0	0	99	0	1	30					Feb-13
	-17.74	-11.29	0.42	30.55		0.5	1.16	12.73	0.81		312.3	0	100	0	0	23					Apr-14
	-17.73	-11.20	0.67	31.53		0.72	0.91	12.71	0.81		312.3	0	100	0	0	23					Apr-14
	-4.92	-0.91	0.91	25.58	40.73	1.23	1.15	8.18	0.82		20.8	1	99	0	0	42					Oct-13
	-4.91	-0.83	1.15	26.58	42.54	1.46	0.9	8.16	0.82		20.8	1	99	0	0	42					Oct-13
	-7.45	-1.91	3.73	29.96	56.20	0.95	0.94	9.96	1		148.7	0	100	0	0	13	26.37	-16.45			Oct-02
	-7.44	-1.94	3.71	30.00	56.25	0.97	0.94	9.97	1		148.7	0	100	0	0	13	26.14	-16.45			Sep-99
500	1.07	17.18	-3.38	42.87	35.54	0	1.76	15.71	1.15	20.73	348.3	5	95	0	0	83			5.75		Dec-11
500	0.88	16.71	-4.13	39.71	30.57	0	2.51	15.69	1.15	20.46	348.3	5	95	0	0	83				1.00	Dec-12
	1.14	17.27	-3.18	43.93	37.29	0	1.51	15.65	1.14	21.18	348.3	5	95	0	0	83					Dec-11
100	5.74	16.09	7.95	18.91	19.65	0.86	2.05	8.57	0.65	13.17	24.7	13	87	0	0	120	17.41	-15.65		1.00	Jan-11
100	5.94	16.63	9.02	22.50	25.88	1.74	1.05	8.55	0.65	13.25	24.7	13	87	0	0	120	17.41	-15.65			Aug-13
50	6.46	17.41	-3.65	48.07	63.12	0.02	1.33	16.88	1.09	26.5	217.8	2	98	0	0	18	27.32	-18.69	5.75		Nov-98
50	6.27	17.00	-4.34	44.99	57.56	0	2.05	16.88	1.09	24.22	217.8	2	98	0	0	18	26.7	-18.96		1.00	Nov-98
	6.56	17.60	-3.39	49.39	65.93	0.3	1.06	16.89	1.09	26.79	217.8	2	98	0	0	18	27.5	-18.58			Mar-08
50	4.61	16.73	11.01	39.11	42.17	0.58	1.26	8.76	0.7	19.17	173.5	8	65	26	0	13	16.42	-10.86	5.75		Nov-92
50	4.49	16.31	10.22	35.30	36.22	0.04	2.01	8.77	0.7	18.59	173.5	8	65	26	0	13	15.7	-11.27		5.00	Jan-87
50	4.43	16.31	10.19	36.09	37.05	0.05	1.98	8.75	0.7	19.31	173.5	8	65	26	0	13	15.93	-11.09		1.00	May-93
	4.73	16.89	11.36	40.29	44.08	0.81	0.97	8.74	0.7	19.15	173.5	8	65	26	0	13	16.58	-10.71			Jul-08
	1.82	11.77	1.82	18.70		0	2.7	8.45	0.6	10.63	47.4	17	72	0	11	262					Mar-16
	1.81	11.74	1.90	19.02		0	2.62	8.45	0.6	10.66	47.4	17	72	0	11	262					Mar-16
	1.83	11.63	1.55	17.70		0	3.02	8.39	0.6	10.55	47.4	17	72	0	11	262					Mar-16
	-2.38	-1.70					1.72			9.83	2.6	5	30	0	65						Dec-18
	-2.28	-1.60					1.57			9.84	2.6	5	30	0	65						Dec-18
	-2.48	-1.80					1.97			9.82	2.6	5	30	0	65						Dec-18
	1.62	8.80	-0.74	16.99	32.09	0	2.35	6.89	0.55	11.24	881.7	17	71	0	12	197					Dec-14
	1.62	8.78	-0.65	17.41	32.69	0	2.24	6.9	0.55	11.27	881.7	17	71	0	12	197					Dec-14
	1.54	8.65	-1.00	15.95	30.23	0	2.63	6.89	0.55	11.17	881.7	17	71	0	12	197					Dec-14
	-1.40	0.38	-0.18	7.74	8.36	0	1.77	6.85	36.25	10.54	62.0	101	0	0	-1	0					Feb-14
	-1.51	0.19	-0.38	6.99	6.99	0	2.02	6.9	37.97	10.39	62.0	101	0	0	-1	0					Feb-14
	-1.82	-3.06	-7.46	7.25	-8.30	0	2.22	8.33	50.61	9.17	10.1	1	88	10	0	586					Jun-14
	-1.95	-3.31	-7.74	6.34	-9.50	0	2.47	8.33	51.36	9.05	10.1	1	88	10	0	586					Jun-14
	-2.08	-1.14	-3.10	-0.61	3.14	0	1.93	5.49	0.32	11.25	201.7	17	0	79	4	36					Dec-11
	-2.21	-1.25	-3.41	-1.34	1.78	0	2.18	5.5	0.12	11.04	201.7	17	0	79	4	36					Dec-11
	1.98	15.01	-7.97			0.2	0.93			10.8	27.4	2	98	0	0	297					Dec-16
	2.07	15.13	-7.90			0.27	0.84			10.8	27.4	2	98	0	0	297					Dec-16
	1.89	14.86	-8.26			0.02	1.24			10.74	27.4	2	98	0	0	297					Dec-16
	1.65	10.02	1.35	16.03	5.93	0.96	1.21	7.39	0.99	12.34	60.8	13	58	27	2	22					Apr-15
	1.79	10.34	1.20	14.36	5.54	0.45	1.41	7.42	1	12.48	60.8	13	58	27	2	22					Apr-12
500	5.06	17.85	14.75	42.51	55.84	1.65	1.09	10.31	0.81	18.68	1,173	3	97	0	0	16			5.50		Jul-12
500	4.86	17.39	13.86	39.30	49.96	1.04	1.84	10.29	0.8	18.5	1,173	3	97	0	0	16				1.00	Jan-13
5,000	5.15	17.99	15.07	43.62	58.02	1.87	0.84	10.31	0.81	18.73	1,173	3	97	0	0	16					Jul-12
500	0.27	7.28	0.97				1.89			9.11	50.0	0	98	0	2				5.50		Dec-18
500	0.08	6.81	0.16				2.64			9.09	50.0	0	98	0	2					1.00	Dec-18
5,000	0.29	7.35	1.17			4.56	1.64			9.09	50.0	0	98	0	2						Dec-17
500	2.02	20.65	10.00	17.23	43.54		1.15	13.5	1.04	34.24	14.0	3	97	0	-1		31.75	-18.1	5.50		Aug-18
5,000	2.07	20.78	10.32	18.16	45.40	2.21	0.9	13.52	1.04	34.5	14.0	3	97	0	-1		31.95	-18.01			Sep-06
	2.76	15.63	6.84			0.72	1.21			11.91	335.3	19	81	0	0						Jun-17

	MARKET			FUND TYPE, CATEGORY & OBJECTIVE	RATINGS				MINIMUMS	
Fund Name	Ticker Symbol	Traded On	Fund Type	Category and (Prospectus Objective)	Overall Rating	Reward Rating	Risk Rating	Recent Up/ Downgrade	Open to New Investors	Min Initial Investment
Aasgard Dividend Growth Small & Mid-Cap Fund No Load Class	AADGX	NAS CM	Open End	US Equity Mid Cap (Growth & Income)	C+	C	B		Y	2,500
AB All China Equity Portfolio Advisor Class	ACEYX	NAS CM	Open End	Greater China Equity (Growth)	D-	D+	C		Y	0
AB All China Equity Portfolio Class A	ACEAX	NAS CM	Open End	Greater China Equity (Growth)	D-	D+	C		Y	2,500
AB All Market Income Portfolio Advisor Class	MRKYX	NAS CM	Open End	Cautious Alloc (Growth)	B-	C	B	Up	Y	0
AB All Market Income Portfolio Class A	MRKAX	NAS CM	Open End	Cautious Alloc (Growth)	B-	C	B	Up	Y	2,500
AB All Market Income Portfolio Class C	MRKCX	NAS CM	Open End	Cautious Alloc (Growth)	C+	C	B	Up	Y	2,500
AB All Market Real Return Portfolio Advisor Class	AMTYX	NAS CM	Open End	Moderate Alloc (Growth & Income)	C	C-	B-		Y	0
AB All Market Real Return Portfolio Class 1	AMTOX	NAS CM	Open End	Moderate Alloc (Growth & Income)	C	C-	B-		Y	5,000
AB All Market Real Return Portfolio Class 2	AMTTX	NAS CM	Open End	Moderate Alloc (Growth & Income)	C	C-	B-		Y	5,000,000
AB All Market Real Return Portfolio Class A	AMTAX	NAS CM	Open End	Moderate Alloc (Growth & Income)	C	C-	B-		Y	2,500
AB All Market Real Return Portfolio Class C	ACMTX	NAS CM	Open End	Moderate Alloc (Growth & Income)	C	C-	C+		Y	2,500
AB All Market Real Return Portfolio Class I	AMTIX	NAS CM	Open End	Moderate Alloc (Growth & Income)	C	C-	B-		Y	2,000,000
AB All Market Real Return Portfolio Class K	AMTKX	NAS CM	Open End	Moderate Alloc (Growth & Income)	C	C-	B-		Y	0
AB All Market Real Return Portfolio Class R	AMTRX	NAS CM	Open End	Moderate Alloc (Growth & Income)	C	C-	B-		Y	0
AB All Market Real Return Portfolio Class Z	AMTZX	NAS CM	Open End	Moderate Alloc (Growth & Income)	C	C-	B-		Y	2,000,000
AB All Market Total Return Portfolio Advisor Class	ABWYX	NAS CM	Open End	Moderate Alloc (Balanced)	B-	C	A-	Up	Y	0
AB All Market Total Return Portfolio Class A	ABWAX	NAS CM	Open End	Moderate Alloc (Balanced)	B-	C	A-	Up	Y	2,500
AB All Market Total Return Portfolio Class B	ABWBX	NAS CM	Open End	Moderate Alloc (Balanced)	B-	C	B+	Up		2,500
AB All Market Total Return Portfolio Class C	ABWCX	NAS CM	Open End	Moderate Alloc (Balanced)	B-	C	B+	Up	Y	2,500
AB All Market Total Return Portfolio Class I	ABWIX	NAS CM	Open End	Moderate Alloc (Balanced)	B-	C	A-	Up	Y	2,000,000
AB All Market Total Return Portfolio Class K	ABWKX	NAS CM	Open End	Moderate Alloc (Balanced)	B-	C	A-	Up	Y	0
AB All Market Total Return Portfolio Class R	ABWRX	NAS CM	Open End	Moderate Alloc (Balanced)	B-	C	B+	Up	Y	0
AB Concentrated Growth Fund Advisor Class	WPSGX	NAS CM	Open End	US Equity Large Cap Growth (Growth)	B	B	B+		Y	0
AB Concentrated Growth Fund Class A	WPASX	NAS CM	Open End	US Equity Large Cap Growth (Growth)	B	B	B+		Y	2,500
AB Concentrated Growth Fund Class C	WPCSX	NAS CM	Open End	US Equity Large Cap Growth (Growth)	B	B-	B+		Y	2,500
AB Concentrated Growth Fund Class I	WPSIX	NAS CM	Open End	US Equity Large Cap Growth (Growth)	B	B	B+		Y	2,000,000
AB Concentrated Growth Fund Class K	WPSKX	NAS CM	Open End	US Equity Large Cap Growth (Growth)	B	B	B+		Y	0
AB Concentrated Growth Fund Class R	WPRSX	NAS CM	Open End	US Equity Large Cap Growth (Growth)	B	B	B+		Y	0
AB Concentrated Growth Fund Class Z	WPSZX	NAS CM	Open End	US Equity Large Cap Growth (Growth)	B	B	B+		Y	2,000,000
AB Concentrated International Growth Portfolio Advisor Cls	CIGYX	NAS CM	Open End	Global Equity Large Cap (Growth)	C	C	C+		Y	0
AB Concentrated International Growth Portfolio Class A	CIAGX	NAS CM	Open End	Global Equity Large Cap (Growth)	C	C	C+		Y	2,500
AB Concentrated International Growth Portfolio Class C	CICGX	NAS CM	Open End	Global Equity Large Cap (Growth)	C	C	C+		Y	2,500
AB Conservative Wealth Strategy Advisor Class	ABPYX	NAS CM	Open End	Cautious Alloc (Balanced)	B-	C	A-	Up	Y	0
AB Conservative Wealth Strategy Class A	ABPAX	NAS CM	Open End	Cautious Alloc (Balanced)	B-	C	A-	Up	Y	2,500
AB Conservative Wealth Strategy Class B	ABPBX	NAS CM	Open End	Cautious Alloc (Balanced)	C+	C	B+	Up		2,500
AB Conservative Wealth Strategy Class C	ABPCX	NAS CM	Open End	Cautious Alloc (Balanced)	C+	C	B+	Up	Y	2,500
AB Conservative Wealth Strategy Class I	APWIX	NAS CM	Open End	Cautious Alloc (Balanced)	B-	C	A-	Up	Y	2,000,000
AB Conservative Wealth Strategy Class K	APWKX	NAS CM	Open End	Cautious Alloc (Balanced)	B-	C	B+	Up	Y	0
AB Conservative Wealth Strategy Class R	APPRX	NAS CM	Open End	Cautious Alloc (Balanced)	B-	C	B+	Up	Y	0
AB Core Opportunities Fund Advisor Class	ADGYX	NAS CM	Open End	US Equity Large Cap Growth (Growth)	B-	C	B+	Down	Y	0
AB Core Opportunities Fund Class A	ADGAX	NAS CM	Open End	US Equity Large Cap Growth (Growth)	B-	C	B+	Down	Y	2,500
AB Core Opportunities Fund Class B	ADGBX	NAS CM	Open End	US Equity Large Cap Growth (Growth)	B-	C	B+	Down		2,500
AB Core Opportunities Fund Class C	ADGCX	NAS CM	Open End	US Equity Large Cap Growth (Growth)	B-	C	B+	Down	Y	2,500
AB Core Opportunities Fund Class I	ADGIX	NAS CM	Open End	US Equity Large Cap Growth (Growth)	B-	C	B+	Down	Y	2,000,000
AB Core Opportunities Fund Class K	ADGKX	NAS CM	Open End	US Equity Large Cap Growth (Growth)	B-	C	B+	Down	Y	0
AB Core Opportunities Fund Class R	ADGRX	NAS CM	Open End	US Equity Large Cap Growth (Growth)	B-	C	B+	Down	Y	0
AB Core Opportunities Fund Class Z	ADGZX	NAS CM	Open End	US Equity Large Cap Growth (Growth)	B-	C	B+	Down	Y	2,000,000
AB Discovery Growth Fund Advisor Class	CHCYX	NAS CM	Open End	US Equity Mid Cap (Growth)	C+	C+	C+	Down	Y	0
AB Discovery Growth Fund Class A	CHCLX	NAS CM	Open End	US Equity Mid Cap (Growth)	C+	C+	C+	Down	Y	2,500
AB Discovery Growth Fund Class B	CHCBX	NAS CM	Open End	US Equity Mid Cap (Growth)	C+	C+	C+	Down		2,500
AB Discovery Growth Fund Class C	CHCCX	NAS CM	Open End	US Equity Mid Cap (Growth)	C+	C+	C+	Down	Y	2,500
AB Discovery Growth Fund Class I	CHCIX	NAS CM	Open End	US Equity Mid Cap (Growth)	C+	C+	C+	Down	Y	2,000,000

★ Expanded analysis of this fund is included in Section II.

Min Additional Investment	TOTAL RETURNS 3-Month Total Return	6-Month Total Return	1-Year Total Return	3-Year Total Return	5-Year Total Return	PERFORMANCE Dividend Yield (TTM)	Expense Ratio	3-Yr Std Deviation	3-Year Beta	ASSETS NAV	Total Assets (MIL)	ASSET ALLOCATION & TURNOVER %Cash	%Stocks	%Bonds	%Other	Turnover Ratio	BULL & BEAR Last Bull Market Total Return	Last Bear Market Total Return	FEES Front End Fee (%)	Back End Fee (%)	Inception Date
500	3.33	15.23	3.36	39.54		0.93	1.33	12.11	0.78	13.22	56.3	1	99	0	0	63					Apr-16
	-1.39	27.21					1.25			9.91	79.7	2	98	0	0	38					Jul-18
50	-1.39	27.12					1.5			9.89	79.7	2	98	0	0	38			4.25		Jul-18
	3.34	12.35	4.84	18.46		4.6	0.75	5.84	0.46	9.79	95.8	19	32	38	2	74					Dec-14
50	3.28	12.35	4.69	17.56		4.36	1	5.82	0.46	9.78	95.8	19	32	38	2	74			4.25		Dec-14
50	3.09	11.94	3.94	14.99		3.66	1.75	5.8	0.46	9.78	95.8	19	32	38	2	74				1.00	Dec-14
	0.00	11.41	-3.88	12.87	-18.40	1.62	1.04	9.95	0.64	8.59	1,160	10	74	16	0	141	13.47	-21.13			Mar-10
	0.00	11.44	-3.87	12.58	-18.82	1.59	1.11	9.94	0.64	8.47	1,160	10	74	16	0	141	13.4	-21.25			Mar-10
	0.11	11.45	-3.64	13.40	-17.75	1.81	0.85	9.94	0.64	8.66	1,160	10	74	16	0	141	13.52	-21.16			Mar-10
50	-0.11	11.22	-4.02	11.95	-19.48	1.35	1.29	9.88	0.63	8.62	1,160	10	74	16	0	141	13.35	-21.26	4.25		Mar-10
50	-0.23	10.79	-4.79	9.41	-22.45	0.37	2.04	9.89	0.63	8.62	1,160	10	74	16	0	141	12.89	-21.49		1.00	Mar-10
	0.00	11.50	-3.59	13.43	-17.84	1.83	0.86	9.91	0.63	8.53	1,160	10	74	16	0	141	13.49	-21.16			Mar-10
	-0.11	11.24	-4.05	11.94	-19.42	1.39	1.29	9.93	0.63	8.51	1,160	10	74	16	0	141	13.43	-21.26			Mar-10
	-0.11	11.09	-4.23	11.11	-20.44	1	1.58	9.96	0.64	8.51	1,160	10	74	16	0	141	13.19	-21.36			Mar-10
	0.00	11.50	-3.60	13.42	-17.86	1.82	0.86	9.93	0.63	8.53	1,160	10	74	16	0	141	13.49	-21.16			Jan-14
	4.04	14.35	6.22	22.64	21.34	0	0.79	6.62	0.54	15.69	729.1	22	61	16	0	38	14.8	-14.55			Sep-03
50	3.94	14.18	6.00	21.72	19.82	0	1.04	6.59	0.54	15.54	729.1	22	61	16	0	38	14.64	-14.72	4.25		Sep-03
50	3.75	13.75	5.23	18.99	15.36	0	1.76	6.59	0.54	15.47	729.1	22	61	16	0	38	14.04	-14.91		4.00	Sep-03
50	3.79	13.75	5.22	18.99	15.40	0	1.78	6.6	0.54	15.3	729.1	22	61	16	0	38	14.22	-14.96		1.00	Sep-03
	4.07	14.27	6.23	22.53	21.17	0	0.82	6.6	0.54	15.85	729.1	22	61	16	0	38	14.84	-14.59			Mar-05
	3.96	14.08	5.88	21.30	19.19	0	1.14	6.6	0.54	15.47	729.1	22	61	16	0	38	14.63	-14.76			Mar-05
	3.91	14.00	5.55	20.26	17.35	0	1.45	6.6	0.54	15.39	729.1	22	61	16	0	38	14.46	-14.86			Feb-04
	7.31	28.87	22.96	77.67	84.73	0	0.96	13.03	1.02	40.93	587.5	4	96	0	0	27	28.13	-11.36			Feb-94
50	7.22	28.70	22.67	76.33	82.44	0	1.21	13.02	1.02	40.35	587.5	4	96	0	0	27	27.95	-11.46	4.25		Feb-14
50	7.04	28.27	21.74	72.44	75.85	0	1.96	13.04	1.02	38.61	587.5	4	96	0	0	27	27.39	-11.73		1.00	Feb-14
	7.32	28.93	22.99	77.74	84.94	0	0.96	13.04	1.02	41	587.5	4	96	0	0	27	28.13	-11.36			Feb-14
	7.25	28.74	22.66	76.37	82.55	0	1.22	13.04	1.02	40.36	587.5	4	96	0	0	27	27.95	-11.46			Feb-14
	7.19	28.58	22.37	75.02	80.26	0	1.45	13.04	1.02	39.76	587.5	4	96	0	0	27	27.76	-11.55			Feb-14
	7.30	28.90	23.00	77.80	84.86	0	0.92	13.05	1.02	40.98	587.5	4	96	0	0	27	28.13	-11.36			Feb-14
	8.00	24.40	3.01	48.71		0.12	1.05	13.56	1.12	11.06	67.2	8	92	0	0	34					Apr-15
50	7.93	24.37	2.71	47.72		0.03	1.3	13.58	1.12	11.02	67.2	8	92	0	0	34			4.25		Apr-15
50	7.80	23.90	1.99	44.60		0	2.05	13.52	1.12	10.78	67.2	8	92	0	0	34				1.00	Apr-15
	3.03	10.56	4.66	15.41	16.87	0.98	1.04	4.82	0.48	12.56	180.8	8	51	40	0	90	8.1	-6.93			Sep-03
50	3.04	10.51	4.48	14.62	15.53	0.74	1.29	4.88	0.49	12.51	180.8	8	51	40	0	90	7.93	-7.09	4.25		Sep-03
50	2.82	10.10	3.65	12.01	11.19	0	2.05	4.8	0.5	12.75	180.8	8	51	40	0	90	7.5	-7.32		4.00	Sep-03
50	2.89	10.07	3.74	12.01	11.25	0	2.02	4.86	0.49	12.46	180.8	8	51	40	0	90	7.52	-7.31		1.00	Sep-03
	3.08	10.53	4.66	15.31	16.72	1.02	0.98	4.78	0.5	12.7	180.8	8	51	40	0	90	8.1	-6.97			Mar-05
	2.97	10.44	4.38	14.21	14.90	0.65	1.4	4.82	0.48	12.48	180.8	8	51	40	0	90	7.85	-7.12			Mar-05
	2.87	10.22	3.99	13.17	13.15	0.39	1.7	4.82	0.49	12.51	180.8	8	51	40	0	90	7.68	-7.26			Feb-04
	3.95	15.89	9.24	51.10	69.31	0.47	0.84	11.28	0.9	19.98	259.1	10	90	0	0	139	26.38	-16.08			Mar-10
50	3.92	15.76	9.00	50.00	67.04	0.26	1.09	11.26	0.9	19.31	259.1	10	90	0	0	139	26.23	-16.21	4.25		Dec-99
50	3.87	15.67	8.81	49.20	65.43	0.1	1.88	11.25	0.9	16.9	259.1	10	90	0	0	139	26.06	-16.33		4.00	Dec-99
50	3.72	15.38	8.21	46.67	61.08	0	1.84	11.27	0.9	15.6	259.1	10	90	0	0	139	25.62	-16.45		1.00	Dec-99
	3.95	15.90	9.25	51.21	69.45	0.49	0.82	11.27	0.9	20.26	259.1	10	90	0	0	139	26.37	-16.04			Mar-05
	3.88	15.78	8.94	49.87	67.04	0.21	1.15	11.26	0.9	19.51	259.1	10	90	0	0	139	26.22	-16.22			Mar-05
	3.86	15.64	8.68	48.82	64.98	0	1.4	11.22	0.9	18.55	259.1	10	90	0	0	139	26.05	-16.23			Nov-03
	3.99	15.99	9.36	51.57	69.86	0.55	0.75	11.26	0.9	20.31	259.1	10	90	0	0	139	26.23	-16.21			Oct-13
	5.41	30.48	7.35	78.86	73.09	0.16	0.72	18.34	1.09	12.07	2,699	1	98	0	0	72	31.52	-22.52			Oct-96
50	5.28	30.22	7.06	77.58	71.15	0	0.96	18.31	1.08	11.16	2,699	1	98	0	0	72	31.27	-22.64	4.25		Jul-38
50	5.05	29.79	6.15	73.27	64.05	0	1.78	18.23	1.08	6.23	2,699	1	98	0	0	72	30.6	-22.71		4.00	Mar-91
50	5.16	29.83	6.26	73.53	64.60	0	1.74	18.24	1.08	6.31	2,699	1	98	0	0	72	30.52	-22.82		1.00	May-93
	5.38	30.38	7.33	78.86	73.03	0.14	0.75	18.36	1.09	11.93	2,699	1	98	0	0	72	31.68	-22.49			Mar-05

	MARKET		FUND TYPE, CATEGORY & OBJECTIVE		RATINGS				MINIMUMS	
Fund Name	Ticker Symbol	Traded On	Fund Type	Category and (Prospectus Objective)	Overall Rating	Reward Rating	Risk Rating	Recent Up/ Downgrade	Open to New Investors	Min Initial Investment
AB Discovery Growth Fund Class K	CHCKX	NAS CM	Open End	US Equity Mid Cap (Growth)	C+	C+	C+	Down	Y	0
AB Discovery Growth Fund Class R	CHCRX	NAS CM	Open End	US Equity Mid Cap (Growth)	C+	C+	C+	Down	Y	0
AB Discovery Growth Fund Class Z	CHCZX	NAS CM	Open End	US Equity Mid Cap (Growth)	C+	C+	C+	Down	Y	2,000,000
AB Discovery Value Fund Advisor Class	ABYSX	NAS CM	Open End	US Equity Mid Cap (Growth)	C	C-	C		Y	0
AB Discovery Value Fund Class A	ABASX	NAS CM	Open End	US Equity Mid Cap (Growth)	C	C-	C		Y	2,500
AB Discovery Value Fund Class B	ABBSX	NAS CM	Open End	US Equity Mid Cap (Growth)	C	C-	C			2,500
AB Discovery Value Fund Class C	ABCSX	NAS CM	Open End	US Equity Mid Cap (Growth)	C	C-	C		Y	2,500
AB Discovery Value Fund Class I	ABSIX	NAS CM	Open End	US Equity Mid Cap (Growth)	C	C-	C		Y	2,000,000
AB Discovery Value Fund Class K	ABSKX	NAS CM	Open End	US Equity Mid Cap (Growth)	C	C-	C		Y	0
AB Discovery Value Fund Class R	ABSRX	NAS CM	Open End	US Equity Mid Cap (Growth)	C	C-	C		Y	0
AB Discovery Value Fund Class Z	ABSZX	NAS CM	Open End	US Equity Mid Cap (Growth)	C	C-	C		Y	2,000,000
AB Emerging Markets Core Portfolio Advisor Class	EMPYX	NAS CM	Open End	Global Emerg Mkts (Div Emerging Mkts)	C	C-	C		Y	0
AB Emerging Markets Core Portfolio Class A	EMPAX	NAS CM	Open End	Global Emerg Mkts (Div Emerging Mkts)	C	C-	C		Y	2,500
AB Emerging Markets Core Portfolio Class C	EMPCX	NAS CM	Open End	Global Emerg Mkts (Div Emerging Mkts)	C-	C-	C	Down	Y	2,500
AB Emerging Markets Multi-Asset Portfolio Advisor Class	ABYEX	NAS CM	Open End	Global Emerg Mkts (Multi-Asset Global)	C	C	B-		Y	0
AB Emerging Markets Multi-Asset Portfolio Class A	ABAEX	NAS CM	Open End	Global Emerg Mkts (Multi-Asset Global)	C	C-	B-		Y	2,500
AB Emerging Markets Multi-Asset Portfolio Class C	ABCEX	NAS CM	Open End	Global Emerg Mkts (Multi-Asset Global)	C	C-	B-		Y	2,500
AB Emerging Markets Multi-Asset Portfolio Class I	ABIEX	NAS CM	Open End	Global Emerg Mkts (Multi-Asset Global)	C	C	B-		Y	2,000,000
AB Emerging Markets Multi-Asset Portfolio Class K	ABKEX	NAS CM	Open End	Global Emerg Mkts (Multi-Asset Global)	C	C-	B-		Y	0
AB Emerging Markets Multi-Asset Portfolio Class R	ABREX	NAS CM	Open End	Global Emerg Mkts (Multi-Asset Global)	C	C-	B-		Y	0
AB Emerging Markets Multi-Asset Portfolio Class Z	ABZEX	NAS CM	Open End	Global Emerg Mkts (Multi-Asset Global)	C	C	B-		Y	2,000,000
AB Emerging Markets Portfolio	SNEMX	NAS CM	Open End	Global Emerg Mkts (Div Emerging Mkts)	C	C	C		Y	5,000
AB Equity Income Fund Advisor Class	AUIYX	NAS CM	Open End	US Equity Large Cap Value (Equity-Income)	B-	C	B+		Y	0
AB Equity Income Fund Class A	AUIAX	NAS CM	Open End	US Equity Large Cap Value (Equity-Income)	B-	C	B		Y	2,500
AB Equity Income Fund Class B	AUIBX	NAS CM	Open End	US Equity Large Cap Value (Equity-Income)	B-	C	B	Up		2,500
AB Equity Income Fund Class C	AUICX	NAS CM	Open End	US Equity Large Cap Value (Equity-Income)	B-	C	B	Up	Y	2,500
AB Equity Income Fund Class I	AUIIX	NAS CM	Open End	US Equity Large Cap Value (Equity-Income)	B-	C	B		Y	2,000,000
AB Equity Income Fund Class K	AUIKX	NAS CM	Open End	US Equity Large Cap Value (Equity-Income)	B-	C	B	Up	Y	0
AB Equity Income Fund Class R	AUIRX	NAS CM	Open End	US Equity Large Cap Value (Equity-Income)	B-	C	B	Up	Y	0
AB Equity Income Fund Class Z	AUIZX	NAS CM	Open End	US Equity Large Cap Value (Equity-Income)	B-	C	B+		Y	2,000,000
AB FlexFee Core Opportunities Portfolio Advisor Class	FFCYX	NAS CM	Open End	US Equity Large Cap Value (Growth)	C	C-	B	Up	Y	0
AB FlexFee Emerging Markets Growth Portfolio Advisor Class	FFEYX	NAS CM	Open End	Global Emerg Mkts (Div Emerging Mkts)	C	C	C	Up	Y	0
AB FlexFee Intl Strategic Core Portfolio Adv Cls	FFSYX	NAS CM	Open End	Global Equity Large Cap (Foreign Stock)	C-	D	B-	Up	Y	0
AB FlexFee Large Cap Growth Portfolio Advisor Class	FFLYX	NAS CM	Open End	US Equity Large Cap Growth (Growth)	C	C-	B	Up	Y	0
AB FlexFee US Thematic Portfolio Advisor Class	FFTYX	NAS CM	Open End	US Equity Large Cap Blend (Growth)	C	C-	B	Up	Y	0
AB Global Core Equity Portfolio Advisor Class	GCEYX	NAS CM	Open End	Global Equity Large Cap (World Stock)	B-	C	B+		Y	0
AB Global Core Equity Portfolio Class A	GCEAX	NAS CM	Open End	Global Equity Large Cap (World Stock)	B-	C	B+		Y	2,500
AB Global Core Equity Portfolio Class C	GCECX	NAS CM	Open End	Global Equity Large Cap (World Stock)	B-	C	B+		Y	2,500
AB Global Real Estate Investment Fund Advisor Class	ARSYX	NAS CM	Open End	Real Estate Sector Equity (Real Estate)	B-	C+	B+		Y	0
AB Global Real Estate Investment Fund Class A	AREAX	NAS CM	Open End	Real Estate Sector Equity (Real Estate)	B-	C	B+		Y	2,500
AB Global Real Estate Investment Fund Class B	AREBX	NAS CM	Open End	Real Estate Sector Equity (Real Estate)	B-	C	B			2,500
AB Global Real Estate Investment Fund Class C	ARECX	NAS CM	Open End	Real Estate Sector Equity (Real Estate)	B-	C	B		Y	2,500
AB Global Real Estate Investment Fund Class I	AEEIX	NAS CM	Open End	Real Estate Sector Equity (Real Estate)	B-	C+	B+		Y	2,000,000
AB Global Real Estate Investment Fund Class K	ARRKX	NAS CM	Open End	Real Estate Sector Equity (Real Estate)	B-	C	B+		Y	0
AB Global Real Estate Investment Fund Class R	ARRRX	NAS CM	Open End	Real Estate Sector Equity (Real Estate)	B-	C	B+		Y	0
AB Global Real Estate Investment Fund II Class I	ARIIX	NAS CM	Open End	Real Estate Sector Equity (Real Estate)	B	C+	B+		Y	2,000,000
AB Global Risk Allocation Fund Class A	CABNX	NAS CM	Open End	Moderate Alloc (Asset Alloc)	B-	C	B+	Up	Y	2,500
AB Global Risk Allocation Fund Class Adv	CBSYX	NAS CM	Open End	Moderate Alloc (Asset Alloc)	B-	C	A-	Up	Y	0
AB Global Risk Allocation Fund Class B	CABBX	NAS CM	Open End	Moderate Alloc (Asset Alloc)	C+	C	B+	Up		2,500
AB Global Risk Allocation Fund Class C	CBACX	NAS CM	Open End	Moderate Alloc (Asset Alloc)	C+	C	B+	Up	Y	2,500
AB Global Risk Allocation Fund Class I	CABIX	NAS CM	Open End	Moderate Alloc (Asset Alloc)	B-	C	A-	Up	Y	2,000,000
AB Global Risk Allocation Fund Class K	CBSKX	NAS CM	Open End	Moderate Alloc (Asset Alloc)	B-	C	B+	Up	Y	0

★ Expanded analysis of this fund is included in Section II.

	TOTAL RETURNS					PERFORMANCE				ASSETS		ASSET ALLOCATION & TURNOVER					BULL & BEAR		FEES		
Min Additional Investment	3-Month Total Return	6-Month Total Return	1-Year Total Return	3-Year Total Return	5-Year Total Return	Dividend Yield (TTM)	Expense Ratio	3-Yr Std Deviation	3-Year Beta	NAV	Total Assets (MIL)	%Cash	%Stocks	%Bonds	%Other	Turnover Ratio	Last Bull Market Total Return	Last Bear Market Total Return	Front End Fee (%)	Back End Fee (%)	Inception Date
	5.25	30.25	6.95	76.90	70.07	0	1.11	18.34	1.09	11.02	2,699	1	98	0	0	72	31.27	-22.53			Mar-05
	5.18	30.02	6.59	75.45	67.65	0	1.39	18.33	1.09	10.35	2,699	1	98	0	0	72	30.98	-22.66			Mar-05
	5.37	30.56	7.41	79.16	73.53	0.21	0.68	18.33	1.09	11.96	2,699	1	98	0	0	72	31.27	-22.64			May-14
	2.01	14.82	-5.49	32.26	30.03	0.54	0.85	16.33	1.07	20.21	2,967	2	98	0	0	42	27.56	-26.49			Mar-01
50	1.96	14.67	-5.74	31.31	28.34	0.28	1.1	16.33	1.07	19.69	2,967	2	98	0	0	42	27.33	-26.55	4.25		Mar-01
50	1.94	14.63	-5.83	30.82	27.66	0.14	1.88	16.34	1.07	18.33	2,967	2	98	0	0	42	27.24	-26.64		4.00	Mar-01
50	1.73	14.27	-6.45	28.36	23.65	0	1.85	16.31	1.07	16.97	2,967	2	98	0	0	42	26.78	-26.8		1.00	Mar-01
	2.03	14.87	-5.49	32.32	30.14	0.54	0.86	16.35	1.07	19.54	2,967	2	98	0	0	42	27.55	-26.49			Mar-05
	1.94	14.67	-5.81	30.93	27.87	0.21	1.21	16.35	1.07	19.38	2,967	2	98	0	0	42	27.39	-26.59			Mar-05
	1.82	14.44	-6.14	29.66	25.90	0	1.52	16.3	1.07	19.01	2,967	2	98	0	0	42	27.14	-26.66			Nov-03
	2.03	14.89	-5.43	32.63	30.62	0.65	0.78	16.36	1.07	19.51	2,967	2	98	0	0	42	27.56	-26.49			Oct-13
	1.70	9.62	-1.55	20.90		1.19	1.1	13.1	0.9	10.14	4.4	1	99	0	0	95					Sep-15
50	1.60	9.40	-1.94	19.86		0.92	1.35	13.08	0.9	10.12	4.4	1	99	0	0	95			4.25		Sep-15
50	1.50	9.07	-2.53	17.31		0.13	2.1	13.07	0.9	10.1	4.4	1	99	0	0	95				1.00	Sep-15
	1.34	12.02	4.23	18.26	14.57	5.63	1	12	0.82	8.95	139.0	1	71	29	0	110	14.59				Aug-11
50	1.29	11.94	3.95	17.42	13.03	5.37	1.25	11.97	0.82	8.93	139.0	1	71	29	0	110	14.48		4.25		Aug-11
50	1.03	11.40	3.12	14.73	8.90	4.72	2	12.02	0.83	8.88	139.0	1	71	29	0	110	14.03			1.00	Aug-11
	1.37	12.03	4.20	18.21	14.45	5.73	1	11.98	0.82	8.87	139.0	1	71	29	0	110	14.65				Aug-11
	1.27	11.92	3.99	17.33	13.07	5.31	1.25	12.04	0.83	8.91	139.0	1	71	29	0	110	14.47				Aug-11
	1.21	11.74	3.66	16.45	11.65	5	1.5	12.01	0.83	8.92	139.0	1	71	29	0	110	14.25				Aug-11
	1.35	11.97	4.23	18.31	14.55	5.65	1	11.98	0.82	8.89	139.0	1	71	29	0	110	14.65				Jul-17
	0.74	16.38	-2.49	26.65	6.29	1.16	1.03	15	1.04	27.13	1,190	4	95	0	0	65	18.83	-30.43			Dec-95
	2.00	15.17	7.99	35.31	38.74	2.81	0.73	10.82	0.86	27.34	539.3	1	99	0	0	68	22.54	-15.94			Oct-96
50	1.92	15.04	7.76	34.34	36.90	2.6	0.98	10.85	0.87	27.05	539.3	1	99	0	0	68	22.35	-16.08	4.25		Oct-93
50	1.72	14.61	6.91	31.30	31.80	1.84	1.77	10.84	0.87	26.69	539.3	1	99	0	0	68	21.83	-16.32		4.00	Oct-93
50	1.71	14.58	6.92	31.31	31.93	1.91	1.73	10.83	0.86	26.65	539.3	1	99	0	0	68	21.83	-16.34		1.00	Oct-93
	1.98	15.19	7.98	35.21	38.64	2.81	0.76	10.82	0.86	26.98	539.3	1	99	0	0	68	22.56	-15.99			Mar-05
	1.89	14.94	7.59	33.87	36.34	2.46	1.09	10.84	0.86	27.05	539.3	1	99	0	0	68	22.32	-16.05			Mar-05
	1.82	14.79	7.29	32.70	34.31	2.2	1.4	10.83	0.86	26.9	539.3	1	99	0	0	68	22.14	-16.17			Mar-05
	1.97	15.21	8.06	35.63	39.27	2.91	0.66	10.82	0.86	26.96	539.3	1	99	0	0	68	22.35	-16.08			Oct-13
	4.23	16.46	8.97			0.43	0.95			11.32	1.1	11	89	0	0	144					Jun-17
	0.19	18.55	-6.63	26.44		1.81	0.15	16.06	1.06	10.34	5.5	6	93	1	0	83					Nov-14
	2.79	13.01	0.44			1.28	1.04			10.66	5.9	2	98	0	0	80					Jun-17
	4.41	22.39	14.36			0	1.1			13.94	228.5	13	87	0	0	38					Jun-17
	5.44	23.61	13.20			0.45	0.43			12.97	91.4	8	92	0	0	31					Jun-17
	4.46	18.35	10.21	51.40		1.09	0.9	12.07	1.04	13.35	797.1	0	100	0	0	45					Nov-14
50	4.47	18.31	9.95	50.31		0.86	1.15	12.08	1.04	13.31	797.1	0	100	0	0	45			4.25		Nov-14
50	4.21	17.80	9.12	46.95		0.66	1.9	12.05	1.04	13.1	797.1	0	100	0	0	45				1.00	Nov-14
	0.05	15.40	8.07	20.45	32.04	3.18	1.1	11.04	0.64	15.07	143.3	0	99	0	1	75	24.86	-21.97			Sep-96
50	0.04	15.33	7.87	19.59	30.46	2.91	1.35	11.04	0.64	15.24	143.3	0	99	0	1	75	24.57	-22.02	4.25		Sep-96
50	-0.17	14.77	6.94	16.72	25.31	2.29	2.16	11.04	0.64	15.04	143.3	0	99	0	1	75	24.03	-22.31		4.00	Sep-96
50	-0.13	14.85	7.05	16.87	25.68	2.2	2.11	11.03	0.64	15.09	143.3	0	99	0	1	75	24.13	-22.34		1.00	Sep-96
	0.12	15.48	8.22	20.81	32.70	3.21	1.04	11.07	0.64	15.18	143.3	0	99	0	1	75	24.9	-21.9			Mar-05
	0.04	15.30	7.84	19.50	30.41	2.91	1.39	11.08	0.64	15.11	143.3	0	99	0	1	75	24.59	-22.03			Mar-05
	-0.10	15.03	7.49	18.39	28.33	2.71	1.7	11.08	0.64	15.03	143.3	0	99	0	1	75	24.44	-22.17			Mar-05
	0.26	15.82	8.78	22.48	35.44	3.96	0.7	11.06	0.56	11.56	331.8	1	98	0	1	70	25.18	-21.42			Dec-97
50	2.76	12.89	3.30	19.46	16.20	0.54	1.29	6.93	0.55	16.72	229.5	1	30	67	0	9	19.34	-10.25	4.25		Jun-32
	2.80	13.00	3.49	20.31	17.64	0.78	1.04	6.91	0.55	16.86	229.5	1	30	67	0	9	19.53	-10.16			Oct-96
50	2.58	12.51	2.51	16.74	11.77	0	2.08	6.95	0.55	15.1	229.5	1	30	67	0	9	18.81	-10.52		4.00	Feb-91
50	2.55	12.45	2.48	16.71	11.85	0	2.05	6.93	0.55	15.26	229.5	1	30	67	0	9	18.84	-10.54		1.00	May-93
	2.86	13.08	3.61	20.70	18.35	0.83	0.99	6.94	0.55	16.85	229.5	1	30	67	0	9	19.6	-10.06			Mar-05
	2.77	12.93	3.23	19.34	16.02	0.52	1.32	6.92	0.55	16.68	229.5	1	30	67	0	9	19.31	-10.22			Mar-05

	MARKET		FUND TYPE, CATEGORY & OBJECTIVE		RATINGS				MINIMUMS	
Fund Name	Ticker Symbol	Traded On	Fund Type	Category and (Prospectus Objective)	Overall Rating	Reward Rating	Risk Rating	Recent Up/ Downgrade	Open to New Investors	Min Initial Investment
AB Global Risk Allocation Fund Class R	CBSRX	NAS CM	Open End	Moderate Alloc (Asset Alloc)	B-	C	B+	Up	Y	0
AB Growth Fund Advisor Class	AGRYX	NAS CM	Open End	US Equity Large Cap Growth (Growth)	B-	C+	B	Down	Y	0
AB Growth Fund Class A	AGRFX	NAS CM	Open End	US Equity Large Cap Growth (Growth)	B-	C+	B	Down	Y	2,500
AB Growth Fund Class B	AGBBX	NAS CM	Open End	US Equity Large Cap Growth (Growth)	B-	C+	B	Down		2,500
AB Growth Fund Class C	AGRCX	NAS CM	Open End	US Equity Large Cap Growth (Growth)	B-	C+	B	Down	Y	2,500
AB Growth Fund Class I	AGFIX	NAS CM	Open End	US Equity Large Cap Growth (Growth)	B-	C+	B	Down	Y	2,000,000
AB Growth Fund Class K	AGFKX	NAS CM	Open End	US Equity Large Cap Growth (Growth)	B-	C+	B	Down	Y	0
AB Growth Fund Class R	AGFRX	NAS CM	Open End	US Equity Large Cap Growth (Growth)	B-	C+	B	Down	Y	0
AB International Portfolio	SIMTX	NAS CM	Open End	Global Equity Large Cap (Foreign Stock)	C	C-	C	Up	Y	10,000
AB International Portfolio Class A	AIZAX	NAS CM	Open End	Global Equity Large Cap (Foreign Stock)	C	C-	C	Up	Y	2,500
AB International Portfolio Class B	AIZBX	NAS CM	Open End	Global Equity Large Cap (Foreign Stock)	C	C-	C	Up		2,500
AB International Portfolio Class C	AIZCX	NAS CM	Open End	Global Equity Large Cap (Foreign Stock)	C	C-	C	Up	Y	2,500
AB International Small Cap Portfolio Advisor Class	IRCYX	NAS CM	Open End	Global Equity Mid/Small Cap (Small Company)	C	C-	C		Y	5,000
AB International Small Cap Portfolio Class Z	IRCZX	NAS CM	Open End	Global Equity Mid/Small Cap (Small Company)	C	C-	C		Y	0
AB International Strategic Core Portfolio Advisor Class	ISRYX	NAS CM	Open End	Global Equity Large Cap (Growth)	C	C	B		Y	0
AB International Strategic Core Portfolio Class A	ISARX	NAS CM	Open End	Global Equity Large Cap (Growth)	C	C	B		Y	2,500
AB International Strategic Core Portfolio Class C	ISCRX	NAS CM	Open End	Global Equity Large Cap (Growth)	C	C	B-		Y	2,500
AB International Strategic Equities Portfolio Advisor Cls	STEYX	NAS CM	Open End	Global Equity Large Cap (Growth)	C	C	C+		Y	10,000
AB International Strategic Equities Portfolio Class Z	STEZX	NAS CM	Open End	Global Equity Large Cap (Growth)	C	C	C+		Y	0
AB International Value Fund Advisor Class	ABIYX	NAS CM	Open End	Global Equity Large Cap (Foreign Stock)	D+	D	C-		Y	0
AB International Value Fund Class A	ABIAX	NAS CM	Open End	Global Equity Large Cap (Foreign Stock)	D+	D	D+		Y	2,500
AB International Value Fund Class B	ABIBX	NAS CM	Open End	Global Equity Large Cap (Foreign Stock)	D+	D	D+			2,500
AB International Value Fund Class C	ABICX	NAS CM	Open End	Global Equity Large Cap (Foreign Stock)	D+	D	D+		Y	2,500
AB International Value Fund Class I	AIVIX	NAS CM	Open End	Global Equity Large Cap (Foreign Stock)	D+	D	C-		Y	2,000,000
AB International Value Fund Class K	AIVKX	NAS CM	Open End	Global Equity Large Cap (Foreign Stock)	D+	D	D+		Y	0
AB International Value Fund Class R	AIVRX	NAS CM	Open End	Global Equity Large Cap (Foreign Stock)	D+	D	D+		Y	0
AB Large Cap Growth Fund Advisor Class	APGYX	NAS CM	Open End	US Equity Large Cap Growth (Growth)	B-	C+	B	Down	Y	0
AB Large Cap Growth Fund Class A	APGAX	NAS CM	Open End	US Equity Large Cap Growth (Growth)	B-	C+	B	Down	Y	2,500
AB Large Cap Growth Fund Class B	APGBX	NAS CM	Open End	US Equity Large Cap Growth (Growth)	B-	C+	B	Down		2,500
AB Large Cap Growth Fund Class C	APGCX	NAS CM	Open End	US Equity Large Cap Growth (Growth)	B-	C+	B	Down	Y	2,500
AB Large Cap Growth Fund Class I	ALLIX	NAS CM	Open End	US Equity Large Cap Growth (Growth)	B-	C+	B	Down	Y	2,000,000
AB Large Cap Growth Fund Class K	ALCKX	NAS CM	Open End	US Equity Large Cap Growth (Growth)	B-	C+	B	Down	Y	0
AB Large Cap Growth Fund Class R	ABPRX	NAS CM	Open End	US Equity Large Cap Growth (Growth)	B-	C+	B	Down	Y	0
AB Large Cap Growth Fund Class Z	APGZX	NAS CM	Open End	US Equity Large Cap Growth (Growth)	B-	C+	B	Down	Y	2,000,000
AB Multi-Manager Select 2010 Fund Advisor Class	TDBYX	NAS CM	Open End	Target Date (Asset Alloc)	B	C	A-	Up	Y	0
AB Multi-Manager Select 2010 Fund Class A	TDBAX	NAS CM	Open End	Target Date (Asset Alloc)	B	C	A-	Up	Y	2,500
AB Multi-Manager Select 2010 Fund Class C	TDBCX	NAS CM	Open End	Target Date (Asset Alloc)	B-	C	B+	Up	Y	2,500
AB Multi-Manager Select 2010 Fund Class I	TDIBX	NAS CM	Open End	Target Date (Asset Alloc)	B	C	A-	Up	Y	2,000,000
AB Multi-Manager Select 2010 Fund Class K	TDBKX	NAS CM	Open End	Target Date (Asset Alloc)	B	C	A-	Up	Y	0
AB Multi-Manager Select 2010 Fund Class R	TDBRX	NAS CM	Open End	Target Date (Asset Alloc)	B-	C	A-	Up	Y	0
AB Multi-Manager Select 2010 Fund Class Z	TDBZX	NAS CM	Open End	Target Date (Asset Alloc)	B	C	A-	Up	Y	2,000,000
AB Multi-Manager Select 2015 Fund Advisor Class	TDCYX	NAS CM	Open End	Target Date (Asset Alloc)	B	C	A-	Up	Y	0
AB Multi-Manager Select 2015 Fund Class A	TDCAX	NAS CM	Open End	Target Date (Asset Alloc)	B-	C	A-	Up	Y	2,500
AB Multi-Manager Select 2015 Fund Class C	TDCCX	NAS CM	Open End	Target Date (Asset Alloc)	B-	C	B+	Up	Y	2,500
AB Multi-Manager Select 2015 Fund Class I	TDCIX	NAS CM	Open End	Target Date (Asset Alloc)	B	C	A-	Up	Y	2,000,000
AB Multi-Manager Select 2015 Fund Class K	TDCKX	NAS CM	Open End	Target Date (Asset Alloc)	B-	C	A-	Up	Y	0
AB Multi-Manager Select 2015 Fund Class R	TDCRX	NAS CM	Open End	Target Date (Asset Alloc)	B-	C	A-	Up	Y	0
AB Multi-Manager Select 2015 Fund Class Z	TDCZX	NAS CM	Open End	Target Date (Asset Alloc)	B	C	A-	Up	Y	2,000,000
AB Multi-Manager Select 2020 Fund Advisor Class	TDDYX	NAS CM	Open End	Target Date (Asset Alloc)	B-	C	A-	Up	Y	0
AB Multi-Manager Select 2020 Fund Class A	TDDAX	NAS CM	Open End	Target Date (Asset Alloc)	B-	C	A-	Up	Y	2,500
AB Multi-Manager Select 2020 Fund Class C	TDDCX	NAS CM	Open End	Target Date (Asset Alloc)	B-	C	A-	Up	Y	2,500
AB Multi-Manager Select 2020 Fund Class I	TDDIX	NAS CM	Open End	Target Date (Asset Alloc)	B-	C	A-	Up	Y	2,000,000

★ Expanded analysis of this fund is included in Section II.

Min Additional Investment	TOTAL RETURNS 3-Month Total Return	6-Month Total Return	1-Year Total Return	3-Year Total Return	5-Year Total Return	PERFORMANCE Dividend Yield (TTM)	Expense Ratio	3-Yr Std Deviation	3-Year Beta	ASSETS NAV	Total Assets (MIL)	ASSET ALLOCATION & TURNOVER %Cash	%Stocks	%Bonds	%Other	Turnover Ratio	BULL & BEAR Last Bull Market Total Return	Last Bear Market Total Return	FEES Front End Fee (%)	Back End Fee (%)	Inception Date
	2.66	12.71	2.90	18.18	14.20	0.22	1.63	6.91	0.55	16.58	229.5	1	30	67	0	9	19.13	-10.37			Nov-03
	4.27	23.25	14.64	77.62	105.54	0	0.94	13.13	0.94	88.88	1,145	9	91	0	0	46	27.83	-16.96			Oct-96
50	4.21	23.10	14.37	76.30	102.97	0	1.2	13.14	0.94	80.56	1,145	9	91	0	0	46	27.59	-17.06	4.25		Sep-90
50	4.01	22.64	13.46	72.25	95.02	0	1.97	13.13	0.94	36.51	1,145	9	91	0	0	46	27	-17.37		4.00	Oct-87
50	4.02	22.65	13.53	72.38	95.42	0	1.95	13.13	0.94	37.25	1,145	9	91	0	0	46	27.05	-17.3		1.00	Aug-93
	4.29	23.30	14.77	78.29	106.72	0	0.83	13.14	0.94	88.56	1,145	9	91	0	0	46	27.99	-16.89			Mar-05
	4.18	23.04	14.27	76.04	102.76	0	1.26	13.13	0.94	82.81	1,145	9	91	0	0	46	27.8	-17.01			Mar-05
	4.11	22.87	13.92	74.44	99.59	0	1.56	13.13	0.94	77.89	1,145	9	91	0	0	46	27.49	-17.12			Mar-05
	2.65	13.57	-3.91	20.89	6.85	1.66	1.06	11.71	1.03	16.23	1,101	3	97	0	0	45	11.87	-25.54			Apr-99
50	2.67	13.60	-3.89	20.97	6.86	0.77	1.18	11.71	1.03	16.12	1,101	3	97	0	0	45	11.22	-25.75	4.25		Jan-04
50	2.49	13.14	-4.62	18.35	3.04	0.46	2.13	11.7	1.03	16.44	1,101	3	97	0	0	45	10.69	-25.97		4.00	Jan-04
50	2.42	13.16	-4.63	18.22	2.94	0.98	1.93	11.71	1.03	16.07	1,101	3	97	0	0	45	10.8	-25.97		1.00	Jan-04
	1.33	11.86	-7.83	25.11		1.95	1.1	12.18	1.01	10.65	1,284	3	97	0	0	81					Dec-15
	1.33	11.86	-7.75	25.13		1.95	1.1	12.13	1	10.65	1,284	3	97	0	0	81					Dec-15
	2.44	12.56	0.06	27.39		1.47	0.95	9.54	0.8	11.74	201.5	3	97	0	0	53					Jul-15
50	2.36	12.39	-0.27	26.45		1.32	1.2	9.5	0.8	11.7	201.5	3	97	0	0	53			4.25		Jul-15
50	2.20	11.96	-1.00	23.63		0.75	1.95	9.49	0.8	11.6	201.5	3	97	0	0	53				1.00	Jul-15
	1.29	11.61	-3.42	29.85		1.79	0.75	11.7	0.98	11.72	4,188	2	98	0	0	69					Dec-15
	1.29	11.60	-3.43	29.79		1.78	0.77	11.65	0.98	11.73	4,188	2	98	0	0	69					Dec-15
	-0.07	9.05	-10.59	12.62	-3.84	0.48	1.18	13.25	1.15	12.65	175.3	0	100	0	0	34	11.9	-27.85			Mar-01
50	-0.16	8.89	-10.80	11.80	-5.08	0.23	1.43	13.21	1.14	12.36	175.3	0	100	0	0	34	11.74	-27.92	4.25		Mar-01
50	-0.41	8.35	-11.58	9.14	-8.83	0	2.24	13.22	1.14	12.06	175.3	0	100	0	0	34	11.26	-28.22		4.00	Mar-01
50	-0.33	8.47	-11.41	9.32	-8.51	0	2.18	13.24	1.15	12.03	175.3	0	100	0	0	34	11.31	-28.18		1.00	Mar-01
	-0.08	9.18	-10.37	13.39	-2.73	0.68	0.99	13.25	1.15	12.36	175.3	0	100	0	0	34	12.01	-27.71			Mar-05
	-0.08	8.92	-10.75	11.99	-4.79	0.23	1.42	13.23	1.14	12.33	175.3	0	100	0	0	34	11.7	-27.85			Mar-05
	-0.16	8.79	-11.03	10.98	-6.26	0	1.73	13.26	1.15	12.25	175.3	0	100	0	0	34	11.52	-27.92			Nov-03
	4.22	21.96	13.76	71.69	102.37	0	0.66	12.26	0.89	58.97	9,074	10	90	0	0	47	27.52	-18.49			Oct-96
50	4.15	21.81	13.47	70.37	99.81	0	0.91	12.24	0.89	53.67	9,074	10	90	0	0	47	27.47	-18.59	4.25		Sep-92
50	3.93	21.31	12.57	66.52	91.95	0	1.7	12.24	0.89	38.3	9,074	10	90	0	0	47	26.74	-18.88		4.00	Sep-92
50	3.95	21.35	12.63	66.61	92.50	0	1.66	12.26	0.89	38.92	9,074	10	90	0	0	47	26.79	-18.86		1.00	May-93
	4.21	21.94	13.76	71.71	102.68	0	0.66	12.26	0.89	58.63	9,074	10	90	0	0	47	27.73	-18.45			Mar-05
	4.11	21.74	13.39	69.97	99.13	0	1	12.25	0.89	54.64	9,074	10	90	0	0	47	27.55	-18.59			Mar-05
	4.03	21.55	13.05	68.46	96.20	0	1.29	12.25	0.89	51.09	9,074	10	90	0	0	47	27.29	-18.65			Nov-03
	4.23	22.02	13.87	72.16	102.62	0	0.57	12.26	0.89	58.79	9,074	10	90	0	0	47	27.47	-18.59			Jun-15
	2.43	8.75	4.91	18.85		2.12	0.7	4.71	1	10.93	18.5	8	34	58	0	85					Dec-14
50	2.41	8.67	4.72	17.96		1.62	0.95	4.75	1.01	11.02	18.5	8	34	58	0	85			4.25		Dec-14
50	2.23	8.26	3.93	15.35		0	1.7	4.66	0.99	11	18.5	8	34	58	0	85				1.00	Dec-14
	2.48	8.85	5.00	18.87		2.69	0.7	4.74	1.01	10.33	18.5	8	34	58	0	85					Dec-14
	2.47	8.71	4.78	18.00		2.32	0.95	4.71	1	10.35	18.5	8	34	58	0	85					Dec-14
	2.36	8.58	4.41	17.03		2	1.2	4.75	1.01	10.37	18.5	8	34	58	0	85					Dec-14
	2.47	8.84	4.98	18.84		2.76	0.7	4.67	1	10.34	18.5	8	34	58	0	85					Dec-14
	2.39	9.54	4.75	21.02		2.57	0.72	5.44	1.01	10.67	47.2	11	39	50	-2	93					Dec-14
50	2.32	9.44	4.41	20.04		2.07	0.97	5.5	1.02	10.54	47.2	11	39	50	-2	93			4.25		Dec-14
50	2.15	9.08	3.66	17.43		1.49	1.72	5.49	1.01	10.45	47.2	11	39	50	-2	93				1.00	Dec-14
	2.48	9.57	4.60	20.93		2.64	0.72	5.45	1.01	10.3	47.2	11	39	50	-2	93					Dec-14
	2.38	9.45	4.40	20.08		2.19	0.97	5.47	1.01	10.3	47.2	11	39	50	-2	93					Dec-14
	2.38	9.34	4.21	19.27		1.86	1.22	5.48	1.01	10.3	47.2	11	39	50	-2	93					Dec-14
	2.39	9.49	4.64	20.90		2.67	0.72	5.52	1.02	10.26	47.2	11	39	50	-2	93					Dec-14
	2.49	10.34	4.69	23.39		2.57	0.7	6.17	1.02	10.67	101.9	9	45	44	2	84					Dec-14
50	2.49	10.12	4.39	22.45		2.22	0.95	6.19	1.02	10.66	101.9	9	45	44	2	84			4.25		Dec-14
50	2.33	9.79	3.62	19.77		1.53	1.7	6.2	1.02	10.54	101.9	9	45	44	2	84				1.00	Dec-14
	2.58	10.28	4.63	23.22		2.52	0.7	6.19	1.02	10.72	101.9	9	45	44	2	84					Dec-14

	MARKET			FUND TYPE, CATEGORY & OBJECTIVE	RATINGS				MINIMUMS	
Fund Name	Ticker Symbol	Traded On	Fund Type	Category and (Prospectus Objective)	Overall Rating	Reward Rating	Risk Rating	Recent Up/ Downgrade	Open to New Investors	Min Initial Investment
AB Multi-Manager Select 2020 Fund Class K	TDDKX	NAS CM	Open End	Target Date (Asset Alloc)	B-	C	A-	Up	Y	0
AB Multi-Manager Select 2020 Fund Class R	TDDRX	NAS CM	Open End	Target Date (Asset Alloc)	B-	C	A-	Up	Y	0
AB Multi-Manager Select 2020 Fund Class Z	TDDZX	NAS CM	Open End	Target Date (Asset Alloc)	B-	C	A-	Up	Y	2,000,000
AB Multi-Manager Select 2025 Fund Advisor Class	TDGYX	NAS CM	Open End	Target Date (Asset Alloc)	B-	C	A-	Up	Y	0
AB Multi-Manager Select 2025 Fund Class A	TDAGX	NAS CM	Open End	Target Date (Asset Alloc)	B-	C	A-	Up	Y	2,500
AB Multi-Manager Select 2025 Fund Class C	TDCGX	NAS CM	Open End	Target Date (Asset Alloc)	B-	C	A-	Up	Y	2,500
AB Multi-Manager Select 2025 Fund Class I	TDIGX	NAS CM	Open End	Target Date (Asset Alloc)	B-	C	A-	Up	Y	2,000,000
AB Multi-Manager Select 2025 Fund Class K	TDGKX	NAS CM	Open End	Target Date (Asset Alloc)	B-	C	A-	Up	Y	0
AB Multi-Manager Select 2025 Fund Class R	TDGRX	NAS CM	Open End	Target Date (Asset Alloc)	B-	C	A-	Up	Y	0
AB Multi-Manager Select 2025 Fund Class Z	TDGZX	NAS CM	Open End	Target Date (Asset Alloc)	B-	C	A-	Up	Y	2,000,000
AB Multi-Manager Select 2030 Fund Advisor Class	TDYHX	NAS CM	Open End	Target Date (Asset Alloc)	B-	C	A-	Up	Y	0
AB Multi-Manager Select 2030 Fund Class A	TDHAX	NAS CM	Open End	Target Date (Asset Alloc)	B-	C	B+	Up	Y	2,500
AB Multi-Manager Select 2030 Fund Class C	TDHCX	NAS CM	Open End	Target Date (Asset Alloc)	B-	C	B+	Up	Y	2,500
AB Multi-Manager Select 2030 Fund Class I	TDIHX	NAS CM	Open End	Target Date (Asset Alloc)	B-	C	A-	Up	Y	2,000,000
AB Multi-Manager Select 2030 Fund Class K	TDHKX	NAS CM	Open End	Target Date (Asset Alloc)	B-	C	B+	Up	Y	0
AB Multi-Manager Select 2030 Fund Class R	TDHRX	NAS CM	Open End	Target Date (Asset Alloc)	B-	C	B+	Up	Y	0
AB Multi-Manager Select 2030 Fund Class Z	TDHZX	NAS CM	Open End	Target Date (Asset Alloc)	B-	C	A-	Up	Y	2,000,000
AB Multi-Manager Select 2035 Fund Advisor Class	TDMYX	NAS CM	Open End	Target Date (Asset Alloc)	B-	C	B+	Up	Y	0
AB Multi-Manager Select 2035 Fund Class A	TDMAX	NAS CM	Open End	Target Date (Asset Alloc)	B-	C	B+	Up	Y	2,500
AB Multi-Manager Select 2035 Fund Class C	TDMCX	NAS CM	Open End	Target Date (Asset Alloc)	B-	C	B+	Up	Y	2,500
AB Multi-Manager Select 2035 Fund Class I	TDIMX	NAS CM	Open End	Target Date (Asset Alloc)	B-	C	B+	Up	Y	2,000,000
AB Multi-Manager Select 2035 Fund Class K	TDMKX	NAS CM	Open End	Target Date (Asset Alloc)	B-	C	B+	Up	Y	0
AB Multi-Manager Select 2035 Fund Class R	TDRMX	NAS CM	Open End	Target Date (Asset Alloc)	B-	C	B+	Up	Y	0
AB Multi-Manager Select 2035 Fund Class Z	TDMZX	NAS CM	Open End	Target Date (Asset Alloc)	B-	C	B+	Up	Y	2,000,000
AB Multi-Manager Select 2040 Fund Advisor Class	TDJYX	NAS CM	Open End	Target Date (Asset Alloc)	B-	C	B+	Up	Y	0
AB Multi-Manager Select 2040 Fund Class A	TDJAX	NAS CM	Open End	Target Date (Asset Alloc)	B-	C	B+	Up	Y	2,500
AB Multi-Manager Select 2040 Fund Class C	TDJCX	NAS CM	Open End	Target Date (Asset Alloc)	B-	C	B+	Up	Y	2,500
AB Multi-Manager Select 2040 Fund Class I	TDJIX	NAS CM	Open End	Target Date (Asset Alloc)	B-	C	B+	Up	Y	2,000,000
AB Multi-Manager Select 2040 Fund Class K	TDJKX	NAS CM	Open End	Target Date (Asset Alloc)	B-	C	B+	Up	Y	0
AB Multi-Manager Select 2040 Fund Class R	TDJRX	NAS CM	Open End	Target Date (Asset Alloc)	B-	C	B+	Up	Y	0
AB Multi-Manager Select 2040 Fund Class Z	TDJZX	NAS CM	Open End	Target Date (Asset Alloc)	B-	C	B+	Up	Y	2,000,000
AB Multi-Manager Select 2045 Fund Advisor Class	TDNYX	NAS CM	Open End	Target Date (Asset Alloc)	B-	C	B+	Up	Y	0
AB Multi-Manager Select 2045 Fund Class A	TDNAX	NAS CM	Open End	Target Date (Asset Alloc)	B-	C	B+	Up	Y	2,500
AB Multi-Manager Select 2045 Fund Class C	TDNCX	NAS CM	Open End	Target Date (Asset Alloc)	B-	C	B	Up	Y	2,500
AB Multi-Manager Select 2045 Fund Class I	TDNIX	NAS CM	Open End	Target Date (Asset Alloc)	B-	C	B+	Up	Y	2,000,000
AB Multi-Manager Select 2045 Fund Class K	TDNKX	NAS CM	Open End	Target Date (Asset Alloc)	B-	C	B+	Up	Y	0
AB Multi-Manager Select 2045 Fund Class R	TDNRX	NAS CM	Open End	Target Date (Asset Alloc)	B-	C	B	Up	Y	0
AB Multi-Manager Select 2045 Fund Class Z	TDNZX	NAS CM	Open End	Target Date (Asset Alloc)	B-	C	B+	Up	Y	2,000,000
AB Multi-Manager Select 2050 Fund Advisor Class	TDLYX	NAS CM	Open End	Target Date (Asset Alloc)	B-	C	B	Up	Y	0
AB Multi-Manager Select 2050 Fund Class A	TDLAX	NAS CM	Open End	Target Date (Asset Alloc)	B-	C	B	Up	Y	2,500
AB Multi-Manager Select 2050 Fund Class C	TDCLX	NAS CM	Open End	Target Date (Asset Alloc)	B-	C	B	Up	Y	2,500
AB Multi-Manager Select 2050 Fund Class I	TDLIX	NAS CM	Open End	Target Date (Asset Alloc)	B-	C	B	Up	Y	2,000,000
AB Multi-Manager Select 2050 Fund Class K	TDLKX	NAS CM	Open End	Target Date (Asset Alloc)	B-	C	B	Up	Y	0
AB Multi-Manager Select 2050 Fund Class R	TDLRX	NAS CM	Open End	Target Date (Asset Alloc)	B-	C	B	Up	Y	0
AB Multi-Manager Select 2050 Fund Class Z	TDLZX	NAS CM	Open End	Target Date (Asset Alloc)	B-	C	B	Up	Y	2,000,000
AB Multi-Manager Select 2055 Fund Advisor Class	TDPYX	NAS CM	Open End	Target Date (Asset Alloc)	B-	C	B	Up	Y	0
AB Multi-Manager Select 2055 Fund Class A	TDAPX	NAS CM	Open End	Target Date (Asset Alloc)	B-	C	B	Up	Y	2,500
AB Multi-Manager Select 2055 Fund Class C	TDCPX	NAS CM	Open End	Target Date (Asset Alloc)	B-	C	B	Up	Y	2,500
AB Multi-Manager Select 2055 Fund Class I	TDIPX	NAS CM	Open End	Target Date (Asset Alloc)	B-	C	B	Up	Y	2,000,000
AB Multi-Manager Select 2055 Fund Class K	TDPKX	NAS CM	Open End	Target Date (Asset Alloc)	B-	C	B	Up	Y	0
AB Multi-Manager Select 2055 Fund Class R	TDPRX	NAS CM	Open End	Target Date (Asset Alloc)	B-	C	B	Up	Y	0
AB Multi-Manager Select 2055 Fund Class Z	TDPZX	NAS CM	Open End	Target Date (Asset Alloc)	B-	C	B	Up	Y	2,000,000

★ Expanded analysis of this fund is included in Section II.

	TOTAL RETURNS					PERFORMANCE				ASSETS		ASSET ALLOCATION & TURNOVER					BULL & BEAR		FEES		
Min Additional Investment	3-Month Total Return	6-Month Total Return	1-Year Total Return	3-Year Total Return	5-Year Total Return	Dividend Yield (TTM)	Expense Ratio	3-Yr Std Deviation	3-Year Beta	NAV	Total Assets (MIL)	%Cash	%Stocks	%Bonds	%Other	Turnover Ratio	Last Bull Market Total Return	Last Bear Market Total Return	Front End Fee (%)	Back End Fee (%)	Inception Date
	2.45	10.12	4.31	22.48		2.2	0.95	6.17	1.02	10.44	101.9	9	45	44	2	84					Dec-14
	2.36	9.95	4.04	21.55		2.22	1.2	6.16	1.02	10.38	101.9	9	45	44	2	84					Dec-14
	2.55	10.38	4.63	23.43		2.65	0.7	6.14	1.01	10.42	101.9	9	45	44	2	84					Dec-14
	2.63	11.33	4.49	26.96		2.5	0.67	7.08	1	10.9	158.2	6	52	37	4	80					Dec-14
50	2.54	11.23	4.29	25.99		2.16	0.92	7.09	1	10.89	158.2	6	52	37	4	80			4.25		Dec-14
50	2.36	10.76	3.41	23.11		1.24	1.67	7.12	1.01	10.8	158.2	6	52	37	4	80				1.00	Dec-14
	2.59	11.26	4.42	26.79		2.49	0.67	7.08	1	10.67	158.2	6	52	37	4	80					Dec-14
	2.50	11.16	4.22	25.99		2.15	0.92	7.05	1	10.65	158.2	6	52	37	4	80					Dec-14
	2.52	11.05	3.96	25.05		2.33	1.17	7.1	1	10.55	158.2	6	52	37	4	80					Dec-14
	2.60	11.30	4.53	26.95		2.58	0.67	7.1	1.01	10.63	158.2	6	52	37	4	80					Dec-14
	2.66	12.17	4.40	30.09		2.38	0.66	8.02	0.98	11.15	136.1	4	60	29	6	73					Dec-14
50	2.57	12.07	4.18	29.08		2.03	0.91	8.02	0.98	11.14	136.1	4	60	29	6	73			4.25		Dec-14
50	2.42	11.68	3.47	26.37		1.72	1.66	8.04	0.99	10.99	136.1	4	60	29	6	73				1.00	Dec-14
	2.72	12.21	4.49	30.18		2.34	0.66	8.03	0.98	10.93	136.1	4	60	29	6	73					Dec-14
	2.63	12.13	4.24	29.18		2.05	0.91	8.02	0.98	10.9	136.1	4	60	29	6	73					Dec-14
	2.55	11.88	3.86	28.10		2.04	1.16	8.02	0.98	10.83	136.1	4	60	29	6	73					Dec-14
	2.63	12.26	4.43	30.17		2.45	0.66	7.98	0.98	10.89	136.1	4	60	29	6	73					Dec-14
	3.05	13.57	4.78	34.27		2.18	0.64	8.95	0.98	11.46	135.5	1	69	23	6	71					Dec-14
50	2.97	13.40	4.50	33.22		1.87	0.89	8.94	0.98	11.42	135.5	1	69	23	6	71			4.25		Dec-14
50	2.73	13.03	3.73	30.22		1.51	1.64	8.94	0.98	11.27	135.5	1	69	23	6	71				1.00	Dec-14
	3.01	13.58	4.74	34.20		2.19	0.64	8.93	0.98	11.29	135.5	1	69	23	6	71					Dec-14
	2.95	13.44	4.46	33.06		1.86	0.89	8.95	0.98	11.14	135.5	1	69	23	6	71					Dec-14
	2.88	13.31	4.26	32.19		1.92	1.14	8.97	0.98	11.06	135.5	1	69	23	6	71					Dec-14
	2.96	13.57	4.66	34.07		2.26	0.64	8.94	0.98	11.13	135.5	1	69	23	6	71					Dec-14
	3.27	14.66	4.87	36.44		1.96	0.63	9.68	0.99	11.34	86.5	-1	78	14	8	85					Dec-14
50	3.19	14.48	4.58	35.35		1.65	0.88	9.69	0.99	11.3	86.5	-1	78	14	8	85			4.25		Dec-14
50	3.05	14.13	3.83	32.44		1.3	1.63	9.72	0.99	11.14	86.5	-1	78	14	8	85				1.00	Dec-14
	3.26	14.58	4.78	36.34		1.99	0.63	9.72	0.99	11.08	86.5	-1	78	14	8	85					Dec-14
	3.18	14.43	4.54	35.35		1.63	0.88	9.72	0.99	11.02	86.5	-1	78	14	8	85					Dec-14
	3.20	14.42	4.35	34.48		1.69	1.13	9.71	0.99	10.95	86.5	-1	78	14	8	85					Dec-14
	3.38	14.68	4.87	36.45		2.05	0.63	9.69	0.99	11.01	86.5	-1	78	14	8	85					Dec-14
	3.46	15.14	5.11	38.07		1.99	0.63	10.02	0.99	11.63	76.0	1	80	11	8	77					Dec-14
50	3.40	15.03	4.75	36.83		1.62	0.88	10.07	0.99	11.55	76.0	1	80	11	8	77			4.25		Dec-14
50	3.13	14.54	3.97	33.82		0.9	1.63	10.03	0.99	11.5	76.0	1	80	11	8	77				1.00	Dec-14
	3.47	15.15	5.01	37.84		2	0.63	10.01	0.99	11.32	76.0	1	80	11	8	77					Dec-14
	3.41	14.95	4.72	36.94		1.67	0.88	10.04	0.99	11.22	76.0	1	80	11	8	77					Dec-14
	3.32	14.90	4.51	35.86		1.27	1.13	10.04	0.99	11.18	76.0	1	80	11	8	77					Dec-14
	3.51	15.22	5.05	37.89		2.08	0.63	10.08	1	11.2	76.0	1	80	11	8	77					Dec-14
	3.51	15.40	4.96	38.32		1.78	0.63	10.15	0.98	12.06	35.5	0	82	10	8	79					Dec-14
50	3.43	15.21	4.77	37.31		1.26	0.88	10.2	0.98	12.04	35.5	0	82	10	8	79			4.25		Dec-14
50	3.30	14.87	3.99	34.26		0.45	1.63	10.23	0.98	11.89	35.5	0	82	10	8	79				1.00	Dec-14
	3.46	15.36	4.97	38.36		1.91	0.63	10.2	0.98	11.64	35.5	0	82	10	8	79					Dec-14
	3.45	15.31	4.72	37.29		1.59	0.88	10.2	0.98	11.37	35.5	0	82	10	8	79					Dec-14
	3.38	15.07	4.43	36.19		1.56	1.13	10.2	0.98	11.3	35.5	0	82	10	8	79					Dec-14
	3.55	15.43	5.02	38.40		1.99	0.63	10.18	0.98	11.37	35.5	0	82	10	8	79					Dec-14
	3.52	15.45	4.95	38.32		1.73	0.63	10.22	0.98	12.03	41.7	1	82	10	8	73					Dec-14
50	3.48	15.33	4.71	37.28		1.43	0.88	10.22	0.98	11.88	41.7	1	82	10	8	73			4.25		Dec-14
50	3.34	14.87	3.95	34.28		0.71	1.63	10.19	0.97	11.74	41.7	1	82	10	8	73				1.00	Dec-14
	3.50	15.43	5.01	38.18		1.9	0.63	10.18	0.97	11.52	41.7	1	82	10	8	73					Dec-14
	3.45	15.31	4.76	37.29		1.59	0.88	10.22	0.98	11.37	41.7	1	82	10	8	73					Dec-14
	3.38	15.18	4.47	36.27		1.57	1.13	10.25	0.98	11.3	41.7	1	82	10	8	73					Dec-14
	3.55	15.43	4.96	38.35		1.98	0.63	10.19	0.97	11.37	41.7	1	82	10	8	73					Dec-14

	MARKET			FUND TYPE, CATEGORY & OBJECTIVE	RATINGS				MINIMUMS	
Fund Name	Ticker Symbol	Traded On	Fund Type	Category and (Prospectus Objective)	Overall Rating	Reward Rating	Risk Rating	Recent Up/ Downgrade	Open to New Investors	Min Initial Investment
AB Multi-Manager Select 2060 Fund Advisor Class	TDQYX	NAS CM	Open End	Target Date (Asset Alloc)	U	U	U		Y	0
AB Multi-Manager Select 2060 Fund Class A	TDQAX	NAS CM	Open End	Target Date (Asset Alloc)	U	U	U		Y	2,500
AB Multi-Manager Select 2060 Fund Class C	TDQCX	NAS CM	Open End	Target Date (Asset Alloc)	U	U	U		Y	2,500
AB Multi-Manager Select 2060 Fund Class I	TDQIX	NAS CM	Open End	Target Date (Asset Alloc)	U	U	U		Y	2,000,000
AB Multi-Manager Select 2060 Fund Class K	TDQKX	NAS CM	Open End	Target Date (Asset Alloc)	U	U	U		Y	0
AB Multi-Manager Select 2060 Fund Class R	TDQRX	NAS CM	Open End	Target Date (Asset Alloc)	U	U	U		Y	0
AB Multi-Manager Select 2060 Fund Class Z	TDQZX	NAS CM	Open End	Target Date (Asset Alloc)	U	U	U		Y	2,000,000
AB Multi-Manager Select Retirement Allocation Advisor Cls	TDAYX	NAS CM	Open End	Target Date (Asset Alloc)	B-	C	A-		Y	0
AB Multi-Manager Select Retirement Allocation Fund Class A	TDAAX	NAS CM	Open End	Target Date (Asset Alloc)	B-	C	A-		Y	2,500
AB Multi-Manager Select Retirement Allocation Fund Class C	TDACX	NAS CM	Open End	Target Date (Asset Alloc)	B-	C	B+	Up	Y	2,500
AB Multi-Manager Select Retirement Allocation Fund Class I	TDAIX	NAS CM	Open End	Target Date (Asset Alloc)	B-	C	A-		Y	2,000,000
AB Multi-Manager Select Retirement Allocation Fund Class K	TDAKX	NAS CM	Open End	Target Date (Asset Alloc)	B-	C	A-		Y	0
AB Multi-Manager Select Retirement Allocation Fund Class R	TDARX	NAS CM	Open End	Target Date (Asset Alloc)	B-	C	B+	Up	Y	0
AB Multi-Manager Select Retirement Allocation Fund Class Z	TDAZX	NAS CM	Open End	Target Date (Asset Alloc)	B-	C	A-		Y	2,000,000
AB Relative Value Fund Advisor Class	CBBYX	NAS CM	Open End	US Equity Large Cap Value (Growth & Income)	B-	C	B+		Y	0
AB Relative Value Fund Class A	CABDX	NAS CM	Open End	US Equity Large Cap Value (Growth & Income)	B-	C	B+		Y	2,500
AB Relative Value Fund Class B	CBBDX	NAS CM	Open End	US Equity Large Cap Value (Growth & Income)	B-	C	B			2,500
AB Relative Value Fund Class C	CBBCX	NAS CM	Open End	US Equity Large Cap Value (Growth & Income)	B-	C	B		Y	2,500
AB Relative Value Fund Class I	CBBIX	NAS CM	Open End	US Equity Large Cap Value (Growth & Income)	B-	C	B+		Y	2,000,000
AB Relative Value Fund Class K	CBBKX	NAS CM	Open End	US Equity Large Cap Value (Growth & Income)	B-	C	B+		Y	0
AB Relative Value Fund Class R	CBBRX	NAS CM	Open End	US Equity Large Cap Value (Growth & Income)	B-	C	B		Y	0
AB Relative Value Fund Class Z	CBBZX	NAS CM	Open End	US Equity Large Cap Value (Growth & Income)	B-	C	B+		Y	2,000,000
AB Select US Equity Portfolio Advisor Class	AUUYX	NAS CM	Open End	US Equity Large Cap Growth (Growth)	B-	C+	B		Y	0
AB Select US Equity Portfolio Class A	AUUAX	NAS CM	Open End	US Equity Large Cap Growth (Growth)	B-	C	B		Y	2,500
AB Select US Equity Portfolio Class C	AUUCX	NAS CM	Open End	US Equity Large Cap Growth (Growth)	B-	C	B	Up	Y	2,500
AB Select US Equity Portfolio Class I	AUUIX	NAS CM	Open End	US Equity Large Cap Growth (Growth)	B-	C+	B		Y	2,000,000
AB Select US Equity Portfolio Class K	AUUKX	NAS CM	Open End	US Equity Large Cap Growth (Growth)	B-	C	B		Y	0
AB Select US Equity Portfolio Class R	AUURX	NAS CM	Open End	US Equity Large Cap Growth (Growth)	B-	C	B	Up	Y	0
AB Select US Long/Short Portfolio Advisor Class	ASYLX	NAS CM	Open End	Long/Short Equity (Growth)	B	C	A-	Up	Y	0
AB Select US Long/Short Portfolio Class A	ASLAX	NAS CM	Open End	Long/Short Equity (Growth)	B	C	A-	Up	Y	2,500
AB Select US Long/Short Portfolio Class C	ASCLX	NAS CM	Open End	Long/Short Equity (Growth)	B-	C	A-	Up	Y	2,500
AB Select US Long/Short Portfolio Class I	ASILX	NAS CM	Open End	Long/Short Equity (Growth)	B	C	A-	Up	Y	2,000,000
AB Select US Long/Short Portfolio Class K	ASLKX	NAS CM	Open End	Long/Short Equity (Growth)	B	C	A-	Up	Y	0
AB Select US Long/Short Portfolio Class R	ASRLX	NAS CM	Open End	Long/Short Equity (Growth)	B-	C	A-		Y	0
AB Small Cap Core Portfolio Advisor Class	SCRYX	NAS CM	Open End	US Equity Small Cap (Small Company)	C	C	C+		Y	5,000
AB Small Cap Core Portfolio Class Z	SCRZX	NAS CM	Open End	US Equity Small Cap (Small Company)	C	C	C+		Y	0
AB Small Cap Growth Portfolio Advisor Class	QUAYX	NAS CM	Open End	US Equity Small Cap (Small Company)	C+	C+	C+	Down		0
AB Small Cap Growth Portfolio Class A	QUASX	NAS CM	Open End	US Equity Small Cap (Small Company)	C+	C+	C+	Down		2,500
AB Small Cap Growth Portfolio Class B	QUABX	NAS CM	Open End	US Equity Small Cap (Small Company)	C+	C+	C+	Down		2,500
AB Small Cap Growth Portfolio Class C	QUACX	NAS CM	Open End	US Equity Small Cap (Small Company)	C+	C+	C+	Down		2,500
AB Small Cap Growth Portfolio Class I	QUAIX	NAS CM	Open End	US Equity Small Cap (Small Company)	C+	C+	C+	Down		2,000,000
AB Small Cap Growth Portfolio Class K	QUAKX	NAS CM	Open End	US Equity Small Cap (Small Company)	C+	C+	C+	Down		0
AB Small Cap Growth Portfolio Class R	QUARX	NAS CM	Open End	US Equity Small Cap (Small Company)	C+	C+	C+	Down		0
AB Small Cap Growth Portfolio Class Z	QUAZX	NAS CM	Open End	US Equity Small Cap (Small Company)	C+	C+	C+	Down	Y	2,000,000
AB Small Cap Value Portfolio Advisor Class	SCYVX	NAS CM	Open End	US Equity Small Cap (Small Company)	C	C-	C		Y	0
AB Small Cap Value Portfolio Class A	SCAVX	NAS CM	Open End	US Equity Small Cap (Small Company)	C	C-	C		Y	2,500
AB Small Cap Value Portfolio Class C	SCCVX	NAS CM	Open End	US Equity Small Cap (Small Company)	C	C-	C		Y	2,500
AB Sustainable Global Thematic Fund Advisor Class	ATEYX	NAS CM	Open End	Global Equity Large Cap (Growth)	C+	C	B		Y	0
AB Sustainable Global Thematic Fund Class A	ALTFX	NAS CM	Open End	Global Equity Large Cap (Growth)	C+	C	B		Y	2,500
AB Sustainable Global Thematic Fund Class B	ATEBX	NAS CM	Open End	Global Equity Large Cap (Growth)	C+	C	B			2,500
AB Sustainable Global Thematic Fund Class C	ATECX	NAS CM	Open End	Global Equity Large Cap (Growth)	C+	C	B		Y	2,500
AB Sustainable Global Thematic Fund Class I	AGTIX	NAS CM	Open End	Global Equity Large Cap (Growth)	C+	C	B		Y	2,000,000

★ Expanded analysis of this fund is included in Section II.

	TOTAL RETURNS					PERFORMANCE				ASSETS		ASSET ALLOCATION & TURNOVER					BULL & BEAR		FEES		
Min Additional Investment	3-Month Total Return	6-Month Total Return	1-Year Total Return	3-Year Total Return	5-Year Total Return	Dividend Yield (TTM)	Expense Ratio	3-Yr Std Deviation	3-Year Beta	NAV	Total Assets (MIL)	%Cash	%Stocks	%Bonds	%Other	Turnover Ratio	Last Bull Market Total Return	Last Bear Market Total Return	Front End Fee (%)	Back End Fee (%)	Inception Date
	3.87						0.63			10.73	0.30	0	82	10	8						Feb-19
50	3.87						0.88			10.72	0.30	0	82	10	8				4.25		Feb-19
50	3.68						1.63			10.69	0.30	0	82	10	8					1.00	Feb-19
	3.87						0.63			10.73	0.30	0	82	10	8						Feb-19
	3.87						0.88			10.72	0.30	0	82	10	8						Feb-19
	3.77						1.13			10.71	0.30	0	82	10	8						Feb-19
	3.87						0.63			10.73	0.30	0	82	10	8						Feb-19
	2.28	7.50	4.85	15.11		1.82	0.68	3.75	0.91	11.18	11.0	9	26	59	4	98					Dec-14
50	2.18	7.36	4.57	14.24		0.24	0.93	3.75	0.92	11.23	11.0	9	26	59	4	98			4.25		Dec-14
50	1.96	6.98	3.75	11.71		0	1.68	3.7	0.9	10.88	11.0	9	26	59	4	98				1.00	Dec-14
	2.22	7.41	4.76	14.99		2.31	0.68	3.72	0.91	10.57	11.0	9	26	59	4	98					Dec-14
	2.17	7.38	4.54	14.24		2.07	0.93	3.7	0.9	10.33	11.0	9	26	59	4	98					Dec-14
	2.08	7.20	4.28	13.28		1.82	1.18	3.66	0.89	10.27	11.0	9	26	59	4	98					Dec-14
	2.27	7.49	4.91	15.17		2.49	0.68	3.72	0.91	10.33	11.0	9	26	59	4	98					Dec-14
	3.57	15.30	8.43	43.05	52.09	1.37	0.65	11.81	0.96	5.5	1,816	11	89	0	0	110	26.83	-15.76			Oct-96
50	3.61	15.22	8.15	42.01	50.17	1.09	0.9	11.74	0.95	5.45	1,816	11	89	0	0	110	26.93	-16.07	4.25		Jul-32
50	3.39	14.64	7.23	38.82	44.51	0.07	1.65	11.79	0.96	5.48	1,816	11	89	0	0	110	25.94	-16.2		4.00	Feb-91
50	3.42	14.79	7.41	38.74	44.87	0.32	1.65	11.72	0.95	5.43	1,816	11	89	0	0	110	26.37	-16.39		1.00	May-93
	3.53	15.11	8.30	43.08	52.25	1.33	0.65	11.76	0.96	5.56	1,816	11	89	0	0	110	26.94	-15.84			Mar-05
	3.46	15.20	8.07	41.98	50.21	1.12	0.9	11.7	0.95	5.38	1,816	11	89	0	0	110	26.54	-15.89			Mar-05
	3.48	15.05	7.89	40.81	48.26	0.79	1.15	11.81	0.96	5.35	1,816	11	89	0	0	110	26.27	-15.97			Nov-03
	3.73	15.35	8.44	43.18	52.28	1.43	0.61	11.74	0.95	5.56	1,816	11	89	0	0	110	26.93	-16.07			Oct-13
	5.26	18.50	9.33	49.54	62.52	0.51	1.22	11.56	0.93	16.78	225.6	4	96	0	0	236					Dec-11
50	5.13	18.30	9.07	48.36	60.50	0.27	1.47	11.58	0.93	16.8	225.6	4	96	0	0	236			4.25		Dec-11
50	4.98	17.84	8.26	45.15	54.65	0	2.23	11.55	0.93	15.78	225.6	4	96	0	0	236				1.00	Dec-11
	5.26	18.48	9.38	49.56	62.59	0.52	1.23	11.56	0.93	16.6	225.6	4	96	0	0	236					Dec-11
	5.19	18.24	8.99	48.04	59.82	0	1.56	11.6	0.94	16.59	225.6	4	96	0	0	236					Dec-11
	5.13	18.10	8.76	47.15	58.26	0.05	1.78	11.58	0.93	16.37	225.6	4	96	0	0	236					Dec-11
	3.56	10.74	6.23	27.87	28.86	0	1.71	7.22	0.57	12.78	1,097	38	65	-3	0	291					Dec-12
50	3.46	10.59	5.93	26.86	27.19	0	1.95	7.22	0.57	12.53	1,097	38	65	-3	0	291			4.25		Dec-12
50	3.31	10.23	5.10	24.02	22.53	0	2.7	7.23	0.57	11.85	1,097	38	65	-3	0	291				1.00	Dec-12
	3.55	10.81	6.22	28.02	29.23	0	1.65	7.2	0.57	12.81	1,097	38	65	-3	0	291					Dec-12
	3.46	10.59	5.93	26.74	27.29	0	1.97	7.26	0.57	12.53	1,097	38	65	-3	0	291					Dec-12
	3.44	10.51	5.69	25.78	25.69	0	2.22	7.22	0.57	12.3	1,097	38	65	-3	0	291					Dec-12
	2.68	17.62	-5.17	33.08		0.23	0.92	17.72	1.03	11.08	963.8	1	99	0	0	102					Dec-15
	2.78	17.74	-5.07	33.20		0.25	0.86	17.73	1.03	11.08	963.8	1	99	0	0	102					Dec-15
	7.08	32.27	10.59	95.34	79.85	0.02	0.9	18.08	1	62.09	2,076	3	97	0	0	65	36.78	-24.26			Oct-96
50	7.02	32.10	10.31	93.92	77.64	0	1.15	18.07	1	56.08	2,076	3	97	0	0	65	36.59	-24.35	4.25		Feb-69
50	6.82	31.60	9.45	89.62	70.58	0	1.95	18.05	1	32.4	2,076	3	97	0	0	65	35.89	-24.58		4.00	Sep-90
50	6.82	31.59	9.50	89.61	71.04	0	1.9	18.05	1	33.03	2,076	3	97	0	0	65	35.96	-24.58		1.00	May-93
	7.10	32.29	10.59	95.40	80.22	0.02	0.91	18.09	1	61.78	2,076	3	97	0	0	65	36.91	-24.24			Mar-05
	7.04	32.15	10.38	94.02	77.80	0	1.11	18.08	1	57.74	2,076	3	97	0	0	65	36.62	-24.33			Mar-05
	6.91	31.83	9.88	91.75	74.56	0	1.55	18.07	1	53.83	2,076	3	97	0	0	65	36.37	-24.43			Mar-05
	7.13	32.33	10.69	95.93	80.22	0.03	0.82	18.09	1	62.05	2,076	3	97	0	0	65	36.59	-24.35			Jun-15
	2.72	15.59	-7.35	31.46		0.2	1	18.06	1.03	12.08	340.3	1	99	0	0	42					Dec-14
50	2.66	15.34	-7.56	30.40		0	1.25	17.99	1.02	11.95	340.3	1	99	0	0	42			4.25		Dec-14
50	2.48	14.95	-8.31	27.56		0	2	17.99	1.02	11.53	340.3	1	99	0	0	42				1.00	Dec-14
	5.98	21.98	9.31	54.65	55.55	0.97	1.03	12.41	1.01	125.67	1,039	6	94	0	0	23	16.83	-29.75			Oct-96
50	5.92	21.83	9.04	53.48	53.58	0.77	1.28	12.41	1.01	118.17	1,039	6	94	0	0	23	16.62	-29.84	4.25		Mar-82
50	5.71	21.34	8.16	49.99	47.49	0.17	1.58	12.4	1	95.32	1,039	6	94	0	0	23	16.07	-30.07		4.00	May-93
50	5.71	21.36	8.23	50.03	47.88	0.27	2.03	12.4	1.01	95.93	1,039	6	94	0	0	23	16.13	-30.06		1.00	May-93
	6.01	22.05	9.42	55.36	56.99	1.07	0.93	12.41	1.01	126.08	1,039	6	94	0	0	23	17.1	-29.67			Mar-05

	MARKET		FUND TYPE, CATEGORY & OBJECTIVE		RATINGS				MINIMUMS	
Fund Name	Ticker Symbol	Traded On	Fund Type	Category and (Prospectus Objective)	Overall Rating	Reward Rating	Risk Rating	Recent Up/ Downgrade	Open to New Investors	Min Initial Investment
AB Sustainable Global Thematic Fund Class K	ATEKX	NAS CM	Open End	Global Equity Large Cap (Growth)	C+	C	B		Y	0
AB Sustainable Global Thematic Fund Class R	ATERX	NAS CM	Open End	Global Equity Large Cap (Growth)	C+	C	B		Y	0
AB Sustainable International Thematic Fund Advisor Class	AWPYX	NAS CM	Open End	Global Equity Large Cap (Foreign Stock)	C	C	C+		Y	0
AB Sustainable International Thematic Fund Class A	AWPAX	NAS CM	Open End	Global Equity Large Cap (Foreign Stock)	C	C	C+		Y	2,500
AB Sustainable International Thematic Fund Class B	AWPBX	NAS CM	Open End	Global Equity Large Cap (Foreign Stock)	C	C-	C+			2,500
AB Sustainable International Thematic Fund Class C	AWPCX	NAS CM	Open End	Global Equity Large Cap (Foreign Stock)	C	C-	C+		Y	2,500
AB Sustainable International Thematic Fund Class I	AWPIX	NAS CM	Open End	Global Equity Large Cap (Foreign Stock)	C	C	C+		Y	2,000,000
AB Sustainable International Thematic Fund Class K	AWPKX	NAS CM	Open End	Global Equity Large Cap (Foreign Stock)	C	C	C+		Y	0
AB Sustainable International Thematic Fund Class R	AWPRX	NAS CM	Open End	Global Equity Large Cap (Foreign Stock)	C	C	C+		Y	0
AB Tax-Managed All Market Income Portfolio Advisor Class	AGIYX	NAS CM	Open End	Cautious Alloc (Balanced)	B-	C+	B		Y	0
AB Tax-Managed All Market Income Portfolio Class A	AGIAX	NAS CM	Open End	Cautious Alloc (Balanced)	B-	C+	B		Y	2,500
AB Tax-Managed All Market Income Portfolio Class B	AGIBX	NAS CM	Open End	Cautious Alloc (Balanced)	B-	C	B	Up		2,500
AB Tax-Managed All Market Income Portfolio Class C	AGICX	NAS CM	Open End	Cautious Alloc (Balanced)	B-	C	B	Up	Y	2,500
AB Tax-Managed International Portfolio	SNIVX	NAS CM	Open End	Global Equity Large Cap (Foreign Stock)	C	C-	C	Up	Y	10,000
AB Tax-Managed International Portfolio Class A	ABXAX	NAS CM	Open End	Global Equity Large Cap (Foreign Stock)	C	C-	C	Up	Y	2,500
AB Tax-Managed International Portfolio Class B	ABXBX	NAS CM	Open End	Global Equity Large Cap (Foreign Stock)	C	C-	C	Up		2,500
AB Tax-Managed International Portfolio Class C	ABXCX	NAS CM	Open End	Global Equity Large Cap (Foreign Stock)	C	C-	C	Up	Y	2,500
AB Tax-Managed Wealth Appreciation Strategy Advisor Class	ATWYX	NAS CM	Open End	Global Equity Large Cap (Growth)	C+	C	B	Up	Y	0
AB Tax-Managed Wealth Appreciation Strategy Class A	ATWAX	NAS CM	Open End	Global Equity Large Cap (Growth)	C+	C	B	Up	Y	2,500
AB Tax-Managed Wealth Appreciation Strategy Class B	ATWBX	NAS CM	Open End	Global Equity Large Cap (Growth)	C+	C	B	Up		2,500
AB Tax-Managed Wealth Appreciation Strategy Class C	ATWCX	NAS CM	Open End	Global Equity Large Cap (Growth)	C+	C	B	Up	Y	2,500
AB Value Fund Advisor Class	ABVYX	NAS CM	Open End	US Equity Large Cap Value (Growth)	C	C-	C+		Y	0
AB Value Fund Class A	ABVAX	NAS CM	Open End	US Equity Large Cap Value (Growth)	C	C-	C+		Y	2,500
AB Value Fund Class B	ABVBX	NAS CM	Open End	US Equity Large Cap Value (Growth)	C	C-	C+			2,500
AB Value Fund Class C	ABVCX	NAS CM	Open End	US Equity Large Cap Value (Growth)	C	C-	C		Y	2,500
AB Value Fund Class I	ABVIX	NAS CM	Open End	US Equity Large Cap Value (Growth)	C	C-	C+		Y	2,000,000
AB Value Fund Class K	ABVKX	NAS CM	Open End	US Equity Large Cap Value (Growth)	C	C-	C+		Y	0
AB Value Fund Class R	ABVRX	NAS CM	Open End	US Equity Large Cap Value (Growth)	C	C-	C+		Y	0
AB Wealth Appreciation Strategy Advisor Class	AWAYX	NAS CM	Open End	Global Equity Large Cap (Growth)	B-	C	B	Up	Y	0
AB Wealth Appreciation Strategy Class A	AWAAX	NAS CM	Open End	Global Equity Large Cap (Growth)	C+	C	B	Up	Y	2,500
AB Wealth Appreciation Strategy Class B	AWABX	NAS CM	Open End	Global Equity Large Cap (Growth)	C+	C	B	Up		2,500
AB Wealth Appreciation Strategy Class C	AWACX	NAS CM	Open End	Global Equity Large Cap (Growth)	C+	C	B	Up	Y	2,500
AB Wealth Appreciation Strategy Class I	AWAIX	NAS CM	Open End	Global Equity Large Cap (Growth)	B-	C	B	Up	Y	2,000,000
AB Wealth Appreciation Strategy Class K	AWAKX	NAS CM	Open End	Global Equity Large Cap (Growth)	C+	C	B	Up	Y	0
AB Wealth Appreciation Strategy Class R	AWARX	NAS CM	Open End	Global Equity Large Cap (Growth)	C+	C	B	Up	Y	0
Abbey Capital Futures Strategy Fund Class A	ABYAX	NAS CM	Open End	Alternative Miscellaneous (Growth)	C-	C-	C	Up	Y	2,500
Abbey Capital Futures Strategy Fund Class C	ABYCX	NAS CM	Open End	Alternative Miscellaneous (Growth)	D+	D	C	Up	Y	2,500
Abbey Capital Futures Strategy Fund Class I	ABYIX	NAS CM	Open End	Alternative Miscellaneous (Growth)	C	C-	C	Up	Y	1,000,000
Abbey Capital Multi Asset Fund Class I	MAFIX	NAS CM	Open End	Alternative Miscellaneous (Growth)	D	D+	B-	Up	Y	1,000,000
Aberdeen Asia Pacific (ex-Japan) Equity Fund Class A	APJAX	NAS CM	Open End	Asia ex-Japan Equity (Pacific Stock)	C	C	B-		Y	1,000
Aberdeen Asia Pacific (ex-Japan) Equity Fund Class C	APJCX	NAS CM	Open End	Asia ex-Japan Equity (Pacific Stock)	C	C	B-		Y	1,000
Aberdeen Asia Pacific (ex-Japan) Equity Fund Class R	APJRX	NAS CM	Open End	Asia ex-Japan Equity (Pacific Stock)	C	C	B-		Y	0
Aberdeen Asia Pacific (ex-Japan) Equity Institutional Cls	AAPIX	NAS CM	Open End	Asia ex-Japan Equity (Pacific Stock)	C	C	B-		Y	1,000,000
Aberdeen Asia Pacific (ex-Japan) Equity Inst Service Cls	AAPEX	NAS CM	Open End	Asia ex-Japan Equity (Pacific Stock)	C	C	B-		Y	1,000,000
Aberdeen Australia Equity Fund Inc	IAF	AMEX	Closed End	Equity Miscellaneous (Pacific Stock)	C	C	C-		Y	
Aberdeen China A Share Equity Fund Class A	GOPAX	NAS CM	Open End	Greater China Equity (Growth)	C+	C	C+	Up	Y	1,000
Aberdeen China A Share Equity Fund Class C	GOPCX	NAS CM	Open End	Greater China Equity (Growth)	C	C	C+		Y	1,000
Aberdeen China A Share Equity Fund Class R	GOPRX	NAS CM	Open End	Greater China Equity (Growth)	C	C	C+		Y	0
Aberdeen China A Share Equity Fund Institutional Class	GOPIX	NAS CM	Open End	Greater China Equity (Growth)	C+	C	C+	Up	Y	1,000,000
Aberdeen China A Share Equity Institutional Service Cls	GOPSX	NAS CM	Open End	Greater China Equity (Growth)	C+	C	C+	Up	Y	1,000,000
Aberdeen Diversified Alternatives Fund Class A	GASAX	NAS CM	Open End	Multialternative (Growth)	C	C	B-		Y	1,000
Aberdeen Diversified Alternatives Fund Class C	GAMCX	NAS CM	Open End	Multialternative (Growth)	C	C-	C+		Y	1,000

★ Expanded analysis of this fund is included in Section II.

Min Additional Investment	TOTAL RETURNS 3-Month Total Return	6-Month Total Return	1-Year Total Return	3-Year Total Return	5-Year Total Return	PERFORMANCE Dividend Yield (TTM)	Expense Ratio	3-Yr Std Deviation	3-Year Beta	ASSETS NAV	Total Assets (MIL)	ASSET ALLOCATION & TURNOVER %Cash	%Stocks	%Bonds	%Other	Turnover Ratio	BULL & BEAR Last Bull Market Total Return	Last Bear Market Total Return	FEES Front End Fee (%)	Back End Fee (%)	Inception Date
	5.91	21.82	9.02	53.60	54.16	0.79	1.29	12.4	1.01	120.84	1,039	6	94	0	0	23	16.85	-29.8			Mar-05
	5.83	21.63	8.68	52.23	51.82	0.34	1.58	12.41	1.01	116.7	1,039	6	94	0	0	23	16.65	-29.88			Nov-03
	5.17	17.31	1.28	26.08	11.52	0	1.15	12.45	0.98	16.87	284.4	6	94	0	0	36	20.35	-26.95			Oct-96
50	5.17	17.16	1.02	25.14	10.15	0	1.4	12.45	0.98	16.45	284.4	6	94	0	0	36	20.17	-27.04	4.25		Jun-94
50	5.00	16.68	0.25	22.12	5.74	0	2.22	12.46	0.98	14.06	284.4	6	94	0	0	36	19.53	-27.22		4.00	Jun-94
50	4.96	16.72	0.31	22.40	6.11	0	2.15	12.46	0.98	14.17	284.4	6	94	0	0	36	19.64	-27.24		1.00	Feb-95
	5.19	17.31	1.40	26.53	12.38	0	1.04	12.48	0.98	16.8	284.4	6	94	0	0	36	20.53	-26.89			Mar-05
	5.14	17.19	1.03	25.20	10.21	0	1.41	12.45	0.98	16.36	284.4	6	94	0	0	36	20.19	-27.03			Mar-05
	5.09	17.01	0.75	23.99	8.58	0	1.71	12.46	0.98	16.09	284.4	6	94	0	0	36	20	-27.12			Mar-05
	3.70	12.17	7.67	20.12	21.29	3.08	0.78	5	0.73	12.65	105.5	0	31	60	2	50	11.17	-8.9			Sep-03
50	3.64	11.95	7.41	19.27	19.73	2.85	1.03	4.95	0.73	12.63	105.5	0	31	60	2	50	11.01	-9.06	4.25		May-92
50	3.51	11.66	6.61	16.63	15.34	2.02	1.78	4.99	0.72	12.96	105.5	0	31	60	2	50	10.64	-9.4		4.00	May-92
50	3.45	11.67	6.69	16.68	15.41	2.06	1.78	5	0.71	12.87	105.5	0	31	60	2	50	10.58	-9.36		1.00	Aug-93
	2.62	13.55	-3.91	20.61	6.79	1.48	1.01	11.69	1.02	16.84	2,915	0	97	0	3	46	11.93	-25.47			Jun-92
50	2.66	13.55	-3.91	20.66	6.85	1.56	1.21	11.69	1.02	16.59	2,915	0	97	0	3	46	11.07	-25.82	4.25		Jan-04
50	2.48	13.21	-4.54	18.06	2.98	0.49	2.12	11.7	1.03	16.88	2,915	0	97	0	3	46	10.54	-26.05		4.00	Jan-04
50	2.44	13.11	-4.64	17.93	2.86	0.75	1.97	11.7	1.03	16.73	2,915	0	97	0	3	46	10.61	-26.08		1.00	Jan-04
	3.15	16.27	4.15	36.96	32.80	1.25	0.78	10.9	0.95	16	718.6	2	98	0	0	25	20.88	-21.58			Sep-03
50	3.10	16.10	3.87	35.90	31.10	1	1.02	10.87	0.95	15.93	718.6	2	98	0	0	25	20.63	-21.66	4.25		Sep-03
50	2.92	15.68	3.08	32.82	26.19	0	1.8	10.85	0.95	15.86	718.6	2	98	0	0	25	20.12	-21.87		4.00	Sep-03
50	2.87	15.66	3.10	32.87	26.28	0	1.78	10.82	0.95	15.73	718.6	2	98	0	0	25	20.23	-21.92		1.00	Sep-03
	0.69	11.80	-2.39	20.79	15.53	1.28	0.72	13.33	1.08	14.58	373.2	2	98	0	0	40	23.28	-21.22			Mar-01
50	0.55	11.65	-2.67	19.83	13.96	1.02	0.97	13.37	1.08	14.56	373.2	2	98	0	0	40	23.02	-21.34	4.25		Mar-01
50	0.54	11.58	-2.80	19.63	13.60	0.87	1.76	13.35	1.07	14.64	373.2	2	98	0	0	40	22.94	-21.37		4.00	Mar-01
50	0.41	11.28	-3.39	17.13	9.81	0	1.73	13.33	1.08	14.59	373.2	2	98	0	0	40	22.54	-21.55		1.00	Mar-01
	0.69	11.84	-2.39	20.94	15.75	1.32	0.68	13.35	1.08	14.45	373.2	2	98	0	0	40	23.31	-21.17			Mar-05
	0.56	11.55	-2.82	19.32	13.31	0.87	1.11	13.31	1.07	14.29	373.2	2	98	0	0	40	23.12	-21.34			Mar-05
	0.48	11.41	-3.14	18.26	11.54	0.52	1.42	13.34	1.07	14.44	373.2	2	98	0	0	40	22.88	-21.48			Nov-03
	3.15	16.26	4.28	36.08	29.86	1.23	0.79	10.85	0.95	16.37	1,303	1	99	0	0	22	20.85	-22.61			Sep-03
50	3.07	16.13	3.96	35.00	28.26	0.97	1.04	10.84	0.95	16.41	1,303	1	99	0	0	22	20.7	-22.72	4.25		Sep-03
50	2.84	15.72	3.21	32.02	23.49	0	1.81	10.84	0.95	16.63	1,303	1	99	0	0	22	20.21	-22.96		4.00	Sep-03
50	2.88	15.71	3.19	32.06	23.54	0.01	1.79	10.82	0.94	16.42	1,303	1	99	0	0	22	20.22	-22.94		1.00	Sep-03
	3.08	16.17	4.16	35.77	29.49	1.08	0.85	10.83	0.95	16.38	1,303	1	99	0	0	22	20.99	-22.68			Mar-05
	3.03	16.01	3.81	34.49	27.37	0.83	1.18	10.82	0.94	16.3	1,303	1	99	0	0	22	20.66	-22.72			Mar-05
	2.90	15.77	3.47	33.19	25.36	0.49	1.49	10.83	0.94	16.29	1,303	1	99	0	0	22	20.38	-22.84			Feb-04
100	4.43	6.65	3.87	-4.15	17.65	0	2.04	8.04	0.3	11.54	668.1	-200	33	288	-21	0			5.75		Aug-14
100	4.17	6.23	3.02	-6.33	13.37	0	2.79	8.03	0.3	11.24	668.1	-200	33	288	-21	0				1.00	Oct-15
1,000	4.48	6.88	4.17	-3.42	19.19	0.13	1.79	8.04	0.3	11.64	668.1	-200	33	288	-21	0					Jul-14
1,000	7.28	14.64	8.57			3.43	1.79			10.02	25.8	-298	96	331	-29						Apr-18
50	3.57	16.13	6.16	44.34	24.32	0.82	1.55	13.63	0.99	13.89	7.3	1	99	0	0	70	19.29	-19.27	5.75		Feb-12
50	3.41	15.69	5.32	41.27	20.04	0	2.26	13.62	0.99	13.64	7.3	1	99	0	0	70	18.81	-19.53		1.00	Feb-12
	3.52	15.95	5.91	43.44	22.99	0.66	1.76	13.62	0.99	13.81	7.3	1	99	0	0	70	19.16	-19.36			Feb-12
	3.62	16.27	6.45	45.58	25.89	1.03	1.26	13.59	0.98	14	7.3	1	99	0	0	70	19.4	-19.11			Nov-09
	3.63	16.23	6.41	45.18	25.58	1.05	1.34	13.59	0.98	13.96	7.3	1	99	0	0	70	19.41	-19.19			Nov-09
	9.06	21.44	7.74	34.61	14.45	2.59	1.32	11.63	0.94	6.01	136.7	3	97	0	0	36	20.95	-25.91			Dec-85
50	3.98	25.00	7.50	55.61	29.95	0.16	1.35	15.34	0.63	25.3	13.1	5	95	0	0	26	19.76	-20.04	5.75		Jun-04
50	3.80	24.51	6.72	52.43	25.51	0	2.02	15.3	0.63	24.28	13.1	5	95	0	0	26	19.28	-20.29		1.00	Jun-04
	3.93	24.79	7.12	54.09	27.66	0	1.67	15.35	0.64	24.81	13.1	5	95	0	0	26	19.53	-20.17			Jun-04
	4.08	25.17	7.81	57.21	31.99	0.33	1.02	15.35	0.64	25.51	13.1	5	95	0	0	26	19.93	-19.97			Jun-04
	4.05	25.11	7.70	56.57	31.40	0.4	1.12	15.33	0.63	25.41	13.1	5	95	0	0	26	19.94	-19.94			Jun-04
50	1.27	4.25	1.55	6.37	2.51	2.06	2.01	3	30.65	12.74	28.8	11	24	50	11	18	15.7	-17.92	5.75		Jun-04
50	1.12	3.86	0.81	4.37	-0.71	1.44	2.63	2.99	30.08	12.23	28.8	11	24	50	11	18	15.2	-18.19		1.00	Jun-04

	MARKET			FUND TYPE, CATEGORY & OBJECTIVE	RATINGS				MINIMUMS	
Fund Name	Ticker Symbol	Traded On	Fund Type	Category and (Prospectus Objective)	Overall Rating	Reward Rating	Risk Rating	Recent Up/ Downgrade	Open to New Investors	Min Initial Investment
Aberdeen Diversified Alternatives Fund Class I	GASIX	NAS CM	Open End	Multialternative (Growth)	C	C	B		Y	1,000,000
Aberdeen Diversified Alternatives Fund Class R	GASRX	NAS CM	Open End	Multialternative (Growth)	C	C-	B-		Y	0
Aberdeen Diversified Income Fund Class A	GMAAX	NAS CM	Open End	Moderate Alloc (Growth & Income)	B-	C	B+	Up	Y	1,000
Aberdeen Diversified Income Fund Class C	GMACX	NAS CM	Open End	Moderate Alloc (Growth & Income)	C+	C	B	Up	Y	1,000
Aberdeen Diversified Income Fund Class I	GMAIX	NAS CM	Open End	Moderate Alloc (Growth & Income)	B-	C	B+	Up	Y	1,000,000
Aberdeen Diversified Income Cls Institutional Service	GAMSX	NAS CM	Open End	Moderate Alloc (Growth & Income)	B-	C	B+	Up	Y	1,000,000
Aberdeen Diversified Income Fund Class R	GMRRX	NAS CM	Open End	Moderate Alloc (Growth & Income)	B-	C	B+	Up	Y	0
Aberdeen Dynamic Allocation Fund Class A	GMMAX	NAS CM	Open End	Moderate Alloc (Growth & Income)	B-	C	B+	Up	Y	1,000
Aberdeen Dynamic Allocation Fund Class C	GMMCX	NAS CM	Open End	Moderate Alloc (Growth & Income)	B-	C	B+	Up	Y	1,000
Aberdeen Dynamic Allocation Cls Institutional Service	GAASX	NAS CM	Open End	Moderate Alloc (Growth & Income)	B-	C	B+	Up	Y	1,000,000
Aberdeen Dynamic Allocation Fund Class R	GAGRX	NAS CM	Open End	Moderate Alloc (Growth & Income)	B-	C	B+	Up	Y	0
Aberdeen Dynamic Allocation Fund Institutional Class	GMMIX	NAS CM	Open End	Moderate Alloc (Growth & Income)	B-	C	B+	Up	Y	1,000,000
Aberdeen Dynamic Dividend Fund Class A	ADAVX	NAS CM	Open End	Global Equity Large Cap (Equity-Income)	C	C	B-		Y	1,000
Aberdeen Dynamic Dividend Fund Institutional Class	ADVDX	NAS CM	Open End	Global Equity Large Cap (Equity-Income)	C+	C	B	Up	Y	1,000,000
Aberdeen Emerging Markets Equity Income Fund, Inc.	AEF	AMEX	Closed End	Global Emerg Mkts (Foreign Stock)	C	C	C+		Y	
Aberdeen Emerging Markets Fund Class A	GEGAX	NAS CM	Open End	Global Emerg Mkts (Div Emerging Mkts)	C	C	C+			1,000
Aberdeen Emerging Markets Fund Class C	GEGCX	NAS CM	Open End	Global Emerg Mkts (Div Emerging Mkts)	C	C	C+			1,000
Aberdeen Emerging Markets Fund Class R	GEMRX	NAS CM	Open End	Global Emerg Mkts (Div Emerging Mkts)	C	C	C+			0
Aberdeen Emerging Markets Fund Institutional Class	ABEMX	NAS CM	Open End	Global Emerg Mkts (Div Emerging Mkts)	C	C	C+			1,000,000
Aberdeen Emerging Markets Fund Institutional Service Class	AEMSX	NAS CM	Open End	Global Emerg Mkts (Div Emerging Mkts)	C	C	C+			1,000,000
Aberdeen Focused U.S. Equity Fund Class A	MLSAX	NAS CM	Open End	US Equity Large Cap Growth (Growth)	B-	C	B	Down	Y	1,000
Aberdeen Focused U.S. Equity Fund Class C	MLSCX	NAS CM	Open End	US Equity Large Cap Growth (Growth)	B-	C	B	Down	Y	1,000
Aberdeen Focused U.S. Equity Fund Class R	GLSRX	NAS CM	Open End	US Equity Large Cap Growth (Growth)	B-	C	B	Down	Y	0
Aberdeen Focused U.S. Equity Fund Institutional Class	GGUIX	NAS CM	Open End	US Equity Large Cap Growth (Growth)	B-	C	B	Down	Y	1,000,000
Aberdeen Focused U.S. Equity Institutional Service Cls	AELSX	NAS CM	Open End	US Equity Large Cap Growth (Growth)	B-	C	B	Down	Y	1,000,000
Aberdeen Global Dynamic Dividend Fund	AGD	NYSE	Closed End	Global Equity Large Cap (World Stock)	C	C	C-		Y	
Aberdeen Global Equity Fund Class A	GLLAX	NAS CM	Open End	Global Equity Large Cap (World Stock)	C+	C	B	Up	Y	1,000
Aberdeen Global Equity Fund Class C	GLLCX	NAS CM	Open End	Global Equity Large Cap (World Stock)	C+	C	B	Up	Y	1,000
Aberdeen Global Equity Fund Class R	GWLRX	NAS CM	Open End	Global Equity Large Cap (World Stock)	C+	C	B	Up	Y	0
Aberdeen Global Equity Fund Institutional Class	GWLIX	NAS CM	Open End	Global Equity Large Cap (World Stock)	C+	C	B	Up	Y	1,000,000
Aberdeen Global Equity Fund Institutional Service Class	GLLSX	NAS CM	Open End	Global Equity Large Cap (World Stock)	C+	C	B	Up	Y	1,000,000
Aberdeen Global Equity Impact Fund Class A	JETAX	NAS CM	Open End	Global Equity Large Cap (World Stock)	C	C	B-		Y	1,000
Aberdeen Global Equity Impact Fund Institutional Class	JETIX	NAS CM	Open End	Global Equity Large Cap (World Stock)	C	C	B-		Y	1,000,000
Aberdeen Global Infrastructure Fund Class A	AIAFX	NAS CM	Open End	Infrastructure Sector Equity (Utility)	B-	B-	B	Down	Y	1,000
Aberdeen Global Infrastructure Fund Institutional Class	AIFRX	NAS CM	Open End	Infrastructure Sector Equity (Utility)	B-	B-	B	Down	Y	1,000,000
Aberdeen Global Premier Property	AWP	NYSE	Closed End	Real Estate Sector Equity (Real Estate)	C+	C+	C+	Up	Y	
Aberdeen Income Builder Fund Class A	AAADX	NAS CM	Open End	Moderate Alloc (Equity-Income)	B	C+	B+	Up	Y	1,000
Aberdeen Income Builder Fund Institutional Class	AADDX	NAS CM	Open End	Moderate Alloc (Equity-Income)	B	C+	B+	Up	Y	1,000,000
Aberdeen International Equity Fund Class A	GIGAX	NAS CM	Open End	Global Equity Large Cap (Foreign Stock)	C	C	B-		Y	1,000
Aberdeen International Equity Fund Class C	GIGCX	NAS CM	Open End	Global Equity Large Cap (Foreign Stock)	C	C	B-		Y	1,000
Aberdeen International Equity Fund Class R	GIRRX	NAS CM	Open End	Global Equity Large Cap (Foreign Stock)	C	C	B-		Y	0
Aberdeen International Equity Fund Institutional Class	GIGIX	NAS CM	Open End	Global Equity Large Cap (Foreign Stock)	C	C	B-		Y	1,000,000
Aberdeen International Equity Institutional Service Cls	GIGSX	NAS CM	Open End	Global Equity Large Cap (Foreign Stock)	C	C	B-		Y	1,000,000
Aberdeen International Real Estate Equity Fund Class A	EGALX	NAS CM	Open End	Real Estate Sector Equity (Real Estate)	C	C	C+		Y	1,000
Aberdeen Intl Real Estate Equity Inst Cls	EGLRX	NAS CM	Open End	Real Estate Sector Equity (Real Estate)	C	C	C+		Y	1,000,000
Aberdeen International Small Cap Fund Class A	WVCCX	NAS CM	Open End	Global Equity Mid/Small Cap (Small Company)	B-	C	B	Up	Y	1,000
Aberdeen International Small Cap Fund Class C	CPVCX	NAS CM	Open End	Global Equity Mid/Small Cap (Small Company)	B-	C	B	Up	Y	1,000
Aberdeen International Small Cap Fund Class R	WPVAX	NAS CM	Open End	Global Equity Mid/Small Cap (Small Company)	B-	C	B	Up	Y	0
Aberdeen International Small Cap Fund Institutional Class	ABNIX	NAS CM	Open End	Global Equity Mid/Small Cap (Small Company)	B-	C	B	Up	Y	1,000,000
Aberdeen International Small Cap Institutional Service Cls	AGISX	NAS CM	Open End	Global Equity Mid/Small Cap (Small Company)	B-	C	B	Up	Y	1,000,000
Aberdeen Japan Equity Fund, Inc.	JEQ	NYSE	Closed End	Japan Equity (Pacific Stock)	D+	D+	C-	Down	Y	
Aberdeen Japanese Equities Fund Class A	AJEAX	NAS CM	Open End	Japan Equity (Foreign Stock)	D+	D+	C-		Y	1,000

★ Expanded analysis of this fund is included in Section II.

Min Additional Investment	TOTAL RETURNS: 3-Month Total Return	6-Month Total Return	1-Year Total Return	3-Year Total Return	5-Year Total Return	PERFORMANCE: Dividend Yield (TTM)	Expense Ratio	3-Yr Std Deviation	3-Year Beta	ASSETS: NAV	Total Assets (MIL)	ASSET ALLOCATION & TURNOVER: %Cash	%Stocks	%Bonds	%Other	Turnover Ratio	BULL & BEAR: Last Bull Market Total Return	Last Bear Market Total Return	FEES: Front End Fee (%)	Back End Fee (%)	Inception Date
	1.41	4.44	1.93	7.56	4.43	2.35	1.63	3.03	30.84	12.89	28.8	11	24	50	11	18	15.84	-17.84			Jun-04
	1.20	4.07	1.20	5.33	1.13	1.8	2.32	2.99	29.66	12.61	28.8	11	24	50	11	18	15.35	-17.99			Jun-04
50	2.50	10.45	4.97	16.76	15.68	3.15	1.08	6.72	0.11	12.26	13.6	4	54	38	0	52	12.2	-12.06	5.75		Jun-04
50	2.36	10.14	4.29	14.50	11.77	2.57	1.76	6.71	0.11	11.99	13.6	4	54	38	0	52	11.83	-12.44		1.00	Jun-04
	2.57	10.66	5.30	17.96	17.45	3.37	0.76	6.75	0.1	12.27	13.6	4	54	38	0	52	12.48	-12.1			Jun-04
	2.59	10.64	5.21	17.65	17.17	3.45	0.76	6.74	0.13	12.21	13.6	4	54	38	0	52	12.48	-12.1			Jun-04
	2.36	10.21	4.60	15.94	13.77	2.88	1.39	6.74	0.11	12.15	13.6	4	54	38	0	52	11.93	-12.31			Jun-04
50	2.87	13.09	3.52	17.54	15.61	2.24	0.98	8.37	0.72	13.67	11.7	3	66	30	0	24	14.61	-14.96	5.75		Jun-04
50	2.73	12.76	2.83	15.17	11.71	1.65	1.65	8.36	0.72	13.38	11.7	3	66	30	0	24	14.14	-15.18		1.00	Jun-04
	2.97	13.32	3.87	18.73	17.40	2.55	0.65	8.4	0.72	13.6	11.7	3	66	30	0	24	14.61	-14.96			Jun-04
	2.80	12.94	3.14	16.37	13.53	1.95	1.29	8.4	0.73	13.59	11.7	3	66	30	0	24	14.48	-15.04			Jun-04
	2.95	13.24	3.82	18.70	17.48	2.51	0.65	8.41	0.73	13.65	11.7	3	66	30	0	24	14.85	-14.89			Jun-04
50	2.56	12.92	2.14	35.89	31.04	5.93	1.61	11.42	0.98	3.88	134.9	5	95	0	0	66	15.7	-29.18	5.75		Dec-11
	2.63	13.07	2.40	36.91	33.01	6.19	1.36	11.28	0.97	3.88	134.9	5	95	0	0	66	15.86	-29.11			Sep-03
	2.71	13.90	7.95	43.02	24.15	1.2	1.77	17.73	0.78	8.28	420.2	1	98	0	1	145	27.54	-27.7			Sep-89
50	3.47	14.98	9.65	26.75	9.54	0.82	1.59	14.07	0.96	15.5	5,471	2	98	0	0	20	20.46	-18.14	5.75		May-12
50	3.35	14.74	9.11	24.78	6.48	0.04	2.1	14.05	0.96	15.41	5,471	2	98	0	0	20	19.94	-18.4		1.00	May-12
	3.43	14.89	9.49	26.06	8.18	0.8	1.75	14.09	0.96	15.35	5,471	2	98	0	0	20	20.29	-18.23			May-12
	3.59	15.24	10.15	28.53	11.93	1.24	1.1	14.04	0.96	15.57	5,471	2	98	0	0	20	20.64	-18.06			May-07
	3.59	15.18	10.08	28.08	11.01	1.24	1.16	14.05	0.96	15.55	5,471	2	98	0	0	20	20.48	-18.24			Nov-09
50	4.19	20.60	11.57	33.18	33.52	0	1.25	11.31	0.87	7.2	20.0	0	100	0	0	113	8.51	-9.13	5.75		Oct-01
50	4.21	20.00	11.07	31.09	29.52	0	1.9	11.34	0.86	1.98	20.0	0	100	0	0	113	7.98	-9.42		1.00	Dec-97
	3.90	20.15	11.10	31.76	31.04	0	1.63	11.28	0.86	6.38	20.0	0	100	0	0	113	8.25	-9.11			Feb-04
	4.16	20.68	11.91	34.50	35.73	0	0.9	11.33	0.87	7.76	20.0	0	100	0	0	113	8.58	-9.02			Jun-04
	4.16	20.57	11.86	33.86	34.46	0	1.01	11.33	0.86	7.5	20.0	0	100	0	0	113	8.41	-9.03			Nov-09
	2.66	12.93	2.73	36.81	32.28	5.05	1.27	11.7	0.9	10.84	136.0	-2	102	0	0	80	17.55	-31.09			Jul-06
50	3.14	14.90	4.55	27.56	8.48	0.64	1.53	10.92	0.91	12.8	32.8	1	99	0	0	22	19.07	-17.62	5.75		Aug-00
50	2.93	14.47	3.85	25.13	4.95	0	2.19	10.94	0.91	11.94	32.8	1	99	0	0	22	18.59	-17.84		1.00	Mar-01
	2.96	14.60	4.06	26.09	6.52	0.23	1.94	10.89	0.91	12.16	32.8	1	99	0	0	22	18.96	-17.62			Oct-03
	3.22	15.10	4.92	28.67	10.20	0.94	1.19	10.97	0.92	12.8	32.8	1	99	0	0	22	19.34	-17.48			Jun-04
	3.18	14.98	4.78	28.56	10.06	0.93	1.26	10.9	0.91	12.97	32.8	1	99	0	0	22	19.13	-17.62			Aug-00
50	4.37	14.37	1.25	25.64	-0.62	1.64	2.03	11.3	0.89	11.22	64.5	1	99	0	0	19	12.98	-27.99			May-05
	4.46	14.57	1.48	26.50	0.69	1.67	1.78	11.26	0.88	11.24	64.5	1	99	0	0	19	13.22	-27.96			May-05
50	4.74	20.37	15.52	37.49	25.84	2.98	1.46	10.59	0.77	21.4	99.8	3	97	0	0	49	21.09	-20.76	5.75		Dec-11
	4.80	20.56	15.79	38.47	27.42	3.21	1.21	10.6	0.77	21.43	99.8	3	97	0	0	49	21.24	-20.68			Nov-08
	2.41	20.66	7.45	36.27	24.15	2.77		11.81	0.67	6.72	573.9	0	100	0	0	83	25.83	-27.66			Apr-07
50	3.01	13.04	7.96	37.54	37.61	2.57	1.43	9.23	0.72	16.42	90.5	3	48	48	0	89	22.09	-17.58	5.75		Dec-11
	3.02	13.12	8.19	38.50	39.20	2.83	1.18	9.22	0.72	16.41	90.5	3	48	48	0	89	22.26	-17.5			Nov-08
50	2.84	14.76	1.63	22.52	-2.06	2.03	1.38	10.95	0.91	14.46	250.5	3	97	0	0	21	17.09	-18.33	5.75		Aug-00
50	2.64	14.32	0.90	19.90	-5.44	1.43	2.1	10.92	0.9	13.57	250.5	3	97	0	0	21	16.59	-18.58		1.00	Mar-01
	2.76	14.55	1.33	21.47	-3.45	1.86	1.64	10.94	0.91	13.77	250.5	3	97	0	0	21	16.89	-18.38			Dec-03
	2.99	14.98	2.00	23.93	-0.32	2.39	1.02	10.94	0.91	14.81	250.5	3	97	0	0	21	17.25	-18.22			Jun-04
	2.93	14.87	1.98	23.73	-0.79	2.37	1.06	10.97	0.91	14.75	250.5	3	97	0	0	21	17.13	-18.18			Aug-00
50	1.34	17.57	2.71	23.69	2.11	2.8	1.62	12.3	0.83	22.55	95.0	2	98	0	0	90	17.18	-31.63	5.75		Dec-11
	1.43	17.68	3.02	24.59	3.38	3.06	1.37	12.29	0.83	22.69	95.0	2	98	0	0	90	17.37	-31.56			Feb-89
50	4.97	17.11	7.36	40.15	35.55	2.06	1.48	10.85	0.85	28.05	101.0	5	92	0	2	18	19.46	-16.35	5.75		Sep-96
50	4.82	16.75	6.66	37.33	31.03	1.28	2.15	10.85	0.85	25.43	101.0	5	92	0	2	18	18.98	-16.6		1.00	Jul-01
	4.88	16.90	7.00	38.73	33.30	1.83	1.79	10.84	0.85	26.42	101.0	5	92	0	2	18	19.26	-16.46			Sep-96
	5.07	17.34	7.74	41.59	37.77	2.3	1.15	10.87	0.85	28.15	101.0	5	92	0	2	18	19.66	-16.22			Jul-09
	5.02	17.22	7.55	40.87	36.39	2.28	1.23	10.85	0.85	28.24	101.0	5	92	0	2	18	19.64	-16.24			Sep-09
	1.85	9.59	-9.03	8.88	27.00	0.79		13.18	1.11	8.22	110.2	1	99	0	0	32	2.09	-7.35			Jul-92
50	1.91	9.68	-9.08	6.91		0.32	1.34	13.17	1.12	10.65	1.5	1	99	0	0	30			5.75		Nov-15

	MARKET			FUND TYPE, CATEGORY & OBJECTIVE	RATINGS				MINIMUMS	
Fund Name	Ticker Symbol	Traded On	Fund Type	Category and (Prospectus Objective)	Overall Rating	Reward Rating	Risk Rating	Recent Up/ Downgrade	Open to New Investors	Min Initial Investment
Aberdeen Japanese Equities Fund Class C	AJECX	NAS CM	Open End	Japan Equity (Foreign Stock)	D+	D+	C-		Y	1,000
Aberdeen Japanese Equities Fund Class R	AJERX	NAS CM	Open End	Japan Equity (Foreign Stock)	D+	D+	C-		Y	0
Aberdeen Japanese Equities Fund Institutional Class	AJEIX	NAS CM	Open End	Japan Equity (Foreign Stock)	D+	D+	C	Down	Y	1,000,000
Aberdeen Japanese Equities Institutional Service Cls	AJESX	NAS CM	Open End	Japan Equity (Foreign Stock)	D+	D+	C	Down	Y	1,000,000
Aberdeen Realty Income & Growth Fund Class A	AIAGX	NAS CM	Open End	Real Estate Sector Equity (Real Estate)	C+	C	B-	Down	Y	1,000
Aberdeen Realty Income & Growth Fund Institutional Class	AIGYX	NAS CM	Open End	Real Estate Sector Equity (Real Estate)	C+	C	B-	Down	Y	1,000,000
Aberdeen Select International Equity Fund Class A	BJBIX	NAS CM	Open End	Global Equity Large Cap (Foreign Stock)	C	C-	B-		Y	1,000
Aberdeen Select International Equity Fund Class I	JIEIX	NAS CM	Open End	Global Equity Large Cap (Foreign Stock)	C	C-	B-		Y	1,000,000
Aberdeen Total Dynamic Dividend Fund	AOD	NYSE	Closed End	Global Equity Large Cap (World Stock)	C	C	C+		Y	
Aberdeen U.S. Mid Cap Equity Fund Class A	GUEAX	NAS CM	Open End	US Equity Mid Cap (Growth)	C+	C	B	Up	Y	1,000
Aberdeen U.S. Mid Cap Equity Fund Class C	GUECX	NAS CM	Open End	US Equity Mid Cap (Growth)	C+	C	B	Up	Y	1,000
Aberdeen U.S. Mid Cap Equity Fund Class R	GUERX	NAS CM	Open End	US Equity Mid Cap (Growth)	C+	C	B	Up	Y	0
Aberdeen U.S. Mid Cap Equity Fund Institutional Class	GUEIX	NAS CM	Open End	US Equity Mid Cap (Growth)	C+	C	B	Up	Y	1,000,000
Aberdeen U.S. Mid Cap Equity Institutional Service Cls	GUESX	NAS CM	Open End	US Equity Mid Cap (Growth)	C+	C	B	Up	Y	1,000,000
Aberdeen U.S. Multi-Cap Equity Fund Class A	GXXAX	NAS CM	Open End	US Equity Large Cap Blend (Growth)	B-	C+	B		Y	1,000
Aberdeen U.S. Multi-Cap Equity Fund Class C	GXXCX	NAS CM	Open End	US Equity Large Cap Blend (Growth)	B-	C+	B		Y	1,000
Aberdeen U.S. Multi-Cap Equity Fund Class R	GGLRX	NAS CM	Open End	US Equity Large Cap Blend (Growth)	B-	C+	B		Y	0
Aberdeen U.S. Multi-Cap Equity Fund Institutional Class	GGLIX	NAS CM	Open End	US Equity Large Cap Blend (Growth)	B-	C+	B		Y	1,000,000
Aberdeen U.S. Multi-Cap Equity Institutional Service Cls	GXXIX	NAS CM	Open End	US Equity Large Cap Blend (Growth)	B-	C+	B		Y	1,000,000
Aberdeen U.S. Small Cap Equity Fund Class A	GSXAX	NAS CM	Open End	US Equity Small Cap (Small Company)	C	C	C+	Down	Y	1,000
Aberdeen U.S. Small Cap Equity Fund Class C	GSXCX	NAS CM	Open End	US Equity Small Cap (Small Company)	C	C	C+		Y	1,000
Aberdeen U.S. Small Cap Equity Fund Class R	GNSRX	NAS CM	Open End	US Equity Small Cap (Small Company)	C	C	C+		Y	0
Aberdeen U.S. Small Cap Equity Fund Institutional Class	GSCIX	NAS CM	Open End	US Equity Small Cap (Small Company)	C	C	B-	Down	Y	1,000,000
Aberdeen U.S. Small Cap Equity Institutional Service Cls	GSXIX	NAS CM	Open End	US Equity Small Cap (Small Company)	C	C	B-	Down	Y	1,000,000
ABR Dynamic Blend Equity & Volatility Institutional Shares	ABRVX	NAS CM	Open End	Long/Short Equity (Growth)	C	C-	B-	Up	Y	100,000
ABR Dynamic Blend Equity & Volatility Fund Investor Shares	ABRTX	NAS CM	Open End	Long/Short Equity (Growth)	C	C-	B-	Up	Y	2,500
ABR Dynamic Short Volatility Fund Institutional Shares	ABRSX	NAS CM	Open End	Multialternative (Growth)	D+	D+	D+	Up		100,000
ABR Dynamic Short Volatility Fund Investor Shares	ABRJX	NAS CM	Open End	Multialternative (Growth)	D+	D+	D+	Up	Y	2,500
Absolute Capital Asset Allocator Fund Class A	AAMAX	NAS CM	Open End	Moderate Alloc (Growth & Income)	C	C	C+		Y	2,500
Absolute Capital Asset Allocator Fund Institutional Class	AAMIX	NAS CM	Open End	Moderate Alloc (Growth & Income)	C	C	C+		Y	100,000
Absolute Capital Asset Allocator Fund Investor Class	AAMCX	NAS CM	Open End	Moderate Alloc (Growth & Income)	C	C-	C		Y	2,500
Absolute Capital Defender Fund Class A	ACMAX	NAS CM	Open End	Moderate Alloc (Growth & Income)	C	C-	C		Y	2,500
Absolute Capital Defender Fund Institutional Class	ACMIX	NAS CM	Open End	Moderate Alloc (Growth & Income)	C	C-	C		Y	100,000
Absolute Capital Defender Fund Investor Class	ACMDX	NAS CM	Open End	Moderate Alloc (Growth & Income)	C	C-	C		Y	2,500
Absolute Capital Opportunities Fund Institutional Shares	CAPOX	NAS CM	Open End	Long/Short Equity (Growth)	B	C	A	Up	Y	25,000
Absolute Convertible Arbitrage Fund Institutional Shares	ARBIX	NAS CM	Open End	Multialternative (Convertible Bond)	C-	D+	B+	Up	Y	25,000
Absolute Strategies Fund Institutional Class	ASFIX	NAS CM	Open End	Multialternative (Growth)	D	D	C-		Y	25,000
AC Alternatives® Disciplined Long Short Fund A Class	ACDQX	NAS CM	Open End	US Equity Large Cap Growth (Growth)	C+	C	B	Down	Y	2,500
AC Alternatives® Disciplined Long Short Fund C Class	ACDHX	NAS CM	Open End	US Equity Large Cap Growth (Growth)	C+	C	B		Y	2,500
AC Alternatives® Disciplined Long Short Fund I Class	ACDKX	NAS CM	Open End	US Equity Large Cap Growth (Growth)	B-	C	B+		Y	5,000,000
AC Alternatives® Disciplined Long Short Investor Cls	ACDJX	NAS CM	Open End	US Equity Large Cap Growth (Growth)	B-	C	B+		Y	2,500
AC Alternatives® Disciplined Long Short Fund R Class	ACDWX	NAS CM	Open End	US Equity Large Cap Growth (Growth)	C+	C	B	Down	Y	2,500
AC Alternatives® Equity Market Neutral Fund A Class	ALIAX	NAS CM	Open End	Market Neutral (Growth)	D+	D	C	Down	Y	2,500
AC Alternatives® Equity Market Neutral Fund C Class	ALICX	NAS CM	Open End	Market Neutral (Growth)	D	D	C	Down	Y	2,500
AC Alternatives® Equity Market Neutral Fund I Class	ALISX	NAS CM	Open End	Market Neutral (Growth)	C-	D+	C	Down	Y	5,000,000
AC Alternatives® Equity Market Neutral Fund Investor Class	ALHIX	NAS CM	Open End	Market Neutral (Growth)	C-	D+	C	Down	Y	2,500
AC Alternatives® Equity Market Neutral Fund R Class	ALIRX	NAS CM	Open End	Market Neutral (Growth)	D+	D	C	Down	Y	2,500
AC Alternatives® Equity Market Neutral Fund R5 Class	ALIGX	NAS CM	Open End	Market Neutral (Growth)	C-	D+	C	Down	Y	0
AC Alternatives® Equity Market Neutral Fund Y Class	ALYIX	NAS CM	Open End	Market Neutral (Growth)	C-	D+	C	Down	Y	0
AC Alternatives® Income Fund A Class	ALNAX	NAS CM	Open End	Cautious Alloc (Income)	C+	C	B	Down	Y	2,500
AC Alternatives® Income Fund C Class	ALNHX	NAS CM	Open End	Cautious Alloc (Income)	C	C	B-	Down	Y	2,500
AC Alternatives® Income Fund I Class	ALNIX	NAS CM	Open End	Cautious Alloc (Income)	C+	C	B	Down	Y	5,000,000

★ Expanded analysis of this fund is included in Section II.

	TOTAL RETURNS					PERFORMANCE				ASSETS		ASSET ALLOCATION & TURNOVER					BULL & BEAR		FEES		
Min Additional Investment	3-Month Total Return	6-Month Total Return	1-Year Total Return	3-Year Total Return	5-Year Total Return	Dividend Yield (TTM)	Expense Ratio	3-Yr Std Deviation	3-Year Beta	NAV	Total Assets (MIL)	%Cash	%Stocks	%Bonds	%Other	Turnover Ratio	Last Bull Market Total Return	Last Bear Market Total Return	Front End Fee (%)	Back End Fee (%)	Inception Date
50	1.84	9.39	-9.61	4.74		0	2	13.16	1.12	10.48	1.5	1	99	0	0	30				1.00	Nov-15
	1.91	9.67	-9.18	6.26		0.05	1.5	13.16	1.11	10.66	1.5	1	99	0	0	30					Nov-15
	2.00	9.96	-8.75	7.88		0.61	1	13.19	1.12	10.7	1.5	1	99	0	0	30					Nov-15
	2.00	9.96	-8.76	7.87		0.6	1.01	13.17	1.12	10.7	1.5	1	99	0	0	30					Nov-15
50	1.59	19.22	11.65	17.01	47.36	2.25	1.25	12.79	0.6	16.57	78.4	0	100	0	0	43	32.46	-18.03	5.75		Dec-11
	1.66	19.30	11.94	17.89	49.23	2.44	1	12.79	0.6	16.61	78.4	0	100	0	0	43	32.62	-17.95			Dec-98
50	0.07	12.21	-1.00	25.55	-1.38	0.79	2.3	12.86	1.04	25.54	148.1	4	96	0	0	19	11.97	-28.37			Oct-93
	0.11	12.36	-0.74	26.49	-0.10	0.81	2.05	12.86	1.04	26.26	148.1	4	96	0	0	19	12.18	-28.31			Nov-99
	2.72	13.66	3.27	35.09	31.17	4.69	1.19	11.58	0.91	9.4	991.1	0	100	0	0	77	15.41	-27.89			Jan-07
50	5.29	21.91	7.96	41.85		0.07	1.25	12.97	0.94	13.13	1.7	2	98	0	0	25			5.75		Feb-16
50	5.16	21.51	7.18	38.75		0	2	13	0.94	12.82	1.7	2	98	0	0	25				1.00	Feb-16
	5.33	21.86	7.79	40.82		0.04	1.5	13.01	0.94	13.04	1.7	2	98	0	0	25					Feb-16
	5.43	22.13	8.32	42.95		0.17	1	13	0.94	13.19	1.7	2	98	0	0	25					Feb-16
	5.35	22.03	8.23	42.85		0.17	1	12.99	0.94	13.18	1.7	2	98	0	0	25					Feb-16
50	4.66	22.17	9.44	48.03	48.70	0.14	1.19	12.62	0.97	12.34	363.3	3	97	0	0	39	23.59	-20.15	5.75		Jun-00
50	4.49	21.79	8.61	44.91	43.40	0	1.9	12.66	0.97	10.45	363.3	3	97	0	0	39	22.98	-20.27		1.00	Mar-01
	4.58	22.03	9.04	46.20	46.15	0	1.6	12.65	0.97	11.41	363.3	3	97	0	0	39	23.43	-20.16			Oct-03
	4.81	22.41	9.84	49.45	50.96	0.35	0.9	12.62	0.97	13.27	363.3	3	97	0	0	39	23.88	-20.07			Jun-04
	4.75	22.40	9.76	48.95	50.25	0.33	0.97	12.65	0.97	13.22	363.3	3	97	0	0	39	23.87	-20.15			Jun-00
50	1.12	16.87	0.93	28.68	55.22	0.01	1.35	17.19	0.97	32.28	1,170	1	99	0	0	38	32.36	-27.67	5.75		Nov-98
50	0.93	16.42	0.18	25.97	49.82	0	2.06	17.17	0.97	27.08	1,170	1	99	0	0	38	31.74	-27.81		1.00	Mar-01
	0.99	16.61	0.52	27.39	52.89	0	1.72	17.17	0.97	29.34	1,170	1	99	0	0	38	32.12	-27.65			Dec-03
	1.20	17.01	1.21	29.84	57.58	0.05	1.07	17.16	0.97	34.39	1,170	1	99	0	0	38	32.52	-27.53			Jun-04
	1.20	17.00	1.18	29.74	57.43	0.05	1.08	17.17	0.97	34.4	1,170	1	99	0	0	38	32.52	-27.53			Nov-98
	2.02	4.46	0.11	16.63		0	2	8.88	1.02	10.07	39.8	96	4	0	0	0					Aug-15
	1.95	4.41	-0.08	15.21		0	2.25	8.86	1.02	9.93	39.8	96	4	0	0	0					Aug-15
	13.24	54.67	11.02			0	2.5			7.61	3.7	21	-2	82	0	748					Oct-17
	13.15	54.48	10.62			0	2.75			7.57	3.7	21	-2	82	0	748					Oct-17
100	0.20	5.25	-0.39	17.12		0	2.19	8.08	0.64	9.81	15.6	6	57	37	0	217			5.75		Dec-15
	0.20	5.25	-0.39	17.12		0	1.94	8.09	0.64	9.81	15.6	6	57	37	0	217					Dec-15
100	0.00	4.92	-1.08	14.66		0	2.94	8.12	0.64	9.58	15.6	6	57	37	0	217					Dec-15
100	-0.10	3.70	-1.12	12.25		0	2.18	7.23	0.56	9.79	14.5	17	50	33	0	249			5.75		Dec-15
	-0.10	3.70	-1.12	12.25		0	1.93	7.27	0.56	9.79	14.5	17	50	33	0	249					Dec-15
100	-0.31	3.13	-1.94	9.67		0	2.93	7.22	0.56	9.55	14.5	17	50	33	0	249					Dec-15
	2.78	4.41	3.17	23.31		0	2.62	6.94	0.53	11.82	56.7	139	-39	0	0	23					Dec-15
	1.30	4.38	4.49			0.62	1.6			10.56	120.8	56	-47	0	0	121					Aug-17
	1.68	-1.71	0.20	-11.96	-7.89	0.08	3.08	4.67	-0.32	8.23	84.3	56	22	0	0	33	0.57	1.92			Jul-05
50	-0.70	5.39	1.28	23.23	31.20	0	2.64	7.84	0.51	17	51.1	48	52	0	0	243			5.75		Oct-11
50	-0.86	4.99	0.49	20.47	26.31	0	3.39	7.81	0.51	15.97	51.1	48	52	0	0	243				1.00	Oct-11
50	-0.57	5.65	1.71	24.93	34.11	0	2.19	7.82	0.51	17.37	51.1	48	52	0	0	243					Oct-11
50	-0.63	5.55	1.49	24.16	32.85	0	2.39	7.85	0.51	17.28	51.1	48	52	0	0	243					Oct-11
50	-0.71	5.29	1.00	22.39	29.61	0	2.89	7.84	0.51	16.69	51.1	48	52	0	0	243					Oct-11
50	-3.32	-4.13	-2.42	-0.15	-3.04	0	3.32	3.66	-11.98	10.19	59.5	100	0	0	0	289	1.67	0.69	5.75		Sep-05
50	-3.56	-4.55	-3.26	-2.39	-6.69	0	4.07	3.65	-12.3	9.21	59.5	100	0	0	0	289	1.22	0.4		1.00	Sep-05
50	-3.31	-4.00	-2.11	1.20	-0.91	0	2.87	3.66	-11.26	10.79	59.5	100	0	0	0	289	1.92	0.87			Sep-05
50	-3.21	-4.01	-2.17	0.67	-1.82	0	3.07	3.64	-10.58	10.52	59.5	100	0	0	0	289	1.84	0.78			Sep-05
50	-3.33	-4.27	-2.68	-0.82	-4.20	0	3.57	3.66	-11.37	9.86	59.5	100	0	0	0	289	1.49	0.59			Sep-05
	-3.31	-3.91	-2.03	1.29	-0.83	0	2.87	3.67	-11.48	10.79	59.5	100	0	0	0	289	1.92	0.87			Apr-17
	-3.22	-3.91	-2.02	1.29	-0.82	0	2.82	3.67	-11.6	10.8	59.5	100	0	0	0	289	1.92	0.87			Apr-17
50	0.44	4.73	2.51	12.48		2.78	2.2	3.15	0.91	9.67	297.0	14	15	64	4	83			5.75		Jul-15
50	0.25	4.50	1.86	10.14		2.04	2.95	3.15	0.91	9.63	297.0	14	15	64	4	83				1.00	Jul-15
50	0.66	5.06	3.08	14.13		3.23	1.75	3.16	0.91	9.68	297.0	14	15	64	4	83					Jul-15

Fund Name	MARKET Ticker Symbol	MARKET Traded On	FUND TYPE Fund Type	Category and (Prospectus Objective)	RATINGS Overall Rating	RATINGS Reward Rating	RATINGS Risk Rating	Recent Up/ Downgrade	Open to New Investors	MINIMUMS Min Initial Investment
AC Alternatives® Income Fund Investor Class	ALNNX	NAS CM	Open End	Cautious Alloc (Income)	C+	C	B	Down	Y	2,500
AC Alternatives® Income Fund R Class	ALNRX	NAS CM	Open End	Cautious Alloc (Income)	C+	C	B-		Y	2,500
AC Alternatives® Income Fund R6 Class	ALNDX	NAS CM	Open End	Cautious Alloc (Income)	C+	C	B	Down	Y	0
AC Alternatives® Income Fund Y Class	ALYNX	NAS CM	Open End	Cautious Alloc (Income)	B-	C	B		Y	0
AC Alternatives® Market Neutral Value Fund A Class	ACVQX	NAS CM	Open End	Market Neutral (Growth)	D	D-	C-	Down	Y	2,500
AC Alternatives® Market Neutral Value Fund C Class	ACVHX	NAS CM	Open End	Market Neutral (Growth)	D	D-	C-		Y	2,500
AC Alternatives® Market Neutral Value Fund I Class	ACVKX	NAS CM	Open End	Market Neutral (Growth)	D	D	C	Down		5,000,000
AC Alternatives® Market Neutral Value Fund Investor Class	ACVVX	NAS CM	Open End	Market Neutral (Growth)	D	D-	C-	Down	Y	2,500
AC Alternatives® Market Neutral Value Fund R Class	ACVWX	NAS CM	Open End	Market Neutral (Growth)	D	D-	C-	Down	Y	2,500
AC One China Fund Institutional Class	ACOIX	NAS CM	Open End	Greater China Equity (Pacific Stock)	C	C-	C		Y	25,000
Acadian Emerging Markets Portfolio Class I	AEMZX	NAS CM	Open End	Global Emerg Mkts (Growth)	C	C	C+		Y	1,000,000
Acadian Emerging Markets Portfolio Class Y	AEMVX	NAS CM	Open End	Global Emerg Mkts (Growth)	C	C	C+		Y	100,000
Acadian Emerging Markets Portfolio Investor Class	AEMGX	NAS CM	Open End	Global Emerg Mkts (Growth)	C	C	C+			2,500
Access Flex Bear High Yield Fund Investor Class	AFBIX	NAS CM	Open End	Trading Tools (Corporate Bond - High Yield)	D	D-	D		Y	15,000
Access Flex Bear High Yield Fund Service Class	AFBSX	NAS CM	Open End	Trading Tools (Corporate Bond - High Yield)	D	D-	D		Y	15,000
Acclivity Small Cap Value Fund Class I Shares	AXVIX	NAS CM	Open End	US Equity Small Cap (Small Company)	U	U	U		Y	100,000
Acclivity Small Cap Value Fund Class N Shares	AXVNX	NAS CM	Open End	US Equity Small Cap (Small Company)	U	U	U		Y	10,000
ACM Dynamic Opportunity Fund Class A	ADOAX	NAS CM	Open End	Long/Short Equity (Growth)	C+	C	B	Up	Y	2,000
ACM Dynamic Opportunity Fund Class I	ADOIX	NAS CM	Open End	Long/Short Equity (Growth)	C+	C	B	Up	Y	10,000
ACM Dynamic Opportunity Fund Class I	IQRAX	NAS CM	Open End	Global Equity Large Cap (Foreign Stock)	C-	D	C	Up	Y	5,000
ACM Dynamic Opportunity Fund Class I	IQRIX	NAS CM	Open End	Global Equity Large Cap (Foreign Stock)	C-	D	C	Up	Y	10,000
ACR Multi-Strategy Quality Return (MQR) Fund Class A	MQRAX	NAS CM	Open End	Flexible Alloc (Growth & Income)	C-	D+	C	Down	Y	5,000
ACR Multi-Strategy Quality Return (MQR) Fund Class I	MQRIX	NAS CM	Open End	Flexible Alloc (Growth & Income)	C-	D+	C	Down	Y	10,000
Acuitas International Small Cap Fund Institutional Shares	AISCX	NAS CM	Open End	Global Equity Mid/Small Cap (Small Company)	D+	D	C-		Y	100,000
Acuitas US Microcap Fund Institutional Shares	AFMCX	NAS CM	Open End	US Equity Small Cap (Small Company)	C-	C-	C	Down	Y	100,000
Adalta International Fund	ADAQX	NAS CM	Open End	Global Equity Mid/Small Cap (World Stock)	D	D	D+		Y	2,500
Adams Diversified Equity Fund	ADX	NYSE	Closed End	US Equity Large Cap Growth (Growth & Income)	C+	C+	C+	Down	Y	
Adams Natural Resources Fund	PEO	NYSE	Closed End	Energy Sector Equity (Natl Res)	D+	D+	C-	Down	Y	
Adara Smaller Companies Fund			Open End	US Equity Small Cap (Small Company)	C+	C	C+		Y	0
Adirondack Small Cap Fund	ADKSX	NAS CM	Open End	US Equity Small Cap (Small Company)	D+	D	D+	Down	Y	3,000
Adler Value Fund Institutional Class	ADLVX	NAS CM	Open End	US Equity Large Cap Value (Growth)	U	U	U		Y	1,000,000
Advent Convertible & Income Fund	AVK	NYSE	Closed End	Convertibles (Convertible Bond)	C+	C	C+	Up	Y	
AdvisorOne CLS Global Aggressive Equity Fund Class N	CLACX	NAS CM	Open End	Global Equity Large Cap (Growth)	C+	C	B	Up	Y	2,500
AdvisorOne CLS Global Aggressive Equity Fund Class T	GLAGX	NAS CM	Open End	Global Equity Large Cap (Growth)	C+	C	B	Up	Y	2,500
AdvisorOne CLS Global Diversified Equity Fund Class N	CLSAX	NAS CM	Open End	Global Equity Large Cap (Growth)	C+	C	B+	Up	Y	2,500
AdvisorOne CLS Global Diversified Equity Fund Class T	GDIVX	NAS CM	Open End	Global Equity Large Cap (Growth)	C+	C	B+	Up	Y	2,500
AdvisorOne CLS Growth and Income Fund Class N	CLERX	NAS CM	Open End	Cautious Alloc (Growth & Income)	B-	C	B+	Up	Y	2,500
AdvisorOne CLS Shelter Fund Class N	CLSHX	NAS CM	Open End	Moderate Alloc (Income)	C+	C	B	Up	Y	2,500
AdvisorOne CLS Shelter Fund Class T	SHELX	NAS CM	Open End	Moderate Alloc (Income)	C+	C	B		Y	2,500
Advisory Research All Cap Value Fund	ADVGX	NAS CM	Open End	US Equity Large Cap Blend (Growth)	B-	C	B+	Down	Y	2,500
Advisory Research Emerging Markets Opportunities Fund	ADVMX	NAS CM	Open End	Global Emerg Mkts (Growth)	D+	D+	C-	Down	Y	2,500
Advisory Research International Small Cap Value Cls I	ADVLX	NAS CM	Open End	Global Equity Mid/Small Cap (Small Company)	C	C	C		Y	500,000
Advy Research Intl Small Cap Value Inv Cls	ADVIX	NAS CM	Open End	Global Equity Mid/Small Cap (Small Company)	C	C	C		Y	2,500
Advisory Research MLP & Energy Income Fund Class A	INFRX	NAS CM	Open End	Energy Sector Equity (Natl Res)	C-	C-	C-	Down	Y	2,500
Advisory Research MLP & Energy Income Fund Class C	INFFX	NAS CM	Open End	Energy Sector Equity (Natl Res)	C-	C-	C-	Down	Y	2,500
Advisory Research MLP & Energy Income Fund Class I	INFIX	NAS CM	Open End	Energy Sector Equity (Natl Res)	C-	C-	C-	Down	Y	1,000,000
Advisory Research MLP & Energy Infrastructure Fund Class I	MLPPX	NAS CM	Open End	Energy Sector Equity (Natl Res)	C-	C-	C-	Down	Y	5,000,000
Advisory Research MLP & Equity Fund Class A	INFJX	NAS CM	Open End	Energy Sector Equity (Natl Res)	D+	D	D+	Down	Y	2,500
Advisory Research MLP & Equity Fund Class C	INFKX	NAS CM	Open End	Energy Sector Equity (Natl Res)	D+	D	D+	Down	Y	2,500
Advisory Research MLP & Equity Fund Class I	INFEX	NAS CM	Open End	Energy Sector Equity (Natl Res)	D+	D+	D+	Down	Y	1,000,000
Aegis Value Fund	AVALX	NAS CM	Open End	US Equity Small Cap (Growth)	C-	C-	C	Down	Y	1,000,000
Aegis Value Fund Class A	AVFAX	NAS CM	Open End	US Equity Small Cap (Growth)	C-	C-	C	Down	Y	2,000

★ Expanded analysis of this fund is included in Section II.

	TOTAL RETURNS					PERFORMANCE				ASSETS		ASSET ALLOCATION & TURNOVER					BULL & BEAR		FEES		
Min Additional Investment	3-Month Total Return	6-Month Total Return	1-Year Total Return	3-Year Total Return	5-Year Total Return	Dividend Yield (TTM)	Expense Ratio	3-Yr Std Deviation	3-Year Beta	NAV	Total Assets (MIL)	%Cash	%Stocks	%Bonds	%Other	Turnover Ratio	Last Bull Market Total Return	Last Bear Market Total Return	Front End Fee (%)	Back End Fee (%)	Inception Date
50	0.50	4.85	2.77	13.33		3.03	1.95	3.15	0.92	9.67	297.0	14	15	64	4	83					Jul-15
50	0.38	4.73	2.36	11.78		2.53	2.45	3.12	0.9	9.66	297.0	14	15	64	4	83					Jul-15
	0.59	5.13	3.23	14.64		3.38	1.6	3.13	0.9	9.68	297.0	14	15	64	4	83					Jul-15
	0.69	5.13	3.23	14.62		3.38	1.6	3.13	0.9	9.68	297.0	14	15	64	4	83					Apr-17
50	0.00	-2.32	-3.00	-3.94	3.45	0	4.09	2.84	2.83	9.26	233.7	100	0	1	0	324			5.75		Oct-11
50	-0.11	-2.58	-3.71	-6.03	-0.35	0	4.84	2.8	2.66	8.68	233.7	100	0	1	0	324				1.00	Oct-11
	0.20	-2.03	-2.50	-2.61	5.84	0	3.64	2.86	3.52	9.63	233.7	100	0	1	0	324					Oct-11
50	0.00	-2.17	-2.84	-3.31	4.64	0	3.84	2.82	2.74	9.45	233.7	100	0	1	0	324					Oct-11
50	-0.10	-2.37	-3.26	-4.69	2.12	0	4.34	2.86	3.32	9.06	233.7	100	0	1	0	324					Oct-11
500	-5.56	11.39	-7.06	35.02	26.50	0	1.51	16.75	1.01	15.45	13.9	4	96	0	0	9					Jul-12
	0.51	10.46	-0.35	33.57	8.82	1.84	1.2	14.66	1.03	19.64	1,254	0	100	0	0	32	18.16	-26.03			Oct-16
	0.46	10.48	-0.39	33.25	8.56	1.81	1.27	14.66	1.03	19.6	1,254	0	100	0	0	32	18.16	-26.03			Oct-16
1,000	0.46	10.40	-0.54	32.93	8.30	1.66	1.4	14.7	1.04	19.63	1,254	0	100	0	0	32	18.16	-26.03			Jun-93
	-3.51	-9.29	-9.88	-17.95	-30.43	0	1.78	4.25	-0.68	34.54	1.0	115	0	-15	0	650	-16.47	4.45			Apr-05
	-3.78	-9.77	-10.81	-19.89	-33.37	0	2.78	4.33	-0.67	30.28	1.0	115	0	-15	0	650	-17.09	3.84			Apr-05
	-0.88	11.50					0.68			11.15	0.62	2	98	0	0						Dec-18
1,000	-0.97	11.40					0.93			11.14	0.62	2	98	0	0						Dec-18
500	-0.99	3.70	0.68	18.39		0	2.04	7.78	0.47	17.92	90.4	25	69	6	0	271			5.75		Jan-15
500	-0.87	3.90	0.95	19.34		0	1.79	7.79	0.47	18.1	90.4	25	69	6	0	271					Jan-15
100	4.35	13.93	-3.90			0.56	1.4			10.3	90.4	38	73	0	-10	52			5.75		Dec-16
100	4.45	14.03	-3.73			0.63	1.25			10.32	90.4	38	73	0	-10	52					Dec-16
100	-0.98	5.46	-6.81	10.94		2.3	1.64	11.66	1.58	10.03	71.2	25	69	2	1	48			5.75		Dec-14
100	-0.88	5.65	-6.60	11.64		2.46	1.42	11.68	1.58	10.09	71.2	25	69	2	1	48					Dec-14
	0.34	11.76	-12.75	9.40		1.36	1.5	12.87	1.02	8.74	1.2	1	98	0	1	144					Jul-14
	-1.85	12.54	-9.67	31.17		0	1.7	16.53	0.91	10.05	77.6	1	99	0	0	48					Jul-14
1,000	-3.30	6.32	-17.81	-5.94	-14.05	0.82	1.61	15.84	1.15	14.03	9.7	6	81	0	13	65	19.08	-21.55			Dec-93
	5.08	20.99	11.80	54.44	63.81	0.87		12.23	1	17.73	1,880	0	99	0	0	58	25.17	-19.08			Oct-29
	-0.73	14.15	-11.23	3.37	-27.82	1.82		18.31		19.9	587.7	1	99	0	0	47	23.17	-27			Jan-29
	4.73	22.06	0.66	58.95		0	0.97	16.29	0.93	13.5	308.7	6	94	0	0	86					Oct-14
50	-2.72	12.85	-14.57	16.79	6.95	0	1.23	18.61	1.01	16.77	131.7	5	93	0	0	31	19.02	-21.93			Apr-05
100	0.69	4.75					1.25			20.26	1.4	65	36	0	0						Aug-18
	4.14	18.81	7.55	34.37	18.92	2.9	0	11.24		16.75	578.3	3	7	46	0	121	13.34	-20.22			Apr-03
250	1.88	13.63	1.57	39.37	32.89	1.52	1.67	12.16	1.06	14.08	149.5	1	98	0	1	28	25.94	-23.41			Oct-09
250	1.88	13.64	1.57	39.37	32.89		1.6	12.16	1.06	14.08	149.5	1	98	0	1	28	25.94	-23.41			Dec-18
250	2.52	12.97	3.38	34.21	26.43	1.85	1.5	10.61	0.92	16.63	443.3	2	94	1	3	24	23.26	-22.36			Jul-97
250	2.52	12.97	3.38	34.21	26.43		1.31	10.61	0.92	16.63	443.3	2	94	1	3	24	23.26	-22.36			Dec-18
250	2.13	10.08	3.26	18.50	17.54	1.69	1.54	6.2	0.53	11.02	416.6	5	52	39	4	23	14.46	-11.65			Jul-97
250	3.13	11.25	2.04	33.50	34.60	0	1.36	9.66	0.82	11.86	217.4	1	99	0	0	172	0.16	-14.73			Dec-09
250	3.13	11.25	2.04	33.50	34.60		1.24	9.66	0.82	11.86	217.4	1	99	0	0	172	0.16	-14.73			Dec-18
500	7.19	19.47	14.26	56.06	52.37	0.47	1	12.4	0.97	11.47	9.8	4	96	0	0	42	20.16	-16.92			Nov-09
500	-0.97	5.91	-3.85	12.92	-4.65	1.4	1.35	11.5		9.13	27.4	4	96	0	1	69					Nov-13
500	1.76	13.00	-6.88	35.87	15.82	1.92	1.15	12.23	0.95	12.69	15.5	4	96	0	1	147	11.05	-20.2			Dec-13
500	1.67	12.96	-6.80	35.83	15.96	1.78	1.22	12.2	0.95	12.72	15.5	4	96	0	1	147	11.05	-20.2			Mar-10
500	-0.51	16.91	-0.42	4.67	-23.96	9.34	1.41	14.13	0.78	7.65	846.2	3	65	33	-2	55	18.71	-9.92	5.50		May-11
500	-0.70	16.43	-1.17	2.30	-26.84	8.52	2.16	14.22	0.79	7.67	846.2	3	65	33	-2	55	18.18	-10.21		1.00	Apr-12
100,000	-0.50	16.97	-0.20	5.39	-23.08	9.62	1.16	14.25	0.79	7.51	846.2	3	65	33	-2	55	18.86	-9.83			Dec-10
500	-1.46	16.10	-0.39	4.99	-26.62	9.91	0.93	13.96	0.77	7.28	89.8	2	38	16	44	73	19.61	-10.42			Sep-10
500	-3.49	17.45	-5.14	-0.93		1.44	1.36	17.28	0.92	8.25	14.2	2	98	0	0	42			5.50		Aug-15
500	-3.59	17.00	-5.91	-3.10		1.12	2.11	17.33	0.92	8.21	14.2	2	98	0	0	42				1.00	Aug-15
100,000	-3.50	17.49	-5.03	-0.31		1.54	1.11	17.35	0.92	8.28	14.2	2	98	0	0	42					Aug-15
250	-2.57	15.29	-10.70	29.28	3.90	0	1.5	19.61	0.77	17.41	111.0	4	96	0	0	62	24.09	-23.66			May-98
250	-2.60	15.18	-10.89	28.43	2.75	0	1.75	19.61	0.77	17.22	111.0	4	96	0	0	62	23.91	-23.74	3.75		Feb-14

	MARKET			FUND TYPE, CATEGORY & OBJECTIVE	RATINGS				MINIMUMS	
Fund Name	Ticker Symbol	Traded On	Fund Type	Category and (Prospectus Objective)	Overall Rating	Reward Rating	Risk Rating	Recent Up/ Downgrade	Open to New Investors	Min Initial Investment
AGF Global Equity Fund Class I	AGXIX	NAS CM	Open End	Global Equity Large Cap (World Stock)	D+	D	C	Up	Y	1,000,000
AGF Global Equity Fund Class R6	AGXRX	NAS CM	Open End	Global Equity Large Cap (World Stock)	D+	D	C	Up	Y	1,000,000
AGF Global Sustainable Growth Equity Fund Class I	AGPIX	NAS CM	Open End	Global Equity Large Cap (World Stock)	D+	D+	C+	Up	Y	1,000,000
AGF Global Sustainable Growth Equity Fund Class R6	AGPRX	NAS CM	Open End	Global Equity Large Cap (World Stock)	D+	D+	C+	Up	Y	1,000,000
AIG Active Allocation Fund Class A	FBAAX	NAS CM	Open End	Moderate Alloc (Asset Alloc)	B-	C	B+	Up	Y	500
AIG Active Allocation Fund Class B	FBABX	NAS CM	Open End	Moderate Alloc (Asset Alloc)	B-	C	B	Up	Y	500
AIG Active Allocation Fund Class C	FBACX	NAS CM	Open End	Moderate Alloc (Asset Alloc)	B-	C	B	Up	Y	500
AIG Commodity Strategy Fund Class A	SUNAX	NAS CM	Open End	Commodities Broad Basket (Growth & Income)	D	D	D+		Y	500
AIG Commodity Strategy Fund Class C	SUNCX	NAS CM	Open End	Commodities Broad Basket (Growth & Income)	D	D	D+		Y	500
AIG Commodity Strategy Fund Class W	SUNWX	NAS CM	Open End	Commodities Broad Basket (Growth & Income)	D	D	C-		Y	50,000
AIG ESG Dividend Fund A Shares	EDFAX	NAS CM	Open End	US Equity Large Cap Value (Growth & Income)	C	C	C+		Y	500
AIG ESG Dividend Fund C Shares	EDFCX	NAS CM	Open End	US Equity Large Cap Value (Growth & Income)	C	C	C		Y	500
AIG ESG Dividend Fund W Shares	EDFWX	NAS CM	Open End	US Equity Large Cap Value (Growth & Income)	C	C	C+		Y	50,000
AIG Focused Alpha Large-Cap Fund Class A	SFLAX	NAS CM	Open End	US Equity Large Cap Growth (Growth)	B-	C+	B	Down	Y	500
AIG Focused Alpha Large-Cap Fund Class C	SFLCX	NAS CM	Open End	US Equity Large Cap Growth (Growth)	B-	C+	B	Down	Y	500
AIG Focused Alpha Large-Cap Fund Class W	SFLWX	NAS CM	Open End	US Equity Large Cap Growth (Growth)	B-	C+	B	Down	Y	50,000
AIG Focused Dividend Strategy Fund Class A	FDSAX	NAS CM	Open End	US Equity Large Cap Value (Growth & Income)	C+	C	B		Y	500
AIG Focused Dividend Strategy Fund Class B	FDSBX	NAS CM	Open End	US Equity Large Cap Value (Growth & Income)	C+	C	B		Y	500
AIG Focused Dividend Strategy Fund Class C	FDSTX	NAS CM	Open End	US Equity Large Cap Value (Growth & Income)	C+	C	B		Y	500
AIG Focused Dividend Strategy Fund Class W	FDSWX	NAS CM	Open End	US Equity Large Cap Value (Growth & Income)	C+	C	B		Y	50,000
AIG Focused Growth Fund Class A	FOCAX	NAS CM	Open End	US Equity Large Cap Growth (Growth)	C+	C	B-	Down	Y	500
AIG Focused Growth Fund Class C	FOCCX	NAS CM	Open End	US Equity Large Cap Growth (Growth)	C+	C	B-	Down	Y	500
AIG Focused Growth Fund Class W	FOCWX	NAS CM	Open End	US Equity Large Cap Growth (Growth)	C+	C	B-	Down	Y	50,000
AIG Income Explorer Fund Class A	IEAAX	NAS CM	Open End	Cautious Alloc (Income)	B-	C	A-	Up	Y	500
AIG Income Explorer Fund Class C	IEACX	NAS CM	Open End	Cautious Alloc (Income)	B-	C	B+	Up	Y	500
AIG Income Explorer Fund Class W	IEAWX	NAS CM	Open End	Cautious Alloc (Income)	B-	C	A-	Up	Y	50,000
AIG International Dividend Strategy Fund Class A	SIEAX	NAS CM	Open End	Global Equity Large Cap (Foreign Stock)	C-	D+	C		Y	500
AIG International Dividend Strategy Fund Class C	SIETX	NAS CM	Open End	Global Equity Large Cap (Foreign Stock)	C-	D+	C		Y	500
AIG International Dividend Strategy Fund Class W	SIEWX	NAS CM	Open End	Global Equity Large Cap (Foreign Stock)	C-	D+	C		Y	50,000
AIG Japan Fund Class A	SAESX	NAS CM	Open End	Japan Equity (Pacific Stock)	C-	C-	C		Y	500
AIG Japan Fund Class C	SAJCX	NAS CM	Open End	Japan Equity (Pacific Stock)	C-	D+	C		Y	500
AIG Japan Fund Class W	SAJWX	NAS CM	Open End	Japan Equity (Pacific Stock)	C-	C-	C		Y	50,000
AIG Multi-Asset Allocation Fund Class A	FASAX	NAS CM	Open End	Moderate Alloc (Asset Alloc)	C+	C	B	Up	Y	500
AIG Multi-Asset Allocation Fund Class B	FMABX	NAS CM	Open End	Moderate Alloc (Asset Alloc)	C	C	B		Y	500
AIG Multi-Asset Allocation Fund Class C	FMATX	NAS CM	Open End	Moderate Alloc (Asset Alloc)	C	C	B		Y	500
AIG Select Dividend Growth Fund Class A	SDVAX	NAS CM	Open End	US Equity Large Cap Value (Growth)	C	C	B-		Y	500
AIG Select Dividend Growth Fund Class C	SDVCX	NAS CM	Open End	US Equity Large Cap Value (Growth)	C	C	B-		Y	500
AIG Select Dividend Growth Fund Class W	SDVWX	NAS CM	Open End	US Equity Large Cap Value (Growth)	C+	C	B-	Up	Y	50,000
AIG Small-Cap Fund Class A	SASAX	NAS CM	Open End	US Equity Small Cap (Small Company)	C	C-	C	Down	Y	500
AIG Small-Cap Fund Class C	SASCX	NAS CM	Open End	US Equity Small Cap (Small Company)	C	C-	C		Y	500
AIG Small-Cap Fund Class W	SASWX	NAS CM	Open End	US Equity Small Cap (Small Company)	C	C-	C	Down	Y	50,000
AIG Strategic Value Fund Class A	SFVAX	NAS CM	Open End	US Equity Large Cap Value (Growth)	C+	C	B	Up	Y	500
AIG Strategic Value Fund Class C	SFVTX	NAS CM	Open End	US Equity Large Cap Value (Growth)	C	C	B-		Y	500
AIG Strategic Value Fund Class W	SFVWX	NAS CM	Open End	US Equity Large Cap Value (Growth)	C+	C	B	Up	Y	50,000
Akre Focus Fund Institutional Class	AKRIX	NAS CM	Open End	US Equity Large Cap Growth (Growth)	B+	B+	A-	Up	Y	250,000
Akre Focus Fund Retail Class	AKREX	NAS CM	Open End	US Equity Large Cap Growth (Growth)	B+	B+	A-	Up	Y	2,000
Akre Focus Fund Supra Institutional Class	AKRSX	NAS CM	Open End	US Equity Large Cap Growth (Growth)	B+	B+	A-	Up	Y	300,000,000
Al Frank Fund Class Advisor	VALAX	NAS CM	Open End	US Equity Large Cap Value (Growth)	C+	C	B		Y	100,000
Al Frank Fund Class Investor	VALUX	NAS CM	Open End	US Equity Large Cap Value (Growth)	C+	C	B		Y	1,000
Alambic Mid Cap Plus Fund	ALMGX	NAS CM	Open End	US Equity Mid Cap (Growth)	C	C	B		Y	5,000
Alambic Mid Cap Value Plus Fund	ALMVX	NAS CM	Open End	US Equity Mid Cap (Growth)	C-	D+	C	Down		5,000
Alambic Small Cap Plus Fund	ALGSX	NAS CM	Open End	US Equity Small Cap (Small Company)	C-	C-	C	Down	Y	5,000

★ Expanded analysis of this fund is included in Section II.

Min Additional Investment	TOTAL RETURNS 3-Month Total Return	6-Month Total Return	1-Year Total Return	3-Year Total Return	5-Year Total Return	PERFORMANCE Dividend Yield (TTM)	Expense Ratio	3-Yr Std Deviation	3-Year Beta	ASSETS NAV	Total Assets (MIL)	ASSET ALLOCATION & TURNOVER %Cash	%Stocks	%Bonds	%Other	Turnover Ratio	BULL & BEAR Last Bull Market Total Return	Last Bear Market Total Return	FEES Front End Fee (%)	Back End Fee (%)	Inception Date
	3.27	17.52	4.12			1.52	0.86			9.79	0.70	-1	101	0	0	11					Nov-17
	3.27	17.52	4.12			1.52	0.86			9.79	0.70	-1	101	0	0	11					Nov-17
	5.00	23.01	7.72			0.46	0.8			10.69	0.85	3	97	0	0	12					Nov-17
	5.00	23.01	7.72			0.46	0.8			10.69	0.85	3	97	0	0	12					Nov-17
100	2.03	10.97	1.96	23.66	24.61	2.53	1.77	8.49	0.67	16.68	130.0	3	65	30	1	17	12.11	-10.01	5.75		Nov-02
100	1.88	10.56	1.32	21.20	20.48	1.93	2.54	8.45	0.67	16.52	130.0	3	65	30	1	17	11.63	-10.25		4.00	Nov-02
100	1.94	10.59	1.32	21.32	20.67	1.93	2.45	8.45	0.67	16.58	130.0	3	65	30	1	17	11.6	-10.2		1.00	Nov-02
100	-0.75	4.43	-9.41	-10.95	-20.77	0.07	1.72	9.05	0.42	6.59	34.5	50	1	12	32	1	-19.84	5.67	5.75		Nov-08
100	-0.94	3.98	-10.04	-12.79	-23.44	0	2.37	8.99	0.42	6.27	34.5	50	1	12	32	1	-20.13	5.34		1.00	Nov-08
	-0.74	4.53	-9.26	-10.37	-19.97	0.25	1.52	8.98	0.42	6.68	34.5	50	1	12	32	1	-19.81	5.75			Nov-08
100	1.09	11.87	2.43			1.79	1.13			14.79	30.5	1	99	0	0	57			5.75		Dec-16
100	0.94	11.55	1.75			1.22	1.78			14.77	30.5	1	99	0	0	57				1.00	Dec-16
	1.22	12.07	2.71			1.99	0.93			14.8	30.5	1	99	0	0	57					Dec-16
100	5.50	21.46	10.44	65.97	75.85	0	1.65	13.89	1.07	28.75	647.6	5	95	0	0	65	26.75	-21.69	5.75		Dec-05
100	5.33	21.04	9.67	62.73	70.21	0	2.33	13.88	1.07	26.86	647.6	5	95	0	0	65	26.27	-21.9		1.00	Jan-12
	5.52	21.52	10.54	66.55	77.04	0	1.52	13.88	1.07	29.24	647.6	5	95	0	0	65	26.8	-21.69			Jan-12
100	0.53	11.87	2.04	27.79	44.18	2.76	1.04	13.63	1.02	16.93	10,317	0	100	0	0	38	22.05	-8.91	5.75		Jun-98
100	0.36	11.45	1.34	25.22	39.52	2.15	1.69	13.59	1.01	16.78	10,317	0	100	0	0	38	21.64	-9.16		4.00	Jun-98
100	0.37	11.47	1.35	25.32	39.59	2.16	1.69	13.6	1.01	16.77	10,317	0	100	0	0	38	21.57	-9.13		1.00	Jun-98
	0.58	11.93	2.19	28.53	45.66	2.96	0.84	13.63	1.01	16.9	10,317	0	100	0	0	38	22.05	-8.91			May-13
100	3.05	16.81	1.79	57.32	65.35	0	1.13	15.3	1.06	26.33	603.5	8	92	0	0	94	25.27	-19.96	5.75		Jul-05
100	2.90	16.46	1.13	54.28	59.97	0	1.78	15.31	1.06	24.47	603.5	8	92	0	0	94	24.77	-20.17		1.00	Jan-12
	3.10	16.92	2.00	58.20	67.00	0	0.93	15.32	1.06	26.88	603.5	8	92	0	0	94	25.26	-19.96			Jan-12
100	3.44	14.69	4.71	25.37	20.82	4.18	2.25	7.66	0.59	15.31	46.3	-4	33	51	-2	51			5.75		Jul-13
100	3.35	14.41	4.11	23.02	16.97	3.57	2.9	7.68	0.59	15.29	46.3	-4	33	51	-2	51				1.00	Jul-13
	3.49	14.82	4.92	26.13	22.02	4.38	2.05	7.65	0.59	15.31	46.3	-4	33	51	-2	51					Jul-13
100	-0.55	9.77	-2.62	12.84	-25.47	2.68	1.9	12.44	1.03	8.18	64.6	1	99	0	0	59	14.36	-25.34	5.75		Nov-96
100	-0.84	9.21	-3.42	10.62	-27.91	2.29	2.55	12.33	1.03	7.39	64.6	1	99	0	0	59	14.03	-25.67		1.00	Mar-97
	-0.58	9.72	-2.62	13.40	-24.95	2.8	1.7	12.41	1.03	8.18	64.6	1	99	0	0	59	14.36	-25.34			Jan-15
100	2.21	9.69	-4.59	26.19	15.52	0	1.9	13.34	1.17	6.45	18.3	3	97	0	0	101	9.29	-24.65	5.75		May-06
100	2.04	9.10	-5.33	23.52	11.65	0	2.55	13.33	1.17	5.99	18.3	3	97	0	0	101	8.97	-24.97		1.00	May-06
	2.21	9.66	-4.46	26.65	15.93	0	1.7	13.33	1.17	6.47	18.3	3	97	0	0	101	9.28	-24.65			Apr-17
100	1.81	11.01	0.26	22.24	22.42	2.52	1.79	9.16	0.72	17.93	229.1	4	64	26	4	7	5.77	-9.56	5.75		Nov-02
100	1.64	10.63	-0.40	19.74	18.31	1.84	2.52	9.16	0.72	17.88	229.1	4	64	26	4	7	5.27	-9.76		4.00	Nov-02
100	1.59	10.58	-0.46	19.84	18.53	1.83	2.45	9.14	0.72	17.86	229.1	4	64	26	4	7	5.33	-9.75		1.00	Nov-02
100	3.14	14.49	1.10	36.57	41.05	1.93	1.13	16.43	1.24	14.38	44.0	1	99	0	0	77			5.75		May-14
100	2.92	14.12	0.43	33.67	35.74	1.37	1.78	16.41	1.24	14.3	44.0	1	99	0	0	77				1.00	May-14
	3.15	14.62	1.26	37.07	41.63	2.14	0.93	16.39	1.23	14.31	44.0	1	99	0	0	77					May-14
100	0.35	13.52	-7.01	44.78	49.76	0	1.26	16.67	0.96	16.96	52.0	2	98	0	0	63			5.75		Feb-14
100	0.18	13.18	-7.60	41.94	44.89	0	1.91	16.67	0.96	16.22	52.0	2	98	0	0	63				1.00	Feb-14
	0.40	13.62	-6.79	45.66	51.23	0	1.06	16.69	0.96	17.18	52.0	2	98	0	0	63					Feb-14
100	2.08	12.59	2.12	25.08	31.38	1.19	1.45	12.01	0.96	27.9	206.5	1	99	0	0	46	22.61	-19.32	5.75		Nov-99
100	1.87	12.14	1.30	22.39	26.88	0.59	2.16	12.01	0.96	25.49	206.5	1	99	0	0	46	22.11	-19.55		1.00	Nov-99
	2.08	12.55	2.08	24.91	31.19	1.15	1.52	12	0.96	27.89	206.5	1	99	0	0	46	22.61	-19.32			Apr-17
25,000	6.03	27.50	23.17	84.63	106.99	0	1.05	10.87	0.79	43.9	11,002	10	90	0	0	4	28.06	-5.89			Aug-09
250	5.92	27.27	22.82	83.12	104.23	0	1.32	10.88	0.79	42.88	11,002	10	90	0	0	4	27.84	-5.99			Aug-09
	6.04	27.53	23.28	85.18	107.69	0	0.95	10.88	0.79	44.05	11,002	10	90	0	0	4	28.06	-5.89			Aug-15
100	3.01	14.38	4.51	42.89	31.39	1.26	1.24	14.28	1.11	23.54	76.5	2	98	0	0	16	23.52	-22.48			May-06
100	2.93	14.20	4.22	41.79	29.74	1	1.49	14.27	1.11	23.47	76.5	2	98	0	0	16	23.35	-22.56			Jan-98
	1.27	18.27	3.37			0.27	0.85			11.12	1.3	18	82	0	0	183					Dec-16
	-4.09	9.26	-4.42			1.53	0.85			10.22	1.1	8	92	0	0	184					Dec-16
	-1.78	9.06	-13.64	33.58		0	0.95	18.31	1.04	9.9	2.6	2	98	0	0	220					Dec-15

	MARKET		FUND TYPE, CATEGORY & OBJECTIVE		RATINGS				MINIMUMS	
Fund Name	Ticker Symbol	Traded On	Fund Type	Category and (Prospectus Objective)	Overall Rating	Reward Rating	Risk Rating	Recent Up/ Downgrade	Open to New Investors	Min Initial Investment
Alambic Small Cap Value Plus Fund	ALAMX	NAS CM	Open End	US Equity Small Cap (Small Company)	D+	D+	D+	Down		5,000
Alger 25 Fund Class P	ATFPX	NAS CM	Open End	US Equity Large Cap Growth (Growth)	D+	C-	C+	Up	Y	500,000
Alger 25 Fund Class P-2	ATFFX	NAS CM	Open End	US Equity Large Cap Growth (Growth)	D+	C-	C+	Up	Y	25,000
Alger 35 Fund Class P	ATVPX	NAS CM	Open End	US Equity Large Cap Growth (Growth)	D	D+	C+	Up	Y	500,000
Alger 35 Fund Class P-2	ATVVX	NAS CM	Open End	US Equity Large Cap Growth (Growth)	D	D+	C+	Up	Y	25,000
Alger Balanced Portfolio Class I-2	ABLOX	NAS CM	Open End	Moderate Alloc (Balanced)	B	C	A-	Up	Y	500,000
Alger Capital Appreciation Fund Class A	ACAAX	NAS CM	Open End	US Equity Large Cap Growth (Aggr Growth)	B-	C+	B	Down	Y	1,000
Alger Capital Appreciation Fund Class B	ACAPX	NAS CM	Open End	US Equity Large Cap Growth (Aggr Growth)	C+	C	B	Down		1,000
Alger Capital Appreciation Fund Class C	ALCCX	NAS CM	Open End	US Equity Large Cap Growth (Aggr Growth)	C+	C	B	Down	Y	1,000
Alger Capital Appreciation Fund Class Z	ACAZX	NAS CM	Open End	US Equity Large Cap Growth (Aggr Growth)	B-	C+	B	Down	Y	500,000
Alger Capital Appreciation Institutional Fund Class I	ALARX	NAS CM	Open End	US Equity Large Cap Growth (Aggr Growth)	B-	C+	B	Down	Y	0
Alger Capital Appreciation Institutional Fund Class R	ACARX	NAS CM	Open End	US Equity Large Cap Growth (Aggr Growth)	B-	C+	B	Down	Y	0
Alger Capital Appreciation Institutional Fund Class Y	ACAYX	NAS CM	Open End	US Equity Large Cap Growth (Aggr Growth)	B-	C+	B	Down	Y	500,000
Alger Capital Appreciation Institutional Fund Class Z-2	ACIZX	NAS CM	Open End	US Equity Large Cap Growth (Aggr Growth)	B-	C+	B	Down	Y	500,000
Alger Capital Appreciation Portfolio Class I-2	ALVOX	NAS CM	Open End	US Equity Large Cap Growth (Aggr Growth)	B-	C+	B	Down	Y	500,000
Alger Capital Appreciation Portfolio Class S			Open End	US Equity Large Cap Growth (Aggr Growth)	B-	C+	B	Down	Y	0
Alger Dynamic Opportunities Fund Class A	SPEDX	NAS CM	Open End	Long/Short Equity (Growth)	B-	C+	B		Y	1,000
Alger Dynamic Opportunities Fund Class C	ADOCX	NAS CM	Open End	Long/Short Equity (Growth)	B-	C+	B	Up	Y	1,000
Alger Dynamic Opportunities Fund Class Z	ADOZX	NAS CM	Open End	Long/Short Equity (Growth)	B-	C+	B		Y	500,000
Alger Emerging Markets Fund Class A	AAEMX	NAS CM	Open End	Global Emerg Mkts (Div Emerging Mkts)	C	C-	C		Y	1,000
Alger Emerging Markets Fund Class C	ACEMX	NAS CM	Open End	Global Emerg Mkts (Div Emerging Mkts)	C	C-	C	Up	Y	1,000
Alger Emerging Markets Fund Class I	AIEMX	NAS CM	Open End	Global Emerg Mkts (Div Emerging Mkts)	C	C-	C		Y	0
Alger Emerging Markets Fund Class Y	AYEMX	NAS CM	Open End	Global Emerg Mkts (Div Emerging Mkts)	C	C	C		Y	500,000
Alger Emerging Markets Fund Class Z	AZEMX	NAS CM	Open End	Global Emerg Mkts (Div Emerging Mkts)	C	C	C		Y	500,000
Alger Focus Equity Fund Class A	ALAFX	NAS CM	Open End	US Equity Large Cap Growth (Growth)	B-	C+	B	Down	Y	1,000
Alger Focus Equity Fund Class C	ALCFX	NAS CM	Open End	US Equity Large Cap Growth (Growth)	B-	C+	B	Down	Y	1,000
Alger Focus Equity Fund Class I	ALGRX	NAS CM	Open End	US Equity Large Cap Growth (Growth)	B-	C+	B	Down	Y	0
Alger Focus Equity Fund Class Y	ALGYX	NAS CM	Open End	US Equity Large Cap Growth (Growth)	B-	C+	B	Down	Y	500,000
Alger Focus Equity Fund Class Z	ALZFX	NAS CM	Open End	US Equity Large Cap Growth (Growth)	B-	C+	B	Down	Y	500,000
Alger Global Focus Fund Class A	CHUSX	NAS CM	Open End	Global Equity Large Cap (Growth)	C	C	C+		Y	1,000
Alger Global Focus Fund Class C	CHUCX	NAS CM	Open End	Global Equity Large Cap (Growth)	C	C	C+		Y	1,000
Alger Global Focus Fund Class I	AFGIX	NAS CM	Open End	Global Equity Large Cap (Growth)	C	C	C+		Y	0
Alger Global Focus Fund Class Z	AFGZX	NAS CM	Open End	Global Equity Large Cap (Growth)	C	C	C+		Y	500,000
Alger Growth & Income Fund Class A	ALBAX	NAS CM	Open End	US Equity Large Cap Blend (Growth & Income)	B-	C	B		Y	1,000
Alger Growth & Income Fund Class C	ALBCX	NAS CM	Open End	US Equity Large Cap Blend (Growth & Income)	B-	C	B		Y	1,000
Alger Growth & Income Fund Class Z	AGIZX	NAS CM	Open End	US Equity Large Cap Blend (Growth & Income)	B-	C	B		Y	500,000
Alger Growth & Income Portfolio I-2	AIGOX	NAS CM	Open End	US Equity Large Cap Blend (Equity-Income)	B-	C	B		Y	500,000
Alger Health Sciences Fund Class A	AHSAX	NAS CM	Open End	Healthcare Sector Equity (Health)	C+	C+	B-	Down	Y	1,000
Alger Health Sciences Fund Class C	AHSCX	NAS CM	Open End	Healthcare Sector Equity (Health)	C+	C+	B-	Down	Y	1,000
Alger Health Sciences Fund Class Z	AHSZX	NAS CM	Open End	Healthcare Sector Equity (Health)	C+	C+	B-	Down	Y	500,000
Alger International Focus Fund Class A	ALGAX	NAS CM	Open End	Global Equity Large Cap (Growth)	C	C-	C	Up	Y	1,000
Alger International Focus Fund Class B	AFGPX	NAS CM	Open End	Global Equity Large Cap (Growth)	C	C-	C	Up		1,000
Alger International Focus Fund Class C	ALGCX	NAS CM	Open End	Global Equity Large Cap (Growth)	C	C-	C	Up	Y	1,000
Alger International Focus Fund Class I	AIGIX	NAS CM	Open End	Global Equity Large Cap (Growth)	C	C-	C+	Up	Y	0
Alger International Focus Fund Class Z	ALCZX	NAS CM	Open End	Global Equity Large Cap (Growth)	C	C-	C+	Up	Y	500,000
Alger Large Cap Growth Portfolio Class I-2	AAGOX	NAS CM	Open End	US Equity Large Cap Growth (Growth)	C+	C	B-	Down	Y	500,000
Alger Large Cap Growth Portfolio Class S			Open End	US Equity Large Cap Growth (Growth)	C+	C	B-	Down	Y	0
Alger Mid Cap Growth Fund Class A	AMGAX	NAS CM	Open End	US Equity Mid Cap (Growth)	C+	C	C+	Down	Y	1,000
Alger Mid Cap Growth Fund Class B	AMCGX	NAS CM	Open End	US Equity Mid Cap (Growth)	C+	C	C+			1,000
Alger Mid Cap Growth Fund Class C	AMGCX	NAS CM	Open End	US Equity Mid Cap (Growth)	C+	C	C+		Y	1,000
Alger Mid Cap Growth Fund Class Z	AMCZX	NAS CM	Open End	US Equity Mid Cap (Growth)	C+	C	C+	Down	Y	500,000
Alger Mid Cap Growth Institutional Fund Class I	ALMRX	NAS CM	Open End	US Equity Mid Cap (Growth)	C+	C	C+	Down	Y	0

★ Expanded analysis of this fund is included in Section II.

	TOTAL RETURNS					PERFORMANCE				ASSETS		ASSET ALLOCATION & TURNOVER					BULL & BEAR		FEES		
Min Additional Investment	3-Month Total Return	6-Month Total Return	1-Year Total Return	3-Year Total Return	5-Year Total Return	Dividend Yield (TTM)	Expense Ratio	3-Yr Std Deviation	3-Year Beta	NAV	Total Assets (MIL)	%Cash	%Stocks	%Bonds	%Other	Turnover Ratio	Last Bull Market Total Return	Last Bear Market Total Return	Front End Fee (%)	Back End Fee (%)	Inception Date
	-6.96	1.10	-19.54	14.70		0.5	0.95	18.14	1.01	9.13	2.6	10	90	0	0	225					Sep-15
	6.97	23.44	8.82			0.31	0.65			12.11	13.0	2	98	0	0	64					Dec-17
	6.96	23.37	8.68				0.81			12.14	13.0	2	98	0	0	64					Oct-18
	6.78	24.62	9.88			0.38	0.65			11.64	9.2	4	96	0	0	31					Apr-18
	6.66	24.52	9.75				0.81			11.68	9.2	4	96	0	0	31					Oct-18
	2.78	11.10	7.61	30.41	41.20	4.15	1.14	7.31	0.59	15.11	44.6	2	63	35	0	5	13.27	-9.26			Sep-89
50	5.25	22.76	9.73	65.61	79.42	0	1.21	14.16	1.04	26.64	2,866	0	99	0	0	67	26.89	-18.79	5.25		Dec-96
50	5.05	22.31	8.92	61.91	72.71	0	1.99	14.16	1.04	20.17	2,866	0	99	0	0	67	26.2	-19.1		5.00	Nov-93
50	5.07	22.30	8.92	61.96	72.83	0	1.94	14.17	1.04	20.29	2,866	0	99	0	0	67	26.31	-19.12		1.00	Jul-97
	5.35	23.00	10.14	67.42	82.51	0	0.87	14.17	1.04	27.54	2,866	0	99	0	0	67	27.05	-18.71			Dec-10
	5.31	22.84	9.90	65.70	79.84	0	1.15	14.16	1.04	34.85	3,523	0	100	0	0	65	27.22	-18.94			Nov-93
	5.19	22.55	9.40	63.40	75.62	0	1.59	14.15	1.03	30.59	3,523	0	100	0	0	65	26.87	-19.13			Jan-03
	5.44	23.10	10.38	67.21	81.48	0	0.75	14.16	1.04	35.22	3,523	0	100	0	0	65	27.22	-18.94			Mar-17
	5.42	23.07	10.29	67.17	81.44	0	0.82	14.15	1.03	35.2	3,523	0	100	0	0	65	27.22	-18.94			Oct-16
	5.54	23.04	10.83	67.23	82.35	0.08	0.95	14.05	1.03	82.97	494.3	0	100	0	0	68	27.25	-18.54			Jan-95
	5.48	22.88	10.55	65.93	79.94	0	1.21	14.05	1.03	78.44	494.3	0	100	0	0	68	26.98	-18.65			May-02
50	1.23	17.60	6.41	38.37	37.25	0	2	11.09	0.69	14.7	116.5	51	48	0	0	182	11.28	-14.77	5.25		Nov-09
50	1.11	17.18	5.62	35.30	32.10	0	2.75	11.13	0.69	13.64	116.5	51	48	0	0	182	10.75	-14.99		1.00	Dec-10
	1.34	17.78	6.68	39.70	39.26	0	1.75	11.1	0.69	15.1	116.5	51	48	0	0	182	11.47	-14.69			Dec-10
50	1.25	12.15	-4.10	24.23	5.56	1.89	1.55	14.68	1.02	9.69	26.6	2	98	0	0	105	15.94	-27.73	5.25		Dec-10
50	0.98	11.68	-4.81	21.50	1.63	1.19	2.3	14.69	1.02	9.27	26.6	2	98	0	0	105	15.27	-27.92		1.00	Dec-10
	1.26	12.25	-4.01	24.39	5.64	2.1	1.45	14.65	1.02	9.62	26.6	2	98	0	0	105	15.73	-27.67			Dec-10
	1.35	12.52	-3.53	26.21	7.32	2.67	0.95	14.71	1.03	9.7	26.6	2	98	0	0	105	15.73	-27.67			May-16
	1.35	12.47	-3.57	25.82	7.86	2.61	0.99	14.68	1.02	9.74	26.6	2	98	0	0	105	15.73	-27.67			Feb-14
50	5.21	22.86	9.50	74.84	92.98	0	1.03	14.08	1.03	36.54	524.3	1	99	0	0	136	23.47	-16.92	5.25		Dec-12
50	5.03	22.43	8.68	70.95	85.83	0	1.8	14.07	1.03	34.65	524.3	1	99	0	0	136	22.94	-17.18		1.00	Dec-12
	5.23	22.94	9.57	74.97	93.58	0	0.89	14.06	1.03	36.76	524.3	1	99	0	0	136	23.65	-16.83			Nov-93
	5.31	23.11	9.92	76.38	95.14	0.21	0.65	14.07	1.03	37.44	524.3	1	99	0	0	136	23.65	-16.83			Mar-17
	5.29	23.09	9.87	76.50	96.30	0.2	0.68	14.07	1.03	37.36	524.3	1	99	0	0	136	23.65	-16.83			Dec-12
50	5.67	18.06	-5.04	27.02	21.22	0.57	1.5	13.73	1.12	21.96	22.5	3	96	0	0	218	20.52	-29.36	5.25		Nov-03
50	5.46	17.65	-5.74	24.15	16.73	0	2.25	13.7	1.12	20.66	22.5	3	96	0	0	218	20.04	-29.61		1.00	Mar-08
	5.80	18.29	-4.76	27.98	22.77	0.56	1.15	13.76	1.12	21.34	22.5	3	96	0	0	218	20.52	-29.36			Jun-13
	5.84	18.33	-4.62	28.60	24.00	0.94	0.99	13.72	1.12	22.46	22.5	3	96	0	0	218	20.52	-29.36			May-13
50	3.53	15.42	9.25	43.98	54.92	1.4	1.06	11.04	0.9	41.24	114.1	3	97	0	0	11	21.87	-12.88	5.25		Dec-96
50	3.32	15.00	8.42	40.74	49.19	0.66	1.82	11.04	0.9	40.67	114.1	3	97	0	0	11	21.37	-13.18		1.00	Jul-97
	3.63	15.63	9.66	45.39	57.28	1.75	0.69	11.05	0.9	41.27	114.1	3	97	0	0	11	21.92	-12.88			Mar-12
	3.99	15.97	9.88	45.47	56.67	1.48	0.96	11.12	0.9	21.16	30.1	2	98	0	0	8	22.6	-13.99			Nov-88
50	4.17	19.94	6.41	92.15	89.03	0	1.15	19.92	1.18	28.45	217.5	0	96	0	3	90	15.45	-12.93	5.25		May-02
50	3.97	19.47	5.58	87.73	81.88	0	1.93	19.9	1.18	21.96	217.5	0	96	0	3	90	14.86	-13.16		1.00	May-02
	4.30	20.23	6.84	94.43	90.24	0	0.75	19.92	1.18	28.58	217.5	0	96	0	3	90	15.45	-12.93			May-15
50	5.81	19.18	-4.68	22.35	8.23	2.76	1.29	12.92	1.02	15.47	139.9	3	97	0	0	207	24.24	-16.67	5.25		Dec-96
50	5.84	19.00	-5.20	19.94	4.71	2.5	2.01	12.9	1.02	13.4	139.9	3	97	0	0	207	23.65	-16.87		5.00	Nov-86
50	5.55	18.62	-5.51	19.39	4.02	1.89	2.09	12.9	1.02	13.12	139.9	3	97	0	0	207	23.41	-16.91		1.00	Jul-97
	5.87	19.33	-4.44	23.07	9.27	2.92	1.1	12.92	1.02	15.49	139.9	3	97	0	0	207	23.65	-16.87			May-13
	5.96	19.49	-4.21	24.02	10.74	3.16	0.89	12.94	1.02	15.63	139.9	3	97	0	0	207	24.39	-16.58			Dec-10
	5.29	21.98	7.44	69.86	66.63	0	0.86	15.77	1.11	62.09	280.6	7	93	0	0	199	24.31	-16.7			Jan-89
	5.16	21.73	6.99	67.73	63.33	0	1.32	15.78	1.11	59.7	280.6	7	93	0	0	199	23.97	-16.83			May-02
50	6.31	29.39	9.05	62.87	55.15	0	1.3	15.99	1.06	15.32	191.0	1	98	0	1	125	28.29	-27.42	5.25		Dec-96
50	6.32	29.08	8.40	59.72	49.93	0	2.05	15.98	1.06	11.94	191.0	1	98	0	1	125	27.46	-27.61		5.00	May-93
50	6.04	28.83	8.05	58.91	48.91	0	2.11	16.02	1.06	11.75	191.0	1	98	0	1	125	27.36	-27.59		1.00	Jul-97
	6.37	29.57	9.38	64.29	55.99	0	1.03	16.01	1.06	15.51	191.0	1	98	0	1	125	27.46	-27.61			May-15
	6.33	29.19	8.60	62.81	56.61	0	1.34	16.01	1.06	32.08	109.0	0	98	0	1	128	27.32	-27.08			Nov-93

	MARKET		FUND TYPE, CATEGORY & OBJECTIVE		RATINGS				MINIMUMS	
Fund Name	Ticker Symbol	Traded On	Fund Type	Category and (Prospectus Objective)	Overall Rating	Reward Rating	Risk Rating	Recent Up/ Downgrade	Open to New Investors	Min Initial Investment
Alger Mid Cap Growth Institutional Fund Class R	AGIRX	NAS CM	Open End	US Equity Mid Cap (Growth)	C+	C	C+		Y	0
Alger Mid Cap Growth Portfolio Class I-2	AMGOX	NAS CM	Open End	US Equity Mid Cap (Growth)	C+	C	C+	Down	Y	500,000
Alger Mid Cap Growth Portfolio Class S			Open End	US Equity Mid Cap (Growth)	C+	C	C+	Down	Y	0
Alger MidCap Growth Institutional Fund Class Z-2	ALMZX	NAS CM	Open End	US Equity Mid Cap (Growth)	C+	C	C+	Down	Y	500,000
Alger Responsible Investing Fund Class A	SPEGX	NAS CM	Open End	US Equity Large Cap Growth (Growth)	C+	C+	B	Down	Y	1,000
Alger Responsible Investing Fund Class C	AGFCX	NAS CM	Open End	US Equity Large Cap Growth (Growth)	C+	C+	B	Down	Y	1,000
Alger Responsible Investing Fund Class I	AGIFX	NAS CM	Open End	US Equity Large Cap Growth (Growth)	C+	C+	B	Down	Y	0
Alger Responsible Investing Fund Class Z	ALGZX	NAS CM	Open End	US Equity Large Cap Growth (Growth)	B-	C+	B		Y	500,000
Alger Small Cap Focus Fund Class A	AOFAX	NAS CM	Open End	US Equity Small Cap (Small Company)	C+	C+	C+	Down	Y	1,000
Alger Small Cap Focus Fund Class C	AOFCX	NAS CM	Open End	US Equity Small Cap (Small Company)	C+	C+	C+	Down	Y	1,000
Alger Small Cap Focus Fund Class I	AOFIX	NAS CM	Open End	US Equity Small Cap (Small Company)	C+	C+	C+	Down	Y	0
Alger Small Cap Focus Fund Class Y	AOFYX	NAS CM	Open End	US Equity Small Cap (Small Company)	C+	C+	C+	Down	Y	500,000
Alger Small Cap Focus Fund Class Z	AGOZX	NAS CM	Open End	US Equity Small Cap (Small Company)	C+	C+	C+	Down	Y	500,000
Alger Small Cap Growth Fund Class A	ALSAX	NAS CM	Open End	US Equity Small Cap (Small Company)	C+	C+	C+	Down	Y	1,000
Alger Small Cap Growth Fund Class B	ALSCX	NAS CM	Open End	US Equity Small Cap (Small Company)	C+	C+	C+	Down		1,000
Alger Small Cap Growth Fund Class C	AGSCX	NAS CM	Open End	US Equity Small Cap (Small Company)	C+	C+	C+	Down	Y	1,000
Alger Small Cap Growth Fund Class Z	ASCZX	NAS CM	Open End	US Equity Small Cap (Small Company)	C+	C+	C+	Down	Y	500,000
Alger Small Cap Growth Institutional Fund Class I	ALSRX	NAS CM	Open End	US Equity Small Cap (Small Company)	C+	C+	C+	Down	Y	0
Alger Small Cap Growth Institutional Fund Class R	ASIRX	NAS CM	Open End	US Equity Small Cap (Small Company)	C+	C+	C+	Down	Y	0
Alger Small Cap Growth Portfolio Class I-2	AASOX	NAS CM	Open End	US Equity Small Cap (Small Company)	C+	C+	C+	Down	Y	500,000
Alger SmallCap Growth Institutional Fund Class Z-2	AISZX	NAS CM	Open End	US Equity Small Cap (Small Company)	C+	C+	C+	Down	Y	500,000
Alger SMid Cap Focus Fund Class A	ALMAX	NAS CM	Open End	US Equity Mid Cap (Growth)	B-	B	C+	Up	Y	1,000
Alger SMid Cap Focus Fund Class C	ALMCX	NAS CM	Open End	US Equity Mid Cap (Growth)	B-	B-	C+	Up	Y	1,000
Alger SMid Cap Focus Fund Class I	ASIMX	NAS CM	Open End	US Equity Mid Cap (Growth)	B-	B	C+	Up	Y	0
Alger SMid Cap Focus Fund Class Y	ASYMX	NAS CM	Open End	US Equity Mid Cap (Growth)	B-	B	C+	Up	Y	500,000
Alger SMid Cap Focus Fund Class Z	ASMZX	NAS CM	Open End	US Equity Mid Cap (Growth)	B-	B	C+	Up	Y	500,000
Alger SMid Cap Focus Portfolio I-2	AAMOX	NAS CM	Open End	US Equity Mid Cap (Growth)	C+	B	C		Y	500,000
Alger Spectra Fund Class A	SPECX	NAS CM	Open End	US Equity Large Cap Growth (Growth)	B-	C+	B	Down	Y	1,000
Alger Spectra Fund Class C	ASPCX	NAS CM	Open End	US Equity Large Cap Growth (Growth)	C+	C	B	Down	Y	1,000
Alger Spectra Fund Class I	ASPIX	NAS CM	Open End	US Equity Large Cap Growth (Growth)	B-	C+	B	Down	Y	0
Alger Spectra Fund Class Y	ASPYX	NAS CM	Open End	US Equity Large Cap Growth (Growth)	B-	C+	B	Down	Y	500,000
Alger Spectra Fund Class Z	ASPZX	NAS CM	Open End	US Equity Large Cap Growth (Growth)	B-	C+	B	Down	Y	500,000
All Asset Growth – Alt 20 Portfolio Class IA			Open End	Moderate Alloc (Growth & Income)	B-	C	B+	Up	Y	0
All Asset Growth – Alt 20 Portfolio Class IB			Open End	Moderate Alloc (Growth & Income)	B-	C	B+	Up	Y	0
All Asset Growth – Alt 20 Portfolio Class K			Open End	Moderate Alloc (Growth & Income)	B-	C	B+	Up	Y	0
All Terrain Opportunity Fund Class Institutional	TERIX	NAS CM	Open End	Global Macro (Growth)	B	C+	A-	Up	Y	2,500
AllianceBernstein Overlay A Portfolio Class 1	SAOOX	NAS CM	Open End	Alloc (Growth & Income)	U	U	U		Y	25,000
AllianceBernstein Overlay A Portfolio Class 2	SAOTX	NAS CM	Open End	Alloc (Growth & Income)	U	U	U		Y	1,500,000
AllianceBernstein Overlay B Portfolio Class 1	SBOOX	NAS CM	Open End	Alloc (Growth & Income)	U	U	U		Y	25,000
AllianceBernstein Overlay B Portfolio Class 2	SBOTX	NAS CM	Open End	Alloc (Growth & Income)	U	U	U		Y	1,500,000
AllianceBernstein Tax-Aware Overlay A Portfolio Class 1	SATOX	NAS CM	Open End	Alloc (Growth & Income)	U	U	U		Y	25,000
AllianceBernstein Tax-Aware Overlay A Portfolio Class 2	SATTX	NAS CM	Open End	Alloc (Growth & Income)	U	U	U		Y	1,500,000
AllianceBernstein Tax-Aware Overlay B Portfolio Class 1	SBTOX	NAS CM	Open End	Alloc (Growth & Income)	U	U	U		Y	25,000
AllianceBernstein Tax-Aware Overlay B Portfolio Class 2	SBTTX	NAS CM	Open End	Alloc (Growth & Income)	U	U	U		Y	1,500,000
AllianceBernstein Tax-Aware Overlay C Portfolio Class 1	SCTOX	NAS CM	Open End	Alloc (Growth & Income)	U	U	U		Y	25,000
AllianceBernstein Tax-Aware Overlay C Portfolio Class 2	SCTTX	NAS CM	Open End	Alloc (Growth & Income)	U	U	U		Y	1,500,000
AllianceBernstein Tax-Aware Overlay N Portfolio Class 1	SNTOX	NAS CM	Open End	Alloc (Growth & Income)	U	U	U		Y	25,000
AllianceBernstein Tax-Aware Overlay N Portfolio Class 2	SNTTX	NAS CM	Open End	Alloc (Growth & Income)	U	U	U		Y	1,500,000
AllianzGI Best Styles Global Equity Fund Class A	ALLGX	NAS CM	Open End	Global Equity Large Cap (World Stock)	C	C	B		Y	1,000
AllianzGI Best Styles Global Equity Fund Class C	ABSGX	NAS CM	Open End	Global Equity Large Cap (World Stock)	C	C	B		Y	1,000
AllianzGI Best Styles Global Equity Cls Institutional	ALLHX	NAS CM	Open End	Global Equity Large Cap (World Stock)	C+	C	B	Up	Y	1,000,000
AllianzGI Best Styles Global Equity Fund Class P	ALGPX	NAS CM	Open End	Global Equity Large Cap (World Stock)	C+	C	B	Up	Y	1,000,000

★ Expanded analysis of this fund is included in Section II.

	TOTAL RETURNS					PERFORMANCE				ASSETS		ASSET ALLOCATION & TURNOVER					BULL & BEAR		FEES		
Min Additional Investment	3-Month Total Return	6-Month Total Return	1-Year Total Return	3-Year Total Return	5-Year Total Return	Dividend Yield (TTM)	Expense Ratio	3-Yr Std Deviation	3-Year Beta	NAV	Total Assets (MIL)	%Cash	%Stocks	%Bonds	%Other	Turnover Ratio	Last Bull Market Total Return	Last Bear Market Total Return	Front End Fee (%)	Back End Fee (%)	Inception Date
	6.17	28.88	8.06	60.28	52.53	0	1.82	16.02	1.06	29.05	109.0	0	98	0	1	128	26.93	-27.23			Jan-03
	6.36	29.50	9.16	63.44	56.36	0	1.01	16.02	1.06	25.06	147.0	0	99	0	1	131	27.61	-27.31			May-93
	6.25	29.26	8.69	61.23	53.10	0	1.46	16.02	1.06	23.28	147.0	0	99	0	1	131	27.36	-27.48			May-02
	6.38	29.37	8.92	64.00	57.76	0	1.05	16.01	1.06	32.33	109.0	0	98	0	1	128	27.32	-27.08			Oct-16
50	4.75	21.65	9.42	60.04	62.39	0	1.35	13.68	1.01	11.01	61.3	4	96	0	0	20	24.08	-17.34	5.25		Dec-00
50	4.44	20.98	8.47	56.11	55.92	0	2.14	13.65	1.01	9.86	61.3	4	96	0	0	20	23.32	-17.53		1.00	Sep-08
	4.67	21.45	9.33	59.83	62.18	0	1.37	13.7	1.01	10.98	61.3	4	96	0	0	20	24.13	-17.37			Sep-08
	4.79	21.85	9.81	61.83	64.20	0	0.95	13.69	1.01	11.15	61.3	4	96	0	0	20	24.08	-17.34			Oct-16
50	9.63	30.49	17.26	108.89	110.96	0	1.18	19.16	0.97	21.74	3,767	3	97	0	0	27	29.43	-26.78	5.25		Mar-08
50	9.35	29.95	16.34	104.29	103.59	0	1.94	19.18	0.98	19.52	3,767	3	97	0	0	27	28.94	-27.04		1.00	Mar-08
	9.58	30.50	17.26	108.95	111.73	0	1.17	19.16	0.97	22.29	3,767	3	97	0	0	27	29.53	-26.75			Mar-08
	9.68	30.69	17.60	110.47	113.27	0	0.85	19.18	0.98	22.65	3,767	3	97	0	0	27	29.53	-26.75			Feb-17
	9.68	30.69	17.66	110.92	114.89	0	0.87	19.15	0.97	22.65	3,767	3	97	0	0	27	29.81	-26.74			Dec-10
50	8.57	31.55	13.33	88.72	71.68	0	1.38	17.88	0.95	9.88	149.6	2	97	0	0	29	29.93	-27.12	5.25		Dec-96
50	8.52	31.30	12.56	84.20	65.24	0	2.23	17.84	0.95	7.13	149.6	2	97	0	0	29	30.27	-27.23		5.00	Nov-86
50	8.35	31.10	12.38	84.14	64.94	0	2.16	17.88	0.95	6.87	149.6	2	97	0	0	29	28.25	-27.23		1.00	Jul-97
	8.73	31.91	13.82	90.79	74.71	0	0.99	17.86	0.95	10.21	149.6	2	97	0	0	29	29.35	-26.88			Dec-10
	8.70	31.71	12.51	88.84	72.01	0	1.32	17.97	0.96	22.72	171.0	2	97	0	1	28	29.01	-26.54			Nov-93
	8.62	31.46	12.05	86.12	67.94	0	1.77	17.96	0.96	18.51	171.0	2	97	0	1	28	28.65	-26.7			Jan-03
	8.88	32.00	13.39	90.21	74.56	0	1.01	17.88	0.95	30.4	225.3	2	98	0	0	26	28.64	-26.69			Sep-88
	8.81	31.93	12.88	90.66	73.67	0	0.99	18	0.96	22.97	171.0	2	97	0	1	28	29.01	-26.54			Aug-16
50	3.58	36.81	12.26	89.96	83.13	0	1.33	19.55	1.07	14.16	557.9	3	96	0	0	43	29.33	-26.1	5.25		May-02
50	3.32	36.26	11.37	85.62	76.12	0	2.08	19.48	1.06	9.62	557.9	3	96	0	0	43	28.69	-26.32		1.00	May-02
	3.63	36.81	12.34	90.08	83.09	0	1.35	19.58	1.07	14.53	557.9	3	96	0	0	43	29.31	-26.03			Aug-07
	3.68	37.07	12.74	91.41	84.53	0	0.87	19.56	1.07	14.64	557.9	3	96	0	0	43	29.33	-26.1			Aug-17
	3.65	37.06	12.61	91.83	86.16	0	0.99	19.58	1.07	15.05	557.9	3	96	0	0	43	29.61	-25.96			Dec-10
	3.62	36.70	12.60	89.74	88.33	0	1.05	19.46	1.06	2.57	1.5	3	96	0	0	56	29.55	-26			Jan-08
50	5.85	23.22	9.78	66.08	80.19	0	1.27	14.22	1.02	22.23	6,218	1	99	0	0	74	26.98	-18.83	5.25		Jul-69
50	5.65	22.77	8.93	62.41	73.43	0	2.01	14.18	1.02	20	6,218	1	99	0	0	74	26.41	-19.08		1.00	Sep-08
	5.88	23.30	9.82	66.26	80.37	0	1.25	14.22	1.02	22.49	6,218	1	99	0	0	74	26.99	-18.8			Sep-08
	5.95	23.53	10.08	66.54	80.69		0.89	14.21	1.02	22.94	6,218	1	99	0	0	74	26.98	-18.83			Dec-18
	5.91	23.41	10.12	67.70	83.06	0	0.94	14.21	1.02	22.93	6,218	1	99	0	0	74	27.09	-18.73			Dec-10
	2.76	12.97	3.69	29.01	23.47	1.73	1.29	8.63		20.91	333.6	4	69	22	4	12	15.39	-15.82			Oct-09
	2.75	12.99	3.73	29.06	23.48	1.73	1.29	8.65		20.97	333.6	4	69	22	4	12	15.28	-15.9			Aug-88
	2.81	13.11	3.99	30.04	25.01	1.98	1.04	8.63		20.89	333.6	4	69	22	4	12	15.28	-15.9			Aug-12
100	1.98	5.24	4.85	16.91		1.77	2.05	2.81	0.58	25.57	30.4	-9	33	75	-1	550			5.75		Nov-14
	-3.10	-3.58	5.21	18.98	27.02	1.3	1.14	7.01	0.67		2,236	4	92	4	0	48	-1.73	-9.43			Feb-10
	-3.02	-3.51	5.44	19.46	27.82	1.53	0.94	7.02	0.67		2,236	4	92	4	0	48	-1.73	-9.34			Feb-10
	-0.72	-0.91	1.55	10.28	7.48	2.13	0.87	3.38	0.53		1,287	10	19	70	0	115	2.04	-2			Feb-10
	-0.72	-0.81	1.64	10.57	7.89	2.31	0.72	3.32	0.5		1,287	10	19	70	0	115	2.04	-1.91			Feb-10
	-3.24	-3.84	4.67	17.86	28.72	2.12	1.13	7	0.67		4,586	2	94	4	0	49	3.06	-13.3			Feb-10
	-3.17	-3.76	4.83	18.36	29.57	2.35	0.93	7.03	0.67		4,586	2	94	4	0	49	2.96	-13.27			Feb-10
	-0.88	-0.88	1.58	10.33	8.00	1.57	0.84	3.02	0.4		1,963	8	24	68	0	115	4.73	-3.91			Feb-10
	-0.79	-0.79	1.73	10.58	8.48	1.71	0.69	3.05	0.4		1,963	8	24	68	0	115	4.63	-3.82			Feb-10
	-0.88	-0.79	1.85	10.81	9.04	1.53	0.89	3.03	0.4		590.5	6	26	69	0	23	5.14	-4.1			Feb-10
	-0.79	-0.61	2.09	11.17	9.52	1.68	0.74	3.03	0.4		590.5	6	26	69	0	23	5.13	-4.1			Feb-10
	-0.89	-0.89	1.55	10.90	9.05	1.57	0.9	3.04	0.42		460.2	10	23	67	0	17	4.77	-4.12			Feb-10
	-0.80	-0.80	1.70	11.25	9.62	1.72	0.75	3.07	0.41		460.2	10	23	67	0	17	4.67	-4.02			Feb-10
50	2.82	15.94	2.17	33.10	27.95	2.33	0.7	11.89	1.04	14.54	485.6	1	99	0	0	87			5.50		Sep-14
50	2.68	15.52	1.48	30.53	23.78	0	1.4	11.9	1.04	14.51	485.6	1	99	0	0	87				1.00	Apr-16
	2.94	16.10	2.56	34.57	29.94	2.82	0.4	11.9	1.04	14.35	485.6	1	99	0	0	87					Sep-14
	2.89	16.01	2.39	34.12	29.39	2.4	0.5	11.9	1.04	14.56	485.6	1	99	0	0	87					Dec-14

	MARKET			FUND TYPE, CATEGORY & OBJECTIVE	RATINGS				MINIMUMS	
Fund Name	Ticker Symbol	Traded On	Fund Type	Category and (Prospectus Objective)	Overall Rating	Reward Rating	Risk Rating	Recent Up/ Downgrade	Open to New Investors	Min Initial Investment
AllianzGI Best Styles Global Equity Fund Class R6	AGERX	NAS CM	Open End	Global Equity Large Cap (World Stock)	C+	C	B	Up	Y	0
AllianzGI Best Styles International Equity Fund Class A	AXABX	NAS CM	Open End	Global Equity Large Cap (World Stock)	C	C-	C		Y	1,000
AllianzGI Best Styles International Equity Fund Class C	AXCBX	NAS CM	Open End	Global Equity Large Cap (World Stock)	C	C-	C	Up	Y	1,000
AllianzGI Best Styles International Equity Fund Class P	ASQPX	NAS CM	Open End	Global Equity Large Cap (World Stock)	C	C-	C		Y	1,000,000
AllianzGI Best Styles International Equity Fund Class R6	ASESX	NAS CM	Open End	Global Equity Large Cap (World Stock)	C	C-	C		Y	0
AllianzGI Best Styles Intl Equity Inst Cls	ASTYX	NAS CM	Open End	Global Equity Large Cap (World Stock)	C	C-	C		Y	1,000,000
AllianzGI Best Styles U.S. Equity Fund Class A	AABUX	NAS CM	Open End	US Equity Large Cap Blend (Growth)	B-	C	B	Up	Y	1,000
AllianzGI Best Styles U.S. Equity Fund Class C	ACBUX	NAS CM	Open End	US Equity Large Cap Blend (Growth)	C+	C	B		Y	1,000
AllianzGI Best Styles U.S. Equity Fund Class P	ALBPX	NAS CM	Open End	US Equity Large Cap Blend (Growth)	B-	C	B		Y	1,000,000
AllianzGI Best Styles U.S. Equity Fund Class R6	ALSEX	NAS CM	Open End	US Equity Large Cap Blend (Growth)	B-	C	B		Y	0
AllianzGI Best Styles U.S. Equity Fund Institutional Class	ABTLX	NAS CM	Open End	US Equity Large Cap Blend (Growth)	B-	C	B		Y	1,000,000
AllianzGI Convertible & Income 2024 Target Term Fund	CBH	NYSE	Closed End	Convertibles (Convertible Bond)	C-	D+	C-		Y	
AllianzGI Convertible & Income Fund	NCV	NYSE	Closed End	Convertibles (Convertible Bond)	C	C	C+		Y	
AllianzGI Convertible & Income Fund II	NCZ	NYSE	Closed End	Convertibles (Convertible Bond)	C	C	C+		Y	
AllianzGI Convertible Fund Administrative Class	ANNAX	NAS CM	Open End	Convertibles (Convertible Bond)	B	C+	A-			1,000,000
AllianzGI Convertible Fund Class A	ANZAX	NAS CM	Open End	Convertibles (Convertible Bond)	B	C+	A-			1,000
AllianzGI Convertible Fund Class C	ANZCX	NAS CM	Open End	Convertibles (Convertible Bond)	B-	C	A-	Down		1,000
AllianzGI Convertible Fund Class P	ANCMX	NAS CM	Open End	Convertibles (Convertible Bond)	B	C+	A-			1,000,000
AllianzGI Convertible Fund Class R	ANZRX	NAS CM	Open End	Convertibles (Convertible Bond)	B	C	A-			0
AllianzGI Convertible Fund Institutional Class	ANNPX	NAS CM	Open End	Convertibles (Convertible Bond)	B	C+	A-			1,000,000
AllianzGI Diversified Income & Convertible Fund	ACV	NYSE	Closed End	Cautious Alloc (Convertible Bond)	C	C	C-	Down	Y	
AllianzGI Emerging Markets Consumer Fund Class A	AMMAX	NAS CM	Open End	Global Emerg Mkts (Growth)	C	C-	C	Up	Y	1,000
AllianzGI Emerging Markets Consumer Institutional Cls	AERIX	NAS CM	Open End	Global Emerg Mkts (Growth)	C	C-	C	Up	Y	1,000,000
AllianzGI Emerging Markets Opportunities Fund Class A	AOTAX	NAS CM	Open End	Global Emerg Mkts (Div Emerging Mkts)	C	C	C+		Y	1,000
AllianzGI Emerging Markets Opportunities Fund Class C	AOTCX	NAS CM	Open End	Global Emerg Mkts (Div Emerging Mkts)	C	C	C+		Y	1,000
AllianzGI Emerging Markets Opportunities Fund Class P	AEMPX	NAS CM	Open End	Global Emerg Mkts (Div Emerging Mkts)	C	C	C+		Y	1,000,000
AllianzGI Emerging Markets Opportunities Institutional Cls	AOTIX	NAS CM	Open End	Global Emerg Mkts (Div Emerging Mkts)	C	C	C+		Y	1,000,000
AllianzGI Emerging Markets Opportunities Fund R6	AEMOX	NAS CM	Open End	Global Emerg Mkts (Div Emerging Mkts)	C	C	C+		Y	0
AllianzGI Emerging Markets Small-Cap Fund Class A	ALMMX	NAS CM	Open End	Global Emerg Mkts (Small Company)	C	C	C+		Y	1,000
AllianzGI Emerging Markets Small-Cap Institutional Cls	ALAIX	NAS CM	Open End	Global Emerg Mkts (Small Company)	C	C	C+		Y	1,000,000
AllianzGI Equity & Convertible Income Fund	NIE	NYSE	Closed End	Aggressive Alloc (Growth & Income)	C	C	C-		Y	
AllianzGI Focused Growth Fund Administrative Class	PGFAX	NAS CM	Open End	US Equity Large Cap Growth (Growth)	C+	C	B-	Down	Y	1,000,000
AllianzGI Focused Growth Fund Class A	PGWAX	NAS CM	Open End	US Equity Large Cap Growth (Growth)	C+	C	B-	Down	Y	1,000
AllianzGI Focused Growth Fund Class C	PGWCX	NAS CM	Open End	US Equity Large Cap Growth (Growth)	C+	C	C+	Down	Y	1,000
AllianzGI Focused Growth Fund Class P	AOGPX	NAS CM	Open End	US Equity Large Cap Growth (Growth)	C+	C	B-	Down	Y	1,000,000
AllianzGI Focused Growth Fund Class R	PPGRX	NAS CM	Open End	US Equity Large Cap Growth (Growth)	C+	C	B-	Down	Y	0
AllianzGI Focused Growth Fund Institutional Class	PGFIX	NAS CM	Open End	US Equity Large Cap Growth (Growth)	C+	C	B-	Down	Y	1,000,000
AllianzGI Focused Growth Fund R6	AFGFX	NAS CM	Open End	US Equity Large Cap Growth (Growth)	C+	C	B-	Down	Y	0
AllianzGI Global Allocation Fund Administrative Class	AGAMX	NAS CM	Open End	Moderate Alloc (Asset Alloc)	B-	C	B+	Up	Y	1,000,000
AllianzGI Global Allocation Fund Class A	PALAX	NAS CM	Open End	Moderate Alloc (Asset Alloc)	B-	C	B+	Up	Y	1,000
AllianzGI Global Allocation Fund Class C	PALCX	NAS CM	Open End	Moderate Alloc (Asset Alloc)	B-	C	B	Up	Y	1,000
AllianzGI Global Allocation Fund Class P	AGAPX	NAS CM	Open End	Moderate Alloc (Asset Alloc)	B-	C	B+	Up	Y	1,000,000
AllianzGI Global Allocation Fund Class R	AGARX	NAS CM	Open End	Moderate Alloc (Asset Alloc)	B-	C	B+	Up	Y	0
AllianzGI Global Allocation Fund Class R6	AGASX	NAS CM	Open End	Moderate Alloc (Asset Alloc)	B-	C	B+	Up	Y	0
AllianzGI Global Allocation Fund Institutional Class	PALLX	NAS CM	Open End	Moderate Alloc (Asset Alloc)	B-	C	B+	Up	Y	1,000,000
AllianzGI Global Dynamic Allocation Administrative Cls	AGFAX	NAS CM	Open End	Moderate Alloc (Asset Alloc)	B-	C	B+	Up	Y	1,000,000
AllianzGI Global Dynamic Allocation Fund Class A	ASGAX	NAS CM	Open End	Moderate Alloc (Asset Alloc)	B-	C	B+	Up	Y	1,000
AllianzGI Global Dynamic Allocation Fund Class C	ASACX	NAS CM	Open End	Moderate Alloc (Asset Alloc)	C+	C	B	Up	Y	1,000
AllianzGI Global Dynamic Allocation Fund Class P	AGSPX	NAS CM	Open End	Moderate Alloc (Asset Alloc)	B-	C	B+	Up	Y	1,000,000
AllianzGI Global Dynamic Allocation Fund Class R	ASFRX	NAS CM	Open End	Moderate Alloc (Asset Alloc)	C+	C	B	Up	Y	0
AllianzGI Global Dynamic Allocation Fund Class R6	ADYFX	NAS CM	Open End	Moderate Alloc (Asset Alloc)	B-	C	B+	Up	Y	0
AllianzGI Global Dynamic Allocation Institutional Cls	AGAIX	NAS CM	Open End	Moderate Alloc (Asset Alloc)	B-	C	B+	Up	Y	1,000,000

★ Expanded analysis of this fund is included in Section II.

	TOTAL RETURNS					PERFORMANCE				ASSETS		ASSET ALLOCATION & TURNOVER					BULL & BEAR		FEES		
Min Additional Investment	3-Month Total Return	6-Month Total Return	1-Year Total Return	3-Year Total Return	5-Year Total Return	Dividend Yield (TTM)	Expense Ratio	3-Yr Std Deviation	3-Year Beta	NAV	Total Assets (MIL)	%Cash	%Stocks	%Bonds	%Other	Turnover Ratio	Last Bull Market Total Return	Last Bear Market Total Return	Front End Fee (%)	Back End Fee (%)	Inception Date
	2.91	16.03	2.46	34.54	30.13	2.78	0.4	11.91	1.04	14.47	485.6	1	99	0	0	87					Dec-13
50	1.77	11.41	-3.68	26.62		3.51	0.7	11.57	1.02	13.76	23.5	1	99	0	0	55			5.50		Apr-16
50	1.63	10.94	-4.41	23.93		2.43	1.45	11.61	1.02	13.68	23.5	1	99	0	0	55				1.00	Apr-16
	1.84	11.49	-3.50	27.36		3.8	0.55	11.59	1.02	13.77	23.5	1	99	0	0	55					Dec-14
	1.83	11.52	-3.45	27.72		3.88	0.45	11.59	1.02	13.84	23.5	1	99	0	0	55					Dec-14
	1.92	11.56	-3.40	27.65		4.01	0.45	11.59	1.02	13.79	23.5	1	99	0	0	55					Dec-14
50	3.86	17.55	7.11	49.07		1.99	0.65	12.15	0.99	16.14	92.2	1	99	0	0	80			5.50		Apr-16
50	3.64	17.17	6.33	45.90		1.69	1.4	12.14	0.99	15.62	92.2	1	99	0	0	80				1.00	Apr-16
	3.89	17.64	7.22	49.84		1.85	0.5	12.13	0.99	16	92.2	1	99	0	0	80					Dec-14
	3.92	17.69	7.35	50.34		1.9	0.4	12.14	0.99	16.16	92.2	1	99	0	0	80					Dec-14
	3.88	17.66	7.24	49.93		1.92	0.4	12.16	0.99	16.05	92.2	1	99	0	0	80					Dec-14
	2.36	10.80	4.89			5.63	2.64			9.81	179.1	4	0	60	0	116					Jun-17
	2.86	14.31	0.85	30.05	9.62	13.26		9.88	0.68	5.6	503.4	3	4	37	0	41	22.17	-19.06			Mar-03
	2.73	14.10	0.53	30.00	9.44	13		9.98	0.68	5.02	380.6	3	4	37	0	41	22.08	-19.17			Jul-03
	5.30	18.04	11.57	49.07	42.56	2.66	0.93	8.95	1.03	29.08	561.1	2	4	1	0	133	16.22	-17.14			Apr-10
50	5.41	18.14	11.66	48.93	42.14	2.78	0.96	8.94	1.02	29.39	561.1	2	4	1	0	133	16.19	-17.13	5.50		Apr-10
50	5.19	17.69	10.80	45.67	37.06	1.64	1.73	8.93	1.02	29.75	561.1	2	4	1	0	133	15.71	-17.42		1.00	Apr-10
	5.44	18.28	11.89	50.03	43.98	3.35	0.74	8.94	1.02	28.58	561.1	2	4	1	0	133	16.31	-17.09			Jun-10
	5.31	18.02	11.52	47.74	39.93	2.7	1.17	8.95	1.02	30.56	561.1	2	4	1	0	133	16.04	-17.26			Apr-10
	5.43	18.28	11.92	50.24	44.32	3.35	0.71	8.94	1.02	28.89	561.1	2	4	1	0	133	16.38	-17.04			Apr-93
	5.42	23.38	10.58	54.62		2.01	2.69	12.9	1	23.54	243.0	3	26	19	0	105					May-15
50	1.73	12.05	-1.90	19.68		0.3	1.4	13.88	0.95	14.04	41.7	2	98	0	0	115			5.50		Dec-14
	1.81	12.23	-1.56	20.95		1.66	1.05	13.92	0.95	14.03	41.7	2	98	0	0	115					Dec-14
50	-0.03	9.86	-3.29	27.28	8.49	1.78	1.26	14.08	0.98	27.06	381.6	3	97	0	0	88	17.36	-29.08	5.50		Aug-06
50	-0.26	9.42	-4.04	24.43	4.44	0.36	2.01	14.08	0.98	26.81	381.6	3	97	0	0	88	16.9	-29.33		1.00	Aug-06
	0.03	9.97	-3.05	28.25	9.83	2.41	1.01	14.09	0.98	26.46	381.6	3	97	0	0	88	17.55	-29.02			Jul-08
	0.03	10.02	-2.96	28.64	10.39	2.56	0.91	14.08	0.98	27.1	381.6	3	97	0	0	88	17.57	-28.97			May-04
	0.03	10.04	-2.96	28.77	10.52	2.6	0.86	14.07	0.98	26.96	381.6	3	97	0	0	88	17.57	-28.97			Dec-15
50	2.33	15.28	2.34	34.30		0.58	1.85	12.29	0.91	16.67	8.9	3	95	0	1	119			5.50		Dec-14
	2.44	15.52	2.75	35.74		1.52	1.5	12.29	0.91	16.37	8.9	3	95	0	1	119					Dec-14
	3.32	17.14	6.55	40.86	42.50	2.11	1.12	11.4		23.48	650.6	5	63	0	0	81	19.83	-17.24			Feb-07
	4.75	23.03	6.85	56.36	75.91	0	0.91	14.99	1.1	45.35	1,042	0	100	0	0	40	26.27	-16.8			Mar-99
50	4.75	22.99	6.79	55.98	75.11	0	0.99	15	1.1	53.33	1,042	0	100	0	0	40	26.22	-16.84	5.50		Oct-90
50	4.52	22.49	5.93	52.41	68.58	0	1.76	14.97	1.1	34.42	1,042	0	100	0	0	40	25.67	-17.12		1.00	Feb-84
	4.80	23.10	7.01	57.09	77.20	0	0.76	14.99	1.1	39.91	1,042	0	100	0	0	40	26.38	-16.74			Jul-08
	4.66	22.78	6.47	54.74	72.84	0	1.26	14.97	1.1	39.01	1,042	0	100	0	0	40	26.04	-16.92			Dec-02
	4.84	23.17	7.14	57.55	78.15	0	0.66	14.99	1.1	48.89	1,042	0	100	0	0	40	26.47	-16.72			Mar-99
	4.83	23.20	7.18	57.79	75.56	0	0.61	14.99	1.1	48.96	1,042	0	100	0	0	40	25.67	-17.12			Dec-15
	3.38	12.20	5.27	21.52	17.32	2.04	0.95	7.58	0.65	11.34	324.5	3	43	27	26	17	14.28	-15.46			May-09
50	3.28	12.13	5.12	21.21	16.92	2.17	1.01	7.5	0.64	11.01	324.5	3	43	27	26	17	14.17	-15.43	5.50		Sep-98
50	3.09	11.76	4.25	18.53	12.65	0.58	1.75	7.54	0.64	11.33	324.5	3	43	27	26	17	13.7	-15.77		1.00	Sep-98
	3.38	12.29	5.36	22.23	18.60	2.53	0.77	7.51	0.64	10.9	324.5	3	43	27	26	17	14.37	-15.4			May-09
	3.26	12.01	4.98	20.54	15.99	1.85	1.21	7.53	0.64	10.9	324.5	3	43	27	26	17	14	-15.59			May-09
	3.44	12.40	5.55	22.45	18.45	2.66	0.7	7.53	0.64	10.75	324.5	3	43	27	26	17	14.17	-15.43			Sep-15
	3.36	12.32	5.44	21.98	18.30	2.53	0.75	7.51	0.64	10.98	324.5	3	43	27	26	17	14.45	-15.37			Feb-99
	3.68	11.73	3.88	20.07	11.99	1.87	0.99	7.73	0.66	19.42	182.3	5	58	37	0	152	18.9	-20.72			Apr-09
50	3.67	11.70	3.87	20.02	11.94	1.82	1.01	7.72	0.66	19.47	182.3	5	58	37	0	152	18.85	-20.72	5.50		Apr-09
50	3.46	11.28	3.05	17.25	7.69	0	1.78	7.72	0.66	19.13	182.3	5	58	37	0	152	18.35	-20.96		1.00	Apr-09
	3.69	11.85	4.05	20.64	12.91	2.02	0.84	7.72	0.66	19.34	182.3	5	58	37	0	152	19	-20.66			Apr-09
	3.58	11.57	3.49	18.77	10.26	1.02	1.38	7.73	0.66	19.38	182.3	5	58	37	0	152	18.7	-20.81			Apr-09
	3.73	11.85	4.13	21.09	13.58	2	0.74	7.7	0.66	19.43	182.3	5	58	37	0	152	19.06	-20.61			Feb-16
	3.72	11.83	4.08	20.97	13.40	0.88	0.74	7.72	0.66	19.75	182.3	5	58	37	0	152	19.06	-20.61			Apr-09

	MARKET			FUND TYPE, CATEGORY & OBJECTIVE	RATINGS				MINIMUMS	
Fund Name	Ticker Symbol	Traded On	Fund Type	Category and (Prospectus Objective)	Overall Rating	Reward Rating	Risk Rating	Recent Up/ Downgrade	Open to New Investors	Min Initial Investment
AllianzGI Global Natural Resources Fund Class A	ARMAX	NAS CM	Open End	Natl Resources Sec Equity (Natl Res)	D+	D	D+	Down	Y	1,000
AllianzGI Global Natural Resources Fund Class C	ARMCX	NAS CM	Open End	Natl Resources Sec Equity (Natl Res)	D	D	D+	Down	Y	1,000
AllianzGI Global Natural Resources Fund Class P	APGPX	NAS CM	Open End	Natl Resources Sec Equity (Natl Res)	D+	D	C-	Down	Y	1,000,000
AllianzGI Global Natural Resources Institutional Cls	RGLIX	NAS CM	Open End	Natl Resources Sec Equity (Natl Res)	D+	D+	C-	Down	Y	1,000,000
AllianzGI Global Small-Cap Fund Class A	RGSAX	NAS CM	Open End	Global Equity Mid/Small Cap (World Stock)	C	C	C+		Y	1,000
AllianzGI Global Small-Cap Fund Class C	RGSCX	NAS CM	Open End	Global Equity Mid/Small Cap (World Stock)	C	C	C+		Y	1,000
AllianzGI Global Small-Cap Fund Class P	ARSPX	NAS CM	Open End	Global Equity Mid/Small Cap (World Stock)	C	C	C+		Y	1,000,000
AllianzGI Global Small-Cap Fund Institutional Class	DGSCX	NAS CM	Open End	Global Equity Mid/Small Cap (World Stock)	C	C	C+		Y	1,000,000
AllianzGI Global Sustainability Fund Class A	ASUAX	NAS CM	Open End	Global Equity Large Cap (Growth)	C+	C	B		Y	1,000
AllianzGI Global Sustainability Fund Class P	ASTPX	NAS CM	Open End	Global Equity Large Cap (Growth)	C+	C	B		Y	1,000,000
AllianzGI Global Sustainability Fund Institutional Class	ASTNX	NAS CM	Open End	Global Equity Large Cap (Growth)	C+	C	B		Y	1,000,000
AllianzGI Global Water Fund Class A	AWTAX	NAS CM	Open End	Natl Resources Sec Equity (Natl Res)	C+	C	B		Y	1,000
AllianzGI Global Water Fund Class C	AWTCX	NAS CM	Open End	Natl Resources Sec Equity (Natl Res)	C+	C	B-		Y	1,000
AllianzGI Global Water Fund Class P	AWTPX	NAS CM	Open End	Natl Resources Sec Equity (Natl Res)	C+	C	B		Y	1,000,000
AllianzGI Global Water Fund Institutional Class	AWTIX	NAS CM	Open End	Natl Resources Sec Equity (Natl Res)	C+	C	B		Y	1,000,000
AllianzGI Health Sciences Fund Class A	RAGHX	NAS CM	Open End	Healthcare Sector Equity (Health)	B-	C	B		Y	1,000
AllianzGI Health Sciences Fund Class C	RCGHX	NAS CM	Open End	Healthcare Sector Equity (Health)	B-	C	B		Y	1,000
AllianzGI Health Sciences Fund Institutional Class	HLHIX	NAS CM	Open End	Healthcare Sector Equity (Health)	B-	C	B		Y	1,000,000
AllianzGI Income & Growth Fund Class A	AZNAX	NAS CM	Open End	Cautious Alloc (Growth & Income)	B-	C	B+		Y	1,000
AllianzGI Income & Growth Fund Class C	AZNCX	NAS CM	Open End	Cautious Alloc (Growth & Income)	B-	C	B+	Up	Y	1,000
AllianzGI Income & Growth Fund Class P	AIGPX	NAS CM	Open End	Cautious Alloc (Growth & Income)	B-	C	B+		Y	1,000,000
AllianzGI Income & Growth Fund Class R	AIGRX	NAS CM	Open End	Cautious Alloc (Growth & Income)	B-	C	B+		Y	0
AllianzGI Income & Growth Fund Institutional Class	AZNIX	NAS CM	Open End	Cautious Alloc (Growth & Income)	B-	C	B+		Y	1,000,000
AllianzGI International Small-Cap Fund Class A	AOPAX	NAS CM	Open End	Global Equity Mid/Small Cap (Foreign Stock)	C-	C-	C		Y	1,000
AllianzGI International Small-Cap Fund Class C	AOPCX	NAS CM	Open End	Global Equity Mid/Small Cap (Foreign Stock)	C-	C-	C-		Y	1,000
AllianzGI International Small-Cap Fund Class P	ALOPX	NAS CM	Open End	Global Equity Mid/Small Cap (Foreign Stock)	C-	C-	C		Y	1,000,000
AllianzGI International Small-Cap Fund Class R	ALORX	NAS CM	Open End	Global Equity Mid/Small Cap (Foreign Stock)	C-	C-	C		Y	0
AllianzGI International Small-Cap Fund Class R6	AIISX	NAS CM	Open End	Global Equity Mid/Small Cap (Foreign Stock)	C-	C-	C		Y	0
AllianzGI International Small-Cap Fund Institutional Class	ALOIX	NAS CM	Open End	Global Equity Mid/Small Cap (Foreign Stock)	C-	C-	C		Y	1,000,000
AllianzGI Micro Cap Fund Class A	GMCAX	NAS CM	Open End	US Equity Small Cap (Growth)	C	C	C		Y	1,000
AllianzGI Micro Cap Fund Class P	AAMPX	NAS CM	Open End	US Equity Small Cap (Growth)	C	C	C		Y	1,000,000
AllianzGI Micro Cap Fund Institutional Class	AMCIX	NAS CM	Open End	US Equity Small Cap (Growth)	C	C	C		Y	1,000,000
AllianzGI Mid-Cap Fund Administrative Class	DRMAX	NAS CM	Open End	US Equity Mid Cap (Growth)	C+	C+	C+		Y	1,000,000
AllianzGI Mid-Cap Fund Class A	RMDAX	NAS CM	Open End	US Equity Mid Cap (Growth)	C+	C	C+		Y	1,000
AllianzGI Mid-Cap Fund Class C	RMDCX	NAS CM	Open End	US Equity Mid Cap (Growth)	C+	C	C+		Y	1,000
AllianzGI Mid-Cap Fund Class P	ARMPX	NAS CM	Open End	US Equity Mid Cap (Growth)	C+	C+	C+		Y	1,000,000
AllianzGI Mid-Cap Fund Class R	PRMRX	NAS CM	Open End	US Equity Mid Cap (Growth)	C+	C	C+		Y	0
AllianzGI Mid-Cap Fund Institutional Class	DRMCX	NAS CM	Open End	US Equity Mid Cap (Growth)	C+	C+	C+		Y	1,000,000
AllianzGI Multi Asset Income Fund Administrative Class	ARAMX	NAS CM	Open End	Target Date (Asset Alloc)	B-	C	B		Y	1,000,000
AllianzGI Multi Asset Income Fund Class A	AGRAX	NAS CM	Open End	Target Date (Asset Alloc)	B-	C+	B		Y	1,000
AllianzGI Multi Asset Income Fund Class C	ARTCX	NAS CM	Open End	Target Date (Asset Alloc)	C+	C	B		Y	1,000
AllianzGI Multi Asset Income Fund Class P	AGRPX	NAS CM	Open End	Target Date (Asset Alloc)	B-	C+	B		Y	1,000,000
AllianzGI Multi Asset Income Fund Class R	ASRRX	NAS CM	Open End	Target Date (Asset Alloc)	B-	C+	B	Up	Y	0
AllianzGI Multi Asset Income Fund Institutional Class	AVRNX	NAS CM	Open End	Target Date (Asset Alloc)	B-	C+	B		Y	1,000,000
AllianzGI Multi Asset Income Fund R6 Class	AVRIX	NAS CM	Open End	Target Date (Asset Alloc)	B-	C+	B		Y	0
AllianzGI NFJ Dividend Interest & Premium Strategy Fund	NFJ	NYSE	Closed End	Aggressive Alloc (Equity-Income)	C	C	C+		Y	
AllianzGI NFJ Dividend Value Fund Administrative Class	ANDAX	NAS CM	Open End	US Equity Large Cap Value (Equity-Income)	C+	C	B	Up	Y	1,000,000
AllianzGI NFJ Dividend Value Fund Class A	PNEAX	NAS CM	Open End	US Equity Large Cap Value (Equity-Income)	C+	C	B	Up	Y	1,000
AllianzGI NFJ Dividend Value Fund Class C	PNECX	NAS CM	Open End	US Equity Large Cap Value (Equity-Income)	C+	C	B	Up	Y	1,000
AllianzGI NFJ Dividend Value Fund Class P	ADJPX	NAS CM	Open End	US Equity Large Cap Value (Equity-Income)	C+	C	B	Up	Y	1,000,000
AllianzGI NFJ Dividend Value Fund Class R	PNERX	NAS CM	Open End	US Equity Large Cap Value (Equity-Income)	C+	C	B	Up	Y	0
AllianzGI NFJ Dividend Value Fund Class R6	ANDVX	NAS CM	Open End	US Equity Large Cap Value (Equity-Income)	C+	C	B	Up	Y	0

★ Expanded analysis of this fund is included in Section II.

	TOTAL RETURNS					PERFORMANCE				ASSETS		ASSET ALLOCATION & TURNOVER					BULL & BEAR		FEES		
Min Additional Investment	3-Month Total Return	6-Month Total Return	1-Year Total Return	3-Year Total Return	5-Year Total Return	Dividend Yield (TTM)	Expense Ratio	3-Yr Std Deviation	3-Year Beta	NAV	Total Assets (MIL)	%Cash	%Stocks	%Bonds	%Other	Turnover Ratio	Last Bull Market Total Return	Last Bear Market Total Return	Front End Fee (%)	Back End Fee (%)	Inception Date
50	0.42	14.05	-9.23	0.35	-28.61	1.69	1.45	17.24	1.08	14.2	12.2	1	99	0	0	113	19.53	-31.02	5.50		Mar-06
50	0.22	13.68	-9.90	-1.83	-31.20	0.88	2.2	17.22	1.08	13.29	12.2	1	99	0	0	113	19.06	-31.24		1.00	Mar-06
	0.55	14.33	-8.88	1.18	-27.63	2.14	1.2	17.27	1.09	14.44	12.2	1	99	0	0	113	19.7	-30.94			Jul-08
	0.48	14.26	-8.92	1.45	-27.33	2.06	1.1	17.21	1.08	14.58	12.2	1	99	0	0	113	19.82	-30.94			Jun-04
50	3.06	18.83	-4.63	31.32	24.25	0	1.62	13.53	0.98	39.37	134.0	4	96	0	0	77	25.96	-23.75	5.50		Feb-02
50	2.85	18.38	-5.37	28.36	19.61	0	2.37	13.52	0.98	33.1	134.0	4	96	0	0	77	25.42	-23.99		1.00	Feb-02
	3.10	18.97	-4.40	32.30	25.79	0	1.37	13.53	0.98	42.51	134.0	4	96	0	0	77	26.13	-23.69			Jul-08
	3.11	19.03	-4.32	32.68	26.39	0	1.27	13.53	0.98	42.97	134.0	4	96	0	0	77	26.21	-23.63			Dec-96
50	5.93	21.46	9.88	44.04		1.54	1.09	11.58	0.98	18.39	21.9	2	98	0	0	20			5.50		Dec-14
	5.95	21.61	10.04	44.72		2.08	0.94	11.56	0.98	18.51	21.9	2	98	0	0	20					Dec-14
	5.95	21.59	10.09	44.97		0.78	0.84	11.57	0.98	18.86	21.9	2	98	0	0	20					Dec-14
50	7.85	23.75	13.24	29.90	30.70	0.79	1.22	12.25	0.96	16.2	602.0	3	97	0	0	34	22.07	-19.84	5.50		Mar-08
50	7.67	23.32	12.40	26.99	25.84	0.06	1.97	12.3	0.96	15.44	602.0	3	97	0	0	34	21.52	-20.17		1.00	Mar-08
	7.99	24.02	13.58	30.98	32.51	1.14	0.94	12.31	0.96	16.21	602.0	3	97	0	0	34	22.16	-19.78			Mar-08
	8.00	23.98	13.56	31.03	32.58	1.12	0.93	12.29	0.96	15.92	602.0	3	97	0	0	34	22.31	-19.8			Jul-08
50	3.19	15.04	13.13	36.77	57.90	0.87	1.47	14.13	1.07	32.27	155.4	4	96	0	0	55	19.88	-14.96	5.50		Feb-02
50	3.04	14.66	12.33	33.74	52.12	0	2.22	14.11	1.07	24.71	155.4	4	96	0	0	55	19.39	-15.23		1.00	Feb-02
	3.31	15.27	13.54	38.19	60.41	1.11	1.12	14.13	1.07	32.76	155.4	4	96	0	0	55	19.88	-14.96			Dec-14
50	2.48	13.63	5.35	32.43	31.11	2.16	1.27	8.52	0.68	11	4,520	4	34	31	0	102	16.01	-14.42	5.50		Feb-07
50	2.33	13.27	4.60	29.56	26.26	1.7	2.02	8.53	0.68	10.07	4,520	4	34	31	0	102	15.4	-14.6		1.00	Feb-07
	2.56	13.82	5.64	33.48	32.81	2.32	1.02	8.62	0.69	11.29	4,520	4	34	31	0	102	16.16	-14.31			Jul-08
	2.42	13.50	5.09	31.46	29.37	1.92	1.52	8.52	0.68	11	4,520	4	34	31	0	102	15.82	-14.43			Feb-11
	2.56	13.84	5.69	33.76	33.41	2.39	0.92	8.58	0.68	11.4	4,520	4	34	31	0	102	16.24	-14.26			Feb-07
50	1.92	14.08	-12.19	21.06	19.47	0.25	1.25	14.51	1.13	32.24	103.5	2	98	0	0	62	17.79	-24.53	5.50		Apr-10
50	1.74	13.65	-12.86	18.20	14.91	0	2	14.57	1.13	30.87	103.5	2	98	0	0	62	17.25	-24.77		1.00	Apr-10
	1.97	14.16	-12.04	21.63	20.42	0.88	1.1	14.56	1.13	31.99	103.5	2	98	0	0	62	17.93	-24.43			Dec-97
	1.84	13.90	-12.46	19.94	17.75	2.25	1.59	14.56	1.13	30.31	103.5	2	98	0	0	62	17.58	-24.61			Apr-10
	2.00	14.21	-11.96	22.05	21.02	1.56	1	14.57	1.13	33.1	103.5	2	98	0	0	62	18.03	-24.41			Feb-16
	1.99	14.20	-11.99	21.84	20.78	1.12	1.04	14.57	1.13	33.29	103.5	2	98	0	0	62	18.03	-24.41			Dec-97
50	3.63	20.60	-9.90	35.98	27.55	0	1.42	18.62	1	11.12	18.6	2	98	0	0	47	38.87	-35.46	5.50		Dec-11
	3.69	20.62	-9.84	36.23	28.09	0	1.34	18.66	1	11.23	18.6	2	98	0	0	47	39	-35.45			Dec-10
	3.66	20.70	-9.83	36.24	27.96	0	1.34	18.6	1	11.31	18.6	2	98	0	0	47	39.08	-35.39			Jul-95
	7.64	33.83	13.60	56.82	66.00	0	1.03	16.7	1.14	4.01	312.3	0	100	0	0	79	25.65	-22.87			Feb-02
50	7.59	33.63	13.58	56.42	64.99	0	1.13	16.85	1.15	3.75	312.3	0	100	0	0	79	25.57	-22.65	5.50		Feb-02
50	7.37	33.25	12.56	53.14	59.07	0	1.88	16.8	1.15	2.98	312.3	0	100	0	0	79	24.86	-22.9		1.00	Feb-02
	7.51	33.89	13.79	57.86	67.50	0	0.88	16.66	1.14	4.36	312.3	0	100	0	0	79	25.84	-22.76			Apr-12
	7.16	33.27	12.96	54.89	62.96	0	1.38	16.63	1.13	3.66	312.3	0	100	0	0	79	25.56	-22.89			Dec-02
	7.45	33.99	13.96	58.25	67.88	0	0.78	16.66	1.14	4.39	312.3	0	100	0	0	79	25.91	-22.72			Nov-79
	2.62	10.76	6.97	15.06	16.42	4.3	0.9	5.58	0.99	17.84	30.0	8	22	68	0	172	9.73	-6.4			Dec-08
50	3.45	11.65	7.73	17.01	18.29	5.02	0.95	5.64	1.01	17.54	30.0	8	22	68	0	172	9.67	-6.41	5.50		Dec-08
50	3.30	11.29	6.96	14.43	13.98	4.29	1.7	5.62	1.01	17.55	30.0	8	22	68	0	172	9.22	-6.68		1.00	Dec-08
	3.54	11.80	8.07	18.07	20.10	5.22	0.65	5.62	1	17.74	30.0	8	22	68	0	172	9.85	-6.3			Dec-08
	3.36	11.46	7.39	15.78	16.30	4.45	1.3	5.6	1	18.38	30.0	8	22	68	0	172	9.52	-6.55			Dec-08
	3.60	11.90	8.17	18.33	20.63	5.42	0.6	5.63	1.01	17.26	30.0	8	22	68	0	172	9.96	-6.32			Feb-18
	3.62	11.92	8.20	18.45	20.75	5.45	0.55	5.64	1.02	17.27	30.0	8	22	68	0	172	9.96	-6.32			Dec-08
	2.67	14.45	4.06	22.96	11.53	6.48		9.98	1.04	13.89	1,317	2	70	0	0	50	18.3	-15.63			Feb-05
	3.17	15.42	4.49	34.58	27.54	1.75	0.94	12.26	0.99	12.41	1,359	1	99	0	0	47	21.46	-16.66			May-00
50	3.24	15.39	4.45	34.27	27.01	1.8	1.04	12.28	0.99	12.11	1,359	1	99	0	0	47	21.46	-16.79	5.50		Oct-01
50	2.97	14.93	3.62	31.22	22.24	0.81	1.79	12.29	0.99	12.32	1,359	1	99	0	0	47	20.89	-17		1.00	Oct-01
	3.19	15.49	4.62	35.18	28.53	2.08	0.79	12.26	0.99	12.21	1,359	1	99	0	0	47	21.65	-16.65			Jul-08
	3.09	15.15	4.13	33.19	25.36	1.29	1.29	12.27	0.99	12.1	1,359	1	99	0	0	47	21.26	-16.79			Dec-02
	3.25	15.56	4.82	35.85	29.47	2.35	0.64	12.27	0.99	12.15	1,359	1	99	0	0	47	21.71	-16.59			Dec-13

	MARKET			FUND TYPE, CATEGORY & OBJECTIVE	RATINGS				MINIMUMS	
Fund Name	Ticker Symbol	Traded On	Fund Type	Category and (Prospectus Objective)	Overall Rating	Reward Rating	Risk Rating	Recent Up/ Downgrade	Open to New Investors	Min Initial Investment
AllianzGI NFJ Dividend Value Fund Institutional Class	NFJEX	NAS CM	Open End	US Equity Large Cap Value (Equity-Income)	C+	C	B	Up	Y	1,000,000
AllianzGI NFJ Emerging Markets Value Fund Class A	AZMAX	NAS CM	Open End	Global Emerg Mkts (Div Emerging Mkts)	C	C	C+		Y	1,000
AllianzGI NFJ Emerging Markets Value Fund Class C	AZMCX	NAS CM	Open End	Global Emerg Mkts (Div Emerging Mkts)	C	C	C		Y	1,000
AllianzGI NFJ Emerging Markets Value Fund Class P	AZMPX	NAS CM	Open End	Global Emerg Mkts (Div Emerging Mkts)	C	C	C+		Y	1,000,000
AllianzGI NFJ Emerging Markets Value Institutional Cls	AZMIX	NAS CM	Open End	Global Emerg Mkts (Div Emerging Mkts)	C	C	C+		Y	1,000,000
AllianzGI NFJ International Value Administrative Cls	AIVAX	NAS CM	Open End	Global Equity Large Cap (Foreign Stock)	C	C-	B-		Y	1,000,000
AllianzGI NFJ International Value Fund Class A	AFJAX	NAS CM	Open End	Global Equity Large Cap (Foreign Stock)	C	C-	B-		Y	1,000
AllianzGI NFJ International Value Fund Class C	AFJCX	NAS CM	Open End	Global Equity Large Cap (Foreign Stock)	C	C-	B-		Y	1,000
AllianzGI NFJ International Value Fund Class P	AFVPX	NAS CM	Open End	Global Equity Large Cap (Foreign Stock)	C	C-	B-		Y	1,000,000
AllianzGI NFJ International Value Fund Class R	ANJRX	NAS CM	Open End	Global Equity Large Cap (Foreign Stock)	C	C-	B-		Y	0
AllianzGI NFJ International Value Fund Class R6	ANAVX	NAS CM	Open End	Global Equity Large Cap (Foreign Stock)	C	C-	B-		Y	0
AllianzGI NFJ International Value Fund Institutional Class	ANJIX	NAS CM	Open End	Global Equity Large Cap (Foreign Stock)	C	C-	B-		Y	1,000,000
AllianzGI NFJ Large-Cap Value Fund Administrative Class	ALNFX	NAS CM	Open End	US Equity Large Cap Value (Growth & Income)	C+	C	B		Y	1,000,000
AllianzGI NFJ Large-Cap Value Fund Class A	PNBAX	NAS CM	Open End	US Equity Large Cap Value (Growth & Income)	C+	C	B		Y	1,000
AllianzGI NFJ Large-Cap Value Fund Class C	PNBCX	NAS CM	Open End	US Equity Large Cap Value (Growth & Income)	C+	C	B	Up	Y	1,000
AllianzGI NFJ Large-Cap Value Fund Class P	ALCPX	NAS CM	Open End	US Equity Large Cap Value (Growth & Income)	C+	C	B		Y	1,000,000
AllianzGI NFJ Large-Cap Value Fund Class R	ANLRX	NAS CM	Open End	US Equity Large Cap Value (Growth & Income)	C+	C	B	Up	Y	0
AllianzGI NFJ Large-Cap Value Fund Institutional Class	ANVIX	NAS CM	Open End	US Equity Large Cap Value (Growth & Income)	C+	C	B		Y	1,000,000
AllianzGI NFJ Mid-Cap Value Fund Administrative Class	PRAAX	NAS CM	Open End	US Equity Mid Cap (Growth & Income)	C+	C	B-	Up	Y	1,000,000
AllianzGI NFJ Mid-Cap Value Fund Class A	PQNAX	NAS CM	Open End	US Equity Mid Cap (Growth & Income)	C+	C	B-	Up	Y	1,000
AllianzGI NFJ Mid-Cap Value Fund Class C	PQNCX	NAS CM	Open End	US Equity Mid Cap (Growth & Income)	C	C	B-		Y	1,000
AllianzGI NFJ Mid-Cap Value Fund Class P	ANRPX	NAS CM	Open End	US Equity Mid Cap (Growth & Income)	C+	C	B-	Up	Y	1,000,000
AllianzGI NFJ Mid-Cap Value Fund Class R	PRNRX	NAS CM	Open End	US Equity Mid Cap (Growth & Income)	C+	C	B-	Up	Y	0
AllianzGI NFJ Mid-Cap Value Fund Class R6	ANPRX	NAS CM	Open End	US Equity Mid Cap (Growth & Income)	C+	C	B	Up	Y	0
AllianzGI NFJ Mid-Cap Value Fund Institutional Class	PRNIX	NAS CM	Open End	US Equity Mid Cap (Growth & Income)	C+	C	B	Up	Y	1,000,000
AllianzGI NFJ Small-Cap Value Fund Administrative Class	PVADX	NAS CM	Open End	US Equity Small Cap (Small Company)	C-	C-	C			1,000,000
AllianzGI NFJ Small-Cap Value Fund Class A	PCVAX	NAS CM	Open End	US Equity Small Cap (Small Company)	C-	D+	C			1,000
AllianzGI NFJ Small-Cap Value Fund Class C	PCVCX	NAS CM	Open End	US Equity Small Cap (Small Company)	C-	D+	C			1,000
AllianzGI NFJ Small-Cap Value Fund Class P	ASVPX	NAS CM	Open End	US Equity Small Cap (Small Company)	C-	C-	C			1,000,000
AllianzGI NFJ Small-Cap Value Fund Class R	PNVRX	NAS CM	Open End	US Equity Small Cap (Small Company)	C-	D+	C			0
AllianzGI NFJ Small-Cap Value Fund Class R6	ANFVX	NAS CM	Open End	US Equity Small Cap (Small Company)	C	C-	C	Up	Y	0
AllianzGI NFJ Small-Cap Value Fund Institutional Class	PSVIX	NAS CM	Open End	US Equity Small Cap (Small Company)	C	C-	C	Up		1,000,000
AllianzGI PerformanceFee Managed Futures Strategy Cls P	APMPX	NAS CM	Open End	Alternative Miscellaneous (Growth)	D+	D	C	Up	Y	1,000,000
AllianzGI PerformanceFee Managed Futures Strategy Cls R6	APMRX	NAS CM	Open End	Alternative Miscellaneous (Growth)	D+	D	C	Up	Y	0
AllianzGI PerformanceFee Managed Futures Strategy Inst Cls	APMIX	NAS CM	Open End	Alternative Miscellaneous (Growth)	D+	D	C	Up	Y	1,000,000
AllianzGI PerformanceFee Structured US Equity Fund Class P	APBPX	NAS CM	Open End	US Equity Large Cap Blend (Growth & Income)	D+	C-	C+	Up	Y	1,000,000
AllianzGI PerformanceFee Structured US Equity Cls R6	APBRX	NAS CM	Open End	US Equity Large Cap Blend (Growth & Income)	D+	C-	C+	Up	Y	0
AllianzGI PerformanceFee Structured US Equity Inst Cls	APBIX	NAS CM	Open End	US Equity Large Cap Blend (Growth & Income)	D+	C-	C+	Up	Y	1,000,000
AllianzGI Preferred Securities and Income Fund Class P	APUPX	NAS CM	Open End	US Fixed Income (Growth & Income)	D	D+	B		Y	1,000,000
AllianzGI Preferred Securities and Income Fund Class R6	ARISX	NAS CM	Open End	US Fixed Income (Growth & Income)	D	D+	B		Y	0
AllianzGI Preferred Securities & Income Institutional Cls	APEIX	NAS CM	Open End	US Fixed Income (Growth & Income)	D	D+	B		Y	1,000,000
AllianzGI Retirement 2020 Fund Administrative Class	AGLMX	NAS CM	Open End	Target Date (Asset Alloc)	B-	C	B+	Up	Y	1,000,000
AllianzGI Retirement 2020 Fund Class A	AGLAX	NAS CM	Open End	Target Date (Asset Alloc)	B-	C	B+	Up	Y	1,000
AllianzGI Retirement 2020 Fund Class C	ABSCX	NAS CM	Open End	Target Date (Asset Alloc)	C+	C	B	Up	Y	1,000
AllianzGI Retirement 2020 Fund Class P	AGLPX	NAS CM	Open End	Target Date (Asset Alloc)	B-	C	B+	Up	Y	1,000,000
AllianzGI Retirement 2020 Fund Class R	AGLRX	NAS CM	Open End	Target Date (Asset Alloc)	C+	C	B	Up	Y	0
AllianzGI Retirement 2020 Fund R6 Class	AGNIX	NAS CM	Open End	Target Date (Asset Alloc)	B-	C	B+	Up	Y	0
AllianzGI Retirement 2025 Fund Administrative Class	GVDAX	NAS CM	Open End	Target Date (Asset Alloc)	B-	C	B+	Up	Y	1,000,000
AllianzGI Retirement 2025 Fund Class A	GVSAX	NAS CM	Open End	Target Date (Asset Alloc)	B-	C	B+	Up	Y	1,000
AllianzGI Retirement 2025 Fund Class P	GVSPX	NAS CM	Open End	Target Date (Asset Alloc)	B-	C	A-	Up	Y	1,000,000
AllianzGI Retirement 2025 Fund Class R	GVSRX	NAS CM	Open End	Target Date (Asset Alloc)	B-	C	B+	Up	Y	0
AllianzGI Retirement 2025 Fund R6 Class	GVSIX	NAS CM	Open End	Target Date (Asset Alloc)	B-	C	A-	Up	Y	0

★ Expanded analysis of this fund is included in Section II.

Min Additional Investment	TOTAL RETURNS: 3-Month Total Return	6-Month Total Return	1-Year Total Return	3-Year Total Return	5-Year Total Return	PERFORMANCE: Dividend Yield (TTM)	Expense Ratio	3-Yr Std Deviation	3-Year Beta	ASSETS: NAV	Total Assets (MIL)	ASSET ALLOCATION & TURNOVER: %Cash	%Stocks	%Bonds	%Other	Turnover Ratio	BULL & BEAR: Last Bull Market Total Return	Last Bear Market Total Return	FEES: Front End Fee (%)	Back End Fee (%)	Inception Date
	3.31	15.56	4.82	35.68	29.23	2.23	0.69	12.29	0.99	12.2	1,359	1	99	0	0	47	21.71	-16.59			May-00
50	1.93	15.41	0.22	34.02	18.66	1.61	1.14	13.79	0.95	16.45	120.9	3	96	0	2	116			5.50		Dec-12
50	1.77	15.03	-0.53	31.08	14.34	1.37	1.89	13.77	0.95	16.44	120.9	3	96	0	2	116				1.00	Dec-12
	1.92	15.47	0.28	34.71	19.56	1.13	0.98	13.79	0.95	16.43	120.9	3	96	0	2	116					Dec-12
	2.01	15.60	0.47	35.16	20.17	2.92	0.89	13.78	0.95	16.38	120.9	3	96	0	2	116					Dec-12
	2.18	15.09	1.67	22.22	-13.93	1.72	1.2	12.29	1.05	18.54	180.0	3	97	0	0	63	19.41	-23.02			May-10
50	2.06	14.91	1.43	21.68	-14.41	1.65	1.3	12.26	1.05	18.47	180.0	3	97	0	0	63	19.39	-23.1	5.50		Apr-05
50	1.95	14.60	0.75	19.06	-17.55	1	2.05	12.26	1.05	18.15	180.0	3	97	0	0	63	18.78	-23.32		1.00	Apr-05
	2.16	15.15	1.75	22.63	-13.31	1.85	1.05	12.26	1.05	18.58	180.0	3	97	0	0	63	19.5	-22.98			Jul-08
	2.04	14.86	1.23	20.82	-15.47	1.4	1.55	12.3	1.05	18.52	180.0	3	97	0	0	63	19.18	-23.16			Nov-09
	2.21	15.22	1.87	23.17	-12.72	2.02	0.9	12.27	1.05	18.59	180.0	3	97	0	0	63	19.61	-22.97			Dec-13
	2.14	15.13	1.83	22.97	-12.90	1.98	0.95	12.26	1.05	18.6	180.0	3	97	0	0	63	19.61	-22.97			Jan-03
	2.33	14.67	4.68	41.49	39.04	1.52	1.01	12.78	1.02	27.28	345.6	1	99	0	0	110	22.26	-16.73			Sep-06
50	2.34	14.65	4.62	41.07	38.31	1.45	1.11	12.81	1.03	26.9	345.6	1	99	0	0	110	22.14	-16.74	5.50		Jul-02
50	2.12	14.19	3.77	37.90	33.17	0.6	1.86	12.78	1.02	27.23	345.6	1	99	0	0	110	21.58	-17		1.00	Jul-02
	2.38	14.73	4.87	42.15	40.06	1.68	0.86	12.8	1.03	27.15	345.6	1	99	0	0	110	22.4	-16.7			Jul-08
	2.25	14.48	4.33	40.07	36.61	1.18	1.36	12.79	1.02	27.18	345.6	1	99	0	0	110	22	-16.86			Jan-06
	2.40	14.83	4.98	42.61	40.79	1.81	0.76	12.79	1.02	26.77	345.6	1	99	0	0	110	22.43	-16.6			May-00
	4.31	19.66	3.56	44.33	44.26	1.08	0.89	14.28	1.03	31.57	1,322	0	100	0	0	31	21.92	-19.79			Aug-98
50	4.27	19.61	3.46	43.88	43.51	1	0.99	14.28	1.03	30.6	1,322	0	100	0	0	31	21.85	-19.85	5.50		Feb-91
50	4.11	19.18	2.68	40.70	38.24	0	1.74	14.29	1.03	25.16	1,322	0	100	0	0	31	21.4	-20.16		1.00	Apr-88
	4.37	19.79	3.75	45.03	45.37	1.51	0.74	14.29	1.03	24.68	1,322	0	100	0	0	31	22.07	-19.75			Feb-11
	4.24	19.50	3.21	42.83	41.77	1.04	1.24	14.31	1.03	26.16	1,322	0	100	0	0	31	21.76	-19.96			Dec-02
	4.38	19.87	3.88	43.16	40.66	1.26	0.59	14.25	1.03	32.75	1,322	0	100	0	0	31	21.4	-20.16			Dec-17
	4.37	19.81	3.82	45.41	46.03	1.21	0.64	14.31	1.03	32.77	1,322	0	100	0	0	31	22.13	-19.75			Dec-97
	2.18	15.47	-7.63	22.43	10.31	3.58	1.06	17.38	0.97	14.48	1,065	0	100	0	0	24	21.24	-18.44			Nov-95
50	2.18	15.40	-7.70	22.07	9.60	3.54	1.16	17.37	0.97	14.53	1,065	0	100	0	0	24	21.12	-18.51	5.50		Jan-97
50	1.96	14.98	-8.34	19.43	5.63	0	1.91	17.38	0.97	12.97	1,065	0	100	0	0	24	20.59	-18.75		1.00	Jan-97
	2.19	15.55	-7.48	22.95	10.93	3.43	0.91	17.39	0.97	16.79	1,065	0	100	0	0	24	21.28	-18.41			Jul-08
	2.06	15.27	-7.97	21.13	8.20	2.92	1.41	17.36	0.97	15.85	1,065	0	100	0	0	24	20.95	-18.6			Dec-02
	2.24	15.64	-7.36	23.54	11.89	3.55	0.76	17.39	0.97	16.85	1,065	0	100	0	0	24	21.42	-18.39			Dec-13
	2.23	15.62	-7.42	23.36	11.61	3.41	0.81	17.39	0.97	16.95	1,065	0	100	0	0	24	21.42	-18.39			Oct-91
	1.91	0.63	2.13			0.85	0.95			9.58	32.0	-4	17	86	1	121					Dec-17
	1.91	0.73	2.16			0.98	0.85			9.58	32.0	-4	17	86	1	121					Dec-17
	1.80	0.63	2.20			0.91	0.9			9.57	32.0	-4	17	86	1	121					Dec-17
	4.82	22.56	10.98			0.81	0.64			10.43	94.3	1	99	0	0	2					Dec-17
	4.90	22.83	11.21			0.53	0.64			10.49	94.3	1	99	0	0	2					Dec-17
	4.71	22.53	11.01			0.77	0.64			10.44	94.3	1	99	0	0	2					Dec-17
0	2.98	12.25	7.11			4.83	0.6			15.28	17.3	1	0	73	0	39					May-18
	3.01	12.31	7.17			4.95	0.5			15.28	17.3	1	0	73	0	39					May-18
0	3.01	12.30	7.12			4.91	0.55			15.28	17.3	1	0	73	0	39					May-18
	3.52	10.56	5.50	19.73	18.66	2.6	0.9	5.86	0.96	19.67	27.3	7	43	32	18	24	11.33	-9.3			Dec-08
50	3.48	10.60	5.52	19.61	18.47	2.28	0.95	5.85	0.96	19.6	27.3	7	43	32	18	24	11.36	-9.34	5.50		Dec-08
50	3.26	10.16	4.70	17.02	14.13	1.07	1.7	5.87	0.97	19.61	27.3	7	43	32	18	24	10.83	-9.6		1.00	Dec-08
	3.57	10.78	5.83	20.70	20.32	2.89	0.65	5.87	0.97	19.72	27.3	7	43	32	18	24	11.56	-9.25			Dec-08
	3.40	10.06	4.83	15.85	13.92	2.36	1.3	6.08	0.97	19.14	27.3	7	43	32	18	24	11.09	-9.43			Dec-08
	3.61	10.82	5.92	21.09	20.88	2.97	0.55	5.86	0.96	19.76	27.3	7	43	32	18	24	11.57	-9.24			Dec-08
	3.41	11.55	4.96	23.37	22.03	2.31	0.9	7.19	1.04	17.57	37.9	10	55	24	11	19					Dec-11
50	3.42	11.59	4.89	23.20	21.77	2.24	0.95	7.17	1.04	17.51	37.9	10	55	24	11	19			5.50		Dec-11
	3.43	11.69	5.19	24.37	23.64	2.6	0.65	7.17	1.04	17.48	37.9	10	55	24	11	19					Dec-11
	3.32	11.33	4.51	21.90	19.63	1.96	1.3	7.14	1.04	17.38	37.9	10	55	24	11	19					Dec-11
	3.48	11.79	5.27	24.69	24.27	2.62	0.55	7.17	1.04	17.53	37.9	10	55	24	11	19					Dec-11

	MARKET			FUND TYPE, CATEGORY & OBJECTIVE	RATINGS				MINIMUMS	
Fund Name	Ticker Symbol	Traded On	Fund Type	Category and (Prospectus Objective)	Overall Rating	Reward Rating	Risk Rating	Recent Up/ Downgrade	Open to New Investors	Min Initial Investment
AllianzGI Retirement 2030 Fund Administrative Class	**ABAMX**	NAS CM	Open End	Target Date (Asset Alloc)	**B-**	C	B+	Up	Y	1,000,000
AllianzGI Retirement 2030 Fund Class A	**ABLAX**	NAS CM	Open End	Target Date (Asset Alloc)	**B-**	C	B+	Up	Y	1,000
AllianzGI Retirement 2030 Fund Class C	**ABLCX**	NAS CM	Open End	Target Date (Asset Alloc)	**B-**	C	B+	Up	Y	1,000
AllianzGI Retirement 2030 Fund Class P	**ABLPX**	NAS CM	Open End	Target Date (Asset Alloc)	**B-**	C	B+	Up	Y	1,000,000
AllianzGI Retirement 2030 Fund Class R	**ABLRX**	NAS CM	Open End	Target Date (Asset Alloc)	**B-**	C	B+	Up	Y	0
AllianzGI Retirement 2030 Fund R6 Class	**ABLIX**	NAS CM	Open End	Target Date (Asset Alloc)	**B-**	C	B+	Up	Y	0
AllianzGI Retirement 2035 Fund Administrative Class	**GVLAX**	NAS CM	Open End	Target Date (Asset Alloc)	**B-**	C	B	Up	Y	1,000,000
AllianzGI Retirement 2035 Fund Class A	**GVRAX**	NAS CM	Open End	Target Date (Asset Alloc)	**B-**	C	B	Up	Y	1,000
AllianzGI Retirement 2035 Fund Class P	**GVPAX**	NAS CM	Open End	Target Date (Asset Alloc)	**B-**	C	B	Up	Y	1,000,000
AllianzGI Retirement 2035 Fund Class R	**GVRRX**	NAS CM	Open End	Target Date (Asset Alloc)	**B-**	C	B	Up	Y	0
AllianzGI Retirement 2035 Fund R6 Class	**GVLIX**	NAS CM	Open End	Target Date (Asset Alloc)	**B-**	C	B	Up	Y	0
AllianzGI Retirement 2040 Fund Administrative Class	**AVAMX**	NAS CM	Open End	Target Date (Asset Alloc)	**B-**	C	B	Up	Y	1,000,000
AllianzGI Retirement 2040 Fund Class A	**AVSAX**	NAS CM	Open End	Target Date (Asset Alloc)	**C+**	C	B	Up	Y	1,000
AllianzGI Retirement 2040 Fund Class C	**AVSCX**	NAS CM	Open End	Target Date (Asset Alloc)	**C+**	C	B	Up	Y	1,000
AllianzGI Retirement 2040 Fund Class P	**AVSPX**	NAS CM	Open End	Target Date (Asset Alloc)	**B-**	C	B	Up	Y	1,000,000
AllianzGI Retirement 2040 Fund Class R	**AVSRX**	NAS CM	Open End	Target Date (Asset Alloc)	**C+**	C	B	Up	Y	0
AllianzGI Retirement 2040 Fund R6 Class	**AVTIX**	NAS CM	Open End	Target Date (Asset Alloc)	**B-**	C	B	Up	Y	0
AllianzGI Retirement 2045 Fund Administrative Class	**GBMAX**	NAS CM	Open End	Target Date (Asset Alloc)	**C+**	C	B	Up	Y	1,000,000
AllianzGI Retirement 2045 Fund Class A	**GBVAX**	NAS CM	Open End	Target Date (Asset Alloc)	**C+**	C	B	Up	Y	1,000
AllianzGI Retirement 2045 Fund Class P	**GBVPX**	NAS CM	Open End	Target Date (Asset Alloc)	**C+**	C	B	Up	Y	1,000,000
AllianzGI Retirement 2045 Fund Class R	**GBVRX**	NAS CM	Open End	Target Date (Asset Alloc)	**C+**	C	B	Up	Y	0
AllianzGI Retirement 2045 Fund R6 Class	**GBVIX**	NAS CM	Open End	Target Date (Asset Alloc)	**C+**	C	B	Up	Y	0
AllianzGI Retirement 2050 Fund Administrative Class	**ANAMX**	NAS CM	Open End	Target Date (Asset Alloc)	**C+**	C	B	Up	Y	1,000,000
AllianzGI Retirement 2050 Fund Class A	**ASNAX**	NAS CM	Open End	Target Date (Asset Alloc)	**C+**	C	B	Up	Y	1,000
AllianzGI Retirement 2050 Fund Class C	**ASNCX**	NAS CM	Open End	Target Date (Asset Alloc)	**C+**	C	B	Up	Y	1,000
AllianzGI Retirement 2050 Fund Class P	**ASNPX**	NAS CM	Open End	Target Date (Asset Alloc)	**C+**	C	B	Up	Y	1,000,000
AllianzGI Retirement 2050 Fund Class R	**ASNRX**	NAS CM	Open End	Target Date (Asset Alloc)	**C+**	C	B	Up	Y	0
AllianzGI Retirement 2050 Fund R6 Class	**ASNIX**	NAS CM	Open End	Target Date (Asset Alloc)	**C+**	C	B	Up	Y	0
AllianzGI Retirement 2055 Fund Administrative Class	**GLRAX**	NAS CM	Open End	Target Date (Asset Alloc)	**C+**	C	B	Up	Y	1,000,000
AllianzGI Retirement 2055 Fund Class A	**GLIAX**	NAS CM	Open End	Target Date (Asset Alloc)	**C+**	C	B	Up	Y	1,000
AllianzGI Retirement 2055 Fund Class P	**GLIPX**	NAS CM	Open End	Target Date (Asset Alloc)	**C+**	C	B	Up	Y	1,000,000
AllianzGI Retirement 2055 Fund Class R	**GLLRX**	NAS CM	Open End	Target Date (Asset Alloc)	**C+**	C	B	Up	Y	0
AllianzGI Retirement 2055 Fund R6 Class	**GBLIX**	NAS CM	Open End	Target Date (Asset Alloc)	**C+**	C	B	Up	Y	0
AllianzGI Small-Cap Fund Class A	**AZBAX**	NAS CM	Open End	US Equity Small Cap (Small Company)	**C+**	C	C+		Y	1,000
AllianzGI Small-Cap Fund Class C	**AZBCX**	NAS CM	Open End	US Equity Small Cap (Small Company)	**C**	C	C+		Y	1,000
AllianzGI Small-Cap Fund Class P	**AZBPX**	NAS CM	Open End	US Equity Small Cap (Small Company)	**C+**	C	C+		Y	1,000,000
AllianzGI Small-Cap Fund Institutional Class	**AZBIX**	NAS CM	Open End	US Equity Small Cap (Small Company)	**C+**	C	C+		Y	1,000,000
AllianzGI Small-Cap Fund R6	**ASCFX**	NAS CM	Open End	US Equity Small Cap (Small Company)	**C+**	C	C+		Y	0
AllianzGI Structured Return Fund Class A	**AZIAX**	NAS CM	Open End	Long/Short Equity (Growth)	**C+**	C	B	Up	Y	1,000
AllianzGI Structured Return Fund Class C	**AZICX**	NAS CM	Open End	Long/Short Equity (Growth)	**C**	C	B-		Y	1,000
AllianzGI Structured Return Fund Class P	**AZIPX**	NAS CM	Open End	Long/Short Equity (Growth)	**C+**	C	B	Up	Y	1,000,000
AllianzGI Structured Return Fund Class R6	**AZIRX**	NAS CM	Open End	Long/Short Equity (Growth)	**C+**	C	B		Y	0
AllianzGI Structured Return Fund Institutional Class	**AZIIX**	NAS CM	Open End	Long/Short Equity (Growth)	**C+**	C	B		Y	1,000,000
AllianzGI Technology Fund Administrative Class	**DGTAX**	NAS CM	Open End	Technology Sector Equity (Technology)	**C+**	C+	B-	Down	Y	1,000,000
AllianzGI Technology Fund Class A	**RAGTX**	NAS CM	Open End	Technology Sector Equity (Technology)	**C+**	C+	B-	Down	Y	1,000
AllianzGI Technology Fund Class C	**RCGTX**	NAS CM	Open End	Technology Sector Equity (Technology)	**C+**	C+	C+	Down	Y	1,000
AllianzGI Technology Fund Class P	**ARTPX**	NAS CM	Open End	Technology Sector Equity (Technology)	**C+**	C+	B-	Down	Y	1,000,000
AllianzGI Technology Fund Institutional Class	**DRGTX**	NAS CM	Open End	Technology Sector Equity (Technology)	**C+**	C+	B-	Down	Y	1,000,000
AllianzGI U.S. Equity-Hedged Fund Class A	**AZUAX**	NAS CM	Open End	Long/Short Equity (Growth)	**B-**	C	B+	Up	Y	1,000
AllianzGI U.S. Equity-Hedged Fund Class C	**AZUCX**	NAS CM	Open End	Long/Short Equity (Growth)	**B-**	C	B	Up	Y	1,000
AllianzGI U.S. Equity-Hedged Fund Class P	**AZUPX**	NAS CM	Open End	Long/Short Equity (Growth)	**B-**	C	B+	Up	Y	1,000,000
AllianzGI U.S. Equity-Hedged Fund Institutional Class	**AZUIX**	NAS CM	Open End	Long/Short Equity (Growth)	**B-**	C	B+	Up	Y	1,000,000

★ Expanded analysis of this fund is included in Section II.

Min Additional Investment	3-Month Total Return	6-Month Total Return	1-Year Total Return	3-Year Total Return	5-Year Total Return	Dividend Yield (TTM)	Expense Ratio	3-Yr Std Deviation	3-Year Beta	NAV	Total Assets (MIL)	%Cash	%Stocks	%Bonds	%Other	Turnover Ratio	Last Bull Market Total Return	Last Bear Market Total Return	Front End Fee (%)	Back End Fee (%)	Inception Date
	TOTAL RETURNS					PERFORMANCE				ASSETS		ASSET ALLOCATION & TURNOVER					BULL & BEAR		FEES		
	3.40	12.71	4.34	26.63	23.10	2.26	0.9	8.4	1.05	21.27	49.9	6	68	22	4	16	13.85	-13.85			Dec-08
50	3.39	12.71	4.34	26.53	22.83	2.15	0.95	8.42	1.06	21.01	49.9	6	68	22	4	16	13.84	-13.89	5.50		Dec-08
50	3.17	12.26	3.52	23.57	18.21	1.27	1.7	8.42	1.05	20.78	49.9	6	68	22	4	16	13.33	-14.12		1.00	Dec-08
	3.45	12.86	4.62	27.57	24.65	2.49	0.65	8.4	1.05	21.23	49.9	6	68	22	4	16	14	-13.75			Dec-08
	3.24	12.41	3.87	25.05	20.63	1.63	1.3	8.41	1.05	21.01	49.9	6	68	22	4	16	13.6	-13.98			Dec-08
	3.49	12.86	4.72	27.95	25.26	2.5	0.55	8.39	1.05	21.32	49.9	6	68	22	4	16	14.1	-13.74			Dec-08
	3.22	13.66	4.01	29.74	24.75	2.64	0.9	9.4	1.03	18.22	39.3	3	79	15	3	19					Dec-11
50	3.13	13.56	3.97	29.49	24.43	2.46	0.95	9.42	1.03	18.08	39.3	3	79	15	3	19			5.50		Dec-11
	3.29	13.78	4.32	30.76	26.35	2.85	0.65	9.42	1.03	18.16	39.3	3	79	15	3	19					Dec-11
	3.09	13.43	3.63	28.17	22.26	2.17	1.3	9.41	1.03	17.99	39.3	3	79	15	3	19					Dec-11
	3.23	13.83	4.35	31.08	26.96	2.97	0.55	9.42	1.04	18.18	39.3	3	79	15	3	19					Dec-11
	3.07	14.47	3.50	31.69	25.01	2.68	0.9	10.37	1.04	21.11	40.9	3	86	10	1	18	16.88	-19.19			Dec-08
50	3.01	14.49	3.48	31.44	24.72	2.43	0.95	10.34	1.04	21.17	40.9	3	86	10	1	18	16.89	-19.26	5.50		Dec-08
50	2.86	14.06	2.72	28.62	20.18	0.86	1.7	10.34	1.04	21.17	40.9	3	86	10	1	18	16.38	-19.5		1.00	Dec-08
	3.15	14.68	3.82	32.70	26.72	2.88	0.65	10.36	1.04	21.24	40.9	3	86	10	1	18	17.09	-19.16			Dec-08
	2.94	14.25	3.11	30.11	22.59	2.07	1.3	10.32	1.04	21	40.9	3	86	10	1	18	16.7	-19.33			Dec-08
	3.14	14.70	3.92	33.12	27.33	3	0.55	10.33	1.04	21.29	40.9	3	86	10	1	18	17.13	-19.11			Dec-08
	2.96	14.91	3.29	33.40	25.90	2.82	0.9	10.84	1.04	18.41	27.2	3	90	7	0	22					Dec-11
50	2.99	14.91	3.22	33.14	25.59	2.35	0.95	10.8	1.04	18.57	27.2	3	90	7	0	22			5.50		Dec-11
	3.05	15.09	3.54	34.38	27.56	3.03	0.65	10.81	1.04	18.53	27.2	3	90	7	0	22					Dec-11
	2.86	14.70	2.85	31.74	23.45	2.31	1.3	10.85	1.04	18.33	27.2	3	90	7	0	22					Dec-11
	3.05	15.11	3.61	34.73	28.22	3.13	0.55	10.84	1.04	18.58	27.2	3	90	7	0	22					Dec-11
	2.99	15.25	3.11	33.55	25.28	2.92	0.9	11.1	1.06	20.63	30.7	3	92	5	0	21	18.31	-20.53			Dec-08
50	3.00	15.22	3.07	33.29	24.99	2.8	0.95	11.1	1.06	20.59	30.7	3	92	5	0	21	18.23	-20.51	5.50		Dec-08
50	2.80	14.78	2.32	30.37	20.43	2.22	1.7	11.07	1.05	20.18	30.7	3	92	5	0	21	17.77	-20.79		1.00	Dec-08
	3.08	15.40	3.37	34.50	26.91	3.14	0.65	11.07	1.05	20.75	30.7	3	92	5	0	21	18.45	-20.42			Dec-08
	2.90	14.98	2.74	31.86	22.75	2.57	1.3	11.06	1.05	20.56	30.7	3	92	5	0	21	18.07	-20.64			Dec-08
	3.06	15.40	3.45	34.93	27.48	3.24	0.55	11.09	1.06	20.83	30.7	3	92	5	0	21	18.57	-20.45			Dec-08
	2.98	15.06	3.16	33.31	24.97	2.85	0.9	10.96	1.04	17.95	16.0	3	92	5	0	31					Dec-11
50	2.92	15.01	3.12	33.06	24.69	2.62	0.95	10.98	1.04	17.93	16.0	3	92	5	0	31			5.50		Dec-11
	2.96	15.17	3.43	34.27	26.59	3.03	0.65	10.97	1.04	18.06	16.0	3	92	5	0	31					Dec-11
	2.87	14.84	2.82	31.72	22.66	2.37	1.3	10.98	1.04	17.87	16.0	3	92	5	0	31					Dec-11
	3.06	15.23	3.55	34.69	27.26	3.13	0.55	10.98	1.04	18.15	16.0	3	92	5	0	31					Dec-11
50	2.69	19.04	-0.62	49.10	46.44	0.09	1.18	15.24	0.87	19.5	110.6	2	98	0	0	126			5.50		Jul-13
50	2.54	18.62	-1.38	45.72	41.02	0	1.93	15.22	0.87	18.68	110.6	2	98	0	0	126				1.00	Jul-13
	2.77	19.19	-0.36	50.21	48.26	0.15	0.93	15.25	0.87	19.74	110.6	2	98	0	0	126					Jul-13
	2.77	19.18	-0.29	50.61	49.01	0.17	0.83	15.24	0.87	19.9	110.6	2	98	0	0	126					Jul-13
	2.77	19.23	-0.24	50.67	49.08		0.78	15.27	0.87	19.9	110.6	2	98	0	0	126					Aug-18
50	1.01	4.51	3.59	11.41	19.80	0.02	1.07	3.18	14.21	15.96	670.7	17	83	0	0	586			5.50		Dec-12
50	0.85	4.15	2.83	8.88	15.39	0	1.82	3.16	13.89	15.3	670.7	17	83	0	0	586				1.00	Dec-12
	1.07	4.66	3.81	12.16	21.03	0.33	0.82	3.14	13.66	15.92	670.7	17	83	0	0	586					Dec-12
	1.13	4.71	3.96	12.54	21.53	0.67	0.76	3.17	13.52	15.98	670.7	17	83	0	0	586					Dec-16
	1.07	4.69	3.87	12.40	21.38	0.72	0.78	3.12	13.48	16.04	670.7	17	83	0	0	586					Dec-12
	3.74	26.02	12.51	111.36	125.08	0	1.47	18.07	1.09	68.67	1,617	4	96	0	0	104	16.28	-22.16			Mar-05
50	3.73	25.97	12.40	110.74	123.99	0	1.57	18.07	1.09	63.92	1,617	4	96	0	0	104	16.23	-22.19	5.50		Feb-02
50	3.54	25.50	11.57	106.10	115.76	0	2.32	18.06	1.09	45.22	1,617	4	96	0	0	104	15.71	-22.43		1.00	Feb-02
	3.79	26.11	12.68	112.34	126.78	0	1.32	18.07	1.09	72.49	1,617	4	96	0	0	104	16.38	-22.09			Jul-08
	3.82	26.19	12.80	112.99	127.95	0	1.22	18.08	1.09	74.1	1,617	4	96	0	0	104	16.43	-22.07			Dec-95
50	2.99	10.64	4.74	23.64	21.47	0.82	1.34	9	0.72	17.56	2.2	0	100	0	0	21			5.50		Dec-12
50	2.87	10.23	4.01	20.89	17.08	0	2.09	9	0.72	16.8	2.2	0	100	0	0	21				1.00	Dec-12
	3.06	10.71	4.95	24.20	22.34	1.76	1.19	8.98	0.72	17.15	2.2	0	100	0	0	21					Dec-12
	3.11	10.78	5.04	24.53	23.03	0.78	1.09	8.99	0.72	17.88	2.2	0	100	0	0	21					Dec-12

	MARKET			FUND TYPE, CATEGORY & OBJECTIVE	RATINGS				MINIMUMS	
Fund Name	Ticker Symbol	Traded On	Fund Type	Category and (Prospectus Objective)	Overall Rating	Reward Rating	Risk Rating	Recent Up/ Downgrade	Open to New Investors	Min Initial Investment
AllianzGI Ultra Micro Cap Fund Class A	GUCAX	NAS CM	Open End	US Equity Small Cap (Growth)	C	C	C	Up		1,000
AllianzGI Ultra Micro Cap Fund Class P	AAUPX	NAS CM	Open End	US Equity Small Cap (Growth)	C	C	C	Up		1,000,000
AllianzGI Ultra Micro Cap Fund Institutional Class	AUMIX	NAS CM	Open End	US Equity Small Cap (Growth)	C	C	C	Up		1,000,000
Alpha Risk Tactical Rotation Fund Institutional Class	ARSAX	NAS CM	Open End	Multialternative (Growth & Income)	D	D	C-		Y	1,000
AlphaCentric Asset Rotation Fund Class A	ROTAX	NAS CM	Open End	Moderate Alloc (Growth)	C-	D+	C-		Y	2,500
AlphaCentric Asset Rotation Fund Class C	ROTCX	NAS CM	Open End	Moderate Alloc (Growth)	D+	D+	C-	Down	Y	2,500
AlphaCentric Asset Rotation Fund Class I	ROTIX	NAS CM	Open End	Moderate Alloc (Growth)	C-	D+	C-	Down	Y	2,500
AlphaCentric Global Innovations Fund Class A	GNXAX	NAS CM	Open End	Technology Sector Equity (Technology)	C-	D	C	Up	Y	2,500
AlphaCentric Global Innovations Fund Class C	GNXCX	NAS CM	Open End	Technology Sector Equity (Technology)	D+	D	C		Y	2,500
AlphaCentric Global Innovations Fund Class I	GNXIX	NAS CM	Open End	Technology Sector Equity (Technology)	C-	D	C	Up	Y	2,500
AlphaCentric Premium Opportunity Fund Class A	HMXAX	NAS CM	Open End	Long/Short Equity (Growth)	C	C	C		Y	2,500
AlphaCentric Premium Opportunity Fund Class C	HMXCX	NAS CM	Open End	Long/Short Equity (Growth)	C	C	C		Y	2,500
AlphaCentric Premium Opportunity Fund Class I	HMXIX	NAS CM	Open End	Long/Short Equity (Growth)	C	C	C		Y	2,500
AlphaCentric Small Cap Opps Fund Class A	SMZAX	NAS CM	Open End	US Equity Small Cap (Growth)	D	D	D+		Y	2,500
AlphaCentric Small Cap Opps Fund Class C	SMZCX	NAS CM	Open End	US Equity Small Cap (Growth)	D	D	D+		Y	2,500
AlphaCentric Small Cap Opps Fund Class I	SMZIX	NAS CM	Open End	US Equity Small Cap (Growth)	D	D	D+		Y	2,500
AlphaMark Large Cap Growth Fund	AMLCX	NAS CM	Open End	US Equity Large Cap Blend (Growth)	C	C	B-	Down	Y	1,000
Alphaone Nextgen Technology Institutional Cls Shares	AONTX	NAS CM	Open End	Technology Sector Equity (Technology)	D+	D+	C+	Up	Y	100,000
Alphaone Nextgen Technology Fund Investor Class Shares	AONAX	NAS CM	Open End	Technology Sector Equity (Technology)	D+	D+	C+	Up	Y	2,500
AlphaOne Small Cap Opportunities Fund Institutional Class	AOMCX	NAS CM	Open End	US Equity Small Cap (Small Company)	C	C-	C		Y	100,000
AlphaOne Small Cap Opportunities Fund Investor Class	AOMAX	NAS CM	Open End	US Equity Small Cap (Small Company)	C	C-	C		Y	2,500
Alphaone Vimco Small Cap Value Institutional Cls Shares	VIMIX	NAS CM	Open End	US Equity Small Cap (Small Company)	D+	D	C-	Up	Y	100,000
Alphaone Vimco Small Cap Value Fund Investor Class Shares	VIMOX	NAS CM	Open End	US Equity Small Cap (Small Company)	D+	D	C-	Up	Y	2,500
ALPS Flat Rock Opportunity Fund USD	FROPX	NAS CM	Closed End	Moderate Alloc (Income)	D-	D+	B		Y	20,000
ALPS/CoreCommodity Mgmt CompleteCommodities Strategy Cls A	JCCSX	NAS CM	Open End	Commodities Broad Basket (Growth & Income)	D+	D+	C-		Y	2,500
ALPS/CoreCommodity Mgmt CompleteCommodities Strategy Cls C	JCRCX	NAS CM	Open End	Commodities Broad Basket (Growth & Income)	D+	D	D+		Y	2,500
ALPS/CoreCommodity Mgmt CompleteCommodities Strategy Cls I	JCRIX	NAS CM	Open End	Commodities Broad Basket (Growth & Income)	D+	D+	C-		Y	100,000
ALPS/CoreCommod Mgmt CompleteCommodities Strat Cls Inv	JCRAX	NAS CM	Open End	Commodities Broad Basket (Growth & Income)	D+	D+	C-		Y	2,500
ALPS/Kotak India Growth Fund Class A	INAAX	NAS CM	Open End	India Equity (Foreign Stock)	C	C	C+		Y	2,500
ALPS/Kotak India Growth Fund Class C	INFCX	NAS CM	Open End	India Equity (Foreign Stock)	C	C	C+		Y	2,500
ALPS/Kotak India Growth Fund Class I	INDIX	NAS CM	Open End	India Equity (Foreign Stock)	C	C	C+		Y	100,000
ALPS/Kotak India Growth Fund Class Investor	INDAX	NAS CM	Open End	India Equity (Foreign Stock)	C	C	C+		Y	2,500
ALPS/Red Rocks Listed Private Equity Fund Class A	LPFAX	NAS CM	Open End	Global Equity Mid/Small Cap (Growth & Income)	C+	C	B	Up	Y	2,500
ALPS/Red Rocks Listed Private Equity Fund Class C	LPFCX	NAS CM	Open End	Global Equity Mid/Small Cap (Growth & Income)	C+	C	B	Up	Y	2,500
ALPS/Red Rocks Listed Private Equity Fund Class I	LPEIX	NAS CM	Open End	Global Equity Mid/Small Cap (Growth & Income)	C+	C	B	Up	Y	100,000
ALPS/Red Rocks Listed Private Equity Fund Class Investor	LPEFX	NAS CM	Open End	Global Equity Mid/Small Cap (Growth & Income)	C+	C	B	Up	Y	2,500
ALPS/Red Rocks Listed Private Equity Fund Class R	LPERX	NAS CM	Open End	Global Equity Mid/Small Cap (Growth & Income)	C+	C	B	Up	Y	0
ALPS/Red Rocks Listed Private Equity Portfolio Class I			Open End	Global Equity Mid/Small Cap (Growth & Income)	C+	C	B	Up	Y	0
ALPS/Red Rocks Listed Private Equity Portfolio Class III	AVPEX	NAS CM	Open End	Global Equity Mid/Small Cap (Growth & Income)	C+	C	B	Up	Y	0
ALPS/Stadion Core ETF Portfolio Class I			Open End	Moderate Alloc (Growth)	B-	C	A-	Up	Y	0
ALPS/Stadion Core ETF Portfolio Class III	ALSTX	NAS CM	Open End	Moderate Alloc (Growth)	B-	C	A-	Up	Y	0
ALPS/Stadion Tactical Growth Portfolio Class I			Open End	Moderate Alloc (Growth)	C+	C	B		Y	0
ALPS/Stadion Tactical Growth Portfolio Class III	ALSGX	NAS CM	Open End	Moderate Alloc (Growth)	C+	C	B	Up	Y	0
ALPS/WMC Research Value Fund Class A	AMWAX	NAS CM	Open End	US Equity Large Cap Blend (Growth)	C+	C	B	Up	Y	2,500
ALPS/WMC Research Value Fund Class C	AMWCX	NAS CM	Open End	US Equity Large Cap Blend (Growth)	C+	C	B	Up	Y	2,500
ALPS/WMC Research Value Fund Class I	AMWIX	NAS CM	Open End	US Equity Large Cap Blend (Growth)	C+	C	B	Up	Y	100,000
ALPS/WMC Research Value Fund Class Investor	AMWYX	NAS CM	Open End	US Equity Large Cap Blend (Growth)	C+	C	B	Up	Y	2,500
Alta Quality Growth Fund Institutional Shares	AQLGX	NAS CM	Open End	US Equity Large Cap Growth (Growth)	U	U	U		Y	10,000
Altegris Futures Evolution Strategy Fund Class A	EVOAX	NAS CM	Open End	Alternative Miscellaneous (Growth)	C	C-	C	Up	Y	2,500
Altegris Futures Evolution Strategy Fund Class C	EVOCX	NAS CM	Open End	Alternative Miscellaneous (Growth)	C-	D+	C	Up	Y	5,000
Altegris Futures Evolution Strategy Fund Class I	EVOIX	NAS CM	Open End	Alternative Miscellaneous (Growth)	C	C-	C	Up	Y	1,000,000
Altegris Futures Evolution Strategy Fund Class N	EVONX	NAS CM	Open End	Alternative Miscellaneous (Growth)	C	C-	C	Up	Y	2,500

★ Expanded analysis of this fund is included in Section II.

	TOTAL RETURNS					PERFORMANCE				ASSETS		ASSET ALLOCATION & TURNOVER					BULL & BEAR		FEES		
Min Additional Investment	3-Month Total Return	6-Month Total Return	1-Year Total Return	3-Year Total Return	5-Year Total Return	Dividend Yield (TTM)	Expense Ratio	3-Yr Std Deviation	3-Year Beta	NAV	Total Assets (MIL)	%Cash	%Stocks	%Bonds	%Other	Turnover Ratio	Last Bull Market Total Return	Last Bear Market Total Return	Front End Fee (%)	Back End Fee (%)	Inception Date
50	3.13	16.94	-14.50	29.93	11.31	0	1.56	19.39	1.03	12.49	21.8	1	99	0	0	41	40.07	-29.46	5.50		Dec-11
	3.19	17.13	-14.28	31.12	13.00	0	1.52	19.38	1.03	12.92	21.8	1	99	0	0	41	40	-29.36			Dec-10
	3.26	17.16	-14.25	31.21	12.86	0	1.49	19.4	1.03	12.97	21.8	1	99	0	0	41	40.23	-29.38			Jan-08
50	-0.33	5.37	-6.63	-4.35	-8.58	0	2.98	9.42	1.1	9.01	0.88	100	0	0	0	368					Sep-12
100	-3.20	-4.73	-7.42	8.12		2.78	1.72	8.77	0.46	8.45	8.0	4	96	0	0	614			5.75		Jul-14
100	-3.41	-5.14	-8.07	5.63		2.1	2.47	8.84	0.46	8.49	8.0	4	96	0	0	614					Jul-14
100	-3.21	-4.64	-7.19	8.92		3.2	1.47	8.8	0.46	8.42	8.0	4	96	0	0	614					Jul-14
100	2.44	24.89	1.15			0	1.68			11.74	25.3	7	93	0	0	297			5.75		May-17
100	2.21	24.43	0.39			0	2.43			11.56	25.3	7	93	0	0	297					May-17
100	2.51	25.10	1.40			0	1.43			11.81	25.3	7	93	0	0	297					May-17
100	2.88	10.75	16.31	11.59	21.95	0	2.61			19.25	9.6	23	-3	80	0	54	15.65		5.75		Sep-16
100	2.72	10.34	15.40	9.20	17.57	0	3.35			18.88	9.6	23	-3	80	0	54	15.15				Sep-16
100	2.95	10.86	16.56	13.07	24.18	0	2.47			19.49	9.6	23	-3	80	0	54	15.82				Sep-16
100	-2.14	16.92	-7.87			0	1.66			9.12	19.8	6	94	0	0	182			5.75		May-18
100	-2.48	16.49	-8.59			0	2.41			9.04	19.8	6	94	0	0	182					May-18
100	-2.14	17.02	-7.67			0	1.41			9.14	19.8	6	94	0	0	182					May-18
100	0.85	15.69	-1.47	33.99	41.76	0.11	1.51	13.72	1.07	13.01	23.7	7	93	0	0	54	25.4	-19.86			Oct-08
10,000	-2.23	17.36	2.33			0	1.4			10.95	1.7	1	99	0	0	732					Dec-17
100	-2.24	17.31	2.05			0	1.65			10.91	1.7	1	99	0	0	732					Jan-18
10,000	3.88	17.20	-8.42	34.15	41.82	0	1.36	19.45	1.09	11.51	25.5	2	98	0	0	23	21.81	-20.66			Mar-11
100	3.68	16.94	-8.74	33.11	40.16	0	1.61	19.39	1.09	11.25	25.5	2	98	0	0	23	21.71	-20.76			Mar-11
10,000	4.55	16.94	-0.64			0	1.4			9.87	3.3	3	97	0	0	34					Dec-17
100	4.46	16.74	-0.94			0	1.65			9.83	3.3	3	97	0	0	34					Jan-18
1,000	3.87	9.08	7.68				5.33			19.78	--										Jul-18
	-1.00	7.44	-10.63	-1.41	-33.71	3.02	1.45	11.11	1.08	6.93	622.0	34	32	33	0	42	8.72	-22.38	5.50		Jun-18
	-1.19	6.96	-11.30	-3.48	-35.92	3.06	2.05	11.02	1.07	6.6	622.0	34	32	33	0	42	8.28	-22.61		1.00	Jun-10
	-0.99	7.56	-10.52	-0.80	-32.97	3.06	1.13	11.14	1.08	6.97	622.0	34	32	33	0	42	8.88	-22.3			Jun-10
	-0.99	7.44	-10.62	-1.36	-33.80	3.02	1.45	11.15	1.08	6.93	622.0	34	32	33	0	42	8.71	-22.44	5.50		Jun-10
	0.62	7.18	3.40	32.08	50.62	0	2	16.41	0.95	12.98	29.1	6	94	0	0	24	0.29	-20.66	5.50		Jun-18
	0.41	6.74	2.70	29.17	45.14	0	2.6	16.38	0.95	12.19	29.1	6	94	0	0	24	-0.04	-20.93		1.00	Feb-11
	0.67	7.28	3.76	33.21	52.67	0	1.6	16.41	0.95	13.4	29.1	6	94	0	0	24	0.44	-20.57			Feb-11
	0.77	7.34	3.64	32.29	50.36	0	2	16.39	0.95	13.01	29.1	6	94	0	0	24	0.19	-20.59	5.50		Feb-11
	6.95	22.12	7.60	51.54	36.34	0.97	1.82	13.02	1.04	7.23	197.1	5	79	0	16	29	16.05	-30.82	5.50		Jun-18
	6.86	21.67	6.87	48.26	31.63	0.12	2.46	13.01	1.04	6.85	197.1	5	79	0	16	29	15.51	-31.03		1.00	Jun-10
	7.11	22.18	7.98	52.84	38.19	1.02	1.49	13	1.04	7.38	197.1	5	79	0	16	29	16.22	-30.75			Dec-07
	6.92	22.01	7.60	51.60	36.19	0.64	1.8	13.06	1.05	7.26	197.1	5	79	0	16	29	15.98	-30.74	5.50		Dec-07
	6.85	21.84	7.43	50.61	35.35	0.85	1.91	13.01	1.05	6.08	197.1	5	79	0	16	29	15.83	-30.87			Dec-07
	7.08	22.38	8.24	48.92		5.75	1.64	12.72	1.04	12.85	27.0	5	79	0	15	20					Oct-14
	7.00	22.16	7.87	47.23		5.31	1.99	12.7	1.04	13.45	27.0	5	79	0	15	20					Oct-14
	2.82	11.90	5.36	32.50	24.02	0.56	0.89	7.82	1.02	12.03	17.4	5	56	39	0	48					Apr-14
	2.76	11.66	5.06	31.04	22.16	0.45	1.24	7.79	1.02	12.25	17.4	5	56	39	0	48					Apr-14
	0.97	9.07	0.74	29.81		0.49	1.15	9.84	0.98	11.42	5.4	16	68	13	3	123					Apr-15
	0.85	8.90	0.48	28.47		0.17	1.5	9.8	0.98	11.74	5.4	16	68	13	3	123					Apr-15
	4.27	18.14	6.16	30.48	33.72	1.06	1.15	11.91	0.97	8.53	85.5	1	100	0	0	74	23.49	-20.48	5.50		Jun-18
	4.03	17.81	5.35	27.68	28.86	1.01	1.9	11.88	0.97	8	85.5	1	100	0	0	74	23.11	-20.76		1.00	Jun-10
	4.37	18.36	6.36	31.51	35.37	1.07	0.9	11.89	0.97	8.83	85.5	1	100	0	0	74	23.64	-20.43			Nov-98
	4.27	18.14	6.16	30.48	33.72	1.06	1.15	11.91	0.97	8.53	85.5	1	100	0	0	74	23.49	-20.48	5.50		Aug-71
100	5.48	20.49					0.79			12.11	25.5	4	96	0	0						Dec-18
250	1.36	2.58	-0.62	-1.99	23.18	4.85	1.94	10.77	56.39	9.3	542.5	6	23	70	0	53			5.75		Oct-11
250	1.60	2.26	-1.41	-4.09	18.78	3.3	2.69	10.77	57.24	9.3	542.5	6	23	70	0	53				1.00	Feb-12
250	1.54	2.81	-0.34	-1.13	24.91	5.37	1.69	10.81	58.03	9.27	542.5	6	23	70	0	53					Oct-11
250	1.36	2.58	-0.62	-1.97	23.33	4.86	1.94	10.79	57.05	9.3	542.5	6	23	70	0	53					Oct-11

	MARKET			FUND TYPE, CATEGORY & OBJECTIVE	RATINGS					MINIMUMS
Fund Name	Ticker Symbol	Traded On	Fund Type	Category and (Prospectus Objective)	Overall Rating	Reward Rating	Risk Rating	Recent Up/ Downgrade	Open to New Investors	Min Initial Investment
Altegris GSA Trend Strategy Fund Class A	TRNAX	NAS CM	Open End	Alternative Miscellaneous (Growth)	D	D	D+		Y	2,500
Altegris GSA Trend Strategy Fund Class I	TRNIX	NAS CM	Open End	Alternative Miscellaneous (Growth)	D	D	D+		Y	1,000,000
Altegris GSA Trend Strategy Fund Class N	TRNNX	NAS CM	Open End	Alternative Miscellaneous (Growth)	D	D	D+		Y	2,500
Altegris Managed Futures Strategy Fund Class A	MFTAX	NAS CM	Open End	Alternative Miscellaneous (Growth)	D+	D	C-	Up	Y	2,500
Altegris Managed Futures Strategy Fund Class C	MFTCX	NAS CM	Open End	Alternative Miscellaneous (Growth)	D+	D	C-	Up	Y	5,000
Altegris Managed Futures Strategy Fund Class I	MFTIX	NAS CM	Open End	Alternative Miscellaneous (Growth)	D+	D	C	Up	Y	1,000,000
Altegris Managed Futures Strategy Fund Class O	MFTOX	NAS CM	Open End	Alternative Miscellaneous (Growth)	D+	D	C	Up	Y	2,500
Altegris/AACA Opportunistic Real Estate Fund A	RAAAX	NAS CM	Open End	Real Estate Sector Equity (Real Estate)	C	C	C+	Down	Y	2,500
Altegris/AACA Opportunistic Real Estate Fund I	RAAIX	NAS CM	Open End	Real Estate Sector Equity (Real Estate)	C+	C+	C+		Y	1,000,000
Altegris/AACA Opportunistic Real Estate Fund N	RAANX	NAS CM	Open End	Real Estate Sector Equity (Real Estate)	C	C	C+	Down	Y	2,500
Altegris/AACA Real Estate Income Fund Class A	INMAX	NAS CM	Open End	US Fixed Income (Real Estate)	D-	D+	C+		Y	2,500
Altegris/AACA Real Estate Income Fund Class I	INMIX	NAS CM	Open End	US Fixed Income (Real Estate)	D-	D+	B-		Y	1,000,000
Altegris/AACA Real Estate Income Fund Class N	INMNX	NAS CM	Open End	US Fixed Income (Real Estate)	D-	D+	B-		Y	2,500
Alternative Strategies Fund Class A	LTAFX	NAS CM	Closed End	Multialternative (Growth)	C+	C	B-		Y	5,000
Alternative Strategies Fund Class C	LTCFX	NAS CM	Closed End	Multialternative (Growth)	C	C	C+		Y	2,500
Amana Mutual Funds Trust Developing World Institutional	AMIDX	NAS CM	Open End	Global Emerg Mkts (Growth)	C-	D+	C	Down	Y	100,000
Amana Mutual Funds Trust Developing World Fund Investor	AMDWX	NAS CM	Open End	Global Emerg Mkts (Growth)	C-	D+	C	Down	Y	250
Amana Mutual Funds Trust Growth Fund Institutional	AMIGX	NAS CM	Open End	US Equity Large Cap Growth (Growth)	B	B-	B+		Y	100,000
Amana Mutual Funds Trust Growth Fund Investor	AMAGX	NAS CM	Open End	US Equity Large Cap Growth (Growth)	B	B-	B+		Y	250
Amana Mutual Funds Trust Income Fund Institutional	AMINX	NAS CM	Open End	US Equity Large Cap Blend (Equity-Income)	B-	C	B	Down	Y	100,000
Amana Mutual Funds Trust Income Fund Investor	AMANX	NAS CM	Open End	US Equity Large Cap Blend (Equity-Income)	B-	C	B	Down	Y	250
AmericaFirst Defensive Growth Fund Class A	DGQAX	NAS CM	Open End	Long/Short Equity (Growth)	D	D	D		Y	1,000
AmericaFirst Defensive Growth Fund Class I	DGQIX	NAS CM	Open End	Long/Short Equity (Growth)	D	D	D+		Y	1,000,000
AmericaFirst Defensive Growth Fund Class U	DGQUX	NAS CM	Open End	Long/Short Equity (Growth)	D	D	D		Y	1,000
AmericaFirst Income Fund Class A	AFPAX	NAS CM	Open End	Moderate Alloc (Income)	C-	D	C	Down	Y	1,000
AmericaFirst Income Fund Class I	AFPIX	NAS CM	Open End	Moderate Alloc (Income)	C-	D	C	Down	Y	1,000,000
AmericaFirst Income Fund Class U	AFPUX	NAS CM	Open End	Moderate Alloc (Income)	D+	D	C	Down	Y	1,000
AmericaFirst Large Cap Share Buyback Fund Class A	SBQAX	NAS CM	Open End	US Equity Large Cap Blend (Growth)	C	C	B		Y	1,000
AmericaFirst Large Cap Share Buyback Fund Class I	SBQIX	NAS CM	Open End	US Equity Large Cap Blend (Growth)	C	C	B		Y	1,000,000
AmericaFirst Large Cap Share Buyback Fund Class U	SBQUX	NAS CM	Open End	US Equity Large Cap Blend (Growth)	C	C	B		Y	1,000
AmericaFirst Seasonal Rotation Fund Class A	STQAX	NAS CM	Open End	Moderate Alloc (Growth)	C-	D+	C		Y	1,000
AmericaFirst Seasonal Rotation Fund Class I	STQIX	NAS CM	Open End	Moderate Alloc (Growth)	C-	D+	C		Y	1,000,000
AmericaFirst Seasonal Rotation Fund Class U	STQUX	NAS CM	Open End	Moderate Alloc (Growth)	D+	D+	C	Down	Y	1,000
AmericaFirst Tactical Alpha Fund Class A	ABRFX	NAS CM	Open End	Moderate Alloc (Growth)	C	C-	C+		Y	1,000
AmericaFirst Tactical Alpha Fund Class I	ABRWX	NAS CM	Open End	Moderate Alloc (Growth)	C	C-	B-		Y	1,000,000
AmericaFirst Tactical Alpha Fund Class U	ABRUX	NAS CM	Open End	Moderate Alloc (Growth)	C	C-	C+		Y	1,000
American Beacon Acadian Emerging Mkts Managed Vol A Cls	ACDAX	NAS CM	Open End	Global Emerg Mkts (Div Emerging Mkts)	B-	C	B+	Up	Y	2,500
American Beacon Acadian Emerging Mkts Managed Vol C Cls	ACDCX	NAS CM	Open End	Global Emerg Mkts (Div Emerging Mkts)	C+	C	B	Up	Y	1,000
American Beacon Acadian Emerging Mkts Managed Vol Inst Cls	ACDIX	NAS CM	Open End	Global Emerg Mkts (Div Emerging Mkts)	B-	C	B+	Up	Y	250,000
American Beacon Acadian Emerging Mkts Managed Vol Inv Cls	ACDPX	NAS CM	Open End	Global Emerg Mkts (Div Emerging Mkts)	B-	C	B+	Up	Y	2,500
American Beacon Acadian Emerging Mkts Managed Vol Y Cls	ACDYX	NAS CM	Open End	Global Emerg Mkts (Div Emerging Mkts)	B-	C	B+	Up	Y	100,000
American Beacon AHL Managed Futures Strategy Fund A Class	AHLAX	NAS CM	Open End	Alternative Miscellaneous (Growth)	C+	C	B	Up	Y	2,500
American Beacon AHL Managed Futures Strategy Fund C Class	AHLCX	NAS CM	Open End	Alternative Miscellaneous (Growth)	C	C	B-	Up	Y	1,000
American Beacon AHL Managed Futures Strategy Inst Cls	AHLIX	NAS CM	Open End	Alternative Miscellaneous (Growth)	C+	C	B	Up	Y	250,000
American Beacon AHL Managed Futures Strategy Investor Cls	AHLPX	NAS CM	Open End	Alternative Miscellaneous (Growth)	C+	C	B	Up	Y	2,500
American Beacon AHL Managed Futures Strategy Fund Y Class	AHLYX	NAS CM	Open End	Alternative Miscellaneous (Growth)	C+	C	B	Up	Y	250,000
American Beacon AHL TargetRisk Fund A	AHTAX	NAS CM	Open End	Fixed Income Miscellaneous (Growth)	U	U	U		Y	2,500
American Beacon AHL TargetRisk Fund C	AHACX	NAS CM	Open End	Fixed Income Miscellaneous (Growth)	U	U	U		Y	1,000
American Beacon AHL TargetRisk Fund Institutional Class	AHTIX	NAS CM	Open End	Fixed Income Miscellaneous (Growth)	U	U	U		Y	250,000
American Beacon AHL TargetRisk Fund Investor Class	AHTPX	NAS CM	Open End	Fixed Income Miscellaneous (Growth)	U	U	U		Y	2,500
American Beacon AHL TargetRisk Fund Y Class	AHTYX	NAS CM	Open End	Fixed Income Miscellaneous (Growth)	U	U	U		Y	100,000
American Beacon Alpha Quant Core Fund Institutional Class	AQCIX	NAS CM	Open End	US Equity Large Cap Blend (Growth)	C	C	C+		Y	250,000

★ Expanded analysis of this fund is included in Section II.

Min Additional Investment	3-Month Total Return	6-Month Total Return	1-Year Total Return	3-Year Total Return	5-Year Total Return	Dividend Yield (TTM)	Expense Ratio	3-Yr Std Deviation	3-Year Beta	NAV	Total Assets (MIL)	%Cash	%Stocks	%Bonds	%Other	Turnover Ratio	Last Bull Market Total Return	Last Bear Market Total Return	Front End Fee (%)	Back End Fee (%)	Inception Date
	TOTAL RETURNS					PERFORMANCE				ASSETS		ASSET ALLOCATION & TURNOVER					BULL & BEAR		FEES		
250	3.24	-3.91	-1.03			0	1.85			8.59	30.2	93	7	0	0	0			5.75		Dec-16
250	3.34	-3.78	-0.80			0	1.6			8.64	30.2	93	7	0	0	0					Dec-16
250	3.24	-3.91	-1.03			0	1.85			8.59	30.2	93	7	0	0	0					Dec-16
250	2.05	0.63	0.26	-8.52	6.96	1.87	1.91	8.38	50.94	7.95	67.0	96	4	0	0	479	-3.12	-4.15	5.75		Aug-10
250	1.87	0.26	-0.51	-10.60	3.00	1.03	2.66	8.31	50.94	7.61	67.0	96	4	0	0	479	-3.54	-4.44		1.00	Feb-11
250	2.02	0.74	0.42	-7.92	8.23	2.12	1.66	8.42	52.51	8.07	67.0	96	4	0	0	479	-2.91	-4.05			Aug-10
250	2.05	0.63	0.26	-8.41	7.09	1.87	1.91	8.37	51.25	7.95	67.0	96	4	0	0	479	-3.05	-4.15			Mar-13
250	5.20	30.48	3.27	33.33	58.88	0.14	2.98	16.46	1.14	16.18	324.0	-3	106	-3	0	36	32.88	-13.79	5.75		Jan-14
250	5.23	30.54	3.57	34.31	60.84	0.2	2.73	16.44	1.14	16.27	324.0	-3	106	-3	0	36	33.08	-13.7			Jan-14
250	5.20	30.48	3.34	33.44	58.94	0.15	2.98	16.42	1.14	16.18	324.0	-3	106	-3	0	36	32.88	-13.79			Jan-14
250	0.43	15.14					1.3			9.52	0.30	5	27	0	0	154			5.75		Jul-18
250	0.47	15.16					1.05			9.54	0.30	5	27	0	0	154					Jul-18
250	0.32	14.93					1.3			9.56	0.30	5	27	0	0	154					Jul-18
1,000	2.03	13.23	6.92	13.95	5.41	8	4.18	9.2		7.27	--	0	94	7	-1	21	11.01	-6.47	4.25		Sep-10
1,000	1.83	12.65	6.07	7.01	-4.68	7.97	4.93	9.62		7.02	--	0	94	7	-1	21	11.01	-6.47		1.00	Jan-15
25	2.67	11.01	2.55	6.11	-7.63	0.55	1.13	10.87	0.7	9.98	32.3	22	78	0	0		9.58	-12.31			Sep-13
25	2.57	10.81	2.35	5.52	-8.72	0.46	1.31	10.87	0.7	9.94	32.3	22	78	0	0		9.58	-12.31			Sep-09
25	3.47	22.94	20.27	69.54	86.81	0.5	0.85	12.61	0.98	42.23	2,119	8	92	0	0		21.48	-15.64			Sep-13
25	3.42	22.78	20.01	68.32	84.68	0.38	1.08	12.62	0.98	42.03	2,119	8	92	0	0		21.48	-15.64			Feb-94
25	1.20	13.94	11.66	35.52	44.13	1.41	0.87	12.26	0.9	50.86	1,340	2	98	0	0		18.19	-15.52			Sep-13
25	1.11	13.78	11.36	34.54	42.35	1.17	1.1	12.26	0.9	51.06	1,340	2	98	0	0		18.19	-15.52			Jun-86
50	2.85	13.52	1.56	-12.48	-12.36	0	3.02	12.73	0.8	9.74	7.5	11	61	17	11	1,020	13.1		5.00		May-11
50	2.98	13.84	2.06	-11.29	-9.23	0	2.53	12.75	0.8	10.36	7.5	11	61	17	11	1,020	13.62				May-11
50	2.76	13.15	1.08	-13.89	-14.68	0	3.53	12.7	0.8	9.29	7.5	11	61	17	11	1,020	12.72		2.50		May-11
50	-3.55	5.10	-6.24	11.99	-7.67	7.23	2.4	9.47	0.05	6.13	11.5	9	74	13	4	332	9.78	-16.27	4.00		Jul-10
50	-3.24	5.41	-5.55	14.81	-3.69	7.28	1.59	9.53	0.02	6.33	11.5	9	74	13	4	332	9.93	-16.02			Jul-10
50	-3.57	4.81	-6.65	10.35	-9.95	6.35	2.92	9.58	0.04	6.18	11.5	9	74	13	4	332	9.45	-16.41	2.00		Jul-10
50	0.17	15.47	5.71			0	1.76			11.49	7.7	3	97	0	0	217			5.00		Jan-17
50	0.17	15.52	5.99			0	1.51			11.68	7.7	3	97	0	0	217					Jan-17
50	-0.08	14.89	5.11			0	2.51			11.34	7.7	3	97	0	0	217			2.50		Jan-17
50	2.30	16.28	-6.22	6.91	4.92	0.69	2.58	13.29	1.92	10.64	6.2	4	38	58	0	357			5.00		Oct-13
50	2.44	16.20	-5.45	9.26	8.36	0.65	1.62	13.34	1.92	10.9	6.2	4	38	58	0	357					Oct-13
50	2.17	16.03	-6.71	5.26	2.25	0.88	3.08	13.32	1.91	10.35	6.2	4	38	58	0	357			2.50		Oct-13
50	2.42	10.46	-3.03	12.07	9.08	0	2.79	9.27	0.6	13.09	13.3	23	48	24	4	794	8.9	-19.82	5.00		Feb-10
50	2.71	11.01	-2.02	15.11	14.74	0	1.84	9.3	0.6	14.01	13.3	23	48	24	4	794	9.17	-19.58			Jul-10
50	2.28	10.21	-3.54	10.40	6.37	0	3.29	9.32	0.6	12.52	13.3	23	48	24	4	794	8.64	-19.96	2.50		Feb-10
50	1.24	7.41	5.69	26.93	7.00	1.5	1.75	10.16	0.69	10.58	21.1	0	99	0	0	28			5.75		Sep-13
50	1.06	7.16	4.88	24.08	3.06	0.39	2.5	10.1	0.68	10.47	21.1	0	99	0	0	28				1.00	Sep-13
50	1.32	7.74	6.12	28.47	9.18	1.65	1.35	10.16	0.69	10.71	21.1	0	99	0	0	28					Sep-13
50	1.24	7.55	5.70	27.01	7.17	1.68	1.73	10.14	0.69	10.54	21.1	0	99	0	0	28					Sep-13
50	1.33	7.68	5.95	28.10	8.63	1.66	1.45	10.14	0.69	10.65	21.1	0	99	0	0	28					Sep-13
50	2.71	0.95	4.68	5.59		0.94	1.94	9.01	28.88	10.6	1,045	49	44	-8	15				5.75		Aug-14
50	2.48	0.68	3.93	3.34		0.14	2.69	8.97	28.23	10.32	1,045	49	44	-8	15					1.00	Aug-14
50	2.77	1.22	5.06	6.90		1.26	1.54	8.93	29	10.76	1,045	49	44	-8	15						Aug-14
50	2.71	1.04	4.72	5.70		0.89	1.92	8.98	29.45	10.6	1,045	49	44	-8	15						Aug-14
50	2.78	1.13	5.02	6.65		1.21	1.64	8.96	28.72	10.71	1,045	49	44	-8	15						Aug-14
50	7.03	19.91					1.45			11.98	34.8	6	15	72	8				5.75		Apr-19
50	6.87	19.51					2.2			11.97	34.8	6	15	72	8					1.00	Apr-19
50	7.13	20.10					1.05			12.01	34.8	6	15	72	8						Dec-18
50	7.05	19.90					1.43			11.99	34.8	6	15	72	8						Dec-18
50	7.04	20.00					1.15			12	34.8	6	15	72	8						Dec-18
50	-0.56	10.74	-0.19			1	0.59			10.62	3.2	1	99	0	0	56					Mar-17

	MARKET		FUND TYPE, CATEGORY & OBJECTIVE		RATINGS				MINIMUMS	
Fund Name	Ticker Symbol	Traded On	Fund Type	Category and (Prospectus Objective)	Overall Rating	Reward Rating	Risk Rating	Recent Up/ Downgrade	Open to New Investors	Min Initial Investment
American Beacon Alpha Quant Core Fund Investor Class	AQCPX	NAS CM	Open End	US Equity Large Cap Blend (Growth)	C	C-	C+		Y	2,500
American Beacon Alpha Quant Core Fund Y Class	AQCYX	NAS CM	Open End	US Equity Large Cap Blend (Growth)	C	C	C+		Y	100,000
American Beacon Alpha Quant Dividend Institutional Cls	AQDIX	NAS CM	Open End	US Equity Large Cap Value (Equity-Income)	C	C	B		Y	250,000
American Beacon Alpha Quant Dividend Fund Investor Class	AQDPX	NAS CM	Open End	US Equity Large Cap Value (Equity-Income)	C	C	B-		Y	2,500
American Beacon Alpha Quant Dividend Fund Y Class	AQDYX	NAS CM	Open End	US Equity Large Cap Value (Equity-Income)	C	C	B		Y	100,000
American Beacon Alpha Quant Quality Institutional Cls	AQQIX	NAS CM	Open End	US Equity Large Cap Blend (Growth)	C	C	B-		Y	250,000
American Beacon Alpha Quant Quality Fund Investor Class	AQQPX	NAS CM	Open End	US Equity Large Cap Blend (Growth)	C	C	B-		Y	2,500
American Beacon Alpha Quant Quality Fund Y Class	AQQYX	NAS CM	Open End	US Equity Large Cap Blend (Growth)	C	C	B-		Y	100,000
American Beacon Alpha Quant Value Fund Institutional Class	AQVVX	NAS CM	Open End	US Equity Large Cap Value (Growth)	C-	D+	C	Down	Y	250,000
American Beacon Alpha Quant Value Fund Investor Class	AQVPX	NAS CM	Open End	US Equity Large Cap Value (Growth)	C-	D+	C	Down	Y	2,500
American Beacon Alpha Quant Value Fund Y Class	AQVYX	NAS CM	Open End	US Equity Large Cap Value (Growth)	C-	D+	C	Down	Y	100,000
American Beacon ARK Transformational Innovation Cls A	ADNAX	NAS CM	Open End	Technology Sector Equity (World Stock)	C	C	C+		Y	2,500
American Beacon ARK Transformational Innovation Cls C	ADNCX	NAS CM	Open End	Technology Sector Equity (World Stock)	C	C	C+		Y	1,000
American Beacon ARK Transformational Innovation Inst Cls	ADNIX	NAS CM	Open End	Technology Sector Equity (World Stock)	C	C	C+		Y	250,000
American Beacon ARK Transformational Innovation Inv Cls	ADNPX	NAS CM	Open End	Technology Sector Equity (World Stock)	C	C	C+		Y	2,500
American Beacon ARK Transformational Innovation Y Cls	ADNYX	NAS CM	Open End	Technology Sector Equity (World Stock)	C	C	C+		Y	100,000
American Beacon Bahl & Gaynor Small Cap Growth A Cls	GBSAX	NAS CM	Open End	US Equity Small Cap (Growth)	C	C	C+		Y	2,500
American Beacon Bahl & Gaynor Small Cap Growth C Cls	GBSCX	NAS CM	Open End	US Equity Small Cap (Growth)	C	C	C+		Y	1,000
American Beacon Bahl & Gaynor Small Cap Growth Inst Cls	GBSIX	NAS CM	Open End	US Equity Small Cap (Growth)	C	C	C+		Y	250,000
American Beacon Bahl & Gaynor Small Cap Growth Inv Cls	GBSPX	NAS CM	Open End	US Equity Small Cap (Growth)	C	C	C+		Y	2,500
American Beacon Bahl & Gaynor Small Cap Growth Y Cls	GBSYX	NAS CM	Open End	US Equity Small Cap (Growth)	C	C	C+		Y	250,000
American Beacon Balanced Fund Advisor Class	ABLSX	NAS CM	Open End	Moderate Alloc (Balanced)	B-	C	B+	Up	Y	2,500
American Beacon Balanced Fund C Class	ABCCX	NAS CM	Open End	Moderate Alloc (Balanced)	B-	C	B+	Up	Y	1,000
American Beacon Balanced Fund Class A	ABFAX	NAS CM	Open End	Moderate Alloc (Balanced)	B-	C	B+	Up	Y	2,500
American Beacon Balanced Fund Class Y	ACBYX	NAS CM	Open End	Moderate Alloc (Balanced)	B-	C	B	Up	Y	100,000
American Beacon Balanced Fund Institutional Class	AADBX	NAS CM	Open End	Moderate Alloc (Balanced)	B-	C	B+	Up	Y	250,000
American Beacon Balanced Fund Investor Class	AABPX	NAS CM	Open End	Moderate Alloc (Balanced)	B-	C	B+	Up	Y	2,500
American Beacon Bridgeway Large Cap Growth Fund A Class	BLYAX	NAS CM	Open End	US Equity Large Cap Growth (Growth)	C+	C	B-	Up	Y	2,500
American Beacon Bridgeway Large Cap Growth Fund C Class	BLYCX	NAS CM	Open End	US Equity Large Cap Growth (Growth)	C+	C	B-	Up	Y	1,000
American Beacon Bridgeway Large Cap Growth Fund Class R6	BLYRX	NAS CM	Open End	US Equity Large Cap Growth (Growth)	C+	C	B-	Up	Y	0
American Beacon Bridgeway Large Cap Growth Inst Cls	BRLGX	NAS CM	Open End	US Equity Large Cap Growth (Growth)	C+	C	B-	Up	Y	250,000
American Beacon Bridgeway Large Cap Growth Investor Cls	BLYPX	NAS CM	Open End	US Equity Large Cap Growth (Growth)	C+	C	B-	Up	Y	2,500
American Beacon Bridgeway Large Cap Growth Fund Y Class	BLYYX	NAS CM	Open End	US Equity Large Cap Growth (Growth)	C+	C	B-	Up	Y	250,000
American Beacon Bridgeway Large Cap Value Fund A Class	BWLAX	NAS CM	Open End	US Equity Large Cap Value (Growth)	C	C	B-		Y	2,500
American Beacon Bridgeway Large Cap Value Fund C Class	BWLCX	NAS CM	Open End	US Equity Large Cap Value (Growth)	C	C	B-		Y	1,000
American Beacon Bridgeway Large Cap Value Inst Cls	BRLVX	NAS CM	Open End	US Equity Large Cap Value (Growth)	C	C	B-		Y	250,000
American Beacon Bridgeway Large Cap Value Investor Cls	BWLIX	NAS CM	Open End	US Equity Large Cap Value (Growth)	C	C	B-		Y	2,500
American Beacon Bridgeway Large Cap Value Fund R6 Class	BWLRX	NAS CM	Open End	US Equity Large Cap Value (Growth)	C	C	B-		Y	0
American Beacon Bridgeway Large Cap Value Fund Y Class	BWLYX	NAS CM	Open End	US Equity Large Cap Value (Growth)	C	C	B-		Y	250,000
American Beacon Continuous Capital Emerging Mkts Inst Cls	CCEIX	NAS CM	Open End	Global Emerg Mkts (Div Emerging Mkts)	U	U	U		Y	250,000
American Beacon Continuous Capital Emerging Mkts Inv Cls	CCEPX	NAS CM	Open End	Global Emerg Mkts (Div Emerging Mkts)	U	U	U		Y	2,500
American Beacon Continuous Capital Emerging Markets Y Cls	CCEYX	NAS CM	Open End	Global Emerg Mkts (Div Emerging Mkts)	U	U	U		Y	100,000
American Beacon International Equity Fund Advisor Class	AAISX	NAS CM	Open End	Global Equity Large Cap (Foreign Stock)	C	C-	C+		Y	2,500
American Beacon International Equity Fund Class A	AIEAX	NAS CM	Open End	Global Equity Large Cap (Foreign Stock)	C	C-	C+		Y	2,500
American Beacon International Equity Fund Class C	AILCX	NAS CM	Open End	Global Equity Large Cap (Foreign Stock)	C	C-	C+		Y	1,000
American Beacon International Equity Fund Class R6	AAERX	NAS CM	Open End	Global Equity Large Cap (Foreign Stock)	C	C-	C+		Y	0
American Beacon International Equity Fund Class Y	ABEYX	NAS CM	Open End	Global Equity Large Cap (Foreign Stock)	C	C-	C+		Y	100,000
American Beacon International Equity Institutional Cls	AAIEX	NAS CM	Open End	Global Equity Large Cap (Foreign Stock)	C	C-	C+		Y	250,000
American Beacon International Equity Fund Investor Class	AAIPX	NAS CM	Open End	Global Equity Large Cap (Foreign Stock)	C	C-	C+		Y	2,500
American Beacon Ionic Strategic Arbitrage Fund Class A	IONAX	NAS CM	Open End	Market Neutral (Growth & Income)	D+	D	C		Y	2,500
American Beacon Ionic Strategic Arbitrage Fund Class C	IONCX	NAS CM	Open End	Market Neutral (Growth & Income)	D	D	C		Y	1,000
American Beacon Ionic Strategic Arbitrage Fund Class Y	IONYX	NAS CM	Open End	Market Neutral (Growth & Income)	C-	D	C	Up	Y	250,000

★ Expanded analysis of this fund is included in Section II.

Min Additional Investment	TOTAL RETURNS 3-Month Total Return	6-Month Total Return	1-Year Total Return	3-Year Total Return	5-Year Total Return	PERFORMANCE Dividend Yield (TTM)	Expense Ratio	3-Yr Std Deviation	3-Year Beta	ASSETS NAV	Total Assets (MIL)	ASSET ALLOCATION & TURNOVER %Cash	%Stocks	%Bonds	%Other	Turnover Ratio	BULL & BEAR Last Bull Market Total Return	Last Bear Market Total Return	FEES Front End Fee (%)	Back End Fee (%)	Inception Date
50	-0.66	10.50	-0.64			1.01	0.97			10.52	3.2	1	99	0	0	56					Mar-17
50	-0.56	10.76	-0.28			1	0.69			10.6	3.2	1	99	0	0	56					Mar-17
50	5.29	19.26	14.93			2.39	0.59			11.08	3.7	1	99	0	0	49					Mar-17
50	5.24	19.08	14.51			2.41	0.97			10.98	3.7	1	99	0	0	49					Mar-17
50	5.31	19.19	14.75			2.39	0.69			11.05	3.7	1	99	0	0	49					Mar-17
50	-0.18	11.55	2.98			0.9	0.59			10.62	2.7	0	100	0	0	62					Mar-17
50	-0.28	11.44	2.64			0.91	0.97			10.52	2.7	0	100	0	0	62					Mar-17
50	-0.18	11.69	2.91			0.9	0.69			10.6	2.7	0	100	0	0	62					Mar-17
50	-1.29	8.75	-5.64			0.99	0.59			10.68	4.0	0	100	0	0	53					Mar-17
50	-1.39	8.61	-5.93			1	0.97			10.59	4.0	0	100	0	0	53					Mar-17
50	-1.29	8.77	-5.73			0.99	0.69			10.66	4.0	0	100	0	0	53					Mar-17
50	2.04	27.12	6.17				1.4			18.42	50.2	0	94	0	6	59			5.75		Jan-19
50	1.83	26.74	5.99				2.15			18.35	50.2	0	94	0	6	59				1.00	Jan-19
50	2.14	27.41	6.54			0	1			18.59	50.2	0	94	0	6	59					Jan-17
50	1.99	27.05	6.07			0	1.38			18.41	50.2	0	94	0	6	59					Jan-17
50	2.09	27.26	6.38			0	1.1			18.53	50.2	0	94	0	6	59					Jan-17
50	2.94	17.43	-3.82	39.39		0.25	1.38	16.46	0.9	13.27	43.8	1	99	0	0	42			5.75		Jul-14
50	2.80	17.04	-4.46	36.36		0	2.13	16.42	0.9	12.84	43.8	1	99	0	0	42				1.00	Jul-14
50	3.04	17.65	-3.41	41.10		0.38	0.98	16.46	0.9	13.53	43.8	1	99	0	0	42					Jul-14
50	2.95	17.44	-3.81	39.44		0.39	1.36	16.46	0.9	13.26	43.8	1	99	0	0	42					Jul-14
50	3.06	17.55	-3.49	40.66		0.38	1.08	16.45	0.9	13.46	43.8	1	99	0	0	42					Jul-14
50	3.78	14.81	5.17	29.31	27.66	1.19	1.12	9.59	-0.49	15.05	273.6	2	62	36	0	28	17.92	-11.24			May-05
50	3.63	14.44	4.53	27.11	23.85	0.88	1.66	9.56	-0.49	14.21	273.6	2	62	36	0	28	17.42	-11.5		1.00	Sep-10
50	3.87	14.91	5.34	29.99	28.57	1.44	0.91	9.56	-0.48	14.08	273.6	2	62	36	0	28	17.9	-11.23	5.75		May-10
50	3.93	15.04	5.63	31.23	30.59	1.38	0.7	9.58	-0.49	16.17	273.6	2	62	36	0	28	18.05	-11.02			Mar-10
50	3.91	15.02	5.54	31.07	30.69	1.45	0.62	9.57	-0.49	16.05	273.6	2	62	36	0	28	18.24	-11.07			Jul-87
50	3.86	14.87	5.41	30.01	28.76	1.38	0.95	9.59	-0.49	14.11	273.6	2	62	36	0	28	18.06	-11.2			Aug-94
50	3.93	22.32	5.35	57.05	73.06	0	1.21	14.29	1.04	30.41	196.0	2	98	0	0	60	27.46	-20.06	5.75		Feb-16
50	3.71	21.86	4.54	53.46	66.60	0	1.96	14.31	1.04	29.6	196.0	2	98	0	0	60	26.91	-20.31		1.00	Feb-16
50	4.03	22.58	5.79	58.81	75.95	0.33	0.76	14.28	1.03	30.67	196.0	2	98	0	0	60	27.65	-19.98			Apr-18
50	4.03	22.55	5.76	58.71	75.84	0.33	0.81	14.26	1.03	30.65	196.0	2	98	0	0	60	27.65	-19.98			Oct-03
50	3.94	22.30	5.34	56.90	73.63	0.08	1.19	14.27	1.03	30.32	196.0	2	98	0	0	60	27.65	-19.98			Feb-16
50	4.01	22.48	5.67	58.33	75.36	0.33	0.91	14.31	1.04	30.56	196.0	2	98	0	0	60	27.65	-19.98			Feb-16
50	4.30	16.69	0.90	30.10	38.28	1.32	1.07	13.5	1.09	25.93	4,233	1	99	0	0	49	23.47	-18.52	5.75		Feb-12
50	4.08	16.28	0.18	27.24	33.20	0.55	1.79	13.47	1.09	25.2	4,233	1	99	0	0	49	22.92	-18.77		1.00	Feb-12
50	4.38	16.91	1.26	31.52	40.72	1.67	0.72	13.47	1.09	26.2	4,233	1	99	0	0	49	23.76	-18.43			Oct-03
50	4.28	16.71	0.94	30.19	38.46	1.26	1.05	13.46	1.09	26.04	4,233	1	99	0	0	49	23.68	-18.43			Feb-12
50	4.38	16.91	1.33	31.55	40.75	1.7	0.7	13.48	1.09	26.19	4,233	1	99	0	0	49	23.76	-18.43			Apr-17
50	4.31	16.82	1.18	31.22	40.32	1.61	0.79	13.48	1.09	26.11	4,233	1	99	0	0	49	23.76	-18.43			Feb-12
	1.97	13.70					1.19			11.37	5.2	8	92	0	0						Dec-18
50	1.79	13.40					1.57			11.34	5.2	8	92	0	0						Dec-18
	1.88	13.70					1.29			11.37	5.2	8	92	0	0						Dec-18
50	2.08	12.20	-3.41	22.93	1.68	1.55	1.21	11.59	1.02	18.11	2,910	5	95	0	0	29	14.67	-25.23			May-03
50	2.08	12.20	-3.35	23.24	2.04	1.68	1.09	11.6	1.02	17.65	2,910	5	95	0	0	29	14.81	-25.2	5.75		May-10
50	1.91	11.81	-4.02	20.55	-1.67	0.99	1.82	11.59	1.02	17.03	2,910	5	95	0	0	29	14.31	-25.5		1.00	Sep-10
50	2.23	12.47	-2.88	24.91	4.22	2.14	0.67	11.62	1.02	17.85	2,910	5	95	0	0	29	15.16	-25.12			Feb-17
50	2.14	12.40	-3.01	24.40	3.62	1.95	0.81	11.59	1.02	18.57	2,910	5	95	0	0	29	15.09	-25.13			Aug-09
50	2.17	12.42	-2.93	24.69	4.04	2.11	0.74	11.61	1.02	17.83	2,910	5	95	0	0	29	15.16	-25.12			Aug-91
50	2.08	12.19	-3.31	23.37	2.23	1.76	1.07	11.58	1.02	17.66	2,910	5	95	0	0	29	14.86	-25.19			Aug-94
50	-0.53	1.09	-2.01	-1.62	3.73	9.45	2.78	2.47	7.59	7.41	25.3	63	-25	10	5	556			4.75		Jun-15
50	-0.80	0.68	-2.90	-3.83	-0.16	7.94	3.57	2.53	7.39	7.36	25.3	63	-25	10	5	556				1.00	Jun-15
50	-0.53	1.21	-1.83	-0.81	5.22	9.54	2.48	2.51	7.77	7.48	25.3	63	-25	10	5	556					Jun-15

	MARKET			FUND TYPE, CATEGORY & OBJECTIVE	RATINGS					MINIMUMS
Fund Name	Ticker Symbol	Traded On	Fund Type	Category and (Prospectus Objective)	Overall Rating	Reward Rating	Risk Rating	Recent Up/ Downgrade	Open to New Investors	Min Initial Investment
American Beacon Ionic Strategic Arbitrage Inst Cls	IONIX	NAS CM	Open End	Market Neutral (Growth & Income)	C-	D	C	Up	Y	250,000
American Beacon Ionic Strategic Arbitrage Investor Cls	IONPX	NAS CM	Open End	Market Neutral (Growth & Income)	D+	D	C		Y	2,500
American Beacon Large Cap Value Fund Advisor Class	AVASX	NAS CM	Open End	US Equity Large Cap Value (Growth & Income)	C+	C	B	Up	Y	2,500
American Beacon Large Cap Value Fund Class A	ALVAX	NAS CM	Open End	US Equity Large Cap Value (Growth & Income)	C+	C	B	Up	Y	2,500
American Beacon Large Cap Value Fund Class C	ALVCX	NAS CM	Open End	US Equity Large Cap Value (Growth & Income)	C+	C	B	Up	Y	1,000
American Beacon Large Cap Value Fund Class R6	AALRX	NAS CM	Open End	US Equity Large Cap Value (Growth & Income)	C+	C	B	Up	Y	0
American Beacon Large Cap Value Fund Class Y	ABLYX	NAS CM	Open End	US Equity Large Cap Value (Growth & Income)	C+	C	B	Up	Y	100,000
American Beacon Large Cap Value Fund Institutional Class	AADEX	NAS CM	Open End	US Equity Large Cap Value (Growth & Income)	C+	C	B	Up	Y	250,000
American Beacon Large Cap Value Fund Investor Class	AAGPX	NAS CM	Open End	US Equity Large Cap Value (Growth & Income)	C+	C	B	Up	Y	2,500
American Beacon Mid-Cap Value Fund Advisor Class	AMCSX	NAS CM	Open End	US Equity Mid Cap (Growth & Income)	C	C	C+		Y	2,500
American Beacon Mid-Cap Value Fund C Class	AMCCX	NAS CM	Open End	US Equity Mid Cap (Growth & Income)	C	C	C+		Y	1,000
American Beacon Mid-Cap Value Fund Class A	ABMAX	NAS CM	Open End	US Equity Mid Cap (Growth & Income)	C	C	C+		Y	2,500
American Beacon Mid-Cap Value Fund Class Y	ACMYX	NAS CM	Open End	US Equity Mid Cap (Growth & Income)	C	C	C+		Y	100,000
American Beacon Mid-Cap Value Fund Institutional Class	AACIX	NAS CM	Open End	US Equity Mid Cap (Growth & Income)	C	C	C+		Y	250,000
American Beacon Mid-Cap Value Fund Investor Class	AMPAX	NAS CM	Open End	US Equity Mid Cap (Growth & Income)	C	C	C+		Y	2,500
American Beacon Mid-Cap Value Fund R6 Class	AMDRX	NAS CM	Open End	US Equity Mid Cap (Growth & Income)	C	C	C+		Y	0
American Beacon Shapiro Equity Opp Inst Cls	SHXIX	NAS CM	Open End	US Equity Large Cap Value (Growth)	C-	D+	C+	Up	Y	250,000
American Beacon Shapiro Equity Opportunities Investor Cls	SHXPX	NAS CM	Open End	US Equity Large Cap Value (Growth)	C-	D+	C+	Up	Y	2,500
American Beacon Shapiro Equity Opportunities Fund Y Class	SHXYX	NAS CM	Open End	US Equity Large Cap Value (Growth)	C-	D+	C+	Up	Y	100,000
American Beacon Shapiro SMID Cap Equity Institutional Cls	SHDIX	NAS CM	Open End	US Equity Mid Cap (Growth)	D+	D	C-		Y	250,000
American Beacon Shapiro SMID Cap Equity Investor Cls	SHDPX	NAS CM	Open End	US Equity Mid Cap (Growth)	D+	D	C-		Y	2,500
American Beacon Shapiro SMID Cap Equity Fund Y Class	SHDYX	NAS CM	Open End	US Equity Mid Cap (Growth)	D+	D	C-		Y	100,000
American Beacon Small Cap Value Fund Advisor Class	AASSX	NAS CM	Open End	US Equity Small Cap (Small Company)	C-	C-	C	Down	Y	2,500
American Beacon Small Cap Value Fund C Class	ASVCX	NAS CM	Open End	US Equity Small Cap (Small Company)	C-	C-	C	Down	Y	1,000
American Beacon Small Cap Value Fund Class A	ABSAX	NAS CM	Open End	US Equity Small Cap (Small Company)	C	C-	C		Y	2,500
American Beacon Small Cap Value Fund Class Institutional	AVFIX	NAS CM	Open End	US Equity Small Cap (Small Company)	C	C-	C		Y	250,000
American Beacon Small Cap Value Fund Class Y	ABSYX	NAS CM	Open End	US Equity Small Cap (Small Company)	C	C-	C		Y	100,000
American Beacon Small Cap Value Fund Investor Class	AVPAX	NAS CM	Open End	US Equity Small Cap (Small Company)	C	C-	C		Y	2,500
American Beacon Small Cap Value Fund R6 Class	AASRX	NAS CM	Open End	US Equity Small Cap (Small Company)	C	C-	C		Y	0
American Beacon SSI Alternative Income Institutional Cls	SSIJX	NAS CM	Open End	Market Neutral (Convertible Bond)	B-	C	B+		Y	250,000
American Beacon SSI Alternative Income Fund --Y Class	PSCIX	NAS CM	Open End	Market Neutral (Convertible Bond)	B-	C	B+		Y	100,000
American Beacon SSI Alternative Income Fund--Investor Cls	PSCAX	NAS CM	Open End	Market Neutral (Convertible Bond)	B-	C	B+		Y	2,500
American Beacon Stephens Mid-Cap Growth Fund A Class	SMFAX	NAS CM	Open End	US Equity Mid Cap (Growth)	B-	C+	B	Down	Y	2,500
American Beacon Stephens Mid-Cap Growth Fund C Class	SMFCX	NAS CM	Open End	US Equity Mid Cap (Growth)	B-	C+	B	Down	Y	1,000
American Beacon Stephens Mid-Cap Growth Fund Class R6	SFMRX	NAS CM	Open End	US Equity Mid Cap (Growth)	B-	C+	B	Down	Y	0
American Beacon Stephens Mid-Cap Growth Institutional Cls	SFMIX	NAS CM	Open End	US Equity Mid Cap (Growth)	B-	C+	B	Down	Y	250,000
American Beacon Stephens Mid-Cap Growth Investor Cls	STMGX	NAS CM	Open End	US Equity Mid Cap (Growth)	B-	C+	B	Down	Y	2,500
American Beacon Stephens Mid-Cap Growth Fund Y Class	SMFYX	NAS CM	Open End	US Equity Mid Cap (Growth)	B-	C+	B	Down	Y	250,000
American Beacon Stephens Small Cap Growth Fund A Class	SPWAX	NAS CM	Open End	US Equity Small Cap (Growth)	C+	C+	C+		Y	2,500
American Beacon Stephens Small Cap Growth Fund C Class	SPWCX	NAS CM	Open End	US Equity Small Cap (Growth)	C+	C	C+		Y	1,000
American Beacon Stephens Small Cap Growth Inst Cls	STSIX	NAS CM	Open End	US Equity Small Cap (Growth)	C+	C+	C+		Y	250,000
American Beacon Stephens Small Cap Growth Investor Cls	STSGX	NAS CM	Open End	US Equity Small Cap (Growth)	C+	C+	C+		Y	2,500
American Beacon Stephens Small Cap Growth Fund R6	STSRX	NAS CM	Open End	US Equity Small Cap (Growth)	C+	C+	C+		Y	0
American Beacon Stephens Small Cap Growth Fund Y Class	SPWYX	NAS CM	Open End	US Equity Small Cap (Growth)	C+	C+	C+		Y	250,000
American Beacon The London Company Income Equity A Cls	ABCAX	NAS CM	Open End	US Equity Large Cap Value (Equity-Income)	B-	C	B+		Y	2,500
American Beacon The London Company Income Equity C Cls	ABECX	NAS CM	Open End	US Equity Large Cap Value (Equity-Income)	B-	C	B		Y	1,000
American Beacon The London Company Income Equity Inst Cls	ABCIX	NAS CM	Open End	US Equity Large Cap Value (Equity-Income)	B-	C+	B+		Y	250,000
American Beacon The London Company Income Equity Inv Cls	ABCVX	NAS CM	Open End	US Equity Large Cap Value (Equity-Income)	B-	C	B+		Y	2,500
American Beacon The London Company Income Equity Y Cls	ABCYX	NAS CM	Open End	US Equity Large Cap Value (Equity-Income)	B-	C	B+		Y	100,000
American Beacon Tocqueville Intl Value Inst Cls	TOVIX	NAS CM	Open End	Global Equity Large Cap (Foreign Stock)	C-	D+	C		Y	250,000
American Beacon Tocqueville Intl Value Inv Cls	TIVFX	NAS CM	Open End	Global Equity Large Cap (Foreign Stock)	C	D+	C+	Up	Y	1,000
American Beacon Tocqueville International Value Y Cls	TOVYX	NAS CM	Open End	Global Equity Large Cap (Foreign Stock)	C-	D+	C		Y	100,000

★ Expanded analysis of this fund is included in Section II.

Min Additional Investment	3-Month Total Return	6-Month Total Return	1-Year Total Return	3-Year Total Return	5-Year Total Return	Dividend Yield (TTM)	Expense Ratio	3-Yr Std Deviation	3-Year Beta	NAV	Total Assets (MIL)	%Cash	%Stocks	%Bonds	%Other	Turnover Ratio	Last Bull Market Total Return	Last Bear Market Total Return	Front End Fee (%)	Back End Fee (%)	Inception Date
	TOTAL RETURNS					PERFORMANCE				ASSETS		ASSET ALLOCATION & TURNOVER					BULL & BEAR		FEES		
50	-0.53	1.35	-1.70	-0.49	5.50	9.52	2.36	2.42	7.24	7.5	25.3	63	-25	10	5	556					Jun-15
50	-0.66	0.95	-2.22	-1.88	3.80	9.38	2.75	2.43	7.34	7.41	25.3	63	-25	10	5	556					Jun-15
50	4.21	18.90	4.35	40.21	33.04	1.48	1.09	14.39	1.17	24.97	5,698	3	97	0	0	23	26.57	-19.73			May-05
50	4.21	18.97	4.47	40.72	33.77	1.76	0.93	14.4	1.17	24.95	5,698	3	97	0	0	23	26.46	-19.73	5.75		May-10
50	4.03	18.51	3.69	37.77	29.00	0.94	1.64	14.38	1.16	24.77	5,698	3	97	0	0	23	25.9	-19.94		1.00	Sep-10
50	4.28	19.16	4.89	42.26	36.29	1.9	0.58	14.43	1.17	27.48	5,698	3	97	0	0	23	26.84	-19.53			Feb-17
50	4.28	19.12	4.72	41.87	35.70	1.79	0.68	14.41	1.17	27.28	5,698	3	97	0	0	23	26.8	-19.59			Aug-09
50	4.28	19.15	4.84	42.20	36.23	1.87	0.62	14.4	1.17	27.49	5,698	3	97	0	0	23	26.84	-19.53			Jul-87
50	4.19	18.98	4.47	40.78	33.95	1.66	0.95	14.38	1.17	25.32	5,698	3	97	0	0	23	26.65	-19.68			Aug-94
50	3.46	18.46	-2.67	29.52	24.18	0.82	1.4	15.93	1.19	14.95	540.6	2	98	0	0	34	29.35	-22.23			Jun-07
50	3.29	18.11	-3.19	27.34	20.56	0.22	1.88	15.92	1.19	14.41	540.6	2	98	0	0	34	28.77	-22.49		1.00	Sep-10
50	3.53	18.49	-2.50	30.07	25.06	0.92	1.26	15.92	1.19	14.93	540.6	2	98	0	0	34	29.29	-22.27	5.75		May-10
50	3.55	18.74	-2.20	31.31	27.05	1.29	0.94	15.95	1.19	15.14	540.6	2	98	0	0	34	29.73	-22.16			Mar-10
50	3.59	18.74	-2.15	31.58	27.48	1.35	0.86	15.94	1.19	15.27	540.6	2	98	0	0	34	29.7	-22.06			Nov-05
50	3.55	18.60	-2.40	30.64	26.01	1.07	1.13	15.96	1.19	15.43	540.6	2	98	0	0	34	29.6	-22.18			Feb-06
50	3.59	18.74	-2.09	31.58	27.48	1.36	0.84	15.94	1.19	15.27	540.6	2	98	0	0	34	29.7	-22.06			Mar-18
50	3.96	20.64	2.97			0.65	0.81			11.28	89.3	4	96	0	0						Sep-17
50	3.79	20.43	2.53			0.65	1.19			11.2	89.3	4	96	0	0						Sep-17
50	3.96	20.64	2.88			0.65	0.91			11.28	89.3	4	96	0	0						Sep-17
50	2.20	18.82	-6.66			0.37	0.9			9.72	6.8	2	98	0	0						Sep-17
50	2.11	18.54	-7.05			0.37	1.28			9.65	6.8	2	98	0	0						Sep-17
50	2.21	18.85	-6.75			0.37	1			9.71	6.8	2	98	0	0						Sep-17
50	1.64	14.74	-8.06	28.67	23.61	0.13	1.29	18.73	1.07	21.63	6,331	3	97	0	0	69	29.76	-26.52			May-03
50	1.44	14.34	-8.66	26.40	19.83	0	1.87	18.71	1.07	20.4	6,331	3	97	0	0	69	29.06	-26.82		1.00	Sep-10
50	1.65	14.80	-7.99	29.02	24.19	0.3	1.21	18.73	1.07	21.48	6,331	3	97	0	0	69	29.64	-26.58	5.75		May-10
50	1.77	15.00	-7.60	30.57	26.68	0.71	0.81	18.73	1.07	22.92	6,331	3	97	0	0	69	30.14	-26.38			Dec-98
50	1.71	14.98	-7.70	30.27	26.17	0.63	0.88	18.73	1.07	22.56	6,331	3	97	0	0	69	30.07	-26.4			Aug-09
50	1.66	14.80	-7.92	29.31	24.63	0.36	1.14	18.74	1.07	21.94	6,331	3	97	0	0	69	29.92	-26.47			Feb-99
50	1.77	15.00	-7.60	30.62	26.72	0.74	0.78	18.72	1.07	22.91	6,331	3	97	0	0	69	30.14	-26.38			Feb-17
							1.7	1.47	17.07	10.27	229.1	7	-33	0	38	76					May-19
50	1.48	4.26	3.76	12.20	9.90	1	1.73	1.47	17.07	10.27	229.1	7	-33	0	38	76					May-12
50	1.38	4.15	3.54	11.32	8.44	0.79	2.02	1.46	16.76	10.27	229.1	7	-33	0	38	76			5.75		May-12
50	6.68	27.43	13.86	78.97	74.01	0	1.29	14.74	1.01	22.34	231.7	3	97	0	0		27.32	-17.14	5.75		Feb-12
50	6.48	26.90	13.04	75.02	67.58	0	2.04	14.75	1.01	20.85	231.7	3	97	0	0		26.65	-17.4		1.00	Feb-12
50	6.80	27.71	14.17	79.68	74.71		0.84	14.76	1.01	26.84	231.7	3	97	0	0		27.36	-17.05			Dec-18
50	6.76	27.64	14.29	81.05	77.46	0	0.89	14.76	1.01	26.83	231.7	3	97	0	0		27.52	-16.94			Aug-06
50	6.70	27.41	13.89	79.26	74.29	0	1.25	14.76	1.01	22.45	231.7	3	97	0	0		27.36	-17.06			Feb-06
50	6.73	27.58	14.17	80.49	76.54	0	0.99	14.75	1.01	26.64	231.7	3	97	0	0		27.38	-17.06			Feb-12
50	6.61	24.20	7.28	66.66	56.99	0	1.38	17.18	0.94	15.14	431.9	2	98	0	0	16	28.26	-21.96	5.75		Feb-12
50	6.45	23.75	6.52	62.96	51.18	0	2.15	17.17	0.94	13.86	431.9	2	98	0	0	16	27.76	-22.2		1.00	Feb-12
50	6.70	24.30	7.61	68.25	59.75	0	1.09	17.17	0.94	17.03	431.9	2	98	0	0	16	28.61	-21.74			Aug-06
50	6.59	24.17	7.32	66.96	57.50	0	1.38	17.17	0.94	15.36	431.9	2	98	0	0	16	28.49	-21.87			Dec-05
50	6.64	24.22	7.37	67.04	57.58		1.05	17.16	0.94	17.04	431.9	2	98	0	0	16	28.49	-21.87			Apr-19
50	6.63	24.30	7.52	67.92	59.09	0	1.15	17.18	0.94	16.88	431.9	2	98	0	0	16	28.57	-21.87			Feb-12
50	2.43	17.08	13.96	34.44	50.09	1.77	1.03	11.42	0.89	18.19	1,114	4	96	0	0	16			5.75		May-12
50	2.25	16.64	13.03	31.40	44.55	1.08	1.81	11.38	0.89	18.05	1,114	4	96	0	0	16				1.00	May-12
50	2.48	17.23	14.31	35.82	52.77	2.05	0.73	11.37	0.89	18.37	1,114	4	96	0	0	16					May-12
50	2.41	17.03	13.92	34.51	50.31	1.74	1.05	11.41	0.89	18.3	1,114	4	96	0	0	16					May-12
50	2.48	17.15	14.18	35.51	52.25	2	0.79	11.38	0.89	18.27	1,114	4	96	0	0	16					May-12
50	2.60	14.38	-4.44	16.80	12.13		0.88	12.07	1.05	15.74	791.8	5	95	0	0	25	7.79	-21.65			Jan-19
100	2.54	14.17	-4.62	16.58	11.92	1.21	1.26	12.06	1.05	15.71	791.8	5	95	0	0	25	7.8	-21.65			Aug-94
50	2.60	14.38	-4.44	16.80	12.13		0.98	12.05	1.05	15.74	791.8	5	95	0	0	25	7.79	-21.65			Jan-19

	MARKET			FUND TYPE, CATEGORY & OBJECTIVE	RATINGS				MINIMUMS	
Fund Name	Ticker Symbol	Traded On	Fund Type	Category and (Prospectus Objective)	Overall Rating	Reward Rating	Risk Rating	Recent Up/ Downgrade	Open to New Investors	Min Initial Investment
American Beacon Zebra Small Cap Equity Fund A Class	AZSAX	NAS CM	Open End	US Equity Small Cap (Small Company)	C	C-	C+	Down	Y	2,500
American Beacon Zebra Small Cap Equity Fund C Class	AZSCX	NAS CM	Open End	US Equity Small Cap (Small Company)	C	C-	C+	Down	Y	1,000
American Beacon Zebra Small Cap Equity Institutional Cls	AZSIX	NAS CM	Open End	US Equity Small Cap (Small Company)	C	C-	C+	Down	Y	250,000
American Beacon Zebra Small Cap Equity Fund Investor Class	AZSPX	NAS CM	Open End	US Equity Small Cap (Small Company)	C	C-	C+	Down	Y	2,500
American Beacon Zebra Small Cap Equity Fund Y Class	AZSYX	NAS CM	Open End	US Equity Small Cap (Small Company)	C	C-	C+	Down	Y	100,000
American Century Adaptive Equity Fund A CLASS	AVDAX	NAS CM	Open End	US Equity Large Cap Blend (Growth)	C+	C	B	Down	Y	2,500
American Century Adaptive Equity Fund I Class	AVDIX	NAS CM	Open End	US Equity Large Cap Blend (Growth)	C+	C	B	Down	Y	5,000,000
American Century Adaptive Equity Fund Investor Class	AMVIX	NAS CM	Open End	US Equity Large Cap Blend (Growth)	C+	C	B	Down	Y	2,500
American Century Adaptive Equity Fund R CLASS	AVDRX	NAS CM	Open End	US Equity Large Cap Blend (Growth)	C+	C	B	Down	Y	2,500
American Century Adaptive Equity Fund R6 CLASS	AVDMX	NAS CM	Open End	US Equity Large Cap Blend (Growth)	C+	C	B	Down	Y	0
American Century Adaptive Small Cap Fund Advisor Class	ACMFX	NAS CM	Open End	US Equity Small Cap (Growth)	C-	C-	C	Down	Y	2,500
American Century Adaptive Small Cap Fund I Class	ACMHX	NAS CM	Open End	US Equity Small Cap (Growth)	C	C-	C		Y	5,000,000
American Century Adaptive Small Cap Fund Investor Class	ACMNX	NAS CM	Open End	US Equity Small Cap (Growth)	C-	C-	C	Down	Y	2,500
American Century Adaptive Small Cap Fund R Class	ACMEX	NAS CM	Open End	US Equity Small Cap (Growth)	C-	C-	C	Down	Y	2,500
American Century Adaptive Small Cap Fund R5 Class	ACMUX	NAS CM	Open End	US Equity Small Cap (Growth)	C	C-	C		Y	0
American Century Adaptive Small Cap Fund R6 Class	ACMMX	NAS CM	Open End	US Equity Small Cap (Growth)	C	C-	C		Y	0
American Century All Cap Growth Fund A Class	ACAQX	NAS CM	Open End	US Equity Large Cap Growth (Growth)	B-	C+	B		Y	2,500
American Century All Cap Growth Fund C Class	ACAHX	NAS CM	Open End	US Equity Large Cap Growth (Growth)	C+	C	B-	Down	Y	2,500
American Century All Cap Growth Fund I Class	ACAJX	NAS CM	Open End	US Equity Large Cap Growth (Growth)	B-	C+	B		Y	5,000,000
American Century All Cap Growth Fund Investor Class	TWGTX	NAS CM	Open End	US Equity Large Cap Growth (Growth)	B-	C+	B		Y	2,500
American Century All Cap Growth Fund R Class	ACAWX	NAS CM	Open End	US Equity Large Cap Growth (Growth)	C+	C+	B	Down	Y	2,500
American Century Balanced Fund I Class	ABINX	NAS CM	Open End	Moderate Alloc (Balanced)	B	C	A-	Up	Y	5,000,000
American Century Balanced Fund Investor Class	TWBIX	NAS CM	Open End	Moderate Alloc (Balanced)	B-	C	A-		Y	2,500
American Century Balanced Fund R5 Class	ABGNX	NAS CM	Open End	Moderate Alloc (Balanced)	B	C	A-	Up	Y	0
American Century Capital Value Fund Class A	ACCVX	NAS CM	Open End	US Equity Large Cap Value (Growth)	B-	C	B	Up	Y	2,500
American Century Capital Value Fund I Class	ACPIX	NAS CM	Open End	US Equity Large Cap Value (Growth)	B-	C	B	Up	Y	5,000,000
American Century Capital Value Fund Investor Class	ACTIX	NAS CM	Open End	US Equity Large Cap Value (Growth)	B-	C	B	Up	Y	2,500
American Century Core Equity Plus Fund Class A	ACPQX	NAS CM	Open End	US Equity Large Cap Blend (Growth)	C+	C	B	Up	Y	2,500
American Century Core Equity Plus Fund Class C	ACPHX	NAS CM	Open End	US Equity Large Cap Blend (Growth)	C+	C	B	Up	Y	2,500
American Century Core Equity Plus Fund Class R	ACPWX	NAS CM	Open End	US Equity Large Cap Blend (Growth)	C+	C	B	Up	Y	2,500
American Century Core Equity Plus Fund I Class	ACPKX	NAS CM	Open End	US Equity Large Cap Blend (Growth)	C+	C	B		Y	5,000,000
American Century Core Equity Plus Fund Investor Class	ACPVX	NAS CM	Open End	US Equity Large Cap Blend (Growth)	C+	C	B	Up	Y	2,500
American Century Disciplined Growth Fund Class A	ADCVX	NAS CM	Open End	US Equity Large Cap Growth (Growth)	C+	C	B-	Down	Y	2,500
American Century Disciplined Growth Fund Class C	ADCCX	NAS CM	Open End	US Equity Large Cap Growth (Growth)	C+	C	B-		Y	2,500
American Century Disciplined Growth Fund Class R	ADRRX	NAS CM	Open End	US Equity Large Cap Growth (Growth)	C+	C	B-	Down	Y	2,500
American Century Disciplined Growth Institutional Cls	ADCIX	NAS CM	Open End	US Equity Large Cap Growth (Growth)	C+	C	B	Down	Y	5,000,000
American Century Disciplined Growth Fund Investor Class	ADSIX	NAS CM	Open End	US Equity Large Cap Growth (Growth)	C+	C	B	Down	Y	2,500
American Century Disciplined Growth Fund R5 Class	ADGGX	NAS CM	Open End	US Equity Large Cap Growth (Growth)	C+	C	B	Down	Y	0
American Century Disciplined Growth Fund Y Class	ADCYX	NAS CM	Open End	US Equity Large Cap Growth (Growth)	C+	C	B	Down	Y	0
American Century Emerging Markets Fund A Class	AEMMX	NAS CM	Open End	Global Emerg Mkts (Div Emerging Mkts)	C	C	C		Y	2,500
American Century Emerging Markets Fund C Class	ACECX	NAS CM	Open End	Global Emerg Mkts (Div Emerging Mkts)	C	C	C		Y	2,500
American Century Emerging Markets Fund I Class	AMKIX	NAS CM	Open End	Global Emerg Mkts (Div Emerging Mkts)	C	C	C		Y	5,000,000
American Century Emerging Markets Fund Investor Class	TWMIX	NAS CM	Open End	Global Emerg Mkts (Div Emerging Mkts)	C	C	C		Y	2,500
American Century Emerging Markets Fund R Class	AEMRX	NAS CM	Open End	Global Emerg Mkts (Div Emerging Mkts)	C	C	C		Y	2,500
American Century Emerging Markets Fund R5 Class	AEGMX	NAS CM	Open End	Global Emerg Mkts (Div Emerging Mkts)	C	C	C		Y	0
American Century Emerging Markets Fund R6 Class	AEDMX	NAS CM	Open End	Global Emerg Mkts (Div Emerging Mkts)	C	C	C		Y	0
American Century Emerging Markets Fund Y Class	AEYMX	NAS CM	Open End	Global Emerg Mkts (Div Emerging Mkts)	C	C	C		Y	0
American Century Emerging Markets Small Cap Fund A Class	AECLX	NAS CM	Open End	Global Emerg Mkts (Div Emerging Mkts)	C	C	C	Up	Y	2,500
American Century Emerging Markets Small Cap Fund C Class	AECHX	NAS CM	Open End	Global Emerg Mkts (Div Emerging Mkts)	C	C	C	Up	Y	2,500
American Century Emerging Markets Small Cap Fund I Class	AECSX	NAS CM	Open End	Global Emerg Mkts (Div Emerging Mkts)	C	C	C	Up	Y	5,000,000
American Century Emerging Markets Small Cap Investor Cls	AECVX	NAS CM	Open End	Global Emerg Mkts (Div Emerging Mkts)	C	C	C	Up	Y	2,500
American Century Emerging Markets Small Cap Fund R Class	AECMX	NAS CM	Open End	Global Emerg Mkts (Div Emerging Mkts)	C	C	C	Up	Y	2,500

★ Expanded analysis of this fund is included in Section II.

	TOTAL RETURNS					PERFORMANCE				ASSETS		ASSET ALLOCATION & TURNOVER					BULL & BEAR		FEES		
Min Additional Investment	3-Month Total Return	6-Month Total Return	1-Year Total Return	3-Year Total Return	5-Year Total Return	Dividend Yield (TTM)	Expense Ratio	3-Yr Std Deviation	3-Year Beta	NAV	Total Assets (MIL)	%Cash	%Stocks	%Bonds	%Other	Turnover Ratio	Last Bull Market Total Return	Last Bear Market Total Return	Front End Fee (%)	Back End Fee (%)	Inception Date
50	1.49	15.78	-3.77	40.72	41.83	0.36	1.29	17.28	0.98	14.96	77.6	2	98	0	0	74	25.07	-20.71	5.75		Jun-10
50	1.29	15.37	-4.48	37.59	36.60	0	2.05	17.27	0.98	14.11	77.6	2	98	0	0	74	24.54	-20.96		1.00	Sep-10
50	1.61	16.02	-3.41	42.42	44.68	0.53	0.9	17.31	0.98	15.13	77.6	2	98	0	0	74	25.45	-20.61			Jun-10
50	1.49	15.81	-3.75	40.80	41.96	0.43	1.28	17.28	0.98	14.94	77.6	2	98	0	0	74	25.05	-20.64			Jun-10
50	1.53	15.98	-3.50	41.97	43.95	0.53	1	17.24	0.97	15.24	77.6	2	98	0	0	74	25.38	-20.58			Jun-10
50	-0.99	11.72	0.31	42.48	48.28	0.77	1.4	12.38	0.97	9.91	100.4	0	100	0	0	112	19.12	-14.01	5.75		Dec-16
	-0.88	11.96	0.72	44.30	51.70	1.17	0.95	12.39	0.97	10.11	100.4	0	100	0	0	112	19.33	-13.69			Aug-00
50	-1.01	11.87	0.51	43.46	50.04	1.01	1.15	12.37	0.96	9.8	100.4	0	100	0	0	112	19.3	-13.92			Nov-99
50	-1.10	11.52	0.03	41.32	46.34	0.54	1.65	12.38	0.97	9.87	100.4	0	100	0	0	112	18.95	-14.1			Dec-16
	-0.86	12.00	0.88	44.93	51.58	1.29	0.8	12.37	0.97	10.26	100.4	0	100	0	0	112	19.29	-13.92			Dec-16
50	1.03	11.47	-9.37	20.17	24.91	0.67	1.41	13.78	0.76	16.61	49.3	0	100	0	0	102	15.13	-12.51			May-06
50	1.07	11.72	-9.00	21.72	27.64	1.07	0.96	13.76	0.76	16.96	49.3	0	100	0	0	102	15.39	-12.31			May-06
50	1.08	11.54	-9.18	21.01	26.44	0.89	1.16	13.78	0.76	16.81	49.3	0	100	0	0	102	15.16	-12.31			May-06
50	0.92	11.29	-9.61	19.22	23.25	0.44	1.66	13.79	0.76	16.36	49.3	0	100	0	0	102	14.89	-12.54			May-06
	1.13	11.71	-8.95	21.76	27.69	1.07	0.96	13.8	0.76	16.98	49.3	0	100	0	0	102	15.39	-12.31			Apr-17
	1.17	11.83	-8.85	22.21	28.16	1.2	0.81	13.78	0.76	17.2	49.3	0	100	0	0	102	15.39	-12.31			Dec-16
50	5.29	23.47	10.01	55.20	70.22	0	1.25	13.85	1.01	33.61	1,189	1	99	0	0	49	27.59	-18.01	5.75		Sep-11
50	5.10	22.99	9.17	51.73	63.92	0	2	13.87	1.01	30.86	1,189	1	99	0	0	49	27.03	-18.26		1.00	Sep-11
50	5.43	23.75	10.54	57.34	74.12	0	0.8	13.87	1.01	35.32	1,189	1	99	0	0	49	27.91	-17.92			Sep-11
50	5.36	23.60	10.28	56.34	72.37	0	1	13.86	1.01	34.56	1,189	1	99	0	0	49	27.79	-17.92			Nov-83
50	5.21	23.28	9.71	53.99	68.10	0	1.5	13.86	1.01	32.67	1,189	1	99	0	0	49	27.43	-18.09			Sep-11
50	3.36	13.79	7.47	30.62	35.34	1.65	0.71	7.62	0.61	18.86	900.6	3	55	42	0	115	16.71	-8.1			May-00
50	3.32	13.69	7.26	29.86	34.02	1.47	0.91	7.63	0.61	18.85	900.6	3	55	42	0	115	16.6	-8.2			Oct-88
	3.36	13.86	7.47	30.49	34.67	1.65	0.71	7.63	0.61	18.86	900.6	3	55	42	0	115	16.6	-8.2			Apr-17
50	3.87	15.55	6.94	32.17	35.31	1.61	1.25	12.37	1.01	8.84	135.8	2	99	0	0	17	24.59	-17.53	5.75		May-03
50	3.97	15.88	7.51	33.96	38.42	2	0.8	12.41	1.01	8.9	135.8	2	99	0	0	17	24.86	-17.35			Mar-02
50	3.86	15.79	7.31	33.24	36.96	1.83	1	12.33	1.01	8.87	135.8	2	99	0	0	17	24.62	-17.35			Mar-99
50	1.52	14.83	3.54	38.36	38.83	0.11	2.1	12.43	1	14.52	170.2	2	98	0	0	101			5.75		Oct-11
50	1.38	14.34	2.76	35.32	33.65	0	2.85	12.46	1	13.95	170.2	2	98	0	0	101				1.00	Oct-11
50	1.48	14.64	3.31	37.38	37.06	0.01	2.35	12.43	1	14.41	170.2	2	98	0	0	101					Oct-11
50	1.72	15.12	4.06	40.40	42.00	0.45	1.65	12.47	1	14.55	170.2	2	98	0	0	101					Oct-11
50	1.63	14.93	3.80	39.46	40.58	0.28	1.85	12.44	1	14.55	170.2	2	98	0	0	101					Oct-11
50	3.74	20.10	6.32	54.03	57.86	0.07	1.27	13.28	0.98	21.53	533.9	0	100	0	0	97	27.89	-16.37	5.75		Sep-05
50	3.57	19.71	5.57	50.58	52.06	0	2.02	13.28	0.98	19.98	533.9	0	100	0	0	97	27.43	-16.69		1.00	Sep-07
50	3.69	19.93	6.03	52.84	55.88	0	1.52	13.29	0.98	21.06	533.9	0	100	0	0	97	27.76	-16.51			Sep-05
50	3.90	20.41	6.82	56.17	61.47	0.35	0.82	13.28	0.98	21.84	533.9	0	100	0	0	97	28.24	-16.26			Sep-05
50	3.82	20.25	6.60	55.21	59.88	0.17	1.02	13.29	0.98	21.76	533.9	0	100	0	0	97	28.09	-16.31			Sep-05
	3.85	20.39	6.81	56.14	61.44	0.35	0.82	13.27	0.98	21.85	533.9	0	100	0	0	97	28.24	-16.26			Apr-17
	3.87	20.42	6.86	56.30	61.61	0.39	0.77	13.28	0.98	21.85	533.9	0	100	0	0	97	28.24	-16.26			Apr-17
50	2.77	13.25	-1.82	36.21	22.64	0.18	1.5	14.32	0.98	10.75	2,503	0	100	0	0	36	23.07	-30.25	5.75		May-99
50	2.52	12.83	-2.59	33.13	18.21	0	2.25	14.36	0.98	9.76	2,503	0	100	0	0	36	22.5	-30.5		1.00	Dec-01
50	2.97	13.51	-1.36	38.11	25.42	0.6	1.05	14.4	0.99	11.44	2,503	0	100	0	0	36	23.25	-30.07			Jan-99
50	2.76	13.35	-1.68	37.16	24.05	0.42	1.25	14.34	0.98	11.14	2,503	0	100	0	0	36	23.13	-30.13			Sep-97
50	2.75	13.08	-2.08	35.31	21.11	0	1.75	14.35	0.98	10.8	2,503	0	100	0	0	36	22.77	-30.35			Sep-07
	2.87	13.50	-1.36	37.89	24.71	0.6	1.05	14.36	0.98	11.45	2,503	0	100	0	0	36	23.13	-30.13			Apr-17
	2.96	13.55	-1.21	38.83	26.32	0.74	0.9	14.36	0.98	11.45	2,503	0	100	0	0	36	23.13	-30.13			Jul-13
	2.96	13.64	-1.21	38.32	25.10	0.74	0.9	14.33	0.98	11.47	2,503	0	100	0	0	36	23.13	-30.13			Apr-17
50	2.73	13.54	-4.08	27.82		0	1.87	13.96	1.01	12.41	8.8	2	97	0	2	75			5.75		Apr-16
50	2.59	13.07	-4.77	25.06		0	2.62	13.97	1.01	12.28	8.8	2	97	0	2	75				1.00	Apr-16
50	2.88	13.76	-3.69	29.57		0	1.42	13.96	1.01	12.48	8.8	2	97	0	2	75					Apr-16
50	2.80	13.69	-3.84	28.75		0	1.62	13.99	1.01	12.45	8.8	2	97	0	2	75					Apr-16
50	2.73	13.47	-4.30	26.88		0	2.12	14.02	1.02	12.38	8.8	2	97	0	2	75					Apr-16

	MARKET			FUND TYPE, CATEGORY & OBJECTIVE	RATINGS				MINIMUMS	
Fund Name	Ticker Symbol	Traded On	Fund Type	Category and (Prospectus Objective)	Overall Rating	Reward Rating	Risk Rating	Recent Up/ Downgrade	Open to New Investors	Min Initial Investment
American Century Emerging Markets Small Cap Fund R6 Class	AECTX	NAS CM	Open End	Global Emerg Mkts (Div Emerging Mkts)	C	C	C	Up	Y	0
American Century Equity Growth Fund A Class	BEQAX	NAS CM	Open End	US Equity Large Cap Blend (Growth)	C+	C	B		Y	2,500
American Century Equity Growth Fund C Class	AEYCX	NAS CM	Open End	US Equity Large Cap Blend (Growth)	C+	C	B		Y	2,500
American Century Equity Growth Fund I Class	AMEIX	NAS CM	Open End	US Equity Large Cap Blend (Growth)	C+	C	B		Y	5,000,000
American Century Equity Growth Fund Investor Class	BEQGX	NAS CM	Open End	US Equity Large Cap Blend (Growth)	C+	C	B		Y	2,500
American Century Equity Growth Fund R Class	AEYRX	NAS CM	Open End	US Equity Large Cap Blend (Growth)	C+	C	B		Y	2,500
American Century Equity Growth Fund R5 Class	AEYGX	NAS CM	Open End	US Equity Large Cap Blend (Growth)	C+	C	B		Y	0
American Century Equity Income Fund A Class	TWEAX	NAS CM	Open End	US Equity Large Cap Value (Equity-Income)	B	C+	A-		Y	2,500
American Century Equity Income Fund C Class	AEYIX	NAS CM	Open End	US Equity Large Cap Value (Equity-Income)	B	C+	A-		Y	2,500
American Century Equity Income Fund I Class	ACIIX	NAS CM	Open End	US Equity Large Cap Value (Equity-Income)	B	C+	A-		Y	5,000,000
American Century Equity Income Fund Investor Class	TWEIX	NAS CM	Open End	US Equity Large Cap Value (Equity-Income)	B	C+	A-		Y	2,500
American Century Equity Income Fund R Class	AEURX	NAS CM	Open End	US Equity Large Cap Value (Equity-Income)	B	C+	A-		Y	2,500
American Century Equity Income Fund R5 Class	AEIUX	NAS CM	Open End	US Equity Large Cap Value (Equity-Income)	B	C+	A-		Y	0
American Century Equity Income Fund R6 Class	AEUDX	NAS CM	Open End	US Equity Large Cap Value (Equity-Income)	B	C+	A-		Y	0
American Century Equity Income Fund Y Class	AEIYX	NAS CM	Open End	US Equity Large Cap Value (Equity-Income)	B	C+	A-		Y	0
American Century Focused International Growth Fund A Class	AFCLX	NAS CM	Open End	Global Equity Large Cap (Growth)	C	C	C+	Up	Y	2,500
American Century Focused International Growth Fund C Class	AFCHX	NAS CM	Open End	Global Equity Large Cap (Growth)	C	C	C+	Up	Y	2,500
American Century Focused International Growth Fund G Class	AFCGX	NAS CM	Open End	Global Equity Large Cap (Growth)	C	C	C+		Y	0
American Century Focused International Growth Fund I Class	AFCSX	NAS CM	Open End	Global Equity Large Cap (Growth)	C	C	C+		Y	5,000,000
American Century Focused International Growth Investor Cls	AFCNX	NAS CM	Open End	Global Equity Large Cap (Growth)	C	C	C+	Up	Y	2,500
American Century Focused International Growth Fund R Class	AFCWX	NAS CM	Open End	Global Equity Large Cap (Growth)	C	C	C+	Up	Y	2,500
American Century Focused International Growth R6 Cls	AFCMX	NAS CM	Open End	Global Equity Large Cap (Growth)	C	C	C+		Y	0
American Century Global Gold Fund A Class	ACGGX	NAS CM	Open End	Precious Metals Sector Equity (Precious Metals)	D+	D	C	Down	Y	2,500
American Century Global Gold Fund C Class	AGYCX	NAS CM	Open End	Precious Metals Sector Equity (Precious Metals)	D+	D	C	Down	Y	2,500
American Century Global Gold Fund I Class	AGGNX	NAS CM	Open End	Precious Metals Sector Equity (Precious Metals)	D+	D	C	Down	Y	5,000,000
American Century Global Gold Fund Investor Class	BGEIX	NAS CM	Open End	Precious Metals Sector Equity (Precious Metals)	D+	D	C	Down	Y	2,500
American Century Global Gold Fund R Class	AGGWX	NAS CM	Open End	Precious Metals Sector Equity (Precious Metals)	D+	D	C	Down	Y	2,500
American Century Global Growth Fund A Class	AGGRX	NAS CM	Open End	Global Equity Large Cap (World Stock)	B-	C+	B	Up	Y	2,500
American Century Global Growth Fund C Class	AGLCX	NAS CM	Open End	Global Equity Large Cap (World Stock)	C+	C	B		Y	2,500
American Century Global Growth Fund I Class	AGGIX	NAS CM	Open End	Global Equity Large Cap (World Stock)	B-	C+	B	Up	Y	5,000,000
American Century Global Growth Fund Investor Class	TWGGX	NAS CM	Open End	Global Equity Large Cap (World Stock)	B-	C+	B	Up	Y	2,500
American Century Global Growth Fund R Class	AGORX	NAS CM	Open End	Global Equity Large Cap (World Stock)	B-	C+	B	Up	Y	2,500
American Century Global Growth Fund R5 Class	AGFGX	NAS CM	Open End	Global Equity Large Cap (World Stock)	B-	C+	B	Up	Y	0
American Century Global Growth Fund R6 Class	AGGDX	NAS CM	Open End	Global Equity Large Cap (World Stock)	B-	C+	B	Up	Y	0
American Century Global Growth Fund Y Class	AGYGX	NAS CM	Open End	Global Equity Large Cap (World Stock)	B-	C+	B	Up	Y	0
American Century Global Real Estate Fund A Class	ARYMX	NAS CM	Open End	Real Estate Sector Equity (Real Estate)	B-	C	B	Up	Y	2,500
American Century Global Real Estate Fund C Class	ARYTX	NAS CM	Open End	Real Estate Sector Equity (Real Estate)	B-	C	B	Up	Y	2,500
American Century Global Real Estate Fund I Class	ARYNX	NAS CM	Open End	Real Estate Sector Equity (Real Estate)	B-	C	B		Y	5,000,000
American Century Global Real Estate Fund Investor Class	ARYVX	NAS CM	Open End	Real Estate Sector Equity (Real Estate)	B-	C	B		Y	2,500
American Century Global Real Estate Fund R Class	ARYWX	NAS CM	Open End	Real Estate Sector Equity (Real Estate)	B-	C	B	Up	Y	2,500
American Century Global Real Estate Fund R5 Class	ARYGX	NAS CM	Open End	Real Estate Sector Equity (Real Estate)	B-	C	B		Y	0
American Century Global Real Estate Fund R6 Class	ARYDX	NAS CM	Open End	Real Estate Sector Equity (Real Estate)	B-	C	B		Y	0
American Century Global Real Estate Fund Y Class	ARYYX	NAS CM	Open End	Real Estate Sector Equity (Real Estate)	B-	C	B		Y	0
American Century Global Small Cap Fund A Class	AGCLX	NAS CM	Open End	Global Equity Mid/Small Cap (Small Company)	C	C	C+		Y	2,500
American Century Global Small Cap Fund C Class	AGCHX	NAS CM	Open End	Global Equity Mid/Small Cap (Small Company)	C	C	C		Y	2,500
American Century Global Small Cap Fund I Class	AGCSX	NAS CM	Open End	Global Equity Mid/Small Cap (Small Company)	C	C	C+		Y	5,000,000
American Century Global Small Cap Fund Investor Class	AGCVX	NAS CM	Open End	Global Equity Mid/Small Cap (Small Company)	C	C	C+		Y	2,500
American Century Global Small Cap Fund R Class	AGCWX	NAS CM	Open End	Global Equity Mid/Small Cap (Small Company)	C	C	C+		Y	2,500
American Century Global Small Cap Fund R6 Class	AGCTX	NAS CM	Open End	Global Equity Mid/Small Cap (Small Company)	C	C	C+		Y	0
American Century Growth Fund A Class	TCRAX	NAS CM	Open End	US Equity Large Cap Growth (Growth)	B-	C+	B	Down	Y	2,500
American Century Growth Fund C Class	TWRCX	NAS CM	Open End	US Equity Large Cap Growth (Growth)	B-	C+	B	Down	Y	2,500
American Century Growth Fund I Class	TWGIX	NAS CM	Open End	US Equity Large Cap Growth (Growth)	B-	C+	B	Down	Y	5,000,000

★ Expanded analysis of this fund is included in Section II.

	TOTAL RETURNS					PERFORMANCE				ASSETS		ASSET ALLOCATION & TURNOVER					BULL & BEAR		FEES		
Min Additional Investment	3-Month Total Return	6-Month Total Return	1-Year Total Return	3-Year Total Return	5-Year Total Return	Dividend Yield (TTM)	Expense Ratio	3-Yr Std Deviation	3-Year Beta	NAV	Total Assets (MIL)	%Cash	%Stocks	%Bonds	%Other	Turnover Ratio	Last Bull Market Total Return	Last Bear Market Total Return	Front End Fee (%)	Back End Fee (%)	Inception Date
	2.96	13.93	-3.46	30.14		0	1.27	13.99	1.01	12.51	8.8	2	97	0	2	75					Apr-16
50	3.53	19.31	6.95	47.45	48.64	0.85	0.91	12.72	1.03	31.69	2,849	2	98	0	0	84	26.3	-15.82	5.75		Oct-97
50	3.33	18.85	6.17	44.16	43.16	0.21	1.66	12.71	1.03	31.34	2,849	2	98	0	0	84	25.75	-16.11		1.00	Jul-01
50	3.61	19.56	7.41	49.40	52.01	1.24	0.46	12.71	1.03	31.76	2,849	2	98	0	0	84	26.65	-15.69			Jan-98
50	3.56	19.42	7.21	48.52	50.51	1.07	0.66	12.71	1.03	31.73	2,849	2	98	0	0	84	26.49	-15.75			May-91
50	3.47	19.16	6.69	46.38	46.82	0.62	1.16	12.73	1.03	31.71	2,849	2	98	0	0	84	26.09	-15.92			Jul-05
	3.64	19.55	7.44	49.17	51.17	1.24	0.46	12.71	1.03	31.77	2,849	2	98	0	0	84	26.49	-15.75			Apr-17
50	4.46	16.23	11.77	33.94	54.23	1.81	1.17	9.18	0.72	9.02	11,975	3	83	6	1	80	16.61	-12.3	5.75		Mar-97
50	4.27	15.82	11.07	31.00	48.61	1.13	1.92	9.21	0.72	9.02	11,975	3	83	6	1	80	16.02	-12.51		1.00	Jul-01
	4.57	16.60	12.25	35.69	57.83	2.22	0.72	9.19	0.72	9.03	11,975	3	83	6	1	80	16.84	-11.97			Jul-98
50	4.53	16.36	12.05	34.93	56.16	2.04	0.92	9.22	0.72	9.02	11,975	3	83	6	1	80	16.75	-12.19			Aug-94
50	4.30	16.03	11.41	32.78	52.36	1.59	1.42	9.2	0.72	8.98	11,975	3	83	6	1	80	16.5	-12.32			Aug-03
	4.46	16.47	12.26	35.50	56.82	2.22	0.72	9.21	0.72	9.02	11,975	3	83	6	1	80	16.75	-12.19			Apr-17
	4.61	16.66	12.53	36.26	58.94	2.35	0.57	9.23	0.72	9.04	11,975	3	83	6	1	80	16.75	-12.19			Jul-13
	4.61	16.66	12.53	36.06	57.46	2.35	0.57	9.25	0.72	9.04	11,975	3	83	6	1	80	16.75	-12.19			Apr-17
50	5.25	20.25	0.14	39.19		0.25	1.48	13.22	1.06	13.42	7.7	1	99	0	0	82			5.75		Mar-16
50	5.09	19.76	-0.52	36.18		0	2.23	13.26	1.06	13.21	7.7	1	99	0	0	82				1.00	Mar-16
	5.53	20.67	0.89	41.83			0	13.23	1.06	13.55	7.7	1	99	0	0	82					Apr-19
50	5.38	20.53	0.59	41.14		0.62	1.03	13.28	1.06	13.5	7.7	1	99	0	0	82					Mar-16
50	5.23	20.28	0.39	40.16		0.46	1.23	13.22	1.06	13.46	7.7	1	99	0	0	82					Mar-16
50	5.18	20.10	-0.10	38.22		0.04	1.73	13.25	1.06	13.38	7.7	1	99	0	0	82					Mar-16
	5.37	20.49	0.74	41.62		0.75	0.88	13.23	1.06	13.52	7.7	1	99	0	0	82					Mar-16
50	14.11	22.78	13.57	-6.21	1.69	0	0.92	25.14	0.24	9.54	449.0	1	99	0	0	37	-14.21	-15	5.75		May-98
50	13.99	22.32	12.57	-8.32	-1.97	0	1.67	25.14	0.24	9.04	449.0	1	99	0	0	37	-14.57	-15.31		1.00	Sep-07
50	14.35	23.03	13.95	-4.93	4.02	0	0.47	25.14	0.24	9.88	449.0	1	99	0	0	37	-13.98	-14.85			Sep-07
50	14.28	22.92	13.75	-5.55	3.00	0	0.67	25.12	0.24	9.76	449.0	1	99	0	0	37	-14.09	-14.93			Aug-88
50	14.04	22.49	13.22	-6.98	0.44	0	1.17	25.16	0.24	9.42	449.0	1	99	0	0	37	-14.36	-15.11			Sep-07
50	6.95	26.36	11.16	53.37	47.67	0	1.32	12.51	1.05	12.46	567.1	0	100	0	0	42	24.86	-20.62	5.75		Feb-99
50	6.70	25.86	10.34	49.88	42.09	0	2.07	12.45	1.05	10.51	567.1	0	100	0	0	42	24.33	-20.9		1.00	Mar-02
50	7.08	26.56	11.69	55.50	50.87	0.25	0.87	12.5	1.05	13.15	567.1	0	100	0	0	42	25.37	-20.56			Aug-00
50	7.06	26.52	11.45	54.47	49.39	0.09	1.07	12.48	1.05	12.88	567.1	0	100	0	0	42	25.08	-20.55			Dec-98
50	6.83	26.16	10.83	52.11	45.66	0	1.57	12.43	1.05	12.2	567.1	0	100	0	0	42	24.8	-20.78			Jul-05
	7.08	26.56	11.60	55.12	50.02	0.25	0.87	12.46	1.05	13.15	567.1	0	100	0	0	42	25.08	-20.55			Apr-17
	7.13	26.75	11.81	56.23	52.07	0.37	0.72	12.46	1.05	13.22	567.1	0	100	0	0	42	25.08	-20.55			Jul-13
	7.12	26.60	11.80	55.64	50.52	0.37	0.72	12.49	1.05	13.23	567.1	0	100	0	0	42	25.08	-20.55			Apr-17
50	2.59	18.96	11.23	18.73	29.64	3.12	1.36	11.24	0.99	12.67	64.9	0	99	0	1	169	20.66	-17.3	5.75		Apr-11
50	2.34	18.46	10.41	16.08	24.83	2.46	2.11	11.24	0.99	12.64	64.9	0	99	0	1	169	20.14	-17.6		1.00	Apr-11
50	2.67	19.28	11.83	20.37	32.63	3.52	0.91	11.26	0.99	12.68	64.9	0	99	0	1	169	20.92	-17.1			Apr-11
50	2.59	19.07	11.51	19.64	31.30	3.35	1.11	11.27	0.99	12.67	64.9	0	99	0	1	169	20.82	-17.2			Apr-11
50	2.50	18.74	10.95	17.82	27.99	2.9	1.61	11.21	0.99	12.67	64.9	0	99	0	1	169	20.5	-17.4			Apr-11
	2.67	19.17	11.73	20.30	32.56	3.52	0.91	11.2	0.99	12.68	64.9	0	99	0	1	169	20.92	-17.09			Apr-17
	2.75	19.28	12.00	20.92	33.65	3.66	0.76	11.26	0.99	12.68	64.9	0	99	0	1	169	20.92	-17.09			Jul-13
	2.67	19.28	11.90	20.72	33.02	3.66	0.76	11.24	0.99	12.68	64.9	0	99	0	1	169	20.92	-17.1			Apr-17
50	7.10	24.43	-2.59	56.21		0	1.75	15.17	1.1	14.92	16.0	1	99	0	0	147			5.75		Mar-16
50	6.91	23.95	-3.36	52.70		0	2.5	15.13	1.1	14.54	16.0	1	99	0	0	147				1.00	Mar-16
50	7.21	24.69	-2.18	58.36		0	1.3	15.19	1.1	15.15	16.0	1	99	0	0	147					Mar-16
50	7.12	24.50	-2.38	57.26		0	1.5	15.16	1.1	15.04	16.0	1	99	0	0	147					Mar-16
50	7.01	24.18	-2.87	54.91		0	2	15.14	1.1	14.79	16.0	1	99	0	0	147					Mar-16
	7.18	24.75	-2.05	58.90		0	1.15	15.14	1.1	15.22	16.0	1	99	0	0	147					Mar-16
50	5.34	23.19	10.92	64.25	76.26	0	1.22	13.74	1.02	33.51	7,952	3	97	0	0	38	27.49	-17.33	5.75		Jun-97
50	5.14	22.71	10.08	60.56	69.74	0	1.97	13.74	1.02	31.5	7,952	3	97	0	0	38	26.94	-17.6		1.00	Mar-10
50	5.47	23.48	11.41	66.48	80.32	0.38	0.77	13.75	1.02	35.44	7,952	3	97	0	0	38	27.82	-17.17			Jun-97

	MARKET		FUND TYPE, CATEGORY & OBJECTIVE		RATINGS				MINIMUMS	
Fund Name	Ticker Symbol	Traded On	Fund Type	Category and (Prospectus Objective)	Overall Rating	Reward Rating	Risk Rating	Recent Up/ Downgrade	Open to New Investors	Min Initial Investment
American Century Growth Fund Investor Class	TWCGX	NAS CM	Open End	US Equity Large Cap Growth (Growth)	B-	C+	B	Down	Y	2,500
American Century Growth Fund R Class	AGWRX	NAS CM	Open End	US Equity Large Cap Growth (Growth)	B-	C+	B	Down	Y	2,500
American Century Growth Fund R5 Class	AGWUX	NAS CM	Open End	US Equity Large Cap Growth (Growth)	B-	C+	B	Down	Y	0
American Century Growth Fund R6 Class	AGRDX	NAS CM	Open End	US Equity Large Cap Growth (Growth)	B-	C+	B	Down	Y	0
American Century Growth Fund Y Class	AGYWX	NAS CM	Open End	US Equity Large Cap Growth (Growth)	B-	C+	B	Down	Y	0
American Century Heritage Fund A Class	ATHAX	NAS CM	Open End	US Equity Mid Cap (Growth)	B-	C+	B		Y	2,500
American Century Heritage Fund C Class	AHGCX	NAS CM	Open End	US Equity Mid Cap (Growth)	B-	C+	B	Up	Y	2,500
American Century Heritage Fund I Class	ATHIX	NAS CM	Open End	US Equity Mid Cap (Growth)	B-	C+	B		Y	5,000,000
American Century Heritage Fund Investor Class	TWHIX	NAS CM	Open End	US Equity Mid Cap (Growth)	B-	C+	B		Y	2,500
American Century Heritage Fund R Class	ATHWX	NAS CM	Open End	US Equity Mid Cap (Growth)	B-	C+	B		Y	2,500
American Century Heritage Fund R5 Class	ATHGX	NAS CM	Open End	US Equity Mid Cap (Growth)	B-	C+	B		Y	0
American Century Heritage Fund R6 Class	ATHDX	NAS CM	Open End	US Equity Mid Cap (Growth)	B-	B-	B		Y	0
American Century Heritage Fund Y Class	ATHYX	NAS CM	Open End	US Equity Mid Cap (Growth)	B-	B-	B		Y	0
American Century Income and Growth Fund C Class	ACGCX	NAS CM	Open End	US Equity Large Cap Value (Growth & Income)	C+	C	B		Y	2,500
American Century Income and Growth Fund Class A	AMADX	NAS CM	Open End	US Equity Large Cap Value (Growth & Income)	C+	C	B		Y	2,500
American Century Income and Growth Fund I Class	AMGIX	NAS CM	Open End	US Equity Large Cap Value (Growth & Income)	C+	C	B		Y	5,000,000
American Century Income and Growth Fund Investor Class	BIGRX	NAS CM	Open End	US Equity Large Cap Value (Growth & Income)	C+	C	B		Y	2,500
American Century Income and Growth Fund R Class	AICRX	NAS CM	Open End	US Equity Large Cap Value (Growth & Income)	C+	C	B		Y	2,500
American Century Income and Growth Fund R5 Class	AICGX	NAS CM	Open End	US Equity Large Cap Value (Growth & Income)	C+	C	B		Y	0
American Century International Core Equity Fund Class A	ACIQX	NAS CM	Open End	Global Equity Large Cap (Foreign Stock)	C	C-	C	Up	Y	2,500
American Century International Core Equity Fund Class C	ACIKX	NAS CM	Open End	Global Equity Large Cap (Foreign Stock)	C-	D+	C		Y	2,500
American Century International Core Equity Fund Class R	ACIRX	NAS CM	Open End	Global Equity Large Cap (Foreign Stock)	C	C-	C	Up	Y	2,500
American Century International Core Equity Fund I Class	ACIUX	NAS CM	Open End	Global Equity Large Cap (Foreign Stock)	C	C-	C+		Y	5,000,000
American Century International Core Equity Investor Cls	ACIMX	NAS CM	Open End	Global Equity Large Cap (Foreign Stock)	C	C-	C		Y	2,500
American Century International Growth Fund A Class	TWGAX	NAS CM	Open End	Global Equity Large Cap (Foreign Stock)	C	C	C+		Y	2,500
American Century International Growth Fund C Class	AIWCX	NAS CM	Open End	Global Equity Large Cap (Foreign Stock)	C	C	C+		Y	2,500
American Century International Growth Fund I Class	TGRIX	NAS CM	Open End	Global Equity Large Cap (Foreign Stock)	C	C	C+		Y	5,000,000
American Century International Growth Fund Investor Class	TWIEX	NAS CM	Open End	Global Equity Large Cap (Foreign Stock)	C	C	C+		Y	2,500
American Century International Growth Fund R Class	ATGRX	NAS CM	Open End	Global Equity Large Cap (Foreign Stock)	C	C	C+		Y	2,500
American Century International Growth Fund R5 Class	ATGGX	NAS CM	Open End	Global Equity Large Cap (Foreign Stock)	C	C	C+		Y	0
American Century International Growth Fund R6 Class	ATGDX	NAS CM	Open End	Global Equity Large Cap (Foreign Stock)	C	C	C+		Y	0
American Century International Growth Fund Y Class	ATYGX	NAS CM	Open End	Global Equity Large Cap (Foreign Stock)	C	C	C+		Y	0
American Century International Opportunities Fund Class A	AIVOX	NAS CM	Open End	Global Equity Mid/Small Cap (Foreign Stock)	C	C	C	Up	Y	10,000
American Century International Opportunities Fund Class C	AIOCX	NAS CM	Open End	Global Equity Mid/Small Cap (Foreign Stock)	C	C-	C	Up	Y	10,000
American Century International Opportunities Fund Class R	AIORX	NAS CM	Open End	Global Equity Mid/Small Cap (Foreign Stock)	C	C	C	Up	Y	10,000
American Century International Opportunities Fund I Class	ACIOX	NAS CM	Open End	Global Equity Mid/Small Cap (Foreign Stock)	C	C	C	Up	Y	5,000,000
American Century International Opportunities Investor Cls	AIOIX	NAS CM	Open End	Global Equity Mid/Small Cap (Foreign Stock)	C	C	C	Up	Y	10,000
American Century International Value Fund A Class	MEQAX	NAS CM	Open End	Global Equity Large Cap (Foreign Stock)	C-	D+	C		Y	2,500
American Century International Value Fund C Class	ACCOX	NAS CM	Open End	Global Equity Large Cap (Foreign Stock)	C-	D+	C		Y	2,500
American Century International Value Fund I Class	ACVUX	NAS CM	Open End	Global Equity Large Cap (Foreign Stock)	C-	D+	C	Down	Y	5,000,000
American Century International Value Fund Investor Class	ACEVX	NAS CM	Open End	Global Equity Large Cap (Foreign Stock)	C-	D+	C	Down	Y	2,500
American Century International Value Fund R Class	ACVRX	NAS CM	Open End	Global Equity Large Cap (Foreign Stock)	C-	D+	C		Y	2,500
American Century International Value Fund R6 Class	ACVDX	NAS CM	Open End	Global Equity Large Cap (Foreign Stock)	C-	D+	C	Down	Y	0
American Century Inv Focused Dynamic Growth Adv Cls	ACFDX	NAS CM	Open End	US Equity Large Cap Growth (Growth)	B-	C+	B		Y	2,500
American Century Investments Focused Dynamic Growth G Cls	ACFGX	NAS CM	Open End	US Equity Large Cap Growth (Growth)	B-	C+	B		Y	0
American Century Investments Focused Dynamic Growth I Cls	ACFSX	NAS CM	Open End	US Equity Large Cap Growth (Growth)	B-	C+	B		Y	5,000,000
American Century Inv Focused Dynamic Growth Inv Cls	ACFOX	NAS CM	Open End	US Equity Large Cap Growth (Growth)	B-	C+	B		Y	2,500
American Century Investments Focused Dynamic Growth R Cls	ACFCX	NAS CM	Open End	US Equity Large Cap Growth (Growth)	C+	C+	B	Down	Y	2,500
American Century Investments Focused Dynamic Growth R6 Cls	ACFNX	NAS CM	Open End	US Equity Large Cap Growth (Growth)	B-	C+	B		Y	0
American Century Inv One Choice 2020 Port A Cls	ARBMX	NAS CM	Open End	Target Date (Asset Alloc)	B	C	A-	Up	Y	2,500
American Century Inv One Choice 2020 Port C Cls	ARNCX	NAS CM	Open End	Target Date (Asset Alloc)	B-	C	A-	Up	Y	2,500
American Century Inv One Choice 2020 Port I Cls	ARBSX	NAS CM	Open End	Target Date (Asset Alloc)	B	C	A-	Up	Y	5,000,000

★ Expanded analysis of this fund is included in Section II.

	TOTAL RETURNS					PERFORMANCE				ASSETS		ASSET ALLOCATION & TURNOVER					BULL & BEAR		FEES		
Min Additional Investment	3-Month Total Return	6-Month Total Return	1-Year Total Return	3-Year Total Return	5-Year Total Return	Dividend Yield (TTM)	Expense Ratio	3-Yr Std Deviation	3-Year Beta	NAV	Total Assets (MIL)	%Cash	%Stocks	%Bonds	%Other	Turnover Ratio	Last Bull Market Total Return	Last Bear Market Total Return	Front End Fee (%)	Back End Fee (%)	Inception Date
50	5.40	23.33	11.19	65.46	78.47	0.21	0.97	13.74	1.02	34.73	7,952	3	97	0	0	38	27.64	-17.21			Jun-71
50	5.27	23.01	10.62	62.97	74.05	0	1.47	13.75	1.02	32.55	7,952	3	97	0	0	38	27.3	-17.42			Aug-03
	5.47	23.45	11.44	66.19	79.25	0.37	0.77	13.74	1.02	35.47	7,952	3	97	0	0	38	27.64	-17.21			Apr-17
	5.51	23.54	11.59	67.24	81.67	0.5	0.62	13.76	1.02	35.42	7,952	3	97	0	0	38	27.64	-17.21			Jul-13
	5.50	23.54	11.58	66.73	79.84	0.5	0.62	13.75	1.02	35.47	7,952	3	97	0	0	38	27.64	-17.21			Apr-17
50	6.88	29.31	15.88	52.62	59.96	0	1.26	13.94	0.96	19.72	4,738	2	98	0	0	85	28.39	-21.45	5.75		Jul-97
50	6.69	28.82	15.00	49.20	54.16	0	2.01	13.98	0.96	14.66	4,738	2	98	0	0	85	27.86	-21.72		1.00	Jun-01
50	7.02	29.58	16.38	54.68	63.65	0	0.81	13.95	0.96	23.61	4,738	2	98	0	0	85	28.73	-21.3			Jun-97
50	6.95	29.38	16.15	53.70	61.96	0	1.01	13.95	0.96	21.84	4,738	2	98	0	0	85	28.57	-21.34			Nov-87
50	6.77	29.09	15.54	51.42	57.94	0	1.51	13.94	0.96	19.7	4,738	2	98	0	0	85	28.22	-21.53			Sep-07
	7.02	29.58	16.38	54.43	62.73	0	0.81	13.96	0.96	23.61	4,738	2	98	0	0	85	28.57	-21.34			Apr-17
	7.07	29.64	16.57	55.39	64.86	0	0.66	13.97	0.96	23.92	4,738	2	98	0	0	85	28.57	-21.34			Jul-13
	7.02	29.64	16.57	54.94	63.26	0	0.66	13.95	0.96	23.92	4,738	2	98	0	0	85	28.57	-21.34			Apr-17
50	1.04	14.34	3.39	36.45	36.75	0.92	1.66	12.48	1.01	36.68	2,216	1	99	0	0	77	24.37	-16.42		1.00	Jun-01
50	1.23	14.78	4.17	39.56	41.95	1.6	0.91	12.49	1.01	36.76	2,216	1	99	0	0	77	24.88	-16.15	5.75		Dec-97
50	1.36	15.03	4.65	41.46	45.19	2	0.46	12.48	1.01	36.88	2,216	1	99	0	0	77	25.19	-15.97			Jan-98
50	1.29	14.92	4.42	40.61	43.74	1.82	0.66	12.48	1.01	36.82	2,216	1	99	0	0	77	25.05	-16.07			Dec-90
50	1.19	14.66	3.94	38.56	40.23	1.37	1.16	12.48	1.01	36.81	2,216	1	99	0	0	77	24.71	-16.21			Aug-03
	1.36	15.03	4.67	41.29	44.43	2	0.46	12.48	1.01	36.89	2,216	1	99	0	0	77	25.05	-16.07			Apr-17
50	2.71	12.40	-3.42	22.01	0.96	2.11	1.41	11.33	1	8.7	27.6	0	100	0	0	99	12.49	-23.88	5.75		Nov-06
50	2.49	11.91	-4.18	19.26	-2.92	1.42	2.16	11.35	1	8.64	27.6	0	100	0	0	99	12.04	-24.21		1.00	Nov-06
50	2.72	12.30	-3.68	21.01	-0.41	1.88	1.66	11.35	1	8.67	27.6	0	100	0	0	99	12.4	-24.03			Nov-06
50	2.83	12.67	-2.97	23.66	3.18	2.52	0.96	11.33	1	8.71	27.6	0	100	0	0	99	12.81	-23.83			Nov-06
50	2.83	12.56	-3.18	22.97	2.03	2.34	1.16	11.32	1	8.69	27.6	0	100	0	0	99	12.76	-23.86			Nov-06
50	4.48	18.68	-2.16	31.32	13.85	0.73	1.42	12.64	1.07	11.88	1,374	0	100	0	0	69	17.49	-24.4	5.75		Oct-96
50	4.27	18.26	-2.87	28.31	9.67	0.09	2.17	12.64	1.07	11.46	1,374	0	100	0	0	69	17.03	-24.66		1.00	Jun-01
50	4.56	18.92	-1.73	33.08	16.41	1.14	0.97	12.68	1.07	11.69	1,374	0	100	0	0	69	17.75	-24.29			Nov-97
50	4.43	18.76	-1.92	32.21	15.26	0.96	1.17	12.66	1.07	11.77	1,374	0	100	0	0	69	17.57	-24.32			May-91
50	4.34	18.44	-2.40	30.20	12.33	0.51	1.67	12.67	1.07	12.01	1,374	0	100	0	0	69	17.35	-24.49			Aug-03
	4.56	18.92	-1.73	32.75	15.74	1.14	0.97	12.66	1.07	11.69	1,374	0	100	0	0	69	17.57	-24.32			Apr-17
	4.56	18.94	-1.65	33.63	17.27	1.27	0.82	12.66	1.07	11.68	1,374	0	100	0	0	69	17.57	-24.32			Jul-13
	4.56	18.92	-1.64	33.16	16.10	1.27	0.82	12.66	1.07	11.69	1,374	0	100	0	0	69	17.57	-24.32			Apr-17
50	3.64	17.80	-11.36	29.32	22.02	0.33	1.72	15.6	1.21	9.66	579.2	0	100	0	0	140	24.18	-25.77	5.75		Mar-10
50	3.46	17.38	-11.98	26.41	17.57	0	2.47	15.58	1.2	9.25	579.2	0	100	0	0	140	23.76	-26.18		1.00	Mar-10
50	3.68	17.71	-11.52	28.35	20.50	0.11	1.97	15.57	1.2	9.57	579.2	0	100	0	0	140	23.99	-25.87			Mar-10
50	3.89	18.22	-10.91	31.06	24.85	0.71	1.27	15.59	1.21	9.86	579.2	0	100	0	0	140	24.59	-25.77			Jan-03
50	3.72	18.03	-11.04	30.34	23.66	0.54	1.47	15.6	1.21	9.75	579.2	0	100	0	0	140	24.4	-25.81			Jun-01
50	1.46	9.26	-5.53	20.29	-7.84	3.49	1.56	11.24	0.96	7.64	40.5	0	100	0	0	80	12.76	-23.17	5.75		Mar-97
50	1.20	8.71	-6.33	17.61	-11.25	2.64	2.31	11.17	0.96	7.57	40.5	0	100	0	0	80	12.4	-23.41		1.00	Apr-06
50	1.60	9.42	-5.15	21.93	-5.79	4.03	1.11	11.23	0.96	7.6	40.5	0	100	0	0	80	13.21	-23.09			Apr-06
50	1.46	9.21	-5.38	21.10	-6.77	3.8	1.31	11.2	0.96	7.6	40.5	0	100	0	0	80	12.95	-23.06			Apr-06
50	1.46	9.10	-5.73	19.38	-8.98	3.21	1.81	11.24	0.96	7.6	40.5	0	100	0	0	80	12.69	-23.25			Apr-06
	1.60	9.61	-4.97	22.39	-5.05	4.21	0.96	11.21	0.96	7.6	40.5	0	100	0	0	80	12.75	-23.17			Jul-13
50	3.72	23.49	10.53	82.96	80.90	0	1.1	15.9	1.13	28.44	195.9	3	97	0	0	29	17.84	-13.58			May-06
	3.93	23.85	11.09	85.55	85.14		0	15.91	1.13	29.48	195.9	3	97	0	0	29	18.19	-13.46			Apr-19
50	3.86	23.78	11.03	85.43	85.03	0	0.65	15.92	1.13	28.99	195.9	3	97	0	0	29	18.19	-13.46			May-06
50	3.78	23.63	10.78	84.37	83.22	0	0.85	15.9	1.13	28.77	195.9	3	97	0	0	29	17.91	-13.5			May-06
50	3.65	23.35	10.23	81.60	78.63	0	1.35	15.91	1.13	28.1	195.9	3	97	0	0	29	17.67	-13.75			May-06
	3.88	23.85	11.17	86.05	85.65	0	0.5	15.92	1.13	29.44	195.9	3	97	0	0	29	18.19	-13.46			Dec-16
50	2.92	10.98	5.30	20.71	22.94	2.29	1.02	5.87	1.18	12.33	1,695	12	45	43	0	15	14.34	-9.29	5.75		May-08
50	2.75	10.59	4.49	18.06	18.41	1.6	1.77	5.82	1.17	12.32	1,695	12	45	43	0	15	13.83	-9.58		1.00	Mar-10
50	3.08	11.25	5.78	22.33	25.74	2.7	0.57	5.81	1.17	12.36	1,695	12	45	43	0	15	14.6	-9.18			May-08

	MARKET			FUND TYPE, CATEGORY & OBJECTIVE	RATINGS					MINIMUMS
Fund Name	Ticker Symbol	Traded On	Fund Type	Category and (Prospectus Objective)	Overall Rating	Reward Rating	Risk Rating	Recent Up/ Downgrade	Open to New Investors	Min Initial Investment
American Century Inv One Choice 2020 Port Inv Cls	ARBVX	NAS CM	Open End	Target Date (Asset Alloc)	B	C	A-	Up	Y	2,500
American Century Inv One Choice 2020 Port R Cls	ARBRX	NAS CM	Open End	Target Date (Asset Alloc)	B-	C	A-	Up	Y	2,500
American Century Inv One Choice 2020 Port R6 Cls	ARBDX	NAS CM	Open End	Target Date (Asset Alloc)	B	C+	A-	Up	Y	0
American Century Inv One Choice 2025 Port A Cls	ARWAX	NAS CM	Open End	Target Date (Asset Alloc)	B-	C	A-	Up	Y	2,500
American Century Inv One Choice 2025 Port C Cls	ARWCX	NAS CM	Open End	Target Date (Asset Alloc)	B-	C	A-	Up	Y	2,500
American Century Inv One Choice 2025 Port I Cls	ARWFX	NAS CM	Open End	Target Date (Asset Alloc)	B	C	A-	Up	Y	5,000,000
American Century Inv One Choice 2025 Port Inv Cls	ARWIX	NAS CM	Open End	Target Date (Asset Alloc)	B	C	A-	Up	Y	2,500
American Century Inv One Choice 2025 Port R Cls	ARWRX	NAS CM	Open End	Target Date (Asset Alloc)	B-	C	A-	Up	Y	2,500
American Century Inv One Choice 2025 Port R6 Cls	ARWDX	NAS CM	Open End	Target Date (Asset Alloc)	B	C	A-	Up	Y	0
American Century Inv One Choice 2030 Port A Cls	ARCMX	NAS CM	Open End	Target Date (Asset Alloc)	B-	C	A-	Up	Y	2,500
American Century Inv One Choice 2030 Port C Cls	ARWOX	NAS CM	Open End	Target Date (Asset Alloc)	B-	C	A-	Up	Y	2,500
American Century Inv One Choice 2030 Port I Cls	ARCSX	NAS CM	Open End	Target Date (Asset Alloc)	B-	C	A-	Up	Y	5,000,000
American Century Inv One Choice 2030 Port Inv Cls	ARCVX	NAS CM	Open End	Target Date (Asset Alloc)	B-	C	A-	Up	Y	2,500
American Century Inv One Choice 2030 Port R Cls	ARCRX	NAS CM	Open End	Target Date (Asset Alloc)	B-	C	A-	Up	Y	2,500
American Century Inv One Choice 2030 Port R6 Cls	ARCUX	NAS CM	Open End	Target Date (Asset Alloc)	B-	C	A-	Up	Y	0
American Century Inv One Choice 2035 Port A Cls	ARYAX	NAS CM	Open End	Target Date (Asset Alloc)	B-	C	B+	Up	Y	2,500
American Century Inv One Choice 2035 Port C Cls	ARLCX	NAS CM	Open End	Target Date (Asset Alloc)	B-	C	B+	Up	Y	2,500
American Century Inv One Choice 2035 Port I Cls	ARLIX	NAS CM	Open End	Target Date (Asset Alloc)	B-	C	B+	Up	Y	5,000,000
American Century Inv One Choice 2035 Port Inv Cls	ARYIX	NAS CM	Open End	Target Date (Asset Alloc)	B-	C	B+	Up	Y	2,500
American Century Inv One Choice 2035 Port R Cls	ARYRX	NAS CM	Open End	Target Date (Asset Alloc)	B-	C	B+	Up	Y	2,500
American Century Inv One Choice 2035 Port R6 Cls	ARLDX	NAS CM	Open End	Target Date (Asset Alloc)	B-	C	A-	Up	Y	0
American Century Inv One Choice 2040 Port A Cls	ARDMX	NAS CM	Open End	Target Date (Asset Alloc)	B-	C	B+	Up	Y	2,500
American Century Inv One Choice 2040 Port C Cls	ARNOX	NAS CM	Open End	Target Date (Asset Alloc)	B-	C	B+	Up	Y	2,500
American Century Inv One Choice 2040 Port I Cls	ARDSX	NAS CM	Open End	Target Date (Asset Alloc)	B-	C	B+	Up	Y	5,000,000
American Century Inv One Choice 2040 Port Inv Cls	ARDVX	NAS CM	Open End	Target Date (Asset Alloc)	B-	C	B+	Up	Y	2,500
American Century Inv One Choice 2040 Port R Cls	ARDRX	NAS CM	Open End	Target Date (Asset Alloc)	B-	C	B+	Up	Y	2,500
American Century Inv One Choice 2040 Port R6 Cls	ARDUX	NAS CM	Open End	Target Date (Asset Alloc)	B-	C	B+	Up	Y	0
American Century Inv One Choice 2045 Port A Cls	AROAX	NAS CM	Open End	Target Date (Asset Alloc)	B-	C	B+	Up	Y	2,500
American Century Inv One Choice 2045 Port C Cls	AROCX	NAS CM	Open End	Target Date (Asset Alloc)	B-	C	B+	Up	Y	2,500
American Century Inv One Choice 2045 Port I Cls	AOOIX	NAS CM	Open End	Target Date (Asset Alloc)	B-	C	B+	Up	Y	5,000,000
American Century Inv One Choice 2045 Port Inv Cls	AROIX	NAS CM	Open End	Target Date (Asset Alloc)	B-	C	B+	Up	Y	2,500
American Century Inv One Choice 2045 Port R Cls	ARORX	NAS CM	Open End	Target Date (Asset Alloc)	B-	C	B+	Up	Y	2,500
American Century Inv One Choice 2045 Port R6 Cls	ARDOX	NAS CM	Open End	Target Date (Asset Alloc)	B-	C	B+	Up	Y	0
American Century Inv One Choice 2050 Port A Cls	ARFMX	NAS CM	Open End	Target Date (Asset Alloc)	B-	C	B	Up	Y	2,500
American Century Inv One Choice 2050 Port C Cls	ARFDX	NAS CM	Open End	Target Date (Asset Alloc)	B-	C	B	Up	Y	2,500
American Century Inv One Choice 2050 Port I Cls	ARFSX	NAS CM	Open End	Target Date (Asset Alloc)	B-	C	B	Up	Y	5,000,000
American Century Inv One Choice 2050 Port Inv Cls	ARFVX	NAS CM	Open End	Target Date (Asset Alloc)	B-	C	B	Up	Y	2,500
American Century Inv One Choice 2050 Port R Cls	ARFWX	NAS CM	Open End	Target Date (Asset Alloc)	B-	C	B	Up	Y	2,500
American Century Inv One Choice 2050 Port R6 Cls	ARFEX	NAS CM	Open End	Target Date (Asset Alloc)	B-	C	B	Up	Y	0
American Century Inv One Choice 2055 Port A Cls	AREMX	NAS CM	Open End	Target Date (Asset Alloc)	B-	C	B	Up	Y	2,500
American Century Inv One Choice 2055 Port C Cls	AREFX	NAS CM	Open End	Target Date (Asset Alloc)	B-	C	B	Up	Y	2,500
American Century Inv One Choice 2055 Port I Cls	ARENX	NAS CM	Open End	Target Date (Asset Alloc)	B-	C	B	Up	Y	5,000,000
American Century Inv One Choice 2055 Port Inv Cls	AREVX	NAS CM	Open End	Target Date (Asset Alloc)	B-	C	B	Up	Y	2,500
American Century Inv One Choice 2055 Port R Cls	AREOX	NAS CM	Open End	Target Date (Asset Alloc)	B-	C	B	Up	Y	2,500
American Century Inv One Choice 2055 Port R6 Cls	AREUX	NAS CM	Open End	Target Date (Asset Alloc)	B-	C	B	Up	Y	0
American Century Inv One Choice 2060 Port A Cls	ARGMX	NAS CM	Open End	Target Date (Asset Alloc)	B-	C	B	Up	Y	2,500
American Century Inv One Choice 2060 Port C Cls	ARGHX	NAS CM	Open End	Target Date (Asset Alloc)	B-	C	B	Up	Y	2,500
American Century Inv One Choice 2060 Port I Cls	ARGNX	NAS CM	Open End	Target Date (Asset Alloc)	B-	C	B	Up	Y	5,000,000
American Century Inv One Choice 2060 Port Inv Cls	ARGVX	NAS CM	Open End	Target Date (Asset Alloc)	B-	C	B	Up	Y	2,500
American Century Inv One Choice 2060 Port R Cls	ARGRX	NAS CM	Open End	Target Date (Asset Alloc)	B-	C	B	Up	Y	2,500
American Century Inv One Choice 2060 Port R6 Cls	ARGDX	NAS CM	Open End	Target Date (Asset Alloc)	B-	C	B	Up	Y	0
American Century Inv One Choice In Retmnt Port A Cls	ARTAX	NAS CM	Open End	Target Date (Asset Alloc)	B	C	A-	Up	Y	2,500

★ Expanded analysis of this fund is included in Section II.

	TOTAL RETURNS					PERFORMANCE				ASSETS		ASSET ALLOCATION & TURNOVER					BULL & BEAR		FEES		
Min Additional Investment	3-Month Total Return	6-Month Total Return	1-Year Total Return	3-Year Total Return	5-Year Total Return	Dividend Yield (TTM)	Expense Ratio	3-Yr Std Deviation	3-Year Beta	NAV	Total Assets (MIL)	%Cash	%Stocks	%Bonds	%Other	Turnover Ratio	Last Bull Market Total Return	Last Bear Market Total Return	Front End Fee (%)	Back End Fee (%)	Inception Date
50	3.00	11.16	5.57	21.60	24.49	2.52	0.77	5.82	1.18	12.35	1,695	12	45	43	0	15	14.49	-9.27			May-08
50	2.92	10.89	5.04	19.81	21.41	2.06	1.27	5.86	1.18	12.32	1,695	12	45	43	0	15	14.18	-9.48			May-08
	3.10	11.35	5.95	22.70	26.50	3.1	0.42	5.81	1.17	11.28	1,695	12	45	43	0	15	14.6	-9.18			Jul-13
50	3.08	11.88	5.38	22.59	24.85	2.21	1.04	6.4	1.05	14.69	2,660	10	50	40	0	14	15.49	-10.58	5.75		Aug-04
50	2.94	11.48	4.64	19.90	20.24	1.53	1.79	6.39	1.05	14.66	2,660	10	50	40	0	14	15.04	-10.9		1.00	Mar-10
50	3.22	12.11	5.86	24.24	27.70	2.62	0.59	6.44	1.06	14.71	2,660	10	50	40	0	14	15.77	-10.4			Aug-04
50	3.15	11.95	5.64	23.51	26.43	2.44	0.79	6.44	1.06	14.7	2,660	10	50	40	0	14	15.66	-10.49			Aug-04
50	3.02	11.65	5.11	21.61	23.22	1.99	1.29	6.44	1.06	14.66	2,660	10	50	40	0	14	15.32	-10.67			Aug-04
	3.24	12.24	5.98	24.57	28.50	3.51	0.44	6.4	1.05	11.46	2,660	10	50	40	0	14	15.77	-10.4			Jul-13
50	3.22	12.68	5.37	24.67	27.01	2.25	1.06	7.1	0.98	12.79	2,280	7	55	37	0	16	16.72	-11.99	5.75		May-08
50	2.98	12.21	4.56	21.92	22.30	1.56	1.81	7.06	0.98	12.77	2,280	7	55	37	0	16	16.2	-12.18		1.00	Mar-10
50	3.30	12.95	5.77	26.33	29.89	2.65	0.61	7.05	0.97	12.82	2,280	7	55	37	0	16	16.95	-11.69			May-08
50	3.22	12.85	5.64	25.67	28.57	2.47	0.81	7.02	0.97	12.82	2,280	7	55	37	0	16	16.85	-11.87			May-08
50	3.14	12.59	5.11	23.74	25.42	2.02	1.31	7.06	0.97	12.78	2,280	7	55	37	0	16	16.55	-12			May-08
	3.42	13.05	6.01	26.78	30.68	3.02	0.46	7.08	0.98	11.78	2,280	7	55	37	0	16	16.95	-11.69			Jul-13
50	3.29	13.54	5.24	26.98	29.14	2.05	1.09	7.83	0.94	16.01	2,383	7	61	31	0	16	18.09	-13.26	5.75		Aug-04
50	3.10	13.04	4.44	24.16	24.33	1.38	1.84	7.78	0.94	15.95	2,383	7	61	31	0	16	17.56	-13.51		1.00	Mar-10
50	3.41	13.74	5.65	28.66	32.07	2.45	0.64	7.78	0.94	16.05	2,383	7	61	31	0	16	18.38	-13.09			Aug-04
50	3.28	13.61	5.44	27.93	30.69	2.28	0.84	7.78	0.94	16.02	2,383	7	61	31	0	16	18.27	-13.17			Aug-04
50	3.22	13.32	4.91	25.96	27.45	1.83	1.34	7.78	0.94	15.99	2,383	7	61	31	0	16	17.92	-13.35			Aug-04
	3.43	13.84	5.86	29.11	32.90	3.48	0.49	7.8	0.94	11.76	2,383	7	61	31	0	16	18.38	-13.09			Jul-13
50	3.31	14.34	5.13	29.40	31.32	2.12	1.11	8.5	0.93	13.39	1,740	7	67	26	0	17	19.56	-14.62	5.75		May-08
50	3.17	13.91	4.40	26.50	26.50	1.45	1.86	8.49	0.93	13.34	1,740	7	67	26	0	17	19.08	-14.84		1.00	Mar-10
50	3.46	14.60	5.68	31.12	34.31	2.52	0.66	8.5	0.93	13.42	1,740	7	67	26	0	17	19.81	-14.42			May-08
50	3.39	14.41	5.39	30.35	32.96	2.34	0.86	8.52	0.93	13.41	1,740	7	67	26	0	17	19.7	-14.51			May-08
50	3.24	14.17	4.86	28.35	29.69	1.9	1.36	8.51	0.93	13.37	1,740	7	67	26	0	17	19.41	-14.65			May-08
	3.51	14.70	5.80	31.56	35.16	2.93	0.51	8.51	0.93	12.09	1,740	7	67	26	0	17	19.81	-14.42			Jul-13
50	3.45	15.15	5.14	31.71	33.62	1.93	1.14	9.23	0.97	16.79	1,690	4	73	22	0	16	20.44	-15.41	5.75		Aug-04
50	3.27	14.74	4.41	28.75	28.67	1.26	1.89	9.22	0.97	16.73	1,690	4	73	22	0	16	19.88	-15.65		1.00	Mar-10
50	3.56	15.42	5.62	33.43	36.62	2.32	0.69	9.25	0.97	16.84	1,690	4	73	22	0	16	20.81	-15.3			Aug-04
50	3.50	15.29	5.41	32.59	35.21	2.15	0.89	9.23	0.97	16.81	1,690	4	73	22	0	16	20.61	-15.39			Aug-04
50	3.38	15.01	4.87	30.64	31.92	1.7	1.39	9.23	0.97	16.78	1,690	4	73	22	0	16	20.26	-15.56			Aug-04
	3.56	15.50	5.69	33.88	37.48	3.4	0.54	9.22	0.97	11.92	1,690	4	73	22	0	16	20.81	-15.3			Jul-13
50	3.53	15.93	5.11	33.31	34.96	1.91	1.17	9.84	1.01	13.75	1,121	2	79	19	0	21	21.11	-15.98	5.75		May-08
50	3.39	15.50	4.38	30.38	30.06	1.25	1.92	9.85	1.01	13.71	1,121	2	79	19	0	21	20.51	-16.27		1.00	Mar-10
50	3.68	16.25	5.66	35.14	38.08	2.3	0.72	9.84	1.01	13.8	1,121	2	79	19	0	21	21.46	-15.85			May-08
50	3.61	16.10	5.38	34.28	36.75	2.13	0.92	9.84	1.01	13.77	1,121	2	79	19	0	21	21.27	-15.96			May-08
50	3.46	15.75	4.84	32.31	33.25	1.69	1.42	9.83	1.01	13.74	1,121	2	79	19	0	21	20.97	-16.17			May-08
	3.66	16.27	5.70	35.63	38.88	2.68	0.57	9.82	1.01	12.43	1,121	2	79	19	0	21	21.46	-15.85			Jul-13
50	3.54	16.25	4.93	34.01	35.70	1.84	1.17	10.15	1.02	14.88	673.8	2	81	16	0	18	21.38	-16.19	5.75		Mar-11
50	3.42	15.83	4.21	31.11	30.73	1.18	1.92	10.11	1.02	14.78	673.8	2	81	16	0	18	20.88	-16.4		1.00	Mar-11
50	3.68	16.47	5.47	35.87	38.74	2.23	0.72	10.12	1.02	14.92	673.8	2	81	16	0	18	21.74	-16			Mar-11
50	3.68	16.39	5.25	35.07	37.36	2.06	0.92	10.16	1.02	14.91	673.8	2	81	16	0	18	21.58	-16.1			Mar-11
50	3.54	16.06	4.73	33.10	33.99	1.62	1.42	10.1	1.02	14.88	673.8	2	81	16	0	18	21.29	-16.29			Mar-11
	3.72	16.55	5.57	36.42	39.68	2.73	0.57	10.12	1.02	12.81	673.8	2	81	16	0	18	21.74	-16			Jul-13
50	3.60	16.47	4.90	34.45		1.84	1.17	10.34	1.04	12.94	138.2	2	83	14	0	12			5.75		Sep-15
50	3.38	16.00	4.14	31.55		1.19	1.92	10.32	1.04	12.83	138.2	2	83	14	0	12				1.00	Sep-15
50	3.75	16.72	5.45	36.29		2.22	0.72	10.34	1.04	12.98	138.2	2	83	14	0	12					Sep-15
50	3.68	16.65	5.16	35.54		2.05	0.92	10.35	1.04	12.96	138.2	2	83	14	0	12					Sep-15
50	3.52	16.29	4.64	33.44		1.62	1.42	10.34	1.04	12.92	138.2	2	83	14	0	12					Sep-15
	3.82	16.87	5.60	36.86		2.35	0.57	10.36	1.04	13.02	138.2	2	83	14	0	12					Sep-15
50	2.93	10.88	5.37	19.67	21.83	2.2	1.02	5.62	1.36	13.17	1,520	12	44	43	0	13	12.45	-7.3	5.75		Aug-04

	MARKET			FUND TYPE, CATEGORY & OBJECTIVE	RATINGS					MINIMUMS
Fund Name	Ticker Symbol	Traded On	Fund Type	Category and (Prospectus Objective)	Overall Rating	Reward Rating	Risk Rating	Recent Up/ Downgrade	Open to New Investors	Min Initial Investment
American Century Inv One Choice In Retmnt Port C Cls	ATTCX	NAS CM	Open End	Target Date (Asset Alloc)	B-	C	A-	Up	Y	2,500
American Century Inv One Choice In Retmnt Port I Cls	ATTIX	NAS CM	Open End	Target Date (Asset Alloc)	B	C	A-	Up	Y	5,000,000
American Century Inv One Choice In Retmnt Port Inv Cls	ARTOX	NAS CM	Open End	Target Date (Asset Alloc)	B	C	A-	Up	Y	2,500
American Century Inv One Choice In Retmnt Port R Cls	ARSRX	NAS CM	Open End	Target Date (Asset Alloc)	B-	C	A-	Up	Y	2,500
American Century Inv One Choice In Retmnt Port R6 Cls	ARDTX	NAS CM	Open End	Target Date (Asset Alloc)	B	C+	A-	Up	Y	0
American Century Inv One Choice Port®: Aggressive Inv Cls	AOGIX	NAS CM	Open End	Aggressive Alloc (Asset Alloc)	B-	C	B	Up	Y	2,500
American Century Inv One Choice Port®: Aggressive R Cls	AORYX	NAS CM	Open End	Aggressive Alloc (Asset Alloc)	B-	C	B	Up	Y	2,500
American Century Inv One Choice Port®: Cons Inv Cls	AOCIX	NAS CM	Open End	Cautious Alloc (Asset Alloc)	B-	C	A-	Up	Y	2,500
American Century Inv One Choice Port®: Conservative R Cls	AORSX	NAS CM	Open End	Cautious Alloc (Asset Alloc)	B-	C	A-	Up	Y	2,500
American Century Inv One Choice Port®: Moderate Inv Cls	AOMIX	NAS CM	Open End	Moderate Alloc (Asset Alloc)	B-	C	B+	Up	Y	2,500
American Century Inv One Choice Port®: Moderate R Cls	AORMX	NAS CM	Open End	Moderate Alloc (Asset Alloc)	B-	C	B+	Up	Y	2,500
American Century Inv One Choice Port®: Very Aggress Inv Cl	AOVIX	NAS CM	Open End	Aggressive Alloc (Asset Alloc)	C+	C	B	Up	Y	2,500
American Century Inv One Choice Port®: Very Aggress R Cls	AORVX	NAS CM	Open End	Aggressive Alloc (Asset Alloc)	C+	C	B	Up	Y	2,500
American Century Inv One Choice Port®: Very Cons Inv Cls	AONIX	NAS CM	Open End	Cautious Alloc (Asset Alloc)	B-	C	A-		Y	2,500
American Century Inv One Choice Port®: Very Cons R Cls	AORHX	NAS CM	Open End	Cautious Alloc (Asset Alloc)	B-	C	B+	Up	Y	2,500
American Century Large Company Value Fund A Class	ALPAX	NAS CM	Open End	US Equity Large Cap Value (Growth)	B-	C	B	Up	Y	2,500
American Century Large Company Value Fund C Class	ALPCX	NAS CM	Open End	US Equity Large Cap Value (Growth)	B-	C	B	Up	Y	2,500
American Century Large Company Value Fund I Class	ALVSX	NAS CM	Open End	US Equity Large Cap Value (Growth)	B-	C	B		Y	5,000,000
American Century Large Company Value Fund Investor Class	ALVIX	NAS CM	Open End	US Equity Large Cap Value (Growth)	B-	C	B	Up	Y	2,500
American Century Large Company Value Fund R Class	ALVRX	NAS CM	Open End	US Equity Large Cap Value (Growth)	B-	C	B	Up	Y	2,500
American Century Large Company Value Fund R5 Class	ALVGX	NAS CM	Open End	US Equity Large Cap Value (Growth)	B-	C	B		Y	0
American Century Large Company Value Fund R6 Class	ALVDX	NAS CM	Open End	US Equity Large Cap Value (Growth)	B-	C	B		Y	0
American Century Mid Cap Value Fund A Class	ACLAX	NAS CM	Open End	US Equity Mid Cap (Growth)	C+	C	B	Up		2,500
American Century Mid Cap Value Fund C Class	ACCLX	NAS CM	Open End	US Equity Mid Cap (Growth)	C+	C	B	Up		2,500
American Century Mid Cap Value Fund I Class	AVUAX	NAS CM	Open End	US Equity Mid Cap (Growth)	C+	C	B	Up		5,000,000
American Century Mid Cap Value Fund Investor Class	ACMVX	NAS CM	Open End	US Equity Mid Cap (Growth)	C+	C	B	Up		2,500
American Century Mid Cap Value Fund R Class	AMVRX	NAS CM	Open End	US Equity Mid Cap (Growth)	C+	C	B	Up		2,500
American Century Mid Cap Value Fund R5 Class	AMVGX	NAS CM	Open End	US Equity Mid Cap (Growth)	C+	C	B	Up	Y	0
American Century Mid Cap Value Fund R6 Class	AMDVX	NAS CM	Open End	US Equity Mid Cap (Growth)	C+	C	B	Up		0
American Century Mid Cap Value Fund Y Class	AMVYX	NAS CM	Open End	US Equity Mid Cap (Growth)	C+	C	B	Up		0
American Century Multi-Asset Income Fund A Class	AMJAX	NAS CM	Open End	Cautious Alloc (Growth & Income)	B-	C	B+		Y	2,500
American Century Multi-Asset Income Fund C Class	AMJCX	NAS CM	Open End	Cautious Alloc (Growth & Income)	C+	C	B		Y	2,500
American Century Multi-Asset Income Fund I Class	AMJIX	NAS CM	Open End	Cautious Alloc (Growth & Income)	B-	C	B+		Y	5,000,000
American Century Multi-Asset Income Fund Investor Class	AMJVX	NAS CM	Open End	Cautious Alloc (Growth & Income)	B-	C	B+		Y	2,500
American Century Multi-Asset Income Fund R Class	AMJWX	NAS CM	Open End	Cautious Alloc (Growth & Income)	B-	C	B	Up	Y	2,500
American Century Multi-Asset Income Fund R5 Class	AMJGX	NAS CM	Open End	Cautious Alloc (Growth & Income)	B-	C	B+		Y	0
American Century Multi-Asset Income Fund R6 Class	AMJRX	NAS CM	Open End	Cautious Alloc (Growth & Income)	B-	C	B+		Y	0
American Century Multi-Asset Income Fund Y Class	AMJYX	NAS CM	Open End	Cautious Alloc (Growth & Income)	B-	C	B+		Y	0
American Century Multi-Asset Real Return Fund A Class	ASIDX	NAS CM	Open End	Cautious Alloc (Growth & Income)	B-	C	B+	Up	Y	2,500
American Century Multi-Asset Real Return Fund C Class	ASIZX	NAS CM	Open End	Cautious Alloc (Growth & Income)	B-	C	B+	Up	Y	2,500
American Century Multi-Asset Real Return Fund I Class	ASINX	NAS CM	Open End	Cautious Alloc (Growth & Income)	B-	C	A-		Y	5,000,000
American Century Multi-Asset Real Return Investor Cls	ASIOX	NAS CM	Open End	Cautious Alloc (Growth & Income)	B-	C	A-		Y	2,500
American Century Multi-Asset Real Return Fund R Class	ASIUX	NAS CM	Open End	Cautious Alloc (Growth & Income)	B-	C	B+	Up	Y	2,500
American Century Multi-Asset Real Return Fund R5 Class	AMRUX	NAS CM	Open End	Cautious Alloc (Growth & Income)	B-	C	A-		Y	0
American Century NT Core Equity Plus Fund G Class	ACNKX	NAS CM	Open End	US Equity Large Cap Blend (Growth)	C+	C	B		Y	0
American Century NT Disciplined Growth Fund G Class	ANDGX	NAS CM	Open End	US Equity Large Cap Growth (Growth)	C+	C	B	Down		0
American Century NT Disciplined Growth Fund Investor Class	ANTDX	NAS CM	Open End	US Equity Large Cap Growth (Growth)	C+	C	B	Down	Y	0
American Century NT Emerging Markets Fund G Class	ACLKX	NAS CM	Open End	Global Emerg Mkts (Div Emerging Mkts)	C	C	C		Y	0
American Century NT Equity Growth Fund G Class	ACLEX	NAS CM	Open End	US Equity Large Cap Blend (Growth)	C+	C	B	Down	Y	0
American Century NT Global Real Estate Fund G Class	ANRHX	NAS CM	Open End	Real Estate Sector Equity (Real Estate)	B-	C+	B			0
American Century NT Global Real Estate Fund Investor Class	ANREX	NAS CM	Open End	Real Estate Sector Equity (Real Estate)	B-	C	B			0
American Century NT Growth Fund G Class	ACLTX	NAS CM	Open End	US Equity Large Cap Growth (Growth)	B-	C+	B	Down	Y	0

★ Expanded analysis of this fund is included in Section II.

Min Additional Investment	TOTAL RETURNS					PERFORMANCE				ASSETS		ASSET ALLOCATION & TURNOVER					BULL & BEAR		FEES		
	3-Month Total Return	6-Month Total Return	1-Year Total Return	3-Year Total Return	5-Year Total Return	Dividend Yield (TTM)	Expense Ratio	3-Yr Std Deviation	3-Year Beta	NAV	Total Assets (MIL)	%Cash	%Stocks	%Bonds	%Other	Turnover Ratio	Last Bull Market Total Return	Last Bear Market Total Return	Front End Fee (%)	Back End Fee (%)	Inception Date
50	2.75	10.53	4.59	17.14	17.39	1.55	1.77	5.63	1.36	13.13	1,520	12	44	43	0	13	11.94	-7.64		1.00	Mar-10
50	3.05	11.12	5.85	21.40	24.54	2.63	0.57	5.7	1.38	13.17	1,520	12	44	43	0	13	12.7	-7.09			Aug-04
50	2.92	10.93	5.64	20.59	23.29	2.44	0.77	5.66	1.37	13.16	1,520	12	44	43	0	13	12.69	-7.27			Aug-04
50	2.87	10.75	5.11	18.90	20.33	1.97	1.27	5.62	1.36	13.16	1,520	12	44	43	0	13	12.32	-7.42			Aug-04
	3.08	11.24	6.02	21.68	25.26	3.35	0.42	5.62	1.36	10.85	1,520	12	44	43	0	13	12.7	-7.09			Jul-13
50	3.53	15.98	4.83	33.79	35.63	2.08	0.97	9.76	0.75	16.69	1,332	3	78	19	0	11	20.63	-15.83			Sep-04
50	3.41	15.76	4.36	31.80	32.33	1.64	1.47	9.75	0.75	16.67	1,332	3	78	19	0	11	20.28	-16			Mar-15
50	3.19	11.31	5.23	20.24	23.68	2.38	0.81	5.83	0.44	13.69	1,239	8	44	47	0	8	12.42	-6.97			Sep-04
50	3.06	11.04	4.78	18.45	20.62	1.9	1.31	5.81	0.43	13.69	1,239	8	44	47	0	8	12.1	-7.17			Mar-15
50	3.28	13.72	5.04	27.59	29.79	2.2	0.9	7.97	0.61	15.57	1,888	6	64	30	0	8	17	-11.95			Sep-04
50	3.15	13.45	4.51	25.69	26.66	1.72	1.4	8.01	0.61	15.57	1,888	6	64	30	0	8	16.66	-12.13			Mar-15
50	3.71	18.27	3.92	40.01	40.57	1.64	1.04	12.05	0.94	17.86	308.6	1	98	0	0	8	23.75	-19.21			Sep-04
50	3.60	17.98	3.39	37.84	37.06	1.21	1.54	12.06	0.94	17.84	308.6	1	98	0	0	8	23.39	-19.38			Mar-15
50	2.84	8.66	5.75	13.79	18.43	2.33	0.71	3.64	0.26	12.13	424.9	9	24	66	0	14	8.03	-2.78			Sep-04
50	2.71	8.39	5.22	12.09	15.49	1.85	1.21	3.63	0.26	12.14	424.9	9	24	66	0	14	7.71	-2.98			Mar-15
50	4.05	17.09	8.41	33.06	36.30	1.51	1.09	12.21	1	10.2	868.8	3	97	0	0	62	24.5	-17.19	5.75		Oct-00
50	3.86	16.69	7.71	30.11	31.34	0.81	1.84	12.3	1	10.2	868.8	3	97	0	0	62	24.06	-17.51		1.00	Nov-01
50	4.16	17.32	8.89	34.82	39.37	1.92	0.64	12.23	1	10.21	868.8	3	97	0	0	62	24.98	-17.13			Aug-01
50	4.22	17.34	8.78	34.18	38.15	1.74	0.84	12.21	1	10.21	868.8	3	97	0	0	62	24.65	-17.22			Jul-99
50	3.98	16.94	8.24	32.03	34.71	1.27	1.34	12.26	1	10.21	868.8	3	97	0	0	62	24.36	-17.43			Aug-03
	4.26	17.43	8.99	34.75	38.74	1.92	0.64	12.26	1	10.22	868.8	3	97	0	0	62	24.65	-17.22			Apr-17
	4.20	17.53	9.16	35.43	40.43	2.06	0.49	12.25	1	10.21	868.8	3	97	0	0	62	24.65	-17.22			Jul-13
50	3.43	17.85	2.53	27.61	43.79	1.08	1.23	13.45	1	15.62	7,872	3	97	0	0	53	21.86	-17.25	5.75		Jan-05
50	3.21	17.33	1.73	24.69	38.40	0.41	1.98	13.43	1	15.43	7,872	3	97	0	0	53	21.21	-17.43		1.00	Mar-10
	3.46	18.04	2.97	29.32	47.02	1.48	0.78	13.46	1	15.66	7,872	3	97	0	0	53	22.16	-17.06			Aug-04
50	3.48	17.94	2.77	28.50	45.52	1.3	0.98	13.43	1	15.65	7,872	3	97	0	0	53	21.95	-17.14			Mar-04
50	3.30	17.69	2.28	26.67	41.95	0.86	1.48	13.41	1	15.57	7,872	3	97	0	0	53	21.57	-17.22			Jul-05
	3.53	18.11	3.03	29.12	46.23	1.48	0.78	13.46	1	15.67	7,872	3	97	0	0	53	21.95	-17.14			Apr-17
	3.57	18.12	3.12	29.90	48.13	1.61	0.63	13.41	1	15.66	7,872	3	97	0	0	53	21.95	-17.14			Jul-13
	3.57	18.20	3.18	29.53	46.69	1.61	0.63	13.39	0.99	15.67	7,872	3	97	0	0	53	21.95	-17.14			Apr-17
50	1.93	10.48	4.16	15.91		4.54	1.14	6.06		9.83	64.3	8	50	33	0	152			5.75		Dec-14
50	1.74	10.10	3.50	13.40		3.82	1.89	6.11		9.83	64.3	8	50	33	0	152				1.00	Dec-14
50	2.05	10.83	4.72	17.57		4.97	0.69	6.06		9.84	64.3	8	50	33	0	152					Dec-14
50	2.00	10.61	4.41	16.77		4.78	0.89	6.06		9.83	64.3	8	50	33	0	152					Dec-14
50	1.87	10.36	4.01	15.07		4.3	1.39	6.15		9.83	64.3	8	50	33	0	152					Dec-14
	2.04	10.81	4.72	17.56		4.97	0.69	6.06		9.85	64.3	8	50	33	0	152					Apr-17
	2.08	10.90	4.87	18.09		5.12	0.54	6.13		9.84	64.3	8	50	33	0	152					Dec-14
	2.08	10.78	4.87	17.97		5.12	0.54	6.08		9.84	64.3	8	50	33	0	152					Apr-17
50	2.23	11.53	5.07	17.67	5.30	2.33	1.18	6.52	0.82	10.53	11.8	9	57	32	3	160	5.91	-10.9	5.75		Apr-10
50	2.02	11.03	4.25	14.99	1.39	1.84	1.93	6.52	0.8	10.09	11.8	9	57	32	3	160	5.5	-11.16		1.00	Apr-10
50	2.39	11.82	5.55	19.29	7.73	2.62	0.73	6.51	0.83	10.69	11.8	9	57	32	3	160	6.17	-10.69			Apr-10
50	2.30	11.66	5.32	18.62	6.68	2.49	0.93	6.56	0.83	10.63	11.8	9	57	32	3	160	6.11	-10.82			Apr-10
50	2.16	11.32	4.73	16.78	4.03	2.17	1.43	6.53	0.8	10.39	11.8	9	57	32	3	160	5.81	-11.08			Apr-10
	2.29	11.71	5.45	19.21	7.66	2.62	0.73	6.56	0.82	10.68	11.8	9	57	32	3	160	6.17	-10.69			Apr-17
	2.02	15.79	5.56	43.44	45.00	1.34	0.44	12.53	1	14.9	474.7	2	98	0	0	100					Dec-11
	4.04	20.89	7.80	58.60		1.09	0.01	13.32	0.98	12.31	485.5	1	99	0	0	105					Mar-15
	3.83	20.38	6.75	55.27		0.3	1.01	13.32	0.98	12.29	485.5	1	99	0	0	105					Mar-15
	3.27	14.30	-0.42	41.90	28.12	1.26	0.01	14.4	0.99	11.35	437.2	1	99	0	0	66	22.61	-29.91			May-06
	3.71	19.81	8.04	50.56	52.70	1.64	0	12.73	1.03	13.09	1,427	2	98	0	0	83	25.94	-15.43			May-06
	2.91	19.66	12.74	22.38		4.1	0	11.26	0.99	10.59	363.9	0	99	0	1	178					Mar-15
	2.63	18.98	11.56	19.42		3.13	1.11	11.22	0.99	10.53	363.9	0	99	0	1	178					Mar-15
	5.59	23.94	12.79	70.19	83.27	1.08	0	13.71	1.01	17.55	1,103	1	99	0	0	53	26.98	-16.93			May-06

	MARKET			FUND TYPE, CATEGORY & OBJECTIVE	RATINGS				MINIMUMS	
Fund Name	Ticker Symbol	Traded On	Fund Type	Category and (Prospectus Objective)	Overall Rating	Reward Rating	Risk Rating	Recent Up/ Downgrade	Open to New Investors	Min Initial Investment
American Century NT Heritage Fund G Class	ACLWX	NAS CM	Open End	US Equity Mid Cap (Growth)	B-	B-	B		Y	0
American Century NT International Growth Fund G Class	ACLNX	NAS CM	Open End	Global Equity Large Cap (Foreign Stock)	C	C	C+		Y	0
American Century NT International Small-Mid Cap G Cls	ANTMX	NAS CM	Open End	Global Equity Mid/Small Cap (Growth)	C	C	C	Up		0
American Century NT Intl Small-Mid Cap Inv Cls	ANTSX	NAS CM	Open End	Global Equity Mid/Small Cap (Growth)	C	C-	C	Up	Y	0
American Century NT International Value Fund G Class	ANTYX	NAS CM	Open End	Global Equity Large Cap (Growth)	C	C-	C			0
American Century NT International Value Investor Cls	ANTVX	NAS CM	Open End	Global Equity Large Cap (Growth)	C-	D+	C	Down	Y	0
American Century NT Large Company Value Fund G Class	ACLLX	NAS CM	Open End	US Equity Large Cap Value (Growth)	B-	C	B		Y	0
American Century NT Mid Cap Value Fund G Class	ACLMX	NAS CM	Open End	US Equity Mid Cap (Growth)	C+	C	B	Up	Y	0
American Century NT Non-U.S. Intrinsic Value Fund G Class	ANTGX	NAS CM	Open End	Global Equity Large Cap (Foreign Stock)	U	U	U		Y	0
American Century NT Non-U.S. Intrinsic Value Investor Cls	ANTUX	NAS CM	Open End	Global Equity Large Cap (Foreign Stock)	U	U	U		Y	0
American Century NT Small Company Fund G Class	ACLOX	NAS CM	Open End	US Equity Small Cap (Small Company)	C	C-	C		Y	0
American Century Real Estate Fund A Class	AREEX	NAS CM	Open End	Real Estate Sector Equity (Real Estate)	C+	C	B-	Down	Y	2,500
American Century Real Estate Fund C Class	ARYCX	NAS CM	Open End	Real Estate Sector Equity (Real Estate)	C	C	C+	Down	Y	2,500
American Century Real Estate Fund I Class	REAIX	NAS CM	Open End	Real Estate Sector Equity (Real Estate)	C+	C	B-	Down	Y	5,000,000
American Century Real Estate Fund Investor Class	REACX	NAS CM	Open End	Real Estate Sector Equity (Real Estate)	C+	C	B-	Down	Y	2,500
American Century Real Estate Fund R Class	AREWX	NAS CM	Open End	Real Estate Sector Equity (Real Estate)	C+	C	B-	Down	Y	2,500
American Century Real Estate Fund R5 Class	ARREX	NAS CM	Open End	Real Estate Sector Equity (Real Estate)	C+	C	B-	Down	Y	0
American Century Real Estate Fund R6 Class	AREDX	NAS CM	Open End	Real Estate Sector Equity (Real Estate)	C+	C	B-	Down	Y	0
American Century Real Estate Fund Y Class	ARYEX	NAS CM	Open End	Real Estate Sector Equity (Real Estate)	C+	C	B-	Down	Y	0
American Century Select Fund A Class	TWCAX	NAS CM	Open End	US Equity Large Cap Growth (Growth)	B-	C+	B	Down	Y	2,500
American Century Select Fund C Class	ACSLX	NAS CM	Open End	US Equity Large Cap Growth (Growth)	C+	C+	B	Down	Y	2,500
American Century Select Fund I Class	TWSIX	NAS CM	Open End	US Equity Large Cap Growth (Growth)	B-	C+	B	Down	Y	5,000,000
American Century Select Fund Investor Class	TWCIX	NAS CM	Open End	US Equity Large Cap Growth (Growth)	B-	C+	B	Down	Y	2,500
American Century Select Fund R Class	ASERX	NAS CM	Open End	US Equity Large Cap Growth (Growth)	B-	C+	B	Down	Y	2,500
American Century Select Fund R5 Class	ASLGX	NAS CM	Open End	US Equity Large Cap Growth (Growth)	B-	C+	B	Down	Y	0
American Century Select Fund R6 Class	ASDEX	NAS CM	Open End	US Equity Large Cap Growth (Growth)	B-	C+	B	Down	Y	0
American Century Select Fund Y Class	ASLWX	NAS CM	Open End	US Equity Large Cap Growth (Growth)	B-	C+	B	Down	Y	0
American Century Small Cap Growth Fund A Class	ANOAX	NAS CM	Open End	US Equity Small Cap (Small Company)	C+	C+	C+	Down	Y	2,500
American Century Small Cap Growth Fund C Class	ANOCX	NAS CM	Open End	US Equity Small Cap (Small Company)	C+	C	C+	Down	Y	2,500
American Century Small Cap Growth Fund G Class	ANOHX	NAS CM	Open End	US Equity Small Cap (Small Company)	C+	C+	C+		Y	0
American Century Small Cap Growth Fund I Class	ANONX	NAS CM	Open End	US Equity Small Cap (Small Company)	C+	C+	C+	Down	Y	5,000,000
American Century Small Cap Growth Fund Investor Class	ANOIX	NAS CM	Open End	US Equity Small Cap (Small Company)	C+	C+	C+	Down	Y	2,500
American Century Small Cap Growth Fund R Class	ANORX	NAS CM	Open End	US Equity Small Cap (Small Company)	C+	C	C+	Down	Y	2,500
American Century Small Cap Growth Fund R5 Class	ANOGX	NAS CM	Open End	US Equity Small Cap (Small Company)	C+	C+	C+	Down	Y	0
American Century Small Cap Growth Fund R6 Class	ANODX	NAS CM	Open End	US Equity Small Cap (Small Company)	C+	C+	C+	Down	Y	0
American Century Small Cap Growth Fund Y Class	ANOYX	NAS CM	Open End	US Equity Small Cap (Small Company)	C+	C+	C+	Down	Y	0
American Century Small Cap Value Fund A Class	ACSCX	NAS CM	Open End	US Equity Small Cap (Small Company)	C	C	C+			2,500
American Century Small Cap Value Fund C Class	ASVNX	NAS CM	Open End	US Equity Small Cap (Small Company)	C	C	C+			2,500
American Century Small Cap Value Fund G Class	ASVHX	NAS CM	Open End	US Equity Small Cap (Small Company)	C	C	C+		Y	0
American Century Small Cap Value Fund I Class	ACVIX	NAS CM	Open End	US Equity Small Cap (Small Company)	C	C	C+			5,000,000
American Century Small Cap Value Fund Investor Class	ASVIX	NAS CM	Open End	US Equity Small Cap (Small Company)	C	C	C+			2,500
American Century Small Cap Value Fund R Class	ASVRX	NAS CM	Open End	US Equity Small Cap (Small Company)	C	C	C+			2,500
American Century Small Cap Value Fund R5 Class	ASVGX	NAS CM	Open End	US Equity Small Cap (Small Company)	C	C	C+		Y	0
American Century Small Cap Value Fund R6 Class	ASVDX	NAS CM	Open End	US Equity Small Cap (Small Company)	C	C	C+			0
American Century Small Cap Value Fund Y Class	ASVYX	NAS CM	Open End	US Equity Small Cap (Small Company)	C	C	C+			0
American Century Small Company Fund A Class	ASQAX	NAS CM	Open End	US Equity Small Cap (Small Company)	C	C-	C		Y	2,500
American Century Small Company Fund C Class	ASQCX	NAS CM	Open End	US Equity Small Cap (Small Company)	C-	C-	C	Down	Y	2,500
American Century Small Company Fund I Class	ASCQX	NAS CM	Open End	US Equity Small Cap (Small Company)	C	C-	C		Y	5,000,000
American Century Small Company Fund Investor Class	ASQIX	NAS CM	Open End	US Equity Small Cap (Small Company)	C	C-	C		Y	2,500
American Century Small Company Fund R Class	ASCRX	NAS CM	Open End	US Equity Small Cap (Small Company)	C	C-	C		Y	2,500
American Century Small Company Fund R5 Class	ASQGX	NAS CM	Open End	US Equity Small Cap (Small Company)	C	C-	C		Y	0
American Century Strategic Allocation: Aggressive A Cls	ACVAX	NAS CM	Open End	Aggressive Alloc (Asset Alloc)	B-	C	B	Up	Y	2,500

★ Expanded analysis of this fund is included in Section II.

Min Additional Investment	TOTAL RETURNS: 3-Month Total Return	6-Month Total Return	1-Year Total Return	3-Year Total Return	5-Year Total Return	PERFORMANCE: Dividend Yield (TTM)	Expense Ratio	3-Yr Std Deviation	3-Year Beta	ASSETS: NAV	Total Assets (MIL)	ASSET ALLOCATION & TURNOVER: %Cash	%Stocks	%Bonds	%Other	Turnover Ratio	BULL & BEAR: Last Bull Market Total Return	Last Bear Market Total Return	FEES: Front End Fee (%)	Back End Fee (%)	Inception Date
	7.27	30.05	17.07	56.70	65.74	0.73	0.01	14.01	0.96	12.98	621.3	2	98	0	0	90	27.07	-21.65			May-06
	5.17	19.51	-0.31	37.01	19.61	1.85	0.01	12.5	1.05	10.78	830.1	0	100	0	0	71	17.51	-24.37			May-06
	4.12	20.34	-10.76	28.45		1.61	0	15.63	1.2	10.35	342.5	2	98	0	0	140					Mar-15
	3.74	19.58	-12.08	24.64		0.35	1.47	15.68	1.21	10.26	342.5	2	98	0	0	140					Mar-15
	2.00	10.12	-3.89	25.30		3.83	0.02	11.18	0.96	9.14	821.8	1	99	0	0	76					Mar-15
	1.67	9.51	-5.05	22.12		2.64	1.3	11.26	0.97	9.09	821.8	1	99	0	0	76					Mar-15
	4.33	17.78	9.56	36.25	39.33	2.55	0.01	12.26	1	11.14	1,603	3	97	0	0	56	24.8	-17.27			May-06
	3.68	18.52	3.83	31.26	49.56	2.18	0.01	13.5	1	11.93	922.7	3	97	0	0	58	22.16	-16.88			May-06
	1.08	7.46					0.01			10.22	377.6	2	98	0	0						Dec-18
	0.69	6.74					1.31			10.13	377.6	2	98	0	0						Dec-18
	0.62	14.67	-6.95	31.39	24.66	1.04	0	17.87	1.03	8.05	395.7	2	98	0	0	99	28	-22.8			May-06
50	2.77	19.39	12.93	12.50	41.17	1.78	1.4	12.14	0.91	29.38	952.0	0	100	0	0	148	31.74	-14.81	5.75		Oct-98
50	2.57	18.92	12.07	9.96	35.97	1.12	2.15	12.14	0.91	28.58	952.0	0	100	0	0	148	31.18	-15.07		1.00	Sep-07
50	1.98	18.62	12.44	14.01	44.36	2.19	0.95	12.15	0.91	29.49	952.0	0	100	0	0	148	32.1	-14.62			Jun-97
50	2.83	19.51	13.19	13.34	42.95	2.01	1.15	12.13	0.91	29.41	952.0	0	100	0	0	148	31.98	-14.73			Sep-95
50	2.72	19.23	12.67	11.66	39.44	1.57	1.65	12.16	0.91	29.16	952.0	0	100	0	0	148	31.57	-14.9			Sep-07
	2.91	19.65	13.46	13.86	43.60	2.19	0.95	12.14	0.91	29.5	952.0	0	100	0	0	148	31.98	-14.73			Apr-17
	2.91	19.75	13.60	14.52	45.46	2.33	0.8	12.16	0.91	29.48	952.0	0	100	0	0	148	31.98	-14.73			Jul-13
	2.95	19.74	13.63	14.23	44.08	2.33	0.8	12.14	0.91	29.49	952.0	0	100	0	0	148	31.98	-14.73			Apr-17
50	4.59	22.11	8.90	61.16	80.03	0	1.22	13.43	0.99	73.33	3,154	0	100	0	0	22	27.76	-15.85	5.75		Aug-97
50	4.39	21.64	8.09	57.59	73.39	0	1.97	13.43	0.99	64.85	3,154	0	100	0	0	22	27.22	-16.11		1.00	Jan-03
50	4.70	22.38	9.39	63.35	84.12	0.21	0.77	13.44	0.99	76.54	3,154	0	100	0	0	22	28.12	-15.7			Mar-97
50	4.64	22.26	9.17	62.37	82.29	0.04	0.97	13.44	0.99	75.18	3,154	0	100	0	0	22	27.93	-15.75			Jun-71
50	4.52	21.95	8.62	59.95	77.78	0	1.47	13.43	0.99	72.55	3,154	0	100	0	0	22	27.59	-15.94			Jul-05
	4.69	22.36	9.35	62.99	82.99	0.21	0.77	13.44	0.99	76.55	3,154	0	100	0	0	22	27.93	-15.75			Apr-17
	4.75	22.47	9.56	64.09	85.50	0.33	0.62	13.43	0.99	76.52	3,154	0	100	0	0	22	27.93	-15.75			Jul-13
	4.74	22.47	9.56	63.61	83.69	0.33	0.62	13.44	0.99	76.61	3,154	0	100	0	0	22	27.93	-15.75			Apr-17
50	7.79	30.00	8.36	76.49	69.00	0	1.52	17.23	0.98	17.29	876.2	2	98	0	0	116	32.53	-28.79	5.75		Jan-03
50	7.61	29.52	7.57	72.48	62.82	0	2.27	17.19	0.97	15.4	876.2	2	98	0	0	116	32.14	-29.07		1.00	Jan-03
	8.15	30.42	8.87	78.21	71.51		0	17.21	0.97	18.76	876.2	2	98	0	0	116	32.79	-28.72			Apr-19
50	7.92	30.23	8.81	78.82	72.87	0	1.07	17.18	0.97	18.52	876.2	2	98	0	0	116	32.94	-28.69			May-07
50	7.90	30.13	8.63	77.81	71.12	0	1.27	17.2	0.97	18.01	876.2	2	98	0	0	116	32.79	-28.72			Jun-01
50	7.76	29.82	8.09	75.12	66.89	0	1.77	17.2	0.97	16.8	876.2	2	98	0	0	116	32.58	-28.92			Sep-07
	7.98	30.30	8.86	78.64	71.92	0	1.07	17.18	0.97	18.53	876.2	2	98	0	0	116	32.79	-28.72			Apr-17
	7.96	30.38	9.01	79.65	74.10	0	0.92	17.2	0.97	18.71	876.2	2	98	0	0	116	32.79	-28.72			Jul-13
	7.96	30.38	8.96	79.20	72.46	0	0.92	17.2	0.97	18.71	876.2	2	98	0	0	116	32.79	-28.72			Apr-17
50	5.97	23.13	-2.48	40.86	37.20	0.23	1.51	18.34	1.02	7.37	1,410	3	97	0	0	90	25.33	-23.62	5.75		Dec-99
50	5.93	22.75	-3.12	37.76	32.23	0	2.26	18.43	1.03	6.96	1,410	3	97	0	0	90	24.71	-23.83		1.00	Mar-10
	6.30	23.47	-1.95	42.26	39.27		0.01	18.38	1.03	7.56	1,410	3	97	0	0	90	25.6	-23.55			Apr-19
50	6.19	23.51	-1.90	42.80	40.37	0.61	1.06	18.36	1.03	7.55	1,410	3	97	0	0	90	25.69	-23.45			Oct-98
50	6.16	23.30	-2.09	42.07	39.08	0.44	1.26	18.4	1.03	7.47	1,410	3	97	0	0	90	25.6	-23.55			Jul-98
50	5.92	22.98	-2.69	39.70	35.62	0.04	1.76	18.44	1.03	7.33	1,410	3	97	0	0	90	25.21	-23.73			Mar-10
	6.04	23.31	-2.01	42.52	39.52	0.61	1.06	18.34	1.02	7.55	1,410	3	97	0	0	90	25.6	-23.55			Apr-17
	6.26	23.59	-1.76	43.44	41.38	0.74	0.91	18.42	1.03	7.55	1,410	3	97	0	0	90	25.6	-23.55			Jul-13
	6.25	23.55	-1.76	43.14	40.13	0.74	0.91	18.39	1.03	7.56	1,410	3	97	0	0	90	25.6	-23.55			Apr-17
50	0.31	14.07	-7.90	28.07	19.78	0	1.11	17.76	1.03	12.89	611.9	1	99	0	0	92	27.9	-23.14	5.75		Sep-00
50	0.16	13.67	-8.59	25.30	15.31	0	1.86	17.74	1.02	12.22	611.9	1	99	0	0	92	27.39	-23.33		1.00	Mar-10
50	0.45	14.28	-7.49	29.86	22.48	0.26	0.66	17.76	1.03	13.36	611.9	1	99	0	0	92	28.14	-22.94			Oct-99
50	0.37	14.18	-7.66	29.13	21.29	0.04	0.86	17.72	1.02	13.28	611.9	1	99	0	0	92	27.96	-22.97			Jul-98
50	0.23	13.88	-8.15	27.12	18.27	0	1.36	17.77	1.03	12.55	611.9	1	99	0	0	92	27.58	-23.1			Aug-03
	0.45	14.27	-7.49	29.65	21.78	0.26	0.66	17.73	1.02	13.37	611.9	1	99	0	0	92	27.96	-22.97			Apr-17
50	3.66	16.29	5.20	33.29	34.03	0.92	1.36	9.8	0.77	7.92	782.1	3	76	22	0	58	20.32	-15.97	5.75		Oct-96

	MARKET			FUND TYPE, CATEGORY & OBJECTIVE	RATINGS					MINIMUMS
Fund Name	Ticker Symbol	Traded On	Fund Type	Category and (Prospectus Objective)	Overall Rating	Reward Rating	Risk Rating	Recent Up/ Downgrade	Open to New Investors	Min Initial Investment
American Century Strategic Allocation: Aggressive C Cls	ASTAX	NAS CM	Open End	Aggressive Alloc (Asset Alloc)	B-	C	B	Up	Y	2,500
American Century Strategic Allocation: Aggressive I Cls	AAAIX	NAS CM	Open End	Aggressive Alloc (Asset Alloc)	B-	C	B	Up	Y	5,000,000
American Century Strategic Allocation: Aggressive Inv Cls	TWSAX	NAS CM	Open End	Aggressive Alloc (Asset Alloc)	B-	C	B	Up	Y	2,500
American Century Strategic Allocation: Aggressive R Cls	AAARX	NAS CM	Open End	Aggressive Alloc (Asset Alloc)	B-	C	B	Up	Y	2,500
American Century Strategic Allocation: Aggressive R5 Cls	ASAUX	NAS CM	Open End	Aggressive Alloc (Asset Alloc)	B-	C	B+	Up	Y	0
American Century Strategic Allocation: Aggressive R6 Cls	AAAUX	NAS CM	Open End	Aggressive Alloc (Asset Alloc)	B-	C	B+	Up	Y	0
American Century Strategic Allocation: Conservative A Cls	ACCAX	NAS CM	Open End	Cautious Alloc (Asset Alloc)	B-	C	A-	Up	Y	2,500
American Century Strategic Allocation: Conservative C Cls	AACCX	NAS CM	Open End	Cautious Alloc (Asset Alloc)	B-	C	B+	Up	Y	2,500
American Century Strategic Allocation: Conservative I Cls	ACCIX	NAS CM	Open End	Cautious Alloc (Asset Alloc)	B	C	A-	Up	Y	2,500
American Century Strategic Alloc: Conservative Inv Cls	TWSCX	NAS CM	Open End	Cautious Alloc (Asset Alloc)	B	C	A-	Up	Y	2,500
American Century Strategic Allocation: Conservative R Cls	AACRX	NAS CM	Open End	Cautious Alloc (Asset Alloc)	B-	C	A-	Up	Y	2,500
American Century Strategic Allocation: Conservative R5 Cls	AACGX	NAS CM	Open End	Cautious Alloc (Asset Alloc)	B	C	A-	Up	Y	0
American Century Strategic Allocation: Conservative R6 Cls	AACDX	NAS CM	Open End	Cautious Alloc (Asset Alloc)	B	C	A-	Up	Y	0
American Century Strategic Allocation: Moderate A Cls	ACOAX	NAS CM	Open End	Moderate Alloc (Asset Alloc)	B-	C	B+	Up	Y	2,500
American Century Strategic Allocation: Moderate C Cls	ASTCX	NAS CM	Open End	Moderate Alloc (Asset Alloc)	B-	C	B+	Up	Y	2,500
American Century Strategic Allocation: Moderate I Cls	ASAMX	NAS CM	Open End	Moderate Alloc (Asset Alloc)	B-	C	B+	Up	Y	5,000,000
American Century Strategic Allocation: Moderate Inv Cls	TWSMX	NAS CM	Open End	Moderate Alloc (Asset Alloc)	B-	C	B+	Up	Y	2,500
American Century Strategic Allocation: Moderate R Cls	ASMRX	NAS CM	Open End	Moderate Alloc (Asset Alloc)	B-	C	B+	Up	Y	2,500
American Century Strategic Allocation: Moderate R5 Cls	ASMUX	NAS CM	Open End	Moderate Alloc (Asset Alloc)	B-	C	B+	Up	Y	0
American Century Strategic Allocation: Moderate R6 Cls	ASMDX	NAS CM	Open End	Moderate Alloc (Asset Alloc)	B-	C	B+	Up	Y	0
American Century Sustainable Equity Fund A Class	AFDAX	NAS CM	Open End	US Equity Large Cap Blend (Growth)	B-	C	B		Y	2,500
American Century Sustainable Equity Fund C Class	AFDCX	NAS CM	Open End	US Equity Large Cap Blend (Growth)	B-	C	B		Y	2,500
American Century Sustainable Equity Fund G Class	AFEGX	NAS CM	Open End	US Equity Large Cap Blend (Growth)	B-	C	B		Y	0
American Century Sustainable Equity Fund I Class	AFEIX	NAS CM	Open End	US Equity Large Cap Blend (Growth)	B-	C+	B		Y	5,000,000
American Century Sustainable Equity Fund Investor Class	AFDIX	NAS CM	Open End	US Equity Large Cap Blend (Growth)	B-	C+	B		Y	2,500
American Century Sustainable Equity Fund R Class	AFDRX	NAS CM	Open End	US Equity Large Cap Blend (Growth)	B-	C	B		Y	2,500
American Century Sustainable Equity Fund R5 Class	AFDGX	NAS CM	Open End	US Equity Large Cap Blend (Growth)	B-	C+	B		Y	0
American Century Sustainable Equity Fund R6 Class	AFEDX	NAS CM	Open End	US Equity Large Cap Blend (Growth)	B-	C	B		Y	0
American Century Sustainable Equity Fund Y Class	AFYDX	NAS CM	Open End	US Equity Large Cap Blend (Growth)	B-	C+	B		Y	0
American Century Ultra® Fund A Class	TWUAX	NAS CM	Open End	US Equity Large Cap Growth (Growth)	C+	C+	B	Down	Y	2,500
American Century Ultra® Fund C Class	TWCCX	NAS CM	Open End	US Equity Large Cap Growth (Growth)	C+	C	B	Down	Y	2,500
American Century Ultra® Fund I Class	TWUIX	NAS CM	Open End	US Equity Large Cap Growth (Growth)	B-	C+	B	Down	Y	5,000,000
American Century Ultra® Fund Investor Class	TWCUX	NAS CM	Open End	US Equity Large Cap Growth (Growth)	B-	C+	B	Down	Y	2,500
American Century Ultra® Fund R Class	AULRX	NAS CM	Open End	US Equity Large Cap Growth (Growth)	C+	C+	B	Down	Y	2,500
American Century Ultra® Fund R5 Class	AULGX	NAS CM	Open End	US Equity Large Cap Growth (Growth)	B-	C+	B	Down	Y	0
American Century Ultra® Fund R6 Class	AULDX	NAS CM	Open End	US Equity Large Cap Growth (Growth)	B-	C+	B	Down	Y	0
American Century Ultra® Fund Y Class	AULYX	NAS CM	Open End	US Equity Large Cap Growth (Growth)	B-	C+	B	Down	Y	0
American Century Utilities Fund Investor Class	BULIX	NAS CM	Open End	Utilities Sector Equity (Utility)	C+	C	C+	Down	Y	2,500
American Century Value Fund A Class	TWADX	NAS CM	Open End	US Equity Large Cap Value (Growth)	C+	C	B	Up	Y	2,500
American Century Value Fund C Class	ACLCX	NAS CM	Open End	US Equity Large Cap Value (Growth)	C+	C	B	Up	Y	2,500
American Century Value Fund I Class	AVLIX	NAS CM	Open End	US Equity Large Cap Value (Growth)	C+	C	B	Up	Y	5,000,000
American Century Value Fund Investor Class	TWVLX	NAS CM	Open End	US Equity Large Cap Value (Growth)	C+	C	B	Up	Y	2,500
American Century Value Fund R Class	AVURX	NAS CM	Open End	US Equity Large Cap Value (Growth)	C+	C	B	Up	Y	2,500
American Century Value Fund R5 Class	AVUGX	NAS CM	Open End	US Equity Large Cap Value (Growth)	C+	C	B	Up	Y	0
American Century Value Fund R6 Class	AVUDX	NAS CM	Open End	US Equity Large Cap Value (Growth)	C+	C	B	Up	Y	0
American Century Value Fund Y Class	AVUYX	NAS CM	Open End	US Equity Large Cap Value (Growth)	C+	C	B		Y	0
American Funds 2010 Target Date Retirement Fund® Class A	AAATX	NAS CM	Open End	Target Date (Asset Alloc)	B	C+	A-	Up	Y	250
American Funds 2010 Target Date Retirement Fund® Class C	CCATX	NAS CM	Open End	Target Date (Asset Alloc)	B-	C	A-		Y	250
American Funds 2010 Target Date Retirement Fund® Class F-1	FAATX	NAS CM	Open End	Target Date (Asset Alloc)	B	C+	A-	Up	Y	250
American Funds 2010 Target Date Retirement Fund® Class F-2	FBATX	NAS CM	Open End	Target Date (Asset Alloc)	B	C+	A		Y	250
American Funds 2010 Target Date Retirement Fund® Class F-3	DJTFX	NAS CM	Open End	Target Date (Asset Alloc)	B	C+	A		Y	1,000,000
American Funds 2010 Target Date Retirement Fund® Class R-1	RAATX	NAS CM	Open End	Target Date (Asset Alloc)	B-	C	A-		Y	250

★ Expanded analysis of this fund is included in Section II.

Min Additional Investment	TOTAL RETURNS 3-Month Total Return	6-Month Total Return	1-Year Total Return	3-Year Total Return	5-Year Total Return	PERFORMANCE Dividend Yield (TTM)	Expense Ratio	3-Yr Std Deviation	3-Year Beta	ASSETS NAV	Total Assets (MIL)	ASSET ALLOCATION & TURNOVER %Cash	%Stocks	%Bonds	%Other	Turnover Ratio	BULL & BEAR Last Bull Market Total Return	Last Bear Market Total Return	FEES Front End Fee (%)	Back End Fee (%)	Inception Date
50	3.48	15.76	4.36	30.40	29.07	0.25	2.11	9.84	0.78	7.71	782.1	3	76	22	0	58	19.94	-16.31		1.00	Nov-01
50	3.72	16.41	5.65	35.00	36.90	1.33	0.91	9.81	0.78	7.8	782.1	3	76	22	0	58	20.79	-15.84			Aug-00
50	3.69	16.29	5.38	34.08	35.57	1.15	1.11	9.79	0.78	7.85	782.1	3	76	22	0	58	20.54	-15.91			Feb-96
50	3.53	16.00	4.80	32.16	32.13	0.69	1.61	9.79	0.77	7.9	782.1	3	76	22	0	58	20.14	-15.97			Mar-05
	3.85	16.56	5.64	34.69	36.19	1.33	0.91	9.84	0.78	7.81	782.1	3	76	22	0	58	20.54	-15.91			Apr-17
	3.73	16.46	5.70	35.53	37.90	1.47	0.76	9.81	0.78	7.78	782.1	3	76	22	0	58	20.55	-15.91			Jul-13
50	2.99	11.20	5.17	18.81	21.17	1.42	1.26	5.82	0.45	5.64	417.3	2	42	56	0	53	12.11	-7.16	5.75		Oct-96
50	2.84	10.83	4.32	16.16	16.79	0.77	2.01	5.81	0.45	5.55	417.3	2	42	56	0	53	11.55	-7.33		1.00	Sep-04
50	3.29	11.41	5.64	20.39	24.05	1.84	0.81	5.83	0.45	5.65	417.3	2	42	56	0	53	12.33	-6.78			Aug-00
50	3.23	11.31	5.44	19.91	22.85	1.65	1.01	5.87	0.45	5.65	417.3	2	42	56	0	53	12.24	-7.04			Feb-96
50	2.93	11.10	4.93	18.01	19.85	1.19	1.51	5.86	0.45	5.63	417.3	2	42	56	0	53	11.98	-7.11			Mar-05
	3.28	11.39	5.64	20.40	23.36	1.83	0.81	5.85	0.45	5.66	417.3	2	42	56	0	53	12.24	-7.04			Apr-17
	3.14	11.49	5.80	20.93	24.97	1.97	0.66	5.84	0.45	5.65	417.3	2	42	56	0	53	12.24	-7.04			Jul-13
50	3.46	13.93	5.28	27.02	28.03	1.23	1.29	8.06	0.64	6.51	909.9	2	60	37	0	55	16.58	-12.04	5.75		Oct-96
50	3.21	13.62	4.63	24.17	23.48	0.62	2.04	8.03	0.63	6.42	909.9	2	60	37	0	55	16.12	-12.33		1.00	Oct-01
50	3.50	14.12	5.72	28.61	30.95	1.63	0.84	8.03	0.63	6.53	909.9	2	60	37	0	55	16.98	-11.97			Aug-00
50	3.40	14.21	5.52	27.88	29.68	1.45	1.04	7.98	0.63	6.53	909.9	2	60	37	0	55	16.87	-12.05			Feb-96
50	3.36	13.89	5.05	25.92	26.43	1.01	1.54	7.97	0.63	6.47	909.9	2	60	37	0	55	16.53	-12.29			Aug-03
	3.65	14.29	5.88	28.42	30.22	1.63	0.84	8.06	0.63	6.54	909.9	2	60	37	0	55	16.87	-12.05			Apr-17
	3.57	14.22	5.88	29.24	31.80	1.77	0.69	8.06	0.64	6.52	909.9	2	60	37	0	55	16.87	-12.05			Jul-13
50	5.15	20.39	10.99	55.17	61.24	0.51	1.04	12.93	1.05	28.99	307.1	1	99	0	0	41	25.8	-16.21	5.75		Nov-04
50	4.92	19.92	10.11	51.66	55.29	0	1.79	12.93	1.05	28.35	307.1	1	99	0	0	41	25.18	-16.43		1.00	Nov-04
	5.29	20.55	11.14	55.38	61.45		0	12.93	1.05	29.21	307.1	1	99	0	0	41	25.8	-16.21			Apr-19
50	5.27	20.66	11.49	57.29	64.89	0.9	0.59	12.93	1.05	29.14	307.1	1	99	0	0	41	26	-15.98			Jul-05
50	5.21	20.52	11.25	56.30	63.29	0.72	0.79	12.93	1.05	29.07	307.1	1	99	0	0	41	25.88	-16.06			Jul-05
50	5.06	20.21	10.68	53.93	59.25	0.29	1.29	12.93	1.05	28.84	307.1	1	99	0	0	41	25.47	-16.24			Jul-05
	5.27	20.64	11.48	56.65	62.77	0.89	0.59	12.93	1.05	29.16	307.1	1	99	0	0	41	25.8	-16.21			Apr-17
	5.25	20.51	11.10	55.33	61.40		0.44	12.93	1.05	29.18	307.1	1	99	0	0	41	25.8	-16.21			Apr-19
	5.30	20.72	11.65	57.16	63.30	1.02	0.44	12.94	1.05	29.18	307.1	1	99	0	0	41	25.8	-16.21			Apr-17
50	3.20	21.81	9.37	70.29	85.55	0	1.22	14.38	1.06	46.4	12,123	2	98	0	0	17	26.12	-15.65	5.75		Oct-96
50	2.98	21.35	8.55	66.49	78.70	0	1.97	14.38	1.06	38.59	12,123	2	98	0	0	17	25.52	-15.88		1.00	Oct-01
50	3.30	22.07	9.87	72.63	89.76	0	0.77	14.38	1.06	50.65	12,123	2	98	0	0	17	26.42	-15.46			Nov-96
50	3.26	21.96	9.63	71.59	87.86	0	0.97	14.39	1.06	48.76	12,123	2	98	0	0	17	26.29	-15.55			Nov-81
50	3.11	21.65	9.09	69.02	83.23	0	1.47	14.38	1.06	45	12,123	2	98	0	0	17	25.94	-15.73			Aug-03
	3.30	22.09	9.86	72.35	88.69	0	0.77	14.38	1.06	50.68	12,123	2	98	0	0	17	26.29	-15.55			Apr-17
	3.34	22.15	10.01	73.40	91.19	0	0.62	14.4	1.06	50.73	12,123	2	98	0	0	17	26.29	-15.55			Jul-13
	3.35	22.17	10.02	72.89	89.29	0	0.62	14.38	1.06	50.79	12,123	2	98	0	0	17	26.29	-15.55			Apr-17
50	1.02	11.38	12.25	15.19	38.84	3.07	0.67	9.38	0.94	17.88	407.0	0	100	0	0	48	8.75	-4.69			Mar-93
50	3.11	15.72	4.31	26.67	33.60	1.39	1.23	13.36	1.08	8.31	2,703	2	98	0	0	48	22.51	-16.85	5.75		Oct-96
50	2.84	15.16	3.48	23.85	28.69	0.72	1.98	13.34	1.08	8.16	2,703	2	98	0	0	48	21.81	-17.01		1.00	Jun-01
	3.09	15.91	4.63	28.44	36.51	1.8	0.78	13.27	1.08	8.33	2,703	2	98	0	0	48	22.73	-16.63			Jul-97
50	3.17	15.83	4.56	27.74	35.41	1.61	0.98	13.36	1.08	8.32	2,703	2	98	0	0	48	22.41	-16.58			Sep-93
50	2.92	15.42	3.93	25.72	31.92	1.16	1.48	13.32	1.08	8.31	2,703	2	98	0	0	48	22.16	-16.79			Jul-05
	3.09	15.91	4.75	28.12	35.80	1.8	0.78	13.28	1.08	8.33	2,703	2	98	0	0	48	22.41	-16.58			Apr-17
	3.12	15.99	4.91	29.02	37.54	1.93	0.63	13.34	1.08	8.33	2,703	2	98	0	0	48	22.41	-16.58			Jul-13
	3.12	15.99	4.91	28.53	36.24	1.93	0.63	13.32	1.08	8.33	2,703	2	98	0	0	48	22.41	-16.58			Apr-17
50	2.49	8.93	6.19	18.77	24.07	1.88	0.67	4.54	0.89	11.09	3,349	6	39	55	0	8	11.3	-6.87	5.75		Feb-07
50	2.34	8.64	5.41	16.10	19.44	1.15	1.43	4.51	0.88	10.93	3,349	6	39	55	0	8	10.93	-7.13		1.00	Feb-14
50	2.41	8.88	6.11	18.59	23.77	1.88	0.7	4.53	0.88	11.03	3,349	6	39	55	0	8	11.41	-6.84			Feb-14
50	2.50	9.06	6.33	19.59	25.41	2.17	0.43	4.52	0.88	11.07	3,349	6	39	55	0	8	11.57	-6.74			Feb-14
50	2.58	9.14	6.48	19.93	26.02	2.22	0.33	4.55	0.89	11.1	3,349	6	39	55	0	8	11.57	-6.74			Jan-17
50	2.31	8.53	5.30	15.98	19.17	0.92	1.46	4.56	0.89	11.06	3,349	6	39	55	0	8	10.79	-7.21			Feb-07

	MARKET			FUND TYPE, CATEGORY & OBJECTIVE	RATINGS				MINIMUMS	
Fund Name	Ticker Symbol	Traded On	Fund Type	Category and (Prospectus Objective)	Overall Rating	Reward Rating	Risk Rating	Recent Up/ Downgrade	Open to New Investors	Min Initial Investment
American Funds 2010 Target Date Retirement Fund® Class R-2	RBATX	NAS CM	Open End	Target Date (Asset Alloc)	B-	C	A-		Y	250
American Funds 2010 Target Date Retirement Fund® Cls R-2E	RBEAX	NAS CM	Open End	Target Date (Asset Alloc)	B	C	A-	Up	Y	250
American Funds 2010 Target Date Retirement Fund® Class R-3	RCATX	NAS CM	Open End	Target Date (Asset Alloc)	B	C+	A-	Up	Y	250
American Funds 2010 Target Date Retirement Fund® Class R-4	RDATX	NAS CM	Open End	Target Date (Asset Alloc)	B	C+	A-	Up	Y	250
American Funds 2010 Target Date Retirement Fund® Class R-5	REATX	NAS CM	Open End	Target Date (Asset Alloc)	B	C+	A-		Y	250
American Funds 2010 Target Date Retirement Fund® Cls R-5E	RHATX	NAS CM	Open End	Target Date (Asset Alloc)	B	C+	A-		Y	250
American Funds 2010 Target Date Retirement Fund® Class R-6	RFTTX	NAS CM	Open End	Target Date (Asset Alloc)	B	C+	A		Y	250
American Funds 2015 Target Date Retirement Fund® Class A	AABTX	NAS CM	Open End	Target Date (Asset Alloc)	B	C+	A-	Up	Y	250
American Funds 2015 Target Date Retirement Fund® Class C	CCBTX	NAS CM	Open End	Target Date (Asset Alloc)	B-	C	A-		Y	250
American Funds 2015 Target Date Retirement Fund® Class F-1	FAKTX	NAS CM	Open End	Target Date (Asset Alloc)	B	C+	A-	Up	Y	250
American Funds 2015 Target Date Retirement Fund® Class F-2	FBBTX	NAS CM	Open End	Target Date (Asset Alloc)	B	C+	A		Y	250
American Funds 2015 Target Date Retirement Fund® Class F-3	FDBTX	NAS CM	Open End	Target Date (Asset Alloc)	B	C+	A		Y	1,000,000
American Funds 2015 Target Date Retirement Fund® Class R-1	RAJTX	NAS CM	Open End	Target Date (Asset Alloc)	B-	C	A-	Up	Y	250
American Funds 2015 Target Date Retirement Fund® Class R-2	RBJTX	NAS CM	Open End	Target Date (Asset Alloc)	B-	C	A-		Y	250
American Funds 2015 Target Date Retirement Fund® Cls R-2E	RBEJX	NAS CM	Open End	Target Date (Asset Alloc)	B	C	A-	Up	Y	250
American Funds 2015 Target Date Retirement Fund® Class R-3	RCJTX	NAS CM	Open End	Target Date (Asset Alloc)	B	C	A-	Up	Y	250
American Funds 2015 Target Date Retirement Fund® Class R-4	RDBTX	NAS CM	Open End	Target Date (Asset Alloc)	B	C+	A-	Up	Y	250
American Funds 2015 Target Date Retirement Fund® Class R-5	REJTX	NAS CM	Open End	Target Date (Asset Alloc)	B	C+	A		Y	250
American Funds 2015 Target Date Retirement Fund® Cls R-5E	RHBTX	NAS CM	Open End	Target Date (Asset Alloc)	B	C+	A		Y	250
American Funds 2015 Target Date Retirement Fund® Class R-6	RFJTX	NAS CM	Open End	Target Date (Asset Alloc)	B	C+	A		Y	250
American Funds 2020 Target Date Retirement Fund® Class A	AACTX	NAS CM	Open End	Target Date (Asset Alloc)	B	C+	A	Up	Y	250
American Funds 2020 Target Date Retirement Fund® Class C	CCCTX	NAS CM	Open End	Target Date (Asset Alloc)	B	C	A-	Up	Y	250
American Funds 2020 Target Date Retirement Fund® Class F-1	FAOTX	NAS CM	Open End	Target Date (Asset Alloc)	B	C+	A	Up	Y	250
American Funds 2020 Target Date Retirement Fund® Class F-2	FBCTX	NAS CM	Open End	Target Date (Asset Alloc)	B	C+	A	Up	Y	250
American Funds 2020 Target Date Retirement Fund® Class F-3	FCCTX	NAS CM	Open End	Target Date (Asset Alloc)	B	C+	A	Up	Y	1,000,000
American Funds 2020 Target Date Retirement Fund® Class R-1	RACTX	NAS CM	Open End	Target Date (Asset Alloc)	B	C	A-	Up	Y	250
American Funds 2020 Target Date Retirement Fund® Class R-2	RBCTX	NAS CM	Open End	Target Date (Asset Alloc)	B	C	A-	Up	Y	250
American Funds 2020 Target Date Retirement Fund® Cls R-2E	RBEHX	NAS CM	Open End	Target Date (Asset Alloc)	B	C	A-	Up	Y	250
American Funds 2020 Target Date Retirement Fund® Class R-3	RCCTX	NAS CM	Open End	Target Date (Asset Alloc)	B	C	A	Up	Y	250
American Funds 2020 Target Date Retirement Fund® Class R-4	RDCTX	NAS CM	Open End	Target Date (Asset Alloc)	B	C+	A	Up	Y	250
American Funds 2020 Target Date Retirement Fund® Class R-5	RECTX	NAS CM	Open End	Target Date (Asset Alloc)	B	C+	A	Up	Y	250
American Funds 2020 Target Date Retirement Fund® Cls R-5E	RHCTX	NAS CM	Open End	Target Date (Asset Alloc)	B	C+	A	Up	Y	250
American Funds 2020 Target Date Retirement Fund® Class R-6	RRCTX	NAS CM	Open End	Target Date (Asset Alloc)	B	C+	A		Y	250
American Funds 2025 Target Date Retirement Fund® Class A	AADTX	NAS CM	Open End	Target Date (Asset Alloc)	B	C	A	Up	Y	250
American Funds 2025 Target Date Retirement Fund® Class C	CCDTX	NAS CM	Open End	Target Date (Asset Alloc)	B	C	A-	Up	Y	250
American Funds 2025 Target Date Retirement Fund® Class F-1	FAPTX	NAS CM	Open End	Target Date (Asset Alloc)	B	C	A	Up	Y	250
American Funds 2025 Target Date Retirement Fund® Class F-2	FBDTX	NAS CM	Open End	Target Date (Asset Alloc)	B	C	A	Up	Y	250
American Funds 2025 Target Date Retirement Fund® Class F-3	FDDTX	NAS CM	Open End	Target Date (Asset Alloc)	B	C	A	Up	Y	1,000,000
American Funds 2025 Target Date Retirement Fund® Class R-1	RADTX	NAS CM	Open End	Target Date (Asset Alloc)	B	C	A-	Up	Y	250
American Funds 2025 Target Date Retirement Fund® Class R-2	RBDTX	NAS CM	Open End	Target Date (Asset Alloc)	B	C	A-	Up	Y	250
American Funds 2025 Target Date Retirement Fund® Cls R-2E	RBEDX	NAS CM	Open End	Target Date (Asset Alloc)	B	C	A	Up	Y	250
American Funds 2025 Target Date Retirement Fund® Class R-3	RCDTX	NAS CM	Open End	Target Date (Asset Alloc)	B	C	A	Up	Y	250
American Funds 2025 Target Date Retirement Fund® Class R-4	RDDTX	NAS CM	Open End	Target Date (Asset Alloc)	B	C	A	Up	Y	250
American Funds 2025 Target Date Retirement Fund® Class R-5	REDTX	NAS CM	Open End	Target Date (Asset Alloc)	B	C	A	Up	Y	250
American Funds 2025 Target Date Retirement Fund® Cls R-5E	RHDTX	NAS CM	Open End	Target Date (Asset Alloc)	B	C	A	Up	Y	250
American Funds 2025 Target Date Retirement Fund® Class R-6	RFDTX	NAS CM	Open End	Target Date (Asset Alloc)	B	C+	A	Up	Y	250
American Funds 2030 Target Date Retirement Fund® Class A	AAETX	NAS CM	Open End	Target Date (Asset Alloc)	B-	C	A-	Up	Y	250
American Funds 2030 Target Date Retirement Fund® Class C	CCETX	NAS CM	Open End	Target Date (Asset Alloc)	B-	C	A-	Up	Y	250
American Funds 2030 Target Date Retirement Fund® Class F-1	FAETX	NAS CM	Open End	Target Date (Asset Alloc)	B-	C	A-	Up	Y	250
American Funds 2030 Target Date Retirement Fund® Class F-2	FBETX	NAS CM	Open End	Target Date (Asset Alloc)	B-	C	A-		Y	250
American Funds 2030 Target Date Retirement Fund® Class F-3	FCETX	NAS CM	Open End	Target Date (Asset Alloc)	B	C	A-	Up	Y	1,000,000
American Funds 2030 Target Date Retirement Fund® Class R-1	RAETX	NAS CM	Open End	Target Date (Asset Alloc)	B-	C	A-	Up	Y	250

★ Expanded analysis of this fund is included in Section II.

	TOTAL RETURNS					PERFORMANCE				ASSETS		ASSET ALLOCATION & TURNOVER					BULL & BEAR		FEES		
Min Additional Investment	3-Month Total Return	6-Month Total Return	1-Year Total Return	3-Year Total Return	5-Year Total Return	Dividend Yield (TTM)	Expense Ratio	3-Yr Std Deviation	3-Year Beta	NAV	Total Assets (MIL)	%Cash	%Stocks	%Bonds	%Other	Turnover Ratio	Last Bull Market Total Return	Last Bear Market Total Return	Front End Fee (%)	Back End Fee (%)	Inception Date
50	2.34	8.54	5.32	16.07	19.57	1.15	1.43	4.47	0.87	10.93	3,349	6	39	55	0	8	11.02	-7.25			Feb-07
50	2.43	8.76	5.72	17.17	21.92	1.5	1.13	4.49	0.88	10.92	3,349	6	39	55	0	8	11.18	-6.97			Aug-14
50	2.41	8.79	5.80	17.62	22.02	1.6	0.99	4.5	0.88	11.01	3,349	6	39	55	0	8	11.11	-7			Feb-07
50	2.49	8.95	6.07	18.68	23.96	1.86	0.69	4.51	0.88	11.07	3,349	6	39	55	0	8	11.31	-6.87			Feb-07
50	2.57	9.19	6.49	19.82	25.90	2.16	0.39	4.55	0.89	11.16	3,349	6	39	55	0	8	11.57	-6.74			Feb-07
50	2.59	9.08	6.37	19.44	25.48	2.11	0.47	4.52	0.88	11.05	3,349	6	39	55	0	8	11.57	-6.74			Nov-15
50	2.67	9.22	6.57	20.07	26.17	2.22	0.33	4.53	0.88	11.13	3,349	6	39	55	0	8	11.54	-6.75			Jul-09
50	2.61	9.49	6.28	20.27	25.70	1.84	0.66	4.9	0.84	11.76	5,129	6	43	51	0	7	12.8	-8.97	5.75		Feb-07
50	2.38	9.14	5.54	17.63	21.09	1.14	1.43	4.93	0.85	11.58	5,129	6	43	51	0	7	12.31	-9.31		1.00	Feb-14
50	2.63	9.55	6.20	20.18	25.61	1.83	0.7	4.93	0.85	11.69	5,129	6	43	51	0	7	12.8	-9.02			Feb-14
50	2.62	9.71	6.52	21.16	27.27	2.12	0.43	4.93	0.85	11.75	5,129	6	43	51	0	7	12.97	-8.93			Feb-14
50	2.70	9.78	6.66	21.50	27.83	2.17	0.33	4.91	0.84	11.78	5,129	6	43	51	0	7	12.97	-8.93			Jan-17
50	2.39	9.15	5.39	17.48	20.84	1	1.46	4.88	0.84	11.56	5,129	6	43	51	0	7	12.31	-9.3			Feb-07
50	2.48	9.15	5.46	17.54	21.28	1.07	1.43	4.94	0.85	11.57	5,129	6	43	51	0	7	12.37	-9.3			Feb-07
50	2.57	9.35	5.81	18.72	23.62	1.45	1.13	4.95	0.85	11.57	5,129	6	43	51	0	7	12.57	-9.16			Aug-14
50	2.54	9.47	5.95	19.17	23.80	1.52	0.99	4.9	0.84	11.67	5,129	6	43	51	0	7	12.79	-9.23			Feb-07
50	2.61	9.60	6.34	20.28	25.79	1.8	0.68	4.93	0.85	11.75	5,129	6	43	51	0	7	12.95	-9.08			Feb-07
50	2.68	9.73	6.57	21.29	27.60	2.11	0.39	4.92	0.85	11.84	5,129	6	43	51	0	7	12.96	-8.93			Feb-07
50	2.62	9.64	6.45	20.99	27.14	2.05	0.47	4.91	0.84	11.71	5,129	6	43	51	0	7	12.97	-8.93			Nov-15
50	2.69	9.76	6.65	21.57	27.93	2.17	0.33	4.95	0.85	11.8	5,129	6	43	51	0	7	13.17	-8.95			Jul-09
50	2.72	10.04	6.16	23.14	28.49	1.6	0.68	5.42	0.78	12.82	15,535	6	46	48	0	2	14.79	-11.27	5.75		Feb-07
50	2.52	9.75	5.38	20.42	23.75	0.94	1.43	5.42	0.78	12.6	15,535	6	46	48	0	2	14.38	-11.49		1.00	Feb-14
50	2.65	10.01	6.11	23.04	28.34	1.61	0.7	5.41	0.78	12.74	15,535	6	46	48	0	2	14.88	-11.21			Feb-14
50	2.80	10.24	6.47	24.07	30.09	1.86	0.44	5.42	0.78	12.81	15,535	6	46	48	0	2	15.05	-11.12			Feb-14
50	2.80	10.21	6.53	24.38	30.60	1.92	0.34	5.44	0.79	12.84	15,535	6	46	48	0	2	15.05	-11.12			Jan-17
50	2.51	9.72	5.34	20.24	23.58	0.84	1.46	5.43	0.78	12.64	15,535	6	46	48	0	2	14.31	-11.51			Feb-07
50	2.52	9.66	5.39	20.38	23.89	0.87	1.44	5.42	0.78	12.59	15,535	6	46	48	0	2	14.36	-11.61			Feb-07
50	2.60	9.84	5.67	21.39	26.16	1.27	1.14	5.37	0.78	12.61	15,535	6	46	48	0	2	14.65	-11.34			Aug-14
50	2.66	9.94	5.84	22.02	26.49	1.29	0.99	5.36	0.78	12.71	15,535	6	46	48	0	2	14.66	-11.43			Feb-07
50	2.72	10.06	6.21	23.09	28.51	1.57	0.69	5.45	0.79	12.8	15,535	6	46	48	0	2	14.8	-11.27			Feb-07
50	2.78	10.23	6.51	24.22	30.43	1.86	0.39	5.4	0.78	12.92	15,535	6	46	48	0	2	15.05	-11.12			Feb-07
50	2.81	10.26	6.42	23.87	30.03	1.81	0.48	5.39	0.78	12.78	15,535	6	46	48	0	2	15.05	-11.12			Nov-15
50	2.79	10.27	6.51	24.38	30.73	1.92	0.34	5.41	0.78	12.88	15,535	6	46	48	0	2	15.02	-11.14			Jul-09
50	2.91	11.39	6.00	27.11	31.87	1.3	0.7	6.53	0.83	13.78	21,272	6	55	38	0	0	17.84	-14.43	5.75		Feb-07
50	2.73	11.00	5.25	24.28	27.00	0.66	1.45	6.48	0.82	13.52	21,272	6	55	38	0	0	17.43	-14.81		1.00	Feb-14
50	2.93	11.39	6.03	27.09	31.83	1.3	0.72	6.5	0.82	13.69	21,272	6	55	38	0	0	17.94	-14.54			Feb-14
50	2.91	11.49	6.30	28.12	33.52	1.55	0.46	6.52	0.83	13.77	21,272	6	55	38	0	0	18.11	-14.45			Feb-14
50	2.98	11.56	6.36	28.33	33.93	1.61	0.36	6.48	0.82	13.8	21,272	6	55	38	0	0	18.11	-14.45			Jan-17
50	2.73	10.98	5.25	24.23	26.82	0.6	1.48	6.46	0.82	13.54	21,272	6	55	38	0	0	17.36	-14.79			Feb-07
50	2.66	10.94	5.18	24.26	27.13	0.59	1.46	6.54	0.83	13.48	21,272	6	55	38	0	0	17.34	-14.72			Feb-07
50	2.80	11.15	5.51	25.41	29.50	0.95	1.16	6.47	0.82	13.55	21,272	6	55	38	0	0	17.7	-14.67			Aug-14
50	2.86	11.25	5.70	25.99	29.84	1.01	1.01	6.46	0.82	13.64	21,272	6	55	38	0	0	17.61	-14.6			Feb-07
50	2.91	11.42	6.06	27.10	31.89	1.28	0.71	6.54	0.83	13.75	21,272	6	55	38	0	0	17.87	-14.53			Feb-07
50	2.96	11.56	6.34	28.23	33.82	1.55	0.41	6.5	0.82	13.89	21,272	6	55	38	0	0	18.11	-14.45			Feb-07
50	2.92	11.52	6.25	27.94	33.37	1.5	0.5	6.52	0.83	13.74	21,272	6	55	38	0	0	18.11	-14.45			Nov-15
50	2.97	11.60	6.34	28.41	34.14	1.6	0.36	6.52	0.83	13.85	21,272	6	55	38	0	0	18.2	-14.4			Jul-09
50	2.99	12.82	5.84	32.64	37.26	1.17	0.72	7.74	0.87	14.78	23,124	7	65	28	0	0	19.04	-15.82	5.75		Feb-07
50	2.83	12.40	5.12	29.65	32.09	0.56	1.47	7.74	0.87	14.5	23,124	7	65	28	0	0	18.59	-16.01		1.00	Feb-14
50	2.94	12.75	5.81	32.53	37.05	1.18	0.74	7.71	0.87	14.67	23,124	7	65	28	0	0	19.1	-15.75			Feb-14
50	3.13	12.99	6.15	33.68	38.94	1.43	0.47	7.73	0.87	14.78	23,124	7	65	28	0	0	19.28	-15.66			Feb-14
50	3.06	12.97	6.21	33.97	39.45	1.49	0.38	7.73	0.87	14.8	23,124	7	65	28	0	0	19.28	-15.66			Jan-17
50	2.75	12.34	5.02	29.51	31.85	0.43	1.5	7.75	0.87	14.56	23,124	7	65	28	0	0	18.42	-16			Feb-07

	MARKET			FUND TYPE, CATEGORY & OBJECTIVE	RATINGS					MINIMUMS
Fund Name	Ticker Symbol	Traded On	Fund Type	Category and (Prospectus Objective)	Overall Rating	Reward Rating	Risk Rating	Recent Up/ Downgrade	Open to New Investors	Min Initial Investment
American Funds 2030 Target Date Retirement Fund® Class R-2	RBETX	NAS CM	Open End	Target Date (Asset Alloc)	B-	C	A-	Up	Y	250
American Funds 2030 Target Date Retirement Fund® Cls R-2E	RBEEX	NAS CM	Open End	Target Date (Asset Alloc)	B-	C	A-	Up	Y	250
American Funds 2030 Target Date Retirement Fund® Class R-3	RCETX	NAS CM	Open End	Target Date (Asset Alloc)	B-	C	A-	Up	Y	250
American Funds 2030 Target Date Retirement Fund® Class R-4	RDETX	NAS CM	Open End	Target Date (Asset Alloc)	B-	C	A-	Up	Y	250
American Funds 2030 Target Date Retirement Fund® Class R-5	REETX	NAS CM	Open End	Target Date (Asset Alloc)	B-	C	A-		Y	250
American Funds 2030 Target Date Retirement Fund® Cls R-5E	RHETX	NAS CM	Open End	Target Date (Asset Alloc)	B-	C	A-	Up	Y	250
American Funds 2030 Target Date Retirement Fund® Class R-6	RFETX	NAS CM	Open End	Target Date (Asset Alloc)	B	C	A-	Up	Y	250
American Funds 2035 Target Date Retirement Fund® Class A	AAFTX	NAS CM	Open End	Target Date (Asset Alloc)	B-	C	B+	Up	Y	250
American Funds 2035 Target Date Retirement Fund® Class C	CCFTX	NAS CM	Open End	Target Date (Asset Alloc)	B-	C	B+	Up	Y	250
American Funds 2035 Target Date Retirement Fund® Class F-1	FAQTX	NAS CM	Open End	Target Date (Asset Alloc)	B-	C	B+	Up	Y	250
American Funds 2035 Target Date Retirement Fund® Class F-2	FBFTX	NAS CM	Open End	Target Date (Asset Alloc)	B-	C	B+	Up	Y	250
American Funds 2035 Target Date Retirement Fund® Class F-3	FDFTX	NAS CM	Open End	Target Date (Asset Alloc)	B-	C	B+	Up	Y	1,000,000
American Funds 2035 Target Date Retirement Fund® Class R-1	RAFTX	NAS CM	Open End	Target Date (Asset Alloc)	B-	C	B+	Up	Y	250
American Funds 2035 Target Date Retirement Fund® Class R-2	RBFTX	NAS CM	Open End	Target Date (Asset Alloc)	B-	C	B+	Up	Y	250
American Funds 2035 Target Date Retirement Fund® Cls R-2E	RBEFX	NAS CM	Open End	Target Date (Asset Alloc)	B-	C	B+	Up	Y	250
American Funds 2035 Target Date Retirement Fund® Class R-3	RCFTX	NAS CM	Open End	Target Date (Asset Alloc)	B-	C	B+	Up	Y	250
American Funds 2035 Target Date Retirement Fund® Class R-4	RDFTX	NAS CM	Open End	Target Date (Asset Alloc)	B-	C	B+	Up	Y	250
American Funds 2035 Target Date Retirement Fund® Class R-5	REFTX	NAS CM	Open End	Target Date (Asset Alloc)	B-	C	B+	Up	Y	250
American Funds 2035 Target Date Retirement Fund® Cls R-5E	RHFTX	NAS CM	Open End	Target Date (Asset Alloc)	B-	C	B+	Up	Y	250
American Funds 2035 Target Date Retirement Fund® Class R-6	RFFTX	NAS CM	Open End	Target Date (Asset Alloc)	B-	C	B+	Up	Y	250
American Funds 2040 Target Date Retirement Fund® Class A	AAGTX	NAS CM	Open End	Target Date (Asset Alloc)	B-	C	B+	Up	Y	250
American Funds 2040 Target Date Retirement Fund® Class C	CCGTX	NAS CM	Open End	Target Date (Asset Alloc)	B-	C	B+	Up	Y	250
American Funds 2040 Target Date Retirement Fund® Class F-1	FAUTX	NAS CM	Open End	Target Date (Asset Alloc)	B-	C	B+	Up	Y	250
American Funds 2040 Target Date Retirement Fund® Class F-2	FBGTX	NAS CM	Open End	Target Date (Asset Alloc)	B-	C	B+	Up	Y	250
American Funds 2040 Target Date Retirement Fund® Class F-3	FCGTX	NAS CM	Open End	Target Date (Asset Alloc)	B-	C	B+	Up	Y	1,000,000
American Funds 2040 Target Date Retirement Fund® Class R-1	RAKTX	NAS CM	Open End	Target Date (Asset Alloc)	B-	C	B+	Up	Y	250
American Funds 2040 Target Date Retirement Fund® Class R-2	RBKTX	NAS CM	Open End	Target Date (Asset Alloc)	B-	C	B+	Up	Y	250
American Funds 2040 Target Date Retirement Fund® Cls R-2E	RBEKX	NAS CM	Open End	Target Date (Asset Alloc)	B-	C	B+	Up	Y	250
American Funds 2040 Target Date Retirement Fund® Class R-3	RCKTX	NAS CM	Open End	Target Date (Asset Alloc)	B-	C	B+	Up	Y	250
American Funds 2040 Target Date Retirement Fund® Class R-4	RDGTX	NAS CM	Open End	Target Date (Asset Alloc)	B-	C	B+	Up	Y	250
American Funds 2040 Target Date Retirement Fund® Class R-5	REGTX	NAS CM	Open End	Target Date (Asset Alloc)	B-	C	B+	Up	Y	250
American Funds 2040 Target Date Retirement Fund® Cls R-5E	RHGTX	NAS CM	Open End	Target Date (Asset Alloc)	B-	C	B+	Up	Y	250
American Funds 2040 Target Date Retirement Fund® Class R-6	RFGTX	NAS CM	Open End	Target Date (Asset Alloc)	B-	C	B+	Up	Y	250
American Funds 2045 Target Date Retirement Fund® Class A	AAHTX	NAS CM	Open End	Target Date (Asset Alloc)	B-	C	B+	Up	Y	250
American Funds 2045 Target Date Retirement Fund® Class C	CCHTX	NAS CM	Open End	Target Date (Asset Alloc)	B-	C	B+	Up	Y	250
American Funds 2045 Target Date Retirement Fund® Class F-1	FATTX	NAS CM	Open End	Target Date (Asset Alloc)	B-	C	B+	Up	Y	250
American Funds 2045 Target Date Retirement Fund® Class F-2	FBHTX	NAS CM	Open End	Target Date (Asset Alloc)	B-	C	B+	Up	Y	250
American Funds 2045 Target Date Retirement Fund® Class F-3	FCHTX	NAS CM	Open End	Target Date (Asset Alloc)	B-	C	B+	Up	Y	1,000,000
American Funds 2045 Target Date Retirement Fund® Class R-1	RAHTX	NAS CM	Open End	Target Date (Asset Alloc)	B-	C	B+	Up	Y	250
American Funds 2045 Target Date Retirement Fund® Class R-2	RBHTX	NAS CM	Open End	Target Date (Asset Alloc)	B-	C	B+	Up	Y	250
American Funds 2045 Target Date Retirement Fund® Cls R-2E	RBHHX	NAS CM	Open End	Target Date (Asset Alloc)	B-	C	B+	Up	Y	250
American Funds 2045 Target Date Retirement Fund® Class R-3	RCHTX	NAS CM	Open End	Target Date (Asset Alloc)	B-	C	B+	Up	Y	250
American Funds 2045 Target Date Retirement Fund® Class R-4	RDHTX	NAS CM	Open End	Target Date (Asset Alloc)	B-	C	B+	Up	Y	250
American Funds 2045 Target Date Retirement Fund® Class R-5	REHTX	NAS CM	Open End	Target Date (Asset Alloc)	B-	C	B+	Up	Y	250
American Funds 2045 Target Date Retirement Fund® Cls R-5E	RHHTX	NAS CM	Open End	Target Date (Asset Alloc)	B-	C	B+	Up	Y	250
American Funds 2045 Target Date Retirement Fund® Class R-6	RFHTX	NAS CM	Open End	Target Date (Asset Alloc)	B-	C	B+	Up	Y	250
American Funds 2050 Target Date Retirement Fund® Class A	AALTX	NAS CM	Open End	Target Date (Asset Alloc)	B-	C	B+	Up	Y	250
American Funds 2050 Target Date Retirement Fund® Class C	CCITX	NAS CM	Open End	Target Date (Asset Alloc)	B-	C	B+	Up	Y	250
American Funds 2050 Target Date Retirement Fund® Class F-1	FAITX	NAS CM	Open End	Target Date (Asset Alloc)	B-	C	B+	Up	Y	250
American Funds 2050 Target Date Retirement Fund® Class F-2	FBITX	NAS CM	Open End	Target Date (Asset Alloc)	B-	C	B+	Up	Y	250
American Funds 2050 Target Date Retirement Fund® Class F-3	DITFX	NAS CM	Open End	Target Date (Asset Alloc)	B-	C	B+	Up	Y	1,000,000
American Funds 2050 Target Date Retirement Fund® Class R-1	RAITX	NAS CM	Open End	Target Date (Asset Alloc)	B-	C	B+	Up	Y	250

★ Expanded analysis of this fund is included in Section II.

	TOTAL RETURNS					PERFORMANCE				ASSETS		ASSET ALLOCATION & TURNOVER					BULL & BEAR		FEES		
Min Additional Investment	3-Month Total Return	6-Month Total Return	1-Year Total Return	3-Year Total Return	5-Year Total Return	Dividend Yield (TTM)	Expense Ratio	3-Yr Std Deviation	3-Year Beta	NAV	Total Assets (MIL.)	%Cash	%Stocks	%Bonds	%Other	Turnover Ratio	Last Bull Market Total Return	Last Bear Market Total Return	Front End Fee (%)	Back End Fee (%)	Inception Date
50	2.84	12.44	5.12	29.63	32.27	0.49	1.48	7.76	0.87	14.46	23,124	7	65	28	0	0	18.53	-15.94			Feb-07
50	2.89	12.52	5.43	30.84	34.60	0.83	1.18	7.75	0.87	14.55	23,124	7	65	28	0	0	18.86	-15.87			Aug-14
50	2.88	12.63	5.56	31.33	35.01	0.89	1.03	7.75	0.87	14.62	23,124	7	65	28	0	0	18.79	-15.92			Feb-07
50	3.00	12.85	5.91	32.62	37.17	1.16	0.73	7.74	0.87	14.75	23,124	7	65	28	0	0	19.06	-15.74			Feb-07
50	3.04	12.96	6.18	33.72	39.19	1.43	0.43	7.77	0.87	14.9	23,124	7	65	28	0	0	19.28	-15.66			Feb-07
50	3.07	12.94	6.11	33.41	38.71	1.38	0.52	7.75	0.87	14.74	23,124	7	65	28	0	0	19.28	-15.66			Nov-15
50	3.12	13.01	6.27	34.07	39.57	1.48	0.38	7.76	0.87	14.85	23,124	7	65	28	0	0	19.26	-15.61			Jul-09
50	3.11	14.66	5.72	37.38	41.48	1.02	0.72	9.18	0.96	15.25	18,453	7	77	16	0	0	19.24	-16.2	5.75		Feb-07
50	2.95	14.27	4.96	34.31	36.21	0.38	1.48	9.17	0.96	14.97	18,453	7	77	16	0	0	18.66	-16.38		1.00	Feb-14
50	3.12	14.66	5.75	37.27	41.35	1.02	0.75	9.15	0.95	15.17	18,453	7	77	16	0	0	19.18	-16.12			Feb-14
50	3.18	14.83	6.04	38.34	43.18	1.28	0.48	9.18	0.96	15.25	18,453	7	77	16	0	0	19.35	-16.03			Feb-14
50	3.17	14.89	6.09	38.72	43.70	1.32	0.39	9.14	0.95	15.27	18,453	7	77	16	0	0	19.35	-16.03			Jan-17
50	2.90	14.18	4.93	34.12	35.99	0.33	1.51	9.18	0.96	14.89	18,453	7	77	16	0	0	18.66	-16.36			Feb-07
50	2.89	14.25	4.99	34.19	36.30	0.33	1.49	9.16	0.96	14.91	18,453	7	77	16	0	0	18.74	-16.41			Feb-07
50	2.95	14.42	5.31	35.45	38.89	0.67	1.19	9.16	0.96	14.99	18,453	7	77	16	0	0	18.94	-16.25			Aug-14
50	3.00	14.50	5.43	36.01	39.25	0.74	1.04	9.17	0.96	15.08	18,453	7	77	16	0	0	19.01	-16.29			Feb-07
50	3.11	14.70	5.79	37.27	41.42	1	0.74	9.19	0.96	15.21	18,453	7	77	16	0	0	19.13	-16.12			Feb-07
50	3.22	14.86	6.06	38.53	43.50	1.26	0.44	9.18	0.96	15.38	18,453	7	77	16	0	0	19.35	-16.03			Feb-07
50	3.11	14.79	5.99	38.17	43.07	1.22	0.53	9.16	0.96	15.21	18,453	7	77	16	0	0	19.35	-16.03			Nov-15
50	3.16	14.84	6.14	38.81	43.81	1.32	0.39	9.15	0.95	15.32	18,453	7	77	16	0	0	19.33	-15.98			Jul-09
50	3.10	15.27	5.71	39.03	42.93	0.92	0.73	9.65	0.94	15.62	16,065	7	81	11	0	0	19.45	-16.46	5.75		Feb-07
50	2.95	14.84	4.91	35.90	37.54	0.31	1.49	9.67	0.94	15.32	16,065	7	81	11	0	0	18.97	-16.73		1.00	Feb-14
50	3.18	15.29	5.70	38.96	42.78	0.95	0.76	9.66	0.94	15.53	16,065	7	81	11	0	0	19.49	-16.47			Feb-14
50	3.23	15.44	5.96	40.11	44.57	1.18	0.49	9.68	0.94	15.62	16,065	7	81	11	0	0	19.66	-16.38			Feb-14
50	3.23	15.49	6.08	40.36	45.03	1.23	0.4	9.67	0.94	15.65	16,065	7	81	11	0	0	19.66	-16.38			Jan-17
50	2.95	14.85	4.89	35.81	37.32	0.23	1.52	9.68	0.94	15.31	16,065	7	81	11	0	0	19.06	-16.78			Feb-07
50	2.96	14.90	4.91	35.91	37.71	0.24	1.5	9.69	0.94	15.26	16,065	7	81	11	0	0	19.07	-16.69			Feb-07
50	3.01	15.04	5.22	37.09	40.20	0.58	1.2	9.67	0.94	15.37	16,065	7	81	11	0	0	19.25	-16.59			Aug-14
50	3.06	15.11	5.41	37.73	40.66	0.64	1.05	9.69	0.94	15.46	16,065	7	81	11	0	0	19.32	-16.56			Feb-07
50	3.11	15.32	5.69	39.02	42.75	0.9	0.75	9.67	0.94	15.58	16,065	7	81	11	0	0	19.58	-16.48			Feb-07
50	3.20	15.45	6.04	40.26	44.93	1.17	0.45	9.71	0.94	15.76	16,065	7	81	11	0	0	19.66	-16.38			Feb-07
50	3.24	15.49	5.91	39.84	44.44	1.13	0.54	9.68	0.94	15.58	16,065	7	81	11	0	0	19.66	-16.38			Nov-15
50	3.22	15.52	6.06	40.44	45.25	1.23	0.4	9.65	0.94	15.7	16,065	7	81	11	0	0	19.64	-16.33			Jul-09
50	3.18	15.56	5.67	39.94	43.92	0.86	0.72	9.88	0.93	15.89	11,753	7	83	10	0	0	19.48	-16.5	5.75		Feb-07
50	2.97	15.07	4.85	36.69	38.38	0.23	1.5	9.86	0.93	15.57	11,753	7	83	10	0	0	19.13	-16.76		1.00	Feb-14
50	3.13	15.50	5.61	39.76	43.63	0.9	0.76	9.87	0.93	15.79	11,753	7	83	10	0	0	19.65	-16.5			Feb-14
50	3.24	15.72	5.99	40.98	45.49	1.12	0.49	9.87	0.93	15.9	11,753	7	83	10	0	0	19.82	-16.42			Feb-14
50	3.24	15.70	6.03	41.14	45.95	1.16	0.4	9.88	0.93	15.91	11,753	7	83	10	0	0	19.82	-16.42			Jan-17
50	2.98	15.01	4.82	36.58	38.23	0.15	1.52	9.83	0.93	15.55	11,753	7	83	10	0	0	18.93	-16.7			Feb-07
50	2.99	15.08	4.88	36.75	38.65	0.18	1.5	9.86	0.93	15.49	11,753	7	83	10	0	0	19.03	-16.73			Feb-07
50	3.09	15.26	5.16	37.97	41.24	0.5	1.2	9.9	0.93	15.63	11,753	7	83	10	0	0	19.4	-16.63			Aug-14
50	3.08	15.36	5.31	38.55	41.53	0.58	1.05	9.85	0.93	15.69	11,753	7	83	10	0	0	19.4	-16.61			Feb-07
50	3.18	15.52	5.66	39.81	43.68	0.84	0.75	9.83	0.93	15.85	11,753	7	83	10	0	0	19.5	-16.41			Feb-07
50	3.28	15.72	5.99	41.10	45.92	1.1	0.46	9.87	0.93	16.04	11,753	7	83	10	0	0	19.82	-16.42			Feb-07
50	3.19	15.63	5.87	40.70	45.34	1.07	0.54	9.86	0.93	15.83	11,753	7	83	10	0	0	19.82	-16.42			Nov-15
50	3.29	15.71	6.08	41.39	46.24	1.16	0.4	9.87	0.93	15.98	11,753	7	83	10	0	0	19.67	-16.37			Jul-09
50	3.17	15.66	5.68	40.43	44.32	0.79	0.74	9.97	0.93	15.58	9,824	7	84	9	0	0	19.41	-16.41	5.75		Feb-07
50	2.97	15.18	4.82	37.14	38.84	0.18	1.51	10.02	0.93	15.25	9,824	7	84	9	0	0	19.09	-16.78		1.00	Feb-14
50	3.19	15.69	5.61	40.34	44.09	0.82	0.77	9.99	0.93	15.48	9,824	7	84	9	0	0	19.61	-16.52			Feb-14
50	3.24	15.76	5.90	41.37	46.01	1.02	0.51	10.04	0.93	15.57	9,824	7	84	9	0	0	19.78	-16.43			Feb-14
50	3.30	15.88	6.04	41.73	46.50	1.09	0.41	9.98	0.93	15.61	9,824	7	84	9	0	0	19.78	-16.43			Jan-17
50	2.97	15.20	4.80	37.08	38.68	0.1	1.54	9.99	0.93	15.23	9,824	7	84	9	0	0	18.94	-16.73			Feb-07

	MARKET			FUND TYPE, CATEGORY & OBJECTIVE	RATINGS				MINIMUMS	
Fund Name	Ticker Symbol	Traded On	Fund Type	Category and (Prospectus Objective)	Overall Rating	Reward Rating	Risk Rating	Recent Up/ Downgrade	Open to New Investors	Min Initial Investment
American Funds 2050 Target Date Retirement Fund® Class R-2	RBITX	NAS CM	Open End	Target Date (Asset Alloc)	B-	C	B+	Up	Y	250
American Funds 2050 Target Date Retirement Fund® Cls R-2E	RBHEX	NAS CM	Open End	Target Date (Asset Alloc)	B-	C	B+	Up	Y	250
American Funds 2050 Target Date Retirement Fund® Class R-3	RCITX	NAS CM	Open End	Target Date (Asset Alloc)	B-	C	B+	Up	Y	250
American Funds 2050 Target Date Retirement Fund® Class R-4	RDITX	NAS CM	Open End	Target Date (Asset Alloc)	B-	C	B+	Up	Y	250
American Funds 2050 Target Date Retirement Fund® Class R-5	REITX	NAS CM	Open End	Target Date (Asset Alloc)	B-	C	B+	Up	Y	250
American Funds 2050 Target Date Retirement Fund® Cls R-5E	RHITX	NAS CM	Open End	Target Date (Asset Alloc)	B-	C	B+	Up	Y	250
American Funds 2050 Target Date Retirement Fund® Class R-6	RFITX	NAS CM	Open End	Target Date (Asset Alloc)	B-	C	B+	Up	Y	250
American Funds 2055 Target Date Retirement Fund® Class A	AAMTX	NAS CM	Open End	Target Date (Asset Alloc)	B-	C	B+	Up	Y	250
American Funds 2055 Target Date Retirement Fund® Class C	CCJTX	NAS CM	Open End	Target Date (Asset Alloc)	B-	C	B+	Up	Y	250
American Funds 2055 Target Date Retirement Fund® Class F-1	FAJTX	NAS CM	Open End	Target Date (Asset Alloc)	B-	C	B+	Up	Y	250
American Funds 2055 Target Date Retirement Fund® Class F-2	FBJTX	NAS CM	Open End	Target Date (Asset Alloc)	B-	C	B+	Up	Y	250
American Funds 2055 Target Date Retirement Fund® Class F-3	FCJTX	NAS CM	Open End	Target Date (Asset Alloc)	B-	C	B+	Up	Y	1,000,000
American Funds 2055 Target Date Retirement Fund® Class R-1	RAMTX	NAS CM	Open End	Target Date (Asset Alloc)	B-	C	B+	Up	Y	250
American Funds 2055 Target Date Retirement Fund® Class R-2	RBMTX	NAS CM	Open End	Target Date (Asset Alloc)	B-	C	B+	Up	Y	250
American Funds 2055 Target Date Retirement Fund® Cls R-2E	RBEMX	NAS CM	Open End	Target Date (Asset Alloc)	B-	C	B+	Up	Y	250
American Funds 2055 Target Date Retirement Fund® Class R-3	RCMTX	NAS CM	Open End	Target Date (Asset Alloc)	B-	C	B+	Up	Y	250
American Funds 2055 Target Date Retirement Fund® Class R-4	RDJTX	NAS CM	Open End	Target Date (Asset Alloc)	B-	C	B+	Up	Y	250
American Funds 2055 Target Date Retirement Fund® Class R-5	REKTX	NAS CM	Open End	Target Date (Asset Alloc)	B-	C	B+	Up	Y	250
American Funds 2055 Target Date Retirement Fund® Cls R-5E	RHJTX	NAS CM	Open End	Target Date (Asset Alloc)	B-	C	B+	Up	Y	250
American Funds 2055 Target Date Retirement Fund® Class R-6	RFKTX	NAS CM	Open End	Target Date (Asset Alloc)	B-	C	B+	Up	Y	250
American Funds 2060 Target Date Retirement Fund® Class A	AANTX	NAS CM	Open End	Target Date (Asset Alloc)	B-	C	B+	Up	Y	250
American Funds 2060 Target Date Retirement Fund® Class C	CCKTX	NAS CM	Open End	Target Date (Asset Alloc)	B-	C	B+	Up	Y	250
American Funds 2060 Target Date Retirement Fund® Class F-1	FAWTX	NAS CM	Open End	Target Date (Asset Alloc)	B-	C	B+	Up	Y	250
American Funds 2060 Target Date Retirement Fund® Class F-2	FBKTX	NAS CM	Open End	Target Date (Asset Alloc)	B-	C	B+	Up	Y	250
American Funds 2060 Target Date Retirement Fund® Class F-3	FCKTX	NAS CM	Open End	Target Date (Asset Alloc)	B-	C	B+	Up	Y	1,000,000
American Funds 2060 Target Date Retirement Fund® Class R-1	RANTX	NAS CM	Open End	Target Date (Asset Alloc)	B-	C	B+	Up	Y	250
American Funds 2060 Target Date Retirement Fund® Class R-2	RBNTX	NAS CM	Open End	Target Date (Asset Alloc)	B-	C	B+	Up	Y	250
American Funds 2060 Target Date Retirement Fund® Cls R-2E	RBENX	NAS CM	Open End	Target Date (Asset Alloc)	B-	C	B+	Up	Y	250
American Funds 2060 Target Date Retirement Fund® Class R-3	RCNTX	NAS CM	Open End	Target Date (Asset Alloc)	B-	C	B+	Up	Y	250
American Funds 2060 Target Date Retirement Fund® Class R-4	RDKTX	NAS CM	Open End	Target Date (Asset Alloc)	B-	C	B+	Up	Y	250
American Funds 2060 Target Date Retirement Fund® Class R-5	REMTX	NAS CM	Open End	Target Date (Asset Alloc)	B-	C	B+	Up	Y	250
American Funds 2060 Target Date Retirement Fund® Cls R-5E	RHKTX	NAS CM	Open End	Target Date (Asset Alloc)	B-	C	B+	Up	Y	250
American Funds 2060 Target Date Retirement Fund® Class R-6	RFUTX	NAS CM	Open End	Target Date (Asset Alloc)	B-	C	B+	Up	Y	250
American Funds AMCAP Fund® Class 529-A	CAFAX	NAS CM	Open End	US Equity Large Cap Growth (Growth)	B-	C	B	Up	Y	250
American Funds AMCAP Fund® Class 529-C	CAFCX	NAS CM	Open End	US Equity Large Cap Growth (Growth)	B-	C	B	Up	Y	250
American Funds AMCAP Fund® Class 529-E	CAFEX	NAS CM	Open End	US Equity Large Cap Growth (Growth)	B-	C	B	Up	Y	250
American Funds AMCAP Fund® Class 529-F-1	CAFFX	NAS CM	Open End	US Equity Large Cap Growth (Growth)	B-	C	B		Y	250
American Funds AMCAP Fund® Class A	AMCPX	NAS CM	Open End	US Equity Large Cap Growth (Growth)	B-	C	B		Y	250
American Funds AMCAP Fund® Class C	AMPCX	NAS CM	Open End	US Equity Large Cap Growth (Growth)	B-	C	B	Up	Y	250
American Funds AMCAP Fund® Class F-1	AMPFX	NAS CM	Open End	US Equity Large Cap Growth (Growth)	B-	C	B	Up	Y	250
American Funds AMCAP Fund® Class F-2	AMCFX	NAS CM	Open End	US Equity Large Cap Growth (Growth)	B-	C	B		Y	250
American Funds AMCAP Fund® Class F-3	FMACX	NAS CM	Open End	US Equity Large Cap Growth (Growth)	B-	C	B		Y	1,000,000
American Funds AMCAP Fund® Class R-1	RAFAX	NAS CM	Open End	US Equity Large Cap Growth (Growth)	B-	C	B	Up	Y	250
American Funds AMCAP Fund® Class R-2	RAFBX	NAS CM	Open End	US Equity Large Cap Growth (Growth)	B-	C	B	Up	Y	250
American Funds AMCAP Fund® Class R-2E	RAEBX	NAS CM	Open End	US Equity Large Cap Growth (Growth)	B-	C	B	Up	Y	250
American Funds AMCAP Fund® Class R-3	RAFCX	NAS CM	Open End	US Equity Large Cap Growth (Growth)	B-	C	B	Up	Y	250
American Funds AMCAP Fund® Class R-4	RAFEX	NAS CM	Open End	US Equity Large Cap Growth (Growth)	B-	C	B	Up	Y	250
American Funds AMCAP Fund® Class R-5	RAFFX	NAS CM	Open End	US Equity Large Cap Growth (Growth)	B-	C	B		Y	250
American Funds AMCAP Fund® Class R-5E	RAEFX	NAS CM	Open End	US Equity Large Cap Growth (Growth)	B-	C	B		Y	250
American Funds AMCAP Fund® Class R-6	RAFGX	NAS CM	Open End	US Equity Large Cap Growth (Growth)	B-	C	B		Y	250
★ American Funds American Balanced Fund® Class 529-A	CLBAX	NAS CM	Open End	Moderate Alloc (Balanced)	B	C	A		Y	250
★ American Funds American Balanced Fund® Class 529-C	CLBCX	NAS CM	Open End	Moderate Alloc (Balanced)	B	C	A	Up	Y	250

★ Expanded analysis of this fund is included in Section II.

Min Additional Investment	TOTAL RETURNS: 3-Month Total Return	6-Month Total Return	1-Year Total Return	3-Year Total Return	5-Year Total Return	PERFORMANCE: Dividend Yield (TTM)	Expense Ratio	3-Yr Std Deviation	3-Year Beta	ASSETS: NAV	Total Assets (MIL)	ASSET ALLOCATION & TURNOVER: %Cash	%Stocks	%Bonds	%Other	Turnover Ratio	BULL & BEAR: Last Bull Market Total Return	Last Bear Market Total Return	FEES: Front End Fee (%)	Back End Fee (%)	Inception Date
50	3.04	15.28	4.88	37.17	39.08	0.11	1.51	9.99	0.93	15.24	9,824	7	84	9	0	0	18.99	-16.71			Feb-07
50	3.09	15.36	5.15	38.47	41.66	0.46	1.21	10	0.93	15.32	9,824	7	84	9	0	0	19.36	-16.64			Aug-14
50	3.14	15.52	5.39	39.09	42.03	0.51	1.07	9.98	0.93	15.4	9,824	7	84	9	0	0	19.32	-16.61			Feb-07
50	3.18	15.71	5.67	40.30	44.21	0.77	0.77	10	0.93	15.54	9,824	7	84	9	0	0	19.57	-16.43			Feb-07
50	3.21	15.85	5.94	41.55	46.32	1.03	0.47	10	0.93	15.71	9,824	7	84	9	0	0	19.78	-16.43			Feb-07
50	3.25	15.79	5.88	41.24	45.93	0.99	0.55	10	0.93	15.54	9,824	7	84	9	0	0	19.78	-16.43			Nov-15
50	3.29	15.90	6.09	41.89	46.81	1.08	0.41	9.98	0.93	15.67	9,824	7	84	9	0	0	19.76	-16.38			Jul-09
50	3.18	15.63	5.62	40.39	44.34	0.76	0.74	10.02	0.93	19.45	5,208	7	84	9	0	1	19.55	-16.5	5.75		Feb-10
50	3.02	15.26	4.89	37.19	38.84	0.14	1.51	9.96	0.92	19.1	5,208	7	84	9	0	1	19.16	-16.79		1.00	Feb-14
50	3.20	15.67	5.64	40.31	44.20	0.8	0.77	9.99	0.92	19.34	5,208	7	84	9	0	1	19.68	-16.53			Feb-14
50	3.23	15.83	5.92	41.36	45.94	1.01	0.51	10	0.92	19.46	5,208	7	84	9	0	1	19.85	-16.44			Feb-14
50	3.28	15.87	6.03	41.73	46.64	1.06	0.42	10	0.92	19.49	5,208	7	84	9	0	1	19.85	-16.44			Jan-17
50	3.03	15.26	4.86	37.14	38.66	0.15	1.54	9.96	0.92	19.03	5,208	7	84	9	0	1	18.99	-16.81			Feb-10
50	2.97	15.19	4.86	37.14	38.98	0.1	1.52	9.98	0.92	19.03	5,208	7	84	9	0	1	19.07	-16.76			Feb-10
50	3.12	15.42	5.22	38.50	41.78	0.47	1.21	9.99	0.92	19.16	5,208	7	84	9	0	1	19.44	-16.65			Aug-14
50	3.10	15.48	5.35	39.02	41.95	0.5	1.07	9.98	0.92	19.24	5,208	7	84	9	0	1	19.31	-16.62			Feb-10
50	3.18	15.67	5.63	40.29	44.13	0.76	0.77	10	0.92	19.41	5,208	7	84	9	0	1	19.63	-16.57			Feb-10
50	3.26	15.83	5.99	41.58	46.28	1	0.47	9.98	0.92	19.61	5,208	7	84	9	0	1	19.71	-16.38			Feb-10
50	3.30	15.82	5.88	41.25	45.93	0.96	0.56	9.97	0.92	19.4	5,208	7	84	9	0	1	19.85	-16.44			Nov-15
50	3.26	15.87	5.99	41.72	46.62	1.05	0.42	10.01	0.93	19.63	5,208	7	84	9	0	1	19.85	-16.44			Feb-10
50	3.19	15.57	5.64	40.27		0.65	0.76	10	0.92	12.91	1,670	7	84	9	0	3			5.75		Mar-15
50	3.07	15.28	4.91	37.18		0.07	1.53	10.03	0.92	12.75	1,670	7	84	9	0	3				1.00	Mar-15
50	3.19	15.66	5.60	40.15		0.69	0.79	10.01	0.92	12.92	1,670	7	84	9	0	3					Mar-15
50	3.26	15.80	5.94	41.20		0.85	0.53	9.99	0.92	12.97	1,670	7	84	9	0	3					Mar-15
50	3.27	15.84	5.94	41.70		0.91	0.44	10	0.92	12.94	1,670	7	84	9	0	3					Jan-17
50	3.05	15.31	4.95	37.27		0.12	1.56	9.99	0.92	12.8	1,670	7	84	9	0	3					Mar-15
50	3.07	15.27	4.89	37.06		0.06	1.54	9.98	0.92	12.75	1,670	7	84	9	0	3					Mar-15
50	3.13	15.49	5.23	38.35		0.36	1.24	9.98	0.92	12.82	1,670	7	84	9	0	3					Mar-15
50	3.13	15.46	5.31	38.86		0.43	1.09	10.02	0.92	12.84	1,670	7	84	9	0	3					Mar-15
50	3.19	15.68	5.63	40.14		0.64	0.79	10	0.92	12.91	1,670	7	84	9	0	3					Mar-15
50	3.25	15.87	5.95	41.53		0.86	0.49	9.97	0.92	12.99	1,670	7	84	9	0	3					Mar-15
50	3.27	15.85	5.93	41.04		0.83	0.58	9.98	0.92	12.93	1,670	7	84	9	0	3					Nov-15
50	3.33	15.86	6.00	41.66		0.9	0.44	9.98	0.92	13	1,670	7	84	9	0	3					Mar-15
50	3.06	17.16	5.07	49.58	56.99	0.46	0.74	12.38	0.98	31.84	67,763	9	91	0	0	32	24.06	-15.79	5.75		Feb-02
50	2.87	16.70	4.29	46.18	51.05	0	1.51	12.36	0.98	28.12	67,763	9	91	0	0	32	23.46	-16.04		1.00	Feb-02
50	2.98	17.01	4.83	48.52	55.15	0.3	0.97	12.37	0.98	30.91	67,763	9	91	0	0	32	23.88	-15.91			Mar-02
50	3.10	17.28	5.31	50.53	58.64	0.66	0.51	12.38	0.98	32.13	67,763	9	91	0	0	32	24.2	-15.72			Sep-02
50	3.09	17.18	5.15	49.91	57.62	0.52	0.66	12.38	0.98	32.23	67,763	9	91	0	0	32	24.13	-15.76	5.75		May-67
50	2.85	16.72	4.32	46.32	51.41	0	1.46	12.35	0.98	27.96	67,763	9	91	0	0	32	23.51	-16.01		1.00	Mar-01
50	3.08	17.15	5.07	49.57	57.15	0.42	0.74	12.38	0.98	31.93	67,763	9	91	0	0	32	24.11	-15.77			Mar-01
50	3.13	17.28	5.36	50.78	59.20	0.68	0.47	12.38	0.98	32.47	67,763	9	91	0	0	32	24.27	-15.68			Aug-08
	3.18	17.39	5.48	51.04	58.80	0.76	0.37	12.37	0.98	32.3	67,763	9	91	0	0	32	24.13	-15.76			Jan-17
50	2.88	16.75	4.34	46.37	51.53	0	1.46	12.36	0.98	28.82	67,763	9	91	0	0	32	23.54	-16.04			Jun-02
50	2.88	16.71	4.33	46.38	51.60	0	1.46	12.37	0.98	28.81	67,763	9	91	0	0	32	23.57	-16.02			May-02
50	2.93	16.90	4.63	47.73	54.48	0.19	1.16	12.38	0.98	31.78	67,763	9	91	0	0	32	23.87	-15.89			Aug-14
50	2.96	16.98	4.78	48.33	54.98	0.23	1.01	12.36	0.98	31.1	67,763	9	91	0	0	32	23.91	-15.87			Jun-02
50	3.08	17.16	5.11	49.68	57.32	0.45	0.71	12.37	0.98	31.92	67,763	9	91	0	0	32	24.13	-15.77			May-02
50	3.14	17.33	5.42	51.05	59.73	0.71	0.41	12.41	0.98	32.73	67,763	9	91	0	0	32	24.31	-15.68			May-02
50	3.11	17.31	5.34	50.71	58.52	0.7	0.5	12.38	0.98	32.29	67,763	9	91	0	0	32	24.13	-15.76			Nov-15
50	3.14	17.38	5.46	51.27	60.10	0.75	0.36	12.38	0.98	32.65	67,763	9	91	0	0	32	24.35	-15.61			May-09
50	2.78	11.45	6.88	29.80	42.22	1.76	0.65	7.01	0.56	27.28	146,710	6	62	32	0	72	17.38	-10.01	5.75		Feb-02
50	2.62	11.03	6.12	26.92	36.89	1.05	1.41	7	0.56	27.29	146,710	6	62	32	0	72	16.81	-10.27		1.00	Feb-02

		MARKET			FUND TYPE, CATEGORY & OBJECTIVE	RATINGS				MINIMUMS	
	Fund Name	Ticker Symbol	Traded On	Fund Type	Category and (Prospectus Objective)	Overall Rating	Reward Rating	Risk Rating	Recent Up/ Downgrade	Open to New Investors	Min Initial Investment
★	American Funds American Balanced Fund® Class 529-E	CLBEX	NAS CM	Open End	Moderate Alloc (Balanced)	B	C	A		Y	250
★	American Funds American Balanced Fund® Class 529-F	CLBFX	NAS CM	Open End	Moderate Alloc (Balanced)	B	C	A		Y	250
★	American Funds American Balanced Fund® Class A	ABALX	NAS CM	Open End	Moderate Alloc (Balanced)	B	C	A		Y	250
★	American Funds American Balanced Fund® Class C	BALCX	NAS CM	Open End	Moderate Alloc (Balanced)	B	C	A	Up	Y	250
★	American Funds American Balanced Fund® Class F-1	BALFX	NAS CM	Open End	Moderate Alloc (Balanced)	B	C	A		Y	250
★	American Funds American Balanced Fund® Class F-2	AMBFX	NAS CM	Open End	Moderate Alloc (Balanced)	B	C	A		Y	250
	American Funds American Balanced Fund® Class F-3	AFMBX	NAS CM	Open End	Moderate Alloc (Balanced)	B	C	A		Y	1,000,000
★	American Funds American Balanced Fund® Class R-1	RLBAX	NAS CM	Open End	Moderate Alloc (Balanced)	B	C	A	Up	Y	250
★	American Funds American Balanced Fund® Class R-2	RLBBX	NAS CM	Open End	Moderate Alloc (Balanced)	B	C	A	Up	Y	250
★	American Funds American Balanced Fund® Class R-2E	RAMHX	NAS CM	Open End	Moderate Alloc (Balanced)	B	C	A		Y	250
★	American Funds American Balanced Fund® Class R-3	RLBCX	NAS CM	Open End	Moderate Alloc (Balanced)	B	C	A		Y	250
★	American Funds American Balanced Fund® Class R-4	RLBEX	NAS CM	Open End	Moderate Alloc (Balanced)	B	C	A		Y	250
★	American Funds American Balanced Fund® Class R-5	RLBFX	NAS CM	Open End	Moderate Alloc (Balanced)	B	C	A		Y	250
★	American Funds American Balanced Fund® Class R-5E	RLEFX	NAS CM	Open End	Moderate Alloc (Balanced)	B	C	A		Y	250
★	American Funds American Balanced Fund® Class R-6	RLBGX	NAS CM	Open End	Moderate Alloc (Balanced)	B	C	A		Y	250
	American Funds American Mutual Fund® Class 529-A	CMLAX	NAS CM	Open End	US Equity Large Cap Value (Growth & Income)	B	C	A-		Y	250
	American Funds American Mutual Fund® Class 529-C	CMLCX	NAS CM	Open End	US Equity Large Cap Value (Growth & Income)	B-	C	A-	Down	Y	250
	American Funds American Mutual Fund® Class 529-E	CMLEX	NAS CM	Open End	US Equity Large Cap Value (Growth & Income)	B-	C	A-	Down	Y	250
	American Funds American Mutual Fund® Class 529-F	CMLFX	NAS CM	Open End	US Equity Large Cap Value (Growth & Income)	B	C	A-		Y	250
	American Funds American Mutual Fund® Class A	AMRMX	NAS CM	Open End	US Equity Large Cap Value (Growth & Income)	B	C	A-		Y	250
	American Funds American Mutual Fund® Class C	AMFCX	NAS CM	Open End	US Equity Large Cap Value (Growth & Income)	B-	C	A-	Down	Y	250
	American Funds American Mutual Fund® Class F-1	AMFFX	NAS CM	Open End	US Equity Large Cap Value (Growth & Income)	B	C	A-		Y	250
	American Funds American Mutual Fund® Class F-2	AMRFX	NAS CM	Open End	US Equity Large Cap Value (Growth & Income)	B	C	A-		Y	250
	American Funds American Mutual Fund® Class F-3	AFMFX	NAS CM	Open End	US Equity Large Cap Value (Growth & Income)	B	C	A-		Y	1,000,000
	American Funds American Mutual Fund® Class R-1	RMFAX	NAS CM	Open End	US Equity Large Cap Value (Growth & Income)	B-	C	A-	Down	Y	250
	American Funds American Mutual Fund® Class R-2	RMFBX	NAS CM	Open End	US Equity Large Cap Value (Growth & Income)	B-	C	A-	Down	Y	250
	American Funds American Mutual Fund® Class R-2E	RMEBX	NAS CM	Open End	US Equity Large Cap Value (Growth & Income)	B-	C	A-	Down	Y	250
	American Funds American Mutual Fund® Class R-3	RMFCX	NAS CM	Open End	US Equity Large Cap Value (Growth & Income)	B-	C	A-	Down	Y	250
	American Funds American Mutual Fund® Class R-4	RMFEX	NAS CM	Open End	US Equity Large Cap Value (Growth & Income)	B	C	A-		Y	250
	American Funds American Mutual Fund® Class R-5	RMFFX	NAS CM	Open End	US Equity Large Cap Value (Growth & Income)	B	C	A-		Y	250
	American Funds American Mutual Fund® Class R-5E	RMFHX	NAS CM	Open End	US Equity Large Cap Value (Growth & Income)	B	C	A-		Y	250
	American Funds American Mutual Fund® Class R-6	RMFGX	NAS CM	Open End	US Equity Large Cap Value (Growth & Income)	B	C	A-		Y	250
	American Funds Capital Income Builder® Class 529-A	CIRAX	NAS CM	Open End	Flexible Alloc (Equity-Income)	C+	C	B		Y	250
	American Funds Capital Income Builder® Class 529-C	CIRCX	NAS CM	Open End	Flexible Alloc (Equity-Income)	C+	C	B	Up	Y	250
★	American Funds Capital Income Builder® Class 529-E	CIREX	NAS CM	Open End	Flexible Alloc (Equity-Income)	C+	C	B		Y	250
	American Funds Capital Income Builder® Class 529-F	CIRFX	NAS CM	Open End	Flexible Alloc (Equity-Income)	C+	C	B		Y	250
★	American Funds Capital Income Builder® Class A	CAIBX	NAS CM	Open End	Flexible Alloc (Equity-Income)	C+	C	B		Y	250
★	American Funds Capital Income Builder® Class C	CIBCX	NAS CM	Open End	Flexible Alloc (Equity-Income)	C+	C	B	Up	Y	250
★	American Funds Capital Income Builder® Class F-1	CIBFX	NAS CM	Open End	Flexible Alloc (Equity-Income)	C+	C	B		Y	250
	American Funds Capital Income Builder® Class F-2	CAIFX	NAS CM	Open End	Flexible Alloc (Equity-Income)	C+	C	B		Y	250
	American Funds Capital Income Builder® Class F-3	CFIHX	NAS CM	Open End	Flexible Alloc (Equity-Income)	B-	C	B	Up	Y	1,000,000
	American Funds Capital Income Builder® Class R-1	RIRAX	NAS CM	Open End	Flexible Alloc (Equity-Income)	C+	C	B	Up	Y	250
	American Funds Capital Income Builder® Class R-2	RIRBX	NAS CM	Open End	Flexible Alloc (Equity-Income)	C+	C	B	Up	Y	250
	American Funds Capital Income Builder® Class R-2E	RCEEX	NAS CM	Open End	Flexible Alloc (Equity-Income)	C+	C	B		Y	250
★	American Funds Capital Income Builder® Class R-3	RIRCX	NAS CM	Open End	Flexible Alloc (Equity-Income)	C+	C	B		Y	250
	American Funds Capital Income Builder® Class R-4	RIREX	NAS CM	Open End	Flexible Alloc (Equity-Income)	C+	C	B		Y	250
	American Funds Capital Income Builder® Class R-5	RIRFX	NAS CM	Open End	Flexible Alloc (Equity-Income)	C+	C	B		Y	250
★	American Funds Capital Income Builder® Class R-5E	RIRHX	NAS CM	Open End	Flexible Alloc (Equity-Income)	C+	C	B		Y	250
	American Funds Capital Income Builder® Class R-6	RIRGX	NAS CM	Open End	Flexible Alloc (Equity-Income)	B-	C	B	Up	Y	250
	American Funds Capital World Growth & Inc Fund® Cls 529-A	CWIAX	NAS CM	Open End	Global Equity Large Cap (Growth & Income)	C+	C	B	Up	Y	250
	American Funds Capital World Growth & Inc Fund® Cls 529-C	CWICX	NAS CM	Open End	Global Equity Large Cap (Growth & Income)	C+	C	B	Up	Y	250
	American Funds Capital World Growth & Inc Fund® Cls 529-E	CWIEX	NAS CM	Open End	Global Equity Large Cap (Growth & Income)	C+	C	B	Up	Y	250

★ Expanded analysis of this fund is included in Section II.

	TOTAL RETURNS					PERFORMANCE				ASSETS		ASSET ALLOCATION & TURNOVER					BULL & BEAR		FEES		
Min Additional Investment	3-Month Total Return	6-Month Total Return	1-Year Total Return	3-Year Total Return	5-Year Total Return	Dividend Yield (TTM)	Expense Ratio	3-Yr Std Deviation	3-Year Beta	NAV	Total Assets (MIL)	%Cash	%Stocks	%Bonds	%Other	Turnover Ratio	Last Bull Market Total Return	Last Bear Market Total Return	Front End Fee (%)	Back End Fee (%)	Inception Date
50	2.76	11.33	6.68	28.95	40.56	1.55	0.89	7.01	0.56	27.27	146,710	6	62	32	0	72	17.24	-10.14			Mar-02
50	2.84	11.59	7.15	30.73	43.89	2	0.41	7	0.56	27.26	146,710	6	62	32	0	72	17.57	-9.91			Sep-02
50	2.79	11.47	7.00	30.14	42.84	1.84	0.57	7.01	0.56	27.33	146,710	6	62	32	0	72	17.46	-9.96	5.75		Jul-75
50	2.62	11.04	6.18	27.08	37.32	1.11	1.36	7	0.56	27.15	146,710	6	62	32	0	72	16.89	-10.23		1.00	Mar-01
50	2.82	11.44	6.93	29.88	42.33	1.77	0.64	7	0.56	27.31	146,710	6	62	32	0	72	17.4	-9.96			Mar-01
50	2.84	11.58	7.17	30.85	44.21	2.02	0.38	7.01	0.56	27.31	146,710	6	62	32	0	72	17.66	-9.91			Aug-08
50	2.90	11.63	7.31	31.09	43.88	2.11	0.29	7.01	0.56	27.32	146,710	6	62	32	0	72	17.46	-9.96			Jan-17
50	2.61	11.04	6.11	27.01	37.25	1.09	1.37	6.98	0.56	27.13	146,710	6	62	32	0	72	16.93	-10.27			May-02
50	2.65	11.08	6.15	27.09	37.43	1.09	1.37	7	0.56	27.15	146,710	6	62	32	0	72	16.93	-10.26			May-02
50	2.68	11.21	6.46	28.17	40.26	1.38	1.08	7.01	0.56	27.22	146,710	6	62	32	0	72	17.22	-10.09			Aug-14
50	2.72	11.25	6.61	28.72	40.31	1.5	0.93	7	0.56	27.18	146,710	6	62	32	0	72	17.22	-10.05			Jun-02
50	2.82	11.46	6.95	29.88	42.49	1.78	0.63	6.99	0.56	27.28	146,710	6	62	32	0	72	17.41	-9.98			Jun-02
50	2.89	11.63	7.25	31.09	44.59	2.06	0.33	7	0.56	27.36	146,710	6	62	32	0	72	17.67	-9.88			May-02
50	2.88	11.55	7.14	30.72	43.57	1.89	0.41	7	0.56	27.31	146,710	6	62	32	0	72	17.46	-9.96			Nov-15
50	2.90	11.67	7.31	31.26	44.98	2.11	0.28	7.01	0.56	27.34	146,710	6	62	32	0	72	17.71	-9.86			May-09
50	3.06	13.05	9.38	37.81	51.27	1.91	0.66	9.27	0.74	41.62	57,149	12	87	1	0	16	19.79	-12.72	5.75		Feb-02
50	2.89	12.65	8.58	34.70	45.62	1.21	1.44	9.27	0.74	41.42	57,149	12	87	1	0	16	19.23	-13.01		1.00	Feb-02
50	3.02	12.96	9.15	36.87	49.52	1.7	0.91	9.26	0.74	41.45	57,149	12	87	1	0	16	19.56	-12.8			Mar-02
50	3.12	13.19	9.63	38.76	52.98	2.13	0.43	9.28	0.74	41.68	57,149	12	87	1	0	16	19.94	-12.65			Sep-02
50	3.10	13.12	9.48	38.18	51.95	1.98	0.57	9.28	0.74	41.73	57,149	12	87	1	0	16	19.85	-12.66	5.75		Feb-50
50	2.87	12.67	8.63	34.91	46.01	1.27	1.37	9.27	0.74	41.1	57,149	12	87	1	0	16	19.33	-13.01		1.00	Mar-01
50	3.07	13.06	9.38	37.79	51.30	1.91	0.67	9.28	0.74	41.53	57,149	12	87	1	0	16	19.86	-12.72			Mar-01
50	3.12	13.23	9.68	38.89	53.28	2.16	0.41	9.28	0.74	41.71	57,149	12	87	1	0	16	19.99	-12.61			Aug-08
50	3.17	13.28	9.79	39.12	52.99	2.25	0.31	9.28	0.74	41.71	57,149	12	87	1	0	16	19.85	-12.66			Jan-17
50	2.87	12.65	8.55	34.72	45.73	1.22	1.42	9.27	0.74	41.26	57,149	12	87	1	0	16	19.27	-12.96			Jun-02
50	2.89	12.68	8.61	34.86	45.96	1.24	1.4	9.27	0.74	41.22	57,149	12	87	1	0	16	19.33	-13.02			May-02
50	2.94	12.82	8.88	36.00	48.59	1.51	1.1	9.28	0.74	41.57	57,149	12	87	1	0	16	19.6	-12.79			Aug-14
50	2.98	12.89	9.07	36.61	49.16	1.65	0.95	9.27	0.74	41.38	57,149	12	87	1	0	16	19.6	-12.81			Jun-02
50	3.07	13.08	9.41	37.86	51.44	1.93	0.65	9.27	0.74	41.58	57,149	12	87	1	0	16	19.84	-12.71			Jun-02
50	3.16	13.25	9.73	39.15	53.79	2.2	0.35	9.26	0.74	41.73	57,149	12	87	1	0	16	20.05	-12.62			May-02
50	3.13	13.22	9.64	38.70	52.60	2.16	0.44	9.26	0.74	41.68	57,149	12	87	1	0	16	19.85	-12.66			Nov-15
50	3.17	13.30	9.79	39.35	54.15	2.25	0.3	9.28	0.74	41.74	57,149	12	87	1	0	16	20.03	-12.56			May-09
50	1.90	10.79	5.63	18.28	20.67	3.43	0.66	7.08	0.58	61.08	104,371	4	71	25	0	73	12.73	-10.01	5.75		Feb-02
50	1.72	10.38	4.86	15.62	16.16	2.68	1.44	7.08	0.58	61.18	104,371	4	71	25	0	73	12.2	-10.3		1.00	Feb-02
50	1.85	10.66	5.41	17.49	19.29	3.21	0.89	7.07	0.58	61.1	104,371	4	71	25	0	73	12.54	-10.09			Mar-02
50	1.96	10.92	5.88	19.09	22.06	3.66	0.43	7.08	0.58	61.08	104,371	4	71	25	0	73	12.85	-9.91			Sep-02
50	1.92	10.83	5.71	18.54	21.19	3.5	0.58	7.08	0.58	61.1	104,371	4	71	25	0	73	12.77	-9.97	5.75		Jul-87
50	1.73	10.39	4.90	15.78	16.47	2.71	1.37	7.07	0.58	61.22	104,371	4	71	25	0	73	12.25	-10.26		1.00	Mar-01
50	1.90	10.78	5.65	18.28	20.73	3.43	0.66	7.08	0.58	61.1	104,371	4	71	25	0	73	12.75	-9.97			Mar-01
50	1.97	10.94	5.92	19.22	22.34	3.69	0.4	7.09	0.58	61.05	104,371	4	71	25	0	73	12.92	-9.88			Aug-08
50	1.99	10.99	6.03	19.37	22.03	3.79	0.29	7.08	0.58	61.08	104,371	4	71	25	0	73	12.77	-9.97			Jan-17
50	1.71	10.37	4.86	15.71	16.40	2.7	1.39	7.07	0.58	61.15	104,371	4	71	25	0	73	12.24	-10.27			Jun-02
50	1.74	10.39	4.88	15.74	16.49	2.71	1.39	7.08	0.58	61.14	104,371	4	71	25	0	73	12.26	-10.27			May-02
50	1.81	10.57	5.20	16.79	18.46	3.03	1.1	7.08	0.58	60.87	104,371	4	71	25	0	73	12.54	-10.1			Aug-14
50	1.83	10.63	5.34	17.30	19.04	3.15	0.95	7.07	0.58	61.11	104,371	4	71	25	0	73	12.55	-10.1			Jun-02
50	1.92	10.81	5.68	18.37	20.87	3.44	0.64	7.08	0.58	61.09	104,371	4	71	25	0	73	12.73	-9.97			May-02
50	2.00	10.98	5.99	19.44	22.69	3.75	0.34	7.08	0.58	61.12	104,371	4	71	25	0	73	12.94	-9.85			May-02
50	1.97	10.93	5.88	19.05	21.77	3.66	0.44	7.09	0.58	61.02	104,371	4	71	25	0	73	12.77	-9.97			Nov-15
50	2.00	10.99	6.03	19.61	23.00	3.8	0.29	7.08	0.58	61.09	104,371	4	71	25	0	73	12.97	-9.85			May-09
50	2.91	16.10	3.05	36.82	31.33	1.98	0.83	10.81	0.94	48.67	97,315	6	94	1	0	49	17.87	-20.79	5.75		Feb-02
50	2.72	15.68	2.27	33.73	26.39	1.27	1.61	10.81	0.94	48.51	97,315	6	94	1	0	49	17.33	-21.07		1.00	Feb-02
50	2.84	15.95	2.80	35.90	29.86	1.78	1.06	10.81	0.94	48.6	97,315	6	94	1	0	49	17.67	-20.87			Mar-02

	MARKET			FUND TYPE, CATEGORY & OBJECTIVE	RATINGS				MINIMUMS	
Fund Name	Ticker Symbol	Traded On	Fund Type	Category and (Prospectus Objective)	Overall Rating	Reward Rating	Risk Rating	Recent Up/ Downgrade	Open to New Investors	Min Initial Investment
American Funds Capital World Growth & Inc Fund® Cls 529-F	CWIFX	NAS CM	Open End	Global Equity Large Cap (Growth & Income)	C+	C	B	Up	Y	250
American Funds Capital World Growth & Income Fund® Cls A	CWGIX	NAS CM	Open End	Global Equity Large Cap (Growth & Income)	C+	C	B	Up	Y	250
American Funds Capital World Growth & Income Fund® Cls C	CWGCX	NAS CM	Open End	Global Equity Large Cap (Growth & Income)	C+	C	B	Up	Y	250
American Funds Capital World Growth & Income Fund® Cls F-1	CWGFX	NAS CM	Open End	Global Equity Large Cap (Growth & Income)	C+	C	B	Up	Y	250
American Funds Capital World Growth & Income Fund® Cls F-2	WGIFX	NAS CM	Open End	Global Equity Large Cap (Growth & Income)	C+	C	B	Up	Y	250
American Funds Capital World Growth & Income Fund® Cls F-3	FWGIX	NAS CM	Open End	Global Equity Large Cap (Growth & Income)	C+	C	B	Up	Y	1,000,000
American Funds Capital World Growth & Income Fund® Cls R-1	RWIAX	NAS CM	Open End	Global Equity Large Cap (Growth & Income)	C+	C	B	Up	Y	250
American Funds Capital World Growth & Income Fund® Cls R-2	RWIBX	NAS CM	Open End	Global Equity Large Cap (Growth & Income)	C+	C	B	Up	Y	250
American Funds Capital World Growth & Inc Fund® Cls R-2E	RWBEX	NAS CM	Open End	Global Equity Large Cap (Growth & Income)	C+	C	B	Up	Y	250
American Funds Capital World Growth & Income Fund® Cls R-3	RWICX	NAS CM	Open End	Global Equity Large Cap (Growth & Income)	C+	C	B	Up	Y	250
American Funds Capital World Growth & Income Fund® Cls R-4	RWIEX	NAS CM	Open End	Global Equity Large Cap (Growth & Income)	C+	C	B	Up	Y	250
American Funds Capital World Growth & Income Fund® Cls R-5	RWIFX	NAS CM	Open End	Global Equity Large Cap (Growth & Income)	C+	C	B	Up	Y	250
American Funds Capital World Growth & Inc Fund® Cls R-5E	RWIHX	NAS CM	Open End	Global Equity Large Cap (Growth & Income)	C+	C	B	Up	Y	250
American Funds Capital World Growth & Income Fund® Cls R-6	RWIGX	NAS CM	Open End	Global Equity Large Cap (Growth & Income)	C+	C	B	Up	Y	250
American Funds College 2021 Fund Class 529-A	CTOAX	NAS CM	Open End	Cautious Alloc (Growth & Income)	B-	C	B	Up	Y	250
American Funds College 2021 Fund Class 529-C	CTOCX	NAS CM	Open End	Cautious Alloc (Growth & Income)	C+	C	B	Up	Y	250
American Funds College 2021 Fund Class 529-E	CTOEX	NAS CM	Open End	Cautious Alloc (Growth & Income)	B-	C	B	Up	Y	250
American Funds College 2021 Fund Class 529F1	CTOFX	NAS CM	Open End	Cautious Alloc (Growth & Income)	B-	C	B+		Y	250
American Funds College 2024 Fund Class 529-A	CFTAX	NAS CM	Open End	Cautious Alloc (Growth & Income)	B	C+	A-		Y	250
American Funds College 2024 Fund Class 529-C	CTFCX	NAS CM	Open End	Cautious Alloc (Growth & Income)	B-	C	B+		Y	250
American Funds College 2024 Fund Class 529-E	CTFEX	NAS CM	Open End	Cautious Alloc (Growth & Income)	B	C+	B+		Y	250
American Funds College 2024 Fund Class 529F1	CTFFX	NAS CM	Open End	Cautious Alloc (Growth & Income)	B	C+	A-		Y	250
American Funds College 2027 Fund Class 529-A	CSTAX	NAS CM	Open End	Cautious Alloc (Growth & Income)	B	C+	A		Y	250
American Funds College 2027 Fund Class 529-C	CTSCX	NAS CM	Open End	Cautious Alloc (Growth & Income)	B	C+	A-	Up	Y	250
American Funds College 2027 Fund Class 529-E	CTSEX	NAS CM	Open End	Cautious Alloc (Growth & Income)	B	C+	A-		Y	250
American Funds College 2027 Fund Class 529F1	CTSFX	NAS CM	Open End	Cautious Alloc (Growth & Income)	B	C+	A		Y	250
American Funds College 2030 Fund Class 529-A	CTHAX	NAS CM	Open End	Aggressive Alloc (Growth & Income)	B	C	A	Up	Y	250
American Funds College 2030 Fund Class 529-C	CTYCX	NAS CM	Open End	Aggressive Alloc (Growth & Income)	B	C	A	Up	Y	250
American Funds College 2030 Fund Class 529-E	CTHEX	NAS CM	Open End	Aggressive Alloc (Growth & Income)	B	C	A	Up	Y	250
American Funds College 2030 Fund Class 529F1	CTHFX	NAS CM	Open End	Aggressive Alloc (Growth & Income)	B	C+	A	Up	Y	250
American Funds College 2033 Fund Class 529-A	CTLAX	NAS CM	Open End	Aggressive Alloc (Growth & Income)	B-	C	A-	Up	Y	250
American Funds College 2033 Fund Class 529-C	CTLCX	NAS CM	Open End	Aggressive Alloc (Growth & Income)	B-	C	B+	Up	Y	250
American Funds College 2033 Fund Class 529-E	CTLEX	NAS CM	Open End	Aggressive Alloc (Growth & Income)	B-	C	A-	Up	Y	250
American Funds College 2033 Fund Class 529-F-1	CTLFX	NAS CM	Open End	Aggressive Alloc (Growth & Income)	B-	C	A-	Up	Y	250
American Funds College 2036 Fund Class 529-A	CCFAX	NAS CM	Open End	Aggressive Alloc (Growth & Income)	D	D+	B-		Y	250
American Funds College 2036 Fund Class 529-C	CTDCX	NAS CM	Open End	Aggressive Alloc (Growth & Income)	D	D+	B-		Y	250
American Funds College 2036 Fund Class 529-E	CTKEX	NAS CM	Open End	Aggressive Alloc (Growth & Income)	D	D+	B-		Y	250
American Funds College 2036 Fund Class 529-F-1	CTAFX	NAS CM	Open End	Aggressive Alloc (Growth & Income)	D	D+	B-		Y	250
American Funds Conservative Growth & Inc Port Cls 529-A	CIPAX	NAS CM	Open End	Moderate Alloc (Growth & Income)	B	C+	A-		Y	250
American Funds Conservative Growth & Inc Port Cls 529-C	CIPCX	NAS CM	Open End	Moderate Alloc (Growth & Income)	B-	C	B+		Y	250
American Funds Conservative Growth & Inc Port Cls 529-E	CIPEX	NAS CM	Open End	Moderate Alloc (Growth & Income)	B	C+	A-	Up	Y	250
American Funds Conservative Growth & Inc Port Cls 529-F-1	CIPFX	NAS CM	Open End	Moderate Alloc (Growth & Income)	B	C+	A-		Y	250
American Funds Conservative Growth & Inc Port Cls A	INPAX	NAS CM	Open End	Moderate Alloc (Growth & Income)	B	C+	A-		Y	250
American Funds Conservative Growth & Inc Port Cls ABLE-A	CIPGX	NAS CM	Open End	Moderate Alloc (Growth & Income)	B	C	A-		Y	250
American Funds Conservative Growth & Inc Port Cls C	INPCX	NAS CM	Open End	Moderate Alloc (Growth & Income)	B-	C	B+		Y	250
American Funds Conservative Growth & Inc Port Cls F-1	INPFX	NAS CM	Open End	Moderate Alloc (Growth & Income)	B	C+	A-		Y	250
American Funds Conservative Growth & Inc Port Cls F-2	INPEX	NAS CM	Open End	Moderate Alloc (Growth & Income)	B	C+	A-		Y	250
American Funds Conservative Growth & Inc Port Cls F-3	INPDX	NAS CM	Open End	Moderate Alloc (Growth & Income)	B	C+	A		Y	1,000,000
American Funds Conservative Growth & Inc Port Cls R-1	RNCAX	NAS CM	Open End	Moderate Alloc (Growth & Income)	B-	C	B+		Y	250
American Funds Conservative Growth & Inc Port Cls R-2	RINBX	NAS CM	Open End	Moderate Alloc (Growth & Income)	B-	C	B+		Y	250
American Funds Conservative Growth & Inc Port Cls R-2E	RNBEX	NAS CM	Open End	Moderate Alloc (Growth & Income)	B	C	A-	Up	Y	250
American Funds Conservative Growth & Inc Port Cls R-3	RNCCX	NAS CM	Open End	Moderate Alloc (Growth & Income)	B	C+	A-	Up	Y	250

★Expanded analysis of this fund is included in Section II.

Min Additional Investment	TOTAL RETURNS: 3-Month Total Return	6-Month Total Return	1-Year Total Return	3-Year Total Return	5-Year Total Return	PERFORMANCE: Dividend Yield (TTM)	Expense Ratio	3-Yr Std Deviation	3-Year Beta	ASSETS: NAV	Total Assets (MIL)	ASSET ALLOCATION & TURNOVER: %Cash	%Stocks	%Bonds	%Other	Turnover Ratio	BULL & BEAR: Last Bull Market Total Return	Last Bear Market Total Return	FEES: Front End Fee (%)	Back End Fee (%)	Inception Date
50	2.97	16.23	3.28	37.77	32.80	2.21	0.6	10.82	0.94	48.7	97,315	6	94	1	0	49	18.02	-20.74			Sep-02
50	2.92	16.16	3.12	37.15	31.86	2.05	0.76	10.81	0.94	48.85	97,315	6	94	1	0	49	17.92	-20.77	5.75		Mar-93
50	2.71	15.67	2.30	33.91	26.71	1.32	1.55	10.81	0.94	48.3	97,315	6	94	1	0	49	17.38	-21.02		1.00	Mar-01
50	2.91	16.11	3.06	36.89	31.50	1.99	0.82	10.82	0.94	48.73	97,315	6	94	1	0	49	17.93	-20.76			Mar-01
50	2.98	16.28	3.35	38.02	33.34	2.26	0.54	10.82	0.94	48.79	97,315	6	94	1	0	49	18.13	-20.7			Aug-08
50	3.00	16.32	3.45	38.19	32.86	2.35	0.44	10.81	0.94	48.83	97,315	6	94	1	0	49	17.92	-20.77			Jan-17
50	2.72	15.68	2.32	33.97	26.85	1.32	1.54	10.8	0.94	48.36	97,315	6	94	1	0	49	17.39	-21.01			Jun-02
50	2.72	15.69	2.32	33.96	26.90	1.33	1.55	10.81	0.94	48.21	97,315	6	94	1	0	49	17.42	-21.03			Jun-02
50	2.81	15.85	2.63	35.18	29.03	1.6	1.24	10.8	0.94	48.66	97,315	6	94	1	0	49	17.68	-20.88			Aug-14
50	2.83	15.97	2.79	35.78	29.72	1.74	1.09	10.81	0.94	48.5	97,315	6	94	1	0	49	17.72	-20.88			Jun-02
50	2.92	16.14	3.09	37.02	31.71	2.02	0.79	10.82	0.94	48.72	97,315	6	94	1	0	49	17.94	-20.77			Jun-02
50	2.98	16.28	3.40	38.23	33.67	2.3	0.49	10.81	0.94	48.85	97,315	6	94	1	0	49	18.14	-20.67			May-02
50	2.97	16.25	3.30	37.82	32.59	2.23	0.58	10.81	0.94	48.76	97,315	6	94	1	0	49	17.92	-20.77			Nov-15
50	3.00	16.32	3.45	38.46	33.99	2.35	0.44	10.81	0.94	48.84	97,315	6	94	1	0	49	18.17	-20.65			May-09
50	1.97	4.99	5.77	8.40	13.28	1.7	0.72	1.92	0.07	11.35	1,949	8	9	83	0	7			4.25		Sep-12
50	1.81	4.57	4.98	6.01	8.98	1.03	1.48	1.92	0.07	11.21	1,949	8	9	83	0	7				1.00	Sep-12
50	1.98	4.92	5.58	7.69	11.97	1.52	0.95	1.95	0.07	11.3	1,949	8	9	83	0	7					Sep-12
50	2.15	5.07	6.11	9.19	14.54	1.94	0.48	1.96	0.07	11.39	1,949	8	9	83	0	7					Sep-12
50	2.44	6.94	6.72	16.09	20.23	1.83	0.71	3.06	0.21	12.17	1,942	7	25	68	0	13			4.25		Sep-12
50	2.29	6.66	6.05	13.48	15.77	1.18	1.47	3.06	0.21	12.01	1,942	7	25	68	0	13				1.00	Sep-12
50	2.45	6.87	6.54	15.25	18.80	1.65	0.94	3.08	0.21	12.12	1,942	7	25	68	0	13					Sep-12
50	2.51	7.19	7.06	16.88	21.67	2.06	0.47	3.07	0.21	12.22	1,942	7	25	68	0	13					Sep-12
50	2.80	9.11	6.83	21.83	25.01	1.77	0.75	4.59	0.34	12.81	1,582	7	40	53	0	11			4.25		Sep-12
50	2.60	8.69	6.02	19.04	20.20	1.08	1.51	4.54	0.34	12.63	1,582	7	40	53	0	11				1.00	Sep-12
50	2.66	8.91	6.58	20.90	23.36	1.6	0.98	4.56	0.34	12.71	1,582	7	40	53	0	11					Sep-12
50	2.87	9.25	7.16	22.61	26.31	1.99	0.51	4.59	0.34	12.87	1,582	7	40	53	0	11					Sep-12
50	2.95	11.02	5.95	27.26	28.95	1.56	0.79	6.27	0.48	13.6	1,785	6	52	41	0	6			4.25		Sep-12
50	2.76	10.66	5.11	24.36	23.90	0.86	1.55	6.25	0.47	13.39	1,785	6	52	41	0	6				1.00	Sep-12
50	2.97	11.00	5.75	26.41	27.31	1.37	1.02	6.26	0.48	13.52	1,785	6	52	41	0	6					Sep-12
50	3.01	11.23	6.20	28.16	30.28	1.79	0.55	6.28	0.48	13.66	1,785	6	52	41	0	6					Sep-12
50	2.95	12.77	4.85	32.65		1.41	0.82	8.02	0.61	11.83	1,073	6	65	29	0				4.25		Mar-15
50	2.80	12.37	4.09	29.51		0.74	1.58	8.05	0.61	11.71	1,073	6	65	29	0					1.00	Mar-15
50	2.88	12.61	4.57	31.57		1.24	1.05	8.05	0.61	11.78	1,073	6	65	29	0						Mar-15
50	3.03	12.92	5.10	33.51		1.63	0.58	8.02	0.61	11.88	1,073	6	65	29	0						Mar-15
50	2.94	14.28	3.99			0.88	0.91			10.48	250.3	6	79	15	0				4.25		Feb-18
50	2.76	13.88	3.25			0.59	1.6			10.42	250.3	6	79	15	0					1.00	Feb-18
50	3.04	14.28	3.85			0.77	1.08			10.48	250.3	6	79	15	0						Feb-18
50	3.03	14.48	4.33			1	0.6			10.51	250.3	6	79	15	0						Feb-18
50	2.40	10.18	6.84	21.92	26.85	3.11	0.69	5.72	0.44	12.62	5,248	6	52	42	0	1			5.75		May-12
50	2.22	9.76	6.17	19.27	22.26	2.41	1.44	5.7	0.44	12.58	5,248	6	52	42	0	1				1.00	May-12
50	2.33	10.06	6.67	21.17	25.52	2.88	0.91	5.72	0.44	12.62	5,248	6	52	42	0	1					May-12
50	2.45	10.29	7.10	22.77	28.35	3.35	0.43	5.7	0.44	12.63	5,248	6	52	42	0	1					May-12
50	2.40	10.19	6.97	22.19	27.37	3.15	0.63	5.72	0.44	12.63	5,248	6	52	42	0	1			5.75		May-12
50	2.39	10.11	6.95	22.19	27.27		0.63	5.74	0.45	12.61	5,248	6	52	42	0	1			5.75		Jul-18
50	2.23	9.88	6.22	19.51	22.69	2.45	1.37	5.71	0.44	12.57	5,248	6	52	42	0	1				1.00	May-12
50	2.39	10.16	6.91	22.01	27.19	3.1	0.67	5.68	0.44	12.64	5,248	6	52	42	0	1					May-12
50	2.45	10.28	7.09	22.97	28.74	3.35	0.41	5.7	0.44	12.64	5,248	6	52	42	0	1					May-12
50	2.48	10.44	7.29	23.43	29.34	3.45	0.31	5.73	0.44	12.63	5,248	6	52	42	0	1					Jan-17
50	2.20	9.74	6.02	19.32	22.48	2.36	1.41	5.72	0.44	12.58	5,248	6	52	42	0	1					May-12
50	2.24	9.81	6.13	19.47	22.58	2.46	1.39	5.7	0.44	12.57	5,248	6	52	42	0	1					May-12
50	2.30	9.97	6.42	20.57	25.87	2.73	1.16	5.76	0.45	12.63	5,248	6	52	42	0	1					Aug-14
50	2.33	10.05	6.62	21.01	25.35	2.83	0.95	5.7	0.44	12.61	5,248	6	52	42	0	1					May-12

	MARKET			FUND TYPE, CATEGORY & OBJECTIVE	RATINGS				MINIMUMS	
Fund Name	Ticker Symbol	Traded On	Fund Type	Category and (Prospectus Objective)	Overall Rating	Reward Rating	Risk Rating	Recent Up/ Downgrade	Open to New Investors	Min Initial Investment
American Funds Conservative Growth & Inc Port Cls R-4	RINEX	NAS CM	Open End	Moderate Alloc (Growth & Income)	B	C+	A-		Y	250
American Funds Conservative Growth & Inc Port Cls R-5	RINFX	NAS CM	Open End	Moderate Alloc (Growth & Income)	B	C+	A-		Y	250
American Funds Conservative Growth & Inc Port Cls R-5E	RGOFX	NAS CM	Open End	Moderate Alloc (Growth & Income)	B	C+	A-		Y	250
American Funds Conservative Growth & Inc Port Cls R-6	RINGX	NAS CM	Open End	Moderate Alloc (Growth & Income)	B	C+	A		Y	250
American Funds Developing World Growth & Income Cls 529-A	CDWAX	NAS CM	Open End	Global Emerg Mkts (Div Emerging Mkts)	C	C	B-		Y	250
American Funds Developing World Growth & Income Cls 529-C	CDWCX	NAS CM	Open End	Global Emerg Mkts (Div Emerging Mkts)	C	C	B-		Y	250
American Funds Developing World Growth & Income Cls 529-E	CDWEX	NAS CM	Open End	Global Emerg Mkts (Div Emerging Mkts)	C	C	B-		Y	250
American Funds Developing World Growth & Inc Cls 529-F-1	CDWFX	NAS CM	Open End	Global Emerg Mkts (Div Emerging Mkts)	C	C	B-		Y	250
American Funds Developing World Growth & Income Cls A	DWGAX	NAS CM	Open End	Global Emerg Mkts (Div Emerging Mkts)	C	C	B-		Y	250
American Funds Developing World Growth & Income Cls C	DWGCX	NAS CM	Open End	Global Emerg Mkts (Div Emerging Mkts)	C	C	B-		Y	250
American Funds Developing World Growth & Income Cls F-1	DWGFX	NAS CM	Open End	Global Emerg Mkts (Div Emerging Mkts)	C	C	B-		Y	250
American Funds Developing World Growth & Income Cls F-2	DWGHX	NAS CM	Open End	Global Emerg Mkts (Div Emerging Mkts)	C	C	B-		Y	250
American Funds Developing World Growth & Income Cls F-3	FDWGX	NAS CM	Open End	Global Emerg Mkts (Div Emerging Mkts)	C	C	B-		Y	1,000,000
American Funds Developing World Growth & Income Cls R-1	RDWAX	NAS CM	Open End	Global Emerg Mkts (Div Emerging Mkts)	C	C	B-		Y	250
American Funds Developing World Growth & Income Cls R-2	RDWBX	NAS CM	Open End	Global Emerg Mkts (Div Emerging Mkts)	C	C	B-		Y	250
American Funds Developing World Growth & Income Cls R-2E	RDEGX	NAS CM	Open End	Global Emerg Mkts (Div Emerging Mkts)	C	C	B-		Y	250
American Funds Developing World Growth & Income Cls R-3	RDWCX	NAS CM	Open End	Global Emerg Mkts (Div Emerging Mkts)	C	C	B-		Y	250
American Funds Developing World Growth & Income Cls R-4	RDWEX	NAS CM	Open End	Global Emerg Mkts (Div Emerging Mkts)	C	C	B-		Y	250
American Funds Developing World Growth & Income Cls R-5	RDWFX	NAS CM	Open End	Global Emerg Mkts (Div Emerging Mkts)	C	C	B-		Y	250
American Funds Developing World Growth & Income Cls R-5E	RDWHX	NAS CM	Open End	Global Emerg Mkts (Div Emerging Mkts)	C	C	B-		Y	250
American Funds Developing World Growth & Income Cls R-6	RDWGX	NAS CM	Open End	Global Emerg Mkts (Div Emerging Mkts)	C	C	B-		Y	250
★ American Funds EuroPacific Growth Fund® Class 529-A	CEUAX	NAS CM	Open End	Global Equity Large Cap (Foreign Stock)	C	C	B-		Y	250
★ American Funds EuroPacific Growth Fund® Class 529-C	CEUCX	NAS CM	Open End	Global Equity Large Cap (Foreign Stock)	C	C	C+		Y	250
★ American Funds EuroPacific Growth Fund® Class 529-E	CEUEX	NAS CM	Open End	Global Equity Large Cap (Foreign Stock)	C	C	B-		Y	250
★ American Funds EuroPacific Growth Fund® Class 529-F-1	CEUFX	NAS CM	Open End	Global Equity Large Cap (Foreign Stock)	C	C	B-		Y	250
★ American Funds EuroPacific Growth Fund® Class A	AEPGX	NAS CM	Open End	Global Equity Large Cap (Foreign Stock)	C	C	B-		Y	250
★ American Funds EuroPacific Growth Fund® Class C	AEPCX	NAS CM	Open End	Global Equity Large Cap (Foreign Stock)	C	C	C+		Y	250
★ American Funds EuroPacific Growth Fund® Class F-1	AEGFX	NAS CM	Open End	Global Equity Large Cap (Foreign Stock)	C	C	B-		Y	250
★ American Funds EuroPacific Growth Fund® Class F-2	AEPFX	NAS CM	Open End	Global Equity Large Cap (Foreign Stock)	C	C	B-		Y	250
American Funds EuroPacific Growth Fund® Class F-3	FEUPX	NAS CM	Open End	Global Equity Large Cap (Foreign Stock)	C	C	B-		Y	1,000,000
★ American Funds EuroPacific Growth Fund® Class R-1	RERAX	NAS CM	Open End	Global Equity Large Cap (Foreign Stock)	C	C	C+		Y	250
★ American Funds EuroPacific Growth Fund® Class R-2	RERBX	NAS CM	Open End	Global Equity Large Cap (Foreign Stock)	C	C	C+		Y	250
★ American Funds EuroPacific Growth Fund® Class R-2E	REEBX	NAS CM	Open End	Global Equity Large Cap (Foreign Stock)	C	C	B-		Y	250
★ American Funds EuroPacific Growth Fund® Class R-3	RERCX	NAS CM	Open End	Global Equity Large Cap (Foreign Stock)	C	C	B-		Y	250
★ American Funds EuroPacific Growth Fund® Class R-4	REREX	NAS CM	Open End	Global Equity Large Cap (Foreign Stock)	C	C	B-		Y	250
★ American Funds EuroPacific Growth Fund® Class R-5	RERFX	NAS CM	Open End	Global Equity Large Cap (Foreign Stock)	C	C	B-		Y	250
★ American Funds EuroPacific Growth Fund® Class R-5E	RERHX	NAS CM	Open End	Global Equity Large Cap (Foreign Stock)	C	C	B-		Y	250
★ American Funds EuroPacific Growth Fund® Class R-6	RERGX	NAS CM	Open End	Global Equity Large Cap (Foreign Stock)	C	C	B-		Y	250
American Funds Fundamental Investors® Class 529-A	CFNAX	NAS CM	Open End	US Equity Large Cap Blend (Growth & Income)	B-	C	B	Up	Y	250
American Funds Fundamental Investors® Class 529-C	CFNCX	NAS CM	Open End	US Equity Large Cap Blend (Growth & Income)	B-	C	B	Up	Y	250
American Funds Fundamental Investors® Class 529-E	CFNEX	NAS CM	Open End	US Equity Large Cap Blend (Growth & Income)	B-	C	B	Up	Y	250
American Funds Fundamental Investors® Class 529-F-1	CFNFX	NAS CM	Open End	US Equity Large Cap Blend (Growth & Income)	B-	C	B	Up	Y	250
American Funds Fundamental Investors® Class A	ANCFX	NAS CM	Open End	US Equity Large Cap Blend (Growth & Income)	B-	C	B	Up	Y	250
American Funds Fundamental Investors® Class C	AFICX	NAS CM	Open End	US Equity Large Cap Blend (Growth & Income)	B-	C	B	Up	Y	250
American Funds Fundamental Investors® Class F-1	AFIFX	NAS CM	Open End	US Equity Large Cap Blend (Growth & Income)	B-	C	B	Up	Y	250
American Funds Fundamental Investors® Class F-2	FINFX	NAS CM	Open End	US Equity Large Cap Blend (Growth & Income)	B-	C	B	Up	Y	250
American Funds Fundamental Investors® Class F-3	FUNFX	NAS CM	Open End	US Equity Large Cap Blend (Growth & Income)	B-	C	B	Up	Y	1,000,000
American Funds Fundamental Investors® Class R-1	RFNAX	NAS CM	Open End	US Equity Large Cap Blend (Growth & Income)	B-	C	B	Up	Y	250
American Funds Fundamental Investors® Class R-2	RFNBX	NAS CM	Open End	US Equity Large Cap Blend (Growth & Income)	B-	C	B	Up	Y	250
American Funds Fundamental Investors® Class R-2E	RFEBX	NAS CM	Open End	US Equity Large Cap Blend (Growth & Income)	B-	C	B	Up	Y	250
American Funds Fundamental Investors® Class R-3	RFNCX	NAS CM	Open End	US Equity Large Cap Blend (Growth & Income)	B-	C	B	Up	Y	250
American Funds Fundamental Investors® Class R-4	RFNEX	NAS CM	Open End	US Equity Large Cap Blend (Growth & Income)	B-	C	B	Up	Y	250

★Expanded analysis of this fund is included in Section II.

Min Additional Investment	3-Month Total Return	6-Month Total Return	1-Year Total Return	3-Year Total Return	5-Year Total Return	Dividend Yield (TTM)	Expense Ratio	3-Yr Std Deviation	3-Year Beta	NAV	Total Assets (MIL)	%Cash	%Stocks	%Bonds	%Other	Turnover Ratio	Last Bull Market Total Return	Last Bear Market Total Return	Front End Fee (%)	Back End Fee (%)	Inception Date
	TOTAL RETURNS					PERFORMANCE				ASSETS		ASSET ALLOCATION & TURNOVER					BULL & BEAR		FEES		
50	2.39	10.17	6.91	22.09	27.24	3.1	0.66	5.74	0.45	12.63	5,248	6	52	42	0	1					May-12
50	2.54	10.39	7.22	23.24	29.13	3.39	0.36	5.69	0.44	12.66	5,248	6	52	42	0	1					May-12
50	2.45	10.28	7.15	22.82	28.72	3.31	0.44	5.71	0.44	12.62	5,248	6	52	42	0	1					Nov-15
50	2.47	10.42	7.28	23.32	29.45	3.44	0.31	5.72	0.44	12.65	5,248	6	52	42	0	1					May-12
50	3.35	13.52	5.87	24.78	1.54	1.94	1.29	11.71	0.8	10.48	2,919	3	95	2	0	31			5.75		Feb-14
50	3.07	13.16	5.07	21.82	-2.59	1.31	2.09	11.69	0.8	10.43	2,919	3	95	2	0	31				1.00	Feb-14
50	3.31	13.56	5.69	24.10	0.58	1.78	1.49	11.72	0.8	10.48	2,919	3	95	2	0	31					Feb-14
50	3.31	13.63	6.10	25.52	2.41	2.15	1.08	11.71	0.8	10.48	2,919	3	95	2	0	31					Feb-14
50	3.37	13.65	5.90	25.06	1.62	1.97	1.24	11.72	0.8	10.49	2,919	3	95	2	0	31			5.75		Feb-14
50	3.08	13.16	5.10	21.92	-2.25	1.33	2.04	11.68	0.8	10.44	2,919	3	95	2	0	31				1.00	Feb-14
50	3.27	13.54	5.92	24.87	1.77	1.99	1.25	11.73	0.81	10.49	2,919	3	95	2	0	31					Feb-14
50	3.33	13.68	6.20	25.89	3.09	2.24	0.98	11.7	0.8	10.49	2,919	3	95	2	0	31					Feb-14
50	3.36	13.76	6.21	26.29	3.53	2.34	0.89	11.67	0.8	10.48	2,919	3	95	2	0	31					Jan-17
50	3.09	13.16	5.13	22.07	-1.95	1.37	1.99	11.67	0.8	10.45	2,919	3	95	2	0	31					Feb-14
50	3.12	13.22	5.09	22.23	-2.20	1.41	1.97	11.72	0.8	10.42	2,919	3	95	2	0	31					Feb-14
50	3.26	13.35	5.49	23.38	0.30	1.59	1.72	11.67	0.8	10.46	2,919	3	95	2	0	31					Aug-14
50	3.31	13.42	5.65	23.96	0.30	1.74	1.53	11.68	0.8	10.47	2,919	3	95	2	0	31					Feb-14
50	3.38	13.69	5.95	25.03	1.89	2.02	1.23	11.71	0.8	10.48	2,919	3	95	2	0	31					Feb-14
50	3.35	13.72	6.27	26.12	3.40	2.3	0.93	11.74	0.81	10.49	2,919	3	95	2	0	31					Feb-14
50	3.33	13.68	6.16	25.92	3.05	2.2	1.02	11.73	0.8	10.47	2,919	3	95	2	0	31					Nov-15
50	3.46	13.87	6.33	26.33	3.67	2.35	0.87	11.77	0.81	10.49	2,919	3	95	2	0	31					Feb-14
50	3.77	17.89	1.49	36.00	22.03	1.18	0.89	12.38	1.06	52.22	161,594	6	94	0	0	35	16.82	-24.05	5.75		Feb-02
50	3.57	17.48	0.75	32.92	17.40	0.55	1.66	12.37	1.06	50.94	161,594	6	94	0	0	35	16.27	-24.31		1.00	Feb-02
50	3.71	17.76	1.29	35.07	20.59	0.96	1.12	12.38	1.06	51.72	161,594	6	94	0	0	35	16.64	-24.14			Mar-02
50	3.83	18.05	1.74	36.92	23.37	1.42	0.65	12.37	1.06	52.19	161,594	6	94	0	0	35	16.95	-23.96			Sep-02
50	3.79	17.95	1.56	36.25	22.37	1.21	0.83	12.38	1.06	52.89	161,594	6	94	0	0	35	16.84	-24.03	5.75		Apr-84
50	3.58	17.48	0.79	33.09	17.68	0.54	1.61	12.37	1.06	51.48	161,594	6	94	0	0	35	16.33	-24.28		1.00	Mar-01
50	3.79	17.91	1.54	36.09	22.19	1.15	0.87	12.38	1.06	52.64	161,594	6	94	0	0	35	16.84	-24.04			Mar-01
50	3.85	18.09	1.82	37.22	23.85	1.46	0.58	12.39	1.06	52.72	161,594	6	94	0	0	35	17.03	-23.96			Aug-08
50	3.86	18.14	1.91	37.34	23.36	1.55	0.49	12.39	1.06	52.87	161,594	6	94	0	0	35	16.84	-24.03			Jan-17
50	3.60	17.50	0.79	33.13	17.77	0.59	1.6	12.36	1.06	50.62	161,594	6	94	0	0	35	16.33	-24.28			Jun-02
50	3.61	17.50	0.79	33.18	17.87	0.6	1.59	12.36	1.05	51.08	161,594	6	94	0	0	35	16.33	-24.29			May-02
50	3.68	17.69	1.07	34.34	19.86	0.25	1.3	12.38	1.06	52.28	161,594	6	94	0	0	35	16.59	-24.14			Aug-14
50	3.71	17.76	1.24	34.97	20.53	0.91	1.14	12.37	1.06	51.71	161,594	6	94	0	0	35	16.64	-24.13			May-02
50	3.77	17.93	1.56	36.19	22.34	1.22	0.84	12.38	1.06	51.76	161,594	6	94	0	0	35	16.84	-24.05			Jun-02
50	3.86	18.11	1.85	37.42	24.19	1.5	0.53	12.38	1.06	52.77	161,594	6	94	0	0	35	17.05	-23.93			May-02
50	3.84	18.05	1.76	37.06	23.20	1.47	0.62	12.37	1.06	52.46	161,594	6	94	0	0	35	16.84	-24.03			Nov-15
50	3.87	18.13	1.91	37.62	24.47	1.55	0.49	12.37	1.06	52.82	161,594	6	94	0	0	35	17.06	-23.91			May-09
50	2.78	15.79	5.32	45.18	58.89	1.49	0.67	11.64	0.93	59.17	100,949	6	94	0	0	34	23.6	-19.71	5.75		Feb-02
50	2.59	15.36	4.53	41.90	52.87	0.77	1.44	11.65	0.93	59.16	100,949	6	94	0	0	34	23.04	-19.97		1.00	Feb-02
50	2.73	15.68	5.08	44.18	57.04	1.28	0.91	11.65	0.93	59.12	100,949	6	94	0	0	34	23.44	-19.79			Mar-02
50	2.86	15.96	5.58	46.16	60.67	1.71	0.44	11.66	0.93	59.12	100,949	6	94	0	0	34	23.75	-19.63			Sep-02
50	2.80	15.85	5.39	45.53	59.56	1.56	0.59	11.64	0.93	59.27	100,949	6	94	0	0	34	23.66	-19.67	5.75		Aug-78
50	2.59	15.39	4.57	42.10	53.33	0.82	1.39	11.64	0.93	58.94	100,949	6	94	0	0	34	23.1	-19.96		1.00	Mar-01
50	2.78	15.80	5.32	45.19	58.99	1.49	0.67	11.65	0.93	59.23	100,949	6	94	0	0	34	23.66	-19.69			Mar-01
50	2.85	15.96	5.60	46.34	61.11	1.74	0.4	11.65	0.93	59.25	100,949	6	94	0	0	34	23.81	-19.6			Aug-08
50	2.87	16.02	5.71	46.52	60.64	1.83	0.31	11.66	0.93	59.25	100,949	6	94	0	0	34	23.66	-19.67			Jan-17
50	2.60	15.38	4.54	42.02	53.26	0.79	1.41	11.64	0.93	58.94	100,949	6	94	0	0	34	23.12	-19.93			Jun-02
50	2.60	15.38	4.54	42.06	53.42	0.81	1.41	11.64	0.93	58.9	100,949	6	94	0	0	34	23.1	-19.93			May-02
50	2.69	15.58	4.87	43.37	56.37	1.1	1.1	11.64	0.93	58.96	100,949	6	94	0	0	34	23.4	-19.79			Aug-14
50	2.72	15.66	5.04	43.97	56.81	1.22	0.95	11.65	0.93	59.11	100,949	6	94	0	0	34	23.43	-19.77			Jun-02
50	2.79	15.82	5.34	45.26	59.16	1.51	0.65	11.65	0.93	59.13	100,949	6	94	0	0	34	23.66	-19.69			Jul-02

	MARKET			FUND TYPE, CATEGORY & OBJECTIVE	RATINGS					MINIMUMS
Fund Name	Ticker Symbol	Traded On	Fund Type	Category and (Prospectus Objective)	Overall Rating	Reward Rating	Risk Rating	Recent Up/ Downgrade	Open to New Investors	Min Initial Investment
American Funds Fundamental Investors® Class R-5	RFNFX	NAS CM	Open End	US Equity Large Cap Blend (Growth & Income)	B-	C	B	Up	Y	250
American Funds Fundamental Investors® Class R-5E	RFNHX	NAS CM	Open End	US Equity Large Cap Blend (Growth & Income)	B-	C	B	Up	Y	250
American Funds Fundamental Investors® Class R-6	RFNGX	NAS CM	Open End	US Equity Large Cap Blend (Growth & Income)	B-	C	B	Up	Y	250
American Funds Global Balanced Fund Class 529-A	CBFAX	NAS CM	Open End	Moderate Alloc (Balanced)	B-	C	A-	Up	Y	250
American Funds Global Balanced Fund Class 529-C	CBFCX	NAS CM	Open End	Moderate Alloc (Balanced)	B-	C	B+	Up	Y	250
American Funds Global Balanced Fund Class 529-E	CBFEX	NAS CM	Open End	Moderate Alloc (Balanced)	B-	C	A-	Up	Y	250
American Funds Global Balanced Fund Class 529-F-1	CBFFX	NAS CM	Open End	Moderate Alloc (Balanced)	B-	C	A-	Up	Y	250
American Funds Global Balanced Fund Class A	GBLAX	NAS CM	Open End	Moderate Alloc (Balanced)	B-	C	A-	Up	Y	250
American Funds Global Balanced Fund Class C	GBLCX	NAS CM	Open End	Moderate Alloc (Balanced)	B-	C	B+	Up	Y	250
American Funds Global Balanced Fund Class F-1	GBLEX	NAS CM	Open End	Moderate Alloc (Balanced)	B-	C	A-	Up	Y	250
American Funds Global Balanced Fund Class F-2	GBLFX	NAS CM	Open End	Moderate Alloc (Balanced)	B-	C	A-	Up	Y	250
American Funds Global Balanced Fund Class F-3	GFBLX	NAS CM	Open End	Moderate Alloc (Balanced)	B-	C	A-	Up	Y	1,000,000
American Funds Global Balanced Fund Class R-1	RGBLX	NAS CM	Open End	Moderate Alloc (Balanced)	B-	C	B+	Up	Y	250
American Funds Global Balanced Fund Class R-2	RGBBX	NAS CM	Open End	Moderate Alloc (Balanced)	B-	C	B+	Up	Y	250
American Funds Global Balanced Fund Class R-2E	RGGHX	NAS CM	Open End	Moderate Alloc (Balanced)	B-	C	B+	Up	Y	250
American Funds Global Balanced Fund Class R-3	RGBCX	NAS CM	Open End	Moderate Alloc (Balanced)	B-	C	A-	Up	Y	250
American Funds Global Balanced Fund Class R-4	RGBEX	NAS CM	Open End	Moderate Alloc (Balanced)	B-	C	A-	Up	Y	250
American Funds Global Balanced Fund Class R-5	RGBFX	NAS CM	Open End	Moderate Alloc (Balanced)	B-	C	A-	Up	Y	250
American Funds Global Balanced Fund Class R-5E	RGBHX	NAS CM	Open End	Moderate Alloc (Balanced)	B-	C	A-	Up	Y	250
American Funds Global Balanced Fund Class R-6	RGBGX	NAS CM	Open End	Moderate Alloc (Balanced)	B-	C	A-	Up	Y	250
American Funds Global Growth Portfolio Class 529-A	CPGAX	NAS CM	Open End	Global Equity Large Cap (Foreign Stock)	C+	C	B	Up	Y	250
American Funds Global Growth Portfolio Class 529-C	CPGCX	NAS CM	Open End	Global Equity Large Cap (Foreign Stock)	C+	C	B	Up	Y	250
American Funds Global Growth Portfolio Class 529-E	CGGEX	NAS CM	Open End	Global Equity Large Cap (Foreign Stock)	C+	C	B	Up	Y	250
American Funds Global Growth Portfolio Class 529-F-1	CGGFX	NAS CM	Open End	Global Equity Large Cap (Foreign Stock)	C+	C	B	Up	Y	250
American Funds Global Growth Portfolio Class A	PGGAX	NAS CM	Open End	Global Equity Large Cap (Foreign Stock)	C+	C	B	Up	Y	250
American Funds Global Growth Portfolio Class ABLE-A	CGGGX	NAS CM	Open End	Global Equity Large Cap (Foreign Stock)	C+	C	B	Up	Y	250
American Funds Global Growth Portfolio Class C	GGPCX	NAS CM	Open End	Global Equity Large Cap (Foreign Stock)	C+	C	B	Up	Y	250
American Funds Global Growth Portfolio Class F-1	PGGFX	NAS CM	Open End	Global Equity Large Cap (Foreign Stock)	C+	C	B	Up	Y	250
American Funds Global Growth Portfolio Class F-2	PGWFX	NAS CM	Open End	Global Equity Large Cap (Foreign Stock)	C+	C	B	Up	Y	250
American Funds Global Growth Portfolio Class F-3	PGXFX	NAS CM	Open End	Global Equity Large Cap (Foreign Stock)	C+	C	B	Up	Y	1,000,000
American Funds Global Growth Portfolio Class R-1	RGGAX	NAS CM	Open End	Global Equity Large Cap (Foreign Stock)	C+	C	B	Up	Y	250
American Funds Global Growth Portfolio Class R-2	RGGBX	NAS CM	Open End	Global Equity Large Cap (Foreign Stock)	C+	C	B	Up	Y	250
American Funds Global Growth Portfolio Class R-2E	REBGX	NAS CM	Open End	Global Equity Large Cap (Foreign Stock)	C+	C	B	Up	Y	250
American Funds Global Growth Portfolio Class R-3	RGLCX	NAS CM	Open End	Global Equity Large Cap (Foreign Stock)	C+	C	B	Up	Y	250
American Funds Global Growth Portfolio Class R-4	RGGEX	NAS CM	Open End	Global Equity Large Cap (Foreign Stock)	C+	C	B	Up	Y	250
American Funds Global Growth Portfolio Class R-5	RGGFX	NAS CM	Open End	Global Equity Large Cap (Foreign Stock)	C+	C	B	Up	Y	250
American Funds Global Growth Portfolio Class R-5E	RGTFX	NAS CM	Open End	Global Equity Large Cap (Foreign Stock)	C+	C	B	Up	Y	250
American Funds Global Growth Portfolio Class R-6	RGGGX	NAS CM	Open End	Global Equity Large Cap (Foreign Stock)	C+	C	B	Up	Y	250
American Funds Growth and Income Portfolio Class 529-A	CGNAX	NAS CM	Open End	Aggressive Alloc (Growth & Income)	B-	C	B+	Up	Y	250
American Funds Growth and Income Portfolio Class 529-C	CGNCX	NAS CM	Open End	Aggressive Alloc (Growth & Income)	B-	C	B+	Up	Y	250
American Funds Growth and Income Portfolio Class 529-E	CGNEX	NAS CM	Open End	Aggressive Alloc (Growth & Income)	B-	C	B+	Up	Y	250
American Funds Growth and Income Portfolio Class 529-F-1	CGNFX	NAS CM	Open End	Aggressive Alloc (Growth & Income)	B-	C	B+	Up	Y	250
American Funds Growth and Income Portfolio Class A	GAIOX	NAS CM	Open End	Aggressive Alloc (Growth & Income)	B-	C	B+	Up	Y	250
American Funds Growth and Income Portfolio Class ABLE-A	CGNGX	NAS CM	Open End	Aggressive Alloc (Growth & Income)	B-	C	B+	Up	Y	250
American Funds Growth and Income Portfolio Class C	GAITX	NAS CM	Open End	Aggressive Alloc (Growth & Income)	B-	C	B+	Up	Y	250
American Funds Growth and Income Portfolio Class F-1	GAIFX	NAS CM	Open End	Aggressive Alloc (Growth & Income)	B-	C	B+	Up	Y	250
American Funds Growth and Income Portfolio Class F-2	GAIEX	NAS CM	Open End	Aggressive Alloc (Growth & Income)	B-	C	B+	Up	Y	250
American Funds Growth and Income Portfolio Class F-3	GAIHX	NAS CM	Open End	Aggressive Alloc (Growth & Income)	B-	C	B+	Up	Y	1,000,000
American Funds Growth and Income Portfolio Class R-1	RGNAX	NAS CM	Open End	Aggressive Alloc (Growth & Income)	B-	C	B+	Up	Y	250
American Funds Growth and Income Portfolio Class R-2	RGNBX	NAS CM	Open End	Aggressive Alloc (Growth & Income)	B-	C	B+	Up	Y	250
American Funds Growth and Income Portfolio Class R-2E	RBEGX	NAS CM	Open End	Aggressive Alloc (Growth & Income)	B-	C	B+	Up	Y	250
American Funds Growth and Income Portfolio Class R-3	RAICX	NAS CM	Open End	Aggressive Alloc (Growth & Income)	B-	C	B+	Up	Y	250

★ Expanded analysis of this fund is included in Section II.

	TOTAL RETURNS					PERFORMANCE				ASSETS		ASSET ALLOCATION & TURNOVER					BULL & BEAR		FEES		
Min Additional Investment	3-Month Total Return	6-Month Total Return	1-Year Total Return	3-Year Total Return	5-Year Total Return	Dividend Yield (TTM)	Expense Ratio	3-Yr Std Deviation	3-Year Beta	NAV	Total Assets (MIL)	%Cash	%Stocks	%Bonds	%Other	Turnover Ratio	Last Bull Market Total Return	Last Bear Market Total Return	Front End Fee (%)	Back End Fee (%)	Inception Date
50	2.88	16.00	5.67	46.61	61.58	1.79	0.35	11.65	0.93	59.32	100,949	6	94	0	0	34	23.86	-19.59			May-02
50	2.84	15.96	5.58	46.18	60.35	1.73	0.44	11.65	0.93	59.16	100,949	6	94	0	0	34	23.66	-19.67			Nov-15
50	2.87	16.02	5.71	46.81	61.96	1.84	0.3	11.65	0.93	59.28	100,949	6	94	0	0	34	23.9	-19.57			May-09
50	2.21	11.47	4.53	19.79	18.85	1.94	0.89	7.14	0.59	32.76	19,381	6	58	36	0	44	13.38	-12.19	5.75		Feb-11
50	1.99	11.02	3.76	17.04	14.30	1.21	1.66	7.13	0.59	32.66	19,381	6	58	36	0	44	12.81	-12.51		1.00	Feb-11
50	2.12	11.33	4.31	18.97	17.49	1.73	1.12	7.13	0.59	32.73	19,381	6	58	36	0	44	13.17	-12.28			Feb-11
50	2.26	11.59	4.81	20.60	20.15	2.16	0.66	7.14	0.59	32.77	19,381	6	58	36	0	44	13.44	-12.1			Feb-11
50	2.23	11.50	4.60	19.97	19.24	2	0.84	7.14	0.59	32.78	19,381	6	58	36	0	44	13.42	-12.22	5.75		Feb-11
50	2.00	11.06	3.79	17.21	14.63	1.24	1.6	7.12	0.58	32.71	19,381	6	58	36	0	44	12.86	-12.47		1.00	Feb-11
50	2.18	11.42	4.53	19.79	18.92	1.93	0.88	7.14	0.59	32.79	19,381	6	58	36	0	44	13.42	-12.2			Feb-11
50	2.27	11.60	4.82	20.76	20.52	2.2	0.61	7.14	0.59	32.79	19,381	6	58	36	0	44	13.53	-12.1			Feb-11
50	2.30	11.67	4.93	21.14	21.12	2.3	0.52	7.14	0.59	32.77	19,381	6	58	36	0	44	13.62	-12.07			Jan-17
50	2.02	11.04	3.78	17.22	14.91	1.23	1.62	7.13	0.59	32.74	19,381	6	58	36	0	44	12.9	-12.44			Feb-11
50	2.01	11.06	3.81	17.25	14.74	1.26	1.6	7.12	0.58	32.67	19,381	6	58	36	0	44	12.99	-12.43			Feb-11
50	2.09	11.21	4.12	18.29	17.24	1.58	1.31	7.13	0.59	32.71	19,381	6	58	36	0	44	13.22	-12.29			Aug-14
50	2.15	11.30	4.27	18.83	17.33	1.69	1.15	7.12	0.58	32.73	19,381	6	58	36	0	44	13.24	-12.3			Feb-11
50	2.19	11.45	4.57	19.87	19.07	1.97	0.86	7.13	0.59	32.77	19,381	6	58	36	0	44	13.44	-12.17			Feb-11
50	2.28	11.62	4.90	20.96	20.85	2.24	0.65	7.13	0.59	32.82	19,381	6	58	36	0	44	13.6	-12.08			Feb-11
50	2.23	11.57	4.76	20.72	20.53	2.18	0.65	7.14	0.59	32.75	19,381	6	58	36	0	44	13.62	-12.07			Nov-15
50	2.30	11.66	4.96	21.16	21.14	2.3	0.52	7.13	0.59	32.8	19,381	6	58	36	0	44	13.62	-12.07			Feb-11
50	3.56	18.07	4.08	44.80	39.47	0.93	0.85	11.79	1.02	16.85	3,676	7	93	0	0	64			5.75		May-12
50	3.36	17.63	3.33	41.45	34.07	0.19	1.63	11.77	1.02	16.61	3,676	7	93	0	0	64				1.00	May-12
50	3.52	17.94	3.85	43.75	37.72	0.74	1.09	11.8	1.02	16.76	3,676	7	93	0	0	64					May-12
50	3.61	18.16	4.35	45.73	40.98	1.16	0.63	11.77	1.02	16.91	3,676	7	93	0	0	64					May-12
50	3.55	18.12	4.14	44.91	39.84	0.93	0.83	11.8	1.02	16.88	3,676	7	93	0	0	64			5.75		May-12
50	3.57	18.13	4.23	45.07	39.82		0.82	11.75	1.02	16.81	3,676	7	93	0	0	64			5.75		Jul-18
50	3.36	17.64	3.37	41.65	34.56	0.27	1.56	11.77	1.02	16.6	3,676	7	93	0	0	64				1.00	May-12
50	3.55	18.09	4.13	44.82	39.54	0.93	0.82	11.8	1.02	16.9	3,676	7	93	0	0	64					May-12
50	3.66	18.28	4.44	46.05	41.45	1.18	0.57	11.82	1.02	16.95	3,676	7	93	0	0	64					May-12
50	3.67	18.33	4.51	46.43	41.98	1.28	0.46	11.77	1.02	16.91	3,676	7	93	0	0	64					Jan-17
50	3.40	17.70	3.46	41.77	34.61	0.26	1.54	11.78	1.02	16.69	3,676	7	93	0	0	64					May-12
50	3.43	17.69	3.39	41.73	34.54	0.28	1.55	11.81	1.02	16.56	3,676	7	93	0	0	64					May-12
50	3.46	17.84	3.74	43.28	38.31	0.79	1.26	11.8	1.02	16.71	3,676	7	93	0	0	64					Aug-14
50	3.52	17.94	3.89	43.67	37.65	0.71	1.11	11.77	1.02	16.76	3,676	7	93	0	0	64					May-12
50	3.62	18.15	4.17	45.00	39.80	0.96	0.81	11.78	1.02	16.86	3,676	7	93	0	0	64					May-12
50	3.65	18.26	4.47	46.27	41.83	1.22	0.52	11.8	1.02	17.03	3,676	7	93	0	0	64					May-12
50	3.69	18.24	4.45	45.98	41.45	1.23	0.61	11.81	1.02	16.85	3,676	7	93	0	0	64					Nov-15
50	3.70	18.37	4.58	46.47	42.22	1.27	0.46	11.78	1.02	17.07	3,676	7	93	0	0	64					May-12
50	2.65	13.64	4.92	31.85	35.58	1.86	0.72	8.99	0.7	15.05	9,679	6	76	17	0	30			5.75		May-12
50	2.47	13.24	4.08	28.91	30.37	1.14	1.49	8.99	0.7	14.98	9,679	6	76	17	0	30				1.00	May-12
50	2.60	13.56	4.70	31.01	33.97	1.65	0.96	9	0.7	15.02	9,679	6	76	17	0	30					May-12
50	2.71	13.75	5.10	32.82	37.02	2.09	0.49	8.96	0.7	15.06	9,679	6	76	17	0	30					May-12
50	2.66	13.73	4.95	32.11	36.08	1.88	0.68	8.98	0.7	15.06	9,679	6	76	17	0	30			5.75		May-12
50	2.67	13.68	4.96	32.05	35.86		0.68	8.98	0.7	15.04	9,679	6	76	17	0	30			5.75		Jul-18
50	2.42	13.20	4.14	29.13	30.88	1.2	1.42	8.97	0.7	14.96	9,679	6	76	17	0	30				1.00	May-12
50	2.65	13.72	4.92	31.96	35.78	1.86	0.71	8.99	0.7	15.06	9,679	6	76	17	0	30					May-12
50	2.71	13.82	5.19	32.95	37.57	2.1	0.45	8.99	0.7	15.08	9,679	6	76	17	0	30					May-12
50	2.74	13.90	5.31	33.34	38.02	2.2	0.34	8.96	0.7	15.06	9,679	6	76	17	0	30					Jan-17
50	2.43	13.21	4.15	29.04	30.82	1.21	1.43	8.96	0.7	14.99	9,679	6	76	17	0	30					May-12
50	2.50	13.32	4.17	29.15	30.86	1.22	1.42	9.02	0.7	14.95	9,679	6	76	17	0	30					May-12
50	2.56	13.48	4.45	30.23	33.83	1.49	1.15	9.01	0.7	15.02	9,679	6	76	17	0	30					Aug-14
50	2.59	13.55	4.65	30.84	33.80	1.6	0.99	9	0.7	15.01	9,679	6	76	17	0	30					May-12

	MARKET		FUND TYPE, CATEGORY & OBJECTIVE		RATINGS				MINIMUMS	
Fund Name	Ticker Symbol	Traded On	Fund Type	Category and (Prospectus Objective)	Overall Rating	Reward Rating	Risk Rating	Recent Up/ Downgrade	Open to New Investors	Min Initial Investment
American Funds Growth and Income Portfolio Class R-4	RGNEX	NAS CM	Open End	Aggressive Alloc (Growth & Income)	B-	C	B+	Up	Y	250
American Funds Growth and Income Portfolio Class R-5	RGNFX	NAS CM	Open End	Aggressive Alloc (Growth & Income)	B-	C	B+	Up	Y	250
American Funds Growth and Income Portfolio Class R-5E	RGQFX	NAS CM	Open End	Aggressive Alloc (Growth & Income)	B-	C	B+	Up	Y	250
American Funds Growth and Income Portfolio Class R-6	RGNGX	NAS CM	Open End	Aggressive Alloc (Growth & Income)	B-	C	B+	Up	Y	250
American Funds Growth Portfolio Class 529-A	CGPAX	NAS CM	Open End	US Equity Large Cap Growth (Growth)	B-	C	B	Up	Y	250
American Funds Growth Portfolio Class 529-C	CGPCX	NAS CM	Open End	US Equity Large Cap Growth (Growth)	C+	C	B	Up	Y	250
American Funds Growth Portfolio Class 529-E	CGPEX	NAS CM	Open End	US Equity Large Cap Growth (Growth)	B-	C	B	Up	Y	250
American Funds Growth Portfolio Class 529-F-1	CGPFX	NAS CM	Open End	US Equity Large Cap Growth (Growth)	B-	C	B	Up	Y	250
American Funds Growth Portfolio Class A	GWPAX	NAS CM	Open End	US Equity Large Cap Growth (Growth)	B-	C	B	Up	Y	250
American Funds Growth Portfolio Class ABLE-A	CGQGX	NAS CM	Open End	US Equity Large Cap Growth (Growth)	B-	C	B	Up	Y	250
American Funds Growth Portfolio Class C	GWPCX	NAS CM	Open End	US Equity Large Cap Growth (Growth)	C+	C	B	Up	Y	250
American Funds Growth Portfolio Class F-1	GWPFX	NAS CM	Open End	US Equity Large Cap Growth (Growth)	B-	C	B	Up	Y	250
American Funds Growth Portfolio Class F-2	GWPEX	NAS CM	Open End	US Equity Large Cap Growth (Growth)	B-	C	B	Up	Y	250
American Funds Growth Portfolio Class F-3	GWPDX	NAS CM	Open End	US Equity Large Cap Growth (Growth)	B-	C	B	Up	Y	1,000,000
American Funds Growth Portfolio Class R-1	RGWAX	NAS CM	Open End	US Equity Large Cap Growth (Growth)	C+	C	B	Up	Y	250
American Funds Growth Portfolio Class R-2	RGWBX	NAS CM	Open End	US Equity Large Cap Growth (Growth)	C+	C	B	Up	Y	250
American Funds Growth Portfolio Class R-2E	RBGEX	NAS CM	Open End	US Equity Large Cap Growth (Growth)	B-	C	B	Up	Y	250
American Funds Growth Portfolio Class R-3	RGPCX	NAS CM	Open End	US Equity Large Cap Growth (Growth)	B-	C	B	Up	Y	250
American Funds Growth Portfolio Class R-4	RGWEX	NAS CM	Open End	US Equity Large Cap Growth (Growth)	B-	C	B	Up	Y	250
American Funds Growth Portfolio Class R-5	RGWFX	NAS CM	Open End	US Equity Large Cap Growth (Growth)	B-	C	B	Up	Y	250
American Funds Growth Portfolio Class R-5E	RGSFX	NAS CM	Open End	US Equity Large Cap Growth (Growth)	B-	C	B	Up	Y	250
American Funds Growth Portfolio Class R-6	RGWGX	NAS CM	Open End	US Equity Large Cap Growth (Growth)	B-	C	B	Up	Y	250
American Funds International Growth & Income Cls 529-A	CGIAX	NAS CM	Open End	Global Equity Large Cap (Foreign Stock)	C	C	B-		Y	250
American Funds International Growth & Income Cls 529-C	CIICX	NAS CM	Open End	Global Equity Large Cap (Foreign Stock)	C	C	B-		Y	250
American Funds International Growth & Income Cls 529-E	CGIEX	NAS CM	Open End	Global Equity Large Cap (Foreign Stock)	C	C	B-		Y	250
American Funds International Growth & Income Cls 529-F-1	CGIFX	NAS CM	Open End	Global Equity Large Cap (Foreign Stock)	C	C	B-		Y	250
American Funds International Growth & Income Cls A	IGAAX	NAS CM	Open End	Global Equity Large Cap (Foreign Stock)	C	C	B-		Y	250
American Funds International Growth & Income Cls C	IGICX	NAS CM	Open End	Global Equity Large Cap (Foreign Stock)	C	C	B-		Y	250
American Funds International Growth & Income Cls F-1	IGIFX	NAS CM	Open End	Global Equity Large Cap (Foreign Stock)	C	C	B-		Y	250
American Funds International Growth & Income Cls F-2	IGFFX	NAS CM	Open End	Global Equity Large Cap (Foreign Stock)	C	C	B-		Y	250
American Funds International Growth & Income Cls F-3	IGAIX	NAS CM	Open End	Global Equity Large Cap (Foreign Stock)	C	C	B-		Y	1,000,000
American Funds International Growth & Income Cls R-1	RIGAX	NAS CM	Open End	Global Equity Large Cap (Foreign Stock)	C	C	B-		Y	250
American Funds International Growth & Income Cls R-2	RIGBX	NAS CM	Open End	Global Equity Large Cap (Foreign Stock)	C	C	B-		Y	250
American Funds International Growth & Income Cls R-2E	RIIEX	NAS CM	Open End	Global Equity Large Cap (Foreign Stock)	C	C	B-		Y	250
American Funds International Growth & Income Cls R-3	RGICX	NAS CM	Open End	Global Equity Large Cap (Foreign Stock)	C	C	B-		Y	250
American Funds International Growth & Income Cls R-4	RIGEX	NAS CM	Open End	Global Equity Large Cap (Foreign Stock)	C	C	B-		Y	250
American Funds International Growth & Income Cls R-5	RIGFX	NAS CM	Open End	Global Equity Large Cap (Foreign Stock)	C	C	B-		Y	250
American Funds International Growth & Income Cls R-5E	RIGIX	NAS CM	Open End	Global Equity Large Cap (Foreign Stock)	C	C	B-		Y	250
American Funds International Growth & Income Cls R-6	RIGGX	NAS CM	Open End	Global Equity Large Cap (Foreign Stock)	C	C	B-		Y	250
American Funds Investment Company of America® Class 529-A	CICAX	NAS CM	Open End	US Equity Large Cap Blend (Equity-Income)	B-	C	B	Up	Y	250
American Funds Investment Company of America® Class 529-C	CICCX	NAS CM	Open End	US Equity Large Cap Blend (Equity-Income)	B-	C	B	Up	Y	250
American Funds Investment Company of America® class 529-E	CICEX	NAS CM	Open End	US Equity Large Cap Blend (Equity-Income)	B-	C	B	Up	Y	250
American Funds Investment Company of America® class 529-F	CICFX	NAS CM	Open End	US Equity Large Cap Blend (Equity-Income)	B-	C	B	Up	Y	250
American Funds Investment Company of America® Class A	AIVSX	NAS CM	Open End	US Equity Large Cap Blend (Equity-Income)	B-	C	B	Up	Y	250
American Funds Investment Company of America® Class C	AICCX	NAS CM	Open End	US Equity Large Cap Blend (Equity-Income)	B-	C	B	Up	Y	250
American Funds Investment Company of America® Class F-1	AICFX	NAS CM	Open End	US Equity Large Cap Blend (Equity-Income)	B-	C	B	Up	Y	250
American Funds Investment Company of America® Class F-2	ICAFX	NAS CM	Open End	US Equity Large Cap Blend (Equity-Income)	B-	C	B	Up	Y	250
American Funds Investment Company of America® Class F-3	FFICX	NAS CM	Open End	US Equity Large Cap Blend (Equity-Income)	B-	C	B	Up	Y	1,000,000
American Funds Investment Company of America® Class R-1	RICAX	NAS CM	Open End	US Equity Large Cap Blend (Equity-Income)	B-	C	B	Up	Y	250
American Funds Investment Company of America® Class R-2	RICBX	NAS CM	Open End	US Equity Large Cap Blend (Equity-Income)	B-	C	B	Up	Y	250
American Funds Investment Company of America® Class R-2E	RIBEX	NAS CM	Open End	US Equity Large Cap Blend (Equity-Income)	B-	C	B	Up	Y	250
American Funds Investment Company of America® Class R-3	RICCX	NAS CM	Open End	US Equity Large Cap Blend (Equity-Income)	B-	C	B	Up	Y	250

★ Expanded analysis of this fund is included in Section II.

	TOTAL RETURNS					PERFORMANCE				ASSETS		ASSET ALLOCATION & TURNOVER					BULL & BEAR		FEES		
Min Additional Investment	3-Month Total Return	6-Month Total Return	1-Year Total Return	3-Year Total Return	5-Year Total Return	Dividend Yield (TTM)	Expense Ratio	3-Yr Std Deviation	3-Year Beta	NAV	Total Assets (MIL)	%Cash	%Stocks	%Bonds	%Other	Turnover Ratio	Last Bull Market Total Return	Last Bear Market Total Return	Front End Fee (%)	Back End Fee (%)	Inception Date
50	2.66	13.65	4.95	31.96	35.86	1.88	0.69	8.96	0.7	15.05	9,679	6	76	17	0	30					May-12
50	2.72	13.91	5.23	33.18	37.85	2.15	0.4	8.98	0.7	15.11	9,679	6	76	17	0	30					May-12
50	2.71	13.77	5.10	32.86	37.31	2.08	0.49	8.96	0.7	15.04	9,679	6	76	17	0	30					Nov-15
50	2.74	13.88	5.23	33.34	38.23	2.2	0.34	9.02	0.7	15.08	9,679	6	76	17	0	30					May-12
50	3.18	17.25	4.30	46.17	48.35	0.8	0.79	11.76	0.93	18.48	8,323	8	92	0	0	33			5.75		May-12
50	2.94	16.78	3.50	42.74	42.51	0.06	1.56	11.79	0.93	18.16	8,323	8	92	0	0	33				1.00	May-12
50	3.08	17.10	4.02	45.14	46.39	0.59	1.02	11.78	0.93	18.35	8,323	8	92	0	0	33					May-12
50	3.22	17.39	4.54	47.20	49.91	1	0.56	11.77	0.93	18.56	8,323	8	92	0	0	33					May-12
50	3.17	17.30	4.33	46.43	48.79	0.82	0.75	11.8	0.93	18.51	8,323	8	92	0	0	33			5.75		May-12
50	3.18	17.30	4.36	46.34	48.56		0.75	11.78	0.93	18.44	8,323	8	92	0	0	33			5.75		Jul-18
50	2.94	16.77	3.50	43.05	43.02	0.15	1.5	11.77	0.93	18.17	8,323	8	92	0	0	33				1.00	May-12
50	3.17	17.31	4.31	46.27	48.42	0.8	0.76	11.81	0.93	18.5	8,323	8	92	0	0	33					May-12
50	3.27	17.43	4.60	47.45	50.39	1.06	0.5	11.8	0.93	18.59	8,323	8	92	0	0	33					May-12
50	3.28	17.55	4.72	47.84	50.98	1.14	0.4	11.79	0.93	18.55	8,323	8	92	0	0	33					Jan-17
50	2.99	16.92	3.57	43.10	43.11	0.3	1.49	11.77	0.93	18.24	8,323	8	92	0	0	33					May-12
50	3.00	16.92	3.60	43.17	43.13	0.18	1.48	11.79	0.93	18.17	8,323	8	92	0	0	33					May-12
50	3.04	17.04	3.88	44.36	46.04	0.47	1.2	11.78	0.93	18.27	8,323	8	92	0	0	33					Aug-14
50	3.08	17.14	4.03	45.01	46.27	0.56	1.04	11.78	0.93	18.38	8,323	8	92	0	0	33					May-12
50	3.18	17.33	4.34	46.37	48.57	0.83	0.74	11.78	0.93	18.48	8,323	8	92	0	0	33					May-12
50	3.26	17.42	4.62	47.58	50.72	1.08	0.45	11.78	0.93	18.67	8,323	8	92	0	0	33					May-12
50	3.24	17.40	4.58	47.32	50.25	1.02	0.54	11.79	0.93	18.48	8,323	8	92	0	0	33					Nov-15
50	3.27	17.46	4.70	47.82	51.11	1.13	0.4	11.75	0.93	18.63	8,323	8	92	0	0	33					May-12
50	3.81	15.95	2.30	29.25	5.59	2.26	0.96	11.38	0.98	33.19	15,349	6	94	0	0	27	12.97	-20.1	5.75		Oct-08
50	3.64	15.52	1.51	26.28	1.53	1.55	1.73	11.38	0.98	33.03	15,349	6	94	0	0	27	12.45	-20.37		1.00	Oct-08
50	3.76	15.83	2.06	28.46	4.45	2.07	1.16	11.37	0.98	33.19	15,349	6	94	0	0	27	12.82	-20.2			Oct-08
50	3.90	16.09	2.53	30.11	6.75	2.48	0.74	11.39	0.98	33.24	15,349	6	94	0	0	27	13.1	-20.03			Oct-08
50	3.82	15.96	2.33	29.49	5.96	2.32	0.9	11.38	0.98	33.23	15,349	6	94	0	0	27	13.02	-20.09	5.75		Oct-08
50	3.67	15.55	1.58	26.49	1.84	1.56	1.69	11.38	0.98	33.16	15,349	6	94	0	0	27	12.49	-20.37		1.00	Oct-08
50	3.81	15.96	2.29	29.29	5.69	2.28	0.94	11.38	0.98	33.27	15,349	6	94	0	0	27	13.02	-20.1			Oct-08
50	3.91	16.12	2.60	30.37	7.13	2.54	0.68	11.38	0.98	33.25	15,349	6	94	0	0	27	13.15	-20.01			Oct-08
50	3.94	16.19	2.70	30.68	7.38	2.64	0.58	11.38	0.98	33.22	15,349	6	94	0	0	27	13.15	-20.01			Jan-17
50	3.66	15.57	1.61	26.63	2.23	1.59	1.69	11.38	0.98	33.16	15,349	6	94	0	0	27	12.66	-20.25			Oct-08
50	3.66	15.56	1.59	26.56	1.80	1.6	1.66	11.38	0.98	33.06	15,349	6	94	0	0	27	12.46	-20.34			Oct-08
50	3.73	15.72	1.85	27.63	4.08	1.9	1.38	11.38	0.98	33.09	15,349	6	94	0	0	27	12.76	-20.21			Aug-14
50	3.79	15.82	2.03	28.28	4.23	2.02	1.22	11.39	0.98	33.17	15,349	6	94	0	0	27	12.76	-20.18			Oct-08
50	3.83	15.97	2.33	29.40	5.85	2.3	0.92	11.38	0.98	33.21	15,349	6	94	0	0	27	13.03	-20.08			Oct-08
50	3.91	16.14	2.64	30.60	7.47	2.58	0.62	11.4	0.98	33.41	15,349	6	94	0	0	27	13.2	-20			Oct-08
50	3.88	16.10	2.56	30.20	6.91	2.54	0.72	11.38	0.98	33.2	15,349	6	94	0	0	27	13.15	-20.01			Nov-15
50	3.94	16.20	2.71	30.82	7.75	2.65	0.57	11.37	0.98	33.23	15,349	6	94	0	0	27	13.2	-19.97			May-09
50	2.16	14.34	4.20	37.70	48.30	1.73	0.65	11.22	0.89	38.05	96,708	7	93	0	0	36	22.41	-17.26	5.75		Feb-02
50	1.98	13.92	3.45	34.62	42.75	1.02	1.42	11.2	0.89	37.96	96,708	7	93	0	0	36	21.82	-17.54		1.00	Feb-02
50	2.11	14.23	3.97	36.74	46.54	1.51	0.9	11.21	0.89	37.92	96,708	7	93	0	0	36	22.23	-17.38			Mar-02
50	2.23	14.49	4.46	38.66	49.98	1.96	0.42	11.21	0.89	38	96,708	7	93	0	0	36	22.56	-17.21			Sep-02
50	2.15	14.38	4.29	38.05	48.97	1.81	0.57	11.21	0.89	38.15	96,708	7	93	0	0	36	22.48	-17.24	5.75		Jan-34
50	1.98	13.95	3.47	34.82	43.15	1.08	1.37	11.2	0.89	37.72	96,708	7	93	0	0	36	21.89	-17.51		1.00	Mar-01
50	2.16	14.33	4.20	37.70	48.30	1.73	0.66	11.2	0.89	38.05	96,708	7	93	0	0	36	22.41	-17.24			Mar-01
50	2.20	14.48	4.48	38.78	50.32	1.98	0.39	11.22	0.89	38.13	96,708	7	93	0	0	36	22.62	-17.15			Aug-08
50	2.25	14.57	4.58	38.98	49.97	2.07	0.3	11.23	0.9	38.14	96,708	7	93	0	0	36	22.48	-17.24			Jan-17
50	1.97	13.93	3.44	34.73	43.05	1.05	1.39	11.19	0.89	37.82	96,708	7	93	0	0	36	21.91	-17.5			Jun-02
50	1.97	13.91	3.43	34.71	43.11	1.05	1.39	11.2	0.89	37.87	96,708	7	93	0	0	36	21.89	-17.52			May-02
50	2.06	14.08	3.76	35.96	45.70	1.33	1.09	11.2	0.89	38.03	96,708	7	93	0	0	36	22.23	-17.36			Aug-14
50	2.10	14.17	3.91	36.55	46.25	1.46	0.94	11.22	0.89	38	96,708	7	93	0	0	36	22.24	-17.36			Jun-02

	MARKET		FUND TYPE, CATEGORY & OBJECTIVE		RATINGS				MINIMUMS	
Fund Name	Ticker Symbol	Traded On	Fund Type	Category and (Prospectus Objective)	Overall Rating	Reward Rating	Risk Rating	Recent Up/ Downgrade	Open to New Investors	Min Initial Investment
American Funds Investment Company of America® Class R-4	RICEX	NAS CM	Open End	US Equity Large Cap Blend (Equity-Income)	B-	C	B	Up	Y	250
American Funds Investment Company of America® Class R-5	RICFX	NAS CM	Open End	US Equity Large Cap Blend (Equity-Income)	B-	C	B	Up	Y	250
American Funds Investment Company of America® Class R-5E	RICHX	NAS CM	Open End	US Equity Large Cap Blend (Equity-Income)	B-	C	B	Up	Y	250
American Funds Investment Company of America® Class R-6	RICGX	NAS CM	Open End	US Equity Large Cap Blend (Equity-Income)	B-	C	B	Up	Y	250
American Funds Moderate Growth & Inc Port Cls 529-A	CBAAX	NAS CM	Open End	Moderate Alloc (Balanced)	B	C	A-	Up	Y	250
American Funds Moderate Growth & Inc Port Cls 529-C	CBPCX	NAS CM	Open End	Moderate Alloc (Balanced)	B-	C	A-	Up	Y	250
American Funds Moderate Growth & Inc Port Cls 529-E	CBAEX	NAS CM	Open End	Moderate Alloc (Balanced)	B	C	A-	Up	Y	250
American Funds Moderate Growth & Inc Port Cls 529-F-1	CBAFX	NAS CM	Open End	Moderate Alloc (Balanced)	B	C	A-	Up	Y	250
American Funds Moderate Growth & Income Portfolio Cls A	BLPAX	NAS CM	Open End	Moderate Alloc (Balanced)	B	C	A-	Up	Y	250
American Funds Moderate Growth & Inc Port Cls ABLE-A	CBAGX	NAS CM	Open End	Moderate Alloc (Balanced)	B	C	A-	Up	Y	250
American Funds Moderate Growth & Income Portfolio Cls C	BLPCX	NAS CM	Open End	Moderate Alloc (Balanced)	B-	C	A-	Up	Y	250
American Funds Moderate Growth & Income Portfolio Cls F-1	BLPFX	NAS CM	Open End	Moderate Alloc (Balanced)	B	C	A-	Up	Y	250
American Funds Moderate Growth & Income Portfolio Cls F-2	BLPEX	NAS CM	Open End	Moderate Alloc (Balanced)	B	C	A-	Up	Y	250
American Funds Moderate Growth & Income Portfolio Cls F-3	BLPDX	NAS CM	Open End	Moderate Alloc (Balanced)	B	C	A-	Up	Y	1,000,000
American Funds Moderate Growth & Income Portfolio Cls R-1	RBAAX	NAS CM	Open End	Moderate Alloc (Balanced)	B-	C	A-	Up	Y	250
American Funds Moderate Growth & Income Portfolio Cls R-2	RBABX	NAS CM	Open End	Moderate Alloc (Balanced)	B-	C	A-	Up	Y	250
American Funds Moderate Growth & Income Portfolio Cls R-2E	RBBEX	NAS CM	Open End	Moderate Alloc (Balanced)	B-	C	A-	Up	Y	250
American Funds Moderate Growth & Income Portfolio Cls R-3	RBACX	NAS CM	Open End	Moderate Alloc (Balanced)	B	C	A-	Up	Y	250
American Funds Moderate Growth & Income Portfolio Cls R-4	RBAEX	NAS CM	Open End	Moderate Alloc (Balanced)	B	C	A-	Up	Y	250
American Funds Moderate Growth & Income Portfolio Cls R-5	RBAFX	NAS CM	Open End	Moderate Alloc (Balanced)	B	C	A-	Up	Y	250
American Funds Moderate Growth & Income Portfolio Cls R-5E	RGPFX	NAS CM	Open End	Moderate Alloc (Balanced)	B	C	A-	Up	Y	250
American Funds Moderate Growth & Income Portfolio Cls R-6	RBAGX	NAS CM	Open End	Moderate Alloc (Balanced)	B	C	A-	Up	Y	250
American Funds New Perspective Fund® Class 529-A	CNPAX	NAS CM	Open End	Global Equity Large Cap (World Stock)	C+	C	B		Y	250
American Funds New Perspective Fund® Class 529-C	CNPCX	NAS CM	Open End	Global Equity Large Cap (World Stock)	C+	C	B	Up	Y	250
American Funds New Perspective Fund® Class 529-E	CNPEX	NAS CM	Open End	Global Equity Large Cap (World Stock)	C+	C	B		Y	250
American Funds New Perspective Fund® Class 529-F	CNPFX	NAS CM	Open End	Global Equity Large Cap (World Stock)	B-	C	B	Up	Y	250
American Funds New Perspective Fund® Class A	ANWPX	NAS CM	Open End	Global Equity Large Cap (World Stock)	B-	C	B	Up	Y	250
American Funds New Perspective Fund® Class C	NPFCX	NAS CM	Open End	Global Equity Large Cap (World Stock)	C+	C	B	Up	Y	250
American Funds New Perspective Fund® Class F-1	NPFFX	NAS CM	Open End	Global Equity Large Cap (World Stock)	C+	C	B		Y	250
American Funds New Perspective Fund® Class F-2	ANWFX	NAS CM	Open End	Global Equity Large Cap (World Stock)	B-	C	B	Up	Y	250
American Funds New Perspective Fund® Class F-3	FNPFX	NAS CM	Open End	Global Equity Large Cap (World Stock)	B-	C	B	Up	Y	1,000,000
American Funds New Perspective Fund® Class R-1	RNPAX	NAS CM	Open End	Global Equity Large Cap (World Stock)	C+	C	B	Up	Y	250
American Funds New Perspective Fund® Class R-2	RNPBX	NAS CM	Open End	Global Equity Large Cap (World Stock)	C+	C	B	Up	Y	250
American Funds New Perspective Fund® Class R-2E	RPEBX	NAS CM	Open End	Global Equity Large Cap (World Stock)	C+	C	B	Up	Y	250
American Funds New Perspective Fund® Class R-3	RNPCX	NAS CM	Open End	Global Equity Large Cap (World Stock)	C+	C	B		Y	250
American Funds New Perspective Fund® Class R-4	RNPEX	NAS CM	Open End	Global Equity Large Cap (World Stock)	C+	C	B		Y	250
American Funds New Perspective Fund® Class R-5	RNPFX	NAS CM	Open End	Global Equity Large Cap (World Stock)	B-	C	B	Up	Y	250
American Funds New Perspective Fund® Class R-5E	RNPHX	NAS CM	Open End	Global Equity Large Cap (World Stock)	B-	C	B	Up	Y	250
American Funds New Perspective Fund® Class R-6	RNPGX	NAS CM	Open End	Global Equity Large Cap (World Stock)	B-	C	B	Up	Y	250
American Funds New World Fund® Class 529-A	CNWAX	NAS CM	Open End	Global Emerg Mkts (Div Emerging Mkts)	C+	C	B	Up	Y	250
American Funds New World Fund® Class 529-C	CNWCX	NAS CM	Open End	Global Emerg Mkts (Div Emerging Mkts)	C+	C	B-	Up	Y	250
American Funds New World Fund® Class 529-E	CNWEX	NAS CM	Open End	Global Emerg Mkts (Div Emerging Mkts)	C+	C	B-	Up	Y	250
American Funds New World Fund® Class 529-F	CNWFX	NAS CM	Open End	Global Emerg Mkts (Div Emerging Mkts)	C+	C	B	Up	Y	250
American Funds New World Fund® Class A	NEWFX	NAS CM	Open End	Global Emerg Mkts (Div Emerging Mkts)	C+	C	B	Up	Y	250
American Funds New World Fund® Class C	NEWCX	NAS CM	Open End	Global Emerg Mkts (Div Emerging Mkts)	C+	C	B-	Up	Y	250
American Funds New World Fund® Class F-1	NWFFX	NAS CM	Open End	Global Emerg Mkts (Div Emerging Mkts)	C+	C	B	Up	Y	250
American Funds New World Fund® Class F-2	NFFFX	NAS CM	Open End	Global Emerg Mkts (Div Emerging Mkts)	C+	C	B	Up	Y	250
American Funds New World Fund® Class F-3	FNWFX	NAS CM	Open End	Global Emerg Mkts (Div Emerging Mkts)	C+	C	B	Up	Y	1,000,000
American Funds New World Fund® Class R-1	RNWAX	NAS CM	Open End	Global Emerg Mkts (Div Emerging Mkts)	C+	C	B-	Up	Y	250
American Funds New World Fund® Class R-2	RNWBX	NAS CM	Open End	Global Emerg Mkts (Div Emerging Mkts)	C+	C	B-	Up	Y	250
American Funds New World Fund® Class R-2E	RNEBX	NAS CM	Open End	Global Emerg Mkts (Div Emerging Mkts)	C+	C	B-	Up	Y	250
American Funds New World Fund® Class R-3	RNWCX	NAS CM	Open End	Global Emerg Mkts (Div Emerging Mkts)	C+	C	B-	Up	Y	250

★ Expanded analysis of this fund is included in Section II.

	TOTAL RETURNS					PERFORMANCE				ASSETS		ASSET ALLOCATION & TURNOVER					BULL & BEAR		FEES		
Min Additional Investment	3-Month Total Return	6-Month Total Return	1-Year Total Return	3-Year Total Return	5-Year Total Return	Dividend Yield (TTM)	Expense Ratio	3-Yr Std Deviation	3-Year Beta	NAV	Total Assets (MIL)	%Cash	%Stocks	%Bonds	%Other	Turnover Ratio	Last Bull Market Total Return	Last Bear Market Total Return	Front End Fee (%)	Back End Fee (%)	Inception Date
50	2.17	14.35	4.22	37.79	48.54	1.75	0.64	11.21	0.89	38.04	96,708	7	93	0	0	36	22.41	-17.24			May-02
50	2.24	14.54	4.56	39.03	50.75	2.03	0.34	11.21	0.89	38.15	96,708	7	93	0	0	36	22.65	-17.13			May-02
50	2.19	14.48	4.44	38.63	49.66	1.95	0.43	11.21	0.89	38.12	96,708	7	93	0	0	36	22.48	-17.24			Nov-15
50	2.25	14.54	4.58	39.24	51.11	2.08	0.29	11.21	0.89	38.14	96,708	7	93	0	0	36	22.68	-17.13			May-09
50	3.02	12.52	6.27	28.33	34.52	1.84	0.77	7.2	0.55	15.01	8,894	6	62	32	0	15			5.75		May-12
50	2.77	12.11	5.43	25.46	29.46	1.13	1.53	7.23	0.55	14.95	8,894	6	62	32	0	15				1.00	May-12
50	2.90	12.43	5.98	27.49	32.94	1.63	1	7.26	0.55	14.98	8,894	6	62	32	0	15					May-12
50	3.08	12.70	6.53	29.28	36.09	2.07	0.53	7.22	0.55	15.03	8,894	6	62	32	0	15					May-12
50	2.96	12.53	6.23	28.52	34.94	1.86	0.73	7.2	0.55	15.01	8,894	6	62	32	0	15			5.75		May-12
50	3.03	12.55	6.32	28.61	34.89		0.73	7.22	0.55	15.01	8,894	6	62	32	0	15			5.75		Jul-18
50	2.79	12.08	5.50	25.71	29.93	1.19	1.46	7.2	0.55	14.92	8,894	6	62	32	0	15				1.00	May-12
50	2.95	12.51	6.20	28.36	34.66	1.84	0.76	7.21	0.55	15.01	8,894	6	62	32	0	15					May-12
50	3.01	12.62	6.47	29.44	36.47	2.08	0.5	7.18	0.55	15.03	8,894	6	62	32	0	15					May-12
50	3.04	12.70	6.59	29.73	36.88	2.18	0.39	7.22	0.55	15.01	8,894	6	62	32	0	15					Jan-17
50	2.78	12.12	5.47	25.57	29.77	1.17	1.49	7.24	0.55	14.95	8,894	6	62	32	0	15					May-12
50	2.79	12.17	5.50	25.74	29.88	1.18	1.48	7.25	0.55	14.93	8,894	6	62	32	0	15					May-12
50	2.92	12.32	5.81	26.72	32.87	1.48	1.23	7.24	0.55	15.01	8,894	6	62	32	0	15					Aug-14
50	2.96	12.41	6.00	27.33	32.77	1.58	1.04	7.21	0.55	14.98	8,894	6	62	32	0	15					May-12
50	2.96	12.53	6.21	28.48	34.84	1.84	0.74	7.21	0.55	15.01	8,894	6	62	32	0	15					May-12
50	3.02	12.64	6.51	29.61	36.76	2.12	0.45	7.2	0.55	15.04	8,894	6	62	32	0	15					May-12
50	3.00	12.61	6.43	29.21	36.23	2.04	0.53	7.19	0.55	15.02	8,894	6	62	32	0	15					Nov-15
50	3.03	12.75	6.64	29.80	37.10	2.17	0.39	7.23	0.55	15.04	8,894	6	62	32	0	15					May-12
50	4.27	19.60	6.95	50.76	53.91	0.88	0.83	12.11	1.03	44.17	89,711	6	94	0	0	23	20.66	-19.76	5.75		Feb-02
50	4.07	19.16	6.17	47.37	48.10	0.14	1.6	12.09	1.03	42.66	89,711	6	94	0	0	23	20.08	-20.01		1.00	Feb-02
50	4.22	19.49	6.72	49.73	52.12	0.66	1.06	12.1	1.03	43.7	89,711	6	94	0	0	23	20.46	-19.85			Mar-02
50	4.33	19.75	7.21	51.81	55.66	1.14	0.6	12.1	1.03	44.07	89,711	6	94	0	0	23	20.8	-19.68			Sep-02
50	4.28	19.65	7.05	51.13	54.55	0.95	0.75	12.1	1.03	44.75	89,711	6	94	0	0	23	20.71	-19.74	5.75		Mar-73
50	4.08	19.20	6.20	47.57	48.50	0.23	1.54	12.08	1.03	42.76	89,711	6	94	0	0	23	20.15	-20		1.00	Mar-01
50	4.29	19.65	6.98	50.78	54.02	0.86	0.82	12.1	1.03	44.45	89,711	6	94	0	0	23	20.71	-19.76			Mar-01
50	4.32	19.79	7.26	52.02	56.12	1.16	0.55	12.09	1.03	44.61	89,711	6	94	0	0	23	20.91	-19.65			Aug-08
50	4.35	19.86	7.36	52.22	55.67	1.23	0.45	12.1	1.03	44.78	89,711	6	94	0	0	23	20.71	-19.74			Jan-17
50	4.07	19.17	6.18	47.52	48.50	0.18	1.55	12.09	1.03	42.39	89,711	6	94	0	0	23	20.17	-19.99			Jun-02
50	4.08	19.20	6.19	47.56	48.58	0.19	1.55	12.09	1.03	42.83	89,711	6	94	0	0	23	20.16	-20			May-02
50	4.17	19.35	6.50	48.92	51.65	0.48	1.25	12.09	1.03	43.96	89,711	6	94	0	0	23	20.46	-19.85			Aug-14
50	4.20	19.45	6.67	49.56	51.90	0.6	1.1	12.09	1.03	43.65	89,711	6	94	0	0	23	20.51	-19.84			Jun-02
50	4.28	19.64	7.02	50.90	54.24	0.9	0.8	12.09	1.03	44.09	89,711	6	94	0	0	23	20.7	-19.76			May-02
50	4.36	19.82	7.31	52.26	56.53	1.19	0.49	12.1	1.03	44.73	89,711	6	94	0	0	23	20.9	-19.64			May-02
50	4.34	19.81	7.26	51.78	55.28	1.25	0.6	12.1	1.03	44.44	89,711	6	94	0	0	23	20.71	-19.74			Nov-15
50	4.35	19.85	7.37	52.50	56.91	1.24	0.45	12.09	1.03	44.8	89,711	6	94	0	0	23	20.94	-19.61			May-09
50	3.74	18.43	6.34	40.76	22.29	0.81	1.06	11.46	0.9	67.08	40,537	8	87	4	0	37	17.54	-21.94	5.75		Feb-02
50	3.56	17.98	5.56	37.53	17.60	0.04	1.85	11.46	0.9	65.42	40,537	8	87	4	0	37	16.99	-22.22		1.00	Feb-02
50	3.70	18.32	6.14	39.91	21.02	0.6	1.28	11.47	0.9	66.58	40,537	8	87	4	0	37	17.35	-22.03			Mar-02
50	3.80	18.54	6.59	41.67	23.59	1.08	0.84	11.46	0.9	67.04	40,537	8	87	4	0	37	17.68	-21.88			Sep-02
50	3.77	18.46	6.42	41.01	22.68	0.85	1	11.46	0.9	67.7	40,537	8	87	4	0	37	17.55	-21.93	5.75		Jun-99
50	3.55	17.99	5.58	37.68	17.86	0.09	1.79	11.45	0.9	65.25	40,537	8	87	4	0	37	17.03	-22.19		1.00	Mar-01
50	3.74	18.46	6.40	41.01	22.73	0.81	1.01	11.47	0.9	67.25	40,537	8	87	4	0	37	17.59	-21.93			Mar-01
50	3.82	18.63	6.71	42.22	24.45	1.15	0.72	11.47	0.9	67.56	40,537	8	87	4	0	37	17.78	-21.84			Aug-08
50	3.86	18.68	6.82	42.28	23.79	1.22	0.63	11.47	0.9	67.77	40,537	8	87	4	0	37	17.55	-21.92			Jan-17
50	3.56	17.99	5.59	37.75	18.02	0.09	1.78	11.46	0.9	65.44	40,537	8	87	4	0	37	17.03	-22.19			Jun-02
50	3.57	18.03	5.65	38.01	18.32	0.14	1.73	11.46	0.9	65.44	40,537	8	87	4	0	37	17.06	-22.18			Jun-02
50	3.64	18.21	5.96	39.25	20.43	0.5	1.44	11.46	0.9	66.77	40,537	8	87	4	0	37	17.31	-22.04			Aug-14
50	3.68	18.29	6.11	39.82	20.98	0.57	1.29	11.46	0.9	66.67	40,537	8	87	4	0	37	17.37	-22.04			Jun-02

Fund Name	MARKET Ticker Symbol	MARKET Traded On	FUND TYPE, CATEGORY & OBJECTIVE Fund Type	Category and (Prospectus Objective)	RATINGS Overall Rating	Reward Rating	Risk Rating	Recent Up/ Downgrade	MINIMUMS Open to New Investors	Min Initial Investment
American Funds New World Fund® Class R-4	RNWEX	NAS CM	Open End	Global Emerg Mkts (Div Emerging Mkts)	C+	C	B	Up	Y	250
American Funds New World Fund® Class R-5	RNWFX	NAS CM	Open End	Global Emerg Mkts (Div Emerging Mkts)	C+	C	B	Up	Y	250
American Funds New World Fund® Class R-5E	RNWHX	NAS CM	Open End	Global Emerg Mkts (Div Emerging Mkts)	C+	C	B	Up	Y	250
American Funds New World Fund® Class R-6	RNWGX	NAS CM	Open End	Global Emerg Mkts (Div Emerging Mkts)	C+	C	B	Up	Y	250
American Funds Retmnt Income Port - Conservative Cls A	NAARX	NAS CM	Open End	Cautious Alloc (Income)	B-	C+	B+		Y	250
American Funds Retmnt Income Port - Conservative Cls C	NGCRX	NAS CM	Open End	Cautious Alloc (Income)	B-	C	B		Y	250
American Funds Retmnt Income Port - Conservative Cls F-1	FAFWX	NAS CM	Open End	Cautious Alloc (Income)	B-	C+	B+		Y	250
American Funds Retmnt Income Port - Conservative Cls F-2	FDFWX	NAS CM	Open End	Cautious Alloc (Income)	B	C+	B+		Y	250
American Funds Retmnt Income Port - Conservative Cls F-3	FICWX	NAS CM	Open End	Cautious Alloc (Income)	B	C+	B+		Y	1,000,000
American Funds Retmnt Income Port - Conservative Cls R-1	RARPX	NAS CM	Open End	Cautious Alloc (Income)	B-	C	B		Y	250
American Funds Retmnt Income Port - Conservative Cls R-2	RDRPX	NAS CM	Open End	Cautious Alloc (Income)	B-	C	B		Y	250
American Funds Retmnt Income Port - Conservative Cls R-2E	RGRPX	NAS CM	Open End	Cautious Alloc (Income)	B	C+	B+		Y	250
American Funds Retmnt Income Port - Conservative Cls R-3	RJRPX	NAS CM	Open End	Cautious Alloc (Income)	B-	C	B+		Y	250
American Funds Retmnt Income Port - Conservative Cls R-4	RMRPX	NAS CM	Open End	Cautious Alloc (Income)	B-	C+	B+		Y	250
American Funds Retmnt Income Port - Conservative Cls R-5	RQRPX	NAS CM	Open End	Cautious Alloc (Income)	B	C+	B+		Y	250
American Funds Retmnt Income Port - Conservative Cls R-5E	RROPX	NAS CM	Open End	Cautious Alloc (Income)	B	C+	B+		Y	250
American Funds Retmnt Income Port - Conservative Cls R-6	RTRPX	NAS CM	Open End	Cautious Alloc (Income)	B	C+	B+		Y	250
American Funds Retmnt Income Portfolio - Enhanced Cls A	NDARX	NAS CM	Open End	Moderate Alloc (Income)	B	C	A-	Up	Y	250
American Funds Retmnt Income Portfolio - Enhanced Cls C	NDCRX	NAS CM	Open End	Moderate Alloc (Income)	B-	C	B+	Up	Y	250
American Funds Retmnt Income Portfolio - Enhanced Cls F-1	FCFWX	NAS CM	Open End	Moderate Alloc (Income)	B	C	A-	Up	Y	250
American Funds Retmnt Income Portfolio - Enhanced Cls F-2	FGFWX	NAS CM	Open End	Moderate Alloc (Income)	B	C	A-	Up	Y	250
American Funds Retmnt Income Portfolio - Enhanced Cls F-3	FIEWX	NAS CM	Open End	Moderate Alloc (Income)	B	C	A-	Up	Y	1,000,000
American Funds Retmnt Income Portfolio - Enhanced Cls R-1	RCRPX	NAS CM	Open End	Moderate Alloc (Income)	B-	C	A-	Up	Y	250
American Funds Retmnt Income Portfolio - Enhanced Cls R-2	RFRPX	NAS CM	Open End	Moderate Alloc (Income)	B-	C	A-	Up	Y	250
American Funds Retmnt Income Portfolio - Enhanced Cls R-2E	RIRPX	NAS CM	Open End	Moderate Alloc (Income)	B	C	A-	Up	Y	250
American Funds Retmnt Income Portfolio - Enhanced Cls R-3	RLRPX	NAS CM	Open End	Moderate Alloc (Income)	B-	C	A-	Up	Y	250
American Funds Retmnt Income Portfolio - Enhanced Cls R-4	RPRPX	NAS CM	Open End	Moderate Alloc (Income)	B	C	A-	Up	Y	250
American Funds Retmnt Income Portfolio - Enhanced Cls R-5	RXRPX	NAS CM	Open End	Moderate Alloc (Income)	B	C	A-	Up	Y	250
American Funds Retmnt Income Portfolio - Enhanced Cls R-5E	RRQPX	NAS CM	Open End	Moderate Alloc (Income)	B	C	A-	Up	Y	250
American Funds Retmnt Income Portfolio - Enhanced Cls R-6	RVRPX	NAS CM	Open End	Moderate Alloc (Income)	B	C	A-	Up	Y	250
American Funds Retmnt Income Portfolio - Moderate Cls A	NBARX	NAS CM	Open End	Moderate Alloc (Income)	B	C+	A-	Up	Y	250
American Funds Retmnt Income Portfolio - Moderate Cls C	NBCRX	NAS CM	Open End	Moderate Alloc (Income)	B-	C	B+	Up	Y	250
American Funds Retmnt Income Portfolio - Moderate Cls F-1	FBFWX	NAS CM	Open End	Moderate Alloc (Income)	B	C	A-	Up	Y	250
American Funds Retmnt Income Portfolio - Moderate Cls F-2	FHFWX	NAS CM	Open End	Moderate Alloc (Income)	B	C+	A-	Up	Y	250
American Funds Retmnt Income Portfolio - Moderate Cls F-3	FIMWX	NAS CM	Open End	Moderate Alloc (Income)	B	C+	A-		Y	1,000,000
American Funds Retmnt Income Portfolio - Moderate Cls R-1	RBRPX	NAS CM	Open End	Moderate Alloc (Income)	B-	C	B+	Up	Y	250
American Funds Retmnt Income Portfolio - Moderate Cls R-2	RERPX	NAS CM	Open End	Moderate Alloc (Income)	B-	C	B+		Y	250
American Funds Retmnt Income Portfolio - Moderate Cls R-2E	RHRPX	NAS CM	Open End	Moderate Alloc (Income)	B	C+	A-	Up	Y	250
American Funds Retmnt Income Portfolio - Moderate Cls R-3	RKRPX	NAS CM	Open End	Moderate Alloc (Income)	B-	C	A-		Y	250
American Funds Retmnt Income Portfolio - Moderate Cls R-4	RNRPX	NAS CM	Open End	Moderate Alloc (Income)	B	C	A-	Up	Y	250
American Funds Retmnt Income Portfolio - Moderate Cls R-5	RRRPX	NAS CM	Open End	Moderate Alloc (Income)	B	C+	A-	Up	Y	250
American Funds Retmnt Income Portfolio - Moderate Cls R-5E	RRPPX	NAS CM	Open End	Moderate Alloc (Income)	B	C+	A-	Up	Y	250
American Funds Retmnt Income Portfolio - Moderate Cls R-6	RURPX	NAS CM	Open End	Moderate Alloc (Income)	B	C+	A-		Y	250
American Funds SMALLCAP World Fund® Class 529-A	CSPAX	NAS CM	Open End	Global Equity Mid/Small Cap (Small Company)	C+	C	B-	Up	Y	250
American Funds SMALLCAP World Fund® Class 529-C	CSPCX	NAS CM	Open End	Global Equity Mid/Small Cap (Small Company)	C+	C	B-	Up	Y	250
American Funds SMALLCAP World Fund® Class 529-E	CSPEX	NAS CM	Open End	Global Equity Mid/Small Cap (Small Company)	C+	C	B-	Up	Y	250
American Funds SMALLCAP World Fund® Class 529-F	CSPFX	NAS CM	Open End	Global Equity Mid/Small Cap (Small Company)	C+	C	B-	Up	Y	250
American Funds SMALLCAP World Fund® Class A	SMCWX	NAS CM	Open End	Global Equity Mid/Small Cap (Small Company)	C+	C	B-	Up	Y	250
American Funds SMALLCAP World Fund® Class C	SCWCX	NAS CM	Open End	Global Equity Mid/Small Cap (Small Company)	C+	C	B-	Up	Y	250
American Funds SMALLCAP World Fund® Class F-1	SCWFX	NAS CM	Open End	Global Equity Mid/Small Cap (Small Company)	C+	C	B-	Up	Y	250
American Funds SMALLCAP World Fund® Class F-2	SMCFX	NAS CM	Open End	Global Equity Mid/Small Cap (Small Company)	C+	C	B	Up	Y	250
American Funds SMALLCAP World Fund® Class F-3	SFCWX	NAS CM	Open End	Global Equity Mid/Small Cap (Small Company)	C+	C	B	Up	Y	1,000,000

★ Expanded analysis of this fund is included in Section II.

	TOTAL RETURNS					PERFORMANCE				ASSETS		ASSET ALLOCATION & TURNOVER					BULL & BEAR		FEES		
Min Additional Investment	3-Month Total Return	6-Month Total Return	1-Year Total Return	3-Year Total Return	5-Year Total Return	Dividend Yield (TTM)	Expense Ratio	3-Yr Std Deviation	3-Year Beta	NAV	Total Assets (MIL)	%Cash	%Stocks	%Bonds	%Other	Turnover Ratio	Last Bull Market Total Return	Last Bear Market Total Return	Front End Fee (%)	Back End Fee (%)	Inception Date
50	3.76	18.49	6.45	41.16	22.93	0.9	0.98	11.46	0.9	67.28	40,537	8	87	4	0	37	17.61	-21.92			Oct-02
50	3.85	18.66	6.78	42.43	24.81	1.2	0.68	11.48	0.9	67.91	40,537	8	87	4	0	37	17.81	-21.82			May-02
50	3.83	18.62	6.67	41.91	23.62	1.15	0.77	11.47	0.9	67.08	40,537	8	87	4	0	37	17.55	-21.92			Nov-15
50	3.86	18.69	6.83	42.66	25.11	1.23	0.62	11.47	0.9	67.74	40,537	8	87	4	0	37	17.84	-21.8			May-09
50	2.50	8.60	6.55	15.63		2.45	0.67	4.08	0.98	11.12	706.9	5	37	57	0	2			5.75		Aug-15
50	2.34	8.31	5.85	13.31		1.8	1.37	4.1	0.98	11.08	706.9	5	37	57	0	2				1.00	Aug-15
50	2.59	8.69	6.64	15.62		2.44	0.69	4.08	0.97	11.13	706.9	5	37	57	0	2					Aug-15
50	2.65	8.80	6.87	16.44		2.66	0.45	4.12	0.98	11.14	706.9	5	37	57	0	2					Aug-15
50	2.58	8.86	6.89	16.56		2.75	0.35	4.12	0.98	11.13	706.9	5	37	57	0	2					Jan-17
50	2.41	8.34	5.86	13.10		1.73	1.44	4.11	0.98	11.12	706.9	5	37	57	0	2					Aug-15
50	2.47	8.36	6.02	13.91		1.97	1.21	4.13	0.99	11.12	706.9	5	37	57	0	2					Aug-15
50	2.64	8.76	6.72	16.27		2.52	1.15	4.09	0.98	11.15	706.9	5	37	57	0	2					Aug-15
50	2.48	8.50	6.25	14.55		2.09	0.98	4.08	0.98	11.14	706.9	5	37	57	0	2					Aug-15
50	2.60	8.70	6.60	15.63		2.4	0.71	4.09	0.98	11.13	706.9	5	37	57	0	2					Aug-15
50	2.67	8.81	6.89	16.44		2.68	0.42	4.17	1	11.15	706.9	5	37	57	0	2					Aug-15
50	2.55	8.68	6.73	16.30		2.61	0.49	4.11	0.98	11.13	706.9	5	37	57	0	2					Nov-15
50	2.58	8.84	6.88	16.74		2.75	0.35	4.11	0.98	11.14	706.9	5	37	57	0	2					Aug-15
50	2.42	10.95	6.16	22.90		2.64	0.68	6.69	1.57	11.68	980.0	5	63	32	0	1			5.75		Aug-15
50	2.26	10.64	5.45	20.42		1.98	1.38	6.73	1.58	11.65	980.0	5	63	32	0	1				1.00	Aug-15
50	2.41	11.02	6.22	22.85		2.61	0.71	6.7	1.57	11.69	980.0	5	63	32	0	1					Aug-15
50	2.47	11.13	6.46	23.73		2.83	0.46	6.68	1.57	11.7	980.0	5	63	32	0	1					Aug-15
50	2.50	11.19	6.58	23.70		2.94	0.46	6.68	1.57	11.69	980.0	5	63	32	0	1					Jan-17
50	2.22	10.53	5.48	21.04		2.18	1.46	6.67	1.57	11.66	980.0	5	63	32	0	1					Aug-15
50	2.25	10.69	5.67	21.11		2.27	1.21	6.64	1.56	11.64	980.0	5	63	32	0	1					Aug-15
50	2.31	10.76	6.07	23.28		2.56	1.16	6.68	1.57	11.7	980.0	5	63	32	0	1					Aug-15
50	2.38	10.87	5.92	21.84		2.5	0.98	6.63	1.56	11.67	980.0	5	63	32	0	1					Aug-15
50	2.44	10.97	6.24	23.13		2.71	0.71	6.73	1.58	11.69	980.0	5	63	32	0	1					Aug-15
50	2.50	11.15	6.50	23.74		2.86	0.42	6.69	1.57	11.71	980.0	5	63	32	0	1					Aug-15
50	2.55	11.10	6.40	23.76		2.77	0.48	6.74	1.58	11.7	980.0	5	63	32	0	1					Nov-15
50	2.50	11.08	6.48	24.07		2.93	0.36	6.68	1.57	11.7	980.0	5	63	32	0	1					Aug-15
50	2.50	9.76	6.45	19.31		2.58	0.66	5.31	1.27	11.38	912.1	5	50	44	0	3			5.75		Aug-15
50	2.23	9.35	5.64	16.80		1.92	1.36	5.34	1.27	11.33	912.1	5	50	44	0	3				1.00	Aug-15
50	2.47	9.73	6.40	19.17		2.54	0.68	5.34	1.27	11.38	912.1	5	50	44	0	3					Aug-15
50	2.45	9.84	6.57	20.03		2.79	0.44	5.31	1.26	11.39	912.1	5	50	44	0	3					Aug-15
50	2.56	9.90	6.77	20.28		2.88	0.34	5.3	1.26	11.38	912.1	5	50	44	0	3					Jan-17
50	2.26	9.27	5.67	16.89		1.97	1.43	5.32	1.27	11.37	912.1	5	50	44	0	3					Aug-15
50	2.35	9.50	5.89	17.61		2.07	1.24	5.32	1.27	11.36	912.1	5	50	44	0	3					Aug-15
50	2.51	9.79	6.55	19.91		2.69	1.14	5.36	1.28	11.4	912.1	5	50	44	0	3					Aug-15
50	2.43	9.53	6.11	18.70		2.36	0.95	5.35	1.28	11.37	912.1	5	50	44	0	3					Aug-15
50	2.47	9.73	6.43	19.55		2.57	0.69	5.34	1.27	11.39	912.1	5	50	44	0	3					Aug-15
50	2.54	9.80	6.64	19.95		2.76	0.41	5.38	1.28	11.4	912.1	5	50	44	0	3					Aug-15
50	2.52	9.80	6.57	20.03		2.7	0.69	5.36	1.28	11.39	912.1	5	50	44	0	3					Nov-15
50	2.55	9.87	6.76	20.44		2.87	0.34	5.32	1.27	11.4	912.1	5	50	44	0	3					Aug-15
50	4.19	21.46	3.95	47.55	46.10	0	1.11	12.43	0.93	55.69	44,800	9	91	0	0	35	23.83	-24.43	5.75		Feb-02
50	3.99	21.00	3.17	44.18	40.54	0	1.9	12.42	0.93	49.49	44,800	9	91	0	0	35	23.27	-24.69		1.00	Feb-02
50	4.11	21.33	3.74	46.63	44.54	0	1.33	12.44	0.93	53.85	44,800	9	91	0	0	35	23.66	-24.53			Mar-02
50	4.21	21.60	4.16	48.47	47.65	0	0.89	12.44	0.93	56.57	44,800	9	91	0	0	35	24	-24.38			Sep-02
50	4.19	21.51	4.01	47.83	46.60	0	1.04	12.43	0.93	56.43	44,800	9	91	0	0	35	23.85	-24.41	5.75		Apr-90
50	3.98	21.02	3.19	44.34	40.87	0	1.84	12.43	0.93	48.53	44,800	9	91	0	0	35	23.33	-24.66		1.00	Mar-01
50	4.19	21.48	3.95	47.63	46.36	0	1.09	12.42	0.93	55.69	44,800	9	91	0	0	35	23.88	-24.41			Mar-01
50	4.24	21.64	4.27	48.96	48.53	0	0.79	12.43	0.93	57.43	44,800	9	91	0	0	35	24.12	-24.34			Aug-08
50	4.28	21.71	4.36	49.07	47.83	0	0.71	12.44	0.93	56.94	44,800	9	91	0	0	35	23.85	-24.41			Jan-17

	MARKET		FUND TYPE, CATEGORY & OBJECTIVE		RATINGS				MINIMUMS	
Fund Name	Ticker Symbol	Traded On	Fund Type	Category and (Prospectus Objective)	Overall Rating	Reward Rating	Risk Rating	Recent Up/ Downgrade	Open to New Investors	Min Initial Investment
American Funds SMALLCAP World Fund® Class R-1	RSLAX	NAS CM	Open End	Global Equity Mid/Small Cap (Small Company)	C+	C	B-	Up	Y	250
American Funds SMALLCAP World Fund® Class R-2	RSLBX	NAS CM	Open End	Global Equity Mid/Small Cap (Small Company)	C+	C	B-	Up	Y	250
American Funds SMALLCAP World Fund® Class R-2E	RSEBX	NAS CM	Open End	Global Equity Mid/Small Cap (Small Company)	C+	C	B-	Up	Y	250
American Funds SMALLCAP World Fund® Class R-3	RSLCX	NAS CM	Open End	Global Equity Mid/Small Cap (Small Company)	C+	C	B-	Up	Y	250
American Funds SMALLCAP World Fund® Class R-4	RSLEX	NAS CM	Open End	Global Equity Mid/Small Cap (Small Company)	C+	C	B-	Up	Y	250
American Funds SMALLCAP World Fund® Class R-5	RSLFX	NAS CM	Open End	Global Equity Mid/Small Cap (Small Company)	C+	C	B	Up	Y	250
American Funds SMALLCAP World Fund® Class R-5E	RSLDX	NAS CM	Open End	Global Equity Mid/Small Cap (Small Company)	C+	C	B-	Up	Y	250
American Funds SMALLCAP World Fund® Class R-6	RLLGX	NAS CM	Open End	Global Equity Mid/Small Cap (Small Company)	C+	C	B	Up	Y	250
American Funds Tax-Advantaged Growth & Inc Port Cls A	TAIAX	NAS CM	Open End	Cautious Alloc (Growth & Income)	B	C+	A		Y	250
American Funds Tax-Advantaged Growth & Inc Port Cls C	TAICX	NAS CM	Open End	Cautious Alloc (Growth & Income)	B	C+	A	Up	Y	250
American Funds Tax-Advantaged Growth & Inc Port Cls F-1	TAIFX	NAS CM	Open End	Cautious Alloc (Growth & Income)	B	C+	A		Y	250
American Funds Tax-Advantaged Growth & Inc Port Cls F-2	TXIFX	NAS CM	Open End	Cautious Alloc (Growth & Income)	B	C+	A		Y	250
American Funds Tax-Advantaged Growth & Inc Port Cls F-3	TYIFX	NAS CM	Open End	Cautious Alloc (Growth & Income)	B	C+	A		Y	1,000,000
★ American Funds The Growth Fund of America® Class 529-A	CGFAX	NAS CM	Open End	US Equity Large Cap Growth (Growth)	C+	C	B		Y	250
★ American Funds The Growth Fund of America® Class 529-C	CGFCX	NAS CM	Open End	US Equity Large Cap Growth (Growth)	C+	C	B		Y	250
★ American Funds The Growth Fund of America® Class 529-E	CGFEX	NAS CM	Open End	US Equity Large Cap Growth (Growth)	C+	C	B		Y	250
★ American Funds The Growth Fund of America® Class 529-F	CGFFX	NAS CM	Open End	US Equity Large Cap Growth (Growth)	B-	C	B		Y	250
★ American Funds The Growth Fund of America® Class A	AGTHX	NAS CM	Open End	US Equity Large Cap Growth (Growth)	B-	C	B		Y	250
★ American Funds The Growth Fund of America® Class C	GFACX	NAS CM	Open End	US Equity Large Cap Growth (Growth)	C+	C	B		Y	250
★ American Funds The Growth Fund of America® Class F-1	GFAFX	NAS CM	Open End	US Equity Large Cap Growth (Growth)	C+	C	B	Down	Y	250
★ American Funds The Growth Fund of America® Class F-2	GFFFX	NAS CM	Open End	US Equity Large Cap Growth (Growth)	B-	C	B		Y	250
American Funds The Growth Fund of America® Class F-3	GAFFX	NAS CM	Open End	US Equity Large Cap Growth (Growth)	B-	C	B		Y	1,000,000
★ American Funds The Growth Fund of America® Class R-1	RGAAX	NAS CM	Open End	US Equity Large Cap Growth (Growth)	C+	C	B		Y	250
★ American Funds The Growth Fund of America® Class R-2	RGABX	NAS CM	Open End	US Equity Large Cap Growth (Growth)	C+	C	B		Y	250
★ American Funds The Growth Fund of America® Class R-2E	RGEBX	NAS CM	Open End	US Equity Large Cap Growth (Growth)	C+	C	B		Y	250
★ American Funds The Growth Fund of America® Class R-3	RGACX	NAS CM	Open End	US Equity Large Cap Growth (Growth)	C+	C	B		Y	250
★ American Funds The Growth Fund of America® Class R-4	RGAEX	NAS CM	Open End	US Equity Large Cap Growth (Growth)	C+	C	B	Down	Y	250
★ American Funds The Growth Fund of America® Class R-5	RGAFX	NAS CM	Open End	US Equity Large Cap Growth (Growth)	B-	C	B		Y	250
★ American Funds The Growth Fund of America® Class R-5E	RGAHX	NAS CM	Open End	US Equity Large Cap Growth (Growth)	B-	C	B		Y	250
★ American Funds The Growth Fund of America® Class R-6	RGAGX	NAS CM	Open End	US Equity Large Cap Growth (Growth)	B-	C	B		Y	250
★ American Funds The Income Fund of America® Class 529-A	CIMAX	NAS CM	Open End	Aggressive Alloc (Income)	B	C	A-	Up	Y	250
★ American Funds The Income Fund of America® Class 529-C	CIMCX	NAS CM	Open End	Aggressive Alloc (Income)	B-	C	A-	Up	Y	250
★ American Funds The Income Fund of America® Class 529-E	CIMEX	NAS CM	Open End	Aggressive Alloc (Income)	B	C	A-	Up	Y	250
★ American Funds The Income Fund of America® Class 529-F-1	CIMFX	NAS CM	Open End	Aggressive Alloc (Income)	B	C	A-	Up	Y	250
★ American Funds The Income Fund of America® Class A	AMECX	NAS CM	Open End	Aggressive Alloc (Income)	B	C	A-	Up	Y	250
★ American Funds The Income Fund of America® Class C	IFACX	NAS CM	Open End	Aggressive Alloc (Income)	B-	C	A-	Up	Y	250
★ American Funds The Income Fund of America® Class F-1	IFAFX	NAS CM	Open End	Aggressive Alloc (Income)	B	C	A-	Up	Y	250
★ American Funds The Income Fund of America® Class F-2	AMEFX	NAS CM	Open End	Aggressive Alloc (Income)	B	C	A-	Up	Y	250
American Funds The Income Fund of America® Class F-3	FIFAX	NAS CM	Open End	Aggressive Alloc (Income)	B	C	A	Up	Y	1,000,000
★ American Funds The Income Fund of America® Class R-1	RIDAX	NAS CM	Open End	Aggressive Alloc (Income)	B-	C	A-	Up	Y	250
★ American Funds The Income Fund of America® Class R-2	RIDBX	NAS CM	Open End	Aggressive Alloc (Income)	B-	C	A-	Up	Y	250
★ American Funds The Income Fund of America® Class R-2E	RIEBX	NAS CM	Open End	Aggressive Alloc (Income)	B-	C	A-	Up	Y	250
★ American Funds The Income Fund of America® Class R-3	RIDCX	NAS CM	Open End	Aggressive Alloc (Income)	B	C	A-	Up	Y	250
★ American Funds The Income Fund of America® Class R-4	RIDEX	NAS CM	Open End	Aggressive Alloc (Income)	B	C	A-	Up	Y	250
★ American Funds The Income Fund of America® Class R-5	RIDFX	NAS CM	Open End	Aggressive Alloc (Income)	B	C	A-	Up	Y	250
★ American Funds The Income Fund of America® Class R-5E	RIDHX	NAS CM	Open End	Aggressive Alloc (Income)	B	C	A-	Up	Y	250
★ American Funds The Income Fund of America® Class R-6	RIDGX	NAS CM	Open End	Aggressive Alloc (Income)	B	C	A	Up	Y	250
American Funds The New Economy Fund® Class 529-A	CNGAX	NAS CM	Open End	US Equity Large Cap Growth (Growth)	B-	C	B	Up	Y	250
American Funds The New Economy Fund® Class 529-C	CNGCX	NAS CM	Open End	US Equity Large Cap Growth (Growth)	C+	C	B	Up	Y	250
American Funds The New Economy Fund® Class 529-E	CNGEX	NAS CM	Open End	US Equity Large Cap Growth (Growth)	B-	C	B	Up	Y	250
American Funds The New Economy Fund® Class 529-F	CNGFX	NAS CM	Open End	US Equity Large Cap Growth (Growth)	B-	C	B	Up	Y	250
American Funds The New Economy Fund® Class A	ANEFX	NAS CM	Open End	US Equity Large Cap Growth (Growth)	B-	C	B	Up	Y	250

★ Expanded analysis of this fund is included in Section II.

	TOTAL RETURNS					PERFORMANCE				ASSETS		ASSET ALLOCATION & TURNOVER					BULL & BEAR		FEES		
Min Additional Investment	3-Month Total Return	6-Month Total Return	1-Year Total Return	3-Year Total Return	5-Year Total Return	Dividend Yield (TTM)	Expense Ratio	3-Yr Std Deviation	3-Year Beta	NAV	Total Assets (MIL)	%Cash	%Stocks	%Bonds	%Other	Turnover Ratio	Last Bull Market Total Return	Last Bear Market Total Return	Front End Fee (%)	Back End Fee (%)	Inception Date
50	3.99	21.03	3.21	44.45	41.13	0	1.82	12.43	0.93	50.23	44,800	9	91	0	0	35	23.34	-24.65			Jun-02
50	3.99	21.04	3.22	44.55	41.26	0	1.8	12.43	0.93	50.27	44,800	9	91	0	0	35	23.34	-24.67			May-02
50	4.06	21.22	3.53	45.84	44.17	0	1.5	12.43	0.93	55.57	44,800	9	91	0	0	35	23.6	-24.53			Aug-14
50	4.12	21.32	3.71	46.52	44.46	0	1.35	12.44	0.93	53.71	44,800	9	91	0	0	35	23.65	-24.51			Jun-02
50	4.20	21.52	4.03	47.87	46.73	0	1.05	12.45	0.93	55.96	44,800	9	91	0	0	35	23.93	-24.4			Jul-02
50	4.27	21.69	4.33	49.19	48.95	0	0.75	12.44	0.93	58.34	44,800	9	91	0	0	35	24.18	-24.32			May-02
50	4.25	21.64	4.24	48.73	47.63	0	0.84	12.44	0.93	56.6	44,800	9	91	0	0	35	23.85	-24.41			Nov-15
50	4.28	21.72	4.37	49.43	49.31	0	0.7	12.44	0.93	57.72	44,800	9	91	0	0	35	24.19	-24.3			May-09
50	2.87	10.14	6.85	24.68	34.09	2.45	0.72	5.14	0.38	13.8	2,661	6	46	49	0	13			3.75		May-12
50	2.64	9.71	6.10	22.03	29.39	1.82	1.42	5.14	0.38	13.71	2,661	6	46	49	0	13				1.00	May-12
50	2.86	10.13	6.89	24.69	34.17	2.41	0.73	5.15	0.39	13.8	2,661	6	46	49	0	13					May-12
50	2.92	10.24	7.08	25.65	35.87	2.66	0.47	5.18	0.39	13.82	2,661	6	46	49	0	13					May-12
50	2.95	10.30	7.19	25.98	36.22	2.76	0.36	5.16	0.39	13.81	2,661	6	46	49	0	13					Jan-17
50	3.45	18.54	4.78	57.05	69.52	0.49	0.69	12.98	1.01	49.74	193,270	6	93	0	0	28	24.13	-19.02	5.75		Feb-02
50	3.24	18.08	4.01	53.50	63.15	0	1.47	12.95	1.01	46.16	193,270	6	93	0	0	28	23.54	-19.3		1.00	Feb-02
50	3.38	18.39	4.54	55.94	67.50	0.25	0.93	12.97	1.01	49.17	193,270	6	93	0	0	28	23.94	-19.13			Mar-02
50	3.50	18.67	5.02	58.08	71.36	0.74	0.47	12.97	1.01	49.62	193,270	6	93	0	0	28	24.26	-18.95			Sep-02
50	3.47	18.58	4.86	57.40	70.19	0.55	0.62	12.97	1.01	50.34	193,270	6	93	0	0	28	24.15	-19.01	5.75		Nov-73
50	3.25	18.12	4.04	53.67	63.57	0	1.42	12.97	1.01	46.02	193,270	6	93	0	0	28	23.6	-19.27		1.00	Mar-01
50	3.43	18.52	4.80	57.06	69.68	0.47	0.69	12.97	1.01	49.97	193,270	6	93	0	0	28	24.17	-18.97			Mar-01
50	3.52	18.71	5.09	58.38	72.02	0.76	0.42	12.97	1.01	50.23	193,270	6	93	0	0	28	24.36	-18.91			Aug-08
50	3.53	18.76	5.19	58.50	71.39	0.84	0.33	12.97	1.01	50.37	193,270	6	93	0	0	28	24.15	-19.01			Jan-17
50	3.26	18.12	4.04	53.66	63.64	0	1.43	12.97	1.01	46.8	193,270	6	93	0	0	28	23.63	-19.26			Jun-02
50	3.27	18.11	4.04	53.71	63.85	0	1.42	12.96	1.01	47.34	193,270	6	93	0	0	28	23.64	-19.22			May-02
50	3.33	18.29	4.35	55.11	66.75	0.18	1.12	12.97	1.01	49.27	193,270	6	93	0	0	28	23.89	-19.13			Aug-14
50	3.37	18.38	4.49	55.74	67.36	0.18	0.98	12.97	1.01	49.27	193,270	6	93	0	0	28	23.96	-19.09			May-02
50	3.46	18.55	4.82	57.18	69.89	0.49	0.68	12.97	1.01	49.84	193,270	6	93	0	0	28	24.14	-19			May-02
50	3.53	18.73	5.13	58.57	72.42	0.78	0.38	12.98	1.01	50.33	193,270	6	93	0	0	28	24.39	-18.89			May-02
50	3.50	18.69	5.03	58.14	71.09	0.79	0.45	12.98	1.01	49.9	193,270	6	93	0	0	28	24.15	-19			Nov-15
50	3.53	18.75	5.18	58.82	72.86	0.84	0.33	12.96	1.01	50.4	193,270	6	93	0	0	28	24.41	-18.89			May-09
50	2.59	11.17	6.43	24.66	30.89	2.88	0.63	7.13	0.56	22.44	109,899	7	66	27	0	70	14.49	-10.13	5.75		Feb-02
50	2.41	10.74	5.64	21.86	26.00	2.17	1.4	7.14	0.56	22.38	109,899	7	66	27	0	70	13.96	-10.41		1.00	Feb-02
50	2.54	11.03	6.16	23.81	29.38	2.67	0.87	7.17	0.56	22.37	109,899	7	66	27	0	70	14.32	-10.21			Feb-02
50	2.65	11.25	6.64	25.55	32.35	3.12	0.4	7.14	0.56	22.43	109,899	7	66	27	0	70	14.61	-10.03			Sep-02
50	2.65	11.23	6.55	25.02	31.51	2.96	0.55	7.16	0.56	22.5	109,899	7	66	27	0	70	14.52	-10.07	5.75		Nov-73
50	2.44	10.80	5.70	22.11	26.42	2.24	1.34	7.14	0.56	22.2	109,899	7	66	27	0	70	13.95	-10.32		1.00	Mar-01
50	2.59	11.11	6.43	24.63	30.89	2.88	0.64	7.12	0.56	22.43	109,899	7	66	27	0	70	14.52	-10.11			Mar-01
50	2.65	11.29	6.70	25.63	32.61	3.13	0.38	7.14	0.56	22.47	109,899	7	66	27	0	70	14.63	-10			Aug-08
50	2.68	11.34	6.80	25.78	32.31	3.22	0.28	7.14	0.56	22.48	109,899	7	66	27	0	70	14.52	-10.07			Jan-17
50	2.46	10.75	5.66	21.99	26.22	2.18	1.38	7.14	0.56	22.36	109,899	7	66	27	0	70	14	-10.38			Jun-02
50	2.44	10.78	5.66	21.94	26.30	2.2	1.37	7.13	0.56	22.23	109,899	7	66	27	0	70	13.99	-10.37			May-02
50	2.53	10.94	5.98	23.06	28.56	2.48	1.08	7.14	0.56	22.44	109,899	7	66	27	0	70	14.28	-10.2			Aug-14
50	2.53	10.98	6.13	23.55	29.07	2.61	0.93	7.17	0.56	22.4	109,899	7	66	27	0	70	14.29	-10.22			Jun-02
50	2.59	11.17	6.43	24.73	31.02	2.89	0.63	7.14	0.56	22.45	109,899	7	66	27	0	70	14.43	-10.06			Jun-02
50	2.67	11.31	6.75	25.87	33.00	3.18	0.33	7.13	0.56	22.49	109,899	7	66	27	0	70	14.72	-9.97			May-02
50	2.69	11.33	6.66	25.42	31.99	3.1	0.42	7.14	0.56	22.47	109,899	7	66	27	0	70	14.52	-10.07			Nov-15
50	2.68	11.33	6.80	26.05	33.32	3.22	0.28	7.14	0.56	22.5	109,899	7	66	27	0	70	14.74	-9.94			May-09
50	1.70	17.59	2.62	62.70	59.43	0.43	0.83	13.09	0.97	44.78	21,429	8	92	0	0	38	24.2	-18.72	5.75		Feb-02
50	1.52	17.15	1.86	58.96	53.30	0	1.62	13.08	0.97	40.7	21,429	8	92	0	0	38	23.62	-18.98		1.00	Feb-02
50	1.63	17.43	2.38	61.59	57.51	0.21	1.08	13.08	0.97	44.05	21,429	8	92	0	0	38	24.01	-18.79			Mar-02
50	1.72	17.68	2.84	63.75	61.06	0.67	0.61	13.1	0.97	44.72	21,429	8	92	0	0	38	24.32	-18.63			Oct-02
50	1.70	17.60	2.69	63.02	59.97	0.48	0.77	13.09	0.97	45.29	21,429	8	92	0	0	38	24.23	-18.66	5.75		Dec-83

Fund Name	MARKET Ticker Symbol	Traded On	FUND TYPE, CATEGORY & OBJECTIVE Fund Type	Category and (Prospectus Objective)	RATINGS Overall Rating	Reward Rating	Risk Rating	Recent Up/ Downgrade	MINIMUMS Open to New Investors	Min Initial Investment
American Funds The New Economy Fund® Class C	ANFCX	NAS CM	Open End	US Equity Large Cap Growth (Growth)	C+	C	B	Up	Y	250
American Funds The New Economy Fund® Class F-1	ANFFX	NAS CM	Open End	US Equity Large Cap Growth (Growth)	B-	C	B	Up	Y	250
American Funds The New Economy Fund® Class F-2	NEFFX	NAS CM	Open End	US Equity Large Cap Growth (Growth)	B-	C	B	Up	Y	250
American Funds The New Economy Fund® Class F-3	FNEFX	NAS CM	Open End	US Equity Large Cap Growth (Growth)	B-	C	B	Up	Y	1,000,000
American Funds The New Economy Fund® Class R-1	RNGAX	NAS CM	Open End	US Equity Large Cap Growth (Growth)	C+	C	B	Up	Y	250
American Funds The New Economy Fund® Class R-2	RNGBX	NAS CM	Open End	US Equity Large Cap Growth (Growth)	C+	C	B	Up	Y	250
American Funds The New Economy Fund® Class R-2E	RNNEX	NAS CM	Open End	US Equity Large Cap Growth (Growth)	C+	C	B	Up	Y	250
American Funds The New Economy Fund® Class R-3	RNGCX	NAS CM	Open End	US Equity Large Cap Growth (Growth)	B-	C	B	Up	Y	250
American Funds The New Economy Fund® Class R-4	RNGEX	NAS CM	Open End	US Equity Large Cap Growth (Growth)	B-	C	B	Up	Y	250
American Funds The New Economy Fund® Class R-5	RNGFX	NAS CM	Open End	US Equity Large Cap Growth (Growth)	B-	C	B	Up	Y	250
American Funds The New Economy Fund® Class R-5E	RNGHX	NAS CM	Open End	US Equity Large Cap Growth (Growth)	B-	C	B	Up	Y	250
American Funds The New Economy Fund® Class R-6	RNGGX	NAS CM	Open End	US Equity Large Cap Growth (Growth)	B-	C	B	Up	Y	250
★ American Funds Washington Mutual Investors Cls 529-A	CWMAX	NAS CM	Open End	US Equity Large Cap Blend (Growth & Income)	B-	C	B+	Down	Y	250
★ American Funds Washington Mutual Investors Cls 529-C	CWMCX	NAS CM	Open End	US Equity Large Cap Blend (Growth & Income)	B-	C	B+	Down	Y	250
★ American Funds Washington Mutual Investors Cls 529-E	CWMEX	NAS CM	Open End	US Equity Large Cap Blend (Growth & Income)	B-	C	B+	Down	Y	250
★ American Funds Washington Mutual Investors Cls 529-F-1	CWMFX	NAS CM	Open End	US Equity Large Cap Blend (Growth & Income)	B-	C	B+	Down	Y	250
★ American Funds Washington Mutual Investors Fund Class A	AWSHX	NAS CM	Open End	US Equity Large Cap Blend (Growth & Income)	B-	C	B+	Down	Y	250
★ American Funds Washington Mutual Investors Fund Class C	WSHCX	NAS CM	Open End	US Equity Large Cap Blend (Growth & Income)	B-	C	B+	Down	Y	250
★ American Funds Washington Mutual Investors Fund Class F-1	WSHFX	NAS CM	Open End	US Equity Large Cap Blend (Growth & Income)	B-	C	B+	Down	Y	250
★ American Funds Washington Mutual Investors Fund Class F-2	WMFFX	NAS CM	Open End	US Equity Large Cap Blend (Growth & Income)	B-	C	B+	Down	Y	250
American Funds Washington Mutual Investors Fund Class F-3	FWMIX	NAS CM	Open End	US Equity Large Cap Blend (Growth & Income)	B-	C	B+	Down	Y	1,000,000
★ American Funds Washington Mutual Investors Fund Class R-1	RWMAX	NAS CM	Open End	US Equity Large Cap Blend (Growth & Income)	B-	C	B+	Down	Y	250
★ American Funds Washington Mutual Investors Fund Class R-2	RWMBX	NAS CM	Open End	US Equity Large Cap Blend (Growth & Income)	B-	C	B+	Down	Y	250
★ American Funds Washington Mutual Investors Fund Class R-2E	RWEBX	NAS CM	Open End	US Equity Large Cap Blend (Growth & Income)	B-	C	B+	Down	Y	250
★ American Funds Washington Mutual Investors Fund Class R-3	RWMCX	NAS CM	Open End	US Equity Large Cap Blend (Growth & Income)	B-	C	B+	Down	Y	250
★ American Funds Washington Mutual Investors Fund Class R-4	RWMEX	NAS CM	Open End	US Equity Large Cap Blend (Growth & Income)	B-	C	B+	Down	Y	250
★ American Funds Washington Mutual Investors Fund Class R-5	RWMFX	NAS CM	Open End	US Equity Large Cap Blend (Growth & Income)	B-	C	B+	Down	Y	250
★ American Funds Washington Mutual Investors Fund Class R-5E	RWMHX	NAS CM	Open End	US Equity Large Cap Blend (Growth & Income)	B-	C	B+	Down	Y	250
★ American Funds Washington Mutual Investors Fund Class R-6	RWMGX	NAS CM	Open End	US Equity Large Cap Blend (Growth & Income)	B-	C	B+	Down	Y	250
American Growth Fund Series One Class A	AMRAX	NAS CM	Open End	US Equity Large Cap Growth (Growth)	C+	C	B		Y	0
American Growth Fund Series One Class B	AMRBX	NAS CM	Open End	US Equity Large Cap Growth (Growth)	C+	C	B		Y	0
American Growth Fund Series One Class C	AMRCX	NAS CM	Open End	US Equity Large Cap Growth (Growth)	C+	C	B		Y	0
American Growth Fund Series One Class D	AMRGX	NAS CM	Open End	US Equity Large Cap Growth (Growth)	C+	C	B		Y	0
American Growth Fund Series Two Class E	AMREX	NAS CM	Open End	US Equity Large Cap Growth (Growth)	D+	D+	D		Y	0
American Growth Fund Series Two Class F	AMRHX	NAS CM	Open End	US Equity Large Cap Growth (Growth)	U	U	U		Y	0
American Independence Global Tactical Allocation Cls A	AARMX	NAS CM	Open End	Moderate Alloc (Growth)	C+	C	B	Up	Y	5,000
American Independence Global Tactical Allocation Inst Cls	RMAIX	NAS CM	Open End	Moderate Alloc (Growth)	C+	C	B+	Up		3,000,000
American Trust Allegiance Fund	ATAFX	NAS CM	Open End	US Equity Large Cap Blend (World Stock)	C+	C	B	Up	Y	2,500
AMG Chicago Equity Partners Balanced Fund Class I	MBESX	NAS CM	Open End	Moderate Alloc (Balanced)	B-	C	B+	Up	Y	100,000
AMG Chicago Equity Partners Balanced Fund Class N	MBEAX	NAS CM	Open End	Moderate Alloc (Balanced)	B-	C	B+	Up	Y	2,000
AMG Chicago Equity Partners Balanced Fund Class Z	MBEYX	NAS CM	Open End	Moderate Alloc (Balanced)	B-	C	B+	Up	Y	5,000,000
AMG FQ Global Risk-Balanced Fund Class I	MMASX	NAS CM	Open End	Moderate Alloc (Growth & Income)	B-	C	B+	Up	Y	100,000
AMG FQ Global Risk-Balanced Fund Class N	MMAVX	NAS CM	Open End	Moderate Alloc (Growth & Income)	B-	C	B	Up	Y	2,000
AMG FQ Global Risk-Balanced Fund Class Z	MMAFX	NAS CM	Open End	Moderate Alloc (Growth & Income)	B-	C	B+	Up	Y	5,000,000
AMG FQ Long-Short Equity Fund Class I	MEQFX	NAS CM	Open End	Long/Short Equity (Growth)	B	C	A-	Up	Y	100,000
AMG FQ Long-Short Equity Fund Class N	FQUAX	NAS CM	Open End	Long/Short Equity (Growth)	B-	C	A-		Y	2,000
AMG FQ Tax-Managed U.S. Equity Fund Class I	MFQTX	NAS CM	Open End	US Equity Large Cap Blend (Growth)	C+	C	B		Y	100,000
AMG FQ Tax-Managed U.S. Equity Fund Class N	MFQAX	NAS CM	Open End	US Equity Large Cap Blend (Growth)	C+	C	B		Y	2,000
AMG Frontier Small Cap Growth Fund Class I	MSSCX	NAS CM	Open End	US Equity Small Cap (Small Company)	C	C	B-	Down		100,000
AMG Frontier Small Cap Growth Fund Class N	MSSVX	NAS CM	Open End	US Equity Small Cap (Small Company)	C	C	C+	Down		2,000
AMG Frontier Small Cap Growth Fund Class Z	MSSYX	NAS CM	Open End	US Equity Small Cap (Small Company)	C	C	B-	Down		5,000,000
AMG GW&K Small Cap Core Fund Class I	GWEIX	NAS CM	Open End	US Equity Small Cap (Small Company)	C	C	C+			100,000

★ Expanded analysis of this fund is included in Section II.

	TOTAL RETURNS					PERFORMANCE				ASSETS		ASSET ALLOCATION & TURNOVER					BULL & BEAR		FEES		
Min Additional Investment	3-Month Total Return	6-Month Total Return	1-Year Total Return	3-Year Total Return	5-Year Total Return	Dividend Yield (TTM)	Expense Ratio	3-Yr Std Deviation	3-Year Beta	NAV	Total Assets (MIL)	%Cash	%Stocks	%Bonds	%Other	Turnover Ratio	Last Bull Market Total Return	Last Bear Market Total Return	Front End Fee (%)	Back End Fee (%)	Inception Date
50	1.51	17.17	1.91	59.18	53.71	0	1.56	13.07	0.97	40.11	21,429	8	92	0	0	38	23.65	-18.94		1.00	Mar-01
50	1.67	17.56	2.62	62.71	59.55	0.38	0.83	13.09	0.97	45.45	21,429	8	92	0	0	38	24.25	-18.69			Mar-01
50	1.75	17.75	2.92	64.07	61.76	0.71	0.55	13.08	0.97	45.23	21,429	8	92	0	0	38	24.45	-18.61			Aug-08
50	1.79	17.82	3.02	64.31	61.25	0.79	0.46	13.1	0.97	45.35	21,429	8	92	0	0	38	24.23	-18.66			Jan-17
50	1.49	17.14	1.89	59.21	53.88	0	1.55	13.08	0.97	41.54	21,429	8	92	0	0	38	23.69	-18.94			Jun-02
50	1.52	17.17	1.90	59.25	53.90	0	1.56	13.06	0.97	41.82	21,429	8	92	0	0	38	23.73	-18.96			May-02
50	1.60	17.32	2.21	60.69	57.39	0.15	1.26	13.09	0.97	44.42	21,429	8	92	0	0	38	23.98	-18.78			Aug-14
50	1.61	17.42	2.34	61.40	57.38	0.13	1.1	13.1	0.97	44.15	21,429	8	92	0	0	38	24.03	-18.81			Jun-02
50	1.70	17.60	2.66	62.87	59.82	0.43	0.8	13.09	0.97	44.83	21,429	8	92	0	0	38	24.24	-18.66			Jul-02
50	1.78	17.77	2.99	64.37	62.25	0.73	0.5	13.09	0.97	45.58	21,429	8	92	0	0	38	24.45	-18.57			May-02
50	1.73	17.71	2.87	63.92	61.01	0.71	0.59	13.08	0.97	45.05	21,429	8	92	0	0	38	24.23	-18.66			Nov-15
50	1.79	17.79	3.02	64.60	62.64	0.79	0.45	13.08	0.97	45.4	21,429	8	92	0	0	38	24.49	-18.56			May-09
50	4.02	15.58	10.04	45.76	57.47	1.74	0.63	10.5	0.84	45.72	118,091	4	96	0	0	25	20.91	-12.56	5.75		Feb-02
50	3.85	15.16	9.26	42.51	51.60	1.04	1.4	10.51	0.84	45.44	118,091	4	96	0	0	25	20.35	-12.85		1.00	Feb-02
50	3.96	15.45	9.80	44.74	55.59	1.52	0.87	10.51	0.84	45.44	118,091	4	96	0	0	25	20.76	-12.67			Mar-02
50	4.09	15.73	10.31	46.79	59.28	1.97	0.4	10.51	0.84	45.6	118,091	4	96	0	0	25	21.04	-12.48			Sep-02
50	4.05	15.64	10.16	46.15	58.16	1.81	0.59	10.51	0.84	45.84	118,091	4	96	0	0	25	20.97	-12.51	5.75		Jul-52
50	3.86	15.19	9.29	42.69	52.03	1.1	1.34	10.51	0.84	45.2	118,091	4	96	0	0	25	20.4	-12.8		1.00	Mar-01
50	4.02	15.58	10.06	45.75	57.48	1.74	0.64	10.52	0.84	45.65	118,091	4	96	0	0	25	20.97	-12.56			Mar-01
50	4.10	15.73	10.35	46.94	59.58	1.99	0.36	10.51	0.84	45.79	118,091	4	96	0	0	25	21.12	-12.44			Aug-08
50	4.12	15.78	10.45	47.08	59.18	2.07	0.28	10.51	0.84	45.81	118,091	4	96	0	0	25	20.97	-12.51			Jan-17
50	3.84	15.19	9.27	42.59	51.89	1.05	1.37	10.51	0.84	45.32	118,091	4	96	0	0	25	20.43	-12.83			May-02
50	3.84	15.18	9.24	42.58	51.99	1.07	1.37	10.49	0.84	45.13	118,091	4	96	0	0	25	20.48	-12.82			May-02
50	3.92	15.33	9.58	43.88	54.98	1.35	1.07	10.52	0.84	45.61	118,091	4	96	0	0	25	20.71	-12.64			Aug-14
50	3.97	15.43	9.74	44.51	55.32	1.47	0.92	10.51	0.84	45.42	118,091	4	96	0	0	25	20.78	-12.67			Jun-02
50	4.03	15.59	10.07	45.82	57.64	1.75	0.62	10.5	0.84	45.57	118,091	4	96	0	0	25	20.95	-12.54			May-02
50	4.11	15.78	10.39	47.14	60.00	2.03	0.32	10.51	0.84	45.81	118,091	4	96	0	0	25	21.19	-12.46			May-02
50	4.09	15.73	10.32	46.74	58.86	1.98	0.41	10.51	0.84	45.77	118,091	4	96	0	0	25	20.97	-12.51			Nov-15
50	4.14	15.82	10.47	47.40	60.43	2.07	0.27	10.52	0.84	45.86	118,091	4	96	0	0	25	21.2	-12.43			May-09
	6.03	24.46	13.28	39.42	44.27	0	5.51	13.35	1.04	5.8	17.9					11	28.44	-24.04	5.75		Mar-96
	4.98	22.53	11.26	34.44	37.49	0	8.95	13.32	1.04	4.84	17.9					11	28.86	-24.51		5.00	Mar-96
	5.84	24.11	12.41	36.59	39.31	0	5.91	13.33	1.04	4.89	17.9					11	27.83	-24.21		1.00	Mar-96
	6.17	24.79	13.57	41.00	46.68	0	4.83	13.32	1.04	6.19	17.9					11	29.07	-24.08	5.75		Jul-58
	-2.81	18.28	3.24	-17.70	-24.87	0	15.17	28.75	1.09	4.14	1.00	12	88	0	0	8	19.5	-23.27	5.75		Feb-11
	5.94	3.21	2.27	12.07	34.68	0	7.57	11.46	0.96		0.90	3	97	0	0	0	19.06	-23.45		1.00	Feb-11
250	2.03	3.69	2.22	15.99	23.38	1.72	1.52	5.9	0.4	9.74	13.3	7	36	57	0				5.75		Sep-13
5,000	2.09	3.92	2.53	17.09	25.64	1.91	1.27	5.89	0.4	9.82	13.3	7	36	57	0						Sep-13
250	3.32	17.85	2.77	38.33	23.78	0	1.45	13.56	1.06	27.99	24.8	7	93	0	0	63	25.3	-18.59			Mar-97
100	3.44	11.71	4.78	29.36	38.54	1.43	0.93	7.53	0.59	17.17	265.6	2	52	46	0	80	15.06	-7.07			Nov-12
100	3.38	11.62	4.60	28.65	37.29	1.29	1.09	7.5	0.58	16.99	265.6	2	52	46	0	80	14.86	-7.11			Jan-97
1,000	3.46	11.77	4.87	29.65	39.03	1.51	0.84	7.52	0.59	17.16	265.6	2	52	46	0	80	15.06	-7.07			Jan-97
100	4.75	16.10	6.23	23.40	24.09	2.04	1.27	8.34	0.5	16.29	54.2	-90	59	121	10	27	10.59	-3.6			Jan-10
100	4.71	16.02	6.01	22.23	21.93	1.79	1.52	8.36	0.51	16.22	54.2	-90	59	121	10	27	10.39	-3.69			Jan-10
1,000	4.76	16.20	6.41	23.81	24.71	2.18	1.12	8.36	0.51	16.28	54.2	-90	59	121	10	27	10.69	-3.52			Nov-88
100	3.24	7.36	6.54	46.79	50.46	0.28	2.55	10.35	0.67	15.79	85.5	-61	163	0	-3	240	25.52	-16.37			Aug-92
100	3.10	7.17	6.21	45.30	48.19	0.1	2.87	10.34	0.67	15.75	85.5	-61	163	0	-3	240	25.36	-16.47			Mar-06
100	3.37	14.67	3.23	43.39	47.95	0.43	0.89	12.86	1	32.43	69.6	1	99	0	0	31	27.79	-18.69			Dec-00
100	3.34	14.56	2.97	42.37	46.14	0.16	1.14	12.86	1	32.48	69.6	1	99	0	0	31	27.55	-18.74			Mar-06
100	-0.95	22.18	3.82	71.31	53.14	0	1.01	19.06	1.04	8.26	19.6	2	98	0	0	233	26.83	-26.8			Sep-97
100	-1.00	21.98	3.53	69.96	50.97	0	1.3	19.07	1.04	7.88	19.6	2	98	0	0	233	26.59	-26.89			Dec-09
1,000	-0.92	22.22	3.89	72.00	54.41	0	0.9	19.1	1.05	8.58	19.6	2	98	0	0	233	26.98	-26.72			Dec-09
100	5.72	20.39	-2.19	39.70	45.72	0.2	0.95	15.49	0.87	25.5	420.2	1	99	0	0	25	25.63	-20.18			Jul-09

	MARKET			FUND TYPE, CATEGORY & OBJECTIVE	RATINGS				MINIMUMS	
Fund Name	Ticker Symbol	Traded On	Fund Type	Category and (Prospectus Objective)	Overall Rating	Reward Rating	Risk Rating	Recent Up/ Downgrade	Open to New Investors	Min Initial Investment
AMG GW&K Small Cap Core Fund Class N	GWETX	NAS CM	Open End	US Equity Small Cap (Small Company)	C	C	C+			2,000
AMG GW&K Small Cap Core Fund Class Z	GWEZX	NAS CM	Open End	US Equity Small Cap (Small Company)	C	C	C+		Y	5,000,000
AMG GW&K Small/Mid Cap Fund Class I	GWGIX	NAS CM	Open End	US Equity Small Cap (Growth)	C+	C	B-		Y	100,000
AMG GW&K Small/Mid Cap Fund Class N	GWGVX	NAS CM	Open End	US Equity Small Cap (Growth)	C+	C	B-		Y	2,000
AMG GW&K Small/Mid Cap Fund Class Z	GWGZX	NAS CM	Open End	US Equity Small Cap (Growth)	C+	C	B-		Y	5,000,000
AMG GW&K Trilogy Emerging Markets Equity Fund - Class I	TLESX	NAS CM	Open End	Global Emerg Mkts (Div Emerging Mkts)	C	C	C+		Y	100,000
AMG GW&K Trilogy Emerging Markets Equity Fund - Class N	TLEVX	NAS CM	Open End	Global Emerg Mkts (Div Emerging Mkts)	C	C	C+		Y	2,000
AMG GW&K Trilogy Emerging Markets Equity Fund - Class Z	TLEIX	NAS CM	Open End	Global Emerg Mkts (Div Emerging Mkts)	C	C	C+		Y	5,000,000
AMG GW&K Trilogy Emerging Wealth Equity Fund - Class I	TYWSX	NAS CM	Open End	Global Emerg Mkts (Div Emerging Mkts)	C	C	C		Y	100,000
AMG GW&K Trilogy Emerging Wealth Equity Fund - Class N	TYWVX	NAS CM	Open End	Global Emerg Mkts (Div Emerging Mkts)	C	C	C		Y	2,000
AMG GW&K Trilogy Emerging Wealth Equity Fund - Class Z	TYWIX	NAS CM	Open End	Global Emerg Mkts (Div Emerging Mkts)	C	C	C		Y	5,000,000
AMG GW&K U.S. Small Cap Growth Fund Class I	ATSIX	NAS CM	Open End	US Equity Small Cap (Small Company)	C+	C	C+		Y	100,000
AMG GW&K U.S. Small Cap Growth Fund Class N	ATASX	NAS CM	Open End	US Equity Small Cap (Small Company)	C+	C	C+		Y	2,000
AMG GW&K U.S. Small Cap Growth Fund Class Z	ATAZX	NAS CM	Open End	US Equity Small Cap (Small Company)	C+	C	C+		Y	5,000,000
AMG Managers Brandywine Advisors Mid Cap Growth Cls N	BWAFX	NAS CM	Open End	US Equity Mid Cap (Growth)	C+	C	C+		Y	2,000
AMG Managers Brandywine Blue Fund Class I	BLUEX	NAS CM	Open End	US Equity Large Cap Growth (Growth)	B-	C+	B-		Y	2,000
AMG Managers Brandywine Fund Class I	BRWIX	NAS CM	Open End	US Equity Mid Cap (Growth)	C+	C+	C+	Down	Y	2,000
AMG Managers Cadence Emerging Companies Fund - Class I	MECIX	NAS CM	Open End	US Equity Small Cap (Small Company)	C	C-	C	Down	Y	100,000
AMG Managers Cadence Emerging Companies Fund - Class N	MECAX	NAS CM	Open End	US Equity Small Cap (Small Company)	C	C-	C	Down	Y	2,000
AMG Managers Cadence Emerging Companies Fund - Class Z	MECZX	NAS CM	Open End	US Equity Small Cap (Small Company)	C	C-	C	Down	Y	5,000,000
AMG Managers Cadence Mid Cap Fund - Class I	MCMYX	NAS CM	Open End	US Equity Mid Cap (Growth)	C+	C	B-		Y	100,000
AMG Managers Cadence Mid Cap Fund - Class N	MCMAX	NAS CM	Open End	US Equity Mid Cap (Growth)	C+	C	B-		Y	2,000
AMG Managers Cadence Mid Cap Fund - Class Z	MCMFX	NAS CM	Open End	US Equity Mid Cap (Growth)	C+	C	B-		Y	5,000,000
AMG Managers CenterSquare Real Estate Fund Class I	MRASX	NAS CM	Open End	Real Estate Sector Equity (Real Estate)	C+	C	B-	Down	Y	100,000
AMG Managers CenterSquare Real Estate Fund Class N	MRESX	NAS CM	Open End	Real Estate Sector Equity (Real Estate)	C+	C	B-	Down	Y	2,000
AMG Managers CenterSquare Real Estate Fund Class Z	MREZX	NAS CM	Open End	Real Estate Sector Equity (Real Estate)	C+	C	B-	Down	Y	5,000,000
AMG Managers Emerging Opportunities Fund Class I	MIMFX	NAS CM	Open End	US Equity Small Cap (Growth)	C+	C	C+	Down	Y	100,000
AMG Managers Emerging Opportunities Fund Class N	MMCFX	NAS CM	Open End	US Equity Small Cap (Growth)	C+	C	C+	Down	Y	2,000
AMG Managers Essex Small/Micro Cap Growth Fund - Class N	MBRSX	NAS CM	Open End	US Equity Small Cap (Growth)	C	C	C+	Down	Y	2,000
AMG Managers Fairpointe ESG Equity Fund Class I	AFFEX	NAS CM	Open End	US Equity Mid Cap (Growth)	C	C-	B-		Y	100,000
AMG Managers Fairpointe ESG Equity Fund Class N	AFPTX	NAS CM	Open End	US Equity Mid Cap (Growth)	C	C-	B-		Y	2,000
AMG Managers Fairpointe Mid Cap Fund Class I	ABMIX	NAS CM	Open End	US Equity Mid Cap (Growth)	C	C-	B-			100,000
AMG Managers Fairpointe Mid Cap Fund Class N	CHTTX	NAS CM	Open End	US Equity Mid Cap (Growth)	C	C-	B-			2,000
AMG Managers Fairpointe Mid Cap Fund Class Z	ABIZX	NAS CM	Open End	US Equity Mid Cap (Growth)	C	C-	B-		Y	5,000,000
AMG Managers LMCG Small Cap Growth Fund Class I	ACWIX	NAS CM	Open End	US Equity Small Cap (Small Company)	C	C	C+	Down	Y	100,000
AMG Managers LMCG Small Cap Growth Fund Class N	ACWDX	NAS CM	Open End	US Equity Small Cap (Small Company)	C	C	C+		Y	2,000
AMG Managers Montag & Caldwell Growth Fund Class I	MCGIX	NAS CM	Open End	US Equity Large Cap Growth (Growth)	B-	C+	B	Down	Y	100,000
AMG Managers Montag & Caldwell Growth Fund Class N	MCGFX	NAS CM	Open End	US Equity Large Cap Growth (Growth)	B-	C+	B	Down	Y	2,000
AMG Managers Pictet International Fund Class I	APCTX	NAS CM	Open End	Global Equity Large Cap (Growth)	C	C-	C+	Up	Y	100,000
AMG Managers Pictet International Fund Class N	APINX	NAS CM	Open End	Global Equity Large Cap (Growth)	C	C-	C+	Up	Y	2,000
AMG Managers Pictet International Fund Class Z	APCZX	NAS CM	Open End	Global Equity Large Cap (Growth)	C	C-	C+	Up	Y	5,000,000
AMG Managers Silvercrest Small Cap Fund Class I	ACRTX	NAS CM	Open End	US Equity Small Cap (Small Company)	C	C	C+		Y	100,000
AMG Managers Silvercrest Small Cap Fund Class N	ASCTX	NAS CM	Open End	US Equity Small Cap (Small Company)	C	C	C+		Y	2,000
AMG Managers Silvercrest Small Cap Fund Class Z	ACZTX	NAS CM	Open End	US Equity Small Cap (Small Company)	C	C	C+		Y	5,000,000
AMG Managers Skyline Special Equities Fund Class I	SKSIX	NAS CM	Open End	US Equity Small Cap (Small Company)	C	C	C+		Y	100,000
AMG Managers Skyline Special Equities Fund Class N	SKSEX	NAS CM	Open End	US Equity Small Cap (Small Company)	C	C-	C+			2,000
AMG Managers Skyline Special Equities Fund Class Z	SKSZX	NAS CM	Open End	US Equity Small Cap (Small Company)	C	C	C+		Y	5,000,000
AMG Managers Special Equity Fund Class I	MSEIX	NAS CM	Open End	US Equity Small Cap (Growth)	C+	C	C+	Down	Y	100,000
AMG Managers Special Equity Fund Class N	MGSEX	NAS CM	Open End	US Equity Small Cap (Growth)	C+	C	C+	Down	Y	2,000
AMG Pantheon Fund, LLC Advisory Class	XPEAX	NAS CM	Closed End	Equity Miscellaneous (Growth & Income)	B	C+	B+	Up	Y	25,000
AMG Pantheon Fund, LLC Brokerage Class	XPEBX	NAS CM	Closed End	Equity Miscellaneous (Growth & Income)	B	C+	B+	Up	Y	25,000
AMG Pantheon Fund, LLC Institutional Class	XPEIX	NAS CM	Closed End	Equity Miscellaneous (Growth & Income)	B	C+	B+	Up	Y	1,000,000

★ Expanded analysis of this fund is included in Section II.

	TOTAL RETURNS					PERFORMANCE				ASSETS		ASSET ALLOCATION & TURNOVER					BULL & BEAR		FEES		
Min Additional Investment	3-Month Total Return	6-Month Total Return	1-Year Total Return	3-Year Total Return	5-Year Total Return	Dividend Yield (TTM)	Expense Ratio	3-Yr Std Deviation	3-Year Beta	NAV	Total Assets (MIL)	%Cash	%Stocks	%Bonds	%Other	Turnover Ratio	Last Bull Market Total Return	Last Bear Market Total Return	Front End Fee (%)	Back End Fee (%)	Inception Date
100	5.60	20.20	-2.51	38.27	42.93	0	1.28	15.48	0.87	25.05	420.2	1	99	0	0	25	25.38	-20.38			Dec-96
1,000	5.76	20.44	-2.16	39.61	44.31	0.25	0.9	15.46	0.87	25.51	420.2	1	99	0	0	25	25.38	-20.38			Feb-17
100	5.68	22.36	5.65	43.28		0.08	0.95	14.47	0.91	12.09	160.0	2	98	0	0	53					Jun-15
100	5.59	22.26	5.55	42.61		0	1.1	14.42	0.91	12.08	160.0	2	98	0	0	53					Feb-17
1,000	5.76	22.44	5.83	43.69		0.15	0.85	14.44	0.91	12.11	160.0	2	98	0	0	53					Feb-17
100	2.06	16.54	3.76	41.21	14.06	1.33	0.99	14.86	1.04	9.86	190.1	3	97	0	0	24	15.56	-27.8			Mar-11
100	1.95	16.35	3.40	39.75	12.14	0.95	1.27	14.89	1.05	9.89	190.1	3	97	0	0	24	15.54	-27.87			Mar-12
1,000	1.97	16.50	3.82	41.68	14.74	1.37	0.87	14.92	1.05	9.81	190.1	3	97	0	0	24	15.58	-27.8			Mar-11
100	0.76	20.26	-0.13	46.51		0.55	1.14	16.31	1.08	11.93	97.0	5	95	0	0	37					Mar-15
100	0.76	20.06	-0.42	45.27		0.52	1.4	16.35	1.08	11.85	97.0	5	95	0	0	37					Mar-15
1,000	0.84	20.34	-0.03	46.90		0.7	1	16.36	1.08	11.89	97.0	5	95	0	0	37					Mar-15
100	5.26	27.65	4.38	59.62	40.03	0	1	16.25	0.91	4.8	30.4	2	98	0	0	36	27.94	-24.27			Jan-05
100	5.11	27.14	4.01	58.12	38.16	0	1.22	16.33	0.91	3.7	30.4	2	98	0	0	36	27.78	-24.36			Nov-00
1,000	5.25	27.58	4.37	59.34	39.22	0	0.9	16.23	0.91	4.81	30.4	2	98	0	0	36	27.78	-24.36			Feb-17
100	1.64	23.76	9.00	46.77	32.02	0	1.13	16.13	1.06	11.77	150.7	4	96	0	0	167	18.47	-29.17			Oct-00
100	6.94	27.57	11.96	62.43	71.99	0	1.16	14.5	1.02	50.38	188.3	4	96	0	0	122	22.79	-21.44			Jan-91
100	4.01	24.89	10.55	57.62	69.38	0	1.1	15.62	1.08	55.39	839.2	3	97	0	0	138	19.36	-28.92			Dec-85
100	-0.73	11.22	-8.15	53.65	74.52	0	0.98	16.82	0.88	55.17	181.0	0	100	0	0	89	36.59	-24.98			Jun-93
100	-0.78	11.12	-8.28	52.97	72.92	0	1.08	16.82	0.88	50.44	181.0	0	100	0	0	89	36.37	-25.07			Apr-96
1,000	-0.71	11.26	-8.06	53.97	74.87	0	0.89	16.82	0.88	55.29	181.0	0	100	0	0	89	36.59	-24.98			May-17
100	1.23	18.46	3.39	44.80	47.65	0.31	0.87	14.46	0.98	27.01	104.2	2	98	0	0	72	26	-19.81			Nov-94
100	1.20	18.33	3.21	43.95	46.38	0.08	1.08	14.43	0.98	25.94	104.2	2	98	0	0	72	25.93	-19.87			Jan-97
1,000	1.27	18.54	3.55	45.53	49.17	0.44	0.72	14.43	0.98	28.57	104.2	2	98	0	0	72	26.24	-19.77			Aug-91
100	1.05	17.21	9.17	12.73	45.77	1.99	0.99	13.01	0.98	11.05	248.1	0	100	0	0	57	30.76	-16.07			Feb-17
100	1.01	17.14	9.02	12.34	45.27	1.86	1.12	13.02	0.98	11.05	248.1	0	100	0	0	57	30.76	-16.07			Dec-97
1,000	1.17	17.28	9.30	12.98	46.09	2.09	0.87	13	0.98	11.05	248.1	0	100	0	0	57	30.76	-16.07			Feb-17
100	4.54	22.32	0.40	72.09	60.85	0	0.95	18.05	0.99	42.58	178.2	4	96	0	0	55	31.89	-25.16			Sep-11
100	4.48	22.18	0.15	70.85	58.88	0	1.2	18.05	0.99	41.74	178.2	4	96	0	0	55	31.86	-25.16			Jun-94
100	1.55	20.37	-0.77	61.58	46.90	0	1.49	18.31	1.01	22.21	21.0	0	100	0	0	47	22.96	-27.95			Jun-02
100	1.13	15.37	-2.70	35.06		1.21	0.9	15.39	1.16	11.63	12.5	3	97	0	0	41					Dec-14
100	1.03	15.27	-2.96	34.13		0.96	1.11	15.33	1.16	11.7	12.5	3	97	0	0	41					Dec-14
100	0.79	16.78	-1.79	33.00	17.75	0.67	0.88	18.15	1.11	37.99	2,184	3	97	0	0	18	27.42	-25.65			Jul-04
100	0.73	16.63	-2.03	32.01	16.28	0.38	1.13	18.15	1.11	36.95	2,184	3	97	0	0	18	27.25	-25.74			Sep-94
1,000	0.82	16.83	-1.71	32.78	16.96	0.78	0.8	18.14	1.11	37.97	2,184	3	97	0	0	18	27.25	-25.74			Sep-17
100	0.91	22.81	3.60	51.25	37.15	0	1.1	18.66	1.03	18.68	78.6	1	99	0	0	161	26.7	-30.21			Jun-11
100	0.88	22.69	3.38	50.36	35.68	0	1.31	18.67	1.03	18.33	78.6	1	99	0	0	161	26.5	-30.23			Nov-10
100	5.38	21.40	13.96	45.95	57.47	0.12	0.98	11.32	0.81	18.6	508.2	5	95	0	0	33	21.3	-11.61			Jun-96
100	5.29	21.32	13.81	45.10	55.75	0	1.17	11.32	0.81	18.49	508.2	5	95	0	0	33	21.06	-11.66			Nov-94
100	2.40	17.24	-5.23	25.26	13.08	1.97	1.01	12.92	1.12	9.38	324.0	3	97	0	0	51					Apr-14
100	2.30	17.06	-5.43	24.21	11.50	1.99	1.28	12.86	1.11	9.33	324.0	3	97	0	0	51					Apr-14
1,000	2.51	17.44	-5.00	25.54	13.33	2.1	0.92	12.86	1.11	9.36	324.0	3	97	0	0	51					Sep-17
100	3.99	16.61	-2.98	32.69	34.78	0.09	1.15	18.58	1.04	15.86	228.0	3	97	0	0	34					Dec-11
100	3.91	16.51	-3.22	31.64	33.05	0.02	1.39	18.54	1.04	15.66	228.0	3	97	0	0	34					Dec-11
1,000	4.00	16.62	-2.93	32.85	34.95	0.19	1.08	18.54	1.04	15.85	228.0	3	97	0	0	34					Sep-17
100	5.71	19.92	-5.33	30.12	23.41	0	1.02	19.75	1.11	37.02	516.9	4	96	0	0	24	32.76	-25.23			Feb-17
100	5.67	19.83	-5.46	29.61	22.92	0	1.18	19.75	1.11	36.85	516.9	4	96	0	0	24	32.76	-25.23			Apr-87
1,000	5.75	19.98	-5.22	30.38	23.65	0	0.93	19.75	1.11	37.1	516.9	4	96	0	0	24	32.76	-25.23			Feb-17
100	5.72	25.29	4.73	66.49	64.44	0	1.12	17.14	0.97	146.9	224.6	3	97	0	0	113	31.02	-23.36			May-04
100	5.65	25.14	4.47	65.26	62.41	0	1.37	17.13	0.97	142.24	224.6	3	97	0	0	113	30.69	-23.44			Jun-84
10,000	3.67	4.46	7.49	40.01		1.88	2.64	6.3			--								3.50		Oct-15
10,000	3.48	4.22	6.98	38.11		1.23	3.14	6.28			--								3.50		Oct-15
10,000	3.72	4.64	7.74	41.24		2.07	2.39	6.23			--										Oct-15

	MARKET			FUND TYPE, CATEGORY & OBJECTIVE	RATINGS					MINIMUMS
Fund Name	Ticker Symbol	Traded On	Fund Type	Category and (Prospectus Objective)	Overall Rating	Reward Rating	Risk Rating	Recent Up/ Downgrade	Open to New Investors	Min Initial Investment
AMG Pantheon Fund, LLC Institutional Plus Class	XPEPX	NAS CM	Closed End	Equity Miscellaneous (Growth & Income)	B	C+	B+	Up	Y	1,000,000
AMG Renaissance Large Cap Growth Fund Class I	MRLSX	NAS CM	Open End	US Equity Large Cap Growth (Growth)	B-	C	B		Y	100,000
AMG Renaissance Large Cap Growth Fund Class N	MRLTX	NAS CM	Open End	US Equity Large Cap Growth (Growth)	B-	C	B		Y	2,000
AMG Renaissance Large Cap Growth Fund Class Z	MRLIX	NAS CM	Open End	US Equity Large Cap Growth (Growth)	B-	C	B	Down	Y	5,000,000
AMG River Road Dividend All Cap Value Fund Class I	ARIDX	NAS CM	Open End	US Equity Large Cap Value (Equity-Income)	B-	C	B			100,000
AMG River Road Dividend All Cap Value Fund Class N	ARDEX	NAS CM	Open End	US Equity Large Cap Value (Equity-Income)	B-	C	B			2,000
AMG River Road Dividend All Cap Value Fund Class Z	ARZDX	NAS CM	Open End	US Equity Large Cap Value (Equity-Income)	B-	C	B		Y	5,000,000
AMG River Road Dividend All Cap Value Fund II Class I	ADIVX	NAS CM	Open End	US Equity Large Cap Value (Equity-Income)	B-	C	B		Y	100,000
AMG River Road Dividend All Cap Value Fund II Class N	ADVTX	NAS CM	Open End	US Equity Large Cap Value (Equity-Income)	B-	C	B		Y	2,000
AMG River Road Dividend All Cap Value Fund II Class Z	ADVZX	NAS CM	Open End	US Equity Large Cap Value (Equity-Income)	B-	C	B		Y	5,000,000
AMG River Road Focused Absolute Value Fund Class I	AFAVX	NAS CM	Open End	US Equity Mid Cap (Growth)	B-	C	B	Up	Y	100,000
AMG River Road Focused Absolute Value Fund Class N	ARRFX	NAS CM	Open End	US Equity Mid Cap (Growth)	B-	C	B+	Up	Y	2,000
AMG River Road Focused Absolute Value Fund Class Z	ARRZX	NAS CM	Open End	US Equity Mid Cap (Growth)	B-	C	B	Up	Y	5,000,000
AMG River Road Long-Short Fund Class I	ALSIX	NAS CM	Open End	Long/Short Equity (Growth & Income)	B-	C+	B+		Y	100,000
AMG River Road Long-Short Fund Class N	ARLSX	NAS CM	Open End	Long/Short Equity (Growth & Income)	B-	C+	B+		Y	2,000
AMG River Road Long-Short Fund Class Z	ARLZX	NAS CM	Open End	Long/Short Equity (Growth & Income)	B-	C+	B+		Y	5,000,000
AMG River Road Small Cap Value Fund Class I	ARSIX	NAS CM	Open End	US Equity Small Cap (Small Company)	B-	C+	B		Y	100,000
AMG River Road Small Cap Value Fund Class N	ARSVX	NAS CM	Open End	US Equity Small Cap (Small Company)	B-	C+	B		Y	2,000
AMG River Road Small Cap Value Fund Class Z	ARZMX	NAS CM	Open End	US Equity Small Cap (Small Company)	B-	C+	B		Y	5,000,000
AMG River Road Small-Mid Cap Value Fund Class I	ARIMX	NAS CM	Open End	US Equity Small Cap (Growth)	B-	C+	B		Y	100,000
AMG River Road Small-Mid Cap Value Fund Class N	ARSMX	NAS CM	Open End	US Equity Small Cap (Growth)	B-	C+	B		Y	2,000
AMG River Road Small-Mid Cap Value Fund Class Z	ARSZX	NAS CM	Open End	US Equity Small Cap (Growth)	B-	C+	B		Y	5,000,000
AMG SouthernSun Small Cap Fund Class I	SSSIX	NAS CM	Open End	US Equity Small Cap (Small Company)	C	C-	C			100,000
AMG SouthernSun Small Cap Fund Class N	SSSFX	NAS CM	Open End	US Equity Small Cap (Small Company)	C	C-	C			2,000
AMG SouthernSun U.S. Equity Fund Class I	SSEIX	NAS CM	Open End	US Equity Mid Cap (Growth)	D+	D+	C	Down	Y	100,000
AMG SouthernSun U.S. Equity Fund Class N	SSEFX	NAS CM	Open End	US Equity Mid Cap (Growth)	D+	D+	C-	Down	Y	2,000
AMG TimesSquare Emerging Markets Small Cap Fund Class I	TQEIX	NAS CM	Open End	Global Emerg Mkts (Div Emerging Mkts)	C	D+	C+	Up	Y	100,000
AMG TimesSquare Emerging Markets Small Cap Fund Class N	TQENX	NAS CM	Open End	Global Emerg Mkts (Div Emerging Mkts)	C	D+	C+	Up	Y	2,000
AMG TimesSquare Emerging Markets Small Cap Fund Class Z	TQEZX	NAS CM	Open End	Global Emerg Mkts (Div Emerging Mkts)	C	D+	C+	Up	Y	5,000,000
AMG TimesSquare Global Small Cap Fund Class I	TSYIX	NAS CM	Open End	Global Equity Mid/Small Cap (Growth)	D	D+	C-		Y	100,000
AMG TimesSquare Global Small Cap Fund Class N	TSYNX	NAS CM	Open End	Global Equity Mid/Small Cap (Growth)	D	D+	C-		Y	2,000
AMG TimesSquare Global Small Cap Fund Class Z	TSYZX	NAS CM	Open End	Global Equity Mid/Small Cap (Growth)	D	D+	C-		Y	5,000,000
AMG TimesSquare International Small Cap Fund Class I	TQTIX	NAS CM	Open End	Global Equity Mid/Small Cap (Small Company)	C	C-	C	Up	Y	100,000
AMG TimesSquare International Small Cap Fund Class N	TCMPX	NAS CM	Open End	Global Equity Mid/Small Cap (Small Company)	C	C-	C	Up	Y	2,000
AMG TimesSquare International Small Cap Fund Class Z	TCMIX	NAS CM	Open End	Global Equity Mid/Small Cap (Small Company)	C	C-	C	Up	Y	5,000,000
AMG TimesSquare Mid Cap Growth Fund Class I	TQMIX	NAS CM	Open End	US Equity Mid Cap (Growth)	B-	B-	B	Down	Y	100,000
AMG TimesSquare Mid Cap Growth Fund Class N	TMDPX	NAS CM	Open End	US Equity Mid Cap (Growth)	B-	B-	B	Down		2,000
AMG TimesSquare Mid Cap Growth Fund Class Z	TMDIX	NAS CM	Open End	US Equity Mid Cap (Growth)	B-	B-	B	Down		5,000,000
AMG TimesSquare Small Cap Growth Fund Class I	TSQIX	NAS CM	Open End	US Equity Small Cap (Small Company)	C+	C	C+	Down	Y	100,000
AMG TimesSquare Small Cap Growth Fund Class N	TSCPX	NAS CM	Open End	US Equity Small Cap (Small Company)	C+	C	C+	Down		2,000
AMG TimesSquare Small Cap Growth Fund Class Z	TSCIX	NAS CM	Open End	US Equity Small Cap (Small Company)	C+	C	C+	Down		5,000,000
AMG Yacktman Focused - Security Selection Only Cls I	YFSIX	NAS CM	Open End	US Equity Large Cap Blend (Growth & Income)	C	C	B+		Y	100,000
AMG Yacktman Focused - Security Selection Only Cls N	YFSNX	NAS CM	Open End	US Equity Large Cap Blend (Growth & Income)	C	C	B+		Y	2,000
AMG Yacktman Focused Fund Class I	YAFIX	NAS CM	Open End	US Equity Large Cap Value (Growth & Income)	B	C+	A		Y	100,000
AMG Yacktman Focused Fund Class N	YAFFX	NAS CM	Open End	US Equity Large Cap Value (Growth & Income)	B	C+	A		Y	2,000
AMG Yacktman Fund Class I	YACKX	NAS CM	Open End	US Equity Large Cap Blend (Growth & Income)	B	C+	A		Y	100,000
AMG Yacktman Special Opportunities Fund Class I	YASSX	NAS CM	Open End	Global Equity Mid/Small Cap (Growth)	C	C-	C+		Y	100,000
AMG Yacktman Special Opportunities Fund Class Z	YASLX	NAS CM	Open End	Global Equity Mid/Small Cap (Growth)	C	C-	C+		Y	5,000,000
AMIDEX35 Israel Fund Class A	AMDAX	NAS CM	Open End	Equity Miscellaneous (Foreign Stock)	D+	D	C	Down	Y	500
AMIDEX35 Israel Fund Class C	AMDCX	NAS CM	Open End	Equity Miscellaneous (Foreign Stock)	D+	D	C		Y	500
AMIDEX35 Israel Mutual Fund	AMDEX	NAS CM	Open End	Equity Miscellaneous (Foreign Stock)	D+	D	C	Down	Y	500
Anchor Tactical Credit Strategies Fund Institutional Class	ATCSX	NAS CM	Open End	Long/Short Credit (Growth & Income)	C	C-	C+	Up	Y	1,000

★ Expanded analysis of this fund is included in Section II.

	TOTAL RETURNS					PERFORMANCE				ASSETS		ASSET ALLOCATION & TURNOVER					BULL & BEAR		FEES		
Min Additional Investment	3-Month Total Return	6-Month Total Return	1-Year Total Return	3-Year Total Return	5-Year Total Return	Dividend Yield (TTM)	Expense Ratio	3-Yr Std Deviation	3-Year Beta	NAV	Total Assets (MIL)	%Cash	%Stocks	%Bonds	%Other	Turnover Ratio	Last Bull Market Total Return	Last Bear Market Total Return	Front End Fee (%)	Back End Fee (%)	Inception Date
10,000	3.77	4.70	8.01	42.15		2.13	2.14	6.26			--										Oct-14
100	5.65	22.99	13.87	55.72	66.26	0.87	0.74	13.56	0.94	12.89	90.1	1	99	0	0	38	30	-21.99			Jun-09
100	5.62	22.92	13.60	54.42	63.83	0.47	1	13.61	0.94	12.76	90.1	1	99	0	0	38	29.82	-22.08			Jun-09
1,000	5.65	23.03	13.88	56.13	67.35	0.94	0.66	13.59	0.94	12.71	90.1	1	99	0	0	38	30.24	-21.97			Jun-09
100	2.69	14.60	6.05	28.41	37.88	2.78	0.85	12.21	0.98	11.91	682.8	2	98	0	0	27	17.73	-11.57			Jun-07
100	2.53	14.35	5.67	27.30	36.00	2.53	1.11	12.29	0.98	11.91	682.8	2	98	0	0	27	17.54	-11.64			Jun-05
1,000	2.62	14.63	6.10	28.09	36.84	2.83	0.79	12.26	0.98	11.91	682.8	2	98	0	0	27	17.54	-11.65			Sep-17
100	2.96	15.02	6.66	29.62	39.39	2.96	0.91	12.2	0.98	12.91	74.6	2	98	0	0	28					Jun-12
100	2.90	14.81	6.37	28.48	37.37	2.71	1.19	12.19	0.98	12.88	74.6	2	98	0	0	28					Jun-12
1,000	2.98	15.06	6.73	29.76	39.54	3.02	0.84	12.24	0.98	12.91	74.6	2	98	0	0	28					Sep-17
100	4.64	21.33	11.84	54.27		0.66	0.96	14.3	1.07	12.17	87.9	2	98	0	0	88					Nov-15
100	4.48	21.22	11.56	53.02		0.43	1.21	14.29	1.07	12.11	87.9	2	98	0	0	88					Nov-15
1,000	4.64	21.33	11.97	54.38		0.7	0.92	14.28	1.07	12.17	87.9	2	98	0	0	88					Sep-17
100	4.03	13.46	11.74	26.97	23.20	0	2.2	8.22	0.52	12.89	22.5	46	55	0	0	189	8.54				Mar-13
100	4.02	13.32	11.58	26.09	21.66	0	2.45	8.25	0.52	12.67	22.5	46	55	0	0	189	8.54				May-11
1,000	4.02	13.44	11.82	26.81	22.36	0	2.12	8.25	0.52	12.91	22.5	46	55	0	0	189	8.54				Sep-17
100	5.91	22.77	9.11	51.68	58.84	0.07	1.32	13.21	0.72	13.26	367.3	7	93	0	0	41	22.16	-18.01			Dec-06
100	5.79	22.58	8.80	50.50	56.79	0	1.57	13.19	0.72	12.97	367.3	7	93	0	0	41	22.01	-18.1			Jun-05
1,000	5.99	22.89	9.26	51.52	57.85	0.17	1.22	13.22	0.72	13.26	367.3	7	93	0	0	41	22.01	-18.1			Sep-17
100	5.34	23.28	10.30	56.28	61.71	0	1.26	13.76	0.85	7.89	103.9	4	96	0	0	46	23.83	-17.5			Jun-07
100	5.33	23.00	10.10	54.99	59.60	0	1.5	13.78	0.85	7.7	103.9	4	96	0	0	46	23.53	-17.65			Mar-07
1,000	5.48	23.28	10.45	55.74	60.37	0	1.21	13.79	0.86	7.89	103.9	4	96	0	0	46	23.54	-17.65			Sep-17
100	3.96	24.56	-5.44	23.47	-3.75	0	0.97	18.71	1.02	23.58	152.2	5	95	0	0	20	33.84	-23.59			Sep-09
100	3.86	24.36	-5.69	22.53	-4.96	0	1.22	18.71	1.02	23.12	152.2	5	95	0	0	20	33.58	-23.67			Oct-03
100	3.48	20.85	-7.86	8.27	-2.31	1.08	0.96	17.18	1.06	12.17	118.3	6	94	0	0	46					Apr-12
100	3.38	20.75	-8.16	7.42	-3.51	0.37	1.21	17.19	1.06	12.22	118.3	6	94	0	0	46					Apr-12
100	-0.95	10.05	-3.49			0.52	1.25			10.4	5.5	1	99	0	0	84					Dec-16
100	-0.95	9.96	-3.86			0.11	1.65			10.37	5.5	1	99	0	0	84					Feb-17
1,000	-0.85	10.16	-3.49			0.52	1.25			10.4	5.5	1	99	0	0	84					Dec-16
100	5.46	24.71	-0.50			0	1			9.84	1.9	1	99	0	0						May-18
100	5.37	24.49	-0.70			0	1.25			9.81	1.9	1	99	0	0						May-18
1,000	5.46	24.71	-0.50			0	1			9.84	1.9	1	99	0	0						May-18
100	3.22	18.90	-10.72	26.22	33.30	1.12	1.06	15.25	1.17	15.03	1,142	2	98	0	0	46					Feb-17
100	3.09	18.77	-10.91	25.48	31.85	0.67	1.23	15.26	1.17	14.99	1,142	2	98	0	0	46					Jan-13
1,000	3.22	18.89	-10.64	26.43	33.52	1.18	0.98	15.22	1.16	15.04	1,142	2	98	0	0	46					Jan-13
100	8.37	27.79	14.28	56.73	62.97	0	1.03	12.87	0.88	19.54	2,001	2	98	0	0	59	30.1	-20.94			Feb-17
100	8.35	27.80	14.13	56.02	61.55	0	1.18	12.85	0.88	18.94	2,001	2	98	0	0	59	30.03	-21.05			Mar-05
1,000	8.36	27.90	14.38	56.94	63.20	0	0.98	12.88	0.88	19.57	2,001	2	98	0	0	59	30.1	-20.94			Mar-05
100	4.33	26.93	8.50	59.93	65.20	0	1.02	16.32	0.9	15.88	1,037	2	96	0	0	63	25.56	-21.5			Feb-17
100	4.35	26.88	8.34	59.26	63.78	0	1.11	16.35	0.9	15.34	1,037	2	96	0	0	63	25.36	-21.49			Jan-00
1,000	4.33	26.99	8.56	60.09	65.36	0	0.98	16.33	0.9	15.9	1,037	2	96	0	0	63	25.56	-21.5			Jan-00
100	3.02	14.54	11.61			0.48	1.09			13.62	68.6	5	92	3	0	2					Jan-17
100	3.02	14.63	11.69			0.48	1.09			13.63	68.6	5	92	3	0	2					Jan-17
100	3.21	12.74	11.64	47.40	55.80	1.51	1.09	8.3	0.54	19.91	3,800	23	75	2	0	16	14.96	-9.39			Jul-12
100	3.15	12.65	11.42	46.63	54.40	1.32	1.27	8.33	0.54	19.94	3,800	23	75	2	0	16	14.96	-9.39			May-97
100	2.82	11.33	10.59	42.11	49.97	1.74	0.75	7.47	0.53	21.11	8,349	30	69	1	0	12	16.05	-10.2			Jul-92
100	-0.18	8.02	-3.64	55.35	30.96	1	1.84	9.83	0.71	10.5	52.4	2	90	0	1	30					Jun-15
1,000	-0.18	8.11	-3.52	55.86	31.56	1.11	1.74	9.8	0.71	10.53	52.4	2	90	0	1	30					Jun-14
250	-1.34	9.57	-3.87	5.70	-9.96	0	4.5	13.57		10.3	7.4	0	100	0	0	11	4.12	-28.81	5.50		Nov-99
250	-1.56	9.14	-4.60	3.27	-13.41	0	5.25	13.52		6.92	7.4	0	100	0	0	11	3.57	-28.96		1.00	May-00
250	-1.31	9.56	-3.87	5.67	-9.93	0	4.5	13.57		13.52	7.4	0	100	0	0	11	4.1	-28.74			Jun-99
100	2.51	3.05	1.72	3.21		0.26	4.18	3.03	0.28	9.79	24.2	0	0	99	0	1,409			4.75		Sep-15

	MARKET		FUND TYPE, CATEGORY & OBJECTIVE		RATINGS				MINIMUMS	
Fund Name	Ticker Symbol	Traded On	Fund Type	Category and (Prospectus Objective)	Overall Rating	Reward Rating	Risk Rating	Recent Up/ Downgrade	Open to New Investors	Min Initial Investment
Anchor Tactical Equity Strategies Fund Institutional Class	ATESX	NAS CM	Open End	Long/Short Equity (Growth & Income)	B-	C	B+	Up	Y	1,000
Anchor Tactical Global Strategies Institutional Cls Shares	ATGSX	NAS CM	Open End	Long/Short Equity (Growth & Income)	U	U	U		Y	1,000
Ancora MicroCap Fund Class I	ANCIX	NAS CM	Open End	US Equity Small Cap (Small Company)	D	D	D+	Down	Y	5,000
Ancora Special Opportunity Fund Class I	ANSIX	NAS CM	Open End	US Equity Small Cap (Growth & Income)	C+	C	B	Down	Y	5,000
Ancora/Thelen Small-Mid Cap Fund Class I	AATIX	NAS CM	Open End	US Equity Small Cap (Growth & Income)	C	C-	B-		Y	5,000
Ancora/Thelen Small-Mid Cap Fund Class S	AATSX	NAS CM	Open End	US Equity Small Cap (Growth & Income)	C	D+	B-		Y	1,500,000
Appleseed Fund Institutional Share	APPIX	NAS CM	Open End	Flexible Alloc (Growth)	C	C-	B-	Down	Y	100,000
Appleseed Fund Investor Share	APPLX	NAS CM	Open End	Flexible Alloc (Growth)	C	C-	B-	Down	Y	2,500
AQR Alternative Risk Premia Fund Class I	QRPIX	NAS CM	Open End	Multialternative (Income)	D	D	C-		Y	5,000,000
AQR Alternative Risk Premia Fund Class N	QRPNX	NAS CM	Open End	Multialternative (Income)	D	D	C-		Y	1,000,000
AQR Alternative Risk Premia Fund Class R6	QRPRX	NAS CM	Open End	Multialternative (Income)	D	D	C-		Y	100,000
AQR Diversified Arbitrage Fund Class I	ADAIX	NAS CM	Open End	Market Neutral (Growth & Income)	B	C+	A-	Up		5,000,000
AQR Diversified Arbitrage Fund Class N	ADANX	NAS CM	Open End	Market Neutral (Growth & Income)	B	C+	A-	Up		1,000,000
AQR Diversified Arbitrage Fund Class R6	QDARX	NAS CM	Open End	Market Neutral (Growth & Income)	B	C+	A-	Up	Y	100,000
AQR Emerging Defensive Style Fund Class I	AZEIX	NAS CM	Open End	Global Emerg Mkts (Div Emerging Mkts)	C	C	B		Y	5,000,000
AQR Emerging Defensive Style Fund Class N	AZENX	NAS CM	Open End	Global Emerg Mkts (Div Emerging Mkts)	C	C	B		Y	1,000,000
AQR Emerging Defensive Style Fund Class R6	AZERX	NAS CM	Open End	Global Emerg Mkts (Div Emerging Mkts)	C	C	B		Y	50,000,000
AQR Emerging Multi-Style Fund Class I	QEELX	NAS CM	Open End	Global Emerg Mkts (Div Emerging Mkts)	C	C	C+		Y	5,000,000
AQR Emerging Multi-Style Fund Class N	QEENX	NAS CM	Open End	Global Emerg Mkts (Div Emerging Mkts)	C	C	C+		Y	1,000,000
AQR Emerging Multi-Style Fund Class R6	QECRX	NAS CM	Open End	Global Emerg Mkts (Div Emerging Mkts)	C	C	C+		Y	50,000,000
AQR Emerging Relaxed Constraint Equity Fund Class I	QERIX	NAS CM	Open End	Global Emerg Mkts (Div Emerging Mkts)	D+	D+	C-		Y	5,000,000
AQR Emerging Relaxed Constraint Equity Fund Class N	QERNX	NAS CM	Open End	Global Emerg Mkts (Div Emerging Mkts)	D+	D+	D+		Y	1,000,000
AQR Emerging Relaxed Constraint Equity Fund Class R6	QERRX	NAS CM	Open End	Global Emerg Mkts (Div Emerging Mkts)	D+	D+	C-		Y	50,000,000
AQR Equity Market Neutral Fund Class I	QMNIX	NAS CM	Open End	Market Neutral (Growth & Income)	D	D	D		Y	5,000,000
AQR Equity Market Neutral Fund Class N	QMNNX	NAS CM	Open End	Market Neutral (Growth & Income)	D	D	D		Y	1,000,000
AQR Equity Market Neutral Fund Class R6	QMNRX	NAS CM	Open End	Market Neutral (Growth & Income)	D	D	D		Y	100,000
AQR Global Equity Fund Class I	AQGIX	NAS CM	Open End	Global Equity Large Cap (World Stock)	C	C	B-		Y	5,000,000
AQR Global Equity Fund Class N	AQGNX	NAS CM	Open End	Global Equity Large Cap (World Stock)	C	C	B-		Y	1,000,000
AQR Global Equity Fund Class R6	AQGRX	NAS CM	Open End	Global Equity Large Cap (World Stock)	C	C	C+		Y	50,000,000
AQR Global Macro Fund Class I	QGMIX	NAS CM	Open End	Global Macro (Growth & Income)	C+	C	B	Up	Y	5,000,000
AQR Global Macro Fund Class N	QGMNX	NAS CM	Open End	Global Macro (Growth & Income)	C+	C	B	Up	Y	1,000,000
AQR Global Macro Fund Class R6	QGMRX	NAS CM	Open End	Global Macro (Growth & Income)	C+	C	B	Up	Y	100,000
AQR International Defensive Style Fund Class I	ANDIX	NAS CM	Open End	Global Equity Large Cap (Foreign Stock)	C+	C	B	Up	Y	5,000,000
AQR International Defensive Style Fund Class N	ANDNX	NAS CM	Open End	Global Equity Large Cap (Foreign Stock)	C+	C-	B	Up	Y	1,000,000
AQR International Defensive Style Fund Class R6	ANDRX	NAS CM	Open End	Global Equity Large Cap (Foreign Stock)	C+	C	B	Up	Y	50,000,000
AQR International Equity Fund Class I	AQIIX	NAS CM	Open End	Global Equity Large Cap (Foreign Stock)	C	C-	C+		Y	5,000,000
AQR International Equity Fund Class N	AQINX	NAS CM	Open End	Global Equity Large Cap (Foreign Stock)	C	C-	C+		Y	1,000,000
AQR International Equity Fund Class R6	AQIRX	NAS CM	Open End	Global Equity Large Cap (Foreign Stock)	C	C-	C+		Y	50,000,000
AQR International Momentum Style Fund Class I	AIMOX	NAS CM	Open End	Global Equity Large Cap (Foreign Stock)	C	C	C+		Y	5,000,000
AQR International Momentum Style Fund Class N	AIONX	NAS CM	Open End	Global Equity Large Cap (Foreign Stock)	C	C-	C+	Up	Y	1,000,000
AQR International Momentum Style Fund Class R6	QIORX	NAS CM	Open End	Global Equity Large Cap (Foreign Stock)	C	C	C+		Y	50,000,000
AQR International Multi-Style Fund Class I	QICLX	NAS CM	Open End	Global Equity Large Cap (Foreign Stock)	C	C	B		Y	5,000,000
AQR International Multi-Style Fund Class N	QICNX	NAS CM	Open End	Global Equity Large Cap (Foreign Stock)	C	C	B-		Y	1,000,000
AQR International Multi-Style Fund Class R6	QICRX	NAS CM	Open End	Global Equity Large Cap (Foreign Stock)	C	C	B		Y	50,000,000
AQR International Relaxed Constraint Equity Fund Class I	QIRIX	NAS CM	Open End	Global Equity Large Cap (Foreign Stock)	C-	D+	C		Y	5,000,000
AQR International Relaxed Constraint Equity Fund Class N	QIRNX	NAS CM	Open End	Global Equity Large Cap (Foreign Stock)	C-	D+	C		Y	1,000,000
AQR International Relaxed Constraint Equity Fund Class R6	QIRRX	NAS CM	Open End	Global Equity Large Cap (Foreign Stock)	C-	D+	C		Y	50,000,000
AQR Large Cap Defensive Style Fund Class I	AUEIX	NAS CM	Open End	US Equity Large Cap Blend (Growth & Income)	B	B-	B+		Y	5,000,000
AQR Large Cap Defensive Style Fund Class N	AUENX	NAS CM	Open End	US Equity Large Cap Blend (Growth & Income)	B	B-	B+		Y	1,000,000
AQR Large Cap Defensive Style Fund Class R6	QUERX	NAS CM	Open End	US Equity Large Cap Blend (Growth & Income)	B	B-	B+		Y	50,000,000
AQR Large Cap Momentum Style Fund Class I	AMOMX	NAS CM	Open End	US Equity Large Cap Growth (Growth)	C+	C	B-	Down	Y	5,000,000
AQR Large Cap Momentum Style Fund Class N	AMONX	NAS CM	Open End	US Equity Large Cap Growth (Growth)	C+	C	B-		Y	1,000,000

★ Expanded analysis of this fund is included in Section II.

Min Additional Investment	TOTAL RETURNS 3-Month Total Return	6-Month Total Return	1-Year Total Return	3-Year Total Return	5-Year Total Return	PERFORMANCE Dividend Yield (TTM)	Expense Ratio	3-Yr Std Deviation	3-Year Beta	ASSETS NAV	Total Assets (MIL)	ASSET ALLOCATION & TURNOVER %Cash	%Stocks	%Bonds	%Other	Turnover Ratio	BULL & BEAR Last Bull Market Total Return	Last Bear Market Total Return	FEES Front End Fee (%)	Back End Fee (%)	Inception Date
100	6.41	11.90	12.50			0	2.32			11.94	128.2	5	95	0	0	1,091					Sep-16
100	4.05						2.6			10.77	9.6	83	17	0	0						Jan-19
1,000	-8.49	5.14	-23.28	15.38	13.78	0	1.79	18.15	0.95	10.02	18.5	4	96	0	0	31	17.82	-23.19			Sep-08
1,000	1.97	20.06	3.03	40.74	39.62	0.52	2.42	14.19	0.96	7.24	16.9	16	80	0	1	71	13.99	-18.5			Jan-04
1,000	-0.34	17.09	-3.01	35.60	29.50	0.19	1.29	14.76	0.92	14.59	128.5	3	97	0	0	52					Jan-13
1,000	-0.33	17.20	-2.75	36.86	31.03	0.35	1.02	14.82	0.92	14.92	128.5	3	97	0	0	52					Jun-15
	-3.43	1.39	2.56	16.61	8.95	0.28	1.16	10.28	0.74	12.38	164.9	4	67	11	18	85	12.9	-11.65			Jan-11
	-3.45	1.31	2.35	16.02	7.84	0.07	1.35	10.25	0.74	12.31	164.9	4	67	11	18	85	12.85	-11.74			Dec-06
	-1.27	0.21	0.62			0.08	3.36			9.29	356.3	-109	26	134	49						Sep-17
	-1.27	0.10	0.39			0.07	3.61			9.26	356.3	-109	26	134	49						Sep-17
	-1.27	0.21	0.73			0.09	3.27			9.31	356.3	-109	26	134	49						Sep-17
	2.21	5.72	4.25	23.01	9.57	6.18	2.05	2.6	5.5	9.24	486.8	18	25	0	21		2.47	-0.53			Jan-09
	2.21	5.59	3.95	22.13	8.36	5.9	2.3	2.6	5.92	9.24	486.8	18	25	0	21		2.35	-0.71			Jan-09
	2.21	5.73	4.25	23.29	10.02	6.29	1.95	2.56	5.57	9.22	486.8	18	25	0	21		2.47	-0.53			Sep-14
	1.38	6.62	3.75	18.73	-2.39	1.76	0.7	11.34	0.76	9.5	86.8	-2	99	0	3						Jul-12
	1.35	6.57	3.47	17.96	-3.37	1.56	0.95	11.32	0.76	9.73	86.8	-2	99	0	3						Jul-12
	1.39	6.64	3.75	18.98	-2.01	1.87	0.6	11.34	0.76	9.47	86.8	-2	99	0	3						Sep-14
	0.60	10.14	-0.59	31.17	6.40	2.24	0.75	14.38	1.02	9.99	240.0	-2	99	0	2						May-14
	0.50	10.02	-0.84	30.19	5.22	1.92	1	14.36	1.02	9.99	240.0	-2	99	0	2						May-14
	0.50	10.25	-0.47	31.54	6.85	2.35	0.65	14.36	1.02	10	240.0	-2	99	0	2						Jul-14
	-1.31	7.11	-9.83			1.99	1.19			11.29	9.0	-11	98	0	13						Dec-16
	-1.39	7.01	-10.07			1.52	1.44			11.29	9.0	-11	98	0	13						Dec-16
	-1.31	7.12	-9.81			2.16	1.09			11.28	9.0	-11	98	0	13						Dec-16
	-6.45	-8.28	-11.62	-9.16		0.53	2.03	6.09	0.02	9.85	489.1	7	15	33	45						Oct-14
	-6.50	-8.42	-11.93	-9.95		0.53	2.31	6.07	1.03	9.78	489.1	7	15	33	45						Oct-14
	-6.45	-8.27	-11.61	-9.03		0.53	1.97	6.1	0.52	9.86	489.1	7	15	33	45						Oct-14
	0.24	14.34	-1.27	33.47	31.26	1.58	0.81	12.65	1.09	8.29	327.8	1	92	0	6	87	19.51	-23.73			Dec-09
	0.00	14.18	-1.65	32.31	29.30	1.58	1.06	12.65	1.09	8.21	327.8	1	92	0	6	87	19.23	-23.83			Dec-09
	0.23	14.38	-1.20	33.79	32.05	1.73	0.71	12.72	1.09	8.35	327.8	1	92	0	6	87	19.23	-23.83			Jan-14
	1.40	3.30	3.21	11.33	13.31	1.61	1.5	6.34	5.84	9.38	28.1	-69	35	94	40						Apr-14
	1.42	3.11	3.07	10.59	11.98	1.56	1.75	6.38	5.87	9.26	28.1	-69	35	94	40						Apr-14
	1.51	3.30	3.37	11.58	13.68	1.65	1.4	6.36	6.06	9.39	28.1	-69	35	94	40						Sep-14
	2.18	11.80	0.55	20.19	15.69	2.16	0.55	9.58	0.8	13.07	242.3	-1	97	0	5						Jul-12
	2.11	11.65	0.26	19.32	14.11	1.17	0.8	9.6	0.81	13.51	242.3	-1	97	0	5						Jul-12
	2.26	11.90	0.70	20.58	16.31	2.22	0.45	9.62	0.81	13.07	242.3	-1	97	0	5						Sep-14
	0.20	12.34	-3.25	23.79	10.32	1.76	0.86	12.61	1.1	9.83	304.5	-2	96	0	6		14.57	-28.03			Sep-09
	0.09	12.24	-3.52	22.91	8.99	1.39	1.11	12.64	1.1	10.08	304.5	-2	96	0	6		14.29	-28.13			Sep-09
	0.19	12.40	-3.24	24.00	10.93	1.71	0.76	12.58	1.1	10.51	304.5	-2	96	0	6		14.57	-28.03			Jan-14
	3.90	16.88	-0.90	21.66	7.70	1.86	0.55	11.7	0.99	15.16	446.5	-2	99	0	3		15.21	-26.89			Jul-09
	3.91	16.82	-1.08	20.79	6.42	1.59	0.8	11.67	0.98	15.14	446.5	-2	99	0	3		15.04	-26.97			Dec-12
	3.98	17.00	-0.78	21.99	8.25	1.97	0.45	11.67	0.98	15.14	446.5	-2	99	0	3		15.21	-26.89			Jul-14
	2.44	15.02	0.52	30.73	6.24	3.31	0.6	11.21	0.99	11.33	300.5	-1	100	0	1						Mar-13
	2.35	14.93	0.27	29.78	4.83	3.1	0.85	11.16	0.98	11.31	300.5	-1	100	0	1						Mar-13
	2.44	15.15	0.63	31.14	6.68	3.41	0.5	11.18	0.98	11.32	300.5	-1	100	0	1						Jul-14
	-1.30	11.86	-5.54			3.57	1.94			11.31	28.1	-2	100	0	2						Dec-16
	-1.30	11.85	-5.72			3.01	2.19			11.32	28.1	-2	100	0	2						Dec-16
	-1.22	11.96	-5.41			3.69	1.84			11.32	28.1	-2	100	0	2						Dec-16
	4.96	19.63	14.69	52.52	87.98	1.02	0.39	10.42	0.81	22.18	4,368	-3	99	0	4						Jul-12
	4.88	19.49	14.40	51.40	85.68	0.78	0.65	10.43	0.82	22.13	4,368	-3	99	0	4						Jul-12
	4.97	19.66	14.79	52.96	88.77	1.08	0.3	10.45	0.82	22.15	4,368	-3	99	0	4						Sep-14
	5.34	22.13	8.83	48.77	60.02	0.91	0.4	12.42	0.95	22.29	965.3	-2	100	0	3		27.52	-20.68			Jul-09
	5.24	22.00	8.53	47.71	58.02	0.66	0.65	12.42	0.95	22.29	965.3	-2	100	0	3		27.34	-20.76			Dec-12

Fund Name	MARKET Ticker Symbol	Traded On	Fund Type	FUND TYPE, CATEGORY & OBJECTIVE Category and (Prospectus Objective)	RATINGS Overall Rating	Reward Rating	Risk Rating	Recent Up/ Downgrade	Open to New Investors	MINIMUMS Min Initial Investment
AQR Large Cap Momentum Style Fund Class R6	QMORX	NAS CM	Open End	US Equity Large Cap Growth (Growth)	C+	C	B		Y	50,000,000
AQR Large Cap Multi-Style Fund Class I	QCELX	NAS CM	Open End	US Equity Large Cap Blend (Growth)	C+	C	B-	Up	Y	5,000,000
AQR Large Cap Multi-Style Fund Class N	QCENX	NAS CM	Open End	US Equity Large Cap Blend (Growth)	C+	C	B-	Up	Y	1,000,000
AQR Large Cap Multi-Style Fund Class R6	QCERX	NAS CM	Open End	US Equity Large Cap Blend (Growth)	C+	C	B-	Up	Y	50,000,000
AQR Large Cap Relaxed Constraint Equity Fund Class I	QLRIX	NAS CM	Open End	US Equity Large Cap Blend (Growth)	C	C-	B-		Y	5,000,000
AQR Large Cap Relaxed Constraint Equity Fund Class N	QLRNX	NAS CM	Open End	US Equity Large Cap Blend (Growth)	C	C-	B-		Y	1,000,000
AQR Large Cap Relaxed Constraint Equity Fund Class R6	QLRRX	NAS CM	Open End	US Equity Large Cap Blend (Growth)	C	C-	B-		Y	50,000,000
AQR Long-Short Equity Fund Class I	QLEIX	NAS CM	Open End	Long/Short Equity (Growth)	D	D	D+	Down	Y	5,000,000
AQR Long-Short Equity Fund Class N	QLENX	NAS CM	Open End	Long/Short Equity (Growth)	D	D	D+	Down	Y	1,000,000
AQR Long-Short Equity Fund Class R6	QLERX	NAS CM	Open End	Long/Short Equity (Growth)	D	D	D+	Down	Y	100,000
AQR Managed Futures Strategy Fund Class I	AQMIX	NAS CM	Open End	Alternative Miscellaneous (Growth & Income)	D	D	D+		Y	5,000,000
AQR Managed Futures Strategy Fund Class N	AQMNX	NAS CM	Open End	Alternative Miscellaneous (Growth & Income)	D	D	D+		Y	1,000,000
AQR Managed Futures Strategy Fund Class R6	AQMRX	NAS CM	Open End	Alternative Miscellaneous (Growth & Income)	D	D	D+		Y	100,000
AQR Managed Futures Strategy HV Fund Class I	QMHIX	NAS CM	Open End	Alternative Miscellaneous (Growth & Income)	D	D	D		Y	5,000,000
AQR Managed Futures Strategy HV Fund Class N	QMHNX	NAS CM	Open End	Alternative Miscellaneous (Growth & Income)	D	D	D		Y	1,000,000
AQR Managed Futures Strategy HV Fund Class R6	QMHRX	NAS CM	Open End	Alternative Miscellaneous (Growth & Income)	D	D	D		Y	100,000
AQR Multi-Asset Fund Class I	AQRIX	NAS CM	Open End	Moderate Alloc (Growth & Income)	B-	C	A-			5,000,000
AQR Multi-Asset Fund Class N	AQRNX	NAS CM	Open End	Moderate Alloc (Growth & Income)	B-	C	A-			1,000,000
AQR Multi-Asset Fund Class R6	AQRRX	NAS CM	Open End	Moderate Alloc (Growth & Income)	B-	C	A-		Y	100,000
AQR Multi-Strategy Alternative Fund Class I	ASAIX	NAS CM	Open End	Multialternative (Growth & Income)	D	D-	D			5,000,000
AQR Multi-Strategy Alternative Fund Class N	ASANX	NAS CM	Open End	Multialternative (Growth & Income)	D	D-	D			1,000,000
AQR Multi-Strategy Alternative Fund Class R6	QSARX	NAS CM	Open End	Multialternative (Growth & Income)	D	D-	D		Y	100,000
AQR Risk Parity II HV Fund Class I	QRHIX	NAS CM	Open End	Moderate Alloc (Growth & Income)	B-	C+	B	Up	Y	5,000,000
AQR Risk Parity II HV Fund Class N	QRHNX	NAS CM	Open End	Moderate Alloc (Growth & Income)	B-	C+	B	Up	Y	1,000,000
AQR Risk Parity II HV Fund Class R6	QRHRX	NAS CM	Open End	Moderate Alloc (Growth & Income)	B-	B-	B	Up	Y	100,000
AQR Risk Parity II MV Fund Class I	QRMIX	NAS CM	Open End	Moderate Alloc (Growth & Income)	B	C+	A-	Up	Y	5,000,000
AQR Risk Parity II MV Fund Class N	QRMNX	NAS CM	Open End	Moderate Alloc (Growth & Income)	B	C+	A-	Up	Y	1,000,000
AQR Risk Parity II MV Fund Class R6	QRMRX	NAS CM	Open End	Moderate Alloc (Growth & Income)	B	C+	A-	Up	Y	100,000
AQR Risk-Balanced Commodities Strategy Fund Class I	ARCIX	NAS CM	Open End	Commodities Broad Basket (Income)	D	D	D+	Down	Y	5,000,000
AQR Risk-Balanced Commodities Strategy Fund Class N	ARCNX	NAS CM	Open End	Commodities Broad Basket (Income)	D	D	D+	Down	Y	1,000,000
AQR Risk-Balanced Commodities Strategy Fund Class R6	QRCRX	NAS CM	Open End	Commodities Broad Basket (Income)	D	D	D+	Down	Y	100,000
AQR Small Cap Momentum Style Fund Class I	ASMOX	NAS CM	Open End	US Equity Small Cap (Small Company)	C	C	C+		Y	5,000,000
AQR Small Cap Momentum Style Fund Class N	ASMNX	NAS CM	Open End	US Equity Small Cap (Small Company)	C	C	C+		Y	1,000,000
AQR Small Cap Momentum Style Fund Class R6	QSMRX	NAS CM	Open End	US Equity Small Cap (Small Company)	C	C	C+		Y	50,000,000
AQR Small Cap Multi-Style Fund Class I	QSMLX	NAS CM	Open End	US Equity Small Cap (Small Company)	C	C-	C		Y	5,000,000
AQR Small Cap Multi-Style Fund Class N	QSMNX	NAS CM	Open End	US Equity Small Cap (Small Company)	C	C-	C		Y	1,000,000
AQR Small Cap Multi-Style Fund Class R6	QSERX	NAS CM	Open End	US Equity Small Cap (Small Company)	C	C-	C		Y	50,000,000
AQR Small Cap Relaxed Constraint Equity Fund Class I	QSRIX	NAS CM	Open End	US Equity Small Cap (Small Company)	D	D	C-	Down	Y	5,000,000
AQR Small Cap Relaxed Constraint Equity Fund Class N	QSRNX	NAS CM	Open End	US Equity Small Cap (Small Company)	D	D	C-	Down	Y	1,000,000
AQR Small Cap Relaxed Constraint Equity Fund Class R6	QSRRX	NAS CM	Open End	US Equity Small Cap (Small Company)	D	D	C-	Down	Y	50,000,000
AQR Style Premia Alternative Fund Class I	QSPIX	NAS CM	Open End	Global Macro (Growth & Income)	D	D	D+			5,000,000
AQR Style Premia Alternative Fund Class N	QSPNX	NAS CM	Open End	Global Macro (Growth & Income)	D	D	D+			1,000,000
AQR Style Premia Alternative Fund Class R6	QSPRX	NAS CM	Open End	Global Macro (Growth & Income)	D	D	D+			100,000
AQR Style Premia Alternative LV Fund Class I	QSLIX	NAS CM	Open End	Global Macro (Growth & Income)	D+	D	C	Down		5,000,000
AQR Style Premia Alternative LV Fund Class N	QSLNX	NAS CM	Open End	Global Macro (Growth & Income)	D+	D	C	Down		1,000,000
AQR Style Premia Alternative LV Fund Class R6	QSLRX	NAS CM	Open End	Global Macro (Growth & Income)	D+	D+	C	Down		100,000
AQR TM Emerging Multi-Style Fund Class I	QTELX	NAS CM	Open End	Global Emerg Mkts (Div Emerging Mkts)	C	C	C+		Y	5,000,000
AQR TM Emerging Multi-Style Fund Class N	QTENX	NAS CM	Open End	Global Emerg Mkts (Div Emerging Mkts)	C	C	C+		Y	1,000,000
AQR TM Emerging Multi-Style Fund Class R6	QTERX	NAS CM	Open End	Global Emerg Mkts (Div Emerging Mkts)	C	C	C+		Y	50,000,000
AQR TM International Momentum Style Fund Class I	ATIMX	NAS CM	Open End	Global Equity Large Cap (Foreign Stock)	C	C-	C+	Up	Y	5,000,000
AQR TM International Momentum Style Fund Class N	ATNNX	NAS CM	Open End	Global Equity Large Cap (Foreign Stock)	C	C-	C+	Up	Y	1,000,000
AQR TM International Momentum Style Fund Class R6	QTIRX	NAS CM	Open End	Global Equity Large Cap (Foreign Stock)	C	C-	C+	Up	Y	50,000,000

★ Expanded analysis of this fund is included in Section II.

Min Additional Investment	3-Month Total Return	6-Month Total Return	1-Year Total Return	3-Year Total Return	5-Year Total Return	Dividend Yield (TTM)	Expense Ratio	3-Yr Std Deviation	3-Year Beta	NAV	Total Assets (MIL)	%Cash	%Stocks	%Bonds	%Other	Turnover Ratio	Last Bull Market Total Return	Last Bear Market Total Return	Front End Fee (%)	Back End Fee (%)	Inception Date
	TOTAL RETURNS					PERFORMANCE				ASSETS		ASSET ALLOCATION & TURNOVER					BULL & BEAR		FEES		
	5.35	22.20	8.95	49.26	60.78	1.03	0.3	12.42	0.95	22.23	965.3	-2	100	0	3		27.52	-20.68			Jul-14
	1.76	15.27	1.06	40.65	42.06	1.55	0.44	12.74	1.02	16.68	1,519	-2	100	0	2						Mar-13
	1.71	15.10	0.78	39.51	40.32	1.27	0.7	12.78	1.03	16.61	1,519	-2	100	0	2						Mar-13
	1.77	15.29	1.10	40.94	42.54	1.64	0.35	12.75	1.02	16.66	1,519	-2	100	0	2						Jul-14
	1.70	14.12	2.34			0.86	1.33			11.96	14.0	0	100	0	0						Dec-16
	1.69	14.00	2.11			0.66	1.58			11.97	14.0	0	100	0	0						Dec-16
	1.70	14.12	2.37			0.96	1.23			11.96	14.0	0	100	0	0						Dec-16
	-4.59	-0.82	-10.08	5.48	35.77	0.35	1.78	8.49		10.8	1,450	40	57	3	0						Jul-13
	-4.72	-1.01	-10.40	4.55	33.88	0.36	2.06	8.5		10.68	1,450	40	57	3	0						Jul-13
	-4.66	-0.82	-10.06	5.69	36.31	0.35	1.71	8.5		10.83	1,450	40	57	3	0						Sep-14
	1.53	1.89	-1.26	-17.45	0.01	0	1.18	7.86	47.33	8.6	5,567	-483	49	500	34	0	-4.01	-5.35			Jan-10
	1.56	1.80	-1.51	-18.02	-1.26	0	1.47	7.78	46.66	8.45	5,567	-483	49	500	34	0	-4.13	-5.36			Jan-10
	1.65	2.01	-1.14	-17.26	0.34	0	1.13	7.83	46.67	8.62	5,567	-483	49	500	34	0	-4.13	-5.36			Sep-14
	2.15	2.54	-3.00	-26.51	-3.79	0	1.67	11.54	69.44	8.06	375.1	7,389	0	0	-7,289	0					Jul-13
	1.92	2.31	-3.28	-27.18	-5.18	0	1.92	11.55	69.15	7.95	375.1	7,389	0	0	-7,289	0					Jul-13
	2.14	2.53	-3.00	-26.40	-3.46	0	1.57	11.55	69.72	8.08	375.1	7,389	0	0	-7,289	0					Sep-14
	3.96	14.38	7.92	22.87	20.23	2.82	1.38	8.05		9.7	181.9	-204	59	212	32	21	10.34	-6.49			Sep-10
	3.98	14.31	7.63	21.81	18.64	2.57	1.65	8.05		9.66	181.9	-204	59	212	32	21	10.13	-6.6			Sep-10
	4.07	14.52	8.05	23.08	20.53	2.93	1.3	8.04		9.7	181.9	-204	59	212	32	21	10.34	-6.49			Sep-14
	-4.55	-6.01	-11.45	-14.35	-2.06	0	2.41	5.14	15.89	7.34	609.6	-204	19	202	53		1.9				Jul-11
	-4.71	-6.19	-11.77	-15.08	-3.36	0	2.68	5.14	16.29	7.27	609.6	-204	19	202	53		1.84				Jul-11
	-4.66	-6.13	-11.44	-14.16	-1.71	0	2.33	5.13	16.02	7.35	609.6	-204	19	202	53		1.9				Sep-14
	7.66	23.65	10.25	27.80	21.29	3.69	1.72	11.2		8.99	29.8	-284	75	262	47						Nov-12
	7.66	23.48	10.02	26.66	19.47	3.12	1.96	11.13		8.99	29.8	-284	75	262	47						Nov-12
	7.79	23.65	10.34	28.13	21.60	3.75	1.62	11.12		8.99	29.8	-284	75	262	47						Sep-14
	5.18	15.54	7.60	19.52	17.18	1.05	0.99	7.41		9.74	109.6	-170	50	177	43	20					Nov-12
	5.22	15.39	7.34	18.69	15.71	0.79	1.24	7.42		9.67	109.6	-170	50	177	43	20					Nov-12
	5.29	15.65	7.83	20.02	17.74	1.14	0.89	7.45		9.75	109.6	-170	50	177	43	20					Sep-14
	0.00	6.01	-9.19	-5.93	-34.42	0.63	1.04	13	1.16	5.99	249.1	26	0	17	58						Jul-12
	-0.16	5.91	-9.36	-6.67	-35.28	0.28	1.3	13.01	1.16	5.91	249.1	26	0	17	58						Jul-12
	0.00	5.99	-9.08	-5.64	-34.12	0.7	0.95	13.01	1.16	6.01	249.1	26	0	17	58						Sep-14
	3.75	20.53	-4.04	42.75	36.64	0.17	0.6	17.03	0.97	19.08	277.3	-1	99	0	2		31.4	-26.17			Jul-09
	3.63	20.36	-4.28	41.71	34.98	0.01	0.85	17.01	0.97	19.09	277.3	-1	99	0	2		31.2	-26.25			Dec-12
	3.76	20.60	-3.97	43.16	37.20	0.3	0.5	17.02	0.97	19.02	277.3	-1	99	0	2		31.4	-26.17			Jul-14
	0.31	13.50	-7.88	28.44	25.88	0.59	0.65	17.01	0.98	12.61	581.5	-2	99	0	3						Mar-13
	0.23	13.34	-8.13	27.40	24.26	0.33	0.9	17	0.98	12.57	581.5	-2	99	0	3						Mar-13
	0.23	13.48	-7.82	28.68	26.46	0.7	0.55	17.01	0.98	12.62	581.5	-2	99	0	3						Jul-14
	-0.10	11.01	-11.12			0	1.73			9.27	2.3	0	99	0	1						Dec-16
	-0.10	10.92	-11.32			0	1.98			9.24	2.3	0	99	0	1						Dec-16
	-0.10	11.00	-11.11			0	1.63			9.28	2.3	0	99	0	1						Dec-16
	-5.00	-5.52	-10.26	-6.70	10.31	1.02	2.32	6.19	-3.4	8.55	2,845	353	0	0	-253						Oct-13
	-5.12	-5.75	-10.61	-7.58	8.79	0.53	2.58	6.18	-2.88	8.52	2,845	353	0	0	-253						Oct-13
	-5.09	-5.62	-10.24	-6.60	10.68	1.14	2.24	6.19	-2.84	8.56	2,845	353	0	0	-253						Sep-14
	-2.38	-2.19	-3.82	-0.58		0.09	1.24	3	-0.03	9.81	307.7	-219	21	219	79						Sep-14
	-2.50	-2.30	-4.13	-1.55		0	1.51	3.03	0.4	9.74	307.7	-219	21	219	79						Sep-14
	-2.28	-2.09	-3.75	-0.44		0.16	1.17	3.02	0.37	9.83	307.7	-219	21	219	79						Sep-14
	-0.09	9.37	-1.20	30.48		2.13	0.75	14.26	1.02	10.27	355.7	-2	99	0	3						Feb-15
	-0.19	9.22	-1.46	29.55		1.62	1	14.25	1.01	10.3	355.7	-2	99	0	3						Feb-15
	-0.09	9.47	-1.12	30.91		2.21	0.65	14.25	1.01	10.28	355.7	-2	99	0	3						Feb-15
	4.30	17.06	-0.62	20.37	5.99	1.96	0.55	11.6	0.99	13.31	114.6	-3	100	0	3						Jan-12
	4.25	16.88	-0.84	19.51	4.89	1.79	0.8	11.64	0.99	13.22	114.6	-3	100	0	3						Dec-12
	4.32	17.01	-0.57	20.73	6.51	2.08	0.45	11.61	0.99	13.27	114.6	-3	100	0	3						Jul-14

	MARKET		FUND TYPE, CATEGORY & OBJECTIVE		RATINGS					MINIMUMS
Fund Name	Ticker Symbol	Traded On	Fund Type	Category and (Prospectus Objective)	Overall Rating	Reward Rating	Risk Rating	Recent Up/ Downgrade	Open to New Investors	Min Initial Investment
AQR TM International Multi-Style Fund Class I	QIMLX	NAS CM	Open End	Global Equity Large Cap (Growth)	C	C	B		Y	5,000,000
AQR TM International Multi-Style Fund Class N	QIMNX	NAS CM	Open End	Global Equity Large Cap (Growth)	C	C	B-		Y	1,000,000
AQR TM International Multi-Style Fund Class R6	QIMRX	NAS CM	Open End	Global Equity Large Cap (Growth)	C	C	B		Y	50,000,000
AQR TM Large Cap Momentum Style Fund Class I	ATMOX	NAS CM	Open End	US Equity Large Cap Growth (Growth)	C+	C	B-		Y	5,000,000
AQR TM Large Cap Momentum Style Fund Class N	ATMNX	NAS CM	Open End	US Equity Large Cap Growth (Growth)	C+	C	B-		Y	1,000,000
AQR TM Large Cap Momentum Style Fund Class R6	QTMRX	NAS CM	Open End	US Equity Large Cap Growth (Growth)	C+	C	B-		Y	50,000,000
AQR TM Large Cap Multi-Style Fund Class I	QTLLX	NAS CM	Open End	US Equity Large Cap Blend (Growth)	C+	C	B	Up	Y	5,000,000
AQR TM Large Cap Multi-Style Fund Class N	QTLNX	NAS CM	Open End	US Equity Large Cap Blend (Growth)	C+	C	B	Up	Y	1,000,000
AQR TM Large Cap Multi-Style Fund Class R6	QTLRX	NAS CM	Open End	US Equity Large Cap Blend (Growth)	C+	C	B	Up	Y	50,000,000
AQR TM Small Cap Momentum Style Fund Class I	ATSMX	NAS CM	Open End	US Equity Small Cap (Small Company)	C	C	C		Y	5,000,000
AQR TM Small Cap Momentum Style Fund Class N	ATSNX	NAS CM	Open End	US Equity Small Cap (Small Company)	C	C	C		Y	1,000,000
AQR TM Small Cap Momentum Style Fund Class R6	QTSRX	NAS CM	Open End	US Equity Small Cap (Small Company)	C	C	C+		Y	50,000,000
AQR TM Small Cap Multi-Style Fund Class I	QSSLX	NAS CM	Open End	US Equity Small Cap (Small Company)	C-	C-	C	Down	Y	5,000,000
AQR TM Small Cap Multi-Style Fund Class N	QSSNX	NAS CM	Open End	US Equity Small Cap (Small Company)	C-	C-	C	Down	Y	1,000,000
AQR TM Small Cap Multi-Style Fund Class R6	QSSRX	NAS CM	Open End	US Equity Small Cap (Small Company)	C-	C-	C	Down	Y	50,000,000
AQR Volatility Risk Premium Fund Class I	QVPIX	NAS CM	Open End	Alternative Miscellaneous (Growth & Income)	U	U	U		Y	5,000,000
AQR Volatility Risk Premium Fund Class N	QVPNX	NAS CM	Open End	Alternative Miscellaneous (Growth & Income)	U	U	U		Y	1,000,000
AQR Volatility Risk Premium Fund Class R6	QVPRX	NAS CM	Open End	Alternative Miscellaneous (Growth & Income)	U	U	U		Y	100,000
Aquarius International Fund			Open End	Global Equity Large Cap (Foreign Stock)	D	D+	C+	Up	Y	0
Aquila Three Peaks Opportunity Growth Fund Class A	ATGAX	NAS CM	Open End	US Equity Mid Cap (Growth)	C+	C	B	Up	Y	1,000
Aquila Three Peaks Opportunity Growth Fund Class C	ATGCX	NAS CM	Open End	US Equity Mid Cap (Growth)	C+	C	B-	Up	Y	1,000
Aquila Three Peaks Opportunity Growth Fund Class Y	ATGYX	NAS CM	Open End	US Equity Mid Cap (Growth)	C+	C	B	Up	Y	0
Aquila Three Peaks Opportunity Growth Institutional Cls	ATRIX	NAS CM	Open End	US Equity Mid Cap (Growth)	C+	C	B	Up	Y	0
Arabesque Systematic USA Fund Institutional Class	ASUIX	NAS CM	Open End	Moderate Alloc (Growth)	C	C-	B-	Up	Y	50,000
Archer Balanced Fund	ARCHX	NAS CM	Open End	Aggressive Alloc (Balanced)	B-	C	B+	Up	Y	2,500
Archer Dividend Growth Fund	ARDGX	NAS CM	Open End	US Equity Large Cap Blend (Equity-Income)	C+	C	B	Up	Y	2,500
Archer Stock Fund	ARSKX	NAS CM	Open End	US Equity Large Cap Blend (Growth)	C	C	B-		Y	2,500
Argent Small Cap Fund Institutional Shares	ACMSX	NAS CM	Open End	US Equity Small Cap (Small Company)	C	C-	C+		Y	250,000
Ariel Appreciation Fund Institutional Class	CAAIX	NAS CM	Open End	US Equity Mid Cap (Growth)	C+	C	B		Y	1,000,000
Ariel Appreciation Fund Investor Class	CAAPX	NAS CM	Open End	US Equity Mid Cap (Growth)	C	C	B-	Down	Y	1,000
Ariel Focus Fund Institutional Class	AFOYX	NAS CM	Open End	US Equity Large Cap Value (Growth)	C	C	B-	Down	Y	1,000,000
Ariel Focus Fund Investor Class	ARFFX	NAS CM	Open End	US Equity Large Cap Value (Growth)	C	C	B-	Down	Y	1,000
Ariel Fund Institutional Class	ARAIX	NAS CM	Open End	US Equity Mid Cap (Growth)	C	C	B-		Y	1,000,000
Ariel Fund Investor Class	ARGFX	NAS CM	Open End	US Equity Mid Cap (Growth)	C	C	B-		Y	1,000
Ariel Global Fund Institutional Class	AGLYX	NAS CM	Open End	Global Equity Large Cap (World Stock)	C+	C	B	Up	Y	1,000,000
Ariel Global Fund Investor Class	AGLOX	NAS CM	Open End	Global Equity Large Cap (World Stock)	C+	C	B	Up	Y	1,000
Ariel International Fund Investor Class	AINTX	NAS CM	Open End	Global Equity Large Cap (Foreign Stock)	C	D+	C+		Y	1,000
Ariel International Institutional Class	AINIX	NAS CM	Open End	Global Equity Large Cap (Foreign Stock)	C	C-	C+		Y	1,000,000
Arin Large Cap Theta Fund Advisor Class	AVOAX	NAS CM	Open End	Long/Short Equity (Growth)	D+	D	C-		Y	25,000
Arin Large Cap Theta Fund Institutional Class	AVOLX	NAS CM	Open End	Long/Short Equity (Growth)	D+	D	C-		Y	25,000
Aristotle Core Equity Fund Class I Shares	ARSLX	NAS CM	Open End	US Equity Large Cap Blend (Growth)	C	C	B-		Y	2,500
Aristotle International Equity Fund Class I	ARSFX	NAS CM	Open End	Global Equity Large Cap (World Stock)	C+	C	B	Up	Y	2,500
Aristotle Small Cap Equity Fund Class I	ARSBX	NAS CM	Open End	US Equity Small Cap (Small Company)	C	C	C+		Y	2,500
Aristotle Value Equity Fund Class I	ARSQX	NAS CM	Open End	US Equity Large Cap Value (Growth)	C+	C	B	Up		2,500
Aristotle/Saul Global Opportunities Fund Class I	ARSOX	NAS CM	Open End	Global Equity Large Cap (Growth & Income)	B-	C	B	Up	Y	2,500
Arrow DWA Balanced Fund Class A	DWAFX	NAS CM	Open End	Moderate Alloc (Balanced)	C	C-	B		Y	5,000
Arrow DWA Balanced Fund Class C	DWATX	NAS CM	Open End	Moderate Alloc (Balanced)	C	C-	B	Up	Y	5,000
Arrow DWA Balanced Fund Institutional Class	DWANX	NAS CM	Open End	Moderate Alloc (Balanced)	C	C-	B		Y	1,000,000
Arrow DWA Tactical Fund Class A	DWTFX	NAS CM	Open End	Moderate Alloc (Growth)	C	C-	C	Up	Y	5,000
Arrow DWA Tactical Fund Class C	DWTTX	NAS CM	Open End	Moderate Alloc (Growth)	C	C-	C	Up	Y	5,000
Arrow DWA Tactical Fund Institutional Class	DWTNX	NAS CM	Open End	Moderate Alloc (Growth)	C	C-	C	Up	Y	1,000,000
Arrow Managed Futures Strategy Fund Class A	MFTFX	NAS CM	Open End	Alternative Miscellaneous (Growth)	C-	D+	C	Up	Y	5,000

★ Expanded analysis of this fund is included in Section II.

	TOTAL RETURNS					PERFORMANCE				ASSETS		ASSET ALLOCATION & TURNOVER					BULL & BEAR		FEES		
Min Additional Investment	3-Month Total Return	6-Month Total Return	1-Year Total Return	3-Year Total Return	5-Year Total Return	Dividend Yield (TTM)	Expense Ratio	3-Yr Std Deviation	3-Year Beta	NAV	Total Assets (MIL)	%Cash	%Stocks	%Bonds	%Other	Turnover Ratio	Last Bull Market Total Return	Last Bear Market Total Return	Front End Fee (%)	Back End Fee (%)	Inception Date
	2.95	15.63	0.75	32.34		2.1	0.6	11.33	1	10.8	196.1	-2	100	0	2						Feb-15
	2.96	15.41	0.54	31.43		1.76	0.85	11.4	1	10.78	196.1	-2	100	0	2						Feb-15
	3.04	15.59	0.86	32.77		2.2	0.5	11.38	1	10.82	196.1	-2	100	0	2						Feb-15
	5.06	21.82	7.74	48.47	59.17	0.83	0.4	12.66	0.97	23.67	227.3	-1	99	0	2						Jan-12
	4.99	21.69	7.47	47.35	57.42	0.56	0.65	12.66	0.97	23.56	227.3	-1	99	0	2						Dec-12
	5.11	21.91	7.87	48.91	59.90	0.92	0.3	12.67	0.97	23.64	227.3	-1	99	0	2						Jul-14
	1.96	15.39	1.88	41.95		1.3	0.45	12.62	1.02	12.97	313.0	-2	99	0	3						Feb-15
	1.88	15.27	1.56	40.86		0.75	0.7	12.6	1.01	12.98	313.0	-2	99	0	3						Feb-15
	1.96	15.48	1.91	42.25		1.39	0.35	12.61	1.01	12.98	313.0	-2	99	0	3						Feb-15
	3.98	21.80	-3.58	42.53	38.01	0.2	0.6	17.13	0.98	18.77	55.5	-1	99	0	2						Jan-12
	3.96	21.68	-3.79	41.54	36.43	0	0.85	17.14	0.98	18.63	55.5	-1	99	0	2						Dec-12
	4.04	21.89	-3.49	43.00	38.71	0.31	0.5	17.13	0.98	18.76	55.5	-1	99	0	2						Jul-14
	-0.09	12.38	-8.96	26.47		0.69	0.66	17.06	0.99	10.89	23.9	-1	99	0	2						Feb-15
	-0.18	12.28	-9.19	25.48		0.26	0.91	17.04	0.98	10.88	23.9	-1	99	0	2						Feb-15
	-0.09	12.47	-8.89	26.77		0.81	0.56	17.06	0.99	10.91	23.9	-1	99	0	2						Feb-15
	0.98	7.89					0.77			10.25	12.0										Nov-18
	0.88	7.79					1.02			10.23	12.0										Nov-18
	1.08	8.00					0.67			10.25	12.0										Nov-18
	3.33	12.08	2.32			1.31	0.82			9.64	163.2	14	86	0	0	36					Apr-18
	6.96	25.95	10.89	33.14	48.15	0	1.42	12.06	0.9	50.86	319.1	4	96	0	0	123	24.32	-20.94	4.25		Jul-94
	6.77	25.52	10.12	30.37	42.94	0	2.12	12.04	0.9	40.32	319.1	4	96	0	0	123	23.74	-21.19		1.00	May-96
	7.04	26.16	11.21	34.36	50.38	0	1.12	12.06	0.9	55.02	319.1	4	96	0	0	123	24.62	-20.89			May-96
	6.97	26.01	10.95	33.44	49.01	0	1.38	12.05	0.9	52.94	319.1	4	96	0	0	123	24.59	-20.84			Dec-05
	1.00	13.10	1.85			0.04	0.95			12	41.9	2	98	0	0	190					May-17
100	4.18	13.99	7.82	25.27	34.86	1.57	1.21	8.47	1.03	13.35	36.7	4	64	28	0	18	12.43	-10.69			Sep-05
100	0.02	10.25	2.41			2.73	0.98			21.64	17.7	3	97	0	0	33					Sep-16
100	3.04	16.81	0.71	32.80	25.98	0.28	1.28	13.6	1.08	46.88	17.8	2	98	0	0	31	23.1	-23.49			Mar-11
	1.38	20.37	-6.91	34.84	38.52		0.86			227.59	121.4	3	97	0	0		34.19	-24.98			Sep-18
100	1.27	17.96	0.35	31.88	29.81	1.22	0.82	15.91	1.15	45.25	1,369	3	97	0	0	11	27.17	-24.84			Dec-11
100	1.18	17.75	0.01	30.65	27.75	0.89	1.13	15.92	1.15	45.16	1,369	3	97	0	0	11	27.05	-24.84			Dec-89
100	3.25	17.66	-0.15	37.20	24.40	1.17	0.75	16.13	1.28	12.99	57.1	4	96	0	0	27	18.37	-17.3			Dec-11
100	3.17	17.54	-0.40	36.22	22.80	0.96	1	16.13	1.28	13	57.1	4	96	0	0	27	18.26	-17.3			Jun-05
100	0.86	19.25	-0.41	43.25	41.22	1.13	0.72	17.81	1.09	65.65	2,187	7	93	0	0	19	30.18	-31.05			Dec-11
100	0.77	19.05	-0.72	41.95	39.11	0.83	1.01	17.8	1.09	65.5515	2,187	7	93	0	0	19	30.05	-31.05			Nov-86
100	0.94	10.67	2.60	25.52	25.74	2.34	0.88	10.49	0.88	15.03	86.5	7	93	0	0	11					Dec-11
100	0.84	10.54	2.36	24.63	24.19	2.07	1.13	10.47	0.88	15.52	86.5	7	93	0	0	11					Dec-11
100	-0.07	7.39	-1.40	12.49	6.29	0.88	1.14	10.19	0.83	13.36	756.9	8	92	0	0	8					Dec-11
100	0.00	7.63	-1.12	13.34	7.63	1.25	0.89	10.19	0.83	13.11	756.9	8	92	0	0	8					Dec-11
100	-0.04	-0.09	-2.10	-2.39	2.16	0.96	1.23	4.5	0.2	9.4	101.3	69	-2	33	0	326					Sep-13
100	0.06	0.04	-1.75	-1.33	4.08	1.31	0.83	4.54	0.2	9.46	101.3	69	-2	33	0	326					Aug-13
100	5.14	23.74	12.02			0.51	0.65			13.08	23.3	5	96	0	-1	32					Mar-17
100	6.55	18.37	4.42	30.48	14.66	1.26	0.8	11.06	0.94	11.21	69.3	3	97	0	0	17					Mar-14
100	4.19	18.83	-2.66	44.25		0.04	0.96	17.38	1	12.68	53.9	3	97	0	0	94					Oct-15
100	6.01	19.74	7.11			0.5	0.78			13.4	60.1	4	96	0	0	18					Aug-16
100	6.00	19.00	6.22	29.16	22.81	1.68	0.8	10.9	0.92	12.71	70.0	3	97	0	0	37					Mar-12
250	2.76	12.25	1.93	12.40	10.99	0	1.86	8.67	0.56	11.91	65.7	4	67	22	3	115	11.7	-12.95	5.75		Aug-06
250	2.62	11.87	1.20	9.88	6.97	0	2.61	8.64	0.56	10.93	65.7	4	67	22	3	115	11.24	-13.28			Aug-06
	2.79	12.43	2.15	13.23	12.42	0	1.61	8.61	0.56	12.12	65.7	4	67	22	3	115	11.7	-12.95			Mar-12
250	1.51	11.88	-4.19	14.10	16.31	0	1.81	11.31	0.84	9.83	121.8	1	99	0	0	108	6.21	-18.36	5.75		May-08
250	1.29	11.44	-4.89	11.53	11.97	0	2.56	11.27	0.84	9.1	121.8	1	99	0	0	108	5.71	-18.59			May-08
	1.62	12.06	-3.85	15.04	17.83	0.03	1.56	11.38	0.85	9.9	121.8	1	99	0	0	108	6.21	-18.36			Mar-12
250	7.39	17.04	5.93	-4.62	11.65	14.84	1.53	22.02	0.6	7.04	116.8	-5	0	37	68	0	-9.17	-9.56	5.75		Apr-10

	MARKET		FUND TYPE, CATEGORY & OBJECTIVE		RATINGS				MINIMUMS	
Fund Name	Ticker Symbol	Traded On	Fund Type	Category and (Prospectus Objective)	Overall Rating	Reward Rating	Risk Rating	Recent Up/ Downgrade	Open to New Investors	Min Initial Investment
Arrow Managed Futures Strategy Fund Class C	MFTTX	NAS CM	Open End	Alternative Miscellaneous (Growth)	C-	D+	C	Up	Y	5,000
Arrow Managed Futures Strategy Fund Institutional Class	MFTNX	NAS CM	Open End	Alternative Miscellaneous (Growth)	C-	D+	C	Up	Y	1,000,000
Artisan Developing World Fund Advisor Shares	APDYX	NAS CM	Open End	Global Emerg Mkts (Growth)	C+	C+	C+	Up	Y	250,000
Artisan Developing World Fund Institutional Shares	APHYX	NAS CM	Open End	Global Emerg Mkts (Growth)	C+	C+	C+	Up	Y	1,000,000
Artisan Developing World Fund Investor Shares	ARTYX	NAS CM	Open End	Global Emerg Mkts (Growth)	C+	C+	C+	Up	Y	1,000
Artisan Global Discovery Fund Investor Shares	APFDX	NAS CM	Open End	Global Equity Large Cap (World Stock)	C-	C-	C+	Up	Y	1,000
Artisan Global Equity Fund Institutional Shares	APHHX	NAS CM	Open End	Global Equity Large Cap (World Stock)	B-	B-	B	Up	Y	1,000,000
Artisan Global Equity Fund Investor Class	ARTHX	NAS CM	Open End	Global Equity Large Cap (World Stock)	B-	C+	B	Up	Y	1,000
Artisan Global Opportunities Fund Advisor Class	APDRX	NAS CM	Open End	Global Equity Large Cap (Growth)	C+	C	B-	Up	Y	250,000
Artisan Global Opportunities Fund Institutional Class	APHRX	NAS CM	Open End	Global Equity Large Cap (Growth)	C+	C	B	Up	Y	1,000,000
Artisan Global Opportunities Fund Investor Class	ARTRX	NAS CM	Open End	Global Equity Large Cap (Growth)	C+	C	B-	Up	Y	1,000
Artisan Global Value Fund Advisor Class	APDGX	NAS CM	Open End	Global Equity Large Cap (World Stock)	C+	C	B	Up		250,000
Artisan Global Value Fund Institutional Class	APHGX	NAS CM	Open End	Global Equity Large Cap (World Stock)	C+	C	B	Up	Y	1,000,000
Artisan Global Value Fund Investor Class	ARTGX	NAS CM	Open End	Global Equity Large Cap (World Stock)	C+	C	B	Up	Y	1,000
Artisan International Fund Advisor Class	APDIX	NAS CM	Open End	Global Equity Large Cap (Foreign Stock)	C+	C	B	Up	Y	250,000
Artisan International Fund Institutional Class	APHIX	NAS CM	Open End	Global Equity Large Cap (Foreign Stock)	C+	C	B	Up	Y	1,000,000
Artisan International Fund Investor Class	ARTIX	NAS CM	Open End	Global Equity Large Cap (Foreign Stock)	C+	C	B	Up	Y	1,000
Artisan International Small-Mid Fund Advisor Shares	APDJX	NAS CM	Open End	Global Equity Mid/Small Cap (Growth)	C	C	C+		Y	250,000
Artisan International Small-Mid Fund Institutional Share	APHJX	NAS CM	Open End	Global Equity Mid/Small Cap (Growth)	C	C	C+		Y	1,000,000
Artisan International Small-Mid Fund Investor Share	ARTJX	NAS CM	Open End	Global Equity Mid/Small Cap (Growth)	C	C	C+			1,000
Artisan International Value Fund Advisor Class	APDKX	NAS CM	Open End	Global Equity Large Cap (Foreign Stock)	C	C	B			250,000
Artisan International Value Fund Institutional Class	APHKX	NAS CM	Open End	Global Equity Large Cap (Foreign Stock)	C	C	B			1,000,000
Artisan International Value Fund Investor Class	ARTKX	NAS CM	Open End	Global Equity Large Cap (Foreign Stock)	C	C	B			1,000
Artisan Mid Cap Fund Advisor Class	APDMX	NAS CM	Open End	US Equity Mid Cap (Growth)	B-	B-	B-			250,000
Artisan Mid Cap Fund Institutional Class	APHMX	NAS CM	Open End	US Equity Mid Cap (Growth)	B-	B-	B-			1,000,000
Artisan Mid Cap Fund Investor Class	ARTMX	NAS CM	Open End	US Equity Mid Cap (Growth)	B-	B-	B-			1,000
Artisan Mid Cap Value Fund Advisor Class	APDQX	NAS CM	Open End	US Equity Mid Cap (Growth)	C+	C	B	Up		250,000
Artisan Mid Cap Value Fund Institutional Class	APHQX	NAS CM	Open End	US Equity Mid Cap (Growth)	C+	C	B	Up		1,000,000
Artisan Mid Cap Value Fund Investor Class	ARTQX	NAS CM	Open End	US Equity Mid Cap (Growth)	C+	C	B	Up		1,000
Artisan Small Cap Fund Advisor Shares	APDSX	NAS CM	Open End	US Equity Small Cap (Small Company)	C+	C+	B-	Down		250,000
Artisan Small Cap Fund Institutional Shares	APHSX	NAS CM	Open End	US Equity Small Cap (Small Company)	C+	C+	B-	Down		1,000,000
Artisan Small Cap Fund Investor Shares	ARTSX	NAS CM	Open End	US Equity Small Cap (Small Company)	C+	C+	B-	Down		1,000
Artisan Sustainable Emerging Markets Institutional Cls	APHEX	NAS CM	Open End	Global Emerg Mkts (Div Emerging Mkts)	C	C	C+		Y	1,000,000
Artisan Sustainable Emerging Markets Fund Investor Class	ARTZX	NAS CM	Open End	Global Emerg Mkts (Div Emerging Mkts)	C	C	C+		Y	1,000
Artisan Thematic Fund Advisor Shares	APDTX	NAS CM	Open End	US Equity Large Cap Blend (Growth)	C	C	B	Up	Y	250,000
Artisan Thematic Fund Investor Shares	ARTTX	NAS CM	Open End	US Equity Large Cap Blend (Growth)	C	C	B	Up	Y	1,000
Artisan Value Fund Advisor Class	APDLX	NAS CM	Open End	US Equity Large Cap Value (Growth)	C+	C	B-	Up	Y	250,000
Artisan Value Fund Institutional Class	APHLX	NAS CM	Open End	US Equity Large Cap Value (Growth)	C+	C	B-	Up	Y	1,000,000
Artisan Value Fund Investor Class	ARTLX	NAS CM	Open End	US Equity Large Cap Value (Growth)	C+	C	B-	Up	Y	1,000
Ashmore Emerging Markets Active Equity Fund Class A	EMQAX	NAS CM	Open End	Global Emerg Mkts (Div Emerging Mkts)	C	C-	B-		Y	1,000
Ashmore Emerging Markets Active Equity Fund Class C	EMQCX	NAS CM	Open End	Global Emerg Mkts (Div Emerging Mkts)	C	C-	B-		Y	1,000
Ashmore Emerging Markets Active Equity Institutional Cls	EMQIX	NAS CM	Open End	Global Emerg Mkts (Div Emerging Mkts)	C	C-	B-		Y	1,000,000
Ashmore Emerging Markets Equity Fund Class A	EMEAX	NAS CM	Open End	Global Emerg Mkts (Growth)	C	C	C+		Y	1,000
Ashmore Emerging Markets Equity Fund Class C	EMECX	NAS CM	Open End	Global Emerg Mkts (Growth)	C	C	C+		Y	1,000
Ashmore Emerging Markets Equity Fund Institutional Class	EMFIX	NAS CM	Open End	Global Emerg Mkts (Growth)	C	C	C+		Y	1,000,000
Ashmore Emerging Markets Frontier Equity Fund Class A	EFEAX	NAS CM	Open End	Global Emerg Mkts (Growth)	C	C-	C+	Up	Y	1,000
Ashmore Emerging Markets Frontier Equity Fund Class C	EFECX	NAS CM	Open End	Global Emerg Mkts (Growth)	C	D+	C+	Up	Y	1,000
Ashmore Emerging Markets Frontier Equity Institutional Cls	EFEIX	NAS CM	Open End	Global Emerg Mkts (Growth)	C	C-	C+		Y	1,000,000
Ashmore Emerging Markets Small Cap Equity Fund Class A	ESSAX	NAS CM	Open End	Global Emerg Mkts (Small Company)	C-	D+	C		Y	1,000
Ashmore Emerging Markets Small Cap Equity Fund Class C	ESSCX	NAS CM	Open End	Global Emerg Mkts (Small Company)	C-	D+	C		Y	1,000
Ashmore Emerging Mkts Small Cap Equity Inst Cls	ESCIX	NAS CM	Open End	Global Emerg Mkts (Small Company)	C-	D+	C			1,000,000
Aspiration Flagship Fund	ASPFX	NAS CM	Open End	Multialternative (Growth)	C	C	C+		Y	10

★ Expanded analysis of this fund is included in Section II.

Min Additional Investment	TOTAL RETURNS 3-Month Total Return	6-Month Total Return	1-Year Total Return	3-Year Total Return	5-Year Total Return	PERFORMANCE Dividend Yield (TTM)	Expense Ratio	3-Yr Std Deviation	3-Year Beta	ASSETS NAV	Total Assets (MIL)	ASSET ALLOCATION & TURNOVER %Cash	%Stocks	%Bonds	%Other	Turnover Ratio	BULL & BEAR Last Bull Market Total Return	Last Bear Market Total Return	FEES Front End Fee (%)	Back End Fee (%)	Inception Date
250	7.26	16.61	5.28	-6.71	7.63	14.47	2.28	21.95	0.6	6.71	116.8	-5	0	37	68	0	-9.54	-9.88			Apr-10
	7.41	17.06	6.29	-4.03	12.85	15.47	1.28	22	0.61	7.1	116.8	-5	0	37	68	0	-9.17	-9.56			Mar-12
	6.48	31.14	18.93	56.10		0.05	1.18	14.39	0.92	14.12	2,404	6	94	0	0	121					Jun-15
	6.54	31.25	19.03	56.53		0.03	1.09	14.33	0.92	14.16	2,404	6	94	0	0	121					Jun-15
	6.51	31.17	18.76	55.29		0.01	1.37	14.42	0.92	14.06	2,404	6	94	0	0	121					Jun-15
	9.19	30.79	14.21			0	1.5			13.42	91.6	8	92	0	0	39					Aug-17
	8.67	23.80	12.54	57.00	56.71	0.39	1.1	11.18	0.91	20.8	242.4	4	95	0	0	120	25.88	-20			Oct-15
	8.60	23.65	12.27	55.85	55.27	0.11	1.36	11.19	0.91	20.7	242.4	4	95	0	0	120	25.88	-20			Mar-10
	6.07	24.50	8.18	55.28	64.58	0	1.01	13.28	1.08	27.08	3,139	4	96	0	0	44	27.63	-19.86			Apr-15
	6.09	24.61	8.32	55.85	65.74	0.01	0.91	13.31	1.08	27.34	3,139	4	96	0	0	44	27.75	-19.92			Jul-11
	6.06	24.48	8.05	54.76	63.79	0	1.15	13.3	1.08	26.95	3,139	4	96	0	0	44	27.63	-19.86			Sep-08
	3.86	16.13	3.88	35.72	30.19	0.96	1.13	12.04	1.02	17.2	2,929	6	94	0	0	28	20.98	-14.73			Apr-15
	3.85	16.16	4.04	36.15	31.04	1.05	1.04	12.03	1.02	17.25	2,929	6	94	0	0	28	20.98	-14.73			Jul-12
	3.79	16.02	3.71	35.18	29.43	0.81	1.28	12.04	1.02	17.23	2,929	6	94	0	0	28	20.98	-14.73			Dec-07
	8.20	19.97	9.03	34.37	17.20	1.24	1.04	11.85	0.98	32.31	10,462	2	96	2	0	55	26.28	-24.17			Apr-15
	8.24	20.05	9.10	34.68	17.80	1.32	0.96	11.85	0.98	32.57	10,462	2	96	2	0	55	26.46	-24.11			Jul-97
	8.18	19.96	8.89	33.84	16.48	1.06	1.18	11.86	0.98	32.39	10,462	2	96	2	0	55	26.28	-24.17			Dec-95
	7.00	24.08	2.81	32.35	14.46		1.27	14.07	1.08	13.91	865.4	2	98	0	0	60	21.51	-23.82			Dec-18
	7.00	24.11	2.86	32.93	15.01	0	1.15	14.05	1.07	14.05	865.4	2	98	0	0	60	21.51	-23.82			Apr-16
	6.92	23.99	2.64	32.14	14.28	0	1.36	14.04	1.07	13.9	865.4	2	98	0	0	60	21.51	-23.82			Dec-01
	3.97	14.87	2.49	29.00	16.80	2.08	1.1	11.6	0.99	35.04	13,397	9	91	0	0	22	17.24	-19.88			Apr-15
	3.99	14.93	2.59	29.33	17.40	2.23	1.01	11.62	0.99	35.18	13,397	9	91	0	0	22	17.37	-19.81			Oct-06
	3.92	14.81	2.34	28.44	16.06	1.79	1.24	11.59	0.99	35.11	13,397	9	91	0	0	22	17.24	-19.88			Sep-02
	10.15	35.61	19.58	59.54	63.50	0	1.05	15.14	1.03	38.95	5,139	2	98	0	0	50	28.22	-16.53			Apr-15
	10.18	35.72	19.76	60.09	64.55	0	0.96	15.12	1.02	43.16	5,139	2	98	0	0	50	28.42	-16.43			Jul-00
	10.11	35.49	19.44	58.93	62.60	0	1.18	15.12	1.02	38.63	5,139	2	98	0	0	50	28.22	-16.53			Jun-97
	5.12	18.68	0.56	30.13	23.50	0.39	1.05	14.67	1.08	19.88	2,347	6	94	0	0	19	22.32	-17.02			Apr-15
	5.17	18.72	0.67	30.49	24.22	0.47	0.99	14.68	1.08	19.91	2,347	6	94	0	0	19	22.32	-17.02			Feb-12
	5.06	18.56	0.44	29.68	22.86	0.2	1.2	14.66	1.08	19.93	2,347	6	94	0	0	19	22.32	-17.02			Mar-01
	6.71	33.46	16.15	79.53	87.64	0	1.06	17.66	0.89	34.34	1,727	2	98	0	0	44	26.04	-16.87			Feb-17
	6.73	33.44	16.21	80.12	89.15	0	1.01	17.65	0.89	34.87	1,727	2	98	0	0	44	26.04	-16.87			May-12
	6.70	33.37	15.99	79.02	87.11	0	1.21	17.65	0.89	34.21	1,727	2	98	0	0	44	26.04	-16.87			Mar-95
	1.02	12.42	2.45	40.58	24.66	0.5	1.2	13.6	0.95	15.74	53.6	3	97	0	0	35	14.53	-30.9			Jun-06
	1.02	12.36	2.33	40.31	24.31	0.87	1.35	13.61	0.95	15.72	53.6	3	97	0	0	35	14.33	-30.97			Jun-08
	5.48	20.95	17.34				1.27			15.18	466.4	4	96	0	0	355					Jul-18
	5.49	20.78	17.27			0	1.52			15.17	466.4	4	96	0	0	355					Apr-17
	4.20	18.79	1.12	33.85	31.92	0.82	0.89	14.98	1.18	12.64	391.8	7	93	0	0	25	22.54	-14.65			Apr-15
	4.19	18.85	1.20	34.12	32.57	0.89	0.8	14.96	1.18	12.67	391.8	7	93	0	0	25	22.65	-14.54			Jul-11
	4.10	18.70	0.95	33.16	31.06	0.68	1.02	14.98	1.18	12.69	391.8	7	93	0	0	25	22.54	-14.64			Mar-06
50	1.91	15.34	4.06			1.56	1.27			10.7	20.2	8	92	0	0	164			5.25		Nov-16
50	1.76	14.89	3.17			0.88	2.02			10.57	20.2	8	92	0	0	164				1.00	Nov-16
5,000	2.00	15.50	4.38			1.68	1.02			10.75	20.2	8	92	0	0	164					Nov-16
50	2.83	17.29	3.43	60.57	20.17	0.62	1.42	15.13	1.03	11.15	34.9	2	98	0	0	140	17.55		5.25		Feb-12
50	2.80	16.92	2.59	57.12	15.87	0.27	2.17	15.15	1.03	10.64	34.9	2	98	0	0	140	17.18			1.00	Aug-12
5,000	2.92	17.32	3.68	61.82	21.73	0.77	1.17	15.16	1.03	10.78	34.9	2	98	0	0	140	17.86				Jun-11
50	3.27	11.09	0.30	20.92	9.33	1.76	1.77	10.72	0.88	8.22	91.6	1	99	0	0	107			5.25		May-14
50	3.19	10.78	-0.46	18.19	4.94	1.39	2.52	10.81	0.88	8.02	91.6	1	99	0	0	107				1.00	May-14
5,000	3.34	11.28	0.76	22.10	11.29	1.61	1.52	10.7	0.88	9.55	91.6	1	99	0	0	107					Nov-13
50	1.00	11.75	-10.42	18.66	2.01	0.1	1.77	14.58	1.02	9.03	29.2	0	100	0	0	126			5.25		Feb-12
50	0.85	11.45	-11.15	16.09	-1.95	0.04	2.52	14.61	1.03	9.44	29.2	0	100	0	0	126				1.00	Aug-12
5,000	1.01	11.89	-10.05	19.57	3.46	0.15	1.52	14.59	1.03	11.63	29.2	0	100	0	0	126					Oct-11
1	0.69	4.62	0.74	8.13		1.09	3.37	3.88	0.31	10.18	14.7	55	37	-2	9	7					Oct-14

Fund Name	MARKET: Ticker Symbol	MARKET: Traded On	FUND TYPE: Fund Type	Category and (Prospectus Objective)	RATINGS: Overall Rating	RATINGS: Reward Rating	RATINGS: Risk Rating	RATINGS: Recent Up/Downgrade	MINIMUMS: Open to New Investors	MINIMUMS: Min Initial Investment
Aspiration Redwood Fund	REDWX	NAS CM	Open End	US Equity Large Cap Blend (Growth & Income)	C+	C	B	Down	Y	10
Aspiriant Defensive Allocation Fund	RMDFX	NAS CM	Open End	Multialternative (Asset Alloc)	B-	C	B+	Up	Y	0
Aspiriant Risk-Managed Equity Allocation Advisor Shares	RMEAX	NAS CM	Open End	Global Equity Large Cap (World Stock)	B-	C	A-		Y	0
Asset Management Fund Large Cap Equity Fund Class AMF	IICAX	NAS CM	Open End	US Equity Large Cap Blend (Growth)	B-	C	B	Down	Y	2,500
Asset Management Fund Large Cap Equity Fund Class H	IICHX	NAS CM	Open End	US Equity Large Cap Blend (Growth)	B-	C	B	Down	Y	3,000,000
Astor Dynamic Allocation Fund Class A	ASTLX	NAS CM	Open End	Moderate Alloc (Growth & Income)	B-	C	B	Up	Y	5,000
Astor Dynamic Allocation Fund Class C	ASTZX	NAS CM	Open End	Moderate Alloc (Growth & Income)	C+	C	B	Up	Y	5,000
Astor Dynamic Allocation Fund Class I	ASTIX	NAS CM	Open End	Moderate Alloc (Growth & Income)	B-	C	B	Up	Y	5,000
Astor Macro Alternative Fund Class I	GBLMX	NAS CM	Open End	Global Macro (Growth & Income)	B-	C	B+		Y	5,000
Astor Sector Allocation Fund Class A	ASPGX	NAS CM	Open End	Moderate Alloc (Growth)	C+	C	B-	Up	Y	5,000
Astor Sector Allocation Fund Class C	CSPGX	NAS CM	Open End	Moderate Alloc (Growth)	C+	C	B-	Up	Y	5,000
Astor Sector Allocation Fund Class I	STARX	NAS CM	Open End	Moderate Alloc (Growth)	C+	C	B	Up	Y	5,000
ATAC Rotation Fund Institutional Class	ATCIX	NAS CM	Open End	Moderate Alloc (Growth & Income)	C	C	C		Y	25,000
ATAC Rotation Fund Investor Class	ATACX	NAS CM	Open End	Moderate Alloc (Growth & Income)	C	C	C		Y	2,500
Athena Behavioral Tactical Fund Class A	ATVAX	NAS CM	Open End	US Equity Mid Cap (Growth)	C	C-	B		Y	2,500
Athena Behavioral Tactical Fund Class I	ATVIX	NAS CM	Open End	US Equity Mid Cap (Growth)	C+	C	B	Up	Y	100,000
ATM International Managed Volatility Portfolio Class K			Open End	Global Equity Large Cap (Foreign Stock)	C	C-	B		Y	0
ATM Large Cap Managed Volatility Portfolio Class K			Open End	US Equity Large Cap Blend (Growth)	B-	C	B	Up	Y	0
ATM Mid Cap Managed Volatility Portfolio Class K			Open End	US Equity Mid Cap (Growth)	C	C	B-		Y	0
ATM Small Cap Managed Volatility Portfolio Class K			Open End	US Equity Small Cap (Small Company)	C	C	C+		Y	0
Auer Growth Fund	AUERX	NAS CM	Open End	US Equity Small Cap (Growth)	C-	D+	C-	Down	Y	2,000
Auxier Focus Fund Class A	AUXAX	NAS CM	Open End	US Equity Large Cap Value (Growth)	B-	C	B+		Y	2,000
Auxier Focus Fund Class Investor	AUXFX	NAS CM	Open End	US Equity Large Cap Value (Growth)	B-	C	B+		Y	5,000
Auxier Focus Fund Institutional	AUXIX	NAS CM	Open End	US Equity Large Cap Value (Growth)	B-	C	B+		Y	250,000
Ave Maria Bond Fund	AVEFX	NAS CM	Open End	Cautious Alloc (Govt Bond)	B	C	A-	Up	Y	2,500
Ave Maria Growth Fund	AVEGX	NAS CM	Open End	US Equity Large Cap Growth (Growth)	B	B	B		Y	2,500
Ave Maria Rising Dividend Fund	AVEDX	NAS CM	Open End	US Equity Large Cap Blend (Growth & Income)	B-	C	B		Y	2,500
Ave Maria Value Fund	AVEMX	NAS CM	Open End	US Equity Mid Cap (Growth)	C+	C	B	Up	Y	2,500
Ave Maria World Equity Fund	AVEWX	NAS CM	Open End	Global Equity Large Cap (World Stock)	B-	C	B	Up	Y	2,500
AXA/Legg Mason Strategic Allocation Portfolio Class K	US29439V5497		Open End	Moderate Alloc (Asset Alloc)	U	U	U		Y	0
AXA/Mutual Large Cap Eq Managed Vol Port Cls K			Open End	US Equity Large Cap Blend (Growth)	B-	C	B+	Down	Y	0
Azzad Ethical Fund	ADJEX	NAS CM	Open End	US Equity Mid Cap (Growth)	C+	C	B	Down	Y	1,000
B. Riley Diversified Equity Fund Class C Shares	BRDCX	NAS CM	Open End	US Equity Small Cap (Growth)	D+	D	D+	Down	Y	0
Baillie Gifford EAFE Choice Fund Class 2	BGCWX	NAS CM	Open End	Global Equity Large Cap (Foreign Stock)	C	C	C+		Y	25,000,000
Baillie Gifford EAFE Choice Fund Class I	BGCSX	NAS CM	Open End	Global Equity Large Cap (Foreign Stock)	C	C	C+		Y	0
Baillie Gifford EAFE Choice Fund Class K	BKGCX	NAS CM	Open End	Global Equity Large Cap (Foreign Stock)	C	C	C+		Y	10,000,000
Baillie Gifford EAFE Fund Class 2	BGETX	NAS CM	Open End	Global Equity Large Cap (Foreign Stock)	C	C	C		Y	25,000,000
Baillie Gifford EAFE Fund Class 3	BGEUX	NAS CM	Open End	Global Equity Large Cap (Foreign Stock)	C	C	C		Y	100,000,000
Baillie Gifford EAFE Fund Class 4	BGEFX	NAS CM	Open End	Global Equity Large Cap (Foreign Stock)	C	C	C		Y	200,000,000
Baillie Gifford EAFE Fund Class 5	BGEVX	NAS CM	Open End	Global Equity Large Cap (Foreign Stock)	C	C	C		Y	500,000,000
Baillie Gifford EAFE Fund Class I	BGESX	NAS CM	Open End	Global Equity Large Cap (Foreign Stock)	C	C	C		Y	0
Baillie Gifford EAFE Fund Class K	BGEKX	NAS CM	Open End	Global Equity Large Cap (Foreign Stock)	C	C	C		Y	10,000,000
Baillie Gifford EAFE Pure Fund Class 2	BGPTX	NAS CM	Open End	Global Equity Large Cap (Foreign Stock)	C	C	C+		Y	25,000,000
Baillie Gifford EAFE Pure Fund Class 3	BGPFX	NAS CM	Open End	Global Equity Large Cap (Foreign Stock)	C	C	C+		Y	100,000,000
Baillie Gifford EAFE Pure Fund Class I	BSGPX	NAS CM	Open End	Global Equity Large Cap (Foreign Stock)	C	C	C+		Y	0
Baillie Gifford EAFE Pure Fund Class K	BGPKX	NAS CM	Open End	Global Equity Large Cap (Foreign Stock)	C	C	C+		Y	10,000,000
Baillie Gifford Emerging Markets Fund Class 2	BGEHX	NAS CM	Open End	Global Emerg Mkts (Div Emerging Mkts)	C+	C	C+	Up	Y	25,000,000
Baillie Gifford Emerging Markets Fund Class 3	BGELX	NAS CM	Open End	Global Emerg Mkts (Div Emerging Mkts)	C+	C	C+	Up	Y	100,000,000
Baillie Gifford Emerging Markets Fund Class 5	BGEDX	NAS CM	Open End	Global Emerg Mkts (Div Emerging Mkts)	C+	C	C+	Up	Y	500,000,000
Baillie Gifford Emerging Markets Fund Class I	BGEGX	NAS CM	Open End	Global Emerg Mkts (Div Emerging Mkts)	C+	C	C+	Up	Y	0
Baillie Gifford Emerging Markets Fund Class K	BGKEX	NAS CM	Open End	Global Emerg Mkts (Div Emerging Mkts)	C+	C	C+	Up	Y	10,000,000
Baillie Gifford Global Alpha Equity Fund Class 2	BGATX	NAS CM	Open End	Global Equity Large Cap (World Stock)	C+	C	B	Up	Y	25,000,000

★ Expanded analysis of this fund is included in Section II.

Min Additional Investment	3-Month Total Return	6-Month Total Return	1-Year Total Return	3-Year Total Return	5-Year Total Return	Dividend Yield (TTM)	Expense Ratio	3-Yr Std Deviation	3-Year Beta	NAV	Total Assets (MIL)	%Cash	%Stocks	%Bonds	%Other	Turnover Ratio	Last Bull Market Total Return	Last Bear Market Total Return	Front End Fee (%)	Back End Fee (%)	Inception Date
	TOTAL RETURNS					PERFORMANCE				ASSETS		ASSET ALLOCATION & TURNOVER					BULL & BEAR		FEES		
1	5.06	24.29	7.53	60.64		0.83	2.51	15.68	1.2	12.86	84.9	1	99	0	0	110					Nov-15
	2.13	7.46	3.23	14.36		2.07	1.01	4.52	1.12	10.51	1,323	16	31	22	31	29					Dec-15
	1.89	10.72	7.52	32.36	29.27	1.86	0.58	8.55	0.72	13.42	1,182	10	85	0	5	79					Apr-13
100	1.54	15.68	7.67	43.38	49.05	0.6	1.81	11.51	0.91	7.96	41.3	3	97	0	0	21	19.21	-8.82			Jun-53
	1.60	15.88	7.93	44.25	50.30	0.79	1.56	11.53	0.91	7.93	41.3	3	97	0	0	21	19.3	-8.75			Feb-09
100	2.30	14.42	2.72	26.06	29.05	0.7	1.64	9.8	0.78	13.41	223.9	8	69	21	1	52	1.26	-11.49	4.75		Nov-11
100	2.06	14.04	1.96	23.23	24.28	0.29	2.39	9.79	0.78	12.83	223.9	8	69	21	1	52	0.88	-11.85		1.00	Mar-10
100	2.35	14.64	2.95	26.98	30.65	0.91	1.39	9.76	0.78	13.45	223.9	8	69	21	1	52	1.37	-11.4			Oct-09
100	4.22	15.53	10.13	22.24		0.9	1.97	8.08	0.61	11.6	6.6	2	85	13	0	194					Jun-15
100	2.74	17.43	1.97	30.79	23.17	0.21	1.68	12.87	1.03	15.36	51.8	3	93	3	0	66			4.75		Nov-11
100	2.55	17.00	1.16	27.82	18.60	0.01	2.43	12.92	1.04	14.45	51.8	3	93	3	0	66				1.00	Nov-11
100	2.76	17.51	2.21	31.67	24.62	0.39	1.43	12.92	1.04	15.55	51.8	3	93	3	0	66					Jan-14
100	9.95	10.83	-5.29	31.55	21.86	0.98	1.7	16.86	0.71	31.6	74.2	1	0	99	0	1,856					Mar-18
100	9.87	10.72	-5.51	31.14	21.48	0.98	1.95	16.87	0.71	31.49	74.2	1	0	99	0	1,856					Sep-12
100	3.78	17.23	0.69	21.21		0.7	1.5	14.33	0.95	9.32	8.4	2	98	0	0	97			5.75		May-15
100	3.89	17.48	0.98	22.25		0.95	1.25	14.36	0.95	9.34	8.4	2	98	0	0	97					May-15
	1.10	5.17	-7.26	20.35	5.70	2.27	0.64	10.42			1,685	0	100	0	0	10	7.44	-24.48			Aug-11
	2.73	6.70	4.11	41.71	58.26	1.37	0.59	11	1.01		3,360	-1	101	0	0	10	19.21	-18.33			Aug-11
	-1.97	2.27	-4.28	31.97	43.79	1.13	0.6	13.77	1.01		218.1	-1	101	0	0	35	20.74	-24.54			Aug-11
	-3.01	2.31	-6.63	39.72	43.85	1.1	0.6	16.03	1		1,098	-1	101	0	0	29	20.25	-26.8			Aug-11
100	2.61	16.83	-15.97	30.01	-15.42	0	2.16	18.64	1.24	7.84	24.2	4	96	0	0	172	24.15	-33.72			Dec-07
50	1.88	12.02	6.80	31.93	35.74	0.92	1.25	10.67	0.84	22.7	231.4	6	94	1	0	3	15.61	-11.57	5.75		Jul-05
50	1.91	12.17	7.07	32.89	36.95	1.27	0.98	10.66	0.84	22.34	231.4	6	94	1	0	3	15.61	-11.63			Jul-99
	1.96	12.24	7.23	33.61	38.16	1.26	0.8	10.65	0.84	22.81	231.4	6	94	1	0	3	15.61	-11.63			May-12
	2.08	5.46	5.74	10.92	16.52	1.77	0.5	2.22	0.17	11.58	347.3	3	18	80	0	26	5.44	-1.83			May-03
	6.31	26.03	15.49	65.88	83.25	0.15	0.97	12.26	0.96	35.19	746.1	3	97	0	0	33	27.88	-19			May-03
	3.70	18.64	10.00	42.10	45.38	1.2	0.94	13.17	1.04	18.5	892.5	3	97	0	0	31	21.09	-16.05			May-05
	4.82	19.75	4.73	45.91	21.43	0	1.1	12.38	0.76	20.43	248.8	14	86	0	0	43	25.51	-19.84			May-01
	5.99	20.89	9.71	38.52	28.65	0.91	1.26	12.06	1.04	15.74	67.1	6	94	0	0	33	19.83	-23.8			Apr-10
	2.75	3.66	10.69			0.8	1				121.6	6	51	42	0	400					Feb-16
	6.47	10.14	10.49	43.14	62.33	1.11	0.8	8.62	0.92		615.7	3	97	1	0	13	18.16	-18.14			Aug-11
50	3.55	23.56	11.24	52.30	45.68	0	0.99	14.6	1	14.84	88.5	1	99	0	0	29	25.95	-17.01			Dec-00
	-3.62	8.28	-18.06	26.60	13.19		2.25	18.27	0.92		9.5	5	95	0	0	186				1.00	Aug-18
	5.91	20.86	0.55	34.48	24.00	0.56	0.68	13.98	1.15	15.8115	383.9	2	98	0	0	12	16.66	-21.89	0.21		Dec-09
	5.85	20.79	0.39	34.08	23.21	0.65	0.78	13.97	1.15	15.74	383.9	2	98	0	0	12	16.55	-21.95			Apr-17
	5.91	20.84	0.53	34.29	23.41	0.71	0.68	13.99	1.15	15.77	383.9	2	98	0	0	12	16.55	-21.95			Apr-17
	3.48	24.31	-3.30	57.67	34.95	0.87	0.6	17.38	1.4	13.2783	2,733	1	99	0	0	14	19.89	-24.92	0.21		Mar-08
	3.50	24.36	-3.23	58.03	35.43	0.93	0.53	17.38	1.4	13.3102	2,733	1	99	0	0	14	19.93	-24.9	0.21		Apr-10
	3.51	24.38	-3.20	58.12	35.34	0.96	0.5	17.38	1.4	13.3218	2,733	1	99	0	0	14	19.89	-24.92	0.21		Oct-13
	3.52	24.41	-3.15	58.41	36.02	1.02	0.45	17.38	1.4	13.3501	2,733	1	99	0	0	14	19.89	-24.92	0.21		Jul-12
	3.51	24.29	-3.34	57.35	34.22	0.92	0.7	17.37	1.4	13.25	2,733	1	99	0	0	14	19.77	-24.97			Apr-17
	3.50	24.36	-3.26	57.48	34.33	0.87	0.6	17.42	1.41	13.27	2,733	1	99	0	0	14	19.77	-24.97			Apr-17
	6.26	20.78	0.64	31.76	22.75	0.23	0.67	13.7	1.12	12.039	461.3	2	98	0	0	14			0.21		Apr-14
	6.28	20.82	0.71	31.96	22.94	0.28	0.6	13.7	1.12	12.161	461.3	2	98	0	0	14			0.21		Mar-17
	6.27	20.80	0.52	31.54	22.13	0.31	0.77	13.67	1.12	12.02	461.3	2	98	0	0	14					Apr-17
	6.27	20.78	0.69	31.65	22.23	0.31	0.67	13.69	1.12	12.03	461.3	2	98	0	0	14					Apr-17
	2.31	17.81	8.41	64.46	35.51	1.05	0.84	16.41	1.12	20.6719	3,051	2	98	0	0	22	25.4	-27.56	0.20		Apr-15
	2.33	17.85	8.48	64.79	32.84	1.12	0.77	16.42	1.12	20.8561	3,051	2	98	0	0	22	25.4	-27.56	0.20		Apr-03
	2.35	17.90	8.57	65.18	36.26	1.17	0.69	16.42	1.12	21.4085	3,051	2	98	0	0	22	25.4	-27.56	0.20		Apr-15
	2.28	17.73	8.27	64.13	31.86	1.17	0.95	16.43	1.13	20.6	3,051	2	98	0	0	22	25.28	-27.61			Apr-17
	2.33	17.82	8.42	64.29	31.99	1.15	0.84	16.4	1.12	20.62	3,051	2	98	0	0	22	25.28	-27.61			Apr-17
	4.76	21.47	5.10	60.15	54.98	0.68	0.68	14.06	1.18	15.8448	741.2	2	98	0	0	18			0.15		Jan-13

	MARKET		FUND TYPE, CATEGORY & OBJECTIVE		RATINGS				MINIMUMS	
Fund Name	Ticker Symbol	Traded On	Fund Type	Category and (Prospectus Objective)	Overall Rating	Reward Rating	Risk Rating	Recent Up/ Downgrade	Open to New Investors	Min Initial Investment
Baillie Gifford Global Alpha Equity Fund Class 3	BGAEX	NAS CM	Open End	Global Equity Large Cap (World Stock)	C+	C	B	Up	Y	100,000,000
Baillie Gifford Global Alpha Equity Fund Class I	BGASX	NAS CM	Open End	Global Equity Large Cap (World Stock)	C+	C	B	Up	Y	0
Baillie Gifford Global Alpha Equity Fund Class K	BGAKX	NAS CM	Open End	Global Equity Large Cap (World Stock)	C+	C	B	Up	Y	10,000,000
Baillie Gifford Global Select Equity Fund Class K	BGSKX	NAS CM	Open End	Global Equity Large Cap (World Stock)	D+	D+	C+	Up	Y	10,000,000
Baillie Gifford Global Select Equity Institutional Cls	BGSSX	NAS CM	Open End	Global Equity Large Cap (World Stock)	D+	D+	C+	Up	Y	0
Baillie Gifford International Concentrated Growth Cls K	BTLKX	NAS CM	Open End	Global Equity Large Cap (Foreign Stock)	D+	D	C	Up	Y	10,000,000
Baillie Gifford Intl Concentrated Growth Inst Cls	BTLSX	NAS CM	Open End	Global Equity Large Cap (Foreign Stock)	D+	D	C	Up	Y	0
Baillie Gifford International Equity Fund Class 2	BGITX	NAS CM	Open End	Global Equity Large Cap (Foreign Stock)	C	C	B-		Y	25,000,000
Baillie Gifford International Equity Fund Class 3	BGIFX	NAS CM	Open End	Global Equity Large Cap (Foreign Stock)	C	C	B-		Y	100,000,000
Baillie Gifford International Equity Fund Class 5	BGIVX	NAS CM	Open End	Global Equity Large Cap (Foreign Stock)	C	C	B-		Y	500,000,000
Baillie Gifford International Equity Fund Class I	BINSX	NAS CM	Open End	Global Equity Large Cap (Foreign Stock)	C	C	B-		Y	0
Baillie Gifford International Smaller Companies Cls K	BICKX	NAS CM	Open End	Global Equity Mid/Small Cap (Small Company)	U	U	U		Y	10,000,000
Baillie Gifford Intl Smaller Companies Inst Cls	BICIX	NAS CM	Open End	Global Equity Mid/Small Cap (Small Company)	U	U	U		Y	0
Baillie Gifford Long Term Global Growth Equity Cls 2	BGLTX	NAS CM	Open End	Global Equity Large Cap (Growth)	C+	C+	C+		Y	25,000,000
Baillie Gifford Long Term Global Growth Equity Cls I	BSGLX	NAS CM	Open End	Global Equity Large Cap (Growth)	C+	C+	C+		Y	0
Baillie Gifford Long Term Global Growth Equity Cls K	BGLKX	NAS CM	Open End	Global Equity Large Cap (Growth)	C+	C+	C+		Y	10,000,000
Baillie Gifford Multi Asset Fund Class K	BGBKX	NAS CM	Open End	Flexible Alloc (Growth)	U	U	U		Y	25,000,000
Baillie Gifford Multi Asset Fund Institutional Class	BGBIX	NAS CM	Open End	Flexible Alloc (Growth)	U	U	U		Y	0
Baillie Gifford Positive Change Equity Fund Class K	BPEKX	NAS CM	Open End	Global Equity Large Cap (Growth)	D+	D+	C	Up	Y	10,000,000
Baillie Gifford Positive Change Equity Institutional Cls	BPESX	NAS CM	Open End	Global Equity Large Cap (Growth)	D+	D+	C	Up	Y	0
Baillie Gifford The International Equity Fund Class K	BGIKX	NAS CM	Open End	Global Equity Large Cap (Foreign Stock)	C	C	B-		Y	10,000,000
Baillie Gifford The U.S. Equity Growth Fund Class I	BGGSX	NAS CM	Open End	US Equity Large Cap Growth (Growth)	C+	C	C+	Up	Y	0
Baillie Gifford The U.S. Equity Growth Fund Class K	BGGKX	NAS CM	Open End	US Equity Large Cap Growth (Growth)	C+	C	C+	Up	Y	10,000,000
Baird MidCap Fund Institutional Class	BMDIX	NAS CM	Open End	US Equity Mid Cap (Growth)	B-	B-	B	Down	Y	25,000
Baird MidCap Fund Investor Class	BMDSX	NAS CM	Open End	US Equity Mid Cap (Growth)	B-	B-	B	Down	Y	2,500
Baird Small/Mid Cap Growth Fund Institutional Class	BSGIX	NAS CM	Open End	US Equity Mid Cap (Growth)	U	U	U		Y	25,000
Baird Small/Mid Cap Growth Fund Investor Class	BSGSX	NAS CM	Open End	US Equity Mid Cap (Growth)	U	U	U		Y	2,500
Baird Small/Mid Cap Value Fund Institutional Class	BMVIX	NAS CM	Open End	US Equity Small Cap (Growth)	C	C	C+		Y	25,000
Baird Small/Mid Cap Value Fund Investor Class	BMVSX	NAS CM	Open End	US Equity Small Cap (Growth)	C	C	C		Y	2,500
Baird SmallCap Value Fund Institutional Class	BSVIX	NAS CM	Open End	US Equity Small Cap (Small Company)	C	C	C		Y	25,000
Baird SmallCap Value Fund Investor Class	BSVSX	NAS CM	Open End	US Equity Small Cap (Small Company)	C	C	C		Y	2,500
Balter European L/S Small Cap Fund Institutional Class	BESMX	NAS CM	Open End	Long/Short Equity (Small Company)	D+	D	C	Down	Y	50,000
Balter European L/S Small Cap Fund Investor Class	BESRX	NAS CM	Open End	Long/Short Equity (Small Company)	D+	D	C-	Down	Y	5,000
Balter L/S Small Cap Equity Fund Institutional Class	BEQIX	NAS CM	Open End	Long/Short Equity (Growth & Income)	B-	C	A-		Y	50,000
Balter L/S Small Cap Equity Fund Investor Class	BEQRX	NAS CM	Open End	Long/Short Equity (Growth & Income)	B-	C	B		Y	5,000
Bancroft Fund	BCV	AMEX	Closed End	Convertibles (Convertible Bond)	C	C+	D+	Down	Y	
Barings Global Emerging Markets Equity Fund Class A	BXQAX	NAS CM	Open End	Global Emerg Mkts (Div Emerging Mkts)	U	U	U		Y	1,000
Barings Global Emerging Markets Equity Fund Class C	BXQCX	NAS CM	Open End	Global Emerg Mkts (Div Emerging Mkts)	U	U	U		Y	1,000
Barings Global Emerging Markets Equity Fund Class I	BXQIX	NAS CM	Open End	Global Emerg Mkts (Div Emerging Mkts)	U	U	U		Y	500,000
Barings Global Emerging Markets Equity Fund Class Y	BXQYX	NAS CM	Open End	Global Emerg Mkts (Div Emerging Mkts)	U	U	U		Y	100,000
Baron Asset Fund Class R6	BARUX	NAS CM	Open End	US Equity Mid Cap (Growth)	B	B	B		Y	5,000,000
Baron Asset Fund Institutional Class	BARIX	NAS CM	Open End	US Equity Mid Cap (Growth)	B	B	B		Y	1,000,000
Baron Asset Fund Retail Class	BARAX	NAS CM	Open End	US Equity Mid Cap (Growth)	B	B	B		Y	2,000
Baron Discovery Fund Institutional Shares	BDFIX	NAS CM	Open End	US Equity Small Cap (Growth)	C	C	C+	Down	Y	1,000,000
Baron Discovery Fund R6 Shares	BDFUX	NAS CM	Open End	US Equity Small Cap (Growth)	C	C	C+	Down	Y	5,000,000
Baron Discovery Fund Retail Shares	BDFFX	NAS CM	Open End	US Equity Small Cap (Growth)	C	C	C+	Down	Y	2,000
Baron Durable Advantage Fund Institutional Shares	BDAIX	NAS CM	Open End	US Equity Large Cap Growth (Growth & Income)	D+	C-	C+	Up	Y	1,000,000
Baron Durable Advantage Fund R6 Shares	BDAUX	NAS CM	Open End	US Equity Large Cap Growth (Growth & Income)	D+	C-	C+	Up	Y	5,000,000
Baron Durable Advantage Fund Retail Shares	BDAFX	NAS CM	Open End	US Equity Large Cap Growth (Growth & Income)	D+	D+	C+	Up	Y	2,000
Baron Emerging Markets Fund Class R6	BEXUX	NAS CM	Open End	Global Emerg Mkts (Div Emerging Mkts)	C	C	C+		Y	5,000,000
Baron Emerging Markets Fund Institutional Shares	BEXIX	NAS CM	Open End	Global Emerg Mkts (Div Emerging Mkts)	C	C	C+		Y	1,000,000
Baron Emerging Markets Fund Retail Shares	BEXFX	NAS CM	Open End	Global Emerg Mkts (Div Emerging Mkts)	C	C	C+		Y	2,000

★ Expanded analysis of this fund is included in Section II.

Min Additional Investment	3-Month Total Return	6-Month Total Return	1-Year Total Return	3-Year Total Return	5-Year Total Return	Dividend Yield (TTM)	Expense Ratio	3-Yr Std Deviation	3-Year Beta	NAV	Total Assets (MIL)	%Cash	%Stocks	%Bonds	%Other	Turnover Ratio	Last Bull Market Total Return	Last Bear Market Total Return	Front End Fee (%)	Back End Fee (%)	Inception Date
TOTAL RETURNS						PERFORMANCE				ASSETS		ASSET ALLOCATION & TURNOVER					BULL & BEAR		FEES		
	4.78	21.52	5.18	60.48	55.82	0.73	0.61	14.06	1.18	16.244	741.2	2	98	0	0	18			0.15		Nov-11
	4.76	21.48	5.10	60.07	54.89	0.69	0.68	14.02	1.18	15.83	741.2	2	98	0	0	18					Apr-17
	4.70	21.42	5.09	59.97	54.80	0.68	0.68	14.05	1.18	15.81	741.2	2	98	0	0	18					Apr-17
	6.27	25.86	5.51			0.16	0.65			11.34	3.4	1	99	0	0	14					Dec-17
	6.27	25.86	5.51			0.16	0.65			11.34	3.4	1	99	0	0	14					Dec-17
	4.41	27.55	0.27			0	0.72			11.11	71.6	1	99	0	0	32					Dec-17
	4.43	27.68	-0.09			0	0.81			11.07	71.6	1	99	0	0	32					Dec-17
	5.44	20.75	3.28	44.89	31.36	1.26	0.62	13.09	1.1	12.9475	2,231	1	99	0	0	33	19.51	-22.73	0.21		Feb-08
	5.46	20.79	3.35	45.20	31.87	1.33	0.55	13.09	1.1	13.124	2,231	1	99	0	0	33	19.56	-22.68	0.21		Sep-10
	5.48	20.84	3.43	45.55	32.44	1.37	0.47	13.09	1.1	13.5773	2,231	1	99	0	0	33	19.51	-22.73	0.21		Apr-14
	5.45	20.78	3.20	44.55	30.60	1.05	0.72	13.1	1.1	12.96	2,231	1	99	0	0	33	19.39	-22.79			Apr-17
	5.06	19.39					0.9			11.82	1.2	2	98	0	0	0					Dec-18
	5.06	19.39					1.05			11.82	1.2	2	98	0	0	0					Dec-18
	1.73	19.77	-0.18	87.79	100.45	0	0.77	19.14	1.44	18.4602	190.8	2	98	0	0	16			0.10		Jun-14
	1.70	19.72	-0.22	87.37	99.33	0	0.86	19.13	1.44	18.45	190.8	2	98	0	0	16					Apr-17
	1.76	19.77	-0.17	87.57	99.53	0	0.77	19.15	1.44	18.47	190.8	2	98	0	0	16					Apr-17
	2.57	10.02					0.8			10.76	10.8	20	31	41	7	14					Dec-18
	2.57	10.02					0.95			10.76	10.8	20	31	41	7	14					Dec-18
	1.98	12.88	1.07			0	0.65			11.3	19.6	1	99	0	0	7					Dec-17
	1.98	12.88	1.07			0	0.65			11.3	19.6	1	99	0	0	7					Dec-17
	5.47	20.76	3.29	44.69	30.73	1.35	0.62	13.06	1.1	12.91	2,231	1	99	0	0	33	19.39	-22.79			Apr-17
	6.42	27.24	7.58			0	0.78			17.89	16.9	1	99	0	0	107					Apr-17
	6.99	27.94	8.47			0	0.65			18.04	16.9	1	99	0	0	107					Apr-17
	6.86	27.95	16.51	64.69	64.43	0	0.81	13.46	0.91	22.43	2,043	3	97	0	0	38	32.5	-16.83			Dec-00
100	6.80	27.74	16.18	63.40	62.36	0	1.06	13.46	0.91	21.18	2,043	3	97	0	0	38	32.13	-16.86			Dec-00
	6.61	28.00					0.85			11.29	13.0	2	98	0	0						Oct-18
100	6.52	27.77					1.1			11.27	13.0	2	98	0	0						Oct-18
	2.22	14.61	-3.72	24.24		0.31	0.85	12.6	0.7	11.92	22.2	6	94	0	0	34					Nov-15
100	2.15	14.46	-3.93	23.41		0.2	1.1	12.62	0.7	11.87	22.2	6	94	0	0	34					Nov-15
	2.06	14.12	-6.87	23.21	19.37	0.37	0.95	13.44	0.66	15.35	33.9	5	95	0	0	36					May-12
100	1.99	13.96	-7.11	22.27	17.89	0	1.2	13.5	0.67	15.34	33.9	5	95	0	0	36					May-12
500	-3.75	2.67	-13.18	17.66	2.80	2.63	3.76	8.7	0.48	9.22	48.9	62	38	0	0	194	12.13	-13.59			Dec-15
500	-3.76	2.56	-13.39	17.07	1.88	2.43	4.06	8.68	0.48	9.2	48.9	62	38	0	0	194	11.97	-13.68			Dec-15
500	0.66	10.80	1.40	33.00	31.83	0	2.44	8.09	0.44		101.7	61	39	0	0	244					Dec-13
500	1.13	11.15	1.53	32.47	30.64	0	2.79	8.04	0.43		101.7	61	39	0	0	244					Nov-17
	5.70	21.54	10.05	43.15	44.24	9.44		10.88	0.8	25.43	134.3	1	3	0	0	43	13.01	-15.33			Oct-71
250	1.97	15.84					1.45			11.104	11.1	7	93	0	0				4.00		Sep-18
250	1.78	15.41					2.2			11.0389	11.1	7	93	0	0						Sep-18
250	2.03	15.99					1.2			11.1257	11.1	7	93	0	0						Sep-18
250	2.03	15.99					1.2			11.1257	11.1	7	93	0	0						Sep-18
	9.90	33.48	19.69	79.23	87.87	0	1.04	14.22	0.94	87.74	4,431	2	98	0	0	10	25.22	-19.8			Jan-16
	9.91	33.49	19.70	79.27	88.71	0	1.04	14.21	0.94	87.76	4,431	2	98	0	0	10	25.42	-19.7			May-09
	9.84	33.31	19.39	77.85	86.19	0	1.3	14.2	0.94	84.35	4,431	2	98	0	0	10	25.22	-19.8			Jun-87
	0.97	22.17	5.46	93.15	76.58	0	1.1	20.02	1.07	20.68	558.7	7	93	0	0	72					Sep-13
	0.97	22.17	5.46	93.18	76.60	0	1.09	20.01	1.07	20.68	558.7	7	93	0	0	72					Aug-16
	0.89	22.03	5.17	91.70	74.34	0	1.35	20	1.07	20.41	558.7	7	93	0	0	72					Sep-13
	8.01	24.97	11.43			0.3	0.7			11.46	4.8	7	93	0	0	6					Dec-17
	8.01	24.97	11.43			0.3	0.7			11.46	4.8	7	93	0	0	6					Dec-17
	7.94	24.80	11.15			0.3	0.95			11.42	4.8	7	93	0	0	6					Dec-17
	0.35	12.98	0.11	28.69	14.77	0.43	1.11	13.09	0.9	14.01	5,178	6	94	0	0	43	14.8	-18.44			Jan-16
	0.28	12.99	0.11	28.71	14.69	0.43	1.1	13.13	0.9	14	5,178	6	94	0	0	43	14.8	-18.44			Dec-10
	0.28	12.85	-0.07	27.81	13.22	0.13	1.36	13.11	0.9	13.96	5,178	6	94	0	0	43	14.71	-18.56			Dec-10

	MARKET		FUND TYPE, CATEGORY & OBJECTIVE		RATINGS				MINIMUMS	
Fund Name	Ticker Symbol	Traded On	Fund Type	Category and (Prospectus Objective)	Overall Rating	Reward Rating	Risk Rating	Recent Up/ Downgrade	Open to New Investors	Min Initial Investment
Baron Fifth Avenue Growth Fund Class R6	BFTUX	NAS CM	Open End	US Equity Large Cap Growth (Growth)	B-	C+	B-	Down	Y	5,000,000
Baron Fifth Avenue Growth Fund Institutional Class	BFTIX	NAS CM	Open End	US Equity Large Cap Growth (Growth)	B-	C+	B-	Down	Y	1,000,000
Baron Fifth Avenue Growth Fund Retail Class	BFTHX	NAS CM	Open End	US Equity Large Cap Growth (Growth)	B-	C+	B-	Down	Y	2,000
Baron Focused Growth Fund Institutional Shares	BFGIX	NAS CM	Open End	US Equity Mid Cap (Growth)	C+	C	B		Y	1,000,000
Baron Focused Growth Fund R6 Shares	BFGUX	NAS CM	Open End	US Equity Mid Cap (Growth)	C+	C	B		Y	5,000,000
Baron Focused Growth Fund Retail Shares	BFGFX	NAS CM	Open End	US Equity Mid Cap (Growth)	C+	C	B		Y	2,000
Baron Global Advantage Fund Institutional Shares	BGAIX	NAS CM	Open End	Global Equity Large Cap (World Stock)	B	B	C+	Up	Y	1,000,000
Baron Global Advantage Fund R6 Shares	BGLUX	NAS CM	Open End	Global Equity Large Cap (World Stock)	B	B	C+	Up	Y	5,000,000
Baron Global Advantage Fund Retail Shares	BGAFX	NAS CM	Open End	Global Equity Large Cap (World Stock)	B	B	C+	Up	Y	2,000
Baron Growth Fund Class R6	BGRUX	NAS CM	Open End	US Equity Mid Cap (Growth)	B	B	B-	Up	Y	5,000,000
Baron Growth Fund Institutional Shares	BGRIX	NAS CM	Open End	US Equity Mid Cap (Growth)	B	B	B-	Up	Y	1,000,000
Baron Growth Fund Retail Shares	BGRFX	NAS CM	Open End	US Equity Mid Cap (Growth)	B	B	B-	Up	Y	2,000
Baron Health Care Fund Institutional Shares	BHCHX	NAS CM	Open End	Healthcare Sector Equity (Health)	D	D+	C	Up	Y	1,000,000
Baron Health Care Fund R6 Shares	BHCUX	NAS CM	Open End	Healthcare Sector Equity (Health)	D	D+	C	Up	Y	5,000,000
Baron Health Care Fund Retail Shares	BHCFX	NAS CM	Open End	Healthcare Sector Equity (Health)	D	D+	C	Up	Y	2,000
Baron International Growth Fund Institutional Shares	BINIX	NAS CM	Open End	Global Equity Large Cap (Foreign Stock)	C	C	C+		Y	1,000,000
Baron International Growth Fund R6 Shares	BIGUX	NAS CM	Open End	Global Equity Large Cap (Foreign Stock)	C	C	C+		Y	5,000,000
Baron International Growth Fund Retail Shares	BIGFX	NAS CM	Open End	Global Equity Large Cap (Foreign Stock)	C	C	C+		Y	2,000
Baron Opportunity Fund Institutional Class	BIOIX	NAS CM	Open End	US Equity Large Cap Growth (Growth)	B-	B-	B	Down	Y	1,000,000
Baron Opportunity Fund R6 Shares	BIOUX	NAS CM	Open End	US Equity Large Cap Growth (Growth)	B-	B-	B	Down	Y	5,000,000
Baron Opportunity Fund Retail Class	BIOPX	NAS CM	Open End	US Equity Large Cap Growth (Growth)	B-	C+	B	Down	Y	2,000
Baron Partners Fund Institutional Shares	BPTIX	NAS CM	Open End	US Equity Mid Cap (Growth)	C+	C	C+		Y	1,000,000
Baron Partners Fund R6 Shares	BPTUX	NAS CM	Open End	US Equity Mid Cap (Growth)	C+	C	C+		Y	5,000,000
Baron Partners Fund Retail Shares	BPTRX	NAS CM	Open End	US Equity Mid Cap (Growth)	C+	C	C+		Y	2,000
Baron Real Estate Fund Class R6	BREUX	NAS CM	Open End	Real Estate Sector Equity (Real Estate)	C	C	C+	Down	Y	5,000,000
Baron Real Estate Fund Institutional Shares	BREIX	NAS CM	Open End	Real Estate Sector Equity (Real Estate)	C	C	C+	Down	Y	1,000,000
Baron Real Estate Fund Retail Shares	BREFX	NAS CM	Open End	Real Estate Sector Equity (Real Estate)	C	C	C+	Down	Y	2,000
Baron Real Estate Income Fund Institutional Shares	BRIIX	NAS CM	Open End	Real Estate Sector Equity (Real Estate)	D+	C-	B-	Up	Y	1,000,000
Baron Real Estate Income Fund R6 Shares	BRIUX	NAS CM	Open End	Real Estate Sector Equity (Real Estate)	D+	C-	B-	Up	Y	5,000,000
Baron Real Estate Income Fund Retail Shares	BRIFX	NAS CM	Open End	Real Estate Sector Equity (Real Estate)	D+	C-	B-	Up	Y	2,000
Baron Small Cap Fund Class R6	BSCUX	NAS CM	Open End	US Equity Small Cap (Small Company)	C+	C+	C+	Down	Y	5,000,000
Baron Small Cap Fund Institutional Class	BSFIX	NAS CM	Open End	US Equity Small Cap (Small Company)	C+	C+	C+	Down	Y	1,000,000
Baron Small Cap Fund Retail Class	BSCFX	NAS CM	Open End	US Equity Small Cap (Small Company)	C+	C+	C+	Down	Y	2,000
Baron WealthBuilder Fund Institutional Shares	BWBIX	NAS CM	Open End	Global Equity Large Cap (Asset Alloc)	D+	C-	C+	Up	Y	1,000,000
Baron WealthBuilder Fund Retail Shares	BWBFX	NAS CM	Open End	Global Equity Large Cap (Asset Alloc)	D+	C-	C+	Up	Y	2,000
Baron WealthBuilder Fund TA Shares	BWBTX	NAS CM	Open End	Global Equity Large Cap (Asset Alloc)	D+	C-	C+	Up	Y	2,000
Barrett Growth Fund	BGRWX	NAS CM	Open End	US Equity Large Cap Growth (Growth)	B	B-	B	Up	Y	2,500
Barrett Opportunity Fund	SAOPX	NAS CM	Open End	US Equity Large Cap Blend (Growth)	C+	C	B		Y	1,000
Baywood ValuePlus Fund Institutional Shares	BVPIX	NAS CM	Open End	US Equity Large Cap Value (Growth)	C+	C	B	Up	Y	100,000
Baywood ValuePlus Fund Investor Shares	BVPNX	NAS CM	Open End	US Equity Large Cap Value (Growth)	C+	C	B	Up	Y	2,500
BBH Core Select Fund Class N	BBTEX	NAS CM	Open End	US Equity Large Cap Blend (Growth)	B-	C	B	Down		10,000
BBH Core Select Retail Class Shares	BBTRX	NAS CM	Open End	US Equity Large Cap Blend (Growth)	B-	C	B			5,000
BBH Global Core Select Fund Class N Shares	BBGNX	NAS CM	Open End	Global Equity Large Cap (Growth)	C+	C	B	Up	Y	10,000
BBH Global Core Select Fund Retail Class Shares	BBGRX	NAS CM	Open End	Global Equity Large Cap (Growth)	C+	C	B	Up	Y	5,000
BBH Partner - International Equity Cls Institutional	BBHLX	NAS CM	Open End	Global Equity Large Cap (Growth & Income)	B-	C	B	Up	Y	10,000
Beacon Accelerated Return Strategy Fund Class A	BARTX	NAS CM	Open End	Long/Short Equity (Growth)	D+	C-	B-	Up	Y	5,000
Beacon Accelerated Return Strategy Institutional Cls	BARLX	NAS CM	Open End	Long/Short Equity (Growth)	C-	C-	B	Up	Y	1,000,000
Beacon Planned Return Strategy Fund Class A	BPRTX	NAS CM	Open End	Long/Short Equity (Growth)	D+	D+	B	Up	Y	5,000
Beacon Planned Return Strategy Fund Institutional Class	BPRLX	NAS CM	Open End	Long/Short Equity (Growth)	C-	C-	B	Up	Y	1,000,000
Beck, Mack & Oliver Partners Fund	BMPEX	NAS CM	Open End	US Equity Large Cap Blend (Growth)	C	C	C+		Y	2,500
Becker Value Equity Fund Institutional Class	BVEIX	NAS CM	Open End	US Equity Large Cap Value (Growth)	C	C	C+		Y	100,000
Becker Value Equity Fund Retail Class	BVEFX	NAS CM	Open End	US Equity Large Cap Value (Growth)	C	C	C+		Y	2,500

★Expanded analysis of this fund is included in Section II.

	TOTAL RETURNS					PERFORMANCE				ASSETS		ASSET ALLOCATION & TURNOVER					BULL & BEAR		FEES		
Min Additional Investment	3-Month Total Return	6-Month Total Return	1-Year Total Return	3-Year Total Return	5-Year Total Return	Dividend Yield (TTM)	Expense Ratio	3-Yr Std Deviation	3-Year Beta	NAV	Total Assets (MIL)	%Cash	%Stocks	%Bonds	%Other	Turnover Ratio	Last Bull Market Total Return	Last Bear Market Total Return	Front End Fee (%)	Back End Fee (%)	Inception Date
	6.60	27.59	11.42	88.06	97.00	0	0.75	15.23	1.05	33.25	310.0	5	95	0	0	9	32.62	-16.69			Jan-16
	6.60	27.60	11.43	88.00	97.76	0	0.75	15.22	1.05	33.24	310.0	5	95	0	0	9	32.86	-16.65			May-09
	6.54	27.39	11.16	86.63	95.26	0	1	15.23	1.05	32.55	310.0	5	95	0	0	9	32.62	-16.69			Apr-04
	1.10	13.44	3.57	52.65	48.11	0	1.09	14.68	0.7	18.31	228.7	0	91	0	0	2	22.73	-20.78			May-09
	1.04	13.44	3.57	52.65	47.31	0	1.1	14.64	0.7	18.31	228.7	0	91	0	0	2	22.62	-20.87			Aug-16
	0.95	13.29	3.29	51.51	46.21	0	1.35	14.65	0.7	17.9	228.7	0	91	0	0	2	22.62	-20.87			Jun-08
	6.84	35.56	15.09	103.69	89.49	0	0.9	15.47	1.13	26.99	215.8	9	91	0	0	20					Apr-12
	6.84	35.59	15.13	103.84	89.63	0	0.9	15.48	1.13	27.01	215.8	9	91	0	0	20					Aug-16
	6.77	35.40	14.79	102.43	87.56	0	1.15	15.47	1.13	26.62	215.8	9	91	0	0	20					Apr-12
	7.02	30.98	14.50	68.80	70.70	0	1.04	16.1	0.84	82.27	6,942	0	99	0	0	3	23.16	-19.29			Jan-16
	7.02	30.98	14.51	68.81	71.41	0	1.03	16.11	0.84	82.26	6,942	0	99	0	0	3	23.33	-19.2			May-09
	6.95	30.81	14.21	67.51	69.22	0	1.29	16.1	0.84	79.55	6,942	0	99	0	0	3	23.16	-19.29			Dec-94
	6.29	24.20	11.05			0	0.85			11.65	11.5	9	91	0	0						Apr-18
	6.39	24.20	11.16			0	0.85			11.65	11.5	9	91	0	0						Apr-18
	6.31	24.14	10.87			0	1.1			11.62	11.5	9	91	0	0						Apr-18
	2.66	20.85	-1.17	38.93	29.86	0	0.95	12.67	1.01	23.12	294.8	6	94	0	0	51	19.66	-22.84			May-09
	2.66	20.85	-1.17	38.93	29.13	0	0.95	12.68	1.01	23.12	294.8	6	94	0	0	51	19.49	-22.93			Aug-16
	2.57	20.70	-1.40	37.93	28.20	0	1.2	12.67	1.01	22.74	294.8	6	94	0	0	51	19.49	-22.93			Dec-08
	6.05	29.90	15.98	98.80	89.63	0	1.11	16.01	1.08	23.46	473.5	5	95	0	0	24	22.23	-19.91			May-09
	6.09	29.92	16.01	98.89	88.70	0	1.09	16.03	1.08	23.49	473.5	5	95	0	0	24	22.06	-20.01			Aug-16
	6.02	29.76	15.73	97.25	87.14	0	1.37	16.02	1.08	22.54	473.5	5	95	0	0	24	22.06	-20.01			Feb-00
	7.49	26.28	6.80	72.71	67.20	0	1.77	17.28	1.06	61.35	2,391	-28	128	0	0	8	29.72	-24.97			May-09
	7.51	26.30	6.82	72.65	66.26	0	1.79	17.28	1.06	61.36	2,391	-28	128	0	0	8	29.51	-25.06			Aug-16
	7.44	26.12	6.54	71.36	65.03	0	2.03	17.28	1.06	59.91	2,391	-28	128	0	0	8	29.51	-25.06			Apr-03
	4.21	25.07	1.05	31.28	27.80	0.26	1.07	15.86	1.15	26.19	587.6	0	100	0	0	56	39.39	-23.08			Jan-16
	4.21	25.07	1.08	31.32	27.78	0.25	1.06	15.85	1.15	26.19	587.6	0	100	0	0	56	39.39	-23.08			Dec-09
	4.16	24.93	0.82	30.27	26.11	0	1.32	15.85	1.15	25.75	587.6	0	100	0	0	56	39.23	-23.08			Dec-09
	2.32	21.49	7.50			2.18	0.8			10.38	3.7	2	98	0	0	67					Dec-17
	2.42	21.46	7.49			2.18	0.8			10.39	3.7	2	98	0	0	67					Dec-17
	2.33	21.45	7.20			2.19	1.05			10.34	3.7	2	98	0	0	67					Dec-17
	4.85	30.51	9.48	66.98	59.88	0	1.05	16.52	0.9	32.21	4,169	2	98	0	0	14	28.61	-22.61			Jan-16
	4.84	30.49	9.48	67.02	60.56	0	1.04	16.54	0.9	32.22	4,169	2	98	0	0	14	28.77	-22.54			May-09
	4.78	30.30	9.17	65.67	58.42	0	1.3	16.52	0.9	30.87	4,169	2	98	0	0	14	28.61	-22.61			Sep-97
	5.85	26.72	9.64			0	1.17			11.76	95.0	-3	102	0	0	1					Dec-17
	5.77	26.67	9.36			0	1.42			11.73	95.0	-3	102	0	0	1					Dec-17
	5.75	26.72	9.64			0	1.17			11.76	95.0	-3	102	0	0	1					Dec-17
50	6.17	22.95	13.69	55.85	69.60	0	1.26	11.99	0.96	22.34	28.1	5	95	0	0	20	23.15	-17.81			Dec-98
50	0.65	11.55	0.74	36.44	39.91	0.84	1.14	12.36	0.95	26.07	58.3	6	94	0	0	4	21.35	-24.59			Feb-79
	2.51	14.23	1.03	33.29	33.95	2.1	0.7	12.57	1.01	16.89	2.8	4	96	0	0	34	21.81	-15.33			Dec-13
100	2.46	14.02	0.73	32.23	32.21	1.87	0.95	12.54	1.01	16.8	2.8	4	96	0	0	34	21.81	-15.33			Dec-13
10,000	7.04	20.03	13.51	40.84	43.23	0.51	1	11.29	0.87	15.34	767.5	1	99	0	0	14	20.95	-11.49			Nov-98
250	7.08	20.17	13.31	39.99	41.71	0	1.25	11.32	0.87	4.23	767.5	1	99	0	0	14	20.83	-11.59			Mar-11
1,000	5.23	20.01	9.43	33.20	28.52	0.54	1.25	10.9	0.9	12.47	55.7	4	96	0	0	19					Mar-13
250	5.08	19.80	9.19	32.19	26.93	0.33	1.5	10.83	0.9	12.4	55.7	4	96	0	0	19					Apr-13
1,000	5.83	23.69	9.70	36.36	25.34	0.98	0.68	12.08	1.02	16.13	1,716	18	82	0	0	124	10.81	-16.63			Oct-02
1,000	4.09	20.53	9.30			0	1.6			9.92	120.5	1	99	0	0				5.00		Jun-18
1,000	4.18	20.87	9.72			0	1.35			9.96	120.5	1	99	0	0						Oct-17
1,000	2.80	13.23	7.67			0	1.56			10.27	305.3	2	98	0	0				5.00		Jun-18
1,000	2.99	13.42	8.08			0	1.31			10.31	305.3	2	98	0	0						Oct-17
1,000	4.62	19.02	-1.50	31.56	1.88	0	1	16.16	1.26	11.76	38.0	1	99	0	0	17	25.7	-15.5			Dec-09
100	3.63	14.72	-0.44	29.35	31.58	2.06	0.68	14.07	1.14	17.69	324.1	2	98	0	0	38	23.56	-18.53			Sep-11
100	3.58	14.70	-0.58	28.92	30.76	1.94	0.78	14.04	1.13	17.63	324.1	2	98	0	0	38	23.48	-18.53			Nov-03

	MARKET		FUND TYPE, CATEGORY & OBJECTIVE		RATINGS				MINIMUMS	
Fund Name	Ticker Symbol	Traded On	Fund Type	Category and (Prospectus Objective)	Overall Rating	Reward Rating	Risk Rating	Recent Up/ Downgrade	Open to New Investors	Min Initial Investment
Beech Hill Total Return Fund Class A	BHTAX	NAS CM	Open End	Moderate Alloc (Growth & Income)	C+	C	B		Y	500
Beech Hill Total Return Fund Class C	BHTCX	NAS CM	Open End	Moderate Alloc (Growth & Income)	C+	C	B	Up	Y	500
Belmont Theta Income Fund Institutional Class	BTIFX	NAS CM	Open End	Long/Short Equity (Income)	D	D+	C	Up	Y	5,000
Berkshire Focus Fund	BFOCX	NAS CM	Open End	Technology Sector Equity (Technology)	B-	B-	C+		Y	5,000
Bernstein International Small Cap Portfolio Class SCB	IRCSX	NAS CM	Open End	Global Equity Mid/Small Cap (Small Company)	C	C-	C		Y	5,000
Bernstein Intl Strategic Equities Portfolio Cls SCB	STESX	NAS CM	Open End	Global Equity Large Cap (Growth)	C	C	C+		Y	10,000
Bernstein Small Cap Core Portfolio Class SCB	SCRSX	NAS CM	Open End	US Equity Small Cap (Small Company)	C	C	C+		Y	5,000
Bernzott US Small Cap Value Fund	BSCVX	NAS CM	Open End	US Equity Small Cap (Small Company)	C+	C	B-		Y	25,000
Berwyn Income Fund	BERIX	NAS CM	Open End	Cautious Alloc (Income)	B-	C	A-		Y	1,000
BFS Equity Fund	BFSAX	NAS CM	Open End	US Equity Large Cap Growth (Growth)	B	B-	B	Up	Y	1,000
Biondo Focus Fund Investor Class	BFONX	NAS CM	Open End	US Equity Large Cap Growth (Growth)	C+	C+	B	Down	Y	1,000
Black Oak Emerging Technology Fund	BOGSX	NAS CM	Open End	Technology Sector Equity (Technology)	C	C	C+	Down	Y	2,000
BlackRock 20/80 Target Allocation Fund Class K	BKCPX	NAS CM	Open End	Cautious Alloc (Asset Alloc)	B	C+	B+	Up	Y	5,000,000
BlackRock 20/80 Target Allocation Institutional Shares	BICPX	NAS CM	Open End	Cautious Alloc (Asset Alloc)	B	C+	B+	Up	Y	2,000,000
BlackRock 20/80 Target Allocation Fund Investor A Shares	BACPX	NAS CM	Open End	Cautious Alloc (Asset Alloc)	B-	C	B+		Y	1,000
BlackRock 20/80 Target Allocation Fund Investor C Shares	BCCPX	NAS CM	Open End	Cautious Alloc (Asset Alloc)	B-	C	B	Up	Y	1,000
BlackRock 20/80 Target Allocation Fund R Shares	BRCPX	NAS CM	Open End	Cautious Alloc (Asset Alloc)	B-	C	B+		Y	100
BlackRock 40/60 Target Allocation Fund Class K	BKMPX	NAS CM	Open End	Cautious Alloc (Asset Alloc)	B	C+	A	Up	Y	5,000,000
BlackRock 40/60 Target Allocation Fund Class R Shares	BRMPX	NAS CM	Open End	Cautious Alloc (Asset Alloc)	B	C	A-	Up	Y	100
BlackRock 40/60 Target Allocation Fund Institutional	BIMPX	NAS CM	Open End	Cautious Alloc (Asset Alloc)	B	C+	A	Up	Y	2,000,000
BlackRock 40/60 Target Allocation Fund Investor A Shares	BAMPX	NAS CM	Open End	Cautious Alloc (Asset Alloc)	B	C+	A-	Up	Y	1,000
BlackRock 40/60 Target Allocation Fund Investor C Shares	BCMPX	NAS CM	Open End	Cautious Alloc (Asset Alloc)	B-	C	A-	Up	Y	1,000
BlackRock 60/40 Target Allocation Fund Class K	BKGPX	NAS CM	Open End	Moderate Alloc (Asset Alloc)	B-	C	A-	Up	Y	5,000,000
BlackRock 60/40 Target Allocation Fund Class R Shares	BRGPX	NAS CM	Open End	Moderate Alloc (Asset Alloc)	B-	C	B+	Up	Y	100
BlackRock 60/40 Target Allocation Institutional Shares	BIGPX	NAS CM	Open End	Moderate Alloc (Asset Alloc)	B-	C	A-	Up	Y	2,000,000
BlackRock 60/40 Target Allocation Fund Investor A Shares	BAGPX	NAS CM	Open End	Moderate Alloc (Asset Alloc)	B-	C	B+	Up	Y	1,000
BlackRock 60/40 Target Allocation Fund Investor C Shares	BCGPX	NAS CM	Open End	Moderate Alloc (Asset Alloc)	B-	C	B+	Up	Y	1,000
BlackRock 80/20 Target Allocation Fund Class A	BAAPX	NAS CM	Open End	Aggressive Alloc (Asset Alloc)	B-	C	B	Up	Y	1,000
BlackRock 80/20 Target Allocation Fund Class C	BCAPX	NAS CM	Open End	Aggressive Alloc (Asset Alloc)	B-	C	B	Up	Y	1,000
BlackRock 80/20 Target Allocation Fund Class Institutional	BIAPX	NAS CM	Open End	Aggressive Alloc (Asset Alloc)	B-	C	B	Up	Y	2,000,000
BlackRock 80/20 Target Allocation Fund Class K	BKAPX	NAS CM	Open End	Aggressive Alloc (Asset Alloc)	B-	C	B	Up	Y	5,000,000
BlackRock 80/20 Target Allocation Fund Class R	BRAPX	NAS CM	Open End	Aggressive Alloc (Asset Alloc)	B-	C	B	Up	Y	100
Blackrock Advantage Emerging Markets Fund Class K	BLSKX	NAS CM	Open End	Global Emerg Mkts (Div Emerging Mkts)	C	C-	C+		Y	5,000,000
BlackRock Advantage Emerging Markets Institutional Shares	BLSIX	NAS CM	Open End	Global Emerg Mkts (Div Emerging Mkts)	C	C-	C+		Y	2,000,000
BlackRock Advantage Emerging Markets Investor A Shares	BLSAX	NAS CM	Open End	Global Emerg Mkts (Div Emerging Mkts)	C	C-	C		Y	1,000
BlackRock Advantage Emerging Markets Investor C Shares	BLSCX	NAS CM	Open End	Global Emerg Mkts (Div Emerging Mkts)	C	C-	C	Up	Y	1,000
BlackRock Advantage Global Fund, Inc.Class K	MKGCX	NAS CM	Open End	Global Equity Large Cap (Growth)	C+	C	B	Up	Y	5,000,000
BlackRock Advantage Global Fund, Inc.Class R	MRGSX	NAS CM	Open End	Global Equity Large Cap (Growth)	C+	C	B	Up	Y	100
BlackRock Advantage Global Fund, Inc.Institutional Shares	MAGCX	NAS CM	Open End	Global Equity Large Cap (Growth)	C+	C	B	Up	Y	2,000,000
BlackRock Advantage Global Fund, Inc.Investor A Shares	MDGCX	NAS CM	Open End	Global Equity Large Cap (Growth)	C+	C	B	Up	Y	1,000
BlackRock Advantage Global Fund, Inc.Investor C Shares	MCGCX	NAS CM	Open End	Global Equity Large Cap (Growth)	C+	C	B	Up	Y	1,000
BlackRock Advantage International Institutional Shares	BROIX	NAS CM	Open End	Global Equity Large Cap (World Stock)	C	C	B		Y	2,000,000
BlackRock Advantage International Fund Investor A Shares	BROAX	NAS CM	Open End	Global Equity Large Cap (World Stock)	C	C	B		Y	1,000
BlackRock Advantage International Fund Investor C Shares	BROCX	NAS CM	Open End	Global Equity Large Cap (World Stock)	C	C	B-		Y	1,000
BlackRock Advantage International Fund K	BROKX	NAS CM	Open End	Global Equity Large Cap (World Stock)	C	C	B		Y	5,000,000
BlackRock Advantage International Fund R Shares	BGORX	NAS CM	Open End	Global Equity Large Cap (World Stock)	C	C	B-			100
BlackRock Advantage Large Cap Core Fund Class K	MLRKX	NAS CM	Open End	US Equity Large Cap Blend (Growth)	B-	C	B		Y	5,000,000
BlackRock Advantage Large Cap Core Fund Class R	MRLRX	NAS CM	Open End	US Equity Large Cap Blend (Growth)	B-	C	B		Y	100
BlackRock Advantage Large Cap Core Institutional Shares	MALRX	NAS CM	Open End	US Equity Large Cap Blend (Growth)	B-	C	B		Y	2,000,000
BlackRock Advantage Large Cap Core Fund Investor A Shares	MDLRX	NAS CM	Open End	US Equity Large Cap Blend (Growth)	B-	C	B		Y	1,000
BlackRock Advantage Large Cap Core Fund Investor C Shares	MCLRX	NAS CM	Open End	US Equity Large Cap Blend (Growth)	B-	C	B	Up	Y	1,000
BlackRock Advantage Large Cap Core Fund Service Shares	MSLRX	NAS CM	Open End	US Equity Large Cap Blend (Growth)	B-	C	B	Up	Y	5,000

★ Expanded analysis of this fund is included in Section II.

Min Additional Investment	3-Month Total Return	6-Month Total Return	1-Year Total Return	3-Year Total Return	5-Year Total Return	Dividend Yield (TTM)	Expense Ratio	3-Yr Std Deviation	3-Year Beta	NAV	Total Assets (MIL)	%Cash	%Stocks	%Bonds	%Other	Turnover Ratio	Last Bull Market Total Return	Last Bear Market Total Return	Front End Fee (%)	Back End Fee (%)	Inception Date
	TOTAL RETURNS					PERFORMANCE				ASSETS		ASSET ALLOCATION & TURNOVER					BULL & BEAR		FEES		
250	1.13	12.73	1.16	29.80	18.25	0.49	1.77	12.29	0.98	12.63	14.1	15	85	0	0	57	13.51	-13.01	4.00		Jan-11
250	0.91	12.32	0.37	26.93	13.88	0.18	2.52	12.24	0.98	12.21	14.1	15	85	0	0	57	12.93	-13.33			Jan-11
1,000	0.20	-0.29	-1.62			0	2.2			19.96	15.8	45	-1	57	0						Apr-18
500	1.69	33.66	18.64	133.77	126.36	0	1.97	20.72	1.22	29.42	293.1	0	94	0	6	596	28.65	-13.33			Jul-97
	1.23	11.77	-7.99	24.28		1.65	1.35	12.15	1	10.63	1,284	3	97	0	0	81					Dec-15
	1.21	11.54	-3.62	28.87		1.53	1.09	11.67	0.98	11.69	4,188	2	98	0	0	69					Dec-15
	2.69	17.55	-5.40	32.14		0.02	1.18	17.73	1.03	11.05	963.8	1	99	0	0	102					Dec-15
5,000	1.31	16.09	1.72	52.50	50.38	0.38	0.95	14.69	0.74	13.85	80.6	4	96	0	0	27					Sep-12
100	2.20	6.25	3.49	14.20	13.91	2.78	0.64	3.52	0.07	13.15	1,146	6	26	60	0	75	9.27	-4.73			Sep-87
	6.31	24.31	15.49	54.29	59.14	0.21	1.25	13.11	1.06	16.67	39.0	5	95	0	0	38					Nov-13
100	3.64	18.70	8.53	99.22	52.99	0	1.58	16.68	1.19	19.61	63.2	5	95	0	0	56	20.3	-28.76			Mar-10
25	1.61	16.97	-1.01	53.21	56.36	0	1.11	17.04	0.98	5.03	36.0	4	96	0	0	19	26.42	-28.69			Dec-00
	2.92	8.53	7.01	15.32	22.26	3.42	0.45	3.39	0.74	11.65	289.4	5	20	74	0	64	11.56	-8.23			Mar-16
	2.92	8.60	6.98	15.14	22.18	3.39	0.47	3.39	0.74	11.65	289.4	5	20	74	0	64	11.56	-8.23			Dec-06
50	2.86	8.39	6.66	14.08	20.05	3.08	0.81	3.38	0.74	11.5	289.4	5	20	74	0	64	11.38	-8.37	5.25		Dec-06
50	2.71	7.97	5.94	11.48	15.65	2.24	1.56	3.37	0.74	11.37	289.4	5	20	74	0	64	10.9	-8.69		1.00	Dec-06
	2.69	8.16	6.32	12.96	18.29	2.76	1.12	3.42	0.76	11.44	289.4	5	20	74	0	64	11.12	-8.42			Dec-06
	3.15	10.89	7.05	21.84	27.84	2.24	0.44	5.2	0.44	11.79	365.6	2	31	58	8	79	15.09	-12.29			Mar-16
	3.01	10.66	6.49	19.91	24.59	1.71	0.96	5.2	0.44	11.63	365.6	2	31	58	8	79	14.9	-12.51			Dec-06
	3.16	10.87	7.04	21.69	27.68	2.22	0.46	5.18	0.44	11.78	365.6	2	31	58	8	79	15.09	-12.29			Dec-06
50	3.09	10.75	6.70	20.57	25.59	1.9	0.8	5.18	0.44	11.68	365.6	2	31	58	8	79	14.97	-12.52	5.25		Dec-06
50	2.86	10.31	5.93	17.84	20.88	1.04	1.55	5.19	0.44	11.53	365.6	2	31	58	8	79	14.45	-12.73		1.00	Dec-06
	3.45	13.55	6.31	27.30	30.37	1.52	0.4	7.44	0.64	13.23	850.9	2	49	38	10	88	18.33	-16.38			Mar-16
	3.27	13.21	5.71	25.25	27.95	1	0.95	7.42	0.64	12.96	850.9	2	49	38	10	88	18.33	-16.38			Dec-06
	3.45	13.55	6.29	27.24	31.41	1.5	0.42	7.42	0.64	13.23	850.9	2	49	38	10	88	18.65	-16.12			Dec-06
50	3.35	13.35	5.96	25.98	29.10	1.23	0.76	7.4	0.64	13	850.9	2	49	38	10	88	18.44	-16.35	5.25		Dec-06
50	3.09	12.93	5.13	23.10	24.46	0.43	1.51	7.38	0.64	12.7	850.9	2	49	38	10	88	18.05	-16.55		1.00	Dec-06
50	3.41	15.65	5.38	31.82	32.61	0.9	0.7	9.5	0.82	12.49	370.0	2	78	19	0	80	22.4	-20.38	5.25		Dec-06
50	3.26	15.20	4.62	28.91	27.81	0.16	1.45	9.49	0.82	12.07	370.0	2	78	19	0	80	21.89	-20.68		1.00	Dec-06
	3.50	15.84	5.67	33.12	34.98	1.21	0.36	9.45	0.82	12.74	370.0	2	78	19	0	80	22.77	-20.35			Dec-06
	3.51	15.87	5.69	33.18	35.05	1.22	0.34	9.44	0.81	12.74	370.0	2	78	19	0	80	22.77	-20.35			Mar-16
	3.34	15.48	5.15	31.04	31.52	0.69	0.86	9.49	0.82	12.4	370.0	2	78	19	0	80	22.46	-20.53			Dec-06
	0.09	10.25	1.06	7.41	5.93	0	0.84	13.12	0.86	10.43	105.0	6	94	0	0	111					Jan-18
	0.19	10.25	1.06	7.41	5.93	0	0.88	13.1	0.86	10.43	105.0	6	94	0	0	111					Oct-11
50	0.09	10.09	0.68	6.54	4.64	0	1.18	13.12	0.86	10.25	105.0	6	94	0	0	111			5.25		Oct-11
50	0.00	9.71	0.00	4.29	0.78	0	1.93	13.06	0.85	9.71	105.0	6	94	0	0	111				1.00	Oct-11
	3.73	17.78	4.09	41.21	20.70	1.5	0.66	12.28	1.04	21.66	452.3	3	97	0	0	189	20.23	-23.79			Jan-18
	3.63	17.51	3.51	39.41	18.29	1.19	1.21	12.3	1.04	18.52	452.3	3	97	0	0	189	19.88	-23.93			Feb-03
	3.73	17.71	4.02	41.95	22.15	1.45	0.71	12.3	1.04	21.66	452.3	3	97	0	0	189	20.43	-23.7			Oct-94
50	3.63	17.56	3.76	40.61	20.18	1.29	0.96	12.28	1.04	20.55	452.3	3	97	0	0	189	20.23	-23.79	5.25		Aug-94
50	3.45	17.16	2.98	37.41	15.57	0.52	1.71	12.28	1.04	16.79	452.3	3	97	0	0	189	19.67	-24.07		1.00	Oct-94
	3.53	15.00	-0.41	28.69	19.82	2.34	0.5	10.76	0.93	16.49	854.5	4	96	0	0	106	17.4	-23.79			Jan-06
50	3.44	14.87	-0.64	27.74	18.30	2.16	0.75	10.79	0.94	16.31	854.5	4	96	0	0	106	17.21	-23.91	5.25		Jan-06
50	3.28	14.47	-1.37	24.81	13.67	0.67	1.5	10.76	0.93	15.83	854.5	4	96	0	0	106	16.66	-24.12		1.00	Jan-06
	3.59	15.07	-0.30	28.83	19.95	2.38	0.45	10.79	0.93	16.49	854.5	4	96	0	0	106	17.4	-23.79			Jan-18
	3.37	14.72	-0.91	26.62	16.27	1.8	1	10.76	0.93	16.3	854.5	4	96	0	0	106	16.99	-23.95			Sep-11
	3.46	18.99	7.90	55.56	60.44	1.14	0.43	12.51	1	16.82	2,736	1	99	0	0	148	25.5	-22.45			Jan-18
	3.39	18.69	7.35	53.13	56.09	0.86	0.98	12.54	1	15	2,736	1	99	0	0	148	25.02	-22.64			Jan-03
	3.52	18.99	7.93	55.50	60.38	1.11	0.48	12.51	1	16.82	2,736	1	99	0	0	148	25.5	-22.45			Dec-99
50	3.41	18.86	7.61	54.33	58.25	0.95	0.73	12.52	1	16.15	2,736	1	99	0	0	148	25.4	-22.5	5.25		Dec-99
50	3.25	18.40	6.82	50.73	52.07	0.18	1.48	12.52	1	13.71	2,736	1	99	0	0	148	24.63	-22.77		1.00	Dec-99
	3.47	18.90	7.70	53.97	57.65	0.9	0.73	12.5	1	16.75	2,736	1	99	0	0	148	25.41	-22.58			Sep-07

	MARKET			FUND TYPE, CATEGORY & OBJECTIVE	RATINGS				MINIMUMS	
Fund Name	Ticker Symbol	Traded On	Fund Type	Category and (Prospectus Objective)	Overall Rating	Reward Rating	Risk Rating	Recent Up/ Downgrade	Open to New Investors	Min Initial Investment
BlackRock Advantage Large Cap Growth Fund Class K	BMCKX	NAS CM	Open End	US Equity Large Cap Growth (Growth)	B-	C+	B		Y	5,000,000
BlackRock Advantage Large Cap Growth Fund Class R	BMCRX	NAS CM	Open End	US Equity Large Cap Growth (Growth)	C+	C+	B	Down		100
BlackRock Advantage Large Cap Growth Institutional Shares	CMVIX	NAS CM	Open End	US Equity Large Cap Growth (Growth)	B-	C+	B		Y	2,000,000
BlackRock Advantage Large Cap Growth Investor A Shares	BMCAX	NAS CM	Open End	US Equity Large Cap Growth (Growth)	B-	C+	B		Y	1,000
BlackRock Advantage Large Cap Growth Investor C Shares	BMCCX	NAS CM	Open End	US Equity Large Cap Growth (Growth)	C+	C	B	Down	Y	1,000
BlackRock Advantage Large Cap Growth Fund Service Shares	CMVSX	NAS CM	Open End	US Equity Large Cap Growth (Growth)	B-	C+	B		Y	5,000
BlackRock Advantage Large Cap Value Fund Class K	MLVKX	NAS CM	Open End	US Equity Large Cap Value (Growth)	B-	C	B	Up	Y	5,000,000
BlackRock Advantage Large Cap Value Fund Class R	MRLVX	NAS CM	Open End	US Equity Large Cap Value (Growth)	B-	C	B	Up	Y	100
BlackRock Advantage Large Cap Value Institutional Shares	MALVX	NAS CM	Open End	US Equity Large Cap Value (Growth)	B-	C	B	Up	Y	2,000,000
BlackRock Advantage Large Cap Value Fund Investor A Shares	MDLVX	NAS CM	Open End	US Equity Large Cap Value (Growth)	B-	C	B	Up	Y	1,000
BlackRock Advantage Large Cap Value Fund Investor C Shares	MCLVX	NAS CM	Open End	US Equity Large Cap Value (Growth)	B-	C	B	Up	Y	1,000
BlackRock Advantage Large Cap Value Fund Service Shares	MSLVX	NAS CM	Open End	US Equity Large Cap Value (Growth)	B-	C	B	Up	Y	5,000
BlackRock Advantage Small Cap Core Fund Class K	BDSKX	NAS CM	Open End	US Equity Small Cap (Growth)	C+	C	C+		Y	5,000,000
BlackRock Advantage Small Cap Core Institutional Shares	BDSIX	NAS CM	Open End	US Equity Small Cap (Growth)	C+	C	C+		Y	2,000,000
BlackRock Advantage Small Cap Core Fund Investor A Shares	BDSAX	NAS CM	Open End	US Equity Small Cap (Growth)	C+	C	C+		Y	1,000
BlackRock Advantage Small Cap Core Fund Investor C Shares	BDSCX	NAS CM	Open End	US Equity Small Cap (Growth)	C	C	C+	Down	Y	1,000
BlackRock Advantage Small Cap Growth Fund Class K	PSGKX	NAS CM	Open End	US Equity Small Cap (Small Company)	C+	C	C+	Down	Y	5,000,000
BlackRock Advantage Small Cap Growth Fund Class R	BSGRX	NAS CM	Open End	US Equity Small Cap (Small Company)	C+	C	C+	Down		100
BlackRock Advantage Small Cap Growth Institutional Shares	PSGIX	NAS CM	Open End	US Equity Small Cap (Small Company)	C+	C	C+	Down	Y	2,000,000
BlackRock Advantage Small Cap Growth Investor A Shares	CSGEX	NAS CM	Open End	US Equity Small Cap (Small Company)	C+	C	C+	Down	Y	1,000
BlackRock Advantage Small Cap Growth Investor C Shares	CGICX	NAS CM	Open End	US Equity Small Cap (Small Company)	C+	C	C+		Y	1,000
BlackRock Advantage Small Cap Growth Fund Service Shares	PCGEX	NAS CM	Open End	US Equity Small Cap (Small Company)	C+	C	C+	Down	Y	5,000
BlackRock Advantage U.S. Total Market Fund, Inc.Class K	MKSPX	NAS CM	Open End	US Equity Small Cap (Growth)	C+	C	B	Down	Y	5,000,000
BlackRock Advantage U.S. Total Market Fund, Inc.Class R	MRSPX	NAS CM	Open End	US Equity Small Cap (Growth)	C+	C	B	Down	Y	100
BlackRock Advantage U.S. Total Mkt Fund, Inc.Inst Shares	MASPX	NAS CM	Open End	US Equity Small Cap (Growth)	C+	C	B	Down	Y	2,000,000
BlackRock Advantage U.S. Total Mkt Fund, Inc.Inv A Shares	MDSPX	NAS CM	Open End	US Equity Small Cap (Growth)	C+	C	B	Down	Y	1,000
BlackRock Advantage U.S. Total Mkt Fund, Inc.Inv C Shares	MCSPX	NAS CM	Open End	US Equity Small Cap (Growth)	C+	C	B		Y	1,000
BlackRock All-Cap Energy & Resources Portfolio Inst Cls	BACIX	NAS CM	Open End	Energy Sector Equity (Natl Res)	C-	D+	C-	Down	Y	2,000,000
BlackRock All-Cap Energy & Resources Portfolio Inv A Cls	BACAX	NAS CM	Open End	Energy Sector Equity (Natl Res)	D+	D+	D+	Down	Y	1,000
BlackRock All-Cap Energy & Resources Portfolio Inv C Cls	BACCX	NAS CM	Open End	Energy Sector Equity (Natl Res)	D+	D+	D+	Down	Y	1,000
BlackRock All-Cap Energy & Resources Portfolio Service Cls	BACSX	NAS CM	Open End	Energy Sector Equity (Natl Res)	D+	D+	D+	Down	Y	5,000
BlackRock Asian Dragon Fund,Inc.Class K	MPCKX	NAS CM	Open End	Asia ex-Japan Equity (Pacific Stock)	C	C-	C+		Y	5,000,000
BlackRock Asian Dragon Fund,Inc.Class R	MRPCX	NAS CM	Open End	Asia ex-Japan Equity (Pacific Stock)	C	C-	C+		Y	100
BlackRock Asian Dragon Fund,Inc.Institutional Shares	MAPCX	NAS CM	Open End	Asia ex-Japan Equity (Pacific Stock)	C	C-	C+		Y	2,000,000
BlackRock Asian Dragon Fund,Inc.Investor A Shares	MDPCX	NAS CM	Open End	Asia ex-Japan Equity (Pacific Stock)	C	C-	C+		Y	1,000
BlackRock Asian Dragon Fund,Inc.Investor C Shares	MCPCX	NAS CM	Open End	Asia ex-Japan Equity (Pacific Stock)	C	C-	C+		Y	1,000
BlackRock Balanced Capital Fund Class K	MKCPX	NAS CM	Open End	Moderate Alloc (Balanced)	B	C+	A-		Y	5,000,000
BlackRock Balanced Capital Fund Class R	MRBPX	NAS CM	Open End	Moderate Alloc (Balanced)	B	C+	A-	Up	Y	100
BlackRock Balanced Capital Fund Institutional Shares	MACPX	NAS CM	Open End	Moderate Alloc (Balanced)	B	C+	A-		Y	2,000,000
BlackRock Balanced Capital Fund Investor A Shares	MDCPX	NAS CM	Open End	Moderate Alloc (Balanced)	B	C+	A-	Up	Y	1,000
BlackRock Balanced Capital Fund Investor C Shares	MCCPX	NAS CM	Open End	Moderate Alloc (Balanced)	B	C+	A-	Up	Y	1,000
BlackRock Basic Value Fund Class K	MBVKX	NAS CM	Open End	US Equity Large Cap Value (Growth)	C+	C	B		Y	5,000,000
BlackRock Basic Value Fund Institutional Shares	MABAX	NAS CM	Open End	US Equity Large Cap Value (Growth)	C+	C	B		Y	2,000,000
BlackRock Basic Value Fund Investor A Shares	MDBAX	NAS CM	Open End	US Equity Large Cap Value (Growth)	C+	C	B		Y	1,000
BlackRock Basic Value Fund Investor C Shares	MCBAX	NAS CM	Open End	US Equity Large Cap Value (Growth)	C+	C	B		Y	1,000
BlackRock Basic Value Fund R Shares	MRBVX	NAS CM	Open End	US Equity Large Cap Value (Growth)	C+	C	B		Y	100
BlackRock Capital Appreciation Fund Institutional Shares	MAFGX	NAS CM	Open End	US Equity Large Cap Growth (Growth)	B-	C+	B	Down	Y	2,000,000
BlackRock Capital Appreciation Fund Investor A Shares	MDFGX	NAS CM	Open End	US Equity Large Cap Growth (Growth)	B-	C+	B	Down	Y	1,000
BlackRock Capital Appreciation Fund Investor C Shares	MCFGX	NAS CM	Open End	US Equity Large Cap Growth (Growth)	B-	C+	B	Down	Y	1,000
BlackRock Capital Appreciation Fund K Shares	BFGBX	NAS CM	Open End	US Equity Large Cap Growth (Growth)	B-	C+	B	Down	Y	5,000,000
BlackRock Capital Appreciation Fund R Shares	MRFGX	NAS CM	Open End	US Equity Large Cap Growth (Growth)	B-	C+	B	Down	Y	100
BlackRock China A Opportunities Fund Class K	CHKLX	NAS CM	Open End	Greater China Equity (Growth & Income)	U	U	U		Y	5,000,000

★ Expanded analysis of this fund is included in Section II.

	TOTAL RETURNS					PERFORMANCE				ASSETS		ASSET ALLOCATION & TURNOVER					BULL & BEAR		FEES		
Min Additional Investment	3-Month Total Return	6-Month Total Return	1-Year Total Return	3-Year Total Return	5-Year Total Return	Dividend Yield (TTM)	Expense Ratio	3-Yr Std Deviation	3-Year Beta	NAV	Total Assets (MIL)	%Cash	%Stocks	%Bonds	%Other	Turnover Ratio	Last Bull Market Total Return	Last Bear Market Total Return	Front End Fee (%)	Back End Fee (%)	Inception Date
	4.25	21.93	9.26	65.14	55.12	0.75	0.57	13.6	0.98	16.47	815.9	1	99	0	0	162	27.26	-24.42			Jan-18
	4.09	21.61	8.63	63.05	52.01	0.09	1.12	13.59	0.98	16.33	815.9	1	99	0	0	162	26.99	-24.53			Jul-10
	4.25	21.93	9.13	65.81	56.73	0.71	0.62	13.62	0.98	16.47	815.9	1	99	0	0	162	27.45	-24.3			Jun-93
50	4.19	21.71	8.86	64.41	54.43	0.51	0.87	13.6	0.98	15.7	815.9	1	99	0	0	162	27.26	-24.42	5.25		Aug-86
50	3.98	21.22	8.02	60.70	48.52	0	1.62	13.62	0.98	13.37	815.9	1	99	0	0	162	26.66	-24.66		1.00	Jun-93
	4.20	21.76	8.89	64.45	54.42	0.45	0.87	13.61	0.98	16.17	815.9	1	99	0	0	162	27.22	-24.41			Jan-05
	2.81	15.93	6.69	44.33	49.16	1.98	0.49	12.22	1	27.92	636.7	1	99	0	0	143	23.97	-24.25			Jan-18
	2.68	15.62	6.07	41.98	45.07	1.51	1.04	12.23	1	26.17	636.7	1	99	0	0	143	23.48	-24.35			Jan-03
	2.81	15.93	6.64	44.26	49.09	1.93	0.54	12.23	1	27.91	636.7	1	99	0	0	143	23.97	-24.25			Dec-99
50	2.72	15.75	6.34	43.14	46.98	1.73	0.79	12.2	0.99	27.3	636.7	1	99	0	0	143	23.57	-24.28	5.25		Dec-99
50	2.57	15.37	5.58	39.96	41.50	0.85	1.54	12.21	1	25.23	636.7	1	99	0	0	143	23.2	-24.53		1.00	Dec-99
	2.76	15.78	6.36	43.16	46.98	1.69	0.79	12.2	1	27.7	636.7	1	99	0	0	143	23.87	-24.25			Oct-06
	1.60	19.11	-2.23	45.63	43.03	0.77	0.45	17.46	1.01	14.14	952.6	1	99	0	0	104					Mar-16
	1.52	19.02	-2.26	45.43	42.82	0.74	0.5	17.37	1.01	14.13	952.6	1	99	0	0	104					Mar-13
50	1.53	18.95	-2.51	44.43	41.00	0.57	0.75	17.4	1.01	14.04	952.6	1	99	0	0	104			5.25		Mar-13
50	1.26	18.48	-3.20	41.16	35.68	0.04	1.5	17.32	1	13.76	952.6	1	99	0	0	104				1.00	Mar-13
	1.89	21.98	1.77	54.66	44.07	0.28	0.45	17.66	1	18.52	656.9	1	98	0	0	129	31.66	-26.86			Jan-18
	2.92	23.04	2.37	54.05	42.08	0	1	17.69	1	13.35	656.9	1	98	0	0	129	31.28	-27.01			Mar-18
	1.83	21.90	1.72	54.58	44.00	0.23	0.5	17.65	1	18.52	656.9	1	98	0	0	129	31.66	-26.86			Sep-93
50	1.77	21.75	1.48	53.38	41.98	0.08	0.75	17.66	1	13.36	656.9	1	98	0	0	129	31.4	-27.02	5.25		Sep-93
50	1.58	21.47	0.74	49.94	36.62	0	1.5	17.66	1	5.84	656.9	1	98	0	0	129	30.75	-27.24		1.00	Sep-96
	1.84	21.77	1.48	53.44	42.05	0.09	0.75	17.65	1	15.1	656.9	1	98	0	0	129	31.38	-26.93			Sep-93
	3.61	18.85	7.39	44.67	36.41	1.4	0.43	15	1.06	28.53	422.9	1	99	0	0	142	27.59	-24.32			Jan-18
	3.49	18.57	6.96	42.47	32.95	1.54	0.98	15	1.06	19.96	422.9	1	99	0	0	142	27.14	-24.57			Feb-03
	3.61	18.88	7.42	44.70	36.43	1.36	0.48	15	1.06	28.54	422.9	1	99	0	0	142	27.59	-24.32			May-78
50	3.54	18.71	7.19	43.56	34.78	1.24	0.73	15.01	1.06	27.3	422.9	1	99	0	0	142	27.37	-24.42	5.25		Oct-94
50	3.38	18.28	6.41	40.31	29.53	1.29	1.48	14.97	1.06	17.49	422.9	1	99	0	0	142	26.69	-24.76		1.00	Oct-94
	-1.25	13.65	-14.46	3.46	-35.43	3.01	0.96	19.38	1.12	10.31	69.3	3	97	0	0	37	15.81	-33.62			Feb-05
50	-1.38	13.30	-14.86	2.19	-36.82	2.53	1.38	19.44	1.12	10.04	69.3	3	97	0	0	37	15.46	-33.74	5.25		Feb-05
50	-1.53	13.07	-15.47	0.07	-39.03	0.61	2.1	19.4	1.12	9.67	69.3	3	97	0	0	37	14.99	-33.92		1.00	Feb-05
	-1.37	13.47	-14.82	2.17	-36.77	2.47	1.38	19.4	1.12	10.09	69.3	3	97	0	0	37	15.54	-33.7			Feb-05
	-1.34	13.68	1.58	27.73	18.06	0.86	0.96	14.94	0.98	15.37	153.9	5	93	0	2	44	15.64	-23.71			Jan-18
	-1.53	13.28	0.88	25.03	13.97	0.22	1.69	14.95	0.98	11.51	153.9	5	93	0	2	44	15.1	-23.98			Jan-03
	-1.34	13.67	1.59	27.66	17.99	0.75	1.02	14.95	0.98	15.38	153.9	5	93	0	2	44	15.64	-23.71			Sep-76
50	-1.36	13.54	1.37	26.86	16.72	0.49	1.27	14.94	0.98	15.17	153.9	5	93	0	2	44	15.46	-23.78	5.25		Oct-94
50	-1.56	13.11	0.57	23.88	12.20	0	2.04	14.98	0.99	10.09	153.9	5	93	0	2	44	14.88	-24.03		1.00	Oct-94
	3.56	14.99	8.71	37.24	45.85	1.84	0.53	7.88	0.63	23.32	1,207	13	53	34	0	140	16.19	-12.84			Jan-18
	3.36	14.61	7.96	34.46	41.08	1.33	1.27	7.91	0.63	21.25	1,207	13	53	34	0	140	15.68	-13.13			Jan-03
	3.56	14.99	8.68	37.08	45.68	1.77	0.63	7.87	0.63	23.31	1,207	13	53	34	0	140	16.19	-12.84			Nov-73
50	3.44	14.79	8.30	35.83	43.53	1.52	0.92	7.9	0.63	23.2	1,207	13	53	34	0	140	16.01	-12.99	5.25		Oct-94
50	3.26	14.35	7.52	32.78	38.19	1.08	1.67	7.88	0.63	19.98	1,207	13	53	34	0	140	15.42	-13.22		1.00	Oct-94
	2.06	14.51	4.60	30.13	30.53	2.09	0.44	13	1.04	21.87	2,131	4	96	0	0	30	25.39	-21.05			Feb-15
	2.11	14.51	4.55	29.76	29.96	1.98	0.55	12.97	1.04	21.86	2,131	4	96	0	0	30	25.39	-21.05			Jul-77
50	2.00	14.27	4.23	28.70	28.14	1.72	0.82	12.97	1.04	21.53	2,131	4	96	0	0	30	25.14	-21.16	5.25		Oct-94
50	1.83	13.90	3.42	25.66	23.18	0.68	1.64	12.96	1.04	18.49	2,131	4	96	0	0	30	24.57	-21.43		1.00	Oct-94
	1.95	14.11	3.88	27.39	26.02	1.41	1.16	12.98	1.04	19.96	2,131	4	96	0	0	30	24.9	-21.28			Jan-03
	5.10	24.11	9.61	75.70	92.72	0	0.76	14.28	1.02	31.3	3,270	1	99	0	0	42	22.93	-20.41			Jun-10
50	5.04	23.93	9.31	74.23	90.07	0	1.04	14.3	1.02	28.73	3,270	1	99	0	0	42	22.7	-20.52	5.25		Dec-97
50	4.81	23.42	8.43	70.13	82.55	0	1.84	14.31	1.02	20.37	3,270	1	99	0	0	42	22.11	-20.78		1.00	Dec-97
	5.14	24.17	9.73	76.31	93.84	0	0.65	14.3	1.02	31.49	3,270	1	99	0	0	42	22.96	-20.4			Dec-97
	4.99	23.78	9.03	72.82	87.57	0	1.3	14.29	1.02	23.27	3,270	1	99	0	0	42	22.47	-20.62			Jun-10
	-0.07	32.33					0.94			13.3	14.7										Dec-18

	MARKET		FUND TYPE, CATEGORY & OBJECTIVE		RATINGS					MINIMUMS
Fund Name	Ticker Symbol	Traded On	Fund Type	Category and (Prospectus Objective)	Overall Rating	Reward Rating	Risk Rating	Recent Up/ Downgrade	Open to New Investors	Min Initial Investment
BlackRock China A Opportunities Fund Institutional	CHILX	NAS CM	Open End	Greater China Equity (Growth & Income)	U	U	U		Y	2,000,000
BlackRock Commodity Strategies Portfolio Class K	BCSKX	NAS CM	Open End	Commodities Broad Basket (Growth & Income)	C-	C-	C		Y	5,000,000
BlackRock Commodity Strategies Portfolio Inst Shares	BICSX	NAS CM	Open End	Commodities Broad Basket (Growth & Income)	C-	C-	C		Y	2,000,000
BlackRock Commodity Strategies Portfolio Investor A Shares	BCSAX	NAS CM	Open End	Commodities Broad Basket (Growth & Income)	C-	C-	C-		Y	1,000
BlackRock Commodity Strategies Portfolio Investor C Shares	BCSCX	NAS CM	Open End	Commodities Broad Basket (Growth & Income)	D+	D+	C-	Down	Y	1,000
BlackRock Dynamic High Income Portfolio Class K	BDHKX	NAS CM	Open End	Cautious Alloc (Growth & Income)	B	C+	A-	Up	Y	5,000,000
BlackRock Dynamic High Income Portfolio Institutional	BDHIX	NAS CM	Open End	Cautious Alloc (Growth & Income)	B	C+	A-	Up	Y	2,000,000
BlackRock Dynamic High Income Portfolio Investor A	BDHAX	NAS CM	Open End	Cautious Alloc (Growth & Income)	B	C+	A-	Up	Y	1,000
BlackRock Dynamic High Income Portfolio Investor C	BDHCX	NAS CM	Open End	Cautious Alloc (Growth & Income)	B-	C	A-	Up	Y	1,000
BlackRock Emerging Markets Equity Strategies Fund Class K	BEFKX	NAS CM	Open End	Global Emerg Mkts (Div Emerging Mkts)	B	C+	B+	Up	Y	5,000,000
BlackRock Emerging Markets Equity Strategies Institutional	BEFIX	NAS CM	Open End	Global Emerg Mkts (Div Emerging Mkts)	B	C+	B+	Up	Y	2,000,000
BlackRock Emerging Markets Equity Strategies Investor A	BEFAX	NAS CM	Open End	Global Emerg Mkts (Div Emerging Mkts)	B-	C+	B+		Y	1,000
BlackRock Emerging Markets Equity Strategies Investor C	BEFCX	NAS CM	Open End	Global Emerg Mkts (Div Emerging Mkts)	B-	C+	B+		Y	1,000
BlackRock Emerging Markets Fund, Inc. Institutional Shares	MADCX	NAS CM	Open End	Global Emerg Mkts (Div Emerging Mkts)	C	C	B-		Y	2,000,000
BlackRock Emerging Markets Fund, Inc. Investor A Shares	MDDCX	NAS CM	Open End	Global Emerg Mkts (Div Emerging Mkts)	C	C	B-		Y	1,000
BlackRock Emerging Markets Fund, Inc. Investor C Shares	MCDCX	NAS CM	Open End	Global Emerg Mkts (Div Emerging Mkts)	C	C	B-		Y	1,000
BlackRock Emerging Markets Fund, Inc. K Shares	MKDCX	NAS CM	Open End	Global Emerg Mkts (Div Emerging Mkts)	C+	C	B-	Up	Y	5,000,000
BlackRock Energy & Resources Portfolio Inst Shares	SGLSX	NAS CM	Open End	Energy Sector Equity (Natl Res)	D	D	D	Down	Y	2,000,000
BlackRock Energy & Resources Portfolio Investor A Shares	SSGRX	NAS CM	Open End	Energy Sector Equity (Natl Res)	D	D	D	Down	Y	1,000
BlackRock Energy & Resources Portfolio Investor C Shares	SSGDX	NAS CM	Open End	Energy Sector Equity (Natl Res)	D	D	D	Down	Y	1,000
BlackRock Energy & Resources Trust	BGR	NYSE	Closed End	Energy Sector Equity (Natl Res)	D+	D+	C-	Down	Y	
BlackRock Enhanced Capital and Income Fund Inc	CII	NYSE	Closed End	Alternative Miscellaneous (Equity-Income)	C	C	C-		Y	
BlackRock Enhanced Equity Dividend Fund	BDJ	NYSE	Closed End	Alternative Miscellaneous (Equity-Income)	C	C	C+		Y	
BlackRock Enhanced Global Dividend Trust	BOE	NYSE	Closed End	Global Equity Large Cap (World Stock)	C	C	C+		Y	
BlackRock Enhanced International Dividend Trust	BGY	NYSE	Closed End	Global Equity Large Cap (Foreign Stock)	C	C	C+		Y	
BlackRock Equity Dividend Fund Institutional Shares	MADVX	NAS CM	Open End	US Equity Large Cap Value (Equity-Income)	B-	C	B	Up	Y	2,000,000
BlackRock Equity Dividend Fund Investor A Shares	MDDVX	NAS CM	Open End	US Equity Large Cap Value (Equity-Income)	B-	C	B	Up	Y	1,000
BlackRock Equity Dividend Fund Investor C Shares	MCDVX	NAS CM	Open End	US Equity Large Cap Value (Equity-Income)	B-	C	B	Up	Y	1,000
BlackRock Equity Dividend Fund Investor C1 Shares	BEDCX	NAS CM	Open End	US Equity Large Cap Value (Equity-Income)	B-	C	B	Up	Y	0
BlackRock Equity Dividend Fund K Shares	MKDVX	NAS CM	Open End	US Equity Large Cap Value (Equity-Income)	B-	C	B	Up	Y	5,000,000
BlackRock Equity Dividend Fund R Shares	MRDVX	NAS CM	Open End	US Equity Large Cap Value (Equity-Income)	B-	C	B	Up	Y	100
BlackRock Equity Dividend Fund Service Shares	MSDVX	NAS CM	Open End	US Equity Large Cap Value (Equity-Income)	B-	C	B	Up	Y	5,000
BlackRock EuroFund Class K	MKEFX	NAS CM	Open End	Europe Equity Large Cap (Europe Stock)	C	D+	C+	Up	Y	5,000,000
BlackRock EuroFund Class R	MREFX	NAS CM	Open End	Europe Equity Large Cap (Europe Stock)	C-	D+	C+		Y	100
BlackRock EuroFund Institutional Shares	MAEFX	NAS CM	Open End	Europe Equity Large Cap (Europe Stock)	C	D+	C+	Up	Y	2,000,000
BlackRock EuroFund Investor A Shares	MDEFX	NAS CM	Open End	Europe Equity Large Cap (Europe Stock)	C-	D+	C+		Y	1,000
BlackRock EuroFund Investor C Shares	MCEFX	NAS CM	Open End	Europe Equity Large Cap (Europe Stock)	C-	D+	C+	Up	Y	1,000
BlackRock Event Driven Equity Fund Institutional Shares	BILPX	NAS CM	Open End	Market Neutral (Growth)	B-	C+	B	Down	Y	2,000,000
BlackRock Event Driven Equity Fund Investor A Shares	BALPX	NAS CM	Open End	Market Neutral (Growth)	B-	C+	B	Down	Y	1,000
BlackRock Event Driven Equity Fund Investor C Shares	BCLPX	NAS CM	Open End	Market Neutral (Growth)	B-	C+	B		Y	1,000
BlackRock Exchange Portfolio BlackRock Shares	STSEX	NAS CM	Open End	US Equity Large Cap Blend (Growth)	B-	C+	B+	Down	Y	0
BlackRock Focus Growth Fund Institutional Shares	MAFOX	NAS CM	Open End	US Equity Large Cap Growth (Growth)	B-	C+	B	Down	Y	2,000,000
BlackRock Focus Growth Fund Investor A Shares	MDFOX	NAS CM	Open End	US Equity Large Cap Growth (Growth)	B-	C+	B	Down	Y	1,000
BlackRock Focus Growth Fund Investor C Shares	MCFOX	NAS CM	Open End	US Equity Large Cap Growth (Growth)	B-	C+	B	Down	Y	1,000
BlackRock GA Disciplined Volatility Equity Fund Class K	BGDVX	NAS CM	Open End	Global Equity Large Cap (Growth & Income)	C	D+	B-	Up	Y	5,000,000
BlackRock GA Disciplined Volatility Equity Institutional	BIDVX	NAS CM	Open End	Global Equity Large Cap (Growth & Income)	C	D+	B-	Up	Y	2,000,000
BlackRock GA Dynamic Equity Fund Class K	BGEEX	NAS CM	Open End	Global Equity Large Cap (Growth & Income)	C-	D	C+	Up	Y	5,000,000
BlackRock GA Dynamic Equity Fund Institutional	BIEEX	NAS CM	Open End	Global Equity Large Cap (Growth & Income)	C-	D	C+	Up	Y	2,000,000
BlackRock Global Allocation Fund, Inc. Class K	MKLOX	NAS CM	Open End	Moderate Alloc (Multi-Asset Global)	B-	C	B+	Up	Y	5,000,000
BlackRock Global Allocation Fund, Inc. Class R	MRLOX	NAS CM	Open End	Moderate Alloc (Multi-Asset Global)	B-	C	B+	Up	Y	100
BlackRock Global Allocation Fund, Inc. Inst Shares	MALOX	NAS CM	Open End	Moderate Alloc (Multi-Asset Global)	B-	C	B+	Up	Y	2,000,000
BlackRock Global Allocation Fund, Inc. Investor A Shares	MDLOX	NAS CM	Open End	Moderate Alloc (Multi-Asset Global)	B-	C	B+	Up	Y	1,000

★ Expanded analysis of this fund is included in Section II.

Min Additional Investment	TOTAL RETURNS 3-Month Total Return	6-Month Total Return	1-Year Total Return	3-Year Total Return	5-Year Total Return	PERFORMANCE Dividend Yield (TTM)	Expense Ratio	3-Yr Std Deviation	3-Year Beta	ASSETS NAV	Total Assets (MIL)	ASSET ALLOCATION & TURNOVER %Cash	%Stocks	%Bonds	%Other	Turnover Ratio	BULL & BEAR Last Bull Market Total Return	Last Bear Market Total Return	FEES Front End Fee (%)	Back End Fee (%)	Inception Date
	-0.15	32.23					0.99			13.29	14.7										Dec-18
	0.27	8.80	-5.82	3.27	-26.08	1.99	0.71	10.19	1.01	7.29	215.5	29	48	25	-2	110					Jan-18
	0.27	8.80	-5.87	3.22	-26.11	1.94	0.76	10.12	1.01	7.29	215.5	29	48	25	-2	110					Oct-11
50	0.27	8.72	-6.03	2.47	-26.91	1.59	1.01	10.11	1.01	7.23	215.5	29	48	25	-2	110			5.25		Oct-11
50	0.00	8.26	-6.83	0.07	-29.70	1.06	1.76	10.17	1.01	6.94	215.5	29	48	25	-2	110				1.00	Oct-11
	3.72	14.80	7.46	30.80		6.34	0.72	7.57	0.64	9.66	985.9	6	39	50	0	75					Mar-16
	3.60	14.65	7.41	30.48		6.29	0.77	7.57	0.64	9.65	985.9	6	39	50	0	75					Nov-14
50	3.55	14.47	7.14	29.50		6.05	1.02	7.5	0.64	9.65	985.9	6	39	50	0	75			5.25		Nov-14
50	3.36	14.07	6.36	26.66		5.32	1.77	7.51	0.64	9.64	985.9	6	39	50	0	75				1.00	Nov-14
	5.40	22.08	21.43	70.13		20.17	1.27	15.06	0.94	11.5	25.1	7	93	0	0	254					Feb-16
	5.31	21.95	21.31	69.92		20.1	1.32	15.09	0.95	11.5	25.1	7	93	0	0	254					Feb-16
50	5.24	21.85	20.99	68.44		20.2	1.57	15.11	0.95	11.43	25.1	7	93	0	0	254			5.25		Feb-16
50	5.04	21.39	20.12	64.87		18.9	2.32	15.07	0.94	11.46	25.1	7	93	0	0	254				1.00	Feb-16
	3.62	15.86	7.99	47.91	21.81	0.85	1	14.88	1.04	24.03	579.5	7	93	0	0	121	21.12	-24.75			Sep-89
50	3.57	15.73	7.72	46.63	19.49	0.57	1.25	14.87	1.03	23.17	579.5	7	93	0	0	121	20.83	-24.8	5.25		Oct-94
50	3.33	15.24	6.90	43.08	14.74	0	2	14.84	1.03	19.5	579.5	7	93	0	0	121	20.31	-25.09		1.00	Oct-94
	3.62	15.86	8.02	48.03	21.91	0.92	0.95	14.87	1.03	24.03	579.5	7	93	0	0	121	21.12	-24.75			Jan-18
	-5.94	12.43	-23.89	-16.69	-60.83	0.5	1.07	24.89	1.04	17.31	98.5	3	97	0	0	26	20.21	-37.19			Jun-93
50	-6.04	12.28	-24.13	-17.47	-61.44	0.31	1.38	24.89	1.04	14.81	98.5	3	97	0	0	26	19.98	-37.29	5.25		Mar-90
50	-6.24	11.82	-24.70	-19.24	-62.81	0	2.1	24.88	1.04	10.34	98.5	3	97	0	0	26	19.48	-37.49		1.00	Jun-93
	-0.56	13.85	-12.25	3.35	-33.83	3.88	0	17.42		13.1	390.7	3	97	0	0	32	24.05	-28.05			Dec-04
	1.86	13.94	4.72	43.29	49.81	1.46		10.76	0.87	16.74	738.6	0	100	0	0	27	20.42	-12.11			Apr-04
	3.87	14.36	5.87	33.07	41.16	2.27		10.3		9.6	1,800	1	99	0	0	34	19.32	-11.44			Aug-05
	0.75	11.62	6.54	21.74	14.15	2.81		8.87	0.7	11.9	820.1	0	98	0	1	28	16.12	-19.89			May-05
	0.84	11.43	4.67	21.15	3.05	2.18		9.32		6.22	678.3	1	96	0	3	60	14.51	-21.09			May-07
	4.66	16.41	7.56	40.75	51.49	1.93	0.73	11.72	0.95	21.46	19,552	7	93	0	0	36	21.49	-13.7			Nov-88
50	4.67	16.34	7.30	39.75	49.58	1.69	0.98	11.74	0.95	21.39	19,552	7	93	0	0	36	21.23	-13.78	5.25		Oct-94
50	4.44	15.84	6.50	36.73	44.29	1.08	1.68	11.73	0.95	20.5	19,552	7	93	0	0	36	20.76	-14.1		1.00	Oct-94
0	4.45	15.90	6.62	37.37	45.50	1.1	1.54	11.74	0.95	20.55	19,552	7	93	0	0	36	20.88	-13.99		1.00	Sep-11
	4.74	16.50	7.70	41.29	52.13	2.04	0.6	11.73	0.95	21.46	19,552	7	93	0	0	36	21.49	-13.7			Mar-16
	4.54	16.09	6.97	38.43	47.21	1.36	1.29	11.74	0.95	21.56	19,552	7	93	0	0	36	21.07	-13.94			Jan-03
	4.62	16.23	7.24	39.70	49.30	1.68	1.02	11.73	0.95	21.36	19,552	7	93	0	0	36	21.34	-13.82			Oct-06
	5.44	19.59	-1.70	18.32	-3.51	2.91	0.96	13.5	0.89	14.34	116.9	0	100	0	0	98	19.34	-28.89			Jan-18
	5.18	18.96	-2.65	15.33	-7.15	2.51	1.81	13.47	0.89	10.54	116.9	0	100	0	0	98	18.76	-29.14			Jan-03
	5.41	19.50	-1.83	18.01	-3.76	2.36	1.11	13.49	0.89	14.4	116.9	0	100	0	0	98	19.34	-28.89			Oct-88
50	5.29	19.37	-2.07	17.18	-4.81	2.23	1.31	13.47	0.89	14.11	116.9	0	100	0	0	98	19.28	-28.94	5.25		Oct-94
50	5.04	18.95	-2.82	14.48	-8.54	2.47	2.08	13.49	0.89	9.79	116.9	0	100	0	0	98	18.66	-29.21		1.00	Oct-94
	1.98	4.61	7.27	20.67	30.52	0.61	1.63	3.35	6.82	9.73	2,617	48	44	9	0	135	25.64	-22.09			Dec-07
50	1.96	4.58	7.00	19.70	28.92	0.44	1.89	3.36	7.14	9.35	2,617	48	44	9	0	135	25.37	-22.16	5.25		Dec-07
50	1.81	4.20	6.23	17.16	24.33	0.03	2.64	3.33	6.99	8.42	2,617	48	44	9	0	135	24.9	-22.38		1.00	Dec-07
	5.97	18.18	15.92	44.85	49.07	1.47	0.63	11.78	0.91	1178.35	178.4	0	100	0	0	0	21.28	-15.14			Dec-76
	5.47	24.31	10.74	76.41	104.02	0	0.67	14.21	1	5.04	218.6	1	97	0	0	51	21.27	-21.24			Mar-00
50	5.49	24.25	10.45	75.33	100.69	0	0.92	14.16	1	4.63	218.6	1	97	0	0	51	21.33	-21.42	5.25		Mar-00
50	5.08	23.58	9.32	70.99	93.30	0	1.67	14.16	1	3.75	218.6	1	97	0	0	51	20.13	-21.34		1.00	Mar-00
	3.48	14.15	9.65			1.58	0.5			10.97	5.5	0	100	0	0	184					Jun-17
	3.39	14.04	9.57				0.55			10.96	5.5	0	100	0	0	184					Nov-18
	2.90	15.70	-2.04			1.36	0.5			10.61	5.4	0	100	0	0	205					Jun-17
	2.82	15.04	-2.31				0.55			10.61	5.4	0	100	0	0	205					Nov-18
	2.88	11.14	4.13	21.91	18.75	0.89	0.74	6.99	0.61	19.24	26,928	2	58	38	1	154	11.67	-13.61			Jun-16
	2.66	10.75	3.36	19.42	14.87	0.24	1.41	6.97	0.61	18.12	26,928	2	58	38	1	154	11.19	-13.8			Jan-03
	2.88	11.08	4.05	21.59	18.44	0.82	0.81	6.97	0.61	19.24	26,928	2	58	38	1	154	11.67	-13.61			Feb-89
50	2.79	10.91	3.72	20.64	16.81	0.55	1.08	6.98	0.61	19.1	26,928	2	58	38	1	154	11.5	-13.7	5.25		Oct-94

	MARKET			FUND TYPE, CATEGORY & OBJECTIVE	RATINGS				MINIMUMS	
Fund Name	Ticker Symbol	Traded On	Fund Type	Category and (Prospectus Objective)	Overall Rating	Reward Rating	Risk Rating	Recent Up/ Downgrade	Open to New Investors	Min Initial Investment
BlackRock Global Allocation Fund, Inc. Investor C Shares	MCLOX	NAS CM	Open End	Moderate Alloc (Multi-Asset Global)	C+	C	B+	Up	Y	1,000
BlackRock Global Dividend Portfolio Class K	BKBDX	NAS CM	Open End	Global Equity Large Cap (Equity-Income)	C+	C	B-		Y	5,000,000
BlackRock Global Dividend Portfolio Insitutional Shares	BIBDX	NAS CM	Open End	Global Equity Large Cap (Equity-Income)	C+	C	B-		Y	2,000,000
BlackRock Global Dividend Portfolio Investor A Shares	BABDX	NAS CM	Open End	Global Equity Large Cap (Equity-Income)	C+	C	B-		Y	1,000
BlackRock Global Dividend Portfolio Investor C Shares	BCBDX	NAS CM	Open End	Global Equity Large Cap (Equity-Income)	C+	C	B-	Up	Y	1,000
BlackRock Global Long/Short Credit Fund Class K	BDMKX	NAS CM	Open End	Long/Short Credit (Growth & Income)	C+	C	B	Up	Y	5,000,000
BlackRock Global Long/Short Credit Institutional Shares	BGCIX	NAS CM	Open End	Long/Short Credit (Growth & Income)	C+	C	B	Up	Y	2,000,000
BlackRock Global Long/Short Credit Fund Investor A Shares	BGCAX	NAS CM	Open End	Long/Short Credit (Growth & Income)	C	C	B-		Y	1,000
BlackRock Global Long/Short Credit Fund Investor C Shares	BGCCX	NAS CM	Open End	Long/Short Credit (Growth & Income)	C	C	B-		Y	1,000
BlackRock Global Long/Short Equity Fund Class K	BGCKX	NAS CM	Open End	Market Neutral (Growth & Income)	B	C	A		Y	5,000,000
BlackRock Global Long/Short Equity Institutional Shares	BDMIX	NAS CM	Open End	Market Neutral (Growth & Income)	B	C	A		Y	2,000,000
BlackRock Global Long/Short Equity Fund Investor A Shares	BDMAX	NAS CM	Open End	Market Neutral (Growth & Income)	B	C	A		Y	1,000
BlackRock Global Long/Short Equity Fund Investor C Shares	BDMCX	NAS CM	Open End	Market Neutral (Growth & Income)	B	C	A-	Up	Y	1,000
BlackRock Health Sciences Opportunities Portfolio Class K	SHSKX	NAS CM	Open End	Healthcare Sector Equity (Health)	B-	C	B+	Down	Y	5,000,000
BlackRock Health Sciences Opportunities Portfolio Class R	BHSRX	NAS CM	Open End	Healthcare Sector Equity (Health)	B-	C	B+	Down	Y	100
BlackRock Health Sciences Opp Portfolio Inst Shares	SHSSX	NAS CM	Open End	Healthcare Sector Equity (Health)	B-	C	B+	Down	Y	2,000,000
BlackRock Health Sciences Opp Portfolio Inv A Shares	SHSAX	NAS CM	Open End	Healthcare Sector Equity (Health)	B-	C	B+	Down	Y	1,000
BlackRock Health Sciences Opp Portfolio Inv C Shares	SHSCX	NAS CM	Open End	Healthcare Sector Equity (Health)	B-	C	B+	Down	Y	1,000
BlackRock Health Sciences Opp Portfolio Service Shares	SHISX	NAS CM	Open End	Healthcare Sector Equity (Health)	B-	C	B+	Down	Y	5,000
BlackRock Health Sciences Trust	BME	NYSE	Closed End	Healthcare Sector Equity (Health)	C	C	C-	Down	Y	
BlackRock High Equity Income Fund Institutional Shares	BMCIX	NAS CM	Open End	US Equity Large Cap Value (Income)	B-	C	B+	Up	Y	2,000,000
BlackRock High Equity Income Fund Investor A Shares	BMEAX	NAS CM	Open End	US Equity Large Cap Value (Income)	B-	C	B+	Up	Y	1,000
BlackRock High Equity Income Fund Investor C Shares	BMECX	NAS CM	Open End	US Equity Large Cap Value (Income)	B-	C	B+	Up	Y	1,000
BlackRock High Equity Income Fund Service Shares	BMCSX	NAS CM	Open End	US Equity Large Cap Value (Income)	B-	C	B+	Up	Y	5,000
BlackRock Impact U.S. Equity Fund Class K	BIRKX	NAS CM	Open End	US Equity Large Cap Blend (Growth & Income)	B-	C	B		Y	5,000,000
BlackRock Impact U.S. Equity Fund Institutional Shares	BIRIX	NAS CM	Open End	US Equity Large Cap Blend (Growth & Income)	B-	C	B		Y	2,000,000
BlackRock Impact U.S. Equity Fund Investor A Shares	BIRAX	NAS CM	Open End	US Equity Large Cap Blend (Growth & Income)	B-	C	B		Y	1,000
BlackRock Impact U.S. Equity Fund Investor C Shares	BIRCX	NAS CM	Open End	US Equity Large Cap Blend (Growth & Income)	C+	C	B	Down	Y	1,000
BlackRock International Dividend Fund Class K	BREKX	NAS CM	Open End	Global Equity Large Cap (Foreign Stock)	C+	C	B-	Up	Y	5,000,000
BlackRock International Dividend Fund Institutional Shares	BISIX	NAS CM	Open End	Global Equity Large Cap (Foreign Stock)	C+	C	B-	Up	Y	2,000,000
BlackRock International Dividend Fund Investor A Shares	BREAX	NAS CM	Open End	Global Equity Large Cap (Foreign Stock)	C+	C	B-	Up	Y	1,000
BlackRock International Dividend Fund Investor C Shares	BRECX	NAS CM	Open End	Global Equity Large Cap (Foreign Stock)	C	C	B-		Y	1,000
BlackRock International Dividend Fund Service Shares	BRESX	NAS CM	Open End	Global Equity Large Cap (Foreign Stock)	C+	C	B-	Up	Y	5,000
BlackRock Intl of BlackRock Series, Inc.Cls K Shares	MKILX	NAS CM	Open End	Global Equity Large Cap (Foreign Stock)	C	C	C+		Y	5,000,000
BlackRock Intl of BlackRock Series, Inc.Cls R Shares	BIFRX	NAS CM	Open End	Global Equity Large Cap (Foreign Stock)	C	C	C+		Y	100
BlackRock Intl of BlackRock Series, Inc.Inst Shares	MAILX	NAS CM	Open End	Global Equity Large Cap (Foreign Stock)	C	C	C+		Y	2,000,000
BlackRock Intl of BlackRock Series, Inc.Inv A Shares	MDILX	NAS CM	Open End	Global Equity Large Cap (Foreign Stock)	C	C	C+		Y	1,000
BlackRock Intl of BlackRock Series, Inc.Inv C Shares	MCILX	NAS CM	Open End	Global Equity Large Cap (Foreign Stock)	C	C	C+		Y	1,000
BlackRock Large Cap Focus Growth Fund Class K	MLHKX	NAS CM	Open End	US Equity Large Cap Growth (Growth)	B-	B-	B	Down	Y	5,000,000
BlackRock Large Cap Focus Growth Fund Class R	MRLHX	NAS CM	Open End	US Equity Large Cap Growth (Growth)	B-	C+	B	Down	Y	100
BlackRock Large Cap Focus Growth Fund Institutional Shares	MALHX	NAS CM	Open End	US Equity Large Cap Growth (Growth)	B-	B-	B	Down	Y	2,000,000
BlackRock Large Cap Focus Growth Fund Investor A Shares	MDLHX	NAS CM	Open End	US Equity Large Cap Growth (Growth)	B-	C+	B	Down	Y	1,000
BlackRock Large Cap Focus Growth Fund Investor C Shares	MCLHX	NAS CM	Open End	US Equity Large Cap Growth (Growth)	B-	C+	B	Down	Y	1,000
BlackRock Large Cap Focus Growth Fund Service Shares	MSLHX	NAS CM	Open End	US Equity Large Cap Growth (Growth)	B-	C+	B	Down	Y	5,000
BlackRock Latin America Fund, Inc. Institutional Shares	MALTX	NAS CM	Open End	Latin America Equity (Foreign Stock)	C	C-	C+		Y	2,000,000
BlackRock Latin America Fund, Inc. Investor A Shares	MDLTX	NAS CM	Open End	Latin America Equity (Foreign Stock)	C	C-	C+		Y	1,000
BlackRock Latin America Fund, Inc. Investor C Shares	MCLTX	NAS CM	Open End	Latin America Equity (Foreign Stock)	C	C-	C+		Y	1,000
BlackRock Latin America Fund, Inc. K Shares	MKLTX	NAS CM	Open End	Latin America Equity (Foreign Stock)	C	C-	C+		Y	5,000,000
BlackRock LifePath Dynamic 2060 Fund Class K Shares	LPDKX	NAS CM	Open End	Target Date (Asset Alloc)	C	D+	B	Up	Y	5,000,000
BlackRock LifePath Dynamic 2060 Fund Class R Shares	LPDRX	NAS CM	Open End	Target Date (Asset Alloc)	C	D+	B	Up	Y	100
BlackRock LifePath Dynamic 2060 Fund Institutional Shares	LPDIX	NAS CM	Open End	Target Date (Asset Alloc)	C	D+	B	Up	Y	2,000,000
BlackRock LifePath Dynamic 2060 Fund Investor A Shares	LPDAX	NAS CM	Open End	Target Date (Asset Alloc)	C	D+	B	Up	Y	1,000

★ Expanded analysis of this fund is included in Section II.

	TOTAL RETURNS					PERFORMANCE				ASSETS		ASSET ALLOCATION & TURNOVER					BULL & BEAR		FEES		
Min Additional Investment	3-Month Total Return	6-Month Total Return	1-Year Total Return	3-Year Total Return	5-Year Total Return	Dividend Yield (TTM)	Expense Ratio	3-Yr Std Deviation	3-Year Beta	NAV	Total Assets (MIL)	%Cash	%Stocks	%Bonds	%Other	Turnover Ratio	Last Bull Market Total Return	Last Bear Market Total Return	Front End Fee (%)	Back End Fee (%)	Inception Date
50	2.64	10.55	3.00	18.02	12.57	0	1.82	6.96	0.61	17.07	26,928	2	58	38	1	154	10.94	-13.97		1.00	Oct-94
	0.95	13.90	8.77	24.84	26.94	2.76	0.66	10.32	0.81	12.71	1,887	0	100	0	0	30	13.64	-9.67			Jun-16
	0.93	13.81	8.71	24.52	26.72	2.7	0.72	10.31	0.81	12.69	1,887	0	100	0	0	30	13.64	-9.67			Apr-08
50	0.87	13.70	8.35	23.59	25.06	2.45	0.99	10.3	0.81	12.64	1,887	0	100	0	0	30	13.49	-9.83	5.25		Apr-08
50	0.70	13.30	7.65	20.84	20.46	1.72	1.73	10.29	0.81	12.54	1,887	0	100	0	0	30	12.99	-10.1		1.00	Apr-08
	1.52	4.27	2.69	9.36	7.33	5.84	1.94	1.9	3.4	10	3,111	19	1	76	1	185	2.41				Mar-16
	1.52	4.17	2.51	9.20	7.06	5.77	2	1.9	3.75	9.99	3,111	19	1	76	1	185	2.41				Sep-11
50	1.42	4.07	2.28	8.27	5.68	5.46	2.25	1.91	2.78	9.97	3,111	19	1	76	1	185	2.21		4.00		Sep-11
50	1.24	3.60	1.50	5.91	1.74	4.66	3.02	1.91	2.73	9.77	3,111	19	1	76	1	185	1.9			1.00	Sep-11
	2.75	3.25	4.67	22.49	13.70	0	1.52	4.5	4.95	12.69	609.0	84	0	16	1	20					Mar-16
	2.67	3.17	4.58	22.29	13.41	0	1.57	4.52	5.08	12.66	609.0	84	0	16	1	20					Dec-12
50	2.62	3.05	4.27	21.33	11.84	0	1.82	4.5	4.33	12.5	609.0	84	0	16	1	20			5.25		Dec-12
50	2.47	2.74	3.56	18.64	7.86	0	2.57	4.55	5.2	12	609.0	84	0	16	1	20				1.00	Dec-12
	1.22	11.74	11.94	46.89	81.52	0.42	0.77	13.81	0.97	62.6	7,136	2	97	0	1	39	17.33	-12.6			Jun-16
	1.03	11.34	11.17	43.81	76.64	0	1.46	13.8	0.96	58.05	7,136	2	97	0	1	39	17.04	-12.69			Sep-11
	1.19	11.67	11.83	46.41	81.98	0.34	0.87	13.8	0.97	62.54	7,136	2	97	0	1	39	17.55	-12.49			Oct-00
50	1.13	11.51	11.52	45.20	79.45	0.09	1.15	13.8	0.97	59.42	7,136	2	97	0	1	39	17.33	-12.6	5.25		Dec-99
50	0.94	11.11	10.72	42.07	73.07	0	1.87	13.8	0.97	51.69	7,136	2	97	0	1	39	16.8	-12.84		1.00	Oct-00
	1.12	11.50	11.50	45.16	79.40	0.07	1.17	13.81	0.97	59.65	7,136	2	97	0	1	39	17.33	-12.61			Jan-05
	2.11	11.59	11.61	42.12	73.80	0.25		12.04		38.26	358.9	4	98	0	-2	37	16.2	-12.29			Mar-05
	2.77	13.00	5.56	34.93	35.66	4.02	0.85	10.36	0.81	26.61	432.9	1	99	0	0	75	22.78	-24.74			May-98
50	2.71	12.88	5.32	33.87	33.52	4.52	1.1	10.38	0.82	22.49	432.9	1	99	0	0	75	22.44	-24.91	5.25		May-98
50	2.46	12.41	4.52	30.84	28.57	6.12	1.85	10.37	0.82	14.47	432.9	1	99	0	0	75	21.92	-25.13		1.00	May-98
	2.71	12.84	5.28	33.84	33.46	4.23	1.1	10.38	0.82	23.96	432.9	1	99	0	0	75	22.45	-24.89			May-98
	3.92	20.33	8.63	53.53		1.23	0.5	12.67	1.01	13.49	80.0	1	99	0	0	118					Mar-16
	3.93	20.24	8.50	53.29		1.18	0.55	12.64	1	13.48	80.0	1	99	0	0	118					Oct-15
50	3.86	20.10	8.27	52.10		0.98	0.8	12.63	1	13.44	80.0	1	99	0	0	118			5.25		Oct-15
50	3.66	19.64	7.47	48.80		0.46	1.55	12.61	1	13.28	80.0	1	99	0	0	118				1.00	Oct-15
	1.27	14.17	6.89	21.50	3.43	2.24	0.79	10.53	0.81	28.98	242.3	1	97	0	2	25	15.52	-25.22			Jan-18
	1.22	14.16	6.83	21.97	4.50	2.19	0.84	10.53	0.81	28.97	242.3	1	97	0	2	25	15.7	-25.11			Sep-97
50	1.22	14.02	6.58	21.01	3.01	2.1	1.09	10.54	0.81	26.99	242.3	1	97	0	2	25	15.52	-25.22	5.25		Sep-97
50	1.00	13.62	5.81	18.31	-0.74	1.71	1.84	10.53	0.81	23.55	242.3	1	97	0	2	25	15.01	-25.46		1.00	Sep-97
	1.16	14.01	6.55	21.00	3.04	2.07	1.09	10.53	0.81	27.44	242.3	1	97	0	2	25	15.35	-25.23			Sep-97
	3.19	18.32	-2.00	30.97	10.41	1.64	0.83	13.84	1.16	16.22	560.9	5	93	0	-2	102	12.8	-24.27			Jan-18
	2.99	17.99	-2.57	28.56	6.85	1.04	1.4	13.86	1.16	15.88	560.9	5	93	0	-2	102	12.41	-24.44			Aug-11
	3.13	18.32	-2.04	30.83	10.30	1.55	0.9	13.84	1.16	16.22	560.9	5	93	0	-2	102	12.8	-24.27			Oct-98
50	3.06	18.20	-2.30	29.54	8.41	1.34	1.15	13.87	1.16	15.86	560.9	5	93	0	-2	102	12.65	-24.43	5.25		Oct-98
50	2.86	17.68	-3.10	26.22	3.55	0.51	1.9	13.85	1.16	14.79	560.9	5	93	0	-2	102	11.98	-24.68		1.00	Oct-98
	5.69	24.65	10.56	82.87	98.13	0	0.62	14.26	1.02	13.63	975.6	2	97	0	1	49	29.69	-20.51			Jan-18
	5.56	24.26	9.97	79.84	92.83	0	1.17	14.22	1.02	11.07	975.6	2	97	0	1	49	29.05	-20.64			Jan-03
	5.69	24.65	10.55	82.84	98.10	0	0.67	14.26	1.02	13.63	975.6	2	97	0	1	49	29.69	-20.51			Dec-99
50	5.61	24.47	10.16	81.17	95.16	0	0.92	14.24	1.02	12.48	975.6	2	97	0	1	49	29.37	-20.58	5.25		Dec-99
50	5.44	23.97	9.30	76.87	87.46	0	1.67	14.19	1.01	9.15	975.6	2	97	0	1	49	28.91	-20.89		1.00	Dec-99
	5.58	24.46	10.21	81.26	95.23	0	0.92	14.25	1.02	13.51	975.6	2	97	0	1	49	29.4	-20.53			Oct-06
	7.38	13.68	25.43	44.94	0.70	1.03	1.34	22.38	1.04	53.83	162.8	3	97	0	0	48	16.86	-28.94			Oct-94
50	7.29	13.52	25.07	43.60	-0.81	0.75	1.64	22.38	1.04	53.13	162.8	3	97	0	0	48	16.71	-29.04	5.25		Sep-91
50	7.08	13.06	24.05	40.12	-4.88	0	2.45	22.37	1.04	48.38	162.8	3	97	0	0	48	16.16	-29.26		1.00	Oct-94
	7.38	13.70	25.47	44.33	-0.31	1.1	1.3	22.37	1.04	53.83	162.8	3	97	0	0	48	16.71	-29.04			Jan-18
	3.17	17.50	5.97			1.97	0.47			10.82	2.5	11	88	1	0	58					May-17
	3.00	17.18	5.30			1.37	1.12			10.82	2.5	11	88	1	0	58					May-17
	3.16	17.49	5.80			1.82	0.67			10.82	2.5	11	88	1	0	58					May-17
50	3.07	17.27	5.47			1.61	0.92			10.81	2.5	11	88	1	0	58			5.25		May-17

	MARKET		FUND TYPE, CATEGORY & OBJECTIVE		RATINGS				MINIMUMS	
Fund Name	Ticker Symbol	Traded On	Fund Type	Category and (Prospectus Objective)	Overall Rating	Reward Rating	Risk Rating	Recent Up/ Downgrade	Open to New Investors	Min Initial Investment
BlackRock LifePath Dynamic 2060 Fund Investor C Shares	LPDCX	NAS CM	Open End	Target Date (Asset Alloc)	C	D+	B	Up	Y	1,000
Blackrock Lifepath Smart Beta 2060 Institutional Shares	BIEGX	NAS CM	Open End	Target Date (Asset Alloc)	C	D	B-	Up	Y	2,000,000
Blackrock Lifepath Smart Beta 2060 Fund Investor A Shares	BAPAX	NAS CM	Open End	Target Date (Asset Alloc)	C	D	B-	Up	Y	1,000
Blackrock Lifepath Smart Beta 2060 Fund K Shares	BKJKX	NAS CM	Open End	Target Date (Asset Alloc)	C	D	B-	Up	Y	5,000,000
Blackrock Lifepath Smart Beta 2060 Fund R Shares	BAPRX	NAS CM	Open End	Target Date (Asset Alloc)	C-	D	B-	Up	Y	100
BlackRock LifePath® Dynamic 2020 Fund Class K Shares	LPSCX	NAS CM	Open End	Target Date (Asset Alloc)	B	C+	A		Y	5,000,000
BlackRock LifePath® Dynamic 2020 Fund Class R Shares	LPRMX	NAS CM	Open End	Target Date (Asset Alloc)	B	C+	A	Up	Y	100
BlackRock LifePath® Dynamic 2020 Fund Institutional Shares	STLCX	NAS CM	Open End	Target Date (Asset Alloc)	B	C+	A	Up	Y	2,000,000
BlackRock LifePath® Dynamic 2020 Fund Investor A Shares	LPRCX	NAS CM	Open End	Target Date (Asset Alloc)	B	C+	A	Up	Y	1,000
BlackRock LifePath® Dynamic 2020 Fund Investor C Shares	LPCMX	NAS CM	Open End	Target Date (Asset Alloc)	B	C	A-	Up	Y	1,000
BlackRock LifePath® Dynamic 2025 Fund Class K Shares	LPBKX	NAS CM	Open End	Target Date (Asset Alloc)	B	C+	A-	Up	Y	5,000,000
BlackRock LifePath® Dynamic 2025 Fund Class R Shares	LPBRX	NAS CM	Open End	Target Date (Asset Alloc)	B	C	A-	Up	Y	100
BlackRock LifePath® Dynamic 2025 Fund Institutional Shares	LPBIX	NAS CM	Open End	Target Date (Asset Alloc)	B	C+	A-	Up	Y	2,000,000
BlackRock LifePath® Dynamic 2025 Fund Investor A Shares	LPBAX	NAS CM	Open End	Target Date (Asset Alloc)	B	C+	A-	Up	Y	1,000
BlackRock LifePath® Dynamic 2025 Fund Investor C Shares	LPBCX	NAS CM	Open End	Target Date (Asset Alloc)	B-	C	A-	Up	Y	1,000
BlackRock LifePath® Dynamic 2030 Fund Class K Shares	LPSDX	NAS CM	Open End	Target Date (Asset Alloc)	B	C+	A-	Up	Y	5,000,000
BlackRock LifePath® Dynamic 2030 Fund Class R Shares	LPRNX	NAS CM	Open End	Target Date (Asset Alloc)	B-	C	A-		Y	100
BlackRock LifePath® Dynamic 2030 Fund Institutional Shares	STLDX	NAS CM	Open End	Target Date (Asset Alloc)	B	C	A-	Up	Y	2,000,000
BlackRock LifePath® Dynamic 2030 Fund Investor A Shares	LPRDX	NAS CM	Open End	Target Date (Asset Alloc)	B-	C	A-		Y	1,000
BlackRock LifePath® Dynamic 2030 Fund Investor C Shares	LPCNX	NAS CM	Open End	Target Date (Asset Alloc)	B-	C	B+	Up	Y	1,000
BlackRock LifePath® Dynamic 2035 Fund Class K Shares	LPJKX	NAS CM	Open End	Target Date (Asset Alloc)	B-	C	B+		Y	5,000,000
BlackRock LifePath® Dynamic 2035 Fund Class R Shares	LPJRX	NAS CM	Open End	Target Date (Asset Alloc)	B-	C	B+	Up	Y	100
BlackRock LifePath® Dynamic 2035 Fund Institutional Shares	LPJIX	NAS CM	Open End	Target Date (Asset Alloc)	B-	C	B+		Y	2,000,000
BlackRock LifePath® Dynamic 2035 Fund Investor A Shares	LPJAX	NAS CM	Open End	Target Date (Asset Alloc)	B-	C	B+	Up	Y	1,000
BlackRock LifePath® Dynamic 2035 Fund Investor C Shares	LPJCX	NAS CM	Open End	Target Date (Asset Alloc)	B-	C	B+	Up	Y	1,000
BlackRock LifePath® Dynamic 2040 Fund Class K Shares	LPSFX	NAS CM	Open End	Target Date (Asset Alloc)	B-	C	B+	Up	Y	5,000,000
BlackRock LifePath® Dynamic 2040 Fund Class R Shares	LPRKX	NAS CM	Open End	Target Date (Asset Alloc)	B-	C	B	Up	Y	100
BlackRock LifePath® Dynamic 2040 Fund Institutional Shares	STLEX	NAS CM	Open End	Target Date (Asset Alloc)	B-	C	B+	Up	Y	2,000,000
BlackRock LifePath® Dynamic 2040 Fund Investor A Shares	LPREX	NAS CM	Open End	Target Date (Asset Alloc)	B-	C	B+	Up	Y	1,000
BlackRock LifePath® Dynamic 2040 Fund Investor C Shares	LPCKX	NAS CM	Open End	Target Date (Asset Alloc)	B-	C	B	Up	Y	1,000
BlackRock LifePath® Dynamic 2045 Fund Class K Shares	LPHKX	NAS CM	Open End	Target Date (Asset Alloc)	B-	C	B	Up	Y	5,000,000
BlackRock LifePath® Dynamic 2045 Fund Class R Shares	LPHRX	NAS CM	Open End	Target Date (Asset Alloc)	B-	C	B	Up	Y	100
BlackRock LifePath® Dynamic 2045 Fund Institutional Shares	LPHIX	NAS CM	Open End	Target Date (Asset Alloc)	B-	C	B	Up	Y	2,000,000
BlackRock LifePath® Dynamic 2045 Fund Investor A Shares	LPHAX	NAS CM	Open End	Target Date (Asset Alloc)	B-	C	B	Up	Y	1,000
BlackRock LifePath® Dynamic 2045 Fund Investor C Shares	LPHCX	NAS CM	Open End	Target Date (Asset Alloc)	B-	C	B	Up	Y	1,000
BlackRock LifePath® Dynamic 2050 Fund Class K Shares	LPSGX	NAS CM	Open End	Target Date (Asset Alloc)	B-	C	B	Up	Y	5,000,000
BlackRock LifePath® Dynamic 2050 Fund Class R Shares	LPRPX	NAS CM	Open End	Target Date (Asset Alloc)	B-	C	B	Up	Y	100
BlackRock LifePath® Dynamic 2050 Fund Institutional Shares	STLFX	NAS CM	Open End	Target Date (Asset Alloc)	B-	C	B	Up	Y	2,000,000
BlackRock LifePath® Dynamic 2050 Fund Investor A Shares	LPRFX	NAS CM	Open End	Target Date (Asset Alloc)	B-	C	B	Up	Y	1,000
BlackRock LifePath® Dynamic 2050 Porfolio Inv C Shares	LPCPX	NAS CM	Open End	Target Date (Asset Alloc)	B-	C	B	Up	Y	1,000
BlackRock LifePath® Dynamic 2055 Fund Class K Shares	LPVKX	NAS CM	Open End	Target Date (Asset Alloc)	B-	C	B	Up	Y	5,000,000
BlackRock LifePath® Dynamic 2055 Fund Class R Shares	LPVRX	NAS CM	Open End	Target Date (Asset Alloc)	B-	C	B	Up	Y	100
BlackRock LifePath® Dynamic 2055 Fund Institutional Shares	LPVIX	NAS CM	Open End	Target Date (Asset Alloc)	B-	C	B	Up	Y	2,000,000
BlackRock LifePath® Dynamic 2055 Fund Investor A Shares	LPVAX	NAS CM	Open End	Target Date (Asset Alloc)	B-	C	B	Up	Y	1,000
BlackRock LifePath® Dynamic 2055 Fund Investor C Shares	LPVCX	NAS CM	Open End	Target Date (Asset Alloc)	B-	C	B	Up	Y	1,000
BlackRock LifePath® Dynamic Retirement Fund Class K Shares	LPSAX	NAS CM	Open End	Target Date (Asset Alloc)	B	C+	A		Y	5,000,000
BlackRock LifePath® Dynamic Retirement Fund Class R Shares	LPRRX	NAS CM	Open End	Target Date (Asset Alloc)	B	C+	A-	Up	Y	100
BlackRock LifePath® Dynamic Retmnt Inst Shares	STLAX	NAS CM	Open End	Target Date (Asset Alloc)	B	C+	A		Y	2,000,000
BlackRock LifePath® Dynamic Retirement Investor A Shares	LPRAX	NAS CM	Open End	Target Date (Asset Alloc)	B	C+	A	Up	Y	1,000
BlackRock LifePath® Dynamic Retirement Investor C Shares	LPCRX	NAS CM	Open End	Target Date (Asset Alloc)	B	C+	A-	Up	Y	1,000
BlackRock LifePath® Index 2020 Fund Class K Shares	LIMKX	NAS CM	Open End	Target Date (Asset Alloc)	B	C+	A-	Up	Y	5,000,000
BlackRock LifePath® Index 2020 Fund Institutional Shares	LIQIX	NAS CM	Open End	Target Date (Asset Alloc)	B	C+	A-	Up	Y	2,000,000

★ Expanded analysis of this fund is included in Section II.

	TOTAL RETURNS					PERFORMANCE				ASSETS		ASSET ALLOCATION & TURNOVER					BULL & BEAR		FEES		
Min Additional Investment	3-Month Total Return	6-Month Total Return	1-Year Total Return	3-Year Total Return	5-Year Total Return	Dividend Yield (TTM)	Expense Ratio	3-Yr Std Deviation	3-Year Beta	NAV	Total Assets (MIL)	%Cash	%Stocks	%Bonds	%Other	Turnover Ratio	Last Bull Market Total Return	Last Bear Market Total Return	Front End Fee (%)	Back End Fee (%)	Inception Date
50	2.77	16.73	4.61			0.93	1.72			10.79	2.5	11	88	1	0	58				1.00	May-17
	1.54	14.31	1.69			3.1	0.35			10.6	1.5	3	94	3	0	36					May-17
50	1.54	14.28	1.53			2.88	0.6			10.59	1.5	3	94	3	0	36			5.25		May-17
	1.54	14.32	1.80			3.2	0.25			10.61	1.5	3	94	3	0	36					May-17
	1.45	14.10	1.25			3.07	0.84			10.53	1.5	3	94	3	0	36					May-17
	3.32	12.68	7.29	26.30	28.94	2.11	0.47	6.02	0.45	15.48	296.3	4	39	56	0	19	13.79	-9.73			May-08
	3.09	12.24	6.54	23.87	24.40	1.56	1.12	6.06	0.45	15.43	296.3	4	39	56	0	19	13.24	-9.98			May-10
	3.25	12.52	7.02	25.62	27.33	1.89	0.67	6.03	0.45	15.55	296.3	4	39	56	0	19	13.57	-9.84			Mar-94
50	3.14	12.35	6.71	24.64	25.78	1.86	0.92	6.02	0.45	14.19	296.3	4	39	56	0	19	13.46	-9.95	5.25		Apr-01
50	2.97	11.94	5.90	21.71	20.95	0.96	1.72	6.02	0.45	15.31	296.3	4	39	56	0	19	12.89	-10.17		1.00	May-10
	3.28	13.91	7.39	30.24	32.01	2.32	0.47	7.17	0.55	13.12	58.5	7	50	43	0	38	15.54	-11.81			Jun-10
	3.11	13.49	6.72	27.62	27.45	1.8	1.12	7.2	0.55	13.1	58.5	7	50	43	0	38	14.91	-12.12			Jun-10
	3.20	13.75	7.10	29.31	30.30	1.44	0.67	7.19	0.55	13.25	58.5	7	50	43	0	38	15.21	-11.94			Jun-10
50	3.17	13.61	6.89	28.43	28.83	1.89	0.92	7.12	0.54	13.13	58.5	7	50	43	0	38	15.19	-12.08	5.25		Jun-10
50	2.91	13.12	6.04	25.37	23.83	1.19	1.72	7.17	0.55	13.05	58.5	7	50	43	0	38	14.57	-12.3		1.00	Jun-10
	3.30	15.23	7.32	34.14	35.25	1.96	0.47	8.29	0.64	13.48	338.3	8	62	31	0	29	16.99	-13.44			May-08
	3.09	14.86	6.64	31.44	30.41	1.46	1.12	8.32	0.64	13.33	338.3	8	62	31	0	29	16.31	-13.77			May-10
	3.17	15.11	7.07	33.23	33.48	1.75	0.67	8.35	0.65	13.5	338.3	8	62	31	0	29	16.7	-13.6			Mar-94
50	3.17	14.98	6.82	32.23	31.84	1.62	0.92	8.33	0.65	12.91	338.3	8	62	31	0	29	16.46	-13.66	5.25		Apr-01
50	2.90	14.48	5.91	29.03	26.72	0.85	1.72	8.33	0.64	13.21	338.3	8	62	31	0	29	15.97	-13.88		1.00	May-10
	3.22	16.17	6.98	36.80	37.10	1.96	0.46	9.31	0.73	14.14	54.4	9	71	21	0	40	18.35	-14.97			Jun-10
	3.06	15.76	6.28	34.15	32.41	1.48	1.11	9.28	0.72	13.88	54.4	9	71	21	0	40	17.79	-15.3			Jun-10
	3.14	16.00	6.79	36.04	35.56	1.56	0.66	9.29	0.72	13.96	54.4	9	71	21	0	40	18.12	-15.05			Jun-10
50	3.09	15.90	6.54	35.08	33.93	1.57	0.91	9.34	0.73	13.9	54.4	9	71	21	0	40	18.01	-15.19	5.25		Jun-10
50	2.93	15.51	5.72	31.88	28.75	0.87	1.71	9.33	0.73	13.75	54.4	9	71	21	0	40	17.44	-15.49		1.00	Jun-10
	3.21	17.31	6.77	39.63	39.17	1.69	0.46	10.31	0.81	16.97	275.9	10	80	10	0	39	19.62	-16.41			May-08
	3.00	16.89	6.06	36.85	34.24	1.18	1.11	10.26	0.8	16.69	275.9	10	80	10	0	39	18.95	-16.75			May-10
	3.18	17.23	6.58	38.89	37.50	1.51	0.66	10.28	0.8	16.88	275.9	10	80	10	0	39	19.28	-16.57			Mar-94
50	3.13	17.04	6.29	37.76	35.77	1.46	0.91	10.26	0.8	15.24	275.9	10	80	10	0	39	19.09	-16.64	5.25		Apr-01
50	2.86	16.57	5.41	34.43	30.46	0.58	1.71	10.25	0.8	16.57	275.9	10	80	10	0	39	18.55	-16.93		1.00	May-10
	3.14	17.74	6.48	40.60	39.50	1.71	0.45	10.86	0.85	14.93	36.7	9	86	5	0	47	20.89	-17.74			Jun-10
	3.01	17.44	5.81	37.95	34.92	1.19	1.1	10.84	0.85	14.7	36.7	9	86	5	0	47	20.22	-18			Jun-10
	3.12	17.62	6.27	39.83	38.05	1.44	0.65	10.88	0.85	14.78	36.7	9	86	5	0	47	20.55	-17.81			Jun-10
50	3.07	17.50	6.01	38.72	36.34	1.31	0.9	10.87	0.85	14.74	36.7	9	86	5	0	47	20.38	-17.86	5.25		Jun-10
50	2.85	17.05	5.15	35.52	31.11	0.62	1.7	10.83	0.85	14.52	36.7	9	86	5	0	47	19.78	-18.11		1.00	Jun-10
	3.21	17.52	6.21	40.90	39.83	1.6	0.45	10.96	0.86	19.88	105.5	10	88	2	0	43	21.84	-18.93			Jun-08
	3.04	17.15	5.54	38.19	34.97	1.07	1.1	10.94	0.86	19.66	105.5	10	88	2	0	43	21.25	-19.21			May-10
	3.17	17.44	5.99	40.15	38.14	1.39	0.65	10.97	0.86	19.82	105.5	10	88	2	0	43	21.62	-19.03			Jun-08
50	3.12	17.25	5.72	39.06	36.40	1.19	0.9	10.97	0.86	19.74	105.5	10	88	2	0	43	21.41	-19.1	5.25		Jun-08
50	2.91	16.79	4.92	35.77	31.20	0.58	1.7	10.95	0.86	19.48	105.5	10	88	2	0	43	20.87	-19.36		1.00	May-10
	3.17	17.39	6.01	40.32	39.04	1.66	0.45	10.92	0.86	15.45	22.7	11	88	1	0	57	22.39	-19.43			Jun-10
	3.05	17.07	5.35	37.65	34.11	1.19	1.1	10.94	0.86	15.14	22.7	11	88	1	0	57	21.77	-19.71			Jun-10
	3.17	17.33	5.82	39.57	37.45	1.39	0.65	10.93	0.86	15.26	22.7	11	88	1	0	57	22.22	-19.58			Jun-10
50	3.12	17.17	5.58	38.51	35.69	1.27	0.9	10.93	0.86	15.18	22.7	11	88	1	0	57	21.95	-19.65	5.25		Jun-10
50	2.90	16.67	4.72	35.27	30.43	0.64	1.7	10.95	0.86	14.96	22.7	11	88	1	0	57	21.4	-19.95		1.00	Jun-10
	3.30	12.20	7.29	23.27	26.84	2.02	0.47	5.54	0.45	10.68	116.3	5	35	60	0	38	10.35	-5.11			May-08
	3.21	11.91	6.70	20.98	22.42	1.48	1.12	5.54	0.46	10.62	116.3	5	35	60	0	38	9.82	-5.52			May-10
	3.23	12.09	7.13	22.51	25.29	1.81	0.67	5.54	0.45	10.73	116.3	5	35	60	0	38	10.13	-5.29			Mar-94
50	3.22	11.91	6.85	21.70	23.79	1.89	0.92	5.55	0.46	9.34	116.3	5	35	60	0	38	9.97	-5.36	5.25		Apr-01
50	2.93	11.51	5.99	18.67	19.01	0.83	1.72	5.54	0.46	10.58	116.3	5	35	60	0	38	9.4	-5.61		1.00	May-10
	3.29	11.23	6.76	22.84	27.58	2.35	0.1	5.53	0.41	13.04	4,737	4	42	54	0	20	13.76				May-11
	3.28	11.19	6.71	22.64	27.26	2.3	0.15	5.51	0.41	13.04	4,737	4	42	54	0	20	13.74				May-11

Fund Name	Ticker Symbol	Traded On	Fund Type	Category and (Prospectus Objective)	Overall Rating	Reward Rating	Risk Rating	Recent Up/ Downgrade	Open to New Investors	Min Initial Investment
	MARKET		FUND TYPE, CATEGORY & OBJECTIVE		RATINGS				MINIMUMS	
BlackRock LifePath® Index 2020 Fund Investor A Shares	LIQAX	NAS CM	Open End	Target Date (Asset Alloc)	B	C+	A-	Up	Y	1,000
BlackRock LifePath® Index 2020 Fund Investor P Shares	LIQPX	NAS CM	Open End	Target Date (Asset Alloc)	B	C+	A-	Up	Y	1,000
BlackRock LifePath® Index 2025 Fund Class K Shares	LIBKX	NAS CM	Open End	Target Date (Asset Alloc)	B	C+	A-	Up	Y	5,000,000
BlackRock LifePath® Index 2025 Fund Institutional Shares	LIBIX	NAS CM	Open End	Target Date (Asset Alloc)	B	C+	A-	Up	Y	2,000,000
BlackRock LifePath® Index 2025 Fund Investor A Shares	LILAX	NAS CM	Open End	Target Date (Asset Alloc)	B	C	A-	Up	Y	1,000
BlackRock LifePath® Index 2025 Fund Investor P Shares	LILPX	NAS CM	Open End	Target Date (Asset Alloc)	B	C	A-	Up	Y	1,000
BlackRock LifePath® Index 2030 Fund Class K Shares	LINKX	NAS CM	Open End	Target Date (Asset Alloc)	B-	C	A-		Y	5,000,000
BlackRock LifePath® Index 2030 Fund Institutional Shares	LINIX	NAS CM	Open End	Target Date (Asset Alloc)	B-	C	A-		Y	2,000,000
BlackRock LifePath® Index 2030 Fund Investor A Shares	LINAX	NAS CM	Open End	Target Date (Asset Alloc)	B-	C+	A-		Y	1,000
BlackRock LifePath® Index 2030 Fund Investor P Shares	LIDPX	NAS CM	Open End	Target Date (Asset Alloc)	B-	C	A-		Y	1,000
BlackRock LifePath® Index 2035 Fund Class K Shares	LIJKX	NAS CM	Open End	Target Date (Asset Alloc)	B-	C	B+		Y	5,000,000
BlackRock LifePath® Index 2035 Fund Institutional Shares	LIJIX	NAS CM	Open End	Target Date (Asset Alloc)	B-	C	B+		Y	2,000,000
BlackRock LifePath® Index 2035 Fund Investor A Shares	LIJAX	NAS CM	Open End	Target Date (Asset Alloc)	B-	C	B+	Up	Y	1,000
BlackRock LifePath® Index 2035 Fund Investor P Shares	LIJPX	NAS CM	Open End	Target Date (Asset Alloc)	B-	C	B+	Up	Y	1,000
BlackRock LifePath® Index 2040 Fund Class K Shares	LIKKX	NAS CM	Open End	Target Date (Asset Alloc)	B-	C	B+	Up	Y	5,000,000
BlackRock LifePath® Index 2040 Fund Institutional Shares	LIKIX	NAS CM	Open End	Target Date (Asset Alloc)	B-	C	B+	Up	Y	2,000,000
BlackRock LifePath® Index 2040 Fund Investor A Shares	LIKAX	NAS CM	Open End	Target Date (Asset Alloc)	B-	C	B+	Up	Y	1,000
BlackRock LifePath® Index 2040 Fund Investor P Shares	LIKPX	NAS CM	Open End	Target Date (Asset Alloc)	B-	C	B+	Up	Y	1,000
BlackRock LifePath® Index 2045 Fund Class K Shares	LIHKX	NAS CM	Open End	Target Date (Asset Alloc)	B-	C	B	Up	Y	5,000,000
BlackRock LifePath® Index 2045 Fund Institutional Shares	LIHIX	NAS CM	Open End	Target Date (Asset Alloc)	B-	C	B	Up	Y	2,000,000
BlackRock LifePath® Index 2045 Fund Investor A Shares	LIHAX	NAS CM	Open End	Target Date (Asset Alloc)	B-	C	B	Up	Y	1,000
BlackRock LifePath® Index 2045 Fund Investor P Shares	LIHPX	NAS CM	Open End	Target Date (Asset Alloc)	B-	C	B	Up	Y	1,000
BlackRock LifePath® Index 2050 Fund Class K Shares	LIPKX	NAS CM	Open End	Target Date (Asset Alloc)	B-	C	B	Up	Y	5,000,000
BlackRock LifePath® Index 2050 Fund Institutional Shares	LIPIX	NAS CM	Open End	Target Date (Asset Alloc)	B-	C	B	Up	Y	2,000,000
BlackRock LifePath® Index 2050 Fund Investor A Shares	LIPAX	NAS CM	Open End	Target Date (Asset Alloc)	B-	C	B	Up	Y	1,000
BlackRock LifePath® Index 2050 Fund Investor P Shares	LIPPX	NAS CM	Open End	Target Date (Asset Alloc)	B-	C	B	Up	Y	1,000
BlackRock LifePath® Index 2055 Fund Class K Shares	LIVKX	NAS CM	Open End	Target Date (Asset Alloc)	B-	C	B	Up	Y	5,000,000
BlackRock LifePath® Index 2055 Fund Institutional Shares	LIVIX	NAS CM	Open End	Target Date (Asset Alloc)	B-	C	B	Up	Y	2,000,000
BlackRock LifePath® Index 2055 Fund Investor A Shares	LIVAX	NAS CM	Open End	Target Date (Asset Alloc)	B-	C	B	Up	Y	1,000
BlackRock LifePath® Index 2055 Fund Investor P Shares	LIVPX	NAS CM	Open End	Target Date (Asset Alloc)	B-	C	B	Up	Y	1,000
BlackRock LifePath® Index 2060 Fund Class K	LIZKX	NAS CM	Open End	Target Date (Asset Alloc)	B-	C	B	Up	Y	5,000,000
BlackRock LifePath® Index 2060 Fund Institutional Shares	LIZIX	NAS CM	Open End	Target Date (Asset Alloc)	B-	C	B	Up	Y	2,000,000
BlackRock LifePath® Index 2060 Fund Investor A Shares	LIZAX	NAS CM	Open End	Target Date (Asset Alloc)	B-	C	B	Up	Y	1,000
BlackRock LifePath® Index 2060 Fund Investor P Shares	LIZPX	NAS CM	Open End	Target Date (Asset Alloc)	B-	C	B	Up	Y	1,000
BlackRock LifePath® Index Retirement Fund Class K Shares	LIRKX	NAS CM	Open End	Target Date (Asset Alloc)	B	C+	A-	Up	Y	5,000,000
BlackRock LifePath® Index Retirement Institutional Shares	LIRIX	NAS CM	Open End	Target Date (Asset Alloc)	B	C+	A-	Up	Y	2,000,000
BlackRock LifePath® Index Retirement Investor A Shares	LIRAX	NAS CM	Open End	Target Date (Asset Alloc)	B	C+	A-	Up	Y	1,000
BlackRock LifePath® Index Retirement Investor P Shares	LIRPX	NAS CM	Open End	Target Date (Asset Alloc)	B	C+	A-	Up	Y	1,000
BlackRock LifePath® Smart Beta 2020 Fund Class K	BIPCX	NAS CM	Open End	Target Date (Asset Alloc)	B	C+	A	Up	Y	5,000,000
BlackRock LifePath® Smart Beta 2020 Fund Class R Shares	BRPCX	NAS CM	Open End	Target Date (Asset Alloc)	B	C+	A-	Up	Y	100
BlackRock LifePath® Smart Beta 2020 Institutional Shares	BLBIX	NAS CM	Open End	Target Date (Asset Alloc)	B	C+	A	Up	Y	2,000,000
BlackRock LifePath® Smart Beta 2020 Fund Investor A Shares	BAPCX	NAS CM	Open End	Target Date (Asset Alloc)	B	C+	A	Up	Y	1,000
BlackRock LifePath® Smart Beta 2025 Fund Class K	BIPDX	NAS CM	Open End	Target Date (Asset Alloc)	B	C	A-	Up	Y	5,000,000
BlackRock LifePath® Smart Beta 2025 Fund Class R Shares	BRPDX	NAS CM	Open End	Target Date (Asset Alloc)	B	C	A-	Up	Y	100
BlackRock LifePath® Smart Beta 2025 Institutional Shares	BLCIX	NAS CM	Open End	Target Date (Asset Alloc)	B	C	A-	Up	Y	2,000,000
BlackRock LifePath® Smart Beta 2025 Fund Investor A Shares	BAPDX	NAS CM	Open End	Target Date (Asset Alloc)	B	C	A-	Up	Y	1,000
BlackRock LifePath® Smart Beta 2030 Fund Class K	BIPEX	NAS CM	Open End	Target Date (Asset Alloc)	B-	C	A-	Up	Y	5,000,000
BlackRock LifePath® Smart Beta 2030 Fund Class R Shares	BRPEX	NAS CM	Open End	Target Date (Asset Alloc)	B-	C	A-	Up	Y	100
BlackRock LifePath® Smart Beta 2030 Institutional Shares	BLEIX	NAS CM	Open End	Target Date (Asset Alloc)	B-	C	A-	Up	Y	2,000,000
BlackRock LifePath® Smart Beta 2030 Fund Investor A Shares	BAPEX	NAS CM	Open End	Target Date (Asset Alloc)	B-	C	A-	Up	Y	1,000
BlackRock LifePath® Smart Beta 2035 Fund Class K	BIPGX	NAS CM	Open End	Target Date (Asset Alloc)	B-	C	B+	Up	Y	5,000,000
BlackRock LifePath® Smart Beta 2035 Fund Class R Shares	BRPGX	NAS CM	Open End	Target Date (Asset Alloc)	B-	C	B+	Up	Y	100

★Expanded analysis of this fund is included in Section II.

Min Additional Investment	3-Month Total Return	6-Month Total Return	1-Year Total Return	3-Year Total Return	5-Year Total Return	Dividend Yield (TTM)	Expense Ratio	3-Yr Std Deviation	3-Year Beta	NAV	Total Assets (MIL)	%Cash	%Stocks	%Bonds	%Other	Turnover Ratio	Last Bull Market Total Return	Last Bear Market Total Return	Front End Fee (%)	Back End Fee (%)	Inception Date
	TOTAL RETURNS					PERFORMANCE				ASSETS		ASSET ALLOCATION & TURNOVER					BULL & BEAR		FEES		
50	3.15	11.01	6.38	21.72	25.71	2.07	0.4	5.48	0.41	13.01	4,737	4	42	54	0	20	13.5				May-11
50	3.15	11.07	6.42	21.84	25.92		0.4	5.47	0.41	13	4,737	4	42	54	0	20	13.59		5.25		Aug-18
	3.21	12.62	6.83	26.58	30.95	2.43	0.1	6.73	0.52	13.67	3,720	3	55	41	0	11	15.29				May-11
	3.28	12.67	6.78	26.38	30.72	2.39	0.15	6.69	0.51	13.67	3,720	3	55	41	0	11	15.39				May-11
50	3.15	12.48	6.52	25.42	29.01	2.15	0.4	6.74	0.52	13.65	3,720	3	55	41	0	11	15.17				May-11
50	3.17	12.44	6.56	25.64	29.32		0.4	6.71	0.51	13.63	3,720	3	55	41	0	11	15.12		5.25		Aug-18
	3.19	13.81	6.82	29.87	33.85	2.34	0.1	7.77	0.6	14.05	6,723	2	67	31	0	15	16.76				May-11
	3.18	13.77	6.77	29.64	33.37	2.3	0.15	7.8	0.61	14.06	6,723	2	67	31	0	15	16.86				May-11
50	3.19	13.65	6.51	28.84	31.91	2.06	0.4	7.82	0.61	14.06	6,723	2	67	31	0	15	16.6				May-11
50	3.19	13.70	6.56	28.90	32.18		0.4	7.79	0.6	14.05	6,723	2	67	31	0	15	16.59		5.25		Aug-18
	3.24	14.92	6.84	33.08	36.56	2.41	0.1	8.83	0.69	14.52	3,312	2	78	20	0	10	18.03				May-11
	3.23	14.86	6.71	32.96	36.19	2.36	0.15	8.82	0.69	14.53	3,312	2	78	20	0	10	18.02				May-11
50	3.18	14.78	6.53	31.99	34.56	2.13	0.4	8.85	0.69	14.5	3,312	2	78	20	0	10	17.77				May-11
50	3.19	14.79	6.54	32.05	34.82		0.4	8.83	0.69	14.48	3,312	2	78	20	0	10	17.86		5.25		Aug-18
	3.20	15.97	6.79	36.00	38.89	2.38	0.1	9.78	0.77	14.88	5,278	2	87	11	0	12	19.26				May-11
	3.19	15.94	6.75	35.80	38.54	2.34	0.15	9.81	0.77	14.88	5,278	2	87	11	0	12	19.37				May-11
50	3.21	15.84	6.49	34.80	36.87	2.1	0.4	9.79	0.77	14.86	5,278	2	87	11	0	12	19.11				May-11
50	3.13	15.73	6.47	34.91	37.09		0.4	9.8	0.77	14.84	5,278	2	87	11	0	12	19.09		5.25		Aug-18
	3.23	16.69	6.81	37.85	40.64	2.43	0.1	10.46	0.82	15.27	2,339	1	94	4	0	8	20.26				May-11
	3.15	16.68	6.69	37.58	40.23	2.38	0.15	10.45	0.82	15.25	2,339	1	94	4	0	8	20.24				May-11
50	3.10	16.51	6.45	36.60	38.47	2.15	0.4	10.48	0.82	15.22	2,339	1	94	4	0	8	20.12				May-11
50	3.17	16.58	6.50	36.76	38.83		0.4	10.48	0.82	15.21	2,339	1	94	4	0	8	20.08		5.25		Aug-18
	3.20	17.02	6.71	38.32	41.03	2.4	0.1	10.78	0.85	15.51	2,524	1	97	1	0	11	21.48				May-11
	3.19	16.97	6.66	38.11	40.67	2.36	0.15	10.77	0.85	15.51	2,524	1	97	1	0	11	21.59				May-11
50	3.14	16.89	6.42	37.15	38.93	2.13	0.4	10.79	0.85	15.48	2,524	1	97	1	0	11	21.33				May-11
50	3.07	16.88	6.39	37.21	39.20		0.4	10.76	0.85	15.46	2,524	1	97	1	0	11	21.3		5.25		Aug-18
	3.21	17.07	6.72	38.35	41.16	2.4	0.09	10.77	0.85	15.82	1,157	1	98	1	0	8	22.07				May-11
	3.20	17.03	6.67	38.14	40.82	2.36	0.14	10.77	0.85	15.82	1,157	1	98	1	0	8	22.04				May-11
50	3.09	16.87	6.36	37.11	39.01	2.14	0.39	10.8	0.85	15.78	1,157	1	98	1	0	8	21.79				May-11
50	3.09	16.85	6.41	37.26	39.34		0.39	10.8	0.85	15.77	1,157	1	98	1	0	8	21.89		5.25		Aug-18
	3.19	17.05	6.75	38.65		2.28	0.1	10.8	0.85	14.02	260.8	1	98	1	0	13					Feb-16
	3.18	17.00	6.70	38.46		2.24	0.15	10.77	0.85	14.02	260.8	1	98	1	0	13					Feb-16
50	3.13	16.85	6.41	37.41		2.04	0.4	10.82	0.85	13.99	260.8	1	98	1	0	13					Feb-16
50	3.06	16.82	6.43	37.55			0.4	10.75	0.84	13.98	260.8	1	98	1	0	13			5.25		Aug-18
	3.21	10.74	6.77	20.31	25.50	2.36	0.1	4.97	0.55	12.58	2,499	4	39	57	0	25	10.33				May-11
	3.20	10.70	6.72	20.10	25.27	2.31	0.15	4.96	0.54	12.59	2,499	4	39	57	0	25	10.42				May-11
50	3.14	10.60	6.55	19.27	23.72	2.07	0.4	4.98	0.55	12.58	2,499	4	39	57	0	25	10.18				May-11
50	3.14	10.65	6.60	19.51	24.05		0.4	4.95	0.55	12.57	2,499	4	39	57	0	25	10.17		5.25		Aug-18
	2.89	11.59	6.79	25.80	27.12	2.96	0.23	5.89	0.42	10.71	19.1	3	48	49	0	103	15.03	-11.93			Apr-07
	2.74	11.29	6.20	23.74	23.48	2.5	0.82	5.9	0.42	10.51	19.1	3	48	49	0	103	14.67	-12.25			Apr-07
	2.88	11.58	6.78	25.58	26.52	2.88	0.33	5.93	0.43	10.73	19.1	3	48	49	0	103	15.03	-11.93			Nov-12
50	2.71	11.43	6.49	24.58	24.98	2.61	0.58	5.9	0.43	10.64	19.1	3	48	49	0	103	14.84	-12.17	5.25		Apr-07
	2.58	12.28	6.37	28.73	29.17	2.52	0.23	7	0.52	10.76	25.0	3	59	38	0	106	16.26	-13.21			Apr-07
	2.43	11.91	5.73	26.61	25.54	2.28	0.82	6.94	0.52	10.55	25.0	3	59	38	0	106	15.77	-13.54			Apr-07
	2.58	12.21	6.20	28.43	28.50	2.46	0.33	6.94	0.52	10.74	25.0	3	59	38	0	106	16.26	-13.21			Nov-12
50	2.60	12.06	6.03	27.63	27.10	2.21	0.58	6.95	0.52	10.67	25.0	3	59	38	0	106	16	-13.45	5.25		Apr-07
	2.49	12.84	5.69	30.88	30.23	2.59	0.23	7.92	0.6	10.33	25.0	3	69	27	0	97	17.74	-15.16			Apr-07
	2.32	12.52	5.07	28.85	26.61	2.3	0.82	7.86	0.6	10.15	25.0	3	69	27	0	97	17.4	-15.5			Apr-07
	2.39	12.66	5.62	30.70	29.69	2.53	0.33	7.88	0.6	10.31	25.0	3	69	27	0	97	17.74	-15.16			Nov-12
50	2.41	12.58	5.38	29.72	28.08	2.22	0.58	7.86	0.6	10.23	25.0	3	69	27	0	97	17.61	-15.43	5.25		Apr-07
	2.23	13.24	5.01	32.99	30.47	2.38	0.23	8.82	0.68	11.01	18.6	3	79	18	0	96	20.63	-18.23			Apr-07
	2.00	12.92	4.37	30.75	26.85	2.2	0.82	8.85	0.68	10.75	18.6	3	79	18	0	96	20.15	-18.47			Apr-07

	MARKET			FUND TYPE, CATEGORY & OBJECTIVE	RATINGS					MINIMUMS
Fund Name	Ticker Symbol	Traded On	Fund Type	Category and (Prospectus Objective)	Overall Rating	Reward Rating	Risk Rating	Recent Up/ Downgrade	Open to New Investors	Min Initial Investment
BlackRock LifePath® Smart Beta 2035 Institutional Shares	BLGIX	NAS CM	Open End	Target Date (Asset Alloc)	B-	C	B+	Up	Y	2,000,000
BlackRock LifePath® Smart Beta 2035 Fund Investor A Shares	BAPGX	NAS CM	Open End	Target Date (Asset Alloc)	B-	C	B+	Up	Y	1,000
BlackRock LifePath® Smart Beta 2040 Fund Class K	BIPHX	NAS CM	Open End	Target Date (Asset Alloc)	B-	C	B+	Up	Y	5,000,000
BlackRock LifePath® Smart Beta 2040 Fund Class R Shares	BRPHX	NAS CM	Open End	Target Date (Asset Alloc)	B-	C	B+	Up	Y	100
BlackRock LifePath® Smart Beta 2040 Institutional Shares	BLHIX	NAS CM	Open End	Target Date (Asset Alloc)	B-	C	B+	Up	Y	2,000,000
BlackRock LifePath® Smart Beta 2040 Fund Investor A Shares	BAPHX	NAS CM	Open End	Target Date (Asset Alloc)	B-	C	B+	Up	Y	1,000
BlackRock LifePath® Smart Beta 2045 Fund Class K	BIPJX	NAS CM	Open End	Target Date (Asset Alloc)	B-	C	B	Up	Y	5,000,000
BlackRock LifePath® Smart Beta 2045 Fund Class R Shares	BRPJX	NAS CM	Open End	Target Date (Asset Alloc)	B-	C	B	Up	Y	100
BlackRock LifePath® Smart Beta 2045 Institutional Shares	BLJIX	NAS CM	Open End	Target Date (Asset Alloc)	B-	C	B	Up	Y	2,000,000
BlackRock LifePath® Smart Beta 2045 Fund Investor A Shares	BAPJX	NAS CM	Open End	Target Date (Asset Alloc)	B-	C	B	Up	Y	1,000
BlackRock LifePath® Smart Beta 2050 Fund Class K	BIPKX	NAS CM	Open End	Target Date (Asset Alloc)	B-	C	B	Up	Y	5,000,000
BlackRock LifePath® Smart Beta 2050 Fund Class R Shares	BRPKX	NAS CM	Open End	Target Date (Asset Alloc)	B-	C	B	Up	Y	100
BlackRock LifePath® Smart Beta 2050 Institutional Shares	BLKIX	NAS CM	Open End	Target Date (Asset Alloc)	B-	C	B	Up	Y	2,000,000
BlackRock LifePath® Smart Beta 2050 Fund Investor A Shares	BAPKX	NAS CM	Open End	Target Date (Asset Alloc)	B-	C	B	Up	Y	1,000
BlackRock LifePath® Smart Beta 2055 Fund Class K Shares	BIPLX	NAS CM	Open End	Target Date (Asset Alloc)	B-	C	B	Up	Y	5,000,000
BlackRock LifePath® Smart Beta 2055 Fund Class R Shares	BRPLX	NAS CM	Open End	Target Date (Asset Alloc)	B-	C	B	Up	Y	100
BlackRock LifePath® Smart Beta 2055 Institutional Shares	BLLIX	NAS CM	Open End	Target Date (Asset Alloc)	B-	C	B	Up	Y	2,000,000
BlackRock LifePath® Smart Beta 2055 Fund Investor A Shares	BAPLX	NAS CM	Open End	Target Date (Asset Alloc)	B-	C	B	Up	Y	1,000
BlackRock LifePath® Smart Beta Retirement Fund Class K	BIPBX	NAS CM	Open End	Target Date (Asset Alloc)	B	C+	A-	Up	Y	5,000,000
BlackRock LifePath® Smart Beta Retirement Cls R Shares	BRPBX	NAS CM	Open End	Target Date (Asset Alloc)	B	C+	A-	Up	Y	100
BlackRock LifePath® Smart Beta Retmnt Inst Shares	BLAIX	NAS CM	Open End	Target Date (Asset Alloc)	B	C+	A-	Up	Y	2,000,000
BlackRock LifePath® Smart Beta Retmnt Inv A Shares	BAPBX	NAS CM	Open End	Target Date (Asset Alloc)	B	C+	A-	Up	Y	1,000
BlackRock Long-Horizon Equity Fund Class R Shares	MREGX	NAS CM	Open End	Global Equity Large Cap (World Stock)	B-	C+	B		Y	100
BlackRock Long-Horizon Equity Fund Institutional Shares	MAEGX	NAS CM	Open End	Global Equity Large Cap (World Stock)	B	C+	B	Up	Y	2,000,000
BlackRock Long-Horizon Equity Fund Investor A Shares	MDEGX	NAS CM	Open End	Global Equity Large Cap (World Stock)	B-	C+	B		Y	1,000
BlackRock Long-Horizon Equity Fund Investor C Shares	MCEGX	NAS CM	Open End	Global Equity Large Cap (World Stock)	B-	C	B		Y	1,000
BlackRock Managed Income Fund Class K Shares	BLDRX	NAS CM	Open End	Cautious Alloc (Income)	B	C+	A		Y	5,000,000
BlackRock Managed Income Fund Institutional Shares	BLDIX	NAS CM	Open End	Cautious Alloc (Income)	B	C+	A-		Y	2,000,000
BlackRock Managed Income Fund Investor A Shares	BLADX	NAS CM	Open End	Cautious Alloc (Income)	B	C+	A-		Y	1,000
BlackRock Managed Income Fund Investor C Shares	BMICX	NAS CM	Open End	Cautious Alloc (Income)	B-	C	B+		Y	1,000
BlackRock Mid Cap Dividend Fund Class K	MJRFX	NAS CM	Open End	US Equity Mid Cap (Growth)	C+	C	B	Up	Y	5,000,000
BlackRock Mid Cap Dividend Fund Class R	MRRFX	NAS CM	Open End	US Equity Mid Cap (Growth)	C+	C	B	Up	Y	100
BlackRock Mid Cap Dividend Fund Institutional Shares	MARFX	NAS CM	Open End	US Equity Mid Cap (Growth)	C+	C	B	Up	Y	2,000,000
BlackRock Mid Cap Dividend Fund Investor A Shares	MDRFX	NAS CM	Open End	US Equity Mid Cap (Growth)	C+	C	B	Up	Y	1,000
BlackRock Mid Cap Dividend Fund Investor C Shares	MCRFX	NAS CM	Open End	US Equity Mid Cap (Growth)	C+	C	B	Up	Y	1,000
BlackRock Mid-Cap Growth Equity Portfolio Class K	BMGKX	NAS CM	Open End	US Equity Mid Cap (Growth)	B	B+	B		Y	5,000,000
BlackRock Mid-Cap Growth Equity Portfolio Class R	BMRRX	NAS CM	Open End	US Equity Mid Cap (Growth)	B	B+	B		Y	100
BlackRock Mid-Cap Growth Equity Portfolio Inst Shares	CMGIX	NAS CM	Open End	US Equity Mid Cap (Growth)	B	B+	B		Y	2,000,000
BlackRock Mid-Cap Growth Equity Portfolio Inv A Shares	BMGAX	NAS CM	Open End	US Equity Mid Cap (Growth)	B	B+	B		Y	1,000
BlackRock Mid-Cap Growth Equity Portfolio Inv C Shares	BMGCX	NAS CM	Open End	US Equity Mid Cap (Growth)	B	B+	B		Y	1,000
BlackRock Mid-Cap Growth Equity Portfolio Service Shares	CMGSX	NAS CM	Open End	US Equity Mid Cap (Growth)	B	B+	B		Y	5,000
BlackRock Multi-Asset Income Portfolio Class K	BKMIX	NAS CM	Open End	Moderate Alloc (Income)	B	C+	A-		Y	5,000,000
BlackRock Multi-Asset Income Portfolio Inst Shares	BIICX	NAS CM	Open End	Moderate Alloc (Income)	B	C+	A-		Y	2,000,000
BlackRock Multi-Asset Income Portfolio Investor A Shares	BAICX	NAS CM	Open End	Moderate Alloc (Income)	B	C+	A-		Y	1,000
BlackRock Multi-Asset Income Portfolio Investor C Shares	BCICX	NAS CM	Open End	Moderate Alloc (Income)	B	C+	B+	Up	Y	1,000
BlackRock Natural Resources Trust Institutional Shares	MAGRX	NAS CM	Open End	Natl Resources Sec Equity (Natl Res)	C	C-	C		Y	2,000,000
BlackRock Natural Resources Trust Investor A Shares	MDGRX	NAS CM	Open End	Natl Resources Sec Equity (Natl Res)	C	C-	C		Y	1,000
BlackRock Natural Resources Trust Investor C Shares	MCGRX	NAS CM	Open End	Natl Resources Sec Equity (Natl Res)	C-	C-	C		Y	1,000
BlackRock Real Estate Securities Fund Institutional Shares	BIREX	NAS CM	Open End	Real Estate Sector Equity (Real Estate)	B-	C+	B-		Y	2,000,000
BlackRock Real Estate Securities Fund Investor A Shares	BAREX	NAS CM	Open End	Real Estate Sector Equity (Real Estate)	C+	C+	B-	Down	Y	1,000
BlackRock Real Estate Securities Fund Investor C Shares	BCREX	NAS CM	Open End	Real Estate Sector Equity (Real Estate)	C+	C	B-	Down	Y	1,000
BlackRock Resources & Commodities Strategy Trust	BCX	NYSE	Closed End	Natl Resources Sec Equity (Growth & Income)	C	C	C+		Y	

★ Expanded analysis of this fund is included in Section II.

Min Additional Investment	TOTAL RETURNS 3-Month Total Return	6-Month Total Return	1-Year Total Return	3-Year Total Return	5-Year Total Return	PERFORMANCE Dividend Yield (TTM)	Expense Ratio	3-Yr Std Deviation	3-Year Beta	ASSETS NAV	Total Assets (MIL)	ASSET ALLOCATION & TURNOVER %Cash	%Stocks	%Bonds	%Other	Turnover Ratio	BULL & BEAR Last Bull Market Total Return	Last Bear Market Total Return	FEES Front End Fee (%)	Back End Fee (%)	Inception Date
	2.14	13.16	4.85	32.63	30.03	2.32	0.33	8.86	0.68	11	18.6	3	79	18	0	96	20.63	-18.23			Nov-12
50	2.16	13.01	4.63	31.69	28.34	2.05	0.58	8.85	0.68	10.91	18.6	3	79	18	0	96	20.26	-18.35	5.25		Apr-07
	1.88	13.50	4.03	33.09	30.68	2.71	0.23	9.79	0.76	10.89	16.8	3	88	9	0	59	20.73	-18.02			Apr-07
	1.72	13.25	3.45	30.93	27.03	2.37	0.82	9.78	0.76	10.7	16.8	3	88	9	0	59	20.22	-18.31			Apr-07
	1.88	13.51	3.93	32.67	30.00	2.63	0.33	9.71	0.75	10.88	16.8	3	88	9	0	59	20.73	-18.02			Nov-12
50	1.80	13.39	3.73	31.85	28.61	2.36	0.58	9.71	0.75	10.78	16.8	3	88	9	0	59	20.32	-18.24	5.25		Apr-07
	1.62	13.66	3.50	34.23	31.04	2.49	0.23	10.32	0.8	11.97	12.8	3	93	3	0	81	20.77	-17.98			Apr-07
	1.49	13.36	2.94	31.93	27.38	2.31	0.82	10.29	0.8	11.59	12.8	3	93	3	0	81	20.15	-18.19			Apr-07
	1.62	13.67	3.40	33.78	30.44	2.41	0.33	10.28	0.8	11.94	12.8	3	93	3	0	81	20.77	-17.98			Nov-12
50	1.65	13.53	3.20	32.81	28.87	2.16	0.58	10.29	0.8	11.75	12.8	3	93	3	0	81	20.49	-18.17	5.25		Apr-07
	1.54	13.64	3.03	33.65	30.42	2.77	0.23	10.51	0.82	11.21	13.4	3	94	3	0	62	20.77	-18.23			Apr-07
	1.39	13.25	2.46	31.29	26.65	2.45	0.82	10.5	0.82	10.96	13.4	3	94	3	0	62	20.2	-18.35			Apr-07
	1.55	13.58	2.95	33.19	29.60	2.7	0.33	10.6	0.82	11.18	13.4	3	94	3	0	62	20.77	-18.23			Nov-12
50	1.48	13.43	2.69	32.18	28.02	2.49	0.58	10.53	0.82	11.04	13.4	3	94	3	0	62	20.42	-18.28	5.25		Apr-07
	1.45	13.62	2.91	33.22	30.81	2.27	0.23	10.67	0.83	11.91	8.6	3	94	3	0	60					Feb-13
	1.30	13.29	2.28	30.88	27.03	2.18	0.82	10.69	0.83	11.69	8.6	3	94	3	0	60					Feb-13
	1.37	13.55	2.83	32.75	30.18	2.2	0.33	10.71	0.83	11.89	8.6	3	94	3	0	60					Feb-13
50	1.37	13.48	2.55	31.85	28.53	1.96	0.58	10.7	0.83	11.85	8.6	3	94	3	0	60			5.25		Feb-13
	2.87	11.35	7.06	22.35	23.67	3.07	0.23	5.44	0.62	10.42	9.6	3	44	53	0	103	14.13	-10.94			Apr-07
	2.69	11.16	6.52	20.41	20.29	2.69	0.82	5.46	0.62	10.32	9.6	3	44	53	0	103	13.65	-11.2			Apr-07
	2.86	11.37	7.07	22.12	23.28	2.83	0.33	5.46	0.61	10.43	9.6	3	44	53	0	103	14.13	-10.94			Nov-12
50	2.89	11.35	6.92	21.29	21.86	2.76	0.58	5.45	0.6	10.34	9.6	3	44	53	0	103	13.79	-11.1	5.25		Apr-07
	3.72	20.79	12.61	40.65	30.46	0	1.64	11.9	0.97	13.94	263.1	1	96	0	3	24	16.14	-19.71			Feb-07
	3.81	21.11	13.28	43.48	34.95	0.7	1	11.85	0.97	13.88	263.1	1	96	0	3	24	16.62	-19.49			Nov-05
50	3.81	21.02	13.05	42.31	33.19	0.45	1.26	11.87	0.97	13.87	263.1	1	96	0	3	24	16.39	-19.58	5.25		Nov-05
50	3.59	20.43	12.17	39.05	28.08	0	2.02	11.88	0.97	13.85	263.1	1	96	0	3	24	15.81	-19.82		1.00	Nov-05
	2.23	6.43	5.88	13.55	22.30	4.11	0.44	2.33	0.16	9.99	378.5	4	6	86	0	79	5.09	15.72			Oct-07
	2.12	6.31	5.84	13.26	21.83	4.07	0.49	2.32	0.17	9.96	378.5	4	6	86	0	79	5.04	15.7			Oct-07
50	2.16	6.28	5.67	12.51	20.11	3.82	0.74	2.29	0.18	9.97	378.5	4	6	86	0	79	4.76	15.5	4.00		Oct-07
50	1.87	5.76	4.77	10.04	16.18	3.07	1.49	2.31	0.16	9.97	378.5	4	6	86	0	79	4.48	15.24		1.00	Oct-16
	5.01	18.28	3.36	35.12	29.23	1.67	0.79	14.74	1.08	17.99	345.6	5	95	0	0	58	26.67	-21.81			Jan-18
	4.87	17.92	2.83	32.84	25.58	1.49	1.35	14.78	1.08	14.64	345.6	5	95	0	0	58	26.02	-22.03			Feb-03
	4.99	18.26	3.36	35.03	29.14	1.62	0.85	14.76	1.08	17.99	345.6	5	95	0	0	58	26.67	-21.82			Feb-95
50	4.95	18.09	3.09	33.92	27.35	1.45	1.1	14.79	1.08	17.1	345.6	5	95	0	0	58	26.31	-21.87	5.25		Feb-95
50	4.76	17.66	2.29	30.92	22.52	1.17	1.85	14.73	1.08	13.34	345.6	5	95	0	0	58	25.69	-22.25		1.00	Feb-95
	9.34	33.48	19.02	93.35	107.40	0	0.75	14.27	0.92	29.74	4,326	2	97	0	1	43	25.85	-21.05			Mar-16
	9.20	33.11	18.38	89.75	101.08	0	1.3	14.26	0.92	25.23	4,326	2	97	0	1	43	25.37	-21.16			Oct-06
	9.32	33.39	18.90	92.77	106.77	0	0.8	14.27	0.92	29.68	4,326	2	97	0	1	43	25.85	-21.05			Dec-96
50	9.22	33.22	18.59	91.17	103.59	0	1.05	14.28	0.92	25.66	4,326	2	97	0	1	43	25.61	-21.19	5.25		Dec-96
50	9.02	32.77	17.70	87.04	96.31	0	1.8	14.25	0.92	19.94	4,326	2	97	0	1	43	24.97	-21.39		1.00	Dec-96
	9.22	33.26	18.63	91.65	103.84	0	1.05	14.27	0.92	26.85	4,326	2	97	0	1	43	25.45	-21.18			Dec-96
	2.77	10.32	7.27	20.33	21.05	5.16	0.53	4.31	0.29	10.85	16,425	4	32	58	0	61	12.69	-6.99			Feb-17
	2.66	10.19	7.22	20.08	20.80	5.11	0.58	4.29	0.31	10.85	16,425	4	32	58	0	61	12.69	-6.98			Apr-08
50	2.60	10.05	6.95	19.19	19.30	4.87	0.83	4.29	0.32	10.84	16,425	4	32	58	0	61	12.36	-7.07	5.25		Apr-08
50	2.50	9.77	6.17	16.68	15.02	4.14	1.58	4.28	0.31	10.83	16,425	4	32	58	0	61	12.06	-7.45		1.00	Apr-08
	1.01	15.65	-5.76	12.27	-26.76	2.67	0.92	15.79	0.98	25.93	156.6	2	98	0	0	75	21.34	-30.69			Oct-88
50	0.95	15.49	-5.99	11.37	-27.72	2.53	1.18	15.8	0.98	24.37	156.6	2	98	0	0	75	21.16	-30.77	5.25		Oct-94
50	0.74	15.05	-6.74	8.80	-30.51	2.36	1.95	15.79	0.98	17.65	156.6	2	98	0	0	75	20.6	-30.99		1.00	Oct-94
	1.90	19.68	13.62	20.01	52.65	2.27	1.05	13.2	0.99	13.61	47.3	1	99	0	0	82					Sep-12
50	1.93	19.56	13.39	19.14	50.74	2.06	1.3	13.23	0.99	13.57	47.3	1	99	0	0	82			5.25		Sep-12
50	1.70	19.14	12.49	16.45	45.24	1.4	2.05	13.13	0.98	13.47	47.3	1	99	0	0	82				1.00	Sep-12
	0.72	14.84	-3.71	22.25	-6.66	4.68	1.1	13.62		9.28	909.8	1	97	1	0	66	11.69	-19.42			Mar-11

	MARKET		FUND TYPE, CATEGORY & OBJECTIVE		RATINGS				MINIMUMS	
Fund Name	Ticker Symbol	Traded On	Fund Type	Category and (Prospectus Objective)	Overall Rating	Reward Rating	Risk Rating	Recent Up/ Downgrade	Open to New Investors	Min Initial Investment
BlackRock Science and Technology Trust	BST	NYSE	Closed End	Technology Sector Equity (Technology)	C	B-	C-	Down	Y	
BlackRock Systematic Multi-Strategy Institutional Shares	BIMBX	NAS CM	Open End	Multialternative (Growth & Income)	B	B-	A+		Y	2,000,000
BlackRock Systematic Multi-Strategy Fund Investor A Shares	BAMBX	NAS CM	Open End	Multialternative (Growth & Income)	B	C+	A+		Y	1,000
BlackRock Systematic Multi-Strategy Fund Investor C Shares	BMBCX	NAS CM	Open End	Multialternative (Growth & Income)	B	C+	A		Y	1,000
BlackRock Tactical Opportunities Fund Class K Shares	PBAKX	NAS CM	Open End	Multialternative (Asset Alloc)	C	C	B	Down	Y	5,000,000
BlackRock Tactical Opportunities Fund Institutional Shares	PBAIX	NAS CM	Open End	Multialternative (Asset Alloc)	C+	C	B+	Down	Y	2,000,000
BlackRock Tactical Opportunities Fund Investor A Shares	PCBAX	NAS CM	Open End	Multialternative (Asset Alloc)	C+	C	B+	Down	Y	1,000
BlackRock Tactical Opportunities Fund Investor C Shares	BRBCX	NAS CM	Open End	Multialternative (Asset Alloc)	C	C-	B	Down	Y	1,000
BlackRock Tactical Opportunities Fund Service Shares	PCBSX	NAS CM	Open End	Multialternative (Asset Alloc)	C+	C	B+	Down	Y	5,000
BlackRock Technology Opportunities Fund Class R Shares	BGSRX	NAS CM	Open End	Technology Sector Equity (Technology)	B-	B-	B-	Down	Y	100
BlackRock Technology Opportunities Institutional Shares	BGSIX	NAS CM	Open End	Technology Sector Equity (Technology)	B-	B	B-	Down	Y	2,000,000
BlackRock Technology Opportunities Fund Investor A Shares	BGSAX	NAS CM	Open End	Technology Sector Equity (Technology)	B-	B	B-	Down	Y	1,000
BlackRock Technology Opportunities Fund Investor C Shares	BGSCX	NAS CM	Open End	Technology Sector Equity (Technology)	B-	B-	B-	Down	Y	1,000
BlackRock Technology Opportunities Fund Service Shares	BSTSX	NAS CM	Open End	Technology Sector Equity (Technology)	B-	B	B-	Down	Y	5,000
BlackRock Total Emerging Markets Fund Institutional	BEEIX	NAS CM	Open End	Global Emerg Mkts (Growth & Income)	C	C	B-		Y	2,000,000
BlackRock Total Emerging Markets Fund Investor A	BEEAX	NAS CM	Open End	Global Emerg Mkts (Growth & Income)	C	C	B-		Y	1,000
BlackRock Total Emerging Markets Fund Investor C	BEECX	NAS CM	Open End	Global Emerg Mkts (Growth & Income)	C	C-	C+		Y	1,000
BlackRock Total Factor Fund Class K	BSTKX	NAS CM	Open End	Multialternative (Multi-Asset Global)	B	C+	A-	Up	Y	5,000,000
BlackRock Total Factor Fund Institutional Shares	BSTIX	NAS CM	Open End	Multialternative (Multi-Asset Global)	B	C+	A-	Up	Y	2,000,000
BlackRock Total Factor Fund Investor A Shares	BSTAX	NAS CM	Open End	Multialternative (Multi-Asset Global)	B	C+	A-	Up	Y	1,000
BlackRock Total Factor Fund Investor C Shares	BSTCX	NAS CM	Open End	Multialternative (Multi-Asset Global)	B-	C	B+	Up	Y	1,000
BlackRock Utilities, Infrastructure & Power Opp Trust	BUI	NYSE	Closed End	Utilities Sector Equity (Equity-Income)	C	B-	C-	Down	Y	
Blackstone Alternative Multi-Strategy Fund Class D	BXMDX	NAS CM	Open End	Multialternative (Growth)	C+	C	B	Down	Y	25,000
Blackstone Alternative Multi-Strategy Fund Class I	BXMIX	NAS CM	Open End	Multialternative (Growth)	C+	C	B	Down	Y	1,000,000
Blackstone Alternative Multi-Strategy Fund Class Y	BXMYX	NAS CM	Open End	Multialternative (Growth)	C+	C	B	Down	Y	0
Blue Chip Investor Fund	BCIFX	NAS CM	Open End	US Equity Large Cap Blend (Growth)	C	C	C+		Y	5,000
Blue Current Global Dividend Fund Institutional Class	BCGDX	NAS CM	Open End	Global Equity Large Cap (Equity-Income)	C+	C	B		Y	100,000
Bluerock Total Income+ Real Estate Fund Class A	TIPRX	NAS CM	Closed End	Real Estate Sector Equity (Real Estate)	B	C+	A		Y	2,500
Bluerock Total Income+ Real Estate Fund Class C	TIPPX	NAS CM	Closed End	Real Estate Sector Equity (Real Estate)	B	C+	A-		Y	2,500
Bluerock Total Income+ Real Estate Fund Class I	TIPWX	NAS CM	Closed End	Real Estate Sector Equity (Real Estate)	B	C+	A		Y	1,000,000
Bluerock Total Income+ Real Estate Fund Class L	TIPLX	NAS CM	Closed End	Real Estate Sector Equity (Real Estate)	B	C+	A-		Y	2,500
BMO Aggressive Allocation Fund Class I	BDSHX	NAS CM	Open End	Aggressive Alloc (Asset Alloc)	B-	C	B	Up	Y	1,000,000
BMO Aggressive Allocation Fund Class R3	BDSRX	NAS CM	Open End	Aggressive Alloc (Asset Alloc)	C+	C	B	Up	Y	0
BMO Aggressive Allocation Fund Class R6	BDSQX	NAS CM	Open End	Aggressive Alloc (Asset Alloc)	B-	C	B	Up	Y	0
BMO Aggressive Allocation Fund Class Y	BDSYX	NAS CM	Open End	Aggressive Alloc (Asset Alloc)	C+	C	B	Up	Y	1,000
BMO Alternative Strategies Fund Class A	BMATX	NAS CM	Open End	Multialternative (Growth)	D	D	C-		Y	1,000
BMO Alternative Strategies Fund Class I	BMASX	NAS CM	Open End	Multialternative (Growth)	D	D	C-	Down	Y	1,000,000
BMO Balanced Allocation Fund Class I	BGRHX	NAS CM	Open End	Moderate Alloc (Balanced)	B-	C	A-	Up	Y	1,000,000
BMO Balanced Allocation Fund Class R3	BGRRX	NAS CM	Open End	Moderate Alloc (Balanced)	B-	C	B+	Up	Y	0
BMO Balanced Allocation Fund Class R6	BGRQX	NAS CM	Open End	Moderate Alloc (Balanced)	B-	C	A-	Up	Y	0
BMO Balanced Allocation Fund Class Y	BGRYX	NAS CM	Open End	Moderate Alloc (Balanced)	B-	C	A-	Up	Y	1,000
BMO Conservative Allocation Fund Class I	BDVIX	NAS CM	Open End	Cautious Alloc (Balanced)	B-	C	B+		Y	1,000,000
BMO Conservative Allocation Fund Class R3	BDVRX	NAS CM	Open End	Cautious Alloc (Balanced)	B-	C	B+	Up	Y	0
BMO Conservative Allocation Fund Class R6	BDVSX	NAS CM	Open End	Cautious Alloc (Balanced)	B-	C	B+		Y	0
BMO Conservative Allocation Fund Class Y	BDVYX	NAS CM	Open End	Cautious Alloc (Balanced)	B-	C	B+		Y	1,000
BMO Disciplined International Equity Fund Class A	BDAQX	NAS CM	Open End	Global Equity Large Cap (Foreign Stock)	C	C-	C+		Y	1,000
BMO Disciplined International Equity Fund Class I	BDIQX	NAS CM	Open End	Global Equity Large Cap (Foreign Stock)	C	C-	C+		Y	1,000,000
BMO Dividend Income Fund Class A	BADIX	NAS CM	Open End	US Equity Large Cap Value (Equity-Income)	B-	C	B		Y	1,000
BMO Dividend Income Fund Class I	MDIVX	NAS CM	Open End	US Equity Large Cap Value (Equity-Income)	B-	C	B	Down	Y	1,000,000
BMO Global Long/Short Equity Fund Class A	BGAQX	NAS CM	Open End	Long/Short Equity (Growth)	D+	D	C-	Down	Y	1,000
BMO Global Long/Short Equity Fund Class I	BGIQX	NAS CM	Open End	Long/Short Equity (Growth)	D+	D	C-	Down	Y	1,000,000
BMO Global Low Volatility Equity Fund Class A	BAEGX	NAS CM	Open End	Global Equity Large Cap (World Stock)	B	C+	A-	Up	Y	1,000

★ Expanded analysis of this fund is included in Section II.

Min Additional Investment	TOTAL RETURNS 3-Month Total Return	6-Month Total Return	1-Year Total Return	3-Year Total Return	5-Year Total Return	PERFORMANCE Dividend Yield (TTM)	Expense Ratio	3-Yr Std Deviation	3-Year Beta	ASSETS NAV	Total Assets (MIL)	ASSET ALLOCATION & TURNOVER %Cash	%Stocks	%Bonds	%Other	Turnover Ratio	BULL & BEAR Last Bull Market Total Return	Last Bear Market Total Return	FEES Front End Fee (%)	Back End Fee (%)	Inception Date
	5.74	29.10	10.82	107.00		0	0.88	15.82	0.94	32.49	726.8	1	97	0	0	53					Oct-14
	2.48	7.70	10.13	20.38		2.57	0.96	2.74	18.35	10.11	122.1	6	12	82	0	426					May-15
50	2.46	7.67	9.93	19.59		2.4	1.21	2.73	17.55	10.1	122.1	6	12	82	0	426			4.00		May-15
50	2.29	7.28	9.01	16.89		1.73	1.96	2.69	17.76	10.09	122.1	6	12	82	0	426				1.00	May-15
	-1.08	0.43	0.03	18.00	12.95	3.96	0.77	4.3	0.15	13.71	906.4	20	66	15	-1	265	12.02	-13.09			Aug-16
	-1.15	0.36	-0.12	17.79	13.41	3.8	0.9	4.31	0.14	13.73	906.4	20	66	15	-1	265	12.18	-12.99			Jun-93
50	-1.23	0.14	-0.44	16.66	11.66	3.52	1.22	4.28	0.14	13.61	906.4	20	66	15	-1	265	12.02	-13.09	5.25		Dec-88
50	-1.41	-0.15	-1.18	14.25	7.87	2.32	1.9	4.29	0.15	13.23	906.4	20	66	15	-1	265	11.54	-13.38		1.00	Jun-93
	-1.16	0.22	-0.41	16.85	11.81	3.54	1.18	4.3	0.15	13.63	906.4	20	66	15	-1	265	12.04	-13.09			Jan-05
	5.69	30.52	13.01	121.49	146.03	0	1.43	17.13	1.06	31.3	1,831	6	94	0	0	49	19.92	-21.5			Sep-08
	5.84	30.85	13.59	125.01	152.86	0	0.93	17.14	1.06	33.46	1,831	6	94	0	0	49	20.32	-21.36			May-00
50	5.78	30.72	13.31	123.22	149.42	0	1.18	17.15	1.06	31.01	1,831	6	94	0	0	49	19.97	-21.43	5.25		May-00
50	5.59	30.24	12.48	118.31	139.77	0	1.93	17.13	1.06	26.15	1,831	6	94	0	0	49	19.54	-21.78		1.00	May-00
	5.79	30.72	13.31	123.47	150.03	0	1.18	17.17	1.06	31.69	1,831	6	94	0	0	49	20.19	-21.36			May-00
	3.38	14.11	6.94	19.69	17.65	5.27	0.91	11.28	0.76	9.78	159.7	-26	67	59	0	61					May-13
50	3.28	13.91	6.65	18.70	16.23	4.83	1.16	11.32	0.77	9.74	159.7	-26	67	59	0	61			5.25		May-13
50	3.09	13.51	5.87	16.07	11.94	4.06	1.91	11.31	0.76	9.66	159.7	-26	67	59	0	61				1.00	May-13
	0.59	5.48	3.80	16.71	18.79	2.33	0.55	5.35	0.23	10.2	218.3	21	18	62	0	64					Feb-17
	0.59	5.58	3.77	16.65	18.73	2.3	0.6	5.4	0.24	10.2	218.3	21	18	62	0	64					Dec-12
50	0.49	5.39	3.48	15.72	17.13	2.12	0.85	5.41	0.24	10.16	218.3	21	18	62	0	64			5.25		Dec-12
50	0.39	4.98	2.73	13.16	12.95	1.23	1.6	5.34	0.24	10.11	218.3	21	18	62	0	64				1.00	Dec-12
	4.56	16.65	11.52	25.57	31.43	3.22	1.15	9.07		21.01	355.5	1	99	0	0	28					Nov-11
5,000	0.93	4.84	4.24	12.59	14.84	0.94	3.24	3.38	0.22	10.83	7,998	-38	26	86	22	203					Nov-14
200,000	1.30	5.31	4.87	14.02	16.79	1.18	2.86	3.39	0.22	10.9	7,998	-38	26	86	22	203					Jun-14
	1.31	5.35	4.88	14.33	17.38	1.26	2.76	3.37	0.22	10.82	7,998	-38	26	86	22	203					Jan-15
100	3.65	12.44	-2.31	25.43	36.04	0	1.16	14.03	1.06	161.52	37.2	3	97	0	0	27	20.68	-15.99			Dec-01
	4.98	19.94	8.25	30.97		1.49	0.99	11.11	1.09	11.84	63.3	5	95	0	0	50					Sep-14
100	1.22	3.26	5.99	21.46	40.53	5.3	2.39	0.91		30.01	--	7	45	-16	63	35			5.75		Oct-12
100	1.14	2.95	5.31	18.85	35.53	5.42	3.14	0.91		28.87	--	7	45	-16	63	35				1.00	Apr-14
	1.25	3.34	6.22	22.30	42.47	5.26	2.17	0.92		30.47	--	7	45	-16	63	35					Apr-14
100	1.17	3.13	5.72	20.88	39.86	5.32	2.67			29.85	--	7	45	-16	63	35			4.25		Jun-17
	2.83	16.62	4.77	40.14	38.26	2.42	0.68	11.32	0.91	8.7	171.7	3	97	0	0		23.49	-20.59			May-14
	2.60	16.19	4.18	38.01	34.64	1.94	1.18	11.36	0.92	8.68	171.7	3	97	0	0		23.13	-20.76			May-14
	2.71	16.62	4.77	40.54	39.15	2.42	0.53	11.37	0.92	8.7	171.7	3	97	0	0		23.49	-20.59			May-14
50	2.71	16.30	4.44	39.03	36.36	2.15	0.93	11.4	0.92	8.7	171.7	3	97	0	0		23.49	-20.59			May-14
50	0.21	0.87	-5.31	-2.26		0	2.02	4.14	19.67	9.26	41.2	85	16	0	-1				5.00		Dec-14
	0.32	1.07	-5.06	-1.34		0	1.77	4.08	19.63	9.37	41.2	85	16	0	-1						Dec-14
	2.76	12.49	4.94	27.28	27.35	2.53	0.69	7.58	0.61	8.55	301.9	12	61	28	0		16.31	-13.75			May-14
	2.51	12.20	4.45	25.33	24.07	2.02	1.19	7.56	0.6	8.55	301.9	12	61	28	0		15.97	-13.93			May-14
	2.76	12.63	5.19	27.78	28.29	2.53	0.54	7.56	0.6	8.56	301.9	12	61	28	0		16.31	-13.75			May-14
50	2.52	12.36	4.64	26.13	25.64	2.27	0.94	7.55	0.6	8.54	301.9	12	61	28	0		16.31	-13.75			May-14
	2.70	8.58	5.80	14.79	17.27	2.48	0.63	3.7	0.53	7.97	39.0	15	23	62	0	40	9.58	-5.34			May-14
	2.62	8.32	5.27	13.02	14.36	2.42	1.13	3.73	0.53	7.81	39.0	15	23	62	0	40	9.26	-5.54			May-14
	2.67	8.48	5.87	15.16	18.05	2.57	0.48	3.63	0.52	7.67	39.0	15	23	62	0	40	9.58	-5.34			May-14
50	2.55	8.36	5.50	13.80	15.75	2.58	0.88	3.64	0.53	7.64	39.0	15	23	62	0	40	9.58	-5.34			May-14
50	-0.19	11.13	-4.60	21.88		1.61	1.15	11.88	1.04	10.38	64.4	0	99	0	0				5.00		Sep-15
	-0.09	11.34	-4.32	22.93		1.87	0.9	11.9	1.04	10.4	64.4	0	99	0	0						Sep-15
50	0.97	13.37	5.74	46.01	53.00	2.06	0.9	12.23	0.98	14.34	236.1	2	98	0	0				5.00		May-14
	1.03	13.54	5.98	47.08	54.88	2.28	0.65	12.25	0.99	14.29	236.1	2	98	0	0						Dec-11
50	-1.62	0.83	-5.63	13.22		1.04	1.66	8.32	0.59	10.89	3.0	3	97	0	0				5.00		Sep-15
	-1.79	0.83	-5.61	13.78		1.04	1.41	8.26	0.58	10.93	3.0	3	97	0	0						Sep-15
50	1.58	11.27	7.67	25.51	36.81	2.74	1.1	8.08	0.64	11.55	34.6	2	98	0	0				5.00		May-14

	MARKET		FUND TYPE, CATEGORY & OBJECTIVE		RATINGS				MINIMUMS	
Fund Name	Ticker Symbol	Traded On	Fund Type	Category and (Prospectus Objective)	Overall Rating	Reward Rating	Risk Rating	Recent Up/ Downgrade	Open to New Investors	Min Initial Investment
BMO Global Low Volatility Equity Fund Class I	BGLBX	NAS CM	Open End	Global Equity Large Cap (World Stock)	B	C+	A-	Up	Y	1,000,000
BMO Growth Allocation Fund Class I	BABHX	NAS CM	Open End	Aggressive Alloc (Asset Alloc)	B-	C	B+	Up	Y	1,000,000
BMO Growth Allocation Fund Class R3	BABRX	NAS CM	Open End	Aggressive Alloc (Asset Alloc)	B-	C	B	Up	Y	0
BMO Growth Allocation Fund Class R6	BABQX	NAS CM	Open End	Aggressive Alloc (Asset Alloc)	B-	C	B+	Up	Y	0
BMO Growth Allocation Fund Class Y	BABYX	NAS CM	Open End	Aggressive Alloc (Asset Alloc)	B-	C	B+	Up	Y	1,000
BMO In-Retirement Fund Class R3	BTRRX	NAS CM	Open End	Target Date (Asset Alloc)	B	C	A-	Up	Y	0
BMO Large-Cap Growth Fund Class A	BALGX	NAS CM	Open End	US Equity Large Cap Growth (Growth)	B-	C	B	Down	Y	1,000
BMO Large-Cap Growth Fund Class I	MLCIX	NAS CM	Open End	US Equity Large Cap Growth (Growth)	B-	C	B	Down	Y	1,000,000
BMO Large-Cap Growth Fund Class R6	BLGRX	NAS CM	Open End	US Equity Large Cap Growth (Growth)	B-	C	B	Down	Y	0
BMO Large-Cap Growth Fund Class Y	MASTX	NAS CM	Open End	US Equity Large Cap Growth (Growth)	B-	C	B	Down	Y	1,000
BMO Large-Cap Value Fund Class A	BALVX	NAS CM	Open End	US Equity Large Cap Value (Growth)	C+	C	B	Up	Y	1,000
BMO Large-Cap Value Fund Class I	MLVIX	NAS CM	Open End	US Equity Large Cap Value (Growth)	C+	C	B	Up	Y	1,000,000
BMO Large-Cap Value Fund Class R6	BLCRX	NAS CM	Open End	US Equity Large Cap Value (Growth)	C+	C	B	Up	Y	0
BMO LGM Emerging Markets Equity Fund Class A	BAEMX	NAS CM	Open End	Global Emerg Mkts (Div Emerging Mkts)	C	C	B-		Y	1,000
BMO LGM Emerging Markets Equity Fund Class I	MIEMX	NAS CM	Open End	Global Emerg Mkts (Div Emerging Mkts)	C	C	B-		Y	1,000,000
BMO LGM Frontier Markets Equity Fund Class I	BLGFX	NAS CM	Closed End	Global Emerg Mkts (Growth)	D	D	D+	Down		5,000
BMO Low Volatility Equity Fund Class A	BLVAX	NAS CM	Open End	US Equity Large Cap Value (Growth)	B	B-	A-		Y	1,000
BMO Low Volatility Equity Fund Class I	MLVEX	NAS CM	Open End	US Equity Large Cap Value (Growth)	B	B-	A-		Y	1,000,000
BMO Mid-Cap Growth Fund Class A	BGMAX	NAS CM	Open End	US Equity Mid Cap (Growth)	C+	C	B	Down	Y	1,000
BMO Mid-Cap Growth Fund Class I	MRMIX	NAS CM	Open End	US Equity Mid Cap (Growth)	C+	C	B	Down	Y	1,000,000
BMO Mid-Cap Growth Fund Class R6	BMGGX	NAS CM	Open End	US Equity Mid Cap (Growth)	C+	C	B	Down	Y	0
BMO Mid-Cap Value Fund Class A	BAMCX	NAS CM	Open End	US Equity Mid Cap (Growth)	C	C-	B-		Y	1,000
BMO Mid-Cap Value Fund Class I	MRVIX	NAS CM	Open End	US Equity Mid Cap (Growth)	C	C-	B-		Y	1,000,000
BMO Mid-Cap Value Fund Class R6	BMVGX	NAS CM	Open End	US Equity Mid Cap (Growth)	C	C-	B-		Y	0
BMO Moderate Allocation Fund Class I	BMBHX	NAS CM	Open End	Cautious Alloc (Balanced)	B	C	A-	Up	Y	1,000,000
BMO Moderate Allocation Fund Class R3	BMBQX	NAS CM	Open End	Cautious Alloc (Balanced)	B-	C	A-	Up	Y	0
BMO Moderate Allocation Fund Class R6	BMBTX	NAS CM	Open End	Cautious Alloc (Balanced)	B	C	A-	Up	Y	0
BMO Moderate Allocation Fund Class Y	BMBYX	NAS CM	Open End	Cautious Alloc (Balanced)	B	C	A-	Up	Y	1,000
BMO Pyrford International Stock Fund Class A	BPIAX	NAS CM	Open End	Global Equity Large Cap (Foreign Stock)	C+	C	B	Up	Y	1,000
BMO Pyrford International Stock Fund Class I	MISNX	NAS CM	Open End	Global Equity Large Cap (Foreign Stock)	C+	C	B	Up	Y	1,000,000
BMO Pyrford International Stock Fund Class R6	BISGX	NAS CM	Open End	Global Equity Large Cap (Foreign Stock)	C+	C	B	Up	Y	0
BMO Small-Cap Core Fund Class A	BCCAX	NAS CM	Open End	US Equity Small Cap (Small Company)	C-	C-	C	Down	Y	1,000
BMO Small-Cap Core Fund Class I	BSCNX	NAS CM	Open End	US Equity Small Cap (Small Company)	C-	C-	C	Down	Y	1,000,000
BMO Small-Cap Growth Fund Class A	BSLAX	NAS CM	Open End	US Equity Small Cap (Small Company)	C	C-	C+	Down	Y	1,000
BMO Small-Cap Growth Fund Class I	MSGIX	NAS CM	Open End	US Equity Small Cap (Small Company)	C	C-	C+		Y	1,000,000
BMO Small-Cap Value Fund Class A	BACVX	NAS CM	Open End	US Equity Small Cap (Small Company)	C	C-	C		Y	1,000
BMO Small-Cap Value Fund Class I	MRSNX	NAS CM	Open End	US Equity Small Cap (Small Company)	C	C-	C		Y	1,000,000
BMO Small-Cap Value Fund Class R6	BSVGX	NAS CM	Open End	US Equity Small Cap (Small Company)	C	C-	C		Y	0
BMO Target Retirement 2020 Fund Class R3	BTRFX	NAS CM	Open End	Target Date (Asset Alloc)	B-	C	A-	Up	Y	0
BMO Target Retirement 2030 Fund Class R3	BTRKX	NAS CM	Open End	Target Date (Asset Alloc)	B-	C	B+	Up	Y	0
BMO Target Retirement 2040 Fund Class R3	BTRPX	NAS CM	Open End	Target Date (Asset Alloc)	B-	C	B	Up	Y	0
BMT Multi-Cap Fund	BMTMX	NAS CM	Open End	US Equity Large Cap Blend (Growth & Income)	C-	C-	B	Up	Y	5,000
BNP Paribas AM Emerging Mkts Equity Inst Shares	BNPOX	NAS CM	Open End	Global Emerg Mkts (Div Emerging Mkts)	U	U	U		Y	5,000,000
BNP Paribas AM Emerging Markets Equity Investor Shares	BNPPX	NAS CM	Open End	Global Emerg Mkts (Div Emerging Mkts)	U	U	U		Y	100,000
BNP Paribas AM Emerging Markets Equity Fund Retail Shares	BNPQX	NAS CM	Open End	Global Emerg Mkts (Div Emerging Mkts)	U	U	U		Y	2,500
BNP Paribas AM U.S. Small Cap Equity Institutional Shares	BNPUX	NAS CM	Open End	US Equity Small Cap (Small Company)	D	D+	C		Y	5,000,000
BNP Paribas AM U.S. Small Cap Equity Fund Investor Shares	BNPVX	NAS CM	Open End	US Equity Small Cap (Small Company)	D	D+	C		Y	100,000
BNP Paribas AM U.S. Small Cap Equity Fund Retail Shares	BNPWX	NAS CM	Open End	US Equity Small Cap (Small Company)	D	D+	C		Y	2,500
BNY Mellon Absolute Insight Multi-Strategy Fund Class A	MAJAX	NAS CM	Open End	Multialternative (Growth & Income)	D+	D	C	Up	Y	1,000
BNY Mellon Absolute Insight Multi-Strategy Fund Class C	MAJCX	NAS CM	Open End	Multialternative (Growth & Income)	D	D	C		Y	1,000
BNY Mellon Absolute Insight Multi-Strategy Fund Class I	MAJIX	NAS CM	Open End	Multialternative (Growth & Income)	D+	D	C		Y	1,000
BNY Mellon Absolute Insight Multi-Strategy Fund Class Y	MAJYX	NAS CM	Open End	Multialternative (Growth & Income)	D+	D	C		Y	1,000,000

★ Expanded analysis of this fund is included in Section II.

	TOTAL RETURNS					PERFORMANCE				ASSETS		ASSET ALLOCATION & TURNOVER					BULL & BEAR		FEES		
Min Additional Investment	3-Month Total Return	6-Month Total Return	1-Year Total Return	3-Year Total Return	5-Year Total Return	Dividend Yield (TTM)	Expense Ratio	3-Yr Std Deviation	3-Year Beta	NAV	Total Assets (MIL)	%Cash	%Stocks	%Bonds	%Other	Turnover Ratio	Last Bull Market Total Return	Last Bear Market Total Return	Front End Fee (%)	Back End Fee (%)	Inception Date
	1.66	11.51	8.02	26.50	38.50	2.83	0.85	8.09	0.64	11.62	34.6	2	98	0	0						Sep-13
	2.60	14.40	4.55	33.72	32.31	2.39	0.69	9.7	0.78	9.45	117.6	10	80	9	0		19.79	-17.51			May-14
	2.48	14.23	4.02	31.84	29.12	1.78	1.19	9.69	0.78	9.47	117.6	10	80	9	0		19.44	-17.68			May-14
	2.71	14.64	4.76	34.42	33.35	2.38	0.54	9.64	0.78	9.47	117.6	10	80	9	0		19.79	-17.51			May-14
50	2.60	14.38	4.32	32.75	30.77	2.11	0.94	9.7	0.78	9.46	117.6	10	80	9	0		19.79	-17.51			May-14
	2.78	10.40	5.09	17.91	17.76	2.87	1.14	4.19	0.94		8.1	10	31	59	0		14.25	-11.14			Aug-13
50	2.35	17.85	8.60	60.99	83.43	0.41	0.79	13.28	0.98	17.82	495.8	2	98	0	0		27.44	-18.54	5.00		May-14
	2.44	17.99	8.92	62.18	85.85	0.6	0.54	13.29	0.98	18.03	495.8	2	98	0	0		27.79	-18.4			Jan-08
	2.49	18.10	9.09	62.98	86.09	0.71	0.39	13.29	0.98	18.07	495.8	2	98	0	0		27.62	-18.46			Dec-15
50	2.35	17.89	8.62	61.02	83.46	0.29	0.79	13.29	0.98	17.85	495.8	2	98	0	0		27.62	-18.46			Nov-92
50	1.31	13.98	2.44	35.45	37.73	1.74	0.79	12.85	1.04	14.29	308.8	2	98	0	0		24.1	-18.92	5.00		May-14
	1.38	14.11	2.63	36.50	39.49	1.98	0.54	12.81	1.04	14.3	308.8	2	98	0	0		24.29	-18.83			Jan-08
	1.40	14.23	2.80	37.12	40.24	2.07	0.39	12.85	1.04	14.31	308.8	2	98	0	0		24.29	-18.83			Dec-15
50	2.84	11.64	2.62	26.29	24.95	0.78	1.41	12.66	0.77	15.92	297.0	2	98	0	0		17.47	-27.38	5.00		May-14
	2.92	11.78	2.89	27.35	26.62	1.17	1.16	12.68	0.77	15.84	297.0	2	98	0	0		17.64	-27.31			Dec-08
100	-4.35	-3.30	-16.07	5.84	-6.76	2.19	2.01	9.93		8.79	--	5	89	0	0	17					Dec-13
50	4.94	17.98	15.67	36.68	60.47	1.33	0.9	9.34	0.67	15.4	182.3	2	98	0	0				5.00		May-14
	5.05	18.13	16.05	37.73	62.74	1.55	0.65	9.42	0.68	15.46	182.3	2	98	0	0						Sep-12
50	1.33	21.20	8.95	57.91	40.53	0	1.24	15.24	1.04	14.46	100.2	2	98	0	0		32.95	-25.77	5.00		May-14
	1.32	21.31	9.16	59.13	42.28	0	0.99	15.21	1.04	15.31	100.2	2	98	0	0		33.14	-25.69			Jan-08
	1.37	21.46	9.30	59.85	43.33	0	0.84	15.23	1.04	15.45	100.2	2	98	0	0		33.14	-25.69			May-14
50	1.06	13.92	-2.19	28.46	24.78	0.91	1.24	14.16	1.05	10.47	153.3	1	99	0	0		26.82	-24.14	5.00		May-14
	1.06	14.16	-1.89	29.46	26.39	1.21	0.99	14.21	1.05	10.4	153.3	1	99	0	0		27.01	-24.06			Jan-08
	1.16	14.26	-1.71	29.97	27.30	1.37	0.83	14.13	1.04	10.41	153.3	1	99	0	0		27.01	-24.06			May-14
	2.69	10.66	5.52	21.05	22.54	2.73	0.63	5.58	0.35	9.13	71.9	13	42	45	0		12.87	-9.61			May-14
	2.58	10.27	5.04	19.21	19.42	2.25	1.13	5.52	0.35	9.12	71.9	13	42	45	0		12.55	-9.8			May-14
	2.69	10.66	5.63	21.64	23.45	2.73	0.48	5.58	0.34	9.13	71.9	13	42	45	0		12.87	-9.61			May-14
50	2.59	10.42	5.25	20.15	20.93	2.61	0.88	5.56	0.36	9.11	71.9	13	42	45	0		12.87	-9.61			May-14
50	3.45	13.37	5.53	19.97	10.24	2.43	1.2	9.49	0.81	13.48	660.1	0	100	0	0				5.00		May-14
	3.52	13.46	5.78	20.95	11.70	2.6	0.95	9.53	0.82	13.23	660.1	0	100	0	0						Dec-11
	3.59	13.55	5.89	21.52	12.55	2.76	0.8	9.55	0.82	13.24	660.1	0	100	0	0						May-14
50	0.59	14.28	-9.79	31.70	35.34	0.04	1.15	18.45	1.06	11.84	15.9	1	99	0	0				5.00		May-14
	0.58	14.32	-9.57	32.71	37.07	0.04	0.9	18.47	1.06	11.97	15.9	1	99	0	0						Dec-13
50	-0.12	16.38	-4.20	41.72	18.13	0	1.24	17.99	1.02	15.91	108.0	2	98	0	0		34.81	-29.26	5.00		May-17
	-0.05	16.51	-3.97	42.85	19.67	0	0.99	17.99	1.02	16.72	108.0	2	98	0	0		35.01	-29.19			Jan-08
50	1.42	13.93	-7.78	29.21	19.95	0.43	1.24	17.89	1.02	12.1	60.1	2	98	0	0		23.99	-22.15	5.00		May-14
	1.48	13.98	-7.59	30.16	21.46	0.7	0.99	17.91	1.02	12.31	60.1	2	98	0	0		24.17	-22.07			Feb-11
	1.55	14.15	-7.38	30.90	22.53	0.71	0.84	17.9	1.02	12.42	60.1	2	98	0	0		24.17	-22.07			May-14
	3.08	13.98	4.77	26.41	24.40	2.12	1.19	6.56	1.14		49.0	8	53	39	0		18.09	-15.28			Aug-13
	3.46	17.51	4.38	32.70	28.69	1.79	1.25	8.65	1.11		65.6	8	74	18	0		20.78	-18.12			Aug-13
	3.58	19.32	4.12	36.56	31.37	1.73	1.24	9.73	1.04		36.4	6	85	8	0		22.06	-19.37			Aug-13
500	4.06	19.22	8.58			0.64	1.02			12.03	206.0	6	94	0	0	8					Aug-17
	0.68	12.29					0.75			10.23	20.5	3	97	0	0						Oct-18
	0.68	12.29					0.9			10.23	20.5	3	97	0	0						Oct-18
	0.59	12.07					1.15			10.21	20.5	3	97	0	0						Oct-18
	2.18	25.25	-1.47			0.23	0.75			9.82	19.7	6	94	0	0						Jan-18
	2.18	25.25	-1.47			0.23	0.75			9.82	19.7	6	94	0	0						Jan-18
	2.08	25.12	-1.66				1.15			9.81	19.7	6	94	0	0						Oct-18
100	0.00	0.58	-2.20	-1.35		0.61	1.77	1.44	11.77	12.12	121.9	100	0	0	0	292			5.75		Dec-15
100	-0.08	0.25	-2.48	-3.12		1.15	2.52	1.4	11.84	11.78	121.9	100	0	0	0	292				1.00	Dec-15
100	0.24	0.92	-1.40	0.00		2.16	1.49	1.39	10.84	12.06	121.9	100	0	0	0	292					Dec-15
	0.24	0.83	-1.40	0.08		2.17	1.49	1.43	11.85	12.06	121.9	100	0	0	0	292					Dec-15

	MARKET			FUND TYPE, CATEGORY & OBJECTIVE	RATINGS				MINIMUMS	
Fund Name	Ticker Symbol	Traded On	Fund Type	Category and (Prospectus Objective)	Overall Rating	Reward Rating	Risk Rating	Recent Up/ Downgrade	Open to New Investors	Min Initial Investment
BNY Mellon Active MidCap Fund - Class A	DNLDX	NAS CM	Open End	US Equity Mid Cap (Growth)	C	C	B-		Y	1,000
BNY Mellon Active MidCap Fund - Class C	DNLCX	NAS CM	Open End	US Equity Mid Cap (Growth)	C	C	B-		Y	1,000
BNY Mellon Active MidCap Fund - Class I	DNLRX	NAS CM	Open End	US Equity Mid Cap (Growth)	C	C	B		Y	1,000
BNY Mellon Active MidCap Fund - Class Y	DNLYX	NAS CM	Open End	US Equity Mid Cap (Growth)	C	C	B		Y	1,000,000
BNY Mellon Alternative Diversifier Strategies - Cls A	DRNAX	NAS CM	Open End	Multialternative (Growth)	C	C	C+	Up	Y	1,000
BNY Mellon Alternative Diversifier Strategies - Cls C	DRNCX	NAS CM	Open End	Multialternative (Growth)	C	D+	C	Up	Y	1,000
BNY Mellon Alternative Diversifier Strategies - Cls I	DRNIX	NAS CM	Open End	Multialternative (Growth)	C	C	B-	Up	Y	1,000
BNY Mellon Alternative Diversifier Strategies - Cls Y	DRYNX	NAS CM	Open End	Multialternative (Growth)	C	C	B-	Up	Y	1,000,000
BNY Mellon Appreciation Fund, Inc. - Class I	DGIGX	NAS CM	Open End	US Equity Large Cap Blend (Growth)	B	B-	B	Up	Y	1,000
BNY Mellon Appreciation Fund, Inc. - Class Y	DGYGX	NAS CM	Open End	US Equity Large Cap Blend (Growth)	B	B-	B	Up	Y	1,000,000
BNY Mellon Appreciation Fund, Inc. - Investor Shares	DGAGX	NAS CM	Open End	US Equity Large Cap Blend (Growth)	B	B-	B	Up	Y	2,500
BNY Mellon Asset Allocation Fund Class M	MPBLX	NAS CM	Open End	Moderate Alloc (Balanced)	B-	C	B+	Up	Y	10,000
BNY Mellon Asset Allocation Fund Investor Class	MIBLX	NAS CM	Open End	Moderate Alloc (Balanced)	B-	C	B+	Up	Y	10,000
BNY Mellon Balanced Opportunity Fund - Class A	DBOAX	NAS CM	Open End	Moderate Alloc (Balanced)	B-	C	B+		Y	1,000
BNY Mellon Balanced Opportunity Fund - Class C	DBOCX	NAS CM	Open End	Moderate Alloc (Balanced)	B-	C	B+	Up	Y	1,000
BNY Mellon Balanced Opportunity Fund - Class J	THPBX	NAS CM	Open End	Moderate Alloc (Balanced)	B-	C	A-			1,000
BNY Mellon Balanced Opportunity Fund - Class Y	DBOYX	NAS CM	Open End	Moderate Alloc (Balanced)	B-	C	A-		Y	1,000,000
BNY Mellon Balanced Opportunity Fund - Class Z	DBOZX	NAS CM	Open End	Moderate Alloc (Balanced)	B-	C	A-			1,000
BNY Mellon Balanced Opportunity Fund- Class I	DBORX	NAS CM	Open End	Moderate Alloc (Balanced)	B-	C	A-		Y	1,000
BNY Mellon Broad Opportunities Fund - Class A	DIOAX	NAS CM	Open End	Multialternative (Multi-Asset Global)	D+	D+	B-	Up	Y	1,000
BNY Mellon Broad Opportunities Fund - Class C	DIOCX	NAS CM	Open End	Multialternative (Multi-Asset Global)	D+	D+	B-	Up	Y	1,000
BNY Mellon Broad Opportunities Fund - Class I	DIOIX	NAS CM	Open End	Multialternative (Multi-Asset Global)	D+	D+	B-	Up	Y	1,000
BNY Mellon Broad Opportunities Fund - Class Y	DIOYX	NAS CM	Open End	Multialternative (Multi-Asset Global)	D+	D+	B-	Up	Y	1,000,000
BNY Mellon Disciplined Stock Fund	DDSTX	NAS CM	Open End	US Equity Large Cap Blend (Growth & Income)	C+	C	B		Y	2,500
BNY Mellon Diversified Emerging Markets Fund Class A	DBEAX	NAS CM	Open End	Global Emerg Mkts (Div Emerging Mkts)	C	C	C+		Y	1,000
BNY Mellon Diversified Emerging Markets Fund Class C	DBECX	NAS CM	Open End	Global Emerg Mkts (Div Emerging Mkts)	C	C	C+		Y	1,000
BNY Mellon Diversified Emerging Markets Fund Class I	SBCEX	NAS CM	Open End	Global Emerg Mkts (Div Emerging Mkts)	C	C	C+		Y	1,000
BNY Mellon Diversified Emerging Markets Fund Class Y	SBYEX	NAS CM	Open End	Global Emerg Mkts (Div Emerging Mkts)	C	C	C+		Y	1,000,000
BNY Mellon Diversified International Fund Class A	DFPAX	NAS CM	Open End	Global Equity Large Cap (Foreign Stock)	C	C	B-		Y	1,000
BNY Mellon Diversified International Fund Class C	DFPCX	NAS CM	Open End	Global Equity Large Cap (Foreign Stock)	C	C	B-		Y	1,000
BNY Mellon Diversified International Fund Class I	DFPIX	NAS CM	Open End	Global Equity Large Cap (Foreign Stock)	C	C	B-		Y	1,000
BNY Mellon Diversified International Fund Class Y	DDIFX	NAS CM	Open End	Global Equity Large Cap (Foreign Stock)	C	C	B-		Y	1,000,000
BNY Mellon Dynamic Total Return Fund Class A	AVGAX	NAS CM	Open End	Global Macro (Growth & Income)	C+	C	B	Up	Y	1,000
BNY Mellon Dynamic Total Return Fund Class C	AVGCX	NAS CM	Open End	Global Macro (Growth & Income)	C+	C	B	Up	Y	1,000
BNY Mellon Dynamic Total Return Fund Class I	AVGRX	NAS CM	Open End	Global Macro (Growth & Income)	C+	C	B	Up	Y	1,000
BNY Mellon Dynamic Total Return Fund Class Y	AVGYX	NAS CM	Open End	Global Macro (Growth & Income)	C+	C	B	Up	Y	1,000,000
BNY Mellon Dynamic Value Fund Class A	DAGVX	NAS CM	Open End	US Equity Large Cap Value (Growth)	C+	C	B	Up	Y	1,000
BNY Mellon Dynamic Value Fund Class C	DCGVX	NAS CM	Open End	US Equity Large Cap Value (Growth)	C+	C	B	Up	Y	1,000
BNY Mellon Dynamic Value Fund Class I	DRGVX	NAS CM	Open End	US Equity Large Cap Value (Growth)	C+	C	B	Up	Y	1,000
BNY Mellon Dynamic Value Fund Class Y	DRGYX	NAS CM	Open End	US Equity Large Cap Value (Growth)	C+	C	B	Up	Y	1,000,000
BNY Mellon Emerging Markets Fund Class Investor	MIEGX	NAS CM	Open End	Global Emerg Mkts (Div Emerging Mkts)	C	C	C		Y	10,000
BNY Mellon Emerging Markets Fund Class M	MEMKX	NAS CM	Open End	Global Emerg Mkts (Div Emerging Mkts)	C	C	C		Y	10,000
BNY Mellon Emerging Markets Securities Fund Class A	DRFMX	NAS CM	Open End	Global Emerg Mkts (Div Emerging Mkts)	C	C-	C+		Y	1,000
BNY Mellon Emerging Markets Securities Fund Class C	DCPEX	NAS CM	Open End	Global Emerg Mkts (Div Emerging Mkts)	C	D+	C+		Y	1,000
BNY Mellon Emerging Markets Securities Fund Class I	DRPEX	NAS CM	Open End	Global Emerg Mkts (Div Emerging Mkts)	C	C-	B-		Y	1,000
BNY Mellon Emerging Markets Securities Fund Class Y	DYPEX	NAS CM	Open End	Global Emerg Mkts (Div Emerging Mkts)	C	C-	B-		Y	1,000,000
BNY Mellon Equity Income Fund Class A	DQIAX	NAS CM	Open End	US Equity Large Cap Value (Equity-Income)	B-	C	B	Up	Y	1,000
BNY Mellon Equity Income Fund Class C	DQICX	NAS CM	Open End	US Equity Large Cap Value (Equity-Income)	B-	C	B	Up	Y	1,000
BNY Mellon Equity Income Fund Class I	DQIRX	NAS CM	Open End	US Equity Large Cap Value (Equity-Income)	B-	C	B	Up	Y	1,000
BNY Mellon Equity Income Fund Class Y	DQIYX	NAS CM	Open End	US Equity Large Cap Value (Equity-Income)	B-	C	B	Up	Y	1,000,000
BNY Mellon Focused Equity Opportunities Cls M Shares	MFOMX	NAS CM	Open End	US Equity Large Cap Growth (Growth)	C+	C	B	Down	Y	10,000
BNY Mellon Focused Equity Opportunities Investor Shares	MFOIX	NAS CM	Open End	US Equity Large Cap Growth (Growth)	C+	C	B	Down	Y	10,000

★ Expanded analysis of this fund is included in Section II.

	TOTAL RETURNS					PERFORMANCE				ASSETS		ASSET ALLOCATION & TURNOVER					BULL & BEAR		FEES		
Min Additional Investment	3-Month Total Return	6-Month Total Return	1-Year Total Return	3-Year Total Return	5-Year Total Return	Dividend Yield (TTM)	Expense Ratio	3-Yr Std Deviation	3-Year Beta	NAV	Total Assets (MIL)	%Cash	%Stocks	%Bonds	%Other	Turnover Ratio	Last Bull Market Total Return	Last Bear Market Total Return	Front End Fee (%)	Back End Fee (%)	Inception Date
100	1.53	15.87	0.11	26.68	35.93	0.5	1.12	13.35	0.97	55.04	475.7	0	100	0	0	68	26.46	-24.02	5.75		Jan-85
100	1.29	15.37	-0.75	23.51	30.29	0	1.96	13.34	0.97	49.88	475.7	0	100	0	0	68	25.84	-24.26		1.00	Nov-02
100	1.58	16.00	0.33	27.54	37.42	0.07	0.89	13.35	0.97	55.64	475.7	0	100	0	0	68	26.63	-24.03			Nov-02
	1.61	16.04	0.38	27.72	37.42	2.12	0.88	13.35	0.97	54.24	475.7	0	100	0	0	68	26.46	-24.02			Sep-15
100	1.93	7.53	1.12	3.54	1.99	0.13	2.14	5.02	0.36	12.63	428.4	-6	38	49	18	19			5.75		Mar-14
100	1.72	7.16	0.27	1.08	-1.74	0.09	2.89	5.07	0.37	12.41	428.4	-6	38	49	18	19				1.00	Mar-14
100	2.02	7.75	1.50	4.70	3.61	0.78	1.72	5.04	0.37	12.61	428.4	-6	38	49	18	19					Mar-14
	2.01	7.80	1.57	4.99	4.32	0.85	1.64	5.04	0.36	12.66	428.4	-6	38	49	18	19					Mar-14
100	5.85	21.52	12.17	50.77	52.20	1.24	0.66	11.33	0.9	32.03	1,640	1	99	0	0	5	21.88	-12.48			Aug-16
	5.86	21.55	12.22	51.19	53.76	1.3	0.59	11.32	0.89	32.1	1,640	1	99	0	0	5	21.88	-12.48			Jul-13
100	5.79	21.41	11.89	49.80	51.22	1.02	0.9	11.33	0.89	32.23	1,640	1	99	0	0	5	21.88	-12.48			Jan-84
100	3.01	13.54	3.80	29.76	29.98	2.1	0.87	8.79	1.26	12.33	465.1	5	66	28	0	21	14.29	-15.02			Oct-00
100	3.02	13.46	3.60	28.79	28.48	1.85	1.12	8.8	1.26	12.43	465.1	5	66	28	0	21	14.13	-15.1			Jul-01
100	3.47	12.99	6.23	29.84	35.28	1.07	1.2	8.72	0.7	22.33	315.4	4	64	32	0	99	16.41	-14.42	5.75		Jan-04
100	3.33	12.56	5.44	26.96	30.30	0.53	1.95	8.71	0.7	22.32	315.4	4	64	32	0	99	15.86	-14.72		1.00	Jan-04
100	3.56	13.11	6.46	30.81	37.00	1.3	0.95	8.72	0.7	22.39	315.4	4	64	32	0	99	16.52	-14.4			Mar-87
	3.51	13.06	6.47	30.85	37.03	1.39	0.95	8.72	0.7	22.37	315.4	4	64	32	0	99	16.52	-14.4			Sep-16
100	3.53	13.07	6.38	30.50	36.50	1.26	1.01	8.72	0.7	22.24	315.4	4	64	32	0	99	16.25	-14.41			Dec-04
100	3.57	13.13	6.52	30.84	37.04	1.73	0.95	8.71	0.7	22.28	315.4	4	64	32	0	99	16.61	-14.34			Jan-04
100	3.37	8.55	6.14			3.7	1.28			12.56	30.2	31	24	39	6				5.75		Nov-17
100	3.12	8.11	5.35			2.92	2.03			12.52	30.2	31	24	39	6					1.00	Nov-17
100	3.37	8.64	6.35			3.97	1.03			12.57	30.2	31	24	39	6						Nov-17
	3.37	8.64	6.36			3.97	1.03			12.57	30.2	31	24	39	6						Nov-17
100	3.55	17.39	6.70	46.79	57.65	1	1	13.09	1.06	33.55	587.9	1	99	0	0	72	23.16	-21.03			Dec-87
100	0.78	11.63	-2.12	29.10	8.63	0.07	1.77	14.2	1	23.13	222.2	1	99	0	0	41	17.59	-29.11	5.75		Mar-09
100	0.55	11.12	-2.86	25.33	4.10	0	2.81	14.17	1	21.67	222.2	1	99	0	0	41	17.03	-29.32		1.00	Mar-09
100	0.92	11.95	-1.50	30.83	11.14	1.06	1.4	14.18	1	22.94	222.2	1	99	0	0	41	18.1	-28.91			Jul-06
	0.92	11.99	-1.48	31.03	11.49	1.16	1.31	14.16	1	22.96	222.2	1	99	0	0	41	18.1	-28.91			Jan-14
100	2.96	14.30	0.01	26.69	12.68	1.38	1.3	11.44	1.01	12.84	879.2	2	98	0	0	4	14.28	-23.25	5.75		Dec-07
100	2.72	14.07	-0.60	24.11	8.69	0.49	2.05	11.49	1.01	12.83	879.2	2	98	0	0	4	13.84	-23.36		1.00	Dec-07
100	3.04	14.56	0.35	28.04	14.60	1.74	0.97	11.48	1.01	12.85	879.2	2	98	0	0	4	14.48	-23.14			Dec-07
	3.13	14.60	0.38	28.13	14.77	1.77	0.93	11.47	1.01	12.84	879.2	2	98	0	0	4	14.48	-23.14			Oct-15
100	1.21	9.82	2.40	9.81	12.44	0.84	1.45	6.56	0.49	15.88	990.2	58	33	9	0	18	11.65	-11.38	5.75		May-06
100	1.02	9.42	1.63	7.36	8.32	0.11	2.2	6.52	0.49	14.74	990.2	58	33	9	0	18	11.16	-11.59		1.00	May-06
100	1.30	9.98	2.72	10.72	13.99	1.16	1.2	6.55	0.49	16.31	990.2	58	33	9	0	18	11.91	-11.21			May-06
	1.30	10.00	2.74	10.81	14.31	1.41	1.15	6.53	0.49	16.28	990.2	58	33	9	0	18	11.91	-11.21			Jul-13
100	4.46	16.14	3.24	39.17	42.75	1.58	0.93	14.19	1.14	35.32	1,500	0	100	0	0	106	25.74	-24.52	5.75		Sep-95
100	4.22	15.68	2.44	36.08	37.48	0.83	1.68	14.18	1.14	32.53	1,500	0	100	0	0	106	25.19	-24.76		1.00	May-01
100	4.50	16.27	3.51	40.26	44.55	1.67	0.68	14.18	1.14	35.5	1,500	0	100	0	0	106	25.87	-24.41			May-01
	4.51	16.27	3.51	40.35	44.64	1.89	0.64	14.18	1.14	35.43	1,500	0	100	0	0	106	25.74	-24.52			Jul-13
100	0.73	11.26	-2.45	31.87	5.02	0.45	1.65	14.75	1.05	10.96	889.5	1	99	0	0	81	17.61	-28.36			Jul-01
100	0.75	11.37	-2.25	32.79	6.28	0.7	1.4	14.72	1.05	10.67	889.5	1	99	0	0	81	17.81	-28.35			Oct-00
100	-0.19	8.99	1.28	26.64	0.09	0.34	1.98	14.16	1	10.06	106.2	0	100	0	0	72	14.43	-28.08	5.75		Jun-96
100	-0.40	8.48	0.61	23.94	-3.62	0	2.73	14.07	0.99	9.84	106.2	0	100	0	0	72	13.87	-28.36		1.00	Nov-02
100	-0.19	9.08	1.51	27.65	1.24	0.67	1.72	14.18	1	10.33	106.2	0	100	0	0	72	14.6	-28.04			Nov-02
	-0.09	9.20	1.73	28.12	2.31	0.85	1.58	14.13	0.99	10.08	106.2	0	100	0	0	72	14.43	-28.08			Jul-13
100	1.17	12.24	3.57	35.74	46.87	2.28	1.03	11.92	0.95	19.27	1,109	1	99	0	0	56	19.91	-10.25	5.75		Jul-06
100	0.94	11.82	2.81	32.73	41.53	1.59	1.78	11.88	0.95	19	1,109	1	99	0	0	56	19.34	-10.54		1.00	Jul-06
100	1.18	12.37	3.81	36.81	48.73	2.51	0.78	11.9	0.95	19.31	1,109	1	99	0	0	56	20.07	-10.13			Jul-06
	1.23	12.43	4.23	37.70	49.57	2.5	0.78	11.95	0.96	19.42	1,109	1	99	0	0	56	20.07	-10.13			Jul-13
100	6.16	18.15	5.40	65.47	66.24	0.69	0.86	13.44	1.05	15.49	440.9	0	100	0	0	45	26.33	-23.1			Sep-09
100	6.10	17.97	5.12	64.10	64.16	0.53	1.11	13.43	1.05	15.29	440.9	0	100	0	0	45	26.16	-23.06			Sep-09

	MARKET			FUND TYPE, CATEGORY & OBJECTIVE	RATINGS				MINIMUMS	
Fund Name	Ticker Symbol	Traded On	Fund Type	Category and (Prospectus Objective)	Overall Rating	Reward Rating	Risk Rating	Recent Up/ Downgrade	Open to New Investors	Min Initial Investment
BNY Mellon Global Emerging Markets Fund - Class A	DGEAX	NAS CM	Open End	Global Emerg Mkts (Growth)	C	C	C		Y	1,000
BNY Mellon Global Emerging Markets Fund - Class C	DGECX	NAS CM	Open End	Global Emerg Mkts (Growth)	C	C-	C	Up	Y	1,000
BNY Mellon Global Emerging Markets Fund - Class I	DGIEX	NAS CM	Open End	Global Emerg Mkts (Growth)	C	C	C		Y	1,000
BNY Mellon Global Emerging Markets Fund - Class Y	DGEYX	NAS CM	Open End	Global Emerg Mkts (Growth)	C	C	C		Y	1,000,000
BNY Mellon Global Equity Income Fund - Class A	DEQAX	NAS CM	Open End	Global Equity Large Cap (Equity-Income)	B	C+	B+	Up	Y	1,000
BNY Mellon Global Equity Income Fund - Class C	DEQCX	NAS CM	Open End	Global Equity Large Cap (Equity-Income)	B-	C	B+	Up	Y	1,000
BNY Mellon Global Equity Income Fund - Class I	DQEIX	NAS CM	Open End	Global Equity Large Cap (Equity-Income)	B	C+	B+	Up	Y	1,000
BNY Mellon Global Equity Income Fund - Class Y	DEQYX	NAS CM	Open End	Global Equity Large Cap (Equity-Income)	B	C+	B+	Up	Y	1,000,000
BNY Mellon Global Real Estate Securities - Class A	DRLAX	NAS CM	Open End	Real Estate Sector Equity (Real Estate)	B-	C	B		Y	1,000
BNY Mellon Global Real Estate Securities Fund - Class C	DGBCX	NAS CM	Open End	Real Estate Sector Equity (Real Estate)	B-	C	B	Up	Y	1,000
BNY Mellon Global Real Estate Securities Fund - Class I	DRLIX	NAS CM	Open End	Real Estate Sector Equity (Real Estate)	B-	C	B		Y	1,000
BNY Mellon Global Real Estate Securities Fund - Class Y	DRLYX	NAS CM	Open End	Real Estate Sector Equity (Real Estate)	B-	C	B		Y	1,000,000
BNY Mellon Global Real Return Fund - Class A	DRRAX	NAS CM	Open End	Global Macro (Growth & Income)	B-	C	B	Up	Y	1,000
BNY Mellon Global Real Return Fund - Class C	DRRCX	NAS CM	Open End	Global Macro (Growth & Income)	C+	C	B	Up	Y	1,000
BNY Mellon Global Real Return Fund - Class I	DRRIX	NAS CM	Open End	Global Macro (Growth & Income)	B-	C	B+	Up	Y	1,000
BNY Mellon Global Real Return Fund - Class Y	DRRYX	NAS CM	Open End	Global Macro (Growth & Income)	B-	C	B+	Up	Y	1,000,000
BNY Mellon Global Stock Fund - Class A	DGLAX	NAS CM	Open End	Global Equity Large Cap (World Stock)	B	C+	B+			1,000
BNY Mellon Global Stock Fund - Class C	DGLCX	NAS CM	Open End	Global Equity Large Cap (World Stock)	B-	C+	B+	Down		1,000
BNY Mellon Global Stock Fund - Class I	DGLRX	NAS CM	Open End	Global Equity Large Cap (World Stock)	B	C+	B+			1,000
BNY Mellon Global Stock Fund - Class Y	DGLYX	NAS CM	Open End	Global Equity Large Cap (World Stock)	B	C+	B+			1,000,000
BNY Mellon Growth and Income Fund, Inc.	DGRIX	NAS CM	Open End	US Equity Large Cap Growth (Growth & Income)	C+	C	B	Down	Y	2,500
BNY Mellon Growth Fund Class I	SSETX	NAS CM	Open End	US Equity Small Cap (Small Company)	C+	C+	C+	Down	Y	1,000
BNY Mellon Income Stock Fund Class A	BMIAX	NAS CM	Open End	US Equity Large Cap Value (Equity-Income)	B-	C	B	Up	Y	1,000
BNY Mellon Income Stock Fund Class C	BMISX	NAS CM	Open End	US Equity Large Cap Value (Equity-Income)	C+	C	B		Y	1,000
BNY Mellon Income Stock Fund Class I	BMIIX	NAS CM	Open End	US Equity Large Cap Value (Equity-Income)	B-	C	B	Up	Y	1,000
BNY Mellon Income Stock Fund Class M	MPISX	NAS CM	Open End	US Equity Large Cap Value (Equity-Income)	B-	C	B	Up	Y	10,000
BNY Mellon Income Stock Fund Class Y	BMIYX	NAS CM	Open End	US Equity Large Cap Value (Equity-Income)	B-	C	B	Up	Y	1,000,000
BNY Mellon Income Stock Fund Investor shares	MIISX	NAS CM	Open End	US Equity Large Cap Value (Equity-Income)	B-	C	B	Up	Y	10,000
BNY Mellon Institutional S&P 500 Stock Index Fund Class I	DSPIX	NAS CM	Open End	US Equity Large Cap Blend (Growth & Income)	B-	C	B		Y	1,000
BNY Mellon International Core Equity Fund Class A	DIEAX	NAS CM	Open End	Global Equity Large Cap (Foreign Stock)	C	C	B-		Y	1,000
BNY Mellon International Core Equity Fund Class C	DIECX	NAS CM	Open End	Global Equity Large Cap (Foreign Stock)	C	C	C+		Y	1,000
BNY Mellon International Core Equity Fund Class I	DIERX	NAS CM	Open End	Global Equity Large Cap (Foreign Stock)	C	C	B-		Y	1,000
BNY Mellon International Core Equity Fund Class Y	DIEYX	NAS CM	Open End	Global Equity Large Cap (Foreign Stock)	C	C	B-		Y	1,000,000
BNY Mellon International Equity Fund Class A	NIEAX	NAS CM	Open End	Global Equity Large Cap (Foreign Stock)	C	C-	B-		Y	1,000
BNY Mellon International Equity Fund Class C	NIECX	NAS CM	Open End	Global Equity Large Cap (Foreign Stock)	C	C-	C+	Up	Y	1,000
BNY Mellon International Equity Fund Class I	SNIEX	NAS CM	Open End	Global Equity Large Cap (Foreign Stock)	C	C-	B-		Y	1,000
BNY Mellon International Equity Fund Class Y	NIEYX	NAS CM	Open End	Global Equity Large Cap (Foreign Stock)	C	C-	B-		Y	1,000,000
BNY Mellon International Equity Income Class M	MLIMX	NAS CM	Open End	Global Equity Large Cap (Foreign Stock)	C	C-	C+		Y	10,000
BNY Mellon International Equity Income Investor	MLIIX	NAS CM	Open End	Global Equity Large Cap (Foreign Stock)	C	C-	C+		Y	10,000
BNY Mellon International Fund Class Investor	MIINX	NAS CM	Open End	Global Equity Large Cap (Foreign Stock)	C	C	B-		Y	10,000
BNY Mellon International Fund Class M	MPITX	NAS CM	Open End	Global Equity Large Cap (Foreign Stock)	C	C	B-		Y	10,000
BNY Mellon International Small Cap Fund Class A	DYAPX	NAS CM	Open End	Global Equity Mid/Small Cap (Small Company)	C	C-	C		Y	1,000
BNY Mellon International Small Cap Fund Class C	DYCPX	NAS CM	Open End	Global Equity Mid/Small Cap (Small Company)	C	C-	C	Up	Y	1,000
BNY Mellon International Small Cap Fund Class I	DYIPX	NAS CM	Open End	Global Equity Mid/Small Cap (Small Company)	C	C-	C		Y	1,000
BNY Mellon International Small Cap Fund Class Y	DYYPX	NAS CM	Open End	Global Equity Mid/Small Cap (Small Company)	C	C-	C		Y	1,000,000
BNY Mellon International Stock Fund Class A	DISAX	NAS CM	Open End	Global Equity Large Cap (Foreign Stock)	B-	C	B	Up		1,000
BNY Mellon International Stock Fund Class C	DISCX	NAS CM	Open End	Global Equity Large Cap (Foreign Stock)	B-	C	B	Up		1,000
BNY Mellon International Stock Fund Class I	DISRX	NAS CM	Open End	Global Equity Large Cap (Foreign Stock)	B-	C	B	Up		1,000
BNY Mellon International Stock Fund Class Y	DISYX	NAS CM	Open End	Global Equity Large Cap (Foreign Stock)	B-	C	B	Up		1,000,000
BNY Mellon International Stock Index Fund Class I	DINIX	NAS CM	Open End	Global Equity Large Cap (Foreign Stock)	C	C	B		Y	1,000
BNY Mellon International Stock Index Fund Investor Shares	DIISX	NAS CM	Open End	Global Equity Large Cap (Foreign Stock)	C	C	B		Y	2,500
BNY Mellon Japan Womenomics Fund Class A	DJWAX	NAS CM	Open End	Japan Equity (Pacific Stock)	U	U	U		Y	1,000

★ Expanded analysis of this fund is included in Section II.

Min Additional Investment	3-Month Total Return	6-Month Total Return	1-Year Total Return	3-Year Total Return	5-Year Total Return	Dividend Yield (TTM)	Expense Ratio	3-Yr Std Deviation	3-Year Beta	NAV	Total Assets (MIL)	%Cash	%Stocks	%Bonds	%Other	Turnover Ratio	Last Bull Market Total Return	Last Bear Market Total Return	Front End Fee (%)	Back End Fee (%)	Inception Date
	TOTAL RETURNS					PERFORMANCE				ASSETS		ASSET ALLOCATION & TURNOVER					BULL & BEAR		FEES		
100	0.12	12.88	-4.79	24.35	13.22	0.77	1.25	15.71	1	15.94	284.0	2	98	0	0	42			5.75		Feb-14
100	-0.12	12.42	-5.55	21.55	8.98	0.1	2	15.7	1	15.47	284.0	2	98	0	0	42				1.00	Feb-14
100	0.12	12.98	-4.62	25.21	14.49	1.17	1	15.72	1	16.01	284.0	2	98	0	0	42					Feb-14
	0.18	13.00	-4.58	25.27	14.75	1.29	0.94	15.72	1	16.07	284.0	2	98	0	0	42					Feb-14
100	6.25	18.51	11.55	31.94	41.35	2.26	1.18	9.87	0.81	13.76	446.0	2	97	0	1	22	15.07	-13.24	5.75		Oct-07
100	6.07	18.12	10.79	29.13	36.28	1.49	1.91	9.83	0.8	14.24	446.0	2	97	0	1	22	14.62	-13.51		1.00	Oct-07
100	6.33	18.72	11.86	33.07	43.27	2.62	0.9	9.88	0.81	13.08	446.0	2	97	0	1	22	15.19	-13.17			Oct-07
	6.27	18.69	11.93	33.26	43.78	2.67	0.83	9.9	0.81	13.06	446.0	2	97	0	1	22	15.19	-13.17			Jul-13
100	0.73	15.57	8.59	16.57	30.47	2	1.3	11.26	1.01	9.58	694.3	1	99	0	1	55	23.96	-19.19	5.75		Dec-06
100	0.42	15.10	7.83	13.85	25.65	1.38	2.05	11.3	1.01	9.38	694.3	1	99	0	1	55	23.33	-19.33		1.00	Sep-08
100	0.74	15.69	8.90	17.35	32.20	2.27	1.05	11.31	1.01	9.44	694.3	1	99	0	1	55	24.04	-18.93			Dec-06
	0.74	15.69	8.93	17.45	32.34	2.3	1.02	11.28	1.01	9.44	694.3	1	99	0	1	55	24.04	-18.93			Jul-13
100	4.03	8.94	9.19	8.79	16.43	3.11	1.13	4.96	4.01	15.22	2,614	7	30	56	3	86	4.04	-7.18	5.75		May-10
100	3.86	8.51	8.41	6.38	12.18	2.42	1.9	5.02	4.57	14.78	2,614	7	30	56	3	86	3.55	-7.45		1.00	May-10
100	4.09	9.07	9.51	9.66	17.99	3.33	0.9	4.96	3.71	15.26	2,614	7	30	56	3	86	4.16	-7.09			May-10
	4.15	9.14	9.59	9.92	18.39	3.41	0.8	4.97	4.06	15.28	2,614	7	30	56	3	86	4.16	-7.09			Jul-13
100	3.77	20.14	13.10	48.20	52.01	0.53	1.2	11.35	0.96	22.02	1,369	3	97	0	0	8	18.95	-14.07	5.75		Dec-06
100	3.54	19.71	12.25	44.91	46.36	0	1.97	11.36	0.96	21.32	1,369	3	97	0	0	8	18.43	-14.36		1.00	Dec-06
100	3.80	20.23	13.39	49.44	54.15	0.73	0.94	11.34	0.96	22.35	1,369	3	97	0	0	8	19.25	-13.98			Dec-06
	3.81	20.34	13.49	49.71	54.47	0.78	0.89	11.32	0.96	22.32	1,369	3	97	0	0	8	19.25	-13.98			Jul-13
100	4.08	19.81	8.21	49.58	58.56	0.85	0.89	13.24	1.07	20.71	899.9	3	97	0	0	62	26.25	-20.41			Dec-91
100	4.16	31.13	7.02	77.55	80.70	0	1	17.7	0.98	31.04	7.3	0	100	0	0	88	27.02	-22.93			Dec-96
100	5.08	16.98	6.20	37.00	46.59	1.88	1.1	12.67	1.13	8.81	1,011	5	95	0	0	68	21.61	-16.11	5.75		May-16
100	4.89	16.58	5.40	33.90	41.06	1.17	1.88	12.63	1.13	8.79	1,011	5	95	0	0	68	21.09	-16.37		1.00	May-16
100	5.16	17.13	6.47	38.05	47.72	2.11	0.83	12.64	1.13	8.81	1,011	5	95	0	0	68	21.61	-16.11			May-16
100	5.17	17.17	6.50	38.13	47.80	2.14	0.8	12.62	1.12	8.81	1,011	5	95	0	0	68	21.61	-16.11			Oct-00
	5.18	17.19	6.49	37.96	47.61	2.14	0.8	12.6	1.12	8.8	1,011	5	95	0	0	68	21.61	-16.11			May-16
100	5.16	17.08	6.27	37.04	45.77	1.89	1.05	12.67	1.13	8.92	1,011	5	95	0	0	68	21.47	-16.18			Jul-01
100	4.26	19.48	10.22	50.07	64.70	1.63	0.2	12.21	1	56.62	2,625	2	98	0	0	3	25.01	-16.31			Sep-93
100	3.11	14.70	-1.92	28.91	8.89	1.85	1.12	12.35	1.1	37.68	687.9	0	100	0	0	55	16.15	-24.88	5.75		Dec-88
100	2.91	14.26	-2.69	25.90	4.70	0.87	1.9	12.33	1.1	38.14	687.9	0	100	0	0	55	15.65	-25.13		1.00	Dec-88
100	3.20	14.85	-1.66	29.96	10.40	2	0.85	12.34	1.1	38.34	687.9	0	100	0	0	55	16.37	-24.83			Dec-88
	3.20	14.86	-1.66	29.94	10.35	2	0.85	12.34	1.1	38.32	687.9	0	100	0	0	55	16.37	-24.83			Jun-15
100	1.82	12.53	-1.80	18.84	6.69	1.76	1.07	11.69	1	20.65	1,145	3	97	0	0	32	14.64	-21.92	5.75		Mar-08
100	1.66	12.11	-2.51	16.13	2.70	0.91	1.82	11.72	1	20.18	1,145	3	97	0	0	32	14.1	-22.16		1.00	Mar-08
100	1.89	12.65	-1.57	19.75	8.15	2.01	0.82	11.71	1	20.47	1,145	3	97	0	0	32	14.82	-21.85			Dec-05
	1.89	12.65	-1.57	19.83	8.44	2.03	0.8	11.74	1.01	20.38	1,145	3	97	0	0	32	14.82	-21.85			Jul-13
100	0.33	9.88	-2.34	23.27	3.42	4.35	1.08	10.98	0.93	12.91	317.1	3	97	0	0	54					Dec-11
100	0.26	9.69	-2.65	21.61	1.66	3.87	1.33	10.92	0.92	13.07	317.1	3	97	0	0	54					Dec-11
100	3.22	14.73	-1.91	28.46	7.38	1.62	1.27	12.31	1.09	13.78	976.1	1	99	0	0	55	11.44	-25.09			Jul-01
100	3.27	14.84	-1.71	29.39	8.72	1.96	1.02	12.33	1.1	12.92	976.1	1	99	0	0	55	11.54	-25.04			Oct-00
100	2.66	14.43	-7.91	27.82		1.26	1.4	13.79	1.1	13.48	619.3	1	99	0	0	71			5.75		Jan-15
100	2.44	13.94	-8.63	25.17		0.54	2.15	13.76	1.09	13.4	619.3	1	99	0	0	71				1.00	Jan-15
100	2.66	14.51	-7.69	28.97		1.62	1.1	13.75	1.09	13.49	619.3	1	99	0	0	71					Jan-15
	2.66	14.61	-7.66	28.98		1.65	1.07	13.76	1.1	13.49	619.3	1	99	0	0	71					Jan-15
100	4.80	17.64	7.92	39.24	31.71	0.76	1.22	10.8	0.88	19.86	4,296	3	97	0	0	7	15.67	-18.47	5.75		Dec-06
100	4.59	17.19	7.11	36.19	26.81	0.07	1.96	10.76	0.87	19.56	4,296	3	97	0	0	7	15.19	-18.75		1.00	Dec-06
100	4.88	17.82	8.27	40.60	33.85	1.06	0.91	10.81	0.88	19.96	4,296	3	97	0	0	7	15.93	-18.4			Dec-06
	4.89	17.81	8.28	40.67	33.94	1.09	0.89	10.8	0.88	19.73	4,296	3	97	0	0	7	15.93	-18.4			Jul-13
100	3.63	14.28	0.88	30.09	10.56	2.61	0.35	11.02	0.99	17.12	650.3	3	97	0	0	7	13.19	-23.39			Aug-16
100	3.50	14.13	0.63	29.09	9.70	2.34	0.6	11.03	0.99	17.12	650.3	3	97	0	0	7	13.19	-23.39			Jun-97
100	-0.52	4.33					1.25			11.3	2.3	8	92	0	0				5.75		Sep-18

	MARKET			FUND TYPE, CATEGORY & OBJECTIVE	RATINGS				MINIMUMS	
Fund Name	Ticker Symbol	Traded On	Fund Type	Category and (Prospectus Objective)	Overall Rating	Reward Rating	Risk Rating	Recent Up/ Downgrade	Open to New Investors	Min Initial Investment
BNY Mellon Japan Womenomics Fund Class C	DJWCX	NAS CM	Open End	Japan Equity (Pacific Stock)	U	U	U		Y	1,000
BNY Mellon Japan Womenomics Fund Class I	DJWIX	NAS CM	Open End	Japan Equity (Pacific Stock)	U	U	U		Y	1,000
BNY Mellon Japan Womenomics Fund Class Y	DJWYX	NAS CM	Open End	Japan Equity (Pacific Stock)	U	U	U		Y	1,000,000
BNY Mellon Large Cap Equity Fund Class A	DLQAX	NAS CM	Open End	US Equity Large Cap Growth (Growth)	C+	C	B		Y	1,000
BNY Mellon Large Cap Equity Fund Class C	DEYCX	NAS CM	Open End	US Equity Large Cap Growth (Growth)	C+	C	B		Y	1,000
BNY Mellon Large Cap Equity Fund Class I	DLQIX	NAS CM	Open End	US Equity Large Cap Growth (Growth)	C+	C	B	Down	Y	1,000
BNY Mellon Large Cap Equity Fund Class Y	DLACX	NAS CM	Open End	US Equity Large Cap Growth (Growth)	C+	C	B	Down	Y	1,000,000
BNY Mellon Large Cap Growth Fund Class A	DAPAX	NAS CM	Open End	US Equity Large Cap Growth (Growth)	C+	C	B-	Down	Y	1,000
BNY Mellon Large Cap Growth Fund Class C	DGTCX	NAS CM	Open End	US Equity Large Cap Growth (Growth)	C+	C	B-		Y	1,000
BNY Mellon Large Cap Growth Fund Class I	DAPIX	NAS CM	Open End	US Equity Large Cap Growth (Growth)	C+	C	B-	Down	Y	1,000
BNY Mellon Large Cap Growth Fund Class Y	DLCGX	NAS CM	Open End	US Equity Large Cap Growth (Growth)	C+	C	B-	Down	Y	1,000,000
BNY Mellon Large Cap Securities Inc	DREVX	NAS CM	Open End	US Equity Large Cap Growth (Growth & Income)	B-	C	B	Down	Y	2,500
BNY Mellon Large Cap Stock Fund Class Investor	MILCX	NAS CM	Open End	US Equity Large Cap Blend (Growth)	C+	C	B		Y	10,000
BNY Mellon Large Cap Stock Fund Class M	MPLCX	NAS CM	Open End	US Equity Large Cap Blend (Growth)	C+	C	B		Y	10,000
BNY Mellon Mid Cap Multi-Strategy Fund Class Investor	MIMSX	NAS CM	Open End	US Equity Mid Cap (Growth)	C+	C	B-	Up	Y	10,000
BNY Mellon Mid Cap Multi-Strategy Fund Class M	MPMCX	NAS CM	Open End	US Equity Mid Cap (Growth)	C+	C	B-		Y	10,000
BNY Mellon MidCap Index Fund Class I	DMIDX	NAS CM	Open End	US Equity Mid Cap (Growth)	C+	C	B-	Up	Y	1,000
BNY Mellon MidCap Index Fund Investor Shares	PESPX	NAS CM	Open End	US Equity Mid Cap (Growth)	C+	C	B-	Up	Y	2,500
BNY Mellon Natural Resources Fund Class A	DNLAX	NAS CM	Open End	Natl Resources Sec Equity (Natl Res)	C-	C-	C-		Y	1,000
BNY Mellon Natural Resources Fund Class C	DLDCX	NAS CM	Open End	Natl Resources Sec Equity (Natl Res)	C-	C-	C-		Y	1,000
BNY Mellon Natural Resources Fund Class I	DLDRX	NAS CM	Open End	Natl Resources Sec Equity (Natl Res)	C-	C-	C-	Down	Y	1,000
BNY Mellon Natural Resources Fund Class Y	DLDYX	NAS CM	Open End	Natl Resources Sec Equity (Natl Res)	C-	C-	C-	Down	Y	1,000,000
BNY Mellon Opportunistic Midcap Value Fund Class A	DMCVX	NAS CM	Open End	US Equity Mid Cap (Growth & Income)	C	C-	C+		Y	1,000
BNY Mellon Opportunistic Midcap Value Fund Class C	DVLCX	NAS CM	Open End	US Equity Mid Cap (Growth & Income)	C	C-	C+		Y	1,000
BNY Mellon Opportunistic Midcap Value Fund Class I	DVLIX	NAS CM	Open End	US Equity Mid Cap (Growth & Income)	C	C-	C+		Y	1,000
BNY Mellon Opportunistic Midcap Value Fund Class Y	DMCYX	NAS CM	Open End	US Equity Mid Cap (Growth & Income)	C	C-	C+		Y	1,000,000
BNY Mellon Opportunistic Small Cap Fund Class I	DOPIX	NAS CM	Open End	US Equity Small Cap (Small Company)	C-	C-	C	Down	Y	1,000
BNY Mellon Opportunistic Small Cap Fund Class Y	DSCYX	NAS CM	Open End	US Equity Small Cap (Small Company)	C-	C-	C	Down		1,000,000
BNY Mellon Opportunistic Small Cap Fund Investor Shares	DSCVX	NAS CM	Open End	US Equity Small Cap (Small Company)	C-	C-	C	Down		2,500
BNY Mellon Research Growth Fund, Inc. Class A	DWOAX	NAS CM	Open End	US Equity Large Cap Growth (Growth)	C+	C+	B	Down	Y	1,000
BNY Mellon Research Growth Fund, Inc. Class C	DWOCX	NAS CM	Open End	US Equity Large Cap Growth (Growth)	C+	C+	B	Down	Y	1,000
BNY Mellon Research Growth Fund, Inc. Class I	DWOIX	NAS CM	Open End	US Equity Large Cap Growth (Growth)	C+	C+	B	Down	Y	1,000
BNY Mellon Research Growth Fund, Inc. Class Y	DRYQX	NAS CM	Open End	US Equity Large Cap Growth (Growth)	B-	C+	B	Down	Y	1,000,000
BNY Mellon Research Growth Fund, Inc. Class Z	DREQX	NAS CM	Open End	US Equity Large Cap Growth (Growth)	B-	C+	B	Down		1,000
BNY Mellon S&P 500 Index Fund	PEOPX	NAS CM	Open End	US Equity Large Cap Blend (Growth & Income)	B-	C	B		Y	2,500
BNY Mellon Select Managers Small Cap Growth Fund Class A	DSGAX	NAS CM	Open End	US Equity Small Cap (Small Company)	C+	C	C+	Up	Y	1,000
BNY Mellon Select Managers Small Cap Growth Fund Class C	DSGCX	NAS CM	Open End	US Equity Small Cap (Small Company)	C+	C	C+	Up	Y	1,000
BNY Mellon Select Managers Small Cap Growth Fund Class I	DSGIX	NAS CM	Open End	US Equity Small Cap (Small Company)	C+	C	C+	Up	Y	1,000
BNY Mellon Select Managers Small Cap Growth Fund Class Y	DSGYX	NAS CM	Open End	US Equity Small Cap (Small Company)	C+	C	C+		Y	1,000,000
BNY Mellon Select Managers Small Cap Value Fund Class A	DMVAX	NAS CM	Open End	US Equity Small Cap (Small Company)	C	C	C+		Y	1,000
BNY Mellon Select Managers Small Cap Value Fund Class C	DMECX	NAS CM	Open End	US Equity Small Cap (Small Company)	C	C-	C+		Y	1,000
BNY Mellon Select Managers Small Cap Value Fund Class I	DMVIX	NAS CM	Open End	US Equity Small Cap (Small Company)	C	C	C+		Y	1,000
BNY Mellon Select Managers Small Cap Value Fund Class Y	DMVYX	NAS CM	Open End	US Equity Small Cap (Small Company)	C	C	C+		Y	1,000,000
BNY Mellon Small Cap Growth Fund Class Y	SSYGX	NAS CM	Open End	US Equity Small Cap (Small Company)	C+	C+	C+	Down	Y	1,000,000
BNY Mellon Small Cap Multi-Strategy Fund Class Investor	MISCX	NAS CM	Open End	US Equity Small Cap (Small Company)	C	C-	C+		Y	10,000
BNY Mellon Small Cap Multi-Strategy Fund Class M	MPSSX	NAS CM	Open End	US Equity Small Cap (Small Company)	C	C-	C+		Y	10,000
BNY Mellon Small Cap Stock Index Fund Class I	DISIX	NAS CM	Open End	US Equity Small Cap (Small Company)	C	C-	C+	Down	Y	1,000
BNY Mellon Small Cap Stock Index Fund Investor Shares	DISSX	NAS CM	Open End	US Equity Small Cap (Small Company)	C	C-	C+		Y	2,500
BNY Mellon Small Cap Value Fund Class A	RUDAX	NAS CM	Open End	US Equity Small Cap (Small Company)	C	C	B-	Down	Y	1,000
BNY Mellon Small Cap Value Fund Class C	BOSCX	NAS CM	Open End	US Equity Small Cap (Small Company)	C	C-	C+	Down	Y	1,000
BNY Mellon Small Cap Value Fund Class I	STSVX	NAS CM	Open End	US Equity Small Cap (Small Company)	C	C	B-	Down		1,000
BNY Mellon Small Cap Value Fund Class Y	BOSYX	NAS CM	Open End	US Equity Small Cap (Small Company)	C	C	B-	Down	Y	1,000,000

★ Expanded analysis of this fund is included in Section II.

	TOTAL RETURNS					PERFORMANCE				ASSETS		ASSET ALLOCATION & TURNOVER					BULL & BEAR		FEES		
Min Additional Investment	3-Month Total Return	6-Month Total Return	1-Year Total Return	3-Year Total Return	5-Year Total Return	Dividend Yield (TTM)	Expense Ratio	3-Yr Std Deviation	3-Year Beta	NAV	Total Assets (MIL)	%Cash	%Stocks	%Bonds	%Other	Turnover Ratio	Last Bull Market Total Return	Last Bear Market Total Return	Front End Fee (%)	Back End Fee (%)	Inception Date
100	-0.61	3.97					2			11.24	2.3	8	92	0	0					1.00	Sep-18
100	-0.43	4.52					1			11.33	2.3	8	92	0	0						Sep-18
	-0.43	4.52					1			11.33	2.3	8	92	0	0						Sep-18
100	5.01	19.49	7.45	54.84	62.05	0.36	1.08	13.31	1.08	19.48	647.6	0	100	0	0	57	25.84	-20.37	5.75		Aug-92
100	4.82	19.03	6.63	51.34	55.84	0	1.9	13.32	1.08	19.56	647.6	0	100	0	0	57	25.05	-20.59		1.00	Sep-08
100	5.11	19.70	7.82	56.30	64.55	0.66	0.78	13.31	1.08	20.76	647.6	0	100	0	0	57	26.1	-20.16			Apr-97
	5.11	19.69	7.84	56.48	64.09	0.71	0.74	13.34	1.08	20.74	647.6	0	100	0	0	57	25.84	-20.37			Oct-15
100	5.77	22.16	7.91	62.23	76.38	0.01	1.15	14.53	1.07	12.82	70.7	1	99	0	0	69	23.17	-18.81	5.75		Dec-86
100	5.65	21.72	7.08	58.62	69.96	0	1.9	14.54	1.08	12.14	70.7	1	99	0	0	69	22.83	-19.24		1.00	Sep-08
100	5.82	22.38	8.13	63.49	78.72	0.2	0.9	14.57	1.08	13.26	70.7	1	99	0	0	69	23.39	-18.73			Apr-97
	5.90	22.36	8.21	63.62	78.37	0.2	0.9	14.57	1.08	13.27	70.7	1	99	0	0	69	23.17	-18.81			Oct-15
100	4.13	18.71	12.38	48.65	59.36	1.11	0.71	11.54	0.93	12.06	1,274	1	99	0	0	32	24.21	-20.24			May-51
100	2.45	16.24	5.27	42.43	50.78	0.89	1.07	12.04	0.98	5.44	204.3	0	100	0	0	46	23.29	-21.27			Jul-01
100	2.51	16.62	5.69	43.50	52.66	1.1	0.82	11.94	0.97	5.44	204.3	0	100	0	0	46	23.46	-21.21			Oct-00
100	3.89	22.78	5.29	43.45	47.48	0.09	1.14	14.35	1.06	17.35	2,810	1	99	0	0	51	24.69	-26.78			Jul-01
100	3.94	22.96	5.51	44.42	49.24	0.28	0.89	14.4	1.06	17.67	2,810	1	99	0	0	51	24.94	-26.68			Oct-00
100	2.96	19.01	1.09	37.97	45.36	1.46	0.25	15.12	1	33.74	2,920	1	99	0	0	16	27.56	-22.73			Aug-16
100	2.92	18.87	0.86	37.03	44.37	1.18	0.5	15.12	1	33.83	2,920	1	99	0	0	16	27.56	-22.73			Jun-91
100	1.59	13.43	-10.30	20.42	-9.64	1.36	1.28	16.72	1.05	29.21	363.6	3	97	0	0	56	16.04	-27.19	5.75		Oct-03
100	1.43	13.08	-10.93	17.91	-12.83	0.79	1.96	16.7	1.04	26.88	363.6	3	97	0	0	56	15.53	-27.44		1.00	Oct-03
100	1.69	13.61	-10.06	21.46	-8.42	1.66	1	16.73	1.05	30.04	363.6	3	97	0	0	56	16.23	-27.17			Oct-03
	1.69	13.69	-9.95	21.84	-8.06	1.78	0.87	16.73	1.05	30.06	363.6	3	97	0	0	56	16.23	-27.17			Sep-15
100	-1.00	18.15	-5.32	30.08	21.04	0	1.16	18.31	1.34	24.53	732.3	1	99	0	0	101	29.55	-27.85	5.75		Sep-95
100	-1.21	17.64	-6.08	27.13	16.58	0	1.91	18.28	1.34	20.27	732.3	1	99	0	0	101	28.98	-28.12		1.00	May-08
100	-0.97	18.26	-5.11	31.08	22.69	0.02	0.89	18.31	1.34	24.41	732.3	1	99	0	0	101	29.73	-27.82			May-08
	-0.93	18.33	-5.03	31.47	23.33	0.15	0.79	18.32	1.34	24.46	732.3	1	99	0	0	101	29.55	-27.85			Jul-13
100	-1.58	13.43	-13.89	37.91	26.40	0	0.87	19.03	1.07	26.09	622.5	1	99	0	0	74	37.59	-34.06			Sep-16
	-1.54	13.54	-13.79	38.17	26.64	0	0.79	19.04	1.07	26.15	622.5	1	99	0	0	74	37.59	-34.06			Sep-16
100	-1.63	13.30	-14.09	37.09	25.66	0	1.09	19.03	1.07	25.89	622.5	1	99	0	0	74	37.59	-34.06			Dec-93
100	3.33	22.20	10.79	54.95	69.42	0.02	1.03	13.8	1.01	15.22	1,710	2	98	0	0	43	26.02	-19.28	5.75		Sep-08
100	3.09	21.74	9.91	51.55	63.20	0	1.78	13.79	1.01	13.63	1,710	2	98	0	0	43	25.41	-19.56		1.00	Sep-08
100	3.34	22.33	11.00	56.10	71.53	0.21	0.78	13.84	1.02	15.24	1,710	2	98	0	0	43	26.26	-19.19			Sep-08
	3.34	22.38	11.02	56.27	71.90	0.21	0.78	13.83	1.02	15.21	1,710	2	98	0	0	43	26.03	-19.14			Jul-13
100	3.40	22.28	10.99	55.84	71.20	0.14	0.85	13.81	1.01	15.55	1,710	2	98	0	0	43	26.03	-19.14			Feb-72
100	4.18	19.29	9.87	48.70	62.19	1.44	0.5	12.2	1	51.99	2,357	1	99	0	0	3	24.76	-16.43			Jan-90
100	5.08	21.70	1.89	58.93	49.12	0	1.29	16.41	0.92	24.78	567.8	3	97	0	0	96	23.72	-20.42	5.75		Jul-10
100	4.88	21.37	1.28	55.51	43.70	0	2.05	16.4	0.92	22.54	567.8	3	97	0	0	96	23.29	-20.71		1.00	Jul-10
100	5.11	21.84	2.15	60.19	51.26	0	0.99	16.44	0.93	25.71	567.8	3	97	0	0	96	23.98	-20.32			Jul-10
	5.10	21.88	2.19	60.38	51.44	0	0.95	16.44	0.93	25.73	567.8	3	97	0	0	96	23.98	-20.32			Jul-13
100	2.53	18.05	-2.76	34.10	24.45	0	1.3	17.31	0.98	21.4	609.7	2	98	0	0	59	27.65	-25.62	5.75		Dec-08
100	2.33	17.60	-3.50	31.18	20.03	0	2.05	17.29	0.98	19.25	609.7	2	98	0	0	59	27.09	-25.78		1.00	Dec-08
100	2.63	18.22	-2.43	35.43	26.49	0.38	0.97	17.3	0.98	21.82	609.7	2	98	0	0	59	27.88	-25.43			Dec-08
	2.63	18.24	-2.43	35.51	26.65	0.42	0.94	17.31	0.98	21.79	609.7	2	98	0	0	59	27.88	-25.43			Jul-13
	4.14	31.25	7.11	77.77	81.02	0	1	17.75	0.98	31.12	7.3	0	100	0	0	88	27.02	-22.93			Jul-13
100	1.40	19.19	-4.59	47.57	41.04	0	1.26	17.53	1.01	16.58	440.0	2	98	0	0	63	28.54	-28.02			Jul-01
100	1.44	19.33	-4.36	48.65	42.82	0	1.01	17.54	1.01	17.59	440.0	2	98	0	0	63	28.7	-27.91			Oct-00
100	1.80	14.23	-5.04	41.99	47.71	1.17	0.25	17.88	1	28.7	2,096	0	100	0	0	20	29.55	-22.16			Aug-16
100	1.77	14.08	-5.29	41.00	46.67	0.9	0.5	17.9	1	28.73	2,096	0	100	0	0	20	29.55	-22.16			Jun-97
100	1.93	14.77	-2.87	38.60	35.03	0.13	1.36	17.07	0.97	20.04	201.8	3	97	0	0	84	33.58	-24.81	5.75		Aug-16
100	1.71	14.38	-3.61	35.12	29.69	0	2.19	17.03	0.97	19.56	201.8	3	97	0	0	84	33	-25.05		1.00	Aug-16
100	2.02	14.94	-2.56	39.85	36.25	0.42	1.01	17.07	0.97	20.15	201.8	3	97	0	0	84	33.58	-24.82			Feb-00
	2.01	15.03	-2.43	40.01	36.41	0.36	0.97	17.05	0.97	20.28	201.8	3	97	0	0	84	33.58	-24.82			Aug-16

Fund Name	MARKET Ticker Symbol	Traded On	Fund Type	FUND TYPE, CATEGORY & OBJECTIVE Category and (Prospectus Objective)	RATINGS Overall Rating	Reward Rating	Risk Rating	Recent Up/ Downgrade	MINIMUMS Open to New Investors	Min Initial Investment
BNY Mellon Small/Mid Cap Growth Fund Class A	DBMAX	NAS CM	Open End	US Equity Mid Cap (Growth)	C+	C+	C+	Down	Y	1,000
BNY Mellon Small/Mid Cap Growth Fund Class C	DBMCX	NAS CM	Open End	US Equity Mid Cap (Growth)	C+	C+	C+	Down	Y	1,000
BNY Mellon Small/Mid Cap Growth Fund Class I	SDSCX	NAS CM	Open End	US Equity Mid Cap (Growth)	C+	C+	C+	Down	Y	1,000
BNY Mellon Small/Mid Cap Growth Fund Class Y	DBMYX	NAS CM	Open End	US Equity Mid Cap (Growth)	C+	C+	C+	Down	Y	1,000,000
BNY Mellon Small/Mid Cap Growth Fund Class Z	DBMZX	NAS CM	Open End	US Equity Mid Cap (Growth)	C+	C+	C+	Down	Y	1,000
BNY Mellon Small/Mid Cap Multi-Strategy Cls M Shares	MMCMX	NAS CM	Open End	US Equity Small Cap (Growth)	C	C	C+	Down	Y	10,000
BNY Mellon Small/Mid Cap Multi-Strategy Investor Shares	MMCIX	NAS CM	Open End	US Equity Small Cap (Growth)	C	C	C+		Y	10,000
BNY Mellon Strategic Beta Emerging Markets Equity Cls A	DOFAX	NAS CM	Open End	Global Emerg Mkts (Growth)	C	C	B		Y	1,000
BNY Mellon Strategic Beta Emerging Markets Equity Cls C	DOFCX	NAS CM	Open End	Global Emerg Mkts (Growth)	C	C	B-		Y	1,000
BNY Mellon Strategic Beta Emerging Markets Equity Cls I	DOFIX	NAS CM	Open End	Global Emerg Mkts (Growth)	C	C	B		Y	1,000
BNY Mellon Strategic Beta Emerging Markets Equity Cls Y	DOFYX	NAS CM	Open End	Global Emerg Mkts (Growth)	C	C	B		Y	1,000,000
BNY Mellon Structured Midcap Fund - Class A	DPSAX	NAS CM	Open End	US Equity Mid Cap (Growth)	C	C-	B-		Y	1,000
BNY Mellon Structured Midcap Fund Class C	DPSCX	NAS CM	Open End	US Equity Mid Cap (Growth)	C	C-	C+		Y	1,000
BNY Mellon Structured Midcap Fund Class I	DPSRX	NAS CM	Open End	US Equity Mid Cap (Growth)	C	C-	B-		Y	1,000
BNY Mellon Structured MidCap Fund Class Y	DPSYX	NAS CM	Open End	US Equity Mid Cap (Growth)	C	C-	B-		Y	1,000,000
BNY Mellon Sustainable Balanced Fund Class K	DRAKX	NAS CM	Open End	Moderate Alloc (Multi-Asset Global)	D+	D	C	Up		1,000,000
BNY Mellon Sustainable Balanced Fund Class Service Class	DRASX	NAS CM	Open End	Moderate Alloc (Multi-Asset Global)	D+	D	C	Up		1,000
BNY Mellon Sustainable U.S. Equity Fund Class A	DTCAX	NAS CM	Open End	US Equity Large Cap Blend (Growth)	B-	C+	B		Y	1,000
BNY Mellon Sustainable U.S. Equity Fund Class C	DTCCX	NAS CM	Open End	US Equity Large Cap Blend (Growth)	B-	C	B		Y	1,000
BNY Mellon Sustainable U.S. Equity Fund Class I	DRTCX	NAS CM	Open End	US Equity Large Cap Blend (Growth)	B-	C+	B		Y	1,000
BNY Mellon Sustainable U.S. Equity Fund Class Y	DTCYX	NAS CM	Open End	US Equity Large Cap Blend (Growth)	B-	C+	B		Y	1,000,000
BNY Mellon Sustainable U.S. Equity Fund Class Z	DRTHX	NAS CM	Open End	US Equity Large Cap Blend (Growth)	B-	C+	B			1,000
BNY Mellon Tax Managed Growth Fund Class A	DTMGX	NAS CM	Open End	US Equity Large Cap Blend (Growth)	B-	C+	B	Down	Y	1,000
BNY Mellon Tax Managed Growth Fund Class C	DPTAX	NAS CM	Open End	US Equity Large Cap Blend (Growth)	B-	C+	B		Y	1,000
BNY Mellon Tax Managed Growth Fund Class I	DPTRX	NAS CM	Open End	US Equity Large Cap Blend (Growth)	B-	C+	B	Down	Y	1,000
BNY Mellon Tax-Sensitive Large Cap Multi-Strategy Cls Inv	MTSIX	NAS CM	Open End	US Equity Large Cap Blend (Growth)	B-	C	B		Y	10,000
BNY Mellon Tax-Sensitive Large Cap Multi-Strategy Cls M	MTSMX	NAS CM	Open End	US Equity Large Cap Blend (Growth)	B-	C	B		Y	10,000
BNY Mellon Technology Growth Fund Class A	DTGRX	NAS CM	Open End	Technology Sector Equity (Technology)	C+	C+	B-	Down	Y	1,000
BNY Mellon Technology Growth Fund Class C	DTGCX	NAS CM	Open End	Technology Sector Equity (Technology)	C+	C+	B-	Down	Y	1,000
BNY Mellon Technology Growth Fund Class I	DGVRX	NAS CM	Open End	Technology Sector Equity (Technology)	C+	C+	B-	Down	Y	1,000
BNY Mellon Technology Growth Fund Class Y	DTEYX	NAS CM	Open End	Technology Sector Equity (Technology)	C+	C+	B-	Down	Y	1,000,000
BNY Mellon U.S. Equity Fund Class A	DPUAX	NAS CM	Open End	US Equity Large Cap Growth (Growth & Income)	B-	C	B	Down		1,000
BNY Mellon U.S. Equity Fund Class C	DPUCX	NAS CM	Open End	US Equity Large Cap Growth (Growth & Income)	B-	C	B	Down		1,000
BNY Mellon U.S. Equity Fund Class I	DPUIX	NAS CM	Open End	US Equity Large Cap Growth (Growth & Income)	B-	C	B	Down		1,000
BNY Mellon U.S. Equity Fund Class Y	DPUYX	NAS CM	Open End	US Equity Large Cap Growth (Growth & Income)	B-	C	B	Down		1,000,000
BNY Mellon Worldwide Growth Fund Class A	PGROX	NAS CM	Open End	Global Equity Large Cap (World Stock)	B-	B-	B		Y	1,000
BNY Mellon Worldwide Growth Fund Class C	PGRCX	NAS CM	Open End	Global Equity Large Cap (World Stock)	B-	C+	B	Up	Y	1,000
BNY Mellon Worldwide Growth Fund Class I	DPWRX	NAS CM	Open End	Global Equity Large Cap (World Stock)	B	B-	B	Up	Y	1,000
BNY Mellon Worldwide Growth Fund Class Y	DPRIX	NAS CM	Open End	Global Equity Large Cap (World Stock)	B	B-	B	Up	Y	1,000,000
Bogle Investment Mgmt Small Cap Growth Inst Cls	BOGIX	NAS CM	Open End	US Equity Small Cap (Small Company)	C	C-	C		Y	10,000
Boston Common ESG Impact International Fund	BCAIX	NAS CM	Open End	Global Equity Large Cap (Foreign Stock)	C	C	B		Y	10,000
Boston Common ESG Impact U.S. Equity Fund	BCAMX	NAS CM	Open End	US Equity Large Cap Growth (Growth)	C+	C	B		Y	10,000
Boston Partners All Cap Value Fund Institutional Class	BPAIX	NAS CM	Open End	US Equity Large Cap Value (Growth & Income)	C+	C	B	Up	Y	100,000
Boston Partners All Cap Value Fund Investor Class	BPAVX	NAS CM	Open End	US Equity Large Cap Value (Growth & Income)	C+	C	B	Up	Y	2,500
Boston Partners Emerging Markets Fund Institutional Class	BPEMX	NAS CM	Open End	Global Emerg Mkts (Div Emerging Mkts)	D+	D	C	Up	Y	100,000
Boston Partners Emerging Mkts Long/Short Inst Cls	BELSX	NAS CM	Open End	Long/Short Equity (Div Emerging Mkts)	C	C-	C+		Y	100,000
Boston Partners Global Equity Institutional Class	BPGIX	NAS CM	Open End	Global Equity Large Cap (World Stock)	C	C	C+		Y	100,000
Boston Partners Global Long/Short Fund Institutional Class	BGLSX	NAS CM	Open End	Long/Short Equity (World Stock)	D+	D	C		Y	100,000
Boston Partners Global Long/Short Fund Investor Class	BGRSX	NAS CM	Open End	Long/Short Equity (World Stock)	D+	D	C		Y	2,500
Boston Partners Long/Short Equity Fund Institutional Class	BPLSX	NAS CM	Open End	Long/Short Equity (Growth)	D+	D	C-			100,000
Boston Partners Long/Short Equity Fund Investor Class	BPLEX	NAS CM	Open End	Long/Short Equity (Growth)	D+	D	C-			2,500
Boston Partners Long/Short Research Institutional Cls	BPIRX	NAS CM	Open End	Long/Short Equity (Growth & Income)	C-	C-	C			100,000

★ Expanded analysis of this fund is included in Section II.

Min Additional Investment	TOTAL RETURNS 3-Month Total Return	6-Month Total Return	1-Year Total Return	3-Year Total Return	5-Year Total Return	PERFORMANCE Dividend Yield (TTM)	Expense Ratio	3-Yr Std Deviation	3-Year Beta	ASSETS NAV	Total Assets (MIL)	ASSET ALLOCATION & TURNOVER %Cash	%Stocks	%Bonds	%Other	Turnover Ratio	BULL & BEAR Last Bull Market Total Return	Last Bear Market Total Return	FEES Front End Fee (%)	Back End Fee (%)	Inception Date
100	4.33	32.31	10.00	73.52	78.00	0	1	17.9	1.04	22.6	2,178	1	99	0	0	57	30.85	-18.14	5.75		Mar-09
100	4.11	31.75	9.11	69.67	71.27	0	1.73	17.89	1.03	19.75	2,178	1	99	0	0	57	30.17	-18.46		1.00	Mar-09
100	4.39	32.46	10.24	74.89	80.26	0	0.74	17.87	1.03	23.5	2,178	1	99	0	0	57	31.14	-18.05			Jan-88
	4.41	32.54	10.31	75.37	81.16	0	0.65	17.84	1.03	23.66	2,178	1	99	0	0	57	31.14	-18.04			Jul-13
100	4.40	32.48	10.24	74.54	79.54	0	0.84	17.88	1.03	23.49	2,178	1	99	0	0	57	31.06	-18.08			Jan-18
100	1.54	21.50	-1.45	48.22	47.36	0	0.93	16.89	1.08	13.11	238.5	1	99	0	0	63	20.64	-27.58			Sep-09
100	1.50	21.40	-1.68	46.91	45.43	0	1.18	16.86	1.08	12.82	238.5	1	99	0	0	63	20.51	-27.7			Sep-09
100	0.54	8.79	2.78	35.57		2.19	1.05	13.45	0.94	12.99	31.9	2	98	0	0	36			5.75		Sep-14
100	0.38	8.36	1.99	32.22		1.62	1.8	13.38	0.94	12.95	31.9	2	98	0	0	36				1.00	Sep-14
100	0.69	9.00	3.15	36.69		2.24	0.8	13.5	0.95	13.07	31.9	2	98	0	0	36					Sep-14
	0.61	8.94	3.08	36.27		2.25	0.8	13.42	0.94	13.03	31.9	2	98	0	0	36					Sep-14
100	-0.22	14.16	-2.46	26.99	29.13	0.05	1.25	15.07	0.97	26.44	148.2	0	100	0	0	67	29.54	-23.16	5.75		Jun-01
100	-0.39	13.70	-3.19	24.25	24.47	0	1.99	15.06	0.97	22.49	148.2	0	100	0	0	67	29.03	-23.38		1.00	Jun-01
100	-0.14	14.31	-2.21	27.99	30.80	0.36	1	15.07	0.98	27.07	148.2	0	100	0	0	67	29.67	-23.09			Jun-01
	-0.14	14.30	-2.14	28.46	31.58	0.48	0.86	15.08	0.98	27	148.2	0	100	0	0	67	29.67	-23.09			Jul-13
	3.41	11.30	0.69			2.8	0.15			12.12	12.3	12	52	36	0						Nov-17
100	3.32	11.20	0.58			2.62	0.4			12.11	12.3	12	52	36	0				5.75		Nov-17
100	5.38	20.93	14.25	45.42	45.36	1.41	0.95	11.24	0.9	12.13	322.8	3	97	0	0	50	24.29	-16.69	5.75		Aug-99
100	5.25	20.37	13.42	42.14	39.95	0.65	1.7	11.29	0.9	10.22	322.8	3	97	0	0	50	23.79	-16.95		1.00	Aug-99
100	5.50	21.10	14.63	46.74	47.56	1.59	0.7	11.25	0.9	12.45	322.8	3	97	0	0	50	24.45	-16.52			Aug-99
	5.51	21.03	14.66	46.64	47.17	1.59	0.7	11.26	0.9	12.43	322.8	3	97	0	0	50	24.43	-16.63			Sep-16
100	5.42	21.01	14.45	46.21	46.73	1.52	0.77	11.25	0.9	12.44	322.8	3	97	0	0	50	24.43	-16.63			Mar-72
100	5.36	20.91	11.31	46.49	45.81	0.91	1.2	11.35	0.9	29.26	106.7	1	99	0	0	6	21.5	-11.03	5.75		Nov-97
100	5.17	20.46	10.50	43.20	40.43	0.3	1.95	11.34	0.89	27.33	106.7	1	99	0	0	6	20.96	-11.36		1.00	Nov-97
100	5.40	21.06	11.64	47.59	47.70	1.14	0.95	11.34	0.89	29.34	106.7	1	99	0	0	6	21.71	-10.96			May-04
100	4.33	18.52	8.13	51.00	59.53	1.05	1.1	12.56	1.02	16.38	321.1	2	83	0	15	15	23.53	-19.18			Jul-10
100	4.38	18.67	8.38	52.06	61.58	1.31	0.85	12.53	1.02	15.95	321.1	2	83	0	15	15	23.7	-18.5			Jul-10
100	1.97	21.16	4.36	80.63	93.56	0	1.22	17.37	1.02	44.94	310.7	1	99	0	0	49	28.02	-19.56	5.75		Oct-97
100	1.78	20.69	3.58	76.57	86.20	0	1.96	17.35	1.02	31.38	310.7	1	99	0	0	49	27.42	-19.82		1.00	Apr-99
100	2.05	21.29	4.60	81.97	95.99	0	0.99	17.38	1.02	51.21	310.7	1	99	0	0	49	28.28	-19.42			Apr-99
	2.06	21.30	4.68	82.38	95.44	0	0.85	17.37	1.02	51.41	310.7	1	99	0	0	49	28.02	-19.56			Sep-16
100	4.66	20.73	13.41	56.06	64.06	0.13	1.15	12.82	1.02	19.95	614.3	3	97	0	0	17	21.89	-14.14	5.75		May-08
100	4.48	20.31	12.57	52.57	57.92	0	1.9	12.82	1.02	18.41	614.3	3	97	0	0	17	21.31	-14.47		1.00	May-08
100	4.76	20.99	13.80	57.65	66.81	0.49	0.82	12.8	1.02	20.01	614.3	3	97	0	0	17	22.24	-14.04			May-08
	4.76	20.97	13.84	57.72	66.96	0.51	0.8	12.82	1.02	20	614.3	3	97	0	0	17	22.24	-14.04			Jul-13
100	6.12	22.18	11.90	46.13	44.96	0.99	1.17	11.31	0.94	52.36	715.0	0	100	0	0	5	22.22	-14.2	5.75		Jul-93
100	5.92	21.74	11.10	42.94	39.73	0.48	1.9	11.31	0.94	45.2	715.0	0	100	0	0	5	21.65	-14.45		1.00	Jun-95
100	6.18	22.34	12.17	47.26	46.88	1.22	0.9	11.31	0.94	52.7	715.0	0	100	0	0	5	22.36	-14.12			Mar-96
	6.21	22.38	12.27	47.62	47.47	1.31	0.82	11.33	0.94	52.64	715.0	0	100	0	0	5	22.22	-14.2			Jul-13
250	1.25	17.86	-6.83	37.07	22.32	0	1.26	18.76	1.03	26.59	72.9	1	99	0	0	349	30.94	-26.8			Oct-99
1,000	3.97	14.38	0.14	28.61	11.03	1.24	1.04	11.79	1.01	29.82	247.8	2	98	0	0	26	16.53	-22.76			Dec-10
1,000	3.11	17.27	7.57	35.64	45.73	0.64	1	11.93	0.96	43.05	37.5	4	96	0	0	27					Apr-12
5,000	5.13	18.41	3.88	39.36	48.73	1.06	0.8	13.75	1.08	25.78	1,978	3	97	0	0	33	26.87	-19.9			Jul-02
100	5.04	18.21	3.59	38.25	46.86	0.8	1.05	13.74	1.08	25.63	1,978	3	97	0	0	33	26.86	-20.08			Jul-02
5,000	2.57	17.42	0.42			0	1.1			9.57	9.9	17	80	0	0	146					Oct-17
5,000	1.53	11.14	-2.57	16.92		0	2.01	11.34	0.78	10.57	59.4	50	47	0	3	222					Feb-15
5,000	1.87	11.61	-1.59	27.13	26.04	1.06	0.95	11.56	1	16.34	754.0	4	96	0	0	80					Dec-11
5,000	0.55	2.95	-2.69	3.26	9.76	0	2.35	5.23	0.42	10.79	676.2	48	53	0	-1	85					Dec-13
100	0.56	2.89	-2.90	2.53	8.58	0	2.6	5.2	0.41	10.67	676.2	48	53	0	-1	85					Apr-14
5,000	0.22	4.57	-6.32	2.53	5.75	0	3.01	10.51	0.61	18.06	283.7	46	55	-1	0	58	14.44	-4.16			Nov-98
100	0.18	4.43	-6.51	1.77	4.44	0	3.26	10.51	0.61	16.47	283.7	46	55	-1	0	58	14.29	-4.23			Nov-98
5,000	1.93	6.55	-1.92	10.15	13.78	0.08	2.1	7.52	0.57	15.28	3,746	52	47	0	0	60	16.97	-10.52			Sep-10

	MARKET		FUND TYPE, CATEGORY & OBJECTIVE		RATINGS				MINIMUMS	
Fund Name	Ticker Symbol	Traded On	Fund Type	Category and (Prospectus Objective)	Overall Rating	Reward Rating	Risk Rating	Recent Up/ Downgrade	Open to New Investors	Min Initial Investment
Boston Partners Long/Short Research Fund Investor Class	BPRRX	NAS CM	Open End	Long/Short Equity (Growth & Income)	C-	D+	C			2,500
Boston Partners Small Cap Value II Institutional Cls	BPSIX	NAS CM	Open End	US Equity Small Cap (Small Company)	C	C	C+		Y	100,000
Boston Partners Small Cap Value Fund II Investor Class	BPSCX	NAS CM	Open End	US Equity Small Cap (Small Company)	C	C	C+		Y	2,500
Boston Trust Asset Management Fund	BTBFX	NAS CM	Open End	Aggressive Alloc (Asset Alloc)	B	C+	A-		Y	100,000
Boston Trust Equity Fund	BTEFX	NAS CM	Open End	US Equity Large Cap Blend (Growth)	B	C+	B+		Y	100,000
Boston Trust Midcap Fund	BTMFX	NAS CM	Open End	US Equity Mid Cap (Growth)	B-	C+	B	Down	Y	100,000
Boston Trust Small Cap Fund	BOSOX	NAS CM	Open End	US Equity Small Cap (Small Company)	C+	C	B	Down		100,000
Boston Trust SMID Cap Fund	BTSMX	NAS CM	Open End	US Equity Small Cap (Growth)	B-	C	B		Y	1,000,000
Boulder Growth & Income Fund	BIF	NYSE	Closed End	US Equity Large Cap Value (Growth & Income)	C+	C	C+		Y	
Boyar Value Fund	BOYAX	NAS CM	Open End	US Equity Large Cap Blend (Growth)	B-	C	B	Up	Y	5,000
Brandes Emerging Markets Value Fund Class A	BEMAX	NAS CM	Open End	Global Emerg Mkts (Div Emerging Mkts)	C	C	B-		Y	2,500
Brandes Emerging Markets Value Fund Class C	BEMCX	NAS CM	Open End	Global Emerg Mkts (Div Emerging Mkts)	C	C	B-		Y	2,500
Brandes Emerging Markets Value Fund Class I	BEMIX	NAS CM	Open End	Global Emerg Mkts (Div Emerging Mkts)	C	C	B-		Y	100,000
Brandes Emerging Markets Value Fund Class R6	BEMRX	NAS CM	Open End	Global Emerg Mkts (Div Emerging Mkts)	C	C	B-		Y	0
Brandes Global Equity Fund Class A	BGEAX	NAS CM	Open End	Global Equity Large Cap (World Stock)	C	C-	B-		Y	2,500
Brandes Global Equity Fund Class C	BGVCX	NAS CM	Open End	Global Equity Large Cap (World Stock)	C	C-	B-		Y	2,500
Brandes Global Equity Fund Class I	BGVIX	NAS CM	Open End	Global Equity Large Cap (World Stock)	C	C-	B-		Y	100,000
Brandes Global Equity Income Fund Class A	BGIAX	NAS CM	Open End	Global Equity Large Cap (World Stock)	C	C-	B		Y	2,500
Brandes Global Equity Income Fund Class C	BGICX	NAS CM	Open End	Global Equity Large Cap (World Stock)	C	C-	B		Y	2,500
Brandes Global Equity Income Fund Class I	BGIIX	NAS CM	Open End	Global Equity Large Cap (World Stock)	C	C-	B		Y	100,000
Brandes Global Opportunities Value Fund Class A	BGOAX	NAS CM	Open End	Global Equity Large Cap (World Stock)	D+	D	C-	Down	Y	2,500
Brandes Global Opportunities Value Fund Class C	BGOCX	NAS CM	Open End	Global Equity Large Cap (World Stock)	D+	D	C-	Down	Y	2,500
Brandes Global Opportunities Value Fund Class I	BGOIX	NAS CM	Open End	Global Equity Large Cap (World Stock)	D+	D	C-	Down	Y	100,000
Brandes International Equity Fund A	BIEAX	NAS CM	Open End	Global Equity Large Cap (Foreign Stock)	C	C-	C+		Y	2,500
Brandes International Equity Fund Class C	BIECX	NAS CM	Open End	Global Equity Large Cap (Foreign Stock)	C	C-	C		Y	2,500
Brandes International Equity Fund Class I	BIIEX	NAS CM	Open End	Global Equity Large Cap (Foreign Stock)	C	C-	C+		Y	100,000
Brandes International Equity Fund Class R6	BIERX	NAS CM	Open End	Global Equity Large Cap (Foreign Stock)	C	C-	C+		Y	0
Brandes International Small Cap Equity Fund Class A	BISAX	NAS CM	Open End	Global Equity Mid/Small Cap (Small Company)	D	D	D+		Y	2,500
Brandes International Small Cap Equity Fund Class C	BINCX	NAS CM	Open End	Global Equity Mid/Small Cap (Small Company)	D	D	D+		Y	2,500
Brandes International Small Cap Equity Fund Class I	BISMX	NAS CM	Open End	Global Equity Mid/Small Cap (Small Company)	D	D	D+		Y	100,000
Brandes International Small Cap Equity Fund Class R6	BISRX	NAS CM	Open End	Global Equity Mid/Small Cap (Small Company)	D	D	D+		Y	0
Brandes Small Cap Value Fund Class A	BSCAX	NAS CM	Open End	US Equity Small Cap (Small Company)	D	D	D+		Y	2,500
Brandes Small Cap Value Fund Class I	BSCMX	NAS CM	Open End	US Equity Small Cap (Small Company)	D	D	D+		Y	100,000
Brandes Small Cap Value Fund Class R6	BSCRX	NAS CM	Open End	US Equity Small Cap (Small Company)	D	D	D+		Y	0
BrandywineGLOBAL - Alternative Credit Fund Class A	LMAPX	NAS CM	Open End	Long/Short Credit (Growth & Income)	B	C+	A	Up	Y	1,000
BrandywineGLOBAL - Alternative Credit Fund Class C	LMAQX	NAS CM	Open End	Long/Short Credit (Growth & Income)	B	C	A-	Up	Y	1,000
BrandywineGLOBAL - Alternative Credit Fund Class FI	LMAOX	NAS CM	Open End	Long/Short Credit (Growth & Income)	B	C+	A	Up	Y	0
BrandywineGLOBAL - Alternative Credit Fund Class I	LMANX	NAS CM	Open End	Long/Short Credit (Growth & Income)	B	C+	A	Up	Y	1,000,000
BrandywineGLOBAL - Alternative Credit Fund Class IS	LMAMX	NAS CM	Open End	Long/Short Credit (Growth & Income)	B-	C+	B+	Up	Y	1,000,000
BrandywineGLOBAL - Diversified US Large Cap Value Cls A	LBWAX	NAS CM	Open End	US Equity Large Cap Value (Growth)	C+	C	B	Up	Y	1,000
BrandywineGLOBAL - Diversified US Large Cap Value Cls A2	LLVAX	NAS CM	Open End	US Equity Large Cap Value (Growth)	C+	C	B	Up	Y	1,000
BrandywineGLOBAL - Diversified US Large Cap Value Cls C	LBWCX	NAS CM	Open End	US Equity Large Cap Value (Growth)	C+	C	B	Up	Y	1,000
BrandywineGLOBAL - Diversified US Large Cap Value Cls I	LBWIX	NAS CM	Open End	US Equity Large Cap Value (Growth)	B-	C	B	Up	Y	1,000,000
BrandywineGLOBAL - Diversified US Large Cap Value Cls IS	LBISX	NAS CM	Open End	US Equity Large Cap Value (Growth)	B-	C	B	Up	Y	1,000,000
BrandywineGLOBAL - Diversified US Large Cap Value Cls R	LBDRX	NAS CM	Open End	US Equity Large Cap Value (Growth)	C+	C	B	Up	Y	0
BrandywineGLOBAL - Dynamic US Large Cap Value Fund Class A	LMBJX	NAS CM	Open End	US Equity Large Cap Value (Growth)	C+	C	B		Y	1,000
BrandywineGLOBAL - Dynamic US Large Cap Value Fund Class C	LMBBX	NAS CM	Open End	US Equity Large Cap Value (Growth)	C+	C	B		Y	1,000
BrandywineGLOBAL - Dynamic US Large Cap Value Fund Class I	LMBEX	NAS CM	Open End	US Equity Large Cap Value (Growth)	C+	C	B		Y	1,000,000
BrandywineGLOBAL - Dynamic US Large Cap Value Cls IS	LMBGX	NAS CM	Open End	US Equity Large Cap Value (Growth)	C+	C	B		Y	1,000,000
BrandywineGLOBAL - Dynamic US Large Cap Value Fund Class R	LMBHX	NAS CM	Open End	US Equity Large Cap Value (Growth)	C+	C	B		Y	0
Bread & Butter Fund	BABFX	NAS CM	Open End	US Equity Large Cap Value (Growth)	C	C	C	Up	Y	3,000
Bretton Fund	BRTNX	NAS CM	Open End	US Equity Large Cap Blend (Growth)	B-	C+	B	Down	Y	2,000

★ Expanded analysis of this fund is included in Section II.

	TOTAL RETURNS					PERFORMANCE				ASSETS		ASSET ALLOCATION & TURNOVER					BULL & BEAR		FEES		
Min Additional Investment	3-Month Total Return	6-Month Total Return	1-Year Total Return	3-Year Total Return	5-Year Total Return	Dividend Yield (TTM)	Expense Ratio	3-Yr Std Deviation	3-Year Beta	NAV	Total Assets (MIL)	%Cash	%Stocks	%Bonds	%Other	Turnover Ratio	Last Bull Market Total Return	Last Bear Market Total Return	Front End Fee (%)	Back End Fee (%)	Inception Date
100	1.90	6.48	-2.10	9.37	12.40	0	2.35	7.49	0.57	14.95	3,746	52	47	0	0	60	16.71	-10.54			Nov-10
5,000	4.08	17.22	-4.83	32.03	28.80	0.48	1.1	16.88	0.96	23.95	559.9	4	96	0	0	40	28.54	-23.52			Jul-98
100	4.05	17.11	-5.02	31.04	27.27	0.24	1.35	16.9	0.96	22.86	559.9	4	96	0	0	40	28.32	-23.65			Jul-98
1,000	3.85	15.85	12.52	37.69	51.66	0.99	0.93	9.2	0.74	50.92	527.2	5	78	17	0	3	17.32	-10.2			Dec-95
1,000	4.65	19.34	14.49	49.62	61.31	0.83	0.92	11.66	0.94	26.78	146.0	0	100	0	0	2	23.51	-15.69			Oct-03
1,000	5.23	20.84	12.99	48.45	65.40	0.41	0.98	12.34	0.89	18.9	109.4	1	99	0	0	19	25.44	-18.01			Sep-07
1,000	4.40	21.90	7.78	47.74	51.46	0.41	1	15.2	0.86	14.47	244.4	1	99	0	0	25	25.71	-21.85			Dec-05
1,000	4.31	20.09	8.00	52.90	58.64	0.65	0.75	13.86	0.86	17.39	88.7	1	99	0	0	15					Nov-11
	5.04	10.95	12.93	46.29	49.29	0.54	2.28	10.88	0.79	13.51	1,427	13	87	0	0	1	12.85	-14.28			Dec-72
1,000	4.46	13.66	5.22	30.68	43.43	0.29	1.8	11.06	0.85	26.45	26.5	13	87	0	0	7	26.55	-16.94	5.00		May-98
500	4.58	13.17	5.54	28.36	-2.26	1.26	1.38	13.71	0.86	8.99	1,484	2	97	0	1	38	18.6	-26.15	5.75		Jan-11
500	4.29	12.66	4.71	25.56	-5.92	0.71	2.11	13.67	0.86	8.94	1,484	2	97	0	1	38	18.22	-26.28		1.00	Jan-13
500	4.49	13.13	5.72	29.24	-1.11	1.45	1.13	13.7	0.87	9.03	1,484	2	97	0	1	38	18.74	-26.05			Jan-11
0	4.61	13.26	5.88	29.85	-0.64	1.49	0.98	13.81	0.87	9.06	1,484	2	97	0	1	38	18.74	-26.05			Jul-16
500	1.21	8.96	-2.18	26.40	10.27	2.04	1.25	11.65	0.93	22.06	37.9	1	99	0	0	9	12.46	-19.09	5.75		Jan-11
500	0.97	8.48	-2.94	23.48	6.19	1.34	2	11.64	0.93	21.9	37.9	1	99	0	0	9	12.09	-19.25		1.00	Jan-13
500	1.25	9.07	-1.95	27.29	11.66	2.23	1	11.64	0.93	22.22	37.9	1	99	0	0	9	12.58	-19			Oct-08
500	-0.37	8.12	-1.52	25.86		2.71	1.25	10.22	0.82	11.17	1.3	0	92	0	0	16			5.75		Dec-14
500	-0.64	7.66	-2.38	21.92		2.27	2	10.05	0.81	10.74	1.3	0	92	0	0	16				1.00	Dec-14
500	-0.34	8.19	-1.28	24.78		3.07	1	10.06	0.81	10.63	1.3	0	92	0	0	16					Dec-14
500	-0.85	5.57	-8.38	14.88		1.57	1.4	12.1	0.94		7.7	3	97	0	0	29			5.75		Dec-14
500	-1.03	5.10	-9.03	12.40		1.04	2.15	12.08	0.94		7.7	3	97	0	0	29				1.00	Dec-14
500	-0.91	5.60	-8.18	15.79		1.77	1.15	12.12	0.94		7.7	3	97	0	0	29					Dec-14
500	-0.44	6.37	-5.00	20.81	3.81	3.47	1.11	11.21	0.92	16.24	725.8	8	92	0	0	20	7.81	-20.63	5.75		Jan-11
500	-0.58	6.00	-5.72	18.14	-0.05	2.92	1.86	11.21	0.92	15.98	725.8	8	92	0	0	20	7.48	-20.99		1.00	Jan-13
500	-0.39	6.46	-4.83	21.52	4.76	3.62	0.85	11.22	0.92	16.29	725.8	8	92	0	0	20	7.95	-20.74			Jan-97
0	-0.37	6.54	-4.71	22.01	5.34	3.65	0.75	11.25	0.92	16.36	725.8	8	92	0	0	20	7.95	-20.74			Feb-16
500	-0.09	3.84	-10.29	-0.99	-6.02	2.59	1.3	10.2	0.73	10.71	587.8	6	94	0	0	22	10.55	-20.13	5.75		Jan-12
500	-0.28	3.44	-10.98	-3.20	-9.45	2.35	2.05	10.17	0.73	10.4	587.8	6	94	0	0	22	10.1	-20.3		1.00	Jan-13
500	-0.09	3.98	-10.16	-0.37	-5.09	2.69	1.1	10.24	0.74	10.75	587.8	6	94	0	0	22	10.65	-20.05			Feb-12
0	0.00	4.08	-9.97	0.04	-4.99	2.71	1	10.22	0.73	10.78	587.8	6	94	0	0	22	11.66	-20.05			Jun-16
500	-1.23	5.85	-7.46			0.79	1.15			8.54	4.5	17	78	3	0	41			5.75		Jan-18
500	-1.02	6.26	-7.01			0.94	0.9			8.57	4.5	17	78	3	0	41					Jan-18
0	-1.25	6.11	-7.17			1.06	0.72			8.59	4.5	17	78	3	0	41					Jan-18
50	2.10	4.06	3.25	19.60	12.68	2.41	1.66	2.97	18.76	10.41	676.3	8	0	92	0	142	9.98	4.66	4.25		Dec-13
50	2.01	3.67	2.48	17.10	8.77	1.47	2.32	2.97	18.83	10.35	676.3	8	0	92	0	142	9.5	4.33		1.00	Dec-13
	2.10	3.96	3.15	19.54	12.46	2.41	1.48	2.91	18.65	10.38	676.3	8	0	92	0	142	9.98	4.66			Dec-13
	2.28	4.21	3.58	20.71	14.44	2.73	1.33	2.97	19.54	10.42	676.3	8	0	92	0	142	10.14	4.77			Dec-13
	2.29	4.25	3.67	21.05	14.90	2.82	1.25	2.94	19.07	10.44	676.3	8	0	92	0	142	10.14	4.77			Dec-13
50	2.72	14.91	5.54	40.38	43.08	1.37	1.08	13.11	1.07	19.57	946.7	1	99	0	0	46	24.3	-15.61	5.75		Sep-10
50	2.71	14.85	5.42	39.79	41.98	1.32	1.16	13.12	1.07	19.33	946.7	1	99	0	0	46	24.57	-15.58	5.75		Oct-12
50	2.36	14.33	4.60	37.01	37.58	1.53	1.86	13.07	1.06	19.06	946.7	1	99	0	0	46	23.84	-15.93		1.00	Sep-10
	2.78	15.10	5.85	41.60	45.11	1.64	0.8	13.1	1.07	19.58	946.7	1	99	0	0	46	24.62	-15.49			Sep-10
	2.77	15.15	5.95	42.01	45.69	1.74	0.7	13.12	1.07	19.6	946.7	1	99	0	0	46	24.75	-15.49			Sep-10
	2.63	14.76	5.22	39.22	41.25	1.23	1.3	13.08	1.06	19.51	946.7	1	99	0	0	46	24.39	-15.67			Jan-14
50	2.02	15.56	6.38	42.17	43.70	1.19	1.1	14.04	1.12	11.58	171.0	1	99	0	0	91	27.82	-17.18	5.75		Nov-14
50	1.86	15.19	5.66	39.08	38.24	0.44	1.82	14.04	1.12	11.45	171.0	1	99	0	0	91	27.27	-17.44		1.00	Nov-14
	2.19	15.83	6.83	43.77	45.86	1.51	0.75	14.01	1.12	11.63	171.0	1	99	0	0	91	28.01	-17.1			Nov-14
	2.10	15.83	6.84	44.06	46.23	1.6	0.65	14.04	1.12	11.63	171.0	1	99	0	0	91	28.01	-17.1			Oct-14
	1.93	15.42	6.14	41.08	41.54	0.75	1.35	14.05	1.12	11.6	171.0	1	99	0	0	91	27.64	-17.27			Nov-14
500	3.99	9.53	2.63	9.97	0.49	0	2.03	9.35	0.63	12.75	1.5	34	59	0	0	48	8.98	-13.06			Oct-05
100	5.70	21.29	13.68	55.05	59.09	0	1.5	13.28	1	36.11	36.6	3	97	0	0	11	33.1	-11.72			Sep-10

Fund Name	MARKET Ticker Symbol	Traded On	FUND TYPE, CATEGORY & OBJECTIVE Fund Type	Category and (Prospectus Objective)	RATINGS Overall Rating	Reward Rating	Risk Rating	Recent Up/ Downgrade	MINIMUMS Open to New Investors	Min Initial Investment
Bridge Builder International Equity Fund	BBIEX	NAS CM	Open End	Global Equity Large Cap (Foreign Stock)	C	C	B		Y	0
Bridge Builder Large Cap Growth Fund	BBGLX	NAS CM	Open End	US Equity Large Cap Growth (Growth)	B-	C+	B	Down	Y	0
Bridge Builder Large Cap Value Fund	BBVLX	NAS CM	Open End	US Equity Large Cap Value (Growth)	B-	C	B	Up	Y	0
Bridge Builder Small/Mid Cap Growth Fund	BBGSX	NAS CM	Open End	US Equity Mid Cap (Growth)	B-	C	B	Down	Y	0
Bridge Builder Small/Mid Cap Value Fund	BBVSX	NAS CM	Open End	US Equity Mid Cap (Growth)	C	C	B-		Y	0
Bridges Investment Fund	BRGIX	NAS CM	Open End	US Equity Large Cap Growth (Growth & Income)	B-	C	B		Y	1,000
Bridgeway Aggressive Investors 1 Fund	BRAGX	NAS CM	Open End	US Equity Mid Cap (Aggr Growth)	C	C	C		Y	2,000
Bridgeway Blue Chip Index Fund	BRLIX	NAS CM	Open End	US Equity Large Cap Blend (Growth & Income)	B	C+	B+		Y	2,000
Bridgeway Managed Volatility Fund	BRBPX	NAS CM	Open End	Long/Short Equity (Balanced)	B-	C	B+	Up	Y	2,000
Bridgeway Omni Small-Cap Value Fund Class N	BOSVX	NAS CM	Open End	US Equity Small Cap (Small Company)	D+	D+	C-	Down	Y	0
Bridgeway Omni Tax-Managed Small-Cap Value Fund Class N	BOTSX	NAS CM	Open End	US Equity Small Cap (Small Company)	D+	D+	C-	Down	Y	0
Bridgeway Small Cap Growth Fund	BRSGX	NAS CM	Open End	US Equity Small Cap (Small Company)	C	C-	C		Y	2,000
Bridgeway Small Cap Value Fund	BRSVX	NAS CM	Open End	US Equity Small Cap (Small Company)	C-	D+	C-	Down	Y	2,000
Bridgeway Ultra Small Company Fund	BRUSX	NAS CM	Open End	US Equity Small Cap (Small Company)	D+	D	C-	Down		2,000
Bridgeway Ultra Small Company Market Fund	BRSIX	NAS CM	Open End	US Equity Small Cap (Small Company)	C-	C-	C-	Down	Y	2,000
Bright Rock Mid Cap Growth Fund Institutional Class	BQMGX	NAS CM	Open End	US Equity Mid Cap (Growth)	B-	C+	B		Y	100,000
Bright Rock Mid Cap Growth Fund Investor Class	BQMIX	NAS CM	Open End	US Equity Mid Cap (Growth)	B-	C+	B		Y	5,000
Bright Rock Quality Large Cap Fund Institutional Class	BQLCX	NAS CM	Open End	US Equity Large Cap Blend (Growth)	B-	C	B		Y	100,000
Bright Rock Quality Large Cap Fund Investor Class	BQLIX	NAS CM	Open End	US Equity Large Cap Blend (Growth)	B-	C	B		Y	5,000
Broadstone Real Estate Access Fund Class I	BDREX	NAS CM	Closed End	Real Estate Sector Equity (Growth & Income)	U	U	U		Y	1,000,000
Broadstone Real Estate Access Fund Class W	BDRWX	NAS CM	Closed End	Real Estate Sector Equity (Growth & Income)	U	U	U		Y	2,500
Broadview Opportunity Fund	BVAOX	NAS CM	Open End	US Equity Small Cap (Growth)	C	C-	C+		Y	1,000
Brookfield Global Listed Infrastructure Fund Class A	BGLAX	NAS CM	Open End	Infrastructure Sector Equity (Growth & Income)	C+	C	B-	Down	Y	1,000
Brookfield Global Listed Infrastructure Fund Class C	BGLCX	NAS CM	Open End	Infrastructure Sector Equity (Growth & Income)	C	C	C+	Down	Y	1,000
Brookfield Global Listed Infrastructure Fund Class I	BGLIX	NAS CM	Open End	Infrastructure Sector Equity (Growth & Income)	C+	C	B-	Down	Y	1,000,000
Brookfield Global Listed Infrastructure Fund Class Y	BGLYX	NAS CM	Open End	Infrastructure Sector Equity (Growth & Income)	C+	C	B-	Down	Y	1,000
Brookfield Global Listed Infrastructure Income Fund	INF	NYSE	Closed End	Infrastructure Sector Equity (Growth & Income)	C	C	C-		Y	
Brookfield Global Listed Real Estate Fund Class A	BLRAX	NAS CM	Open End	Real Estate Sector Equity (Real Estate)	B-	C	B	Up	Y	1,000
Brookfield Global Listed Real Estate Fund Class C	BLRCX	NAS CM	Open End	Real Estate Sector Equity (Real Estate)	C+	C	B		Y	1,000
Brookfield Global Listed Real Estate Fund Class I	BLRIX	NAS CM	Open End	Real Estate Sector Equity (Real Estate)	B-	C	B	Up	Y	1,000,000
Brookfield Global Listed Real Estate Fund Class Y	BLRYX	NAS CM	Open End	Real Estate Sector Equity (Real Estate)	B-	C	B	Up	Y	1,000
Brookfield Real Assets Securities Fund Class A	RASAX	NAS CM	Open End	Flexible Alloc (Growth & Income)	C+	C	B	Down	Y	1,000
Brookfield Real Assets Securities Fund Class C	RASCX	NAS CM	Open End	Flexible Alloc (Growth & Income)	C+	C	B-	Down	Y	1,000
Brookfield Real Assets Securities Fund Class I	RASIX	NAS CM	Open End	Flexible Alloc (Growth & Income)	C+	C	B	Down	Y	1,000,000
Brookfield Real Assets Securities Fund Class Y	RASYX	NAS CM	Open End	Flexible Alloc (Growth & Income)	C+	C	B	Down	Y	1,000
Brookfield U.S. Listed Real Estate Fund Class A	BRUAX	NAS CM	Open End	Real Estate Sector Equity (Real Estate)	C	C	C	Down	Y	1,000
Brookfield U.S. Listed Real Estate Fund Class C	BRUCX	NAS CM	Open End	Real Estate Sector Equity (Real Estate)	C	C	C	Down	Y	1,000
Brookfield U.S. Listed Real Estate Fund Class I	BRUIX	NAS CM	Open End	Real Estate Sector Equity (Real Estate)	C	C	C+	Down	Y	1,000,000
Brookfield U.S. Listed Real Estate Fund Class Y	BRUYX	NAS CM	Open End	Real Estate Sector Equity (Real Estate)	C	C	C+	Down	Y	1,000
Brown Advy - Beutel Goodman Large-Cap Value Inst Shares	BVALX	NAS CM	Open End	US Equity Large Cap Value (Growth)	D	C-	B-		Y	1,000,000
Brown Advisory Equity Income Fund Advisor Shares	BADAX	NAS CM	Open End	US Equity Large Cap Blend (Equity-Income)	B-	C+	B	Down	Y	100
Brown Advisory Equity Income Fund Inst Shares	BAFDX	NAS CM	Open End	US Equity Large Cap Blend (Equity-Income)	B	C+	B+		Y	1,000,000
Brown Advisory Equity Income Fund Investor Shares	BIADX	NAS CM	Open End	US Equity Large Cap Blend (Equity-Income)	B	C+	B		Y	100
Brown Advisory Flexible Equity Fund Advisor Shares	BAFAX	NAS CM	Open End	US Equity Large Cap Growth (Growth)	B-	C+	B		Y	100
Brown Advisory Flexible Equity Fund Institutional Shares	BAFFX	NAS CM	Open End	US Equity Large Cap Growth (Growth)	B-	C+	B		Y	1,000,000
Brown Advisory Flexible Equity Fund Investor Shares	BIAFX	NAS CM	Open End	US Equity Large Cap Growth (Growth)	B-	C+	B		Y	100
Brown Advisory Global Leaders Fund Institutional Shares	BAFLX	NAS CM	Open End	Global Equity Large Cap (World Stock)	B	B-	B	Up	Y	1,000,000
Brown Advisory Global Leaders Fund Investor Shares	BIALX	NAS CM	Open End	Global Equity Large Cap (World Stock)	B-	B-	B		Y	100
Brown Advisory Growth Equity Fund Advisor Shares	BAGAX	NAS CM	Open End	US Equity Large Cap Growth (Growth)	B-	B-	B	Down	Y	100
Brown Advisory Growth Equity Fund Institutional Shares	BAFGX	NAS CM	Open End	US Equity Large Cap Growth (Growth)	B	B-	B		Y	1,000,000
Brown Advisory Growth Equity Fund Investor Shares	BIAGX	NAS CM	Open End	US Equity Large Cap Growth (Growth)	B	B-	B		Y	100
Brown Advisory Mid-Cap Growth Fund Institutional Class	BAFMX	NAS CM	Open End	US Equity Small Cap (Growth)	C-	C-	B-	Up	Y	1,000,000

★ Expanded analysis of this fund is included in Section II.

Min Additional Investment	TOTAL RETURNS 3-Month Total Return	6-Month Total Return	1-Year Total Return	3-Year Total Return	5-Year Total Return	PERFORMANCE Dividend Yield (TTM)	Expense Ratio	3-Yr Std Deviation	3-Year Beta	ASSETS NAV	Total Assets (MIL)	ASSET ALLOCATION & TURNOVER %Cash	%Stocks	%Bonds	%Other	Turnover Ratio	BULL & BEAR Last Bull Market Total Return	Last Bear Market Total Return	FEES Front End Fee (%)	Back End Fee (%)	Inception Date
	3.26	14.83	1.57	30.72		1.87	0.39	11.43	1.01	11.38	10,640	3	97	0	0	20					Jul-15
	4.49	22.00	13.75	59.91		0.91	0.25	12.24	0.9	14.64	6,997	2	98	0	0	54					Apr-15
	4.58	18.87	8.45	40.72		1.82	0.28	12.35	1.01	12.71	8,688	3	97	0	0	23					Apr-15
	5.24	24.34	11.65	61.73		0.32	0.42	14.1	0.84	14.25	4,023	2	98	0	0	26					Apr-15
	4.33	18.94	1.22	32.47		1.16	0.5	14.65	0.96	11.55	4,808	3	97	0	0	38					Apr-15
	4.68	20.02	8.70	54.64	54.46	0.49	0.79	12.94	0.94	68.16	180.3	7	93	0	0	3	27.75	-16.09			Jul-63
100	4.13	19.39	-6.66	29.00	23.23	0.53	0.96	16.68	1.26	62	181.5	0	100	0	0	105	30.5	-30.95			Aug-94
100	5.19	19.34	16.25	50.56	67.67	1.91	0.15	12.15		14.99	505.2	0	100	0	0	14	24.19	-13.18			Jul-97
100	1.89	9.05	1.74	14.78	16.20	0.85	0.95	5.92	0.45	15.05	30.7	39	61	0	0	50	14.01	-10.64			Jun-01
	-3.04	7.23	-16.81	23.68	14.71	1.04	0.6	19.94	1.13	14.97	987.8	0	100	0	0	24	30.35				Aug-11
	-2.49	6.80	-16.48	23.79	15.96	1.29	0.6	19.53	1.11	14.43	608.9	1	100	0	0	27	28.33	-26.06			Dec-10
100	0.91	10.76	-10.81	35.91	46.24	0.37	0.94	18.84	1.05	24.28	42.1	0	100	0	0	122	34.51	-27.76			Oct-03
100	-2.50	6.69	-17.12	22.37	11.78	0.98	0.94	18.07	1	20.24	49.7	1	99	0	0	78	30.06	-24.02			Oct-03
100	-5.21	8.63	-14.48	11.16	-12.29	0.04	2.03	18.1		24.16	74.0	1	97	0	2	89	35.36	-30			Aug-94
100	-2.66	12.05	-16.97	28.34	18.22	0.59	0.86	18.45		11.34	236.5	0	100	0	0	35	30.64	-26			Jul-97
5,000	6.51	22.08	9.75	45.76	66.06	0	1.18	11.98	0.78	19.46	69.6	2	98	0	0	11	23.25	-23.4			May-10
1,000	6.43	21.92	9.42	44.64	64.10	0	1.43	12	0.78	19.85	69.6	2	98	0	0	11	23.45	-23.48			Jan-12
5,000	4.58	18.25	11.39	31.14	44.93	1.26	0.89	11.34	0.87	17.46	246.6	1	99	0	0	43	26.86	-15.8			May-10
1,000	4.50	18.12	11.07	30.07	42.98	0.99	1.14	11.31	0.87	17.9	246.6	1	99	0	0	43	26.96	-15.88			Jan-12
1,000	1.78	12.18					2.5			10.59	--	-30	118	12	0						Oct-18
1,000	1.69	12.00					2.75			10.59	--	-30	118	12	0						Oct-18
100	0.90	17.78	-4.58	30.84	22.70	0	1.23	16.19	0.92	29.08	284.6	12	88	0	0	49	28.21	-24.46			Dec-96
100	3.19	20.58	11.04	18.57	2.80	3.58	1.35	10.52	1.02	13.23	202.2	0	100	0	0	75			4.75		Dec-11
100	3.05	20.15	10.22	15.89	-1.00	2.94	2.1	10.49	1.02	13.06	202.2	0	100	0	0	75				1.00	Apr-12
	3.25	20.78	11.30	19.39	4.05	3.82	1.1	10.5	1.02	13.26	202.2	0	100	0	0	75					Nov-11
100	3.26	20.79	11.31	19.40	4.12	3.82	1.1	10.5	1.02	13.25	202.2	0	100	0	0	75					Nov-11
	3.42	28.48	13.10	21.49	-14.23	2.36	2.41	15.85		14.97	201.8	2	98	0	0	36	28.6				Aug-11
100	-0.25	15.16	5.33	14.70	24.92	3.69	1.2	11.46	1	13.29	1,839	0	98	0	2	82			4.75		Apr-12
100	-0.36	14.74	4.55	12.20	20.44	3.02	1.95	11.44	1	13.22	1,839	0	98	0	2	82				1.00	Apr-12
	-0.12	15.27	5.59	15.59	26.49	3.93	0.95	11.47	1.01	13.3	1,839	0	98	0	2	82					Nov-11
100	-0.12	15.34	5.58	15.66	26.56	3.92	0.95	11.47	1	13.32	1,839	0	98	0	2	82					Nov-11
100	2.22	17.80	8.25	17.85		3.31	1.35	9.33	0.62	9.55	67.2	0	78	19	0	83			4.75		Nov-14
100	2.01	17.33	7.57	15.70		3.02	2.1	9.28	0.62	9.56	67.2	0	78	19	0	83				1.00	Nov-14
	2.30	17.93	8.47	18.21		3.87	1.1	9.3	0.61	9.41	67.2	0	78	19	0	83					Nov-14
100	2.41	18.03	8.57	18.18		3.86	1.1	9.31	0.62	9.43	67.2	0	78	19	0	83					Nov-14
100	1.93	19.14	9.99	11.97	26.99	3.53	1.2	13.54	1	10.73	10.8	0	100	0	0	107			4.75		Dec-13
100	1.80	18.83	9.21	9.65	22.62	2.84	1.95	13.56	1	10.71	10.8	0	100	0	0	107				1.00	Dec-13
	2.05	19.36	10.28	12.90	28.67	3.85	0.95	13.55	1	10.66	10.8	0	100	0	0	107					Dec-13
100	2.04	19.40	10.35	13.07	29.07	3.83	0.95	13.57	1	10.7	10.8	0	100	0	0	107					Dec-13
100	4.49	16.85	11.61			1.01	0.67			10.47	295.9	3	97	0	0						Feb-18
100	4.76	20.19	12.67	40.86	43.13	1.38	1.17	10.96	0.87	14.14	89.7	4	96	0	0						Dec-11
100	4.86	20.41	13.11	42.47	45.95	1.73	0.77	10.92	0.87	14.15	89.7	4	96	0	0						Oct-12
100	4.82	20.32	13.03	41.90	45.02	1.6	0.92	10.94	0.87	14.15	89.7	4	96	0	0						Dec-11
100	4.66	20.46	8.51	58.79	62.00	0	0.98	13.34	1.07	22.9	483.5	2	98	0	0		26.39	-15.49			Jan-07
100	4.75	20.69	8.94	60.78	65.25	0.35	0.58	13.31	1.07	22.92	483.5	2	98	0	0		26.58	-15.41			Oct-12
100	4.71	20.61	8.76	59.97	64.11	0.22	0.73	13.32	1.07	22.88	483.5	2	98	0	0		26.58	-15.41			Nov-06
100	4.88	21.14	10.56	60.26			0.75	12.24	1.02	15.24	232.9	4	96	0	0						Oct-18
100	4.88	21.06	10.49	60.15		0.21	0.9	12.23	1.02	15.23	232.9	4	96	0	0						Jul-15
100	5.43	27.35	16.21	70.51	85.27	0	1.11	13.97	0.98	23.09	2,359	3	97	0	0		30.1	-18.48			May-06
100	5.57	27.63	16.68	72.58	89.02	0	0.71	13.98	0.98	24.8	2,359	3	97	0	0		30.27	-18.41			Oct-12
100	5.51	27.53	16.49	71.81	87.55	0	0.86	13.98	0.98	24.5	2,359	3	97	0	0		30.27	-18.41			Jun-99
100	8.50	32.72	16.97				0.71			13.14	45.0	3	97	0	0						Jul-18

Fund Name	MARKET Ticker Symbol	Traded On	Fund Type	FUND TYPE, CATEGORY & OBJECTIVE Category and (Prospectus Objective)	RATINGS Overall Rating	Reward Rating	Risk Rating	Recent Up/ Downgrade	MINIMUMS Open to New Investors	Min Initial Investment
Brown Advisory Mid-Cap Growth Fund Investor Class	BMIDX	NAS CM	Open End	US Equity Small Cap (Growth)	D+	C-	B-	Up	Y	100
Brown Advisory Small-Cap Fundamental Value Advisor Shares	BAUAX	NAS CM	Open End	US Equity Small Cap (Small Company)	C	C	C+		Y	100
Brown Advy Small-Cap Fundamental Value Inst Shares	BAUUX	NAS CM	Open End	US Equity Small Cap (Small Company)	C	C-	B-		Y	1,000,000
Brown Advisory Small-Cap Fundamental Value Investor Shares	BIAUX	NAS CM	Open End	US Equity Small Cap (Small Company)	C	C-	C+		Y	100
Brown Advisory Small-Cap Growth Fund Advisor Shares	BASAX	NAS CM	Open End	US Equity Small Cap (Small Company)	B-	B-	B-	Down	Y	100
Brown Advisory Small-Cap Growth Fund Institutional Shares	BAFSX	NAS CM	Open End	US Equity Small Cap (Small Company)	B-	B-	B-	Down	Y	1,000,000
Brown Advisory Small-Cap Growth Fund Investor Shares	BIASX	NAS CM	Open End	US Equity Small Cap (Small Company)	B-	B-	B-	Down	Y	100
Brown Advisory Sustainable Growth Fund Advisor Shares	BAWAX	NAS CM	Open End	US Equity Large Cap Growth (Growth)	B	B-	B		Y	100
Brown Advisory Sustainable Growth Institutional Shares	BAFWX	NAS CM	Open End	US Equity Large Cap Growth (Growth)	B	B	B		Y	1,000,000
Brown Advisory Sustainable Growth Fund Investor Shares	BIAWX	NAS CM	Open End	US Equity Large Cap Growth (Growth)	B	B	B		Y	100
Brown Advy WMC Strategic European Equity Adv Shares	BAHAX	NAS CM	Open End	Europe Equity Large Cap (Europe Stock)	C	C	C+		Y	100
Brown Advy WMC Strategic European Equity Inst Shares	BAFHX	NAS CM	Open End	Europe Equity Large Cap (Europe Stock)	C	C	C+		Y	1,000,000
Brown Advy WMC Strategic European Equity Inv Shares	BIAHX	NAS CM	Open End	Europe Equity Large Cap (Europe Stock)	C	C	C+		Y	100
Brown Capital Mgmt Intl Equity Inst Shares	BCISX	NAS CM	Open End	Global Equity Large Cap (Foreign Stock)	C+	C	B	Up	Y	500,000
Brown Capital Mgmt Intl Equity Inv Shares	BCIIX	NAS CM	Open End	Global Equity Large Cap (Foreign Stock)	C+	C	B	Up	Y	5,000
Brown Capital Mgmt Intl Small Company Inst Shares	BCSFX	NAS CM	Open End	Global Equity Mid/Small Cap (Small Company)	C+	C	C+	Up	Y	500,000
Brown Capital Mgmt Intl Small Company Inv Shares	BCSVX	NAS CM	Open End	Global Equity Mid/Small Cap (Small Company)	C+	C	C+	Up	Y	5,000
Brown Capital Management Mid Company Institutional Shares	BCMIX	NAS CM	Open End	US Equity Mid Cap (Growth)	B-	B	B-	Up	Y	500,000
Brown Capital Management Mid Company Fund Investor Shares	BCMSX	NAS CM	Open End	US Equity Mid Cap (Growth)	B-	B-	B-	Up	Y	5,000
Brown Capital Mgmt Small Company Inst Shares	BCSSX	NAS CM	Open End	US Equity Small Cap (Small Company)	C+	C+	C			500,000
Brown Capital Management Small Company Investor Shares	BCSIX	NAS CM	Open End	US Equity Small Cap (Small Company)	C+	C+	C			5,000
Bruce Fund	BRUFX	NAS CM	Open End	Moderate Alloc (Growth)	B-	C	B		Y	1,000
Buffalo Discovery Fund	BUFTX	NAS CM	Open End	US Equity Mid Cap (Growth)	B-	B-	B		Y	2,500
Buffalo Dividend Focus Fund	BUFDX	NAS CM	Open End	US Equity Large Cap Blend (Equity-Income)	B-	C	B		Y	2,500
Buffalo Emerging Opportunities Fund	BUFOX	NAS CM	Open End	US Equity Small Cap (Growth)	C+	C+	C+	Down		2,500
Buffalo Flexible Income Fund	BUFBX	NAS CM	Open End	Aggressive Alloc (Balanced)	B-	C	B		Y	2,500
Buffalo Growth Fund	BUFGX	NAS CM	Open End	US Equity Large Cap Growth (Growth)	B-	B-	B	Down	Y	2,500
Buffalo International Fund	BUFIX	NAS CM	Open End	Global Equity Large Cap (Foreign Stock)	C+	C	B	Up	Y	2,500
Buffalo Large Cap Fund	BUFEX	NAS CM	Open End	US Equity Large Cap Growth (Growth)	B-	C+	B	Down	Y	2,500
Buffalo Mid Cap Fund	BUFMX	NAS CM	Open End	US Equity Mid Cap (Growth)	C+	C	B-		Y	2,500
Buffalo Small Cap Fund	BUFSX	NAS CM	Open End	US Equity Small Cap (Small Company)	C+	C	C+	Down		2,500
Bullfinch Greater Western New York Series	BWNYX	NAS CM	Open End	US Equity Mid Cap (Growth)	C+	C	B	Down	Y	2,500
Calamos Convertible & High Income Fund	CHY	NAS CM	Closed End	Convertibles (Convertible Bond)	C	C	C+	Down	Y	
Calamos Convertible Fund Class A	CCVIX	NAS CM	Open End	Convertibles (Convertible Bond)	B	C	A-		Y	2,500
Calamos Convertible Fund Class C	CCVCX	NAS CM	Open End	Convertibles (Convertible Bond)	B-	C	A-	Down	Y	2,500
Calamos Convertible Fund Institutional Class	CICVX	NAS CM	Open End	Convertibles (Convertible Bond)	B	C	A-		Y	1,000,000
Calamos Convertible Opportunities and Income Fund	CHI	NAS CM	Closed End	Convertibles (Convertible Bond)	C+	C	C+	Down	Y	
Calamos Dividend Growth Fund Class A	CADVX	NAS CM	Open End	US Equity Large Cap Value (Equity-Income)	B-	C	B		Y	2,500
Calamos Dividend Growth Fund Class C	CCDVX	NAS CM	Open End	US Equity Large Cap Value (Equity-Income)	B-	C	B		Y	2,500
Calamos Dividend Growth Fund Class I	CIDVX	NAS CM	Open End	US Equity Large Cap Value (Equity-Income)	B-	C	B		Y	1,000,000
Calamos Dynamic Convertible and Income Fund	CCD	NAS CM	Closed End	Convertibles (Convertible Bond)	C	C	C-		Y	
Calamos Emerging Market Equity Fund Class A	CEGAX	NAS CM	Open End	Global Emerg Mkts (Div Emerging Mkts)	C	C-	C	Up	Y	2,500
Calamos Emerging Market Equity Fund Class C	CEGCX	NAS CM	Open End	Global Emerg Mkts (Div Emerging Mkts)	C	C-	C	Up	Y	2,500
Calamos Emerging Market Equity Fund Class I	CIEIX	NAS CM	Open End	Global Emerg Mkts (Div Emerging Mkts)	C	C-	C		Y	1,000,000
Calamos Evolving World Growth Fund Class A	CNWGX	NAS CM	Open End	Global Emerg Mkts (Growth)	C	C	C+		Y	2,500
Calamos Evolving World Growth Fund Class C	CNWDX	NAS CM	Open End	Global Emerg Mkts (Growth)	C	C-	C		Y	2,500
Calamos Evolving World Growth Fund Class I	CNWIX	NAS CM	Open End	Global Emerg Mkts (Growth)	C	C	C+		Y	1,000,000
Calamos Global Convertible Fund Class A	CAGCX	NAS CM	Open End	Convertibles (Growth & Income)	B-	C	A-	Up	Y	2,500
Calamos Global Convertible Fund Class C	CCGCX	NAS CM	Open End	Convertibles (Growth & Income)	B-	C	A-	Up	Y	2,500
Calamos Global Convertible Fund Class I	CXGCX	NAS CM	Open End	Convertibles (Growth & Income)	B	C	A	Up	Y	1,000,000
Calamos Global Dynamic Income Fund	CHW	NAS CM	Closed End	Alloc Miscellaneous (Multi-Asset Global)	C	C	C+		Y	
Calamos Global Equity Fund Class A	CAGEX	NAS CM	Open End	Global Equity Large Cap (World Stock)	C	C	C+		Y	2,500

★Expanded analysis of this fund is included in Section II.

Min Additional Investment	TOTAL RETURNS: 3-Month Total Return	6-Month Total Return	1-Year Total Return	3-Year Total Return	5-Year Total Return	PERFORMANCE: Dividend Yield (TTM)	Expense Ratio	3-Yr Std Deviation	3-Year Beta	ASSETS: NAV	Total Assets (MIL)	ASSET ALLOCATION & TURNOVER: %Cash	%Stocks	%Bonds	%Other	Turnover Ratio	BULL & BEAR: Last Bull Market Total Return	Last Bear Market Total Return	FEES: Front End Fee (%)	Back End Fee (%)	Inception Date
100	8.51	32.65	16.79			0	0.86			13.12	45.0	3	97	0	0						Oct-17
100	1.73	15.35	-3.27	30.96	31.48	0.32	1.55	14.95	0.84	24.64	1,033	5	95	0	0	32	22.45	-20.6			Jul-11
100	1.85	15.58	-2.90	32.56	34.13	0.75	1.15	14.96	0.84	24.77	1,033	5	95	0	0	32	22.64	-20.57			Oct-12
100	1.81	15.49	-3.04	31.95	33.13	0.58	1.3	14.96	0.84	24.75	1,033	5	95	0	0	32	22.64	-20.57			Dec-08
100	7.74	32.43	14.07	57.79	77.74	0.2	1.39	14.64	0.79	21.15	1,347	8	92	0	0		28.16	-24.49			Apr-06
100	7.84	32.69	14.55	59.71	81.26	0.39	0.99	14.67	0.79	44.24	1,347	8	92	0	0		28.37	-24.3			Sep-02
100	7.79	32.59	14.40	59.02	79.90	0.33	1.14	14.66	0.79	22.13	1,347	8	92	0	0		28.34	-24.33			Jun-99
100	6.22	26.55	18.38	74.12	108.67	0	1.13	12.65	0.92	25.59	1,373	2	98	0	0						Jun-12
100	6.32	26.87	18.89	76.24	112.84	0	0.73	12.66	0.92	26.39	1,373	2	98	0	0						Jun-12
100	6.27	26.73	18.68	75.43	111.21	0	0.88	12.67	0.92	26.07	1,373	2	98	0	0						Jun-12
100	6.36	16.84	0.41	30.02	21.91	1.28	1.47	12.65	0.95	11.03	496.6	3	97	0	0						Oct-13
100	6.49	17.12	0.84	31.69	24.40	1.62	1.07	12.61	0.94	11.15	496.6	3	97	0	0						Oct-13
100	6.41	16.92	0.57	30.91	23.40	1.55	1.22	12.58	0.94	11.12	496.6	3	97	0	0						Oct-13
500	4.36	16.49	1.95	26.49	17.84	0.87	1.01	10.56	0.88	14.34	36.8	3	93	0	0	28	16.67	-25.21			Aug-14
500	4.30	16.26	1.67	25.40	16.33	0.7	1.26	10.54	0.88	14.3	36.8	3	93	0	0	28	16.67	-25.21			May-99
500	4.08	24.55	4.75	66.26		0	1.16	14.76	1.08	17.6	600.6	10	90	0	0	7					Sep-15
500	3.99	24.41	4.49	64.97		0	1.41	14.75	1.08	17.43	600.6	10	90	0	0	7					Sep-15
500	8.38	34.54	19.73	62.58	42.16	0	0.91	15.64	0.95	12.93	26.6	4	96	0	0	25	22.97	-20.78			Dec-11
500	8.42	34.34	19.45	61.39	40.43	0	1.16	15.63	0.95	12.36	26.6	4	96	0	0	25	22.91	-20.78			Sep-02
500	7.30	29.83	8.54	79.61	103.47	0	1.06	19.38	0.97	108.8	5,414	3	97	0	0	17	22.99	-18.77			Dec-11
500	7.26	29.70	8.32	78.51	101.44	0	1.26	19.38	0.97	106.77	5,414	3	97	0	0	17	22.89	-18.77			Jul-92
500	3.00	13.12	8.81	17.96	27.46	2.21	0.69	8.12	0.55	555	521.1	1	75	17	0	20	13.69	-10.34			Mar-68
100	6.32	28.16	13.11	59.79	71.10	0	1.02	13.13	0.9	26.89	1,797	4	96	0	0	77	31.74	-19.13			Apr-01
100	4.05	16.25	8.39	41.74	56.36	1.47	0.96	11.17	0.9	17.26	60.3	3	90	0	0	20					Dec-12
100	6.79	26.17	6.58	76.46	53.11	0	1.5	15.71	0.84	16.34	87.9	13	87	0	0	40	40.57	-20.94			May-04
100	0.37	12.91	3.79	26.19	25.13	2.5	1.01	11.09		15.24	600.4	8	88	2	0	6	14.47	-6.69			Aug-94
100	6.85	24.39	12.19	59.08	70.03	0.02	0.92	12.76	0.89	26.82	177.2	2	98	0	0	16	26.47	-18.13			May-95
100	6.84	19.56	5.35	47.16	37.70	0.48	1.06	11.75	0.97	15.77	377.4	9	91	0	0	16	19.39	-23.5			Sep-07
100	4.77	21.68	12.46	60.62	86.03	0.33	0.94	12.67	0.9	32.49	72.5	5	95	0	0	10	22.39	-19.57			May-95
100	6.68	29.29	11.80	47.23	42.49	0	1.02	14.3	0.96	15.49	159.2	1	99	0	0	36	23.82	-19.97			Dec-01
100	6.43	31.16	5.30	74.61	54.27	0	1.01	19.69	1.12	13.72	527.9	5	95	0	0	57	35.67	-25.5			Apr-98
250	1.74	15.75	4.76	17.30	22.56	0.14	1.61	13.25		22.78	0.73	10	90	0	0	2	18.17	-15.81			Dec-97
	4.10	17.91	7.11	38.59	26.84	3.15	1.23	10.13	0.16	11.41	834.8	2	6	37	0	58	13.61	-8.91			May-03
50	3.32	12.60	6.18	37.27	29.50	1.9	1.17	7.88	0.91	17.33	712.6	2	6	2	0	73	7.83	-13.85	2.25		Jun-85
50	3.06	12.17	5.33	34.17	24.63	1.19	1.92	7.86	0.91	17.14	712.6	2	6	2	0	73	7.33	-14.1		1.00	Jul-96
	3.37	12.66	6.40	38.29	31.06	2.39	0.92	7.85	0.9	15.27	712.6	2	6	2	0	73	7.93	-13.73			Jun-97
	4.08	17.83	7.30	39.42	27.81	3.67	1.44	9.91	0.74	10.85	769.0	2	5	37	0	58	13.27	-9.01			Jun-02
50	4.25	18.89	9.96	47.24	44.81	0.5	1.36	11.8	0.96	12.98	17.1	-1	101	0	0	11			4.75		Aug-13
50	4.09	18.35	9.09	44.05	39.56	0	2.11	11.79	0.96	12.7	17.1	-1	101	0	0	11				1.00	Aug-13
	4.32	18.94	10.16	48.36	46.60	0.73	1.11	11.82	0.97	12.96	17.1	-1	101	0	0	11					Aug-13
	4.37	18.77	6.91	42.38		2.33	1.82	11.28	0.26	20.31	496.1	1	6	16	0	67					Mar-15
50	1.86	14.45	-1.89	20.25	-4.26	0	1.77	15.34	1.06	9.82	15.5	1	99	0	0	100			4.75		Dec-13
50	1.71	14.02	-2.66	17.69	-7.75	0	2.52	15.35	1.06	9.51	15.5	1	99	0	0	100				1.00	Dec-13
	1.96	14.63	-1.73	21.22	-3.07	0.05	1.52	15.34	1.06	9.87	15.5	1	99	0	0	100					Dec-13
50	2.88	14.18	0.21	22.76	0.11	0	1.63	13.25	0.91	14.25	179.4	0	79	1	0	97	14.02	-21.47	4.75		Aug-08
50	2.69	13.84	-0.52	20.10	-3.59	0	2.38	13.3	0.92	13.32	179.4	0	79	1	0	97	13.57	-21.73		1.00	Aug-08
	2.93	14.39	0.41	23.75	1.35	0	1.38	13.29	0.92	14.38	179.4	0	79	1	0	97	14.2	-21.38			Aug-08
50	2.43	9.15	3.17	25.94		1.93	1.36	6.38	0.86	10.92	136.8	9	5	14	1	32			2.25		Dec-14
50	2.18	8.77	2.36	23.14		1.42	2.11	6.4	0.86	10.78	136.8	9	5	14	1	32				1.00	Dec-14
	2.50	9.28	3.45	26.82		2.19	1.11	6.39	0.86	10.92	136.8	9	5	14	1	32					Dec-14
	4.79	19.44	3.83	38.33	26.74	2.18	4.28	12.01		8.21	486.0	8	41	25	0	93	20.49	-19.85			Jun-07
50	4.83	22.00	2.62	44.42	40.76	0	1.4	13.88	1.14	11.7	89.1	5	95	0	0	81	18.61	-17.65	4.75		Mar-07

	MARKET			FUND TYPE, CATEGORY & OBJECTIVE	RATINGS				MINIMUMS	
Fund Name	Ticker Symbol	Traded On	Fund Type	Category and (Prospectus Objective)	Overall Rating	Reward Rating	Risk Rating	Recent Up/ Downgrade	Open to New Investors	Min Initial Investment
Calamos Global Equity Fund Class C	CCGEX	NAS CM	Open End	Global Equity Large Cap (World Stock)	C	C	C+		Y	2,500
Calamos Global Equity Fund Institutional Class	CIGEX	NAS CM	Open End	Global Equity Large Cap (World Stock)	C	C	B-		Y	1,000,000
Calamos Global Growth & Income Fund Class A	CVLOX	NAS CM	Open End	Moderate Alloc (Multi-Asset Global)	C+	C	B	Up	Y	2,500
Calamos Global Growth & Income Fund Class C	CVLCX	NAS CM	Open End	Moderate Alloc (Multi-Asset Global)	C+	C	B	Up	Y	2,500
Calamos Global Growth & Income Fund Class I	CGCIX	NAS CM	Open End	Moderate Alloc (Multi-Asset Global)	C+	C	B	Up	Y	1,000,000
Calamos Global Total Return Fund	CGO	NAS CM	Closed End	Alloc Miscellaneous (Multi-Asset Global)	C	C	C-	Up	Y	
Calamos Growth & Income Fund Class A	CVTRX	NAS CM	Open End	Aggressive Alloc (Growth & Income)	B-	C	B+		Y	2,500
Calamos Growth & Income Fund Class C	CVTCX	NAS CM	Open End	Aggressive Alloc (Growth & Income)	B-	C	B+	Up	Y	2,500
Calamos Growth & Income Fund Institutional Class	CGIIX	NAS CM	Open End	Aggressive Alloc (Growth & Income)	B-	C	B+		Y	1,000,000
Calamos Growth Fund Class A	CVGRX	NAS CM	Open End	US Equity Large Cap Growth (Growth)	C+	C	B		Y	2,500
Calamos Growth Fund Class C	CVGCX	NAS CM	Open End	US Equity Large Cap Growth (Growth)	C+	C	B		Y	2,500
Calamos Growth Fund Institutional Class	CGRIX	NAS CM	Open End	US Equity Large Cap Growth (Growth)	C+	C	B		Y	1,000,000
Calamos Hedged Equity Fund Class A	CAHEX	NAS CM	Open End	Long/Short Equity (Income)	B-	C	B+	Up	Y	2,500
Calamos Hedged Equity Fund Class C	CCHEX	NAS CM	Open End	Long/Short Equity (Income)	B-	C	B	Up	Y	2,500
Calamos Hedged Equity Fund Class I	CIHEX	NAS CM	Open End	Long/Short Equity (Income)	B-	C	B+		Y	1,000,000
Calamos International Growth Fund Class A	CIGRX	NAS CM	Open End	Global Equity Large Cap (Foreign Stock)	C	C	C		Y	2,500
Calamos International Growth Fund Class C	CIGCX	NAS CM	Open End	Global Equity Large Cap (Foreign Stock)	C	C	C		Y	2,500
Calamos International Growth Fund Class R6	CIGOX	NAS CM	Open End	Global Equity Large Cap (Foreign Stock)	C	C	C		Y	0
Calamos International Growth Fund Institutional Class	CIGIX	NAS CM	Open End	Global Equity Large Cap (Foreign Stock)	C	C	C		Y	1,000,000
Calamos Market Neutral Income Fund Class A	CVSIX	NAS CM	Open End	Market Neutral (Income)	B-	C	B+		Y	2,500
Calamos Market Neutral Income Fund Class C	CVSCX	NAS CM	Open End	Market Neutral (Income)	B-	C	B	Up	Y	2,500
Calamos Market Neutral Income Fund Institutional Class	CMNIX	NAS CM	Open End	Market Neutral (Income)	B-	C	B+		Y	1,000,000
Calamos Opportunistic Value Fund Class A	CVAAX	NAS CM	Open End	US Equity Large Cap Blend (Growth)	B-	C	B	Up	Y	2,500
Calamos Opportunistic Value Fund Class C	CVACX	NAS CM	Open End	US Equity Large Cap Blend (Growth)	B-	C	B	Up	Y	2,500
Calamos Opportunistic Value Fund Institutional Class	CVAIX	NAS CM	Open End	US Equity Large Cap Blend (Growth)	B-	C	B	Up	Y	1,000,000
Calamos Phineus Long/Short Fund Class A	CPLSX	NAS CM	Open End	Long/Short Equity (Growth & Income)	C	C	B-		Y	2,500
Calamos Phineus Long/Short Fund Class C	CPCLX	NAS CM	Open End	Long/Short Equity (Growth & Income)	C	C-	B-		Y	2,500
Calamos Phineus Long/Short Fund Class I	CPLIX	NAS CM	Open End	Long/Short Equity (Growth & Income)	C	C	B-		Y	1,000,000
Calamos Strategic Total Return Fund	CSQ	NAS CM	Closed End	Moderate Alloc (Growth & Income)	C+	C	C+		Y	
Calamos Timpani Small Cap Growth Fund Class A	CTASX	NAS CM	Open End	US Equity Small Cap (Small Company)	C+	C+	C+		Y	2,500
Calamos Timpani Small Cap Growth Fund Class I	CTSIX	NAS CM	Open End	US Equity Small Cap (Small Company)	C+	C+	C+		Y	1,000,000
Calamos Timpani Small Cap Growth Fund Class R6	CTSOX	NAS CM	Open End	US Equity Small Cap (Small Company)	C+	C+	C+			0
Calamos® Growth & Income Portfolio			Open End	Aggressive Alloc (Growth & Income)	B-	C	B+		Y	0
Caldwell & Orkin - Gator Capital Long/Short Fund	COAGX	NAS CM	Open End	Long/Short Equity (Asset Alloc)	D+	D	C		Y	5,000
Calvert Aggressive Allocation Fund Class A	CAAAX	NAS CM	Open End	Aggressive Alloc (Asset Alloc)	B-	C	B	Up	Y	1,000
Calvert Aggressive Allocation Fund Class C	CAACX	NAS CM	Open End	Aggressive Alloc (Asset Alloc)	B-	C	B	Up	Y	1,000
Calvert Balanced Fund Class A	CSIFX	NAS CM	Open End	Moderate Alloc (Balanced)	B	C+	A-		Y	1,000
Calvert Balanced Fund Class C	CSGCX	NAS CM	Open End	Moderate Alloc (Balanced)	B	C+	A-		Y	1,000
Calvert Balanced Fund Class I	CBAIX	NAS CM	Open End	Moderate Alloc (Balanced)	B	B-	A-		Y	250,000
Calvert Balanced Fund Class R6	CBARX	NAS CM	Open End	Moderate Alloc (Balanced)	B	C+	A-		Y	1,000,000
Calvert Conservative Allocation Fund Class A	CCLAX	NAS CM	Open End	Cautious Alloc (Asset Alloc)	B	C+	A		Y	1,000
Calvert Conservative Allocation Fund Class C	CALCX	NAS CM	Open End	Cautious Alloc (Asset Alloc)	B	C+	A-	Up	Y	1,000
Calvert Conservative Allocation Fund Class I	CFAIX	NAS CM	Open End	Cautious Alloc (Asset Alloc)	B	C+	B+	Up	Y	250,000
Calvert Emerging Markets Equity Fund Class A	CVMAX	NAS CM	Open End	Global Emerg Mkts (Div Emerging Mkts)	C	C	C+		Y	1,000
Calvert Emerging Markets Equity Fund Class C	CVMCX	NAS CM	Open End	Global Emerg Mkts (Div Emerging Mkts)	C	C	C+		Y	1,000
Calvert Emerging Markets Equity Fund Class I	CVMIX	NAS CM	Open End	Global Emerg Mkts (Div Emerging Mkts)	C	C	C+		Y	250,000
Calvert Emerging Markets Equity Fund Class R6	CVMRX	NAS CM	Open End	Global Emerg Mkts (Div Emerging Mkts)	C	C	C+		Y	1,000,000
Calvert Equity Fund Class A	CSIEX	NAS CM	Open End	US Equity Large Cap Growth (Growth)	B+	B	A-	Up	Y	1,000
Calvert Equity Fund Class C	CSECX	NAS CM	Open End	US Equity Large Cap Growth (Growth)	B+	B	A-	Up	Y	1,000
Calvert Equity Fund Class I	CEYIX	NAS CM	Open End	US Equity Large Cap Growth (Growth)	B+	B+	A-	Up	Y	250,000
Calvert Equity Fund Class R6	CEYRX	NAS CM	Open End	US Equity Large Cap Growth (Growth)	B+	B	A-	Up	Y	1,000,000
Calvert Global Energy Solutions Fund Class A	CGAEX	NAS CM	Open End	Global Equity Mid/Small Cap (Natl Res)	C	C	C+		Y	1,000

★ Expanded analysis of this fund is included in Section II.

Min Additional Investment	TOTAL RETURNS 3-Month Total Return	6-Month Total Return	1-Year Total Return	3-Year Total Return	5-Year Total Return	PERFORMANCE Dividend Yield (TTM)	Expense Ratio	3-Yr Std Deviation	3-Year Beta	ASSETS NAV	Total Assets (MIL)	ASSET ALLOCATION & TURNOVER %Cash	%Stocks	%Bonds	%Other	Turnover Ratio	BULL & BEAR Last Bull Market Total Return	Last Bear Market Total Return	FEES Front End Fee (%)	Back End Fee (%)	Inception Date
50	4.70	21.61	1.90	41.21	35.65	0	2.15	13.94	1.15	10.24	89.1	5	95	0	0	81	18.02	-17.93		1.00	Mar-07
	4.95	22.14	2.94	45.46	42.56	0	1.15	13.91	1.15	12.08	89.1	5	95	0	0	81	18.68	-17.49			Mar-07
50	3.67	14.01	2.19	26.36	20.75	0.73	1.5	9.66	0.82	8.59	163.6	3	60	10	0	75	9.27	-12.54	4.75		Sep-96
50	3.43	13.57	1.41	23.44	16.33	0	2.25	9.64	0.82	7.53	163.6	3	60	10	0	75	8.86	-12.79		1.00	Sep-96
	3.73	14.05	2.48	27.34	22.26	0.93	1.5	9.64	0.82	8.87	163.6	3	60	10	0	75	9.5	-12.42			Sep-97
	5.16	21.00	4.00	34.05	27.45	1.6	1.61	13.01		12.06	104.4	5	49	24	0	119	14.42	-15.73			Oct-05
50	4.00	16.66	8.30	38.96	44.34	1.48	1.1	10.31	0.84	32.72	2,018	2	75	5	0	25	13.12	-13.74	4.75		Sep-88
50	3.80	16.24	7.51	35.93	38.96	0.62	1.85	10.32	0.84	32.98	2,018	2	75	5	0	25	12.64	-13.99		1.00	Aug-96
	4.08	16.81	8.56	40.05	46.12	1.78	0.85	10.31	0.84	31.35	2,018	2	75	5	0	25	13.28	-13.63			Sep-97
50	5.76	23.37	8.74	51.25	55.57	0	1.29	12.67	0.98	31.93	1,458	8	92	0	0	72	22.83	-22.64	4.75		Sep-90
50	5.64	22.98	8.01	48.04	49.94	0	2.04	12.72	0.99	18.14	1,458	8	92	0	0	72	22.3	-22.88		1.00	Sep-96
	5.83	23.52	9.01	52.41	57.50	0	1.04	12.69	0.99	43.68	1,458	8	92	0	0	72	23.01	-22.55			Sep-97
50	1.99	8.62	4.62	23.33		0.27	1.26	5.7	0.45	11.65	203.4	2	98	0	0	141			4.75		Dec-14
50	1.76	8.18	3.82	20.71		0.07	2.01	5.67	0.45	11.5	203.4	2	98	0	0	141				1.00	Dec-14
	2.03	8.74	4.89	24.38		0.67	1.01	5.7	0.45	11.63	203.4	2	98	0	0	141					Dec-14
50	5.68	20.78	-1.37	31.66	16.79	0	1.1	14.29	1.16	17.84	213.2	2	98	0	0	112	16.77	-19.95	4.75		Mar-05
50	5.53	20.38	-2.10	28.72	12.48	0	1.85	14.28	1.16	15.83	213.2	2	98	0	0	112	16.29	-20.17		1.00	Mar-05
	5.82	21.04	-1.02	32.76	18.38		0.75	14.3	1.16	18.52	213.2	2	98	0	0	112	16.95	-19.84			Sep-18
	5.81	21.00	-1.09	32.67	18.30	0	0.85	14.3	1.16	18.38	213.2	2	98	0	0	112	16.95	-19.84			Mar-05
50	1.39	4.34	3.67	14.20	17.49	1.46	1.26	2.03	-0.07	13.32	7,940	38	14	3	0	67	8.39	-4.51	2.25		Sep-90
50	1.18	3.91	2.87	11.62	13.15	0.66	2.01	2.06	-0.07	13.55	7,940	38	14	3	0	67	7.93	-4.84		1.00	Feb-00
	1.47	4.50	3.89	15.07	18.95	1.77	1	2.04	-0.08	13.15	7,940	38	14	3	0	67	8.52	-4.42			May-00
50	3.30	15.75	6.77	38.73	33.09	0.39	1.16	11.92	0.88	13.74	44.7	1	99	0	0	119	17.76	-17.42	4.75		Jan-02
50	3.09	15.30	6.04	35.69	28.20	0.45	1.91	11.9	0.88	11.98	44.7	1	99	0	0	119	17.26	-17.67		1.00	Jan-02
	3.36	15.83	7.05	39.69	34.71	0.9	0.91	11.88	0.87	14.12	44.7	1	99	0	0	119	17.91	-17.29			Mar-02
50	2.06	5.60	-0.99	29.78	34.18	0	2.32	7.43	0.3	11.88	900.4	98	-2	4	0	229	17.37	-14.1	4.75		Apr-16
50	1.93	5.26	-1.67	26.87	29.18	0	3.07	7.37	0.3	11.59	900.4	98	-2	4	0	229	16.86	-14.37		1.00	Apr-16
	2.21	5.82	-0.64	30.70	36.05	0.02	2.04	7.41	0.3	11.99	900.4	98	-2	4	0	229	17.54	-14.01			Apr-16
	4.87	23.70	9.79	51.84	52.26	2.23	1.91	13.9		12.94	1,999	1	66	18	0	27	21.72	-18.83			Mar-04
50	5.82	25.80	4.27	81.56	63.78	0	1.3	18.38	0.98	24.33	80.8	1	99	0	0	126	35.81	-27.94	4.75		Jan-14
	5.91	26.02	4.64	83.82	67.00	0	1.05	18.4	0.98	24.89	80.8	1	99	0	0	126	36.01	-27.87			Mar-11
							0.95	18.78	1	24.89	80.8	1	99	0	0	126					May-19
	3.93	16.56	7.92	36.61	40.11	2.05	1.36	10.27	0.84	16.03	26.7	3	74	4	0	22	13.26	-14.75			May-99
100	4.28	18.17	-1.54	-5.06	0.40	0	2.54	12.4	0.82	20.42	21.8	53	52	0	-4	240	4.52	0.4			Aug-92
	4.04	17.50	7.44	40.39	40.87	1.69	0.89	10.79	0.84	20.34	163.8	1	91	8	0	64	19.06	-17.54	4.75		Jun-05
	3.85	17.09	6.68	37.33	34.90	1.26	1.64	10.8	0.85	17.26	163.8	1	91	8	0	64	18.2	-18.03		1.00	Jun-05
	4.77	16.30	10.96	31.45	36.17	1.3	0.93	7.14	0.56	33.63	785.2	2	61	36	0	76	16.64	-8.24	4.75		Oct-82
	4.57	15.88	10.12	28.43	30.97	0.64	1.68	7.13	0.56	32.52	785.2	2	61	36	0	76	16.07	-8.55		1.00	Mar-94
	4.82	16.45	11.26	32.76	38.72	1.49	0.68	7.13	0.56	34.31	785.2	2	61	36	0	76	17.01	-8.03			Feb-99
	4.85	16.42	11.07	31.59	36.31		0.64	7.14	0.56	34.32	785.2	2	61	36	0	76	16.64	-8.24			Feb-19
	3.27	10.90	7.41	21.45	26.13	2.37	0.96	4.59	0.32	17.41	206.1	4	34	63	0	94	9	-3.06	4.75		Apr-05
	3.05	10.49	6.61	18.70	20.99	1.67	1.71	4.55	0.32	17.2	206.1	4	34	63	0	94	8.35	-3.58		1.00	Apr-05
	3.33	11.03	7.79	22.66	27.42	2.61	0.71	4.56	0.32	17.42	206.1	4	34	63	0	94	9.01	-3.06			May-16
	1.29	13.32	4.87	42.98	27.54	0.72	1.24	14.13	0.98	16.41	1,927	2	98	0	0	27			4.75		Oct-12
	1.13	12.84	4.06	39.70	22.55	0.39	1.99	14.13	0.98	15.99	1,927	2	98	0	0	27				1.00	Oct-12
	1.40	13.49	5.20	44.32	29.78	1.1	0.99	14.15	0.98	16.57	1,927	2	98	0	0	27					Oct-12
	1.40	13.52	5.19	44.22	29.69	1.2	0.92	14.18	0.98	16.54	1,927	2	98	0	0	27					Feb-18
	7.11	26.50	24.67	71.16	89.28	0.02	0.99	10.51	0.73	52.22	2,937	2	97	1	0	18	21.82	-16	4.75		Aug-87
	6.90	26.00	23.74	67.30	82.25	0	1.74	10.5	0.73	28.78	2,937	2	97	1	0	18	21.28	-16.24		1.00	Mar-94
	7.16	26.64	25.00	72.86	93.00	0.19	0.74	10.51	0.73	60.84	2,937	2	97	1	0	18	22.18	-15.79			Nov-99
	7.18	26.67	25.05	72.01	90.23	0.28	0.67	10.51	0.73	60.74	2,937	2	97	1	0	18	21.82	-16			Oct-17
	4.73	19.79	3.15	25.86	-5.77	1.42	1.24	14.43		7.08	80.4	0	97	2	0	38	1.97	-38.7	4.75		May-07

	MARKET		FUND TYPE, CATEGORY & OBJECTIVE		RATINGS					MINIMUMS
Fund Name	Ticker Symbol	Traded On	Fund Type	Category and (Prospectus Objective)	Overall Rating	Reward Rating	Risk Rating	Recent Up/ Downgrade	Open to New Investors	Min Initial Investment
Calvert Global Energy Solutions Fund Class C	CGACX	NAS CM	Open End	Global Equity Mid/Small Cap (Natl Res)	C	C-	C+		Y	1,000
Calvert Global Energy Solutions Fund Class I	CAEIX	NAS CM	Open End	Global Equity Mid/Small Cap (Natl Res)	C	C	C+		Y	250,000
Calvert Global Water Fund Class A	CFWAX	NAS CM	Open End	Natl Resources Sec Equity (Natl Res)	C+	C	B	Up	Y	1,000
Calvert Global Water Fund Class C	CFWCX	NAS CM	Open End	Natl Resources Sec Equity (Natl Res)	C+	C	B	Up	Y	1,000
Calvert Global Water Fund Class I	CFWIX	NAS CM	Open End	Natl Resources Sec Equity (Natl Res)	C+	C	B	Up	Y	250,000
Calvert International Equity Fund Class A	CWVGX	NAS CM	Open End	Global Equity Large Cap (Foreign Stock)	C+	C	B	Up	Y	1,000
Calvert International Equity Fund Class C	CWVCX	NAS CM	Open End	Global Equity Large Cap (Foreign Stock)	C+	C	B	Up	Y	1,000
Calvert International Equity Fund Class I	CWVIX	NAS CM	Open End	Global Equity Large Cap (Foreign Stock)	C+	C	B	Up	Y	250,000
Calvert International Equity Fund Class R6	CIESX	NAS CM	Open End	Global Equity Large Cap (Foreign Stock)	C+	C	B	Up	Y	1,000,000
Calvert International Opportunities Fund Class A	CIOAX	NAS CM	Open End	Global Equity Mid/Small Cap (Foreign Stock)	C	C	C+		Y	1,000
Calvert International Opportunities Fund Class C	COICX	NAS CM	Open End	Global Equity Mid/Small Cap (Foreign Stock)	C	C	C+		Y	1,000
Calvert International Opportunities Fund Class I	COIIX	NAS CM	Open End	Global Equity Mid/Small Cap (Foreign Stock)	C	C	C+		Y	250,000
Calvert International Opportunities Fund Class R6	COIRX	NAS CM	Open End	Global Equity Mid/Small Cap (Foreign Stock)	C	C	C+		Y	1,000,000
Calvert International Responsible Index Fund Class A	CDHAX	NAS CM	Open End	Global Equity Large Cap (Growth & Income)	C	C	B		Y	5,000
Calvert International Responsible Index Fund Class I	CDHIX	NAS CM	Open End	Global Equity Large Cap (Growth & Income)	C	C	B		Y	100,000
Calvert International Responsible Index Fund Class R6	CDHRX	NAS CM	Open End	Global Equity Large Cap (Growth & Income)	C	C	B		Y	1,000,000
Calvert Mid-Cap Fund Class A	CCAFX	NAS CM	Open End	US Equity Mid Cap (Growth)	B-	C	B		Y	1,000
Calvert Mid-Cap Fund Class C	CCACX	NAS CM	Open End	US Equity Mid Cap (Growth)	B-	C	B		Y	1,000
Calvert Mid-Cap Fund Class I	CCPIX	NAS CM	Open End	US Equity Mid Cap (Growth)	B-	C+	B		Y	250,000
Calvert Moderate Allocation Fund Class A	CMAAX	NAS CM	Open End	Moderate Alloc (Asset Alloc)	B	C+	A-	Up	Y	1,000
Calvert Moderate Allocation Fund Class C	CMACX	NAS CM	Open End	Moderate Alloc (Asset Alloc)	B-	C	A-	Up	Y	1,000
Calvert Small-Cap Fund Class A	CCVAX	NAS CM	Open End	US Equity Small Cap (Small Company)	C+	C	B	Down	Y	1,000
Calvert Small-Cap Fund Class C	CSCCX	NAS CM	Open End	US Equity Small Cap (Small Company)	C+	C	B-		Y	1,000
Calvert Small-Cap Fund Class I	CSVIX	NAS CM	Open End	US Equity Small Cap (Small Company)	C+	C	B	Down	Y	250,000
Calvert Small-Cap Fund Class R6	CALRX	NAS CM	Open End	US Equity Small Cap (Small Company)	C+	C	B	Down	Y	1,000,000
Calvert US Large Cap Core Responsible Index Fund Class A	CSXAX	NAS CM	Open End	US Equity Large Cap Blend (Growth)	B-	C	B	Down	Y	5,000
Calvert US Large Cap Core Responsible Index Fund Class C	CSXCX	NAS CM	Open End	US Equity Large Cap Blend (Growth)	B-	C	B		Y	5,000
Calvert US Large Cap Core Responsible Index Fund Class I	CISIX	NAS CM	Open End	US Equity Large Cap Blend (Growth)	B-	C	B	Down	Y	100,000
Calvert US Large Cap Core Responsible Index Fund Class R6	CSXRX	NAS CM	Open End	US Equity Large Cap Blend (Growth)	B-	C	B	Down	Y	1,000,000
Calvert US Large Cap Growth Responsible Index Fund Class A	CGJAX	NAS CM	Open End	US Equity Large Cap Growth (Growth)	B-	C+	B	Down	Y	5,000
Calvert US Large Cap Growth Responsible Index Fund Class I	CGJIX	NAS CM	Open End	US Equity Large Cap Growth (Growth)	B-	C+	B	Down	Y	100,000
Calvert US Large Cap Value Responsible Index Fund Class A	CFJAX	NAS CM	Open End	US Equity Large Cap Value (Growth)	B-	C	B	Up	Y	5,000
Calvert US Large Cap Value Responsible Index Fund Class I	CFJIX	NAS CM	Open End	US Equity Large Cap Value (Growth)	B-	C	B	Up	Y	100,000
Calvert US Mid Cap Core Responsible Index Fund Class A	CMJAX	NAS CM	Open End	US Equity Mid Cap (Growth & Income)	C+	C	B		Y	5,000
Calvert US Mid Cap Core Responsible Index Fund Class I	CMJIX	NAS CM	Open End	US Equity Mid Cap (Growth & Income)	C+	C	B		Y	100,000
Cambiar Global Equity Fund Investor Class	CAMGX	NAS CM	Open End	Global Equity Large Cap (World Stock)	C	C	B		Y	2,500
Cambiar Global Ultra Focus Fund Investor Class	CAMAX	NAS CM	Open End	Global Equity Large Cap (World Stock)	C-	D+	C+		Y	2,500
Cambiar International Equity Fund Investor Class	CAMIX	NAS CM	Open End	Global Equity Large Cap (Foreign Stock)	C	C-	C	Up	Y	2,500
Cambiar International Equity Institutional	CAMYX	NAS CM	Open End	Global Equity Large Cap (Foreign Stock)	C	C-	C	Up	Y	5,000,000
Cambiar International Small Cap Fund Institutional Class	CAMFX	NAS CM	Open End	Global Equity Mid/Small Cap (Small Company)	C	C	B		Y	100,000
Cambiar Opportunity Fund Class Institutional	CAMWX	NAS CM	Open End	US Equity Large Cap Blend (Growth & Income)	C+	C	B	Up	Y	5,000,000
Cambiar Opportunity Fund Class Investor	CAMOX	NAS CM	Open End	US Equity Large Cap Blend (Growth & Income)	C+	C	B	Up	Y	2,500
Cambiar Small Cap Fund Class Investor	CAMSX	NAS CM	Open End	US Equity Small Cap (Small Company)	C	C	C+			2,500
Cambiar Small Cap Institutional Class	CAMZX	NAS CM	Open End	US Equity Small Cap (Small Company)	C	C	C+		Y	5,000,000
Cambiar SMID Fund Institutional Class	CAMUX	NAS CM	Open End	US Equity Mid Cap (Growth)	B-	C	B+	Down	Y	5,000,000
Cambiar SMID Fund Investor Class Shares	CAMMX	NAS CM	Open End	US Equity Mid Cap (Growth)	B-	C	B+	Down	Y	2,500
Camelot Event Driven Fund Class A	EVDAX	NAS CM	Open End	Multialternative (Growth)	B	C	A		Y	2,000
Camelot Event Driven Fund Institutional Class	EVDIX	NAS CM	Open End	Multialternative (Growth)	B	C	A		Y	1,000,000
Camelot Excalibur Small Cap Income Fund Class A	CEXAX	NAS CM	Open End	US Equity Small Cap (Income)	C+	C	B-		Y	2,500
Camelot Excalibur Small Cap Income Fund Class I	CEXIX	NAS CM	Open End	US Equity Small Cap (Income)	C+	C	B-	Down	Y	100,000
Camelot Premium Return Fund Class A	CPRFX	NAS CM	Open End	Long/Short Equity (Income)	C	C	C+		Y	2,500
Camelot Premium Return Fund Class I	CPRIX	NAS CM	Open End	Long/Short Equity (Income)	C	C	C+		Y	100,000

★ Expanded analysis of this fund is included in Section II.

	TOTAL RETURNS					PERFORMANCE				ASSETS		ASSET ALLOCATION & TURNOVER					BULL & BEAR		FEES		
Min Additional Investment	3-Month Total Return	6-Month Total Return	1-Year Total Return	3-Year Total Return	5-Year Total Return	Dividend Yield (TTM)	Expense Ratio	3-Yr Std Deviation	3-Year Beta	NAV	Total Assets (MIL)	%Cash	%Stocks	%Bonds	%Other	Turnover Ratio	Last Bull Market Total Return	Last Bear Market Total Return	Front End Fee (%)	Back End Fee (%)	Inception Date
	4.40	19.24	2.37	22.91	-9.71	0.7	1.99	14.47		6.63	80.4	0	97	2	0	38	1.35	-38.88		1.00	Jul-07
	4.81	19.83	3.45	27.23	-3.85	1.68	0.99	14.45		7.19	80.4	0	97	2	0	38	2.09	-38.5			May-07
	5.01	18.12	5.58	26.10	8.18	1.11	1.24	11.84		20.53	410.2	0	99	0	0	40	22.02	-19.03	4.75		Sep-08
	4.83	17.72	4.85	23.34	4.34	0.44	1.99	11.87		18.86	410.2	0	99	0	0	40	21.31	-19.37		1.00	Sep-08
	5.13	18.31	5.95	27.41	10.45	1.39	0.99	11.85		20.67	410.2	0	99	0	0	40	22.02	-19.03			Jan-14
	6.27	19.47	7.65	32.80	12.00	0.98	1.26	10.95	0.92	18.28	231.9	0	98	2	0	48	15.08	-23.31	4.75		Jul-92
	6.02	19.01	6.81	29.82	7.66	0.45	2.01	10.93	0.92	15.65	231.9	0	98	2	0	48	14.52	-23.54		1.00	Mar-94
	6.37	19.66	8.04	34.28	14.41	1.17	1.01	10.92	0.92	19.53	231.9	0	98	2	0	48	15.59	-23.07			Feb-99
	6.37	19.58	7.75	32.92	12.10		0.97	10.96	0.92	19.53	231.9	0	98	2	0	48	15.08	-23.31			Mar-19
	3.05	14.33	-3.69	41.98	25.06	1.3	1.35	12.31	0.98	16.51	332.7	2	97	0	1	60	18.79	-23.46	4.75		May-07
	2.87	13.95	-4.39	38.72	19.97	0.59	2.1	12.29	0.98	16.09	332.7	2	97	0	1	60	18.16	-23.74		1.00	Jul-07
	3.19	14.51	-3.42	43.29	27.40	1.59	1.1	12.34	0.99	16.17	332.7	2	97	0	1	60	19.03	-23.25			May-07
	3.19	14.59	-3.36	43.38	27.48		1.06	12.34	0.99	16.17	332.7	2	97	0	1	60	19.03	-23.25			Feb-19
	4.24	15.46	2.45	29.13		1.82	0.54	11.32		22.85	118.1	1	99	0	0	24			4.75		Oct-15
	4.28	15.58	2.74	30.37		1.96	0.29	11.34		23.14	118.1	1	99	0	0	24					Oct-15
	4.28	15.58	2.74	30.37			0.26	11.34		23.14	118.1	1	99	0	0	24					Feb-19
	5.35	22.05	9.95	40.64	36.78	0.22	1.18	11.92	0.87	34.04	217.9	2	97	1	0	62	29.64	-23.97	4.75		Oct-94
	5.16	21.59	9.13	37.52	31.63	0	1.93	11.92	0.87	23.42	217.9	2	97	1	0	62	29.03	-24.26		1.00	Oct-94
	5.39	22.17	10.24	42.09	39.76	0.37	0.93	11.92	0.87	40.44	217.9	2	97	1	0	62	30.15	-23.74			Feb-99
	3.45	14.17	7.50	31.76	34.10	2.01	0.91	7.77	0.61	19.39	325.1	2	62	36	0	73	14.73	-11.62	4.75		Apr-05
	3.27	13.72	6.71	28.81	29.15	1.43	1.66	7.76	0.61	18.42	325.1	2	62	36	0	73	14.19	-11.86		1.00	Apr-05
	6.73	23.40	6.65	52.75	57.64	0	1.21	15.29	0.87	25.52	563.0	2	98	0	0	51	21.5	-23.67	4.75		Oct-04
	6.54	22.94	5.84	49.30	51.76	0	1.96	15.28	0.87	21.81	563.0	2	98	0	0	51	20.77	-23.95		1.00	Apr-05
	6.75	23.54	6.93	54.46	60.81	0.2	0.96	15.26	0.87	27.65	563.0	2	98	0	0	51	22.03	-23.41			Apr-05
	6.79	23.49	6.74	52.87	57.76		0.9	15.28	0.87	27.66	563.0	2	98	0	0	51	21.5	-23.67			Feb-19
	4.45	20.36	11.75	51.22	64.72	0.86	0.49	12.61	0.99	24.41	1,843	1	99	0	0	28	26.34	-15.85	4.75		Jun-00
	4.28	19.95	10.93	47.85	58.68	0.3	1.24	12.6	0.99	22.9	1,843	1	99	0	0	28	25.63	-16.21		1.00	Jun-00
	4.54	20.54	12.07	52.72	67.92	1.09	0.24	12.64	1	25.05	1,843	1	99	0	0	28	26.73	-15.7			Jun-00
	4.55	20.56	12.10	52.69	67.88	1.15	0.19	12.62	1	25.03	1,843	1	99	0	0	28	26.73	-15.7			Oct-17
	4.20	22.06	13.73	62.50		0.65	0.49	13.24	1	29.26	88.6	0	100	0	0	54			4.75		Jun-15
	4.24	22.24	14.06	64.12		0.81	0.24	13.23	1	29.46	88.6	0	100	0	0	54					Jun-15
	4.77	18.28	7.95	37.97		1.46	0.49	13.2	0.99	23.03	378.8	0	100	0	0	67			4.75		Jun-15
	4.84	18.45	8.26	39.39		1.68	0.24	13.19	0.99	23.17	378.8	0	100	0	0	67					Jun-15
	4.80	23.12	8.56	46.47		0.89	0.49	14.43		27.05	58.1	0	100	0	0	39			4.75		Oct-15
	4.92	23.32	8.94	47.96		1.08	0.24	14.46		27.28	58.1	0	100	0	0	39					Oct-15
100	5.15	18.89	1.73	28.67	21.15	1.32	0.8	12.62	1.07	12.65	11.5	2	98	0	0	54					Nov-11
100	7.99	20.44	-5.81	23.04	0.34	0.79	0.98	17.44	1.34	18.38	58.8	1	99	0	0	87	18.06	-39.93			Aug-07
100	2.62	12.52	-5.21	17.48	8.79	0.61	1.03	12.47	1.08	25.79	2,700	1	99	0	0	54	20.24	-24.08			Sep-02
	2.62	12.55	-5.13	17.90	9.47	0.85	0.9	12.46	1.08	25.82	2,700	1	99	0	0	54	20.24	-24.08			Nov-12
	2.38	14.10	0.40	35.96		0.61	0.95	11.36	0.87	11.57	2.5	7	93	0	0	68					Nov-14
	6.87	18.89	4.01	36.37	37.85	1.21	0.65	13.79	1.1	21.46	235.7	1	99	0	0	47	20.51	-26.56			Nov-05
100	6.84	18.87	3.86	35.54	36.32	1.03	0.85	13.77	1.1	21.54	235.7	1	99	0	0	47	20.27	-26.59			Jun-98
100	4.34	20.79	1.29	34.49	10.90	0.06	0.97	17.78	0.99	16.09	95.0	7	93	0	0	45	34.37	-26.92			Aug-04
	4.41	20.94	1.51	35.15	11.98	0.15	0.9	17.81	0.99	16.57	95.0	7	93	0	0	45	34.51	-26.83			Oct-08
	4.22	22.17	12.78	59.39	40.23	0.46	0.85	14	0.88	18.51	47.1	9	91	0	0	61	36.76				Nov-14
100	4.16	22.09	12.71	59.16	40.01	0.46	0.85	13.94	0.88	18.51	47.1	9	91	0	0	61	36.76				May-11
100	2.08	11.46	4.86	29.46	24.68	1.31	2	7.55	0.48	14.19	30.1	27	54	14	0	391	10.22	-11.82	5.50		Nov-03
	2.21	11.70	5.24	30.51	26.34	1.6	1.75	7.52	0.48	14.32	30.1	27	54	14	0	391	10.37	-11.81			Jun-10
50	1.95	22.21	-0.75	27.02	9.93	3.53	2.1	16.74	0.88	8.29	10.9	14	55	18	-6	36			5.75		Dec-13
50	2.04	22.38	-0.50	27.12	10.02	3.81	1.85	16.81	0.88	8.23	10.9	14	55	18	-6	36					Dec-16
50	3.55	25.96	0.63	27.09	19.16	2.47	2.28	18.66	1.34	9.5	44.1	1	69	23	-4	44	23.95	-17.18	5.75		Dec-10
50	3.63	26.16	0.80	27.93	19.95	2.73	2.03	18.63	1.34	9.49	44.1	1	69	23	-4	44	23.95	-17.18			Dec-16

	MARKET			FUND TYPE, CATEGORY & OBJECTIVE	RATINGS				MINIMUMS	
Fund Name	Ticker Symbol	Traded On	Fund Type	Category and (Prospectus Objective)	Overall Rating	Reward Rating	Risk Rating	Recent Up/ Downgrade	Open to New Investors	Min Initial Investment
Campbell Dynamic Trend Fund Institutional Shares	CDRTX	NAS CM	Open End	Alternative Miscellaneous (Growth)	C	D+	C+	Up	Y	2,500
CAN SLIM Select Growth Fund	CANGX	NAS CM	Open End	Aggressive Alloc (Growth)	C	C	B-		Y	2,500
Cannabis Growth Fund Institutional Class	CANIX	NAS CM	Open End	Equity Miscellaneous (Growth)	U	U	U		Y	100,000
Cannabis Growth Fund Investor Class	CANNX	NAS CM	Open End	Equity Miscellaneous (Growth)	U	U	U		Y	2,500
Canterbury Portfolio Thermostat Fund Class I Shares	CAPTX	NAS CM	Open End	Aggressive Alloc (Growth)	C	D+	C+	Up	Y	5,000
Capital Advisors Growth Fund Investor Class	CIAOX	NAS CM	Open End	US Equity Large Cap Growth (Growth)	C+	C	B	Down	Y	5,000
Capital Emerging Markets Growth Fund, Inc.	EMRGX	NAS CM	Open End	Global Emerg Mkts (Div Emerging Mkts)	C	C	C+		Y	1,000,000
Capital Group Emerging Markets Growth Fund, Inc. Class F-3	EMGEX	NAS CM	Open End	Global Emerg Mkts (Div Emerging Mkts)	C	C	C+		Y	1,000,000
Capital Group Emerging Markets Growth Fund, Inc. Class R-6	REFGX	NAS CM	Open End	Global Emerg Mkts (Div Emerging Mkts)	C	C	C+		Y	1,000,000
Capital Group Emerging Markets Total Opportunities Cls F-2	CTPFX	NAS CM	Open End	Global Emerg Mkts (Div Emerging Mkts)	C+	C	B	Up	Y	1,000,000
Capital Group Emerging Markets Total Opportunities Cls F-3	ETPFX	NAS CM	Open End	Global Emerg Mkts (Div Emerging Mkts)	C+	C	B	Up	Y	1,000,000
Capital Group Emerging Markets Total Opportunities Cls R-6	REPGX	NAS CM	Open End	Global Emerg Mkts (Div Emerging Mkts)	C+	C	B	Up	Y	1,000,000
Capital Group Global Equity Fund	CGLOX	NAS CM	Open End	Global Equity Large Cap (World Stock)	B-	C	B	Up	Y	25,000
Capital Group International Equity Fund	CNUSX	NAS CM	Open End	Global Equity Large Cap (Foreign Stock)	C+	C	B	Up	Y	25,000
Capital Group U.S. Equity Fund	CUSEX	NAS CM	Open End	US Equity Large Cap Growth (Growth)	B	C+	B+		Y	25,000
Caravan Frontier Mkts Opp Inst Shares	CFROX	NAS CM	Open End	Global Emerg Mkts (Growth)	D	D	D		Y	100,000
Caravan Frontier Mkts Opp Supra Inst Shares	CSFOX	NAS CM	Open End	Global Emerg Mkts (Growth)	D	D	D		Y	10,000,000
Cardinal Small Cap Value Fund Institutional Class	CCMSX	NAS CM	Open End	US Equity Small Cap (Small Company)	C	C	C		Y	1,000,000
Cargile Fund	CFNDX	NAS CM	Open End	Alloc Miscellaneous (Growth)	D-	D+	C		Y	5,000
Carillon ClariVest Capital Appreciation Fund Class A	HRCPX	NAS CM	Open End	US Equity Large Cap Growth (Growth)	C+	C	B-		Y	1,000
Carillon ClariVest Capital Appreciation Fund Class C	HRCCX	NAS CM	Open End	US Equity Large Cap Growth (Growth)	C+	C	B-		Y	1,000
Carillon ClariVest Capital Appreciation Fund Class I	HRCIX	NAS CM	Open End	US Equity Large Cap Growth (Growth)	C+	C	B-		Y	10,000
Carillon ClariVest Capital Appreciation Fund Class R3	HRCLX	NAS CM	Open End	US Equity Large Cap Growth (Growth)	C+	C	B-		Y	0
Carillon ClariVest Capital Appreciation Fund Class R5	HRCMX	NAS CM	Open End	US Equity Large Cap Growth (Growth)	C+	C	B-		Y	0
Carillon ClariVest Capital Appreciation Fund Class R6	HRCUX	NAS CM	Open End	US Equity Large Cap Growth (Growth)	C+	C	B-		Y	0
Carillon ClariVest Capital Appreciation Fund Class Y	HRCYX	NAS CM	Open End	US Equity Large Cap Growth (Growth)	C+	C	B-		Y	1,000
Carillon ClariVest International Stock Fund Class A	EISAX	NAS CM	Open End	Global Equity Large Cap (Foreign Stock)	C	C-	C		Y	1,000
Carillon ClariVest International Stock Fund Class C	EISDX	NAS CM	Open End	Global Equity Large Cap (Foreign Stock)	C	C-	C	Up	Y	1,000
Carillon ClariVest International Stock Fund Class I	EISIX	NAS CM	Open End	Global Equity Large Cap (Foreign Stock)	C	C-	C		Y	10,000
Carillon ClariVest International Stock Fund Class R-3	EISRX	NAS CM	Open End	Global Equity Large Cap (Foreign Stock)	C	C-	C		Y	0
Carillon ClariVest International Stock Fund Class R-5	EISSX	NAS CM	Open End	Global Equity Large Cap (Foreign Stock)	C	C-	C		Y	0
Carillon ClariVest International Stock Fund Class R-6	EISVX	NAS CM	Open End	Global Equity Large Cap (Foreign Stock)	C	C-	C		Y	0
Carillon ClariVest International Stock Fund Class Y	EISYX	NAS CM	Open End	Global Equity Large Cap (Foreign Stock)	C	C-	C		Y	1,000
Carillon Cougar Tactical Allocation Fund Class A	ETAFX	NAS CM	Open End	Moderate Alloc (Growth & Income)	C+	C	B	Up	Y	1,000
Carillon Cougar Tactical Allocation Fund Class C	ETDFX	NAS CM	Open End	Moderate Alloc (Growth & Income)	C	C	B-		Y	1,000
Carillon Cougar Tactical Allocation Fund Class I	ETIFX	NAS CM	Open End	Moderate Alloc (Growth & Income)	C+	C	B	Up	Y	10,000
Carillon Cougar Tactical Allocation Fund Class R-3	ETRFX	NAS CM	Open End	Moderate Alloc (Growth & Income)	C+	C	B	Up	Y	0
Carillon Cougar Tactical Allocation Fund Class R-5	ETSFX	NAS CM	Open End	Moderate Alloc (Growth & Income)	C+	C	B	Up	Y	0
Carillon Cougar Tactical Allocation Fund Class R-6	ETUFX	NAS CM	Open End	Moderate Alloc (Growth & Income)	C+	C	B	Up	Y	0
Carillon Cougar Tactical Allocation Fund Class Y	ETYFX	NAS CM	Open End	Moderate Alloc (Growth & Income)	C+	C	B	Up	Y	1,000
Carillon Eagle Growth & Income Fund Class A	HRCVX	NAS CM	Open End	US Equity Large Cap Value (Growth & Income)	B	C+	A-		Y	1,000
Carillon Eagle Growth & Income Fund Class C	HIGCX	NAS CM	Open End	US Equity Large Cap Value (Growth & Income)	B	C+	B+		Y	1,000
Carillon Eagle Growth & Income Fund Class I	HIGJX	NAS CM	Open End	US Equity Large Cap Value (Growth & Income)	B	C+	A-		Y	10,000
Carillon Eagle Growth & Income Fund Class R3	HIGRX	NAS CM	Open End	US Equity Large Cap Value (Growth & Income)	B	C+	A-		Y	0
Carillon Eagle Growth & Income Fund Class R5	HIGSX	NAS CM	Open End	US Equity Large Cap Value (Growth & Income)	B	C+	A-		Y	0
Carillon Eagle Growth & Income Fund Class R6	HIGUX	NAS CM	Open End	US Equity Large Cap Value (Growth & Income)	B	C+	A-		Y	0
Carillon Eagle Growth & Income Fund Class Y	HIGYX	NAS CM	Open End	US Equity Large Cap Value (Growth & Income)	B	C+	A-		Y	1,000
Carillon Eagle Mid Cap Growth Fund Class A	HAGAX	NAS CM	Open End	US Equity Mid Cap (Growth)	C+	C	B-		Y	1,000
Carillon Eagle Mid Cap Growth Fund Class C	HAGCX	NAS CM	Open End	US Equity Mid Cap (Growth)	C+	C	C+		Y	1,000
Carillon Eagle Mid Cap Growth Fund Class I	HAGIX	NAS CM	Open End	US Equity Mid Cap (Growth)	C+	C	B-		Y	10,000
Carillon Eagle Mid Cap Growth Fund Class R3	HAREX	NAS CM	Open End	US Equity Mid Cap (Growth)	C+	C	B-		Y	0
Carillon Eagle Mid Cap Growth Fund Class R5	HARSX	NAS CM	Open End	US Equity Mid Cap (Growth)	C+	C	B-		Y	0

★ Expanded analysis of this fund is included in Section II.

	TOTAL RETURNS					PERFORMANCE				ASSETS		ASSET ALLOCATION & TURNOVER					BULL & BEAR		FEES		
Min Additional Investment	3-Month Total Return	6-Month Total Return	1-Year Total Return	3-Year Total Return	5-Year Total Return	Dividend Yield (TTM)	Expense Ratio	3-Yr Std Deviation	3-Year Beta	NAV	Total Assets (MIL)	%Cash	%Stocks	%Bonds	%Other	Turnover Ratio	Last Bull Market Total Return	Last Bear Market Total Return	Front End Fee (%)	Back End Fee (%)	Inception Date
500	4.20	6.31	2.95	-0.89		0.38	1.25	6.17	0.86	8.92	24.2	45	2	53	0	0					Dec-14
100	3.15	13.36	-0.23	29.15	28.26	0	1.43	10.67	0.83	13.74	46.9	4	80	15	0	183	11.02	-15.78			Sep-05
5,000	-10.28						1.1			8.98	1.4	20	78	0	2						May-19
100	-10.37						1.35			8.98	1.4	20	78	0	2						Feb-19
1,000	0.82	8.84	0.54	13.81		0.38	1.74			11.03	28.7	16	72	11	0	185					Aug-16
250	5.68	21.59	8.26	40.73	47.03	0.15	1.02	12.22	0.98	27.7	60.3	10	91	0	0	46	19.24	-12.82			Dec-99
	1.51	14.65	4.70	44.59	18.64	1.14	0.89	13.84	0.95	8.06	2,258	2	97	0	1	37	15.53	-28.15			May-86
	1.51	14.67	4.55	44.38	18.47	1.12	0.95	13.79	0.95	8.05	2,258	2	97	0	1	37	15.53	-28.15			Sep-17
	1.51	14.67	4.59	44.19	18.31	1.04	0.95	13.82	0.95	8.05	2,258	2	97	0	1	37	15.53	-28.15			Sep-17
	3.32	10.56	6.30	19.32	3.76	2.87	1.1	7.84	0.52	11.2	60.2	7	45	45	3	61					Jan-12
	3.32	10.56	6.30	19.44	3.86	2.95	0.98	7.84	0.52	11.2	60.2	7	45	45	3	61					Sep-17
	3.41	10.65	6.34	19.48	3.90	2.82	0.98	7.88	0.53	11.22	60.2	7	45	45	3	61					Sep-17
	4.08	18.35	8.43	46.11	45.00	1.1	0.65	10.91	0.93	15.8	661.2	5	95	0	0	28	18.7	-18.86			Apr-11
	4.76	18.53	6.95	36.00	26.18	2.59	0.65	11.29	0.96	14.07	963.4	5	95	0	0	22	15.85	-20.01			Apr-11
	4.80	20.80	12.70	48.76	61.46	1.36	0.43	10.98	0.88	23.7	240.5	3	97	0	0	22	21.94	-17.63			Apr-11
10,000	4.03	8.83	-8.35			1.04	1.65			8.5	18.0	4	94	0	3						Nov-17
1 Million	4.16	9.10	-8.02			1.36	1.35			8.51	18.0	4	94	0	3						Nov-17
	4.61	14.25	-6.29	26.85	31.39	0.42	1.01	14.4	0.79	11.78	105.9	4	96	0	0	45					Apr-14
100	3.34	3.99					1.78			9.9	11.0	63	20	17	0						Jul-18
	3.32	19.28	4.62	54.59	74.20	0.14	1	13.33	0.99	41.62	541.2	1	99	0	0	45	27.77	-17.63	4.75		Dec-85
	3.14	18.83	3.85	51.08	67.61	0	1.75	13.31	0.99	28.89	541.2	1	99	0	0	45	27.28	-17.84		1.00	Apr-95
	3.41	19.46	4.94	56.03	76.79	0.43	0.7	13.32	0.99	43.88	541.2	1	99	0	0	45	28.02	-17.48			Mar-06
	3.27	19.11	4.36	53.26	71.52	0	1.25	13.33	0.99	39.76	541.2	1	99	0	0	45	27.51	-17.69			Sep-07
	3.40	19.44	4.93	56.03	76.72	0.45	0.7	13.33	0.99	43.73	541.2	1	99	0	0	45	27.99	-17.48			Oct-06
	3.42	19.50	5.05	56.42	76.61	0.52	0.6	13.33	0.99	43.51	541.2	1	99	0	0	45	27.77	-17.63			Jul-15
	3.32	19.27	4.63	54.62	74.23	0.02	1	13.34	0.99	43.82	541.2	1	99	0	0	45	27.77	-17.63			Nov-17
	2.19	12.93	-3.17	26.26	10.46	1.27	1.45	12.13	1.07	17.2	12.6	2	98	0	0	49			4.75		Feb-13
	1.99	12.43	-3.89	23.49	6.24	0.28	2.2	12.12	1.07	16.91	12.6	2	98	0	0	49				1.00	Feb-13
	2.26	13.04	-2.92	27.61	12.59	1.61	1.15	12.11	1.06	17.16	12.6	2	98	0	0	49					Feb-13
	2.16	12.79	-3.38	25.57	9.50	1.18	1.7	12.13	1.07	17.01	12.6	2	98	0	0	49					Feb-13
	2.26	13.02	-2.93	27.48	12.52	1.6	1.15	12.12	1.06	17.18	12.6	2	98	0	0	49					Feb-13
	2.31	13.07	-2.77	28.01	13.16	1.69	1.05	12.13	1.07	17.21	12.6	2	98	0	0	49					Feb-13
	2.09	12.83	-3.29	26.64	11.40	1.6	1.45	12.11	1.06	17.06	12.6	2	98	0	0	49					Nov-17
	2.01	10.47	1.18	15.60		0.48	1.25	8.21		15.71	21.2	3	55	42	0	88			4.75		Dec-15
	1.77	10.11	0.39	12.94		0.17	2	8.14		15.46	21.2	3	55	42	0	88				1.00	Dec-15
	2.01	10.63	1.45	16.57		0.78	0.95	8.2		15.71	21.2	3	55	42	0	88					Dec-15
	1.94	10.41	0.92	14.76		0.25	1.5	8.17		15.69	21.2	3	55	42	0	88					Dec-15
	2.01	10.61	1.48	16.63		0.74	0.95	8.17		15.73	21.2	3	55	42	0	88					Dec-15
	2.07	10.75	1.59	17.00		0.84	0.85	8.17		15.75	21.2	3	55	42	0	88					Dec-15
	2.01	10.50	1.18	15.85		0.48	1.25	8.16		15.68	21.2	3	55	42	0	88					Nov-17
	3.58	15.23	12.94	42.63	48.51	1.33	0.97	9.82	0.77	21.29	812.9	4	96	0	0	10	20.65	-14.29	4.75		Dec-86
	3.42	14.79	12.11	39.46	42.95	0.89	1.73	9.82	0.77	20.28	812.9	4	96	0	0	10	20.06	-14.53		1.00	Apr-95
	3.71	15.41	13.28	43.91	50.56	1.54	0.72	9.83	0.77	21.25	812.9	4	96	0	0	10	20.84	-14.11			Mar-09
	3.51	15.03	12.64	41.42	45.98	1.14	1.3	9.82	0.77	21.19	812.9	4	96	0	0	10	20.39	-14.34			Sep-09
	3.67	15.41	13.15	43.75	49.69	1.49	0.78	9.83	0.77	21.27	812.9	4	96	0	0	10	20.74	-14.26			Dec-09
	3.73	15.46	13.37	44.23	50.80	1.59	0.64	9.82	0.77	21.2	812.9	4	96	0	0	10	20.82	-14.35			Aug-11
	3.59	15.18	12.77	42.26	48.12	1.34	1.25	9.84	0.77	21.2	812.9	4	96	0	0	10	20.65	-14.29			Nov-17
	8.05	28.38	10.20	67.04	74.24	0	1.04	16.08	1.1	63.55	5,673	1	99	0	0	44	27.97	-24.05	4.75		Aug-98
	7.88	27.93	9.46	63.50	68.16	0	1.74	16.09	1.1	49.83	5,673	1	99	0	0	44	27.54	-24.25		1.00	Aug-98
	8.13	28.57	10.54	68.60	77.10	0	0.75	16.08	1.1	67.41	5,673	1	99	0	0	44	28.25	-23.91			Jun-06
	7.98	28.21	9.94	65.67	71.87	0	1.32	16.08	1.1	61.39	5,673	1	99	0	0	44	27.8	-24.13			Jan-09
	8.13	28.57	10.53	68.62	76.86	0	0.75	16.09	1.1	67.23	5,673	1	99	0	0	44	28.23	-23.89			Dec-09

Fund Name	Ticker Symbol (MARKET)	Traded On	Fund Type (FUND TYPE, CATEGORY & OBJECTIVE)	Category and (Prospectus Objective)	Overall Rating (RATINGS)	Reward Rating	Risk Rating	Recent Up/ Downgrade	Open to New Investors (MINIMUMS)	Min Initial Investment
Carillon Eagle Mid Cap Growth Fund Class R6	HRAUX	NAS CM	Open End	US Equity Mid Cap (Growth)	C+	C	B-		Y	0
Carillon Eagle Mid Cap Growth Fund Class Y	HRAYX	NAS CM	Open End	US Equity Mid Cap (Growth)	C+	C	B-		Y	1,000
Carillon Eagle Small Cap Growth Fund Class A	HRSCX	NAS CM	Open End	US Equity Small Cap (Small Company)	C	C	C+		Y	1,000
Carillon Eagle Small Cap Growth Fund Class C	HSCCX	NAS CM	Open End	US Equity Small Cap (Small Company)	C	C	C+		Y	1,000
Carillon Eagle Small Cap Growth Fund Class I	HSIIX	NAS CM	Open End	US Equity Small Cap (Small Company)	C	C	C+	Down	Y	10,000
Carillon Eagle Small Cap Growth Fund Class R3	HSRRX	NAS CM	Open End	US Equity Small Cap (Small Company)	C	C	C+		Y	0
Carillon Eagle Small Cap Growth Fund Class R5	HSRSX	NAS CM	Open End	US Equity Small Cap (Small Company)	C	C	C+	Down	Y	0
Carillon Eagle Small Cap Growth Fund Class R6	HSRUX	NAS CM	Open End	US Equity Small Cap (Small Company)	C	C	C+	Down	Y	0
Carillon Eagle Small Cap Growth Fund Class Y	HSRYX	NAS CM	Open End	US Equity Small Cap (Small Company)	C	C	C+		Y	1,000
Carillon Scout International Fund Class A	CSIGX	NAS CM	Open End	Global Equity Large Cap (Foreign Stock)	C	C	B-		Y	1,000
Carillon Scout International Fund Class C	CSIHX	NAS CM	Open End	Global Equity Large Cap (Foreign Stock)	C	C-	C+		Y	1,000
Carillon Scout International Fund Class I	UMBWX	NAS CM	Open End	Global Equity Large Cap (Foreign Stock)	C	C	B-		Y	10,000
Carillon Scout International Fund Class R-3	CSIQX	NAS CM	Open End	Global Equity Large Cap (Foreign Stock)	C	C	B-		Y	0
Carillon Scout International Fund Class R-5	CSIUX	NAS CM	Open End	Global Equity Large Cap (Foreign Stock)	C	C	B-		Y	0
Carillon Scout International Fund Class R-6	CSIWX	NAS CM	Open End	Global Equity Large Cap (Foreign Stock)	C	C	B-		Y	0
Carillon Scout International Fund Class Y	CSIZX	NAS CM	Open End	Global Equity Large Cap (Foreign Stock)	C	C	B-		Y	1,000
Carillon Scout Mid Cap Fund Class A	CSMEX	NAS CM	Open End	US Equity Mid Cap (Growth)	C+	C	B	Up	Y	1,000
Carillon Scout Mid Cap Fund Class C	CSMFX	NAS CM	Open End	US Equity Mid Cap (Growth)	C+	C	B-	Up	Y	1,000
Carillon Scout Mid Cap Fund Class I	UMBMX	NAS CM	Open End	US Equity Mid Cap (Growth)	C+	C	B		Y	10,000
Carillon Scout Mid Cap Fund Class R-3	CSMRX	NAS CM	Open End	US Equity Mid Cap (Growth)	C+	C	B	Up	Y	0
Carillon Scout Mid Cap Fund Class R-5	CSMSX	NAS CM	Open End	US Equity Mid Cap (Growth)	C+	C	B	Up	Y	0
Carillon Scout Mid Cap Fund Class R-6	CSMUX	NAS CM	Open End	US Equity Mid Cap (Growth)	C+	C	B		Y	0
Carillon Scout Mid Cap Fund Class Y	CSMZX	NAS CM	Open End	US Equity Mid Cap (Growth)	C+	C	B	Up	Y	1,000
Carillon Scout Small Cap Fund Class A	CSSAX	NAS CM	Open End	US Equity Small Cap (Small Company)	C+	C	B-	Down	Y	1,000
Carillon Scout Small Cap Fund Class C	CSSJX	NAS CM	Open End	US Equity Small Cap (Small Company)	C+	C	C+	Down	Y	1,000
Carillon Scout Small Cap Fund Class I	UMBHX	NAS CM	Open End	US Equity Small Cap (Small Company)	C+	C	B-	Down	Y	10,000
Carillon Scout Small Cap Fund Class R-3	CSSQX	NAS CM	Open End	US Equity Small Cap (Small Company)	C+	C	B-	Down	Y	0
Carillon Scout Small Cap Fund Class R-5	CSSSX	NAS CM	Open End	US Equity Small Cap (Small Company)	C+	C	B-	Down	Y	0
Carillon Scout Small Cap Fund Class R-6	CSSVX	NAS CM	Open End	US Equity Small Cap (Small Company)	C+	C	B-	Down	Y	0
Carillon Scout Small Cap Fund Class Y	CSSWX	NAS CM	Open End	US Equity Small Cap (Small Company)	C+	C	B-	Down	Y	1,000
Castle Focus Fund Class C	CASTX	NAS CM	Open End	US Equity Large Cap Value (Growth)	C+	C	B		Y	2,000
Castle Focus Fund Class Investor	MOATX	NAS CM	Open End	US Equity Large Cap Value (Growth)	B-	C	B+	Up	Y	4,000
Castle Tandem Fund Institutional Shares	TANDX	NAS CM	Open End	US Equity Large Cap Blend (Growth)	U	U	U		Y	10,000
Catalyst Buyback Strategy Fund Class A	BUYAX	NAS CM	Open End	US Equity Mid Cap (Growth)	C+	C	B	Down	Y	2,500
Catalyst Buyback Strategy Fund Class C	BUYCX	NAS CM	Open End	US Equity Mid Cap (Growth)	C+	C	B	Down	Y	2,500
Catalyst Buyback Strategy Fund Class I	BUYIX	NAS CM	Open End	US Equity Mid Cap (Growth)	C+	C	B	Down	Y	2,500
Catalyst Dynamic Alpha Fund Class A	CPEAX	NAS CM	Open End	US Equity Large Cap Growth (Growth)	C+	C	B	Down	Y	2,500
Catalyst Dynamic Alpha Fund Class C	CPECX	NAS CM	Open End	US Equity Large Cap Growth (Growth)	C+	C	B	Down	Y	2,500
Catalyst Dynamic Alpha Fund Class I	CPEIX	NAS CM	Open End	US Equity Large Cap Growth (Growth)	C+	C	B	Down	Y	2,500
Catalyst Growth of Income Fund Class A	CGGAX	NAS CM	Open End	US Equity Large Cap Blend (Growth & Income)	C	C	B	Down	Y	2,500
Catalyst Growth of Income Fund Class C	CGGCX	NAS CM	Open End	US Equity Large Cap Blend (Growth & Income)	C	C-	B	Down	Y	2,500
Catalyst Growth of Income Fund Class I	CGGIX	NAS CM	Open End	US Equity Large Cap Blend (Growth & Income)	C+	C	B	Down	Y	2,500
Catalyst Hedged Commodity Strategy Fund Class A	CFHAX	NAS CM	Open End	Commodities Broad Basket (Growth)	C	D+	B-	Down	Y	2,500
Catalyst Hedged Commodity Strategy Fund Class C	CFHCX	NAS CM	Open End	Commodities Broad Basket (Growth)	C-	D	C+	Down	Y	2,500
Catalyst Hedged Commodity Strategy Fund Class I	CFHIX	NAS CM	Open End	Commodities Broad Basket (Growth)	C	D+	B-	Down	Y	2,500
Catalyst Hedged Futures Strategy Fund Class A	HFXAX	NAS CM	Open End	Long/Short Equity (Growth)	D	D	D		Y	2,500
Catalyst Hedged Futures Strategy Fund Class C	HFXCX	NAS CM	Open End	Long/Short Equity (Growth)	D	D	D		Y	2,500
Catalyst Hedged Futures Strategy Fund Class I	HFXIX	NAS CM	Open End	Long/Short Equity (Growth)	D	D	D		Y	2,500
Catalyst Insider Buying Fund Class A	INSAX	NAS CM	Open End	US Equity Large Cap Growth (Growth)	C+	C	B-	Down	Y	2,500
Catalyst Insider Buying Fund Class C	INSCX	NAS CM	Open End	US Equity Large Cap Growth (Growth)	C+	C	B-	Down	Y	2,500
Catalyst Insider Buying Fund Class I	INSIX	NAS CM	Open End	US Equity Large Cap Growth (Growth)	C+	C	B-	Down	Y	2,500
Catalyst IPOx Allocation Fund Class A	OIPAX	NAS CM	Open End	US Equity Mid Cap (Growth)	B-	B-	B-	Down	Y	2,500

★ Expanded analysis of this fund is included in Section II.

Min Additional Investment	TOTAL RETURNS: 3-Month Total Return	6-Month Total Return	1-Year Total Return	3-Year Total Return	5-Year Total Return	PERFORMANCE: Dividend Yield (TTM)	Expense Ratio	3-Yr Std Deviation	3-Year Beta	ASSETS: NAV	Total Assets (MIL)	ASSET ALLOCATION & TURNOVER: %Cash	%Stocks	%Bonds	%Other	Turnover Ratio	BULL & BEAR: Last Bull Market Total Return	Last Bear Market Total Return	FEES: Front End Fee (%)	Back End Fee (%)	Inception Date
	8.17	28.63	10.65	69.08	77.99	0	0.66	16.09	1.1	67.92	5,673	1	99	0	0	44	28.3	-24.02			Aug-11
	8.07	28.43	10.23	66.91	74.10	0	1.13	16.09	1.1	67.03	5,673	1	99	0	0	44	27.97	-24.05			Nov-17
	2.51	22.09	0.65	46.82	51.05	0	1.04	17.65	0.98	50.62	4,573	0	100	0	0	35	26.49	-21.84	4.75		May-93
	2.28	21.66	-0.05	43.78	45.80	0	1.74	17.62	0.98	33.58	4,573	0	100	0	0	35	26	-22.08		1.00	Apr-95
	2.57	22.29	0.95	48.27	53.51	0	0.75	17.65	0.98	54.14	4,573	0	100	0	0	35	26.35	-21.72			Jun-06
	2.43	21.94	0.37	45.68	49.07	0	1.32	17.63	0.98	48.34	4,573	0	100	0	0	35	26.3	-21.79			Sep-06
	2.56	22.28	0.95	48.25	53.59	0	0.75	17.65	0.98	54.43	4,573	0	100	0	0	35	26.68	-21.71			Oct-06
	2.58	22.34	1.06	48.75	54.46	0	0.65	17.66	0.98	55.08	4,573	0	100	0	0	35	26.79	-21.84			Aug-11
	2.44	22.03	0.58	46.55	50.78	0	1.12	17.66	0.98	53.72	4,573	0	100	0	0	35	26.49	-21.84			Nov-17
	3.96	16.22	-1.17	26.68	12.06	3.36	1.31	12.14	1.06	18.34	754.2	2	98	0	0	13	18.96	-24.31	4.75		Nov-17
	3.74	15.83	-1.95	23.83	7.92	2.57	2.2	12.16	1.06	18.29	754.2	2	98	0	0	13	18.44	-24.55		1.00	Nov-17
	4.06	16.48	-0.87	27.78	13.59	3.34	1.07	12.15	1.06	18.44	754.2	2	98	0	0	13	19.13	-24.23			Sep-93
	3.89	16.07	-1.48	25.62	10.57	2.65	1.7	12.15	1.06	18.41	754.2	2	98	0	0	13	18.78	-24.39			Nov-17
	4.06	16.41	-0.90	27.64	13.47	3.23	1.15	12.16	1.06	18.44	754.2	2	98	0	0	13	19.13	-24.23			Nov-17
	4.06	16.50	-0.79	27.90	13.70	3.49	0.99	12.17	1.06	18.42	754.2	2	98	0	0	13	19.13	-24.23			Nov-17
	3.95	16.28	-1.19	26.60	11.98	2.94	1.45	12.16	1.06	18.42	754.2	2	98	0	0	13	18.96	-24.31			Nov-17
	1.10	16.92	2.69	47.39	52.35	0.48	1.19	14.14	1.02	18.31	2,876	0	100	0	0	106	21.67	-15.77	4.75		Nov-17
	0.88	16.40	1.87	44.06	46.70	0.16	1.94	14.13	1.02	18.16	2,876	0	100	0	0	106	21.14	-16.03		1.00	Nov-17
	1.10	17.00	2.81	48.29	54.05	0.45	0.98	14.11	1.02	18.37	2,876	0	100	0	0	106	21.84	-15.68			Oct-06
	0.99	16.68	2.32	46.04	50.20	0.32	1.44	14.14	1.02	18.25	2,876	0	100	0	0	106	21.49	-15.86			Nov-17
	1.10	16.94	2.62	47.90	53.64	0.56	0.99	14.14	1.02	18.29	2,876	0	100	0	0	106	21.84	-15.68			Nov-17
	1.15	17.09	2.98	48.48	54.25	0.59	0.9	14.14	1.02	18.36	2,876	0	100	0	0	106	21.84	-15.68			Nov-17
	1.10	16.93	2.70	47.32	52.28	0.49	1.19	14.12	1.02	18.3	2,876	0	100	0	0	106	21.67	-15.77			Nov-17
	2.73	21.19	4.99	71.19	73.73	0	1.23	18.31	1.02	29.33	347.2	0	100	0	0	22	30.22	-26.66	4.75		Nov-17
	2.51	20.71	4.19	67.38	67.36	0	1.97	18.28	1.01	28.96	347.2	0	100	0	0	22	29.66	-26.89		1.00	Nov-17
	2.79	21.38	5.23	72.52	75.97	0	0.92	18.31	1.02	29.46	347.2	0	100	0	0	22	30.41	-26.59			Nov-86
	2.63	21.01	4.67	69.85	71.52	0	1.5	18.32	1.02	29.19	347.2	0	100	0	0	22	30.03	-26.74			Nov-17
	2.79	21.33	5.23	72.52	75.97	0	0.95	18.31	1.02	29.46	347.2	0	100	0	0	22	30.41	-26.59			Nov-17
	2.78	21.39	5.33	72.81	76.26	0	0.85	18.31	1.02	29.51	347.2	0	100	0	0	22	30.41	-26.59			Nov-17
	2.69	21.16	4.92	71.07	73.62	0	1.25	18.31	1.02	29.31	347.2	0	100	0	0	22	30.22	-26.66			Nov-17
100	4.08	11.42	4.13	17.30	21.99	0	2.4	7.24	0.54	19.6	115.6	34	66	0	0	39	9.12	-6.12		1.00	Jun-10
100	4.32	11.98	5.19	20.82	28.21	0.46	1.4	7.25	0.54	21.21	115.6	34	66	0	0	39	9.8	-5.69			Jun-10
100	3.54						1.18			26.28	3.7										Mar-19
50	2.44	14.00	2.91	44.99	39.37	0	1.53	14.1	1.06	10.91	25.0	2	98	0	0	836			5.75		Dec-13
50	2.23	13.60	2.23	41.72	34.21	0	2.28	14.13	1.06	10.52	25.0	2	98	0	0	836					Dec-13
50	2.51	14.19	3.17	46.04	41.00	0	1.28	14.14	1.06	11.02	25.0	2	98	0	0	836					Dec-13
50	-0.81	11.36	3.04	45.79	72.42	0.24	1.38	12.44	0.93	19.5	340.0	1	99	0	0	87			5.75		Dec-11
50	-1.03	10.90	2.25	42.55	66.05	0	2.13	12.46	0.93	18.21	340.0	1	99	0	0	87					Dec-11
50	-0.75	11.54	3.31	46.91	74.47	0.49	1.13	12.46	0.93	19.71	340.0	1	99	0	0	87					Jun-14
50	-0.82	9.86	0.79	30.27	27.66	2.8	1.38	12.37	0.93	9.26	1.8	4	96	0	0	16	20.64	-11.11	5.75		Dec-09
50	-0.99	9.53	0.08	27.47	23.12	2.27	2.13	12.41	0.93	8.98	1.8	4	96	0	0	16	20.12	-11.35			Dec-09
50	-0.74	10.26	1.22	31.91	29.93	3.11	1.13	12.43	0.93	9.33	1.8	4	96	0	0	16	20.78	-11			Nov-10
50	0.73	-0.45	2.10	3.37		0.33	2.57	8.27	-0.18	10.94	50.0	28	15	57	0	0			5.75		Sep-15
50	0.56	-0.82	1.41	1.19		0	3.32	8.25	-0.18	10.76	50.0	28	15	57	0	0					Sep-15
50	0.82	-0.36	2.39	4.21		0.96	2.32	8.24	-0.18	10.94	50.0	28	15	57	0	0					Sep-15
50	-1.25	-0.38	-2.60	-23.67	-17.15	0	2.44	12.42	-0.25	7.86	430.9	71	-1	19	10	0	6.12	8.52	5.75		Aug-13
50	-1.44	-0.79	-3.35	-25.40	-20.26	0	3.2	12.36	-0.25	7.5	430.9	71	-1	19	10	0	5.65	8.18			Aug-13
50	-1.11	-0.24	-2.32	-23.03	-16.11	0	2.2	12.46	-0.25	7.98	430.9	71	-1	19	10	0	6.12	8.52			Aug-13
50	-0.10	19.23	4.04	46.83	26.58	0	1.53	14.74	1.09	19.28	52.3	1	99	0	0	153	22.83		5.75		Jul-11
50	-0.31	18.75	3.22	43.60	21.90	0	2.28	14.68	1.09	18.87	52.3	1	99	0	0	153	22.26				Jul-11
50	-0.10	19.32	4.27	48.02	28.21	0	1.28	14.73	1.09	19.51	52.3	1	99	0	0	153	22.83				Jun-14
50	4.97	25.89	8.88	66.77		0	2.2	14.62	1	14.34	3.3	13	87	0	0	149			5.75		Sep-15

	MARKET		FUND TYPE, CATEGORY & OBJECTIVE		RATINGS				MINIMUMS	
Fund Name	Ticker Symbol	Traded On	Fund Type	Category and (Prospectus Objective)	Overall Rating	Reward Rating	Risk Rating	Recent Up/ Downgrade	Open to New Investors	Min Initial Investment
Catalyst IPOx Allocation Fund Class C	OIPCX	NAS CM	Open End	US Equity Mid Cap (Growth)	B-	C+	B-		Y	2,500
Catalyst IPOx Allocation Fund Class I	OIPIX	NAS CM	Open End	US Equity Mid Cap (Growth)	B-	B-	B-	Down	Y	2,500
Catalyst MLP & Infrastructure Fund Class A	MLXAX	NAS CM	Open End	Energy Sector Equity (Growth & Income)	D+	D+	D+	Down	Y	2,500
Catalyst MLP & Infrastructure Fund Class C	MLXCX	NAS CM	Open End	Energy Sector Equity (Growth & Income)	D+	D+	D+	Down	Y	2,500
Catalyst MLP & Infrastructure Fund Class I	MLXIX	NAS CM	Open End	Energy Sector Equity (Growth & Income)	D+	D+	D+	Down	Y	2,500
Catalyst Multi-Strategy Fund Class A	ACXAX	NAS CM	Open End	Alternative Miscellaneous (Growth)	C-	D+	C	Up	Y	2,500
Catalyst Multi-Strategy Fund Class C	ACXCX	NAS CM	Open End	Alternative Miscellaneous (Growth)	C-	D+	C	Up	Y	2,500
Catalyst Multi-Strategy Fund Class I	ACXIX	NAS CM	Open End	Alternative Miscellaneous (Growth)	C	D+	C+	Up	Y	2,500
Catalyst Small Cap Insider Buying Fund Class A	CTVAX	NAS CM	Open End	US Equity Small Cap (Growth)	C-	C-	C-	Down	Y	2,500
Catalyst Small Cap Insider Buying Fund Class C	CTVCX	NAS CM	Open End	US Equity Small Cap (Growth)	C-	C-	C-	Down	Y	2,500
Catalyst Small Cap Insider Buying Fund Class I	CTVIX	NAS CM	Open End	US Equity Small Cap (Growth)	C-	C-	C	Down	Y	2,500
Catalyst Systematic Alpha Fund Class A	ATRAX	NAS CM	Open End	Long/Short Equity (Growth & Income)	D	D	D+		Y	2,500
Catalyst Systematic Alpha Fund Class C	ATRCX	NAS CM	Open End	Long/Short Equity (Growth & Income)	D	D	D+		Y	2,500
Catalyst Systematic Alpha Fund Class I	ATRFX	NAS CM	Open End	Long/Short Equity (Growth & Income)	D	D	D+		Y	2,500
Catalyst/Exceed Defined Risk Fund Class A	CLPAX	NAS CM	Open End	Alternative Miscellaneous (Growth)	B	C	A-	Up	Y	2,500
Catalyst/Exceed Defined Risk Fund Class C	CLPCX	NAS CM	Open End	Alternative Miscellaneous (Growth)	B-	C	A-	Up	Y	2,500
Catalyst/Exceed Defined Risk Fund Class I	CLPFX	NAS CM	Open End	Alternative Miscellaneous (Growth)	B	C	A-	Up	Y	2,500
Catalyst/Exceed Defined Shield Fund Class A	SHIEX	NAS CM	Open End	Long/Short Equity (Growth)	B-	C	B+	Up	Y	2,500
Catalyst/Exceed Defined Shield Fund Class C	SHINX	NAS CM	Open End	Long/Short Equity (Growth)	B-	C	B+	Up	Y	2,500
Catalyst/Exceed Defined Shield Fund Class I	SHIIX	NAS CM	Open End	Long/Short Equity (Growth)	B-	C	B+	Up	Y	2,500
Catalyst/Lyons Tactical Allocation Fund Class A	CLTAX	NAS CM	Open End	Flexible Alloc (Asset Alloc)	C	C	C	Up	Y	2,500
Catalyst/Lyons Tactical Allocation Fund Class C	CLTCX	NAS CM	Open End	Flexible Alloc (Asset Alloc)	C	C	C	Up	Y	2,500
Catalyst/Lyons Tactical Allocation Fund Class I	CLTIX	NAS CM	Open End	Flexible Alloc (Asset Alloc)	C	C	C	Up	Y	2,500
Catalyst/MAP Global Balanced Fund Class A	TRXAX	NAS CM	Open End	Moderate Alloc (Multi-Asset Global)	B	C	A	Up	Y	2,500
Catalyst/MAP Global Balanced Fund Class C	TRXCX	NAS CM	Open End	Moderate Alloc (Multi-Asset Global)	B-	C	A-	Up	Y	2,500
Catalyst/MAP Global Balanced Fund Class I	TRXIX	NAS CM	Open End	Moderate Alloc (Multi-Asset Global)	B	C	A	Up	Y	2,500
Catalyst/MAP Global Equity Fund Class A	CAXAX	NAS CM	Open End	Global Equity Large Cap (World Stock)	B-	C	A-	Up	Y	2,500
Catalyst/MAP Global Equity Fund Class C	CAXCX	NAS CM	Open End	Global Equity Large Cap (World Stock)	B-	C	A-	Up	Y	2,500
Catalyst/MAP Global Equity Fund Class I	CAXIX	NAS CM	Open End	Global Equity Large Cap (World Stock)	B-	C	A-		Y	2,500
Catalyst/Millburn Hedge Strategy Fund Class A	MBXAX	NAS CM	Open End	Multialternative (Growth & Income)	B-	C	B+	Down	Y	2,500
Catalyst/Millburn Hedge Strategy Fund Class C	MBXCX	NAS CM	Open End	Multialternative (Growth & Income)	C+	C	B	Down	Y	2,500
Catalyst/Millburn Hedge Strategy Fund Class I	MBXIX	NAS CM	Open End	Multialternative (Growth & Income)	B-	C	B+	Down	Y	2,500
Catalyst/SMH Total Return Income Fund Class A	TRIFX	NAS CM	Open End	Moderate Alloc (Growth & Income)	C+	C+	B-		Y	2,500
Catalyst/SMH Total Return Income Fund Class C	TRICX	NAS CM	Open End	Moderate Alloc (Growth & Income)	C+	C+	B-		Y	2,500
Catalyst/SMH Total Return Income Fund Class I	TRIIX	NAS CM	Open End	Moderate Alloc (Growth & Income)	C+	C+	B-		Y	2,500
Catholic Investor International Equity Fund Class S	KCISX	NAS CM	Open End	Global Equity Large Cap (World Stock)	C	C	B		Y	0
Catholic Investor International Equity Fund I Class	KCIIX	NAS CM	Open End	Global Equity Large Cap (World Stock)	C	C	B		Y	25,000
Catholic Investor International Equity Investor Shares	KCIVX	NAS CM	Open End	Global Equity Large Cap (World Stock)	C	C	B		Y	1,000
Catholic Investor Large Cap Growth Fund Class S	KCGSX	NAS CM	Open End	US Equity Large Cap Growth (Growth)	C+	C	B-	Down	Y	0
Catholic Investor Large Cap Growth Fund I Class	KCGIX	NAS CM	Open End	US Equity Large Cap Growth (Growth)	C+	C	B-		Y	25,000
Catholic Investor Large Cap Growth Fund Investor Shares	KCGVX	NAS CM	Open End	US Equity Large Cap Growth (Growth)	C+	C	B-		Y	1,000
Catholic Investor Large Cap Value Fund Class S	KCVSX	NAS CM	Open End	US Equity Large Cap Value (Growth)	C+	C	B		Y	0
Catholic Investor Large Cap Value Fund I Class	KCVIX	NAS CM	Open End	US Equity Large Cap Value (Growth)	C+	C	B		Y	25,000
Catholic Investor Large Cap Value Fund Investor Shares	KCVVX	NAS CM	Open End	US Equity Large Cap Value (Growth)	C+	C	B		Y	1,000
Catholic Investor Small Cap Fund Class S	KCSSX	NAS CM	Open End	US Equity Small Cap (Small Company)	C	C	C+		Y	0
Catholic Investor Small Cap Fund I Class	KCSIX	NAS CM	Open End	US Equity Small Cap (Small Company)	C	C	C+		Y	25,000
Catholic Investor Small Cap Fund Investor Shares	KCSVX	NAS CM	Open End	US Equity Small Cap (Small Company)	C	C	C+		Y	1,000
Causeway Emerging Markets Fund Class Institutional	CEMIX	NAS CM	Open End	Global Emerg Mkts (Div Emerging Mkts)	C	C	C+		Y	1,000,000
Causeway Emerging Markets Fund Investor Class	CEMVX	NAS CM	Open End	Global Emerg Mkts (Div Emerging Mkts)	C	C	C+		Y	5,000
Causeway Global Absolute Return Fund Institutional Class	CGAIX	NAS CM	Open End	Market Neutral (Growth)	D	D	D	Down	Y	1,000,000
Causeway Global Absolute Return Fund Investor Class	CGAVX	NAS CM	Open End	Market Neutral (Growth)	D	D	D	Down	Y	5,000
Causeway Global Value Fund Institutional Class	CGVIX	NAS CM	Open End	Global Equity Large Cap (Growth & Income)	C	C-	C+		Y	1,000,000

★ Expanded analysis of this fund is included in Section II.

	TOTAL RETURNS					PERFORMANCE				ASSETS		ASSET ALLOCATION & TURNOVER					BULL & BEAR		FEES		
Min Additional Investment	3-Month Total Return	6-Month Total Return	1-Year Total Return	3-Year Total Return	5-Year Total Return	Dividend Yield (TTM)	Expense Ratio	3-Yr Std Deviation	3-Year Beta	NAV	Total Assets (MIL)	%Cash	%Stocks	%Bonds	%Other	Turnover Ratio	Last Bull Market Total Return	Last Bear Market Total Return	Front End Fee (%)	Back End Fee (%)	Inception Date
50	4.75	25.40	8.07	62.94		0	2.95	14.62	1	13.87	3.3	13	87	0	0	149					Sep-15
50	5.07	26.13	9.18	67.88		0	1.95	14.61	1	14.48	3.3	13	87	0	0	149					Sep-15
50	-4.06	19.66	-4.59	2.63		13.86	1.68	20.89	1.1	4.59	199.8	0	100	0	0	49			5.75		Dec-14
50	-4.44	18.97	-5.48	0.28		13.1	2.43	20.77	1.1	4.58	199.8	0	100	0	0	49					Dec-14
50	-4.00	19.74	-4.54	3.35		14.09	1.43	20.81	1.1	4.6	199.8	0	100	0	0	49					Dec-14
50	0.81	2.20	1.57	-3.68	4.26	0	2.44	6.01	7.23	14.85	4.4	82	18	0	0	0	-0.73	-4.41	5.75		Aug-15
50	0.55	1.76	0.76	-5.86	0.30	0	3.19	6.01	7.36	14.44	4.4	82	18	0	0	0	-1.16	-4.71			Aug-15
50	0.81	2.33	1.84	-3.00	5.54	0	2.19	6.01	7.63	14.91	4.4	82	18	0	0	0	-0.59	-4.31			Aug-15
50	1.63	7.48	-11.01	23.93	-17.11	0	1.79	19.6	0.98	14.94	12.1	0	100	0	0	188	22	-32.88	5.75		Jul-06
50	1.43	6.98	-11.70	21.13	-20.20	0	2.54	19.59	0.98	14.1	12.1	0	100	0	0	188	21.47	-33.09			Jul-06
50	1.68	7.57	-10.78	24.80	-16.06	0	1.54	19.58	0.98	15.05	12.1	0	100	0	0	188	22.12	-32.76			Mar-09
50	5.08	17.13	2.38	-6.75		0.01	2.43	10.86		9.09	2.6	10	16	27	47	116			5.75		Jul-14
50	4.91	16.64	1.48	-9.00		0.38	3.18	10.82		8.76	2.6	10	16	27	47	116					Jul-14
50	5.16	17.27	2.51	-6.09		1.18	2.18	10.81		8.96	2.6	10	16	27	47	116					Jul-14
50	3.17	13.17	6.54	30.26	22.02	0.26	1.57	8.33	0.61	10.74	12.2	13	5	82	0	177			5.75		Dec-13
50	2.91	12.76	5.64	26.93	17.10	0.07	2.32	8.33	0.61	10.25	12.2	13	5	82	0	177					Dec-13
50	3.14	13.19	6.72	30.82	23.19	0.46	1.32	8.25	0.6	10.81	12.2	13	5	82	0	177					Jun-14
50	3.65	13.48	5.75	29.12		0.85	1.49	8.81	0.72	9.87	31.2	17	3	80	0	160			5.75		Apr-15
50	2.85	12.47	4.33	25.56		0.5	2.24	8.82	0.72	9.74	31.2	17	3	80	0	160					Sep-17
50	2.49	12.28	4.73	28.60		1.09	1.24	8.86	0.72	9.93	31.2	17	3	80	0	160					Apr-15
50	2.19	3.29	-6.71	28.39	30.49	0.57	1.53	10.96		15.38	66.9	3	0	97	0	146			5.75		Jul-12
50	1.89	2.86	-7.43	25.45	25.67	0.05	2.28	10.91		15.08	66.9	3	0	97	0	146					Jul-12
50	2.19	3.37	-6.52	29.29	32.17	1.04	1.28	10.96		15.33	66.9	3	0	97	0	146					Jun-14
50	1.91	8.25	4.28	19.39	18.61	1.49	1.24	5	0.39	11.65	23.4	14	50	32	1	42	9.18		5.75		Jul-11
50	1.67	7.81	3.44	16.71	14.22	0.94	1.99	5.05	0.39	11.52	23.4	14	50	32	1	42	8.79				Jul-11
50	1.97	8.46	4.54	20.38	20.39	1.73	0.99	5.09	0.4	11.67	23.4	14	50	32	1	42	9.18				Jun-14
50	3.36	13.19	5.39	38.32	32.57	0	1.24	9.22	0.73	14.75	62.7	8	89	0	3	30	12.94		5.75		Jul-11
50	3.15	12.76	4.57	35.11	27.48	0	1.99	9.2	0.72	14.4	62.7	8	89	0	3	30	12.41				Jul-11
50	3.43	13.36	5.70	39.39	34.33	0.14	0.99	9.2	0.72	14.76	62.7	8	89	0	3	30	12.94				Jun-14
50	0.34	7.22	6.13	23.70	61.03	1.38	2.25	9.3	37.68	32.07	4,924	24	51	24	0	12	7.6	-17.85	5.75		Dec-15
50	0.19	6.82	5.36	20.93	54.97	0.84	3	9.29	37.93	31.47	4,924	24	51	24	0	12	7.13	-18.11			Dec-15
50	0.40	7.32	6.41	24.59	63.00	1.63	2	9.28	37.82	32.23	4,924	24	51	24	0	12	7.76	-17.77			Dec-15
50	1.37	12.61	4.32	38.70	-2.32	5.81	3.43	10.01	0.64	4.32	18.2	11	46	40	0	11	13.64	-19.62	5.75		May-08
50	1.18	12.20	3.79	35.68	-5.74	5.07	4.18	9.88	0.64	4.32	18.2	11	46	40	0	11	13.16	-19.87			May-08
50	1.43	13.04	4.83	39.78	-0.86	6.06	3.18	10.11	0.65	4.32	18.2	11	46	40	0	11	13.64	-19.62			Jul-13
	0.33	12.37	-1.52	39.85		1.64	1.24	11.54	0.98	11.21	79.1	6	92	0	2	45					Jul-15
250	0.27	12.41	-1.43	40.27		1.72	1.1	11.51	0.98	11.22	79.1	6	92	0	2	45					Feb-15
	0.30	12.39	-1.59	39.15		1.48	1.35	11.5	0.98	11.22	79.1	6	92	0	2	45					Jun-16
	5.03	21.58	6.62	54.26		0.06	0.97	13.8	1.02	12.73	68.0	2	98	0	0	118					Jul-15
250	5.05	21.69	6.75	54.60		0.1	0.9	13.79	1.02	12.75	68.0	2	98	0	0	118					Feb-15
	4.96	21.57	6.46	53.28		0.04	1.15	13.77	1.02	12.68	68.0	2	98	0	0	118					Jun-16
	3.67	17.50	5.76	43.96		1.47	1.04	13.64	1.1	12.31	65.3	5	95	0	0	56					Jul-15
250	3.70	17.55	5.87	44.28		1.56	0.9	13.6	1.1	12.31	65.3	5	95	0	0	56					Feb-15
	3.55	17.42	5.64	43.07		1.35	1.15	13.6	1.1	12.3	65.3	5	95	0	0	56					Jun-16
	4.31	20.65	-2.77	37.53		0.02	1.2	17.83	1.01	10.63	88.3	2	98	0	0	92					Jul-15
250	4.31	20.74	-2.62	38.03		0.07	1.05	17.86	1.02	10.66	88.3	2	98	0	0	92					Feb-15
	4.23	20.61	-2.89	36.99		0	1.3	17.84	1.02	10.59	88.3	2	98	0	0	92					Jun-16
	0.40	9.51	-1.90	31.82	8.33	1.85	1.15	14.42	1.02	12.43	4,153	3	96	0	1	49	21	-27.43			Mar-07
	0.40	9.51	-2.02	30.93	7.12	1.42	1.4	14.39	1.02	12.55	4,153	3	96	0	1	49	20.84	-27.41			Mar-07
	-6.03	-12.45	-2.39	-5.98	-6.59	11.06	1.52	9.05	-39.66	7.94	42.8	104	0	0	-4		4.4	-0.67			Jan-11
	-6.10	-12.58	-2.68	-6.55	-7.62	11	1.77	9.05	-39.61	7.85	42.8	104	0	0	-4		4.25	-0.77			Jan-11
	0.39	11.67	-0.32	28.48	16.55	1.7	1.05	12.83	1.07	10.04	86.6	3	97	0	0	50	21.6	-22.83			Apr-08

Fund Name	Ticker Symbol	Traded On	Fund Type	Category and (Prospectus Objective)	Overall Rating	Reward Rating	Risk Rating	Recent Up/ Downgrade	Open to New Investors	Min Initial Investment
	MARKET			FUND TYPE, CATEGORY & OBJECTIVE	RATINGS				MINIMUMS	
Causeway Global Value Fund Investor	CGVVX	NAS CM	Open End	Global Equity Large Cap (Growth & Income)	C	C-	B-		Y	5,000
Causeway International Opportunities Institutional Cls	CIOIX	NAS CM	Open End	Global Equity Large Cap (Foreign Stock)	C	C-	C+		Y	1,000,000
Causeway International Opportunities Fund Investor Class	CIOVX	NAS CM	Open End	Global Equity Large Cap (Foreign Stock)	C	C-	C+		Y	5,000
Causeway International Small Cap Fund Institutional Class	CIISX	NAS CM	Open End	Global Equity Mid/Small Cap (Small Company)	C	C-	C	Up	Y	1,000,000
Causeway International Small Cap Fund Investor Class	CVISX	NAS CM	Open End	Global Equity Mid/Small Cap (Small Company)	C	C-	C	Up	Y	5,000
Causeway International Value Fund Class Institutional	CIVIX	NAS CM	Open End	Global Equity Large Cap (Foreign Stock)	C	C-	C+		Y	1,000,000
Causeway International Value Fund Class Investor	CIVVX	NAS CM	Open End	Global Equity Large Cap (Foreign Stock)	C	C-	C+		Y	5,000
Cavalier Fundamental Growth Fund A Class	CFDAX	NAS CM	Open End	US Equity Mid Cap (Growth)	C	C	C		Y	1,000
Cavalier Fundamental Growth Fund C Class	CFGAX	NAS CM	Open End	US Equity Mid Cap (Growth)	C	C	C		Y	1,000
Cavalier Fundamental Growth Fund Institutional Class	CAFGX	NAS CM	Open End	US Equity Mid Cap (Growth)	C	C	C		Y	1,000
Cavalier Growth Opportunities Fund Class A	CAGOX	NAS CM	Open End	Moderate Alloc (Growth)	C+	C	B	Up	Y	1,000
Cavalier Growth Opportunities Fund Class C	CATDX	NAS CM	Open End	Moderate Alloc (Growth)	C+	C	B	Up	Y	1,000
Cavalier Growth Opportunities Fund Institutional Class	CATEX	NAS CM	Open End	Moderate Alloc (Growth)	C+	C	B	Up	Y	1,000
Cavalier Tactical Economic Fund A Class	CAVMX	NAS CM	Open End	Flexible Alloc (Growth & Income)	B-	C	B+		Y	1,000
Cavalier Tactical Economic Fund C Class	CMSYX	NAS CM	Open End	Flexible Alloc (Growth & Income)	B-	C	B+	Up	Y	1,000
Cavalier Tactical Economic Fund Institutional Class	CMSFX	NAS CM	Open End	Flexible Alloc (Growth & Income)	B-	C	B+		Y	1,000
Cavalier Tactical Rotation Fund C Class	CATOX	NAS CM	Open End	Moderate Alloc (Growth)	C	D+	C+		Y	1,000
Cavalier Tactical Rotation Fund Class A	CAVTX	NAS CM	Open End	Moderate Alloc (Growth)	C	C-	B-		Y	1,000
Cavalier Tactical Rotation Fund Institutional Class	CTROX	NAS CM	Open End	Moderate Alloc (Growth)	C	C-	B-		Y	1,000
Cavanal Hill Active Core Fund Class A	AABAX	NAS CM	Open End	Moderate Alloc (Balanced)	B	C	A-	Up	Y	0
Cavanal Hill Active Core Fund Class C	AACBX	NAS CM	Open End	Moderate Alloc (Balanced)	B-	C	A-	Up	Y	0
Cavanal Hill Active Core Fund Institutional Class	AIBLX	NAS CM	Open End	Moderate Alloc (Balanced)	B	C	A-	Up	Y	1,000
Cavanal Hill Active Core Fund Investor Class	APBAX	NAS CM	Open End	Moderate Alloc (Balanced)	B	C	A-	Up	Y	100
Cavanal Hill Opportunistic Fund Class A	AAOPX	NAS CM	Open End	Aggressive Alloc (Growth)	C	C-	C+		Y	0
Cavanal Hill Opportunistic Fund Class C	AACOX	NAS CM	Open End	Aggressive Alloc (Growth)	C	C-	C		Y	0
Cavanal Hill Opportunistic Fund Institutional	AIOPX	NAS CM	Open End	Aggressive Alloc (Growth)	C	C-	C+		Y	1,000
Cavanal Hill Opportunistic Fund Investor	APOPX	NAS CM	Open End	Aggressive Alloc (Growth)	C	C-	C+		Y	100
Cavanal Hill World Energy Fund A	AAWEX	NAS CM	Open End	Energy Sector Equity (Growth & Income)	D	D	D	Down	Y	0
Cavanal Hill World Energy Fund C	ACWEX	NAS CM	Open End	Energy Sector Equity (Growth & Income)	D	D	D	Down	Y	0
Cavanal Hill World Energy Fund Institutional	AIWEX	NAS CM	Open End	Energy Sector Equity (Growth & Income)	D	D	D	Down	Y	1,000
Cavanal Hill World Energy Fund Investor	APWEX	NAS CM	Open End	Energy Sector Equity (Growth & Income)	D	D	D	Down	Y	100
Cavanal Mid Cap Core Equity Fund Class A	AAWVX	NAS CM	Open End	US Equity Mid Cap (Growth & Income)	C+	C	B	Up	Y	0
Cavanal Mid Cap Core Equity Fund Class C	ACWVX	NAS CM	Open End	US Equity Mid Cap (Growth & Income)	C	C	B		Y	0
Cavanal Mid Cap Core Equity Fund Institutional Shares	AIWVX	NAS CM	Open End	US Equity Mid Cap (Growth & Income)	C+	C	B	Up	Y	1,000
Cavanal Mid Cap Core Equity Fund Investor Shares	APWVX	NAS CM	Open End	US Equity Mid Cap (Growth & Income)	C+	C	B	Up	Y	100
CBOE Vest S&P 500 Dividend Aristocrats Target Income Cls A	KNGAX	NAS CM	Open End	US Equity Large Cap Blend (Growth & Income)	C-	C-	B-	Up	Y	1,000
CBOE Vest S&P 500 Dividend Aristocrats Target Income Cls C	KNGCX	NAS CM	Open End	US Equity Large Cap Blend (Growth & Income)	C-	C-	B-	Up	Y	1,000
CBOE Vest S&P 500 Dividend Aristocrats Target Income Cls Y	KNGYX	NAS CM	Open End	US Equity Large Cap Blend (Growth & Income)	C-	C-	B-	Up	Y	10,000,000
CBOE Vest S&P 500 Div Aristocrats Target Income Inst Cls	KNGIX	NAS CM	Open End	US Equity Large Cap Blend (Growth & Income)	C-	C-	B-	Up	Y	100,000
CBOE Vest S&P 500 Div Aristocrats Target Income Inv Cls	KNGLX	NAS CM	Open End	US Equity Large Cap Blend (Growth & Income)	C-	C-	B-	Up	Y	1,000
CBOE Vest S&P 500 Enhanced Growth Strategy Cls Y Shares	ENGYX	NAS CM	Open End	Long/Short Equity (Growth & Income)	C+	C	B	Up	Y	10,000,000
CBOE Vest S&P 500® Buffer Strategy Fund Class A Shares	BUAGX	NAS CM	Open End	Long/Short Equity (Growth & Income)	C+	C	B	Up	Y	1,000
CBOE Vest S&P 500® Buffer Strategy Fund Class C Shares	BUCGX	NAS CM	Open End	Long/Short Equity (Growth & Income)	C+	C	B	Up	Y	1,000
CBOE Vest S&P 500® Buffer Strategy Cls Inst Shares	BUIGX	NAS CM	Open End	Long/Short Equity (Growth & Income)	C+	C	B	Up	Y	100,000
CBOE Vest S&P 500® Buffer Strategy Cls Investor Shares	BUMGX	NAS CM	Open End	Long/Short Equity (Growth & Income)	C+	C	B	Up	Y	1,000
CBOE Vest S&P 500® Buffer Strategy Fund Class Y Shares	BUYGX	NAS CM	Open End	Long/Short Equity (Growth & Income)	D-	D+	B		Y	10,000,000
CBOE Vest S&P 500® Enhanced Growth Strategy Cls A Shares	ENGAX	NAS CM	Open End	Long/Short Equity (Growth & Income)	C+	C	B	Up	Y	1,000
CBOE Vest S&P 500® Enhanced Growth Strategy Cls C Shares	ENGCX	NAS CM	Open End	Long/Short Equity (Growth & Income)	C+	C	B	Up	Y	1,000
CBOE Vest S&P 500® Enhanced Growth Strat Inst Cls Shares	ENGIX	NAS CM	Open End	Long/Short Equity (Growth & Income)	C+	C	B	Up	Y	100,000
CBOE Vest S&P 500® Enhanced Growth Strategy Inv Cls Shares	ENGLX	NAS CM	Open End	Long/Short Equity (Growth & Income)	C+	C	B	Up	Y	1,000
CBRE Clarion Global Real Estate Income Fund	IGR	NYSE	Closed End	Real Estate Sector Equity (Real Estate)	C	C	C+	Down	Y	
CC Real Estate Capital Income Fund C	XNCFX	NAS CM	Closed End	Real Estate Sector Equity (Real Estate)	D	D+	C		Y	4,000

★ Expanded analysis of this fund is included in Section II.

Min Additional Investment	3-Month Total Return	6-Month Total Return	1-Year Total Return	3-Year Total Return	5-Year Total Return	Dividend Yield (TTM)	Expense Ratio	3-Yr Std Deviation	3-Year Beta	NAV	Total Assets (MIL)	%Cash	%Stocks	%Bonds	%Other	Turnover Ratio	Last Bull Market Total Return	Last Bear Market Total Return	Front End Fee (%)	Back End Fee (%)	Inception Date
	TOTAL RETURNS					PERFORMANCE				ASSETS		ASSET ALLOCATION & TURNOVER					BULL & BEAR		FEES		
	0.40	11.62	-0.36	27.83	15.32	1.58	1.3	12.85	1.07	9.99	86.6	3	97	0	0	50	21.47	-22.88			Jan-11
	1.25	12.15	-3.17	28.11	5.55	2.24	1.05	11.86	1.01	12.92	193.4	3	97	0	0	35	19.13	-26.14			Dec-09
	1.26	12.05	-3.39	27.28	4.36	2.01	1.3	11.86	1.01	12.83	193.4	3	97	0	0	35	18.97	-26.26			Dec-09
	-0.62	11.59	-7.50	24.95		2.86	1.17	13.17	1.03	11.07	66.9	2	97	0	1	86					Oct-14
	-0.71	11.48	-7.74	24.10		2.62	1.42	13.1	1.03	11.07	66.9	2	97	0	1	86					Oct-14
	0.06	10.84	-4.72	23.70	2.51	2.48	0.88	12.35	1.06	15.02	6,685	2	98	0	0	30	18.76	-25.79			Oct-01
	0.00	10.69	-4.95	22.93	1.34	2.26	1.13	12.34	1.06	14.9	6,685	2	98	0	0	30	18.61	-25.94			Oct-01
50	3.76	22.51	-5.53	28.47	30.18	0	1.47	17.83	1.31	8	87.9	2	98	0	0	124			4.50		Mar-18
50	3.59	22.13	-6.23	25.62	25.34	0	2.25	17.79	1.31	12.69	87.9	2	98	0	0	124				1.00	Nov-13
50	3.81	22.74	-5.39	29.36	31.74	0	1.25	17.78	1.31	13.33	87.9	2	98	0	0	124					Oct-13
50	1.89	16.41	2.66	43.94	40.97	8.77	1.95	12.75	1.03	9.15	59.4	12	88	0	0				4.50		Apr-18
50	1.73	16.67	2.10	41.12	36.08	5.12	2.7	12.71	1.03	15.81	59.4	12	88	0	0					1.00	Sep-12
50	2.02	17.26	3.16	45.40	43.11	4.86	1.7	12.74	1.03	16.64	59.4	12	88	0	0						Sep-12
50	2.38	9.87	5.70	33.47	27.79		1.8	8.86	0.66	8.57	16.4	2	88	10	0	163			4.50		Oct-18
50	2.26	9.51	4.98	30.71	23.28	0.33	2.55	8.81	0.65	11.74	16.4	2	88	10	0	163				1.00	Sep-12
50	2.37	10.02	6.00	34.52	29.44	0.31	1.55	8.84	0.66	12.51	16.4	2	88	10	0	163					Sep-12
50	-2.57	5.38	-4.06	16.16	14.59	0.78	2.41	9.79	0.75	10.95	72.5	0	100	0	0	80				1.00	Sep-12
50	-2.42	5.74	-3.41	20.87	20.89	0.97	1.66	9.93	0.75	8.46	72.5	0	100	0	0	80			4.50		Apr-18
50	-2.34	5.90	-3.17	19.67	20.30	0.73	1.41	9.79	0.75	11.66	72.5	0	100	0	0	80					Sep-12
	2.92	12.05	6.08	23.14	29.24	1.12	1.24	6.52	0.51	13.36	47.4	3	54	43	0	37	14.07	-9.37	2.00		May-11
	2.83	11.76	5.42	20.63	24.81	0.62	1.91	6.54	0.52	13.36	47.4	3	54	43	0	37	13.57	-9.6		1.00	Dec-14
	3.06	12.33	6.48	24.36	31.22	1.58	0.88	6.51	0.51	13.44	47.4	3	54	43	0	37	14.25	-9.25			Dec-05
	2.93	12.14	6.22	23.40	29.83	1.34	1.14	6.53	0.52	13.4	47.4	3	54	43	0	37	14.06	-9.32			Jun-95
	-0.07	11.39	-8.30	18.37	14.89	1.1	1.28	10.73	0.75	13.08	41.3	24	48	24	0	157	26.03		2.00		Sep-11
	-0.23	10.97	-9.03	15.58	10.64	0.37	2.03	10.74	0.76	12.72	41.3	24	48	24	0	157	25.51			1.00	Dec-14
	0.00	11.53	-8.04	19.32	16.44	1.37	1.03	10.74	0.76	13.18	41.3	24	48	24	0	157	26.25				Sep-11
	-0.08	11.42	-8.34	18.25	14.79	1.1	1.28	10.73	0.75	13.03	41.3	24	48	24	0	157	26.14				Sep-11
	-5.84	7.06	-22.47	-10.65	-32.60	1.53	1.16	20.23	1.17	7.38	32.5	2	89	8	0	130			2.00		Feb-14
	-6.09	6.56	-23.11	-12.68	-35.09	0.66	1.91	20.18	1.16	7.31	32.5	2	89	8	0	130				1.00	Feb-14
	-5.90	7.03	-22.34	-9.96	-31.74	1.78	0.91	20.27	1.17	7.39	32.5	2	89	8	0	130					Feb-14
	-5.97	6.90	-22.49	-10.69	-32.74	1.51	1.16	20.16	1.16	7.38	32.5	2	89	8	0	130					Feb-14
	3.11	19.38	4.24			0.37	1.06			11.42	1.3	3	97	0	0	74			2.00		Dec-16
	3.24	19.14	3.45			0.07	1.81			11.14	1.3	3	97	0	0	74				1.00	Dec-16
	3.17	19.53	4.46			0.64	0.81			11.36	1.3	3	97	0	0	74					Dec-16
	3.08	19.45	4.27			0.28	1.06			11.36	1.3	3	97	0	0	74					Dec-16
100	2.67	15.64	12.17			1.4	1.2			11.12	61.7	0	100	0	0	206			5.75		Sep-17
100	2.41	15.08	11.08			0.56	1.95			11.08	61.7	0	100	0	0	206					Sep-17
	2.81	15.93	12.79				0.7			11.14	61.7	0	100	0	0	206					Jul-18
100	2.72	15.75	12.41			1.34	0.95			11.13	61.7	0	100	0	0	206					Sep-17
100	2.68	15.65	12.24			1.17	1.2			11.11	61.7	0	100	0	0	206					Sep-17
	4.86	21.95	9.82				0.71			12.5	38.2	1	99	0	0	0					Jul-18
100	3.00	11.57	6.35				1.2			12.34	67.4	0	100	0	0	0			5.75		Jul-18
100	2.78	11.22	4.99				1.95			12.19	67.4	0	100	0	0	0					Jul-18
100	2.99	11.74	6.54			0	0.95			12.37	67.4	0	100	0	0	0					Aug-16
100	2.93	11.52	6.31			0	1.2			12.29	67.4	0	100	0	0	0					Dec-16
	3.07	11.82					0.7			12.39	67.4	0	100	0	0	0					Jul-18
100	4.74	21.75	9.46			0	1.21			12.37	38.2	1	99	0	0	0			5.75		Jan-17
100	4.56	21.29	8.53				1.96			12.36	38.2	1	99	0	0	0					Jul-18
100	4.87	21.87	9.65			0	0.96			12.48	38.2	1	99	0	0	0					Dec-16
100	4.81	21.80	9.44			0	1.21			12.4	38.2	1	99	0	0	0					Jan-17
	1.51	19.04	8.99	12.16	17.97	2.13	0	11.33	0.99	8.64	1,007	0	94	0	-16	70	21.71	-15.27			Feb-04
100	-8.21	-3.54	-4.35			4.74	4.37			8.33	--										Feb-18

Fund Name	Ticker Symbol	Traded On	Fund Type	Category and (Prospectus Objective)	Overall Rating	Reward Rating	Risk Rating	Recent Up/ Downgrade	Open to New Investors	Min Initial Investment
	MARKET		FUND TYPE, CATEGORY & OBJECTIVE		RATINGS				MINIMUMS	
CC Real Estate Capital Income Fund Class A	XNAFX	NAS CM	Closed End	Real Estate Sector Equity (Real Estate)	C	C-	C+		Y	4,000
CC Real Estate Capital Income Fund Class I			Closed End	Real Estate Sector Equity (Real Estate)	C	C	B			100,000
CC Real Estate Capital Income Fund Class T	XNTFX	NAS CM	Closed End	Real Estate Sector Equity (Real Estate)	C	C-	C		Y	4,000
CC Real Estate Capital Income Master Fund			Closed End	Real Estate Sector Equity (Real Estate)	C-	C-	C		Y	0
CCA Aggressive Return Fund Institutional Class Shares	RSKIX	NAS CM	Open End	Moderate Alloc (Growth)	C+	C	B	Up	Y	100,000
CCM Alternative Income Fund Institutional Shares	CCMNX	NAS CM	Open End	Multialternative (Income)	B-	C	B		Y	1,000
Centaur Total Return Fund	TILDX	NAS CM	Open End	Cautious Alloc (Growth & Income)	C	C	B-		Y	1,500
Center Coast Brookfield Energy Infrastructure Fund Class Y	BEIYX	NAS CM	Open End	Energy Sector Equity (Growth & Income)	U	U	U		Y	1,000
Center Coast Brookfield MLP & NRG Inf Fd	CEN	NYSE	Closed End	Energy Sector Equity (Growth & Income)	D+	C-	D+	Down	Y	
Center Coast Brookfield MLP Focus Fund Class A	CCCAX	NAS CM	Open End	Energy Sector Equity (Growth & Income)	C-	D+	C-	Down	Y	1,000
Center Coast Brookfield MLP Focus Fund Class C	CCCCX	NAS CM	Open End	Energy Sector Equity (Growth & Income)	D+	D+	C-	Down	Y	1,000
Center Coast Brookfield MLP Focus Fund Class I	CCCZX	NAS CM	Open End	Energy Sector Equity (Growth & Income)	C-	C-	C-	Down	Y	1,000,000
Center Coast Brookfield MLP Focus Fund Class Y	CCCNX	NAS CM	Open End	Energy Sector Equity (Growth & Income)	C-	C-	C-	Down	Y	1,000
Centerstone International Fund Class A	CSIAX	NAS CM	Open End	Global Equity Large Cap (Growth)	C	D+	B-		Y	2,500
Centerstone International Fund Class C	CSINX	NAS CM	Open End	Global Equity Large Cap (Growth)	C	D+	B-	Up	Y	2,500
Centerstone International Fund Class I	CINTX	NAS CM	Open End	Global Equity Large Cap (Growth)	C	D+	B		Y	2,500
Centerstone Investors Fund Class A	CETAX	NAS CM	Open End	Moderate Alloc (Growth & Income)	C+	C	B	Up	Y	2,500
Centerstone Investors Fund Class C	CENNX	NAS CM	Open End	Moderate Alloc (Growth & Income)	C	C-	B		Y	2,500
Centerstone Investors Fund Class I	CENTX	NAS CM	Open End	Moderate Alloc (Growth & Income)	C+	C	B	Up	Y	2,500
Central Securities Corporation	CET	AMEX	Closed End	US Equity Large Cap Blend (Growth & Income)	B-	B	C-	Up	Y	
Centre American Select Equity Fund Institutional Class	DHANX	NAS CM	Open End	US Equity Large Cap Blend (Growth)	B-	C	B	Up	Y	1,000,000
Centre American Select Equity Fund Investor Class	DHAMX	NAS CM	Open End	US Equity Large Cap Blend (Growth)	B-	C	B	Up	Y	5,000
Centre Global Infrastructure Fund Institutional Class	DHINX	NAS CM	Open End	Infrastructure Sector Equity (World Stock)	D	C-	B-		Y	1,000,000
Centre Global Infrastructure Fund Investor Class	DHIVX	NAS CM	Open End	Infrastructure Sector Equity (World Stock)	D	C-	B-		Y	5,000
CG Core Total Return Fund Institutional Class	CGBNX	NAS CM	Open End	Aggressive Alloc (Growth)	C+	C	B	Up	Y	100,000
CGM Focus Fund	CGMFX	NAS CM	Open End	US Equity Large Cap Blend (Growth)	D	D	D	Down	Y	2,500
CGM Mutual Fund	LOMMX	NAS CM	Open End	Aggressive Alloc (Balanced)	C-	D+	C	Down	Y	2,500
CGM Realty Fund	CGMRX	NAS CM	Open End	US Equity Large Cap Blend (Real Estate)	C	C	C+	Down	Y	2,500
Chadwick & D'Amato Fund	CDFFX	NAS CM	Open End	Moderate Alloc (Growth)	C-	D+	C	Up	Y	250
Champlain Emerging Markets Fund Advisor Shares	CIPDX	NAS CM	Open End	Global Emerg Mkts (Div Emerging Mkts)	C	C	C		Y	10,000
Champlain Mid Cap Fund Advisor Class	CIPMX	NAS CM	Open End	US Equity Mid Cap (Growth)	B-	C+	B	Down	Y	10,000
Champlain Mid Cap Fund Institutional Class	CIPIX	NAS CM	Open End	US Equity Mid Cap (Growth)	B-	C+	B	Down	Y	1,000,000
Champlain Small Company Fund Class Advisor	CIPSX	NAS CM	Open End	US Equity Small Cap (Small Company)	C+	C	B-			10,000
Champlain Small Company Fund Institutional Class	CIPNX	NAS CM	Open End	US Equity Small Cap (Small Company)	C+	C	B-		Y	1,000,000
Charter Aggressive Growth Portfolio Class B			Open End	Aggressive Alloc (Asset Alloc)	B-	C	B	Up	Y	0
Charter Conservative Portfolio Class B			Open End	Cautious Alloc (Asset Alloc)	B	C	A-	Up	Y	0
Charter Growth Portfolio Class B			Open End	Moderate Alloc (Asset Alloc)	B-	C	B+	Up	Y	0
Charter Moderate Growth Portfolio Class B			Open End	Moderate Alloc (Asset Alloc)	B-	C	A-	Up	Y	0
Charter Moderate Portfolio Class B			Open End	Cautious Alloc (Asset Alloc)	B-	C	A-	Up	Y	0
Charter Small Cap Growth Portfolio Class A			Open End	US Equity Small Cap (Small Company)	C+	C+	C+	Down	Y	0
Charter Small Cap Growth Portfolio Class B			Open End	US Equity Small Cap (Small Company)	C+	C+	C+	Down	Y	0
Charter Small Cap Value Portfolio Class A			Open End	US Equity Small Cap (Small Company)	C	D+	C+		Y	0
Charter Small Cap Value Portfolio Class B			Open End	US Equity Small Cap (Small Company)	C	C-	C+		Y	0
Chartwell Mid Cap Value Fund	BERCX	NAS CM	Open End	US Equity Large Cap Value (Growth)	C+	C	B		Y	1,000
Chartwell Small Cap Growth Fund	CWSGX	NAS CM	Open End	US Equity Small Cap (Small Company)	C-	D+	C		Y	1,000
Chartwell Small Cap Value Fund	CWSIX	NAS CM	Open End	US Equity Small Cap (Small Company)	C	C	C+		Y	1,000
Chase Growth Fund Class Institutional	CHAIX	NAS CM	Open End	US Equity Large Cap Growth (Growth)	C+	C	B	Down	Y	1,000,000
Chase Growth Fund Class N Shares	CHASX	NAS CM	Open End	US Equity Large Cap Growth (Growth)	C+	C	B	Down	Y	2,000
Chase Mid Cap Growth Fund Class N	CHAMX	NAS CM	Open End	US Equity Mid Cap (Growth)	C+	C	B-	Down	Y	2,000
Chase Mid Cap Growth Fund Institutional Class	CHIMX	NAS CM	Open End	US Equity Mid Cap (Growth)	C+	C	B-	Down	Y	1,000,000
Chautauqua Global Growth Fund Institutional Class	CCGIX	NAS CM	Open End	Global Equity Large Cap (Growth)	C	C	C+		Y	25,000
Chautauqua Global Growth Fund Investor Class	CCGSX	NAS CM	Open End	Global Equity Large Cap (Growth)	C	C	C+		Y	2,500

★ Expanded analysis of this fund is included in Section II.

Min Additional Investment	TOTAL RETURNS 3-Month Total Return	6-Month Total Return	1-Year Total Return	3-Year Total Return	5-Year Total Return	PERFORMANCE Dividend Yield (TTM)	Expense Ratio	3-Yr Std Deviation	3-Year Beta	ASSETS NAV	Total Assets (MIL)	ASSET ALLOCATION & TURNOVER %Cash	%Stocks	%Bonds	%Other	Turnover Ratio	BULL & BEAR Last Bull Market Total Return	Last Bear Market Total Return	FEES Front End Fee (%)	Back End Fee (%)	Inception Date
100	-8.02	-3.25	-4.96			4.81	2.99			8.2	--								8.00		Jan-17
100	-0.44	3.85	2.85			4.98	2.99				--								0.00		Jan-17
100	-8.37	-3.79	-6.07			4.42	5.21			8.05	--										Jan-17
	-8.20	-3.60	-5.71			4.41	4.11			5.45	--										Jan-17
100	3.36	6.09	4.38	23.32	11.57	0.81	0.99	9.77	0.95	11.67	32.2	2	56	42	0	474					Dec-12
	0.76	4.65	3.21	13.00	8.89	4.92	1.85	3.5	32.44	9.28	55.5	3	27	32	0	71					May-13
100	0.96	8.13	-0.98	24.77	27.79	0	1.64	7.33	1.27	11.56	10.9	3	56	41	0	142	16.62	-15.4			Mar-05
100	-2.35	19.24					1.25			9.54	4.8	0	100	0	0						Sep-18
	-1.88	27.78	3.83	0.44	-31.00	0	2.45	25.3		7.96	268.3	1	89	0	11	33					Sep-13
100	-1.78	20.35	3.78	0.76	-17.60	10.67	1.46	17.74	1.05	6.41	2,409	1	99	0	0	35	10.68	-4.49	4.75		Dec-10
100	-1.96	19.71	2.95	-1.63	-20.73	11.79	2.21	17.8	1.06	5.8	2,409	1	99	0	0	35	10.14	-4.8		1.00	Dec-10
	-2.67	18.62	3.31	2.16	-17.84	10.43	1.21	17.69	1.05	6.56	2,409	1	99	0	0	35	10.8	-4.4			Feb-18
100	-1.59	20.63	4.01	1.43	-16.56	10.41	1.21	17.76	1.06	6.57	2,409	1	99	0	0	35	10.8	-4.4			Dec-10
100	3.92	12.43	2.94	20.17		1.07	1.37	9.58	0.8	11.39	201.9	6	82	7	5	34			5.00		May-16
100	3.77	12.03	2.16	18.11		0.44	2.12	9.6	0.81	11.26	201.9	6	82	7	5	34				1.00	May-16
100	3.91	12.53	3.13	21.10		1.33	1.12	9.59	0.8	11.4	201.9	6	82	7	5	34					May-16
100	4.12	14.73	4.69	21.06		0.81	1.37	9.09	0.76	11.6	420.1	6	77	8	6	34			5.00		May-16
100	3.98	14.35	3.94	18.86		0.36	2.12	9.07	0.76	11.47	420.1	6	77	8	6	34				1.00	May-16
100	4.20	14.89	4.90	22.07		1.01	1.12	9.1	0.76	11.65	420.1	6	77	8	6	34					May-16
	7.31	24.04	13.91	71.92	69.08	1.63		11.97	0.89	36.72	935.7	5	95	0	0	8	13.02	-18.34			Oct-29
10,000	0.27	12.44	2.07	37.87	45.06	0	0.93	11	0.84	10.84	114.5	1	99	0	0						Jan-14
1,000	0.09	12.22	1.50	36.52	43.35	0	1.45	11.01	0.84	10.74	114.5	1	99	0	0						Dec-11
10,000	3.80	17.94	8.16			2.46	1.17			10.1	12.1	1	99	0	0						Jan-18
1,000	3.65	17.60	7.86			2.29	1.34			10.08	12.1	1	99	0	0						Jan-18
100	2.46	15.18	1.86	49.98	42.31	0.4	1.03	13.18	-0.61	13.73	6.8	13	77	9	0	84					Dec-13
50	-8.18	-13.72	-21.15	1.75	-13.74	0.42	2.45	17.54	0.73	34.31	491.5	1	99	0	0	403	20.04	-27.53			Sep-97
50	-2.42	5.39	-0.62	23.14	15.63	1.02	1.15	12.63	0.72	27.71	324.0	4	72	24	0	362	20.61	-18.89			Nov-29
50	-1.13	9.64	-3.76	23.94	29.13	1.94	0.98	13.61	0.62	27.47	695.1	3	97	0	0	239	33.35	-22.49			May-94
50	0.60	10.78	-3.99	5.57	-5.58	0	2.72	12.22	2.1	9.96	43.6	-4	64	38	1	70	6.45	-14.6			Jun-10
	1.02	15.55	-2.37	26.21		0	1.5	14.39	0.91	9.88	4.0	3	97	0	0	35					Sep-14
	2.90	21.01	14.22	63.92	81.41	0	1.15	12.14	0.86	19.81	3,493	5	95	0	0	33	24.79	-18.44			Jun-08
	3.00	21.19	14.57	65.16	83.77	0	0.9	12.21	0.87	20.24	3,493	5	95	0	0	33	24.94	-18.28			Jan-11
	3.43	20.27	1.47	56.30	66.99	0	1.3	15.22	0.86	20.17	1,936	5	95	0	0	35	23.71	-18.95			Nov-04
	3.45	20.35	1.70	57.42	68.19	0	1.05	15.23	0.86	20.34	1,936	5	95	0	0	35	23.71	-18.95			Aug-16
	2.39	14.16	2.72	30.68	19.40	1.31	1.45	9.77		11.19	8.0	0	79	16	2	26					Oct-13
	2.43	8.55	4.95	16.68	14.39	1.85	1.25	4.16		10.55	38.7	3	23	65	0	12					Oct-13
	2.54	12.86	3.38	27.51	19.05	1.42	1.4	8.32		10.94	18.2	-1	66	29	1	10					Oct-13
	2.53	11.55	3.96	24.38	18.88	1.61	1.35	7.01		10.96	33.7	-1	53	42	1	14					Oct-13
	2.57	10.34	4.51	21.41	17.34	1.77	1.25	5.77		10.81	35.7	1	40	52	1	13					Oct-13
	3.73	28.42	5.95	74.25	58.96	3.2	1.45	17.9	1	15.79	111.3	1	99	0	0	10	21.33	-29.33			Jan-08
	3.60	28.06	5.28	72.72	57.73	3.25	1.45	17.87	1	15.49	111.3	1	99	0	0	10	21.4	-29.61			Dec-98
	-0.05	18.29	-5.25	42.93	14.38	1.23	1.45	17.3	0.95	17.96	159.8	1	99	0	0	12	25.06	-26.26			Oct-02
	-0.11	18.28	-5.30	42.89	14.37	1.23	1.45	17.31	0.95	17.97	159.8	1	99	0	0	12	25.01	-26.34			Jan-98
100	4.60	18.24	5.13	43.41	26.87	0.71	1.05	13.82	0.98	15.23	24.2	5	95	0	0	65	25.94	-18.66			May-02
100	3.65	24.30	3.09			0	1.06			12.48	22.0	6	94	0	0	97					Jun-17
100	3.01	14.77	-4.72	34.84	30.42	0.39	1.05	16.65	0.95	18.1	175.8	4	96	0	0	19					Mar-12
1,000	5.38	20.58	7.90	48.86	60.76	0	1.11	11.85	0.86	13.71	71.7	3	97	0	0	62	24.59	-15.76			Jan-07
250	5.39	20.55	7.79	48.40	59.49	0	1.26	11.83	0.86	13.08	71.7	3	97	0	0	62	24.41	-15.88			Dec-97
250	4.23	24.59	8.01	52.17	56.33	0	1.34	13.72	0.93	40.12	22.1	3	97	0	0	87	23.2	-15.13			Aug-02
1,000	4.26	24.68	8.14	52.81	57.73	0	1.19	13.73	0.93	41.07	22.1	3	97	0	0	87	23.23	-15.13			Feb-12
	5.01	22.97	3.57	50.59		0.02	0.8	15.3	1.21	13.81	50.2	5	95	0	0	38					Apr-16
100	4.98	22.86	3.33	49.38		0	1.05	15.23	1.2	13.7	50.2	5	95	0	0	38					Apr-16

	MARKET		FUND TYPE, CATEGORY & OBJECTIVE		RATINGS				MINIMUMS	
Fund Name	Ticker Symbol	Traded On	Fund Type	Category and (Prospectus Objective)	Overall Rating	Reward Rating	Risk Rating	Recent Up/ Downgrade	Open to New Investors	Min Initial Investment
Chautauqua International Growth Fund Institutional Class	CCWIX	NAS CM	Open End	Global Equity Large Cap (Growth)	C	C-	C+	Up	Y	25,000
Chautauqua International Growth Fund Investor Class	CCWSX	NAS CM	Open End	Global Equity Large Cap (Growth)	C	C-	C+	Up	Y	2,500
Chesapeake Growth Fund	CHCGX	NAS CM	Open End	US Equity Large Cap Growth (Growth)	C+	C	B-		Y	2,500
China Fund, Inc.	CHN	NYSE	Closed End	Greater China Equity (Pacific Stock)	C-	C-	C-	Down	Y	
Chiron Capital Allocation Fund Class I	CCAPX	NAS CM	Open End	Moderate Alloc (Growth & Income)	C	C-	C+		Y	100,000
Chiron SMid Opportunities Fund Class I Shares	CSMOX	NAS CM	Open End	Global Equity Mid/Small Cap (Growth)	C-	D	C+	Up	Y	100,000
Chou Income Fund	CHOIX	NAS CM	Open End	Cautious Alloc (Income)	D	D	D+	Down	Y	5,000
Chou Opportunity Fund	CHOEX	NAS CM	Open End	Moderate Alloc (Growth)	D	D	D	Down	Y	5,000
Christopher Weil & Company Core Investment Fund	CWCFX	NAS CM	Open End	US Equity Large Cap Growth (Growth)	B-	C	B		Y	3,500
CIBC Atlas All Cap Growth Fund Institutional Class	AWGIX	NAS CM	Open End	US Equity Large Cap Growth (Growth)	B-	B-	B-	Down	Y	250,000
CIBC Atlas Disciplined Equity Fund Institutional Class	AWEIX	NAS CM	Open End	US Equity Large Cap Blend (World Stock)	B-	C+	B+	Down	Y	250,000
CIBC Atlas Equity Income Fund Institutional Class	AWYIX	NAS CM	Open End	US Equity Large Cap Growth (Equity-Income)	B	C+	B+		Y	250,000
CIBC Atlas Income Opportunities Fund Institutional Class	AWIIX	NAS CM	Open End	Moderate Alloc (Income)	B	C+	A-		Y	250,000
CIBC Atlas Mid Cap Equity Fund Institutional Class	AWMIX	NAS CM	Open End	US Equity Mid Cap (Equity-Income)	B-	C+	B		Y	250,000
City National Rochdale Dividend & Income Fund Class N	RIMHX	NAS CM	Open End	US Equity Large Cap Value (Equity-Income)	C+	C	B		Y	0
City National Rochdale Select Strategies Fund Class 1	CNRLX	NAS CM	Closed End	Equity Miscellaneous (Growth & Income)	C-	D+	B-	Up	Y	1,000,000
City National Rochdale U.S. Core Equity Cls Institutional	CNRUX	NAS CM	Open End	US Equity Large Cap Growth (Growth)	B	B	B+		Y	1,000,000
City National Rochdale U.S. Core Equity Fund Class N	CNRWX	NAS CM	Open End	US Equity Large Cap Growth (Growth)	B	B-	B+		Y	0
City National Rochdale U.S. Core Equity Cls Servicing	CNRVX	NAS CM	Open End	US Equity Large Cap Growth (Growth)	B	B-	B+		Y	0
Clarkston Founders Fund Institutional Class	CIMDX	NAS CM	Open End	US Equity Mid Cap (Growth)	C	C	B		Y	10,000
Clarkston Fund Institutional Class	CILGX	NAS CM	Open End	US Equity Large Cap Blend (Growth)	B-	C	B+		Y	10,000
Clarkston Partners Fund Founders Class	CFSMX	NAS CM	Open End	US Equity Mid Cap (Growth)	B-	C	B+	Up	Y	100,000,000
Clarkston Partners Fund Institutional Class	CISMX	NAS CM	Open End	US Equity Mid Cap (Growth)	B-	C	B+	Up	Y	25,000
ClearBridge Aggressive Growth Fund Class A	SHRAX	NAS CM	Open End	US Equity Large Cap Growth (Aggr Growth)	C	C	B-	Down	Y	1,000
ClearBridge Aggressive Growth Fund Class C	SAGCX	NAS CM	Open End	US Equity Large Cap Growth (Aggr Growth)	C	C	B-	Down	Y	1,000
ClearBridge Aggressive Growth Fund Class FI	LMPFX	NAS CM	Open End	US Equity Large Cap Growth (Aggr Growth)	C	C	B-	Down	Y	0
ClearBridge Aggressive Growth Fund Class I	SAGYX	NAS CM	Open End	US Equity Large Cap Growth (Aggr Growth)	C+	C	B-		Y	1,000,000
ClearBridge Aggressive Growth Fund Class IS	LSIFX	NAS CM	Open End	US Equity Large Cap Growth (Aggr Growth)	C+	C	B-		Y	1,000,000
ClearBridge Aggressive Growth Fund Class R	LMPRX	NAS CM	Open End	US Equity Large Cap Growth (Aggr Growth)	C	C	B-	Down	Y	0
ClearBridge All Cap Value Fund Class A	SHFVX	NAS CM	Open End	US Equity Large Cap Value (Growth)	C+	C	B-	Up	Y	1,000
ClearBridge All Cap Value Fund Class C	SFVCX	NAS CM	Open End	US Equity Large Cap Value (Growth)	C+	C	B-	Up	Y	1,000
ClearBridge All Cap Value Fund Class I	SFVYX	NAS CM	Open End	US Equity Large Cap Value (Growth)	C+	C	B-	Up	Y	1,000,000
ClearBridge All Cap Value Fund Class IS	LSISX	NAS CM	Open End	US Equity Large Cap Value (Growth)	C+	C	B-	Up	Y	1,000,000
ClearBridge Appreciation Fund Class A	SHAPX	NAS CM	Open End	US Equity Large Cap Blend (Growth)	B	C+	B+		Y	1,000
ClearBridge Appreciation Fund Class C	SAPCX	NAS CM	Open End	US Equity Large Cap Blend (Growth)	B-	C+	B+	Down	Y	1,000
ClearBridge Appreciation Fund Class FI	LMPIX	NAS CM	Open End	US Equity Large Cap Blend (Growth)	B	C+	B+		Y	0
ClearBridge Appreciation Fund Class I	SAPYX	NAS CM	Open End	US Equity Large Cap Blend (Growth)	B	B-	B+		Y	1,000,000
ClearBridge Appreciation Fund Class IS	LMESX	NAS CM	Open End	US Equity Large Cap Blend (Growth)	B	B-	B+		Y	1,000,000
ClearBridge Appreciation Fund Class R	LMPPX	NAS CM	Open End	US Equity Large Cap Blend (Growth)	B	C+	B+		Y	0
ClearBridge Dividend Strategy Fund Class 1	LCBOX	NAS CM	Open End	US Equity Large Cap Blend (Equity-Income)	B	B-	B+		Y	0
ClearBridge Dividend Strategy Fund Class A	SOPAX	NAS CM	Open End	US Equity Large Cap Blend (Equity-Income)	B	B-	B+		Y	1,000
ClearBridge Dividend Strategy Fund Class C	SBPLX	NAS CM	Open End	US Equity Large Cap Blend (Equity-Income)	B	B-	B+		Y	1,000
ClearBridge Dividend Strategy Fund Class FI	LBRIX	NAS CM	Open End	US Equity Large Cap Blend (Equity-Income)	B	B-	B+		Y	0
ClearBridge Dividend Strategy Fund Class I	SOPYX	NAS CM	Open End	US Equity Large Cap Blend (Equity-Income)	B	B-	B+		Y	1,000,000
ClearBridge Dividend Strategy Fund Class IS	LCBEX	NAS CM	Open End	US Equity Large Cap Blend (Equity-Income)	B	B-	B+		Y	1,000,000
ClearBridge Dividend Strategy Fund Class R	LMMRX	NAS CM	Open End	US Equity Large Cap Blend (Equity-Income)	B	B-	B+		Y	0
ClearBridge Energy Midstream Opportunity Fund	EMO	NYSE	Closed End	Energy Sector Equity (Natl Res)	C-	D+	C-	Down	Y	
ClearBridge International Growth Fund Class A	LGGAX	NAS CM	Open End	Global Equity Large Cap (Growth)	C+	C	B	Up	Y	1,000
ClearBridge International Growth Fund Class C	LMGTX	NAS CM	Open End	Global Equity Large Cap (Growth)	C+	C	B-	Up	Y	1,000
ClearBridge International Growth Fund Class FI	LMGFX	NAS CM	Open End	Global Equity Large Cap (Growth)	C+	C	B	Up	Y	0
ClearBridge International Growth Fund Class I	LMGNX	NAS CM	Open End	Global Equity Large Cap (Growth)	C+	C	B	Up	Y	1,000,000
ClearBridge International Growth Fund Class IS	LMGPX	NAS CM	Open End	Global Equity Large Cap (Growth)	C+	C	B-	Up	Y	1,000,000

★ Expanded analysis of this fund is included in Section II.

Min Additional Investment	3-Month Total Return	6-Month Total Return	1-Year Total Return	3-Year Total Return	5-Year Total Return	Dividend Yield (TTM)	Expense Ratio	3-Yr Std Deviation	3-Year Beta	NAV	Total Assets (MIL)	%Cash	%Stocks	%Bonds	%Other	Turnover Ratio	Last Bull Market Total Return	Last Bear Market Total Return	Front End Fee (%)	Back End Fee (%)	Inception Date
TOTAL RETURNS						PERFORMANCE				ASSETS		ASSET ALLOCATION & TURNOVER					BULL & BEAR		FEES		
	5.88	20.59	-0.82	34.79		0.46	0.8	14.89	1.14	12.24	155.4	7	93	0	0	42					Apr-16
100	5.81	20.43	-1.12	33.93		0.21	1.05	14.83	1.14	12.2	155.4	7	93	0	0	42					Apr-16
500	3.88	18.04	2.68	55.27	60.40	0	1.9	14.21	1.09	36.38	36.7	10	90	0	0	122	29.22	-22.85			Sep-97
	-1.43	22.13	2.01	49.50	34.01	0.73	0	18.42	1.1	22.7	249.8	1	99	0	0	50	6.12	-24.29			Jul-92
	2.28	8.19	-3.55	20.94		1.3	1.11	7.42	0.56	11.68	1,509	14	36	45	5						Nov-15
	4.17	16.90	0.22			0.5	1.2			10.78	11.6	5	95	0	0						Oct-17
500	-9.60	2.04	-10.77	-4.77	-26.12	4.08	1.2	10.39	0.95	5.63	7.1	35	9	34	0	11	10.07	-11.18			Jul-10
500	-21.18	-6.32	-22.42	-5.75	-38.32	4.28	1.2	20.87	1.01	6.66	17.5	7	65	28	0	13	16.23	-25.64			Jul-10
100	6.42	18.21	6.75	45.71	42.03	0	1.23	12.31	0.92	14.41	40.1	12	88	0	0	50					Dec-11
	7.45	28.08	12.65	73.24	84.60	0	1.1	14.75	1.04	29.83	185.4	5	95	0	0	4	22.31	-18.71			Sep-07
	5.28	19.94	14.17	56.12	73.61	1.43	0.76	12.35	1	21.11	1,146	3	97	0	0	19	24.12	-13.59			Dec-05
	5.78	19.41	14.87	48.80	44.55	0.87	1.1	10.72	0.84	40.33	127.5	3	97	0	0	3	22.72	-13.1			Apr-10
	4.11	15.07	10.77	35.22	39.40	2.44	0.75	8.44	0.67	12.06	404.1	4	65	29	0	19					Jun-14
	5.15	25.44	13.36	45.56	64.34	0	0.85	13.46	0.91	16.12	715.6	3	97	0	0	9					Jun-14
	2.55	14.35	9.98	14.34	35.31	2.75	1.14	9.01	0.63	39.41	235.8	3	92	0	0	10	14.73	-8.54			Jun-99
	-0.48	-0.48	5.27			0	1			10.18	--	100	0	0	0						Jul-17
	7.27	23.41	15.14	60.95	72.38	0.94	0.52	10.96	0.88	18.76	314.9	2	98	0	0	18					Dec-12
	7.17	23.20	14.63	58.60	68.05	0.51	1.02	10.97	0.88	18.55	314.9	2	98	0	0	18					Dec-12
	7.22	23.30	14.88	59.75	70.21	0.73	0.77	10.96	0.88	18.58	314.9	2	98	0	0	18					Dec-12
	2.71	14.51	3.98			0.71	0.95			11.36	41.9	26	74	0	0	9					Jan-17
	4.90	20.28	11.99	32.29		2.1	0.7	10.08	0.79	12.19	52.2	8	92	0	0	11					Apr-16
	3.18	15.14	2.87	34.38		0.71	0.85	10.45	0.64	12.62	919.6	22	78	0	0	23					Sep-15
	3.11	15.10	2.76	33.85		0.68	1	10.39	0.64	12.57	919.6	22	78	0	0	23					Sep-15
50	1.79	14.19	-1.95	30.40	22.44	0.19	1.12	16.26	1.08	179.85	7,898	0	100	0	0	0	28.57	-19.64	5.75		Oct-83
50	1.61	13.79	-2.64	27.72	18.25	0	1.79	16.25	1.08	137.07	7,898	0	100	0	0	0	28.09	-19.85		1.00	May-93
	1.82	14.20	-1.92	30.46	22.46	0.17	1.11	16.26	1.08	181.01	7,898	0	100	0	0	0	28.55	-19.64			Apr-07
	1.88	14.38	-1.62	31.66	24.37	0.42	0.8	16.27	1.08	201.92	7,898	0	100	0	0	0	28.88	-19.49			Jan-96
	1.90	14.42	-1.56	32.00	24.99	0.5	0.71	16.27	1.08	204.37	7,898	0	100	0	0	0	28.97	-19.45			Aug-08
	1.73	14.03	-2.23	29.25	20.65	0	1.41	16.26	1.08	174.98	7,898	0	100	0	0	0	28.42	-19.71			Dec-06
50	1.93	16.92	1.01	36.27	32.24	0.73	1.19	14.68	1.17	12.8	1,612	0	100	0	0	16	24.75	-24.3	5.75		Nov-81
50	1.91	16.75	0.38	33.68	28.03	0.22	1.82	14.69	1.17	10.82	1,612	0	100	0	0	16	24.44	-24.56		1.00	Aug-93
	2.03	17.13	1.28	37.85	34.82	1.05	0.81	14.67	1.17	13.69	1,612	0	100	0	0	16	25.15	-24.21			Jan-96
	1.96	17.16	1.36	37.18	33.13	1.12	0.71	14.67	1.17	13.67	1,612	0	100	0	0	16	24.75	-24.3			Sep-17
50	5.90	19.13	14.59	46.52	61.29	0.91	0.97	11.01	0.88	25.65	6,450	2	98	0	0	8	23.36	-15.31	5.75		Mar-70
50	5.70	18.69	13.80	43.44	55.70	0.29	1.65	11	0.88	24.63	6,450	2	98	0	0	8	22.75	-15.53		1.00	Feb-93
	5.87	19.06	14.49	46.31	61.01	0.81	1	10.99	0.88	25.79	6,450	2	98	0	0	8	23.28	-15.29			Dec-08
	5.94	19.27	14.91	47.81	63.62	1.2	0.67	10.98	0.88	25.49	6,450	2	98	0	0	8	23.57	-15.18			Jan-96
	5.96	19.31	15.02	48.20	64.38	1.27	0.58	11.01	0.88	25.57	6,450	2	98	0	0	8	23.64	-15.15			Aug-08
	5.83	18.92	14.27	45.11	58.73	0.55	1.28	10.99	0.88	25.58	6,450	2	98	0	0	8	23.22	-15.45			Dec-06
	5.56	20.53	15.48	46.02	58.51	1.61	0.77	10.81	0.86	24.54	6,398	2	98	0	0	14	21.12	-11.4			Apr-11
50	5.50	20.38	15.18	44.80	56.34	1.36	1.06	10.79	0.86	24.53	6,398	2	98	0	0	14	20.98	-11.51	5.75		Nov-92
50	5.32	19.89	14.36	41.79	51.01	0.74	1.75	10.81	0.86	24.16	6,398	2	98	0	0	14	20.4	-11.71		1.00	Jun-98
	5.55	20.37	15.25	44.76	56.25	1.43	1.07	10.78	0.86	24.48	6,398	2	98	0	0	14	20.98	-11.51			May-13
	5.59	20.52	15.52	46.15	58.72	1.6	0.74	10.8	0.86	25.22	6,398	2	98	0	0	14	21.24	-11.34			Feb-96
	5.60	20.58	15.61	46.46	59.35	1.65	0.68	10.8	0.86	25.25	6,398	2	98	0	0	14	20.98	-11.51			Apr-13
	5.41	20.12	14.77	43.53	54.17	1.08	1.38	10.77	0.86	24.36	6,398	2	98	0	0	14	20.83	-11.6			Feb-12
	-1.91	26.29	0.85	1.46	-39.39	2.7	1.78	21.01		10.55	756.6	0	100	0	0	14	23.46				Jun-11
50	6.38	22.00	4.93	54.82	46.94	0.02	1.16	12.28	1.01	46.8	1,681	1	99	0	0	31	25.63	-17.54	5.75		Feb-09
50	6.17	21.54	4.14	51.32	41.52	0	1.91	12.27	1.01	43.49	1,681	1	99	0	0	31	25.05	-17.8		1.00	Apr-95
	6.38	21.99	4.93	54.79	46.94	0.01	1.16	12.29	1.01	48.8	1,681	1	99	0	0	31	25.65	-17.57			Jan-04
	6.46	22.19	5.23	56.04	48.86	0.19	0.89	12.3	1.02	50.59	1,681	1	99	0	0	31	25.83	-17.48			Mar-04
	6.48	22.22	5.04	52.63	42.75		0.81	12.26	1.01	50.59	1,681	1	99	0	0	31	25.05	-17.8			Sep-18

	MARKET			FUND TYPE, CATEGORY & OBJECTIVE	RATINGS				MINIMUMS	
Fund Name	Ticker Symbol	Traded On	Fund Type	Category and (Prospectus Objective)	Overall Rating	Reward Rating	Risk Rating	Recent Up/ Downgrade	Open to New Investors	Min Initial Investment
ClearBridge International Growth Fund Class R	LMGRX	NAS CM	Open End	Global Equity Large Cap (Growth)	C+	C	B-	Up	Y	0
ClearBridge International Small Cap Fund Class A	LCOAX	NAS CM	Open End	Global Equity Mid/Small Cap (Small Company)	D+	D	C-	Down	Y	1,000
ClearBridge International Small Cap Fund Class A2	LCRNX	NAS CM	Open End	Global Equity Mid/Small Cap (Small Company)	D+	D	C-	Down	Y	1,000
ClearBridge International Small Cap Fund Class C	LCOCX	NAS CM	Open End	Global Equity Mid/Small Cap (Small Company)	D+	D	D+	Down	Y	1,000
ClearBridge International Small Cap Fund Class I	LCOIX	NAS CM	Open End	Global Equity Mid/Small Cap (Small Company)	D+	D	C-	Down	Y	1,000,000
ClearBridge International Small Cap Fund Class IS	CBISX	NAS CM	Open End	Global Equity Mid/Small Cap (Small Company)	D+	D	C-	Down	Y	1,000,000
ClearBridge International Value Fund Class A	SBIEX	NAS CM	Open End	Global Equity Large Cap (Foreign Stock)	D+	D	C-		Y	1,000
ClearBridge International Value Fund Class C	SBICX	NAS CM	Open End	Global Equity Large Cap (Foreign Stock)	D+	D	D+		Y	1,000
ClearBridge International Value Fund Class I	SBIYX	NAS CM	Open End	Global Equity Large Cap (Foreign Stock)	D+	D	C-		Y	1,000,000
ClearBridge International Value Fund Class IS	LSIUX	NAS CM	Open End	Global Equity Large Cap (Foreign Stock)	D+	D	C-		Y	1,000,000
ClearBridge International Value Fund Class R	LIORX	NAS CM	Open End	Global Equity Large Cap (Foreign Stock)	D+	D	C-		Y	0
ClearBridge Large Cap Growth Fund Class A	SBLGX	NAS CM	Open End	US Equity Large Cap Growth (Growth)	B-	C+	B	Down	Y	1,000
ClearBridge Large Cap Growth Fund Class C	SLCCX	NAS CM	Open End	US Equity Large Cap Growth (Growth)	B-	C+	B	Down	Y	1,000
ClearBridge Large Cap Growth Fund Class I	SBLYX	NAS CM	Open End	US Equity Large Cap Growth (Growth)	B-	C+	B	Down	Y	1,000,000
ClearBridge Large Cap Growth Fund Class IS	LSITX	NAS CM	Open End	US Equity Large Cap Growth (Growth)	B-	C+	B	Down	Y	1,000,000
ClearBridge Large Cap Growth Fund Class O	LCMMX	NAS CM	Open End	US Equity Large Cap Growth (Growth)	B-	C+	B	Down	Y	0
ClearBridge Large Cap Growth Fund Class R	LMPLX	NAS CM	Open End	US Equity Large Cap Growth (Growth)	B-	C+	B	Down	Y	0
ClearBridge Large Cap Value Fund Class 1	LCLIX	NAS CM	Open End	US Equity Large Cap Value (Growth & Income)	B-	C	B		Y	0
ClearBridge Large Cap Value Fund Class A	SINAX	NAS CM	Open End	US Equity Large Cap Value (Growth & Income)	B-	C	B	Up	Y	1,000
ClearBridge Large Cap Value Fund Class A2	LIVVX	NAS CM	Open End	US Equity Large Cap Value (Growth & Income)	B-	C	B	Up	Y	1,000
ClearBridge Large Cap Value Fund Class C	SINOX	NAS CM	Open End	US Equity Large Cap Value (Growth & Income)	B-	C	B	Up	Y	1,000
ClearBridge Large Cap Value Fund Class I	SAIFX	NAS CM	Open End	US Equity Large Cap Value (Growth & Income)	B-	C	B		Y	1,000,000
ClearBridge Large Cap Value Fund Class IS	LMLSX	NAS CM	Open End	US Equity Large Cap Value (Growth & Income)	B-	C	B		Y	1,000,000
ClearBridge Large Cap Value Fund Class R	LCBVX	NAS CM	Open End	US Equity Large Cap Value (Growth & Income)	B-	C	B	Up	Y	0
ClearBridge Mid Cap Fund Class 1	SMCPX	NAS CM	Open End	US Equity Mid Cap (Growth)	C+	C	B			0
ClearBridge Mid Cap Fund Class A	SBMAX	NAS CM	Open End	US Equity Mid Cap (Growth)	C+	C	B		Y	1,000
ClearBridge Mid Cap Fund Class C	SBMLX	NAS CM	Open End	US Equity Mid Cap (Growth)	C+	C	B	Up	Y	1,000
ClearBridge Mid Cap Fund Class I	SMBYX	NAS CM	Open End	US Equity Mid Cap (Growth)	C+	C	B		Y	1,000,000
ClearBridge Mid Cap Fund Class IS	LSIRX	NAS CM	Open End	US Equity Mid Cap (Growth)	C+	C	B		Y	1,000,000
ClearBridge Mid Cap Fund Class R	LMREX	NAS CM	Open End	US Equity Mid Cap (Growth)	C+	C	B		Y	0
ClearBridge Mid Cap Growth Fund Class A	LBGAX	NAS CM	Open End	US Equity Mid Cap (Growth)	C+	C	B	Down	Y	1,000
ClearBridge Mid Cap Growth Fund Class A2	LCBGX	NAS CM	Open End	US Equity Mid Cap (Growth)	C+	C+	B	Down	Y	1,000
ClearBridge Mid Cap Growth Fund Class C	LBGCX	NAS CM	Open End	US Equity Mid Cap (Growth)	C+	C	B		Y	1,000
ClearBridge Mid Cap Growth Fund Class I	LBGIX	NAS CM	Open End	US Equity Mid Cap (Growth)	C+	C+	B	Down	Y	1,000,000
ClearBridge Mid Cap Growth Fund Class IS	LCMIX	NAS CM	Open End	US Equity Mid Cap (Growth)	C+	C+	B	Down	Y	1,000,000
ClearBridge Mid Cap Growth Fund Class R	LCMRX	NAS CM	Open End	US Equity Mid Cap (Growth)	C+	C	B		Y	0
ClearBridge MLP and Midstream Fund Inc.	CEM	NYSE	Closed End	Energy Sector Equity (Natl Res)	C	C-	C		Y	
ClearBridge MLP and Midstream TR Fund Inc.	CTR	NYSE	Closed End	Energy Sector Equity (Growth & Income)	C-	C-	D+	Down	Y	
ClearBridge Select Fund Class A	LCLAX	NAS CM	Open End	US Equity Mid Cap (Growth)	B-	C+	B	Down	Y	1,000
ClearBridge Select Fund Class A2	LCLTX	NAS CM	Open End	US Equity Mid Cap (Growth)	B-	C+	B	Down	Y	1,000
ClearBridge Select Fund Class C	LCLCX	NAS CM	Open End	US Equity Mid Cap (Growth)	B-	C+	B	Down	Y	1,000
ClearBridge Select Fund Class FI	LCBSX	NAS CM	Open End	US Equity Mid Cap (Growth)	B-	C+	B	Down	Y	0
ClearBridge Select Fund Class I	LBFIX	NAS CM	Open End	US Equity Mid Cap (Growth)	B-	C+	B	Down	Y	1,000,000
ClearBridge Select Fund Class IS	LCSSX	NAS CM	Open End	US Equity Mid Cap (Growth)	B-	C+	B	Down	Y	1,000,000
ClearBridge Small Cap Fund Class A	LMSAX	NAS CM	Open End	US Equity Small Cap (Small Company)	C+	C	B-	Down	Y	1,000
ClearBridge Small Cap Fund Class A2	LBRTX	NAS CM	Open End	US Equity Small Cap (Small Company)	C+	C	B-	Down	Y	1,000
ClearBridge Small Cap Fund Class C	LMASX	NAS CM	Open End	US Equity Small Cap (Small Company)	C+	C	B-		Y	1,000
ClearBridge Small Cap Fund Class FI	LGASX	NAS CM	Open End	US Equity Small Cap (Small Company)	C+	C	B-	Down	Y	0
ClearBridge Small Cap Fund Class I	LMNSX	NAS CM	Open End	US Equity Small Cap (Small Company)	C+	C	B	Down	Y	1,000,000
ClearBridge Small Cap Fund Class IS	LISGX	NAS CM	Open End	US Equity Small Cap (Small Company)	C+	C	B	Down	Y	1,000,000
ClearBridge Small Cap Fund Class R	LMARX	NAS CM	Open End	US Equity Small Cap (Small Company)	C+	C	B-		Y	0
ClearBridge Small Cap Growth Fund Class 1	LMPMX	NAS CM	Open End	US Equity Small Cap (Small Company)	C+	C+	C+	Down		0

★ Expanded analysis of this fund is included in Section II.

	TOTAL RETURNS					PERFORMANCE				ASSETS		ASSET ALLOCATION & TURNOVER					BULL & BEAR		FEES		
Min Additional Investment	3-Month Total Return	6-Month Total Return	1-Year Total Return	3-Year Total Return	5-Year Total Return	Dividend Yield (TTM)	Expense Ratio	3-Yr Std Deviation	3-Year Beta	NAV	Total Assets (MIL)	%Cash	%Stocks	%Bonds	%Other	Turnover Ratio	Last Bull Market Total Return	Last Bear Market Total Return	Front End Fee (%)	Back End Fee (%)	Inception Date
	6.32	21.87	4.67	53.70	45.09	0	1.41	12.28	1.01	47.25	1,681	1	99	0	0	31	25.47	-17.65			Dec-06
50	-1.03	6.79	-12.63	13.61	-1.84	1.77	1.42	13.52	1.05	12.41	74.7	3	97	0	0	43	15.5	-20.9	5.75		Oct-10
50	-1.05	6.71	-12.78	12.92	-2.68	2.11	1.62	13.56	1.05	12.24	74.7	3	97	0	0	43	15.5	-20.89	5.75		Aug-14
50	-1.21	6.39	-13.23	11.11	-5.42	1.37	2.17	13.5	1.05	12.15	74.7	3	97	0	0	43	14.99	-21.1		1.00	Oct-10
	-0.95	7.04	-12.30	14.68	-0.32	2.61	1.07	13.54	1.05	12.46	74.7	3	97	0	0	43	15.67	-20.81			Oct-10
	-0.95	7.04	-12.23	15.00	0.11	2.78	0.97	13.49	1.04	12.46	74.7	3	97	0	0	43	15.67	-20.81			May-15
50	-0.10	8.34	-9.70	14.04	-10.57	1.36	1.26	14.76	1.24	9.74	335.3	1	99	0	0	24	14.2	-21.48	5.75		Feb-86
50	-0.25	7.85	-10.37	11.40	-13.86	0.85	2.01	14.7	1.24	7.96	335.3	1	99	0	0	24	13.64	-21.68		1.00	Jan-93
	-0.10	8.38	-9.50	15.07	-8.96	1.85	0.91	14.72	1.24	9.57	335.3	1	99	0	0	24	14.57	-21.35			Dec-06
	0.00	8.42	-9.43	15.50	-8.52	1.87	0.81	14.7	1.24	9.78	335.3	1	99	0	0	24	14.47	-21.3			Aug-08
	-0.20	8.12	-10.00	13.16	-11.63	0.45	1.51	14.71	1.24	9.71	335.3	1	99	0	0	24	14.03	-21.56			Jan-14
50	5.09	22.65	13.28	62.86	90.06	0	1.05	13.09	0.94	47.42	14,233	4	96	0	0	20	24.63	-15.48	5.75		Aug-97
50	4.92	22.21	12.48	59.42	83.29	0	1.74	13.11	0.94	37.52	14,233	4	96	0	0	20	24.09	-15.77		1.00	Aug-97
	5.20	22.85	13.63	64.34	93.01	0.24	0.76	13.11	0.94	52.78	14,233	4	96	0	0	20	24.87	-15.4			Oct-97
	5.21	22.91	13.75	64.78	93.73	0.33	0.66	13.1	0.94	52.84	14,233	4	96	0	0	20	24.63	-15.48			Mar-13
50	5.21	22.88	13.68	64.55	93.05	0.28	0.71	13.1	0.94	52.83	14,233	4	96	0	0	20	24.63	-15.48			Dec-14
	5.02	22.48	12.93	61.46	87.30	0	1.36	13.09	0.94	45.32	14,233	4	96	0	0	20	24.39	-15.61			Dec-06
	5.36	19.40	9.90	37.47	41.51	1.57	0.6	12.21	0.99	33.04	1,676	5	95	0	0	10	26.33	-16.62			Aug-13
50	5.31	19.28	9.66	36.62	40.09	1.37	0.81	12.2	0.99	33.06	1,676	5	95	0	0	10	26.12	-16.74	5.75		Jan-95
50	5.27	19.17	9.51	36.02	38.98	1.24	0.95	12.22	0.99	33.03	1,676	5	95	0	0	10	26.14	-16.71	5.75		Aug-13
50	5.11	18.86	8.87	33.61	34.90	0.7	1.54	12.2	0.99	32.06	1,676	5	95	0	0	10	25.55	-17		1.00	Jan-95
	5.36	19.40	9.96	37.81	42.15	1.64	0.52	12.2	0.99	32.98	1,676	5	95	0	0	10	26.33	-16.62			May-58
	5.37	19.43	10.01	38.01	42.57	1.69	0.47	12.21	0.99	32.99	1,676	5	95	0	0	10	26.33	-16.62			Oct-13
	5.19	18.97	9.03	34.96	36.78	0.78	1.19	12.17	0.98	33.1	1,676	5	95	0	0	10	25.96	-16.79			Dec-13
	4.56	23.21	7.10	37.57	37.61	0.45	0.82	14.72	1.07	35.61	1,972	1	99	0	0	21	33.24	-24.44			Sep-00
50	4.49	23.05	6.76	36.25	35.51	0.16	1.15	14.7	1.07	34.05	1,972	1	99	0	0	21	33.05	-24.52	5.75		Sep-98
50	4.33	22.66	6.05	33.48	30.91	0	1.82	14.71	1.07	26.79	1,972	1	99	0	0	21	32.45	-24.72		1.00	Sep-98
	4.55	23.23	7.10	37.61	37.78	0.4	0.83	14.7	1.07	37.97	1,972	1	99	0	0	21	33.31	-24.38			Dec-98
	4.59	23.29	7.21	38.04	38.50	0.5	0.73	14.72	1.07	38.32	1,972	1	99	0	0	21	33.31	-24.36			Aug-08
	4.42	22.87	6.47	35.15	33.71	0	1.43	14.71	1.07	33.14	1,972	1	99	0	0	21	32.74	-24.63			Sep-08
50	6.28	27.93	14.57	56.97	55.96	0	1.2	15.65	1.07	30.27	90.8	4	96	0	0	21	41.94	-25.1	5.75		Aug-10
50	6.25	27.88	14.39	56.05	54.48	0	1.4	15.66	1.07	29.9	90.8	4	96	0	0	21	42	-25.15	5.75		Dec-13
50	6.10	27.50	13.73	53.31	50.10	0	1.95	15.66	1.07	28	90.8	4	96	0	0	21	41.44	-25.4		1.00	Aug-10
	6.36	28.12	14.89	58.21	58.11	0	0.85	15.66	1.07	31.07	90.8	4	96	0	0	21	42.2	-25.07			Aug-10
	6.39	28.15	14.98	58.34	58.39	0	0.75	15.68	1.07	31.13	90.8	4	96	0	0	21	42.2	-25.07			Sep-13
	6.25	27.84	14.28	55.02	53.18	0	1.45	15.63	1.07	29.57	90.8	4	96	0	0	21	41.79	-25.23			Sep-13
	-1.25	23.67	0.66	6.45	-32.41	3.36	5.63	20.7	1.2	13.43	945.7	0	100	0	0	14	18.61	-8.58			Jun-10
	-0.90	27.95	-0.44	0.07	-37.07	2.54	1.78	21.53		10.69	410.5	1	99	0	0	15					Jun-12
50	4.31	23.55	11.15	107.41	109.90	0	1.59	14.72	0.98	27.07	603.6	19	81	0	0	27			5.75		Sep-13
50	4.31	23.48	11.21	107.47	110.34		1.58	14.72	0.98	27.08	603.6	19	81	0	0	27			5.75		Sep-18
50	4.15	23.07	10.38	102.75	102.03	0	2.34	14.68	0.98	25.82	603.6	19	81	0	0	27				1.00	Sep-13
	4.32	23.57	11.16	107.10	109.88	0	1.59	14.72	0.98	27.05	603.6	19	81	0	0	27					Nov-12
	4.43	23.73	11.50	109.04	112.99	0	1.24	14.72	0.98	27.79	603.6	19	81	0	0	27					Nov-12
	4.40	23.76	11.56	109.44	113.71	0	1.14	14.74	0.98	27.76	603.6	19	81	0	0	27					Nov-12
50	2.64	21.14	3.41	45.70	52.57	0	1.23	16.72	0.95	39.65	1,249	3	97	0	0	48	27.53	-30.24	5.75		Feb-09
50	2.61	21.04	3.24	44.87	50.99	0	1.27	16.7	0.95	39.22	1,249	3	97	0	0	48	26.97	-30.49	5.75		Aug-14
50	2.44	20.69	2.67	42.49	46.84	0	1.94	16.7	0.95	36.92	1,249	3	97	0	0	48	26.97	-30.49		1.00	Dec-85
	2.61	21.09	3.34	45.19	51.47	0	1.36	16.71	0.95	58.37	1,249	3	97	0	0	48	27.47	-30.3			Jul-04
	2.69	21.29	3.69	46.75	54.29	0	0.98	16.71	0.95	61.68	1,249	3	97	0	0	48	27.74	-30.19			Dec-94
	2.70	21.34	3.78	45.18	49.60	0	0.87	16.69	0.95	61.8	1,249	3	97	0	0	48	26.97	-30.49			Sep-17
	2.56	20.94	3.06	44.45	49.96	0	1.55	16.71	0.95	56.82	1,249	3	97	0	0	48	27.2	-30.37			Dec-06
	4.91	21.58	5.94	78.26	67.92	0	0.93	16.42	0.9	36.95	3,963	3	97	0	0	15	37.5	-22.6			Mar-07

	MARKET		FUND TYPE, CATEGORY & OBJECTIVE		RATINGS				MINIMUMS	
Fund Name	Ticker Symbol	Traded On	Fund Type	Category and (Prospectus Objective)	Overall Rating	Reward Rating	Risk Rating	Recent Up/ Downgrade	Open to New Investors	Min Initial Investment
ClearBridge Small Cap Growth Fund Class A	SASMX	NAS CM	Open End	US Equity Small Cap (Small Company)	C+	C+	C+	Down		1,000
ClearBridge Small Cap Growth Fund Class C	SCSMX	NAS CM	Open End	US Equity Small Cap (Small Company)	C+	C+	C+	Down		1,000
ClearBridge Small Cap Growth Fund Class FI	LMPSX	NAS CM	Open End	US Equity Small Cap (Small Company)	C+	C+	C+	Down		0
ClearBridge Small Cap Growth Fund Class I	SBPYX	NAS CM	Open End	US Equity Small Cap (Small Company)	C+	C+	C+	Down		1,000,000
ClearBridge Small Cap Growth Fund Class IS	LMOIX	NAS CM	Open End	US Equity Small Cap (Small Company)	C+	C+	C+	Down		1,000,000
ClearBridge Small Cap Growth Fund Class R	LMPOX	NAS CM	Open End	US Equity Small Cap (Small Company)	C+	C+	C+	Down		0
ClearBridge Small Cap Value Fund Class A	SBVAX	NAS CM	Open End	US Equity Small Cap (Small Company)	C	C-	C		Y	1,000
ClearBridge Small Cap Value Fund Class C	SBVLX	NAS CM	Open End	US Equity Small Cap (Small Company)	C-	C-	C		Y	1,000
ClearBridge Small Cap Value Fund Class I	SMCYX	NAS CM	Open End	US Equity Small Cap (Small Company)	C	C-	C		Y	1,000,000
ClearBridge Small Cap Value Fund Class IS	LCBIX	NAS CM	Open End	US Equity Small Cap (Small Company)	C	C-	C		Y	1,000,000
ClearBridge Sustainability Leaders Fund Class A	CLSUX	NAS CM	Open End	US Equity Large Cap Growth (Growth)	B-	C+	B	Down	Y	1,000
ClearBridge Sustainability Leaders Fund Class FI	LCSTX	NAS CM	Open End	US Equity Large Cap Growth (Growth)	B-	C+	B	Down	Y	0
ClearBridge Sustainability Leaders Fund Class I	LCISX	NAS CM	Open End	US Equity Large Cap Growth (Growth)	B-	C+	B	Down	Y	1,000,000
ClearBridge Sustainability Leaders Fund Class IS	LCILX	NAS CM	Open End	US Equity Large Cap Growth (Growth)	B-	C+	B	Down	Y	1,000,000
ClearBridge Tactical Dividend Income Fund Class A	CFLGX	NAS CM	Open End	US Equity Large Cap Value (Equity-Income)	C+	C	B	Down	Y	1,000
ClearBridge Tactical Dividend Income Fund Class A2	LBDAX	NAS CM	Open End	US Equity Large Cap Value (Equity-Income)	C+	C	B	Down	Y	1,000
ClearBridge Tactical Dividend Income Fund Class C	SMDLX	NAS CM	Open End	US Equity Large Cap Value (Equity-Income)	C+	C	B		Y	1,000
ClearBridge Tactical Dividend Income Fund Class I	LADIX	NAS CM	Open End	US Equity Large Cap Value (Equity-Income)	C+	C	B	Down	Y	1,000,000
ClearBridge Tactical Dividend Income Fund Class IS	LCBDX	NAS CM	Open End	US Equity Large Cap Value (Equity-Income)	C+	C	B	Down	Y	1,000,000
ClearBridge Value Trust Class A	LGVAX	NAS CM	Open End	US Equity Large Cap Blend (Growth)	C+	C	B		Y	1,000
ClearBridge Value Trust Class C	LMVTX	NAS CM	Open End	US Equity Large Cap Blend (Growth)	C+	C	B		Y	1,000
ClearBridge Value Trust Class FI	LMVFX	NAS CM	Open End	US Equity Large Cap Blend (Growth)	C+	C	B		Y	0
ClearBridge Value Trust Class I	LMNVX	NAS CM	Open End	US Equity Large Cap Blend (Growth)	C+	C	B		Y	1,000,000
ClearBridge Value Trust Class R	LMVRX	NAS CM	Open End	US Equity Large Cap Blend (Growth)	C+	C	B		Y	0
Clifford Capital Partners Fund Institutional Class	CLIFX	NAS CM	Open End	US Equity Mid Cap (Growth)	C	C-	B	Down	Y	100,000
Clifford Capital Partners Fund Investor Class	CLFFX	NAS CM	Open End	US Equity Mid Cap (Growth)	C	C-	B	Down	Y	2,500
Clipper Fund	CFIMX	NAS CM	Open End	US Equity Large Cap Blend (Growth)	C	C	B-		Y	2,500
Clough China Fund Class A	CHCAX	NAS CM	Open End	Greater China Equity (Pacific Stock)	C-	D+	C		Y	2,500
Clough China Fund Class C	CHNCX	NAS CM	Open End	Greater China Equity (Pacific Stock)	C-	D+	C		Y	2,500
Clough China Fund Class I	CHNIX	NAS CM	Open End	Greater China Equity (Pacific Stock)	C-	D+	C		Y	100,000
Clough China Fund Class Investor	CHNAX	NAS CM	Open End	Greater China Equity (Pacific Stock)	C-	D+	C		Y	2,500
Clough Global Dividend and Income Fund	GLV	AMEX	Closed End	Moderate Alloc (Multi-Asset Global)	C	C	C-		Y	
Clough Global Equity Fund	GLQ	AMEX	Closed End	Global Equity Large Cap (World Stock)	C	C	C-		Y	
Clough Global Long/Short Fund Class A	CLOVX	NAS CM	Open End	Long/Short Equity (Growth)	C	C	C+		Y	2,500
Clough Global Long/Short Fund Class C	CLOCX	NAS CM	Open End	Long/Short Equity (Growth)	C	C-	C	Up	Y	2,500
Clough Global Long/Short Fund Class I	CLOIX	NAS CM	Open End	Long/Short Equity (Growth)	C	C	C+		Y	1,000,000
Clough Global Long/Short Fund Investor Class	CLOAX	NAS CM	Open End	Long/Short Equity (Growth)	C	C	C+		Y	2,500
Clough Global Opportunities Fund	GLO	AMEX	Closed End	Moderate Alloc (Multi-Asset Global)	C	C	C+		Y	
CM Advisors Small Cap Value Fund	CMOVX	NAS CM	Open End	US Equity Small Cap (Small Company)	D+	D+	C-	Down	Y	2,500
CMG Mauldin Core Fund Class A Shares	GEFAX	NAS CM	Open End	Global Equity Large Cap (Growth)	C+	C	B	Up	Y	5,000
CMG Mauldin Core Fund Class I Shares	GEFIX	NAS CM	Open End	Global Equity Large Cap (Growth)	C+	C	B	Up	Y	15,000
CMG Tactical All Asset Strategy Fund Class A Shares	CMGQX	NAS CM	Open End	Multialternative (Growth)	D+	D	C	Down	Y	5,000
CMG Tactical All Asset Strategy Fund Class I Shares	CMGHX	NAS CM	Open End	Multialternative (Growth)	C-	D+	C		Y	15,000
Cognios Large Cap Growth Fund Institutional Class	COGEX	NAS CM	Open End	US Equity Large Cap Growth (Growth)	C+	C	B	Up	Y	100,000
Cognios Large Cap Growth Fund Investor Class	COGGX	NAS CM	Open End	US Equity Large Cap Growth (Growth)	C+	C	B	Up	Y	1,000
Cognios Large Cap Value Fund Institutional Class	COGVX	NAS CM	Open End	US Equity Large Cap Value (Growth)	B-	C	B	Up	Y	100,000
Cognios Large Cap Value Fund Investor Class	COGLX	NAS CM	Open End	US Equity Large Cap Value (Growth)	B-	C	B	Up	Y	1,000
Cognios Market Neutral Large Cap Fund Institutional Class	COGIX	NAS CM	Open End	Market Neutral (Growth)	C-	C-	C	Down	Y	100,000
Cognios Market Neutral Large Cap Fund Investor Class	COGMX	NAS CM	Open End	Market Neutral (Growth)	C-	C-	C	Down	Y	1,000
Cohen & Steers Alternative Income Fund Class A	DVFAX	NAS CM	Open End	US Equity Large Cap Value (Equity-Income)	B-	C	B		Y	0
Cohen & Steers Alternative Income Fund Class C	DVFCX	NAS CM	Open End	US Equity Large Cap Value (Equity-Income)	B-	C	B	Up	Y	0
Cohen & Steers Alternative Income Fund Class Institutional	DVFIX	NAS CM	Open End	US Equity Large Cap Value (Equity-Income)	B-	C	B		Y	100,000

★ Expanded analysis of this fund is included in Section II.

	TOTAL RETURNS					PERFORMANCE				ASSETS		ASSET ALLOCATION & TURNOVER					BULL & BEAR		FEES		
Min Additional Investment	3-Month Total Return	6-Month Total Return	1-Year Total Return	3-Year Total Return	5-Year Total Return	Dividend Yield (TTM)	Expense Ratio	3-Yr Std Deviation	3-Year Beta	NAV	Total Assets (MIL)	%Cash	%Stocks	%Bonds	%Other	Turnover Ratio	Last Bull Market Total Return	Last Bear Market Total Return	Front End Fee (%)	Back End Fee (%)	Inception Date
50	4.88	21.45	5.69	77.11	66.10	0	1.19	16.42	0.9	35.83	3,963	3	97	0	0	15	37.33	-22.7	5.75		Jul-98
50	4.65	20.99	4.91	73.36	60.30	0	1.89	16.41	0.9	27.66	3,963	3	97	0	0	15	36.54	-22.98		1.00	Jul-98
	4.85	21.40	5.67	77.22	66.25	0	1.19	16.42	0.9	36.07	3,963	3	97	0	0	15	37.29	-22.66			Dec-07
	4.91	21.60	5.95	78.65	68.68	0	0.9	16.43	0.9	38.67	3,963	3	97	0	0	15	37.71	-22.53			Nov-04
	4.95	21.68	6.09	79.30	69.84	0	0.78	16.44	0.9	39.17	3,963	3	97	0	0	15	37.72	-22.54			Aug-08
	4.80	21.24	5.36	75.64	63.91	0	1.47	16.42	0.9	34.7	3,963	3	97	0	0	15	37.16	-22.72			Dec-06
50	1.86	18.12	-9.71	23.88	12.55	0.24	1.35	19.68	1.12	16.19	129.7	2	97	0	0	30	28.46	-26.96	5.75		Feb-99
50	1.74	17.81	-10.30	21.49	8.80	0	2.01	19.62	1.11	12.07	129.7	2	97	0	0	30	27.83	-27.24		1.00	Feb-99
	1.99	18.37	-9.38	25.19	14.60	0.46	1	19.67	1.12	17.75	129.7	2	97	0	0	30	28.62	-26.83			Apr-03
	1.98	18.38	-9.31	25.58	15.16	0.55	0.9	19.65	1.11	17.8	129.7	2	97	0	0	30	28.46	-26.96			May-13
50	6.56	22.16	14.78	56.00		0.21	1.2	12.61	0.98	14.44	10.4	0	100	0	0	14			5.75		Nov-15
	6.54	22.09	14.75	56.29		0.15	1.2	12.55	0.98	14.48	10.4	0	100	0	0	14					Mar-15
	6.66	22.45	15.23	57.90		0.45	0.85	12.61	0.98	14.56	10.4	0	100	0	0	14					Mar-15
	6.65	22.41	15.22	57.98		0.46	0.75	12.58	0.98	14.58	10.4	0	100	0	0	14					Mar-15
50	4.10	19.19	13.63	23.11	12.35	4.49	1.67	10.81	0.92	17.41	349.0	1	93	0	1	21	20.51	-21.45	5.75		Oct-90
50	4.09	19.15	13.52	22.67	11.68	4.42	1.76	10.83	0.92	17.35	349.0	1	93	0	1	21	20.51	-21.45	5.75		Jun-13
50	3.94	18.74	12.79	20.37	8.30	4.03	2.4	10.84	0.92	16.5	349.0	1	93	0	1	21	20.11	-21.74		1.00	Sep-00
	4.14	19.35	13.94	24.03	13.75	4.74	1.4	10.8	0.92	17.53	349.0	1	93	0	1	21	20.77	-21.42			May-08
	4.15	19.40	13.96	24.02	13.82	4.76	1.38	10.82	0.92	17.52	349.0	1	93	0	1	21	20.51	-21.45			May-13
50	2.44	19.19	4.69	34.18	35.50	0.46	1.06	14.72	1.14	82.58	1,870	1	99	0	0	27	24	-18.11	5.75		Feb-09
50	2.25	18.78	3.97	31.42	30.77	0	1.74	14.71	1.14	80.64	1,870	1	99	0	0	27	23.44	-18.4		0.95	Apr-82
	2.40	19.12	4.60	33.85	34.93	0.39	1.13	14.72	1.14	94.05	1,870	1	99	0	0	27	23.99	-18.16			Mar-01
	2.48	19.33	4.93	35.16	37.07	0.65	0.8	14.72	1.14	97.29	1,870	1	99	0	0	27	24.12	-18			Dec-94
	2.33	18.98	4.32	32.83	33.11	0	1.4	14.71	1.14	92.82	1,870	1	99	0	0	27	23.66	-18.29			Dec-06
1,000	-2.65	15.69	1.33	45.12	53.44	0.99	0.91	14.76	1.1	14.67	27.4	6	94	0	0	20					Jan-14
100	-2.72	15.64	1.14	44.38	51.84	0.71	1.11	14.76	1.1	14.64	27.4	6	94	0	0	20					Jan-14
25	3.82	17.61	-0.63	38.04	50.22	0.27	0.71	14.87	1.14	112.32	1,065	3	94	0	3	24	18.57	-13.97			Feb-84
	-5.49	9.42	-14.07	21.47	12.97	0	1.95	19.3	0.96	21.48	38.1	7	93	0	0	131	15.67	-24.21	5.50		Jun-18
	-5.64	9.08	-14.68	18.81	8.47	0	2.7	19.31	0.96	20.06	38.1	7	93	0	0	131	15.17	-24.44		1.00	Dec-05
	-5.42	9.61	-13.83	22.42	14.42	0	1.7	19.31	0.96	22.12	38.1	7	93	0	0	131	15.84	-24.13			Dec-05
	-5.54	9.42	-14.07	21.48	12.65	0	1.95	19.3	0.96	21.48	38.1	7	93	0	0	131	15.69	-24.21	5.50		Dec-05
	2.12	11.18	2.94	19.79	10.93	0.84	0	8.46	0.98	12.43	87.1	-9	68	32	2	109	18.09	-20.89			Jul-04
	2.78	19.78	1.03	42.27	24.90	0.18	0	14.16	0.95	13.66	150.6	-6	97	2	2	115	18.62	-21.92			Apr-05
0	1.91	12.24	-5.57	20.75		0	2.42	10.17	0.72	11.18	52.8	45	54	1	0	156			5.50		Jun-18
	1.76	11.86	-6.25	18.01		0	3.07	10.14	0.72	10.94	52.8	45	54	1	0	156				1.00	Sep-15
	2.07	12.42	-5.27	21.74		0	2.07	10.2	0.72	11.31	52.8	45	54	1	0	156					Sep-15
	1.91	12.24	-5.57	20.60		0	2.42	10.17	0.72	11.18	52.8	45	54	1	0	156			5.50		Sep-15
	2.65	17.69	-0.25	27.79	15.35	0.06	0	12.48		10.72	345.4	-13	91	17	2	120	17.81	-21.16			Apr-06
	-0.37	16.15	-20.88	10.99	-13.81	0	1.26	27.33	1.34	10.57	77.3	8	92	0	0	31	25.51	-22.22			Apr-11
1,000	1.57	5.97	1.49	12.08	3.63	0	1.74	5.78	0.43	10.99	65.9	6	48	39	5	220			5.75		May-13
1,000	1.65	6.14	1.73	12.82	4.76	0.06	1.55	5.76	0.43	11.05	65.9	6	48	39	5	220					May-13
1,000	-0.99	0.10	-2.94	1.85		0	1.54	4.84	0.45	9.9	32.3	9	30	50	0	627			5.75		Apr-16
1,000	-0.99	0.20	-2.73	2.41		0	1.45	4.91	0.45	9.94	32.3	9	30	50	0	627					Apr-16
	3.37	20.26	9.63			0.13	0.9			13.47	45.5	4	96	0	0	221					Oct-16
	3.31	20.14	9.41			0	1.15			13.42	45.5	4	96	0	0	221					Oct-16
	4.08	22.30	12.55			1.73	0.85			9.43	20.5	3	97	0	0	84					Oct-16
	4.07	22.59	12.89			1.69	1.1			9.44	20.5	3	97	0	0	84					Oct-16
	-2.49	-2.77	-2.77	-1.05	16.55	0	3.24	7.15	0.23	10.17	92.4	68	32	0	0	104					Dec-12
	-2.53	-2.91	-3.00	-1.75	15.04	0	3.49	7.13	0.23	10	92.4	68	32	0	0	104					Dec-12
	3.87	17.72	9.27	41.28	44.74	1.3	1	12.68		11.89	49.9	1	99	0	0	158	23.83	-16.83	4.50		Aug-05
	3.69	17.32	8.55	38.51	40.03	0.58	1.65	12.66		11.8	49.9	1	99	0	0	158	23.32	-17.04		1.00	Aug-05
	3.96	17.96	9.69	42.81	47.33	1.6	0.65	12.67		11.92	49.9	1	99	0	0	158	24.14	-16.67			Aug-05

	MARKET			FUND TYPE, CATEGORY & OBJECTIVE	RATINGS				MINIMUMS	
Fund Name	Ticker Symbol	Traded On	Fund Type	Category and (Prospectus Objective)	Overall Rating	Reward Rating	Risk Rating	Recent Up/ Downgrade	Open to New Investors	Min Initial Investment
Cohen & Steers Alternative Income Fund Class R	DVFRX	NAS CM	Open End	US Equity Large Cap Value (Equity-Income)	B-	C	B	Up	Y	0
Cohen & Steers Alternative Income Fund Class Z	DVFZX	NAS CM	Open End	US Equity Large Cap Value (Equity-Income)	B-	C	B		Y	0
Cohen & Steers Closed-End Opportunity Fund	FOF	NYSE	Closed End	Moderate Alloc (Growth & Income)	C	C+	C-		Y	
Cohen & Steers Global Income Builder Inc	INB	NYSE	Closed End	Global Equity Large Cap (World Stock)	C	C	C-		Y	
Cohen & Steers Global Infrastructure Fund, Inc. Class A	CSUAX	NAS CM	Open End	Infrastructure Sector Equity (Utility)	B	B-	B		Y	0
Cohen & Steers Global Infrastructure Fund, Inc. Class C	CSUCX	NAS CM	Open End	Infrastructure Sector Equity (Utility)	B-	C+	B	Down	Y	0
Cohen & Steers Global Infrastructure Fund, Inc. Class I	CSUIX	NAS CM	Open End	Infrastructure Sector Equity (Utility)	B	B-	B		Y	100,000
Cohen & Steers Global Infrastructure Fund, Inc. Class R	CSURX	NAS CM	Open End	Infrastructure Sector Equity (Utility)	B	B-	B		Y	0
Cohen & Steers Global Infrastructure Fund, Inc. Class Z	CSUZX	NAS CM	Open End	Infrastructure Sector Equity (Utility)	B	B-	B		Y	0
Cohen & Steers Global Realty Shares, Inc. Class A	CSFAX	NAS CM	Open End	Real Estate Sector Equity (Real Estate)	B	C+	B+		Y	0
Cohen & Steers Global Realty Shares, Inc. Class C	CSFCX	NAS CM	Open End	Real Estate Sector Equity (Real Estate)	B-	C+	B+		Y	0
Cohen & Steers Global Realty Shares, Inc. Class I	CSSPX	NAS CM	Open End	Real Estate Sector Equity (Real Estate)	B	C+	B+		Y	100,000
Cohen & Steers Global Realty Shares, Inc. Class R	GRSRX	NAS CM	Open End	Real Estate Sector Equity (Real Estate)	B	C+	B+		Y	0
Cohen & Steers Global Realty Shares, Inc. Class Z	CSFZX	NAS CM	Open End	Real Estate Sector Equity (Real Estate)	B	C+	B+		Y	0
Cohen & Steers Infrastructure Fund	UTF	NYSE	Closed End	Infrastructure Sector Equity (Utility)	B	B	C+		Y	
Cohen & Steers Institutional Realty Shares	CSRIX	NAS CM	Open End	Real Estate Sector Equity (Real Estate)	B-	C+	B-		Y	1,000,000
Cohen & Steers International Realty Fund Class A	IRFAX	NAS CM	Open End	Real Estate Sector Equity (Real Estate)	B	C+	B+	Up	Y	0
Cohen & Steers International Realty Fund Class C	IRFCX	NAS CM	Open End	Real Estate Sector Equity (Real Estate)	B	C+	B+	Up	Y	0
Cohen & Steers International Realty Fund Class I	IRFIX	NAS CM	Open End	Real Estate Sector Equity (Real Estate)	B	B-	B+	Up	Y	100,000
Cohen & Steers International Realty Fund Class R	IRFRX	NAS CM	Open End	Real Estate Sector Equity (Real Estate)	B	C+	B+	Up	Y	0
Cohen & Steers International Realty Fund Class Z	IRFZX	NAS CM	Open End	Real Estate Sector Equity (Real Estate)	B	B-	B+	Up	Y	0
Cohen & Steers Limited Dur Preferred & Income Fund, Inc	LDP	NYSE	Closed End	US Fixed Income (Growth & Income)	C	C+	C-	Up	Y	
Cohen & Steers Low Duration Preferred & Income Cls A	LPXAX	NAS CM	Open End	US Fixed Income (Income)	B	C+	A-	Up	Y	0
Cohen & Steers Low Duration Preferred & Income Cls C	LPXCX	NAS CM	Open End	US Fixed Income (Income)	B-	C	B+	Up	Y	0
Cohen & Steers Low Duration Preferred & Income Cls I	LPXIX	NAS CM	Open End	US Fixed Income (Income)	B	C+	A-		Y	100,000
Cohen & Steers Low Duration Preferred & Income Cls R	LPXRX	NAS CM	Open End	US Fixed Income (Income)	B	C+	A-	Up	Y	0
Cohen & Steers Low Duration Preferred & Income Cls Z	LPXZX	NAS CM	Open End	US Fixed Income (Income)	B	C+	A-		Y	0
Cohen & Steers MLP & Energy Opportunity Fund, Inc. Class A	MLOAX	NAS CM	Open End	Energy Sector Equity (Growth & Income)	C	C-	C+	Down	Y	0
Cohen & Steers MLP & Energy Opportunity Fund, Inc. Class C	MLOCX	NAS CM	Open End	Energy Sector Equity (Growth & Income)	C	C-	C	Down	Y	0
Cohen & Steers MLP & Energy Opportunity Fund, Inc. Class I	MLOIX	NAS CM	Open End	Energy Sector Equity (Growth & Income)	C	C-	C+	Down	Y	100,000
Cohen & Steers MLP & Energy Opportunity Fund, Inc. Class R	MLORX	NAS CM	Open End	Energy Sector Equity (Growth & Income)	C	C-	C+	Down	Y	0
Cohen & Steers MLP & Energy Opportunity Fund, Inc. Class Z	MLOZX	NAS CM	Open End	Energy Sector Equity (Growth & Income)	C	C-	C+	Down	Y	0
Cohen & Steers MLP Income & Energy Opportunity Fund, Inc.	MIE	NYSE	Closed End	Energy Sector Equity (Natl Res)	C-	C-	C	Down	Y	
Cohen & Steers Preferred Sec & Income Fund, Inc. Cls A	CPXAX	NAS CM	Open End	US Fixed Income (Growth & Income)	B	B-	B	Up	Y	0
Cohen & Steers Preferred Sec & Income Fund, Inc. Cls C	CPXCX	NAS CM	Open End	US Fixed Income (Growth & Income)	B-	C+	B	Up	Y	0
Cohen & Steers Preferred Sec & Income Fund, Inc. Cls F	CPXFX	NAS CM	Open End	US Fixed Income (Growth & Income)	B	B-	B	Up	Y	0
Cohen & Steers Preferred Sec & Income Fund, Inc. Cls I	CPXIX	NAS CM	Open End	US Fixed Income (Growth & Income)	B	B-	B	Up	Y	100,000
Cohen & Steers Preferred Sec & Income Fund, Inc. Cls R	CPRRX	NAS CM	Open End	US Fixed Income (Growth & Income)	B	B-	B	Up	Y	0
Cohen & Steers Preferred Sec & Income Fund, Inc. Cls Z	CPXZX	NAS CM	Open End	US Fixed Income (Growth & Income)	B	B-	B	Up	Y	0
Cohen & Steers Preferred Securities and Income SMA Shares	PISHX	NAS CM	Open End	US Fixed Income (Growth & Income)	U	U	U		Y	0
Cohen & Steers Quality Income Realty Fund	RQI	NYSE	Closed End	Real Estate Sector Equity (Real Estate)	C+	C	C+		Y	
Cohen & Steers Real Assets Fund Inc Class A	RAPAX	NAS CM	Open End	Moderate Alloc (Asset Alloc)	C+	C	B		Y	0
Cohen & Steers Real Assets Fund Inc Class C	RAPCX	NAS CM	Open End	Moderate Alloc (Asset Alloc)	C+	C	B	Up	Y	0
Cohen & Steers Real Assets Fund Inc Class I	RAPIX	NAS CM	Open End	Moderate Alloc (Asset Alloc)	C+	C	B+		Y	100,000
Cohen & Steers Real Assets Fund Inc Class R	RAPRX	NAS CM	Open End	Moderate Alloc (Asset Alloc)	C+	C	B		Y	0
Cohen & Steers Real Assets Fund Inc Class Z	RAPZX	NAS CM	Open End	Moderate Alloc (Asset Alloc)	C+	C	B+		Y	0
Cohen & Steers Real Estate Securities Fund, Inc. Class A	CSEIX	NAS CM	Open End	Real Estate Sector Equity (Real Estate)	C+	C+	B-	Down	Y	0
Cohen & Steers Real Estate Securities Fund, Inc. Class C	CSCIX	NAS CM	Open End	Real Estate Sector Equity (Real Estate)	C+	C	B-	Down	Y	0
Cohen & Steers Real Estate Securities Fund, Inc. Class F	CREFX	NAS CM	Open End	Real Estate Sector Equity (Real Estate)	B-	C+	B-		Y	0
Cohen & Steers Real Estate Securities Fund, Inc. Cls Inst	CSDIX	NAS CM	Open End	Real Estate Sector Equity (Real Estate)	B-	C+	B-		Y	100,000
Cohen & Steers Real Estate Securities Fund, Inc. Class R	CIRRX	NAS CM	Open End	Real Estate Sector Equity (Real Estate)	C+	C+	B-	Down	Y	0
Cohen & Steers Real Estate Securities Fund, Inc. Class Z	CSZIX	NAS CM	Open End	Real Estate Sector Equity (Real Estate)	B-	C+	B-		Y	0

★ Expanded analysis of this fund is included in Section II.

Min Additional Investment	TOTAL RETURNS: 3-Month Total Return	6-Month Total Return	1-Year Total Return	3-Year Total Return	5-Year Total Return	PERFORMANCE: Dividend Yield (TTM)	Expense Ratio	3-Yr Std Deviation	3-Year Beta	ASSETS: NAV	Total Assets (MIL)	ASSET ALLOCATION & TURNOVER: %Cash	%Stocks	%Bonds	%Other	Turnover Ratio	BULL & BEAR: Last Bull Market Total Return	Last Bear Market Total Return	FEES: Front End Fee (%)	Back End Fee (%)	Inception Date
	3.83	17.69	9.17	40.69	43.72	1.16	1.15	12.69		11.91	49.9	1	99	0	0	158	23.78	-16.85			Oct-14
	3.94	17.94	9.68	42.79	47.31	1.6	0.65	12.67		11.92	49.9	1	99	0	0	158	24.14	-16.67			Oct-14
	3.40	18.87	6.99	31.00	29.71	3.01	0.95	10.4		13.28	361.3	-10	60	44	-1	37	16.36	-15.09			Nov-06
	3.28	16.81	3.95	26.30	15.47	3.16	1.8	10.61	0.77	9.54	220.8	1	90	4	0	102	25.08	-18.44			Jul-07
	3.87	17.51	14.30	28.66	28.67	1.54	1.32	9.12	0.46	20.51	307.8	3	97	0	0	56	10.4	-8.09	4.50		May-04
	3.70	17.11	13.53	26.14	24.51	0.87	1.97	9.09	0.46	20.47	307.8	3	97	0	0	56	9.96	-8.35		1.00	May-04
	3.92	17.70	14.70	29.99	30.67	1.86	0.97	9.11	0.46	20.57	307.8	3	97	0	0	56	10.57	-7.97			May-04
	3.81	17.34	14.06	28.02	27.57	0.97	1.47	9.08	0.46	20.63	307.8	3	97	0	0	56	10.25	-8.16			Oct-14
	3.97	17.76	14.76	30.06	30.96	1.86	0.97	9.1	0.46	20.58	307.8	3	97	0	0	56	10.57	-7.97			Oct-14
	0.94	16.22	10.89	22.88	35.08	2.36	1.23	10.71	0.95	56.19	1,429	0	99	0	1	76	23.3	-22.25	4.50		Sep-04
	0.78	15.84	10.16	20.50	30.78	1.66	1.88	10.72	0.95	55.88	1,429	0	99	0	1	76	22.87	-22.47		1.00	Sep-04
	1.03	16.41	11.26	24.15	37.45	2.65	0.9	10.72	0.95	56.47	1,429	0	99	0	1	76	23.55	-22.12			May-97
	0.89	16.14	10.73	22.33	34.36	2.23	1.38	10.73	0.95	56.6	1,429	0	99	0	1	76	23.19	-22.28			Oct-14
	1.03	16.43	11.29	24.20	37.54	2.68	0.88	10.72	0.95	56.48	1,429	0	99	0	1	76	23.55	-22.12			Oct-14
	5.18	25.62	20.12	41.37	40.22	3.52	0	11.65	0.58	26.56	2,266	1	84	6	0	37	19.25	-15.27			Mar-04
10,000	3.46	21.66	14.67	21.72	54.44	3.18	0.75	12.54	0.94	44.92	3,331	1	99	0	0	68	30.16	-17.69			Feb-00
	-0.78	12.90	7.79	29.50	25.66	3.14	1.35	10.96	0.98	12.37	631.9	1	99	0	0	76	16.95	-23.02	4.50		Mar-05
	-0.88	12.73	7.22	27.16	21.77	1.93	2	10.95	0.98	12.35	631.9	1	99	0	0	76	16.46	-23.23		1.00	Mar-05
	-0.69	13.19	8.20	30.91	27.89	3.45	1	10.99	0.98	12.45	631.9	1	99	0	0	76	17.1	-22.92			Mar-05
	-0.88	12.84	7.59	29.36	25.15	2.83	1.5	10.96	0.98	12.5	631.9	1	99	0	0	76	16.76	-23.08			Oct-15
	-0.70	13.19	8.21	30.91	28.00	3.45	1	10.97	0.98	12.45	631.9	1	99	0	0	76	17.11	-22.92			Oct-15
	3.99	12.90	6.25	26.03	36.43	5.78	1.8	6.27	0.76	25.22	727.5	0	0	61	0	35					Jul-12
	2.35	6.78	5.25	14.73		4.26	0.9	2.64	1.62	10	1,461	1	0	76	0	34			2.00		Nov-15
	2.17	6.41	4.53	12.37		3.58	1.55	2.65	1.64	9.98	1,461	1	0	76	0	34				1.00	Nov-15
	2.35	6.97	5.51	15.73		4.6	0.55	2.65	1.61	9.99	1,461	1	0	76	0	34					Nov-15
	2.29	6.75	4.99	13.93		4.02	1.05	2.61	1.6	10.01	1,461	1	0	76	0	34					Nov-15
	2.45	6.98	5.51	15.73		4.6	0.55	2.62	1.6	9.99	1,461	1	0	76	0	34					Nov-15
	-2.44	19.06	-0.78	13.88	-23.02	3.78	1.25	16.16	0.97	8	239.6	2	98	0	0	75			4.50		Dec-13
	-2.62	18.60	-1.43	11.59	-25.50	3.12	1.9	16.17	0.97	7.97	239.6	2	98	0	0	75				1.00	Dec-13
	-2.49	19.22	-0.44	14.98	-21.73	4.12	0.9	16.21	0.97	8.01	239.6	2	98	0	0	75					Dec-13
	-2.54	18.88	-0.88	13.37	-23.65	3.55	1.4	16.18	0.97	8.01	239.6	2	98	0	0	75					Oct-14
	-2.49	19.22	-0.44	14.98	-21.73	4.12	0.9	16.23	0.97	8.01	239.6	2	98	0	0	75					Dec-13
	-1.74	27.42	1.79	7.37	-35.57	0	2.53	22.4		9.88	264.7	1	90	3	0	58					Mar-13
	3.87	11.05	8.11	18.26	30.95	5.15	1.16	4.58	0.77	13.77	7,347	1	0	52	0	51	11.95	-5	3.75		May-10
	3.72	10.76	7.38	15.94	26.77	4.55	1.81	4.57	0.77	13.69	7,347	1	0	52	0	51	11.49	-5.26		1.00	May-10
	3.87	11.22	8.40	19.39	33.14	5.49	0.81	4.57	0.77	13.79	7,347	1	0	52	0	51	12.14	-4.87			Apr-17
	3.94	11.27	8.42	19.36	33.11	5.43	0.86	4.58	0.77	13.8	7,347	1	0	52	0	51	12.14	-4.87			May-10
	3.75	10.96	7.87	17.63	29.92	5.01	1.31	4.55	0.76	13.78	7,347	1	0	52	0	51	11.82	-5.07			Oct-14
	3.95	11.30	8.48	19.50	33.27	5.48	0.81	4.55	0.77	13.8	7,347	1	0	52	0	51	12.14	-4.87			Oct-14
	4.24						0			10.36	10.1	2	0	58	0						Mar-19
	3.28	24.59	15.92	20.05	60.11	1.52	0	14.51	1.14	14.03	1,532	0	82	3	0	26	38.4	-20.97			Feb-02
	1.73	11.99	3.00	9.04	-5.59	1.71	1.16	7.51	0.54	9.13	121.9	4	58	11	25	99			4.50		Jan-12
	1.61	11.77	2.35	6.94	-8.70	1.09	1.81	7.51	0.54	9.11	121.9	4	58	11	25	99				1.00	Jan-12
	1.79	12.17	3.40	10.10	-4.09	2.09	0.81	7.55	0.54	9.14	121.9	4	58	11	25	99					Jan-12
	1.75	11.92	2.86	8.44	-6.34	1.59	1.31	7.56	0.54	9.21	121.9	4	58	11	25	99					Jan-12
	1.90	12.32	3.40	10.24	-4.01	2.09	0.81	7.51	0.54	9.13	121.9	4	58	11	25	99					Jan-12
	2.77	20.24	13.34	20.50	59.59	3.03	1.14	12.56	0.94	15.72	5,566	1	99	0	0	75	29.76	-17.17	4.50		Sep-97
	2.63	19.86	12.64	18.24	54.56	2.72	1.79	12.53	0.94	14.15	5,566	1	99	0	0	75	29.31	-17.39		1.00	Jan-98
	2.89	20.40	13.73	21.43	60.82	3.17	0.79	12.56	0.94	16.62	5,566	1	99	0	0	75	29.76	-17.17			Apr-17
	2.86	20.35	13.64	21.52	61.85	3.09	0.87	12.56	0.94	16.62	5,566	1	99	0	0	75	30.12	-17.04			Jul-98
	2.78	20.14	13.18	20.06	58.49	2.73	1.29	12.54	0.94	16.56	5,566	1	99	0	0	75	29.57	-17.25			Oct-14
	2.89	20.40	13.73	21.82	62.33	3.17	0.79	12.58	0.94	16.62	5,566	1	99	0	0	75	29.76	-17.17			Oct-14

Fund Name	Ticker Symbol	Traded On	Fund Type	Category and (Prospectus Objective)	Overall Rating	Reward Rating	Risk Rating	Recent Up/ Downgrade	Open to New Investors	Min Initial Investment
	MARKET			FUND TYPE, CATEGORY & OBJECTIVE	RATINGS				MINIMUMS	
Cohen & Steers Realty Shares Fund Class L	CSRSX	NAS CM	Open End	Real Estate Sector Equity (Real Estate)	C+	C+	B-	Down	Y	10,000
Cohen & Steers REIT & Preferred Income Fund	RNP	NYSE	Closed End	Moderate Alloc (Income)	B-	B	C+	Up	Y	
Cohen & Steers Select Preferred and Income Fund	PSF	NYSE	Closed End	US Fixed Income (Growth)	C+	B	C-	Up	Y	
Cohen & Steers Total Return Realty	RFI	NYSE	Closed End	Real Estate Sector Equity (Real Estate)	C	C+	C-	Down	Y	
Coho Relative Value Equity Fund Advisor Class	COHOX	NAS CM	Open End	US Equity Large Cap Blend (Equity-Income)	B-	C	B+		Y	5,000
Coho Relative Value Equity Fund Institutional Class	COHIX	NAS CM	Open End	US Equity Large Cap Blend (Equity-Income)	B-	C	B+		Y	1,000,000
Columbia Acorn Emerging Markets Fund Advisor Class	CAERX	NAS CM	Open End	Global Emerg Mkts (Div Emerging Mkts)	C	C-	C			2,000
Columbia Acorn Emerging Markets Fund Class A	CAGAX	NAS CM	Open End	Global Emerg Mkts (Div Emerging Mkts)	C	C-	C			2,000
Columbia Acorn Emerging Markets Fund Class C	CGMCX	NAS CM	Open End	Global Emerg Mkts (Div Emerging Mkts)	C	C-	C			2,000
Columbia Acorn Emerging Markets Fund Institutional 2 Class	CANRX	NAS CM	Open End	Global Emerg Mkts (Div Emerging Mkts)	C	C-	C+			0
Columbia Acorn Emerging Markets Fund Institutional 3 Class	CPHRX	NAS CM	Open End	Global Emerg Mkts (Div Emerging Mkts)	C	C-	C+			1,000,000
Columbia Acorn Emerging Markets Fund Institutional Class	CEFZX	NAS CM	Open End	Global Emerg Mkts (Div Emerging Mkts)	C	C-	C			2,000
Columbia Acorn European Fund Advisor Class	CLOFX	NAS CM	Open End	Europe Equity Large Cap (Europe Stock)	C	C	C+		Y	2,000
Columbia Acorn European Fund Class A	CAEAX	NAS CM	Open End	Europe Equity Large Cap (Europe Stock)	C	C	C+		Y	2,000
Columbia Acorn European Fund Class C	CAECX	NAS CM	Open End	Europe Equity Large Cap (Europe Stock)	C	C	C+		Y	2,000
Columbia Acorn European Fund Institutional 2 Class	CAEEX	NAS CM	Open End	Europe Equity Large Cap (Europe Stock)	C	C	C+		Y	0
Columbia Acorn European Fund Institutional 3 Class	CAEYX	NAS CM	Open End	Europe Equity Large Cap (Europe Stock)	C	C	C+		Y	1,000,000
Columbia Acorn European Fund Institutional Class	CAEZX	NAS CM	Open End	Europe Equity Large Cap (Europe Stock)	C	C	C+		Y	2,000
Columbia Acorn Fund Advisor Class	CEARX	NAS CM	Open End	US Equity Mid Cap (Growth)	C+	C	C+		Y	2,000
Columbia Acorn Fund Class A	LACAX	NAS CM	Open End	US Equity Mid Cap (Growth)	C+	C	C+		Y	2,000
Columbia Acorn Fund Class C	LIACX	NAS CM	Open End	US Equity Mid Cap (Growth)	C+	C	C+		Y	2,000
Columbia Acorn Fund Institutional 2 Class	CRBRX	NAS CM	Open End	US Equity Mid Cap (Growth)	C+	C	C+		Y	0
Columbia Acorn Fund Institutional 3 Class	CRBYX	NAS CM	Open End	US Equity Mid Cap (Growth)	C+	C	C+		Y	1,000,000
Columbia Acorn Fund Institutional Class	ACRNX	NAS CM	Open End	US Equity Mid Cap (Growth)	C+	C	C+		Y	2,000
Columbia Acorn International Fund Advisor Class	CCIRX	NAS CM	Open End	Global Equity Mid/Small Cap (Foreign Stock)	C	C	C+		Y	2,000
Columbia Acorn International Fund Class A	LAIAX	NAS CM	Open End	Global Equity Mid/Small Cap (Foreign Stock)	C	C	C+		Y	2,000
Columbia Acorn International Fund Class C	LAICX	NAS CM	Open End	Global Equity Mid/Small Cap (Foreign Stock)	C	C	C+		Y	2,000
Columbia Acorn International Fund Class R	CACRX	NAS CM	Open End	Global Equity Mid/Small Cap (Foreign Stock)	C	C	C+		Y	0
Columbia Acorn International Fund Institutional 2 Class	CAIRX	NAS CM	Open End	Global Equity Mid/Small Cap (Foreign Stock)	C	C	C+		Y	0
Columbia Acorn International Fund Institutional 3 Class	CCYIX	NAS CM	Open End	Global Equity Mid/Small Cap (Foreign Stock)	C	C	C+		Y	1,000,000
Columbia Acorn International Fund Institutional Class	ACINX	NAS CM	Open End	Global Equity Mid/Small Cap (Foreign Stock)	C	C	C+		Y	2,000
Columbia Acorn International Select Fund Advisor Class	CILRX	NAS CM	Open End	Global Equity Large Cap (Foreign Stock)	C+	C	B-	Up	Y	2,000
Columbia Acorn International Select Fund Class A	LAFAX	NAS CM	Open End	Global Equity Large Cap (Foreign Stock)	C+	C	B-	Up	Y	2,000
Columbia Acorn International Select Fund Class C	LFFCX	NAS CM	Open End	Global Equity Large Cap (Foreign Stock)	C+	C	B-	Up	Y	2,000
Columbia Acorn International Select Institutional 2 Cls	CRIRX	NAS CM	Open End	Global Equity Large Cap (Foreign Stock)	C+	C	B-	Up	Y	0
Columbia Acorn International Select Institutional 3 Cls	CSIRX	NAS CM	Open End	Global Equity Large Cap (Foreign Stock)	C+	C	B-	Up	Y	1,000,000
Columbia Acorn International Select Institutional Cls	ACFFX	NAS CM	Open End	Global Equity Large Cap (Foreign Stock)	C+	C	B-	Up	Y	2,000
Columbia Acorn Select Fund Advisor Class	CSSRX	NAS CM	Open End	US Equity Mid Cap (Growth)	C	C	C+	Down	Y	2,000
Columbia Acorn Select Fund Class A	LTFAX	NAS CM	Open End	US Equity Mid Cap (Growth)	C	C	C+	Down	Y	2,000
Columbia Acorn Select Fund Class C	LTFCX	NAS CM	Open End	US Equity Mid Cap (Growth)	C	C	C+	Down	Y	2,000
Columbia Acorn Select Fund Institutional 2 Class	CSLRX	NAS CM	Open End	US Equity Mid Cap (Growth)	C	C	C+	Down	Y	0
Columbia Acorn Select Fund Institutional 3 Class	CSLYX	NAS CM	Open End	US Equity Mid Cap (Growth)	C	C	C+	Down	Y	1,000,000
Columbia Acorn Select Fund Institutional Class	ACTWX	NAS CM	Open End	US Equity Mid Cap (Growth)	C	C	C+	Down	Y	2,000
Columbia Acorn USA Fund Advisor Class	CUSAX	NAS CM	Open End	US Equity Small Cap (Growth)	C+	C	C+	Down	Y	2,000
Columbia Acorn USA Fund Class A	LAUAX	NAS CM	Open End	US Equity Small Cap (Growth)	C+	C	C+	Down	Y	2,000
Columbia Acorn USA Fund Class C	LAUCX	NAS CM	Open End	US Equity Small Cap (Growth)	C	C	C+	Down	Y	2,000
Columbia Acorn USA Fund Institutional 2 Class	CYSRX	NAS CM	Open End	US Equity Small Cap (Growth)	C+	C	C+	Down	Y	0
Columbia Acorn USA Fund Institutional 3 Class	CUSYX	NAS CM	Open End	US Equity Small Cap (Growth)	C+	C	C+	Down	Y	1,000,000
Columbia Acorn USA Fund Institutional Class	AUSAX	NAS CM	Open End	US Equity Small Cap (Growth)	C+	C	C+	Down	Y	2,000
Columbia Adaptive Retirement 2020 Fund Advisor Class	CARGX	NAS CM	Open End	Target Date (Asset Alloc)	D+	D+	B	Up	Y	2,000
Columbia Adaptive Retirement 2020 Institutional 3 Cls	CARHX	NAS CM	Open End	Target Date (Asset Alloc)	D+	D+	B	Up	Y	1,000,000
Columbia Adaptive Retirement 2025 Fund Advisor Class	CAAHX	NAS CM	Open End	Target Date (Asset Alloc)	D	D+	B	Up	Y	2,000

★ Expanded analysis of this fund is included in Section II.

Min Additional Investment	TOTAL RETURNS 3-Month Total Return	6-Month Total Return	1-Year Total Return	3-Year Total Return	5-Year Total Return	PERFORMANCE Dividend Yield (TTM)	Expense Ratio	3-Yr Std Deviation	3-Year Beta	ASSETS NAV	Total Assets (MIL)	ASSET ALLOCATION & TURNOVER %Cash	%Stocks	%Bonds	%Other	Turnover Ratio	BULL & BEAR Last Bull Market Total Return	Last Bear Market Total Return	FEES Front End Fee (%)	Back End Fee (%)	Inception Date
500	3.43	21.70	14.56	20.89	52.81	3.06	0.88	12.63	0.99	65.64	4,397	1	99	0	0	63	30.18	-17.67			Jul-91
	4.13	20.85	14.47	24.44	57.33	2.43	0	10.25	0.78	23.25	1,106	1	51	23	0	39	30.51	-16.63			Jun-03
	4.78	14.48	9.04	26.49	41.99	6.13	2.08	6		26.13	313.6	2	0	50	2	56	17.33	-8.29			Nov-10
	2.84	18.95	13.27	18.16	48.93	2.32	0	11.02	0.86	13.58	355.0	0	83	1	0	29	26.34	-14.98			Sep-93
100	-0.42	9.95	4.19	28.76	45.08	1.53	0.95	11.5	0.82	14.03	573.3	4	96	0	0						Aug-13
100	-0.42	10.00	4.36	29.32	45.98	1.62	0.8	11.55	0.82	14.07	573.3	4	96	0	0						May-14
	2.11	11.36	-3.03	19.68	-7.67	1.58	1.3	13.36	0.96	12.05	59.3	3	97	0	0	53	23.41				Nov-12
	2.05	11.30	-3.26	18.80	-8.95	1.33	1.55	13.39	0.96	11.91	59.3	3	97	0	0	53	22.96		5.75		Aug-11
	1.82	10.85	-4.01	16.16	-12.27	0.55	2.3	13.37	0.96	11.74	59.3	3	97	0	0	53	22.53			1.00	Aug-11
	2.11	11.46	-2.94	20.01	-7.38	1.65	1.24	13.39	0.96	12.06	59.3	3	97	0	0	53	23.41				Nov-12
	2.22	11.46	-2.91	20.17	-7.07	1.72	1.19	13.42	0.96	11.96	59.3	3	97	0	0	53	23.41				Jun-13
	2.13	11.44	-2.96	19.80	-7.69	1.59	1.3	13.39	0.96	11.98	59.3	3	97	0	0	53	23.41				Aug-11
	11.39	30.80	4.89	48.74	33.96	0	1.2	15.39	1.03	20.34	80.5	2	97	0	1	39	19.84				Jun-14
	11.31	30.65	4.61	47.53	32.20	0	1.45	15.39	1.03	20.16	80.5	2	97	0	1	39	19.51		5.75		Aug-11
	11.12	30.13	3.83	44.27	27.40	0	2.2	15.36	1.02	19.78	80.5	2	97	0	1	39	19.08			1.00	Aug-11
	11.43	30.88	4.97	48.98	34.16	0	1.14	15.36	1.02	20.47	80.5	2	97	0	1	39	19.84				Nov-12
	11.38	30.84	5.00	49.00	34.13	0	1.09	15.39	1.03	20.15	80.5	2	97	0	1	39	19.84				Mar-17
	11.39	30.83	4.92	48.78	33.93	0	1.2	15.38	1.03	20.24	80.5	2	97	0	1	39	19.84				Aug-11
	3.96	22.29	4.26	61.66	53.96	0	0.86	15.69	0.94	15.83	4,365	2	98	0	0	66	26.21	-22.11			Nov-12
	3.95	22.18	4.08	60.56	52.39	0	1.11	15.67	0.94	12.2	4,365	2	98	0	0	66	25.97	-22.19	5.75		Oct-00
	3.67	21.77	3.27	56.97	46.78	0	1.86	15.69	0.94	4.97	4,365	2	98	0	0	66	25.45	-22.46		1.00	Oct-00
	3.93	22.30	4.28	61.78	54.47	0	0.82	15.69	0.94	15.99	4,365	2	98	0	0	66	26.21	-22.11			Nov-12
	3.95	22.38	4.36	62.15	54.99	0	0.78	15.7	0.94	16.16	4,365	2	98	0	0	66	26.21	-22.11			Nov-12
	3.96	22.32	4.27	61.73	54.32	0	0.86	15.7	0.94	15.05	4,365	2	98	0	0	66	26.21	-22.11			Jun-70
	5.32	19.24	-0.41	32.07	15.32	0.62	0.99	12.96	1.04	33.24	2,756	0	100	0	0	32	17.63	-21.34			Nov-12
	5.26	19.10	-0.65	31.12	14.07	0.37	1.24	12.98	1.04	32.78	2,756	0	100	0	0	32	17.36	-21.45	5.75		Oct-00
	5.07	18.61	-1.41	28.17	9.84	0	1.99	12.97	1.04	30.58	2,756	0	100	0	0	32	16.84	-21.68		1.00	Oct-00
	5.18	18.91	-0.93	30.07	12.32	0.07	1.49	12.96	1.04	32.77	2,756	0	100	0	0	32	17.13	-21.49			Aug-11
	5.35	19.26	-0.36	32.26	15.81	0.69	0.92	12.98	1.04	32.84	2,756	0	100	0	0	32	17.66	-21.34			Aug-11
	5.38	19.31	-0.29	32.50	16.13	0.74	0.88	12.98	1.04	33.26	2,756	0	100	0	0	32	17.63	-21.34			Nov-12
	5.35	19.25	-0.41	32.07	15.56	0.63	0.99	12.98	1.04	32.86	2,756	0	100	0	0	32	17.63	-21.34			Sep-92
	6.69	23.92	6.26	53.24	25.72	0.37	1.15	13.25	1.04	29.23	137.3	2	98	0	0	48	15.68	-18.46			Nov-12
	6.61	23.74	5.95	52.03	24.09	0.14	1.4	13.25	1.04	28.57	137.3	2	98	0	0	48	15.46	-18.58	5.75		Oct-00
	6.41	23.33	5.21	48.69	19.49	0	2.15	13.24	1.04	26.1	137.3	2	98	0	0	48	14.94	-18.85		1.00	Oct-00
	6.71	23.99	6.32	53.59	26.21	0.45	1.06	13.26	1.04	29.22	137.3	2	98	0	0	48	15.68	-18.46			Nov-12
	6.72	24.00	6.40	53.86	26.54	0.49	1.01	13.25	1.04	29.21	137.3	2	98	0	0	48	15.68	-18.46			Nov-12
	6.67	23.90	6.24	53.16	25.79	0.37	1.15	13.28	1.04	28.99	137.3	2	98	0	0	48	15.68	-18.46			Nov-98
	2.84	17.41	-4.07	47.93	45.53	0	0.92	16.21	0.95	14.39	271.2	3	97	0	0	60	26.43	-27.19			Nov-12
	2.77	17.31	-4.38	46.81	43.72	0	1.17	16.2	0.95	11.75	271.2	3	97	0	0	60	26.17	-27.28	5.75		Oct-00
	2.43	16.77	-5.13	43.38	38.44	0	1.92	16.19	0.95	6.65	271.2	3	97	0	0	60	25.66	-27.53		1.00	Oct-00
	2.89	17.46	-4.05	48.20	46.05	0	0.84	16.21	0.95	14.49	271.2	3	97	0	0	60	26.43	-27.19			Nov-12
	2.85	17.50	-3.95	48.44	46.48	0	0.79	16.23	0.95	14.66	271.2	3	97	0	0	60	26.43	-27.19			Nov-12
	2.90	17.47	-4.05	47.94	45.70	0	0.92	16.22	0.95	13.74	271.2	3	97	0	0	60	26.43	-27.19			Nov-98
	2.47	20.79	1.75	59.80	58.25	0.05	1.17	17.19	0.96	15.9	306.8	4	96	0	0	86	27.79	-24.71			Nov-12
	2.39	20.58	1.49	58.52	56.30	0.07	1.42	17.18	0.96	11.7	306.8	4	96	0	0	86	27.6	-24.83	5.75		Oct-00
	2.04	20.04	0.62	54.87	50.67	0	2.17	17.07	0.96	4.8	306.8	4	96	0	0	86	27.06	-25.05		1.00	Oct-00
	2.51	20.86	1.83	60.19	59.04	0.05	1.08	17.2	0.96	16.03	306.8	4	96	0	0	86	27.79	-24.71			Nov-12
	2.49	20.86	1.86	60.36	59.38	0.05	1.04	17.19	0.96	16.2	306.8	4	96	0	0	86	27.79	-24.71			Nov-12
	2.44	20.78	1.73	59.71	58.26	0.06	1.17	17.2	0.96	14.86	306.8	4	96	0	0	86	27.79	-24.71			Sep-96
	2.65	9.89	7.14			3.42	0.68			10.44	7.8	-11	46	59	6	26					Oct-17
	2.65	9.89	7.14			3.42	0.5			10.44	7.8	-11	46	59	6	26					Oct-17
	2.95	11.06	7.54			3.57	0.68			10.44	3.7	-20	53	61	6	28					Apr-18

	MARKET			FUND TYPE, CATEGORY & OBJECTIVE	RATINGS				MINIMUMS	
Fund Name	Ticker Symbol	Traded On	Fund Type	Category and (Prospectus Objective)	Overall Rating	Reward Rating	Risk Rating	Recent Up/ Downgrade	Open to New Investors	Min Initial Investment
Columbia Adaptive Retirement 2025 Institutional 3 Cls	CAIDX	NAS CM	Open End	Target Date (Asset Alloc)	D	D+	B	Up	Y	1,000,000
Columbia Adaptive Retirement 2030 Fund Advisor Class	CARLX	NAS CM	Open End	Target Date (Asset Alloc)	D+	D+	B	Up	Y	2,000
Columbia Adaptive Retirement 2030 Institutional 3 Cls	CARMX	NAS CM	Open End	Target Date (Asset Alloc)	D+	D+	B	Up	Y	1,000,000
Columbia Adaptive Retirement 2035 Fund Advisor Class	CARJX	NAS CM	Open End	Target Date (Asset Alloc)	D	D+	B-	Up	Y	2,000
Columbia Adaptive Retirement 2035 Institutional 3 Cls	CAIEX	NAS CM	Open End	Target Date (Asset Alloc)	D	D+	B-	Up	Y	1,000,000
Columbia Adaptive Retirement 2040 Fund Advisor Class	CAROX	NAS CM	Open End	Target Date (Asset Alloc)	D+	D+	B-	Up	Y	2,000
Columbia Adaptive Retirement 2040 Institutional 3 Cls	CARQX	NAS CM	Open End	Target Date (Asset Alloc)	D+	C-	B-	Up	Y	1,000,000
Columbia Adaptive Retirement 2045 Fund Advisor Class	CARPX	NAS CM	Open End	Target Date (Asset Alloc)	D	D+	B-	Up	Y	2,000
Columbia Adaptive Retirement 2045 Institutional 3 Cls	CAIHX	NAS CM	Open End	Target Date (Asset Alloc)	D	D+	B-	Up	Y	1,000,000
Columbia Adaptive Retirement 2050 Fund Advisor Class	CARSX	NAS CM	Open End	Target Date (Asset Alloc)	D+	C-	B-	Up	Y	2,000
Columbia Adaptive Retirement 2050 Institutional 3 Cls	CARUX	NAS CM	Open End	Target Date (Asset Alloc)	D+	C-	B-	Up	Y	1,000,000
Columbia Adaptive Retirement 2055 Fund Advisor Class	CARFX	NAS CM	Open End	Target Date (Asset Alloc)	D	D+	B-	Up	Y	2,000
Columbia Adaptive Retirement 2055 Institutional 3 Cls	CAIJX	NAS CM	Open End	Target Date (Asset Alloc)	D	D+	B-	Up	Y	1,000,000
Columbia Adaptive Retirement 2060 Fund Advisor Class	CARKX	NAS CM	Open End	Target Date (Asset Alloc)	D+	C-	B-	Up	Y	2,000
Columbia Adaptive Retirement 2060 Institutional 3 Cls	CARVX	NAS CM	Open End	Target Date (Asset Alloc)	D+	C-	B-	Up	Y	1,000,000
Columbia Adaptive Risk Allocation Fund Advisor Class	CARRX	NAS CM	Open End	Moderate Alloc (Growth & Income)	B	C	A		Y	2,000
Columbia Adaptive Risk Allocation Fund Class A	CRAAX	NAS CM	Open End	Moderate Alloc (Growth & Income)	B	C	A		Y	2,000
Columbia Adaptive Risk Allocation Fund Class C	CRACX	NAS CM	Open End	Moderate Alloc (Growth & Income)	B	C	A-	Up	Y	2,000
Columbia Adaptive Risk Allocation Fund Class R	CRKRX	NAS CM	Open End	Moderate Alloc (Growth & Income)	B	C	A-	Up	Y	0
Columbia Adaptive Risk Allocation Institutional 2 Cls	CRDRX	NAS CM	Open End	Moderate Alloc (Growth & Income)	B	C	A		Y	0
Columbia Adaptive Risk Allocation Institutional 3 Cls	CARYX	NAS CM	Open End	Moderate Alloc (Growth & Income)	B	C	A		Y	1,000,000
Columbia Adaptive Risk Allocation Fund Institutional Class	CRAZX	NAS CM	Open End	Moderate Alloc (Growth & Income)	B	C	A		Y	2,000
Columbia Alternative Beta Fund Advisor Class	CLFUX	NAS CM	Open End	Multialternative (Growth & Income)	D	D-	D		Y	2,000
Columbia Alternative Beta Fund Class A	CLAAX	NAS CM	Open End	Multialternative (Growth & Income)	D	D-	D		Y	2,000
Columbia Alternative Beta Fund Class C	CLABX	NAS CM	Open End	Multialternative (Growth & Income)	D	D-	D		Y	2,000
Columbia Alternative Beta Fund Class R	CRRLX	NAS CM	Open End	Multialternative (Growth & Income)	D	D-	D		Y	0
Columbia Alternative Beta Fund Institutional 2 Class	CLIVX	NAS CM	Open End	Multialternative (Growth & Income)	D	D-	D		Y	0
Columbia Alternative Beta Fund Institutional 3 Class	CLAYX	NAS CM	Open End	Multialternative (Growth & Income)	D	D-	D		Y	1,000,000
Columbia Alternative Beta Fund Institutional Class	CLAZX	NAS CM	Open End	Multialternative (Growth & Income)	D	D-	D		Y	2,000
Columbia Balanced Fund Advisor Class	CBDRX	NAS CM	Open End	Moderate Alloc (Balanced)	B-	C	A-		Y	2,000
Columbia Balanced Fund Class A	CBLAX	NAS CM	Open End	Moderate Alloc (Balanced)	B-	C	B+	Up	Y	2,000
Columbia Balanced Fund Class C	CBLCX	NAS CM	Open End	Moderate Alloc (Balanced)	B-	C	B+	Up	Y	2,000
Columbia Balanced Fund Class R	CBLRX	NAS CM	Open End	Moderate Alloc (Balanced)	B-	C	B+	Up	Y	0
Columbia Balanced Fund Institutional 2 Class	CLREX	NAS CM	Open End	Moderate Alloc (Balanced)	B-	C	A-		Y	0
Columbia Balanced Fund Institutional 3 Class	CBDYX	NAS CM	Open End	Moderate Alloc (Balanced)	B-	C	A-		Y	1,000,000
Columbia Balanced Fund Institutional Class	CBALX	NAS CM	Open End	Moderate Alloc (Balanced)	B-	C	A-		Y	2,000
Columbia Capital Allocation Aggressive Portfolio Adv Cls	CPDAX	NAS CM	Open End	Aggressive Alloc (Growth & Income)	B-	C	B	Up	Y	2,000
Columbia Capital Allocation Aggressive Portfolio Class A	AXBAX	NAS CM	Open End	Aggressive Alloc (Growth & Income)	B-	C	B	Up	Y	2,000
Columbia Capital Allocation Aggressive Portfolio Class C	RBGCX	NAS CM	Open End	Aggressive Alloc (Growth & Income)	C+	C	B	Up	Y	2,000
Columbia Capital Allocation Aggressive Portfolio Class R	CPARX	NAS CM	Open End	Aggressive Alloc (Growth & Income)	B-	C	B	Up	Y	0
Columbia Capital Alloc Aggressive Port Inst 2 Cls	CPANX	NAS CM	Open End	Aggressive Alloc (Growth & Income)	B-	C	B	Up	Y	0
Columbia Capital Alloc Aggressive Port Inst 3 Cls	CPDIX	NAS CM	Open End	Aggressive Alloc (Growth & Income)	B-	C	B	Up	Y	1,000,000
Columbia Capital Allocation Aggressive Portfolio Inst Cls	CPAZX	NAS CM	Open End	Aggressive Alloc (Growth & Income)	B-	C	B	Up	Y	2,000
Columbia Capital Allocation Conservative Portfolio Adv Cls	CPCYX	NAS CM	Open End	Cautious Alloc (Growth & Income)	B-	C	B+		Y	2,000
Columbia Capital Allocation Conservative Portfolio Class A	ABDAX	NAS CM	Open End	Cautious Alloc (Growth & Income)	B-	C	B+	Up	Y	2,000
Columbia Capital Allocation Conservative Portfolio Class C	RPCCX	NAS CM	Open End	Cautious Alloc (Growth & Income)	C+	C	B	Up	Y	2,000
Columbia Capital Allocation Conservative Portfolio Class R	CBVRX	NAS CM	Open End	Cautious Alloc (Growth & Income)	B-	C	B+	Up	Y	0
Columbia Capital Alloc Conservative Port Inst 2 Cls	CPAOX	NAS CM	Open End	Cautious Alloc (Growth & Income)	B-	C	B+		Y	0
Columbia Capital Alloc Conservative Port Inst 3 Cls	CPDHX	NAS CM	Open End	Cautious Alloc (Growth & Income)	B-	C	B+		Y	1,000,000
Columbia Capital Alloc Conservative Port Inst Cls	CBVZX	NAS CM	Open End	Cautious Alloc (Growth & Income)	B-	C	B+		Y	2,000
Columbia Capital Alloc Moderate Aggressive Port Adv Cls	CGBRX	NAS CM	Open End	Moderate Alloc (Growth & Income)	B-	C	B+	Up	Y	2,000
Columbia Capital Alloc Moderate Aggressive Port Cls A	NBIAX	NAS CM	Open End	Moderate Alloc (Growth & Income)	B-	C	B+	Up	Y	2,000

★ Expanded analysis of this fund is included in Section II.

Min Additional Investment	3-Month Total Return	6-Month Total Return	1-Year Total Return	3-Year Total Return	5-Year Total Return	Dividend Yield (TTM)	Expense Ratio	3-Yr Std Deviation	3-Year Beta	NAV	Total Assets (MIL)	%Cash	%Stocks	%Bonds	%Other	Turnover Ratio	Last Bull Market Total Return	Last Bear Market Total Return	Front End Fee (%)	Back End Fee (%)	Inception Date
	TOTAL RETURNS					PERFORMANCE				ASSETS		ASSET ALLOCATION & TURNOVER					BULL & BEAR		FEES		
	2.95	11.06	7.54			3.57	0.5			10.44	3.7	-20	53	61	6	28					Apr-18
	3.33	12.77	8.11			3.92	0.68			10.24	1.2	-31	62	63	6	23					Oct-17
	3.32	12.76	8.12			3.93	0.5			10.25	1.2	-31	62	63	6	23					Oct-17
	3.65	14.50	8.56			4.03	0.68			10.5	1.1	-45	73	66	6	32					Apr-18
	3.65	14.50	8.56			4.03	0.5			10.5	1.1	-45	73	66	6	32					Apr-18
	4.13	16.66	9.31			4.27	0.68			10.57	1.1	-58	83	68	7	30					Oct-17
	4.13	16.66	9.32			4.28	0.5			10.57	1.1	-58	83	68	7	30					Oct-17
	4.34	17.98	9.56			4.42	0.68			10.56	1.1	-70	92	71	7	30					Apr-18
	4.34	17.98	9.56			4.42	0.5			10.56	1.1	-70	92	71	7	30					Apr-18
	4.53	19.07	10.10			4.58	0.68			10.61	1.1	-77	98	72	7	27					Oct-17
	4.53	19.07	10.10			4.58	0.5			10.61	1.1	-77	98	72	7	27					Oct-17
	4.54	18.87	9.93			4.52	0.68			10.58	1.1	-77	98	72	7	29					Apr-18
	4.54	18.87	9.93			4.52	0.5			10.58	1.1	-77	98	72	7	29					Apr-18
	4.63	19.19	10.13			4.58	0.68			10.62	1.1	-77	98	72	7	26					Oct-17
	4.63	19.19	10.13			4.58	0.5			10.62	1.1	-77	98	72	7	26					Oct-17
	3.00	12.50	7.05	23.74	25.77	3.33	0.82	6.43		10.98	2,996	-76	59	105	12	210					Oct-14
	2.93	12.30	6.73	22.70	24.06	3.12	1.07	6.41		10.86	2,996	-76	59	105	12	210			5.75		Jun-12
	2.75	11.88	5.90	20.06	19.55	2.48	1.82	6.45		10.45	2,996	-76	59	105	12	210				1.00	Jun-12
	2.97	12.22	6.52	21.95	22.64	2.9	1.32	6.43		10.74	2,996	-76	59	105	12	210					Jun-12
	2.99	12.37	6.92	23.62	25.91	3.31	0.83	6.42		10.99	2,996	-76	59	105	12	210					Jun-12
	2.98	12.44	7.03	24.00	26.17	3.32	0.79	6.4		11.02	2,996	-76	59	105	12	210					Oct-14
	3.00	12.39	6.95	23.63	25.66	3.33	0.82	6.39		10.97	2,996	-76	59	105	12	210					Jun-12
	-2.46	-2.08	-12.96	-17.55		0	1.02	6.04	23.46	7.52	603.3	-392	-1	0	493	0					Jan-15
	-2.48	-2.22	-13.25	-18.20		0	1.27	6.01	22.84	7.46	603.3	-392	-1	0	493	0			5.75		Jan-15
	-2.66	-2.53	-13.91	-20.00		0	2.02	6.07	23.16	7.3	603.3	-392	-1	0	493	0				1.00	Jan-15
	-2.63	-2.37	-13.55	-18.84		0	1.52	6.02	23.24	7.4	603.3	-392	-1	0	493	0					Jan-15
	-2.46	-2.08	-13.04	-17.43		0	0.89	6.04	23.24	7.53	603.3	-392	-1	0	493	0					Jan-15
	-2.45	-2.07	-12.91	-17.18		0	0.83	6.08	24.5	7.55	603.3	-392	-1	0	493	0					Jan-15
	-2.34	-1.95	-12.97	-17.46		0	1.02	6.08	22.72	7.51	603.3	-392	-1	0	493	0					Jan-15
	4.02	14.68	8.79	27.91	39.41	1.62	0.7	8		42.18	6,831	3	55	42	0	76	17.17	-10.86			Nov-12
	3.91	14.51	8.51	26.93	37.66	1.4	0.95	8		41.85	6,831	3	55	42	0	76	16.98	-10.92	5.75		Nov-02
	3.73	14.07	7.70	24.10	32.60	0.7	1.7	7.99		41.75	6,831	3	55	42	0	76	16.51	-11.22		1.00	Oct-03
	3.84	14.37	8.24	25.99	35.96	1.17	1.2	8		41.86	6,831	3	55	42	0	76	16.85	-11.01			Sep-10
	3.99	14.68	8.83	28.09	39.91	1.69	0.65	8.01		41.79	6,831	3	55	42	0	76	17.24	-10.8			Mar-11
	4.02	14.70	8.87	28.28	40.23	1.71	0.6	8.01		42.18	6,831	3	55	42	0	76	17.17	-10.86			Nov-12
	4.01	14.65	8.80	27.91	39.40	1.64	0.7	8.01		41.77	6,831	3	55	42	0	76	17.17	-10.86			Oct-91
	3.28	16.07	4.54	36.77	40.03	2.04	0.86	10.87		12.05	719.8	-1	80	17	4	20	18.6	-16.45			Jun-13
	3.19	15.98	4.30	35.75	38.27	1.75	1.11	10.89		12.31	719.8	-1	80	17	4	20	18.6	-16.45	5.75		Mar-04
	2.96	15.46	3.49	32.71	33.06	1.04	1.86	10.82		11.96	719.8	-1	80	17	4	20	18.07	-16.71		1.00	Mar-04
	3.11	15.81	3.95	34.74	36.49	1.52	1.36	10.88		12.19	719.8	-1	80	17	4	20	18.23	-16.42			Sep-10
	3.28	16.08	4.56	36.96	40.37	2.07	0.84	10.85		12.04	719.8	-1	80	17	4	20	18.6	-16.45			Jun-13
	3.20	16.10	4.54	37.08	40.63	2.12	0.79	10.82		12.03	719.8	-1	80	17	4	20	18.6	-16.45			Jun-13
	3.22	16.08	4.55	36.82	39.95	2.02	0.86	10.82		12.26	719.8	-1	80	17	4	20	18.66	-16.3			Sep-10
	2.58	8.04	5.22	13.51	17.93	2.44	0.76	3.45		10.05	227.6	-6	20	76	8	21	7.51	-4.15			Jun-13
	2.60	7.96	5.02	12.80	16.60	2.17	1.01	3.54		10.13	227.6	-6	20	76	8	21	7.51	-4.15	4.75		Mar-04
	2.43	7.50	4.16	10.25	12.26	1.46	1.76	3.52		10.07	227.6	-6	20	76	8	21	7.16	-4.52		1.00	Mar-04
	2.54	7.72	4.66	11.85	15.04	1.93	1.26	3.48		10.12	227.6	-6	20	76	8	21	7.47	-4.36			Sep-10
	2.59	8.05	5.24	13.63	18.21	2.46	0.73	3.47		10.05	227.6	-6	20	76	8	21	7.52	-4.15			Jun-13
	2.71	8.09	5.30	13.82	18.50	2.51	0.68	3.54		10.04	227.6	-6	20	76	8	21	7.51	-4.15			Jun-13
	2.67	8.10	5.29	13.66	18.06	2.42	0.76	3.48		10.12	227.6	-6	20	76	8	21	7.64	-4.11			Sep-10
	3.25	14.55	5.14	31.57	36.04	2.22	0.83	8.98		12.19	2,027	-2	65	34	2	18	16.18	-13.32			Nov-12
	3.22	14.35	4.84	30.55	34.45	2	1.08	8.98		12.08	2,027	-2	65	34	2	18	16.02	-13.43	5.75		Oct-96

	MARKET			FUND TYPE, CATEGORY & OBJECTIVE	RATINGS					MINIMUMS
Fund Name	Ticker Symbol	Traded On	Fund Type	Category and (Prospectus Objective)	Overall Rating	Reward Rating	Risk Rating	Recent Up/ Downgrade	Open to New Investors	Min Initial Investment
Columbia Capital Alloc Moderate Aggressive Port Cls C	NBICX	NAS CM	Open End	Moderate Alloc (Growth & Income)	B-	C	B+	Up	Y	2,000
Columbia Capital Alloc Moderate Aggressive Port Cls R	CLBRX	NAS CM	Open End	Moderate Alloc (Growth & Income)	B-	C	B+	Up	Y	0
Columbia Capital Alloc Moderate Aggressive Port Cls V	CGGTX	NAS CM	Open End	Moderate Alloc (Growth & Income)	B-	C	B+	Up		2,000
Columbia Capital Alloc Moderate Aggressive Port Inst 2 Cls	CLHRX	NAS CM	Open End	Moderate Alloc (Growth & Income)	B-	C	B+	Up	Y	0
Columbia Capital Alloc Moderate Aggressive Port Inst 3 Cls	CPHNX	NAS CM	Open End	Moderate Alloc (Growth & Income)	B-	C	B+	Up	Y	1,000,000
Columbia Capital Alloc Moderate Aggressive Port Inst Cls	NBGPX	NAS CM	Open End	Moderate Alloc (Growth & Income)	B-	C	B+	Up	Y	2,000
Columbia Capital Alloc Moderate Conservative Port Adv Cls	CHWRX	NAS CM	Open End	Cautious Alloc (Growth & Income)	B	C+	A-	Up	Y	2,000
Columbia Capital Alloc Moderate Conservative Port Cls A	NLGAX	NAS CM	Open End	Cautious Alloc (Growth & Income)	B	C	A-	Up	Y	2,000
Columbia Capital Alloc Moderate Conservative Port Cls C	NIICX	NAS CM	Open End	Cautious Alloc (Growth & Income)	B-	C	B+	Up	Y	2,000
Columbia Capital Alloc Moderate Conservative Port Cls R	CLIRX	NAS CM	Open End	Cautious Alloc (Growth & Income)	B-	C	A-	Up	Y	0
Columbia Capital Alloc Mod Cons Port Inst 2 Cls	CLRRX	NAS CM	Open End	Cautious Alloc (Growth & Income)	B	C+	A-	Up	Y	0
Columbia Capital Alloc Mod Cons Port Inst 3 Cls	CPDGX	NAS CM	Open End	Cautious Alloc (Growth & Income)	B	C+	A-	Up	Y	1,000,000
Columbia Capital Alloc Moderate Conservative Port Inst Cls	NIPAX	NAS CM	Open End	Cautious Alloc (Growth & Income)	B	C+	A-	Up	Y	2,000
Columbia Capital Allocation Moderate Portfolio Advisor Cls	CPCZX	NAS CM	Open End	Cautious Alloc (Growth & Income)	B-	C	A-	Up	Y	2,000
Columbia Capital Allocation Moderate Portfolio Class A	ABUAX	NAS CM	Open End	Cautious Alloc (Growth & Income)	B-	C	A-	Up	Y	2,000
Columbia Capital Allocation Moderate Portfolio Class C	AMTCX	NAS CM	Open End	Cautious Alloc (Growth & Income)	B-	C	A-	Up	Y	2,000
Columbia Capital Allocation Moderate Portfolio Class R	CBMRX	NAS CM	Open End	Cautious Alloc (Growth & Income)	B-	C	A-	Up	Y	0
Columbia Capital Allocation Moderate Portfolio Inst 2 Cls	CPAMX	NAS CM	Open End	Cautious Alloc (Growth & Income)	B-	C	A-	Up	Y	0
Columbia Capital Allocation Moderate Portfolio Inst 3 Cls	CPDMX	NAS CM	Open End	Cautious Alloc (Growth & Income)	B-	C	A-	Up	Y	1,000,000
Columbia Capital Allocation Moderate Portfolio Inst Cls	CBMZX	NAS CM	Open End	Cautious Alloc (Growth & Income)	B-	C	A-	Up	Y	2,000
Columbia Commodity Strategy Fund Advisor Class	CCOMX	NAS CM	Open End	Commodities Broad Basket ()	D	D	C-		Y	2,000
Columbia Commodity Strategy Fund Class A	CCSAX	NAS CM	Open End	Commodities Broad Basket ()	D	D	C-		Y	2,000
Columbia Commodity Strategy Fund Class C	CCSCX	NAS CM	Open End	Commodities Broad Basket ()	D	D	D+		Y	2,000
Columbia Commodity Strategy Fund Class R	CCSRX	NAS CM	Open End	Commodities Broad Basket ()	D	D	C-		Y	0
Columbia Commodity Strategy Fund Institutional 2 Class	CADLX	NAS CM	Open End	Commodities Broad Basket ()	D	D	C-		Y	0
Columbia Commodity Strategy Fund Institutional 3 Class	CCFYX	NAS CM	Open End	Commodities Broad Basket ()	D	D	C-		Y	1,000,000
Columbia Commodity Strategy Fund Institutional Class	CCSZX	NAS CM	Open End	Commodities Broad Basket ()	D	D	C-		Y	2,000
Columbia Contrarian Asia Pacific Fund Class A	CAJAX	NAS CM	Open End	Asia ex-Japan Equity (Pacific Stock)	C	C-	C		Y	2,000
Columbia Contrarian Asia Pacific Fund Class C	CAJCX	NAS CM	Open End	Asia ex-Japan Equity (Pacific Stock)	C	C-	C		Y	2,000
Columbia Contrarian Asia Pacific Fund Class R	CAJRX	NAS CM	Open End	Asia ex-Japan Equity (Pacific Stock)	C	C-	C		Y	0
Columbia Contrarian Asia Pacific Institutional 2 Cls	TAPRX	NAS CM	Open End	Asia ex-Japan Equity (Pacific Stock)	C	C-	C		Y	100,000
Columbia Contrarian Asia Pacific Institutional 3 Cls	CAPYX	NAS CM	Open End	Asia ex-Japan Equity (Pacific Stock)	C	C-	C		Y	0
Columbia Contrarian Asia Pacific Fund Institutional Class	CAJZX	NAS CM	Open End	Asia ex-Japan Equity (Pacific Stock)	C	C-	C		Y	2,000
Columbia Contrarian Core Fund Advisor Class	CORRX	NAS CM	Open End	US Equity Large Cap Blend (Growth & Income)	C+	C	B		Y	2,000
Columbia Contrarian Core Fund Class A	LCCAX	NAS CM	Open End	US Equity Large Cap Blend (Growth & Income)	C+	C	B		Y	2,000
Columbia Contrarian Core Fund Class C	LCCCX	NAS CM	Open End	US Equity Large Cap Blend (Growth & Income)	C+	C	B		Y	2,000
Columbia Contrarian Core Fund Class R	CCCRX	NAS CM	Open End	US Equity Large Cap Blend (Growth & Income)	C+	C	B		Y	0
Columbia Contrarian Core Fund Class V	SGIEX	NAS CM	Open End	US Equity Large Cap Blend (Growth & Income)	C+	C	B			2,000
Columbia Contrarian Core Fund Institutional 2 Class	COFRX	NAS CM	Open End	US Equity Large Cap Blend (Growth & Income)	C+	C	B		Y	0
Columbia Contrarian Core Fund Institutional 3 Class	COFYX	NAS CM	Open End	US Equity Large Cap Blend (Growth & Income)	B-	C	B	Up	Y	1,000,000
Columbia Contrarian Core Fund Institutional Class	SMGIX	NAS CM	Open End	US Equity Large Cap Blend (Growth & Income)	C+	C	B		Y	2,000
Columbia Contrarian Europe Fund Advisor Class	CADJX	NAS CM	Open End	Europe Equity Large Cap (Europe Stock)	C	C-	C+	Up	Y	0
Columbia Contrarian Europe Fund Class A	AXEAX	NAS CM	Open End	Europe Equity Large Cap (Europe Stock)	C	C-	C+	Up	Y	2,000
Columbia Contrarian Europe Fund Class C	REECX	NAS CM	Open End	Europe Equity Large Cap (Europe Stock)	C	C-	C+	Up	Y	2,000
Columbia Contrarian Europe Fund Institutional 2 Class	CADKX	NAS CM	Open End	Europe Equity Large Cap (Europe Stock)	C	C	C+		Y	100,000
Columbia Contrarian Europe Fund Institutional 3 Class	CEEUX	NAS CM	Open End	Europe Equity Large Cap (Europe Stock)	C	C	C+		Y	0
Columbia Contrarian Europe Fund Institutional Class	CEEZX	NAS CM	Open End	Europe Equity Large Cap (Europe Stock)	C	C-	C+	Up	Y	2,000
Columbia Convertible Securities Fund Advisor Class	COVRX	NAS CM	Open End	Convertibles (Convertible Bond)	B	C+	A-	Down	Y	2,000
Columbia Convertible Securities Fund Class A	PACIX	NAS CM	Open End	Convertibles (Convertible Bond)	B	C+	A-	Down	Y	2,000
Columbia Convertible Securities Fund Class C	PHIKX	NAS CM	Open End	Convertibles (Convertible Bond)	B	C	A-		Y	2,000
Columbia Convertible Securities Fund Class R	CVBRX	NAS CM	Open End	Convertibles (Convertible Bond)	B	C+	A-		Y	0
Columbia Convertible Securities Fund Institutional 2 Class	COCRX	NAS CM	Open End	Convertibles (Convertible Bond)	B	C+	A-	Down	Y	0

★ Expanded analysis of this fund is included in Section II.

	TOTAL RETURNS					PERFORMANCE				ASSETS		ASSET ALLOCATION & TURNOVER					BULL & BEAR		FEES		
Min Additional Investment	3-Month Total Return	6-Month Total Return	1-Year Total Return	3-Year Total Return	5-Year Total Return	Dividend Yield (TTM)	Expense Ratio	3-Yr Std Deviation	3-Year Beta	NAV	Total Assets (MIL)	%Cash	%Stocks	%Bonds	%Other	Turnover Ratio	Last Bull Market Total Return	Last Bear Market Total Return	Front End Fee (%)	Back End Fee (%)	Inception Date
	3.02	13.89	4.03	27.71	29.37	1.27	1.83	9.01		12.11	2,027	-2	65	34	2	18	15.5	-13.7		1.00	Oct-96
	3.16	14.22	4.57	29.71	32.81	1.76	1.33	9		12.07	2,027	-2	65	34	2	18	15.9	-13.55			Jan-06
	3.22	14.35	4.84	30.55	34.43	2	1.08	8.98		12.08	2,027	-2	65	34	2	18	16	-13.45	5.75		Mar-11
	3.35	14.59	5.20	31.84	36.61	2.27	0.73	9		12.18	2,027	-2	65	34	2	18	16.18	-13.32			Nov-12
	3.36	14.60	5.30	32.07	36.96	2.37	0.73	9.01		11.88	2,027	-2	65	34	2	18	16.18	-13.32			Jun-13
	3.29	14.52	5.11	31.61	36.12	2.24	0.83	9.04		12.05	2,027	-2	65	34	2	18	16.18	-13.32			Oct-96
	2.88	10.17	5.44	19.35	23.84	2.41	0.74	5.15		10.64	529.9	-5	35	65	4	21	10.83	-6.19			Nov-12
	2.79	9.94	5.12	18.39	22.19	2.15	0.99	5.13		10.74	529.9	-5	35	65	4	21	10.69	-6.34	5.75		Oct-96
	2.64	9.57	4.40	15.89	17.73	1.45	1.74	5.12		10.59	529.9	-5	35	65	4	21	10.18	-6.59		1.00	Oct-96
	2.72	9.78	4.85	17.59	20.64	1.91	1.24	5.12		10.76	529.9	-5	35	65	4	21	10.54	-6.45			Jan-06
	2.88	10.20	5.37	19.48	24.04	2.44	0.71	5.12		10.63	529.9	-5	35	65	4	21	10.83	-6.19			Nov-12
	2.84	10.15	5.39	19.58	24.35	2.51	0.67	5.1		10.48	529.9	-5	35	65	4	21	10.83	-6.19			Jun-13
	2.89	10.12	5.37	19.34	23.73	2.43	0.74	5.15		10.58	529.9	-5	35	65	4	21	10.83	-6.19			Oct-96
	3.22	12.76	5.53	25.91	31.01	2.53	0.76	7.21		10.99	1,492	-3	50	50	2	20	13.26	-10.44			Jun-13
	3.12	12.45	5.19	24.96	29.33	2.26	1.01	7.23		11.13	1,492	-3	50	50	2	20	13.26	-10.44	5.75		Mar-04
	2.95	12.15	4.44	22.15	24.54	1.55	1.76	7.2		11.04	1,492	-3	50	50	2	20	12.82	-10.75		1.00	Mar-04
	3.06	12.35	4.94	23.99	27.68	2.03	1.26	7.13		11.1	1,492	-3	50	50	2	20	13.03	-10.49			Sep-10
	3.23	12.67	5.54	26.02	31.22	2.55	0.75	7.21		10.98	1,492	-3	50	50	2	20	13.26	-10.44			Jun-13
	3.24	12.69	5.49	26.20	31.63	2.59	0.7	7.19		10.98	1,492	-3	50	50	2	20	13.26	-10.44			Jun-13
	3.28	12.71	5.47	25.94	31.00	2.51	0.76	7.16		11.12	1,492	-3	50	50	2	20	13.3	-10.31			Sep-10
	-0.67	3.79	-8.95	-10.29	-41.38	17.49	0.83	8.62	1	4.38	362.0	-36	-2	32	106	0	8.36				Mar-13
	-0.69	3.63	-9.03	-10.96	-42.21	17.57	1.08	8.62	1	4.28	362.0	-36	-2	32	106	0	8.2		5.75		Jun-12
	-1.21	3.04	-9.96	-13.08	-44.44	17.49	1.83	8.57	0.99	4.06	362.0	-36	-2	32	106	0	7.73			1.00	Jun-12
	-0.94	3.43	-9.29	-11.55	-42.94	17.52	1.33	8.62	1	4.21	362.0	-36	-2	32	106	0	8.04				Jun-12
	-0.67	3.77	-8.84	-10.14	-41.28	17.52	0.75	8.7	1	4.4	362.0	-36	-2	32	106	0	8.36				Jan-14
	-0.89	3.52	-8.90	-10.02	-41.16	17.57	0.69	8.62	1	4.41	362.0	-36	-2	32	106	0	8.36				Oct-14
	-0.68	3.57	-8.84	-10.35	-41.63	17.67	0.83	8.6	0.99	4.34	362.0	-36	-2	32	106	0	8.36				Jun-12
	-1.99	14.64	-4.36	34.85	20.77	1.83	1.55	15.99	1.17	12.29	17.8	5	95	0	0	150	20.03	-27.16	5.75		Sep-10
	-2.17	14.23	-5.08	31.78	16.19	1.05	2.3	15.93	1.17	12.12	17.8	5	95	0	0	150	19.33	-27.47		1.00	Sep-10
	-2.09	14.48	-4.63	33.66	19.20	1.58	1.8	15.99	1.17	12.17	17.8	5	95	0	0	150	19.76	-27.31			Sep-10
	-1.98	14.79	-4.01	36.14	22.91	2.2	1.17	15.97	1.17	12.34	17.8	5	95	0	0	150	20.13	-26.99			Jul-09
	-1.92	14.87	-3.98	36.29	23.05	2.29	1.11	15.98	1.17	12.2	17.8	5	95	0	0	150	20.13	-26.99			Mar-17
	-1.99	14.75	-4.22	35.60	22.11	2.1	1.3	15.94	1.17	12.29	17.8	5	95	0	0	150	20.04	-27.19			Sep-10
	4.64	20.34	9.58	42.45	57.61	1.03	0.77	12.7	1.02	26.15	9,914	2	98	0	0	63	26.12	-18.05			Nov-12
	4.60	20.20	9.32	41.38	55.61	0.82	1.02	12.7	1.02	25.46	9,914	2	98	0	0	63	25.96	-18.19	5.75		Oct-98
	4.38	19.75	8.52	38.27	49.88	0.11	1.77	12.71	1.02	22.85	9,914	2	98	0	0	63	25.37	-18.44		1.00	Dec-02
	4.51	20.02	9.06	40.31	53.73	0.58	1.27	12.71	1.02	25.47	9,914	2	98	0	0	63	25.79	-18.25			Sep-10
	4.56	20.18	9.33	41.36	55.56	0.82	1.02	12.7	1.02	25.19	9,914	2	98	0	0	63	25.84	-18.14	5.75		Feb-93
	4.68	20.40	9.73	42.91	58.47	1.11	0.68	12.71	1.02	26.14	9,914	2	98	0	0	63	26.12	-18.05			Nov-12
	4.68	20.45	9.74	43.08	58.89	1.16	0.63	12.7	1.02	26.15	9,914	2	98	0	0	63	26.12	-18.05			Nov-12
	4.64	20.33	9.63	42.46	57.65	1.05	0.77	12.73	1.02	25.68	9,914	2	98	0	0	63	26.12	-18.05			Dec-92
	5.94	20.45	-0.24	27.29	7.37	1.18	1.1	14.1	1.08	6.95	282.6	3	94	0	3	63	17.48	-25.56			Jan-14
	5.91	20.13	-0.53	26.17	6.09	0.93	1.35	14.12	1.08	6.98	282.6	3	94	0	3	63	17.48	-25.56	5.75		Jun-00
	5.75	19.93	-1.17	23.44	2.25	0.18	2.1	14.14	1.08	6.8	282.6	3	94	0	3	63	16.8	-25.72		1.00	Jun-00
	6.05	20.48	-0.13	27.63	8.08	1.26	1.01	14.15	1.08	7	282.6	3	94	0	3	63	17.48	-25.56			Jan-14
	6.07	20.53	-0.06	27.91	7.41	1.36	0.95	14.15	1.09	6.81	282.6	3	94	0	3	63	17.48	-25.56			Mar-16
	5.94	20.45	-0.38	27.04	7.34	1.18	1.1	14.12	1.08	6.95	282.6	3	94	0	3	63	17.46	-25.37			Sep-10
	5.29	18.48	11.23	49.31	42.58	2.16	0.88	9.04	1.04	21.89	1,276	3	7	0	0	60	15.05	-16.72			Nov-12
	5.23	18.31	10.97	48.15	40.79	1.96	1.13	9.05	1.04	21.67	1,276	3	7	0	0	60	15.05	-16.72	5.75		Sep-87
	5.05	17.87	10.12	44.88	35.60	1.26	1.88	9.05	1.04	21.61	1,276	3	7	0	0	60	14.57	-16.97		1.00	Oct-96
	5.17	18.24	10.70	47.09	39.08	1.73	1.38	9.05	1.04	21.66	1,276	3	7	0	0	60	14.97	-16.81			Nov-11
	5.32	18.54	11.32	49.63	43.20	2.23	0.81	9.06	1.04	21.87	1,276	3	7	0	0	60	15.05	-16.72			Nov-12

	MARKET			FUND TYPE, CATEGORY & OBJECTIVE	RATINGS				MINIMUMS	
Fund Name	Ticker Symbol	Traded On	Fund Type	Category and (Prospectus Objective)	Overall Rating	Reward Rating	Risk Rating	Recent Up/ Downgrade	Open to New Investors	Min Initial Investment
Columbia Convertible Securities Fund Institutional 3 Class	CSFYX	NAS CM	Open End	Convertibles (Convertible Bond)	B	C+	A-	Down	Y	1,000,000
Columbia Convertible Securities Fund Institutional Class	NCIAX	NAS CM	Open End	Convertibles (Convertible Bond)	B	C+	A-	Down	Y	2,000
Columbia Disciplined Core Fund Advisor Class	CLCQX	NAS CM	Open End	US Equity Large Cap Blend (Growth)	B-	C	B		Y	2,000
Columbia Disciplined Core Fund Class A	AQEAX	NAS CM	Open End	US Equity Large Cap Blend (Growth)	B-	C	B		Y	2,000
Columbia Disciplined Core Fund Class C	RDCEX	NAS CM	Open End	US Equity Large Cap Blend (Growth)	B-	C	B		Y	2,000
Columbia Disciplined Core Fund Class R	CLQRX	NAS CM	Open End	US Equity Large Cap Blend (Growth)	B-	C	B		Y	0
Columbia Disciplined Core Fund Institutional 2 Class	RSIPX	NAS CM	Open End	US Equity Large Cap Blend (Growth)	B-	C	B		Y	0
Columbia Disciplined Core Fund Institutional 3 Class	CCQYX	NAS CM	Open End	US Equity Large Cap Blend (Growth)	B-	C	B		Y	1,000,000
Columbia Disciplined Core Fund Institutional Class	CCRZX	NAS CM	Open End	US Equity Large Cap Blend (Growth)	B-	C	B		Y	2,000
Columbia Disciplined Growth Fund Advisor Class	CGQFX	NAS CM	Open End	US Equity Large Cap Growth (Growth)	C+	C	B	Down	Y	0
Columbia Disciplined Growth Fund Class A	RDLAX	NAS CM	Open End	US Equity Large Cap Growth (Growth)	C+	C	B	Down	Y	2,000
Columbia Disciplined Growth Fund Class C	RDLCX	NAS CM	Open End	US Equity Large Cap Growth (Growth)	C+	C	B	Down	Y	2,000
Columbia Disciplined Growth Fund Class R	CGQRX	NAS CM	Open End	US Equity Large Cap Growth (Growth)	C+	C	B	Down	Y	0
Columbia Disciplined Growth Fund Institutional 2 Class	CQURX	NAS CM	Open End	US Equity Large Cap Growth (Growth)	C+	C	B	Down	Y	0
Columbia Disciplined Growth Fund Institutional 3 Class	CGQYX	NAS CM	Open End	US Equity Large Cap Growth (Growth)	C+	C	B	Down	Y	0
Columbia Disciplined Growth Fund Institutional Class	CLQZX	NAS CM	Open End	US Equity Large Cap Growth (Growth)	C+	C	B	Down	Y	2,000
Columbia Disciplined Small Core Fund Advisor Class	CFFRX	NAS CM	Open End	US Equity Small Cap (Small Company)	C-	D+	C		Y	2,000
Columbia Disciplined Small Core Fund Class A	LSMAX	NAS CM	Open End	US Equity Small Cap (Small Company)	C-	D+	C		Y	2,000
Columbia Disciplined Small Core Fund Class C	LSMCX	NAS CM	Open End	US Equity Small Cap (Small Company)	D+	D	C-	Down	Y	2,000
Columbia Disciplined Small Core Fund Class V	SSCEX	NAS CM	Open End	US Equity Small Cap (Small Company)	C-	D+	C			2,000
Columbia Disciplined Small Core Fund Institutional 2 Class	CLLRX	NAS CM	Open End	US Equity Small Cap (Small Company)	C-	D+	C		Y	0
Columbia Disciplined Small Core Fund Institutional 3 Class	CPFRX	NAS CM	Open End	US Equity Small Cap (Small Company)	C-	D+	C		Y	1,000,000
Columbia Disciplined Small Core Fund Institutional Class	SMCEX	NAS CM	Open End	US Equity Small Cap (Small Company)	C-	D+	C		Y	2,000
Columbia Disciplined Value Fund Advisor Class	COLEX	NAS CM	Open End	US Equity Large Cap Value (Growth)	C+	C	B		Y	0
Columbia Disciplined Value Fund Class A	RLCAX	NAS CM	Open End	US Equity Large Cap Value (Growth)	C+	C	B		Y	2,000
Columbia Disciplined Value Fund Class C	RDCCX	NAS CM	Open End	US Equity Large Cap Value (Growth)	C+	C	B	Up	Y	2,000
Columbia Disciplined Value Fund Class R	RLCOX	NAS CM	Open End	US Equity Large Cap Value (Growth)	C+	C	B	Up	Y	0
Columbia Disciplined Value Fund Class V	CVQTX	NAS CM	Open End	US Equity Large Cap Value (Growth)	C+	C	B			2,000
Columbia Disciplined Value Fund Institutional 2 Class	COLVX	NAS CM	Open End	US Equity Large Cap Value (Growth)	C+	C	B		Y	100,000
Columbia Disciplined Value Fund Institutional 3 Class	COLYX	NAS CM	Open End	US Equity Large Cap Value (Growth)	C+	C	B		Y	0
Columbia Disciplined Value Fund Institutional Class	CVQZX	NAS CM	Open End	US Equity Large Cap Value (Growth)	C+	C	B		Y	2,000
Columbia Dividend Income Fund Advisor Class	CVIRX	NAS CM	Open End	US Equity Large Cap Value (Equity-Income)	B	C+	B+		Y	2,000
Columbia Dividend Income Fund Class A	LBSAX	NAS CM	Open End	US Equity Large Cap Value (Equity-Income)	B-	C+	B+	Down	Y	2,000
Columbia Dividend Income Fund Class C	LBSCX	NAS CM	Open End	US Equity Large Cap Value (Equity-Income)	B-	C+	B+	Down	Y	2,000
Columbia Dividend Income Fund Class R	CDIRX	NAS CM	Open End	US Equity Large Cap Value (Equity-Income)	B-	C+	B+	Down	Y	0
Columbia Dividend Income Fund Class V	GEQAX	NAS CM	Open End	US Equity Large Cap Value (Equity-Income)	B	C+	B+			2,000
Columbia Dividend Income Fund Institutional 2 Class	CDDRX	NAS CM	Open End	US Equity Large Cap Value (Equity-Income)	B	C+	B+		Y	0
Columbia Dividend Income Fund Institutional 3 Class	CDDYX	NAS CM	Open End	US Equity Large Cap Value (Equity-Income)	B	C+	B+		Y	1,000,000
Columbia Dividend Income Fund Institutional Class	GSFTX	NAS CM	Open End	US Equity Large Cap Value (Equity-Income)	B	C+	B+		Y	2,000
Columbia Dividend Opportunity Fund Advisor Class	CDORX	NAS CM	Open End	US Equity Large Cap Value (Equity-Income)	B-	C	B+	Down	Y	2,000
Columbia Dividend Opportunity Fund Class A	INUTX	NAS CM	Open End	US Equity Large Cap Value (Equity-Income)	B-	C	B+	Down	Y	2,000
Columbia Dividend Opportunity Fund Class C	ACUIX	NAS CM	Open End	US Equity Large Cap Value (Equity-Income)	B-	C	B+		Y	2,000
Columbia Dividend Opportunity Fund Class R	RSOOX	NAS CM	Open End	US Equity Large Cap Value (Equity-Income)	B-	C	B+		Y	0
Columbia Dividend Opportunity Fund Institutional 2 Class	RSDFX	NAS CM	Open End	US Equity Large Cap Value (Equity-Income)	B-	C	B+	Down	Y	0
Columbia Dividend Opportunity Fund Institutional 3 Class	CDOYX	NAS CM	Open End	US Equity Large Cap Value (Equity-Income)	B-	C	B+	Down	Y	1,000,000
Columbia Dividend Opportunity Fund Institutional Class	CDOZX	NAS CM	Open End	US Equity Large Cap Value (Equity-Income)	B-	C	B+	Down	Y	2,000
Columbia Emerging Markets Fund Advisor Class	CEMHX	NAS CM	Open End	Global Emerg Mkts (Div Emerging Mkts)	C	C	C		Y	2,000
Columbia Emerging Markets Fund Class A	EEMAX	NAS CM	Open End	Global Emerg Mkts (Div Emerging Mkts)	C	C	C		Y	2,000
Columbia Emerging Markets Fund Class C	EEMCX	NAS CM	Open End	Global Emerg Mkts (Div Emerging Mkts)	C	C	C		Y	2,000
Columbia Emerging Markets Fund Class R	CEMRX	NAS CM	Open End	Global Emerg Mkts (Div Emerging Mkts)	C	C	C		Y	0
Columbia Emerging Markets Fund Institutional 2 Class	CEKRX	NAS CM	Open End	Global Emerg Mkts (Div Emerging Mkts)	C	C	C		Y	0
Columbia Emerging Markets Fund Institutional 3 Class	CEKYX	NAS CM	Open End	Global Emerg Mkts (Div Emerging Mkts)	C	C	C		Y	1,000,000

★Expanded analysis of this fund is included in Section II.

	TOTAL RETURNS					PERFORMANCE				ASSETS		ASSET ALLOCATION & TURNOVER					BULL & BEAR		FEES		
Min Additional Investment	3-Month Total Return	6-Month Total Return	1-Year Total Return	3-Year Total Return	5-Year Total Return	Dividend Yield (TTM)	Expense Ratio	3-Yr Std Deviation	3-Year Beta	NAV	Total Assets (MIL)	%Cash	%Stocks	%Bonds	%Other	Turnover Ratio	Last Bull Market Total Return	Last Bear Market Total Return	Front End Fee (%)	Back End Fee (%)	Inception Date
	5.34	18.53	11.33	49.79	43.35	2.26	0.77	9.06	1.04	22.04	1,276	3	7	0	0	60	15.05	-16.72			Oct-14
	5.29	18.48	11.22	49.24	42.56	2.18	0.88	9.04	1.04	21.7	1,276	3	7	0	0	60	15.26	-16.66			May-99
	1.99	16.05	7.14	49.55	63.08	1.11	0.74	12.45	1.01	12.29	4,509	0	100	0	0	71	27.42	-14.62			Mar-13
	2.01	15.91	6.93	48.52	61.13	0.88	0.99	12.45	1.01	12.16	4,509	0	100	0	0	71	27.42	-14.62	5.75		Apr-03
	1.79	15.45	6.11	45.10	55.19	0.16	1.74	12.43	1.01	11.88	4,509	0	100	0	0	71	26.85	-14.84		1.00	Apr-03
	1.84	15.72	6.56	47.39	58.95	0.64	1.24	12.44	1.01	12.14	4,509	0	100	0	0	71	27.29	-14.78			Dec-06
	2.09	16.07	7.22	49.79	63.65	1.14	0.71	12.44	1.01	12.2	4,509	0	100	0	0	71	27.68	-14.42			Dec-06
	1.99	16.11	7.25	50.03	63.33	1.19	0.66	12.43	1.01	12.25	4,509	0	100	0	0	71	27.43	-14.62			Jun-15
	2.08	16.12	7.17	49.67	63.09	1.12	0.74	12.48	1.01	12.24	4,509	0	100	0	0	71	27.71	-14.69			Sep-10
	2.46	17.76	6.38	57.74	76.76	0.11	0.92	13.49	1	9.15	462.9	0	100	0	0	82	27.97	-15.89			Jun-15
	2.37	17.63	6.09	56.73	75.21	0	1.17	13.55	1	9.07	462.9	0	100	0	0	82	27.97	-15.89	5.75		May-07
	2.26	17.26	5.33	53.30	68.82	0	1.92	13.56	1	8.56	462.9	0	100	0	0	82	27.45	-16.17		1.00	May-07
	2.25	17.48	5.84	55.49	73.07	0	1.42	13.47	0.99	9.07	462.9	0	100	0	0	82	27.82	-16			May-07
	2.47	17.79	6.44	58.18	78.40	0.17	0.86	13.52	1	9.53	462.9	0	100	0	0	82	27.97	-15.89			Nov-12
	2.42	17.91	6.55	58.43	77.83	0.22	0.81	13.55	1	9.28	462.9	0	100	0	0	82	27.97	-15.89			Jun-15
	2.45	17.69	6.36	57.71	77.42	0.11	0.92	13.52	1	9.18	462.9	0	100	0	0	82	28.11	-15.8			Sep-10
	-0.80	13.94	-11.16	20.96	3.81	0	1.08	17.81	1.03	6.13	95.8	0	100	0	0	87	26.3	-23.61			Nov-12
	-0.78	13.93	-11.33	20.20	2.66	0	1.33	17.86	1.03	5.07	95.8	0	100	0	0	87	26.06	-23.6	5.75		Nov-98
	-1.10	13.29	-11.89	17.56	-1.00	0	2.08	17.66	1.02	1.79	95.8	0	100	0	0	87	25.53	-23.86		1.00	Nov-02
	-0.85	13.75	-11.45	20.00	2.52	0	1.33	17.77	1.02	4.63	95.8	0	100	0	0	87	26.06	-23.65	5.75		Feb-93
	-0.79	14.15	-11.04	21.39	4.54	0	0.96	17.83	1.03	6.21	95.8	0	100	0	0	87	26.3	-23.61			Nov-12
	-0.63	14.10	-10.93	21.55	4.79	0	0.91	17.83	1.03	6.31	95.8	0	100	0	0	87	26.3	-23.61			Nov-12
	-0.66	14.20	-11.07	21.18	3.98	0	1.08	17.94	1.03	5.95	95.8	0	100	0	0	87	26.3	-23.61			Dec-92
	2.41	12.99	4.40	35.02	39.97	1.75	0.9	12.82	1.04	9.74	719.1	-1	101	0	0	86	25.11	-18.56			Jun-15
	2.33	12.86	4.14	34.08	38.59	1.51	1.15	12.81	1.04	9.65	719.1	-1	101	0	0	86	25.11	-18.56	5.75		Aug-08
	2.17	12.45	3.46	31.17	33.44	0.76	1.9	12.75	1.04	9.39	719.1	-1	101	0	0	86	24.6	-18.93		1.00	Aug-08
	2.32	12.83	3.95	33.02	36.95	1.25	1.4	12.85	1.04	9.67	719.1	-1	101	0	0	86	24.85	-18.66			Aug-08
	2.34	12.91	4.16	34.05	38.48	1.51	1.15	12.8	1.04	9.62	719.1	-1	101	0	0	86	25.19	-18.58	5.75		Mar-11
	2.42	13.13	4.55	35.51	40.49	1.88	0.76	12.76	1.04	9.73	719.1	-1	101	0	0	86	25.11	-18.56			Jun-15
	2.41	13.10	4.61	35.79	40.87	1.93	0.71	12.79	1.04	9.75	719.1	-1	101	0	0	86	25.11	-18.56			Jun-15
	2.41	12.97	4.40	34.98	40.19	1.74	0.9	12.85	1.04	9.75	719.1	-1	101	0	0	86	25.18	-18.47			Sep-10
	4.09	17.51	12.95	44.58	62.82	1.83	0.71	10.74	0.84	23.09	14,746	4	96	0	0	15	22.72	-12.43			Nov-12
	4.05	17.38	12.65	43.49	60.81	1.63	0.96	10.75	0.84	22.68	14,746	4	96	0	0	15	22.59	-12.56	5.75		Nov-02
	3.84	16.92	11.86	40.34	54.92	0.97	1.71	10.75	0.84	21.95	14,746	4	96	0	0	15	22.07	-12.84		1.00	Nov-02
	3.98	17.22	12.42	42.46	58.85	1.4	1.21	10.74	0.84	22.7	14,746	4	96	0	0	15	22.42	-12.66			Mar-08
	4.05	17.37	12.65	43.46	60.72	1.63	0.96	10.75	0.84	22.69	14,746	4	96	0	0	15	22.54	-12.51	5.75		Mar-98
	4.11	17.57	13.05	44.96	63.72	1.91	0.63	10.76	0.84	23.07	14,746	4	96	0	0	15	22.72	-12.43			Nov-12
	4.12	17.58	13.08	45.23	64.16	1.95	0.58	10.76	0.84	23.1	14,746	4	96	0	0	15	22.72	-12.43			Nov-12
	4.11	17.50	12.92	44.59	62.84	1.86	0.71	10.74	0.84	22.7	14,746	4	96	0	0	15	22.72	-12.43			Mar-98
	2.62	16.30	10.09	31.29	41.93	3.09	0.73	10.76	0.97	9.47	2,777	0	95	0	0	65	21.26	-14.28			Nov-12
	2.50	16.11	9.79	30.25	40.24	2.92	0.98	10.75	0.97	9.28	2,777	0	95	0	0	65	21.26	-14.28	5.75		Aug-88
	2.25	15.70	8.84	27.21	34.92	2.27	1.73	10.75	0.97	9.05	2,777	0	95	0	0	65	20.88	-14.6		1.00	Jun-00
	2.55	16.11	9.52	29.30	38.52	2.69	1.23	10.78	0.97	9.28	2,777	0	95	0	0	65	21.09	-14.31			Aug-08
	2.67	16.42	10.16	31.51	42.55	3.18	0.68	10.72	0.97	9.35	2,777	0	95	0	0	65	21.58	-14.17			Aug-08
	2.53	16.31	10.18	31.63	42.84	3.18	0.63	10.73	0.97	9.49	2,777	0	95	0	0	65	21.26	-14.28			Nov-12
	2.66	16.44	10.13	31.35	42.09	3.14	0.73	10.73	0.97	9.33	2,777	0	95	0	0	65	21.5	-14.22			Sep-10
	2.80	17.81	0.19	37.69	20.00	0.1	1.29	15.09	1.04	12.83	1,347	4	96	0	0	39	18.23	-25.72			Mar-13
	2.77	17.77	0.00	36.74	18.50	0	1.54	15.16	1.05	12.59	1,347	4	96	0	0	39	18.01	-25.8	5.75		Sep-07
	2.61	17.31	-0.75	33.67	14.24	0	2.29	15.12	1.04	11.79	1,347	4	96	0	0	39	17.51	-25.97		1.00	Sep-07
	2.73	17.64	-0.24	35.66	17.09	0	1.79	15.16	1.04	12.4	1,347	4	96	0	0	39	18.04	-25.83			Sep-10
	2.88	18.03	0.43	38.37	21.02	0.24	1.16	15.17	1.05	12.83	1,347	4	96	0	0	39	18.23	-25.72			Nov-12
	2.87	17.94	0.42	38.45	21.19	0.3	1.11	15.11	1.04	12.88	1,347	4	96	0	0	39	18.23	-25.72			Nov-12

	MARKET		FUND TYPE, CATEGORY & OBJECTIVE		RATINGS				MINIMUMS	
Fund Name	Ticker Symbol	Traded On	Fund Type	Category and (Prospectus Objective)	Overall Rating	Reward Rating	Risk Rating	Recent Up/ Downgrade	Open to New Investors	Min Initial Investment
Columbia Emerging Markets Fund Institutional Class	UMEMX	NAS CM	Open End	Global Emerg Mkts (Div Emerging Mkts)	C	C	C		Y	2,000
Columbia Flexible Capital Income Fund Advisor Class	CFCRX	NAS CM	Open End	Cautious Alloc (Income)	B-	C+	B	Up	Y	2,000
Columbia Flexible Capital Income Fund Class A	CFIAX	NAS CM	Open End	Cautious Alloc (Income)	B-	C	B	Up	Y	2,000
Columbia Flexible Capital Income Fund Class C	CFIGX	NAS CM	Open End	Cautious Alloc (Income)	B-	C	B	Up	Y	2,000
Columbia Flexible Capital Income Fund Class R	CFIRX	NAS CM	Open End	Cautious Alloc (Income)	B-	C	B	Up	Y	0
Columbia Flexible Capital Income Institutional 2 Cls	CFXRX	NAS CM	Open End	Cautious Alloc (Income)	B-	C+	B	Up	Y	0
Columbia Flexible Capital Income Institutional 3 Cls	CFCYX	NAS CM	Open End	Cautious Alloc (Income)	B-	C+	B	Up	Y	1,000,000
Columbia Flexible Capital Income Fund Institutional Class	CFIZX	NAS CM	Open End	Cautious Alloc (Income)	B-	C	B	Up	Y	2,000
Columbia Global Dividend Opportunity Fund Advisor Class	CGOLX	NAS CM	Open End	Global Equity Large Cap (Equity-Income)	C+	C	B	Up	Y	2,000
Columbia Global Dividend Opportunity Fund Class A	CSVAX	NAS CM	Open End	Global Equity Large Cap (Equity-Income)	C+	C	B	Up	Y	2,000
Columbia Global Dividend Opportunity Fund Class C	CSRCX	NAS CM	Open End	Global Equity Large Cap (Equity-Income)	C+	C	B	Up	Y	2,000
Columbia Global Dividend Opportunity Fund Class R	CSGRX	NAS CM	Open End	Global Equity Large Cap (Equity-Income)	C+	C	B	Up	Y	0
Columbia Global Dividend Opportunity Institutional 2 Cls	CADPX	NAS CM	Open End	Global Equity Large Cap (Equity-Income)	C+	C	B	Up	Y	0
Columbia Global Dividend Opportunity Institutional 3 Cls	CLSYX	NAS CM	Open End	Global Equity Large Cap (Equity-Income)	C+	C	B	Up	Y	1,000,000
Columbia Global Dividend Opportunity Institutional Cls	CSVFX	NAS CM	Open End	Global Equity Large Cap (Equity-Income)	C+	C	B	Up	Y	2,000
Columbia Global Energy & Natural Resources Advisor Cls	CENRX	NAS CM	Open End	Natl Resources Sec Equity (Natl Res)	C-	C-	C	Down	Y	2,000
Columbia Global Energy and Natural Resources Fund Class A	EENAX	NAS CM	Open End	Natl Resources Sec Equity (Natl Res)	C-	C-	C	Down	Y	2,000
Columbia Global Energy and Natural Resources Fund Class C	EENCX	NAS CM	Open End	Natl Resources Sec Equity (Natl Res)	C-	C-	C-	Down	Y	2,000
Columbia Global Energy and Natural Resources Fund Class R	CETRX	NAS CM	Open End	Natl Resources Sec Equity (Natl Res)	C-	C-	C	Down	Y	0
Columbia Global Energy & Natural Resources Inst 2 Cls	CNRRX	NAS CM	Open End	Natl Resources Sec Equity (Natl Res)	C-	C-	C	Down	Y	0
Columbia Global Energy & Natural Resources Inst 3 Cls	CGEYX	NAS CM	Open End	Natl Resources Sec Equity (Natl Res)	C-	C-	C	Down	Y	1,000,000
Columbia Global Energy & Natural Resources Inst Cls	UMESX	NAS CM	Open End	Natl Resources Sec Equity (Natl Res)	C-	C-	C	Down	Y	2,000
Columbia Global Equity Value Fund Advisor Class	RSEVX	NAS CM	Open End	Global Equity Large Cap (Growth & Income)	B-	C	B	Up	Y	2,000
Columbia Global Equity Value Fund Class A	IEVAX	NAS CM	Open End	Global Equity Large Cap (Growth & Income)	B-	C	B	Up	Y	2,000
Columbia Global Equity Value Fund Class C	REVCX	NAS CM	Open End	Global Equity Large Cap (Growth & Income)	B-	C	B	Up	Y	2,000
Columbia Global Equity Value Fund Class R	REVRX	NAS CM	Open End	Global Equity Large Cap (Growth & Income)	B-	C	B	Up	Y	0
Columbia Global Equity Value Fund Institutional 2 Class	RSEYX	NAS CM	Open End	Global Equity Large Cap (Growth & Income)	B-	C	B	Up	Y	0
Columbia Global Equity Value Fund Institutional 3 Class	CEVYX	NAS CM	Open End	Global Equity Large Cap (Growth & Income)	B-	C	B	Up	Y	1,000,000
Columbia Global Equity Value Fund Institutional Class	CEVZX	NAS CM	Open End	Global Equity Large Cap (Growth & Income)	B-	C	B	Up	Y	2,000
Columbia Global Infrastructure Fund Advisor Class	CRRIX	NAS CM	Open End	Infrastructure Sector Equity (Utility)	C+	C	B		Y	2,000
Columbia Global Infrastructure Fund Class A	RRIAX	NAS CM	Open End	Infrastructure Sector Equity (Utility)	C+	C	B		Y	2,000
Columbia Global Infrastructure Fund Class C	RRICX	NAS CM	Open End	Infrastructure Sector Equity (Utility)	C+	C	B		Y	2,000
Columbia Global Infrastructure Fund Class R	RRIRX	NAS CM	Open End	Infrastructure Sector Equity (Utility)	C+	C	B		Y	0
Columbia Global Infrastructure Fund Institutional 2 Class	RRIZX	NAS CM	Open End	Infrastructure Sector Equity (Utility)	C+	C	B		Y	0
Columbia Global Infrastructure Fund Institutional 3 Class	CGLYX	NAS CM	Open End	Infrastructure Sector Equity (Utility)	C+	C	B		Y	1,000,000
Columbia Global Infrastructure Fund Institutional Class	CRIZX	NAS CM	Open End	Infrastructure Sector Equity (Utility)	C+	C	B		Y	2,000
Columbia Global Opportunities Fund Advisor Class	CSDRX	NAS CM	Open End	Moderate Alloc (Growth & Income)	B-	C	A-	Up	Y	2,000
Columbia Global Opportunities Fund Class A	IMRFX	NAS CM	Open End	Moderate Alloc (Growth & Income)	B-	C	A-	Up	Y	2,000
Columbia Global Opportunities Fund Class C	RSSCX	NAS CM	Open End	Moderate Alloc (Growth & Income)	C+	C	B+	Up	Y	2,000
Columbia Global Opportunities Fund Class R	CSARX	NAS CM	Open End	Moderate Alloc (Growth & Income)	B-	C	B+	Up	Y	0
Columbia Global Opportunities Fund Institutional 2 Class	CLNRX	NAS CM	Open End	Moderate Alloc (Growth & Income)	B-	C	A-	Up	Y	0
Columbia Global Opportunities Fund Institutional 3 Class	CGOYX	NAS CM	Open End	Moderate Alloc (Growth & Income)	B-	C	A-	Up	Y	1,000,000
Columbia Global Opportunities Fund Institutional Class	CSAZX	NAS CM	Open End	Moderate Alloc (Growth & Income)	B-	C	A-	Up	Y	2,000
Columbia Global Strategic Equity Fund Advisor Class	CWPRX	NAS CM	Open End	Global Equity Large Cap (Growth)	C+	C	B	Up	Y	2,000
Columbia Global Strategic Equity Fund Class A	NLGIX	NAS CM	Open End	Global Equity Large Cap (Growth)	C+	C	B	Up	Y	2,000
Columbia Global Strategic Equity Fund Class C	NLGCX	NAS CM	Open End	Global Equity Large Cap (Growth)	C+	C	B	Up	Y	2,000
Columbia Global Strategic Equity Fund Class R	CLGRX	NAS CM	Open End	Global Equity Large Cap (Growth)	C+	C	B	Up	Y	0
Columbia Global Strategic Equity Institutional 2 Cls	CGPRX	NAS CM	Open End	Global Equity Large Cap (Growth)	C+	C	B	Up	Y	0
Columbia Global Strategic Equity Institutional 3 Cls	CGSYX	NAS CM	Open End	Global Equity Large Cap (Growth)	C+	C	B	Up	Y	1,000,000
Columbia Global Strategic Equity Fund Institutional Class	NGPAX	NAS CM	Open End	Global Equity Large Cap (Growth)	C+	C	B	Up	Y	2,000
Columbia Global Technology Growth Fund Advisor Class	CTYRX	NAS CM	Open End	Technology Sector Equity (Technology)	B-	C+	B-	Down	Y	2,000
Columbia Global Technology Growth Fund Class A	CTCAX	NAS CM	Open End	Technology Sector Equity (Technology)	B-	C+	B-	Down	Y	2,000

★ Expanded analysis of this fund is included in Section II.

Min Additional Investment	3-Month Total Return	6-Month Total Return	1-Year Total Return	3-Year Total Return	5-Year Total Return	Dividend Yield (TTM)	Expense Ratio	3-Yr Std Deviation	3-Year Beta	NAV	Total Assets (MIL)	%Cash	%Stocks	%Bonds	%Other	Turnover Ratio	Last Bull Market Total Return	Last Bear Market Total Return	Front End Fee (%)	Back End Fee (%)	Inception Date
	TOTAL RETURNS					PERFORMANCE				ASSETS		ASSET ALLOCATION & TURNOVER					BULL & BEAR		FEES		
	2.82	17.85	0.27	37.76	19.94	0.1	1.29	15.16	1.05	12.74	1,347	4	96	0	0	39	18.23	-25.72			Jan-98
	3.03	14.86	5.68	35.07	31.71	4.29	0.92	8.56		13.09	930.6	0	42	28	0	50	19.03				Nov-12
	2.99	14.75	5.38	34.15	30.13	4.08	1.17	8.56		12.99	930.6	0	42	28	0	50	18.79		5.75		Jul-11
	2.82	14.22	4.62	31.15	25.30	3.36	1.92	8.55		12.92	930.6	0	42	28	0	50	18.35			1.00	Jul-11
	2.93	14.52	5.12	33.18	28.44	3.84	1.42	8.55		12.98	930.6	0	42	28	0	50	18.64				Jul-11
	3.04	14.87	5.72	35.32	32.07	4.33	0.89	8.55		13.1	930.6	0	42	28	0	50	19.03				Nov-12
	3.01	14.81	5.76	35.42	32.03	4.43	0.84	8.58		12.93	930.6	0	42	28	0	50	19.03				Mar-17
	2.98	14.80	5.65	35.04	31.66	4.33	0.92	8.59		12.98	930.6	0	42	28	0	50	19.03				Jul-11
	4.53	17.20	6.16	26.42	13.83	2.85	1.08	10.48	1.04	18.63	511.9	4	96	0	0	39	23.48	-24.42			Mar-13
	4.44	17.01	5.89	25.43	12.34	2.64	1.33	10.48	1.04	18.47	511.9	4	96	0	0	39	23.3	-24.49	5.75		Nov-02
	4.24	16.59	5.14	22.66	8.25	2.05	2.08	10.49	1.04	17.27	511.9	4	96	0	0	39	22.76	-24.76		1.00	Oct-03
	4.38	16.89	5.63	24.52	10.95	2.4	1.58	10.48	1.04	18.45	511.9	4	96	0	0	39	23.09	-24.58			Sep-10
	4.54	17.22	6.29	26.90	14.69	3	0.95	10.5	1.04	18.48	511.9	4	96	0	0	39	23.48	-24.42			Jan-14
	4.55	17.22	6.34	27.13	15.02	3.05	0.89	10.49	1.04	18.51	511.9	4	96	0	0	39	23.58	-24.42			Jul-09
	4.49	17.16	6.13	26.35	13.77	2.87	1.08	10.51	1.04	18.53	511.9	4	96	0	0	39	23.48	-24.42			Nov-00
	-0.54	13.69	-11.08	14.13	-19.77	2.05	1.07	16.16		18.26	184.7	0	100	0	0	37	17.6	-30.41			Nov-12
	-0.56	13.59	-11.27	13.26	-20.76	1.83	1.32	16.17		17.71	184.7	0	100	0	0	37	17.43	-30.51	5.75		Sep-07
	-0.71	13.23	-11.90	10.80	-23.67	1.27	2.07	16.16		16.68	184.7	0	100	0	0	37	16.95	-30.71		1.00	Sep-07
	-0.67	13.42	-11.50	12.44	-21.75	1.56	1.57	16.15		17.57	184.7	0	100	0	0	37	17.31	-30.58			Sep-10
	-0.48	13.82	-10.91	14.66	-19.10	2.18	0.93	16.19		18.36	184.7	0	100	0	0	37	17.6	-30.41			Nov-12
	-0.50	13.81	-10.90	14.60	-19.43	2.3	0.88	16.16		17.79	184.7	0	100	0	0	37	17.6	-30.41			Mar-17
	-0.49	13.76	-11.04	14.12	-19.76	2.08	1.07	16.2		17.94	184.7	0	100	0	0	37	17.6	-30.41			Dec-92
	3.27	15.77	6.53	40.25	28.45	1.59	0.89	11.23	1.01	12.92	752.8	1	99	0	0	33	23.23	-22.35			Dec-06
	3.22	15.72	6.29	39.28	26.89	1.43	1.14	11.2	1	12.86	752.8	1	99	0	0	33	23.23	-22.28	5.75		Mar-95
	3.07	15.34	5.55	36.20	22.21	0.91	1.89	11.22	1	12.68	752.8	1	99	0	0	33	22.74	-22.55		1.00	Jun-00
	3.16	15.53	6.03	38.22	25.27	1.25	1.39	11.2	1	12.82	752.8	1	99	0	0	33	23.09	-22.35			Dec-06
	3.31	15.91	6.63	40.74	29.08	1.66	0.83	11.19	1	12.85	752.8	1	99	0	0	33	23.56	-22.15			Dec-06
	3.33	15.92	6.68	40.95	29.54	1.73	0.78	11.2	1	12.5	752.8	1	99	0	0	33	23.23	-22.28			Feb-13
	3.28	15.83	6.55	40.27	28.46	1.6	0.89	11.18	1	12.88	752.8	1	99	0	0	33	23.5	-22.2			Sep-10
	5.91	23.67	11.18	29.17	18.58	2	0.94	11.12	0.93	13.79	170.3	4	96	0	0	45	30.31	-32.66			Mar-13
	5.84	23.52	10.87	28.19	17.11	1.82	1.19	11.1	0.93	13.39	170.3	4	96	0	0	45	29.97	-32.77	5.75		Feb-09
	5.62	23.16	10.25	28.18	16.45	1.95	1.94	11.12	0.92	12.39	170.3	4	96	0	0	45	29.39	-32.96		1.00	Feb-09
	5.70	23.38	10.56	27.18	15.61	1.64	1.44	11.13	0.93	12.98	170.3	4	96	0	0	45	29.81	-32.82			Feb-09
	5.95	23.77	11.27	29.53	19.05	2.07	0.88	11.13	0.93	13.69	170.3	4	96	0	0	45	30.31	-32.66			Feb-09
	5.90	23.77	11.28	29.55	19.06	2.12	0.83	11.13	0.93	13.64	170.3	4	96	0	0	45	30.31	-32.66			Mar-17
	5.88	23.71	11.11	29.15	18.53	2.02	0.94	11.13	0.93	13.67	170.3	4	96	0	0	45	30.14	-32.66			Sep-10
	3.04	11.45	3.30	24.62	24.20	0.56	0.93	7.38		14.2	559.2	-5	47	55	3	97	17.09	-11.78			Nov-12
	2.92	11.22	2.98	23.61	22.67	0.32	1.18	7.32		14.07	559.2	-5	47	55	3	97	17.09	-11.78	5.75		Jan-85
	2.74	10.86	2.27	20.95	18.24	0	1.93	7.35		13.47	559.2	-5	47	55	3	97	16.71	-12.2		1.00	Jun-00
	2.88	11.18	2.81	22.74	21.08	0.08	1.43	7.37		13.92	559.2	-5	47	55	3	97	16.99	-11.9			Dec-06
	2.96	11.42	3.26	24.79	24.68	0.59	0.9	7.34		14.24	559.2	-5	47	55	3	97	17.09	-11.78			Nov-12
	2.97	11.39	3.31	24.48	23.54	0.63	0.85	7.33		14.18	559.2	-5	47	55	3	97	17.09	-11.78			Mar-17
	2.98	11.40	3.24	24.59	24.28	0.56	0.93	7.36		14.16	559.2	-5	47	55	3	97	17.38	-11.72			Sep-10
	4.03	18.56	5.13	42.69	41.88	1.49	0.95	11.89	1.04	15.3	634.3	1	95	0	0	18	22.64	-19.97			Nov-12
	3.88	18.38	4.83	41.55	40.12	1.39	1.2	11.91	1.04	14.56	634.3	1	95	0	0	18	22.46	-20.02	5.75		Oct-96
	3.76	17.99	4.09	38.57	35.00	1.23	1.95	11.89	1.04	12.19	634.3	1	95	0	0	18	22.04	-20.28		1.00	Oct-96
	3.90	18.35	4.58	40.64	38.43	1.24	1.45	11.86	1.03	14.29	634.3	1	95	0	0	18	22.29	-20.11			Jan-06
	4.03	18.64	5.22	42.97	42.52	1.52	0.91	11.91	1.04	15.33	634.3	1	95	0	0	18	22.64	-19.97			Nov-12
	4.03	18.68	5.26	43.06	42.23	1.57	0.85	11.88	1.04	15.13	634.3	1	95	0	0	18	22.64	-19.97			Mar-17
	3.96	18.58	5.08	42.70	41.88	1.52	0.95	11.89	1.04	15.03	634.3	1	95	0	0	18	22.64	-19.97			Oct-96
	5.14	26.88	10.99	104.86	142.19	0	1	15.97	1.02	37.38	1,512	2	98	0	0	28	21.6	-24.74			Nov-12
	5.10	26.72	10.73	103.45	139.20	0	1.25	15.98	1.02	35.42	1,512	2	98	0	0	28	21.42	-24.83	5.75		Nov-02

	MARKET			FUND TYPE, CATEGORY & OBJECTIVE	RATINGS				MINIMUMS	
Fund Name	Ticker Symbol	Traded On	Fund Type	Category and (Prospectus Objective)	Overall Rating	Reward Rating	Risk Rating	Recent Up/ Downgrade	Open to New Investors	Min Initial Investment
Columbia Global Technology Growth Fund Class C	CTHCX	NAS CM	Open End	Technology Sector Equity (Technology)	C+	C+	B-	Down	Y	2,000
Columbia Global Technology Growth Institutional 2 Cls	CTHRX	NAS CM	Open End	Technology Sector Equity (Technology)	B-	C+	B-	Down	Y	0
Columbia Global Technology Growth Institutional 3 Cls	CGTUX	NAS CM	Open End	Technology Sector Equity (Technology)	B-	C+	B-	Down	Y	1,000,000
Columbia Global Technology Growth Fund Institutional Class	CMTFX	NAS CM	Open End	Technology Sector Equity (Technology)	B-	C+	B-	Down	Y	2,000
Columbia Greater China Fund Advisor Class	CGCHX	NAS CM	Open End	Greater China Equity (Pacific Stock)	C	C	C		Y	2,000
Columbia Greater China Fund Class A	NGCAX	NAS CM	Open End	Greater China Equity (Pacific Stock)	C	C	C		Y	2,000
Columbia Greater China Fund Class C	NGCCX	NAS CM	Open End	Greater China Equity (Pacific Stock)	C	C	C		Y	2,000
Columbia Greater China Fund Institutional 2 Class	CGCRX	NAS CM	Open End	Greater China Equity (Pacific Stock)	C	C	C		Y	0
Columbia Greater China Fund Institutional 3 Class	CGCYX	NAS CM	Open End	Greater China Equity (Pacific Stock)	C	C	C		Y	1,000,000
Columbia Greater China Fund Institutional Class	LNGZX	NAS CM	Open End	Greater China Equity (Pacific Stock)	C	C	C		Y	2,000
Columbia Income Builder Fund Advisor Class	CNMRX	NAS CM	Open End	Cautious Alloc (Growth & Income)	B	C+	B+		Y	2,000
Columbia Income Builder Fund Class A	RBBAX	NAS CM	Open End	Cautious Alloc (Growth & Income)	B	C+	B+	Up	Y	2,000
Columbia Income Builder Fund Class C	RBBCX	NAS CM	Open End	Cautious Alloc (Growth & Income)	B-	C+	B		Y	2,000
Columbia Income Builder Fund Class R	CBURX	NAS CM	Open End	Cautious Alloc (Growth & Income)	B-	C+	B		Y	0
Columbia Income Builder Fund Institutional 2 Class	CKKRX	NAS CM	Open End	Cautious Alloc (Growth & Income)	B	C+	B+		Y	0
Columbia Income Builder Fund Institutional 3 Class	CIBYX	NAS CM	Open End	Cautious Alloc (Growth & Income)	B	C+	B+		Y	1,000,000
Columbia Income Builder Fund Institutional Class	CBUZX	NAS CM	Open End	Cautious Alloc (Growth & Income)	B	C+	B+		Y	2,000
Columbia Large Cap Enhanced Core Fund Advisor Class	CECFX	NAS CM	Open End	US Equity Large Cap Blend (Growth)	B-	C	B		Y	2,000
Columbia Large Cap Enhanced Core Fund Class A	NMIAX	NAS CM	Open End	US Equity Large Cap Blend (Growth)	B-	C	B		Y	2,000
Columbia Large Cap Enhanced Core Fund Class R	CCERX	NAS CM	Open End	US Equity Large Cap Blend (Growth)	B-	C	B		Y	0
Columbia Large Cap Enhanced Core Institutional 2 Cls	CLNCX	NAS CM	Open End	US Equity Large Cap Blend (Growth)	B-	C	B		Y	0
Columbia Large Cap Enhanced Core Institutional 3 Cls	CECYX	NAS CM	Open End	US Equity Large Cap Blend (Growth)	B-	C	B		Y	1,000,000
Columbia Large Cap Enhanced Core Fund Institutional Class	NMIMX	NAS CM	Open End	US Equity Large Cap Blend (Growth)	B-	C	B		Y	2,000
Columbia Large Cap Growth Fund Advisor Class	CCGRX	NAS CM	Open End	US Equity Large Cap Growth (Growth)	C+	C	B	Down	Y	2,000
Columbia Large Cap Growth Fund Class A	LEGAX	NAS CM	Open End	US Equity Large Cap Growth (Growth)	C+	C	B	Down	Y	2,000
Columbia Large Cap Growth Fund Class C	LEGCX	NAS CM	Open End	US Equity Large Cap Growth (Growth)	C+	C	B-	Down	Y	2,000
Columbia Large Cap Growth Fund Class E	CLGEX	NAS CM	Open End	US Equity Large Cap Growth (Growth)	C+	C	B	Down		0
Columbia Large Cap Growth Fund Class R	CGWRX	NAS CM	Open End	US Equity Large Cap Growth (Growth)	C+	C	B-	Down	Y	0
Columbia Large Cap Growth Fund Class V	GAEGX	NAS CM	Open End	US Equity Large Cap Growth (Growth)	C+	C	B	Down		2,000
Columbia Large Cap Growth Fund III Advisor Class	CSFRX	NAS CM	Open End	US Equity Large Cap Growth (Growth)	C+	C	B	Down	Y	2,000
Columbia Large Cap Growth Fund III Class A	NFEAX	NAS CM	Open End	US Equity Large Cap Growth (Growth)	C+	C	B-	Down	Y	2,000
Columbia Large Cap Growth Fund III Class C	NFECX	NAS CM	Open End	US Equity Large Cap Growth (Growth)	C+	C	B-	Down	Y	2,000
Columbia Large Cap Growth Fund III Class R	CLGPX	NAS CM	Open End	US Equity Large Cap Growth (Growth)	C+	C	B-	Down	Y	0
Columbia Large Cap Growth Fund III Institutional 2 Class	CADRX	NAS CM	Open End	US Equity Large Cap Growth (Growth)	C+	C	B	Down	Y	0
Columbia Large Cap Growth Fund III Institutional 3 Class	CLRYX	NAS CM	Open End	US Equity Large Cap Growth (Growth)	C+	C	B	Down	Y	1,000,000
Columbia Large Cap Growth Fund III Institutional Class	NFEPX	NAS CM	Open End	US Equity Large Cap Growth (Growth)	C+	C	B	Down	Y	2,000
Columbia Large Cap Growth Fund Institutional 2 Class	CLWFX	NAS CM	Open End	US Equity Large Cap Growth (Growth)	C+	C	B	Down	Y	0
Columbia Large Cap Growth Fund Institutional 3 Class	CGFYX	NAS CM	Open End	US Equity Large Cap Growth (Growth)	C+	C	B	Down	Y	1,000,000
Columbia Large Cap Growth Fund Institutional Class	GEGTX	NAS CM	Open End	US Equity Large Cap Growth (Growth)	C+	C	B	Down	Y	2,000
Columbia Large Cap Index Fund Class A	NEIAX	NAS CM	Open End	US Equity Large Cap Blend (Growth & Income)	B-	C	B		Y	2,000
Columbia Large Cap Index Fund Institutional 2 Class	CLXRX	NAS CM	Open End	US Equity Large Cap Blend (Growth & Income)	B-	C	B		Y	0
Columbia Large Cap Index Fund Institutional 3 Class	CLPYX	NAS CM	Open End	US Equity Large Cap Blend (Growth & Income)	B-	C	B		Y	1,000,000
Columbia Large Cap Index Fund Institutional Class	NINDX	NAS CM	Open End	US Equity Large Cap Blend (Growth & Income)	B-	C	B		Y	2,000
Columbia Large Cap Value Fund Advisor Class	RDERX	NAS CM	Open End	US Equity Large Cap Value (Equity-Income)	B-	C	B	Up	Y	2,000
Columbia Large Cap Value Fund Class A	INDZX	NAS CM	Open End	US Equity Large Cap Value (Equity-Income)	B-	C	B	Up	Y	2,000
Columbia Large Cap Value Fund Class C	ADECX	NAS CM	Open End	US Equity Large Cap Value (Equity-Income)	C+	C	B		Y	2,000
Columbia Large Cap Value Fund Class R	RDEIX	NAS CM	Open End	US Equity Large Cap Value (Equity-Income)	B-	C	B	Up	Y	0
Columbia Large Cap Value Fund Institutional 2 Class	RSEDX	NAS CM	Open End	US Equity Large Cap Value (Equity-Income)	B-	C	B	Up	Y	0
Columbia Large Cap Value Fund Institutional 3 Class	CDEYX	NAS CM	Open End	US Equity Large Cap Value (Equity-Income)	B-	C	B	Up	Y	1,000,000
Columbia Large Cap Value Fund Institutional Class	CDVZX	NAS CM	Open End	US Equity Large Cap Value (Equity-Income)	B-	C	B	Up	Y	2,000
Columbia Mid Cap Growth Fund Advisor Class	CPGRX	NAS CM	Open End	US Equity Mid Cap (Growth)	B-	B-	B-		Y	2,000
Columbia Mid Cap Growth Fund Class A	CBSAX	NAS CM	Open End	US Equity Mid Cap (Growth)	B-	B-	B-		Y	2,000

★ Expanded analysis of this fund is included in Section II.

Min Additional Investment	TOTAL RETURNS 3-Month Total Return	6-Month Total Return	1-Year Total Return	3-Year Total Return	5-Year Total Return	PERFORMANCE Dividend Yield (TTM)	Expense Ratio	3-Yr Std Deviation	3-Year Beta	ASSETS NAV	Total Assets (MIL)	ASSET ALLOCATION & TURNOVER %Cash	%Stocks	%Bonds	%Other	Turnover Ratio	BULL & BEAR Last Bull Market Total Return	Last Bear Market Total Return	FEES Front End Fee (%)	Back End Fee (%)	Inception Date
	4.90	26.26	9.92	98.88	130.43	0	2	15.96	1.01	31.68	1,512	2	98	0	0	28	20.81	-25		1.00	Oct-03
	5.17	26.95	11.08	105.39	143.42	0	0.93	15.98	1.02	37.63	1,512	2	98	0	0	28	21.6	-24.74			Nov-12
	5.18	26.95	11.14	105.67	143.28	0	0.88	15.98	1.02	37.73	1,512	2	98	0	0	28	21.6	-24.74			Mar-16
	5.13	26.87	10.98	104.89	142.21	0	1	15.99	1.02	36.87	1,512	2	98	0	0	28	21.6	-24.74			Nov-00
	0.25	21.20	-4.25	60.28	53.80	0	1.26	20.21	1	51.62	116.5	0	100	0	0	26	19.85	-32.11			Mar-13
	0.19	21.04	-4.50	59.06	51.88	0	1.51	20.2	1	46.3	116.5	0	100	0	0	26	19.68	-32.2	5.75		May-97
	0.00	20.60	-5.21	55.54	46.30	0	2.26	20.19	1	42.2	116.5	0	100	0	0	26	19.16	-32.41		1.00	May-97
	0.27	21.22	-4.17	60.70	54.70	0	1.19	20.22	1	51.8	116.5	0	100	0	0	26	19.85	-32.11			Nov-12
	0.29	21.29	-4.11	60.77	54.30	0	1.13	20.21	1	50.46	116.5	0	100	0	0	26	19.85	-32.11			Mar-17
	0.25	21.18	-4.26	60.25	53.81	0	1.26	20.21	1	50.63	116.5	0	100	0	0	26	19.85	-32.11			May-97
	2.75	10.12	7.51	21.19	24.52	3.19	0.75	4.03		12.09	1,315	-8	19	84	0	13	11.59	-5.93			Nov-12
	2.69	10.02	7.27	20.26	22.96	2.95	1	4.05		12.05	1,315	-8	19	84	0	13	11.59	-5.93	4.75		Feb-06
	2.49	9.57	6.44	17.51	18.45	2.22	1.75	4.05		12.1	1,315	-8	19	84	0	13	11.08	-6.2		1.00	Feb-06
	2.61	9.82	6.96	19.34	21.40	2.7	1.25	4.02		12.12	1,315	-8	19	84	0	13	11.53	-6.01			Sep-10
	2.75	10.13	7.43	21.16	24.62	3.2	0.74	4		12.09	1,315	-8	19	84	0	13	11.59	-5.93			Nov-12
	2.77	10.17	7.50	21.18	23.90	3.26	0.68	4.01		12.08	1,315	-8	19	84	0	13	11.59	-5.93			Mar-17
	2.76	10.16	7.44	21.16	24.49	3.2	0.75	4.05		12.05	1,315	-8	19	84	0	13	11.87	-5.83			Sep-10
	1.95	15.89	6.65	48.87	61.02	1	0.63	12.59	1.02	23.51	552.5	0	100	0	0	99	26.02	-15.15			Jul-15
	1.88	15.73	6.38	47.81	58.97	0.78	0.88	12.6	1.02	23.79	552.5	0	100	0	0	99	25.89	-15.23			Jul-96
	1.80	15.57	6.07	46.71	57.05	0.58	1.13	12.58	1.02	23.72	552.5	0	100	0	0	99	25.7	-15.35			Jan-06
	1.94	15.90	6.71	49.27	61.77	1.08	0.54	12.59	1.02	23.65	552.5	0	100	0	0	99	26.03	-15.16			Jun-14
	1.97	15.98	6.77	49.45	62.07	1.12	0.49	12.58	1.02	23.76	552.5	0	100	0	0	99	26.03	-15.13			Jul-09
	1.93	15.88	6.63	48.87	60.98	0.99	0.63	12.59	1.02	23.75	552.5	0	100	0	0	99	26.03	-15.15			Jul-96
	4.87	23.37	9.32	59.56	78.60	0	0.8	14.47	1.07	45.6	3,611	2	98	0	0	32	26.92	-18.6			Nov-12
	4.81	23.22	9.06	58.39	76.41	0	1.05	14.46	1.07	42.66	3,611	2	98	0	0	32	26.97	-18.59	5.75		Oct-98
	4.62	22.77	8.25	54.89	69.94	0	1.8	14.44	1.06	34.83	3,611	2	98	0	0	32	26.33	-18.82		1.00	Nov-02
	4.79	23.18	8.98	57.95	75.51	0	1.15	14.46	1.06	42.4	3,611	2	98	0	0	32	26.87	-18.59	4.50		Sep-06
	4.77	23.08	8.79	57.23	74.25	0	1.3	14.46	1.06	42.17	3,611	2	98	0	0	32	26.74	-18.69			Sep-10
	4.83	23.24	9.09	58.44	76.41	0	1.05	14.47	1.07	42.26	3,611	2	98	0	0	32	26.92	-18.6	5.75		Dec-90
	4.92	23.53	9.36	59.57	66.33	0	0.8	14.6	1.08	20.27	1,551	1	99	0	0	23	27.72	-17.52			Nov-12
	4.89	23.34	9.06	58.30	64.28	0	1.05	14.58	1.08	18.03	1,551	1	99	0	0	23	27.54	-17.58	5.75		Dec-97
	4.68	22.86	8.26	54.88	58.18	0	1.8	14.59	1.08	12.11	1,551	1	99	0	0	23	26.98	-17.88		1.00	Dec-97
	4.86	23.25	8.82	57.22	62.33	0	1.3	14.56	1.07	18.14	1,551	1	99	0	0	23	27.35	-17.69			Oct-16
	4.97	23.59	9.43	59.88	67.22	0	0.73	14.57	1.07	20.49	1,551	1	99	0	0	23	27.72	-17.52			Dec-13
	4.95	23.56	9.46	59.94	66.80	0	0.69	14.57	1.07	19.73	1,551	1	99	0	0	23	27.71	-17.52			Mar-17
	4.97	23.55	9.33	59.56	66.40	0	0.8	14.6	1.08	19.63	1,551	1	99	0	0	23	27.72	-17.52			Dec-97
	4.91	23.42	9.41	59.94	79.43	0	0.74	14.46	1.06	44.63	3,611	2	98	0	0	32	27.27	-18.44			Mar-11
	4.92	23.43	9.45	60.17	79.89	0	0.69	14.47	1.07	44.77	3,611	2	98	0	0	32	27.29	-18.44			Jul-09
	4.89	23.39	9.34	59.60	78.63	0	0.8	14.45	1.06	44.57	3,611	2	98	0	0	32	27.14	-18.52			Dec-90
	4.18	19.28	9.91	48.85	62.61	1.63	0.45	12.2	1	48.6	3,370	0	100	0	0	6	24.76	-16.39			Oct-95
	4.25	19.44	10.19	49.98	64.66	1.83	0.2	12.2	1	49.69	3,370	0	100	0	0	6	25	-16.32			Nov-12
	4.24	19.43	10.18	49.99	64.66	1.89	0.2	12.2	1	48.11	3,370	0	100	0	0	6	25	-16.32			Mar-17
	4.25	19.43	10.17	49.98	64.65	1.86	0.2	12.2	1	48.91	3,370	0	100	0	0	6	25	-16.32			Dec-93
	4.46	19.05	8.54	38.10	44.00	1.62	0.76	12.56	1.03	13.57	1,984	1	98	0	0	21	22.71	-21.68			Dec-06
	4.40	18.89	8.26	37.06	42.19	1.39	1.01	12.58	1.03	13.58	1,984	1	98	0	0	21	22.75	-21.6	5.75		Oct-90
	4.21	18.51	7.48	34.02	36.98	0.71	1.76	12.56	1.03	13.55	1,984	1	98	0	0	21	22.22	-21.88		1.00	Jun-00
	4.36	18.79	8.04	36.09	40.41	1.17	1.26	12.6	1.03	13.49	1,984	1	98	0	0	21	22.47	-21.62			Dec-06
	4.48	19.07	8.61	38.36	44.54	1.69	0.71	12.55	1.03	13.58	1,984	1	98	0	0	21	22.99	-21.39			Dec-06
	4.51	19.13	8.68	38.55	44.83	1.68	0.68	12.58	1.03	13.74	1,984	1	98	0	0	21	22.75	-21.6			Nov-12
	4.55	19.07	8.62	38.14	43.93	1.62	0.76	12.58	1.03	13.56	1,984	1	98	0	0	21	22.95	-21.47			Sep-10
	6.41	27.17	11.54	54.89	64.08	0	0.92	13.96	0.95	27.05	1,744	3	97	0	0	140	24.31	-23.02			Nov-12
	6.38	27.03	11.30	53.76	62.08	0	1.17	13.97	0.95	24.01	1,744	3	97	0	0	140	24.14	-23.12	5.75		Nov-02

	MARKET			FUND TYPE, CATEGORY & OBJECTIVE	RATINGS				MINIMUMS	
Fund Name	Ticker Symbol	Traded On	Fund Type	Category and (Prospectus Objective)	Overall Rating	Reward Rating	Risk Rating	Recent Up/ Downgrade	Open to New Investors	Min Initial Investment
Columbia Mid Cap Growth Fund Class C	CMCCX	NAS CM	Open End	US Equity Mid Cap (Growth)	B-	C+	B-	Up	Y	2,000
Columbia Mid Cap Growth Fund Class R	CMGRX	NAS CM	Open End	US Equity Mid Cap (Growth)	B-	C+	B-		Y	0
Columbia Mid Cap Growth Fund Class V	CBSTX	NAS CM	Open End	US Equity Mid Cap (Growth)	B-	B-	B-			2,000
Columbia Mid Cap Growth Fund Institutional 2 Class	CMGVX	NAS CM	Open End	US Equity Mid Cap (Growth)	B-	B-	B		Y	0
Columbia Mid Cap Growth Fund Institutional 3 Class	CMGYX	NAS CM	Open End	US Equity Mid Cap (Growth)	B-	B-	B		Y	1,000,000
Columbia Mid Cap Growth Fund Institutional Class	CLSPX	NAS CM	Open End	US Equity Mid Cap (Growth)	B-	B-	B		Y	2,000
Columbia Mid Cap Index Fund Class A	NTIAX	NAS CM	Open End	US Equity Mid Cap (Growth & Income)	C+	C	B-	Up	Y	2,000
Columbia Mid Cap Index Fund Institutional 2 Class	CPXRX	NAS CM	Open End	US Equity Mid Cap (Growth & Income)	C+	C	B-	Up	Y	0
Columbia Mid Cap Index Fund Institutional 3 Class	CMDYX	NAS CM	Open End	US Equity Mid Cap (Growth & Income)	C+	C	B-	Up	Y	1,000,000
Columbia Mid Cap Index Fund Institutional Class	NMPAX	NAS CM	Open End	US Equity Mid Cap (Growth & Income)	C+	C	B-	Up	Y	2,000
Columbia Multi-Asset Income Fund Advisor Class	CLNFX	NAS CM	Open End	Moderate Alloc (Asset Alloc)	B-	C	B+	Up	Y	2,000
Columbia Multi-Asset Income Fund Class A	CLNAX	NAS CM	Open End	Moderate Alloc (Asset Alloc)	B-	C	B+	Up	Y	2,000
Columbia Multi-Asset Income Fund Class C	CLCNX	NAS CM	Open End	Moderate Alloc (Asset Alloc)	C+	C	B	Up	Y	2,000
Columbia Multi-Asset Income Fund Institutional 2 Class	CLNVX	NAS CM	Open End	Moderate Alloc (Asset Alloc)	B-	C	B+	Up	Y	0
Columbia Multi-Asset Income Fund Institutional 3 Class	CMUYX	NAS CM	Open End	Moderate Alloc (Asset Alloc)	B-	C	B+	Up	Y	1,000,000
Columbia Multi-Asset Income Fund Institutional Class	CLNZX	NAS CM	Open End	Moderate Alloc (Asset Alloc)	B-	C	B+	Up	Y	2,000
Columbia Overseas Core Fund Advisor Class	COSDX	NAS CM	Open End	Global Equity Large Cap (Foreign Stock)	D	D	C		Y	2,000
Columbia Overseas Core Fund Class A	COSAX	NAS CM	Open End	Global Equity Large Cap (Foreign Stock)	D	D	C		Y	2,000
Columbia Overseas Core Fund Class C	COSCX	NAS CM	Open End	Global Equity Large Cap (Foreign Stock)	D	D	C		Y	2,000
Columbia Overseas Core Fund Class R	COSRX	NAS CM	Open End	Global Equity Large Cap (Foreign Stock)	D	D	C		Y	0
Columbia Overseas Core Fund Institutional 2 Class	COSTX	NAS CM	Open End	Global Equity Large Cap (Foreign Stock)	D	D	C		Y	0
Columbia Overseas Core Fund Institutional 3 Class	COSOX	NAS CM	Open End	Global Equity Large Cap (Foreign Stock)	D	D	C		Y	2,000
Columbia Overseas Core Fund Institutional Class	COSNX	NAS CM	Open End	Global Equity Large Cap (Foreign Stock)	D	D	C		Y	2,000
Columbia Overseas Value Fund Advisor Class	COSVX	NAS CM	Open End	Global Equity Large Cap (Foreign Stock)	C	C	C+		Y	2,000
Columbia Overseas Value Fund Class A	COAVX	NAS CM	Open End	Global Equity Large Cap (Foreign Stock)	C	C	C+		Y	2,000
Columbia Overseas Value Fund Class C	COCVX	NAS CM	Open End	Global Equity Large Cap (Foreign Stock)	C	C	C+		Y	2,000
Columbia Overseas Value Fund Class R	COVUX	NAS CM	Open End	Global Equity Large Cap (Foreign Stock)	C	C	C+			0
Columbia Overseas Value Fund Institutional 2 Class	COSSX	NAS CM	Open End	Global Equity Large Cap (Foreign Stock)	C	C	C+		Y	0
Columbia Overseas Value Fund Institutional 3 Class	COSYX	NAS CM	Open End	Global Equity Large Cap (Foreign Stock)	C	C	C+		Y	1,000,000
Columbia Overseas Value Fund Institutional Class	COSZX	NAS CM	Open End	Global Equity Large Cap (Foreign Stock)	C	C	C+			2,000
Columbia Pacific/Asia Fund Advisor Class	CPRAX	NAS CM	Open End	Asia Equity (Pacific Stock)	C	C	C+		Y	2,000
Columbia Pacific/Asia Fund Class A	CASAX	NAS CM	Open End	Asia Equity (Pacific Stock)	C	C	C+		Y	2,000
Columbia Pacific/Asia Fund Class C	CASCX	NAS CM	Open End	Asia Equity (Pacific Stock)	C	C	C+		Y	2,000
Columbia Pacific/Asia Fund Institutional 3 Class	CPAYX	NAS CM	Open End	Asia Equity (Pacific Stock)	C	C	C+		Y	1,000,000
Columbia Pacific/Asia Fund Institutional Class	USPAX	NAS CM	Open End	Asia Equity (Pacific Stock)	C	C	C+		Y	2,000
Columbia Real Estate Equity Fund Advisor Class	CRERX	NAS CM	Open End	Real Estate Sector Equity (Real Estate)	C	C	C+	Down	Y	2,000
Columbia Real Estate Equity Fund Class A	CREAX	NAS CM	Open End	Real Estate Sector Equity (Real Estate)	C	C	C+	Down	Y	2,000
Columbia Real Estate Equity Fund Class C	CRECX	NAS CM	Open End	Real Estate Sector Equity (Real Estate)	C	C	C+	Down	Y	2,000
Columbia Real Estate Equity Fund Class R	CRSRX	NAS CM	Open End	Real Estate Sector Equity (Real Estate)	C	C	C+	Down	Y	0
Columbia Real Estate Equity Fund Institutional 2 Class	CRRVX	NAS CM	Open End	Real Estate Sector Equity (Real Estate)	C	C	C+	Down	Y	0
Columbia Real Estate Equity Fund Institutional 3 Class	CREYX	NAS CM	Open End	Real Estate Sector Equity (Real Estate)	C	C	C+	Down	Y	1,000,000
Columbia Real Estate Equity Fund Institutional Class	CREEX	NAS CM	Open End	Real Estate Sector Equity (Real Estate)	C	C	C+	Down	Y	2,000
Columbia Select Global Equity Fund Advisor Class	CSGVX	NAS CM	Open End	Global Equity Large Cap (World Stock)	B	B-	B		Y	2,000
Columbia Select Global Equity Fund Class A	IGLGX	NAS CM	Open End	Global Equity Large Cap (World Stock)	B	B-	B		Y	2,000
Columbia Select Global Equity Fund Class C	RGCEX	NAS CM	Open End	Global Equity Large Cap (World Stock)	B-	B-	B	Down	Y	2,000
Columbia Select Global Equity Fund Class R	CGERX	NAS CM	Open End	Global Equity Large Cap (World Stock)	B	B-	B		Y	0
Columbia Select Global Equity Fund Institutional 2 Class	RGERX	NAS CM	Open End	Global Equity Large Cap (World Stock)	B	B-	B		Y	100,000
Columbia Select Global Equity Fund Institutional 3 Class	CSEYX	NAS CM	Open End	Global Equity Large Cap (World Stock)	B	B-	B		Y	0
Columbia Select Global Equity Fund Institutional Class	CGEZX	NAS CM	Open End	Global Equity Large Cap (World Stock)	B	B-	B		Y	2,000
Columbia Select Global Growth Fund Advisor Class	CADHX	NAS CM	Open End	Global Equity Large Cap (World Stock)	C	C	C		Y	2,000
Columbia Select Global Growth Fund Class A	COGAX	NAS CM	Open End	Global Equity Large Cap (World Stock)	C	C	C		Y	2,000
Columbia Select Global Growth Fund Class C	COGCX	NAS CM	Open End	Global Equity Large Cap (World Stock)	C	C	C		Y	2,000

★ Expanded analysis of this fund is included in Section II.

Min Additional Investment	TOTAL RETURNS 3-Month Total Return	6-Month Total Return	1-Year Total Return	3-Year Total Return	5-Year Total Return	PERFORMANCE Dividend Yield (TTM)	Expense Ratio	3-Yr Std Deviation	3-Year Beta	ASSETS NAV	Total Assets (MIL)	ASSET ALLOCATION & TURNOVER %Cash	%Stocks	%Bonds	%Other	Turnover Ratio	BULL & BEAR Last Bull Market Total Return	Last Bear Market Total Return	FEES Front End Fee (%)	Back End Fee (%)	Inception Date
	6.16	26.50	10.42	50.32	56.06	0	1.92	13.97	0.95	18.95	1,744	3	97	0	0	140	23.55	-23.37		1.00	Oct-03
	6.30	26.86	10.99	52.58	60.02	0	1.42	13.98	0.95	22.76	1,744	3	97	0	0	140	23.95	-23.18			Jan-13
	6.36	27.00	11.26	53.77	62.03	0	1.17	13.98	0.95	23.89	1,744	3	97	0	0	140	24.08	-23.14	5.75		Nov-02
	6.46	27.22	11.62	55.32	64.92	0	0.84	13.98	0.95	26.36	1,744	3	97	0	0	140	24.46	-23.01			Mar-11
	6.45	27.26	11.69	55.51	65.39	0	0.79	13.98	0.95	26.37	1,744	3	97	0	0	140	24.34	-23.01			Jul-09
	6.44	27.20	11.54	54.90	64.10	0	0.92	13.98	0.95	26.09	1,744	3	97	0	0	140	24.31	-23.02			Nov-85
	2.92	18.93	0.91	37.07	44.32	1.04	0.45	15.14	1	15.51	4,091	0	100	0	0	17	27.52	-22.66			May-00
	2.97	19.03	1.16	38.06	46.17	1.26	0.2	15.15	1	15.78	4,091	0	100	0	0	17	27.76	-22.6			Nov-12
	3.03	19.04	1.15	38.11	46.17	1.31	0.2	15.15	1	15.15	4,091	0	100	0	0	17	27.76	-22.6			Mar-17
	3.04	19.07	1.19	38.10	46.16	1.29	0.2	15.18	1	15.44	4,091	0	100	0	0	17	27.76	-22.6			Mar-00
	3.06	12.37	5.61	17.31		6.76	0.74	6.17		9.44	151.8	-14	23	72	0	76					Mar-15
	3.00	12.23	5.34	16.54		6.51	0.99	6.14		9.44	151.8	-14	23	72	0	76			4.75		Mar-15
	2.81	11.69	4.56	13.96		5.78	1.74	6.12		9.44	151.8	-14	23	72	0	76				1.00	Mar-15
	3.07	12.27	5.65	17.45		6.81	0.68	6.08		9.44	151.8	-14	23	72	0	76					Mar-15
	3.10	12.33	5.73	17.62		6.88	0.62	6.06		9.42	151.8	-14	23	72	0	76					Mar-17
	3.06	12.24	5.60	17.28		6.76	0.74	6.05		9.44	151.8	-14	23	72	0	76					Mar-15
100	1.44	15.18	-1.58			1.21	1.03			9.47	254.9	1	99	0	0	71					Mar-18
100	1.40	14.99	-1.75			0.96	1.28			9.47	254.9	1	99	0	0	71			5.75		Mar-18
100	1.28	14.74	-2.46			0.21	2.03			9.46	254.9	1	99	0	0	71				1.00	Mar-18
	1.36	14.83	-2.12			0.71	1.53			9.46	254.9	1	99	0	0	71					Mar-18
	1.56	15.30	-1.41			1.18	0.9			9.49	254.9	1	99	0	0	71					Mar-18
100	1.57	15.31	-1.44			1.24	0.84			9.49	254.9	1	99	0	0	71					Mar-18
100	1.54	15.16	-1.48			1.21	1.03			9.48	254.9	1	99	0	0	71					Mar-18
	1.58	12.91	-4.03	34.25	16.83	1.45	0.97	12.1	1.01	9.31	1,798	0	100	0	0	58	13.32	-22.47			Jul-15
	1.54	12.83	-4.30	33.17	15.31	1.17	1.22	12.01	1.01	9.33	1,798	0	100	0	0	58	13.15	-22.55	5.75		Feb-13
	1.31	12.36	-4.95	30.34	11.13	0.5	1.97	12.09	1.01	9.27	1,798	0	100	0	0	58	12.66	-22.79		1.00	Feb-13
	1.44	12.62	-4.55	32.19	13.84	0.97	1.47	12.11	1.01	9.1	1,798	0	100	0	0	58	12.99	-22.63			Mar-16
	1.49	12.96	-4.02	34.74	17.28	1.56	0.86	12.06	1.01	9.29	1,798	0	100	0	0	58	13.32	-22.47			Jul-15
	1.50	12.95	-3.98	34.84	17.49	1.59	0.83	12.03	1.01	9.3	1,798	0	100	0	0	58	13.32	-22.47			Jul-15
	1.47	12.86	-4.12	34.11	16.64	1.43	0.97	12.04	1.01	9.34	1,798	0	100	0	0	58	13.32	-22.47			Mar-08
	2.89	16.35	0.15	35.77	40.30	1.31	1.25	13.21	1.05	9.87	158.3	3	97	0	0	44	12.63	-18.67			Mar-13
	2.85	16.15	-0.01	34.73	38.49	1	1.5	13.2	1.05	9.8	158.3	3	97	0	0	44	12.44	-18.85	5.75		Mar-08
	2.64	15.65	-0.84	31.68	33.33	0.63	2.25	13.2	1.05	9.52	158.3	3	97	0	0	44	11.85	-19.02		1.00	Mar-08
	2.98	16.40	0.42	36.20	40.69	1.57	1.06	13.17	1.04	9.73	158.3	3	97	0	0	44	12.63	-18.67			Mar-17
	2.90	16.26	0.15	35.71	40.19	1.31	1.25	13.21	1.05	9.85	158.3	3	97	0	0	44	12.63	-18.67			Dec-92
	1.53	19.50	9.65	10.06	40.78	1.86	1.04	12.43	0.92	14.4	293.2	0	100	0	0	18	30.84	-16.56			Nov-12
	1.50	19.38	9.37	9.32	39.11	1.67	1.29	12.43	0.92	14.08	293.2	0	100	0	0	18	30.64	-16.43	5.75		Nov-02
	1.24	18.87	8.57	6.83	33.92	0.96	2.04	12.46	0.93	14.07	293.2	0	100	0	0	18	29.98	-16.7		1.00	Oct-03
	1.37	19.17	9.11	8.45	37.33	1.44	1.54	12.46	0.93	14.06	293.2	0	100	0	0	18	30.43	-16.54			Sep-10
	1.53	19.55	9.80	10.53	41.79	2.04	0.89	12.42	0.92	14.06	293.2	0	100	0	0	18	30.94	-16.29			Mar-11
	1.60	19.62	9.82	10.63	41.51	2.06	0.85	12.46	0.93	14.22	293.2	0	100	0	0	18	30.84	-16.56			Mar-17
	1.48	19.48	9.62	10.11	40.85	1.9	1.04	12.44	0.93	14.11	293.2	0	100	0	0	18	30.84	-16.56			Apr-94
	7.38	23.94	14.80	56.46	58.29	0	1.09	12.6	0.98	14.39	473.6	1	99	0	0	74	21.71	-23.01			Mar-18
	7.36	23.78	14.48	55.89	57.71	0	1.34	12.61	0.98	14	473.6	1	99	0	0	74	21.71	-23.01	5.75		May-90
	7.13	23.34	13.65	52.33	52.00	0	2.09	12.56	0.98	12.31	473.6	1	99	0	0	74	21.29	-23.29		1.00	Jun-00
	7.30	23.64	14.20	54.75	55.86	0	1.59	12.6	0.98	13.96	473.6	1	99	0	0	74	21.65	-23.18			Dec-06
	7.46	24.00	14.87	57.47	60.80	0	1.01	12.58	0.98	14.26	473.6	1	99	0	0	74	22.05	-23.06			Dec-06
	7.47	24.03	14.97	57.30	59.14	0	0.96	12.62	0.98	14.09	473.6	1	99	0	0	74	21.71	-23.01			Mar-17
	7.41	23.93	14.77	56.98	59.82	0	1.09	12.59	0.98	14.19	473.6	1	99	0	0	74	21.93	-23.09			Sep-10
	3.34	26.95	-0.66	40.46	38.86	0	1.03	17.97	1.43	16.39	66.7	7	93	0	0	46	29.82	-23.61			Jan-14
	3.22	26.80	-0.92	39.44	37.28	0	1.28	18	1.43	15.99	66.7	7	93	0	0	46	29.56	-23.56	5.75		Apr-08
	3.05	26.34	-1.64	36.41	32.14	0	2.03	17.97	1.43	14.82	66.7	7	93	0	0	46	29.03	-23.88		1.00	Apr-08

	MARKET			FUND TYPE, CATEGORY & OBJECTIVE	RATINGS				MINIMUMS	
Fund Name	Ticker Symbol	Traded On	Fund Type	Category and (Prospectus Objective)	Overall Rating	Reward Rating	Risk Rating	Recent Up/ Downgrade	Open to New Investors	Min Initial Investment
Columbia Select Global Growth Fund Class R	COGRX	NAS CM	Open End	Global Equity Large Cap (World Stock)	C	C	C		Y	0
Columbia Select Global Growth Fund Institutional 2 Class	CADIX	NAS CM	Open End	Global Equity Large Cap (World Stock)	C	C	C		Y	0
Columbia Select Global Growth Fund Institutional 3 Class	CGGYX	NAS CM	Open End	Global Equity Large Cap (World Stock)	C	C	C		Y	1,000,000
Columbia Select Global Growth Fund Institutional Class	COGZX	NAS CM	Open End	Global Equity Large Cap (World Stock)	C	C	C		Y	2,000
Columbia Select International Equity Fund Advisor Class	CQYRX	NAS CM	Open End	Global Equity Large Cap (Foreign Stock)	C	C	B-		Y	2,000
Columbia Select International Equity Fund Class A	NIIAX	NAS CM	Open End	Global Equity Large Cap (Foreign Stock)	C	C	B-		Y	2,000
Columbia Select International Equity Fund Class C	NITRX	NAS CM	Open End	Global Equity Large Cap (Foreign Stock)	C	C	B-		Y	2,000
Columbia Select International Equity Fund Class R	CIERX	NAS CM	Open End	Global Equity Large Cap (Foreign Stock)	C	C	B-		Y	0
Columbia Select International Equity Institutional 2 Cls	CQQRX	NAS CM	Open End	Global Equity Large Cap (Foreign Stock)	C	C	B-		Y	0
Columbia Select International Equity Institutional 3 Cls	CMIYX	NAS CM	Open End	Global Equity Large Cap (Foreign Stock)	C	C	B-		Y	1,000,000
Columbia Select International Equity Institutional Cls	NIEQX	NAS CM	Open End	Global Equity Large Cap (Foreign Stock)	C	C	B-		Y	2,000
Columbia Select Large Cap Equity Fund Advisor Class	CLSRX	NAS CM	Open End	US Equity Large Cap Blend (Growth)	B-	C	B		Y	2,000
Columbia Select Large Cap Equity Fund Class A	NSGAX	NAS CM	Open End	US Equity Large Cap Blend (Growth)	B-	C	B		Y	2,000
Columbia Select Large Cap Equity Fund Class C	NSGCX	NAS CM	Open End	US Equity Large Cap Blend (Growth)	B-	C	B		Y	2,000
Columbia Select Large Cap Equity Institutional 2 Cls	CLCRX	NAS CM	Open End	US Equity Large Cap Blend (Growth)	B-	C	B		Y	0
Columbia Select Large Cap Equity Institutional 3 Cls	CLEYX	NAS CM	Open End	US Equity Large Cap Blend (Growth)	B-	C	B		Y	1,000,000
Columbia Select Large Cap Equity Fund Institutional Class	NSEPX	NAS CM	Open End	US Equity Large Cap Blend (Growth)	B-	C	B		Y	2,000
Columbia Select Large Cap Growth Fund Advisor Class	CSRRX	NAS CM	Open End	US Equity Large Cap Growth (World Stock)	C+	C	C+	Down	Y	2,000
Columbia Select Large Cap Growth Fund Class A	ELGAX	NAS CM	Open End	US Equity Large Cap Growth (World Stock)	C+	C	C+	Down	Y	2,000
Columbia Select Large Cap Growth Fund Class C	ELGCX	NAS CM	Open End	US Equity Large Cap Growth (World Stock)	C+	C	C+	Down	Y	2,000
Columbia Select Large Cap Growth Fund Class R	URLGX	NAS CM	Open End	US Equity Large Cap Growth (World Stock)	C+	C	C+	Down	Y	0
Columbia Select Large Cap Growth Institutional 2 Cls	CGTRX	NAS CM	Open End	US Equity Large Cap Growth (World Stock)	C+	C	C+	Down	Y	0
Columbia Select Large Cap Growth Institutional 3 Cls	CCWRX	NAS CM	Open End	US Equity Large Cap Growth (World Stock)	C+	C	C+	Down	Y	1,000,000
Columbia Select Large Cap Growth Fund Institutional Class	UMLGX	NAS CM	Open End	US Equity Large Cap Growth (World Stock)	C+	C	C+	Down	Y	2,000
Columbia Select Large Cap Value Fund Advisor Class	CSERX	NAS CM	Open End	US Equity Large Cap Value (Growth)	C+	C	B	Up	Y	2,000
Columbia Select Large Cap Value Fund Class A	SLVAX	NAS CM	Open End	US Equity Large Cap Value (Growth)	C+	C	B	Up	Y	2,000
Columbia Select Large Cap Value Fund Class C	SVLCX	NAS CM	Open End	US Equity Large Cap Value (Growth)	C+	C	B	Up	Y	2,000
Columbia Select Large Cap Value Fund Class R	SLVRX	NAS CM	Open End	US Equity Large Cap Value (Growth)	C+	C	B	Up	Y	0
Columbia Select Large Cap Value Fund Institutional 2 Class	SLVIX	NAS CM	Open End	US Equity Large Cap Value (Growth)	C+	C	B		Y	0
Columbia Select Large Cap Value Fund Institutional 3 Class	CSRYX	NAS CM	Open End	US Equity Large Cap Value (Growth)	C+	C	B		Y	1,000,000
Columbia Select Large Cap Value Fund Institutional Class	CSVZX	NAS CM	Open End	US Equity Large Cap Value (Growth)	C+	C	B		Y	2,000
Columbia Select Mid Cap Value Fund Advisor Class	CFDRX	NAS CM	Open End	US Equity Mid Cap (Growth)	C+	C	B		Y	2,000
Columbia Select Mid Cap Value Fund Class A	CMUAX	NAS CM	Open End	US Equity Mid Cap (Growth)	C+	C	B		Y	2,000
Columbia Select Mid Cap Value Fund Class C	CMUCX	NAS CM	Open End	US Equity Mid Cap (Growth)	C+	C	B		Y	2,000
Columbia Select Mid Cap Value Fund Class R	CMVRX	NAS CM	Open End	US Equity Mid Cap (Growth)	C+	C	B		Y	0
Columbia Select Mid Cap Value Fund Institutional 2 Class	CVERX	NAS CM	Open End	US Equity Mid Cap (Growth)	C+	C	B		Y	0
Columbia Select Mid Cap Value Fund Institutional 3 Class	CMVYX	NAS CM	Open End	US Equity Mid Cap (Growth)	C+	C	B		Y	1,000,000
Columbia Select Mid Cap Value Fund Institutional Class	NAMAX	NAS CM	Open End	US Equity Mid Cap (Growth)	C+	C	B		Y	2,000
Columbia Select Small Cap Value Fund Advisor Class	CSPRX	NAS CM	Open End	US Equity Small Cap (Small Company)	C	C-	B-		Y	2,000
Columbia Select Small Cap Value Fund Class A	SSCVX	NAS CM	Open End	US Equity Small Cap (Small Company)	C	C-	C+		Y	2,000
Columbia Select Small Cap Value Fund Class C	SVMCX	NAS CM	Open End	US Equity Small Cap (Small Company)	C	C-	C+		Y	2,000
Columbia Select Small Cap Value Fund Class R	SSVRX	NAS CM	Open End	US Equity Small Cap (Small Company)	C	C-	C+		Y	0
Columbia Select Small Cap Value Fund Institutional 2 Class	SSVIX	NAS CM	Open End	US Equity Small Cap (Small Company)	C	C-	B-		Y	0
Columbia Select Small Cap Value Fund Institutional 3 Class	CSSYX	NAS CM	Open End	US Equity Small Cap (Small Company)	C	C-	B-		Y	1,000,000
Columbia Select Small Cap Value Fund Institutional Class	CSSZX	NAS CM	Open End	US Equity Small Cap (Small Company)	C	C-	B-		Y	2,000
Columbia Seligman Communications & Information Advisor Cls	SCIOX	NAS CM	Open End	Technology Sector Equity (Technology)	C+	C+	B-	Down	Y	2,000
Columbia Seligman Communications & Information Cls A	SLMCX	NAS CM	Open End	Technology Sector Equity (Technology)	C+	C+	B-		Y	2,000
Columbia Seligman Communications & Information Cls C	SCICX	NAS CM	Open End	Technology Sector Equity (Technology)	C+	C	B-		Y	2,000
Columbia Seligman Communications & Information Cls R	SCIRX	NAS CM	Open End	Technology Sector Equity (Technology)	C+	C	B-		Y	0
Columbia Seligman Communications & Information Inst 2 Cls	SCMIX	NAS CM	Open End	Technology Sector Equity (Technology)	C+	C+	B-	Down	Y	0
Columbia Seligman Communications & Information Inst 3 Cls	CCOYX	NAS CM	Open End	Technology Sector Equity (Technology)	C+	C+	B-	Down	Y	1,000,000
Columbia Seligman Communications & Information Inst Cls	CCIZX	NAS CM	Open End	Technology Sector Equity (Technology)	C+	C+	B-	Down	Y	2,000

★Expanded analysis of this fund is included in Section II.

	TOTAL RETURNS					PERFORMANCE				ASSETS		ASSET ALLOCATION & TURNOVER					BULL & BEAR		FEES		
Min Additional Investment	3-Month Total Return	6-Month Total Return	1-Year Total Return	3-Year Total Return	5-Year Total Return	Dividend Yield (TTM)	Expense Ratio	3-Yr Std Deviation	3-Year Beta	NAV	Total Assets (MIL)	%Cash	%Stocks	%Bonds	%Other	Turnover Ratio	Last Bull Market Total Return	Last Bear Market Total Return	Front End Fee (%)	Back End Fee (%)	Inception Date
	3.17	26.72	-1.13	38.47	35.54	0	1.53	17.98	1.43	15.6	66.7	7	93	0	0	46	29.33	-23.69			Apr-08
	3.32	27.02	-0.60	40.73	39.33	0	0.97	18	1.43	16.45	66.7	7	93	0	0	46	29.82	-23.61			Jan-14
	3.36	27.04	-0.54	40.78	39.27	0	0.91	17.97	1.43	16.3	66.7	7	93	0	0	46	29.82	-23.61			Mar-17
	3.33	27.03	-0.66	40.55	39.04	0	1.03	17.99	1.43	16.4	66.7	7	93	0	0	46	29.82	-23.61			Apr-08
	5.40	19.45	3.11	34.54	12.95	1.55	1.06	12.51	1.08	14.91	268.4	5	94	0	1	34	19.81	-25.11			Nov-12
	5.39	19.41	2.88	33.62	11.59	1.36	1.31	12.47	1.08	14.51	268.4	5	94	0	1	34	19.58	-25.21	5.75		Jun-92
	5.20	18.89	2.09	30.63	7.46	0.71	2.06	12.52	1.08	12.7	268.4	5	94	0	1	34	19.12	-25.42		1.00	Jun-92
	5.31	19.27	2.64	32.60	10.25	1.12	1.56	12.49	1.08	14.41	268.4	5	94	0	1	34	19.42	-25.3			Jan-06
	5.50	19.67	3.36	35.24	13.97	1.66	0.93	12.47	1.08	14.99	268.4	5	94	0	1	34	19.81	-25.11			Nov-12
	5.45	19.63	3.37	35.39	14.20	1.73	0.86	12.51	1.08	14.94	268.4	5	94	0	1	34	19.87	-25.01			Mar-11
	5.36	19.50	3.13	34.55	12.95	1.56	1.06	12.5	1.08	14.82	268.4	5	94	0	1	34	19.81	-25.11			Dec-91
	4.47	19.32	9.75	52.06	68.09	1.22	0.55	12.53	1.02	14.13	726.8	0	100	0	0	62	25.74	-18.09			Jul-17
	4.38	19.21	9.51	51.03	66.01	0.98	0.8	12.52	1.02	14.3	726.8	0	100	0	0	62	25.49	-18.14	5.75		Aug-99
	4.21	18.83	8.69	47.67	60.02	0.3	1.55	12.52	1.02	13.01	726.8	0	100	0	0	62	24.97	-18.4		1.00	Aug-99
	4.47	19.41	9.86	52.39	68.78	1.25	0.46	12.53	1.02	14.64	726.8	0	100	0	0	62	25.74	-18.09			Nov-12
	4.54	19.49	9.92	52.62	68.71	1.35	0.42	12.5	1.02	13.98	726.8	0	100	0	0	62	25.74	-18.09			Mar-17
	4.45	19.33	9.78	52.10	68.13	1.22	0.55	12.49	1.02	14.19	726.8	0	100	0	0	62	25.74	-18.09			Oct-98
	4.93	28.37	8.83	62.67	73.19	0	0.82	18.25	1.27	14.18	2,494	8	92	0	0	27	26.34	-18.55			Nov-12
	4.83	28.14	8.52	61.44	71.05	0	1.07	18.18	1.27	12.96	2,494	8	92	0	0	27	26.13	-18.62	5.75		Sep-07
	4.67	27.64	7.70	57.87	64.77	0	1.82	18.2	1.27	10.83	2,494	8	92	0	0	27	25.66	-18.85		1.00	Sep-07
	4.82	28.06	8.29	60.24	68.91	0	1.32	18.24	1.27	11.72	2,494	8	92	0	0	27	26.05	-18.69			Dec-04
	4.95	28.39	8.89	63.24	74.20	0	0.71	18.23	1.27	14.3	2,494	8	92	0	0	27	26.34	-18.55			Nov-12
	4.96	28.41	8.97	63.36	74.55	0	0.71	18.22	1.27	14.52	2,494	8	92	0	0	27	26.34	-18.55			Nov-12
	4.91	28.35	8.81	62.70	73.23	0	0.82	18.24	1.27	13.6	2,494	8	92	0	0	27	26.34	-18.55			Oct-97
	3.33	16.14	3.23	43.15	43.95	1.59	0.55	14.61	1.18	26.62	1,145	1	99	0	0	9	28.43	-22.6			Nov-12
	3.26	16.02	2.98	42.07	42.17	1.41	0.8	14.6	1.18	25.27	1,145	1	99	0	0	9	28.43	-22.6	5.75		Apr-97
	3.08	15.58	2.22	38.87	36.87	0.7	1.55	14.58	1.18	23.06	1,145	1	99	0	0	9	27.85	-22.85		1.00	May-99
	3.19	15.85	2.73	41.04	40.39	1.17	1.05	14.6	1.18	24.85	1,145	1	99	0	0	9	28.24	-22.66			Apr-03
	3.38	16.18	3.30	43.41	44.51	1.67	0.51	14.6	1.18	26.28	1,145	1	99	0	0	9	28.72	-22.47			Nov-01
	3.32	16.19	3.33	43.56	44.72	1.68	0.46	14.62	1.18	26.69	1,145	1	99	0	0	9	28.43	-22.6			Oct-14
	3.34	16.18	3.23	43.13	43.93	1.61	0.55	14.61	1.18	26.27	1,145	1	99	0	0	9	28.6	-22.5			Sep-10
	3.88	22.10	5.75	32.89	31.15	0.77	0.92	13.48	1.01	11.1	1,558	0	100	0	0	79	26.28	-23.12			Nov-12
	3.77	21.93	5.52	31.88	29.48	0.58	1.17	13.49	1.01	10.67	1,558	0	100	0	0	79	26.15	-23.19	5.75		Nov-01
	3.65	21.44	4.72	28.91	24.73	0.09	1.92	13.43	1	9.61	1,558	0	100	0	0	79	25.62	-23.44		1.00	Nov-01
	3.73	21.76	5.29	30.94	27.93	0.38	1.42	13.56	1.01	10.62	1,558	0	100	0	0	79	26.03	-23.32			Jan-06
	3.91	22.04	5.87	33.35	31.97	0.87	0.8	13.54	1.01	11.1	1,558	0	100	0	0	79	26.28	-23.12			Nov-12
	3.89	22.06	5.96	33.43	32.24	0.94	0.76	13.53	1.01	10.66	1,558	0	100	0	0	79	26.39	-23.11			Jul-09
	3.83	22.00	5.76	32.76	31.09	0.8	0.92	13.48	1.01	10.7	1,558	0	100	0	0	79	26.28	-23.12			Nov-01
	1.59	16.08	-1.58	30.93	22.76	0.16	1.03	15.86	0.86	19.7	518.0	0	100	0	0	20	30.9	-27.67			Nov-12
	1.57	15.98	-1.80	29.95	21.27	0.08	1.28	15.88	0.86	16.76	518.0	0	100	0	0	20	30.9	-27.67	5.75		Apr-97
	1.38	15.51	-2.57	27.07	16.75	0	2.03	15.86	0.86	11.69	518.0	0	100	0	0	20	30.38	-27.96		1.00	May-99
	1.50	15.77	-2.08	28.96	19.73	0	1.53	15.86	0.86	15.56	518.0	0	100	0	0	20	30.67	-27.73			Apr-03
	1.60	16.12	-1.55	31.20	23.38	0.19	0.96	15.87	0.86	19.66	518.0	0	100	0	0	20	31.34	-27.57			Nov-01
	1.64	16.15	-1.48	31.42	23.45	0.2	0.91	15.87	0.86	20.35	518.0	0	100	0	0	20	30.9	-27.67			Oct-14
	1.62	16.11	-1.56	30.98	22.82	0.16	1.03	15.86	0.86	19.38	518.0	0	100	0	0	20	31.06	-27.58			Sep-10
	2.89	26.93	9.99	85.63	118.81	0	0.98	18.16	1.04	71.06	6,009	2	98	0	0	39	27.03	-17.5			Aug-09
	2.83	26.76	9.71	84.26	116.10	0	1.23	18.15	1.04	73.37	6,009	2	98	0	0	39	27.09	-17.47	5.75		Jun-83
	2.64	26.28	8.91	80.15	108.11	0	1.98	18.14	1.04	47.76	6,009	2	98	0	0	39	26.54	-17.72		1.00	May-99
	2.75	26.60	9.45	82.85	113.39	0	1.48	18.15	1.04	69.29	6,009	2	98	0	0	39	26.92	-17.56			Apr-03
	2.90	26.96	10.05	85.95	119.75	0	0.94	18.16	1.04	81.22	6,009	2	98	0	0	39	27.39	-17.33			Nov-01
	2.92	26.99	10.10	85.71	117.80	0	0.89	18.15	1.04	80.53	6,009	2	98	0	0	39	27.09	-17.47			Mar-17
	2.88	26.93	9.99	85.62	118.81	0	0.98	18.16	1.04	80.82	6,009	2	98	0	0	39	27.3	-17.35			Sep-10

	MARKET			FUND TYPE, CATEGORY & OBJECTIVE	RATINGS					MINIMUMS
Fund Name	Ticker Symbol	Traded On	Fund Type	Category and (Prospectus Objective)	Overall Rating	Reward Rating	Risk Rating	Recent Up/ Downgrade	Open to New Investors	Min Initial Investment
Columbia Seligman Global Technology Fund Advisor Class	CCHRX	NAS CM	Open End	Technology Sector Equity (Technology)	C+	C	B-		Y	0
Columbia Seligman Global Technology Fund Class A	SHGTX	NAS CM	Open End	Technology Sector Equity (Technology)	C+	C	B-		Y	2,000
Columbia Seligman Global Technology Fund Class C	SHTCX	NAS CM	Open End	Technology Sector Equity (Technology)	C+	C	B-		Y	2,000
Columbia Seligman Global Technology Fund Class R	SGTRX	NAS CM	Open End	Technology Sector Equity (Technology)	C+	C	B-		Y	0
Columbia Seligman Global Technology Institutional 2 Cls	SGTTX	NAS CM	Open End	Technology Sector Equity (Technology)	C+	C	B-		Y	100,000
Columbia Seligman Global Technology Institutional 3 Cls	CGTYX	NAS CM	Open End	Technology Sector Equity (Technology)	C+	C	B-		Y	0
Columbia Seligman Global Technology Institutional Cls	CSGZX	NAS CM	Open End	Technology Sector Equity (Technology)	C+	C	B-		Y	2,000
Columbia Seligman Premium Technology Growth Fund	STK	NYSE	Closed End	Technology Sector Equity (Technology)	C	C	C-		Y	
Columbia Small Cap Growth Fund I Advisor Class	CHHRX	NAS CM	Open End	US Equity Small Cap (Small Company)	C+	C+	B-	Down		2,000
Columbia Small Cap Growth Fund I Class A	CGOAX	NAS CM	Open End	US Equity Small Cap (Small Company)	C+	C+	B-	Down		2,000
Columbia Small Cap Growth Fund I Class C	CGOCX	NAS CM	Open End	US Equity Small Cap (Small Company)	C+	C+	B-	Down		2,000
Columbia Small Cap Growth Fund I Class R	CCRIX	NAS CM	Open End	US Equity Small Cap (Small Company)	C+	C+	B-	Down		0
Columbia Small Cap Growth Fund I Institutional 2 Class	CSCRX	NAS CM	Open End	US Equity Small Cap (Small Company)	C+	C+	B-	Down		0
Columbia Small Cap Growth Fund I Institutional 3 Class	CSGYX	NAS CM	Open End	US Equity Small Cap (Small Company)	B-	C+	B-	Down		1,000,000
Columbia Small Cap Growth Fund I Institutional Class	CMSCX	NAS CM	Open End	US Equity Small Cap (Small Company)	C+	C+	B-	Down		2,000
Columbia Small Cap Index Fund Class A	NMSAX	NAS CM	Open End	US Equity Small Cap (Small Company)	C	C-	C+		Y	2,000
Columbia Small Cap Index Fund Institutional 2 Class	CXXRX	NAS CM	Open End	US Equity Small Cap (Small Company)	C	C-	C+	Down	Y	0
Columbia Small Cap Index Fund Institutional 3 Class	CSPYX	NAS CM	Open End	US Equity Small Cap (Small Company)	C	C-	C+	Down	Y	1,000,000
Columbia Small Cap Index Fund Institutional Class	NMSCX	NAS CM	Open End	US Equity Small Cap (Small Company)	C	C-	C+	Down	Y	2,000
Columbia Small Cap Value Fund I Advisor Class	CVVRX	NAS CM	Open End	US Equity Small Cap (Small Company)	C-	C-	C	Down	Y	2,000
Columbia Small Cap Value Fund I Class A	CSMIX	NAS CM	Open End	US Equity Small Cap (Small Company)	C-	C-	C	Down	Y	2,000
Columbia Small Cap Value Fund I Class C	CSSCX	NAS CM	Open End	US Equity Small Cap (Small Company)	C-	C-	C	Down	Y	2,000
Columbia Small Cap Value Fund I Class R	CSVRX	NAS CM	Open End	US Equity Small Cap (Small Company)	C-	C-	C	Down	Y	0
Columbia Small Cap Value Fund I Institutional 2 Class	CUURX	NAS CM	Open End	US Equity Small Cap (Small Company)	C-	C-	C	Down	Y	0
Columbia Small Cap Value Fund I Institutional 3 Class	CSVYX	NAS CM	Open End	US Equity Small Cap (Small Company)	C-	C-	C	Down	Y	1,000,000
Columbia Small Cap Value Fund I Institutional Class	CSCZX	NAS CM	Open End	US Equity Small Cap (Small Company)	C-	C-	C	Down	Y	2,000
Columbia Small Cap Value Fund II Advisor Class	CLURX	NAS CM	Open End	US Equity Small Cap (Growth)	C	C-	C+			0
Columbia Small Cap Value Fund II Class A	COVAX	NAS CM	Open End	US Equity Small Cap (Growth)	C	C-	C			2,000
Columbia Small Cap Value Fund II Class C	COVCX	NAS CM	Open End	US Equity Small Cap (Growth)	C	C-	C			2,000
Columbia Small Cap Value Fund II Class R	CCTRX	NAS CM	Open End	US Equity Small Cap (Growth)	C	C-	C			0
Columbia Small Cap Value Fund II Institutional 2 Class	CRRRX	NAS CM	Open End	US Equity Small Cap (Growth)	C	C-	C+			100,000
Columbia Small Cap Value Fund II Institutional 3 Class	CRRYX	NAS CM	Open End	US Equity Small Cap (Growth)	C	C-	C+			0
Columbia Small Cap Value Fund II Institutional Class	NSVAX	NAS CM	Open End	US Equity Small Cap (Growth)	C	C-	C+			2,000
Columbia Small/Mid Cap Value Fund Advisor Class	RMCRX	NAS CM	Open End	US Equity Small Cap (Growth)	C	C	C+		Y	2,000
Columbia Small/Mid Cap Value Fund Class A	AMVAX	NAS CM	Open End	US Equity Small Cap (Growth)	C	C	C+		Y	2,000
Columbia Small/Mid Cap Value Fund Class C	AMVCX	NAS CM	Open End	US Equity Small Cap (Growth)	C	C-	C+		Y	2,000
Columbia Small/Mid Cap Value Fund Class R	RMVTX	NAS CM	Open End	US Equity Small Cap (Growth)	C	C	C+		Y	0
Columbia Small/Mid Cap Value Fund Institutional 2 Class	RSCMX	NAS CM	Open End	US Equity Small Cap (Growth)	C	C	C+		Y	0
Columbia Small/Mid Cap Value Fund Institutional 3 Class	CPHPX	NAS CM	Open End	US Equity Small Cap (Growth)	C	C	C+		Y	1,000,000
Columbia Small/Mid Cap Value Fund Institutional Class	CMOZX	NAS CM	Open End	US Equity Small Cap (Growth)	C	C	C+		Y	2,000
Columbia Thermostat Fund Advisor Class	CTORX	NAS CM	Open End	Cautious Alloc (Growth)	B	C+	A		Y	2,000
Columbia Thermostat Fund Class A	CTFAX	NAS CM	Open End	Cautious Alloc (Growth)	B	C+	A-		Y	2,000
Columbia Thermostat Fund Class C	CTFDX	NAS CM	Open End	Cautious Alloc (Growth)	B-	C	B+	Down	Y	2,000
Columbia Thermostat Fund Institutional 2 Class	CQTRX	NAS CM	Open End	Cautious Alloc (Growth)	B	C+	A		Y	0
Columbia Thermostat Fund Institutional 3 Class	CYYYX	NAS CM	Open End	Cautious Alloc (Growth)	B	C+	A		Y	1,000,000
Columbia Thermostat Fund Institutional Class	COTZX	NAS CM	Open End	Cautious Alloc (Growth)	B	C+	A		Y	2,000
Commerce Growth Fund	CFGRX	NAS CM	Open End	US Equity Large Cap Growth (Growth)	B	B-	B		Y	1,000
Commerce MidCap Growth Fund	CFAGX	NAS CM	Open End	US Equity Mid Cap (Growth)	B	B	B		Y	1,000
Commerce Value Fund	CFVLX	NAS CM	Open End	US Equity Large Cap Value (Growth & Income)	B-	C	B+	Down	Y	1,000
Commonwealth Africa Fund	CAFRX	NAS CM	Open End	Equity Miscellaneous (Foreign Stock)	C-	D+	C		Y	200
Commonwealth Australia/New Zealand Fund	CNZLX	NAS CM	Open End	Equity Miscellaneous (Foreign Stock)	C	C	C+		Y	200
Commonwealth Global Fund	CNGLX	NAS CM	Open End	Global Equity Large Cap (World Stock)	C	C	B		Y	200

★ Expanded analysis of this fund is included in Section II.

	TOTAL RETURNS					PERFORMANCE				ASSETS		ASSET ALLOCATION & TURNOVER					BULL & BEAR		FEES		
Min Additional Investment	3-Month Total Return	6-Month Total Return	1-Year Total Return	3-Year Total Return	5-Year Total Return	Dividend Yield (TTM)	Expense Ratio	3-Yr Std Deviation	3-Year Beta	NAV	Total Assets (MIL)	%Cash	%Stocks	%Bonds	%Other	Turnover Ratio	Last Bull Market Total Return	Last Bear Market Total Return	Front End Fee (%)	Back End Fee (%)	Inception Date
	2.66	27.49	9.68	86.02	122.03	0	1.07	18.35	1.08	41.92	1,110	1	99	0	0	42	25.4	-17.78			Nov-12
	2.61	27.35	9.40	84.58	119.31	0	1.32	18.38	1.08	40.37	1,110	1	99	0	0	42	25.4	-17.78	5.75		May-94
	2.41	26.88	8.58	80.50	111.26	0	2.07	18.38	1.08	30.16	1,110	1	99	0	0	42	24.8	-18.05		1.00	May-99
	2.54	27.15	9.13	83.24	116.61	0	1.57	18.37	1.08	38.72	1,110	1	99	0	0	42	25.19	-17.87			Apr-03
	2.70	27.53	9.75	86.35	123.15	0	1.01	18.4	1.08	41.45	1,110	1	99	0	0	42	25.53	-17.63			Aug-09
	2.71	27.56	9.82	86.13	121.16	0	0.97	18.37	1.08	41.19	1,110	1	99	0	0	42	25.4	-17.78			Mar-17
	2.66	27.50	9.66	86.01	122.08	0	1.07	18.37	1.08	41.21	1,110	1	99	0	0	42	25.6	-17.67			Sep-10
	1.36	24.35	8.19	77.30	103.17	0	1.26	17.36	0.98	20	312.6	46	54	0	0	34	24.5	-19.47			Nov-09
	8.98	35.34	19.83	90.63	100.47	0	1.1	17.71	0.97	22.44	634.0	7	93	0	0	156	27.57	-28.38			Nov-12
	8.96	35.20	19.58	89.23	98.08	0	1.35	17.72	0.97	19.7	634.0	7	93	0	0	156	27.42	-28.46	5.75		Nov-05
	8.71	34.67	18.64	84.89	90.63	0	2.1	17.72	0.97	15.34	634.0	7	93	0	0	156	26.87	-28.7		1.00	Nov-05
	8.84	35.02	19.25	87.80	95.51	0	1.6	17.69	0.97	19.2	634.0	7	93	0	0	156	27.24	-28.56			Sep-10
	9.05	35.52	20.08	91.33	102.43	0	0.99	17.72	0.97	21.44	634.0	7	93	0	0	156	27.57	-28.38			Feb-13
	9.04	35.45	20.05	91.64	102.16	0	0.94	17.72	0.97	21.7	634.0	7	93	0	0	156	27.72	-28.33			Jul-09
	9.01	35.38	19.85	90.63	100.50	0	1.1	17.71	0.97	21.16	634.0	7	93	0	0	156	27.57	-28.38			Oct-96
	1.71	14.10	-5.28	41.47	46.73	0.89	0.45	17.87	1	22.61	4,072	0	100	0	0	22	29.24	-22.15			Oct-96
	1.83	14.32	-5.02	42.59	48.65	1.08	0.2	17.87	1	23.33	4,072	0	100	0	0	22	29.47	-22.08			Nov-12
	1.84	14.29	-5.03	42.63	48.73	1.13	0.2	17.86	1	22.18	4,072	0	100	0	0	22	29.47	-22.08			Mar-17
	1.83	14.31	-5.02	42.55	48.64	1.11	0.2	17.87	1	22.78	4,072	0	100	0	0	22	29.47	-22.08			Oct-96
	0.27	13.38	-10.84	36.68	28.34	0.47	1.07	19.22	1.1	39.97	576.9	0	100	0	0	51	23.34	-23.99			Nov-12
	0.20	13.27	-11.06	35.63	26.69	0.34	1.32	19.21	1.1	34.39	576.9	0	100	0	0	51	23.34	-23.99	5.75		Jul-86
	0.00	12.85	-11.71	32.64	22.04	0	2.07	19.19	1.1	21.88	576.9	0	100	0	0	51	22.8	-24.25		1.00	Jan-96
	0.11	13.07	-11.31	34.59	25.11	0.15	1.57	19.2	1.1	34.26	576.9	0	100	0	0	51	23.2	-24.04			Sep-10
	0.32	13.46	-10.72	37.24	29.24	0.56	0.94	19.23	1.1	40.01	576.9	0	100	0	0	51	23.34	-23.99			Nov-12
	0.30	13.48	-10.67	37.41	29.55	0.61	0.89	19.22	1.1	38.95	576.9	0	100	0	0	51	23.68	-23.87			Jul-09
	0.25	13.38	-10.84	36.66	28.30	0.49	1.07	19.22	1.1	38.71	576.9	0	100	0	0	51	23.54	-23.93			Jul-95
	1.94	16.67	-5.99	30.11	27.11	0.41	1.04	17.7	1.01	15.27	1,321	4	96	0	0	38	30.6	-26.75			Nov-12
	1.84	16.46	-6.27	29.13	25.54	0.16	1.29	17.67	1.01	14.63	1,321	4	96	0	0	38	30.37	-26.81	5.75		May-02
	1.69	16.11	-6.93	26.24	20.84	0	2.04	17.65	1.01	12.49	1,321	4	96	0	0	38	29.81	-27.06		1.00	May-02
	1.77	16.35	-6.48	28.15	23.94	0.07	1.54	17.65	1.01	14.32	1,321	4	96	0	0	38	30.17	-26.94			Jan-06
	2.02	16.74	-5.83	30.72	28.06	0.55	0.89	17.66	1.01	15.31	1,321	4	96	0	0	38	30.6	-26.75			Nov-12
	1.95	16.77	-5.86	30.87	28.38	0.6	0.84	17.62	1.01	15.36	1,321	4	96	0	0	38	30.6	-26.75			Nov-12
	1.92	16.62	-6.02	30.10	27.04	0.42	1.04	17.69	1.01	14.89	1,321	4	96	0	0	38	30.6	-26.75			May-02
	1.32	18.73	-2.86	31.19	23.05	0.54	0.98	16.04	1.05	9.19	674.5	4	96	0	0	46	26.05	-25.37			Dec-06
	1.21	18.52	-3.16	30.16	21.45	0.28	1.23	16.02	1.04	9.15	674.5	4	96	0	0	46	26.16	-25.37	5.75		Feb-02
	1.00	18.18	-3.90	27.20	16.88	0	1.98	16.09	1.05	8.06	674.5	4	96	0	0	46	25.44	-25.57		1.00	Feb-02
	1.13	18.43	-3.42	29.15	19.87	0.02	1.48	16.08	1.05	8.93	674.5	4	96	0	0	46	25.82	-25.35			Dec-06
	1.29	18.80	-2.83	31.53	23.58	0.61	0.89	16.11	1.05	9.35	674.5	4	96	0	0	46	26.45	-25.2			Dec-06
	1.32	18.88	-2.73	31.64	23.76	0.66	0.85	16.1	1.05	9.19	674.5	4	96	0	0	46	26.16	-25.37			Jun-13
	1.39	18.74	-2.89	31.20	22.97	0.52	0.98	16.11	1.05	9.44	674.5	4	96	0	0	46	26.3	-25.22			Sep-10
	3.42	10.00	9.18	17.31	23.57	1.89	0.65	3.5	0.21	14.93	683.7	-1	39	62	0	122	17.07	-7.98			Nov-12
	3.32	9.83	8.82	16.44	21.99	1.64	0.9	3.49	0.21	15.05	683.7	-1	39	62	0	122	16.87	-8.12	5.75		Mar-03
	3.17	9.47	8.10	13.90	17.52	0.94	1.65	3.48	0.21	15.11	683.7	-1	39	62	0	122	16.39	-8.37		1.00	Mar-03
	3.42	10.06	9.21	17.45	23.67	1.93	0.61	3.48	0.21	14.95	683.7	-1	39	62	0	122	17.07	-7.98			Nov-12
	3.49	10.08	9.29	17.66	24.02	1.98	0.57	3.46	0.2	14.93	683.7	-1	39	62	0	122	17.07	-7.98			Nov-12
	3.37	9.98	9.08	17.25	23.47	1.9	0.65	3.46	0.2	14.84	683.7	-1	39	62	0	122	17.06	-7.98			Sep-02
250	6.75	23.95	16.09	62.19	92.36	0.58	0.77	12.2	0.9	36.02	156.6	1	99	0	0	45	28.21	-18.01			Dec-94
250	8.46	29.40	17.93	59.15	80.35	0.35	0.84	12.42	0.84	43.83	210.1	1	99	0	0	71	25.4	-22.12			Dec-94
250	3.16	15.10	12.51	36.96	53.61	2.31	0.71	11.08	0.88	30.53	256.6	1	99	0	0	49	20.42	-11.81			Mar-97
	1.79	4.79	-5.25	15.56	-17.09	0.48	1.86	17.98	0.9	8.53	2.8	2	98	0	0	4					Nov-11
	2.17	8.15	-0.56	24.21	14.49	0.64	2.41	12.13	0.75	13.13	16.4	2	98	0	0	14	17.71	-13.04			Nov-91
	2.84	14.02	0.30	18.93	0.05	0	2.39	10.91	0.93	15.53	15.8	1	99	0	0	6	15.79	-23.14			Dec-02

	MARKET			FUND TYPE, CATEGORY & OBJECTIVE	RATINGS					MINIMUMS
Fund Name	Ticker Symbol	Traded On	Fund Type	Category and (Prospectus Objective)	Overall Rating	Reward Rating	Risk Rating	Recent Up/ Downgrade	Open to New Investors	Min Initial Investment
Commonwealth Japan Fund	CNJFX	NAS CM	Open End	Japan Equity (Pacific Stock)	C	C-	C+		Y	200
Commonwealth Real Estate Securities Fund	CNREX	NAS CM	Open End	Real Estate Sector Equity (Real Estate)	C+	C	B-		Y	200
Communication Services UltraSector ProFund Investor Class	WCPIX	NAS CM	Open End	Trading Tools (Comm)	C	C+	C	Down	Y	15,000
Communication Services UltraSector ProFund Service Class	WCPSX	NAS CM	Open End	Trading Tools (Comm)	C	C+	C	Down	Y	15,000
Comstock Capital Value Fund AAA Class	COMVX	NAS CM	Open End	Alternative Miscellaneous (Multi-Asset Global)	D	D-	D		Y	1,000
Comstock Capital Value Fund Class A	DRCVX	NAS CM	Open End	Alternative Miscellaneous (Multi-Asset Global)	D	D-	D		Y	1,000
Comstock Capital Value Fund Class C	CPCCX	NAS CM	Open End	Alternative Miscellaneous (Multi-Asset Global)	D	D-	D		Y	1,000
Comstock Capital Value Fund Class I	CPCRX	NAS CM	Open End	Alternative Miscellaneous (Multi-Asset Global)	D	D-	D		Y	500,000
Concorde Wealth Management Fund	CONWX	NAS CM	Open End	US Equity Large Cap Blend (Growth)	B-	C	A-		Y	500
Conductor Global Equity Value Fund Class A	RAALX	NAS CM	Open End	Global Equity Mid/Small Cap (Growth & Income)	C	C-	C		Y	2,500
Conductor Global Equity Value Fund Class C	RACLX	NAS CM	Open End	Global Equity Mid/Small Cap (Growth & Income)	C-	C-	C	Down	Y	2,500
Conductor Global Equity Value Fund Class I	RAILX	NAS CM	Open End	Global Equity Mid/Small Cap (Growth & Income)	C	C-	C		Y	100,000
Conductor Global Equity Value Fund Class Y	RAYLX	NAS CM	Open End	Global Equity Mid/Small Cap (Growth & Income)	C	C-	C		Y	10,000,000
Conestoga Small Cap Fund Investors Class	CCASX	NAS CM	Open End	US Equity Small Cap (Small Company)	C+	C+	B-		Y	2,500
Conestoga Small Cap Institutional Class	CCALX	NAS CM	Open End	US Equity Small Cap (Small Company)	C+	C+	B-		Y	250,000
Conestoga SMid Cap Fund Institutional Class	CCSGX	NAS CM	Open End	US Equity Mid Cap (Growth)	B-	B	C+		Y	250,000
Conestoga SMid Cap Fund Investors Class	CCSMX	NAS CM	Open End	US Equity Mid Cap (Growth)	B-	B	C+		Y	2,500
Congress Large Cap Growth Fund Institutional Class	CMLIX	NAS CM	Open End	US Equity Large Cap Growth (Growth)	B	B-	B		Y	500,000
Congress Large Cap Growth Fund Retail Class	CAMLX	NAS CM	Open End	US Equity Large Cap Growth (Growth)	B	B-	B		Y	2,000
Congress Mid Cap Growth Fund Institutional Class	IMIDX	NAS CM	Open End	US Equity Mid Cap (Growth)	B-	C+	B	Down	Y	500,000
Congress Mid Cap Growth Fund Retail Class	CMIDX	NAS CM	Open End	US Equity Mid Cap (Growth)	B-	C	B	Down	Y	2,000
Congress Small Cap Growth Fund Institutional Class	CSMCX	NAS CM	Open End	US Equity Small Cap (Small Company)	C+	C	B-	Down	Y	500,000
Congress Small Cap Growth Fund Retail Class	CSMVX	NAS CM	Open End	US Equity Small Cap (Small Company)	C+	C	B-	Down	Y	2,000
Convergence Core Plus Fund Institutional Class	MARNX	NAS CM	Open End	US Equity Large Cap Blend (Growth)	C+	C	B-	Up	Y	15,000
Convergence Market Neutral Fund Institutional Class	CPMNX	NAS CM	Open End	Market Neutral (Growth & Income)	C-	D+	C		Y	15,000
Convergence Opportunities Fund Institutional Class	CIPOX	NAS CM	Open End	US Equity Small Cap (Growth)	C-	C-	C-	Down	Y	15,000
Copeland Intl Risk Managed Dividend Growth Cls A Shares	IDVGX	NAS CM	Open End	Global Equity Large Cap (Growth & Income)	C	C-	C	Up	Y	2,500
Copeland Intl Risk Managed Dividend Growth Cls C Shares	IDVCX	NAS CM	Open End	Global Equity Large Cap (Growth & Income)	C	C-	C	Up	Y	2,500
Copeland Intl Risk Managed Dividend Growth Cls I Shares	IDVIX	NAS CM	Open End	Global Equity Large Cap (Growth & Income)	C	C-	C	Up	Y	25,000
Copeland Risk Managed Dividend Growth Fund Class A Shares	CDGRX	NAS CM	Open End	US Equity Large Cap Blend (Growth & Income)	C+	C	B-	Up	Y	1,000
Copeland Risk Managed Dividend Growth Fund Class C Shares	CDCRX	NAS CM	Open End	US Equity Large Cap Blend (Growth & Income)	C	C	B-		Y	1,000
Copeland Risk Managed Dividend Growth Fund Class I Shares	CDIVX	NAS CM	Open End	US Equity Large Cap Blend (Growth & Income)	C+	C	B-	Up	Y	25,000
Copeland SMID Cap Dividend Growth Fund Class A Shares	CSDGX	NAS CM	Open End	US Equity Mid Cap (Equity-Income)	C	C	B-		Y	5,000
Copeland SMID Cap Dividend Growth Fund Class I Shares	CSMDX	NAS CM	Open End	US Equity Mid Cap (Equity-Income)	C	C	B		Y	5,000
Copley Fund	COPLX	NAS CM	Open End	US Equity Large Cap Value (Equity-Income)	B	B	A		Y	1,000
Core Market Neutral Fund Class N	STTKX	NAS CM	Open End	Market Neutral (Growth)	D	D	D		Y	5,000
Core Market Neutral Fund Institutional Class	STAKX	NAS CM	Open End	Market Neutral (Growth)	D	D	D		Y	500,000
CornerCap Balanced Fund	CBLFX	NAS CM	Open End	Moderate Alloc (Balanced)	B-	C	B+	Up	Y	2,000
CornerCap Large/Mid-Cap Value Fund	CMCRX	NAS CM	Open End	US Equity Large Cap Value (Growth)	C+	C	B	Up	Y	2,000
CornerCap Small-Cap Value Fund Institutional Shares	CSCJX	NAS CM	Open End	US Equity Small Cap (Small Company)	C	C	C+		Y	1,000,000
CornerCap Small-Cap Value Fund Investor Shares	CSCVX	NAS CM	Open End	US Equity Small Cap (Small Company)	C	C	C+		Y	2,000
Cornerstone Advs Global Public Equity Inst Shares	CAGLX	NAS CM	Open End	Global Equity Large Cap (Growth)	C+	C	B	Up	Y	2,000
Cornerstone Strategic Value Fund	CLM	AMEX	Closed End	US Equity Large Cap Blend (Growth)	B	B	C+	Up	Y	
Cornerstone Total Return Fund Inc	CRF	AMEX	Closed End	US Equity Large Cap Blend (Growth)	B	B	C+	Up	Y	
Counterpoint Long-Short Equity Fund Class A Shares	CPQAX	NAS CM	Open End	Long/Short Equity (Growth)	D+	D	C-	Up	Y	5,000
Counterpoint Long-Short Equity Fund Class C Shares	CPQCX	NAS CM	Open End	Long/Short Equity (Growth)	D+	D	C	Up	Y	5,000
Counterpoint Long-Short Equity Fund Class I Shares	CPQIX	NAS CM	Open End	Long/Short Equity (Growth)	D+	D	C	Up	Y	100,000
Counterpoint Tactical Equity Fund Class A	CPAEX	NAS CM	Open End	Long/Short Equity (Growth)	D+	D	C-	Down	Y	5,000
Counterpoint Tactical Equity Fund Class C	CPCEX	NAS CM	Open End	Long/Short Equity (Growth)	D+	D	C-		Y	5,000
Counterpoint Tactical Equity Fund Class I	CPIEX	NAS CM	Open End	Long/Short Equity (Growth)	D+	D	C-	Down	Y	100,000
Cove Street Capital Small Cap Value Inst Cls Shares	CSCAX	NAS CM	Open End	US Equity Small Cap (Small Company)	C+	C	B	Up	Y	10,000
Crawford Dividend Growth Fund Class C	CDGCX	NAS CM	Open End	US Equity Large Cap Blend (Growth)	B-	C	B+	Down	Y	2,500

★ Expanded analysis of this fund is included in Section II.

Min Additional Investment	3-Month Total Return	6-Month Total Return	1-Year Total Return	3-Year Total Return	5-Year Total Return	Dividend Yield (TTM)	Expense Ratio	3-Yr Std Deviation	3-Year Beta	NAV	Total Assets (MIL)	%Cash	%Stocks	%Bonds	%Other	Turnover Ratio	Last Bull Market Total Return	Last Bear Market Total Return	Front End Fee (%)	Back End Fee (%)	Inception Date
	TOTAL RETURNS					PERFORMANCE				ASSETS		ASSET ALLOCATION & TURNOVER					BULL & BEAR		FEES		
	1.31	8.78	-3.27	14.97	23.47	0	1.77	10.46	0.83	3.84	6.0	4	96	0	0	1	-0.72	-0.35			Jul-89
	2.34	17.78	4.02	18.55	23.43	0.21	2.5	10.9	0.72	17.02	11.7	3	97	0	0	20	27.57	-22.53			Jan-04
	0.05	10.90	28.07	69.22	58.68	0	1.78	21.84		88.96	14.4	43	57	0	0	818	18.54	-29.81			Jun-00
	-0.19	10.36	26.77	64.27	50.95	0	2.78	21.83		73.38	14.4	43	57	0	0	818	17.9	-30.08			Jun-00
	-3.78	-19.10	-9.24	-41.46	-52.52	0	3	15.63	-1.23	4.32	18.9	85	-25	38	3	39	-25	21.95			Dec-08
	-3.80	-19.17	-9.28	-41.65	-52.22	0	3	15.71	-1.24	4.3	18.9	85	-25	38	3	39	-25.37	22.56	5.75		Oct-85
	-4.15	-19.60	-9.99	-42.87	-53.87	0	3.75	15.66	-1.24	3.69	18.9	85	-25	38	3	39	-26.22	22.81		1.00	Aug-95
	-3.90	-19.16	-9.22	-41.08	-51.84	0	2.75	15.74	-1.24	4.43	18.9	85	-25	38	3	39	-25.24	22.42			Aug-95
100	2.66	12.54	5.55	24.44	19.86	0.37	1.84	7.96	0.56	15.79	26.0	5	55	35	5	20	21.96	-21.31			Dec-87
500	-0.71	7.99	-10.84	29.34	30.24	0.49	1.87	11.49	0.92	11.81	86.3	4	96	0	0	141			5.75	1.00	Apr-14
500	-0.85	7.58	-11.53	26.50	25.44	0	2.61	11.5	0.92	11.63	86.3	4	96	0	0	141				1.00	Sep-15
1,000	-0.57	8.18	-10.57	30.27	31.82	0.79	1.61	11.49	0.93	11.88	86.3	4	96	0	0	141					Dec-13
1,000	-0.48	8.40	-10.15	32.47	34.04	0.78	1.31	11.5	0.93	12.1	86.3	4	96	0	0	141					Apr-16
	9.33	24.58	10.53	81.18	95.57	0	1.1	16.5	0.88	59.95	2,727	4	96	0	0	9	23.86	-17.95			Oct-02
	9.38	24.69	10.73	82.27	97.50	0	0.9	16.5	0.88	60.6	2,727	4	96	0	0	9	23.86	-17.95			Aug-14
	8.67	28.05	11.69	87.69	84.11	0	0.85	15.71	0.9	17.16	113.5	5	95	0	0	8					Dec-14
	8.64	27.90	11.40	86.33	82.18	0	1.1	15.69	0.9	16.96	113.5	5	95	0	0	8					Jan-14
	5.10	23.52	13.90	61.14	81.37	0.47	0.74	12.37	0.9	31.5	326.0	2	98	0	0	17	26.32	-17.33			Mar-28
	5.02	23.35	13.59	60.28	69.96	0.43	0.99	12.12	0.89	31.37	326.0	2	98	0	0	17	26.52	-15.34			Mar-09
	4.50	23.91	15.14	45.63	67.98	0.01	0.83	13.73	0.9	21.35	1,106	2	98	0	0	44					Oct-12
	4.50	23.81	14.89	44.57	65.86	0	1.08	13.72	0.9	21.11	1,106	2	98	0	0	44					Oct-12
	5.50	21.85	12.07	66.77	55.07	0	1	17.26	0.94	29.5	82.8	5	95	0	0	35	30.88	-24.24			Dec-99
	5.44	21.73	11.83	65.57	52.95	0	1.25	17.27	0.94	26.94	82.8	5	95	0	0	35	30.6	-24.32			Feb-00
5,000	3.69	8.72	2.10	46.14	46.49	0.37	2.2	11.96	0.87	18.81	98.2	35	65	0	0	194	29.8	-19.56			Dec-09
5,000	0.94	-4.28	-2.88	13.20		0.02	2.7	5.55	10.05	10.73	60.5	78	22	0	0	220					Jan-16
5,000	1.65	9.41	-7.41	23.59	23.22	0	2.71	16.77	0.91	11.04	16.4	33	67	0	0	253					Nov-13
500	1.36	6.24	-4.03	14.35	0.05	0	1.6	9.34	0.7	11.9	17.1	1	56	42	0	96			5.75		Dec-12
500	1.14	5.80	-4.80	11.71	-3.69	0	2.35	9.34	0.7	11.48	17.1	1	56	42	0	96					Dec-12
500	1.36	6.35	-3.95	14.73	0.67	0	1.45	9.36	0.7	11.89	17.1	1	56	42	0	96					Dec-12
500	2.56	6.49	0.40	27.16	23.22	0.09	1.45	9.06	0.57	13.61	138.0	1	30	69	0	30	11.01	-7.83	5.75		Dec-10
500	2.33	6.04	-0.33	24.37	18.69	0	2.2	9.05	0.57	13.16	138.0	1	30	69	0	30	10.57	-8.12			Jan-12
500	2.66	6.64	0.56	27.80	24.23	0.38	1.3	9.05	0.57	13.48	138.0	1	30	69	0	30	11.01	-7.83			Mar-13
500	7.65	22.61	10.15				1.2			12.23	4.3	4	96	0	0	26			5.75		Feb-19
500	7.74	22.76	10.42			0.66	0.95			12.24	4.3	4	96	0	0	26					Feb-17
100	3.37	13.28	14.41	43.80	70.69	0	2.71	12.22	0.63	115.32	100.4	-18	118	0	0	0	11.69	-3.17			Sep-78
100	1.66	5.33	-6.82			0	2.19			12.83	28.4	48	0	52	0	0					Dec-17
100	1.81	5.57	-6.59			0	1.94			12.88	28.4	48	0	52	0	0					Aug-17
250	1.96	11.70	3.68	25.06	23.31	1.56	1.02	8.67		14.03	34.1	4	60	37	0	64	13.73	-13.29			May-97
250	2.27	16.80	2.68	37.41	30.90	1.11	1	14.28	1.16	12.58	36.1	1	99	0	0	89	21.27	-22.98			Jul-00
	4.18	18.82	-2.62	36.49	43.16	0.53	1	17.51	1	13.7	123.7	0	100	0	0	117	27.64	-28.03			Dec-15
250	4.19	18.66	-2.82	35.37	41.68	0.27	1.3	17.5	1	13.67	123.7	0	100	0	0	117	27.64	-28.03			Sep-92
	3.02	15.56	1.00	36.64	32.68	2.12	0.88	11.47	1	12.62	517.1	2	97	0	0	56					Aug-12
	4.13	18.94	11.62	55.30	53.52	1.31	2.01	11.74	0.95	11.09	805.0	1	98	2	-1	58	20.6	-13.67			Jun-87
	3.85	19.02	11.12	54.11	65.59	1	1.84	11.82	0.95	10.73	411.6	1	98	1	0	57	23.98	-14.67			May-73
250	4.45	4.30	-1.17			0.76	2.04			14.55	12.6	34	57	25	-16				5.75		Oct-17
250	4.99	5.29	0.76			1.13	2.79			14.72	12.6	34	57	25	-16						Oct-17
1,000	4.45	4.45	-0.92			1.14	1.79			14.55	12.6	34	57	25	-16						Oct-17
250	0.14	-5.54	-8.72	11.39		0	2.85	8.45	0.13	13.46	23.5	37	69	14	-21				5.75		Nov-15
250	-0.07	-5.97	-9.45	8.85		0	3.6	8.42	0.13	13.07	23.5	37	69	14	-21						Nov-15
10,000	0.14	-5.49	-8.53	12.15		0	2.6	8.48	0.13	13.58	23.5	37	69	14	-21						Nov-15
100	3.52	20.74	6.53	23.72	23.06	0	1.17	14.8	0.81	36.72	130.3	4	90	4	0	59	42.49	-19.74			Oct-01
	5.28	19.18	12.51	36.67	34.65	0.68	1.98	11.59	0.92	11.48	49.4	2	98	0	0	14	21.9	-17.15		1.00	Jan-04

	MARKET		FUND TYPE, CATEGORY & OBJECTIVE		RATINGS				MINIMUMS	
Fund Name	Ticker Symbol	Traded On	Fund Type	Category and (Prospectus Objective)	Overall Rating	Reward Rating	Risk Rating	Recent Up/ Downgrade	Open to New Investors	Min Initial Investment
Crawford Dividend Growth Fund Class Institutional	CDGIX	NAS CM	Open End	US Equity Large Cap Blend (Growth)	B-	C+	B+	Down	Y	10,000
Crawford Dividend Opportunity Fund	CDOFX	NAS CM	Open End	US Equity Small Cap (Small Company)	C+	C	B		Y	10,000
Crawford Dividend Opportunity Fund Class C	CDOCX	NAS CM	Open End	US Equity Small Cap (Small Company)	C+	C	B		Y	2,500
Crawford Multi-Asset Income Fund	CMALX	NAS CM	Open End	Moderate Alloc (Multi-Asset Global)	C-	D+	B	Up	Y	10,000
Credit Suisse Commodity Return Strategy Fund Class A	CRSAX	NAS CM	Open End	Commodities Broad Basket (Growth & Income)	D	D	C-	Down	Y	2,500
Credit Suisse Commodity Return Strategy Fund Class C	CRSCX	NAS CM	Open End	Commodities Broad Basket (Growth & Income)	D	D	C-	Down	Y	2,500
Credit Suisse Commodity Return Strategy Fund Class I	CRSOX	NAS CM	Open End	Commodities Broad Basket (Growth & Income)	D	D	C-	Down	Y	250,000
Credit Suisse Managed Futures Strategy Fund Class A	CSAAX	NAS CM	Open End	Alternative Miscellaneous (Growth & Income)	D+	D+	C-		Y	2,500
Credit Suisse Managed Futures Strategy Fund Class C	CSACX	NAS CM	Open End	Alternative Miscellaneous (Growth & Income)	D+	D	C-	Up	Y	2,500
Credit Suisse Managed Futures Strategy Fund Class I	CSAIX	NAS CM	Open End	Alternative Miscellaneous (Growth & Income)	D+	D+	C-		Y	250,000
Credit Suisse Multialternative Strategy Cls A Shares	CSQAX	NAS CM	Open End	Multialternative (Growth & Income)	C+	C	B	Up	Y	2,500
Credit Suisse Multialternative Strategy Cls C Shares	CSQCX	NAS CM	Open End	Multialternative (Growth & Income)	U	U	U		Y	2,500
Credit Suisse Multialternative Strategy Cls I Shares	CSQIX	NAS CM	Open End	Multialternative (Growth & Income)	C+	C	B	Up	Y	250,000
Credit Suisse Trust Commodity Return Strategy Portfolio	CCRSX	NAS CM	Open End	Commodities Broad Basket (Growth & Income)	D	D	C-	Down	Y	0
CRM All Cap Value Fund Class Institutional	CRIEX	NAS CM	Open End	US Equity Large Cap Blend (Growth)	C	C	B-		Y	1,000,000
CRM All Cap Value Fund Class Investor	CRMEX	NAS CM	Open End	US Equity Large Cap Blend (Growth)	C	C	C+		Y	2,500
CRM Long/Short Opportunities Fund Institutional Shares	CRIHX	NAS CM	Open End	Long/Short Equity (Growth)	C	D+	C		Y	100,000,000
CRM Mid Cap Value Fund Class Institutional	CRIMX	NAS CM	Open End	US Equity Mid Cap (Growth & Income)	C+	C	B-	Down	Y	1,000,000
CRM Mid Cap Value Fund Class Investor	CRMMX	NAS CM	Open End	US Equity Mid Cap (Growth & Income)	C+	C	B-	Down	Y	2,500
CRM Small Cap Value Fund Class Institutional	CRISX	NAS CM	Open End	US Equity Small Cap (Small Company)	C	C	B-		Y	1,000,000
CRM Small Cap Value Fund Class Investor	CRMSX	NAS CM	Open End	US Equity Small Cap (Small Company)	C	C	B-		Y	2,500
CRM Small/Mid Cap Value Fund Class Institutional	CRIAX	NAS CM	Open End	US Equity Mid Cap (Growth)	C+	C	B-	Down	Y	1,000,000
CRM Small/Mid Cap Value Fund Class Investor	CRMAX	NAS CM	Open End	US Equity Mid Cap (Growth)	C+	C	B-		Y	2,500
Cross Shore Discovery Fund Institutional Shares			Closed End	Long/Short Equity (Growth)	U	U	U		Y	50,000
CrossingBridge Long/Short Credit Fund Institutional Class	CCLIX	NAS CM	Open End	Long/Short Credit (Growth & Income)	C	C-	C+		Y	250,000
Crossmark Steward Covered Call Income Fund Class A	SCJAX	NAS CM	Open End	Long/Short Equity (Equity-Income)	D+	D+	B-	Up	Y	2,000
Crossmark Steward Covered Call Income Fund Class C	SCJCX	NAS CM	Open End	Long/Short Equity (Equity-Income)	D+	D+	B-	Up	Y	2,000
Crossmark Steward Covered Call Income Fund Class R6	SCJKX	NAS CM	Open End	Long/Short Equity (Equity-Income)	D+	D+	B-	Up	Y	0
Crossmark Steward Covered Call Income Institutional Cls	SCJIX	NAS CM	Open End	Long/Short Equity (Equity-Income)	D+	D+	B-	Up	Y	100,000
Crossmark Steward Global Equity Income Fund Class A	SGIDX	NAS CM	Open End	Global Equity Large Cap (Equity-Income)	B-	C	B	Up	Y	2,000
Crossmark Steward Global Equity Income Fund Class C	SGIFX	NAS CM	Open End	Global Equity Large Cap (Equity-Income)	B-	C	B	Up	Y	2,000
Crossmark Steward Global Equity Income Cls Institutional	SGISX	NAS CM	Open End	Global Equity Large Cap (Equity-Income)	B-	C	B	Up	Y	100,000
Crossmark Steward Global Equity Income Fund Class R6	SGIGX	NAS CM	Open End	Global Equity Large Cap (Equity-Income)	B-	C	B	Up	Y	0
Crossmark Steward International Enhanced Index Cls A	SNTKX	NAS CM	Open End	Global Equity Large Cap (Foreign Stock)	C	C	B		Y	2,000
Crossmark Steward International Enhanced Index Cls C	SNTDX	NAS CM	Open End	Global Equity Large Cap (Foreign Stock)	C	C	B		Y	2,000
Crossmark Steward Intl Enhanced Index Cls Inst	SNTCX	NAS CM	Open End	Global Equity Large Cap (Foreign Stock)	C+	C	B	Up	Y	100,000
Crossmark Steward International Enhanced Index Cls R6	SNTFX	NAS CM	Open End	Global Equity Large Cap (Foreign Stock)	C	C	B		Y	0
Crossmark Steward Large Cap Enhanced Index Fund Class A	SEEKX	NAS CM	Open End	US Equity Large Cap Blend (Growth)	C+	C	B		Y	2,000
Crossmark Steward Large Cap Enhanced Index Fund Class C	SEEBX	NAS CM	Open End	US Equity Large Cap Blend (Growth)	C+	C	B	Up	Y	2,000
Crossmark Steward Large Cap Enhanced Index Cls Inst	SEECX	NAS CM	Open End	US Equity Large Cap Blend (Growth)	C+	C	B		Y	100,000
Crossmark Steward Large Cap Enhanced Index Fund Class R6	SEEHX	NAS CM	Open End	US Equity Large Cap Blend (Growth)	C+	C	B	Up	Y	0
Crossmark Steward Small-Mid Cap Enhanced Index Cls A	TRDFX	NAS CM	Open End	US Equity Small Cap (Growth)	C	C-	C+		Y	2,000
Crossmark Steward Small-Mid Cap Enhanced Index Cls C	SSMEX	NAS CM	Open End	US Equity Small Cap (Growth)	C	C-	C+		Y	2,000
Crossmark Steward Small-Mid Cap Enhanced Index Cls R6	SSMOX	NAS CM	Open End	US Equity Small Cap (Growth)	C	C-	C+		Y	0
Crossmark Steward Small-Mid Cap Enhanced Index Inst Cls	SCECX	NAS CM	Open End	US Equity Small Cap (Growth)	C	C-	C+		Y	100,000
Crow Point Global Tactical Allocation Inst Cls Shares	CGHIX	NAS CM	Open End	Flexible Alloc (Equity-Income)	B-	C	B+		Y	1,000
Crow Point Global Tactical Allocation Investor Cls Shares	CGHAX	NAS CM	Open End	Flexible Alloc (Equity-Income)	B-	C	B+		Y	500
Crow Point Growth Fund Institutional Class	GAMIX	NAS CM	Open End	US Equity Small Cap (Growth)	D+	D	C-	Down	Y	100,000
Cullen Emerging Markets High Dividend Fund Class C	CEMGX	NAS CM	Open End	Global Emerg Mkts (Div Emerging Mkts)	C	C-	C+		Y	1,000
Cullen Emerging Markets High Dividend Fund Class I	CEMFX	NAS CM	Open End	Global Emerg Mkts (Div Emerging Mkts)	C	C	C+		Y	1,000,000
Cullen Emerging Markets High Dividend Fund Retail Class	CEMDX	NAS CM	Open End	Global Emerg Mkts (Div Emerging Mkts)	C	C	C+		Y	1,000
Cullen Enhanced Equity Income Fund Class C	ENHCX	NAS CM	Open End	Long/Short Equity (Equity-Income)	C+	C	B	Down	Y	1,000

★ Expanded analysis of this fund is included in Section II.

	TOTAL RETURNS					PERFORMANCE				ASSETS		ASSET ALLOCATION & TURNOVER					BULL & BEAR		FEES		
Min Additional Investment	3-Month Total Return	6-Month Total Return	1-Year Total Return	3-Year Total Return	5-Year Total Return	Dividend Yield (TTM)	Expense Ratio	3-Yr Std Deviation	3-Year Beta	NAV	Total Assets (MIL)	%Cash	%Stocks	%Bonds	%Other	Turnover Ratio	Last Bull Market Total Return	Last Bear Market Total Return	Front End Fee (%)	Back End Fee (%)	Inception Date
	5.51	19.70	13.67	40.89	41.51	1.63	0.98	11.65	0.93	11.57	49.4	2	98	0	0	14	22.61	-16.77			Jan-04
	3.76	15.78	1.19	44.47	55.18	1.08	1.05	14.51	0.82	41.49	225.1	2	98	0	0	33					Sep-12
	3.50	15.19	0.16	40.19	47.58	0.24	2.05	14.51	0.82	41.26	225.1	2	98	0	0	33				1.00	Apr-15
0	1.75	13.76	6.13			4.22	1.15			25.08	69.8	5	50	17	0	28					Sep-17
100	-1.53	3.53	-7.30	-7.84	-39.36	1	1.03	8.42	0.98	4.47	1,898	4	0	79	17	90	0.15	-19.96	4.75		Dec-04
100	-1.83	2.84	-8.28	-10.08	-41.64	0.23	1.78	8.36	0.97	4.2	1,898	4	0	79	17	90	-0.34	-20.12		1.00	Dec-04
100,000	-1.44	3.58	-7.10	-7.11	-38.55	1.24	0.78	8.48	0.98	4.57	1,898	4	0	79	17	90	0.27	-19.82			Dec-04
100	2.02	-1.08	2.44	-8.78	18.58	0	1.55	9.07	1	10.06	352.0	-73	-61	228	6				5.25		Sep-12
100	1.80	-1.43	1.69	-10.84	14.19	0	2.3	9.12	1	9.6	352.0	-73	-61	228	6					1.00	Sep-12
100,000	2.00	-0.97	2.72	-8.19	20.02	0	1.3	9.14	1	10.18	352.0	-73	-61	228	6						Sep-12
100	0.80	6.49	1.75	6.93	7.73	0	1.19	3.9	0.84	10	77.8	58	-38	71	8	1,373			5.25		Mar-12
100	1.54	2.87	1.44	1.90	9.18	0	1.86	3.75	0.9		106.1	61	21	11	7	586				1.00	Mar-12
100,000	0.89	6.52	2.03	7.78	9.06	0	0.94	3.87	0.84	10.12	77.8	58	-38	71	8	1,373					Mar-12
	-1.42	3.60	-7.29	-7.93	-39.25	0.92	1.04	8.47	0.98	3.61	429.2	4	0	80	16	105	0.14	-20.01			Feb-06
	1.70	18.15	-0.50	31.33	39.13	0.14	1.21	13.64	1.04	7.16	36.1	4	96	0	0	72	22.69	-24.53			Oct-06
50	1.59	18.07	-0.71	30.35	37.35	0	1.46	13.64	1.04	6.99	36.1	4	96	0	0	72	22.47	-24.64			Oct-06
	0.98	11.14	-2.27			0	2.81			10.27	482.0	35	65	0	0	251					Aug-16
	4.28	21.22	3.60	44.25	53.13	0.35	0.92	13.17	0.94	22.16	464.1	4	96	0	0	58	22.72	-23.07			Jan-98
50	4.22	21.11	3.39	43.33	51.59	0.18	1.12	13.17	0.94	21.22	464.1	4	96	0	0	58	22.57	-23.15			Sep-00
	1.75	18.94	0.11	39.65	44.51	0.41	0.9	16.21	0.91	17.96	325.2	5	95	0	0	49	22.11	-28.05			Jan-98
50	1.65	18.73	-0.16	38.68	42.85	0.22	1.14	16.21	0.91	15.34	325.2	5	95	0	0	49	21.96	-28.11			Sep-95
	1.29	19.38	2.12	41.47	34.20	0.23	0.92	14.52	0.92	11.7	278.3	3	97	0	0	48	30.84	-24.3			Sep-04
50	1.24	19.20	1.90	40.48	32.67	0	1.14	14.49	0.92	11.36	278.3	3	97	0	0	48	30.65	-24.34			Sep-04
5,000	1.61	4.53	-3.95	7.30		0	9.3	9.74	0.84		--										Jan-15
1,000	0.06	0.84	0.63	5.11		1.8	2.14	1.5	-0.01	9.56	60.5	46	0	41	11						Feb-15
1,000	1.14	12.20	5.96			0.79	1.25			9.64	29.0	2	98	0	0						Dec-17
1,000	1.03	12.00	5.89			0.23	2			9.72	29.0	2	98	0	0						Dec-17
	1.13	11.98	5.82			0.18	0.9			9.69	29.0	2	98	0	0						Dec-17
50,000	1.31	12.32	6.36			1.04	1			9.63	29.0	2	98	0	0						Dec-17
1,000	2.93	14.70	3.78	37.81	45.28	1.92	0.99	11.12	0.88	31.18	312.4	0	100	0	0		19.52	-13.07			Apr-08
1,000	2.68	14.27	3.10	35.69	41.16	9.68	1.68	11.06	0.88	5.13	312.4	0	100	0	0		19.06	-13.33			Dec-17
50,000	3.00	14.90	4.05	39.11	47.63	2.19	0.68	11.12	0.88	31.26	312.4	0	100	0	0		19.75	-12.97			Apr-08
	3.14	15.01	4.16	38.58	47.06	10.72	0.58	11.16	0.89	4.83	312.4	0	100	0	0		19.75	-12.97			Dec-17
1,000	2.18	13.29	0.81	29.74	3.16	2.3	1.02	11.78	1.03	21.68	150.3	2	98	0	0		12.88	-24.26			Feb-06
1,000	1.40	12.30	-0.79	26.08	-1.22	1.88	1.71	11.86	1.04	9.43	150.3	2	98	0	0		12.39	-24.5			Dec-17
50,000	2.29	13.44	1.09	30.99	4.87	2.56	0.71	11.79	1.03	21.75	150.3	2	98	0	0		13.1	-24.14			Mar-06
	1.62	12.45	-0.68	27.76	1.59	1.89	0.61	11.87	1.04	9.42	150.3	2	98	0	0		12.88	-24.26			Dec-17
1,000	3.96	18.98	7.19	44.64	49.56	0.84	0.84	12.78	1.04	43.19	429.3	1	99	0	0		23.98	-17.83			Oct-04
1,000	3.41	17.86	5.20	39.79	42.70	0.74	1.54	12.76	1.04	8.61	429.3	1	99	0	0		23.5	-18.05			Dec-17
50,000	4.05	19.16	7.53	45.96	51.99	1.02	0.54	12.78	1.04	43.06	429.3	1	99	0	0		24.22	-17.71			Oct-04
	3.98	19.09	6.35	43.15	49.07	2.72	0.44	12.8	1.04	8.46	429.3	1	99	0	0		24.22	-17.71			Dec-17
1,000	0.51	14.34	-5.62	33.80	35.23	0.6	0.83	17.08	1.08	13.54	221.5	1	99	0	0		27.53	-22.36			Jan-52
1,000	0.64	14.97	-6.11	30.82	30.26	0.26	1.57	17.19	1.08	6.6	221.5	1	99	0	0		26.97	-22.6			Dec-17
	0.65	15.02	-6.04	32.32	33.73	0.26	0.47	17.21	1.08	6.58	221.5	1	99	0	0		27.53	-22.36			Dec-17
50,000	0.58	14.54	-5.42	35.04	37.21	0.82	0.57	17.05	1.07	13.78	221.5	1	99	0	0		27.79	-22.3			Apr-06
	1.43	11.57	4.81	19.87	8.04	0.83	1.83	8.69	0.65	9.16	20.9	8	59	21	12	73					Apr-13
250	1.44	11.61	5.03	19.44	7.04	0.49	2.08	8.73	0.65	9.13	20.9	8	59	21	12	73			2.25		Jun-12
100	-3.32	15.64	-6.22	3.04	-19.26	0	1.35	22.57	1.07	8.13	13.9	0	100	0	0	264	16.44	-15.82			Jul-14
100	-0.15	12.01	-0.07	19.69	2.62	2.97	2	12.65	0.88	10.14	350.0	5	95	0	0	48					Aug-12
100	0.08	12.54	0.93	23.39	7.98	3.65	1	12.65	0.88	10.33	350.0	5	95	0	0	48					Aug-12
100	0.02	12.38	0.66	22.47	6.47	3.49	1.25	12.67	0.88	10.26	350.0	5	95	0	0	48					Aug-12
100	0.26	10.54	7.96	18.80		4.6	1.76	9.5	1	10.18	52.5	4	96	0	0	157					Dec-15

	MARKET			FUND TYPE, CATEGORY & OBJECTIVE	RATINGS					MINIMUMS
Fund Name	Ticker Symbol	Traded On	Fund Type	Category and (Prospectus Objective)	Overall Rating	Reward Rating	Risk Rating	Recent Up/ Downgrade	Open to New Investors	Min Initial Investment
Cullen Enhanced Equity Income Fund Class I	ENHNX	NAS CM	Open End	Long/Short Equity (Equity-Income)	C+	C	B	Down	Y	1,000,000
Cullen Enhanced Equity Income Fund Retail Class	ENHRX	NAS CM	Open End	Long/Short Equity (Equity-Income)	C+	C	B	Down	Y	1,000
Cullen High Dividend Equity Fund Class C	CHVCX	NAS CM	Open End	US Equity Large Cap Value (Equity-Income)	B-	C	B+		Y	1,000
Cullen High Dividend Equity Fund Class Institutional	CHDVX	NAS CM	Open End	US Equity Large Cap Value (Equity-Income)	B-	C	B+	Down	Y	1,000,000
Cullen High Dividend Equity Fund Class R1	CHDRX	NAS CM	Open End	US Equity Large Cap Value (Equity-Income)	B-	C	B+	Down	Y	0
Cullen High Dividend Equity Fund Class R2	CHDPX	NAS CM	Open End	US Equity Large Cap Value (Equity-Income)	B-	C	B+	Down	Y	0
Cullen High Dividend Equity Fund Retail Class	CHDEX	NAS CM	Open End	US Equity Large Cap Value (Equity-Income)	B-	C	B+	Down	Y	1,000
Cullen International High Dividend Fund Class C	CIHCX	NAS CM	Open End	Global Equity Large Cap (Equity-Income)	C-	D+	C+		Y	1,000
Cullen International High Dividend Cls Institutional	CIHIX	NAS CM	Open End	Global Equity Large Cap (Equity-Income)	C	D+	B-	Up	Y	1,000,000
Cullen International High Dividend Fund Class R1	CIHRX	NAS CM	Open End	Global Equity Large Cap (Equity-Income)	C	D+	C+	Up	Y	0
Cullen International High Dividend Fund Class R2	CIHPX	NAS CM	Open End	Global Equity Large Cap (Equity-Income)	C	D+	B-	Up	Y	0
Cullen International High Dividend Fund Retail Class	CIHDX	NAS CM	Open End	Global Equity Large Cap (Equity-Income)	C	D+	B-	Up	Y	1,000
Cullen Small Cap Value Fund Class C	CUSCX	NAS CM	Open End	US Equity Small Cap (Small Company)	C	C-	C+		Y	1,000
Cullen Small Cap Value Fund Class I	CUSIX	NAS CM	Open End	US Equity Small Cap (Small Company)	C	C-	B-		Y	1,000,000
Cullen Small Cap Value Fund Class Retail Class	CUSRX	NAS CM	Open End	US Equity Small Cap (Small Company)	C	C-	B-		Y	1,000
Cullen Value Fund Class C	CVLFX	NAS CM	Open End	US Equity Large Cap Value (Growth & Income)	B-	C	B+		Y	1,000
Cullen Value Fund Class I	CVLVX	NAS CM	Open End	US Equity Large Cap Value (Growth & Income)	B-	C	B+		Y	1,000,000
Cullen Value Fund Retail Class	CVLEX	NAS CM	Open End	US Equity Large Cap Value (Growth & Income)	B-	C	B+		Y	1,000
Cushing® MLP & Infrastructure Total Return Fund	SRV	NYSE	Closed End	Energy Sector Equity (Natl Res)	C-	C-	C-	Down	Y	
Cushing® MLP Infrastructure Fund Class A Shares	PAPEX	NAS CM	Open End	Energy Sector Equity (Natl Res)	D+	D	C-	Down	Y	2,000
Cushing® MLP Infrastructure Fund Class C Shares	PCPEX	NAS CM	Open End	Energy Sector Equity (Natl Res)	D+	D	C-	Down	Y	2,000
Cushing® MLP Infrastructure Fund Class I Shares	PIPEX	NAS CM	Open End	Energy Sector Equity (Natl Res)	D+	D	C-	Down	Y	250,000
Cutler Emerging Markets Fund	CUTDX	NAS CM	Open End	Global Emerg Mkts (Div Emerging Mkts)	C	C-	B-		Y	2,500
Cutler Equity Fund	CALEX	NAS CM	Open End	US Equity Large Cap Value (Growth)	B-	C	B+	Down	Y	2,500
CVR Dynamic Allocation Fund Institutional Shares	CVRAX	NAS CM	Open End	Moderate Alloc (Growth)	C	D+	C+		Y	5,000
Dana Epiphany ESG Equity Fund Institutional Class Shares	ESGIX	NAS CM	Open End	US Equity Large Cap Blend (Growth)	C+	C	B		Y	100,000
Dana Epiphany ESG Equity Fund Investor Class Shares	ESGAX	NAS CM	Open End	US Equity Large Cap Blend (Growth)	C+	C	B		Y	1,000
Dana Large Cap Equity Fund Institutional Class	DLCIX	NAS CM	Open End	US Equity Large Cap Blend (Growth)	C+	C	B		Y	1,000,000
Dana Large Cap Equity Fund Investor Class	DLCEX	NAS CM	Open End	US Equity Large Cap Blend (Growth)	C+	C	B		Y	1,000
Dana Small Cap Equity Fund Institutional Class	DSCIX	NAS CM	Open End	US Equity Small Cap (Small Company)	C	C	C		Y	1,000,000
Dana Small Cap Equity Fund Investor Class	DSCEX	NAS CM	Open End	US Equity Small Cap (Small Company)	C	C	C		Y	1,000
Davenport Balanced Income Fund	DBALX	NAS CM	Open End	Moderate Alloc (Growth & Income)	B-	C	B+	Up	Y	5,000
Davenport Core Fund	DAVPX	NAS CM	Open End	US Equity Large Cap Growth (Growth)	B-	C+	B		Y	5,000
Davenport Equity Opportunities Fund	DEOPX	NAS CM	Open End	US Equity Mid Cap (Growth)	B-	B-	B	Up	Y	5,000
Davenport Small Cap Focus Fund	DSCPX	NAS CM	Open End	US Equity Small Cap (Small Company)	C+	C	B-	Up	Y	5,000
Davenport Value & Income Fund	DVIPX	NAS CM	Open End	US Equity Large Cap Value (Growth & Income)	B-	C	B	Up	Y	5,000
Davidson Multi-Cap Equity Fund Class A	DFMAX	NAS CM	Open End	US Equity Large Cap Blend (Growth)	B-	C	B		Y	2,500
Davidson Multi-Cap Equity Fund Class I	DFMIX	NAS CM	Open End	US Equity Large Cap Blend (Growth)	B-	C	B		Y	250,000
Davis Appreciation & Income Fund Class A	RPFCX	NAS CM	Open End	Aggressive Alloc (Growth & Income)	B-	C	B	Up	Y	1,000
Davis Appreciation & Income Fund Class C	DCSCX	NAS CM	Open End	Aggressive Alloc (Growth & Income)	C+	C	B	Up	Y	1,000
Davis Appreciation & Income Fund Class Y	DCSYX	NAS CM	Open End	Aggressive Alloc (Growth & Income)	B-	C	B	Up	Y	5,000,000
Davis Financial Fund Class A	RPFGX	NAS CM	Open End	Financials Sector Equity (Financial)	C	C	B-		Y	1,000
Davis Financial Fund Class C	DFFCX	NAS CM	Open End	Financials Sector Equity (Financial)	C	C	B-		Y	1,000
Davis Financial Fund Class Y	DVFYX	NAS CM	Open End	Financials Sector Equity (Financial)	C	C	B		Y	5,000,000
Davis Global Fund Class A	DGFAX	NAS CM	Open End	Global Equity Large Cap (World Stock)	C	C-	C		Y	1,000
Davis Global Fund Class C	DGFCX	NAS CM	Open End	Global Equity Large Cap (World Stock)	C	C-	C		Y	1,000
Davis Global Fund Class Y	DGFYX	NAS CM	Open End	Global Equity Large Cap (World Stock)	C	C-	C		Y	5,000,000
Davis International Fund Class A	DILAX	NAS CM	Open End	Global Equity Large Cap (Foreign Stock)	C	C-	C		Y	1,000
Davis International Fund Class C	DILCX	NAS CM	Open End	Global Equity Large Cap (Foreign Stock)	C	C-	C		Y	1,000
Davis International Fund Class Y	DILYX	NAS CM	Open End	Global Equity Large Cap (Foreign Stock)	C	C-	C		Y	5,000,000
Davis New York Venture Fund Class A	NYVTX	NAS CM	Open End	US Equity Large Cap Blend (Growth)	C+	C	B-	Up	Y	1,000
Davis New York Venture Fund Class B	NYVBX	NAS CM	Open End	US Equity Large Cap Blend (Growth)	C	C	C+		Y	1,000

★ Expanded analysis of this fund is included in Section II.

Min Additional Investment	3-Month Total Return	6-Month Total Return	1-Year Total Return	3-Year Total Return	5-Year Total Return	Dividend Yield (TTM)	Expense Ratio	3-Yr Std Deviation	3-Year Beta	NAV	Total Assets (MIL)	%Cash	%Stocks	%Bonds	%Other	Turnover Ratio	Last Bull Market Total Return	Last Bear Market Total Return	Front End Fee (%)	Back End Fee (%)	Inception Date
	TOTAL RETURNS					PERFORMANCE				ASSETS		ASSET ALLOCATION & TURNOVER					BULL & BEAR		FEES		
100	0.50	11.02	9.02	22.36		5.59	0.76	9.54	1	10.21	52.5	4	96	0	0	157					Dec-15
100	0.35	10.84	8.68	21.43		5.36	1.01	9.52	1	10.15	52.5	4	96	0	0	157					Dec-15
100	0.56	12.41	8.88	26.99	36.35	1.37	1.75	9.88	0.72	16.69	1,603	3	97	0	0	16	16.51	-8.75			Oct-04
100	0.88	12.95	10.01	30.87	43.35	2.19	0.75	9.88	0.73	16.92	1,603	3	97	0	0	16	17.19	-8.42			Oct-04
	0.72	12.57	9.21	28.03	38.12	1.84	1.5	9.9	0.73	14.34	1,603	3	97	0	0	16	16.74	-8.76			Mar-10
	0.75	12.73	9.44	28.91	39.85	2	1.25	9.85	0.72	14.57	1,603	3	97	0	0	16	16.93	-8.6			Mar-10
100	0.76	12.82	9.67	29.90	41.53	1.96	1	9.9	0.73	16.91	1,603	3	97	0	0	16	17.04	-8.5			Aug-03
100	3.40	12.12	-0.70	10.40	-7.73	2.63	2	10.92	0.95	9.53	158.6	6	94	0	0	31	13.35	-21.05			Dec-05
100	3.75	12.68	0.33	13.82	-3.01	3.62	1	10.96	0.95	9.63	158.6	6	94	0	0	31	14.02	-20.74			Dec-05
	3.50	12.24	-0.42	11.27	-6.35	2.42	1.71	10.99	0.96	11.17	158.6	6	94	0	0	31	13.53	-21			Mar-10
	3.59	12.50	-0.18	12.17	-5.17	2.68	1.46	10.93	0.95	11.06	158.6	6	94	0	0	31	13.7	-20.88			Mar-10
100	3.70	12.63	0.06	12.91	-4.21	3.38	1.25	11	0.96	9.55	158.6	6	94	0	0	31	13.84	-20.92			Dec-05
100	2.36	14.01	-3.00	25.72	-3.35	0	2.01	16.96	1.06	10.41	4.3	6	94	0	0	34	27.04	-23.39			Oct-09
100	2.64	14.53	-2.06	29.53	1.24	0	1.01	16.93	1.06	11.66	4.3	6	94	0	0	34	27.82	-23.13			Oct-09
100	2.61	14.51	-2.28	28.65	0.27	0	1.26	16.87	1.06	11.36	4.3	6	94	0	0	34	27.55	-23.24			Oct-09
100	3.70	14.42	8.64	36.06	35.72	0.67	1.76	11.11	0.86	16.55	40.3	9	91	0	0	2					Aug-12
100	3.95	14.97	9.73	40.19	42.58	1.62	0.76	11.09	0.86	16.55	40.3	9	91	0	0	2					Aug-12
100	3.89	14.82	9.47	39.19	40.97	1.4	1.01	11.14	0.86	16.56	40.3	9	91	0	0	2					Aug-12
	-0.06	25.39	-2.40	4.66	-51.21	2.32	2.84	22.05		11.67	78.6	1	93	4	0	96	13.32	-18.12			Aug-07
100	-3.07	14.75	-9.05	-3.90	-28.82	5.93	1.75	16.8	0.93	17.84	26.7	1	99	0	0				5.50		Dec-17
100	-3.38	14.10	-9.88	-6.16	-31.52	6.01	2.5	16.81	0.93	17.6	26.7	1	99	0	0					1.00	Dec-17
100	-2.95	15.08	-8.64	-2.97	-27.77	5.89	1.5	16.82	0.93	17.95	26.7	1	99	0	0						Aug-12
	0.20	8.25	0.80	18.69		1.23	1.68	11.48	0.83	9.57	14.2	2	98	0	0	2					Jul-15
	4.80	15.09	10.36	36.00	46.04	1.47	1.15	11.96	0.91	20.67	159.8	2	98	0	0	10	21.06	-12.97			Dec-92
	2.90	13.58	-1.88	17.31	3.53	0	1.65	14.26	2.07	10.62	15.2	6	95	0	0	129					Dec-13
250	4.09	17.26	5.10	42.83	35.49	0.79	0.85	12.4	1	11.14	12.8	2	98	0	0	23	21.19	-18.04		1.00	Feb-08
250	4.06	17.98	5.56	41.77	39.51	0.57	1.1	12.37	1	11.46	12.8	2	98	0	0	23	21.56	-17.79	5.00		Jan-07
1,000	4.69	19.67	7.37	47.30	51.06	1.64	0.73	12.3	1	21.4	127.5	1	99	0	0	58	24.45	-18.04			Oct-13
250	4.62	19.52	7.09	46.16	49.04	1.44	0.98	12.26	0.99	21.4	127.5	1	99	0	0	58	24.45	-18.04			Mar-10
1,000	3.24	19.06	-2.50	25.57		0	0.95	17.67	1.01	10.49	16.0	1	99	0	0	78					Nov-15
250	3.17	18.87	-2.79	24.58		0	1.2	17.68	1.01	10.39	16.0	1	99	0	0	78					Nov-15
	2.57	11.27	5.75	18.44		2.1	0.97	7.35	0.58	11.56	148.8	4	59	37	0	30					Dec-15
	6.05	22.23	11.79	48.50	56.55	0.43	0.9	12.21	0.98	25.04	548.4	2	99	0	0	21	25.41	-16.22			Jan-98
	8.82	30.23	19.01	50.70	53.57	0	0.91	12.64	0.85	20	448.6	4	96	0	0	19	28.2	-17.1			Dec-10
	7.21	26.72	5.61	50.97		0.45	1	15.28	0.84	14.12	178.6	5	95	0	0	60					Dec-14
	2.50	14.68	5.34	29.52	42.28	2.16	0.9	11.44	0.92	16.68	686.4	6	94	0	0	18	24.33	-12.73			Dec-10
	3.22	17.42	7.71	40.01	44.80	1.31	1.15	12.16	0.95	25.27	112.0	3	97	0	0	32	24.11	-19.3	5.00		Aug-08
	3.31	17.53	7.96	41.06	46.62	1.69	0.9	12.16	0.95	25.27	112.0	3	97	0	0	32	24.1	-19.3			Oct-13
25	2.03	11.56	0.82	28.10	14.34	1.1	1.01	10.03	0.79	40.05	189.7	5	70	25	0	54	19.19	-21.6	4.75		May-92
25	1.81	11.12	0.00	25.17	9.83	0.37	1.76	10.01	0.79	40.16	189.7	5	70	25	0	54	18.62	-21.88		1.00	Aug-97
25	2.08	11.75	1.13	29.31	15.87	1.42	0.68	10.03	0.79	40.22	189.7	5	70	25	0	54	19.25	-21.52			Nov-96
25	4.88	13.29	0.90	41.89	48.15	1	0.94	13.52	0.98	47.45	1,099	0	100	0	0	18	21.19	-19.77	4.75		May-91
25	4.66	12.81	0.11	38.66	42.23	0.22	1.7	13.51	0.98	38.82	1,099	0	100	0	0	18	20.56	-20.06		1.00	Aug-97
25	4.94	13.41	1.12	42.93	49.73	1.25	0.7	13.51	0.98	49.02	1,099	0	100	0	0	18	21.38	-19.73			Mar-97
25	1.15	18.74	-6.42	38.00	34.86	0.22	0.96	15.94	1.3	22.68	1,069	1	94	0	1	37	18.49	-26.01	4.75		Dec-04
25	0.96	18.27	-7.17	34.87	29.66	0	1.71	15.94	1.3	21.03	1,069	1	94	0	1	37	17.97	-26.34		1.00	Dec-04
25	1.20	18.86	-6.25	38.99	36.54	0.49	0.7	15.93	1.3	22.75	1,069	1	94	0	1	37	18.77	-25.93			Jul-07
25	-0.41	16.08	-8.65	31.63	14.26	0.54	1.04	15.63	1.23	11.91	324.6	5	92	0	0	17	19.25	-31.52	4.75		Dec-06
25	-0.62	15.50	-9.37	27.97	8.63	0	1.85	15.61	1.23	11.1	324.6	5	92	0	0	17	18.78	-32.94		1.00	Dec-06
25	-0.33	16.20	-8.40	32.79	15.99	0.9	0.72	15.64	1.23	11.76	324.6	5	92	0	0	17	19.67	-32.5			Dec-09
25	3.45	18.40	0.13	43.05	47.13	0.63	0.88	14.96	1.16	27.56	8,912	1	96	0	0	25	22.99	-20.21	4.75		Feb-69
25	3.19	17.89	-0.75	38.98	40.23	0.09	1.86	14.95	1.16	23.36	8,912	1	96	0	0	25	22.37	-20.54		4.00	Dec-94

Fund Name	MARKET Ticker Symbol	Traded On	FUND TYPE, CATEGORY & OBJECTIVE Fund Type	Category and (Prospectus Objective)	RATINGS Overall Rating	Reward Rating	Risk Rating	Recent Up/ Downgrade	MINIMUMS Open to New Investors	Min Initial Investment
Davis New York Venture Fund Class C	NYVCX	NAS CM	Open End	US Equity Large Cap Blend (Growth)	C	C	C+		Y	1,000
Davis New York Venture Fund Class R	NYVRX	NAS CM	Open End	US Equity Large Cap Blend (Growth)	C+	C	B-	Up	Y	500,000
Davis New York Venture Fund Class Y	DNVYX	NAS CM	Open End	US Equity Large Cap Blend (Growth)	C+	C	B-	Up	Y	5,000,000
Davis Opportunity Fund Class A	RPEAX	NAS CM	Open End	US Equity Large Cap Growth (Growth)	C	C-	C		Y	1,000
Davis Opportunity Fund Class C	DGOCX	NAS CM	Open End	US Equity Large Cap Growth (Growth)	C	C-	C		Y	1,000
Davis Opportunity Fund Class Y	DGOYX	NAS CM	Open End	US Equity Large Cap Growth (Growth)	C	C-	C+		Y	5,000,000
Davis Real Estate Fund Class A	RPFRX	NAS CM	Open End	Real Estate Sector Equity (Real Estate)	B-	C+	B		Y	1,000
Davis Real Estate Fund Class C	DRECX	NAS CM	Open End	Real Estate Sector Equity (Real Estate)	B-	C	B		Y	1,000
Davis Real Estate Fund Class Y	DREYX	NAS CM	Open End	Real Estate Sector Equity (Real Estate)	B-	C+	B		Y	5,000,000
Day Hagan Logix Tactical Dividend Fund Class A	DHQAX	NAS CM	Open End	US Equity Large Cap Value (Equity-Income)	C+	C	B-	Up	Y	1,000
Day Hagan Logix Tactical Dividend Fund Class C	DHQCX	NAS CM	Open End	US Equity Large Cap Value (Equity-Income)	C	C	C+		Y	1,000
Day Hagan Logix Tactical Dividend Fund Class I	DHQIX	NAS CM	Open End	US Equity Large Cap Value (Equity-Income)	C+	C	B	Up	Y	1,000
Day Hagan Tactical Allocation Fund Class A	DHAAX	NAS CM	Open End	Moderate Alloc (Growth)	C	C-	C	Up	Y	1,000
Day Hagan Tactical Allocation Fund Class C	DHACX	NAS CM	Open End	Moderate Alloc (Growth)	C-	C-	C		Y	1,000
Day Hagan Tactical Allocation Fund Class I	DHAIX	NAS CM	Open End	Moderate Alloc (Growth)	C	C-	C	Up	Y	1,000
Dean Mid Cap Value Fund	DALCX	NAS CM	Open End	US Equity Mid Cap (Growth & Income)	B-	C	B	Up	Y	1,000
Dean Small Cap Value Fund	DASCX	NAS CM	Open End	US Equity Small Cap (Small Company)	C	D+	B-		Y	1,000
Dearborn Partners Rising Dividend Fund Class A Shares	DRDAX	NAS CM	Open End	US Equity Large Cap Blend (Equity-Income)	B	C+	B+		Y	5,000
Dearborn Partners Rising Dividend Fund Class C Shares	DRDCX	NAS CM	Open End	US Equity Large Cap Blend (Equity-Income)	B	C+	B+		Y	5,000
Dearborn Partners Rising Dividend Fund Class I Shares	DRDIX	NAS CM	Open End	US Equity Large Cap Blend (Equity-Income)	B	B-	B+		Y	500,000
Delaware Emerging Markets Fund Class A	DEMAX	NAS CM	Open End	Global Emerg Mkts (Div Emerging Mkts)	C	C-	C+		Y	1,000
Delaware Emerging Markets Fund Class C	DEMCX	NAS CM	Open End	Global Emerg Mkts (Div Emerging Mkts)	C	C-	C+		Y	1,000
Delaware Emerging Markets Fund Class R	DEMRX	NAS CM	Open End	Global Emerg Mkts (Div Emerging Mkts)	C	C-	C+		Y	0
Delaware Emerging Markets Fund Class R6	DEMZX	NAS CM	Open End	Global Emerg Mkts (Div Emerging Mkts)	C	C-	C+		Y	0
Delaware Emerging Markets Fund Institutional Class	DEMIX	NAS CM	Open End	Global Emerg Mkts (Div Emerging Mkts)	C	C-	C+		Y	0
Delaware Enhanced Global Dividend & Income	DEX	NYSE	Closed End	Alloc Miscellaneous (World Stock)	C	C	C-	Up	Y	
Delaware Global Real Estate Opportunities Fund Class A	DGRPX	NAS CM	Open End	Real Estate Sector Equity (Real Estate)	C+	C	B		Y	1,000
Delaware Global Real Estate Opportunities Fund Class C	DLPCX	NAS CM	Open End	Real Estate Sector Equity (Real Estate)	C+	C	B		Y	1,000
Delaware Global Real Estate Opportunities Fund Class R	DLPRX	NAS CM	Open End	Real Estate Sector Equity (Real Estate)	C+	C	B		Y	0
Delaware Global Real Estate Opp Inst Cls	DGROX	NAS CM	Open End	Real Estate Sector Equity (Real Estate)	C+	C	B		Y	0
Delaware Global Value Fund Class A	DABAX	NAS CM	Open End	Global Equity Large Cap (World Stock)	C	C	B-		Y	1,000
Delaware Global Value Fund Class C	DABCX	NAS CM	Open End	Global Equity Large Cap (World Stock)	C	C-	B-		Y	1,000
Delaware Global Value Fund Institutional Class	DABIX	NAS CM	Open End	Global Equity Large Cap (World Stock)	C	C	B-		Y	0
Delaware Healthcare Fund Class A	DLHAX	NAS CM	Open End	Healthcare Sector Equity (Health)	C+	C	B	Down	Y	1,000
Delaware Healthcare Fund Class C	DLHCX	NAS CM	Open End	Healthcare Sector Equity (Health)	C+	C	B-	Down	Y	1,000
Delaware Healthcare Fund Class I	DLHIX	NAS CM	Open End	Healthcare Sector Equity (Health)	C+	C	B	Down	Y	0
Delaware Healthcare Fund Class R	DLRHX	NAS CM	Open End	Healthcare Sector Equity (Health)	C+	C	B	Down	Y	0
Delaware International Small Cap Fund Class A	DGGAX	NAS CM	Open End	Global Equity Mid/Small Cap (Small Company)	C	C	C-	Up	Y	1,000
Delaware International Small Cap Fund Class C	DGGCX	NAS CM	Open End	Global Equity Mid/Small Cap (Small Company)	C-	C	C-		Y	1,000
Delaware International Small Cap Fund Class R	DGGRX	NAS CM	Open End	Global Equity Mid/Small Cap (Small Company)	C-	C	C-		Y	0
Delaware International Small Cap Fund Class R6	DGRRX	NAS CM	Open End	Global Equity Mid/Small Cap (Small Company)	C	C	C	Up	Y	0
Delaware International Small Cap Fund Institutional Class	DGGIX	NAS CM	Open End	Global Equity Mid/Small Cap (Small Company)	C	C	C	Up	Y	0
Delaware International Value Equity Fund Class A	DEGIX	NAS CM	Open End	Global Equity Large Cap (Foreign Stock)	C	C-	B-		Y	1,000
Delaware International Value Equity Fund Class C	DEGCX	NAS CM	Open End	Global Equity Large Cap (Foreign Stock)	C	C-	B-		Y	1,000
Delaware International Value Equity Fund Class R	DIVRX	NAS CM	Open End	Global Equity Large Cap (Foreign Stock)	C	C-	B-		Y	0
Delaware International Value Equity Fund Class R6	DEQRX	NAS CM	Open End	Global Equity Large Cap (Foreign Stock)	C	C-	B-		Y	0
Delaware International Value Equity Institutional Cls	DEQIX	NAS CM	Open End	Global Equity Large Cap (Foreign Stock)	C	C-	B-		Y	0
Delaware Investments Dividend and Income Fund	DDF	NYSE	Closed End	US Equity Large Cap Value (Income)	C	C	C-	Down	Y	
Delaware Mid Cap Value Fund Class A	DLMAX	NAS CM	Open End	US Equity Mid Cap (Growth)	C	C	B-		Y	1,000
Delaware Mid Cap Value Fund Class C	DLMCX	NAS CM	Open End	US Equity Mid Cap (Growth)	C	C	B-		Y	1,000
Delaware Mid Cap Value Fund Class R	DLMRX	NAS CM	Open End	US Equity Mid Cap (Growth)	C	C	B-		Y	0
Delaware Mid Cap Value Fund Institutional Class	DLMIX	NAS CM	Open End	US Equity Mid Cap (Growth)	C	C	B-		Y	0

★ Expanded analysis of this fund is included in Section II.

	TOTAL RETURNS					PERFORMANCE				ASSETS		ASSET ALLOCATION & TURNOVER					BULL & BEAR		FEES		
Min Additional Investment	3-Month Total Return	6-Month Total Return	1-Year Total Return	3-Year Total Return	5-Year Total Return	Dividend Yield (TTM)	Expense Ratio	3-Yr Std Deviation	3-Year Beta	NAV	Total Assets (MIL)	%Cash	%Stocks	%Bonds	%Other	Turnover Ratio	Last Bull Market Total Return	Last Bear Market Total Return	Front End Fee (%)	Back End Fee (%)	Inception Date
25	3.24	17.97	-0.61	39.75	41.49	0.2	1.65	14.97	1.16	24.29	8,912	1	96	0	0	25	22.43	-20.47		1.00	Dec-94
25	3.34	18.22	-0.13	41.79	44.98	0.42	1.17	14.95	1.16	27.66	8,912	1	96	0	0	25	22.74	-20.33			Aug-03
25	3.51	18.59	0.42	44.19	49.02	0.89	0.62	14.96	1.16	28.31	8,912	1	96	0	0	25	23.2	-20.14			Oct-96
25	1.90	12.98	-4.72	33.54	42.35	0	0.94	13.65	1	31.58	525.4	3	97	0	0	44	17.27	-18.33	4.75		Dec-94
25	1.68	12.53	-5.48	30.40	36.83	0	1.71	13.64	1	24.78	525.4	3	97	0	0	44	16.75	-18.65		1.00	Aug-97
25	1.95	13.10	-4.48	34.48	44.05	0	0.69	13.64	1	33.41	525.4	3	97	0	0	44	17.45	-18.28			Sep-97
25	1.64	18.95	10.57	19.57	51.04	2.06	0.97	12.31	0.59	42.12	261.5	4	95	0	0	44	30.03	-14.3	4.75		Jan-94
25	1.42	18.42	9.62	16.54	44.62	1.28	1.8	12.28	0.59	42.1	261.5	4	95	0	0	44	29.42	-14.63		1.00	Aug-97
25	1.72	19.08	10.81	20.42	52.73	2.28	0.74	12.29	0.59	42.73	261.5	4	95	0	0	44	30.2	-14.2			Nov-96
50	1.81	12.31	0.08	15.80	27.76	1.34	1.6	11.76	0.92	10.32	79.3	6	84	9	0	84			5.75		Jul-14
50	1.54	11.92	-0.69	13.19	22.96	0.62	2.35	11.71	0.91	10.1	79.3	6	84	9	0	84					Jul-14
50	1.87	12.42	0.34	16.61	29.37	1.59	1.35	11.78	0.92	10.35	79.3	6	84	9	0	84					Jul-14
50	-0.28	5.99	-3.39	9.56	4.77	0.65	1.8	8.04	0.67	10.43	18.2	18	55	23	4	303	13.11	-13.95	5.75		Oct-09
50	-0.41	5.54	-4.07	7.14	0.92	0	2.55	8.01	0.67	9.7	18.2	18	55	23	4	303	12.69	-14.18			Oct-09
50	-0.09	6.17	-3.04	10.47	6.32	0.89	1.55	8.08	0.68	10.49	18.2	18	55	23	4	303	13.11	-13.95			Jul-14
	3.98	18.09	7.47	33.14	44.33	0.74	1.1	12.48	0.92	20.62	43.7	4	96	0	0	46	31.17	-23.86			May-97
	-0.14	13.63	-3.64	26.33	26.41	1.39	1.18	16.79	0.94	14.17	321.9	2	98	0	0	120	32.71	-25.81			May-97
500	4.97	19.90	18.32	37.67	53.57	0.91	1.25	10.79	0.83	16.66	257.3	5	95	0	0	14			5.00		Apr-13
500	4.81	19.52	17.40	34.66	47.93	0.31	2	10.81	0.83	16.59	257.3	5	95	0	0	14				1.00	Apr-13
500	5.10	20.01	18.59	38.75	55.53	1.14	1	10.84	0.83	16.68	257.3	5	95	0	0	14					Apr-13
100	-1.24	9.88	-0.90	41.47	12.66	0.31	1.62	16.04	1.11	18.23	5,298	0	100	0	0	11	17.15	-30.41	5.75		Jun-96
100	-1.45	9.46	-1.68	38.29	8.49	0	2.37	16	1.11	16.89	5,298	0	100	0	0	11	16.61	-30.66		1.00	Jun-96
	-1.29	9.74	-1.16	40.39	11.26	0.02	1.87	16	1.11	18.36	5,298	0	100	0	0	11	16.94	-30.5			Aug-09
	-1.13	10.07	-0.57	43.00	14.45	0.69	1.25	16.02	1.11	18.35	5,298	0	100	0	0	11	17.27	-30.33			May-16
	-1.18	10.01	-0.68	42.54	14.08	0.59	1.37	15.98	1.11	18.35	5,298	0	100	0	0	11	17.27	-30.33			Jun-96
	3.24	16.02	3.36	24.69	13.01	3.04	0	10.44		11.11	140.7	-39	60	60	4	34	16.65	-16.68			Jun-07
100	1.19	14.69	7.70	12.13	24.58	2.2	1.4	11.31	1	7.94	30.2	3	96	0	1	187	23.47	-18.05	5.75		Jan-07
100	0.88	14.11	6.74	9.55	19.93	1.45	2.15	11.26	1	7.93	30.2	3	96	0	1	187	22.8	-18.19		1.00	Sep-12
	1.13	14.54	7.42	11.38	23.14	1.95	1.65	11.26	1	7.94	30.2	3	96	0	1	187	23.16	-18.02			Sep-12
	1.13	14.71	7.85	12.90	26.08	2.46	1.15	11.32	1	7.92	30.2	3	96	0	1	187	23.52	-17.85			Jan-07
100	4.03	16.65	2.25	24.02	10.76	1.4	1.4	11.14	0.93	12.12	14.1	0	101	0	-1	19	16.93	-23.65	5.75		Dec-97
100	3.81	16.22	1.48	21.22	6.65	0	2.15	11.07	0.92	11.96	14.1	0	101	0	-1	19	16.26	-23.89		1.00	Sep-01
	4.10	16.81	2.47	25.00	12.16	1.65	1.15	11.08	0.92	12.16	14.1	0	101	0	-1	19	17.04	-23.58			Dec-97
100	1.13	15.59	2.99	48.31	64.79	0.59	1.31	15.75	1.02	24.9	1,002	0	104	0	-4	33	25.09	-17.52	5.75		Sep-07
100	0.93	15.17	2.23	45.04	58.72	0.03	2.06	15.75	1.03	23.68	1,002	0	104	0	-4	33	24.53	-17.75		1.00	Jan-10
	1.17	15.71	3.24	49.41	66.84	0.79	1.06	15.73	1.02	25.04	1,002	0	104	0	-4	33	25.19	-17.43			Sep-07
	1.02	15.39	2.71	47.21	62.64	0.35	1.56	15.73	1.02	24.59	1,002	0	104	0	-4	33	24.84	-17.57			Jan-10
100	1.92	14.83	-12.89	32.26	24.83	0	1.37	15.33	1.22	6.89	90.3	4	95	0	1	106	24.07	-16.78	5.75		Dec-08
100	1.76	14.45	-13.60	29.40	20.30	0	2.12	15.34	1.21	5.78	90.3	4	95	0	1	106	23.49	-17.02		1.00	Dec-10
	1.71	14.58	-13.18	31.24	23.22	0	1.62	15.31	1.21	6.52	90.3	4	95	0	1	106	23.79	-16.86			Dec-10
	1.96	15.07	-12.65	33.56	26.69	0	1	15.26	1.21	7.25	90.3	4	95	0	1	106	24.17	-16.69			Jun-17
	1.83	14.94	-12.68	33.20	26.34	0	1.12	15.3	1.21	7.23	90.3	4	95	0	1	106	24.17	-16.69			Dec-08
100	3.16	15.45	0.21	23.54	5.68	2.03	1.33	11.26	0.99	14.34	299.3	1	98	0	1	13	13.33	-28.13	5.75		Oct-91
100	2.97	14.97	-0.57	20.71	1.74	0.7	2.08	11.26	0.99	14.2	299.3	1	98	0	1	13	12.83	-28.32		1.00	Nov-95
	3.10	15.24	-0.02	22.57	4.31	1.77	1.58	11.24	0.99	14.29	299.3	1	98	0	1	13	13.1	-28.14			Jun-03
	3.22	15.58	0.51	23.92	6.01	2.33	1.02	11.24	0.99	14.39	299.3	1	98	0	1	13	13.33	-28.13			Mar-18
	3.22	15.58	0.44	24.40	6.97	2.28	1.08	11.25	0.99	14.39	299.3	1	98	0	1	13	13.56	-28.03			Nov-92
	0.97	15.79	6.70	29.22	38.92	1.94	0	12.61	0.98	10.94	84.1	-40	92	39	1	29	26.24	-16.29			Mar-93
100	2.16	19.72	0.11	34.20	37.09	0.28	1.14	15.32	1.13	6.13	27.1	4	96	0	0	20	29.21	-25.14	5.75		Feb-08
100	1.98	19.15	-0.75	30.97	31.95	0	1.89	15.35	1.13	5.66	27.1	4	96	0	0	20	28.6	-25.39		1.00	Jul-08
	2.34	19.53	-0.01	33.24	35.46	0.17	1.39	15.35	1.13	6.12	27.1	4	96	0	0	20	28.51	-25.21			Jul-08
	2.33	19.92	0.40	35.14	38.80	0.51	0.89	15.33	1.13	6.14	27.1	4	96	0	0	20	29.34	-25.02			Feb-08

	MARKET			FUND TYPE, CATEGORY & OBJECTIVE	RATINGS				MINIMUMS	
Fund Name	Ticker Symbol	Traded On	Fund Type	Category and (Prospectus Objective)	Overall Rating	Reward Rating	Risk Rating	Recent Up/ Downgrade	Open to New Investors	Min Initial Investment
Delaware REIT Fund Class A	DPREX	NAS CM	Open End	Real Estate Sector Equity (Real Estate)	C	C	C	Down	Y	1,000
Delaware REIT Fund Class C	DPRCX	NAS CM	Open End	Real Estate Sector Equity (Real Estate)	C	C	C	Down	Y	1,000
Delaware REIT Fund Class R	DPRRX	NAS CM	Open End	Real Estate Sector Equity (Real Estate)	C	C	C	Down	Y	0
Delaware REIT Fund Class R6	DPRDX	NAS CM	Open End	Real Estate Sector Equity (Real Estate)	C	C	C+	Down	Y	0
Delaware REIT Fund Institutional Class	DPRSX	NAS CM	Open End	Real Estate Sector Equity (Real Estate)	C	C	C	Down	Y	0
Delaware Select Growth Fund Class A	DVEAX	NAS CM	Open End	US Equity Large Cap Growth (Growth)	B-	C	B			1,000
Delaware Select Growth Fund Class C	DVECX	NAS CM	Open End	US Equity Large Cap Growth (Growth)	B-	C	B			1,000
Delaware Select Growth Fund Class R	DFSRX	NAS CM	Open End	US Equity Large Cap Growth (Growth)	B-	C	B			0
Delaware Select Growth Fund Institutional Class	VAGGX	NAS CM	Open End	US Equity Large Cap Growth (Growth)	B-	C	B			0
Delaware Small Cap Core Fund Class A	DCCAX	NAS CM	Open End	US Equity Small Cap (Small Company)	C	C	C+		Y	1,000
Delaware Small Cap Core Fund Class C	DCCCX	NAS CM	Open End	US Equity Small Cap (Small Company)	C	C	C+		Y	1,000
Delaware Small Cap Core Fund Class R	DCCRX	NAS CM	Open End	US Equity Small Cap (Small Company)	C	C	C+		Y	0
Delaware Small Cap Core Fund Class R6	DCZRX	NAS CM	Open End	US Equity Small Cap (Small Company)	C	C	C+		Y	0
Delaware Small Cap Core Fund Institutional Class	DCCIX	NAS CM	Open End	US Equity Small Cap (Small Company)	C	C	C+		Y	0
Delaware Small Cap Growth Fund Class A	DSGDX	NAS CM	Open End	US Equity Small Cap (Small Company)	C+	C	C+	Up	Y	1,000
Delaware Small Cap Growth Fund Class C	DSGEX	NAS CM	Open End	US Equity Small Cap (Small Company)	C+	C	C+	Up	Y	1,000
Delaware Small Cap Growth Fund Class R	DSGFX	NAS CM	Open End	US Equity Small Cap (Small Company)	C+	C	C+	Up	Y	0
Delaware Small Cap Growth Fund Institutional Class	DSGGX	NAS CM	Open End	US Equity Small Cap (Small Company)	C+	C	C+	Up	Y	0
Delaware Small Cap Value Fund Class A	DEVLX	NAS CM	Open End	US Equity Small Cap (Small Company)	C	C-	C+		Y	1,000
Delaware Small Cap Value Fund Class C	DEVCX	NAS CM	Open End	US Equity Small Cap (Small Company)	C	C-	C+		Y	1,000
Delaware Small Cap Value Fund Class R	DVLRX	NAS CM	Open End	US Equity Small Cap (Small Company)	C	C-	C+		Y	0
Delaware Small Cap Value Fund Class R6	DVZRX	NAS CM	Open End	US Equity Small Cap (Small Company)	C	C-	C+		Y	0
Delaware Small Cap Value Fund Institutional Class	DEVIX	NAS CM	Open End	US Equity Small Cap (Small Company)	C	C-	C+		Y	0
Delaware Smid Cap Growth Fund Class A	DFCIX	NAS CM	Open End	US Equity Mid Cap (Growth)	C+	C+	C+	Up		1,000
Delaware Smid Cap Growth Fund Class C	DEEVX	NAS CM	Open End	US Equity Mid Cap (Growth)	C+	C+	C+	Up		1,000
Delaware Smid Cap Growth Fund Class R	DFRIX	NAS CM	Open End	US Equity Mid Cap (Growth)	C+	C+	C+	Up		0
Delaware Smid Cap Growth Fund Class R6	DFZRX	NAS CM	Open End	US Equity Mid Cap (Growth)	C+	C+	C+	Up		0
Delaware Smid Cap Growth Fund Institutional Class	DFDIX	NAS CM	Open End	US Equity Mid Cap (Growth)	C+	C+	C+	Up		0
Delaware Strategic Allocation Class A	DFBAX	NAS CM	Open End	Moderate Alloc (Asset Alloc)	B-	C	B+	Up	Y	1,000
Delaware Strategic Allocation Class C	DFBCX	NAS CM	Open End	Moderate Alloc (Asset Alloc)	B-	C	B+	Up	Y	1,000
Delaware Strategic Allocation Class R	DFBRX	NAS CM	Open End	Moderate Alloc (Asset Alloc)	B-	C	B+	Up	Y	0
Delaware Strategic Allocation Institutional Class	DFFIX	NAS CM	Open End	Moderate Alloc (Asset Alloc)	B-	C	B+	Up	Y	0
Delaware U.S. Growth Fund Class A	DUGAX	NAS CM	Open End	US Equity Large Cap Growth (Growth)	C+	C	B	Down	Y	1,000
Delaware U.S. Growth Fund Class C	DEUCX	NAS CM	Open End	US Equity Large Cap Growth (Growth)	C+	C	B	Down	Y	1,000
Delaware U.S. Growth Fund Class R	DEURX	NAS CM	Open End	US Equity Large Cap Growth (Growth)	C+	C	B	Down	Y	0
Delaware U.S. Growth Fund Class R6	DUZRX	NAS CM	Open End	US Equity Large Cap Growth (Growth)	B-	C	B		Y	0
Delaware U.S. Growth Fund Institutional Class	DEUIX	NAS CM	Open End	US Equity Large Cap Growth (Growth)	B-	C	B		Y	0
Delaware Value® Fund Class A	DDVAX	NAS CM	Open End	US Equity Large Cap Value (Growth)	B-	C	B+			1,000
Delaware Value® Fund Class C	DDVCX	NAS CM	Open End	US Equity Large Cap Value (Growth)	B-	C	B+			1,000
Delaware Value® Fund Class R	DDVRX	NAS CM	Open End	US Equity Large Cap Value (Growth)	B-	C	B+		Y	0
Delaware Value® Fund Class R6	DDZRX	NAS CM	Open End	US Equity Large Cap Value (Growth)	B-	C	B+		Y	0
Delaware Value® Fund Institutional Class	DDVIX	NAS CM	Open End	US Equity Large Cap Value (Growth)	B-	C	B+			0
Delaware Wealth Builder Fund Class A	DDIAX	NAS CM	Open End	Moderate Alloc (Equity-Income)	B-	C	B	Up	Y	1,000
Delaware Wealth Builder Fund Class C	DDICX	NAS CM	Open End	Moderate Alloc (Equity-Income)	C+	C	B	Up	Y	1,000
Delaware Wealth Builder Fund Class R	DDDRX	NAS CM	Open End	Moderate Alloc (Equity-Income)	C+	C	B		Y	0
Delaware Wealth Builder Fund Institutional Class	DDIIX	NAS CM	Open End	Moderate Alloc (Equity-Income)	B-	C	B+	Up	Y	0
Destinations Equity Income Fund Class I	DGEFX	NAS CM	Open End	US Equity Large Cap Value (Income)	C	C	B		Y	0
Destinations Equity Income Fund Class Z	DGEZX	NAS CM	Open End	US Equity Large Cap Value (Income)	C	C	B		Y	0
Destinations International Equity Fund Class I	DIEFX	NAS CM	Open End	Global Equity Large Cap (Foreign Stock)	C	D+	B-	Up	Y	0
Destinations International Equity Fund Class Z	DIEZX	NAS CM	Open End	Global Equity Large Cap (Foreign Stock)	C	D+	B-	Up	Y	0
Destinations Large Cap Equity Fund Class I	DLCFX	NAS CM	Open End	US Equity Large Cap Blend (Growth)	C	C	B		Y	0
Destinations Large Cap Equity Fund Class Z	DLCZX	NAS CM	Open End	US Equity Large Cap Blend (Growth)	C	C	B-		Y	0

★ Expanded analysis of this fund is included in Section II.

Min Additional Investment	3-Month Total Return	6-Month Total Return	1-Year Total Return	3-Year Total Return	5-Year Total Return	Dividend Yield (TTM)	Expense Ratio	3-Yr Std Deviation	3-Year Beta	NAV	Total Assets (MIL)	%Cash	%Stocks	%Bonds	%Other	Turnover Ratio	Last Bull Market Total Return	Last Bear Market Total Return	Front End Fee (%)	Back End Fee (%)	Inception Date
	TOTAL RETURNS					PERFORMANCE				ASSETS		ASSET ALLOCATION & TURNOVER					BULL & BEAR		FEES		
100	2.36	18.11	9.43	5.90	31.16	2.08	1.4	13.1	0.98	11.96	75.7	2	98	0	0	120	31.18	-15.36	5.75		Dec-95
100	2.25	17.70	8.57	3.59	26.35	1.4	2.15	13.09	0.98	11.94	75.7	2	98	0	0	120	30.52	-15.55		1.00	Nov-97
	2.30	17.99	9.10	5.12	29.54	1.87	1.65	13.11	0.98	11.95	75.7	2	98	0	0	120	30.79	-15.38			Jun-03
	2.53	18.38	9.88	7.10	32.66	2.4	1	13.1	0.98	11.99	75.7	2	98	0	0	120	31.18	-15.36			Aug-16
	2.41	18.29	9.65	6.72	32.81	2.3	1.15	13.12	0.98	12.01	75.7	2	98	0	0	120	31.28	-15.22			Nov-97
100	6.11	24.57	11.35	57.16	49.79	0	1.24	14.68	1.01	34.52	312.8	2	98	0	0	51	25.98	-11.97	5.75		May-94
100	5.87	24.09	10.49	53.64	44.22	0	1.99	14.66	1.01	20.91	312.8	2	98	0	0	51	25.42	-12.23		1.00	May-94
	6.02	24.39	11.08	55.95	47.90	0	1.49	14.69	1.01	31.67	312.8	2	98	0	0	51	25.77	-12.06			Jun-03
	6.17	24.68	11.62	58.33	51.66	0	0.99	14.7	1.01	38.69	312.8	2	98	0	0	51	26.14	-11.87			Aug-97
100	3.26	19.52	-3.23	44.31	44.33	0.1	1.12	17.5	1.01	22.16	4,780	3	97	0	0	38	32.16	-24.22	5.75		Dec-98
100	3.06	19.12	-3.95	41.11	39.04	0	1.87	17.51	1.01	19.5	4,780	3	97	0	0	38	31.5	-24.48		1.00	Aug-05
	3.19	19.40	-3.47	43.28	42.55	0	1.37	17.54	1.01	21.35	4,780	3	97	0	0	38	31.82	-24.25			Aug-05
	3.36	19.74	-2.85	45.95	46.80	0.47	0.74	17.53	1.01	22.74	4,780	3	97	0	0	38	32.2	-24.14			May-16
	3.31	19.64	-2.98	45.41	46.17	0.37	0.87	17.54	1.01	22.72	4,780	3	97	0	0	38	32.2	-24.14			Dec-98
100	4.33	32.51	11.77	75.28		0	1.3	22.83	1.18	10.84	13.4	3	99	0	-2	158			5.75		Jun-16
100	4.06	32.07	10.94	71.25		0	2.05	22.84	1.18	10.5	13.4	3	99	0	-2	158				1.00	Jun-16
	4.18	32.38	11.42	73.73		0	1.55	22.85	1.18	10.71	13.4	3	99	0	-2	158					Jun-16
	4.29	32.64	11.99	76.19		0	1.05	22.83	1.18	10.93	13.4	3	99	0	-2	158					Jun-16
100	3.34	18.09	-4.69	34.12	31.26	0.67	1.15	17.48	0.98	58.41	4,122	3	97	0	0	18	28.26	-22.44	5.75		Jun-87
100	3.14	17.67	-5.39	31.14	26.43	0	1.9	17.48	0.98	47.53	4,122	3	97	0	0	18	27.67	-22.67		1.00	Nov-95
	3.28	17.97	-4.92	33.11	29.63	0.42	1.4	17.49	0.98	56.52	4,122	3	97	0	0	18	28.08	-22.52			Jun-03
	3.45	18.36	-4.28	35.88	33.02	1.07	0.72	17.49	0.98	61.94	4,122	3	97	0	0	18	28.26	-22.44			May-16
	3.42	18.25	-4.44	35.14	32.93	0.92	0.9	17.49	0.98	61.87	4,122	3	97	0	0	18	28.44	-22.37			Nov-92
100	5.40	33.15	11.89	70.90	95.54	0	1.17	22.16	1.2	25.14	1,666	0	100	0	0	96	25.49	-15.71	5.75		Mar-86
100	5.16	32.71	11.02	66.95	88.23	0	1.92	22.16	1.2	10.79	1,666	0	100	0	0	96	25.02	-15.97		1.00	Nov-95
	5.31	33.00	11.59	69.58	93.02	0	1.42	22.13	1.2	22.77	1,666	0	100	0	0	96	25.35	-15.81			Jun-03
	5.50	33.43	12.28	72.55	97.53	0	0.84	22.16	1.2	35.24	1,666	0	100	0	0	96	25.49	-15.71			May-16
	5.45	33.35	12.17	72.14	97.92	0	0.92	22.16	1.2	35.18	1,666	0	100	0	0	96	25.7	-15.63			Nov-92
100	1.72	9.94	2.98	21.00	20.17	1.86	1.14	7.12	0.56	10.63	266.4	0	58	44	-2	97	13.94	-12.33	5.75		Dec-97
100	1.53	9.41	2.21	18.24	15.55	1.13	1.9	7.11	0.56	10.63	266.4	0	58	44	-2	97	13.3	-12.53		1.00	Dec-97
	1.67	9.73	2.80	20.05	18.49	1.6	1.4	7.1	0.56	10.58	266.4	0	58	44	-2	97	13.72	-12.4			Jun-03
	1.78	10.06	3.32	21.85	21.58	2.09	0.9	7.13	0.56	10.64	266.4	0	58	44	-2	97	14.08	-12.23			Dec-97
100	7.67	21.40	10.39	52.82	57.57	0	1.09	13.63	0.96	21.89	2,446	1	99	0	0	39	28.08	-12.42	5.75		Dec-93
100	7.43	20.93	9.53	49.36	51.68	0	1.84	13.59	0.96	17.91	2,446	1	99	0	0	39	27.54	-12.7		1.00	May-94
	7.61	21.26	10.11	51.65	55.54	0	1.34	13.61	0.96	20.64	2,446	1	99	0	0	39	27.9	-12.53			Jun-03
	7.81	21.69	10.91	54.79	59.66	0	0.62	13.64	0.96	24.57	2,446	1	99	0	0	39	28.08	-12.42			May-16
	7.75	21.57	10.65	53.95	59.53	0	0.84	13.65	0.96	24.46	2,446	1	99	0	0	39	28.24	-12.3			Feb-94
100	0.49	11.77	5.86	27.88	45.06	1.55	0.93	11.63	0.92	21.51	14,534	1	99	0	0	20	24.12	-14.44	5.75		Sep-98
100	0.35	11.38	5.12	25.05	39.77	0.83	1.68	11.64	0.92	21.48	14,534	1	99	0	0	20	23.58	-14.67		1.00	May-02
	0.47	11.68	5.62	26.95	43.29	1.29	1.18	11.64	0.92	21.51	14,534	1	99	0	0	20	23.97	-14.54			Sep-05
	0.63	12.03	6.29	29.29	47.33	1.89	0.58	11.66	0.92	21.51	14,534	1	99	0	0	20	24.27	-14.34			May-16
	0.60	11.91	6.18	28.84	46.87	1.8	0.68	11.65	0.92	21.51	14,534	1	99	0	0	20	24.27	-14.34			Sep-98
100	2.00	10.83	4.45	16.13	20.03	2.5	1.09	7.34		13.59	530.2	8	49	27	4	57	16.5	-13.26	5.75		Dec-96
100	1.81	10.40	3.72	13.54	15.61	1.77	1.84	7.36		13.62	530.2	8	49	27	4	57	15.99	-13.61		1.00	Oct-03
	2.01	10.69	4.25	15.29	18.59	2.25	1.34	7.4		13.6	530.2	8	49	27	4	57	16.44	-13.44			Oct-03
	2.07	10.98	4.72	17.01	21.56	2.75	0.84	7.34		13.59	530.2	8	49	27	4	57	16.8	-13.26			Dec-96
	1.64	12.96	9.35			2.62	0.89			10.4	413.9	2	97	0	0						Mar-17
	1.63	12.96	9.66				0.74			10.09	413.9	2	97	0	0						Jul-18
	3.70	16.68	2.56			1.04	1.2			11.47	1,764	4	96	0	0						Mar-17
	3.83	16.78	2.89				1.05			10.02	1,764	4	96	0	0						Jul-18
	3.58	19.00	6.96			0.77	0.85			12.15	3,706	3	97	0	0						Mar-17
	3.55	18.96	7.05				0.7			9.91	3,706	3	97	0	0						Jul-18

	MARKET			FUND TYPE, CATEGORY & OBJECTIVE	RATINGS				MINIMUMS	
Fund Name	Ticker Symbol	Traded On	Fund Type	Category and (Prospectus Objective)	Overall Rating	Reward Rating	Risk Rating	Recent Up/ Downgrade	Open to New Investors	Min Initial Investment
Destinations Multi Strategy Alternatives Fund Class I	DMSFX	NAS CM	Open End	Multialternative (Growth)	C	C	B-	Up	Y	0
Destinations Multi Strategy Alternatives Fund Class Z	DMSZX	NAS CM	Open End	Multialternative (Growth)	C	C	B-	Up	Y	0
Destinations Real Assets Fund Class I	DRAFX	NAS CM	Open End	Aggressive Alloc (Growth)	D	D	D		Y	0
Destinations Real Assets Fund Class Z	DRAZX	NAS CM	Open End	Aggressive Alloc (Growth)	D	D	D		Y	0
Destinations Small-Mid Cap Equity Fund Class I	DSMFX	NAS CM	Open End	US Equity Mid Cap (Growth)	C	C	B-	Up	Y	0
Destinations Small-Mid Cap Equity Fund Class Z	DSMZX	NAS CM	Open End	US Equity Mid Cap (Growth)	C	C	B-	Up	Y	0
Destra Flaherty & Crumrine Preferred & Income Cls A	DPIAX	NAS CM	Open End	US Fixed Income (Income)	B	B-	B	Up	Y	2,500
Destra Flaherty & Crumrine Preferred & Income Cls C	DPICX	NAS CM	Open End	US Fixed Income (Income)	B-	B-	B	Up	Y	2,500
Destra Flaherty & Crumrine Preferred & Income Cls I	DPIIX	NAS CM	Open End	US Fixed Income (Income)	B	B-	B	Up	Y	100,000
Destra Multi-Alternative Fund Class A Shares	MSFDX	NAS CM	Closed End	Multialternative (Growth & Income)	C-	D+	C+		Y	2,500
Destra Multi-Alternative Fund Class C Shares	MCFDX	NAS CM	Closed End	Multialternative (Growth & Income)	C-	D+	C	Up	Y	2,500
Destra Multi-Alternative Fund Class I Shares	MSFIX	NAS CM	Closed End	Multialternative (Growth & Income)	C	D+	C+	Up	Y	1,000,000
Destra Multi-Alternative Fund Class T Shares	MSFYX	NAS CM	Closed End	Multialternative (Growth & Income)	C-	D+	C	Up	Y	2,500
Destra Wolverine Dynamic Asset Fund Class A	DWAAX	NAS CM	Open End	Alloc Miscellaneous (Growth & Income)	C	C-	C		Y	2,500
Destra Wolverine Dynamic Asset Fund Class C	DWACX	NAS CM	Open End	Alloc Miscellaneous (Growth & Income)	C	C-	C	Up	Y	2,500
Destra Wolverine Dynamic Asset Fund Class I	DWAIX	NAS CM	Open End	Alloc Miscellaneous (Growth & Income)	C	C-	C		Y	100,000
DF Dent Midcap Growth Fund Institutional Shares	DFMGX	NAS CM	Open End	US Equity Mid Cap (Growth)	B	B+	B		Y	500,000
DF Dent Midcap Growth Fund Investor Shares	DFDMX	NAS CM	Open End	US Equity Mid Cap (Growth)	B	B+	B		Y	2,500
DF Dent Premier Growth Fund Investor Shares	DFDPX	NAS CM	Open End	US Equity Large Cap Growth (Growth)	B	B+	B		Y	2,500
DF Dent Small Cap Growth Fund Institutional Shares	DFSGX	NAS CM	Open End	US Equity Small Cap (Small Company)	B-	B-	B-		Y	500,000
DF Dent Small Cap Growth Fund Investor Shares	DFDSX	NAS CM	Open End	US Equity Small Cap (Small Company)	B-	B-	B-		Y	2,500
DFA Asia Pacific Small Company Portfolio Institutional Cls	DFRSX	NAS CM	Open End	Asia ex-Japan Equity (Pacific Stock)	C	C-	B-		Y	0
DFA Commodity Strategy Portfolio Institutional Cls Shares	DCMSX	NAS CM	Open End	Commodities Broad Basket (Growth & Income)	D+	D	C-		Y	0
DFA Continental Small Company Portfolio Institutional Cls	DFCSX	NAS CM	Open End	Europe Equity Large Cap (Small Company)	C	C	C+		Y	0
DFA CSTG&E U.S. Social Core Equity 2 Portfolio	DFCUX	NAS CM	Open End	US Equity Mid Cap (Growth)	D	D+	D			0
DFA Emerging Mkts Core Equity Portfolio Inst Cls	DFCEX	NAS CM	Open End	Global Emerg Mkts (Div Emerging Mkts)	C	C	C+		Y	0
DFA Emerging Markets Portfolio II	DFETX	NAS CM	Open End	Global Emerg Mkts (Div Emerging Mkts)	C	C	B-			0
DFA Emerging Markets Portfolio Institutional Class	DFEMX	NAS CM	Open End	Global Emerg Mkts (Div Emerging Mkts)	C	C	B-		Y	0
DFA Emerging Markets Small Cap Portfolio Institutional Cls	DEMSX	NAS CM	Open End	Global Emerg Mkts (Div Emerging Mkts)	C	C	C+		Y	0
DFA Emerging Markets Social Core Portfolio	DFESX	NAS CM	Open End	Global Emerg Mkts (Growth)	C	C	C+		Y	0
DFA Emerging Mkts Sustainability Core 1 Portfolio Inst Cls	DESIX	NAS CM	Open End	Global Emerg Mkts (Growth)	D	D	C-		Y	0
DFA Emerging Mkts Targeted Value Portfolio Inst Cls	DEMGX	NAS CM	Open End	Global Emerg Mkts (Div Emerging Mkts)	U	U	U		Y	0
DFA Emerging Markets Value Portfolio Class R2	DFEPX	NAS CM	Open End	Global Emerg Mkts (Div Emerging Mkts)	C	C	B-		Y	0
DFA Emerging Markets Value Portfolio Institutional Class	DFEVX	NAS CM	Open End	Global Emerg Mkts (Div Emerging Mkts)	C	C	B-		Y	0
DFA Enhanced U.S. Large Company Portfolio Inst Cls	DFELX	NAS CM	Open End	US Equity Large Cap Blend (Growth)	B-	C+	B		Y	0
DFA Global Allocation 25/75 Portfolio Class R2	DFGPX	NAS CM	Open End	Cautious Alloc (Growth & Income)	B-	C	A-		Y	0
DFA Global Allocation 25/75 Portfolio Institutional Class	DGTSX	NAS CM	Open End	Cautious Alloc (Growth & Income)	B-	C	A-		Y	0
DFA Global Allocation 60/40 Portfolio Class R2	DFPRX	NAS CM	Open End	Moderate Alloc (Growth & Income)	B-	C	A-	Up	Y	0
DFA Global Allocation 60/40 Portfolio Institutional Class	DGSIX	NAS CM	Open End	Moderate Alloc (Growth & Income)	B-	C	A-	Up	Y	0
DFA Global Equity Portfolio Class Retirement 2	DGERX	NAS CM	Open End	Global Equity Large Cap (World Stock)	C+	C	B	Up	Y	0
DFA Global Equity Portfolio Institutional Class	DGEIX	NAS CM	Open End	Global Equity Large Cap (World Stock)	C+	C	B	Up	Y	0
DFA Global Real Estate Securities Portfolio	DFGEX	NAS CM	Open End	Real Estate Sector Equity (Real Estate)	B-	C	B		Y	0
DFA Global Small Company Portfolio Institutional Class	DGLIX	NAS CM	Open End	Global Equity Mid/Small Cap (Small Company)	C-	D+	C		Y	0
DFA International Core Equity Portfolio Institutional Cls	DFIEX	NAS CM	Open End	Global Equity Large Cap (Growth)	C	C	C+		Y	0
DFA Intl High Relative Profitability Portfolio Inst Cls	DIHRX	NAS CM	Open End	Global Equity Large Cap (Foreign Stock)	C-	D	B-	Up	Y	0
DFA International Large Cap Growth Portfolio	DILRX	NAS CM	Open End	Global Equity Large Cap (Growth)	C	C	B		Y	0
DFA Intl Real Estate Securities Portfolio Inst Cls	DFITX	NAS CM	Open End	Real Estate Sector Equity (Real Estate)	B-	C	B	Up	Y	0
DFA International Small Cap Growth Portfolio	DISMX	NAS CM	Open End	Global Equity Mid/Small Cap (Small Company)	C	C	C+		Y	0
DFA Intl Small Cap Value Portfolio Inst Cls	DISVX	NAS CM	Open End	Global Equity Mid/Small Cap (Foreign Stock)	D+	D+	C-	Down	Y	0
DFA Intl Small Company Portfolio Inst Cls	DFISX	NAS CM	Open End	Global Equity Mid/Small Cap (Foreign Stock)	C	C-	C		Y	0
DFA Intl Social Core Equity Portfolio Inst Cls Shares	DSCLX	NAS CM	Open End	Global Equity Large Cap (Growth)	C	C	C+		Y	0
DFA International Sustainability Core 1 Portfolio	DFSPX	NAS CM	Open End	Global Equity Large Cap (Growth)	C	C	B-		Y	0

★ Expanded analysis of this fund is included in Section II.

	TOTAL RETURNS					PERFORMANCE				ASSETS		ASSET ALLOCATION & TURNOVER					BULL & BEAR		FEES		
Min Additional Investment	3-Month Total Return	6-Month Total Return	1-Year Total Return	3-Year Total Return	5-Year Total Return	Dividend Yield (TTM)	Expense Ratio	3-Yr Std Deviation	3-Year Beta	NAV	Total Assets (MIL)	%Cash	%Stocks	%Bonds	%Other	Turnover Ratio	Last Bull Market Total Return	Last Bear Market Total Return	Front End Fee (%)	Back End Fee (%)	Inception Date
	1.08	7.49	1.19			4.13	1.59			9.69	918.4	25	17	57	0						Mar-17
	1.15	7.61	1.24				1.44			9.47	918.4	25	17	57	0						Jul-18
	-17.20	-5.27	-45.79			0.06	1.21			5.39	183.5	4	96	0	0						Mar-17
	-17.02	-5.04	-45.60				1.06			5.46	183.5	4	96	0	0						Jul-18
	4.27	21.62	3.88			0.45	1.04			11.7	1,024	4	96	0	0						Mar-17
	4.49	21.71	4.15				0.89			9.53	1,024	4	96	0	0						Jul-18
	3.47	11.71	6.88	17.97	32.74	4.55	1.43	5.14		18	231.7	3	0	32	1	7	9.94	-1.1	4.50		Apr-11
	3.26	11.24	6.06	15.36	27.97	3.81	2.18	5.11		18.08	231.7	3	0	32	1	7	9.5	-1.43		1.00	Nov-11
	3.54	11.89	7.18	18.93	34.95	4.81	1.18	5.15		17.94	231.7	3	0	32	1	7	10.17	-1.02			Apr-11
100	0.32	4.91	-1.53	3.77	7.17	6.14	3.57	4.77		13.49	--	1	49	-8	57	49			5.75		Mar-12
100	0.13	4.49	-2.27	1.48	3.27	6.16	4.32	4.73		13.04	--	1	49	-8	57	49					Jul-14
	0.41	5.04	-1.21	5.07	8.62	6.13	3.38	4.82		13.72	--	1	49	-8	57	49					Jul-14
100	0.14	4.63	-1.97	2.25	4.57	6.16	4.07	4.76		13.19	--	1	49	-8	57	49			2.00		Jul-14
	0.39	4.86	-3.57	13.23		0	2.23	8.22	1.92	10.14	61.2	6	84	10	-1	224			4.50		Oct-15
	0.20	4.52	-4.26	10.81		0	2.98	8.18	1.91	9.94	61.2	6	84	10	-1	224				1.00	Oct-15
	0.39	4.95	-3.29	14.13		0.18	1.98	8.19	1.91	10.16	61.2	6	84	10	-1	224					Oct-15
0	10.36	32.85	20.44	78.04	88.16	0	0.85	13.71	0.91	25.88	101.3	2	98	0	0	32	30.1				Nov-17
500	10.29	32.73	20.27	77.70	87.81	0	0.98	13.69	0.91	25.83	101.3	2	98	0	0	32	30.11				Jul-11
500	9.83	32.94	21.13	84.80	94.20	0	1.1	13.46	1.01	35.75	209.4	2	98	0	0	16	28.2	-18.87			Jul-01
0	11.30	31.66	15.20	63.10	72.55	0	0.95	14.28	0.76	17.13	19.1	4	96	0	0	40					Nov-17
500	11.25	31.53	15.00	62.82	72.26	0	1.05	14.23	0.75	17.1	19.1	4	96	0	0	40					Nov-13
	-0.64	11.24	-4.38	21.71	9.88	3.15	0.54	11.65	0.95	21.56	326.4	1	99	0	0	14	23.19	-27.94			Jan-93
	-1.87	3.73	-6.99	-5.76	-35.86	2.06	0.32	8.29	0.96	5.44	1,641	-46	0	91	55	78	1.22	-19.69			Nov-10
	5.34	16.75	-4.05	38.40	25.60	2.09	0.54	14.47	0.98	24.71	644.6	1	99	0	0	13	12.65	-32.88			Apr-88
	-43.23	-46.23	-44.67	-12.68	-13.94	2.09	0.32	12.61	1.08		83.7	0	100	0	0	10	27.21	-22.43			Aug-07
	0.85	9.99	1.29	31.67	12.32	2.37	0.52	13.49	0.96	20.93	28,955	1	99	0	0	4	17.58	-27.36			Apr-05
	0.91	9.55	2.06	34.17	13.49	2.74	0.34	13.42	0.96	25.34	69.2	1	99	0	0	8	17.67	-25.69			Aug-97
	0.85	9.48	1.94	33.56	12.44	2.09	0.47	13.41	0.96	28	6,053	1	99	0	0	8	17.5	-25.72			Apr-94
	0.76	10.34	-1.30	25.88	15.94	2.1	0.7	13.74	0.94	20.51	6,880	1	99	0	0	15	17.6	-27.08			Mar-98
	1.17	10.75	1.96	34.50	14.31	2.31	0.53	13.53	0.96	13.6	1,475	1	99	0	0	11	17.75	-28.06			Aug-06
	1.03	10.14	1.25			1.55	0.65			8.97	232.2	1	99	0	0	6					Mar-18
	-0.09	8.71					0.85			10.85	119.7	1	99	0	0						Nov-18
	0.20	7.80	1.70	38.29	9.44	2.12	0.8	13.6	0.95	28.62	18,322	1	99	0	0	21	15.62	-31.19			Jan-08
	0.28	7.96	1.95	39.23	10.80	2.5	0.54	13.6	0.95	28.8	18,322	1	99	0	0	21	15.79	-31.13			Apr-98
	4.52	20.78	11.33	49.53	65.86	2.41	0.15	12.36	1.01	13.51	349.9	-100	103	95	2	91	25.36	-16.11			Jul-96
	1.94	6.62	4.01	13.12	14.43	2.31	0.51	3.2	0.27	13.55	888.2	8	24	68	0		6.72	-4.87			Dec-03
	1.92	6.73	4.26	13.88	16.20	2.54	0.26	3.15	0.27	13.59	888.2	8	24	68	0		6.86	-4.66			Dec-03
	2.69	11.75	3.95	25.48	24.28	2.15	0.53	7.48	0.65	18.33	4,253	6	58	35	0		14.3	-13.95			Dec-03
	2.71	11.91	4.14	26.30	25.75	2.48	0.28	7.5	0.65	18.2	4,253	6	58	35	0		14.43	-13.82			Dec-03
	3.07	16.75	2.27	38.74	33.71	1.7	0.55	12.48	1.08	23.24	7,301	1	99	0	0		22.08	-23.11			Dec-03
	3.16	16.95	2.56	39.83	35.42	1.96	0.3	12.49	1.08	23.1	7,301	1	99	0	0		22.24	-23.04			Dec-03
	1.82	17.53	11.91	17.45	39.04	4.34	0.24	11.26	0.98	11.73	8,527	0	99	0	0	3	24.88	-17.23			Jun-08
	1.94	14.10	-5.60			0.97	0.49			11	37.5	1	99	0	0						Jan-17
	2.44	13.43	-4.03	29.50	11.50	3.04	0.3	12.19	1.09	12.97	29,710	2	98	0	0	4	13.83	-25.04			Sep-05
	3.68	16.16	1.49			2.19	0.35			10.49	531.3	3	97	0	0	9					May-17
	4.83	17.83	2.86	30.11	16.98	2.14	0.3	11.43	0.98	12.98	370.7	1	99	0	0	19					Dec-12
	2.15	14.47	7.58	15.53	19.07	5.24	0.28	10.68	0.99	5.22	5,881	1	98	0	1	5	16.43	-18.78			Mar-07
	3.56	16.35	-5.30	31.70	29.38	1.93	0.55	12.86	0.97	14.14	200.8	1	99	0	0	30					Dec-12
	0.15	9.53	-11.54	21.25	5.75	2.71	0.68	13.38	1.05	17.98	13,314	1	98	0	0	23	15.02	-26.05			Dec-94
	2.17	13.16	-7.33	26.94	16.41	2.42	0.53	12.44	1.01	17.8	12,484	1	99	0	0	22	14.45	-23.33			Sep-96
	2.37	13.23	-4.45	29.61	10.12	2.98	0.33	12.13	1.08	12.47	1,174	1	99	0	0	8					Nov-12
	3.64	15.28	-0.72	32.03	12.74	2.56	0.37	11.66	1.04	10.28	1,245	1	99	0	0	8	13.64	-24.43			Mar-08

Fund Name	Ticker Symbol	Traded On	Fund Type	Category and (Prospectus Objective)	Overall Rating	Reward Rating	Risk Rating	Recent Up/ Downgrade	Open to New Investors	Min Initial Investment
	MARKET			FUND TYPE, CATEGORY & OBJECTIVE	RATINGS				MINIMUMS	
DFA International Value Portfolio Class R2	DFIPX	NAS CM	Open End	Global Equity Large Cap (Foreign Stock)	C	C-	C		Y	0
DFA International Value Portfolio III	DFVIX	NAS CM	Open End	Global Equity Large Cap (Foreign Stock)	C	C-	C			0
DFA International Value Portfolio Institutional Class	DFIVX	NAS CM	Open End	Global Equity Large Cap (Foreign Stock)	C	C-	C		Y	0
DFA Intl Vector Equity Portfolio Inst Cls	DFVQX	NAS CM	Open End	Global Equity Mid/Small Cap (Foreign Stock)	C	C-	C		Y	0
DFA Japanese Small Company Portfolio Institutional Class	DFJSX	NAS CM	Open End	Japan Equity (Pacific Stock)	C-	C-	C-		Y	0
DFA Large Cap International Portfolio Institutional Class	DFALX	NAS CM	Open End	Global Equity Large Cap (Foreign Stock)	C	C	B		Y	0
DFA Real Estate Securities Portfolio Institutional Class	DFREX	NAS CM	Open End	Real Estate Sector Equity (Real Estate)	C+	C+	B-	Down	Y	0
DFA Selectively Hedged Global Eq Port Inst Cls Shares	DSHGX	NAS CM	Open End	Global Equity Large Cap (Growth)	C+	C	B	Up	Y	0
DFA T.A. U.S. Core Equity 2 Portfolio Institutional Class	DFTCX	NAS CM	Open End	US Equity Large Cap Blend (Growth)	C+	C	B	Up	Y	0
DFA T.A. World ex U.S. Core Equity Portfolio Inst Cls	DFTWX	NAS CM	Open End	Global Equity Large Cap (Growth)	C	C	C+		Y	0
DFA Tax Managed International Value Portfolio	DTMIX	NAS CM	Open End	Global Equity Large Cap (World Stock)	C	C	C		Y	0
DFA Tax Managed U.S. Equity Portfolio	DTMEX	NAS CM	Open End	US Equity Large Cap Blend (Growth)	B-	C	B		Y	0
DFA Tax Managed U.S. Small Cap Portfolio	DFTSX	NAS CM	Open End	US Equity Small Cap (Small Company)	C	C-	C		Y	0
DFA Tax-Managed U.S. Marketwide Value Portfolio	DTMMX	NAS CM	Open End	US Equity Large Cap Value (Growth)	C+	C	B	Up	Y	0
DFA Tax-Managed U.S. Marketwide Value Portfolio II	DFMVX	NAS CM	Open End	US Equity Large Cap Value (Growth)	C+	C	B	Up		0
DFA Tax-Managed U.S. Targeted Value Portfolio	DTMVX	NAS CM	Open End	US Equity Small Cap (Growth)	C	C-	C		Y	0
DFA U.S. Core Equity 1 Portfolio Institutional Class	DFEOX	NAS CM	Open End	US Equity Large Cap Blend (Growth)	C+	C	B		Y	0
DFA U.S. Core Equity II Portfolio Institutional Class	DFQTX	NAS CM	Open End	US Equity Large Cap Blend (Growth)	C+	C	B	Up	Y	0
DFA U.S. Large Cap Equity Portfolio Institutional Class	DUSQX	NAS CM	Open End	US Equity Large Cap Blend (Growth)	B-	C	B		Y	0
DFA U.S. Large Cap Growth Portfolio Institutional Class	DUSLX	NAS CM	Open End	US Equity Large Cap Growth (Growth)	B-	C+	B	Down	Y	0
DFA U.S. Large Cap Growth Portfolio Institutional Class	DFCVX	NAS CM	Open End	US Equity Large Cap Value (Growth)	C+	C	B	Up		0
DFA U.S. Large Cap Value III Portfolio	DFUVX	NAS CM	Open End	US Equity Large Cap Value (Growth)	C+	C	B	Up		0
DFA U.S. Large Cap Value Portfolio Institutional Class	DFLVX	NAS CM	Open End	US Equity Large Cap Value (Growth & Income)	C+	C	B	Up	Y	0
DFA U.S. Large Company Portfolio	DFUSX	NAS CM	Open End	US Equity Large Cap Blend (Growth & Income)	B-	C	B		Y	0
DFA U.S. Micro Cap Portfolio Institutional Class	DFSCX	NAS CM	Open End	US Equity Small Cap (Small Company)	C	C-	C		Y	0
DFA U.S. Small Cap Growth Portfolio Institutional Class	DSCGX	NAS CM	Open End	US Equity Small Cap (Small Company)	C	C	C+		Y	0
DFA U.S. Small Cap Portfolio Institutional Class	DFSTX	NAS CM	Open End	US Equity Small Cap (Small Company)	C	C-	C+		Y	0
DFA U.S. Small Cap Value Portfolio Institutional Class	DFSVX	NAS CM	Open End	US Equity Small Cap (Small Company)	C-	C-	C	Down	Y	0
DFA U.S. Social Core Equity 2 Portfolio	DFUEX	NAS CM	Open End	US Equity Large Cap Blend (Growth)	C+	C	B	Up	Y	0
DFA U.S. Sustainability Core 1 Portfolio	DFSIX	NAS CM	Open End	US Equity Large Cap Blend (Growth)	C+	C	B		Y	0
DFA U.S. Targeted Value Portfolio Class R1	DFTVX	NAS CM	Open End	US Equity Small Cap (Growth & Income)	C	C-	C		Y	0
DFA U.S. Targeted Value Portfolio Class R2	DFTPX	NAS CM	Open End	US Equity Small Cap (Growth & Income)	C-	C-	C	Down	Y	0
DFA U.S. Targeted Value Portfolio Institutional Class	DFFVX	NAS CM	Open End	US Equity Small Cap (Growth & Income)	C	C-	C		Y	0
DFA U.S. Vector Equity Portfolio Institutional Class	DFVEX	NAS CM	Open End	US Equity Mid Cap (Growth)	C	C	B-		Y	0
DFA United Kingdom Small Company Portfolio Inst Cls	DFUKX	NAS CM	Open End	Equity Miscellaneous (Europe Stock)	C	D+	C+	Up	Y	0
DFA US High Relative Profitability Portfolio Inst Cls	DURPX	NAS CM	Open End	US Equity Large Cap Blend (Growth)	C	C-	B-	Up	Y	0
DFA World Core Equity Portfolio Institutional Class	DREIX	NAS CM	Open End	Global Equity Large Cap (Growth)	C+	C	B	Up	Y	0
DFA World ex U.S. Core Equity Portfolio Inst Cls Shares	DFWIX	NAS CM	Open End	Global Equity Large Cap (World Stock)	C	C	C+		Y	0
DFA World ex U.S. Targeted Value Portfolio Inst Cls Shares	DWUSX	NAS CM	Open End	Global Equity Mid/Small Cap (Foreign Stock)	C-	D+	C	Down	Y	0
DFA World ex U.S. Value Port Institution Class	DFWVX	NAS CM	Open End	Global Equity Large Cap (Foreign Stock)	C	C-	C		Y	0
DGHM MicroCap Value Fund Institutional Class	DGMIX	NAS CM	Open End	US Equity Small Cap (Growth)	C	C	C		Y	100,000
DGHM MicroCap Value Fund Investor Class	DGMMX	NAS CM	Open End	US Equity Small Cap (Growth)	C	C	C		Y	2,500
DGHM V2000 SmallCap Value Fund Institutional Class	DGIVX	NAS CM	Open End	US Equity Small Cap (Small Company)	C	C-	C		Y	100,000
DGHM V2000 SmallCap Value Fund Investor Class	DGSMX	NAS CM	Open End	US Equity Small Cap (Small Company)	C	C-	C		Y	2,500
Diamond Hill All Cap Select Fund Class A	DHTAX	NAS CM	Open End	US Equity Large Cap Blend (Growth)	C+	C	B	Up	Y	2,500
Diamond Hill All Cap Select Fund Class C	DHTCX	NAS CM	Open End	US Equity Large Cap Blend (Growth)	C+	C	B-	Up	Y	2,500
Diamond Hill All Cap Select Fund Class I	DHLTX	NAS CM	Open End	US Equity Large Cap Blend (Growth)	C+	C	B	Up	Y	2,500
Diamond Hill All Cap Select Fund Class Y	DHTYX	NAS CM	Open End	US Equity Large Cap Blend (Growth)	C+	C	B	Up	Y	500,000
Diamond Hill Global Fund Class A	DHGBX	NAS CM	Open End	Global Equity Large Cap (World Stock)	D+	D	C	Up	Y	2,500
Diamond Hill Global Fund Class I	DHGIX	NAS CM	Open End	Global Equity Large Cap (World Stock)	D+	D	C	Up	Y	2,500
Diamond Hill Global Fund Class Y	DHGYX	NAS CM	Open End	Global Equity Large Cap (World Stock)	D+	D	C	Up	Y	500,000
Diamond Hill Large Cap Fund Class A	DHLAX	NAS CM	Open End	US Equity Large Cap Value (Growth)	B-	C+	B	Up	Y	2,500

★ Expanded analysis of this fund is included in Section II.

	TOTAL RETURNS					PERFORMANCE				ASSETS		ASSET ALLOCATION & TURNOVER					BULL & BEAR		FEES		
Min Additional Investment	3-Month Total Return	6-Month Total Return	1-Year Total Return	3-Year Total Return	5-Year Total Return	Dividend Yield (TTM)	Expense Ratio	3-Yr Std Deviation	3-Year Beta	NAV	Total Assets (MIL)	%Cash	%Stocks	%Bonds	%Other	Turnover Ratio	Last Bull Market Total Return	Last Bear Market Total Return	Front End Fee (%)	Back End Fee (%)	Inception Date
	1.39	10.35	-5.12	31.19	1.55	2.86	0.68	12.99	1.11	17.09	9,362	2	98	0	0	17	10.52	-26.96			Apr-08
	1.52	10.59	-4.66	32.75	3.68	3.4	0.24	12.97	1.11	14.62	2,553	2	98	0	0	17	10.8	-26.8			Feb-95
	1.46	10.47	-4.83	32.24	2.86	3.14	0.43	13	1.11	17.14	9,362	2	98	0	0	17	10.67	-26.87			Feb-94
	1.97	12.35	-6.57	28.45	9.78	2.9	0.48	12.54	1.11	11.43	2,497	0	100	0	0	12	13.54	-25.81			Aug-08
	0.00	6.43	-12.38	25.48	35.51	1.16	0.53	12.93	1.05	23.17	576.8	0	100	0	0	13	2.72	3.5			Jan-86
	3.27	14.68	0.32	31.11	10.81	2.95	0.23	11.4	1.02	22.4	5,204	2	98	0	0	4	13.7	-23.5			Jul-91
	1.73	19.33	14.28	17.98	51.37	3.56	0.18	12.81	0.56	38.59	9,710	0	100	0	0	3	31	-16.08			Jan-93
	2.67	15.53	2.16	40.07	33.68	2.72	0.34	11.62	1.01	16.14	419.9	6	94	0	0						Nov-11
	3.92	18.89	4.49	45.06	48.16	1.63	0.24	13.91	1.09	18.8	9,769	0	100	0	0	1	26.95	-22.02			Oct-07
	1.66	12.25	-3.19	30.07	11.37	2.8	0.36	12.12	1.05	10.56	3,903	0	100	0	0	6	14.78	-25.97			Mar-08
	1.47	10.50	-4.75	31.90	2.22	3.38	0.53	12.83	1.1	14.56	3,828	1	99	0	0	21	11.09	-26.97			Apr-99
	4.21	19.58	8.80	50.68	62.06	1.73	0.22	12.67	1.01	31.7	3,900	0	100	0	0	8	25.16	-17.4			Sep-01
	2.35	15.48	-5.20	36.41	36.19	0.9	0.47	17.19	1	42.03	3,076	1	99	0	0	11	28.4	-24.63			Dec-98
	3.60	16.63	5.04	39.90	43.55	1.71	0.37	13.73	1.1	30.2	5,220	0	100	0	0	7	26.68	-23.77			Dec-98
	3.62	16.73	5.17	40.50	44.59	1.91	0.22	13.72	1.1	28.03	1,858	0	100	0	0	7	26.71	-23.72			Dec-98
	1.49	14.34	-7.60	30.41	26.20	1.16	0.44	17.77	1.01	33.77	4,637	1	99	0	0	14	29.3	-26.56			Dec-98
	3.89	19.27	5.87	48.45	54.74	1.61	0.19	13.52	1.07	24.11	25,923	1	99	0	0	3	26.31	-20.17			Sep-05
	3.67	18.66	4.14	44.64	46.86	1.64	0.22	13.94	1.09	22.15	27,191	1	99	0	0	1	27.11	-21.99			Sep-05
	4.28	19.96	8.90	50.74	59.10	1.69	0.17	12.86	1.04	18.09	1,626	0	100	0	0	7					Jun-13
	4.19	20.61	12.25	57.22	74.07	1.68	0.19	12.79	0.93	21.27	2,140	0	100	0	0	19					Dec-12
	3.11	15.21	3.12	39.81	42.23	2.23	0.14	13.9	1.14	16.78	2,140	0	100	0	0	15	26.06	-23.92			Aug-94
	3.10	15.18	3.09	39.84	42.37	2.05	0.13	13.92	1.14	24.67	3,817	0	100	0	0	15	26.07	-23.96			Feb-95
	3.09	15.11	2.96	39.26	41.42	1.94	0.27	13.93	1.14	36.32	25,603	0	100	0	0	15	25.91	-23.99			Feb-93
	4.29	19.50	10.33	50.70	65.78	1.83	0.08	12.22	1	22.68	9,457	0	100	0	0	5	25.07	-16.26			Sep-99
	0.85	13.24	-7.48	37.85	36.43	0.84	0.52	17.91	1.03	20.73	6,428	1	99	0	0	19	28.05	-23.94			Dec-81
	3.76	19.53	-0.53	40.31	43.14	0.8	0.38	16.76	0.94	18.36	621.7	0	100	0	0	23					Dec-12
	1.93	15.40	-5.52	35.10	34.88	1.02	0.37	17.37	1.01	33.92	17,484	0	100	0	0	13	28.39	-24.71			Mar-92
	-0.79	11.14	-10.84	27.43	18.30	1.1	0.52	19.09	1.09	33.01	14,127	0	100	0	0	27	29.63	-27.77			Mar-93
	3.97	19.46	3.99	47.14	45.23	1.46	0.28	14.38	1.12	16.53	1,201	1	100	0	0	9	27.54	-22.88			Oct-07
	4.73	20.69	7.55	52.58	57.68	1.29	0.25	13.64	1.08	22.89	1,947	0	100	0	0	4	26.54	-20.08			Mar-08
	0.92	13.95	-8.12	29.60	21.83	1.14	0.47	18.58	1.06	22.3	10,734	1	99	0	0	23	29.1	-27.48			Jan-08
	0.88	13.88	-8.29	29.00	20.88	0.97	0.62	18.59	1.06	22.18	10,734	1	99	0	0	23	28.99	-27.49			Jun-08
	0.94	14.00	-8.07	29.94	22.41	1.25	0.37	18.56	1.06	22.3	10,734	1	99	0	0	23	29.16	-27.42			Feb-00
	3.05	16.94	-1.61	37.75	33.76	1.43	0.32	15.8	1.18	18.44	4,618	1	99	0	0	10	28.02	-24.76			Dec-05
	0.30	15.09	-8.25	23.80	4.31	1.7	0.58	14.83	0.98	26.62	29.5	0	100	0	0	9	26.84	-22.75			Mar-86
	3.93	20.53	10.13			1.52	0.25			12.93	1,338	1	99	0	0	7					May-17
	3.05	16.10	1.72	39.27	31.49	2.08	0.32	12.17	1.07	16.15	846.1	1	99	0	0						Mar-12
	1.82	12.48	-3.01	30.01	10.93	2.99	0.39	12.15	1.06	11.07	3,585	1	99	0	0	4					Apr-13
	0.39	9.31	-7.80	26.23	9.18	2.34	0.66	12.96	1.06	12.36	543.8	1	99	0	0	24					Nov-12
	1.00	9.68	-3.78	32.67	5.01	3.1	0.52	12.62	1.07	11.06	281.2	2	98	0	0	2	12.05	-27.79			Aug-10
500	4.83	13.68	-10.76	36.43	49.65	0.42	1.24	15.66	0.85	11.7	43.6	2	97	0	0	36	30.68	-20.37			May-16
500	4.83	13.55	-10.91	35.17	47.50	0.18	1.69	15.72	0.85	11.71	43.6	2	97	0	0	36	30.49	-20.45			Jul-16
500	0.49	14.54	-5.78	25.00	18.76	0.68	1.03	16.8	0.95	12.13	27.7	1	99	0	0	39	24.11	-22.25			Jun-10
500	0.43	14.31	-6.19	23.39	16.35	0.28	1.43	16.76	0.94	11.42	27.7	1	99	0	0	39	23.93	-22.19			Jun-10
	4.17	17.27	1.49	45.96	37.90	0.39	1.16	15.8	1.18	14.73	223.5	2	98	0	0	84	20.28	-18.47	5.00		Dec-05
	3.93	16.86	0.72	42.60	32.85	0	1.91	15.77	1.18	13.72	223.5	2	98	0	0	84	19.79	-18.8		1.00	Dec-05
	4.21	17.40	1.81	47.14	39.95	0.71	0.87	15.78	1.18	14.84	223.5	2	98	0	0	84	20.38	-18.38			Dec-05
	4.20	17.45	1.89	47.60	40.63	0.83	0.75	15.78	1.18	14.87	223.5	2	98	0	0	84	20.49	-18.38			Dec-11
	4.90	17.81	-0.11			0.4	1.13			13.69	18.2	1	99	0	0	84			5.00		Dec-17
	4.96	17.95	0.15			0.5	0.84			13.73	18.2	1	99	0	0	84					Dec-17
	5.04	18.02	0.26			0.54	0.72			13.75	18.2	1	99	0	0	84					Dec-17
	6.87	21.79	12.25	48.35	54.10	0.92	0.96	13.19	1.03	27.66	6,056	2	98	0	0	29	23.39	-17.08	5.00		Jun-01

	MARKET		FUND TYPE, CATEGORY & OBJECTIVE		RATINGS				MINIMUMS	
Fund Name	Ticker Symbol	Traded On	Fund Type	Category and (Prospectus Objective)	Overall Rating	Reward Rating	Risk Rating	Recent Up/ Downgrade	Open to New Investors	Min Initial Investment
Diamond Hill Large Cap Fund Class C	DHLCX	NAS CM	Open End	US Equity Large Cap Value (Growth)	B-	C	B	Up	Y	2,500
Diamond Hill Large Cap Fund Class I	DHLRX	NAS CM	Open End	US Equity Large Cap Value (Growth)	B-	C+	B	Up	Y	2,500
Diamond Hill Large Cap Fund Class Y	DHLYX	NAS CM	Open End	US Equity Large Cap Value (Growth)	B-	C+	B	Up	Y	500,000
Diamond Hill Long Short Fund Class A	DIAMX	NAS CM	Open End	Long/Short Equity (Growth)	B-	C	B	Up		2,500
Diamond Hill Long Short Fund Class C	DHFCX	NAS CM	Open End	Long/Short Equity (Growth)	C+	C	B	Up		2,500
Diamond Hill Long Short Fund Class I	DHLSX	NAS CM	Open End	Long/Short Equity (Growth)	B-	C	B	Up		2,500
Diamond Hill Long-Short Fund Class Y	DIAYX	NAS CM	Open End	Long/Short Equity (Growth)	B-	C	B	Up		500,000
Diamond Hill Mid Cap Fund Class A	DHPAX	NAS CM	Open End	US Equity Mid Cap (Growth)	C+	C	B		Y	2,500
Diamond Hill Mid Cap Fund Class I	DHPIX	NAS CM	Open End	US Equity Mid Cap (Growth)	C+	C	B		Y	2,500
Diamond Hill Mid Cap Fund Class Y	DHPYX	NAS CM	Open End	US Equity Mid Cap (Growth)	C+	C	B		Y	500,000
Diamond Hill Research Opportunities Fund Class A	DHROX	NAS CM	Open End	Long/Short Equity (Growth)	C	C	C+		Y	2,500
Diamond Hill Research Opportunities Fund Class C	DROCX	NAS CM	Open End	Long/Short Equity (Growth)	C	C-	C+		Y	2,500
Diamond Hill Research Opportunities Fund Class I	DROIX	NAS CM	Open End	Long/Short Equity (Growth)	C	C	C+		Y	2,500
Diamond Hill Research Opportunities Fund Class Y	DROYX	NAS CM	Open End	Long/Short Equity (Growth)	C	C	B-		Y	500,000
Diamond Hill Small Cap Fund Class A	DHSCX	NAS CM	Open End	US Equity Small Cap (Small Company)	C	C-	C		Y	2,500
Diamond Hill Small Cap Fund Class C	DHSMX	NAS CM	Open End	US Equity Small Cap (Small Company)	C-	C-	C	Down	Y	2,500
Diamond Hill Small Cap Fund Class I	DHSIX	NAS CM	Open End	US Equity Small Cap (Small Company)	C	C-	C			2,500
Diamond Hill Small Cap Fund Class Y	DHSYX	NAS CM	Open End	US Equity Small Cap (Small Company)	C	C-	C		Y	500,000
Diamond Hill Small Mid Cap Fund Class A	DHMAX	NAS CM	Open End	US Equity Mid Cap (Growth)	C+	C	B	Up		2,500
Diamond Hill Small Mid Cap Fund Class C	DHMCX	NAS CM	Open End	US Equity Mid Cap (Growth)	C+	C	B	Up		2,500
Diamond Hill Small Mid Cap Fund Class I	DHMIX	NAS CM	Open End	US Equity Mid Cap (Growth)	C+	C	B	Up		2,500
Diamond Hill Small-Mid Cap Fund Class Y	DHMYX	NAS CM	Open End	US Equity Mid Cap (Growth)	C+	C	B	Up		500,000
Dimensional 2005 Target Date Retmnt Income Inst Cls	DRIMX	NAS CM	Open End	Target Date (Asset Alloc)	B	C	A-	Up	Y	0
Dimensional 2010 Target Date Retmnt Income Inst Cls	DRIBX	NAS CM	Open End	Target Date (Asset Alloc)	B	C+	A-	Up	Y	0
Dimensional 2015 Target Date Retmnt Income Inst Cls	DRIQX	NAS CM	Open End	Target Date (Asset Alloc)	B	C+	B+	Up	Y	0
Dimensional 2020 Target Date Retmnt Income Inst Cls	DRIRX	NAS CM	Open End	Target Date (Asset Alloc)	B	C+	A-	Up	Y	0
Dimensional 2025 Target Date Retmnt Income Inst Cls	DRIUX	NAS CM	Open End	Target Date (Asset Alloc)	B	C+	A-	Up	Y	0
Dimensional 2030 Target Date Retmnt Income Inst Cls	DRIWX	NAS CM	Open End	Target Date (Asset Alloc)	B-	C	B+	Up	Y	0
Dimensional 2035 Target Date Retmnt Income Inst Cls	DRIGX	NAS CM	Open End	Target Date (Asset Alloc)	B-	C	B+	Up	Y	0
Dimensional 2040 Target Date Retmnt Income Inst Cls	DRIHX	NAS CM	Open End	Target Date (Asset Alloc)	B-	C	B+	Up	Y	0
Dimensional 2045 Target Date Retmnt Income Inst Cls	DRIIX	NAS CM	Open End	Target Date (Asset Alloc)	B-	C	B	Up	Y	0
Dimensional 2050 Target Date Retmnt Income Inst Cls	DRIJX	NAS CM	Open End	Target Date (Asset Alloc)	B-	C	B	Up	Y	0
Dimensional 2055 Target Date Retmnt Income Inst Cls	DRIKX	NAS CM	Open End	Target Date (Asset Alloc)	B-	C	B	Up	Y	0
Dimensional 2060 Target Date Retmnt Income Inst Cls	DRILX	NAS CM	Open End	Target Date (Asset Alloc)	B-	C	B	Up	Y	0
Dimensional Retirement Income Fund Institutional Class	TDIFX	NAS CM	Open End	Target Date (Asset Alloc)	B-	C	A-		Y	0
Direxion Indexed Commodity & Income Strategy Inst Cls	DXCIX	NAS CM	Open End	Commodities Broad Basket (Growth)	D	D	C-	Down	Y	2,500,000
Direxion Indexed Commodity & Income Strategy Investor Cls	DXCTX	NAS CM	Open End	Commodities Broad Basket (Growth)	D	D	D+	Down	Y	2,500
Direxion Monthly 25+ Year Treasury Bear 1.35X Investor Cls	DXSTX	NAS CM	Open End	Trading Tools (Growth & Income)	D	D	D	Down	Y	25,000
Direxion Monthly 25+ Year Treasury Bull 1.35X Investor Cls	DXLTX	NAS CM	Open End	Trading Tools (Growth & Income)	C	C	C	Up	Y	25,000
Direxion Monthly 7-10 Year Treasury Bear 2X Fund	DXKSX	NAS CM	Open End	Trading Tools (Growth)	D+	D	D		Y	25,000
Direxion Monthly 7-10 Year Treasury Bull 2X Fund	DXKLX	NAS CM	Open End	Trading Tools (Growth)	C	C	C		Y	25,000
Direxion Monthly Emerging Markets Bull 2X Fund	DXELX	NAS CM	Open End	Trading Tools (Div Emerging Mkts)	C-	C-	D+		Y	25,000
Direxion Monthly High Yield Bull 1.2X Fund Investor Class	DXHYX	NAS CM	Open End	Trading Tools (Growth & Income)	C+	C	B		Y	25,000
Direxion Monthly NASDAQ-100 Bull 2X Fund Investor Class	DXQLX	NAS CM	Open End	Trading Tools (Growth)	C	B-	C	Down	Y	25,000
Direxion Monthly NASDAQ-100® Bear 1.25X Fund	DXNSX	NAS CM	Open End	Trading Tools (Growth & Income)	D	D-	D		Y	25,000
Direxion Monthly NASDAQ-100® Bull 1.25X Fund	DXNLX	NAS CM	Open End	Trading Tools (Growth & Income)	C+	C+	C+	Up	Y	25,000
Direxion Monthly S&P 500 Bear 2X Fund Investor Class	DXSSX	NAS CM	Open End	Alternative Miscellaneous (Growth)	D	D-	D		Y	25,000
Direxion Monthly S&P 500 Bull 2X Fund Investor Class	DXSLX	NAS CM	Open End	Trading Tools (Growth)	C	C+	C		Y	25,000
Direxion Monthly Small Cap Bear 2X Fund	DXRSX	NAS CM	Open End	Alternative Miscellaneous (Small Company)	D	D-	D		Y	25,000
Direxion Monthly Small Cap Bull 2X Fund	DXRLX	NAS CM	Open End	Trading Tools (Small Company)	C-	C-	D+		Y	25,000
Dividend and Income Fund	DNI	NYSE	Closed End	Moderate Alloc (Income)	C	C	C-		Y	
DNP Select Income Fund	DNP	NYSE	Closed End	Utilities Sector Equity (Utility)	B	B	C+		Y	

★ Expanded analysis of this fund is included in Section II.

Min Additional Investment	TOTAL RETURNS: 3-Month Total Return	6-Month Total Return	1-Year Total Return	3-Year Total Return	5-Year Total Return	PERFORMANCE: Dividend Yield (TTM)	Expense Ratio	3-Yr Std Deviation	3-Year Beta	ASSETS: NAV	Total Assets (MIL)	ASSET ALLOCATION & TURNOVER: %Cash	%Stocks	%Bonds	%Other	Turnover Ratio	BULL & BEAR: Last Bull Market Total Return	Last Bear Market Total Return	FEES: Front End Fee (%)	Back End Fee (%)	Inception Date
	6.66	21.34	11.39	45.05	48.41	0.24	1.71	13.16	1.03	26.09	6,056	2	98	0	0	29	22.87	-17.32		1.00	Sep-01
	6.94	21.96	12.57	49.70	56.31	1.18	0.67	13.16	1.03	27.87	6,056	2	98	0	0	29	23.59	-17.01			Jan-05
	6.97	22.04	12.68	50.18	57.21	1.31	0.55	13.17	1.03	27.9	6,056	2	98	0	0	29	23.59	-17.08			Dec-11
	6.81	16.75	9.75	28.27	25.48	0.27	1.74	10.04	0.75	26.48	3,377	35	63	2	0	64	16.96	-12.08	5.00		Jun-00
	6.56	16.33	8.90	25.41	20.84	0	2.49	10.01	0.75	23.36	3,377	35	63	2	0	64	16.5	-12.37		1.00	Feb-01
	6.88	16.92	10.06	29.42	27.35	0.66	1.45	10.03	0.75	27.15	3,377	35	63	2	0	64	17.17	-12.05			Jan-05
	6.89	16.98	10.15	29.84	28.03	0.76	1.33	10.03	0.75	27.27	3,377	35	63	2	0	64	17.14	-12.08			Dec-11
	3.70	18.64	3.86	32.37	38.92	0.43	1.07	13.35	0.96	14	185.7	7	92	1	0	20			5.00		Dec-13
	3.91	18.93	4.26	33.68	41.01	0.71	0.78	13.41	0.96	14.07	185.7	7	92	1	0	20					Dec-13
	3.90	18.97	4.32	34.10	41.71	0.82	0.66	13.4	0.96	14.11	185.7	7	92	1	0	20					Dec-13
	3.70	14.54	-1.42	25.27	18.06	0	1.8	14.39	1.07	22.37	79.5	12	88	0	0	88	21.14	-10.28	5.00		Dec-11
	3.45	14.08	-2.18	22.43	13.66	0	2.55	14.42	1.07	20.98	79.5	12	88	0	0	88	20.59	-10.69		1.00	Dec-11
	3.74	14.63	-1.16	26.29	19.67	0.06	1.51	14.42	1.07	22.71	79.5	12	88	0	0	88	21.24	-10.22			Dec-11
	3.77	14.74	-1.01	26.80	20.42	0.08	1.39	14.4	1.07	22.8	79.5	12	88	0	0	88	21.34	-10.17			Dec-11
	1.78	12.24	-5.52	18.93	12.12	0	1.27	14.55	0.81	30.79	842.8	4	96	0	0	23	18.93	-21.7	5.00		Dec-00
	1.59	11.79	-6.25	16.22	7.94	0	2.02	14.51	0.8	26.06	842.8	4	96	0	0	23	18.45	-21.96		1.00	Feb-01
	1.85	12.41	-5.27	19.98	13.70	0.27	0.98	14.53	0.8	31.33	842.8	4	96	0	0	23	19.08	-21.6			Apr-05
	1.91	12.47	-5.13	20.34	14.35	0.34	0.86	14.55	0.81	31.38	842.8	4	96	0	0	23	19.08	-21.7			Dec-11
	3.50	18.40	1.08	26.51	32.58	0.16	1.22	13.84	0.86	21.87	2,343	5	94	2	0	26	22.16	-21.36	5.00		Dec-05
	3.34	17.93	0.32	23.73	27.70	0	1.97	13.83	0.86	19.79	2,343	5	94	2	0	26	21.57	-21.58		1.00	Dec-05
	3.60	18.55	1.38	27.73	34.49	0.45	0.93	13.84	0.86	22.11	2,343	5	94	2	0	26	22.32	-21.19			Dec-05
	3.59	18.62	1.47	28.11	35.33	0.57	0.81	13.82	0.86	22.16	2,343	5	94	2	0	26	22.41	-21.19			Dec-11
	2.61	7.64	4.91	13.61		2.05	0.19	3.38	0.24	10.81	6.7	9	20	72	0						Nov-15
	3.23	9.39	5.64	14.97		2.12	0.2	4.22	0.29	11.03	19.8	1	24	76	0						Nov-15
	3.41	9.96	5.53	15.25		2.12	0.19	4.59	0.3	11.13	50.8	1	24	76	0						Nov-15
	3.55	10.83	5.41	18.12		2.14	0.21	5.3	0.35	11.37	114.8	1	25	74	0						Nov-15
	3.66	12.55	5.26	23.03		2.17	0.21	6.51	0.49	11.76	156.7	1	38	61	0						Nov-15
	3.55	13.54	5.06	27.66		2.19	0.24	7.36	0.6	12.01	155.9	2	52	46	0						Nov-15
	3.34	13.98	5.10	32.22		2.16	0.25	8.35	0.72	12.14	124.1	3	66	32	0						Nov-15
	3.03	14.25	4.68	36.30		2.12	0.26	9.73	0.85	12.41	102.9	3	79	17	0						Nov-15
	3.35	16.20	4.74	39.78		2.05	0.26	11.2	0.98	12.67	74.3	2	93	5	0						Nov-15
	3.37	16.37	4.84	39.98		2.09	0.26	11.24	0.98	12.63	61.1	1	94	4	0						Nov-15
	3.29	16.18	4.73	39.73		2.05	0.26	11.22	0.98	12.61	28.7	2	94	4	0						Nov-15
	3.36	16.21	4.88	39.95		2.05	0.26	11.21	0.98	12.67	19.8	2	94	5	0						Nov-15
	2.29	7.04	4.66	12.44		2.08	0.21	3.09	0.23	10.75	17.8	12	19	69	0						Nov-15
100	-3.62	-3.97	-5.68	-12.78	-25.54	0	1.08	6.93	1	13.28	13.4	87	0	0	13		-7.94	-25.38			May-09
100	-3.76	-4.11	-5.97	-13.45	-26.47	0	1.33	6.95	1	13.05	13.4	87	0	0	13		-8.1	-25.44	5.50		Jun-08
500	-7.67	-13.60	-14.51	-11.44		0	1.18	13.18		15.1424	0.30	165	-65	0	0	0					Nov-15
500	7.06	13.34	12.40	-2.70		0.13	1.2	13.67		22.7014	5.5	46	54	0	0	0					Nov-15
500	-6.25	-11.09	-14.70	-5.71	-31.33	0	1.47	9.48		26.21	2.4	346	0	0	-246	0	-5.35	-26.38			May-04
500	6.31	11.77	16.17	-1.98	19.04	0	1.46	9.61		38.06	33.3	33	0	0	67	0	0.48	27.98			Mar-05
500	-0.86	15.94	-5.96	50.14	-11.18	0	1.47	29.96		46.83	11.4	31	69	0	0	0	38.08	-53.83			Nov-05
500	1.70	10.06	6.44	19.56		10.9	1.7	5.12		22.0172	120.3	33	0	65	2	1,218					Feb-16
500	5.49	43.28	9.91	171.07	233.85	0	1.45	30.23		25	204.5	34	43	0	23	0	58.38	-21.33			May-06
500	-6.46	-24.05	-13.98	-55.23		0	1.21	18.93		9.1452	0.14	243	-143	0	0	0					Mar-16
500	4.29	26.79	8.71	92.78		0.31	1.23	18.87		32.4536	27.7	45	55	0	0	0					Mar-16
500	-9.62	-31.54	-21.75	-58.44	-69.40	0	1.46	24.42		10.61	8.3	345	-245	0	0	0	-40.11	37.8			May-06
500	6.29	37.19	11.95	92.21	116.37	0.01	1.46	24.36		27.79	86.5	34	66	0	0	0	51.62	-31.44			May-06
500	-6.06	-31.71	-4.83	-61.16	-67.23	0	1.46	34.33		12.4	4.2	307	-207	0	0	0	-45.71	64.81			Dec-99
500	1.73	32.75	-16.06	71.04	50.70	0.09	1.45	34.23		68.41	15.5	34	66	0	0	0	58.24	-45.76			Feb-99
	4.32	21.60	2.67	43.12	25.60	2.11	0	15.88	1.23	15.09	186.4	0	96	0	0	59	30.97	-15.77			Jun-98
	4.17	22.44	20.61	30.50	51.20	2.24	1.86	11.77	0.89	10.2277	2,921	-9	116	15	-22	13	14.71	-0.93			Jan-87

	MARKET			FUND TYPE, CATEGORY & OBJECTIVE	RATINGS					MINIMUMS
Fund Name	Ticker Symbol	Traded On	Fund Type	Category and (Prospectus Objective)	Overall Rating	Reward Rating	Risk Rating	Recent Up/ Downgrade	Open to New Investors	Min Initial Investment
Dodge & Cox Balanced Fund	DODBX	NAS CM	Open End	Moderate Alloc (Balanced)	B-	C	A-		Y	2,500
Dodge & Cox Global Stock Fund	DODWX	NAS CM	Open End	Global Equity Large Cap (World Stock)	C	C	B-		Y	2,500
Dodge & Cox International Stock Fund	DODFX	NAS CM	Open End	Global Equity Large Cap (Foreign Stock)	C	C-	B-			2,500
Dodge & Cox Stock Fund	DODGX	NAS CM	Open End	US Equity Large Cap Value (Growth & Income)	B-	C	B	Up	Y	2,500
Domini Impact Equity Fund A Shares	DSEPX	NAS CM	Open End	US Equity Large Cap Blend (Growth & Income)	C+	C	B	Up	Y	2,500
Domini Impact Equity Fund Institutional Shares	DIEQX	NAS CM	Open End	US Equity Large Cap Blend (Growth & Income)	C+	C	B		Y	500,000
Domini Impact Equity Fund Investor Shares	DSEFX	NAS CM	Open End	US Equity Large Cap Blend (Growth & Income)	C+	C	B	Up	Y	2,500
Domini Impact Equity Fund R Shares	DSFRX	NAS CM	Open End	US Equity Large Cap Blend (Growth & Income)	C+	C	B		Y	0
Domini Impact International Equity Fund A Shares	DOMAX	NAS CM	Open End	Global Equity Large Cap (Foreign Stock)	C	C-	B-		Y	2,500
Domini Impact International Equity Fund Class Y	DOMYX	NAS CM	Open End	Global Equity Large Cap (Foreign Stock)	C	C-	B-		Y	0
Domini Impact International Equity Institutional Shares	DOMOX	NAS CM	Open End	Global Equity Large Cap (Foreign Stock)	C	C-	B-		Y	500,000
Domini Impact International Equity Fund Investor Shares	DOMIX	NAS CM	Open End	Global Equity Large Cap (Foreign Stock)	C	C-	B-		Y	2,500
DoubleLine Colony Real Estate and Income Fund Class I	DBRIX	NAS CM	Open End	Real Estate Sector Equity (Real Estate)	U	U	U		Y	100,000
DoubleLine Colony Real Estate and Income Fund Class N	DLREX	NAS CM	Open End	Real Estate Sector Equity (Real Estate)	U	U	U		Y	2,000
DoubleLine Multi-Asset Growth Fund Class A	DMLAX	NAS CM	Open End	Moderate Alloc (Asset Alloc)	C+	C	B	Up	Y	2,000
DoubleLine Multi-Asset Growth Fund Class I	DMLIX	NAS CM	Open End	Moderate Alloc (Asset Alloc)	C+	C	B	Up	Y	100,000
DoubleLine Shiller Enhanced CAPE® Class I	DSEEX	NAS CM	Open End	US Equity Large Cap Blend (Growth)	B-	B-	B	Down	Y	100,000
DoubleLine Shiller Enhanced CAPE® Class N	DSENX	NAS CM	Open End	US Equity Large Cap Blend (Growth)	B-	B-	B		Y	2,000
DoubleLine Shiller Enhanced International CAPE® Class I	DSEUX	NAS CM	Open End	Europe Equity Large Cap (Growth & Income)	C	C	C+	Up	Y	100,000
DoubleLine Shiller Enhanced International CAPE® Class N	DLEUX	NAS CM	Open End	Europe Equity Large Cap (Growth & Income)	C	C	C+	Up	Y	2,000
DoubleLine Strategic Commodity Fund Class I	DBCMX	NAS CM	Open End	Commodities Broad Basket (Growth)	C-	D+	C	Down	Y	100,000
DoubleLine Strategic Commodity Fund Class N	DLCMX	NAS CM	Open End	Commodities Broad Basket (Growth)	C-	D+	C	Down	Y	2,000
Driehaus Active Income Fund	LCMAX	NAS CM	Open End	Long/Short Credit (Income)	C	C	B			25,000
Driehaus Emerging Markets Growth Fund Institutional Class	DIEMX	NAS CM	Open End	Global Emerg Mkts (Div Emerging Mkts)	C	C	C+		Y	500,000
Driehaus Emerging Markets Growth Fund Investor Class	DREGX	NAS CM	Open End	Global Emerg Mkts (Div Emerging Mkts)	C	C	C+		Y	10,000
Driehaus Emerging Markets Small Cap Growth Fund	DRESX	NAS CM	Open End	Global Emerg Mkts (Div Emerging Mkts)	C	C-	C	Up	Y	10,000
Driehaus Event Driven Fund	DEVDX	NAS CM	Open End	Multialternative (Growth)	B	B-	B	Up	Y	10,000
Driehaus International Small Cap Growth Fund	DRIOX	NAS CM	Open End	Global Equity Mid/Small Cap (Small Company)	C	C	C+			10,000
Driehaus Micro Cap Growth Fund	DMCRX	NAS CM	Open End	US Equity Small Cap (Growth)	C+	C+	C+	Down	Y	10,000
Driehaus Multi-Asset Growth Economies Fund	DMAGX	NAS CM	Open End	Global Macro (Multi-Asset Global)	C	C-	B-	Up	Y	10,000
Driehaus Small Cap Growth Fund Institutional Class	DNSMX	NAS CM	Open End	US Equity Small Cap (Small Company)	C-	C-	C	Up	Y	500,000
Driehaus Small Cap Growth Fund Investor Class	DVSMX	NAS CM	Open End	US Equity Small Cap (Small Company)	C-	C-	C	Up	Y	10,000
Duff & Phelps Global Utility Income	DPG	NYSE	Closed End	Utilities Sector Equity (Utility)	C	C	C	Down	Y	
Duff & Phelps Select Energy MLP & Midstream Energy Inc.	DSE	NYSE	Closed End	Energy Sector Equity (Growth)	D+	D+	D+	Down	Y	
DUNDAS International Equity Growth Institutional Cls	DUNIX	NAS CM	Open End	Global Equity Large Cap (Growth)	C-	C-	C	Down	Y	100,000
Dunham Dynamic Macro Fund Class A	DAAVX	NAS CM	Open End	Global Macro (Growth & Income)	C	C	B-		Y	5,000
Dunham Dynamic Macro Fund Class C	DCAVX	NAS CM	Open End	Global Macro (Growth & Income)	C	C	C+	Up	Y	5,000
Dunham Dynamic Macro Fund Class N	DNAVX	NAS CM	Open End	Global Macro (Growth & Income)	C	C	B-		Y	100,000
Dunham Emerging Markets Stock Fund Class A	DAEMX	NAS CM	Open End	Global Emerg Mkts (Div Emerging Mkts)	C	C	C		Y	5,000
Dunham Emerging Markets Stock Fund Class C	DCEMX	NAS CM	Open End	Global Emerg Mkts (Div Emerging Mkts)	C	C-	C		Y	5,000
Dunham Emerging Markets Stock Fund Class N	DNEMX	NAS CM	Open End	Global Emerg Mkts (Div Emerging Mkts)	C	C	C		Y	100,000
Dunham Focused Large Cap Growth Fund Class A	DAFGX	NAS CM	Open End	US Equity Large Cap Growth (Growth)	B-	C+	B	Down	Y	5,000
Dunham Focused Large Cap Growth Fund Class C	DCFGX	NAS CM	Open End	US Equity Large Cap Growth (Growth)	C+	C+	B-	Down	Y	5,000
Dunham Focused Large Cap Growth Fund Class N	DNFGX	NAS CM	Open End	US Equity Large Cap Growth (Growth)	B-	C+	B	Down	Y	100,000
Dunham International Stock Fund Class A	DAINX	NAS CM	Open End	Global Equity Large Cap (Foreign Stock)	C	C	B-		Y	5,000
Dunham International Stock Fund Class C	DCINX	NAS CM	Open End	Global Equity Large Cap (Foreign Stock)	C	C	C+		Y	5,000
Dunham International Stock Fund Class N	DNINX	NAS CM	Open End	Global Equity Large Cap (Foreign Stock)	C	C	B-		Y	100,000
Dunham Large Cap Value Fund Class A	DALVX	NAS CM	Open End	US Equity Large Cap Value (Growth & Income)	B-	C	B	Up	Y	5,000
Dunham Large Cap Value Fund Class C	DCLVX	NAS CM	Open End	US Equity Large Cap Value (Growth & Income)	B-	C	B	Up	Y	5,000
Dunham Large Cap Value Fund Class N	DNLVX	NAS CM	Open End	US Equity Large Cap Value (Growth & Income)	B-	C	B	Up	Y	100,000
Dunham Long/Short Credit Fund Class A	DAAIX	NAS CM	Open End	Long/Short Credit (Growth & Income)	B	C+	A		Y	5,000
Dunham Long/Short Credit Fund Class C	DCAIX	NAS CM	Open End	Long/Short Credit (Growth & Income)	B	C+	A		Y	5,000

★ Expanded analysis of this fund is included in Section II.

	TOTAL RETURNS					PERFORMANCE				ASSETS		ASSET ALLOCATION & TURNOVER					BULL & BEAR		FEES		
Min Additional Investment	3-Month Total Return	6-Month Total Return	1-Year Total Return	3-Year Total Return	5-Year Total Return	Dividend Yield (TTM)	Expense Ratio	3-Yr Std Deviation	3-Year Beta	NAV	Total Assets (MIL)	%Cash	%Stocks	%Bonds	%Other	Turnover Ratio	Last Bull Market Total Return	Last Bear Market Total Return	Front End Fee (%)	Back End Fee (%)	Inception Date
100	2.68	11.25	5.57	36.68	37.98	2.05	0.53	8.91	0.68	99.55	14,775	4	61	34	0	24	19.12	-16.16			Jun-31
100	2.31	12.64	1.48	42.08	26.40	1.92	0.62	12.9	1.06	12.38	9,189	1	99	0	0	31	19.6	-24.32			May-08
100	2.81	12.99	-0.30	32.30	2.46	2.59	0.63	13.7	1.14	41.66	47,577	2	97	0	0	17	14.7	-25.68			May-01
100	2.59	14.02	4.14	51.77	48.73	1.66	0.52	13.78	1.05	187.1	67,165	3	97	0	0	20	24.41	-21.54			Jan-65
100	4.34	19.59	8.71	41.14	34.24	0.87	1.09	12.52	1	22.1	766.9	0	100	0	0	78	24.71	-16.11	4.75		Nov-08
	4.41	19.79	9.12	42.80	36.77	1.41	0.72	12.5	1	22.04	766.9	0	100	0	0	78	24.99	-15.93			Nov-08
100	4.31	19.53	8.74	41.28	34.37	0.86	1.06	12.51	1	22.11	766.9	0	100	0	0	78	24.68	-16.07			Jun-91
	4.39	19.74	9.05	42.44	36.40	1.32	0.8	12.53	1	22.05	766.9	0	100	0	0	78	24.93	-15.93			Nov-03
100	2.37	13.27	-1.40	25.63	15.87	0.89	1.43	11.89	1.05	8.5	1,251	1	99	0	0	68	12.02	-24.4	4.75		Nov-08
	2.40	13.45	-1.07	26.17	16.46		1.13	11.99	1.06	7.96	1,251	1	99	0	0	68	11.95	-24.46			Jul-18
	2.43	13.34	-0.94	27.18	18.23	2.23	1.02	11.89	1.05	7.95	1,251	1	99	0	0	68	11.95	-24.46			Nov-12
100	2.04	12.99	-1.58	25.51	15.85	1.39	1.41	11.85	1.05	8	1,251	1	99	0	0	68	11.95	-24.46			Dec-06
100	1.73	19.84					0.66			11.41	129.1	2	53	45	0						Dec-18
100	1.75	19.72					0.91			11.41	129.1	2	53	45	0						Dec-18
100	2.29	11.19	2.23	22.31	22.24	2.47	1.54	7.84		9.27	222.0	15	44	38	4	45	1.71	-0.06	4.25		Dec-10
100	2.34	11.35	2.48	23.32	23.87	2.7	1.29	7.79		9.31	222.0	15	44	38	4	45	1.72	0.03			Dec-10
100	4.93	22.88	13.63	61.94	89.04	2.79	0.56	13.36		15.42	6,666	5	50	45	0	55					Oct-13
100	4.80	22.74	13.29	60.69	86.55	2.57	0.81	13.33		15.4	6,666	5	50	45	0	55					Oct-13
100	5.35	16.73	6.73			3.63	0.68			10.62	64.0	3	50	47	0	72					Dec-16
100	5.29	16.56	6.56			3.39	0.92			10.62	64.0	3	50	47	0	72					Dec-16
100	-5.75	3.11	-10.41	2.69		1.17	1.12	12.36	1.15	9.17	458.8	56	19	25	0	0					May-15
100	-5.69	2.97	-10.63	1.87		0.91	1.37	12.34	1.15	9.1	458.8	56	19	25	0	0					May-15
5,000	0.95	3.29	0.98	7.46	5.44	5.18	1.1	2.94	2.1	9.28	487.3	0	1	78	18	74	7.14	-9.07			Nov-05
	3.97	15.57	2.61	39.54	18.77	0.66	1.18	12.94	0.9	36.58	1,687	7	92	0	1	218	16.09	-22.2			Jul-17
2,000	3.91	15.49	2.41	39.03	18.34	0.43	1.39	12.96	0.9	36.6	1,687	7	92	0	1	218	16.09	-22.2			Dec-97
2,000	5.61	20.98	-2.11	13.85	-3.41	0	1.45	13.16	0.89	12.97	61.0	4	96	0	0	207	12.29	-18.03			Aug-11
2,000	4.45	18.26	9.64	26.36	12.59	3.04	1.9	8.23	0.26	11.72	68.0	0	30	30	38	101					Aug-13
2,000	3.26	17.88	-5.10	33.39	32.21	0	1.23	13.28	0.99	9.49	260.0	6	94	0	0	118	12.58	-22.35			Sep-07
2,000	6.82	30.40	8.93	105.86	113.97	0	1.44	20.17	1.04	14.24	273.6	5	96	0	0	156	33.09	-35.11			Nov-13
2,000	4.14	14.24	5.21			0	1.01			11.31	36.7	0	61	31	8	169					Apr-17
	8.72	36.01	15.21			0	0.95			15.71	172.9	1	99	0	0	193					Aug-17
2,000	8.61	35.79	14.88			0	1.2			15.63	172.9	1	99	0	0	193					Aug-17
	2.80	25.70	14.69	11.01	0.04	1.27	2.26	15.15		16.98	644.0	-38	138	0	0	46	10.48				Jul-11
	-3.87	28.89	-0.49	-0.02	-50.63	0	2.25	27.7	1.62	5.19	136.0	0	131	0	-31	33					Jun-14
	0.00	0.00	0.00	0.00		0	0.65	0		10	0.00	3	97	0	0						Mar-16
100	1.34	8.87	1.48	6.44	4.27	2.02	2.22	6.53	1.67	9.81	40.5	63	29	8	0	11	11.03	-7.88	5.75		Apr-10
100	1.07	8.43	0.71	3.90	0.34	1.35	2.97	6.52	1.66	9.38	40.5	63	29	8	0	11	10.62	-8.13			Apr-10
	1.43	9.05	1.81	7.20	5.64	2.23	1.97	6.48	1.65	9.88	40.5	63	29	8	0	11	11.16	-7.66			Apr-10
100	2.27	14.09	-0.83	27.97	2.93	1.57	1.77	14.42	1	13.92	73.9	6	94	0	0	66	17.38	-30.64	5.75		Jan-07
100	2.09	13.73	-1.53	25.12	-0.95	0.88	2.52	14.4	1	13.17	73.9	6	94	0	0	66	16.84	-30.86			Dec-04
	2.29	14.28	-0.56	28.99	4.22	1.76	1.52	14.42	1	14.24	73.9	6	94	0	0	66	17.55	-30.57			Dec-04
100	5.75	27.84	17.22	77.61	90.95	0	1.55	16.66	1.17	24.24	109.5	2	98	0	0	25			5.75		Dec-11
100	5.55	27.37	16.31	73.73	84.13	0	2.3	16.65	1.17	22.8	109.5	2	98	0	0	25					Dec-11
	5.81	28.03	17.51	79.00	93.52	0	1.3	16.66	1.17	24.75	109.5	2	98	0	0	25					Dec-11
100	2.20	12.43	-0.47	26.97	8.66	0.85	1.92	11.73	0.99	15.28	126.9	1	98	0	1	113	10.23	-23.55	5.75		Jan-07
100	2.04	12.06	-1.13	24.12	4.70	0.1	2.67	11.71	0.99	14.49	126.9	1	98	0	1	113	9.73	-23.78			Dec-04
	2.25	12.58	-0.20	27.90	10.04	1.08	1.67	11.72	0.99	15.39	126.9	1	98	0	1	113	10.32	-23.42			Dec-04
100	4.16	16.62	8.00	32.88	31.93	0.8	1.55	11.91	0.97	14.52	82.9	3	97	0	0	45	20.64	-18.41	5.75		Jan-07
100	3.89	16.17	7.19	29.89	27.06	0.09	2.3	11.89	0.97	13.86	82.9	3	97	0	0	45	20.1	-18.71			Dec-04
	4.21	16.81	8.31	33.91	33.66	1.02	1.3	11.87	0.97	14.59	82.9	3	97	0	0	45	20.79	-18.38			Dec-04
100	1.19	4.05	4.00	28.97	17.10	2.69	1.91	5.24		9.23	71.6	46	0	47	7	275	11.8	-14.49	5.75		Jan-07
100	0.69	3.45	2.95	25.91	12.40	2.29	2.66	5.2		8.98	71.6	46	0	47	7	275	11.34	-14.86			Dec-04

	MARKET		FUND TYPE, CATEGORY & OBJECTIVE		RATINGS				MINIMUMS	
Fund Name	Ticker Symbol	Traded On	Fund Type	Category and (Prospectus Objective)	Overall Rating	Reward Rating	Risk Rating	Recent Up/ Downgrade	Open to New Investors	Min Initial Investment
Dunham Long/Short Credit Fund Class N	DNAIX	NAS CM	Open End	Long/Short Credit (Growth & Income)	B	C+	A		Y	100,000
Dunham Monthly Distribution Fund Class A	DAMDX	NAS CM	Open End	Multialternative (Growth)	C+	C	B		Y	5,000
Dunham Monthly Distribution Fund Class C	DCMDX	NAS CM	Open End	Multialternative (Growth)	C	C	B-		Y	5,000
Dunham Monthly Distribution Fund Class N	DNMDX	NAS CM	Open End	Multialternative (Growth)	C+	C	B		Y	100,000
Dunham Real Estate Stock Fund Class A	DAREX	NAS CM	Open End	Real Estate Sector Equity (Real Estate)	C	C	C+	Down	Y	5,000
Dunham Real Estate Stock Fund Class C	DCREX	NAS CM	Open End	Real Estate Sector Equity (Real Estate)	C	C	C+	Down	Y	5,000
Dunham Real Estate Stock Fund Class N	DNREX	NAS CM	Open End	Real Estate Sector Equity (Real Estate)	C	C	C+	Down	Y	100,000
Dunham Small Cap Growth Fund Class A	DADGX	NAS CM	Open End	US Equity Small Cap (Small Company)	C+	C+	C+	Down	Y	5,000
Dunham Small Cap Growth Fund Class C	DCDGX	NAS CM	Open End	US Equity Small Cap (Small Company)	C+	C+	C+	Down	Y	5,000
Dunham Small Cap Growth Fund Class N	DNDGX	NAS CM	Open End	US Equity Small Cap (Small Company)	C+	C+	C+	Down	Y	100,000
Dunham Small Cap Value Fund Class A	DASVX	NAS CM	Open End	US Equity Small Cap (Small Company)	C	C-	B-		Y	5,000
Dunham Small Cap Value Fund Class C	DCSVX	NAS CM	Open End	US Equity Small Cap (Small Company)	C	C-	C+		Y	5,000
Dunham Small Cap Value Fund Class N	DNSVX	NAS CM	Open End	US Equity Small Cap (Small Company)	C	C-	B-		Y	100,000
DuPont Capital Emerging Markets Fund Class I	DCMEX	NAS CM	Open End	Global Emerg Mkts (Div Emerging Mkts)	C	C	C+		Y	1,000,000
DWS Capital Growth Fund - Class A	SDGAX	NAS CM	Open End	US Equity Large Cap Growth (Growth)	B-	B-	B	Down	Y	1,000
DWS Capital Growth Fund - Class C	SDGCX	NAS CM	Open End	US Equity Large Cap Growth (Growth)	B-	C+	B	Down	Y	1,000
DWS Capital Growth Fund - Class Institutional	SDGTX	NAS CM	Open End	US Equity Large Cap Growth (Growth)	B-	B-	B	Down	Y	1,000,000
DWS Capital Growth Fund - Class R	SDGRX	NAS CM	Open End	US Equity Large Cap Growth (Growth)	B-	B-	B	Down	Y	0
DWS Capital Growth Fund - Class R6	SDGZX	NAS CM	Open End	US Equity Large Cap Growth (Growth)	B-	B-	B	Down	Y	0
DWS Capital Growth Fund - Class S	SCGSX	NAS CM	Open End	US Equity Large Cap Growth (Growth)	B-	B-	B	Down	Y	2,500
DWS Communications Fund - Class A	TISHX	NAS CM	Open End	Communications Sector Equity (Comm)	C+	C	B-	Down	Y	1,000
DWS Communications Fund - Class C	FTICX	NAS CM	Open End	Communications Sector Equity (Comm)	C+	C	B-		Y	1,000
DWS Communications Fund - Class Inst	FLICX	NAS CM	Open End	Communications Sector Equity (Comm)	C+	C	B-	Down	Y	1,000,000
DWS Core Equity Fund - Class A	SUWAX	NAS CM	Open End	US Equity Large Cap Blend (Growth & Income)	C+	C	B	Down	Y	1,000
DWS Core Equity Fund - Class C	SUWCX	NAS CM	Open End	US Equity Large Cap Blend (Growth & Income)	C+	C	B		Y	1,000
DWS Core Equity Fund - Class Inst	SUWIX	NAS CM	Open End	US Equity Large Cap Blend (Growth & Income)	B-	C	B		Y	1,000,000
DWS Core Equity Fund - Class R	SUWTX	NAS CM	Open End	US Equity Large Cap Blend (Growth & Income)	C+	C	B		Y	0
DWS Core Equity Fund - Class R6	SUWZX	NAS CM	Open End	US Equity Large Cap Blend (Growth & Income)	B-	C	B		Y	0
DWS Core Equity Fund - Class S	SCDGX	NAS CM	Open End	US Equity Large Cap Blend (Growth & Income)	B-	C	B		Y	2,500
DWS Core Equity Fund - Class T	SUWUX	NAS CM	Open End	US Equity Large Cap Blend (Growth & Income)	C+	C	B	Down	Y	1,000
DWS CROCI Equity Dividend Fund - Class A	KDHAX	NAS CM	Open End	US Equity Large Cap Value (Growth & Income)	B-	C	B+	Down	Y	1,000
DWS CROCI Equity Dividend Fund - Class C	KDHCX	NAS CM	Open End	US Equity Large Cap Value (Growth & Income)	B-	C	B+	Down	Y	1,000
DWS CROCI Equity Dividend Fund - Class Inst	KDHIX	NAS CM	Open End	US Equity Large Cap Value (Growth & Income)	B-	C	B+	Down	Y	1,000,000
DWS CROCI Equity Dividend Fund - Class R	KDHRX	NAS CM	Open End	US Equity Large Cap Value (Growth & Income)	B-	C	B+	Down	Y	0
DWS CROCI Equity Dividend Fund - Class R6	KDHTX	NAS CM	Open End	US Equity Large Cap Value (Growth & Income)	B-	C	B+	Down	Y	0
DWS CROCI Equity Dividend Fund - Class S	KDHSX	NAS CM	Open End	US Equity Large Cap Value (Growth & Income)	B-	C	B+	Down	Y	2,500
DWS CROCI Equity Dividend Fund - Class T	KDHUX	NAS CM	Open End	US Equity Large Cap Value (Growth & Income)	B-	C	B+	Down	Y	1,000
DWS CROCI International Fund - Class A	SUIAX	NAS CM	Open End	Global Equity Large Cap (Foreign Stock)	C	C-	B-		Y	1,000
DWS CROCI International Fund - Class C	SUICX	NAS CM	Open End	Global Equity Large Cap (Foreign Stock)	C	D+	C+		Y	1,000
DWS CROCI International Fund - Class Inst	SUIIX	NAS CM	Open End	Global Equity Large Cap (Foreign Stock)	C	C-	B-		Y	1,000,000
DWS CROCI International Fund - Class R6	SUIRX	NAS CM	Open End	Global Equity Large Cap (Foreign Stock)	C	C-	B-		Y	0
DWS CROCI International Fund - Class S	SCINX	NAS CM	Open End	Global Equity Large Cap (Foreign Stock)	C	C-	B-		Y	2,500
DWS CROCI International Fund - Class T	SUITX	NAS CM	Open End	Global Equity Large Cap (Foreign Stock)	C	C-	B-		Y	1,000
DWS CROCI U.S. Fund - Class A	DCUAX	NAS CM	Open End	US Equity Large Cap Value (Growth)	C+	C	B		Y	1,000
DWS CROCI U.S. Fund - Class C	DCUCX	NAS CM	Open End	US Equity Large Cap Value (Growth)	C+	C	B		Y	1,000
DWS CROCI U.S. Fund - Class Inst	DCUIX	NAS CM	Open End	US Equity Large Cap Value (Growth)	C+	C	B		Y	1,000,000
DWS CROCI U.S. Fund - Class R	DCUTX	NAS CM	Open End	US Equity Large Cap Value (Growth)	C+	C	B		Y	0
DWS CROCI U.S. Fund - Class R6	DCURX	NAS CM	Open End	US Equity Large Cap Value (Growth)	C+	C	B		Y	0
DWS CROCI U.S. Fund - Class S	DCUSX	NAS CM	Open End	US Equity Large Cap Value (Growth)	C+	C	B		Y	2,500
DWS CROCI U.S. Fund - Class T	DCUUX	NAS CM	Open End	US Equity Large Cap Value (Growth)	C+	C	B		Y	1,000
DWS EAFE Equity Index Fund - Class Inst	BTAEX	NAS CM	Open End	Global Equity Large Cap (Foreign Stock)	C	C	B		Y	1,000,000
DWS Emerging Markets Equity Fund - Class A	SEKAX	NAS CM	Open End	Global Emerg Mkts (Div Emerging Mkts)	C	C	B-		Y	1,000

★ Expanded analysis of this fund is included in Section II.

	TOTAL RETURNS					PERFORMANCE				ASSETS		ASSET ALLOCATION & TURNOVER					BULL & BEAR		FEES		
Min Additional Investment	3-Month Total Return	6-Month Total Return	1-Year Total Return	3-Year Total Return	5-Year Total Return	Dividend Yield (TTM)	Expense Ratio	3-Yr Std Deviation	3-Year Beta	NAV	Total Assets (MIL)	%Cash	%Stocks	%Bonds	%Other	Turnover Ratio	Last Bull Market Total Return	Last Bear Market Total Return	Front End Fee (%)	Back End Fee (%)	Inception Date
	1.01	3.95	4.00	29.75	18.31	2.93	1.66	5.24		9.25	71.6	46	0	47	7	275	11.87	-14.45			Dec-04
100	0.45	2.80	1.51	10.02	5.27	0	2.42	2.68	0.79	33.14	271.5	62	36	2	0	453	8.51	-6.3	5.75		Aug-08
100	0.26	2.41	0.74	7.55	1.33	0	3.17	2.67	0.79	26.13	271.5	62	36	2	0	453	8.02	-6.59			Aug-08
	0.06	2.48	1.32	10.35	6.11	0	2.17	2.68	0.79	34.28	271.5	62	36	2	0	453	8.68	-6.21			Sep-08
100	1.22	18.42	11.92	9.63	38.09	1.48	1.35	12.27	0.98	17.29	56.3	2	98	0	0	74	30.67	-17.85	5.75		Jan-07
100	1.11	18.03	11.09	7.14	32.96	0.91	2.1	12.31	0.98	16.3	56.3	2	98	0	0	74	30.05	-18.11			Dec-04
	1.35	18.67	12.23	10.45	39.80	1.7	1.1	12.32	0.99	17.16	56.3	2	98	0	0	74	30.83	-17.75			Dec-04
100	6.59	30.27	5.22	76.63	67.17	0	2.2	18.47	1	16.48	52.7	4	96	0	0	190	26.93	-27.77	5.75		Jan-07
100	6.40	29.80	4.42	72.68	60.98	0	2.95	18.44	1	12.63	52.7	4	96	0	0	190	26.35	-27.98			Dec-04
	6.65	30.49	5.46	77.91	69.25	0	1.95	18.42	1	17.46	52.7	4	96	0	0	190	27.13	-27.73			Dec-04
100	1.60	13.77	-3.09	36.29	31.80	0	1.79	16.88	0.96	13.96	51.1	1	99	0	0	101	23.31	-20.51	5.75		Jan-07
100	1.42	13.28	-3.79	33.29	26.88	0	2.54	16.84	0.96	12.11	51.1	1	99	0	0	101	22.84	-20.72			Dec-04
	1.72	13.91	-2.80	37.40	33.46	0	1.54	16.89	0.96	14.16	51.1	1	99	0	0	101	23.42	-20.38			Dec-04
100,000	0.11	10.37	2.73	39.45	3.19	1.85	1.28	14.35	1.01	8.72	25.1	1	99	0	0	65	19.01	-24.54			Dec-10
50	5.78	25.74	13.27	65.71	84.63	0	0.94	13.29	0.98	80.84	1,562	1	99	0	0	27	27.04	-19.54	5.75		Jun-01
50	5.57	25.22	12.35	61.60	77.18	0	1.72	13.29	0.98	67.21	1,562	1	99	0	0	27	26.49	-19.8		1.00	Jun-01
	5.85	25.88	13.51	66.85	86.91	0.19	0.71	13.3	0.98	81.7	1,562	1	99	0	0	27	27.28	-19.41			Aug-02
	5.76	25.61	12.88	63.73	80.96	0	1.39	13.31	0.98	79.1	1,562	1	99	0	0	27	26.94	-19.42			Nov-03
	5.86	25.93	13.61	67.27	87.02	0.26	0.63	13.29	0.98	81.44	1,562	1	99	0	0	27	27.23	-19.43			Aug-14
50	5.86	25.91	13.55	66.96	87.00	0.2	0.7	13.3	0.98	81.83	1,562	1	99	0	0	27	27.23	-19.43			Jul-00
50	3.23	17.46	10.30	16.08	24.75	1.34	1.63	11.83	0.86	23.94	88.5	4	87	8	0	70	14.44	-15.27	5.75		Jan-84
50	3.05	17.00	9.46	13.50	20.13	0.66	2.38	11.79	0.86	21.6	88.5	4	87	8	0	70	13.96	-15.53		1.00	Oct-98
	3.28	17.58	10.56	16.96	26.32	1.57	1.38	11.83	0.86	24.54	88.5	4	87	8	0	70	14.49	-15.28			Jun-98
50	4.03	19.17	7.31	48.85	63.66	0.96	0.86	12.54	1.01	26.52	3,784	0	100	0	0	46	23.53	-19.32	5.75		Aug-99
50	3.82	18.73	6.50	45.47	57.49	0.24	1.62	12.54	1.01	25.22	3,784	0	100	0	0	46	22.93	-19.57		1.00	Dec-00
	4.10	19.37	7.64	50.25	66.27	1.24	0.55	12.57	1.01	26.88	3,784	0	100	0	0	46	23.81	-19.16			Aug-02
	3.93	18.96	6.89	47.03	60.43	0.59	1.28	12.56	1.01	26.8	3,784	0	100	0	0	46	23.35	-19.4			May-12
	4.08	19.37	7.66	50.49	66.35	1.29	0.5	12.54	1.01	26.85	3,784	0	100	0	0	46	23.7	-19.24			Aug-14
50	4.10	19.35	7.58	50.12	65.98	1.22	0.58	12.54	1.01	26.82	3,784	0	100	0	0	46	23.7	-19.24			May-29
50	4.03	19.17	7.33	48.92	63.82	0.98	0.83	12.53	1.01	26.53	3,784	0	100	0	0	46	23.52	-19.32	2.50		Jun-17
50	2.51	16.30	13.01	44.63	51.85	1.65	1.03	11.67	0.9	55.16	1,160	1	99	0	0	69	25.04	-19.47	5.75		Mar-88
50	2.42	15.92	12.31	41.54	46.38	0.94	1.81	11.66	0.9	55.08	1,160	1	99	0	0	69	24.44	-19.73		1.00	Sep-95
	2.58	16.45	13.34	45.77	53.82	1.9	0.78	11.66	0.9	55.18	1,160	1	99	0	0	69	25.28	-19.35			Aug-02
	2.47	16.13	12.70	43.46	49.87	1.39	1.34	11.66	0.9	55.02	1,160	1	99	0	0	69	24.8	-19.54			Oct-03
	2.60	16.50	13.39	46.07	53.85	1.99	0.68	11.66	0.9	55.18	1,160	1	99	0	0	69	25.04	-19.47			Mar-15
50	2.57	16.44	13.26	45.65	53.70	1.87	0.8	11.67	0.9	55.14	1,160	1	99	0	0	69	25.24	-19.43			Feb-05
50	2.53	16.30	13.06	44.70	51.89	1.69	1.09	11.66	0.9	55.16	1,160	1	99	0	0	69	25.03	-19.47	2.50		Jun-17
50	0.44	8.86	-4.04	24.54	4.32	3.18	1.17	10.97	0.9	43.34	605.0	0	100	0	0	53	16.71	-26.25	5.75		Aug-99
50	0.25	8.48	-4.72	21.80	0.51	2.5	1.88	10.97	0.9	42.98	605.0	0	100	0	0	53	16.14	-26.49		1.00	Dec-00
	0.48	9.03	-3.74	25.69	5.90	3.49	0.85	10.96	0.9	43.33	605.0	0	100	0	0	53	17.04	-26.13			Dec-00
	0.51	9.07	-3.66	26.01	6.12	3.58	0.76	10.97	0.9	43.26	605.0	0	100	0	0	53	16.9	-26.15			Dec-14
50	0.50	9.01	-3.77	25.50	5.57	3.44	0.9	10.98	0.9	43.54	605.0	0	100	0	0	53	16.9	-26.15			Jun-53
50	0.41	8.86	-4.00	24.59	4.28	3.24	1.11	10.98	0.9	43.34	605.0	0	100	0	0	53	16.73	-26.22	2.50		Jun-17
50	4.86	19.60	6.95	35.98		2.09	1.01	14.19	1.11	11.65	822.8	0	100	0	0	98			5.75		Apr-15
50	4.72	19.25	6.18	32.96		1.43	1.75	14.18	1.1	11.52	822.8	0	100	0	0	98				1.00	Apr-15
	4.95	19.83	7.23	37.17		2.39	0.68	14.21	1.11	11.66	822.8	0	100	0	0	98					Apr-15
	4.76	19.38	6.64	34.76		1.84	1.29	14.2	1.11	11.64	822.8	0	100	0	0	98					Dec-16
	5.04	19.81	7.42	37.49		2.47	0.59	14.22	1.11	11.67	822.8	0	100	0	0	98					Apr-15
50	5.04	19.93	7.33	37.31		2.4	0.67	14.22	1.11	11.67	822.8	0	100	0	0	98					Apr-15
50	4.95	19.71	7.04	36.08		2.16	0.93	14.2	1.1	11.66	822.8	0	100	0	0	98			2.50		Jun-17
	3.59	14.35	0.96	30.53	10.98	2.84	0.27	11.03	0.99	5.77	43.9	1	97	0	0	4	13.17	-23.36			Jan-96
50	1.01	12.03	3.74	43.30	20.36	0.49	1.18	13.56	0.96	19.83	449.1	11	89	0	0	34	18.07	-29.96	5.75		May-01

Fund Name	Ticker Symbol	Traded On	Fund Type	Category and (Prospectus Objective)	Overall Rating	Reward Rating	Risk Rating	Recent Up/ Downgrade	Open to New Investors	Min Initial Investment
	MARKET			FUND TYPE, CATEGORY & OBJECTIVE	RATINGS				MINIMUMS	
DWS Emerging Markets Equity Fund - Class C	SEKCX	NAS CM	Open End	Global Emerg Mkts (Div Emerging Mkts)	C	C	B-		Y	1,000
DWS Emerging Markets Equity Fund - Class Inst	SEKIX	NAS CM	Open End	Global Emerg Mkts (Div Emerging Mkts)	C	C	B-		Y	1,000,000
DWS Emerging Markets Equity Fund - Class R6	SEKRX	NAS CM	Open End	Global Emerg Mkts (Div Emerging Mkts)	C	C	B-		Y	0
DWS Emerging Markets Equity Fund - Class S	SEMGX	NAS CM	Open End	Global Emerg Mkts (Div Emerging Mkts)	C	C	B-		Y	2,500
DWS Emerging Markets Equity Fund - Class T	SEKTX	NAS CM	Open End	Global Emerg Mkts (Div Emerging Mkts)	C	C	B-		Y	1,000
DWS Enhanced Commodity Strategy Fund - Class A	SKNRX	NAS CM	Open End	Commodities Broad Basket (Growth & Income)	D	D	C-	Down	Y	1,000
DWS Enhanced Commodity Strategy Fund - Class C	SKCRX	NAS CM	Open End	Commodities Broad Basket (Growth & Income)	D	D	C-	Down	Y	1,000
DWS Enhanced Commodity Strategy Fund - Class Inst	SKIRX	NAS CM	Open End	Commodities Broad Basket (Growth & Income)	D	D	C-	Down	Y	1,000,000
DWS Enhanced Commodity Strategy Fund - Class R6	SKRRX	NAS CM	Open End	Commodities Broad Basket (Growth & Income)	D	D	C-	Down	Y	0
DWS Enhanced Commodity Strategy Fund - Class S	SKSRX	NAS CM	Open End	Commodities Broad Basket (Growth & Income)	D	D	C-	Down	Y	2,500
DWS Enhanced Commodity Strategy Fund - Class T	SKSTX	NAS CM	Open End	Commodities Broad Basket (Growth & Income)	D	D	C-	Down	Y	1,000
DWS Equity 500 Index Fund - Class Inst	BTIIX	NAS CM	Open End	US Equity Large Cap Blend (Growth)	B-	C	B	Down	Y	1,000,000
DWS Equity 500 Index Fund - Class R6	BTIRX	NAS CM	Open End	US Equity Large Cap Blend (Growth)	B-	C	B	Down	Y	0
DWS Equity 500 Index Fund - Class S	BTIEX	NAS CM	Open End	US Equity Large Cap Blend (Growth)	B-	C	B		Y	2,500
DWS European Equity Fund - Class A	DURAX	NAS CM	Open End	Europe Equity Large Cap (Europe Stock)	C	C	C+	Up	Y	1,000
DWS European Equity Fund - Class C	DURCX	NAS CM	Open End	Europe Equity Large Cap (Europe Stock)	C	C-	C+	Up	Y	1,000
DWS European Equity Fund - Class Institutional	DURIX	NAS CM	Open End	Europe Equity Large Cap (Europe Stock)	C	C	C+	Up	Y	1,000,000
DWS European Equity Fund - Class S	DURSX	NAS CM	Open End	Europe Equity Large Cap (Europe Stock)	C	C	C+	Up	Y	2,500
DWS Global Income Builder Fund - Class A	KTRAX	NAS CM	Open End	Moderate Alloc (Balanced)	B-	C	A-	Up	Y	1,000
DWS Global Income Builder Fund - Class C	KTRCX	NAS CM	Open End	Moderate Alloc (Balanced)	B-	C	B+	Up	Y	1,000
DWS Global Income Builder Fund - Class Inst	KTRIX	NAS CM	Open End	Moderate Alloc (Balanced)	B	C+	A-	Up	Y	1,000,000
DWS Global Income Builder Fund - Class R6	KTRZX	NAS CM	Open End	Moderate Alloc (Balanced)	B	C+	A-	Up	Y	0
DWS Global Income Builder Fund - Class S	KTRSX	NAS CM	Open End	Moderate Alloc (Balanced)	B	C+	A-	Up	Y	2,500
DWS Global Macro Fund - Class A	DBISX	NAS CM	Open End	Global Macro (World Stock)	B-	C	A-	Down	Y	1,000
DWS Global Macro Fund - Class C	DBICX	NAS CM	Open End	Global Macro (World Stock)	B-	C	B+		Y	1,000
DWS Global Macro Fund - Class Inst	MGINX	NAS CM	Open End	Global Macro (World Stock)	B-	C	A-	Down	Y	1,000,000
DWS Global Macro Fund - Class R	DBITX	NAS CM	Open End	Global Macro (World Stock)	B-	C	B+		Y	0
DWS Global Macro Fund - Class S	DBIVX	NAS CM	Open End	Global Macro (World Stock)	B-	C	A-	Down	Y	2,500
DWS Global Small Cap Fund - Class A	KGDAX	NAS CM	Open End	Global Equity Mid/Small Cap (World Stock)	D+	D+	C	Down	Y	1,000
DWS Global Small Cap Fund - Class C	KGDCX	NAS CM	Open End	Global Equity Mid/Small Cap (World Stock)	D+	D	C-		Y	1,000
DWS Global Small Cap Fund - Class Inst	KGDIX	NAS CM	Open End	Global Equity Mid/Small Cap (World Stock)	C-	D+	C		Y	1,000,000
DWS Global Small Cap Fund - Class R6	KGDZX	NAS CM	Open End	Global Equity Mid/Small Cap (World Stock)	C-	D+	C		Y	0
DWS Global Small Cap Fund - Class S	SGSCX	NAS CM	Open End	Global Equity Mid/Small Cap (World Stock)	C-	D+	C		Y	2,500
DWS Global Small Cap Fund - Class T	KGDTX	NAS CM	Open End	Global Equity Mid/Small Cap (World Stock)	D+	D+	C	Down	Y	1,000
DWS Health and Wellness Fund - Class A	SUHAX	NAS CM	Open End	Healthcare Sector Equity (Health)	B-	C	B		Y	1,000
DWS Health and Wellness Fund - Class C	SUHCX	NAS CM	Open End	Healthcare Sector Equity (Health)	C+	C	B	Down	Y	1,000
DWS Health and Wellness Fund - Class Inst	SUHIX	NAS CM	Open End	Healthcare Sector Equity (Health)	B-	C	B		Y	1,000,000
DWS Health and Wellness Fund - Class S	SCHLX	NAS CM	Open End	Healthcare Sector Equity (Health)	B-	C	B		Y	2,500
DWS International Growth Fund - Class A	SGQAX	NAS CM	Open End	Global Equity Large Cap (World Stock)	C	C	B-		Y	1,000
DWS International Growth Fund - Class C	SGQCX	NAS CM	Open End	Global Equity Large Cap (World Stock)	C	C	B-		Y	1,000
DWS International Growth Fund - Class Inst	SGQIX	NAS CM	Open End	Global Equity Large Cap (World Stock)	C	C	B-		Y	1,000,000
DWS International Growth Fund - Class R	SGQRX	NAS CM	Open End	Global Equity Large Cap (World Stock)	C	C	B-		Y	0
DWS International Growth Fund - Class R6	SGQTX	NAS CM	Open End	Global Equity Large Cap (World Stock)	C	C	B-		Y	0
DWS International Growth Fund - Class S	SCOBX	NAS CM	Open End	Global Equity Large Cap (World Stock)	C	C	B-		Y	2,500
DWS Large Cap Focus Growth Fund - Class A	SGGAX	NAS CM	Open End	US Equity Large Cap Growth (Growth)	B-	B-	B	Down	Y	1,000
DWS Large Cap Focus Growth Fund - Class C	SGGCX	NAS CM	Open End	US Equity Large Cap Growth (Growth)	B-	B-	B	Down	Y	1,000
DWS Large Cap Focus Growth Fund - Class Inst	SGGIX	NAS CM	Open End	US Equity Large Cap Growth (Growth)	B-	B-	B	Down	Y	1,000,000
DWS Large Cap Focus Growth Fund - Class S	SCQGX	NAS CM	Open End	US Equity Large Cap Growth (Growth)	B-	B-	B	Down	Y	2,500
DWS Latin America Equity Fund - Class A	SLANX	NAS CM	Open End	Latin America Equity (Foreign Stock)	C+	C	C+	Down	Y	1,000
DWS Latin America Equity Fund - Class C	SLAPX	NAS CM	Open End	Latin America Equity (Foreign Stock)	C+	C	C+		Y	1,000
DWS Latin America Equity Fund - Class Inst	SLARX	NAS CM	Open End	Latin America Equity (Foreign Stock)	C+	C	C+	Down	Y	1,000,000
DWS Latin America Equity Fund - Class S	SLAFX	NAS CM	Open End	Latin America Equity (Foreign Stock)	C+	C	C+	Down	Y	2,500

★Expanded analysis of this fund is included in Section II.

	TOTAL RETURNS					PERFORMANCE				ASSETS		ASSET ALLOCATION & TURNOVER					BULL & BEAR		FEES		
Min Additional Investment	3-Month Total Return	6-Month Total Return	1-Year Total Return	3-Year Total Return	5-Year Total Return	Dividend Yield (TTM)	Expense Ratio	3-Yr Std Deviation	3-Year Beta	NAV	Total Assets (MIL)	%Cash	%Stocks	%Bonds	%Other	Turnover Ratio	Last Bull Market Total Return	Last Bear Market Total Return	Front End Fee (%)	Back End Fee (%)	Inception Date
50	0.85	11.64	2.97	40.11	15.88	0	1.93	13.56	0.96	17.64	449.1	11	89	0	0	34	17.49	-30.17		1.00	May-01
	1.10	12.17	3.96	44.36	21.81	0.71	0.93	13.57	0.96	20.08	449.1	11	89	0	0	34	18.35	-29.8			Mar-08
	1.10	12.17	4.05	44.23	21.80		0.93	13.58	0.97	20.09	449.1	11	89	0	0	34	18.16	-29.85			Sep-18
50	1.05	12.10	3.93	44.06	21.66	0.64	1.01	13.56	0.96	20.1	449.1	11	89	0	0	34	18.16	-29.85			May-96
50	1.07	12.03	3.74	43.24	20.36	0.49	1.18	13.57	0.96	19.83	449.1	11	89	0	0	34	17.99	-29.92	2.50		Jun-17
50	-3.18	2.12	-9.76	-10.80	-26.93	11.87	1.33	7.85	0.73	9.47	2,769	10	19	70	0	79	1.28	-20.13	5.75		Feb-05
50	-3.42	1.69	-10.47	-12.76	-29.63	11.05	2.08	7.84	0.73	8.49	2,769	10	19	70	0	79	0.94	-20.35		1.00	Feb-05
	-3.04	2.28	-9.46	-9.83	-25.69	12.26	0.99	7.84	0.73	9.62	2,769	10	19	70	0	79	1.36	-19.91			Feb-05
	-3.14	2.30	-9.45	-9.75	-25.62	12.31	0.95	7.85	0.73	9.61	2,769	10	19	70	0	79	1.36	-19.91			Jun-16
50	-3.09	2.20	-9.57	-10.23	-26.16	12.11	1.13	7.86	0.73	9.59	2,769	10	19	70	0	79	1.3	-19.91			Feb-05
50	-3.18	2.12	-9.72	-10.55	-26.54	11.9	1.33	7.84	0.73	9.48	2,769	10	19	70	0	79	1.25	-19.97	2.50		Jun-17
	4.24	19.44	10.60	50.33	64.78	1.58	0.24	12.09	0.99	197.47	624.3	1	99	0	0	3	25	-16.32			Dec-92
	4.24	19.45	10.60	50.33	64.77	1.58	0.23	12.09	0.99	197.44	624.3	1	99	0	0	3	25	-16.32			Mar-17
50	4.23	19.41	10.54	50.11	64.37	1.53	0.29	12.09	0.99	194.23	624.3	1	99	0	0	3	24.96	-16.35			Dec-92
50	6.54	19.75	-2.98	28.78		1.76	1.12	13.49	1.04	11.55	34.5	1	99	0	0	93			5.75		Nov-14
50	6.39	19.21	-3.75	25.93		1.12	1.87	13.43	1.03	11.32	34.5	1	99	0	0	93				1.00	Nov-14
	6.59	19.83	-2.70	29.72		1.98	0.87	13.47	1.04	11.63	34.5	1	99	0	0	93					Nov-14
50	6.71	19.89	-2.76	29.46		1.93	0.92	13.51	1.04	11.6	34.5	1	99	0	0	93					Nov-14
50	3.15	13.94	6.61	28.82	20.93	3.88	0.92	7.83	1.47	9.37	747.7	5	54	33	0	67	14.01	-12.47	5.75		Mar-64
50	3.07	13.51	5.80	25.80	16.24	3.13	1.67	7.78	1.46	9.37	747.7	5	54	33	0	67	13.44	-12.84		1.00	May-94
	3.22	13.97	6.87	29.61	22.29	4.12	0.68	7.79	1.45	9.35	747.7	5	54	33	0	67	14.08	-12.49			Jul-95
	3.24	14.02	6.98	30.09	22.42	4.22	0.58	7.75	1.45	9.35	747.7	5	54	33	0	67	14.01	-12.47			Aug-14
50	3.32	14.06	6.84	29.63	22.19	4.09	0.71	7.82	1.46	9.37	747.7	5	54	33	0	67	14.13	-12.47			Mar-05
50	1.96	6.59	6.00	25.36	20.89	4.17	1.42	5.56	0.21	9.86	32.4	33	32	34	0	80	12.04	-23.13	5.75		Feb-01
50	1.76	6.21	5.17	22.58	16.45	3.42	2.17	5.59	0.51	9.23	32.4	33	32	34	0	80	11.56	-23.42		1.00	Feb-01
	2.11	6.85	6.32	26.34	22.45	4.42	1.17	5.64	0.98	9.67	32.4	33	32	34	0	80	12.17	-23.01			May-95
	1.93	6.50	5.68	24.45	19.30	3.92	1.67	5.57	0.6	9.49	32.4	33	32	34	0	80	12.13	-23.27			Jul-03
50	2.01	6.75	6.27	26.19	22.15	4.37	1	5.55	-0.24	9.64	32.4	33	32	34	0	80	12.28	-23.07			Feb-05
50	1.33	14.92	-12.06	16.16	1.76	0	1.39	15.19	1.12	27.33	213.8	1	98	0	0	33	17.08	-21.04	5.75		Apr-98
50	1.16	14.48	-12.70	13.60	-1.96	0	2.14	15.18	1.11	20.86	213.8	1	98	0	0	33	16.59	-21.29		1.00	Apr-98
	1.37	15.05	-11.76	17.28	3.36	0	1.07	15.16	1.11	29.42	213.8	1	98	0	0	33	17.34	-20.91			Aug-08
	1.44	15.16	-11.71	17.52	3.58	0	1.04	15.19	1.12	29.47	213.8	1	98	0	0	33	17.28	-20.96			Aug-14
50	1.38	15.05	-11.85	17.06	3.09	0	1.14	15.2	1.12	29.34	213.8	1	98	0	0	33	17.28	-20.96			Sep-91
50	1.37	14.95	-12.04	16.27	1.88	0	1.36	15.18	1.12	27.36	213.8	1	98	0	0	33	17.11	-21.05	2.50		Jun-17
50	1.77	12.55	10.01	32.36	48.72	0	1.35	14.26	0.92	36.14	289.4	4	96	0	0	27	22.12	-13.76	5.75		Dec-00
50	1.60	12.12	9.17	29.44	43.26	0	2.07	14.26	0.92	27.2	289.4	4	96	0	0	27	21.69	-14.05		1.00	Dec-00
	1.84	12.67	10.28	33.43	50.62	0.21	1.07	14.26	0.92	40.81	289.4	4	96	0	0	27	22.27	-13.63			Dec-00
50	1.85	12.70	10.29	33.42	50.63	0.19	1.08	14.27	0.92	39.04	289.4	4	96	0	0	27	22.31	-13.64			Mar-98
50	6.50	23.36	4.21	31.76	18.24	0.8	1.24	13.06	1.07	35.37	560.2	3	96	0	0	73	17.09	-26.06	5.75		Jun-01
50	6.28	22.88	3.45	28.86	13.86	0.2	1.97	13.04	1.07	33.29	560.2	3	96	0	0	73	16.59	-26.27		1.00	Jun-01
	6.59	23.60	4.58	33.11	20.08	1.11	0.85	13.06	1.07	35.4	560.2	3	96	0	0	73	17.29	-25.96			Aug-08
	6.39	23.20	3.94	30.68	16.70	0.57	1.49	13.04	1.07	35.1	560.2	3	96	0	0	73	16.92	-26.21			Nov-03
	6.59	23.60	4.62	33.11	19.98	1.14	0.87	13.06	1.07	35.4	560.2	3	96	0	0	73	17.28	-25.93			Jun-16
50	6.56	23.54	4.51	32.85	19.78	1.05	0.93	13.07	1.07	35.37	560.2	3	96	0	0	73	17.28	-25.93			Jul-86
50	6.48	25.78	14.18	62.43	84.99	0	1.14	13.67	0.99	49.61	255.0	4	96	0	0	36	27.75	-20.05	5.75		Aug-99
50	6.28	25.28	13.34	58.79	78.14	0	1.89	13.66	0.99	41.12	255.0	4	96	0	0	36	27.15	-20.29		1.00	Dec-00
	6.53	25.89	14.45	63.61	87.29	0.09	0.89	13.65	0.99	52.66	255.0	4	96	0	0	36	27.96	-19.96			Dec-00
50	6.54	25.93	14.49	63.69	87.32	0.08	0.89	13.66	0.99	51.95	255.0	4	96	0	0	36	27.88	-19.97			May-91
50	10.23	21.57	39.36	54.09	14.10	0	1.66	22.2	0.95	30.48	320.3	2	98	0	0	203	19.41	-27.73	5.75		May-01
50	10.03	21.11	38.32	50.75	9.96	0	2.41	22.19	0.95	28.62	320.3	2	98	0	0	203	18.9	-27.97		1.00	May-01
	10.32	21.70	39.73	55.36	15.61	0	1.41	22.19	0.95	30.56	320.3	2	98	0	0	203	19.62	-27.65			Feb-15
50	10.32	21.71	39.68	55.31	15.57	0	1.41	22.19	0.95	30.55	320.3	2	98	0	0	203	19.62	-27.65			Dec-92

	MARKET		FUND TYPE, CATEGORY & OBJECTIVE		RATINGS				MINIMUMS	
Fund Name	Ticker Symbol	Traded On	Fund Type	Category and (Prospectus Objective)	Overall Rating	Reward Rating	Risk Rating	Recent Up/ Downgrade	Open to New Investors	Min Initial Investment
DWS Mid Cap Value Fund - Class A	MIDVX	NAS CM	Open End	US Equity Mid Cap (Growth)	C	C-	C+		Y	1,000
DWS Mid Cap Value Fund - Class C	MIDZX	NAS CM	Open End	US Equity Mid Cap (Growth)	C	C-	C		Y	1,000
DWS Mid Cap Value Fund - Class Institutional	MIDIX	NAS CM	Open End	US Equity Mid Cap (Growth)	C	C-	C+		Y	1,000,000
DWS Mid Cap Value Fund - Class R	MIDQX	NAS CM	Open End	US Equity Mid Cap (Growth)	C	C-	C+		Y	0
DWS Mid Cap Value Fund - Class R6	MIDUX	NAS CM	Open End	US Equity Mid Cap (Growth)	C	C-	C+		Y	0
DWS Mid Cap Value Fund - Class S	MIDTX	NAS CM	Open End	US Equity Mid Cap (Growth)	C	C-	C+		Y	2,500
DWS Multi-Asset Conservative Allocation Fund - Class A	SPDAX	NAS CM	Open End	Cautious Alloc (Asset Alloc)	B-	C	B+	Up	Y	1,000
DWS Multi-Asset Conservative Allocation Fund - Class C	SPDCX	NAS CM	Open End	Cautious Alloc (Asset Alloc)	B-	C	B+	Up	Y	1,000
DWS Multi-Asset Conservative Allocation Fund - Class S	SPBAX	NAS CM	Open End	Cautious Alloc (Asset Alloc)	B-	C	A-	Up	Y	2,500
DWS Multi-Asset Global Allocation Fund - Class A	SUPAX	NAS CM	Open End	Moderate Alloc (Asset Alloc)	C+	C	B	Up	Y	1,000
DWS Multi-Asset Global Allocation Fund - Class C	SUPCX	NAS CM	Open End	Moderate Alloc (Asset Alloc)	C+	C-	B	Up	Y	1,000
DWS Multi-Asset Global Allocation Fund - Class S	SPGRX	NAS CM	Open End	Moderate Alloc (Asset Alloc)	C+	C	B+	Up	Y	2,500
DWS Multi-Asset Moderate Allocation Fund - Class A	PLUSX	NAS CM	Open End	Moderate Alloc (Asset Alloc)	B-	C	B+	Up	Y	1,000
DWS Multi-Asset Moderate Allocation Fund - Class C	PLSCX	NAS CM	Open End	Moderate Alloc (Asset Alloc)	B-	C	B+	Up	Y	1,000
DWS Multi-Asset Moderate Allocation Fund - Class S	PPLSX	NAS CM	Open End	Moderate Alloc (Asset Alloc)	B-	C	B+	Up	Y	2,500
DWS RREEF Global Infrastructure Fund - Class A	TOLLX	NAS CM	Open End	Infrastructure Sector Equity (Growth & Income)	C	C	C+	Down	Y	1,000
DWS RREEF Global Infrastructure Fund - Class C	TOLCX	NAS CM	Open End	Infrastructure Sector Equity (Growth & Income)	C	C	C+	Down	Y	1,000
DWS RREEF Global Infrastructure Fund - Class Inst	TOLIX	NAS CM	Open End	Infrastructure Sector Equity (Growth & Income)	C	C	C+	Down	Y	1,000,000
DWS RREEF Global Infrastructure Fund - Class R6	TOLZX	NAS CM	Open End	Infrastructure Sector Equity (Growth & Income)	C+	C	B-		Y	0
DWS RREEF Global Infrastructure Fund - Class S	TOLSX	NAS CM	Open End	Infrastructure Sector Equity (Growth & Income)	C	C	C+	Down	Y	2,500
DWS RREEF Global Infrastructure Fund - Class T	TOLTX	NAS CM	Open End	Infrastructure Sector Equity (Growth & Income)	C	C	C+	Down	Y	1,000
DWS RREEF Global Real Estate Securities Fund - Class A	RRGAX	NAS CM	Open End	Real Estate Sector Equity (Real Estate)	B-	C	B+		Y	1,000
DWS RREEF Global Real Estate Securities Fund - Class C	RRGCX	NAS CM	Open End	Real Estate Sector Equity (Real Estate)	B-	C	B+		Y	1,000
DWS RREEF Global Real Estate Securities Fund - Class Inst	RRGIX	NAS CM	Open End	Real Estate Sector Equity (Real Estate)	B-	C+	B+		Y	1,000,000
DWS RREEF Global Real Estate Securities Fund - Class R6	RRGRX	NAS CM	Open End	Real Estate Sector Equity (Real Estate)	B-	C+	B+		Y	0
DWS RREEF Global Real Estate Securities Fund - Class S	RRGTX	NAS CM	Open End	Real Estate Sector Equity (Real Estate)	B-	C	B+		Y	2,500
DWS RREEF Global Real Estate Securities Fund - Class T	RRGUX	NAS CM	Open End	Real Estate Sector Equity (Real Estate)	B-	C	B+		Y	1,000
DWS RREEF MLP & Energy Infrastructure Fund - Class A	DMPAX	NAS CM	Open End	Energy Sector Equity (Growth & Income)	C	C	C	Down	Y	1,000
DWS RREEF MLP & Energy Infrastructure Fund - Class C	DMPCX	NAS CM	Open End	Energy Sector Equity (Growth & Income)	C	C	C	Down	Y	1,000
DWS RREEF MLP & Energy Infrastructure Fund - Class Inst	DMPIX	NAS CM	Open End	Energy Sector Equity (Growth & Income)	C	C	C	Down	Y	1,000,000
DWS RREEF MLP & Energy Infrastructure Fund - Class S	DMPSX	NAS CM	Open End	Energy Sector Equity (Growth & Income)	C	C	C	Down	Y	2,500
DWS RREEF Real Assets Fund - Class A	AAAAX	NAS CM	Open End	Moderate Alloc (Growth & Income)	B	C+	A-		Y	1,000
DWS RREEF Real Assets Fund - Class C	AAAPX	NAS CM	Open End	Moderate Alloc (Growth & Income)	B-	C	B+		Y	1,000
DWS RREEF Real Assets Fund - Class Inst	AAAZX	NAS CM	Open End	Moderate Alloc (Growth & Income)	B	C+	A-		Y	1,000,000
DWS RREEF Real Assets Fund - Class R	AAAQX	NAS CM	Open End	Moderate Alloc (Growth & Income)	B-	C	A-	Down	Y	0
DWS RREEF Real Assets Fund - Class R6	AAAVX	NAS CM	Open End	Moderate Alloc (Growth & Income)	B	C+	A-		Y	0
DWS RREEF Real Assets Fund - Class S	AAASX	NAS CM	Open End	Moderate Alloc (Growth & Income)	B	C+	A-		Y	2,500
DWS RREEF Real Assets Fund - Class T	AAAWX	NAS CM	Open End	Moderate Alloc (Growth & Income)	B	C+	A-		Y	1,000
DWS RREEF Real Estate Securities Fund - Class A	RRRAX	NAS CM	Open End	Real Estate Sector Equity (Real Estate)	C+	C	B	Down	Y	1,000
DWS RREEF Real Estate Securities Fund - Class C	RRRCX	NAS CM	Open End	Real Estate Sector Equity (Real Estate)	C+	C	B-	Down	Y	1,000
DWS RREEF Real Estate Securities Fund - Class Instl	RRRRX	NAS CM	Open End	Real Estate Sector Equity (Real Estate)	C+	C	B	Down	Y	1,000,000
DWS RREEF Real Estate Securities Fund - Class R	RRRSX	NAS CM	Open End	Real Estate Sector Equity (Real Estate)	C+	C	B	Down	Y	0
DWS RREEF Real Estate Securities Fund - Class R6	RRRZX	NAS CM	Open End	Real Estate Sector Equity (Real Estate)	C+	C+	B	Down	Y	0
DWS RREEF Real Estate Securities Fund - Class S	RRREX	NAS CM	Open End	Real Estate Sector Equity (Real Estate)	C+	C	B	Down	Y	2,500
DWS RREEF Real Estate Securities Fund - Class T	RRRTX	NAS CM	Open End	Real Estate Sector Equity (Real Estate)	C+	C	B	Down	Y	1,000
DWS S&P 500 Index Fund - Class A	SXPAX	NAS CM	Open End	US Equity Large Cap Blend (Growth & Income)	B-	C	B		Y	1,000
DWS S&P 500 Index Fund - Class C	SXPCX	NAS CM	Open End	US Equity Large Cap Blend (Growth & Income)	B-	C	B		Y	1,000
DWS S&P 500 Index Fund - Class R6	SXPRX	NAS CM	Open End	US Equity Large Cap Blend (Growth & Income)	B-	C	B		Y	0
DWS S&P 500 Index Fund - Class S	SCPIX	NAS CM	Open End	US Equity Large Cap Blend (Growth & Income)	B-	C	B		Y	2,500
DWS Science and Technology Fund - Class A	KTCAX	NAS CM	Open End	Technology Sector Equity (Technology)	C+	C+	B-	Down	Y	1,000
DWS Science and Technology Fund - Class C	KTCCX	NAS CM	Open End	Technology Sector Equity (Technology)	C+	C+	B-	Down	Y	1,000
DWS Science and Technology Fund - Class Inst	KTCIX	NAS CM	Open End	Technology Sector Equity (Technology)	C+	C+	B-	Down	Y	1,000,000

★ Expanded analysis of this fund is included in Section II.

Min Additional Investment	3-Month Total Return	6-Month Total Return	1-Year Total Return	3-Year Total Return	5-Year Total Return	Dividend Yield (TTM)	Expense Ratio	3-Yr Std Deviation	3-Year Beta	NAV	Total Assets (MIL)	%Cash	%Stocks	%Bonds	%Other	Turnover Ratio	Last Bull Market Total Return	Last Bear Market Total Return	Front End Fee (%)	Back End Fee (%)	Inception Date
	TOTAL RETURNS					PERFORMANCE				ASSETS		ASSET ALLOCATION & TURNOVER					BULL & BEAR		FEES		
50	1.87	14.64	-1.95	18.13	21.60	0.95	1.24	13.11	0.97	14.64	197.7	1	99	0	0	114	22.23	-23.69	5.75		Aug-05
50	1.72	14.26	-2.62	15.59	17.19	0.25	1.99	13.1	0.97	14.18	197.7	1	99	0	0	114	21.68	-23.86		1.00	Aug-05
	1.95	14.82	-1.61	19.19	23.26	1.19	0.98	13.14	0.97	14.64	197.7	1	99	0	0	114	22.47	-23.59			Aug-05
	1.81	14.48	-2.17	17.24	20.10	0.71	1.49	13.16	0.98	14.62	197.7	1	99	0	0	114	22.2	-23.79			Mar-11
	1.95	14.77	-1.64	19.33	23.55	1.28	0.88	13.14	0.97	14.6	197.7	1	99	0	0	114	22.47	-23.59			Aug-14
50	1.95	14.83	-1.62	19.12	23.18	1.18	0.99	13.13	0.97	14.63	197.7	1	99	0	0	114	22.35	-23.61			Aug-05
50	2.88	11.09	5.06	17.23	16.18	1.92	1.13	5.87	1.36	13.32	84.4	5	37	57	0	45	13.32	-12.24	5.75		Dec-00
50	2.69	10.68	4.28	14.61	11.89	1.19	1.88	5.86	1.36	13.32	84.4	5	37	57	0	45	12.89	-12.49		1.00	Dec-00
50	2.96	11.16	5.26	18.05	17.58	2.16	0.88	5.85	1.35	13.29	84.4	5	37	57	0	45	13.59	-12.15			Nov-96
50	3.38	13.76	2.87	20.70	11.92	1.85	1.15	8.47	1.64	15.87	83.6	5	49	42	0	35	15.11	-14.19	5.75		Dec-00
50	3.20	13.38	2.10	17.99	7.79	1.17	1.9	8.47	1.64	15.76	83.6	5	49	42	0	35	14.63	-14.5		1.00	Dec-00
50	3.45	13.91	3.13	21.53	13.37	2.07	0.9	8.44	1.63	15.88	83.6	5	49	42	0	35	15.29	-14.11			Nov-96
50	2.87	12.85	4.16	24.50	19.94	1.26	1.22	8.02	1.51	9.66	27.8	4	61	34	0	45	18.5	-18.49	5.75		Nov-04
50	2.66	12.48	3.37	21.69	15.48	0.59	1.97	7.95	1.5	9.64	27.8	4	61	34	0	45	18.06	-18.72		1.00	Nov-04
50	2.87	12.99	4.44	25.35	21.42	1.49	0.97	7.99	1.5	9.65	27.8	4	61	34	0	45	18.78	-18.39			Nov-04
50	4.60	20.87	10.27	15.18	15.39	1.97	1.37	9.73	0.61	15.57	1,593	1	99	0	0	78	14.29	-3.71	5.75		Jun-08
50	4.46	20.43	9.39	12.61	11.16	1.26	2.12	9.72	0.61	15.38	1,593	1	99	0	0	78	13.8	-4.09		1.00	Jun-08
	4.69	21.04	10.51	16.03	16.97	2.21	1.12	9.74	0.61	15.5	1,593	1	99	0	0	78	14.56	-3.63			Jun-08
	4.77	21.14	10.58	16.45	17.27	2.28	1.07	9.77	0.61	15.52	1,593	1	99	0	0	78	14.56	-3.63			Aug-14
50	4.67	20.98	10.50	15.92	16.56	2.14	1.2	9.74	0.61	15.51	1,593	1	99	0	0	78	14.58	-3.72			Jun-08
50	4.68	20.88	10.31	15.26	15.61	2.01	1.37	9.76	0.61	15.58	1,593	1	99	0	0	78	14.4	-3.73	2.50		Jun-17
50	0.63	15.74	9.75	17.57	31.39	1.57	1.2	11.04	0.6	9.49	750.9	1	98	0	1	116	23.44	-20.42	5.75		Jul-06
50	0.53	15.37	9.03	14.95	26.59	1.37	1.95	10.97	0.6	9.47	750.9	1	98	0	1	116	23.06	-20.66		1.00	Jul-06
	0.74	15.92	10.05	18.41	33.14	1.8	0.95	11.04	0.6	9.47	750.9	1	98	0	1	116	23.75	-20.29			Jul-06
	0.74	15.90	10.16	18.39	33.12	1.8	0.95	10.9	0.6	9.48	750.9	1	98	0	1	116	23.76	-20.29			Nov-16
50	0.74	15.90	10.05	18.06	32.02	1.71	1.05	10.97	0.61	9.48	750.9	1	98	0	1	116	23.97	-20.34			Jul-06
50	0.63	15.76	9.76	17.59	31.56	1.58	1.2	10.98	0.6	9.48	750.9	1	98	0	1	116	23.57	-20.37	2.50		Jun-17
50	2.79	25.75	8.63	7.57		5.41	1.59	16.12	0.94	7.43	11.5	0	100	0	0				5.75		Feb-15
50	2.59	25.44	7.95	5.28		4.65	2.34	16.08	0.94	7.44	11.5	0	100	0	0					1.00	Feb-15
	2.86	26.09	8.91	8.54		5.66	1.34	16.06	0.94	7.44	11.5	0	100	0	0						Feb-15
50	2.83	26.06	8.80	8.20		5.56	1.44	16.07	0.94	7.43	11.5	0	100	0	0						Feb-15
50	2.22	15.69	7.48	20.00	14.13	1.9	1.22	8.51	0.58	10.14	541.6	6	59	17	18	72	8.11	-11.22	5.75		Jul-07
50	2.04	15.22	6.60	17.27	9.81	1.2	1.97	8.47	0.58	10.06	541.6	6	59	17	18	72	7.68	-11.47		1.00	Jul-07
	2.30	15.90	7.82	20.90	15.86	2.16	0.95	8.44	0.58	10.06	541.6	6	59	17	18	72	8.3	-11.14			Jul-07
	2.16	15.53	7.17	18.99	12.77	1.67	1.47	8.47	0.58	10.2	541.6	6	59	17	18	72	8.07	-11.34			Jun-11
	2.30	15.77	7.71	20.89	15.85	2.16	0.95	8.44	0.58	10.06	541.6	6	59	17	18	72	8.3	-11.14			Nov-14
50	2.27	15.87	7.69	20.56	14.96	2.04	1.07	8.49	0.58	10.06	541.6	6	59	17	18	72	8.17	-11.04			Jul-07
50	2.22	15.69	7.59	20.14	14.64	1.9	1.22	8.5	0.58	10.14	541.6	6	59	17	18	72	8.16	-11.22	2.50		Jun-17
50	2.12	19.18	13.42	16.26	47.87	1.91	0.97	12.61	0.55	22.23	1,246	0	100	0	0	166	31.9	-17.25	5.75		Sep-02
50	1.95	18.78	12.67	13.89	42.87	1.24	1.69	12.59	0.54	22.52	1,246	0	100	0	0	166	31.29	-17.46		1.00	Sep-02
	2.20	19.41	13.79	17.47	50.42	2.24	0.65	12.62	0.55	22.19	1,246	0	100	0	0	166	32.04	-17.07			Dec-99
	2.08	19.05	13.13	15.22	45.59	1.63	1.27	12.58	0.55	22.24	1,246	0	100	0	0	166	31.38	-17.16			Oct-03
	2.28	19.53	13.91	17.90	51.25	2.35	0.54	12.6	0.54	22.2	1,246	0	100	0	0	166	32.04	-17.07			Aug-14
50	2.22	19.33	13.71	17.17	49.81	2.16	0.72	12.61	0.55	22.36	1,246	0	100	0	0	166	32.05	-17.12			May-05
50	2.18	19.28	13.54	16.58	48.54	2.01	0.88	12.6	0.54	22.24	1,246	0	100	0	0	166	31.85	-17.16	2.50		Jun-17
50	4.14	19.26	10.25	48.82	61.88	1.29	0.57	12.08	0.99	31.49	1,006	1	99	0	0	3	24.74	-16.5	4.50		Feb-05
50	3.97	18.80	9.44	45.62	56.29	0.62	1.28	12.08	0.99	31.42	1,006	1	99	0	0	3	24.19	-16.73		1.00	Feb-05
	4.22	19.41	10.57	50.18	64.61	1.61	0.24	12.09	0.99	31.56	1,006	1	99	0	0	3	25	-16.32			Mar-17
50	4.23	19.41	10.51	49.99	64.08	1.53	0.32	12.09	0.99	31.56	1,006	1	99	0	0	3	24.86	-16.34			Aug-97
50	5.22	26.11	9.66	88.74	98.86	0	0.93	15.57	1.08	23.37	875.4	4	96	0	0	34	28.57	-16.76	5.75		Sep-48
50	5.00	25.54	8.69	83.76	90.30	0	1.78	15.54	1.07	14.89	875.4	4	96	0	0	34	28.02	-17.09		1.00	May-94
	5.30	26.25	9.89	89.97	101.16	0	0.72	15.56	1.08	25.82	875.4	4	96	0	0	34	28.86	-16.63			Aug-02

	MARKET			FUND TYPE, CATEGORY & OBJECTIVE	RATINGS					MINIMUMS
Fund Name	Ticker Symbol	Traded On	Fund Type	Category and (Prospectus Objective)	Overall Rating	Reward Rating	Risk Rating	Recent Up/ Downgrade	Open to New Investors	Min Initial Investment
DWS Science and Technology Fund - Class S	KTCSX	NAS CM	Open End	Technology Sector Equity (Technology)	C+	C+	B-	Down	Y	2,500
DWS Small Cap Core Fund - Class A	SZCAX	NAS CM	Open End	US Equity Small Cap (Small Company)	C-	C-	C	Down	Y	1,000
DWS Small Cap Core Fund - Class C	SZCCX	NAS CM	Open End	US Equity Small Cap (Small Company)	C-	C-	C	Down	Y	1,000
DWS Small Cap Core Fund - Class Inst	SZCIX	NAS CM	Open End	US Equity Small Cap (Small Company)	C-	C-	C	Down	Y	1,000,000
DWS Small Cap Core Fund - Class R6	SZCRX	NAS CM	Open End	US Equity Small Cap (Small Company)	C-	C-	C	Down	Y	0
DWS Small Cap Core Fund - Class S	SSLCX	NAS CM	Open End	US Equity Small Cap (Small Company)	C-	C-	C	Down	Y	2,500
DWS Small Cap Core Fund - Class T	SZCTX	NAS CM	Open End	US Equity Small Cap (Small Company)	C-	C-	C	Down	Y	1,000
DWS Small Cap Growth Fund - Class A	SSDAX	NAS CM	Open End	US Equity Small Cap (Small Company)	C	C	C+		Y	1,000
DWS Small Cap Growth Fund - Class C	SSDCX	NAS CM	Open End	US Equity Small Cap (Small Company)	C	C-	C+		Y	1,000
DWS Small Cap Growth Fund - Class Inst	SSDIX	NAS CM	Open End	US Equity Small Cap (Small Company)	C	C	C+		Y	1,000,000
DWS Small Cap Growth Fund - Class R	SSDGX	NAS CM	Open End	US Equity Small Cap (Small Company)	C	C	C+		Y	0
DWS Small Cap Growth Fund - Class R6	SSDZX	NAS CM	Open End	US Equity Small Cap (Small Company)	C	C	C+		Y	0
DWS Small Cap Growth Fund - Class S	SSDSX	NAS CM	Open End	US Equity Small Cap (Small Company)	C	C	C+		Y	2,500
DWS U.S. Multi-Factor Fund - Class Inst	DMFJX	NAS CM	Open End	US Equity Large Cap Blend (Growth)	C	C	B-	Up	Y	1,000,000
DWS U.S. Multi-Factor Fund - Class R6	DMFRX	NAS CM	Open End	US Equity Large Cap Blend (Growth)	C	C	B-	Up	Y	0
DWS World Dividend Fund - Class A	SERAX	NAS CM	Open End	Global Equity Large Cap (Equity-Income)	C	D+	B		Y	1,000
DWS World Dividend Fund - Class C	SERCX	NAS CM	Open End	Global Equity Large Cap (Equity-Income)	C	D+	B	Up	Y	1,000
DWS World Dividend Fund - Class Inst	SERNX	NAS CM	Open End	Global Equity Large Cap (Equity-Income)	C	C-	B		Y	1,000,000
DWS World Dividend Fund - Class R6	SERZX	NAS CM	Open End	Global Equity Large Cap (Equity-Income)	C	C-	B		Y	0
DWS World Dividend Fund - Class S	SCGEX	NAS CM	Open End	Global Equity Large Cap (Equity-Income)	C	C-	B		Y	2,500
DWS World Dividend Fund - Class T	SERTX	NAS CM	Open End	Global Equity Large Cap (Equity-Income)	C	D+	B		Y	1,000
Dynamic International Opportunity Fund Class I	ICCIX	NAS CM	Open End	Global Equity Large Cap (Growth)	C	C-	B		Y	100,000
Dynamic International Opportunity Fund Class N	ICCNX	NAS CM	Open End	Global Equity Large Cap (Growth)	C	C-	B		Y	5,000
Dynamic U.S. Opportunity Fund Class I	ICSIX	NAS CM	Open End	Moderate Alloc (Growth)	C+	C	B	Up	Y	100,000
Dynamic U.S. Opportunity Fund Class N	ICSNX	NAS CM	Open End	Moderate Alloc (Growth)	C+	C	B	Up	Y	5,000
Eagle Capital Growth Fund, Inc.	GRF	AMEX	Closed End	US Equity Large Cap Blend (Growth)	C	C+	D+	Down	Y	
Eagle Growth and Income Opportunities Fund	EGIF	NYSE	Closed End	Cautious Alloc (Growth & Income)	C	C	C-	Up	Y	
Eagle MLP Strategy Fund Class A Shares	EGLAX	NAS CM	Open End	Energy Sector Equity (Growth & Income)	D+	D+	D+	Down	Y	2,500
Eagle MLP Strategy Fund Class C Shares	EGLCX	NAS CM	Open End	Energy Sector Equity (Growth & Income)	D+	D+	D+	Down	Y	2,500
Eagle MLP Strategy Fund Class I Shares	EGLIX	NAS CM	Open End	Energy Sector Equity (Growth & Income)	C-	C-	C-	Down	Y	100,000
Eagle MLP Strategy Fund Class N Shares	EGLNX	NAS CM	Open End	Energy Sector Equity (Growth & Income)	C-	C-	C-	Down	Y	10,000,000
EAS Crow Point Alternatives Fund Institutional Class	EASIX	NAS CM	Open End	Multialternative (Growth)	C	C-	C		Y	1,000
EAS Crow Point Alternatives Fund Investor Class	EASAX	NAS CM	Open End	Multialternative (Growth)	C	C-	C	Up	Y	500
Eaton Vance Atlanta Capital Focused Growth Fund Class C	EAGCX	NAS CM	Open End	US Equity Large Cap Growth (Growth)	B+	B+	A-	Up	Y	1,000
Eaton Vance Atlanta Capital Select Equity Fund Class A	ESEAX	NAS CM	Open End	US Equity Large Cap Growth (Growth)	B	B	B+		Y	1,000
Eaton Vance Atlanta Capital Select Equity Fund Class C	ESECX	NAS CM	Open End	US Equity Large Cap Growth (Growth)	B	B	B+		Y	1,000
Eaton Vance Atlanta Capital Select Equity Fund Class I	ESEIX	NAS CM	Open End	US Equity Large Cap Growth (Growth)	B	B	B+		Y	250,000
Eaton Vance Atlanta Capital Select Equity Fund Class R6	ESERX	NAS CM	Open End	US Equity Large Cap Growth (Growth)	B	B	B+		Y	1,000,000
Eaton Vance Atlanta Capital SMID-Cap Fund Class A	EAASX	NAS CM	Open End	US Equity Mid Cap (Growth)	B-	B-	B			1,000
Eaton Vance Atlanta Capital SMID-Cap Fund Class C	ECASX	NAS CM	Open End	US Equity Mid Cap (Growth)	B-	B-	B-			1,000
Eaton Vance Atlanta Capital SMID-Cap Fund Class I	EISMX	NAS CM	Open End	US Equity Mid Cap (Growth)	B	B	B	Up		250,000
Eaton Vance Atlanta Capital SMID-Cap Fund Class R	ERSMX	NAS CM	Open End	US Equity Mid Cap (Growth)	B-	B-	B-			1,000
Eaton Vance Atlanta Capital SMID-Cap Fund Class R6	ERASX	NAS CM	Open End	US Equity Mid Cap (Growth)	B	B	B	Up	Y	1,000,000
Eaton Vance Balanced Fund Class A	EVIFX	NAS CM	Open End	Moderate Alloc (Balanced)	B	C+	A-		Y	1,000
Eaton Vance Balanced Fund Class B	EMIFX	NAS CM	Open End	Moderate Alloc (Balanced)	B	C	A-	Up		1,000
Eaton Vance Balanced Fund Class C	ECIFX	NAS CM	Open End	Moderate Alloc (Balanced)	B	C	A-	Up	Y	1,000
Eaton Vance Balanced Fund Class I	EIIFX	NAS CM	Open End	Moderate Alloc (Balanced)	B	C+	A-		Y	250,000
Eaton Vance Balanced Fund Class R	ERIFX	NAS CM	Open End	Moderate Alloc (Balanced)	B	C+	A-	Up	Y	1,000
Eaton Vance Balanced Fund Class R6	ESIFX	NAS CM	Open End	Moderate Alloc (Balanced)	B	C+	A-		Y	1,000,000
Eaton Vance Dividend Builder Fund Class A	EVTMX	NAS CM	Open End	US Equity Large Cap Blend (Equity-Income)	B-	C+	B		Y	1,000
Eaton Vance Dividend Builder Fund Class C	ECTMX	NAS CM	Open End	US Equity Large Cap Blend (Equity-Income)	B-	C	B		Y	1,000
Eaton Vance Dividend Builder Fund Class I	EIUTX	NAS CM	Open End	US Equity Large Cap Blend (Equity-Income)	B-	C+	B		Y	250,000

★ Expanded analysis of this fund is included in Section II.

Min Additional Investment	3-Month Total Return	6-Month Total Return	1-Year Total Return	3-Year Total Return	5-Year Total Return	Dividend Yield (TTM)	Expense Ratio	3-Yr Std Deviation	3-Year Beta	NAV	Total Assets (MIL)	%Cash	%Stocks	%Bonds	%Other	Turnover Ratio	Last Bull Market Total Return	Last Bear Market Total Return	Front End Fee (%)	Back End Fee (%)	Inception Date
	TOTAL RETURNS					PERFORMANCE				ASSETS		ASSET ALLOCATION & TURNOVER					BULL & BEAR		FEES		
50	5.27	26.26	9.83	89.68	100.38	0	0.77	15.56	1.08	23.75	875.4	4	96	0	0	34	28.66	-16.73			Dec-04
50	-0.76	13.79	-9.96	30.56	32.00	0.19	1.09	18.38	1.06	27.23	369.3	4	96	0	0	44	30.92	-25.39	5.75		Jun-01
50	-0.97	13.36	-10.66	27.64	27.16	0	1.84	18.4	1.06	22.39	369.3	4	96	0	0	44	30.36	-25.67		1.00	Jun-01
	-0.69	13.94	-9.73	31.62	33.79	0.41	0.84	18.4	1.06	28.52	369.3	4	96	0	0	44	31.13	-25.3			Jun-16
	-0.69	13.93	-9.71	31.67	33.83	0.46	0.79	18.39	1.06	28.53	369.3	4	96	0	0	44	31.13	-25.3			Jun-16
50	-0.73	13.88	-9.77	31.41	33.57	0.37	0.89	18.4	1.06	28.54	369.3	4	96	0	0	44	31.13	-25.3			Jul-00
50	-0.76	13.80	-9.97	30.58	32.07	0.19	1.09	18.39	1.06	27.2	369.3	4	96	0	0	44	30.94	-25.37	2.50		Jun-17
50	2.00	16.68	-4.44	37.66	31.69	0	1.21	16.76	0.95	27.48	370.1	2	98	0	0	43	26.14	-21.27	5.75		Jun-02
50	1.79	16.22	-5.19	34.48	26.80	0	1.96	16.73	0.94	22.06	370.1	2	98	0	0	43	25.53	-21.46		1.00	Jun-02
	2.07	16.84	-4.20	38.65	33.44	0	0.94	16.76	0.95	29.55	370.1	2	98	0	0	43	26.41	-21.08			Dec-04
	1.94	16.53	-4.70	36.57	29.97	0	1.46	16.75	0.95	26.78	370.1	2	98	0	0	43	25.94	-21.36			May-12
	2.08	16.85	-4.12	38.82	33.43	0	0.86	16.76	0.95	27.94	370.1	2	98	0	0	43	26.14	-21.27			Aug-14
50	2.10	16.86	-4.20	38.69	33.37	0	0.95	16.76	0.95	29.1	370.1	2	98	0	0	43	26.27	-21.18			Dec-04
	4.64	20.05	7.41			1.3	0.35			11.66	295.8	1	99	0	0	54					May-17
	4.66	20.08	7.47			1.34	0.3			11.66	295.8	1	99	0	0	54					May-17
50	2.72	15.19	1.12	12.18	7.30	1.04	1.22	10.45	0.99	30.25	176.8	8	88	0	0	30	13.79	-15.61	5.75		Mar-01
50	2.55	14.79	0.40	9.72	3.40	0.33	1.97	10.45	0.99	30.01	176.8	8	88	0	0	30	13.34	-15.86		1.00	Mar-01
	2.76	15.35	1.38	13.00	8.75	1.28	0.97	10.47	0.99	30.53	176.8	8	88	0	0	30	14.05	-15.49			Mar-05
	2.76	15.35	1.43	13.18	8.76	1.33	0.96	10.48	0.99	30.27	176.8	8	88	0	0	30	13.95	-15.56			Aug-14
50	2.80	15.36	1.40	12.96	8.58	1.24	0.97	10.47	0.99	30.29	176.8	8	88	0	0	30	13.95	-15.56			Oct-94
50	2.72	15.23	1.16	12.15	7.27	1.04	1.22	10.47	0.99	30.23	176.8	8	88	0	0	30	13.78	-15.65	2.50		Jun-17
	1.76	10.07	2.63	23.32	11.76	1.8	1.77	11.62	0.94	10.93	99.1	2	98	0	0	189					Dec-11
1,000	1.67	9.84	2.32	22.46	10.37	1.43	2.02	11.64	0.95	10.93	99.1	2	98	0	0	189					Dec-11
	3.50	19.00	3.37	33.01	34.18	0.7	1.4	11.17	0.85	11.52	51.0	0	100	0	0	352					Dec-11
1,000	3.49	18.84	3.17	32.14	32.60	0.41	1.65	11.16	0.85	11.54	51.0	0	100	0	0	352					Dec-11
	4.75	7.48	13.55	38.07	55.02	0.77	1.61	9.82	0.56	9.48	35.3	8	92	0	0	42	18.24	-14.07			Jul-90
	0.83	16.79	2.24	7.76		4.77	2.71	10.84		18.09	129.9	1	81	29	-35	30					Jun-15
100	-2.11	19.81	-2.56	0.91	-41.38	7.19	1.66	18.72	1.02	6.48	486.5	5	89	0	6	29			5.75		Sep-12
100	-2.30	19.43	-3.18	-1.38	-43.51	6.4	2.41	18.72	1.02	6.46	486.5	5	89	0	6	29					Feb-13
100	-2.05	19.92	-2.31	1.57	-40.62	7.44	1.41	18.75	1.03	6.49	486.5	5	89	0	6	29					Sep-12
100	-2.05	20.10	-2.16	1.72	-40.53		1.26	18.68	1.02	6.5	486.5	5	89	0	6	29					Aug-18
	0.10	5.71	-2.14	9.37	6.35	0	3.26	6.71	2.36	9.25	36.1	15	50	6	29	66	5.05	-11.37			Aug-08
500	0.00	5.53	-2.48	8.45	4.92	0	3.51	6.7	2.36	9.15	36.1	15	50	6	29	66	4.85	-11.44	5.50		Aug-08
	6.70	26.83	25.19	79.16	86.40	0	1.8	10.88	0.75	10.35	71.7	4	96	0	0	14	23.38	-18.36		1.00	May-11
	8.31	27.13	22.60	55.09	78.59	0	1.05	10.97	0.83	24.74	489.2	4	96	0	0	3			5.75		Jan-12
	8.13	26.65	21.70	51.67	71.93	0	1.8	10.98	0.83	23.52	489.2	4	96	0	0	3				1.00	Mar-13
	8.39	27.30	22.97	56.26	80.87	0	0.8	10.95	0.83	25.18	489.2	4	96	0	0	3					Jan-12
	8.42	27.30	23.02	56.38	81.02	0	0.75	10.99	0.83	25.22	489.2	4	96	0	0	3					Feb-17
	8.91	27.41	13.73	56.78	87.89	0	1.16	13.68	0.82	33.83	12,862	2	98	0	0	5	29.89	-19.15	5.75		Nov-03
100	8.75	26.95	12.93	53.35	81.06	0	1.91	13.67	0.82	30.94	12,862	2	98	0	0	5	29.31	-19.38		1.00	Oct-09
	8.99	27.59	14.02	57.98	90.25	0	0.91	13.68	0.82	37.68	12,862	2	98	0	0	5	30.09	-19.02			Apr-02
	8.84	27.27	13.46	55.65	85.56	0	1.41	13.68	0.82	32.85	12,862	2	98	0	0	5	29.72	-19.17			Aug-09
	9.00	27.66	14.13	58.42	91.19	0	0.82	13.69	0.82	37.89	12,862	2	98	0	0	5	30.09	-19.02			Jul-14
	4.87	16.25	10.55	29.56	39.22	1.46	0.98	7.16	0.56	9.5	885.8	1	62	37	0	7	15.59	-10.59	5.75		Apr-32
	4.56	15.75	9.60	26.60	33.96	0.59	1.73	7.12	0.56	9.54	885.8	1	62	37	0	7	15.15	-10.94		5.00	Nov-93
	4.65	15.88	9.67	26.54	34.15	0.75	1.73	7.1	0.56	9.54	885.8	1	62	37	0	7	15.09	-10.9		1.00	Nov-93
	4.82	16.40	10.71	30.37	40.92	1.7	0.73	7.19	0.56	9.5	885.8	1	62	37	0	7	15.59	-10.59			Sep-12
	4.72	16.05	10.24	28.56	37.63	1.29	1.23	7.16	0.56	9.47	885.8	1	62	37	0	7	15.42	-10.69			May-16
	4.83	16.41	10.75	30.60	40.43	1.74	0.69	7.16	0.56	9.5	885.8	1	62	37	0	7	15.59	-10.59			May-16
	4.70	18.45	10.09	40.01	54.07	1.69	1.02	11.11	0.9	14.56	895.2	0	100	0	0	41	21.45	-14.62	5.75		Dec-81
	4.47	17.94	9.24	36.88	48.31	0.96	1.77	11.12	0.9	14.65	895.2	0	100	0	0	41	20.96	-14.86		1.00	Nov-93
	4.77	18.61	10.37	41.11	55.96	1.92	0.77	11.12	0.9	14.55	895.2	0	100	0	0	41	21.76	-14.54			Jun-05

Fund Name	MARKET: Ticker Symbol	MARKET: Traded On	FUND TYPE: Fund Type	CATEGORY & OBJECTIVE: Category and (Prospectus Objective)	RATINGS: Overall Rating	RATINGS: Reward Rating	RATINGS: Risk Rating	RATINGS: Recent Up/ Downgrade	Open to New Investors	MINIMUMS: Min Initial Investment
Eaton Vance Emerging & Frontier Countries Equity Cls A	EACOX	NAS CM	Open End	Global Emerg Mkts (Growth & Income)	C	C	C+		Y	1,000
Eaton Vance Emerging & Frontier Countries Equity Cls I	EICOX	NAS CM	Open End	Global Emerg Mkts (Growth & Income)	C	C	B-		Y	250,000
Eaton Vance Enhanced Equity Income Fund	EOI	NYSE	Closed End	Long/Short Equity (Equity-Income)	C+	C	C+		Y	
Eaton Vance Enhanced Equity Income Fund II	EOS	NYSE	Closed End	Long/Short Equity (Equity-Income)	C+	C	C+	Down	Y	
Eaton Vance Focused Global Opportunities Fund Class I	EFGIX	NAS CM	Open End	Global Equity Large Cap (World Stock)	C+	C	B	Up	Y	250,000
Eaton Vance Focused Growth Opportunities Fund Class A	EAFGX	NAS CM	Open End	US Equity Large Cap Growth (Growth)	B-	C	B	Down	Y	1,000
Eaton Vance Focused Growth Opportunities Fund Class C	ECFGX	NAS CM	Open End	US Equity Large Cap Growth (Growth)	C+	C	B	Down	Y	1,000
Eaton Vance Focused Growth Opportunities Fund Class I	EIFGX	NAS CM	Open End	US Equity Large Cap Growth (Growth)	B-	C	B	Down	Y	250,000
Eaton Vance Focused Value Opportunities Fund Class A	EAFVX	NAS CM	Open End	US Equity Large Cap Value (Growth & Income)	B-	C+	B		Y	1,000
Eaton Vance Focused Value Opportunities Fund Class C	ECFVX	NAS CM	Open End	US Equity Large Cap Value (Growth & Income)	B-	C+	B		Y	1,000
Eaton Vance Focused Value Opportunities Fund Class I	EIFVX	NAS CM	Open End	US Equity Large Cap Value (Growth & Income)	B-	C+	B		Y	250,000
Eaton Vance Global Income Builder Fund Class A	EDIAX	NAS CM	Open End	Moderate Alloc (Growth & Income)	B-	C	B+	Up	Y	1,000
Eaton Vance Global Income Builder Fund Class C	EDICX	NAS CM	Open End	Moderate Alloc (Growth & Income)	B-	C	B+	Up	Y	1,000
Eaton Vance Global Income Builder Fund Class I	EDIIX	NAS CM	Open End	Moderate Alloc (Growth & Income)	B-	C	B+	Up	Y	250,000
Eaton Vance Global Income Builder Fund Class R	EDIRX	NAS CM	Open End	Moderate Alloc (Growth & Income)	B-	C	B+	Up	Y	1,000
Eaton Vance Global Small-Cap Equity Fund Class A	ESVAX	NAS CM	Open End	Global Equity Mid/Small Cap (Small Company)	C+	C	B	Up	Y	1,000
Eaton Vance Global Small-Cap Equity Fund Class C	ESVCX	NAS CM	Open End	Global Equity Mid/Small Cap (Small Company)	C+	C	B	Up	Y	1,000
Eaton Vance Global Small-Cap Equity Fund Class I	ESVIX	NAS CM	Open End	Global Equity Mid/Small Cap (Small Company)	C+	C	B	Up	Y	250,000
Eaton Vance Greater China Growth Fund Class A	EVCGX	NAS CM	Open End	Greater China Equity (Foreign Stock)	C+	C	B-	Up	Y	1,000
Eaton Vance Greater China Growth Fund Class C	ECCGX	NAS CM	Open End	Greater China Equity (Foreign Stock)	C	C	C+		Y	1,000
Eaton Vance Greater China Growth Fund Class I	EICGX	NAS CM	Open End	Greater China Equity (Foreign Stock)	C+	C	B-	Up	Y	250,000
Eaton Vance Greater India Fund Class A	ETGIX	NAS CM	Open End	India Equity (Foreign Stock)	C	C	C+		Y	1,000
Eaton Vance Greater India Fund Class B	EMGIX	NAS CM	Open End	India Equity (Foreign Stock)	C	C	C+			1,000
Eaton Vance Greater India Fund Class C	ECGIX	NAS CM	Open End	India Equity (Foreign Stock)	C	C	C+		Y	1,000
Eaton Vance Greater India Fund Class I	EGIIX	NAS CM	Open End	India Equity (Foreign Stock)	C	C	C+		Y	250,000
Eaton Vance Growth Fund Class A	EALCX	NAS CM	Open End	US Equity Large Cap Growth (Growth & Income)	C+	C	B	Down	Y	1,000
Eaton Vance Growth Fund Class C	ECLCX	NAS CM	Open End	US Equity Large Cap Growth (Growth & Income)	C+	C	B	Down	Y	1,000
Eaton Vance Growth Fund Class I	ELCIX	NAS CM	Open End	US Equity Large Cap Growth (Growth & Income)	C+	C	B	Down	Y	250,000
Eaton Vance Growth Fund Class R	ELCRX	NAS CM	Open End	US Equity Large Cap Growth (Growth & Income)	C+	C	B	Down	Y	1,000
Eaton Vance Hexavest Global Equity Fund Class A	EHGAX	NAS CM	Open End	Global Equity Large Cap (World Stock)	B-	C	B	Up	Y	1,000
Eaton Vance Hexavest Global Equity Fund Class C	EHGCX	NAS CM	Open End	Global Equity Large Cap (World Stock)	C+	C	B	Up	Y	1,000
Eaton Vance Hexavest Global Equity Fund Class I	EHGIX	NAS CM	Open End	Global Equity Large Cap (World Stock)	B-	C	B+	Up	Y	250,000
Eaton Vance Hexavest International Equity Fund Class A	EHIAX	NAS CM	Open End	Global Equity Large Cap (Foreign Stock)	C	C-	B		Y	1,000
Eaton Vance Hexavest International Equity Fund Class I	EHIIX	NAS CM	Open End	Global Equity Large Cap (Foreign Stock)	C	C-	B		Y	250,000
Eaton Vance International Small-Cap Fund Class A	EILAX	NAS CM	Open End	Global Equity Mid/Small Cap (Small Company)	C	C	C+		Y	1,000
Eaton Vance International Small-Cap Fund Class I	EILIX	NAS CM	Open End	Global Equity Mid/Small Cap (Small Company)	C	C	C+		Y	250,000
Eaton Vance Large-Cap Value Fund Class A	EHSTX	NAS CM	Open End	US Equity Large Cap Value (Growth & Income)	B-	C+	B		Y	1,000
Eaton Vance Large-Cap Value Fund Class C	ECSTX	NAS CM	Open End	US Equity Large Cap Value (Growth & Income)	C+	C	B		Y	1,000
Eaton Vance Large-Cap Value Fund Class I	EILVX	NAS CM	Open End	US Equity Large Cap Value (Growth & Income)	B-	C+	B		Y	250,000
Eaton Vance Large-Cap Value Fund Class R	ERSTX	NAS CM	Open End	US Equity Large Cap Value (Growth & Income)	B-	C	B		Y	1,000
Eaton Vance Large-Cap Value Fund Class R6	ERLVX	NAS CM	Open End	US Equity Large Cap Value (Growth & Income)	B-	C+	B		Y	1,000,000
Eaton Vance Real Estate Fund Class A	EAREX	NAS CM	Open End	Real Estate Sector Equity (Real Estate)	C+	C	B-	Down	Y	1,000
Eaton Vance Real Estate Fund Class I	EIREX	NAS CM	Open End	Real Estate Sector Equity (Real Estate)	C+	C	B	Down	Y	250,000
Eaton Vance Richard Bernstein All Asset Strategy Cls A	EARAX	NAS CM	Open End	Moderate Alloc (Asset Alloc)	C	C	B		Y	1,000
Eaton Vance Richard Bernstein All Asset Strategy Cls C	ECRAX	NAS CM	Open End	Moderate Alloc (Asset Alloc)	C	C-	B-		Y	1,000
Eaton Vance Richard Bernstein All Asset Strategy Cls I	EIRAX	NAS CM	Open End	Moderate Alloc (Asset Alloc)	C	C	B		Y	250,000
Eaton Vance Richard Bernstein Equity Strategy Fund Class A	ERBAX	NAS CM	Open End	Global Equity Large Cap (Growth)	C+	C	B	Up	Y	1,000
Eaton Vance Richard Bernstein Equity Strategy Fund Class C	ERBCX	NAS CM	Open End	Global Equity Large Cap (Growth)	C	C	B		Y	1,000
Eaton Vance Richard Bernstein Equity Strategy Fund Class I	ERBIX	NAS CM	Open End	Global Equity Large Cap (Growth)	C+	C	B	Up	Y	250,000
Eaton Vance Risk-Managed Diversified Equity Income Fund	ETJ	NYSE	Closed End	Long/Short Equity (Equity-Income)	C+	C+	C+		Y	
Eaton Vance Small-Cap Fund Class A	ETEGX	NAS CM	Open End	US Equity Small Cap (Small Company)	C+	C	B	Down	Y	1,000
Eaton Vance Small-Cap Fund Class C	ECSMX	NAS CM	Open End	US Equity Small Cap (Small Company)	C+	C	B	Down	Y	1,000

★ Expanded analysis of this fund is included in Section II.

Min Additional Investment	TOTAL RETURNS 3-Month Total Return	6-Month Total Return	1-Year Total Return	3-Year Total Return	5-Year Total Return	PERFORMANCE Dividend Yield (TTM)	Expense Ratio	3-Yr Std Deviation	3-Year Beta	ASSETS NAV	Total Assets (MIL)	ASSET ALLOCATION & TURNOVER %Cash	%Stocks	%Bonds	%Other	Turnover Ratio	BULL & BEAR Last Bull Market Total Return	Last Bear Market Total Return	FEES Front End Fee (%)	Back End Fee (%)	Inception Date
	2.17	10.36	-0.83	30.27		2.54	1.65	10.78	0.74	10.33	175.8	8	91	0	0	39			5.75		Nov-14
	2.26	10.54	-0.56	31.28		2.68	1.4	10.78	0.74	10.38	175.8	8	91	0	0	39					Nov-14
	4.13	18.34	9.34	42.56	47.61	0.66	0	11.04	0.89	15.2	596.3	0	100	0	0	46	20.33	-15.99			Oct-04
	2.41	17.91	7.15	52.10	64.29	0	0	12.39	0.9	16.66	797.6	1	99	0	0	44	21.06	-14.18			Jan-05
	4.86	20.12	7.22	39.91		0.97	0.95	12.29	1.05	11.64	4.9	2	98	0	0	82					Dec-15
	1.55	20.16	8.55	59.02	76.87	0	1.05	14.48	1.04	22.23	262.9	3	97	0	0	79	24.57	-20.66	5.75		Mar-11
	1.36	19.71	7.74	55.54	70.43	0	1.8	14.49	1.04	20.83	262.9	3	97	0	0	79	24.07	-20.97		1.00	Mar-11
	1.61	20.34	8.81	60.22	79.02	0	0.8	14.5	1.04	22.6	262.9	3	97	0	0	79	24.8	-20.56			Mar-11
	6.56	20.93	10.93	45.58	49.93	0.98	1.05	13.04	1.03	16.23	104.5	0	100	0	0	98	24.39	-19.9	5.75		Mar-11
	6.42	20.52	10.17	42.33	44.51	0.36	1.8	13.06	1.04	15.91	104.5	0	100	0	0	98	23.86	-20.13		1.00	Mar-11
	6.61	21.11	11.23	46.67	51.86	1.13	0.8	13.04	1.03	16.29	104.5	0	100	0	0	98	24.69	-19.9			Mar-11
	3.64	14.86	5.84	26.67	26.76	3.56	1.17	8.52	0.73	9.09	302.5	2	58	38	0	143	17.63	-18.79	5.75		Nov-05
	3.37	14.48	4.99	23.88	22.15	2.87	1.92	8.56	0.74	8.99	302.5	2	58	38	0	143	17.1	-19.06		1.00	Nov-05
	3.71	15.04	6.14	27.74	28.60	3.83	0.92	8.52	0.73	9.08	302.5	2	58	38	0	143	17.79	-18.71			Jan-06
	3.59	14.78	5.47	25.62	25.14	3.32	1.42	8.53	0.73	9.06	302.5	2	58	38	0	143	17.52	-18.89			Jan-06
	5.46	19.63	3.27	46.59	31.40	0.2	1.35	11.71	0.86	13.89	38.1	0	99	0	1	41	24.36	-21.24	5.75		Mar-02
	5.31	19.18	2.50	43.37	26.58	0	2.1	11.75	0.86	10.5	38.1	0	99	0	1	41	23.83	-21.48		1.00	Mar-02
	5.57	19.80	3.55	47.68	33.10	0.4	1.1	11.72	0.86	14.4	38.1	0	99	0	1	41	24.55	-21.11			Oct-09
	-0.86	16.63	2.58	62.13	49.05	0.59	1.82	14.33	0.84	23.98	110.9	8	92	0	0	12	19.98	-28.27	5.75		Oct-92
	-1.05	16.20	1.86	58.77	43.87	0	2.52	14.32	0.84	22.44	110.9	8	92	0	0	12	19.56	-28.52		1.00	Dec-93
	-0.81	16.80	2.88	63.56	51.25	0.89	1.52	14.33	0.84	24.19	110.9	8	92	0	0	12	20.22	-28.21			Oct-09
	-0.17	6.16	1.75	31.23	46.25	1.11	1.62	16.35	0.96	33.9	218.7	1	99	0	0	29	-1.83	-23.33	5.75		May-94
	-0.37	5.76	1.01	28.44	41.17	1.28	2.32	16.32	0.96	29.36	218.7	1	99	0	0	29	-2.25	-23.53		5.00	May-94
	-0.34	5.80	1.02	28.46	41.24	1.29	2.32	16.36	0.96	29.14	218.7	1	99	0	0	29	-2.25	-23.56		1.00	Jul-06
	-0.11	6.31	2.04	32.38	48.45	1.09	1.32	16.36	0.96	34.69	218.7	1	99	0	0	29	-1.67	-23.23			Oct-09
	2.77	20.48	8.36	57.94	74.87	0	1.05	13.94	1.02	28.11	346.9	1	99	0	0	28	23.11	-17.76	5.75		Sep-02
	2.59	20.02	7.56	54.46	68.41	0	1.8	13.94	1.02	23.32	346.9	1	99	0	0	28	22.57	-17.97		1.00	Sep-02
	2.86	20.63	8.66	59.12	77.08	0	0.8	13.95	1.02	29.06	346.9	1	99	0	0	28	23.36	-17.66			May-07
	2.70	20.34	8.08	56.77	72.67	0	1.3	13.94	1.02	27.33	346.9	1	99	0	0	28	22.95	-17.83			Aug-09
	2.29	11.58	4.69	21.46	28.86	2.37	1.16	9.34	0.79	12.04	65.4	7	93	0	0	95			5.75		Aug-12
	2.04	11.15	3.91	18.74	24.16	1.61	1.91	9.31	0.78	11.96	65.4	7	93	0	0	95				1.00	Dec-16
	2.28	11.66	4.93	22.33	30.48	2.64	0.91	9.31	0.78	12.06	65.4	7	93	0	0	95					Aug-12
	1.60	10.33	1.44	17.25	5.07	0.07	1.16	9.96	0.85	11.42	50.2	10	90	0	0	98			5.75		Aug-12
	1.68	10.50	1.73	18.27	6.44	0.33	0.91	9.95	0.85	11.47	50.2	10	90	0	0	98					Aug-12
	2.90	13.69	-4.11	36.91		0.77	1.41	12.26	0.98	12.04	42.3	1	98	0	1	65			5.75		Dec-15
	2.98	13.86	-3.90	37.80		1.09	1.16	12.25	0.98	12.07	42.3	1	98	0	1	65					Dec-15
	5.78	20.20	10.88	39.75	41.88	1.14	1.06	12.64	1.02	19.54	1,726	0	100	0	0	48	22.42	-18.96	5.75		Sep-31
	5.54	19.79	10.07	36.59	36.56	0.3	1.81	12.65	1.02	19.59	1,726	0	100	0	0	48	21.88	-19.2		1.00	Nov-94
	5.82	20.39	11.17	40.79	43.60	1.36	0.81	12.66	1.03	19.62	1,726	0	100	0	0	48	22.65	-18.9			Dec-04
	5.67	20.04	10.63	38.66	40.02	0.91	1.31	12.66	1.03	19.48	1,726	0	100	0	0	48	22.3	-19.05			Feb-04
	5.78	20.42	11.24	41.11	44.17	1.42	0.72	12.62	1.02	19.63	1,726	0	100	0	0	48	22.42	-18.96			Jul-14
	1.75	18.35	10.80	13.92	45.12	1.59	1.25	12.66	0.96	15.11	49.8	0	100	0	0	35	30.05	-15.13	5.75		Jun-10
	1.81	18.50	11.07	14.82	46.99	1.82	1	12.72	0.96	15.11	49.8	0	100	0	0	35	30.31	-15.04			Apr-06
	1.55	8.38	0.41	21.42	19.60	0.49	1.32	7.7	0.11	14.34	680.4	6	50	43	0	44	8.78		5.75		Sep-11
	1.37	8.01	-0.26	18.67	15.20	0	2.07	7.71	0.11	14.02	680.4	6	50	43	0	44	8.24			1.00	Sep-11
	1.55	8.51	0.68	22.26	21.03	0.74	1.07	7.71	0.12	14.4	680.4	6	50	43	0	44	8.9				Sep-11
	2.49	15.99	1.77	36.23	30.50	0.02	1.28	11.86	1.01	16.46	817.6	2	98	0	0	43	14.98	-19.58	5.75		Oct-10
	2.27	15.56	1.03	33.18	25.64	0	2.03	11.87	1.01	16.19	817.6	2	98	0	0	43	14.43	-19.86		1.00	Oct-10
	2.55	16.13	2.05	37.27	32.12	0.27	1.03	11.89	1.02	16.48	817.6	2	98	0	0	43	15.04	-19.48			Oct-10
	2.21	10.87	6.99	23.46	20.63	2.85	0	7.12	0.54	9.41	599.2	0	100	0	0	53	4.44	-7.59			Jul-07
	7.14	24.09	7.41	56.19	55.63	0	1.21	14.18	0.81	13.65	84.4	2	98	0	0	44	22.87	-25.29	5.75		Jan-97
	6.90	23.61	6.66	52.81	49.87	0	1.96	14.16	0.81	11.15	84.4	2	98	0	0	44	22.28	-25.5		1.00	May-02

	MARKET		FUND TYPE, CATEGORY & OBJECTIVE		RATINGS				MINIMUMS	
Fund Name	Ticker Symbol	Traded On	Fund Type	Category and (Prospectus Objective)	Overall Rating	Reward Rating	Risk Rating	Recent Up/ Downgrade	Open to New Investors	Min Initial Investment
Eaton Vance Small-Cap Fund Class I	EISGX	NAS CM	Open End	US Equity Small Cap (Small Company)	C+	C	B	Down	Y	250,000
Eaton Vance Small-Cap Fund Class R	ERSGX	NAS CM	Open End	US Equity Small Cap (Small Company)	C+	C	B	Down	Y	1,000
Eaton Vance Special Equities Fund Class A	EVSEX	NAS CM	Open End	US Equity Mid Cap (Growth)	B-	C+	B		Y	1,000
Eaton Vance Special Equities Fund Class C	ECSEX	NAS CM	Open End	US Equity Mid Cap (Growth)	B-	C+	B		Y	1,000
Eaton Vance Special Equities Fund Class I	EISEX	NAS CM	Open End	US Equity Mid Cap (Growth)	B-	C+	B		Y	250,000
Eaton Vance Stock Fund Class A	EAERX	NAS CM	Open End	US Equity Large Cap Blend (Growth)	B-	C+	B		Y	1,000
Eaton Vance Stock Fund Class C	ECERX	NAS CM	Open End	US Equity Large Cap Blend (Growth)	B-	C	B		Y	1,000
Eaton Vance Stock Fund Institutional Class	EIERX	NAS CM	Open End	US Equity Large Cap Blend (Growth)	B-	C+	B		Y	250,000
Eaton Vance Tax-Advantaged Dividend Income Fund	EVT	NYSE	Closed End	Aggressive Alloc (Equity-Income)	C+	C+	C+		Y	
Eaton Vance Tax-Advantaged Global Dividend Income Fund	ETG	NYSE	Closed End	Alloc Miscellaneous (World Stock)	C	C	C+		Y	
Eaton Vance Tax-Advantaged Global Dividend Opp Fund	ETO	NYSE	Closed End	Alloc Miscellaneous (World Stock)	C	C	C-		Y	
Eaton Vance Tax-Managed Buy-Write Income Fund	ETB	NYSE	Closed End	Long/Short Equity (Equity-Income)	C	C	C-		Y	
Eaton Vance Tax-Managed Buy-Write Opportunities Fund	ETV	NYSE	Closed End	Long/Short Equity (Equity-Income)	C	C	C+	Down	Y	
Eaton Vance Tax-Managed Buy-Write Strategy Fund	EXD	NYSE	Closed End	Multialternative (Growth)	D+	D+	C-		Y	
Eaton Vance Tax-Managed Diversified Equity Income Fund	ETY	NYSE	Closed End	Long/Short Equity (Equity-Income)	C+	C	C+		Y	
Eaton Vance Tax-Managed Equity Asset Allocation Cls A	EAEAX	NAS CM	Open End	Aggressive Alloc (Asset Alloc)	B-	C	B		Y	1,000
Eaton Vance Tax-Managed Equity Asset Allocation Cls B	EBEAX	NAS CM	Open End	Aggressive Alloc (Asset Alloc)	B-	C	B	Up		1,000
Eaton Vance Tax-Managed Equity Asset Allocation Cls C	ECEAX	NAS CM	Open End	Aggressive Alloc (Asset Alloc)	B-	C	B	Up	Y	1,000
Eaton Vance Tax-Managed Equity Asset Allocation Cls I	EIEAX	NAS CM	Open End	Aggressive Alloc (Asset Alloc)	B-	C	B		Y	250,000
Eaton Vance Tax-Managed Global Buy-Write Opp Fund	ETW	NYSE	Closed End	Long/Short Equity (World Stock)	C	C	C+		Y	
Eaton Vance Tax-Managed Global Diversified Eq Income Fund	EXG	NYSE	Closed End	Long/Short Equity (World Stock)	C	C	C+		Y	
Eaton Vance Tax-Managed Global Dividend Income Cls A	EADIX	NAS CM	Open End	Global Equity Large Cap (Equity-Income)	C+	C	B	Up	Y	1,000
Eaton Vance Tax-Managed Global Dividend Income Cls B	EBDIX	NAS CM	Open End	Global Equity Large Cap (Equity-Income)	C+	C	B	Up		1,000
Eaton Vance Tax-Managed Global Dividend Income Cls C	ECDIX	NAS CM	Open End	Global Equity Large Cap (Equity-Income)	C+	C	B	Up	Y	1,000
Eaton Vance Tax-Managed Global Dividend Income Cls I	EIDIX	NAS CM	Open End	Global Equity Large Cap (Equity-Income)	C+	C	B	Up	Y	250,000
Eaton Vance Tax-Managed Growth 1.0 Fund	CAPEX	NAS CM	Open End	US Equity Large Cap Blend (Growth)	B-	C	B			0
Eaton Vance Tax-Managed Growth 1.1 Fund Class A	ETTGX	NAS CM	Open End	US Equity Large Cap Growth (Growth)	B-	C	B			1,000
Eaton Vance Tax-Managed Growth 1.1 Fund Class B	EMTGX	NAS CM	Open End	US Equity Large Cap Growth (Growth)	C+	C	B	Down		1,000
Eaton Vance Tax-Managed Growth 1.1 Fund Class C	ECTGX	NAS CM	Open End	US Equity Large Cap Growth (Growth)	C+	C	B			1,000
Eaton Vance Tax-Managed Growth 1.1 Fund Class I	EITMX	NAS CM	Open End	US Equity Large Cap Growth (Growth)	B-	C	B			250,000
Eaton Vance Tax-Managed Growth 1.2 Fund Class A	EXTGX	NAS CM	Open End	US Equity Large Cap Growth (Growth)	B-	C	B		Y	1,000
Eaton Vance Tax-Managed Growth 1.2 Fund Class B	EYTGX	NAS CM	Open End	US Equity Large Cap Growth (Growth)	C+	C	B			1,000
Eaton Vance Tax-Managed Growth 1.2 Fund Class C	EZTGX	NAS CM	Open End	US Equity Large Cap Growth (Growth)	C+	C	B		Y	1,000
Eaton Vance Tax-Managed Growth 1.2 Institutional Cls	EITGX	NAS CM	Open End	US Equity Large Cap Growth (Growth)	B-	C	B		Y	250,000
Eaton Vance Tax-Managed Multi-Cap Growth Fund Class A	EACPX	NAS CM	Open End	US Equity Large Cap Growth (Growth)	C+	C	B-	Down	Y	1,000
Eaton Vance Tax-Managed Multi-Cap Growth Fund Class C	ECCPX	NAS CM	Open End	US Equity Large Cap Growth (Growth)	C+	C	B-	Down	Y	1,000
Eaton Vance Tax-Managed Small-Cap Fund Class A	ETMGX	NAS CM	Open End	US Equity Small Cap (Small Company)	C+	C	B	Down	Y	1,000
Eaton Vance Tax-Managed Small-Cap Fund Class C	ECMGX	NAS CM	Open End	US Equity Small Cap (Small Company)	C+	C	B	Down	Y	1,000
Eaton Vance Tax-Managed Small-Cap Fund Class I	EIMGX	NAS CM	Open End	US Equity Small Cap (Small Company)	C+	C	B	Down	Y	250,000
Eaton Vance Tax-Managed Value Fund Class A	EATVX	NAS CM	Open End	US Equity Large Cap Value (Growth)	B-	C+	B		Y	1,000
Eaton Vance Tax-Managed Value Fund Class C	ECTVX	NAS CM	Open End	US Equity Large Cap Value (Growth)	B-	C	B		Y	1,000
Eaton Vance Tax-Managed Value Fund Class I	EITVX	NAS CM	Open End	US Equity Large Cap Value (Growth)	B-	C+	B		Y	250,000
Eaton Vance Worldwide Health Sciences Fund Class A	ETHSX	NAS CM	Open End	Healthcare Sector Equity (Health)	B-	C	B		Y	1,000
Eaton Vance Worldwide Health Sciences Fund Class B	EMHSX	NAS CM	Open End	Healthcare Sector Equity (Health)	B-	C	B			1,000
Eaton Vance Worldwide Health Sciences Fund Class C	ECHSX	NAS CM	Open End	Healthcare Sector Equity (Health)	B-	C	B		Y	1,000
Eaton Vance Worldwide Health Sciences Fund Class I	EIHSX	NAS CM	Open End	Healthcare Sector Equity (Health)	B-	C	B		Y	250,000
Eaton Vance Worldwide Health Sciences Fund Class R	ERHSX	NAS CM	Open End	Healthcare Sector Equity (Health)	B-	C	B		Y	1,000
Eaton Vance-Atlanta Capital Focused Growth Fund Class A	EAALX	NAS CM	Open End	US Equity Large Cap Growth (Growth)	B+	B+	A-	Up	Y	1,000
Eaton Vance-Atlanta Capital Focused Growth Fund Class I	EILGX	NAS CM	Open End	US Equity Large Cap Growth (Growth)	B+	B+	A-	Up	Y	250,000
Edgar Lomax Value Fund	LOMAX	NAS CM	Open End	US Equity Large Cap Value (Growth & Income)	B-	C	B+		Y	2,500
Edgewood Growth Fund Class Institutional	EGFIX	NAS CM	Open End	US Equity Large Cap Growth (Growth)	B-	B-	B	Down	Y	100,000
Edgewood Growth Fund Retail Class	EGFFX	NAS CM	Open End	US Equity Large Cap Growth (Growth)	B-	C+	B	Down	Y	3,000

★ Expanded analysis of this fund is included in Section II.

Min Additional Investment	TOTAL RETURNS: 3-Month Total Return	6-Month Total Return	1-Year Total Return	3-Year Total Return	5-Year Total Return	PERFORMANCE: Dividend Yield (TTM)	Expense Ratio	3-Yr Std Deviation	3-Year Beta	ASSETS: NAV	Total Assets (MIL)	ASSET ALLOCATION & TURNOVER: %Cash	%Stocks	%Bonds	%Other	Turnover Ratio	BULL & BEAR: Last Bull Market Total Return	Last Bear Market Total Return	FEES: Front End Fee (%)	Back End Fee (%)	Inception Date
	7.11	24.26	7.63	57.27	57.46	0	0.96	14.17	0.81	15.21	84.4	2	98	0	0	44	23.04	-25.22			Sep-08
	7.06	23.95	7.16	55.05	53.64	0	1.46	14.17	0.81	13.04	84.4	2	98	0	0	44	22.64	-25.34			Aug-09
	6.55	24.08	9.12	52.01	50.12	0	1.35	13.3	0.84	24.37	48.8	1	99	0	0	41	20.17	-21.21	5.75		Apr-68
	6.36	23.57	8.28	48.58	44.58	0	2.1	13.27	0.84	21.23	48.8	1	99	0	0	41	19.66	-21.46		1.00	Nov-94
	6.64	24.27	9.42	53.22	52.09	0	1.1	13.28	0.84	25.03	48.8	1	99	0	0	41	20.46	-21.21			Jul-11
	6.19	23.61	12.31	46.27	59.21	0.74	0.98	11.53	0.93	18.01	95.1	0	100	0	0	90	24.34	-17.85	5.75		Nov-01
100	5.92	23.10	11.45	43.02	53.34	0.05	1.73	11.55	0.93	17.53	95.1	0	100	0	0	90	23.72	-18		1.00	Oct-09
	6.24	23.74	12.57	47.38	61.19	0.98	0.73	11.54	0.93	18.03	95.1	0	100	0	0	90	24.46	-17.7			Sep-08
	5.64	22.14	12.15	43.66	51.40	2.46	0	12.44	1	23.78	1,735	1	74	14	0	4	24.75	-20.14			Sep-03
	3.96	20.33	4.66	37.17	32.09	3.33	1.28	13.79	1.19	17.36	1,325	1	82	9	0	110	22.96	-22.78			Jan-04
	6.45	25.57	9.18	43.30	41.33	2.04	0	13.29	1.15	23.62	355.9	2	79	8	0	56	23.17	-24.56			Apr-04
	2.28	11.03	2.49	25.57	35.75	0.99	0	8.83	0.69	14.79	392.7	0	100	0	0	4	23.82	-11.79			Apr-05
	2.23	11.79	4.11	35.38	48.91	0.58	0	9.01	0.7	14.13	1,151	0	100	0	0	9	24.22	-10.74			Jun-05
	2.22	4.59	1.90	-6.74	0.68	0.74	1.45	8.03	0.08	10.12	98.5	0	100	0	0	59	6.04	3.98			Jun-10
	3.79	16.60	7.58	38.98	46.49	0.77	1.2	10.3	0.82	11.96	1,791	0	100	0	0	48	19.44	-17.62			Nov-06
	3.75	18.34	7.12	42.00	44.87	0.74	1.32	11.28	0.9	21.8	515.6	1	91	3	0	6	23.58	-20.16	5.75		Mar-02
	3.58	17.91	6.31	38.82	39.49	0	2.07	11.29	0.9	20.54	515.6	1	91	3	0	6	22.99	-20.48		5.00	Mar-02
	3.58	17.90	6.28	38.83	39.53	0.03	2.07	11.27	0.9	20.22	515.6	1	91	3	0	6	23.1	-20.49		1.00	Mar-02
	3.86	18.50	7.38	43.08	46.20	0.98	1.07	11.28	0.9	21.77	515.6	1	91	3	0	6	23.58	-20.16			Sep-15
	1.85	11.19	2.10	28.04	25.69	1.27	0	8.76	0.67	10.26	1,093	0	100	0	0	4	19.27	-15.04			Sep-05
	4.19	17.55	5.47	29.72	28.45	0.95	1.2	10.45	0.89	8.7	2,625	-1	101	0	0	66	18.16	-20			Feb-07
	3.86	17.24	4.46	29.62	27.07	3.45	1.18	11.6	1	12.52	647.7	0	99	1	0	136	16.63	-16.68	5.75		May-03
	3.66	16.82	3.73	26.84	22.46	2.69	1.93	11.62	1.01	12.5	647.7	0	99	1	0	136	16.16	-16.9		5.00	May-03
	3.67	16.84	3.67	26.80	22.34	2.71	1.93	11.61	1.01	12.49	647.7	0	99	1	0	136	16.16	-16.98		1.00	May-03
	4.00	17.47	4.80	30.80	28.75	3.69	0.93	11.58	1	12.54	647.7	0	99	1	0	136	16.91	-16.59			Aug-07
	3.26	18.58	8.82	50.00	62.57	1.2		12.9	1.05	1256.92	967.7	1	99	0	0	1	24.9	-16.06			Mar-66
	3.17	18.41	8.49	48.62	60.06	0.79	0.79	12.92	1.05	56.52	1,653	1	99	0	0	1	24.66	-16.17	5.75		Mar-96
	2.98	17.99	7.69	45.33	54.18	0	1.54	12.91	1.05	55.53	1,653	1	99	0	0	1	24.15	-16.48		5.00	Mar-96
	2.97	17.92	7.65	45.29	54.13	0.14	1.54	12.87	1.05	50.59	1,653	1	99	0	0	1	24.11	-16.43		1.00	Aug-96
	3.24	18.57	8.77	49.75	62.07	1.11	0.54	12.92	1.05	52.79	1,653	1	99	0	0	1	24.89	-16.12			Jul-99
	3.16	18.35	8.34	47.97	58.82	0.64	0.94	12.92	1.05	25.4	836.5	1	99	0	0	1	24.45	-16.2	5.75		Feb-01
	2.94	17.92	7.57	44.67	52.94	0	1.69	12.91	1.05	25.13	836.5	1	99	0	0	1	23.94	-16.53		5.00	Feb-01
	2.92	17.89	7.55	44.68	52.95	0	1.69	12.86	1.05	24.64	836.5	1	99	0	0	1	23.96	-16.53		1.00	Feb-01
	3.24	18.51	8.62	49.12	60.89	0.88	0.69	12.92	1.05	25.48	836.5	1	99	0	0	1	24.72	-16.16			Feb-01
	3.90	22.88	6.21	60.73	71.24	0	1.31	14.82	1.06	31.9	97.0	1	99	0	0	18	28.91	-20.68	5.75		Jun-00
	3.68	22.39	5.40	57.11	64.85	0	2.06	14.8	1.06	27.27	97.0	1	99	0	0	18	28.25	-20.89		1.00	Jul-00
	7.01	23.91	7.13	55.69	53.83	0.11	1.17	14.2	0.81	27.15	124.2	3	97	0	0	51	23.05	-25.12	5.75		Sep-97
	6.76	23.41	6.33	52.20	48.14	0	1.92	14.18	0.81	21.61	124.2	3	97	0	0	51	22.5	-25.35		1.00	Sep-97
	7.08	24.05	7.40	56.91	55.79	0.34	0.92	14.19	0.81	27.95	124.2	3	97	0	0	51	23.3	-25.06			Oct-09
	3.61	17.90	9.14	40.95	43.02	0.97	1.17	11.64	0.94	28.64	620.9	0	100	0	0	10	22.94	-18.28	5.75		Dec-99
	3.42	17.45	8.31	37.81	37.70	0.24	1.92	11.63	0.94	27.45	620.9	0	100	0	0	10	22.39	-18.51		1.00	Jan-00
	3.67	18.04	9.39	41.99	44.68	1.22	0.92	11.64	0.94	28.52	620.9	0	100	0	0	10	23.09	-18.19			Nov-07
	1.90	14.73	15.90	29.97	45.49	0.28	1	13.92	1.07	11.76	1,026	1	99	0	0	37	17.5	-9.67	5.75		Jul-85
	1.69	14.24	15.04	27.03	40.17	0	1.76	13.86	1.07	12.03	1,026	1	99	0	0	37	17.04	-10.05		5.00	Sep-96
	1.71	14.25	15.01	27.00	40.23	0	1.75	13.84	1.07	11.86	1,026	1	99	0	0	37	17.04	-10.05		1.00	Jan-98
	1.94	14.82	16.16	30.91	47.31	0.51	0.75	13.91	1.07	12.08	1,026	1	99	0	0	37	17.76	-9.63			Oct-09
	1.86	14.58	15.61	28.97	43.73	0.04	1.25	13.9	1.07	12.57	1,026	1	99	0	0	37	17.37	-9.77			Sep-03
	6.83	27.40	26.22	83.15	93.59	0	1.05	10.92	0.76	11.25	71.7	4	96	0	0	14	23.95	-18.17	5.75		Nov-03
	6.90	27.58	26.52	84.57	96.01	0	0.8	10.91	0.76	9.76	71.7	4	96	0	0	14	24.24	-18.15			Apr-02
100	2.64	13.02	10.56	40.46	52.86	1.99	0.7	10.83	0.83	13.97	115.3	4	96	0	0	41	17.73	-10.29			Dec-97
	5.34	23.56	9.80	84.10	105.95	0	1	13.76	1.05	35.29	15,209	1	99	0	0	19	25.3	-11.91			Feb-06
	5.20	23.26	9.34	81.96	101.95	0	1.4	13.75	1.05	33.75	15,209	1	99	0	0	19	25.71	-12.38			Feb-06

	MARKET			FUND TYPE, CATEGORY & OBJECTIVE	RATINGS				MINIMUMS	
Fund Name	Ticker Symbol	Traded On	Fund Type	Category and (Prospectus Objective)	Overall Rating	Reward Rating	Risk Rating	Recent Up/ Downgrade	Open to New Investors	Min Initial Investment
EIC Value Fund Class A	EICVX	NAS CM	Open End	US Equity Large Cap Value (Growth)	B-	C	B+	Up	Y	2,500
EIC Value Fund Class C	EICCX	NAS CM	Open End	US Equity Large Cap Value (Growth)	B-	C	B	Up	Y	2,500
EIC Value Fund Institutional Class	EICIX	NAS CM	Open End	US Equity Large Cap Value (Growth)	B-	C	B+	Up	Y	100,000
EIP Growth and Income Fund Class I	EIPIX	NAS CM	Open End	Energy Sector Equity (Natl Res)	C	C	C		Y	1,000,000
EIP Growth and Income Fund Investor Class	EIPFX	NAS CM	Open End	Energy Sector Equity (Natl Res)	C	C	C		Y	2,500
Elfun Diversified Fund	ELDFX	NAS CM	Open End	Moderate Alloc (Asset Alloc)	B	C	A-	Up	Y	500
Elfun International Equity Fund	EGLBX	NAS CM	Open End	Global Equity Large Cap (World Stock)	C	C	B-		Y	500
Elfun Trusts	ELFNX	NAS CM	Open End	US Equity Large Cap Growth (Growth)	B-	C+	B	Down	Y	500
Ellsworth Growth and Income Fund Ltd	ECF	AMEX	Closed End	Convertibles (Convertible Bond)	C	C+	C-		Y	
Emerald Banking and Finance Fund Class A	HSSAX	NAS CM	Open End	Financials Sector Equity (Financial)	C-	C-	C-		Y	2,000
Emerald Banking and Finance Fund Class C	HSSCX	NAS CM	Open End	Financials Sector Equity (Financial)	C-	C-	C-		Y	2,000
Emerald Banking and Finance Fund Institutional Class	HSSIX	NAS CM	Open End	Financials Sector Equity (Financial)	C-	C-	C-		Y	1,000,000
Emerald Banking and Finance Fund Investor Class	FFBFX	NAS CM	Open End	Financials Sector Equity (Financial)	C-	C-	C-		Y	2,000
Emerald Growth Fund Class A	HSPGX	NAS CM	Open End	US Equity Small Cap (Growth)	C	C	C+	Down	Y	2,000
Emerald Growth Fund Class C	HSPCX	NAS CM	Open End	US Equity Small Cap (Growth)	C	C	C+	Down	Y	2,000
Emerald Growth Fund Institutional Class	FGROX	NAS CM	Open End	US Equity Small Cap (Growth)	C+	C	C+		Y	1,000,000
Emerald Growth Fund Investor Class	FFGRX	NAS CM	Open End	US Equity Small Cap (Growth)	C	C	C+	Down	Y	2,000
Emerald Insights Fund Class A	EFCAX	NAS CM	Open End	US Equity Mid Cap (Growth)	C+	C	C+		Y	2,000
Emerald Insights Fund Class C	EFCCX	NAS CM	Open End	US Equity Mid Cap (Growth)	C	C	C+	Down	Y	2,000
Emerald Insights Fund Institutional Class	EFCIX	NAS CM	Open End	US Equity Mid Cap (Growth)	C+	C	C+		Y	1,000,000
Emerald Insights Fund Investor Class	EFCNX	NAS CM	Open End	US Equity Mid Cap (Growth)	C+	C	C+		Y	2,000
Emerald Small Cap Value Fund Class A	ELASX	NAS CM	Open End	US Equity Small Cap (Small Company)	C	C	C		Y	2,000
Emerald Small Cap Value Fund Class C	ELCSX	NAS CM	Open End	US Equity Small Cap (Small Company)	C	C	C		Y	2,000
Emerald Small Cap Value Fund Institutional Class	LSRYX	NAS CM	Open End	US Equity Small Cap (Small Company)	C	C	C		Y	1,000,000
Emerald Small Cap Value Fund Investor Class	LSRIX	NAS CM	Open End	US Equity Small Cap (Small Company)	C	C	C		Y	2,000
Empiric 2500 Fund Class A	EMCAX	NAS CM	Open End	US Equity Small Cap (Growth)	C	C	C+	Down	Y	2,500
Empiric 2500 Fund Class C	EMCCX	NAS CM	Open End	US Equity Small Cap (Growth)	C	C	C+	Down	Y	2,500
Ensemble Fund	ENSBX	NAS CM	Open End	US Equity Large Cap Growth (Growth)	B-	C+	B	Down	Y	5,000
EnTrust Global - Alternative Core Fund Class A	LPTAX	NAS CM	Open End	Multialternative (Asset Alloc)	D+	D	C		Y	1,000
EnTrust Global - Alternative Core Fund Class C	LPTCX	NAS CM	Open End	Multialternative (Asset Alloc)	D+	D	C		Y	1,000
EnTrust Global - Alternative Core Fund Class FI	LPTFX	NAS CM	Open End	Multialternative (Asset Alloc)	D+	D	C		Y	0
EnTrust Global - Alternative Core Fund Class I	LPTIX	NAS CM	Open End	Multialternative (Asset Alloc)	D+	D	C		Y	1,000,000
EnTrust Global - Alternative Core Fund Class IS	LPTSX	NAS CM	Open End	Multialternative (Asset Alloc)	D+	D	C		Y	1,000,000
EP Emerging Markets Small Companies Fund Class A	EPASX	NAS CM	Open End	Global Emerg Mkts (Small Company)	C-	D+	C		Y	2,500
EP Emerging Markets Small Companies Fund Class I	EPEIX	NAS CM	Open End	Global Emerg Mkts (Small Company)	C-	D+	C		Y	5,000
EQ/2000 Managed Volatility Portfolio Class IB			Open End	US Equity Small Cap (Growth)	C	C	C+		Y	0
EQ/2000 Managed Volatility Portfolio Class K			Open End	US Equity Small Cap (Growth)	C	C	C+		Y	0
EQ/400 Managed Volatility Portfolio Class IB			Open End	US Equity Mid Cap (Growth)	C	C	B-		Y	0
EQ/400 Managed Volatility Portfolio Class K			Open End	US Equity Mid Cap (Growth)	C	C	B-		Y	0
EQ/500 Managed Volatility Portfolio Class IB			Open End	US Equity Large Cap Blend (Growth)	B-	C	B	Up	Y	0
EQ/500 Managed Volatility Portfolio Class K			Open End	US Equity Large Cap Blend (Growth)	B-	C	B	Up	Y	0
EQ/AB Dynamic Aggressive Growth Portfolio Class IB			Open End	Aggressive Alloc (Aggr Growth)	D+	D+	C	Up	Y	0
EQ/AB Dynamic Aggressive Growth Portfolio Class K			Open End	Aggressive Alloc (Aggr Growth)	D+	D+	C	Up	Y	0
EQ/AB Dynamic Growth Portfolio Class IB			Open End	Moderate Alloc (Growth)	B-	C	B+	Up	Y	0
EQ/AB Dynamic Moderate Growth Portfolio Class IB			Open End	Moderate Alloc (Growth)	B-	C	B+	Up	Y	0
EQ/AB Small Cap Growth Portfolio Class IA			Open End	US Equity Small Cap (Small Company)	C	C	C+	Down	Y	0
EQ/AB Small Cap Growth Portfolio Class IB			Open End	US Equity Small Cap (Small Company)	C	C	C+	Down	Y	0
EQ/AB Small Cap Growth Portfolio Class K			Open End	US Equity Small Cap (Small Company)	C	C	C+	Down	Y	0
EQ/Aggressive Allocation Portfolio Class K			Open End	Aggressive Alloc (Asset Alloc)	C+	C	B	Up	Y	0
EQ/Aggressive Strategy Growth Portfolio Class IB			Open End	Aggressive Alloc (Growth & Income)	B-	C	B	Up	Y	0
EQ/American Century Mid Cap Value Portfolio Class IB			Open End	US Equity Mid Cap (Growth)	U	U	U		Y	0
EQ/American Century Moderate Growth Alloc Port Cls IB			Open End	Moderate Alloc (Asset Alloc)	U	U	U		Y	0

★ Expanded analysis of this fund is included in Section II.

	TOTAL RETURNS					PERFORMANCE				ASSETS		ASSET ALLOCATION & TURNOVER					BULL & BEAR		FEES		
Min Additional Investment	3-Month Total Return	6-Month Total Return	1-Year Total Return	3-Year Total Return	5-Year Total Return	Dividend Yield (TTM)	Expense Ratio	3-Yr Std Deviation	3-Year Beta	NAV	Total Assets (MIL)	%Cash	%Stocks	%Bonds	%Other	Turnover Ratio	Last Bull Market Total Return	Last Bear Market Total Return	Front End Fee (%)	Back End Fee (%)	Inception Date
250	2.20	13.84	4.86	28.93	30.75	1.08	1.21	10.94	0.86	13.9	206.0	11	85	3	0	33	17.06	-8.6	5.50		May-11
250	2.02	13.48	4.09	25.99	25.98	0.55	1.96	10.95	0.86	13.63	206.0	11	85	3	0	33	16.54	-8.9		1.00	Jul-11
	2.28	14.03	5.15	29.91	32.43	1.66	0.96	10.94	0.86	13.89	206.0	11	85	3	0	33	17.2	-8.5			Apr-11
	2.37	20.93	10.61	7.27	-2.23	3.41	2.95	11.36	0.66	15.44	158.5	2	98	1	0		21.83	-6.29			Aug-06
100	2.28	20.72	10.24	6.09	-3.78	3.02	3.41	11.36	0.66	15.43	158.5	2	98	1	0		21.65	-6.39			Oct-16
	3.40	12.92	6.94	28.10	28.78	2.25	0.33	7.38	0.57	19.13	194.8	13	50	36	0	72	15.87	-13.76			Jan-88
	5.82	19.43	2.88	29.42	12.62	2.09	0.36	11.91	1.04	22	207.9	2	98	0	0	27	16.45	-25.88			Jan-88
	6.35	21.29	11.70	57.70	71.17	1.12	0.19	12.88	1.02	60.38	2,789	2	98	0	0	18	28.83	-17.03			May-35
	5.04	22.06	11.29	42.29	43.32	4.54	0	10.95		11.46	148.2	1	28	0	0	35	13.78	-14.73			Jun-86
100	7.00	14.07	-13.87	43.03	57.18	0	1.42	19.4	1.03	32.98	317.2	0	100	0	0	62	30.66	-20.17	4.75		Feb-97
100	6.85	13.73	-14.43	40.26	52.23	0	2.07	19.4	1.03	28.07	317.2	0	100	0	0	62	30.18	-20.29		1.00	Jul-00
	7.12	14.29	-13.56	44.46	59.81	0	1.12	19.41	1.03	33.99	317.2	0	100	0	0	62	30.66	-20.17			Mar-12
100	7.03	14.11	-13.89	43.14	57.26	0	1.47	19.41	1.03	31.21	317.2	0	100	0	0	62	30.94	-19.98			Mar-10
100	2.65	25.70	2.51	63.14	65.82	0	1.03	18.05	1	25.87	1,350	2	98	0	0	66	38.81	-26.92	4.75		Oct-92
100	2.53	25.27	1.87	59.95	60.62	0	1.68	18.04	1	21.46	1,350	2	98	0	0	66	38.25	-27.13		1.00	Jul-00
	2.73	25.88	2.89	64.67	68.56	0	0.73	18.06	1	27.04	1,350	2	98	0	0	66	39.01	-26.81			Oct-08
100	2.67	25.67	2.52	62.93	65.61	0	1.08	18.07	1	25.75	1,350	2	98	0	0	66	38.76	-26.94			May-11
100	4.16	25.68	4.55	52.89		0	1.35	17.39	1.17	11.5	11.1	1	99	0	0	138			4.75		Aug-14
100	3.95	25.34	3.88	49.92		0	2	17.31	1.17	11.03	11.1	1	99	0	0	138				1.00	Aug-14
	4.18	25.83	4.83	54.29		0	1.05	17.34	1.17	11.69	11.1	1	99	0	0	138					Aug-14
100	4.09	25.71	4.50	52.58		0	1.4	17.36	1.17	11.44	11.1	1	99	0	0	138					Aug-14
100	5.30	18.93	-10.31	33.95	27.13	0	1.35	17.61	0.99	7.35	3.6	1	99	0	0	71			4.75		Jun-15
100	5.09	18.61	-10.82	31.40	23.01	0	2	17.6	0.99	7.01	3.6	1	99	0	0	71				1.00	Jun-15
	5.46	19.33	-9.93	35.46	29.44	0	1	17.6	0.99	7.53	3.6	1	99	0	0	71					Oct-12
100	5.27	19.00	-10.18	34.68	28.23	0	1.25	17.58	0.99	7.39	3.6	1	99	0	0	71					Oct-12
50	1.69	16.72	-1.41	52.25	33.91	0	1.99	16.06	0.95	43.27	26.2	1	99	0	0	11	19.8	-23.98	5.75		Nov-95
50	1.49	16.26	-2.16	48.81	28.90	0	2.74	16.05	0.95	38.81	26.2	1	99	0	0	11	19.31	-24.22			Oct-05
100	6.61	26.26	11.71	67.44		0.06	1	13.86	1.04	14.18	30.2	0	100	0	0	63					Nov-15
50	0.59	3.49	-3.96	-2.40	-0.17	1.94	1.58	4.3	0.77	12.88	76.6	36	64	0	0	190	9.81	-12.34	5.75		Apr-09
50	0.36	3.10	-4.69	-4.55	-3.82	0.89	2.32	4.28	0.76	12.76	76.6	36	64	0	0	190	9.4	-12.62		1.00	Apr-09
	0.58	3.48	-3.89	-2.32	-0.11	1.45	1.57	4.32	0.77	13.22	76.6	36	64	0	0	190	9.82	-12.35			Apr-09
	0.67	3.65	-3.63	-1.59	1.16	2.14	1.31	4.32	0.77	12.89	76.6	36	64	0	0	190	9.93	-12.22			Apr-09
	0.74	3.68	-3.60	-1.46	1.22	2.3	1.21	4.36	0.78	13.06	76.6	36	64	0	0	190	9.93	-12.22			Apr-09
250	0.75	9.28	-4.78	15.60	-1.91	0	1.75	12.65	0.9	10.71	58.1	2	98	0	0	43	25.19	-25.04	4.50		Dec-10
250	0.73	9.43	-4.54	16.42	-0.71	0	1.5	12.62	0.9	10.9	58.1	2	98	0	0	43	25.19	-25.04			Jul-13
	-3.04	2.34	-6.70	39.23	42.30	0.77	0.83	15.96	1		3,582	-1	101	0	0	20	21.57	-26.42			Oct-09
	-2.97	2.48	-6.50	40.23	44.03	1.03	0.58	16.04	1		3,582	-1	101	0	0	20	21.62	-26.37			Aug-11
	-2.01	2.43	-4.29	31.32	42.61	0.94	0.85	13.73	1		630.2	-1	101	0	0	20	22.12	-24.27			Oct-09
	-1.95	2.56	-4.07	32.35	44.37	1.18	0.6	13.75	1.01		630.2	-1	101	0	0	20	22.24	-24.26			Aug-11
	2.67	6.93	4.21	41.45	57.40	1.05	0.82	10.97	1.01		9,448	-1	101	0	0	4	20.15	-17.87			Oct-09
	2.73	7.10	4.49	42.52	59.37	1.28	0.57	10.98	1.01		9,448	-1	101	0	0	4	20.39	-17.89			Aug-11
	1.49	5.16	-0.92			1.06	1.2				138.6	20	68	13	0	3					Nov-17
	1.59	5.33	-0.66			1.3	0.95				138.6	20	68	13	0	3					Nov-17
	1.47	4.92	-0.40	21.51		0.95	1.2	6.87			694.6	18	61	22	0	7					Apr-15
	1.33	4.69	0.21	19.29	21.63	1.15	1.13	5.91			2,674	2	65	33	0	12	10.55	-9.63			Feb-11
	-0.64	8.99	-2.28	53.84	58.75	0.12	0.92	16.33	0.99		1,985	1	99	0	0	46	29.97	-24.12			May-97
	-0.59	9.00	-2.21	53.86	58.87	0.12	0.92	16.35	0.99		1,985	1	99	0	0	46	29.83	-24.21			May-97
	-0.59	9.13	-2.04	54.96	60.74	0.35	0.67	16.34	0.99		1,985	1	99	0	0	46	30.04	-24.12			Aug-11
	3.36	15.77	4.04	39.14	35.66	1.75	0.92	11.16		11.74	3,326	1	91	8	0	11	16.87	-19.63			Dec-11
	3.10	14.09	4.04	33.81	33.94	1.15	1.06	10.02		15.38	4,054	0	82	18	0	6					Apr-12
	0.91	4.93					1				316.7	3	97	0	0	11					Oct-18
	2.26						1.2				13.9	0	63	37	0						Jan-19

Fund Name	MARKET Ticker Symbol	Traded On	FUND TYPE, CATEGORY & OBJECTIVE Fund Type	Category and (Prospectus Objective)	RATINGS Overall Rating	Reward Rating	Risk Rating	Recent Up/ Downgrade	MINIMUMS Open to New Investors	Min Initial Investment
EQ/American Century Moderate Growth Alloc Port Cls K			Open End	Moderate Alloc (Asset Alloc)	U	U	U		Y	0
EQ/AXA Inv Managers Moderate Alloc Port Cls IB			Open End	Moderate Alloc (Asset Alloc)	U	U	U		Y	0
EQ/AXA Inv Managers Moderate Alloc Port Cls K			Open End	Moderate Alloc (Asset Alloc)	U	U	U		Y	0
EQ/Balanced Strategy Fund Class IA			Open End	Moderate Alloc (Balanced)	B-	C	A-	Up	Y	0
EQ/Balanced Strategy Fund Class IB			Open End	Moderate Alloc (Balanced)	B-	C	A-	Up	Y	0
EQ/BlackRock Basic Value Equity Portfolio Class IA			Open End	US Equity Large Cap Value (Growth & Income)	C+	C	B		Y	0
EQ/BlackRock Basic Value Equity Portfolio Class IB			Open End	US Equity Large Cap Value (Growth & Income)	C+	C	B		Y	0
EQ/BlackRock Basic Value Equity Portfolio Class K			Open End	US Equity Large Cap Value (Growth & Income)	C+	C	B		Y	0
EQ/Capital Guardian Research Portfolio Class IA			Open End	US Equity Large Cap Growth (Growth)	B-	C	B	Down	Y	0
EQ/Capital Guardian Research Portfolio Class IB			Open End	US Equity Large Cap Growth (Growth)	B-	C	B	Down	Y	0
EQ/Capital Guardian Research Portfolio Class K			Open End	US Equity Large Cap Growth (Growth)	B-	C	B	Down	Y	0
EQ/ClearBridge Large Cap Growth Portfolio Class IA			Open End	US Equity Large Cap Growth (Growth)	B-	C	B	Down	Y	0
EQ/ClearBridge Large Cap Growth Portfolio Class IB			Open End	US Equity Large Cap Growth (Growth)	B-	C	B	Down	Y	0
EQ/ClearBridge Large Cap Growth Portfolio Class K			Open End	US Equity Large Cap Growth (Growth)	B-	C	B	Down	Y	0
EQ/ClearBridge Select Eq Managed Vol Port Cls IA			Open End	US Equity Large Cap Blend (Growth)	C+	C	B		Y	0
EQ/ClearBridge Select Eq Managed Vol Port Cls IB			Open End	US Equity Large Cap Blend (Growth)	C+	C	B		Y	0
EQ/Common Stock Index Portfolio Class IA			Open End	US Equity Large Cap Blend (Growth)	B-	C	B		Y	0
EQ/Common Stock Index Portfolio Class IB			Open End	US Equity Large Cap Blend (Growth)	B-	C	B		Y	0
EQ/Conservative Allocation Portfolio Class K			Open End	Cautious Alloc (Asset Alloc)	B-	C	B+		Y	0
EQ/Conservative Growth Strategy Fund Class IB			Open End	Cautious Alloc (Growth & Income)	B-	C	A-		Y	0
EQ/Conservative Growth Strategy Fund Class IB			Open End	Cautious Alloc (Income)	B-	C	B+	Up	Y	0
EQ/Conservative-Plus Allocation Portfolio Class K			Open End	Cautious Alloc (Asset Alloc)	B	C	A-	Up	Y	0
EQ/Emerging Markets Equity PLUS Portfolio Class IB			Open End	Global Emerg Mkts (Div Emerging Mkts)	C	C-	C+		Y	0
EQ/Emerging Markets Equity PLUS Portfolio Class K			Open End	Global Emerg Mkts (Div Emerging Mkts)	C	C-	C+		Y	0
EQ/Equity 500 Index Portfolio Class IA			Open End	US Equity Large Cap Blend (Growth & Income)	B-	C	B		Y	0
EQ/Equity 500 Index Portfolio Class IB			Open End	US Equity Large Cap Blend (Growth & Income)	B-	C	B		Y	0
EQ/Equity 500 Index Portfolio Class K			Open End	US Equity Large Cap Blend (Growth & Income)	B-	C	B		Y	0
EQ/Fidelity Institutional AM Large Cap Portfolio Class IB			Open End	US Equity Large Cap Blend (Growth)	U	U	U		Y	0
EQ/Fidelity Institutional AM Large Cap Portfolio Class K			Open End	US Equity Large Cap Blend (Growth)	U	U	U		Y	0
EQ/First Trust Moderate Growth Allocation Portfolio Cls IB			Open End	Moderate Alloc (Asset Alloc)	U	U	U		Y	0
EQ/First Trust Moderate Growth Allocation Portfolio Cls K			Open End	Moderate Alloc (Asset Alloc)	U	U	U		Y	0
EQ/Franklin Balanced Managed Volatility Portfolio Class IA			Open End	Moderate Alloc (Growth & Income)	B-	C	A-		Y	0
EQ/Franklin Balanced Managed Volatility Portfolio Class IB			Open End	Moderate Alloc (Growth & Income)	B-	C	A-		Y	0
EQ/Franklin Balanced Managed Volatility Portfolio Class K			Open End	Moderate Alloc (Growth & Income)	B-	C	A-		Y	0
EQ/Franklin Rising Dividends Portfolio Class IB			Open End	US Equity Large Cap Blend (Growth)	U	U	U		Y	0
EQ/Franklin Small Cap Value Managed Vol Port Cls IA			Open End	US Equity Small Cap (Small Company)	C	C-	C+		Y	0
EQ/Franklin Small Cap Value Managed Vol Port Cls IB			Open End	US Equity Small Cap (Small Company)	C	C-	C+		Y	0
EQ/Franklin Small Cap Value Managed Vol Port Cls K			Open End	US Equity Small Cap (Small Company)	C	C-	C+		Y	0
EQ/Franklin Templeton Alloc Managed Vol Port Cls IA			Open End	Aggressive Alloc (Growth & Income)	B-	C	B+	Up	Y	0
EQ/Franklin Templeton Alloc Managed Vol Port Cls IB			Open End	Aggressive Alloc (Growth & Income)	B-	C	B	Up	Y	0
EQ/Global Equity Managed Volatility Portfolio Class IA			Open End	Global Equity Large Cap (World Stock)	C+	C	B	Up	Y	0
EQ/Global Equity Managed Volatility Portfolio Class IB			Open End	Global Equity Large Cap (World Stock)	C+	C	B	Up	Y	0
EQ/Global Equity Managed Volatility Portfolio Class K			Open End	Global Equity Large Cap (World Stock)	C+	C	B	Up	Y	0
EQ/Goldman Sachs Growth Allocation Portfolio Class IB			Open End	Aggressive Alloc (Asset Alloc)	U	U	U		Y	0
EQ/Goldman Sachs Growth Allocation Portfolio Class K			Open End	Aggressive Alloc (Asset Alloc)	U	U	U		Y	0
EQ/Goldman Sachs Mid Cap Value Portfolio Class IB			Open End	US Equity Mid Cap (Growth)	U	U	U		Y	0
EQ/Goldman Sachs Moderate Growth Alloc Port Cls IB			Open End	Moderate Alloc (Asset Alloc)	B-	C	B+	Up	Y	0
EQ/Growth Strategy Fund Class IA			Open End	Aggressive Alloc (Growth & Income)	B-	C	B+	Up	Y	0
EQ/Growth Strategy Fund Class IB			Open End	Aggressive Alloc (Growth & Income)	B-	C	B+	Up	Y	0
EQ/International Core Managed Volatility Portfolio Cls IA			Open End	Global Equity Large Cap (Foreign Stock)	C	C-	B		Y	0
EQ/International Core Managed Volatility Portfolio Cls IB			Open End	Global Equity Large Cap (Foreign Stock)	C	C-	B		Y	0
EQ/International Core Managed Volatility Portfolio Class K			Open End	Global Equity Large Cap (Foreign Stock)	C	C-	B		Y	0

★Expanded analysis of this fund is included in Section II.

Min Additional Investment	TOTAL RETURNS 3-Month Total Return	6-Month Total Return	1-Year Total Return	3-Year Total Return	5-Year Total Return	PERFORMANCE Dividend Yield (TTM)	Expense Ratio	3-Yr Std Deviation	3-Year Beta	ASSETS NAV	Total Assets (MIL)	ASSET ALLOCATION & TURNOVER %Cash	%Stocks	%Bonds	%Other	Turnover Ratio	BULL & BEAR Last Bull Market Total Return	Last Bear Market Total Return	FEES Front End Fee (%)	Back End Fee (%)	Inception Date
	2.26						0.95				13.9	0	63	37	0						Jan-19
	2.07						1.2				11.6	1	53	45	0						Jan-19
	2.07						0.95				11.6	1	53	45	0						Jan-19
	2.60	10.23	4.59	21.42	23.15	1.18	1.01	6.17		15.78	3,544	1	51	47	0	10	9.79	-10.08			Sep-09
	2.60	10.21	4.59	21.47	23.12	1.18	1.01	6.16		15.8	3,544	1	51	47	0	10	9.7	-10.23			Apr-09
	0.93	3.59	1.07	25.90	30.85	1.61	0.95	11.76	1.05		1,649	2	98	0	0	36	25.06	-20.93			Oct-02
	0.97	3.62	1.11	25.94	30.82	1.61	0.95	11.8	1.06		1,649	2	98	0	0	36	24.98	-20.97			May-97
	1.02	3.75	1.35	26.91	32.51	1.86	0.7	11.78	1.06		1,649	2	98	0	0	36	25.15	-20.98			Aug-11
	3.53	11.56	7.62	53.21	74.22	0.53	0.97	12.08	1.07		422.3	2	98	0	0	31	25.53	-15.82			Mar-02
	3.48	11.54	7.61	53.13	74.19	0.53	0.97	12.08	1.07		422.3	2	98	0	0	31	25.3	-15.88			May-99
	3.57	11.72	7.89	54.33	76.41	0.76	0.72	12.08	1.07		422.3	2	98	0	0	31	25.3	-15.88			Oct-13
	5.40	13.81	9.57	55.46	63.95	0.15	1.04	12.04	0.94		381.2	3	97	0	0	18	32.07	-22.91			Oct-02
	5.42	13.85	9.47	55.45	63.85	0.16	1.04	12.01	0.94		381.2	3	97	0	0	18	32.05	-23.01			Jan-99
	5.49	14.00	9.81	56.60	65.86	0.37	0.79	12.06	0.94		381.2	3	97	0	0	18	32.05	-23.01			Aug-12
	3.31	10.65	4.18	34.23	40.51	3.9	1.05	11.63	1.05		197.7	3	97	0	0	44	18.03	-18.14			Sep-06
	3.32	10.78	4.22	34.33	40.62	3.91	1.05	11.61	1.05		197.7	3	97	0	0	44	17.91	-18.18			Sep-06
	2.18	7.78	4.38	43.49	58.44	1.27	0.7	11.16	1		5,878	0	100	0	0	3	25.31	-17.73			Jan-76
	2.17	7.76	4.38	43.51	58.42	1.28	0.7	11.16	1		5,878	0	100	0	0	3	25.16	-17.79			Oct-96
	2.26	6.62	5.30	11.66	14.71	1.73	0.75	2.71		9.5	1,062	2	21	77	0	12	4.81	-2.49			Aug-12
	2.38	8.88	4.69	17.51	19.63	1.18	0.99	4.96		14.64	1,530	2	41	57	0	8	7.95	-7.9			Apr-09
	2.07	6.23	4.80	9.85	12.52	1.2	0.95	2.63		12.3	1,530	3	21	76	0	10	4.59	-3.16			Apr-09
	2.60	9.21	4.96	19.03	20.59	1.69	0.85	5.01		9.87	1,235	2	41	57	0	14	8.26	-7.65			Dec-11
	-5.41	1.63	-11.25	29.32	-0.95	1.33	1.3	13.62	1.02		60.7	0	100	0	0	8					Feb-13
	-5.42	1.69	-11.00	30.32	0.21	1.59	1.05	13.68	1.02		60.7	0	100	0	0	8					Feb-13
	2.74	7.99	5.42	44.33	61.65	1.37	0.58	10.83	1		5,977	0	100	0	0	3	24.62	-16.32			Mar-94
	2.73	7.99	5.43	44.30	61.64	1.38	0.58	10.83	1		5,977	0	100	0	0	3	24.62	-16.45			May-97
	2.79	8.10	5.67	45.40	63.55	1.61	0.33	10.84	1		5,977	0	100	0	0	3	24.72	-16.32			Aug-11
	2.12	7.83					0.87				768.4	1	99	0	0	88					Oct-18
	2.17	7.96					0.62				768.4	1	99	0	0	88					Oct-18
	1.47						1.2				14.0	0	59	41	0						Jan-19
	1.57						0.95				14.0	0	59	41	0						Jan-19
	1.49	4.59	3.30	21.96	23.77	2.91	1.05	5.8	0.51		1,145	0	48	51	0	30	11.3	-10.48			Sep-06
	1.58	4.68	3.39	22.07	23.88	2.91	1.05	5.74	0.51		1,145	0	48	51	0	30	11.29	-10.6			Sep-06
	1.58	4.77	3.57	22.88	25.35	3.16	0.8	5.76	0.51		1,145	0	48	51	0	30	11.43	-10.48			Aug-11
	2.54	7.10					0.87				165.3	2	98	0	0	5					Oct-18
	-3.66	1.20	-7.88	33.08	33.82	0.63	1.11	14.94	0.91		289.4	1	98	0	0	36	24.27	-26.72			Sep-06
	-3.65	1.27	-7.86	33.14	33.78	0.63	1.11	14.93	0.91		289.4	1	98	0	0	36	24.36	-26.8			Sep-06
	-3.59	1.38	-7.65	34.12	35.44	0.89	0.86	14.91	0.91		289.4	1	98	0	0	36	24.4	-26.72			Aug-11
	2.85	13.45	3.94	30.51	24.87	2.28	1.2	9.97	0.8	9.06	1,100	1	83	16	0	44	15.06	-16.9			Apr-07
	2.85	13.45	3.94	30.64	24.87	2.28	1.2	9.92	0.8	9.06	1,100	1	83	16	0	44	14.94	-17.02			Apr-07
	1.04	5.68	-3.85	30.23	25.00	1.06	1.1	10.35			2,076	0	100	0	0	13	14.93	-21.64			Oct-02
	1.04	5.70	-3.86	30.22	25.06	1.06	1.1	10.34			2,076	0	100	0	0	13	14.79	-21.7			Aug-97
	1.04	5.79	-3.63	31.20	26.58	1.31	0.85	10.35			2,076	0	100	0	0	13	15.03	-21.74			Aug-11
	1.95						1.2				21.8	-18	65	53	0						Jan-19
	2.05						0.95				21.8	-18	65	53	0						Jan-19
	2.27	7.47					1.09				98.7	3	97	0	0	16					Oct-18
	1.90	5.37	2.29	18.64		0.89	1.2	5.68			582.5	-1	61	40	0	183					Apr-15
	2.92	12.84	4.26	29.57	30.33	1.16	1.02	8.76		18.72	5,349	1	72	27	0	10	13.3	-14.53			Sep-09
	2.86	12.76	4.20	29.55	30.22	1.16	1.02	8.75		18.74	5,349	1	72	27	0	10	13.2	-14.61			Apr-09
	1.06	5.36	-7.79	22.19	3.92	1.78	1.06	10.76			1,544	1	99	0	0	10	12.58	-26.32			Mar-02
	0.96	5.35	-7.86	22.17	3.91	1.77	1.06	10.77			1,544	1	99	0	0	10	12.57	-26.41			May-99
	1.16	5.53	-7.58	23.17	5.27	2.03	0.81	10.77			1,544	1	99	0	0	10	12.71	-26.4			Aug-11

	MARKET		FUND TYPE, CATEGORY & OBJECTIVE		RATINGS				MINIMUMS	
Fund Name	Ticker Symbol	Traded On	Fund Type	Category and (Prospectus Objective)	Overall Rating	Reward Rating	Risk Rating	Recent Up/ Downgrade	Open to New Investors	Min Initial Investment
EQ/International Equity Index Portfolio Class IA Shares			Open End	Global Equity Large Cap (Foreign Stock)	C	C-	B-		Y	0
EQ/International Equity Index Portfolio Class IB Shares			Open End	Global Equity Large Cap (Foreign Stock)	C	C-	B-		Y	0
EQ/International Equity Index Portfolio Class K			Open End	Global Equity Large Cap (Foreign Stock)	C	C-	B-		Y	0
EQ/International Managed Volatility Portfolio Class IB			Open End	Global Equity Large Cap (Foreign Stock)	C	C-	B		Y	0
EQ/International Managed Volatility Portfolio Class K			Open End	Global Equity Large Cap (Foreign Stock)	C	C-	B		Y	0
EQ/International Value Managed Volatility Portfolio Cls IA			Open End	Global Equity Large Cap (Growth & Income)	C	C-	B-		Y	0
EQ/International Value Managed Volatility Portfolio Cls IB			Open End	Global Equity Large Cap (Growth & Income)	C	C-	B-		Y	0
EQ/International Value Managed Volatility Portfolio Cls K			Open End	Global Equity Large Cap (Growth & Income)	C	C-	B-		Y	0
EQ/Invesco Comstock Portfolio Class IA			Open End	US Equity Large Cap Value (Growth & Income)	C+	C	B	Up	Y	0
EQ/Invesco Comstock Portfolio Class IB			Open End	US Equity Large Cap Value (Growth & Income)	C+	C	B	Up	Y	0
EQ/Invesco Comstock Portfolio Class K			Open End	US Equity Large Cap Value (Growth & Income)	C+	C	B	Up	Y	0
EQ/Invesco Global Real Estate Portfolio Class IB			Open End	Real Estate Sector Equity (Real Estate)	U	U	U		Y	0
EQ/Invesco International Growth Portfolio Class IB			Open End	Global Equity Large Cap (Foreign Stock)	U	U	U		Y	0
EQ/Invesco Moderate Allocation Portfolio Class IB			Open End	Cautious Alloc (Asset Alloc)	B-	C	B+	Up	Y	0
EQ/Invesco Moderate Growth Allocation Portfolio Class IB			Open End	Moderate Alloc (Asset Alloc)	U	U	U		Y	0
EQ/Invesco Moderate Growth Allocation Portfolio Class K			Open End	Moderate Alloc (Asset Alloc)	U	U	U		Y	0
EQ/Ivy Energy Portfolio Class IB			Open End	Energy Sector Equity ()	U	U	U		Y	0
EQ/Ivy Mid Cap Growth Portfolio Class IB			Open End	US Equity Mid Cap (Growth)	U	U	U		Y	0
EQ/Ivy Science and Technology Portfolio Class IB			Open End	Technology Sector Equity (Technology)	U	U	U		Y	0
EQ/Janus Enterprise Portfolio Class IA			Open End	US Equity Mid Cap (Growth)	B-	C	B	Down	Y	0
EQ/Janus Enterprise Portfolio Class IB			Open End	US Equity Mid Cap (Growth)	B-	C	B	Down	Y	0
EQ/Janus Enterprise Portfolio Class K			Open End	US Equity Mid Cap (Growth)	B-	C	B	Down	Y	0
EQ/JPMorgan Growth Allocation Portfolio Class IB			Open End	Moderate Alloc (Growth & Income)	D+	D+	C	Up	Y	0
EQ/JPMorgan Growth Allocation Portfolio Class K			Open End	Moderate Alloc (Growth & Income)	D+	D+	C	Up	Y	0
EQ/JPMorgan Value Opportunities Portfolio Class IA			Open End	US Equity Large Cap Value (Growth & Income)	C	C	B-		Y	0
EQ/JPMorgan Value Opportunities Portfolio Class IB			Open End	US Equity Large Cap Value (Growth & Income)	C	C	B-		Y	0
EQ/JPMorgan Value Opportunities Portfolio Class K			Open End	US Equity Large Cap Value (Growth & Income)	C+	C	B-	Up	Y	0
EQ/Large Cap Core Managed Volatility Portfolio Class IA			Open End	US Equity Large Cap Blend (Growth & Income)	C+	C	B		Y	0
EQ/Large Cap Core Managed Volatility Portfolio Class IB			Open End	US Equity Large Cap Blend (Growth & Income)	C+	C	B		Y	0
EQ/Large Cap Core Managed Volatility Portfolio Class K			Open End	US Equity Large Cap Blend (Growth & Income)	B-	C	B	Up	Y	0
EQ/Large Cap Growth Index Portfolio Class IA			Open End	US Equity Large Cap Growth (Growth)	C+	C	B	Down	Y	0
EQ/Large Cap Growth Index Portfolio Class IB			Open End	US Equity Large Cap Growth (Growth)	C+	C	B	Down	Y	0
EQ/Large Cap Growth Index Portfolio Class K			Open End	US Equity Large Cap Growth (Growth)	C+	C	B	Down	Y	0
EQ/Large Cap Growth Managed Volatility Portfolio Class IA			Open End	US Equity Large Cap Growth (Growth)	B-	C	B		Y	0
EQ/Large Cap Growth Managed Volatility Portfolio Class IB			Open End	US Equity Large Cap Growth (Growth)	B-	C	B		Y	0
EQ/Large Cap Growth Managed Volatility Portfolio Class K			Open End	US Equity Large Cap Growth (Growth)	B-	C	B		Y	0
EQ/Large Cap Value Index Portfolio Class IA			Open End	US Equity Large Cap Value (Growth & Income)	B-	C	B	Up	Y	0
EQ/Large Cap Value Index Portfolio Class IB			Open End	US Equity Large Cap Value (Growth & Income)	B-	C	B	Up	Y	0
EQ/Large Cap Value Index Portfolio Class K			Open End	US Equity Large Cap Value (Growth & Income)	B-	C	B	Up	Y	0
EQ/Large Cap Value Managed Volatility Portfolio Class IA			Open End	US Equity Large Cap Value (Growth)	C+	C	B	Up	Y	0
EQ/Large Cap Value Managed Volatility Portfolio Class IB			Open End	US Equity Large Cap Value (Growth)	C+	C	B	Up	Y	0
EQ/Large Cap Value Managed Volatility Portfolio Class K			Open End	US Equity Large Cap Value (Growth)	C+	C	B	Up	Y	0
EQ/Lazard Emerging Markets Equity Portfolio Class IB			Open End	Global Emerg Mkts (Div Emerging Mkts)	U	U	U		Y	0
EQ/Legg Mason Growth Allocation Portfolio Class IB			Open End	Moderate Alloc (Asset Alloc)	U	U	U		Y	0
EQ/Legg Mason Growth Allocation Portfolio Class K			Open End	Moderate Alloc (Asset Alloc)	U	U	U		Y	0
EQ/Legg Mason Moderate Allocation Portfolio Class IB			Open End	Moderate Alloc (Asset Alloc)	C+	C	B+	Up	Y	0
EQ/Loomis Sayles Growth Portfolio Class IA			Open End	US Equity Large Cap Growth (Growth)	B-	C	B		Y	0
EQ/Loomis Sayles Growth Portfolio Class IB			Open End	US Equity Large Cap Growth (Growth)	B-	C	B		Y	0
EQ/Loomis Sayles Growth Portfolio Class K			Open End	US Equity Large Cap Growth (Growth)	B-	C	B		Y	0
EQ/MFS International Growth Portfolio Class IA			Open End	Global Equity Large Cap (Foreign Stock)	C+	C	B	Up	Y	0
EQ/MFS International Growth Portfolio Class IB			Open End	Global Equity Large Cap (Foreign Stock)	C+	C	B	Up	Y	0
EQ/MFS International Growth Portfolio Class K			Open End	Global Equity Large Cap (Foreign Stock)	C+	C	B	Up	Y	0

★ Expanded analysis of this fund is included in Section II.

	TOTAL RETURNS					PERFORMANCE				ASSETS		ASSET ALLOCATION & TURNOVER					BULL & BEAR		FEES		
Min Additional Investment	3-Month Total Return	6-Month Total Return	1-Year Total Return	3-Year Total Return	5-Year Total Return	Dividend Yield (TTM)	Expense Ratio	3-Yr Std Deviation	3-Year Beta	NAV	Total Assets (MIL)	%Cash	%Stocks	%Bonds	%Other	Turnover Ratio	Last Bull Market Total Return	Last Bear Market Total Return	Front End Fee (%)	Back End Fee (%)	Inception Date
	1.33	4.90	-8.65	20.50	5.06	2.53	0.81	10.62			1,612	0	100	0	0	8	10.93	-23.48			Apr-95
	1.35	4.99	-8.59	20.52	5.12	2.57	0.81	10.64			1,612	0	100	0	0	8	10.76	-23.45			May-97
	1.33	4.98	-8.48	21.30	6.33	2.8	0.56	10.62			1,612	0	100	0	0	8	10.93	-23.48			Aug-11
	1.03	5.10	-7.52	19.95	4.49	1.89	0.88	10.41			2,311	-1	101	0	0	5	8.77	-24.13			Oct-09
	1.10	5.19	-7.29	20.85	5.79	2.14	0.63	10.42			2,311	-1	101	0	0	5	8.94	-24.12			Aug-11
	0.40	4.33	-10.19	15.77	-0.10	1.81	1.02	11.23			982.3	0	100	0	0	42	10.92	-25.08			Mar-02
	0.40	4.33	-10.25	15.77	-0.10	1.81	1.02	11.19			982.3	0	100	0	0	42	10.87	-25.18			May-97
	0.47	4.44	-10.03	16.71	1.16	2.06	0.77	11.21			982.3	0	100	0	0	42	11.02	-25.17			Aug-11
	0.58	3.09	-4.04	38.28	36.35	1.55	1	13.11	1.17		239.7	6	94	0	0	18	24.84	-19.97			Apr-05
	0.58	3.09	-4.09	38.25	36.33	1.55	1	13.12	1.17		239.7	6	94	0	0	18	24.79	-20.07			Apr-05
	0.64	3.20	-3.83	39.31	38.07	1.8	0.75	13.12	1.17		239.7	6	94	0	0	18	24.84	-19.97			Oct-13
	2.77	10.03					1.27				219.5	1	98	0	1	8					Oct-18
	1.96	9.27					1.18				184.7	3	95	2	0	9					Oct-18
	1.44	4.18	1.10	13.75		0.77	1.2	5			282.1	-1	51	50	0	78					Apr-15
	2.36						1.2				15.1	-18	56	62	0						Jan-19
	2.36						0.95				15.1	-18	56	62	0						Jan-19
	-3.57	-9.89					1.19				88.1	0	100	0	0	5					Oct-18
	1.77	12.28					1.1				309.8	2	98	0	0	7					Oct-18
	5.85	16.66					1.15				158.8	3	96	2	0	2					Oct-18
	3.18	14.22	9.34	61.85	47.27	0	1.05	13.63	0.96		1,035	2	98	0	0	13	17.71	-21.43			Apr-05
	3.17	14.20	9.31	61.90	47.24	0	1.05	13.63	0.96		1,035	2	98	0	0	13	17.75	-21.58			Apr-05
	3.27	14.41	9.60	63.10	49.15	0	0.8	13.63	0.96		1,035	2	98	0	0	13	17.85	-21.43			Dec-11
	1.58	4.10	0.43			0.51	1.2				116.5	9	54	37	0	1					Nov-17
	1.58	4.16	0.59			0.76	0.95				116.5	9	54	37	0	1					Nov-17
	-1.57	1.89	-4.04	32.66	48.79	1.01	0.98	14.59	1.28		631.5	3	97	0	0	151	25.6	-21.77			Oct-02
	-1.62	1.83	-4.09	32.57	48.65	1.01	0.98	14.6	1.29		631.5	3	97	0	0	151	25.5	-21.83			May-97
	-1.57	1.96	-3.82	33.60	50.60	1.26	0.73	14.59	1.28		631.5	3	97	0	0	151	25.53	-21.83			Dec-11
	2.69	6.91	3.54	42.46	57.28	0.99	0.91	11.27	1.04		2,468	1	99	0	0	16	20.68	-18.74			Mar-02
	2.59	6.91	3.54	42.46	57.28	0.99	0.91	11.27	1.04		2,468	1	99	0	0	16	20.57	-18.87			Jan-99
	2.69	7.10	3.82	43.67	59.24	1.23	0.66	11.27	1.04		2,468	1	99	0	0	16	20.85	-18.86			Aug-11
	4.03	12.02	7.24	57.63	80.75	0.57	0.74	12.23	1		1,504	0	100	0	0	13	26.23	-15.4			May-99
	4.10	12.04	7.26	57.67	80.87	0.59	0.74	12.26	1		1,504	0	100	0	0	13	26.1	-15.52			May-99
	4.17	12.22	7.58	58.98	83.11	0.8	0.48	12.2	1		1,504	0	100	0	0	13	26.36	-15.4			Aug-11
	4.19	11.15	6.99	55.85	76.75	0.44	0.86	12.1	0.98		5,030	0	100	0	0	20	22.94	-16.94			Nov-98
	4.22	11.18	7.00	55.88	76.80	0.46	0.86	12.1	0.98		5,030	0	100	0	0	20	22.84	-17.28			May-97
	4.25	11.30	7.27	57.05	79.00	0.67	0.61	12.09	0.98		5,030	0	100	0	0	20	23	-17.24			Aug-11
	0.91	4.22	2.49	30.45	39.58	2	0.74	10.73	1		666.2	0	100	0	0	16	24.01	-19.07			Oct-05
	0.91	4.23	2.50	30.39	39.54	2.01	0.74	10.65	0.99		666.2	0	100	0	0	16	24.01	-19.13			Oct-05
	1.03	4.40	2.77	31.40	40.95	2.25	0.49	10.68	1		666.2	0	100	0	0	16	24	-19.06			Aug-11
	0.97	3.35	0.95	28.62	37.54	2.53	0.85	11	1.02		4,502	0	100	0	0	19	19.98	-19.71			May-01
	0.91	3.35	0.89	28.53	37.46	2.54	0.85	11.03	1.03		4,502	0	100	0	0	19	19.73	-19.76			Jan-98
	1.02	3.46	1.16	29.49	39.28	2.78	0.6	11	1.02		4,502	0	100	0	0	19	19.97	-19.82			Aug-11
	-5.61	1.19					1.38				388.4	5	96	0	0	0					Oct-18
	1.66						1.2				13.7	0	64	36	0						Jan-19
	1.66						0.95				13.7	0	64	36	0						Jan-19
	0.96	4.03	-0.22	14.15		1.25	1.2	5.38			187.2	6	52	43	0	510					Feb-16
	5.13	12.98	9.05	63.54	97.80	0.08	1.05	13.5	1.02		674.6	1	99	0	0	9	21.14	-11.82			Dec-04
	5.10	12.92	8.88	63.39	97.45	0.08	1.05	13.42	1.02		674.6	1	99	0	0	9	20.98	-11.81			Dec-98
	5.13	13.03	9.22	64.76	99.34	0.31	0.8	13.46	1.02		674.6	1	99	0	0	9	20.98	-11.8			Feb-15
	2.56	9.66	-0.73	36.72	28.76	0.85	1.15	10.68	0.93		1,262	1	99	0	0	20	20.24	-21.73			Sep-08
	2.42	9.50	-0.85	36.66	28.72	0.84	1.15	10.7	0.93		1,262	1	99	0	0	20	20.31	-21.84			Nov-94
	2.42	9.67	-0.58	37.74	30.39	1.09	0.9	10.75	0.93		1,262	1	99	0	0	20	20.43	-21.84			Aug-11

Fund Name	MARKET Ticker Symbol	Traded On	FUND TYPE, CATEGORY & OBJECTIVE Fund Type	Category and (Prospectus Objective)	RATINGS Overall Rating	Reward Rating	Risk Rating	Recent Up/ Downgrade	MINIMUMS Open to New Investors	Min Initial Investment
EQ/MFS International Value Portfolio Class IB			Open End	Global Equity Large Cap (Foreign Stock)	U	U	U		Y	0
EQ/MFS Technology Portfolio Class IB			Open End	Technology Sector Equity (Technology)	U	U	U		Y	0
EQ/MFS Utilities Series Portfolio Class IB			Open End	Utilities Sector Equity (Utility)	U	U	U		Y	0
EQ/MFS Utilities Series Portfolio Class K			Open End	Utilities Sector Equity (Utility)	U	U	U		Y	0
EQ/Mid Cap Index Portfolio Class IA			Open End	US Equity Mid Cap (Growth)	C+	C	B-	Up	Y	0
EQ/Mid Cap Index Portfolio Class IB			Open End	US Equity Mid Cap (Growth)	C+	C	B-	Up	Y	0
EQ/Mid Cap Index Portfolio Class K			Open End	US Equity Mid Cap (Growth)	C+	C	B-	Up	Y	0
EQ/Mid Cap Value Managed Volatility Portfolio Class IA			Open End	US Equity Mid Cap (Growth)	C+	C	B	Up	Y	0
EQ/Mid Cap Value Managed Volatility Portfolio Class IB			Open End	US Equity Mid Cap (Growth)	C+	C	B	Up	Y	0
EQ/Mid Cap Value Managed Volatility Portfolio Class K			Open End	US Equity Mid Cap (Growth)	C+	C	B	Up	Y	0
EQ/Moderate Allocation Portfolio Class K			Open End	Moderate Alloc (Asset Alloc)	B-	C	A-	Up	Y	0
EQ/Moderate Growth Strategy Fund Class IB			Open End	Moderate Alloc (Growth & Income)	B-	C	A-	Up	Y	0
EQ/Moderate-Plus Allocation Portfolio Class K			Open End	Aggressive Alloc (Asset Alloc)	B-	C	B+	Up	Y	0
EQ/Morgan Stanley Small Cap Growth Portfolio Class IB			Open End	US Equity Small Cap (Small Company)	C+	C	C+	Down	Y	0
EQ/Morgan Stanley Small Cap Growth Portfolio Class K			Open End	US Equity Small Cap (Small Company)	C+	C+	C+	Down	Y	0
EQ/Oppenheimer Global Portfolio Class IA			Open End	Global Equity Large Cap (Growth)	C	C	B-		Y	0
EQ/Oppenheimer Global Portfolio Class IB			Open End	Global Equity Large Cap (Growth)	C	C	B-		Y	0
EQ/Premier VIP Aggressive Allocation Fund Class A			Open End	Aggressive Alloc (Asset Alloc)	C+	C	B	Up	Y	0
EQ/Premier VIP Aggressive Allocation Fund Class B			Open End	Aggressive Alloc (Asset Alloc)	C+	C	B	Up	Y	0
EQ/Premier VIP Conservative Allocation Fund Class A			Open End	Cautious Alloc (Asset Alloc)	B-	C	B+	Up	Y	0
EQ/Premier VIP Conservative Allocation Fund Class B			Open End	Cautious Alloc (Asset Alloc)	B-	C	B+	Up	Y	0
EQ/Premier VIP Conservative-Plus Allocation Fund Class A			Open End	Cautious Alloc (Asset Alloc)	B-	C	A-		Y	0
EQ/Premier VIP Conservative-Plus Allocation Fund Class B			Open End	Cautious Alloc (Asset Alloc)	B-	C	A-		Y	0
EQ/Premier VIP Moderate Allocation Fund Class A			Open End	Moderate Alloc (Asset Alloc)	B-	C	A-	Up	Y	0
EQ/Premier VIP Moderate Allocation Fund Class B			Open End	Moderate Alloc (Asset Alloc)	B-	C	A-	Up	Y	0
EQ/Premier VIP Moderate-Plus Allocation Fund Class A			Open End	Aggressive Alloc (Asset Alloc)	B-	C	B+	Up	Y	0
EQ/Premier VIP Moderate-Plus Allocation Fund Class B			Open End	Aggressive Alloc (Asset Alloc)	B-	C	B+	Up	Y	0
EQ/Small Company Index Class K			Open End	US Equity Small Cap (Small Company)	C	C	C+		Y	0
EQ/Small Company Index Portfolio Class IA			Open End	US Equity Small Cap (Small Company)	C	C	C+		Y	0
EQ/Small Company Index Portfolio Class IB			Open End	US Equity Small Cap (Small Company)	C	C	C+		Y	0
EQ/T. Rowe Price Growth Stock Portfolio Class IA			Open End	US Equity Large Cap Growth (Growth)	B-	C	B	Down	Y	0
EQ/T. Rowe Price Growth Stock Portfolio Class IB			Open End	US Equity Large Cap Growth (Growth)	B-	C	B	Down	Y	0
EQ/T. Rowe Price Growth Stock Portfolio Class K			Open End	US Equity Large Cap Growth (Growth)	B-	C	B	Down	Y	0
EQ/T. Rowe Price Health Sciences Portfolio Class IB			Open End	Healthcare Sector Equity (Health)	U	U	U		Y	0
EQ/Templeton Global Eq Managed Vol Port Cls IA			Open End	Global Equity Large Cap (Growth)	C	C-	B-		Y	0
EQ/Templeton Global Eq Managed Vol Port Cls IB			Open End	Global Equity Large Cap (Growth)	C	C-	B		Y	0
EQ/Templeton Global Eq Managed Vol Port Cls K			Open End	Global Equity Large Cap (Growth)	C	C-	B		Y	0
EQ/UBS Growth and Income Portfolio Class IB			Open End	US Equity Large Cap Blend (Growth & Income)	C+	C	B-	Up	Y	0
Equable Shares Small Cap Fund	EQSIX	NAS CM	Open End	Long/Short Equity (Small Company)	U	U	U			100,000
Equinox Ampersand Strategy Fund Class A	EEHAX	NAS CM	Open End	Long/Short Equity (Growth)	C+	C	B	Up	Y	2,500
Equinox Ampersand Strategy Fund Class I	EEHIX	NAS CM	Open End	Long/Short Equity (Growth)	C+	C	B	Up	Y	1,000,000
Equinox Aspect Core Diversified Strategy Fund Class A	EQAAX	NAS CM	Open End	Alternative Miscellaneous (Growth)	D+	D	C-	Up	Y	2,500
Equinox Aspect Core Diversified Strategy Fund Class C	EQACX	NAS CM	Open End	Alternative Miscellaneous (Growth)	D	D	C-		Y	2,500
Equinox Aspect Core Diversified Strategy Fund Class I	EQAIX	NAS CM	Open End	Alternative Miscellaneous (Growth)	D+	D	C-	Up	Y	100,000
Equinox Campbell Strategy Fund Class A	EBSAX	NAS CM	Open End	Alternative Miscellaneous (Growth)	C	C-	C+	Up	Y	2,500
Equinox Campbell Strategy Fund Class C	EBSCX	NAS CM	Open End	Alternative Miscellaneous (Growth)	C	C-	C	Up	Y	2,500
Equinox Campbell Strategy Fund Class I	EBSIX	NAS CM	Open End	Alternative Miscellaneous (Growth)	C	C-	C+	Up	Y	100,000
Equinox Campbell Strategy Fund Class P	EBSPX	NAS CM	Open End	Alternative Miscellaneous (Growth)	C	C-	C+	Up	Y	2,500
Equinox Chesapeake Strategy Fund Class A	ECHAX	NAS CM	Open End	Alternative Miscellaneous (Growth)	D	D	D+		Y	2,500
Equinox Chesapeake Strategy Fund Class C	ECHCX	NAS CM	Open End	Alternative Miscellaneous (Growth)	D	D	D+		Y	2,500
Equinox Chesapeake Strategy Fund Class I	EQCHX	NAS CM	Open End	Alternative Miscellaneous (Growth)	D	D	D+		Y	100,000
Equinox IPM Systematic Macro Fund Class I	EQIPX	NAS CM	Open End	Alternative Miscellaneous (Growth)	D+	D	C	Down	Y	200,000,000

★ Expanded analysis of this fund is included in Section II.

Min Additional Investment	TOTAL RETURNS 3-Month Total Return	6-Month Total Return	1-Year Total Return	3-Year Total Return	5-Year Total Return	PERFORMANCE Dividend Yield (TTM)	Expense Ratio	3-Yr Std Deviation	3-Year Beta	ASSETS NAV	Total Assets (MIL)	ASSET ALLOCATION & TURNOVER %Cash	%Stocks	%Bonds	%Other	Turnover Ratio	BULL & BEAR Last Bull Market Total Return	Last Bear Market Total Return	FEES Front End Fee (%)	Back End Fee (%)	Inception Date
	3.87	9.88					1.15				922.6	3	97	0	0	1					Oct-18
	6.15	19.40					1.14				243.4	2	98	0	0	5					Oct-18
	4.17	11.82					1.05				189.7	4	94	0	0	10					Oct-18
	4.25	11.94					0.8				189.7	4	94	0	0	10					Oct-18
	-1.97	3.12	-3.53	32.99	45.08	1.06	0.72	13.68	1		1,978	0	100	0	0	18	27.64	-22.75			Mar-02
	-1.93	3.17	-3.45	32.97	45.08	1.08	0.72	13.64	1		1,978	0	100	0	0	18	27.45	-22.77			Sep-00
	-1.96	3.26	-3.26	34.00	46.91	1.31	0.47	13.68	1		1,978	0	100	0	0	18	27.64	-22.83			Aug-11
	-0.75	3.55	-2.56	25.58	34.68	1.23	0.96	12.5	1.04		1,905	0	100	0	0	25	22.28	-23.74			Nov-98
	-0.75	3.52	-2.53	25.50	34.67	1.24	0.96	12.52	1.04		1,905	0	100	0	0	25	22.2	-23.94			May-97
	-0.68	3.71	-2.23	26.52	36.47	1.47	0.71	12.5	1.04		1,905	0	100	0	0	25	22.33	-23.94			Dec-11
	2.73	10.45	4.67	22.86	23.01	1.75	0.84	6.18		14.31	7,296	1	51	47	0	12	9.73	-10.25			Dec-11
	2.72	11.50	4.41	25.46	26.73	1.16	1.01	7.5		17.43	7,250	1	62	37	0	9	11.34	-12.31			Apr-09
	3.02	13.17	4.11	30.93	29.30	1.78	0.88	8.78		11.31	8,764	1	71	28	0	8	13.26	-15.11			Dec-11
	2.33	18.02	7.30	69.48	67.05	0	1.15	17.12	1		329.5	3	97	0	0	62					Apr-14
	2.40	18.13	7.59	70.82	69.18	0	0.9	17.18	1.01		329.5	3	97	0	0	62					Apr-14
	1.72	9.02	-4.02	44.43	39.45	0.35	1.15	12.86	1.22		308.0	2	98	0	0	18	17.8	-22.94			Aug-06
	1.72	8.97	-4.02	44.36	39.48	0.35	1.15	12.89	1.22		308.0	2	98	0	0	18	17.77	-23.04			Aug-06
	3.28	15.57	3.74	38.14	33.86	1.5	1.17	11.16		11.73	3,326	1	91	8	0	11	16.75	-19.63			Jul-03
	3.36	15.67	3.74	38.25	33.97	1.5	1.17	11.16		11.73	3,326	1	91	8	0	11	16.73	-19.74			Jul-03
	2.15	6.38	5.02	10.68	13.25	1.48	1	2.69		9.51	1,062	2	21	77	0	12	4.81	-2.49			Jul-03
	2.26	6.50	5.01	10.79	13.25	1.48	1	2.71		9.51	1,062	2	21	77	0	12	4.76	-2.49			Jul-03
	2.39	8.98	4.58	18.02	18.97	1.45	1.1	5.01		9.85	1,235	2	41	57	0	14	8.14	-7.65			Jul-03
	2.50	8.97	4.68	18.01	19.08	1.45	1.1	5		9.86	1,235	2	41	57	0	14	8.1	-7.66			Jul-03
	2.66	10.30	4.39	21.86	21.40	1.51	1.09	6.2		14.29	7,296	1	51	47	0	12	9.65	-10.25			Jan-86
	2.61	10.31	4.35	21.86	21.37	1.52	1.09	6.2		14.17	7,296	1	51	47	0	12	9.52	-10.39			Jul-98
	2.93	13.07	3.91	29.96	27.70	1.54	1.13	8.73		11.29	8,764	1	71	28	0	8	13.15	-15.11			Jul-03
	2.93	13.07	3.91	29.95	27.69	1.54	1.13	8.73		11.3	8,764	1	71	28	0	8	13.1	-15.12			Jul-03
	-2.99	3.04	-5.63	41.34	46.69	1.23	0.39	15.92	1		1,169	0	100	0	0	15	27.51	-24.88			Aug-11
	-2.99	2.92	-5.90	40.38	44.93	0.98	0.64	15.96	1		1,169	0	100	0	0	15	27.38	-24.87			Mar-02
	-2.98	2.92	-5.82	40.34	45.02	0.98	0.64	15.97	1		1,169	0	100	0	0	15	27.32	-24.89			Jan-98
	2.93	13.22	5.44	64.17	89.48	0	1	13.2	1.03		1,584	2	98	0	0	45	30.92	-16.9			May-07
	2.91	13.21	5.43	64.14	89.45	0	1	13.19	1.02		1,584	2	98	0	0	45	30.77	-16.96			Aug-88
	2.97	13.36	5.69	65.37	91.82	0.09	0.75	13.18	1.02		1,584	2	98	0	0	45	30.88	-16.96			Dec-11
	-4.40	1.63					1.2				176.3	1	99	0	0	8					Oct-18
	-1.11	1.85	-5.55	24.41	15.92	2.96	1.1	10.34			713.8	1	99	0	0	18	15.9	-21.5			Sep-06
	-1.11	1.85	-5.55	24.40	15.92	2.96	1.1	10.34			713.8	1	99	0	0	18	15.76	-21.53			Sep-06
	-1.02	1.99	-5.26	25.47	17.41	3.22	0.85	10.36			713.8	1	99	0	0	18	16.04	-21.5			Aug-11
	3.57	9.84	0.69	42.13	52.63	0.33	1.05	13.95	1.22		104.7	0	100	0	0	47	24.88	-19.25			Dec-98
25,000	1.13	6.83					1.39			8.91	14.4										Aug-18
500	11.03	28.58	15.74	36.81	55.56	0.04	1.24	12.65	0.9	11.47	6.6	18	0	59	23	69			5.75	1.00	Sep-13
	11.19	28.82	16.19	38.43	58.21	0.41	0.99	12.64	0.9	11.62	6.6	18	0	59	23	69					Sep-13
500	3.86	7.40	-0.21	-8.43		0	1.7	9.64	1.34	9.14	21.2	20	2	77	0	20			5.75		Aug-15
500	3.74	7.00	-0.89	-10.54		0	2.45	9.62	1.34	8.86	21.2	20	2	77	0	20				1.00	Aug-15
	3.85	7.51	0.00	-7.90		0	1.45	9.6	1.34	9.16	21.2	20	2	77	0	20					Nov-14
500	6.77	11.46	9.22	-0.57	15.35	12.39	2.14	12.3	1.69	9.14	73.0	30	5	65	0	122			5.75		Mar-13
	6.60	11.13	8.43	-2.80	11.18	11.7	2.89	12.29	1.69	8.88	73.0	30	5	65	0	122				1.00	Feb-14
	6.82	11.59	9.50	0.14	16.88	12.58	1.89	12.26	1.69	9.24	73.0	30	5	65	0	122					Mar-13
	6.80	11.49	8.77	-0.62	15.98	9.99	2.14	12.35	1.7	9.41	73.0	30	5	65	0	122					Mar-13
500	-0.27	-1.00	-6.34	-7.91	10.62	0.46	2.04	13.46	1.5	10.87	93.1	7	5	88	0	13			5.75		Aug-15
500	-0.37	-1.39	-6.99	-9.90	6.66	0	2.81	13.4	1.49	10.62	93.1	7	5	88	0	13				1.00	Aug-15
	-0.09	-0.81	-6.03	-7.06	12.16	0.73	1.81	13.42	1.49	10.96	93.1	7	5	88	0	13					Sep-12
	-0.10	-1.00	-3.33	-1.26		1.38	1.85	8	-0.16	9.88	358.3	15	0	74	11	0					Jul-15

	MARKET		FUND TYPE, CATEGORY & OBJECTIVE		RATINGS				MINIMUMS	
Fund Name	Ticker Symbol	Traded On	Fund Type	Category and (Prospectus Objective)	Overall Rating	Reward Rating	Risk Rating	Recent Up/ Downgrade	Open to New Investors	Min Initial Investment
Equinox MutualHedge Futures Strategy Fund - Class A	MHFAX	NAS CM	Open End	Alternative Miscellaneous (Growth)	C	D+	B-	Up	Y	2,500
Equinox MutualHedge Futures Strategy Fund - Class C	MHFCX	NAS CM	Open End	Alternative Miscellaneous (Growth)	C	D+	C+	Up	Y	2,500
Equinox MutualHedge Futures Strategy Fund - Class I	MHFIX	NAS CM	Open End	Alternative Miscellaneous (Growth)	C	C-	B-	Up	Y	1,000,000
EquityCompass Quality Dividend Fund Class A	QDVAX	NAS CM	Open End	US Equity Large Cap Value (Equity-Income)	B-	C	B		Y	1,000
EquityCompass Quality Dividend Fund Class C	QDVCX	NAS CM	Open End	US Equity Large Cap Value (Equity-Income)	C+	C	B	Down	Y	1,000
EquityCompass Quality Dividend Fund Institutional Class	QDVIX	NAS CM	Open End	US Equity Large Cap Value (Equity-Income)	B-	C	B		Y	1,000,000
ERShares Global Fund™ Institutional Class	ENTIX	NAS CM	Open End	Global Equity Large Cap (Growth)	C+	C	B-	Up	Y	2,500
ERShares US Large Cap Fund™ Institutionall Class	IMPLX	NAS CM	Open End	US Equity Large Cap Growth (Growth)	C+	C	B-	Down	Y	2,500
ERShares US Small Cap Fund™ Institutional Class	IMPAX	NAS CM	Open End	US Equity Small Cap (Growth)	C	C	C+	Down	Y	2,500
Essential 40 Stock Fund Class I	ESSIX	NAS CM	Open End	US Equity Large Cap Blend (Growth)	C+	C	B		Y	10,000
Essex Environmental Opportunities Fund Institutional Class	GEOSX	NAS CM	Open End	Global Equity Large Cap (Growth)	C-	D+	C	Up	Y	100,000
Essex Environmental Opportunities Fund Investor Class	EEOFX	NAS CM	Open End	Global Equity Large Cap (Growth)	C-	D+	C	Up	Y	2,000
EuroPac Gold Fund Class A	EPGFX	NAS CM	Open End	Precious Metals Sector Equity (Precious Metals)	D+	D+	C	Down	Y	2,500
EuroPac Gold Fund Class I	EPGIX	NAS CM	Open End	Precious Metals Sector Equity (Precious Metals)	D+	D+	C	Down	Y	5,000
EuroPac International Dividend Income Fund Class A	EPDPX	NAS CM	Open End	Global Equity Large Cap (Equity-Income)	C	C-	C		Y	2,500
EuroPac International Dividend Income Fund Class I	EPDIX	NAS CM	Open End	Global Equity Large Cap (Equity-Income)	C	C-	C		Y	15,000
EuroPac International Value Fund Class A	EPIVX	NAS CM	Open End	Global Equity Large Cap (Foreign Stock)	D+	D	C-	Down	Y	2,500
EuroPac International Value Fund Class I	EPVIX	NAS CM	Open End	Global Equity Large Cap (Foreign Stock)	D+	D	C-	Down	Y	15,000
E-Valuator Aggressive Growth (85%-99%) RMS R4 Cls Shares	EVFGX	NAS CM	Open End	Aggressive Alloc (Aggr Growth)	C+	C	B	Up	Y	10,000
E-Valuator Aggressive Growth (85%-99%) RMS Serv Cls Shares	EVAGX	NAS CM	Open End	Aggressive Alloc (Aggr Growth)	C+	C	B	Up	Y	10,000
E-Valuator Conservative (15%-30%) RMS Fund R4 Class	EVFCX	NAS CM	Open End	Cautious Alloc (Growth & Income)	B-	C	A-	Up	Y	10,000
E-Valuator Conservative (15%-30%) RMS Fund Service Class	EVCLX	NAS CM	Open End	Cautious Alloc (Growth & Income)	B-	C	A-	Up	Y	10,000
E-Valuator Conservative/Moderate (30%-50%) RMS R4 Cls	EVFTX	NAS CM	Open End	Cautious Alloc (Growth & Income)	C+	C	B+	Up	Y	10,000
E-Valuator Conservative/Moderate (30%-50%) RMS Service Cls	EVTTX	NAS CM	Open End	Cautious Alloc (Growth & Income)	C+	C	B+	Up	Y	10,000
E-Valuator Growth (70%-85%) RMS Fund R4 Class Shares	EVGRX	NAS CM	Open End	Aggressive Alloc (Growth)	C+	C	B	Up	Y	10,000
E-Valuator Growth (70%-85%) RMS Fund Service Class Shares	EVGLX	NAS CM	Open End	Aggressive Alloc (Growth)	C+	C	B	Up	Y	10,000
E-Valuator Moderate (50%-70%) RMS Fund R4 Class Shares	EVFMX	NAS CM	Open End	Moderate Alloc (Growth & Income)	B-	C	B	Up	Y	10,000
E-Valuator Moderate (50%-70%) RMS Service Cls Shares	EVMLX	NAS CM	Open End	Moderate Alloc (Growth & Income)	B-	C	B	Up	Y	10,000
E-Valuator Very Conservative (0%-15%) RMS Fund R4 Class	EVVCX	NAS CM	Open End	Cautious Alloc (Growth & Income)	B-	C	B	Up	Y	10,000
E-Valuator Very Conservative (0%-15%) RMS Service Cls	EVVLX	NAS CM	Open End	Cautious Alloc (Growth & Income)	B-	C	B+	Up	Y	10,000
Eventide Gilead Class A	ETAGX	NAS CM	Open End	US Equity Mid Cap (Growth)	B	B	B		Y	1,000
Eventide Gilead Class C	ETCGX	NAS CM	Open End	US Equity Mid Cap (Growth)	B	B	B-		Y	1,000
Eventide Gilead Class I	ETILX	NAS CM	Open End	US Equity Mid Cap (Growth)	B	B	B		Y	100,000
Eventide Gilead Class N	ETGLX	NAS CM	Open End	US Equity Mid Cap (Growth)	B	B	B		Y	1,000
Eventide Global Dividend Opportunities Fund Class A Shares	ETADX	NAS CM	Open End	Global Equity Large Cap (Growth & Income)	C-	D+	C+	Up	Y	1,000
Eventide Global Dividend Opportunities Fund Class C Shares	ETCDX	NAS CM	Open End	Global Equity Large Cap (Growth & Income)	C-	D+	C+	Up	Y	1,000
Eventide Global Dividend Opportunities Fund Class I Shares	ETIDX	NAS CM	Open End	Global Equity Large Cap (Growth & Income)	C-	D+	C+	Up	Y	100,000
Eventide Global Dividend Opportunities Fund Class N Shares	ETNDX	NAS CM	Open End	Global Equity Large Cap (Growth & Income)	C-	D+	C+	Up	Y	1,000
Eventide Healthcare & Life Sciences Fund Class A Shares	ETAHX	NAS CM	Open End	Healthcare Sector Equity (Health)	C+	C+	C+		Y	1,000
Eventide Healthcare & Life Sciences Fund CLASS C SHARES	ETCHX	NAS CM	Open End	Healthcare Sector Equity (Health)	C+	C+	C+		Y	1,000
Eventide Healthcare & Life Sciences Fund CLASS I SHARES	ETIHX	NAS CM	Open End	Healthcare Sector Equity (Health)	C+	C+	C+		Y	100,000
Eventide Healthcare & Life Sciences Fund CLASS N SHARES	ETNHX	NAS CM	Open End	Healthcare Sector Equity (Health)	C+	C+	C+		Y	1,000
Eventide Multi-Asset Income Fund Class A	ETAMX	NAS CM	Open End	Moderate Alloc (Income)	C+	C	B		Y	1,000
Eventide Multi-Asset Income Fund Class C	ETCMX	NAS CM	Open End	Moderate Alloc (Income)	C+	C	B	Up	Y	1,000
Eventide Multi-Asset Income Fund Class I	ETIMX	NAS CM	Open End	Moderate Alloc (Income)	B-	C+	B	Up	Y	100,000
Eventide Multi-Asset Income Fund Class N	ETNMX	NAS CM	Open End	Moderate Alloc (Income)	C+	C	B		Y	1,000
Evercore Equity Fund	EWMCX	NAS CM	Open End	US Equity Large Cap Growth (Growth)	C+	C	B	Down	Y	1,000
Evermore Global Value Fund Institutional Class	EVGIX	NAS CM	Open End	Global Equity Mid/Small Cap (World Stock)	C-	D+	C	Up	Y	1,000,000
Evermore Global Value Fund Investor Class	EVGBX	NAS CM	Open End	Global Equity Mid/Small Cap (World Stock)	C-	D+	C	Up	Y	5,000
Fairholme Allocation Fund	FAAFX	NAS CM	Open End	Cautious Alloc (Asset Alloc)	C-	C-	C	Up		10,000
Fairholme Fund	FAIRX	NAS CM	Open End	US Equity Large Cap Value (Growth)	C	C	C	Up	Y	10,000
Fallen Angels Income Fund	FAINX	NAS CM	Open End	Aggressive Alloc (Income)	B	C+	A-		Y	10,000

★ Expanded analysis of this fund is included in Section II.

Min Additional Investment	TOTAL RETURNS 3-Month Total Return	6-Month Total Return	1-Year Total Return	3-Year Total Return	5-Year Total Return	PERFORMANCE Dividend Yield (TTM)	Expense Ratio	3-Yr Std Deviation	3-Year Beta	ASSETS NAV	Total Assets (MIL)	ASSET ALLOCATION & TURNOVER %Cash	%Stocks	%Bonds	%Other	Turnover Ratio	BULL & BEAR Last Bull Market Total Return	Last Bear Market Total Return	FEES Front End Fee (%)	Back End Fee (%)	Inception Date
500	7.37	10.86	6.47	2.32	24.89	0	1.95	10.37	0.13	8.88	251.8	-90	0	64	127	75	-3.62	-0.18	5.75		Dec-09
500	7.10	10.47	5.76	0.04	20.28	0	2.7	10.42	0.12	8.44	251.8	-90	0	64	127	75	-3.98	-0.56		1.00	Dec-09
	7.40	10.98	6.64	3.02	26.42	0	1.7	10.43	0.13	8.99	251.8	-90	0	64	127	75	-3.47	-0.19			May-11
100	0.81	13.83	9.26	29.43	35.91	2.88	1.24	10.94	0.86	12.76	70.0	0	100	0	0	51			5.75		Sep-13
100	0.62	13.31	8.40	26.53	30.87	2.14	1.99	10.91	0.85	12.82	70.0	0	100	0	0	51				1.00	Oct-13
	0.88	13.95	9.58	30.37	36.90	3.12	0.99	10.93	0.85	12.76	70.0	0	100	0	0	51					Oct-16
	2.60	19.90	1.11	50.46	50.10	0	1.71	13.95	1.16	15.78	63.8	5	95	0	0	38	21.77	-24.83			Nov-10
	1.88	22.43	5.09	64.63	74.39	0	0.75	14.82	1.13	15.17	133.3	6	94	0	0	43					Jun-14
	-1.70	20.70	1.57	79.69	71.95	0	0.86	17.87	0.97	12.71	160.7	7	93	0	0	72					Dec-13
1,000	1.87	14.28	5.42	20.62	13.39	1.2	0.7	12.12		10.88	31.4	0	100	0	0	63					Jun-14
	6.48	23.63	6.06			0	1			10.67	7.3	15	85	0	0	23					Sep-17
	6.41	23.34	5.67			0	1.25			10.62	7.3	15	85	0	0	23					Sep-17
250	7.08	19.09	2.76	-6.14	5.09	0	1.5	21.78	0.82	8.92	89.5	0	100	0	0	21			4.50		Jul-13
250	7.19	19.35	2.99	-5.92	5.33		1.25	21.78	0.82	8.94	89.5	0	100	0	0	21					Nov-18
250	2.21	10.09	7.29	5.73	-14.74	2.71	1.5	11.02	0.95	7.86	56.1	6	95	0	-1	15	14.6	-17.58	4.50		Jan-14
2,000	2.27	10.07	7.56	6.50	-13.68	2.95	1.25	11.14	0.96	7.86	56.1	6	95	0	-1	15	14.77	-17.49			Jan-14
250	1.50	10.29	3.55	-2.04	-24.11	1.49	1.75	13.48	0.84	7.18	57.1	6	93	0	1	23	15.52	-23.6	4.50		Apr-10
2,500	1.56	10.25	3.66	-1.39	-23.33	1.73	1.5	13.43	0.83	7.18	57.1	6	93	0	1	23	15.52	-23.6			Jul-13
100	3.16	16.84	1.15	33.20	33.55	0.86	1.07	11.92	0.95	11.1	92.6	2	96	2	0	298					Feb-12
100	3.25	16.98	1.36	34.40	34.77	1.11	0.82	11.92	0.95	11.09	92.6	2	96	2	0	298					May-16
100	3.05	10.10	4.88	16.68	20.30	2.56	1.04	5.1	0.26	10.46	56.0	6	29	60	1	322					Feb-12
100	3.06	10.26	5.13	17.61	21.27	3.03	0.78	5.14	0.27	10.42	56.0	6	29	60	1	322					May-16
100	3.05	11.68	2.81	16.39	15.38	0.72	1.23	7.06	0.54	10.13	12.9	5	47	43	1	237					May-16
100	2.98	11.73	2.90	17.10	16.66	1.12	0.92	7.02	0.53	10	12.9	5	47	43	1	237					May-16
100	3.29	15.63	2.52	31.51	33.89	1.35	1.03	10.65	0.85	10.65	234.7	3	82	14	1	303					Feb-12
100	3.31	15.82	2.77	32.66	35.06	1.63	0.78	10.64	0.85	10.61	234.7	3	82	14	1	303					May-16
100	3.28	14.46	3.99	26.81	29.86	1.73	1.03	9.06	0.72	10.68	173.9	2	68	27	1	303					Feb-12
100	3.39	14.62	4.22	27.99	31.07	2.07	0.78	9.09	0.73	10.66	173.9	2	68	27	1	303					May-16
100	2.68	7.05	4.22	10.71	12.68	2.51	1.16	3.19	0.24	10.32	14.3	12	14	70	1	389					May-16
100	2.71	7.12	4.40	11.52	14.06	3.79	0.94	3.18	0.24	10.22	14.3	12	14	70	1	389					May-16
50	3.10	33.75	16.35	90.85	80.06	0	1.45	16.84	1.13	41.57	2,652	15	84	0	1	24	34.76	-25.45	5.75		Oct-09
50	2.89	33.27	15.50	86.63	73.38	0	2.2	16.8	1.13	38.37	2,652	15	84	0	1	24	34.18	-25.69		1.00	Oct-09
50	3.17	33.93	16.66	92.29	82.31	0	1.2	16.83	1.13	42.59	2,652	15	84	0	1	24	34.81	-25.38			Feb-10
50	3.13	33.80	16.43	91.18	80.47	0	1.4	16.82	1.13	41.76	2,652	15	84	0	1	24	34.72	-25.43			Jul-08
50	4.51	17.46	9.15			1.62	1.22			10.36	16.6	13	82	0	0				5.75		Sep-17
50	4.44	17.11	8.33			1.09	1.97			10.35	16.6	13	82	0	0				5.75		Sep-17
50	4.67	17.70	9.40			1.93	0.97			10.37	16.6	13	82	0	0						Sep-17
50	4.62	17.59	9.20			1.67	1.17			10.37	16.6	13	82	0	0						Sep-17
50	-0.89	36.93	10.40	107.65	122.34	0	1.56	24.14	1.25	35.33	1,083	5	92	0	3	43			5.75		Dec-12
50	-1.06	36.49	9.62	103.11	114.22	0	2.31	24.13	1.25	33.55	1,083	5	92	0	3	43				1.00	Dec-12
50	-0.82	37.11	10.72	109.27	125.09	0	1.31	24.14	1.25	35.98	1,083	5	92	0	3	43					Dec-12
50	-0.86	36.99	10.51	107.96	122.88	0	1.51	24.14	1.25	35.51	1,083	5	92	0	3	43					Dec-12
50	3.41	13.09	6.56	18.79		2.92	1.24	7.09	0.57	10.89	111.5	6	52	33	0	29			5.75		Jul-15
50	3.22	12.73	5.73	16.11		2.25	1.99	7.02	0.57	10.86	111.5	6	52	33	0	29					Jul-15
50	3.57	13.34	6.81	19.70		3.15	0.99	7.01	0.56	10.9	111.5	6	52	33	0	29					Jul-15
50	3.51	13.23	6.61	19.08		2.96	1.19	7.07	0.57	10.9	111.5	6	52	33	0	29					Jul-15
100	4.50	21.81	7.38	58.77	59.02	0.19	1	14.18	1.14	19.49	175.9	5	95	0	0	14	27.59	-16.78			Dec-45
100	6.61	13.88	-9.80	29.20	27.33	0.44	1.19	13.68	0.92	13.37	577.6	5	93	2	0	29	14.04	-30.04			Dec-09
100	6.50	13.70	-10.05	28.17	25.82	0.04	1.44	13.66	0.91	13.27	577.6	5	93	2	0	29	13.96	-30.06			Dec-09
1,000	2.90	14.43	6.28	0.25	-25.83	0.99	1.01	17.22	-0.77	7.45	78.3	66	17	0	0	24	36.73	-25.6			Dec-10
1,000	5.68	26.75	6.14	12.85	-8.62	1.76	1	22.2	0.62	19.14	1,143	36	38	9	0	16	29.98	-30.59			Dec-99
1,000	5.76	15.98	13.13	35.23	34.65	0.5	2.09	8.56	1.04	13.11	9.0	8	73	16	0	19	15.53	-11.01			Nov-06

	MARKET			FUND TYPE, CATEGORY & OBJECTIVE	RATINGS				MINIMUMS	
Fund Name	Ticker Symbol	Traded On	Fund Type	Category and (Prospectus Objective)	Overall Rating	Reward Rating	Risk Rating	Recent Up/ Downgrade	Open to New Investors	Min Initial Investment
FAM Equity-Income Fund Investor Class	FAMEX	NAS CM	Open End	US Equity Mid Cap (Equity-Income)	B	B-	B+		Y	500
FAM Small Cap Fund Institutional Class	FAMDX	NAS CM	Open End	US Equity Small Cap (Small Company)	C	C	C+	Down	Y	500,000
FAM Small Cap Fund Investor Class	FAMFX	NAS CM	Open End	US Equity Small Cap (Small Company)	C	C	C+	Down	Y	500
FAM Value Fund Institutional Class	FAMWX	NAS CM	Open End	US Equity Mid Cap (Growth)	B-	C+	B			500,000
FAM Value Fund Investor Class	FAMVX	NAS CM	Open End	US Equity Mid Cap (Growth)	B-	C+	B		Y	500
FBP Appreciation & Income Opportunities Fund	FBPBX	NAS CM	Open End	Aggressive Alloc (Growth & Income)	C+	C	B		Y	5,000
FBP Equity & Dividend Plus Fund	FBPEX	NAS CM	Open End	US Equity Large Cap Value (Equity-Income)	B-	C	B	Up	Y	5,000
FDP BlackRock Capital Appreciation Institutional Shares	MADDX	NAS CM	Open End	US Equity Large Cap Growth (Growth)	B-	C+	B	Down	Y	2,000,000
FDP BlackRock Capital Appreciation Fund Investor A Shares	MDDDX	NAS CM	Open End	US Equity Large Cap Growth (Growth)	B-	C+	B	Down	Y	1,000
FDP BlackRock Capital Appreciation Fund Investor C Shares	MCDDX	NAS CM	Open End	US Equity Large Cap Growth (Growth)	C+	C+	B	Down	Y	1,000
FDP BlackRock Equity Dividend Fund Institutional Shares	MAVVX	NAS CM	Open End	US Equity Large Cap Value (Growth & Income)	B-	C	B	Up	Y	2,000,000
FDP BlackRock Equity Dividend Fund Investor A Shares	MDVVX	NAS CM	Open End	US Equity Large Cap Value (Growth & Income)	B-	C	B	Up	Y	1,000
FDP BlackRock Equity Dividend Fund Investor C Shares	MCVVX	NAS CM	Open End	US Equity Large Cap Value (Growth & Income)	B-	C	B	Up	Y	1,000
FDP BlackRock International Fund Institutional Shares	MAIQX	NAS CM	Open End	Global Equity Large Cap (Growth)	C	C-	C+		Y	2,000,000
FDP BlackRock International Fund Investor A Shares	MDIQX	NAS CM	Open End	Global Equity Large Cap (Growth)	C	C-	C+	Up	Y	1,000
FDP BlackRock International Fund Investor C Shares	MCIQX	NAS CM	Open End	Global Equity Large Cap (Growth)	C	C-	C+	Up	Y	1,000
Federated Absolute Return Fund Class A Shares	FMAAX	NAS CM	Open End	Market Neutral (Growth)	D	D	C-	Down	Y	1,500
Federated Absolute Return Fund Class B Shares	FMBBX	NAS CM	Open End	Market Neutral (Growth)	D	D	D+	Down		1,500
Federated Absolute Return Fund Class C Shares	FMRCX	NAS CM	Open End	Market Neutral (Growth)	D	D	D+	Down	Y	1,500
Federated Absolute Return Fund Class Institutional Shares	FMIIX	NAS CM	Open End	Market Neutral (Growth)	D	D	C-	Down	Y	1,000,000
Federated Capital Income Fund Class A Shares	CAPAX	NAS CM	Open End	Cautious Alloc (Income)	B-	C	B+	Up	Y	1,500
Federated Capital Income Fund Class B Shares	CAPBX	NAS CM	Open End	Cautious Alloc (Income)	C+	C	B+	Up		1,500
Federated Capital Income Fund Class C Shares	CAPCX	NAS CM	Open End	Cautious Alloc (Income)	C+	C	B+	Up	Y	1,500
Federated Capital Income Fund Class F Shares	CAPFX	NAS CM	Open End	Cautious Alloc (Income)	B-	C	B+	Up	Y	1,500
Federated Capital Income Fund Class R	CAPRX	NAS CM	Open End	Cautious Alloc (Income)	B-	C	B+	Up	Y	0
Federated Capital Income Fund Institutional Class	CAPSX	NAS CM	Open End	Cautious Alloc (Income)	B-	C	B+	Up	Y	1,000,000
Federated Clover Small Value Fund Class A	VSFAX	NAS CM	Open End	US Equity Small Cap (Small Company)	C-	C-	C	Down	Y	1,500
Federated Clover Small Value Fund Class C	VSFCX	NAS CM	Open End	US Equity Small Cap (Small Company)	C-	C-	C		Y	1,500
Federated Clover Small Value Fund Class R	VSFRX	NAS CM	Open End	US Equity Small Cap (Small Company)	C-	C-	C	Down	Y	0
Federated Clover Small Value Fund Class R6	VSFSX	NAS CM	Open End	US Equity Small Cap (Small Company)	C	C-	C		Y	0
Federated Clover Small Value Fund Institutional Shares	VSFIX	NAS CM	Open End	US Equity Small Cap (Small Company)	C	C-	C		Y	1,000,000
Federated Equity Advantage Fund Class A	FEKAX	NAS CM	Open End	US Equity Small Cap (Growth)	C	C-	C+		Y	1,500
Federated Equity Advantage Fund Institutional Shares	FEKIX	NAS CM	Open End	US Equity Small Cap (Growth)	C	C-	C+		Y	1,000,000
Federated Equity Income Fund, Inc. Class A Shares	LEIFX	NAS CM	Open End	US Equity Large Cap Value (Equity-Income)	C	C	B-		Y	1,500
Federated Equity Income Fund, Inc. Class B Shares	LEIBX	NAS CM	Open End	US Equity Large Cap Value (Equity-Income)	C	C	B-			1,500
Federated Equity Income Fund, Inc. Class C Shares	LEICX	NAS CM	Open End	US Equity Large Cap Value (Equity-Income)	C	C	B-		Y	1,500
Federated Equity Income Fund, Inc. Class F Shares	LFEIX	NAS CM	Open End	US Equity Large Cap Value (Equity-Income)	C	C	B-		Y	1,500
Federated Equity Income Fund, Inc. Class R Shares	FDERX	NAS CM	Open End	US Equity Large Cap Value (Equity-Income)	C	C	B-		Y	0
Federated Equity Income Fund, Inc. Institutional Shares	LEISX	NAS CM	Open End	US Equity Large Cap Value (Equity-Income)	C	C	B-		Y	1,000,000
Federated Global Allocation Fund Class A Shares	FSTBX	NAS CM	Open End	Flexible Alloc (Asset Alloc)	B-	C	B+	Up	Y	1,500
Federated Global Allocation Fund Class B Shares	FSBBX	NAS CM	Open End	Flexible Alloc (Asset Alloc)	C+	C	B+	Up		1,500
Federated Global Allocation Fund Class C Shares	FSBCX	NAS CM	Open End	Flexible Alloc (Asset Alloc)	C+	C	B+	Up	Y	1,500
Federated Global Allocation Fund Class R Shares	FSBKX	NAS CM	Open End	Flexible Alloc (Asset Alloc)	B-	C	B+	Up	Y	0
Federated Global Allocation Fund Class R6	FSBLX	NAS CM	Open End	Flexible Alloc (Asset Alloc)	B-	C	B+	Up	Y	0
Federated Global Allocation Fund Institutional Shares	SBFIX	NAS CM	Open End	Flexible Alloc (Asset Alloc)	B-	C	B+	Up	Y	1,000,000
Federated Global Strategic Value Dividend Cls A Shares	GVDSX	NAS CM	Open End	Global Equity Large Cap (Equity-Income)	C	C	C+		Y	1,500
Federated Global Strategic Value Dividend Cls C Shares	GVDCX	NAS CM	Open End	Global Equity Large Cap (Equity-Income)	C	C	C		Y	1,500
Federated Global Strategic Value Dividend Cls R6 Shares	GVDLX	NAS CM	Open End	Global Equity Large Cap (Equity-Income)	C	C	C+		Y	0
Federated Global Strategic Value Dividend Inst Shares	GVDIX	NAS CM	Open End	Global Equity Large Cap (Equity-Income)	C	C	C+		Y	1,000,000
Federated Hermes SDG Engagement Equity Inst Shares	FHESX	NAS CM	Open End	Global Equity Mid/Small Cap (Growth)	U	U	U		Y	1,000,000
Federated International Dividend Strategy Portfolio	FIDPX	NAS CM	Open End	Global Equity Large Cap (Equity-Income)	C	C	C+		Y	0
Federated International Leaders Fund Class A Shares	FGFAX	NAS CM	Open End	Global Equity Large Cap (World Stock)	C	C-	C+	Up	Y	1,500

★ Expanded analysis of this fund is included in Section II.

	TOTAL RETURNS					PERFORMANCE				ASSETS		ASSET ALLOCATION & TURNOVER					BULL & BEAR		FEES		
Min Additional Investment	3-Month Total Return	6-Month Total Return	1-Year Total Return	3-Year Total Return	5-Year Total Return	Dividend Yield (TTM)	Expense Ratio	3-Yr Std Deviation	3-Year Beta	NAV	Total Assets (MIL)	%Cash	%Stocks	%Bonds	%Other	Turnover Ratio	Last Bull Market Total Return	Last Bear Market Total Return	Front End Fee (%)	Back End Fee (%)	Inception Date
50	6.96	24.71	19.64	57.94	72.24	0.58	1.24	12.4	0.87	36.61	358.4	8	93	0	0	18	24.27	-14.37			Apr-96
	3.86	16.78	-0.57	29.23	38.68	0	1.18	14.46	0.8	17.46	181.2	5	95	0	0	31					Jan-16
50	3.82	16.73	-0.68	28.79	38.03	0	1.29	14.41	0.8	17.37	181.2	5	95	0	0	31					Mar-12
	7.52	21.88	12.62	47.74	61.19	0.26	1	12.54	0.89	79.99	1,337	7	93	0	0	12	24.48	-18.36			Jan-17
50	7.48	21.77	12.43	47.11	60.52	0.09	1.19	12.54	0.89	79.8	1,337	7	93	0	0	12	24.48	-18.36			Jan-87
	0.04	9.32	1.18	28.60	22.44	1.91	1.13	10.21	0.79	18.82	32.9	9	74	17	0	21	17.91	-18.08			Jul-89
	0.66	10.15	2.62	33.83	32.00	2.39	1.24	11.04	0.84	25.19	28.7	9	91	0	0	18	21.78	-25.25			Jul-93
	5.86	24.98	10.32	63.67	65.74	0	1.03	14.25	1.03	16.06	69.4	0	100	0	0	106	28.44	-18.23			Jul-05
50	5.81	24.81	10.03	62.45	63.62	0	1.28	14.22	1.03	15.29	69.4	0	100	0	0	106	28.28	-18.26	5.25		Jul-05
50	5.64	24.42	9.30	58.92	57.60	0	2.04	14.28	1.03	13.09	69.4	0	100	0	0	106	27.63	-18.5		1.00	Jul-05
	4.58	16.21	7.17	47.60	39.25	1.2	0.96	12.53	0.99	12.54	60.7	7	93	0	0	81	24.77	-19.79			Jul-05
50	4.57	16.18	6.87	46.51	37.59	0.99	1.21	12.55	1	12.35	60.7	7	93	0	0	81	24.69	-19.93	5.25		Jul-05
50	4.37	15.71	6.12	43.22	32.49	0.31	1.96	12.52	1	11.93	60.7	7	93	0	0	81	24.03	-20.16		1.00	Jul-05
	3.52	18.90	-1.92	23.49	3.69	1.33	1.23	13.68	1.15	12.64	61.1	1	94	0	0	144	13.56	-22.03			Jul-05
50	3.54	18.80	-2.16	22.54	2.49	0.88	1.48	13.73	1.16	12.57	61.1	1	94	0	0	144	13.39	-22.13	5.25		Jul-05
50	3.30	18.38	-2.91	19.79	-1.33	0	2.24	13.73	1.16	12.49	61.1	1	94	0	0	144	12.85	-22.4		1.00	Jul-05
100	0.11	2.85	-5.14	-10.39	-12.10	0	2.4	6.27	11.39	8.66	65.2	54	76	-30	0	192	-0.98	-0.5	5.50		Dec-00
100	0.00	2.44	-5.84	-12.35	-15.28	0	3.15	6.24	10.84	8.37	65.2	54	76	-30	0	192	-1.33	-0.81		5.50	Dec-00
100	0.00	2.58	-5.76	-12.31	-15.34	0	3.15	6.27	12.04	8.33	65.2	54	76	-30	0	192	-1.44	-0.81		1.00	Dec-00
	0.22	3.05	-4.87	-9.66	-10.96	0	2.15	6.28	10.87	8.78	65.2	54	76	-30	0	192	-0.79	-0.4			Jun-07
100	2.64	10.90	3.29	16.74	9.33	3.82	0.9	6.32	0.5	7.86	1,239	-2	38	59	0	105	12.28	-7.23	5.50		May-88
100	2.29	10.43	2.47	14.03	5.08	3.03	1.75	6.29	0.5	7.87	1,239	-2	38	59	0	105	11.76	-7.51		5.50	Sep-94
100	2.30	10.45	2.48	14.06	5.21	3.04	1.73	6.28	0.49	7.86	1,239	-2	38	59	0	105	11.78	-7.51		1.00	Apr-93
100	2.51	10.91	3.29	16.72	9.28	3.81	0.91	6.34	0.5	7.85	1,239	-2	38	59	0	105	12.29	-7.23	1.00		May-96
	2.59	10.77	3.23	16.14	8.21	3.63	1.15	6.3	0.5	7.87	1,239	-2	38	59	0	105	11.96	-7.42			Jun-13
	2.70	11.02	3.68	17.75	10.70	4.06	0.65	6.27	0.49	7.87	1,239	-2	38	59	0	105	12.43	-7.23			Mar-12
100	2.01	14.17	-8.28	26.29	16.66	0.06	1.27	17.01	0.96	19.73	344.1	4	96	0	0	84	24.65	-24.87	5.50		Feb-96
100	1.77	13.69	-8.99	23.40	12.34	0	2.02	17	0.96	18.35	344.1	4	96	0	0	84	24.16	-25.13		1.00	Feb-96
	2.00	14.11	-8.32	26.15	16.32	0.12	1.41	17.02	0.96	19.32	344.1	4	96	0	0	84	24.5	-24.96			Dec-10
	2.07	14.33	-7.99	27.46	17.74	0.46	0.95	16.99	0.96	19.7	344.1	4	96	0	0	84	24.65	-24.87			Mar-16
	2.06	14.26	-8.09	27.18	18.13	0.41	1.02	16.99	0.96	19.78	344.1	4	96	0	0	84	24.83	-24.77			Mar-09
100	2.60	17.07	-5.35	24.42		0.89	1.23	18.64	0.98	9.46	2.1	3	97	0	0	69			5.50		Feb-16
	2.59	17.16	-5.16	25.09		1.22	0.98	18.63	0.98	9.49	2.1	3	97	0	0	69					Feb-16
100	2.19	13.59	-0.29	29.50	21.24	1.75	1.12	12.56	1.02	20.78	926.5	0	96	4	0	133	21.84	-12.19	5.50		Dec-86
100	1.99	13.14	-1.10	26.42	16.50	1	1.91	12.57	1.02	20.7	926.5	0	96	4	0	133	21.24	-12.46		5.50	Sep-94
100	2.01	13.14	-1.04	26.54	16.70	1.01	1.88	12.55	1.02	20.74	926.5	0	96	4	0	133	21.29	-12.5		1.00	May-93
100	2.18	13.49	-0.54	28.52	19.79	1.51	1.37	12.58	1.02	20.8	926.5	0	96	4	0	133	21.62	-12.3	1.00		Nov-93
	2.21	13.55	-0.43	28.85	20.29	1.58	1.36	12.58	1.02	20.79	926.5	0	96	4	0	133	21.49	-12.37			Jan-13
	2.26	13.72	-0.06	30.41	22.78	1.96	0.89	12.57	1.02	20.77	926.5	0	96	4	0	133	21.79	-12.19			Mar-12
100	2.69	12.61	3.72	24.11	18.49	1.79	1.16	8.39	0.64	19.39	355.7	0	64	36	0	66	14.66	-13.4	5.50		Dec-68
100	2.48	12.17	2.88	21.22	13.82	1.02	1.99	8.37	0.63	18.91	355.7	0	64	36	0	66	14.15	-13.7		5.50	Aug-96
100	2.51	12.20	2.96	21.36	14.13	1.09	1.95	8.39	0.63	18.83	355.7	0	64	36	0	66	14.21	-13.69		1.00	Apr-93
	2.60	12.41	3.30	22.57	16.04	1.39	1.59	8.4	0.64	19.26	355.7	0	64	36	0	66	14.41	-13.54			Apr-03
	2.77	12.77	4.07	25.22	19.55	2.11	0.85	8.38	0.63	19.39	355.7	0	64	36	0	66	14.66	-13.4			Jun-16
	2.80	12.81	4.05	25.28	20.27	2.06	0.87	8.4	0.64	19.51	355.7	0	64	36	0	66	14.91	-13.29			Jun-09
100	1.33	12.19	6.26			3.83	1.11			5.1	1.6	1	99	0	0	25			5.50		Jan-17
100	0.93	11.63	5.37			3.01	1.89			5.1	1.6	1	99	0	0	25				1.00	Jan-17
	1.40	12.33	6.54			4.08	0.85			5.1	1.6	1	99	0	0	25					Jan-17
	1.19	12.32	6.52			4.07	0.86			5.1	1.6	1	99	0	0	25					Jan-17
	5.45	18.38					0.95			10.82	28.9	0	99	0	1						Nov-18
	4.94	13.62	10.31	11.47		4.87	0	9.72	0.7	8.19	89.2	0	100	0	0	38					Feb-15
100	5.14	17.62	-2.87	32.70	5.12	2.4	1.24	13.9	1.22	33.71	1,233	9	91	0	0	37	23.27	-29.47	5.50		Sep-98

Fund Name	Ticker Symbol	Traded On	Fund Type	Category and (Prospectus Objective)	Overall Rating	Reward Rating	Risk Rating	Recent Up/ Downgrade	Open to New Investors	Min Initial Investment
	MARKET			FUND TYPE, CATEGORY & OBJECTIVE	RATINGS				MINIMUMS	
Federated International Leaders Fund Class B Shares	FGFBX	NAS CM	Open End	Global Equity Large Cap (World Stock)	C	C-	C+	Up		1,500
Federated International Leaders Fund Class C Shares	FGFCX	NAS CM	Open End	Global Equity Large Cap (World Stock)	C	C-	C+	Up	Y	1,500
Federated International Leaders Fund Class R	FGFRX	NAS CM	Open End	Global Equity Large Cap (World Stock)	C	C-	C+	Up	Y	0
Federated International Leaders Fund Class R6 Shares	FGRSX	NAS CM	Open End	Global Equity Large Cap (World Stock)	C	C-	C+	Up	Y	0
Federated International Leaders Fund Institutional Class	FGFLX	NAS CM	Open End	Global Equity Large Cap (World Stock)	C	C-	C+	Up	Y	1,000,000
Federated International Small-Mid Company Fund Class A	ISCAX	NAS CM	Open End	Global Equity Mid/Small Cap (Growth)	C	C	C+		Y	1,500
Federated International Small-Mid Company Fund Class C	ISCCX	NAS CM	Open End	Global Equity Mid/Small Cap (Growth)	C	C	C+		Y	1,500
Federated Intl Small-Mid Company Inst Cls	ISCIX	NAS CM	Open End	Global Equity Mid/Small Cap (Growth)	C	C	C+		Y	1,000,000
Federated Intl Strategic Value Dividend Cls A Shares	IVFAX	NAS CM	Open End	Global Equity Large Cap (Growth & Income)	C	C-	C		Y	1,500
Federated Intl Strategic Value Dividend Cls C Shares	IVFCX	NAS CM	Open End	Global Equity Large Cap (Growth & Income)	C-	D+	C	Down	Y	1,500
Federated Intl Strategic Value Dividend Cls R6 Shares	IVFLX	NAS CM	Open End	Global Equity Large Cap (Growth & Income)	C	C-	C+		Y	0
Federated Intl Strategic Value Dividend Inst Shares	IVFIX	NAS CM	Open End	Global Equity Large Cap (Growth & Income)	C	C-	C+		Y	1,000,000
Federated Kaufmann Fund Class A Shares	KAUAX	NAS CM	Open End	US Equity Mid Cap (Growth)	B-	B-	B	Down	Y	1,500
Federated Kaufmann Fund Class B Shares	KAUBX	NAS CM	Open End	US Equity Mid Cap (Growth)	B-	C+	B	Down		1,500
Federated Kaufmann Fund Class C Shares	KAUCX	NAS CM	Open End	US Equity Mid Cap (Growth)	B-	C+	B	Down	Y	1,500
Federated Kaufmann Fund Class R Shares	KAUFX	NAS CM	Open End	US Equity Mid Cap (Growth)	B-	C+	B	Down	Y	0
Federated Kaufmann Fund Institutional Shares	KAUIX	NAS CM	Open End	US Equity Mid Cap (Growth)	B-	C+	B	Down	Y	1,000,000
Federated Kaufmann Large Cap Fund Class A	KLCAX	NAS CM	Open End	US Equity Large Cap Growth (Growth)	B	B-	B		Y	1,500
Federated Kaufmann Large Cap Fund Class C	KLCCX	NAS CM	Open End	US Equity Large Cap Growth (Growth)	B	B-	B		Y	1,500
Federated Kaufmann Large Cap Fund Class R Shares	KLCKX	NAS CM	Open End	US Equity Large Cap Growth (Growth)	B	B-	B		Y	0
Federated Kaufmann Large Cap Fund Class R6	KLCSX	NAS CM	Open End	US Equity Large Cap Growth (Growth)	B	B-	B		Y	0
Federated Kaufmann Large Cap Fund Institutional Shares	KLCIX	NAS CM	Open End	US Equity Large Cap Growth (Growth)	B	B-	B		Y	1,000,000
Federated Kaufmann Small Cap Fund Class A Shares	FKASX	NAS CM	Open End	US Equity Small Cap (Small Company)	B	B	B		Y	1,500
Federated Kaufmann Small Cap Fund Class B Shares	FKBSX	NAS CM	Open End	US Equity Small Cap (Small Company)	B	B	B			1,500
Federated Kaufmann Small Cap Fund Class C Shares	FKCSX	NAS CM	Open End	US Equity Small Cap (Small Company)	B	B	B		Y	1,500
Federated Kaufmann Small Cap Fund Class R Shares	FKKSX	NAS CM	Open End	US Equity Small Cap (Small Company)	B	B	B		Y	0
Federated Kaufmann Small Cap Fund Class R6 Shares	FKALX	NAS CM	Open End	US Equity Small Cap (Small Company)	B	B	B		Y	0
Federated Kaufmann Small Cap Fund Institutional Shares	FKAIX	NAS CM	Open End	US Equity Small Cap (Small Company)	B	B	B		Y	1,000,000
Federated Max-Cap Index Fund Class C Shares	MXCCX	NAS CM	Open End	US Equity Large Cap Blend (Growth & Income)	B-	C	B		Y	1,500
Federated Max-Cap Index Fund Class R Shares	FMXKX	NAS CM	Open End	US Equity Large Cap Blend (Growth & Income)	B-	C	B		Y	0
Federated Max-Cap Index Fund Institutional Shares	FISPX	NAS CM	Open End	US Equity Large Cap Blend (Growth & Income)	B-	C	B		Y	1,000,000
Federated Max-Cap Index Fund Service Shares	FMXSX	NAS CM	Open End	US Equity Large Cap Blend (Growth & Income)	B-	C	B		Y	1,000,000
Federated MDT All Cap Core Fund Class A Shares	QAACX	NAS CM	Open End	US Equity Large Cap Value (Growth)	B-	C	B	Down	Y	1,500
Federated MDT All Cap Core Fund Class C Shares	QCACX	NAS CM	Open End	US Equity Large Cap Value (Growth)	B-	C	B	Down	Y	1,500
Federated MDT All Cap Core Fund Class R6 Shares	QKACX	NAS CM	Open End	US Equity Large Cap Value (Growth)	B-	C	B	Down	Y	0
Federated MDT All Cap Core Fund Institutional Shares	QIACX	NAS CM	Open End	US Equity Large Cap Value (Growth)	B-	C	B	Down	Y	1,000,000
Federated MDT Balanced Fund Class A Shares	QABGX	NAS CM	Open End	Moderate Alloc (Balanced)	B-	C	B+		Y	1,500
Federated MDT Balanced Fund Class C Shares	QCBGX	NAS CM	Open End	Moderate Alloc (Balanced)	B-	C	B+	Up	Y	1,500
Federated MDT Balanced Fund Class R6 Shares	QKBGX	NAS CM	Open End	Moderate Alloc (Balanced)	B-	C	B+		Y	0
Federated MDT Balanced Fund Institutional Shares	QIBGX	NAS CM	Open End	Moderate Alloc (Balanced)	B-	C	B+		Y	1,000,000
Federated MDT Large Cap Growth Fund Class A Shares	QALGX	NAS CM	Open End	US Equity Large Cap Growth (Growth)	B-	C+	B	Down	Y	1,500
Federated MDT Large Cap Growth Fund Class B Shares	QBLGX	NAS CM	Open End	US Equity Large Cap Growth (Growth)	B-	C+	B	Down	Y	1,500
Federated MDT Large Cap Growth Fund Class C Shares	QCLGX	NAS CM	Open End	US Equity Large Cap Growth (Growth)	B-	C+	B	Down	Y	1,500
Federated MDT Large Cap Growth Fund Institutional Shares	QILGX	NAS CM	Open End	US Equity Large Cap Growth (Growth)	B-	C+	B	Down	Y	1,000,000
Federated MDT Large Cap Value Fund Class A	FSTRX	NAS CM	Open End	US Equity Large Cap Value (Growth & Income)	B-	C	B	Up	Y	1,500
Federated MDT Large Cap Value Fund Class B	QBLVX	NAS CM	Open End	US Equity Large Cap Value (Growth & Income)	B-	C	B	Up	Y	1,500
Federated MDT Large Cap Value Fund Class C	QCLVX	NAS CM	Open End	US Equity Large Cap Value (Growth & Income)	B-	C	B	Up	Y	1,500
Federated MDT Large Cap Value Fund Class R	QRLVX	NAS CM	Open End	US Equity Large Cap Value (Growth & Income)	B-	C	B	Up	Y	0
Federated MDT Large Cap Value Fund Class R6	FSTLX	NAS CM	Open End	US Equity Large Cap Value (Growth & Income)	B-	C	B		Y	0
Federated MDT Large Cap Value Fund Institutional Shares	FMSTX	NAS CM	Open End	US Equity Large Cap Value (Growth & Income)	B-	C	B	Up	Y	1,000,000
Federated MDT Large Cap Value Fund Service Shares	FSTKX	NAS CM	Open End	US Equity Large Cap Value (Growth & Income)	B-	C	B	Up	Y	1,000,000
Federated MDT Mid Cap Growth Fund Class A Shares	FGSAX	NAS CM	Open End	US Equity Mid Cap (Growth)	C+	C+	B-	Down	Y	1,500

★ Expanded analysis of this fund is included in Section II.

Min Additional Investment	3-Month Total Return	6-Month Total Return	1-Year Total Return	3-Year Total Return	5-Year Total Return	Dividend Yield (TTM)	Expense Ratio	3-Yr Std Deviation	3-Year Beta	NAV	Total Assets (MIL)	%Cash	%Stocks	%Bonds	%Other	Turnover Ratio	Last Bull Market Total Return	Last Bear Market Total Return	Front End Fee (%)	Back End Fee (%)	Inception Date
TOTAL RETURNS						PERFORMANCE				ASSETS		ASSET ALLOCATION & TURNOVER					BULL & BEAR		FEES		
100	4.89	17.15	-3.62	29.70	1.20	1.32	2.1	13.88	1.21	31.49	1,233	9	91	0	0	37	22.71	-29.69		5.50	Sep-98
100	4.91	17.12	-3.64	29.75	1.21	1.32	2.09	13.88	1.21	31.39	1,233	9	91	0	0	37	22.69	-29.7		1.00	Sep-98
	5.10	17.52	-3.04	31.98	4.15	2.16	1.43	13.88	1.21	33.53	1,233	9	91	0	0	37	22.91	-29.62			Jun-13
	5.21	17.82	-2.54	34.02	6.80	2.8	0.93	13.9	1.22	33.71	1,233	9	91	0	0	37	23.27	-29.47			Aug-13
	5.20	17.80	-2.60	33.78	6.49	2.71	0.98	13.88	1.21	33.75	1,233	9	91	0	0	37	23.38	-29.36			Jun-10
100	5.26	21.03	1.20	36.69	22.49	0.86	1.87	12.93	1.04	33.78	118.7	5	95	0	0	28	24.17	-29.35	5.50		Feb-96
100	5.06	20.53	0.39	33.44	17.70	0	2.67	12.93	1.04	25.12	118.7	5	95	0	0	28	23.6	-29.58		1.00	Feb-96
	5.32	21.16	1.41	37.54	23.76	1.05	1.67	12.93	1.04	34.63	118.7	5	95	0	0	28	24.25	-29.28			Mar-08
100	1.13	10.36	3.37	5.37	-9.16	4.13	1.11	10.25	0.78	3.4	444.0	1	99	0	0	24	12.4	-15.92	5.50		Jun-08
100	0.95	10.05	2.67	3.23	-12.46	3.46	1.86	10.18	0.77	3.37	444.0	1	99	0	0	24	12.02	-16.27		1.00	Jun-08
	1.20	10.51	3.65	6.17	-8.27	4.4	0.85	10.43	0.79	3.4	444.0	1	99	0	0	24	12.84	-15.82			Jan-17
	1.49	10.82	3.93	6.44	-8.04	4.37	0.86	10.46	0.79	3.41	444.0	1	99	0	0	24	12.84	-15.82			Jun-08
100	5.47	27.71	14.58	77.58	91.09	0	1.98	14.44	0.94	6.36	6,797	22	78	0	0	33	26.19	-25.63	5.50		Apr-01
100	5.17	27.31	13.71	75.03	86.22	0	2.53	14.45	0.94	5.08	6,797	22	78	0	0	33	25.85	-25.71		5.50	Apr-01
100	5.40	27.38	13.96	74.84	86.14	0	2.53	14.56	0.95	5.07	6,797	22	78	0	0	33	25.84	-25.71		1.00	Apr-01
	5.46	27.65	14.37	77.40	91.17	0	1.98	14.59	0.95	6.37	6,797	22	78	0	0	33	26.2	-25.63			Feb-86
	5.54	27.86	15.07	79.77	93.73	0	1.53	14.57	0.95	6.47	6,797	22	78	0	0	33	26.2	-25.63			Dec-16
100	7.19	28.09	17.59	65.05	77.98	0	1.09	13.16	0.95	26.81	3,453	2	98	0	0	35	33.29	-20.36	5.50		Dec-07
100	6.95	27.57	16.66	61.22	71.11	0	1.87	13.15	0.95	24.29	3,453	2	98	0	0	35	32.74	-20.65		1.00	Dec-07
	7.08	27.89	17.13	63.18	74.47	0	1.48	13.14	0.95	25.4	3,453	2	98	0	0	35	33.04	-20.53			Dec-07
	7.28	28.31	17.97	66.62	80.76	0	0.78	13.17	0.95	27.69	3,453	2	98	0	0	35	33.54	-20.28			Dec-13
	7.27	28.26	17.85	66.34	80.17	0	0.84	13.16	0.95	27.59	3,453	2	98	0	0	35	33.54	-20.28			Dec-07
100	5.30	30.76	18.44	113.51	118.39	0	1.37	15.78	0.85	41.91	3,149	16	84	0	0	39	40.09	-29.15	5.50		Dec-02
100	5.10	30.34	17.72	109.61	112.15	0	2.04	15.78	0.85	35.61	3,149	16	84	0	0	39	39.64	-29.33		5.50	Dec-02
100	5.13	30.36	17.71	109.72	112.27	0	2.02	15.8	0.85	35.63	3,149	16	84	0	0	39	39.64	-29.33		1.00	Dec-02
	5.29	30.76	18.50	113.80	118.85	0	1.37	15.79	0.85	42.12	3,149	16	84	0	0	39	40.07	-29.14			Nov-05
	5.41	31.06	19.03	115.24	120.16	0	0.9	15.79	0.85	42.28	3,149	16	84	0	0	39	40.09	-29.15			Sep-17
	5.41	31.06	19.00	116.48	121.92	0	0.91	15.78	0.85	42.65	3,149	16	84	0	0	39	40.09	-29.15			Dec-15
100	-0.04	14.18	4.84	39.77	49.92	0.44	1.44	12.2	1	9.59	321.0	0	100	0	0	30	24.02	-16.73		1.00	Nov-97
	0.14	14.39	5.25	41.17	52.43	0.66	1.11	12.23	1	9.79	321.0	0	100	0	0	30	24.17	-16.62			Apr-03
	0.31	14.80	6.06	44.30	58.15	1.21	0.36	12.21	1	9.97	321.0	0	100	0	0	30	24.68	-16.3			Jul-90
	0.13	14.54	5.64	42.87	55.74	0.99	0.66	12.16	1	9.81	321.0	0	100	0	0	30	24.54	-16.5			Sep-93
100	4.13	21.33	10.16	60.22	57.97	0.22	1.05	13.28	1.04	29.69	314.2	2	98	0	0	82	26.21	-23.03	5.50		Feb-03
100	3.96	20.90	9.35	56.61	52.10	0	1.8	13.28	1.04	27.82	314.2	2	98	0	0	82	25.66	-23.3		1.00	Sep-05
	4.23	21.56	10.50	61.41	57.75	0.48	0.74	13.3	1.04	29.54	314.2	2	98	0	0	82	25.95	-23.23			Dec-06
	4.22	21.53	10.49	61.64	60.31	0.42	0.75	13.28	1.04	30.08	314.2	2	98	0	0	82	26.53	-23.02			Oct-02
100	3.09	14.27	7.07	33.48	33.60	0.95	1.35	8.37	0.67	18.65	160.1	-2	64	38	0	89	15.91	-14.77	5.50		Sep-05
100	2.90	13.88	6.24	30.48	28.62	0	2.1	8.36	0.67	18.45	160.1	-2	64	38	0	89	15.31	-15.04		1.00	Sep-05
	3.20	14.46	7.30	34.34	33.81	1.17	1.09	8.41	0.67	18.67	160.1	-2	64	38	0	89	15.54	-14.96			Dec-06
	3.14	14.43	7.34	34.48	35.18	1.14	1.1	8.4	0.67	18.71	160.1	-2	64	38	0	89	16.02	-14.73			Oct-02
100	5.00	24.35	13.00	73.70	67.99	0	1.52	14.22	1.04	20.58	128.8	2	98	0	0	104	26.31	-18.77	5.50		Sep-05
100	4.82	23.89	12.17	69.78	61.69	0	2.27	14.23	1.04	18.46	128.8	2	98	0	0	104	25.7	-18.93		5.50	Mar-07
100	4.79	23.85	12.11	69.72	61.79	0	2.27	14.23	1.04	17.91	128.8	2	98	0	0	104	25.68	-19.05		1.00	Sep-05
	5.06	24.52	13.25	75.02	70.15	0	1.27	14.25	1.04	21.58	128.8	2	98	0	0	104	26.39	-18.65			Sep-05
100	1.98	14.27	5.21	39.13	36.28	1.3	0.99	12.3	1	27.17	1,161	2	98	0	0	95	30.17	-22.29	5.50		May-14
100	2.37	15.11	5.55	34.79	32.54	0.47	1.86	12.29	1	27.22	1,161	2	98	0	0	95	29.6	-22.53		5.50	Dec-17
100	2.38	15.14	5.59	34.86	32.61	0.51	1.81	12.34	1	27.21	1,161	2	98	0	0	95	29.6	-22.53		1.00	Dec-17
	2.48	15.31	5.96	36.09	34.49	0.9	1.44	12.31	1	27.19	1,161	2	98	0	0	95	29.79	-22.45			Dec-17
	2.61	15.73	6.72	39.16	38.90	1.57	0.7	12.28	1	27.2	1,161	2	98	0	0	95	30.17	-22.29			Jun-16
	2.63	15.70	6.65	38.99	39.29	1.51	0.77	12.33	1	27.19	1,161	2	98	0	0	95	30.31	-22.23			Jan-10
	2.57	15.56	6.41	38.04	37.78	1.3	0.99	12.32	1	27.21	1,161	2	98	0	0	95	30.17	-22.29			Mar-82
100	5.48	26.79	12.81	76.16	69.38	0	1.15	15.94	1.07	42.11	597.9	2	98	0	0	171	18.77	-22.71	5.50		Aug-84

	MARKET			FUND TYPE, CATEGORY & OBJECTIVE	RATINGS				MINIMUMS	
Fund Name	Ticker Symbol	Traded On	Fund Type	Category and (Prospectus Objective)	Overall Rating	Reward Rating	Risk Rating	Recent Up/ Downgrade	Open to New Investors	Min Initial Investment
Federated MDT Mid Cap Growth Fund Class C Shares	FGSCX	NAS CM	Open End	US Equity Mid Cap (Growth)	C+	C	B-	Down	Y	1,500
Federated MDT Mid Cap Growth Fund Class R6 Shares	FGSKX	NAS CM	Open End	US Equity Mid Cap (Growth)	C+	C+	B-	Down	Y	0
Federated MDT Mid Cap Growth Fund Institutional Shares	FGSIX	NAS CM	Open End	US Equity Mid Cap (Growth)	C+	C+	B-	Down	Y	1,000,000
Federated MDT Small Cap Core Fund Class A	QASCX	NAS CM	Open End	US Equity Small Cap (Small Company)	C	C-	C		Y	1,500
Federated MDT Small Cap Core Fund Class C	QCSCX	NAS CM	Open End	US Equity Small Cap (Small Company)	C	C-	C		Y	1,500
Federated MDT Small Cap Core Fund Class R6	QLSCX	NAS CM	Open End	US Equity Small Cap (Small Company)	C	C-	C		Y	0
Federated MDT Small Cap Core Fund Institutional Class	QISCX	NAS CM	Open End	US Equity Small Cap (Small Company)	C	C-	C		Y	1,000,000
Federated MDT Small Cap Growth Fund Class A Shares	QASGX	NAS CM	Open End	US Equity Small Cap (Small Company)	C	C	C+		Y	1,500
Federated MDT Small Cap Growth Fund Class C Shares	QCSGX	NAS CM	Open End	US Equity Small Cap (Small Company)	C	C	C+	Down	Y	1,500
Federated MDT Small Cap Growth Fund Class R6	QLSGX	NAS CM	Open End	US Equity Small Cap (Small Company)	C	C	C+		Y	0
Federated MDT Small Cap Growth Fund Institutional Shares	QISGX	NAS CM	Open End	US Equity Small Cap (Small Company)	C	C	C+		Y	1,000,000
Federated Mid-Cap Index Fund Class R6 Shares	FMCLX	NAS CM	Open End	US Equity Mid Cap (Growth & Income)	C+	C	B-	Up	Y	0
Federated Mid-Cap Index Fund Institutional Shares	FMCRX	NAS CM	Open End	US Equity Mid Cap (Growth & Income)	C+	C	B-	Up	Y	1,000,000
Federated Mid-Cap Index Fund Service Shares	FMDCX	NAS CM	Open End	US Equity Mid Cap (Growth & Income)	C+	C	B-	Up	Y	1,000,000
Federated Muni and Stock Advantage Fund Class A Shares	FMUAX	NAS CM	Open End	Cautious Alloc (Income)	B-	C	B+	Up	Y	1,500
Federated Muni and Stock Advantage Fund Class B Shares	FMNBX	NAS CM	Open End	Cautious Alloc (Income)	B-	C	B+	Up		1,500
Federated Muni and Stock Advantage Fund Class C Shares	FMUCX	NAS CM	Open End	Cautious Alloc (Income)	B-	C	B+	Up	Y	1,500
Federated Muni and Stock Advantage Fund Class F Shares	FMUFX	NAS CM	Open End	Cautious Alloc (Income)	B-	C	B+	Up	Y	1,500
Federated Muni & Stock Advantage Institutional Shares	FMUIX	NAS CM	Open End	Cautious Alloc (Income)	B-	C	A-	Up	Y	1,000,000
Federated Prudent Bear Fund Class A Shares	BEARX	NAS CM	Open End	Alternative Miscellaneous (Growth)	D-	D-	D-	Down	Y	1,500
Federated Prudent Bear Fund Class C Shares	PBRCX	NAS CM	Open End	Alternative Miscellaneous (Growth)	D-	D-	D-	Down	Y	1,500
Federated Prudent Bear Fund Institutional Shares	PBRIX	NAS CM	Open End	Alternative Miscellaneous (Growth)	D-	D-	D	Down	Y	1,000,000
Federated Strategic Value Dividend Fund Class A Shares	SVAAX	NAS CM	Open End	US Equity Large Cap Value (Equity-Income)	C+	C	B		Y	1,500
Federated Strategic Value Dividend Fund Class C Shares	SVACX	NAS CM	Open End	US Equity Large Cap Value (Equity-Income)	C+	C	B-		Y	1,500
Federated Strategic Value Dividend Fund Class R6	SVALX	NAS CM	Open End	US Equity Large Cap Value (Equity-Income)	C+	C	B		Y	0
Federated Strategic Value Dividend Institutional Shares	SVAIX	NAS CM	Open End	US Equity Large Cap Value (Equity-Income)	C+	C	B		Y	1,000,000
Fidelity Advisor Asset Manager® 20% Fund Class A	FTAWX	NAS CM	Open End	Cautious Alloc (Asset Alloc)	B-	C	B+		Y	0
Fidelity Advisor Asset Manager® 20% Fund Class C	FTCWX	NAS CM	Open End	Cautious Alloc (Asset Alloc)	B-	C	B+	Up	Y	0
Fidelity Advisor Asset Manager® 20% Fund Class M	FTDWX	NAS CM	Open End	Cautious Alloc (Asset Alloc)	B-	C	B+		Y	0
Fidelity Advisor Asset Manager® 20% Fund Class Z	FIKVX	NAS CM	Open End	Cautious Alloc (Asset Alloc)	B-	C	A-		Y	0
Fidelity Advisor Asset Manager® 20% Fund I Class	FTIWX	NAS CM	Open End	Cautious Alloc (Asset Alloc)	B-	C	A-		Y	0
Fidelity Advisor Asset Manager® 30% Fund Class A	FTAAX	NAS CM	Open End	Cautious Alloc (Asset Alloc)	B-	C	A-		Y	0
Fidelity Advisor Asset Manager® 30% Fund Class C	FCANX	NAS CM	Open End	Cautious Alloc (Asset Alloc)	B-	C	B+	Up	Y	0
Fidelity Advisor Asset Manager® 30% Fund Class M	FTTNX	NAS CM	Open End	Cautious Alloc (Asset Alloc)	B-	C	A-		Y	0
Fidelity Advisor Asset Manager® 30% Fund Class Z	FIKWX	NAS CM	Open End	Cautious Alloc (Asset Alloc)	B	C	A-	Up	Y	0
Fidelity Advisor Asset Manager® 30% Fund I Class	FTINX	NAS CM	Open End	Cautious Alloc (Asset Alloc)	B	C	A-	Up	Y	0
Fidelity Advisor Asset Manager® 40% Fund Class A	FFNAX	NAS CM	Open End	Cautious Alloc (Asset Alloc)	B-	C	A-	Up	Y	0
Fidelity Advisor Asset Manager® 40% Fund Class C	FFNCX	NAS CM	Open End	Cautious Alloc (Asset Alloc)	B-	C	B+	Up	Y	0
Fidelity Advisor Asset Manager® 40% Fund Class M	FFNTX	NAS CM	Open End	Cautious Alloc (Asset Alloc)	B-	C	A-	Up	Y	0
Fidelity Advisor Asset Manager® 40% Fund Class Z	FIKYX	NAS CM	Open End	Cautious Alloc (Asset Alloc)	B	C	A-	Up	Y	0
Fidelity Advisor Asset Manager® 40% Fund I Class	FFNIX	NAS CM	Open End	Cautious Alloc (Asset Alloc)	B	C	A-	Up	Y	0
Fidelity Advisor Asset Manager® 50% Fund Class A	FFAMX	NAS CM	Open End	Cautious Alloc (Asset Alloc)	B-	C	A-	Up	Y	0
Fidelity Advisor Asset Manager® 50% Fund Class C	FFCMX	NAS CM	Open End	Cautious Alloc (Asset Alloc)	B-	C	B+	Up	Y	0
Fidelity Advisor Asset Manager® 50% Fund Class M	FFTMX	NAS CM	Open End	Cautious Alloc (Asset Alloc)	B-	C	A-	Up	Y	0
Fidelity Advisor Asset Manager® 50% Fund Class Z	FIKZX	NAS CM	Open End	Cautious Alloc (Asset Alloc)	B-	C	A-	Up	Y	0
Fidelity Advisor Asset Manager® 50% Fund I Class	FFIMX	NAS CM	Open End	Cautious Alloc (Asset Alloc)	B-	C	A-	Up	Y	0
Fidelity Advisor Asset Manager® 60% Fund Class A	FSAAX	NAS CM	Open End	Moderate Alloc (Asset Alloc)	B-	C	B+	Up	Y	0
Fidelity Advisor Asset Manager® 60% Fund Class C	FSCNX	NAS CM	Open End	Moderate Alloc (Asset Alloc)	B-	C	B+	Up	Y	0
Fidelity Advisor Asset Manager® 60% Fund Class M	FSATX	NAS CM	Open End	Moderate Alloc (Asset Alloc)	B-	C	B+	Up	Y	0
Fidelity Advisor Asset Manager® 60% Fund Class Z	FIQAX	NAS CM	Open End	Moderate Alloc (Asset Alloc)	B-	C	B+	Up	Y	0
Fidelity Advisor Asset Manager® 60% Fund I Class	FSNIX	NAS CM	Open End	Moderate Alloc (Asset Alloc)	B-	C	B+	Up	Y	0
Fidelity Advisor Asset Manager® 70% Fund Class A	FAASX	NAS CM	Open End	Moderate Alloc (Asset Alloc)	B-	C	B+	Up	Y	0

★ Expanded analysis of this fund is included in Section II.

	TOTAL RETURNS					PERFORMANCE				ASSETS		ASSET ALLOCATION & TURNOVER					BULL & BEAR		FEES		
Min Additional Investment	3-Month Total Return	6-Month Total Return	1-Year Total Return	3-Year Total Return	5-Year Total Return	Dividend Yield (TTM)	Expense Ratio	3-Yr Std Deviation	3-Year Beta	NAV	Total Assets (MIL)	%Cash	%Stocks	%Bonds	%Other	Turnover Ratio	Last Bull Market Total Return	Last Bear Market Total Return	Front End Fee (%)	Back End Fee (%)	Inception Date
100	5.26	26.31	11.93	72.25	63.15	0	1.89	15.91	1.07	27.79	597.9	2	98	0	0	171	18.23	-22.93		1.00	Aug-95
	5.54	27.00	13.11	77.34	68.85	0	0.84	15.93	1.07	39.41	597.9	2	98	0	0	171	18.43	-22.85			Dec-06
	5.53	26.97	13.12	77.53	71.51	0	0.85	15.92	1.07	43.5	597.9	2	98	0	0	171	18.95	-22.61			Jan-10
100	1.30	14.01	-7.33	47.69	53.09	0	1.14	18.48	1.07	18.63	981.4	2	98	0	0	88	29.52	-29.24	5.50		Sep-05
100	1.11	13.59	-8.03	44.34	47.40	0	1.89	18.46	1.07	16.38	981.4	2	98	0	0	88	28.98	-29.45		1.00	Sep-05
	1.36	14.16	-7.10	48.86	55.08	0.11	0.88	18.49	1.07	19.34	981.4	2	98	0	0	88	29.79	-29.17			Jun-16
	1.36	14.10	-7.15	48.77	54.99	0.11	0.89	18.5	1.07	19.33	981.4	2	98	0	0	88	29.79	-29.17			Sep-05
100	2.67	17.60	-2.81	63.96	70.11	0	1.14	18.35	1.04	23.05	886.8	2	98	0	0	129	33.43	-27.18	5.50		Sep-05
100	2.49	17.18	-3.55	60.32	63.85	0	1.89	18.34	1.04	20.12	886.8	2	98	0	0	129	32.78	-27.4		1.00	Sep-05
	2.77	17.79	-2.54	65.11	72.28	0	0.88	18.38	1.04	24.1	886.8	2	98	0	0	129	33.54	-27.1			Jun-16
	2.72	17.73	-2.58	65.11	72.27	0	0.89	18.36	1.04	24.1	886.8	2	98	0	0	129	33.54	-27.1			Sep-05
	-0.30	15.17	-2.18	33.65	40.47	1.16	0.3	15.14	1	20.58	574.9	0	100	0	0	29	27.57	-22.72			Oct-16
	2.89	18.89	0.98	37.99	45.74	1.14	0.31	15.12	1	20.55	574.9	0	100	0	0	29	27.59	-22.72			Jan-12
	-0.42	14.99	-2.47	32.66	39.42	0.94	0.56	15.12	1	20.57	574.9	0	100	0	0	29	27.57	-22.72			Nov-92
100	4.00	10.66	4.81	17.83	20.86	2.14	1	5.46	0.17	12.86	1,565	0	43	57	0	87	10.89	-0.53	5.50		Sep-03
100	3.89	10.34	4.10	15.22	16.53	1.42	1.75	5.52	0.17	12.86	1,565	0	43	57	0	87	10.4	-0.84		5.50	Sep-03
100	3.89	10.26	4.11	15.23	16.45	1.42	1.75	5.51	0.16	12.85	1,565	0	43	57	0	87	10.4	-0.84		1.00	Sep-03
100	4.00	10.66	4.81	17.83	20.86	2.14	1	5.48	0.17	12.86	1,565	0	43	57	0	87	10.89	-0.53	1.00		May-07
	4.15	10.89	5.16	18.72	22.47	2.38	0.75	5.52	0.18	12.86	1,565	0	43	57	0	87	11.04	-0.42			Dec-10
100	-4.61	-14.55	-12.11	-39.00	-48.48	0	3.55	10.17	-0.78	12.62	156.0	386	-477	191	0	284	-21.68	16.08	5.50		Dec-95
100	-4.74	-14.88	-12.72	-40.35	-50.49	0	4.3	10.17	-0.78	11.04	156.0	386	-477	191	0	284	-21.9	15.53		1.00	Feb-99
	-4.56	-14.46	-11.90	-38.56	-47.99	0	3.27	10.2	-0.79	12.95	156.0	386	-477	191	0	284	-21.55	15.97			Dec-08
100	-0.74	10.63	5.71	12.98	30.69	3.47	1.06	10.08	0.6	5.63	9,727	1	99	0	0	9	11.47	-4.1	5.50		Mar-05
100	-0.92	10.20	4.90	10.43	25.84	2.73	1.81	10.13	0.6	5.64	9,727	1	99	0	0	9	10.98	-4.39		1.00	Mar-05
	-0.67	10.72	5.96	13.83	32.46	3.71	0.79	10.13	0.6	5.66	9,727	1	99	0	0	9	11.82	-4.2			Jun-16
	-0.67	10.71	5.94	13.77	32.39	3.69	0.81	10.12	0.6	5.66	9,727	1	99	0	0	9	11.82	-4.2			Mar-05
	2.06	6.74	4.58	12.58	15.88	1.9	0.85	3.08	0.47	13.4	5,044	29	21	49	1	24	6.39	-3.36	5.75		Oct-06
	1.87	6.36	3.78	10.02	11.55	1.14	1.6	3.08	0.49	13.32	5,044	29	21	49	1	24	5.86	-3.57		1.00	Oct-06
	2.01	6.58	4.32	11.74	14.42	1.66	1.11	3.06	0.48	13.37	5,044	29	21	49	1	24	6.24	-3.46	3.50		Oct-06
	2.14	6.88	4.86	13.67	17.70		0.5	3.06	0.48	13.42	5,044	29	21	49	1	24	6.57	-3.23			Oct-18
	2.20	6.92	4.86	13.58	17.52	2.16	0.56	3.06	0.48	13.42	5,044	29	21	49	1	24	6.54	-3.16			Oct-06
	2.45	8.50	4.79	16.47	19.86	1.78	0.85	4.19	0.47	11.16	1,679	19	32	48	1	18	8.46	-5.69	5.75		Oct-07
	2.27	8.03	3.93	13.84	15.34	1.06	1.62	4.22	0.48	11.08	1,679	19	32	48	1	18	8.01	-5.99		1.00	Oct-07
	2.40	8.32	4.44	15.53	18.31	1.55	1.11	4.19	0.47	11.14	1,679	19	32	48	1	18	8.3	-5.78	3.50		Oct-07
	2.55	8.57	5.07	17.56	21.73		0.52	4.22	0.46	11.15	1,679	19	32	48	1	18	8.75	-5.56			Oct-18
	2.52	8.62	4.97	17.25	21.28	2.03	0.62	4.22	0.47	11.15	1,679	19	32	48	1	18	8.71	-5.59			Oct-07
	2.70	9.99	4.58	20.08	23.03	1.61	0.86	5.37	0.41	11.75	1,776	13	42	43	1	17	10.56	-8.19	5.75		Oct-07
	2.51	9.62	3.88	17.37	18.44	0.87	1.62	5.36	0.43	11.69	1,776	13	42	43	1	17	10.01	-8.45		1.00	Oct-07
	2.64	9.83	4.37	19.13	21.37	1.33	1.12	5.34	0.42	11.73	1,776	13	42	43	1	17	10.36	-8.25	3.50		Oct-07
	2.69	10.08	4.84	21.13	24.83		0.53	5.37	0.42	11.75	1,776	13	42	43	1	17	10.77	-8.03			Oct-18
	2.76	10.16	4.88	21.10	24.71	1.88	0.58	5.32	0.41	11.75	1,776	13	42	43	1	17	10.75	-8.13			Oct-07
	2.90	11.48	4.32	23.54	25.62	1.43	0.96	6.57	0.51	18.15	9,299	8	52	38	1	15	12.36	-10.68	5.75		Oct-06
	2.68	10.98	3.51	20.66	20.85	0.73	1.72	6.54	0.5	17.98	9,299	8	52	38	1	15	11.89	-11		1.00	Oct-06
	2.84	11.36	4.11	22.57	24.02	1.19	1.21	6.55	0.51	18.13	9,299	8	52	38	1	15	12.24	-10.79	3.50		Oct-06
	2.98	11.68	4.69	24.67	27.55		0.57	6.56	0.51	18.19	9,299	8	52	38	1	15	12.59	-10.58			Oct-18
	2.96	11.59	4.59	24.50	27.27	1.69	0.69	6.55	0.5	18.19	9,299	8	52	38	1	15	12.49	-10.57			Oct-06
	3.02	12.91	4.08	26.91	28.15	1.13	1.04	7.76	0.61	12.59	3,051	3	62	33	1	18	14.27	-13.18	5.75		Oct-07
	2.91	12.56	3.34	24.25	23.48	0.53	1.81	7.76	0.61	12.36	3,051	3	62	33	1	18	13.88	-13.47		1.00	Oct-07
	3.04	12.79	3.78	26.10	26.57	0.93	1.3	7.72	0.6	12.52	3,051	3	62	33	1	18	14.1	-13.31	3.50		Oct-07
	3.26	13.23	4.46	28.30	30.38		0.66	7.74	0.6	12.66	3,051	3	62	33	1	18	14.49	-13.04			Oct-18
	3.09	13.13	4.32	28.02	29.99	1.34	0.77	7.76	0.61	12.66	3,051	3	62	33	1	18	14.5	-13.14			Oct-07
	3.17	14.21	3.59	30.63	30.70	1.06	1.02	8.97	0.71	22.1	5,301	3	72	23	1	21	16.33	-15.83	5.75		Sep-08

	MARKET			FUND TYPE, CATEGORY & OBJECTIVE	RATINGS				MINIMUMS	
Fund Name	Ticker Symbol	Traded On	Fund Type	Category and (Prospectus Objective)	Overall Rating	Reward Rating	Risk Rating	Recent Up/ Downgrade	Open to New Investors	Min Initial Investment
Fidelity Advisor Asset Manager® 70% Fund Class C	FCASX	NAS CM	Open End	Moderate Alloc (Asset Alloc)	B-	C	B	Up	Y	0
Fidelity Advisor Asset Manager® 70% Fund Class M	FTASX	NAS CM	Open End	Moderate Alloc (Asset Alloc)	B-	C	B+	Up	Y	0
Fidelity Advisor Asset Manager® 70% Fund Class Z	FIQBX	NAS CM	Open End	Moderate Alloc (Asset Alloc)	B-	C	B+	Up	Y	0
Fidelity Advisor Asset Manager® 70% Fund I Class	FAAIX	NAS CM	Open End	Moderate Alloc (Asset Alloc)	B-	C	B+	Up	Y	0
Fidelity Advisor Asset Manager® 85% Fund Class A	FEYAX	NAS CM	Open End	Aggressive Alloc (Asset Alloc)	C+	C	B	Up	Y	0
Fidelity Advisor Asset Manager® 85% Fund Class C	FEYCX	NAS CM	Open End	Aggressive Alloc (Asset Alloc)	C+	C	B	Up	Y	0
Fidelity Advisor Asset Manager® 85% Fund Class M	FEYTX	NAS CM	Open End	Aggressive Alloc (Asset Alloc)	C+	C	B	Up	Y	0
Fidelity Advisor Asset Manager® 85% Fund Class Z	FIQCX	NAS CM	Open End	Aggressive Alloc (Asset Alloc)	C+	C	B	Up	Y	0
Fidelity Advisor Asset Manager® 85% Fund I Class	FEYIX	NAS CM	Open End	Aggressive Alloc (Asset Alloc)	C+	C	B	Up	Y	0
Fidelity Advisor Freedom® 2005 Fund Class A	FFAVX	NAS CM	Open End	Target Date (Asset Alloc)	B	C+	A-	Up	Y	0
Fidelity Advisor Freedom® 2005 Fund Class C	FCFVX	NAS CM	Open End	Target Date (Asset Alloc)	B	C	A-	Up	Y	0
Fidelity Advisor Freedom® 2005 Fund Class I	FFIVX	NAS CM	Open End	Target Date (Asset Alloc)	B	C+	A		Y	0
Fidelity Advisor Freedom® 2005 Fund Class M	FFTVX	NAS CM	Open End	Target Date (Asset Alloc)	B	C+	A-	Up	Y	0
Fidelity Advisor Freedom® 2005 Fund Class Z	FIJHX	NAS CM	Open End	Target Date (Asset Alloc)	B	C+	A	Up	Y	0
Fidelity Advisor Freedom® 2005 Fund Class Z6	FYGLX	NAS CM	Open End	Target Date (Asset Alloc)	B	C+	A		Y	0
Fidelity Advisor Freedom® 2010 Fund Class A	FACFX	NAS CM	Open End	Target Date (Asset Alloc)	B	C+	A	Up	Y	0
Fidelity Advisor Freedom® 2010 Fund Class C	FCFCX	NAS CM	Open End	Target Date (Asset Alloc)	B	C	A-	Up	Y	0
Fidelity Advisor Freedom® 2010 Fund Class I	FCIFX	NAS CM	Open End	Target Date (Asset Alloc)	B	C+	A	Up	Y	0
Fidelity Advisor Freedom® 2010 Fund Class M	FCFTX	NAS CM	Open End	Target Date (Asset Alloc)	B	C+	A-	Up	Y	0
Fidelity Advisor Freedom® 2010 Fund Class Z	FIJJX	NAS CM	Open End	Target Date (Asset Alloc)	B	C+	A	Up	Y	0
Fidelity Advisor Freedom® 2010 Fund Class Z6	FUGLX	NAS CM	Open End	Target Date (Asset Alloc)	B	C+	A	Up	Y	0
Fidelity Advisor Freedom® 2015 Fund Class A	FFVAX	NAS CM	Open End	Target Date (Asset Alloc)	B	C+	A	Up	Y	0
Fidelity Advisor Freedom® 2015 Fund Class C	FFVCX	NAS CM	Open End	Target Date (Asset Alloc)	B	C	A-	Up	Y	0
Fidelity Advisor Freedom® 2015 Fund Class I	FFVIX	NAS CM	Open End	Target Date (Asset Alloc)	B	C+	A	Up	Y	0
Fidelity Advisor Freedom® 2015 Fund Class M	FFVTX	NAS CM	Open End	Target Date (Asset Alloc)	B	C	A	Up	Y	0
Fidelity Advisor Freedom® 2015 Fund Class Z	FIJKX	NAS CM	Open End	Target Date (Asset Alloc)	B	C+	A	Up	Y	0
Fidelity Advisor Freedom® 2015 Fund Class Z6	FIGLX	NAS CM	Open End	Target Date (Asset Alloc)	B	C+	A	Up	Y	0
Fidelity Advisor Freedom® 2020 Fund Class A	FDAFX	NAS CM	Open End	Target Date (Asset Alloc)	B	C	A-	Up	Y	0
Fidelity Advisor Freedom® 2020 Fund Class C	FDCFX	NAS CM	Open End	Target Date (Asset Alloc)	B-	C	A-	Up	Y	0
Fidelity Advisor Freedom® 2020 Fund Class I	FDIFX	NAS CM	Open End	Target Date (Asset Alloc)	B	C	A-	Up	Y	0
Fidelity Advisor Freedom® 2020 Fund Class M	FDTFX	NAS CM	Open End	Target Date (Asset Alloc)	B	C	A-	Up	Y	0
Fidelity Advisor Freedom® 2020 Fund Class Z	FIJLX	NAS CM	Open End	Target Date (Asset Alloc)	B	C+	A-	Up	Y	0
Fidelity Advisor Freedom® 2020 Fund Class Z6	FOGLX	NAS CM	Open End	Target Date (Asset Alloc)	B	C+	A-	Up	Y	0
Fidelity Advisor Freedom® 2025 Fund Class A	FATWX	NAS CM	Open End	Target Date (Asset Alloc)	B-	C	A-	Up	Y	0
Fidelity Advisor Freedom® 2025 Fund Class C	FCTWX	NAS CM	Open End	Target Date (Asset Alloc)	B-	C	A-	Up	Y	0
Fidelity Advisor Freedom® 2025 Fund Class I	FITWX	NAS CM	Open End	Target Date (Asset Alloc)	B	C	A-	Up	Y	0
Fidelity Advisor Freedom® 2025 Fund Class M	FTTWX	NAS CM	Open End	Target Date (Asset Alloc)	B-	C	A-	Up	Y	0
Fidelity Advisor Freedom® 2025 Fund Class Z	FIJMX	NAS CM	Open End	Target Date (Asset Alloc)	B	C	A-	Up	Y	0
Fidelity Advisor Freedom® 2025 Fund Class Z6	FPGLX	NAS CM	Open End	Target Date (Asset Alloc)	B	C	A-	Up	Y	0
Fidelity Advisor Freedom® 2030 Fund Class A	FAFEX	NAS CM	Open End	Target Date (Asset Alloc)	B-	C	B+	Up	Y	0
Fidelity Advisor Freedom® 2030 Fund Class C	FCFEX	NAS CM	Open End	Target Date (Asset Alloc)	B-	C	B+	Up	Y	0
Fidelity Advisor Freedom® 2030 Fund Class I	FEFIX	NAS CM	Open End	Target Date (Asset Alloc)	B-	C	B+	Up	Y	0
Fidelity Advisor Freedom® 2030 Fund Class M	FTFEX	NAS CM	Open End	Target Date (Asset Alloc)	B-	C	B+	Up	Y	0
Fidelity Advisor Freedom® 2030 Fund Class Z	FIJNX	NAS CM	Open End	Target Date (Asset Alloc)	B-	C	B+	Up	Y	0
Fidelity Advisor Freedom® 2030 Fund Class Z6	FDGLX	NAS CM	Open End	Target Date (Asset Alloc)	B-	C	B+	Up	Y	0
Fidelity Advisor Freedom® 2035 Fund Class A	FATHX	NAS CM	Open End	Target Date (Asset Alloc)	B-	C	B	Up	Y	0
Fidelity Advisor Freedom® 2035 Fund Class C	FCTHX	NAS CM	Open End	Target Date (Asset Alloc)	B-	C	B	Up	Y	0
Fidelity Advisor Freedom® 2035 Fund Class I	FITHX	NAS CM	Open End	Target Date (Asset Alloc)	B-	C	B	Up	Y	0
Fidelity Advisor Freedom® 2035 Fund Class M	FTTHX	NAS CM	Open End	Target Date (Asset Alloc)	B-	C	B	Up	Y	0
Fidelity Advisor Freedom® 2035 Fund Class Z	FIJOX	NAS CM	Open End	Target Date (Asset Alloc)	B-	C	B	Up	Y	0
Fidelity Advisor Freedom® 2035 Fund Class Z6	FHGLX	NAS CM	Open End	Target Date (Asset Alloc)	B-	C	B	Up	Y	0
Fidelity Advisor Freedom® 2040 Fund Class A	FAFFX	NAS CM	Open End	Target Date (Asset Alloc)	B-	C	B	Up	Y	0

★ Expanded analysis of this fund is included in Section II.

Min Additional Investment	TOTAL RETURNS					PERFORMANCE				ASSETS		ASSET ALLOCATION & TURNOVER					BULL & BEAR		FEES		
	3-Month Total Return	6-Month Total Return	1-Year Total Return	3-Year Total Return	5-Year Total Return	Dividend Yield (TTM)	Expense Ratio	3-Yr Std Deviation	3-Year Beta	NAV	Total Assets (MIL)	%Cash	%Stocks	%Bonds	%Other	Turnover Ratio	Last Bull Market Total Return	Last Bear Market Total Return	Front End Fee (%)	Back End Fee (%)	Inception Date
	3.00	13.83	2.86	27.72	25.83	0.32	1.77	8.96	0.71	21.97	5,301	3	72	23	1	21	15.73	-16.06		1.00	Sep-08
	3.12	14.09	3.34	29.67	29.05	0.81	1.27	8.99	0.71	22.1	5,301	3	72	23	1	21	16.13	-15.9	3.50		Sep-08
	3.26	14.48	3.99	32.01	32.80		0.64	8.97	0.71	22.13	5,301	3	72	23	1	21	16.54	-15.69			Oct-18
	3.26	14.41	3.89	31.73	32.48	1.32	0.74	8.96	0.71	22.15	5,301	3	72	23	1	21	16.5	-15.68			Sep-08
	3.49	16.43	3.28	36.30	34.84	0.87	1.04	10.8	0.86	19.27	2,589	4	81	12	2	24	19.07	-19.41	5.75		Oct-06
	3.27	16.00	2.46	33.27	29.85	0.11	1.79	10.81	0.86	18.92	2,589	4	81	12	2	24	18.63	-19.67		1.00	Oct-06
	3.40	16.27	3.00	35.24	32.89	0.63	1.31	10.82	0.86	19.15	2,589	4	81	12	2	24	18.8	-19.41	3.50		Oct-06
	3.58	16.67	3.69	37.69	37.04		0.65	10.79	0.86	19.38	2,589	4	81	12	2	24	19.23	-19.22			Oct-18
	3.52	16.58	3.53	37.38	36.74	1.04	0.77	10.8	0.86	19.4	2,589	4	81	12	2	24	19.21	-19.26			Oct-06
	2.77	8.50	5.65	19.10	21.68	1.92	0.73	3.88	0.48	11.49	171.1	20	24	56	0	28	9.71	-8.46	5.75		Nov-03
	2.57	8.09	4.80	16.45	17.09	1.01	1.48	3.83	0.49	11.49	171.1	20	24	56	0	28	9.3	-8.83		1.00	Nov-03
	2.71	8.59	5.83	19.96	23.08	2.1	0.48	3.83	0.48	11.57	171.1	20	24	56	0	28	9.94	-8.44			Nov-03
	2.61	8.34	5.30	18.14	20.04	1.68	0.98	3.87	0.48	11.47	171.1	20	24	56	0	28	9.58	-8.6	3.50		Nov-03
	2.75	8.56	5.88	20.02	23.15		0.42	3.84	0.48	11.52	171.1	20	24	56	0	28	9.94	-8.44			Oct-18
	2.85	8.75	5.98	20.30	23.43	2.31	0.37	3.85	0.48	11.55	171.1	20	24	56	0	28	9.94	-8.44			Jun-17
	2.98	9.88	5.81	22.48	24.68	1.76	0.77	4.84	0.44	11.86	420.8	17	33	50	0	24	11.88	-10.37	5.75		Jul-03
	2.77	9.43	4.94	19.66	19.96	0.9	1.52	4.78	0.44	11.74	420.8	17	33	50	0	24	11.3	-10.63		1.00	Jul-03
	3.03	10.01	6.01	23.26	26.15	2.02	0.52	4.79	0.44	11.9	420.8	17	33	50	0	24	12.04	-10.34			Jul-03
	2.83	9.66	5.41	21.51	23.08	1.56	1.02	4.8	0.43	11.8	420.8	17	33	50	0	24	11.69	-10.47	3.50		Jul-03
	3.08	9.99	6.07	23.33	26.22		0.46	4.8	0.44	11.85	420.8	17	33	50	0	24	12.04	-10.35			Oct-18
	2.99	10.07	6.07	23.59	26.49	2.23	0.39	4.77	0.44	11.88	420.8	17	33	50	0	24	12.04	-10.34			Jun-17
	3.19	11.21	5.83	25.70	27.65	1.72	0.81	5.78	0.4	11.83	970.4	14	42	44	0	21	12.12	-10.57	5.75		Nov-03
	2.88	10.74	5.03	22.83	22.85	1	1.56	5.78	0.38	11.71	970.4	14	42	44	0	21	11.66	-10.94		1.00	Nov-03
	3.22	11.27	6.08	26.62	29.15	1.97	0.56	5.81	0.37	11.93	970.4	14	42	44	0	21	12.34	-10.55			Nov-03
	3.13	11.06	5.58	24.73	26.04	1.49	1.06	5.77	0.38	11.8	970.4	14	42	44	0	21	12	-10.72	3.50		Nov-03
	3.18	11.36	6.13	26.68	29.21		0.49	5.81	0.39	11.87	970.4	14	42	44	0	21	12.34	-10.55			Oct-18
	3.19	11.35	6.24	27.01	29.55	2.17	0.41	5.75	0.38	11.9	970.4	14	42	44	0	21	12.34	-10.55			Jun-17
	3.25	12.25	5.86	27.92	29.49	1.64	0.85	6.55	0.51	12.97	2,303	12	49	38	0	22	13.69	-12.61	5.75		Jul-03
	3.11	11.90	5.14	25.16	24.82	1	1.6	6.58	0.51	12.85	2,303	12	49	38	0	22	13.21	-12.87		1.00	Jul-03
	3.36	12.39	6.20	28.94	31.19	1.9	0.6	6.58	0.51	13.08	2,303	12	49	38	0	22	13.91	-12.56			Jul-03
	3.19	12.10	5.61	27.01	27.94	1.43	1.1	6.59	0.51	12.96	2,303	12	49	38	0	22	13.55	-12.68	3.50		Jul-03
	3.37	12.44	6.25	28.99	31.24		0.53	6.57	0.51	13.01	2,303	12	49	38	0	22	13.91	-12.56			Oct-18
	3.35	12.50	6.33	29.37	31.63	2.13	0.43	6.56	0.51	13.04	2,303	12	49	38	0	22	13.91	-12.56			Jun-17
	3.45	13.21	5.98	30.24	31.25	1.57	0.9	7.32	0.57	12.97	2,966	10	56	34	0	24	15.67	-14.98	5.75		Nov-03
	3.25	12.86	5.14	27.35	26.44	0.94	1.65	7.28	0.57	12.76	2,966	10	56	34	0	24	15.16	-15.19		1.00	Nov-03
	3.47	13.33	6.15	31.23	32.90	1.82	0.65	7.28	0.57	13.09	2,966	10	56	34	0	24	15.87	-14.91			Nov-03
	3.38	13.12	5.64	29.26	29.64	1.39	1.15	7.28	0.57	12.99	2,966	10	56	34	0	24	15.51	-15.09	3.50		Nov-03
	3.57	13.48	6.31	31.43	33.11		0.56	7.31	0.57	13.02	2,966	10	56	34	0	24	15.87	-14.91			Oct-18
	3.55	13.54	6.43	31.84	33.53	2.11	0.45	7.33	0.57	13.06	2,966	10	56	34	0	24	15.87	-14.91			Jun-17
	3.62	14.85	5.93	35.49	35.32	1.56	0.94	8.67	0.68	13.92	3,066	7	67	26	0	22	16.33	-15.82	5.75		Jul-03
	3.49	14.48	5.18	32.51	30.32	1.04	1.69	8.65	0.68	13.64	3,066	7	67	26	0	22	15.81	-16.06		1.00	Jul-03
	3.73	15.08	6.21	36.47	37.02	1.76	0.69	8.65	0.68	14.01	3,066	7	67	26	0	22	16.46	-15.7			Jul-03
	3.59	14.71	5.65	34.44	33.68	1.41	1.19	8.66	0.68	13.84	3,066	7	67	26	0	22	16.13	-15.85	3.50		Jul-03
	3.76	15.08	6.30	36.58	37.14		0.6	8.69	0.68	13.93	3,066	7	67	26	0	22	16.46	-15.7			Oct-18
	3.81	15.21	6.44	37.11	37.67	1.99	0.47	8.65	0.68	13.97	3,066	7	67	26	0	22	16.46	-15.7			Jun-17
	3.80	16.59	5.58	39.15	38.14	1.47	0.98	10.18	0.81	13.43	2,474	7	80	12	0	23	18.1	-18.06	5.75		Nov-03
	3.55	16.04	4.78	36.06	33.06	0.9	1.73	10.16	0.81	13.01	2,474	7	80	12	0	23	17.47	-18.29		1.00	Nov-03
	3.83	16.71	5.84	40.21	39.94	1.66	0.73	10.18	0.81	13.54	2,474	7	80	12	0	23	18.21	-17.93			Nov-03
	3.72	16.36	5.32	38.07	36.40	1.34	1.23	10.14	0.81	13.28	2,474	7	80	12	0	23	17.84	-18.13	3.50		Nov-03
	3.79	16.72	5.88	40.27	40.00		0.63	10.16	0.81	13.45	2,474	7	80	12	0	23	18.21	-17.93			Oct-18
	3.91	16.82	6.11	40.86	40.59	1.93	0.49	10.14	0.81	13.52	2,474	7	80	12	0	23	18.21	-17.93			Jun-17
	3.81	17.12	5.52	39.27	38.24	1.44	1	10.64	0.85	14.33	2,233	6	86	7	0	21	18.24	-18.29	5.75		Jul-03

Fund Name	MARKET Ticker Symbol	Traded On	FUND TYPE, CATEGORY & OBJECTIVE Fund Type	Category and (Prospectus Objective)	RATINGS Overall Rating	Reward Rating	Risk Rating	Recent Up/ Downgrade	MINIMUMS Open to New Investors	Min Initial Investment
Fidelity Advisor Freedom® 2040 Fund Class C	FCFFX	NAS CM	Open End	Target Date (Asset Alloc)	B-	C	B	Up	Y	0
Fidelity Advisor Freedom® 2040 Fund Class I	FIFFX	NAS CM	Open End	Target Date (Asset Alloc)	B-	C	B	Up	Y	0
Fidelity Advisor Freedom® 2040 Fund Class M	FTFFX	NAS CM	Open End	Target Date (Asset Alloc)	B-	C	B	Up	Y	0
Fidelity Advisor Freedom® 2040 Fund Class Z	FIJPX	NAS CM	Open End	Target Date (Asset Alloc)	B-	C	B	Up	Y	0
Fidelity Advisor Freedom® 2040 Fund Class Z6	FKGLX	NAS CM	Open End	Target Date (Asset Alloc)	B-	C	B	Up	Y	0
Fidelity Advisor Freedom® 2045 Fund Class A	FFFZX	NAS CM	Open End	Target Date (Asset Alloc)	B-	C	B	Up	Y	0
Fidelity Advisor Freedom® 2045 Fund Class C	FFFJX	NAS CM	Open End	Target Date (Asset Alloc)	B-	C	B	Up	Y	0
Fidelity Advisor Freedom® 2045 Fund Class I	FFFIX	NAS CM	Open End	Target Date (Asset Alloc)	B-	C	B	Up	Y	0
Fidelity Advisor Freedom® 2045 Fund Class M	FFFTX	NAS CM	Open End	Target Date (Asset Alloc)	B-	C	B	Up	Y	0
Fidelity Advisor Freedom® 2045 Fund Class Z	FIJQX	NAS CM	Open End	Target Date (Asset Alloc)	B-	C	B	Up	Y	0
Fidelity Advisor Freedom® 2045 Fund Class Z6	FCGLX	NAS CM	Open End	Target Date (Asset Alloc)	B-	C	B	Up	Y	0
Fidelity Advisor Freedom® 2050 Fund Class A	FFFLX	NAS CM	Open End	Target Date (Asset Alloc)	B-	C	B	Up	Y	0
Fidelity Advisor Freedom® 2050 Fund Class C	FFFYX	NAS CM	Open End	Target Date (Asset Alloc)	B-	C	B	Up	Y	0
Fidelity Advisor Freedom® 2050 Fund Class I	FFFPX	NAS CM	Open End	Target Date (Asset Alloc)	B-	C	B	Up	Y	0
Fidelity Advisor Freedom® 2050 Fund Class M	FFFQX	NAS CM	Open End	Target Date (Asset Alloc)	B-	C	B	Up	Y	0
Fidelity Advisor Freedom® 2050 Fund Class Z	FIJRX	NAS CM	Open End	Target Date (Asset Alloc)	B-	C	B	Up	Y	0
Fidelity Advisor Freedom® 2050 Fund Class Z6	FVGLX	NAS CM	Open End	Target Date (Asset Alloc)	B-	C	B	Up	Y	0
Fidelity Advisor Freedom® 2055 Fund Class A	FHFAX	NAS CM	Open End	Target Date (Asset Alloc)	B-	C	B	Up	Y	0
Fidelity Advisor Freedom® 2055 Fund Class C	FHFCX	NAS CM	Open End	Target Date (Asset Alloc)	B-	C	B	Up	Y	0
Fidelity Advisor Freedom® 2055 Fund Class I	FHFIX	NAS CM	Open End	Target Date (Asset Alloc)	B-	C	B	Up	Y	0
Fidelity Advisor Freedom® 2055 Fund Class M	FHFTX	NAS CM	Open End	Target Date (Asset Alloc)	B-	C	B	Up	Y	0
Fidelity Advisor Freedom® 2055 Fund Class Z	FIJSX	NAS CM	Open End	Target Date (Asset Alloc)	B-	C	B	Up	Y	0
Fidelity Advisor Freedom® 2055 Fund Class Z6	FBGLX	NAS CM	Open End	Target Date (Asset Alloc)	B-	C	B	Up	Y	0
Fidelity Advisor Freedom® 2060 Fund Class A	FDKPX	NAS CM	Open End	Target Date (Asset Alloc)	B-	C	B	Up	Y	0
Fidelity Advisor Freedom® 2060 Fund Class C	FDKSX	NAS CM	Open End	Target Date (Asset Alloc)	B-	C	B	Up	Y	0
Fidelity Advisor Freedom® 2060 Fund Class I	FDKQX	NAS CM	Open End	Target Date (Asset Alloc)	B-	C	B	Up	Y	0
Fidelity Advisor Freedom® 2060 Fund Class M	FDKTX	NAS CM	Open End	Target Date (Asset Alloc)	B-	C	B	Up	Y	0
Fidelity Advisor Freedom® 2060 Fund Class Z	FIJTX	NAS CM	Open End	Target Date (Asset Alloc)	B-	C	B	Up	Y	0
Fidelity Advisor Freedom® 2060 Fund Class Z6	FNGLX	NAS CM	Open End	Target Date (Asset Alloc)	B-	C	B	Up	Y	0
Fidelity Advisor Freedom® Blend 2005 Fund Class A	FHAGX	NAS CM	Open End	Target Date (Asset Alloc)	U	U	U		Y	0
Fidelity Advisor Freedom® Blend 2005 Fund Class C	FHAAX	NAS CM	Open End	Target Date (Asset Alloc)	U	U	U		Y	0
Fidelity Advisor Freedom® Blend 2005 Fund Class I	FHADX	NAS CM	Open End	Target Date (Asset Alloc)	U	U	U		Y	0
Fidelity Advisor Freedom® Blend 2005 Fund Class M	FHAFX	NAS CM	Open End	Target Date (Asset Alloc)	U	U	U		Y	0
Fidelity Advisor Freedom® Blend 2005 Fund Class Z	FHACX	NAS CM	Open End	Target Date (Asset Alloc)	U	U	U		Y	0
Fidelity Advisor Freedom® Blend 2005 Fund Class Z6	FHJHX	NAS CM	Open End	Target Date (Asset Alloc)	U	U	U		Y	0
Fidelity Advisor Freedom® Blend 2010 Fund Class A	FHABX	NAS CM	Open End	Target Date (Asset Alloc)	U	U	U		Y	0
Fidelity Advisor Freedom® Blend 2010 Fund Class C	FJAYX	NAS CM	Open End	Target Date (Asset Alloc)	U	U	U		Y	0
Fidelity Advisor Freedom® Blend 2010 Fund Class I	FJAWX	NAS CM	Open End	Target Date (Asset Alloc)	U	U	U		Y	0
Fidelity Advisor Freedom® Blend 2010 Fund Class M	FJAZX	NAS CM	Open End	Target Date (Asset Alloc)	U	U	U		Y	0
Fidelity Advisor Freedom® Blend 2010 Fund Class Z	FJAVX	NAS CM	Open End	Target Date (Asset Alloc)	U	U	U		Y	0
Fidelity Advisor Freedom® Blend 2010 Fund Class Z6	FHZCX	NAS CM	Open End	Target Date (Asset Alloc)	U	U	U		Y	0
Fidelity Advisor Freedom® Blend 2015 Fund Class A	FJAUX	NAS CM	Open End	Target Date (Asset Alloc)	U	U	U		Y	0
Fidelity Advisor Freedom® Blend 2015 Fund Class C	FJASX	NAS CM	Open End	Target Date (Asset Alloc)	U	U	U		Y	0
Fidelity Advisor Freedom® Blend 2015 Fund Class I	FJAQX	NAS CM	Open End	Target Date (Asset Alloc)	U	U	U		Y	0
Fidelity Advisor Freedom® Blend 2015 Fund Class M	FJATX	NAS CM	Open End	Target Date (Asset Alloc)	U	U	U		Y	0
Fidelity Advisor Freedom® Blend 2015 Fund Class Z	FJAPX	NAS CM	Open End	Target Date (Asset Alloc)	U	U	U		Y	0
Fidelity Advisor Freedom® Blend 2015 Fund Class Z6	FHXCX	NAS CM	Open End	Target Date (Asset Alloc)	U	U	U		Y	0
Fidelity Advisor Freedom® Blend 2020 Fund Class A	FJAOX	NAS CM	Open End	Target Date (Asset Alloc)	U	U	U		Y	0
Fidelity Advisor Freedom® Blend 2020 Fund Class C	FJALX	NAS CM	Open End	Target Date (Asset Alloc)	U	U	U		Y	0
Fidelity Advisor Freedom® Blend 2020 Fund Class I	FJAJX	NAS CM	Open End	Target Date (Asset Alloc)	U	U	U		Y	0
Fidelity Advisor Freedom® Blend 2020 Fund Class M	FJANX	NAS CM	Open End	Target Date (Asset Alloc)	U	U	U		Y	0
Fidelity Advisor Freedom® Blend 2020 Fund Class Z	FJAIX	NAS CM	Open End	Target Date (Asset Alloc)	U	U	U		Y	0

★ Expanded analysis of this fund is included in Section II.

Min Additional Investment	TOTAL RETURNS: 3-Month Total Return	6-Month Total Return	1-Year Total Return	3-Year Total Return	5-Year Total Return	PERFORMANCE: Dividend Yield (TTM)	Expense Ratio	3-Yr Std Deviation	3-Year Beta	ASSETS: NAV	Total Assets (MIL)	ASSET ALLOCATION & TURNOVER: %Cash	%Stocks	%Bonds	%Other	Turnover Ratio	BULL & BEAR: Last Bull Market Total Return	Last Bear Market Total Return	FEES: Front End Fee (%)	Back End Fee (%)	Inception Date
	3.51	16.62	4.63	36.11	33.06	0.91	1.75	10.63	0.85	13.9	2,233	6	86	7	0	21	17.8	-18.55		1.00	Jul-03
	3.84	17.24	5.70	40.34	39.92	1.62	0.75	10.64	0.85	14.43	2,233	6	86	7	0	21	18.47	-18.25			Jul-03
	3.72	16.92	5.26	38.27	36.52	1.31	1.25	10.63	0.85	14.24	2,233	6	86	7	0	21	18.15	-18.38	3.50		Jul-03
	3.81	17.26	5.79	40.46	40.04		0.65	10.64	0.85	14.34	2,233	6	86	7	0	21	18.47	-18.25			Oct-18
	3.87	17.37	5.99	41.14	40.72	1.89	0.5	10.65	0.85	14.4	2,233	6	86	7	0	21	18.47	-18.25			Jun-17
	3.72	17.05	5.45	39.18	38.26	1.47	1	10.63	0.85	11.18	1,452	6	86	7	0	22	18.77	-18.87	5.75		Jun-06
	3.58	16.64	4.69	36.16	33.18	0.97	1.75	10.64	0.85	10.9	1,452	6	86	7	0	22	18.28	-19.16		1.00	Jun-06
	3.76	17.22	5.72	40.21	39.91	1.66	0.75	10.62	0.85	11.26	1,452	6	86	7	0	22	18.89	-18.75			Jun-06
	3.71	16.94	5.17	38.22	36.47	1.33	1.25	10.61	0.84	11.07	1,452	6	86	7	0	22	18.59	-18.9	3.50		Jun-06
	3.84	17.27	5.80	40.31	40.02		0.65	10.67	0.85	11.19	1,452	6	86	7	0	22	18.89	-18.75			Oct-18
	3.93	17.44	6.06	41.07	40.77	1.93	0.5	10.62	0.85	11.25	1,452	6	86	7	0	22	18.89	-18.75			Jun-17
	3.81	17.06	5.53	39.27	38.33	1.45	1	10.68	0.85	11.17	1,178	6	86	7	0	23	19.44	-19.73	5.75		Jun-06
	3.52	16.65	4.71	36.12	33.18	0.94	1.75	10.65	0.85	10.93	1,178	6	86	7	0	23	18.92	-20.01		1.00	Jun-06
	3.83	17.21	5.70	40.25	40.04	1.63	0.75	10.66	0.85	11.25	1,178	6	86	7	0	23	19.57	-19.68			Jun-06
	3.66	16.86	5.20	38.11	36.53	1.3	1.25	10.65	0.85	11.09	1,178	6	86	7	0	23	19.28	-19.85	3.50		Jun-06
	3.87	17.32	5.73	40.30	40.08		0.65	10.61	0.84	11.19	1,178	6	86	7	0	23	19.57	-19.68			Oct-18
	3.91	17.33	6.03	40.94	40.73	1.91	0.5	10.65	0.85	11.23	1,178	6	86	7	0	23	19.57	-19.68			Jun-17
	3.83	17.15	5.47	39.28	38.35	1.43	1	10.63	0.85	12.45	672.2	6	86	7	0	27	19.79		5.75		Jun-11
	3.54	16.67	4.71	36.13	33.12	0.98	1.75	10.65	0.85	12.28	672.2	6	86	7	0	27	19.29			1.00	Jun-11
	3.79	17.24	5.70	40.27	40.00	1.65	0.75	10.63	0.85	12.5	672.2	6	86	7	0	27	19.92				Jun-11
	3.63	16.90	5.12	38.12	36.44	1.31	1.25	10.65	0.85	12.36	672.2	6	86	7	0	27	19.47		3.50		Jun-11
	3.87	17.30	5.83	40.44	40.17		0.65	10.64	0.85	12.43	672.2	6	86	7	0	27	19.92				Oct-18
	3.87	17.35	5.95	40.96	40.69	1.92	0.5	10.62	0.85	12.48	672.2	6	86	7	0	27	19.92				Jun-17
	3.80	17.17	5.55	39.34		1.45	1	10.63	0.85	11.24	172.8	7	86	7	0	27			5.75		Aug-14
	3.62	16.63	4.67	36.11		1.03	1.75	10.64	0.85	11.21	172.8	7	86	7	0	27				1.00	Aug-14
	3.84	17.26	5.79	40.28		1.61	0.75	10.68	0.85	11.29	172.8	7	86	7	0	27					Aug-14
	3.74	16.89	5.21	38.18		1.3	1.25	10.63	0.85	11.22	172.8	7	86	7	0	27			3.50		Aug-14
	3.81	17.28	5.84	40.34			0.65	10.64	0.85	11.24	172.8	7	86	7	0	27					Oct-18
	3.90	17.44	6.02	40.97		1.82	0.5	10.62	0.85	11.29	172.8	7	86	7	0	27					Jun-17
	2.64	8.16					0.71			10.25	11.4	19	23	57	0	11			5.75		Aug-18
	2.44	7.73					1.46			10.22	11.4	19	23	57	0	11				1.00	Aug-18
	2.63	8.26					0.46			10.27	11.4	19	23	57	0	11					Aug-18
	2.64	8.05					0.96			10.25	11.4	19	23	57	0	11			3.50		Aug-18
	2.76	8.40					0.36			10.28	11.4	19	23	57	0	11					Aug-18
	2.78	8.42					0.26			10.28	11.4	19	23	57	0	11					Aug-18
	2.82	9.54					0.72			10.21	42.2	16	32	51	0	98			5.75		Aug-18
	2.62	9.11					1.47			10.18	42.2	16	32	51	0	98				1.00	Aug-18
	2.91	9.64					0.47			10.23	42.2	16	32	51	0	98					Aug-18
	2.82	9.32					0.97			10.2	42.2	16	32	51	0	98			3.50		Aug-18
	3.01	9.75					0.37			10.24	42.2	16	32	51	0	98					Aug-18
	2.91	9.75					0.27			10.24	42.2	16	32	51	0	98					Aug-18
	2.92	10.74					0.74			10.2	151.9	14	41	44	0	52			5.75		Aug-18
	2.73	10.33					1.49			10.14	151.9	14	41	44	0	52				1.00	Aug-18
	3.02	10.96					0.49			10.22	151.9	14	41	44	0	52					Aug-18
	2.92	10.64					0.99			10.19	151.9	14	41	44	0	52			3.50		Aug-18
	3.02	10.96					0.39			10.22	151.9	14	41	44	0	52					Aug-18
	3.12	11.07					0.29			10.23	151.9	14	41	44	0	52					Aug-18
	3.12	11.92					0.76			10.23	460.1	12	49	39	0	78			5.75		Aug-18
	2.92	11.36					1.51			10.19	460.1	12	49	39	0	78				1.00	Aug-18
	3.21	12.00					0.51			10.26	460.1	12	49	39	0	78					Aug-18
	3.12	11.68					1.01			10.23	460.1	12	49	39	0	78			3.50		Aug-18
	3.21	12.00					0.41			10.26	460.1	12	49	39	0	78					Aug-18

	MARKET			FUND TYPE, CATEGORY & OBJECTIVE	RATINGS				MINIMUMS	
Fund Name	Ticker Symbol	Traded On	Fund Type	Category and (Prospectus Objective)	Overall Rating	Reward Rating	Risk Rating	Recent Up/ Downgrade	Open to New Investors	Min Initial Investment
Fidelity Advisor Freedom® Blend 2020 Fund Class Z6	FHWCX	NAS CM	Open End	Target Date (Asset Alloc)	U	U	U		Y	0
Fidelity Advisor Freedom® Blend 2025 Fund Class A	FJAHX	NAS CM	Open End	Target Date (Asset Alloc)	U	U	U		Y	0
Fidelity Advisor Freedom® Blend 2025 Fund Class C	FJAEX	NAS CM	Open End	Target Date (Asset Alloc)	U	U	U		Y	0
Fidelity Advisor Freedom® Blend 2025 Fund Class I	FJADX	NAS CM	Open End	Target Date (Asset Alloc)	U	U	U		Y	0
Fidelity Advisor Freedom® Blend 2025 Fund Class M	FJAGX	NAS CM	Open End	Target Date (Asset Alloc)	U	U	U		Y	0
Fidelity Advisor Freedom® Blend 2025 Fund Class Z	FJABX	NAS CM	Open End	Target Date (Asset Alloc)	U	U	U		Y	0
Fidelity Advisor Freedom® Blend 2025 Fund Class Z6	FHSPX	NAS CM	Open End	Target Date (Asset Alloc)	U	U	U		Y	0
Fidelity Advisor Freedom® Blend 2030 Fund Class A	FJAMX	NAS CM	Open End	Target Date (Asset Alloc)	U	U	U		Y	0
Fidelity Advisor Freedom® Blend 2030 Fund Class C	FJTMX	NAS CM	Open End	Target Date (Asset Alloc)	U	U	U		Y	0
Fidelity Advisor Freedom® Blend 2030 Fund Class I	FJEFX	NAS CM	Open End	Target Date (Asset Alloc)	U	U	U		Y	0
Fidelity Advisor Freedom® Blend 2030 Fund Class M	FTYJX	NAS CM	Open End	Target Date (Asset Alloc)	U	U	U		Y	0
Fidelity Advisor Freedom® Blend 2030 Fund Class Z	FJLMX	NAS CM	Open End	Target Date (Asset Alloc)	U	U	U		Y	0
Fidelity Advisor Freedom® Blend 2030 Fund Class Z6	FHRCX	NAS CM	Open End	Target Date (Asset Alloc)	U	U	U		Y	0
Fidelity Advisor Freedom® Blend 2035 Fund Class A	FHJGX	NAS CM	Open End	Target Date (Asset Alloc)	U	U	U		Y	0
Fidelity Advisor Freedom® Blend 2035 Fund Class C	FHVCX	NAS CM	Open End	Target Date (Asset Alloc)	U	U	U		Y	0
Fidelity Advisor Freedom® Blend 2035 Fund Class I	FHGDX	NAS CM	Open End	Target Date (Asset Alloc)	U	U	U		Y	0
Fidelity Advisor Freedom® Blend 2035 Fund Class M	FHBCX	NAS CM	Open End	Target Date (Asset Alloc)	U	U	U		Y	0
Fidelity Advisor Freedom® Blend 2035 Fund Class Z	FHSDX	NAS CM	Open End	Target Date (Asset Alloc)	U	U	U		Y	0
Fidelity Advisor Freedom® Blend 2035 Fund Class Z6	FHQCX	NAS CM	Open End	Target Date (Asset Alloc)	U	U	U		Y	0
Fidelity Advisor Freedom® Blend 2040 Fund Class A	FHDEX	NAS CM	Open End	Target Date (Asset Alloc)	U	U	U		Y	0
Fidelity Advisor Freedom® Blend 2040 Fund Class C	FHZEX	NAS CM	Open End	Target Date (Asset Alloc)	U	U	U		Y	0
Fidelity Advisor Freedom® Blend 2040 Fund Class I	FHJFX	NAS CM	Open End	Target Date (Asset Alloc)	U	U	U		Y	0
Fidelity Advisor Freedom® Blend 2040 Fund Class M	FHOEX	NAS CM	Open End	Target Date (Asset Alloc)	U	U	U		Y	0
Fidelity Advisor Freedom® Blend 2040 Fund Class Z	FHHFX	NAS CM	Open End	Target Date (Asset Alloc)	U	U	U		Y	0
Fidelity Advisor Freedom® Blend 2040 Fund Class Z6	FHOCX	NAS CM	Open End	Target Date (Asset Alloc)	U	U	U		Y	0
Fidelity Advisor Freedom® Blend 2045 Fund Class A	FHGFX	NAS CM	Open End	Target Date (Asset Alloc)	U	U	U		Y	0
Fidelity Advisor Freedom® Blend 2045 Fund Class C	FHDFX	NAS CM	Open End	Target Date (Asset Alloc)	U	U	U		Y	0
Fidelity Advisor Freedom® Blend 2045 Fund Class I	FHCFX	NAS CM	Open End	Target Date (Asset Alloc)	U	U	U		Y	0
Fidelity Advisor Freedom® Blend 2045 Fund Class M	FHEFX	NAS CM	Open End	Target Date (Asset Alloc)	U	U	U		Y	0
Fidelity Advisor Freedom® Blend 2045 Fund Class Z	FHBFX	NAS CM	Open End	Target Date (Asset Alloc)	U	U	U		Y	0
Fidelity Advisor Freedom® Blend 2045 Fund Class Z6	FHLCX	NAS CM	Open End	Target Date (Asset Alloc)	U	U	U		Y	0
Fidelity Advisor Freedom® Blend 2050 Fund Class A	FHJKX	NAS CM	Open End	Target Date (Asset Alloc)	U	U	U		Y	0
Fidelity Advisor Freedom® Blend 2050 Fund Class C	FHXEX	NAS CM	Open End	Target Date (Asset Alloc)	U	U	U		Y	0
Fidelity Advisor Freedom® Blend 2050 Fund Class I	FHWEX	NAS CM	Open End	Target Date (Asset Alloc)	U	U	U		Y	0
Fidelity Advisor Freedom® Blend 2050 Fund Class M	FHYEX	NAS CM	Open End	Target Date (Asset Alloc)	U	U	U		Y	0
Fidelity Advisor Freedom® Blend 2050 Fund Class Z	FHVEX	NAS CM	Open End	Target Date (Asset Alloc)	U	U	U		Y	0
Fidelity Advisor Freedom® Blend 2050 Fund Class Z6	FHJCX	NAS CM	Open End	Target Date (Asset Alloc)	U	U	U		Y	0
Fidelity Advisor Freedom® Blend 2055 Fund Class A	FHUEX	NAS CM	Open End	Target Date (Asset Alloc)	U	U	U		Y	0
Fidelity Advisor Freedom® Blend 2055 Fund Class C	FHREX	NAS CM	Open End	Target Date (Asset Alloc)	U	U	U		Y	0
Fidelity Advisor Freedom® Blend 2055 Fund Class I	FHQEX	NAS CM	Open End	Target Date (Asset Alloc)	U	U	U		Y	0
Fidelity Advisor Freedom® Blend 2055 Fund Class M	FHTEX	NAS CM	Open End	Target Date (Asset Alloc)	U	U	U		Y	0
Fidelity Advisor Freedom® Blend 2055 Fund Class Z	FHPEX	NAS CM	Open End	Target Date (Asset Alloc)	U	U	U		Y	0
Fidelity Advisor Freedom® Blend 2055 Fund Class Z6	FHGCX	NAS CM	Open End	Target Date (Asset Alloc)	U	U	U		Y	0
Fidelity Advisor Freedom® Blend 2060 Fund Class A	FHNEX	NAS CM	Open End	Target Date (Asset Alloc)	U	U	U		Y	0
Fidelity Advisor Freedom® Blend 2060 Fund Class C	FHLEX	NAS CM	Open End	Target Date (Asset Alloc)	U	U	U		Y	0
Fidelity Advisor Freedom® Blend 2060 Fund Class I	FHKEX	NAS CM	Open End	Target Date (Asset Alloc)	U	U	U		Y	0
Fidelity Advisor Freedom® Blend 2060 Fund Class M	FHMEX	NAS CM	Open End	Target Date (Asset Alloc)	U	U	U		Y	0
Fidelity Advisor Freedom® Blend 2060 Fund Class Z	FHJEX	NAS CM	Open End	Target Date (Asset Alloc)	U	U	U		Y	0
Fidelity Advisor Freedom® Blend 2060 Fund Class Z6	FHDCX	NAS CM	Open End	Target Date (Asset Alloc)	U	U	U		Y	0
Fidelity Advisor Freedom® Blend Income Fund Class A	FHAMX	NAS CM	Open End	Target Date (Asset Alloc)	U	U	U		Y	0
Fidelity Advisor Freedom® Blend Income Fund Class C	FHAKX	NAS CM	Open End	Target Date (Asset Alloc)	U	U	U		Y	0
Fidelity Advisor Freedom® Blend Income Fund Class I	FHAJX	NAS CM	Open End	Target Date (Asset Alloc)	U	U	U		Y	0

★ Expanded analysis of this fund is included in Section II.

Min Additional Investment	TOTAL RETURNS 3-Month Total Return	6-Month Total Return	1-Year Total Return	3-Year Total Return	5-Year Total Return	PERFORMANCE Dividend Yield (TTM)	Expense Ratio	3-Yr Std Deviation	3-Year Beta	ASSETS NAV	Total Assets (MIL)	ASSET ALLOCATION & TURNOVER %Cash	%Stocks	%Bonds	%Other	Turnover Ratio	BULL & BEAR Last Bull Market Total Return	Last Bear Market Total Return	FEES Front End Fee (%)	Back End Fee (%)	Inception Date
	3.32	12.11					0.31			10.27	460.1	12	49	39	0	78					Aug-18
	3.25	12.91					0.77			10.14	558.5	10	55	34	0	23			5.75		Aug-18
	3.05	12.45					1.52			10.11	558.5	10	55	34	0	23				1.00	Aug-18
	3.35	13.01					0.52			10.16	558.5	10	55	34	0	23					Aug-18
	3.15	12.68					1.02			10.13	558.5	10	55	34	0	23			3.50		Aug-18
	3.35	13.01					0.42			10.16	558.5	10	55	34	0	23					Aug-18
	3.35	13.12					0.32			10.17	558.5	10	55	34	0	23					Aug-18
	3.51	14.38					0.78			10.02	533.0	7	66	26	0	29			5.75		Aug-18
	3.31	14.05					1.53			9.98	533.0	7	66	26	0	29					Aug-18
	3.61	14.61					0.53			10.04	533.0	7	66	26	0	29					Aug-18
	3.40	14.26					1.03			10.01	533.0	7	66	26	0	29			3.50		Aug-18
	3.50	14.61					0.43			10.04	533.0	7	66	26	0	29					Aug-18
	3.60	14.72					0.33			10.05	533.0	7	66	26	0	29					Aug-18
	3.64	16.10					0.79			9.95	513.1	6	80	13	0	16			5.75		Aug-18
	3.44	15.75					1.54			9.92	513.1	6	80	13	0	16					Aug-18
	3.64	16.21					0.54			9.96	513.1	6	80	13	0	16					Aug-18
	3.54	16.00					1.04			9.93	513.1	6	80	13	0	16			3.50		Aug-18
	3.74	16.33					0.44			9.97	513.1	6	80	13	0	16					Aug-18
	3.63	16.33					0.34			9.97	513.1	6	80	13	0	16					Aug-18
	3.45	16.62					0.8			9.89	464.3	6	86	7	0	17			5.75		Aug-18
	3.35	16.13					1.55			9.86	464.3	6	86	7	0	17					Aug-18
	3.66	16.72					0.55			9.91	464.3	6	86	7	0	17					Aug-18
	3.45	16.37					1.05			9.88	464.3	6	86	7	0	17			3.50		Aug-18
	3.87	16.84					0.45			9.92	464.3	6	86	7	0	17					Aug-18
	3.65	16.84					0.35			9.92	464.3	6	86	7	0	17					Aug-18
	3.57	16.50					0.8			9.89	392.3	6	86	7	0	19			5.75		Aug-18
	3.36	16.14					1.55			9.86	392.3	6	86	7	0	19				1.00	Aug-18
	3.67	16.73					0.55			9.91	392.3	6	86	7	0	19					Aug-18
	3.57	16.38					1.05			9.88	392.3	6	86	7	0	19			3.50		Aug-18
	3.67	16.73					0.45			9.91	392.3	6	86	7	0	19					Aug-18
	3.66	16.85					0.35			9.92	392.3	6	86	7	0	19					Aug-18
	3.48	16.46					0.8			9.84	281.4	6	86	7	0	12			5.75		Aug-18
	3.27	15.97					1.55			9.81	281.4	6	86	7	0	12				1.00	Aug-18
	3.58	16.69					0.55			9.86	281.4	6	86	7	0	12					Aug-18
	3.37	16.34					1.05			9.83	281.4	6	86	7	0	12			3.50		Aug-18
	3.58	16.69					0.45			9.86	281.4	6	86	7	0	12					Aug-18
	3.68	16.81					0.35			9.87	281.4	6	86	7	0	12					Aug-18
	3.49	16.47					0.8			9.84	104.8	6	86	7	0	14			5.75		Aug-18
	3.39	16.11					1.55			9.81	104.8	6	86	7	0	14				1.00	Aug-18
	3.59	16.71					0.55			9.86	104.8	6	86	7	0	14					Aug-18
	3.38	16.35					1.05			9.83	104.8	6	86	7	0	14			3.50		Aug-18
	3.59	16.71					0.45			9.86	104.8	6	86	7	0	14					Aug-18
	3.69	16.82					0.35			9.87	104.8	6	86	7	0	14					Aug-18
	3.58	16.54					0.8			9.86	20.0	6	86	7	0	11			5.75		Aug-18
	3.26	16.07					1.55			9.82	20.0	6	86	7	0	11				1.00	Aug-18
	3.57	16.66					0.55			9.87	20.0	6	86	7	0	11					Aug-18
	3.47	16.42					1.05			9.85	20.0	6	86	7	0	11			3.50		Aug-18
	3.57	16.66					0.45			9.87	20.0	6	86	7	0	11					Aug-18
	3.68	16.78					0.35			9.88	20.0	6	86	7	0	11					Aug-18
	2.48	6.97					0.71			10.25	26.2	21	16	63	0	48			5.75		Aug-18
	2.33	6.56					1.46			10.23	26.2	21	16	63	0	48				1.00	Aug-18
	2.44	7.46					0.46			10.26	26.2	21	16	63	0	48					Aug-18

Fund Name	MARKET Ticker Symbol	Traded On	FUND TYPE, CATEGORY & OBJECTIVE Fund Type	Category and (Prospectus Objective)	RATINGS Overall Rating	Reward Rating	Risk Rating	Recent Up/ Downgrade	MINIMUMS Open to New Investors	Min Initial Investment
Fidelity Advisor Freedom® Blend Income Fund Class M	FHALX	NAS CM	Open End	Target Date (Asset Alloc)	U	U	U		Y	0
Fidelity Advisor Freedom® Blend Income Fund Class Z	FHAHX	NAS CM	Open End	Target Date (Asset Alloc)	U	U	U		Y	0
Fidelity Advisor Freedom® Blend Income Fund Class Z6	FHBDX	NAS CM	Open End	Target Date (Asset Alloc)	U	U	U		Y	0
Fidelity Advisor Freedom® Income Fund Class A	FAFAX	NAS CM	Open End	Target Date (Asset Alloc)	B	C+	A-	Up	Y	0
Fidelity Advisor Freedom® Income Fund Class C	FCAFX	NAS CM	Open End	Target Date (Asset Alloc)	B-	C	B+		Y	0
Fidelity Advisor Freedom® Income Fund Class I	FIAFX	NAS CM	Open End	Target Date (Asset Alloc)	B	C+	A-	Up	Y	0
Fidelity Advisor Freedom® Income Fund Class M	FTAFX	NAS CM	Open End	Target Date (Asset Alloc)	B	C	A-	Up	Y	0
Fidelity Advisor Freedom® Income Fund Class Z	FIJUX	NAS CM	Open End	Target Date (Asset Alloc)	B	C+	A-	Up	Y	0
Fidelity Advisor Freedom® Income Fund Class Z6	FEGLX	NAS CM	Open End	Target Date (Asset Alloc)	B	C+	A-		Y	0
Fidelity Advisor Managed Retirement 2005 Fund Class A	FIOAX	NAS CM	Open End	Target Date (Asset Alloc)	B	C+	A-	Up	Y	2,500
Fidelity Advisor Managed Retirement 2005 Fund Class C	FIOCX	NAS CM	Open End	Target Date (Asset Alloc)	B	C	A-	Up	Y	2,500
Fidelity Advisor Managed Retirement 2005 Fund Class I	FIOIX	NAS CM	Open End	Target Date (Asset Alloc)	B	C+	A		Y	2,500
Fidelity Advisor Managed Retirement 2005 Fund Class M	FIOTX	NAS CM	Open End	Target Date (Asset Alloc)	B	C+	A-	Up	Y	2,500
Fidelity Advisor Managed Retirement 2010 Fund Class A	FRQAX	NAS CM	Open End	Target Date (Asset Alloc)	B	C+	A-	Up	Y	2,500
Fidelity Advisor Managed Retirement 2010 Fund Class C	FRQCX	NAS CM	Open End	Target Date (Asset Alloc)	B	C	A-	Up	Y	2,500
Fidelity Advisor Managed Retirement 2010 Fund Class I	FRQIX	NAS CM	Open End	Target Date (Asset Alloc)	B	C+	A	Up	Y	2,500
Fidelity Advisor Managed Retirement 2010 Fund Class M	FRQTX	NAS CM	Open End	Target Date (Asset Alloc)	B	C+	A-	Up	Y	2,500
Fidelity Advisor Managed Retirement 2015 Fund Class A	FARSX	NAS CM	Open End	Target Date (Asset Alloc)	B	C	A	Up	Y	2,500
Fidelity Advisor Managed Retirement 2015 Fund Class C	FCRSX	NAS CM	Open End	Target Date (Asset Alloc)	B-	C	A-	Up	Y	2,500
Fidelity Advisor Managed Retirement 2015 Fund Class I	FRASX	NAS CM	Open End	Target Date (Asset Alloc)	B	C+	A	Up	Y	2,500
Fidelity Advisor Managed Retirement 2015 Fund Class M	FTRSX	NAS CM	Open End	Target Date (Asset Alloc)	B	C	A-	Up	Y	2,500
Fidelity Advisor Managed Retirement Income Fund Class A	FRAMX	NAS CM	Open End	Target Date (Asset Alloc)	B	C	A-	Up	Y	2,500
Fidelity Advisor Managed Retirement Income Fund Class C	FRCMX	NAS CM	Open End	Target Date (Asset Alloc)	B-	C	A-	Up	Y	2,500
Fidelity Advisor Managed Retirement Income Fund Class I	FRIMX	NAS CM	Open End	Target Date (Asset Alloc)	B	C+	A-	Up	Y	2,500
Fidelity Advisor Managed Retirement Income Fund Class M	FRTMX	NAS CM	Open End	Target Date (Asset Alloc)	B	C	A-	Up	Y	2,500
Fidelity Advisor Simplicity RMD 2005 Fund Class A	FARPX	NAS CM	Open End	Target Date (Asset Alloc)	B	C+	A-	Up	Y	2,500
Fidelity Advisor Simplicity RMD 2005 Fund Class C	FCRPX	NAS CM	Open End	Target Date (Asset Alloc)	B	C	A-	Up	Y	2,500
Fidelity Advisor Simplicity RMD 2005 Fund Class I	FRAPX	NAS CM	Open End	Target Date (Asset Alloc)	B	C+	A		Y	2,500
Fidelity Advisor Simplicity RMD 2005 Fund Class M	FTRPX	NAS CM	Open End	Target Date (Asset Alloc)	B	C+	A-	Up	Y	2,500
Fidelity Advisor Simplicity RMD 2010 Fund Class A	FIARX	NAS CM	Open End	Target Date (Asset Alloc)	B	C+	A-	Up	Y	2,500
Fidelity Advisor Simplicity RMD 2010 Fund Class C	FICRX	NAS CM	Open End	Target Date (Asset Alloc)	B	C	A-	Up	Y	2,500
Fidelity Advisor Simplicity RMD 2010 Fund Class I	FIIRX	NAS CM	Open End	Target Date (Asset Alloc)	B	C+	A	Up	Y	2,500
Fidelity Advisor Simplicity RMD 2010 Fund Class M	FTIRX	NAS CM	Open End	Target Date (Asset Alloc)	B	C+	A-	Up	Y	2,500
Fidelity Advisor Simplicity RMD 2015 Fund Class A	FURAX	NAS CM	Open End	Target Date (Asset Alloc)	B	C	A	Up	Y	2,500
Fidelity Advisor Simplicity RMD 2015 Fund Class C	FURCX	NAS CM	Open End	Target Date (Asset Alloc)	B-	C	A-	Up	Y	2,500
Fidelity Advisor Simplicity RMD 2015 Fund Class I	FURIX	NAS CM	Open End	Target Date (Asset Alloc)	B	C+	A	Up	Y	2,500
Fidelity Advisor Simplicity RMD 2015 Fund Class M	FURTX	NAS CM	Open End	Target Date (Asset Alloc)	B	C	A-	Up	Y	2,500
Fidelity Advisor Simplicity RMD 2020 Fund Class A	FARWX	NAS CM	Open End	Target Date (Asset Alloc)	B	C	A-	Up	Y	2,500
Fidelity Advisor Simplicity RMD 2020 Fund Class C	FCRWX	NAS CM	Open End	Target Date (Asset Alloc)	B-	C	A-	Up	Y	2,500
Fidelity Advisor Simplicity RMD 2020 Fund Class I	FIIWX	NAS CM	Open End	Target Date (Asset Alloc)	B	C	A	Up	Y	2,500
Fidelity Advisor Simplicity RMD 2020 Fund Class M	FTRWX	NAS CM	Open End	Target Date (Asset Alloc)	B-	C	A-	Up	Y	2,500
Fidelity Advisor Simplicity RMD Income Fund Class A	FRNAX	NAS CM	Open End	Target Date (Asset Alloc)	B	C+	A-	Up	Y	2,500
Fidelity Advisor Simplicity RMD Income Fund Class C	FRNCX	NAS CM	Open End	Target Date (Asset Alloc)	B-	C	A-	Up	Y	2,500
Fidelity Advisor Simplicity RMD Income Fund Class I	FRNIX	NAS CM	Open End	Target Date (Asset Alloc)	B	C+	A-		Y	2,500
Fidelity Advisor Simplicity RMD Income Fund Class M	FRNTX	NAS CM	Open End	Target Date (Asset Alloc)	B	C	A-	Up	Y	2,500
Fidelity Advisor® Balanced Fund Class A	FABLX	NAS CM	Open End	Moderate Alloc (Balanced)	B-	C	B+		Y	0
Fidelity Advisor® Balanced Fund Class C	FABCX	NAS CM	Open End	Moderate Alloc (Balanced)	B-	C	B+	Up	Y	0
Fidelity Advisor® Balanced Fund Class M	FAIGX	NAS CM	Open End	Moderate Alloc (Balanced)	B-	C	B+	Up	Y	0
Fidelity Advisor® Balanced Fund Class Z	FZAAX	NAS CM	Open End	Moderate Alloc (Balanced)	B-	C	B+		Y	0
Fidelity Advisor® Balanced Fund I Class	FAIOX	NAS CM	Open End	Moderate Alloc (Balanced)	B-	C	B+		Y	0
Fidelity Advisor® Biotechnology Fund Class A	FBTAX	NAS CM	Open End	Healthcare Sector Equity (Health)	C	C	C+		Y	0
Fidelity Advisor® Biotechnology Fund Class C	FBTCX	NAS CM	Open End	Healthcare Sector Equity (Health)	C	C	C+		Y	0

★ Expanded analysis of this fund is included in Section II.

	TOTAL RETURNS					PERFORMANCE				ASSETS		ASSET ALLOCATION & TURNOVER					BULL & BEAR		FEES		
Min Additional Investment	3-Month Total Return	6-Month Total Return	1-Year Total Return	3-Year Total Return	5-Year Total Return	Dividend Yield (TTM)	Expense Ratio	3-Yr Std Deviation	3-Year Beta	NAV	Total Assets (MIL)	%Cash	%Stocks	%Bonds	%Other	Turnover Ratio	Last Bull Market Total Return	Last Bear Market Total Return	Front End Fee (%)	Back End Fee (%)	Inception Date
	2.39	6.82					0.96			10.25	26.2	21	16	63	0	48			3.50		Aug-18
	2.50	7.16					0.36			10.26	26.2	21	16	63	0	48					Aug-18
	2.51	7.17					0.26			10.26	26.2	21	16	63	0	48					Aug-18
	2.47	7.25	5.34	15.06	17.95	1.81	0.72	2.99	0.52	10.89	229.1	23	16	61	0	36	6.14	-3.86	5.75		Jul-03
	2.33	6.89	4.68	12.57	13.70	1.02	1.47	2.99	0.53	10.87	229.1	23	16	61	0	36	5.7	-4.17		1.00	Jul-03
	2.62	7.44	5.69	15.98	19.47	2.04	0.47	2.97	0.5	10.93	229.1	23	16	61	0	36	6.27	-3.76			Jul-03
	2.51	7.05	5.18	14.21	16.49	1.57	0.97	3	0.51	10.88	229.1	23	16	61	0	36	6.02	-3.97	3.50		Jul-03
	2.56	7.37	5.70	16.00	19.49		0.42	2.97	0.52	10.92	229.1	23	16	61	0	36	6.27	-3.76			Oct-18
	2.56	7.40	5.76	16.16	19.66	2.19	0.37	2.96	0.52	10.91	229.1	23	16	61	0	36	6.27	-3.76			Jun-17
	2.47	7.28	5.11	18.26	21.12	1.77	0.7	3.28	0.41	58.63	5.4	21	17	62	0	24	12.54	-10.62	5.75		Aug-07
	2.29	6.87	4.34	15.64	16.68	1.01	1.45	3.27	0.41	58.34	5.4	21	17	62	0	24	12.03	-10.89		1.00	Aug-07
	2.55	7.41	5.38	19.17	22.64	2.01	0.45	3.28	0.41	58.62	5.4	21	17	62	0	24	12.69	-10.51			Aug-07
	2.43	7.15	4.87	17.40	19.62	1.52	0.95	3.27	0.41	58.66	5.4	21	17	62	0	24	12.36	-10.7	3.50		Aug-07
	2.63	8.38	5.10	21.17	23.79	1.72	0.71	4.09	0.36	56.35	9.3	18	25	56	0	21	13.37	-11.54	5.75		Aug-07
	2.44	7.97	4.31	18.49	19.24	0.97	1.46	4.1	0.37	55.9	9.3	18	25	56	0	21	12.9	-11.82		1.00	Aug-07
	2.70	8.52	5.36	22.08	25.36	1.94	0.46	4.09	0.37	56.37	9.3	18	25	56	0	21	13.56	-11.45			Aug-07
	2.57	8.25	4.85	20.27	22.26	1.46	0.96	4.1	0.36	56.48	9.3	18	25	56	0	21	13.16	-11.63	3.50		Aug-07
	2.76	9.44	5.06	23.29	25.68	1.61	0.72	4.89	0.32	53.13	4.5	16	32	51	0	20	13.99	-12.31	5.75		Aug-07
	2.55	9.00	4.28	20.52	21.03	0.91	1.47	4.88	0.33	52.82	4.5	16	32	51	0	20	13.5	-12.59		1.00	Aug-07
	2.82	9.57	5.32	24.21	27.26	1.84	0.47	4.89	0.32	53.12	4.5	16	32	51	0	20	14.16	-12.22			Aug-07
	2.69	9.30	4.80	22.36	24.11	1.37	0.97	4.88	0.33	53.22	4.5	16	32	51	0	20	13.82	-12.4	3.50		Aug-07
	2.46	7.04	5.14	14.49	17.53	1.8	0.7	2.89	0.43	57.75	6.4	21	16	63	0	19	11.21	-9.16	5.75		Aug-07
	2.27	6.65	4.37	11.94	13.22	1.02	1.45	2.87	0.43	57.59	6.4	21	16	63	0	19	10.71	-9.45		1.00	Aug-07
	2.51	7.19	5.42	15.37	19.02	2.03	0.45	2.88	0.43	57.72	6.4	21	16	63	0	19	11.36	-9.05			Aug-07
	2.39	6.92	4.89	13.65	16.08	1.49	0.95	2.88	0.43	57.83	6.4	21	16	63	0	19	11.04	-9.25	3.50		Aug-07
	2.43	7.22	5.05	19.34	22.05	1.79	0.73	3.37	0.4	58.24	17.9	22	17	60	0	32	12.98	-11.11	5.75		Aug-07
	2.22	6.81	4.25	16.66	17.53	1.06	1.48	3.37	0.4	57.92	17.9	22	17	60	0	32	12.5	-11.38		1.00	Aug-07
	2.50	7.36	5.33	20.24	23.58	2.02	0.48	3.37	0.39	58.22	17.9	22	17	60	0	32	13.15	-11.01			Aug-07
	2.36	7.08	4.79	18.42	20.52	1.54	0.98	3.37	0.4	58.19	17.9	22	17	60	0	32	12.81	-11.19	3.50		Aug-07
	2.58	8.40	5.02	21.83	24.36	1.65	0.78	4.2	0.35	53.51	10.6	20	25	55	0	44	13.67	-11.9	5.75		Aug-07
	2.38	7.96	4.22	19.10	19.76	0.92	1.53	4.2	0.35	53.14	10.6	20	25	55	0	44	13.18	-12.18		1.00	Aug-07
	2.62	8.51	5.26	22.72	25.91	1.89	0.53	4.21	0.35	53.52	10.6	20	25	55	0	44	13.84	-11.8			Aug-07
	2.51	8.24	4.75	20.91	22.81	1.41	1.03	4.21	0.35	53.54	10.6	20	25	55	0	44	13.49	-12	3.50		Aug-07
	2.68	9.52	4.94	23.89	26.15	1.57	0.82	5.08	0.3	59.42	20.9	17	34	48	0	44	14.3	-12.73	5.75		Aug-07
	2.49	8.60	3.66	20.56	20.95	0.88	1.57	5.07	0.27	58.47	20.9	17	34	48	0	44	13.8	-13		1.00	Aug-07
	2.76	9.66	5.20	24.86	27.90	1.82	0.57	5.08	0.3	59.5	20.9	17	34	48	0	44	14.46	-12.64			Aug-07
	2.64	9.40	4.68	22.95	24.58	1.29	1.07	5.08	0.3	59.38	20.9	17	34	48	0	44	14.14	-12.82	3.50		Aug-07
	2.82	10.68	4.83	25.83	27.85	1.48	0.86	6.01	0.26	59.94	42.6	15	43	42	0	29	15.28	-13.79	5.75		Dec-07
	2.62	10.26	4.06	23.00	23.14	0.93	1.61	6	0.26	59.04	42.6	15	43	42	0	29	14.77	-14.07		1.00	Dec-07
	2.87	10.81	5.10	26.75	29.43	1.72	0.61	6.01	0.26	59.85	42.6	15	43	42	0	29	15.46	-13.71			Dec-07
	2.75	10.54	4.58	24.86	26.25	1.22	1.11	6	0.26	59.98	42.6	15	43	42	0	29	15.1	-13.88	3.50		Dec-07
	2.41	6.99	5.08	16.35	19.28	1.76	0.72	3	0.41	58.51	19.7	23	16	61	0	46	12.04	-9.99	5.75		Aug-07
	2.22	6.31	4.05	13.48	14.61	1.03	1.47	2.98	0.4	58.09	19.7	23	16	61	0	46	11.53	-10.27		1.00	Aug-07
	2.48	7.13	5.35	17.24	20.81	1.96	0.47	3	0.42	58.54	19.7	23	16	61	0	46	12.18	-9.89			Aug-07
	2.34	6.86	4.83	15.48	17.81	1.5	0.97	3	0.42	58.5	19.7	23	16	61	0	46	11.87	-10.07	3.50		Aug-07
	3.60	15.03	6.17	33.87	40.98	1.24	0.87	8.93	0.72	21.19	3,732	6	64	30	0	62	15.64	-10.52	5.75		Sep-96
	3.37	14.64	5.37	30.89	35.81	0.55	1.62	8.9	0.72	21.01	3,732	6	64	30	0	62	15.09	-10.79		1.00	Nov-97
	3.49	14.88	5.87	32.91	39.27	0.99	1.12	8.9	0.72	21.44	3,732	6	64	30	0	62	15.46	-10.6	3.50		Jan-87
	3.70	15.31	6.57	35.44	43.86	1.55	0.49	8.92	0.72	21.65	3,732	6	64	30	0	62	15.46	-10.6			Aug-13
	3.62	15.22	6.45	34.95	42.85	1.44	0.61	8.95	0.72	21.64	3,732	6	64	30	0	62	15.74	-10.37			Jul-95
	-1.70	14.67	0.03	41.76	41.35	0	1.06	22.7	1.3	26.49	2,300	1	99	0	0	45	37.41	-12.02	5.75		Dec-00
	-1.86	14.26	-0.69	38.61	36.21	0	1.8	22.68	1.3	22.59	2,300	1	99	0	0	45	36.71	-12.21		1.00	Dec-00

	MARKET			FUND TYPE, CATEGORY & OBJECTIVE	RATINGS				MINIMUMS	
Fund Name	Ticker Symbol	Traded On	Fund Type	Category and (Prospectus Objective)	Overall Rating	Reward Rating	Risk Rating	Recent Up/ Downgrade	Open to New Investors	Min Initial Investment
Fidelity Advisor® Biotechnology Fund Class M	FBTTX	NAS CM	Open End	Healthcare Sector Equity (Health)	C	C	C+		Y	0
Fidelity Advisor® Biotechnology Fund Class Z	FIJYX	NAS CM	Open End	Healthcare Sector Equity (Health)	C	C	B-		Y	0
Fidelity Advisor® Biotechnology Fund I Class	FBTIX	NAS CM	Open End	Healthcare Sector Equity (Health)	C	C	B-		Y	0
Fidelity Advisor® Canada Fund Class A	FACNX	NAS CM	Open End	Equity Miscellaneous (Foreign Stock)	C+	C	B		Y	0
Fidelity Advisor® Canada Fund Class C	FCCNX	NAS CM	Open End	Equity Miscellaneous (Foreign Stock)	C+	C	B		Y	0
Fidelity Advisor® Canada Fund Class M	FTCNX	NAS CM	Open End	Equity Miscellaneous (Foreign Stock)	C+	C	B		Y	0
Fidelity Advisor® Canada Fund Class Z	FIQEX	NAS CM	Open End	Equity Miscellaneous (Foreign Stock)	C+	C	B		Y	0
Fidelity Advisor® Canada Fund I Class	FICCX	NAS CM	Open End	Equity Miscellaneous (Foreign Stock)	C+	C	B		Y	0
Fidelity Advisor® Capital Development Fund Class A	FDTTX	NAS CM	Open End	US Equity Large Cap Blend (World Stock)	C+	C	B		Y	0
Fidelity Advisor® Capital Development Fund Class C	FDECX	NAS CM	Open End	US Equity Large Cap Blend (World Stock)	C+	C	B	Up	Y	0
Fidelity Advisor® Capital Development Fund Class M	FDTZX	NAS CM	Open End	US Equity Large Cap Blend (World Stock)	C+	C	B		Y	0
Fidelity Advisor® Capital Development Fund Class O	FDETX	NAS CM	Open End	US Equity Large Cap Blend (World Stock)	C+	C	B			0
Fidelity Advisor® Capital Development Fund I Class	FDEIX	NAS CM	Open End	US Equity Large Cap Blend (World Stock)	C+	C	B		Y	0
Fidelity Advisor® China Region Fund Class A	FHKAX	NAS CM	Open End	Greater China Equity (Pacific Stock)	C	C-	C		Y	0
Fidelity Advisor® China Region Fund Class C	FCHKX	NAS CM	Open End	Greater China Equity (Pacific Stock)	C	C-	C		Y	0
Fidelity Advisor® China Region Fund Class M	FHKTX	NAS CM	Open End	Greater China Equity (Pacific Stock)	C	C-	C		Y	0
Fidelity Advisor® China Region Fund Class Z	FIQFX	NAS CM	Open End	Greater China Equity (Pacific Stock)	C	C-	C		Y	0
Fidelity Advisor® China Region Fund I Class	FHKIX	NAS CM	Open End	Greater China Equity (Pacific Stock)	C	C-	C		Y	0
Fidelity Advisor® Communication Services Class A	FGDMX	NAS CM	Open End	Consumer Goods Sec Equity (Comm)	B-	C+	B		Y	0
Fidelity Advisor® Communication Services Class C	FGHMX	NAS CM	Open End	Consumer Goods Sec Equity (Comm)	B-	C	B		Y	0
Fidelity Advisor® Communication Services Class I	FGJMX	NAS CM	Open End	Consumer Goods Sec Equity (Comm)	B-	C+	B		Y	0
Fidelity Advisor® Communication Services Class M	FGEMX	NAS CM	Open End	Consumer Goods Sec Equity (Comm)	B-	C+	B		Y	0
Fidelity Advisor® Communication Services Class Z	FGKMX	NAS CM	Open End	Consumer Goods Sec Equity (Comm)	B-	C+	B		Y	0
Fidelity Advisor® Communications Equipment Fund Class A	FDMAX	NAS CM	Open End	Technology Sector Equity (Comm)	C+	C-	B		Y	0
Fidelity Advisor® Communications Equipment Fund Class C	FDMCX	NAS CM	Open End	Technology Sector Equity (Comm)	C+	C-	B		Y	0
Fidelity Advisor® Communications Equipment Fund Class M	FDMTX	NAS CM	Open End	Technology Sector Equity (Comm)	C+	C-	B		Y	0
Fidelity Advisor® Communications Equipment Fund I Class	FDMIX	NAS CM	Open End	Technology Sector Equity (Comm)	C+	C-	B		Y	0
Fidelity Advisor® Consumer Discretionary Fund Class A	FCNAX	NAS CM	Open End	Consumer Goods Sec Equity ()	B-	C+	B		Y	0
Fidelity Advisor® Consumer Discretionary Fund Class C	FCECX	NAS CM	Open End	Consumer Goods Sec Equity ()	B-	C+	B		Y	0
Fidelity Advisor® Consumer Discretionary Fund Class M	FACPX	NAS CM	Open End	Consumer Goods Sec Equity ()	B-	C+	B		Y	0
Fidelity Advisor® Consumer Discretionary Fund Class Z	FIJZX	NAS CM	Open End	Consumer Goods Sec Equity ()	B-	C+	B		Y	0
Fidelity Advisor® Consumer Discretionary Fund I Class	FCNIX	NAS CM	Open End	Consumer Goods Sec Equity ()	B-	C+	B		Y	0
Fidelity Advisor® Consumer Staples Fund Class A	FDAGX	NAS CM	Open End	Consumer Goods Sec Equity ()	C	C	C		Y	0
Fidelity Advisor® Consumer Staples Fund Class C	FDCGX	NAS CM	Open End	Consumer Goods Sec Equity ()	C	C	C		Y	0
Fidelity Advisor® Consumer Staples Fund Class M	FDTGX	NAS CM	Open End	Consumer Goods Sec Equity ()	C	C	C		Y	0
Fidelity Advisor® Consumer Staples Fund I Class	FDIGX	NAS CM	Open End	Consumer Goods Sec Equity ()	C	C	C		Y	0
Fidelity Advisor® Consumer Staples Portfolio Class Z	FIJCX	NAS CM	Open End	Consumer Goods Sec Equity ()	C	C	C		Y	0
Fidelity Advisor® Convertible Securities Fund Class A	FACVX	NAS CM	Open End	Convertibles (Convertible Bond)	B	C	A-		Y	0
Fidelity Advisor® Convertible Securities Fund Class C	FCCVX	NAS CM	Open End	Convertibles (Convertible Bond)	B	C	A-		Y	0
Fidelity Advisor® Convertible Securities Fund Class M	FTCVX	NAS CM	Open End	Convertibles (Convertible Bond)	B	C	A-		Y	0
Fidelity Advisor® Convertible Securities Fund Class Z	FIQVX	NAS CM	Open End	Convertibles (Convertible Bond)	B	C	A-		Y	0
Fidelity Advisor® Convertible Securities Fund I Class	FICVX	NAS CM	Open End	Convertibles (Convertible Bond)	B	C	A-		Y	0
Fidelity Advisor® Diversified International Fund Class A	FDVAX	NAS CM	Open End	Global Equity Large Cap (Foreign Stock)	C	C	B-		Y	0
Fidelity Advisor® Diversified International Fund Class C	FADCX	NAS CM	Open End	Global Equity Large Cap (Foreign Stock)	C	C	B-		Y	0
Fidelity Advisor® Diversified International Fund Class M	FADIX	NAS CM	Open End	Global Equity Large Cap (Foreign Stock)	C	C	B-		Y	0
Fidelity Advisor® Diversified International Fund Class Z	FZABX	NAS CM	Open End	Global Equity Large Cap (Foreign Stock)	C	C	B-		Y	0
Fidelity Advisor® Diversified International Fund I Class	FDVIX	NAS CM	Open End	Global Equity Large Cap (Foreign Stock)	C	C	B-		Y	0
Fidelity Advisor® Diversified Stock Fund Class A	FDTOX	NAS CM	Open End	US Equity Large Cap Blend (World Stock)	C+	C	B		Y	0
Fidelity Advisor® Diversified Stock Fund Class C	FDTCX	NAS CM	Open End	US Equity Large Cap Blend (World Stock)	C+	C	B-	Up	Y	0
Fidelity Advisor® Diversified Stock Fund Class M	FDTEX	NAS CM	Open End	US Equity Large Cap Blend (World Stock)	C+	C	B		Y	0
Fidelity Advisor® Diversified Stock Fund Class O	FDESX	NAS CM	Open End	US Equity Large Cap Blend (World Stock)	C+	C	B			0
Fidelity Advisor® Diversified Stock Fund Class Z	FZACX	NAS CM	Open End	US Equity Large Cap Blend (World Stock)	C+	C	B		Y	0

★ Expanded analysis of this fund is included in Section II.

	TOTAL RETURNS					PERFORMANCE				ASSETS		ASSET ALLOCATION & TURNOVER					BULL & BEAR		FEES		
Min Additional Investment	3-Month Total Return	6-Month Total Return	1-Year Total Return	3-Year Total Return	5-Year Total Return	Dividend Yield (TTM)	Expense Ratio	3-Yr Std Deviation	3-Year Beta	NAV	Total Assets (MIL)	%Cash	%Stocks	%Bonds	%Other	Turnover Ratio	Last Bull Market Total Return	Last Bear Market Total Return	Front End Fee (%)	Back End Fee (%)	Inception Date
	-1.80	14.48	-0.31	40.34	39.08	0	1.38	22.67	1.3	24.97	2,300	1	99	0	0	45	37.05	-12.02	3.50		Dec-00
	-1.64	14.89	0.35	42.95	43.36		0.66	22.71	1.3	28.16	2,300	1	99	0	0	45	37.53	-11.86			Oct-18
	-1.64	14.81	0.28	42.85	43.25	0	0.79	22.72	1.3	28.14	2,300	1	99	0	0	45	37.53	-11.86			Dec-00
	5.73	20.71	5.71	23.93	4.57	0.71	1.21	11.8	0.89	52.33	1,034	1	99	0	0	29	12.65	-23.87	5.75		May-07
	5.55	20.29	4.95	21.28	0.82	0	1.94	11.79	0.89	51.1	1,034	1	99	0	0	29	12.15	-24.11		1.00	May-07
	5.65	20.52	5.40	22.84	3.02	0.41	1.51	11.8	0.89	52.09	1,034	1	99	0	0	29	12.48	-23.97	3.50		May-07
	5.86	21.00	6.14	25.24	6.29		0.8	11.82	0.89	52.36	1,034	1	99	0	0	29	12.86	-23.78			Oct-18
	5.83	20.94	6.09	25.26	6.36	1.08	0.86	11.81	0.89	52.43	1,034	1	99	0	0	29	12.85	-23.78			May-07
	2.64	17.70	4.99	45.50	45.37	1.39	0.87	13.78	1.09	14.76	3,108	3	97	0	0	36	20.37	-19.55	5.75		Apr-99
	2.31	17.06	3.92	41.19	38.28	0.55	1.84	13.7	1.08	13.72	3,108	3	97	0	0	36	19.75	-19.8		1.00	Jul-05
	2.43	17.29	4.39	43.06	41.43	0.88	1.41	13.77	1.09	14.31	3,108	3	97	0	0	36	20.04	-19.72	3.50		Jul-05
	2.67	17.89	5.27	46.81	47.50	1.62	0.58	13.77	1.09	15.35	3,108	3	97	0	0	36	20.58	-19.41			Dec-85
	2.59	17.72	5.11	46.08	46.29	1.5	0.72	13.75	1.09	15.41	3,108	3	97	0	0	36	20.33	-19.48			Jul-05
	-1.49	17.50	-2.41	51.73	37.81	0.34	1.27	18.16	1.08	34.17	1,218	1	99	0	0	60	17.55	-27.15	5.75		May-08
	-1.66	17.09	-3.09	48.47	32.79	0	2.01	18.16	1.08	33.16	1,218	1	99	0	0	60	17	-27.38		1.00	May-08
	-1.56	17.35	-2.68	50.25	35.51	0	1.62	18.16	1.08	34.02	1,218	1	99	0	0	60	17.34	-27.23	3.50		May-08
	-1.38	17.81	-2.00	53.31	40.04		0.91	18.16	1.08	34.26	1,218	1	99	0	0	60	17.74	-27.07			Oct-18
	-1.40	17.69	-2.10	53.16	39.99	0.68	0.98	18.16	1.08	34.32	1,218	1	99	0	0	60	17.75	-27.06			May-08
	4.50	20.81	13.67	45.77	46.96		1.08	14.54	0.9	61.83	628.4	0	100	0	0	107	30.57	-22.58	5.75		Nov-18
	4.27	20.32	12.77	42.49	41.53		1.81	14.54	0.9	61.54	628.4	0	100	0	0	107	30	-22.82		1.00	Nov-18
	4.58	21.02	14.00	46.94	48.88		0.79	14.55	0.9	61.95	628.4	0	100	0	0	107	30.76	-22.49			Nov-18
	4.42	20.64	13.36	44.66	45.12		1.38	14.55	0.9	61.73	628.4	0	100	0	0	107	30.38	-22.66	3.50		Nov-18
	4.61	21.07	14.06	47.01	48.95		0.64	14.55	0.9	61.98	628.4	0	100	0	0	107	30.76	-22.49			Nov-18
	-4.24	12.78	3.96	51.68	43.67	0	1.4	14.58	0.89	15.35	33.6	6	94	0	0	60	14.21	-32.37	5.75		Dec-00
	-4.37	12.38	3.14	48.28	38.44	0	2.15	14.56	0.89	13.34	33.6	6	94	0	0	60	13.65	-32.57		1.00	Dec-00
	-4.23	12.72	3.77	50.65	41.95	0	1.65	14.55	0.88	14.71	33.6	6	94	0	0	60	14.09	-32.52	3.50		Dec-00
	-4.18	12.96	4.25	52.90	45.56	0	1.15	14.58	0.89	16.03	33.6	6	94	0	0	60	14.44	-32.35			Dec-00
	4.29	21.34	7.81	51.34	68.83	0	1.12	14.86	1.13	29.62	422.9	0	100	0	0	60	31.4	-16.55	5.75		Sep-96
	4.10	20.91	7.04	48.01	62.64	0	1.87	14.85	1.13	23.82	422.9	0	100	0	0	60	30.89	-16.85		1.00	Nov-97
	4.23	21.16	7.54	50.15	66.45	0	1.38	14.83	1.13	27.59	422.9	0	100	0	0	60	31.17	-16.65	3.50		Sep-96
	4.39	21.61	8.25	52.78	71.38		0.7	14.84	1.13	32.07	422.9	0	100	0	0	60	31.72	-16.44			Oct-18
	4.33	21.50	8.11	52.59	71.17	0	0.84	14.83	1.13	32.03	422.9	0	100	0	0	60	31.72	-16.44			Sep-96
	3.01	21.22	11.42	8.83	27.43	2.24	1.05	12.65	0.73	82.29	1,485	1	99	0	0	41	17.63	-6.73	5.75		Dec-06
	2.81	20.76	10.58	6.42	22.75	1.63	1.79	12.64	0.73	79.85	1,485	1	99	0	0	41	17.12	-7.02		1.00	Dec-06
	2.94	21.05	11.11	7.95	25.70	2.05	1.33	12.65	0.73	81.41	1,485	1	99	0	0	41	17.43	-6.84	3.50		Dec-06
	3.09	21.40	11.74	9.74	29.17	2.47	0.77	12.65	0.73	82.98	1,485	1	99	0	0	41	17.78	-6.64			Dec-06
	3.10	21.47	11.83	9.87	29.35		0.63	12.65	0.73	82.91	1,485	1	99	0	0	41	17.81	-6.63			Oct-18
	5.82	18.63	10.93	34.69	23.64	2.43	0.76	8.55	0.96	29.43	1,533	6	11	0	0	176	15.92	-19.86	5.75		Feb-09
	5.61	18.16	10.13	31.71	19.07	1.73	1.5	8.54	0.96	29.22	1,533	6	11	0	0	176	15.33	-20.1		1.00	Feb-09
	5.74	18.44	10.60	33.50	21.82	2.14	1.04	8.55	0.96	29.44	1,533	6	11	0	0	176	15.68	-19.96	3.50		Feb-09
	5.93	18.86	11.34	35.97	25.51		0.37	8.56	0.96	29.51	1,533	6	11	0	0	176	16.06	-19.75			Oct-18
	5.87	18.75	11.22	35.80	25.31	2.69	0.48	8.54	0.96	29.5	1,533	6	11	0	0	176	16.03	-19.79			Feb-09
	5.69	18.10	2.28	29.43	19.03	0.75	1.19	11.73	1.02	22.44	1,832	4	96	0	0	32	16.95	-24.67	5.75		Dec-98
	5.50	17.66	1.50	26.50	14.61	0	1.95	11.72	1.02	21.45	1,832	4	96	0	0	32	16.4	-24.85		1.00	Dec-98
	5.59	17.94	1.96	28.40	17.45	0.47	1.46	11.73	1.02	22.28	1,832	4	96	0	0	32	16.78	-24.72	3.50		Dec-98
	5.75	18.33	2.67	31.02	21.56	1.17	0.78	11.72	1.02	22.78	1,832	4	96	0	0	32	17.13	-24.56			Aug-13
	5.79	18.30	2.59	30.54	20.69	1.03	0.92	11.74	1.02	22.81	1,832	4	96	0	0	32	17.13	-24.56			Dec-98
	3.84	18.75	4.89	52.60	49.64	0.3	0.82	13.48	1.07	24.32	2,093	2	97	0	1	103	26.62	-18.31	5.75		Apr-99
	3.62	18.23	3.95	48.41	42.89	0	1.74	13.49	1.07	23.41	2,093	2	97	0	1	103	26.01	-18.66		1.00	Jul-05
	3.74	18.55	4.55	50.84	46.80	0	1.19	13.46	1.07	24.09	2,093	2	97	0	1	103	26.32	-18.45	3.50		Jul-05
	3.89	18.97	5.28	54.16	52.28	0.63	0.47	13.47	1.07	25.08	2,093	2	97	0	1	103	26.92	-18.22			Jul-70
	3.91	18.92	5.24	54.01	52.06	0.59	0.51	13.47	1.07	25.76	2,093	2	97	0	1	103	26.92	-18.22			Aug-13

Fund Name	Ticker Symbol	Traded On	Fund Type	Category and (Prospectus Objective)	Overall Rating	Reward Rating	Risk Rating	Recent Up/ Downgrade	Open to New Investors	Min Initial Investment
Fidelity Advisor® Diversified Stock Fund I Class	FDTIX	NAS CM	Open End	US Equity Large Cap Blend (World Stock)	C+	C	B	Up	Y	0
Fidelity Advisor® Dividend Growth Fund Class A	FADAX	NAS CM	Open End	US Equity Large Cap Blend (Growth)	B-	C	B		Y	0
Fidelity Advisor® Dividend Growth Fund Class C	FDGCX	NAS CM	Open End	US Equity Large Cap Blend (Growth)	B-	C	B	Up	Y	0
Fidelity Advisor® Dividend Growth Fund Class M	FDGTX	NAS CM	Open End	US Equity Large Cap Blend (Growth)	B-	C	B		Y	0
Fidelity Advisor® Dividend Growth Fund Class Z	FZADX	NAS CM	Open End	US Equity Large Cap Blend (Growth)	B-	C	B+		Y	0
Fidelity Advisor® Dividend Growth Fund I Class	FDGIX	NAS CM	Open End	US Equity Large Cap Blend (Growth)	B-	C	B+		Y	0
Fidelity Advisor® Emerging Asia Fund Class A	FEAAX	NAS CM	Open End	Asia ex-Japan Equity (Pacific Stock)	C	C	C+		Y	0
Fidelity Advisor® Emerging Asia Fund Class C	FERCX	NAS CM	Open End	Asia ex-Japan Equity (Pacific Stock)	C	C	C+		Y	0
Fidelity Advisor® Emerging Asia Fund Class M	FEATX	NAS CM	Open End	Asia ex-Japan Equity (Pacific Stock)	C	C	C+		Y	0
Fidelity Advisor® Emerging Asia Fund Class Z	FIQPX	NAS CM	Open End	Asia ex-Japan Equity (Pacific Stock)	C	C	C+		Y	0
Fidelity Advisor® Emerging Asia Fund I Class	FERIX	NAS CM	Open End	Asia ex-Japan Equity (Pacific Stock)	C+	C	C+	Up	Y	0
Fidelity Advisor® Emerg Eur, Mid East, Afr (EMEA) Cls A	FMEAX	NAS CM	Open End	Global Emerg Mkts (Foreign Stock)	C	C	B-		Y	0
Fidelity Advisor® Emerg Eur, Mid East, Afr (EMEA) Cls C	FEMCX	NAS CM	Open End	Global Emerg Mkts (Foreign Stock)	C	C	B-		Y	0
Fidelity Advisor® Emerg Eur, Mid East, Afr (EMEA) Cls M	FEMTX	NAS CM	Open End	Global Emerg Mkts (Foreign Stock)	C	C	B-		Y	0
Fidelity Advisor® Emerg Eur, Mid East, Afr (EMEA) I Cls	FIEMX	NAS CM	Open End	Global Emerg Mkts (Foreign Stock)	C+	C	B-	Up	Y	0
Fidelity Advisor® Emerging Markets Discovery Fund Class A	FEDAX	NAS CM	Open End	Global Emerg Mkts (Div Emerging Mkts)	C	C	C		Y	0
Fidelity Advisor® Emerging Markets Discovery Fund Class C	FEDGX	NAS CM	Open End	Global Emerg Mkts (Div Emerging Mkts)	C	C-	C		Y	0
Fidelity Advisor® Emerging Markets Discovery Fund Class M	FEDTX	NAS CM	Open End	Global Emerg Mkts (Div Emerging Mkts)	C	C	C		Y	0
Fidelity Advisor® Emerging Markets Discovery Fund Class Z	FIQGX	NAS CM	Open End	Global Emerg Mkts (Div Emerging Mkts)	C	C	C		Y	0
Fidelity Advisor® Emerging Markets Discovery Fund I Class	FEDIX	NAS CM	Open End	Global Emerg Mkts (Div Emerging Mkts)	C	C	C		Y	0
Fidelity Advisor® Emerging Markets Fund Class A	FAMKX	NAS CM	Open End	Global Emerg Mkts (Div Emerging Mkts)	C	C	C+		Y	0
Fidelity Advisor® Emerging Markets Fund Class C	FMCKX	NAS CM	Open End	Global Emerg Mkts (Div Emerging Mkts)	C	C	C		Y	0
Fidelity Advisor® Emerging Markets Fund Class M	FTMKX	NAS CM	Open End	Global Emerg Mkts (Div Emerging Mkts)	C	C	C+		Y	0
Fidelity Advisor® Emerging Markets Fund Class Z	FZAEX	NAS CM	Open End	Global Emerg Mkts (Div Emerging Mkts)	C	C	C+		Y	0
Fidelity Advisor® Emerging Markets Fund I Class	FIMKX	NAS CM	Open End	Global Emerg Mkts (Div Emerging Mkts)	C	C	C+		Y	0
Fidelity Advisor® Energy Fund Class A	FANAX	NAS CM	Open End	Energy Sector Equity (Natl Res)	D	D	D	Down	Y	0
Fidelity Advisor® Energy Fund Class C	FNRCX	NAS CM	Open End	Energy Sector Equity (Natl Res)	D	D	D	Down	Y	0
Fidelity Advisor® Energy Fund Class M	FAGNX	NAS CM	Open End	Energy Sector Equity (Natl Res)	D	D	D	Down	Y	0
Fidelity Advisor® Energy Fund Class Z	FIKAX	NAS CM	Open End	Energy Sector Equity (Natl Res)	D	D	D	Down	Y	0
Fidelity Advisor® Energy Fund I Class	FANIX	NAS CM	Open End	Energy Sector Equity (Natl Res)	D	D	D+	Down	Y	0
Fidelity Advisor® Equity Growth Fund Class A	EPGAX	NAS CM	Open End	US Equity Large Cap Growth (Growth)	B-	C+	B	Down	Y	0
Fidelity Advisor® Equity Growth Fund Class C	EPGCX	NAS CM	Open End	US Equity Large Cap Growth (Growth)	B-	C+	B	Down	Y	0
Fidelity Advisor® Equity Growth Fund Class M	FAEGX	NAS CM	Open End	US Equity Large Cap Growth (Growth)	B-	C+	B	Down	Y	0
Fidelity Advisor® Equity Growth Fund Class Z	FZAFX	NAS CM	Open End	US Equity Large Cap Growth (Growth)	B-	C+	B	Down	Y	0
Fidelity Advisor® Equity Growth Fund I Class	EQPGX	NAS CM	Open End	US Equity Large Cap Growth (Growth)	B-	C+	B	Down	Y	0
Fidelity Advisor® Equity Income Fund Class A	FEIAX	NAS CM	Open End	US Equity Large Cap Value (Equity-Income)	C+	C	B	Up	Y	0
Fidelity Advisor® Equity Income Fund Class C	FEICX	NAS CM	Open End	US Equity Large Cap Value (Equity-Income)	C+	C	B	Up	Y	0
Fidelity Advisor® Equity Income Fund Class M	FEIRX	NAS CM	Open End	US Equity Large Cap Value (Equity-Income)	C+	C	B	Up	Y	0
Fidelity Advisor® Equity Income Fund Class Z	FZAGX	NAS CM	Open End	US Equity Large Cap Value (Equity-Income)	C+	C	B	Up	Y	0
Fidelity Advisor® Equity Income Fund I Class	EQPIX	NAS CM	Open End	US Equity Large Cap Value (Equity-Income)	C+	C	B	Up	Y	0
Fidelity Advisor® Equity Value Fund Class A	FAVAX	NAS CM	Open End	US Equity Large Cap Value (Growth)	B-	C	B	Up	Y	0
Fidelity Advisor® Equity Value Fund Class C	FAVCX	NAS CM	Open End	US Equity Large Cap Value (Growth)	B-	C	B	Up	Y	0
Fidelity Advisor® Equity Value Fund Class M	FAVTX	NAS CM	Open End	US Equity Large Cap Value (Growth)	B-	C	B	Up	Y	0
Fidelity Advisor® Equity Value Fund Class Z	FAEVX	NAS CM	Open End	US Equity Large Cap Value (Growth)	B-	C	B	Up	Y	0
Fidelity Advisor® Equity Value Fund I Class	FAIVX	NAS CM	Open End	US Equity Large Cap Value (Growth)	B-	C	B	Up	Y	0
Fidelity Advisor® Europe Fund Class A	FHJUX	NAS CM	Open End	Europe Equity Large Cap (Europe Stock)	C	C-	C+		Y	0
Fidelity Advisor® Europe Fund Class C	FHJTX	NAS CM	Open End	Europe Equity Large Cap (Europe Stock)	C	C-	C+	Up	Y	0
Fidelity Advisor® Europe Fund Class M	FHJVX	NAS CM	Open End	Europe Equity Large Cap (Europe Stock)	C	C-	C+		Y	0
Fidelity Advisor® Europe Fund Class Z	FIQHX	NAS CM	Open End	Europe Equity Large Cap (Europe Stock)	C	C	C+		Y	0
Fidelity Advisor® Europe Fund I Class	FHJMX	NAS CM	Open End	Europe Equity Large Cap (Europe Stock)	C	C	C+		Y	0
Fidelity Advisor® Event Driven Opportunities Fund Class A	FCHSX	NAS CM	Open End	US Equity Small Cap (Growth)	D	D	D+	Down	Y	0
Fidelity Advisor® Event Driven Opportunities Fund Class C	FATJX	NAS CM	Open End	US Equity Small Cap (Growth)	D	D	D+	Down	Y	0

★ Expanded analysis of this fund is included in Section II.

	TOTAL RETURNS					PERFORMANCE				ASSETS		ASSET ALLOCATION & TURNOVER					BULL & BEAR		FEES		
Min Additional Investment	3-Month Total Return	6-Month Total Return	1-Year Total Return	3-Year Total Return	5-Year Total Return	Dividend Yield (TTM)	Expense Ratio	3-Yr Std Deviation	3-Year Beta	NAV	Total Assets (MIL)	%Cash	%Stocks	%Bonds	%Other	Turnover Ratio	Last Bull Market Total Return	Last Bear Market Total Return	Front End Fee (%)	Back End Fee (%)	Inception Date
	3.87	18.85	5.12	53.50	51.22	0.47	0.62	13.47	1.07	26.03	2,093	2	97	0	1	103	26.67	-18.24			Jul-05
	3.54	16.31	8.91	38.88	43.48	1.49	0.84	12.21	0.96	15.76	999.5	1	99	0	0	110	27.21	-24.67	5.75		Dec-98
	3.29	15.86	8.03	35.70	38.04	0.8	1.61	12.14	0.96	14.75	999.5	1	99	0	0	110	26.7	-24.88		1.00	Dec-98
	3.43	16.17	8.57	37.77	41.70	1.27	1.09	12.19	0.96	15.66	999.5	1	99	0	0	110	26.97	-24.7	3.50		Dec-98
	3.58	16.51	9.31	40.49	46.30	1.78	0.45	12.17	0.96	17.07	999.5	1	99	0	0	110	27.48	-24.61			Aug-13
	3.64	16.52	9.19	39.93	45.23	1.64	0.6	12.2	0.96	16.78	999.5	1	99	0	0	110	27.48	-24.61			Dec-98
	1.94	18.69	5.37	51.68	42.73	0.48	1.32	14.83	0.97	38.8	295.4	5	95	0	0	34	18.38	-25.51	5.75		Mar-94
	1.74	18.29	4.60	48.38	37.55	0	2.06	14.82	0.97	34.92	295.4	5	95	0	0	34	17.88	-25.76		1.00	Jun-99
	1.84	18.51	5.04	50.28	40.57	0.14	1.61	14.82	0.97	37.63	295.4	5	95	0	0	34	18.2	-25.6	3.50		Jun-99
	2.04	18.95	5.67	52.11	43.14		0.97	14.83	0.97	39.98	295.4	5	95	0	0	34	18.38	-25.51			Oct-18
	1.98	18.84	5.67	52.99	44.84	0.79	1.03	14.84	0.97	40.04	295.4	5	95	0	0	34	18.62	-25.43			Jun-99
	8.55	15.99	8.16	41.98	15.03	1.81	1.59	14.53	0.9	10.15	110.1	3	97	0	0	39	19.71	-26.75	5.75		May-08
	8.35	15.52	7.30	38.66	10.63	0.9	2.39	14.51	0.89	10.12	110.1	3	97	0	0	39	19.19	-26.96		1.00	May-08
	8.48	15.82	7.81	40.74	13.25	1.59	1.9	14.52	0.9	10.1	110.1	3	97	0	0	39	19.6	-26.8	3.50		May-08
	8.57	16.03	8.40	43.26	16.84	2.19	1.25	14.52	0.89	10.13	110.1	3	97	0	0	39	20.01	-26.67			May-08
	1.18	12.65	-3.08	29.39	13.31	1.32	1.52	13.38	1	13.62	325.7	4	96	0	0	98			5.75		Nov-11
	0.98	12.24	-3.84	26.55	9.17	0.38	2.28	13.32	1	13.29	325.7	4	96	0	0	98				1.00	Nov-11
	1.11	12.58	-3.39	28.38	11.86	0.72	1.79	13.32	1	13.6	325.7	4	96	0	0	98			3.50		Nov-11
	1.25	12.93	-2.66	30.77	15.15		1.17	13.33	1	13.71	325.7	4	96	0	0	98					Oct-18
	1.25	12.90	-2.75	30.65	15.05	1.59	1.22	13.35	1	13.74	325.7	4	96	0	0	98					Nov-11
	3.84	20.04	4.82	40.89	25.98	0.12	1.44	14.31	0.98	29.46	861.4	5	95	0	0	87	16.5	-28.44	5.75		Mar-04
	3.65	19.57	4.00	37.69	21.29	0	2.22	14.3	0.98	27.8	861.4	5	95	0	0	87	16.03	-28.7		1.00	Mar-04
	3.77	19.89	4.51	39.74	24.27	0	1.73	14.32	0.98	29.17	861.4	5	95	0	0	87	16.32	-28.55	3.50		Mar-04
	3.97	20.30	5.29	42.93	29.09	0.63	0.98	14.31	0.98	29.57	861.4	5	95	0	0	87	16.69	-28.35			Aug-13
	3.89	20.23	5.15	42.32	28.15	0.49	1.12	14.31	0.98	29.59	861.4	5	95	0	0	87	16.69	-28.35			Mar-04
	-2.74	13.19	-21.19	-5.96	-34.72	0.72	1.11	23.69	1.34	28.73	634.4	2	98	0	0	56	21.69	-31.01	5.75		Sep-96
	-2.87	12.82	-21.73	-7.97	-37.03	0	1.84	23.69	1.34	26.39	634.4	2	98	0	0	56	21.18	-31.2		1.00	Nov-97
	-2.77	13.06	-21.37	-6.70	-35.56	0.36	1.38	23.68	1.34	29.42	634.4	2	98	0	0	56	21.56	-31.07	3.50		Dec-87
	-2.57	13.50	-20.98	-6.23	-35.23		0.67	23.69	1.34	30.25	634.4	2	98	0	0	56	21.56	-31.07			Oct-18
	-2.63	13.36	-20.95	-5.14	-33.81	1.05	0.83	23.7	1.34	30.28	634.4	2	98	0	0	56	21.97	-30.93			Jul-95
	4.31	22.58	10.15	70.90	78.46	0	1.02	13.7	0.98	12.32	3,243	0	99	0	0	37	27.7	-18.21	5.75		Sep-96
	4.04	22.03	9.32	66.94	71.70	0	1.78	13.68	0.98	10.3	3,243	0	99	0	0	37	27.16	-18.45		1.00	Nov-97
	4.14	22.45	9.91	69.67	76.37	0	1.25	13.66	0.98	12.05	3,243	0	99	0	0	37	27.56	-18.25	3.50		Sep-92
	4.33	22.82	10.59	72.90	82.05	0	0.62	13.71	0.99	13.72	3,243	0	99	0	0	37	27.95	-18.08			Aug-13
	4.29	22.72	10.42	72.20	80.85	0	0.75	13.71	0.99	13.61	3,243	0	99	0	0	37	27.95	-18.08			Nov-83
	3.04	15.92	5.27	31.06	30.84	2.23	0.94	12.01	0.96	28.45	1,612	1	98	0	0	59	22.43	-17.86	5.75		Sep-96
	2.86	15.47	4.45	28.05	25.91	1.29	1.71	12	0.96	28.71	1,612	1	98	0	0	59	21.89	-18.14		1.00	Nov-97
	3.00	15.79	5.02	30.11	29.30	1.92	1.17	12.01	0.96	29.19	1,612	1	98	0	0	59	22.3	-17.93	3.50		Sep-92
	3.15	16.16	5.70	32.64	33.51	2.48	0.54	12.01	0.96	29.95	1,612	1	98	0	0	59	22.63	-17.78			Aug-13
	3.11	16.07	5.53	32.08	32.54	2.34	0.68	12.02	0.96	29.97	1,612	1	98	0	0	59	22.63	-17.78			Apr-83
	2.80	13.61	3.80	31.18	33.12	1.51	1	11.04	0.88	17.61	233.2	4	96	0	0	33	25.73	-21.17	5.75		May-01
	2.56	13.10	3.01	28.13	28.04	0.71	1.78	11.04	0.88	17.17	233.2	4	96	0	0	33	25.12	-21.4		1.00	May-01
	2.68	13.40	3.51	30.06	31.29	1.22	1.27	11.03	0.88	17.6	233.2	4	96	0	0	33	25.51	-21.21	3.50		May-01
	2.92	13.85	4.22	32.72	35.47	1.93	0.59	11.05	0.88	17.92	233.2	4	96	0	0	33	25.89	-21.1			Feb-17
	2.87	13.71	4.08	32.26	35.01	1.76	0.73	11.04	0.88	17.91	233.2	4	96	0	0	33	25.89	-21.1			May-01
	4.80	16.96	0.20	26.75	8.26	0.27	1.28	13.64	1.05	36.61	954.6	1	98	0	1	57	17.82	-29.4	5.75		Mar-14
	4.58	16.50	-0.58	23.78	4.07	0	2.06	13.64	1.05	36.28	954.6	1	98	0	1	57	17.31	-29.62		1.00	Mar-14
	4.71	16.78	-0.09	25.55	6.61	0	1.61	13.64	1.05	36.67	954.6	1	98	0	1	57	17.65	-29.48	3.50		Mar-14
	4.91	17.22	0.60	28.07	10.10		0.91	13.66	1.05	36.47	954.6	1	98	0	1	57	17.99	-29.33			Oct-18
	4.88	17.15	0.53	28.05	10.17	0.81	0.95	13.66	1.05	36.53	954.6	1	98	0	1	57	17.99	-29.33			Mar-14
	-2.21	3.61	-21.19	15.01	13.73	0.36	1.55	15.21	0.97	10.61	15.8	1	99	0	0	97			5.75		Dec-13
	-2.44	3.18	-21.79	12.33	9.49	0	2.3	15.23	0.96	10.38	15.8	1	99	0	0	97				1.00	Dec-13

	MARKET			FUND TYPE, CATEGORY & OBJECTIVE	RATINGS				MINIMUMS	
Fund Name	Ticker Symbol	Traded On	Fund Type	Category and (Prospectus Objective)	Overall Rating	Reward Rating	Risk Rating	Recent Up/ Downgrade	Open to New Investors	Min Initial Investment
Fidelity Advisor® Event Driven Opportunities Fund Class M	FJPDX	NAS CM	Open End	US Equity Small Cap (Growth)	D	D	D+	Down	Y	0
Fidelity Advisor® Event Driven Opportunities Fund Class Z	FIJVX	NAS CM	Open End	US Equity Small Cap (Growth)	D+	D	D+		Y	0
Fidelity Advisor® Event Driven Opportunities Fund I Class	FMRMX	NAS CM	Open End	US Equity Small Cap (Growth)	D+	D	D+		Y	0
Fidelity Advisor® Financial Services Fund Class A	FAFDX	NAS CM	Open End	Financials Sector Equity (Financial)	C	C	B-		Y	0
Fidelity Advisor® Financial Services Fund Class C	FAFCX	NAS CM	Open End	Financials Sector Equity (Financial)	C	C	B-		Y	0
Fidelity Advisor® Financial Services Fund Class M	FAFSX	NAS CM	Open End	Financials Sector Equity (Financial)	C	C	B-		Y	0
Fidelity Advisor® Financial Services Fund Class Z	FIKBX	NAS CM	Open End	Financials Sector Equity (Financial)	C	C	B-		Y	0
Fidelity Advisor® Financial Services Fund I Class	FFSIX	NAS CM	Open End	Financials Sector Equity (Financial)	C	C	B-		Y	0
Fidelity Advisor® Founders Fund Class A	FIFOX	NAS CM	Open End	US Equity Large Cap Blend (Growth)	U	U	U		Y	0
Fidelity Advisor® Founders Fund Class C	FIFQX	NAS CM	Open End	US Equity Large Cap Blend (Growth)	U	U	U		Y	0
Fidelity Advisor® Founders Fund Class I	FIFVX	NAS CM	Open End	US Equity Large Cap Blend (Growth)	U	U	U		Y	0
Fidelity Advisor® Founders Fund Class M	FIFPX	NAS CM	Open End	US Equity Large Cap Blend (Growth)	U	U	U		Y	0
Fidelity Advisor® Founders Fund Class Z	FIFWX	NAS CM	Open End	US Equity Large Cap Blend (Growth)	U	U	U		Y	0
Fidelity Advisor® Global Capital Appreciation Fund Class A	FGEAX	NAS CM	Open End	Global Equity Mid/Small Cap (World Stock)	C	C	C+		Y	0
Fidelity Advisor® Global Capital Appreciation Fund Class C	FEUCX	NAS CM	Open End	Global Equity Mid/Small Cap (World Stock)	C	C	C		Y	0
Fidelity Advisor® Global Capital Appreciation Fund Class M	FGETX	NAS CM	Open End	Global Equity Mid/Small Cap (World Stock)	C	C	C+		Y	0
Fidelity Advisor® Global Capital Appreciation Fund I Class	FEUIX	NAS CM	Open End	Global Equity Mid/Small Cap (World Stock)	C	C	C+		Y	0
Fidelity Advisor® Global Commodity Stock Fund Class A	FFGAX	NAS CM	Open End	Natl Resources Sec Equity (Growth)	C	C	C		Y	0
Fidelity Advisor® Global Commodity Stock Fund Class C	FCGCX	NAS CM	Open End	Natl Resources Sec Equity (Growth)	C	C	C		Y	0
Fidelity Advisor® Global Commodity Stock Fund Class M	FFGTX	NAS CM	Open End	Natl Resources Sec Equity (Growth)	C	C	C		Y	0
Fidelity Advisor® Global Commodity Stock Fund Class Z	FIQRX	NAS CM	Open End	Natl Resources Sec Equity (Growth)	C	C	C		Y	0
Fidelity Advisor® Global Commodity Stock Fund I Class	FFGIX	NAS CM	Open End	Natl Resources Sec Equity (Growth)	C	C	C		Y	0
Fidelity Advisor® Global Equity Income Fund Class A	FBLYX	NAS CM	Open End	Global Equity Large Cap (Equity-Income)	B-	C	B	Up	Y	0
Fidelity Advisor® Global Equity Income Fund Class C	FGTNX	NAS CM	Open End	Global Equity Large Cap (Equity-Income)	C+	C	B	Up	Y	0
Fidelity Advisor® Global Equity Income Fund Class M	FGABX	NAS CM	Open End	Global Equity Large Cap (Equity-Income)	C+	C	B	Up	Y	0
Fidelity Advisor® Global Equity Income Fund Class Z	FIQQX	NAS CM	Open End	Global Equity Large Cap (Equity-Income)	B-	C	B	Up	Y	0
Fidelity Advisor® Global Equity Income Fund I Class	FBUSX	NAS CM	Open End	Global Equity Large Cap (Equity-Income)	B-	C	B	Up	Y	0
Fidelity Advisor® Global Real Estate Fund Class A	FWRAX	NAS CM	Open End	Real Estate Sector Equity (Real Estate)	C+	C	B		Y	0
Fidelity Advisor® Global Real Estate Fund Class C	FWRCX	NAS CM	Open End	Real Estate Sector Equity (Real Estate)	C+	C	B		Y	0
Fidelity Advisor® Global Real Estate Fund Class I	FWRIX	NAS CM	Open End	Real Estate Sector Equity (Real Estate)	B-	C	B	Up	Y	0
Fidelity Advisor® Global Real Estate Fund Class M	FWRTX	NAS CM	Open End	Real Estate Sector Equity (Real Estate)	C+	C	B		Y	0
Fidelity Advisor® Global Real Estate Fund Class Z	FIKKX	NAS CM	Open End	Real Estate Sector Equity (Real Estate)	B-	C	B	Up	Y	0
Fidelity Advisor® Growth & Income Fund Class A	FGIRX	NAS CM	Open End	US Equity Large Cap Blend (Growth & Income)	C+	C	B		Y	0
Fidelity Advisor® Growth & Income Fund Class C	FGIUX	NAS CM	Open End	US Equity Large Cap Blend (Growth & Income)	C+	C	B	Up	Y	0
Fidelity Advisor® Growth & Income Fund Class M	FGITX	NAS CM	Open End	US Equity Large Cap Blend (Growth & Income)	C+	C	B		Y	0
Fidelity Advisor® Growth & Income Fund Class Z	FGIZX	NAS CM	Open End	US Equity Large Cap Blend (Growth & Income)	C+	C	B		Y	0
Fidelity Advisor® Growth & Income Fund I Class	FGIOX	NAS CM	Open End	US Equity Large Cap Blend (Growth & Income)	C+	C	B		Y	0
Fidelity Advisor® Growth Opportunities Fund Class A	FAGAX	NAS CM	Open End	US Equity Large Cap Growth (Growth)	B	C+	B	Down	Y	0
Fidelity Advisor® Growth Opportunities Fund Class C	FACGX	NAS CM	Open End	US Equity Large Cap Growth (Growth)	B-	C+	B	Down	Y	0
Fidelity Advisor® Growth Opportunities Fund Class M	FAGOX	NAS CM	Open End	US Equity Large Cap Growth (Growth)	B	C+	B	Down	Y	0
Fidelity Advisor® Growth Opportunities Fund Class Z	FZAHX	NAS CM	Open End	US Equity Large Cap Growth (Growth)	B	C+	B	Down	Y	0
Fidelity Advisor® Growth Opportunities Fund I Class	FAGCX	NAS CM	Open End	US Equity Large Cap Growth (Growth)	B	C+	B	Down	Y	0
Fidelity Advisor® Health Care Fund Class A	FACDX	NAS CM	Open End	Healthcare Sector Equity (Health)	C+	C	B	Down	Y	0
Fidelity Advisor® Health Care Fund Class C	FHCCX	NAS CM	Open End	Healthcare Sector Equity (Health)	C	C	B	Down	Y	0
Fidelity Advisor® Health Care Fund Class M	FACTX	NAS CM	Open End	Healthcare Sector Equity (Health)	C+	C	B	Down	Y	0
Fidelity Advisor® Health Care Fund Class Z	FIKCX	NAS CM	Open End	Healthcare Sector Equity (Health)	C+	C	B	Down	Y	0
Fidelity Advisor® Health Care Fund I Class	FHCIX	NAS CM	Open End	Healthcare Sector Equity (Health)	C+	C	B	Down	Y	0
Fidelity Advisor® Industrials Fund Class A	FCLAX	NAS CM	Open End	Industrials Sector Equity ()	C+	C	C+	Down	Y	0
Fidelity Advisor® Industrials Fund Class C	FCLCX	NAS CM	Open End	Industrials Sector Equity ()	C+	C	C+	Down	Y	0
Fidelity Advisor® Industrials Fund Class M	FCLTX	NAS CM	Open End	Industrials Sector Equity ()	C+	C	C+	Down	Y	0
Fidelity Advisor® Industrials Fund Class Z	FIKEX	NAS CM	Open End	Industrials Sector Equity ()	C+	C	C+	Down	Y	0
Fidelity Advisor® Industrials Fund I Class	FCLIX	NAS CM	Open End	Industrials Sector Equity ()	C+	C	C+	Down	Y	0

★ Expanded analysis of this fund is included in Section II.

	TOTAL RETURNS					PERFORMANCE				ASSETS		ASSET ALLOCATION & TURNOVER					BULL & BEAR		FEES		
Min Additional Investment	3-Month Total Return	6-Month Total Return	1-Year Total Return	3-Year Total Return	5-Year Total Return	Dividend Yield (TTM)	Expense Ratio	3-Yr Std Deviation	3-Year Beta	NAV	Total Assets (MIL)	%Cash	%Stocks	%Bonds	%Other	Turnover Ratio	Last Bull Market Total Return	Last Bear Market Total Return	Front End Fee (%)	Back End Fee (%)	Inception Date
	-2.31	3.42	-21.39	14.02	12.26	0.14	1.8	15.22	0.96	10.56	15.8	1	99	0	0	97			3.50		Dec-13
	-2.20	3.69	-20.91	15.99	15.27		1.16	15.19	0.96	10.66	15.8	1	99	0	0	97					Oct-18
	-2.29	3.59	-21.08	15.74	15.02	0.48	1.3	15.21	0.96	10.66	15.8	1	99	0	0	97					Dec-13
	7.28	19.08	2.96	47.54	46.05	0.85	1.1	15.63	1.07	20.9	384.4	1	99	0	0	46	29.79	-28.14	5.75		Sep-96
	7.13	18.66	2.22	44.37	40.68	0.13	1.86	15.64	1.07	19.52	384.4	1	99	0	0	46	29.09	-28.3		1.00	Nov-97
	7.20	18.92	2.70	46.35	43.97	0.6	1.37	15.62	1.07	20.67	384.4	1	99	0	0	46	29.58	-28.27	3.50		Sep-96
	7.39	19.32	3.38	48.97	48.30		0.69	15.65	1.07	21.49	384.4	1	99	0	0	46	29.87	-28.02			Oct-18
	7.38	19.29	3.30	48.86	48.20	1.11	0.83	15.64	1.07	21.52	384.4	1	99	0	0	46	29.87	-28.02			Sep-96
	4.39						1.25			10.92	23.1	2	98	0	0	4			5.75		Feb-19
	4.59						2			10.89	23.1	2	98	0	0	4				1.00	Feb-19
	4.20						1			10.93	23.1	2	98	0	0	4					Feb-19
	4.11						1.5			10.91	23.1	2	98	0	0	4			3.50		Feb-19
	4.39						0.85			10.93	23.1	2	98	0	0	4					Feb-19
	2.33	16.32	-5.81	30.04	29.00	0.13	1.39	13.51	1.16	15.75	108.3	0	100	0	0	99	14.64	-23.04	5.75		Dec-98
	2.16	15.87	-6.54	27.09	24.23	0	2.14	13.53	1.16	13.21	108.3	0	100	0	0	99	14.16	-23.31		1.00	Dec-98
	2.33	16.18	-6.08	29.04	27.37	0	1.67	13.52	1.16	14.93	108.3	0	100	0	0	99	14.45	-23.1	3.50		Dec-98
	2.39	16.50	-5.52	31.26	30.82	0.42	1.09	13.53	1.16	16.66	108.3	0	100	0	0	99	14.83	-22.93			Dec-98
	1.28	13.29	-5.90	30.68	-10.07	1.57	1.28	14.67	1.04	12.61	547.7	1	99	0	0	70	14.17	-29.68	5.75		Mar-09
	1.13	12.94	-6.57	27.75	-13.34	0.84	2	14.71	1.04	12.48	547.7	1	99	0	0	70	13.66	-29.92		1.00	Mar-09
	1.28	13.20	-6.15	29.51	-11.33	1.25	1.59	14.76	1.04	12.6	547.7	1	99	0	0	70	14.04	-29.79	3.50		Mar-09
	1.44	13.60	-5.45	32.14	-8.46		0.89	14.71	1.04	12.61	547.7	1	99	0	0	70	14.35	-29.62			Oct-18
	1.44	13.59	-5.46	32.13	-8.47	1.99	0.93	14.7	1.04	12.62	547.7	1	99	0	0	70	14.35	-29.62			Mar-09
	3.50	17.03	5.51	30.54	31.51	1.41	1.45	10.24	0.88	14.73	18.0	2	98	0	0	37			5.75		May-12
	3.33	16.67	4.72	27.65	26.70	0.68	2.2	10.25	0.88	14.63	18.0	2	98	0	0	37				1.00	May-12
	3.37	16.90	5.17	29.52	29.83	1.17	1.7	10.23	0.88	14.71	18.0	2	98	0	0	37			3.50		May-12
	3.54	17.23	5.83	31.65	33.27		1.05	10.22	0.88	14.76	18.0	2	98	0	0	37					Oct-18
	3.54	17.24	5.75	31.55	33.17	1.69	1.2	10.23	0.88	14.75	18.0	2	98	0	0	37					May-12
	1.51	16.23	9.20			1.4	1.4			10.74	6.4	2	98	0	0	46			5.75		Aug-16
	1.33	15.76	8.36			1.11	2.15			10.65	6.4	2	98	0	0	46				1.00	Aug-16
	1.60	16.32	9.40			1.57	1.15			10.76	6.4	2	98	0	0	46					Aug-16
	1.41	16.01	8.80			1.16	1.65			10.72	6.4	2	98	0	0	46			3.50		Aug-16
	1.60	16.43	9.50				1			10.77	6.4	2	98	0	0	46					Oct-18
	2.85	17.01	5.08	41.88	43.14	1.62	0.96	13.16	1.04	25.93	534.9	5	95	0	0	40	26.76	-16.92	5.75		Dec-96
	2.64	16.49	4.24	38.66	37.80	0.95	1.72	13.18	1.04	24.08	534.9	5	95	0	0	40	26.24	-17.2		1.00	Nov-97
	2.81	16.83	4.82	40.84	41.37	1.36	1.21	13.18	1.04	25.95	534.9	5	95	0	0	40	26.6	-17.03	3.50		Dec-96
	2.98	17.23	5.52	43.53	45.57	1.85	0.56	13.18	1.04	26.59	534.9	5	95	0	0	40	27.01	-16.8			Feb-17
	2.94	17.17	5.34	43.06	45.09	1.85	0.69	13.2	1.04	26.54	534.9	5	95	0	0	40	27.01	-16.8			Dec-96
	3.80	26.49	21.80	105.57	116.44	0	1.05	14.4	1	82.68	6,286	1	96	0	0	46	28.41	-16.24	5.75		Sep-96
	3.61	26.02	20.88	100.98	108.48	0	1.81	14.39	1	70.5	6,286	1	96	0	0	46	27.87	-16.49		1.00	Nov-97
	3.76	26.36	21.53	104.17	113.99	0	1.28	14.4	1	81.87	6,286	1	96	0	0	46	28.27	-16.3	3.50		Nov-87
	3.92	26.75	22.29	108.07	120.89	0	0.66	14.41	1	90.29	6,286	1	96	0	0	46	28.27	-16.3			Aug-13
	3.88	26.68	22.14	107.31	119.51	0	0.78	14.41	1	89.53	6,286	1	96	0	0	46	28.66	-16.12			Jul-95
	2.09	14.17	6.60	45.56	62.71	0	1.05	16.79	1.06	49.22	4,057	2	97	0	0	81	22.31	-14.88	5.75		Sep-96
	1.92	13.74	5.84	42.35	56.75	0	1.8	16.79	1.06	38.74	4,057	2	97	0	0	81	21.77	-15.12		1.00	Nov-97
	2.02	13.99	6.32	44.41	60.55	0	1.32	16.8	1.06	45.77	4,057	2	97	0	0	81	22.11	-14.97	3.50		Sep-96
	2.18	14.38	6.97	46.84	64.99		0.65	16.8	1.06	53.83	4,057	2	97	0	0	81	22.47	-14.75			Oct-18
	2.16	14.32	6.89	46.73	64.87	0	0.79	16.8	1.06	53.78	4,057	2	97	0	0	81	22.47	-14.75			Sep-96
	5.24	25.35	8.66	41.79	43.91	0.44	1.06	16.38	1.22	39.3	667.7	0	100	0	0	61	30.66	-26.12	5.75		Sep-96
	5.03	24.86	7.85	38.61	38.58	0	1.82	16.37	1.22	34.6	667.7	0	100	0	0	61	30.15	-26.35		1.00	Nov-97
	5.18	25.21	8.39	40.70	42.06	0.17	1.32	16.37	1.22	38.34	667.7	0	100	0	0	61	30.52	-26.2	3.50		Sep-96
	5.35	25.60	9.06	43.08	46.00		0.66	16.38	1.22	41.5	667.7	0	100	0	0	61	30.9	-26.02			Oct-18
	5.32	25.52	8.96	42.94	45.86	0.67	0.8	16.39	1.22	41.56	667.7	0	100	0	0	61	30.9	-26.02			Sep-96

	MARKET			FUND TYPE, CATEGORY & OBJECTIVE	RATINGS					MINIMUMS
Fund Name	Ticker Symbol	Traded On	Fund Type	Category and (Prospectus Objective)	Overall Rating	Reward Rating	Risk Rating	Recent Up/ Downgrade	Open to New Investors	Min Initial Investment
Fidelity Advisor® International Capital Appreciation Cls A	FCPAX	NAS CM	Open End	Global Equity Large Cap (Foreign Stock)	C+	C	B-	Up	Y	0
Fidelity Advisor® International Capital Appreciation Cls C	FCPCX	NAS CM	Open End	Global Equity Large Cap (Foreign Stock)	C+	C	B-	Up	Y	0
Fidelity Advisor® International Capital Appreciation Cls M	FIATX	NAS CM	Open End	Global Equity Large Cap (Foreign Stock)	C+	C	B-	Up	Y	0
Fidelity Advisor® International Capital Appreciation Cls Z	FIDZX	NAS CM	Open End	Global Equity Large Cap (Foreign Stock)	C+	C	B-	Up	Y	0
Fidelity Advisor® International Capital Appreciation I Cls	FCPIX	NAS CM	Open End	Global Equity Large Cap (Foreign Stock)	C+	C	B-	Up	Y	0
Fidelity Advisor® International Discovery Fund Class A	FAIDX	NAS CM	Open End	Global Equity Large Cap (Foreign Stock)	C	C	C+		Y	0
Fidelity Advisor® International Discovery Fund Class C	FCADX	NAS CM	Open End	Global Equity Large Cap (Foreign Stock)	C	C-	C+	Up	Y	0
Fidelity Advisor® International Discovery Fund Class I	FIADX	NAS CM	Open End	Global Equity Large Cap (Foreign Stock)	C	C	C+		Y	0
Fidelity Advisor® International Discovery Fund Class M	FTADX	NAS CM	Open End	Global Equity Large Cap (Foreign Stock)	C	C	C+		Y	0
Fidelity Advisor® International Discovery Fund Class Z	FZAIX	NAS CM	Open End	Global Equity Large Cap (Foreign Stock)	C	C	C+		Y	0
Fidelity Advisor® International Growth Fund Class A	FIAGX	NAS CM	Open End	Global Equity Large Cap (Foreign Stock)	C+	C	B	Up	Y	0
Fidelity Advisor® International Growth Fund Class C	FIGCX	NAS CM	Open End	Global Equity Large Cap (Foreign Stock)	C+	C	B	Up	Y	0
Fidelity Advisor® International Growth Fund Class M	FITGX	NAS CM	Open End	Global Equity Large Cap (Foreign Stock)	C+	C	B	Up	Y	0
Fidelity Advisor® International Growth Fund Class Z	FZAJX	NAS CM	Open End	Global Equity Large Cap (Foreign Stock)	C+	C	B	Up	Y	0
Fidelity Advisor® International Growth Fund I Class	FIIIX	NAS CM	Open End	Global Equity Large Cap (Foreign Stock)	C+	C	B	Up	Y	0
Fidelity Advisor® International Real Estate Fund Class A	FIRAX	NAS CM	Open End	Real Estate Sector Equity (Real Estate)	B	C+	B+	Up	Y	0
Fidelity Advisor® International Real Estate Fund Class C	FIRCX	NAS CM	Open End	Real Estate Sector Equity (Real Estate)	B	C+	B+	Up	Y	0
Fidelity Advisor® International Real Estate Fund Class I	FIRIX	NAS CM	Open End	Real Estate Sector Equity (Real Estate)	B	B-	B+	Up	Y	0
Fidelity Advisor® International Real Estate Fund Class M	FIRTX	NAS CM	Open End	Real Estate Sector Equity (Real Estate)	B	C+	B+	Up	Y	0
Fidelity Advisor® International Real Estate Fund Class Z	FIKLX	NAS CM	Open End	Real Estate Sector Equity (Real Estate)	B	B-	B+	Up	Y	0
Fidelity Advisor® International Small Cap Fund Class A	FIASX	NAS CM	Open End	Global Equity Mid/Small Cap (Foreign Stock)	C	C	C+		Y	0
Fidelity Advisor® International Small Cap Fund Class C	FICSX	NAS CM	Open End	Global Equity Mid/Small Cap (Foreign Stock)	C	C	C+		Y	0
Fidelity Advisor® International Small Cap Fund Class I	FIXIX	NAS CM	Open End	Global Equity Mid/Small Cap (Foreign Stock)	C	C	C+		Y	0
Fidelity Advisor® International Small Cap Fund Class M	FTISX	NAS CM	Open End	Global Equity Mid/Small Cap (Foreign Stock)	C	C	C+		Y	0
Fidelity Advisor® International Small Cap Fund Class Z	FIQIX	NAS CM	Open End	Global Equity Mid/Small Cap (Foreign Stock)	C	C	C+		Y	0
Fidelity Advisor® Intl Small Cap Opp Cls A	FOPAX	NAS CM	Open End	Global Equity Mid/Small Cap (Small Company)	C	C	C+		Y	0
Fidelity Advisor® Intl Small Cap Opp Cls C	FOPCX	NAS CM	Open End	Global Equity Mid/Small Cap (Small Company)	C	C	C+		Y	0
Fidelity Advisor® Intl Small Cap Opp Cls M	FOPTX	NAS CM	Open End	Global Equity Mid/Small Cap (Small Company)	C	C	C+		Y	0
Fidelity Advisor® Intl Small Cap Opp Cls Z	FIQJX	NAS CM	Open End	Global Equity Mid/Small Cap (Small Company)	C	C	B-		Y	0
Fidelity Advisor® Intl Small Cap Opp I Cls	FOPIX	NAS CM	Open End	Global Equity Mid/Small Cap (Small Company)	C	C	B-		Y	0
Fidelity Advisor® International Value Fund Class A	FIVMX	NAS CM	Open End	Global Equity Large Cap (Foreign Stock)	C-	D+	C		Y	0
Fidelity Advisor® International Value Fund Class C	FIVOX	NAS CM	Open End	Global Equity Large Cap (Foreign Stock)	C-	D+	C		Y	0
Fidelity Advisor® International Value Fund Class M	FIVPX	NAS CM	Open End	Global Equity Large Cap (Foreign Stock)	C-	D+	C		Y	0
Fidelity Advisor® International Value Fund Class Z	FIQKX	NAS CM	Open End	Global Equity Large Cap (Foreign Stock)	C	D+	C+	Up	Y	0
Fidelity Advisor® International Value Fund I Class	FIVQX	NAS CM	Open End	Global Equity Large Cap (Foreign Stock)	C-	D+	C		Y	0
Fidelity Advisor® Japan Fund Class A	FPJAX	NAS CM	Open End	Japan Equity (Pacific Stock)	C	C	C+		Y	0
Fidelity Advisor® Japan Fund Class C	FJPCX	NAS CM	Open End	Japan Equity (Pacific Stock)	C	C	C+		Y	0
Fidelity Advisor® Japan Fund Class I	FJPIX	NAS CM	Open End	Japan Equity (Pacific Stock)	C	C	C+		Y	0
Fidelity Advisor® Japan Fund Class M	FJPTX	NAS CM	Open End	Japan Equity (Pacific Stock)	C	C	C+		Y	0
Fidelity Advisor® Japan Fund Class Z	FIQLX	NAS CM	Open End	Japan Equity (Pacific Stock)	C	C	C+		Y	0
Fidelity Advisor® Large Cap Fund Class A	FALAX	NAS CM	Open End	US Equity Large Cap Blend (Growth)	C+	C	B		Y	0
Fidelity Advisor® Large Cap Fund Class C	FLCCX	NAS CM	Open End	US Equity Large Cap Blend (Growth)	C+	C	B	Up	Y	0
Fidelity Advisor® Large Cap Fund Class M	FALGX	NAS CM	Open End	US Equity Large Cap Blend (Growth)	C+	C	B		Y	0
Fidelity Advisor® Large Cap Fund Class Z	FIDLX	NAS CM	Open End	US Equity Large Cap Blend (Growth)	C+	C	B		Y	0
Fidelity Advisor® Large Cap Fund I Class	FALIX	NAS CM	Open End	US Equity Large Cap Blend (Growth)	C+	C	B		Y	0
Fidelity Advisor® Latin America Fund Class A	FLFAX	NAS CM	Open End	Latin America Equity (Foreign Stock)	C	C	C		Y	0
Fidelity Advisor® Latin America Fund Class C	FLFCX	NAS CM	Open End	Latin America Equity (Foreign Stock)	C	C	C		Y	0
Fidelity Advisor® Latin America Fund Class I	FLFIX	NAS CM	Open End	Latin America Equity (Foreign Stock)	C	C	C		Y	0
Fidelity Advisor® Latin America Fund Class M	FLFTX	NAS CM	Open End	Latin America Equity (Foreign Stock)	C	C	C		Y	0
Fidelity Advisor® Latin America Fund Class Z	FIQMX	NAS CM	Open End	Latin America Equity (Foreign Stock)	C	C	C		Y	0
Fidelity Advisor® Leveraged Company Stock Fund Class A	FLSAX	NAS CM	Open End	US Equity Mid Cap (Growth)	C	D+	C+		Y	0
Fidelity Advisor® Leveraged Company Stock Fund Class C	FLSCX	NAS CM	Open End	US Equity Mid Cap (Growth)	C	D+	C+		Y	0

★ Expanded analysis of this fund is included in Section II.

	TOTAL RETURNS					PERFORMANCE				ASSETS		ASSET ALLOCATION & TURNOVER					BULL & BEAR		FEES		
Min Additional Investment	3-Month Total Return	6-Month Total Return	1-Year Total Return	3-Year Total Return	5-Year Total Return	Dividend Yield (TTM)	Expense Ratio	3-Yr Std Deviation	3-Year Beta	NAV	Total Assets (MIL)	%Cash	%Stocks	%Bonds	%Other	Turnover Ratio	Last Bull Market Total Return	Last Bear Market Total Return	Front End Fee (%)	Back End Fee (%)	Inception Date
	6.80	23.54	7.80	39.30	41.91	0.18	1.29	12.38	0.97	21.04	2,430	2	98	0	0	151	26.59	-26.03	5.75		Nov-97
	6.58	23.08	6.95	36.16	36.66	0	2.04	12.37	0.97	18.45	2,430	2	98	0	0	151	26	-26.27		1.00	Nov-97
	6.71	23.34	7.49	38.13	40.02	0	1.55	12.4	0.97	20.5	2,430	2	98	0	0	151	26.41	-26.11	3.50		Nov-97
	6.89	23.77	8.21	40.84	44.17	0.55	0.89	12.4	0.97	22.49	2,430	2	98	0	0	151	26.79	-25.95			Feb-17
	6.89	23.73	8.07	40.42	43.75	0.44	1.02	12.39	0.97	22.47	2,430	2	98	0	0	151	26.79	-25.95			Nov-97
	4.51	17.21	-0.43	28.51	15.58	0.76	1.22	11.84	1.02	42.36	9,261	3	96	0	0	45	15.39	-24.59	5.75		Jan-05
	4.31	16.76	-1.19	25.57	11.24	0	2	11.85	1.02	41.78	9,261	3	96	0	0	45	14.86	-24.82		1.00	Jan-05
	4.60	17.39	-0.12	29.77	17.48	1.11	0.91	11.85	1.02	42.52	9,261	3	96	0	0	45	15.62	-24.5			Jan-05
	4.44	17.04	-0.69	27.58	14.19	0.52	1.46	11.84	1.02	42.1	9,261	3	96	0	0	45	15.21	-24.68	3.50		Jan-05
	4.62	17.46	0.03	30.33	18.33	1.25	0.77	11.86	1.02	42.5	9,261	3	96	0	0	45	15.57	-24.47			Aug-13
	6.82	21.02	7.38	35.78	30.82	0.5	1.24	12.04	1.01	14.39	2,943	2	98	0	0	34	21.26	-22.04	5.75		Nov-07
	6.66	20.63	6.58	32.75	25.75	0	1.99	12.06	1.01	14.09	2,943	2	98	0	0	34	20.69	-22.32		1.00	Nov-07
	6.76	20.87	7.04	34.52	28.79	0.22	1.54	12.02	1	14.36	2,943	2	98	0	0	34	21.11	-22.15	3.50		Nov-07
	7.01	21.35	7.87	37.65	33.73	0.86	0.8	12.05	1	14.49	2,943	2	98	0	0	34	21.45	-21.99			Aug-13
	6.87	21.20	7.67	37.00	32.76	0.75	0.93	12.02	1	14.46	2,943	2	98	0	0	34	21.45	-21.99			Nov-07
	3.09	16.57	8.63	35.01	32.21	1.34	1.36	9.79	0.67	12.31	578.4	4	96	0	0	56	19.51	-25.3	5.75		Apr-07
	2.83	16.00	7.75	32.10	27.51	0.98	2.05	9.79	0.67	11.96	578.4	4	96	0	0	56	18.94	-25.48		1.00	Apr-07
	3.16	16.76	9.02	36.57	34.76	1.55	0.96	9.82	0.67	12.4	578.4	4	96	0	0	56	19.66	-25.17			Apr-07
	2.95	16.31	8.20	33.77	30.29	1.15	1.65	9.8	0.67	12.19	578.4	4	96	0	0	56	19.29	-25.29	3.50		Apr-07
	3.15	16.74	8.98	36.27	34.00		0.86	9.81	0.67	12.41	578.4	4	96	0	0	56	19.61	-25.14			Oct-18
	3.32	12.79	-3.53	32.30	31.33	1.41	1.49	10.8	0.89	26.1	2,267	5	95	0	0	25	14.13	-21.69	5.75		May-03
	3.11	12.34	-4.24	29.31	26.36	0.64	2.24	10.78	0.89	25.12	2,267	5	95	0	0	25	13.54	-21.9		1.00	May-03
	3.39	12.94	-3.28	33.41	33.35	1.65	1.21	10.8	0.89	26.78	2,267	5	95	0	0	25	14.38	-21.6			May-03
	3.25	12.60	-3.82	31.20	29.41	1.02	1.77	10.79	0.89	25.99	2,267	5	95	0	0	25	13.92	-21.77	3.50		May-03
	3.40	13.00	-3.17	33.59	33.32		1.15	10.78	0.89	26.76	2,267	5	95	0	0	25	14.26	-21.6			Oct-18
	4.35	16.23	-1.03	37.26	34.66	0.6	1.39	11.88	0.92	18.47	1,282	7	93	0	0	19	19.76	-20.48	5.75		Aug-05
	4.20	15.77	-1.78	34.14	29.53	0	2.16	11.87	0.92	17.83	1,282	7	93	0	0	19	19.13	-20.73		1.00	Aug-05
	4.26	16.02	-1.33	36.05	32.64	0.31	1.68	11.88	0.92	18.32	1,282	7	93	0	0	19	19.51	-20.55	3.50		Aug-05
	4.43	16.38	-0.69	38.49	36.73		1.04	11.85	0.91	18.61	1,282	7	93	0	0	19	19.79	-20.37			Oct-18
	4.42	16.35	-0.78	38.36	36.61	0.85	1.13	11.87	0.92	18.64	1,282	7	93	0	0	19	19.79	-20.37			Aug-05
	3.30	11.84	-3.33	15.98	-2.24	2.62	1.23	11.68	0.99	8.12	468.7	0	100	0	0	55	10.82	-27.71	5.75		May-06
	3.04	11.40	-4.14	13.30	-5.96	1.63	2.04	11.67	0.99	8.11	468.7	0	100	0	0	55	10.27	-27.98		1.00	May-06
	3.04	11.55	-3.70	14.86	-3.68	2.27	1.56	11.62	0.98	8.11	468.7	0	100	0	0	55	10.76	-27.85	3.50		May-06
	3.31	12.01	-2.89	17.15	-0.86		0.84	11.64	0.98	8.11	468.7	0	100	0	0	55	11.06	-27.65			Oct-18
	3.30	11.84	-3.14	16.85	-1.11	2.92	0.97	11.66	0.99	8.12	468.7	0	100	0	0	55	11.06	-27.65			May-06
	3.34	13.22	-3.32	29.26	25.96	0	1.33	12.04	1.04	14.81	689.0	1	99	0	0	40	5.64	-10.39	5.75		Dec-10
	3.19	12.79	-4.02	26.50	21.55	0	2.04	12.02	1.04	14.55	689.0	1	99	0	0	40	5.22	-10.7		1.00	Dec-10
	3.48	13.37	-2.96	30.62	28.08	0.28	0.98	12.02	1.04	14.83	689.0	1	99	0	0	40	5.9	-10.28			Dec-10
	3.29	13.03	-3.65	27.98	23.80	0	1.67	12.04	1.04	14.74	689.0	1	99	0	0	40	5.43	-10.49	3.50		Dec-10
	3.49	13.47	-3.06	30.38	27.83		0.96	12.03	1.04	14.82	689.0	1	99	0	0	40	5.77	-10.28			Oct-18
	2.66	17.91	4.94	46.38	45.25	1.33	0.92	13.88	1.1	30.01	1,151	2	97	0	1	37	27.79	-19.28	5.75		Sep-96
	2.45	17.46	4.15	43.06	39.83	0.7	1.69	13.87	1.1	26.7	1,151	2	97	0	1	37	27.23	-19.57		1.00	Nov-97
	2.57	17.74	4.65	45.17	43.31	1.07	1.18	13.87	1.1	29.93	1,151	2	97	0	1	37	27.6	-19.37	3.50		Feb-96
	2.72	18.11	5.33	47.92	47.57	1.68	0.53	13.88	1.1	31.63	1,151	2	97	0	1	37	28	-19.17			Feb-17
	2.72	18.05	5.21	47.48	47.13	1.52	0.66	13.87	1.1	31.64	1,151	2	97	0	1	37	28	-19.17			Feb-96
	12.12	22.25	28.64	40.11	-6.35	1.61	1.38	22.5	1.02	26.26	554.1	0	100	0	0	53	18.57	-24.85	5.75		Sep-10
	11.90	21.78	27.69	37.02	-9.79	0.78	2.13	22.48	1.02	26.61	554.1	0	100	0	0	53	18.06	-25.09		1.00	Sep-10
	12.23	22.48	29.09	41.72	-4.69	1.92	1.01	22.5	1.02	26.15	554.1	0	100	0	0	53	18.8	-24.76			Sep-10
	12.04	22.12	28.30	39.01	-7.63	1.33	1.66	22.49	1.02	26.33	554.1	0	100	0	0	53	18.39	-24.94	3.50		Sep-10
	12.25	22.59	29.14	41.52	-4.89		0.95	22.5	1.02	26.1	554.1	0	100	0	0	53	18.79	-24.75			Oct-18
	-0.47	18.96	-2.98	31.17	17.84	0	1.07	16.95	1.3	37.95	1,319	5	95	0	0	32	33.44	-30.13	5.75		Dec-00
	-0.66	18.49	-3.71	28.25	13.48	0	1.82	16.94	1.3	33.06	1,319	5	95	0	0	32	32.9	-30.36		1.00	Dec-00

Fund Name	Ticker Symbol	Traded On	Fund Type	Category and (Prospectus Objective)	Overall Rating	Reward Rating	Risk Rating	Recent Up/ Downgrade	Open to New Investors	Min Initial Investment
	MARKET			FUND TYPE, CATEGORY & OBJECTIVE	RATINGS				MINIMUMS	
Fidelity Advisor® Leveraged Company Stock Fund Class M	FLSTX	NAS CM	Open End	US Equity Mid Cap (Growth)	C	D+	C+		Y	0
Fidelity Advisor® Leveraged Company Stock Fund Class Z	FZAKX	NAS CM	Open End	US Equity Mid Cap (Growth)	C	C-	C+		Y	0
Fidelity Advisor® Leveraged Company Stock Fund I Class	FLVIX	NAS CM	Open End	US Equity Mid Cap (Growth)	C	C-	C+		Y	0
Fidelity Advisor® Managed Retirement 2020 Fund Class A	FARVX	NAS CM	Open End	Target Date (Asset Alloc)	B	C	A-	Up	Y	2,500
Fidelity Advisor® Managed Retirement 2020 Fund Class C	FCRVX	NAS CM	Open End	Target Date (Asset Alloc)	B-	C	A-	Up	Y	2,500
Fidelity Advisor® Managed Retirement 2020 Fund Class I	FIIVX	NAS CM	Open End	Target Date (Asset Alloc)	B	C	A	Up	Y	2,500
Fidelity Advisor® Managed Retirement 2020 Fund Class M	FTRVX	NAS CM	Open End	Target Date (Asset Alloc)	B	C	A-	Up	Y	2,500
Fidelity Advisor® Managed Retirement 2025 Fund Class A	FARFX	NAS CM	Open End	Target Date (Asset Alloc)	B	C	A-	Up	Y	2,500
Fidelity Advisor® Managed Retirement 2025 Fund Class C	FCRFX	NAS CM	Open End	Target Date (Asset Alloc)	B-	C	A-	Up	Y	2,500
Fidelity Advisor® Managed Retirement 2025 Fund Class I	FIRFX	NAS CM	Open End	Target Date (Asset Alloc)	B	C	A	Up	Y	2,500
Fidelity Advisor® Managed Retirement 2025 Fund Class M	FITTX	NAS CM	Open End	Target Date (Asset Alloc)	B-	C	A-	Up	Y	2,500
Fidelity Advisor® Materials Fund Class A	FMFAX	NAS CM	Open End	Natl Resources Sec Equity (Natl Res)	C-	D+	C	Down	Y	0
Fidelity Advisor® Materials Fund Class C	FMFCX	NAS CM	Open End	Natl Resources Sec Equity (Natl Res)	D+	D+	C-	Down	Y	0
Fidelity Advisor® Materials Fund Class I	FMFEX	NAS CM	Open End	Natl Resources Sec Equity (Natl Res)	C-	D+	C	Down	Y	0
Fidelity Advisor® Materials Fund Class M	FMFTX	NAS CM	Open End	Natl Resources Sec Equity (Natl Res)	D+	D+	C-	Down	Y	0
Fidelity Advisor® Materials Fund Class Z	FIJFX	NAS CM	Open End	Natl Resources Sec Equity (Natl Res)	C-	D+	C	Down	Y	0
Fidelity Advisor® Mega Cap Stock Fund Class A	FGTAX	NAS CM	Open End	US Equity Large Cap Blend (Growth)	C+	C	B		Y	0
Fidelity Advisor® Mega Cap Stock Fund Class C	FGRCX	NAS CM	Open End	US Equity Large Cap Blend (Growth)	C+	C	B		Y	0
Fidelity Advisor® Mega Cap Stock Fund Class I	FTRIX	NAS CM	Open End	US Equity Large Cap Blend (Growth)	C+	C	B		Y	0
Fidelity Advisor® Mega Cap Stock Fund Class M	FTGRX	NAS CM	Open End	US Equity Large Cap Blend (Growth)	C+	C	B		Y	0
Fidelity Advisor® Mega Cap Stock Fund Class Z	FZALX	NAS CM	Open End	US Equity Large Cap Blend (Growth)	C+	C	B		Y	0
Fidelity Advisor® Mid Cap II Fund Class A	FIIAX	NAS CM	Open End	US Equity Mid Cap (Growth)	C	C	C+		Y	0
Fidelity Advisor® Mid Cap II Fund Class C	FIICX	NAS CM	Open End	US Equity Mid Cap (Growth)	C	C	C+		Y	0
Fidelity Advisor® Mid Cap II Fund Class I	FIIMX	NAS CM	Open End	US Equity Mid Cap (Growth)	C	C	C+		Y	0
Fidelity Advisor® Mid Cap II Fund Class M	FITIX	NAS CM	Open End	US Equity Mid Cap (Growth)	C	C	C+		Y	0
Fidelity Advisor® Mid Cap II Fund Class Z	FZAMX	NAS CM	Open End	US Equity Mid Cap (Growth)	C	C	C+		Y	0
Fidelity Advisor® Mid Cap Value Fund Class A	FMPAX	NAS CM	Open End	US Equity Mid Cap (Growth)	C	C-	B-		Y	0
Fidelity Advisor® Mid Cap Value Fund Class C	FMPEX	NAS CM	Open End	US Equity Mid Cap (Growth)	C	C-	C+		Y	0
Fidelity Advisor® Mid Cap Value Fund Class I	FMPOX	NAS CM	Open End	US Equity Mid Cap (Growth)	C	C-	B-		Y	0
Fidelity Advisor® Mid Cap Value Fund Class M	FMPTX	NAS CM	Open End	US Equity Mid Cap (Growth)	C	C-	C+		Y	0
Fidelity Advisor® Mid Cap Value Fund Class Z	FIDFX	NAS CM	Open End	US Equity Mid Cap (Growth)	C	C-	B-		Y	0
Fidelity Advisor® Multi-Asset Income Fund Class A	FWATX	NAS CM	Open End	Cautious Alloc (Growth & Income)	B-	C+	B+	Down	Y	0
Fidelity Advisor® Multi-Asset Income Fund Class C	FWBTX	NAS CM	Open End	Cautious Alloc (Growth & Income)	B-	C	B+	Down	Y	0
Fidelity Advisor® Multi-Asset Income Fund Class I	FAYZX	NAS CM	Open End	Cautious Alloc (Growth & Income)	B-	C+	B+	Down	Y	0
Fidelity Advisor® Multi-Asset Income Fund Class M	FAZYX	NAS CM	Open End	Cautious Alloc (Growth & Income)	B-	C+	B+	Down	Y	0
Fidelity Advisor® Multi-Asset Income Fund Class Z	FIWBX	NAS CM	Open End	Cautious Alloc (Growth & Income)	B-	C+	B+	Down	Y	0
Fidelity Advisor® Municipal Income 2019 Fund Class A	FAPAX	NAS CM	Open End	US Muni Fixed Income (Municipal Bond - Natl)	C	C-	C+		Y	10,000
Fidelity Advisor® Municipal Income 2019 Fund I Class	FACIX	NAS CM	Open End	US Muni Fixed Income (Municipal Bond - Natl)	C	C-	C+		Y	10,000
Fidelity Advisor® Municipal Income 2021 Fund Class A	FOMAX	NAS CM	Open End	US Muni Fixed Income (Municipal Bond - Natl)	C	C	B-		Y	0
Fidelity Advisor® Municipal Income 2021 Fund I Class	FOMIX	NAS CM	Open End	US Muni Fixed Income (Municipal Bond - Natl)	C	C	B-		Y	0
Fidelity Advisor® Municipal Income 2023 Fund Class A	FSODX	NAS CM	Open End	US Muni Fixed Income (Municipal Bond - Natl)	C+	C	B		Y	0
Fidelity Advisor® Municipal Income 2023 Fund I Class	FSWTX	NAS CM	Open End	US Muni Fixed Income (Municipal Bond - Natl)	C+	C	B		Y	0
Fidelity Advisor® Municipal Income 2025 Fund Class A	FAMHX	NAS CM	Open End	US Muni Fixed Income (Municipal Bond - Natl)	C	D+	B		Y	0
Fidelity Advisor® Municipal Income 2025 Fund Class I	FAMYX	NAS CM	Open End	US Muni Fixed Income (Municipal Bond - Natl)	C	D+	B		Y	0
Fidelity Advisor® New Insights Fund Class A	FNIAX	NAS CM	Open End	US Equity Large Cap Growth (Growth)	C+	C	B	Down	Y	0
Fidelity Advisor® New Insights Fund Class C	FNICX	NAS CM	Open End	US Equity Large Cap Growth (Growth)	C+	C	B		Y	0
Fidelity Advisor® New Insights Fund Class I	FINSX	NAS CM	Open End	US Equity Large Cap Growth (Growth)	C+	C	B		Y	0
Fidelity Advisor® New Insights Fund Class M	FNITX	NAS CM	Open End	US Equity Large Cap Growth (Growth)	C+	C	B		Y	0
Fidelity Advisor® New Insights Fund Class Z	FZANX	NAS CM	Open End	US Equity Large Cap Growth (Growth)	C+	C	B		Y	0
Fidelity Advisor® Overseas Fund Class A	FAOAX	NAS CM	Open End	Global Equity Large Cap (Foreign Stock)	C	C	B-		Y	0
Fidelity Advisor® Overseas Fund Class C	FAOCX	NAS CM	Open End	Global Equity Large Cap (Foreign Stock)	C	C	B-		Y	0
Fidelity Advisor® Overseas Fund Class I	FAOIX	NAS CM	Open End	Global Equity Large Cap (Foreign Stock)	C	C	B-		Y	0

★ Expanded analysis of this fund is included in Section II.

	TOTAL RETURNS					PERFORMANCE				ASSETS		ASSET ALLOCATION & TURNOVER					BULL & BEAR		FEES		
Min Additional Investment	3-Month Total Return	6-Month Total Return	1-Year Total Return	3-Year Total Return	5-Year Total Return	Dividend Yield (TTM)	Expense Ratio	3-Yr Std Deviation	3-Year Beta	NAV	Total Assets (MIL)	%Cash	%Stocks	%Bonds	%Other	Turnover Ratio	Last Bull Market Total Return	Last Bear Market Total Return	Front End Fee (%)	Back End Fee (%)	Inception Date
	-0.54	18.80	-3.22	30.22	16.41	0	1.31	16.94	1.3	36.45	1,319	5	95	0	0	32	33.29	-30.21	3.50		Dec-00
	-0.38	19.16	-2.59	32.73	20.17	0.1	0.68	16.95	1.3	39.05	1,319	5	95	0	0	32	33.65	-30.05			Aug-13
	-0.40	19.14	-2.70	32.25	19.41	0.05	0.81	16.95	1.3	39.02	1,319	5	95	0	0	32	33.65	-30.05			Dec-00
	2.88	10.46	5.02	25.05	27.20	1.54	0.72	5.65	0.3	51.33	4.6	14	40	45	0	19	14.75	-13.24	5.75		Dec-07
	2.70	10.04	4.24	22.25	22.52	0.92	1.47	5.65	0.29	50.67	4.6	14	40	45	0	19	14.27	-13.51		1.00	Dec-07
	2.96	10.58	5.28	25.99	28.81	1.77	0.47	5.67	0.29	51.34	4.6	14	40	45	0	19	14.92	-13.13			Dec-07
	2.81	10.30	4.74	24.09	25.62	1.29	0.97	5.66	0.3	51.29	4.6	14	40	45	0	19	14.58	-13.31	3.50		Dec-07
	2.95	11.19	4.98	26.37	28.28	1.48	0.73	6.23	0.48	52.87	20.7	13	45	42	0	19	15.66	-14.13	5.75		Dec-07
	2.77	10.76	4.19	23.57	23.56	0.94	1.48	6.23	0.48	52.12	20.7	13	45	42	0	19	15.15	-14.39		1.00	Dec-07
	3.03	11.32	5.24	27.35	29.91	1.71	0.48	6.23	0.48	52.98	20.7	13	45	42	0	19	15.8	-14.03			Dec-07
	2.89	11.06	4.71	25.44	26.69	1.24	0.98	6.22	0.48	52.86	20.7	13	45	42	0	19	15.47	-14.22	3.50		Dec-07
	1.22	13.46	-10.41	19.54	2.49	0.82	1.06	17.32	1.24	69.61	996.0	0	99	1	0	77	29.81	-28.36	5.75		Dec-06
	1.02	13.04	-11.09	16.89	-1.28	0.06	1.81	17.3	1.24	67	996.0	0	99	1	0	77	29.24	-28.58		1.00	Dec-06
	1.29	13.64	-10.15	20.57	3.95	1.11	0.78	17.32	1.24	69.81	996.0	0	99	1	0	77	30.02	-28.26			Dec-06
	1.14	13.30	-10.67	18.50	0.96	0.58	1.35	17.32	1.24	68.96	996.0	0	99	1	0	77	29.59	-28.45	3.50		Dec-06
	1.33	13.71	-10.08	20.66	3.97		0.63	17.32	1.24	69.72	996.0	0	99	1	0	77	30.02	-28.27			Oct-18
	3.26	16.88	6.98	44.34	46.93	1.42	0.93	12.55	1	15.51	1,953	6	93	0	0	39	27.98	-16.12	5.75		Feb-08
	3.05	16.38	6.23	41.16	41.68	0.73	1.68	12.54	1	15.2	1,953	6	93	0	0	39	27.47	-16.36		1.00	Feb-08
	3.35	17.05	7.33	45.56	49.06	1.65	0.67	12.56	1	15.72	1,953	6	93	0	0	39	28.13	-15.99			Feb-08
	3.19	16.71	6.79	43.33	45.27	1.15	1.19	12.54	1	15.5	1,953	6	93	0	0	39	27.81	-16.15	3.50		Feb-08
	3.36	17.14	7.47	46.19	50.15	1.73	0.53	12.52	0.99	15.65	1,953	6	93	0	0	39	28.24	-16.02			Aug-13
	2.15	18.54	-2.79	34.85	32.92	0.19	1.04	14.92	0.96	18.49	1,811	4	96	0	0	49	18.04	-20.5	5.75		Aug-04
	1.96	18.06	-3.57	31.81	27.91	0	1.81	14.92	0.96	16.1	1,811	4	96	0	0	49	17.59	-20.75		1.00	Aug-04
	2.18	18.68	-2.57	35.96	34.78	0.47	0.76	14.89	0.96	19.14	1,811	4	96	0	0	49	18.25	-20.44			Aug-04
	2.10	18.41	-3.03	33.88	31.35	0	1.28	14.91	0.96	17.96	1,811	4	96	0	0	49	17.92	-20.54	3.50		Aug-04
	2.24	18.81	-2.43	36.52	35.73	0.6	0.63	14.9	0.96	19.15	1,811	4	96	0	0	49	18.25	-20.44			Aug-13
	0.98	14.83	-3.49	19.93	23.17	1.63	0.82	14.4	1.07	21.44	1,823	2	98	0	0	80	26.62	-23.2	5.75		Feb-07
	0.83	14.41	-4.18	17.29	18.70	0.86	1.56	14.38	1.06	20.64	1,823	2	98	0	0	80	26.09	-23.46		1.00	Feb-07
	1.07	15.02	-3.16	20.94	24.96	1.91	0.53	14.41	1.07	21.59	1,823	2	98	0	0	80	26.87	-23.14			Feb-07
	0.94	14.68	-3.75	18.95	21.47	1.37	1.1	14.4	1.07	21.32	1,823	2	98	0	0	80	26.46	-23.3	3.50		Feb-07
	1.12	15.09	-3.07	21.35	25.38	2.07	0.4	14.4	1.07	21.58	1,823	2	98	0	0	80	26.86	-23.1			Feb-17
	4.66	13.52	10.23	22.03		2.11	1.1	6.23	0.34	10.92	82.7	3	49	43	0	367			4.00		Sep-15
	4.47	13.12	9.49	19.33		1.46	1.85	6.26	0.35	10.91	82.7	3	49	43	0	367				1.00	Sep-15
	4.72	13.55	10.50	22.96		2.35	0.85	6.24	0.34	10.92	82.7	3	49	43	0	367					Sep-15
	4.66	13.52	10.23	22.04		2.11	1.1	6.23	0.35	10.92	82.7	3	49	43	0	367			4.00		Sep-15
	4.74	13.60	10.57	23.03			0.76	6.27	0.34	10.92	82.7	3	49	43	0	367					Oct-18
	0.26	0.59	1.05	1.30	4.86	1.05	0.65	1.03	0.21	10.57	55.7	82	0	18	0	7	5.34		2.75		May-11
	0.32	0.72	1.30	2.06	6.18	1.3	0.4	1.02	0.21	10.57	55.7	82	0	18	0	7	5.49				May-11
	0.92	1.88	2.67	2.19	9.73	1.81	0.65	2.36	0.6	10.83	52.7	0	0	100	0	8	5.91		2.75		May-11
	0.98	2.10	2.93	2.95	11.11	2.06	0.4	2.36	0.6	10.83	52.7	0	0	100	0	8	6.06				May-11
	1.44	3.45	4.48	3.56	14.62	1.82	0.65	3.4	0.94	10.34	35.1	0	0	100	0	12			2.75		Apr-13
	1.50	3.58	4.74	4.34	16.05	2.07	0.4	3.42	0.95	10.34	35.1	0	0	100	0	12					Apr-13
	2.10	5.23	7.23			1.76	0.65			10.29	23.8	0	0	100	0	44			2.75		May-17
	2.16	5.26	7.50			2	0.4			10.29	23.8	0	0	100	0	44					May-17
	5.49	22.66	7.79	58.67	66.55	0	1.05	13.18	1.03	32.04	27,055	2	95	0	2	36	23.44	-14.48	5.75		Jul-03
	5.31	22.20	6.99	55.16	60.41	0	1.8	13.17	1.03	27.35	27,055	2	95	0	2	36	22.95	-14.76		1.00	Jul-03
	5.55	22.84	8.09	59.93	68.70	0.2	0.79	13.18	1.03	32.85	27,055	2	95	0	2	36	23.6	-14.38			Jul-03
	5.44	22.53	7.55	57.53	64.52	0	1.3	13.17	1.03	30.77	27,055	2	95	0	2	36	23.24	-14.56	3.50		Jul-03
	5.61	22.89	8.24	60.55	69.80	0.32	0.67	13.18	1.03	32.9	27,055	2	95	0	2	36	23.6	-14.38			Aug-13
	6.73	19.22	2.86	33.72	18.51	0.84	1.21	11.86	1.03	23.94	631.2	1	99	0	0	39	18	-27.57	5.75		Sep-96
	6.47	18.73	2.00	30.47	13.78	0	2.03	11.84	1.03	23.2	631.2	1	99	0	0	39	17.5	-27.8		1.00	Nov-97
	6.77	19.40	3.17	34.93	20.34	1.26	0.92	11.88	1.03	24.43	631.2	1	99	0	0	39	18.27	-27.46			Jul-95

	MARKET		FUND TYPE, CATEGORY & OBJECTIVE		RATINGS				MINIMUMS	
Fund Name	Ticker Symbol	Traded On	Fund Type	Category and (Prospectus Objective)	Overall Rating	Reward Rating	Risk Rating	Recent Up/ Downgrade	Open to New Investors	Min Initial Investment
Fidelity Advisor® Overseas Fund Class M	FAERX	NAS CM	Open End	Global Equity Large Cap (Foreign Stock)	C	C	B-		Y	0
Fidelity Advisor® Overseas Fund Class Z	FAOSX	NAS CM	Open End	Global Equity Large Cap (Foreign Stock)	C	C	B-		Y	0
Fidelity Advisor® Real Estate Fund Class A	FHEAX	NAS CM	Open End	Real Estate Sector Equity (Real Estate)	C+	C	B-	Down	Y	0
Fidelity Advisor® Real Estate Fund Class C	FHECX	NAS CM	Open End	Real Estate Sector Equity (Real Estate)	C	C	C+	Down	Y	0
Fidelity Advisor® Real Estate Fund Class M	FHETX	NAS CM	Open End	Real Estate Sector Equity (Real Estate)	C+	C	B-	Down	Y	0
Fidelity Advisor® Real Estate Fund Class Z	FIKJX	NAS CM	Open End	Real Estate Sector Equity (Real Estate)	C+	C	B-	Down	Y	0
Fidelity Advisor® Real Estate Fund I Class	FHEIX	NAS CM	Open End	Real Estate Sector Equity (Real Estate)	C+	C	B-	Down	Y	0
Fidelity Advisor® Real Estate Income Fund Class A	FRINX	NAS CM	Open End	Real Estate Sector Equity (Real Estate)	B	B-	B		Y	0
Fidelity Advisor® Real Estate Income Fund Class C	FRIOX	NAS CM	Open End	Real Estate Sector Equity (Real Estate)	B	B-	B		Y	0
Fidelity Advisor® Real Estate Income Fund Class I	FRIRX	NAS CM	Open End	Real Estate Sector Equity (Real Estate)	B	B-	B		Y	0
Fidelity Advisor® Real Estate Income Fund Class M	FRIQX	NAS CM	Open End	Real Estate Sector Equity (Real Estate)	B	B-	B		Y	0
Fidelity Advisor® Real Estate Income Fund Class Z	FIKMX	NAS CM	Open End	Real Estate Sector Equity (Real Estate)	B	B-	B		Y	0
Fidelity Advisor® Semiconductors Fund Class A	FELAX	NAS CM	Open End	Technology Sector Equity (Technology)	C	C	C+	Down	Y	0
Fidelity Advisor® Semiconductors Fund Class C	FELCX	NAS CM	Open End	Technology Sector Equity (Technology)	C	C	C+	Down	Y	0
Fidelity Advisor® Semiconductors Fund Class I	FELIX	NAS CM	Open End	Technology Sector Equity (Technology)	C	C	C+	Down	Y	0
Fidelity Advisor® Semiconductors Fund Class M	FELTX	NAS CM	Open End	Technology Sector Equity (Technology)	C	C	C+	Down	Y	0
Fidelity Advisor® Semiconductors Fund Class Z	FIKGX	NAS CM	Open End	Technology Sector Equity (Technology)	C	C	C+	Down	Y	0
Fidelity Advisor® Series Equity Growth Fund	FMFMX	NAS CM	Open End	US Equity Large Cap Growth (Growth)	B-	C+	B	Down	Y	0
Fidelity Advisor® Series Growth Opportunities Fund	FAOFX	NAS CM	Open End	US Equity Large Cap Growth (World Stock)	B	B-	B+	Down	Y	0
Fidelity Advisor® Series Small Cap Fund	FSSFX	NAS CM	Open End	US Equity Small Cap (Small Company)	C	C	C+		Y	0
Fidelity Advisor® Small Cap Fund Class A	FSCDX	NAS CM	Open End	US Equity Small Cap (Small Company)	C	C	C+		Y	0
Fidelity Advisor® Small Cap Fund Class C	FSCEX	NAS CM	Open End	US Equity Small Cap (Small Company)	C	C	C+		Y	0
Fidelity Advisor® Small Cap Fund Class M	FSCTX	NAS CM	Open End	US Equity Small Cap (Small Company)	C	C	C+		Y	0
Fidelity Advisor® Small Cap Fund Class Z	FZAOX	NAS CM	Open End	US Equity Small Cap (Small Company)	C	C	C+		Y	0
Fidelity Advisor® Small Cap Fund I Class	FSCIX	NAS CM	Open End	US Equity Small Cap (Small Company)	C	C	C+		Y	0
Fidelity Advisor® Small Cap Growth Fund Class A	FCAGX	NAS CM	Open End	US Equity Small Cap (Small Company)	C+	C+	C+	Down	Y	0
Fidelity Advisor® Small Cap Growth Fund Class C	FCCGX	NAS CM	Open End	US Equity Small Cap (Small Company)	C+	C	C+		Y	0
Fidelity Advisor® Small Cap Growth Fund Class M	FCTGX	NAS CM	Open End	US Equity Small Cap (Small Company)	C+	C	C+		Y	0
Fidelity Advisor® Small Cap Growth Fund Class Z	FIDGX	NAS CM	Open End	US Equity Small Cap (Small Company)	C+	C+	C+	Down	Y	0
Fidelity Advisor® Small Cap Growth Fund I Class	FCIGX	NAS CM	Open End	US Equity Small Cap (Small Company)	C+	C+	C+	Down	Y	0
Fidelity Advisor® Small Cap Value Fund Class A	FCVAX	NAS CM	Open End	US Equity Small Cap (Small Company)	C	C-	C+			0
Fidelity Advisor® Small Cap Value Fund Class C	FCVCX	NAS CM	Open End	US Equity Small Cap (Small Company)	C	C-	C+			0
Fidelity Advisor® Small Cap Value Fund Class I	FCVIX	NAS CM	Open End	US Equity Small Cap (Small Company)	C	C-	C+			0
Fidelity Advisor® Small Cap Value Fund Class M	FCVTX	NAS CM	Open End	US Equity Small Cap (Small Company)	C	C-	C+			0
Fidelity Advisor® Small Cap Value Fund Class Z	FIKNX	NAS CM	Open End	US Equity Small Cap (Small Company)	C	C-	C+		Y	0
Fidelity Advisor® Stock Selector All Cap Fund Class A	FMAMX	NAS CM	Open End	US Equity Large Cap Growth (Growth)	C+	C	B-	Up	Y	0
Fidelity Advisor® Stock Selector All Cap Fund Class C	FLACX	NAS CM	Open End	US Equity Large Cap Growth (Growth)	C+	C	B-	Up	Y	0
Fidelity Advisor® Stock Selector All Cap Fund Class K	FSSKX	NAS CM	Open End	US Equity Large Cap Growth (Growth)	C+	C	B-	Up	Y	0
Fidelity Advisor® Stock Selector All Cap Fund Class M	FSJHX	NAS CM	Open End	US Equity Large Cap Growth (Growth)	C+	C	B-	Up	Y	0
Fidelity Advisor® Stock Selector All Cap Fund Class Z	FZAPX	NAS CM	Open End	US Equity Large Cap Growth (Growth)	C+	C	B-	Up	Y	0
Fidelity Advisor® Stock Selector All Cap Fund I Class	FBRNX	NAS CM	Open End	US Equity Large Cap Growth (Growth)	C+	C	B-	Up	Y	0
Fidelity Advisor® Stock Selector Large Cap Value Cls A	FLUAX	NAS CM	Open End	US Equity Large Cap Value (Growth)	B-	C	B	Up	Y	0
Fidelity Advisor® Stock Selector Large Cap Value Cls C	FLUEX	NAS CM	Open End	US Equity Large Cap Value (Growth)	C+	C	B	Up	Y	0
Fidelity Advisor® Stock Selector Large Cap Value Cls I	FLUIX	NAS CM	Open End	US Equity Large Cap Value (Growth)	B-	C	B	Up	Y	0
Fidelity Advisor® Stock Selector Large Cap Value Cls M	FLUTX	NAS CM	Open End	US Equity Large Cap Value (Growth)	B-	C	B	Up	Y	0
Fidelity Advisor® Stock Selector Large Cap Value Cls Z	FSCZX	NAS CM	Open End	US Equity Large Cap Value (Growth)	B-	C	B	Up	Y	0
Fidelity Advisor® Stock Selector Mid Cap Fund Class A	FMCDX	NAS CM	Open End	US Equity Mid Cap (Growth)	C+	C	B		Y	0
Fidelity Advisor® Stock Selector Mid Cap Fund Class C	FMCEX	NAS CM	Open End	US Equity Mid Cap (Growth)	C+	C	B		Y	0
Fidelity Advisor® Stock Selector Mid Cap Fund Class M	FMCAX	NAS CM	Open End	US Equity Mid Cap (Growth)	C+	C	B		Y	0
Fidelity Advisor® Stock Selector Mid Cap Fund Class Z	FSLZX	NAS CM	Open End	US Equity Mid Cap (Growth)	C+	C	B		Y	0
Fidelity Advisor® Stock Selector Mid Cap Fund I Class	FMCCX	NAS CM	Open End	US Equity Mid Cap (Growth)	C+	C	B		Y	0
Fidelity Advisor® Stock Selector Small Cap Fund Class A	FCDAX	NAS CM	Open End	US Equity Small Cap (Small Company)	C+	C	C+		Y	0

★ Expanded analysis of this fund is included in Section II.

Min Additional Investment	TOTAL RETURNS: 3-Month Total Return	6-Month Total Return	1-Year Total Return	3-Year Total Return	5-Year Total Return	PERFORMANCE: Dividend Yield (TTM)	Expense Ratio	3-Yr Std Deviation	3-Year Beta	ASSETS: NAV	Total Assets (MIL)	ASSET ALLOCATION & TURNOVER: %Cash	%Stocks	%Bonds	%Other	Turnover Ratio	BULL & BEAR: Last Bull Market Total Return	Last Bear Market Total Return	FEES: Front End Fee (%)	Back End Fee (%)	Inception Date
	6.67	19.10	2.65	32.87	17.25	0.6	1.44	11.85	1.03	24.62	631.2	1	99	0	0	39	17.91	-27.64	3.50		Apr-90
	6.82	19.47	3.33	34.87	19.02	1.43	0.79	11.88	1.03	24.42	631.2	1	99	0	0	39	17.91	-27.64			Feb-17
	0.96	17.46	7.80	9.03	35.43	1.85	1.1	13.14	0.65	22.51	545.2	2	98	0	0	41	33.56	-18.89	5.75		Sep-02
	0.73	16.99	6.96	6.51	30.29	1.41	1.88	13.11	0.65	21.89	545.2	2	98	0	0	41	33.01	-19.18		1.00	Sep-02
	0.91	17.33	7.58	8.26	33.87	1.69	1.33	13.12	0.65	22.48	545.2	2	98	0	0	41	33.32	-18.99	3.50		Sep-02
	1.06	17.70	8.27	10.08	37.41		0.66	13.11	0.65	22.75	545.2	2	98	0	0	41	33.74	-18.8			Oct-18
	1.07	17.68	8.17	9.97	37.28	2.06	0.82	13.11	0.65	22.75	545.2	2	98	0	0	41	33.74	-18.8			Sep-02
	2.89	11.46	9.64	20.95	35.70	4.1	1.02	5.31	0.25	12.28	6,194	9	30	38	0	27	14.08	-6.48	4.00		Apr-10
	2.72	11.15	8.82	18.28	30.75	3.41	1.76	5.31	0.25	12.15	6,194	9	30	38	0	27	13.59	-6.74		1.00	Apr-10
	2.95	11.65	9.92	21.92	37.50	4.35	0.75	5.26	0.24	12.3	6,194	9	30	38	0	27	14.22	-6.38			Apr-10
	2.88	11.53	9.61	20.86	35.51	4.07	1.04	5.3	0.25	12.29	6,194	9	30	38	0	27	14.05	-6.49	4.00		Apr-10
	2.98	11.70	10.03	21.95	37.44		0.62	5.3	0.25	12.3	6,194	9	30	38	0	27	14.26	-6.41			Oct-18
	4.08	28.16	4.71	93.83	127.77	0.42	1.15	23.07	1.53	21.66	251.7	0	100	0	0	133	22.97	-23.47	5.75		Dec-00
	3.88	27.61	3.90	89.46	119.32	0	1.91	23.03	1.53	18.44	251.7	0	100	0	0	133	22.22	-23.63		1.00	Dec-00
	4.17	28.32	5.01	95.68	131.31	0.61	0.86	23.05	1.53	22.97	251.7	0	100	0	0	133	23.06	-23.39			Dec-00
	4.04	27.95	4.41	92.06	124.08	0.26	1.48	23.04	1.53	20.6	251.7	0	100	0	0	133	22.69	-23.57	3.50		Dec-00
	4.18	28.40	5.07	95.78	131.43		0.73	23.08	1.54	22.92	251.7	0	100	0	0	133	23.06	-23.39			Oct-18
	4.66	23.35	11.07	76.28	85.12	0.83	0.01	13.75	0.99	14.58	982.5	1	99	0	0	38					Jun-14
	3.87	27.39	24.09	113.52	126.10	0.61	0.01	14.54	0.99	15.02	650.7	1	95	0	0	47					Nov-13
	4.86	24.18	1.25	32.95	30.04	0.99	0.01	15.22	0.86	10.99	464.1	2	98	0	0	82					Nov-13
	4.71	23.95	0.20	29.33	26.69	0	0.97	15.33	0.86	22.87	1,856	1	99	0	0	74	22.24	-23.87	5.75		Sep-98
	4.51	23.47	-0.54	26.40	21.98	0	1.74	15.34	0.86	16.2	1,856	1	99	0	0	74	21.72	-24.14		1.00	Sep-98
	4.67	23.84	0.00	28.48	25.29	0	1.2	15.34	0.86	20.83	1,856	1	99	0	0	74	22.05	-23.93	3.50		Sep-98
	4.83	24.24	0.66	30.99	29.42	0	0.56	15.33	0.86	25.57	1,856	1	99	0	0	74	22.43	-23.78			Aug-13
	4.80	24.17	0.51	30.41	28.43	0	0.71	15.34	0.86	25.53	1,856	1	99	0	0	74	22.43	-23.78			Sep-98
	5.35	27.79	5.39	73.22	84.57	0	1.31	16.11	0.89	25.56	4,093	1	98	0	0	106	26.2	-24.61	5.75		Nov-04
	5.18	27.33	4.59	69.35	77.53	0	2.07	16.11	0.89	22.5	4,093	1	98	0	0	106	25.64	-24.84		1.00	Nov-04
	5.34	27.65	5.13	71.89	82.06	0	1.58	16.1	0.89	24.65	4,093	1	98	0	0	106	25.99	-24.7	3.50		Nov-04
	5.48	28.06	5.82	75.31	87.81	0	0.9	16.12	0.89	26.92	4,093	1	98	0	0	106	26.42	-24.47			Feb-17
	5.45	28.02	5.71	74.73	87.17	0	1.04	16.11	0.89	26.86	4,093	1	98	0	0	106	26.46	-24.53			Nov-04
	1.75	13.40	-4.66	25.96	30.78	0.51	1.18	14.38	0.8	14.47	2,076	2	98	0	0	55	30.67	-23.75	5.75		Nov-04
	1.59	12.94	-5.39	23.09	25.90	0.09	1.93	14.39	0.8	12.74	2,076	2	98	0	0	55	30.11	-23.96		1.00	Nov-04
	1.85	13.55	-4.39	27.02	32.58	0.75	0.91	14.41	0.8	14.83	2,076	2	98	0	0	55	30.88	-23.59			Nov-04
	1.66	13.24	-4.88	25.04	29.21	0.29	1.42	14.4	0.8	14.02	2,076	2	98	0	0	55	30.48	-23.76	3.50		Nov-04
	1.85	13.63	-4.27	27.08	32.63		0.77	14.41	0.8	14.83	2,076	2	98	0	0	55	30.92	-23.61			Oct-18
	4.09	20.60	4.20	48.13	52.41	0.35	0.99	13.34	1.05	46.06	9,367	2	98	0	0	12	24.53	-21.23	5.75		Oct-12
	3.90	20.13	3.40	44.72	46.64	0	1.77	13.32	1.05	45.46	9,367	2	98	0	0	12	23.99	-21.47		1.00	Oct-12
	4.20	20.85	4.63	49.94	55.60	0.6	0.59	13.34	1.05	46.13	9,367	2	98	0	0	12	24.82	-21.05			May-08
	4.04	20.46	3.96	47.00	50.48	0.09	1.25	13.34	1.05	46.04	9,367	2	98	0	0	12	24.35	-21.31	3.50		Oct-12
	4.19	20.83	4.62	49.92	55.61	0.77	0.59	13.34	1.05	45.93	9,367	2	98	0	0	12	24.76	-21.12			Aug-13
	4.16	20.76	4.49	49.32	54.48	0.62	0.73	13.34	1.05	46.06	9,367	2	98	0	0	12	24.71	-21.14			Oct-12
	4.03	16.32	6.48	30.05	34.50	1.12	0.97	12.06	0.99	20.09	981.9	2	98	0	0	92	24.72	-20.26	5.75		Feb-07
	3.82	15.80	5.59	26.74	28.98	0.39	1.8	11.98	0.98	19.56	981.9	2	98	0	0	92	24.24	-20.47		1.00	Feb-07
	4.13	16.42	6.76	30.93	36.25	1.37	0.7	12.02	0.98	20.13	981.9	2	98	0	0	92	24.94	-20.2			Feb-07
	3.99	16.11	6.14	28.76	32.37	0.87	1.29	12.04	0.99	20.03	981.9	2	98	0	0	92	24.56	-20.33	3.50		Feb-07
	4.13	16.53	6.93	31.55	36.85	1.51	0.55	12.03	0.99	20.16	981.9	2	98	0	0	92	24.88	-20.13			Feb-17
	3.97	21.49	4.18	47.51	45.37	0.62	0.93	14.26	0.93	34.54	2,120	3	97	0	0	81	27.57	-21.09	5.75		Sep-96
	3.79	21.04	3.40	44.26	39.99	0	1.69	14.27	0.93	30.89	2,120	3	97	0	0	81	27.12	-21.37		1.00	Nov-97
	3.88	21.34	3.93	46.45	43.63	0.34	1.17	14.25	0.92	34.79	2,120	3	97	0	0	81	27.51	-21.18	3.50		Feb-96
	4.08	21.78	4.60	49.18	47.55	0.98	0.53	14.27	0.93	36.45	2,120	3	97	0	0	81	27.84	-21.01			Feb-17
	4.01	21.67	4.41	48.59	46.96	0.72	0.69	14.27	0.93	36.49	2,120	3	97	0	0	81	27.84	-21.01			Feb-96
	3.67	21.51	2.72	41.10	41.04	0.04	0.97	15.59	0.89	23.44	1,193	3	97	0	0	68	27.27	-25.51	5.75		May-07

	MARKET			FUND TYPE, CATEGORY & OBJECTIVE	RATINGS				MINIMUMS	
Fund Name	Ticker Symbol	Traded On	Fund Type	Category and (Prospectus Objective)	Overall Rating	Reward Rating	Risk Rating	Recent Up/ Downgrade	Open to New Investors	Min Initial Investment
Fidelity Advisor® Stock Selector Small Cap Fund Class C	FCDCX	NAS CM	Open End	US Equity Small Cap (Small Company)	C+	C	C+	Up	Y	0
Fidelity Advisor® Stock Selector Small Cap Fund Class M	FCDTX	NAS CM	Open End	US Equity Small Cap (Small Company)	C+	C	C+		Y	0
Fidelity Advisor® Stock Selector Small Cap Fund Class Z	FSSZX	NAS CM	Open End	US Equity Small Cap (Small Company)	C+	C	B-		Y	0
Fidelity Advisor® Stock Selector Small Cap Fund I Class	FCDIX	NAS CM	Open End	US Equity Small Cap (Small Company)	C+	C	B-		Y	0
Fidelity Advisor® Strategic Dividend & Income® Cls A	FASDX	NAS CM	Open End	Aggressive Alloc (Equity-Income)	B	C+	A-		Y	0
Fidelity Advisor® Strategic Dividend & Income® Cls C	FCSDX	NAS CM	Open End	Aggressive Alloc (Equity-Income)	B-	C	B+	Down	Y	0
Fidelity Advisor® Strategic Dividend & Income® Cls M	FTSDX	NAS CM	Open End	Aggressive Alloc (Equity-Income)	B	C+	B+		Y	0
Fidelity Advisor® Strategic Dividend & Income® Cls Z	FIQWX	NAS CM	Open End	Aggressive Alloc (Equity-Income)	B	C+	A-		Y	0
Fidelity Advisor® Strategic Dividend & Income® I Cls	FSIDX	NAS CM	Open End	Aggressive Alloc (Equity-Income)	B	C+	A-		Y	0
Fidelity Advisor® Strategic Real Return Fund Class A	FSRAX	NAS CM	Open End	Cautious Alloc (Growth & Income)	B-	C	B+	Up	Y	0
Fidelity Advisor® Strategic Real Return Fund Class C	FCSRX	NAS CM	Open End	Cautious Alloc (Growth & Income)	C+	C	B		Y	0
Fidelity Advisor® Strategic Real Return Fund Class M	FSRTX	NAS CM	Open End	Cautious Alloc (Growth & Income)	B-	C	B+	Up	Y	0
Fidelity Advisor® Strategic Real Return Fund Class Z	FIQDX	NAS CM	Open End	Cautious Alloc (Growth & Income)	B-	C	B+		Y	0
Fidelity Advisor® Strategic Real Return Fund I Class	FSIRX	NAS CM	Open End	Cautious Alloc (Growth & Income)	B-	C	B+		Y	0
Fidelity Advisor® Technology Fund Class A	FADTX	NAS CM	Open End	Technology Sector Equity (Technology)	C+	C+	C+		Y	0
Fidelity Advisor® Technology Fund Class C	FTHCX	NAS CM	Open End	Technology Sector Equity (Technology)	C+	C+	C+		Y	0
Fidelity Advisor® Technology Fund Class M	FATEX	NAS CM	Open End	Technology Sector Equity (Technology)	C+	C+	C+		Y	0
Fidelity Advisor® Technology Fund Class Z	FIKHX	NAS CM	Open End	Technology Sector Equity (Technology)	C+	C+	C+		Y	0
Fidelity Advisor® Technology Fund I Class	FATIX	NAS CM	Open End	Technology Sector Equity (Technology)	C+	C+	C+		Y	0
Fidelity Advisor® Telecommunications Fund Class A	FTUAX	NAS CM	Open End	Communications Sector Equity (Comm)	C	C	C	Down	Y	0
Fidelity Advisor® Telecommunications Fund Class C	FTUCX	NAS CM	Open End	Communications Sector Equity (Comm)	C	C	C		Y	0
Fidelity Advisor® Telecommunications Fund Class M	FTUTX	NAS CM	Open End	Communications Sector Equity (Comm)	C	C	C	Down	Y	0
Fidelity Advisor® Telecommunications Fund Class Z	FIJGX	NAS CM	Open End	Communications Sector Equity (Comm)	C	C	C+	Down	Y	0
Fidelity Advisor® Telecommunications Fund I Class	FTUIX	NAS CM	Open End	Communications Sector Equity (Comm)	C	C	C+	Down	Y	0
Fidelity Advisor® Total Emerging Markets Fund Class A	FTEDX	NAS CM	Open End	Global Emerg Mkts (Div Emerging Mkts)	C	C	B-		Y	0
Fidelity Advisor® Total Emerging Markets Fund Class C	FTEFX	NAS CM	Open End	Global Emerg Mkts (Div Emerging Mkts)	C	C	B-		Y	0
Fidelity Advisor® Total Emerging Markets Fund Class M	FTEHX	NAS CM	Open End	Global Emerg Mkts (Div Emerging Mkts)	C	C	B-		Y	0
Fidelity Advisor® Total Emerging Markets Fund Class Z	FIQNX	NAS CM	Open End	Global Emerg Mkts (Div Emerging Mkts)	C	C	B-		Y	0
Fidelity Advisor® Total Emerging Markets Fund I Class	FTEJX	NAS CM	Open End	Global Emerg Mkts (Div Emerging Mkts)	C	C	B-		Y	0
Fidelity Advisor® Total International Equity Fund Class A	FTAEX	NAS CM	Open End	Global Equity Large Cap (Foreign Stock)	C	C	B-		Y	0
Fidelity Advisor® Total International Equity Fund Class C	FTCEX	NAS CM	Open End	Global Equity Large Cap (Foreign Stock)	C	C	B-		Y	0
Fidelity Advisor® Total International Equity Fund Class M	FTTEX	NAS CM	Open End	Global Equity Large Cap (Foreign Stock)	C	C	B-		Y	0
Fidelity Advisor® Total International Equity Fund Class Z	FIEZX	NAS CM	Open End	Global Equity Large Cap (Foreign Stock)	C	C	B-		Y	0
Fidelity Advisor® Total International Equity Fund I Class	FTEIX	NAS CM	Open End	Global Equity Large Cap (Foreign Stock)	C	C	B-		Y	0
Fidelity Advisor® Utilities Fund Class A	FUGAX	NAS CM	Open End	Utilities Sector Equity (Utility)	B	B	A-	Up	Y	0
Fidelity Advisor® Utilities Fund Class C	FUGCX	NAS CM	Open End	Utilities Sector Equity (Utility)	B	B	A-	Up	Y	0
Fidelity Advisor® Utilities Fund Class M	FAUFX	NAS CM	Open End	Utilities Sector Equity (Utility)	B	B	A-	Up	Y	0
Fidelity Advisor® Utilities Fund Class Z	FIKIX	NAS CM	Open End	Utilities Sector Equity (Utility)	B+	B	A-	Up	Y	0
Fidelity Advisor® Utilities Fund I Class	FUGIX	NAS CM	Open End	Utilities Sector Equity (Utility)	B+	B	A-	Up	Y	0
Fidelity Advisor® Value Fund Class A	FAVFX	NAS CM	Open End	US Equity Mid Cap (Growth)	C	C	C+		Y	0
Fidelity Advisor® Value Fund Class C	FCVFX	NAS CM	Open End	US Equity Mid Cap (Growth)	C	C	C+		Y	0
Fidelity Advisor® Value Fund Class M	FTVFX	NAS CM	Open End	US Equity Mid Cap (Growth)	C	C	C+		Y	0
Fidelity Advisor® Value Fund Class Z	FVLZX	NAS CM	Open End	US Equity Mid Cap (Growth)	C	C	B-		Y	0
Fidelity Advisor® Value Fund I Class	FVIFX	NAS CM	Open End	US Equity Mid Cap (Growth)	C	C	B-		Y	0
Fidelity Advisor® Value Leaders Fund Class A	FVLAX	NAS CM	Open End	US Equity Large Cap Value (Growth)	C+	C	B	Up	Y	0
Fidelity Advisor® Value Leaders Fund Class C	FVLCX	NAS CM	Open End	US Equity Large Cap Value (Growth)	C+	C	B-	Up	Y	0
Fidelity Advisor® Value Leaders Fund Class M	FVLTX	NAS CM	Open End	US Equity Large Cap Value (Growth)	C+	C	B	Up	Y	0
Fidelity Advisor® Value Leaders Fund I Class	FVLIX	NAS CM	Open End	US Equity Large Cap Value (Growth)	C+	C	B	Up	Y	0
Fidelity Advisor® Value Strategies Fund Class A	FSOAX	NAS CM	Open End	US Equity Large Cap Value (Growth)	C	C	C+		Y	0
Fidelity Advisor® Value Strategies Fund Class C	FVCSX	NAS CM	Open End	US Equity Large Cap Value (Growth)	C	C	C+		Y	0
Fidelity Advisor® Value Strategies Fund Class I	FASOX	NAS CM	Open End	US Equity Large Cap Value (Growth)	C+	C	C+	Up	Y	0
Fidelity Advisor® Value Strategies Fund Class K	FVSKX	NAS CM	Open End	US Equity Large Cap Value (Growth)	C+	C	C+	Up	Y	0

★ Expanded analysis of this fund is included in Section II.

	TOTAL RETURNS					PERFORMANCE				ASSETS		ASSET ALLOCATION & TURNOVER					BULL & BEAR		FEES		
Min Additional Investment	3-Month Total Return	6-Month Total Return	1-Year Total Return	3-Year Total Return	5-Year Total Return	Dividend Yield (TTM)	Expense Ratio	3-Yr Std Deviation	3-Year Beta	NAV	Total Assets (MIL)	%Cash	%Stocks	%Bonds	%Other	Turnover Ratio	Last Bull Market Total Return	Last Bear Market Total Return	Front End Fee (%)	Back End Fee (%)	Inception Date
	3.47	21.00	1.90	37.63	35.30	0	1.79	15.59	0.89	21.14	1,193	3	97	0	0	68	26.69	-25.73		1.00	May-07
	3.56	21.31	2.40	39.63	38.59	0	1.33	15.58	0.89	22.65	1,193	3	97	0	0	68	27.1	-25.6	3.50		May-07
	3.78	21.75	3.18	42.83	43.41	0.36	0.55	15.6	0.9	24.12	1,193	3	97	0	0	68	27.46	-25.4			Feb-17
	3.74	21.68	3.02	42.34	43.06	0.2	0.69	15.61	0.9	24.13	1,193	3	97	0	0	68	27.74	-25.45			May-07
	2.44	14.70	8.61	27.28	39.17	2.56	1.01	8.37	0.65	15.18	4,835	3	65	10	0	49	18.9	-11.67	5.75		Dec-03
	2.31	14.29	7.84	24.43	34.05	1.81	1.76	8.33	0.65	15.1	4,835	3	65	10	0	49	18.35	-11.94		1.00	Dec-03
	2.45	14.55	8.34	26.35	37.44	2.32	1.26	8.33	0.65	15.17	4,835	3	65	10	0	49	18.79	-11.74	3.50		Dec-03
	2.59	14.89	9.01	28.38	41.15		0.65	8.35	0.65	15.25	4,835	3	65	10	0	49	19.11	-11.51			Oct-18
	2.56	14.86	8.93	28.29	41.05	2.79	0.75	8.32	0.65	15.25	4,835	3	65	10	0	49	19.11	-11.51			Dec-03
	0.86	6.93	1.40	7.55	0.93	3.24	1.09	4.21	0.52	8.35	373.1	16	14	55	12	23	8.3	-7.81	4.00		Sep-05
	0.73	6.60	0.67	5.10	-2.81	2.67	1.85	4.24	0.53	8.23	373.1	16	14	55	12	23	7.76	-8.14		1.00	Sep-05
	0.84	7.04	1.39	7.51	0.88	3.21	1.12	4.19	0.54	8.36	373.1	16	14	55	12	23	8.29	-7.9	4.00		Sep-05
	0.94	7.27	1.74	8.56	2.37		0.72	4.2	0.55	8.37	373.1	16	14	55	12	23	8.47	-7.75			Oct-18
	0.92	7.12	1.69	8.50	2.31	3.49	0.81	4.21	0.55	8.37	373.1	16	14	55	12	23	8.47	-7.75			Sep-05
	6.03	28.78	5.77	101.10	116.62	0	1.05	17.51	1.16	51.14	2,108	0	99	0	0	84	25.54	-21.71	5.75		Sep-96
	5.81	28.28	4.96	96.59	108.54	0	1.81	17.51	1.16	41.64	2,108	0	99	0	0	84	25.05	-21.99		1.00	Nov-97
	5.94	28.58	5.49	99.57	113.83	0	1.31	17.5	1.16	47.91	2,108	0	99	0	0	84	25.39	-21.81	3.50		Sep-96
	6.11	29.01	6.13	102.99	120.03		0.65	17.52	1.17	55.71	2,108	0	99	0	0	84	25.84	-21.64			Oct-18
	6.10	28.93	6.04	102.81	119.84	0.01	0.78	17.52	1.16	55.79	2,108	0	99	0	0	84	25.84	-21.64			Sep-96
	2.49	12.27	6.80	10.24	29.15	1.7	1.18	11.92	0.7	58.01	285.7	4	96	0	0	64	12.09	-16.68	5.75		Dec-06
	2.30	11.87	6.05	7.89	24.57	0.93	1.88	11.9	0.7	57.7	285.7	4	96	0	0	64	11.61	-16.93		1.00	Dec-06
	2.41	12.11	6.49	9.14	27.06	1.43	1.5	11.91	0.7	57.69	285.7	4	96	0	0	64	11.89	-16.77	3.50		Dec-06
	2.60	12.55	7.28	11.46	31.46		0.68	11.93	0.7	58.23	285.7	4	96	0	0	64	12.29	-16.57			Oct-18
	2.55	12.41	7.08	11.27	31.21	2.01	0.91	11.93	0.7	58.2	285.7	4	96	0	0	64	12.27	-16.59			Dec-06
	2.70	13.86	5.14	31.55	18.99	1.88	1.4	11.4	0.8	12.89	738.0	5	70	24	0	94			5.75		Nov-11
	2.48	13.39	4.36	28.56	14.57	1.19	2.14	11.4	0.8	12.78	738.0	5	70	24	0	94				1.00	Nov-11
	2.62	13.68	4.83	30.25	17.25	1.61	1.74	11.4	0.8	12.88	738.0	5	70	24	0	94			3.50		Nov-11
	2.79	14.09	5.44	32.47	20.51		1.07	11.4	0.8	12.87	738.0	5	70	24	0	94					Oct-18
	2.70	13.97	5.36	32.52	20.48	2.2	1.12	11.38	0.8	12.89	738.0	5	70	24	0	94					Nov-11
	4.79	17.99	2.99	31.49	19.68	0.56	1.45	11.89	1.02	9.18	99.3	2	98	0	0	52	16.31	-25.3	5.75		Nov-07
	4.56	17.43	2.11	28.56	15.14	0	2.2	11.8	1.01	9.16	99.3	2	98	0	0	52	15.86	-25.58		1.00	Nov-07
	4.76	17.88	2.79	30.55	18.17	0.21	1.7	11.88	1.02	9.23	99.3	2	98	0	0	52	16.22	-25.33	3.50		Nov-07
	4.91	18.14	3.36	32.84	21.46	0.96	1.05	11.85	1.01	9.18	99.3	2	98	0	0	52	16.52	-25.24			Feb-17
	4.79	18.16	3.19	32.52	21.16	0.72	1.2	11.86	1.01	9.17	99.3	2	98	0	0	52	16.52	-25.24			Nov-07
	2.83	12.92	12.93	36.79	47.41	1.39	1.12	9.94	0.3	31.9	638.2	1	99	0	0	106	11.31	-2.6	5.75		Sep-96
	2.60	12.48	12.05	33.69	41.92	0.77	1.87	9.94	0.3	31.08	638.2	1	99	0	0	106	10.85	-2.87		1.00	Nov-97
	2.76	12.77	12.58	35.58	45.26	1.13	1.41	9.94	0.3	31.95	638.2	1	99	0	0	106	11.17	-2.66	3.50		Sep-96
	2.90	13.14	13.33	38.02	49.62		0.69	9.94	0.3	32.63	638.2	1	99	0	0	106	11.53	-2.47			Oct-18
	2.90	13.06	13.22	37.88	49.47	1.63	0.84	9.94	0.3	32.63	638.2	1	99	0	0	106	11.53	-2.47			Sep-96
	3.11	21.08	-0.32	27.81	25.14	0.49	1.13	15.46	1.15	22.17	88.3	1	99	0	0	98	26.59	-24.82	5.75		Dec-03
	2.94	20.59	-1.09	24.74	20.38	0	1.94	15.46	1.15	20.96	88.3	1	99	0	0	98	25.93	-24.98		1.00	Dec-03
	3.05	20.88	-0.59	26.74	23.54	0.22	1.4	15.45	1.15	21.94	88.3	1	99	0	0	98	26.37	-24.86	3.50		Dec-03
	3.22	21.35	0.09	29.24	27.33	0.98	0.71	15.49	1.16	22.39	88.3	1	99	0	0	98	26.72	-24.68			Feb-17
	3.22	21.26	0.00	28.96	27.05	0.82	0.82	15.48	1.16	22.41	88.3	1	99	0	0	98	26.72	-24.68			Dec-03
	2.02	10.90	2.13	28.61	31.82	1	1.25	11.32	0.88	18.1	26.7	1	99	0	0	35	20.66	-23.85	5.75		Jun-03
	1.85	10.52	1.40	25.76	27.00	0.2	2	11.34	0.89	17.53	26.7	1	99	0	0	35	20.11	-24.09		1.00	Jun-03
	1.96	10.79	1.88	27.66	30.20	0.67	1.5	11.33	0.88	18.17	26.7	1	99	0	0	35	20.4	-23.89	3.50		Jun-03
	2.12	11.08	2.46	29.64	33.60	1.31	0.96	11.35	0.89	18.24	26.7	1	99	0	0	35	20.81	-23.77			Jun-03
	3.58	22.67	1.24	31.63	29.16	0.83	0.91	14.54	1.06	30.95	870.4	2	98	0	0	72	29.06	-26.82	5.75		Sep-96
	3.42	22.21	0.49	28.68	24.34	0.11	1.68	14.53	1.06	26.24	870.4	2	98	0	0	72	28.48	-27.07		1.00	Aug-01
	3.65	22.81	1.48	32.61	30.77	0.96	0.67	14.54	1.07	34.34	870.4	2	98	0	0	72	29.28	-26.75			Jul-95
	3.71	22.93	1.65	33.29	31.89	1.07	0.5	14.56	1.07	36.88	870.4	2	98	0	0	72	29.39	-26.68			May-08

Fund Name	MARKET Ticker Symbol	Traded On	FUND TYPE, CATEGORY & OBJECTIVE Fund Type	Category and (Prospectus Objective)	RATINGS Overall Rating	Reward Rating	Risk Rating	Recent Up/ Downgrade	MINIMUMS Open to New Investors	Min Initial Investment
Fidelity Advisor® Value Strategies Fund Class M	FASPX	NAS CM	Open End	US Equity Large Cap Value (Growth)	C	C	C+		Y	0
Fidelity Advisor® Worldwide Fund Class A	FWAFX	NAS CM	Open End	Global Equity Large Cap (World Stock)	C+	C	B		Y	0
Fidelity Advisor® Worldwide Fund Class C	FWCFX	NAS CM	Open End	Global Equity Large Cap (World Stock)	C+	C	B	Up	Y	0
Fidelity Advisor® Worldwide Fund Class M	FWTFX	NAS CM	Open End	Global Equity Large Cap (World Stock)	C+	C	B		Y	0
Fidelity Advisor® Worldwide Fund Class Z	FIQOX	NAS CM	Open End	Global Equity Large Cap (World Stock)	C+	C	B		Y	0
Fidelity Advisor® Worldwide Fund I Class	FWIFX	NAS CM	Open End	Global Equity Large Cap (World Stock)	C+	C	B		Y	0
Fidelity Asset Manager® 20% Fund	FASIX	NAS CM	Open End	Cautious Alloc (Asset Alloc)	B-	C	A-		Y	0
Fidelity Asset Manager® 30% Fund	FTANX	NAS CM	Open End	Cautious Alloc (Asset Alloc)	B	C	A-	Up	Y	0
Fidelity Asset Manager® 40% Fund	FFANX	NAS CM	Open End	Cautious Alloc (Asset Alloc)	B	C	A-	Up	Y	0
Fidelity Asset Manager® 50% Fund	FASMX	NAS CM	Open End	Cautious Alloc (Asset Alloc)	B-	C	A-	Up	Y	0
Fidelity Asset Manager® 60% Fund	FSANX	NAS CM	Open End	Moderate Alloc (Asset Alloc)	B-	C	B+	Up	Y	0
Fidelity Asset Manager® 70% Fund	FASGX	NAS CM	Open End	Moderate Alloc (Asset Alloc)	B-	C	B+	Up	Y	0
Fidelity Asset Manager® 85% Fund	FAMRX	NAS CM	Open End	Aggressive Alloc (Asset Alloc)	C+	C	B	Up	Y	0
Fidelity Flex Freedom 2005 Fund	FERNX	NAS CM	Open End	Target Date (Asset Alloc)	C	D+	B	Up	Y	0
Fidelity Flex Freedom 2010 Fund	FISNX	NAS CM	Open End	Target Date (Asset Alloc)	C	D+	B	Up	Y	0
Fidelity Flex Freedom 2015 Fund	FILSX	NAS CM	Open End	Target Date (Asset Alloc)	C	D+	B	Up	Y	0
Fidelity Flex Freedom 2020 Fund	FULSX	NAS CM	Open End	Target Date (Asset Alloc)	C	D+	B	Up	Y	0
Fidelity Flex Freedom 2025 Fund	FELSX	NAS CM	Open End	Target Date (Asset Alloc)	C	D+	B	Up	Y	0
Fidelity Flex Freedom 2030 Fund	FVLSX	NAS CM	Open End	Target Date (Asset Alloc)	C	D+	B	Up	Y	0
Fidelity Flex Freedom 2035 Fund	FJLSX	NAS CM	Open End	Target Date (Asset Alloc)	C	D+	B	Up	Y	0
Fidelity Flex Freedom 2040 Fund	FCLSX	NAS CM	Open End	Target Date (Asset Alloc)	C	D+	B	Up	Y	0
Fidelity Flex Freedom 2045 Fund	FOLSX	NAS CM	Open End	Target Date (Asset Alloc)	C	D+	B	Up	Y	0
Fidelity Flex Freedom 2050 Fund	FYLSX	NAS CM	Open End	Target Date (Asset Alloc)	C	D+	B	Up	Y	0
Fidelity Flex Freedom 2055 Fund	FQLSX	NAS CM	Open End	Target Date (Asset Alloc)	C	D+	B	Up	Y	0
Fidelity Flex Freedom 2060 Fund	FWLSX	NAS CM	Open End	Target Date (Asset Alloc)	C	D+	B	Up	Y	0
Fidelity Flex Freedom Income Fund	FTLSX	NAS CM	Open End	Target Date (Asset Alloc)	C	D+	B	Up	Y	0
Fidelity Freedom® 2005 Fund	FFFVX	NAS CM	Open End	Target Date (Asset Alloc)	B	C+	A-	Up	Y	0
Fidelity Freedom® 2005 Fund Class K6	FITKX	NAS CM	Open End	Target Date (Asset Alloc)	B	C+	A	Up	Y	0
Fidelity Freedom® 2010 Fund	FFFCX	NAS CM	Open End	Target Date (Asset Alloc)	B	C+	A	Up	Y	0
Fidelity Freedom® 2010 Fund Class K6	FOTKX	NAS CM	Open End	Target Date (Asset Alloc)	B	C+	A	Up	Y	0
Fidelity Freedom® 2015 Fund	FFVFX	NAS CM	Open End	Target Date (Asset Alloc)	B	C	A	Up	Y	0
Fidelity Freedom® 2015 Fund Class K6	FPTKX	NAS CM	Open End	Target Date (Asset Alloc)	B	C	A	Up	Y	0
Fidelity Freedom® 2020 Fund	FFFDX	NAS CM	Open End	Target Date (Asset Alloc)	B-	C	A-	Up	Y	0
Fidelity Freedom® 2020 Fund Class K6	FATKX	NAS CM	Open End	Target Date (Asset Alloc)	B	C	A-	Up	Y	0
Fidelity Freedom® 2025 Fund	FFTWX	NAS CM	Open End	Target Date (Asset Alloc)	B-	C	A-	Up	Y	0
Fidelity Freedom® 2025 Fund Class K6	FDTKX	NAS CM	Open End	Target Date (Asset Alloc)	B-	C	A-	Up	Y	0
Fidelity Freedom® 2030 Fund	FFFEX	NAS CM	Open End	Target Date (Asset Alloc)	B-	C	B+	Up	Y	0
Fidelity Freedom® 2030 Fund Class K6	FGTKX	NAS CM	Open End	Target Date (Asset Alloc)	B-	C	B+	Up	Y	0
Fidelity Freedom® 2035 Fund	FFTHX	NAS CM	Open End	Target Date (Asset Alloc)	B-	C	B	Up	Y	0
Fidelity Freedom® 2035 Fund Class K6	FWTKX	NAS CM	Open End	Target Date (Asset Alloc)	B-	C	B	Up	Y	0
Fidelity Freedom® 2040 Fund	FFFFX	NAS CM	Open End	Target Date (Asset Alloc)	B-	C	B	Up	Y	0
Fidelity Freedom® 2040 Fund Class K6	FHTKX	NAS CM	Open End	Target Date (Asset Alloc)	B-	C	B	Up	Y	0
Fidelity Freedom® 2045 Fund	FFFGX	NAS CM	Open End	Target Date (Asset Alloc)	B-	C	B	Up	Y	0
Fidelity Freedom® 2045 Fund Class K6	FJTKX	NAS CM	Open End	Target Date (Asset Alloc)	B-	C	B	Up	Y	0
Fidelity Freedom® 2050 Fund	FFFHX	NAS CM	Open End	Target Date (Asset Alloc)	B-	C	B	Up	Y	0
Fidelity Freedom® 2050 Fund Class K6	FZTKX	NAS CM	Open End	Target Date (Asset Alloc)	B-	C	B	Up	Y	0
Fidelity Freedom® 2055 Fund	FDEEX	NAS CM	Open End	Target Date (Asset Alloc)	B-	C	B	Up	Y	0
Fidelity Freedom® 2055 Fund Class K6	FCTKX	NAS CM	Open End	Target Date (Asset Alloc)	B-	C	B	Up	Y	0
Fidelity Freedom® 2060 Fund	FDKVX	NAS CM	Open End	Target Date (Asset Alloc)	B-	C	B	Up	Y	0
Fidelity Freedom® 2060 Fund Class K6	FVTKX	NAS CM	Open End	Target Date (Asset Alloc)	B-	C	B	Up	Y	0
Fidelity Freedom® Blend 2005 Fund	FHAZX	NAS CM	Open End	Target Date (Asset Alloc)	U	U	U		Y	0
Fidelity Freedom® Blend 2005 Fund Class K	FHGEX	NAS CM	Open End	Target Date (Asset Alloc)	U	U	U		Y	0

★ Expanded analysis of this fund is included in Section II.

Min Additional Investment	TOTAL RETURNS 3-Month Total Return	6-Month Total Return	1-Year Total Return	3-Year Total Return	5-Year Total Return	PERFORMANCE Dividend Yield (TTM)	Expense Ratio	3-Yr Std Deviation	3-Year Beta	ASSETS NAV	Total Assets (MIL)	ASSET ALLOCATION & TURNOVER %Cash	%Stocks	%Bonds	%Other	Turnover Ratio	BULL & BEAR Last Bull Market Total Return	Last Bear Market Total Return	FEES Front End Fee (%)	Back End Fee (%)	Inception Date
	3.52	22.52	1.01	30.77	27.74	0.52	1.14	14.53	1.06	32.85	870.4	2	98	0	0	72	28.89	-26.87	3.50		Aug-86
	4.03	19.26	6.81	49.75	44.33	0.05	1.23	12.36	1.02	27.05	2,580	4	96	0	0	117	19.17	-20.04	5.75		Feb-09
	3.81	18.79	5.96	46.34	38.80	0	2.01	12.34	1.02	26.1	2,580	4	96	0	0	117	18.68	-20.29		1.00	Feb-09
	3.95	19.09	6.52	48.49	42.21	0	1.52	12.37	1.02	26.82	2,580	4	96	0	0	117	19.01	-20.17	3.50		Feb-09
	4.16	19.52	7.23	51.28	46.66		0.88	12.37	1.02	27.24	2,580	4	96	0	0	117	19.45	-19.94			Oct-18
	4.12	19.42	7.10	51.08	46.31	0.32	0.96	12.35	1.02	27.24	2,580	4	96	0	0	117	19.32	-19.93			Feb-09
	2.21	6.94	4.91	13.73	17.76	2.21	0.53	3.04	0.48	13.43	5,044	29	21	49	1	24	6.57	-3.23			Oct-92
	2.53	8.65	5.04	17.53	21.70	2.1	0.54	4.19	0.46	11.15	1,679	19	32	48	1	18	8.75	-5.56			Oct-07
	2.77	10.17	4.92	21.22	24.92	1.91	0.55	5.36	0.42	11.75	1,776	13	42	43	1	17	10.77	-8.03			Oct-07
	2.95	11.63	4.67	24.66	27.54	1.71	0.65	6.55	0.5	18.23	9,299	8	52	38	1	15	12.59	-10.58			Dec-88
	3.18	13.14	4.37	28.19	30.26	1.38	0.72	7.73	0.6	12.65	3,051	3	62	33	1	18	14.49	-13.04			Oct-07
	3.31	14.47	3.95	31.95	32.74	1.36	0.71	8.98	0.71	22.15	5,301	3	72	23	1	21	16.54	-15.69			Dec-91
	3.51	16.60	3.57	37.53	36.88	1.13	0.73	10.79	0.86	19.45	2,589	4	81	12	2	24	19.23	-19.22			Sep-99
	2.69	8.40	5.75			2.4	0			10.17	0.11	20	23	56	0	23					Jun-17
	2.82	9.68	5.78			2.38	0			10.17	0.11	17	32	51	0	23					Jun-17
	2.98	10.89	5.77			2.34	0			10.17	0.11	15	40	44	0	23					Jun-17
	3.06	11.81	5.71			2.32	0			10.16	0.11	13	48	39	0	22					Jun-17
	3.26	12.86	5.65			2.27	0			10.16	0.11	11	54	34	0	22					Jun-17
	3.29	14.22	5.45			2.24	0			10.12	0.12	8	65	27	0	20					Jun-17
	3.36	15.67	4.96			2.1	0			10.09	0.12	8	79	13	0	20					Jun-17
	3.35	16.07	4.65			2.07	0			10.05	0.12	7	85	7	0	20					Jun-17
	3.34	16.05	4.66			2.07	0			10.05	0.12	7	85	7	0	20					Jun-17
	3.36	16.08	4.65			2.07	0			10.05	0.12	7	85	7	0	20					Jun-17
	3.35	16.07	4.67			2.07	0			10.05	0.12	7	85	7	0	20					Jun-17
	3.36	16.08	4.67			2.07	0			10.05	0.12	7	85	7	0	20					Jun-17
	2.58	7.41	5.84			2.48	0			10.15	0.11	23	16	61	0	23					Jun-17
	2.63	8.22	5.33	19.75	23.31	1.95	0.48	3.81	0.46	12.32	971.9	20	24	56	0	26	9.87	-8.45			Nov-03
	2.60	8.29	5.44	19.86	23.43	2.2	0.37	3.81	0.47	12.28	971.9	20	24	56	0	26	9.87	-8.45			Jun-17
	2.75	9.38	5.27	22.90	26.20	1.92	0.52	4.77	0.42	15.47	5,806	17	32	50	0	20	12.02	-10.33			Oct-96
	2.81	9.46	5.38	23.22	26.52	2.19	0.39	4.77	0.42	15.42	5,806	17	32	50	0	20	12.02	-10.33			Jun-17
	2.87	10.54	5.20	25.97	29.16	1.84	0.56	5.76	0.36	12.73	8,745	15	41	44	0	19	12.21	-10.53			Nov-03
	2.93	10.63	5.31	26.35	29.55	2.15	0.41	5.76	0.37	12.69	8,745	15	41	44	0	19	12.21	-10.53			Jun-17
	2.96	11.56	5.10	28.19	31.09	1.76	0.6	6.55	0.5	15.86	27,514	13	48	38	0	19	13.9	-12.61			Oct-96
	3.09	11.65	5.29	28.63	31.54	2.09	0.43	6.51	0.5	15.82	27,514	13	48	38	0	19	13.9	-12.61			Jun-17
	3.08	12.42	4.98	30.35	32.75	1.65	0.65	7.22	0.56	13.85	27,510	11	55	34	0	19	15.83	-14.91			Nov-03
	3.16	12.53	5.26	30.87	33.28	2.02	0.45	7.27	0.56	13.82	27,510	11	55	34	0	19	15.83	-14.91			Jun-17
	3.19	13.78	4.71	35.34	36.80	1.57	0.69	8.61	0.67	17.15	32,616	8	66	26	0	18	16.47	-15.8			Oct-96
	3.21	13.89	4.90	35.98	37.44	1.93	0.47	8.58	0.67	17.11	32,616	8	66	26	0	18	16.47	-15.8			Jun-17
	3.28	15.18	4.08	38.82	39.40	1.42	0.73	10.07	0.8	14.32	22,552	8	80	12	0	18	18.28	-18.08			Nov-03
	3.29	15.31	4.35	39.50	40.08	1.75	0.49	10.05	0.79	14.28	22,552	8	80	12	0	18	18.28	-18.08			Jun-17
	3.13	15.62	3.92	38.76	39.30	1.42	0.75	10.54	0.84	9.98	22,805	7	85	7	0	17	18.43	-18.4			Sep-00
	3.21	15.75	4.09	39.43	39.97	1.76	0.5	10.55	0.84	9.95	22,805	7	85	7	0	17	18.44	-18.4			Jun-17
	3.23	15.67	3.92	38.88	39.39	1.4	0.75	10.59	0.84	11.33	14,123	7	85	7	0	18	18.94	-18.96			Jun-06
	3.23	15.81	4.16	39.63	40.15	1.76	0.5	10.56	0.84	11.29	14,123	7	85	7	0	18	18.94	-18.96			Jun-17
	3.19	15.64	3.91	38.85	39.36	1.4	0.75	10.55	0.84	11.41	12,207	7	85	7	0	18	19.66	-19.85			Jun-06
	3.27	15.77	4.14	39.60	40.11	1.74	0.5	10.55	0.84	11.38	12,207	7	85	7	0	18	19.66	-19.85			Jun-17
	3.13	15.57	3.84	38.70	39.26	1.35	0.75	10.51	0.83	12.99	5,480	7	85	7	0	18	19.84				Jun-11
	3.22	15.79	4.17	39.44	40.01	1.69	0.5	10.57	0.84	12.97	5,480	7	85	7	0	18	19.84				Jun-17
	3.10	15.58	3.83	38.60		1.31	0.75	10.54	0.84	11.71	1,450	7	85	7	0	16					Aug-14
	3.17	15.79	4.09	39.32		1.61	0.5	10.49	0.83	11.7	1,450	7	85	7	0	16					Jun-17
	2.65	8.27					0.46			10.26	11.4	19	23	57	0	11					Aug-18
	2.76	8.40					0.36			10.28	11.4	19	23	57	0	11					Aug-18

	MARKET		FUND TYPE, CATEGORY & OBJECTIVE		RATINGS				MINIMUMS	
Fund Name	Ticker Symbol	Traded On	Fund Type	Category and (Prospectus Objective)	Overall Rating	Reward Rating	Risk Rating	Recent Up/ Downgrade	Open to New Investors	Min Initial Investment
Fidelity Freedom® Blend 2005 Fund Class K6	FHQDX	NAS CM	Open End	Target Date (Asset Alloc)	U	U	U		Y	0
Fidelity Freedom® Blend 2010 Fund	FHAYX	NAS CM	Open End	Target Date (Asset Alloc)	U	U	U		Y	0
Fidelity Freedom® Blend 2010 Fund Class K	FHFEX	NAS CM	Open End	Target Date (Asset Alloc)	U	U	U		Y	0
Fidelity Freedom® Blend 2010 Fund Class K6	FHPDX	NAS CM	Open End	Target Date (Asset Alloc)	U	U	U		Y	0
Fidelity Freedom® Blend 2015 Fund	FHAWX	NAS CM	Open End	Target Date (Asset Alloc)	U	U	U		Y	0
Fidelity Freedom® Blend 2015 Fund Class K	FHEEX	NAS CM	Open End	Target Date (Asset Alloc)	U	U	U		Y	0
Fidelity Freedom® Blend 2015 Fund Class K6	FHODX	NAS CM	Open End	Target Date (Asset Alloc)	U	U	U		Y	0
Fidelity Freedom® Blend 2020 Fund	FHAVX	NAS CM	Open End	Target Date (Asset Alloc)	U	U	U		Y	0
Fidelity Freedom® Blend 2020 Fund Class K	FHCEX	NAS CM	Open End	Target Date (Asset Alloc)	U	U	U		Y	0
Fidelity Freedom® Blend 2020 Fund Class K6	FHNDX	NAS CM	Open End	Target Date (Asset Alloc)	U	U	U		Y	0
Fidelity Freedom® Blend 2025 Fund	FHAUX	NAS CM	Open End	Target Date (Asset Alloc)	U	U	U		Y	0
Fidelity Freedom® Blend 2025 Fund Class K	FHBEX	NAS CM	Open End	Target Date (Asset Alloc)	U	U	U		Y	0
Fidelity Freedom® Blend 2025 Fund Class K6	FHLDX	NAS CM	Open End	Target Date (Asset Alloc)	U	U	U		Y	0
Fidelity Freedom® Blend 2030 Fund	FHATX	NAS CM	Open End	Target Date (Asset Alloc)	U	U	U		Y	0
Fidelity Freedom® Blend 2030 Fund Class K	FHAEX	NAS CM	Open End	Target Date (Asset Alloc)	U	U	U		Y	0
Fidelity Freedom® Blend 2030 Fund Class K6	FHKDX	NAS CM	Open End	Target Date (Asset Alloc)	U	U	U		Y	0
Fidelity Freedom® Blend 2035 Fund	FHASX	NAS CM	Open End	Target Date (Asset Alloc)	U	U	U		Y	0
Fidelity Freedom® Blend 2035 Fund Class K	FHZDX	NAS CM	Open End	Target Date (Asset Alloc)	U	U	U		Y	0
Fidelity Freedom® Blend 2035 Fund Class K6	FHJDX	NAS CM	Open End	Target Date (Asset Alloc)	U	U	U		Y	0
Fidelity Freedom® Blend 2040 Fund	FHARX	NAS CM	Open End	Target Date (Asset Alloc)	U	U	U		Y	0
Fidelity Freedom® Blend 2040 Fund Class K	FHYDX	NAS CM	Open End	Target Date (Asset Alloc)	U	U	U		Y	0
Fidelity Freedom® Blend 2040 Fund Class K6	FHHDX	NAS CM	Open End	Target Date (Asset Alloc)	U	U	U		Y	0
Fidelity Freedom® Blend 2045 Fund	FHAQX	NAS CM	Open End	Target Date (Asset Alloc)	U	U	U		Y	0
Fidelity Freedom® Blend 2045 Fund Class K	FHXDX	NAS CM	Open End	Target Date (Asset Alloc)	U	U	U		Y	0
Fidelity Freedom® Blend 2045 Fund Class K6	FHFDX	NAS CM	Open End	Target Date (Asset Alloc)	U	U	U		Y	0
Fidelity Freedom® Blend 2050 Fund	FHAPX	NAS CM	Open End	Target Date (Asset Alloc)	U	U	U		Y	0
Fidelity Freedom® Blend 2050 Fund Class K	FHWDX	NAS CM	Open End	Target Date (Asset Alloc)	U	U	U		Y	0
Fidelity Freedom® Blend 2050 Fund Class K6	FHEDX	NAS CM	Open End	Target Date (Asset Alloc)	U	U	U		Y	0
Fidelity Freedom® Blend 2055 Fund	FHAOX	NAS CM	Open End	Target Date (Asset Alloc)	U	U	U		Y	0
Fidelity Freedom® Blend 2055 Fund Class K	FHVDX	NAS CM	Open End	Target Date (Asset Alloc)	U	U	U		Y	0
Fidelity Freedom® Blend 2055 Fund Class K6	FHDDX	NAS CM	Open End	Target Date (Asset Alloc)	U	U	U		Y	0
Fidelity Freedom® Blend 2060 Fund	FHANX	NAS CM	Open End	Target Date (Asset Alloc)	U	U	U		Y	0
Fidelity Freedom® Blend 2060 Fund Class K	FHTDX	NAS CM	Open End	Target Date (Asset Alloc)	U	U	U		Y	0
Fidelity Freedom® Blend 2060 Fund Class K6	FHCDX	NAS CM	Open End	Target Date (Asset Alloc)	U	U	U		Y	0
Fidelity Freedom® Blend Income Fund	FHBZX	NAS CM	Open End	Target Date (Asset Alloc)	U	U	U		Y	0
Fidelity Freedom® Blend Income Fund Class K	FHHEX	NAS CM	Open End	Target Date (Asset Alloc)	U	U	U		Y	0
Fidelity Freedom® Blend Income Fund Class K6	FHRDX	NAS CM	Open End	Target Date (Asset Alloc)	U	U	U		Y	0
Fidelity Freedom® Income Fund	FFFAX	NAS CM	Open End	Target Date (Asset Alloc)	B	C+	A-	Up	Y	0
Fidelity Freedom® Income Fund Class K6	FYTKX	NAS CM	Open End	Target Date (Asset Alloc)	B	C+	A-	Up	Y	0
Fidelity Freedom® Index 2005 Institutional Premium Cls	FFGFX	NAS CM	Open End	Target Date (Asset Alloc)	B	C+	A		Y	100,000,000
Fidelity Freedom® Index 2005 Fund Investor Class	FJIFX	NAS CM	Open End	Target Date (Asset Alloc)	B	C+	A		Y	0
Fidelity Freedom® Index 2010 Institutional Premium Cls	FFWTX	NAS CM	Open End	Target Date (Asset Alloc)	B	C+	A		Y	100,000,000
Fidelity Freedom® Index 2010 Fund Investor Class	FKIFX	NAS CM	Open End	Target Date (Asset Alloc)	B	C+	A		Y	0
Fidelity Freedom® Index 2015 Institutional Premium Cls	FIWFX	NAS CM	Open End	Target Date (Asset Alloc)	B	C+	A	Up	Y	100,000,000
Fidelity Freedom® Index 2015 Fund Investor Class	FLIFX	NAS CM	Open End	Target Date (Asset Alloc)	B	C+	A	Up	Y	0
Fidelity Freedom® Index 2020 Institutional Premium Cls	FIWTX	NAS CM	Open End	Target Date (Asset Alloc)	B	C+	A	Up	Y	100,000,000
Fidelity Freedom® Index 2020 Fund Investor Class	FPIFX	NAS CM	Open End	Target Date (Asset Alloc)	B	C+	A	Up	Y	0
Fidelity Freedom® Index 2025 Institutional Premium Cls	FFEDX	NAS CM	Open End	Target Date (Asset Alloc)	B	C+	A-	Up	Y	100,000,000
Fidelity Freedom® Index 2025 Fund Investor Class	FQIFX	NAS CM	Open End	Target Date (Asset Alloc)	B	C+	A-	Up	Y	0
Fidelity Freedom® Index 2030 Institutional Premium Cls	FFEGX	NAS CM	Open End	Target Date (Asset Alloc)	B-	C	B+		Y	100,000,000
Fidelity Freedom® Index 2030 Fund Investor Class	FXIFX	NAS CM	Open End	Target Date (Asset Alloc)	B-	C	B+		Y	0
Fidelity Freedom® Index 2035 Institutional Premium Cls	FFEZX	NAS CM	Open End	Target Date (Asset Alloc)	B-	C	B+	Up	Y	100,000,000

★Expanded analysis of this fund is included in Section II.

	TOTAL RETURNS					PERFORMANCE				ASSETS		ASSET ALLOCATION & TURNOVER					BULL & BEAR		FEES		
Min Additional Investment	3-Month Total Return	6-Month Total Return	1-Year Total Return	3-Year Total Return	5-Year Total Return	Dividend Yield (TTM)	Expense Ratio	3-Yr Std Deviation	3-Year Beta	NAV	Total Assets (MIL)	%Cash	%Stocks	%Bonds	%Other	Turnover Ratio	Last Bull Market Total Return	Last Bear Market Total Return	Front End Fee (%)	Back End Fee (%)	Inception Date
	2.75	8.38					0.26			10.27	11.4	19	23	57	0	11					Aug-18
	2.95	9.68					0.47			10.23	42.2	16	32	51	0	98					Aug-18
	3.01	9.75					0.37			10.24	42.2	16	32	51	0	98					Aug-18
	2.98	9.83					0.27			10.24	42.2	16	32	51	0	98					Aug-18
	3.02	10.85					0.49			10.21	151.9	14	41	44	0	52					Aug-18
	3.02	10.96					0.39			10.22	151.9	14	41	44	0	52					Aug-18
	3.07	11.02					0.29			10.22	151.9	14	41	44	0	52					Aug-18
	3.32	12.14					0.51			10.25	460.1	12	49	39	0	78					Aug-18
	3.21	12.00					0.41			10.26	460.1	12	49	39	0	78					Aug-18
	3.27	12.06					0.31			10.26	460.1	12	49	39	0	78					Aug-18
	3.35	13.02					0.52			10.15	558.5	10	55	34	0	23					Aug-18
	3.35	13.01					0.42			10.16	558.5	10	55	34	0	23					Aug-18
	3.39	13.17					0.32			10.17	558.5	10	55	34	0	23					Aug-18
	3.61	14.61					0.53			10.04	533.0	7	66	26	0	29					Aug-18
	3.50	14.61					0.43			10.04	533.0	7	66	26	0	29					Aug-18
	3.64	14.76					0.33			10.05	533.0	7	66	26	0	29					Aug-18
	3.64	16.35					0.54			9.96	513.1	6	80	13	0	16					Aug-18
	3.74	16.33					0.44			9.97	513.1	6	80	13	0	16					Aug-18
	3.77	16.37					0.34			9.97	513.1	6	80	13	0	16					Aug-18
	3.66	16.74					0.55			9.9	464.3	6	86	7	0	17					Aug-18
	3.65	16.84					0.45			9.92	464.3	6	86	7	0	17					Aug-18
	3.68	16.87					0.35			9.92	464.3	6	86	7	0	17					Aug-18
	3.56	16.62					0.55			9.9	392.3	6	86	7	0	19					Aug-18
	3.67	16.73					0.45			9.91	392.3	6	86	7	0	19					Aug-18
	3.68	16.87					0.35			9.92	392.3	6	86	7	0	19					Aug-18
	3.58	16.58					0.55			9.85	281.4	6	86	7	0	12					Aug-18
	3.58	16.69					0.45			9.86	281.4	6	86	7	0	12					Aug-18
	3.70	16.84					0.35			9.87	281.4	6	86	7	0	12					Aug-18
	3.70	16.71					0.55			9.86	104.8	6	86	7	0	14					Aug-18
	3.59	16.71					0.45			9.86	104.8	6	86	7	0	14					Aug-18
	3.61	16.73					0.35			9.86	104.8	6	86	7	0	14					Aug-18
	3.47	16.54					0.55			9.86	20.0	6	86	7	0	11					Aug-18
	3.57	16.66					0.45			9.87	20.0	6	86	7	0	11					Aug-18
	3.71	16.81					0.35			9.88	20.0	6	86	7	0	11					Aug-18
	2.58	7.08					0.46			10.26	26.2	21	16	63	0	48					Aug-18
	2.50	7.16					0.36			10.26	26.2	21	16	63	0	48					Aug-18
	2.52	7.19					0.26			10.26	26.2	21	16	63	0	48					Aug-18
	2.45	7.16	5.33	15.72	19.51	2.03	0.47	2.95	0.51	11.59	3,400	23	16	61	0	22	6.35	-3.87			Oct-96
	2.49	7.14	5.40	15.90	19.70	2.18	0.37	2.96	0.52	11.57	3,400	23	16	61	0	22	6.35	-3.87			Jun-17
	2.90	8.52	6.67	18.49	21.96	2.05	0.08	3.62	0.44	13.82	141.1	13	8	18	61	52	8.59	-6.91			Jun-15
	2.88	8.51	6.60	18.32	21.70	1.99	0.12	3.59	0.44	13.82	141.1	13	8	18	61	52	8.59	-6.91			Oct-09
	3.08	9.83	6.91	21.91	25.29	2.1	0.08	4.55	0.39	14.53	605.6	10	10	15	64	45	10.69	-8.56			Jun-15
	3.08	9.82	6.86	21.72	25.00	2.06	0.12	4.57	0.4	14.53	605.6	10	10	15	64	45	10.69	-8.56			Oct-09
	3.29	11.18	7.06	25.42	28.59	2.08	0.08	5.56	0.34	15.5	1,404	8	13	13	67	36	10.94	-8.79			Jun-15
	3.21	11.09	7.00	25.11	28.19	2.03	0.12	5.57	0.33	15.5	1,404	8	13	13	67	36	10.94	-8.79			Oct-09
	3.38	12.22	7.21	27.79	30.76	2.05	0.08	6.36	0.5	16.49	4,742	5	15	11	69	26	12.38	-10.57			Jun-15
	3.43	12.27	7.15	27.57	30.53	2	0.12	6.38	0.5	16.5	4,742	5	15	11	69	26	12.38	-10.57			Oct-09
	3.54	13.23	7.30	30.14	32.87	1.99	0.08	7.08	0.56	17.59	5,167	3	17	9	71	19	14.27	-12.7			Jun-15
	3.52	13.22	7.24	29.94	32.58	1.94	0.12	7.09	0.56	17.59	5,167	3	17	9	71	19	14.27	-12.7			Oct-09
	3.66	14.75	7.33	35.66	37.28	2.01	0.08	8.43	0.67	18.6	6,278	0	20	5	74	14	14.8	-13.49			Jun-15
	3.71	14.74	7.34	35.46	36.98	1.96	0.12	8.43	0.67	18.6	6,278	0	20	5	74	14	14.8	-13.49			Oct-09
	3.76	16.38	7.06	39.89	40.73	1.93	0.08	9.97	0.8	19.74	4,405	0	25	3	72	10	16.63	-15.72			Jun-15

Fund Name	MARKET Ticker Symbol	Traded On	FUND TYPE, CATEGORY & OBJECTIVE Fund Type	Category and (Prospectus Objective)	RATINGS Overall Rating	Reward Rating	Risk Rating	Recent Up/ Downgrade	MINIMUMS Open to New Investors	Min Initial Investment
Fidelity Freedom® Index 2035 Fund Investor Class	FIHFX	NAS CM	Open End	Target Date (Asset Alloc)	B-	C	B+	Up	Y	0
Fidelity Freedom® Index 2040 Institutional Premium Cls	FFIZX	NAS CM	Open End	Target Date (Asset Alloc)	B-	C	B	Up	Y	100,000,000
Fidelity Freedom® Index 2040 Fund Investor Class	FBIFX	NAS CM	Open End	Target Date (Asset Alloc)	B-	C	B	Up	Y	0
Fidelity Freedom® Index 2045 Institutional Premium Cls	FFOLX	NAS CM	Open End	Target Date (Asset Alloc)	B-	C	B	Up	Y	100,000,000
Fidelity Freedom® Index 2045 Fund Investor Class	FIOFX	NAS CM	Open End	Target Date (Asset Alloc)	B-	C	B	Up	Y	0
Fidelity Freedom® Index 2050 Institutional Premium Cls	FFOPX	NAS CM	Open End	Target Date (Asset Alloc)	B-	C	B	Up	Y	100,000,000
Fidelity Freedom® Index 2050 Fund Investor Class	FIPFX	NAS CM	Open End	Target Date (Asset Alloc)	B-	C	B	Up	Y	0
Fidelity Freedom® Index 2055 Institutional Premium Cls	FFLDX	NAS CM	Open End	Target Date (Asset Alloc)	B-	C	B	Up	Y	100,000,000
Fidelity Freedom® Index 2055 Fund Investor Class	FDEWX	NAS CM	Open End	Target Date (Asset Alloc)	B-	C	B	Up	Y	0
Fidelity Freedom® Index 2060 Institutional Premium Cls	FFLEX	NAS CM	Open End	Target Date (Asset Alloc)	B-	C	B	Up	Y	100,000,000
Fidelity Freedom® Index 2060 Fund Investor Class	FDKLX	NAS CM	Open End	Target Date (Asset Alloc)	B-	C	B	Up	Y	0
Fidelity Freedom® Index Income Institutional Premium Cls	FFGZX	NAS CM	Open End	Target Date (Asset Alloc)	B	C+	A-		Y	100,000,000
Fidelity Freedom® Index Income Fund Investor Class	FIKFX	NAS CM	Open End	Target Date (Asset Alloc)	B	C+	A-		Y	0
Fidelity Managed Retirement 2005 Fund	FIROX	NAS CM	Open End	Target Date (Asset Alloc)	B	C+	A		Y	2,500
Fidelity Managed Retirement 2010 Fund	FIRQX	NAS CM	Open End	Target Date (Asset Alloc)	B	C+	A	Up	Y	2,500
Fidelity Managed Retirement 2015 Fund	FIRSX	NAS CM	Open End	Target Date (Asset Alloc)	B	C+	A	Up	Y	2,500
Fidelity Managed Retirement 2020 Fund	FIRVX	NAS CM	Open End	Target Date (Asset Alloc)	B	C	A	Up	Y	2,500
Fidelity Managed Retirement 2025 Fund	FIXRX	NAS CM	Open End	Target Date (Asset Alloc)	B	C	A	Up	Y	2,500
Fidelity Managed Retirement Income Fund	FIRMX	NAS CM	Open End	Target Date (Asset Alloc)	B	C+	A-	Up	Y	2,500
Fidelity SAI Inflation-Focused Fund	FIFGX	NAS CM	Open End	Commodities Broad Basket (Income)	U	U	U		Y	0
Fidelity Select Advisor® Gold Fund Class A	FGDAX	NAS CM	Open End	Precious Metals Sector Equity (Precious Metals)	D+	D	C-	Down	Y	0
Fidelity Select Advisor® Gold Fund Class C	FGDCX	NAS CM	Open End	Precious Metals Sector Equity (Precious Metals)	D	D	C-	Down	Y	0
Fidelity Select Advisor® Gold Fund Class I	FGDIX	NAS CM	Open End	Precious Metals Sector Equity (Precious Metals)	D+	D	C-	Down	Y	0
Fidelity Select Advisor® Gold Fund Class M	FGDTX	NAS CM	Open End	Precious Metals Sector Equity (Precious Metals)	D+	D	C-	Down	Y	0
Fidelity Select Advisor® Gold Fund Class Z	FIJDX	NAS CM	Open End	Precious Metals Sector Equity (Precious Metals)	D+	D	C-	Down	Y	0
Fidelity Simplicity RMD 2005 Fund	FIRPX	NAS CM	Open End	Target Date (Asset Alloc)	B	C+	A		Y	0
Fidelity Simplicity RMD 2010 Fund	FIRRX	NAS CM	Open End	Target Date (Asset Alloc)	B	C+	A	Up	Y	0
Fidelity Simplicity RMD 2015 Fund	FIRUX	NAS CM	Open End	Target Date (Asset Alloc)	B	C+	A	Up	Y	0
Fidelity Simplicity RMD 2020 Fund	FIRWX	NAS CM	Open End	Target Date (Asset Alloc)	B	C	A	Up	Y	0
Fidelity Simplicity RMD Income Fund	FIRNX	NAS CM	Open End	Target Date (Asset Alloc)	B	C+	A-		Y	0
Fidelity ZERO Extended Market Index Fund	FZIPX	NAS CM	Open End	US Equity Mid Cap (Growth & Income)	U	U	U		Y	0
Fidelity ZERO International Index Fund	FZILX	NAS CM	Open End	Global Equity Large Cap (Foreign Stock)	U	U	U		Y	0
Fidelity ZERO Large Cap Index Fund	FNILX	NAS CM	Open End	US Equity Large Cap Blend (Growth & Income)	U	U	U		Y	0
Fidelity ZERO Total Market Index Fund	FZROX	NAS CM	Open End	US Equity Large Cap Blend (Growth & Income)	U	U	U		Y	0
Fidelity® 500 Index Fund	FXAIX	NAS CM	Open End	US Equity Large Cap Blend (Growth & Income)	B-	C	B		Y	0
Fidelity® Balanced Fund	FBALX	NAS CM	Open End	Moderate Alloc (Balanced)	B-	C	B+		Y	0
Fidelity® Balanced Fund Class K	FBAKX	NAS CM	Open End	Moderate Alloc (Balanced)	B-	C+	B+		Y	0
Fidelity® Blue Chip Growth Fund	FBGRX	NAS CM	Open End	US Equity Large Cap Growth (Growth)	C+	C+	B	Down	Y	0
Fidelity® Blue Chip Growth Fund Class K	FBGKX	NAS CM	Open End	US Equity Large Cap Growth (Growth)	C+	C+	B	Down	Y	0
Fidelity® Blue Chip Growth K6 Fund	FBCGX	NAS CM	Open End	US Equity Large Cap Growth (Growth)	C	C-	C+	Up	Y	0
Fidelity® Blue Chip Value Fund	FBCVX	NAS CM	Open End	US Equity Large Cap Value (Growth)	C+	C	B		Y	0
Fidelity® Canada Fund	FICDX	NAS CM	Open End	Equity Miscellaneous (Foreign Stock)	C+	C	B		Y	0
Fidelity® Capital Appreciation Fund	FDCAX	NAS CM	Open End	US Equity Large Cap Growth (Aggr Growth)	C+	C	B		Y	0
Fidelity® Capital Appreciation Fund Class K	FCAKX	NAS CM	Open End	US Equity Large Cap Growth (Aggr Growth)	C+	C	B		Y	0
Fidelity® China Region Fund	FHKCX	NAS CM	Open End	Greater China Equity (Pacific Stock)	C	C-	C		Y	0
Fidelity® Commodity Strategy Fund	FYHTX	NAS CM	Open End	Commodities Broad Basket (Growth & Income)	D+	D	C-	Up	Y	0
★ Fidelity® Contrafund® Fund	FCNTX	NAS CM	Open End	US Equity Large Cap Growth (Growth)	C+	C	B	Down	Y	0
★ Fidelity® Contrafund® Fund Class K	FCNKX	NAS CM	Open End	US Equity Large Cap Growth (Growth)	C+	C	B	Down	Y	0
Fidelity® Contrafund® K6	FLCNX	NAS CM	Open End	US Equity Large Cap Growth (World Stock)	C	C-	C+	Up	Y	0
Fidelity® Convertible Securities Fund	FCVSX	NAS CM	Open End	Convertibles (Convertible Bond)	B	C	A-		Y	0
Fidelity® Disciplined Equity Fund	FDEQX	NAS CM	Open End	US Equity Large Cap Blend (Growth)	C+	C	B	Up	Y	0
Fidelity® Disciplined Equity Fund Class K	FDEKX	NAS CM	Open End	US Equity Large Cap Blend (Growth)	C+	C	B	Up	Y	0

★ Expanded analysis of this fund is included in Section II.

	TOTAL RETURNS					PERFORMANCE				ASSETS		ASSET ALLOCATION & TURNOVER					BULL & BEAR		FEES		
Min Additional Investment	3-Month Total Return	6-Month Total Return	1-Year Total Return	3-Year Total Return	5-Year Total Return	Dividend Yield (TTM)	Expense Ratio	3-Yr Std Deviation	3-Year Beta	NAV	Total Assets (MIL)	%Cash	%Stocks	%Bonds	%Other	Turnover Ratio	Last Bull Market Total Return	Last Bear Market Total Return	Front End Fee (%)	Back End Fee (%)	Inception Date
	3.79	16.43	7.06	39.67	40.43	1.88	0.12	9.97	0.8	19.74	4,405	0	25	3	72	10	16.63	-15.72			Oct-09
	3.81	16.98	6.99	40.15	40.84	1.93	0.08	10.42	0.84	19.88	4,515	0	26	3	70	10	16.69	-15.89			Jun-15
	3.80	16.97	6.88	39.84	40.53	1.88	0.12	10.43	0.84	19.88	4,515	0	26	3	70	10	16.69	-15.89			Oct-09
	3.84	16.98	7.01	40.10	40.86	1.92	0.08	10.42	0.84	20.03	2,954	0	26	3	70	10	16.99	-16.31			Jun-15
	3.78	16.97	6.89	39.90	40.56	1.87	0.12	10.42	0.84	20.02	2,954	0	26	3	70	10	16.99	-16.31			Oct-09
	3.81	16.95	6.98	40.11	40.99	1.92	0.08	10.43	0.84	20.11	2,652	0	26	3	70	12	17.57	-17.18			Jun-15
	3.80	16.94	6.87	39.82	40.60	1.88	0.12	10.45	0.84	20.11	2,652	0	26	3	70	12	17.57	-17.18			Oct-09
	3.81	16.93	6.97	40.12	40.77	1.89	0.08	10.41	0.84	15.89	1,167	0	26	3	70	11	17.86				Jun-15
	3.80	16.92	6.92	39.88	40.58	1.85	0.12	10.42	0.84	15.88	1,167	0	26	3	70	11	17.86				Jun-11
	3.83	17.04	6.97	40.11		1.83	0.08	10.44	0.84	12.95	362.1	0	26	3	70	15					Jun-15
	3.83	16.93	6.93	39.86		1.8	0.12	10.44	0.84	12.94	362.1	0	26	3	70	15					Aug-14
	2.68	7.30	6.44	14.45	17.98	2.2	0.08	2.75	0.48	12.21	395.4	16	5	20	59	51	5.06	-2.57			Jun-15
	2.66	7.35	6.44	14.32	17.78	2.12	0.12	2.78	0.49	12.23	395.4	16	5	20	59	51	5.06	-2.57			Oct-09
	2.54	7.40	5.37	19.17	22.64	2	0.45	3.28	0.41	58.65	5.4	21	17	62	0	24	12.69	-10.51			Aug-07
	2.69	8.52	5.36	22.08	25.35	1.94	0.46	4.1	0.36	56.38	9.3	18	25	56	0	21	13.56	-11.45			Aug-07
	2.80	9.55	5.31	24.19	27.24	1.85	0.47	4.89	0.33	53.11	4.5	16	32	51	0	20	14.16	-12.22			Aug-07
	2.95	10.60	5.29	25.97	28.79	1.78	0.47	5.66	0.29	51.34	4.6	14	40	45	0	19	14.92	-13.13			Dec-07
	3.04	11.34	5.24	27.33	29.92	1.71	0.48	6.22	0.48	52.91	20.7	13	45	42	0	19	15.83	-14.05			Dec-07
	2.51	7.18	5.41	15.36	19.01	2.03	0.45	2.88	0.43	57.74	6.4	21	16	63	0	19	11.36	-9.07			Aug-07
	-1.32	5.78					0.5			10.42	1,222	7	0	78	15						Dec-18
	12.88	21.84	13.18	-12.21	-3.82	0	1.19	24.17	-0.06	21.03	1,440	3	96	0	1	37	-15.15	-13.71	5.75		Dec-06
	12.75	21.51	12.49	-13.90	-7.07	0	1.84	24.16	-0.06	19.54	1,440	3	96	0	1	37	-15.51	-13.97		1.00	Dec-06
	13.03	22.07	13.62	-11.29	-2.23	0	0.84	24.18	-0.05	21.68	1,440	3	96	0	1	37	-14.99	-13.58			Dec-06
	12.85	21.74	12.91	-12.93	-5.17	0	1.48	24.18	-0.06	20.55	1,440	3	96	0	1	37	-15.3	-13.82	3.50		Dec-06
	13.07	22.18	13.73	-11.24	-2.23		0.68	24.17	-0.05	21.7	1,440	3	96	0	1	37	-15.04	-13.6			Oct-18
	2.48	7.35	5.30	20.22	23.56	2.03	0.48	3.36	0.39	58.2	17.9	22	17	60	0	32	13.15	-11.01			Aug-07
	2.63	8.52	5.28	22.72	25.91	1.9	0.53	4.2	0.35	53.51	10.6	20	25	55	0	44	13.84	-11.8			Aug-07
	2.76	9.66	5.19	24.82	27.73	1.83	0.57	5.08	0.3	59.38	20.9	17	34	48	0	44	14.46	-12.64			Aug-07
	2.87	10.82	5.09	26.75	29.43	1.74	0.61	6.01	0.26	59.85	42.6	15	43	42	0	29	15.46	-13.69			Dec-07
	2.47	7.12	5.36	17.23	20.79	2	0.47	3	0.42	58.51	19.7	23	16	61	0	46	12.18	-9.89			Aug-07
	2.34	19.02					0			9.59	394.5	0	100	0	0	0					Sep-18
	3.00	13.72					0			9.94	1,077	6	94	0	0	0					Aug-18
	4.38	19.62					0			10.24	797.2	1	99	0	0	1					Sep-18
	4.09	19.63					0			10.42	3,477	0	100	0	0	0					Aug-18
	4.29	19.55	10.40	50.84	66.20	1.8	0.02	12.2	1	102.66	198,287	0	100	0	0	4	25.1	-16.26			May-11
	3.69	15.41	6.61	35.28	43.39	1.56	0.53	8.92	0.72	23.6	33,544	3	66	31	0	66	15.77	-10.4			Nov-86
	3.66	15.43	6.71	35.64	44.04	1.64	0.45	8.92	0.72	23.6	33,544	3	66	31	0	66	15.82	-10.32			May-08
	3.28	21.34	8.02	79.08	91.28	0.1	0.72	14.54	1.05	101.01	27,915	0	95	0	0	41	26.11	-17.2			Dec-87
	3.30	21.40	8.14	79.65	92.33	0.18	0.62	14.54	1.05	101.19	27,915	0	95	0	0	41	26.2	-17.11			May-08
	3.39	22.13	6.44			0.38	0.45			13.41	2,236	0	98	0	1	40					May-17
	1.99	11.12	2.70	31.11	34.87	1.46	0.7	11.35	0.88	19.38	473.8	2	98	0	0	45	20.64	-23.89			Jun-03
	5.82	20.89	6.04	25.13	6.19	1.05	0.89	11.81	0.89	52.53	1,034	1	99	0	0	29	12.86	-23.78			Nov-87
	5.19	20.61	5.33	53.28	57.02	0.69	0.54	13.02	1.01	35.45	6,278	1	99	0	0	101	27.89	-16.97			Nov-86
	5.21	20.64	5.41	53.68	57.81	0.78	0.45	13.02	1.01	35.53	6,278	1	99	0	0	101	28.02	-16.91			May-08
	-1.39	17.71	-2.06	53.21	39.96	0.71	0.96	18.17	1.08	34.56	1,218	1	99	0	0	60	17.74	-27.07			Nov-95
	-1.47	3.44	-7.60			2.19	0.6			8.71	524.1	51	0	0	49	0					May-17
	5.43	21.87	7.91	64.96	80.53	0	0.82	13.74	1.04	13.18	121,774	2	97	0	0	32	24.33	-14.42			May-67
	5.51	21.97	8.01	65.44	81.41	0	0.73	13.75	1.04	13.19	121,774	2	97	0	0	32	24.41	-14.38			May-08
	5.50	22.22	8.13			0.28	0.45			13.42	8,753	3	97	0	0	54					May-17
	5.86	18.76	11.25	35.86	25.41	2.69	0.46	8.53	0.95	29.55	1,533	6	11	0	0	176	16.06	-19.75			Jan-87
	5.57	20.88	7.64	40.86	47.25	1.31	0.53	12.31	1	36.53	1,280	1	99	0	0	181	24.88	-21.87			Dec-88
	5.61	20.96	7.71	41.23	47.95	1.4	0.43	12.3	1	36.47	1,280	1	99	0	0	181	25.04	-21.86			May-08

	MARKET		FUND TYPE, CATEGORY & OBJECTIVE		RATINGS				MINIMUMS	
Fund Name	Ticker Symbol	Traded On	Fund Type	Category and (Prospectus Objective)	Overall Rating	Reward Rating	Risk Rating	Recent Up/ Downgrade	Open to New Investors	Min Initial Investment
Fidelity® Diversified International Fund	FDIVX	NAS CM	Open End	Global Equity Large Cap (Foreign Stock)	C	C	B-		Y	0
Fidelity® Diversified International Fund Class K	FDIKX	NAS CM	Open End	Global Equity Large Cap (Foreign Stock)	C	C	B-		Y	0
Fidelity® Diversified International K6 Fund	FKIDX	NAS CM	Open End	Global Equity Large Cap (Foreign Stock)	C-	D	C+	Up	Y	0
Fidelity® Dividend Growth Fund	FDGFX	NAS CM	Open End	US Equity Large Cap Blend (Equity-Income)	B-	C	B		Y	0
Fidelity® Dividend Growth Fund Class K	FDGKX	NAS CM	Open End	US Equity Large Cap Blend (Equity-Income)	B-	C	B		Y	0
Fidelity® Emerging Asia Fund	FSEAX	NAS CM	Open End	Asia ex-Japan Equity (Pacific Stock)	C	C	C+		Y	0
Fidelity® Emerging Europe, Middle East, Africa (EMEA) Fund	FEMEX	NAS CM	Open End	Global Emerg Mkts (Foreign Stock)	C+	C	B-	Up	Y	0
Fidelity® Emerging Markets Discovery Fund	FEDDX	NAS CM	Open End	Global Emerg Mkts (Div Emerging Mkts)	C	C	C		Y	0
Fidelity® Emerging Markets Fund	FEMKX	NAS CM	Open End	Global Emerg Mkts (Div Emerging Mkts)	C	C	C+		Y	0
Fidelity® Emerging Markets Fund Class K	FKEMX	NAS CM	Open End	Global Emerg Mkts (Div Emerging Mkts)	C	C	C+		Y	0
Fidelity® Emerging Markets Index Fund	FPADX	NAS CM	Open End	Global Emerg Mkts (Div Emerging Mkts)	C	C	C+		Y	0
Fidelity® Equity Dividend Income Fund	FEQTX	NAS CM	Open End	US Equity Large Cap Value (Equity-Income)	C+	C	B		Y	0
Fidelity® Equity Dividend Income Fund Class K	FETKX	NAS CM	Open End	US Equity Large Cap Value (Equity-Income)	C+	C	B		Y	0
Fidelity® Equity-Income Fund	FEQIX	NAS CM	Open End	US Equity Large Cap Value (Equity-Income)	B-	C	B		Y	0
Fidelity® Equity-Income Fund Class K	FEIKX	NAS CM	Open End	US Equity Large Cap Value (Equity-Income)	B-	C	B		Y	0
Fidelity® Europe Fund	FIEUX	NAS CM	Open End	Europe Equity Large Cap (Europe Stock)	C	C	C+		Y	0
Fidelity® Event Driven Opportunities Fund	FARNX	NAS CM	Open End	US Equity Small Cap (Growth)	D+	D	D+		Y	0
Fidelity® Export and Multinational Fund	FEXPX	NAS CM	Open End	US Equity Large Cap Blend (Growth)	B-	C	B		Y	0
Fidelity® Export and Multinational Fund Class K	FEXKX	NAS CM	Open End	US Equity Large Cap Blend (Growth)	B-	C	B		Y	0
Fidelity® Extended Market Index Fund	FSMAX	NAS CM	Open End	US Equity Mid Cap (Growth & Income)	C+	C	B-		Y	0
Fidelity® Flex 500 Index Fund	FDFIX	NAS CM	Open End	US Equity Large Cap Blend (Growth & Income)	C	C	B		Y	0
Fidelity® Flex International Fund	FULTX	NAS CM	Open End	Global Equity Large Cap (Foreign Stock)	C	C-	B	Up	Y	0
Fidelity® Flex International Index Fund	FITFX	NAS CM	Open End	Global Equity Large Cap (Foreign Stock)	C	D+	B-	Up	Y	0
Fidelity® Flex Intrinsic Opportunities Fund	FFNPX	NAS CM	Open End	US Equity Large Cap Blend (Growth)	C-	D+	C		Y	0
Fidelity® Flex Large Cap Growth Fund	FLCLX	NAS CM	Open End	US Equity Large Cap Growth (Growth)	C	C	B-		Y	0
Fidelity® Flex Large Cap Value Fund	FVCLX	NAS CM	Open End	US Equity Large Cap Value (Growth)	C	C	B-		Y	0
Fidelity® Flex Mid Cap Growth Fund	FFMGX	NAS CM	Open End	US Equity Mid Cap (Growth)	C	C	B		Y	0
Fidelity® Flex Mid Cap Index Fund	FLAPX	NAS CM	Open End	US Equity Mid Cap (Growth & Income)	C	C	B-		Y	0
Fidelity® Flex Mid Cap Value Fund	FFMVX	NAS CM	Open End	US Equity Mid Cap (Growth)	C	C	B-	Up	Y	0
Fidelity® Flex Opportunistic Insights Fund	FFPIX	NAS CM	Open End	US Equity Large Cap Blend (Growth)	C	C	B		Y	0
Fidelity® Flex Real Estate Fund	FFERX	NAS CM	Open End	Real Estate Sector Equity (Real Estate)	C	C	B-		Y	0
Fidelity® Flex Small Cap Fund	FCUTX	NAS CM	Open End	US Equity Small Cap (Small Company)	C	C	B-	Up	Y	0
Fidelity® Flex Small Cap Index Fund	FLXSX	NAS CM	Open End	US Equity Small Cap (Small Company)	C	C-	C+	Up	Y	0
Fidelity® Focused Stock Fund	FTQGX	NAS CM	Open End	US Equity Large Cap Growth (Growth)	B-	C+	B	Down	Y	0
Fidelity® Founders Fund	FIFNX	NAS CM	Open End	US Equity Large Cap Blend (Growth)	U	U	U		Y	0
Fidelity® Four-in-One Index Fund	FFNOX	NAS CM	Open End	Aggressive Alloc (Asset Alloc)	B-	C	B+	Up	Y	0
Fidelity® Fund	FFIDX	NAS CM	Open End	US Equity Large Cap Growth (Growth)	C+	C	B		Y	0
Fidelity® Fund Class K	FFDKX	NAS CM	Open End	US Equity Large Cap Growth (Growth)	C+	C	B		Y	0
Fidelity® Global Commodity Stock Fund	FFGCX	NAS CM	Open End	Natl Resources Sec Equity (Growth)	C	C	C		Y	0
Fidelity® Global Equity Income Fund	FGILX	NAS CM	Open End	Global Equity Large Cap (Equity-Income)	B-	C	B	Up	Y	0
Fidelity® Global ex U.S. Index Fund	FSGGX	NAS CM	Open End	Global Equity Large Cap (Foreign Stock)	C	C	B		Y	0
Fidelity® Growth & Income Portfolio	FGRIX	NAS CM	Open End	US Equity Large Cap Blend (Growth & Income)	C+	C	B		Y	0
Fidelity® Growth & Income Portfolio Class K	FGIKX	NAS CM	Open End	US Equity Large Cap Blend (Growth & Income)	C+	C	B		Y	0
Fidelity® Growth Company	FDGRX	NAS CM	Open End	US Equity Large Cap Growth (Growth)	C+	C+	C+			2,500
Fidelity® Growth Company Fund Class K	FGCKX	NAS CM	Open End	US Equity Large Cap Growth (Growth)	C+	C+	C+			0
Fidelity® Growth Discovery Fund	FDSVX	NAS CM	Open End	US Equity Large Cap Growth (Growth)	B-	C+	B	Down	Y	0
Fidelity® Growth Discovery Fund Class K	FGDKX	NAS CM	Open End	US Equity Large Cap Growth (Growth)	B-	C+	B	Down	Y	0
Fidelity® Growth Strategies Fund	FDEGX	NAS CM	Open End	US Equity Mid Cap (Aggr Growth)	C+	C	B	Down	Y	0
Fidelity® Growth Strategies Fund Class K	FAGKX	NAS CM	Open End	US Equity Mid Cap (Aggr Growth)	C+	C	B	Down	Y	0
Fidelity® Growth Strategies K6 Fund	FSKGX	NAS CM	Open End	US Equity Mid Cap (World Stock)	C	C-	B-	Up	Y	0
Fidelity® Independence Fund	FDFFX	NAS CM	Open End	US Equity Large Cap Growth (Growth)	C+	C	B-		Y	0
Fidelity® Independence Fund Class K	FDFKX	NAS CM	Open End	US Equity Large Cap Growth (Growth)	C+	C	B-		Y	0

★ Expanded analysis of this fund is included in Section II.

	TOTAL RETURNS					PERFORMANCE				ASSETS		ASSET ALLOCATION & TURNOVER					BULL & BEAR		FEES		
Min Additional Investment	3-Month Total Return	6-Month Total Return	1-Year Total Return	3-Year Total Return	5-Year Total Return	Dividend Yield (TTM)	Expense Ratio	3-Yr Std Deviation	3-Year Beta	NAV	Total Assets (MIL)	%Cash	%Stocks	%Bonds	%Other	Turnover Ratio	Last Bull Market Total Return	Last Bear Market Total Return	Front End Fee (%)	Back End Fee (%)	Inception Date
	5.82	18.28	2.49	29.65	18.21	1.09	0.81	11.77	1.02	37.26	13,571	3	97	0	0	30	16.78	-24.53			Dec-91
	5.89	18.39	2.63	30.17	19.00	1.21	0.69	11.77	1.02	37.2	13,571	3	97	0	0	30	16.84	-24.48			May-08
	5.84	18.27	2.49			1.17	0.6			10.68	2,848	3	97	0	0	48					May-17
	3.67	16.62	9.03	40.01	45.47	1.74	0.5	12.33	0.97	29.32	6,902	1	99	0	0	115	27.42	-24.6			Apr-93
	3.75	16.68	9.15	40.47	46.33	1.83	0.4	12.33	0.97	29.3	6,902	1	99	0	0	115	27.51	-24.51			May-08
	2.11	18.87	5.55	51.74	44.49	0.87	1.02	14.81	0.97	43.84	1,080	4	96	0	0	36	18.63	-25.38			Apr-93
	8.67	16.13	8.39	42.94	16.42	2.1	1.34	14.54	0.9	10.15	110.1	3	97	0	0	39	19.87	-26.67			May-08
	1.25	12.85	-2.79	30.55	14.90	1.62	1.22	13.34	1	13.7	325.7	4	96	0	0	98					Nov-11
	4.48	21.12	5.88	43.91	29.95	0.67	0.96	14.44	0.99	32.17	4,733	3	97	0	0	86	16.52	-28.26			Nov-90
	4.51	21.19	6.02	44.53	30.99	0.82	0.82	14.44	0.99	32.19	4,733	3	97	0	0	86	16.68	-28.19			May-08
	0.85	10.92	1.42	36.25	14.93	1.99	0.08	14.09	1.01	10.56	2,671	1	99	0	0	4	15.83				Sep-11
	3.10	15.94	5.76	31.14	39.15	2.3	0.62	11.8	0.94	25.1	4,983	3	97	0	0	56	25.87	-22.33			Aug-90
	3.16	16.06	5.91	31.54	39.91	2.39	0.52	11.81	0.94	25.11	4,983	3	97	0	0	56	26.02	-22.3			May-08
	3.72	17.20	9.26	36.82	37.93	2.21	0.61	11.63	0.92	58.36	6,371	6	94	0	0	24	23.58	-22.28			May-66
	3.75	17.27	9.37	37.25	38.69	2.3	0.51	11.63	0.92	58.33	6,371	6	94	0	0	24	23.7	-22.23			May-08
	4.87	17.14	0.52	27.96	10.00	0.8	0.96	13.65	1.05	36.55	954.6	1	98	0	1	57	17.99	-29.33			Oct-86
	-1.90	4.63	-19.90	18.91	19.96	0.61	1.05	15.38	0.98	10.84	160.7	1	99	0	0	95					Dec-13
	3.52	16.01	8.59	38.82	50.99	1.41	0.74	12.55	0.99	20.86	1,680	1	99	0	0	99	22.88	-18.47			Oct-94
	3.53	16.06	8.69	39.30	51.89	1.52	0.63	12.51	0.98	20.81	1,680	1	99	0	0	99	22.96	-18.39			May-08
	3.02	20.58	2.02	47.27	46.38	1.41	0.05	15.22	1	62.47	24,011	0	100	0	0	13	28.68	-23.57			Sep-11
	4.32	19.52	10.42			1.71	0			12.58	663.1	1	99	0	0	8					Mar-17
	5.22	18.78	4.33			2.31	0			12.08	42.9	3	97	0	0	69					Mar-17
	2.97	13.98	1.35			1.69	0			11.41	346.3	6	94	0	0	4					Mar-17
	-0.97	6.05	-3.56			2.48	0			11.21	17.1	2	98	0	0	6					Mar-17
	3.87	22.54	7.75			0.72	0			14.46	25.3	2	96	0	1	65					Mar-17
	4.95	17.29	8.09			2.39	0				25.1	3	97	0	0	130					Mar-17
	8.07	26.55	12.14			0.63	0			13.25	10.1	6	94	0	0	88					Mar-17
	4.11	22.50	7.88			1.66	0			12.24	80.5	0	100	0	0	25					Mar-17
	3.80	23.47	1.82			1.98	0			10.36	4.2	2	98	0	0	218					Mar-17
	5.71	23.14	8.68			1.03	0			14.42	17.9	4	95	0	0	93					Mar-17
	2.03	18.58	11.94			2.89	0			11.18	1.5	1	99	0	0	91					Mar-17
	4.59	22.94	3.62			1.01	0			11.84	12.5	4	96	0	0	163					Mar-17
	2.10	17.83	-3.28			1.33	0			11.5	76.1	1	99	0	0	23					Mar-17
	4.39	21.74	14.00	70.45	73.49	0.1	0.82	13.9	1.02	25.19	2,876	4	96	0	0	138	24.8	-17.3			Nov-96
	4.39						1			10.93	23.1	2	98	0	0	4					Feb-19
	3.86	16.39	6.87	38.37	40.91	1.95	0.11	9.87		46.42	6,296	1	83	16	0	12	18.88	-16.03			Jun-99
	4.86	19.38	8.27	47.19	59.36	0.87	0.5	12.23	0.98	47.6	4,349	1	99	0	0	38	22.11	-18.42			Apr-30
	4.89	19.44	8.37	47.63	60.21	0.95	0.41	12.22	0.98	47.6	4,349	1	99	0	0	38	22.21	-18.36			May-08
	1.36	13.50	-5.70	31.43	-9.01	1.83	1.08	14.68	1.04	12.61	547.7	1	99	0	0	70	14.28	-29.62			Mar-09
	3.40	16.72	5.75	32.21	33.59	1.88	1.06	10.2	0.88	14.08	69.2	5	95	0	0	34					May-12
	3.03	14.05	1.43	31.99	11.69	2.34	0.06	11.37	0.99	12.9	5,969	8	92	0	0	19	14.5				Sep-11
	2.92	16.88	5.44	43.30	45.62	2.1	0.61	13.12	1.04	38.64	6,402	5	95	0	0	38	26.97	-16.93			Dec-85
	2.94	16.96	5.52	43.77	46.44	2.2	0.51	13.13	1.04	38.61	6,402	5	95	0	0	38	27.08	-16.85			May-08
	2.34	23.42	4.94	79.62	96.49	0	0.85	16.29	1.17	19.6	44,105	0	98	0	0	18	29.31	-16.92			Jan-83
	2.34	23.47	5.02	80.10	97.44	0	0.76	16.3	1.17	19.62	44,105	0	98	0	0	18	29.41	-16.87			May-08
	4.42	22.57	10.33	71.41	80.51	0.16	0.74	13.56	0.98	37.74	2,073	1	98	0	0	45	27.37	-17.56			Mar-98
	4.48	22.62	10.46	71.98	81.59	0.25	0.63	13.56	0.98	37.78	2,073	1	98	0	0	45	27.5	-17.53			May-08
	7.65	26.38	12.02	47.17	61.38	0.6	0.59	12.55	0.84	47.56	2,818	1	99	0	0	43	21.89	-23.67			Dec-90
	7.68	26.47	12.17	47.78	62.57	0.72	0.46	12.55	0.84	47.91	2,818	1	99	0	0	43	22.05	-23.56			May-08
	7.77	26.71	12.40			0.67	0.45			12.76	141.7	1	99	0	0	51					May-17
	5.40	22.03	6.68	54.41	42.32	0.54	0.5	13.48	1.07	37.27	3,721	2	97	0	0	46	27.89	-25.49			Mar-83
	5.39	22.06	6.76	54.80	42.92	0.62	0.42	13.47	1.07	37.29	3,721	2	97	0	0	46	27.98	-25.42			May-08

Fund Name	MARKET: Ticker Symbol	MARKET: Traded On	FUND TYPE, CATEGORY & OBJECTIVE: Fund Type	FUND TYPE, CATEGORY & OBJECTIVE: Category and (Prospectus Objective)	RATINGS: Overall Rating	RATINGS: Reward Rating	RATINGS: Risk Rating	RATINGS: Recent Up/ Downgrade	MINIMUMS: Open to New Investors	MINIMUMS: Min Initial Investment
Fidelity® International Capital Appreciation Fund	FIVFX	NAS CM	Open End	Global Equity Large Cap (Foreign Stock)	C+	C	B-	Up	Y	0
Fidelity® International Capital Appreciation K6 Fund	FAPCX	NAS CM	Open End	Global Equity Large Cap (Foreign Stock)	C	D+	B-	Up	Y	0
Fidelity® International Discovery Fund	FIGRX	NAS CM	Open End	Global Equity Large Cap (Foreign Stock)	C	C	C+		Y	0
Fidelity® International Discovery Fund Class K	FIDKX	NAS CM	Open End	Global Equity Large Cap (Foreign Stock)	C	C	C+		Y	0
Fidelity® International Enhanced Index Fund	FIENX	NAS CM	Open End	Global Equity Large Cap (Growth)	C	C	B-		Y	0
Fidelity® International Growth Fund	FIGFX	NAS CM	Open End	Global Equity Large Cap (Foreign Stock)	C+	C	B	Up	Y	0
Fidelity® International Index Fund	FSPSX	NAS CM	Open End	Global Equity Large Cap (Foreign Stock)	C	C	B		Y	0
Fidelity® International Real Estate Fund	FIREX	NAS CM	Open End	Real Estate Sector Equity (Real Estate)	B	B-	B+	Up	Y	0
Fidelity® International Small Cap Fund	FISMX	NAS CM	Open End	Global Equity Mid/Small Cap (Foreign Stock)	C	C	C+		Y	0
Fidelity® International Small Cap Opportunities Fund	FSCOX	NAS CM	Open End	Global Equity Mid/Small Cap (Small Company)	C	C	B-		Y	0
Fidelity® International Sustainability Index Fd	FNIDX	NAS CM	Open End	Global Equity Large Cap (Growth & Income)	C-	D	C+	Up	Y	0
Fidelity® International Value Fund	FIVLX	NAS CM	Open End	Global Equity Large Cap (Foreign Stock)	C-	D+	C		Y	0
Fidelity® Japan Fund	FJPNX	NAS CM	Open End	Japan Equity (Pacific Stock)	C	C	C+		Y	0
Fidelity® Japan Smaller Companies Fund	FJSCX	NAS CM	Open End	Japan Equity (Pacific Stock)	C	C	C		Y	0
Fidelity® Large Cap Core Enhanced Index Fund	FLCEX	NAS CM	Open End	US Equity Large Cap Blend (Growth)	B-	C	B		Y	0
Fidelity® Large Cap Growth Enhanced Index Fund	FLGEX	NAS CM	Open End	US Equity Large Cap Growth (Growth)	C+	C	B	Down	Y	0
Fidelity® Large Cap Growth Index Fund	FSPGX	NAS CM	Open End	US Equity Large Cap Growth (Growth)	C+	C	B		Y	0
Fidelity® Large Cap Stock Fund	FLCSX	NAS CM	Open End	US Equity Large Cap Blend (Growth)	C+	C	B		Y	0
Fidelity® Large Cap Stock K6 Fund	FCLKX	NAS CM	Open End	US Equity Large Cap Blend (Growth)	C	D+	B-	Up	Y	0
Fidelity® Large Cap Value Enhanced Index Fund	FLVEX	NAS CM	Open End	US Equity Large Cap Value (Growth)	B-	C	B	Up	Y	0
Fidelity® Large Cap Value Index Fund	FLCOX	NAS CM	Open End	US Equity Large Cap Value (Growth)	C+	C	B	Up	Y	0
Fidelity® Latin America Fund	FLATX	NAS CM	Open End	Latin America Equity (Foreign Stock)	C	C	C		Y	0
Fidelity® Leveraged Company Stock Fund	FLVCX	NAS CM	Open End	US Equity Mid Cap (Growth)	C	C	C+		Y	0
Fidelity® Leveraged Company Stock Fund Class K	FLCKX	NAS CM	Open End	US Equity Mid Cap (Growth)	C	C	C+		Y	0
Fidelity® Low-Priced Stock Fund	FLPSX	NAS CM	Open End	US Equity Mid Cap (Growth)	C	C	B		Y	0
Fidelity® Low-Priced Stock Fund Class K	FLPKX	NAS CM	Open End	US Equity Mid Cap (Growth)	C	C	B		Y	0
Fidelity® Low-Priced Stock K6 Fund	FLKSX	NAS CM	Open End	US Equity Mid Cap (World Stock)	C-	D	C+		Y	0
Fidelity® Magellan® Fund Class K	FMGKX	NAS CM	Open End	US Equity Large Cap Growth (Growth)	C+	C	B		Y	0
Fidelity® Mega Cap Stock Fund	FGRTX	NAS CM	Open End	US Equity Large Cap Blend (Growth)	C+	C	B		Y	0
Fidelity® Mid Cap Enhanced Index Fund	FMEIX	NAS CM	Open End	US Equity Mid Cap (Growth)	C+	C	B	Up	Y	0
Fidelity® Mid Cap Index Fund	FSMDX	NAS CM	Open End	US Equity Mid Cap (Growth)	C+	C	B	Down	Y	0
Fidelity® Mid Cap Value Fund	FSMVX	NAS CM	Open End	US Equity Mid Cap (Growth)	C	C-	B-		Y	0
Fidelity® Mid Cap Value K6 Fund	FCMVX	NAS CM	Open End	US Equity Mid Cap (World Stock)	D+	D	C-		Y	0
Fidelity® Mid-Cap Stock Fund	FMCSX	NAS CM	Open End	US Equity Mid Cap (Growth)	B-	C	B	Up	Y	0
Fidelity® Mid-Cap Stock Fund Class K	FKMCX	NAS CM	Open End	US Equity Mid Cap (Growth)	B-	C	B		Y	0
Fidelity® Multi-Asset Income Fund	FMSDX	NAS CM	Open End	Cautious Alloc (Growth & Income)	B	C+	B+		Y	0
Fidelity® Municipal Income 2019 Fund	FMCFX	NAS CM	Open End	US Muni Fixed Income (Municipal Bond - Natl)	C	C-	C+		Y	10,000
Fidelity® Municipal Income 2021 Fund	FOCFX	NAS CM	Open End	US Muni Fixed Income (Municipal Bond - Natl)	C	C	B-		Y	0
Fidelity® Municipal Income 2023 Fund	FCHPX	NAS CM	Open End	US Muni Fixed Income (Municipal Bond - Natl)	C+	C	B		Y	0
Fidelity® Municipal Income 2025 Fund	FIMSX	NAS CM	Open End	US Muni Fixed Income (Municipal Bond - Natl)	C	D+	B		Y	0
Fidelity® NASDAQ Composite Index® Fund	FNCMX	NAS CM	Open End	US Equity Large Cap Growth (Growth)	C+	C	B	Down	Y	0
Fidelity® New Millennium Fund®	FMILX	NAS CM	Open End	US Equity Large Cap Growth (Aggr Growth)	C+	C	B		Y	0
Fidelity® Nordic Fund	FNORX	NAS CM	Open End	Equity Miscellaneous (Europe Stock)	C	C-	C+		Y	0
Fidelity® OTC Portfolio	FOCPX	NAS CM	Open End	US Equity Large Cap Growth (Growth)	C+	C+	C+	Down	Y	0
Fidelity® OTC Portfolio Class K	FOCKX	NAS CM	Open End	US Equity Large Cap Growth (Growth)	C+	C+	C+	Down	Y	0
Fidelity® Overseas Fund	FOSFX	NAS CM	Open End	Global Equity Large Cap (Foreign Stock)	C	C	B-		Y	0
Fidelity® Overseas Fund Class K	FOSKX	NAS CM	Open End	Global Equity Large Cap (Foreign Stock)	C	C	B-		Y	0
Fidelity® Pacific Basin Fund	FPBFX	NAS CM	Open End	Asia Equity (Pacific Stock)	C	C	C+		Y	0
Fidelity® Puritan® Fund	FPURX	NAS CM	Open End	Moderate Alloc (Growth & Income)	B-	C	B+	Up	Y	0
Fidelity® Puritan® Fund Class K	FPUKX	NAS CM	Open End	Moderate Alloc (Growth & Income)	B-	C	B+	Up	Y	0
Fidelity® Real Estate Income Fund	FRIFX	NAS CM	Open End	Real Estate Sector Equity (Real Estate)	B	B-	B		Y	0
Fidelity® Real Estate Index Fund	FSRNX	NAS CM	Open End	Real Estate Sector Equity (Real Estate)	C+	C	B-		Y	0

★ Expanded analysis of this fund is included in Section II.

Min Additional Investment	3-Month Total Return	6-Month Total Return	1-Year Total Return	3-Year Total Return	5-Year Total Return	Dividend Yield (TTM)	Expense Ratio	3-Yr Std Deviation	3-Year Beta	NAV	Total Assets (MIL)	%Cash	%Stocks	%Bonds	%Other	Turnover Ratio	Last Bull Market Total Return	Last Bear Market Total Return	Front End Fee (%)	Back End Fee (%)	Inception Date
	TOTAL RETURNS					PERFORMANCE				ASSETS		ASSET ALLOCATION & TURNOVER					BULL & BEAR		FEES		
	6.96	23.87	8.17	41.00	44.87	0.37	1.06	12.46	0.98	21.95	2,937	2	98	0	0	157	26.68	-25.87			Nov-94
	6.96	24.15	8.58			0.66	0.66			12.13	452.9	1	99	0	0	158					May-17
	4.61	17.43	-0.07	29.87	17.61	1.13	0.88	11.85	1.02	42.64	9,261	3	96	0	0	45	15.57	-24.47			Dec-86
	4.62	17.48	0.00	30.32	18.31	1.25	0.77	11.84	1.02	42.53	9,261	3	96	0	0	45	15.72	-24.43			May-08
	2.81	12.96	-1.30	31.34	14.57	2.11	0.59	11.28	1.01	9.5	1,522	0	99	0	0	66	12.73	-22.44			Dec-07
	6.85	21.15	7.63	36.84	32.56	0.73	0.95	11.99	1	14.49	2,943	2	98	0	0	34	21.42	-21.89			Nov-07
	3.70	14.49	1.20	31.42	12.47	2.58	0.05	11.01	0.99	41.37	27,595	1	99	0	0	3	13.11	-23.02			Sep-11
	3.14	16.63	8.88	36.15	33.88	1.48	1.05	9.79	0.67	12.48	578.4	4	96	0	0	56	19.61	-25.14			Sep-04
	3.37	12.94	-3.26	33.47	33.20	1.64	1.2	10.8	0.89	26.61	2,267	5	95	0	0	25	14.26	-21.6			Sep-02
	4.42	16.33	-0.79	38.39	36.59	0.9	1.11	11.87	0.92	18.66	1,282	7	93	0	0	19	19.79	-20.38			Aug-05
	3.20	13.58	1.76			2.02	0.2			10.62	58.6	7	93	0	0	10					May-17
	3.31	12.01	-3.07	17.21	-0.48	2.98	0.89	11.67	0.99	8.11	468.7	0	100	0	0	55	11.04	-27.71			May-06
	3.41	13.36	-3.09	30.34	27.78	0.34	1.05	12.05	1.04	14.84	689.0	1	99	0	0	40	5.77	-10.28			Sep-92
	1.78	9.12	-6.15	26.50	44.48	0.65	0.94	11.16	0.91	16.51	660.2	2	98	0	0	17	5.37	-6.41			Nov-95
	3.10	16.66	8.47	49.56	60.06	1.48	0.39	12.08	0.98	15.26	833.4	2	97	0	0	92	24.34	-15.12			Apr-07
	3.94	19.88	8.57	58.19	74.36	1.06	0.39	13.19	0.98	20.02	1,112	1	99	0	0	100	26.38	-15.12			Apr-07
	4.66	22.65	11.46	66.19		1.02	0.04	13.41	1	15.72	2,351	0	100	0	0	14					Jun-16
	2.72	17.98	5.13	46.88	46.73	1.64	0.63	13.88	1.1	30.83	2,674	2	98	0	0	35	28.09	-19.28			Jun-95
	2.62	17.87	5.47			2	0.45			11.34	82.8	1	98	0	0	49					May-17
	2.60	14.76	6.31	38.37	44.52	2.26	0.39	12.23	1	12.98	3,738	2	98	0	0	99	23.45	-17.48			Apr-07
	3.80	17.21	8.50	35.86		2.14	0.04	12.09	1	12.51	2,205	0	100	0	0	15					Jun-16
	12.17	22.46	29.00	41.36	-5.00	1.92	1.07	22.48	1.02	26.17	554.1	0	100	0	0	53	18.79	-24.75			Apr-93
	2.63	23.27	-0.24	37.55	22.79	0	0.78	15.74	1.19	29.24	2,276	2	98	0	0	67	33.13	-30.1			Dec-00
	2.65	23.32	-0.14	38.02	23.48	0	0.67	15.72	1.19	29.34	2,276	2	98	0	0	67	33.31	-30.07			May-08
	1.41	12.73	-0.92	32.16	34.25	1.57	0.62	11.13	0.58	48.59	30,090	7	93	0	0	11	23.38	-17.6			Dec-89
	1.44	12.79	-0.83	32.53	34.87	1.66	0.53	11.14	0.58	48.56	30,090	7	93	0	0	11	23.49	-17.56			May-08
	1.46	12.60	-0.40			1.56	0.5			11.08	1,947	9	91	0	0	23					May-17
	5.46	21.51	7.75	55.45	68.93	0.64	0.59	13.02	1.04	10.66	16,853	2	97	0	0	42	24.33	-24.22			May-08
	3.35	17.06	7.32	45.58	49.03	1.64	0.68	12.56	1	15.71	1,953	6	93	0	0	39	28.24	-16.02			Dec-98
	2.83	19.71	4.53	39.76	45.33	1.55	0.59	13.71	1.01	14.88	1,212	1	99	0	0	108	25.54	-21.49			Dec-07
	4.13	22.47	7.88	43.35	51.66	1.5	0.03	13.41	1	22.53	10,321	0	100	0	0	12	26.44				Sep-11
	1.06	14.98	-3.17	20.96	24.97	1.89	0.53	14.39	1.07	21.79	1,823	2	98	0	0	80	26.86	-23.1			Nov-01
	1.19	15.13	-3.03			2.16	0.45			10.12	50.6	4	96	0	0	89					May-17
	4.81	18.39	6.22	44.31	45.83	0.84	0.73	11.08	0.71	35.23	7,698	8	90	0	3	29	23.35	-18.77			Mar-94
	4.85	18.50	6.34	44.86	46.69	0.94	0.62	11.06	0.71	35.25	7,698	8	90	0	3	29	23.46	-18.71			May-08
	4.81	13.65	10.59	23.05		2.34	0.85	6.31	0.35	10.93	82.7	3	49	43	0	367					Feb-18
	0.32	0.72	1.30	2.06	6.18	1.3	0.4	1.02	0.21	10.57	55.7	82	0	18	0	7	5.49				May-11
	0.98	2.10	2.93	2.95	11.11	2.06	0.4	2.36	0.6	10.83	52.7	0	0	100	0	8	6.07				May-11
	1.50	3.58	4.74	4.34	16.05	2.07	0.4	3.41	0.94	10.34	35.1	0	0	100	0	12					Apr-13
	2.16	5.37	7.50			2	0.4			10.29	23.8	0	0	100	0	44					May-17
	3.99	22.26	7.64	71.89	91.11	0.77	0.3	14.61	1	104.43	6,702	13	87	1	0	15	26.87	-15.56			Sep-03
	4.83	19.15	5.43	48.97	46.75	0.93	0.67	11.7	0.93	36.89	3,056	4	93	0	2	37	22.93	-15.37			Dec-92
	5.75	11.63	0.55	22.59	15.67	0.1	0.98	14.16		47.22	274.5	1	97	0	2	56	20.95	-31.79			Nov-95
	4.01	22.98	5.12	82.34	104.49	0	0.88	16.01	1.06	12.14	19,587	0	97	0	0	38	19.51	-17.41			Dec-84
	3.96	22.95	5.21	82.83	105.51	0	0.78	16.01	1.06	12.32	19,587	0	97	0	0	38	19.61	-17.37			May-08
	7.17	19.88	3.50	36.24	31.10	1.34	0.97	11.76	1.02	48.71	7,723	3	97	0	0	33	21.23	-27.53			Dec-84
	7.18	19.96	3.62	36.75	31.92	1.46	0.86	11.76	1.02	48.61	7,723	3	97	0	0	33	21.35	-27.48			May-08
	4.16	18.94	1.00	34.70	43.29	0.57	1.07	13.58	1.04	31.26	874.2	1	99	0	0	37	14.83	-21.34			Oct-86
	3.34	14.06	5.24	34.96	43.30	1.45	0.54	8.8	0.7	22.12	27,345	2	64	33	0	44	16.96	-11.82			Apr-47
	3.36	14.15	5.34	35.35	44.02	1.53	0.45	8.8	0.7	22.11	27,345	2	64	33	0	44	17.07	-11.75			May-08
	2.94	11.69	9.96	21.88	37.35	4.32	0.75	5.34	0.25	12.35	6,194	9	30	38	0	27	14.26	-6.41			Feb-03
	0.77	16.94	9.68	12.69	43.56	3.01	0.07	13.1	1	16.55	2,152	0	100	0	0	6	31.16				Sep-11

	MARKET			FUND TYPE, CATEGORY & OBJECTIVE	RATINGS					MINIMUMS
Fund Name	Ticker Symbol	Traded On	Fund Type	Category and (Prospectus Objective)	Overall Rating	Reward Rating	Risk Rating	Recent Up/ Downgrade	Open to New Investors	Min Initial Investment
Fidelity® Real Estate Investment Portfolio	FRESX	NAS CM	Open End	Real Estate Sector Equity (Real Estate)	C+	C	B-	Down	Y	0
Fidelity® SAI Emerging Markets Index Fund	FERGX	NAS CM	Open End	Global Emerg Mkts (Div Emerging Mkts)	C	C	C+		Y	0
Fidelity® SAI Emerging Markets Low Volatility Index Fund	FGKPX	NAS CM	Open End	Global Emerg Mkts (Growth & Income)	U	U	U		Y	0
Fidelity® SAI International Index Fund	FIONX	NAS CM	Open End	Global Equity Large Cap (Foreign Stock)	C	C	B		Y	0
Fidelity® SAI International Low Volatility Index Fund	FSKLX	NAS CM	Open End	Global Equity Large Cap (Foreign Stock)	B-	C	A-	Up	Y	0
Fidelity® SAI International Value Index Fund	FIWCX	NAS CM	Open End	Global Equity Large Cap (Foreign Stock)	D	D	D+		Y	0
Fidelity® SAI Real Estate Index Fund	FESIX	NAS CM	Open End	Real Estate Sector Equity (Real Estate)	C+	C	B-	Up	Y	0
Fidelity® SAI Small-Mid Cap 500 Index Fund	FZFLX	NAS CM	Open End	US Equity Mid Cap (Growth)	C+	C	B-	Down	Y	0
Fidelity® SAI U.S. Large Cap Index Fund	FLCPX	NAS CM	Open End	US Equity Large Cap Blend (Growth)	B-	C	B	Up	Y	0
Fidelity® SAI U.S. Low Volatility Index Fund	FSUVX	NAS CM	Open End	US Equity Large Cap Blend (Growth)	B	B-	A-		Y	0
Fidelity® SAI U.S. Momentum Index Fund	FUMIX	NAS CM	Open End	US Equity Large Cap Growth (Growth & Income)	C	C	B		Y	0
Fidelity® SAI U.S. Quality Index Fund	FUQIX	NAS CM	Open End	US Equity Large Cap Growth (Growth)	B-	C+	B	Down	Y	0
Fidelity® SAI U.S. Value Index Fund	FSWCX	NAS CM	Open End	US Equity Large Cap Value (Growth & Income)	D+	D+	C	Up	Y	0
Fidelity® Select Automotive Portfolio	FSAVX	NAS CM	Open End	Consumer Goods Sec Equity ()	C	C	C+	Down	Y	2,500
Fidelity® Select Banking Portfolio	FSRBX	NAS CM	Open End	Financials Sector Equity (Financial)	C	C	C+	Down	Y	0
Fidelity® Select Biotechnology Portfolio	FBIOX	NAS CM	Open End	Healthcare Sector Equity (Health)	C	C	C		Y	0
Fidelity® Select Brokerage & Invmt Mgmt Portfolio	FSLBX	NAS CM	Open End	Financials Sector Equity (Financial)	C	C	C+	Down	Y	0
Fidelity® Select Chemicals Portfolio	FSCHX	NAS CM	Open End	Natl Resources Sec Equity ()	C	C-	C		Y	0
Fidelity® Select Communication Services Portfolio	FBMPX	NAS CM	Open End	Consumer Goods Sec Equity (Comm)	B-	C+	B		Y	2,500
Fidelity® Select Communications Equip Portfolio	FSDCX	NAS CM	Open End	Technology Sector Equity (Comm)	C+	C-	B		Y	0
Fidelity® Select Computers Portfolio	FDCPX	NAS CM	Open End	Technology Sector Equity (Technology)	C+	C	B-		Y	0
Fidelity® Select Construction & Housing Portfolio	FSHOX	NAS CM	Open End	Consumer Goods Sec Equity ()	C	C	C+	Down	Y	2,500
Fidelity® Select Consumer Discretionary Portfolio	FSCPX	NAS CM	Open End	Consumer Goods Sec Equity ()	B-	C+	B		Y	2,500
Fidelity® Select Consumer Finance Portfolio	FSVLX	NAS CM	Open End	Financials Sector Equity (Financial)	B	B-	B	Up	Y	0
Fidelity® Select Consumer Staples Portfolio	FDFAX	NAS CM	Open End	Consumer Goods Sec Equity ()	C	C	C		Y	0
Fidelity® Select Defense & Aerospace Portfolio	FSDAX	NAS CM	Open End	Industrials Sector Equity ()	C+	C+	B-	Down	Y	0
Fidelity® Select Energy Portfolio	FSENX	NAS CM	Open End	Energy Sector Equity (Natl Res)	D	D	D+	Down	Y	0
Fidelity® Select Energy Service Portfolio	FSESX	NAS CM	Open End	Energy Sector Equity (Natl Res)	D	D-	D		Y	0
Fidelity® Select Envir and Alt Energy Portfolio	FSLEX	NAS CM	Open End	Industrials Sector Equity ()	C+	C	B	Down	Y	0
Fidelity® Select Financial Services Portfolio	FIDSX	NAS CM	Open End	Financials Sector Equity (Financial)	C	C	B-		Y	0
Fidelity® Select Gold Portfolio	FSAGX	NAS CM	Open End	Precious Metals Sector Equity (Precious Metals)	D+	D	C-	Down	Y	0
Fidelity® Select Health Care Portfolio	FSPHX	NAS CM	Open End	Healthcare Sector Equity (Health)	C+	C	B	Down	Y	0
Fidelity® Select Health Care Services Portfolio	FSHCX	NAS CM	Open End	Healthcare Sector Equity (Health)	C	C-	C+	Down	Y	0
Fidelity® Select Industrials Portfolio	FCYIX	NAS CM	Open End	Industrials Sector Equity ()	C+	C	C+	Down	Y	0
Fidelity® Select Insurance Portfolio	FSPCX	NAS CM	Open End	Financials Sector Equity (Financial)	B-	B-	B	Up	Y	0
Fidelity® Select IT Services Portfolio	FBSOX	NAS CM	Open End	Technology Sector Equity (Technology)	B	B+	B		Y	0
Fidelity® Select Leisure Portfolio	FDLSX	NAS CM	Open End	Consumer Goods Sec Equity ()	B	B-	B+		Y	2,500
Fidelity® Select Materials Portfolio	FSDPX	NAS CM	Open End	Natl Resources Sec Equity (Natl Res)	C-	D+	C	Down	Y	0
Fidelity® Select Medical Technology and Devices Portfolio	FSMEX	NAS CM	Open End	Healthcare Sector Equity (Health)	B-	C+	B	Down	Y	0
Fidelity® Select Natural Gas Portfolio	FSNGX	NAS CM	Open End	Energy Sector Equity (Natl Res)	D	D	D	Down	Y	0
Fidelity® Select Natural Resources Portfolio	FNARX	NAS CM	Open End	Energy Sector Equity (Natl Res)	D+	D	D+	Down	Y	0
Fidelity® Select Pharmaceuticals Portfolio	FPHAX	NAS CM	Open End	Healthcare Sector Equity (Health)	C+	C	B		Y	0
Fidelity® Select Portfolios Air Transportation Portfolio	FSAIX	NAS CM	Open End	Industrials Sector Equity ()	C+	C	B	Down	Y	0
Fidelity® Select Retailing Portfolio	FSRPX	NAS CM	Open End	Consumer Goods Sec Equity ()	C+	C+	B-	Down	Y	2,500
Fidelity® Select Semiconductors Portfolio	FSELX	NAS CM	Open End	Technology Sector Equity (Utility)	C	C	C+	Down	Y	0
Fidelity® Select Software & IT Services Portfolio	FSCSX	NAS CM	Open End	Technology Sector Equity (Technology)	B	B-	B		Y	0
Fidelity® Select Technology Portfolio	FSPTX	NAS CM	Open End	Technology Sector Equity (Technology)	C+	C+	C+		Y	0
Fidelity® Select Telecommunications Portfolio	FSTCX	NAS CM	Open End	Communications Sector Equity (Comm)	C	C	C+	Down	Y	0
Fidelity® Select Transportation Portfolio	FSRFX	NAS CM	Open End	Industrials Sector Equity ()	C	C	B-	Down	Y	0
Fidelity® Select Utilities Portfolio	FSUTX	NAS CM	Open End	Utilities Sector Equity (Utility)	B+	B	A-	Up	Y	0
Fidelity® Select Wireless Portfolio	FWRLX	NAS CM	Open End	Communications Sector Equity (Comm)	B	B-	B	Up	Y	0
Fidelity® Series All-Sector Equity Fund	FSAEX	NAS CM	Open End	US Equity Large Cap Growth (Growth)	C+	C	B	Down		0

★ Expanded analysis of this fund is included in Section II.

Min Additional Investment	TOTAL RETURNS 3-Month Total Return	6-Month Total Return	1-Year Total Return	3-Year Total Return	5-Year Total Return	PERFORMANCE Dividend Yield (TTM)	Expense Ratio	3-Yr Std Deviation	3-Year Beta	ASSETS NAV	Total Assets (MIL)	ASSET ALLOCATION & TURNOVER %Cash	%Stocks	%Bonds	%Other	Turnover Ratio	BULL & BEAR Last Bull Market Total Return	Last Bear Market Total Return	FEES Front End Fee (%)	Back End Fee (%)	Inception Date
	1.85	18.25	11.21	14.13	48.96	2.26	0.76	12.67	0.6	44.96	4,255	3	97	0	0	20	33.4	-16.94			Nov-86
	0.87	11.09	1.54	36.38		2.33	0.08	14.09	1.01	13.82	3,908	0	100	0	0	3					Jan-16
	0.98						0.25			10.21	634.8										Jan-19
	3.66	14.54	1.16	30.75		2.63	0.05	10.97	0.98	11.89	6,499	0	100	0	0	7					Jan-16
	3.20	11.03	6.29	22.99		2.14	0.2	8.25	0.99	11.27	2,010	4	95	0	0	43					May-15
	0.55	9.57	-4.21			1.95	0.2			9.04	692.4	2	98	0	0	54					Dec-17
	0.83	17.00	9.69	12.68		3.16	0.07	13.12	1	11.7	103.1	0	100	0	0	8					Feb-16
	3.61	22.28	5.90	43.61		1.33	0.1	14.49		12.62	1,869	0	100	0	0	39					Aug-15
	4.34	19.60	10.42	50.82		1.77	0.02	12.2	1	15.86	13,172	0	100	0	0	26					Feb-16
	5.05	18.40	17.01	42.66		1.33	0.15	9.57	1.02	14.54	3,432	1	99	0	0	39					May-15
	4.94	18.39	8.05			0.85	0.15			13.58	3,609	0	99	0	0	153					Feb-17
	2.47	20.14	11.51	58.09		1.26	0.15	12.07	0.95	14.91	8,393	0	100	0	0	34					Oct-15
	1.96	15.57	2.47			1.9	0.15			9.87	1,764	0	100	0	0	113					Dec-17
	2.94	12.01	-3.49	33.62	10.00	1.02	0.97	15.84	1.06	33.31	35.0	0	100	0	0	31	24.96	-33.09			Jun-86
	6.26	19.93	-2.52	53.46	45.10	1.44	0.77	21.29	1.36	25.81	455.1	0	100	0	0	44	39.28	-25.92			Jun-86
	-1.19	21.23	-2.57	39.78	44.00	0	0.72	24.21	1.44	20.3	7,077	1	97	0	2	37	36.69	-12.52			Dec-85
	7.07	16.92	-0.13	61.17	32.07	1.1	0.78	15.62	0.96	73.03	317.2	2	98	0	0	30	24.31	-30.13			Jul-85
	0.86	11.39	-10.92	26.71	23.67	1.46	0.77	18.46	1.3	13.03	1,048	0	99	1	0	62	39.76	-26.7			Jul-85
	4.58	20.97	13.97	46.89	48.83	0.18	0.82	14.55	0.9	61.93	628.4	0	100	0	0	107	30.76	-22.5			Jun-86
	-4.12	13.16	4.77	54.81	47.45	0.4	0.84	14.62	0.89	38.33	205.7	4	96	0	0	71	15.37	-31.85			Jun-90
	3.83	17.12	3.08	75.66	59.91	0.96	0.77	16.41	1.11	72.88	485.8	1	99	0	0	81	33.79	-20.42			Jul-85
	7.18	27.50	10.52	39.59	68.47	0.8	0.8	15.9	1.12	58.11	257.0	1	99	0	0	90	49.73	-23.37			Sep-86
	4.35	21.52	8.22	52.98	73.72	0.28	0.78	14.85	1.13	46.81	462.2	0	100	0	0	46	31.52	-16.18			Jun-90
	6.63	26.64	12.33	69.47	58.80	1.2	0.87	14.58	1.06	16.93	153.4	3	97	0	0	32	30.31	-15.88			Dec-85
	3.08	21.41	11.74	9.78	29.24	2.46	0.77	12.65	0.73	83.17	1,485	1	99	0	0	41	17.81	-6.63			Jul-85
	8.30	28.48	12.48	83.15	99.75	0.4	0.75	17.78	1.2	17.86	2,836	1	99	0	0	44	24.46	-15.39			May-84
	-2.71	13.23	-21.19	-5.19	-33.83	1.42	0.78	23.74	1.34	37.16	1,079	2	98	0	0	59	21.86	-30.86			Jul-81
	-12.26	6.21	-40.37	-33.93	-66.74	1.19	0.84	31.88	1.83	26.68	244.1	1	99	0	0	80	23.26	-36.39			Dec-85
	3.99	21.29	11.70	53.40	44.35	0.74	0.87	15.84	1.18	25.56	169.0	4	96	0	0	62	13.34	-29.03			Jun-89
	7.43	19.48	3.44	49.14	47.74	1.1	0.76	15.71	1.08	10.12	547.1	1	99	0	0	49	29.62	-28.26			Dec-81
	13.03	22.07	13.62	-11.33	-2.32	0	0.86	24.16	-0.05	21.68	1,440	3	96	0	1	37	-15.04	-13.6			Dec-85
	2.24	14.93	7.31	46.64	64.53	0.06	0.71	16.93	1.07	25.01	7,256	1	97	0	0	60	23.29	-14.87			Jul-81
	1.99	1.97	2.52	38.36	74.20	0.11	0.76	17.67	0.97	88.59	1,070	2	98	0	0	60	25.93	-17.59			Jun-86
	5.32	25.52	9.06	43.15	45.49	0.53	0.76	16.34	1.22	35.6	639.9	1	99	0	0	88	30.71	-26.07			Mar-97
	10.81	24.37	17.32	47.89	64.32	1.31	0.82	12.23	0.82	63.1	260.3	2	98	0	0	9	26.56	-22.51			Dec-85
	5.68	33.93	20.91	99.10	139.65	0.04	0.74	14.2	1.04	71.43	3,670	2	98	0	0	26	30.74	-17.3			Feb-98
	8.23	24.81	16.71	60.50	70.77	0.67	0.76	13.42	0.92	15.96	511.3	0	100	0	0	46	34.21	-12.07			May-84
	1.30	13.62	-10.17	20.54	3.87	1.12	0.79	17.32	1.24	69.95	996.0	0	99	1	0	77	30.02	-28.27			Sep-86
	5.07	21.14	17.75	72.31	129.16	0	0.73	16.52	0.98	56.48	6,711	2	98	0	0	43	14.18	-15.89			Apr-98
	-4.80	13.19	-21.57	-15.62	-52.73	0	0.89	23.97	1.31	19.99	181.3	0	100	0	0	86	18.45	-27.97			Apr-93
	0.93	17.88	-14.81	-0.33	-32.88	1	0.81	20.77	1.18	26.25	425.7	0	100	0	0	26	18.12	-30.94			Mar-97
	1.39	13.79	15.12	20.63	27.98	1.37	0.8	14.22	0.83	21.12	720.7	1	99	0	0	55	19.93	-10.42			Jun-01
	3.00	16.40	6.35	58.24	58.22	0.61	0.81	18.21	1.28	75.22	289.2	3	97	0	0	32	22.07	-18.05			Dec-85
	3.20	19.81	6.29	63.42	123.53	0.15	0.76	15.9	1.16	15.84	3,113	0	100	0	0	34	30.64	-8.42			Dec-85
	4.23	28.39	5.51	97.31	132.09	0.6	0.73	23.04	1.53	10.02	3,212	1	99	0	0	130	23.03	-22.9			Jul-85
	6.23	27.05	15.44	101.09	134.79	0.08	0.72	14.32	0.97	18.52	7,272	5	95	0	0	48	30.74	-15.42			Jul-85
	5.99	29.11	5.31	99.77	117.10	0.1	0.72	17.63	1.17	17.16	5,602	1	98	0	0	126	25.83	-21.57			Jul-81
	2.57	12.46	7.16	11.34	31.32	1.95	0.84	11.92	0.7	58.42	285.7	4	96	0	0	64	12.29	-16.57			Jul-85
	0.05	13.95	4.32	55.60	48.39	0.79	0.79	18.69	1.27	92.09	424.4	3	97	0	0	58	26.05	-23.34			Sep-86
	2.96	13.44	13.63	38.74	50.46	1.3	0.78	9.89	0.3	90.62	1,209	1	99	0	0	97	11.56	-2.42			Dec-81
	4.86	18.72	12.74	49.55	48.91	1.61	0.83	12.1	0.79	9.7	261.5	0	100	0	0	54	11.91	-15.61			Sep-00
	4.15	19.66	7.10	48.32	57.88	1.7	0	13.16	1.06	10.03	3,758	3	97	0	0	65	23.46	-18.65			Oct-08

	MARKET		FUND TYPE, CATEGORY & OBJECTIVE		RATINGS				MINIMUMS	
Fund Name	Ticker Symbol	Traded On	Fund Type	Category and (Prospectus Objective)	Overall Rating	Reward Rating	Risk Rating	Recent Up/ Downgrade	Open to New Investors	Min Initial Investment
Fidelity® Series Blue Chip Growth Fund	FSBDX	NAS CM	Open End	US Equity Large Cap Growth (Growth)	B-	C+	B	Down	Y	0
Fidelity® Series Canada Fund	FCNSX	NAS CM	Open End	Global Equity Large Cap (Growth)	C-	D+	C+	Up	Y	0
Fidelity® Series Commodity Strategy Fund	FCSSX	NAS CM	Open End	Commodities Broad Basket (Growth)	D+	D	C-			0
Fidelity® Series Emerging Markets Fund	FHKFX	NAS CM	Open End	Global Emerg Mkts (Div Emerging Mkts)	U	U	U		Y	0
Fidelity® Series Emerging Markets Opportunities Fund	FEMSX	NAS CM	Open End	Global Emerg Mkts (Div Emerging Mkts)	C	C	C+			0
Fidelity® Series Global ex U.S. Index Fund	FSGEX	NAS CM	Open End	Global Equity Large Cap (Foreign Stock)	C	C	B		Y	0
Fidelity® Series Growth Company Fund	FCGSX	NAS CM	Open End	US Equity Large Cap Growth (Growth)	C+	C+	C+		Y	0
Fidelity® Series International Growth Fund	FIGSX	NAS CM	Open End	Global Equity Large Cap (Foreign Stock)	C+	C	B	Up		0
Fidelity® Series International Index Fund	FHLFX	NAS CM	Open End	Global Equity Large Cap (Foreign Stock)	U	U	U		Y	0
Fidelity® Series International Small Cap Fund	FSTSX	NAS CM	Open End	Global Equity Mid/Small Cap (Small Company)	C	C	B-			0
Fidelity® Series International Value Fund	FINVX	NAS CM	Open End	Global Equity Large Cap (Foreign Stock)	C	C-	C+	Up		0
Fidelity® Series Intrinsic Opportunities Fund	FDMLX	NAS CM	Open End	US Equity Mid Cap (Growth)	C	C-	C+		Y	0
Fidelity® Series Large Cap Growth Index Fund	FHOFX	NAS CM	Open End	US Equity Large Cap Blend (Growth & Income)	U	U	U		Y	0
Fidelity® Series Large Cap Stock Fund	FGLGX	NAS CM	Open End	US Equity Large Cap Blend (Growth & Income)	C+	C	B		Y	0
Fidelity® Series Large Cap Value Index Fund	FIOOX	NAS CM	Open End	US Equity Large Cap Value (Equity-Income)	B-	C	B		Y	0
Fidelity® Series Opportunistic Insights Fund	FVWSX	NAS CM	Open End	US Equity Large Cap Growth (Growth)	C+	C	B	Down	Y	0
Fidelity® Series Real Estate Income Fund	FSREX	NAS CM	Open End	Real Estate Sector Equity (Real Estate)	B	B-	A-			0
Fidelity® Series Small Cap Discovery Fund	FJACX	NAS CM	Open End	US Equity Small Cap (Small Company)	C+	C	B	Up	Y	0
Fidelity® Series Small Cap Opportunities Fund	FSOPX	NAS CM	Open End	US Equity Small Cap (Small Company)	C+	C	B-			0
Fidelity® Series Stock Selector Large Cap Value Fund	FBLEX	NAS CM	Open End	US Equity Large Cap Value (Growth)	B-	C	B	Up	Y	0
Fidelity® Series Value Discovery Fund	FNKLX	NAS CM	Open End	US Equity Large Cap Value (Growth)	B-	C	B+	Up	Y	0
Fidelity® Small Cap Discovery Fund	FSCRX	NAS CM	Open End	US Equity Small Cap (Small Company)	C	C	B			0
Fidelity® Small Cap Enhanced Index Fund	FCPEX	NAS CM	Open End	US Equity Small Cap (Growth)	C	C	C+		Y	0
Fidelity® Small Cap Growth Fund	FCPGX	NAS CM	Open End	US Equity Small Cap (Small Company)	C+	C+	C+	Down	Y	0
Fidelity® Small Cap Growth K6 Fund	FOCSX	NAS CM	Open End	US Equity Small Cap (Small Company)	C-	D+	C			0
Fidelity® Small Cap Index Fund	FSSNX	NAS CM	Open End	US Equity Small Cap (Small Company)	C	C	C+		Y	0
Fidelity® Small Cap Stock Fund	FSLCX	NAS CM	Open End	US Equity Small Cap (Small Company)	C+	C	B-	Up	Y	0
Fidelity® Small Cap Stock K6 Fund	FKICX	NAS CM	Open End	US Equity Small Cap (Small Company)	C	D+	C+	Up	Y	0
Fidelity® Small Cap Value Fund	FCPVX	NAS CM	Open End	US Equity Small Cap (Small Company)	C	C-	C+			0
Fidelity® Stock Selector All Cap Fund	FDSSX	NAS CM	Open End	US Equity Large Cap Growth (Growth)	C+	C	B-	Up	Y	0
Fidelity® Stock Selector Large Cap Value Fund	FSLVX	NAS CM	Open End	US Equity Large Cap Value (Growth)	B-	C	B	Up	Y	0
Fidelity® Stock Selector Mid Cap Fund	FSSMX	NAS CM	Open End	US Equity Mid Cap (Growth)	C+	C	B		Y	0
Fidelity® Stock Selector Small Cap Fund	FDSCX	NAS CM	Open End	US Equity Small Cap (Small Company)	C+	C	B-		Y	0
Fidelity® Strategic Dividend & Income® Fund	FSDIX	NAS CM	Open End	Aggressive Alloc (Equity-Income)	B	C+	A-		Y	0
Fidelity® Strategic Real Return Fund	FSRRX	NAS CM	Open End	Cautious Alloc (Growth & Income)	B-	C	B+		Y	0
Fidelity® Telecom and Utilities Fund	FIUIX	NAS CM	Open End	Utilities Sector Equity (Utility)	B	B-	A-	Up	Y	0
Fidelity® Total Emerging Markets Fund	FTEMX	NAS CM	Open End	Global Emerg Mkts (Div Emerging Mkts)	C	C	B-		Y	0
Fidelity® Total International Equity Fund	FTIEX	NAS CM	Open End	Global Equity Large Cap (Foreign Stock)	C	C	B-		Y	0
Fidelity® Total International Index Fund	FTIHX	NAS CM	Open End	Global Equity Large Cap (Foreign Stock)	C	D+	B	Up	Y	0
Fidelity® Total Market Index Fund	FSKAX	NAS CM	Open End	US Equity Large Cap Blend (Growth & Income)	B-	C	B		Y	0
Fidelity® Trend Fund	FTRNX	NAS CM	Open End	US Equity Large Cap Growth (Growth)	C+	C	B-	Down	Y	0
Fidelity® US Sustainability Index Fund	FITLX	NAS CM	Open End	US Equity Large Cap Blend (Growth & Income)	C	C-	B	Up	Y	0
Fidelity® Value Discovery Fund	FVDFX	NAS CM	Open End	US Equity Large Cap Value (Growth)	B-	C	B	Up	Y	0
Fidelity® Value Discovery Fund Class K	FVDKX	NAS CM	Open End	US Equity Large Cap Value (Growth)	B-	C	B	Up	Y	0
Fidelity® Value Discovery K6 Fund	FDVKX	NAS CM	Open End	US Equity Large Cap Value (World Stock)	C	D+	B-	Up	Y	0
Fidelity® Value Fund	FDVLX	NAS CM	Open End	US Equity Mid Cap (Growth)	C	C	B-		Y	0
Fidelity® Value Fund Class K	FVLKX	NAS CM	Open End	US Equity Mid Cap (Growth)	C	C	B-		Y	0
Fidelity® Value Strategies Fund	FSLSX	NAS CM	Open End	US Equity Large Cap Value (Growth)	C+	C	C+	Up	Y	0
Fidelity® Var Ins Products Extended Mkt Ind Port Serv Cls	FVIMX	NAS CM	Open End	US Equity Mid Cap (Growth & Income)	D	D+	C		Y	0
Fidelity® Var Ins Products Health Care Port Serv Cls 2	FVINX	NAS CM	Open End	Healthcare Sector Equity (Health)	C	C	B		Y	0
Fidelity® Var Ins Products Intl Index Port Serv Cls	FVIRX	NAS CM	Open End	Global Equity Large Cap (Foreign Stock)	D	D+	C+		Y	0
Fidelity® Var Ins Products Total Mkt Index Port Serv Cls	FVIUX	NAS CM	Open End	US Equity Large Cap Blend (Growth & Income)	D	D+	C+		Y	0

★ Expanded analysis of this fund is included in Section II.

Min Additional Investment	3-Month Total Return	6-Month Total Return	1-Year Total Return	3-Year Total Return	5-Year Total Return	Dividend Yield (TTM)	Expense Ratio	3-Yr Std Deviation	3-Year Beta	NAV	Total Assets (MIL)	%Cash	%Stocks	%Bonds	%Other	Turnover Ratio	Last Bull Market Total Return	Last Bear Market Total Return	Front End Fee (%)	Back End Fee (%)	Inception Date
	TOTAL RETURNS					PERFORMANCE				ASSETS		ASSET ALLOCATION & TURNOVER					BULL & BEAR		FEES		
	3.32	21.24	10.66	85.40	99.55	0.69	0	14.21	1.01	15.24	6,162	1	94	0	0	41					Nov-13
	5.91	21.73	5.68			2.08	0			10.92	1,680	2	98	0	0	36					Aug-17
	-1.25	3.74	-6.95	-7.80	-40.26	1.87	0.05	8.52	0.99	4.71	5,983	107	0	0	-7	0	0.78	-20.53			Oct-09
	-1.83	5.95					0.01			9.61	1,735	3	97	0	0	15					Aug-18
	3.02	16.68	5.12	44.55	20.22	2.01	0.01	14.3	1.01	19.09	15,994	3	96	0	0	64	20.8	-28.26			Dec-08
	3.02	14.03	1.37	32.18	11.59	2.52	0.06	11.42	1	12.59	7,900	3	97	0	0	2	14.17	-24.16			Sep-09
	2.48	23.87	5.53	82.20	99.80	0.79	0	16.35	1.18	17.33	11,764	1	98	0	0	23					Nov-13
	7.17	22.03	8.62	38.96	35.14	1.66	0.01	12.06	1.01	16.28	15,822	2	98	0	0	33	21.28	-22.34			Dec-09
	3.56	14.27					0.01			10.17	78.7	1	99	0	0	1					Aug-18
	4.50	15.92	-0.30	38.25	33.25	2.1	0.01	11.4	0.88	16.23	3,502	8	92	0	0	14	19.73	-20.86			Dec-09
	3.54	12.50	-2.31	19.53	1.44	3.61	0.01	11.64	0.98	9.63	15,048	1	99	0	0	43	11.11	-27.58			Dec-09
	-0.18	6.76	-3.22	34.43	42.84	2.43	0.01	9.92	0.72	16.42	13,939	13	87	0	0	13					Dec-12
	4.69	22.71					0.01			10.54	266.9	1	99	0	0	21					Aug-18
	2.94	17.54	5.83	44.60	46.46	2.42	0	13.32	1.05	14.98	14,498	4	95	0	0	44					Dec-12
	3.86	17.18	8.60	36.03	43.22	2.46	0	12.15	1	12.89	4,259	0	100	0	0	19					Nov-13
	5.89	23.67	9.18	65.71	84.46	0.64	0	14.13	1.02	18.51	7,375	5	93	0	0	32					Dec-12
	3.10	10.43	9.52	22.22	35.95	5.48	0	3.91	0.18	11.09	966.2	3	15	51	0	27					Oct-11
	1.96	18.97	1.18	34.06	32.76	1.69	0	15.56	0.88	11.08	1,646	2	98	0	0	41					Nov-13
	3.56	22.17	3.46	44.66	43.43	0.92	0	15.44	0.89	13.94	5,892	2	98	0	0	68	27.07	-25.36			Mar-07
	4.32	16.79	7.60	32.08	38.05	2.12	0	12.02	0.99	12.31	10,814	3	97	0	0	87					Dec-12
	2.80	13.72	4.45	30.43	33.92	2.28	0	10.85	0.86	12.84	8,022	4	96	0	0	40					Dec-12
	1.56	17.08	-1.01	27.40	26.44	0.92	0.61	15.55	0.88	22.27	2,815	1	99	0	0	32	33.13	-24.35			Sep-00
	2.47	17.28	-4.79	34.25	35.36	0.8	0.64	18.09	1.04	12.42	651.2	1	99	0	0	88	29.29	-23.49			Dec-07
	5.47	28.01	5.70	74.69	87.15	0	1.02	16.1	0.89	26.78	4,093	1	98	0	0	106	26.43	-24.47			Nov-04
	5.70	27.74	5.73			0	0.61			13.72	835.6	5	95	0	0	114					May-17
	2.13	17.96	-3.21	44.80	42.49	1.17	0.03	17.12	1	20.1	9,399	1	99	0	0	18	27.55				Sep-11
	5.84	22.00	2.78	38.17	45.03	0.27	0.67	14.94	0.84	17.02	1,502	1	99	0	0	66	26.12	-32.43			Mar-98
	5.78	22.22	2.70			0.71	0.6			11.2	87.6	1	99	0	0	75					May-17
	1.85	13.55	-4.34	26.98	32.53	0.74	0.91	14.41	0.8	14.83	2,076	2	98	0	0	55	30.92	-23.61			Nov-04
	4.16	20.78	4.52	49.52	54.88	0.67	0.63	13.33	1.05	46.02	9,367	2	98	0	0	12	24.76	-21.12			Sep-90
	4.11	16.50	6.79	31.16	36.45	1.38	0.68	12.01	0.98	20.26	981.9	2	98	0	0	92	24.88	-20.13			Nov-01
	4.00	21.61	4.36	48.35	46.87	0.75	0.77	14.26	0.92	36.35	2,120	3	97	0	0	81	27.84	-21.01			Jun-12
	3.75	21.71	3.05	42.38	42.96	0.19	0.68	15.59	0.89	24.05	1,193	3	97	0	0	68	27.46	-25.4			Jun-93
	2.55	14.90	8.93	28.35	41.13	2.8	0.72	8.3	0.65	15.29	4,835	3	65	10	0	49	19.05	-11.48			Dec-03
	0.90	7.07	1.66	8.41	2.26	3.46	0.83	4.21	0.56	8.39	373.1	16	14	55	12	23	8.48	-7.72			Sep-05
	3.23	12.99	12.27	28.45	43.28	2.16	0.7	9.33	0.44	27.44	1,054	0	100	0	0	77	12.28	-5.75			Nov-87
	2.70	14.04	5.39	32.40	20.44	2.16	1.13	11.42	0.8	12.91	738.0	5	70	24	0	94					Nov-11
	4.90	18.09	3.22	32.44	21.40	0.85	1.2	11.91	1.02	9.2	99.3	2	98	0	0	52	16.46	-25.18			Nov-07
	2.85	13.76	0.39	30.83		1.95	0.06	11.41	0.99	11.9	2,833	8	92	0	0	3					Jun-16
	4.08	19.74	8.88	50.30	62.30	1.72	0.02	12.55	1	83.41	48,079	0	100	0	0	8	25.77	-17.7			Sep-11
	6.16	24.14	10.33	65.17	80.06	0.2	0.67	13.71	1	106.29	1,948	0	99	0	1	88	24.13	-16.98			Jun-58
	3.95	19.16	11.69			1.15	0.11			12.62	155.8	0	100	0	0	15					May-17
	2.86	13.73	4.35	32.76	36.09	1.96	0.69	10.9	0.86	28.4	2,431	5	95	0	0	33	26.09	-21.01			Dec-02
	2.86	13.77	4.43	33.22	36.91	2.1	0.57	10.91	0.87	28.41	2,431	5	95	0	0	33	26.21	-20.96			May-08
	2.96	13.86	4.42			2.49	0.45			10.76	219.7	5	95	0	0	38					May-17
	3.15	21.22	-0.02	29.72	27.79	1.03	0.59	15.45	1.15	10.45	6,980	1	99	0	0	100	26.86	-24.68			Dec-78
	3.15	21.20	0.09	30.08	28.44	1.12	0.49	15.51	1.16	10.46	6,980	1	99	0	0	100	26.95	-24.63			May-08
	3.67	22.85	1.52	32.78	31.00	0.92	0.63	14.56	1.07	36.93	870.4	2	98	0	0	72	29.28	-26.76			Dec-83
	1.27	17.10	-0.33				0.23			10.39	48.9	1	99	0	0	11					Apr-19
	-4.85	4.96	-0.66	40.81	59.78		0.9	16.37	1.05		780.8	1	98	0	0	65	23.14	-15			Apr-19
	3.12	13.38	1.88				0.27			9.57	88.1	4	96	0	0	5					Apr-19
	4.01	18.64	7.89				0.22			10.93	127.1	2	98	0	0	4					Apr-19

	MARKET			FUND TYPE, CATEGORY & OBJECTIVE	RATINGS					MINIMUMS
Fund Name	Ticker Symbol	Traded On	Fund Type	Category and (Prospectus Objective)	Overall Rating	Reward Rating	Risk Rating	Recent Up/ Downgrade	Open to New Investors	Min Initial Investment
Fidelity® Worldwide Fund	FWWFX	NAS CM	Open End	Global Equity Large Cap (World Stock)	C+	C	B		Y	0
Fiduciary/Claymore Energy Infrastructure Fund	FMO	NYSE	Closed End	Energy Sector Equity (Natl Res)	D+	D+	C-	Down	Y	
Fiera Capital Diversified Alternatives Institutional Cls	FCAIX	NAS CM	Open End	Multialternative (Income)	C-	D+	C	Up	Y	10,000
Fiera Capital Diversified Alternatives Fund Investor Class	FCARX	NAS CM	Open End	Multialternative (Income)	C-	D+	C	Up	Y	2,000
Fiera Capital Emerging Markets Fund Institutional Class	CNRYX	NAS CM	Open End	Global Emerg Mkts (Div Emerging Mkts)	C	C-	C		Y	0
Fiera Capital Emerging Markets Fund Investor Class	RIMIX	NAS CM	Open End	Global Emerg Mkts (Div Emerging Mkts)	C	C-	C		Y	0
Fiera Capital Equity Allocation Fund Bel Air Advisor Class	FCEAX	NAS CM	Open End	US Equity Large Cap Blend (Growth)	U	U	U		Y	10,000
Fiera Capital Global Equity Fund Institutional Class	FCGIX	NAS CM	Open End	Global Equity Large Cap (Growth)	C	C	B-	Up	Y	1,000,000
Fiera Capital Global Equity Fund Investor Class	FCGEX	NAS CM	Open End	Global Equity Large Cap (Growth)	C	C	B-	Up	Y	1,000
FIERA CAPITAL INTERNATIONAL EQUITY FUND Class Z	FCIWX	NAS CM	Open End	Global Equity Large Cap (Foreign Stock)	C-	D+	B-	Up	Y	100,000,000
FIERA CAPITAL INTERNATIONAL EQUITY Institutional Cls	FCIUX	NAS CM	Open End	Global Equity Large Cap (Foreign Stock)	C-	D+	C+	Up	Y	1,000,000
FIERA CAPITAL INTERNATIONAL EQUITY FUND Investor Class	FCIRX	NAS CM	Open End	Global Equity Large Cap (Foreign Stock)	C-	D+	C+	Up	Y	1,000
Fiera Capital Small/Mid-Cap Growth Fund Investor Class	APSRX	NAS CM	Open End	US Equity Mid Cap (Growth)	C+	C	C+		Y	1,000
Fintrust Income and Opportunity Fund Class A	HROAX	NAS CM	Open End	Long/Short Equity (Growth & Income)	B-	C	B+	Up	Y	1,000
Fintrust Income and Opportunity Fund Institutional Class	HIOIX	NAS CM	Open End	Long/Short Equity (Growth & Income)	B-	C	B+	Up	Y	2,000
First Eagle Fund of America Class A	FEFAX	NAS CM	Open End	US Equity Mid Cap (Growth)	C	C-	C		Y	2,500
First Eagle Fund of America Class C	FEAMX	NAS CM	Open End	US Equity Mid Cap (Growth)	C-	D+	C	Down	Y	2,500
First Eagle Fund of America Class I	FEAIX	NAS CM	Open End	US Equity Mid Cap (Growth)	C	C-	C		Y	1,000,000
First Eagle Fund of America Class R3	EARFX	NAS CM	Open End	US Equity Mid Cap (Growth)	C	D+	C		Y	0
First Eagle Fund of America Class R6	FEFRX	NAS CM	Open End	US Equity Mid Cap (Growth)	C	C-	C		Y	0
First Eagle Fund of America Class Y	FEAFX	NAS CM	Open End	US Equity Mid Cap (Growth)	C	C-	C			2,500
First Eagle Global Fund Class A	SGENX	NAS CM	Open End	Flexible Alloc (Multi-Asset Global)	B-	C	A-	Up	Y	2,500
First Eagle Global Fund Class C	FESGX	NAS CM	Open End	Flexible Alloc (Multi-Asset Global)	B-	C	B+	Up	Y	2,500
First Eagle Global Fund Class I	SGIIX	NAS CM	Open End	Flexible Alloc (Multi-Asset Global)	B-	C	A-	Up	Y	1,000,000
First Eagle Global Fund Class R3	EARGX	NAS CM	Open End	Flexible Alloc (Multi-Asset Global)	B-	C	B+	Up	Y	0
First Eagle Global Fund Class R4	EAGRX	NAS CM	Open End	Flexible Alloc (Multi-Asset Global)	B-	C	A-	Up	Y	0
First Eagle Global Fund Class R6	FEGRX	NAS CM	Open End	Flexible Alloc (Multi-Asset Global)	B-	C	A-	Up	Y	0
First Eagle Global Income Builder Fund Class A	FEBAX	NAS CM	Open End	Moderate Alloc (Multi-Asset Global)	B-	C	A-	Up	Y	2,500
First Eagle Global Income Builder Fund Class C	FEBCX	NAS CM	Open End	Moderate Alloc (Multi-Asset Global)	B-	C	B+	Up	Y	2,500
First Eagle Global Income Builder Fund Class I	FEBIX	NAS CM	Open End	Moderate Alloc (Multi-Asset Global)	B-	C	A-	Up	Y	1,000,000
First Eagle Global Income Builder Fund Class R3	FBRRX	NAS CM	Open End	Moderate Alloc (Multi-Asset Global)	B-	C	A-	Up	Y	0
First Eagle Global Income Builder Fund Class R6	FEBRX	NAS CM	Open End	Moderate Alloc (Multi-Asset Global)	B-	C	A-	Up	Y	0
First Eagle Gold Fund Class A	SGGDX	NAS CM	Open End	Precious Metals Sector Equity (Precious Metals)	D+	D	C-		Y	2,500
First Eagle Gold Fund Class C	FEGOX	NAS CM	Open End	Precious Metals Sector Equity (Precious Metals)	D	D	C-	Down	Y	2,500
First Eagle Gold Fund Class I	FEGIX	NAS CM	Open End	Precious Metals Sector Equity (Precious Metals)	D+	D	C-		Y	1,000,000
First Eagle Gold Fund Class R3	EAURX	NAS CM	Open End	Precious Metals Sector Equity (Precious Metals)	D+	D	C-		Y	0
First Eagle Gold Fund Class R6	FEURX	NAS CM	Open End	Precious Metals Sector Equity (Precious Metals)	D+	D	C-		Y	0
First Eagle Overseas Fund Class A	SGOVX	NAS CM	Open End	Global Equity Large Cap (Foreign Stock)	C+	C-	B	Up		2,500
First Eagle Overseas Fund Class C	FESOX	NAS CM	Open End	Global Equity Large Cap (Foreign Stock)	C	C-	B			2,500
First Eagle Overseas Fund Class I	SGOIX	NAS CM	Open End	Global Equity Large Cap (Foreign Stock)	C+	C-	B	Up		1,000,000
First Eagle Overseas Fund Class R3	EAROX	NAS CM	Open End	Global Equity Large Cap (Foreign Stock)	C	C-	B		Y	0
First Eagle Overseas Fund Class R4	FIORX	NAS CM	Open End	Global Equity Large Cap (Foreign Stock)	C+	C-	B	Up	Y	0
First Eagle Overseas Fund Class R5	FEROX	NAS CM	Open End	Global Equity Large Cap (Foreign Stock)	C+	C-	B	Up	Y	0
First Eagle Overseas Fund Class R6	FEORX	NAS CM	Open End	Global Equity Large Cap (Foreign Stock)	C+	C-	B	Up		0
First Eagle U.S. Value Fund Class A	FEVAX	NAS CM	Open End	US Equity Large Cap Blend (Growth)	B-	C	A-		Y	2,500
First Eagle U.S. Value Fund Class C	FEVCX	NAS CM	Open End	US Equity Large Cap Blend (Growth)	B-	C	A-		Y	2,500
First Eagle U.S. Value Fund Class I	FEVIX	NAS CM	Open End	US Equity Large Cap Blend (Growth)	B-	C	A-		Y	1,000,000
First Eagle U.S. Value Fund Class R3	EARVX	NAS CM	Open End	US Equity Large Cap Blend (Growth)	B-	C	A-		Y	0
First Eagle U.S. Value Fund Class R6	FEVRX	NAS CM	Open End	US Equity Large Cap Blend (Growth)	B-	C	A-		Y	0
First Investors Covered Call Strategy Fund Class A	FRCCX	NAS CM	Open End	Long/Short Equity (Growth)	C+	C	B	Up	Y	1,000
First Investors Covered Call Strategy Fund Class Advisor	FRCDX	NAS CM	Open End	Long/Short Equity (Growth)	C+	C	B	Up	Y	1,000
First Investors Covered Call Strategy Cls Institutional	FRCEX	NAS CM	Open End	Long/Short Equity (Growth)	C+	C	B	Up	Y	2,000,000

★ Expanded analysis of this fund is included in Section II.

	TOTAL RETURNS					PERFORMANCE				ASSETS		ASSET ALLOCATION & TURNOVER					BULL & BEAR		FEES		
Min Additional Investment	3-Month Total Return	6-Month Total Return	1-Year Total Return	3-Year Total Return	5-Year Total Return	Dividend Yield (TTM)	Expense Ratio	3-Yr Std Deviation	3-Year Beta	NAV	Total Assets (MIL)	%Cash	%Stocks	%Bonds	%Other	Turnover Ratio	Last Bull Market Total Return	Last Bear Market Total Return	Front End Fee (%)	Back End Fee (%)	Inception Date
	4.14	19.44	7.15	51.16	46.54	0.29	0.94	12.37	1.02	27.4	2,580	4	96	0	0	117	19.45	-19.94			May-90
	-4.58	19.64	-3.52	-0.09	-36.83	0	11.57	22.75	1.25	10.45	370.4	0	100	0	0	41	18.53	-11.03			Dec-04
	2.81	7.70	5.32	-1.04		0	3.32	5.1	22.76	9.5	50.8	-233	12	320	0	221					Jul-14
	2.62	7.45	4.92	-1.78		0	3.57	5.06	21.41	9.37	50.8	-233	12	320	0	221					Jul-14
	-1.43	14.60	-3.73	25.97	26.95	0.19	1.38	14.68	0.93	45.21	1,956	7	93	0	0						Jun-16
	-1.48	14.46	-3.96	25.01	25.98	0	1.63	14.67	0.93	45.02	1,956	7	93	0	0						Dec-11
100	0.85	15.26					1.25			10.57	17.5	1	99	0	0						Nov-18
100	5.57	23.73	15.76			0.65	0.9			13.45	16.2	1	99	0	0						Apr-17
100	5.49	23.55	15.54			0.49	1.15			13.43	16.2	1	99	0	0						Apr-17
	6.65	20.38	9.98			0.94	0.8			11.22	103.0	0	99	0	1						Sep-17
100	6.67	20.21	9.79			0.94	1			11.18	103.0	0	99	0	1						Sep-17
100	6.58	20.10	9.57			0.68	1.25			11.17	103.0	0	99	0	1						Sep-17
100	5.14	26.22	6.26	53.35	44.01	0	1.31	16.33	0.97	17.57	193.3	0	99	0	1						Feb-18
100	1.93	9.45	2.50	18.91		0	2.22	8.21	0.6	10.53	10.2	0	86	14	0	281			5.50		Jan-16
100	1.91	9.59	2.67	19.71		0	1.97	8.22	0.6	10.62	10.2	0	86	14	0	281					Jan-16
100	2.09	22.38	-5.71	19.95	8.49	0	1.32	16.27	1.22	26.3	1,138	6	94	0	0	60	26.66	-19.88	5.00		Nov-98
100	1.89	21.90	-6.41	17.26	4.50	0	2.06	16.26	1.22	19.31	1,138	6	94	0	0	60	26.11	-20.13		1.00	Mar-98
100	2.16	22.59	-5.45	20.99	10.08	0	1.02	16.27	1.22	27.35	1,138	6	94	0	0	60	26.68	-19.92			Mar-13
	1.94	22.24	-5.86	19.48	7.86	0	1.38	16.25	1.22	27.2	1,138	6	94	0	0	60	26.61	-19.95			May-18
	2.20	22.67	-5.34	20.86	9.33	0	0.98	16.26	1.22	27.38	1,138	6	94	0	0	60	26.68	-19.92			Mar-17
100	2.10	22.41	-5.71	19.92	8.48	0	1.33	16.29	1.22	27.14	1,138	6	94	0	0	60	26.68	-19.92			Apr-87
100	3.63	14.34	5.56	23.92	25.80	0.71	1.11	8.72	0.74	57.95	50,427	15	76	1	9		12.73	-11.43	5.00		Apr-70
100	3.43	13.91	4.76	21.14	21.13	0	1.86	8.72	0.74	55.68	50,427	15	76	1	9		12.23	-11.69		1.00	Jun-00
100	3.70	14.50	5.82	24.88	27.48	0.98	0.84	8.72	0.74	58.26	50,427	15	76	1	9		12.88	-11.32			Jul-98
	3.59	14.28	5.42	23.48	25.11	0.75	1.25	8.73	0.74	58.16	50,427	15	76	1	9		12.66	-11.47			May-18
	3.66	14.43	5.70	24.18	26.06	0.85	1.02	8.73	0.74	58.26	50,427	15	76	1	9		12.73	-11.43			Jan-18
	3.71	14.54	5.91	24.82	26.72	1.04	0.78	8.72	0.74	58.28	50,427	15	76	1	9		12.73	-11.43			Mar-17
100	2.40	10.28	3.91	21.69	16.43	2.2	1.18	6.36		12.04	1,501	10	56	28	6	22			5.00		May-12
100	2.13	9.81	3.06	18.94	12.05	1.47	1.93	6.34		12	1,501	10	56	28	6	22				1.00	May-12
100	2.47	10.45	4.10	22.68	17.92	2.45	0.92	6.32		12.01	1,501	10	56	28	6	22					May-12
	2.27	10.15	3.63	21.25	15.73	2.01	1.27	6.31		12.01	1,501	10	56	28	6	22					May-18
	2.47	10.37	4.13	22.78	18.02	2.48	0.88	6.32		12	1,501	10	56	28	6	22					Mar-17
100	11.74	20.78	8.81	-12.66	-5.38	0	1.29	20.86	0.31	17.03	1,122	6	72	0	22	9	-11.18	-11.27	5.00		Aug-93
100	11.53	20.36	8.07	-14.65	-9.05	0	2.05	20.9	0.31	15.66	1,122	6	72	0	22	9	-11.55	-11.55		1.00	May-03
100	11.86	20.97	9.15	-11.90	-4.05	0	1	20.9	0.31	17.53	1,122	6	72	0	22	9	-11.07	-11.16			May-03
	12.13	21.27	9.27	-12.53	-5.43	0	1.32	20.88	0.31	17.56	1,122	6	72	0	22	9	-11.23	-11.3			May-18
	12.03	21.21	9.45	-11.70	-4.35	0	0.91	20.88	0.31	17.6	1,122	6	72	0	22	9	-11.18	-11.27			Mar-17
100	4.09	12.69	3.75	15.86	15.13	1.1	1.15	8.02	0.68	24.14	13,924	14	77	1	9	12	7.98	-11.71	5.00		Aug-93
100	3.85	12.22	2.98	13.26	10.96	0.38	1.88	7.99	0.68	23.14	13,924	14	77	1	9	12	7.52	-11.97		1.00	Jun-00
100	4.13	12.79	4.04	16.77	16.75	1.4	0.86	7.99	0.68	24.69	13,924	14	77	1	9	12	8.14	-11.62			Jul-98
	4.05	12.61	3.65	15.47	14.52	1.21	1.21	7.98	0.68	24.64	13,924	14	77	1	9	12	7.92	-11.75			May-18
	4.09	12.70	3.79	16.02	15.29	1.27	1.03	8.01	0.68	24.66	13,924	14	77	1	9	12	7.98	-11.71			Jan-18
	4.13	12.73	3.78	15.90	15.17		0.95	8.02	0.68	24.68	13,924	14	77	1	9	12	7.98	-11.71			Mar-19
	4.21	12.88	4.12	16.78	16.05	1.47	0.8	7.99	0.68	24.7	13,924	14	77	1	9	12	7.98	-11.71			Mar-17
100	3.32	14.68	6.77	31.13	33.07	0.57	1.1	9.92	0.78	18.67	1,655	17	71	2	10	9	16.9	-10.31	5.00		Sep-01
100	3.07	14.20	5.91	28.10	28.06	0	1.85	9.88	0.77	17.77	1,655	17	71	2	10	9	16.42	-10.58		1.00	Sep-01
100	3.37	14.79	7.00	32.13	34.79	0.84	0.82	9.89	0.77	19.01	1,655	17	71	2	10	9	17.08	-10.2			Sep-01
	3.21	14.55	6.60	30.68	32.39	0.64	1.19	9.93	0.78	18.97	1,655	17	71	2	10	9	16.84	-10.33			May-18
	3.42	14.85	7.09	32.22	34.89	0.87	0.81	9.9	0.77	19.02	1,655	17	71	2	10	9	17.08	-10.2			Mar-17
	3.15	15.42	4.76	19.26		1.09	1.3	10.75	0.85	11.61	314.9	1	99	0	0	107			5.75		Apr-16
	3.36	15.59	5.09	20.40		1.38	1.03	10.76	0.85	11.58	314.9	1	99	0	0	107					Apr-16
	3.29	15.60	5.20	20.88		1.55	0.89	10.76	0.85	11.5	314.9	1	99	0	0	107					Apr-16

Fund Name	MARKET Ticker Symbol	Traded On	FUND TYPE, CATEGORY & OBJECTIVE Fund Type	Category and (Prospectus Objective)	RATINGS Overall Rating	Reward Rating	Risk Rating	Recent Up/ Downgrade	Open to New Investors	MINIMUMS Min Initial Investment
First Investors Equity Income Fund Advisor Class	FIUUX	NAS CM	Open End	US Equity Large Cap Value (Equity-Income)	B-	C	B	Up	Y	1,000
First Investors Equity Income Fund Class A	FIUTX	NAS CM	Open End	US Equity Large Cap Value (Equity-Income)	B-	C	B	Up	Y	1,000
First Investors Equity Income Fund Class B	FIUBX	NAS CM	Open End	US Equity Large Cap Value (Equity-Income)	C+	C	B	Up	Y	1,000
First Investors Equity Income Fund Institutional Class	FIUVX	NAS CM	Open End	US Equity Large Cap Value (Equity-Income)	B-	C	B	Up	Y	2,000,000
First Investors Global Fund Advisor Class	FIITX	NAS CM	Open End	Global Equity Large Cap (World Stock)	C+	C	B	Up	Y	1,000
First Investors Global Fund Class A	FIISX	NAS CM	Open End	Global Equity Large Cap (World Stock)	C+	C	B	Up	Y	1,000
First Investors Global Fund Class B	FIBGX	NAS CM	Open End	Global Equity Large Cap (World Stock)	C	C	B-		Y	1,000
First Investors Global Fund Institutional Class	FIIUX	NAS CM	Open End	Global Equity Large Cap (World Stock)	C+	C	B	Up	Y	2,000,000
First Investors Growth and Income Fund Advisor Class	FGIPX	NAS CM	Open End	US Equity Large Cap Value (Growth & Income)	C+	C	B	Up	Y	1,000
First Investors Growth and Income Fund Class A	FGINX	NAS CM	Open End	US Equity Large Cap Value (Growth & Income)	C+	C	B	Up	Y	1,000
First Investors Growth and Income Fund Class B	FGIBX	NAS CM	Open End	US Equity Large Cap Value (Growth & Income)	C+	C	B	Up	Y	1,000
First Investors Growth and Income Fund Institutional Class	FGIQX	NAS CM	Open End	US Equity Large Cap Value (Growth & Income)	C+	C	B	Up	Y	2,000,000
First Investors Hedged U.S. Equity Opportunities A Cls	FHEJX	NAS CM	Open End	Long/Short Equity (Growth & Income)	C+	C	B		Y	1,000
First Invs Hedged U.S. Equity Opp Adv Cls	FHEKX	NAS CM	Open End	Long/Short Equity (Growth & Income)	B-	C	B	Up	Y	1,000
First Invs Hedged U.S. Equity Opp Inst Cls	FHELX	NAS CM	Open End	Long/Short Equity (Growth & Income)	B-	C	B	Up	Y	2,000,000
First Investors International Fund Advisor Class	FIIPX	NAS CM	Open End	Global Equity Large Cap (Foreign Stock)	C+	C	B-	Up	Y	1,000
First Investors International Fund Class A	FIINX	NAS CM	Open End	Global Equity Large Cap (Foreign Stock)	C+	C	B-	Up	Y	1,000
First Investors International Fund Class B	FIIOX	NAS CM	Open End	Global Equity Large Cap (Foreign Stock)	C	C	B-		Y	1,000
First Investors International Fund Institutional Class	FIIQX	NAS CM	Open End	Global Equity Large Cap (Foreign Stock)	C+	C	B-	Up	Y	2,000,000
First Investors Opportunity Fund Advisor Class	FIVUX	NAS CM	Open End	US Equity Mid Cap (Growth)	C+	C	B-	Up	Y	1,000
First Investors Opportunity Fund Class A	FIUSX	NAS CM	Open End	US Equity Mid Cap (Growth)	C	C	B-		Y	1,000
First Investors Opportunity Fund Class B	FIMBX	NAS CM	Open End	US Equity Mid Cap (Growth)	C	C	B-		Y	1,000
First Investors Opportunity Fund Institutional Class	FIVVX	NAS CM	Open End	US Equity Mid Cap (Growth)	C+	C	B-	Up	Y	2,000,000
First Investors Premium Income Fund Advisor Class	FPILX	NAS CM	Open End	Long/Short Equity (Income)	D	D+	C+	Up	Y	1,000
First Investors Premium Income Fund Class A	FPIKX	NAS CM	Open End	Long/Short Equity (Income)	D	D+	C+	Up	Y	1,000
First Investors Premium Income Fund Institutional Class	FPIMX	NAS CM	Open End	Long/Short Equity (Income)	D	D+	B-	Up	Y	2,000,000
First Investors Select Growth Fund Advisor Class	FICHX	NAS CM	Open End	US Equity Large Cap Growth (Growth)	C+	C	B	Down	Y	1,000
First Investors Select Growth Fund Class A	FICGX	NAS CM	Open End	US Equity Large Cap Growth (Growth)	C+	C	B	Down	Y	1,000
First Investors Select Growth Fund Class B	FIGBX	NAS CM	Open End	US Equity Large Cap Growth (Growth)	C	C-	B	Down	Y	1,000
First Investors Select Growth Fund Institutional Class	FICIX	NAS CM	Open End	US Equity Large Cap Growth (Growth)	C+	C	B	Down	Y	2,000,000
First Investors Special Situations Class A	FISSX	NAS CM	Open End	US Equity Small Cap (Aggr Growth)	C-	C-	C	Down	Y	1,000
First Investors Special Situations Class B	FISBX	NAS CM	Open End	US Equity Small Cap (Aggr Growth)	C-	C-	C	Down	Y	1,000
First Investors Special Situations Fund Advisor Class	FISTX	NAS CM	Open End	US Equity Small Cap (Aggr Growth)	C	C-	C		Y	1,000
First Investors Special Situations Institutional Cls	FISUX	NAS CM	Open End	US Equity Small Cap (Aggr Growth)	C	C-	C		Y	2,000,000
First Investors Total Return Fund Advisor Class	FITUX	NAS CM	Open End	Moderate Alloc (Asset Alloc)	B-	C	B+	Up	Y	1,000
First Investors Total Return Fund Institutional Class	FITVX	NAS CM	Open End	Moderate Alloc (Asset Alloc)	B-	C	B+	Up	Y	2,000,000
First Investors Total Return Series Class A	FITRX	NAS CM	Open End	Moderate Alloc (Asset Alloc)	B-	C	B+	Up	Y	1,000
First Investors Total Return Series Class B	FBTRX	NAS CM	Open End	Moderate Alloc (Asset Alloc)	B-	C	B	Up	Y	1,000
First State Global Listed Infrastructure Fund Class I	FLIIX	NAS CM	Open End	Infrastructure Sector Equity ()	C	C	B-		Y	1,000,000
First Trust Dynamic Europe Equity Income	FDEU	NYSE	Closed End	Europe Equity Large Cap (Equity-Income)	D+	D+	C-	Down	Y	
First Trust Energy Income and Growth Fund	FEN	AMEX	Closed End	Energy Sector Equity (Natl Res)	C	C	C-		Y	
First Trust Energy Infrastructure Fund	FIF	NYSE	Closed End	Energy Sector Equity (Equity-Income)	C	C	C-		Y	
First Trust Enhanced Equity Income Fund	FFA	NYSE	Closed End	Alternative Miscellaneous (Equity-Income)	C	C	C-		Y	
First Trust Intermediate Duration Preferred & Income Fund	FPF	NYSE	Closed End	US Fixed Income (Income)	B-	B-	C+	Up	Y	
First Trust MLP and Energy Income Fund Common	FEI	NYSE	Closed End	Energy Sector Equity (Growth & Income)	C	C	C		Y	
First Trust New Opps MLP & Energy Fund	FPL	NYSE	Closed End	Energy Sector Equity (Income)	C	C	C-		Y	
First Trust Preferred Securities and Income Fund Class A	FPEAX	NAS CM	Open End	US Fixed Income (Income)	B	B-	B+	Up	Y	2,500
First Trust Preferred Securities and Income Fund Class C	FPECX	NAS CM	Open End	US Fixed Income (Income)	B	C+	B+	Up	Y	2,500
First Trust Preferred Securities and Income Fund Class F	FPEFX	NAS CM	Open End	US Fixed Income (Income)	B	B-	B+	Up	Y	2,500
First Trust Preferred Securities and Income Fund Class I	FPEIX	NAS CM	Open End	US Fixed Income (Income)	B	B-	B+	Up	Y	1,000,000
First Trust Preferred Securities and Income Fund Class R3	FPERX	NAS CM	Open End	US Fixed Income (Income)	B	B-	B+	Up	Y	0
First Trust Special Finance & Financial Opportunities Fund	FGB	NYSE	Closed End	Financials Sector Equity (Financial)	C	C+	C-	Down	Y	

★ Expanded analysis of this fund is included in Section II.

Min Additional Investment	TOTAL RETURNS 3-Month Total Return	6-Month Total Return	1-Year Total Return	3-Year Total Return	5-Year Total Return	PERFORMANCE Dividend Yield (TTM)	Expense Ratio	3-Yr Std Deviation	3-Year Beta	ASSETS NAV	Total Assets (MIL)	ASSET ALLOCATION & TURNOVER %Cash	%Stocks	%Bonds	%Other	Turnover Ratio	BULL & BEAR Last Bull Market Total Return	Last Bear Market Total Return	FEES Front End Fee (%)	Back End Fee (%)	Inception Date
	3.36	14.00	5.09	30.56	36.60	2.89	0.86	10.92	0.93	9.59	503.2	7	90	0	0	27	23.06	-17.75			Apr-13
	3.44	13.96	4.90	29.40	34.43	2.52	1.16	10.9	0.92	9.54	503.2	7	90	0	0	27	23.06	-17.75	5.75		Feb-93
	1.01	9.50	0.22	24.10	27.78	1.78	2.05	10.32	0.92		479.4	7	90	0	0	27	22.5	-17.97		4.00	Jan-95
	3.51	14.27	5.31	31.03	37.01	3.13	0.81	10.9	0.92	9.53	503.2	7	90	0	0	27	23.06	-17.75			Apr-13
	4.74	17.65	2.88	38.34	37.87	0	1.1	11.69	1	7.73	654.5	4	96	0	0	154	21.79	-22.62			Apr-13
	4.60	17.39	2.57	36.73	35.08	0	1.43	11.68	1	7.49	654.5	4	96	0	0	154	21.79	-22.62	5.75		Nov-81
	1.91	11.75	-4.14	28.48	26.96	0	2.28	11.43	1.02		628.4	4	96	0	0	154	21.15	-22.79		4.00	Jan-95
	4.71	17.70	2.97	38.30	38.05	0	1.05	11.66	1	7.78	654.5	4	96	0	0	154	21.79	-22.62			Apr-13
	4.22	16.33	6.06	35.45	33.86	1.39	0.8	11.94	1	19.65	1,707	6	95	0	0	22	29.31	-18.78			Apr-13
	4.21	16.14	5.73	34.01	31.43	1.13	1.1	11.93	1	19.48	1,707	6	95	0	0	22	29.31	-18.78	5.75		Oct-93
	1.80	10.48	0.75	27.82	25.32	0.4	1.94	11.51	1.01		1,624	6	95	0	0	22	28.87	-19.06		4.00	Jan-95
	4.27	16.35	6.16	35.62	34.11	1.55	0.75	11.97	1	19.56	1,707	6	95	0	0	22	29.31	-18.78			Apr-13
	4.97	16.12	9.30	25.32		0	1.76			12.24	315.8	7	93	0	0	7			5.75		Aug-16
	5.10	16.38	9.68	26.56		0	1.42			12.36	315.8	7	93	0	0	7					Aug-16
	5.08	16.43	9.85	26.97		0.01	1.39			12.4	315.8	7	93	0	0	7					Aug-16
	6.34	19.46	5.59	31.53	28.68	0.23	1.18	11.48	0.92	16.08	432.0	4	96	0	0	36	19.65	-14.2			Apr-13
	6.27	19.31	5.21	30.05	26.23	0.17	1.51	11.49	0.92	15.75	432.0	4	96	0	0	36	19.65	-14.2	5.75		Jun-06
	3.55	14.35	0.04	22.88	17.43	0.01	2.38	11.13	0.9		414.1	4	96	0	0	36	19.21	-14.44		4.00	Jun-06
	6.38	19.62	5.68	31.96	29.40	0.27	1.09	11.53	0.92	16.15	432.0	4	96	0	0	36	19.65	-14.2			Apr-13
	3.58	20.25	1.22	34.13	30.57	0.97	0.9	13.96	0.9	38.17	1,026	4	96	0	0	34	29.41	-20.87			Apr-13
	3.52	20.10	0.92	32.89	28.62	0.93	1.16	13.94	0.9	37.27	1,026	4	96	0	0	34	29.41	-20.87	5.75		Aug-92
	1.66	14.56	-4.05	25.59	23.16	1.17	1.97	13.63	0.91		978.2	4	96	0	0	34	28.87	-21.11		4.00	Jan-95
	3.61	20.39	1.37	34.63	31.39	1.05	0.78	13.94	0.9	38.14	1,026	4	96	0	0	34	29.41	-20.87			Apr-13
	0.79	7.76	3.88			1.84	1.06			10.15	116.1	2	98	0	0	77					Apr-18
	0.74	7.69	3.56			1.82	1.3			10.14	116.1	2	98	0	0	77			5.75		Apr-18
	0.86	7.99	4.08			80.58	0.99			5.52	116.1	2	98	0	0	77					Apr-18
	-0.39	15.06	3.46	56.60	67.25	0.06	0.83	13.99	0.99	12.6	686.1	2	98	0	0	33	26.78	-16.53			Apr-13
	-0.40	14.92	3.12	54.94	64.10	0	1.17	13.94	0.99	12.32	686.1	2	98	0	0	33	26.78	-16.53	5.75		Oct-00
	-2.10	10.53	-3.43	47.80	56.11	0	1.98	13.66	0.99		652.3	2	98	0	0	33	26.34	-16.85		4.00	Oct-00
	-0.39	15.06	3.48	56.75	67.65	0.1	0.8	13.93	0.99	12.68	686.1	2	98	0	0	33	26.78	-16.53			Apr-13
	1.16	12.82	-8.36	28.40	24.37	0.28	1.24	15.63	0.96	25.25	574.7	4	96	0	0	55	24.96	-19.73	5.75		Sep-90
	-2.77	6.94	-13.27	20.85	17.59	0.23	2.07	15.24	0.95		542.1	4	96	0	0	55	24.52	-19.98		4.00	Jan-95
	1.22	12.95	-8.11	29.55	26.29	0.35	0.95	15.65	0.96	25.64	574.7	4	96	0	0	55	24.96	-19.73			Apr-13
	1.29	13.06	-7.96	30.08	27.16	0.39	0.86	15.64	0.96	25.87	574.7	4	96	0	0	55	24.96	-19.73			Apr-13
	4.51	13.64	6.96	23.17	25.01	2.07	0.84	7.45	0.59	18.9	881.0	7	56	37	0	44	19.07	-10.59			Apr-13
	4.47	13.74	7.13	23.49	25.39	2.33	0.77	7.49	0.59	18.94	881.0	7	56	37	0	44	19.07	-10.59			Apr-13
	4.37	13.49	6.69	21.98	22.86	1.75	1.13	7.46	0.59	18.8	881.0	7	56	37	0	44	19.07	-10.59	5.75		Apr-90
	2.69	9.67	2.45	16.91	16.97	1	1.94	7.12	0.59		850.2	7	56	37	0	44	18.5	-10.79		4.00	Jan-95
	4.37	19.23	13.84			1.46	0.95			11.22	24.2	0	100	0	0	60					Feb-17
	-0.54	10.50	-4.55	16.83		7.28	1.99	13.28	0.88	15.38	265.0	9	128	-37	0	44					Sep-15
	1.44	22.14	7.83	13.89	-10.29	0	13.3	16.04	0.88	22.14	442.5	4	96	0	0	42	21	-8.85			Jun-04
	2.51	25.76	13.08	13.48	1.91	1.77		14.16		17.94	314.9	2	98	0	0	58	23.94				Sep-11
	3.55	19.54	7.82	34.44	39.20	1.21	0	11.41	1.47	15.9	317.6	1	99	0	0	45	24.69	-16.94			Aug-04
	4.39	12.82	9.14	28.82	41.43	7.25	1.92	5.68		23.58	1,433	1	0	12	0	29					May-13
	1.20	23.09	6.53	6.12	-16.82	2.4	2.17	14.45		12.6	590.4	1	99	0	0	45					Nov-12
	2.44	28.83	10.78	5.08	-20.83	3.95	2.14	17.33	0.95	10.26	260.6	2	98	0	0	64					Mar-14
50	3.36	10.07	7.50	19.88	31.66	5.34	1.37	4.15	0.67	21.51	257.4	1	0	39	0	33	10.93	-0.58	4.50		Feb-11
50	3.21	9.73	6.82	17.48	27.16	4.58	2.02	4.15	0.67	21.61	257.4	1	0	39	0	33	10.54	-0.69		1.00	Feb-11
50	3.40	10.17	7.62	20.40	32.46	5.37	1.3	4.17	0.67	21.75	257.4	1	0	39	0	33	11.86	-0.78			Mar-11
	3.45	10.24	7.81	21.11	33.63	5.54	1.02	4.13	0.67	21.66	257.4	1	0	39	0	33	11.22	-0.77			Jan-11
	3.31	9.96	7.20	18.96	29.89	5.1	1.65	4.14	0.67	21.47	257.4	1	0	39	0	33	10.95	-1.01			Mar-11
	1.61	16.65	8.58	25.44	17.42	9.04	0	15.41		5.81	83.4	2	91	0	7	12	23.9	-19.82			May-07

	MARKET		FUND TYPE, CATEGORY & OBJECTIVE		RATINGS					MINIMUMS
Fund Name	Ticker Symbol	Traded On	Fund Type	Category and (Prospectus Objective)	Overall Rating	Reward Rating	Risk Rating	Recent Up/ Downgrade	Open to New Investors	Min Initial Investment
First Trust/Aberdeen Emerging Opportunity Fund	FEO	NYSE	Closed End	Global Emerg Mkts (Multi-Asset Global)	C	C	D+	Up	Y	
First Trust/Confluence Small Cap Value Fund Class A	FOVAX	NAS CM	Open End	US Equity Small Cap (Small Company)	C	C	C+		Y	2,500
First Trust/Confluence Small Cap Value Fund Class C	FOVCX	NAS CM	Open End	US Equity Small Cap (Small Company)	C	C	C+		Y	2,500
First Trust/Confluence Small Cap Value Fund Class I	FOVIX	NAS CM	Open End	US Equity Small Cap (Small Company)	C	C	C+	Down	Y	1,000,000
Firsthand Alternative Energy Fund	ALTEX	NAS CM	Open End	Technology Sector Equity (Natl Res)	C	C	C+		Y	2,000
Firsthand Technology Opportunities Fund	TEFQX	NAS CM	Open End	Technology Sector Equity (Technology)	C+	C+	C+	Up	Y	2,000
Flaherty & Crumrine Dynamic Preferred and Income Fund	DFP	NYSE	Closed End	US Fixed Income (Growth & Income)	C+	B	C-	Up	Y	
Flaherty & Crumrine Preferred Income Fund	PFD	NYSE	Closed End	US Fixed Income (Income)	C+	B	C-	Up	Y	
Flaherty & Crumrine Preferred Income Opportunity Fund	PFO	NYSE	Closed End	US Fixed Income (Income)	C+	B	C-	Up	Y	
Flaherty & Crumrine Preferred Securities Income Fund	FFC	NYSE	Closed End	US Fixed Income (Income)	B-	B	C-	Up	Y	
Flaherty & CrumrineTotal Return Fund	FLC	NYSE	Closed End	US Fixed Income (Income)	C+	B	C-	Up	Y	
FMI Common Stock Fund	FMIMX	NAS CM	Open End	US Equity Mid Cap (Growth)	B-	C+	B			1,000
FMI Common Stock Fund Institutional Class	FMIUX	NAS CM	Open End	US Equity Mid Cap (Growth)	B-	C+	B		Y	100,000
FMI International Fund	FMIJX	NAS CM	Open End	Global Equity Large Cap (Foreign Stock)	B-	C	B+	Up	Y	2,500
FMI International Fund Institutional Class	FMIYX	NAS CM	Open End	Global Equity Large Cap (Foreign Stock)	B-	C	B+	Up	Y	100,000
FMI Large Cap Fund	FMIHX	NAS CM	Open End	US Equity Large Cap Blend (Growth)	B	C+	B+			1,000
FMI Large Cap Fund Institutional Class	FMIQX	NAS CM	Open End	US Equity Large Cap Blend (Growth)	B	C+	B+		Y	100,000
Footprints Discover Value Fund	ABSOX	NAS CM	Open End	Cautious Alloc (Growth & Income)	D	D	D		Y	10,000
Forester Discovery Fund	INTLX	NAS CM	Open End	Global Equity Large Cap (Growth)	D+	D	C-		Y	2,500
Forester Value Fund Class I	FVILX	NAS CM	Open End	Long/Short Equity (Growth)	C	C-	C		Y	25,000
Forester Value Fund Class N	FVALX	NAS CM	Open End	Long/Short Equity (Growth)	C-	C-	C	Down	Y	2,500
Forester Value Fund Class R	FVRLX	NAS CM	Open End	Long/Short Equity (Growth)	C-	D+	C	Down	Y	2,500
FormulaFolios US Equity Fund Institutional Class	FFILX	NAS CM	Open End	US Equity Large Cap Blend (Growth)	C	C-	B-		Y	50,000
FormulaFolios US Equity Fund Investor Class	FFIOX	NAS CM	Open End	US Equity Large Cap Blend (Growth)	C	C-	C+		Y	2,000
FormulaFolios US Equity Portfolio Class 1			Open End	US Equity Large Cap Blend (Growth)	C	C-	C+		Y	0
Fort Pitt Capital Total Return Fund	FPCGX	NAS CM	Open End	US Equity Large Cap Blend (Growth & Income)	B-	C	B+	Down	Y	2,500
Foundry Partners Fundamental Small Cap Value Inst Cls	DRISX	NAS CM	Open End	US Equity Small Cap (Small Company)	C	C-	C		Y	100,000
Foundry Partners Fundamental Small Cap Value Investor Cls	DRSVX	NAS CM	Open End	US Equity Small Cap (Small Company)	C	C-	C		Y	2,500
Foxby Corp	FXBY	OTC BB	Closed End	US Equity Large Cap Blend (Multi-Asset Global)	C	C	D+	Up	Y	
FPA Capital Fund	FPPTX	NAS CM	Open End	US Equity Mid Cap (Growth)	C-	D	C			1,500
FPA Crescent Fund	FPACX	NAS CM	Open End	Moderate Alloc (Growth)	B-	C	B+	Up	Y	1,500
FPA International Value Fund	FPIVX	NAS CM	Open End	Global Equity Mid/Small Cap (Foreign Stock)	C+	C	B	Up	Y	1,500
FPA Paramount Fund	FPRAX	NAS CM	Open End	Global Equity Large Cap (Growth & Income)	B-	C	B	Up	Y	1,500
FPA U.S. Value Fund	FPPFX	NAS CM	Open End	US Equity Large Cap Blend (Growth & Income)	C+	C	B-			1,500
Frank Value Fund Class C	FNKCX	NAS CM	Open End	US Equity Mid Cap (Growth)	D	D	C	Down	Y	1,500
Frank Value Fund Institutional Class	FNKIX	NAS CM	Open End	US Equity Mid Cap (Growth)	D+	D	C		Y	1,000,000
Frank Value Fund Investor Class	FRNKX	NAS CM	Open End	US Equity Mid Cap (Growth)	D+	D	C		Y	1,500
Franklin Biotechnology Discovery Fund Advisor Class	FTDZX	NAS CM	Open End	Healthcare Sector Equity (Health)	C	C	C+			100,000
Franklin Biotechnology Discovery Fund Class A	FBDIX	NAS CM	Open End	Healthcare Sector Equity (Health)	C	C	C+			1,000
Franklin Biotechnology Discovery Fund Class C	FBTDX	NAS CM	Open End	Healthcare Sector Equity (Health)	C	C	C			1,000
Franklin Biotechnology Discovery Fund Class R6	FRBRX	NAS CM	Open End	Healthcare Sector Equity (Health)	C	C	C+			1,000,000
Franklin Conservative Allocation Fund Advisor Class	FTCZX	NAS CM	Open End	Cautious Alloc (Asset Alloc)	B	C	A	Up	Y	100,000
Franklin Conservative Allocation Fund Class A	FTCIX	NAS CM	Open End	Cautious Alloc (Asset Alloc)	B	C	A-	Up	Y	1,000
Franklin Conservative Allocation Fund Class C	FTCCX	NAS CM	Open End	Cautious Alloc (Asset Alloc)	B-	C	A-	Up	Y	1,000
Franklin Conservative Allocation Fund Class R	FTCRX	NAS CM	Open End	Cautious Alloc (Asset Alloc)	B	C	A-	Up	Y	1,000
Franklin Conservative Allocation Fund Class R6			Open End	Cautious Alloc (Asset Alloc)	B	C	A	Up	Y	1,000,000
Franklin Convertible Securities Fund Advisor Class	FCSZX	NAS CM	Open End	Convertibles (Convertible Bond)	B	C+	B		Y	100,000
Franklin Convertible Securities Fund Class A	FISCX	NAS CM	Open End	Convertibles (Convertible Bond)	B	C+	A-		Y	1,000
Franklin Convertible Securities Fund Class C	FROTX	NAS CM	Open End	Convertibles (Convertible Bond)	B	C+	A-		Y	1,000
Franklin Convertible Securities Fund Class R6	FCSKX	NAS CM	Open End	Convertibles (Convertible Bond)	B	C+	B		Y	1,000,000
Franklin Corefolio Allocation Fund Advisor Class	FCAZX	NAS CM	Open End	Aggressive Alloc (Growth)	B-	C	B	Up	Y	100,000
Franklin Corefolio Allocation Fund Class A	FTCOX	NAS CM	Open End	Aggressive Alloc (Growth)	C+	C	B		Y	1,000

★ Expanded analysis of this fund is included in Section II.

Min Additional Investment	TOTAL RETURNS: 3-Month Total Return	6-Month Total Return	1-Year Total Return	3-Year Total Return	5-Year Total Return	PERFORMANCE: Dividend Yield (TTM)	Expense Ratio	3-Yr Std Deviation	3-Year Beta	ASSETS: NAV	Total Assets (MIL)	ASSET ALLOCATION & TURNOVER: %Cash	%Stocks	%Bonds	%Other	Turnover Ratio	BULL & BEAR: Last Bull Market Total Return	Last Bear Market Total Return	FEES: Front End Fee (%)	Back End Fee (%)	Inception Date
	5.15	13.11	10.79	20.98	10.50	3.35	1.3	10.49		15.59	78.9	2	44	54	0	48	17.62	-12.83			Aug-06
50	3.72	18.34	-1.88	38.24	50.03	0	1.6	15.02	0.8	30.64	27.9	3	97	0	0	35	20.82	-19.31	5.50		Feb-11
50	3.59	18.15	-2.38	35.34	44.38	0	2.35	15.04	0.8	27.07	27.9	3	97	0	0	35	19.21	-19.27		1.00	Mar-11
	3.79	18.68	-1.48	38.46	50.58	0	1.35	15.04	0.8	31.44	27.9	3	97	0	0	35	21.44	-17.27			Jan-11
50	15.45	34.80	14.24	45.37	-4.28	0.03	1.98	16.92	1.11	7.32	5.7	6	94	0	0	7	-7.15	-40.74			Oct-07
50	-0.29	30.14	12.38	135.78	129.15	0	1.85	19.24	1.18	13.34	346.0	22	78	0	0	25	12.06	-17.98			Sep-99
	4.82	16.62	9.70	27.48	47.02	6.95	1.75	7.15		25.11	481.1	1	0	29	0	10					May-13
	4.85	15.56	9.26	27.29	44.31	6.66		6.46	0.93	13.78	154.6	2	0	30	0	11	15.34	-3.4			Jan-91
	4.78	15.43	9.11	26.89	44.10	6.75		6.41	0.92	11.43	143.9	2	0	30	0	11	15.81	-3.38			Feb-92
	5.06	15.94	9.47	29.41	47.35	6.92	0	6.56	0.94	19.6	868.2	2	0	33	0	12	15.7	-3.31			Jan-03
	5.17	16.13	9.38	27.79	44.83	6.75	0	6.61	0.99	20.81	207.2	1	0	32	0	13	14.55	-2.76			Aug-03
100	4.83	21.62	9.41	44.60	40.42	0.34	0.99	13.04	0.72	26.66	999.0	15	85	0	0	26	26.95	-17.61			Dec-81
100	4.83	21.65	9.53	44.97	40.78	0.47	0.89	13.04	0.72	26.68	999.0	15	85	0	0	26	26.95	-17.61			Oct-16
100	2.73	11.89	1.74	25.97	30.84	4.03	0.9	8.47		31.88	7,290	10	90	0	0	21	20.22	-13.71			Dec-10
1,000	2.76	11.96	1.87	26.42	31.30	4.22	0.76	8.46		31.91	7,290	10	90	0	0	21	20.22	-13.71			Oct-16
100	5.34	17.55	9.72	46.56	53.86	1.22	0.8	10.86	0.84	20.09	5,115	8	92	0	0	25	22.61	-15.37			Dec-01
100	5.40	17.64	9.89	47.03	54.35	1.39	0.66	10.85	0.84	20.07	5,115	8	92	0	0	25	22.61	-15.37			Oct-16
100	-21.41	-14.05	-32.68			0	2.01			6	3.0	14	81	5	0				5.75		Dec-17
100	0.78	3.14	-4.96	-0.45	-5.99	1.82	1.37	7.39	0.59	12.78	2.7	23	77	0	0	9	5.19	-10.05			Sep-99
100	-1.63	2.60	2.37	-2.86	-5.48	1.69	1.01	4.78	0.22	11.42	18.0	26	74	0	0	38	1.81	-5.27			Jun-09
100	-1.75	2.37	2.10	-3.69	-6.70	0.98	1.27	4.81	0.22	11.19	18.0	26	74	0	0	38	1.58	-5.43			Sep-99
100	-1.70	2.30	1.88	-4.31	-7.54	0.63	1.52	4.8	0.22	11.56	18.0	26	74	0	0	38	2.06	-5.55			Dec-10
500	1.79	13.93	-0.08	18.61		0.53	1.15	12.23	0.95	10.22	330.3	0	100	0	0	367					Dec-15
500	1.53	13.37	-1.08	14.76		0.02	2.15	12.32	0.95	9.92	330.3	0	100	0	0	367					Dec-15
	1.92	12.94	0.07	13.65		1.63	2.14	11.79	0.89	6.37	0.19	0	100	0	0	429					Nov-15
100	2.63	17.84	9.65	55.46	57.91	0.93	1.24	13.43	1.02	26.88	73.5	5	95	0	0	4	18.3	-11.79			Dec-01
1,000	2.34	14.58	-5.85	26.09	24.22	0.68	1.07	16.99	0.96	20.51	192.8	5	95	0	0	34	26.71	-26.84			Aug-07
1,000	2.25	14.39	-6.09	25.14	22.68	0.38	1.32	16.97	0.96	20.42	192.8	5	95	0	0	34	26.69	-27			Dec-03
	2.67	18.07	1.32	30.00	15.06	0	0	17.98	0.89	3.07	8.0	-1	98	1	0	59	26.82	-8.37			Oct-99
100	-0.34	15.70	-5.47	10.01	-18.02	1.03	0.83	16.84	0.96	30.92	258.8	17	69	12	1	82	22.18	-22.15			Jul-84
100	3.33	14.80	6.69	30.24	28.22	1.16	1.18	9.93	0.76	33.19	14,445	26	66	7	0	64	15.46	-11.58			Jun-93
100	4.08	13.68	3.67	40.47	15.63	0.91	1.29	10.52	0.84	15.29	252.2	22	73	0	5	120					Dec-11
100	5.08	17.06	5.70	48.66	31.57	0.52	1.29	11.93	0.99	21.06	165.6	0	98	0	2	79	28.82	-24.14			Jul-78
100	4.97	21.83	7.71	25.87	21.96	0.07	1.2	14.28	0.82	10.67	68.9	5	91	0	5	79	28.85	-24.83			Apr-84
100	-0.44	1.09	-1.76	-4.79	-7.32	0	2.27	4.43	0.24	11.06	12.4	41	25	31	3	68	22.49	-14.66			Sep-10
500	-0.24	1.59	-0.78	-1.96	-2.59	0.36	1.27	4.49	0.25	12.07	12.4	41	25	31	3	68	23.07	-14.44			Nov-10
100	-0.25	1.44	-0.98	-2.72	-3.83	0.1	1.52	4.49	0.25	11.91	12.4	41	25	31	3	68	22.93	-14.43			Jul-04
	3.84	27.07	1.27	35.25	34.22	0	0.77	22.97	1.01	155.74	1,088	3	97	0	0	27	34.31	-15.49			Sep-09
	3.77	26.91	1.02	34.24	32.59	0	1.02	22.96	1.01	151.62	1,088	3	97	0	0	27	34.08	-15.59	5.50		Sep-97
	3.57	26.43	0.27	31.27	27.75	0	1.77	22.94	1	145.6	1,088	3	97	0	0	27	33.5	-15.85		1.00	Mar-14
	3.88	27.15	1.39	35.84	35.23	0	0.64	22.96	1.01	157.15	1,088	3	97	0	0	27	34.08	-15.59			May-13
	2.33	9.82	5.72	21.70	20.36	3.06	0.88	5.21	0.45	14.43	1,196	6	36	56	1	31	9.18	-8.27			Dec-05
	2.26	9.70	5.46	20.72	18.80	2.81	1.13	5.23	0.46	14.43	1,196	6	36	56	1	31	8.96	-8.38	5.50		Dec-96
	2.03	9.28	4.65	18.04	14.44	2.09	1.88	5.21	0.45	14.13	1,196	6	36	56	1	31	8.55	-8.65		1.00	Dec-96
	2.20	9.53	5.19	19.86	17.35	2.56	1.38	5.21	0.45	14.37	1,196	6	36	56	1	31	8.87	-8.52			Jan-02
	2.35	9.88	5.82	21.93	20.89	3.14	0.8	5.22	0.45	14.41	1,196	6	36	56	1	31	8.96	-8.38			May-13
	5.56	20.99	15.09	55.53	58.54	2.37	0.6	9.75	1.02	22.73	3,864	2	6	0	0	36	14.92	-18.31			May-08
	5.54	20.81	14.81	54.39	56.55	2.15	0.85	9.73	1.02	22.73	3,864	2	6	0	0	36	14.77	-18.37	5.50		Apr-87
	5.34	20.38	13.93	50.96	50.83	1.46	1.6	9.73	1.02	22.37	3,864	2	6	0	0	36	14.19	-18.65		1.00	Oct-95
	5.60	21.01	15.22	56.02	59.40	2.46	0.51	9.74	1.02	22.87	3,864	2	6	0	0	36	14.77	-18.37			Mar-14
	3.73	18.31	5.69	44.52	41.43	0.96	0.74	12.14	0.97	19.31	763.2	3	95	1	0	4	22	-18.79			Aug-03
	3.69	18.17	5.43	43.37	39.54	0.74	0.99	12.11	0.97	19.25	763.2	3	95	1	0	4	21.81	-18.92	5.50		Aug-03

	MARKET		FUND TYPE, CATEGORY & OBJECTIVE		RATINGS				MINIMUMS	
Fund Name	Ticker Symbol	Traded On	Fund Type	Category and (Prospectus Objective)	Overall Rating	Reward Rating	Risk Rating	Recent Up/ Downgrade	Open to New Investors	Min Initial Investment
Franklin Corefolio Allocation Fund Class C	FTCLX	NAS CM	Open End	Aggressive Alloc (Growth)	C+	C	B	Up	Y	1,000
Franklin Corefolio Allocation Fund Class R			Open End	Aggressive Alloc (Growth)	C+	C	B	Up	Y	1,000
Franklin Corefolio Allocation Fund Class R6	FTLQX	NAS CM	Open End	Aggressive Alloc (Growth)	B-	C	B	Up	Y	1,000,000
Franklin DynaTech Fund Advisor Class	FDYZX	NAS CM	Open End	US Equity Large Cap Growth (Technology)	B-	B	B-	Down	Y	100,000
Franklin DynaTech Fund Class A	FKDNX	NAS CM	Open End	US Equity Large Cap Growth (Technology)	B-	B-	B-	Down	Y	1,000
Franklin DynaTech Fund Class C	FDYNX	NAS CM	Open End	US Equity Large Cap Growth (Technology)	B-	B-	B-	Down	Y	1,000
Franklin DynaTech Fund Class R	FDNRX	NAS CM	Open End	US Equity Large Cap Growth (Technology)	B-	B-	B-	Down	Y	1,000
Franklin DynaTech Fund Class R6	FDTRX	NAS CM	Open End	US Equity Large Cap Growth (Technology)	B-	B	B-	Down	Y	1,000,000
Franklin Equity Income Fund Advisor Class	FEIFX	NAS CM	Open End	US Equity Large Cap Value (Equity-Income)	B-	C	B+	Down	Y	100,000
Franklin Equity Income Fund Class A	FISEX	NAS CM	Open End	US Equity Large Cap Value (Equity-Income)	B-	C	B+	Down	Y	1,000
Franklin Equity Income Fund Class C	FRETX	NAS CM	Open End	US Equity Large Cap Value (Equity-Income)	B-	C	B+		Y	1,000
Franklin Equity Income Fund Class R	FREIX	NAS CM	Open End	US Equity Large Cap Value (Equity-Income)	B-	C	B+	Down	Y	1,000
Franklin Equity Income Fund Class R6	FEIQX	NAS CM	Open End	US Equity Large Cap Value (Equity-Income)	B-	C	B+	Down	Y	1,000,000
Franklin Founding Funds Allocation Fund Advisor Class	FFAAX	NAS CM	Open End	Aggressive Alloc (Asset Alloc)	C+	C	B	Up	Y	100,000
Franklin Founding Funds Allocation Fund Class A	FFALX	NAS CM	Open End	Aggressive Alloc (Asset Alloc)	C+	C	B	Up	Y	1,000
Franklin Founding Funds Allocation Fund Class C	FFACX	NAS CM	Open End	Aggressive Alloc (Asset Alloc)	C	C	B-		Y	1,000
Franklin Founding Funds Allocation Fund Class R	FFARX	NAS CM	Open End	Aggressive Alloc (Asset Alloc)	C	C	B-		Y	1,000
Franklin Founding Funds Allocation Fund Class R6	FFAQX	NAS CM	Open End	Aggressive Alloc (Asset Alloc)	C+	C	B	Up	Y	1,000,000
Franklin Global Listed Infrastructure Fund Advisor Class	FLGZX	NAS CM	Open End	Infrastructure Sector Equity (World Stock)	B	B	B	Up	Y	100,000
Franklin Global Listed Infrastructure Fund Class A	FLGIX	NAS CM	Open End	Infrastructure Sector Equity (World Stock)	B	B	B	Up	Y	1,000
Franklin Global Listed Infrastructure Fund Class C	FLGDX	NAS CM	Open End	Infrastructure Sector Equity (World Stock)	B-	B-	B		Y	1,000
Franklin Global Listed Infrastructure Fund Class R	FLGRX	NAS CM	Open End	Infrastructure Sector Equity (World Stock)	B	B	B	Up	Y	1,000
Franklin Global Listed Infrastructure Fund Class R6	FILGX	NAS CM	Open End	Infrastructure Sector Equity (World Stock)	B	B	B	Up	Y	1,000,000
Franklin Gold and Precious Metals Fund Advisor Class	FGADX	NAS CM	Open End	Precious Metals Sector Equity (Precious Metals)	D	D	D	Down	Y	100,000
Franklin Gold and Precious Metals Fund Class A	FKRCX	NAS CM	Open End	Precious Metals Sector Equity (Precious Metals)	D	D	D	Down	Y	1,000
Franklin Gold and Precious Metals Fund Class C	FRGOX	NAS CM	Open End	Precious Metals Sector Equity (Precious Metals)	D	D	D		Y	1,000
Franklin Gold and Precious Metals Fund Class R6	FGPMX	NAS CM	Open End	Precious Metals Sector Equity (Precious Metals)	D	D	D	Down	Y	1,000,000
Franklin Growth Allocation Fund Advisor Class	FGTZX	NAS CM	Open End	Aggressive Alloc (Asset Alloc)	B-	C	B+	Up	Y	100,000
Franklin Growth Allocation Fund Class A	FGTIX	NAS CM	Open End	Aggressive Alloc (Asset Alloc)	B-	C	B+	Up	Y	1,000
Franklin Growth Allocation Fund Class C	FTGTX	NAS CM	Open End	Aggressive Alloc (Asset Alloc)	B-	C	B+	Up	Y	1,000
Franklin Growth Allocation Fund Class R	FGTRX	NAS CM	Open End	Aggressive Alloc (Asset Alloc)	B-	C	B+	Up	Y	1,000
Franklin Growth Allocation Fund Class R6			Open End	Aggressive Alloc (Asset Alloc)	B-	C	B+	Up	Y	1,000,000
Franklin Growth Fund Advisor Class	FCGAX	NAS CM	Open End	US Equity Large Cap Growth (Growth)	B-	C+	B	Down	Y	100,000
Franklin Growth Opportunities Fund Advisor Class	FRAAX	NAS CM	Open End	US Equity Large Cap Growth (Aggr Growth)	B-	C+	B-		Y	100,000
Franklin Growth Opportunities Fund Class A	FGRAX	NAS CM	Open End	US Equity Large Cap Growth (Aggr Growth)	B-	C+	B-		Y	1,000
Franklin Growth Opportunities Fund Class C	FKACX	NAS CM	Open End	US Equity Large Cap Growth (Aggr Growth)	C+	C+	B-	Down	Y	1,000
Franklin Growth Opportunities Fund Class R	FKARX	NAS CM	Open End	US Equity Large Cap Growth (Aggr Growth)	B-	C+	B-		Y	1,000
Franklin Growth Opportunities Fund Class R6	FOPPX	NAS CM	Open End	US Equity Large Cap Growth (Aggr Growth)	B-	B-	B-		Y	1,000,000
Franklin Growth Series Class A	FKGRX	NAS CM	Open End	US Equity Large Cap Growth (Growth)	B-	C+	B	Down	Y	1,000
Franklin Growth Series Class C	FRGSX	NAS CM	Open End	US Equity Large Cap Growth (Growth)	B-	C+	B		Y	1,000
Franklin Growth Series Class R	FGSRX	NAS CM	Open End	US Equity Large Cap Growth (Growth)	B-	C+	B	Down	Y	1,000
Franklin Growth Series Class R6	FIFRX	NAS CM	Open End	US Equity Large Cap Growth (Growth)	B-	C+	B	Down	Y	1,000,000
Franklin Income Fund Advisor Class	FRIAX	NAS CM	Open End	Cautious Alloc (Balanced)	B-	C	A-	Down	Y	100,000
Franklin Income Fund Class A	FKIQX	NAS CM	Open End	Cautious Alloc (Balanced)	B-	C+	B		Y	1,000
Franklin Income Fund Class A1	FKINX	NAS CM	Open End	Cautious Alloc (Balanced)	B	C	A-		Y	1,000
Franklin Income Fund Class C	FCISX	NAS CM	Open End	Cautious Alloc (Balanced)	B-	C+	B		Y	1,000
Franklin Income Fund Class R	FISRX	NAS CM	Open End	Cautious Alloc (Balanced)	B-	C	B		Y	1,000
Franklin Income Fund Class R6	FNCFX	NAS CM	Open End	Cautious Alloc (Balanced)	B-	C+	B	Down	Y	1,000,000
Franklin India Growth Fund Advisor Class	FIGZX	NAS CM	Open End	India Equity (Foreign Stock)	C	C	C+		Y	100,000
Franklin India Growth Fund Class A	FINGX	NAS CM	Open End	India Equity (Foreign Stock)	C	C-	C		Y	1,000
Franklin India Growth Fund Class C	FINDX	NAS CM	Open End	India Equity (Foreign Stock)	C	D+	C		Y	1,000
Franklin India Growth Fund Class R6	FIGEX	NAS CM	Open End	India Equity (Foreign Stock)	C	C	C+		Y	1,000,000

★ Expanded analysis of this fund is included in Section II.

Min Additional Investment	TOTAL RETURNS 3-Month Total Return	6-Month Total Return	1-Year Total Return	3-Year Total Return	5-Year Total Return	PERFORMANCE Dividend Yield (TTM)	Expense Ratio	3-Yr Std Deviation	3-Year Beta	ASSETS NAV	Total Assets (MIL)	ASSET ALLOCATION & TURNOVER %Cash	%Stocks	%Bonds	%Other	Turnover Ratio	BULL & BEAR Last Bull Market Total Return	Last Bear Market Total Return	FEES Front End Fee (%)	Back End Fee (%)	Inception Date
	3.48	17.69	4.62	40.21	34.44	0.07	1.74	12.1	0.97	18.91	763.2	3	95	1	0	4	21.38	-19.14		1.00	Aug-03
	3.58	17.97	5.13	42.35	37.87	0.46	1.24	12.1	0.97	19.24	763.2	3	95	1	0	4	21.64	-18.94			Aug-03
	3.78	18.38	5.78	44.82	41.73	1.03	0.66	12.12	0.97	19.31	763.2	3	95	1	0	4	22	-18.79			Aug-17
	6.70	31.38	17.42	98.68	118.27	0	0.62	15.87	1.11	87.86	7,895	4	96	0	0	17	25.88	-16.77			May-08
	6.64	31.22	17.13	97.19	115.57	0	0.87	15.86	1.11	85.11	7,895	4	96	0	0	17	25.66	-16.83	5.50		Jan-68
	6.45	30.73	16.24	92.83	107.65	0	1.62	15.86	1.11	70.61	7,895	4	96	0	0	17	25.11	-17.09		1.00	Sep-96
	6.57	31.05	16.84	95.73	112.91	0	1.12	15.86	1.11	82.5	7,895	4	96	0	0	17	25.5	-16.92			Dec-08
	6.73	31.46	17.53	99.50	119.90	0	0.51	15.87	1.11	88.74	7,895	4	96	0	0	17	25.66	-16.83			May-13
	3.89	15.83	10.11	39.01	46.49	2.52	0.59	10.42	0.83	25.51	2,260	1	89	2	0	28	21.33	-15.46			May-08
	3.83	15.69	9.84	37.96	44.70	2.29	0.84	10.42	0.83	25.47	2,260	1	89	2	0	28	21.18	-15.56	5.50		Mar-88
	3.61	15.26	8.98	34.85	39.33	1.54	1.59	10.44	0.84	25.27	2,260	1	89	2	0	28	20.64	-15.8		1.00	Oct-95
	3.77	15.58	9.58	37.02	42.96	2.07	1.09	10.42	0.83	25.47	2,260	1	89	2	0	28	20.93	-15.6			Aug-02
	3.90	15.86	10.20	39.44	47.35	2.6	0.51	10.42	0.83	25.51	2,260	1	89	2	0	28	21.18	-15.56			May-13
	1.57	11.60	1.66	25.51	15.27	3.2	0.73	10.15	0.78	13.93	3,733	5	72	19	0	1	17.19	-17.38			Aug-03
	1.46	11.37	1.35	24.53	13.83	2.98	1.04	10.17	0.78	13.84	3,733	5	72	19	0	1	16.91	-17.42	5.50		Aug-03
	1.31	11.04	0.62	21.75	9.64	1.51	1.79	10.15	0.78	13.74	3,733	5	72	19	0	1	16.36	-17.66		1.00	Aug-03
	1.42	11.29	1.18	23.62	12.41	2.68	1.29	10.13	0.77	13.89	3,733	5	72	19	0	1	16.88	-17.59			Aug-03
	1.59	11.57	1.73	25.64	15.40	1.43	0.7	10.18	0.78	14.21	3,733	5	72	19	0	1	17.19	-17.38			Aug-17
	7.10	22.25	12.89	33.86	32.45	1.74	0.99	10.43	0.99	14.88	63.2	1	99	0	0	97					Sep-13
	7.02	22.09	12.56	32.95	30.55	1.52	1.24	10.44	0.99	14.85	63.2	1	99	0	0	97			5.50		Sep-13
	6.89	21.67	11.72	30.05	25.94	0.79	1.99	10.44	0.99	14.77	63.2	1	99	0	0	97				1.00	Sep-13
	7.00	21.99	12.30	32.06	29.18	1.31	1.49	10.4	0.99	14.84	63.2	1	99	0	0	97					Sep-13
	7.17	22.41	13.09	34.72	33.38	1.91	0.82	10.43	0.99	14.89	63.2	1	99	0	0	97					Sep-13
	11.17	23.93	11.84	-20.10	-14.08	0	0.73	25.54	0.89	16.62	753.9	0	100	0	0	8	-11.69	-21.06			Dec-96
	11.15	23.83	11.55	-20.68	-15.12	0	0.98	25.55	0.89	15.64	753.9	0	100	0	0	8	-11.8	-21.14	5.50		May-69
	10.93	23.38	10.76	-22.43	-18.22	0	1.73	25.57	0.89	14.3	753.9	0	100	0	0	8	-12.2	-21.37		1.00	May-95
	11.19	24.02	12.01	-19.65	-13.05	0	0.56	25.57	0.89	16.78	753.9	0	100	0	0	8	-11.8	-21.14			May-13
	3.10	15.36	6.58	35.76	34.85	1.79	0.93	9.38	0.82	18.92	1,221	6	76	17	1	31	15.13	-15			Dec-05
	3.06	15.24	6.33	34.71	33.23	1.56	1.18	9.38	0.82	18.82	1,221	6	76	17	1	31	14.97	-15.05	5.50		Dec-96
	2.81	14.77	5.48	31.68	28.29	0.57	1.93	9.35	0.82	18.26	1,221	6	76	17	1	31	14.42	-15.31		1.00	Dec-96
	2.99	15.06	6.05	33.70	31.56	1.24	1.43	9.36	0.82	18.56	1,221	6	76	17	1	31	14.75	-15.1			Jan-02
	3.10	15.37	6.66	36.21	35.77	1.9	0.8	9.36	0.82	18.91	1,221	6	76	17	1	31	14.97	-15.05			May-13
	5.80	23.23	12.85	63.13	79.08	0.62	0.59	13.12	1.05	109.91	15,253	2	98	0	0	6	24.31	-15.87			Dec-96
	6.08	27.72	11.39	68.03	74.30	0	0.74	14.41	1.02	43.44	3,802	1	96	0	3	23	27.59	-19.9			Jun-99
	6.00	27.53	11.12	66.79	72.05	0	0.99	14.39	1.02	40.07	3,802	1	96	0	3	23	27.33	-19.97	5.75		Jun-99
	5.79	27.04	10.36	63.15	65.86	0	1.74	14.37	1.02	32.84	3,802	1	96	0	3	23	26.83	-20.17		1.00	Jun-99
	5.93	27.40	10.88	65.60	70.06	0	1.24	14.4	1.02	38.03	3,802	1	96	0	3	23	27.21	-20.03			Jan-02
	6.10	27.75	11.48	68.82	75.74	0	0.59	14.41	1.02	44	3,802	1	96	0	3	23	27.59	-19.9			May-13
	5.73	23.07	12.58	61.92	76.87	0.4	0.84	13.12	1.05	109.61	15,253	2	98	0	0	6	24.16	-15.97	5.50		Apr-48
	5.54	22.62	11.75	58.31	70.33	0	1.59	13.11	1.05	100.01	15,253	2	98	0	0	6	23.6	-16.24		1.00	May-95
	5.67	22.92	12.31	60.71	74.65	0.13	1.09	13.12	1.05	109.13	15,253	2	98	0	0	6	23.96	-16.06			Jan-02
	5.82	23.29	12.96	63.76	80.41	0.71	0.48	13.12	1.05	109.83	15,253	2	98	0	0	6	24.16	-15.97			May-13
	1.34	12.01	6.01	26.26	17.66	5.32	0.47	7.33	0.54	2.3	72,795	5	33	51	0	50	13.7	-11.64			Dec-96
	1.72	11.79	5.75	25.19	16.17		0.72	7.48	0.56	2.32	72,795	5	33	51	0	50	13.99	-11.68	3.75		Sep-18
	1.31	11.84	5.85	25.57	16.75	5.17	0.62	7.33	0.54	2.32	72,795	5	33	51	0	50	14.05	-11.64	3.75		Aug-48
	1.59	11.85	5.67	23.78	14.04	4.58	1.12	7.25	0.54	2.36	72,795	5	33	51	0	50	13.6	-11.73		1.00	May-95
	1.24	11.86	6.03	24.12	14.98	4.89	0.97	7.11	0.52	2.28	72,795	5	33	51	0	50	13.44	-11.48			Jan-02
	1.80	12.00	6.53	26.42	18.56	5.35	0.4	7.34	0.55	2.31	72,795	5	33	51	0	50	14.04	-11.64			May-13
	2.92	8.17	2.68	23.46	40.05	0	1.4	16.48	0.95	14.43	103.9	1	5	0	94	26	-2.06	-18.36			Jan-08
	2.86	8.02	2.40	22.66	38.34	0	1.65	16.46	0.95	14	103.9	1	5	0	94	26	-2.08	-18.51	5.50		Jan-08
	2.62	7.69	1.66	19.82	33.25	0	2.4	16.47	0.95	12.88	103.9	1	5	0	94	26	-2.48	-18.71		1.00	Jan-08
	2.96	8.23	2.87	24.26	41.42	0	1.25	16.49	0.95	14.59	103.9	1	5	0	94	26	-2.06	-18.36			May-13

	MARKET			FUND TYPE, CATEGORY & OBJECTIVE	RATINGS					MINIMUMS
Fund Name	Ticker Symbol	Traded On	Fund Type	Category and (Prospectus Objective)	Overall Rating	Reward Rating	Risk Rating	Recent Up/ Downgrade	Open to New Investors	Min Initial Investment
Franklin International Growth Fund Class A	FNGAX	NAS CM	Open End	Global Equity Large Cap (Foreign Stock)	C	C	C+		Y	1,000
Franklin International Growth Fund Class Adv	FNGZX	NAS CM	Open End	Global Equity Large Cap (Foreign Stock)	C	C	C+		Y	100,000
Franklin International Growth Fund Class C	FNGDX	NAS CM	Open End	Global Equity Large Cap (Foreign Stock)	C	C	C+		Y	1,000
Franklin International Growth Fund Class R	FNGRX	NAS CM	Open End	Global Equity Large Cap (Foreign Stock)	C	C	C+		Y	1,000
Franklin International Growth Fund Class R6	FILRX	NAS CM	Open End	Global Equity Large Cap (Foreign Stock)	C	C	C+		Y	1,000,000
Franklin International Small Cap Fund Advisor Class	FKSCX	NAS CM	Open End	Global Equity Mid/Small Cap (Small Company)	C	C-	C	Up		100,000
Franklin International Small Cap Fund Class A	FINAX	NAS CM	Open End	Global Equity Mid/Small Cap (Small Company)	C	C-	C	Up		1,000
Franklin International Small Cap Fund Class C	FCSMX	NAS CM	Open End	Global Equity Mid/Small Cap (Small Company)	C-	D+	C			1,000
Franklin International Small Cap Fund Class R	FISDX	NAS CM	Open End	Global Equity Mid/Small Cap (Small Company)	C-	C-	C			1,000
Franklin International Small Cap Fund Class R6	FCAPX	NAS CM	Open End	Global Equity Mid/Small Cap (Small Company)	C	C-	C	Up		1,000,000
Franklin K2 Alternative Strategies Fund Advisor Class	FABZX	NAS CM	Open End	Multialternative (Growth)	B-	C	A-	Up	Y	100,000
Franklin K2 Alternative Strategies Fund Class A	FAAAX	NAS CM	Open End	Multialternative (Growth)	B-	C	A-	Up	Y	1,000
Franklin K2 Alternative Strategies Fund Class C	FASCX	NAS CM	Open End	Multialternative (Growth)	C+	C	B+	Up	Y	1,000
Franklin K2 Alternative Strategies Fund Class R	FSKKX	NAS CM	Open End	Multialternative (Growth)	B-	C	B+	Up	Y	1,000
Franklin K2 Alternative Strategies Fund Class R6	FASRX	NAS CM	Open End	Multialternative (Growth)	B-	C	A-	Up	Y	1,000,000
Franklin K2 Global Macro Opportunities Fund Advisor Class	FKMZX	NAS CM	Open End	Global Macro (Growth)	C	C	C+	Up	Y	100,000
Franklin K2 Global Macro Opportunities Fund Class A	FKMAX	NAS CM	Open End	Global Macro (Growth)	C	C	C+	Up	Y	1,000
Franklin K2 Global Macro Opportunities Fund Class C	FKMDX	NAS CM	Open End	Global Macro (Growth)	C	C	C	Up	Y	1,000
Franklin K2 Global Macro Opportunities Fund Class R	FKMRX	NAS CM	Open End	Global Macro (Growth)	C	C	C+	Up	Y	1,000
Franklin K2 Global Macro Opportunities Fund Class R6	FKMQX	NAS CM	Open End	Global Macro (Growth)	C	C	C+	Up	Y	1,000,000
Franklin K2 Long Short Credit Fund Advisor Class	FKLZX	NAS CM	Open End	Long/Short Credit (Income)	B	C+	A-		Y	100,000
Franklin K2 Long Short Credit Fund Class A	FKLSX	NAS CM	Open End	Long/Short Credit (Income)	B	C+	A-		Y	1,000
Franklin K2 Long Short Credit Fund Class C	FKLCX	NAS CM	Open End	Long/Short Credit (Income)	B-	C	B+		Y	1,000
Franklin K2 Long Short Credit Fund Class R	FKLRX	NAS CM	Open End	Long/Short Credit (Income)	B-	C	B+		Y	1,000
Franklin K2 Long Short Credit Fund Class R6	FKLQX	NAS CM	Open End	Long/Short Credit (Income)	B	C+	A-		Y	1,000,000
Franklin LifeSmart™ 2020 Retirement Target Advisor Cls	FLROX	NAS CM	Open End	Target Date (Asset Alloc)	B	C	A-	Up	Y	100,000
Franklin LifeSmart™ 2020 Retirement Target Fund Class A	FLRMX	NAS CM	Open End	Target Date (Asset Alloc)	B-	C	A-	Up	Y	1,000
Franklin LifeSmart™ 2020 Retirement Target Fund Class C	FLRQX	NAS CM	Open End	Target Date (Asset Alloc)	B-	C	A-	Up	Y	1,000
Franklin LifeSmart™ 2020 Retirement Target Fund Class R	FLRVX	NAS CM	Open End	Target Date (Asset Alloc)	B-	C	A-	Up	Y	1,000
Franklin LifeSmart™ 2020 Retirement Target Fund Class R6	FRTSX	NAS CM	Open End	Target Date (Asset Alloc)	B	C	A-	Up	Y	1,000,000
Franklin LifeSmart™ 2025 Retirement Target Advisor Cls	FLRFX	NAS CM	Open End	Target Date (Asset Alloc)	B-	C	A-	Up	Y	100,000
Franklin LifeSmart™ 2025 Retirement Target Fund Class A	FTRTX	NAS CM	Open End	Target Date (Asset Alloc)	B-	C	A-	Up	Y	1,000
Franklin LifeSmart™ 2025 Retirement Target Fund Class C	FTTCX	NAS CM	Open End	Target Date (Asset Alloc)	B-	C	A-	Up	Y	1,000
Franklin LifeSmart™ 2025 Retirement Target Fund Class R	FRELX	NAS CM	Open End	Target Date (Asset Alloc)	B-	C	A-	Up	Y	1,000
Franklin LifeSmart™ 2025 Retirement Target Fund Class R6	FTLMX	NAS CM	Open End	Target Date (Asset Alloc)	B-	C	A-	Up	Y	1,000,000
Franklin LifeSmart™ 2030 Retirement Target Advisor Cls	FLRZX	NAS CM	Open End	Target Date (Asset Alloc)	B-	C	A-	Up	Y	100,000
Franklin LifeSmart™ 2030 Retirement Target Fund Class A	FLRSX	NAS CM	Open End	Target Date (Asset Alloc)	B-	C	A-	Up	Y	1,000
Franklin LifeSmart™ 2030 Retirement Target Fund Class C	FLRTX	NAS CM	Open End	Target Date (Asset Alloc)	B-	C	B+	Up	Y	1,000
Franklin LifeSmart™ 2030 Retirement Target Fund Class R	FLRWX	NAS CM	Open End	Target Date (Asset Alloc)	B-	C	A-	Up	Y	1,000
Franklin LifeSmart™ 2030 Retirement Target Fund Class R6	FLERX	NAS CM	Open End	Target Date (Asset Alloc)	B-	C	A-	Up	Y	1,000,000
Franklin LifeSmart™ 2035 Retirement Target Advisor Cls	FLRHX	NAS CM	Open End	Target Date (Asset Alloc)	B-	C	B+	Up	Y	100,000
Franklin LifeSmart™ 2035 Retirement Target Fund Class A	FRTAX	NAS CM	Open End	Target Date (Asset Alloc)	B-	C	B+	Up	Y	1,000
Franklin LifeSmart™ 2035 Retirement Target Fund Class C	FTRCX	NAS CM	Open End	Target Date (Asset Alloc)	B-	C	B+	Up	Y	1,000
Franklin LifeSmart™ 2035 Retirement Target Fund Class R	FLRGX	NAS CM	Open End	Target Date (Asset Alloc)	B-	C	B+	Up	Y	1,000
Franklin LifeSmart™ 2035 Retirement Target Fund Class R6	FMTLX	NAS CM	Open End	Target Date (Asset Alloc)	B-	C	B+	Up	Y	1,000,000
Franklin LifeSmart™ 2040 Retirement Target Advisor Cls	FLSHX	NAS CM	Open End	Target Date (Asset Alloc)	B-	C	B+	Up	Y	100,000
Franklin LifeSmart™ 2040 Retirement Target Fund Class A	FLADX	NAS CM	Open End	Target Date (Asset Alloc)	B-	C	B+	Up	Y	1,000
Franklin LifeSmart™ 2040 Retirement Target Fund Class C	FLOLX	NAS CM	Open End	Target Date (Asset Alloc)	B-	C	B+	Up	Y	1,000
Franklin LifeSmart™ 2040 Retirement Target Fund Class R	FLSGX	NAS CM	Open End	Target Date (Asset Alloc)	B-	C	B+	Up	Y	1,000
Franklin LifeSmart™ 2040 Retirement Target Fund Class R6	FLREX	NAS CM	Open End	Target Date (Asset Alloc)	B-	C	B+	Up	Y	1,000,000
Franklin LifeSmart™ 2045 Retirement Target Advisor Cls	FLRLX	NAS CM	Open End	Target Date (Asset Alloc)	B-	C	B+	Up	Y	100,000
Franklin LifeSmart™ 2045 Retirement Target Fund Class A	FTTAX	NAS CM	Open End	Target Date (Asset Alloc)	B-	C	B+	Up	Y	1,000

★ Expanded analysis of this fund is included in Section II.

Min Additional Investment	TOTAL RETURNS 3-Month Total Return	6-Month Total Return	1-Year Total Return	3-Year Total Return	5-Year Total Return	PERFORMANCE Dividend Yield (TTM)	Expense Ratio	3-Yr Std Deviation	3-Year Beta	ASSETS NAV	Total Assets (MIL)	ASSET ALLOCATION & TURNOVER %Cash	%Stocks	%Bonds	%Other	Turnover Ratio	BULL & BEAR Last Bull Market Total Return	Last Bear Market Total Return	FEES Front End Fee (%)	Back End Fee (%)	Inception Date
	3.94	20.54	-2.60	45.79	30.67	0.23	1.12	13.85	1.14	14.49	1,312	5	95	0	0	58	20.88	-25.04	5.50		Jun-08
	4.00	20.78	-2.35	46.82	32.39	0.32	0.87	13.85	1.15	14.53	1,312	5	95	0	0	58	21.13	-24.97			Jun-08
	3.73	20.15	-3.31	42.51	25.92	0	1.87	13.82	1.14	13.89	1,312	5	95	0	0	58	20.34	-25.23		1.00	Jun-08
	3.90	20.45	-2.85	44.72	29.15	0.19	1.37	13.83	1.14	14.37	1,312	5	95	0	0	58	20.66	-25.09			Jun-08
	4.00	20.74	-2.23	47.61	33.49	0.37	0.69	13.84	1.14	14.55	1,312	5	95	0	0	58	21.13	-24.97			May-13
	-0.80	12.57	-7.93	25.94	7.20	1.73	1.13	13.28	0.98	17.19	856.4	3	97	0	0	27	14.21	-20.17			Oct-02
	-0.81	12.46	-8.15	24.99	5.88	1.55	1.38	13.28	0.98	17.14	856.4	3	97	0	0	27	14.02	-20.32	5.50		May-08
	-1.05	12.06	-8.87	22.22	1.97	0.89	2.13	13.25	0.98	16.91	856.4	3	97	0	0	27	13.53	-20.52		1.00	May-08
	-0.86	12.36	-8.40	24.06	4.53	1.37	1.63	13.27	0.98	17.17	856.4	3	97	0	0	27	13.85	-20.34			May-08
	-0.75	12.71	-7.78	26.50	7.97	1.83	1.01	13.27	0.98	17.2	856.4	3	97	0	0	27	14.21	-20.17			May-13
	1.94	6.75	3.04	14.01	15.10	0	2.36	3.58	0.82	11.54	1,238	50	24	17	0	235					Oct-13
	1.95	6.68	2.87	13.09	13.53	0	2.61	3.54	0.81	11.49	1,238	50	24	17	0	235			5.50		Oct-13
	1.71	6.23	2.01	10.59	9.50	0	3.36	3.51	0.81	11.25	1,238	50	24	17	0	235				1.00	Oct-13
	1.86	6.48	2.51	12.28	11.73	0	2.86	3.51	0.81	11.49	1,238	50	24	17	0	235					Oct-13
	1.94	6.83	3.13	14.31	15.58	0	2.28	3.57	0.82	11.56	1,238	50	24	17	0	235					Oct-13
	1.28	4.29	4.64	-3.11		0.33	2.02			9.48	23.8	48	23	26	0	240					Jul-16
	1.17	4.18	4.40	-3.77		0.09	2.27			9.45	23.8	48	23	26	0	240			5.50		Jul-16
	0.87	3.58	3.47	-6.04		0	3.02			9.24	23.8	48	23	26	0	240				1.00	Jul-16
	1.18	4.08	4.28	-3.87		0.08	2.52			9.43	23.8	48	23	26	0	240					Jul-16
	1.17	4.18	4.54	-3.20		0.33	2.02			9.47	23.8	48	23	26	0	240					Jul-16
	1.44	3.84	3.89	15.51		3.11	2.86	1.26	0.36	10.52	117.9	29	1	68	0	252					Sep-15
	1.35	3.75	3.71	15.05		2.94	3.11	1.3	0.37	10.51	117.9	29	1	68	0	252			5.50		Sep-15
	1.17	3.30	2.71	11.84		2.36	3.86	1.3	0.36	10.31	117.9	29	1	68	0	252				1.00	Sep-15
	1.36	3.58	3.31	14.03		2.65	3.36	1.25	0.37	10.41	117.9	29	1	68	0	252					Sep-15
	1.44	3.85	3.82	15.45		3.14	2.84	1.24	0.35	10.51	117.9	29	1	68	0	252					Sep-15
	2.09	9.30	4.93	21.59	19.94	3.27	0.45	5.47	0.48	11.84	43.2	7	47	45	1	57					Jul-13
	2.03	9.21	4.78	20.64	18.33	3.04	0.7	5.43	0.47	11.81	43.2	7	47	45	1	57			5.50		Jul-13
	1.93	8.79	4.00	18.01	14.06	2.3	1.45	5.46	0.48	11.74	43.2	7	47	45	1	57				1.00	Jul-13
	1.96	9.07	4.49	19.69	16.84	2.77	0.95	5.48	0.48	11.8	43.2	7	47	45	1	57					Jul-13
	2.10	9.33	5.07	21.77	20.23	3.32	0.4	5.45	0.48	11.84	43.2	7	47	45	1	57					Jul-13
	2.58	11.91	5.42	26.66	24.25	2.91	0.45	7.1	0.62	12.66	122.8	6	56	36	1	53	14.09	-14.21			Aug-06
	2.52	11.72	5.17	25.64	22.61	2.68	0.7	7.14	0.62	12.63	122.8	6	56	36	1	53	13.92	-14.36	5.50		Aug-06
	2.36	11.36	4.37	22.86	18.21	1.98	1.45	7.05	0.62	12.42	122.8	6	56	36	1	53	13.46	-14.64		1.00	Aug-06
	2.46	11.63	4.91	24.69	21.18	2.43	0.95	7.1	0.62	12.58	122.8	6	56	36	1	53	13.79	-14.48			Aug-06
	2.59	11.93	5.47	26.85	24.54	2.96	0.4	7.12	0.62	12.67	122.8	6	56	36	1	53	14.09	-14.21			May-13
	2.73	13.07	5.42	29.14	27.81	2.61	0.45	8.12	0.71	12.75	53.2	6	68	25	1	47					Jul-13
	2.68	12.99	5.18	28.18	26.13	2.38	0.7	8.12	0.71	12.71	53.2	6	68	25	1	47			5.50		Jul-13
	2.43	12.58	4.36	25.40	21.54	1.67	1.45	8.07	0.71	12.56	53.2	6	68	25	1	47				1.00	Jul-13
	2.54	12.79	4.84	27.17	24.58	2.14	0.95	8.1	0.71	12.69	53.2	6	68	25	1	47					Jul-13
	2.74	13.18	5.47	29.33	28.08	2.66	0.4	8.09	0.71	12.76	53.2	6	68	25	1	47					Jul-13
	2.83	13.97	5.45	31.13	28.36	2.86	0.45	8.78	0.77	13.52	116.5	6	75	17	1	48	15.05	-15.26			Aug-06
	2.74	13.79	5.20	30.03	26.70	2.54	0.7	8.77	0.77	13.4	116.5	6	75	17	1	48	14.82	-15.34	5.50		Aug-06
	2.54	13.39	4.41	27.19	22.12	1.52	1.45	8.76	0.77	13.08	116.5	6	75	17	1	48	14.38	-15.66		1.00	Aug-06
	2.71	13.69	4.91	29.15	25.23	2.19	0.95	8.78	0.77	13.38	116.5	6	75	17	1	48	14.67	-15.52			Aug-06
	2.78	13.92	5.46	31.18	28.68	2.94	0.4	8.7	0.76	13.5	116.5	6	75	17	1	48	15.05	-15.26			May-13
	2.83	14.21	5.41	31.89	30.30	2.7	0.45	9.16	0.8	13.04	44.4	6	83	10	1	42					Jul-13
	2.73	14.16	5.24	31.09	28.64	2.38	0.7	9.17	0.8	12.98	44.4	6	83	10	1	42			5.50		Jul-13
	2.46	13.68	4.39	28.03	23.98	1.39	1.45	9.16	0.8	12.75	44.4	6	83	10	1	42				1.00	Jul-13
	2.63	13.97	4.99	30.09	27.26	2	0.95	9.16	0.8	12.96	44.4	6	83	10	1	42					Jul-13
	2.77	14.31	5.56	32.13	30.71	2.77	0.4	9.23	0.81	13.06	44.4	6	83	10	1	42					Jul-13
	2.89	14.64	5.41	32.24	29.29	2.64	0.45	9.48	0.83	13.6	82.2	6	90	4	1	43	15.24	-15.51			Aug-06
	2.80	14.46	5.15	31.26	27.60	2.32	0.7	9.49	0.83	13.49	82.2	6	90	4	1	43	15.01	-15.58	5.50		Aug-06

	MARKET		FUND TYPE, CATEGORY & OBJECTIVE		RATINGS				MINIMUMS	
Fund Name	Ticker Symbol	Traded On	Fund Type	Category and (Prospectus Objective)	Overall Rating	Reward Rating	Risk Rating	Recent Up/ Downgrade	Open to New Investors	Min Initial Investment
Franklin LifeSmart™ 2045 Retirement Target Fund Class C	FLRIX	NAS CM	Open End	Target Date (Asset Alloc)	B-	C	B+	Up	Y	1,000
Franklin LifeSmart™ 2045 Retirement Target Fund Class R	FLRJX	NAS CM	Open End	Target Date (Asset Alloc)	B-	C	B+	Up	Y	1,000
Franklin LifeSmart™ 2045 Retirement Target Fund Class R6	FMLTX	NAS CM	Open End	Target Date (Asset Alloc)	B-	C	B+	Up	Y	1,000,000
Franklin LifeSmart™ 2050 Retirement Target Advisor Cls	FLSOX	NAS CM	Open End	Target Date (Asset Alloc)	B-	C	B+	Up	Y	100,000
Franklin LifeSmart™ 2050 Retirement Target Fund Class A	FLSJX	NAS CM	Open End	Target Date (Asset Alloc)	B-	C	B+	Up	Y	1,000
Franklin LifeSmart™ 2050 Retirement Target Fund Class C	FLSKX	NAS CM	Open End	Target Date (Asset Alloc)	B-	C	B+	Up	Y	1,000
Franklin LifeSmart™ 2050 Retirement Target Fund Class R	FLSNX	NAS CM	Open End	Target Date (Asset Alloc)	B-	C	B+	Up	Y	1,000
Franklin LifeSmart™ 2050 Retirement Target Fund Class R6	FRLEX	NAS CM	Open End	Target Date (Asset Alloc)	B-	C	B+	Up	Y	1,000,000
Franklin LifeSmart™ 2055 Retirement Target Advisor Cls	FLTKX	NAS CM	Open End	Target Date (Asset Alloc)	B-	C	B+	Up	Y	100,000
Franklin LifeSmart™ 2055 Retirement Target Fund Class A	FLTFX	NAS CM	Open End	Target Date (Asset Alloc)	B-	C	B+	Up	Y	1,000
Franklin LifeSmart™ 2055 Retirement Target Fund Class C	FLTNX	NAS CM	Open End	Target Date (Asset Alloc)	B-	C	B+	Up	Y	1,000
Franklin LifeSmart™ 2055 Retirement Target Fund Class R	FLSBX	NAS CM	Open End	Target Date (Asset Alloc)	B-	C	B+	Up	Y	1,000
Franklin LifeSmart™ 2055 Retirement Target Fund Class R6	FLSZX	NAS CM	Open End	Target Date (Asset Alloc)	B-	C	B+	Up	Y	1,000,000
Franklin LifeSmart™ Retirement Income Fund Advisor Class	FLRDX	NAS CM	Open End	Target Date (Asset Alloc)	B-	C	B		Y	100,000
Franklin LifeSmart™ Retirement Income Fund Class A	FTRAX	NAS CM	Open End	Target Date (Asset Alloc)	B-	C	B		Y	1,000
Franklin LifeSmart™ Retirement Income Fund Class C	FRTCX	NAS CM	Open End	Target Date (Asset Alloc)	C+	C	B		Y	1,000
Franklin LifeSmart™ Retirement Income Fund Class R	FBRLX	NAS CM	Open End	Target Date (Asset Alloc)	C+	C	B	Down	Y	1,000
Franklin LifeSmart™ Retirement Income Fund Class R6	FLMTX	NAS CM	Open End	Target Date (Asset Alloc)	B-	C	B		Y	1,000,000
Franklin Managed Income Fund Advisor Class	FBFZX	NAS CM	Open End	Moderate Alloc (Balanced)	B	C+	A		Y	100,000
Franklin Managed Income Fund Class A	FBLAX	NAS CM	Open End	Moderate Alloc (Balanced)	B	C+	A		Y	1,000
Franklin Managed Income Fund Class C	FBMCX	NAS CM	Open End	Moderate Alloc (Balanced)	B	C+	A-		Y	1,000
Franklin Managed Income Fund Class R	FBFQX	NAS CM	Open End	Moderate Alloc (Balanced)	B	C+	A		Y	1,000
Franklin Managed Income Fund Class R6	FBFRX	NAS CM	Open End	Moderate Alloc (Balanced)	B	C+	A		Y	1,000,000
Franklin MicroCap Value Fund Advisor Class	FVRMX	NAS CM	Open End	US Equity Small Cap (Growth & Income)	C-	D+	C-	Down		100,000
Franklin MicroCap Value Fund Class A	FRMCX	NAS CM	Open End	US Equity Small Cap (Growth & Income)	D+	D+	C-	Down		1,000
Franklin MicroCap Value Fund Class R6	FMCVX	NAS CM	Open End	US Equity Small Cap (Growth & Income)	C-	D+	C-	Down		1,000,000
Franklin Moderate Allocation Fund Advisor Class	FMTZX	NAS CM	Open End	Moderate Alloc (Asset Alloc)	B	C	A-	Up	Y	100,000
Franklin Moderate Allocation Fund Class A	FMTIX	NAS CM	Open End	Moderate Alloc (Asset Alloc)	B	C	A-	Up	Y	1,000
Franklin Moderate Allocation Fund Class C	FTMTX	NAS CM	Open End	Moderate Alloc (Asset Alloc)	B-	C	A-	Up	Y	1,000
Franklin Moderate Allocation Fund Class R	FTMRX	NAS CM	Open End	Moderate Alloc (Asset Alloc)	B-	C	A-	Up	Y	1,000
Franklin Moderate Allocation Fund Class R6			Open End	Moderate Alloc (Asset Alloc)	B	C	A-	Up	Y	1,000,000
Franklin Mutual Beacon Fund Class A	TEBIX	NAS CM	Open End	Global Equity Large Cap (Growth & Income)	C+	C	B		Y	1,000
Franklin Mutual Beacon Fund Class C	TEMEX	NAS CM	Open End	Global Equity Large Cap (Growth & Income)	B-	C	B+	Up	Y	1,000
Franklin Mutual Beacon Fund Class R			Open End	Global Equity Large Cap (Growth & Income)	C+	C	B		Y	1,000
Franklin Mutual Beacon Fund Class R6	FMBRX	NAS CM	Open End	Global Equity Large Cap (Growth & Income)	B-	C	B	Up	Y	1,000,000
Franklin Mutual Beacon Fund Class Z	BEGRX	NAS CM	Open End	Global Equity Large Cap (Growth & Income)	B-	C	B+	Up	Y	100,000
Franklin Mutual European Fund Class A	TEMIX	NAS CM	Open End	Europe Equity Large Cap (Europe Stock)	C+	C-	B	Up	Y	1,000
Franklin Mutual European Fund Class C	TEURX	NAS CM	Open End	Europe Equity Large Cap (Europe Stock)	C	C-	B		Y	1,000
Franklin Mutual European Fund Class R	FMURX	NAS CM	Open End	Europe Equity Large Cap (Europe Stock)	C+	C-	B	Up	Y	1,000
Franklin Mutual European Fund Class R6	FMEUX	NAS CM	Open End	Europe Equity Large Cap (Europe Stock)	C+	C-	B	Up	Y	1,000,000
Franklin Mutual European Fund Class Z	MEURX	NAS CM	Open End	Europe Equity Large Cap (Europe Stock)	C+	C-	B	Up	Y	100,000
Franklin Mutual Financial Services Fund Class A	TFSIX	NAS CM	Open End	Financials Sector Equity (Financial)	C	C-	C+	Up	Y	1,000
Franklin Mutual Financial Services Fund Class C	TMFSX	NAS CM	Open End	Financials Sector Equity (Financial)	C	C-	C+	Up	Y	1,000
Franklin Mutual Financial Services Fund Class R6	FMFVX	NAS CM	Open End	Financials Sector Equity (Financial)	C	C-	C+		Y	1,000,000
Franklin Mutual Financial Services Fund Class Z	TEFAX	NAS CM	Open End	Financials Sector Equity (Financial)	C	C-	C+		Y	100,000
Franklin Mutual Global Discovery Fund Class A	TEDIX	NAS CM	Open End	Global Equity Large Cap (World Stock)	C+	C	B	Up	Y	1,000
Franklin Mutual Global Discovery Fund Class C	TEDSX	NAS CM	Open End	Global Equity Large Cap (World Stock)	C+	C	B	Up	Y	1,000
Franklin Mutual Global Discovery Fund Class R	TEDRX	NAS CM	Open End	Global Equity Large Cap (World Stock)	C+	C	B	Up	Y	1,000
Franklin Mutual Global Discovery Fund Class R6	FMDRX	NAS CM	Open End	Global Equity Large Cap (World Stock)	C+	C	B	Up	Y	1,000,000
Franklin Mutual Global Discovery Fund Class Z	MDISX	NAS CM	Open End	Global Equity Large Cap (World Stock)	C+	C	B	Up	Y	100,000
Franklin Mutual International Fund Class A	FMIAX	NAS CM	Open End	Global Equity Large Cap (Foreign Stock)	D+	D	C-		Y	1,000
Franklin Mutual International Fund Class C	FCMIX	NAS CM	Open End	Global Equity Large Cap (Foreign Stock)	D+	D	C-		Y	1,000

★ Expanded analysis of this fund is included in Section II.

	TOTAL RETURNS					PERFORMANCE				ASSETS		ASSET ALLOCATION & TURNOVER					BULL & BEAR		FEES		
Min Additional Investment	3-Month Total Return	6-Month Total Return	1-Year Total Return	3-Year Total Return	5-Year Total Return	Dividend Yield (TTM)	Expense Ratio	3-Yr Std Deviation	3-Year Beta	NAV	Total Assets (MIL)	%Cash	%Stocks	%Bonds	%Other	Turnover Ratio	Last Bull Market Total Return	Last Bear Market Total Return	Front End Fee (%)	Back End Fee (%)	Inception Date
	2.61	14.02	4.37	28.37	23.03	1.3	1.45	9.49	0.83	13.13	82.2	6	90	4	1	43	14.53	-15.86		1.00	Aug-06
	2.70	14.22	4.86	30.14	26.01	1.97	0.95	9.47	0.83	13.42	82.2	6	90	4	1	43	14.73	-15.7			Aug-06
	2.84	14.59	5.40	32.39	29.57	2.72	0.4	9.5	0.83	13.59	82.2	6	90	4	1	43	15.24	-15.51			May-13
	2.82	14.68	5.48	32.47	31.41	2.56	0.45	9.56	0.84	13.26	40.5	6	90	3	1	36					Jul-13
	2.81	14.56	5.24	31.50	29.75	2.25	0.7	9.55	0.84	13.18	40.5	6	90	3	1	36			5.50		Jul-13
	2.57	14.01	4.40	28.47	24.99	1.23	1.45	9.57	0.84	13.08	40.5	6	90	3	1	36				1.00	Jul-13
	2.62	14.35	4.87	30.47	28.07	1.9	0.95	9.54	0.84	13.17	40.5	6	90	3	1	36					Jul-13
	2.84	14.71	5.56	32.70	31.73	2.63	0.4	9.58	0.84	13.26	40.5	6	90	3	1	36					Jul-13
	2.78	14.52	5.32	32.77		2.49	0.45	9.53	0.83	11.11	15.0	7	90	3	1	43					May-15
	2.75	14.51	5.15	31.83		2.16	0.7	9.51	0.83	11.1	15.0	7	90	3	1	43			5.50		May-15
	2.57	14.03	4.33	29.02		1.27	1.45	9.52	0.83	10.95	15.0	7	90	3	1	43				1.00	May-15
	2.67	14.35	4.82	30.93		1.84	0.95	9.49	0.83	11.06	15.0	7	90	3	1	43					May-15
	2.88	14.63	5.47	33.09		2.55	0.4	9.54	0.84	11.12	15.0	7	90	3	1	43					May-15
	1.92	8.52	5.49	15.62	14.35	4.09	0.46	3.96	0.33	11.02	51.6	11	16	65	0	46	10.99	-10.34			Aug-06
	1.87	8.31	5.24	14.79	12.93	3.85	0.71	3.94	0.32	10.98	51.6	11	16	65	0	46	10.86	-10.5	5.50		Aug-06
	1.70	8.01	4.48	12.29	8.85	3.12	1.46	3.97	0.33	10.85	51.6	11	16	65	0	46	10.38	-10.73		1.00	Aug-06
	1.81	8.21	4.98	13.92	11.56	3.6	0.96	3.93	0.32	10.94	51.6	11	16	65	0	46	10.67	-10.53			Aug-06
	1.93	8.54	5.54	15.79	14.64	4.14	0.41	3.93	0.32	11.03	51.6	11	16	65	0	46	10.99	-10.34			May-13
	2.97	11.84	8.96	26.74	30.11	3.25	0.68	5.85	0.04	12.57	3,561	7	40	45	0	64	17.01	-10.75			Jul-06
	2.92	11.74	8.72	25.78	28.41	3.02	0.93	5.86	0.05	12.54	3,561	7	40	45	0	64	16.72	-10.79	5.50		Jul-06
	2.68	11.37	7.93	22.96	23.85	2.35	1.68	5.85	0.06	12.42	3,561	7	40	45	0	64	16.39	-11.14		1.00	Jul-06
	2.85	11.67	8.52	24.85	26.91	2.78	1.18	5.86	0.04	12.58	3,561	7	40	45	0	64	16.68	-10.95			Jul-06
	2.99	11.88	9.14	27.20	30.94	3.32	0.6	5.85	0.05	12.58	3,561	7	40	45	0	64	17.01	-10.75			May-13
	0.49	8.67	-11.32	18.86	13.55	0	0.92	17.44	0.95	28.56	207.6	4	96	0	0	4	19.05	-15.8			Nov-05
	0.46	8.59	-11.54	18.03	12.20	0	1.17	17.45	0.95	28.31	207.6	4	96	0	0	4	18.86	-15.88	5.50		Dec-95
	0.52	8.78	-11.23	19.25	14.30	0	0.83	17.44	0.95	28.73	207.6	4	96	0	0	4	18.86	-15.88			May-13
	2.70	12.57	6.25	28.75	27.81	2.98	1.14	7.25	0.63	15.6	1,895	6	56	37	1	34	11.49	-10.8			Dec-05
	2.63	12.45	6.05	27.82	26.18	2.62	1.24	7.26	0.64	15.59	1,895	6	56	37	1	34	11.27	-10.85	5.50		Dec-96
	2.45	12.00	5.19	24.95	21.55	1.56	1.89	7.22	0.63	15.12	1,895	6	56	37	1	34	10.8	-11.15		1.00	Dec-96
	2.57	12.27	5.76	26.79	24.62	2.22	1.39	7.22	0.63	15.56	1,895	6	56	37	1	34	11.18	-11			Jan-02
	2.66	12.56	6.32	29.07	28.38	3.11	0.8	7.23	0.63	15.58	1,895	6	56	37	1	34	11.27	-10.85			May-13
	2.44	14.70	6.33	33.53	31.18	1.63	1.06	10.67	0.88	15.52	3,440	3	94	3	0	47	19.49	-17.25	5.50		Jun-62
	2.31	14.30	5.56	30.52	26.37	0.09	1.81	10.7	0.88	15.5	3,440	3	94	3	0	47	19.03	-17.49		1.00	Jun-62
	2.40	14.58	6.10	32.54	29.66	1.4	1.31	10.64	0.87	15.32	3,440	3	94	3	0	47	19.34	-17.3			Oct-09
	2.54	14.94	6.70	34.87	33.45	1.91	0.74	10.68	0.88	15.69	3,440	3	94	3	0	47	19.64	-17.12			May-13
	2.54	14.86	6.62	34.55	32.95	1.84	0.81	10.67	0.88	15.69	3,440	3	94	3	0	47	19.64	-17.12			Jun-62
	2.96	12.31	1.01	23.10	6.96	3.49	1.29	11.07		19.43	1,553	7	93	1	0	35	14.29	-20.79	5.50		Jul-96
	2.72	11.82	0.22	20.33	3.02	1.99	2.04	11.04		19.57	1,553	7	93	1	0	35	13.84	-21.02		1.00	Jul-96
	2.86	12.13	0.75	22.15	5.63	3.31	1.54	11.05		19.04	1,553	7	93	1	0	35	14.14	-20.83			Oct-09
	3.03	12.52	1.41	24.54	9.17	3.77	0.91	11.06		20.03	1,553	7	93	1	0	35	14.46	-20.67			May-13
	3.03	12.45	1.25	24.08	8.38	3.63	1.04	11.06		20.04	1,553	7	93	1	0	35	14.46	-20.67			Jul-96
	3.05	11.44	-3.19	28.71	34.11	0.53	1.34	11.64	0.79	21.62	480.2	8	90	2	0	33	14.8	-19.82	5.50		Aug-97
	2.89	11.03	-3.91	25.87	29.27	0.27	2.09	11.65	0.79	21.33	480.2	8	90	2	0	33	14.41	-20.08		1.00	Aug-97
	3.17	11.65	-2.83	30.20	36.80	0.91	0.97	11.66	0.8	21.74	480.2	8	90	2	0	33	14.97	-19.72			May-13
	3.15	11.57	-2.92	29.72	35.92	0.77	1.09	11.65	0.79	21.59	480.2	8	90	2	0	33	14.97	-19.72			Aug-97
	3.35	15.64	3.85	27.52	20.19	1.78	1.23	10.72	0.88	30.23	15,179	3	94	3	0	15	16.82	-17.26	5.50		Dec-92
	3.15	15.18	3.04	24.65	15.77	0.33	1.98	10.73	0.88	30.04	15,179	3	94	3	0	15	16.31	-17.49		1.00	Dec-92
	3.29	15.50	3.60	26.60	18.77	1.5	1.48	10.73	0.88	29.79	15,179	3	94	3	0	15	16.66	-17.33			Jan-02
	3.44	15.86	4.24	28.95	22.57	2.1	0.88	10.72	0.88	30.9	15,179	3	94	3	0	15	17.01	-17.14			May-13
	3.44	15.81	4.14	28.50	21.80	1.99	0.98	10.72	0.88	30.9	15,179	3	94	3	0	15	17.01	-17.14			Dec-92
	-0.65	7.45	-8.82	12.06	0.41	1.54	1.22	10.76		13.69	129.5	6	94	0	0	29	16.29	-21.14	5.50		May-09
	-0.80	7.11	-9.44	9.58	-3.18	0.26	1.97	10.78		13.55	129.5	6	94	0	0	29	15.83	-21.37		1.00	May-09

	MARKET		FUND TYPE, CATEGORY & OBJECTIVE		RATINGS				MINIMUMS	
Fund Name	Ticker Symbol	Traded On	Fund Type	Category and (Prospectus Objective)	Overall Rating	Reward Rating	Risk Rating	Recent Up/ Downgrade	Open to New Investors	Min Initial Investment
Franklin Mutual International Fund Class R	FRMIX	NAS CM	Open End	Global Equity Large Cap (Foreign Stock)	D+	D	C-		Y	1,000
Franklin Mutual International Fund Class R6	FIMFX	NAS CM	Open End	Global Equity Large Cap (Foreign Stock)	D+	D	C		Y	1,000,000
Franklin Mutual International Fund Class Z	FMIZX	NAS CM	Open End	Global Equity Large Cap (Foreign Stock)	D+	D	C		Y	100,000
Franklin Mutual Quest Fund Class A	TEQIX	NAS CM	Open End	Moderate Alloc (World Stock)	C	C-	B		Y	1,000
Franklin Mutual Quest Fund Class C	TEMQX	NAS CM	Open End	Moderate Alloc (World Stock)	C	D+	B-		Y	1,000
Franklin Mutual Quest Fund Class R	FMQSX	NAS CM	Open End	Moderate Alloc (World Stock)	C	C-	B		Y	1,000
Franklin Mutual Quest Fund Class R6	FMQRX	NAS CM	Open End	Moderate Alloc (World Stock)	C	C-	B		Y	1,000,000
Franklin Mutual Quest Fund Class Z	MQIFX	NAS CM	Open End	Moderate Alloc (World Stock)	C	C-	B		Y	100,000
Franklin Mutual Shares Fund Class A	TESIX	NAS CM	Open End	Aggressive Alloc (Growth & Income)	B-	C	B	Up	Y	1,000
Franklin Mutual Shares Fund Class C	TEMTX	NAS CM	Open End	Aggressive Alloc (Growth & Income)	C+	C	B	Up	Y	1,000
Franklin Mutual Shares Fund Class R	TESRX	NAS CM	Open End	Aggressive Alloc (Growth & Income)	C+	C	B	Up	Y	1,000
Franklin Mutual Shares Fund Class R6	FMSHX	NAS CM	Open End	Aggressive Alloc (Growth & Income)	C+	C	B	Up	Y	1,000,000
Franklin Mutual Shares Fund Class Z	MUTHX	NAS CM	Open End	Aggressive Alloc (Growth & Income)	B-	C	B	Up	Y	100,000
Franklin Mutual U.S. Value Fund Advisor Class	FBSAX	NAS CM	Open End	US Equity Mid Cap (Growth & Income)	C	C	B-		Y	100,000
Franklin Mutual U.S. Value Fund Class A	FRBSX	NAS CM	Open End	US Equity Mid Cap (Growth & Income)	C	C	B-		Y	1,000
Franklin Mutual U.S. Value Fund Class C	FCBSX	NAS CM	Open End	US Equity Mid Cap (Growth & Income)	C	C	B-		Y	1,000
Franklin Mutual U.S. Value Fund Class R	FBSRX	NAS CM	Open End	US Equity Mid Cap (Growth & Income)	C	C	B-		Y	1,000
Franklin Mutual U.S. Value Fund Class R6	FBSIX	NAS CM	Open End	US Equity Mid Cap (Growth & Income)	C	C	B-		Y	1,000,000
Franklin Natural Resources Fund Advisor Class	FNRAX	NAS CM	Open End	Natl Resources Sec Equity (Natl Res)	D	D	D+	Down	Y	100,000
Franklin Natural Resources Fund Class A	FRNRX	NAS CM	Open End	Natl Resources Sec Equity (Natl Res)	D	D	D+	Down	Y	1,000
Franklin Natural Resources Fund Class C	FNCRX	NAS CM	Open End	Natl Resources Sec Equity (Natl Res)	D	D	D+	Down	Y	1,000
Franklin Natural Resources Fund Class R6	FNCSX	NAS CM	Open End	Natl Resources Sec Equity (Natl Res)	D	D	D+	Down	Y	1,000,000
Franklin NextStep Conservative Fund Advisor Class	FNCVX	NAS CM	Open End	Cautious Alloc (Growth & Income)	B-	C	B+	Up	Y	100,000
Franklin NextStep Conservative Fund Class A	FNCAX	NAS CM	Open End	Cautious Alloc (Growth & Income)	B-	C	B+	Up	Y	1,000
Franklin NextStep Conservative Fund Class C	FNCDX	NAS CM	Open End	Cautious Alloc (Growth & Income)	C+	C	B	Up	Y	1,000
Franklin NextStep Growth Fund Advisor Class	FNGVX	NAS CM	Open End	Aggressive Alloc (Growth)	B-	C	B+	Up	Y	100,000
Franklin NextStep Growth Fund Class A	FNGBX	NAS CM	Open End	Aggressive Alloc (Growth)	B-	C	B+	Up	Y	1,000
Franklin NextStep Growth Fund Class C	FNGCX	NAS CM	Open End	Aggressive Alloc (Growth)	B-	C	B+	Up	Y	1,000
Franklin NextStep Moderate Fund Advisor Class	FNMZX	NAS CM	Open End	Moderate Alloc (Growth & Income)	B-	C	A-	Up	Y	100,000
Franklin NextStep Moderate Fund Class A	FNMDX	NAS CM	Open End	Moderate Alloc (Growth & Income)	B-	C	A-	Up	Y	1,000
Franklin NextStep Moderate Fund Class C	FNMFX	NAS CM	Open End	Moderate Alloc (Growth & Income)	B-	C	B+	Up	Y	1,000
Franklin Payout 2019 Fund Advisor Class	FPOFX	NAS CM	Open End	US Fixed Income (Growth & Income)	C	C	B-		Y	1,000,000
Franklin Payout 2019 Fund Class R6	FPOEX	NAS CM	Open End	US Fixed Income (Growth & Income)	C	C	B-		Y	1,000,000
Franklin Payout 2020 Fund Advisor Class	FPOHX	NAS CM	Open End	US Fixed Income (Growth & Income)	C	C	B-		Y	1,000,000
Franklin Payout 2020 Fund Class R6	FPOGX	NAS CM	Open End	US Fixed Income (Growth & Income)	C	C	B-		Y	1,000,000
Franklin Payout 2021 Fund Advisor Class	FPOJX	NAS CM	Open End	US Fixed Income (Growth & Income)	C	C	C+		Y	1,000,000
Franklin Payout 2021 Fund Class R6	FPOMX	NAS CM	Open End	US Fixed Income (Growth & Income)	C	C	C+		Y	1,000,000
Franklin Payout 2022 Fund Advisor Class	FPOQX	NAS CM	Open End	US Fixed Income (Growth & Income)	D	D+	B+		Y	1,000,000
Franklin Payout 2022 Fund Class R6	FPONX	NAS CM	Open End	US Fixed Income (Growth & Income)	D	D+	B+		Y	1,000,000
Franklin Pelagos Commodities Strategy Fund Advisor Class	FSLPX	NAS CM	Open End	Commodities Broad Basket (Growth & Income)	D	D	D+	Down	Y	100,000
Franklin Pelagos Commodities Strategy Fund Class A	FLSQX	NAS CM	Open End	Commodities Broad Basket (Growth & Income)	D	D	D+	Down	Y	1,000
Franklin Pelagos Commodities Strategy Fund Class C	FLSVX	NAS CM	Open End	Commodities Broad Basket (Growth & Income)	D	D	D+		Y	1,000
Franklin Pelagos Commodities Strategy Fund Class R	FLSWX	NAS CM	Open End	Commodities Broad Basket (Growth & Income)	D	D	D+	Down	Y	1,000
Franklin Pelagos Commodities Strategy Fund Class R6	FPELX	NAS CM	Open End	Commodities Broad Basket (Growth & Income)	D	D	D+	Down	Y	1,000,000
Franklin Real Estate Securities Fund Advisor Class	FRLAX	NAS CM	Open End	Real Estate Sector Equity (Real Estate)	C+	C	C+	Down	Y	100,000
Franklin Real Estate Securities Fund Class A	FREEX	NAS CM	Open End	Real Estate Sector Equity (Real Estate)	C	C	C+	Down	Y	1,000
Franklin Real Estate Securities Fund Class C	FRRSX	NAS CM	Open End	Real Estate Sector Equity (Real Estate)	C	C	C+	Down	Y	1,000
Franklin Real Estate Securities Fund Class R6	FSERX	NAS CM	Open End	Real Estate Sector Equity (Real Estate)	C+	C	B-	Down	Y	1,000,000
Franklin Rising Dividends Fund Advisor Class	FRDAX	NAS CM	Open End	US Equity Large Cap Blend (Equity-Income)	B-	C+	B	Down	Y	100,000
Franklin Rising Dividends Fund Class A	FRDPX	NAS CM	Open End	US Equity Large Cap Blend (Equity-Income)	B-	C+	B	Down	Y	1,000
Franklin Rising Dividends Fund Class C	FRDTX	NAS CM	Open End	US Equity Large Cap Blend (Equity-Income)	B-	C+	B	Down	Y	1,000
Franklin Rising Dividends Fund Class R	FRDRX	NAS CM	Open End	US Equity Large Cap Blend (Equity-Income)	B-	C+	B	Down	Y	1,000

★ Expanded analysis of this fund is included in Section II.

	TOTAL RETURNS					PERFORMANCE				ASSETS		ASSET ALLOCATION & TURNOVER					BULL & BEAR		FEES		
Min Additional Investment	3-Month Total Return	6-Month Total Return	1-Year Total Return	3-Year Total Return	5-Year Total Return	Dividend Yield (TTM)	Expense Ratio	3-Yr Std Deviation	3-Year Beta	NAV	Total Assets (MIL)	%Cash	%Stocks	%Bonds	%Other	Turnover Ratio	Last Bull Market Total Return	Last Bear Market Total Return	Front End Fee (%)	Back End Fee (%)	Inception Date
	-0.65	7.43	-8.97	11.34	-0.70	1.33	1.47	10.77		13.59	129.5	6	94	0	0	29	16.21	-21.21			May-09
	-0.50	7.74	-8.40	13.42	2.53	2.02	0.81	10.76		13.77	129.5	6	94	0	0	29	16.52	-21.07			May-13
	-0.57	7.66	-8.55	12.96	1.76	1.82	0.97	10.75		13.76	129.5	6	94	0	0	29	16.52	-21.07			May-09
	-1.36	7.69	-3.16	18.09	11.87	3.65	1.03	8.46	0.65	13.71	4,451	15	60	25	0	116	15.46	-14.94	5.50		Sep-80
	-1.52	7.21	-3.96	15.40	7.76	2.08	1.78	8.43	0.65	13.53	4,451	15	60	25	0	116	15.05	-15.18		1.00	Sep-80
	-1.39	7.58	-3.38	17.22	10.59	3.55	1.28	8.44	0.65	13.47	4,451	15	60	25	0	116	15.38	-15.01			May-09
	-1.27	7.90	-2.91	19.17	13.74	3.9	0.72	8.45	0.65	13.93	4,451	15	60	25	0	116	15.7	-14.82			May-13
	-1.27	7.81	-2.97	18.96	13.35	3.83	0.78	8.46	0.65	13.94	4,451	15	60	25	0	116	15.7	-14.82			Sep-80
	3.21	14.33	4.22	25.73	23.29	1.62	1.02	11.05	0.85	27.27	12,661	5	89	6	0	21	19.91	-17.62	5.50		Jul-49
	3.03	13.93	3.41	22.91	18.76	0.09	1.77	11.04	0.85	27.14	12,661	5	89	6	0	21	19.46	-17.9		1.00	Jul-49
	3.15	14.22	3.97	24.84	21.81	1.27	1.27	11.03	0.85	27.14	12,661	5	89	6	0	21	19.82	-17.73			Jan-02
	3.33	14.53	4.55	27.06	25.57	1.91	0.7	11.03	0.85	27.58	12,661	5	89	6	0	21	20.12	-17.51			May-13
	3.29	14.48	4.50	26.68	24.92	1.83	0.77	11.03	0.85	27.59	12,661	5	89	6	0	21	20.12	-17.51			Jul-49
	3.07	15.51	0.48	36.94	21.41	1.4	0.66	14.79	1.16	35.21	813.2	13	86	1	0	30	23.74	-22.59			Mar-01
	3.01	15.36	0.22	35.91	19.90	1.21	0.91	14.78	1.16	33.86	813.2	13	86	1	0	30	23.56	-22.67	5.50		Apr-90
	2.79	14.92	-0.54	32.89	15.48	0	1.66	14.76	1.16	32.34	813.2	13	86	1	0	30	23.05	-22.92		1.00	Mar-01
	2.93	15.22	-0.04	34.91	18.42	0.93	1.16	14.76	1.16	33.98	813.2	13	86	1	0	30	23.42	-22.76			Jan-02
	3.11	15.60	0.58	37.41	22.25	1.53	0.55	14.76	1.16	35.12	813.2	13	86	1	0	30	23.56	-22.67			May-13
	-4.14	12.69	-18.55	-3.62	-41.59	2.12	0.81	21.17	1.1	24.06	322.1	2	98	0	0	30	19.87	-32.51			Dec-96
	-4.21	12.55	-18.74	-4.33	-42.36	2.18	1.06	21.18	1.1	22.5	322.1	2	98	0	0	30	19.65	-32.6	5.50		Jun-95
	-4.39	12.11	-19.39	-6.47	-44.46	1.82	1.81	21.17	1.1	21.75	322.1	2	98	0	0	30	19.18	-32.8		1.00	Sep-05
	-4.10	12.78	-18.40	-2.89	-40.80	2.22	0.58	21.18	1.1	24.08	322.1	2	98	0	0	30	19.65	-32.6			Sep-13
	2.70	8.37	6.58	14.09		2.75	0.75	3.55	0.4	10.96	3.7	6	22	71	1	40					Jun-16
	2.56	8.17	6.36	13.24		2.55	1	3.56	0.41	10.96	3.7	6	22	71	1	40			5.50		Feb-16
	2.39	7.75	5.52	10.72		1.77	1.75	3.5	0.4	10.91	3.7	6	22	71	1	40				1.00	Feb-16
	3.32	14.29	5.97	27.67		1.86	0.85	8.8	0.7	12.54	7.2	4	72	23	1	75					Jun-16
	3.23	14.02	5.63	26.61		1.62	1.1	8.76	0.69	12.5	7.2	4	72	23	1	75			5.50		Feb-16
	3.04	13.55	4.81	23.83		0.92	1.85	8.79	0.69	12.36	7.2	4	72	23	1	75				1.00	Feb-16
	3.02	12.31	5.88	23.56		2.19	0.84	7.19	0.56	11.97	12.5	5	57	37	1	66					Jun-16
	2.97	12.13	5.55	22.52		1.96	1.09	7.2	0.56	11.94	12.5	5	57	37	1	66			5.50		Feb-16
	2.74	11.67	4.78	19.83		1.24	1.84	7.23	0.56	11.85	12.5	5	57	37	1	66				1.00	Feb-16
	0.70	1.51	2.62	3.63		1.88	0.45	0.81		10.06	4.1	11	0	89	0	1					Jun-15
	0.70	1.51	2.63	3.65		1.89	0.3	0.8		10.06	4.1	11	0	89	0	1					Jun-15
	1.10	2.43	3.63	3.86		2.03	0.45	1.42		10.09	4.1	5	0	95	0	1					Jun-15
	1.10	2.43	3.64	3.99		2.05	0.3	1.41		10.09	4.1	5	0	95	0	1					Jun-15
	1.49	3.45	4.74	3.88		2.22	0.45	2		10.18	4.1	7	0	93	0						Jun-15
	1.49	3.45	4.75	3.91		2.24	0.3	1.99		10.18	4.1	7	0	93	0						Jun-15
	1.97	4.87	6.41			2.26	0.44			10.32	3.6	2	0	98	0						Jan-18
	1.97	4.87	6.43			2.28	0.29			10.32	3.6	2	0	98	0						Jan-18
	-4.28	0.18	-11.08	-13.02	-38.31	7.54	0.95	9.3	1.06	5.58	158.4	52	0	28	20	42					Dec-11
	-4.22	0.18	-11.25	-13.48	-39.01	7.5	1.2	9.23	1.05	5.44	158.4	52	0	28	20	42			5.50		Jan-14
	-4.33	0.00	-11.73	-15.32	-41.12	6.08	1.95	9.37	1.07	5.3	158.4	52	0	28	20	42				1.00	Jan-14
	-4.42	0.00	-11.47	-14.10	-39.65	7.06	1.45	9.26	1.05	5.4	158.4	52	0	28	20	42					Jan-14
	-4.13	0.54	-10.69	-12.02	-37.40	7.9	0.58	9.28	1.05	5.56	158.4	52	0	28	20	42					Jan-14
	1.30	18.39	10.52	9.63	39.92	1.86	0.8	12.92	0.96	22.22	456.1	1	99	0	0	20	31.06	-15.37			Dec-96
	1.24	18.23	10.27	8.78	38.19	1.7	1.05	12.91	0.96	21.97	456.1	1	99	0	0	20	30.88	-15.5	5.75		Jan-94
	1.10	17.84	9.46	6.37	33.10	1.18	1.8	12.88	0.96	20.92	456.1	1	99	0	0	20	30.32	-15.77		1.00	May-95
	1.35	18.49	10.75	10.35	41.40	1.97	0.61	12.91	0.96	22.26	456.1	1	99	0	0	20	30.88	-15.5			May-13
	5.06	21.98	13.98	47.62	60.94	1.29	0.63	12.38	0.98	66.59	19,187	1	99	0	0	2	19.77	-11.85			Oct-05
	4.99	21.83	13.69	46.50	58.92	1.06	0.88	12.36	0.98	66.62	19,187	1	99	0	0	2	19.56	-11.92	5.50		Jan-87
	4.80	21.37	12.84	43.24	53.05	0.4	1.63	12.37	0.98	65.27	19,187	1	99	0	0	2	19.04	-12.19		1.00	May-95
	4.92	21.68	13.40	45.41	56.95	0.84	1.13	12.37	0.98	66.37	19,187	1	99	0	0	2	19.41	-12.03			Jan-02

	MARKET			FUND TYPE, CATEGORY & OBJECTIVE	RATINGS					MINIMUMS
Fund Name	Ticker Symbol	Traded On	Fund Type	Category and (Prospectus Objective)	Overall Rating	Reward Rating	Risk Rating	Recent Up/ Downgrade	Open to New Investors	Min Initial Investment
Franklin Rising Dividends Fund R6 Class	FRISX	NAS CM	Open End	US Equity Large Cap Blend (Equity-Income)	B-	C+	B	Down	Y	1,000,000
Franklin Select U.S. Equity Fund Advisor Class	FCEZX	NAS CM	Open End	US Equity Large Cap Growth (Growth)	C+	C	B	Down	Y	100,000
Franklin Select U.S. Equity Fund Class A	FCEQX	NAS CM	Open End	US Equity Large Cap Growth (Growth)	C+	C	B	Down	Y	1,000
Franklin Select U.S. Equity Fund Class C	FCEDX	NAS CM	Open End	US Equity Large Cap Growth (Growth)	C+	C	B		Y	1,000
Franklin Select U.S. Equity Fund Class R	FCERX	NAS CM	Open End	US Equity Large Cap Growth (Growth)	C+	C	B	Down	Y	1,000
Franklin Select U.S. Equity Fund Class R6	FEFCX	NAS CM	Open End	US Equity Large Cap Growth (Growth)	C+	C	B	Down	Y	1,000,000
Franklin Small Cap Growth Fund Advisor Class	FSSAX	NAS CM	Open End	US Equity Small Cap (Small Company)	C+	C	B-	Down		100,000
Franklin Small Cap Growth Fund Class A	FSGRX	NAS CM	Open End	US Equity Small Cap (Small Company)	C+	C	B-	Down		1,000
Franklin Small Cap Growth Fund Class C	FCSGX	NAS CM	Open End	US Equity Small Cap (Small Company)	C+	C	B-	Down		1,000
Franklin Small Cap Growth Fund Class R	FSSRX	NAS CM	Open End	US Equity Small Cap (Small Company)	C+	C	B-	Down		1,000
Franklin Small Cap Growth Fund Class R6	FSMLX	NAS CM	Open End	US Equity Small Cap (Small Company)	C+	C	B-	Down		1,000,000
Franklin Small Cap Value Fund Advisor Class	FVADX	NAS CM	Open End	US Equity Small Cap (Small Company)	C	C-	B-		Y	100,000
Franklin Small Cap Value Fund Class A	FRVLX	NAS CM	Open End	US Equity Small Cap (Small Company)	C	C-	B-		Y	1,000
Franklin Small Cap Value Fund Class C	FRVFX	NAS CM	Open End	US Equity Small Cap (Small Company)	C	C-	C+		Y	1,000
Franklin Small Cap Value Fund Class R	FVFRX	NAS CM	Open End	US Equity Small Cap (Small Company)	C	C-	C+		Y	1,000
Franklin Small Cap Value Fund Class R6	FRCSX	NAS CM	Open End	US Equity Small Cap (Small Company)	C	C-	B-		Y	1,000,000
Franklin Small-Mid Cap Growth Fund Advisor Class	FSGAX	NAS CM	Open End	US Equity Mid Cap (Growth)	B-	C+	B		Y	100,000
Franklin Small-Mid Cap Growth Fund Class A	FRSGX	NAS CM	Open End	US Equity Mid Cap (Growth)	B-	C+	B		Y	1,000
Franklin Small-Mid Cap Growth Fund Class C	FRSIX	NAS CM	Open End	US Equity Mid Cap (Growth)	B-	C+	B		Y	1,000
Franklin Small-Mid Cap Growth Fund Class R	FSMRX	NAS CM	Open End	US Equity Mid Cap (Growth)	B-	C+	B		Y	1,000
Franklin Small-Mid Cap Growth Fund Class R6	FMGGX	NAS CM	Open End	US Equity Mid Cap (Growth)	B-	C+	B	Down	Y	1,000,000
Franklin Universal Trust	FT	NYSE	Closed End	Moderate Alloc (Balanced)	C+	B	C-		Y	
Franklin Utilities Fund Advisor Class	FRUAX	NAS CM	Open End	Utilities Sector Equity (Utility)	B	B	B-		Y	100,000
Franklin Utilities Fund Class A USD	FKUQX	NAS CM	Open End	Utilities Sector Equity (Utility)	B	B	B-		Y	1,000
Franklin Utilities Fund Class A1	FKUTX	NAS CM	Open End	Utilities Sector Equity (Utility)	B	B	B-		Y	1,000
Franklin Utilities Fund Class C	FRUSX	NAS CM	Open End	Utilities Sector Equity (Utility)	B	B	B-		Y	1,000
Franklin Utilities Fund Class R	FRURX	NAS CM	Open End	Utilities Sector Equity (Utility)	B	B	B-		Y	1,000
Franklin Utilities Fund Class R6	FUFRX	NAS CM	Open End	Utilities Sector Equity (Utility)	B	B	B-		Y	1,000,000
Free Market International Equity Fund Institutional Class	FMNEX	NAS CM	Open End	Global Equity Mid/Small Cap (Foreign Stock)	C	C-	C		Y	0
Friess Small Cap Growth Fund Institutional Class	SCGFX	NAS CM	Open End	US Equity Small Cap (Small Company)	C	C-	C+	Up	Y	100,000
Friess Small Cap Growth Fund Investor Class	SCGNX	NAS CM	Open End	US Equity Small Cap (Small Company)	C	C-	C+	Up	Y	2,000
Frontier MFG Core Infrastructure Fund Institutional Class	FMGIX	NAS CM	Open End	Infrastructure Sector Equity (Utility)	B-	B-	B		Y	100,000
Frontier MFG Core Infrastructure Fund Service Class	FCIVX	NAS CM	Open End	Infrastructure Sector Equity (Utility)	B-	B-	B		Y	10,000
Frontier MFG Global Equity Fund Institutional Class	FMGEX	NAS CM	Open End	US Equity Large Cap Growth (World Stock)	B	B-	A-			1,000,000
Frontier MFG Global Plus Fund Institutional Class	FMGPX	NAS CM	Open End	US Equity Large Cap Blend (Growth)	B	B-	A-		Y	1,000,000
Frontier MFG Global Plus Fund Service Class	FMPSX	NAS CM	Open End	US Equity Large Cap Blend (Growth)	B	B-	A-		Y	10,000
Frontier MFG Select Infrastructure Institutional Cls	FMSIX	NAS CM	Open End	Infrastructure Sector Equity (Utility)	D-	D+	B		Y	1,000,000
Frontier MFG Select Infrastructure Fund Service Class	FMSSX	NAS CM	Open End	Infrastructure Sector Equity (Utility)	D-	D+	B		Y	10,000
Frontier Phocas Small Cap Value Fund Institutional Class	FPSVX	NAS CM	Open End	US Equity Small Cap (Small Company)	C	C-	C		Y	100,000
Frontier Phocas Small Cap Value Fund Service Class	FPVSX	NAS CM	Open End	US Equity Small Cap (Small Company)	C	C-	C		Y	10,000
Frost Growth Equity Fund Class Institutional	FICEX	NAS CM	Open End	US Equity Large Cap Growth (Growth)	B-	C+	B	Down	Y	1,000,000
Frost Growth Equity Fund Investor Class Shares	FACEX	NAS CM	Open End	US Equity Large Cap Growth (Growth)	B-	C+	B	Down	Y	2,500
Frost Mid Cap Equity Fund Class Institutional	FIKSX	NAS CM	Open End	US Equity Mid Cap (Growth)	B-	C	B	Up	Y	1,000,000
Frost Mid Cap Equity Fund Investor Class Shares	FAKSX	NAS CM	Open End	US Equity Mid Cap (Growth)	B-	C	B	Up	Y	2,500
Frost Value Equity Fund Class Institutional	FIDVX	NAS CM	Open End	US Equity Large Cap Value (Growth & Income)	C	C	B		Y	1,000,000
Frost Value Equity Fund Investor Class Shares	FADVX	NAS CM	Open End	US Equity Large Cap Value (Growth & Income)	C	C	B		Y	2,500
FS Energy Total Return Fund A	XFEAX	NAS CM	Closed End	Natl Resources Sec Equity (Natl Res)	C	C	C-	Up	Y	2,500
FS Energy Total Return Fund I	XFEYX	NAS CM	Closed End	Natl Resources Sec Equity (Natl Res)	C	C	C	Up	Y	1,000,000
FS Event Driven Fund Class A	FSDDX	NAS CM	Open End	Market Neutral (Growth)	U	U	U		Y	2,500
FS Event Driven Fund Class I	FSDFX	NAS CM	Open End	Market Neutral (Growth)	U	U	U		Y	1,000,000
FS Global Macro Fund Class A	FGMCX	NAS CM	Open End	Multialternative (World Stock)	U	U	U		Y	2,500
FS Global Macro Fund Class I	FGMIX	NAS CM	Open End	Multialternative (World Stock)	U	U	U		Y	1,000,000

★ Expanded analysis of this fund is included in Section II.

	TOTAL RETURNS					PERFORMANCE				ASSETS		ASSET ALLOCATION & TURNOVER					BULL & BEAR		FEES		
Min Additional Investment	3-Month Total Return	6-Month Total Return	1-Year Total Return	3-Year Total Return	5-Year Total Return	Dividend Yield (TTM)	Expense Ratio	3-Yr Std Deviation	3-Year Beta	NAV	Total Assets (MIL)	%Cash	%Stocks	%Bonds	%Other	Turnover Ratio	Last Bull Market Total Return	Last Bear Market Total Return	Front End Fee (%)	Back End Fee (%)	Inception Date
	5.08	22.03	14.03	48.09	61.96	1.36	0.53	12.38	0.98	66.59	19,187	1	99	0	0	2	19.56	-11.92			May-13
	3.65	20.21	7.39	43.13	36.46	0	1	12.87	1.01	15.88	104.2	5	95	0	0	93	23.73	-20.63			Dec-07
	3.59	20.07	7.13	42.08	34.71	0	1.25	12.87	1.01	15.55	104.2	5	95	0	0	93	23.47	-20.77	5.75		Dec-07
	3.37	19.58	6.37	38.95	29.82	0	2	12.84	1.01	14.41	104.2	5	95	0	0	93	23.22	-21		1.00	Dec-07
	3.46	19.82	6.79	41.09	33.24	0	1.5	12.89	1.01	15.23	104.2	5	95	0	0	93	23.56	-20.87			Dec-07
	3.69	20.24	7.54	43.69	37.45	0	0.88	12.88	1.01	15.98	104.2	5	95	0	0	93	23.73	-20.63			May-13
	5.25	26.89	8.41	67.42	50.87	0	0.84	18.02	1.01	23.45	2,505	1	98	0	0	30	27.59	-22.43			May-00
	5.18	26.66	8.20	66.21	48.96	0	1.09	18.03	1.01	21.52	2,505	1	98	0	0	30	27.38	-22.58	5.50		May-00
	4.94	26.23	7.53	62.72	43.70	0	1.84	17.98	1	17.18	2,505	1	98	0	0	30	26.86	-22.71		1.00	May-00
	5.09	26.56	7.94	65.06	47.27	0	1.34	18	1	20.2	2,505	1	98	0	0	30	27.21	-22.57			Jan-02
	5.26	26.91	8.59	68.35	52.43	0	0.65	18.05	1.01	23.81	2,505	1	98	0	0	30	27.59	-22.43			May-13
	0.86	12.92	-4.09	29.13	26.03	0.99	0.8	15.34	0.86	48.74	2,245	5	95	0	0	53	31.95	-25.56			Dec-96
	0.83	12.79	-4.31	28.18	24.40	0.82	1.05	15.34	0.86	46.1	2,245	5	95	0	0	53	31.72	-25.66	5.50		Mar-96
	0.62	12.38	-5.01	25.35	19.91	0	1.8	15.32	0.86	40.02	2,245	5	95	0	0	53	31.18	-25.88		1.00	Sep-96
	0.75	12.65	-4.55	27.24	22.93	0.49	1.3	15.32	0.86	45.58	2,245	5	95	0	0	53	31.58	-25.72			Aug-02
	0.93	13.03	-3.90	29.88	27.39	1.21	0.62	15.34	0.86	48.65	2,245	5	95	0	0	53	31.72	-25.66			May-13
	5.46	28.50	14.59	57.22	56.23	0	0.68	14.16	0.97	41.48	3,324	4	96	0	0	38	28.26	-23.82			Dec-96
	5.42	28.37	14.38	56.09	54.36	0	0.93	14.14	0.97	37.51	3,324	4	96	0	0	38	28.06	-23.89	5.50		Feb-92
	5.22	27.88	13.65	52.73	48.78	0	1.68	14.1	0.97	25.18	3,324	4	96	0	0	38	27.51	-24.15		1.00	Oct-95
	5.33	28.21	14.12	54.95	52.46	0	1.18	14.12	0.97	33.95	3,324	4	96	0	0	38	27.89	-23.99			Feb-92
	5.52	28.62	14.75	58.19	57.94	0	0.49	14.16	0.97	42.24	3,324	4	96	0	0	38	28.06	-23.89			May-13
	2.98	15.34	12.36	30.13	31.03	4.55	0	6.89	1.24	8.44	212.1	2	41	88	-31	23	14.7	-5.23			Sep-88
	4.01	17.48	20.03	29.84	55.82	2.5	0.59	10.56	0.95	21.14	6,287	1	98	0	0	5	11.53	1.68			Dec-96
	3.93	17.25	19.67	28.81	53.82		0.84	10.58	0.95	20.96	6,287	1	98	0	0	5	11.36	1.57	3.75		Sep-18
	4.00	17.37	19.85	29.26	54.67	2.39	0.74	10.58	0.95	20.97	6,287	1	98	0	0	5	11.43	1.61	3.75		Sep-48
	3.85	17.07	19.26	27.31	50.77	1.95	1.24	10.54	0.95	20.85	6,287	1	98	0	0	5	11.04	1.46		1.00	May-95
	3.88	17.12	19.40	27.91	51.98	2.08	1.09	10.56	0.95	20.88	6,287	1	98	0	0	5	11.19	1.45			Jan-02
	4.03	17.48	20.08	30.23	56.55	2.58	0.5	10.58	0.95	21.13	6,287	1	98	0	0	5	11.43	1.61			May-13
	0.83	10.05	-7.10	25.24	4.51	1.8	1.03	12.52	1.1	9.63	2,288	1	85	0	14	3	13.6	-26.31			Dec-07
100	1.85	18.69	8.17			0	1.2			23.55	161.3	0	100	0	0	220					May-17
100	1.78	18.53	7.89			0	1.45			23.41	161.3	0	100	0	0	220					May-17
1,000	5.39	18.50	14.65	25.68	42.60	2.58	0.72	10.51	0.48	17.16	510.9	3	91	0	5	19					Jan-12
1,000	5.42	18.56	14.59	25.65	42.57	2.5	0.87	10.47	0.47	17.2	510.9	3	91	0	5	19					Jul-16
1,000	6.30	18.86	15.06	57.84	64.21	0.8	0.82	9.92	0.81	19.72	1,125	14	86	0	0	28					Dec-11
1,000	6.36	18.86	15.22	57.30		1.12	0.82	9.92	0.81	13.04	330.9	13	86	0	1	59					Mar-15
1,000	6.36	18.77	15.08	56.94		1.07	0.97	9.98	0.82	13.03	330.9	13	86	0	1	59					May-16
1,000	5.79	19.20	13.90				0.8			11.18	89.1	8	87	0	4						Jul-18
1,000	5.77	19.29	13.98				0.95			11.19	89.1	8	87	0	4						Feb-19
1,000	2.15	17.00	-7.34	25.85	23.35	0.48	0.95	17.86	1.02	30.82	26.3	4	96	0	0	68	24.34	-24.48			Sep-06
1,000	2.12	16.93	-7.35	25.58	23.08	0.49	1.1	17.86	1.02	30.72	26.3	4	96	0	0	68	24.35	-24.48			Jul-16
	4.45	21.97	11.51	73.08	85.52	0.25	0.64	13.43	0.98	13.6	327.2	5	95	0	0	15	25.26	-17.1			Apr-08
500	4.44	21.92	11.30	71.75	83.30	0.05	0.89	13.4	0.98	13.4	327.2	5	95	0	0	15	25.08	-17.12			Jun-08
	2.94	18.38	5.80	47.31	37.11	0.25	1.33	12.04	0.86	7.34	4.8	1	99	0	0	55	27.46	-24.14			Apr-08
500	3.00	18.64	5.61	47.02	36.10	0.08	1.51	12.17	0.87	7.19	4.8	1	99	0	0	55	27.33	-24.22			Feb-12
	2.14	15.19	-0.11	31.17	33.81	1.86	0.69	13.13	1.05	7.65	31.0	2	98	0	0	26	16.86	-17.9			Apr-08
500	2.22	15.08	-0.23	30.30	32.26	1.63	0.94	13.08	1.04	7.64	31.0	2	98	0	0	26	16.57	-17.98			Jun-08
100	-0.88	20.25	0.44			5.32	2.86			11.24	--								5.75		May-17
	-0.88	20.32	0.53			5.56	2.61			11.24	--										Mar-17
100	3.15	1.40					1.7			10.14	2.0	100	0	0	0				5.75		Dec-18
0	3.15	1.50					1.45			10.15	2.0	100	0	0	0						Dec-18
100	0.49	2.50					1.69			10.25	2.1	92	0	7	2				5.75		Dec-18
0	0.58	2.70					1.44			10.27	2.1	92	0	7	2						Dec-18

	MARKET		FUND TYPE, CATEGORY & OBJECTIVE		RATINGS				MINIMUMS	
Fund Name	Ticker Symbol	Traded On	Fund Type	Category and (Prospectus Objective)	Overall Rating	Reward Rating	Risk Rating	Recent Up/ Downgrade	Open to New Investors	Min Initial Investment
FS Long/Short Equity Fund Class A	FSYAX	NAS CM	Open End	Long/Short Equity (Growth)	U	U	U		Y	2,500
FS Long/Short Equity Fund Class I	FSYIX	NAS CM	Open End	Long/Short Equity (Growth)	U	U	U		Y	1,000,000
FS Managed Futures Fund Class A	FMFFX	NAS CM	Open End	Global Macro (Growth & Income)	U	U	U		Y	2,500
FS Managed Futures Fund Class I	FMGFX	NAS CM	Open End	Global Macro (Growth & Income)	U	U	U		Y	1,000,000
FS Market Neutral Fund Class A	FANFX	NAS CM	Open End	Market Neutral (Growth)	U	U	U		Y	2,500
FS Market Neutral Fund Class I	FSNFX	NAS CM	Open End	Market Neutral (Growth)	U	U	U		Y	1,000,000
FS Multi-Strategy Alternatives Fund Class A	FSMMX	NAS CM	Open End	Multialternative (Growth & Income)	C	D+	B-	Up	Y	2,500
FS Multi-Strategy Alternatives Fund Class I	FSMSX	NAS CM	Open End	Multialternative (Growth & Income)	C	D+	B-	Up	Y	1,000,000
FS Real Asset Fund Class A	FARLX	NAS CM	Open End	Flexible Alloc (Growth & Income)	U	U	U		Y	2,500
FS Real Asset Fund Class I	FSRLX	NAS CM	Open End	Flexible Alloc (Growth & Income)	U	U	U		Y	1,000,000
Fulcrum Diversified Absolute Return Institutional Cls	FARIX	NAS CM	Open End	Global Macro (Growth & Income)	C	C	B	Down	Y	1,000,000
Fulcrum Diversified Absolute Return Super Inst Cls	FARYX	NAS CM	Open End	Global Macro (Growth & Income)	C	C	B	Down	Y	25,000,000
Fuller & Thaler Behavioral Micro-Cap Equity Inst Shares	FTMSX	NAS CM	Open End	US Equity Small Cap (Growth)	U	U	U		Y	100,000
Fuller & Thaler Behavioral Mid-Cap Value Inst Shares	FTVSX	NAS CM	Open End	US Equity Mid Cap (Growth)	D+	D+	C+	Up	Y	100,000
Fuller & Thaler Behavioral Mid-Cap Value Investor Shares	FTVNX	NAS CM	Open End	US Equity Mid Cap (Growth)	D+	D+	C+	Up	Y	1,000
Fuller & Thaler Behavioral Mid-Cap Value Fund R6 Shares	FTVZX	NAS CM	Open End	US Equity Mid Cap (Growth)	D+	D+	C+	Up	Y	1,000,000
Fuller & Thaler Behavioral Small-Cap Equity Fund A Shares	FTHAX	NAS CM	Open End	US Equity Small Cap (Growth)	C	C	C+		Y	1,000
Fuller & Thaler Behavioral Small-Cap Equity Fund C Shares	FTYCX	NAS CM	Open End	US Equity Small Cap (Growth)	C	C	C+		Y	1,000
Fuller & Thaler Behavioral Small-Cap Growth Fund A Shares	FTXAX	NAS CM	Open End	US Equity Small Cap (Small Company)	D+	D+	C-	Up	Y	1,000
Fuller & Thaler Behavioral Small-Cap Growth Fund C Shares	FTXCX	NAS CM	Open End	US Equity Small Cap (Small Company)	D+	D	C-	Up	Y	1,000
Fuller & Thaler Behavioral Small-Cap Growth Inst Shares	FTXSX	NAS CM	Open End	US Equity Small Cap (Small Company)	D+	D+	C-	Up	Y	100,000
Fuller & Thaler Behavioral Small-Cap Growth Inv Shares	FTXNX	NAS CM	Open End	US Equity Small Cap (Small Company)	D+	D	C-	Up	Y	1,000
Fuller & Thaler Behavioral Small-Cap Growth Fund R6 Shares	FTXFX	NAS CM	Open End	US Equity Small Cap (Small Company)	D+	D+	C-	Up	Y	1,000,000
Fuller & Thaler Behavioral Small-Mid Core Eq Inst Shares	FTSIX	NAS CM	Open End	US Equity Mid Cap (Growth)	U	U	U		Y	100,000
Fuller & Thaler Behavioral Unconstrained Eq Inst Shares	FTZIX	NAS CM	Open End	US Equity Large Cap Blend (Growth)	U	U	U		Y	100,000
Fuller & Thaler Behavioral Unconstrained Equity R6 Shares	FTZFX	NAS CM	Open End	US Equity Large Cap Blend (Growth)	U	U	U		Y	1,000,000
FundX Aggressive Upgrader Fund	HOTFX	NAS CM	Open End	US Equity Large Cap Growth (Growth)	C+	C	B-	Up	Y	1,000
FundX Conservative Upgrader Fund	RELAX	NAS CM	Open End	Moderate Alloc (Growth & Income)	B-	C	B+	Up	Y	1,000
FundX Sustainable Impact Fund	SRIFX	NAS CM	Open End	US Equity Large Cap Growth (Growth)	C	C	B-		Y	1,000
FundX Tactical Upgrader Fund	TACTX	NAS CM	Open End	Long/Short Equity (Growth)	B-	C	A-	Down	Y	1,000
FundX Upgrader Fund	FUNDX	NAS CM	Open End	Aggressive Alloc (Growth)	C+	C	B		Y	1,000
Gabelli ABC Fund Class AAA	GABCX	NAS CM	Open End	Market Neutral (Growth & Income)	C+	C	B		Y	10,000
Gabelli ABC Fund Class Advisor	GADVX	NAS CM	Open End	Market Neutral (Growth & Income)	C	C	B	Down	Y	10,000
Gabelli Asset Fund Class A	GATAX	NAS CM	Open End	US Equity Large Cap Blend (Growth)	B-	C	B	Up	Y	1,000
Gabelli Asset Fund Class AAA	GABAX	NAS CM	Open End	US Equity Large Cap Blend (Growth)	B-	C	B	Up	Y	1,000
Gabelli Asset Fund Class C	GATCX	NAS CM	Open End	US Equity Large Cap Blend (Growth)	B-	C	B	Up	Y	1,000
Gabelli Asset Fund Class I	GABIX	NAS CM	Open End	US Equity Large Cap Blend (Growth)	B-	C	B	Up	Y	500,000
Gabelli Convertible & Income Securities	GCV	NYSE	Closed End	Aggressive Alloc (Convertible Bond)	C	C+	C-		Y	
Gabelli Dividend & Income Trust	GDV	NYSE	Closed End	US Equity Large Cap Value (Equity-Income)	C	C	C+		Y	
Gabelli Dividend Growth Fund Class A	GBCAX	NAS CM	Open End	US Equity Large Cap Blend (Growth)	C+	C	B	Up	Y	1,000
Gabelli Dividend Growth Fund Class AAA	GABBX	NAS CM	Open End	US Equity Large Cap Blend (Growth)	C+	C	B	Up	Y	1,000
Gabelli Dividend Growth Fund Class C	GBCCX	NAS CM	Open End	US Equity Large Cap Blend (Growth)	C+	C	B	Up	Y	1,000
Gabelli Dividend Growth Fund Class Institutional	GBCIX	NAS CM	Open End	US Equity Large Cap Blend (Growth)	C+	C	B		Y	500,000
Gabelli Enterprise Mergers and Acquisitions Fund Class A	EMAAX	NAS CM	Open End	Market Neutral (Aggr Growth)	B-	C	B+		Y	1,000
Gabelli Enterprise Mergers and Acquisitions Fund Class AAA	EAAAX	NAS CM	Open End	Market Neutral (Aggr Growth)	B-	C	B+		Y	1,000
Gabelli Enterprise Mergers and Acquisitions Fund Class C	EMACX	NAS CM	Open End	Market Neutral (Aggr Growth)	C+	C	B		Y	1,000
Gabelli Enterprise Mergers and Acquisitions Fund Class Y	EMAYX	NAS CM	Open End	Market Neutral (Aggr Growth)	B-	C	A-		Y	500,000
Gabelli Equity Income Fund Class A	GCAEX	NAS CM	Open End	US Equity Large Cap Blend (Equity-Income)	C+	C	B	Up	Y	1,000
Gabelli Equity Income Fund Class AAA	GABEX	NAS CM	Open End	US Equity Large Cap Blend (Equity-Income)	C+	C	B	Up	Y	1,000
Gabelli Equity Income Fund Class C	GCCEX	NAS CM	Open End	US Equity Large Cap Blend (Equity-Income)	C+	C	B	Up	Y	1,000
Gabelli Equity Income Fund Class Institutional	GCIEX	NAS CM	Open End	US Equity Large Cap Blend (Equity-Income)	C+	C	B	Up	Y	500,000
Gabelli Equity Trust	GAB	NYSE	Closed End	US Equity Large Cap Blend (Growth)	C	C	C+		Y	

★Expanded analysis of this fund is included in Section II.

	TOTAL RETURNS					PERFORMANCE				ASSETS		ASSET ALLOCATION & TURNOVER					BULL & BEAR		FEES		
Min Additional Investment	3-Month Total Return	6-Month Total Return	1-Year Total Return	3-Year Total Return	5-Year Total Return	Dividend Yield (TTM)	Expense Ratio	3-Yr Std Deviation	3-Year Beta	NAV	Total Assets (MIL)	%Cash	%Stocks	%Bonds	%Other	Turnover Ratio	Last Bull Market Total Return	Last Bear Market Total Return	Front End Fee (%)	Back End Fee (%)	Inception Date
100	11.21	16.00					1.7			11.6	2.3	83	0	0	17				5.75		Dec-18
0	11.20	16.10					1.45			11.61	2.3	83	0	0	17						Dec-18
100	1.18	2.10					1.65			10.21	2.1	99	0	0	1				5.75		Dec-18
0	1.38	2.30					1.4			10.23	2.1	99	0	0	1						Dec-18
100	-0.19	2.50					1.7			10.25	2.1	100	0	0	0				5.75		Dec-18
0	-0.09	2.60					1.45			10.26	2.1	100	0	0	0						Dec-18
100	3.36	8.29	4.84			0	2.11			10.45	121.6	47	25	23	4	317			5.75		May-17
0	3.44	8.35	5.03			0	1.86			10.5	121.6	47	25	23	4	317					May-17
100	-1.12	5.60					1.76			10.56	3.2	77	0	20	4				5.75		Dec-18
0	-0.93	5.80					1.51			10.58	3.2	77	0	20	4						Dec-18
100	0.00	4.41	1.08	6.79		8.54	1.16	4.8	35.3	8.99	186.0	27	36	34	1	11					Jul-15
1,000	0.11	4.52	1.21	6.92		8.54	1.06	4.75	33.89	9	186.0	27	36	34	1	11					Jul-15
50	-4.90	15.40					1.75			23.58	3.1	2	98	0	0						Dec-18
50	5.33	19.94	6.91			0.5	0.9			21.11	15.9	8	92	0	0	0					Dec-17
50	5.30	19.87	6.66			0.36	1.15			21.05	15.9	8	92	0	0	0					Dec-17
50	5.43	20.05	7.06			0.54	0.8			21.13	15.9	8	92	0	0	0					Dec-17
50	4.52	18.15	-1.64	45.63	57.15		1.25	16.68	0.95	24.93	1,802	9	91	0	0	35	30.14		5.75		Dec-18
50	4.36	17.78	-2.36	42.42	51.41		1.75	16.66	0.95	24.84	1,802	9	91	0	0	35	29.58			1.00	Dec-18
50	-0.89	12.32	-8.18				1.3			22.41	15.9	4	96	0	0	71			5.75		Dec-18
50	-1.03	12.07	-8.77				1.8			22.35	15.9	4	96	0	0	71				1.00	Dec-18
50	0.40	14.32	-6.25			0	0.99			22.5	15.9	4	96	0	0	71					Dec-17
50	0.31	14.16	-6.50			0	1.25			22.41	15.9	4	96	0	0	71					Dec-17
50	0.40	14.31	-6.20			0	0.9			22.52	15.9	4	96	0	0	71					Dec-17
50	3.01	17.39					0.95			23.89	2.5	4	96	0	0						Dec-18
50	2.80	21.90					0.99			24.88	3.9	2	98	0	0						Dec-18
50	2.80	21.89					0.9			24.89	3.9	2	98	0	0						Dec-18
100	3.03	17.50	2.99	29.07	29.46	0	2.08	12.62	1.01	58.71	37.5	0	96	4	0	144	21.18	-22.16			Jul-02
100	2.94	13.08	5.31	27.81	30.98	0.39	1.99	8.28	0.68	39.54	54.4	5	60	33	0	92	13.22	-14.31			Jul-02
100	4.23	19.66	9.03			0	2.13			27.54	20.8	4	95	0	0	161					Mar-17
100	0.39	0.22	1.87	25.46	29.79	0	1.63	5.03	0.07	25.17	49.9	40	43	14	0	524	7.36	-3.7			Feb-08
100	4.11	19.86	8.13	41.31	44.91	0	1.89	12.68	1.03	60.98	216.2	3	96	0	0	83	20.73	-20.95			Nov-01
	0.78	2.79	2.30	7.34	10.68	2.26	0.57	1.75	5.07	10.3	1,007	36	44	21	0	231	5.06	-3.14			May-93
	0.69	2.62	2.06	6.56	9.35	1.93	0.82	1.75	4.49	10.18	1,007	36	44	21	0	231	4.98	-3.36			May-07
	3.75	16.51	5.64	37.09	34.36	0.27	1.35	11.81	0.94	56.44	2,316	0	100	0	0	2	21.92	-18.99	5.75		Dec-03
	3.74	16.48	5.64	37.09	34.36	0.28	1.35	11.81	0.93	57.08	2,316	0	100	0	0	2	21.9	-18.98			Mar-86
	3.56	16.08	4.86	34.05	29.41	0	2.1	11.8	0.93	51.66	2,316	0	100	0	0	2	21.4	-19.26		1.00	Dec-03
	3.82	16.63	5.90	38.11	36.04	0.54	1.1	11.81	0.93	56.99	2,316	0	100	0	0	2	22.11	-18.92			Jan-08
	3.01	16.72	5.60	37.56	26.05	8.86	1.8	9.94	0.77	5.42	101.7	1	24	6	0	42	15.12	-13.56			Mar-95
	1.64	17.83	2.17	29.64	25.89	5.63	1.38	14.96	1.19	23.45	1,933	2	98	0	0	0	23.87	-20.51			Nov-03
	5.36	18.89	6.21	32.45	22.44	0.01	2	12.34	0.98	16.11	23.2	2	98	0	0	25	23.76	-19.33	5.75		Dec-03
	5.34	18.83	6.19	32.42	22.39	0.02	2	12.33	0.98	16.15	23.2	2	98	0	0	25	23.85	-19.39			Aug-99
	5.16	18.42	5.36	29.50	17.91	0	2.75	12.33	0.98	14.46	23.2	2	98	0	0	25	23.35	-19.6		1.00	Dec-03
	5.63	19.50	7.29	36.23	26.57	1.04	1	12.37	0.98	16.3	23.2	2	98	0	0	25	24.05	-19.3			Jun-04
	1.27	6.24	2.76	15.11	16.87	0.25	1.7	5.91	0.41	14.3	145.2	30	67	3	0	159	7.24	-6.66	5.75		Feb-01
	1.32	6.35	2.99	15.83	18.21	0.5	1.5	5.94	0.41	14.55	145.2	30	67	3	0	159	7.41	-6.47			Feb-10
	1.16	5.95	2.26	13.29	13.75	0	2.24	5.94	0.41	12.98	145.2	30	67	3	0	159	6.9	-6.81		1.00	Feb-01
	1.38	6.52	3.27	16.75	19.64	0.74	1.24	5.93	0.41	15.35	145.2	30	67	3	0	159	7.54	-6.44			Feb-01
	2.10	15.68	3.60	25.19	24.66	3.22	1.41	11.76	0.93	17.96	864.1	0	100	0	0	0	20.6	-16.28	5.75		Dec-03
	2.08	15.64	3.58	25.17	24.70	3.21	1.41	11.74	0.93	18.08	864.1	0	100	0	0	0	20.66	-16.34			Jan-92
	1.82	15.17	2.78	22.33	20.03	3.94	2.14	11.74	0.93	13.94	864.1	0	100	0	0	0	20.14	-16.59		1.00	Dec-03
	2.07	15.75	3.80	26.06	26.19	3.06	1.14	11.76	0.93	19.14	864.1	0	100	0	0	0	20.9	-16.28			Jan-08
	1.88	18.58	3.91	42.53	34.80	10.83	0	14.58	1.15	5.91	1,497	1	99	0	0	17	29.69	-25.03			Aug-86

	MARKET			FUND TYPE, CATEGORY & OBJECTIVE	RATINGS					MINIMUMS
Fund Name	Ticker Symbol	Traded On	Fund Type	Category and (Prospectus Objective)	Overall Rating	Reward Rating	Risk Rating	Recent Up/ Downgrade	Open to New Investors	Min Initial Investment
Gabelli ESG Fund Class A	SRIAX	NAS CM	Open End	US Equity Large Cap Blend (Growth)	C+	C	B-	Up	Y	1,000
Gabelli ESG Fund Class AAA	SRIGX	NAS CM	Open End	US Equity Large Cap Blend (Growth)	C+	C	B-	Up	Y	1,000
Gabelli ESG Fund Class C	SRICX	NAS CM	Open End	US Equity Large Cap Blend (Growth)	C	C	C+		Y	1,000
Gabelli ESG Fund Class I	SRIDX	NAS CM	Open End	US Equity Large Cap Blend (Growth)	C+	C	B-	Up	Y	100,000
Gabelli Focus Five Fund Class A	GWSAX	NAS CM	Open End	US Equity Mid Cap (Growth)	D	D	C-	Down	Y	1,000
Gabelli Focus Five Fund Class AAA	GWSVX	NAS CM	Open End	US Equity Mid Cap (Growth)	D	D	C-	Down	Y	1,000
Gabelli Focus Five Fund Class C	GWSCX	NAS CM	Open End	US Equity Mid Cap (Growth)	D	D	C-	Down	Y	1,000
Gabelli Focus Five Fund Class Institutional	GWSIX	NAS CM	Open End	US Equity Mid Cap (Growth)	D+	D	C-	Down	Y	500,000
Gabelli Global Content & Connectivity Fund Class A	GTCAX	NAS CM	Open End	Communications Sector Equity (Comm)	C	C	C+		Y	1,000
Gabelli Global Content & Connectivity Fund Class AAA	GABTX	NAS CM	Open End	Communications Sector Equity (Comm)	C	C	C+		Y	1,000
Gabelli Global Content & Connectivity Fund Class C	GTCCX	NAS CM	Open End	Communications Sector Equity (Comm)	C	C	C		Y	1,000
Gabelli Global Content & Connectivity Fund Class I	GTTIX	NAS CM	Open End	Communications Sector Equity (Comm)	C	C	B-		Y	500,000
Gabelli Global Deal Fund	GDL	NYSE	Closed End	US Equity Mid Cap (Income)	C	C	C-		Y	
Gabelli Global Financial Services Fund Class A	GGFSX	NAS CM	Open End	Financials Sector Equity (Growth)	U	U	U		Y	1,000
Gabelli Global Financial Services Fund Class AAA	GAFSX	NAS CM	Open End	Financials Sector Equity (Growth)	U	U	U		Y	1,000
Gabelli Global Financial Services Fund Class C	GCFSX	NAS CM	Open End	Financials Sector Equity (Growth)	U	U	U		Y	1,000
Gabelli Global Financial Services Fund Class I	GFSIX	NAS CM	Open End	Financials Sector Equity (Growth)	U	U	U		Y	500,000
Gabelli Global Mini MitesTM Fund Class A	GMNAX	NAS CM	Open End	Global Equity Mid/Small Cap (Growth)	U	U	U		Y	10,000
Gabelli Global Mini MitesTM Fund Class AAA	GAMNX	NAS CM	Open End	Global Equity Mid/Small Cap (Growth)	U	U	U		Y	10,000
Gabelli Global Mini MitesTM Fund Class C	GMNCX	NAS CM	Open End	Global Equity Mid/Small Cap (Growth)	U	U	U		Y	10,000
Gabelli Global Mini MitesTM Fund Class I	GGMMX	NAS CM	Open End	Global Equity Mid/Small Cap (Growth)	U	U	U		Y	100,000
Gabelli Global Rising Income and Dividend Fund Class A	GAGAX	NAS CM	Open End	Moderate Alloc (Growth & Income)	C	C-	C+		Y	1,000
Gabelli Global Rising Income and Dividend Fund Class C	GACCX	NAS CM	Open End	Moderate Alloc (Growth & Income)	C	C-	C		Y	1,000
Gabelli Global Rising Income and Dividend Fund Class I	GAGIX	NAS CM	Open End	Moderate Alloc (Growth & Income)	C	C	B-		Y	500,000
Gabelli Global Utility & Income Trust	GLU	AMEX	Closed End	Utilities Sector Equity (Utility)	C	C	C-	Up	Y	
Gabelli Go Anywhere Trust	GGO	AMEX	Closed End	Moderate Alloc (Equity-Income)	D	D	D		Y	
Gabelli Gold Fund Class A	GLDAX	NAS CM	Open End	Precious Metals Sector Equity (Precious Metals)	D	D	C-	Down	Y	1,000
Gabelli Gold Fund Class AAA	GOLDX	NAS CM	Open End	Precious Metals Sector Equity (Precious Metals)	D	D	C-	Down	Y	1,000
Gabelli Gold Fund Class C	GLDCX	NAS CM	Open End	Precious Metals Sector Equity (Precious Metals)	D	D	D+	Down	Y	1,000
Gabelli Gold Fund Class I	GLDIX	NAS CM	Open End	Precious Metals Sector Equity (Precious Metals)	D	D	C-	Down	Y	500,000
Gabelli Healthcare & WellnessRx Trust	GRX	NYSE	Closed End	Healthcare Sector Equity (Health)	C	C	C-		Y	
Gabelli International Small Cap Fund Class A	GOCAX	NAS CM	Open End	Global Equity Large Cap (World Stock)	C-	D+	C		Y	1,000
Gabelli International Small Cap Fund Class AAA	GABOX	NAS CM	Open End	Global Equity Large Cap (World Stock)	C-	D+	C		Y	1,000
Gabelli International Small Cap Fund Class C	GGLCX	NAS CM	Open End	Global Equity Large Cap (World Stock)	C-	D+	C	Up	Y	1,000
Gabelli International Small Cap Fund Class Institutional	GLOIX	NAS CM	Open End	Global Equity Large Cap (World Stock)	C-	D+	C		Y	500,000
Gabelli Media Mogul Fund	MOGLX	NAS CM	Open End	Communications Sector Equity ()	U	U	U		Y	5,000
Gabelli Pet Parents'™ Fund	PETZX	NAS CM	Open End	Equity Miscellaneous ()	U	U	U		Y	5,000
Gabelli Small Cap Growth Fund Class A	GCASX	NAS CM	Open End	US Equity Small Cap (Small Company)	C	C	B-		Y	1,000
Gabelli Small Cap Growth Fund Class AAA	GABSX	NAS CM	Open End	US Equity Small Cap (Small Company)	C	C	B-		Y	1,000
Gabelli Small Cap Growth Fund Class C	GCCSX	NAS CM	Open End	US Equity Small Cap (Small Company)	C	C-	C+		Y	1,000
Gabelli Small Cap Growth Fund Class I	GACIX	NAS CM	Open End	US Equity Small Cap (Small Company)	C	C	B-		Y	500,000
Gabelli Utilities Fund Class A	GAUAX	NAS CM	Open End	Utilities Sector Equity (Utility)	B-	C+	B	Down	Y	1,000
Gabelli Utilities Fund Class AAA	GABUX	NAS CM	Open End	Utilities Sector Equity (Utility)	B-	C+	B	Down	Y	1,000
Gabelli Utilities Fund Class C	GAUCX	NAS CM	Open End	Utilities Sector Equity (Utility)	C+	C+	B	Down	Y	1,000
Gabelli Utilities Fund Class Institutional	GAUIX	NAS CM	Open End	Utilities Sector Equity (Utility)	B-	C+	B	Down	Y	500,000
Gabelli Utility Trust	GUT	NYSE	Closed End	Utilities Sector Equity (Utility)	C+	C	C+		Y	
Gabelli Value 25 Fund Class A	GABVX	NAS CM	Open End	US Equity Mid Cap (Growth)	B-	C	B	Up	Y	1,000
Gabelli Value 25 Fund Class AAA	GVCAX	NAS CM	Open End	US Equity Mid Cap (Growth)	B-	C	B	Up	Y	1,000
Gabelli Value 25 Fund Class C	GVCCX	NAS CM	Open End	US Equity Mid Cap (Growth)	C+	C	B		Y	1,000
Gabelli Value 25 Fund Class I	GVCIX	NAS CM	Open End	US Equity Mid Cap (Growth)	B-	C	B	Up	Y	250,000
GAMCO Global Gold, Natural Resources & Income Trust	GGN	AMEX	Closed End	Natl Resources Sec Equity (Natl Res)	C-	D+	C+	Down	Y	
GAMCO Global Growth Fund Class A	GGGAX	NAS CM	Open End	Global Equity Large Cap (World Stock)	B-	C+	B		Y	1,000

★ Expanded analysis of this fund is included in Section II.

Min Additional Investment	TOTAL RETURNS 3-Month Total Return	6-Month Total Return	1-Year Total Return	3-Year Total Return	5-Year Total Return	PERFORMANCE Dividend Yield (TTM)	Expense Ratio	3-Yr Std Deviation	3-Year Beta	ASSETS NAV	Total Assets (MIL)	ASSET ALLOCATION & TURNOVER %Cash	%Stocks	%Bonds	%Other	Turnover Ratio	BULL & BEAR Last Bull Market Total Return	Last Bear Market Total Return	FEES Front End Fee (%)	Back End Fee (%)	Inception Date
	4.06	17.47	3.90	17.07	23.45	0	1.27	12.32	1.01	14.59	41.3	11	89	0	0	29	12.75	-28.47	5.75		Jun-07
	4.06	17.45	3.82	17.05	23.42	0	1.27	12.33	1.01	14.6	41.3	11	89	0	0	29	12.84	-28.52			Jun-07
	3.90	17.07	3.10	14.48	18.87	0	2.02	12.34	1.01	13.3	41.3	11	89	0	0	29	12.35	-28.78		1.00	Jun-07
	4.10	17.59	4.08	17.91	24.92	0	1.02	12.32	1.01	14.97	41.3	11	89	0	0	29	13	-28.43			Jun-07
	2.91	16.42	-8.89	2.07	-12.37	0	1.53	18.31	0.94	12.69	53.2	5	94	1	0	105	28.83	-27.79	5.75		Dec-02
	2.95	16.40	-8.91	2.09	-12.42	0	1.53	18.27	0.94	12.56	53.2	5	94	1	0	105	28.71	-27.84			Dec-02
	2.75	15.87	-9.61	-0.19	-15.63	0	2.28	18.28	0.94	10.8	53.2	5	94	1	0	105	28.21	-28.05		1.00	Dec-02
	3.01	16.53	-8.65	2.83	-11.31	0	1.28	18.31	0.94	12.97	53.2	5	94	1	0	105	28.91	-27.77			Jan-08
	3.42	11.57	2.93	9.47	6.41	0.5	1.73	11.31	0.8	20.25	80.0	1	99	0	0	19	9.44	-18.57	5.75		Mar-00
	3.40	11.50	2.91	9.61	6.50	0.56	1.73	11.28	0.8	20.07	80.0	1	99	0	0	19	9.46	-18.6			Nov-93
	3.20	11.11	2.14	7.18	2.59	0	2.48	11.26	0.8	19.3	80.0	1	99	0	0	19	9.02	-18.84		1.00	Jun-00
	3.61	11.92	3.67	11.81	9.18	1.34	1.01	11.27	0.8	20.09	80.0	1	99	0	0	19	9.61	-18.51			Jan-08
	-0.08	3.28	3.07	7.64	12.06	3.6	0	3.4		11.12	202.9	13	73	14	0	390	5.36	-5.81			Jan-07
	2.31	10.21					1.25			9.28	13.0								5.75		Oct-18
	2.31	10.22					1.25			9.27	13.0										Oct-18
	2.10	9.73					2			9.24	13.0									1.00	Oct-18
	2.31	10.34					1			9.28	13.0										Oct-18
	-2.83	6.67					1.25			9.27	1.5	2	98	0	0	6			5.75		Oct-18
	-4.07	5.63					1.25			9.28	1.5	2	98	0	0	6					Oct-18
	-2.94	6.45					2			9.24	1.5	2	98	0	0	6				1.00	Oct-18
	-2.72	6.78					1			9.28	1.5	2	98	0	0	6					Oct-18
	2.80	10.61	-1.90	18.85	19.40	0.83	1.67	10.67	1.52	25.32	51.2	1	99	0	0	20	2.97	-11.32	5.75		May-01
	2.61	10.19	-2.63	16.18	15.05	0.16	2.42	10.66	1.52	21.19	51.2	1	99	0	0	20	2.6	-11.58		1.00	Nov-01
	2.99	11.03	-1.19	21.06	22.27	1.57	1	10.66	1.52	25.46	51.2	1	99	0	0	20	3.37	-11.16			Jan-08
	0.76	9.17	2.07	10.04	11.57	5.41	1.37	12.04	0.78	19.88	106.7	11	78	11	0	13	8.72	-9.68			May-04
	-3.92	12.80	-10.27			4.69	8.45			17.06	27.5	11	89	0	0	102					Nov-16
	12.63	23.35	12.48	-13.54	2.89	0.27	1.55	25.41	0.04	14.26	268.4	0	100	0	0	6	-12.15	-12.23	5.75		Dec-02
	12.65	23.39	12.50	-13.49	2.85	0.28	1.55	25.41	0.04	14.24	268.4	0	100	0	0	6	-12.39	-12.26			Jul-94
	12.40	22.88	11.53	-15.45	-0.89	0	2.3	25.39	0.04	13.05	268.4	0	100	0	0	6	-12.73	-12.53		1.00	Dec-02
	12.73	23.46	12.72	-12.84	4.18	0.5	1.3	25.44	0.05	14.52	268.4	0	100	0	0	6	-12.26	-12.14			Jan-08
	-0.89	13.32	5.82	14.02	35.04	4.46	1.99	14.96	0.97	12.1	226.0	3	95	1	0	32	24.65	-11.96			Jun-07
	0.82	11.97	-9.30	11.41	4.97	0	2	12.24	0.96	12.25	7.6	2	97	0	0	26	19.58	-22.66	5.75		Mar-00
	1.06	12.47	-8.37	13.40	6.91	1.25	1	12.21	0.96	12.35	7.6	2	97	0	0	26	19.58	-22.63			May-98
	0.63	11.59	-9.96	9.33	1.58	0	2.75	12.23	0.96	11.07	7.6	2	97	0	0	26	19.05	-22.88		1.00	Nov-01
	1.03	12.50	-8.33	14.21	9.55	1.18	1	12.24	0.96	12.69	7.6	2	97	0	0	26	19.74	-22.56			Jan-08
	1.35						0.91			11.22	4.7										Apr-19
	4.96						0.96			9.94	1.7										Apr-19
	1.27	15.77	-2.75	31.76	30.52	0.16	1.36	14.59	0.78	54.1	2,648	0	100	0	0	3	22.6	-20.98	5.75		Dec-03
	1.25	15.76	-2.76	31.75	30.51	0.16	1.36	14.59	0.78	54.12	2,648	0	100	0	0	3	22.56	-20.95			Oct-91
	1.07	15.34	-3.47	28.82	25.71	0	2.11	14.58	0.78	46.9	2,648	0	100	0	0	3	22.07	-21.2		1.00	Dec-03
	1.33	15.92	-2.50	32.74	32.18	0.43	1.11	14.6	0.78	55.47	2,648	0	100	0	0	3	22.76	-20.88			Jan-08
	2.83	14.43	12.19	22.19	30.47	6.3	1.37	9.02	0.68	9.06	2,176	0	99	0	0	1	9.98	-8.66	5.75		Dec-02
	2.77	14.30	12.03	22.05	30.31	6.42	1.37	9.1	0.69	8.89	2,176	0	99	0	0	1	9.89	-8.69			Aug-99
	2.62	14.04	11.33	19.38	25.65	9.68	2.12	9.03	0.68	5.87	2,176	0	99	0	0	1	9.49	-9.01		1.00	Dec-02
	2.83	14.52	12.35	22.99	31.92	6.07	1.12	9.08	0.69	9.4	2,176	0	99	0	0	1	10.13	-8.63			Jan-08
	2.44	15.57	11.74	19.01	34.70	10.98	1.45	11.1	0.88	5.02	269.1	11	81	8	0	26	15.37	-8.1			Jul-99
	4.11	15.90	4.08	26.98	19.90	0.02	1.44	11.63	0.83	14.94	372.6	1	99	0	0	2	20.93	-19.68	5.75		Sep-89
	4.12	15.97	4.16	27.00	19.94	0.01	1.44	11.59	0.83	14.88	372.6	1	99	0	0	2	20.97	-19.65			Apr-10
	3.87	15.48	3.37	24.15	15.50	0	2.19	11.62	0.83	11.26	372.6	1	99	0	0	2	20.39	-19.89		1.00	Mar-00
	4.18	16.18	4.58	28.49	21.92	0.47	1	11.61	0.83	14.93	372.6	1	99	0	0	2	21.2	-19.58			Jan-08
	2.12	14.08	-0.85	1.13	-22.40	11.37	1.31	10.79	0.41	4.45	606.2	13	84	2	0	146	8.91	-22.1			Mar-05
	5.45	23.13	10.19	58.83	52.53	0	1.25	12.36	1	36.51	105.4	0	100	0	0	58	29.71	-22.46	5.75		Mar-00

	MARKET		FUND TYPE, CATEGORY & OBJECTIVE		RATINGS				MINIMUMS	
Fund Name	Ticker Symbol	Traded On	Fund Type	Category and (Prospectus Objective)	Overall Rating	Reward Rating	Risk Rating	Recent Up/ Downgrade	Open to New Investors	Min Initial Investment
GAMCO Global Growth Fund Class AAA	GICPX	NAS CM	Open End	Global Equity Large Cap (World Stock)	B-	C+	B		Y	1,000
GAMCO Global Growth Fund Class C	GGGCX	NAS CM	Open End	Global Equity Large Cap (World Stock)	C+	C	B		Y	1,000
GAMCO Global Growth Fund Class Institutional	GGGIX	NAS CM	Open End	Global Equity Large Cap (World Stock)	B-	C+	B		Y	500,000
GAMCO Growth Fund Class A	GGCAX	NAS CM	Open End	US Equity Large Cap Growth (Growth)	B-	B-	B	Down	Y	1,000
GAMCO Growth Fund Class AAA	GABGX	NAS CM	Open End	US Equity Large Cap Growth (Growth)	B-	B-	B	Down	Y	1,000
GAMCO Growth Fund Class C	GGCCX	NAS CM	Open End	US Equity Large Cap Growth (Growth)	B-	C+	B	Down	Y	1,000
GAMCO Growth Fund Class I	GGCIX	NAS CM	Open End	US Equity Large Cap Growth (Growth)	B-	B-	B	Down	Y	500,000
GAMCO International Growth Fund Class A	GAIGX	NAS CM	Open End	Global Equity Large Cap (Foreign Stock)	C+	C	B	Up	Y	1,000
GAMCO International Growth Fund Class AAA	GIGRX	NAS CM	Open End	Global Equity Large Cap (Foreign Stock)	C+	C	B	Up	Y	1,000
GAMCO International Growth Fund Class C	GCIGX	NAS CM	Open End	Global Equity Large Cap (Foreign Stock)	C	C	B-		Y	1,000
GAMCO International Growth Fund Class I	GIIGX	NAS CM	Open End	Global Equity Large Cap (Foreign Stock)	C+	C	B	Up	Y	500,000
GAMCO Natural Resources Gold & Income Trust	GNT	NYSE	Closed End	Natl Resources Sec Equity (Natl Res)	C-	C-	C-		Y	
Gateway Equity Call Premium Fund Class A	GCPAX	NAS CM	Open End	Long/Short Equity (Growth & Income)	C+	C	B		Y	2,500
Gateway Equity Call Premium Fund Class C	GCPCX	NAS CM	Open End	Long/Short Equity (Growth & Income)	C+	C	B	Up	Y	2,500
Gateway Equity Call Premium Fund Class N	GCPNX	NAS CM	Open End	Long/Short Equity (Growth & Income)	C+	C	B		Y	1,000,000
Gateway Equity Call Premium Fund Class Y	GCPYX	NAS CM	Open End	Long/Short Equity (Growth & Income)	C+	C	B		Y	100,000
Gateway Fund Class A Shares	GATEX	NAS CM	Open End	Long/Short Equity (Growth & Income)	C+	C	B		Y	2,500
Gateway Fund Class C Shares	GTECX	NAS CM	Open End	Long/Short Equity (Growth & Income)	C	C	C+		Y	2,500
Gateway Fund Class N	GTENX	NAS CM	Open End	Long/Short Equity (Growth & Income)	C+	C	B	Up	Y	1,000,000
Gateway Fund Class Y Shares	GTEYX	NAS CM	Open End	Long/Short Equity (Growth & Income)	C+	C	B	Up	Y	100,000
Gator Focus Fund Institutional Shares	GFFIX	NAS CM	Open End	US Equity Small Cap (Small Company)	C	C-	C+		Y	5,000
GE RSP U.S. Equity Fund	GESSX	NAS CM	Open End	US Equity Large Cap Blend (Growth)	B-	C	B	Down	Y	0
General American Investors Co. Inc.	GAM	NYSE	Closed End	US Equity Large Cap Blend (Growth)	C	C	C-		Y	
George Putnam Balanced Fund Class A	PGEOX	NAS CM	Open End	Moderate Alloc (Balanced)	B	C+	A-		Y	0
George Putnam Balanced Fund Class B	PGEBX	NAS CM	Open End	Moderate Alloc (Balanced)	B	C+	A-		Y	0
George Putnam Balanced Fund Class C	PGPCX	NAS CM	Open End	Moderate Alloc (Balanced)	B	C+	A-		Y	0
George Putnam Balanced Fund Class M	PGEMX	NAS CM	Open End	Moderate Alloc (Balanced)	B	C+	A-		Y	0
George Putnam Balanced Fund Class R	PGPRX	NAS CM	Open End	Moderate Alloc (Balanced)	B	C+	A-		Y	0
George Putnam Balanced Fund Class R5	PGELX	NAS CM	Open End	Moderate Alloc (Balanced)	B	C+	A-		Y	0
George Putnam Balanced Fund Class R6	PGEJX	NAS CM	Open End	Moderate Alloc (Balanced)	B	C+	A-		Y	0
George Putnam Balanced Fund Class Y	PGEYX	NAS CM	Open End	Moderate Alloc (Balanced)	B	C+	A-		Y	0
Gerstein Fisher Multi-Factor Global Real Estate Sec Fund	GFMRX	NAS CM	Open End	Real Estate Sector Equity (Equity-Income)	B-	C	B		Y	250
Gerstein Fisher Multi-Factor Growth Equity Fund	GFMGX	NAS CM	Open End	US Equity Large Cap Growth (Growth)	C+	C	B-	Down	Y	250
Gerstein Fisher Multi-Factor Intl Growth Equity Fund	GFIGX	NAS CM	Open End	Global Equity Large Cap (Foreign Stock)	C	C	C+		Y	250
Glenmede Alternative Risk Premia Portfolio	GLARX	NAS CM	Open End	Multialternative (Income)	U	U	U		Y	0
Glenmede Equity Income Portfolio	GEQIX	NAS CM	Open End	US Equity Large Cap Value (Growth & Income)	C+	C	B	Up	Y	0
Glenmede Global Secured Options Portfolio	NOVIX	NAS CM	Open End	Long/Short Equity (Growth)	C+	C	B	Up	Y	0
Glenmede Large Cap Value Portfolio	GTMEX	NAS CM	Open End	US Equity Large Cap Value (Growth)	C+	C	B		Y	0
Glenmede Quantitative International Equity Portfolio	GTCIX	NAS CM	Open End	Global Equity Large Cap (Foreign Stock)	C	C-	C+		Y	0
Glenmede Quantitative U.S. Large Cap Core Equity Portfolio	GTLOX	NAS CM	Open End	US Equity Large Cap Blend (Growth)	B-	C	B	Up	Y	0
Glenmede Quantitative U.S. Large Cap Core Eq Inst Shares	GTLIX	NAS CM	Open End	US Equity Large Cap Blend (Growth)	B-	C	B	Up	Y	10,000,000
Glenmede Quantitative U.S. Large Cap Growth Eq Port	GTLLX	NAS CM	Open End	US Equity Large Cap Growth (Growth)	B-	C+	B	Down	Y	0
Glenmede Quantitative U.S. Large Cap Growth Eq Inst Shares	GTILX	NAS CM	Open End	US Equity Large Cap Growth (Growth)	B-	C+	B	Down	Y	10,000,000
Glenmede Quantitative U.S. Large Cap Value Eq Port	GQLVX	NAS CM	Open End	US Equity Large Cap Value (Growth)	D+	D	C-	Up	Y	0
Glenmede Quantitative U.S. Long/Short Equity Portfolio	GTAPX	NAS CM	Open End	Long/Short Equity (Growth & Income)	D+	D	C	Down	Y	0
Glenmede Quantitative U.S. Long/Short Eq Port Inst Shares	GTLSX	NAS CM	Open End	Long/Short Equity (Growth & Income)	D+	D	C	Down	Y	10,000,000
Glenmede Quantitative U.S. Small Cap Equity Portfolio	GQSCX	NAS CM	Open End	US Equity Small Cap (Small Company)	D	D	C-		Y	0
Glenmede Quantitative U.S. Total Market Equity Portfolio	GTTMX	NAS CM	Open End	US Equity Mid Cap (Growth)	C	C	B-		Y	0
Glenmede Responsible ESG U.S. Equity Portfolio	RESGX	NAS CM	Open End	US Equity Large Cap Blend (Growth)	B-	C	B	Up	Y	0
Glenmede Secured Options Portfolio	GTSOX	NAS CM	Open End	Long/Short Equity (Growth)	C+	C	B	Up	Y	0
Glenmede Secured Options Portfolio Institutional Class	GLSOX	NAS CM	Open End	Long/Short Equity (Growth)	C+	C	B		Y	10,000,000
Glenmede Small Cap Equity Portfolio Class Advisor	GTCSX	NAS CM	Open End	US Equity Small Cap (Small Company)	C	C-	C		Y	0

★ Expanded analysis of this fund is included in Section II.

Min Additional Investment	TOTAL RETURNS					PERFORMANCE				ASSETS		ASSET ALLOCATION & TURNOVER					BULL & BEAR		FEES		
	3-Month Total Return	6-Month Total Return	1-Year Total Return	3-Year Total Return	5-Year Total Return	Dividend Yield (TTM)	Expense Ratio	3-Yr Std Deviation	3-Year Beta	NAV	Total Assets (MIL)	%Cash	%Stocks	%Bonds	%Other	Turnover Ratio	Last Bull Market Total Return	Last Bear Market Total Return	Front End Fee (%)	Back End Fee (%)	Inception Date
	5.48	23.16	10.22	58.83	52.57	0	1.25	12.36	1	36.53	105.4	0	100	0	0	58	29.66	-22.43			Feb-94
	5.26	22.69	9.39	55.28	46.95	0	2	12.36	1	30.6	105.4	0	100	0	0	58	29.13	-22.68		1.00	Mar-00
	5.54	23.33	10.52	61.38	57.09	0	1	12.39	1	37.32	105.4	0	100	0	0	58	29.85	-22.33			Jan-08
	4.26	23.37	11.90	68.57	83.37	0	1.4	13.62	1	66.77	707.3	1	99	0	0	65	29.46	-19.86	5.75		Dec-03
	4.26	23.35	11.91	68.56	83.37	0	1.4	13.61	1	66.75	707.3	1	99	0	0	65	29.44	-19.86			Apr-87
	4.07	22.93	11.07	64.85	76.65	0	2.15	13.61	1	57.73	707.3	1	99	0	0	65	28.94	-20.14		1.00	Dec-03
	4.33	23.52	12.18	69.83	85.70	0	1.15	13.62	1	68.42	707.3	1	99	0	0	65	29.64	-19.8			Jan-08
	4.51	17.37	4.32	29.69	15.49	0	2.38	11.55	0.93	23.37	21.4	0	100	0	0	5	18.65	-20.89	5.75		Jul-01
	4.85	18.04	5.68	31.45	17.07	0.35	1.25	11.52	0.93	23.09	21.4	0	100	0	0	5	18.61	-20.88			Jun-95
	4.31	16.91	3.59	26.85	11.30	0	3.13	11.54	0.93	20.32	21.4	0	100	0	0	5	18.09	-21.13		1.00	Dec-00
	4.93	18.26	5.95	34.64	22.52	1.03	1	11.53	0.93	23.38	21.4	0	100	0	0	5	18.84	-20.79			Jan-08
	2.52	13.83	0.36	5.44	-13.10	8.94	1.18	9.6		6.18	129.1	17	79	4	0	167	9.02	-23.88			Jan-11
50	2.11	10.04	3.20	22.54		0.83	1.2	7.3	0.89	12.3	58.0	2	98	0	0	58			5.75		Sep-14
50	1.91	9.67	2.38	19.77		0.13	1.95	7.29	0.89	12.26	58.0	2	98	0	0	58				1.00	Sep-14
	2.18	10.21	3.38	23.58		1.17	0.9	7.26	0.89	12.29	58.0	2	98	0	0	58					May-17
50	2.26	10.27	3.50	23.55		1.12	0.95	7.31	0.9	12.3	58.0	2	98	0	0	58					Sep-14
50	0.82	6.45	1.37	15.98	20.58	1.12	0.94	5.53	0.43	33.29	8,099	2	98	0	0	10	8.86	-6.02	5.75		Dec-77
50	0.63	6.00	0.62	13.36	16.08	0.35	1.7	5.53	0.43	33.14	8,099	2	98	0	0	10	8.38	-6.3		1.00	Feb-08
	0.89	6.57	1.65	16.65	21.28	1.42	0.65	5.52	0.43	33.27	8,099	2	98	0	0	10	8.86	-6.02			May-17
50	0.88	6.54	1.63	16.80	22.05	1.37	0.7	5.54	0.43	33.27	8,099	2	98	0	0	10	9.03	-5.94			Feb-08
1,000	2.26	22.93	-3.36	39.06	-5.14	0	1.49	18.89	1.28	12.65	3.3	1	95	0	0	54					Apr-13
	5.50	20.33	12.05	53.63	58.75	1.38	0.14	12.36	1	54.98	5,348	2	98	0	0	40	26.59	-18.59			Jan-80
	6.62	23.66	3.69	35.14	30.35	0.68	1.17	13.73	1.05	42.33	1,079	-7	103	0	4	23	28.81	-21.86			Feb-27
	4.67	15.73	10.10	35.29	42.42	1.28	0.99	7.76	0.62	20.37	1,292	2	63	35	0	179	15.42	-10.52	5.75		Nov-37
	4.53	15.30	9.31	32.30	37.19	0.59	1.74	7.79	0.62	20.14	1,292	2	63	35	0	179	14.96	-10.85		5.00	Apr-92
	4.49	15.30	9.25	32.27	37.21	0.65	1.74	7.79	0.62	20.21	1,292	2	63	35	0	179	14.89	-10.84		1.00	Jul-99
	4.57	15.46	9.59	33.30	38.95	0.84	1.49	7.79	0.62	20.07	1,292	2	63	35	0	179	15.06	-10.73	3.50		Dec-94
	4.63	15.60	9.82	34.27	40.68	1.07	1.24	7.8	0.63	20.3	1,292	2	63	35	0	179	15.23	-10.66			Jan-03
	4.80	15.96	10.46	36.54	44.54	1.51	0.73	7.79	0.62	20.56	1,292	2	63	35	0	179	15.42	-10.52			Dec-13
	4.80	15.98	10.51	36.76	45.05	1.61	0.63	7.79	0.62	20.46	1,292	2	63	35	0	179	15.42	-10.52			Dec-13
	4.72	15.86	10.39	36.29	44.24	1.51	0.74	7.81	0.63	20.45	1,292	2	63	35	0	179	15.61	-10.52			Mar-94
	0.39	15.86	8.90	17.05	36.67	2.52	0.9	11.18	0.99	11.73	144.5	0	99	0	1	17					Apr-13
	2.20	15.50	0.66	48.12	57.98	0.55	1	14.26	1.03	21.83	279.5	0	100	0	0	12	27.2	-16.81			Jan-10
	1.29	14.07	-2.55	28.05	14.21	1.01	1.11	11.76	0.97	14.83	194.9	1	98	0	1	26					Jan-12
	0.67	3.48					1.64			10.38	5.6	32	49	18	0						Dec-18
	4.34	17.16	10.46			1.93	0.85			12.06	23.5	2	98	0	0	6					Dec-16
	4.34	13.29	1.65	21.84	5.51	0.03	1.09	9.23	0.73	0.48	1.2	34	3	63	0	224					Sep-12
	3.24	16.17	6.62	37.91	40.03	1.7	0.91	13.51	1.1	9.89	56.1	1	99	0	0	71	25.47	-26.53			Jan-93
	2.47	11.44	-3.74	18.63	0.35	2.61	1	11.63	1.02	13.96	281.0	0	100	0	0	78	15.1	-27.66			Nov-88
	2.34	14.12	3.65	43.51	56.58	1.16	0.85	12.66	1.01	26.6	2,596	0	100	0	0	71	27	-18.36			Feb-04
	2.39	14.21	3.86	44.37	57.68	1.36	0.65	12.68	1.01	26.62	2,596	0	100	0	0	71	27	-18.36			Dec-15
	5.59	22.43	11.32	59.18	80.09	0.52	0.85	12.71	0.92	31.88	3,492	0	100	0	0	63	27.67	-18.42			Feb-04
	5.63	22.57	11.55	60.14	81.39	0.71	0.65	12.69	0.92	31.9	3,492	0	100	0	0	63	27.67	-18.42			Nov-15
	3.69	16.22	1.34			2.05	0.85			10.15	2.0	1	99	0	0	61					Nov-17
	-0.76	1.90	-6.07	7.30	11.00	0.39	2.26	6.56	0.45	12.06	268.8	70	30	0	0	84	9.12	-5.03			Sep-06
	-1.14	1.51	-6.43	6.89	10.58		2.06	6.56	0.44	12.06	268.8	70	30	0	0	84	9.12	-5.03			Feb-19
	0.54	14.05	-5.79			0.73	0.85			10.35	1.4	1	99	0	0	80					Nov-17
	2.21	16.09	1.03	41.87	44.21	0.47	1.96	14.55	1.12	17.85	76.3	0	100	0	0	82	23.72	-21.03			Dec-06
	2.24	14.33	5.39	49.21		0.95	0.85	13.07	1.03	14.28	22.5	0	100	0	0	61					Dec-15
	3.15	12.17	2.34	18.90	28.35	0	0.84	7.95	0.96	12.44	675.7	24	76	0	0	0	20.5	-10.31			Jun-10
	3.13	12.30	2.50	19.46	28.95	0	0.64	8.03	0.97	12.5	675.7	24	76	0	0	0	20.5	-10.31			Nov-16
	1.44	14.78	-8.47	31.58	26.53	0.25	0.9	18.22	1.05	24.34	2,386	2	98	0	0	44	26.67	-23.64			Mar-91

	MARKET		FUND TYPE, CATEGORY & OBJECTIVE		RATINGS				MINIMUMS	
Fund Name	Ticker Symbol	Traded On	Fund Type	Category and (Prospectus Objective)	Overall Rating	Reward Rating	Risk Rating	Recent Up/ Downgrade	Open to New Investors	Min Initial Investment
Glenmede Small Cap Equity Portfolio Institutional Class	GTSCX	NAS CM	Open End	US Equity Small Cap (Small Company)	C	C-	C		Y	10,000,000
Glenmede Strategic Equity Portfolio	GTCEX	NAS CM	Open End	US Equity Large Cap Blend (Growth)	B-	C	B		Y	0
Glenmede Women in Leadership U.S. Equity Portfolio	GWILX	NAS CM	Open End	US Equity Large Cap Blend (Growth)	B-	C	B	Up	Y	0
GMO Alpha Only Fund Class III	GGHEX	NAS CM	Open End	Market Neutral (World Stock)	D	D	C-	Down	Y	5,000,000
GMO Alpha Only Fund Class IV	GAPOX	NAS CM	Open End	Market Neutral (World Stock)	D	D	C-	Down	Y	125,000,000
GMO Benchmark-Free Allocation Fund Class III	GBMFX	NAS CM	Open End	Cautious Alloc (Asset Alloc)	B-	C	B+	Up	Y	5,000,000
GMO Benchmark-Free Allocation Fund Class IV	GBMBX	NAS CM	Open End	Cautious Alloc (Asset Alloc)	B-	C	B+	Up	Y	125,000,000
GMO Benchmark-Free Allocation Fund Class MF			Open End	Cautious Alloc (Asset Alloc)	C	C-	B-		Y	0
GMO Benchmark-Free Allocation Series Fund Class PS	GBFPX	NAS CM	Open End	Cautious Alloc (Growth)	B-	C	B+	Up	Y	10,000,000
GMO Benchmark-Free Allocation Series Fund Class R6	GBMRX	NAS CM	Open End	Cautious Alloc (Growth)	B-	C	B+	Up	Y	10,000,000
GMO Benchmark-Free Fund Class III	GBFFX	NAS CM	Open End	Cautious Alloc (Income)	C+	C	B+	Up	Y	5,000,000
GMO Climate Change Fund Class III	GCCHX	NAS CM	Open End	Global Equity Mid/Small Cap (Growth & Income)	C	C-	C+	Up	Y	5,000,000
GMO Climate Change Series Fund Class PS	GCHPX	NAS CM	Open End	Global Equity Mid/Small Cap (Growth & Income)	U	U	U		Y	10,000,000
GMO Emerging Domestic Opportunities Fund Class II	GEDTX	NAS CM	Open End	Global Emerg Mkts (Div Emerging Mkts)	C	C	C		Y	5,000,000
GMO Emerging Domestic Opportunities Fund Class III	GEDSX	NAS CM	Open End	Global Emerg Mkts (Div Emerging Mkts)	C	C	C		Y	50,000,000
GMO Emerging Domestic Opportunities Fund Class V	GEDOX	NAS CM	Open End	Global Emerg Mkts (Div Emerging Mkts)	C	C	C		Y	250,000,000
GMO Emerging Domestic Opportunities Series Fund Class PS	GEDAX	NAS CM	Open End	Global Emerg Mkts (Growth & Income)	U	U	U		Y	10,000,000
GMO Emerging Markets Fund Class II	GMEMX	NAS CM	Open End	Global Emerg Mkts (Div Emerging Mkts)	C	C	B-		Y	5,000,000
GMO Emerging Markets Fund Class III	GMOEX	NAS CM	Open End	Global Emerg Mkts (Div Emerging Mkts)	C	C	B-		Y	50,000,000
GMO Emerging Markets Fund Class IV	GMEFX	NAS CM	Open End	Global Emerg Mkts (Div Emerging Mkts)	C	C	C		Y	250,000,000
GMO Emerging Markets Fund Class V	GEMVX	NAS CM	Open End	Global Emerg Mkts (Div Emerging Mkts)	C	C	C		Y	500,000,000
GMO Emerging Markets Fund Class VI	GEMMX	NAS CM	Open End	Global Emerg Mkts (Div Emerging Mkts)	C	C	B-		Y	300,000,000
GMO Emerging Markets Series Fund Class PS	GECPX	NAS CM	Open End	Global Emerg Mkts (Div Emerging Mkts)	C	C	B-		Y	0
GMO Emerging Markets Series Fund Class R6	GECRX	NAS CM	Open End	Global Emerg Mkts (Div Emerging Mkts)	C	C	B-		Y	10,000,000
GMO Foreign Small Companies Fund Class III	GMFSX	NAS CM	Open End	Global Equity Mid/Small Cap (Foreign Stock)	D+	D+	C-	Down	Y	5,000,000
GMO Foreign Small Companies Fund Class IV	GFSFX	NAS CM	Open End	Global Equity Mid/Small Cap (Foreign Stock)	U	U	U		Y	250,000,000
GMO Global Asset Allocation Fund Class III	GMWAX	NAS CM	Open End	Cautious Alloc (Asset Alloc)	B-	C	A-	Up	Y	5,000,000
GMO Global Asset Allocation Series Fund Class PS	GLAPX	NAS CM	Open End	Cautious Alloc (Multi-Asset Global)	B-	C	A-	Up	Y	10,000,000
GMO Global Asset Allocation Series Fund Class R6	GATRX	NAS CM	Open End	Cautious Alloc (Multi-Asset Global)	B-	C	A-	Up	Y	10,000,000
GMO Global Developed Equity Allocation Fund Class III	GWOAX	NAS CM	Open End	Global Equity Large Cap (Asset Alloc)	C+	C	B	Up	Y	5,000,000
GMO Global Equity Allocation Fund Class III	GMGEX	NAS CM	Open End	Global Equity Large Cap (World Stock)	C+	C	B	Up	Y	5,000,000
GMO Global Equity Allocation Series Fund Class R6	GGASX	NAS CM	Open End	Global Equity Large Cap (World Stock)	C+	C	B	Up	Y	10,000,000
GMO Implementation Fund	GIMFX	NAS CM	Open End	Moderate Alloc (Growth)	B-	C	B+	Up	Y	5,000,000
GMO International Developed Equity Allocation Cls III	GIOTX	NAS CM	Open End	Global Equity Large Cap (Growth & Income)	C	C-	C+		Y	5,000,000
GMO Intl Developed Equity Allocation Series Cls R6	GIDRX	NAS CM	Open End	Global Equity Large Cap (Growth & Income)	C	C-	C+		Y	10,000,000
GMO International Equity Allocation Fund Class III	GIEAX	NAS CM	Open End	Global Equity Large Cap (Foreign Stock)	C	C	C+		Y	5,000,000
GMO International Equity Allocation Series Fund Class R6	GEARX	NAS CM	Open End	Global Equity Large Cap (Foreign Stock)	C	C	C+		Y	10,000,000
GMO International Equity Fund Class II	GMICX	NAS CM	Open End	Global Equity Large Cap (Foreign Stock)	C	C-	C	Up	Y	5,000,000
GMO International Equity Fund Class III	GMOIX	NAS CM	Open End	Global Equity Large Cap (Foreign Stock)	C	C-	C	Up	Y	35,000,000
GMO International Equity Fund Class IV	GMCFX	NAS CM	Open End	Global Equity Large Cap (Foreign Stock)	C	C-	C	Up	Y	125,000,000
GMO Quality Fund Class III	GQETX	NAS CM	Open End	US Equity Large Cap Blend (Growth)	B-	C+	B+	Down	Y	5,000,000
GMO Quality Fund Class IV	GQEFX	NAS CM	Open End	US Equity Large Cap Blend (Growth)	B	C+	B+		Y	125,000,000
GMO Quality Fund Class V	GQLFX	NAS CM	Open End	US Equity Large Cap Blend (Growth)	C+	C	B	Down	Y	500,000,000
GMO Quality Fund Class VI	GQLOX	NAS CM	Open End	US Equity Large Cap Blend (Growth)	B	C+	B+		Y	300,000,000
GMO Quality Series Fund Class PS	GQPSX	NAS CM	Open End	US Equity Large Cap Blend (Growth & Income)	B-	C+	B+	Down	Y	10,000,000
GMO Quality Series Fund Class R6	GQURX	NAS CM	Open End	US Equity Large Cap Blend (Growth & Income)	B-	C+	B+	Down	Y	10,000,000
GMO Resources Fund Class III	GOFIX	NAS CM	Open End	Natl Resources Sec Equity (Natl Res)	C+	C	B		Y	5,000,000
GMO Resources Fund Class IV	GOVIX	NAS CM	Open End	Natl Resources Sec Equity (Natl Res)	C+	C	B		Y	125,000,000
GMO Resources Series Fund Class PS	GREPX	NAS CM	Open End	Natl Resources Sec Equity (Natl Res)	D	D	C		Y	10,000,000
GMO Resources Series Fund Class R6	GREDX	NAS CM	Open End	Natl Resources Sec Equity (Natl Res)	D	D	C		Y	10,000,000
GMO Risk Premium Fund Class III	GMRPX	NAS CM	Open End	Cautious Alloc (Growth)	C+	C	B-		Y	5,000,000
GMO Risk Premium Fund Class VI	GMOKX	NAS CM	Open End	Cautious Alloc (Growth)	C+	C	B-		Y	300,000,000

★Expanded analysis of this fund is included in Section II.

	TOTAL RETURNS					PERFORMANCE				ASSETS		ASSET ALLOCATION & TURNOVER					BULL & BEAR		FEES		
Min Additional Investment	3-Month Total Return	6-Month Total Return	1-Year Total Return	3-Year Total Return	5-Year Total Return	Dividend Yield (TTM)	Expense Ratio	3-Yr Std Deviation	3-Year Beta	NAV	Total Assets (MIL)	%Cash	%Stocks	%Bonds	%Other	Turnover Ratio	Last Bull Market Total Return	Last Bear Market Total Return	Front End Fee (%)	Back End Fee (%)	Inception Date
	1.49	14.91	-8.30	32.38	27.81	0.44	0.7	18.21	1.05	25.78	2,386	2	98	0	0	44	26.83	-23.56			Jan-98
	3.35	19.25	8.56	50.65	67.32	0.84	0.83	12.56	0.98	26.16	255.7	2	98	0	0	6	27.14	-18.32			Jul-89
	3.29	15.64	5.89	44.72		1.01	0.85	12.3	0.97	13.61	20.1	0	100	0	0	81					Dec-15
	-1.64	-6.35	-3.57	-5.06	-8.30	4.15	0.7	5.31	0.87	19.17	82.6	0	77	24	-2	90	-2.6	6.05			Jul-94
	-1.58	-6.29	-3.50	-4.93	-8.06	4.17	0.64	5.3	0.98	19.19	82.6	0	77	24	-2	90	-2.59	6.04			Mar-06
	1.58	7.44	3.06	18.23	9.74	3.34	0.93	5.89	0.78	26.84	10,633	11	50	32	6	18	8.53	-3.99	0.20		Jul-03
	1.62	7.48	3.12	18.38	10.02	3.4	0.88	5.91	0.78	26.84	10,633	11	50	32	6	18	8.53	-3.99	0.20		Dec-12
	1.62	7.52	-0.55	14.19	6.17	0	0.88	6.58	0.74	26.87	10,633	11	50	32	6	18	8.53	-3.99	0.20		Mar-12
	1.46	7.24	2.83	18.00	9.52	3.19	1.03	5.86	0.78	10.36	630.3	6	48	21	25	10	8.53	-3.99			Jan-18
	1.56	7.35	2.94	17.72	9.15	3.2	0.98	5.82	0.78	10.37	630.3	6	48	21	25	10	8.53	-3.99	0.18		Jan-13
	1.98	8.75	3.28	22.16	11.92	3.61	0.37	6.98	0.94	20.01	2,945	6	57	18	18	59	6.56		0.25		Jun-11
	3.93	14.08	0.20			1.13	0.77			22.44	112.8	0	89	4	3						Apr-17
	3.96	14.02					0.87			10.49	9.0	0	89	3	4	1					Nov-18
	2.36	12.28	-0.05	21.81	13.38	0.66	1.18	13.31	0.92	22.48	1,431	0	82	2	14	238	19.53	-17.93	0.40		Mar-11
	2.36	12.34	0.00	22.03	13.78	0.74	1.11	13.3	0.92	22.48	1,431	0	82	2	14	238	19.53	-17.93	0.40		Jun-12
	2.41	12.34	0.08	22.33	14.19	0.77	1.05	13.3	0.92	22.48	1,431	0	82	2	14	238	19.53	-17.93	0.40		Mar-11
	2.27						1.21			10.34	4.5	0	82	2	15	1					Feb-19
	2.77	13.70	6.27	36.68	13.44	2.93	0.94	13.8	0.96	33.36	3,542	0	95	2	3	98	15	-26.5	0.40		Nov-96
	2.79	13.73	6.34	36.79	13.70	2.97	0.89	13.8	0.96	33.46	3,542	0	95	2	3	98	15.02	-26.49	0.40		Dec-93
	8.46	3.89	-8.38	56.49	23.81	3.06	0.86	15.35	1		3,515	0	94	0	4	87	15.12	-26.53	0.40		Jan-98
	8.48	3.82	-8.37	56.65	24.03	3.08	0.81	15.38	1		3,515	0	94	0	4	87	15.21	-26.51	0.40		Aug-03
	2.82	13.77	6.47	37.31	14.46	3.11	0.76	13.82	0.96	33.13	3,542	0	95	2	3	98	15.11	-26.45	0.40		Jun-03
	2.57	13.51	6.13	36.52	13.48		0.99	13.78	0.96	9.94	22.8	0	94	2	4	11	15.02	-26.49			Feb-19
	2.57	13.32	6.03	38.92	17.43	2.89	0.94	13.65	0.95	9.95	22.8	0	94	2	4	11	15.02	-26.49			May-14
	2.77	10.61	-10.20	16.26	-0.38	0.94	1.19	13.21	1.02	10.73	17.6	0	96	2	1	35	14.2	-24.16	0.50		Jan-95
	-3.93	2.41	13.18	19.09	38.26	1.68	0.71	11	0.92		57.4	0	95	1	3	106	14.3	-24.18	0.50		Jun-02
	2.67	10.61	4.95	22.65	14.91	3.42	0.56	6.93		32.63	1,789	5	56	34	5	21	9.19	-7.89	0.15		Oct-96
	2.57	10.39	4.75	22.50	14.76	3.32	0.66	6.85		9.56	191.8	8	55	32	5	4	9.19	-7.89			May-18
	2.68	10.50	4.85	22.16	14.20	3.31	0.61	6.85		9.57	191.8	8	55	32	5	4	9.19	-7.89	0.14		Jul-12
	2.66	15.39	3.16	34.25	18.72	2.63	0.52	11.65	1.01	21.96	458.6	0	97	1	1	6	15.22	-14.19	0.08		Jun-05
	2.65	14.98	3.45	34.19	18.17	2.75	0.61	11.73	1.01	25.48	1,611	0	97	1	1	11	14.76	-15.64	0.18		Nov-96
	2.66	14.77	3.35	33.15	17.05	2.69	0.66	11.64	1	10.8	5.6	0	96	1	2	8	14.76	-15.64	0.19		Sep-12
	1.88	8.00	3.88	20.37	10.59	4.26	0.11	6.48	0.85	13.5	8,451	5	66	26	3	112			0.20		Mar-12
	1.82	13.15	-2.87	22.03	-4.61	3.46	0.62	12.76	1.11	15.05	575.9	0	97	1	1	8	10.37	-20.32	0.08		Jun-06
	1.78	13.05	-2.78	21.85	-4.73	3.35	0.67	12.68	1.1	9.7	12.9	0	96	1	2	6	10.37	-20.32	0.08		Jan-15
	2.05	13.31	-0.40	25.92	0.01	3.36	0.7	12.67	1.08	28.77	914.3	0	97	1	1	8	11.58	-21.86	0.25		Oct-96
	1.95	12.99	-0.51	25.11	-0.48	3.26	0.75	12.52	1.07	9.39	241.1	0	95	1	3	7	11.36	-21.86	0.27		Mar-12
	1.64	12.99	-4.08	19.80	-7.53	3.27	0.73	12.8	1.12	20.43	3,637	0	98	2	0	41	7.37	-21.82			Sep-96
	1.62	12.99	-4.03	20.03	-7.23	3.32	0.66	12.8	1.12	20.69	3,637	0	98	2	0	41	7.42	-21.79			Mar-87
	1.67	13.08	-3.94	20.30	-6.89	3.38	0.6	12.81	1.12	20.66	3,637	0	98	2	0	41	7.4	-21.75			Jan-98
	3.64	18.19	14.09	58.54	79.85	1.41	0.48	11.54	0.89	23.91	6,700	0	99	1	0	18	20.44	-6.85			Feb-04
	3.63	18.21	14.13	58.70	80.27	1.45	0.44	11.54	0.89	23.95	6,700	0	99	1	0	18	20.46	-6.79			Feb-04
	3.50	-1.81	6.77	59.00	78.95	1.57	0.42	10.9	0.91		6,348	1	99	0	0	10	20.54	-6.83			Dec-06
	3.68	18.24	14.19	59.00	80.75	1.49	0.39	11.54	0.89	23.92	6,700	0	99	1	0	18	20.52	-6.78			Dec-06
	3.54	17.70	13.72	57.48	78.89	1.53	0.58	11.45	0.88	11.1	78.6	1	98	1	1	11	20.46	-6.78			Jan-18
	3.64	17.83	13.75	57.93	79.40	1.56	0.53	11.47	0.88	11.1	78.6	1	98	1	1	11	20.47	-6.79			May-18
	1.47	14.09	3.92	65.51	12.87	3.58	0.74	15.37	0.91	20.64	534.2	0	88	1	2	35			0.30		Dec-11
	1.52	14.14	3.97	65.74	13.10	3.57	0.7	15.39	0.91	20.58	534.2	0	88	1	2	35			0.30		Mar-13
	1.49	13.89	3.34			3.42	0.84			9.51	134.8	0	86	1	4	7					Feb-18
	1.49	13.89	3.34				0.79			9.51	134.8	0	86	1	4	7					Jan-19
	2.25	10.59	2.81	27.13	29.76	0.97	0.4	7.71		27.66	393.0	23	0	77	0	16			0.15		Dec-12
	2.31	10.65	2.92	27.46	30.35	1.02	0.31	7.71		27.83	393.0	23	0	77	0	16			0.15		Nov-12

Fund Name	MARKET Ticker Symbol	Traded On	FUND TYPE, CATEGORY & OBJECTIVE Fund Type	Category and (Prospectus Objective)	RATINGS Overall Rating	Reward Rating	Risk Rating	Recent Up/ Downgrade	MINIMUMS Open to New Investors	Min Initial Investment
GMO SGM Major Markets Fund Class III	GSMFX	NAS CM	Open End	Global Macro (Growth & Income)	C	C	B	Down	Y	5,000,000
GMO SGM Major Markets Fund Class IV	GSMJX	NAS CM	Open End	Global Macro (Growth & Income)	C	C	B	Down	Y	125,000,000
GMO SGM Major Markets Fund Class VI	GSMHX	NAS CM	Open End	Global Macro (Growth & Income)	C	C	B	Down	Y	300,000,000
GMO SGM Major Markets Series Fund Class PS	GBPSX	NAS CM	Open End	Global Macro (Growth)	C	C-	B	Down	Y	10,000,000
GMO Special Opportunities Fund Class VI	GSOFX	NAS CM	Open End	Multialternative (Income)	C+	C	B-	Up	Y	300,000,000
GMO Strategic Opportunities Allocation Fund Class III	GBATX	NAS CM	Open End	Moderate Alloc (Growth)	B-	C	B+	Up	Y	5,000,000
GMO Tax-Managed International Equities Fund Class III	GTMIX	NAS CM	Open End	Global Equity Large Cap (Foreign Stock)	C	C-	C	Up	Y	5,000,000
GMO U.S. Equity Fund Class III	GMUEX	NAS CM	Open End	US Equity Large Cap Blend (Growth & Income)	C+	C	B	Up	Y	5,000,000
GMO U.S. Equity Fund Class IV	GMRTX	NAS CM	Open End	US Equity Large Cap Blend (Growth & Income)	C	C	C		Y	250,000,000
GMO U.S. Equity Fund Class V	GMEQX	NAS CM	Open End	US Equity Large Cap Blend (Growth & Income)	C	C	C		Y	500,000,000
GMO U.S. Equity Fund Class VI	GMCQX	NAS CM	Open End	US Equity Large Cap Blend (Growth & Income)	C+	C	B	Up	Y	300,000,000
Goehring & Rozencwajg Resources Fund Institutional Class	GRHIX	NAS CM	Open End	Natl Resources Sec Equity (Natl Res)	D	D	D		Y	100,000
Goehring & Rozencwajg Resources Fund Retail Class	GRHAX	NAS CM	Open End	Natl Resources Sec Equity (Natl Res)	D	D	D		Y	3,000
Goldman Sachs Absolute Return Multi-Asset Fund Class A	GARDX	NAS CM	Open End	Global Macro (Multi-Asset Global)	C	C	B-	Up	Y	1,000
Goldman Sachs Absolute Return Multi-Asset Fund Class C	GAREX	NAS CM	Open End	Global Macro (Multi-Asset Global)	C	D+	C+	Up	Y	1,000
Goldman Sachs Absolute Return Multi-Asset Fund Class P	GARPX	NAS CM	Open End	Global Macro (Multi-Asset Global)	C	C	B		Y	0
Goldman Sachs Absolute Return Multi-Asset Fund Class R	GARRX	NAS CM	Open End	Global Macro (Multi-Asset Global)	C	D+	B-	Up	Y	0
Goldman Sachs Absolute Return Multi-Asset Fund Class R6	GARNX	NAS CM	Open End	Global Macro (Multi-Asset Global)	C	C	B		Y	5,000,000
Goldman Sachs Absolute Return Multi-Asset Inst Cls	GARFX	NAS CM	Open End	Global Macro (Multi-Asset Global)	C	C	B-		Y	1,000,000
Goldman Sachs Absolute Return Multi-Asset Investor Cls	GARMX	NAS CM	Open End	Global Macro (Multi-Asset Global)	C	C	B-		Y	0
Goldman Sachs Absolute Return Tracker Fund Class A	GARTX	NAS CM	Open End	Multialternative (Growth & Income)	B-	C	A-	Up	Y	1,000
Goldman Sachs Absolute Return Tracker Fund Class C	GCRTX	NAS CM	Open End	Multialternative (Growth & Income)	B-	C	B+	Up	Y	1,000
Goldman Sachs Absolute Return Tracker Fund Class P	GSGPX	NAS CM	Open End	Multialternative (Growth & Income)	B-	C	B	Up	Y	0
Goldman Sachs Absolute Return Tracker Fund Class R	GRRTX	NAS CM	Open End	Multialternative (Growth & Income)	B-	C	B+	Up	Y	0
Goldman Sachs Absolute Return Tracker Fund Class R6	GARUX	NAS CM	Open End	Multialternative (Growth & Income)	B-	C	A-	Up	Y	5,000,000
Goldman Sachs Absolute Return Tracker Institutional Cls	GJRTX	NAS CM	Open End	Multialternative (Growth & Income)	B-	C	B	Up	Y	1,000,000
Goldman Sachs Absolute Return Tracker Fund Investor Class	GSRTX	NAS CM	Open End	Multialternative (Growth & Income)	B-	C	A-	Up	Y	0
Goldman Sachs Alternative Premia Class P	GSSPX	NAS CM	Open End	Multialternative (Growth & Income)	C	C-	C+	Down	Y	0
Goldman Sachs Alternative Premia Fund Class A	GDAFX	NAS CM	Open End	Multialternative (Growth & Income)	C	C-	C+	Down	Y	1,000
Goldman Sachs Alternative Premia Fund Class C	GDCFX	NAS CM	Open End	Multialternative (Growth & Income)	C	D+	C		Y	1,000
Goldman Sachs Alternative Premia Fund Class R	GDRFX	NAS CM	Open End	Multialternative (Growth & Income)	C	D+	C+		Y	0
Goldman Sachs Alternative Premia Fund Class R6	GDHUX	NAS CM	Open End	Multialternative (Growth & Income)	C	C-	B-	Down	Y	5,000,000
Goldman Sachs Alternative Premia Fund Institutional Class	GDIFX	NAS CM	Open End	Multialternative (Growth & Income)	C	C-	B-	Down	Y	1,000,000
Goldman Sachs Alternative Premia Fund Investor Class	GDHFX	NAS CM	Open End	Multialternative (Growth & Income)	C	C-	B-	Down	Y	0
Goldman Sachs Asia Equity Fund Class A	GSAGX	NAS CM	Open End	Asia ex-Japan Equity (Pacific Stock)	C	C	C		Y	1,000
Goldman Sachs Asia Equity Fund Class C	GSACX	NAS CM	Open End	Asia ex-Japan Equity (Pacific Stock)	C	C	C		Y	1,000
Goldman Sachs Asia Equity Fund Class P	GMEPX	NAS CM	Open End	Asia ex-Japan Equity (Pacific Stock)	C	C	C+		Y	0
Goldman Sachs Asia Equity Fund Class R6	GSAFX	NAS CM	Open End	Asia ex-Japan Equity (Pacific Stock)	C	C	C+		Y	5,000,000
Goldman Sachs Asia Equity Fund Institutional Class	GSAIX	NAS CM	Open End	Asia ex-Japan Equity (Pacific Stock)	C	C	C+		Y	1,000,000
Goldman Sachs Asia Equity Fund Investor Class	GSAEX	NAS CM	Open End	Asia ex-Japan Equity (Pacific Stock)	C	C	C+		Y	0
Goldman Sachs Balanced Strategy Portfolio Class A	GIPAX	NAS CM	Open End	Moderate Alloc (Asset Alloc)	B-	C	B+	Up	Y	1,000
Goldman Sachs Balanced Strategy Portfolio Class C	GIPCX	NAS CM	Open End	Moderate Alloc (Asset Alloc)	C+	C	B+	Up	Y	1,000
Goldman Sachs Balanced Strategy Portfolio Class P	GAOPX	NAS CM	Open End	Moderate Alloc (Asset Alloc)	B-	C	A-	Up	Y	0
Goldman Sachs Balanced Strategy Portfolio Class R	GIPRX	NAS CM	Open End	Moderate Alloc (Asset Alloc)	B-	C	B+	Up	Y	0
Goldman Sachs Balanced Strategy Portfolio Class R6	GIPUX	NAS CM	Open End	Moderate Alloc (Asset Alloc)	B-	C	A-	Up	Y	5,000,000
Goldman Sachs Balanced Strategy Portfolio Inst Cls	GIPIX	NAS CM	Open End	Moderate Alloc (Asset Alloc)	B-	C	A-	Up	Y	1,000,000
Goldman Sachs Balanced Strategy Portfolio Investor Class	GIPTX	NAS CM	Open End	Moderate Alloc (Asset Alloc)	B-	C	A-	Up	Y	0
Goldman Sachs Balanced Strategy Portfolio Service Class	GIPSX	NAS CM	Open End	Moderate Alloc (Asset Alloc)	B-	C	B+	Up	Y	0
Goldman Sachs Blue Chip Fund Class A	GAGVX	NAS CM	Open End	US Equity Large Cap Growth (Growth)	B-	C+	B+	Down	Y	1,000
Goldman Sachs Blue Chip Fund Class C	GCGVX	NAS CM	Open End	US Equity Large Cap Growth (Growth)	B-	C+	B	Down	Y	1,000
Goldman Sachs Blue Chip Fund Class P	GALPX	NAS CM	Open End	US Equity Large Cap Growth (Growth)	B-	C+	B+	Down	Y	0
Goldman Sachs Blue Chip Fund Class R	GRGVX	NAS CM	Open End	US Equity Large Cap Growth (Growth)	B-	C+	B+	Down	Y	0

★ Expanded analysis of this fund is included in Section II.

	TOTAL RETURNS					PERFORMANCE				ASSETS		ASSET ALLOCATION & TURNOVER					BULL & BEAR		FEES		
Min Additional Investment	3-Month Total Return	6-Month Total Return	1-Year Total Return	3-Year Total Return	5-Year Total Return	Dividend Yield (TTM)	Expense Ratio	3-Yr Std Deviation	3-Year Beta	NAV	Total Assets (MIL)	%Cash	%Stocks	%Bonds	%Other	Turnover Ratio	Last Bull Market Total Return	Last Bear Market Total Return	Front End Fee (%)	Back End Fee (%)	Inception Date
	-0.64	2.81	-0.76	3.90	10.63	0.36	1	4.84	8.45	32.15	1,128	19	0	81	0	49					Oct-11
	-0.62	2.85	-0.67	4.08	10.82	0.39	0.95	4.84	8.76	32.06	1,128	19	0	81	0	49					Oct-16
	-0.61	2.85	-0.65	4.19	11.00	0.41	0.91	4.85	8.38	32.09	1,128	19	0	81	0	49					Dec-15
	-0.67	2.72	-0.85	3.81	10.53		1.1	4.82	8.74	10.25	10.8	19	0	80	1	1					Jan-19
	2.73	19.89	-0.63	50.98		0	1.21	17.24	-0.06	19.16	372.9	5	81	11	3	30			0.50		Jul-14
	2.54	11.70	4.21	25.74	16.37	3.15	0.55	8.62		20.13	913.5	3	72	23	3	35	12.17	-9.79	0.20		May-05
			-3.97	21.69	-7.98	2.33	0.79	12.66	1.1	14.23	46.8	0	97	2	0	63	9.87	-21.34			Jul-98
	3.90	18.60	6.67	39.96	48.47	1.63	0.46	12.7	0.98	13.58	918.5	0	97	2	0	89	21.75	-10.31			Sep-85
	6.42	-2.81	1.27	42.99	52.39	1.81	0.41	11.62	0.98		879.7	0	99	1	0	79	21.75	-10.31			Jan-98
	6.41	-2.80	1.24	43.02	52.18	1.71	0.4	11.61	0.98		879.7	0	99	1	0	79	21.75	-10.31			Aug-16
	3.85	18.67	6.67	40.32	49.13	1.72	0.37	12.71	0.98	13.47	918.5	0	97	2	0	89	21.81	-10.24			Jun-03
	-7.44	5.71	-27.82			1.12	0.92			7.21	34.8	4	96	0	0	15					Dec-16
	-7.48	5.44	-28.08			0.84	1.25			7.17	34.8	4	96	0	0	15					Dec-16
50	1.79	6.50	2.61	4.60		3.05	1.43	3.84	16.29	9.66	4.1	125	13	-62	23	228			5.50		Sep-15
50	1.59	6.09	1.87	2.36		2.37	2.18	3.8	16.39	9.58	4.1	125	13	-62	23	228				1.00	Sep-15
	1.88	6.70	3.08	5.99		3.49	1.03	3.88	16.37	9.71	4.1	125	13	-62	23	228					Apr-18
	1.68	6.39	2.38	3.93		2.84	1.68	3.89	16.58	9.65	4.1	125	13	-62	23	228					Sep-15
	1.89	6.59	3.07	5.87		3.48	1.03	3.8	16.16	9.7	4.1	125	13	-62	23	228					Sep-15
	1.88	6.68	3.14	5.89		3.14	1.04	3.85	16.56	9.74	4.1	125	13	-62	23	228					Sep-15
	1.89	6.71	2.91	5.45		3.33	1.18	3.77	16.48	9.7	4.1	125	13	-62	23	228					Sep-15
50	1.93	7.36	3.57	15.64	14.40	0.69	1.12	4.33	1.03	9.47	2,979	29	30	41	0	137	3.94	-8.3	5.50		May-08
50	1.75	6.88	2.66	13.01	10.13	0.19	1.87	4.32	1.03	8.69	2,979	29	30	41	0	137	3.56	-8.59		1.00	May-08
	1.98	7.48	3.86	17.05	16.73	1.03	0.72	4.35	1.04	9.76	2,979	29	30	41	0	137	4.12	-8.11			Apr-18
	1.87	7.21	3.28	14.84	12.96	0.46	1.37	4.32	1.03	9.21	2,979	29	30	41	0	137	3.85	-8.46			May-08
	2.09	7.60	3.96	16.98	16.69	1.02	0.72	4.33	1.04	9.76	2,979	29	30	41	0	137	4.12	-8.11			Jul-15
	2.08	7.59	3.94	17.03	16.70	1.01	0.73	4.32	1.04	9.77	2,979	29	30	41	0	137	4.12	-8.11			May-08
	2.00	7.44	3.78	16.56	15.87	0.94	0.87	4.36	1.04	9.67	2,979	29	30	41	0	137	4.02	-8.15			May-08
	-2.39	0.86	-3.88	15.03	6.68	0	0.93	5.46	13.18	8.15	77.9	-43	-19	119	43	349	6.84	-9.73			Apr-18
50	-2.45	0.63	-4.31	13.41	4.40	0	1.33	5.49	13.58	7.95	77.9	-43	-19	119	43	349	6.63	-9.79	5.50		Jan-10
50	-2.64	0.27	-5.12	10.96	0.57	0	2.08	5.53	13.12	7.35	77.9	-43	-19	119	43	349	6.16	-10.15		1.00	Jan-10
	-2.50	0.64	-4.51	12.70	3.26	0	1.58	5.52	13.68	7.78	77.9	-43	-19	119	43	349	6.4	-9.91			Jan-10
	-2.28	0.99	-3.89	14.78	6.48	0	0.93	5.43	13.18	8.14	77.9	-43	-19	119	43	349	6.84	-9.73			Jul-15
	-2.39	0.86	-3.88	14.90	6.56	0	0.94	5.46	13.06	8.16	77.9	-43	-19	119	43	349	6.84	-9.73			Jan-10
	-2.29	0.87	-4.02	14.39	5.79	0	1.08	5.5	13.52	8.09	77.9	-43	-19	119	43	349	6.76	-9.67			Jan-10
50	0.35	14.41	-1.07	40.32	33.14	0.15	1.5	15.04	0.99	25.24	73.6	2	98	0	0	39	16.51	-24.58	5.50		Jul-94
50	0.22	13.99	-1.76	37.24	28.33	0	2.25	15.02	0.99	22.64	73.6	2	98	0	0	39	16.02	-24.83		1.00	Aug-97
	0.44	14.64	-0.65	41.02	33.81	0.57	1.14	15.02	0.99	26.85	73.6	2	98	0	0	39	16.51	-24.58			Apr-18
	0.44	14.60	-0.71	41.02	33.81	0.55	1.14	15.02	0.99	26.84	73.6	2	98	0	0	39	16.51	-24.58			Feb-18
	0.44	14.64	-0.69	41.94	35.83	0.29	1.15	15.03	0.99	26.93	73.6	2	98	0	0	39	16.8	-24.46			Feb-96
	0.45	14.59	-0.79	41.40	34.85	0.18	1.25	15.04	0.99	26.77	73.6	2	98	0	0	39	16.51	-24.58			Feb-14
50	2.95	10.54	4.99	17.69	16.59	2.22	1.25	5.85		11.31	517.7	38	63	-22	21	45	9.18	-10.04	5.50		Jan-98
50	2.84	10.10	4.27	15.00	12.28	1.3	2	5.85		11.33	517.7	38	63	-22	21	45	8.54	-10.3		1.00	Jan-98
	3.05	10.75	5.40	18.91	18.74	2.6	0.85	5.87		11.31	517.7	38	63	-22	21	45	9.39	-9.92			Apr-18
	2.90	10.45	4.75	16.74	15.32	1.99	1.5	5.89		11.27	517.7	38	63	-22	21	45	8.87	-10.09			Nov-07
	3.05	10.75	5.41	19.03	18.87	2.6	0.85	5.9		11.31	517.7	38	63	-22	21	45	9.39	-9.92			Jul-15
	3.05	10.74	5.40	18.99	18.83	2.59	0.86	5.85		11.31	517.7	38	63	-22	21	45	9.39	-9.92			Jan-98
	3.03	10.61	5.27	18.55	18.03	2.46	1	5.87		11.26	517.7	38	63	-22	21	45	9.25	-9.92			Nov-07
	2.89	10.46	4.90	17.19	16.74	2.08	1.36	5.84		11.44	517.7	38	63	-22	21	45	9.09	-10.06			Jan-98
50	4.20	19.14	12.45	49.01	49.82	0.58	1.03	11.22	0.9	13.38	11.3	4	96	0	0	71	24.63	-19.85	5.50		Nov-09
50	4.00	18.65	11.64	45.63	44.26	0.28	1.78	11.23	0.9	12.72	11.3	4	96	0	0	71	24.03	-20.08		1.00	Nov-09
	4.32	19.25	12.86	50.47	52.57	0.77	0.66	11.23	0.9	13.5	11.3	4	96	0	0	71	24.99	-19.72			Apr-18
	4.10	18.92	12.11	47.74	47.91	0.39	1.28	11.22	0.9	13.45	11.3	4	96	0	0	71	24.38	-19.87			Nov-09

Fund Name	MARKET Ticker Symbol	Traded On	FUND TYPE, CATEGORY & OBJECTIVE Fund Type	Category and (Prospectus Objective)	RATINGS Overall Rating	Reward Rating	Risk Rating	Recent Up/ Downgrade	Open to New Investors	MINIMUMS Min Initial Investment
Goldman Sachs Blue Chip Fund Class R6	GDEUX	NAS CM	Open End	US Equity Large Cap Growth (Growth)	B-	C+	B+	Down	Y	5,000,000
Goldman Sachs Blue Chip Fund Institutional Class	GINGX	NAS CM	Open End	US Equity Large Cap Growth (Growth)	B-	C+	B+	Down	Y	1,000,000
Goldman Sachs Blue Chip Fund Investor Class	GIRGX	NAS CM	Open End	US Equity Large Cap Growth (Growth)	B-	C+	B+	Down	Y	0
Goldman Sachs Capital Growth Fund Class A	GSCGX	NAS CM	Open End	US Equity Large Cap Growth (Growth)	B-	C+	B		Y	1,000
Goldman Sachs Capital Growth Fund Class C	GSPCX	NAS CM	Open End	US Equity Large Cap Growth (Growth)	B-	C+	B		Y	1,000
Goldman Sachs Capital Growth Fund Class P	GGGPX	NAS CM	Open End	US Equity Large Cap Growth (Growth)	B-	C+	B	Down	Y	0
Goldman Sachs Capital Growth Fund Class R	GSPRX	NAS CM	Open End	US Equity Large Cap Growth (Growth)	B-	C+	B		Y	0
Goldman Sachs Capital Growth Fund Class R6	GSPUX	NAS CM	Open End	US Equity Large Cap Growth (Growth)	B-	C+	B		Y	5,000,000
Goldman Sachs Capital Growth Fund Institutional Class	GSPIX	NAS CM	Open End	US Equity Large Cap Growth (Growth)	B-	C+	B		Y	1,000,000
Goldman Sachs Capital Growth Fund Investor Class	GSPTX	NAS CM	Open End	US Equity Large Cap Growth (Growth)	B-	C+	B		Y	0
Goldman Sachs Capital Growth Fund Service Class	GSPSX	NAS CM	Open End	US Equity Large Cap Growth (Growth)	B-	C+	B		Y	0
Goldman Sachs Commodity Strategy Fund Class A	GSCAX	NAS CM	Open End	Commodities Broad Basket (Growth & Income)	C-	D+	C		Y	1,000
Goldman Sachs Commodity Strategy Fund Class C	GSCCX	NAS CM	Open End	Commodities Broad Basket (Growth & Income)	C-	D+	C	Up	Y	1,000
Goldman Sachs Commodity Strategy Fund Class P	GGRPX	NAS CM	Open End	Commodities Broad Basket (Growth & Income)	C-	D+	C		Y	0
Goldman Sachs Commodity Strategy Fund Class R	GCCRX	NAS CM	Open End	Commodities Broad Basket (Growth & Income)	C-	D+	C		Y	0
Goldman Sachs Commodity Strategy Fund Class R6	GCCUX	NAS CM	Open End	Commodities Broad Basket (Growth & Income)	C-	D+	C		Y	5,000,000
Goldman Sachs Commodity Strategy Fund Institutional Class	GCCIX	NAS CM	Open End	Commodities Broad Basket (Growth & Income)	C-	D+	C		Y	1,000,000
Goldman Sachs Commodity Strategy Fund Investor Class	GCCTX	NAS CM	Open End	Commodities Broad Basket (Growth & Income)	C-	D+	C		Y	0
Goldman Sachs Concentrated Growth Fund Class A	GCGAX	NAS CM	Open End	US Equity Large Cap Growth (Growth)	B-	C+	B	Down	Y	1,000
Goldman Sachs Concentrated Growth Fund Class C	GCGCX	NAS CM	Open End	US Equity Large Cap Growth (Growth)	C+	C+	B	Down	Y	1,000
Goldman Sachs Concentrated Growth Fund Class P	GACPX	NAS CM	Open End	US Equity Large Cap Growth (Growth)	B-	C+	B	Down	Y	0
Goldman Sachs Concentrated Growth Fund Class R	GGCRX	NAS CM	Open End	US Equity Large Cap Growth (Growth)	C+	C+	B	Down	Y	0
Goldman Sachs Concentrated Growth Fund Class R6	GCGUX	NAS CM	Open End	US Equity Large Cap Growth (Growth)	B-	C+	B	Down	Y	5,000,000
Goldman Sachs Concentrated Growth Fund Institutional Class	GCRIX	NAS CM	Open End	US Equity Large Cap Growth (Growth)	B-	C+	B	Down	Y	1,000,000
Goldman Sachs Concentrated Growth Fund Investor Class	GGCTX	NAS CM	Open End	US Equity Large Cap Growth (Growth)	B-	C+	B	Down	Y	0
Goldman Sachs Dynamic Global Equity Fund Class A	GAPAX	NAS CM	Open End	Global Equity Large Cap (Growth)	C+	C	B	Up	Y	1,000
Goldman Sachs Dynamic Global Equity Fund Class C	GAXCX	NAS CM	Open End	Global Equity Large Cap (Growth)	C+	C	B	Up	Y	1,000
Goldman Sachs Dynamic Global Equity Fund Class P	GADPX	NAS CM	Open End	Global Equity Large Cap (Growth)	C+	C	B	Up	Y	0
Goldman Sachs Dynamic Global Equity Fund Class R	GAPRX	NAS CM	Open End	Global Equity Large Cap (Growth)	C+	C	B	Up	Y	0
Goldman Sachs Dynamic Global Equity Fund Class R6	GAPUX	NAS CM	Open End	Global Equity Large Cap (Growth)	C+	C	B	Up	Y	5,000,000
Goldman Sachs Dynamic Global Equity Institutional Cls	GAPIX	NAS CM	Open End	Global Equity Large Cap (Growth)	C+	C	B	Up	Y	1,000,000
Goldman Sachs Dynamic Global Equity Fund Investor Class	GAPTX	NAS CM	Open End	Global Equity Large Cap (Growth)	C+	C	B	Up	Y	0
Goldman Sachs Dynamic Global Equity Fund Service Class	GAPSX	NAS CM	Open End	Global Equity Large Cap (Growth)	C+	C	B	Up	Y	0
Goldman Sachs Emerging Markets Equity Fund Class A	GEMAX	NAS CM	Open End	Global Emerg Mkts (Div Emerging Mkts)	C	C	C		Y	1,000
Goldman Sachs Emerging Markets Equity Fund Class C	GEMCX	NAS CM	Open End	Global Emerg Mkts (Div Emerging Mkts)	C	C	C		Y	1,000
Goldman Sachs Emerging Markets Equity Fund Class P	GAHPX	NAS CM	Open End	Global Emerg Mkts (Div Emerging Mkts)	C	C	C		Y	0
Goldman Sachs Emerging Markets Equity Fund Class R6	GEMUX	NAS CM	Open End	Global Emerg Mkts (Div Emerging Mkts)	C	C	C		Y	5,000,000
Goldman Sachs Emerging Markets Equity Institutional Cls	GEMIX	NAS CM	Open End	Global Emerg Mkts (Div Emerging Mkts)	C	C	C		Y	1,000,000
Goldman Sachs Emerging Markets Equity Fund Investor Class	GIRMX	NAS CM	Open End	Global Emerg Mkts (Div Emerging Mkts)	C	C	C		Y	0
Goldman Sachs Emerging Markets Equity Fund Service Class	GEMSX	NAS CM	Open End	Global Emerg Mkts (Div Emerging Mkts)	C	C	C		Y	0
Goldman Sachs Emerging Markets Equity Insights Cls A	GERAX	NAS CM	Open End	Global Emerg Mkts (Div Emerging Mkts)	C	C	C+		Y	1,000
Goldman Sachs Emerging Markets Equity Insights Cls C	GERCX	NAS CM	Open End	Global Emerg Mkts (Div Emerging Mkts)	C	C	C+		Y	1,000
Goldman Sachs Emerging Markets Equity Insights Cls P	GAGPX	NAS CM	Open End	Global Emerg Mkts (Div Emerging Mkts)	C	C	C+		Y	0
Goldman Sachs Emerging Markets Equity Insights Cls R	GRRPX	NAS CM	Open End	Global Emerg Mkts (Div Emerging Mkts)	C	C	C+		Y	0
Goldman Sachs Emerging Markets Equity Insights Cls R6	GERUX	NAS CM	Open End	Global Emerg Mkts (Div Emerging Mkts)	C	C	C+		Y	5,000,000
Goldman Sachs Emerging Mkts Equity Insights Intl	GERIX	NAS CM	Open End	Global Emerg Mkts (Div Emerging Mkts)	C	C	C+		Y	1,000,000
Goldman Sachs Emerging Mkts Equity Insights Inv Cls	GIRPX	NAS CM	Open End	Global Emerg Mkts (Div Emerging Mkts)	C	C	C+		Y	0
Goldman Sachs Enhanced Div Global Eq Port Cls A	GADGX	NAS CM	Open End	Global Equity Large Cap (Growth & Income)	B-	C	B+	Up	Y	1,000
Goldman Sachs Enhanced Div Global Eq Port Cls P	GAFPX	NAS CM	Open End	Global Equity Large Cap (Growth & Income)	B-	C	B	Up	Y	0
Goldman Sachs Enhanced Div Global Eq Port Cls R6 Shares	GRGDX	NAS CM	Open End	Global Equity Large Cap (Growth & Income)	B-	C	B	Up	Y	5,000,000
Goldman Sachs Enhanced Div Global Eq Port Inst Cls	GIDGX	NAS CM	Open End	Global Equity Large Cap (Growth & Income)	B-	C	B	Up	Y	1,000,000
Goldman Sachs Equity Income Fund Class A	GSGRX	NAS CM	Open End	US Equity Large Cap Value (Growth & Income)	B-	C	B+		Y	1,000

★ Expanded analysis of this fund is included in Section II.

Min Additional Investment	TOTAL RETURNS 3-Month Total Return	6-Month Total Return	1-Year Total Return	3-Year Total Return	5-Year Total Return	PERFORMANCE Dividend Yield (TTM)	Expense Ratio	3-Yr Std Deviation	3-Year Beta	ASSETS NAV	Total Assets (MIL)	ASSET ALLOCATION & TURNOVER %Cash	%Stocks	%Bonds	%Other	Turnover Ratio	BULL & BEAR Last Bull Market Total Return	Last Bear Market Total Return	FEES Front End Fee (%)	Back End Fee (%)	Inception Date
	4.32	19.25	12.84	50.59	52.72	0.75	0.66	11.23	0.9	13.5	11.3	4	96	0	0	71	24.99	-19.72			Jul-15
	4.32	19.25	12.91	50.54	52.64	0.74	0.67	11.22	0.9	13.5	11.3	4	96	0	0	71	24.99	-19.72			Nov-09
	4.32	19.25	12.76	50.07	51.59	0.7	0.78	11.2	0.9	13.5	11.3	4	96	0	0	71	24.69	-19.69			Nov-09
50	4.90	21.51	9.83	60.90	73.55	0.02	1.14	12.61	0.97	22.87	904.0	1	99	0	0	93	29.04	-16.71	5.50		Apr-90
50	4.70	21.05	9.13	57.46	67.23	0	1.89	12.58	0.97	14.03	904.0	1	99	0	0	93	28.41	-16.94		1.00	Aug-97
	4.99	21.79	10.32	61.69	74.40	0.26	0.74	12.62	0.97	26.26	904.0	1	99	0	0	93	29.04	-16.71			Apr-18
	4.80	21.37	9.61	59.72	71.37	0	1.39	12.6	0.97	21.58	904.0	1	99	0	0	93	28.82	-16.8			Nov-07
	4.95	21.74	10.27	62.83	76.34	0.26	0.74	12.61	0.97	26.26	904.0	1	99	0	0	93	29.04	-16.71			Jul-15
	4.98	21.75	10.29	62.84	77.05	0.2	0.75	12.61	0.97	26.3	904.0	1	99	0	0	93	29.33	-16.56			Aug-97
	4.94	21.66	10.13	62.10	75.75	0.17	0.89	12.61	0.97	23.36	904.0	1	99	0	0	93	29.18	-16.6			Nov-07
	4.88	21.45	9.74	60.41	72.66	0	1.25	12.61	0.97	21.68	904.0	1	99	0	0	93	28.9	-16.7			Aug-97
50	-1.87	12.63	-12.12	-0.72	-51.03	1.12	0.95	15.91	1	10.83	320.1	60	0	20	20	46	13.53	-22.9	4.50		Mar-07
50	-2.04	12.25	-12.78	-2.96	-52.87	0.43	1.7	15.93	1	10.28	320.1	60	0	20	20	46	13.16	-23.23		1.00	Mar-07
	-1.77	12.80	-11.82	0.25	-50.21	1.54	0.6	15.94	1	10.94	320.1	60	0	20	20	46	13.69	-22.76			Apr-18
	-1.92	12.51	-12.33	-1.51	-51.65	0.95	1.2	15.93	1	10.65	320.1	60	0	20	20	46	13.29	-22.99			Nov-07
	-1.77	12.78	-11.83	0.26	-50.19	1.45	0.6	15.93	1	10.95	320.1	60	0	20	20	46	13.69	-22.76			Jul-15
	-1.78	12.80	-11.84	0.22	-50.23	1.53	0.61	15.93	1	10.93	320.1	60	0	20	20	46	13.69	-22.76			Mar-07
	-1.76	12.82	-11.86	-0.01	-50.38	1.42	0.7	15.93	1	10.94	320.1	60	0	20	20	46	13.79	-22.83			Nov-07
50	5.47	24.78	11.03	58.26	68.26	0	1.16	13.63	0.99	17.52	149.1	1	99	0	0	44	27.81	-16.84	5.50		Sep-02
50	5.23	24.30	10.15	54.60	61.91	0	1.91	13.62	0.99	13.86	149.1	1	99	0	0	44	27.28	-17.1		1.00	Sep-02
	5.54	25.03	11.46	59.96	71.52	0.26	0.79	13.61	0.99	18.83	149.1	1	99	0	0	44	28.16	-16.72			Apr-18
	5.39	24.61	10.76	57.00	66.07	0	1.41	13.57	0.99	16.81	149.1	1	99	0	0	44	27.72	-16.97			Nov-07
	5.54	24.95	11.45	59.91	71.50	0.25	0.79	13.62	0.99	18.83	149.1	1	99	0	0	44	28.16	-16.72			Jul-15
	5.59	25.03	11.44	59.91	71.47	0.09	0.8	13.6	0.99	18.88	149.1	1	99	0	0	44	28.16	-16.72			Sep-02
	5.55	24.89	11.29	59.41	70.36	0.15	0.91	13.61	0.99	17.86	149.1	1	99	0	0	44	27.98	-16.73			Nov-07
50	3.46	16.45	3.20	39.42	34.99	2.28	0.83	11.66	1.02	18.83	838.0	14	86	0	0	11	20.38	-22.16	5.50		Jan-98
50	3.29	16.07	2.47	36.41	30.13	0.39	1.58	11.69	1.02	18.2	838.0	14	86	0	0	11	19.74	-22.39		1.00	Jan-98
	3.52	16.69	3.59	41.11	37.69	2.62	0.43	11.69	1.02	19.08	838.0	14	86	0	0	11	20.61	-22.06			Apr-18
	3.37	16.33	2.94	38.40	33.32	2.06	1.08	11.7	1.02	18.66	838.0	14	86	0	0	11	20.16	-22.24			Nov-07
	3.52	16.63	3.61	41.22	37.74	2.63	0.43	11.69	1.02	19.07	838.0	14	86	0	0	11	20.61	-22.06			Jul-15
	3.52	16.70	3.60	41.11	37.70	2.48	0.44	11.68	1.02	19.07	838.0	14	86	0	0	11	20.61	-22.06			Jan-98
	3.50	16.56	3.45	40.48	36.63	2.53	0.58	11.68	1.02	18.58	838.0	14	86	0	0	11	20.43	-22.02			Nov-07
	3.41	16.38	3.11	39.03	34.32	2.11	0.94	11.68	1.02	18.75	838.0	14	86	0	0	11	20.22	-22.15			Jan-98
50	1.68	15.64	1.09	37.66	23.82	0.42	1.58	14.64	1.01	19.96	1,704	0	100	0	0	52	15.21	-26.38	5.50		Dec-97
50	1.53	15.26	0.39	34.73	19.33	0	2.33	14.65	1.01	17.82	1,704	0	100	0	0	52	14.58	-26.57		1.00	Dec-97
	1.80	15.91	1.50	39.33	26.24	0.72	1.18	14.64	1.01	21.49	1,704	0	100	0	0	52	15.47	-26.27			Apr-18
	1.80	15.91	1.54	39.47	26.39	0.71	1.18	14.65	1.01	21.49	1,704	0	100	0	0	52	15.47	-26.27			Jul-15
	1.80	15.92	1.51	39.36	26.27	0.69	1.19	14.65	1.01	21.4	1,704	0	100	0	0	52	15.47	-26.27			Dec-97
	1.77	15.82	1.40	38.78	25.37	0.59	1.33	14.67	1.01	21.23	1,704	0	100	0	0	52	15.27	-26.3			Aug-10
	1.68	15.62	0.98	37.23	23.11	0.21	1.69	14.62	1.01	19.31	1,704	0	100	0	0	52	15.1	-26.44			Dec-97
50	0.62	9.34	-2.39	33.52	17.74	1.6	1.48	14.06	1	9.59	1,968	2	98	0	0	147	21.4	-26.76	5.50		Oct-07
50	0.42	8.85	-3.12	30.50	13.29	0.88	2.23	14.06	1	9.46	1,968	2	98	0	0	147	20.93	-27.03		1.00	Oct-07
	0.73	9.49	-1.95	35.12	20.04	2.1	1.08	14.06	1	9.57	1,968	2	98	0	0	147	21.69	-26.68			Apr-18
	0.53	9.11	-2.60	32.46	16.19	1.46	1.73	14.08	1	9.46	1,968	2	98	0	0	147	21.33	-26.84			Feb-14
	0.73	9.49	-1.97	35.04	20.02	2.09	1.08	14.08	1	9.57	1,968	2	98	0	0	147	21.69	-26.68			Jul-15
	0.63	9.49	-2.09	34.95	19.89	2.07	1.09	14.06	1	9.57	1,968	2	98	0	0	147	21.69	-26.68			Oct-07
	0.73	9.50	-2.11	34.47	19.21	1.96	1.23	14.05	1	9.56	1,968	2	98	0	0	147	21.62	-26.78			Aug-10
50	2.23	13.45	2.84	28.45	24.51	2.28	1.34	9.25		11.7	621.7	0	90	0	10	20	18.56	-17.16	5.50		Apr-08
	2.32	13.55	3.23	29.83	26.90	2.64	0.94	9.26		11.79	621.7	0	90	0	10	20	18.71	-16.94			Apr-18
	2.31	13.64	3.22	29.92	26.98	2.63	0.94	9.26		11.8	621.7	0	90	0	10	20	18.71	-16.94			Dec-17
	2.31	13.61	3.21	29.88	26.95	2.62	0.95	9.25		11.82	621.7	0	90	0	10	20	18.71	-16.94			Apr-08
50	3.99	16.29	10.28	32.86	36.29	1.69	1.08	10.57	0.85	38.98	366.2	0	100	0	0	69	23.99	-21.81	5.50		Feb-93

Fund Name	MARKET Ticker Symbol	Traded On	FUND TYPE, CATEGORY & OBJECTIVE Fund Type	Category and (Prospectus Objective)	RATINGS Overall Rating	Reward Rating	Risk Rating	Recent Up/ Downgrade	Open to New Investors	MINIMUMS Min Initial Investment
Goldman Sachs Equity Income Fund Class C	GSGCX	NAS CM	Open End	US Equity Large Cap Value (Growth & Income)	B-	C	B+		Y	1,000
Goldman Sachs Equity Income Fund Class P	GABPX	NAS CM	Open End	US Equity Large Cap Value (Growth & Income)	B-	C	B+		Y	0
Goldman Sachs Equity Income Fund Class R	GRGRX	NAS CM	Open End	US Equity Large Cap Value (Growth & Income)	B-	C	B+		Y	0
Goldman Sachs Equity Income Fund Class R6	GRGUX	NAS CM	Open End	US Equity Large Cap Value (Growth & Income)	B-	C	B+		Y	5,000,000
Goldman Sachs Equity Income Fund Institutional Class	GSIIX	NAS CM	Open End	US Equity Large Cap Value (Growth & Income)	B-	C	B+		Y	1,000,000
Goldman Sachs Equity Income Fund Investor Class	GRGTX	NAS CM	Open End	US Equity Large Cap Value (Growth & Income)	B-	C	B+		Y	0
Goldman Sachs Equity Income Fund Service Class	GSGSX	NAS CM	Open End	US Equity Large Cap Value (Growth & Income)	B-	C	B+		Y	0
Goldman Sachs ESG Emerging Markets Equity Cls A Shares	GEBAX	NAS CM	Open End	Global Emerg Mkts (Div Emerging Mkts)	D	D+	C		Y	1,000
Goldman Sachs ESG Emerging Markets Equity Cls C Shares	GEBCX	NAS CM	Open End	Global Emerg Mkts (Div Emerging Mkts)	D	D+	C		Y	1,000
Goldman Sachs ESG Emerging Mkts Equity Cls Inv Shares	GEBNX	NAS CM	Open End	Global Emerg Mkts (Div Emerging Mkts)	D	D+	C		Y	0
Goldman Sachs ESG Emerging Markets Equity Cls R Shares	GEBRX	NAS CM	Open End	Global Emerg Mkts (Div Emerging Mkts)	D	D+	C		Y	0
Goldman Sachs ESG Emerging Markets Equity Cls R6 Shares	GEBSX	NAS CM	Open End	Global Emerg Mkts (Div Emerging Mkts)	D	D+	C		Y	5,000,000
Goldman Sachs ESG Emerging Mkts Equity Inst Shares	GEBIX	NAS CM	Open End	Global Emerg Mkts (Div Emerging Mkts)	D	D+	C		Y	1,000,000
Goldman Sachs Flexible Cap Fund Class A	GALLX	NAS CM	Open End	US Equity Large Cap Growth (Growth)	B-	C+	B		Y	1,000
Goldman Sachs Flexible Cap Fund Class C	GCLLX	NAS CM	Open End	US Equity Large Cap Growth (Growth)	C+	C	B		Y	1,000
Goldman Sachs Flexible Cap Fund Class P	GGZPX	NAS CM	Open End	US Equity Large Cap Growth (Growth)	B-	C+	B		Y	0
Goldman Sachs Flexible Cap Fund Class R	GRLLX	NAS CM	Open End	US Equity Large Cap Growth (Growth)	B-	C+	B		Y	0
Goldman Sachs Flexible Cap Fund Class R6	GFCUX	NAS CM	Open End	US Equity Large Cap Growth (Growth)	B-	C+	B		Y	5,000,000
Goldman Sachs Flexible Cap Fund Institutional Class	GILLX	NAS CM	Open End	US Equity Large Cap Growth (Growth)	B-	C+	B		Y	1,000,000
Goldman Sachs Flexible Cap Fund Investor Class	GSLLX	NAS CM	Open End	US Equity Large Cap Growth (Growth)	B-	C+	B		Y	0
Goldman Sachs Focused Value Fund Class A	GFVAX	NAS CM	Open End	US Equity Large Cap Value (Growth)	C+	C	B		Y	1,000
Goldman Sachs Focused Value Fund Class C	GFVCX	NAS CM	Open End	US Equity Large Cap Value (Growth)	C+	C	B		Y	1,000
Goldman Sachs Focused Value Fund Class P	GGYPX	NAS CM	Open End	US Equity Large Cap Value (Growth)	C+	C	B	Down	Y	0
Goldman Sachs Focused Value Fund Class R	GFVRX	NAS CM	Open End	US Equity Large Cap Value (Growth)	C+	C	B		Y	0
Goldman Sachs Focused Value Fund Class R6	GFVUX	NAS CM	Open End	US Equity Large Cap Value (Growth)	C+	C	B	Down	Y	5,000,000
Goldman Sachs Focused Value Fund Institutional Class	GFVSX	NAS CM	Open End	US Equity Large Cap Value (Growth)	C+	C	B	Down	Y	1,000,000
Goldman Sachs Focused Value Fund Investor Class	GFVIX	NAS CM	Open End	US Equity Large Cap Value (Growth)	C+	C	B	Down	Y	0
Goldman Sachs Global Infrastructure Fund Class A	GGIAX	NAS CM	Open End	Infrastructure Sector Equity (Utility)	C	C	C+	Down	Y	1,000
Goldman Sachs Global Infrastructure Fund Class C	GGICX	NAS CM	Open End	Infrastructure Sector Equity (Utility)	C	C	C+	Down	Y	1,000
Goldman Sachs Global Infrastructure Fund Class P	GGWPX	NAS CM	Open End	Infrastructure Sector Equity (Utility)	C	C	C+	Down	Y	0
Goldman Sachs Global Infrastructure Fund Class R	GGIEX	NAS CM	Open End	Infrastructure Sector Equity (Utility)	C	C	C+	Down	Y	0
Goldman Sachs Global Infrastructure Fund Class R6	GGIJX	NAS CM	Open End	Infrastructure Sector Equity (Utility)	C	C	C+	Down	Y	5,000,000
Goldman Sachs Global Infrastructure Institutional Cls	GGIDX	NAS CM	Open End	Infrastructure Sector Equity (Utility)	C	C	C+	Down	Y	1,000,000
Goldman Sachs Global Infrastructure Fund Investor Class	GGINX	NAS CM	Open End	Infrastructure Sector Equity (Utility)	C	C	C+	Down	Y	0
Goldman Sachs Global Real Estate Securities Fund Class A	GARGX	NAS CM	Open End	Real Estate Sector Equity (Real Estate)	C+	C	B		Y	1,000
Goldman Sachs Global Real Estate Securities Fund Class C	GARKX	NAS CM	Open End	Real Estate Sector Equity (Real Estate)	C+	C	B		Y	1,000
Goldman Sachs Global Real Estate Securities Fund Class P	GGUPX	NAS CM	Open End	Real Estate Sector Equity (Real Estate)	B-	C	B	Up	Y	0
Goldman Sachs Global Real Estate Securities Fund Class R	GARHX	NAS CM	Open End	Real Estate Sector Equity (Real Estate)	C+	C	B		Y	0
Goldman Sachs Global Real Estate Securities Fund Class R6	GARVX	NAS CM	Open End	Real Estate Sector Equity (Real Estate)	B-	C	B	Up	Y	5,000,000
Goldman Sachs Global Real Estate Securities Inst Cls	GARSX	NAS CM	Open End	Real Estate Sector Equity (Real Estate)	B-	C	B	Up	Y	1,000,000
Goldman Sachs Global Real Estate Securities Investor Cls	GARJX	NAS CM	Open End	Real Estate Sector Equity (Real Estate)	B-	C	B	Up	Y	0
Goldman Sachs GQG Partners Intl Opp Cls A	GSIHX	NAS CM	Open End	Global Equity Large Cap (Foreign Stock)	C+	C	B	Up	Y	1,000
Goldman Sachs GQG Partners Intl Opp Cls C	GSILX	NAS CM	Open End	Global Equity Large Cap (Foreign Stock)	C+	C	B	Up	Y	1,000
Goldman Sachs GQG Partners Intl Opp Cls P	GGIPX	NAS CM	Open End	Global Equity Large Cap (Foreign Stock)	C+	C	B	Up	Y	0
Goldman Sachs GQG Partners Intl Opp Cls R	GSIQX	NAS CM	Open End	Global Equity Large Cap (Foreign Stock)	C+	C	B	Up	Y	0
Goldman Sachs GQG Partners Intl Opp Cls R6	GSIYX	NAS CM	Open End	Global Equity Large Cap (Foreign Stock)	C+	C	B	Up	Y	5,000,000
Goldman Sachs GQG Partners Intl Opp Inst Shares	GSIMX	NAS CM	Open End	Global Equity Large Cap (Foreign Stock)	C+	C	B	Up	Y	1,000,000
Goldman Sachs GQG Partners Intl Opp Inv Shares	GSINX	NAS CM	Open End	Global Equity Large Cap (Foreign Stock)	C+	C	B	Up	Y	0
Goldman Sachs Growth and Income Strategy Portfolio Class A	GOIAX	NAS CM	Open End	Moderate Alloc (Growth & Income)	B-	C	B+	Up	Y	1,000
Goldman Sachs Growth and Income Strategy Portfolio Class C	GOICX	NAS CM	Open End	Moderate Alloc (Growth & Income)	C+	C	B+	Up	Y	1,000
Goldman Sachs Growth and Income Strategy Portfolio Class P	GGSPX	NAS CM	Open End	Moderate Alloc (Growth & Income)	B-	C	B+	Up	Y	0
Goldman Sachs Growth and Income Strategy Portfolio Class R	GPIRX	NAS CM	Open End	Moderate Alloc (Growth & Income)	B-	C	B+	Up	Y	0

★ Expanded analysis of this fund is included in Section II.

	TOTAL RETURNS					PERFORMANCE				ASSETS		ASSET ALLOCATION & TURNOVER					BULL & BEAR		FEES		
Min Additional Investment	3-Month Total Return	6-Month Total Return	1-Year Total Return	3-Year Total Return	5-Year Total Return	Dividend Yield (TTM)	Expense Ratio	3-Yr Std Deviation	3-Year Beta	NAV	Total Assets (MIL)	%Cash	%Stocks	%Bonds	%Other	Turnover Ratio	Last Bull Market Total Return	Last Bear Market Total Return	Front End Fee (%)	Back End Fee (%)	Inception Date
50	3.79	15.81	9.52	29.97	31.34	0.89	1.83	10.54	0.85	37.18	366.2	0	100	0	0	69	23.46	-22.04		1.00	Aug-97
	4.10	16.46	10.70	33.48	36.93	2.01	0.72	10.57	0.85	39.64	366.2	0	100	0	0	69	23.99	-21.81			Apr-18
	3.92	16.12	9.98	31.82	34.57	1.46	1.33	10.57	0.85	38.77	366.2	0	100	0	0	69	23.75	-21.84			Nov-07
	4.10	16.50	10.69	34.44	38.45	2.01	0.72	10.59	0.86	39.65	366.2	0	100	0	0	69	23.99	-21.81			Jul-15
	4.07	16.46	10.65	34.37	38.96	2	0.73	10.58	0.86	39.64	366.2	0	100	0	0	69	24.29	-21.68			Jun-96
	4.04	16.39	10.52	33.84	37.98	1.92	0.83	10.58	0.86	38.9	366.2	0	100	0	0	69	24.15	-21.72			Nov-07
	3.96	16.16	10.13	32.41	35.56	1.55	1.23	10.58	0.86	39.12	366.2	0	100	0	0	69	23.89	-21.82			Feb-93
50	2.29	16.90	3.07			0.2	1.62			9.82	8.1	1	99	0	0	23			5.50		May-18
50	1.98	16.32	2.19			0	2.37			9.76	8.1	1	99	0	0	23				1.00	May-18
	2.28	17.02	3.23			0.34	1.37			9.83	8.1	1	99	0	0	23					May-18
	2.18	16.78	2.80			0.07	1.87			9.81	8.1	1	99	0	0	23					May-18
	2.28	17.02	3.33			0.42	1.22			9.83	8.1	1	99	0	0	23					May-18
	2.28	17.02	3.33			0.42	1.23			9.83	8.1	1	99	0	0	23					May-18
50	4.48	20.48	9.37	54.13	66.74	0.81	0.98	12.38	0.97	11.88	18.6	1	99	0	0	157	28.53	-19.12	5.50		Jan-08
50	4.40	19.99	8.61	50.62	60.52	0.26	1.73	12.43	0.98	10.2	18.6	1	99	0	0	157	27.95	-19.38		1.00	Jan-08
	4.64	20.65	9.77	55.75	69.92	1.07	0.58	12.43	0.98	12.85	18.6	1	99	0	0	157	28.79	-19			Apr-18
	4.41	20.23	9.09	52.96	64.64	0.67	1.23	12.4	0.97	11.35	18.6	1	99	0	0	157	28.3	-19.24			Jan-08
	4.56	20.56	9.75	55.72	69.87	1.06	0.58	12.4	0.97	12.84	18.6	1	99	0	0	157	28.79	-19			Jul-15
	4.63	20.61	9.77	55.75	69.91	0.88	0.59	12.43	0.98	12.87	18.6	1	99	0	0	157	28.79	-19			Jan-08
	4.57	20.49	9.64	55.11	68.71	0.97	0.73	12.41	0.97	12.58	18.6	1	99	0	0	157	28.62	-19.01			Jan-08
50	4.05	18.20	8.96	35.48		0.46	1.08	12.81	1.02	10.78	5.0	2	98	0	0	204			5.50		Jul-15
50	3.78	17.71	8.10	32.41		0.08	1.83	12.73	1.01	10.7	5.0	2	98	0	0	204				1.00	Jul-15
	4.15	18.31	9.38	37.04		1.12	0.72	12.77	1.01	10.79	5.0	2	98	0	0	204					Apr-18
	3.96	18.02	8.76	34.48		0.52	1.33	12.78	1.01	10.74	5.0	2	98	0	0	204					Jul-15
	4.15	18.44	9.48	37.17		1.11	0.72	12.78	1.01	10.79	5.0	2	98	0	0	204					Jul-15
	4.14	18.40	9.42	37.07		0.91	0.73	12.8	1.01	10.81	5.0	2	98	0	0	204					Jul-15
	4.15	18.33	9.31	36.43		0.97	0.83	12.83	1.02	10.78	5.0	2	98	0	0	204					Jul-15
50	4.81	22.66	13.08	21.25		1.73	1.35	9.91	0.98	11.68	198.9	1	99	0	0	67			5.50		Jun-16
50	4.57	22.15	12.25	18.54		1.18	2.1	9.85	0.97	11.63	198.9	1	99	0	0	67				1.00	Jun-16
	4.91	22.88	13.64	22.67		2.1	0.98	9.89	0.98	11.68	198.9	1	99	0	0	67					Apr-18
	4.65	22.40	12.80	20.29		1.51	1.6	9.89	0.98	11.68	198.9	1	99	0	0	67					Jun-16
	4.81	22.88	13.53	22.66		2.09	0.98	9.87	0.97	11.68	198.9	1	99	0	0	67					Jun-16
	4.89	22.80	13.48	22.67		2.08	0.99	9.9	0.98	11.71	198.9	1	99	0	0	67					Jun-16
	4.88	22.81	13.37	22.13		1.97	1.1	9.87	0.97	11.68	198.9	1	99	0	0	67					Jun-16
50	1.26	15.66	8.28	12.94		1.87	1.36	10.89	0.97	11.2	239.5	3	94	0	4	67			5.50		Aug-15
50	1.13	15.25	7.47	10.52		1.25	2.11	10.86	0.97	11.19	239.5	3	94	0	4	67				1.00	Aug-15
	1.38	15.88	8.74	14.40		2.28	0.96	10.89	0.97	11.21	239.5	3	94	0	4	67					Apr-18
	1.31	15.54	8.04	12.29		1.67	1.61	10.84	0.97	11.21	239.5	3	94	0	4	67					Aug-15
	1.47	15.98	8.73	14.49		2.28	0.96	10.88	0.97	11.22	239.5	3	94	0	4	67					Aug-15
	1.47	15.94	8.71	14.47		2.27	0.97	10.88	0.97	11.24	239.5	3	94	0	4	67					Aug-15
	1.43	15.90	8.57	13.96		2.14	1.11	10.86	0.97	11.22	239.5	3	94	0	4	67					Aug-15
50	7.44	19.93	9.42			0.15	1.28			14.44	2,792	4	93	0	2	90			5.50		Dec-16
50	7.25	19.52	8.64			0	2.03			14.2	2,792	4	93	0	2	90				1.00	Dec-16
	7.49	20.14	9.80			0.47	0.87			14.49	2,792	4	93	0	2	90					Apr-18
	7.40	19.86	9.20			0.07	1.53			14.36	2,792	4	93	0	2	90					Dec-16
	7.56	20.13	9.87			0.46	0.87			14.5	2,792	4	93	0	2	90					Dec-16
	7.48	20.13	9.84			0.44	0.89			14.5	2,792	4	93	0	2	90					Dec-16
	7.58	20.08	9.75			0.36	1.03			14.47	2,792	4	93	0	2	90					Dec-16
50	2.88	12.20	3.63	24.18	21.30	2.28	1.23	8.05		13.65	898.0	38	118	-83	27	32	12.63	-14.19	5.50		Jan-98
50	2.69	11.83	2.87	21.39	16.79	1.61	1.98	8.04		13.33	898.0	38	118	-83	27	32	12.21	-14.51		1.00	Jan-98
	3.05	12.46	4.11	25.60	23.68	2.65	0.83	8.06		13.69	898.0	38	118	-83	27	32	12.93	-14.05			Apr-18
	2.92	12.08	3.40	23.22	19.73	2.05	1.48	8.04		13.55	898.0	38	118	-83	27	32	12.44	-14.26			Nov-07

	MARKET		FUND TYPE, CATEGORY & OBJECTIVE		RATINGS				MINIMUMS	
Fund Name	Ticker Symbol	Traded On	Fund Type	Category and (Prospectus Objective)	Overall Rating	Reward Rating	Risk Rating	Recent Up/ Downgrade	Open to New Investors	Min Initial Investment
Goldman Sachs Growth & Income Strategy Portfolio Cls R6	GOIUX	NAS CM	Open End	Moderate Alloc (Growth & Income)	B-	C	B+	Up	Y	5,000,000
Goldman Sachs Growth & Income Strategy Portfolio Inst Cls	GOIIX	NAS CM	Open End	Moderate Alloc (Growth & Income)	B-	C	B+	Up	Y	1,000,000
Goldman Sachs Growth & Income Strategy Portfolio Inv Cls	GPITX	NAS CM	Open End	Moderate Alloc (Growth & Income)	B-	C	B+	Up	Y	0
Goldman Sachs Growth & Inc Strategy Port Serv Cls	GOISX	NAS CM	Open End	Moderate Alloc (Growth & Income)	B-	C	B+	Up	Y	0
Goldman Sachs Growth Opportunities Fund Class A	GGOAX	NAS CM	Open End	US Equity Mid Cap (Growth)	B-	C+	B		Y	1,000
Goldman Sachs Growth Opportunities Fund Class C	GGOCX	NAS CM	Open End	US Equity Mid Cap (Growth)	B-	C+	B		Y	1,000
Goldman Sachs Growth Opportunities Fund Class P	GGQPX	NAS CM	Open End	US Equity Mid Cap (Growth)	B-	B-	B		Y	0
Goldman Sachs Growth Opportunities Fund Class R	GGORX	NAS CM	Open End	US Equity Mid Cap (Growth)	B-	C+	B		Y	0
Goldman Sachs Growth Opportunities Fund Class R6	GGOUX	NAS CM	Open End	US Equity Mid Cap (Growth)	B-	B-	B		Y	5,000,000
Goldman Sachs Growth Opportunities Institutional Cls	GGOIX	NAS CM	Open End	US Equity Mid Cap (Growth)	B-	B-	B		Y	1,000,000
Goldman Sachs Growth Opportunities Fund Investor Class	GGOTX	NAS CM	Open End	US Equity Mid Cap (Growth)	B-	B-	B		Y	0
Goldman Sachs Growth Opportunities Fund Service Class	GGOSX	NAS CM	Open End	US Equity Mid Cap (Growth)	B-	C+	B		Y	0
Goldman Sachs Growth Strategy Portfolio Class A	GGSAX	NAS CM	Open End	Aggressive Alloc (Growth & Income)	C+	C	B	Up	Y	1,000
Goldman Sachs Growth Strategy Portfolio Class C	GGSCX	NAS CM	Open End	Aggressive Alloc (Growth & Income)	C+	C	B	Up	Y	1,000
Goldman Sachs Growth Strategy Portfolio Class P	GGPPX	NAS CM	Open End	Aggressive Alloc (Growth & Income)	C+	C	B	Up	Y	0
Goldman Sachs Growth Strategy Portfolio Class R	GGSRX	NAS CM	Open End	Aggressive Alloc (Growth & Income)	C+	C	B	Up	Y	0
Goldman Sachs Growth Strategy Portfolio Class R6	GGSUX	NAS CM	Open End	Aggressive Alloc (Growth & Income)	C+	C	B	Up	Y	5,000,000
Goldman Sachs Growth Strategy Portfolio Institutional Cls	GGSIX	NAS CM	Open End	Aggressive Alloc (Growth & Income)	C+	C	B	Up	Y	1,000,000
Goldman Sachs Growth Strategy Portfolio Investor Class	GGSTX	NAS CM	Open End	Aggressive Alloc (Growth & Income)	C+	C	B	Up	Y	0
Goldman Sachs Growth Strategy Portfolio Service Class	GGSSX	NAS CM	Open End	Aggressive Alloc (Growth & Income)	C+	C	B	Up	Y	0
Goldman Sachs Income Builder Fund Class A	GSBFX	NAS CM	Open End	Cautious Alloc (Balanced)	B	C+	B+		Y	1,000
Goldman Sachs Income Builder Fund Class C	GSBCX	NAS CM	Open End	Cautious Alloc (Balanced)	B-	C+	B+		Y	1,000
Goldman Sachs Income Builder Fund Class P	GGKPX	NAS CM	Open End	Cautious Alloc (Balanced)	B	C+	B+		Y	0
Goldman Sachs Income Builder Fund Class R6	GSBUX	NAS CM	Open End	Cautious Alloc (Balanced)	B	C+	A-		Y	5,000,000
Goldman Sachs Income Builder Fund Institutional Class	GSBIX	NAS CM	Open End	Cautious Alloc (Balanced)	B	C+	A-		Y	1,000,000
Goldman Sachs Income Builder Fund Investor Class	GKIRX	NAS CM	Open End	Cautious Alloc (Balanced)	B	C+	B+		Y	0
Goldman Sachs Intl Equity Dividend & Premium Cls A	GIDAX	NAS CM	Open End	Global Equity Large Cap (Foreign Stock)	C	C-	C+		Y	1,000
Goldman Sachs Intl Equity Dividend & Premium Cls C	GIDCX	NAS CM	Open End	Global Equity Large Cap (Foreign Stock)	C	C-	C+		Y	1,000
Goldman Sachs Intl Equity Dividend & Premium Cls P	GGHPX	NAS CM	Open End	Global Equity Large Cap (Foreign Stock)	C	C-	C+		Y	0
Goldman Sachs Intl Equity Dividend & Premium Cls R6	GIDUX	NAS CM	Open End	Global Equity Large Cap (Foreign Stock)	C	C-	C+		Y	5,000,000
Goldman Sachs Intl Equity Dividend & Premium Inst Cls	GIDHX	NAS CM	Open End	Global Equity Large Cap (Foreign Stock)	C	C-	C+		Y	1,000,000
Goldman Sachs Intl Equity Dividend & Premium Inv Cls	GIRVX	NAS CM	Open End	Global Equity Large Cap (Foreign Stock)	C	C-	C+		Y	0
Goldman Sachs International Equity ESG Fund Class A	GSIFX	NAS CM	Open End	Global Equity Large Cap (Foreign Stock)	C	C	B-		Y	1,000
Goldman Sachs International Equity ESG Fund Class C	GSICX	NAS CM	Open End	Global Equity Large Cap (Foreign Stock)	C	C-	B-		Y	1,000
Goldman Sachs International Equity ESG Fund Class P	GTFPX	NAS CM	Open End	Global Equity Large Cap (Foreign Stock)	C	C	B-		Y	0
Goldman Sachs International Equity ESG Fund Class R6	GSIWX	NAS CM	Open End	Global Equity Large Cap (Foreign Stock)	C	C	B		Y	5,000,000
Goldman Sachs International Equity ESG Institutional Cls	GSIEX	NAS CM	Open End	Global Equity Large Cap (Foreign Stock)	C	C	B-		Y	1,000,000
Goldman Sachs International Equity ESG Fund Investor Class	GIRNX	NAS CM	Open End	Global Equity Large Cap (Foreign Stock)	C	C	B-		Y	0
Goldman Sachs International Equity ESG Fund Service Class	GSISX	NAS CM	Open End	Global Equity Large Cap (Foreign Stock)	C	C	B-		Y	0
Goldman Sachs International Equity Income Fund Class A	GSAKX	NAS CM	Open End	Global Equity Large Cap (Foreign Stock)	C+	C	B	Up	Y	1,000
Goldman Sachs International Equity Income Fund Class C	GSCKX	NAS CM	Open End	Global Equity Large Cap (Foreign Stock)	C	C	B		Y	1,000
Goldman Sachs Intl Equity Income Cls Inst	GSIKX	NAS CM	Open End	Global Equity Large Cap (Foreign Stock)	C+	C	B	Up	Y	1,000,000
Goldman Sachs International Equity Income Fund Class P	GSNPX	NAS CM	Open End	Global Equity Large Cap (Foreign Stock)	C+	C	B	Up	Y	0
Goldman Sachs International Equity Income Fund Class R	GSRKX	NAS CM	Open End	Global Equity Large Cap (Foreign Stock)	C+	C	B	Up	Y	0
Goldman Sachs International Equity Income Fund Class R6	GSUKX	NAS CM	Open End	Global Equity Large Cap (Foreign Stock)	C+	C	B	Up	Y	5,000,000
Goldman Sachs International Equity Income Investor Cls	GSTKX	NAS CM	Open End	Global Equity Large Cap (Foreign Stock)	C+	C	B	Up	Y	0
Goldman Sachs International Equity Insights Fund Class A	GCIAX	NAS CM	Open End	Global Equity Large Cap (Foreign Stock)	C	C	C		Y	1,000
Goldman Sachs International Equity Insights Fund Class C	GCICX	NAS CM	Open End	Global Equity Large Cap (Foreign Stock)	C	C-	C		Y	1,000
Goldman Sachs International Equity Insights Fund Class P	GGFPX	NAS CM	Open End	Global Equity Large Cap (Foreign Stock)	C	C	C+		Y	0
Goldman Sachs International Equity Insights Fund Class R	GCIRX	NAS CM	Open End	Global Equity Large Cap (Foreign Stock)	C	C	C		Y	0
Goldman Sachs International Equity Insights Fund Class R6	GCIUX	NAS CM	Open End	Global Equity Large Cap (Foreign Stock)	C	C	C+		Y	5,000,000
Goldman Sachs International Equity Insights Fund Class S	GCISX	NAS CM	Open End	Global Equity Large Cap (Foreign Stock)	C	C	C		Y	0

★Expanded analysis of this fund is included in Section II.

	TOTAL RETURNS					PERFORMANCE				ASSETS		ASSET ALLOCATION & TURNOVER					BULL & BEAR		FEES		
Min Additional Investment	3-Month Total Return	6-Month Total Return	1-Year Total Return	3-Year Total Return	5-Year Total Return	Dividend Yield (TTM)	Expense Ratio	3-Yr Std Deviation	3-Year Beta	NAV	Total Assets (MIL)	%Cash	%Stocks	%Bonds	%Other	Turnover Ratio	Last Bull Market Total Return	Last Bear Market Total Return	Front End Fee (%)	Back End Fee (%)	Inception Date
	3.05	12.46	4.03	25.62	23.70	2.65	0.83	8.04		13.69	898.0	38	118	-83	27	32	12.92	-14.05			Jul-15
	3.12	12.54	4.09	25.66	23.73	2.64	0.84	8.03		13.7	898.0	38	118	-83	27	32	12.93	-14.05			Jan-98
	3.03	12.39	3.90	25.16	22.87	2.52	0.98	8.02		13.59	898.0	38	118	-83	27	32	12.72	-14.1			Nov-07
	2.93	12.17	3.51	23.73	20.63	2.17	1.34	8.02		13.62	898.0	38	118	-83	27	32	12.61	-14.27			Jan-98
50	6.92	27.61	15.15	52.21	53.64	0	1.24	13.03	0.88	18.07	1,315	1	99	0	0	60	32.76	-23.27	5.50		May-99
50	6.74	27.10	14.29	48.86	47.98	0	1.99	13.02	0.88	10.13	1,315	1	99	0	0	60	32.18	-23.52		1.00	May-99
	7.01	27.83	15.60	53.85	56.49	0	0.89	13.05	0.88	22.87	1,315	1	99	0	0	60	33.06	-23.12			Apr-18
	6.90	27.51	14.89	51.18	51.79	0	1.49	13.06	0.88	16.87	1,315	1	99	0	0	60	32.52	-23.34			Nov-07
	7.02	27.85	15.61	53.91	56.54	0	0.89	13.06	0.88	22.86	1,315	1	99	0	0	60	33.06	-23.12			Jul-15
	7.02	27.81	15.57	53.81	56.45	0	0.9	13.06	0.88	22.84	1,315	1	99	0	0	60	33.06	-23.12			May-99
	7.00	27.81	15.49	53.45	55.62	0	0.99	13.06	0.88	19.39	1,315	1	99	0	0	60	32.95	-23.18			Nov-07
	6.85	27.50	14.96	51.53	52.60	0	1.4	13.05	0.88	16.83	1,315	1	99	0	0	60	32.68	-23.29			May-99
50	3.30	14.33	3.29	31.00	26.68	2.31	1.27	10		15.63	789.4	36	259	-235	40	29	16.41	-18.94	5.50		Jan-98
50	3.05	13.94	2.52	28.11	21.98	0	2.02	9.93		15.85	789.4	36	259	-235	40	29	15.94	-19.24		1.00	Jan-98
	3.30	14.57	3.60	32.54	29.14	2.68	0.87	9.94		15.64	789.4	36	259	-235	40	29	16.71	-18.87			Apr-18
	3.19	14.19	2.97	30.00	25.07	2.13	1.52	9.94		15.2	789.4	36	259	-235	40	29	16.21	-19.05			Nov-07
	3.37	14.57	3.67	32.61	29.24	2.68	0.87	9.94		15.64	789.4	36	259	-235	40	29	16.71	-18.87			Jul-15
	3.30	14.50	3.62	32.48	29.08	2.65	0.88	9.98		15.63	789.4	36	259	-235	40	29	16.71	-18.87			Jan-98
	3.28	14.48	3.45	31.91	28.21	2.49	1.02	9.93		15.41	789.4	36	259	-235	40	29	16.58	-18.84			Nov-07
	3.24	14.31	3.12	30.57	25.97	2.15	1.38	9.92		15.57	789.4	36	259	-235	40	29	16.24	-18.92			Jan-98
50	3.88	13.99	9.35	23.14	20.17	3.58	0.98	5.93	0.44	23.25	1,587	9	37	50	2	42	15.11	-8.38	5.50		Oct-94
50	3.67	13.53	8.52	20.35	15.75	2.93	1.73	5.91	0.44	22.84	1,587	9	37	50	2	42	14.58	-8.66		1.00	Aug-97
	3.66	13.83	9.42	23.30	20.33	3.88	0.58	5.9	0.44	23.77	1,587	9	37	50	2	42	15.11	-8.38			Apr-18
	3.99	14.19	9.76	24.62	22.05	3.88	0.58	5.9	0.44	23.77	1,587	9	37	50	2	42	15.11	-8.38			Jul-15
	3.98	14.18	9.75	24.54	22.54	3.87	0.59	5.92	0.44	23.77	1,587	9	37	50	2	42	15.38	-8.21			Aug-97
	3.96	14.10	9.58	24.03	21.68	3.74	0.73	5.9	0.44	23.7	1,587	9	37	50	2	42	15.29	-8.3			Aug-10
50	2.66	9.67	-1.23	22.18	-0.51	2.8	1.33	9.63	0.84	7	311.0	-1	101	0	0	14	10.36	-22.18	5.50		Jan-08
50	2.38	9.26	-2.06	19.27	-4.34	1.96	2.08	9.67	0.84	6.75	311.0	-1	101	0	0	14	9.86	-22.43		1.00	Jan-08
	2.65	9.90	-0.83	23.45	1.34	3.27	0.93	9.76	0.85	6.87	311.0	-1	101	0	0	14	10.56	-22.04			Apr-18
	2.66	9.91	-0.83	23.44	1.33	3.28	0.93	9.77	0.85	6.86	311.0	-1	101	0	0	14	10.56	-22.04			Apr-18
	2.80	9.89	-0.85	23.58	1.45	3.26	0.94	9.65	0.84	6.87	311.0	-1	101	0	0	14	10.56	-22.04			Jan-08
	2.77	9.86	-0.97	22.99	0.67	3.15	1.08	9.6	0.83	6.85	311.0	-1	101	0	0	14	10.55	-22.12			Aug-10
50	3.36	14.36	-0.16	27.21	5.67	1.28	1.24	11.9	1.04	19.35	135.9	2	98	0	0	38	13.07	-24.91	5.50		Dec-92
50	3.15	13.94	-0.90	24.42	1.83	0.22	1.99	11.92	1.04	17.98	135.9	2	98	0	0	38	12.6	-25.14		1.00	Aug-97
	3.46	14.54	0.22	27.56	5.77	1.68	0.89	11.9	1.04	19.69	135.9	2	98	0	0	38	13.1	-24.98			Apr-18
	3.46	14.60	0.25	28.78	6.89	1.66	0.89	11.94	1.04	19.7	135.9	2	98	0	0	38	13.1	-24.98			Feb-16
	3.44	14.51	0.18	28.63	7.73	1.2	0.9	11.89	1.04	19.8	135.9	2	98	0	0	38	13.42	-24.83			Feb-96
	3.41	14.46	0.03	28.09	6.98	1.43	0.99	11.94	1.04	19.7	135.9	2	98	0	0	38	13.25	-24.85			Aug-10
	3.31	14.26	-0.25	26.85	5.18	1.14	1.4	11.91	1.04	20.26	135.9	2	98	0	0	38	13.1	-24.98			Dec-92
50	3.79	15.41	4.05	29.76	11.38	2.6	1.24	10.88	0.93	12.84	52.5	1	99	0	0	87	14.25	-23.75	5.50		Jun-07
50	3.65	14.89	3.25	26.84	7.26	2.28	1.99	10.85	0.93	11.34	52.5	1	99	0	0	87	13.72	-23.95		1.00	Jun-07
	3.91	15.51	4.38	31.17	13.56	2.55	0.85	10.9	0.94	13.55	52.5	1	99	0	0	87	14.54	-23.64			Jun-07
	3.92	15.55	4.40	31.13	13.52	2.62	0.84	10.89	0.93	13.52	52.5	1	99	0	0	87	14.54	-23.64			Apr-18
	3.70	15.08	3.70	28.55	9.87	2.52	1.49	10.83	0.93	12.89	52.5	1	99	0	0	87	14.2	-23.85			Nov-07
	3.91	15.54	4.40	31.17	13.56	2.62	0.84	10.88	0.93	13.53	52.5	1	99	0	0	87	14.54	-23.64			Feb-16
	3.80	15.37	4.22	30.63	12.71	2.68	0.99	10.85	0.93	12.83	52.5	1	99	0	0	87	14.47	-23.62			Nov-07
50	2.08	12.11	-4.33	29.59	17.26	1.42	1.19	11.68	1.03	12.22	3,069	0	99	0	1	124	14.25	-26.49	5.50		Aug-97
50	1.96	11.70	-4.99	26.63	12.97	0.72	1.94	11.68	1.03	11.93	3,069	0	99	0	1	124	13.73	-26.71		1.00	Aug-97
	2.28	12.35	-3.95	30.99	19.57	1.76	0.79	11.69	1.03	12.55	3,069	0	99	0	1	124	14.44	-26.34			Apr-18
	2.06	11.97	-4.51	28.55	15.83	1.26	1.44	11.71	1.03	11.88	3,069	0	99	0	1	124	14.06	-26.55			Nov-07
	2.27	12.34	-3.95	31.03	19.65	1.75	0.79	11.7	1.03	12.56	3,069	0	99	0	1	124	14.44	-26.34			Jul-15
	2.06	11.98	-4.51	28.90	16.52	1.27	1.3	11.68	1.03	12.33	3,069	0	99	0	1	124	14.14	-26.5			Aug-97

	MARKET			FUND TYPE, CATEGORY & OBJECTIVE	RATINGS					MINIMUMS
Fund Name	Ticker Symbol	Traded On	Fund Type	Category and (Prospectus Objective)	Overall Rating	Reward Rating	Risk Rating	Recent Up/ Downgrade	Open to New Investors	Min Initial Investment
Goldman Sachs Intl Equity Insights Inst Cls	GCIIX	NAS CM	Open End	Global Equity Large Cap (Foreign Stock)	C	C	C+		Y	1,000,000
Goldman Sachs International Equity Insights Investor Cls	GCITX	NAS CM	Open End	Global Equity Large Cap (Foreign Stock)	C	C	C+		Y	0
Goldman Sachs International Real Estate Securities Cls A	GIRAX	NAS CM	Open End	Real Estate Sector Equity (Real Estate)	B-	C	B	Up	Y	1,000
Goldman Sachs International Real Estate Securities Cls C	GIRCX	NAS CM	Open End	Real Estate Sector Equity (Real Estate)	B-	C	B	Up	Y	1,000
Goldman Sachs International Real Estate Securities Cls P	GGEPX	NAS CM	Open End	Real Estate Sector Equity (Real Estate)	B-	C	B	Up	Y	0
Goldman Sachs International Real Estate Securities Cls R6	GIRUX	NAS CM	Open End	Real Estate Sector Equity (Real Estate)	B-	C	B	Up	Y	5,000,000
Goldman Sachs Intl Real Estate Securities Inst Cls	GIRIX	NAS CM	Open End	Real Estate Sector Equity (Real Estate)	B-	C	B	Up	Y	1,000,000
Goldman Sachs Intl Real Estate Securities Inv Cls	GIRTX	NAS CM	Open End	Real Estate Sector Equity (Real Estate)	B-	C	B	Up	Y	0
Goldman Sachs International Small Cap Insights Cls A	GICAX	NAS CM	Open End	Global Equity Mid/Small Cap (Small Company)	C	C-	C		Y	1,000
Goldman Sachs International Small Cap Insights Cls C	GICCX	NAS CM	Open End	Global Equity Mid/Small Cap (Small Company)	C	C-	C	Up	Y	1,000
Goldman Sachs International Small Cap Insights Cls P	GGDPX	NAS CM	Open End	Global Equity Mid/Small Cap (Small Company)	C	C	C		Y	0
Goldman Sachs International Small Cap Insights Cls R6	GICUX	NAS CM	Open End	Global Equity Mid/Small Cap (Small Company)	C	C	C		Y	5,000,000
Goldman Sachs Intl Small Cap Insights Inst Cls	GICIX	NAS CM	Open End	Global Equity Mid/Small Cap (Small Company)	C	C	C		Y	1,000,000
Goldman Sachs Intl Small Cap Insights Inv Cls	GIRLX	NAS CM	Open End	Global Equity Mid/Small Cap (Small Company)	C	C	C		Y	0
Goldman Sachs International Tax-Managed Equity Cls A	GATMX	NAS CM	Open End	Global Equity Large Cap (Foreign Stock)	C	C-	C		Y	1,000
Goldman Sachs International Tax-Managed Equity Cls C	GCTMX	NAS CM	Open End	Global Equity Large Cap (Foreign Stock)	C	C-	C	Up	Y	1,000
Goldman Sachs International Tax-Managed Equity Cls P	GGCPX	NAS CM	Open End	Global Equity Large Cap (Foreign Stock)	C	C	C		Y	0
Goldman Sachs International Tax-Managed Equity Cls R6	GHTRX	NAS CM	Open End	Global Equity Large Cap (Foreign Stock)	C	C	C		Y	5,000,000
Goldman Sachs Intl Tax-Managed Equity Inst Cls	GHTMX	NAS CM	Open End	Global Equity Large Cap (Foreign Stock)	C	C	C		Y	1,000,000
Goldman Sachs Intl Tax-Managed Equity Inv Cls	GITRX	NAS CM	Open End	Global Equity Large Cap (Foreign Stock)	C	C	C		Y	0
Goldman Sachs Large Cap Growth Insights Fund Class A	GLCGX	NAS CM	Open End	US Equity Large Cap Growth (Growth & Income)	C+	C	B		Y	1,000
Goldman Sachs Large Cap Growth Insights Fund Class C	GLCCX	NAS CM	Open End	US Equity Large Cap Growth (Growth & Income)	C+	C	B-		Y	1,000
Goldman Sachs Large Cap Growth Insights Fund Class P	GMZPX	NAS CM	Open End	US Equity Large Cap Growth (Growth & Income)	C+	C	B	Down	Y	0
Goldman Sachs Large Cap Growth Insights Fund Class R	GLCRX	NAS CM	Open End	US Equity Large Cap Growth (Growth & Income)	C+	C	B-	Down	Y	0
Goldman Sachs Large Cap Growth Insights Fund Class R6	GLCUX	NAS CM	Open End	US Equity Large Cap Growth (Growth & Income)	C+	C	B	Down	Y	5,000,000
Goldman Sachs Large Cap Growth Insights Institutional Cls	GCGIX	NAS CM	Open End	US Equity Large Cap Growth (Growth & Income)	C+	C	B	Down	Y	1,000,000
Goldman Sachs Large Cap Growth Insights Investor Cls	GLCTX	NAS CM	Open End	US Equity Large Cap Growth (Growth & Income)	C+	C	B	Down	Y	0
Goldman Sachs Large Cap Growth Insights Fund Service Class	GSCLX	NAS CM	Open End	US Equity Large Cap Growth (Growth & Income)	C+	C	B-	Down	Y	0
Goldman Sachs Large Cap Value Fund Class A	GSLAX	NAS CM	Open End	US Equity Large Cap Value (Growth)	B-	C	B	Up	Y	1,000
Goldman Sachs Large Cap Value Fund Class C	GSVCX	NAS CM	Open End	US Equity Large Cap Value (Growth)	C+	C	B	Up	Y	1,000
Goldman Sachs Large Cap Value Fund Class P	GMYPX	NAS CM	Open End	US Equity Large Cap Value (Growth)	B-	C	B	Up	Y	0
Goldman Sachs Large Cap Value Fund Class R	GSVRX	NAS CM	Open End	US Equity Large Cap Value (Growth)	C+	C	B		Y	0
Goldman Sachs Large Cap Value Fund Class R6	GSVUX	NAS CM	Open End	US Equity Large Cap Value (Growth)	B-	C	B	Up	Y	5,000,000
Goldman Sachs Large Cap Value Fund Institutional Class	GSLIX	NAS CM	Open End	US Equity Large Cap Value (Growth)	B-	C	B	Up	Y	1,000,000
Goldman Sachs Large Cap Value Fund Investor Class	GSVTX	NAS CM	Open End	US Equity Large Cap Value (Growth)	B-	C	B	Up	Y	0
Goldman Sachs Large Cap Value Fund Service Class	GSVSX	NAS CM	Open End	US Equity Large Cap Value (Growth)	C+	C	B		Y	0
Goldman Sachs Large Cap Value Insights Fund Class A	GCVAX	NAS CM	Open End	US Equity Large Cap Value (Growth & Income)	C+	C	B		Y	1,000
Goldman Sachs Large Cap Value Insights Fund Class C	GCVCX	NAS CM	Open End	US Equity Large Cap Value (Growth & Income)	C+	C	B	Up	Y	1,000
Goldman Sachs Large Cap Value Insights Fund Class P	GMXPX	NAS CM	Open End	US Equity Large Cap Value (Growth & Income)	C+	C	B		Y	0
Goldman Sachs Large Cap Value Insights Fund Class R	GCVRX	NAS CM	Open End	US Equity Large Cap Value (Growth & Income)	C+	C	B		Y	0
Goldman Sachs Large Cap Value Insights Fund Class R6	GCVUX	NAS CM	Open End	US Equity Large Cap Value (Growth & Income)	C+	C	B		Y	5,000,000
Goldman Sachs Large Cap Value Insights Institutional Cls	GCVIX	NAS CM	Open End	US Equity Large Cap Value (Growth & Income)	C+	C	B		Y	1,000,000
Goldman Sachs Large Cap Value Insights Fund Investor Class	GCVTX	NAS CM	Open End	US Equity Large Cap Value (Growth & Income)	C+	C	B		Y	0
Goldman Sachs Large Cap Value Insights Fund Service Class	GCLSX	NAS CM	Open End	US Equity Large Cap Value (Growth & Income)	C+	C	B		Y	0
Goldman Sachs Long Short Credit Strategies Fund Class P	GMUPX	NAS CM	Open End	Long/Short Credit (Growth & Income)	C	C	B-		Y	0
Goldman Sachs Long Short Credit Strategies Fund Class R6	GSSAX	NAS CM	Open End	Long/Short Credit (Growth & Income)	C	C	B-		Y	5,000,000
Goldman Sachs Long Short Credit Strategies Inst Shares	GSAWX	NAS CM	Open End	Long/Short Credit (Growth & Income)	C+	C	B-	Up	Y	1,000,000
Goldman Sachs Managed Futures Strategy Fund Class A	GMSAX	NAS CM	Open End	Alternative Miscellaneous (Growth & Income)	C	C	C+	Up	Y	1,000
Goldman Sachs Managed Futures Strategy Fund Class C	GMSCX	NAS CM	Open End	Alternative Miscellaneous (Growth & Income)	C	C-	C+	Up	Y	1,000
Goldman Sachs Managed Futures Strategy Fund Class P	GMQPX	NAS CM	Open End	Alternative Miscellaneous (Growth & Income)	C	C	B-	Up	Y	0
Goldman Sachs Managed Futures Strategy Fund Class R	GFFRX	NAS CM	Open End	Alternative Miscellaneous (Growth & Income)	C	C	C+	Up	Y	0
Goldman Sachs Managed Futures Strategy Fund Class R6	GMSWX	NAS CM	Open End	Alternative Miscellaneous (Growth & Income)	C	C	B-	Up	Y	5,000,000

★ Expanded analysis of this fund is included in Section II.

Min Additional Investment	TOTAL RETURNS 3-Month Total Return	6-Month Total Return	1-Year Total Return	3-Year Total Return	5-Year Total Return	PERFORMANCE Dividend Yield (TTM)	Expense Ratio	3-Yr Std Deviation	3-Year Beta	ASSETS NAV	Total Assets (MIL)	ASSET ALLOCATION & TURNOVER %Cash	%Stocks	%Bonds	%Other	Turnover Ratio	BULL & BEAR Last Bull Market Total Return	Last Bear Market Total Return	FEES Front End Fee (%)	Back End Fee (%)	Inception Date
	2.19	12.24	-3.98	30.95	19.54	1.73	0.8	11.74	1.04	12.56	3,069	0	99	0	1	124	14.44	-26.34			Aug-97
	2.13	12.17	-4.08	30.46	18.72	1.75	0.94	11.72	1.03	11.98	3,069	0	99	0	1	124	14.28	-26.41			Nov-07
50	-0.17	13.38	5.17	20.46	13.81	1.44	1.38	11.04	0.99	6.62	84.6	3	92	0	5	43	19.52	-24.4	5.50		Jul-06
50	-0.34	13.12	4.31	17.81	9.77	0.25	2.13	10.99	0.98	6.68	84.6	3	92	0	5	43	18.77	-24.43		1.00	Jul-06
	0.01	13.75	5.49	22.03	16.09	1.91	0.98	10.99	0.98	6.39	84.6	3	92	0	5	43	19.76	-24.22			Apr-18
	0.01	13.71	5.63	22.22	16.29	1.9	0.98	11.07	0.99	6.4	84.6	3	92	0	5	43	19.76	-24.22			Jul-15
	-0.14	13.71	5.46	21.96	16.02	1.9	0.99	11.03	0.98	6.4	84.6	3	92	0	5	43	19.76	-24.22			Jul-06
	-0.05	13.64	5.49	21.53	15.40	1.7	1.13	11.06	0.99	6.57	84.6	3	92	0	5	43	19.56	-24.21			Nov-07
50	1.50	13.11	-7.33	28.44	21.57	0.99	1.26	12.69	1.02	11.47	3,904	1	99	0	0	110	13.89	-21.91	5.50		Sep-07
50	1.28	12.61	-8.06	25.49	17.07	0.21	2.01	12.66	1.01	11.07	3,904	1	99	0	0	110	13.47	-22.11		1.00	Sep-07
	1.50	13.32	-6.99	29.98	24.02	1.51	0.86	12.76	1.02	11.48	3,904	1	99	0	0	110	14.26	-21.81			Apr-18
	1.59	13.42	-6.91	30.06	24.38	1.51	0.86	12.74	1.02	11.49	3,904	1	99	0	0	110	14.26	-21.81			Jul-15
	1.59	13.35	-7.02	29.93	23.97	1.5	0.87	12.69	1.02	11.46	3,904	1	99	0	0	110	14.26	-21.81			Sep-07
	1.51	13.30	-7.10	29.43	23.21	1.32	1.01	12.74	1.02	11.41	3,904	1	99	0	0	110	14.13	-21.83			Aug-10
50	1.73	11.92	-5.37	24.94	12.16	1.54	1.24	11.74	1.02	9.95	729.3	-1	101	0	0	177	13.01	-23.8	5.50		Jan-08
50	1.58	11.58	-6.12	22.08	8.08	0.7	1.99	11.71	1.02	9.63	729.3	-1	101	0	0	177	12.4	-24.03		1.00	Jan-08
	1.85	12.14	-5.06	26.51	14.54	2.05	0.89	11.72	1.02	9.88	729.3	-1	101	0	0	177	13.19	-23.54			Apr-18
	1.85	12.14	-5.06	26.39	14.44	2.04	0.89	11.73	1.02	9.88	729.3	-1	101	0	0	177	13.19	-23.55			Apr-18
	1.84	12.06	-5.09	26.35	14.40	1.48	0.9	11.72	1.02	9.94	729.3	-1	101	0	0	177	13.19	-23.54			Jan-08
	1.84	12.06	-5.20	25.83	13.49	1.87	0.99	11.75	1.03	9.94	729.3	-1	101	0	0	177	13.11	-23.66			Aug-10
50	3.46	19.50	6.03	56.77	74.27	0.27	0.92	13.82	1.02	30.76	2,046	1	99	0	0	188	25.85	-15.13	5.50		May-97
50	3.30	19.10	5.26	53.37	67.86	0	1.67	13.82	1.02	27.18	2,046	1	99	0	0	188	25.41	-15.44		1.00	Aug-97
	3.57	19.75	6.48	58.72	77.75	0.62	0.52	13.81	1.02	31.89	2,046	1	99	0	0	188	26.23	-14.94			Apr-18
	3.41	19.37	5.79	55.62	72.10	0	1.17	13.83	1.02	30	2,046	1	99	0	0	188	25.75	-15.2			Nov-07
	3.60	19.78	6.50	58.78	77.87	0.6	0.52	13.82	1.02	31.91	2,046	1	99	0	0	188	26.23	-14.94			Jul-15
	3.56	19.77	6.48	58.71	77.74	0.59	0.53	13.82	1.02	31.92	2,046	1	99	0	0	188	26.23	-14.94			May-97
	3.54	19.68	6.33	57.99	76.39	0.49	0.67	13.82	1.02	30.34	2,046	1	99	0	0	188	26.14	-15.08			Nov-07
	3.45	19.50	5.96	56.33	73.35	0.03	1.03	13.82	1.02	30.27	2,046	1	99	0	0	188	25.84	-15.13			May-97
50	3.59	16.87	8.00	29.09	26.45	0.85	1.11	12.15	0.98	14.68	496.0	1	99	0	0	171	24.17	-22.56	5.50		Dec-99
50	3.42	16.42	7.13	26.17	21.76	0	1.86	12.16	0.98	13.89	496.0	1	99	0	0	171	23.74	-22.89		1.00	Dec-99
	3.69	17.05	8.28	30.33	28.73	1.13	0.78	12.14	0.98	15.17	496.0	1	99	0	0	171	24.53	-22.49			Apr-18
	3.49	16.74	7.67	28.00	24.85	0.66	1.36	12.16	0.98	14.22	496.0	1	99	0	0	171	24.07	-22.65			Nov-07
	3.62	17.05	8.27	30.61	29.06	1.12	0.78	12.13	0.98	15.17	496.0	1	99	0	0	171	24.53	-22.49			Jul-15
	3.70	17.04	8.32	30.32	28.72	1.09	0.79	12.19	0.99	14.83	496.0	1	99	0	0	171	24.53	-22.49			Dec-99
	3.67	16.98	8.20	29.94	28.00	1.06	0.86	12.18	0.99	14.67	496.0	1	99	0	0	171	24.46	-22.54			Nov-07
	3.54	16.77	7.79	28.47	25.59	0.33	1.29	12.16	0.98	14.62	496.0	1	99	0	0	171	24.27	-22.67			Dec-99
50	1.08	13.58	1.84	37.67	42.35	1.25	0.95	13.15	1.07	20.92	497.8	3	97	0	0	202	23.01	-17.41	5.50		Dec-98
50	0.90	13.14	1.07	34.57	37.03	0.52	1.7	13.14	1.07	20.73	497.8	3	97	0	0	202	22.54	-17.67		1.00	Dec-98
	1.13	13.77	2.20	39.23	45.04	1.64	0.55	13.16	1.07	20.87	497.8	3	97	0	0	202	23.39	-17.32			Apr-18
	1.02	13.43	1.60	36.61	40.50	1.02	1.2	13.15	1.07	20.78	497.8	3	97	0	0	202	22.87	-17.51			Nov-07
	1.18	13.75	2.25	39.28	45.10	1.63	0.55	13.18	1.07	20.88	497.8	3	97	0	0	202	23.39	-17.32			Jul-15
	1.13	13.76	2.20	39.21	45.01	1.63	0.56	13.15	1.07	20.88	497.8	3	97	0	0	202	23.39	-17.32			Dec-98
	1.15	13.66	2.08	38.65	44.03	1.51	0.7	13.17	1.07	20.83	497.8	3	97	0	0	202	23.22	-17.31			Nov-07
	1.09	13.50	1.75	37.19	41.55	1.13	1.06	13.16	1.07	21.01	497.8	3	97	0	0	202	22.96	-17.46			Dec-98
	0.89	5.19	1.01	5.31	3.49	6.28	1.12	3.06	13.17	8.73	114.1	28	1	72	0	220	9.86	-2.61			Apr-18
	0.89	5.18	1.01	5.43	3.60	6.28	1.12	3.08	13.47	8.74	114.1	28	1	72	0	220	9.86	-2.61			Nov-17
	1.15	8.84	1.26	5.69	3.86	6.27	1.13	3.06	13.56	8.74	114.1	28	1	72	0	220	9.86	-2.61			Jun-09
50	4.46	4.46	5.68	3.00	15.34	0	1.59	6.99	48.14	10.52	236.4	983	53	-956	20	529			5.50		Feb-12
50	4.17	4.06	4.89	0.68	11.10	0	2.34	7.03	48.64	9.98	236.4	983	53	-956	20	529				1.00	Feb-12
	4.55	4.75	6.15	4.22	17.63	0	1.19	7.01	48.66	10.8	236.4	983	53	-956	20	529					Apr-18
	4.44	4.44	5.46	2.34	13.94	0	1.84	6.98	48.7	10.34	236.4	983	53	-956	20	529					Feb-12
	4.54	4.74	6.14	4.32	17.73	0	1.19	7.01	48.56	10.81	236.4	983	53	-956	20	529					Apr-18

	MARKET			FUND TYPE, CATEGORY & OBJECTIVE	RATINGS				MINIMUMS	
Fund Name	Ticker Symbol	Traded On	Fund Type	Category and (Prospectus Objective)	Overall Rating	Reward Rating	Risk Rating	Recent Up/ Downgrade	Open to New Investors	Min Initial Investment
Goldman Sachs Managed Futures Strategy Institutional Cls	GMSSX	NAS CM	Open End	Alternative Miscellaneous (Growth & Income)	C	C	B-	Up	Y	1,000,000
Goldman Sachs Managed Futures Strategy Fund Investor Class	GFIRX	NAS CM	Open End	Alternative Miscellaneous (Growth & Income)	C	C	B-	Up	Y	0
Goldman Sachs Mid Cap Value Fund Class A	GCMAX	NAS CM	Open End	US Equity Mid Cap (Growth)	C+	C	B		Y	1,000
Goldman Sachs Mid Cap Value Fund Class C	GCMCX	NAS CM	Open End	US Equity Mid Cap (Growth)	C+	C	B	Up	Y	1,000
Goldman Sachs Mid Cap Value Fund Class P	GMPPX	NAS CM	Open End	US Equity Mid Cap (Growth)	C+	C	B		Y	0
Goldman Sachs Mid Cap Value Fund Class R	GCMRX	NAS CM	Open End	US Equity Mid Cap (Growth)	C+	C	B	Up	Y	0
Goldman Sachs Mid Cap Value Fund Class R6	GCMUX	NAS CM	Open End	US Equity Mid Cap (Growth)	C+	C	B		Y	5,000,000
Goldman Sachs Mid Cap Value Fund Institutional Class	GSMCX	NAS CM	Open End	US Equity Mid Cap (Growth)	C+	C	B		Y	1,000,000
Goldman Sachs Mid Cap Value Fund Investor Class	GCMTX	NAS CM	Open End	US Equity Mid Cap (Growth)	C+	C	B		Y	0
Goldman Sachs Mid Cap Value Fund Service Class	GSMSX	NAS CM	Open End	US Equity Mid Cap (Growth)	C+	C	B	Up	Y	0
Goldman Sachs MLP & Energy Fund Class A Shares	GLEAX	NAS CM	Open End	Energy Sector Equity (Growth & Income)	C-	D+	C+	Up	Y	1,000
Goldman Sachs MLP & Energy Fund Class C Shares	GLECX	NAS CM	Open End	Energy Sector Equity (Growth & Income)	C-	D+	C	Up	Y	1,000
Goldman Sachs MLP & Energy Fund Class P	GAMPX	NAS CM	Open End	Energy Sector Equity (Growth & Income)	C-	D+	C+	Up	Y	0
Goldman Sachs MLP & Energy Fund Class R Shares	GLERX	NAS CM	Open End	Energy Sector Equity (Growth & Income)	C-	D+	C+	Up	Y	0
Goldman Sachs MLP & Energy Fund Class R6 Shares	GLESX	NAS CM	Open End	Energy Sector Equity (Growth & Income)	C-	D+	C+	Up	Y	5,000,000
Goldman Sachs MLP & Energy Fund Institutional Shares	GLEPX	NAS CM	Open End	Energy Sector Equity (Growth & Income)	C-	D+	C+	Up	Y	1,000,000
Goldman Sachs MLP & Energy Fund Investor Shares	GLEIX	NAS CM	Open End	Energy Sector Equity (Growth & Income)	C-	D+	C+	Up	Y	0
Goldman Sachs MLP and Energy Renaissance Fund	GER	NYSE	Closed End	Energy Sector Equity (Income)	D+	D+	C-	Down	Y	
Goldman Sachs MLP Energy Infrastructure Fund Class A	GLPAX	NAS CM	Open End	Energy Sector Equity (Growth & Income)	C-	C-	C	Down	Y	1,000
Goldman Sachs MLP Energy Infrastructure Fund Class C	GLPCX	NAS CM	Open End	Energy Sector Equity (Growth & Income)	C-	C-	C-	Down	Y	1,000
Goldman Sachs MLP Energy Infrastructure Fund Class P	GMNPX	NAS CM	Open End	Energy Sector Equity (Growth & Income)	C	C-	C		Y	0
Goldman Sachs MLP Energy Infrastructure Fund Class R	GLPRX	NAS CM	Open End	Energy Sector Equity (Growth & Income)	C-	C-	C-	Down	Y	0
Goldman Sachs MLP Energy Infrastructure Fund Class R6	GLPSX	NAS CM	Open End	Energy Sector Equity (Growth & Income)	C-	C-	C	Down	Y	5,000,000
Goldman Sachs MLP Energy Infrastructure Institutional Cls	GMLPX	NAS CM	Open End	Energy Sector Equity (Growth & Income)	C-	C-	C	Down	Y	1,000,000
Goldman Sachs MLP Energy Infrastructure Investor Cls	GLPIX	NAS CM	Open End	Energy Sector Equity (Growth & Income)	C-	C-	C	Down	Y	0
Goldman Sachs MLP Income Opportunities Fund	GMZ	NYSE	Closed End	Energy Sector Equity (Income)	C-	D+	C-	Down	Y	
Goldman Sachs Multi-Manager Alternatives Fund Class A	GMAMX	NAS CM	Open End	Multialternative (Growth)	C	C	B-		Y	1,000
Goldman Sachs Multi-Manager Alternatives Fund Class C	GMCMX	NAS CM	Open End	Multialternative (Growth)	C	C-	C+	Up	Y	1,000
Goldman Sachs Multi-Manager Alternatives Fund Class P	GMMPX	NAS CM	Open End	Multialternative (Growth)	C	C	B		Y	0
Goldman Sachs Multi-Manager Alternatives Fund Class R	GRMMX	NAS CM	Open End	Multialternative (Growth)	C	C-	B-	Up	Y	0
Goldman Sachs Multi-Manager Alternatives Fund Class R6	GMMFX	NAS CM	Open End	Multialternative (Growth)	C	C	B		Y	5,000,000
Goldman Sachs Multi-Manager Alternatives Institutional Cls	GSMMX	NAS CM	Open End	Multialternative (Growth)	C	C	B		Y	1,000,000
Goldman Sachs Multi-Manager Alternatives Investor Cls	GIMMX	NAS CM	Open End	Multialternative (Growth)	C	C	B		Y	0
Goldman Sachs N-11 Equity Fund Class A	GSYAX	NAS CM	Open End	Global Emerg Mkts (Growth)	D+	D	C-	Down		1,000
Goldman Sachs N-11 Equity Fund Class C	GSYCX	NAS CM	Open End	Global Emerg Mkts (Growth)	D	D	C-	Down		1,000
Goldman Sachs N-11 Equity Fund Class P	GMKPX	NAS CM	Open End	Global Emerg Mkts (Growth)	D+	D	C-	Down	Y	0
Goldman Sachs N-11 Equity Fund Class R6	GSYFX	NAS CM	Open End	Global Emerg Mkts (Growth)	D+	D	C-	Down	Y	5,000,000
Goldman Sachs N-11 Equity Fund Institutional Class	GSYIX	NAS CM	Open End	Global Emerg Mkts (Growth)	D+	D	C-	Down		1,000,000
Goldman Sachs N-11 Equity Fund Investor Class	GSYRX	NAS CM	Open End	Global Emerg Mkts (Growth)	D+	D	C-	Down		0
Goldman Sachs Real Estate Securities Fund Class A	GREAX	NAS CM	Open End	Real Estate Sector Equity (Real Estate)	C+	C	B-	Down	Y	1,000
Goldman Sachs Real Estate Securities Fund Class C	GRECX	NAS CM	Open End	Real Estate Sector Equity (Real Estate)	C+	C	B-	Down	Y	1,000
Goldman Sachs Real Estate Securities Fund Class P	GMJPX	NAS CM	Open End	Real Estate Sector Equity (Real Estate)	C+	C	B-	Down	Y	0
Goldman Sachs Real Estate Securities Fund Class R	GRERX	NAS CM	Open End	Real Estate Sector Equity (Real Estate)	C+	C	B-	Down	Y	0
Goldman Sachs Real Estate Securities Fund Class R6	GREUX	NAS CM	Open End	Real Estate Sector Equity (Real Estate)	C+	C	B-	Down	Y	5,000,000
Goldman Sachs Real Estate Securities Institutional Cls	GREIX	NAS CM	Open End	Real Estate Sector Equity (Real Estate)	C+	C	B-	Down	Y	1,000,000
Goldman Sachs Real Estate Securities Fund Investor Class	GRETX	NAS CM	Open End	Real Estate Sector Equity (Real Estate)	C+	C	B-	Down	Y	0
Goldman Sachs Real Estate Securities Fund Service Class	GRESX	NAS CM	Open End	Real Estate Sector Equity (Real Estate)	C+	C	B-	Down	Y	0
Goldman Sachs Rising Dividend Growth Fund Class A	GSRAX	NAS CM	Open End	US Equity Large Cap Blend (Equity-Income)	C+	C	B	Down	Y	1,000
Goldman Sachs Rising Dividend Growth Fund Class C	GSRCX	NAS CM	Open End	US Equity Large Cap Blend (Equity-Income)	C+	C	B		Y	1,000
Goldman Sachs Rising Dividend Growth Fund Class P	GMHPX	NAS CM	Open End	US Equity Large Cap Blend (Equity-Income)	C+	C	B	Down	Y	0
Goldman Sachs Rising Dividend Growth Fund Class R	GSRRX	NAS CM	Open End	US Equity Large Cap Blend (Equity-Income)	C+	C	B	Down	Y	0
Goldman Sachs Rising Dividend Growth Fund Class R6	GSRFX	NAS CM	Open End	US Equity Large Cap Blend (Equity-Income)	C+	C	B	Down	Y	5,000,000

★ Expanded analysis of this fund is included in Section II.

	TOTAL RETURNS					PERFORMANCE				ASSETS		ASSET ALLOCATION & TURNOVER					BULL & BEAR		FEES		
Min Additional Investment	3-Month Total Return	6-Month Total Return	1-Year Total Return	3-Year Total Return	5-Year Total Return	Dividend Yield (TTM)	Expense Ratio	3-Yr Std Deviation	3-Year Beta	NAV	Total Assets (MIL)	%Cash	%Stocks	%Bonds	%Other	Turnover Ratio	Last Bull Market Total Return	Last Bear Market Total Return	Front End Fee (%)	Back End Fee (%)	Inception Date
	4.44	4.65	6.14	4.22	17.63	0	1.2	6.99	49.51	10.8	236.4	983	53	-956	20	529					Feb-12
	4.49	4.69	6.00	3.85	16.81	0	1.34	7	49.83	10.7	236.4	983	53	-956	20	529					Feb-12
50	5.30	22.01	7.23	31.88	27.42	0.38	1.22	12.26	0.92	32.37	1,251	2	98	0	0	137	23.76	-22.25	5.50		Aug-97
50	5.11	21.57	6.43	28.96	22.74	0	1.97	12.24	0.92	28.18	1,251	2	98	0	0	137	23.2	-22.49		1.00	Aug-97
	5.40	22.24	7.67	33.51	30.02	0.76	0.82	12.28	0.92	32.75	1,251	2	98	0	0	137	24	-22.12			Apr-18
	5.25	21.87	6.97	30.92	25.85	0.16	1.47	12.26	0.92	31.26	1,251	2	98	0	0	137	23.57	-22.34			Jan-09
	5.40	22.28	7.66	33.48	30.05	0.73	0.82	12.27	0.92	32.76	1,251	2	98	0	0	137	24	-22.12			Jul-15
	5.40	22.26	7.68	33.48	30.00	0.72	0.83	12.26	0.92	32.78	1,251	2	98	0	0	137	24	-22.12			Aug-95
	5.37	22.16	7.53	32.89	29.05	0.62	0.97	12.27	0.92	31.58	1,251	2	98	0	0	137	23.92	-22.19			Nov-07
	5.29	21.98	7.14	31.48	26.79	0.27	1.33	12.28	0.92	31.63	1,251	2	98	0	0	137	23.67	-22.28			Jul-97
50	-0.65	22.36	1.60			2.95	1.61			9.84	54.4	0	100	0	0	67			5.50		Sep-17
50	-0.90	21.80	0.80			2.17	2.36			9.84	54.4	0	100	0	0	67				1.00	Sep-17
	-0.56	22.60	2.00			3.33	1.21			9.84	54.4	0	100	0	0	67					Apr-18
	-0.72	22.15	1.32			2.67	1.86			9.84	54.4	0	100	0	0	67					Sep-17
	-0.46	22.72	2.09			3.31	1.21			9.85	54.4	0	100	0	0	67					Sep-17
	-0.46	22.71	2.08			3.3	1.22			9.85	54.4	0	100	0	0	67					Sep-17
	-0.54	22.61	1.93			3.16	1.36			9.85	54.4	0	100	0	0	67					Sep-17
	-1.57	31.99	0.53	6.85		0	2.44	28.42	1.64	5.85	463.6	0	100	0	0	61					Sep-14
50	-0.73	19.28	-0.33	0.08	-32.21	7.66	1.71	17.33	1.01	6.51	2,152	1	99	0	0	68			5.50		Mar-13
50	-0.94	18.79	-1.11	-2.19	-34.75	8.11	2.46	17.39	1.01	6.15	2,152	1	99	0	0	68				1.00	Mar-13
	-0.71	21.70	1.83	2.92	-29.67	11.1	1.31	17.72	1.02	6.72	2,152	1	99	0	0	68					Apr-18
	-0.75	19.27	-0.48	-0.61	-33.08	7.81	1.96	17.36	1.01	6.39	2,152	1	99	0	0	68					Mar-13
	-0.57	19.65	0.10	1.18	-30.87	7.43	1.31	17.33	1.01	6.71	2,152	1	99	0	0	68					Apr-18
	-0.57	19.65	0.10	1.18	-30.87	7.43	1.32	17.37	1.01	6.71	2,152	1	99	0	0	68					Mar-13
	-0.72	19.68	-0.04	0.77	-31.36	7.51	1.46	17.37	1.01	6.64	2,152	1	99	0	0	68					Mar-13
	-3.20	26.33	-1.98	7.42	-43.05	0	1.75	26.05	1.5	8.22	365.2	2	98	0	0	64					Nov-13
50	2.14	6.50	4.17	5.49	0.51	0	2.17	3.2	20.99	10.48	318.8	59	36	4	0	232			5.50		Apr-13
50	2.01	6.17	3.46	3.17	-3.10	0	2.92	3.15	20.76	10.14	318.8	59	36	4	0	232				1.00	Apr-13
	2.31	6.74	4.53	6.69	2.45	0	1.83	3.19	20.48	10.61	318.8	59	36	4	0	232					Apr-18
	2.16	6.46	4.00	4.75	-0.68	0	2.42	3.17	19.96	10.38	318.8	59	36	4	0	232					Apr-13
	2.31	6.84	4.63	6.79	2.54	0	1.83	3.19	20.73	10.62	318.8	59	36	4	0	232					Feb-18
	2.21	6.74	4.53	6.69	2.45	0	1.84	3.19	20.9	10.61	318.8	59	36	4	0	232					Apr-13
	2.32	6.77	4.55	6.35	1.86	0	1.92	3.2	20.41	10.56	318.8	59	36	4	0	232					Apr-13
50	0.68	8.49	-1.08	1.87	-22.69	0.66	1.74	14.28		8.81	29.4	1	99	0	0	11	12.8	-19.89	5.50		Feb-11
50	0.47	8.11	-1.87	-0.35	-25.55	0	2.49	14.29		8.39	29.4	1	99	0	0	11	12.3	-20.18		1.00	Feb-11
	0.79	8.73	-0.72	3.04	-21.23	1.4	1.34	14.28		8.84	29.4	1	99	0	0	11	13.11	-19.78			Apr-18
	0.79	8.72	-0.63	3.14	-21.16	1.38	1.34	14.24		8.85	29.4	1	99	0	0	11	13.11	-19.78			Feb-18
	0.79	8.72	-0.72	3.04	-21.23	1.29	1.35	14.26		8.85	29.4	1	99	0	0	11	13.11	-19.78			Feb-11
	0.79	8.57	-0.90	2.65	-21.76	0.82	1.49	14.32		8.86	29.4	1	99	0	0	11	13.01	-19.8			Feb-11
50	2.06	18.18	10.05	10.09	36.21	2.05	1.3	13.01	0.99	14.74	168.1	3	97	0	0	43	32.45	-16.14	5.50		Jul-98
50	1.88	17.75	9.16	7.60	31.16	1.51	2.05	13	0.99	14.01	168.1	3	97	0	0	43	31.82	-16.4		1.00	Jul-98
	2.16	18.40	10.45	11.39	38.86	2.24	0.9	13.01	0.99	15.25	168.1	3	97	0	0	43	32.76	-15.97			Apr-18
	2.02	18.10	9.80	9.29	34.50	1.9	1.55	12.97	0.99	14.57	168.1	3	97	0	0	43	32.29	-16.24			Nov-07
	2.22	18.48	10.44	11.48	38.99	2.23	0.9	12.99	0.99	15.26	168.1	3	97	0	0	43	32.76	-15.97			Jul-15
	2.22	18.47	10.50	11.43	38.91	2.22	0.91	12.98	0.99	15.26	168.1	3	97	0	0	43	32.76	-15.97			Jul-98
	2.17	18.38	10.35	10.92	37.86	2.18	1.05	12.98	0.99	14.88	168.1	3	97	0	0	43	32.57	-16.11			Nov-07
	2.02	18.14	9.87	9.72	35.46	1.96	1.41	13.04	1	14.86	168.1	3	97	0	0	43	32.37	-16.16			Jul-98
50	4.45	19.05	9.04	34.23	34.89	1.87	1.1	12.88	1.02	11.14	808.3	2	98	0	0	101	19.34	-12.36	5.50		Mar-04
50	4.16	18.51	8.17	31.19	29.39	1.28	1.85	12.85	1.02	11.32	808.3	2	98	0	0	101	18.99	-12.46		1.00	Apr-05
	4.49	19.15	9.43	34.77	35.43	2.08	0.76	12.86	1.02	11.71	808.3	2	98	0	0	101	19.34	-12.36			Apr-18
	4.31	18.89	8.72	33.15	32.49	1.68	1.35	12.85	1.02	11.09	808.3	2	98	0	0	101	19.2	-12.45			Feb-12
	4.49	19.16	9.45	34.87	35.53	2.08	0.76	12.85	1.02	11.71	808.3	2	98	0	0	101	19.34	-12.36			Feb-18

	MARKET		FUND TYPE, CATEGORY & OBJECTIVE		RATINGS				MINIMUMS	
Fund Name	Ticker Symbol	Traded On	Fund Type	Category and (Prospectus Objective)	Overall Rating	Reward Rating	Risk Rating	Recent Up/ Downgrade	Open to New Investors	Min Initial Investment
Goldman Sachs Rising Dividend Growth Institutional Cls	GSRLX	NAS CM	Open End	US Equity Large Cap Blend (Equity-Income)	C+	C	B	Down	Y	1,000,000
Goldman Sachs Rising Dividend Growth Fund Investor Class	GSRIX	NAS CM	Open End	US Equity Large Cap Blend (Equity-Income)	C+	C	B	Down	Y	0
Goldman Sachs Satellite Strategies Portfolio Class A	GXSAX	NAS CM	Open End	Moderate Alloc (Growth)	C+	C	B	Up	Y	1,000
Goldman Sachs Satellite Strategies Portfolio Class C	GXSCX	NAS CM	Open End	Moderate Alloc (Growth)	C+	C	B	Up	Y	1,000
Goldman Sachs Satellite Strategies Portfolio Class P	GMFPX	NAS CM	Open End	Moderate Alloc (Growth)	B-	C	B	Up	Y	0
Goldman Sachs Satellite Strategies Portfolio Class R	GXSRX	NAS CM	Open End	Moderate Alloc (Growth)	C+	C	B	Up	Y	0
Goldman Sachs Satellite Strategies Portfolio Class R6	GXSUX	NAS CM	Open End	Moderate Alloc (Growth)	B-	C	B	Up	Y	5,000,000
Goldman Sachs Satellite Strategies Portfolio Inst Cls	GXSIX	NAS CM	Open End	Moderate Alloc (Growth)	B-	C	B	Up	Y	1,000,000
Goldman Sachs Satellite Strategies Portfolio Investor Cls	GXSTX	NAS CM	Open End	Moderate Alloc (Growth)	B-	C	B	Up	Y	0
Goldman Sachs Satellite Strategies Portfolio Service Class	GXSSX	NAS CM	Open End	Moderate Alloc (Growth)	C+	C	B	Up	Y	0
Goldman Sachs Small Cap Equity Insights Fund Class A	GCSAX	NAS CM	Open End	US Equity Small Cap (Small Company)	C	C	C+		Y	1,000
Goldman Sachs Small Cap Equity Insights Fund Class C	GCSCX	NAS CM	Open End	US Equity Small Cap (Small Company)	C	C	C+		Y	1,000
Goldman Sachs Small Cap Equity Insights Fund Class P	GMAPX	NAS CM	Open End	US Equity Small Cap (Small Company)	C	C	C+		Y	0
Goldman Sachs Small Cap Equity Insights Fund Class R	GDSRX	NAS CM	Open End	US Equity Small Cap (Small Company)	C	C	C+		Y	0
Goldman Sachs Small Cap Equity Insights Fund Class R6	GCSUX	NAS CM	Open End	US Equity Small Cap (Small Company)	C	C	C+		Y	5,000,000
Goldman Sachs Small Cap Equity Insights Institutional Cls	GCSIX	NAS CM	Open End	US Equity Small Cap (Small Company)	C	C	C+		Y	1,000,000
Goldman Sachs Small Cap Equity Insights Investor Cls	GDSTX	NAS CM	Open End	US Equity Small Cap (Small Company)	C	C	C+		Y	0
Goldman Sachs Small Cap Equity Insights Fund Service Class	GCSSX	NAS CM	Open End	US Equity Small Cap (Small Company)	C	C	C+		Y	0
Goldman Sachs Small Cap Growth Insights Fund Class A	GSAOX	NAS CM	Open End	US Equity Small Cap (Small Company)	C	C	C+	Down	Y	1,000
Goldman Sachs Small Cap Growth Insights Fund Class C	GSCOX	NAS CM	Open End	US Equity Small Cap (Small Company)	C	C	C+	Down	Y	1,000
Goldman Sachs Small Cap Growth Insights Fund Class P	GSZPX	NAS CM	Open End	US Equity Small Cap (Small Company)	C	C	C+	Down	Y	0
Goldman Sachs Small Cap Growth Insights Fund Class R	GSROX	NAS CM	Open End	US Equity Small Cap (Small Company)	C	C	C+	Down	Y	0
Goldman Sachs Small Cap Growth Insights Fund Class R6	GINUX	NAS CM	Open End	US Equity Small Cap (Small Company)	C	C	C+	Down	Y	5,000,000
Goldman Sachs Small Cap Growth Insights Institutional Cls	GSIOX	NAS CM	Open End	US Equity Small Cap (Small Company)	C	C	C+	Down	Y	1,000,000
Goldman Sachs Small Cap Growth Insights Investor Cls	GSTOX	NAS CM	Open End	US Equity Small Cap (Small Company)	C	C	C+	Down	Y	0
Goldman Sachs Small Cap Value Fund Class A	GSSMX	NAS CM	Open End	US Equity Small Cap (Small Company)	C	C	C+			1,000
Goldman Sachs Small Cap Value Fund Class C	GSSCX	NAS CM	Open End	US Equity Small Cap (Small Company)	C	C	C+			1,000
Goldman Sachs Small Cap Value Fund Class P	GSYPX	NAS CM	Open End	US Equity Small Cap (Small Company)	C	C	B-		Y	0
Goldman Sachs Small Cap Value Fund Class R	GSQRX	NAS CM	Open End	US Equity Small Cap (Small Company)	C	C	C+			0
Goldman Sachs Small Cap Value Fund Class R6	GSSUX	NAS CM	Open End	US Equity Small Cap (Small Company)	C	C	B-		Y	5,000,000
Goldman Sachs Small Cap Value Fund Institutional Class	GSSIX	NAS CM	Open End	US Equity Small Cap (Small Company)	C	C	B-			1,000,000
Goldman Sachs Small Cap Value Fund Investor Class	GSQTX	NAS CM	Open End	US Equity Small Cap (Small Company)	C	C	C+			0
Goldman Sachs Small Cap Value Fund Service Class	GSSSX	NAS CM	Open End	US Equity Small Cap (Small Company)	C	C	C+			0
Goldman Sachs Small Cap Value Insights Fund Class A	GSATX	NAS CM	Open End	US Equity Small Cap (Small Company)	C	C-	C		Y	1,000
Goldman Sachs Small Cap Value Insights Fund Class C	GSCTX	NAS CM	Open End	US Equity Small Cap (Small Company)	C	C-	C		Y	1,000
Goldman Sachs Small Cap Value Insights Fund Class P	GSXPX	NAS CM	Open End	US Equity Small Cap (Small Company)	C	C-	C+		Y	0
Goldman Sachs Small Cap Value Insights Fund Class R	GTTRX	NAS CM	Open End	US Equity Small Cap (Small Company)	C	C-	C		Y	0
Goldman Sachs Small Cap Value Insights Fund Class R6	GTTUX	NAS CM	Open End	US Equity Small Cap (Small Company)	C	C-	C+		Y	5,000,000
Goldman Sachs Small Cap Value Insights Institutional Cls	GSITX	NAS CM	Open End	US Equity Small Cap (Small Company)	C	C-	C+		Y	1,000,000
Goldman Sachs Small Cap Value Insights Fund Investor Class	GTTTX	NAS CM	Open End	US Equity Small Cap (Small Company)	C	C-	C		Y	0
Goldman Sachs Small/Mid Cap Growth Fund Class A	GSMAX	NAS CM	Open End	US Equity Mid Cap (Growth)	C+	C+	B-	Down	Y	1,000
Goldman Sachs Small/Mid Cap Growth Fund Class C	GSMGX	NAS CM	Open End	US Equity Mid Cap (Growth)	C+	C	B-	Down	Y	1,000
Goldman Sachs Small/Mid Cap Growth Fund Class P	GSWPX	NAS CM	Open End	US Equity Mid Cap (Growth)	C+	C+	B-	Down	Y	0
Goldman Sachs Small/Mid Cap Growth Fund Class R	GTMRX	NAS CM	Open End	US Equity Mid Cap (Growth)	C+	C+	B-	Down	Y	0
Goldman Sachs Small/Mid Cap Growth Fund Class R6	GTMUX	NAS CM	Open End	US Equity Mid Cap (Growth)	C+	C+	B-	Down	Y	5,000,000
Goldman Sachs Small/Mid Cap Growth Institutional Cls	GSMYX	NAS CM	Open End	US Equity Mid Cap (Growth)	C+	C+	B-	Down	Y	1,000,000
Goldman Sachs Small/Mid Cap Growth Fund Investor Class	GTMTX	NAS CM	Open End	US Equity Mid Cap (Growth)	C+	C+	B-	Down	Y	0
Goldman Sachs Small/Mid Cap Growth Fund Service Class	GSMQX	NAS CM	Open End	US Equity Mid Cap (Growth)	C+	C+	B-	Down	Y	0
Goldman Sachs Small/Mid Cap Value Fund Class A	GMVAX	NAS CM	Open End	US Equity Mid Cap (Growth)	C	C	B-		Y	1,000
Goldman Sachs Small/Mid Cap Value Fund Class C	GMVCX	NAS CM	Open End	US Equity Mid Cap (Growth)	C	C	B-		Y	1,000
Goldman Sachs Small/Mid Cap Value Fund Class P	GSVPX	NAS CM	Open End	US Equity Mid Cap (Growth)	C	C	B-		Y	0
Goldman Sachs Small/Mid Cap Value Fund Class R	GMVRX	NAS CM	Open End	US Equity Mid Cap (Growth)	C	C	B-		Y	0

★ Expanded analysis of this fund is included in Section II.

	TOTAL RETURNS					PERFORMANCE				ASSETS		ASSET ALLOCATION & TURNOVER					BULL & BEAR		FEES		
Min Additional Investment	3-Month Total Return	6-Month Total Return	1-Year Total Return	3-Year Total Return	5-Year Total Return	Dividend Yield (TTM)	Expense Ratio	3-Yr Std Deviation	3-Year Beta	NAV	Total Assets (MIL)	%Cash	%Stocks	%Bonds	%Other	Turnover Ratio	Last Bull Market Total Return	Last Bear Market Total Return	Front End Fee (%)	Back End Fee (%)	Inception Date
	4.49	19.14	9.42	35.72	36.83	2.07	0.77	12.86	1.02	11.71	808.3	2	98	0	0	101	19.65	-12.11			Mar-07
	4.47	19.05	9.28	35.13	35.83	1.97	0.85	12.85	1.02	11.69	808.3	2	98	0	0	101	19.44	-12.36			Feb-12
50	2.54	13.15	5.13	17.21	10.70	2.56	1.42	7.84		8.23	364.7	4	58	36	1	17	14.18	-13.56	5.50		Mar-07
50	2.40	12.84	4.34	14.78	6.59	1.69	2.17	7.9		8.2	364.7	4	58	36	1	17	13.84	-13.95		1.00	Mar-07
	2.64	13.37	5.55	18.71	12.90	2.94	1.02	7.89		8.22	364.7	4	58	36	1	17	14.57	-13.5			Apr-18
	2.47	13.04	4.85	16.55	9.37	2.29	1.67	7.85		8.2	364.7	4	58	36	1	17	14.24	-13.69			Nov-07
	2.64	13.53	5.55	18.74	13.09	2.94	1.02	7.92		8.22	364.7	4	58	36	1	17	14.57	-13.5			Jul-15
	2.64	13.38	5.54	18.69	12.88	2.93	1.03	7.9		8.21	364.7	4	58	36	1	17	14.57	-13.5			Mar-07
	2.72	13.44	5.51	18.30	12.16	2.78	1.17	7.96		8.22	364.7	4	58	36	1	17	14.49	-13.55			Nov-07
	2.51	13.09	4.99	16.99	10.09	2.42	1.53	7.87		8.22	364.7	4	58	36	1	17	14.19	-13.64			Aug-08
50	2.24	17.30	-4.38	42.23	45.63	0	1.23	16.86	0.97	25.01	644.6	3	97	0	0	111	27.47	-22.81	5.50		Aug-97
50	2.06	16.91	-5.08	39.13	40.24	0	1.98	16.83	0.97	21.29	644.6	3	97	0	0	111	27.01	-23.11		1.00	Aug-97
	2.35	17.53	-3.98	43.98	48.56	0.23	0.83	16.87	0.98	26.07	644.6	3	97	0	0	111	27.8	-22.71			Apr-18
	2.17	17.20	-4.59	41.18	43.80	0	1.48	16.86	0.98	24.39	644.6	3	97	0	0	111	27.31	-22.95			Nov-07
	2.35	17.53	-3.99	44.02	48.66	0.22	0.83	16.86	0.98	26.07	644.6	3	97	0	0	111	27.8	-22.71			Jul-15
	2.31	17.53	-4.01	43.94	48.52	0.2	0.84	16.87	0.98	26.07	644.6	3	97	0	0	111	27.8	-22.71			Aug-97
	2.30	17.47	-4.15	43.35	47.46	0.19	0.98	16.87	0.98	24.87	644.6	3	97	0	0	111	27.64	-22.73			Nov-07
	2.20	17.27	-4.48	41.77	44.83	0	1.34	16.88	0.98	24.58	644.6	3	97	0	0	111	27.37	-22.87			Aug-97
50	2.57	20.37	-1.85	51.44	53.08	0	1.23	17.2	0.97	35.09	1,156	3	97	0	0	127	28.92	-23.35	5.50		Jun-07
50	2.38	19.93	-2.56	48.06	47.48	0	1.98	17.19	0.97	26.23	1,156	3	97	0	0	127	28.34	-23.61		1.00	Jun-07
	2.67	20.61	-1.44	53.17	56.12	0	0.83	17.21	0.98	41.9	1,156	3	97	0	0	127	29.19	-23.22			Apr-18
	2.50	20.20	-2.09	50.26	51.18	0	1.48	17.2	0.97	33.61	1,156	3	97	0	0	127	28.74	-23.46			Nov-07
	2.67	20.61	-1.46	53.22	56.22	0	0.83	17.2	0.97	41.9	1,156	3	97	0	0	127	29.19	-23.22			Jul-15
	2.67	20.62	-1.46	53.17	56.12	0	0.84	17.21	0.98	41.88	1,156	3	97	0	0	127	29.19	-23.22			Jun-07
	2.64	20.54	-1.60	52.56	55.02	0	0.98	17.2	0.97	36.14	1,156	3	97	0	0	127	29.15	-23.29			Nov-07
50	3.10	16.75	-2.17	34.02	31.82	0.03	1.33	16.02	0.91	49.47	5,988	2	98	0	0	55	30.56	-22.84	5.50		Oct-92
50	2.91	16.31	-2.91	31.05	26.98	0	2.08	16.01	0.91	35.65	5,988	2	98	0	0	55	29.99	-23.08		1.00	Aug-97
	3.21	16.97	-1.78	34.66	32.46	0.39	0.93	16.02	0.91	53.97	5,988	2	98	0	0	55	30.56	-22.84			Apr-18
	3.03	16.60	-2.42	33.02	30.19	0	1.58	16.02	0.91	48.18	5,988	2	98	0	0	55	30.39	-22.93			Nov-07
	3.21	16.97	-1.79	35.68	33.95	0.38	0.93	16.02	0.91	53.97	5,988	2	98	0	0	55	30.56	-22.84			Jul-15
	3.21	16.98	-1.79	35.63	34.48	0.37	0.94	16.02	0.91	54	5,988	2	98	0	0	55	30.88	-22.71			Aug-97
	3.17	16.88	-1.92	35.04	33.48	0.27	1.08	16.03	0.91	49.07	5,988	2	98	0	0	55	30.78	-22.76			Nov-07
	3.06	16.68	-2.29	33.60	31.14	0	1.44	16.02	0.91	47.69	5,988	2	98	0	0	55	30.51	-22.9			Aug-97
50	1.90	14.60	-6.69	36.92	38.25	0.44	1.23	17.12	0.98	38.44	477.7	3	97	0	0	130	25.72	-21.91	5.50		Jun-07
50	1.73	14.15	-7.36	33.91	33.23	0	1.98	17.1	0.98	26.45	477.7	3	97	0	0	130	25.15	-22.14		1.00	Jun-07
	2.00	14.80	-6.33	38.54	41.02	0.61	0.83	17.11	0.98	51.96	477.7	3	97	0	0	130	25.99	-21.77			Apr-18
	1.83	14.42	-6.93	35.86	36.49	0.31	1.48	17.1	0.98	37.76	477.7	3	97	0	0	130	25.5	-21.97			Nov-07
	2.00	14.80	-6.32	38.57	41.05	0.61	0.83	17.1	0.98	51.96	477.7	3	97	0	0	130	25.99	-21.77			Jul-15
	2.00	14.79	-6.33	38.52	41.00	0.58	0.84	17.1	0.98	51.98	477.7	3	97	0	0	130	25.99	-21.77			Jun-07
	1.94	14.69	-6.48	37.91	39.97	0.74	0.98	17.1	0.98	38.24	477.7	3	97	0	0	130	25.86	-21.81			Nov-07
50	7.08	29.92	12.83	57.90	59.62	0	1.24	15.05	0.88	20.71	2,102	4	96	0	0	59	30.83	-22.87	5.50		Jun-05
50	6.95	29.39	11.99	54.37	53.79	0	1.99	15.1	0.89	17.08	2,102	4	96	0	0	59	30.26	-23.06		1.00	Jun-05
	7.16	30.08	13.24	59.62	62.70	0	0.91	15.07	0.88	22.57	2,102	4	96	0	0	59	31.11	-22.76			Apr-18
	7.04	29.74	12.53	56.63	57.63	0	1.49	15.06	0.88	19.76	2,102	4	96	0	0	59	30.61	-22.93			Nov-07
	7.22	30.16	13.24	59.67	62.76	0	0.91	15.09	0.89	22.57	2,102	4	96	0	0	59	31.11	-22.76			Jul-15
	7.17	30.12	13.19	59.56	62.64	0	0.92	15.08	0.89	22.55	2,102	4	96	0	0	59	31.11	-22.76			Jun-05
	7.15	30.07	13.13	59.05	61.71	0	0.99	15.08	0.89	21.71	2,102	4	96	0	0	59	31	-22.73			Nov-07
	7.05	29.74	12.65	57.17	58.58	0	1.42	15.08	0.89	20.02	2,102	4	96	0	0	59	30.75	-22.91			Jun-05
50	3.45	18.55	0.41	31.55	28.50	0.18	1.23	14.06	0.92	12.27	124.0	3	97	0	0	105			5.50		Jan-14
50	3.19	18.08	-0.36	28.57	23.91	0	1.98	14.08	0.92	11.95	124.0	3	97	0	0	105				1.00	Jan-14
	3.58	18.92	0.88	33.19	31.25	0.43	0.83	14.11	0.92	12.44	124.0	3	97	0	0	105					Apr-18
	3.37	18.49	0.17	30.54	26.91	0.05	1.48	14.08	0.92	12.24	124.0	3	97	0	0	105					Jan-14

	MARKET			FUND TYPE, CATEGORY & OBJECTIVE	RATINGS				MINIMUMS	
Fund Name	Ticker Symbol	Traded On	Fund Type	Category and (Prospectus Objective)	Overall Rating	Reward Rating	Risk Rating	Recent Up/ Downgrade	Open to New Investors	Min Initial Investment
Goldman Sachs Small/Mid Cap Value Fund Class R6	GMCUX	NAS CM	Open End	US Equity Mid Cap (Growth)	C	C	B-		Y	5,000,000
Goldman Sachs Small/Mid Cap Value Fund Institutional Class	GSMVX	NAS CM	Open End	US Equity Mid Cap (Growth)	C	C	B-		Y	1,000,000
Goldman Sachs Small/Mid Cap Value Fund Investor Class	GMVIX	NAS CM	Open End	US Equity Mid Cap (Growth)	C	C	B-		Y	0
Goldman Sachs Strategic Factor Allocation Fund Class P	GSQPX	NAS CM	Open End	Moderate Alloc (Growth & Income)	D+	D	C-	Up	Y	0
Goldman Sachs Strategic Factor Allocation Cls R6 Shares	SRAFX	NAS CM	Open End	Moderate Alloc (Growth & Income)	D+	D	C-	Up	Y	5,000,000
Goldman Sachs Strategic Factor Allocation Inst Shares	SFAFX	NAS CM	Open End	Moderate Alloc (Growth & Income)	C	C-	B		Y	1,000,000
Goldman Sachs Strategic Growth Fund Class A	GGRAX	NAS CM	Open End	US Equity Large Cap Growth (Growth)	B-	C+	B	Down	Y	1,000
Goldman Sachs Strategic Growth Fund Class C	GGRCX	NAS CM	Open End	US Equity Large Cap Growth (Growth)	C+	C+	B	Down	Y	1,000
Goldman Sachs Strategic Growth Fund Class P	GSPPX	NAS CM	Open End	US Equity Large Cap Growth (Growth)	B-	C+	B	Down	Y	0
Goldman Sachs Strategic Growth Fund Class R	GSTRX	NAS CM	Open End	US Equity Large Cap Growth (Growth)	B-	C+	B	Down	Y	0
Goldman Sachs Strategic Growth Fund Class R6	GGRUX	NAS CM	Open End	US Equity Large Cap Growth (Growth)	B-	C+	B	Down	Y	5,000,000
Goldman Sachs Strategic Growth Fund Institutional Class	GSTIX	NAS CM	Open End	US Equity Large Cap Growth (Growth)	B-	C+	B	Down	Y	1,000,000
Goldman Sachs Strategic Growth Fund Investor Class	GSTTX	NAS CM	Open End	US Equity Large Cap Growth (Growth)	B-	C+	B	Down	Y	0
Goldman Sachs Strategic Growth Fund Service Class	GSTSX	NAS CM	Open End	US Equity Large Cap Growth (Growth)	C+	C+	B	Down	Y	0
Goldman Sachs Tactical Exposure Fund Class P	GSMPX	NAS CM	Open End	Alloc Miscellaneous (Growth & Income)	D	D+	C	Up		0
Goldman Sachs Tactical Tilt Overlay Fund Class P	GSLPX	NAS CM	Open End	Moderate Alloc (Growth & Income)	B-	C	B+		Y	0
Goldman Sachs Tactical Tilt Overlay Institutional Shares	TTIFX	NAS CM	Open End	Moderate Alloc (Growth & Income)	B-	C	B+		Y	1,000,000
Goldman Sachs Target Date 2020 Portfolio A Shares	GTAHX	NAS CM	Open End	Target Date (Asset Alloc)	B	C+	A-		Y	1,000
Goldman Sachs Target Date 2020 Portfolio Inst Shares	GTIHX	NAS CM	Open End	Target Date (Asset Alloc)	B	C+	A-		Y	1,000,000
Goldman Sachs Target Date 2020 Portfolio Investor Shares	GTMHX	NAS CM	Open End	Target Date (Asset Alloc)	B	C+	A-		Y	0
Goldman Sachs Target Date 2020 Portfolio R Shares	GTRHX	NAS CM	Open End	Target Date (Asset Alloc)	B	C+	B+		Y	0
Goldman Sachs Target Date 2020 Portfolio R6 Shares	GTZHX	NAS CM	Open End	Target Date (Asset Alloc)	B	C+	A-		Y	5,000,000
Goldman Sachs Target Date 2020 Portfolio Service Shares	GTVHX	NAS CM	Open End	Target Date (Asset Alloc)	B	C+	A-		Y	0
Goldman Sachs Target Date 2025 Portfolio A Shares	GTADX	NAS CM	Open End	Target Date (Asset Alloc)	C+	C	B		Y	1,000
Goldman Sachs Target Date 2025 Portfolio Inst Shares	GTIFX	NAS CM	Open End	Target Date (Asset Alloc)	C+	C	B+		Y	1,000,000
Goldman Sachs Target Date 2025 Portfolio Investor Shares	GTMFX	NAS CM	Open End	Target Date (Asset Alloc)	C+	C	B+		Y	0
Goldman Sachs Target Date 2025 Portfolio R Shares	GTRDX	NAS CM	Open End	Target Date (Asset Alloc)	C+	C	B		Y	0
Goldman Sachs Target Date 2025 Portfolio R6 Shares	GTZFX	NAS CM	Open End	Target Date (Asset Alloc)	C+	C	B+		Y	5,000,000
Goldman Sachs Target Date 2025 Portfolio Service Shares	GTVFX	NAS CM	Open End	Target Date (Asset Alloc)	C+	C	B		Y	0
Goldman Sachs Target Date 2030 Portfolio A Shares	GTAJX	NAS CM	Open End	Target Date (Asset Alloc)	B	C	A-	Up	Y	1,000
Goldman Sachs Target Date 2030 Portfolio Inst Shares	GTIJX	NAS CM	Open End	Target Date (Asset Alloc)	B	C	A-	Up	Y	1,000,000
Goldman Sachs Target Date 2030 Portfolio Investor Shares	GTMJX	NAS CM	Open End	Target Date (Asset Alloc)	B	C	A-	Up	Y	0
Goldman Sachs Target Date 2030 Portfolio R Shares	GTRJX	NAS CM	Open End	Target Date (Asset Alloc)	B	C	A-	Up	Y	0
Goldman Sachs Target Date 2030 Portfolio R6 Shares	GTZJX	NAS CM	Open End	Target Date (Asset Alloc)	B	C+	A-	Up	Y	5,000,000
Goldman Sachs Target Date 2030 Portfolio Service Shares	GTVJX	NAS CM	Open End	Target Date (Asset Alloc)	B	C	A-	Up	Y	0
Goldman Sachs Target Date 2035 Portfolio A Shares	GTALX	NAS CM	Open End	Target Date (Asset Alloc)	C+	C	B+		Y	1,000
Goldman Sachs Target Date 2035 Portfolio Inst Shares	GTIOX	NAS CM	Open End	Target Date (Asset Alloc)	C+	C	B+		Y	1,000,000
Goldman Sachs Target Date 2035 Portfolio Investor Shares	GTMPX	NAS CM	Open End	Target Date (Asset Alloc)	C+	C	B+		Y	0
Goldman Sachs Target Date 2035 Portfolio R Shares	GTROX	NAS CM	Open End	Target Date (Asset Alloc)	C+	C	B		Y	0
Goldman Sachs Target Date 2035 Portfolio R6 Shares	GTZLX	NAS CM	Open End	Target Date (Asset Alloc)	C+	C	B+		Y	5,000,000
Goldman Sachs Target Date 2035 Portfolio Service Shares	GTVOX	NAS CM	Open End	Target Date (Asset Alloc)	C+	C	B		Y	0
Goldman Sachs Target Date 2040 Portfolio A Shares	GTAMX	NAS CM	Open End	Target Date (Asset Alloc)	B-	C	B+		Y	1,000
Goldman Sachs Target Date 2040 Portfolio Inst Shares	GTIMX	NAS CM	Open End	Target Date (Asset Alloc)	B-	C	B+		Y	1,000,000
Goldman Sachs Target Date 2040 Portfolio Investor Shares	GTMMX	NAS CM	Open End	Target Date (Asset Alloc)	B-	C	B+		Y	0
Goldman Sachs Target Date 2040 Portfolio R Shares	GTRMX	NAS CM	Open End	Target Date (Asset Alloc)	B-	C	B+		Y	0
Goldman Sachs Target Date 2040 Portfolio R6 Shares	GTZMX	NAS CM	Open End	Target Date (Asset Alloc)	B-	C	A-		Y	5,000,000
Goldman Sachs Target Date 2040 Portfolio Service Shares	GTVMX	NAS CM	Open End	Target Date (Asset Alloc)	B-	C	B+		Y	0
Goldman Sachs Target Date 2045 Portfolio A Shares	GTAQX	NAS CM	Open End	Target Date (Asset Alloc)	C+	C	B		Y	1,000
Goldman Sachs Target Date 2045 Portfolio Inst Shares	GTIQX	NAS CM	Open End	Target Date (Asset Alloc)	C+	C	B		Y	1,000,000
Goldman Sachs Target Date 2045 Portfolio Investor Shares	GTMQX	NAS CM	Open End	Target Date (Asset Alloc)	C+	C	B		Y	0
Goldman Sachs Target Date 2045 Portfolio R Shares	GTREX	NAS CM	Open End	Target Date (Asset Alloc)	C+	C	B	Up	Y	0
Goldman Sachs Target Date 2045 Portfolio R6 Shares	GTZQX	NAS CM	Open End	Target Date (Asset Alloc)	C+	C	B		Y	5,000,000

★ Expanded analysis of this fund is included in Section II.

Min Additional Investment	3-Month Total Return	6-Month Total Return	1-Year Total Return	3-Year Total Return	5-Year Total Return	Dividend Yield (TTM)	Expense Ratio	3-Yr Std Deviation	3-Year Beta	NAV	Total Assets (MIL)	%Cash	%Stocks	%Bonds	%Other	Turnover Ratio	Last Bull Market Total Return	Last Bear Market Total Return	Front End Fee (%)	Back End Fee (%)	Inception Date
	TOTAL RETURNS					PERFORMANCE				ASSETS		ASSET ALLOCATION & TURNOVER					BULL & BEAR		FEES		
	3.57	18.92	0.86	33.17	31.37	0.42	0.83	14.13	0.92	12.44	124.0	3	97	0	0	105					Jul-15
	3.57	18.79	0.85	33.16	31.21	0.28	0.84	14.08	0.92	12.45	124.0	3	97	0	0	105					Jan-14
	3.51	18.82	0.68	32.58	30.11	0.27	0.98	14.13	0.92	12.37	124.0	3	97	0	0	105					Jan-14
	0.32	-3.36	-3.97				0.84				1,555					725					Apr-18
	0.30	-3.38	-3.99			0.85	0.84				1,555					725					Dec-17
	5.44	5.44	5.44			0	0.98				2,005					725					May-16
50	4.52	23.23	10.28	62.44	77.26	0	1.14	13.52	1	9.23	164.7	2	98	0	0	40	27.24	-15.7	5.50		May-99
50	4.28	22.58	9.28	58.58	70.47	0	1.89	13.48	0.99	6.08	164.7	2	98	0	0	40	26.6	-15.87		1.00	May-99
	4.66	23.44	10.68	64.29	80.66	0.26	0.74	13.53	1	10.32	164.7	2	98	0	0	40	27.41	-15.5			Apr-18
	4.48	23.05	9.94	61.28	75.20	0	1.39	13.52	0.99	8.86	164.7	2	98	0	0	40	27	-15.73			Jan-09
	4.55	23.41	10.65	64.45	80.73	0.25	0.74	13.55	1	10.33	164.7	2	98	0	0	40	27.41	-15.5			Jul-15
	4.54	23.36	10.61	64.30	80.67	0.18	0.75	13.54	1	10.35	164.7	2	98	0	0	40	27.41	-15.5			May-99
	4.56	23.32	10.48	63.59	79.40	0.19	0.89	13.52	0.99	10.31	164.7	2	98	0	0	40	27.33	-15.71			Jan-09
	4.49	23.09	10.13	61.92	76.27	0	1.25	13.52	0.99	9.06	164.7	2	98	0	0	40	27.16	-15.65			May-99
	-0.42	2.97	-0.36			1.23	0.9			9.36	137.5					132					Apr-18
	0.40	5.82	3.20	8.65		2.63	0.81	3.81	20.4	9.81	3,298	49	22	28	1	41					Apr-18
	0.49	5.98	3.27	8.73		0	0.82	3.85	20.57	10.1	3,298	49	22	28	1	41					Jul-14
50	3.54	11.69	7.99	17.59	24.51	2.2	0.68	4.7	0.9	9.36	7.2	3	37	60	0	200	10.84	-8.21	5.50		Aug-16
	3.63	12.02	8.48	19.08	26.71	2.42	0.29	4.79	0.92	9.41	7.2	3	37	60	0	200	11	-8.11			Aug-16
	3.64	11.91	8.34	18.59	26.19	2.3	0.43	4.8	0.92	9.39	7.2	3	37	60	0	200	11	-8.11			Aug-16
	3.53	11.68	7.83	16.95	23.21	1.87	0.93	4.78	0.91	9.37	7.2	3	37	60	0	200	10.68	-8.3			Aug-16
	3.63	11.89	8.48	19.09	26.72	2.43	0.27	4.73	0.91	9.41	7.2	3	37	60	0	200	11	-8.11			Oct-07
	3.53	11.66	7.93	17.43	24.33	1.96	0.79	4.76	0.92	9.38	7.2	3	37	60	0	200	10.84	-8.21			Aug-16
50	3.48	12.51	7.43			2.61	0.67			10.7	7.7	3	46	51	0	177			5.50		Aug-16
	3.57	12.73	7.86			2.89	0.28			10.71	7.7	3	46	51	0	177					Aug-16
	3.58	12.65	7.67			2.8	0.42			10.68	7.7	3	46	51	0	177					Aug-16
	3.49	12.43	7.19			2.32	0.92			10.67	7.7	3	46	51	0	177					Aug-16
	3.58	12.74	7.82			2.94	0.26			10.7	7.7	3	46	51	0	177					Aug-16
	3.49	12.43	7.27			2.47	0.78			10.67	7.7	3	46	51	0	177					Aug-16
50	3.50	13.30	7.08	25.61	31.48	1.57	0.68	6.86	0.94	9.45	5.5	4	54	41	0	156	13.11	-10.52	5.50		Aug-16
	3.60	13.51	7.51	27.20	33.81	1.95	0.29	6.89	0.94	9.49	5.5	4	54	41	0	156	13.28	-10.43			Aug-16
	3.61	13.54	7.45	26.67	33.25	1.8	0.43	6.82	0.94	9.47	5.5	4	54	41	0	156	13.28	-10.43			Aug-16
	3.50	13.19	6.85	24.83	30.01	1.37	0.93	6.85	0.94	9.44	5.5	4	54	41	0	156	12.95	-10.61			Aug-16
	3.60	13.51	7.51	27.23	33.84	1.96	0.27	6.86	0.94	9.49	5.5	4	54	41	0	156	13.28	-10.43			Oct-07
	3.50	13.29	7.00	25.40	31.26	1.51	0.79	6.78	0.93	9.46	5.5	4	54	41	0	156	13.11	-10.52			Aug-16
50	3.35	13.95	7.34			2.62	0.67			10.78	7.4	3	64	32	0	139			5.50		Aug-16
	3.53	14.22	7.88			2.74	0.28			10.84	7.4	3	64	32	0	139					Aug-16
	3.44	14.16	7.61			2.67	0.42			10.8	7.4	3	64	32	0	139					Aug-16
	3.35	13.93	7.12			2.2	0.92			10.79	7.4	3	64	32	0	139					Aug-16
	3.53	14.23	7.85			2.8	0.26			10.83	7.4	3	64	32	0	139					Aug-16
	3.44	13.92	7.28			2.34	0.78			10.8	7.4	3	64	32	0	139					Aug-16
50	3.40	15.00	7.09	29.59	35.45	1.58	0.66	8.58	0.94	9.12	7.8	3	76	20	0	143	14.7	-12.34	5.50		Aug-16
	3.49	15.20	7.54	31.06	37.67	1.87	0.27	8.57	0.94	9.17	7.8	3	76	20	0	143	14.86	-12.25			Aug-16
	3.39	15.11	7.28	30.51	37.09	1.75	0.41	8.56	0.93	9.14	7.8	3	76	20	0	143	14.86	-12.25			Aug-16
	3.17	14.75	6.77	28.52	33.67	1.31	0.91	8.53	0.93	9.1	7.8	3	76	20	0	143	14.53	-12.43			Aug-16
	3.49	15.20	7.43	31.06	37.67	1.88	0.25	8.56	0.93	9.17	7.8	3	76	20	0	143	14.87	-12.25			Oct-07
	3.28	14.84	6.88	29.16	35.01	1.41	0.77	8.53	0.93	9.13	7.8	3	76	20	0	143	14.7	-12.34			Aug-16
50	3.15	15.75	6.83			2.26	0.65			10.8	8.0	7	85	7	0	145			5.50		Aug-16
	3.33	16.04	7.26			2.54	0.26			10.85	8.0	7	85	7	0	145					Aug-16
	3.24	15.84	7.08			2.47	0.4			10.82	8.0	7	85	7	0	145					Aug-16
	3.15	15.64	6.65			2.04	0.9			10.79	8.0	7	85	7	0	145					Aug-16
	3.23	15.93	7.23			2.59	0.24			10.84	8.0	7	85	7	0	145					Aug-16

Fund Name	MARKET Ticker Symbol	Traded On	Fund Type	FUND TYPE, CATEGORY & OBJECTIVE Category and (Prospectus Objective)	RATINGS Overall Rating	Reward Rating	Risk Rating	Recent Up/ Downgrade	Open to New Investors	MINIMUMS Min Initial Investment
Goldman Sachs Target Date 2045 Portfolio Service Shares	GTVEX	NAS CM	Open End	Target Date (Asset Alloc)	C+	C	B	Up	Y	0
Goldman Sachs Target Date 2050 Portfolio A Shares	GTASX	NAS CM	Open End	Target Date (Asset Alloc)	B-	C	B+	Up	Y	1,000
Goldman Sachs Target Date 2050 Portfolio Inst Shares	GTIPX	NAS CM	Open End	Target Date (Asset Alloc)	B-	C	B+	Up	Y	1,000,000
Goldman Sachs Target Date 2050 Portfolio Investor Shares	GTMAX	NAS CM	Open End	Target Date (Asset Alloc)	B-	C	B+	Up	Y	0
Goldman Sachs Target Date 2050 Portfolio R Shares	GTRSX	NAS CM	Open End	Target Date (Asset Alloc)	B-	C	B+	Up	Y	0
Goldman Sachs Target Date 2050 Portfolio R6 Shares	GTZSX	NAS CM	Open End	Target Date (Asset Alloc)	B-	C	B+	Up	Y	5,000,000
Goldman Sachs Target Date 2050 Portfolio Service Shares	GTVSX	NAS CM	Open End	Target Date (Asset Alloc)	B-	C	B+	Up	Y	0
Goldman Sachs Target Date 2055 Portfolio A Shares	GTANX	NAS CM	Open End	Target Date (Asset Alloc)	C+	C	B	Up	Y	1,000
Goldman Sachs Target Date 2055 Portfolio Inst Shares	GTIWX	NAS CM	Open End	Target Date (Asset Alloc)	C+	C	B	Up	Y	1,000,000
Goldman Sachs Target Date 2055 Portfolio Investor Shares	GTMWX	NAS CM	Open End	Target Date (Asset Alloc)	C+	C	B	Up	Y	0
Goldman Sachs Target Date 2055 Portfolio R Shares	GTRZX	NAS CM	Open End	Target Date (Asset Alloc)	C+	C	B	Up	Y	0
Goldman Sachs Target Date 2055 Portfolio R6 Shares	GTZWX	NAS CM	Open End	Target Date (Asset Alloc)	C+	C	B	Up	Y	5,000,000
Goldman Sachs Target Date 2055 Portfolio Service Shares	GTVIX	NAS CM	Open End	Target Date (Asset Alloc)	C+	C	B	Up	Y	0
Goldman Sachs Target Date 2060 Portfolio Class A	GTBAX	NAS CM	Open End	Target Date (Asset Alloc)	D	D+	B-	Up	Y	1,000
Goldman Sachs Target Date 2060 Portfolio Class R	GTBRX	NAS CM	Open End	Target Date (Asset Alloc)	D	D+	B-	Up	Y	0
Goldman Sachs Target Date 2060 Portfolio Class R6	GTBBX	NAS CM	Open End	Target Date (Asset Alloc)	D	D+	B-	Up	Y	5,000,000
Goldman Sachs Target Date 2060 Portfolio Inst Shares	GTBCX	NAS CM	Open End	Target Date (Asset Alloc)	D	D+	B-	Up	Y	1,000,000
Goldman Sachs Target Date 2060 Portfolio Investor Shares	GTBIX	NAS CM	Open End	Target Date (Asset Alloc)	D	D+	B-	Up	Y	0
Goldman Sachs Target Date 2060 Portfolio Service Shares	GTBSX	NAS CM	Open End	Target Date (Asset Alloc)	D	D+	B-	Up	Y	0
Goldman Sachs Tax-Advantaged Global Equity Portfolio Cls A	TAGGX	NAS CM	Open End	Aggressive Alloc (Growth)	C+	C	B	Up	Y	1,000
Goldman Sachs Tax-Advantaged Global Equity Portfolio Cls P	GSKPX	NAS CM	Open End	Aggressive Alloc (Growth)	C+	C	B	Up	Y	0
Goldman Sachs Tax-Advantaged Global Eq Port Cls R6 Shares	TRGGX	NAS CM	Open End	Aggressive Alloc (Growth)	C+	C	B	Up	Y	5,000,000
Goldman Sachs Tax-Advantaged Global Eq Port Inst Cls	TIGGX	NAS CM	Open End	Aggressive Alloc (Growth)	C+	C	B	Up	Y	1,000,000
Goldman Sachs Technology Opportunities Fund Class A	GITAX	NAS CM	Open End	Technology Sector Equity (Technology)	B-	B-	B	Down	Y	1,000
Goldman Sachs Technology Opportunities Fund Class C	GITCX	NAS CM	Open End	Technology Sector Equity (Technology)	B-	B-	B	Down	Y	1,000
Goldman Sachs Technology Opportunities Fund Class P	GSJPX	NAS CM	Open End	Technology Sector Equity (Technology)	B-	B-	B	Down	Y	0
Goldman Sachs Technology Opportunities Cls R6 Shares	GTORX	NAS CM	Open End	Technology Sector Equity (Technology)	B-	B-	B	Down	Y	5,000,000
Goldman Sachs Technology Opportunities Institutional Cls	GITIX	NAS CM	Open End	Technology Sector Equity (Technology)	B-	B-	B	Down	Y	1,000,000
Goldman Sachs Technology Opportunities Fund Investor Class	GISTX	NAS CM	Open End	Technology Sector Equity (Technology)	B-	B-	B	Down	Y	0
Goldman Sachs Technology Opportunities Fund Service Class	GITSX	NAS CM	Open End	Technology Sector Equity (Technology)	B-	B-	B	Down	Y	0
Goldman Sachs U.S. Equity Dividend & Premium Cls A	GSPAX	NAS CM	Open End	US Equity Large Cap Blend (Equity-Income)	B-	C	B	Up	Y	1,000
Goldman Sachs U.S. Equity Dividend & Premium Cls C	GSPQX	NAS CM	Open End	US Equity Large Cap Blend (Equity-Income)	B-	C	B	Up	Y	1,000
Goldman Sachs U.S. Equity Dividend & Premium Cls P	GSFPX	NAS CM	Open End	US Equity Large Cap Blend (Equity-Income)	B-	C	B		Y	0
Goldman Sachs U.S. Equity Dividend & Premium Cls R6	GIDWX	NAS CM	Open End	US Equity Large Cap Blend (Equity-Income)	B-	C	B		Y	5,000,000
Goldman Sachs U.S. Equity Dividend & Premium Inst Cls	GSPKX	NAS CM	Open End	US Equity Large Cap Blend (Equity-Income)	B-	C	B		Y	1,000,000
Goldman Sachs U.S. Equity Dividend & Premium Investor Cls	GVIRX	NAS CM	Open End	US Equity Large Cap Blend (Equity-Income)	B-	C	B		Y	0
Goldman Sachs U.S. Equity Insights Fund Class A	GSSQX	NAS CM	Open End	US Equity Large Cap Blend (Growth)	C+	C	B		Y	1,000
Goldman Sachs U.S. Equity Insights Fund Class C	GSUSX	NAS CM	Open End	US Equity Large Cap Blend (Growth)	C+	C	B		Y	1,000
Goldman Sachs U.S. Equity Insights Fund Class P	GSEPX	NAS CM	Open End	US Equity Large Cap Blend (Growth)	C+	C	B		Y	0
Goldman Sachs U.S. Equity Insights Fund Class R	GSURX	NAS CM	Open End	US Equity Large Cap Blend (Growth)	C+	C	B		Y	0
Goldman Sachs U.S. Equity Insights Fund Class R6	GSEUX	NAS CM	Open End	US Equity Large Cap Blend (Growth)	C+	C	B		Y	5,000,000
Goldman Sachs U.S. Equity Insights Institutional Cls	GSELX	NAS CM	Open End	US Equity Large Cap Blend (Growth)	C+	C	B		Y	1,000,000
Goldman Sachs U.S. Equity Insights Fund Investor Class	GSUTX	NAS CM	Open End	US Equity Large Cap Blend (Growth)	C+	C	B		Y	0
Goldman Sachs U.S. Equity Insights Fund Service Class	GSESX	NAS CM	Open End	US Equity Large Cap Blend (Growth)	C+	C	B		Y	0
Goldman Sachs U.S. Tax-Managed Equity Fund Class A	GCTAX	NAS CM	Open End	US Equity Large Cap Blend (Growth)	C+	C	B	Up	Y	1,000
Goldman Sachs U.S. Tax-Managed Equity Fund Class C	GCTCX	NAS CM	Open End	US Equity Large Cap Blend (Growth)	C+	C	B-	Up	Y	1,000
Goldman Sachs U.S. Tax-Managed Equity Fund Class P	GSDPX	NAS CM	Open End	US Equity Large Cap Blend (Growth)	C+	C	B		Y	0
Goldman Sachs U.S. Tax-Managed Equity Fund Class R6	GCTRX	NAS CM	Open End	US Equity Large Cap Blend (Growth)	C+	C	B		Y	5,000,000
Goldman Sachs U.S. Tax-Managed Equity Institutional Cls	GCTIX	NAS CM	Open End	US Equity Large Cap Blend (Growth)	C+	C	B		Y	1,000,000
Goldman Sachs U.S. Tax-Managed Equity Fund Investor Class	GQIRX	NAS CM	Open End	US Equity Large Cap Blend (Growth)	C+	C	B		Y	0
Goldman Sachs U.S. Tax-Managed Equity Fund Service Class	GCTSX	NAS CM	Open End	US Equity Large Cap Blend (Growth)	C+	C	B	Up	Y	0
Golub Group Equity Fund	GGEFX	NAS CM	Open End	US Equity Large Cap Blend (Growth)	C+	C	B	Down	Y	1,000

★ Expanded analysis of this fund is included in Section II.

	TOTAL RETURNS					PERFORMANCE				ASSETS		ASSET ALLOCATION & TURNOVER					BULL & BEAR		FEES		
Min Additional Investment	3-Month Total Return	6-Month Total Return	1-Year Total Return	3-Year Total Return	5-Year Total Return	Dividend Yield (TTM)	Expense Ratio	3-Yr Std Deviation	3-Year Beta	NAV	Total Assets (MIL)	%Cash	%Stocks	%Bonds	%Other	Turnover Ratio	Last Bull Market Total Return	Last Bear Market Total Return	Front End Fee (%)	Back End Fee (%)	Inception Date
	3.24	15.72	6.76			2.13	0.76			10.82	8.0	7	85	7	0	145					Aug-16
50	3.22	15.70	6.18	32.24	39.82	1.59	0.66	9.72	1	10.24	7.2	6	86	8	0	155	16.55	-14.31	5.50		Aug-16
	3.31	15.86	6.62	33.82	42.23	1.89	0.27	9.73	1	10.3	7.2	6	86	8	0	155	16.72	-14.22			Aug-16
	3.31	15.89	6.47	33.30	41.68	1.76	0.41	9.75	1	10.28	7.2	6	86	8	0	155	16.72	-14.22			Aug-16
	3.11	15.54	5.91	31.28	38.09	1.27	0.91	9.74	1	10.26	7.2	6	86	8	0	155	16.38	-14.4			Aug-16
	3.31	15.86	6.63	33.86	42.27	1.9	0.25	9.74	1	10.3	7.2	6	86	8	0	155	16.72	-14.22			Jan-11
	3.21	15.65	6.07	31.91	39.47	1.41	0.77	9.69	0.99	10.27	7.2	6	86	8	0	155	16.55	-14.31			Aug-16
50	3.18	15.69	6.21			2.24	0.65			10.69	7.4	6	86	8	0	177			5.50		Aug-16
	3.36	15.96	6.63			2.51	0.26			10.75	7.4	6	86	8	0	177					Aug-16
	3.27	15.89	6.46			2.45	0.4			10.72	7.4	6	86	8	0	177					Aug-16
	3.09	15.61	5.94			2.01	0.9			10.66	7.4	6	86	8	0	177					Aug-16
	3.26	15.98	6.61			2.56	0.24			10.74	7.4	6	86	8	0	177					Aug-16
	3.17	15.65	6.05			2.11	0.76			10.71	7.4	6	86	8	0	177					Aug-16
50	3.23	15.58	5.98			0.94	0.65			10.53	7.6	6	87	8	0	56			5.50		Apr-18
	3.13	15.47	5.69			0.78	0.9			10.52	7.6	6	87	8	0	56					Apr-18
	3.32	15.93	6.40			1.2	0.24			10.55	7.6	6	87	8	0	56					Apr-18
	3.33	15.93	6.38			1.19	0.26			10.55	7.6	6	87	8	0	56					Apr-18
	3.23	15.82	6.28			1.1	0.4			10.54	7.6	6	87	8	0	56					Apr-18
	3.13	15.47	5.80			0.87	0.76			10.52	7.6	6	87	8	0	56					Apr-18
50	1.74	13.98	0.86	32.00	27.17	0.84	1.32	10.98		15.73	2,827	-1	91	0	10	17	20.27	-18.45	5.50		Apr-08
	1.88	14.30	1.31	33.71	29.80	1.3	0.92	10.95		15.66	2,827	-1	91	0	10	17	20.64	-18.36			Apr-18
	1.82	14.23	1.22	33.58	29.68	1.27	0.92	10.94		15.65	2,827	-1	91	0	10	17	20.64	-18.36			Dec-17
	1.86	14.26	1.22	33.59	29.68	0.11	0.93	10.95		15.86	2,827	-1	91	0	10	17	20.64	-18.36			Apr-08
50	5.93	26.51	13.34	91.13	115.08	0	1.33	15.11	0.97	23.19	484.2	0	100	0	0	46	31.43	-23.64	5.50		Oct-99
50	5.76	26.06	12.55	87.00	107.32	0	2.08	15.09	0.96	17.99	484.2	0	100	0	0	46	30.8	-23.91		1.00	Oct-99
	6.04	26.68	13.80	93.46	119.44	0	0.97	15.12	0.97	26.3	484.2	0	100	0	0	46	31.64	-23.45			Apr-18
	6.04	26.68	13.80	93.46	119.44	0	0.97	15.1	0.97	26.3	484.2	0	100	0	0	46	31.64	-23.45			Dec-17
	6.00	26.69	13.76	93.41	119.38	0	0.98	15.12	0.97	26.29	484.2	0	100	0	0	46	31.64	-23.46			Oct-99
	6.04	26.65	13.67	92.58	117.84	0	1.08	15.11	0.97	25.8	484.2	0	100	0	0	46	31.52	-23.54			Sep-10
	5.86	26.35	13.19	90.48	113.96	0	1.48	15.12	0.97	22.58	484.2	0	100	0	0	46	31.32	-23.62			Oct-99
50	2.88	15.67	6.09	33.12	48.02	1.58	1.12	10.32	0.84	13.04	2,934	0	100	0	0	37	21.66	-13.02	5.50		Aug-05
50	2.78	15.33	5.30	30.16	42.59	0.86	1.87	10.37	0.84	12.99	2,934	0	100	0	0	37	21.16	-13.36		1.00	Aug-05
	3.07	16.03	6.54	34.55	50.83	1.96	0.73	10.36	0.84	13.01	2,934	0	100	0	0	37	21.91	-12.86			Apr-18
	3.00	15.94	6.46	34.55	50.83	1.96	0.73	10.36	0.84	13	2,934	0	100	0	0	37	21.91	-12.86			Apr-18
	3.07	15.92	6.52	34.62	50.90	1.95	0.74	10.37	0.84	13.01	2,934	0	100	0	0	37	21.91	-12.86			Aug-05
	3.04	15.94	6.38	34.12	49.91	1.82	0.87	10.38	0.84	13.02	2,934	0	100	0	0	37	21.83	-13			Aug-10
50	2.18	16.56	3.90	46.45	55.64	0.33	0.94	13.25	1.07	48.21	1,059	1	99	0	0	168	23.35	-15.33	5.50		May-91
50	2.01	16.14	3.19	43.28	49.98	0	1.69	13.23	1.07	43.03	1,059	1	99	0	0	168	22.83	-15.61		1.00	Aug-97
	2.30	16.79	4.34	46.92	55.78	0.68	0.54	13.24	1.07	49.78	1,059	1	99	0	0	168	23.27	-15.37			Apr-18
	2.13	16.42	3.67	45.41	53.74	0.05	1.19	13.25	1.07	47.28	1,059	1	99	0	0	168	23.14	-15.42			Nov-07
	2.28	16.78	4.33	48.25	57.95	0.69	0.54	13.26	1.07	49.76	1,059	1	99	0	0	168	23.27	-15.37			Jul-15
	2.28	16.76	4.32	48.21	58.74	0.68	0.55	13.26	1.07	49.79	1,059	1	99	0	0	168	23.65	-15.24			Jun-95
	2.25	16.68	4.17	47.56	57.62	0.62	0.69	13.25	1.07	47.55	1,059	1	99	0	0	168	23.56	-15.27			Nov-07
	2.17	16.49	3.82	46.04	54.85	0.16	1.05	13.26	1.07	47.96	1,059	1	99	0	0	168	23.27	-15.37			May-91
50	2.25	16.30	2.31	40.64	44.90	0.48	1.1	13.56	1.07	23.54	1,727	1	99	0	0	152	24.65	-16.69	5.50		Apr-00
50	2.06	15.90	1.50	37.47	39.58	0	1.85	13.57	1.07	22.23	1,727	1	99	0	0	152	24.03	-16.95		1.00	Apr-00
	2.35	16.49	2.69	42.19	47.75	0.81	0.74	13.58	1.07	23.94	1,727	1	99	0	0	152	24.85	-16.49			Apr-18
	2.35	16.55	2.68	42.25	47.81	0.81	0.74	13.58	1.07	23.94	1,727	1	99	0	0	152	24.85	-16.5			Apr-18
	2.37	16.55	2.70	42.27	47.83	0.09	0.75	13.56	1.07	24.15	1,727	1	99	0	0	152	24.85	-16.49			Apr-00
	2.30	16.45	2.51	41.65	46.75	0.67	0.85	13.59	1.07	23.92	1,727	1	99	0	0	152	24.63	-16.49			Aug-10
	2.24	16.24	2.20	40.15	44.14	0.33	1.25	13.56	1.07	23.69	1,727	1	99	0	0	152	24.48	-16.74			Apr-00
	5.44	18.70	7.90	39.90	44.14	0	1.27	13.42	1.07	18.4	57.9	7	93	0	0	31	23.87	-13.47			Apr-09

	MARKET			FUND TYPE, CATEGORY & OBJECTIVE	RATINGS				MINIMUMS	
Fund Name	Ticker Symbol	Traded On	Fund Type	Category and (Prospectus Objective)	Overall Rating	Reward Rating	Risk Rating	Recent Up/ Downgrade	Open to New Investors	Min Initial Investment
Good Harbor Tactical Core US Fund Class A Shares	GHUAX	NAS CM	Open End	Moderate Alloc (Growth & Income)	C	D+	C		Y	2,500
Good Harbor Tactical Core US Fund Class C Shares	GHUCX	NAS CM	Open End	Moderate Alloc (Growth & Income)	C-	D+	C		Y	2,500
Good Harbor Tactical Core US Fund Class I Shares	GHUIX	NAS CM	Open End	Moderate Alloc (Growth & Income)	C	D+	C		Y	250,000
Good Harbor Tactical Select Fund Class A	GHSAX	NAS CM	Open End	Moderate Alloc (Growth & Income)	C	C-	C		Y	2,500
Good Harbor Tactical Select Fund Class C	GHSCX	NAS CM	Open End	Moderate Alloc (Growth & Income)	C-	D+	C		Y	2,500
Good Harbor Tactical Select Fund Class I	GHSIX	NAS CM	Open End	Moderate Alloc (Growth & Income)	C	C-	C		Y	250,000
GoodHaven Fund	GOODX	NAS CM	Open End	US Equity Mid Cap (Growth)	C	C-	C		Y	10,000
Gotham Absolute 500 Core Fund Institutional Class	GACFX	NAS CM	Open End	Long/Short Equity (Growth)	C+	C	B		Y	250,000
Gotham Absolute 500 Fund Institutional Class	GFIVX	NAS CM	Open End	Long/Short Equity (Growth)	C+	C	B	Down	Y	250,000
Gotham Absolute Return Fund Institutional Class Shares	GARIX	NAS CM	Open End	Long/Short Equity (Growth)	B-	C	B	Up	Y	250,000
Gotham Defensive Long 500 Fund Institutional Class	GDLFX	NAS CM	Open End	Long/Short Equity (Growth)	B-	C	B		Y	250,000
Gotham Defensive Long Fund Institutional Class	GDLIX	NAS CM	Open End	Long/Short Equity (Growth)	C+	C	B	Up	Y	250,000
Gotham Enhanced 500 Fund Institutional Class	GENFX	NAS CM	Open End	US Equity Large Cap Blend (Growth)	B-	C	B		Y	250,000
Gotham Enhanced 500 Plus Fund Institutional Class	GEFPX	NAS CM	Open End	US Equity Large Cap Blend (Growth)	B-	C	B		Y	250,000
Gotham Enhanced Index Plus Fund Institutional Class	GENDX	NAS CM	Open End	US Equity Large Cap Blend (Growth)	B-	C	B	Up	Y	250,000
Gotham Enhanced Return Fund Institutional Class Shares	GENIX	NAS CM	Open End	US Equity Mid Cap (Growth)	B-	C	B	Up	Y	250,000
Gotham Enhanced S&P 500 Index Fund Institutional Class	GSPFX	NAS CM	Open End	US Equity Large Cap Blend (Growth)	C+	C	B	Up	Y	250,000
Gotham Hedged Core Fund Institutional Class	GCHDX	NAS CM	Open End	Long/Short Equity (Growth)	C+	C	B		Y	250,000
Gotham Hedged Plus Fund Institutional Class	GHPLX	NAS CM	Open End	Long/Short Equity (Growth)	C+	C	B	Up	Y	250,000
Gotham Index Plus All-Cap Fund Institutional Class	GANDX	NAS CM	Open End	US Equity Large Cap Blend (Growth)	D+	D+	C+	Up	Y	250,000
Gotham Index Plus Fund Institutional Class	GINDX	NAS CM	Open End	US Equity Large Cap Blend (Growth)	B-	C	B		Y	250,000
Gotham Index Plus Fund Investor Class	GNNDX	NAS CM	Open End	US Equity Large Cap Blend (Growth)	B-	C	B		Y	2,500
Gotham Large Value Fund Institutional Class	GVALX	NAS CM	Open End	US Equity Large Cap Value (Growth)	B-	C	B	Down	Y	100,000
Gotham Master Index Plus Fund Institutional Class	GMIDX	NAS CM	Open End	US Equity Large Cap Blend (Growth)	C	C	B-	Up	Y	250,000
Gotham Master Neutral Fund Institutional Class Shares	GMNFX	NAS CM	Open End	Market Neutral (Growth)	D+	D	C	Down	Y	250,000
Gotham Neutral 500 Fund Institutional Class	GONFX	NAS CM	Open End	Market Neutral (Growth)	C-	D+	C	Down	Y	250,000
Gotham Neutral Fund Institutional Class	GONIX	NAS CM	Open End	Market Neutral (Growth)	D+	D	C	Down	Y	250,000
Gotham Short Strategies Fund Institutional Shares	GSSFX	NAS CM	Open End	Long/Short Equity (Growth)	D	D	D	Down	Y	250,000
Gotham Total Return Fund Institutional Class	GTRFX	NAS CM	Open End	Long/Short Equity (Growth)	B-	C	B+		Y	250,000
Gotham Total Return Fund Investor Class	GTRNX	NAS CM	Open End	Long/Short Equity (Growth)	B-	C	B		Y	2,500
Government Street Equity Fund	GVEQX	NAS CM	Open End	US Equity Large Cap Growth (Growth)	B-	C	B	Up	Y	5,000
Government Street Mid-Cap Fund	GVMCX	NAS CM	Open End	US Equity Mid Cap (Growth)	B-	C	B	Up	Y	5,000
GQG Partners Emerging Markets Equity Institutional Shares	GQGIX	NAS CM	Open End	Global Emerg Mkts (Div Emerging Mkts)	C	C-	C+	Up	Y	500,000
GQG Partners Emerging Markets Equity Fund Investor Shares	GQGPX	NAS CM	Open End	Global Emerg Mkts (Div Emerging Mkts)	C	C-	C+	Up	Y	2,500
GQG Partners Emerging Markets Equity Fund R6 Shares	GQGRX	NAS CM	Open End	Global Emerg Mkts (Div Emerging Mkts)	C	C-	C+	Up	Y	0
GQG Partners Global Quality Equity Institutional Shares	GQRIX	NAS CM	Open End	Global Equity Large Cap (World Stock)	U	U	U		Y	500,000
GQG Partners Global Quality Equity Fund Investor Shares	GQRPX	NAS CM	Open End	Global Equity Large Cap (World Stock)	U	U	U		Y	2,500
GQG Partners Global Quality Equity Fund R6 Shares	GQRRX	NAS CM	Open End	Global Equity Large Cap (World Stock)	U	U	U		Y	0
GQG Partners US Select Quality Equity Institutional Shares	GQEIX	NAS CM	Open End	US Equity Large Cap Growth (Growth)	U	U	U		Y	500,000
GQG Partners US Select Quality Equity Fund Investor Shares	GQEPX	NAS CM	Open End	US Equity Large Cap Growth (Growth)	U	U	U		Y	2,500
GQG Partners US Select Quality Equity Fund R6 Shares	GQERX	NAS CM	Open End	US Equity Large Cap Growth (Growth)	U	U	U		Y	0
Grandeur Peak Emerging Mkts Opp Inst Cls	GPEIX	NAS CM	Open End	Global Emerg Mkts (Div Emerging Mkts)	C	C-	C+			2,000
Grandeur Peak Emerging Markets Opportunities Investor Cls	GPEOX	NAS CM	Open End	Global Emerg Mkts (Div Emerging Mkts)	C	C-	C+			2,000
Grandeur Peak Global Micro Cap Fund Institutional Class	GPMCX	NAS CM	Open End	Global Equity Mid/Small Cap (Growth)	C	C	C			2,000
Grandeur Peak Global Opportunities Institutional Cls	GPGIX	NAS CM	Open End	Global Equity Mid/Small Cap (World Stock)	C	C	C+			2,000
Grandeur Peak Global Opportunities Fund Investor Class	GPGOX	NAS CM	Open End	Global Equity Mid/Small Cap (World Stock)	C	C	C+			2,000
Grandeur Peak Global Reach Fund Institutional Class	GPRIX	NAS CM	Open End	Global Equity Mid/Small Cap (World Stock)	C	C	B-			2,000
Grandeur Peak Global Reach Fund Investor Class	GPROX	NAS CM	Open End	Global Equity Mid/Small Cap (World Stock)	C	C	B-			2,000
Grandeur Peak Global Stalwarts Fund Institutional Class	GGSYX	NAS CM	Open End	Global Equity Mid/Small Cap (World Stock)	C	C	C+		Y	2,000
Grandeur Peak Global Stalwarts Fund Investor Class	GGSOX	NAS CM	Open End	Global Equity Mid/Small Cap (World Stock)	C	C	C+		Y	2,000
Grandeur Peak Intl Opp Inst Cls	GPIIX	NAS CM	Open End	Global Equity Mid/Small Cap (Foreign Stock)	C	C	C+			2,000
Grandeur Peak International Opportunities Investor Cls	GPIOX	NAS CM	Open End	Global Equity Mid/Small Cap (Foreign Stock)	C	C	C+			2,000

★ Expanded analysis of this fund is included in Section II.

Min Additional Investment	TOTAL RETURNS 3-Month Total Return	6-Month Total Return	1-Year Total Return	3-Year Total Return	5-Year Total Return	PERFORMANCE Dividend Yield (TTM)	Expense Ratio	3-Yr Std Deviation	3-Year Beta	ASSETS NAV	Total Assets (MIL)	ASSET ALLOCATION & TURNOVER %Cash	%Stocks	%Bonds	%Other	Turnover Ratio	BULL & BEAR Last Bull Market Total Return	Last Bear Market Total Return	FEES Front End Fee (%)	Back End Fee (%)	Inception Date
250	-1.55	4.00	-6.46	16.43	-5.56	0	1.88	10.57	0.71	10.13	36.6	-19	93	26	0	466			5.75		Dec-12
250	-1.62	3.75	-7.02	13.91	-8.92	0	2.63	10.58	0.71	9.66	36.6	-19	93	26	0	466				1.00	Jan-13
10,000	-1.43	4.25	-6.19	17.31	-4.33	0	1.63	10.6	0.71	10.3	36.6	-19	93	26	0	466					Dec-12
250	0.00	2.68	-4.53	14.12	7.08	0.35	2.18	8.45	0.55	9.93	9.8	-7	93	10	4	402			5.75		Aug-15
250	-0.30	2.20	-5.33	11.67	3.54	0	2.93	8.43	0.55	9.73	9.8	-7	93	10	4	402				1.00	Aug-15
10,000	0.00	2.79	-4.30	15.12	8.57	0.67	1.93	8.5	0.56	9.94	9.8	-7	93	10	4	402					May-14
1,000	2.31	9.37	-2.21	9.76	-14.03	1.17	1.1	10.76	0.72	23.44	85.8	13	80	6	0	13	17.74	-6.06			Apr-11
5,000	0.63	6.36	4.71			0.22	1.93			11.03	2.5	39	61	0	0	239					Sep-16
5,000	0.00	3.74	3.06	31.27		0.29	2.76	8.58	1.08	11.35	15.2	40	60	0	0	243					Jul-14
5,000	0.88	7.08	2.84	20.58	12.64	0	2.56	8.12	1.19	14.82	925.7	40	60	0	0	258					Aug-12
5,000	1.11	8.67	7.92			0.53	3.36			12.65	12.7	1	99	0	0	220					Sep-16
5,000	2.23	10.18	7.01			0	3.63			11.9	2.4	1	99	0	0	225					Sep-16
5,000	0.00	9.23	4.47	50.54		0.45	3.61	13.34	0.96	11.71	27.7	1	99	0	0	216					Dec-14
5,000	1.85	13.80	7.87			0.91	2.1			11.54	2.9	1	99	0	0	224					Sep-16
5,000	1.93	15.30	6.55			0.76	1.96			12.13	3.3	1	99	0	0	347					Sep-16
5,000	2.28	13.89	6.99	41.42	35.98	0	3.63	13.01	1	14.34	554.0	1	99	0	0	197					May-13
5,000	3.00	17.57	9.06			1.54	0.5			11.64	3.7	1	99	0	0	230					Dec-16
5,000	1.48	7.76	4.79			0.54	1.16			10.97	2.5	39	61	0	0	221					Sep-16
5,000	0.00	3.36	1.72	33.56		0.49	2.71	9.09	1.15	11.07	2.9	40	60	0	0	227					Mar-16
5,000	2.41	15.36	5.61			0.39	2.49			10.59	2.4	2	98	0	0						Dec-17
5,000	1.85	9.21	5.26	54.60		0.38	3.39	13.26	0.97	14.82	746.7	0	100	0	0	218					Mar-15
500	1.78	9.07	5.07	53.54		0.27	3.64	13.25	0.97	14.79	746.7	0	100	0	0	218					Dec-17
2,000	3.07	18.03	9.00	50.70		0.11	0.75	13.74	1.09	13.09	57.2	0	100	0	0	670					Dec-15
5,000	2.43	15.27	7.02			1.19	2.06			10.94	1.2	-5	105	0	0	62					Apr-17
5,000	-1.38	-1.96	-1.26			0.64	1.68			9.96	20.1	83	15	2	0	170					Apr-17
5,000	-1.51	-2.98	-0.10			0.37	2.28			11.05	9.3	75	25	0	0	269					Sep-16
5,000	-0.88	-0.88	-1.46	2.01	-6.04	0	2.61	4.69	7.32	10.12	202.7	75	25	0	0	274					Aug-13
5,000	-4.40	-12.75	-8.49			0	1.35			8.69	27.7	3	99	0	-2	591					Jul-17
5,000	0.54	6.34	4.59	38.11		0.37	3.12	9.88	1.32	12.9	33.2	20	80	0	0						Mar-15
500	0.54	6.27	4.40	37.13		0.17	3.37	9.89	1.32	12.88	33.2	20	80	0	0						Dec-17
100	4.13	17.10	7.91	41.95	47.38	0.91	0.88	11.86	0.95	76.19	57.8	4	96	0	0	9	23.42	-16.33			Jun-91
100	3.45	18.82	6.26	41.42	54.69	0.56	1.09	12.47	0.8	27.67	47.6	6	94	0	0	6	22.13	-18.81			Nov-03
	6.98	19.44	8.45			0.68	0.98			13.33	1,790	5	92	0	1	94					Dec-16
100	6.91	19.40	8.25			0.5	1.16			13.29	1,790	5	92	0	1	94					Dec-16
	6.98	19.44	8.45			0.68	0.98			13.33	1,790	5	92	0	1	94					Dec-16
	3.90						0.75			10.39	13.5	7	93	0	0						Mar-19
100	3.90						1			10.39	13.5	7	93	0	0						Mar-19
	3.90						0.75			10.39	13.5	7	93	0	0						Mar-19
	3.45	15.27					0.59			10.49	44.0	11	89	0	0						Sep-18
100	3.45	15.29					0.84			10.48	44.0	11	89	0	0						Sep-18
	3.34	15.27					0.59			10.49	44.0	11	89	0	0						Sep-18
	2.65	16.50	-2.17	23.17	17.82	0.31	1.55	11.35	0.8	12	450.9	7	93	0	0	33					Dec-13
	2.57	16.38	-2.38	22.37	16.62	0.14	1.8	11.35	0.8	11.93	450.9	7	93	0	0	33					Dec-13
	4.41	13.62	-5.81	32.99		0	2	10.68	0.71	11.59	35.8	0	99	0	0	46					Oct-15
	4.43	20.06	-1.55	40.81	39.29	0.19	1.36	13.1	0.97	3.53	648.1	3	97	0	0	29					Oct-11
	4.50	19.99	-1.83	39.81	37.35	0	1.61	12.96	0.96	3.48	648.1	3	97	0	0	29					Oct-11
	5.01	19.49	-1.64	42.31	39.73	0.18	1.28	12.24	0.9	15.08	330.8	1	98	0	1	43					Jun-13
	4.89	19.31	-1.93	41.23	38.00	0.01	1.53	12.26	0.91	15.01	330.8	1	98	0	1	43					Jun-13
	3.67	21.55	-0.81	43.45		0.14	1.1	13.89	1.11	14.66	189.3	2	97	0	0	30					Sep-15
	3.62	21.41	-0.99	42.43		0	1.35	13.9	1.11	14.57	189.3	2	97	0	0	30					Sep-15
	3.71	17.95	-6.09	31.59	29.48	0.47	1.37	12.72	1.02	3.35	660.2	8	92	0	0	26					Oct-11
	3.73	17.66	-6.30	30.68	28.11	0.29	1.62	12.8	1.02	3.33	660.2	8	92	0	0	26					Oct-11

Fund Name	MARKET Ticker Symbol	Traded On	FUND TYPE, CATEGORY & OBJECTIVE Fund Type	Category and (Prospectus Objective)	RATINGS Overall Rating	Reward Rating	Risk Rating	Recent Up/ Downgrade	MINIMUMS Open to New Investors	Min Initial Investment
Grandeur Peak International Stalwarts Institutional Cls	GISYX	NAS CM	Open End	Global Equity Large Cap (Foreign Stock)	C	C	C+		Y	2,000
Grandeur Peak International Stalwarts Fund Investor Class	GISOX	NAS CM	Open End	Global Equity Large Cap (Foreign Stock)	C	C	C+		Y	2,000
Grant Park Multi Alternative Strategies Fund Class A	GPAAX	NAS CM	Open End	Multialternative (Growth & Income)	C+	C	B	Up	Y	2,500
Grant Park Multi Alternative Strategies Fund Class C	GPACX	NAS CM	Open End	Multialternative (Growth & Income)	C	C	B-	Up	Y	2,500
Grant Park Multi Alternative Strategies Fund Class I	GPAIX	NAS CM	Open End	Multialternative (Growth & Income)	C+	C	B	Up	Y	100,000
Grant Park Multi Alternative Strategies Fund Class N	GPANX	NAS CM	Open End	Multialternative (Growth & Income)	C+	C	B	Up	Y	2,500
Great Lakes Disciplined Equity Fund Institutional Class	GLDNX	NAS CM	Open End	US Equity Large Cap Blend (Growth & Income)	B-	C	B		Y	1,000
Great Lakes Disciplined Intl Smaller Company Inst Cls	GLISX	NAS CM	Open End	Global Equity Mid/Small Cap (Small Company)	C-	D+	C		Y	100,000
Great Lakes Large Cap Value Institutional Cls Shares	GLLIX	NAS CM	Open End	US Equity Large Cap Value (Growth & Income)	C+	C	B	Up	Y	1,000
Great Lakes Small Cap Opportunity Fund Institutional Class	GLSIX	NAS CM	Open End	US Equity Small Cap (Small Company)	C+	C	B	Down	Y	100,000
Great Lakes Small Cap Opportunity Fund Investor Class	GLSCX	NAS CM	Open End	US Equity Small Cap (Small Company)	C+	C	B	Down	Y	1,000
Great-West Aggressive Profile Fund Class L	MXEPX	NAS CM	Open End	Aggressive Alloc (Aggr Growth)	C+	C	B	Up	Y	0
Great-West Aggressive Profile Fund Institutional Class	MXGTX	NAS CM	Open End	Aggressive Alloc (Aggr Growth)	C+	C	B	Up	Y	0
Great-West Aggressive Profile Fund Investor Class	MXAPX	NAS CM	Open End	Aggressive Alloc (Aggr Growth)	C+	C	B	Up	Y	0
Great-West Ariel Mid Cap Value Fund Class L	MXAMX	NAS CM	Open End	US Equity Mid Cap (Growth)	C	C	B-	Down	Y	0
Great-West Ariel Mid Cap Value Fund Institutional Class	MXOAX	NAS CM	Open End	US Equity Mid Cap (Growth)	C+	C	B-		Y	0
Great-West Ariel Mid Cap Value Fund Investor Class	MXMCX	NAS CM	Open End	US Equity Mid Cap (Growth)	C	C	B-	Down	Y	0
Great-West Conservative Profile Fund Class L	MXIPX	NAS CM	Open End	Cautious Alloc (Growth)	B-	C	A-		Y	0
Great-West Conservative Profile Fund Institutional Class	MXKVX	NAS CM	Open End	Cautious Alloc (Growth)	B	C	A-	Up	Y	0
Great-West Conservative Profile Fund Investor Class	MXCPX	NAS CM	Open End	Cautious Alloc (Growth)	B-	C	A-		Y	0
Great-West Core Strategies: International Equity Cls L	MXEJX	NAS CM	Open End	Global Equity Large Cap (Growth)	D	D+	C		Y	0
Great-West Core Strategies: Intl Equity Inst Cls	MXECX	NAS CM	Open End	Global Equity Large Cap (Growth)	D	D+	C+		Y	0
Great-West Core Strategies: U.S. Equity Fund Class L	MXEHX	NAS CM	Open End	US Equity Large Cap Blend (Growth)	D	D+	C		Y	0
Great-West Core Strategies: U.S. Equity Institutional Cls	MXEBX	NAS CM	Open End	US Equity Large Cap Blend (Growth)	D	D+	C		Y	0
Great-West Emerging Markets Equity Fund Class L	MXEKX	NAS CM	Open End	Global Emerg Mkts (Div Emerging Mkts)	D	D	D+		Y	0
Great-West Emerging Markets Equity Institutional Cls	MXENX	NAS CM	Open End	Global Emerg Mkts (Div Emerging Mkts)	D	D	C-		Y	0
Great-West Emerging Markets Equity Fund Investor Class	MXEOX	NAS CM	Open End	Global Emerg Mkts (Div Emerging Mkts)	D	D	C-		Y	0
Great-West International Growth Fund Institutional Class	MXHTX	NAS CM	Open End	Global Equity Large Cap (Foreign Stock)	C	C	C+		Y	0
Great-West International Growth Fund Investor Class	MXIGX	NAS CM	Open End	Global Equity Large Cap (Foreign Stock)	C	C	C+		Y	0
Great-West International Index Fund Class L	MXGHX	NAS CM	Open End	Global Equity Large Cap (Growth)	C	C	B		Y	0
Great-West International Index Fund Institutional Class	MXPBX	NAS CM	Open End	Global Equity Large Cap (Growth)	C	C	B		Y	0
Great-West International Index Fund Investor Class	MXINX	NAS CM	Open End	Global Equity Large Cap (Growth)	C	C	B		Y	0
Great-West International Value Fund Class L	MXMIX	NAS CM	Open End	Global Equity Large Cap (Foreign Stock)	C	C	B-		Y	0
Great-West International Value Fund Institutional Class	MXJVX	NAS CM	Open End	Global Equity Large Cap (Foreign Stock)	C	C	B		Y	0
Great-West International Value Fund Investor Class	MXIVX	NAS CM	Open End	Global Equity Large Cap (Foreign Stock)	C	C	B-		Y	0
Great-West Invesco Small Cap Value Institutional Cls	MXMYX	NAS CM	Open End	US Equity Small Cap (Small Company)	C-	C-	C	Down	Y	0
Great-West Invesco Small Cap Value Fund Investor Class	MXSVX	NAS CM	Open End	US Equity Small Cap (Small Company)	C-	C-	C	Down	Y	0
Great-West Large Cap Growth Fund Institutional Class	MXGSX	NAS CM	Open End	US Equity Large Cap Growth (Growth)	B-	B-	B	Down	Y	0
Great-West Large Cap Growth Fund Investor Class	MXLGX	NAS CM	Open End	US Equity Large Cap Growth (Growth)	B-	B-	B	Down	Y	0
Great-West Lifetime 2015 Fund Class L	MXABX	NAS CM	Open End	Target Date (Asset Alloc)	B	C	A-	Up	Y	0
Great-West Lifetime 2020 Fund Class L	MXAJX	NAS CM	Open End	Target Date (Asset Alloc)	C+	C	B	Up	Y	0
Great-West Lifetime 2020 Fund Institutional Class	MXAKX	NAS CM	Open End	Target Date (Asset Alloc)	C+	C	B+	Up	Y	0
Great-West Lifetime 2020 Fund Investor Class	MXAGX	NAS CM	Open End	Target Date (Asset Alloc)	C+	C	B	Up	Y	0
Great-West Lifetime 2020 Fund Service Class	MXAHX	NAS CM	Open End	Target Date (Asset Alloc)	C+	C	B	Up	Y	0
Great-West Lifetime 2025 Fund Class L	MXANX	NAS CM	Open End	Target Date (Asset Alloc)	B-	C	A-	Up	Y	0
Great-West Lifetime 2030 Fund Class L	MXAWX	NAS CM	Open End	Target Date (Asset Alloc)	C+	C	B	Up	Y	0
Great-West Lifetime 2030 Fund Institutional Class	MXAYX	NAS CM	Open End	Target Date (Asset Alloc)	C+	C	B	Up	Y	0
Great-West Lifetime 2030 Fund Investor Class	MXATX	NAS CM	Open End	Target Date (Asset Alloc)	C+	C	B	Up	Y	0
Great-West Lifetime 2030 Fund Service Class	MXAUX	NAS CM	Open End	Target Date (Asset Alloc)	C+	C	B	Up	Y	0
Great-West Lifetime 2035 Fund Class L	MXAZX	NAS CM	Open End	Target Date (Asset Alloc)	B-	C	B+	Up	Y	0
Great-West Lifetime 2040 Fund Class L	MXBFX	NAS CM	Open End	Target Date (Asset Alloc)	C+	C	B	Up	Y	0
Great-West Lifetime 2040 Fund Institutional Class	MXBGX	NAS CM	Open End	Target Date (Asset Alloc)	C+	C	B	Up	Y	0

★ Expanded analysis of this fund is included in Section II.

Min Additional Investment	TOTAL RETURNS: 3-Month Total Return	6-Month Total Return	1-Year Total Return	3-Year Total Return	5-Year Total Return	PERFORMANCE: Dividend Yield (TTM)	Expense Ratio	3-Yr Std Deviation	3-Year Beta	ASSETS: NAV	Total Assets (MIL)	ASSET ALLOCATION & TURNOVER: %Cash	%Stocks	%Bonds	%Other	Turnover Ratio	BULL & BEAR: Last Bull Market Total Return	Last Bear Market Total Return	FEES: Front End Fee (%)	Back End Fee (%)	Inception Date
	3.70	20.01	-3.74	37.60		0.47	0.94	13.53	1.07	14.57	665.2	5	95	0	0	24					Sep-15
	3.64	19.90	-3.94	36.71		0.32	1.19	13.53	1.07	14.52	665.2	5	95	0	0	24					Sep-15
100	5.36	11.13	8.07	8.60	24.67	0	1.94	9.52	2.61	11.58	180.3	42	12	45	0	89			5.75		Dec-13
100	5.24	10.73	7.31	6.21	20.14	0	2.69	9.51	2.56	11.24	180.3	42	12	45	0	89					Dec-13
1,000	5.40	11.21	8.28	9.33	26.21	0	1.69	9.53	2.62	11.7	180.3	42	12	45	0	89					Dec-13
100	5.35	11.11	8.06	8.59	24.75	0	1.94	9.51	2.6	11.6	180.3	42	12	45	0	89					Dec-13
100	4.20	20.54	10.27	44.78	58.59	0.76	0.85	12.24	0.98	15.57	43.7	2	98	0	0	107	24.88	-15.07			Jun-09
100	1.71	9.41	-6.88	16.33		0	1.46	12.07	0.98	10.69	14.2	8	92	0	0	113					Dec-15
100	5.32	17.60	5.75	36.95	42.99	1.6	0.86	13.92	1.13	13.38	49.2	4	96	0	0	42					Sep-12
100	1.36	18.67	4.88	44.21	31.02	0.2	0.86	16.69	0.93	17.03	78.2	4	96	0	0	115	32.89	-25.15			Dec-08
200	1.27	18.51	4.60	43.22	29.41	0	1.11	16.69	0.93	16.71	78.2	4	96	0	0	115	32.63	-25.24			Dec-08
	3.04	16.35	3.16	37.96	38.57	1.08	1.4	11.78	0.92	12.61	700.3	2	97	0	0	40	22.53	-20.54			Jul-11
	3.17	16.80	3.76	40.47	42.48	1.96	0.8	11.78	0.92	9.94	700.3	2	97	0	0	40	22.87	-20.6			May-15
	3.14	16.64	3.40	39.11	40.43	2.56	1.15	11.75	0.92	6.43	700.3	2	97	0	0	40	22.87	-20.6			Sep-99
	0.79	16.46	-1.69	30.60	25.35	0	1.3	15.85	1.15	12.88	133.2	2	98	0	0	19	27.14	-25.26			Dec-13
	0.95	16.80	-1.09	32.86	29.00	0	0.7	15.93	1.15	11.75	133.2	2	98	0	0	19	27.33	-25.18			May-15
	0.94	16.84	-1.33	31.50	26.49	0.93	1.05	16.15	1.17	1.71	133.2	2	98	0	0	19	27.33	-25.18			Jan-94
	1.94	7.66	4.18	15.43	17.13	2.09	1.04	4.04	0.18	9.34	796.9	3	30	44	23	25	9.23	-6.55			Jul-11
	2.19	8.17	4.85	17.69	20.58	2.7	0.44	4.01	0.18	9.9	796.9	3	30	44	23	25	9.36	-6.52			May-15
	2.03	7.90	4.45	16.34	18.60	2.87	0.79	4	0.18	7.99	796.9	3	30	44	23	25	9.36	-6.52			Sep-99
	2.42	13.04	-1.65				1.26			9.92	133.9	0	97	0	0	29					Sep-18
	2.57	13.50	-1.14			0.68	0.66			9.79	133.9	0	97	0	0	29					Jun-18
	4.23	19.55	4.19				1.16			9.85	8.6	0	100	0	0	34					Sep-18
	4.36	19.94	4.81			0.65	0.56			10.42	8.6	0	100	0	0	34					Jun-18
	1.64	12.37	-0.06			1.69	1.48			8.62	401.7	0	100	0	0						Jan-18
	1.74	12.64	0.37			1.05	0.88			8.72	401.7	0	100	0	0						Jan-18
	1.63	12.35	0.01			0.72	1.23			8.72	401.7	0	100	0	0						Jan-18
	5.76	20.74	0.72	36.44	17.66	0.61	0.85	12.35	1.02	8.5	458.2	1	96	0	0	124	18.55	-23.16			May-15
	5.60	20.46	0.28	34.77	16.31	0	1.2	12.32	1.02	11.39	458.2	1	96	0	0	124	18.55	-23.16			May-03
	3.38	13.62	0.78	30.16	7.49		0.9	11.12	1	9.8	1,047	2	96	0	0	10	12.62	-23.49			Sep-18
	3.58	13.93	1.34	32.50	10.29	2.58	0.3	11.12	1	9.85	1,047	2	96	0	0	10	12.78	-23.41			May-15
	3.43	13.73	1.01	31.12	8.82	1.87	0.65	11.1	0.99	11.48	1,047	2	96	0	0	10	12.78	-23.41			Jan-11
	2.48	12.92	0.38	21.82	25.68	0.03	1.32	11.66	0.84	10.35	1,118	2	96	0	0	76	13	-13.43			Apr-13
	2.71	13.26	1.05	24.33	29.48	2.36	0.71	11.55	0.84	7.97	1,118	2	96	0	0	76	13.16	-13.34			May-15
	2.52	13.04	0.69	22.93	27.56	1.31	1.06	11.6	0.84	10.62	1,118	2	96	0	0	76	13.16	-13.34			Dec-93
	-1.57	10.06	-9.99	28.61	18.70	4.82	0.83	17.29	0.97	8.53	106.8	4	96	0	0	94	27.26	-24.54			May-15
	-1.73	9.85	-10.26	27.29	16.96	3.36	1.18	17.35	0.98	9.88	106.8	4	96	0	0	94	27.26	-24.53			May-08
	6.54	24.79	13.96	73.98	90.36	0.37	0.65	12.8	0.94	10.73	784.2	2	98	0	0	42	25.1	-20.34			May-15
	6.56	24.62	13.64	72.25	86.87	0.24	1	12.76	0.94	10.17	784.2	2	98	0	0	42	25.1	-20.34			May-03
	2.55	10.10	4.96	21.30	22.90	2.65	1.07	5.61	1.04	10.1	849.7	3	43	43	11	43	15.71	-12.44			Apr-16
	2.68	10.81	4.96	23.86		2.41	1.13	6.26	1.04	11.02	231.4	3	48	40	8	46					Apr-16
	2.83	11.16	5.59	25.77		3.05	0.53	6.24	1.04	11.04	231.4	3	48	40	8	46					Apr-16
	2.75	11.01	5.21	24.59		2.63	0.88	6.27	1.04	11.01	231.4	3	48	40	8	46					Apr-16
	2.80	10.93	5.19	24.24		2.53	0.98	6.25	1.04	11.04	231.4	3	48	40	8	46					Apr-16
	2.93	11.99	5.04	26.81	27.29	2.81	1.11	7.11	1.04	9.86	1,710	3	56	35	6	39	19.37	-16.99			Apr-16
	2.94	13.04	4.79	30.55		2.33	1.14	8.3	1.05	11.4	225.9	3	66	27	4	40					Apr-16
	3.18	13.50	5.50	32.51		2.93	0.54	8.3	1.05	11.42	225.9	3	66	27	4	40					Apr-16
	3.03	13.15	5.06	31.17		2.57	0.89	8.2	1.04	11.38	225.9	3	66	27	4	40					Apr-16
	3.05	13.26	5.02	31.04		2.45	0.99	8.25	1.04	11.42	225.9	3	66	27	4	40					Apr-16
	3.10	14.46	4.62	33.69	32.11	2.45	1	9.39	1.04	9.85	1,556	2	77	18	2	37	21.42	-19.31			Apr-16
	3.21	15.21	4.23	35.69		2.38	1.16	10.26	1.03	11.41	150.3	3	84	11	1	36					Apr-16
	3.27	15.56	4.84	37.61		2.9	0.56	10.29	1.04	11.45	150.3	3	84	11	1	36					Apr-16

Fund Name	MARKET Ticker Symbol	Traded On	FUND TYPE, CATEGORY & OBJECTIVE Fund Type	Category and (Prospectus Objective)	RATINGS Overall Rating	Reward Rating	Risk Rating	Recent Up/ Downgrade	MINIMUMS Open to New Investors	Min Initial Investment
Great-West Lifetime 2040 Fund Investor Class	MXBDX	NAS CM	Open End	Target Date (Asset Alloc)	C+	C	B	Up	Y	0
Great-West Lifetime 2040 Fund Service Class	MXBEX	NAS CM	Open End	Target Date (Asset Alloc)	C+	C	B	Up	Y	0
Great-West Lifetime 2045 Fund Class L	MXBHX	NAS CM	Open End	Target Date (Asset Alloc)	B-	C	B	Up	Y	0
Great-West Lifetime 2050 Fund Class L	MXBRX	NAS CM	Open End	Target Date (Asset Alloc)	C+	C	B	Up	Y	0
Great-West Lifetime 2050 Fund Institutional Class	MXBSX	NAS CM	Open End	Target Date (Asset Alloc)	C+	C	B	Up	Y	0
Great-West Lifetime 2050 Fund Investor Class	MXBOX	NAS CM	Open End	Target Date (Asset Alloc)	C+	C	B	Up	Y	0
Great-West Lifetime 2050 Fund Service Class	MXBQX	NAS CM	Open End	Target Date (Asset Alloc)	C+	C	B	Up	Y	0
Great-West Lifetime 2055 Fund Class L	MXBTX	NAS CM	Open End	Target Date (Asset Alloc)	B-	C	B	Up	Y	0
Great-West Lifetime Conservative 2015 Institutional Cls	MXMAX	NAS CM	Open End	Target Date (Asset Alloc)	B	C+	A-	Up	Y	0
Great-West Lifetime Conservative 2015 Fund Investor Class	MXLTX	NAS CM	Open End	Target Date (Asset Alloc)	B	C	A-	Up	Y	0
Great-West Lifetime Conservative 2015 Fund Service Class	MXLUX	NAS CM	Open End	Target Date (Asset Alloc)	B	C	A-	Up	Y	0
Great-West Lifetime Conservative 2020 Institutional Cls	MXAFX	NAS CM	Open End	Target Date (Asset Alloc)	C+	C	B		Y	0
Great-West Lifetime Conservative 2020 Fund Investor Class	MXACX	NAS CM	Open End	Target Date (Asset Alloc)	C+	C	B		Y	0
Great-West Lifetime Conservative 2020 Fund Service Class	MXAEX	NAS CM	Open End	Target Date (Asset Alloc)	C+	C	B		Y	0
Great-West Lifetime Conservative 2025 Institutional Cls	MXOZX	NAS CM	Open End	Target Date (Asset Alloc)	B	C+	A	Up	Y	0
Great-West Lifetime Conservative 2025 Fund Investor Class	MXALX	NAS CM	Open End	Target Date (Asset Alloc)	B	C	A-	Up	Y	0
Great-West Lifetime Conservative 2025 Fund Service Class	MXBLX	NAS CM	Open End	Target Date (Asset Alloc)	B	C	A-	Up	Y	0
Great-West Lifetime Conservative 2030 Institutional Cls	MXARX	NAS CM	Open End	Target Date (Asset Alloc)	C+	C	B+	Up	Y	0
Great-West Lifetime Conservative 2030 Fund Investor Class	MXAOX	NAS CM	Open End	Target Date (Asset Alloc)	C+	C	B	Up	Y	0
Great-West Lifetime Conservative 2030 Fund Service Class	MXAQX	NAS CM	Open End	Target Date (Asset Alloc)	C+	C	B	Up	Y	0
Great-West Lifetime Conservative 2035 Institutional Cls	MXRCX	NAS CM	Open End	Target Date (Asset Alloc)	B	C	A-	Up	Y	0
Great-West Lifetime Conservative 2035 Fund Investor Class	MXGLX	NAS CM	Open End	Target Date (Asset Alloc)	B-	C	A-	Up	Y	0
Great-West Lifetime Conservative 2035 Fund Service Class	MXHLX	NAS CM	Open End	Target Date (Asset Alloc)	B-	C	A-	Up	Y	0
Great-West Lifetime Conservative 2040 Institutional Cls	MXBCX	NAS CM	Open End	Target Date (Asset Alloc)	C+	C	B	Up	Y	0
Great-West Lifetime Conservative 2040 Fund Investor Class	MXBAX	NAS CM	Open End	Target Date (Asset Alloc)	C+	C	B	Up	Y	0
Great-West Lifetime Conservative 2040 Fund Service Class	MXBBX	NAS CM	Open End	Target Date (Asset Alloc)	C+	C	B	Up	Y	0
Great-West Lifetime Conservative 2045 Institutional Cls	MXUCX	NAS CM	Open End	Target Date (Asset Alloc)	B-	C	B+	Up	Y	0
Great-West Lifetime Conservative 2045 Fund Investor Class	MXMLX	NAS CM	Open End	Target Date (Asset Alloc)	B-	C	B+	Up	Y	0
Great-West Lifetime Conservative 2045 Fund Service Class	MXNLX	NAS CM	Open End	Target Date (Asset Alloc)	B-	C	B+	Up	Y	0
Great-West Lifetime Conservative 2050 Institutional Cls	MXBNX	NAS CM	Open End	Target Date (Asset Alloc)	C+	C	B	Up	Y	0
Great-West Lifetime Conservative 2050 Fund Investor Class	MXBKX	NAS CM	Open End	Target Date (Asset Alloc)	C+	C	B	Up	Y	0
Great-West Lifetime Conservative 2050 Fund Service Class	MXBMX	NAS CM	Open End	Target Date (Asset Alloc)	C+	C	B	Up	Y	0
Great-West Lifetime Conservative 2055 Institutional Cls	MXXFX	NAS CM	Open End	Target Date (Asset Alloc)	B-	C	B+	Up	Y	0
Great-West Lifetime Conservative 2055 Fund Investor Class	MXSLX	NAS CM	Open End	Target Date (Asset Alloc)	B-	C	B	Up	Y	0
Great-West Lifetime Conservative 2055 Fund Service Class	MXTLX	NAS CM	Open End	Target Date (Asset Alloc)	B-	C	B	Up	Y	0
Great-West Loomis Sayles Small Cap Value Institutional Cls	MXTFX	NAS CM	Open End	US Equity Small Cap (Small Company)	C	C	C+		Y	0
Great-West Loomis Sayles Small Cap Value Investor Cls	MXLSX	NAS CM	Open End	US Equity Small Cap (Small Company)	C	C	C+		Y	0
Great-West Mid Cap Value Fund Class L	MXGFX	NAS CM	Open End	US Equity Mid Cap (Growth)	C+	C	B	Up	Y	0
Great-West Mid Cap Value Fund Institutional Class	MXKJX	NAS CM	Open End	US Equity Mid Cap (Growth)	C+	C	B	Up	Y	0
Great-West Mid Cap Value Fund Investor Class	MXMVX	NAS CM	Open End	US Equity Mid Cap (Growth)	C+	C	B	Up	Y	0
Great-West Moderate Profile Fund Class L	MXGPX	NAS CM	Open End	Moderate Alloc (Growth)	B-	C	A-	Up	Y	0
Great-West Moderate Profile Fund Institutional Class	MXITX	NAS CM	Open End	Moderate Alloc (Growth)	B-	C	A-	Up	Y	0
Great-West Moderate Profile Fund Investor Class	MXMPX	NAS CM	Open End	Moderate Alloc (Growth)	B-	C	A-	Up	Y	0
Great-West Moderately Aggressive Profile Fund Class L	MXFPX	NAS CM	Open End	Aggressive Alloc (Aggr Growth)	B-	C	B+	Up	Y	0
Great-West Moderately Aggressive Profile Institutional Cls	MXHRX	NAS CM	Open End	Aggressive Alloc (Aggr Growth)	B-	C	B+	Up	Y	0
Great-West Moderately Aggressive Profile Investor Cls	MXBPX	NAS CM	Open End	Aggressive Alloc (Aggr Growth)	B-	C	B+	Up	Y	0
Great-West Moderately Conservative Profile Fund Class L	MXHPX	NAS CM	Open End	Cautious Alloc (Growth & Income)	B-	C	A-	Up	Y	0
Great-West Moderately Conservative Profile Inst Cls	MXJUX	NAS CM	Open End	Cautious Alloc (Growth & Income)	B	C	A-	Up	Y	0
Great-West Moderately Conservative Profile Investor Cls	MXDPX	NAS CM	Open End	Cautious Alloc (Growth & Income)	B-	C	A-		Y	0
Great-West Putnam Equity Income Fund Institutional Class	MXQCX	NAS CM	Open End	US Equity Large Cap Value (Equity-Income)	C+	C	B		Y	0
Great-West Putnam Equity Income Fund Investor Class	MXQIX	NAS CM	Open End	US Equity Large Cap Value (Equity-Income)	C+	C	B		Y	0
Great-West Real Estate Index Fund Class L	MXGIX	NAS CM	Open End	Real Estate Sector Equity (Real Estate)	C+	C	B-		Y	0

★Expanded analysis of this fund is included in Section II.

	TOTAL RETURNS					PERFORMANCE				ASSETS		ASSET ALLOCATION & TURNOVER					BULL & BEAR		FEES		
Min Additional Investment	3-Month Total Return	6-Month Total Return	1-Year Total Return	3-Year Total Return	5-Year Total Return	Dividend Yield (TTM)	Expense Ratio	3-Yr Std Deviation	3-Year Beta	NAV	Total Assets (MIL)	%Cash	%Stocks	%Bonds	%Other	Turnover Ratio	Last Bull Market Total Return	Last Bear Market Total Return	Front End Fee (%)	Back End Fee (%)	Inception Date
	3.31	15.37	4.54	36.37		2.74	0.91	10.31	1.04	11.37	150.3	3	84	11	1	36					Apr-16
	3.25	15.38	4.45	35.83		2.58	1.01	10.27	1.04	11.41	150.3	3	84	11	1	36					Apr-16
	3.14	15.67	3.93	36.27	32.63	2.21	1.17	10.77	1.04	10.11	908.6	2	89	8	1	33	21.45	-19.73			Apr-16
	3.14	15.75	3.83	36.62		2.34	1.18	10.83	1.04	11.77	84.5	2	90	7	0	33					Apr-16
	3.29	16.09	4.47	38.83		2.95	0.58	10.85	1.04	11.81	84.5	2	90	7	0	33					Apr-16
	3.33	15.98	4.22	37.42		2.59	0.93	10.87	1.04	11.77	84.5	2	90	7	0	33					Apr-16
	3.18	15.78	4.01	37.14		2.5	1.03	10.87	1.04	11.79	84.5	2	90	7	0	33					Apr-16
	3.20	15.67	3.78	36.35	31.84	2.69	1.18	10.9	1.04	9.86	389.0	2	90	6	0	36	21.28	-19.88			Apr-16
	2.54	8.59	5.53	18.43	21.55	3.59	0.43	3.97	0.95	9.46	58.4	3	28	55	13	46	11.61	-7.71			May-15
	2.44	8.31	5.16	17.22	19.80	2.5	0.78	3.98	0.95	12.2	58.4	3	28	55	13	46	11.61	-7.71			May-09
	2.46	8.30	5.00	16.92	19.19	2.21	0.88	4	0.96	12.29	58.4	3	28	55	13	46	11.57	-7.79			May-09
	2.70	9.22	5.78	20.54		4.13	0.46	4.54	0.97	10.57	5.9	3	32	53	11	64					Apr-16
	2.52	9.05	5.20	19.21		2.96	0.81	4.51	0.96	10.7	5.9	3	32	53	11	64					Apr-16
	2.52	8.99	5.16	18.72		2.73	0.91	4.52	0.96	10.65	5.9	3	32	53	11	64					Apr-16
	2.77	9.95	5.74	22.58	25.10	4.31	0.47	5.1	0.98	8.7	142.8	3	38	50	9	39	14.4	-11.38			May-15
	2.71	9.83	5.48	21.38	23.31	2.43	0.82	5.1	0.98	12.9	142.8	3	38	50	9	39	14.4	-11.38			May-09
	2.64	9.73	5.34	20.93	22.69	2.16	0.92	5.12	0.98	12.95	142.8	3	38	50	9	39	14.38	-11.46			May-09
	2.84	10.89	5.67	25.58		4.63	0.5	5.96	1.01	10.7	9.6	3	45	45	6	53					Apr-16
	2.80	10.70	5.30	24.22		5.12	0.85	5.98	1.01	10.61	9.6	3	45	45	6	53					Apr-16
	2.75	10.61	5.25	23.84		4.72	0.95	5.97	1.01	10.65	9.6	3	45	45	6	53					Apr-16
	3.03	12.07	5.67	29.14	30.25	4.47	0.53	7.07	1.03	7.7	138.2	3	55	37	4	39	18.02	-15.61			May-15
	2.89	11.95	5.36	27.86	28.39	2.04	0.88	7.1	1.03	13.83	138.2	3	55	37	4	39	18.02	-15.61			May-09
	2.91	11.94	5.19	27.46	27.77	1.78	0.98	7.08	1.03	13.89	138.2	3	55	37	4	39	18.02	-15.63			May-09
	3.11	13.48	5.40	32.73		3.32	0.55	8.29	1.04	11.36	5.5	2	66	28	3	56					Apr-16
	3.03	13.25	5.09	31.29		2.91	0.9	8.27	1.04	11.39	5.5	2	66	28	3	56					Apr-16
	3.01	13.19	4.87	30.92		2.86	1	8.29	1.04	11.32	5.5	2	66	28	3	56					Apr-16
	3.23	14.50	5.11	35.13	34.23	4.38	0.56	9.2	1.03	7.18	88.2	3	75	20	1	38	19.56	-17.5			May-15
	3.16	14.35	4.80	33.75	32.28	1.74	0.91	9.25	1.04	14.56	88.2	3	75	20	1	38	19.55	-17.5			May-09
	3.11	14.28	4.66	33.30	31.63	1.52	1.01	9.22	1.03	14.57	88.2	3	75	20	1	38	19.46	-17.51			May-09
	3.29	14.93	4.82	35.91		3.08	0.57	9.76	1.04	11.51	4.6	3	80	16	1	32					Apr-16
	3.12	14.76	4.49	34.52		2.9	0.93	9.78	1.04	11.49	4.6	3	80	16	1	32					Apr-16
	3.19	14.79	4.40	34.27		2.74	1.02	9.8	1.04	11.54	4.6	3	80	16	1	32					Apr-16
	3.25	15.04	4.65	36.33	33.92	4.23	0.57	9.91	1.03	7.81	44.2	3	82	14	1	48	19.61	-17.92			May-15
	3.21	14.94	4.40	34.88	32.07	1.83	0.92	10	1.04	14.69	44.2	3	82	14	1	48	19.61	-17.92			May-09
	3.10	14.88	4.22	34.46	31.33	1.63	1.02	9.94	1.03	14.71	44.2	3	82	14	1	48	19.55	-17.94			May-09
	2.67	18.17	-2.45	34.81	33.84	0.58	0.74	16.57	0.94	7.58	291.8	2	98	0	0	35	29.28	-23.68			May-15
	2.58	17.95	-2.81	33.36	31.84	0	1.09	16.56	0.94	26.92	291.8	2	98	0	0	35	29.28	-23.68			Nov-94
	0.05	13.23	-1.33	34.32	38.90		1.35	14.16	1.06	8.75	725.2	0	100	0	0	204	24.84	-20.55			Sep-18
	0.19	13.70	-0.76	36.94	42.99	7.17	0.8	14.14	1.06	8.8	725.2	0	100	0	0	204	25.02	-20.47			May-15
	0.09	13.40	-1.04	35.39	40.71	4.64	1.15	14.11	1.06	11.87	725.2	0	100	0	0	204	25.02	-20.47			May-08
	2.36	11.29	3.73	24.81	26.31	1.52	1.17	7.3	0.01	10.48	1,632	3	58	22	16	31	14.64	-12.65			Jul-11
	2.47	11.65	4.37	27.07	29.75	2.35	0.57	7.33	0	9.95	1,632	3	58	22	16	31	14.83	-12.51			May-15
	2.37	11.48	3.97	25.73	27.89	2.88	0.92	7.34	0.01	6.86	1,632	3	58	22	16	31	14.83	-12.51			Sep-99
	2.62	12.98	3.58	29.08	30.27	1.83	1.26	8.72	-0.04	9.3	679.5	2	71	17	9	38	17.48	-15.28			Jul-11
	2.83	13.31	4.31	31.50	33.89	2.45	0.66	8.74	-0.04	9.88	679.5	2	71	17	9	38	17.63	-15.29			May-15
	2.75	13.18	3.95	30.05	32.04	2.58	1.01	8.75	-0.06	7.8	679.5	2	71	17	9	38	17.62	-15.29			Sep-99
	2.08	9.40	3.83	20.00	21.65	2.11	1.09	5.66	0.09	9.58	458.6	3	44	30	22	31	12.01	-9.69			Jul-11
	2.28	9.75	4.47	22.26	25.04	2.82	0.49	5.62	0.08	9.87	458.6	3	44	30	22	31	12.09	-9.54			May-15
	2.22	9.64	4.18	20.98	23.27	2.69	0.84	5.62	0.09	8.56	458.6	3	44	30	22	31	12.09	-9.54			Sep-99
	3.67	16.30	5.69	42.76	44.04	3.27	0.75	12.09	0.98	9.26	570.9	2	97	0	0	22	25.67				May-15
	3.71	16.16	5.44	41.36	41.82	1.21	1.1	12.09	0.98	15	570.9	2	97	0	0	22	25.67				Jun-11
	-0.47	15.88	8.32	10.43	36.34		0.91	13.07	0.99	10.03	404.6	0	100	0	0	21					Sep-18

Fund Name	MARKET Ticker Symbol	Traded On	FUND TYPE, CATEGORY & OBJECTIVE Fund Type	Category and (Prospectus Objective)	RATINGS Overall Rating	Reward Rating	Risk Rating	Recent Up/ Downgrade	Open to New Investors	MINIMUMS Min Initial Investment
Great-West Real Estate Index Fund Institutional Class	MXSFX	NAS CM	Open End	Real Estate Sector Equity (Real Estate)	C+	C	B-		Y	0
Great-West Real Estate Index Fund Investor Class	MXREX	NAS CM	Open End	Real Estate Sector Equity (Real Estate)	C+	C	B-		Y	0
Great-West S&P 500® Index Fund Class L	MXVJX	NAS CM	Open End	US Equity Large Cap Blend (Growth)	B-	C	B		Y	0
Great-West S&P 500® Index Fund Institutional Class	MXKWX	NAS CM	Open End	US Equity Large Cap Blend (Growth)	B-	C	B		Y	0
Great-West S&P 500® Index Fund Investor Class	MXVIX	NAS CM	Open End	US Equity Large Cap Blend (Growth)	B-	C	B		Y	0
Great-West S&P Mid Cap 400® Index Fund Class L	MXBUX	NAS CM	Open End	US Equity Mid Cap (Growth)	C+	C	B-	Up	Y	0
Great-West S&P Mid Cap 400® Index Fund Institutional Class	MXNZX	NAS CM	Open End	US Equity Mid Cap (Growth)	C+	C	B-	Up	Y	0
Great-West S&P Mid Cap 400® Index Fund Investor Class	MXMDX	NAS CM	Open End	US Equity Mid Cap (Growth)	C+	C	B-	Up	Y	0
Great-West S&P Small Cap 600® Index Fund Class L	MXNSX	NAS CM	Open End	US Equity Small Cap (Small Company)	C	C-	C+		Y	0
Great-West S&P Small Cap 600® Index Institutional Cls	MXERX	NAS CM	Open End	US Equity Small Cap (Small Company)	C	C-	C+	Down	Y	0
Great-West S&P Small Cap 600® Index Fund Investor Class	MXISX	NAS CM	Open End	US Equity Small Cap (Small Company)	C	C-	C+		Y	0
Great-West SecureFoundation® Balanced ETF Fund Class A	SFBPX	NAS CM	Open End	Moderate Alloc (Balanced)	B-	C	A-	Up	Y	10,000
Great-West SecureFoundation® Balanced Fund Class L	MXLDX	NAS CM	Open End	Moderate Alloc (Balanced)	B-	C	A-	Up	Y	0
Great-West SecureFoundation® Balanced Institutional Cls	MXCJX	NAS CM	Open End	Moderate Alloc (Balanced)	B-	C	A-		Y	0
Great-West SecureFoundation® Balanced Fund Investor Class	MXSBX	NAS CM	Open End	Moderate Alloc (Balanced)	B-	C	A-	Up	Y	0
Great-West SecureFoundation® Balanced Fund Service Class	MXSHX	NAS CM	Open End	Moderate Alloc (Balanced)	B-	C	A-	Up	Y	0
Great-West SecureFoundation® Lifetime 2020 Fund Class L	MXLFX	NAS CM	Open End	Target Date (Asset Alloc)	B-	C	A-	Up	Y	0
Great-West SecureFoundation® Lifetime 2020 Investor Cls	MXSMX	NAS CM	Open End	Target Date (Asset Alloc)	B-	C	A-	Up	Y	0
Great-West SecureFoundation® Lifetime 2020 Service Cls	MXSPX	NAS CM	Open End	Target Date (Asset Alloc)	B-	C	A-	Up	Y	0
Great-West SecureFoundation® Lifetime 2025 Fund Class L	MXLHX	NAS CM	Open End	Target Date (Asset Alloc)	B-	C	A-	Up	Y	0
Great-West SecureFoundation® Lifetime 2025 Investor Cls	MXSNX	NAS CM	Open End	Target Date (Asset Alloc)	B-	C	A-	Up	Y	0
Great-West SecureFoundation® Lifetime 2025 Service Cls	MXSOX	NAS CM	Open End	Target Date (Asset Alloc)	B-	C	A-	Up	Y	0
Great-West SecureFoundation® Lifetime 2030 Fund Class L	MXLIX	NAS CM	Open End	Target Date (Asset Alloc)	B-	C	A-	Up	Y	0
Great-West SecureFoundation® Lifetime 2030 Investor Cls	MXSQX	NAS CM	Open End	Target Date (Asset Alloc)	B-	C	A-	Up	Y	0
Great-West SecureFoundation® Lifetime 2030 Service Cls	MXASX	NAS CM	Open End	Target Date (Asset Alloc)	B-	C	A-	Up	Y	0
Great-West SecureFoundation® Lifetime 2035 Fund Class L	MXLJX	NAS CM	Open End	Target Date (Asset Alloc)	B-	C	B+	Up	Y	0
Great-West SecureFoundation® Lifetime 2035 Investor Cls	MXSRX	NAS CM	Open End	Target Date (Asset Alloc)	B-	C	B+	Up	Y	0
Great-West SecureFoundation® Lifetime 2035 Service Cls	MXSSX	NAS CM	Open End	Target Date (Asset Alloc)	B-	C	B+	Up	Y	0
Great-West SecureFoundation® Lifetime 2040 Fund Class L	MXLKX	NAS CM	Open End	Target Date (Asset Alloc)	B-	C	B+	Up	Y	0
Great-West SecureFoundation® Lifetime 2040 Investor Cls	MXDSX	NAS CM	Open End	Target Date (Asset Alloc)	B-	C	B+	Up	Y	0
Great-West SecureFoundation® Lifetime 2040 Service Cls	MXESX	NAS CM	Open End	Target Date (Asset Alloc)	B-	C	B+	Up	Y	0
Great-West SecureFoundation® Lifetime 2045 Fund Class L	MXLNX	NAS CM	Open End	Target Date (Asset Alloc)	B-	C	B	Up	Y	0
Great-West SecureFoundation® Lifetime 2045 Investor Cls	MXSTX	NAS CM	Open End	Target Date (Asset Alloc)	B-	C	B	Up	Y	0
Great-West SecureFoundation® Lifetime 2045 Service Cls	MXSWX	NAS CM	Open End	Target Date (Asset Alloc)	B-	C	B	Up	Y	0
Great-West SecureFoundation® Lifetime 2050 Fund Class L	MXLOX	NAS CM	Open End	Target Date (Asset Alloc)	B-	C	B	Up	Y	0
Great-West SecureFoundation® Lifetime 2050 Investor Cls	MXFSX	NAS CM	Open End	Target Date (Asset Alloc)	B-	C	B	Up	Y	0
Great-West SecureFoundation® Lifetime 2050 Service Cls	MXHSX	NAS CM	Open End	Target Date (Asset Alloc)	B-	C	B	Up	Y	0
Great-West SecureFoundation® Lifetime 2055 Fund Class L	MXLPX	NAS CM	Open End	Target Date (Asset Alloc)	B-	C	B	Up	Y	0
Great-West SecureFoundation® Lifetime 2055 Investor Cls	MXSYX	NAS CM	Open End	Target Date (Asset Alloc)	B-	C	B	Up	Y	0
Great-West SecureFoundation® Lifetime 2055 Service Cls	MXSZX	NAS CM	Open End	Target Date (Asset Alloc)	B-	C	B	Up	Y	0
Great-West Small Cap Growth Fund Institutional	MXMSX	NAS CM	Open End	US Equity Small Cap (Small Company)	C+	C	C+	Down	Y	0
Great-West Small Cap Growth Fund Investor	MXMTX	NAS CM	Open End	US Equity Small Cap (Small Company)	C+	C	C+	Down	Y	0
Great-West T. Rowe Price Equity Income Fund Class L	MXTQX	NAS CM	Open End	US Equity Large Cap Value (Equity-Income)	B-	C	B	Up	Y	0
Great-West T. Rowe Price Equity Income Institutional Cls	MXVHX	NAS CM	Open End	US Equity Large Cap Value (Equity-Income)	B-	C	B	Up	Y	0
Great-West T. Rowe Price Equity Income Fund Investor Class	MXEQX	NAS CM	Open End	US Equity Large Cap Value (Equity-Income)	B-	C	B	Up	Y	0
Great-West T. Rowe Price Mid Cap Growth Fund Class L	MXTMX	NAS CM	Open End	US Equity Mid Cap (Growth)	B-	C+	B	Down	Y	0
Great-West T. Rowe Price Mid Cap Growth Institutional Cls	MXYKX	NAS CM	Open End	US Equity Mid Cap (Growth)	B-	C+	B	Down	Y	0
Great-West T. Rowe Price Mid Cap Growth Investor Cls	MXMGX	NAS CM	Open End	US Equity Mid Cap (Growth)	B-	C+	B	Down	Y	0
Green Century Balanced Fund	GCBLX	NAS CM	Open End	Moderate Alloc (Balanced)	B	C+	A		Y	2,500
Green Century Equity Fund Individual Investor Class	GCEQX	NAS CM	Open End	US Equity Large Cap Growth (Growth & Income)	B-	C	B	Down	Y	2,500
Green Century Equity Fund Institutional Class	GCEUX	NAS CM	Open End	US Equity Large Cap Growth (Growth & Income)	B-	C	B	Down	Y	250,000
Green Century MSCI International Index Individual Investor	GCINX	NAS CM	Open End	Global Equity Large Cap (Growth & Income)	C	D+	B	Up	Y	2,500

★ Expanded analysis of this fund is included in Section II.

Min Additional Investment	TOTAL RETURNS 3-Month Total Return	6-Month Total Return	1-Year Total Return	3-Year Total Return	5-Year Total Return	PERFORMANCE Dividend Yield (TTM)	Expense Ratio	3-Yr Std Deviation	3-Year Beta	ASSETS NAV	Total Assets (MIL)	ASSET ALLOCATION & TURNOVER %Cash	%Stocks	%Bonds	%Other	Turnover Ratio	BULL & BEAR Last Bull Market Total Return	Last Bear Market Total Return	FEES Front End Fee (%)	Back End Fee (%)	Inception Date
	-0.33	16.17	9.00	12.38	40.13	3.23	0.35	13.13	1	9.25	404.6	0	100	0	0	21					May-15
	-0.37	15.99	8.58	11.25	38.04	1.79	0.7	13.1	1	12.31	404.6	0	100	0	0	21					Nov-12
	4.26	18.45	9.04	49.06	58.70	0.65	0.78	12.2	1	17.42	2,973	1	99	0	0	4	24.52	-16.47			Jul-11
	4.34	18.88	9.67	51.81	63.08	2.76	0.16	12.16	1	9.9	2,973	1	99	0	0	4	24.66	-16.44			May-15
	4.31	18.63	9.31	50.21	60.71	0.68	0.51	12.2	1	22.77	2,973	1	99	0	0	4	24.66	-16.44			Sep-03
	1.97	17.26	-0.57	36.54	40.18	1.99	0.78	15.12	1	9.28	809.3	1	99	0	0	25	27.15	-22.8			Apr-17
	2.03	17.61	0.01	39.04	44.04	2.24	0.19	15.13	1	8.97	809.3	1	99	0	0	25	27.34	-22.72			May-15
	1.99	17.41	-0.28	37.52	41.89	0.63	0.55	15.13	1	16.15	809.3	1	99	0	0	25	27.34	-22.72			Jan-11
	0.36	12.40	-7.16	41.03	42.51	0.52	0.81	17.84	1	16.32	907.2	0	100	0	0	21	28.85	-22.22			Aug-11
	0.48	12.80	-6.59	43.60	46.43	2.56	0.2	17.9	1	8.14	907.2	0	100	0	0	21	29.16	-22.2			May-15
	0.44	12.61	-6.81	42.22	44.41	1.15	0.56	17.92	1	12.2	907.2	0	100	0	0	21	29.15	-22.2			Dec-93
500	2.89	12.29	4.93	27.41	30.68	1.95	0.35	7.58	0.59	13.58	34.2	2	59	39	0	39			5.00		Jan-12
	2.67	11.42	4.16	25.45	28.26	2.03	0.85	7.38	0.58	11.87	934.0	2	58	35	5	18	14.7	-11.21			Jan-11
	2.77	11.71	4.79	27.79	31.84	3.42	0.25	7.36	0.58	9.69	934.0	2	58	35	5	18	14.83	-11.15			May-15
	2.65	11.50	4.39	26.34	29.79	1.97	0.6	7.38	0.58	13.55	934.0	2	58	35	5	18	14.83	-11.15			Nov-09
	2.66	11.47	4.31	26.01	29.20	1.8	0.7	7.39	0.58	13.74	934.0	2	58	35	5	18	14.75	-11.2			Nov-09
	2.72	10.85	4.63	23.44	25.75	1.89	0.86	6.72		12.01	52.2	1	54	36	8	22	13.61	-10.68			Jan-11
	2.76	11.07	4.86	24.42	27.30	2.21	0.61	6.71		11.9	52.2	1	54	36	8	22	13.72	-10.65			Jan-11
	2.78	10.96	4.80	24.08	26.77	2.02	0.71	6.72		11.95	52.2	1	54	36	8	22	13.58	-10.67			Jan-11
	2.62	10.86	4.55	23.46	25.51	2.38	0.86	6.74		9.63	61.4	1	54	36	8	33	14.73	-13.44			Jan-11
	2.74	10.98	4.77	24.37	27.09	2.3	0.61	6.7		11.03	61.4	1	54	36	8	33	14.96	-13.38			Nov-09
	2.71	10.93	4.69	23.92	26.44	1.94	0.71	6.74		11.2	61.4	1	54	36	8	33	14.9	-13.44			Nov-09
	2.76	11.41	4.65	27.08	27.62	1.84	0.88	7.29		12.68	78.9	2	58	33	7	30	17.24	-15.82			Jan-11
	2.73	11.51	4.86	27.99	29.03	2.2	0.63	7.31		12.48	78.9	2	58	33	7	30	17.23	-15.79			Jan-11
	2.74	11.38	4.72	27.67	28.46	2.02	0.73	7.29		12.55	78.9	2	58	33	7	30	17.14	-15.8			Jan-11
	2.93	12.70	4.29	31.89	30.94	2.37	0.89	8.7		10.17	53.4	2	70	24	4	32	18.87	-17.68			Jan-11
	2.88	12.69	4.35	32.24	31.55	2.24	0.64	8.74		11.8	53.4	2	70	24	4	32	18.91	-17.67			Nov-09
	2.83	12.69	4.26	31.90	30.91	1.9	0.74	8.73		11.98	53.4	2	70	24	4	32	18.81	-17.72			Nov-09
	2.86	13.75	3.81	35.37	32.99	2.12	0.91	9.9		12.78	64.0	2	80	16	2	28	19.64	-18.52			Jan-11
	2.90	13.71	3.86	35.59	33.19	2.16	0.66	9.92		12.66	64.0	2	80	16	2	28	19.74	-18.59			Jan-11
	2.83	13.70	3.76	35.14	32.51	1.94	0.76	9.91		12.7	64.0	2	80	16	2	28	19.64	-18.6			Jan-11
	2.95	14.40	3.51	36.61	33.14	2.17	0.91	10.65		10.16	26.9	2	86	10	1	36	19.93	-18.98			Jan-11
	2.90	14.25	3.40	36.93	33.61	2.49	0.66	10.68		12.02	26.9	2	86	10	1	36	19.91	-18.99			Nov-09
	2.91	14.30	3.35	36.60	32.97	2.21	0.76	10.63		11.99	26.9	2	86	10	1	36	19.93	-18.98			Nov-09
	2.93	14.41	3.16	36.75	32.85	2.03	0.92	10.89		12.82	21.1	2	88	8	1	37	19.91	-19.19			Jan-11
	2.90	14.44	3.24	37.42	33.44	2.17	0.66	10.91		12.76	21.1	2	88	8	1	37	20.02	-19.26			Jan-11
	2.89	14.42	3.15	36.97	32.73	1.89	0.76	10.89		12.78	21.1	2	88	8	1	37	19.93	-19.27			Jan-11
	2.93	14.43	3.07	37.21	32.64	2.58	0.91	10.97		10.44	10.5	2	89	8	1	39	19.94	-19.44			Jan-11
	2.88	14.42	3.10	37.39	32.86	2.22	0.66	10.99		12.35	10.5	2	89	8	1	39	19.93	-19.41			Nov-09
	2.86	14.43	3.06	37.09	32.18	1.92	0.76	11		12.43	10.5	2	89	8	1	39	19.91	-19.47			Nov-09
	2.88	20.49	1.15	66.17		5.27	0.84	18.04	1.02	10.89	83.3	0	100	0	0	86					Sep-15
	2.91	20.34	0.85	64.64		5.01	1.19	18.01	1.02	10.77	83.3	0	100	0	0	86					Sep-15
	3.85	15.64	4.48	38.77	33.10	1.61	1.07	12.32	1	9.15	742.5	3	95	1	0	22	23.48	-18.28			Jul-11
	4.00	15.91	5.12	41.40	37.18	2.93	0.47	12.3	1	7.73	742.5	3	95	1	0	22	23.65	-18.26			May-15
	3.92	15.75	4.72	40.02	35.22	0.23	0.82	12.33	1.01	20.76	742.5	3	95	1	0	22	23.65	-18.26			Nov-94
	6.48	24.19	14.48	60.05	77.60	1.92	1.27	12.96	0.88	6.55	1,864	7	92	0	1	38	24.83	-20.36			Aug-11
	6.70	24.51	15.14	63.01	82.72	1.94	0.67	12.88	0.87	8.5	1,864	7	92	0	1	38	25.03	-20.33			May-15
	6.54	24.23	14.65	61.27	79.96	0.07	1.02	12.92	0.88	29.78	1,864	7	92	0	1	38	25.03	-20.33			Jul-97
100	4.24	15.17	11.42	33.86	36.22	0.37	1.48	7.65		28.73	272.0	4	65	31	0	18	16.74	-11.72			Mar-92
100	4.18	19.32	10.66	49.98	62.45	0.46	1.25	12.22		45.23	295.0	0	100	0	0		22.48	-15.2			Sep-95
100	4.26	19.50	11.01	50.53	63.05	0.86	0.95	12.2		45.17	295.0	0	100	0	0		22.48	-15.2			Apr-18
100	5.67	15.62	2.81			1.45	1.28			11.29	64.0	0	94	0	1	28					Sep-16

	MARKET		FUND TYPE, CATEGORY & OBJECTIVE		RATINGS					MINIMUMS
Fund Name	Ticker Symbol	Traded On	Fund Type	Category and (Prospectus Objective)	Overall Rating	Reward Rating	Risk Rating	Recent Up/ Downgrade	Open to New Investors	Min Initial Investment
Green Century MSCI International Index Fund Institutional	GCIFX	NAS CM	Open End	Global Equity Large Cap (Growth & Income)	C	D+	B	Up	Y	250,000
Green Owl Intrinsic Value Fund	GOWLX	NAS CM	Open End	US Equity Large Cap Blend (Growth)	C+	C	B	Down	Y	2,500
Greenspring Fund	GRSPX	NAS CM	Open End	Moderate Alloc (Growth)	C+	C	B	Up	Y	2,500
Griffin Institutional Access Real Estate Fund Class A	GIREX	NAS CM	Closed End	Real Estate Sector Equity (Real Estate)	B	C+	A-		Y	2,500
Griffin Institutional Access Real Estate Fund Class C	GCREX	NAS CM	Closed End	Real Estate Sector Equity (Real Estate)	B	C+	A+		Y	2,500
Griffin Institutional Access Real Estate Fund Class I	GRIFX	NAS CM	Closed End	Real Estate Sector Equity (Real Estate)	B	C+	A		Y	1,000,000
Griffin Institutional Access Real Estate Fund Class L	GLREX	NAS CM	Closed End	Real Estate Sector Equity (Real Estate)	B	C+	A+		Y	2,500
Griffin Institutional Access Real Estate Fund Class M	GMREX	NAS CM	Closed End	Real Estate Sector Equity (Real Estate)	B	C+	A-		Y	25,000
Grizzly Short Fund	GRZZX	NAS CM	Open End	Alternative Miscellaneous (Growth)	D	D-	D-		Y	10,000
Guggenheim Alpha Opportunity Fund Class A	SAOAX	NAS CM	Open End	Long/Short Equity (Growth)	D	D	D+	Down	Y	2,500
Guggenheim Alpha Opportunity Fund Class C	SAOCX	NAS CM	Open End	Long/Short Equity (Growth)	D	D	D+	Down	Y	2,500
Guggenheim Alpha Opportunity Fund Class P	SAOSX	NAS CM	Open End	Long/Short Equity (Growth)	D	D	D+	Down	Y	0
Guggenheim Alpha Opportunity Fund Institutional Class	SAOIX	NAS CM	Open End	Long/Short Equity (Growth)	D	D	D+	Down	Y	2,000,000
Guggenheim Directional Allocation Fund Class A	TVRAX	NAS CM	Open End	US Equity Large Cap Growth (Growth & Income)	C+	C	B	Up	Y	2,500
Guggenheim Directional Allocation Fund Class C	TVRCX	NAS CM	Open End	US Equity Large Cap Growth (Growth & Income)	C+	C	B-	Up	Y	2,500
Guggenheim Directional Allocation Fund Class I	TVRIX	NAS CM	Open End	US Equity Large Cap Growth (Growth & Income)	C+	C	B		Y	2,000,000
Guggenheim Directional Allocation Fund Class P	TVFRX	NAS CM	Open End	US Equity Large Cap Growth (Growth & Income)	C+	C	B	Up	Y	0
Guggenheim Diversified Income Fund Class A	GUDAX	NAS CM	Open End	Cautious Alloc (Income)	B	C+	B+	Up	Y	2,500
Guggenheim Diversified Income Fund Class C	GUDCX	NAS CM	Open End	Cautious Alloc (Income)	B-	C	B+	Up	Y	2,500
Guggenheim Diversified Income Fund Class P	GUDPX	NAS CM	Open End	Cautious Alloc (Income)	B	C+	B+	Up	Y	0
Guggenheim Diversified Income Fund Institutional	GUDIX	NAS CM	Open End	Cautious Alloc (Income)	B	C+	B+	Up	Y	2,000,000
Guggenheim Enhanced Equity Income	GPM	NYSE	Closed End	Alternative Miscellaneous (Growth & Income)	C	C	C+		Y	
Guggenheim Large Cap Value Fund Class A	SECIX	NAS CM	Open End	US Equity Large Cap Value (Growth)	C+	C	B		Y	2,500
Guggenheim Large Cap Value Fund Class C	SEGIX	NAS CM	Open End	US Equity Large Cap Value (Growth)	C+	C	B-	Up	Y	2,500
Guggenheim Large Cap Value Fund Class Institutional	GILCX	NAS CM	Open End	US Equity Large Cap Value (Growth)	C+	C	B		Y	2,000,000
Guggenheim Large Cap Value Fund Class P	SEGPX	NAS CM	Open End	US Equity Large Cap Value (Growth)	C+	C	B		Y	0
Guggenheim Long Short Equity Fund Class A	RYAMX	NAS CM	Open End	Long/Short Equity (Growth)	D+	D+	C-	Down	Y	2,500
Guggenheim Long Short Equity Fund Class C	RYISX	NAS CM	Open End	Long/Short Equity (Growth)	D+	D	C-	Down	Y	2,500
Guggenheim Long Short Equity Fund Class P	RYSRX	NAS CM	Open End	Long/Short Equity (Growth)	D+	D+	C-	Down	Y	0
Guggenheim Long Short Equity Institutional Cls Shares	RYQTX	NAS CM	Open End	Long/Short Equity (Growth)	C-	D+	C-	Down	Y	2,000,000
Guggenheim Managed Futures Strategy Fund Class P	RYMFX	NAS CM	Open End	Alternative Miscellaneous (Growth & Income)	C-	D+	C	Up	Y	0
Guggenheim Market Neutral Real Estate Fund Class A	GUMAX	NAS CM	Open End	Market Neutral (Real Estate)	B	C+	A-	Up	Y	2,500
Guggenheim Market Neutral Real Estate Fund Class C	GUMCX	NAS CM	Open End	Market Neutral (Real Estate)	B-	C	B+	Up	Y	2,500
Guggenheim Market Neutral Real Estate Fund Class P	GUMPX	NAS CM	Open End	Market Neutral (Real Estate)	B	C+	A-	Up	Y	0
Guggenheim Market Neutral Real Estate Fund Institutional	GUMNX	NAS CM	Open End	Market Neutral (Real Estate)	B	C+	A-	Up	Y	2,000,000
Guggenheim Mid Cap Value Fund Class A	SEVAX	NAS CM	Open End	US Equity Mid Cap (Growth)	C	C	C+		Y	2,500
Guggenheim Mid Cap Value Fund Class C	SEVSX	NAS CM	Open End	US Equity Mid Cap (Growth)	C	C	C+		Y	2,500
Guggenheim Mid Cap Value Fund Class P	SEVPX	NAS CM	Open End	US Equity Mid Cap (Growth)	C	C	C+		Y	0
Guggenheim Mid Cap Value Institutional Fund	SVUIX	NAS CM	Open End	US Equity Mid Cap (Growth)	C	C	C+		Y	2,000,000
Guggenheim Multi-Hedge Strategies Fund Class A	RYMQX	NAS CM	Open End	Global Macro (Growth)	C	C	C+		Y	2,500
Guggenheim Multi-Hedge Strategies Fund Class C	RYMRX	NAS CM	Open End	Global Macro (Growth)	C	C	C	Up	Y	2,500
Guggenheim Multi-Hedge Strategies Fund Class I	RYIMX	NAS CM	Open End	Global Macro (Growth)	C	C	B-		Y	2,000,000
Guggenheim Multi-Hedge Strategies Fund Class P	RYMSX	NAS CM	Open End	Global Macro (Growth)	C	C	C+		Y	0
Guggenheim RBP® Dividend Fund Class A	TVEAX	NAS CM	Open End	US Equity Mid Cap (Growth & Income)	B-	C	B	Up	Y	2,500
Guggenheim RBP® Dividend Fund Class C	TVECX	NAS CM	Open End	US Equity Mid Cap (Growth & Income)	C+	C	B		Y	2,500
Guggenheim RBP® Dividend Fund Class I	TVEIX	NAS CM	Open End	US Equity Mid Cap (Growth & Income)	B-	C	B	Up	Y	2,000,000
Guggenheim RBP® Dividend Fund Class P	TVEFX	NAS CM	Open End	US Equity Mid Cap (Growth & Income)	B-	C	B	Up	Y	0
Guggenheim RBP® Large-Cap Defensive Fund Class A	TVDAX	NAS CM	Open End	US Equity Large Cap Growth (Growth & Income)	B-	C+	B		Y	2,500
Guggenheim RBP® Large-Cap Defensive Fund Class C	TVDCX	NAS CM	Open End	US Equity Large Cap Growth (Growth & Income)	B-	C+	B		Y	2,500
Guggenheim RBP® Large-Cap Defensive Fund Class I	TVIDX	NAS CM	Open End	US Equity Large Cap Growth (Growth & Income)	B-	C+	B		Y	2,000,000
Guggenheim RBP® Large-Cap Defensive Fund Class P	TVFDX	NAS CM	Open End	US Equity Large Cap Growth (Growth & Income)	B-	C+	B		Y	0
Guggenheim RBP® Large-Cap Market Fund Class A	TVMAX	NAS CM	Open End	US Equity Large Cap Growth (Growth & Income)	B-	C	B		Y	2,500

★ Expanded analysis of this fund is included in Section II.

Min Additional Investment	TOTAL RETURNS					PERFORMANCE				ASSETS		ASSET ALLOCATION & TURNOVER					BULL & BEAR		FEES		
	3-Month Total Return	6-Month Total Return	1-Year Total Return	3-Year Total Return	5-Year Total Return	Dividend Yield (TTM)	Expense Ratio	3-Yr Std Deviation	3-Year Beta	NAV	Total Assets (MIL)	%Cash	%Stocks	%Bonds	%Other	Turnover Ratio	Last Bull Market Total Return	Last Bear Market Total Return	Front End Fee (%)	Back End Fee (%)	Inception Date
100	5.76	15.82	3.13			1.83	0.98			11.28	64.0	0	94	0	1	28					Sep-16
	6.08	20.40	8.88	53.24	45.60	0.26	1.1	15.05	1.14	18.65	83.2	0	100	0	0	33					Dec-11
100	3.42	14.97	0.46	26.83	19.70	1.59	1.02	10.56	0.8	22.65	202.5	4	71	26	0	30	11.67	-10.02			Jul-83
100	1.47	5.09	6.77	19.85	41.37	5.24	2.11	2.12		27.24	--	2	98	0	0	29			5.75		Jun-14
100	1.28	4.72	6.00	17.21	37.48	5.26	2.86	2.12		26.48	--	2	98	0	0	29				1.00	Aug-15
100	1.50	5.22	7.03	20.76	42.72	5.24	1.86	2.13		27.51	--	2	98	0	0	29					Aug-15
	1.40	4.94	6.54	19.36	40.80	5.25	2.35			27.12	--	2	98	0	0	29			4.25		Apr-17
10,000	1.36	4.84	6.31	18.35	39.61	5.25	2.59			26.9	--	2	98	0	0	29					Nov-16
100	-4.06	-21.76	-12.61	-42.05	-44.47	0.7	2.79	14.47	-1.06	15.88	87.5	221	-121	0	0	0	-26.88	30.16			Jun-00
100	-3.59	-3.37	-5.99	1.00	2.73	1.22	1.54	7.95	16.57	17.44	90.9	9	94	0	-3	255	30.85	-24.46	4.75		Jul-03
100	-3.73	-3.73	-6.74	-1.26	-1.06	0	2.34	7.96	16.22	15.21	90.9	9	94	0	-3	255	30.2	-24.66		1.00	Jul-03
	-3.56	-3.30	-5.97	1.38	3.16	0.79	1.58	7.93	16	17.58	90.9	9	94	0	-3	255	30.85	-24.46			May-15
	-3.49	-3.16	-5.59	2.70	4.97	1.22	1.12	7.94	16.71	25.37	90.9	9	94	0	-3	255	30.96	-24.37			Nov-08
100	4.13	21.45	5.43	47.01	42.47	0	1.48	13.94	1.12	16.36	576.9	0	100	0	0	92			4.75		Jun-12
100	3.95	21.11	4.60	43.82	37.58	0	2.11	13.93	1.12	15.49	576.9	0	100	0	0	92				1.00	Jun-12
	4.22	21.68	5.67	48.12	44.57	0	1.11	13.93	1.12	16.78	576.9	0	100	0	0	92					Jun-12
	4.17	21.58	5.41	47.15	42.84	0	1.36	13.94	1.12	16.45	576.9	0	100	0	0	92					Jun-12
100	2.32	7.86	4.43	16.24		2.92	1.42	3.58	0.3	26.7	7.2	15	25	59	-1	37			4.00		Jan-16
100	2.10	7.46	3.68	13.68		2.03	2.17	3.58	0.3	26.73	7.2	15	25	59	-1	37				1.00	Jan-16
	2.29	7.87	4.45	16.24		2.94	1.42	3.58	0.3	26.7	7.2	15	25	59	-1	37					Jan-16
	2.35	7.98	4.69	17.09		3.16	1.18	3.57	0.3	26.71	7.2	15	25	59	-1	37					Jan-16
	3.76	20.56	4.73	36.71	45.40	0.74	0	13.41	1.07	7.86	378.6	0	100	0	0	25	27.79	-15.02			Aug-05
100	0.87	12.77	2.12	34.11	34.85	0.79	1.15	13.31	1.09	43.86	60.9	3	97	0	1	24	25.11	-22.16	4.75		Aug-44
100	0.70	12.38	1.39	31.08	29.87	0	1.9	13.3	1.09	40.12	60.9	3	97	0	1	24	24.56	-22.42		1.00	Jan-99
	0.93	12.92	2.39	35.06	36.48	1.06	0.9	13.31	1.09	43.35	60.9	3	97	0	1	24	25.11	-22.16			Jun-13
	0.87	12.78	2.15	34.08	34.94	0.84	1.15	13.31	1.09	43.76	60.9	3	97	0	1	24	25.11	-22.16			May-15
	-2.34	1.93	-4.17	4.13	6.54	0	1.77	10.09	0.74	15.82	21.3	4	96	0	0	170	11.81	-19.05	4.75		Mar-04
	-2.53	1.53	-4.92	1.78	2.59	0	2.52	10.08	0.74	13.85	21.3	4	96	0	0	170	11.34	-19.32		1.00	Mar-02
	-2.33	1.92	-4.21	4.11	6.52	0	1.76	10.08	0.74	15.87	21.3	4	96	0	0	170	11.77	-19.06			Mar-02
	-2.28	2.07	-3.96	4.95	7.90	0	1.5	10.05	0.74	16.22	21.3	4	96	0	0	170	11.85	-19.06			Nov-11
	2.46	5.87	0.26	-2.19	-0.57	0	1.81	9.3	35.64	18.73	31.5	33	0	40	26	21	-8.56	-7.81			Mar-07
100	3.97	6.47	7.68	17.42		0.02	1.65	4.4	-7.21	26.97	8.6	21	89	0	-11	216			4.75		Feb-16
100	3.77	6.04	6.70	14.68		0.43	2.4	4.41	-7.34	26.14	8.6	21	89	0	-11	216				1.00	Feb-16
	3.98	6.48	7.36	16.98		2.7	1.65	4.41	-6.99	26.12	8.6	21	89	0	-11	216					Feb-16
	4.04	6.61	7.80	18.07		1.42	1.4	4.4	-6.89	26.75	8.6	21	89	0	-11	216					Feb-16
100	2.59	15.58	-4.19	34.57	25.47	0.1	1.26	14.73	0.96	29.67	388.5	1	99	0	-1	54	20.97	-24.15	4.75		May-97
100	2.41	15.10	-4.96	31.38	20.75	0	2.03	14.72	0.96	19.96	388.5	1	99	0	-1	54	20.43	-24.39		1.00	Jan-99
	2.58	15.50	-4.26	34.47	25.07	0.07	1.32	14.7	0.96	29.42	388.5	1	99	0	-1	54	20.97	-24.15			May-15
	2.58	15.69	-4.09	35.05	27.69	0.64	1.14	14.64	0.96	9.51	58.6	2	99	0	-1	63	21.3	-24.35			Jul-08
	1.23	4.31	3.52	3.37	8.02	0.16	1.91	4.32	0.24	24.64	38.6	49	14	8	29	172	0.33	1.48	4.75		Sep-05
	1.04	3.92	2.86	1.20	4.14	0	2.69	4.36	0.24	22.24	38.6	49	14	8	29	172	-0.06	1.17		1.00	Sep-05
	1.29	4.44	3.85	4.13	9.35	0.56	1.74	4.35	0.24	25.12	38.6	49	14	8	29	172	0.51	1.61			May-10
	1.27	4.35	3.61	3.55	8.20	0.17	1.93	4.3	0.24	24.7	38.6	49	14	8	29	172	0.38	1.48			Sep-05
100	2.65	16.79	5.66	35.21	43.63	2.54	1.22	12.79		11.83	22.3	1	99	0	0	97	23.01	-16.3	4.75		Apr-11
100	2.36	16.18	4.77	32.15	38.62	1.28	1.97	12.77		11.88	22.3	1	99	0	0	97	22.6	-16.49		1.00	Apr-11
	2.69	16.87	5.93	36.33	45.87	2.87	0.97	12.78		11.54	22.3	1	99	0	0	97	23.27	-16.11			Feb-11
	2.66	16.71	5.67	35.22	44.02	2.51	1.22	12.75		11.96	22.3	1	99	0	0	97	23.2	-16.29			Apr-11
100	6.33	21.74	11.29	44.48	52.15	0.28	1.21	11.22		10.75	15.4	1	99	0	0	117	21.97	-11.62	4.75		Apr-10
100	6.13	21.40	10.54	41.36	46.95	0	1.96	11.24		10.38	15.4	1	99	0	0	117	21.47	-11.71		1.00	Apr-11
	6.36	21.89	11.56	45.60	54.47	0.51	0.96	11.27		11.19	15.4	1	99	0	0	117	22.23	-11.43			Feb-11
	6.32	21.73	11.22	44.48	52.67	0.18	1.21	11.27		11.09	15.4	1	99	0	0	117	22.01	-11.52			Apr-10
100	4.89	22.82	9.14	51.51	54.74	0	1.21	12.66		10.71	15.4	1	99	0	0	93	22.92	-16.87	4.75		Apr-10

Fund Name	MARKET Ticker Symbol	Traded On	Fund Type	FUND TYPE, CATEGORY & OBJECTIVE Category and (Prospectus Objective)	RATINGS Overall Rating	Reward Rating	Risk Rating	Recent Up/ Downgrade	MINIMUMS Open to New Investors	Min Initial Investment
Guggenheim RBP® Large-Cap Market Fund Class C	TVMCX	NAS CM	Open End	US Equity Large Cap Growth (Growth & Income)	C+	C	B	Down	Y	2,500
Guggenheim RBP® Large-Cap Market Fund Class I	TVIMX	NAS CM	Open End	US Equity Large Cap Growth (Growth & Income)	B-	C	B		Y	2,000,000
Guggenheim RBP® Large-Cap Market Fund Class P	TVFMX	NAS CM	Open End	US Equity Large Cap Growth (Growth & Income)	B-	C	B		Y	0
Guggenheim RBP® Large-Cap Value Fund Class A	TVVAX	NAS CM	Open End	US Equity Mid Cap (Growth & Income)	C+	C	B		Y	2,500
Guggenheim RBP® Large-Cap Value Fund Class C	TVVCX	NAS CM	Open End	US Equity Mid Cap (Growth & Income)	C+	C	B		Y	2,500
Guggenheim RBP® Large-Cap Value Fund Class I	TVVIX	NAS CM	Open End	US Equity Mid Cap (Growth & Income)	C+	C	B		Y	2,000,000
Guggenheim RBP® Large-Cap Value Fund Class P	TVVFX	NAS CM	Open End	US Equity Mid Cap (Growth & Income)	C+	C	B		Y	0
Guggenheim Risk Managed Real Estate Fund Class A	GURAX	NAS CM	Open End	Real Estate Sector Equity (Real Estate)	B	B	B		Y	2,500
Guggenheim Risk Managed Real Estate Fund Class C	GURCX	NAS CM	Open End	Real Estate Sector Equity (Real Estate)	B-	B-	B		Y	2,500
Guggenheim Risk Managed Real Estate Fund Class P	GURPX	NAS CM	Open End	Real Estate Sector Equity (Real Estate)	B	B-	B		Y	0
Guggenheim Risk Managed Real Estate Fund Institutional	GURIX	NAS CM	Open End	Real Estate Sector Equity (Real Estate)	B	B	B		Y	2,000,000
Guggenheim Series Trust Managed Futures Strategy Cls A	RYMTX	NAS CM	Open End	Alternative Miscellaneous (Growth & Income)	C-	D+	C	Up	Y	2,500
Guggenheim Series Trust Managed Futures Strategy Cls C	RYMZX	NAS CM	Open End	Alternative Miscellaneous (Growth & Income)	C-	D+	C	Up	Y	2,500
Guggenheim Series Trust Managed Futures Strategy Cls I	RYIFX	NAS CM	Open End	Alternative Miscellaneous (Growth & Income)	C-	D+	C	Up	Y	2,000,000
Guggenheim Small Cap Value Fund Class A	SSUAX	NAS CM	Open End	US Equity Small Cap (Small Company)	C	C-	C		Y	2,500
Guggenheim Small Cap Value Fund Class C	SSVCX	NAS CM	Open End	US Equity Small Cap (Small Company)	C-	D+	C	Down	Y	2,500
Guggenheim Small Cap Value Fund Class P	SSUPX	NAS CM	Open End	US Equity Small Cap (Small Company)	C	C-	C		Y	0
Guggenheim Small Cap Value Institutional Fund	SSUIX	NAS CM	Open End	US Equity Small Cap (Small Company)	C	C-	C		Y	2,000,000
Guggenheim StylePlus - Large Core Fund Class A	SECEX	NAS CM	Open End	US Equity Large Cap Blend (Growth)	C+	C	B		Y	2,500
Guggenheim StylePlus - Large Core Fund Class C	SFECX	NAS CM	Open End	US Equity Large Cap Blend (Growth)	C+	C	B		Y	2,500
Guggenheim StylePlus - Large Core Fund Class P	SFEPX	NAS CM	Open End	US Equity Large Cap Blend (Growth)	C+	C	B		Y	0
Guggenheim StylePlus - Large Core Fund Institutional	GILIX	NAS CM	Open End	US Equity Large Cap Blend (Growth)	B-	C	B	Up	Y	2,000,000
Guggenheim StylePlus - Mid Growth Fund Class A	SECUX	NAS CM	Open End	US Equity Mid Cap (Growth)	C+	C	B	Down	Y	2,500
Guggenheim StylePlus - Mid Growth Fund Class C	SUFCX	NAS CM	Open End	US Equity Mid Cap (Growth)	C+	C	B-		Y	2,500
Guggenheim StylePlus - Mid Growth Fund Class P	SEUPX	NAS CM	Open End	US Equity Mid Cap (Growth)	C+	C	B-	Down	Y	0
Guggenheim StylePlus - Mid Growth Fund Institutional	GIUIX	NAS CM	Open End	US Equity Mid Cap (Growth)	C+	C	B	Down	Y	2,000,000
Guggenheim World Equity Income Fund Class A	SEQAX	NAS CM	Open End	Global Equity Large Cap (World Stock)	B-	C	B	Up	Y	2,500
Guggenheim World Equity Income Fund Class C	SFGCX	NAS CM	Open End	Global Equity Large Cap (World Stock)	C+	C	B	Up	Y	2,500
Guggenheim World Equity Income Fund Class P	SEQPX	NAS CM	Open End	Global Equity Large Cap (World Stock)	B-	C	B	Up	Y	0
Guggenheim World Equity Income Fund Institutional Class	SEWIX	NAS CM	Open End	Global Equity Large Cap (World Stock)	B-	C	B	Up	Y	2,000,000
GuideMark® Emerging Markets Fund Service Shares	GMLVX	NAS CM	Open End	Global Emerg Mkts (Div Emerging Mkts)	C	C	C+		Y	0
GuideMark® Large Cap Core Fund Institutional Shares	GILGX	NAS CM	Open End	US Equity Large Cap Blend (Growth)	C+	C	B	Down	Y	0
GuideMark® Large Cap Core Fund Service Shares	GMLGX	NAS CM	Open End	US Equity Large Cap Blend (Growth)	C+	C	B		Y	0
GuideMark® Small/Mid Cap Core Fund Institutional Shares	GISMX	NAS CM	Open End	US Equity Small Cap (Growth)	B-	C	B+	Down	Y	0
GuideMark® Small/Mid Cap Core Fund Service Shares	GMSMX	NAS CM	Open End	US Equity Small Cap (Growth)	C	C	B-	Down	Y	0
GuideMark® World ex-US Fund Institutional Shares	GIWEX	NAS CM	Open End	Global Equity Large Cap (Foreign Stock)	C	C	B-		Y	0
GuideMark® World ex-US Fund Service Shares	GMWEX	NAS CM	Open End	Global Equity Large Cap (Foreign Stock)	C	C	B-		Y	0
GuidePath® Absolute Return Allocation Institutional Shares	GIARX	NAS CM	Open End	Cautious Alloc (Asset Alloc)	B-	C	B		Y	0
GuidePath® Absolute Return Allocation Fund Service Shares	GPARX	NAS CM	Open End	Cautious Alloc (Asset Alloc)	B-	C	B+	Down	Y	0
GuidePath® Conservative Allocation Institutional Shares	GITTX	NAS CM	Open End	Cautious Alloc (Asset Alloc)	B	C+	A-	Up	Y	0
GuidePath® Conservative Allocation Fund Service Shares	GPTCX	NAS CM	Open End	Cautious Alloc (Asset Alloc)	B-	C	B+		Y	0
GuidePath® Conservative Allocation Fund Service Shares	GIXFX	NAS CM	Open End	US Fixed Income (Income)	C+	C	B		Y	0
GuidePath® Conservative Allocation Fund Service Shares	GPIFX	NAS CM	Open End	US Fixed Income (Income)	C	C	B-		Y	0
GuidePath® Growth Allocation Fund Institutional Shares	GISRX	NAS CM	Open End	Global Equity Large Cap (Asset Alloc)	C+	C	B	Up	Y	0
GuidePath® Growth Allocation Fund Service Shares	GPSTX	NAS CM	Open End	Global Equity Large Cap (Asset Alloc)	C+	C	B	Up	Y	0
Guidepath® Growth and Income Fund	GPIGX	NAS CM	Open End	US Equity Large Cap Value (Growth & Income)	D	D+	C-	Up	Y	0
GuidePath® Managed Futures Strategy Institutional Shares	GIFMX	NAS CM	Open End	Alternative Miscellaneous (Growth & Income)	D+	D	C-	Up	Y	0
GuidePath® Managed Futures Strategy Fund Service Shares	GPMFX	NAS CM	Open End	Alternative Miscellaneous (Growth & Income)	D	D	C-		Y	0
GuidePath® Multi-Asset Income Allocation Service Shares	GPMIX	NAS CM	Open End	Cautious Alloc (Multi-Asset Global)	B-	C	B		Y	0
GuidePath® Tactical Allocation Fund Institutional Shares	GITUX	NAS CM	Open End	Moderate Alloc (Balanced)	B-	C	B	Up	Y	0
GuidePath® Tactical Allocation Fund Service Shares	GPTUX	NAS CM	Open End	Moderate Alloc (Balanced)	C+	C	B	Up	Y	0
GuideStone Funds Aggressive Allocation Institutional Cls	GAGYX	NAS CM	Open End	Global Equity Large Cap (Asset Alloc)	C+	C	B	Up	Y	1,000,000

★ Expanded analysis of this fund is included in Section II.

	TOTAL RETURNS					PERFORMANCE				ASSETS		ASSET ALLOCATION & TURNOVER					BULL & BEAR		FEES		
Min Additional Investment	3-Month Total Return	6-Month Total Return	1-Year Total Return	3-Year Total Return	5-Year Total Return	Dividend Yield (TTM)	Expense Ratio	3-Yr Std Deviation	3-Year Beta	NAV	Total Assets (MIL)	%Cash	%Stocks	%Bonds	%Other	Turnover Ratio	Last Bull Market Total Return	Last Bear Market Total Return	Front End Fee (%)	Back End Fee (%)	Inception Date
100	4.67	22.18	8.31	47.97	49.43	0	1.96	12.64		10.08	15.4	1	99	0	0	93	22.56	-17.06		1.00	Apr-11
	4.95	22.90	9.43	52.60	57.13	0	0.96	12.67		11.43	15.4	1	99	0	0	93	23.22	-16.87			Feb-11
	4.83	22.77	9.15	51.25	55.10	0	1.21	12.67		11.05	15.4	1	99	0	0	93	23.05	-16.96			Apr-10
100	1.82	17.11	5.82	36.58	41.09	0.58	1.21	12.81		10.06	3.5	1	98	0	1	104	26.25	-18.86	4.75		Apr-11
100	1.63	16.80	5.01	33.44	35.85	0.47	1.96	12.78		9.94	3.5	1	98	0	1	104	25.79	-19.15		1.00	Apr-11
	1.90	17.39	6.11	37.65	43.19	1.13	0.96	12.79		10.19	3.5	1	98	0	1	104	26.61	-18.85			Feb-11
	1.71	17.14	5.74	36.55	41.42	0.79	1.21	12.78		10.11	3.5	1	98	0	1	104	26.3	-18.86			Apr-11
100	3.64	19.17	14.34	25.04	59.50	1.86	1.77	9.77	0.7	32.15	204.4	19	81	0	0	107			4.75		Mar-14
100	3.44	18.75	13.50	22.24	53.59	1.16	2.53	9.78	0.7	31.94	204.4	19	81	0	0	107				1.00	Mar-14
	3.67	19.21	14.35	24.97	59.53	1.77	1.78	9.78	0.7	32.35	204.4	19	81	0	0	107					May-15
	3.73	19.37	14.63	26.11	61.83	2.07	1.49	9.78	0.7	32.53	204.4	19	81	0	0	107					Mar-14
	2.46	5.95	0.32	-2.39	-0.77	0	1.81	9.33	36.79	18.69	31.5	33	0	40	26	21	-8.56	-7.81	4.75		Mar-07
	2.30	5.57	-0.41	-4.55	-4.40	0	2.56	9.29	36.57	16.85	31.5	33	0	40	26	21	-8.98	-8.06		1.00	Mar-07
	2.56	6.08	0.57	-1.65	0.46	0	1.56	9.32	37.05	19.18	31.5	33	0	40	26	21	-8.44	-7.71			May-10
100	1.68	12.51	-5.87	22.37	12.39	1.33	1.3	16.23	0.93	12.68	15.5	3	97	0	0	18	29.9	-25.87	4.75		Jul-08
100	1.48	12.06	-6.56	19.63	8.28	0.28	2.05	16.21	0.92	11.61	15.5	3	97	0	0	18	29.45	-26.13		1.00	Jul-08
	1.66	12.53	-5.85	22.34	12.35	1.34	1.3	16.23	0.93	12.84	15.5	3	97	0	0	18	29.97	-25.88			May-15
	1.69	12.61	-5.68	23.22	13.69	1.76	1.05	16.19	0.92	11.43	15.5	3	97	0	0	18	30.16	-25.8			Jul-08
100	3.69	18.40	7.77	46.81	61.24	1.23	1.34	12.62	1.03	20.2	202.8	23	21	31	25	46	25.4	-20.65	4.75		Sep-62
100	3.45	17.95	6.78	42.98	54.04	0	2.24	12.64	1.04	14.06	202.8	23	21	31	25	46	24.78	-20.88		1.00	Jan-99
	3.63	18.33	7.67	46.12	60.14	1.1	1.56	12.66	1.04	19.94	202.8	23	21	31	25	46	25.4	-20.65			May-15
	3.67	18.46	7.95	48.09	63.84	1.52	1.06	12.64	1.04	20.02	202.8	23	21	31	25	46	25.4	-20.65			Mar-12
100	4.65	25.41	10.52	53.65	60.91	0.84	1.55	14.54	1.01	40.02	88.6	21	20	29	30	52	27.97	-20.55	4.75		Sep-69
100	4.42	24.85	9.51	49.75	54.17	0	2.33	14.52	1.01	25.97	88.6	21	20	29	30	52	27.41	-20.83		1.00	Jan-99
	4.62	25.34	10.38	52.88	59.76	0.54	1.68	14.53	1.01	39.57	88.6	21	20	29	30	52	27.97	-20.55			May-15
	4.65	25.34	10.62	54.55	61.79	1.07	1.26	14.51	1.01	40.01	88.6	21	20	29	30	52	28.04	-20.55			Mar-12
100	2.37	13.01	2.96	23.02	21.20	2.25	1.22	9.54	0.82	15.13	79.0	1	99	0	0	125	10.26	-21.2	4.75		Oct-93
100	2.36	12.20	1.96	21.47	16.35	1.52	1.97	9.56	0.82	12.95	79.0	1	99	0	0	125	9.84	-21.48		1.00	Jan-99
	2.55	12.65	2.75	24.73	21.78	2.27	1.22	9.55	0.82	15.25	79.0	1	99	0	0	125	10.26	-21.2			May-15
	2.61	12.73	2.95	25.17	22.32	2.61	0.97	9.57	0.82	15.05	79.0	1	99	0	0	125	9.6	-21.2			May-11
	0.54	10.40	-0.53	34.69	31.11	8.53	1.64	14.34	1.02	13.35	83.1	0	100	0	0	47	24.33	-20.72			Jun-01
	3.10	18.56	6.75	44.74	57.98	0.98	0.65	12.97	1.04	19.229	347.2	1	99	0	0	45	27.51	-20.05			Apr-11
	2.95	18.21	6.13	42.27	53.64	0.39	1.21	12.97	1.05	18.945	347.2	1	99	0	0	45	27.12	-20.34			Jun-01
	0.00	0.00	1.49	48.11	39.36		0.97	8.43	0.28	18.8801	66.0	1	99	0	0	39	32.37	-27.1			Apr-11
	1.36	16.34	-2.43	39.32	33.75	0	1.55	15.7	1.01	14.582	66.0	1	99	0	0	39	32.37	-27.1			Jun-01
	3.05	14.39	-1.44	31.16	11.42	1.85	0.82	11.3	1.01	9.378	224.1	1	99	0	0	59	16.23	-25.48			Apr-11
	2.91	14.04	-2.02	27.75	7.11	1.42	1.41	11.3	1.01	9.113	224.1	1	99	0	0	59	15.98	-25.6			Jun-01
	2.00	5.99	5.78	15.16	19.86	2.6	0.59	2.36	33.22	10.611	324.6	8	6	85	0	147	2.96	-2			Sep-12
	1.86	5.67	5.15	13.15	16.35	2.15	1.19	2.32	33.26	10.596	324.6	8	6	85	0	147	2.96	-2			Apr-11
	3.09	10.97	6.52	19.13	15.92	2.05	0.4	5.66	1.34	9.977	363.8	4	45	51	0	69	16.12	-15.9			Sep-12
	2.94	10.65	5.88	17.00	12.43	1.54	1	5.67	1.34	9.9	363.8	4	45	51	0	69	16.12	-15.9			Apr-11
	0.37	3.07	3.58	8.13	13.46	4.37	0.49	3.63	0.3	9.337	363.8	3	0	96	0	380					Sep-12
	0.22	2.76	2.97	6.33	9.31	3.86	1.12	3.63	0.3	9.279	363.8	3	0	96	0	380					Aug-12
	3.04	16.58	4.08	36.76	28.57	1.62	0.51	11.58	1.26	11.905	850.6	3	96	0	0	54	20.31	-21.29			Sep-12
	2.88	16.23	3.45	34.30	24.79	1.11	1.1	11.61	1.26	11.808	850.6	3	96	0	0	54	20.31	-21.3			Apr-11
	1.40	8.28	0.53			2.35	0.99			9.89	16.3	23	72	5	0	124					Apr-18
	4.48	6.54	-0.75	-10.99		0	1.34	10.68	126.96	8.429	168.0	73	1	22	4	0					Jan-16
	4.33	6.22	-1.33	-12.52		0	1.94	10.72	127.06	8.257	168.0	73	1	22	4	0					Jan-16
	2.47	11.55	6.15	17.36	16.17	3.21	1.51	6.16	0.98	10.857	136.5	3	49	42	0	45					Aug-12
	1.41	11.02	3.65	32.05	21.77	1.11	0.62	9.93	0.86	11.117	357.9	-2	68	34	0	337	9.48	-13.5			Sep-12
	1.26	10.69	3.04	29.71	18.22	0.57	1.2	9.92	0.86	11.057	357.9	-2	68	34	0	337	9.48	-13.5			Apr-11
	3.99	18.59	4.89	45.12	37.41	3.18	0.95	12.44	0.94	12.5	1,034	0	100	0	0	9	22.89	-20.59			Nov-15

	MARKET		FUND TYPE, CATEGORY & OBJECTIVE		RATINGS				MINIMUMS	
Fund Name	Ticker Symbol	Traded On	Fund Type	Category and (Prospectus Objective)	Overall Rating	Reward Rating	Risk Rating	Recent Up/ Downgrade	Open to New Investors	Min Initial Investment
GuideStone Funds Aggressive Allocation Fund Investor Class	GGBZX	NAS CM	Open End	Global Equity Large Cap (Asset Alloc)	C+	C	B	Up	Y	1,000
GuideStone Funds Balanced Allocation Institutional Cls	GBAYX	NAS CM	Open End	Cautious Alloc (Balanced)	B	C+	A	Up	Y	1,000,000
GuideStone Funds Balanced Allocation Fund Investor Class	GGIZX	NAS CM	Open End	Cautious Alloc (Balanced)	B	C	A	Up	Y	1,000
GuideStone Funds Conservative Allocation Institutional Cls	GCAYX	NAS CM	Open End	Cautious Alloc (Asset Alloc)	B	C	A-	Up	Y	1,000,000
GuideStone Funds Conservative Allocation Investor Cls	GFIZX	NAS CM	Open End	Cautious Alloc (Asset Alloc)	B	C	A-	Up	Y	1,000
GuideStone Funds Defensive Mkt Strategies Inst Cls	GDMYX	NAS CM	Open End	Moderate Alloc (Growth)	B	C+	A		Y	1,000,000
GuideStone Funds Defensive Market Strategies Investor Cls	GDMZX	NAS CM	Open End	Moderate Alloc (Growth)	B	C+	A		Y	1,000
GuideStone Funds Emerging Markets Equity Institutional Cls	GEMYX	NAS CM	Open End	Global Emerg Mkts (Div Emerging Mkts)	C	C	C		Y	1,000,000
GuideStone Funds Emerging Markets Equity Investor Cls	GEMZX	NAS CM	Open End	Global Emerg Mkts (Div Emerging Mkts)	C	C	C		Y	1,000
GuideStone Funds Equity Index Fund Institutional Class	GEQYX	NAS CM	Open End	US Equity Large Cap Blend (Growth)	B-	C	B		Y	1,000,000
GuideStone Funds Equity Index Fund Investor Class	GEQZX	NAS CM	Open End	US Equity Large Cap Blend (Growth)	B-	C	B		Y	1,000
GuideStone Funds Global Real Estate Securities Inst Cls	GREYX	NAS CM	Open End	Real Estate Sector Equity (Real Estate)	B-	C	B+		Y	1,000,000
GuideStone Funds Global Real Estate Securities Inv Cls	GREZX	NAS CM	Open End	Real Estate Sector Equity (Real Estate)	B-	C	B+		Y	1,000
GuideStone Funds Growth Allocation Institutional Cls	GGRYX	NAS CM	Open End	Aggressive Alloc (Asset Alloc)	B-	C	B+	Up	Y	1,000,000
GuideStone Funds Growth Allocation Fund Investor Class	GCOZX	NAS CM	Open End	Aggressive Alloc (Asset Alloc)	B-	C	B+	Up	Y	1,000
GuideStone Funds Growth Equity Fund Institutional Class	GGEYX	NAS CM	Open End	US Equity Large Cap Growth (Growth)	B-	C+	B	Down	Y	1,000,000
GuideStone Funds Growth Equity Fund Investor Class	GGEZX	NAS CM	Open End	US Equity Large Cap Growth (Growth)	B-	C+	B	Down	Y	1,000
GuideStone Funds International Equity Institutional Cls	GIEYX	NAS CM	Open End	Global Equity Large Cap (Foreign Stock)	C	C	B-		Y	1,000,000
GuideStone Funds International Equity Fund Investor Class	GIEZX	NAS CM	Open End	Global Equity Large Cap (Foreign Stock)	C	C	B-		Y	1,000
GuideStone Funds Intl Equity Index Inst Cls	GIIYX	NAS CM	Open End	Global Equity Large Cap (Foreign Stock)	C+	C	B	Up	Y	1,000,000
GuideStone Funds MyDestination 2015 Fund Institutional	GMTYX	NAS CM	Open End	Target Date (Asset Alloc)	B	C+	A	Up	Y	1,000,000
GuideStone Funds MyDestination 2015 Fund Investor Class	GMTZX	NAS CM	Open End	Target Date (Asset Alloc)	B	C+	A	Up	Y	1,000
GuideStone Funds MyDestination 2025 Fund Institutional	GMWYX	NAS CM	Open End	Target Date (Asset Alloc)	B	C	A-	Up	Y	1,000,000
GuideStone Funds MyDestination 2025 Fund Investor Class	GMWZX	NAS CM	Open End	Target Date (Asset Alloc)	B	C	A-	Up	Y	1,000
GuideStone Funds MyDestination 2035 Fund Institutional	GMHYX	NAS CM	Open End	Target Date (Asset Alloc)	B-	C	B+	Up	Y	1,000,000
GuideStone Funds MyDestination 2035 Fund Investor Class	GMHZX	NAS CM	Open End	Target Date (Asset Alloc)	B-	C	B+	Up	Y	1,000
GuideStone Funds MyDestination 2045 Fund Institutional	GMYYX	NAS CM	Open End	Target Date (Asset Alloc)	B-	C	B	Up	Y	1,000,000
GuideStone Funds MyDestination 2045 Fund Investor Class	GMFZX	NAS CM	Open End	Target Date (Asset Alloc)	B-	C	B	Up	Y	1,000
GuideStone Funds MyDestination 2055 Fund Institutional	GMGYX	NAS CM	Open End	Target Date (Asset Alloc)	B-	C	B	Up	Y	1,000,000
GuideStone Funds MyDestination 2055 Fund Investor Class	GMGZX	NAS CM	Open End	Target Date (Asset Alloc)	B-	C	B	Up	Y	1,000
GuideStone Funds Small Cap Equity Fund Institutional Class	GSCYX	NAS CM	Open End	US Equity Small Cap (Small Company)	C	C	C+		Y	1,000,000
GuideStone Funds Small Cap Equity Fund Investor Class	GSCZX	NAS CM	Open End	US Equity Small Cap (Small Company)	C	C	C+		Y	1,000
GuideStone Funds Strategic Alternatives Fund Institutional	GFSYX	NAS CM	Open End	Multialternative (Income)	C	D+	B-	Up	Y	1,000,000
GuideStone Funds Strategic Alternatives Fund Investor	GFSZX	NAS CM	Open End	Multialternative (Income)	C	D+	B-	Up	Y	1,000
GuideStone Funds Value Equity Fund Institutional Class	GVEYX	NAS CM	Open End	US Equity Large Cap Value (Growth)	C+	C	B	Up	Y	1,000,000
GuideStone Funds Value Equity Fund Investor Class	GVEZX	NAS CM	Open End	US Equity Large Cap Value (Growth)	C+	C	B	Up	Y	1,000
Guinness Atkinson Alternative Energy Fund	GAAEX	NAS CM	Open End	Global Equity Mid/Small Cap (Growth)	C	C-	C+		Y	5,000
Guinness Atkinson Asia Focus Fund	IASMX	NAS CM	Open End	Asia ex-Japan Equity (Pacific Stock)	C	C-	C		Y	5,000
Guinness Atkinson Asia Pacific Dividend Builder Fund	GAADX	NAS CM	Open End	Asia ex-Japan Equity (Growth & Income)	C	C-	B-		Y	5,000
Guinness Atkinson China And Hong Kong Fund	ICHKX	NAS CM	Open End	Greater China Equity (Pacific Stock)	C	C-	C		Y	5,000
Guinness Atkinson Dividend Builder Fund	GAINX	NAS CM	Open End	Global Equity Large Cap (Equity-Income)	B	C+	B+	Up	Y	10,000
Guinness Atkinson Global Energy Fund	GAGEX	NAS CM	Open End	Energy Sector Equity (Growth)	D+	D+	D+	Down	Y	5,000
Guinness Atkinson™ Global Innovators Institutional Cls	GINNX	NAS CM	Open End	US Equity Large Cap Growth (Growth)	C	C	C+	Down	Y	100,000
Guinness Atkinson™ Global Innovators Fund Investor Class	IWIRX	NAS CM	Open End	US Equity Large Cap Growth (Growth)	C	C	C+	Down	Y	5,000
Hamlin High Dividend Equity Institutional Cls Shares	HHDFX	NAS CM	Open End	US Equity Large Cap Value (Equity-Income)	B-	C	B+	Up	Y	100,000
Hamlin High Dividend Equity Fund Investor Class Shares	HHDVX	NAS CM	Open End	US Equity Large Cap Value (Equity-Income)	B-	C	B+	Up	Y	2,500
Hancock Horizon Burkenroad Small Cap Fund Class D	HYBUX	NAS CM	Open End	US Equity Small Cap (Small Company)	C-	C-	C	Down	Y	1,000
Hancock Horizon Burkenroad Small Cap Institutional Cls	HIBUX	NAS CM	Open End	US Equity Small Cap (Small Company)	C-	C-	C	Down	Y	1,000
Hancock Horizon Burkenroad Small Cap Fund Investor Class	HHBUX	NAS CM	Open End	US Equity Small Cap (Small Company)	C-	C-	C	Down	Y	1,000
Hancock Horizon Diversified Income Institutional Cls	HHIIX	NAS CM	Open End	Moderate Alloc (Income)	C+	C	B		Y	1,000
Hancock Horizon Diversified Income Fund Investor Class	HHIAX	NAS CM	Open End	Moderate Alloc (Income)	C+	C	B		Y	1,000
Hancock Horizon Diversified Intl Inst Cls	HHDTX	NAS CM	Open End	Global Equity Large Cap (Foreign Stock)	C	C	B		Y	1,000

★ Expanded analysis of this fund is included in Section II.

	TOTAL RETURNS					PERFORMANCE				ASSETS		ASSET ALLOCATION & TURNOVER					BULL & BEAR		FEES		
Min Additional Investment	3-Month Total Return	6-Month Total Return	1-Year Total Return	3-Year Total Return	5-Year Total Return	Dividend Yield (TTM)	Expense Ratio	3-Yr Std Deviation	3-Year Beta	NAV	Total Assets (MIL)	%Cash	%Stocks	%Bonds	%Other	Turnover Ratio	Last Bull Market Total Return	Last Bear Market Total Return	Front End Fee (%)	Back End Fee (%)	Inception Date
100	3.92	18.45	4.70	44.08	36.25	2.95	1.19	12.42	0.94	12.45	1,034	0	100	0	0	9	22.89	-20.59			Aug-01
	3.51	12.34	6.74	24.37	22.27	3.98	0.77	6.24	0.38	12.38	1,576	-4	46	54	0	13	12.39	-9.11			Nov-15
100	3.43	12.15	6.45	23.34	21.13	3.74	1.02	6.23	0.39	12.36	1,576	-4	46	54	0	13	12.39	-9.11			Aug-01
	2.27	7.65	5.13	15.62	15.02	3.18	0.72	3.48	-0.32	11.67	514.6	-26	26	97	1	12	6.69	-4.15			Nov-15
100	2.28	7.56	4.98	14.83	14.10	2.96	0.95	3.52	-0.36	11.66	514.6	-26	26	97	1	12	6.69	-4.15			Aug-01
	3.63	13.60	9.15	32.17	48.31	1.26	0.69	6.93	0.56	13.07	1,161	16	45	14	0	65	12.25				Sep-11
100	3.59	13.45	8.94	31.14	46.45	1.02	0.97	6.94	0.56	13.08	1,161	16	45	14	0	65	12.06				Sep-11
	0.72	11.87	-2.90	26.95	-0.60	0.61	1.28	14.49	1.04	9.7	486.7	-2	103	1	-1	155					Oct-13
100	0.72	11.75	-3.09	26.09	-1.84	0.26	1.57	14.56	1.04	9.7	486.7	-2	103	1	-1	155					Oct-13
	4.40	19.57	10.43	51.78	65.98	1.6	0.13	12.21	1	32.36	1,905	0	100	0	0	3	24.73	-15.18			Aug-01
100	4.35	19.42	10.12	50.56	64.01	1.35	0.38	12.21	1	32.38	1,905	0	100	0	0	3	24.71	-15.33			Aug-01
	0.76	16.09	9.41	18.58	32.78	2.48	0.87	10.96	0.98	10.13	242.1	0	100	0	1	128	32.34	-17.74			Apr-15
100	0.63	15.89	9.06	17.52	31.35	2.21	1.15	10.94	0.98	10.16	242.1	0	100	0	1	128	32.34	-17.74			Dec-06
	3.68	15.60	5.87	34.29	27.91	3.63	0.87	9.38	0.24	12.67	1,207	-1	75	25	0	9	18.14	-15.45			Nov-15
100	3.60	15.41	5.66	33.35	26.76	3.39	1.12	9.42	0.24	12.65	1,207	-1	75	25	0	9	18.14	-15.45			Aug-01
	5.26	25.19	14.29	72.64	85.44	0.09	0.72	14.54	1.05	26.25	1,613	0	100	0	0	19	29.39	-15.81			Aug-01
100	5.19	25.02	14.00	71.28	83.05	0	0.98	14.53	1.04	26.09	1,613	0	100	0	0	19	29.28	-15.89			Aug-01
	3.51	15.73	0.31	36.59	16.99	2.16	1.14	12.22	1.09	13.53	1,242	1	99	0	0	73	14.34	-24.88			Aug-01
100	3.43	15.52	0.06	35.51	15.42	1.91	1.41	12.18	1.08	13.54	1,242	1	99	0	0	73	14.16	-24.98			Aug-01
	3.85	14.11	1.37	32.40		1.27	0.23	10.69	0.96	10.51	641.5	0	100	0	0	4					Jun-15
	3.19	10.46	6.54	23.19	23.40	3.56	0.5	5.09		10.34	648.9	-8	38	66	0	32	13.61	-10.19			May-17
100	3.09	10.24	6.27	22.48	22.69	3.33	0.75	5.07		10.33	648.9	-8	38	66	0	32	13.61	-10.19			Dec-06
	3.43	12.29	6.61	28.60	26.73	2.68	0.5	6.6		10.23	1,301	-3	52	48	0	37	17.36	-13.96			May-17
100	3.33	12.17	6.34	27.97	26.11	2.45	0.75	6.65		10.23	1,301	-3	52	48	0	37	17.36	-13.96			Dec-06
	3.67	14.76	6.18	35.17	28.03	2.83	0.5	8.88		9.87	815.6	-1	74	25	0	50	21.8	-18.61			May-17
100	3.57	14.65	5.81	34.40	27.31	2.61	0.75	8.87		9.86	815.6	-1	74	25	0	50	21.81	-18.61			Dec-06
	3.72	15.93	5.70	39.17	30.02	2.64	0.5	10.07		9.46	615.3	0	87	12	0	58	22.89	-20.1			May-17
100	3.73	15.80	5.44	38.37	29.28	2.42	0.75	10.1		9.45	615.3	0	87	12	0	58	22.89	-20.1			Dec-06
	3.75	16.21	5.51	40.49	31.18	2.26	0.5	10.47		13.26	180.3	0	90	9	0	62					May-17
100	3.68	16.14	5.30	39.86	30.59	2.09	0.75	10.45		13.24	180.3	0	90	9	0	62					Dec-11
	3.16	21.22	-0.62	40.91	35.08	0	1	17.1	0.99	15.65	575.4	0	100	0	0	172	28.84	-23.72			Aug-01
100	3.04	21.04	-0.86	39.86	33.31	0	1.26	17.1	0.99	15.59	575.4	0	100	0	0	172	28.87	-23.82			Aug-01
	0.89	3.34	2.68			1.77	1.03			10.18	403.3	37	8	55	0	172					Jun-17
100	0.79	3.25	2.35			1.46	1.38			10.16	403.3	37	8	55	0	172					Jun-17
	4.53	17.46	4.90	37.14	37.25	1.7	0.61	13.21	1.08	19.4	1,162	0	100	0	0	38	26.16	-19.81			Aug-01
100	4.41	17.24	4.62	36.11	35.44	1.47	0.87	13.18	1.08	19.41	1,162	0	100	0	0	38	26.12	-19.92			Aug-01
250	4.82	19.21	4.20	17.37	-31.57	0.08	1.98	17.83	1.18	3.04	8.9	2	98	0	0	37	-9.66	-48.34			Mar-06
250	-0.77	16.14	-3.15	42.99	27.21	1.26	1.99	16.22	1	19.21	16.5	4	96	0	0	32	17.13	-31.5			Apr-96
250	-0.36	13.65	1.29	33.29	37.19	4.52	1.12	13.31	0.9	15.85	4.8	1	99	0	0	23	20.78	-22.54			Mar-06
250	-1.94	15.76	-5.92	49.32	29.85	1.32	1.54	16.78		21.66	62.6	1	99	0	0	22	23.33	-34.42			Jun-94
1,000	2.76	15.74	10.47	38.65	34.07	2.46	0.68	10.02	0.83	19.2	11.4	1	99	0	0	24					Mar-12
250	-2.34	13.22	-18.08	0.18	-43.82	1.53	1.45	20.79	1.19	20.38	19.6	2	98	0	0	14	18.1	-34.12			Jun-04
5,000	2.85	21.97	0.85	56.22	48.91	0.54	1	15.72	1.3	42.46	177.5	1	99	0	0	29	24.44	-21.04			Dec-15
250	2.79	21.80	0.60	55.06	47.61	0.34	1.25	15.72	1.3	42.29	177.5	1	99	0	0	29	24.44	-21.04			Dec-98
	3.59	14.21	6.17	31.47	31.51	2.91	0.86	10.45	0.81	22.14	765.8	10	90	0	0	58					Mar-12
	3.51	13.99	5.83	29.98	28.42	2.57	1.24	10.45	0.8	22.18	765.8	10	90	0	0	58					Mar-12
100	-0.30	12.75	-9.17	21.65	15.56	0.88	1.5	18.1	1.03	45.18	322.5	1	99	0	0	31	28.67	-19.79			Dec-01
100	-0.18	13.00	-9.23	22.50	16.97	1.05	1	18.12	1.03	47.63	322.5	1	99	0	0	31	28.86	-19.7			May-16
100	-0.23	12.89	-9.37	21.83	16.31	0.79	1.25	18.13	1.03	47.45	322.5	1	99	0	0	31	28.86	-19.7	5.25		Dec-01
100	1.54	10.87	4.22	12.04	2.15	4.14	0.97	6.27	0.5	13.04	44.8	7	41	42	0	69					Sep-12
100	1.48	10.76	3.96	11.19	0.86	3.91	1.22	6.29	0.51	13.01	44.8	7	41	42	0	69			4.25		Sep-12
100	2.24	13.49	-0.65	34.12	5.87	1.13	1.13	11.94	1.02	23.64	230.2	3	97	0	0	10	12.96	-24.76			Sep-08

	MARKET			FUND TYPE, CATEGORY & OBJECTIVE	RATINGS					MINIMUMS
Fund Name	Ticker Symbol	Traded On	Fund Type	Category and (Prospectus Objective)	Overall Rating	Reward Rating	Risk Rating	Recent Up/ Downgrade	Open to New Investors	Min Initial Investment
Hancock Horizon Diversified International Investor Cls	HHDAX	NAS CM	Open End	Global Equity Large Cap (Foreign Stock)	C	C	B		Y	1,000
Hancock Horizon Dynamic Asset Allocation Institutional Cls	HDAIX	NAS CM	Open End	Moderate Alloc (Asset Alloc)	C	C-	B-		Y	1,000
Hancock Horizon Dynamic Asset Allocation Investor Cls	HDAAX	NAS CM	Open End	Moderate Alloc (Asset Alloc)	C	C-	B-		Y	1,000
Hancock Horizon International Small Cap Institutional Cls	HICIX	NAS CM	Open End	Global Equity Mid/Small Cap (Small Company)	C-	D+	C-		Y	1,000
Hancock Horizon International Small Cap Investor Cls	HISAX	NAS CM	Open End	Global Equity Mid/Small Cap (Small Company)	D+	D+	C-	Down	Y	1,000
Hancock Horizon Microcap Fund Institutional Class	HMIIX	NAS CM	Open End	US Equity Small Cap (Growth)	D+	D	D+		Y	1,000
Hancock Horizon Microcap Fund Investor Class	HMIAX	NAS CM	Open End	US Equity Small Cap (Growth)	D+	D	D+		Y	1,000
Hancock Horizon Quantitative Long/Short Institutional Cls	HHQTX	NAS CM	Open End	Long/Short Equity (Growth)	C	C-	C+		Y	1,000
Hancock Horizon Quantitative Long/Short Investor Cls	HHQAX	NAS CM	Open End	Long/Short Equity (Growth)	C	C-	C+		Y	1,000
Hancock Horizon U.S. Small Cap Fund Institutional Class	HSCIX	NAS CM	Open End	US Equity Small Cap (Small Company)	D+	D	D+		Y	1,000
Hancock Horizon U.S. Small Cap Fund Investor Class	HSCAX	NAS CM	Open End	US Equity Small Cap (Small Company)	D+	D	D+		Y	1,000
Hanlon Tactical Dividend and Momentum Fund Class A	HTDAX	NAS CM	Open End	Moderate Alloc (Growth & Income)	C+	C	B-	Up	Y	2,500
Hanlon Tactical Dividend and Momentum Fund Class C	HTDCX	NAS CM	Open End	Moderate Alloc (Growth & Income)	C	C	C+	Up	Y	2,500
Hanlon Tactical Dividend and Momentum Fund Class I	HTDIX	NAS CM	Open End	Moderate Alloc (Growth & Income)	C+	C	B-	Up	Y	100,000
Hanlon Tactical Dividend and Momentum Fund Class R	HTDRX	NAS CM	Open End	Moderate Alloc (Growth & Income)	C	C	B-		Y	2,500
Harbor Capital Appreciation Fund Administrative Class	HRCAX	NAS CM	Open End	US Equity Large Cap Growth (Growth)	C+	C+	B	Down	Y	50,000
Harbor Capital Appreciation Fund Institutional Class	HACAX	NAS CM	Open End	US Equity Large Cap Growth (Growth)	C+	C+	B	Down	Y	50,000
Harbor Capital Appreciation Fund Investor Class	HCAIX	NAS CM	Open End	US Equity Large Cap Growth (Growth)	C+	C+	B	Down	Y	2,500
Harbor Capital Appreciation Fund Retirement Class	HNACX	NAS CM	Open End	US Equity Large Cap Growth (Growth)	C+	C+	B	Down	Y	1,000,000
Harbor Convertible Securities Fund Administrative Class	HRCSX	NAS CM	Open End	Convertibles (Convertible Bond)	B	C	A		Y	50,000
Harbor Convertible Securities Fund Institutional Class	HACSX	NAS CM	Open End	Convertibles (Convertible Bond)	B-	C	B+	Down	Y	1,000
Harbor Convertible Securities Fund Investor Class	HICSX	NAS CM	Open End	Convertibles (Convertible Bond)	B	C	A		Y	2,500
Harbor Convertible Securities Fund Retirement Class	HNCVX	NAS CM	Open End	Convertibles (Convertible Bond)	B	C	A		Y	1,000,000
Harbor Diversified Intl All Cap Admin Cls	HRIDX	NAS CM	Open End	Global Equity Large Cap (Growth)	C	C	B		Y	50,000
Harbor Diversified International All Cap Institutional Cls	HAIDX	NAS CM	Open End	Global Equity Large Cap (Growth)	C	C	B		Y	50,000
Harbor Diversified International All Cap Investor Cls	HIIDX	NAS CM	Open End	Global Equity Large Cap (Growth)	C	C	B		Y	2,500
Harbor Diversified International All Cap Retirement Cls	HNIDX	NAS CM	Open End	Global Equity Large Cap (Growth)	C	C	B		Y	1,000,000
Harbor Emerging Markets Equity Fund Administrative Class	HREMX	NAS CM	Open End	Global Emerg Mkts (Growth)	C	C	B-		Y	50,000
Harbor Emerging Markets Equity Fund Institutional Class	HAEMX	NAS CM	Open End	Global Emerg Mkts (Growth)	C	C	B-		Y	50,000
Harbor Emerging Markets Equity Fund Investor Class	HIEEX	NAS CM	Open End	Global Emerg Mkts (Growth)	C	C	B-		Y	2,500
Harbor Emerging Markets Equity Fund Retirement Class	HNEMX	NAS CM	Open End	Global Emerg Mkts (Growth)	C	C	B-		Y	1,000,000
Harbor Global Leaders Fund Administrative Class	HRGAX	NAS CM	Open End	Global Equity Large Cap (World Stock)	B	B-	B		Y	50,000
Harbor Global Leaders Fund Institutional Class	HGGAX	NAS CM	Open End	Global Equity Large Cap (World Stock)	B	B-	B		Y	50,000
Harbor Global Leaders Fund Investor Class	HGGIX	NAS CM	Open End	Global Equity Large Cap (World Stock)	B	B-	B		Y	2,500
Harbor Global Leaders Fund Retirement Class	HNGIX	NAS CM	Open End	Global Equity Large Cap (World Stock)	B	B-	B		Y	1,000,000
Harbor International Fund Administrative Class	HRINX	NAS CM	Open End	Global Equity Large Cap (Foreign Stock)	C-	D+	C+		Y	50,000
Harbor International Fund Institutional Class	HAINX	NAS CM	Open End	Global Equity Large Cap (Foreign Stock)	C	D+	C+	Up	Y	50,000
Harbor International Fund Investor Class	HIINX	NAS CM	Open End	Global Equity Large Cap (Foreign Stock)	C-	D+	C+		Y	2,500
Harbor International Fund Retirement Class	HNINX	NAS CM	Open End	Global Equity Large Cap (Foreign Stock)	C	D+	C+	Up	Y	1,000,000
Harbor International Growth Fund Administrative Class	HRIGX	NAS CM	Open End	Global Equity Large Cap (Foreign Stock)	C	C	C+		Y	50,000
Harbor International Growth Fund Institutional Class	HAIGX	NAS CM	Open End	Global Equity Large Cap (Foreign Stock)	C	C	C+		Y	50,000
Harbor International Growth Fund Investor Class	HIIGX	NAS CM	Open End	Global Equity Large Cap (Foreign Stock)	C	C	C+		Y	2,500
Harbor International Growth Fund Retirement Class	HNGFX	NAS CM	Open End	Global Equity Large Cap (Foreign Stock)	C	C	C+		Y	1,000,000
Harbor International Small Cap Fund Administrative Class	HRISX	NAS CM	Open End	Global Equity Mid/Small Cap (Small Company)	C	C-	C		Y	50,000
Harbor International Small Cap Fund Institutional Class	HAISX	NAS CM	Open End	Global Equity Mid/Small Cap (Small Company)	C	C-	C		Y	50,000
Harbor International Small Cap Fund Investor Class	HIISX	NAS CM	Open End	Global Equity Mid/Small Cap (Small Company)	C	C-	C		Y	2,500
Harbor International Small Cap Fund Retirement Class	HNISX	NAS CM	Open End	Global Equity Mid/Small Cap (Small Company)	C	C-	C		Y	1,000,000
Harbor Large Cap Value Fund Administrative Class	HRLVX	NAS CM	Open End	US Equity Large Cap Blend (Growth & Income)	B-	C	B	Up	Y	50,000
Harbor Large Cap Value Fund Institutional Class	HAVLX	NAS CM	Open End	US Equity Large Cap Blend (Growth & Income)	B-	C	B	Up	Y	50,000
Harbor Large Cap Value Fund Investor Class	HILVX	NAS CM	Open End	US Equity Large Cap Blend (Growth & Income)	C+	C	B		Y	2,500
Harbor Large Cap Value Fund Retirement Class	HNLVX	NAS CM	Open End	US Equity Large Cap Blend (Growth & Income)	B-	C	B	Up	Y	1,000,000
Harbor Mid Cap Growth Fund Administrative Class	HRMGX	NAS CM	Open End	US Equity Mid Cap (Growth)	B-	B-	B-	Down	Y	50,000

★ Expanded analysis of this fund is included in Section II.

	TOTAL RETURNS					PERFORMANCE				ASSETS		ASSET ALLOCATION & TURNOVER					BULL & BEAR		FEES		
Min Additional Investment	3-Month Total Return	6-Month Total Return	1-Year Total Return	3-Year Total Return	5-Year Total Return	Dividend Yield (TTM)	Expense Ratio	3-Yr Std Deviation	3-Year Beta	NAV	Total Assets (MIL)	%Cash	%Stocks	%Bonds	%Other	Turnover Ratio	Last Bull Market Total Return	Last Bear Market Total Return	Front End Fee (%)	Back End Fee (%)	Inception Date
100	2.19	13.40	-0.68	33.36	4.69	0.88	1.38	11.91	1.02	23.69	230.2	3	97	0	0	10	12.75	-24.8	5.25		Sep-08
100	1.70	7.78	0.21	12.27		1.82	1.7	6.71	0.54	15.51	14.2	5	58	34	0	310					May-15
100	1.64	7.64	-0.05	11.43		1.56	1.95	6.71	0.54	15.49	14.2	5	58	34	0	310			5.25		May-15
100	1.46	8.99	-12.14	16.46		1.54	1.25	12.27	0.96	14.54	13.8	4	96	0	0	86					May-15
100	1.39	8.91	-12.33	15.68		1.23	1.5	12.27	0.96	14.54	13.8	4	96	0	0	86			5.25		May-15
100	1.11	12.88	-16.80	16.85		0.07	1.3	17.31	0.93	16.3	15.4	1	99	0	0	143					May-15
100	1.06	12.75	-17.01	15.96		0	1.55	17.3	0.93	16.18	15.4	1	99	0	0	143			5.25		May-15
100	1.41	6.75	-1.26	13.51	17.91	0.52	1.25	8.3	1.22	17.87	144.5	40	60	0	0	84	21.02	-20.09			Sep-08
100	1.39	6.66	-1.44	13.21	16.99	0.39	1.5	8.35	1.22	17.44	144.5	40	60	0	0	84	20.79	-20.15	5.25		Sep-08
100	-0.19	12.18	-13.50	5.30	6.64	0.06	1.1	18.82	1.07	15.28	25.0	1	99	0	0	113					Dec-13
100	-0.19	12.03	-13.64	4.61	5.43	0	1.35	18.8	1.07	15.17	25.0	1	99	0	0	113			5.25		Dec-13
500	1.03	6.97	-0.42	13.65		0.03	1.76	9.14	0.66	10.73	129.8	3	97	0	0	48			5.75		Sep-15
500	0.77	6.56	-1.23	11.05		0	2.51	9.13	0.65	10.39	129.8	3	97	0	0	48				1.00	Sep-15
500	1.04	7.07	-0.19	14.52		0.34	1.51	9.12	0.65	10.59	129.8	3	97	0	0	48					Sep-15
500	1.05	6.99	-0.56	13.22		0	1.91	9.17	0.66	10.56	129.8	3	97	0	0	48					Sep-15
	2.97	22.17	7.76	73.26	87.13	0	0.91	15	1.08	73.49	30,609	0	100	0	0	40	26.75	-13.86			Nov-02
	3.03	22.33	8.03	74.58	89.47	0.18	0.66	15	1.08	75.04	30,609	0	100	0	0	40	26.94	-13.77			Dec-87
	2.92	22.10	7.64	72.65	86.01	0	1.03	15.01	1.08	71.86	30,609	0	100	0	0	40	26.67	-13.9			Nov-02
	3.04	22.37	8.12	74.92	89.88	0.25	0.58	15	1.08	75.03	30,609	0	100	0	0	40	26.94	-13.77			Mar-16
	3.22	13.26	6.43	26.53	22.64	1.15	1.03	7.04	0.79	10.75	135.0	0	0	1	0	94	9				May-11
	3.28	13.37	7.01	27.73	24.54	1.49	0.78	6.92	0.77	10.77	135.0	0	0	1	0	94	9.01				May-11
	3.20	13.21	6.63	26.39	22.22	1.15	1.15	6.96	0.78	10.75	135.0	0	0	1	0	94	8.83				May-11
	3.30	13.43	7.00	28.02	24.72	1.56	0.7	6.99	0.78	10.76	135.0	0	0	1	0	94	9.01				Mar-16
	3.49	14.67	1.28	28.32		0.91	1.05	10.79	0.93	10.94	762.2	1	99	0	0	42					Nov-15
	3.49	14.88	1.59	29.17		1.1	0.8	10.74	0.92	10.96	762.2	1	99	0	0	42					Nov-15
	3.41	14.63	1.19	27.94		0.75	1.17	10.75	0.93	10.89	762.2	1	99	0	0	42					Nov-15
	3.59	14.88	1.67	29.58		1.17	0.72	10.79	0.93	10.96	762.2	1	99	0	0	42					Mar-16
	1.47	16.56	8.24	48.11	9.82	0.48	1.41	15.18	1.05	10.98	99.0	2	98	0	0	58					Nov-13
	1.59	15.19	7.16	47.26	9.85	0.81	1.16	15.12	1.05	10.84	99.0	2	98	0	0	58					Nov-13
	1.59	15.10	6.80	45.75	7.83	0.42	1.53	15.12	1.05	10.82	99.0	2	98	0	0	58					Nov-13
	1.59	15.31	7.24	47.75	10.07	0.88	1.08	15.13	1.05	10.84	99.0	2	98	0	0	58					Mar-16
	6.48	24.44	16.56	64.99	61.74	0	1.16	12.52	1	29.22	89.9	2	98	0	0	20	30.3	-24.36			Mar-09
	6.54	24.60	16.88	66.26	63.80	0	0.91	12.5	1	29.78	89.9	2	98	0	0	20	30.5	-24.26			Mar-09
	6.42	24.32	16.40	64.40	60.75	0	1.28	12.5	1	28.83	89.9	2	98	0	0	20	30.23	-24.4			Mar-09
	6.57	24.60	16.94	66.55	64.17	0	0.83	12.51	1	29.83	89.9	2	98	0	0	20	30.5	-24.27			Mar-16
	2.79	13.20	-6.36	16.09	-3.18	0.69	1.02	12	1.02	38.24	6,970	2	98	0	0	64	21.26	-25.72			Nov-02
	2.86	13.36	-6.13	16.96	-1.95	1.41	0.77	12.01	1.02	38.08	6,970	2	98	0	0	64	21.44	-25.64			Dec-87
	2.75	13.15	-6.46	15.68	-3.74	0.84	1.14	12.01	1.02	37.67	6,970	2	98	0	0	64	21.18	-25.77			Nov-02
	2.87	13.41	-6.05	17.22	-1.73	1.65	0.69	12.01	1.02	37.95	6,970	2	98	0	0	64	21.44	-25.64			Mar-16
	5.54	20.09	-0.13	31.31	20.52	0.42	1.1	13.75	1.11	15.6	566.1	2	98	0	0	17	20.83	-24.48			Nov-02
	5.61	20.16	0.12	32.28	21.98	0.64	0.85	13.74	1.11	15.61	566.1	2	98	0	0	17	20.95	-24.4			Nov-93
	5.51	19.95	-0.24	30.88	19.83	0.33	1.22	13.7	1.11	15.51	566.1	2	98	0	0	17	20.75	-24.55			Nov-02
	5.61	20.24	0.20	32.64	22.32	0.7	0.77	13.75	1.11	15.62	566.1	2	98	0	0	17	20.95	-24.4			Mar-16
	0.82	12.38	-7.51	27.70		0.41	1.21	12.83	1.01	12.25	54.8	5	95	0	0	53					Feb-16
	0.82	12.57	-7.26	28.71		0.71	0.96	12.85	1.01	12.26	54.8	5	95	0	0	53					Feb-16
	0.82	12.38	-7.54	27.40		0.31	1.33	12.84	1.01	12.25	54.8	5	95	0	0	53					Feb-16
	0.90	12.67	-7.12	29.04		0.77	0.88	12.81	1.01	12.27	54.8	5	95	0	0	53					Feb-16
	6.07	19.89	7.54	48.23	60.04	0.71	0.94	12.9	1.03	15.67	1,146	5	95	0	0	15	24	-17.07			Nov-02
	6.13	20.05	7.76	49.45	62.17	0.96	0.69	12.86	1.03	15.66	1,146	5	95	0	0	15	24.11	-16.95			Dec-87
	6.07	19.84	7.42	47.80	59.23	0.55	1.06	12.89	1.03	15.83	1,146	5	95	0	0	15	23.95	-17.16			Nov-02
	6.17	20.10	7.91	49.75	62.70	1.02	0.61	12.9	1.03	15.66	1,146	5	95	0	0	15	24.11	-16.95			Mar-16
	6.09	33.50	15.37	77.86	74.29	0	1.14	17.09	1.14	10.44	257.7	11	89	0	0	85	24.15	-24.07			Nov-02

	MARKET			FUND TYPE, CATEGORY & OBJECTIVE	RATINGS				MINIMUMS	
Fund Name	Ticker Symbol	Traded On	Fund Type	Category and (Prospectus Objective)	Overall Rating	Reward Rating	Risk Rating	Recent Up/ Downgrade	Open to New Investors	Min Initial Investment
Harbor Mid Cap Growth Fund Institutional Class	HAMGX	NAS CM	Open End	US Equity Mid Cap (Growth)	B-	B-	B-	Down	Y	50,000
Harbor Mid Cap Growth Fund Investor Class	HIMGX	NAS CM	Open End	US Equity Mid Cap (Growth)	B-	B-	B-	Down	Y	2,500
Harbor Mid Cap Growth Fund Retirement Class	HNMGX	NAS CM	Open End	US Equity Mid Cap (Growth)	B-	B-	B-	Down	Y	1,000,000
Harbor Mid Cap Value Fund Administrative Class	HRMVX	NAS CM	Open End	US Equity Mid Cap (Growth & Income)	C	C-	C+		Y	50,000
Harbor Mid Cap Value Fund Institutional Class	HAMVX	NAS CM	Open End	US Equity Mid Cap (Growth & Income)	C	C-	C+		Y	50,000
Harbor Mid Cap Value Fund Investor Class	HIMVX	NAS CM	Open End	US Equity Mid Cap (Growth & Income)	C	C-	C+		Y	2,500
Harbor Mid Cap Value Fund Retirement Class	HNMVX	NAS CM	Open End	US Equity Mid Cap (Growth & Income)	C	C-	C+		Y	1,000,000
Harbor Overseas Fund Institutional Class	HAOSX	NAS CM	Open End	Global Equity Large Cap (Growth)	U	U	U		Y	50,000
Harbor Overseas Fund Investor Class	HAONX	NAS CM	Open End	Global Equity Large Cap (Growth)	U	U	U		Y	2,500
Harbor Overseas Fund Retirement Class	HAORX	NAS CM	Open End	Global Equity Large Cap (Growth)	U	U	U		Y	1,000,000
Harbor Small Cap Growth Fund Administrative Class	HRSGX	NAS CM	Open End	US Equity Small Cap (Small Company)	C+	C	C+			50,000
Harbor Small Cap Growth Fund Institutional Class	HASGX	NAS CM	Open End	US Equity Small Cap (Small Company)	C+	C	C+			50,000
Harbor Small Cap Growth Fund Investor Class	HISGX	NAS CM	Open End	US Equity Small Cap (Small Company)	C+	C	C+			2,500
Harbor Small Cap Growth Fund Retirement Class	HNSGX	NAS CM	Open End	US Equity Small Cap (Small Company)	C+	C	C+		Y	1,000,000
Harbor Small Cap Growth Opportunities Administrative Cls	HRSOX	NAS CM	Open End	US Equity Small Cap (Small Company)	C	C-	C+		Y	50,000
Harbor Small Cap Growth Opportunities Institutional Cls	HASOX	NAS CM	Open End	US Equity Small Cap (Small Company)	C	C-	C+		Y	50,000
Harbor Small Cap Growth Opportunities Fund Investor Class	HISOX	NAS CM	Open End	US Equity Small Cap (Small Company)	C	C-	C+		Y	2,500
Harbor Small Cap Growth Opportunities Retirement Cls	HNSOX	NAS CM	Open End	US Equity Small Cap (Small Company)	C	C-	C+		Y	1,000,000
Harbor Small Cap Value Fund Administrative Class	HSVRX	NAS CM	Open End	US Equity Small Cap (Small Company)	C	C	C+		Y	50,000
Harbor Small Cap Value Fund Institutional Class	HASCX	NAS CM	Open End	US Equity Small Cap (Small Company)	C	C	C+		Y	50,000
Harbor Small Cap Value Fund Investor Class	HISVX	NAS CM	Open End	US Equity Small Cap (Small Company)	C	C	C+		Y	2,500
Harbor Small Cap Value Fund Retirement Class	HNVRX	NAS CM	Open End	US Equity Small Cap (Small Company)	C	C	C+		Y	1,000,000
Harbor Small Cap Value Opportunities Administrative Cls	HSAVX	NAS CM	Open End	US Equity Small Cap (Small Company)	D	D	D+		Y	50,000
Harbor Small Cap Value Opportunities Institutional Cls	HSOVX	NAS CM	Open End	US Equity Small Cap (Small Company)	D	D	D+		Y	50,000
Harbor Small Cap Value Opportunities Fund Investor Class	HSIVX	NAS CM	Open End	US Equity Small Cap (Small Company)	D	D	D+		Y	2,500
Harbor Small Cap Value Opportunities Fund Retirement Class	HSRVX	NAS CM	Open End	US Equity Small Cap (Small Company)	D	D	D+		Y	1,000,000
Harbor Strategic Growth Fund Administrative Class	HSRGX	NAS CM	Open End	US Equity Large Cap Growth (Growth)	B	B-	B		Y	50,000
Harbor Strategic Growth Fund Institutional Class	MVSGX	NAS CM	Open End	US Equity Large Cap Growth (Growth)	B	B-	B		Y	50,000
Harbor Strategic Growth Fund Investor Class	HISWX	NAS CM	Open End	US Equity Large Cap Growth (Growth)	B-	C+	B	Down	Y	2,500
Harbor Strategic Growth Fund Retirement Class	HNGSX	NAS CM	Open End	US Equity Large Cap Growth (Growth)	B	B-	B		Y	1,000,000
Harbor Target Retirement 2015 Fund Institutional Class	HARGX	NAS CM	Open End	Target Date (Asset Alloc)	B	C+	A-	Up	Y	1,000
Harbor Target Retirement 2020 Fund Institutional Class	HARJX	NAS CM	Open End	Target Date (Asset Alloc)	B	C+	A	Up	Y	1,000
Harbor Target Retirement 2025 Fund Institutional Class	HARMX	NAS CM	Open End	Target Date (Asset Alloc)	B	C	A-	Up	Y	1,000
Harbor Target Retirement 2030 Fund Institutional Class	HARPX	NAS CM	Open End	Target Date (Asset Alloc)	B-	C	A-	Up	Y	1,000
Harbor Target Retirement 2035 Fund Institutional Class	HARUX	NAS CM	Open End	Target Date (Asset Alloc)	B-	C	B+	Up	Y	1,000
Harbor Target Retirement 2040 Fund Institutional Class	HARYX	NAS CM	Open End	Target Date (Asset Alloc)	B-	C	B+	Up	Y	1,000
Harbor Target Retirement 2045 Fund Institutional Class	HACCX	NAS CM	Open End	Target Date (Asset Alloc)	B-	C	B	Up	Y	1,000
Harbor Target Retirement 2050 Fund Institutional Class	HAFFX	NAS CM	Open End	Target Date (Asset Alloc)	C+	C	B	Up	Y	1,000
Harbor Target Retirement 2055 Fund Institutional Class	HATRX	NAS CM	Open End	Target Date (Asset Alloc)	C+	C	B	Up	Y	1,000
Harbor Target Retirement Income Fund Institutional Class	HARAX	NAS CM	Open End	Target Date (Asset Alloc)	B	C+	A-	Up	Y	1,000
Harding Loevner Emerging Markets Portfolio Advisor Class	HLEMX	NAS CM	Open End	Global Emerg Mkts (Div Emerging Mkts)	C	C	C+		Y	5,000
Harding Loevner Emerging Mkts Research Portfolio Inst Cls	HLREX	NAS CM	Open End	Global Emerg Mkts (Div Emerging Mkts)	C	C-	B-		Y	100,000
Harding Loevner Frontier Emerging Mkts Inst Cls	HLFMX	NAS CM	Open End	Global Emerg Mkts (Div Emerging Mkts)	C	C-	C+		Y	100,000
Harding Loevner Frontier Emerging Mkts Inst Cls II	HLFFX	NAS CM	Open End	Global Emerg Mkts (Div Emerging Mkts)	C	C-	C+		Y	10,000,000
Harding Loevner Frontier Emerging Markets Investor Cls	HLMOX	NAS CM	Open End	Global Emerg Mkts (Div Emerging Mkts)	C	C-	C+		Y	5,000
Harding Loevner Global Equity Portfolio Advisor Class	HLMGX	NAS CM	Open End	Global Equity Large Cap (World Stock)	C+	C	B	Up	Y	5,000
Harding Loevner Global Equity Portfolio Institutional Cls	HLMVX	NAS CM	Open End	Global Equity Large Cap (World Stock)	C+	C	B	Up	Y	100,000
Harding Loevner Global Equity Portfolio Inst Cls Z	HLGZX	NAS CM	Open End	Global Equity Large Cap (World Stock)	C+	C	B	Up	Y	10,000,000
Harding Loevner Global Equity Research Portfolio Inst Cls	HLRGX	NAS CM	Open End	Global Equity Large Cap (World Stock)	B-	C	B	Up	Y	100,000
Harding Loevner Inst Emerging Mkts Portfolio Cls I	HLMEX	NAS CM	Open End	Global Emerg Mkts (Div Emerging Mkts)	C	C	C+		Y	500,000
Harding Loevner Inst Emerging Mkts Portfolio Cls Z	HLEZX	NAS CM	Open End	Global Emerg Mkts (Div Emerging Mkts)	C	C	C+			10,000,000
Harding Loevner Intl Equity Portfolio Inst Cls	HLMIX	NAS CM	Open End	Global Equity Large Cap (Foreign Stock)	C	C	B-		Y	100,000

★ Expanded analysis of this fund is included in Section II.

Min Additional Investment	TOTAL RETURNS 3-Month Total Return	6-Month Total Return	1-Year Total Return	3-Year Total Return	5-Year Total Return	PERFORMANCE Dividend Yield (TTM)	Expense Ratio	3-Yr Std Deviation	3-Year Beta	ASSETS NAV	Total Assets (MIL)	ASSET ALLOCATION & TURNOVER %Cash	%Stocks	%Bonds	%Other	Turnover Ratio	BULL & BEAR Last Bull Market Total Return	Last Bear Market Total Return	FEES Front End Fee (%)	Back End Fee (%)	Inception Date
	6.14	33.57	15.55	79.18	76.48	0	0.89	17.11	1.14	11.06	257.7	11	89	0	0	85	24.36	-23.98			Nov-00
	6.11	33.42	15.13	77.23	73.24	0	1.26	17.1	1.14	10.06	257.7	11	89	0	0	85	24.01	-24.11			Nov-02
	6.12	33.61	15.62	79.56	76.85	0	0.81	17.08	1.14	11.09	257.7	11	89	0	0	85	24.36	-23.98			Mar-16
	0.88	14.15	-5.40	23.70	21.51	1.34	1.09	16.3	1.2	20.49	820.7	2	98	0	0	24	29.22	-25.19			Nov-02
	0.94	14.22	-5.17	24.63	23.03	1.64	0.84	16.28	1.2	20.31	820.7	2	98	0	0	24	29.4	-25.11			Mar-02
	0.84	14.04	-5.46	23.32	20.83	1.17	1.21	16.27	1.2	20.3	820.7	2	98	0	0	24	29.01	-25.19			Nov-02
	0.94	14.29	-5.08	24.89	23.29	1.72	0.76	16.3	1.2	20.31	820.7	2	98	0	0	24	29.4	-25.11			Mar-16
	1.49						0.85			10.18	26.0	1	99	0	0						Mar-19
	1.29						1.22			10.16	26.0	1	99	0	0						Mar-19
	1.49						0.77			10.18	26.0	1	99	0	0						Mar-19
	4.97	29.46	5.42	58.64	56.34	0	1.13	16.69	0.93	11.82	716.2	3	97	0	0	99	27.76	-28.65			Nov-02
	5.11	29.75	5.67	60.33	58.83	0	0.88	16.67	0.92	12.95	716.2	3	97	0	0	99	27.84	-28.58			Nov-00
	4.90	29.41	5.29	58.52	55.88	0	1.25	16.66	0.92	11.13	716.2	3	97	0	0	99	27.51	-28.69			Nov-02
	5.09	29.64	5.73	60.71	59.06	0	0.8	16.68	0.93	12.99	716.2	3	97	0	0	99	27.84	-28.58			Mar-16
	1.10	17.59	-4.90	44.70	34.40	0	1.14	18.04	0.99	10.09	218.5	2	98	0	0	71					Feb-14
	1.09	17.66	-4.71	45.94	35.13	0	0.89	18.08	1	10.19	218.5	2	98	0	0	71					Feb-14
	1.01	17.53	-5.05	44.39	32.73	0	1.26	18.08	1	9.92	218.5	2	98	0	0	71					Feb-14
	1.08	17.74	-4.61	46.14	35.46	0	0.81	18.08	1	10.22	218.5	2	98	0	0	71					Mar-16
	5.65	20.59	-1.69	44.43	49.27	0.11	1.13	17.72	0.96	32.68	1,552	4	96	0	0	22	27.37	-22.55			Nov-02
	5.72	20.71	-1.42	45.52	51.15	0.34	0.88	17.72	0.96	32.87	1,552	4	96	0	0	22	27.63	-22.5			Dec-01
	5.61	20.51	-1.80	43.88	48.38	0	1.25	17.7	0.96	31.96	1,552	4	96	0	0	22	27.36	-22.6			Nov-02
	5.72	20.74	-1.36	45.75	51.46	0.42	0.8	17.7	0.96	32.88	1,552	4	96	0	0	22	27.63	-22.49			Mar-16
	-2.15	16.13	-10.76			0.31	1.14			9.07	32.3	3	97	0	0	73					Aug-17
	-2.15	16.13	-10.64			0.58	0.89			9.07	32.3	3	97	0	0	73					Aug-17
	-2.15	15.98	-10.88			0.18	1.26			9.07	32.3	3	97	0	0	73					Aug-17
	-2.04	16.26	-10.46			0.66	0.81			9.08	32.3	3	97	0	0	73					Aug-17
	5.97	22.31	12.34	49.44	65.28	0.07	0.96	11.87	0.85	21.65	105.1	2	98	0	0	15					Mar-17
	6.01	22.48	12.61	50.59	67.39	0.28	0.71	11.86	0.85	21.68	105.1	2	98	0	0	15					Nov-11
	5.96	22.33	10.73	47.18	62.78	0.06	1.08	12.24	0.87	21.31	105.1	2	98	0	0	15					Mar-17
	6.06	22.52	12.69	50.90	67.74	0.35	0.63	11.88	0.85	21.7	105.1	2	98	0	0	15					Mar-17
	3.02	9.20	5.70	18.67	19.00	2.95	0.7	3.88	0.52	10.91	3.9	4	20	76	0	29	12.53	-8.97			Jan-09
	3.30	11.11	5.58	22.41	22.05	2.83	0.71	5.12	0.45	9.7	25.8	4	31	65	0	31	13.74	-10.39			Jan-09
	3.61	12.82	5.78	25.10	23.64	2.99	0.74	6.22	0.39	12.32	19.6	-2	41	61	0	36	15.02	-12.6			Jan-09
	3.69	13.65	5.47	27.39	24.90	2.69	0.75	7.04	0.32	8.99	32.0	-1	49	52	0	31	16.84	-14.82			Jan-09
	3.85	14.96	5.12	30.64	27.32	2.37	0.76	8.21	0.27	14.29	19.4	0	58	42	0	29	18.84	-16.83			Jan-09
	4.08	16.29	4.77	33.59	30.23	2.12	0.75	9.28	0.21	8.92	28.6	2	68	30	0	30	20.48	-18.97			Jan-09
	4.14	16.97	4.43	36.54	32.32	1.81	0.76	10.07	0.18	15.09	14.9	2	72	26	0	22	22.07	-20.81			Jan-09
	4.20	18.23	4.01	39.40	34.74	1.56	0.78	11.2	0.13	9.92	26.3	2	82	16	0	23	23.07	-21.52			Jan-09
	4.38	19.22	3.72	40.88		1.32	0.79	11.97	0.12	11.66	5.6	2	91	7	0	29					Nov-14
	2.96	9.03	5.78	16.98	18.77	3.01	0.7	3.64	0.53	9.08	13.5	4	19	76	0	28	9.94	-5.08			Jan-09
	1.42	16.27	-1.25	33.35	14.74	0.76	1.4	14.92	1.03	55.44	4,337	2	98	0	0	24	21.64	-24.08			Nov-98
	1.15	14.07	2.08			0.77	1.15			11.35	7.2	3	96	0	0	55					Dec-16
	3.10	13.40	1.33	17.25	-8.42	1.19	1.62	10.06	0.84	8.29	369.9					20	10	-19.66			May-08
	3.10	13.54	1.60	17.98	-7.85	1.32	1.35	10.07	0.84	8.3	369.9					20	10	-19.66			Mar-17
	2.99	13.32	1.09	16.09	-10.16	0.76	2	10.05	0.84	8.25	369.9					20	9.87	-19.81			Dec-10
	3.59	18.45	2.17	46.37	48.68	0.11	1.14	12.76	1.09	34.86	969.9	1	99	0	0	42	21.34	-18.51			Nov-96
	3.65	18.61	2.45	47.48	50.55	0.31	0.94	12.75	1.09	34.92	969.9	1	99	0	0	42	21.52	-18.41			Nov-09
0	3.65	18.63	2.47	47.04	49.37	0.36	0.9	12.73	1.09	34.89	969.9	1	99	0	0	42	21.34	-18.52			Aug-17
	4.03	18.14	8.48			0.69	0.8			12.37	6.8	1	99	0	0	45					Dec-16
	1.34	16.20	-1.30	33.45	14.95	0.84	1.27	14.91	1.03	21.15	5,250	2	98	0	0	28	22.32	-24.13			Oct-05
	1.34	16.26	-1.18	34.38	16.01	0.95	1.11	14.91	1.03	21.16	5,250	2	98	0	0	28	22.32	-24.13			Mar-14
	4.45	16.87	0.69	34.21	28.11	1.29	0.81	12.32	1.04	22.51	15,983	4	96	0	0	10	17.02	-22.16			May-94

	MARKET			FUND TYPE, CATEGORY & OBJECTIVE	RATINGS				MINIMUMS	
Fund Name	Ticker Symbol	Traded On	Fund Type	Category and (Prospectus Objective)	Overall Rating	Reward Rating	Risk Rating	Recent Up/ Downgrade	Open to New Investors	Min Initial Investment
Harding Loevner Intl Equity Portfolio Inst Cls Z	HLIZX	NAS CM	Open End	Global Equity Large Cap (Foreign Stock)	C	C	B-		Y	10,000,000
Harding Loevner Intl Equity Portfolio Inv Cls	HLMNX	NAS CM	Open End	Global Equity Large Cap (Foreign Stock)	C	C	B-		Y	5,000
Harding Loevner Intl Equity Research Portfolio Inst Cls	HLIRX	NAS CM	Open End	Global Equity Large Cap (Foreign Stock)	C	C	B		Y	100,000
Harding Loevner Intl Small Companies Portfolio Inst	HLMRX	NAS CM	Open End	Global Equity Mid/Small Cap (Small Company)	C	C	C+		Y	100,000
Harding Loevner Intl Small Companies Portfolio Inv	HLMSX	NAS CM	Open End	Global Equity Mid/Small Cap (Small Company)	C	C	C+		Y	5,000
Hartford Balanced HLS Fund Class IA	HADAX	NAS CM	Open End	Moderate Alloc (Asset Alloc)	B-	C	B+	Up	Y	0
Hartford Balanced HLS Fund Class IB	HAIBX	NAS CM	Open End	Moderate Alloc (Asset Alloc)	B-	C	B+	Up	Y	0
Hartford Capital Appreciation HLS Fund Class IA	HIACX	NAS CM	Open End	US Equity Large Cap Growth (Growth)	B-	C+	B		Y	0
Hartford Capital Appreciation HLS Fund Class IB	HIBCX	NAS CM	Open End	US Equity Large Cap Growth (Growth)	B-	C+	B	Up	Y	0
Hartford Capital Appreciation HLS Fund Class IC	HCPCX	NAS CM	Open End	US Equity Large Cap Growth (Growth)	B-	C	B	Up	Y	0
Hartford Checks and Balances Fund Class A	HCKAX	NAS CM	Open End	Moderate Alloc (Growth & Income)	B	C+	A-		Y	2,000
Hartford Checks and Balances Fund Class C	HCKCX	NAS CM	Open End	Moderate Alloc (Growth & Income)	B	C+	A-	Up	Y	2,000
Hartford Checks and Balances Fund Class F	HCKFX	NAS CM	Open End	Moderate Alloc (Growth & Income)	B	C+	A-		Y	1,000,000
Hartford Checks and Balances Fund Class I	HCKIX	NAS CM	Open End	Moderate Alloc (Growth & Income)	B	C+	A-		Y	2,000
Hartford Checks and Balances Fund Class R3	HCKRX	NAS CM	Open End	Moderate Alloc (Growth & Income)	B	C+	A-		Y	0
Hartford Checks and Balances Fund Class R4	HCKSX	NAS CM	Open End	Moderate Alloc (Growth & Income)	B	C+	A-		Y	0
Hartford Checks and Balances Fund Class R5	HCKTX	NAS CM	Open End	Moderate Alloc (Growth & Income)	B	C+	A-		Y	0
Hartford Conservative Allocation Fund Class A	HCVAX	NAS CM	Open End	Cautious Alloc (Asset Alloc)	B	C	A-	Up	Y	2,000
Hartford Conservative Allocation Fund Class C	HCVCX	NAS CM	Open End	Cautious Alloc (Asset Alloc)	B-	C	A-	Up	Y	2,000
Hartford Conservative Allocation Fund Class F	HCVFX	NAS CM	Open End	Cautious Alloc (Asset Alloc)	B	C+	A-	Up	Y	1,000,000
Hartford Conservative Allocation Fund Class I	HCVIX	NAS CM	Open End	Cautious Alloc (Asset Alloc)	B	C+	A-	Up	Y	2,000
Hartford Conservative Allocation Fund Class R3	HCVRX	NAS CM	Open End	Cautious Alloc (Asset Alloc)	B	C	A-	Up	Y	0
Hartford Conservative Allocation Fund Class R4	HCVSX	NAS CM	Open End	Cautious Alloc (Asset Alloc)	B	C	A-	Up	Y	0
Hartford Conservative Allocation Fund Class R5	HCVTX	NAS CM	Open End	Cautious Alloc (Asset Alloc)	B	C+	A	Up	Y	0
Hartford Core Equity Fund Class A	HAIAX	NAS CM	Open End	US Equity Large Cap Blend (Growth)	B-	C+	B	Down	Y	2,000
Hartford Core Equity Fund Class C	HGICX	NAS CM	Open End	US Equity Large Cap Blend (Growth)	B-	C+	B		Y	2,000
Hartford Core Equity Fund Class F	HGIFX	NAS CM	Open End	US Equity Large Cap Blend (Growth)	B-	C+	B	Down	Y	1,000,000
Hartford Core Equity Fund Class I	HGIIX	NAS CM	Open End	US Equity Large Cap Blend (Growth)	B-	C+	B	Down	Y	2,000
Hartford Core Equity Fund Class R3	HGIRX	NAS CM	Open End	US Equity Large Cap Blend (Growth)	B-	C+	B	Down	Y	0
Hartford Core Equity Fund Class R4	HGISX	NAS CM	Open End	US Equity Large Cap Blend (Growth)	B-	C+	B	Down	Y	0
Hartford Core Equity Fund Class R5	HGITX	NAS CM	Open End	US Equity Large Cap Blend (Growth)	B-	C+	B	Down	Y	0
Hartford Core Equity Fund Class R6	HAITX	NAS CM	Open End	US Equity Large Cap Blend (Growth)	B-	C+	B	Down	Y	0
Hartford Core Equity Fund Class Y	HGIYX	NAS CM	Open End	US Equity Large Cap Blend (Growth)	B-	C+	B	Down	Y	250,000
Hartford Disciplined Equity HLS Fund Class IA	HIAGX	NAS CM	Open End	US Equity Large Cap Blend (Growth)	B-	C+	B	Down	Y	0
Hartford Disciplined Equity HLS Fund Class IB	HBGIX	NAS CM	Open End	US Equity Large Cap Blend (Growth)	B-	C+	B	Down	Y	0
Hartford Dividend and Growth HLS Fund Class IA	HIADX	NAS CM	Open End	US Equity Large Cap Value (Growth & Income)	B-	C	B+		Y	0
Hartford Dividend and Growth HLS Fund Class IB	HDGBX	NAS CM	Open End	US Equity Large Cap Value (Growth & Income)	B-	C	B		Y	0
Hartford Emerging Markets Equity Fund Class A	HERAX	NAS CM	Open End	Global Emerg Mkts (Div Emerging Mkts)	C	C	C+		Y	2,000
Hartford Emerging Markets Equity Fund Class C	HERCX	NAS CM	Open End	Global Emerg Mkts (Div Emerging Mkts)	C	C	C+		Y	2,000
Hartford Emerging Markets Equity Fund Class F	HERFX	NAS CM	Open End	Global Emerg Mkts (Div Emerging Mkts)	C	C	C+		Y	1,000,000
Hartford Emerging Markets Equity Fund Class I	HERIX	NAS CM	Open End	Global Emerg Mkts (Div Emerging Mkts)	C	C	C+		Y	2,000
Hartford Emerging Markets Equity Fund Class R3	HERRX	NAS CM	Open End	Global Emerg Mkts (Div Emerging Mkts)	C	C	C+		Y	0
Hartford Emerging Markets Equity Fund Class R4	HERSX	NAS CM	Open End	Global Emerg Mkts (Div Emerging Mkts)	C	C	C+		Y	0
Hartford Emerging Markets Equity Fund Class R5	HERTX	NAS CM	Open End	Global Emerg Mkts (Div Emerging Mkts)	C	C	C+		Y	0
Hartford Emerging Markets Equity Fund Class R6	HERVX	NAS CM	Open End	Global Emerg Mkts (Div Emerging Mkts)	C	C	C+		Y	0
Hartford Emerging Markets Equity Fund Class Y	HERYX	NAS CM	Open End	Global Emerg Mkts (Div Emerging Mkts)	C	C	C+		Y	250,000
Hartford Environmental Opportunities Fund Class A	HEOMX	NAS CM	Open End	Global Equity Mid/Small Cap (Growth & Income)	C	C	B-		Y	5,000
Hartford Environmental Opportunities Fund Class C	HEONX	NAS CM	Open End	Global Equity Mid/Small Cap (Growth & Income)	C	C	B-		Y	5,000
Hartford Environmental Opportunities Fund Class F	HEOFX	NAS CM	Open End	Global Equity Mid/Small Cap (Growth & Income)	C	C	B-		Y	1,000,000
Hartford Environmental Opportunities Fund Class I	HEOIX	NAS CM	Open End	Global Equity Mid/Small Cap (Growth & Income)	C	C	B-		Y	5,000
Hartford Environmental Opportunities Fund Class R3	HEORX	NAS CM	Open End	Global Equity Mid/Small Cap (Growth & Income)	C	C	B-		Y	0
Hartford Environmental Opportunities Fund Class R4	HEOSX	NAS CM	Open End	Global Equity Mid/Small Cap (Growth & Income)	C	C	B-		Y	0

★ Expanded analysis of this fund is included in Section II.

	TOTAL RETURNS					PERFORMANCE				ASSETS		ASSET ALLOCATION & TURNOVER					BULL & BEAR		FEES		
Min Additional Investment	3-Month Total Return	6-Month Total Return	1-Year Total Return	3-Year Total Return	5-Year Total Return	Dividend Yield (TTM)	Expense Ratio	3-Yr Std Deviation	3-Year Beta	NAV	Total Assets (MIL)	%Cash	%Stocks	%Bonds	%Other	Turnover Ratio	Last Bull Market Total Return	Last Bear Market Total Return	Front End Fee (%)	Back End Fee (%)	Inception Date
	4.50	16.99	0.78	34.50	28.38	1.37	0.74	12.34	1.04	22.51	15,983	4	96	0	0	10	17.02	-22.16			Jul-17
	4.41	16.71	0.38	32.89	26.01	0.83	1.14	12.34	1.04	22.48	15,983	4	96	0	0	10	16.77	-22.32			Sep-05
	3.58	15.73	1.03	34.41		1.01	0.75	11.56	0.98	11.84	12.2	2	97	0	1	43					Dec-15
	4.75	19.86	-1.11	34.17	24.31	0.76	1.15	12.71	1	15.63	251.8	4	95	0	0	52	19.45	-23.15			Jun-11
	4.73	19.70	-1.30	33.21	22.74	0.61	1.4	12.69	1	15.49	251.8	4	95	0	0	52	19.32	-23.23			Mar-07
	3.72	13.88	7.28	28.31	36.93	1.87	0.63	8.4		31.17	2,064	1	64	34	0	31	18.53	-12.11			Mar-83
	3.70	13.77	7.03	27.37	35.24	1.59	0.88	8.4		31.64	2,064	1	64	34	0	31	18.36	-12.2			Apr-98
	4.77	22.43	9.46	49.51	49.94	0.81	0.67	12.49	0.98	48.46	4,447	3	96	0	0	73	24.25	-24.7			Apr-84
	4.70	22.26	9.19	48.40	48.07	0.59	0.92	12.48	0.98	47.66	4,447	3	96	0	0	73	24.07	-24.77			Apr-98
	4.65	22.12	8.92	47.27	46.26	0.39	1.17	12.5	0.98	47.92	4,447	3	96	0	0	73	24.07	-24.77			Apr-14
50	4.01	15.26	9.54	34.08	38.79	3.21	0.95	7.86		9.4	1,555	4	62	33	0	28	16.22	-13.83	5.50		May-07
50	3.94	14.91	8.71	31.06	33.71	2.46	1.72	7.91		9.34	1,555	4	62	33	0	28	15.7	-14.12		1.00	May-07
	4.20	15.55	9.89	35.22	39.97	3.52	0.61	7.92		9.42	1,555	4	62	33	0	28	16.22	-13.83			Feb-17
50	4.18	15.50	9.79	35.08	40.52	3.44	0.7	7.92		9.42	1,555	4	62	33	0	28	16.36	-13.8			Feb-08
	3.93	15.13	9.19	32.64	36.25	2.88	1.33	7.91		9.36	1,555	4	62	33	0	28	16.06	-14.07			Aug-08
	4.01	15.29	9.50	33.78	38.43	3.16	1.03	7.91		9.37	1,555	4	62	33	0	28	16.22	-13.95			Aug-08
	4.17	15.55	9.75	35.04	40.56	3.4	0.73	7.92		9.42	1,555	4	62	33	0	28	16.36	-13.79			Aug-08
50	2.98	10.21	6.00	19.27	12.05	2.93	1.18	4.76		10.68	133.8	5	35	59	1	32	11.49	-8.16	5.50		May-04
50	2.71	9.63	5.10	16.46	7.80	1.66	1.94	4.77		10.58	133.8	5	35	59	1	32	10.98	-8.42		1.00	May-04
	2.98	10.30	6.34	20.18	12.90	3.23	0.81	4.72		10.7	133.8	5	35	59	1	32	11.49	-8.16			Feb-17
50	2.98	10.20	6.21	20.07	13.41	3.12	0.94	4.78		10.69	133.8	5	35	59	1	32	11.76	-8.04			Aug-06
	2.88	9.97	5.61	18.25	10.47	2.41	1.44	4.78		10.69	133.8	5	35	59	1	32	11.29	-8.28			Dec-06
	2.88	10.09	5.94	19.36	12.13	2.88	1.14	4.74		10.69	133.8	5	35	59	1	32	11.48	-8.1			Dec-06
	2.97	10.28	6.29	20.42	13.77	3.19	0.84	4.76		10.72	133.8	5	35	59	1	32	11.63	-8.04			Dec-06
50	5.31	20.75	13.11	49.41	73.69	0.63	0.75	11.58	0.93	32.11	4,986	2	98	0	0	22	23.64	-16.17	5.50		Apr-98
50	5.14	20.32	12.25	46.12	67.43	0	1.49	11.56	0.93	29.25	4,986	2	98	0	0	22	23.11	-16.48	2.50	1.00	Jul-98
	5.40	20.93	13.48	50.97	76.79	0.92	0.39	11.58	0.93	32.18	4,986	2	98	0	0	22	24.04	-16.03			Feb-17
50	5.40	20.89	13.39	50.51	76.17	0.85	0.47	11.58	0.93	32.17	4,986	2	98	0	0	22	24.04	-16.03			Mar-15
	5.23	20.52	12.70	47.88	70.92	0.2	1.1	11.57	0.93	32.59	4,986	2	98	0	0	22	23.55	-16.3			Dec-06
	5.34	20.75	13.10	49.31	73.67	0.51	0.79	11.58	0.93	33.11	4,986	2	98	0	0	22	23.75	-16.16			Dec-06
	5.36	20.88	13.37	50.55	76.12	0.83	0.49	11.59	0.93	32.41	4,986	2	98	0	0	22	23.98	-16.04			Dec-06
	5.44	20.95	13.49	51.03	76.80	0.91	0.39	11.58	0.93	32.56	4,986	2	98	0	0	22	24.04	-16.03			Mar-15
	5.37	20.91	13.43	50.83	76.63	0.88	0.45	11.58	0.93	32.55	4,986	2	98	0	0	22	24.04	-16.03			Apr-98
	5.36	21.02	13.29	50.03	75.84	0.64	0.78	11.77	0.95	16.29	633.2	1	99	0	0	22	24.3	-16.35			May-98
	5.30	20.88	12.98	48.93	73.69	0.42	1.03	11.74	0.95	16.09	633.2	1	99	0	0	22	24.12	-16.44			May-98
	3.60	16.44	10.06	45.10	53.36	1.71	0.68	11.59	0.92	23.01	3,214	2	98	0	0	28	22.82	-17.47			Mar-94
	3.48	16.32	9.79	44.00	51.43	1.49	0.93	11.59	0.92	22.87	3,214	2	98	0	0	28	22.64	-17.55			Apr-98
50	1.90	11.77	0.13	38.90	13.65	1.69	1.46	14.45	1.03	9.11	308.4	11	89	0	0	85	17.63		5.50		May-11
50	1.70	11.45	-0.66	35.62	9.49	0.5	2.21	14.44	1.03	8.95	308.4	11	89	0	0	85	17.08			1.00	May-11
	2.14	12.14	0.64	40.62	16.11	2.15	0.99	14.52	1.03	9.05	308.4	11	89	0	0	85	17.8				Feb-17
50	2.02	12.08	0.51	40.08	15.67	2.03	1.21	14.45	1.03	9.09	308.4	11	89	0	0	85	17.8				May-11
	1.90	11.77	-0.10	37.89	12.24	1.38	1.71	14.51	1.03	9.11	308.4	11	89	0	0	85	17.33				May-11
	2.00	11.98	0.23	39.27	13.81	1.77	1.46	14.45	1.03	9.16	308.4	11	89	0	0	85	17.59				May-11
	2.02	12.14	0.60	40.94	14.96	2.02	1.16	14.53	1.03	9.05	308.4	11	89	0	0	85	17.76				May-11
	2.01	12.06	0.64	40.41	15.94	2.05	0.99	14.46	1.03	9.1	308.4	11	89	0	0	85	17.8				Mar-18
	2.02	12.09	0.56	40.46	16.05	2.08	1.11	14.54	1.04	9.08	308.4	11	89	0	0	85	17.8				May-11
50	5.94	20.94	5.92	24.99		0.93	1.19	13.13	1.06	10.51	17.4	1	99	0	0	44			5.50		Feb-16
50	6.45	21.54	6.42	25.14		0.98	1.94	13.17	1.07	10.55	17.4	1	99	0	0	44				1.00	Feb-16
	6.01	21.07	6.17	26.06		1.19	0.69	13.09	1.06	10.57	17.4	1	99	0	0	44					Feb-17
50	6.03	21.16	6.30	26.06		2.19	0.89	13.12	1.06	10.36	17.4	1	99	0	0	44					Feb-16
	6.36	21.31	6.33	25.26		0.99	1.41	13.2	1.07	10.53	17.4	1	99	0	0	44					Feb-16
	6.16	21.08	6.20	25.39		1.05	1.11	13.14	1.06	10.51	17.4	1	99	0	0	44					Feb-16

	MARKET			FUND TYPE, CATEGORY & OBJECTIVE	RATINGS					MINIMUMS
Fund Name	Ticker Symbol	Traded On	Fund Type	Category and (Prospectus Objective)	Overall Rating	Reward Rating	Risk Rating	Recent Up/ Downgrade	Open to New Investors	Min Initial Investment
Hartford Environmental Opportunities Fund Class R5	HEOTX	NAS CM	Open End	Global Equity Mid/Small Cap (Growth & Income)	C	C	B-		Y	0
Hartford Environmental Opportunities Fund Class R6	HEOVX	NAS CM	Open End	Global Equity Mid/Small Cap (Growth & Income)	C	C	B-		Y	0
Hartford Environmental Opportunities Fund Class Y	HEOYX	NAS CM	Open End	Global Equity Mid/Small Cap (Growth & Income)	C	C	B-		Y	250,000
Hartford Global All-Asset Fund Class C	HLACX	NAS CM	Open End	Moderate Alloc (Asset Alloc)	C+	C	B+	Up	Y	5,000
Hartford Global All-Asset Fund Class F	HLAFX	NAS CM	Open End	Moderate Alloc (Asset Alloc)	C+	C	B+	Up	Y	1,000,000
Hartford Global All-Asset Fund Class I	HLAIX	NAS CM	Open End	Moderate Alloc (Asset Alloc)	C+	C	B+	Up	Y	5,000
Hartford Global All-Asset Fund Class R3	HLARX	NAS CM	Open End	Moderate Alloc (Asset Alloc)	C+	C	B+	Up	Y	0
Hartford Global All-Asset Fund Class R4	HLASX	NAS CM	Open End	Moderate Alloc (Asset Alloc)	C+	C	B+	Up	Y	0
Hartford Global All-Asset Fund Class R5	HLATX	NAS CM	Open End	Moderate Alloc (Asset Alloc)	C+	C	B+	Up	Y	0
Hartford Global All-Asset Fund Class R6	HLAUX	NAS CM	Open End	Moderate Alloc (Asset Alloc)	C+	C	B+	Up	Y	0
Hartford Global Growth HLS Fund Class IA	HIALX	NAS CM	Open End	Global Equity Large Cap (World Stock)	C+	C	B	Down	Y	0
Hartford Global Growth HLS Fund Class IB	HBGLX	NAS CM	Open End	Global Equity Large Cap (World Stock)	C+	C	B	Down	Y	0
Hartford Global Impact Fund Class A	HGXAX	NAS CM	Open End	Global Equity Mid/Small Cap (World Stock)	C	C	B	Up	Y	5,000
Hartford Global Impact Fund Class C	HGXCX	NAS CM	Open End	Global Equity Mid/Small Cap (World Stock)	C	C	B	Up	Y	5,000
Hartford Global Impact Fund Class F	HGXFX	NAS CM	Open End	Global Equity Mid/Small Cap (World Stock)	C	C	B	Up	Y	1,000,000
Hartford Global Impact Fund Class I	HGXIX	NAS CM	Open End	Global Equity Mid/Small Cap (World Stock)	C	C	B	Up	Y	5,000
Hartford Global Impact Fund Class R3	HGXRX	NAS CM	Open End	Global Equity Mid/Small Cap (World Stock)	C	C	B	Up	Y	0
Hartford Global Impact Fund Class R4	HGXSX	NAS CM	Open End	Global Equity Mid/Small Cap (World Stock)	C	C	B	Up	Y	0
Hartford Global Impact Fund Class R5	HGXTX	NAS CM	Open End	Global Equity Mid/Small Cap (World Stock)	C	C	B	Up	Y	0
Hartford Global Impact Fund Class R6	HGXVX	NAS CM	Open End	Global Equity Mid/Small Cap (World Stock)	C	C	B	Up	Y	0
Hartford Global Impact Fund Class Y	HGXYX	NAS CM	Open End	Global Equity Mid/Small Cap (World Stock)	C	C	B	Up	Y	250,000
Hartford Global Real Asset Fund Class A	HRLAX	NAS CM	Open End	Moderate Alloc (Asset Alloc)	C	C-	B-		Y	5,000
Hartford Global Real Asset Fund Class F	HRLFX	NAS CM	Open End	Moderate Alloc (Asset Alloc)	C	C-	B-		Y	1,000,000
Hartford Global Real Asset Fund Class I	HRLIX	NAS CM	Open End	Moderate Alloc (Asset Alloc)	C	C-	B-		Y	5,000
Hartford Global Real Asset Fund Class R3	HRLRX	NAS CM	Open End	Moderate Alloc (Asset Alloc)	C	C-	B-		Y	0
Hartford Global Real Asset Fund Class R4	HRLSX	NAS CM	Open End	Moderate Alloc (Asset Alloc)	C	C-	B-		Y	0
Hartford Global Real Asset Fund Class R5	HRLTX	NAS CM	Open End	Moderate Alloc (Asset Alloc)	C	C-	B-		Y	0
Hartford Global Real Asset Fund Class Y	HRLYX	NAS CM	Open End	Moderate Alloc (Asset Alloc)	C	C-	B-		Y	250,000
Hartford Growth Allocation Fund Class A	HRAAX	NAS CM	Open End	Aggressive Alloc (Asset Alloc)	B-	C	B+	Up	Y	2,000
Hartford Growth Allocation Fund Class C	HRACX	NAS CM	Open End	Aggressive Alloc (Asset Alloc)	B-	C	B	Up	Y	2,000
Hartford Growth Allocation Fund Class F	HRAFX	NAS CM	Open End	Aggressive Alloc (Asset Alloc)	B-	C	B+	Up	Y	1,000,000
Hartford Growth Allocation Fund Class I	HRAIX	NAS CM	Open End	Aggressive Alloc (Asset Alloc)	B-	C	B+	Up	Y	2,000
Hartford Growth Allocation Fund Class R3	HRARX	NAS CM	Open End	Aggressive Alloc (Asset Alloc)	B-	C	B+	Up	Y	0
Hartford Growth Allocation Fund Class R4	HRASX	NAS CM	Open End	Aggressive Alloc (Asset Alloc)	B-	C	B+	Up	Y	0
Hartford Growth Allocation Fund Class R5	HRATX	NAS CM	Open End	Aggressive Alloc (Asset Alloc)	B-	C	B+	Up	Y	0
Hartford Growth Opportunities HLS Fund Class IA	HAGOX	NAS CM	Open End	US Equity Large Cap Growth (Growth)	B-	B-	B-	Down	Y	0
Hartford Growth Opportunities HLS Fund Class IB	HBGOX	NAS CM	Open End	US Equity Large Cap Growth (Growth)	B-	B-	B-	Down	Y	0
Hartford Growth Opportunities HLS Fund Class IC	HCGOX	NAS CM	Open End	US Equity Large Cap Growth (Growth)	B-	B-	B-	Down	Y	0
Hartford Healthcare HLS Fund Class IA	HIAHX	NAS CM	Open End	Healthcare Sector Equity (Health)	C+	C	B		Y	0
Hartford Healthcare HLS Fund Class IB	HBGHX	NAS CM	Open End	Healthcare Sector Equity (Health)	C+	C	B-		Y	0
Hartford International Equity Fund Class A	HDVAX	NAS CM	Open End	Global Equity Large Cap (Growth)	C	C	C+		Y	2,000
Hartford International Equity Fund Class C	HDVCX	NAS CM	Open End	Global Equity Large Cap (Growth)	C	C-	C+		Y	2,000
Hartford International Equity Fund Class F	HDVFX	NAS CM	Open End	Global Equity Large Cap (Growth)	C	C	B-		Y	1,000,000
Hartford International Equity Fund Class I	HDVIX	NAS CM	Open End	Global Equity Large Cap (Growth)	C	C	B-		Y	2,000
Hartford International Equity Fund Class R3	HDVRX	NAS CM	Open End	Global Equity Large Cap (Growth)	C	C	C+		Y	0
Hartford International Equity Fund Class R4	HDVSX	NAS CM	Open End	Global Equity Large Cap (Growth)	C	C	C+		Y	0
Hartford International Equity Fund Class R5	HDVTX	NAS CM	Open End	Global Equity Large Cap (Growth)	C	C	B-		Y	0
Hartford International Equity Fund Class R6	HDVVX	NAS CM	Open End	Global Equity Large Cap (Growth)	C	C	B-			0
Hartford International Equity Fund Class Y	HDVYX	NAS CM	Open End	Global Equity Large Cap (Growth)	C	C	B-		Y	250,000
Hartford International Growth Fund Class A	HNCAX	NAS CM	Open End	Global Equity Large Cap (Foreign Stock)	C	C	C+		Y	2,000
Hartford International Growth Fund Class C	HNCCX	NAS CM	Open End	Global Equity Large Cap (Foreign Stock)	C	C	C+		Y	2,000
Hartford International Growth Fund Class F	HNCFX	NAS CM	Open End	Global Equity Large Cap (Foreign Stock)	C	C	C+		Y	1,000,000

★ Expanded analysis of this fund is included in Section II.

	TOTAL RETURNS					PERFORMANCE				ASSETS		ASSET ALLOCATION & TURNOVER					BULL & BEAR		FEES		
Min Additional Investment	3-Month Total Return	6-Month Total Return	1-Year Total Return	3-Year Total Return	5-Year Total Return	Dividend Yield (TTM)	Expense Ratio	3-Yr Std Deviation	3-Year Beta	NAV	Total Assets (MIL)	%Cash	%Stocks	%Bonds	%Other	Turnover Ratio	Last Bull Market Total Return	Last Bear Market Total Return	Front End Fee (%)	Back End Fee (%)	Inception Date
	6.16	21.22	6.20	25.80		1.12	0.81	13.15	1.07	10.51	17.4	1	99	0	0	44					Feb-16
	6.15	21.19	6.33	26.27		1.22	0.69	13.13	1.06	10.52	17.4	1	99	0	0	44					Feb-16
	6.16	21.22	6.30	26.20		1.2	0.79	13.06	1.06	10.51	17.4	1	99	0	0	44					Feb-16
50	3.09	11.43	1.30	20.97	14.61	8.3	1.99	7.06		9.65	156.8	14	49	36	0	62	11.12	-15.9		1.00	May-10
	3.47	12.08	2.53	25.12	21.17	9.58	0.74	7.04		9.83	156.8	14	49	36	0	62	11.72	-15.51			Feb-17
50	3.47	11.95	2.40	24.77	20.60	9.46	0.94	7.06		9.83	156.8	14	49	36	0	62	11.72	-15.52			May-10
	3.27	11.75	1.78	22.66	17.34	8.74	1.46	7.08		9.79	156.8	14	49	36	0	62	11.49	-15.8			May-10
	3.32	11.79	2.11	23.86	19.17	8.84	1.16	7.06		9.95	156.8	14	49	36	0	62	11.61	-15.69			May-10
	3.39	12.06	2.37	24.98	20.14	9.5	0.86	7.03		9.75	156.8	14	49	36	0	62	11.65	-15.51			May-10
	3.47	12.07	2.49	25.15	21.20	9.54	0.74	7		9.84	156.8	14	49	36	0	62	11.71	-15.51			Mar-18
	5.46	23.84	9.43	62.70	75.89	0.47	0.8	13.65	1.08	30.12	515.7	1	100	0	0	55	24.64	-24.78			Oct-98
	5.41	23.68	9.16	61.49	73.72	0.25	1.05	13.65	1.08	29.77	515.7	1	100	0	0	55	24.46	-24.86			Sep-98
50	4.49	17.92	5.92			0.52	1.19			10.92	43.0	13	87	0	0	79			5.50		Feb-17
50	4.47	17.74	5.61			0.23	1.94			10.75	43.0	13	87	0	0	79				1.00	Feb-17
	4.68	18.24	6.50			1.05	0.69			10.95	43.0	13	87	0	0	79					Feb-17
50	4.71	18.24	6.46			0.63	0.89			10.89	43.0	13	87	0	0	79					Feb-17
	4.56	17.98	6.08			0.82	1.41			10.76	43.0	13	87	0	0	79					Feb-17
	4.61	18.00	6.14			0.75	1.11			10.88	43.0	13	87	0	0	79					Feb-17
	4.66	18.22	6.27			0.95	0.81			10.77	43.0	13	87	0	0	79					Feb-17
	4.65	18.29	6.47			0.89	0.69			10.8	43.0	13	87	0	0	79					Feb-17
	4.76	18.22	6.43			1	0.79			10.77	43.0	13	87	0	0	79					Feb-17
50	1.11	10.04	-2.93	15.19	-11.85	1.9	1.27	9.28		9.09	296.5	8	65	13	15	111	8.02	-20.22	5.50		May-10
	1.11	10.20	-2.66	16.29	-10.39	2.26	0.92	9.32		9.07	296.5	8	65	13	15	111	8.28	-20.09			Feb-17
50	1.11	10.19	-2.63	16.19	-10.65	2.18	1.02	9.32		9.08	296.5	8	65	13	15	111	8.15	-20.11			May-10
	0.99	9.85	-3.15	14.16	-12.99	1.66	1.52	9.35		9.14	296.5	8	65	13	15	111	7.86	-20.3			May-10
	1.11	10.02	-2.83	15.41	-11.69	1.89	1.22	9.34		9.11	296.5	8	65	13	15	111	7.96	-20.19			May-10
	1.12	10.13	-2.65	16.24	-10.53	2.89	0.97	9.34		9.02	296.5	8	65	13	15	111	8.22	-20.09			May-10
	1.11	10.19	-2.54	16.38	-10.32	2.27	0.92	9.34		9.08	296.5	8	65	13	15	111	8.28	-20.09			May-10
50	3.35	15.53	5.21	33.63	24.04	2.24	1.17	9.83		12.64	619.3	3	80	16	1	32	18.84	-17.59	5.50		May-04
50	3.12	15.03	4.33	30.63	19.46	0.57	1.93	9.82		12.55	619.3	3	80	16	1	32	18.29	-17.88		1.00	May-04
	3.37	15.74	5.57	34.81	25.13	2.6	0.78	9.8		12.57	619.3	3	80	16	1	32	18.85	-17.59			Feb-17
50	3.45	15.74	5.55	34.86	26.08	2.52	0.87	9.84		12.57	619.3	3	80	16	1	32	19.04	-17.49			Aug-06
	3.26	15.34	4.84	32.32	22.06	1.95	1.5	9.82		12.33	619.3	3	80	16	1	32	18.61	-17.67			Dec-06
	3.36	15.51	5.17	33.60	23.91	2.13	1.19	9.84		12.58	619.3	3	80	16	1	32	18.77	-17.59			Dec-06
	3.34	15.63	5.49	34.74	25.81	2.48	0.89	9.81		12.65	619.3	3	80	16	1	32	19.03	-17.5			Dec-06
	6.08	30.13	12.61	72.05	100.93	0	0.65	16.01	1.12	43.44	1,655	4	92	0	2	118	27.19	-22.88			Mar-87
	6.02	30.00	12.33	70.73	98.40	0	0.9	16.02	1.12	41.33	1,655	4	92	0	2	118	27	-22.96			May-02
	5.95	29.81	12.06	69.49	95.99	0	1.15	16	1.12	42.19	1,655	4	92	0	2	118	27	-22.96			Apr-14
	1.70	18.03	7.04	36.33	62.32	0.1	0.89	16.1	1.09	23.89	231.2	2	98	0	0	29	23.17	-12.53			May-00
	1.66	17.85	6.76	35.35	60.29	0	1.14	16.1	1.09	22.57	231.2	2	98	0	0	29	22.99	-12.63			May-00
50	2.51	13.36	-1.66	27.21	12.99	0.23	1.05	11.72	1.01	10.6	990.1	2	97	0	1	125	15.19	-23.47	5.50		Jun-08
50	2.26	12.90	-2.50	24.18	8.84	0	1.8	11.7	1.01	10.41	990.1	2	97	0	1	125	14.86	-23.72		1.00	Jun-08
	2.66	13.69	-1.06	28.99	15.49	0.33	0.55	11.65	1.01	10.79	990.1	2	97	0	1	125	15.49	-23.37			Feb-17
50	2.58	13.54	-1.37	28.37	14.93	0.31	0.75	11.68	1.01	10.73	990.1	2	97	0	1	125	15.49	-23.37			Jun-08
	2.43	13.22	-2.08	25.99	11.54	0.19	1.27	11.75	1.01	10.53	990.1	2	97	0	1	125	15.03	-23.55			Jun-08
	2.51	13.47	-1.74	27.11	13.06	0.24	0.97	11.74	1.01	10.61	990.1	2	97	0	1	125	15.4	-23.52			Jun-08
	2.51	13.57	-1.04	29.06	14.62	0.36	0.67	11.62	1	9.37	990.1	2	97	0	1	125	15.61	-23.4			Jun-08
	2.56	13.59	-0.60	29.36	15.81	0.34	0.55	11.54	1	10.78	990.1	2	97	0	1	125	15.49	-23.37			Mar-18
	2.58	13.54	-1.01	28.95	15.70	0.38	0.66	11.62	1	10.73	990.1	2	97	0	1	125	15.52	-23.37			Jun-08
50	4.02	18.41	0.84	32.91	21.71	0.51	1.3	13.16	1.06	14.21	340.2	3	97	0	0	76	17.23	-24.21	5.50		Apr-01
50	3.83	17.99	0.16	30.03	17.44	0	2.05	13.19	1.06	12.98	340.2	3	97	0	0	76	16.74	-24.49		1.00	Apr-01
	4.20	18.77	1.38	34.57	24.46	0.89	0.85	13.2	1.06	14.11	340.2	3	97	0	0	76	17.49	-23.98			Feb-17

	MARKET			FUND TYPE, CATEGORY & OBJECTIVE	RATINGS				MINIMUMS	
Fund Name	Ticker Symbol	Traded On	Fund Type	Category and (Prospectus Objective)	Overall Rating	Reward Rating	Risk Rating	Recent Up/ Downgrade	Open to New Investors	Min Initial Investment
Hartford International Growth Fund Class I	HNCJX	NAS CM	Open End	Global Equity Large Cap (Foreign Stock)	C	C	C+		Y	2,000
Hartford International Growth Fund Class R3	HNCRX	NAS CM	Open End	Global Equity Large Cap (Foreign Stock)	C	C	C+		Y	0
Hartford International Growth Fund Class R4	HNCSX	NAS CM	Open End	Global Equity Large Cap (Foreign Stock)	C	C	C+		Y	0
Hartford International Growth Fund Class R5	HNCTX	NAS CM	Open End	Global Equity Large Cap (Foreign Stock)	C	C	C+		Y	0
Hartford International Growth Fund Class R6	HNCUX	NAS CM	Open End	Global Equity Large Cap (Foreign Stock)	C	C	C+		Y	0
Hartford International Growth Fund Class Y	HNCYX	NAS CM	Open End	Global Equity Large Cap (Foreign Stock)	C	C	C+		Y	250,000
Hartford International Opportunities HLS Fund Class IA	HIAOX	NAS CM	Open End	Global Equity Large Cap (Foreign Stock)	C	C	C+		Y	0
Hartford International Opportunities HLS Fund Class IB	HBIOX	NAS CM	Open End	Global Equity Large Cap (Foreign Stock)	C	C	C+		Y	0
Hartford International Small Company Fund Class A	HNSAX	NAS CM	Open End	Global Equity Mid/Small Cap (Foreign Stock)	D+	D	C-		Y	2,000
Hartford International Small Company Fund Class C	HNSCX	NAS CM	Open End	Global Equity Mid/Small Cap (Foreign Stock)	D+	D	C-	Up	Y	2,000
Hartford International Small Company Fund Class F	HNSFX	NAS CM	Open End	Global Equity Mid/Small Cap (Foreign Stock)	D+	D+	C-			1,000,000
Hartford International Small Company Fund Class I	HNSJX	NAS CM	Open End	Global Equity Mid/Small Cap (Foreign Stock)	D+	D+	C-		Y	2,000
Hartford International Small Company Fund Class R3	HNSRX	NAS CM	Open End	Global Equity Mid/Small Cap (Foreign Stock)	D+	D	C-		Y	0
Hartford International Small Company Fund Class R4	HNSSX	NAS CM	Open End	Global Equity Mid/Small Cap (Foreign Stock)	D+	D+	C-		Y	0
Hartford International Small Company Fund Class R5	HNSTX	NAS CM	Open End	Global Equity Mid/Small Cap (Foreign Stock)	D+	D+	C-		Y	0
Hartford International Small Company Fund Class Y	HNSYX	NAS CM	Open End	Global Equity Mid/Small Cap (Foreign Stock)	D+	D+	C-		Y	250,000
Hartford International Value Fund Class A	HILAX	NAS CM	Open End	Global Equity Large Cap (Foreign Stock)	C	C-	C			2,000
Hartford International Value Fund Class C	HILCX	NAS CM	Open End	Global Equity Large Cap (Foreign Stock)	C-	D+	C	Down		2,000
Hartford International Value Fund Class F	HILDX	NAS CM	Open End	Global Equity Large Cap (Foreign Stock)	C	C-	C		Y	1,000,000
Hartford International Value Fund Class I	HILIX	NAS CM	Open End	Global Equity Large Cap (Foreign Stock)	C	C-	C			2,000
Hartford International Value Fund Class R3	HILRX	NAS CM	Open End	Global Equity Large Cap (Foreign Stock)	C-	C-	C	Down		0
Hartford International Value Fund Class R4	HILSX	NAS CM	Open End	Global Equity Large Cap (Foreign Stock)	C-	C-	C	Down		0
Hartford International Value Fund Class R5	HILTX	NAS CM	Open End	Global Equity Large Cap (Foreign Stock)	C	C-	C			0
Hartford International Value Fund Class R6	HILUX	NAS CM	Open End	Global Equity Large Cap (Foreign Stock)	C	C-	C		Y	0
Hartford Long/Short Global Equity Fund Class A	HLOAX	NAS CM	Open End	Long/Short Equity (Growth)	C-	D+	C		Y	5,000
Hartford Long/Short Global Equity Fund Class C	HLOCX	NAS CM	Open End	Long/Short Equity (Growth)	C-	D+	C		Y	5,000
Hartford Long/Short Global Equity Fund Class F	HLOFX	NAS CM	Open End	Long/Short Equity (Growth)	C-	D+	C			1,000,000
Hartford Long/Short Global Equity Fund Class I	HLOIX	NAS CM	Open End	Long/Short Equity (Growth)	C-	D+	C		Y	5,000
Hartford Long/Short Global Equity Fund Class Y	HLOYX	NAS CM	Open End	Long/Short Equity (Growth)	C-	D+	C		Y	250,000
Hartford MidCap Growth HLS Fund Class IA	HMCSX	NAS CM	Open End	US Equity Mid Cap (Growth & Income)	C+	C+	B-		Y	0
Hartford MidCap Growth HLS Fund Class IB	HMCVX	NAS CM	Open End	US Equity Mid Cap (Growth & Income)	C+	C+	B-		Y	0
Hartford MidCap HLS Fund Class IA	HIMCX	NAS CM	Open End	US Equity Mid Cap (Growth)	C+	C	B-	Down	Y	0
Hartford MidCap HLS Fund Class IB	HBMCX	NAS CM	Open End	US Equity Mid Cap (Growth)	C+	C	B-		Y	0
Hartford MidCap Value Fund Class A	HMVAX	NAS CM	Open End	US Equity Mid Cap (Growth)	C	C	B-		Y	2,000
Hartford MidCap Value Fund Class C	HMVCX	NAS CM	Open End	US Equity Mid Cap (Growth)	C	C	B-		Y	2,000
Hartford MidCap Value Fund Class F	HMVFX	NAS CM	Open End	US Equity Mid Cap (Growth)	C	C	B-		Y	1,000,000
Hartford MidCap Value Fund Class I	HMVJX	NAS CM	Open End	US Equity Mid Cap (Growth)	C	C	B-		Y	2,000
Hartford MidCap Value Fund Class R3	HMVRX	NAS CM	Open End	US Equity Mid Cap (Growth)	C	C	B-		Y	0
Hartford MidCap Value Fund Class R4	HMVSX	NAS CM	Open End	US Equity Mid Cap (Growth)	C	C	B-		Y	0
Hartford MidCap Value Fund Class R5	HMVTX	NAS CM	Open End	US Equity Mid Cap (Growth)	C	C	B-		Y	0
Hartford MidCap Value Fund Class Y	HMVYX	NAS CM	Open End	US Equity Mid Cap (Growth)	C	C	B-		Y	250,000
Hartford MidCap Value HLS Fund Class IA	HMVIX	NAS CM	Open End	US Equity Mid Cap (Growth)	C	C	B-		Y	0
Hartford MidCap Value HLS Fund Class IB	HBMVX	NAS CM	Open End	US Equity Mid Cap (Growth)	C	C	B-		Y	0
Hartford Moderate Allocation Fund Class A	HBAAX	NAS CM	Open End	Moderate Alloc (Balanced)	B-	C	A-	Up	Y	2,000
Hartford Moderate Allocation Fund Class C	HBACX	NAS CM	Open End	Moderate Alloc (Balanced)	B-	C	A-	Up	Y	2,000
Hartford Moderate Allocation Fund Class F	HBADX	NAS CM	Open End	Moderate Alloc (Balanced)	B-	C	A-	Up	Y	1,000,000
Hartford Moderate Allocation Fund Class I	HBAIX	NAS CM	Open End	Moderate Alloc (Balanced)	B-	C	A-	Up	Y	2,000
Hartford Moderate Allocation Fund Class R3	HBARX	NAS CM	Open End	Moderate Alloc (Balanced)	B-	C	A-	Up	Y	0
Hartford Moderate Allocation Fund Class R4	HBASX	NAS CM	Open End	Moderate Alloc (Balanced)	B-	C	A-	Up	Y	0
Hartford Moderate Allocation Fund Class R5	HBATX	NAS CM	Open End	Moderate Alloc (Balanced)	B-	C	A-	Up	Y	0
Hartford Multi-Asset Income and Growth Fund Class A	ITTAX	NAS CM	Open End	Moderate Alloc (Balanced)	B-	C	B+	Up	Y	2,000
Hartford Multi-Asset Income and Growth Fund Class C	HAFCX	NAS CM	Open End	Moderate Alloc (Balanced)	B-	C	B+	Up	Y	2,000

★ Expanded analysis of this fund is included in Section II.

Min Additional Investment	TOTAL RETURNS 3-Month Total Return	6-Month Total Return	1-Year Total Return	3-Year Total Return	5-Year Total Return	PERFORMANCE Dividend Yield (TTM)	Expense Ratio	3-Yr Std Deviation	3-Year Beta	ASSETS NAV	Total Assets (MIL)	ASSET ALLOCATION & TURNOVER %Cash	%Stocks	%Bonds	%Other	Turnover Ratio	BULL & BEAR Last Bull Market Total Return	Last Bear Market Total Return	FEES Front End Fee (%)	Back End Fee (%)	Inception Date
50	4.13	18.70	1.28	34.20	23.78	0.8	1	13.19	1.06	14.09	340.2	3	97	0	0	76	17.37	-24.09			Aug-06
	3.96	18.29	0.61	31.88	20.24	0.21	1.57	13.16	1.06	14.42	340.2	3	97	0	0	76	17.01	-24.24			Dec-06
	4.05	18.44	0.89	33.02	22.14	0.39	1.27	13.17	1.06	14.64	340.2	3	97	0	0	76	17.44	-24.16			Dec-06
	4.16	18.66	1.22	34.23	23.99	0.76	1	13.2	1.06	14.75	340.2	3	97	0	0	76	17.47	-24.04			Dec-06
	4.21	18.73	1.41	34.60	24.49	0.82	0.85	13.19	1.06	14.83	340.2	3	97	0	0	76	17.49	-23.98			Mar-18
	4.15	18.68	1.30	34.45	24.35	0.83	0.95	13.18	1.06	14.8	340.2	3	97	0	0	76	17.49	-23.98			Apr-01
	4.16	19.27	0.00	27.88	16.29	1.96	0.73	13.08	1.12	16.52	1,238	3	97	0	0	80	18.43	-23.52			Jul-90
	4.11	19.10	-0.27	26.91	14.83	1.67	0.98	13.07	1.11	16.71	1,238	3	97	0	0	80	18.26	-23.6			Apr-98
50	1.64	12.77	-14.70	12.31	0.21	0.53	1.46	15.07	1.16	11.74	190.9	1	99	0	0	38	17.2	-21.44	5.50		Apr-01
50	1.47	12.43	-15.35	9.73	-3.42	0	2.24	15.04	1.16	10.31	190.9	1	99	0	0	38	16.71	-21.72		1.00	Apr-01
	1.83	13.13	-14.28	14.00	2.72	1.04	0.99	15.08	1.16	11.63	190.9	1	99	0	0	38	17.53	-21.28			Feb-17
50	1.74	12.91	-14.45	13.52	2.04	0.82	1.08	15.09	1.17	11.63	190.9	1	99	0	0	38	17.5	-21.26			May-07
	1.62	12.74	-14.87	11.67	-0.72	0.25	1.65	15.07	1.16	11.85	190.9	1	99	0	0	38	17.07	-21.41			May-10
	1.70	12.89	-14.63	12.63	0.82	0.58	1.35	15.08	1.16	11.91	190.9	1	99	0	0	38	17.36	-21.36			May-10
	1.78	13.01	-14.36	13.72	2.29	0.95	1.05	15.03	1.16	11.98	190.9	1	99	0	0	38	17.47	-21.22			May-10
	1.78	13.11	-14.30	13.89	2.61	1	1	15.1	1.17	11.99	190.9	1	99	0	0	38	17.53	-21.28			Apr-01
50	1.58	9.19	-5.70	30.94	12.11	2.32	1.21	12.66	1.08	14.13	2,473	5	95	0	0	22	14.29	-22.76	5.50		May-10
50	1.38	8.81	-6.38	28.29	8.42	1.48	1.93	12.68	1.09	13.95	2,473	5	95	0	0	22	13.81	-22.94		1.00	May-10
	1.63	9.42	-5.35	32.56	14.33	2.75	0.84	12.67	1.08	14.28	2,473	5	95	0	0	22	14.56	-22.58			Feb-17
50	1.63	9.34	-5.46	32.22	14.03	2.65	0.91	12.67	1.08	14.27	2,473	5	95	0	0	22	14.56	-22.58			May-10
	1.49	9.04	-6.04	29.71	10.46	1.89	1.56	12.66	1.08	14.23	2,473	5	95	0	0	22	14.07	-22.78			May-10
	1.57	9.13	-5.74	31.00	12.23	2.29	1.26	12.69	1.09	14.22	2,473	5	95	0	0	22	14.42	-22.74			May-10
	1.63	9.31	-5.43	32.16	13.96	2.66	0.94	12.67	1.08	14.31	2,473	5	95	0	0	22	14.47	-22.58			May-10
	1.67	9.45	-5.37	32.35	14.14		0.84	12.67	1.08	14.6	2,473	5	95	0	0	22	14.56	-22.58			Feb-19
50	3.08	8.51	-3.85	16.37		0.78	2.29	9.18	0.72	10.71	17.7	39	61	0	0	31			5.50		Aug-14
50	3.13	8.45	-4.02	15.25		0.36	3.04	9.22	0.72	10.52	17.7	39	61	0	0	31				1.00	Aug-14
	3.15	8.66	-3.65	16.96		0.94	2.04	9.14	0.71	10.78	17.7	39	61	0	0	31					Feb-17
50	3.15	8.66	-3.69	16.84		0.99	2.04	9.14	0.72	10.78	17.7	39	61	0	0	31					Aug-14
	3.16	8.70	-3.62	17.08		1.31	2.04	9.21	0.72	10.74	17.7	39	61	0	0	31					Aug-14
	6.88	28.83	10.40	54.40	47.90	0.63	0.91	15.24	0.98	9.16	95.6	0	100	0	0	160	24.88	-22.28			May-98
	6.69	28.61	10.05	53.15	45.92	0.38	1.16	15.29	0.98	9.08	95.6	0	100	0	0	160	24.69	-22.36			Mar-08
	4.85	27.69	8.50	60.66	66.06	0.02	0.69	14.98	0.96	42.56	2,182	0	100	0	0	35	29.46	-25.59			Jul-97
	4.79	27.55	8.23	59.44	64.00	0	0.94	14.97	0.96	41.34	2,182	0	100	0	0	35	29.27	-25.67			Nov-99
50	3.37	17.86	-0.78	27.62	23.58	0.29	1.22	15.23	1.12	13.79	679.6	0	98	0	2	49	31.58	-25.59	5.50		Apr-01
50	3.18	17.48	-1.57	24.84	19.12	0	1.98	15.2	1.12	11.02	679.6	0	98	0	2	49	30.99	-25.78	2.50	1.00	Apr-01
	3.49	18.15	-0.40	29.31	26.37	0.64	0.8	15.25	1.12	13.93	679.6	0	98	0	2	49	31.96	-25.43			Feb-17
50	3.41	18.05	-0.46	28.61	25.36	0.54	0.9	15.22	1.12	13.93	679.6	0	98	0	2	49	31.84	-25.45			May-10
	3.26	17.70	-1.08	26.53	21.85	0	1.52	15.24	1.12	14.56	679.6	0	98	0	2	49	31.4	-25.6			May-10
	3.33	17.90	-0.84	27.70	23.74	0.23	1.22	15.23	1.12	14.88	679.6	0	98	0	2	49	31.59	-25.52			May-10
	3.35	17.98	-0.59	28.77	25.58	0.48	0.91	15.22	1.12	15.09	679.6	0	98	0	2	49	31.89	-25.43			May-10
	3.41	18.09	-0.47	29.04	26.11	0.52	0.85	15.23	1.12	15.14	679.6	0	98	0	2	49	31.96	-25.43			Apr-01
	3.55	18.37	-0.47	29.14	26.36	1	0.81	15.3	1.13	11.66	306.7	2	98	0	0	42	31.65	-25.24			Apr-01
	3.39	18.16	-0.82	28.20	24.73	0.48	1.06	15.28	1.12	11.58	306.7	2	98	0	0	42	31.46	-25.31			Apr-01
50	3.16	13.01	5.38	26.92	18.80	2.51	1.14	7.53		11.72	415.4	4	59	36	1	32	15.36	-13.01	5.50		May-04
50	2.93	12.52	4.58	23.99	14.38	0.98	1.89	7.49		11.59	415.4	4	59	36	1	32	14.93	-13.3		1.00	May-04
	3.24	13.18	5.74	27.86	19.69	2.82	0.77	7.49		11.76	415.4	4	59	36	1	32	15.36	-13.01			Feb-17
50	3.24	13.18	5.65	27.93	20.56	2.74	0.86	7.51		11.76	415.4	4	59	36	1	32	15.55	-12.88			Aug-06
	3.03	12.81	4.99	25.52	16.73	2.14	1.48	7.44		11.53	415.4	4	59	36	1	32	15.19	-13.14			Dec-06
	3.17	13.03	5.40	26.65	18.52	2.45	1.19	7.49		11.71	415.4	4	59	36	1	32	15.36	-13.03			Dec-06
	3.24	13.17	5.68	27.76	20.35	2.69	0.88	7.51		11.77	415.4	4	59	36	1	32	15.51	-12.89			Dec-06
50	2.27	11.58	5.28	25.34	32.04	2.27	1.05	7.34		23.13	982.4	3	35	59	0	65	17.84	-12.15	5.50		Jul-96
50	2.14	11.22	4.57	22.68	27.50	1.55	1.76	7.35		23.15	982.4	3	35	59	0	65	17.32	-12.42		1.00	Jul-98

	MARKET			FUND TYPE, CATEGORY & OBJECTIVE	RATINGS				MINIMUMS	
Fund Name	Ticker Symbol	Traded On	Fund Type	Category and (Prospectus Objective)	Overall Rating	Reward Rating	Risk Rating	Recent Up/ Downgrade	Open to New Investors	Min Initial Investment
Hartford Multi-Asset Income and Growth Fund Class F	ITTFX	NAS CM	Open End	Moderate Alloc (Balanced)	B-	C	A-	Up	Y	1,000,000
Hartford Multi-Asset Income and Growth Fund Class I	ITTIX	NAS CM	Open End	Moderate Alloc (Balanced)	B-	C	A-	Up	Y	2,000
Hartford Multi-Asset Income and Growth Fund Class R3	ITTRX	NAS CM	Open End	Moderate Alloc (Balanced)	B-	C	B+	Up	Y	0
Hartford Multi-Asset Income and Growth Fund Class R4	ITTSX	NAS CM	Open End	Moderate Alloc (Balanced)	B-	C	B+	Up	Y	0
Hartford Multi-Asset Income and Growth Fund Class R5	ITTTX	NAS CM	Open End	Moderate Alloc (Balanced)	B-	C	B+	Up	Y	0
Hartford Multi-Asset Income and Growth Fund Class R6	ITTVX	NAS CM	Open End	Moderate Alloc (Balanced)	B-	C	A-	Up	Y	0
Hartford Multi-Asset Income and Growth Fund Class Y	IHAYX	NAS CM	Open End	Moderate Alloc (Balanced)	B-	C	A-	Up	Y	250,000
Hartford Multi-Asset Income Fund Class A	HAFAX	NAS CM	Open End	Cautious Alloc (Income)	B	C+	A	Up	Y	2,000
Hartford Multi-Asset Income Fund Class C	HAICX	NAS CM	Open End	Cautious Alloc (Income)	B	C+	A	Up	Y	2,000
Hartford Multi-Asset Income Fund Class F	HAFDX	NAS CM	Open End	Cautious Alloc (Income)	B	C+	B+	Up	Y	1,000,000
Hartford Multi-Asset Income Fund Class I	HAFIX	NAS CM	Open End	Cautious Alloc (Income)	B	C+	A	Up	Y	2,000
Hartford Multi-Asset Income Fund Class R3	HAFRX	NAS CM	Open End	Cautious Alloc (Income)	B	C+	A	Up	Y	0
Hartford Multi-Asset Income Fund Class R4	HAFSX	NAS CM	Open End	Cautious Alloc (Income)	B	C+	A	Up	Y	0
Hartford Multi-Asset Income Fund Class R5	HAFTX	NAS CM	Open End	Cautious Alloc (Income)	B	C+	A	Up	Y	0
Hartford Multi-Asset Income Fund Class R6	HAFVX	NAS CM	Open End	Cautious Alloc (Income)	B	C+	B+	Up	Y	0
Hartford Multi-Asset Income Fund Class Y	HAFYX	NAS CM	Open End	Cautious Alloc (Income)	B	C+	A	Up	Y	250,000
Hartford Quality Value Fund Class A	HVOAX	NAS CM	Open End	US Equity Large Cap Value (Growth)	B-	C	B	Up	Y	2,000
Hartford Quality Value Fund Class C	HVOCX	NAS CM	Open End	US Equity Large Cap Value (Growth)	C+	C	B	Up	Y	2,000
Hartford Quality Value Fund Class F	HVOFX	NAS CM	Open End	US Equity Large Cap Value (Growth)	B-	C	B	Up	Y	1,000,000
Hartford Quality Value Fund Class I	HVOIX	NAS CM	Open End	US Equity Large Cap Value (Growth)	B-	C	B	Up	Y	2,000
Hartford Quality Value Fund Class R3	HVORX	NAS CM	Open End	US Equity Large Cap Value (Growth)	B-	C	B	Up	Y	0
Hartford Quality Value Fund Class R4	HVOSX	NAS CM	Open End	US Equity Large Cap Value (Growth)	B-	C	B	Up	Y	0
Hartford Quality Value Fund Class R5	HVOTX	NAS CM	Open End	US Equity Large Cap Value (Growth)	B-	C	B	Up	Y	0
Hartford Quality Value Fund Class R6	HVOVX	NAS CM	Open End	US Equity Large Cap Value (Growth)	B-	C	B	Up	Y	0
Hartford Quality Value Fund Class Y	HVOYX	NAS CM	Open End	US Equity Large Cap Value (Growth)	B-	C	B	Up	Y	250,000
Hartford Schroders Emerging Markets Equity Fund Class A	SEMVX	NAS CM	Open End	Global Emerg Mkts (Div Emerging Mkts)	C	C	C+		Y	2,000
Hartford Schroders Emerging Markets Equity Fund Class C	HHHCX	NAS CM	Open End	Global Emerg Mkts (Div Emerging Mkts)	C	C	C+		Y	2,000
Hartford Schroders Emerging Markets Equity Fund Class F	HHHFX	NAS CM	Open End	Global Emerg Mkts (Div Emerging Mkts)	C	C	C+		Y	1,000,000
Hartford Schroders Emerging Markets Equity Fund Class I	SEMNX	NAS CM	Open End	Global Emerg Mkts (Div Emerging Mkts)	C	C	C+		Y	2,000
Hartford Schroders Emerging Markets Equity Fund Class R3	HHHRX	NAS CM	Open End	Global Emerg Mkts (Div Emerging Mkts)	C	C	C+		Y	0
Hartford Schroders Emerging Markets Equity Fund Class R4	HHHSX	NAS CM	Open End	Global Emerg Mkts (Div Emerging Mkts)	C	C	C+		Y	0
Hartford Schroders Emerging Markets Equity Fund Class R5	HHHTX	NAS CM	Open End	Global Emerg Mkts (Div Emerging Mkts)	C	C	C+		Y	0
Hartford Schroders Emerging Markets Equity Fund Class SDR	SEMTX	NAS CM	Open End	Global Emerg Mkts (Div Emerging Mkts)	C	C	C+		Y	5,000,000
Hartford Schroders Emerging Markets Equity Fund Class Y	HHHYX	NAS CM	Open End	Global Emerg Mkts (Div Emerging Mkts)	C	C	C+		Y	250,000
Hartford Schroders International Multi-Cap Value Cls A	SIDVX	NAS CM	Open End	Global Equity Large Cap (Foreign Stock)	C	C-	C+		Y	2,000
Hartford Schroders International Multi-Cap Value Cls C	HFYCX	NAS CM	Open End	Global Equity Large Cap (Foreign Stock)	C	C-	C+		Y	2,000
Hartford Schroders International Multi-Cap Value Cls F	HFYFX	NAS CM	Open End	Global Equity Large Cap (Foreign Stock)	C	C-	B-		Y	1,000,000
Hartford Schroders International Multi-Cap Value Cls I	SIDNX	NAS CM	Open End	Global Equity Large Cap (Foreign Stock)	C	C-	B-		Y	2,000
Hartford Schroders International Multi-Cap Value Cls R3	HFYRX	NAS CM	Open End	Global Equity Large Cap (Foreign Stock)	C	C-	C+		Y	0
Hartford Schroders International Multi-Cap Value Cls R4	HFYSX	NAS CM	Open End	Global Equity Large Cap (Foreign Stock)	C	C-	C+		Y	0
Hartford Schroders International Multi-Cap Value Cls R5	HFYTX	NAS CM	Open End	Global Equity Large Cap (Foreign Stock)	C	C-	B-		Y	0
Hartford Schroders International Multi-Cap Value Cls SDR	SIDRX	NAS CM	Open End	Global Equity Large Cap (Foreign Stock)	C	C-	B-		Y	5,000,000
Hartford Schroders International Multi-Cap Value Cls Y	HFYYX	NAS CM	Open End	Global Equity Large Cap (Foreign Stock)	C	C-	B-		Y	250,000
Hartford Schroders International Stock Fund Class A	SCVEX	NAS CM	Open End	Global Equity Large Cap (Foreign Stock)	C	C	B		Y	2,000
Hartford Schroders International Stock Fund Class C	HSWCX	NAS CM	Open End	Global Equity Large Cap (Foreign Stock)	C	C	B		Y	2,000
Hartford Schroders International Stock Fund Class F	HSWFX	NAS CM	Open End	Global Equity Large Cap (Foreign Stock)	C+	C	B	Up	Y	1,000,000
Hartford Schroders International Stock Fund Class I	SCIEX	NAS CM	Open End	Global Equity Large Cap (Foreign Stock)	C+	C	B	Up	Y	2,000
Hartford Schroders International Stock Fund Class R3	HSWRX	NAS CM	Open End	Global Equity Large Cap (Foreign Stock)	C	C	B		Y	0
Hartford Schroders International Stock Fund Class R4	HSWSX	NAS CM	Open End	Global Equity Large Cap (Foreign Stock)	C	C	B		Y	0
Hartford Schroders International Stock Fund Class R5	HSWTX	NAS CM	Open End	Global Equity Large Cap (Foreign Stock)	C+	C	B	Up	Y	0
Hartford Schroders International Stock Fund Class SDR	SCIJX	NAS CM	Open End	Global Equity Large Cap (Foreign Stock)	C+	C	B	Up	Y	5,000,000
Hartford Schroders International Stock Fund Class Y	HSWYX	NAS CM	Open End	Global Equity Large Cap (Foreign Stock)	C+	C	B	Up	Y	250,000

★ Expanded analysis of this fund is included in Section II.

	TOTAL RETURNS					PERFORMANCE				ASSETS		ASSET ALLOCATION & TURNOVER					BULL & BEAR		FEES		
Min Additional Investment	3-Month Total Return	6-Month Total Return	1-Year Total Return	3-Year Total Return	5-Year Total Return	Dividend Yield (TTM)	Expense Ratio	3-Yr Std Deviation	3-Year Beta	NAV	Total Assets (MIL)	%Cash	%Stocks	%Bonds	%Other	Turnover Ratio	Last Bull Market Total Return	Last Bear Market Total Return	Front End Fee (%)	Back End Fee (%)	Inception Date
	2.37	11.80	5.73	26.79	34.69	2.63	0.65	7.36		23.11	982.4	3	35	59	0	65	18.17	-11.99			Feb-17
50	2.35	11.76	5.66	26.44	34.16	2.57	0.72	7.34		23.12	982.4	3	35	59	0	65	18.17	-11.99			Mar-15
	2.22	11.46	4.98	24.28	30.27	1.99	1.37	7.36		23.39	982.4	3	35	59	0	65	17.76	-12.28			Dec-06
	2.28	11.60	5.31	25.31	32.20	2.17	1.07	7.34		23.46	982.4	3	35	59	0	65	17.82	-12.16			Dec-06
	2.36	11.71	5.57	26.43	34.13	2.49	0.77	7.36		23.47	982.4	3	35	59	0	65	18.14	-12.02			Dec-06
	2.38	11.80	5.69	26.72	34.62	2.59	0.65	7.38		23.48	982.4	3	35	59	0	65	18.17	-11.99			Mar-18
	2.36	11.78	5.63	26.64	34.54	2.54	0.71	7.36		23.48	982.4	3	35	59	0	65	18.17	-11.99			Jul-96
50	2.75	10.48	5.59	22.43	16.47	6.86	1.08	4.8		9.18	85.6	11	25	54	0	61			4.50		Apr-14
50	2.55	10.06	4.88	19.89	12.37	6.09	1.83	4.77		9.19	85.6	11	25	54	0	61				1.00	Apr-14
	2.84	10.67	5.88	23.26	17.95	7.83	0.62	4.79		9.11	85.6	11	25	54	0	61					Feb-17
50	2.79	10.45	5.74	22.87	17.49	7.01	0.78	4.77		9.17	85.6	11	25	54	0	61					Apr-14
	2.83	10.52	5.61	22.14	15.51	6.88	1.34	4.81		9.19	85.6	11	25	54	0	61					Apr-14
	2.80	10.42	5.66	22.44	16.45	6.93	1.04	4.75		9.18	85.6	11	25	54	0	61					Apr-14
	2.80	10.46	5.74	22.80	17.24	7.01	0.74	4.8		9.17	85.6	11	25	54	0	61					Apr-14
	2.82	10.60	5.82	23.14	17.84		0.62	4.76		9.17	85.6	11	25	54	0	61					Feb-19
	2.81	10.63	5.85	23.19	17.88	7.11	0.68	4.76		9.17	85.6	11	25	54	0	61					Apr-14
50	3.68	18.31	7.84	36.11	31.46	1.3	0.96	12.71	1.03	20.28	207.8	2	97	0	0	85	24.5	-22.13	5.50		Feb-02
50	3.51	17.91	7.06	33.09	26.67	0	1.71	12.7	1.03	17.38	207.8	2	97	0	0	85	24.02	-22.39	2.50	1.00	Feb-02
	3.79	18.57	8.34	37.41	32.71	1.74	0.46	12.7	1.03	19.98	207.8	2	97	0	0	85	24.5	-22.13			Feb-17
50	3.78	18.54	8.26	37.43	33.66	1.64	0.64	12.7	1.03	20.01	207.8	2	97	0	0	85	24.72	-22.01			Aug-06
	3.66	18.22	7.61	34.94	29.58	0.99	1.18	12.7	1.03	20.63	207.8	2	97	0	0	85	24.4	-22.21			Dec-06
	3.68	18.36	7.94	36.16	31.63	1.25	0.88	12.7	1.03	20.82	207.8	2	97	0	0	85	24.62	-22.09			Dec-06
	3.80	18.52	8.26	37.43	33.56	1.5	0.63	12.72	1.03	20.99	207.8	2	97	0	0	85	24.86	-22.04			Dec-06
	3.79	18.60	8.38	36.91	32.22	1.65	0.46	12.72	1.03	21.04	207.8	2	97	0	0	85	24.5	-22.13			Mar-18
	3.80	18.61	8.31	37.73	34.12	1.59	0.57	12.71	1.03	21.03	207.8	2	97	0	0	85	24.87	-22			Feb-02
50	2.08	13.13	1.32	41.37	17.87	0.88	1.47	14.31	1.01	15.68	3,694	2	98	0	0	24	21.91	-27.29	5.50		Mar-06
50	1.84	12.78	0.59	38.50	13.72	0.47	2.21	14.31	1.02	15.44	3,694	2	98	0	0	24	21.19	-27.5		1.00	Oct-16
	2.15	13.39	1.73	42.85	19.65	1.24	1.1	14.31	1.02	15.66	3,694	2	98	0	0	24	21.89	-27.19			Feb-17
50	2.15	13.31	1.55	42.41	19.28	1.08	1.25	14.33	1.02	15.66	3,694	2	98	0	0	24	21.89	-27.19			Mar-06
	2.03	13.06	1.07	40.93	16.87	0.78	1.82	14.34	1.02	15.58	3,694	2	98	0	0	24	21.54	-27.35			Oct-16
	2.10	12.99	1.14	41.28	17.75	1.13	1.5	14.29	1.01	15.56	3,694	2	98	0	0	24	21.72	-27.27			Oct-16
	2.15	13.31	1.55	42.68	19.51	1.14	1.21	14.28	1.01	15.66	3,694	2	98	0	0	24	21.89	-27.19			Oct-16
	2.14	13.36	1.73	43.03	20.09	1.24	1.1	14.32	1.02	15.69	3,694	2	98	0	0	24	21.89	-27.19			Dec-14
	2.15	13.37	1.64	43.13	19.89	1.22	1.15	14.32	1.02	15.68	3,694	2	98	0	0	24	21.89	-27.19			Oct-16
50	1.28	11.30	-1.94	22.88	6.49	2.74	1.12	11.86	1.02	8.98	2,047	1	99	0	0	87	12.82	-22.26	5.50		Aug-06
50	1.09	10.93	-2.53	20.26	2.69	1.95	1.87	11.88	1.02	8.93	2,047	1	99	0	0	87	12.12	-22.49		1.00	Oct-16
	1.37	11.47	-1.51	24.22	8.20	3.05	0.77	11.91	1.02	8.98	2,047	1	99	0	0	87	12.77	-22.16			Feb-17
50	1.34	11.56	-1.62	23.98	7.99	2.95	0.86	11.93	1.03	8.98	2,047	1	99	0	0	87	12.77	-22.16			Aug-06
	1.28	11.35	-2.09	22.01	5.23	2.49	1.49	11.91	1.02	8.96	2,047	1	99	0	0	87	12.44	-22.32			Oct-16
	1.17	11.31	-1.98	22.86	6.49	2.7	1.19	11.91	1.02	8.96	2,047	1	99	0	0	87	12.6	-22.24			Oct-16
	1.34	11.56	-1.63	23.93	7.95	2.95	0.87	11.87	1.02	8.97	2,047	1	99	0	0	87	12.77	-22.16			Oct-16
	1.37	11.49	-1.51	24.36	8.56	3.06	0.77	11.85	1.02	8.97	2,047	1	99	0	0	87	12.77	-22.16			Dec-14
	1.36	11.46	-1.56	24.31	8.28	3.01	0.82	11.93	1.03	8.97	2,047	1	99	0	0	87	12.77	-22.16			Oct-16
50	3.01	14.89	2.23	34.37	17.65	1.13	1.15	12.52	1.06	12.65	375.1	2	98	0	0	65	17.29	-27.17	5.50		May-06
50	2.90	14.44	1.41	31.51	13.42	0.75	1.93	12.5	1.06	12.04	375.1	2	98	0	0	65	16.71	-27.34		1.00	Oct-16
	3.19	15.11	2.58	35.74	19.42	1.33	0.75	12.55	1.06	12.26	375.1	2	98	0	0	65	17.39	-27.04			Feb-17
50	3.11	15.03	2.50	35.43	19.15	1.32	0.85	12.5	1.06	12.24	375.1	2	98	0	0	65	17.39	-27.04			Dec-85
	3.03	14.83	2.24	34.47	17.13	1.18	1.45	12.54	1.06	12.23	375.1	2	98	0	0	65	17.05	-27.19			Oct-16
	3.03	14.93	2.36	34.92	18.11	1.22	1.15	12.52	1.06	12.24	375.1	2	98	0	0	65	17.22	-27.12			Oct-16
	3.11	15.02	2.45	35.51	19.22	1.29	0.85	12.47	1.06	12.25	375.1	2	98	0	0	65	17.39	-27.04			Oct-16
	3.11	15.02	2.56	35.83	19.69	1.38	0.75	12.52	1.06	12.25	375.1	2	98	0	0	65	17.39	-27.04			Dec-14
	3.11	15.00	2.51	35.76	19.44	1.34	0.85	12.52	1.06	12.26	375.1	2	98	0	0	65	17.39	-27.04			Oct-16

	MARKET			FUND TYPE, CATEGORY & OBJECTIVE	RATINGS				MINIMUMS	
Fund Name	Ticker Symbol	Traded On	Fund Type	Category and (Prospectus Objective)	Overall Rating	Reward Rating	Risk Rating	Recent Up/ Downgrade	Open to New Investors	Min Initial Investment
Hartford Schroders US MidCap Opportunities Fund Class A	SMDVX	NAS CM	Open End	US Equity Mid Cap (Growth)	C+	C	B	Up	Y	2,000
Hartford Schroders US MidCap Opportunities Fund Class C	HFDCX	NAS CM	Open End	US Equity Mid Cap (Growth)	C+	C	B	Up	Y	2,000
Hartford Schroders US MidCap Opportunities Fund Class F	HFDFX	NAS CM	Open End	US Equity Mid Cap (Growth)	C+	C	B	Up	Y	1,000,000
Hartford Schroders US MidCap Opportunities Fund Class I	SMDIX	NAS CM	Open End	US Equity Mid Cap (Growth)	C+	C	B	Up	Y	2,000
Hartford Schroders US MidCap Opportunities Fund Class R3	HFDRX	NAS CM	Open End	US Equity Mid Cap (Growth)	C+	C	B	Up	Y	0
Hartford Schroders US MidCap Opportunities Fund Class R4	HFDSX	NAS CM	Open End	US Equity Mid Cap (Growth)	C+	C	B	Up	Y	0
Hartford Schroders US MidCap Opportunities Fund Class R5	HFDTX	NAS CM	Open End	US Equity Mid Cap (Growth)	C+	C	B	Up	Y	0
Hartford Schroders US MidCap Opportunities Fund Class SDR	SMDRX	NAS CM	Open End	US Equity Mid Cap (Growth)	C+	C	B	Up	Y	5,000,000
Hartford Schroders US MidCap Opportunities Fund Class Y	HFDYX	NAS CM	Open End	US Equity Mid Cap (Growth)	C+	C	B	Up	Y	250,000
Hartford Schroders US Small Cap Opportunities Fund Class A	SCUVX	NAS CM	Open End	US Equity Small Cap (Growth)	C+	C	B-	Up	Y	2,000
Hartford Schroders US Small Cap Opportunities Fund Class C	HOOCX	NAS CM	Open End	US Equity Small Cap (Growth)	C+	C	B-	Up	Y	2,000
Hartford Schroders US Small Cap Opportunities Fund Class F	HOOFX	NAS CM	Open End	US Equity Small Cap (Growth)	C+	C	B	Up	Y	1,000,000
Hartford Schroders US Small Cap Opportunities Fund Class I	SCUIX	NAS CM	Open End	US Equity Small Cap (Growth)	C+	C	B	Up	Y	2,000
Hartford Schroders US Small Cap Opportunities Cls R3	HOORX	NAS CM	Open End	US Equity Small Cap (Growth)	C+	C	B-	Up	Y	0
Hartford Schroders US Small Cap Opportunities Cls R4	HOOSX	NAS CM	Open End	US Equity Small Cap (Growth)	C+	C	B	Up	Y	0
Hartford Schroders US Small Cap Opportunities Cls R5	HOOTX	NAS CM	Open End	US Equity Small Cap (Growth)	C+	C	B	Up	Y	0
Hartford Schroders US Small Cap Opportunities Cls SDR	SCURX	NAS CM	Open End	US Equity Small Cap (Growth)	C+	C	B	Up	Y	5,000,000
Hartford Schroders US Small Cap Opportunities Fund Class Y	HOOYX	NAS CM	Open End	US Equity Small Cap (Growth)	C+	C	B	Up	Y	250,000
Hartford Small Cap Growth Fund Class A	HSLAX	NAS CM	Open End	US Equity Small Cap (Small Company)	C	C	C+			2,000
Hartford Small Cap Growth Fund Class C	HSLCX	NAS CM	Open End	US Equity Small Cap (Small Company)	C	C	C+			2,000
Hartford Small Cap Growth Fund Class F	HSLFX	NAS CM	Open End	US Equity Small Cap (Small Company)	C	C	C+		Y	1,000,000
Hartford Small Cap Growth Fund Class I	HSLIX	NAS CM	Open End	US Equity Small Cap (Small Company)	C	C	C+			2,000
Hartford Small Cap Growth Fund Class R3	HSLRX	NAS CM	Open End	US Equity Small Cap (Small Company)	C	C	C+			0
Hartford Small Cap Growth Fund Class R4	HSLSX	NAS CM	Open End	US Equity Small Cap (Small Company)	C	C	C+			0
Hartford Small Cap Growth Fund Class R5	HSLTX	NAS CM	Open End	US Equity Small Cap (Small Company)	C	C	C+			0
Hartford Small Cap Growth Fund Class R6	HSLVX	NAS CM	Open End	US Equity Small Cap (Small Company)	C	C	C+			0
Hartford Small Cap Growth Fund Class Y	HSLYX	NAS CM	Open End	US Equity Small Cap (Small Company)	C	C	C+			250,000
Hartford Small Cap Growth HLS Fund Class IA	HISCX	NAS CM	Open End	US Equity Small Cap (Small Company)	C	C	C+			0
Hartford Small Cap Growth HLS Fund Class IB	HBSGX	NAS CM	Open End	US Equity Small Cap (Small Company)	C	C	C+			0
Hartford Small Cap Value Fund Class A	HSMAX	NAS CM	Open End	US Equity Small Cap (Small Company)	C	D+	C+		Y	2,000
Hartford Small Cap Value Fund Class C	HTSCX	NAS CM	Open End	US Equity Small Cap (Small Company)	C	D+	C+		Y	2,000
Hartford Small Cap Value Fund Class F	HSMFX	NAS CM	Open End	US Equity Small Cap (Small Company)	C	D+	C+		Y	1,000,000
Hartford Small Cap Value Fund Class I	HSEIX	NAS CM	Open End	US Equity Small Cap (Small Company)	C	D+	B-		Y	2,000
Hartford Small Cap Value Fund Class R3	HSMRX	NAS CM	Open End	US Equity Small Cap (Small Company)	C	D+	C+		Y	0
Hartford Small Cap Value Fund Class R4	HSMSX	NAS CM	Open End	US Equity Small Cap (Small Company)	C	D+	C+		Y	0
Hartford Small Cap Value Fund Class R5	HSMTX	NAS CM	Open End	US Equity Small Cap (Small Company)	C	D+	C+		Y	0
Hartford Small Cap Value Fund Class R6	HSMVX	NAS CM	Open End	US Equity Small Cap (Small Company)	C	D+	B-		Y	0
Hartford Small Cap Value Fund Class Y	HSMYX	NAS CM	Open End	US Equity Small Cap (Small Company)	C	D+	B-		Y	250,000
Hartford Small Company HLS Fund Class IA	HIASX	NAS CM	Open End	US Equity Small Cap (Small Company)	C+	C+	C+	Down		0
Hartford Small Company HLS Fund Class IB	HDMBX	NAS CM	Open End	US Equity Small Cap (Small Company)	C+	C+	C+	Down		0
Hartford Stock HLS Fund Class IA	HSTAX	NAS CM	Open End	US Equity Large Cap Blend (Growth)	B	B	B+		Y	0
Hartford Stock HLS Fund Class IB	HIBSX	NAS CM	Open End	US Equity Large Cap Blend (Growth)	B	B	B+		Y	0
Hartford Value HLS Fund Class IA	HIAVX	NAS CM	Open End	US Equity Large Cap Value (Growth)	C+	C	B	Up	Y	0
Hartford Value HLS Fund Class IB	HBVLX	NAS CM	Open End	US Equity Large Cap Value (Growth)	C+	C	B	Up	Y	0
Harvest Edge Absolute Fund Institutional Class	HEAIX	NAS CM	Open End	Long/Short Equity (Growth & Income)	D	D	D		Y	25,000
Harvest Edge Absolute Fund Investor Class	HEANX	NAS CM	Open End	Long/Short Equity (Growth & Income)	D	D	D		Y	2,500
Harvest Edge Bond Fund Institutional Class	HEBIX	NAS CM	Open End	Multialternative (Growth & Income)	D+	D+	C	Up	Y	25,000
Harvest Edge Bond Fund Investor Class	HEBNX	NAS CM	Open End	Multialternative (Growth & Income)	D+	D+	C	Up	Y	2,500
Harvest Edge Equity Fund Institutional Class	HEEIX	NAS CM	Open End	Long/Short Equity (Growth & Income)	D+	D	C-	Up	Y	25,000
Harvest Edge Equity Fund Investor Class	HEENX	NAS CM	Open End	Long/Short Equity (Growth & Income)	D+	D	C-	Up	Y	2,500
Haverford Quality Growth Stock Fund	HAVGX	NAS CM	Open End	US Equity Large Cap Blend (Growth)	C+	C	B	Down	Y	2,500
HC The ESG Growth Portfolio HC Advisors Shares	HCSGX	NAS CM	Open End	Alloc (Growth & Income)	U	U	U		Y	0

★ Expanded analysis of this fund is included in Section II.

Min Additional Investment	3-Month Total Return	6-Month Total Return	1-Year Total Return	3-Year Total Return	5-Year Total Return	Dividend Yield (TTM)	Expense Ratio	3-Yr Std Deviation	3-Year Beta	NAV	Total Assets (MIL)	%Cash	%Stocks	%Bonds	%Other	Turnover Ratio	Last Bull Market Total Return	Last Bear Market Total Return	Front End Fee (%)	Back End Fee (%)	Inception Date
	TOTAL RETURNS					PERFORMANCE				ASSETS		ASSET ALLOCATION & TURNOVER					BULL & BEAR		FEES		
50	4.14	18.90	5.13	34.65	50.99	0	1.32	13.06	0.96	14.59	939.2	5	95	0	0	37	23.92	-21.04	5.50		Mar-06
50	3.92	18.45	4.32	31.69	45.60	0	2.08	13.08	0.96	14.83	939.2	5	95	0	0	37	23.39	-21.32		1.00	Oct-16
	4.25	19.04	5.50	36.01	53.40	0.34	0.97	13.13	0.96	15.19	939.2	5	95	0	0	37	24.11	-20.99			Feb-17
50	4.25	19.04	5.40	35.78	53.14	0.26	1.05	13.11	0.96	15.19	939.2	5	95	0	0	37	24.11	-20.99			Mar-06
	4.09	18.75	4.84	33.43	49.00	0	1.69	13.1	0.96	15.01	939.2	5	95	0	0	37	23.75	-21.16			Oct-16
	4.13	18.80	5.05	34.49	50.93	0.14	1.39	13.1	0.96	15.1	939.2	5	95	0	0	37	23.93	-21.07			Oct-16
	4.12	18.90	5.30	35.58	52.92	0.29	1.09	13.12	0.96	15.16	939.2	5	95	0	0	37	24.11	-20.99			Oct-16
	4.24	19.09	5.49	36.05	53.70	0.34	0.97	13.07	0.96	15.22	939.2	5	95	0	0	37	24.11	-20.99			Dec-14
	4.18	19.05	5.48	35.89	53.26	0.33	1.04	13.09	0.96	15.18	939.2	5	95	0	0	37	24.11	-20.99			Oct-16
50	5.90	20.82	3.44	41.32	47.27	0.02	1.42	14.73	0.84	25.12	182.3	7	93	0	0	42	23.93	-23.02	5.50		May-06
50	5.67	20.37	2.67	38.17	41.87	0	2.17	14.72	0.84	25.7	182.3	7	93	0	0	42	23.38	-23.25		1.00	Oct-16
	6.02	21.11	3.88	42.91	49.69	0.3	1.02	14.73	0.84	26.39	182.3	7	93	0	0	42	24.09	-22.92			Feb-17
50	5.98	21.01	3.77	42.65	49.41	0.22	1.17	14.75	0.84	26.37	182.3	7	93	0	0	42	24.09	-22.92			Aug-93
	5.87	20.72	3.20	40.57	45.78	0	1.72	14.71	0.84	26.15	182.3	7	93	0	0	42	23.73	-23.09			Oct-16
	5.95	20.89	3.61	41.89	47.88	0.15	1.42	14.73	0.84	26.33	182.3	7	93	0	0	42	23.91	-23.01			Oct-16
	5.99	20.98	3.74	42.49	49.25	0.22	1.12	14.72	0.84	26.35	182.3	7	93	0	0	42	24.09	-22.92			Oct-16
	6.01	21.08	3.86	43.01	49.91	0.33	1.02	14.72	0.84	26.42	182.3	7	93	0	0	42	24.09	-22.92			Sep-15
	5.98	21.01	3.81	42.82	49.59	0.31	1.12	14.71	0.84	26.37	182.3	7	93	0	0	42	24.09	-22.92			Oct-16
50	2.24	25.17	-0.18	48.85	47.24	0	1.22	17.92	1.02	45.95	1,103	3	97	0	0	68	28.77	-24.07	5.50		Feb-02
50	2.09	24.72	-0.86	45.78	42.24	0	1.9	17.9	1.02	31.12	1,103	3	97	0	0	68	28.22	-24.31	2.50	1.00	Feb-02
	2.39	25.47	0.27	50.85	50.62	0	0.76	17.92	1.02	48.41	1,103	3	97	0	0	68	29.11	-23.89			Feb-17
50	2.35	25.40	0.18	50.25	49.50	0	0.84	17.93	1.02	48.23	1,103	3	97	0	0	68	28.99	-23.95			Aug-06
	2.18	25.02	-0.43	47.59	45.27	0	1.48	17.92	1.02	45.32	1,103	3	97	0	0	68	28.6	-24.11			Dec-06
	2.28	25.20	-0.12	49.01	47.62	0	1.17	17.93	1.02	47.93	1,103	3	97	0	0	68	28.85	-24.04			Dec-06
	2.33	25.39	0.15	50.33	49.85	0	0.87	17.92	1.02	50.76	1,103	3	97	0	0	68	29.04	-23.92			Dec-06
	2.38	25.45	0.27	50.80	50.42	0	0.77	17.92	1.02	51.55	1,103	3	97	0	0	68	29.11	-23.89			Nov-14
	2.38	25.43	0.22	50.70	50.47	0	0.8	17.92	1.02	51.58	1,103	3	97	0	0	68	29.11	-23.89			Feb-02
	2.41	25.22	0.49	51.11	51.99	0	0.65	17.85	1.01	33.11	1,313	3	97	0	0	86	29.3	-23.51			May-94
	2.36	25.07	0.26	50.02	50.12	0	0.9	17.85	1.01	32.07	1,313	3	97	0	0	86	29.11	-23.59			May-02
50	0.00	13.29	-5.55	32.29	23.92	0.22	1.3	17.5	0.98	10.14	107.2	5	95	0	0	68	24.57	-22.38	5.50		Dec-04
50	-0.11	12.94	-6.25	29.39	19.46	0	2.05	17.49	0.98	8.81	107.2	5	95	0	0	68	24.17	-22.69	2.50	1.00	Dec-04
	0.19	13.64	-5.08	34.19	26.81	0.58	0.8	17.5	0.98	10.16	107.2	5	95	0	0	68	24.97	-22.23			Feb-17
50	0.09	13.51	-5.19	33.60	26.13	0.49	0.98	17.51	0.98	10.16	107.2	5	95	0	0	68	24.97	-22.23			Mar-15
	0.00	13.34	-5.61	31.59	22.82	0.13	1.5	17.46	0.97	10.53	107.2	5	95	0	0	68	24.53	-22.37			Sep-11
	0.09	13.37	-5.42	32.65	24.54	0.17	1.2	17.47	0.97	10.68	107.2	5	95	0	0	68	24.76	-22.29			Sep-11
	0.09	13.55	-5.20	33.87	26.35	0.5	0.9	17.48	0.98	10.64	107.2	5	95	0	0	68	24.95	-22.23			Sep-11
	0.18	13.67	-5.05	34.17	26.79	0.55	0.8	17.46	0.97	10.64	107.2	5	95	0	0	68	24.97	-22.23			Mar-18
	0.09	13.56	-5.16	34.10	26.73	0.58	0.85	17.48	0.98	10.63	107.2	5	95	0	0	68	24.97	-22.23			Dec-04
	4.48	29.42	8.66	70.86	49.32	0	0.78	18.31	1.02	23.53	636.2	4	95	0	0	86	27.07	-24.54			Aug-96
	4.43	29.29	8.38	69.62	47.48	0	1.03	18.33	1.02	21.67	636.2	4	95	0	0	86	26.88	-24.62			Apr-98
	5.95	21.69	18.43	49.25	70.73	1.41	0.51	10.79	0.82	94.42	1,496	1	99	0	0	22	26.88	-19.42			Aug-77
	5.89	21.54	18.14	48.14	68.61	1.17	0.76	10.79	0.82	94.31	1,496	1	99	0	0	22	26.69	-19.51			Apr-98
	3.89	17.37	5.93	33.87	39.50	1.5	0.71	12.57	1.03	14.93	439.0	1	99	0	0	28	27.44	-20.51			Apr-01
	3.83	17.32	5.69	32.90	37.76	1.26	0.96	12.6	1.03	14.9	439.0	1	99	0	0	28	27.25	-20.6			Apr-01
	-0.29	3.59	-14.99			0.94	1.24			8.55	5.8	107	-7	0	0						Dec-17
100	-0.46	3.33	-15.21			0.31	1.55			8.57	5.8	107	-7	0	0						Dec-17
	2.43	6.33	2.05			2.1	0.79			9.7	1.1	7	-2	94	0						Dec-17
100	2.42	6.13	1.89			1.41	1.03			9.35	1.1	7	-2	94	0						Dec-17
	3.47	20.02	-1.60			0.75	1.11			9.83	1.2	4	96	0	0						Dec-17
100	3.37	19.82	-1.83			0.81	1.36			9.79	1.2	4	96	0	0						Dec-17
	5.19	18.86	9.94	38.54	44.38	1.2	0.82	12.58	1.01	17.49	209.4	1	99	0	0	21	22.09	-17.11			Jun-04
	-4.97						0.56				117.7										Jul-15

	MARKET		FUND TYPE, CATEGORY & OBJECTIVE		RATINGS				MINIMUMS	
Fund Name	Ticker Symbol	Traded On	Fund Type	Category and (Prospectus Objective)	Overall Rating	Reward Rating	Risk Rating	Recent Up/ Downgrade	Open to New Investors	Min Initial Investment
HC The ESG Growth Portfolio HC Strategic Shares	HCESX	NAS CM	Open End	Alloc (Growth & Income)	U	U	U		Y	0
HCM Dividend Sector Plus Fund Class A	HCMNX	NAS CM	Open End	US Equity Large Cap Value (Equity-Income)	C	C-	C+		Y	2,500
HCM Dividend Sector Plus Fund Class A1	HCMWX	NAS CM	Open End	US Equity Large Cap Value (Equity-Income)	C	C-	C+		Y	2,500
HCM Dividend Sector Plus Fund Class I	HCMQX	NAS CM	Open End	US Equity Large Cap Value (Equity-Income)	C	C-	C+		Y	500,000
HCM Dividend Sector Plus Fund Class R	HCMZX	NAS CM	Open End	US Equity Large Cap Value (Equity-Income)	C	C-	C+		Y	0
HCM Dividend Sector Plus Fund Investor Class	HCMPX	NAS CM	Open End	US Equity Large Cap Value (Equity-Income)	C	C-	C+		Y	2,500
HCM Income Plus Fund Class A Shares	HCMEX	NAS CM	Open End	Cautious Alloc (Income)	C	C-	B-	Up	Y	2,500
HCM Income Plus Fund Investor Class Shares	HCMKX	NAS CM	Open End	Cautious Alloc (Income)	C	C-	C+	Up	Y	2,500
HCM Tactical Growth Fund Class A	HCMGX	NAS CM	Open End	US Equity Large Cap Blend (Growth)	C	C-	C		Y	2,500
HCM Tactical Growth Fund Class I	HCMIX	NAS CM	Open End	US Equity Large Cap Blend (Growth)	C	C-	C		Y	100,000
HCM Tactical Growth Fund Class R	HCMSX	NAS CM	Open End	US Equity Large Cap Blend (Growth)	C	C-	C		Y	2,500
HCM Tactical Growth Fund Investor Class	HCMDX	NAS CM	Open End	US Equity Large Cap Blend (Growth)	C	C-	C		Y	2,500
Heartland Mid Cap Value Fund Institutional Class	HNMDX	NAS CM	Open End	US Equity Mid Cap (Growth & Income)	B-	C	B	Up	Y	500,000
Heartland Mid Cap Value Fund Investor Class	HRMDX	NAS CM	Open End	US Equity Mid Cap (Growth & Income)	B-	C	B	Up	Y	1,000
Heartland Select Value Fund Institutional Class	HNSVX	NAS CM	Open End	US Equity Large Cap Value (Growth)	B-	C	B+		Y	500,000
Heartland Select Value Fund Investor Class	HRSVX	NAS CM	Open End	US Equity Large Cap Value (Growth)	B-	C	B+		Y	1,000
Heartland Value Fund Institutional Class	HNTVX	NAS CM	Open End	US Equity Small Cap (Small Company)	C	C-	B-		Y	500,000
Heartland Value Fund Investor Class	HRTVX	NAS CM	Open End	US Equity Small Cap (Small Company)	C	C-	B-		Y	1,000
Heartland Value Plus Fund Institutional Class	HNVIX	NAS CM	Open End	US Equity Small Cap (Equity-Income)	C	C	C+			500,000
Heartland Value Plus Fund Investor Class	HRVIX	NAS CM	Open End	US Equity Small Cap (Equity-Income)	C	C	C+			1,000
Hedeker Strategic Appreciation Fund Institutional Shares	SAFFX	NAS CM	Open End	Convertibles (Convertible Bond)	C	C-	B-		Y	1,000
Heitman US Real Estate Securities Fund Institutional Class	HTMIX	NAS CM	Open End	Real Estate Sector Equity (Real Estate)	D+	C	B	Up	Y	25,000
Heitman US Real Estate Securities Fund Investor Class	HTMNX	NAS CM	Open End	Real Estate Sector Equity (Real Estate)	D+	C	B	Up	Y	2,500
Hennessy Balanced Fund Investor Class	HBFBX	NAS CM	Open End	Moderate Alloc (Balanced)	B	C	A		Y	2,500
Hennessy BP Energy Fund Institutional Class	HNRIX	NAS CM	Open End	Energy Sector Equity (Natl Res)	D	D	D	Down	Y	250,000
Hennessy BP Energy Fund Investor Class	HNRGX	NAS CM	Open End	Energy Sector Equity (Natl Res)	D	D	D	Down	Y	2,500
Hennessy BP Midstream Fund Institutional Class	HMSIX	NAS CM	Open End	Energy Sector Equity (Natl Res)	D+	D+	D+	Down	Y	250,000
Hennessy BP Midstream Fund Investor Class	HMSFX	NAS CM	Open End	Energy Sector Equity (Natl Res)	D+	D+	D+	Down	Y	2,500
Hennessy Cornerstone Growth Fund Class Institutional	HICGX	NAS CM	Open End	US Equity Mid Cap (Growth)	C-	C-	C-	Down	Y	250,000
Hennessy Cornerstone Growth Fund Investor Class	HFCGX	NAS CM	Open End	US Equity Mid Cap (Growth)	C-	C-	C-	Down	Y	2,500
Hennessy Cornerstone Large Growth Fund Institutional Class	HILGX	NAS CM	Open End	US Equity Large Cap Value (Growth)	B-	C	B	Up	Y	250,000
Hennessy Cornerstone Large Growth Fund Investor Class	HFLGX	NAS CM	Open End	US Equity Large Cap Value (Growth)	B-	C	B	Up	Y	2,500
Hennessy Cornerstone Mid Cap 30 Fund Institutional Class	HIMDX	NAS CM	Open End	US Equity Mid Cap (Growth)	D+	D+	C-	Down	Y	250,000
Hennessy Cornerstone Mid Cap 30 Fund Investor Class	HFMDX	NAS CM	Open End	US Equity Mid Cap (Growth)	D+	D	C-	Down	Y	2,500
Hennessy Cornerstone Value Fund Class Institutional	HICVX	NAS CM	Open End	US Equity Large Cap Value (Equity-Income)	C+	C	B		Y	250,000
Hennessy Cornerstone Value Fund Investor Class	HFCVX	NAS CM	Open End	US Equity Large Cap Value (Equity-Income)	C+	C	B		Y	2,500
Hennessy Equity and Income Fund Institutional Class	HEIIX	NAS CM	Open End	Moderate Alloc (Balanced)	B	C	A-	Up	Y	250,000
Hennessy Equity and Income Fund Investor Class	HEIFX	NAS CM	Open End	Moderate Alloc (Balanced)	B-	C	A-		Y	2,500
Hennessy Focus Fund Institutional Class	HFCIX	NAS CM	Open End	US Equity Mid Cap (Growth)	B-	C+	B	Up	Y	250,000
Hennessy Focus Fund Investor Class	HFCSX	NAS CM	Open End	US Equity Mid Cap (Growth)	B-	C+	B	Up	Y	2,500
Hennessy Gas Utility Fund Institutional Class	HGASX	NAS CM	Open End	Utilities Sector Equity (Utility)	C+	B-	C+	Down	Y	250,000
Hennessy Gas Utility Fund Investor Class	GASFX	NAS CM	Open End	Utilities Sector Equity (Utility)	C+	B-	C+	Down	Y	2,500
Hennessy Japan Fund Institutional Class	HJPIX	NAS CM	Open End	Japan Equity (Pacific Stock)	C+	C	B	Up	Y	250,000
Hennessy Japan Fund Investor Class	HJPNX	NAS CM	Open End	Japan Equity (Pacific Stock)	C+	C	B	Up	Y	2,500
Hennessy Japan Small Cap Fund Institutional Class	HJSIX	NAS CM	Open End	Japan Equity (Pacific Stock)	C	C	C		Y	250,000
Hennessy Japan Small Cap Fund Investor Class	HJPSX	NAS CM	Open End	Japan Equity (Pacific Stock)	C	C	C		Y	2,500
Hennessy Large Cap Financial Fund Institutional Class	HILFX	NAS CM	Open End	Financials Sector Equity (Financial)	C+	C	B-	Down	Y	250,000
Hennessy Large Cap Financial Fund Investor Class	HLFNX	NAS CM	Open End	Financials Sector Equity (Financial)	C+	C	B-	Down	Y	2,500
Hennessy Small Cap Financial Fund Institutional Class	HISFX	NAS CM	Open End	Financials Sector Equity (Financial)	C-	C-	C	Down	Y	250,000
Hennessy Small Cap Financial Fund Investor Class	HSFNX	NAS CM	Open End	Financials Sector Equity (Financial)	C-	D+	C	Down	Y	2,500
Hennessy Technology Fund Institutional Class	HTCIX	NAS CM	Open End	Technology Sector Equity (Technology)	C+	C	B-	Down	Y	250,000
Hennessy Technology Fund Investor Class	HTECX	NAS CM	Open End	Technology Sector Equity (Technology)	C+	C	B-	Down	Y	2,500

★ Expanded analysis of this fund is included in Section II.

	TOTAL RETURNS					PERFORMANCE				ASSETS		ASSET ALLOCATION & TURNOVER					BULL & BEAR		FEES		
Min Additional Investment	3-Month Total Return	6-Month Total Return	1-Year Total Return	3-Year Total Return	5-Year Total Return	Dividend Yield (TTM)	Expense Ratio	3-Yr Std Deviation	3-Year Beta	NAV	Total Assets (MIL)	%Cash	%Stocks	%Bonds	%Other	Turnover Ratio	Last Bull Market Total Return	Last Bear Market Total Return	Front End Fee (%)	Back End Fee (%)	Inception Date
	-4.97						0.31				117.7										Jul-15
500	-0.09	10.29	-4.79	36.77		1.98	2.55	16.83	1.26	10.93	430.2	-30	130	0	0	127			5.75		Mar-15
500	-0.09	10.19	-4.94	36.28		1.1	2.7	16.86	1.26	11.02	430.2	-30	130	0	0	127			5.75		Mar-15
500	-0.09	10.29	-4.79	36.77		1.98	2.3	16.83	1.26	10.93	430.2	-30	130	0	0	127					Mar-15
	-0.09	10.29	-4.79	36.77		1.98	1.86	16.83	1.26	10.93	430.2	-30	130	0	0	127					Mar-15
500	-0.18	9.90	-5.48	33.87		1.37	3.3	16.86	1.26	10.76	430.2	-30	130	0	0	127					Mar-15
500	1.99	7.66	-0.25			1.3	1.84			10.25	188.8	3	50	29	0	65			5.75		Nov-16
500	1.80	7.29	-0.95			0.76	2.59			10.15	188.8	3	50	29	0	65					Nov-16
500	-3.83	7.20	-8.35	56.97		0	2.72	17.1	1.3	12.8	238.4	-47	135	0	12	18			5.75		Jul-14
500	-3.82	7.19	-8.35	56.91		0	2.47	17.09	1.3	12.81	238.4	-47	135	0	12	18					Jul-14
500	-3.82	7.19	-8.35	56.91		0	2.25	17.09	1.3	12.81	238.4	-47	135	0	12	18					Jul-14
500	-4.01	6.88	-9.04	53.59		0	3.47	17.09	1.3	12.42	238.4	-47	135	0	12	18					Jul-14
100	3.00	17.40	5.19	40.75		1.27	0.99	14.43	1.04	11.67	13.1	-1	98	3	0	49					Oct-14
100	3.00	17.20	4.95	39.68		1.07	1.25	14.48	1.04	11.65	13.1	-1	98	3	0	49					Oct-14
100	3.32	15.26	6.18	43.31	40.52	1.34	0.98	12.75	1	25.82	216.7	0	99	0	1	37	21.26	-21.85			May-08
100	3.22	15.11	5.93	42.28	38.77	1.1	1.2	12.73	1	25.9	216.7	0	99	0	1	37	20.99	-21.96			Oct-96
100	0.25	15.26	-4.50	30.80	7.62	0.32	0.9	14.37	0.79	39.18	669.3	3	92	5	0	37	20.29	-24.05			May-08
100	0.20	15.13	-4.68	30.12	6.71	0.15	1.07	14.38	0.79	38.34	669.3	3	92	5	0	37	20.16	-24.11			Dec-84
100	3.70	18.81	-4.28	45.93	10.66	1.22	0.95	18.78	1.05	33.59	341.6	0	98	0	2	71	24.91	-25.02			May-08
100	3.65	18.71	-4.49	44.98	9.53	0.96	1.18	18.77	1.05	33.74	341.6	0	98	0	2	71	24.7	-25.1			Oct-93
100	0.47	9.96	0.00			2.98	1.46			24.73	64.8	5	2	0	0	163					Dec-16
0	1.97	18.53	11.41			1.53	0.77			10.87	24.1					148					Dec-17
0	1.97	18.43	11.25			1.31	1.17			10.86	24.1					148					Dec-17
	0.94	7.32	7.34	20.88	27.08	1	1.85	5.38	0.39	12.4	12.4	7	49	44	0	21	8.97	-3.66			Mar-96
	-4.32	13.53	-24.39	-5.65	-29.59	0	1.57	24.54	1.53	16.36	63.6	3	97	0	0	72					Dec-13
	-4.43	13.31	-24.65	-6.47	-30.53	0	1.82	24.56	1.54	16.17	63.6	3	97	0	0	72			5.75		Dec-13
	-3.08	18.24	-1.58	-5.24	-26.48	8.37	1.52	17.17	1.02	12.3	48.2	0	100	0	0	64					Dec-13
	-3.12	18.12	-1.76	-5.83	-27.38	8.51	1.78	17.2	1.02	12.11	48.2	0	100	0	0	64			5.75		Dec-13
	3.85	13.87	-9.94	15.43	21.22	0	0.96	16.49	0.88	20.19	151.1	3	97	0	0	133	42.73	-32.63			Mar-08
	3.77	13.68	-10.27	14.27	19.42	0	1.3	16.52	0.88	19.52	151.1	3	97	0	0	133	42.4	-32.73			Nov-96
	1.60	13.78	3.88	43.65	38.93	0.95	0.96	14.78	1.1	10.15	134.4	1	99	0	0	70	21.92	-16.46			Mar-09
	1.51	13.55	3.50	42.44	37.34	0.71	1.24	14.84	1.11	10.05	134.4	1	99	0	0	70	21.68	-16.54			Mar-09
	-0.47	12.42	-11.97	13.34	13.29	0	0.95	15.89	1.12	12.67	435.2	2	98	0	0	181	25.36	-20.23			Mar-08
	-0.56	12.20	-12.34	12.04	11.45	0	1.31	15.9	1.12	12.23	435.2	2	98	0	0	181	25.06	-20.33			Sep-03
	0.59	11.42	0.75	34.25	34.58	2.34	0.99	12.1	0.93	16.97	260.7	2	98	0	0	41	17.42	-11.16			Mar-08
	0.59	11.28	0.60	33.40	33.33	2.14	1.22	12.1	0.93	16.96	260.7	2	98	0	0	41	17.14	-11.23			Nov-96
	2.02	10.77	6.92	25.46	31.25	1.51	1.09	7.34	0.58	14.46	183.1	1	58	38	0	18	15.14	-5.08			Jun-97
	2.01	10.57	6.53	24.04	28.83	0.98	1.49	7.31	0.58	15.36	183.1	1	58	38	0	18	15.02	-5.2			Sep-01
	8.30	24.06	10.14	41.90	59.98	0	1.1	11.81	0.88	82.85	1,794	2	98	0	0	13	31.28	-15.39			May-08
	8.21	23.85	9.75	40.31	57.10	0	1.48	11.81	0.88	80.38	1,794	2	98	0	0	13	31.07	-15.47			Jan-97
	2.76	17.88	13.28	21.90	27.12	2.49	0.65	9.7		29.32	907.9	0	100	0	0	14	17.82	-3.79			Mar-17
	2.69	17.70	12.88	20.97	26.15	2.13	1.01	9.7		29.4	907.9	0	100	0	0	14	17.82	-3.79			May-89
	1.94	9.49	0.28	39.51	75.01	0.29	1.02	12.05	0.93	36.66	661.5	8	92	0	0	1	4.24	-2.6			Oct-03
	1.86	9.28	-0.13	37.84	72.04	0.03	1.44	12.05	0.93	35.56	661.5	8	92	0	0	1	4.08	-2.69			Oct-03
	3.71	9.42	-5.69	50.81	71.00	0.3	1.05	12.31	0.97	14.52	140.5	3	97	0	0	35	7.59	-0.37			Jun-15
	3.60	9.07	-6.19	49.10	68.58	0	1.47	12.29	0.96	14.67	140.5	3	97	0	0	35	7.59	-0.37			Aug-07
	9.49	23.19	6.64	72.39	49.34	0	1.35	16.89	1.14	22.84	34.2	1	99	0	0	64	31.81	-25.05			Jun-15
	9.39	22.95	6.19	70.48	46.97	0	1.7	16.88	1.14	22.82	34.2	1	99	0	0	64	31.81	-25.05			Jan-97
	5.91	12.66	-9.13	32.96	43.39	1.33	1.16	18.97	0.97	12.72	123.9	2	98	0	0	28	25.46	-27.54			May-08
	5.86	12.52	-9.47	31.43	40.72	0.31	1.55	18.98	0.97	21.29	123.9	2	98	0	0	28	25.43	-27.65			Jan-97
	1.94	24.59	12.05	56.49	53.49	0	0.99	17.62	1.11	18.39	4.9	3	97	0	0	225	25.23	-23.1			Mar-10
	1.87	24.34	11.74	55.19	51.15	0	1.24	17.6	1.11	17.93	4.9	3	97	0	0	225	24.89	-23.16			Feb-02

	MARKET			FUND TYPE, CATEGORY & OBJECTIVE	RATINGS					MINIMUMS
Fund Name	Ticker Symbol	Traded On	Fund Type	Category and (Prospectus Objective)	Overall Rating	Reward Rating	Risk Rating	Recent Up/ Downgrade	Open to New Investors	Min Initial Investment
Hennessy Total Return Fund Investor Class	HDOGX	NAS CM	Open End	Aggressive Alloc (Balanced)	B	C	A		Y	2,500
Herzfeld Caribbean Basin Fund	CUBA	NAS CM	Closed End	US Equity Mid Cap (World Stock)	C-	D+	C-	Down	Y	
High Income Securities Fund	PCF	NYSE	Closed End	Convertibles (Convertible Bond)	C	C+	C-		Y	
Highland Energy MLP Fund Class A	HEFAX	NAS CM	Open End	Energy Sector Equity (Natl Res)	D	D	D+	Down	Y	1,000
Highland Energy MLP Fund Class C	HEFCX	NAS CM	Open End	Energy Sector Equity (Natl Res)	D	D	D+	Down	Y	1,000
Highland Energy MLP Fund Class Y	HEFYX	NAS CM	Open End	Energy Sector Equity (Natl Res)	D	D	D+	Down	Y	0
Highland Global Allocation Fund	HGLB	NYSE	Closed End	Moderate Alloc (Growth & Income)	C-	C-	C-	Down	Y	
Highland Long/Short Equity Fund Class A	HEOAX	NAS CM	Open End	Long/Short Equity (Equity-Income)	C	D+	B		Y	2,500
Highland Long/Short Equity Fund Class C	HEOCX	NAS CM	Open End	Long/Short Equity (Equity-Income)	C	D+	B		Y	2,500
Highland Long/Short Equity Fund Class Z	HEOZX	NAS CM	Open End	Long/Short Equity (Equity-Income)	C	D+	B		Y	2,500
Highland Long/Short Healthcare Fund Class A	HHCAX	NAS CM	Open End	Long/Short Equity (Health)	C	C-	B-		Y	2,500
Highland Long/Short Healthcare Fund Class C	HHCCX	NAS CM	Open End	Long/Short Equity (Health)	C	C-	C+		Y	2,500
Highland Long/Short Healthcare Fund Class Z	HHCZX	NAS CM	Open End	Long/Short Equity (Health)	C	C-	B-		Y	2,500
Highland Merger Arbitrage Fund Class A	HMEAX	NAS CM	Open End	Market Neutral (Growth & Income)	B-	C+	B		Y	2,500
Highland Merger Arbitrage Fund Class C	HMECX	NAS CM	Open End	Market Neutral (Growth & Income)	B-	C	B	Down	Y	2,500
Highland Merger Arbitrage Fund Class Z	HMEZX	NAS CM	Open End	Market Neutral (Growth & Income)	B-	C+	B		Y	2,500
Highland Premier Growth Equity Fund Class A	HPEAX	NAS CM	Open End	US Equity Large Cap Growth (Growth)	C	C	C+		Y	1,000
Highland Premier Growth Equity Fund Class C	HPECX	NAS CM	Open End	US Equity Large Cap Growth (Growth)	C	C	C		Y	1,000
Highland Premier Growth Equity Fund Class Y	HPEYX	NAS CM	Open End	US Equity Large Cap Growth (Growth)	C	C	C+		Y	0
Highland Resolute Fund Class I	RMRGX	NAS CM	Open End	Multialternative (Growth)	C	C-	B		Y	1,000,000
Highland Small-Cap Equity Fund Class A	HSZAX	NAS CM	Open End	US Equity Small Cap (Small Company)	C	C	C+	Down	Y	1,000
Highland Small-Cap Equity Fund Class C	HSZCX	NAS CM	Open End	US Equity Small Cap (Small Company)	C	C	C+	Down	Y	1,000
Highland Small-Cap Equity Fund Class Y	HSZYX	NAS CM	Open End	US Equity Small Cap (Small Company)	C	C	C+	Down	Y	0
Highland Total Return Fund Class A	HTAAX	NAS CM	Open End	Moderate Alloc (Asset Alloc)	C+	C	B	Up	Y	1,000
Highland Total Return Fund Class C	HTACX	NAS CM	Open End	Moderate Alloc (Asset Alloc)	C+	C	B	Up	Y	1,000
Highland Total Return Fund Class Y	HTAYX	NAS CM	Open End	Moderate Alloc (Asset Alloc)	C+	C	B	Up	Y	0
Hillman Fund No Load Shares	HCMAX	NAS CM	Open End	US Equity Large Cap Value (Aggr Growth)	B	B-	B+	Up	Y	5,000
Hilton Tactical Income Fund Institutional Class	HCYIX	NAS CM	Open End	Moderate Alloc (Growth & Income)	B	B-	A		Y	50,000
Hilton Tactical Income Fund Investor Class	HCYAX	NAS CM	Open End	Moderate Alloc (Growth & Income)	B	C+	A		Y	2,500
Hodges Blue Chip Equity Income Fund Retail Class	HDPBX	NAS CM	Open End	US Equity Large Cap Blend (Growth & Income)	C+	C	B	Down	Y	1,000
Hodges Fund Institutional Class	HDPIX	NAS CM	Open End	US Equity Mid Cap (Growth)	D+	D	C-	Down	Y	1,000,000
Hodges Fund Retail Class	HDPMX	NAS CM	Open End	US Equity Mid Cap (Growth)	D+	D	C-	Down	Y	1,000
Hodges Small Cap Fund Institutional Class	HDSIX	NAS CM	Open End	US Equity Small Cap (Small Company)	C	C-	C		Y	1,000,000
Hodges Small Cap Fund Retail Class	HDPSX	NAS CM	Open End	US Equity Small Cap (Small Company)	C	C-	C		Y	1,000
Hodges Small Intrinsic Value Fund Retail Class	HDSVX	NAS CM	Open End	US Equity Small Cap (Growth)	D+	D+	D+	Down	Y	1,000
Hodges Small-Mid Cap Fund Retail Class	HDSMX	NAS CM	Open End	US Equity Mid Cap (Growth)	C	C-	C		Y	1,000
Holland Balanced Fund	HOLBX	NAS CM	Open End	Moderate Alloc (Balanced)	B-	C	B+		Y	1,000
Homestead Funds Value Fund	HOVLX	NAS CM	Open End	US Equity Large Cap Value (Growth & Income)	B-	C	B	Down	Y	500
Homestead Growth Fund	HNASX	NAS CM	Open End	US Equity Large Cap Growth (Growth)	B-	C+	B	Down	Y	500
Homestead International Equity Fund	HISIX	NAS CM	Open End	Global Equity Large Cap (Foreign Stock)	C	C	B-		Y	500
Homestead Small Company Stock Fund	HSCSX	NAS CM	Open End	US Equity Small Cap (Small Company)	C-	D+	C	Down	Y	500
Homestead Stock Index Fund	HSTIX	NAS CM	Open End	US Equity Large Cap Blend (Growth)	B-	C	B		Y	500
Hood River Small-Cap Growth Fund Class Institutional	HRSMX	NAS CM	Open End	US Equity Small Cap (Growth)	C+	C	C+		Y	25,000
Hood River Small-Cap Growth Fund Investor Shares	HRSRX	NAS CM	Open End	US Equity Small Cap (Growth)	C+	C	C+		Y	1,000
Hood River Small-Cap Growth Fund Retirement Shares	HRSIX	NAS CM	Open End	US Equity Small Cap (Growth)	C+	C	C+		Y	0
Horizon Active Asset Allocation Fund Class A	HASAX	NAS CM	Open End	Moderate Alloc (Asset Alloc)	C+	C	B-	Up	Y	2,500
Horizon Active Asset Allocation Fund Class I	HASIX	NAS CM	Open End	Moderate Alloc (Asset Alloc)	C+	C	B	Up	Y	10,000,000
Horizon Active Asset Allocation Fund Investor Class	AAANX	NAS CM	Open End	Moderate Alloc (Asset Alloc)	C+	C	B	Up	Y	2,500
Horizon Active Dividend Fund Advisor Class	HADUX	NAS CM	Open End	US Equity Large Cap Value (Equity-Income)	C	C	B-		Y	2,500
Horizon Active Dividend Fund Investor Class	HNDDX	NAS CM	Open End	US Equity Large Cap Value (Equity-Income)	C	C	B-		Y	2,500
Horizon Active Risk Assist® Fund Class A	ARAAX	NAS CM	Open End	Aggressive Alloc (Asset Alloc)	C	C	C		Y	2,500
Horizon Active Risk Assist® Fund Class I	ACRIX	NAS CM	Open End	Aggressive Alloc (Asset Alloc)	C	C	C+		Y	10,000,000

★ Expanded analysis of this fund is included in Section II.

	TOTAL RETURNS					PERFORMANCE				ASSETS		ASSET ALLOCATION & TURNOVER					BULL & BEAR		FEES		
Min Additional Investment	3-Month Total Return	6-Month Total Return	1-Year Total Return	3-Year Total Return	5-Year Total Return	Dividend Yield (TTM)	Expense Ratio	3-Yr Std Deviation	3-Year Beta	NAV	Total Assets (MIL)	%Cash	%Stocks	%Bonds	%Other	Turnover Ratio	Last Bull Market Total Return	Last Bear Market Total Return	Front End Fee (%)	Back End Fee (%)	Inception Date
	1.12	9.87	10.34	27.25	40.68	1.69	1.96	7.28	0.51	13.97	76.4	52	48	0	0	10	14.88	-5.72			Jul-98
	1.77	15.63	-2.54	26.20	-1.67	0	3.35	14.64	1.04	7.59	46.6	0	100	0	0	19	21.9	-20.43			May-94
	0.84	2.46	3.87	27.14	22.20	0.08		3.44	0.24	9.55	53.1	1	5	40	0	49	11.23	-11.94			Jul-87
1,000	-1.95	32.26	-6.57	-7.64	-60.67	11.03	7.51	27.68	1.56	3.08	25.1	-24	124	0	0	15			5.75		Dec-11
1,000	-1.84	31.90	-7.29	-9.66	-62.05	10.23	8.26	27.65	1.56	3.07	25.1	-24	124	0	0	15				1.00	Dec-11
	-1.58	32.57	-6.08	-6.66	-60.32	11.34	7.26	27.66	1.56	3.07	25.1	-24	124	0	0	15					Dec-11
	-4.75	4.47	5.12	19.06	1.61	4.05	2.67	10.61		14.09	328.1	-24	77	39	2		24.53	-19.28			Jan-98
50	-1.96	10.45	-1.89	14.67	11.00	0	2.88	9.42	0.64	10.99	152.2	8	92	0	0	247	8.21	-6.78	5.50		Dec-06
50	-2.15	10.03	-2.52	12.34	7.44	0	3.53	9.4	0.64	9.98	152.2	8	92	0	0	247	8.05	-7.12		1.00	Dec-06
50	-1.95	10.32	-1.81	15.48	12.65	0	2.53	9.34	0.63	11.54	152.2	8	92	0	0	247	8.26	-6.52			Dec-06
50	-4.98	4.51	8.78	23.35	2.92	0	2.64	17.05	0.39	14.11	44.2	46	54	0	0	489	-1.15	0	5.50		May-08
50	-5.10	4.18	8.11	21.00	-0.12	0	3.3	17.07	0.39	13.19	44.2	46	54	0	0	489	-1.51	-0.23		1.00	May-08
50	-4.87	4.71	9.16	24.74	4.88	0	2.36	17.1	0.39	14.65	44.2	46	54	0	0	489	-1.05	0.23			May-08
50	1.14	2.66	5.77	18.81		13.74	3.97			18.5	29.3	54	46	0	0				5.50		Aug-16
50	0.98	2.33	5.05	16.51		13.27	4.72			18.37	29.3	54	46	0	0					1.00	Aug-16
50	1.19	2.81	6.06	20.00		14.22	3.8			18.65	29.3	54	46	0	0						Aug-16
1,000	1.82	10.24	-4.38	32.66	43.77	0	1.3	12.36	0.7	15.61	107.0	5	94	0	0	258	28.21	-17.17	5.75		Dec-96
1,000	1.56	9.81	-5.11	29.64	38.43	0	2.06	12.32	0.7	7.16	107.0	5	94	0	0	258	27.64	-17.42		1.00	Sep-99
	1.88	10.34	-4.14	33.65	45.59	0	1.05	12.36	0.7	17.28	107.0	5	94	0	0	258	28.38	-17.08			Dec-96
	0.59	6.36	-0.75	11.64	9.97	1.4	1.27	4.85	1.12	10.19	298.1	7	10	63	18	79					Dec-11
1,000	3.50	28.30	1.89	55.93	58.88	0	2.41	16.78	0.68	13.01	48.4	23	97	-29	0	38	26.31	-20.64	5.75		Sep-98
1,000	3.28	27.75	1.15	52.52	53.26	0	3.16	16.67	0.68	7.87	48.4	23	97	-29	0	38	25.72	-20.9		1.00	Sep-99
	3.53	28.42	2.09	56.95	60.69	0	2.17	16.74	0.68	14.64	48.4	23	97	-29	0	38	26.45	-20.55			Sep-98
1,000	3.89	13.78	2.49	19.43	20.11	0.1	1.23	8.68	0.6	22.95	78.7	12	66	20	-1	105	14.93	-14.46	5.75		Feb-93
1,000	3.72	13.32	1.71	16.77	15.64	0	1.99	8.71	0.6	20.33	78.7	12	66	20	-1	105	14.41	-14.71		1.00	Sep-99
	3.96	13.91	2.71	20.33	21.54	0.33	0.98	8.68	0.6	23.33	78.7	12	66	20	-1	105	15.13	-14.36			Nov-93
500	4.05	21.94	14.88	55.58	65.26	0.64	1.53	12.11	0.96	26.95	44.8	12	88	0	0	51	27.22	-21.84			Dec-00
100	3.60	11.30	7.43	22.73	26.99	2.68	1.43	5.09	0.35	17.1	132.6	1	40	34	0	64					Sep-13
100	3.48	11.12	7.14	21.80	25.33	2.47	1.68	5.06	0.34	17.07	132.6	1	40	34	0	64			5.50		Sep-13
100	4.13	18.84	7.23	41.76	45.81	0.74	1.3	13.54	1.07	16.45	24.7	0	100	0	0	76	21.23	-14.63			Sep-09
100	-2.17	25.33	-16.92	19.72	13.04	0	0.93	24.98	1.8	37.84	182.6	0	100	0	0	119	21.46	-24.68			Dec-08
100	-2.25	25.11	-17.15	18.63	11.16	0	1.18	24.96	1.8	36.91	182.6	0	100	0	0	119	21.27	-24.81			Oct-92
100	2.01	19.96	-5.96	30.62	13.61	0	1.05	20.26	1.11	19.23	446.0	0	100	0	0	81	31.62	-18.94			Dec-08
100	1.93	19.84	-6.18	29.60	12.03	0	1.3	20.22	1.11	18.48	446.0	0	100	0	0	81	31.4	-19.05			Dec-07
100	-0.08	14.40	-15.39	18.34	14.31	0	1.29	19.9	1.13	11.12	12.4	0	100	0	0	137					Dec-13
100	2.15	18.83	-9.31	24.53	19.10	0	1.4	20.28	1.25	11.86	12.9	0	100	0	0	76					Dec-13
500	3.88	11.55	8.57	21.89	28.22	0.09	2.03	8.16	0.63	21.12	31.2	6	71	24	0	0	17.36	-10.06			Oct-95
	3.71	17.24	11.19	45.42	54.39	1.57	0.6	13.14	0.95	53.31	938.5	2	98	0	0	1	26.16	-20.64			Nov-90
	3.01	19.23	9.63	86.92	99.08	0.12	0.86	13.81	0.98	11.34	228.0	3	97	0	0	34	29.43	-16.9			Jan-01
	5.42	18.09	1.64	35.77	16.33	1.51	0.99	12.16	1.05	8.55	75.4	3	91	0	2	16	9.38	-24.31			Jan-01
	4.98	18.70	-11.70	16.61	15.81	0.41	0.99	18.53	1.03	27.77	391.3	4	96	0	0	5	28.82	-24.35			Mar-98
	4.01	19.00	9.58	48.13	61.45	1.44	0.56	12.22	1	22.04	153.3	1	99	0	0	11	24.79	-16.46			Oct-99
	4.11	24.88	4.51	66.22	69.60	0	1.1	18.51	1.01	41.7	576.7	0	100	0	0	102	33.14	-25.33			Jan-03
	4.07	24.77	4.29	65.28	68.03	0	1.27	18.51	1.01	41.35	576.7	0	100	0	0	102	33.01	-25.38			Jul-15
	4.16	24.94	4.58	66.52	69.91	0	1	18.51	1.01	41.78	576.7	0	100	0	0	102	33.14	-25.33			Mar-17
250	1.25	13.49	0.49	31.95	29.10	0.55	1.59	12.86	1.03	12.11	550.5	2	98	0	0	256			5.75		Sep-15
	1.32	13.60	0.73	32.89	30.43	0.74	1.33	12.83	1.02	12.19	550.5	2	98	0	0	256					Sep-16
250	1.33	13.63	0.70	32.44	29.99	0.65	1.44	12.86	1.02	12.17	550.5	2	98	0	0	256					Jan-12
250	2.55	12.26	1.31			1.71	1.31			57.75	124.6	12	88	0	0	320					Jun-17
250	2.59	12.35	1.48			1.86	1.15			57.76	124.6	12	88	0	0	320					Dec-16
250	0.92	7.09	-2.99	22.60		0.4	1.57	10.54	0.82	20.82	909.4	7	88	5	0	275			5.75		Sep-15
	0.87	7.19	-2.80	23.44		0.66	1.33	10.52	0.82	20.85	909.4	7	88	5	0	275					Sep-16

	MARKET		FUND TYPE, CATEGORY & OBJECTIVE		RATINGS				MINIMUMS	
Fund Name	Ticker Symbol	Traded On	Fund Type	Category and (Prospectus Objective)	Overall Rating	Reward Rating	Risk Rating	Recent Up/ Downgrade	Open to New Investors	Min Initial Investment
Horizon Active Risk Assist® Fund Investor Class	ARANX	NAS CM	Open End	Aggressive Alloc (Asset Alloc)	C	C	C+		Y	2,500
Horizon Defined Risk Fund Advisor Class	HADRX	NAS CM	Open End	Long/Short Equity (Growth)	D+	D+	C+	Up	Y	2,500
Horizon Defined Risk Fund Investor Class	HNDRX	NAS CM	Open End	Long/Short Equity (Growth)	D+	D+	C+	Up	Y	2,500
Hotchkis & Wiley Capital Income Fund Class A	HWIAX	NAS CM	Open End	Moderate Alloc (Income)	C	C	C+		Y	2,500
Hotchkis & Wiley Capital Income Fund Class I	HWIIX	NAS CM	Open End	Moderate Alloc (Income)	C	C	C+		Y	250,000
Hotchkis & Wiley Diversified Value Fund Class A	HWCAX	NAS CM	Open End	US Equity Large Cap Value (Growth)	C+	C	B-	Up	Y	2,500
Hotchkis & Wiley Diversified Value Fund Class C	HWCCX	NAS CM	Open End	US Equity Large Cap Value (Growth)	C	C	B-		Y	2,500
Hotchkis & Wiley Diversified Value Cls Institutional	HWCIX	NAS CM	Open End	US Equity Large Cap Value (Growth)	C+	C	B-	Up	Y	250,000
Hotchkis & Wiley Global Value Fund Class A	HWGAX	NAS CM	Open End	Global Equity Large Cap (World Stock)	C	C	C+		Y	2,500
Hotchkis & Wiley Global Value Fund Class I	HWGIX	NAS CM	Open End	Global Equity Large Cap (World Stock)	C	C	C+		Y	250,000
Hotchkis & Wiley International Value Fund Class I	HWNIX	NAS CM	Open End	Global Equity Large Cap (Foreign Stock)	C-	D+	C		Y	250,000
Hotchkis & Wiley Large Cap Value Fund Class A	HWLAX	NAS CM	Open End	US Equity Large Cap Value (Equity-Income)	C+	C	B-	Up	Y	2,500
Hotchkis & Wiley Large Cap Value Fund Class C	HWLCX	NAS CM	Open End	US Equity Large Cap Value (Equity-Income)	C	C	B-		Y	2,500
Hotchkis & Wiley Large Cap Value Fund Class I	HWLIX	NAS CM	Open End	US Equity Large Cap Value (Equity-Income)	C+	C	B-	Up	Y	250,000
Hotchkis & Wiley Large Cap Value Fund Class R	HWLRX	NAS CM	Open End	US Equity Large Cap Value (Equity-Income)	C+	C	B-	Up	Y	2,500
Hotchkis & Wiley Mid-Cap Value Fund Class A	HWMAX	NAS CM	Open End	US Equity Mid Cap (Growth)	C-	D+	C-	Down		2,500
Hotchkis & Wiley Mid-Cap Value Fund Class C	HWMCX	NAS CM	Open End	US Equity Mid Cap (Growth)	D+	D+	C-	Down		2,500
Hotchkis & Wiley Mid-Cap Value Fund Class I	HWMIX	NAS CM	Open End	US Equity Mid Cap (Growth)	C-	D+	C	Down		250,000
Hotchkis & Wiley Mid-Cap Value Fund Class R	HWMRX	NAS CM	Open End	US Equity Mid Cap (Growth)	C-	D+	C-	Down		2,500
Hotchkis & Wiley Small Cap Diversified Value Fund Class A	HWVAX	NAS CM	Open End	US Equity Small Cap (Small Company)	C-	C-	C	Down	Y	2,500
Hotchkis & Wiley Small Cap Diversified Value Fund Class I	HWVIX	NAS CM	Open End	US Equity Small Cap (Small Company)	C	C-	C		Y	250,000
Hotchkis & Wiley Small Cap Value Fund Class A	HWSAX	NAS CM	Open End	US Equity Small Cap (Small Company)	C-	C-	C	Down		2,500
Hotchkis & Wiley Small Cap Value Fund Class C	HWSCX	NAS CM	Open End	US Equity Small Cap (Small Company)	C-	C-	C	Down		2,500
Hotchkis & Wiley Small Cap Value Fund Class I	HWSIX	NAS CM	Open End	US Equity Small Cap (Small Company)	C-	C-	C	Down		250,000
Hotchkis & Wiley Value Opportunities Fund Class A	HWAAX	NAS CM	Open End	Aggressive Alloc (Growth)	C+	C	B	Up	Y	2,500
Hotchkis & Wiley Value Opportunities Fund Class C	HWACX	NAS CM	Open End	Aggressive Alloc (Growth)	C+	C	B-	Up	Y	2,500
Hotchkis & Wiley Value Opportunities Cls Institutional	HWAIX	NAS CM	Open End	Aggressive Alloc (Growth)	C+	C	B	Up	Y	250,000
HSBC Asia ex-Japan Smaller Companies Equity Fund Class A	HAJAX	NAS CM	Open End	Asia ex-Japan Equity (Growth)	D+	D	C-	Down	Y	1,000
HSBC Asia ex-Japan Smaller Companies Equity Fund Class I	HAJIX	NAS CM	Open End	Asia ex-Japan Equity (Growth)	D+	D	C-	Down	Y	1,000,000
HSBC Asia ex-Japan Smaller Companies Equity Fund Class S	HAJSX	NAS CM	Open End	Asia ex-Japan Equity (Growth)	U	U	U		Y	25,000,000
HSBC Frontier Markets Fund Class A	HSFAX	NAS CM	Open End	Global Emerg Mkts (Growth)	C	D+	C+	Up		1,000
HSBC Frontier Markets Fund Class I	HSFIX	NAS CM	Open End	Global Emerg Mkts (Growth)	C	C-	C+			1,000,000
HSBC Opportunity Fund Class A	HSOAX	NAS CM	Open End	US Equity Mid Cap (Growth)	C	C	C+		Y	1,000
HSBC Opportunity Fund Class B	HOPBX	NAS CM	Open End	US Equity Mid Cap (Growth)	C	C	C+			1,000
HSBC Opportunity Fund Class C	HOPCX	NAS CM	Open End	US Equity Mid Cap (Growth)	C	C	C+		Y	1,000
HSBC Opportunity Fund Class I	RESCX	NAS CM	Open End	US Equity Mid Cap (Growth)	C+	C	C+	Up	Y	1,000,000
Huber Capital Diversified Large Cap Value Inst Cls	HUDEX	NAS CM	Open End	US Equity Large Cap Value (Growth & Income)	C+	C	B-		Y	1,000,000
Huber Capital Diversified Large Cap Value Investor Cls	HUDIX	NAS CM	Open End	US Equity Large Cap Value (Growth & Income)	C+	C	B-		Y	5,000
Huber Capital Equity Income Fund Institutional Class	HULEX	NAS CM	Open End	US Equity Large Cap Value (Equity-Income)	C+	C	B-	Down	Y	1,000,000
Huber Capital Equity Income Fund Investor Class	HULIX	NAS CM	Open End	US Equity Large Cap Value (Equity-Income)	C+	C	B-	Down	Y	5,000
Huber Capital Mid Cap Value Fund Institutional Class	HUMEX	NAS CM	Open End	US Equity Small Cap (Growth & Income)	C-	C-	C	Down	Y	1,000,000
Huber Capital Mid Cap Value Fund Investor Class	HUMDX	NAS CM	Open End	US Equity Small Cap (Growth & Income)	C-	C-	C	Down	Y	5,000
Huber Capital Small Cap Value Fund Institutional Class	HUSEX	NAS CM	Open End	US Equity Small Cap (Small Company)	C	C	C		Y	1,000,000
Huber Capital Small Cap Value Fund Investor Class	HUSIX	NAS CM	Open End	US Equity Small Cap (Small Company)	C	C	C		Y	5,000
Hundredfold Select Alternative Fund Investor Class	HFSAX	NAS CM	Open End	Moderate Alloc (Growth & Income)	B-	C	B+		Y	1,000,000
Hundredfold Select Alternative Fund Service Class	SFHYX	NAS CM	Open End	Moderate Alloc (Growth & Income)	B	C	A	Up	Y	5,000
Hussman Strategic Growth Fund	HSGFX	NAS CM	Open End	Market Neutral (Growth)	D	D	D	Down	Y	1,000
Hussman Strategic International Fund	HSIEX	NAS CM	Open End	Market Neutral (Foreign Stock)	D	D	C-		Y	1,000
Hussman Strategic Total Return Fund	HSTRX	NAS CM	Open End	Moderate Alloc (Growth & Income)	C+	C	B	Down	Y	1,000
HVIA Equity Fund Institutional Class	HVEIX	NAS CM	Open End	US Equity Large Cap Growth (Growth)	B-	C	B		Y	25,000
ICM Small Company Portfolio	ICSCX	NAS CM	Open End	US Equity Small Cap (Small Company)	C	C	C+		Y	2,500,000
ICON Consumer Discretionary Fund Class A	ICCAX	NAS CM	Open End	Consumer Goods Sec Equity ()	C-	D+	C	Down	Y	1,000

★ Expanded analysis of this fund is included in Section II.

	TOTAL RETURNS					PERFORMANCE				ASSETS		ASSET ALLOCATION & TURNOVER					BULL & BEAR		FEES		
Min Additional Investment	3-Month Total Return	6-Month Total Return	1-Year Total Return	3-Year Total Return	5-Year Total Return	Dividend Yield (TTM)	Expense Ratio	3-Yr Std Deviation	3-Year Beta	NAV	Total Assets (MIL)	%Cash	%Stocks	%Bonds	%Other	Turnover Ratio	Last Bull Market Total Return	Last Bear Market Total Return	Front End Fee (%)	Back End Fee (%)	Inception Date
250	0.87	7.09	-2.93	22.87		0.58	1.44	10.49	0.82	20.82	909.4	7	88	5	0	275					Aug-14
250	2.25	7.98	4.85			0.19	1.19			52.07	97.5										Feb-18
250	2.29	8.07	5.00			0.32	1.04			52.06	97.5										Dec-17
100	1.87	12.09	-3.21	28.19	21.38	2.97	1.13	11.06	0.78	12.56	26.7	0	59	39	0	46	18.59	-10.09	4.75		Feb-11
100	1.93	12.30	-3.17	29.01	22.37	3.37	0.88	11.08	0.78	12.03	26.7	0	59	39	0	46	18.01	-9.99			Dec-10
100	4.29	20.24	1.77	44.83	36.33	1.09	1.05	16.4	1.23	18.95	101.3	1	99	0	0	28	27.8	-21.53	5.25		Aug-04
100	4.10	19.78	0.97	41.63	31.31	0.25	1.8	16.41	1.24	18.77	101.3	1	99	0	0	28	27.37	-21.84		1.00	Aug-04
100	4.41	20.45	2.07	45.97	38.14	1.36	0.8	16.42	1.24	18.9	101.3	1	99	0	0	28	28.09	-21.5			Aug-04
100	3.86	15.96	-4.85	35.27	17.69	0.7	1.2	15.04	1.18	11.55	39.8	3	97	0	0	43			5.25		Aug-13
100	3.96	16.19	-4.57	36.22	19.10	1.09	0.95	15.02	1.18	11.55	39.8	3	97	0	0	43					Dec-12
100	2.08	9.16	-9.03	20.85		1.32	0.95	13.06	0.99	9.77	2.3	2	98	0	0	33					Dec-15
100	4.14	20.15	2.24	43.63	38.21	1.52	1.2	16.08	1.21	33.14	494.3	2	98	0	0	41	26.98	-20.48	5.25		Oct-01
100	3.92	19.68	1.48	40.40	33.10	0.51	1.95	16.07	1.21	32.59	494.3	2	98	0	0	41	26.41	-20.71		1.00	Feb-02
100	4.19	20.31	2.50	44.69	39.97	1.92	0.95	16.07	1.21	33.29	494.3	2	98	0	0	41	27.21	-20.39			Jun-87
100	4.03	19.98	1.97	42.51	36.47	0.87	1.45	16.06	1.21	33.5	494.3	2	98	0	0	41	26.88	-20.57			Aug-03
100	-3.47	12.91	-14.48	22.15	3.10	0.83	1.24	21.4	1.43	32.53	1,236	3	97	0	0	32	44.3	-31.12	5.25		Jan-01
100	-3.66	12.43	-15.14	19.39	-0.70	0.37	1.99	21.38	1.43	28.12	1,236	3	97	0	0	32	43.68	-31.36		1.00	Jan-01
100	-3.44	13.00	-14.29	23.01	4.39	1	0.99	21.4	1.43	33.1	1,236	3	97	0	0	32	44.57	-31.09			Jan-97
100	-3.55	12.74	-14.70	21.20	1.82	0.47	1.49	21.38	1.43	32.56	1,236	3	97	0	0	32	44.1	-31.23			Aug-03
100	0.70	13.58	-9.35	43.64	36.04	0.54	1.15	18.91	1.08	10.03	97.6	2	98	0	0	95			5.25		Jun-14
100	0.80	13.64	-9.23	44.62	37.77	0.77	0.9	18.94	1.08	10.08	97.6	2	98	0	0	95					Jun-14
100	1.20	13.56	-9.19	33.27	15.66	0.23	1.27	19.45	1.09	52.98	721.9	7	93	0	0	29	30.39	-29.19	5.25		Oct-00
100	1.03	13.14	-9.86	30.29	11.40	0	2.02	19.43	1.09	42.94	721.9	7	93	0	0	29	29.83	-29.42		1.00	Feb-02
100	1.27	13.70	-8.96	34.25	17.11	0.57	1.02	19.45	1.09	53.27	721.9	7	93	0	0	29	30.54	-29.11			Sep-85
100	4.69	19.25	2.17	49.16	39.99	0.73	1.22	15.17	1.11	28.12	766.5	2	89	8	0	55	31.09	-23.67	5.25		Dec-02
100	4.51	18.82	1.44	45.90	34.87	0.03	1.97	15.16	1.11	25.94	766.5	2	89	8	0	55	30.47	-23.92		1.00	Aug-03
100	4.77	19.43	2.45	50.29	41.77	1.02	0.97	15.17	1.11	28.08	766.5	2	89	8	0	55	31.21	-23.59			Dec-02
100	-3.68	5.91	-16.35	13.72		0.65	1.26	14.15	1.03	9.67	18.1	1	99	0	0				5.00		Nov-14
0	-3.61	5.96	-16.08	14.89		1.83	0.91	14.12	1.03	9.59	18.1	1	99	0	0						Nov-14
0	10.02	5.34	34.25			1.56	1.33				12.0	2	96	0	2	93					Nov-14
100	4.93	17.14	3.64	17.79	3.18	1.27	1.85	11.43	0.87	12.98	8.4	2	98	0	0	62	14.1		5.00		Sep-11
0	5.00	17.32	3.99	19.08	4.99	1.9	1.5	11.48	0.88	13	8.4	2	98	0	0	62	14.32				Sep-11
100	3.94	22.45	0.73	55.01	41.47	0	1.65	15.71	0.92	9.49	144.8	1	99	0	0	77	29.48	-24.85	5.00		Sep-96
100	3.92	22.28	0.11	51.60	36.31	0	2.4	15.65	0.92	4.5	144.8	1	99	0	0	77	28.75	-25.04		4.00	Jan-98
100	3.81	22.19	0.00	51.70	36.38	0	2.4	15.67	0.92	4.9	144.8	1	99	0	0	77	28.82	-25.11		1.00	Nov-98
0	3.96	22.59	1.19	57.04	44.94	0	1.1	15.64	0.92	12.86	144.8	1	99	0	0	77	29.79	-24.67			Sep-96
5,000	4.08	19.06	4.89	40.45	27.64	1.52	0.76	13.99	1.09	15.05	4.9	7	93	0	0	39					Dec-12
100	4.23	19.14	4.79	39.86	26.20	1.3	1.16	14	1.09	15	4.9	7	93	0	0	39					Dec-12
5,000	6.67	23.02	8.50	43.80	27.14	1.38	0.99	14.07	1.09	16.94	63.8	4	96	0	0	20	24.56	-16.1			Oct-11
100	6.59	22.86	8.24	42.50	24.91	1.13	1.39	14.07	1.09	16.98	63.8	4	96	0	0	20	24.39	-16.1			Jun-07
5,000	2.07	15.18	-11.45	28.59		1.27	1.11	18.39	1.29	11.83	1.8	8	92	0	0	43					Dec-15
100	2.16	15.09	-11.57	27.82		1.01	1.41	18.29	1.28	11.82	1.8	8	92	0	0	43					Dec-15
5,000	5.05	19.80	-9.32	33.95	-2.88	0.46	1.36	18.38	1.03	17.24	43.1	6	94	0	0	39	37.54	-24.08			Oct-11
100	4.98	19.64	-9.57	33.02	-4.33	0.16	1.76	18.36	1.03	17.05	43.1	6	94	0	0	39	37.2	-24.08			Jun-07
0	2.32	8.26	5.83	23.19	27.43	0.87	2	4.88	0.19	23.21	57.7	26	7	66	1	505	8.85	-3.05			Oct-12
1,000	2.13	7.80	4.90	19.93	21.83	0.28	2.9	4.85	0.18	22.08	57.7	26	7	66	1	505	8.85	-3.05			Sep-04
100	-6.52	-13.15	-8.04	-24.69	-37.71	1.37	1.29	7.64	-0.46	5.87	293.8	57	42	0	1	142	-12.24	9.02			Jul-00
100	-0.11	-0.75	-5.67	-8.86	-13.82	0.08	2	2.83	0.02	8.35	22.0	2	89	0	9	61	-2.45	-1.99			Dec-09
100	3.48	7.60	9.71	5.97	14.82	1.35	0.8	4.39	1.04	12.83	221.3	8	25	66	1	63	1.26	2.34			Sep-02
	4.12	21.13	11.78			0.53	0.99			14.13	19.5	5	95	0	0	29					Oct-16
1,000	2.84	18.04	-5.84	42.44	44.34	0.37	0.93	18.93	1.08	28.15	881.8	4	96	0	0	31	31.19	-24.97			Apr-89
100	-3.70	10.09	0.16	3.54	9.12	0	1.99	15.35	0.86	12.22	20.6	0	100	0	0	137	30.17	-9.13	5.75		Sep-10

	MARKET		FUND TYPE, CATEGORY & OBJECTIVE		RATINGS				MINIMUMS	
Fund Name	Ticker Symbol	Traded On	Fund Type	Category and (Prospectus Objective)	Overall Rating	Reward Rating	Risk Rating	Recent Up/ Downgrade	Open to New Investors	Min Initial Investment
ICON Consumer Discretionary Fund Class S	ICCCX	NAS CM	Open End	Consumer Goods Sec Equity ()	C-	D+	C	Down	Y	1,000
ICON Consumer Staples Fund Class A	ICRAX	NAS CM	Open End	Consumer Goods Sec Equity ()	C	C	C+	Down	Y	1,000
ICON Consumer Staples Fund Class S	ICLEX	NAS CM	Open End	Consumer Goods Sec Equity ()	C	C	C+	Down	Y	1,000
ICON Emerging Markets Fund Class A	IPCAX	NAS CM	Open End	Global Emerg Mkts (Div Emerging Mkts)	C	C-	B-		Y	1,000
ICON Emerging Markets Fund Class S	ICARX	NAS CM	Open End	Global Emerg Mkts (Div Emerging Mkts)	C	C-	B-		Y	1,000
ICON Energy Fund Class A	ICEAX	NAS CM	Open End	Energy Sector Equity ()	D	D	D	Down	Y	1,000
ICON Energy Fund Class S	ICENX	NAS CM	Open End	Energy Sector Equity ()	D	D	D	Down	Y	1,000
ICON Equity Income Fund Class A	IEQAX	NAS CM	Open End	Aggressive Alloc (Equity-Income)	B-	C	B	Up	Y	1,000
ICON Equity Income Fund Class C	IOECX	NAS CM	Open End	Aggressive Alloc (Equity-Income)	B-	C	B	Up	Y	1,000
ICON Equity Income Fund Class S	IOEZX	NAS CM	Open End	Aggressive Alloc (Equity-Income)	B-	C	B	Up	Y	1,000
ICON Financial Fund Class A	ICFAX	NAS CM	Open End	Financials Sector Equity (Financial)	C	C	C+	Down	Y	1,000
ICON Financial Fund Class S	ICFSX	NAS CM	Open End	Financials Sector Equity (Financial)	C	C	C+	Down	Y	1,000
ICON Fund Class A	ICNAX	NAS CM	Open End	US Equity Large Cap Growth (Growth & Income)	C	C	C+	Down	Y	1,000
ICON Fund Class C	ICNCX	NAS CM	Open End	US Equity Large Cap Growth (Growth & Income)	C	C	C+	Down	Y	1,000
ICON Fund Class S	ICNZX	NAS CM	Open End	US Equity Large Cap Growth (Growth & Income)	C	C	C+	Down	Y	1,000
ICON Healthcare Fund Class A	ICHAX	NAS CM	Open End	Healthcare Sector Equity (Health)	C	C-	C	Down	Y	1,000
ICON Healthcare Fund Class S	ICHCX	NAS CM	Open End	Healthcare Sector Equity (Health)	C	C-	C+	Down	Y	1,000
ICON Industrials Fund Class A	ICIAX	NAS CM	Open End	Industrials Sector Equity ()	C	C	C+	Down	Y	1,000
ICON Industrials Fund Class S	ICTRX	NAS CM	Open End	Industrials Sector Equity ()	C	C	C+	Down	Y	1,000
ICON Information Technology Fund Class A	ICTTX	NAS CM	Open End	Technology Sector Equity (Technology)	C+	C	C+	Down	Y	1,000
ICON Information Technology Fund Class S	ICTEX	NAS CM	Open End	Technology Sector Equity (Technology)	C+	C	C+	Down	Y	1,000
ICON International Equity Fund Class A	IIQAX	NAS CM	Open End	Global Equity Large Cap (Foreign Stock)	D+	D	C-		Y	1,000
ICON International Equity Fund Class C	IIQCX	NAS CM	Open End	Global Equity Large Cap (Foreign Stock)	D+	D	C-		Y	1,000
ICON International Equity Fund Class S	ICNEX	NAS CM	Open End	Global Equity Large Cap (Foreign Stock)	D+	D+	C		Y	1,000
ICON Long/Short Fund Class A	ISTAX	NAS CM	Open End	US Equity Large Cap Growth (Growth)	C	C	C+	Down	Y	1,000
ICON Long/Short Fund Class C	IOLCX	NAS CM	Open End	US Equity Large Cap Growth (Growth)	C	C	C+	Down	Y	1,000
ICON Long/Short Fund Class S	IOLZX	NAS CM	Open End	US Equity Large Cap Growth (Growth)	C	C	C+	Down	Y	1,000
ICON Natural Resources Fund Class A	ICBAX	NAS CM	Open End	Natl Resources Sec Equity (Natl Res)	C	C-	C		Y	1,000
ICON Natural Resources Fund Class C	ICBCX	NAS CM	Open End	Natl Resources Sec Equity (Natl Res)	C	C-	C		Y	1,000
ICON Natural Resources Fund Class S	ICBMX	NAS CM	Open End	Natl Resources Sec Equity (Natl Res)	C	C	C		Y	1,000
ICON Opportunities Fund	ICONX	NAS CM	Open End	US Equity Small Cap (Small Company)	C	C-	C	Down	Y	1,000
ICON Risk-Managed Balanced Fund Class A	IOCAX	NAS CM	Open End	Moderate Alloc (Growth & Income)	C+	C	B	Up	Y	1,000
ICON Risk-Managed Balanced Fund Class C	IOCCX	NAS CM	Open End	Moderate Alloc (Growth & Income)	C	C-	B		Y	1,000
ICON Risk-Managed Balanced Fund Class S	IOCZX	NAS CM	Open End	Moderate Alloc (Growth & Income)	C+	C	B	Up	Y	1,000
ICON Utilities Fund Class A	ICTVX	NAS CM	Open End	Utilities Sector Equity (Utility)	B-	B-	B	Down	Y	1,000
ICON Utilities Fund Class S	ICTUX	NAS CM	Open End	Utilities Sector Equity (Utility)	B	B-	B		Y	1,000
Iman Fund Class K	IMANX	NAS CM	Open End	US Equity Large Cap Growth (Growth)	C+	C	B-	Down	Y	250
IMS Capital Value Fund	IMSCX	NAS CM	Open End	US Equity Mid Cap (Growth)	C+	C	B-		Y	5,000
IMS Dividend Growth Fund	IMSAX	NAS CM	Open End	US Equity Large Cap Value (Growth)	C+	C	B	Down	Y	5,000
IMS Strategic Income Fund	IMSIX	NAS CM	Open End	Moderate Alloc (Equity-Income)	C-	D+	C		Y	5,000
Independent Franchise Partners US Equity Fund	IFPUX	NAS CM	Open End	US Equity Large Cap Blend (Income)	B	C+	B+	Up	Y	3,000,000
Index Funds S&P 500® Equal Weight No Load Shares	INDEX	NAS CM	Open End	US Equity Large Cap Blend (Growth & Income)	B-	C	B		Y	1,000
Infinity Q Diversified Alpha Fund Institutional Class	IQDNX	NAS CM	Open End	Multialternative (Growth & Income)	B	C	A+			1,000,000
Infinity Q Diversified Alpha Fund Investor Class	IQDAX	NAS CM	Open End	Multialternative (Growth & Income)	B	C	A+			100,000
Innovative Dividend Performers Fund Class A	INDPX	NAS CM	Open End	Alternative Miscellaneous (Equity-Income)	U	U	U		Y	5,000
Innovative Dividend Performers Fund Class I	IPDPX	NAS CM	Open End	Alternative Miscellaneous (Equity-Income)	U	U	U		Y	100,000
Innovative Preferred Plus Fund Class A	INPPX	NAS CM	Open End	US Fixed Income (Income)	U	U	U		Y	5,000
Innovative Preferred Plus Fund Class I	IPPPX	NAS CM	Open End	US Fixed Income (Income)	U	U	U		Y	100,000
Insignia Macro Fund Class A	IGMFX	NAS CM	Open End	Alternative Miscellaneous (Growth & Income)	C-	D	C	Up	Y	2,500
Insignia Macro Fund Class I	IGMLX	NAS CM	Open End	Alternative Miscellaneous (Growth & Income)	C-	D	C	Up	Y	250,000
Integrity Dividend Harvest Fund Class A Shares	IDIVX	NAS CM	Open End	US Equity Large Cap Value (Equity-Income)	B-	C+	B	Down	Y	1,000
Integrity Dividend Harvest Fund Class C	IDHCX	NAS CM	Open End	US Equity Large Cap Value (Equity-Income)	B-	C	B	Down	Y	1,000

★ Expanded analysis of this fund is included in Section II.

	TOTAL RETURNS					PERFORMANCE				ASSETS		ASSET ALLOCATION & TURNOVER					BULL & BEAR		FEES		
Min Additional Investment	3-Month Total Return	6-Month Total Return	1-Year Total Return	3-Year Total Return	5-Year Total Return	Dividend Yield (TTM)	Expense Ratio	3-Yr Std Deviation	3-Year Beta	NAV	Total Assets (MIL)	%Cash	%Stocks	%Bonds	%Other	Turnover Ratio	Last Bull Market Total Return	Last Bear Market Total Return	Front End Fee (%)	Back End Fee (%)	Inception Date
100	-3.59	10.27	0.46	4.99	11.72	0	1.6	15.39	0.86	12.88	20.6	0	100	0	0	137	30.14	-8.72			Jul-97
100	1.05	13.13	5.28	9.82	34.47	0.96	1.77	11.21	0.91	6.72	11.9	12	88	0	0	58	14.45	-6.66	5.75		Sep-10
100	1.04	13.25	5.51	10.52	35.95	1.32	1.51	11.2	0.91	6.75	11.9	12	88	0	0	58	14.68	-7.51			May-97
100	1.16	10.62	1.33	20.60	18.11	1.43	1.8	14.03	0.93	15.62	51.3	4	94	0	0	63	20.62	-26.49	5.75		May-06
100	1.22	10.79	1.56	21.46	19.67	1.92	1.55	13.97	0.92	15.7	51.3	4	94	0	0	63	20.76	-26.45			Feb-97
100	-4.53	8.56	-22.81	-16.69	-47.56	0.34	1.75	22.08	1.03	9.89	116.5	1	99	0	0	69	15.49	-28.18	5.75		Sep-10
100	-4.49	8.70	-22.58	-15.95	-46.82	0.41	1.5	22.15	1.03	9.99	116.5	1	99	0	0	69	15.71	-27.99			Nov-97
100	4.46	18.23	5.76	33.26	41.03	2.93	1.3	12.09	0.9	18.13	83.2	1	90	8	0	171	20.01	-16.72	5.75		May-06
100	4.27	17.84	5.02	30.35	35.81	2.18	2.05	12.12	0.9	18.35	83.2	1	90	8	0	171	19.61	-17.03		1.00	Nov-02
100	4.57	18.39	6.08	34.38	42.85	3.18	1.05	12.13	0.9	18.18	83.2	1	90	8	0	171	20.23	-16.6			May-04
100	8.00	22.52	2.32	52.44	34.74	0.56	1.75	19.32	1.11	10.66	37.8	1	99	0	0	44	28.83	-25.47	5.75		Sep-10
100	8.00	22.67	2.48	53.69	36.82	0.62	1.44	19.35	1.12	10.66	37.8	1	99	0	0	44	29.32	-25.43			Jul-97
100	4.72	24.69	-0.62	50.54	30.16	0	1.5	17.39	1.32	18.38	43.6	0	100	0	0	25	27.06	-21.37	5.75		May-06
100	4.47	24.22	-1.37	47.08	25.30	0	2.25	17.39	1.32	16.82	43.6	0	100	0	0	25	26.8	-21.29		1.00	Nov-00
100	4.74	24.85	-0.33	52.23	32.66	0	1.1	17.38	1.32	19.64	43.6	0	100	0	0	25	27.09	-20.82			May-04
100	-3.09	6.10	1.26	25.45	37.77	0	1.75	15.69	1.08	15.64	65.1	1	99	0	0	63	19.42	-11.74	5.75		Sep-10
100	-3.00	6.26	1.56	26.64	39.95	0	1.45	15.68	1.08	16.46	65.1	1	99	0	0	63	19.66	-11.54			Feb-97
100	5.33	24.69	8.72	31.03	26.03	0	1.75	18.53	1.07	15.2	12.4	1	99	0	0	87	26.29	-26.2	5.75		Sep-10
100	5.38	24.87	9.02	32.02	27.48	0	1.5	18.57	1.07	15.46	12.4	1	99	0	0	87	27.9	-25.92			May-97
100	6.31	28.05	7.66	69.27	102.84	0	1.75	15.84	0.96	14.65	57.2	1	99	0	0	98	29.39	-13.59	5.75		Sep-10
100	6.37	28.13	7.95	70.87	106.19	0	1.41	15.83	0.96	15.35	57.2	1	99	0	0	98	29.8	-13.47			Feb-97
100	1.12	11.49	-6.28	6.55	-8.53	1.36	1.8	13.72	1.16	11.64	34.7	1	99	0	0	92	17.75	-33.18	5.75		May-06
100	0.87	10.95	-7.12	4.12	-11.96	1.35	2.55	13.71	1.16	10.33	34.7	1	99	0	0	92	17.29	-33.43		1.00	Feb-04
100	1.19	11.52	-6.10	7.42	-7.09	1.39	1.49	13.68	1.16	11.9	34.7	1	99	0	0	92	18.01	-33.09			Feb-97
100	3.74	24.47	0.45	54.87	40.64	0	1.55	17.5	1.32	25.73	19.3	0	100	0	0	36	24.82	-16.25	5.75		May-06
100	3.54	23.97	-0.30	51.43	35.45	0	2.3	17.47	1.32	23.06	19.3	0	100	0	0	36	24.24	-16.48		1.00	Oct-02
100	3.80	24.56	0.70	56.21	42.74	0	1.25	17.51	1.32	26.72	19.3	0	100	0	0	36	24.97	-16.05			May-04
100	3.35	14.79	-4.85	25.32	6.99	1.72	1.75	14.93	0.99	12.34	58.9	6	94	0	0	117	26.23	-27.13	5.75		Sep-10
100	3.06	14.27	-5.62	22.30	2.90	0.94	2.5	14.9	0.98	11.77	58.9	6	94	0	0	117	25.61	-27.3		1.00	Sep-10
100	3.40	14.94	-4.60	26.10	8.39	2.29	1.5	14.96	0.99	12.46	58.9	6	94	0	0	117	26.53	-27			May-97
100	1.53	19.83	-5.69	38.76	31.51	0	1.3	21.53	1.15	13.23	16.9	0	100	0	0	87					Sep-12
100	2.87	15.66	1.40	16.94	18.61	0.84	1.56	10.42	0.81	15.61	28.2	5	64	30	-1	87	10.72	-10.65	5.75		May-06
100	2.68	15.22	0.61	14.32	14.28	0.32	2.31	10.43	0.81	14.61	28.2	5	64	30	-1	87	10.33	-10.98		1.00	Nov-02
100	2.93	15.77	1.60	17.78	20.06	1.09	1.31	10.4	0.81	16	28.2	5	64	30	-1	87	11.01	-10.59			May-04
100	2.13	14.12	15.44	24.95	55.69	2.85	1.47	10.08	0.88	9.54	45.3	2	98	0	0	156	6.95	-0.16	5.75		Sep-10
100	2.26	14.35	15.81	25.87	57.84	3.03	1.22	10.12	0.89	9.72	45.3	2	98	0	0	156	7.1	0.02			Jul-97
50	5.84	26.58	11.48	65.36	77.65	0	1.33	15.16	1.21	13.76	124.0	0	100	0	0	72	22.44	-20.28			Jun-00
100	3.80	22.43	6.99	27.08	28.05	0	1.74	15.24	1.2	23.47	30.4	1	99	0	0	40	27.24	-29.29			Aug-96
100	4.95	17.70	7.53	37.30	39.18	0.6	1.96	12.43	0.97	16.71	10.0	8	92	0	0	23	19.06	-14.67			Nov-02
100	1.16	14.19	12.21	-3.96	-35.16	4.98	2.02	8.07	0.07	2.61	5.9	25	34	41	0	759	9.43	-10.47			Nov-02
250,000	2.34	20.96	10.19	41.64	66.30	1.6	0.76	11.49	0.78	18.35	2,161	0	94	0	6	39					Dec-11
1,000	3.62	20.00	7.97	43.46		1.51	0.25	13.06	1	32.33	43.0	0	100	0	0	83					Apr-15
10,000	0.84	1.19	7.40	23.24		0	2.23	5.24	-0.39	11.88	626.0	65	29	3	2	8					Sep-14
100	0.76	1.02	7.18	22.33		0	2.48	5.21	-0.39	11.77	626.0	65	29	3	2	8			5.00		Sep-14
100	3.26	16.25					1.75			11.71	9.1	18	83	0	0						Dec-18
100	3.61	16.72					1.5			11.75	9.1	18	83	0	0						Dec-18
100	3.73	11.30					1.8			10.9	6.1	4	0	10	1						Dec-18
100	2.43	10.26					1.55			10.92	6.1	4	0	10	1						Dec-18
	-0.73	-2.75	-1.28	-3.84	4.08	0.06	2	5.48	0.8	9.52	11.4	32	0	67	0	70			5.50		Dec-13
	-0.73	-2.75	-1.21	-3.63	4.42	0.14	1.75	5.46	0.8	9.52	11.4	32	0	67	0	70					Dec-13
50	1.55	13.61	12.87	27.30	49.88	2.89	0.95	9.92	0.69	14.05	135.1	0	100	0	0				5.00		May-12
50	1.37	13.16	12.03	24.48	44.40	2.21	1.7	9.9	0.69	13.96	135.1	0	100	0	0					1.00	Aug-15

	MARKET			FUND TYPE, CATEGORY & OBJECTIVE	RATINGS				MINIMUMS	
Fund Name	Ticker Symbol	Traded On	Fund Type	Category and (Prospectus Objective)	Overall Rating	Reward Rating	Risk Rating	Recent Up/ Downgrade	Open to New Investors	Min Initial Investment
Integrity Dividend Harvest Fund Class I	IDHIX	NAS CM	Open End	US Equity Large Cap Value (Equity-Income)	B-	C+	B	Down	Y	1,000
Integrity Energized Dividend Fund Class A	NRGDX	NAS CM	Open End	Energy Sector Equity (Equity-Income)	C	C	B-		Y	1,000
Integrity Energized Dividend Fund Class C	NRGUX	NAS CM	Open End	Energy Sector Equity (Equity-Income)	C	C	C+		Y	1,000
Integrity Energized Dividend Fund Class I	NRIGX	NAS CM	Open End	Energy Sector Equity (Equity-Income)	C	C	B-		Y	1,000
Integrity Growth & Income Fund Class A	IGIAX	NAS CM	Open End	US Equity Large Cap Blend (Growth & Income)	B	C+	B+		Y	1,000
Integrity Growth & Income Fund Class C	IGIUX	NAS CM	Open End	US Equity Large Cap Blend (Growth & Income)	B	C+	B+		Y	1,000
Integrity Growth & Income Fund Class I	IGIVX	NAS CM	Open End	US Equity Large Cap Blend (Growth & Income)	B	C+	B+		Y	1,000
Intrepid Capital Fund Institutional Class	ICMVX	NAS CM	Open End	Moderate Alloc (Growth & Income)	D+	D	C	Down	Y	250,000
Intrepid Capital Fund Investor Class	ICMBX	NAS CM	Open End	Moderate Alloc (Growth & Income)	D+	D	C		Y	2,500
Intrepid Endurance Fund Institutional Class	ICMZX	NAS CM	Open End	US Equity Small Cap (Small Company)	C-	D	C		Y	250,000
Intrepid Endurance Fund Investor Class	ICMAX	NAS CM	Open End	US Equity Small Cap (Small Company)	D+	D	C	Down	Y	2,500
Intrepid International Fund Investor Class	ICMIX	NAS CM	Open End	Global Equity Mid/Small Cap (Foreign Stock)	D+	D+	C-		Y	2,500
Invenomic Fund Institutional Class shares	BIVIX	NAS CM	Open End	Long/Short Equity (Growth)	C	D+	B+	Up	Y	50,000
Invenomic Fund Investor Class shares	BIVRX	NAS CM	Open End	Long/Short Equity (Growth)	C	D+	B+	Up	Y	5,000
Invenomic Fund Super Institutional Class shares	BIVSX	NAS CM	Open End	Long/Short Equity (Growth)	C	D+	B+		Y	50,000,000
Invesco All Cap Market Neutral Fund Class A	CPNAX	NAS CM	Open End	Market Neutral (Growth & Income)	D	D	D		Y	1,000
Invesco All Cap Market Neutral Fund Class C	CPNCX	NAS CM	Open End	Market Neutral (Growth & Income)	D	D	D		Y	1,000
Invesco All Cap Market Neutral Fund Class R	CPNRX	NAS CM	Open End	Market Neutral (Growth & Income)	D	D	D		Y	0
Invesco All Cap Market Neutral Fund Class R5	CPNFX	NAS CM	Open End	Market Neutral (Growth & Income)	D	D	D+		Y	10,000,000
Invesco All Cap Market Neutral Fund Class R6	CPNSX	NAS CM	Open End	Market Neutral (Growth & Income)	D	D	D+		Y	10,000,000
Invesco All Cap Market Neutral Fund Class Y	CPNYX	NAS CM	Open End	Market Neutral (Growth & Income)	D	D	D+		Y	1,000
Invesco Alternative Strategies Fund Class A	LQLAX	NAS CM	Open End	Multialternative (Growth)	C-	D+	C		Y	1,000
Invesco Alternative Strategies Fund Class C	LQLCX	NAS CM	Open End	Multialternative (Growth)	D+	D	C		Y	1,000
Invesco Alternative Strategies Fund Class R	LQLRX	NAS CM	Open End	Multialternative (Growth)	C-	D	C		Y	0
Invesco Alternative Strategies Fund Class R5	LQLFX	NAS CM	Open End	Multialternative (Growth)	C-	D+	C		Y	10,000,000
Invesco Alternative Strategies Fund Class R6	LQLSX	NAS CM	Open End	Multialternative (Growth)	C-	D+	C		Y	10,000,000
Invesco Alternative Strategies Fund Class Y	LQLYX	NAS CM	Open End	Multialternative (Growth)	C-	D+	C		Y	1,000
Invesco American Franchise Fund Class A	VAFAX	NAS CM	Open End	US Equity Large Cap Growth (Growth)	C+	C	B-	Down	Y	1,000
Invesco American Franchise Fund Class C	VAFCX	NAS CM	Open End	US Equity Large Cap Growth (Growth)	C+	C	B-		Y	1,000
Invesco American Franchise Fund Class R	VAFRX	NAS CM	Open End	US Equity Large Cap Growth (Growth)	C+	C	B-		Y	0
Invesco American Franchise Fund Class R6	VAFFX	NAS CM	Open End	US Equity Large Cap Growth (Growth)	C+	C	B-	Down	Y	10,000,000
Invesco American Franchise Fund Class Y	VAFIX	NAS CM	Open End	US Equity Large Cap Growth (Growth)	C+	C	B-	Down	Y	1,000
Invesco American Franchise Fund R5 Class	VAFNX	NAS CM	Open End	US Equity Large Cap Growth (Growth)	C+	C	B-	Down	Y	10,000,000
Invesco American Value Fund Class A	MSAVX	NAS CM	Open End	US Equity Mid Cap (Growth & Income)	C	C-	C+		Y	1,000
Invesco American Value Fund Class C	MSVCX	NAS CM	Open End	US Equity Mid Cap (Growth & Income)	C	C-	C+		Y	1,000
Invesco American Value Fund Class R	MSARX	NAS CM	Open End	US Equity Mid Cap (Growth & Income)	C	C-	C+		Y	0
Invesco American Value Fund Class R6	MSAFX	NAS CM	Open End	US Equity Mid Cap (Growth & Income)	C	C-	B-		Y	10,000,000
Invesco American Value Fund Class Y	MSAIX	NAS CM	Open End	US Equity Mid Cap (Growth & Income)	C	C-	C+		Y	1,000
Invesco American Value Fund R5 Class	MSAJX	NAS CM	Open End	US Equity Mid Cap (Growth & Income)	C	C-	C+		Y	10,000,000
Invesco Asia Pacific Growth Fund Class A	ASIAX	NAS CM	Open End	Asia ex-Japan Equity (Pacific Stock)	C+	C	B	Up	Y	1,000
Invesco Asia Pacific Growth Fund Class C	ASICX	NAS CM	Open End	Asia ex-Japan Equity (Pacific Stock)	C+	C	B	Up	Y	1,000
Invesco Asia Pacific Growth Fund Class R6	ASISX	NAS CM	Open End	Asia ex-Japan Equity (Pacific Stock)	C+	C	B	Up	Y	10,000,000
Invesco Asia Pacific Growth Fund Class Y	ASIYX	NAS CM	Open End	Asia ex-Japan Equity (Pacific Stock)	C+	C	B	Up	Y	1,000
Invesco Balanced-Risk Allocation Fund Class A	ABRZX	NAS CM	Open End	Flexible Alloc (Growth & Income)	B-	C	A-	Up	Y	1,000
Invesco Balanced-Risk Allocation Fund Class C	ABRCX	NAS CM	Open End	Flexible Alloc (Growth & Income)	B-	C	B+	Up	Y	1,000
Invesco Balanced-Risk Allocation Fund Class R	ABRRX	NAS CM	Open End	Flexible Alloc (Growth & Income)	B-	C	B+	Up	Y	0
Invesco Balanced-Risk Allocation Fund Class R6	ALLFX	NAS CM	Open End	Flexible Alloc (Growth & Income)	B-	C	A-	Up	Y	10,000,000
Invesco Balanced-Risk Allocation Fund Class Y	ABRYX	NAS CM	Open End	Flexible Alloc (Growth & Income)	B-	C	A-	Up	Y	1,000
Invesco Balanced-Risk Allocation Fund R5 Class	ABRIX	NAS CM	Open End	Flexible Alloc (Growth & Income)	B-	C	A-	Up	Y	10,000,000
Invesco Balanced-Risk Commodity Strategy Fund Class A	BRCAX	NAS CM	Open End	Commodities Broad Basket (Growth & Income)	D	D	C-	Down	Y	1,000
Invesco Balanced-Risk Commodity Strategy Fund Class C	BRCCX	NAS CM	Open End	Commodities Broad Basket (Growth & Income)	D	D	C-	Down	Y	1,000
Invesco Balanced-Risk Commodity Strategy Fund Class R	BRCRX	NAS CM	Open End	Commodities Broad Basket (Growth & Income)	D	D	C-	Down	Y	0

★ Expanded analysis of this fund is included in Section II.

	TOTAL RETURNS					PERFORMANCE				ASSETS		ASSET ALLOCATION & TURNOVER					BULL & BEAR		FEES		
Min Additional Investment	3-Month Total Return	6-Month Total Return	1-Year Total Return	3-Year Total Return	5-Year Total Return	Dividend Yield (TTM)	Expense Ratio	3-Yr Std Deviation	3-Year Beta	NAV	Total Assets (MIL)	%Cash	%Stocks	%Bonds	%Other	Turnover Ratio	Last Bull Market Total Return	Last Bear Market Total Return	Front End Fee (%)	Back End Fee (%)	Inception Date
50	1.69	13.72	13.14	28.21	50.96	3.13	0.7	9.88	0.69	14.06	135.1	0	100	0	0						Aug-16
50	-0.28	18.69	-1.97	38.88		4.7	1.05	15.99	0.94	10.95	5.9	0	100	0	0				5.00		May-16
50	-0.45	18.28	-2.74	35.69		3.95	1.8	15.98	0.94	10.92	5.9	0	100	0	0					1.00	May-16
50	-0.22	18.80	-1.72	39.86		4.94	0.8	16.02	0.94	10.95	5.9	0	100	0	0						Aug-16
50	5.25	19.45	16.63	47.63	44.07	0.53	1.25	12.36	0.99	58.27	38.7	0	100	0	0		24.44	-20.89	5.00		Jan-95
50	5.13	19.18	16.13	45.01	39.71	0.74	2	12.36	0.99	57.71	38.7	0	100	0	0		23.9	-21.13		1.00	Aug-15
50	5.32	19.60	16.92	48.78	45.20	0.76	1	12.36	0.99	58.32	38.7	0	100	0	0		24.44	-20.89			Aug-16
100	0.12	5.48	-6.75	6.55	6.36	2.26	1.16	7.41	0.54	10.49	141.5	4	64	28	0	46	13.23	-9.52			Apr-10
100	0.05	5.45	-6.94	5.77	5.10	2.06	1.41	7.43	0.54	10.48	141.5	4	64	28	0	46	13	-9.56			Jan-05
100	0.78	3.07	-0.90	1.72	-0.06	0.56	1.16	4.06	0.14	14.08	89.8	39	36	21	3	44	13.63	-10.55			Nov-09
100	0.73	3.00	-1.05	1.04	-1.23	0.52	1.38	4.01	0.14	13.71	89.8	39	36	21	3	44	13.5	-10.6			Oct-05
100	1.54	9.49	-8.42	4.26		0.96	1.4	9.19	0.52	8.53	14.3	12	76	6	0	55					Dec-14
500	0.00	5.66	8.17			0	2.73			11.2	219.7	75	25	0	0	106					Jun-17
500	0.00	5.49	7.91			0	2.98			11.14	219.7	75	25	0	0	106					Jun-17
500	0.00	5.66	8.17				2.48			11.2	219.7	75	25	0	0	106					May-19
50	-1.54	-9.52	-6.40	-11.03	-1.30	0	1.51	7.78	35.96	7.03	68.3	101	-1	0	0	125			5.50		Dec-13
50	-1.75	-9.82	-7.06	-13.00	-4.87	0	2.26	7.81	35.63	6.7	68.3	101	-1	0	0	125				1.00	Dec-13
	-1.70	-9.54	-6.50	-11.64	-2.52	0	1.76	7.79	36.22	6.92	68.3	101	-1	0	0	125					Dec-13
	-1.51	-9.36	-6.07	-10.10	0.12	0	1.13	7.73	34.74	7.16	68.3	101	-1	0	0	125					Dec-13
	-1.37	-9.25	-5.94	-10.08	0.15	0	1.13	7.75	36.63	7.16	68.3	101	-1	0	0	125					Dec-13
50	-1.51	-9.27	-6.08	-10.32	-0.11	0	1.26	7.81	35.02	7.14	68.3	101	-1	0	0	125					Dec-13
50	-0.65	1.00	-2.63	3.53		1.37	1.44	3.59	33.02	9.04	3.5	28	18	41	12	30			5.50		Oct-14
50	-0.77	0.67	-3.33	1.25		0.49	2.19	3.55	32.42	8.95	3.5	28	18	41	12	30				1.00	Oct-14
	-0.66	0.89	-2.93	2.80		1.08	1.69	3.55	32.48	9.01	3.5	28	18	41	12	30					Oct-14
	-0.54	1.11	-2.40	4.30		1.58	1.19	3.58	32.53	9.07	3.5	28	18	41	12	30					Oct-14
	-0.54	1.11	-2.40	4.30		1.58	1.19	3.54	32.25	9.07	3.5	28	18	41	12	30					Oct-14
50	-0.54	1.11	-2.40	4.30		1.58	1.19	3.5	32.12	9.08	3.5	28	18	41	12	30					Oct-14
50	4.96	23.48	7.16	60.69	66.68	0	1.01	15.27	1.1	21.14	10,922	0	100	0	0	44	23.17	-19.31	5.50		Jun-05
50	4.76	23.03	6.40	57.22	60.50	0	1.76	15.25	1.1	19.12	10,922	0	100	0	0	44	22.65	-19.61		1.00	Jun-05
	4.88	23.31	6.92	59.61	64.60	0	1.26	15.27	1.1	20.63	10,922	0	100	0	0	44	23	-19.48			May-11
	5.03	23.71	7.56	62.71	70.21	0	0.62	15.28	1.1	21.91	10,922	0	100	0	0	44	23.32	-19.28			Sep-12
50	5.03	23.57	7.43	61.96	68.74	0	0.76	15.26	1.1	21.7	10,922	0	100	0	0	44	23.32	-19.28			Jun-05
	5.06	23.69	7.51	62.32	69.52	0	0.71	15.28	1.1	21.77	10,922	0	100	0	0	44	23.39	-19.2			Dec-10
50	2.05	17.27	-3.74	27.02	18.71	0.38	1.19	16.66	1.23	33.2	1,106	2	98	0	0	44	32.64	-21.77	5.50		Oct-93
50	1.88	16.86	-4.43	24.28	14.48	0	1.92	16.65	1.23	26.47	1,106	2	98	0	0	44	32.03	-21.97		1.00	Oct-93
	2.00	17.16	-3.95	26.07	17.28	0	1.44	16.66	1.23	33.04	1,106	2	98	0	0	44	32.4	-21.85			Mar-07
	2.16	17.53	-3.34	28.62	21.35	0.87	0.77	16.67	1.23	33.51	1,106	2	98	0	0	44	32.64	-21.77			Sep-12
50	2.13	17.39	-3.50	27.94	20.21	0.66	0.94	16.66	1.23	33.47	1,106	2	98	0	0	44	32.82	-21.69			Feb-06
	2.16	17.50	-3.40	28.35	20.85	0.76	0.86	16.68	1.23	33.5	1,106	2	98	0	0	44	33	-21.58			Jun-10
50	0.60	13.12	7.32	31.07	30.44	0.97	1.46	11.74	0.84	33.1	763.5	11	89	0	0	21	24.53	-19.8	5.50		Nov-97
50	0.39	12.69	6.54	28.14	25.61	0.23	2.21	11.72	0.84	30.28	763.5	11	89	0	0	21	24.04	-20.08		1.00	Nov-97
	0.69	13.36	7.78	32.30	31.67	1.44	1.03	11.72	0.84	33.16	763.5	11	89	0	0	21	24.53	-19.8			Apr-17
50	0.66	13.24	7.60	32.04	32.06	1.24	1.21	11.73	0.84	33.17	763.5	11	89	0	0	21	24.75	-19.72			Oct-08
50	2.10	10.62	3.33	14.79	17.98	0	1.31	5.93	0.35	11.14	3,369	-74	43	108	23	116	11.89	1.39	5.50		Jun-09
50	1.93	10.14	2.53	12.23	13.57	0	2.06	5.92	0.35	10.53	3,369	-74	43	108	23	116	11.45	1.05		1.00	Jun-09
	2.05	10.52	3.11	13.88	16.49	0	1.56	5.95	0.35	10.92	3,369	-74	43	108	23	116	11.78	1.31			Jun-09
	2.24	10.80	3.73	16.07	20.26	0	0.96	5.93	0.35	11.38	3,369	-74	43	108	23	116	12.01	1.56			Sep-12
50	2.16	10.74	3.56	15.62	19.42	0	1.06	5.91	0.35	11.34	3,369	-74	43	108	23	116	12.01	1.56			Jun-09
	2.25	10.82	3.74	15.79	19.77	0	1.02	5.92	0.35	11.36	3,369	-74	43	108	23	116	12.01	1.56			Jun-09
50	-2.03	2.11	-8.58	-9.27	-29.36	0.15	1.4	9.08	0.88	6.27	1,448	59	0	18	23	96	14.37	-17.17	5.50		Nov-10
50	-2.31	1.54	-9.30	-11.28	-31.99	0.03	2.15	9.09	0.87	5.92	1,448	59	0	18	23	96	13.94	-17.47		1.00	Nov-10
	-2.06	1.81	-8.74	-9.95	-30.20	0.11	1.65	9.12	0.88	6.17	1,448	59	0	18	23	96	14.38	-17.26			Nov-10

	MARKET			FUND TYPE, CATEGORY & OBJECTIVE	RATINGS				MINIMUMS	
Fund Name	Ticker Symbol	Traded On	Fund Type	Category and (Prospectus Objective)	Overall Rating	Reward Rating	Risk Rating	Recent Up/ Downgrade	Open to New Investors	Min Initial Investment
Invesco Balanced-Risk Commodity Strategy Fund Class R6	IBRFX	NAS CM	Open End	Commodities Broad Basket (Growth & Income)	D	D	C-	Down	Y	10,000,000
Invesco Balanced-Risk Commodity Strategy Fund Class Y	BRCYX	NAS CM	Open End	Commodities Broad Basket (Growth & Income)	D	D	C-	Down	Y	1,000
Invesco Balanced-Risk Commodity Strategy Fund R5 Class	BRCNX	NAS CM	Open End	Commodities Broad Basket (Growth & Income)	D	D	C-	Down	Y	10,000,000
Invesco Balanced-Risk Retirement 2020 Fund Class A	AFTAX	NAS CM	Open End	Target Date (Asset Alloc)	B-	C	A-	Up	Y	1,000
Invesco Balanced-Risk Retirement 2020 Fund Class AX	VRCAX	NAS CM	Open End	Target Date (Asset Alloc)	B-	C	A-	Up		1,000
Invesco Balanced-Risk Retirement 2020 Fund Class C	AFTCX	NAS CM	Open End	Target Date (Asset Alloc)	C+	C	B+	Up	Y	1,000
Invesco Balanced-Risk Retirement 2020 Fund Class CX	VRCCX	NAS CM	Open End	Target Date (Asset Alloc)	C+	C	B+	Up		1,000
Invesco Balanced-Risk Retirement 2020 Fund Class R	ATFRX	NAS CM	Open End	Target Date (Asset Alloc)	B-	C	B+	Up	Y	0
Invesco Balanced-Risk Retirement 2020 Fund Class R6	VRCFX	NAS CM	Open End	Target Date (Asset Alloc)	B-	C	A-		Y	10,000,000
Invesco Balanced-Risk Retirement 2020 Fund Class RX	VRCRX	NAS CM	Open End	Target Date (Asset Alloc)	B-	C	B+	Up		0
Invesco Balanced-Risk Retirement 2020 Fund Class Y	AFTYX	NAS CM	Open End	Target Date (Asset Alloc)	B-	C	A-		Y	1,000
Invesco Balanced-Risk Retirement 2020 Fund R5 Class	AFTSX	NAS CM	Open End	Target Date (Asset Alloc)	B-	C	A-		Y	10,000,000
Invesco Balanced-Risk Retirement 2030 Fund Class A	TNAAX	NAS CM	Open End	Target Date (Asset Alloc)	B-	C	A-	Up	Y	1,000
Invesco Balanced-Risk Retirement 2030 Fund Class AX	VREAX	NAS CM	Open End	Target Date (Asset Alloc)	B-	C	A-	Up		1,000
Invesco Balanced-Risk Retirement 2030 Fund Class C	TNACX	NAS CM	Open End	Target Date (Asset Alloc)	B-	C	B+	Up	Y	1,000
Invesco Balanced-Risk Retirement 2030 Fund Class CX	VRECX	NAS CM	Open End	Target Date (Asset Alloc)	B-	C	B+	Up		1,000
Invesco Balanced-Risk Retirement 2030 Fund Class R	TNARX	NAS CM	Open End	Target Date (Asset Alloc)	B-	C	B+	Up	Y	0
Invesco Balanced-Risk Retirement 2030 Fund Class R6	TNAFX	NAS CM	Open End	Target Date (Asset Alloc)	B-	C	A-	Up	Y	10,000,000
Invesco Balanced-Risk Retirement 2030 Fund Class RX	VRERX	NAS CM	Open End	Target Date (Asset Alloc)	B-	C	B+	Up		0
Invesco Balanced-Risk Retirement 2030 Fund Class Y	TNAYX	NAS CM	Open End	Target Date (Asset Alloc)	B-	C	A-	Up	Y	1,000
Invesco Balanced-Risk Retirement 2030 Fund R5 Class	TNAIX	NAS CM	Open End	Target Date (Asset Alloc)	B-	C	A-	Up	Y	10,000,000
Invesco Balanced-Risk Retirement 2040 Fund Class A	TNDAX	NAS CM	Open End	Target Date (Asset Alloc)	B-	C	B+	Up	Y	1,000
Invesco Balanced-Risk Retirement 2040 Fund Class AX	VRGAX	NAS CM	Open End	Target Date (Asset Alloc)	B-	C	B+	Up		1,000
Invesco Balanced-Risk Retirement 2040 Fund Class C	TNDCX	NAS CM	Open End	Target Date (Asset Alloc)	B-	C	B+	Up	Y	1,000
Invesco Balanced-Risk Retirement 2040 Fund Class CX	VRGCX	NAS CM	Open End	Target Date (Asset Alloc)	B-	C	B+	Up		1,000
Invesco Balanced-Risk Retirement 2040 Fund Class R	TNDRX	NAS CM	Open End	Target Date (Asset Alloc)	B-	C	B+	Up	Y	0
Invesco Balanced-Risk Retirement 2040 Fund Class R6	TNDFX	NAS CM	Open End	Target Date (Asset Alloc)	B-	C	B+	Up	Y	10,000,000
Invesco Balanced-Risk Retirement 2040 Fund Class RX	VRGRX	NAS CM	Open End	Target Date (Asset Alloc)	B-	C	B+	Up		0
Invesco Balanced-Risk Retirement 2040 Fund Class Y	TNDYX	NAS CM	Open End	Target Date (Asset Alloc)	B-	C	B+	Up	Y	1,000
Invesco Balanced-Risk Retirement 2040 Fund R5 Class	TNDIX	NAS CM	Open End	Target Date (Asset Alloc)	B-	C	B+	Up	Y	10,000,000
Invesco Balanced-Risk Retirement 2050 Fund Class A	TNEAX	NAS CM	Open End	Target Date (Asset Alloc)	B-	C	B+	Up	Y	1,000
Invesco Balanced-Risk Retirement 2050 Fund Class AX	VRIAX	NAS CM	Open End	Target Date (Asset Alloc)	B-	C	B+	Up		1,000
Invesco Balanced-Risk Retirement 2050 Fund Class C	TNECX	NAS CM	Open End	Target Date (Asset Alloc)	B-	C	B	Up	Y	1,000
Invesco Balanced-Risk Retirement 2050 Fund Class CX	VRICX	NAS CM	Open End	Target Date (Asset Alloc)	B-	C	B	Up		1,000
Invesco Balanced-Risk Retirement 2050 Fund Class R	TNERX	NAS CM	Open End	Target Date (Asset Alloc)	B-	C	B+	Up	Y	0
Invesco Balanced-Risk Retirement 2050 Fund Class R5	TNEIX	NAS CM	Open End	Target Date (Asset Alloc)	B-	C	B+	Up	Y	10,000,000
Invesco Balanced-Risk Retirement 2050 Fund Class R6	TNEFX	NAS CM	Open End	Target Date (Asset Alloc)	B-	C	B+	Up	Y	10,000,000
Invesco Balanced-Risk Retirement 2050 Fund Class RX	VRIRX	NAS CM	Open End	Target Date (Asset Alloc)	B-	C	B+	Up		0
Invesco Balanced-Risk Retirement 2050 Fund Class Y	TNEYX	NAS CM	Open End	Target Date (Asset Alloc)	B-	C	B+	Up	Y	1,000
Invesco Balanced-Risk Retirement Now Fund Class A	IANAX	NAS CM	Open End	Target Date (Asset Alloc)	B-	C	A-	Up	Y	1,000
Invesco Balanced-Risk Retirement Now Fund Class AX	VIRAX	NAS CM	Open End	Target Date (Asset Alloc)	B-	C	A-	Up		1,000
Invesco Balanced-Risk Retirement Now Fund Class C	IANCX	NAS CM	Open End	Target Date (Asset Alloc)	C+	C	B+	Up	Y	1,000
Invesco Balanced-Risk Retirement Now Fund Class CX	VIRCX	NAS CM	Open End	Target Date (Asset Alloc)	B-	C	B+	Up		1,000
Invesco Balanced-Risk Retirement Now Fund Class R	IANRX	NAS CM	Open End	Target Date (Asset Alloc)	B-	C	B+	Up	Y	0
Invesco Balanced-Risk Retirement Now Fund Class R6	IANFX	NAS CM	Open End	Target Date (Asset Alloc)	B-	C	A-		Y	10,000,000
Invesco Balanced-Risk Retirement Now Fund Class RX	VIRRX	NAS CM	Open End	Target Date (Asset Alloc)	B-	C	B+	Up		0
Invesco Balanced-Risk Retirement Now Fund Class Y	IANYX	NAS CM	Open End	Target Date (Asset Alloc)	B-	C	A-		Y	1,000
Invesco Balanced-Risk Retirement Now Fund R5 Class	IANIX	NAS CM	Open End	Target Date (Asset Alloc)	B-	C	A-		Y	10,000,000
Invesco Charter Fund Class A	CHTRX	NAS CM	Open End	US Equity Large Cap Blend (Growth)	C+	C	B		Y	1,000
Invesco Charter Fund Class C	CHTCX	NAS CM	Open End	US Equity Large Cap Blend (Growth)	C+	C	B		Y	1,000
Invesco Charter Fund Class R	CHRRX	NAS CM	Open End	US Equity Large Cap Blend (Growth)	C+	C	B		Y	0
Invesco Charter Fund Class R6	CHFTX	NAS CM	Open End	US Equity Large Cap Blend (Growth)	C+	C	B		Y	10,000,000

★ Expanded analysis of this fund is included in Section II.

Min Additional Investment	TOTAL RETURNS: 3-Month Total Return	6-Month Total Return	1-Year Total Return	3-Year Total Return	5-Year Total Return	PERFORMANCE: Dividend Yield (TTM)	Expense Ratio	3-Yr Std Deviation	3-Year Beta	ASSETS: NAV	Total Assets (MIL)	ASSET ALLOCATION & TURNOVER: %Cash	%Stocks	%Bonds	%Other	Turnover Ratio	BULL & BEAR: Last Bull Market Total Return	Last Bear Market Total Return	FEES: Front End Fee (%)	Back End Fee (%)	Inception Date
	-1.97	2.22	-8.20	-8.19	-27.82	0.33	1.12	9.01	0.87	6.44	1,448	59	0	18	23	96	14.73	-17.06			Sep-12
50	-1.99	2.23	-8.35	-8.58	-28.51	0.22	1.15	9.08	0.88	6.4	1,448	59	0	18	23	96	14.73	-17.06			Nov-10
	-1.98	2.06	-8.29	-8.48	-28.15	0.26	1.15	9.12	0.88	6.42	1,448	59	0	18	23	96	14.85	-17.14			Nov-10
50	1.55	7.15	2.88	11.62	14.24	1.64	0.89	4.03		9.13	46.3	-11	21	74	16	0	11.09	1.47	5.50		Jan-07
50	1.55	7.15	2.88	11.75	14.24	1.64	0.89	4.05		9.13	46.3	-11	21	74	16	0	11.09	1.47	5.50		Jun-10
50	1.36	6.82	2.01	9.29	10.20	1.68	1.64	4.06		8.92	46.3	-11	21	74	16	0	10.72	1.03		1.00	Jan-07
50	1.36	6.82	2.13	9.29	10.08	1.68	1.64	4.09		8.92	46.3	-11	21	74	16	0	10.6	1.15		1.00	Jun-10
	1.45	7.09	2.55	10.86	12.93	1.65	1.14	4.06		9.06	46.3	-11	21	74	16	0	11.01	1.25			Jan-07
	1.65	7.33	3.19	12.47	15.64	1.62	0.64	4.02		9.22	46.3	-11	21	74	16	0	11.29	1.58			Sep-12
	1.45	6.96	2.55	10.86	12.93	1.65	1.14	4.04		9.06	46.3	-11	21	74	16	0	11.01	1.25			Jun-10
50	1.66	7.38	3.10	12.43	15.73	1.63	0.64	4.04		9.16	46.3	-11	21	74	16	0	11.34	1.47			Oct-08
	1.65	7.33	3.19	12.60	15.89	1.62	0.64	4.06		9.22	46.3	-11	21	74	16	0	11.29	1.58			Jan-07
50	2.22	10.78	3.53	15.55	19.45	2.44	1.11	6.08		8.73	56.5	-71	33	114	25	3	11.79	1.43	5.50		Jan-07
50	2.22	10.77	3.52	15.54	19.56	2.44	1.11	6.08		8.74	56.5	-71	33	114	25	3	11.78	1.43	5.50		Jun-10
50	1.90	10.33	2.62	13.17	15.21	2.5	1.86	6.04		8.54	56.5	-71	33	114	25	3	11.29	1.08		1.00	Jan-07
50	2.02	10.46	2.74	13.31	15.35	2.49	1.86	6.1		8.55	56.5	-71	33	114	25	3	11.29	1.08		1.00	Jun-10
	2.12	10.61	3.19	14.77	18.01	2.46	1.36	6.07		8.65	56.5	-71	33	114	25	3	11.6	1.31			Jan-07
	2.32	10.95	3.74	16.44	20.91	2.42	0.86	6.07		8.81	56.5	-71	33	114	25	3	11.98	1.54			Sep-12
	2.12	10.61	3.20	14.92	18.16	2.46	1.36	6.04		8.65	56.5	-71	33	114	25	3	11.48	1.44			Jun-10
50	2.21	10.99	3.75	16.36	20.95	2.43	0.86	6.1		8.78	56.5	-71	33	114	25	3	12.01	1.42			Oct-08
	2.32	10.95	3.74	16.44	20.90	2.42	0.86	6.03		8.81	56.5	-71	33	114	25	3	11.98	1.54			Jan-07
50	2.45	12.46	3.81	17.58	22.39	2.82	1.14	7.03		7.94	42.2	-86	37	126	24	6	11.84	1.37	5.50		Jan-07
50	2.45	12.48	3.82	17.61	22.41	2.82	1.14	7.07		7.93	42.2	-86	37	126	24	6	11.86	1.37	5.50		Jun-10
50	2.23	12.13	3.09	15.34	18.25	2.88	1.89	7.02		7.76	42.2	-86	37	126	24	6	11.37	1.13		1.00	Jan-07
50	2.24	12.01	3.10	15.22	18.13	2.89	1.89	7.1		7.74	42.2	-86	37	126	24	6	11.24	1.13		1.00	Jun-10
	2.47	12.42	3.58	16.95	21.06	2.84	1.39	7.07		7.87	42.2	-86	37	126	24	6	11.64	1.25			Jan-07
	2.43	12.51	4.05	18.36	23.87	2.8	0.89	7.09		8	42.2	-86	37	126	24	6	11.92	1.49			Sep-12
	2.34	12.42	3.58	16.79	20.91	2.84	1.39	7.07		7.87	42.2	-86	37	126	24	6	11.77	1.25			Jun-10
50	2.56	12.69	4.06	18.55	23.92	2.8	0.89	7.05		7.99	42.2	-86	37	126	24	6	11.8	1.61			Oct-08
	2.56	12.67	4.05	18.37	23.87	2.8	0.89	7.01		8	42.2	-86	37	126	24	6	11.92	1.49			Jan-07
50	2.63	14.05	4.20	19.65	25.15	1.59	1.16	8.04		7.79	31.5	-101	40	138	23	10	11.63	1.52	5.50		Jan-07
50	2.63	14.03	4.19	19.62	25.13	1.58	1.16	8		7.8	31.5	-101	40	138	23	10	11.75	1.4	5.50		Jun-10
50	2.56	13.77	3.33	17.30	20.80	1.63	1.91	7.97		7.6	31.5	-101	40	138	23	10	11.28	1.15		1.00	Jan-07
50	2.56	13.77	3.46	17.31	20.96	1.63	1.91	7.95		7.6	31.5	-101	40	138	23	10	11.15	1.15		1.00	Jun-10
	2.65	14.03	3.96	18.88	23.86	1.6	1.41	7.95		7.72	31.5	-101	40	138	23	10	11.46	1.4			Jan-07
	2.74	14.26	4.30	20.39	26.75	1.57	0.91	7.91		7.85	31.5	-101	40	138	23	10	11.93	1.52			Jan-07
	2.87	14.39	4.56	20.51	26.73	1.57	0.91	7.99		7.87	31.5	-101	40	138	23	10	11.93	1.52			Sep-12
	2.65	14.01	3.96	18.87	23.85	1.6	1.41	7.99		7.73	31.5	-101	40	138	23	10	11.59	1.27			Jun-10
50	2.88	14.26	4.44	20.57	26.79	1.57	0.91	7.99		7.85	31.5	-101	40	138	23	10	11.81	1.52			Oct-08
50	1.56	6.82	2.99	10.48	12.44	0.3	0.83	3.6		8.45	18.9	-4	20	69	15	1	7.07	0.92	5.50		Jan-07
50	1.56	6.83	2.99	10.49	12.58	0.3	0.83	3.6		8.44	18.9	-4	20	69	15	1	7.08	0.8	5.50		Jun-10
50	1.38	6.32	2.15	8.04	8.52	0.12	1.58	3.57		8.07	18.9	-4	20	69	15	1	6.58	0.57		1.00	Jan-07
50	1.38	6.46	2.28	8.18	8.65	0.12	1.58	3.65		8.07	18.9	-4	20	69	15	1	6.47	0.57		1.00	Jun-10
	1.46	6.53	2.59	9.68	10.93	0.24	1.08	3.58		8.32	18.9	-4	20	69	15	1	6.83	0.8			Jan-07
	1.53	6.85	3.14	11.16	13.84	0.36	0.58	3.59		8.57	18.9	-4	20	69	15	1	7.19	1.03			Sep-12
	1.46	6.66	2.72	9.69	11.19	0.24	1.08	3.58		8.32	18.9	-4	20	69	15	1	6.84	0.69			Jun-10
50	1.53	6.84	3.14	11.28	13.84	0.36	0.58	3.56		8.58	18.9	-4	20	69	15	1	7.19	1.03			Oct-08
	1.53	6.85	3.14	11.16	13.72	0.36	0.58	3.56		8.57	18.9	-4	20	69	15	1	7.19	1.03			Jan-07
50	4.09	18.98	7.09	29.15	24.43	0.35	1.08	12.73	1	17.3	3,245	0	100	0	0	46	18.22	-15.11	5.50		Nov-68
50	3.88	18.52	6.29	26.26	19.86	0	1.83	12.71	1	16.06	3,245	0	100	0	0	46	17.78	-15.44		1.00	Aug-97
	4.06	18.84	6.83	28.24	22.87	0	1.33	12.7	1	17.15	3,245	0	100	0	0	46	18.07	-15.26			Jun-02
	4.18	19.16	7.46	30.63	26.91	0.71	0.7	12.74	1	18.17	3,245	0	100	0	0	46	18.22	-15.11			Sep-12

	MARKET			FUND TYPE, CATEGORY & OBJECTIVE	RATINGS				MINIMUMS	
Fund Name	Ticker Symbol	Traded On	Fund Type	Category and (Prospectus Objective)	Overall Rating	Reward Rating	Risk Rating	Recent Up/ Downgrade	Open to New Investors	Min Initial Investment
Invesco Charter Fund Class S	CHRSX	NAS CM	Open End	US Equity Large Cap Blend (Growth)	C+	C	B		Y	0
Invesco Charter Fund Class Y	CHTYX	NAS CM	Open End	US Equity Large Cap Blend (Growth)	C+	C	B		Y	1,000
Invesco Charter Fund R5 Class	CHTVX	NAS CM	Open End	US Equity Large Cap Blend (Growth)	C+	C	B		Y	10,000,000
Invesco Comstock Fund Class A	ACSTX	NAS CM	Open End	US Equity Large Cap Value (Growth & Income)	C+	C	B	Up	Y	1,000
Invesco Comstock Fund Class C	ACSYX	NAS CM	Open End	US Equity Large Cap Value (Growth & Income)	C	C	B-		Y	1,000
Invesco Comstock Fund Class R	ACSRX	NAS CM	Open End	US Equity Large Cap Value (Growth & Income)	C+	C	B-	Up	Y	0
Invesco Comstock Fund Class R6	ICSFX	NAS CM	Open End	US Equity Large Cap Value (Growth & Income)	C+	C	B	Up	Y	10,000,000
Invesco Comstock Fund Class Y	ACSDX	NAS CM	Open End	US Equity Large Cap Value (Growth & Income)	C+	C	B	Up	Y	1,000
Invesco Comstock Fund R5 Class	ACSHX	NAS CM	Open End	US Equity Large Cap Value (Growth & Income)	C+	C	B	Up	Y	10,000,000
Invesco Conservative Allocation Fund Class A	CAAMX	NAS CM	Open End	Cautious Alloc (Asset Alloc)	B-	C	A-		Y	1,000
Invesco Conservative Allocation Fund Class C	CACMX	NAS CM	Open End	Cautious Alloc (Asset Alloc)	B-	C	B+	Up	Y	1,000
Invesco Conservative Allocation Fund Class R	CMARX	NAS CM	Open End	Cautious Alloc (Asset Alloc)	B-	C	A-	Up	Y	0
Invesco Conservative Allocation Fund Class R6	CNSSX	NAS CM	Open End	Cautious Alloc (Asset Alloc)	B	C+	A-	Up	Y	10,000,000
Invesco Conservative Allocation Fund Class S	CMASX	NAS CM	Open End	Cautious Alloc (Asset Alloc)	B	C	A-	Up	Y	0
Invesco Conservative Allocation Fund Class Y	CAAYX	NAS CM	Open End	Cautious Alloc (Asset Alloc)	B	C+	A-	Up	Y	1,000
Invesco Conservative Allocation Fund R5 Class	CMAIX	NAS CM	Open End	Cautious Alloc (Asset Alloc)	B	C+	A-	Up	Y	10,000,000
Invesco Convertible Securities Fund Class A	CNSAX	NAS CM	Open End	Convertibles (Convertible Bond)	B-	C	B+	Down	Y	1,000
Invesco Convertible Securities Fund Class C	CNSCX	NAS CM	Open End	Convertibles (Convertible Bond)	B-	C	B+		Y	1,000
Invesco Convertible Securities Fund Class R6	CNSFX	NAS CM	Open End	Convertibles (Convertible Bond)	B-	C	B+	Down	Y	10,000,000
Invesco Convertible Securities Fund Class Y	CNSDX	NAS CM	Open End	Convertibles (Convertible Bond)	B-	C	B+	Down	Y	1,000
Invesco Convertible Securities Fund R5 Shares	CNSIX	NAS CM	Open End	Convertibles (Convertible Bond)	B-	C	B+	Down	Y	10,000,000
Invesco Developing Markets Fund Class A	GTDDX	NAS CM	Open End	Global Emerg Mkts (Div Emerging Mkts)	C	C	C+			1,000
Invesco Developing Markets Fund Class C	GTDCX	NAS CM	Open End	Global Emerg Mkts (Div Emerging Mkts)	C	C	C+			1,000
Invesco Developing Markets Fund Class R6	GTDFX	NAS CM	Open End	Global Emerg Mkts (Div Emerging Mkts)	C	C	C+			10,000,000
Invesco Developing Markets Fund Class Y	GTDYX	NAS CM	Open End	Global Emerg Mkts (Div Emerging Mkts)	C	C	C+			1,000
Invesco Developing Markets Fund R5 Class	GTDIX	NAS CM	Open End	Global Emerg Mkts (Div Emerging Mkts)	C	C	C+			10,000,000
Invesco Diversified Dividend Fund Class A	LCEAX	NAS CM	Open End	US Equity Large Cap Value (Equity-Income)	C+	C	B	Down	Y	1,000
Invesco Diversified Dividend Fund Class C	LCEVX	NAS CM	Open End	US Equity Large Cap Value (Equity-Income)	C+	C	B		Y	1,000
Invesco Diversified Dividend Fund Class R	DDFRX	NAS CM	Open End	US Equity Large Cap Value (Equity-Income)	C+	C	B	Down	Y	0
Invesco Diversified Dividend Fund Class R6	LCEFX	NAS CM	Open End	US Equity Large Cap Value (Equity-Income)	C+	C	B	Down	Y	10,000,000
Invesco Diversified Dividend Fund Class Y	LCEYX	NAS CM	Open End	US Equity Large Cap Value (Equity-Income)	C+	C	B	Down	Y	1,000
Invesco Diversified Dividend Fund Investor Class	LCEIX	NAS CM	Open End	US Equity Large Cap Value (Equity-Income)	C+	C	B	Down	Y	1,000
Invesco Diversified Dividend Fund R5 Class	DDFIX	NAS CM	Open End	US Equity Large Cap Value (Equity-Income)	C+	C	B	Down	Y	10,000,000
Invesco Dividend Income Fund Class A	IAUTX	NAS CM	Open End	US Equity Large Cap Value (Equity-Income)	C+	C	B	Down	Y	1,000
Invesco Dividend Income Fund Class C	IUTCX	NAS CM	Open End	US Equity Large Cap Value (Equity-Income)	C+	C	B	Down	Y	1,000
Invesco Dividend Income Fund Class R6	IFUTX	NAS CM	Open End	US Equity Large Cap Value (Equity-Income)	C+	C	B	Down	Y	10,000,000
Invesco Dividend Income Fund Class Y	IAUYX	NAS CM	Open End	US Equity Large Cap Value (Equity-Income)	C+	C	B	Down	Y	1,000
Invesco Dividend Income Fund Investor Class	FSTUX	NAS CM	Open End	US Equity Large Cap Value (Equity-Income)	C+	C	B	Down		1,000
Invesco Dividend Income Fund R5 Class	FSIUX	NAS CM	Open End	US Equity Large Cap Value (Equity-Income)	C+	C	B	Down	Y	10,000,000
Invesco Emerging Markets Select Equity Fund Class A	IEMAX	NAS CM	Open End	Global Emerg Mkts (Div Emerging Mkts)	C	C-	C		Y	1,000
Invesco Emerging Markets Select Equity Fund Class C	IEMCX	NAS CM	Open End	Global Emerg Mkts (Div Emerging Mkts)	C	C-	C		Y	1,000
Invesco Emerging Markets Select Equity Fund Class R	IEMRX	NAS CM	Open End	Global Emerg Mkts (Div Emerging Mkts)	C	C-	C		Y	0
Invesco Emerging Markets Select Equity Fund Class R6	EMEFX	NAS CM	Open End	Global Emerg Mkts (Div Emerging Mkts)	C	C-	C		Y	10,000,000
Invesco Emerging Markets Select Equity Fund Class Y	IEMYX	NAS CM	Open End	Global Emerg Mkts (Div Emerging Mkts)	C	C-	C		Y	1,000
Invesco Emerging Markets Select Equity Fund R5 Class	IEMIX	NAS CM	Open End	Global Emerg Mkts (Div Emerging Mkts)	C	C-	C		Y	10,000,000
Invesco Endeavor Fund Class A	ATDAX	NAS CM	Open End	US Equity Mid Cap (Growth)	C	C-	B-		Y	1,000
Invesco Endeavor Fund Class C	ATDCX	NAS CM	Open End	US Equity Mid Cap (Growth)	C	C-	B-		Y	1,000
Invesco Endeavor Fund Class R	ATDRX	NAS CM	Open End	US Equity Mid Cap (Growth)	C	C-	B-		Y	0
Invesco Endeavor Fund Class R6	ATDFX	NAS CM	Open End	US Equity Mid Cap (Growth)	C	C	B-		Y	10,000,000
Invesco Endeavor Fund Class Y	ATDYX	NAS CM	Open End	US Equity Mid Cap (Growth)	C	C	B-		Y	1,000
Invesco Endeavor Fund R5 Class	ATDIX	NAS CM	Open End	US Equity Mid Cap (Growth)	C	C	B-		Y	10,000,000
Invesco Energy Fund Class A	IENAX	NAS CM	Open End	Energy Sector Equity (Natl Res)	D	D	D	Down	Y	1,000

★ Expanded analysis of this fund is included in Section II.

	TOTAL RETURNS					PERFORMANCE				ASSETS		ASSET ALLOCATION & TURNOVER					BULL & BEAR		FEES		
Min Additional Investment	3-Month Total Return	6-Month Total Return	1-Year Total Return	3-Year Total Return	5-Year Total Return	Dividend Yield (TTM)	Expense Ratio	3-Yr Std Deviation	3-Year Beta	NAV	Total Assets (MIL)	%Cash	%Stocks	%Bonds	%Other	Turnover Ratio	Last Bull Market Total Return	Last Bear Market Total Return	Front End Fee (%)	Back End Fee (%)	Inception Date
	4.15	18.98	7.22	29.56	25.01	0.46	0.98	12.74	1	17.3	3,245	0	100	0	0	46	18.31	-15.1			Sep-09
50	4.19	19.05	7.39	30.08	25.97	0.61	0.83	12.74	1	17.37	3,245	0	100	0	0	46	18.41	-15.07			Oct-08
	4.24	19.13	7.43	30.45	26.52	0.64	0.77	12.74	1	18.18	3,245	0	100	0	0	46	18.52	-14.98			Jul-91
50	2.83	15.85	0.98	42.29	35.16	1.64	0.82	14.65	1.17	24.55	11,704	6	94	0	0	14	25.08	-20.2	5.50		Oct-68
50	2.61	15.38	0.19	39.09	30.23	0.93	1.56	14.6	1.17	24.55	11,704	6	94	0	0	14	24.52	-20.44		1.00	Oct-93
	2.77	15.76	0.73	41.28	33.52	1.4	1.07	14.62	1.17	24.56	11,704	6	94	0	0	14	24.92	-20.25			Oct-02
	2.93	16.10	1.39	44.12	38.10	2.03	0.42	14.62	1.17	24.53	11,704	6	94	0	0	14	25.08	-20.2			Sep-12
50	2.89	15.99	1.23	43.35	36.91	1.88	0.57	14.62	1.17	24.55	11,704	6	94	0	0	14	25.23	-20.1			Oct-04
	2.90	16.04	1.29	43.64	37.44	1.94	0.51	14.63	1.17	24.53	11,704	6	94	0	0	14	25.45	-20.03			Jun-10
50	2.92	10.33	6.05	16.78	16.29	2.41	1.03	4.66	0.35	11.63	297.0	-3	33	67	2	23	11.07	-4.92	5.50		Apr-05
50	2.76	9.91	5.19	14.15	12.00	1.68	1.78	4.68	0.35	11.51	297.0	-3	33	67	2	23	10.6	-5.24		1.00	Apr-05
	2.96	10.22	5.80	15.93	14.94	2.17	1.28	4.71	0.36	11.59	297.0	-3	33	67	2	23	10.91	-4.93			Apr-05
	3.08	10.56	6.36	17.88	18.14	2.7	0.74	4.69	0.36	11.68	297.0	-3	33	67	2	23	11.19	-4.71			Apr-17
	3.04	10.37	6.15	17.11	16.97	2.51	0.93	4.64	0.35	11.65	297.0	-3	33	67	2	23	11.1	-4.74			Jun-11
50	3.08	10.48	6.32	17.67	17.86	2.66	0.78	4.68	0.36	11.62	297.0	-3	33	67	2	23	11.15	-4.82			Oct-08
	3.08	10.45	6.36	17.78	18.04	2.71	0.74	4.62	0.35	11.68	297.0	-3	33	67	2	23	11.19	-4.71			Apr-05
50	4.68	16.65	8.42	33.88	26.16	1.47	0.91	8.56	0.97	24.69	1,156	2	6	0	0	62	12.57	-14.81	5.50		Jul-97
50	4.47	16.21	7.60	30.94	21.72	0.77	1.67	8.55	0.97	24.56	1,156	2	6	0	0	62	12.03	-15.04		1.00	Jul-97
	4.77	16.84	8.80	35.31	28.39	1.79	0.57	8.56	0.97	24.7	1,156	2	6	0	0	62	12.75	-14.73			Sep-12
50	4.73	16.82	8.68	34.89	27.69	1.69	0.67	8.57	0.98	24.72	1,156	2	6	0	0	62	12.75	-14.73			Jul-97
	4.75	16.80	8.71	34.98	27.93	1.72	0.65	8.56	0.97	24.7	1,156	2	6	0	0	62	12.78	-14.65			May-11
50	5.34	18.17	10.30	26.96	8.99	1.3	1.41	14	0.9	35.5	2,236	5	95	0	0	20	19.91	-20.27	5.50		Jan-94
50	5.12	17.73	9.49	24.19	5.00	0.42	2.16	14.01	0.9	34.65	2,236	5	95	0	0	20	19.38	-20.55		1.00	Mar-99
	5.41	18.39	10.75	28.51	11.27	1.79	1.01	14	0.9	35.4	2,236	5	95	0	0	20	19.91	-20.27			Sep-12
50	5.40	18.32	10.57	27.95	10.36	1.59	1.16	14.01	0.9	35.51	2,236	5	95	0	0	20	20.09	-20.18			Oct-08
	5.38	18.34	10.66	28.34	11.02	1.72	1.06	14	0.9	35.41	2,236	5	95	0	0	20	20.21	-20.13			Oct-05
50	3.28	15.92	8.68	22.88	39.25	2.4	0.81	9.25	0.73	19.9	19,194	6	94	0	0	10	21.17	-15.87	5.50		Dec-01
50	3.08	15.45	7.84	20.18	34.09	1.69	1.56	9.29	0.73	19.64	19,194	6	94	0	0	10	20.66	-16.15		1.00	Dec-01
	3.21	15.79	8.44	21.97	37.49	2.17	1.06	9.25	0.73	19.97	19,194	6	94	0	0	10	20.96	-16			Oct-05
	3.43	16.15	9.17	24.42	42.04	2.78	0.42	9.3	0.73	19.9	19,194	6	94	0	0	10	21.17	-15.87			Sep-12
50	3.39	16.11	9.00	23.85	40.97	2.64	0.56	9.3	0.73	19.92	19,194	6	94	0	0	10	21.3	-15.81			Oct-08
50	3.30	15.96	8.78	23.09	39.60	2.44	0.76	9.3	0.73	19.89	19,194	6	94	0	0	10	21.21	-15.91			Jul-05
	3.41	16.16	9.07	24.06	41.36	2.69	0.52	9.29	0.73	19.9	19,194	6	94	0	0	10	21.5	-15.8			Oct-05
50	1.58	12.34	8.37	18.87	42.51	2.53	1.02	9.18	0.67	22.58	1,453	6	94	0	0	11	7.02	0.21	5.50		Mar-02
50	1.42	11.92	7.54	16.22	37.22	1.83	1.77	9.18	0.67	22.89	1,453	6	94	0	0	11	6.55	-0.08		1.00	Feb-00
	1.68	12.54	8.77	20.21	45.16	2.88	0.65	9.18	0.67	22.6	1,453	6	94	0	0	11	6.97	0.28			Sep-12
50	1.68	12.51	8.63	19.79	44.28	2.76	0.77	9.17	0.67	22.82	1,453	6	94	0	0	11	7.17	0.34			Oct-08
50	1.62	12.33	8.37	18.85	42.51	2.53	1.02	9.17	0.67	22.81	1,453	6	94	0	0	11	6.97	0.28			Jun-86
	1.70	12.50	8.69	19.93	44.61	2.8	0.73	9.18	0.67	22.59	1,453	6	94	0	0	11	7.26	0.46			Oct-05
50	-0.92	18.80	-1.45	37.62	17.00	0.36	1.33	17.02	1.32	8.53	68.3	5	95	0	0	104	15.71		5.50		May-11
50	-0.96	18.44	-2.17	34.49	12.75	0	2.08	16.96	1.32	8.22	68.3	5	95	0	0	104	15.28			1.00	May-11
	-0.82	18.84	-1.65	36.56	15.42	0.11	1.58	16.93	1.32	8.45	68.3	5	95	0	0	104	15.46				May-11
	-0.81	19.08	-1.24	38.49	18.18	0.63	1.08	16.99	1.32	8.55	68.3	5	95	0	0	104	15.79				Sep-12
50	-0.81	19.05	-1.24	38.63	18.46	0.63	1.08	16.98	1.32	8.56	68.3	5	95	0	0	104	15.79				May-11
	-0.81	19.05	-1.24	38.64	18.46	0.63	1.08	16.98	1.32	8.56	68.3	5	95	0	0	104	15.79				May-11
50	0.88	17.49	-0.58	36.43	24.72	0	1.34	15.56	1.1	18.27	166.6	7	93	0	0	34	18.86	-18.15	5.50		Nov-03
50	0.65	16.95	-1.42	33.29	20.08	0	2.09	15.55	1.1	15.45	166.6	7	93	0	0	34	18.31	-18.38		1.00	Nov-03
	0.75	17.31	-0.89	35.36	23.10	0	1.59	15.56	1.1	17.41	166.6	7	93	0	0	34	18.69	-18.21			Apr-04
	0.97	17.73	-0.20	38.21	27.56	0	0.91	15.54	1.1	19.72	166.6	7	93	0	0	34	18.86	-18.15			Sep-12
50	0.90	17.56	-0.41	37.43	26.22	0	1.09	15.58	1.1	18.94	166.6	7	93	0	0	34	19.06	-18.04			Oct-08
	0.97	17.72	-0.29	37.91	27.01	0	0.99	15.54	1.1	19.59	166.6	7	93	0	0	34	19.23	-18			Apr-04
50	-6.71	9.63	-25.49	-20.16	-54.37	2.78	1.33	23.18	1.31	19.58	383.1	1	99	0	0	9	20.14	-31.31	5.50		Mar-02

Fund Name	MARKET Ticker Symbol	Traded On	Fund Type	FUND TYPE, CATEGORY & OBJECTIVE Category and (Prospectus Objective)	RATINGS Overall Rating	Reward Rating	Risk Rating	Recent Up/ Downgrade	MINIMUMS Open to New Investors	Min Initial Investment
Invesco Energy Fund Class C	IEFCX	NAS CM	Open End	Energy Sector Equity (Natl Res)	D	D	D	Down	Y	1,000
Invesco Energy Fund Class Y	IENYX	NAS CM	Open End	Energy Sector Equity (Natl Res)	D	D	D	Down	Y	1,000
Invesco Energy Fund Investor Class	FSTEX	NAS CM	Open End	Energy Sector Equity (Natl Res)	D	D	D	Down		1,000
Invesco Energy Fund R5 Class	IENIX	NAS CM	Open End	Energy Sector Equity (Natl Res)	D	D	D	Down	Y	10,000,000
Invesco Equally-Weighted S&P 500 Fund Class A	VADAX	NAS CM	Open End	US Equity Large Cap Blend (Growth & Income)	B-	C	B		Y	1,000
Invesco Equally-Weighted S&P 500 Fund Class C	VADCX	NAS CM	Open End	US Equity Large Cap Blend (Growth & Income)	C+	C	B		Y	1,000
Invesco Equally-Weighted S&P 500 Fund Class R	VADRX	NAS CM	Open End	US Equity Large Cap Blend (Growth & Income)	C+	C	B	Down	Y	0
Invesco Equally-Weighted S&P 500 Fund Class R6	VADFX	NAS CM	Open End	US Equity Large Cap Blend (Growth & Income)	B-	C	B		Y	10,000,000
Invesco Equally-Weighted S&P 500 Fund Class Y	VADDX	NAS CM	Open End	US Equity Large Cap Blend (Growth & Income)	B-	C	B		Y	1,000
Invesco Equity and Income Fund Class A	ACEIX	NAS CM	Open End	Moderate Alloc (Equity-Income)	B-	C	B+	Up	Y	1,000
Invesco Equity and Income Fund Class C	ACERX	NAS CM	Open End	Moderate Alloc (Equity-Income)	B-	C	B	Up	Y	1,000
Invesco Equity and Income Fund Class R	ACESX	NAS CM	Open End	Moderate Alloc (Equity-Income)	B-	C	B+	Up	Y	0
Invesco Equity and Income Fund Class R6	IEIFX	NAS CM	Open End	Moderate Alloc (Equity-Income)	B-	C	B+	Up	Y	10,000,000
Invesco Equity and Income Fund Class Y	ACETX	NAS CM	Open End	Moderate Alloc (Equity-Income)	B-	C	B+	Up	Y	1,000
Invesco Equity and Income Fund R5 Class	ACEKX	NAS CM	Open End	Moderate Alloc (Equity-Income)	B-	C	B+	Up	Y	10,000,000
Invesco European Growth Fund Class A	AEDAX	NAS CM	Open End	Europe Equity Large Cap (Europe Stock)	C	C-	B-	Up	Y	1,000
Invesco European Growth Fund Class C	AEDCX	NAS CM	Open End	Europe Equity Large Cap (Europe Stock)	C	C-	C+	Up	Y	1,000
Invesco European Growth Fund Class R	AEDRX	NAS CM	Open End	Europe Equity Large Cap (Europe Stock)	C	C-	C+	Up	Y	0
Invesco European Growth Fund Class R6	AEGSX	NAS CM	Open End	Europe Equity Large Cap (Europe Stock)	C	C-	B-		Y	10,000,000
Invesco European Growth Fund Class Y	AEDYX	NAS CM	Open End	Europe Equity Large Cap (Europe Stock)	C	C-	B-		Y	1,000
Invesco European Growth Fund Investor Class	EGINX	NAS CM	Open End	Europe Equity Large Cap (Europe Stock)	C	C-	B-			1,000
Invesco European Small Company Fund Class A	ESMAX	NAS CM	Open End	Europe Equity Large Cap (Europe Stock)	C	C	C			1,000
Invesco European Small Company Fund Class C	ESMCX	NAS CM	Open End	Europe Equity Large Cap (Europe Stock)	C	C-	C			1,000
Invesco European Small Company Fund Class R6	ESMSX	NAS CM	Open End	Europe Equity Large Cap (Europe Stock)	C	C	C+		Y	10,000,000
Invesco European Small Company Fund Class Y	ESMYX	NAS CM	Open End	Europe Equity Large Cap (Europe Stock)	C	C	C+			1,000
Invesco Exchange Fund	ACEHX	NAS CM	Open End	US Equity Large Cap Value (Growth)	B-	C	B+			0
Invesco Funds - Invesco Energy Fund Class R6	IENSX	NAS CM	Open End	Energy Sector Equity (Natl Res)	D	D	D	Down	Y	10,000,000
Invesco Global Core Equity Fund Class A	AWSAX	NAS CM	Open End	Global Equity Large Cap (World Stock)	C	C	B		Y	1,000
Invesco Global Core Equity Fund Class C	AWSCX	NAS CM	Open End	Global Equity Large Cap (World Stock)	C	C	B		Y	1,000
Invesco Global Core Equity Fund Class R6	AWSSX	NAS CM	Open End	Global Equity Large Cap (World Stock)	C	C	B		Y	10,000,000
Invesco Global Core Equity Fund Class Y	AWSYX	NAS CM	Open End	Global Equity Large Cap (World Stock)	C	C	B		Y	1,000
Invesco Global Core Equity Fund ClassR	AWSRX	NAS CM	Open End	Global Equity Large Cap (World Stock)	C	C	B		Y	0
Invesco Global Core Equity Fund R5 Class	AWSIX	NAS CM	Open End	Global Equity Large Cap (World Stock)	C	C	B		Y	10,000,000
Invesco Global Growth Fund Class A	AGGAX	NAS CM	Open End	Global Equity Large Cap (World Stock)	C+	C	B	Up	Y	1,000
Invesco Global Growth Fund Class C	AGGCX	NAS CM	Open End	Global Equity Large Cap (World Stock)	C+	C	B	Up	Y	1,000
Invesco Global Growth Fund Class R5	GGAIX	NAS CM	Open End	Global Equity Large Cap (World Stock)	C+	C	B	Up	Y	10,000,000
Invesco Global Growth Fund Class R6	AGGFX	NAS CM	Open End	Global Equity Large Cap (World Stock)	C+	C	B	Up	Y	10,000,000
Invesco Global Growth Fund Class Y	AGGYX	NAS CM	Open End	Global Equity Large Cap (World Stock)	C+	C	B	Up	Y	1,000
Invesco Global Infrastructure Fund Class A	GIZAX	NAS CM	Open End	Infrastructure Sector Equity (World Stock)	B-	B-	B	Down	Y	1,000
Invesco Global Infrastructure Fund Class C	GIZCX	NAS CM	Open End	Infrastructure Sector Equity (World Stock)	B-	C+	B		Y	1,000
Invesco Global Infrastructure Fund Class R	GIZRX	NAS CM	Open End	Infrastructure Sector Equity (World Stock)	B-	B-	B	Down	Y	0
Invesco Global Infrastructure Fund Class R5	GIZFX	NAS CM	Open End	Infrastructure Sector Equity (World Stock)	B-	B-	B	Down	Y	10,000,000
Invesco Global Infrastructure Fund Class R6	GIZSX	NAS CM	Open End	Infrastructure Sector Equity (World Stock)	B-	B-	B	Down	Y	10,000,000
Invesco Global Infrastructure Fund Class Y	GIZYX	NAS CM	Open End	Infrastructure Sector Equity (World Stock)	B-	B-	B	Down	Y	1,000
Invesco Global Low Volatility Equity Yield Fund Class A	GTNDX	NAS CM	Open End	Global Equity Mid/Small Cap (World Stock)	C	C-	B-		Y	1,000
Invesco Global Low Volatility Equity Yield Fund Class C	GNDCX	NAS CM	Open End	Global Equity Mid/Small Cap (World Stock)	C	C-	C+		Y	1,000
Invesco Global Low Volatility Equity Yield Fund Class R	GTNRX	NAS CM	Open End	Global Equity Mid/Small Cap (World Stock)	C	C-	B-		Y	0
Invesco Global Low Volatility Equity Yield Fund Class R6	GNDSX	NAS CM	Open End	Global Equity Mid/Small Cap (World Stock)	C	C-	B-		Y	10,000,000
Invesco Global Low Volatility Equity Yield Fund Class Y	GTNYX	NAS CM	Open End	Global Equity Mid/Small Cap (World Stock)	C	C-	B-		Y	1,000
Invesco Global Low Volatility Equity Yield Fund R5 Class	GNDIX	NAS CM	Open End	Global Equity Mid/Small Cap (World Stock)	C	C-	B-		Y	10,000,000
Invesco Global Market Neutral Fund Class A	MKNAX	NAS CM	Open End	Market Neutral (Growth & Income)	D	D	D		Y	1,000
Invesco Global Market Neutral Fund Class C	MKNCX	NAS CM	Open End	Market Neutral (Growth & Income)	D	D-	D		Y	1,000

★Expanded analysis of this fund is included in Section II.

	TOTAL RETURNS					PERFORMANCE				ASSETS		ASSET ALLOCATION & TURNOVER					BULL & BEAR		FEES		
Min Additional Investment	3-Month Total Return	6-Month Total Return	1-Year Total Return	3-Year Total Return	5-Year Total Return	Dividend Yield (TTM)	Expense Ratio	3-Yr Std Deviation	3-Year Beta	NAV	Total Assets (MIL)	%Cash	%Stocks	%Bonds	%Other	Turnover Ratio	Last Bull Market Total Return	Last Bear Market Total Return	Front End Fee (%)	Back End Fee (%)	Inception Date
50	-6.85	9.28	-26.05	-21.90	-56.04	2.1	2.08	23.2	1.31	16.72	383.1	1	99	0	0	9	19.64	-31.56		1.00	Feb-00
50	-6.67	9.75	-25.31	-19.55	-53.79	3.13	1.08	23.21	1.31	19.58	383.1	1	99	0	0	9	20.28	-31.24			Oct-08
50	-6.69	9.67	-25.46	-20.13	-54.35	2.79	1.33	23.2	1.31	19.5	383.1	1	99	0	0	9	20.12	-31.31			Jan-84
	-6.56	9.91	-25.15	-19.08	-53.37	3.27	0.91	23.21	1.31	20.06	383.1	1	99	0	0	9	20.41	-31.22			Jan-06
50	3.59	19.87	7.63	41.95	50.82	1.28	0.53	13.06	1.05	61.46	7,665	0	100	0	0	20	25.31	-19.88	5.50		Jul-97
50	3.40	19.40	6.81	38.83	45.44	0.66	1.21	13.05	1.05	58.63	7,665	0	100	0	0	20	24.76	-20.14		1.00	Jul-97
	3.50	19.71	7.35	40.86	48.90	1.05	0.78	13.07	1.05	61.08	7,665	0	100	0	0	20	25.06	-19.97			Mar-08
	3.68	20.10	8.03	43.53	53.67	1.61	0.16	13.08	1.05	62.2	7,665	0	100	0	0	20	25.49	-19.79			Sep-12
50	3.65	20.02	7.90	43.00	52.70	1.5	0.28	13.07	1.05	62.1	7,665	0	100	0	0	20	25.49	-19.79			Jul-97
50	3.30	13.75	3.47	29.18	30.89	1.98	0.78	10.11	0.82	10.25	13,588	7	62	23	0	129	17.71	-15.36	5.50		Aug-60
50	3.07	13.38	2.65	26.34	26.02	1.29	1.52	10.12	0.82	10.05	13,588	7	62	23	0	129	17.11	-15.57		1.00	Jul-93
	3.22	13.65	3.20	28.20	29.26	1.74	1.03	10.08	0.82	10.31	13,588	7	62	23	0	129	17.36	-15.39			Oct-02
	3.40	13.99	3.89	30.78	33.49	2.36	0.39	10.08	0.82	10.24	13,588	7	62	23	0	129	17.71	-15.36			Sep-12
50	3.36	13.89	3.73	30.17	32.54	2.22	0.53	10.16	0.82	10.25	13,588	7	62	23	0	129	17.87	-15.25			Dec-04
	3.38	13.93	3.80	30.40	32.87	2.28	0.48	10.17	0.82	10.25	13,588	7	62	23	0	129	17.79	-15.16			Jun-10
50	4.39	16.13	-0.74	23.45	8.55	1.23	1.36	11.92	0.9	38.22	1,332	7	93	0	0	16	18.22	-20.63	5.50		Nov-97
50	4.22	15.71	-1.49	20.73	4.56	0.42	2.11	11.91	0.9	35.56	1,332	7	93	0	0	16	17.71	-20.88		1.00	Nov-97
	4.35	16.02	-0.98	22.57	7.22	0.95	1.61	11.91	0.9	38.09	1,332	7	93	0	0	16	18.06	-20.73			Jun-02
	4.53	16.38	-0.35	24.51	9.48	1.65	1.01	11.92	0.9	38.28	1,332	7	93	0	0	16	18.22	-20.63			Apr-17
50	4.47	16.28	-0.49	24.41	9.94	1.52	1.11	11.93	0.9	38.28	1,332	7	93	0	0	16	18.39	-20.54			Oct-08
50	4.40	16.17	-0.67	23.71	8.84	1.3	1.31	11.93	0.9	38.13	1,332	7	93	0	0	16	18.23	-20.64			Sep-03
50	1.48	9.05	-5.30	30.13	18.82	1.96	1.39	10.18	0.73	14.33	494.0	10	86	0	4	11	14.54	-19.14	5.50		Aug-00
50	1.21	8.63	-6.00	27.21	14.38	1.14	2.14	10.21	0.73	13.34	494.0	10	86	0	4	11	14.12	-19.5		1.00	Aug-00
	1.55	9.25	-5.00	30.96	19.58	2.34	1.08	10.18	0.73	14.4	494.0	10	86	0	4	11	14.54	-19.14			Apr-17
50	1.48	9.18	-5.09	31.08	20.24	2.26	1.14	10.21	0.73	14.39	494.0	10	86	0	4	11	14.77	-19.14			Oct-08
	2.21	16.30	10.66	30.76	28.84	1.68	0.54	11.39		625.69	59.0	1	99	0	0	0	17.71	-18.62			Dec-76
	-6.61	9.92	-25.15	-19.38	-53.93	3.29	0.9	23.2	1.31	20.04	383.1	1	99	0	0	9	20.12	-31.31			Apr-17
50	2.37	15.45	0.79	29.25	20.55	1.1	1.22	12.85	1.1	14.64	759.4	1	99	0	0	30	16.23	-24.01	5.50		Dec-00
50	2.20	15.09	0.08	26.45	16.24	0.31	1.97	12.86	1.1	13.88	759.4	1	99	0	0	30	15.72	-24.19		1.00	Dec-00
	2.41	15.64	1.09	30.03	21.28	1.42	0.91	12.84	1.1	14.86	759.4	1	99	0	0	30	16.23	-24.01			Apr-17
50	2.44	15.54	0.97	30.09	22.07	1.37	0.97	12.9	1.11	14.64	759.4	1	99	0	0	30	16.32	-23.92			Oct-08
	2.30	15.29	0.55	28.26	19.03	0.83	1.47	12.88	1.1	14.62	759.4	1	99	0	0	30	16.03	-24.09			May-11
	2.48	15.64	1.03	30.23	22.42	1.36	0.97	12.86	1.1	14.86	759.4	1	99	0	0	30	16.53	-23.86			Oct-05
50	3.78	20.93	7.02	26.56	23.05	0.4	1.23	12.14	1.04	31.54	457.9	5	95	0	0	32	20.01	-19.5	5.50		Sep-94
50	3.57	20.52	6.23	23.78	18.55	0	1.98	12.14	1.04	28.66	457.9	5	95	0	0	32	19.55	-19.74		1.00	Aug-97
	3.87	21.13	7.37	27.91	25.32	0.75	0.89	12.14	1.04	31.35	457.9	5	95	0	0	32	20.32	-19.29			Sep-07
	3.84	21.14	7.37	27.87	25.37	0.75	0.89	12.12	1.04	31.34	457.9	5	95	0	0	32	20.01	-19.5			Sep-12
50	3.81	21.07	7.26	27.48	24.60	0.66	0.98	12.11	1.04	31.6	457.9	5	95	0	0	32	20.18	-19.38			Oct-08
50	4.78	21.59	11.18	28.73	21.23	1.41	1.28	10.22	1.02	11.52	20.2	1	99	0	0	114			5.50		May-14
50	4.60	21.07	10.39	25.81	16.68	0.72	2.03	10.19	1.01	11.5	20.2	1	99	0	0	114				1.00	May-14
	4.81	21.44	10.91	27.78	19.72	1.18	1.53	10.18	1.01	11.52	20.2	1	99	0	0	114					May-14
	4.93	21.84	11.55	29.67	22.86	1.64	1.03	10.18	1.01	11.53	20.2	1	99	0	0	114					May-14
	4.93	21.84	11.55	29.80	22.86	1.64	1.03	10.22	1.02	11.53	20.2	1	99	0	0	114					May-14
50	4.93	21.84	11.55	29.80	22.86	1.64	1.03	10.17	1.01	11.53	20.2	1	99	0	0	114					May-14
50	1.83	11.13	-3.35	14.63	-1.65	1.65	1.59	9.54	0.75	13.42	84.7	1	99	0	0	111	18	-18.31	5.50		Sep-97
50	1.64	10.70	-4.06	12.11	-5.25	0.91	2.34	9.55	0.75	12.69	84.7	1	99	0	0	111	17.41	-18.54		1.00	Jan-98
	1.76	10.98	-3.59	13.76	-2.92	1.4	1.84	9.55	0.75	13.44	84.7	1	99	0	0	111	17.81	-18.39			Oct-05
	1.93	11.34	-2.95	15.63	-0.78	2.07	1.2	9.56	0.75	13.58	84.7	1	99	0	0	111	18	-18.31			Apr-17
50	1.88	11.24	-3.10	15.48	-0.43	1.9	1.34	9.55	0.75	13.45	84.7	1	99	0	0	111	18.2	-18.25			Oct-08
	1.93	11.35	-2.95	15.98	0.26	2.07	1.21	9.55	0.75	13.58	84.7	1	99	0	0	111	18.44	-18.12			Apr-04
50	-4.27	-9.70	-11.25	-11.65	-14.69	3	1.5	5.3	9.92	6.05	8.3	7	93	0	0	64			5.50		Dec-13
50	-4.42	-10.16	-11.92	-13.72	-17.81	1.75	2.25	5.31	10.48	5.83	8.3	7	93	0	0	64				1.00	Dec-13

Fund Name	Ticker Symbol	Traded On	Fund Type	Category and (Prospectus Objective)	Overall Rating	Reward Rating	Risk Rating	Recent Up/ Downgrade	Open to New Investors	Min Initial Investment
	MARKET		FUND TYPE, CATEGORY & OBJECTIVE		RATINGS				MINIMUMS	
Invesco Global Market Neutral Fund Class R	**MKNRX**	NAS CM	Open End	Market Neutral (Growth & Income)	**D**	D	D		Y	0
Invesco Global Market Neutral Fund Class R5	**MKNFX**	NAS CM	Open End	Market Neutral (Growth & Income)	**D**	D	D		Y	10,000,000
Invesco Global Market Neutral Fund Class R6	**MKNSX**	NAS CM	Open End	Market Neutral (Growth & Income)	**D**	D	D		Y	10,000,000
Invesco Global Market Neutral Fund Class Y	**MKNYX**	NAS CM	Open End	Market Neutral (Growth & Income)	**D**	D	D		Y	1,000
Invesco Global Opportunities Fund Class A	**IAOPX**	NAS CM	Open End	Global Equity Large Cap (World Stock)	**C**	D+	C		Y	1,000
Invesco Global Opportunities Fund Class C	**ICOPX**	NAS CM	Open End	Global Equity Large Cap (World Stock)	**C-**	D+	C	Down	Y	1,000
Invesco Global Opportunities Fund Class R	**IROPX**	NAS CM	Open End	Global Equity Large Cap (World Stock)	**C**	D+	C		Y	0
Invesco Global Opportunities Fund Class R6	**IFOPX**	NAS CM	Open End	Global Equity Large Cap (World Stock)	**C**	C-	C		Y	10,000,000
Invesco Global Opportunities Fund Class Y	**IYOPX**	NAS CM	Open End	Global Equity Large Cap (World Stock)	**C**	C-	C		Y	1,000
Invesco Global Opportunities Fund R5 Class	**IIOPX**	NAS CM	Open End	Global Equity Large Cap (World Stock)	**C**	C-	C		Y	10,000,000
Invesco Global Real Estate Fund Class A	**AGREX**	NAS CM	Open End	Real Estate Sector Equity (Real Estate)	**B-**	C	B		Y	1,000
Invesco Global Real Estate Fund Class C	**CGREX**	NAS CM	Open End	Real Estate Sector Equity (Real Estate)	**B-**	C	B	Up	Y	1,000
Invesco Global Real Estate Fund Class R	**RGREX**	NAS CM	Open End	Real Estate Sector Equity (Real Estate)	**B-**	C	B		Y	0
Invesco Global Real Estate Fund Class R6	**FGREX**	NAS CM	Open End	Real Estate Sector Equity (Real Estate)	**B-**	C	B+		Y	10,000,000
Invesco Global Real Estate Fund Class Y	**ARGYX**	NAS CM	Open End	Real Estate Sector Equity (Real Estate)	**B-**	C	B+		Y	1,000
Invesco Global Real Estate Fund R5 Class	**IGREX**	NAS CM	Open End	Real Estate Sector Equity (Real Estate)	**B-**	C	B+		Y	10,000,000
Invesco Global Real Estate Income Fund Class A	**ASRAX**	NAS CM	Open End	Real Estate Sector Equity (Real Estate)	**B-**	C+	B+		Y	1,000
Invesco Global Real Estate Income Fund Class C	**ASRCX**	NAS CM	Open End	Real Estate Sector Equity (Real Estate)	**B-**	C	B		Y	1,000
Invesco Global Real Estate Income Fund Class R5	**ASRIX**	NAS CM	Open End	Real Estate Sector Equity (Real Estate)	**B**	C+	B+		Y	10,000,000
Invesco Global Real Estate Income Fund Class R6	**ASRFX**	NAS CM	Open End	Real Estate Sector Equity (Real Estate)	**B**	C+	B+		Y	10,000,000
Invesco Global Real Estate Income Fund Class Y	**ASRYX**	NAS CM	Open End	Real Estate Sector Equity (Real Estate)	**B**	C+	B+		Y	1,000
Invesco Global Responsibility Equity Fund Class A	**VSQAX**	NAS CM	Open End	Global Equity Large Cap (Growth)	**C**	D+	C	Up	Y	1,000
Invesco Global Responsibility Equity Fund Class C	**VSQCX**	NAS CM	Open End	Global Equity Large Cap (Growth)	**C-**	D+	C		Y	1,000
Invesco Global Responsibility Equity Fund Class R	**VSQRX**	NAS CM	Open End	Global Equity Large Cap (Growth)	**C**	D+	C	Up	Y	0
Invesco Global Responsibility Equity Fund Class R5	**VSQFX**	NAS CM	Open End	Global Equity Large Cap (Growth)	**C**	D+	C+	Up	Y	10,000,000
Invesco Global Responsibility Equity Fund Class R6	**VSQSX**	NAS CM	Open End	Global Equity Large Cap (Growth)	**C**	D+	C+	Up	Y	10,000,000
Invesco Global Responsibility Equity Fund Class Y	**VSQYX**	NAS CM	Open End	Global Equity Large Cap (Growth)	**C**	D+	C+	Up	Y	1,000
Invesco Global Small & Mid Cap Growth Fund Class A	**AGAAX**	NAS CM	Open End	Global Equity Mid/Small Cap (World Stock)	**C+**	C	B	Up	Y	1,000
Invesco Global Small & Mid Cap Growth Fund Class C	**AGACX**	NAS CM	Open End	Global Equity Mid/Small Cap (World Stock)	**C**	C	B		Y	1,000
Invesco Global Small & Mid Cap Growth Fund Class R5	**GAIIX**	NAS CM	Open End	Global Equity Mid/Small Cap (World Stock)	**C+**	C	B	Up	Y	10,000,000
Invesco Global Small & Mid Cap Growth Fund Class R6	**AGSSX**	NAS CM	Open End	Global Equity Mid/Small Cap (World Stock)	**C+**	C	B	Up	Y	10,000,000
Invesco Global Small & Mid Cap Growth Fund Class Y	**AGAYX**	NAS CM	Open End	Global Equity Mid/Small Cap (World Stock)	**C+**	C	B	Up	Y	1,000
Invesco Global Targeted Returns Fund Class A	**GLTAX**	NAS CM	Open End	Global Macro (Growth & Income)	**C-**	D	C+		Y	1,000
Invesco Global Targeted Returns Fund Class C	**GLTCX**	NAS CM	Open End	Global Macro (Growth & Income)	**D+**	D	C		Y	1,000
Invesco Global Targeted Returns Fund Class R	**GLTRX**	NAS CM	Open End	Global Macro (Growth & Income)	**C-**	D	C	Up	Y	0
Invesco Global Targeted Returns Fund Class R5	**GLTFX**	NAS CM	Open End	Global Macro (Growth & Income)	**C**	C-	C+	Up	Y	10,000,000
Invesco Global Targeted Returns Fund Class R6	**GLTSX**	NAS CM	Open End	Global Macro (Growth & Income)	**C**	C-	C+	Up	Y	10,000,000
Invesco Global Targeted Returns Fund Class Y	**GLTYX**	NAS CM	Open End	Global Macro (Growth & Income)	**C**	C-	C+	Up	Y	1,000
Invesco Gold & Precious Metals Fund Class R6	**IGDSX**	NAS CM	Open End	Precious Metals Sector Equity (Precious Metals)	**D**	D	D+	Down	Y	10,000,000
Invesco Gold and Precious Metals Fund Class A	**IGDAX**	NAS CM	Open End	Precious Metals Sector Equity (Precious Metals)	**D**	D	D	Down	Y	1,000
Invesco Gold and Precious Metals Fund Class C	**IGDCX**	NAS CM	Open End	Precious Metals Sector Equity (Precious Metals)	**D**	D	D	Down	Y	1,000
Invesco Gold and Precious Metals Fund Class Investor	**FGLDX**	NAS CM	Open End	Precious Metals Sector Equity (Precious Metals)	**D**	D	D	Down		1,000
Invesco Gold and Precious Metals Fund Class Y	**IGDYX**	NAS CM	Open End	Precious Metals Sector Equity (Precious Metals)	**D**	D	D+	Down	Y	1,000
Invesco Greater China Fund Class A	**AACFX**	NAS CM	Open End	Greater China Equity (Pacific Stock)	**C**	C-	C+		Y	1,000
Invesco Greater China Fund Class C	**CACFX**	NAS CM	Open End	Greater China Equity (Pacific Stock)	**C**	C-	C+		Y	1,000
Invesco Greater China Fund Class R5	**IACFX**	NAS CM	Open End	Greater China Equity (Pacific Stock)	**C**	C-	C+		Y	10,000,000
Invesco Greater China Fund Class R6	**CACSX**	NAS CM	Open End	Greater China Equity (Pacific Stock)	**C**	C-	C+		Y	10,000,000
Invesco Greater China Fund Class Y	**AMCYX**	NAS CM	Open End	Greater China Equity (Pacific Stock)	**C**	C-	C+		Y	1,000
Invesco Growth Allocation Fund Class A	**AADAX**	NAS CM	Open End	Aggressive Alloc (Asset Alloc)	**B-**	C	B+	Up	Y	1,000
Invesco Growth Allocation Fund Class C	**AADCX**	NAS CM	Open End	Aggressive Alloc (Asset Alloc)	**B-**	C	B+	Up	Y	1,000
Invesco Growth Allocation Fund Class R	**AADRX**	NAS CM	Open End	Aggressive Alloc (Asset Alloc)	**B-**	C	B+	Up	Y	0
Invesco Growth Allocation Fund Class R6	**AAESX**	NAS CM	Open End	Aggressive Alloc (Asset Alloc)	**B-**	C	B+	Up	Y	10,000,000

★ Expanded analysis of this fund is included in Section II.

Min Additional Investment	TOTAL RETURNS 3-Month Total Return	6-Month Total Return	1-Year Total Return	3-Year Total Return	5-Year Total Return	PERFORMANCE Dividend Yield (TTM)	Expense Ratio	3-Yr Std Deviation	3-Year Beta	ASSETS NAV	Total Assets (MIL)	ASSET ALLOCATION & TURNOVER %Cash	%Stocks	%Bonds	%Other	Turnover Ratio	BULL & BEAR Last Bull Market Total Return	Last Bear Market Total Return	FEES Front End Fee (%)	Back End Fee (%)	Inception Date
	-4.47	-9.95	-11.55	-12.41	-15.83	2.62	1.75	5.25	8.72	5.97	8.3	7	93	0	0	64					Dec-13
	-4.38	-9.74	-11.17	-11.10	-13.80	3.38	1.25	5.29	6.1	6.11	8.3	7	93	0	0	64					Dec-13
	-4.22	-9.60	-11.02	-10.96	-13.66	3.37	1.25	5.26	9.64	6.12	8.3	7	93	0	0	64					Dec-13
50	-4.38	-9.74	-11.07	-11.10	-13.79	3.38	1.25	5.31	9.14	6.11	8.3	7	93	0	0	64					Dec-13
50	0.43	12.69	-10.79	28.32	18.30	1.88	1.02	15.36	1.21	13.85	36.6	0	100	0	0	92			5.50		Aug-12
50	0.22	12.16	-11.50	25.47	13.93	1.08	1.77	15.38	1.21	13.55	36.6	0	100	0	0	92				1.00	Aug-12
	0.43	12.52	-11.02	27.24	16.65	1.62	1.27	15.36	1.21	13.75	36.6	0	100	0	0	92					Aug-12
	0.50	12.73	-10.60	29.23	19.73	2.14	0.77	15.36	1.21	13.9	36.6	0	100	0	0	92					Sep-12
50	0.50	12.82	-10.60	29.33	19.73	2.14	0.77	15.39	1.21	13.9	36.6	0	100	0	0	92					Aug-12
	0.50	12.81	-10.53	29.32	19.81	2.14	0.77	15.39	1.21	13.91	36.6	0	100	0	0	92					Aug-12
50	0.46	15.75	8.42	17.52	24.64	4.48	1.26	11.32	0.68	13.07	798.6	1	98	0	1	47	23.9	-20.05	5.50		Apr-05
50	0.20	15.32	7.52	14.82	19.91	3.77	2.01	11.3	0.68	13.08	798.6	1	98	0	1	47	23.31	-20.29		1.00	Apr-05
	0.40	15.61	8.15	16.56	23.02	4.24	1.51	11.28	0.68	13.07	798.6	1	98	0	1	47	23.62	-20.16			Apr-05
	0.57	16.10	8.87	19.05	27.85	4.94	0.83	11.34	0.68	13.02	798.6	1	98	0	1	47	24.17	-19.77			Sep-12
50	0.44	15.91	8.61	18.33	26.10	4.72	1.01	11.31	0.68	13.06	798.6	1	98	0	1	47	24.03	-19.93			Oct-08
	0.55	15.95	8.78	18.78	27.37	4.86	0.92	11.3	0.68	13.02	798.6	1	98	0	1	47	24.16	-19.77			Apr-05
50	1.22	13.19	7.47	15.49	24.12	3.32	1.25	7.8	0.46	9.37	743.0	4	64	18	1	59	14.45	-8.21	5.50		May-02
50	0.92	12.78	6.68	12.92	19.54	2.59	2	7.82	0.46	9.36	743.0	4	64	18	1	59	13.9	-8.46		1.00	Mar-07
	1.30	13.41	7.88	16.69	26.22	3.68	0.93	7.78	0.46	9.36	743.0	4	64	18	1	59	14.84	-8.16			Mar-07
	1.33	13.46	7.98	17.01	26.63	3.77	0.83	7.78	0.46	9.36	743.0	4	64	18	1	59	14.45	-8.21			Sep-12
50	1.28	13.37	7.75	16.38	25.71	3.56	1	7.77	0.46	9.34	743.0	4	64	18	1	59	14.64	-8.12			Oct-08
50	3.02	12.47	-3.31	19.90		1.53	0.85			11.9	8.7	2	98	0	0	89			5.50		Jul-16
50	2.87	12.03	-4.14	17.28		0.62	1.6			11.82	8.7	2	98	0	0	89				1.00	Jul-16
	2.95	12.31	-3.63	18.87		1.25	1.1			11.86	8.7	2	98	0	0	89					Jul-16
	3.02	12.54	-3.16	20.68		1.74	0.6			11.93	8.7	2	98	0	0	89					Jul-16
	3.02	12.54	-3.16	20.68		1.74	0.6			11.93	8.7	2	98	0	0	89					Jul-16
50	3.02	12.54	-3.16	20.67		1.74	0.6			11.93	8.7	2	98	0	0	89					Jul-16
50	4.55	17.73	2.26	28.32	17.31	0.51	1.36	11.31	0.87	17.66	449.6	5	94	0	1	33	18.6	-21.94	5.50		Sep-94
50	4.35	17.29	1.50	25.43	12.97	0	2.11	11.31	0.87	13.9	449.6	5	94	0	1	33	18.12	-22.19		1.00	Aug-97
	4.72	17.97	2.61	29.65	19.45	0.88	1.02	11.31	0.87	17.52	449.6	5	94	0	1	33	18.97	-21.78			Sep-07
	4.72	18.05	2.71	29.52	18.41	0.96	0.94	11.29	0.87	17.52	449.6	5	94	0	1	33	18.6	-21.94			Apr-17
50	4.67	17.92	2.53	29.32	18.80	0.78	1.11	11.32	0.87	17.7	449.6	5	94	0	1	33	18.83	-21.89			Oct-08
50	0.31	2.75	0.21	0.40	3.30	1.8	1.44	3.09	20.76	9.7	67.1	58	1	29	12	67			5.50		Dec-13
50	0.10	2.37	-0.48	-1.70	-0.44	0.85	2.19	3.15	22.12	9.49	67.1	58	1	29	12	67				1.00	Dec-13
	0.31	2.66	-0.01	-0.25	2.04	1.49	1.69	3.14	22.78	9.64	67.1	58	1	29	12	67					Dec-13
	0.41	2.95	0.45	1.22	4.74	2.13	1.19	3.12	22.52	9.76	67.1	58	1	29	12	67					Dec-13
	0.30	2.84	0.46	1.22	4.64	2.13	1.19	3.15	22.36	9.75	67.1	58	1	29	12	67					Dec-13
50	0.30	2.84	0.46	1.21	4.63	2.13	1.19	3.16	21.66	9.75	67.1	58	1	29	12	67					Dec-13
	9.24	20.72	6.35	-17.94	-16.54	0	1.01	22.71	0.78	4.02	213.8	1	91	0	8	20	-9.75	-17.11			Apr-17
50	8.91	20.30	5.67	-18.66	-17.27	0	1.45	22.81	0.78	3.91	213.8	1	91	0	8	20	-9.8	-17.11	5.50		Mar-02
50	8.65	19.69	4.85	-20.52	-20.38	0	2.2	22.74	0.78	3.89	213.8	1	91	0	8	20	-10.16	-17.36		1.00	Feb-00
50	9.14	20.48	5.91	-18.55	-17.17	0	1.45	22.83	0.78	3.94	213.8	1	91	0	8	20	-9.75	-17.1			Jan-84
50	9.26	20.42	6.08	-17.87	-16.18	0	1.2	22.85	0.78	4.01	213.8	1	91	0	8	20	-9.75	-17.04			Oct-08
50	-2.36	11.91	-6.01	35.67	45.00	0.79	1.79	15.63	0.91	23.11	83.0	0	100	0	0	45	16.68	-29.92	5.50		Mar-06
50	-2.53	11.45	-6.70	32.65	39.69	0	2.54	15.63	0.91	22.28	83.0	0	100	0	0	45	16.18	-30.14		1.00	Mar-06
	-2.28	12.12	-5.61	37.44	48.18	1.24	1.4	15.64	0.91	23.11	83.0	0	100	0	0	45	17.07	-29.8			Mar-06
	-2.24	12.13	-5.58	37.43	48.16	1.24	1.4	15.64	0.91	23.1	83.0	0	100	0	0	45	17.07	-29.8			Apr-17
50	-2.28	12.07	-5.76	36.72	46.86	1.08	1.54	15.63	0.91	23.12	83.0	0	100	0	0	45	16.91	-29.86			Oct-08
50	3.21	14.47	4.69	28.90	23.62	1.21	1.05	9.1	0.72	16.37	988.8	2	77	20	1	16	17.34	-13.55	5.50		Apr-04
50	2.99	14.02	3.82	26.08	19.09	0.45	1.8	9.08	0.72	16.18	988.8	2	77	20	1	16	16.92	-13.86		1.00	Apr-04
	3.16	14.36	4.40	27.97	22.12	0.95	1.3	9.09	0.72	16.32	988.8	2	77	20	1	16	17.26	-13.67			Apr-04
	3.32	14.70	5.05	30.32	25.88	1.52	0.71	9.12	0.73	16.46	988.8	2	77	20	1	16	17.5	-13.4			Apr-17

	MARKET		FUND TYPE, CATEGORY & OBJECTIVE		RATINGS					MINIMUMS
Fund Name	Ticker Symbol	Traded On	Fund Type	Category and (Prospectus Objective)	Overall Rating	Reward Rating	Risk Rating	Recent Up/ Downgrade	Open to New Investors	Min Initial Investment
Invesco Growth Allocation Fund Class S	AADSX	NAS CM	Open End	Aggressive Alloc (Asset Alloc)	B-	C	B+	Up	Y	0
Invesco Growth Allocation Fund Class Y	AADYX	NAS CM	Open End	Aggressive Alloc (Asset Alloc)	B-	C	B+	Up	Y	1,000
Invesco Growth Allocation Fund R5 Class	AADIX	NAS CM	Open End	Aggressive Alloc (Asset Alloc)	B-	C	B+	Up	Y	10,000,000
Invesco Growth and Income Fund Class A	ACGIX	NAS CM	Open End	US Equity Large Cap Value (Growth & Income)	C+	C	B	Up	Y	1,000
Invesco Growth and Income Fund Class C	ACGKX	NAS CM	Open End	US Equity Large Cap Value (Growth & Income)	C+	C	B	Up	Y	1,000
Invesco Growth and Income Fund Class R	ACGLX	NAS CM	Open End	US Equity Large Cap Value (Growth & Income)	C+	C	B	Up	Y	0
Invesco Growth and Income Fund Class R6	GIFFX	NAS CM	Open End	US Equity Large Cap Value (Growth & Income)	C+	C	B	Up	Y	10,000,000
Invesco Growth and Income Fund Class Y	ACGMX	NAS CM	Open End	US Equity Large Cap Value (Growth & Income)	C+	C	B	Up	Y	1,000
Invesco Growth and Income Fund R5 Class	ACGQX	NAS CM	Open End	US Equity Large Cap Value (Growth & Income)	C+	C	B	Up	Y	10,000,000
Invesco Health Care Fund Class A	GGHCX	NAS CM	Open End	Healthcare Sector Equity (Health)	C+	C	B	Down	Y	1,000
Invesco Health Care Fund Class C	GTHCX	NAS CM	Open End	Healthcare Sector Equity (Health)	C+	C	B	Down	Y	1,000
Invesco Health Care Fund Class R6	GGHSX	NAS CM	Open End	Healthcare Sector Equity (Health)	B-	C	B		Y	10,000,000
Invesco Health Care Fund Class Y	GGHYX	NAS CM	Open End	Healthcare Sector Equity (Health)	B-	C	B		Y	1,000
Invesco Health Care Fund Investor Class	GTHIX	NAS CM	Open End	Healthcare Sector Equity (Health)	C+	C	B	Down	Y	1,000
Invesco Income Allocation Fund Class A	ALAAX	NAS CM	Open End	Cautious Alloc (Asset Alloc)	B-	C+	B	Down	Y	1,000
Invesco Income Allocation Fund Class C	CLIAX	NAS CM	Open End	Cautious Alloc (Asset Alloc)	B-	C+	B		Y	1,000
Invesco Income Allocation Fund Class R	RLIAX	NAS CM	Open End	Cautious Alloc (Asset Alloc)	B-	C+	B	Down	Y	0
Invesco Income Allocation Fund Class R6	IIASX	NAS CM	Open End	Cautious Alloc (Asset Alloc)	B-	C+	B+	Down	Y	10,000,000
Invesco Income Allocation Fund Class Y	ALAYX	NAS CM	Open End	Cautious Alloc (Asset Alloc)	B	C+	B+		Y	1,000
Invesco Income Allocation Fund R5 Class	ILAAX	NAS CM	Open End	Cautious Alloc (Asset Alloc)	B-	C+	B+	Down	Y	10,000,000
Invesco International Allocation Fund Class A	AINAX	NAS CM	Open End	Global Equity Large Cap (Growth)	C	C	B-		Y	1,000
Invesco International Allocation Fund Class C	INACX	NAS CM	Open End	Global Equity Large Cap (Growth)	C	C	B-		Y	1,000
Invesco International Allocation Fund Class R	RINAX	NAS CM	Open End	Global Equity Large Cap (Growth)	C	C	B-		Y	0
Invesco International Allocation Fund Class R6	INASX	NAS CM	Open End	Global Equity Large Cap (Growth)	C	C	B-		Y	10,000,000
Invesco International Allocation Fund Class Y	AINYX	NAS CM	Open End	Global Equity Large Cap (Growth)	C	C	B-		Y	1,000
Invesco International Allocation Fund R5 Class	INAIX	NAS CM	Open End	Global Equity Large Cap (Growth)	C	C	B-		Y	10,000,000
Invesco International Core Equity Fund Class A	IBVAX	NAS CM	Open End	Global Equity Large Cap (Foreign Stock)	C	C-	C+	Up	Y	1,000
Invesco International Core Equity Fund Class C	IBVCX	NAS CM	Open End	Global Equity Large Cap (Foreign Stock)	C	D+	C+	Up	Y	1,000
Invesco International Core Equity Fund Class R	IIBRX	NAS CM	Open End	Global Equity Large Cap (Foreign Stock)	C	C-	C+	Up	Y	0
Invesco International Core Equity Fund Class R5	IBVIX	NAS CM	Open End	Global Equity Large Cap (Foreign Stock)	C	C-	C+	Up	Y	10,000,000
Invesco International Core Equity Fund Class R6	IBVFX	NAS CM	Open End	Global Equity Large Cap (Foreign Stock)	C	C-	C+	Up	Y	10,000,000
Invesco International Core Equity Fund Class Y	IBVYX	NAS CM	Open End	Global Equity Large Cap (Foreign Stock)	C	C-	C+	Up	Y	1,000
Invesco International Core Equity Fund Investor Class	IIBCX	NAS CM	Open End	Global Equity Large Cap (Foreign Stock)	C	C-	C+	Up		1,000
Invesco International Growth Fund Class A	AIIEX	NAS CM	Open End	Global Equity Large Cap (Foreign Stock)	C+	C	B-	Up		1,000
Invesco International Growth Fund Class C	AIECX	NAS CM	Open End	Global Equity Large Cap (Foreign Stock)	C+	C	B-	Up		1,000
Invesco International Growth Fund Class R	AIERX	NAS CM	Open End	Global Equity Large Cap (Foreign Stock)	C+	C	B-	Up		0
Invesco International Growth Fund Class R6	IGFRX	NAS CM	Open End	Global Equity Large Cap (Foreign Stock)	C+	C	B	Up		10,000,000
Invesco International Growth Fund Class Y	AIIYX	NAS CM	Open End	Global Equity Large Cap (Foreign Stock)	C+	C	B	Up		1,000
Invesco International Growth Fund R5 Class	AIEVX	NAS CM	Open End	Global Equity Large Cap (Foreign Stock)	C+	C	B	Up		10,000,000
Invesco International Select Equity Fund Class A	IZIAX	NAS CM	Open End	Global Equity Large Cap (Growth)	C	C-	C+		Y	1,000
Invesco International Select Equity Fund Class C	IZICX	NAS CM	Open End	Global Equity Large Cap (Growth)	C	C-	C+		Y	1,000
Invesco International Select Equity Fund Class R	IZIRX	NAS CM	Open End	Global Equity Large Cap (Growth)	C	C-	C+		Y	0
Invesco International Select Equity Fund Class R5	IZIFX	NAS CM	Open End	Global Equity Large Cap (Growth)	C	C-	C+		Y	10,000,000
Invesco International Select Equity Fund Class R6	IZISX	NAS CM	Open End	Global Equity Large Cap (Growth)	C	C-	C+		Y	10,000,000
Invesco International Select Equity Fund Class Y	IZIYX	NAS CM	Open End	Global Equity Large Cap (Growth)	C	C-	C+		Y	1,000
Invesco International Small Company Fund Class A	IEGAX	NAS CM	Open End	Global Equity Mid/Small Cap (Foreign Stock)	C	C-	C		Y	1,000
Invesco International Small Company Fund Class C	IEGCX	NAS CM	Open End	Global Equity Mid/Small Cap (Foreign Stock)	C-	C-	C	Down	Y	1,000
Invesco International Small Company Fund Class R6	IEGFX	NAS CM	Open End	Global Equity Mid/Small Cap (Foreign Stock)	C	C-	C		Y	10,000,000
Invesco International Small Company Fund Class Y	IEGYX	NAS CM	Open End	Global Equity Mid/Small Cap (Foreign Stock)	C	C-	C		Y	1,000
Invesco International Small Company Fund R5 Class	IEGIX	NAS CM	Open End	Global Equity Mid/Small Cap (Foreign Stock)	C	C-	C		Y	10,000,000
Invesco Long/Short Equity Fund Class A	LSQAX	NAS CM	Open End	Long/Short Equity (Growth)	D	D	D	Down	Y	1,000
Invesco Long/Short Equity Fund Class C	LSQCX	NAS CM	Open End	Long/Short Equity (Growth)	D	D	D	Down	Y	1,000

★ Expanded analysis of this fund is included in Section II.

	TOTAL RETURNS					PERFORMANCE				ASSETS		ASSET ALLOCATION & TURNOVER					BULL & BEAR		FEES		
Min Additional Investment	3-Month Total Return	6-Month Total Return	1-Year Total Return	3-Year Total Return	5-Year Total Return	Dividend Yield (TTM)	Expense Ratio	3-Yr Std Deviation	3-Year Beta	NAV	Total Assets (MIL)	%Cash	%Stocks	%Bonds	%Other	Turnover Ratio	Last Bull Market Total Return	Last Bear Market Total Return	Front End Fee (%)	Back End Fee (%)	Inception Date
	3.28	14.56	4.75	29.33	24.29	1.31	0.95	9.1	0.72	16.36	988.8	2	77	20	1	16	17.44	-13.47			Sep-09
50	3.28	14.65	4.93	29.96	25.20	1.46	0.8	9.1	0.72	16.35	988.8	2	77	20	1	16	17.49	-13.47			Oct-08
	3.32	14.62	4.99	30.32	25.88	1.52	0.71	9.09	0.72	16.46	988.8	2	77	20	1	16	17.5	-13.4			Apr-04
50	3.40	17.18	2.12	38.69	37.88	1.63	0.8	14.53	1.17	23.63	7,105	5	95	0	0	29	23.21	-19.71	5.50		Aug-46
50	3.17	16.78	1.35	35.69	32.88	0.95	1.53	14.53	1.17	23.32	7,105	5	95	0	0	29	22.73	-20		1.00	Aug-93
	3.34	17.07	1.87	37.67	36.18	1.4	1.05	14.53	1.17	23.66	7,105	5	95	0	0	29	23.05	-19.8			Oct-02
	3.50	17.45	2.52	40.45	40.86	2.02	0.38	14.53	1.17	23.67	7,105	5	95	0	0	29	23.21	-19.71			Sep-12
50	3.41	17.31	2.34	39.71	39.60	1.87	0.55	14.54	1.17	23.64	7,105	5	95	0	0	29	23.43	-19.65			Oct-04
	3.48	17.39	2.46	40.06	40.25	1.93	0.48	14.56	1.17	23.67	7,105	5	95	0	0	29	23.49	-19.61			Jun-10
50	3.09	16.87	12.17	32.05	33.18	0	1.1	14.8	0.98	37.96	1,381	3	95	0	1	36	19.89	-13.83	5.50		Aug-89
50	2.90	16.45	11.34	29.13	28.27	0	1.85	14.78	0.98	25.13	1,381	3	95	0	1	36	19.38	-14.1		1.00	Mar-99
	3.18	17.04	12.53	32.91	34.04	0	0.8	14.8	0.98	38.93	1,381	3	95	0	1	36	19.89	-13.83			Apr-17
50	3.18	17.00	12.46	33.02	34.84	0	0.85	14.8	0.98	38.87	1,381	3	95	0	1	36	20.06	-13.74			Oct-08
50	3.09	16.86	12.17	32.04	33.17	0	1.1	14.79	0.98	37.97	1,381	3	95	0	1	36	19.89	-13.85			Jul-05
50	2.67	10.37	7.35	16.89	24.18	4.09	0.81	4.5	0.3	11.6	540.0	-5	30	68	1	20	9.37	-5.05	5.50		Oct-05
50	2.47	10.05	6.64	14.38	19.60	3.36	1.56	4.55	0.31	11.62	540.0	-5	30	68	1	20	8.84	-5.3		1.00	Oct-05
	2.60	10.33	7.17	16.01	22.63	3.84	1.06	4.51	0.31	11.61	540.0	-5	30	68	1	20	9.23	-5.17			Oct-05
	2.73	10.51	7.61	17.77	25.63	4.33	0.56	4.55	0.31	11.6	540.0	-5	30	68	1	20	9.51	-4.93			Apr-17
50	2.73	10.51	7.62	17.77	25.75	4.33	0.56	4.47	0.3	11.6	540.0	-5	30	68	1	20	9.51	-4.92			Oct-08
	2.73	10.51	7.61	17.77	25.63	4.33	0.56	4.55	0.31	11.6	540.0	-5	30	68	1	20	9.51	-4.92			Oct-05
50	4.19	16.21	2.27	27.67	7.64	1.28	1.4	11.72	1.02	11.68	119.5	2	97	0	0	10	13.69	-20.18	5.50		Oct-05
50	3.91	15.74	1.49	24.82	3.66	0.39	2.15	11.73	1.02	11.69	119.5	2	97	0	0	10	13.13	-20.4		1.00	Oct-05
	4.09	16.08	2.10	26.84	6.39	0.98	1.65	11.78	1.02	11.69	119.5	2	97	0	0	10	13.5	-20.27			Oct-05
	4.37	16.56	2.88	29.54	10.17	1.79	0.92	11.74	1.02	11.68	119.5	2	97	0	0	10	13.86	-20.16			Apr-17
50	4.30	16.39	2.60	28.71	9.07	1.55	1.15	11.77	1.02	11.64	119.5	2	97	0	0	10	13.77	-20.07			Oct-08
	4.28	16.45	2.77	29.28	9.95	1.7	1.01	11.77	1.02	11.68	119.5	2	97	0	0	10	13.86	-20.16			Oct-05
50	3.14	15.52	-3.16	20.62	5.11	1.38	1.12	12.93	1.12	10.49	77.1	3	97	0	0	73	10.06	-22.46	5.50		Mar-02
50	2.80	15.03	-3.95	17.85	1.16	0.45	1.87	12.93	1.12	10.25	77.1	3	97	0	0	73	9.53	-22.74		1.00	Feb-00
	2.93	15.35	-3.50	19.64	3.64	1.07	1.37	12.94	1.12	10.52	77.1	3	97	0	0	73	9.83	-22.52			Nov-03
	3.17	15.66	-2.98	21.54	6.91	1.65	0.87	12.96	1.12	10.41	77.1	3	97	0	0	73	10.53	-22.31			Apr-04
	3.07	15.55	-2.99	21.43	6.84	1.65	0.87	12.9	1.11	10.4	77.1	3	97	0	0	73	10.02	-22.54			Sep-12
50	3.08	15.58	-2.99	21.52	6.28	1.61	0.87	12.94	1.12	10.68	77.1	3	97	0	0	73	10.33	-22.46			Oct-08
50	3.08	15.45	-3.19	20.59	5.03	1.36	1.12	13	1.12	10.68	77.1	3	97	0	0	73	10.02	-22.54			Oct-98
50	4.85	20.03	7.70	25.65	13.28	0.8	1.31	11.87	1	33.49	5,713	5	95	0	0	26	16.89	-20.29	5.50		Apr-92
50	4.66	19.58	6.88	22.84	9.11	0.05	2.06	11.85	1	30.53	5,713	5	95	0	0	26	16.36	-20.51		1.00	Aug-97
	4.75	19.83	7.43	24.68	11.86	0.55	1.56	11.84	1	33.05	5,713	5	95	0	0	26	16.72	-20.36			Jun-02
	4.93	20.24	8.14	27.22	15.68	1.27	0.9	11.87	1	34.03	5,713	5	95	0	0	26	16.89	-20.29			Sep-12
50	4.87	20.15	7.96	26.55	14.69	1.09	1.06	11.85	1	33.56	5,713	5	95	0	0	26	17.1	-20.21			Oct-08
	4.92	20.20	8.07	26.88	15.18	1.07	0.98	11.86	1	34.09	5,713	5	95	0	0	26	17.18	-20.14			Mar-02
50	-0.36	19.97	-0.91	26.71		0.58	1.12	14.98	1.2	10.99	120.2	7	93	0	0	46			5.50		Dec-15
50	-0.55	19.55	-1.70	23.91		0	1.87	14.97	1.2	10.82	120.2	7	93	0	0	46				1.00	Dec-15
	-0.36	19.84	-1.15	25.80		0.38	1.37	14.95	1.19	10.93	120.2	7	93	0	0	46					Dec-15
	-0.27	20.08	-0.74	27.61		0.94	0.87	14.96	1.19	11	120.2	7	93	0	0	46					Dec-15
	-0.27	20.08	-0.65	27.62		0.94	0.87	14.94	1.19	11	120.2	7	93	0	0	46					Dec-15
50	-0.27	20.21	-0.73	27.62		0.94	0.87	14.91	1.19	11	120.2	7	93	0	0	46					Dec-15
50	1.22	9.35	-7.79	26.20	2.85	2.03	1.57	11.77	0.92	16.48	286.6	11	87	0	2	15	15.61	-17.59	5.50		Aug-00
50	1.03	8.92	-8.47	23.42	-0.90	1.2	2.32	11.75	0.92	15.62	286.6	11	87	0	2	15	15.07	-17.86		1.00	Aug-00
	1.36	9.57	-7.37	27.85	5.09	2.52	1.16	11.79	0.92	16.36	286.6	11	87	0	2	15	15.61	-17.59			Sep-12
50	1.34	9.54	-7.54	27.20	4.18	2.31	1.32	11.75	0.92	16.52	286.6	11	87	0	2	15	15.76	-17.53			Oct-08
	1.36	9.57	-7.44	27.59	4.75	2.44	1.23	11.79	0.92	16.37	286.6	11	87	0	2	15	15.85	-17.44			Oct-05
50	-0.90	-2.11	-14.94	8.71	2.31	0	1.57	13.93	89.44	8.78	60.4	5	95	0	0	92			5.50		Dec-13
50	-1.04	-2.52	-15.60	6.37	-1.43	0	2.32	13.89	88.9	8.48	60.4	5	95	0	0	92				1.00	Dec-13

	MARKET			FUND TYPE, CATEGORY & OBJECTIVE	RATINGS				MINIMUMS	
Fund Name	Ticker Symbol	Traded On	Fund Type	Category and (Prospectus Objective)	Overall Rating	Reward Rating	Risk Rating	Recent Up/ Downgrade	Open to New Investors	Min Initial Investment
Invesco Long/Short Equity Fund Class R	LSQRX	NAS CM	Open End	Long/Short Equity (Growth)	D	D	D	Down	Y	0
Invesco Long/Short Equity Fund Class R5	LSQFX	NAS CM	Open End	Long/Short Equity (Growth)	D	D	D	Down	Y	10,000,000
Invesco Long/Short Equity Fund Class R6	LSQSX	NAS CM	Open End	Long/Short Equity (Growth)	D	D	D	Down	Y	10,000,000
Invesco Long/Short Equity Fund Class Y	LSQYX	NAS CM	Open End	Long/Short Equity (Growth)	D	D	D	Down	Y	1,000
Invesco Low Volatility Emerging Markets Fund Class A	LVLAX	NAS CM	Open End	Global Emerg Mkts (Growth)	C-	D+	C		Y	1,000
Invesco Low Volatility Emerging Markets Fund Class C	LVLCX	NAS CM	Open End	Global Emerg Mkts (Growth)	D+	D+	C-	Down	Y	1,000
Invesco Low Volatility Emerging Markets Fund Class R	LVLRX	NAS CM	Open End	Global Emerg Mkts (Growth)	C-	D+	C		Y	0
Invesco Low Volatility Emerging Markets Fund Class R5	LVLFX	NAS CM	Open End	Global Emerg Mkts (Growth)	C-	D+	C	Down	Y	10,000,000
Invesco Low Volatility Emerging Markets Fund Class R6	LVLSX	NAS CM	Open End	Global Emerg Mkts (Growth)	C-	D+	C	Down	Y	10,000,000
Invesco Low Volatility Emerging Markets Fund Class Y	LVLYX	NAS CM	Open End	Global Emerg Mkts (Growth)	C-	D+	C	Down	Y	1,000
Invesco Low Volatility Equity Yield Fund Class A	SCAUX	NAS CM	Open End	US Equity Large Cap Value (Growth & Income)	C	C-	C		Y	1,000
Invesco Low Volatility Equity Yield Fund Class C	SCCUX	NAS CM	Open End	US Equity Large Cap Value (Growth & Income)	C	C-	C		Y	1,000
Invesco Low Volatility Equity Yield Fund Class R	SCRUX	NAS CM	Open End	US Equity Large Cap Value (Growth & Income)	C	C-	C		Y	0
Invesco Low Volatility Equity Yield Fund Class R6	SLESX	NAS CM	Open End	US Equity Large Cap Value (Growth & Income)	C	C-	C		Y	10,000,000
Invesco Low Volatility Equity Yield Fund Class Y	SCAYX	NAS CM	Open End	US Equity Large Cap Value (Growth & Income)	C	C-	C		Y	1,000
Invesco Low Volatility Equity Yield Fund Investor Class	SCNUX	NAS CM	Open End	US Equity Large Cap Value (Growth & Income)	C	C-	C		Y	1,000
Invesco Low Volatility Equity Yield Fund R5 Class	SCIUX	NAS CM	Open End	US Equity Large Cap Value (Growth & Income)	C	C-	C		Y	10,000,000
Invesco Macro Allocation Strategy Fund Class A	GMSDX	NAS CM	Open End	Moderate Alloc (Multi-Asset Global)	C+	C-	B	Up	Y	1,000
Invesco Macro Allocation Strategy Fund Class C	GMSEX	NAS CM	Open End	Moderate Alloc (Multi-Asset Global)	C	C-	B		Y	1,000
Invesco Macro Allocation Strategy Fund Class R	GMSJX	NAS CM	Open End	Moderate Alloc (Multi-Asset Global)	C+	C-	B	Up	Y	0
Invesco Macro Allocation Strategy Fund Class R5	GMSKX	NAS CM	Open End	Moderate Alloc (Multi-Asset Global)	C+	C-	B+	Up	Y	10,000,000
Invesco Macro Allocation Strategy Fund Class R6	GMSLX	NAS CM	Open End	Moderate Alloc (Multi-Asset Global)	C+	C-	B+	Up	Y	10,000,000
Invesco Macro Allocation Strategy Fund Class Y	GMSHX	NAS CM	Open End	Moderate Alloc (Multi-Asset Global)	C+	C-	B	Up	Y	1,000
Invesco Mid Cap Core Equity Fund Class A	GTAGX	NAS CM	Open End	US Equity Mid Cap (Growth)	C+	C	B	Up	Y	1,000
Invesco Mid Cap Core Equity Fund Class C	GTACX	NAS CM	Open End	US Equity Mid Cap (Growth)	C+	C	B	Up	Y	1,000
Invesco Mid Cap Core Equity Fund Class R	GTARX	NAS CM	Open End	US Equity Mid Cap (Growth)	C+	C	B	Up	Y	0
Invesco Mid Cap Core Equity Fund Class R6	GTAFX	NAS CM	Open End	US Equity Mid Cap (Growth)	C+	C	B	Up	Y	10,000,000
Invesco Mid Cap Core Equity Fund Class Y	GTAYX	NAS CM	Open End	US Equity Mid Cap (Growth)	C+	C	B	Up	Y	1,000
Invesco Mid Cap Core Equity Fund R5 Class	GTAVX	NAS CM	Open End	US Equity Mid Cap (Growth)	C+	C	B	Up	Y	10,000,000
Invesco Mid Cap Growth Fund Class A	VGRAX	NAS CM	Open End	US Equity Mid Cap (Growth)	C+	C	B-		Y	1,000
Invesco Mid Cap Growth Fund Class C	VGRCX	NAS CM	Open End	US Equity Mid Cap (Growth)	C+	C	B-		Y	1,000
Invesco Mid Cap Growth Fund Class R	VGRRX	NAS CM	Open End	US Equity Mid Cap (Growth)	C+	C	B-		Y	0
Invesco Mid Cap Growth Fund Class R5	VGRJX	NAS CM	Open End	US Equity Mid Cap (Growth)	C+	C	B-	Down	Y	10,000,000
Invesco Mid Cap Growth Fund Class R6	VGRFX	NAS CM	Open End	US Equity Mid Cap (Growth)	C+	C	B-	Down	Y	10,000,000
Invesco Mid Cap Growth Fund Class Y	VGRDX	NAS CM	Open End	US Equity Mid Cap (Growth)	C+	C	B-		Y	1,000
Invesco MLP Fund Class A	ILPAX	NAS CM	Open End	Energy Sector Equity (Growth & Income)	C-	C-	C-	Down	Y	1,000
Invesco MLP Fund Class C	ILPCX	NAS CM	Open End	Energy Sector Equity (Growth & Income)	C-	C-	C-	Down	Y	1,000
Invesco MLP Fund Class R	ILPRX	NAS CM	Open End	Energy Sector Equity (Growth & Income)	C-	C-	C-	Down	Y	0
Invesco MLP Fund Class R5	ILPFX	NAS CM	Open End	Energy Sector Equity (Growth & Income)	C-	C-	C	Down	Y	10,000,000
Invesco MLP Fund Class R6	ILPQX	NAS CM	Open End	Energy Sector Equity (Growth & Income)	C-	C-	C	Down	Y	10,000,000
Invesco MLP Fund Class Y	ILPYX	NAS CM	Open End	Energy Sector Equity (Growth & Income)	C-	C-	C	Down	Y	1,000
Invesco Moderate Allocation Fund Class A	AMKAX	NAS CM	Open End	Moderate Alloc (Asset Alloc)	B-	C	A-	Up	Y	1,000
Invesco Moderate Allocation Fund Class C	AMKCX	NAS CM	Open End	Moderate Alloc (Asset Alloc)	B-	C	B+	Up	Y	1,000
Invesco Moderate Allocation Fund Class R	AMKRX	NAS CM	Open End	Moderate Alloc (Asset Alloc)	B-	C	A-	Up	Y	0
Invesco Moderate Allocation Fund Class R6	AMLSX	NAS CM	Open End	Moderate Alloc (Asset Alloc)	B-	C	A-	Up	Y	10,000,000
Invesco Moderate Allocation Fund Class S	AMKSX	NAS CM	Open End	Moderate Alloc (Asset Alloc)	B-	C	A-	Up	Y	0
Invesco Moderate Allocation Fund Class Y	ABKYX	NAS CM	Open End	Moderate Alloc (Asset Alloc)	B-	C	A-	Up	Y	1,000
Invesco Moderate Allocation Fund R5 Class	AMLIX	NAS CM	Open End	Moderate Alloc (Asset Alloc)	B-	C	A-	Up	Y	10,000,000
Invesco Multi-Asset Income Fund Class A	PIAFX	NAS CM	Open End	Cautious Alloc (Income)	B-	C+	B	Down	Y	1,000
Invesco Multi-Asset Income Fund Class C	PICFX	NAS CM	Open End	Cautious Alloc (Income)	B-	C+	B		Y	1,000
Invesco Multi-Asset Income Fund Class R	PIRFX	NAS CM	Open End	Cautious Alloc (Income)	B-	C+	B		Y	0
Invesco Multi-Asset Income Fund Class R5	IPNFX	NAS CM	Open End	Cautious Alloc (Income)	B-	B-	B	Down	Y	10,000,000

★ Expanded analysis of this fund is included in Section II.

	TOTAL RETURNS					PERFORMANCE				ASSETS		ASSET ALLOCATION & TURNOVER					BULL & BEAR		FEES		
Min Additional Investment	3-Month Total Return	6-Month Total Return	1-Year Total Return	3-Year Total Return	5-Year Total Return	Dividend Yield (TTM)	Expense Ratio	3-Yr Std Deviation	3-Year Beta	NAV	Total Assets (MIL)	%Cash	%Stocks	%Bonds	%Other	Turnover Ratio	Last Bull Market Total Return	Last Bear Market Total Return	Front End Fee (%)	Back End Fee (%)	Inception Date
	-0.91	-2.25	-15.16	7.97	1.09	0	1.82	13.91	90.38	8.68	60.4	5	95	0	0	92					Dec-13
	-0.78	-1.98	-14.62	9.82	3.93	0	1.24	13.9	88.94	8.89	60.4	5	95	0	0	92					Dec-13
	-0.78	-1.98	-14.61	9.93	4.04	0	1.17	13.94	89.08	8.9	60.4	5	95	0	0	92					Dec-13
50	-0.89	-2.09	-14.74	9.48	3.60	0	1.32	13.88	89.08	8.87	60.4	5	95	0	0	92					Dec-13
50	0.00	6.49	-3.60	16.15	-9.45	2.3	1.33	12.27	0.83	6.39	33.2	2	98	0	0	61			5.50		Dec-13
50	-0.15	5.96	-4.32	13.41	-12.91	0.87	2.08	12.2	0.83	6.39	33.2	2	98	0	0	61				1.00	Dec-13
	0.00	6.14	-3.93	15.26	-10.65	1.86	1.58	12.22	0.83	6.39	33.2	2	98	0	0	61					Dec-13
	0.15	6.52	-3.36	16.98	-8.38	2.9	1.08	12.24	0.83	6.37	33.2	2	98	0	0	61					Dec-13
	0.15	6.53	-3.36	17.00	-8.48	2.91	1.08	12.26	0.83	6.36	33.2	2	98	0	0	61					Dec-13
50	0.15	6.52	-3.36	16.98	-8.38	2.9	1.08	12.24	0.83	6.37	33.2	2	98	0	0	61					Dec-13
50	-0.46	9.46	-5.05	16.99	14.89	1.17	1.21	12.31	0.95	10.69	225.9	0	100	0	0	119	25.44	-17.64	5.50		Mar-06
50	-0.65	8.89	-5.78	14.24	10.60	0.41	1.96	12.32	0.95	10.51	225.9	0	100	0	0	119	25	-17.84		1.00	Mar-06
	-0.52	9.37	-5.23	16.16	13.58	0.91	1.46	12.36	0.95	10.65	225.9	0	100	0	0	119	25.29	-17.71			Mar-06
	-0.34	9.76	-4.60	18.50	17.40	1.61	0.75	12.33	0.95	10.75	225.9	0	100	0	0	119	25.64	-17.48			Apr-17
50	-0.39	9.55	-4.79	17.81	16.34	1.42	0.96	12.32	0.95	10.74	225.9	0	100	0	0	119	25.63	-17.48			Oct-08
50	-0.45	9.43	-5.03	16.94	14.89	1.17	1.21	12.36	0.95	10.73	225.9	0	100	0	0	119	25.51	-17.7			Apr-08
	-0.34	9.65	-4.62	18.43	17.33	1.6	0.79	12.36	0.95	10.75	225.9	0	100	0	0	119	25.64	-17.48			Mar-06
50	-0.74	2.20	-2.25	11.25	15.24	0.16	1.47	7.07	2.76	9.29	33.4	-88	60	105	23	94			5.50		Aug-13
50	-0.97	1.78	-3.02	8.84	11.08	0.04	2.22	7.09	2.65	9.15	33.4	-88	60	105	23	94				1.00	Aug-13
	-0.85	1.98	-2.50	10.39	13.88	0.12	1.72	7.04	2.71	9.26	33.4	-88	60	105	23	94					Aug-13
	-0.74	2.29	-1.99	12.15	16.79	0.29	1.22	7.05	1.75	9.36	33.4	-88	60	105	23	94					Aug-13
	-0.63	2.29	-2.00	12.16	16.81	0.29	1.22	7.07	3.02	9.35	33.4	-88	60	105	23	94					Aug-13
50	-0.74	2.29	-2.10	12.03	16.79	0.29	1.22	7.1	2.28	9.35	33.4	-88	60	105	23	94					Sep-12
50	1.54	16.75	5.21	28.96	22.24	0.1	1.24	12.17	0.88	19.72	953.7	21	79	0	0	29	18.54	-20.83	5.50		Jun-87
50	1.32	16.23	4.41	26.11	17.76	0	1.99	12.19	0.88	10.67	953.7	21	79	0	0	29	18.07	-21.11		1.00	May-99
	1.51	16.66	5.01	28.09	20.81	0	1.49	12.18	0.88	18.76	953.7	21	79	0	0	29	18.37	-20.9			Jun-02
	1.67	17.02	5.68	30.67	25.02	0.89	0.82	12.18	0.88	21.86	953.7	21	79	0	0	29	18.54	-20.83			Sep-12
50	1.61	16.88	5.48	29.96	23.81	0.49	0.99	12.19	0.88	20.14	953.7	21	79	0	0	29	18.75	-20.75			Oct-08
	1.67	17.01	5.61	30.42	24.59	0.72	0.89	12.17	0.88	21.87	953.7	21	79	0	0	29	18.84	-20.71			Mar-02
50	6.13	26.28	9.12	49.65	50.21	0	1.17	13.55	0.92	39.11	2,982	1	99	0	0	51	23.62	-25.9	5.50		Dec-95
50	5.90	25.83	8.33	46.44	44.91	0	1.88	13.51	0.92	27.62	2,982	1	99	0	0	51	23.11	-26.15		1.00	Dec-95
	6.06	26.16	8.84	48.53	48.38	0	1.42	13.52	0.92	37.61	2,982	1	99	0	0	51	23.41	-25.95			Jul-08
	6.22	26.54	9.51	51.31	52.97	0	0.82	13.54	0.92	41.81	2,982	1	99	0	0	51	23.93	-25.74			Jun-10
	6.23	26.59	9.58	51.68	53.66	0	0.73	13.53	0.92	42.08	2,982	1	99	0	0	51	23.62	-25.9			Jul-13
50	6.20	26.48	9.39	50.81	52.14	0	0.92	13.54	0.92	41.26	2,982	1	99	0	0	51	23.8	-25.8			Aug-05
50	-0.89	18.46	1.06	-0.81		6.07	1.69	16.8	1	5.29	11.6	1	99	0	0	97			5.50		Aug-14
50	-1.26	17.80	0.12	-3.08		5.3	2.44	16.81	1	5.28	11.6	1	99	0	0	97				1.00	Aug-14
	-1.13	18.09	0.62	-1.75		5.82	1.94	16.74	0.99	5.28	11.6	1	99	0	0	97					Aug-14
	-1.01	18.38	1.12	-0.24		6.34	1.44	16.83	1	5.28	11.6	1	99	0	0	97					Aug-14
	-0.83	18.38	1.12	-0.24		6.34	1.44	16.81	1	5.28	11.6	1	99	0	0	97					Aug-14
50	-1.01	18.38	1.12	-0.23		6.34	1.44	16.72	0.99	5.28	11.6	1	99	0	0	97					Aug-14
50	3.02	12.53	5.25	23.98	20.70	1.99	1.02	7.1	0.56	13.33	712.0	-1	58	41	1	20	14.42	-9.6	5.50		Apr-04
50	2.84	12.11	4.48	21.24	16.30	1.27	1.77	7.08	0.56	13.23	712.0	-1	58	41	1	20	13.81	-9.85		1.00	Apr-04
	2.96	12.32	4.99	22.99	19.21	1.75	1.27	7.12	0.56	13.3	712.0	-1	58	41	1	20	14.28	-9.71			Apr-04
	3.09	12.74	5.56	25.24	22.30	2.29	0.72	7.1	0.56	13.39	712.0	-1	58	41	1	20	14.53	-9.48			Apr-17
	3.12	12.59	5.36	24.36	21.31	2.09	0.92	7.1	0.56	13.33	712.0	-1	58	41	1	20	14.43	-9.52			Sep-09
50	3.08	12.65	5.51	24.90	22.22	2.23	0.77	7.09	0.56	13.35	712.0	-1	58	41	1	20	14.55	-9.42			Oct-08
	3.08	12.64	5.56	25.14	22.21	2.29	0.72	7.08	0.56	13.39	712.0	-1	58	41	1	20	14.53	-9.48			Apr-04
50	2.86	12.36	7.85	21.33	32.44	5.23	0.86	6.09	1.04	10.75	658.5	-27	31	65	9	59			5.50		Dec-11
50	2.67	11.95	7.05	18.63	27.56	4.5	1.61	6.1	1.03	10.74	658.5	-27	31	65	9	59				1.00	Dec-11
	2.70	12.11	7.48	20.31	30.67	4.99	1.11	6.08	1.03	10.74	658.5	-27	31	65	9	59					Dec-11
	2.92	12.38	8.02	22.11	33.98	5.47	0.61	6.07	1.03	10.75	658.5	-27	31	65	9	59					Dec-11

	MARKET			FUND TYPE, CATEGORY & OBJECTIVE	RATINGS				MINIMUMS	
Fund Name	Ticker Symbol	Traded On	Fund Type	Category and (Prospectus Objective)	Overall Rating	Reward Rating	Risk Rating	Recent Up/ Downgrade	Open to New Investors	Min Initial Investment
Invesco Multi-Asset Income Fund Class R6	PIFFX	NAS CM	Open End	Cautious Alloc (Income)	B-	B-	B	Down	Y	10,000,000
Invesco Multi-Asset Income Fund Class Y	PIYFX	NAS CM	Open End	Cautious Alloc (Income)	B-	C+	B	Down	Y	1,000
Invesco Multi-Asset Inflation Fund Class A	MIZAX	NAS CM	Open End	Cautious Alloc (Growth & Income)	C	C-	B		Y	1,000
Invesco Multi-Asset Inflation Fund Class C	MIZCX	NAS CM	Open End	Cautious Alloc (Growth & Income)	C	C-	B-		Y	1,000
Invesco Multi-Asset Inflation Fund Class R	MIZRX	NAS CM	Open End	Cautious Alloc (Growth & Income)	C	C-	B		Y	0
Invesco Multi-Asset Inflation Fund Class R5	MIZFX	NAS CM	Open End	Cautious Alloc (Growth & Income)	C	C-	B		Y	10,000,000
Invesco Multi-Asset Inflation Fund Class R6	MIZSX	NAS CM	Open End	Cautious Alloc (Growth & Income)	C	C-	B		Y	10,000,000
Invesco Multi-Asset Inflation Fund Class Y	MIZYX	NAS CM	Open End	Cautious Alloc (Growth & Income)	C	C-	B		Y	1,000
Invesco OFI Pictet Global Environmental Solutions Cls A	IOGDX	NAS CM	Open End	Global Equity Large Cap (Growth)	D+	D+	C		Y	1,000
Invesco OFI Pictet Global Environmental Solutions Cls C	IOGEX	NAS CM	Open End	Global Equity Large Cap (Growth)	D+	D+	C		Y	1,000
Invesco OFI Pictet Global Environmental Solutions Cls R	IOGFX	NAS CM	Open End	Global Equity Large Cap (Growth)	D+	D+	C		Y	0
Invesco OFI Pictet Global Environmental Solutions Cls R5	IOGGX	NAS CM	Open End	Global Equity Large Cap (Growth)	D+	D+	C		Y	1,000,000
Invesco OFI Pictet Global Environmental Solutions Fund R6	OPEIX	NAS CM	Open End	Global Equity Large Cap (Growth)	D+	D+	C	Up	Y	1,000,000
Invesco OFI Pictet Global Environmental Solutions Fund Y	OPEYX	NAS CM	Open End	Global Equity Large Cap (Growth)	D+	D+	C	Up	Y	1,000
Invesco Oppenheimer Capital Appreciation Fund Class A	OPTFX	NAS CM	Open End	US Equity Large Cap Growth (Growth)	C+	C+	B-	Down	Y	1,000
Invesco Oppenheimer Capital Appreciation Fund Class C	OTFCX	NAS CM	Open End	US Equity Large Cap Growth (Growth)	C+	C	B-	Down	Y	1,000
Invesco Oppenheimer Capital Appreciation Fund Class R	OTCNX	NAS CM	Open End	US Equity Large Cap Growth (Growth)	C+	C+	B-	Down	Y	0
Invesco Oppenheimer Capital Appreciation Fund Class R5	CPTUX	NAS CM	Open End	US Equity Large Cap Growth (Growth)	C+	C+	B-		Y	1,000,000
Invesco Oppenheimer Capital Appreciation Fund Class R6	OPTIX	NAS CM	Open End	US Equity Large Cap Growth (Growth)	C+	C+	B-	Down	Y	1,000,000
Invesco Oppenheimer Capital Appreciation Fund Class Y	OTCYX	NAS CM	Open End	US Equity Large Cap Growth (Growth)	C+	C+	B-	Down	Y	1,000
Invesco Oppenheimer Capital Income Fund Class A	OPPEX	NAS CM	Open End	Cautious Alloc (Equity-Income)	B-	C	B+	Up	Y	1,000
Invesco Oppenheimer Capital Income Fund Class C	OPECX	NAS CM	Open End	Cautious Alloc (Equity-Income)	B-	C	B+	Up	Y	1,000
Invesco Oppenheimer Capital Income Fund Class R	OCINX	NAS CM	Open End	Cautious Alloc (Equity-Income)	B-	C	B+	Up	Y	0
Invesco Oppenheimer Capital Income Fund Class R5	CPIFX	NAS CM	Open End	Cautious Alloc (Equity-Income)	B-	C	B+		Y	1,000,000
Invesco Oppenheimer Capital Income Fund Class R6	OCIIX	NAS CM	Open End	Cautious Alloc (Equity-Income)	B-	C	B	Up	Y	1,000,000
Invesco Oppenheimer Capital Income Fund Class Y	OCIYX	NAS CM	Open End	Cautious Alloc (Equity-Income)	B-	C	B	Up	Y	1,000
Invesco Oppenheimer Developing Markets Fund Class A	ODMAX	NAS CM	Open End	Global Emerg Mkts (Div Emerging Mkts)	C	C	B-			1,000
Invesco Oppenheimer Developing Markets Fund Class C	ODVCX	NAS CM	Open End	Global Emerg Mkts (Div Emerging Mkts)	C	C	B-			1,000
Invesco Oppenheimer Developing Markets Fund Class R	ODVNX	NAS CM	Open End	Global Emerg Mkts (Div Emerging Mkts)	C	C	B-			0
Invesco Oppenheimer Developing Markets Fund Class R5	DVMFX	NAS CM	Open End	Global Emerg Mkts (Div Emerging Mkts)	C	C	B-		Y	1,000,000
Invesco Oppenheimer Developing Markets Fund Class R6	ODVIX	NAS CM	Open End	Global Emerg Mkts (Div Emerging Mkts)	C	C	B-			1,000,000
Invesco Oppenheimer Developing Markets Fund Class Y	ODVYX	NAS CM	Open End	Global Emerg Mkts (Div Emerging Mkts)	C	C	B-			1,000
Invesco Oppenheimer Discovery Fund Class A	OPOCX	NAS CM	Open End	US Equity Small Cap (Small Company)	C+	C+	C+	Down		1,000
Invesco Oppenheimer Discovery Fund Class C	ODICX	NAS CM	Open End	US Equity Small Cap (Small Company)	C+	C	C+	Down		1,000
Invesco Oppenheimer Discovery Fund Class R	ODINX	NAS CM	Open End	US Equity Small Cap (Small Company)	C+	C+	C+	Down		0
Invesco Oppenheimer Discovery Fund Class R5	DIGGX	NAS CM	Open End	US Equity Small Cap (Small Company)	C+	C+	C+		Y	1,000,000
Invesco Oppenheimer Discovery Fund Class R6	ODIIX	NAS CM	Open End	US Equity Small Cap (Small Company)	C+	C+	C+	Down		1,000,000
Invesco Oppenheimer Discovery Fund Class Y	ODIYX	NAS CM	Open End	US Equity Small Cap (Small Company)	C+	C+	C+	Down		1,000
Invesco Oppenheimer Discovery Mid Cap Growth Fund A	OEGAX	NAS CM	Open End	US Equity Mid Cap (Growth)	B-	B-	C+	Up	Y	1,000
Invesco Oppenheimer Discovery Mid Cap Growth Fund C	OEGCX	NAS CM	Open End	US Equity Mid Cap (Growth)	C+	C+	C+		Y	1,000
Invesco Oppenheimer Discovery Mid Cap Growth Fund Class R5	DMCFX	NAS CM	Open End	US Equity Mid Cap (Growth)	B-	B-	B-		Y	1,000,000
Invesco Oppenheimer Discovery Mid Cap Growth Fund R	OEGNX	NAS CM	Open End	US Equity Mid Cap (Growth)	C+	C+	C+		Y	0
Invesco Oppenheimer Discovery Mid Cap Growth Fund R6	OEGIX	NAS CM	Open End	US Equity Mid Cap (Growth)	B-	B-	B-		Y	1,000,000
Invesco Oppenheimer Discovery Mid Cap Growth Fund Y	OEGYX	NAS CM	Open End	US Equity Mid Cap (Growth)	B-	B-	C+		Y	1,000
Invesco Oppenheimer Dividend Opportunity Fund Class A	OSVAX	NAS CM	Open End	US Equity Large Cap Value (Growth & Income)	B-	C	B+	Up	Y	1,000
Invesco Oppenheimer Dividend Opportunity Fund Class C	OSCVX	NAS CM	Open End	US Equity Large Cap Value (Growth & Income)	B-	C	B+	Up	Y	1,000
Invesco Oppenheimer Dividend Opportunity Fund Class R	OSVNX	NAS CM	Open End	US Equity Large Cap Value (Growth & Income)	B-	C	B+	Up	Y	0
Invesco Oppenheimer Dividend Opportunity Fund Class R5	DVOPX	NAS CM	Open End	US Equity Large Cap Value (Growth & Income)	B-	C	B+		Y	1,000,000
Invesco Oppenheimer Dividend Opportunity Fund Class R6	OSVIX	NAS CM	Open End	US Equity Large Cap Value (Growth & Income)	B-	C	B+	Up	Y	1,000,000
Invesco Oppenheimer Dividend Opportunity Fund Class Y	OSVYX	NAS CM	Open End	US Equity Large Cap Value (Growth & Income)	B-	C	B+	Up	Y	1,000
Invesco Oppenheimer Emerging Markets Innovators Cls A	EMIAX	NAS CM	Open End	Global Emerg Mkts (Div Emerging Mkts)	C	C-	C	Up	Y	1,000
Invesco Oppenheimer Emerging Markets Innovators Cls C	EMVCX	NAS CM	Open End	Global Emerg Mkts (Div Emerging Mkts)	C	C-	C	Up	Y	1,000

★Expanded analysis of this fund is included in Section II.

Min Additional Investment	TOTAL RETURNS 3-Month Total Return	6-Month Total Return	1-Year Total Return	3-Year Total Return	5-Year Total Return	PERFORMANCE Dividend Yield (TTM)	Expense Ratio	3-Yr Std Deviation	3-Year Beta	ASSETS NAV	Total Assets (MIL)	ASSET ALLOCATION & TURNOVER %Cash	%Stocks	%Bonds	%Other	Turnover Ratio	BULL & BEAR Last Bull Market Total Return	Last Bear Market Total Return	FEES Front End Fee (%)	Back End Fee (%)	Inception Date
	2.92	12.50	8.12	22.24	33.98	5.47	0.61	6.1	1.04	10.75	658.5	-27	31	65	9	59					Sep-12
50	2.92	12.50	8.12	22.12	33.98	5.47	0.61	6.09	1.03	10.75	658.5	-27	31	65	9	59					Dec-11
50	0.88	10.80	-0.31	7.74		2.28	1.02	7.57	51.68	9.13	1.3	11	43	37	7	44			5.50		Oct-14
50	0.77	10.36	-0.98	5.36		1.49	1.77	7.55	51.98	9.05	1.3	11	43	37	7	44				1.00	Oct-14
	0.99	10.67	-0.38	7.10		2.02	1.27	7.55	51.18	9.12	1.3	11	43	37	7	44					Oct-14
	0.99	10.89	0.00	8.58		2.57	0.77	7.52	51.04	9.16	1.3	11	43	37	7	44					Oct-14
	1.10	11.01	0.11	8.70		2.56	0.77	7.56	51.34	9.17	1.3	11	43	37	7	44					Oct-14
50	0.99	11.01	0.00	8.69		2.56	0.77	7.55	51.48	9.17	1.3	11	43	37	7	44					Oct-14
	5.76	27.97	8.07				1.2			10.56	31.8	1	99	0	0	20			5.50		May-19
	5.63	27.56	7.33				1.95			10.56	31.8	1	99	0	0	20				1.00	May-19
	5.72	27.83	7.82				1.45			10.56	31.8	1	99	0	0	20					May-19
	5.91	28.22	8.42				0.9			10.57	31.8	1	99	0	0	20					May-19
	5.79	28.08	8.30			0.15	0.85			10.58	31.8	1	99	0	0	20					Dec-17
50	5.70	27.84	8.06			0.12	0.95			10.56	31.8	1	99	0	0	20					Dec-17
50	5.60	23.30	9.93	53.23	58.86	0	1.03	14.31	1.12	61.79	4,041	4	96	0	0	29	24.5	-16.56	5.50		Jan-81
50	5.40	22.81	9.07	49.71	52.88	0	1.78	14.3	1.12	44.84	4,041	4	96	0	0	29	23.93	-16.85		1.00	Dec-93
	5.53	23.12	9.63	52.01	56.79	0	1.28	14.3	1.12	57.76	4,041	4	96	0	0	29	24.32	-16.65			Mar-01
	5.64	23.34	9.96	53.28	58.91		0.66	14.32	1.12	61.81	4,041	4	96	0	0	29	24.5	-16.55			May-19
	5.71	23.88	10.66	55.48	62.60	0.2	0.61	14.32	1.12	67.9	4,041	4	96	0	0	29	24.7	-16.56			Dec-11
50	5.67	23.43	10.17	54.26	60.68	0.02	0.78	14.31	1.12	67.41	4,041	4	96	0	0	29	24.79	-16.41			Nov-97
	2.19	8.63	5.22	14.63	18.43	2.67	0.95	4.62	0.35	10.24	2,283	4	28	64	1	88	8.43	-4.87	5.50		Dec-70
	1.86	8.10	4.28	11.97	13.91	2.01	1.7	4.56	0.34	9.89	2,283	4	28	64	1	88	7.95	-5.18		1.00	Nov-95
	2.16	8.52	4.92	13.81	16.95	2.46	1.2	4.62	0.35	10.09	2,283	4	28	64	1	88	8.23	-5.09			Mar-01
	2.19	8.63	5.22	14.64	18.43		0.62	4.62	0.35	10.23	2,283	4	28	64	1	88	8.43	-4.87			May-19
	2.27	8.82	5.62	16.17	20.94	3.05	0.57	4.6	0.35	10.23	2,283	4	28	64	1	88	8.43	-4.87			Dec-13
	2.25	8.75	5.46	15.46	19.76	2.9	0.7	4.61	0.35	10.23	2,283	4	28	64	1	88	8.59	-4.68			Jan-11
50	2.75	15.58	2.71	42.50	13.12	0.24	1.26	13.34	0.93	44.05	42,250	4	91	0	4	36	18.46	-23.19	5.50		Nov-96
50	2.53	15.13	1.92	39.29	8.90	0	2.01	13.34	0.93	40.84	42,250	4	91	0	4	36	17.97	-23.41		1.00	Nov-96
	2.67	15.42	2.44	41.41	11.69	0	1.51	13.34	0.93	42.29	42,250	4	91	0	4	36	18.2	-23.3			Mar-01
	2.80	15.64	2.76	42.56	13.17		0.9	13.35	0.93	44.06	42,250	4	91	0	4	36	18.46	-23.19			May-19
	2.86	15.80	3.13	44.28	15.56	0.69	0.85	13.36	0.93	43.46	42,250	4	91	0	4	36	18.59	-23.19			Dec-11
50	2.81	15.71	2.95	43.54	14.54	0.53	1.01	13.35	0.93	43.44	42,250	4	91	0	4	36	18.69	-23.1			Sep-05
50	9.69	32.56	12.58	71.42	78.37	0	1.08	16.37	0.89	82.8	2,721	2	98	0	0	91	27.59	-22.32	5.50		Sep-86
50	9.47	32.04	11.73	67.57	71.72	0	1.84	16.36	0.89	54.76	2,721	2	98	0	0	91	27.02	-22.56		1.00	Oct-95
	9.61	32.37	12.28	70.10	76.08	0	1.33	16.36	0.89	75.35	2,721	2	98	0	0	91	27.36	-22.4			Mar-01
	9.72	32.59	12.61	71.47	78.42		0.71	16.38	0.89	82.82	2,721	2	98	0	0	91	27.59	-22.32			May-19
	9.80	32.81	13.03	73.55	82.16	0	0.66	16.37	0.89	97.41	2,721	2	98	0	0	91	27.75	-22.32			Jan-12
50	9.74	32.70	12.85	72.63	80.51	0	0.84	16.37	0.89	95.48	2,721	2	98	0	0	91	27.92	-22.19			Jun-94
50	8.96	31.26	14.69	58.20	77.12	0	1.12	14.43	0.96	22	1,557	3	97	0	0	108	27.32	-19.66	5.50		Nov-00
50	8.73	30.75	13.76	54.54	70.39	0	1.86	14.41	0.96	17.56	1,557	3	97	0	0	108	26.84	-19.95		1.00	Nov-00
	9.04	31.45	14.95	59.35	79.28		0.74	14.44	0.96	22	1,557	3	97	0	0	108	27.73	-19.48			May-19
	8.87	31.08	14.38	56.92	74.85	0	1.37	14.41	0.96	20.37	1,557	3	97	0	0	108	27.21	-19.77			Mar-01
	9.04	31.54	15.12	60.10	80.88	0	0.69	14.41	0.96	25.31	1,557	3	97	0	0	108	27.73	-19.48			Feb-13
50	9.00	31.41	14.91	59.30	79.23	0	0.87	14.43	0.96	24.93	1,557	3	97	0	0	108	27.73	-19.48			Nov-00
50	4.10	15.48	5.89	31.14	35.37	2.35	1.14	10.73	0.85	23.91	258.4	3	94	0	0	63	16.19	-24.66	5.50		Nov-02
50	3.88	15.08	5.11	28.21	30.42	1.72	1.88	10.74	0.85	23.03	258.4	3	94	0	0	63	15.7	-24.95		1.00	Feb-04
	4.04	15.33	5.61	30.17	33.68	2.14	1.37	10.73	0.85	23.65	258.4	3	94	0	0	63	16.11	-24.75			Feb-04
	4.12	15.51	5.92	31.17	35.40		0.76	10.73	0.85	23.9	258.4	3	94	0	0	63	16.19	-24.66			May-19
	4.22	15.73	6.35	32.82	38.34	2.76	0.71	10.75	0.85	23.88	258.4	3	94	0	0	63	16.19	-24.66			Aug-14
50	4.17	15.63	6.17	32.12	37.11	2.6	0.88	10.72	0.85	23.88	258.4	3	94	0	0	63	16.49	-24.54			Feb-04
50	-0.49	13.54	-7.31	20.95	1.75	0	1.7	14.47	0.97	10.14	640.4	8	92	0	0	24			5.50		Jun-14
50	-0.60	13.04	-7.98	18.23	-2.04	0	2.45	14.47	0.97	9.79	640.4	8	92	0	0	24				1.00	Jun-14

	MARKET		FUND TYPE, CATEGORY & OBJECTIVE		RATINGS				MINIMUMS	
Fund Name	Ticker Symbol	Traded On	Fund Type	Category and (Prospectus Objective)	Overall Rating	Reward Rating	Risk Rating	Recent Up/ Downgrade	Open to New Investors	Min Initial Investment
Invesco Oppenheimer Emerging Markets Innovators Cls R	EMIRX	NAS CM	Open End	Global Emerg Mkts (Div Emerging Mkts)	C	C-	C	Up	Y	0
Invesco Oppenheimer Emerging Markets Innovators Cls R5	EMIMX	NAS CM	Open End	Global Emerg Mkts (Div Emerging Mkts)	C	C-	C		Y	1,000,000
Invesco Oppenheimer Emerging Markets Innovators Cls R6	EMVIX	NAS CM	Open End	Global Emerg Mkts (Div Emerging Mkts)	C	C-	C	Up	Y	1,000,000
Invesco Oppenheimer Emerging Markets Innovators Cls Y	EMIYX	NAS CM	Open End	Global Emerg Mkts (Div Emerging Mkts)	C	C-	C	Up	Y	1,000
Invesco Oppenheimer Equity Income Fund Class A	OAEIX	NAS CM	Open End	US Equity Large Cap Value (Equity-Income)	B-	C	B	Up	Y	1,000
Invesco Oppenheimer Equity Income Fund Class C	OCEIX	NAS CM	Open End	US Equity Large Cap Value (Equity-Income)	C+	C	B	Up	Y	1,000
Invesco Oppenheimer Equity Income Fund Class R	ONEIX	NAS CM	Open End	US Equity Large Cap Value (Equity-Income)	B-	C	B	Up	Y	0
Invesco Oppenheimer Equity Income Fund Class R5	ETYIX	NAS CM	Open End	US Equity Large Cap Value (Equity-Income)	B-	C	B		Y	1,000,000
Invesco Oppenheimer Equity Income Fund Class R6	OEIIX	NAS CM	Open End	US Equity Large Cap Value (Equity-Income)	B-	C	B	Up	Y	1,000,000
Invesco Oppenheimer Equity Income Fund Class Y	OYEIX	NAS CM	Open End	US Equity Large Cap Value (Equity-Income)	B-	C	B	Up	Y	1,000
Invesco Oppenheimer Fundamental Alternatives Fund A	QVOPX	NAS CM	Open End	Multialternative (Asset Alloc)	C	C	C+	Up	Y	1,000
Invesco Oppenheimer Fundamental Alternatives Fund C	QOPCX	NAS CM	Open End	Multialternative (Asset Alloc)	C-	C-	C		Y	1,000
Invesco Oppenheimer Fundamental Alternatives Fund Class R5	FDATX	NAS CM	Open End	Multialternative (Asset Alloc)	C	C	C+		Y	1,000,000
Invesco Oppenheimer Fundamental Alternatives Fund R	QOPNX	NAS CM	Open End	Multialternative (Asset Alloc)	C	C	C	Up	Y	0
Invesco Oppenheimer Fundamental Alternatives Fund R6	QOPIX	NAS CM	Open End	Multialternative (Asset Alloc)	C	C	C+		Y	1,000,000
Invesco Oppenheimer Fundamental Alternatives Fund Y	QOPYX	NAS CM	Open End	Multialternative (Asset Alloc)	C	C	C+		Y	1,000
Invesco Oppenheimer Global Allocation Fund Class A	QVGIX	NAS CM	Open End	Moderate Alloc (Asset Alloc)	C+	C-	B	Up	Y	1,000
Invesco Oppenheimer Global Allocation Fund Class C	QGRCX	NAS CM	Open End	Moderate Alloc (Asset Alloc)	C	C-	B		Y	1,000
Invesco Oppenheimer Global Allocation Fund Class R	QGRNX	NAS CM	Open End	Moderate Alloc (Asset Alloc)	C+	C-	B	Up	Y	0
Invesco Oppenheimer Global Allocation Fund Class R5	GLALX	NAS CM	Open End	Moderate Alloc (Asset Alloc)	C+	C-	B		Y	1,000,000
Invesco Oppenheimer Global Allocation Fund Class R6	QGRIX	NAS CM	Open End	Moderate Alloc (Asset Alloc)	C+	C	B	Up	Y	1,000,000
Invesco Oppenheimer Global Allocation Fund Class Y	QGRYX	NAS CM	Open End	Moderate Alloc (Asset Alloc)	C+	C	B	Up	Y	1,000
Invesco Oppenheimer Global Focus Fund Class A	GLVAX	NAS CM	Open End	Global Equity Large Cap (World Stock)	C+	C	B-	Up	Y	1,000
Invesco Oppenheimer Global Focus Fund Class C	GLVCX	NAS CM	Open End	Global Equity Large Cap (World Stock)	C+	C	C+	Up	Y	1,000
Invesco Oppenheimer Global Focus Fund Class R	GLVNX	NAS CM	Open End	Global Equity Large Cap (World Stock)	C+	C	B-	Up	Y	0
Invesco Oppenheimer Global Focus Fund Class R5	GFFDX	NAS CM	Open End	Global Equity Large Cap (World Stock)	C+	C	B-		Y	1,000,000
Invesco Oppenheimer Global Focus Fund Class R6	GLVIX	NAS CM	Open End	Global Equity Large Cap (World Stock)	C+	C	B-	Up	Y	1,000,000
Invesco Oppenheimer Global Focus Fund Class Y	GLVYX	NAS CM	Open End	Global Equity Large Cap (World Stock)	C+	C	B-	Up	Y	1,000
Invesco Oppenheimer Global Fund Class A	OPPAX	NAS CM	Open End	Global Equity Large Cap (World Stock)	C+	C	B-	Up	Y	1,000
Invesco Oppenheimer Global Fund Class C	OGLCX	NAS CM	Open End	Global Equity Large Cap (World Stock)	C	C	B-		Y	1,000
Invesco Oppenheimer Global Fund Class Fund Class Y	OGLYX	NAS CM	Open End	Global Equity Large Cap (World Stock)	C+	C	B-	Up	Y	1,000
Invesco Oppenheimer Global Fund Class R	OGLNX	NAS CM	Open End	Global Equity Large Cap (World Stock)	C+	C	B-	Up	Y	0
Invesco Oppenheimer Global Fund Class R5	GFDDX	NAS CM	Open End	Global Equity Large Cap (World Stock)	C+	C	B-		Y	1,000,000
Invesco Oppenheimer Global Fund Class R6	OGLIX	NAS CM	Open End	Global Equity Large Cap (World Stock)	C+	C	B-	Up	Y	1,000,000
Invesco Oppenheimer Global Multi-Asset Growth Fund Class A	QMGAX	NAS CM	Open End	Flexible Alloc (Multi-Asset Global)	C	C	B		Y	1,000
Invesco Oppenheimer Global Multi-Asset Growth Fund Class C	QMGCX	NAS CM	Open End	Flexible Alloc (Multi-Asset Global)	C	C-	B		Y	1,000
Invesco Oppenheimer Global Multi-Asset Growth Fund Class R	QMGRX	NAS CM	Open End	Flexible Alloc (Multi-Asset Global)	C	C	B		Y	0
Invesco Oppenheimer Global Multi-Asset Growth Cls R5	GMAGX	NAS CM	Open End	Flexible Alloc (Multi-Asset Global)	C	C	B		Y	1,000,000
Invesco Oppenheimer Global Multi-Asset Growth Cls R6	QMGIX	NAS CM	Open End	Flexible Alloc (Multi-Asset Global)	C	C	B		Y	1,000,000
Invesco Oppenheimer Global Multi-Asset Growth Fund Class Y	QMGYX	NAS CM	Open End	Flexible Alloc (Multi-Asset Global)	C	C	B		Y	1,000
Invesco Oppenheimer Global Multi-Asset Income Fund Class A	QMAAX	NAS CM	Open End	Cautious Alloc (Growth & Income)	C+	C	B	Up	Y	1,000
Invesco Oppenheimer Global Multi-Asset Income Fund Class C	QMACX	NAS CM	Open End	Cautious Alloc (Growth & Income)	C	C	B-		Y	1,000
Invesco Oppenheimer Global Multi-Asset Income Fund Class R	QMARX	NAS CM	Open End	Cautious Alloc (Growth & Income)	C	C	B-		Y	0
Invesco Oppenheimer Global Multi-Asset Income Cls R5	GMUAX	NAS CM	Open End	Cautious Alloc (Growth & Income)	C+	C	B		Y	1,000,000
Invesco Oppenheimer Global Multi-Asset Income Cls R6	QMAIX	NAS CM	Open End	Cautious Alloc (Growth & Income)	C+	C	B	Up	Y	1,000,000
Invesco Oppenheimer Global Multi-Asset Income Fund Class Y	QMAYX	NAS CM	Open End	Cautious Alloc (Growth & Income)	C+	C	B	Up	Y	1,000
Invesco Oppenheimer Global Opportunities Fund Class A	OPGIX	NAS CM	Open End	Global Equity Mid/Small Cap (World Stock)	C	C	C		Y	1,000
Invesco Oppenheimer Global Opportunities Fund Class C	OGICX	NAS CM	Open End	Global Equity Mid/Small Cap (World Stock)	C	C	C		Y	1,000
Invesco Oppenheimer Global Opportunities Fund Class R	OGINX	NAS CM	Open End	Global Equity Mid/Small Cap (World Stock)	C	C	C		Y	0
Invesco Oppenheimer Global Opportunities Fund Class R5	GOFFX	NAS CM	Open End	Global Equity Mid/Small Cap (World Stock)	C	C	C		Y	1,000,000
Invesco Oppenheimer Global Opportunities Fund Class R6	OGIIX	NAS CM	Open End	Global Equity Mid/Small Cap (World Stock)	C	C	C		Y	1,000,000
Invesco Oppenheimer Global Opportunities Fund Class Y	OGIYX	NAS CM	Open End	Global Equity Mid/Small Cap (World Stock)	C	C	C		Y	1,000

★ Expanded analysis of this fund is included in Section II.

	TOTAL RETURNS					PERFORMANCE				ASSETS		ASSET ALLOCATION & TURNOVER					BULL & BEAR		FEES		
Min Additional Investment	3-Month Total Return	6-Month Total Return	1-Year Total Return	3-Year Total Return	5-Year Total Return	Dividend Yield (TTM)	Expense Ratio	3-Yr Std Deviation	3-Year Beta	NAV	Total Assets (MIL)	%Cash	%Stocks	%Bonds	%Other	Turnover Ratio	Last Bull Market Total Return	Last Bear Market Total Return	Front End Fee (%)	Back End Fee (%)	Inception Date
	-0.49	13.33	-7.55	19.91	0.42	0	1.95	14.44	0.96	10.03	640.4	8	92	0	0	24					Jun-14
	-0.38	13.76	-6.94	22.61	4.13		1.3	14.48	0.97	10.14	640.4	8	92	0	0	24					May-19
	-0.38	13.76	-6.93	22.61	4.13	0	1.25	14.48	0.97	10.33	640.4	8	92	0	0	24					Jun-14
50	-0.38	13.76	-6.98	21.91	3.11	0	1.45	14.49	0.97	10.25	640.4	8	92	0	0	24					Jun-14
50	2.98	15.27	5.09	34.11	21.76	2.02	1	12.03	0.98	29.95	2,936	4	93	0	0	104	24.24	-22.15	5.50		Feb-87
50	2.81	14.85	4.32	31.11	17.25	1.94	1.75	12.01	0.97	23.1	2,936	4	93	0	0	104	23.65	-22.36		1.00	Mar-97
	2.90	15.12	4.80	33.06	20.19	1.89	1.25	11.99	0.97	28.48	2,936	4	93	0	0	104	23.9	-22.3			Mar-01
	3.02	15.31	5.13	34.16	21.80		0.66	12.03	0.98	29.93	2,936	4	93	0	0	104	24.24	-22.15			May-19
	3.11	15.54	5.54	35.75	24.35	2.39	0.61	12.03	0.98	29.89	2,936	4	93	0	0	104	24.35	-22.15			Feb-12
50	3.05	15.41	5.35	35.10	23.26	2.25	0.75	12.03	0.98	29.91	2,936	4	93	0	0	104	24.37	-22.05			Feb-11
50	1.47	4.15	2.65	3.35	6.80	1.71	1.97	3.78	0.56	26.82	1,016	41	20	32	4	155	0.87	-10.17	5.50		Jan-89
50	1.28	3.77	1.86	0.98	2.80	1.12	2.72	3.78	0.56	23.66	1,016	41	20	32	4	155	0.43	-10.45		1.00	Sep-93
	1.51	4.19	2.69	3.39	6.84		1.6	3.79	0.57	26.83	1,016	41	20	32	4	155	0.87	-10.17			May-19
	1.42	4.02	2.39	2.52	5.42	1.53	2.22	3.79	0.56	25.61	1,016	41	20	32	4	155	0.72	-10.28			Mar-01
	1.54	4.35	3.06	4.62	9.05	2.08	1.55	3.77	0.56	27.55	1,016	41	20	32	4	155	0.87	-10.17			Feb-13
50	1.51	4.25	2.85	4.04	8.05	1.92	1.72	3.78	0.56	27.43	1,016	41	20	32	4	155	1.06	-10.06			Dec-96
50	2.73	11.11	1.21	18.08	18.84	2.01	1.29	7.32	0.61	18	1,388	3	63	32	0	151	9.03	-14.95	5.50		Nov-91
50	2.51	10.66	0.45	15.38	14.45	1.3	2.04	7.31	0.61	17.12	1,388	3	63	32	0	151	8.55	-15.23		1.00	Sep-93
	2.68	10.96	0.96	17.22	17.44	1.81	1.54	7.31	0.61	17.61	1,388	3	63	32	0	151	8.82	-15.03			Mar-01
	2.73	11.11	1.21	18.08	18.84		0.9	7.32	0.61	18	1,388	3	63	32	0	151	9.03	-14.95			May-19
	2.80	11.33	1.56	19.53	21.39	2.46	0.85	7.3	0.61	17.98	1,388	3	63	32	0	151	9.08	-14.95			Feb-12
50	2.74	11.19	1.41	18.88	20.26	2.24	1.04	7.28	0.61	17.98	1,388	3	63	32	0	151	9.25	-14.82			May-00
50	4.02	22.01	3.25	47.79	31.59	0	1.27	15.22	1.26	52.98	606.7	0	100	0	0	63	19.11	-22.05	5.50		Oct-07
50	3.83	21.55	2.45	44.45	26.66	0	2.01	15.21	1.26	49.06	606.7	0	100	0	0	63	18.6	-22.29		1.00	Oct-07
	3.95	21.85	2.98	46.69	29.91	0	1.52	15.2	1.26	51.57	606.7	0	100	0	0	63	18.99	-22.14			Oct-07
	4.10	22.18	3.50	48.89	33.23		0.9	15.22	1.26	53	606.7	0	100	0	0	63	19.36	-21.94			May-19
	4.14	22.26	3.68	49.66	34.43	0	0.85	15.22	1.26	54.8	606.7	0	100	0	0	63	19.36	-21.94			Aug-12
50	4.09	22.17	3.49	48.88	33.21	0	1.02	15.22	1.26	54.16	606.7	0	100	0	0	63	19.36	-21.94			Oct-07
50	3.96	22.41	3.32	57.54	45.43	0.41	1.08	14.21	1.22	89.78	11,105	0	100	0	0	14	17.76	-23.19	5.50		Dec-69
50	3.74	21.95	2.53	53.95	39.97	0	1.83	14.2	1.22	81.38	11,105	0	100	0	0	14	17.25	-23.41		1.00	Oct-95
50	4.00	22.54	3.55	58.63	47.14	0.67	0.83	14.2	1.22	89.89	11,105	0	100	0	0	14	17.95	-23.11			Nov-98
	3.88	22.26	3.04	56.29	43.53	0.15	1.33	14.21	1.22	89.25	11,105	0	100	0	0	14	17.52	-23.29			Mar-01
	3.97	22.42	3.33	57.56	45.45		0.72	14.21	1.22	89.8	11,105	0	100	0	0	14	17.76	-23.19			May-19
	4.04	22.65	3.72	59.45	48.47	0.83	0.67	14.21	1.22	89.92	11,105	0	100	0	0	14	17.91	-23.19			Jan-12
50	3.26	13.89	1.28	21.55		0	1.29	9.96	0.84	10.74	70.9	14	65	16	2	126			5.50		Aug-15
50	3.13	13.45	0.65	18.96		0	2.04	10	0.85	10.54	70.9	14	65	16	2	126				1.00	Aug-15
	3.18	13.73	1.10	20.72		0	1.54	9.99	0.84	10.68	70.9	14	65	16	2	126					Aug-15
	3.37	14.08	1.58	22.54			1.09	10.01	0.84	10.75	70.9	14	65	16	2	126					May-19
	3.35	14.05	1.56	22.52		0	1.04	10	0.84	10.79	70.9	14	65	16	2	126					Aug-15
50	3.25	13.93	1.46	22.29		0	1.14	9.96	0.84	10.79	70.9	14	65	16	2	126					Aug-15
	2.00	9.96	2.59	10.49		4.98	0.95	5.88	0.48	9.14	89.3	8	21	57	11	68			4.25		Dec-14
	1.71	9.44	1.78	7.91		4.2	1.75	5.86	0.48	9.12	89.3	8	21	57	11	68				1.00	Dec-14
	1.82	9.69	2.29	9.46		4.69	1.25	5.83	0.47	9.13	89.3	8	21	57	11	68					Dec-14
	2.06	10.09	2.85	11.30			0.75	5.92	0.48	9.14	89.3	8	21	57	11	68					May-19
	2.07	10.09	2.85	11.30		5.23	0.7	5.92	0.48	9.14	89.3	8	21	57	11	68					Dec-14
50	2.05	10.06	2.79	11.14		5.18	0.75	5.87	0.48	9.14	89.3	8	21	57	11	68					Dec-14
50	4.35	20.01	-4.69	68.00	79.05	0	1.1	21.09	1.56	60.56	8,161	1	99	0	0	21	16.64	-19.52	5.50		Oct-90
50	4.16	19.55	-5.41	64.27	72.43	0	1.85	21.08	1.56	52.21	8,161	1	99	0	0	21	16.16	-19.78		1.00	Dec-93
	4.29	19.85	-4.92	66.77	76.80	0	1.35	21.08	1.56	57.82	8,161	1	99	0	0	21	16.44	-19.65			Mar-01
	4.39	20.05	-4.66	68.06	79.11		0.74	21.09	1.56	60.58	8,161	1	99	0	0	21	16.64	-19.52			May-19
	4.46	20.24	-4.30	70.12	82.91	0	0.69	21.1	1.56	62	8,161	1	99	0	0	21	16.77	-19.52			Jan-12
50	4.42	20.16	-4.45	69.26	81.27	0	0.85	21.1	1.56	61.57	8,161	1	99	0	0	21	16.85	-19.44			Feb-01

	MARKET			FUND TYPE, CATEGORY & OBJECTIVE	RATINGS				MINIMUMS	
Fund Name	Ticker Symbol	Traded On	Fund Type	Category and (Prospectus Objective)	Overall Rating	Reward Rating	Risk Rating	Recent Up/ Downgrade	Open to New Investors	Min Initial Investment
Invesco Oppenheimer Gold & Special Minerals Fund Class A	OPGSX	NAS CM	Open End	Precious Metals Sector Equity (Precious Metals)	C	C-	C	Up	Y	1,000
Invesco Oppenheimer Gold & Special Minerals Fund Class C	OGMCX	NAS CM	Open End	Precious Metals Sector Equity (Precious Metals)	D+	D	C	Down	Y	1,000
Invesco Oppenheimer Gold & Special Minerals Fund Class R	OGMNX	NAS CM	Open End	Precious Metals Sector Equity (Precious Metals)	C-	C-	C		Y	0
Invesco Oppenheimer Gold & Special Minerals Fund Class R5	IOGYX	NAS CM	Open End	Precious Metals Sector Equity (Precious Metals)	C	C-	C		Y	1,000,000
Invesco Oppenheimer Gold & Special Minerals Fund Class R6	OGMIX	NAS CM	Open End	Precious Metals Sector Equity (Precious Metals)	C	C	C	Up	Y	1,000,000
Invesco Oppenheimer Gold & Special Minerals Fund Class Y	OGMYX	NAS CM	Open End	Precious Metals Sector Equity (Precious Metals)	C	C-	C	Up	Y	1,000
Invesco Oppenheimer International Diversified Fund Class A	OIDAX	NAS CM	Open End	Global Equity Large Cap (Growth)	C	C	B-		Y	1,000
Invesco Oppenheimer International Diversified Fund Class C	OIDCX	NAS CM	Open End	Global Equity Large Cap (Growth)	C	C	C+		Y	1,000
Invesco Oppenheimer International Diversified Fund Class R	OIDNX	NAS CM	Open End	Global Equity Large Cap (Growth)	C	C	B-		Y	0
Invesco Oppenheimer International Diversified Cls R5	INDFX	NAS CM	Open End	Global Equity Large Cap (Growth)	C	C	B-		Y	1,000,000
Invesco Oppenheimer International Diversified Cls R6	OIDIX	NAS CM	Open End	Global Equity Large Cap (Growth)	C	C	B-		Y	1,000,000
Invesco Oppenheimer International Diversified Fund Class Y	OIDYX	NAS CM	Open End	Global Equity Large Cap (Growth)	C	C	B-		Y	1,000
Invesco Oppenheimer International Equity Fund Class A	QIVAX	NAS CM	Open End	Global Equity Large Cap (Foreign Stock)	C	C-	C+		Y	1,000
Invesco Oppenheimer International Equity Fund Class C	QIVCX	NAS CM	Open End	Global Equity Large Cap (Foreign Stock)	C	C-	C	Up	Y	1,000
Invesco Oppenheimer International Equity Fund Class R	QIVNX	NAS CM	Open End	Global Equity Large Cap (Foreign Stock)	C	C-	C+		Y	0
Invesco Oppenheimer International Equity Fund Class R5	INEQX	NAS CM	Open End	Global Equity Large Cap (Foreign Stock)	C	C-	C+		Y	1,000,000
Invesco Oppenheimer International Equity Fund Class R6	QIVIX	NAS CM	Open End	Global Equity Large Cap (Foreign Stock)	C	C	C+		Y	1,000,000
Invesco Oppenheimer International Equity Fund Class Y	QIVYX	NAS CM	Open End	Global Equity Large Cap (Foreign Stock)	C	C	C+		Y	1,000
Invesco Oppenheimer International Growth Fund Class A	OIGAX	NAS CM	Open End	Global Equity Large Cap (Foreign Stock)	C	C-	C+	Up	Y	1,000
Invesco Oppenheimer International Growth Fund Class C	OIGCX	NAS CM	Open End	Global Equity Large Cap (Foreign Stock)	C	C-	C+	Up	Y	1,000
Invesco Oppenheimer International Growth Fund Class R	OIGNX	NAS CM	Open End	Global Equity Large Cap (Foreign Stock)	C	C-	C+	Up	Y	0
Invesco Oppenheimer International Growth Fund Class R5	INGFX	NAS CM	Open End	Global Equity Large Cap (Foreign Stock)	C	C-	C+		Y	1,000,000
Invesco Oppenheimer International Growth Fund Class R6	OIGIX	NAS CM	Open End	Global Equity Large Cap (Foreign Stock)	C	C-	C+	Up	Y	1,000,000
Invesco Oppenheimer International Growth Fund Class Y	OIGYX	NAS CM	Open End	Global Equity Large Cap (Foreign Stock)	C	C-	C+	Up	Y	1,000
Invesco Oppenheimer International Small-Mid Company Cls A	OSMAX	NAS CM	Open End	Global Equity Mid/Small Cap (Growth)	C+	C	B-	Up	Y	1,000
Invesco Oppenheimer International Small-Mid Company Cls C	OSMCX	NAS CM	Open End	Global Equity Mid/Small Cap (Growth)	C	C	B-		Y	1,000
Invesco Oppenheimer International Small-Mid Company Cls R	OSMNX	NAS CM	Open End	Global Equity Mid/Small Cap (Growth)	C+	C	B-	Up		0
Invesco Oppenheimer International Small-Mid Company Cls R5	INSLX	NAS CM	Open End	Global Equity Mid/Small Cap (Growth)	C+	C	B-		Y	1,000,000
Invesco Oppenheimer International Small-Mid Company Cls R6	OSCIX	NAS CM	Open End	Global Equity Mid/Small Cap (Growth)	C+	C	B-	Up		1,000,000
Invesco Oppenheimer International Small-Mid Company Cls Y	OSMYX	NAS CM	Open End	Global Equity Mid/Small Cap (Growth)	C+	C	B-	Up		0
Invesco Oppenheimer Macquarie Global Infrastructure Cls A	OQGAX	NAS CM	Open End	Infrastructure Sector Equity (Growth & Income)	C	C	C+		Y	1,000
Invesco Oppenheimer Macquarie Global Infrastructure Cls C	OQGCX	NAS CM	Open End	Infrastructure Sector Equity (Growth & Income)	C	C	C+		Y	1,000
Invesco Oppenheimer Macquarie Global Infrastructure Cls R	OQGRX	NAS CM	Open End	Infrastructure Sector Equity (Growth & Income)	C	C	C+		Y	0
Invesco Oppenheimer Macquarie Global Infrastructure Cls R5	GBITX	NAS CM	Open End	Infrastructure Sector Equity (Growth & Income)	C	C	C+		Y	1,000,000
Invesco Oppenheimer Macquarie Global Infrastructure Cls R6	OQGIX	NAS CM	Open End	Infrastructure Sector Equity (Growth & Income)	C	C	C+	Down	Y	1,000,000
Invesco Oppenheimer Macquarie Global Infrastructure Cls Y	OQGYX	NAS CM	Open End	Infrastructure Sector Equity (Growth & Income)	C	C	C+	Down	Y	1,000
Invesco Oppenheimer Main Street All Cap Fund Class A	OMSOX	NAS CM	Open End	US Equity Large Cap Blend (Growth)	C+	C	B-	Up	Y	1,000
Invesco Oppenheimer Main Street All Cap Fund Class C	OMSCX	NAS CM	Open End	US Equity Large Cap Blend (Growth)	C+	C	B-	Up	Y	1,000
Invesco Oppenheimer Main Street All Cap Fund Class R	OMSNX	NAS CM	Open End	US Equity Large Cap Blend (Growth)	C+	C	B-	Up	Y	0
Invesco Oppenheimer Main Street All Cap Fund Class R5	MSAZX	NAS CM	Open End	US Equity Large Cap Blend (Growth)	C+	C	B-		Y	1,000
Invesco Oppenheimer Main Street All Cap Fund Class R6	IOAPX	NAS CM	Open End	US Equity Large Cap Blend (Growth)	C+	C	B		Y	0
Invesco Oppenheimer Main Street All Cap Fund Class Y	OMSYX	NAS CM	Open End	US Equity Large Cap Blend (Growth)	C+	C	B	Up	Y	1,000
Invesco Oppenheimer Main Street Fund Class A	MSIGX	NAS CM	Open End	US Equity Large Cap Blend (Growth & Income)	B-	C	B		Y	1,000
Invesco Oppenheimer Main Street Fund Class C	MIGCX	NAS CM	Open End	US Equity Large Cap Blend (Growth & Income)	C+	C	B	Down	Y	1,000
Invesco Oppenheimer Main Street Fund Class R	OMGNX	NAS CM	Open End	US Equity Large Cap Blend (Growth & Income)	B-	C	B		Y	0
Invesco Oppenheimer Main Street Fund Class R5	MSJFX	NAS CM	Open End	US Equity Large Cap Blend (Growth & Income)	B-	C	B		Y	1,000,000
Invesco Oppenheimer Main Street Fund Class R6	OMSIX	NAS CM	Open End	US Equity Large Cap Blend (Growth & Income)	B-	C+	B		Y	0
Invesco Oppenheimer Main Street Fund Class Y	MIGYX	NAS CM	Open End	US Equity Large Cap Blend (Growth & Income)	B-	C+	B		Y	1,000
Invesco Oppenheimer Main Street Mid Cap Fund Class A	OPMSX	NAS CM	Open End	US Equity Mid Cap (Growth)	C+	C	B-	Up	Y	1,000
Invesco Oppenheimer Main Street Mid Cap Fund Class C	OPMCX	NAS CM	Open End	US Equity Mid Cap (Growth)	C+	C	B-	Up	Y	1,000
Invesco Oppenheimer Main Street Mid Cap Fund Class R	OPMNX	NAS CM	Open End	US Equity Mid Cap (Growth)	C+	C	B-	Up	Y	0
Invesco Oppenheimer Main Street Mid Cap Fund Class R5	MSMJX	NAS CM	Open End	US Equity Mid Cap (Growth)	C+	C	B-		Y	1,000,000

★ Expanded analysis of this fund is included in Section II.

	TOTAL RETURNS					PERFORMANCE				ASSETS		ASSET ALLOCATION & TURNOVER					BULL & BEAR		FEES		
Min Additional Investment	3-Month Total Return	6-Month Total Return	1-Year Total Return	3-Year Total Return	5-Year Total Return	Dividend Yield (TTM)	Expense Ratio	3-Yr Std Deviation	3-Year Beta	NAV	Total Assets (MIL)	%Cash	%Stocks	%Bonds	%Other	Turnover Ratio	Last Bull Market Total Return	Last Bear Market Total Return	Front End Fee (%)	Back End Fee (%)	Inception Date
50	14.33	26.73	15.21	0.35	3.50	0	1.17	24.98	0.4	17.87	1,099	2	98	0	0	44	-13.91	-21.07	5.50		Jul-83
50	14.08	26.26	14.32	-1.89	-0.34	0	1.92	24.94	0.4	16.2	1,099	2	98	0	0	44	-14.25	-21.29		1.00	Nov-95
	14.26	26.62	14.96	-0.41	2.17	0	1.42	24.96	0.4	16.98	1,099	2	98	0	0	44	-14.08	-21.17			Mar-01
	14.33	26.73	15.21	0.35	3.50		0.8	24.98	0.4	17.87	1,099	2	98	0	0	44	-13.91	-21.07			May-19
	14.47	27.06	15.72	1.64	5.72	0	0.75	24.94	0.4	18.03	1,099	2	98	0	0	44	-13.91	-21.07			Oct-12
50	14.39	26.98	15.50	1.08	4.75	0	0.92	24.97	0.4	17.88	1,099	2	98	0	0	44	-13.86	-20.92			Sep-10
50	3.87	16.40	-0.16	34.05	22.03	0.71	1.29	12.48	1.05	17.95	4,950	5	95	0	0	30	12.91	-21.25	5.50		Sep-05
50	3.75	15.97	-0.85	31.17	17.60	0	2.04	12.49	1.05	17.42	4,950	5	95	0	0	30	12.47	-21.49		1.00	Sep-05
	3.86	16.27	-0.38	33.10	20.51	0.49	1.54	12.49	1.05	17.72	4,950	5	95	0	0	30	12.78	-21.33			Sep-05
	4.01	16.59	0.14	35.17	23.63		0.91	12.51	1.05	17.96	4,950	5	95	0	0	30	13.13	-21.2			May-19
	4.00	16.66	0.28	35.78	24.70	1.13	0.86	12.47	1.05	18.2	4,950	5	95	0	0	30	13.13	-21.2			Aug-12
50	4.01	16.59	0.14	35.17	23.63	1.02	0.99	12.51	1.05	18.13	4,950	5	95	0	0	30	13.13	-21.2			Sep-05
50	2.82	12.27	-2.85	24.32	12.68	1.1	1.23	12.38	1.04	20.4	1,879	8	92	0	0	85	6.95	-26.82	5.50		Jul-90
50	2.60	11.91	-3.56	21.58	8.50	0.44	1.98	12.4	1.04	18.13	1,879	8	92	0	0	85	6.44	-27.04		1.00	Sep-93
	2.70	12.15	-3.10	23.37	11.22	0.96	1.48	12.38	1.04	20.12	1,879	8	92	0	0	85	6.72	-26.91			Mar-01
	2.87	12.32	-2.80	24.38	12.74		0.82	12.39	1.04	20.41	1,879	8	92	0	0	85	6.95	-26.82			May-19
	2.93	12.52	-2.43	25.98	15.14	1.56	0.79	12.4	1.04	20.31	1,879	8	92	0	0	85	6.95	-26.82			Mar-13
50	2.89	12.51	-2.46	25.59	14.36	1.52	0.85	12.38	1.04	20.59	1,879	8	92	0	0	85	7.25	-26.59			Nov-08
50	5.93	18.47	-2.13	21.92	10.11	0.91	1.1	13.38	1.1	41.23	17,750	3	97	0	0	18	18.05	-20.36	5.50		Mar-96
50	5.71	18.01	-2.88	19.16	6.05	0.17	1.85	13.36	1.1	39.04	17,750	3	97	0	0	18	17.54	-20.56		1.00	Mar-96
	5.86	18.36	-2.37	21.01	8.76	0.71	1.35	13.37	1.1	40.42	17,750	3	97	0	0	18	17.87	-20.41			Mar-01
	5.96	18.50	-2.10	21.95	10.14		0.72	13.38	1.1	41.24	17,750	3	97	0	0	18	18.05	-20.36			May-19
	6.05	18.74	-1.73	23.48	12.50	1.41	0.67	13.36	1.1	40.99	17,750	3	97	0	0	18	18.16	-20.36			Mar-12
50	6.00	18.65	-1.90	22.82	11.48	1.22	0.85	13.38	1.1	40.97	17,750	3	97	0	0	18	18.34	-20.19			Sep-05
	4.23	19.60	1.39	52.28	60.92	0.41	1.32	12.95	1.01	48.2	8,915	3	96	0	1	27	14.05	-18.89	5.50		Nov-97
	4.04	19.18	0.63	48.88	54.99	0	2.07	12.93	1.01	43.74	8,915	3	96	0	1	27	13.58	-19.19		1.00	Nov-97
	4.16	19.48	1.14	51.13	58.92	0.29	1.57	12.94	1.01	45.75	8,915	3	96	0	1	27	13.78	-19			Mar-01
	4.26	19.62	1.41	52.32	60.95		0.98	12.96	1.01	48.21	8,915	3	96	0	1	27	14.05	-18.89			May-19
	4.33	19.86	1.80	54.21	64.38	0.93	0.93	12.96	1.01	47.85	8,915	3	96	0	1	27	14.22	-18.89			Dec-11
	4.28	19.75	1.62	53.40	62.86	0.76	1.07	12.95	1.01	47.71	8,915	3	96	0	1	27	14.36	-18.79			Sep-05
50	4.28	17.84	8.87	24.27		2.21	1.35	9.58	0.9	11.5	136.9	4	96	0	0	37			5.50		May-16
50	4.00	17.36	7.90	21.30		1.51	2.15	9.58	0.9	11.44	136.9	4	96	0	0	37				1.00	May-16
	4.13	17.60	8.46	23.24		1.94	1.65	9.57	0.9	11.48	136.9	4	96	0	0	37					May-16
	4.29	18.00	9.16	25.59			1.05	9.56	0.9	11.49	136.9	4	96	0	0	37					May-19
	4.29	18.00	9.15	25.58		2.48	1	9.56	0.9	11.52	136.9	4	96	0	0	37					May-16
50	4.35	18.06	9.12	25.20		2.44	1.1	9.64	0.91	11.52	136.9	4	96	0	0	37					May-16
50	4.90	22.32	6.37	36.55	38.26	0.39	1.12	12.77	1	17.97	1,144	2	98	0	0	48	25.97	-14.5	5.50		Sep-00
50	4.78	21.87	5.67	33.59	33.26	0	1.87	12.74	1	16.21	1,144	2	98	0	0	48	25.51	-14.76		1.00	Sep-00
	4.88	22.19	6.16	35.59	36.65	0.17	1.37	12.74	1	17.4	1,144	2	98	0	0	48	25.66	-14.58			Mar-01
50	1.07	16.14	-4.66	25.80	17.57		1.32	12.76	1	17.98	1,144	2	98	0	0	48	32.64	-21.77	2.50		May-19
	4.94	22.45	6.67	37.54	40.01		0.74	12.76	1	17.98	1,144	2	98	0	0	48	26.2	-14.41			May-19
50	4.95	22.45	6.67	37.55	40.02	0.61	0.87	12.76	1	18.43	1,144	2	98	0	0	48	26.2	-14.41			Sep-00
50	5.81	22.33	11.72	41.07	55.83	0.89	0.87	12.38	0.99	48.04	9,574	2	98	0	0	56	26.45	-15.14	5.50		Feb-88
50	5.61	21.86	10.86	37.85	50.02	0.21	1.62	12.37	0.99	44.97	9,574	2	98	0	0	56	25.93	-15.39		1.00	Dec-93
	5.73	22.17	11.41	39.95	53.83	0.64	1.12	12.38	0.99	46.99	9,574	2	98	0	0	56	26.26	-15.22			Mar-01
	5.81	22.33	11.72	41.06	55.83		0.53	12.38	0.99	48.05	9,574	2	98	0	0	56	26.45	-15.14			May-19
	5.90	22.57	12.16	42.79	59.09	1.28	0.48	12.39	1	47.51	9,574	2	98	0	0	56	26.61	-15.14			Dec-11
50	5.87	22.47	11.98	42.03	57.68	1.1	0.62	12.38	0.99	47.58	9,574	2	98	0	0	56	26.77	-14.99			Nov-96
	4.30	22.41	2.49	32.71	33.00	0	1.1	14.14	1.02	25.18	2,245	1	99	0	0	60	29.9	-23.58	5.50		Aug-99
	4.11	21.95	1.74	29.72	28.13	0	1.84	14.13	1.02	20	2,245	1	99	0	0	60	29.36	-23.83		1.00	Aug-99
	4.23	22.24	2.27	31.72	31.34	0	1.34	14.16	1.02	23.63	2,245	1	99	0	0	60	29.71	-23.68			Mar-01
	4.34	22.57	2.74	33.66	34.68		0.71	14.15	1.02	25.19	2,245	1	99	0	0	60	30.2	-23.44			May-19

	MARKET			FUND TYPE, CATEGORY & OBJECTIVE	RATINGS				MINIMUMS	
Fund Name	Ticker Symbol	Traded On	Fund Type	Category and (Prospectus Objective)	Overall Rating	Reward Rating	Risk Rating	Recent Up/ Downgrade	Open to New Investors	Min Initial Investment
Invesco Oppenheimer Main Street Mid Cap Fund Class R6	**OPMIX**	NAS CM	Open End	US Equity Mid Cap (Growth)	**C+**	C	B-	Up	Y	0
Invesco Oppenheimer Main Street Mid Cap Fund Class Y	**OPMYX**	NAS CM	Open End	US Equity Mid Cap (Growth)	**C+**	C	B-	Up	Y	1,000
Invesco Oppenheimer Main Street Small Cap Fund Class A	**OSCAX**	NAS CM	Open End	US Equity Small Cap (Small Company)	**C**	C	C+		Y	1,000
Invesco Oppenheimer Main Street Small Cap Fund Class C	**OSCCX**	NAS CM	Open End	US Equity Small Cap (Small Company)	**C**	C	C+		Y	1,000
Invesco Oppenheimer Main Street Small Cap Fund Class R	**OSCNX**	NAS CM	Open End	US Equity Small Cap (Small Company)	**C**	C	C+		Y	0
Invesco Oppenheimer Main Street Small Cap Fund Class R5	**MNSQX**	NAS CM	Open End	US Equity Small Cap (Small Company)	**C**	C	C+		Y	1,000,000
Invesco Oppenheimer Main Street Small Cap Fund Class R6	**OSSIX**	NAS CM	Open End	US Equity Small Cap (Small Company)	**C**	C	C+		Y	1,000,000
Invesco Oppenheimer Main Street Small Cap Fund Class Y	**OSCYX**	NAS CM	Open End	US Equity Small Cap (Small Company)	**C**	C	C+		Y	1,000
Invesco Oppenheimer Mid Cap Value Fund Class A	**QVSCX**	NAS CM	Open End	US Equity Mid Cap (Growth)	**C**	C	C+		Y	1,000
Invesco Oppenheimer Mid Cap Value Fund Class C	**QSCCX**	NAS CM	Open End	US Equity Mid Cap (Growth)	**C**	C	C+		Y	1,000
Invesco Oppenheimer Mid Cap Value Fund Class R	**QSCNX**	NAS CM	Open End	US Equity Mid Cap (Growth)	**C**	C	C+		Y	0
Invesco Oppenheimer Mid Cap Value Fund Class R5	**MCVDX**	NAS CM	Open End	US Equity Mid Cap (Growth)	**C**	C	C+		Y	1,000,000
Invesco Oppenheimer Mid Cap Value Fund Class R6	**QSCIX**	NAS CM	Open End	US Equity Mid Cap (Growth)	**C**	C	C+		Y	0
Invesco Oppenheimer Mid Cap Value Fund Class Y	**QSCYX**	NAS CM	Open End	US Equity Mid Cap (Growth)	**C**	C	C+		Y	1,000
Invesco Oppenheimer Port Series: Active Alloc Cls A	**OAAAX**	NAS CM	Open End	Aggressive Alloc (Asset Alloc)	**B-**	C	B	Up	Y	1,000
Invesco Oppenheimer Port Series: Active Alloc Cls C	**OAACX**	NAS CM	Open End	Aggressive Alloc (Asset Alloc)	**B-**	C	B	Up	Y	1,000
Invesco Oppenheimer Port Series: Active Alloc Cls R	**OAANX**	NAS CM	Open End	Aggressive Alloc (Asset Alloc)	**B-**	C	B	Up	Y	0
Invesco Oppenheimer Port Series: Active Alloc Cls R5	**PAAJX**	NAS CM	Open End	Aggressive Alloc (Asset Alloc)	**B-**	C	B		Y	1,000,000
Invesco Oppenheimer Port Series: Active Alloc Cls R6	**PAAQX**	NAS CM	Open End	Aggressive Alloc (Asset Alloc)	**B-**	C	B		Y	0
Invesco Oppenheimer Port Series: Active Alloc Cls Y	**OAAYX**	NAS CM	Open End	Aggressive Alloc (Asset Alloc)	**B-**	C	B	Up	Y	1,000
Invesco Oppenheimer Port Series: Conservative Inv Cls A	**OACIX**	NAS CM	Open End	Cautious Alloc (Asset Alloc)	**B-**	C	A-		Y	1,000
Invesco Oppenheimer Port Series: Conservative Inv Cls C	**OCCIX**	NAS CM	Open End	Cautious Alloc (Asset Alloc)	**B-**	C	B+	Up	Y	1,000
Invesco Oppenheimer Port Series: Conservative Inv Cls R	**ONCIX**	NAS CM	Open End	Cautious Alloc (Asset Alloc)	**B-**	C	B+	Up	Y	0
Invesco Oppenheimer Port Series: Conservative Inv Cls R5	**PXCIX**	NAS CM	Open End	Cautious Alloc (Asset Alloc)	**B**	C+	A-		Y	1,000,000
Invesco Oppenheimer Port Series: Conservative Inv Cls R6	**PXCCX**	NAS CM	Open End	Cautious Alloc (Asset Alloc)	**B**	C+	A-		Y	0
Invesco Oppenheimer Port Series: Conservative Inv Cls Y	**OYCIX**	NAS CM	Open End	Cautious Alloc (Asset Alloc)	**B**	C+	A-	Up	Y	1,000
Invesco Oppenheimer Portfolio Series: Growth Inv Cls A	**OAAIX**	NAS CM	Open End	Aggressive Alloc (Growth)	**C**	C	B		Y	1,000
Invesco Oppenheimer Portfolio Series: Growth Inv Cls C	**OCAIX**	NAS CM	Open End	Aggressive Alloc (Growth)	**C**	C	B		Y	1,000
Invesco Oppenheimer Portfolio Series: Growth Inv Cls R	**ONAIX**	NAS CM	Open End	Aggressive Alloc (Growth)	**C**	C	B		Y	0
Invesco Oppenheimer Portfolio Series: Growth Inv Cls R5	**PXQIX**	NAS CM	Open End	Aggressive Alloc (Growth)	**C+**	C	B		Y	1,000,000
Invesco Oppenheimer Portfolio Series: Growth Inv Cls R6	**PXGGX**	NAS CM	Open End	Aggressive Alloc (Growth)	**C+**	C	B		Y	0
Invesco Oppenheimer Portfolio Series: Growth Inv Cls Y	**OYAIX**	NAS CM	Open End	Aggressive Alloc (Growth)	**C+**	C	B	Up	Y	1,000
Invesco Oppenheimer Portfolio Series: Moderate Inv Cls A	**OAMIX**	NAS CM	Open End	Moderate Alloc (Asset Alloc)	**B-**	C	B+	Up	Y	1,000
Invesco Oppenheimer Portfolio Series: Moderate Inv Cls C	**OCMIX**	NAS CM	Open End	Moderate Alloc (Asset Alloc)	**B-**	C	B+	Up	Y	1,000
Invesco Oppenheimer Portfolio Series: Moderate Inv Cls R	**ONMIX**	NAS CM	Open End	Moderate Alloc (Asset Alloc)	**B-**	C	B+	Up	Y	0
Invesco Oppenheimer Portfolio Series: Moderate Inv Cls R5	**PXMQX**	NAS CM	Open End	Moderate Alloc (Asset Alloc)	**B-**	C	B+		Y	1,000,000
Invesco Oppenheimer Portfolio Series: Moderate Inv Cls R6	**PXMMX**	NAS CM	Open End	Moderate Alloc (Asset Alloc)	**B-**	C	B+		Y	0
Invesco Oppenheimer Portfolio Series: Moderate Inv Cls Y	**OYMIX**	NAS CM	Open End	Moderate Alloc (Asset Alloc)	**B-**	C	B+	Up	Y	1,000
Invesco Oppenheimer Preferred Securities & Income Cls A	**OPRAX**	NAS CM	Open End	US Fixed Income (Growth & Income)	**D**	D+	B		Y	1,000
Invesco Oppenheimer Preferred Securities & Income Cls C	**PSTHX**	NAS CM	Open End	US Fixed Income (Growth & Income)	**D**	D+	B		Y	1,000
Invesco Oppenheimer Preferred Securities & Income Cls R	**PSTJX**	NAS CM	Open End	US Fixed Income (Growth & Income)	**D**	D+	B		Y	0
Invesco Oppenheimer Preferred Securities & Income Cls R5	**PSTVX**	NAS CM	Open End	US Fixed Income (Growth & Income)	**D**	D+	B		Y	1,000,000
Invesco Oppenheimer Preferred Securities & Income Cls R6	**OPRIX**	NAS CM	Open End	US Fixed Income (Growth & Income)	**D**	D+	B		Y	0
Invesco Oppenheimer Preferred Securities & Income Cls Y	**OPRYX**	NAS CM	Open End	US Fixed Income (Growth & Income)	**D**	D+	B		Y	1,000
Invesco Oppenheimer Real Estate Fund Class A	**OREAX**	NAS CM	Open End	Real Estate Sector Equity (Real Estate)	**C**	C	C+	Down	Y	1,000
Invesco Oppenheimer Real Estate Fund Class C	**ORECX**	NAS CM	Open End	Real Estate Sector Equity (Real Estate)	**C**	C	C+	Down	Y	1,000
Invesco Oppenheimer Real Estate Fund Class R	**ORENX**	NAS CM	Open End	Real Estate Sector Equity (Real Estate)	**C**	C	C+	Down	Y	0
Invesco Oppenheimer Real Estate Fund Class R5	**IOREX**	NAS CM	Open End	Real Estate Sector Equity (Real Estate)	**C**	C	C+		Y	1,000,000
Invesco Oppenheimer Real Estate Fund Class R6	**OREIX**	NAS CM	Open End	Real Estate Sector Equity (Real Estate)	**C+**	C	C+	Down	Y	0
Invesco Oppenheimer Real Estate Fund Class Y	**OREYX**	NAS CM	Open End	Real Estate Sector Equity (Real Estate)	**C+**	C	C+	Down	Y	1,000
Invesco Oppenheimer Rising Dividends Fund Class A	**OARDX**	NAS CM	Open End	US Equity Large Cap Blend (Growth)	**C+**	C	B		Y	1,000
Invesco Oppenheimer Rising Dividends Fund Class C	**OCRDX**	NAS CM	Open End	US Equity Large Cap Blend (Growth)	**C+**	C	B		Y	1,000

★ Expanded analysis of this fund is included in Section II.

	TOTAL RETURNS					PERFORMANCE				ASSETS		ASSET ALLOCATION & TURNOVER					BULL & BEAR		FEES		
Min Additional Investment	3-Month Total Return	6-Month Total Return	1-Year Total Return	3-Year Total Return	5-Year Total Return	Dividend Yield (TTM)	Expense Ratio	3-Yr Std Deviation	3-Year Beta	NAV	Total Assets (MIL)	%Cash	%Stocks	%Bonds	%Other	Turnover Ratio	Last Bull Market Total Return	Last Bear Market Total Return	Front End Fee (%)	Back End Fee (%)	Inception Date
	4.37	22.63	2.92	34.35	35.87	0.36	0.66	14.16	1.02	27.41	2,245	1	99	0	0	60	30.2	-23.45			Oct-12
	4.32	22.55	2.73	33.64	34.66	0.18	0.84	14.14	1.02	27.49	2,245	1	99	0	0	60	30.2	-23.45			Aug-99
50	3.28	16.25	-4.24	36.86	38.30	0	1.2	16.58	0.95	14.45	647.0	2	98	0	0	52			5.75		May-13
50	3.12	15.81	-4.92	33.81	33.03	0	1.94	16.55	0.95	13.84	647.0	2	98	0	0	52				1.00	May-13
	3.25	16.12	-4.47	35.72	36.39	0	1.45	16.56	0.95	14.26	647.0	2	98	0	0	52					May-13
	3.38	16.44	-3.90	38.50	41.22		0.91	16.57	0.95	14.45	647.0	2	98	0	0	52					May-19
	3.40	16.48	-3.88	38.53	41.26	0.37	0.77	16.58	0.95	14.56	647.0	2	98	0	0	52					May-13
50	3.34	16.42	-4.01	37.94	40.39	0.26	0.9	16.5	0.94	14.53	647.0	2	98	0	0	52					May-13
50	4.91	20.52	-0.35	28.78	27.90	0.49	1.16	14.59	1.08	50.86	1,107	4	96	0	0	71	18.01	-24.25	5.50		Jan-89
50	4.70	20.09	-1.10	25.92	23.17	0.06	1.9	14.58	1.08	40.78	1,107	4	96	0	0	71	17.46	-24.51		1.00	Sep-93
	4.81	20.34	-0.63	27.79	26.26	0.29	1.4	14.59	1.08	48.42	1,107	4	96	0	0	71	17.8	-24.35			Mar-01
	4.94	20.55	-0.32	28.82	27.94		0.8	14.6	1.08	50.82	1,107	4	96	0	0	71	18.01	-24.25			May-19
	4.99	20.76	0.04	30.43	30.69	0.86	0.75	14.6	1.08	51.84	1,107	4	96	0	0	71	18.11	-24.25			Feb-12
50	4.94	20.63	-0.12	29.76	29.49	0.7	0.91	14.58	1.08	52.35	1,107	4	96	0	0	71	18.24	-24.17			Oct-05
50	3.25	15.77	4.02	30.66	27.94	1.6	1.16	9.75	0.85	14.9	2,355	5	74	20	0	38	13.89	-15.74	5.50		Apr-05
50	3.04	15.30	3.21	27.64	23.17	0.87	1.91	9.74	0.85	14.54	2,355	5	74	20	0	38	13.4	-16.07		1.00	Apr-05
	3.20	15.62	3.70	29.61	26.28	1.38	1.41	9.74	0.85	14.8	2,355	5	74	20	0	38	13.7	-15.83			Apr-05
	3.35	15.95	4.34	31.68	29.54		0.82	9.73	0.85	14.91	2,355	5	74	20	0	38	14.14	-15.65			May-19
	3.35	15.95	4.34	31.68	29.54		0.77	9.73	0.85	14.91	2,355	5	74	20	0	38	14.14	-15.65			May-19
50	3.34	15.95	4.34	31.67	29.54	1.59	0.91	9.73	0.85	15.12	2,355	5	74	20	0	38	14.14	-15.65			Apr-05
50	3.16	9.39	6.11	16.19	18.13	2.11	0.95	4.41	0.63	9.78	578.8	10	20	68	0	45	8.93	-7.3	5.50		Apr-05
50	2.99	9.04	5.34	13.57	13.84	1.39	1.7	4.42	0.63	9.64	578.8	10	20	68	0	45	8.4	-7.5		1.00	Apr-05
	3.06	9.30	5.88	15.34	16.70	1.9	1.2	4.46	0.64	9.75	578.8	10	20	68	0	45	8.7	-7.33			Apr-05
	3.26	9.60	6.40	17.05	19.65		0.65	4.45	0.63	9.79	578.8	10	20	68	0	45	9.08	-7.15			May-19
	3.26	9.60	6.40	17.05	19.65		0.6	4.45	0.63	9.79	578.8	10	20	68	0	45	9.08	-7.15			May-19
50	3.25	9.58	6.39	17.03	19.64	2.37	0.7	4.45	0.63	9.83	578.8	10	20	68	0	45	9.08	-7.15			Apr-05
50	3.50	17.78	2.15	34.91	28.71	0.99	1.16	11.79	1.03	17.42	858.4	4	91	4	0	38	19.24	-20.98	5.50		Apr-05
50	3.29	17.33	1.36	31.87	23.94	0.23	1.91	11.74	1.02	16.92	858.4	4	91	4	0	38	18.72	-21.16		1.00	Apr-05
	3.45	17.57	1.93	33.89	27.11	0.76	1.41	11.77	1.02	17.39	858.4	4	91	4	0	38	19.02	-20.98			Apr-05
	3.58	17.86	2.37	35.88	30.23		0.84	11.77	1.02	17.42	858.4	4	91	4	0	38	19.48	-20.81			May-19
	3.64	17.93	2.43	35.96	30.30		0.79	11.78	1.02	17.43	858.4	4	91	4	0	38	19.48	-20.81			May-19
50	3.60	17.90	2.40	35.91	30.26	1.24	0.91	11.77	1.02	17.52	858.4	4	91	4	0	38	19.48	-20.81			Apr-05
50	3.39	13.53	5.33	25.79	25.72	1.63	0.99	7.65	0.66	12.5	1,571	7	55	37	0	40	12.38	-11.86	5.50		Apr-05
50	3.20	13.14	4.55	22.94	21.05	0.91	1.74	7.65	0.66	12.22	1,571	7	55	37	0	40	12.01	-12.18		1.00	Apr-05
	3.33	13.43	5.10	24.74	24.07	1.41	1.24	7.7	0.67	12.41	1,571	7	55	37	0	40	12.38	-11.95			Apr-05
	3.48	13.77	5.59	26.72	27.24		0.7	7.69	0.67	12.51	1,571	7	55	37	0	40	12.49	-11.7			May-19
	3.48	13.77	5.59	26.72	27.24		0.65	7.69	0.67	12.51	1,571	7	55	37	0	40	12.49	-11.7			May-19
50	3.45	13.74	5.56	26.69	27.20	1.84	0.74	7.69	0.67	12.58	1,571	7	55	37	0	40	12.49	-11.7			Apr-05
50	3.19	11.64	6.46			4.7	1.19			9.9	19.9	2	0	32	0	23			4.25		Feb-18
50	3.04	11.21	5.78				1.94			9.9	19.9	2	0	32	0	23					May-19
	3.16	11.48	6.30				1.44			9.9	19.9	2	0	32	0	23					May-19
	3.39	11.86	6.93				0.8			9.91	19.9	2	0	32	0	23					May-19
	3.39	11.87	6.93			5.14	0.75			9.9	19.9	2	0	32	0	23					Feb-18
50	3.26	11.79	6.74			4.96	0.94			9.9	19.9	2	0	32	0	23					Feb-18
50	1.10	18.13	11.31	9.82	39.98	1.85	1.34	12.56	0.94	26.03	1,001	0	100	0	0	84	30.53	-17.05	5.50		Mar-02
50	0.95	17.72	10.48	7.38	34.78	1.2	2.09	12.55	0.94	25.26	1,001	0	100	0	0	84	29.94	-17.31		1.00	Oct-03
	1.05	18.01	11.05	9.01	38.22	1.62	1.59	12.57	0.94	25.89	1,001	0	100	0	0	84	30.33	-17.16			Oct-03
	1.14	18.17	11.35	9.86	40.02		0.97	12.56	0.94	26.01	1,001	0	100	0	0	84	30.53	-17.05			May-19
	1.20	18.35	11.79	11.20	42.99	2.22	0.92	12.56	0.94	26.3	1,001	0	100	0	0	84	30.53	-17.05			Aug-12
50	1.19	18.27	11.57	10.65	41.67	2.05	1.09	12.56	0.94	26.34	1,001	0	100	0	0	84	30.75	-16.9			Oct-03
50	4.79	19.17	8.26	36.51	41.28	1.06	1.02	11.41	0.92	19.59	2,865	2	98	0	0	58	23.82	-15.84	5.50		Apr-80
50	4.62	18.74	7.49	33.47	36.07	0.63	1.77	11.38	0.92	16.28	2,865	2	98	0	0	58	23.22	-16.14		1.00	Sep-93

	MARKET		FUND TYPE, CATEGORY & OBJECTIVE		RATINGS				MINIMUMS	
Fund Name	Ticker Symbol	Traded On	Fund Type	Category and (Prospectus Objective)	Overall Rating	Reward Rating	Risk Rating	Recent Up/ Downgrade	Open to New Investors	Min Initial Investment
Invesco Oppenheimer Rising Dividends Fund Class R	ONRDX	NAS CM	Open End	US Equity Large Cap Blend (Growth)	C+	C	B		Y	0
Invesco Oppenheimer Rising Dividends Fund Class R5	RSDQX	NAS CM	Open End	US Equity Large Cap Blend (Growth)	C+	C	B		Y	1,000,000
Invesco Oppenheimer Rising Dividends Fund Class R6	OIRDX	NAS CM	Open End	US Equity Large Cap Blend (Growth)	C+	C	B		Y	0
Invesco Oppenheimer Rising Dividends Fund Class Y	OYRDX	NAS CM	Open End	US Equity Large Cap Blend (Growth)	C+	C	B		Y	1,000
Invesco Oppenheimer Small Cap Value Fund A	OVSAX	NAS CM	Open End	US Equity Small Cap (Small Company)	D+	D	C-	Down	Y	1,000
Invesco Oppenheimer Small Cap Value Fund C	OVSCX	NAS CM	Open End	US Equity Small Cap (Small Company)	D+	D	C-	Down	Y	1,000
Invesco Oppenheimer Small Cap Value Fund Class R5	IOSDX	NAS CM	Open End	US Equity Small Cap (Small Company)	D+	D	C-		Y	1,000,000
Invesco Oppenheimer Small Cap Value Fund R	OVSRX	NAS CM	Open End	US Equity Small Cap (Small Company)	D+	D	C-	Down	Y	0
Invesco Oppenheimer Small Cap Value Fund R6	OVSIX	NAS CM	Open End	US Equity Small Cap (Small Company)	D+	D	C-	Down	Y	0
Invesco Oppenheimer Small Cap Value Fund Y	OVSYX	NAS CM	Open End	US Equity Small Cap (Small Company)	D+	D	C-	Down	Y	1,000
Invesco Oppenheimer SteelPath MLP & Energy Infrastr Cls R	SPNMX	NAS CM	Open End	Energy Sector Equity (Natl Res)	D+	D+	C		Y	0
Invesco Oppenheimer SteelPath MLP & Energy Infrastr Cls R5	SPMKX	NAS CM	Open End	Energy Sector Equity (Natl Res)	D+	D+	C		Y	1,000,000
Invesco Oppenheimer SteelPath MLP Alpha Fund Class A	MLPAX	NAS CM	Open End	Energy Sector Equity ()	D+	C-	D+	Down	Y	1,000
Invesco Oppenheimer SteelPath MLP Alpha Fund Class C	MLPGX	NAS CM	Open End	Energy Sector Equity ()	D+	D+	D+	Down	Y	1,000
Invesco Oppenheimer SteelPath MLP Alpha Fund Class R	SPMGX	NAS CM	Open End	Energy Sector Equity ()	D+	C-	D+		Y	0
Invesco Oppenheimer SteelPath MLP Alpha Fund Class R5	SPMHX	NAS CM	Open End	Energy Sector Equity ()	D+	C-	D+		Y	1,000,000
Invesco Oppenheimer SteelPath MLP Alpha Fund Class R6	OSPAX	NAS CM	Open End	Energy Sector Equity ()	D+	C-	D+	Down	Y	1,000,000
Invesco Oppenheimer SteelPath MLP Alpha Fund Class Y	MLPOX	NAS CM	Open End	Energy Sector Equity ()	D+	C-	D+	Down	Y	1,000
Invesco Oppenheimer SteelPath MLP Alpha Plus Fund Class A	MLPLX	NAS CM	Open End	Energy Sector Equity ()	D+	C-	D+	Down	Y	1,000
Invesco Oppenheimer SteelPath MLP Alpha Plus Fund Class C	MLPMX	NAS CM	Open End	Energy Sector Equity ()	D+	D+	D+	Down	Y	1,000
Invesco Oppenheimer SteelPath MLP Alpha Plus Fund Class R	SPMJX	NAS CM	Open End	Energy Sector Equity ()	D+	D+	D+		Y	0
Invesco Oppenheimer SteelPath MLP Alpha Plus Fund Class R5	SPMPX	NAS CM	Open End	Energy Sector Equity ()	D+	D+	D+		Y	1,000,000
Invesco Oppenheimer SteelPath MLP Alpha Plus Fund Class R6	OSPPX	NAS CM	Open End	Energy Sector Equity ()	D+	C-	D+	Down	Y	1,000,000
Invesco Oppenheimer SteelPath MLP Alpha Plus Fund Class Y	MLPNX	NAS CM	Open End	Energy Sector Equity ()	D+	C-	D+	Down	Y	1,000
Invesco Oppenheimer SteelPath MLP & Energy Infrastr A	OMLPX	NAS CM	Open End	Energy Sector Equity (Natl Res)	D+	D+	C	Up	Y	1,000
Invesco Oppenheimer SteelPath MLP & Energy Infrastr C	OMLCX	NAS CM	Open End	Energy Sector Equity (Natl Res)	D+	D+	C	Up	Y	1,000
Invesco Oppenheimer SteelPath MLP & Energy Infrastr R6	OMLIX	NAS CM	Open End	Energy Sector Equity (Natl Res)	D+	D+	C	Up	Y	0
Invesco Oppenheimer SteelPath MLP & Energy Infrastr Y	OMLYX	NAS CM	Open End	Energy Sector Equity (Natl Res)	D+	D+	C	Up	Y	1,000
Invesco Oppenheimer SteelPath MLP Income Fund Class A	MLPDX	NAS CM	Open End	Energy Sector Equity ()	C-	C-	C-	Down		1,000
Invesco Oppenheimer SteelPath MLP Income Cls C Shares	MLPRX	NAS CM	Open End	Energy Sector Equity ()	C-	C-	D+	Down		1,000
Invesco Oppenheimer SteelPath MLP Income Fund Class R	SPNNX	NAS CM	Open End	Energy Sector Equity ()	C-	C-	C-		Y	0
Invesco Oppenheimer SteelPath MLP Income Fund Class R5	SPMQX	NAS CM	Open End	Energy Sector Equity ()	C-	C-	C-		Y	1,000,000
Invesco Oppenheimer SteelPath MLP Income Fund Class R6	OSPMX	NAS CM	Open End	Energy Sector Equity ()	C-	C-	C-	Down		1,000,000
Invesco Oppenheimer SteelPath MLP Income Fund Class Y	MLPZX	NAS CM	Open End	Energy Sector Equity ()	C-	C-	C-	Down		1,000
Invesco Oppenheimer SteelPath MLP Select 40 Fund Class A	MLPFX	NAS CM	Open End	Energy Sector Equity ()	C-	C-	C-	Down	Y	1,000
Invesco Oppenheimer SteelPath MLP Select 40 Fund Class C	MLPEX	NAS CM	Open End	Energy Sector Equity ()	C-	C-	C-	Down	Y	1,000
Invesco Oppenheimer SteelPath MLP Select 40 Fund Class R	SPMWX	NAS CM	Open End	Energy Sector Equity ()	C-	C-	C-		Y	0
Invesco Oppenheimer SteelPath MLP Select 40 Fund Class R5	SPMVX	NAS CM	Open End	Energy Sector Equity ()	C-	C-	C-		Y	1,000,000
Invesco Oppenheimer SteelPath MLP Select 40 Fund Class R6	OSPSX	NAS CM	Open End	Energy Sector Equity ()	C-	C-	C-	Down	Y	1,000,000
Invesco Oppenheimer SteelPath MLP Select 40 Fund Class Y	MLPTX	NAS CM	Open End	Energy Sector Equity ()	C-	C-	C-	Down	Y	1,000
Invesco Oppenheimer SteelPath Panoramic Fund Class A	EESAX	NAS CM	Open End	Energy Sector Equity (Growth & Income)	D	D	D	Down	Y	1,000
Invesco Oppenheimer SteelPath Panoramic Fund Class C	EESCX	NAS CM	Open End	Energy Sector Equity (Growth & Income)	D	D	D	Down	Y	1,000
Invesco Oppenheimer SteelPath Panoramic Fund Class R	EESRX	NAS CM	Open End	Energy Sector Equity (Growth & Income)	D	D	D	Down	Y	0
Invesco Oppenheimer SteelPath Panoramic Fund Class R5	SPMNX	NAS CM	Open End	Energy Sector Equity (Growth & Income)	D	D	D		Y	1,000,000
Invesco Oppenheimer SteelPath Panoramic Fund Class R6	EESIX	NAS CM	Open End	Energy Sector Equity (Growth & Income)	D	D	D	Down	Y	1,000,000
Invesco Oppenheimer SteelPath Panoramic Fund Class Y	EESYX	NAS CM	Open End	Energy Sector Equity (Growth & Income)	D	D	D	Down	Y	1,000
Invesco Oppenheimer Value Fund Class A	CGRWX	NAS CM	Open End	US Equity Large Cap Value (Growth)	C+	C	B	Up	Y	1,000
Invesco Oppenheimer Value Fund Class C	CGRCX	NAS CM	Open End	US Equity Large Cap Value (Growth)	C+	C	B	Up	Y	1,000
Invesco Oppenheimer Value Fund Class R	CGRNX	NAS CM	Open End	US Equity Large Cap Value (Growth)	C+	C	B	Up	Y	0
Invesco Oppenheimer Value Fund Class R5	IOVVX	NAS CM	Open End	US Equity Large Cap Value (Growth)	C+	C	B		Y	1,000,000
Invesco Oppenheimer Value Fund Class R6	OGRIX	NAS CM	Open End	US Equity Large Cap Value (Growth)	C+	C	B	Up	Y	1,000,000
Invesco Oppenheimer Value Fund Class Y	CGRYX	NAS CM	Open End	US Equity Large Cap Value (Growth)	C+	C	B	Up	Y	1,000

★ Expanded analysis of this fund is included in Section II.

Min Additional Investment	TOTAL RETURNS: 3-Month Total Return	6-Month Total Return	1-Year Total Return	3-Year Total Return	5-Year Total Return	PERFORMANCE: Dividend Yield (TTM)	Expense Ratio	3-Yr Std Deviation	3-Year Beta	ASSETS: NAV	Total Assets (MIL)	ASSET ALLOCATION & TURNOVER: %Cash	%Stocks	%Bonds	%Other	Turnover Ratio	BULL & BEAR: Last Bull Market Total Return	Last Bear Market Total Return	FEES: Front End Fee (%)	Back End Fee (%)	Inception Date
	4.70	19.06	8.00	35.46	39.58	0.84	1.27	11.42	0.92	19.45	2,865	2	98	0	0	58	23.51	-15.96			Mar-01
	4.84	19.23	8.32	36.58	41.35		0.68	11.42	0.93	19.58	2,865	2	98	0	0	58	23.82	-15.84			May-19
	4.86	19.39	8.70	38.21	44.29	1.38	0.63	11.37	0.92	20.32	2,865	2	98	0	0	58	23.86	-15.84			Feb-12
50	4.86	19.38	8.56	37.52	43.13	1.23	0.77	11.42	0.93	20.38	2,865	2	98	0	0	58	23.98	-15.81			Dec-96
	-0.62	11.57	-13.95	15.31		0.99	1.25	18.3	1.03	10.83	33.2	0	100	0	0	73			5.50		Dec-15
50	-0.82	11.16	-14.60	12.76		0.32	2	18.29	1.03	10.75	33.2	0	100	0	0	73				1.00	Dec-15
	-0.57	11.58	-13.70	16.40			0.98	18.3	1.03	10.82	33.2	0	100	0	0	73					May-19
	-0.68	11.33	-14.23	14.46		0.73	1.5	18.33	1.03	10.83	33.2	0	100	0	0	73					Dec-15
	-0.55	11.60	-13.68	16.41		1.3	0.93	18.3	1.03	10.83	33.2	0	100	0	0	73					Dec-15
50	-0.55	11.69	-13.77	16.20		1.25	1	18.32	1.03	10.84	33.2	0	100	0	0	73					Dec-15
	-1.05	21.94	1.71				1.62			9.63	12.9	0	100	0	0	51					May-19
	-1.01	21.99	1.75				0.98			9.63	12.9	0	100	0	0	51					May-19
50	-1.10	17.69	2.14	-5.08	-26.07	9.51	2.13	15.59	0.83	6.88	1,763	0	96	0	3	36	10.44	-5.84	5.50		Mar-10
50	-1.33	17.13	1.21	-7.32	-28.86	10.24	2.88	15.54	0.83	6.39	1,763	0	96	0	3	36	9.89	-6.14		1.00	Aug-11
	-1.08	17.62	1.94	-5.82	-26.96		2.38	15.52	0.83	6.88	1,763	0	96	0	3	36	10.27	-5.93			May-19
	-1.00	17.87	2.41	-4.44	-25.14		1.65	15.52	0.83	6.88	1,763	0	96	0	3	36	10.59	-5.73			May-19
	-1.06	17.87	2.33	-4.26	-24.86	9.15	1.82	15.54	0.83	7.15	1,763	0	96	0	3	36	10.59	-5.73			Jun-13
50	-1.06	17.79	2.34	-4.50	-25.19	9.2	1.88	15.52	0.83	7.11	1,763	0	96	0	3	36	10.59	-5.73			Mar-10
50	-1.54	24.98	2.21	-8.80	-39.45	12.04	3.55	22.53	1.15	5.46	180.5	0	125	0	-26	44			5.75		Feb-12
50	-1.65	24.56	1.41	-10.89	-41.63	12.94	4.32	22.54	1.15	5.08	180.5	0	125	0	-26	44				1.00	May-12
	-1.70	24.58	1.75	-9.67	-40.26		3.8	22.6	1.15	5.46	180.5	0	125	0	-26	44					May-19
	-1.43	25.07	2.40	-8.17	-38.67		3.23	22.62	1.16	5.47	180.5	0	125	0	-26	44					May-19
	-1.32	25.20	2.66	-7.77	-38.09	11.6	3.18	22.56	1.15	5.67	180.5	0	125	0	-26	44					Jun-13
50	-1.33	25.21	2.51	-8.07	-38.60	11.7	3.33	22.62	1.16	5.62	180.5	0	125	0	-26	44					Dec-11
50	-1.14	21.70	1.26			5.18	1.37			9.62	12.9	0	100	0	0	51			5.50		Nov-17
50	-1.33	21.31	0.53			4.45	2.12			9.61	12.9	0	100	0	0	51				1.00	Nov-17
	-1.01	21.98	1.74			5.98	0.93			9.59	12.9	0	100	0	0	51					Nov-17
50	-0.99	21.93	1.55			5.36	1.12			9.62	12.9	0	100	0	0	51					Nov-17
50	-0.88	20.37	6.07	-0.13	-20.71	12.27	1.91	15.47	0.81	5.56	3,270	0	94	0	3	30	10.19	-9.61	5.50		Mar-10
50	-0.95	20.01	5.58	-2.18	-23.47	13.35	2.66	15.47	0.8	5.11	3,270	0	94	0	3	30	9.77	-9.91		1.00	Jun-11
	-0.91	20.29	5.95	-0.82	-21.61		2.16	15.55	0.81	5.56	3,270	0	94	0	3	30	10.15	-9.77			May-19
	-0.83	20.55	6.43	0.62	-19.67		1.63	15.56	0.81	5.56	3,270	0	94	0	3	30	10.47	-9.58			May-19
	-0.84	20.60	6.55	0.77	-19.41	11.76	1.58	15.52	0.81	5.8	3,270	0	94	0	3	30	10.47	-9.58			Jun-13
50	-0.85	20.52	6.41	0.60	-19.68	11.84	1.66	15.56	0.81	5.76	3,270	0	94	0	3	30	10.47	-9.58			Mar-10
50	-0.32	13.50	3.87	2.22	-18.41	9.46	1.12	12.12	0.65	7.46	3,473	3	97	0	-2	24	10.78	-7.41	5.50		Mar-10
50	-0.48	13.13	3.12	-0.04	-21.37	10.14	1.87	12.05	0.65	6.96	3,473	3	97	0	-2	24	10.55	-7.7		1.00	Jul-11
	-0.35	13.28	3.57	1.42	-19.40		1.37	12.08	0.65	7.47	3,473	3	97	0	-2	24	10.7	-7.48			May-19
	-0.26	13.52	4.05	2.91	-17.39		0.84	12.08	0.65	7.47	3,473	3	97	0	-2	24	11.02	-7.29			May-19
	-0.18	13.70	4.25	3.22	-17.04	9.07	0.79	12.07	0.65	7.78	3,473	3	97	0	-2	24	11.02	-7.29			Jun-13
50	-0.18	13.61	4.14	3.00	-17.32	9.12	0.87	12.09	0.65	7.74	3,473	3	97	0	-2	24	11.02	-7.28			Mar-10
50	-3.00	13.84	-24.05	-16.77		0.07	1.55	23.61	1.1	8.06	18.3	1	99	0	0	48			5.50		Nov-15
50	-3.20	13.58	-24.56	-18.54		0	2.3	23.61	1.1	7.86	18.3	1	99	0	0	48				1.00	Nov-15
	-3.02	13.77	-24.21	-17.33		0	1.8	23.59	1.1	8.01	18.3	1	99	0	0	48					Nov-15
	-2.89	14.23	-23.70	-15.61			1.15	23.58	1.1	8.07	18.3	1	99	0	0	48					May-19
	-2.85	14.28	-23.67	-15.57		0.52	1.1	23.58	1.1	8.16	18.3	1	99	0	0	48					Nov-15
50	-2.98	14.04	-23.85	-16.08		0.28	1.3	23.6	1.1	8.12	18.3	1	99	0	0	48					Nov-15
50	4.52	18.11	5.07	35.70	33.87	1.4	0.92	12.37	1.01	33.62	1,382	4	95	0	0	45	19.25	-20.87	5.50		Sep-85
50	4.30	17.66	4.29	32.67	28.88	0.76	1.67	12.37	1.01	31.85	1,382	4	95	0	0	45	18.73	-21.16		1.00	May-96
	4.43	17.97	4.81	34.69	32.23	1.2	1.17	12.38	1.01	32.86	1,382	4	95	0	0	45	19.04	-20.98			Mar-01
	4.57	18.17	5.12	35.76	33.94		0.54	12.38	1.01	33.6	1,382	4	95	0	0	45	19.25	-20.87			May-19
	4.62	18.34	5.52	37.41	36.74	1.73	0.49	12.38	1.01	34.42	1,382	4	95	0	0	45	19.34	-20.87			Feb-12
50	4.59	18.26	5.32	36.69	35.49	1.56	0.67	12.37	1.01	34.49	1,382	4	95	0	0	45	19.52	-20.71			Dec-96

	MARKET		FUND TYPE, CATEGORY & OBJECTIVE		RATINGS				MINIMUMS	
Fund Name	Ticker Symbol	Traded On	Fund Type	Category and (Prospectus Objective)	Overall Rating	Reward Rating	Risk Rating	Recent Up/ Downgrade	Open to New Investors	Min Initial Investment
Invesco Pacific Growth Fund Class A	TGRAX	NAS CM	Open End	Asia Equity (Pacific Stock)	C	C-	C+		Y	1,000
Invesco Pacific Growth Fund Class C	TGRCX	NAS CM	Open End	Asia Equity (Pacific Stock)	C	C-	C		Y	1,000
Invesco Pacific Growth Fund Class R	TGRRX	NAS CM	Open End	Asia Equity (Pacific Stock)	C	C-	C+		Y	0
Invesco Pacific Growth Fund Class R6	TGRUX	NAS CM	Open End	Asia Equity (Pacific Stock)	C	C-	C+		Y	10,000,000
Invesco Pacific Growth Fund Class Y	TGRDX	NAS CM	Open End	Asia Equity (Pacific Stock)	C	C-	C+		Y	1,000
Invesco Pacific Growth Fund R5 Shares	TGRSX	NAS CM	Open End	Asia Equity (Pacific Stock)	C	C-	C+		Y	10,000,000
Invesco Peak Retirement 2015 Fund Class A	PKTMX	NAS CM	Open End	Target Date (Asset Alloc)	D+	D+	B	Up	Y	1,000
Invesco Peak Retirement 2015 Fund Class C	PKTNX	NAS CM	Open End	Target Date (Asset Alloc)	D+	D+	B	Up	Y	1,000
Invesco Peak Retirement 2015 Fund Class R	PKTPX	NAS CM	Open End	Target Date (Asset Alloc)	D+	D+	B	Up	Y	0
Invesco Peak Retirement 2015 Fund Class R5	PKTQX	NAS CM	Open End	Target Date (Asset Alloc)	D+	D+	B	Up	Y	10,000,000
Invesco Peak Retirement 2015 Fund Class R6	PKTRX	NAS CM	Open End	Target Date (Asset Alloc)	D+	D+	B	Up	Y	10,000,000
Invesco Peak Retirement 2015 Fund Class Y	PKTOX	NAS CM	Open End	Target Date (Asset Alloc)	D+	D+	B	Up	Y	1,000
Invesco Peak Retirement 2020 Fund Class A	PKTGX	NAS CM	Open End	Target Date (Asset Alloc)	D+	D+	B	Up	Y	1,000
Invesco Peak Retirement 2020 Fund Class C	PKTHX	NAS CM	Open End	Target Date (Asset Alloc)	D+	D+	B	Up	Y	1,000
Invesco Peak Retirement 2020 Fund Class R	PKTJX	NAS CM	Open End	Target Date (Asset Alloc)	D+	D+	B	Up	Y	0
Invesco Peak Retirement 2020 Fund Class R5	PKTKX	NAS CM	Open End	Target Date (Asset Alloc)	D+	D+	B	Up	Y	10,000,000
Invesco Peak Retirement 2020 Fund Class R6	PKTLX	NAS CM	Open End	Target Date (Asset Alloc)	D+	D+	B	Up	Y	10,000,000
Invesco Peak Retirement 2020 Fund Class Y	PKTIX	NAS CM	Open End	Target Date (Asset Alloc)	D+	D+	B	Up	Y	1,000
Invesco Peak Retirement 2025 Fund Class A	PKTAX	NAS CM	Open End	Target Date (Asset Alloc)	D+	D+	B-	Up	Y	1,000
Invesco Peak Retirement 2025 Fund Class C	PKTBX	NAS CM	Open End	Target Date (Asset Alloc)	D+	D+	B-	Up	Y	1,000
Invesco Peak Retirement 2025 Fund Class R	PKTDX	NAS CM	Open End	Target Date (Asset Alloc)	D+	D+	B-	Up	Y	0
Invesco Peak Retirement 2025 Fund Class R5	PKTEX	NAS CM	Open End	Target Date (Asset Alloc)	D+	D+	B-	Up	Y	10,000,000
Invesco Peak Retirement 2025 Fund Class R6	PKTFX	NAS CM	Open End	Target Date (Asset Alloc)	D+	D+	B	Up	Y	10,000,000
Invesco Peak Retirement 2025 Fund Class Y	PKTCX	NAS CM	Open End	Target Date (Asset Alloc)	D+	D+	B-	Up	Y	1,000
Invesco Peak Retirement 2030 Fund Class A	PKKSX	NAS CM	Open End	Target Date (Asset Alloc)	D+	D+	B-	Up	Y	1,000
Invesco Peak Retirement 2030 Fund Class C	PKKTX	NAS CM	Open End	Target Date (Asset Alloc)	D+	D+	B-	Up	Y	1,000
Invesco Peak Retirement 2030 Fund Class R	PKKVX	NAS CM	Open End	Target Date (Asset Alloc)	D+	D+	B-	Up	Y	0
Invesco Peak Retirement 2030 Fund Class R5	PKKWX	NAS CM	Open End	Target Date (Asset Alloc)	D+	D+	B-	Up	Y	10,000,000
Invesco Peak Retirement 2030 Fund Class R6	PKKZX	NAS CM	Open End	Target Date (Asset Alloc)	D+	D+	B-	Up	Y	10,000,000
Invesco Peak Retirement 2030 Fund Class Y	PKKUX	NAS CM	Open End	Target Date (Asset Alloc)	D+	D+	B-	Up	Y	1,000
Invesco Peak Retirement 2035 Fund Class A	PKKMX	NAS CM	Open End	Target Date (Asset Alloc)	D+	D+	B-	Up	Y	1,000
Invesco Peak Retirement 2035 Fund Class C	PKKNX	NAS CM	Open End	Target Date (Asset Alloc)	D+	D+	B-	Up	Y	1,000
Invesco Peak Retirement 2035 Fund Class R	PKKPX	NAS CM	Open End	Target Date (Asset Alloc)	D+	D+	B-	Up	Y	0
Invesco Peak Retirement 2035 Fund Class R5	PKKQX	NAS CM	Open End	Target Date (Asset Alloc)	D+	D+	B-	Up	Y	10,000,000
Invesco Peak Retirement 2035 Fund Class R6	PKKRX	NAS CM	Open End	Target Date (Asset Alloc)	D+	D+	B-	Up	Y	10,000,000
Invesco Peak Retirement 2035 Fund Class Y	PKKOX	NAS CM	Open End	Target Date (Asset Alloc)	D+	D+	B-	Up	Y	1,000
Invesco Peak Retirement 2040 Fund Class A	PKKGX	NAS CM	Open End	Target Date (Asset Alloc)	D+	D+	B-	Up	Y	1,000
Invesco Peak Retirement 2040 Fund Class C	PKKHX	NAS CM	Open End	Target Date (Asset Alloc)	D+	D+	B-	Up	Y	1,000
Invesco Peak Retirement 2040 Fund Class R	PKKJX	NAS CM	Open End	Target Date (Asset Alloc)	D+	D+	B-	Up	Y	0
Invesco Peak Retirement 2040 Fund Class R5	PKKKX	NAS CM	Open End	Target Date (Asset Alloc)	D+	D+	B-	Up	Y	10,000,000
Invesco Peak Retirement 2040 Fund Class R6	PKKLX	NAS CM	Open End	Target Date (Asset Alloc)	D+	D+	B-	Up	Y	10,000,000
Invesco Peak Retirement 2040 Fund Class Y	PKKIX	NAS CM	Open End	Target Date (Asset Alloc)	D+	D+	B-	Up	Y	1,000
Invesco Peak Retirement 2045 Fund Class A	PKKAX	NAS CM	Open End	Target Date (Asset Alloc)	D+	D+	B-	Up	Y	1,000
Invesco Peak Retirement 2045 Fund Class C	PKKBX	NAS CM	Open End	Target Date (Asset Alloc)	D+	D+	B-	Up	Y	1,000
Invesco Peak Retirement 2045 Fund Class R	PKKDX	NAS CM	Open End	Target Date (Asset Alloc)	D+	D+	B-	Up	Y	0
Invesco Peak Retirement 2045 Fund Class R5	PKKEX	NAS CM	Open End	Target Date (Asset Alloc)	D+	D+	B-	Up	Y	10,000,000
Invesco Peak Retirement 2045 Fund Class R6	PKKFX	NAS CM	Open End	Target Date (Asset Alloc)	D+	D+	B-	Up	Y	10,000,000
Invesco Peak Retirement 2045 Fund Class Y	PKKCX	NAS CM	Open End	Target Date (Asset Alloc)	D+	D+	B-	Up	Y	1,000
Invesco Peak Retirement 2050 Fund Class A	PKRSX	NAS CM	Open End	Target Date (Asset Alloc)	D+	D+	B-	Up	Y	1,000
Invesco Peak Retirement 2050 Fund Class C	PKRTX	NAS CM	Open End	Target Date (Asset Alloc)	D+	D+	C+	Up	Y	1,000
Invesco Peak Retirement 2050 Fund Class R	PKRVX	NAS CM	Open End	Target Date (Asset Alloc)	D+	D+	B-	Up	Y	0
Invesco Peak Retirement 2050 Fund Class R5	PKRWX	NAS CM	Open End	Target Date (Asset Alloc)	D+	D+	B-	Up	Y	10,000,000

★ Expanded analysis of this fund is included in Section II.

	TOTAL RETURNS					PERFORMANCE				ASSETS		ASSET ALLOCATION & TURNOVER					BULL & BEAR		FEES		
Min Additional Investment	3-Month Total Return	6-Month Total Return	1-Year Total Return	3-Year Total Return	5-Year Total Return	Dividend Yield (TTM)	Expense Ratio	3-Yr Std Deviation	3-Year Beta	NAV	Total Assets (MIL)	%Cash	%Stocks	%Bonds	%Other	Turnover Ratio	Last Bull Market Total Return	Last Bear Market Total Return	Front End Fee (%)	Back End Fee (%)	Inception Date
50	-0.78	13.03	-4.59	25.31	30.35	0.7	1.54	14.67	0.93	29.23	82.3	2	98	0	0	54	11.31	-22.21	5.50		Jul-97
50	-1.03	12.55	-5.35	22.46	25.54	0	2.3	14.66	0.93	26.72	82.3	2	98	0	0	54	10.86	-22.47		1.00	Jul-97
	-0.82	12.92	-4.81	24.36	28.73	0.47	1.8	14.67	0.93	28.83	82.3	2	98	0	0	54	11.18	-22.33			Mar-08
	-0.69	13.22	-4.29	26.40	32.17	1.06	1.22	14.69	0.94	29.88	82.3	2	98	0	0	54	11.54	-22.17			Apr-17
50	-0.69	13.20	-4.37	26.20	31.96	0.97	1.3	14.68	0.94	29.83	82.3	2	98	0	0	54	11.54	-22.17			Jul-97
	-0.73	13.22	-4.29	26.48	32.69	1.06	1.22	14.67	0.93	29.88	82.3	2	98	0	0	54	11.58	-22.03			May-11
50	2.71	9.53	6.61			2.7	0.81			10.22	0.60	5	26	64	1	5			5.50		Dec-17
50	2.53	9.15	5.91			2.54	1.56			10.13	0.60	5	26	64	1	5				1.00	Dec-17
	2.61	9.45	6.32			2.64	1.06			10.19	0.60	5	26	64	1	5					Dec-17
	2.80	9.62	6.94			2.81	0.56			10.25	0.60	5	26	64	1	5					Dec-17
	2.80	9.74	6.94			2.81	0.56			10.25	0.60	5	26	64	1	5					Dec-17
50	2.80	9.62	6.94			2.81	0.56			10.25	0.60	5	26	64	1	5					Dec-17
50	2.60	9.28	6.17			2.46	0.81			10.24	0.99	7	27	64	1	5			5.50		Dec-17
50	2.41	8.86	5.36			1.84	1.56			10.19	0.99	7	27	64	1	5				1.00	Dec-17
	2.60	9.17	5.92			2.24	1.06			10.23	0.99	7	27	64	1	5					Dec-17
	2.69	9.48	6.41			2.58	0.56			10.27	0.99	7	27	64	1	5					Dec-17
	2.69	9.48	6.41			2.58	0.56			10.27	0.99	7	27	64	1	5					Dec-17
50	2.69	9.48	6.41			2.58	0.56			10.27	0.99	7	27	64	1	5					Dec-17
50	2.60	10.08	6.03			2.18	0.81			10.26	1.8	9	32	58	1	10			5.50		Dec-17
50	2.51	9.67	5.31			1.71	1.56			10.2	1.8	9	32	58	1	10				1.00	Dec-17
	2.50	9.87	5.85			2.01	1.06			10.24	1.8	9	32	58	1	10					Dec-17
	2.69	10.17	6.38			2.29	0.56			10.29	1.8	9	32	58	1	10					Dec-17
	2.69	10.17	6.38			2.29	0.56			10.29	1.8	9	32	58	1	10					Dec-17
50	2.69	10.17	6.38			2.29	0.56			10.29	1.8	9	32	58	1	10					Dec-17
50	2.70	11.27	5.69			1.94	0.81			10.26	1.8	12	41	45	1	5			5.50		Dec-17
50	2.50	10.85	4.85			1.3	1.56			10.21	1.8	12	41	45	1	5				1.00	Dec-17
	2.60	11.06	5.32			1.71	1.06			10.24	1.8	12	41	45	1	5					Dec-17
	2.79	11.36	6.00			2.03	0.56			10.29	1.8	12	41	45	1	5					Dec-17
	2.79	11.48	6.00			2.03	0.56			10.29	1.8	12	41	45	1	5					Dec-17
50	2.79	11.36	6.00			2.03	0.56			10.29	1.8	12	41	45	1	5					Dec-17
50	2.81	12.32	5.23			2.02	0.81			10.21	1.2	11	53	35	1	6			5.50		Dec-17
50	2.62	11.89	4.36			1.45	1.56			10.16	1.2	11	53	35	1	6				1.00	Dec-17
	2.72	12.22	5.02			1.93	1.06			10.19	1.2	11	53	35	1	6					Dec-17
	2.91	12.52	5.46			2.14	0.56			10.24	1.2	11	53	35	1	6					Dec-17
	2.91	12.52	5.46			2.14	0.56			10.24	1.2	11	53	35	1	6					Dec-17
50	2.91	12.52	5.46			2.14	0.56			10.24	1.2	11	53	35	1	6					Dec-17
50	2.92	13.57	4.97			1.84	0.81			10.21	1.1	9	65	25	0	5			5.50		Dec-17
50	2.72	13.12	4.13			1.12	1.56			10.17	1.1	9	65	25	0	5				1.00	Dec-17
	2.82	13.45	4.79			1.6	1.06			10.2	1.1	9	65	25	0	5					Dec-17
	2.91	13.65	5.27			1.93	0.56			10.24	1.1	9	65	25	0	5					Dec-17
	3.01	13.65	5.27			1.93	0.56			10.24	1.1	9	65	25	0	5					Dec-17
50	2.91	13.65	5.27			1.93	0.56			10.24	1.1	9	65	25	0	5					Dec-17
50	2.90	14.50	5.20			1.82	0.81			10.26	0.97	9	73	18	0	3			5.50		Dec-17
50	2.83	14.26	4.34			1.61	1.56			10.17	0.97	9	73	18	0	3				1.00	Dec-17
	2.91	14.54	5.00			1.74	1.06			10.24	0.97	9	73	18	0	3					Dec-17
	3.10	14.71	5.57			1.96	0.56			10.29	0.97	9	73	18	0	3					Dec-17
	3.10	14.71	5.57			1.96	0.56			10.29	0.97	9	73	18	0	3					Dec-17
50	3.10	14.71	5.57			1.96	0.56			10.29	0.97	9	73	18	0	3					Dec-17
50	3.18	15.60	5.82			1.58	0.81			10.37	1.3	8	79	13	0	10			5.50		Dec-17
50	3.10	15.24	5.13			1.43	1.56			10.28	1.3	8	79	13	0	10				1.00	Dec-17
	3.19	15.53	5.54			1.51	1.06			10.34	1.3	8	79	13	0	10					Dec-17
	3.37	15.79	6.19			1.64	0.56			10.41	1.3	8	79	13	0	10					Dec-17

	MARKET			FUND TYPE, CATEGORY & OBJECTIVE	RATINGS				MINIMUMS	
Fund Name	Ticker Symbol	Traded On	Fund Type	Category and (Prospectus Objective)	Overall Rating	Reward Rating	Risk Rating	Recent Up/ Downgrade	Open to New Investors	Min Initial Investment
Invesco Peak Retirement 2050 Fund Class R6	PKRZX	NAS CM	Open End	Target Date (Asset Alloc)	D+	D+	B-	Up	Y	10,000,000
Invesco Peak Retirement 2050 Fund Class Y	PKRUX	NAS CM	Open End	Target Date (Asset Alloc)	D+	D+	B-	Up	Y	1,000
Invesco Peak Retirement 2055 Fund Class A	PKRMX	NAS CM	Open End	Target Date (Asset Alloc)	D+	D+	B-	Up	Y	1,000
Invesco Peak Retirement 2055 Fund Class C	PKRNX	NAS CM	Open End	Target Date (Asset Alloc)	D+	D+	C+	Up	Y	1,000
Invesco Peak Retirement 2055 Fund Class R	PKRPX	NAS CM	Open End	Target Date (Asset Alloc)	D+	D+	C+	Up	Y	0
Invesco Peak Retirement 2055 Fund Class R5	PKRQX	NAS CM	Open End	Target Date (Asset Alloc)	D+	D+	B-	Up	Y	10,000,000
Invesco Peak Retirement 2055 Fund Class R6	PKRRX	NAS CM	Open End	Target Date (Asset Alloc)	D+	D+	B-	Up	Y	10,000,000
Invesco Peak Retirement 2055 Fund Class Y	PKROX	NAS CM	Open End	Target Date (Asset Alloc)	D+	D+	B-	Up	Y	1,000
Invesco Peak Retirement 2060 Fund Class A	PKRGX	NAS CM	Open End	Target Date (Asset Alloc)	D+	D+	C+	Up	Y	1,000
Invesco Peak Retirement 2060 Fund Class C	PKRHX	NAS CM	Open End	Target Date (Asset Alloc)	D+	D+	C+	Up	Y	1,000
Invesco Peak Retirement 2060 Fund Class R	PKRJX	NAS CM	Open End	Target Date (Asset Alloc)	D+	D+	C+	Up	Y	0
Invesco Peak Retirement 2060 Fund Class R5	PKRKX	NAS CM	Open End	Target Date (Asset Alloc)	D+	D+	C+	Up	Y	10,000,000
Invesco Peak Retirement 2060 Fund Class R6	PKRLX	NAS CM	Open End	Target Date (Asset Alloc)	D+	D+	C+	Up	Y	10,000,000
Invesco Peak Retirement 2060 Fund Class Y	PKRIX	NAS CM	Open End	Target Date (Asset Alloc)	D+	D+	C+	Up	Y	1,000
Invesco Peak Retirement 2065 Fund Class A	PKRAX	NAS CM	Open End	Target Date (Asset Alloc)	D+	D+	B-	Up	Y	1,000
Invesco Peak Retirement 2065 Fund Class C	PKRBX	NAS CM	Open End	Target Date (Asset Alloc)	D+	D+	C+	Up	Y	1,000
Invesco Peak Retirement 2065 Fund Class R	PKRDX	NAS CM	Open End	Target Date (Asset Alloc)	D+	D+	C+	Up	Y	0
Invesco Peak Retirement 2065 Fund Class R5	PKREX	NAS CM	Open End	Target Date (Asset Alloc)	D+	D+	B-	Up	Y	10,000,000
Invesco Peak Retirement 2065 Fund Class R6	PKRFX	NAS CM	Open End	Target Date (Asset Alloc)	D+	D+	B-	Up	Y	10,000,000
Invesco Peak Retirement 2065 Fund Class Y	PKRCX	NAS CM	Open End	Target Date (Asset Alloc)	D+	D+	B-	Up	Y	1,000
Invesco Peak Retirement Now Fund Class A	PKTSX	NAS CM	Open End	Target Date (Asset Alloc)	D+	D+	B	Up	Y	1,000
Invesco Peak Retirement Now Fund Class C	PKTTX	NAS CM	Open End	Target Date (Asset Alloc)	D+	D+	B	Up	Y	1,000
Invesco Peak Retirement Now Fund Class R	PKTVX	NAS CM	Open End	Target Date (Asset Alloc)	D+	D+	B	Up	Y	0
Invesco Peak Retirement Now Fund Class R5	PKTWX	NAS CM	Open End	Target Date (Asset Alloc)	D+	D+	B	Up	Y	10,000,000
Invesco Peak Retirement Now Fund Class R6	PKTZX	NAS CM	Open End	Target Date (Asset Alloc)	D+	D+	B	Up	Y	10,000,000
Invesco Peak Retirement Now Fund Class Y	PKTUX	NAS CM	Open End	Target Date (Asset Alloc)	D+	D+	B	Up	Y	1,000
Invesco Real Estate Fund Class A	IARAX	NAS CM	Open End	Real Estate Sector Equity (Real Estate)	C+	C	B-	Down	Y	1,000
Invesco Real Estate Fund Class C	IARCX	NAS CM	Open End	Real Estate Sector Equity (Real Estate)	C+	C	B-		Y	1,000
Invesco Real Estate Fund Class R	IARRX	NAS CM	Open End	Real Estate Sector Equity (Real Estate)	C+	C	B-		Y	0
Invesco Real Estate Fund Class R6	IARFX	NAS CM	Open End	Real Estate Sector Equity (Real Estate)	C+	C+	B	Down	Y	10,000,000
Invesco Real Estate Fund Class Y	IARYX	NAS CM	Open End	Real Estate Sector Equity (Real Estate)	C+	C	B	Down	Y	1,000
Invesco Real Estate Fund Investor Class	REINX	NAS CM	Open End	Real Estate Sector Equity (Real Estate)	C+	C	B	Down		1,000
Invesco Real Estate Fund R5 Class	IARIX	NAS CM	Open End	Real Estate Sector Equity (Real Estate)	C+	C+	B	Down	Y	10,000,000
Invesco S&P 500 Index Fund Class A	SPIAX	NAS CM	Open End	US Equity Large Cap Blend (Growth & Income)	B-	C	B		Y	1,000
Invesco S&P 500 Index Fund Class C	SPICX	NAS CM	Open End	US Equity Large Cap Blend (Growth & Income)	B-	C	B		Y	1,000
Invesco S&P 500 Index Fund Class Y	SPIDX	NAS CM	Open End	US Equity Large Cap Blend (Growth & Income)	B-	C	B		Y	1,000
Invesco S&P 500 Index Fund ClassR6	SPISX	NAS CM	Open End	US Equity Large Cap Blend (Growth & Income)	B-	C	B		Y	10,000,000
Invesco Select Companies Fund Class A	ATIAX	NAS CM	Open End	US Equity Small Cap (Small Company)	C+	C	B			1,000
Invesco Select Companies Fund Class C	ATICX	NAS CM	Open End	US Equity Small Cap (Small Company)	C+	C	B-			1,000
Invesco Select Companies Fund Class R	ATIRX	NAS CM	Open End	US Equity Small Cap (Small Company)	C+	C	B-			0
Invesco Select Companies Fund Class R6	ATISX	NAS CM	Open End	US Equity Small Cap (Small Company)	C+	C	B		Y	10,000,000
Invesco Select Companies Fund Class Y	ATIYX	NAS CM	Open End	US Equity Small Cap (Small Company)	C+	C	B			1,000
Invesco Select Companies Fund R5 Class	ATIIX	NAS CM	Open End	US Equity Small Cap (Small Company)	C+	C	B			10,000,000
Invesco Select Opportunities Fund Class A	IZSAX	NAS CM	Open End	Global Equity Mid/Small Cap (Small Company)	C	D+	C+		Y	1,000
Invesco Select Opportunities Fund Class C	IZSCX	NAS CM	Open End	Global Equity Mid/Small Cap (Small Company)	C-	D	C	Down	Y	1,000
Invesco Select Opportunities Fund Class R	IZSRX	NAS CM	Open End	Global Equity Mid/Small Cap (Small Company)	C-	D+	C+	Down	Y	0
Invesco Select Opportunities Fund Class R6	IZFSX	NAS CM	Open End	Global Equity Mid/Small Cap (Small Company)	C	D+	C+		Y	10,000,000
Invesco Select Opportunities Fund Class Y	IZSYX	NAS CM	Open End	Global Equity Mid/Small Cap (Small Company)	C	D+	C+		Y	1,000
Invesco Select Opportunities Fund R5 Class	IZSIX	NAS CM	Open End	Global Equity Mid/Small Cap (Small Company)	C	D+	C+		Y	10,000,000
Invesco Small Cap Discovery Fund Class A	VASCX	NAS CM	Open End	US Equity Small Cap (Small Company)	C+	C	C+	Down	Y	1,000
Invesco Small Cap Discovery Fund Class C	VCSCX	NAS CM	Open End	US Equity Small Cap (Small Company)	C+	C	C+	Down	Y	1,000
Invesco Small Cap Discovery Fund Class R5	VESCX	NAS CM	Open End	US Equity Small Cap (Small Company)	C+	C	C+	Down	Y	10,000,000

★ Expanded analysis of this fund is included in Section II.

	TOTAL RETURNS					PERFORMANCE				ASSETS		ASSET ALLOCATION & TURNOVER					BULL & BEAR		FEES		
Min Additional Investment	3-Month Total Return	6-Month Total Return	1-Year Total Return	3-Year Total Return	5-Year Total Return	Dividend Yield (TTM)	Expense Ratio	3-Yr Std Deviation	3-Year Beta	NAV	Total Assets (MIL)	%Cash	%Stocks	%Bonds	%Other	Turnover Ratio	Last Bull Market Total Return	Last Bear Market Total Return	Front End Fee (%)	Back End Fee (%)	Inception Date
	3.27	15.68	6.09			1.64	0.56			10.4	1.3	8	79	13	0	10					Dec-17
50	3.37	15.79	6.19			1.64	0.56			10.41	1.3	8	79	13	0	10					Dec-17
50	3.29	16.31	5.50			1.81	0.81			10.34	0.61	7	85	8	0	6			5.50		Dec-17
50	3.11	16.04	4.75			1.43	1.56			10.27	0.61	7	85	8	0	6				1.00	Dec-17
	3.09	16.10	5.12			1.66	1.06			10.31	0.61	7	85	8	0	6					Dec-17
	3.29	16.53	5.82			1.99	0.56			10.36	0.61	7	85	8	0	6					Dec-17
	3.29	16.53	5.82			1.99	0.56			10.36	0.61	7	85	8	0	6					Dec-17
50	3.29	16.53	5.82			1.99	0.56			10.36	0.61	7	85	8	0	6					Dec-17
50	3.39	16.70	5.54			1.75	0.81			10.34	0.79	7	87	5	0	6			5.50		Dec-17
50	3.21	16.28	4.67			1.19	1.56			10.28	0.79	7	87	5	0	6				1.00	Dec-17
	3.40	16.61	5.20			1.56	1.06			10.32	0.79	7	87	5	0	6					Dec-17
	3.49	16.92	5.89			1.95	0.56			10.36	0.79	7	87	5	0	6					Dec-17
	3.49	16.92	5.89			1.95	0.56			10.36	0.79	7	87	5	0	6					Dec-17
50	3.49	16.92	5.89			1.95	0.56			10.36	0.79	7	87	5	0	6					Dec-17
50	3.16	16.42	5.18			1.76	0.81			10.42	0.58	7	87	6	0	165			5.50		Dec-17
50	3.01	16.08	4.44			1.45	1.56			10.25	0.58	7	87	6	0	165				1.00	Dec-17
	3.10	16.38	4.87			1.64	1.06			10.3	0.58	7	87	6	0	165					Dec-17
	3.19	16.57	5.49			1.99	0.56			10.34	0.58	7	87	6	0	165					Dec-17
	3.19	16.57	5.49			1.99	0.56			10.34	0.58	7	87	6	0	165					Dec-17
50	3.19	16.57	5.49			1.99	0.56			10.34	0.58	7	87	6	0	165					Dec-17
50	2.75	9.76	7.23			4.2	0.81			9.97	0.52	1	26	67	1	4			5.50		Dec-17
50	2.56	9.36	6.43			3.46	1.56			9.97	0.52	1	26	67	1	4				1.00	Dec-17
	2.69	9.63	6.96			3.95	1.06			9.97	0.52	1	26	67	1	4					Dec-17
	2.82	9.90	7.39			4.44	0.56			9.97	0.52	1	26	67	1	4					Dec-17
	2.82	9.90	7.39			4.44	0.56			9.97	0.52	1	26	67	1	4					Dec-17
50	2.82	9.90	7.39			4.44	0.56			9.97	0.52	1	26	67	1	4					Dec-17
50	1.99	19.56	11.67	17.93	44.68	1.36	1.27	12.3	0.96	22.2	1,492	2	98	0	0	47	29.78	-16.21	5.50		Dec-96
50	1.82	19.14	10.80	15.28	39.32	0.67	2.02	12.26	0.96	22.07	1,492	2	98	0	0	47	29.21	-16.51		1.00	May-95
	1.93	19.39	11.38	17.03	42.89	1.13	1.52	12.25	0.96	22.23	1,492	2	98	0	0	47	29.61	-16.31			Apr-04
	2.10	19.87	12.17	19.54	48.03	1.78	0.8	12.26	0.96	22.17	1,492	2	98	0	0	47	29.21	-16.51			Sep-12
50	2.10	19.72	12.00	18.83	46.52	1.59	1.02	12.27	0.96	22.19	1,492	2	98	0	0	47	29.96	-16.14			Oct-08
50	2.00	19.58	11.72	17.99	44.80	1.39	1.23	12.26	0.96	22.14	1,492	2	98	0	0	47	29.73	-16.23			Sep-03
	2.13	19.82	12.13	19.23	47.38	1.7	0.88	12.24	0.96	22.18	1,492	2	98	0	0	47	30.09	-16.07			Apr-04
50	4.17	19.23	9.84	48.40	61.61	1.32	0.57	12.21	1	31.68	1,394	0	100	0	0	4	24.64	-16.48	5.50		Sep-97
50	3.95	18.78	8.98	45.08	55.71	0.72	1.29	12.19	1	30.48	1,394	0	100	0	0	4	24.15	-16.74		1.00	Sep-97
50	4.22	19.34	10.05	49.43	63.60	1.52	0.32	12.21	1	32.08	1,394	0	100	0	0	4	24.88	-16.44			Sep-97
	4.22	19.38	10.12	49.57	63.76	1.55	0.29	12.22	1	32.09	1,394	0	100	0	0	4	24.88	-16.44			Apr-17
50	1.18	19.86	1.52	46.57	29.58	0	1.25	14.96	0.8	17.86	380.0	5	95	0	0	12	18.75	-14.77	5.50		Nov-03
50	1.03	19.33	0.76	43.22	24.72	0	2	14.98	0.8	14.69	380.0	5	95	0	0	12	18.19	-15.03		1.00	Nov-03
	1.14	19.67	1.25	45.47	27.94	0	1.5	15	0.8	16.85	380.0	5	95	0	0	12	18.58	-14.89			Apr-04
	1.30	20.08	1.96	47.93	30.77	0	0.85	14.97	0.8	19.43	380.0	5	95	0	0	12	18.75	-14.77			Apr-17
50	1.26	19.98	1.79	47.60	31.19	0	1	15.01	0.8	18.43	380.0	5	95	0	0	12	18.93	-14.69			Oct-08
	1.25	20.06	1.86	48.01	31.72	0	0.93	15.01	0.8	19.39	380.0	5	95	0	0	12	18.99	-14.63			Apr-04
50	-0.84	12.20	-3.93	25.21	0.00	0.27	1.03	13.27	0.92	14.16	49.7	4	96	0	0	23			5.50		Aug-12
50	-0.95	11.85	-4.61	22.48	-3.66	0	1.78	13.26	0.91	13.49	49.7	4	96	0	0	23				1.00	Aug-12
	-0.85	12.03	-4.16	24.25	-1.24	0.04	1.28	13.25	0.91	13.96	49.7	4	96	0	0	23					Aug-12
	-0.76	12.38	-3.66	26.19	1.22	0.65	0.78	13.24	0.91	14.34	49.7	4	96	0	0	23					Sep-12
50	-0.69	12.37	-3.66	26.17	1.29	0.65	0.78	13.26	0.91	14.35	49.7	4	96	0	0	23					Aug-12
	-0.76	12.37	-3.66	26.17	1.22	0.65	0.78	13.24	0.91	14.35	49.7	4	96	0	0	23					Aug-12
50	5.65	27.55	6.93	61.50	56.34	0	1.37	15.97	0.88	9.72	602.2	3	97	0	0	49	28.36	-25.01	5.50		Nov-00
50	5.60	27.20	6.34	58.18	50.89	0	2.08	16.01	0.89	6.78	602.2	3	97	0	0	49	27.67	-25.14		1.00	Nov-00
	5.85	27.81	7.33	63.56	59.77	0	0.98	15.96	0.88	10.66	602.2	3	97	0	0	49	28.37	-25.01			Sep-12

	MARKET			FUND TYPE, CATEGORY & OBJECTIVE	RATINGS				MINIMUMS	
Fund Name	Ticker Symbol	Traded On	Fund Type	Category and (Prospectus Objective)	Overall Rating	Reward Rating	Risk Rating	Recent Up/ Downgrade	Open to New Investors	Min Initial Investment
Invesco Small Cap Discovery Fund Class R6	VFSCX	NAS CM	Open End	US Equity Small Cap (Small Company)	C+	C	C+	Down	Y	10,000,000
Invesco Small Cap Discovery Fund Class Y	VISCX	NAS CM	Open End	US Equity Small Cap (Small Company)	C+	C	C+	Down	Y	1,000
Invesco Small Cap Equity Fund Class A	SMEAX	NAS CM	Open End	US Equity Small Cap (Small Company)	C	C	C+		Y	1,000
Invesco Small Cap Equity Fund Class C	SMECX	NAS CM	Open End	US Equity Small Cap (Small Company)	C	C	C+		Y	1,000
Invesco Small Cap Equity Fund Class R	SMERX	NAS CM	Open End	US Equity Small Cap (Small Company)	C	C	C+		Y	0
Invesco Small Cap Equity Fund Class R6	SMEFX	NAS CM	Open End	US Equity Small Cap (Small Company)	C	C	C+		Y	10,000,000
Invesco Small Cap Equity Fund Class Y	SMEYX	NAS CM	Open End	US Equity Small Cap (Small Company)	C	C	C+		Y	1,000
Invesco Small Cap Equity Fund R5 Class	SMEIX	NAS CM	Open End	US Equity Small Cap (Small Company)	C	C	C+		Y	10,000,000
Invesco Small Cap Growth Fund Class A	GTSAX	NAS CM	Open End	US Equity Small Cap (Small Company)	C	C	C+	Down		1,000
Invesco Small Cap Growth Fund Class C	GTSDX	NAS CM	Open End	US Equity Small Cap (Small Company)	C	C	C+			1,000
Invesco Small Cap Growth Fund Class R	GTSRX	NAS CM	Open End	US Equity Small Cap (Small Company)	C	C	C+	Down		0
Invesco Small Cap Growth Fund Class R6	GTSFX	NAS CM	Open End	US Equity Small Cap (Small Company)	C	C	C+	Down		10,000,000
Invesco Small Cap Growth Fund Class Y	GTSYX	NAS CM	Open End	US Equity Small Cap (Small Company)	C	C	C+	Down		1,000
Invesco Small Cap Growth Fund Investor Class	GTSIX	NAS CM	Open End	US Equity Small Cap (Small Company)	C	C	C+			1,000
Invesco Small Cap Growth Fund R5 Class	GTSVX	NAS CM	Open End	US Equity Small Cap (Small Company)	C	C	C+	Down		10,000,000
Invesco Small Cap Value Fund Class A	VSCAX	NAS CM	Open End	US Equity Small Cap (Small Company)	C	C-	C			1,000
Invesco Small Cap Value Fund Class C	VSMCX	NAS CM	Open End	US Equity Small Cap (Small Company)	C	C-	C			1,000
Invesco Small Cap Value Fund Class R6	SMVSX	NAS CM	Open End	US Equity Small Cap (Small Company)	C	C-	C		Y	10,000,000
Invesco Small Cap Value Fund Class Y	VSMIX	NAS CM	Open End	US Equity Small Cap (Small Company)	C	C-	C			1,000
Invesco Summit Fund Class A	ASMMX	NAS CM	Open End	US Equity Large Cap Growth (Growth)	C+	C+	B-	Down	Y	1,000
Invesco Summit Fund Class C	CSMMX	NAS CM	Open End	US Equity Large Cap Growth (Growth)	C+	C	B-	Down	Y	1,000
Invesco Summit Fund Class P	SMMIX	NAS CM	Open End	US Equity Large Cap Growth (Growth)	C+	C+	B-	Down		0
Invesco Summit Fund Class R6	SMISX	NAS CM	Open End	US Equity Large Cap Growth (Growth)	C+	C+	B-	Down	Y	10,000,000
Invesco Summit Fund Class S	SMMSX	NAS CM	Open End	US Equity Large Cap Growth (Growth)	C+	C+	B-	Down	Y	0
Invesco Summit Fund Class Y	ASMYX	NAS CM	Open End	US Equity Large Cap Growth (Growth)	C+	C+	B-	Down	Y	1,000
Invesco Summit Fund R5 Class	SMITX	NAS CM	Open End	US Equity Large Cap Growth (Growth)	C+	C+	B-	Down	Y	10,000,000
Invesco Technology Fund Class A	ITYAX	NAS CM	Open End	Technology Sector Equity (Technology)	C+	C+	B-	Down	Y	1,000
Invesco Technology Fund Class C	ITHCX	NAS CM	Open End	Technology Sector Equity (Technology)	C+	C	B-	Down	Y	1,000
Invesco Technology Fund Class R6	FTPSX	NAS CM	Open End	Technology Sector Equity (Technology)	C+	C+	B-	Down	Y	10,000,000
Invesco Technology Fund Class Y	ITYYX	NAS CM	Open End	Technology Sector Equity (Technology)	C+	C+	B-	Down	Y	1,000
Invesco Technology Fund Investor Class	FTCHX	NAS CM	Open End	Technology Sector Equity (Technology)	C+	C+	B-	Down		1,000
Invesco Technology Fund R5 Class	FTPIX	NAS CM	Open End	Technology Sector Equity (Technology)	C+	C+	B-	Down	Y	10,000,000
Invesco Technology Sector Fund Class A	IFOAX	NAS CM	Open End	Technology Sector Equity (Technology)	C+	C+	B-	Down		1,000
Invesco Technology Sector Fund Class C	IFOCX	NAS CM	Open End	Technology Sector Equity (Technology)	C+	C	B-	Down		1,000
Invesco Technology Sector Fund Class Y	IFODX	NAS CM	Open End	Technology Sector Equity (Technology)	C+	C+	B-	Down		1,000
Invesco U.S. Managed Volatility Fund Class R6	USMVX	NAS CM	Open End	US Equity Large Cap Blend (Growth)	D+	D+	C+	Up	Y	10,000,000
Invesco Value Opportunities Fund Class A	VVOAX	NAS CM	Open End	US Equity Large Cap Value (Growth & Income)	C	C-	C+		Y	1,000
Invesco Value Opportunities Fund Class C	VVOCX	NAS CM	Open End	US Equity Large Cap Value (Growth & Income)	C	C-	C+		Y	1,000
Invesco Value Opportunities Fund Class R	VVORX	NAS CM	Open End	US Equity Large Cap Value (Growth & Income)	C	C-	C+		Y	0
Invesco Value Opportunities Fund Class R5	VVONX	NAS CM	Open End	US Equity Large Cap Value (Growth & Income)	C	C-	C+		Y	10,000,000
Invesco Value Opportunities Fund Class R6	VVOSX	NAS CM	Open End	US Equity Large Cap Value (Growth & Income)	C	C-	C+		Y	10,000,000
Invesco Value Opportunities Fund Class Y	VVOIX	NAS CM	Open End	US Equity Large Cap Value (Growth & Income)	C	C-	C+		Y	1,000
Investec Emerging Markets Equity Fund A Shares	ZEMAX	NAS CM	Open End	Global Emerg Mkts (Div Emerging Mkts)	U	U	U		Y	0
Investec Emerging Markets Equity Fund I Shares	ZEMIX	NAS CM	Open End	Global Emerg Mkts (Div Emerging Mkts)	U	U	U		Y	0
Investec Global Franchise Fund A Shares	ZGFAX	NAS CM	Open End	Global Equity Large Cap (Growth)	D+	C-	B-	Up	Y	0
Investec Global Franchise Fund Institutional Shares	ZGFIX	NAS CM	Open End	Global Equity Large Cap (Growth)	D+	C-	B-	Up	Y	0
InvestEd Aggressive Portfolio	WAGPX	NAS CM	Open End	Aggressive Alloc (Growth)	C-	D+	B-	Up	Y	250
InvestEd Balanced Portfolio	WBLAX	NAS CM	Open End	Moderate Alloc (Growth & Income)	B	C	A-	Up	Y	250
InvestEd Conservative Portfolio	WICAX	NAS CM	Open End	Moderate Alloc (Income)	B	C	A-	Up	Y	250
InvestEd Growth Portfolio	WAGRX	NAS CM	Open End	Aggressive Alloc (Growth)	B-	C	B+	Up	Y	250
InvestEd Income Portfolio	WICPX	NAS CM	Open End	Cautious Alloc (Income)	C-	D+	B	Up	Y	250
IPS Strategic Capital Absolute Return Inst Cls Shares	IPSAX	NAS CM	Open End	Long/Short Equity (Growth)	C	C	B		Y	5,000

★ Expanded analysis of this fund is included in Section II.

	TOTAL RETURNS					PERFORMANCE				ASSETS		ASSET ALLOCATION & TURNOVER					BULL & BEAR		FEES		
Min Additional Investment	3-Month Total Return	6-Month Total Return	1-Year Total Return	3-Year Total Return	5-Year Total Return	Dividend Yield (TTM)	Expense Ratio	3-Yr Std Deviation	3-Year Beta	NAV	Total Assets (MIL)	%Cash	%Stocks	%Bonds	%Other	Turnover Ratio	Last Bull Market Total Return	Last Bear Market Total Return	Front End Fee (%)	Back End Fee (%)	Inception Date
	5.83	27.95	7.49	63.97	60.15	0	0.89	15.94	0.88	10.71	602.2	3	97	0	0	49	28.37	-25.01			Sep-12
50	5.85	27.80	7.25	62.75	58.35	0	1.12	15.98	0.88	10.48	602.2	3	97	0	0	49	28.45	-24.9			Feb-06
50	4.03	20.31	-3.35	29.18	24.23	0	1.28	16.36	0.94	13.15	961.2	3	97	0	0	22	28.99	-24.87	5.50		Aug-00
50	3.84	19.92	-4.01	26.37	19.67	0	2.03	16.28	0.93	9.99	961.2	3	97	0	0	22	28.33	-25.03		1.00	Aug-00
	4.01	20.23	-3.58	28.27	22.70	0	1.53	16.34	0.94	12.18	961.2	3	97	0	0	22	28.68	-24.87			Jun-02
	4.19	20.61	-2.87	31.12	27.40	0	0.8	16.35	0.94	14.92	961.2	3	97	0	0	22	28.99	-24.87			Sep-12
50	4.09	20.45	-3.10	30.12	25.75	0	1.03	16.34	0.94	13.72	961.2	3	97	0	0	22	29.12	-24.76			Oct-08
	4.15	20.61	-2.90	30.81	26.86	0	0.87	16.36	0.94	14.8	961.2	3	97	0	0	22	29.38	-24.68			Apr-05
50	3.64	21.79	-0.08	52.03	54.02	0	1.18	16.84	0.95	37.27	2,926	1	99	0	0	21	28.88	-23.65	5.50		Oct-95
50	3.46	21.29	-0.86	48.59	48.29	0	1.93	16.83	0.95	23.87	2,926	1	99	0	0	21	28.32	-23.88		1.00	May-99
	3.57	21.66	-0.34	50.85	52.08	0	1.43	16.83	0.95	34.15	2,926	1	99	0	0	21	28.66	-23.72			Jun-02
	3.74	22.09	0.37	54.16	57.71	0	0.71	16.84	0.95	42.93	2,926	1	99	0	0	21	28.88	-23.65			Sep-12
50	3.70	21.96	0.16	53.15	55.97	0	0.93	16.85	0.95	38.65	2,926	1	99	0	0	21	29.07	-23.56			Oct-08
50	3.63	21.81	-0.08	52.06	54.06	0	1.18	16.84	0.95	39.36	2,926	1	99	0	0	21	28.84	-23.63			Apr-06
	3.74	22.05	0.28	53.73	57.03	0	0.81	16.85	0.95	42.67	2,926	1	99	0	0	21	29.18	-23.49			Mar-02
50	2.78	23.37	-6.96	38.87	15.82	0	1.12	22.89	1.25	13.67	1,504	4	96	0	0	28	36.31	-29	5.50		Jun-99
50	2.48	22.86	-7.68	35.69	11.50	0	1.86	22.8	1.25	8.65	1,504	4	96	0	0	28	35.76	-29.21		1.00	Jun-99
	2.82	23.47	-6.62	40.08	16.83	0	0.69	22.83	1.25	14.57	1,504	4	96	0	0	28	36.31	-29			Feb-17
50	2.83	23.48	-6.73	39.91	17.28	0	0.87	22.84	1.25	14.51	1,504	4	96	0	0	28	36.49	-28.88			Aug-05
50	5.43	24.95	9.78	67.31	78.42	0	1.02	14.98	1.09	21.13	2,385	0	100	0	0	35	23.96	-18.36	5.50		Oct-05
50	5.26	24.53	8.99	63.57	71.86	0	1.77	14.95	1.09	18.78	2,385	0	100	0	0	35	23.33	-18.65		1.00	Oct-05
	5.49	25.07	9.97	68.04	79.75	0	0.87	14.99	1.09	21.5	2,385	0	100	0	0	35	24.09	-18.33			Nov-82
	5.52	25.18	10.15	68.63	80.38	0	0.72	14.99	1.09	21.57	2,385	0	100	0	0	35	24.09	-18.33			Apr-17
	5.49	25.05	9.96	67.78	79.33	0	0.92	14.98	1.09	21.31	2,385	0	100	0	0	35	24.06	-18.33			Sep-09
50	5.50	25.07	10.05	68.49	80.71	0	0.77	14.96	1.09	21.45	2,385	0	100	0	0	35	24.22	-18.33			Oct-08
	5.48	25.07	10.06	68.65	81.17	0	0.72	14.98	1.09	21.55	2,385	0	100	0	0	35	24.29	-18.31			Oct-08
50	5.90	24.13	8.38	80.39	81.44	0	1.28	16.45	1.08	49.84	974.5	1	99	0	0	47	26.02	-17.4	5.50		Mar-02
50	5.70	23.67	7.55	76.32	74.69	0	2.03	16.44	1.08	39.29	974.5	1	99	0	0	47	25.48	-17.61		1.00	Feb-00
	6.01	24.40	8.82	82.19	83.57	0	0.85	16.45	1.08	59.43	974.5	1	99	0	0	47	26.05	-17.39			Apr-17
50	5.95	24.27	8.63	81.75	83.67	0	1.03	16.45	1.08	50.73	974.5	1	99	0	0	47	26.21	-17.29			Oct-08
50	5.91	24.18	8.49	80.90	82.27	0	1.2	16.46	1.08	49.6	974.5	1	99	0	0	47	26.05	-17.39			Jan-84
	5.99	24.39	8.80	82.80	85.73	0	0.85	16.46	1.08	59.41	974.5	1	99	0	0	47	26.52	-17.15			Dec-98
50	5.85	24.01	8.11	79.77	80.91	0	1.33	16.52	1.09	24.94	98.7	1	99	0	0	46	27.94	-18.13	5.50		Jul-97
50	5.67	23.53	7.27	75.74	74.20	0	2.07	16.47	1.08	20.47	98.7	1	99	0	0	46	27.62	-18.51		1.00	Jul-97
50	5.91	24.19	8.38	81.04	83.04	0	1.08	16.5	1.09	26.49	98.7	1	99	0	0	46	28.29	-18.1			Jul-97
	3.81	16.44	7.40			1.75	0.15			10.62	6.8	1	99	0	0						Dec-17
50	2.30	22.44	0.84	43.97	22.31	0	1.22	20.18	1.45	12.44	724.7	3	97	0	0	30	27.06	-20.82	5.50		Jun-01
50	2.19	22.01	0.17	40.96	18.05	0	1.92	20.18	1.45	11.64	724.7	3	97	0	0	30	26.45	-21		1.00	Jun-01
	2.24	22.28	0.62	42.97	20.83	0	1.47	20.22	1.46	12.29	724.7	3	97	0	0	30	26.87	-20.9			May-12
	2.44	22.77	1.23	45.69	24.77	0	0.85	20.21	1.46	12.56	724.7	3	97	0	0	30	27.63	-20.7			May-11
	2.44	22.73	1.29	45.41	23.53	0	0.78	20.15	1.45	12.58	724.7	3	97	0	0	30	27.06	-20.82			Apr-17
50	2.38	22.61	1.07	45.10	23.84	0	0.97	20.17	1.45	12.47	724.7	3	97	0	0	30	27.29	-20.8			Mar-05
	0.93	12.66					1.1			10.76	47.7	2	98	0	0				5.75		Nov-18
	0.93	12.77					0.85			10.77	47.7	2	98	0	0						Nov-18
	3.35	18.76	11.89				1.1			11.39	55.0	9	91	0	0	9			5.75		Sep-18
	3.44	18.97	12.21			0.68	0.85			11.41	55.0	9	91	0	0	9					Dec-17
	3.47	16.10	6.04			0.57	0.98			11.03	25.3	3	88	9	0	23			2.50		Sep-17
	3.05	12.21	6.33	29.48	29.24	1.54	0.88	7.33		10.47	80.0	5	59	35	0	39	15.15	-13.71	2.50		Oct-01
	2.77	9.54	6.46	19.03	18.09	1.98	0.87	4.83		11.13	76.2	6	40	53	0	43	5.66	-0.27	2.50		Oct-01
	3.30	14.00	6.05	36.73	37.44	0.93	0.96	9.26		11.56	117.4	4	74	22	0	34	17.89	-18.08	2.50		Oct-01
	2.51	7.39	6.07			0.69	0.78			10.6	108.1	11	25	63	0	42			2.50		Sep-17
200	1.35	8.12	2.12	16.05		0	1.8	9.38	0.72	9.75	61.4	59	27	14	0	0					Apr-16

	MARKET		FUND TYPE, CATEGORY & OBJECTIVE		RATINGS				MINIMUMS	
Fund Name	Ticker Symbol	Traded On	Fund Type	Category and (Prospectus Objective)	Overall Rating	Reward Rating	Risk Rating	Recent Up/ Downgrade	Open to New Investors	Min Initial Investment
Ironclad Managed Risk Fund	IRONX	NAS CM	Open End	Long/Short Equity (Growth)	C	C	B-		Y	2,500
iShares Developed Real Estate Index Fund Class K	BKRDX	NAS CM	Open End	Real Estate Sector Equity (Real Estate)	B-	C	B+		Y	5,000,000
iShares Developed Real Estate Index Institutional Shares	BIRDX	NAS CM	Open End	Real Estate Sector Equity (Real Estate)	B-	C	B+		Y	2,000,000
iShares Developed Real Estate Index Fund Investor A Shares	BARDX	NAS CM	Open End	Real Estate Sector Equity (Real Estate)	B-	C	B+		Y	1,000
iShares Edge MSCI Min Vol EAFE Index Fund Class K	BKEVX	NAS CM	Open End	Global Equity Large Cap (Growth & Income)	C+	C	B	Up	Y	5,000,000
iShares Edge MSCI Min Vol EAFE Index Institutional Shares	BIEVX	NAS CM	Open End	Global Equity Large Cap (Growth & Income)	C+	C	B	Up	Y	2,000,000
iShares Edge MSCI Min Vol USA Index Fund Class K	BKMVX	NAS CM	Open End	US Equity Large Cap Blend (Growth & Income)	B-	C	B+		Y	5,000,000
iShares Edge MSCI Min Vol USA Index Institutional Shares	BIMVX	NAS CM	Open End	US Equity Large Cap Blend (Growth & Income)	B-	C	B+		Y	2,000,000
iShares Edge MSCI Multifactor Intl Index Fund Class K	BKIMX	NAS CM	Open End	Global Equity Large Cap (Growth & Income)	C	D+	C+	Up	Y	5,000,000
iShares Edge MSCI Multifactor Intl Index Inst Shares	BIIMX	NAS CM	Open End	Global Equity Large Cap (Growth & Income)	C	D+	C+	Up	Y	2,000,000
iShares Edge MSCI Multifactor USA Index Fund Class K	BKMFX	NAS CM	Open End	US Equity Large Cap Blend (Growth & Income)	C	C-	B-		Y	5,000,000
iShares Edge MSCI Multifactor USA Index Inst Shares	BIMFX	NAS CM	Open End	US Equity Large Cap Blend (Growth & Income)	C	C-	B-		Y	2,000,000
iShares MSCI EAFE International Index Fund Class K	BTMKX	NAS CM	Open End	Global Equity Large Cap (Foreign Stock)	C	C	B		Y	5,000,000
iShares MSCI EAFE International Index Institutional Shares	MAIIX	NAS CM	Open End	Global Equity Large Cap (Foreign Stock)	C	C	B		Y	2,000,000
iShares MSCI EAFE International Index Investor A Shares	MDIIX	NAS CM	Open End	Global Equity Large Cap (Foreign Stock)	C	C	B		Y	1,000
iShares MSCI EAFE International Index Investor P Shares	BTMPX	NAS CM	Open End	Global Equity Large Cap (Foreign Stock)	C	C	B		Y	1,000
iShares MSCI Total International Index Fund Class K	BDOKX	NAS CM	Open End	Global Equity Large Cap (Foreign Stock)	C	C	B		Y	5,000,000
iShares MSCI Total Intl Index Inst Shares	BDOIX	NAS CM	Open End	Global Equity Large Cap (Foreign Stock)	C	C	B		Y	2,000,000
iShares MSCI Total International Index Investor A Shares	BDOAX	NAS CM	Open End	Global Equity Large Cap (Foreign Stock)	C	C	B		Y	1,000
iShares Russell 1000 Large-Cap Index Fund Class K	BRGKX	NAS CM	Open End	US Equity Large Cap Blend (Growth)	B-	C	B		Y	5,000,000
iShares Russell 1000 Large-Cap Index Institutional Shares	BRGNX	NAS CM	Open End	US Equity Large Cap Blend (Growth)	B-	C	B		Y	2,000,000
iShares Russell 1000 Large-Cap Index Investor A Shares	BRGAX	NAS CM	Open End	US Equity Large Cap Blend (Growth)	B-	C	B		Y	1,000
iShares Russell 2000 Small-Cap Index Fund Class K	BDBKX	NAS CM	Open End	US Equity Small Cap (Small Company)	C	C	C+		Y	5,000,000
iShares Russell 2000 Small-Cap Index Institutional Shares	MASKX	NAS CM	Open End	US Equity Small Cap (Small Company)	C	C	C+		Y	2,000,000
iShares Russell 2000 Small-Cap Index Investor A Shares	MDSKX	NAS CM	Open End	US Equity Small Cap (Small Company)	C	C	C+		Y	1,000
iShares Russell 2000 Small-Cap Index Investor P Shares	BDBPX	NAS CM	Open End	US Equity Small Cap (Small Company)	C	C	C+		Y	1,000
iShares Russell Mid-Cap Index Fund Class K	BRMKX	NAS CM	Open End	US Equity Mid Cap (Growth)	C+	C	B	Down	Y	5,000,000
iShares Russell Mid-Cap Index Fund Institutional Shares	BRMIX	NAS CM	Open End	US Equity Mid Cap (Growth)	C+	C	B	Down	Y	2,000,000
iShares Russell Mid-Cap Index Fund Investor A Shares	BRMAX	NAS CM	Open End	US Equity Mid Cap (Growth)	C+	C	B		Y	1,000
iShares Russell Small/Mid-Cap Index Fund Class K	BSMKX	NAS CM	Open End	US Equity Small Cap (Growth & Income)	C+	C	B-		Y	5,000,000
iShares Russell Small/Mid-Cap Index Institutional Shares	BSMIX	NAS CM	Open End	US Equity Small Cap (Growth & Income)	C+	C	B-		Y	2,000,000
iShares Russell Small/Mid-Cap Index Fund Investor A Shares	BSMAX	NAS CM	Open End	US Equity Small Cap (Growth & Income)	C+	C	B-		Y	1,000
iShares S&P 500 Index Fund Class K	WFSPX	NAS CM	Open End	US Equity Large Cap Blend (Growth & Income)	B-	C	B		Y	5,000,000
iShares S&P 500 Index Fund Institutional Shares	BSPIX	NAS CM	Open End	US Equity Large Cap Blend (Growth & Income)	B-	C	B		Y	2,000,000
iShares S&P 500 Index Fund Investor A Shares	BSPAX	NAS CM	Open End	US Equity Large Cap Blend (Growth & Income)	B-	C	B		Y	1,000
iShares S&P 500 Index Fund Investor C1 Shares	BSPZX	NAS CM	Open End	US Equity Large Cap Blend (Growth & Income)	B-	C	B		Y	1,000
iShares S&P 500 Index Fund Investor P Shares	BSPPX	NAS CM	Open End	US Equity Large Cap Blend (Growth & Income)	B-	C	B		Y	1,000
iShares S&P 500 Index Fund Service Shares	BSPSX	NAS CM	Open End	US Equity Large Cap Blend (Growth & Income)	B-	C	B		Y	5,000
iShares Total U.S. Stock Market Index Fund Class K	BKTSX	NAS CM	Open End	US Equity Large Cap Blend (Growth)	B-	C	B		Y	5,000,000
iShares Total U.S. Stock Market Index Institutional Shares	BITSX	NAS CM	Open End	US Equity Large Cap Blend (Growth)	B-	C	B		Y	2,000,000
iShares Total U.S. Stock Market Index Investor A Shares	BASMX	NAS CM	Open End	US Equity Large Cap Blend (Growth)	B-	C	B		Y	1,000
Issachar Fund Class N	LIONX	NAS CM	Open End	Moderate Alloc (Growth)	D+	D	C	Down	Y	1,000
IVA International Fund Class A	IVIOX	NAS CM	Open End	Global Equity Large Cap (Growth)	C	C-	B-			5,000
IVA International Fund Class C	IVICX	NAS CM	Open End	Global Equity Large Cap (Growth)	C	D+	C+	Up		5,000
IVA International Fund Class I	IVIQX	NAS CM	Open End	Global Equity Large Cap (Growth)	C	C-	B-			1,000,000
IVA Worldwide Fund Class A	IVWAX	NAS CM	Open End	Moderate Alloc (Growth)	C+	C	B+	Up		5,000
IVA Worldwide Fund Class C	IVWCX	NAS CM	Open End	Moderate Alloc (Growth)	C+	C	B	Up		5,000
IVA Worldwide Fund Class I	IVWIX	NAS CM	Open End	Moderate Alloc (Growth)	C+	C	B+	Up		1,000,000
Ivy Accumulative Fund Class A	IATAX	NAS CM	Open End	US Equity Large Cap Growth (Growth)	B-	C	B			750
Ivy Accumulative Fund Class B	IATBX	NAS CM	Open End	US Equity Large Cap Growth (Growth)	C+	C	B	Down		750
Ivy Accumulative Fund Class C	IATCX	NAS CM	Open End	US Equity Large Cap Growth (Growth)	C+	C	B	Down		750
Ivy Accumulative Fund Class I	IATIX	NAS CM	Open End	US Equity Large Cap Growth (Growth)	B-	C	B		Y	0

★ Expanded analysis of this fund is included in Section II.

	TOTAL RETURNS					PERFORMANCE				ASSETS		ASSET ALLOCATION & TURNOVER					BULL & BEAR		FEES		
Min Additional Investment	3-Month Total Return	6-Month Total Return	1-Year Total Return	3-Year Total Return	5-Year Total Return	Dividend Yield (TTM)	Expense Ratio	3-Yr Std Deviation	3-Year Beta	NAV	Total Assets (MIL)	%Cash	%Stocks	%Bonds	%Other	Turnover Ratio	Last Bull Market Total Return	Last Bear Market Total Return	Front End Fee (%)	Back End Fee (%)	Inception Date
500	1.11	4.16	-0.18	12.40	14.64	0	1.25	4.77	0.36	10.01	101.8	100	0	0	0	0	10.28	-3.66			Oct-10
	0.05	15.13	8.54	16.55		4.02	0.15	11.09	0.99	10.89	2,013	5	94	0	1	23					Aug-15
	0.04	15.08	8.46	16.38		3.96	0.2	11.07	0.99	10.91	2,013	5	94	0	1	23					Aug-15
50	-0.01	14.91	8.24	15.46		3.67	0.49	11.1	0.99	10.9	2,013	5	94	0	1	23					Aug-15
	2.86	11.27	5.00	19.88		2.98	0.18			10.82	155.5	1	99	0	0	25					Jul-16
	2.85	11.27	4.95	19.76		2.94	0.23			10.82	155.5	1	99	0	0	25					Jul-16
	5.48	19.93	18.50	39.87		1.81	0.13			12.98	22.3	1	99	0	0	32					Jul-16
	5.56	19.81	18.45	39.72		1.77	0.18			12.98	22.3	1	99	0	0	32					Jul-16
	1.95	13.06	-2.17	26.60		2.95	0.3			10.71	10.8	1	98	0	1	50					Jul-16
	1.94	13.04	-2.15	26.43		2.89	0.35			10.71	10.8	1	98	0	1	50					Jul-16
	2.78	15.96	2.45	35.97		2.79	0.2			11.96	13.4	0	100	0	0	52					Jul-16
	2.85	16.06	2.41	35.81		2.75	0.25			11.96	13.4	0	100	0	0	52					Jul-16
	3.70	14.68	1.48	31.51	11.45	4.01	0.06	11.1	1	13.43	7,970	0	98	0	1	43	13.19	-23.36			Mar-11
	3.71	14.51	1.35	31.28	11.14	3.97	0.09	11.09	0.99	13.41	7,970	0	98	0	1	43	13.33	-23.44			Apr-97
50	3.65	14.43	1.13	30.34	9.78	3.72	0.36	11.06	0.99	13.32	7,970	0	98	0	1	43	13.13	-23.51			Apr-97
50	3.59	14.39	1.12	30.32	9.77		0.36	11.08	0.99	13.27	7,970	0	98	0	1	43	13.17	-23.52			Aug-18
	2.90	13.95	1.41	32.07	11.06	2.98	0.11	11.53	1	9.16	888.9	1	99	0	0	40	13.13				Jun-11
	2.86	13.97	1.40	31.97	10.78	3.02	0.16	11.6	1.01	8.89	888.9	1	99	0	0	40	13.12				Jun-11
50	2.68	13.74	1.04	30.84	9.40	2.79	0.41	11.52	1	8.86	888.9	1	99	0	0	40	12.92				Jun-11
	4.26	19.88	9.98	50.47	63.87	1.88	0.08	12.29	1	19.37	352.0	1	99	0	0	12	25.45	-17.15			Mar-11
	4.17	19.76	9.89	50.23	63.43	1.82	0.13	12.3	1	19.44	352.0	1	99	0	0	12	25.42	-17.17			Mar-11
50	4.14	19.68	9.67	49.09	61.33	1.59	0.38	12.3	1	19.33	352.0	1	99	0	0	12	25.26	-17.27			Mar-11
	2.11	17.93	-3.25	44.27	41.51	1	0.07	17.11	1	19.79	2,094	1	99	0	0	28	27.79	-25.26			Mar-11
	2.12	17.93	-3.30	44.00	41.12	0.97	0.12	17.09	1	19.73	2,094	1	99	0	0	28	27.66	-25.28			Apr-97
50	2.06	17.79	-3.53	43.01	39.44	0.71	0.37	17.1	1	19.73	2,094	1	99	0	0	28	27.44	-25.3			Apr-97
50	2.02	17.71	-3.54	42.92	39.37		0.37	17.09	1	19.67	2,094	1	99	0	0	28	27.48	-25.35			Aug-18
	4.13	22.44	7.93	43.32		1.3	0.07	13.42	1	10.89	1,100	1	99	0	0	75					May-15
	4.03	22.22	7.80	42.97		1.27	0.12	13.35	0.99	10.86	1,100	1	99	0	0	75					May-15
50	3.99	22.26	7.63	41.98		1.1	0.35	13.37	1	10.82	1,100	1	99	0	0	75					Nov-15
	2.92	20.40	1.47	43.70		1.4	0.07	15.52	1	12.64	201.6	1	99	0	0	54					Aug-15
	2.90	20.27	1.42	43.53		1.35	0.12	15.51	1	12.64	201.6	1	99	0	0	54					Aug-15
50	2.86	20.15	1.18	42.51		1.13	0.37	15.5	1	12.61	201.6	1	99	0	0	54					Aug-15
	4.29	19.52	10.41	50.78	66.02	1.85	0.04	12.18	1	349.13	19,490	1	99	0	0	12	25	-16.31			Jul-93
	4.27	19.47	10.33	50.46	65.44	1.78	0.11	12.18	1	349.05	19,490	1	99	0	0	12	25	-16.31			Apr-13
50	4.20	19.32	10.05	49.34	63.38	1.55	0.36	12.18	1	348.95	19,490	1	99	0	0	12	24.82	-16.39			Apr-13
50	4.02	18.90	9.23	46.11	57.56	0.65	1.08	12.17	1	350.28	19,490	1	99	0	0	12	24.35	-16.62		1.00	Apr-13
50	4.21	19.33	10.07	49.58	63.88		0.36	12.18	1	348.69	19,490	1	99	0	0	12	24.82	-16.39	5.25		Aug-18
	4.24	19.40	10.20	49.93	64.46	1.67	0.23	12.18	1	349.04	19,490	1	99	0	0	12	24.89	-16.36			Apr-13
	4.16	19.89	9.06	50.08		1.78	0.03	12.5	1	13.99	1,073	1	99	0	0	14					Aug-15
	4.14	19.77	9.00	49.92		1.73	0.08	12.51	1	13.99	1,073	1	99	0	0	14					Aug-15
50	4.02	19.66	8.69	48.72		1.52	0.33	12.51	1	13.96	1,073	1	99	0	0	14					Aug-15
100	-0.30	-2.07	-3.01	1.47	6.24	0	2.57	4.69	0.45	9.93	10.6	18	3	78	0	3,108					Feb-14
100	2.13	10.01	-2.13	13.74	12.51	1.27	1.25	8.6	0.73	15.82	3,045	13	77	2	7	19	5.89	-9.69	5.00		Oct-08
100	1.90	9.63	-2.88	11.23	8.39	0.58	2	8.6	0.72	15.48	3,045	13	77	2	7	19	5.37	-9.97		1.00	Oct-08
100	2.12	10.14	-1.88	14.56	13.92	1.51	1	8.61	0.73	15.85	3,045	13	77	2	7	19	5.96	-9.56			Oct-08
100	2.07	8.78	1.65	19.38	15.86	0.81	1.25	7.45	0.63	17.22	6,482	31	61	2	6	25	8.8	-11.74	5.00		Oct-08
100	1.88	8.39	0.93	16.70	11.59	0.1	2	7.44	0.63	16.78	6,482	31	61	2	6	25	8.39	-12.05		1.00	Oct-08
100	2.12	8.94	1.91	20.26	17.33	1.04	1	7.42	0.63	17.29	6,482	31	61	2	6	25	9.02	-11.67			Oct-08
	5.59	25.38	13.86	46.85	56.26	0.43	1.1	12.39	0.87	10.57	1,338	1	99	0	0	79	24.96	-17.57	5.75		Oct-40
	5.29	24.63	12.47	41.56	47.11	0	2.29	12.28	0.86	8.55	1,338	1	99	0	0	79	24.09	-18.1		5.00	Oct-99
	5.38	24.78	12.87	42.59	48.92	0	2.06	12.31	0.86	8.81	1,338	1	99	0	0	79	24.3	-18.04		1.00	Oct-99
	5.65	25.44	14.07	47.78	57.97	0.66	0.87	12.36	0.86	10.65	1,338	1	99	0	0	79	25.44	-17.65			Jul-95

	MARKET			FUND TYPE, CATEGORY & OBJECTIVE	RATINGS				MINIMUMS	
Fund Name	Ticker Symbol	Traded On	Fund Type	Category and (Prospectus Objective)	Overall Rating	Reward Rating	Risk Rating	Recent Up/ Downgrade	Open to New Investors	Min Initial Investment
Ivy Accumulative Fund Class N	IATNX	NAS CM	Open End	US Equity Large Cap Growth (Growth)	B-	C	B		Y	0
Ivy Accumulative Fund Class R	IATLX	NAS CM	Open End	US Equity Large Cap Growth (Growth)	B-	C	B		Y	0
Ivy Accumulative Fund Class Y	IATYX	NAS CM	Open End	US Equity Large Cap Growth (Growth)	B-	C	B		Y	0
Ivy Apollo Multi-Asset Income Fund Class A	IMAAX	NAS CM	Open End	Moderate Alloc (Income)	B	C	A-	Up	Y	750
Ivy Apollo Multi-Asset Income Fund Class C	IMACX	NAS CM	Open End	Moderate Alloc (Income)	B-	C	A-	Up	Y	750
Ivy Apollo Multi-Asset Income Fund Class I	IMAIX	NAS CM	Open End	Moderate Alloc (Income)	B	C	A-	Up	Y	0
Ivy Apollo Multi-Asset Income Fund Class N	IMURX	NAS CM	Open End	Moderate Alloc (Income)	B	C+	A	Up	Y	1,000,000
Ivy Apollo Multi-Asset Income Fund Class Y	IMAYX	NAS CM	Open End	Moderate Alloc (Income)	B	C	A-	Up	Y	0
Ivy Asset Strategy Fund Class A	WASAX	NAS CM	Open End	Moderate Alloc (Asset Alloc)	B-	C	B+	Up	Y	750
Ivy Asset Strategy Fund Class B	WASBX	NAS CM	Open End	Moderate Alloc (Asset Alloc)	B-	C	B+	Up		750
Ivy Asset Strategy Fund Class C	WASCX	NAS CM	Open End	Moderate Alloc (Asset Alloc)	B-	C	B+	Up	Y	750
Ivy Asset Strategy Fund Class E	IASEX	NAS CM	Open End	Moderate Alloc (Asset Alloc)	B-	C	B+	Up	Y	250
Ivy Asset Strategy Fund Class I	IVAEX	NAS CM	Open End	Moderate Alloc (Asset Alloc)	B-	C	B+	Up	Y	0
Ivy Asset Strategy Fund Class N	IASTX	NAS CM	Open End	Moderate Alloc (Asset Alloc)	B-	C	B+	Up	Y	1,000,000
Ivy Asset Strategy Fund Class R	IASRX	NAS CM	Open End	Moderate Alloc (Asset Alloc)	B-	C	B+	Up	Y	0
Ivy Asset Strategy Fund Class Y	WASYX	NAS CM	Open End	Moderate Alloc (Asset Alloc)	B-	C	B+	Up	Y	0
Ivy Balanced Fund Class A	IBNAX	NAS CM	Open End	Moderate Alloc (Balanced)	B-	C	A-		Y	750
Ivy Balanced Fund Class B	IBNBX	NAS CM	Open End	Moderate Alloc (Balanced)	B-	C	B+			750
Ivy Balanced Fund Class C	IBNCX	NAS CM	Open End	Moderate Alloc (Balanced)	B-	C	B+		Y	750
Ivy Balanced Fund Class I	IYBIX	NAS CM	Open End	Moderate Alloc (Balanced)	B-	C	A-		Y	0
Ivy Balanced Fund Class N	IBARX	NAS CM	Open End	Moderate Alloc (Balanced)	B-	C	A-		Y	1,000,000
Ivy Balanced Fund Class R	IYBFX	NAS CM	Open End	Moderate Alloc (Balanced)	B-	C	B+		Y	0
Ivy Balanced Fund Class Y	IBNYX	NAS CM	Open End	Moderate Alloc (Balanced)	B-	C	A-		Y	0
Ivy Core Equity Fund Class A	WCEAX	NAS CM	Open End	US Equity Large Cap Growth (Growth)	C+	C	B		Y	750
Ivy Core Equity Fund Class B	WCEBX	NAS CM	Open End	US Equity Large Cap Growth (Growth)	C+	C	B			750
Ivy Core Equity Fund Class C	WTRCX	NAS CM	Open End	US Equity Large Cap Growth (Growth)	C+	C	B		Y	750
Ivy Core Equity Fund Class E	ICFEX	NAS CM	Open End	US Equity Large Cap Growth (Growth)	C+	C	B		Y	250
Ivy Core Equity Fund Class I	ICIEX	NAS CM	Open End	US Equity Large Cap Growth (Growth)	C+	C	B		Y	0
Ivy Core Equity Fund Class N	ICEQX	NAS CM	Open End	US Equity Large Cap Growth (Growth)	C+	C	B	Down	Y	1,000,000
Ivy Core Equity Fund Class R	IYCEX	NAS CM	Open End	US Equity Large Cap Growth (Growth)	C+	C	B		Y	0
Ivy Core Equity Fund Class Y	WCEYX	NAS CM	Open End	US Equity Large Cap Growth (Growth)	C+	C	B		Y	0
Ivy Emerging Markets Equity Fund Class A	IPOAX	NAS CM	Open End	Global Emerg Mkts (Div Emerging Mkts)	C	C	C		Y	750
Ivy Emerging Markets Equity Fund Class B	IPOBX	NAS CM	Open End	Global Emerg Mkts (Div Emerging Mkts)	C	C	C			750
Ivy Emerging Markets Equity Fund Class C	IPOCX	NAS CM	Open End	Global Emerg Mkts (Div Emerging Mkts)	C	C	C		Y	750
Ivy Emerging Markets Equity Fund Class I	IPOIX	NAS CM	Open End	Global Emerg Mkts (Div Emerging Mkts)	C	C	C		Y	0
Ivy Emerging Markets Equity Fund Class N	IMEGX	NAS CM	Open End	Global Emerg Mkts (Div Emerging Mkts)	C	C	C		Y	1,000,000
Ivy Emerging Markets Equity Fund Class R	IYPCX	NAS CM	Open End	Global Emerg Mkts (Div Emerging Mkts)	C	C	C		Y	0
Ivy Emerging Markets Equity Fund Class T	IPOTX	NAS CM	Open End	Global Emerg Mkts (Div Emerging Mkts)	C	C	C		Y	0
Ivy Emerging Markets Equity Fund Class Y	IPOYX	NAS CM	Open End	Global Emerg Mkts (Div Emerging Mkts)	C	C	C		Y	0
Ivy Energy Fund Class A	IEYAX	NAS CM	Open End	Energy Sector Equity (Natl Res)	D	D	D	Down	Y	750
Ivy Energy Fund Class B	IEYBX	NAS CM	Open End	Energy Sector Equity (Natl Res)	D	D	D	Down		750
Ivy Energy Fund Class C	IEYCX	NAS CM	Open End	Energy Sector Equity (Natl Res)	D	D	D	Down	Y	750
Ivy Energy Fund Class I	IVEIX	NAS CM	Open End	Energy Sector Equity (Natl Res)	D	D	D	Down	Y	0
Ivy Energy Fund Class N	IENRX	NAS CM	Open End	Energy Sector Equity (Natl Res)	D	D	D	Down	Y	1,000,000
Ivy Energy Fund Class R	IYEFX	NAS CM	Open End	Energy Sector Equity (Natl Res)	D	D	D	Down	Y	0
Ivy Energy Fund Class Y	IEYYX	NAS CM	Open End	Energy Sector Equity (Natl Res)	D	D	D	Down	Y	0
Ivy Global Equity Income Fund Class A	IBIAX	NAS CM	Open End	Global Equity Large Cap (Growth & Income)	C+	C	B	Up	Y	750
Ivy Global Equity Income Fund Class B	IBIBX	NAS CM	Open End	Global Equity Large Cap (Growth & Income)	C+	C	B	Up		750
Ivy Global Equity Income Fund Class C	IBICX	NAS CM	Open End	Global Equity Large Cap (Growth & Income)	C+	C	B	Up	Y	750
Ivy Global Equity Income Fund Class E	IBIEX	NAS CM	Open End	Global Equity Large Cap (Growth & Income)	C+	C	B	Up	Y	250
Ivy Global Equity Income Fund Class I	IBIIX	NAS CM	Open End	Global Equity Large Cap (Growth & Income)	B-	C	B	Up	Y	0
Ivy Global Equity Income Fund Class N	IICNX	NAS CM	Open End	Global Equity Large Cap (Growth & Income)	B-	C	B	Up	Y	1,000,000

★ Expanded analysis of this fund is included in Section II.

	TOTAL RETURNS					PERFORMANCE				ASSETS		ASSET ALLOCATION & TURNOVER					BULL & BEAR		FEES		
Min Additional Investment	3-Month Total Return	6-Month Total Return	1-Year Total Return	3-Year Total Return	5-Year Total Return	Dividend Yield (TTM)	Expense Ratio	3-Yr Std Deviation	3-Year Beta	NAV	Total Assets (MIL)	%Cash	%Stocks	%Bonds	%Other	Turnover Ratio	Last Bull Market Total Return	Last Bear Market Total Return	Front End Fee (%)	Back End Fee (%)	Inception Date
	5.79	25.62	14.30	47.57	57.02	0.69	0.74	12.39	0.86	10.59	1,338	1	99	0	0	79	24.96	-17.57			Feb-18
	5.60	25.14	13.51	45.52	54.07	0.17	1.49	12.35	0.86	10.55	1,338	1	99	0	0	79	24.78	-17.66			Feb-18
	5.59	25.23	13.87	46.87	56.28	0.44	1.08	12.3	0.86	10.57	1,338	1	99	0	0	79	24.96	-17.57			Feb-18
	1.91	10.30	4.81	20.12		4.15	1.25	5.98		10.59	459.8	8	46	45	0	59			5.75		Oct-15
	1.72	9.91	4.14	17.36		3.44	1.99	6.01		10.59	459.8	8	46	45	0	59				1.00	Oct-15
	2.02	10.53	5.33	21.31		4.55	0.76	5.98		10.59	459.8	8	46	45	0	59					Oct-15
	2.12	10.52	5.37	21.85		4.58	0.76	5.96		10.6	459.8	8	46	45	0	59					Oct-15
	1.91	10.31	4.83	20.28		4.18	1.2	5.95		10.59	459.8	8	46	45	0	59					Oct-15
	5.19	15.59	7.25	28.26	6.51	1.39	1.13	9.36	0.79	21.65	2,947	1	67	22	5	52	23.32	-22.07	5.75		Jul-00
	4.97	15.10	6.39	25.37	2.54	0.68	1.89	9.37	0.8	20.09	2,947	1	67	22	5	52	22.77	-22.34		5.00	Jul-00
	4.99	15.17	6.53	25.59	2.77	0.76	1.86	9.35	0.79	20.28	2,947	1	67	22	5	52	22.81	-22.31		1.00	Apr-95
	5.26	15.71	7.36	28.79	6.88	1.5	1.03	9.38	0.8	21.74	2,947	1	67	22	5	52	23.31	-22.09	2.50		Apr-07
	5.28	15.78	7.53	29.33	7.95	1.64	0.84	9.38	0.8	21.97	2,947	1	67	22	5	52	23.52	-22.02			Apr-07
	5.30	15.81	7.65	29.90	8.55	1.76	0.69	9.39	0.8	22.03	2,947	1	67	22	5	52	22.81	-22.31			Jul-14
	5.13	15.42	6.89	27.06	4.76	1.08	1.44	9.36	0.79	21.36	2,947	1	67	22	5	52	23.1	-22.2			Jul-08
	5.23	15.62	7.31	28.44	6.66	1.41	1.08	9.37	0.79	21.72	2,947	1	67	22	5	52	23.33	-22.1			Dec-95
	3.01	13.33	7.12	24.83	25.41	1.36	1.11	8.82	0.7	24.21	2,490	1	64	35	0	53	18.74	-11.74	5.75		Nov-87
	2.85	12.94	6.35	22.14	20.90	0.67	1.86	8.82	0.7	23.93	2,490	1	64	35	0	53	18.25	-12.04		5.00	Dec-03
	2.87	12.91	6.39	22.24	21.11	0.73	1.83	8.82	0.7	24.02	2,490	1	64	35	0	53	18.22	-11.96		1.00	Dec-03
	3.12	13.47	7.43	25.77	27.02	1.59	0.87	8.83	0.7	24.21	2,490	1	64	35	0	53	18.93	-11.62			Apr-07
	3.15	13.58	7.58	26.41	27.96	1.72	0.72	8.82	0.7	24.26	2,490	1	64	35	0	53	18.74	-11.74			Jul-14
	2.93	13.12	6.77	23.58	23.31	1.05	1.46	8.82	0.7	24.17	2,490	1	64	35	0	53	18.57	-11.83			Dec-12
	3.05	13.33	7.17	24.92	25.51	1.36	1.11	8.82	0.7	24.22	2,490	1	64	35	0	53	18.77	-11.72			Dec-03
	5.56	18.89	6.94	42.67	43.15	0.56	1.03	12.98	1.02	14.22	3,949	1	99	0	0	97	26.64	-17.25	5.75		Jul-00
	5.26	18.27	5.83	38.39	36.27	0	2.1	12.99	1.02	11.39	3,949	1	99	0	0	97	25.75	-17.57		5.00	Jul-00
	5.30	18.38	6.03	39.23	37.62	0	1.89	13.02	1.03	11.91	3,949	1	99	0	0	97	25.94	-17.44		1.00	Sep-92
	5.51	18.80	6.86	42.55	42.51	0.47	1.1	13.01	1.02	14.15	3,949	1	99	0	0	97	26.62	-17.27	2.50		Apr-07
	5.56	18.96	7.11	43.69	45.10	0.7	0.83	12.95	1.02	16.12	3,949	1	99	0	0	97	26.83	-17.12			Apr-07
	5.62	19.08	7.35	44.29	45.80	0.85	0.73	12.98	1.02	16.16	3,949	1	99	0	0	97	25.94	-17.44			Jul-14
	5.46	18.60	6.55	41.09	40.59	0.21	1.46	12.97	1.02	14.09	3,949	1	99	0	0	97	25.94	-17.44			Dec-12
	5.54	18.90	7.07	43.70	45.03	0.72	0.84	12.97	1.02	15.6	3,949	1	99	0	0	97	26.65	-17.13			Dec-95
	-0.20	14.36	1.73	38.50	24.47	0.6	1.44	15.6	1.08	19.11	1,816	1	99	0	0	59	17.25	-30.01	5.75		Oct-93
	-0.44	13.83	0.75	34.65	18.61	0.09	2.4	15.63	1.08	15.55	1,816	1	99	0	0	59	16.44	-30.31		5.00	Oct-93
	-0.36	13.95	1.01	35.65	19.78	0.24	2.13	15.64	1.08	16.33	1,816	1	99	0	0	59	16.74	-30.21		1.00	Apr-96
	-0.10	14.61	2.16	40.29	26.73	0.97	0.99	15.61	1.08	19.76	1,816	1	99	0	0	59	17.57	-29.82			Apr-07
	-0.10	14.59	2.16	40.49	27.26	1.02	0.95	15.63	1.08	19.86	1,816	1	99	0	0	59	17.25	-30.01			Jul-14
	-0.26	14.19	1.38	37.40	22.61	0.43	1.7	15.58	1.08	18.9	1,816	1	99	0	0	59	17.08	-30.08			Dec-12
	-0.10	14.53	1.98	39.10	25.01	0.82	1.2	15.59	1.08	19.15	1,816	1	99	0	0	59	17.25	-30.01	2.50		Jul-17
	-0.20	14.37	1.75	38.79	24.73	0.63	1.36	15.62	1.08	19.49	1,816	1	99	0	0	59	17.37	-29.9			Jul-03
	-5.50	11.06	-30.39	-26.99	-51.36	0	1.41	28.68	1.31	8.93	299.2	2	98	0	0	31	23.31	-31.66	5.75		Apr-06
	-5.75	10.62	-30.98	-28.90	-53.45	0	2.29	28.6	1.31	8.02	299.2	2	98	0	0	31	22.62	-31.87		5.00	Apr-06
	-5.63	10.64	-30.89	-28.48	-52.97	0	2.11	28.58	1.3	8.21	299.2	2	98	0	0	31	22.75	-31.84		1.00	Apr-06
	-5.48	11.23	-30.15	-26.28	-50.49	0	0.99	28.65	1.31	9.31	299.2	2	98	0	0	31	23.53	-31.51			Apr-07
	-5.45	11.29	-30.14	-25.98	-50.18	0	0.94	28.66	1.31	9.36	299.2	2	98	0	0	31	23.35	-31.61			Jul-14
	-5.56	10.94	-30.60	-27.58	-51.93	0	1.69	28.6	1.31	8.82	299.2	2	98	0	0	31	23.17	-31.68			Dec-12
	-5.52	11.02	-30.41	-26.88	-51.15	0	1.34	28.58	1.3	9.06	299.2	2	98	0	0	31	23.35	-31.61			Apr-06
	2.62	14.31	4.04	25.73	22.22	2.36	1.24	10.43	0.98	12.09	760.9	2	98	0	0	28			5.75		Jun-12
	2.52	13.91	3.39	23.35	18.32	1.72	1.93	10.48	0.98	12.09	760.9	2	98	0	0	28				5.00	Jun-12
	2.45	13.91	3.39	23.39	18.37	1.72	1.89	10.47	0.98	12.09	760.9	2	98	0	0	28				1.00	Jun-12
	2.65	14.36	4.14	26.10	22.75	2.45	1.13	10.46	0.98	12.09	760.9	2	98	0	0	28					Feb-18
	2.72	14.48	4.45	27.07	24.31	2.66	0.92	10.5	0.98	12.1	760.9	2	98	0	0	28					Jun-12
	2.75	14.54	4.60	27.62	25.17	2.79	0.8	10.51	0.98	12.11	760.9	2	98	0	0	28					Jul-14

	MARKET		FUND TYPE, CATEGORY & OBJECTIVE		RATINGS					MINIMUMS
Fund Name	Ticker Symbol	Traded On	Fund Type	Category and (Prospectus Objective)	Overall Rating	Reward Rating	Risk Rating	Recent Up/ Downgrade	Open to New Investors	Min Initial Investment
Ivy Global Equity Income Fund Class R	IYGEX	NAS CM	Open End	Global Equity Large Cap (Growth & Income)	C+	C	B	Up	Y	0
Ivy Global Equity Income Fund Class Y	IBIYX	NAS CM	Open End	Global Equity Large Cap (Growth & Income)	C+	C	B	Up	Y	0
Ivy Global Growth Fund Class A	IVINX	NAS CM	Open End	Global Equity Large Cap (Growth)	C+	C	B	Up	Y	750
Ivy Global Growth Fund Class B	IVIBX	NAS CM	Open End	Global Equity Large Cap (Growth)	C+	C	B	Up		750
Ivy Global Growth Fund Class C	IVNCX	NAS CM	Open End	Global Equity Large Cap (Growth)	C+	C	B	Up	Y	750
Ivy Global Growth Fund Class I	IGIIX	NAS CM	Open End	Global Equity Large Cap (Growth)	C+	C	B	Up	Y	0
Ivy Global Growth Fund Class N	ITGRX	NAS CM	Open End	Global Equity Large Cap (Growth)	C+	C	B	Up	Y	1,000,000
Ivy Global Growth Fund Class R	IYIGX	NAS CM	Open End	Global Equity Large Cap (Growth)	C+	C	B	Up	Y	0
Ivy Global Growth Fund Class Y	IVIYX	NAS CM	Open End	Global Equity Large Cap (Growth)	C+	C	B	Up	Y	0
Ivy International Core Equity Fund Class A	IVIAX	NAS CM	Open End	Global Equity Large Cap (Foreign Stock)	C	C-	C		Y	750
Ivy International Core Equity Fund Class B	IIFBX	NAS CM	Open End	Global Equity Large Cap (Foreign Stock)	C-	D+	C			750
Ivy International Core Equity Fund Class C	IVIFX	NAS CM	Open End	Global Equity Large Cap (Foreign Stock)	C-	D+	C		Y	750
Ivy International Core Equity Fund Class E	IICEX	NAS CM	Open End	Global Equity Large Cap (Foreign Stock)	C	C-	C		Y	250
Ivy International Core Equity Fund Class I	ICEIX	NAS CM	Open End	Global Equity Large Cap (Foreign Stock)	C	C-	C+		Y	0
Ivy International Core Equity Fund Class N	IINCX	NAS CM	Open End	Global Equity Large Cap (Foreign Stock)	C	C-	C+		Y	1,000,000
Ivy International Core Equity Fund Class R	IYITX	NAS CM	Open End	Global Equity Large Cap (Foreign Stock)	C	D+	C		Y	0
Ivy International Core Equity Fund Class T	IICTX	NAS CM	Open End	Global Equity Large Cap (Foreign Stock)	C	C-	C		Y	0
Ivy International Core Equity Fund Class Y	IVVYX	NAS CM	Open End	Global Equity Large Cap (Foreign Stock)	C	C-	C		Y	0
Ivy International Small Cap Fund Class A	IVJAX	NAS CM	Open End	Global Equity Mid/Small Cap (Small Company)	C-	D+	C	Up	Y	750
Ivy International Small Cap Fund Class C	IVJCX	NAS CM	Open End	Global Equity Mid/Small Cap (Small Company)	C-	D+	C-	Up	Y	750
Ivy International Small Cap Fund Class I	IVJIX	NAS CM	Open End	Global Equity Mid/Small Cap (Small Company)	C-	D+	C	Up	Y	0
Ivy International Small Cap Fund Class N	IVJRX	NAS CM	Open End	Global Equity Mid/Small Cap (Small Company)	C-	D+	C	Up	Y	1,000,000
Ivy International Small Cap Fund Class Y	IVJYX	NAS CM	Open End	Global Equity Mid/Small Cap (Small Company)	C-	D+	C	Up	Y	0
Ivy Large Cap Growth Fund Class A	WLGAX	NAS CM	Open End	US Equity Large Cap Growth (Growth)	B	B-	B		Y	750
Ivy Large Cap Growth Fund Class B	WLGBX	NAS CM	Open End	US Equity Large Cap Growth (Growth)	B-	B-	B	Down		750
Ivy Large Cap Growth Fund Class C	WLGCX	NAS CM	Open End	US Equity Large Cap Growth (Growth)	B-	B-	B	Down	Y	750
Ivy Large Cap Growth Fund Class E	ILCEX	NAS CM	Open End	US Equity Large Cap Growth (Growth)	B	B-	B		Y	250
Ivy Large Cap Growth Fund Class I	IYGIX	NAS CM	Open End	US Equity Large Cap Growth (Growth)	B	B-	B		Y	0
Ivy Large Cap Growth Fund Class N	ILGRX	NAS CM	Open End	US Equity Large Cap Growth (Growth)	B	B-	B		Y	1,000,000
Ivy Large Cap Growth Fund Class R	WLGRX	NAS CM	Open End	US Equity Large Cap Growth (Growth)	B-	B-	B	Down	Y	0
Ivy Large Cap Growth Fund Class Y	WLGYX	NAS CM	Open End	US Equity Large Cap Growth (Growth)	B	B-	B		Y	0
Ivy LaSalle Global Real Estate Fund Class A	IREAX	NAS CM	Open End	Real Estate Sector Equity (Real Estate)	B-	C	B+	Up	Y	750
Ivy LaSalle Global Real Estate Fund Class B	IREBX	NAS CM	Open End	Real Estate Sector Equity (Real Estate)	B-	C	B	Up		750
Ivy LaSalle Global Real Estate Fund Class C	IRECX	NAS CM	Open End	Real Estate Sector Equity (Real Estate)	B-	C	B	Up	Y	750
Ivy LaSalle Global Real Estate Fund Class I	IRESX	NAS CM	Open End	Real Estate Sector Equity (Real Estate)	B-	C	B+		Y	0
Ivy LaSalle Global Real Estate Fund Class N	IRENX	NAS CM	Open End	Real Estate Sector Equity (Real Estate)	B-	C	B+	Up	Y	1,000,000
Ivy LaSalle Global Real Estate Fund Class R	IRERX	NAS CM	Open End	Real Estate Sector Equity (Real Estate)	B-	C	B+	Up	Y	0
Ivy LaSalle Global Real Estate Fund Class Y	IREYX	NAS CM	Open End	Real Estate Sector Equity (Real Estate)	B-	C	B+	Up	Y	0
Ivy Managed International Opportunities Fund Class A	IVTAX	NAS CM	Open End	Global Equity Large Cap (Growth)	C	C-	C+		Y	750
Ivy Managed International Opportunities Fund Class B	IVTBX	NAS CM	Open End	Global Equity Large Cap (Growth)	C	C-	C+			750
Ivy Managed International Opportunities Fund Class C	IVTCX	NAS CM	Open End	Global Equity Large Cap (Growth)	C	C-	C+		Y	750
Ivy Managed International Opportunities Fund Class I	IVTIX	NAS CM	Open End	Global Equity Large Cap (Growth)	C	C	C+		Y	0
Ivy Managed International Opportunities Fund Class N	IVTNX	NAS CM	Open End	Global Equity Large Cap (Growth)	C	C	C+		Y	1,000,000
Ivy Managed International Opportunities Fund Class R	IYMGX	NAS CM	Open End	Global Equity Large Cap (Growth)	C	C-	C+		Y	0
Ivy Managed International Opportunities Fund Class Y	IVTYX	NAS CM	Open End	Global Equity Large Cap (Growth)	C	C-	C+		Y	0
Ivy Mid Cap Growth Fund Class A	WMGAX	NAS CM	Open End	US Equity Mid Cap (Growth)	B-	C+	B	Down	Y	750
Ivy Mid Cap Growth Fund Class B	WMGBX	NAS CM	Open End	US Equity Mid Cap (Growth)	C+	C+	B-	Down		750
Ivy Mid Cap Growth Fund Class C	WMGCX	NAS CM	Open End	US Equity Mid Cap (Growth)	C+	C+	B-	Down	Y	750
Ivy Mid Cap Growth Fund Class E	IMCEX	NAS CM	Open End	US Equity Mid Cap (Growth)	B-	C+	B	Down	Y	250
Ivy Mid Cap Growth Fund Class I	IYMIX	NAS CM	Open End	US Equity Mid Cap (Growth)	B-	C+	B	Down	Y	0
Ivy Mid Cap Growth Fund Class N	IGRFX	NAS CM	Open End	US Equity Mid Cap (Growth)	B-	C+	B	Down	Y	1,000,000
Ivy Mid Cap Growth Fund Class R	WMGRX	NAS CM	Open End	US Equity Mid Cap (Growth)	C+	C+	B	Down	Y	0

★Expanded analysis of this fund is included in Section II.

	TOTAL RETURNS					PERFORMANCE				ASSETS		ASSET ALLOCATION & TURNOVER					BULL & BEAR		FEES		
Min Additional Investment	3-Month Total Return	6-Month Total Return	1-Year Total Return	3-Year Total Return	5-Year Total Return	Dividend Yield (TTM)	Expense Ratio	3-Yr Std Deviation	3-Year Beta	NAV	Total Assets (MIL)	%Cash	%Stocks	%Bonds	%Other	Turnover Ratio	Last Bull Market Total Return	Last Bear Market Total Return	Front End Fee (%)	Back End Fee (%)	Inception Date
	2.55	14.14	3.82	24.82	20.56	2.11	1.54	10.48	0.98	12.1	760.9	2	98	0	0	28					Dec-12
	2.65	14.35	4.08	26.03	22.82	2.4	1.19	10.48	0.98	12.09	760.9	2	98	0	0	28					Jun-12
	4.26	18.72	4.37	42.59	30.17	0.16	1.36	13.12	1.11	44.96	906.6	1	98	1	0	54	20.21	-21.94	5.75		Apr-86
	3.96	17.86	3.19	37.97	23.40	0	2.38	13.07	1.11	36.69	906.6	1	98	1	0	54	19.53	-22.27		5.00	Oct-93
	4.04	18.22	3.54	39.28	25.31	0	2.17	13.12	1.11	37.3	906.6	1	98	1	0	54	19.6	-22.27		1.00	Apr-96
	4.35	18.88	4.68	43.91	32.38	0.42	1.06	13.12	1.11	46.02	906.6	1	98	1	0	54	20.48	-21.84			Apr-07
	4.37	18.99	4.82	44.56	33.35	0.57	0.94	13.11	1.11	46.3	906.6	1	98	1	0	54	20.21	-21.94			Jul-14
	4.16	18.51	4.05	41.37	28.50	0	1.68	13.12	1.11	44.48	906.6	1	98	1	0	54	20.02	-22.03			Dec-12
	4.24	18.72	4.39	42.78	30.65	0.18	1.35	13.11	1.11	45.2	906.6	1	98	1	0	54	20.32	-21.91			Jul-03
	1.55	12.12	-5.68	22.52	5.76	1.98	1.25	12.78	1.12	17.01	5,261	3	94	3	1	52	14.41	-24.58	5.75		May-97
	1.36	11.69	-6.46	19.39	1.22	1.35	2.11	12.75	1.12	14.9	5,261	3	94	3	1	52	13.75	-24.87		5.00	May-97
	1.35	11.73	-6.27	20.07	2.24	1.52	1.93	12.75	1.12	14.95	5,261	3	94	3	1	52	13.93	-24.8		1.00	May-97
	1.54	12.09	-5.70	22.37	5.33	1.91	1.28	12.78	1.12	17.14	5,261	3	94	3	1	52	14.35	-24.59	2.50		Apr-07
	1.72	12.38	-5.20	23.89	7.62	2.34	0.79	12.78	1.12	17.15	5,261	3	94	3	1	52	14.66	-24.44			Apr-07
	1.65	12.35	-5.23	24.24	8.22	2.45	0.79	12.78	1.12	17.19	5,261	3	94	3	1	52	14.41	-24.58			Jul-14
	1.49	11.98	-5.90	21.50	4.34	1.68	1.53	12.77	1.12	17	5,261	3	94	3	1	52	14.24	-24.66			Dec-12
	1.61	12.20	-5.53	23.03	6.20	2.34	1.02	12.79	1.12	17.01	5,261	3	94	3	1	52	14.41	-24.58	2.50		Jul-17
	1.60	12.17	-5.58	22.70	6.07	2.03	1.19	12.77	1.12	17.14	5,261	3	94	3	1	52	14.49	-24.5			Jul-03
	2.10	10.37	-10.91			1.25	1.45			11.17	161.0	2	97	0	1	60			5.75		Jan-17
	1.83	9.92	-11.61			0.38	2.22			11.08	161.0	2	97	0	1	60				1.00	Jan-17
	2.09	10.56	-10.57			1.57	0.99			11.2	161.0	2	97	0	1	60					Jan-17
	2.18	10.67	-10.58			1.56	0.99			11.2	161.0	2	97	0	1	60					Jan-17
	2.01	10.38	-10.99			1.25	1.45			11.16	161.0	2	97	0	1	60					Jan-17
	6.86	24.94	14.62	73.36	88.13	0	1.12	12.92	0.94	24.29	4,284	0	100	0	0	37	27.14	-14.81	5.75		Jun-00
	6.65	24.38	13.61	68.80	79.94	0	1.99	12.95	0.94	17.8	4,284	0	100	0	0	37	26.36	-15.2		5.00	Jul-00
	6.66	24.48	13.69	69.52	81.33	0	1.86	12.91	0.94	19.52	4,284	0	100	0	0	37	26.58	-15.14		1.00	Jul-00
	6.83	24.90	14.50	73.01	87.78	0	1.15	12.94	0.94	24.22	4,284	0	100	0	0	37	27.16	-14.82	2.50		Apr-07
	6.93	25.17	14.97	74.73	90.71	0	0.69	12.93	0.94	25.76	4,284	0	100	0	0	37	27.29	-14.74			Apr-07
	6.92	25.14	14.99	75.39	91.99	0	0.69	12.92	0.94	25.93	4,284	0	100	0	0	37	27.14	-14.81			Jul-14
	6.72	24.71	14.18	71.58	84.99	0	1.46	12.92	0.94	23.16	4,284	0	100	0	0	37	27	-14.98			Dec-05
	6.84	24.91	14.58	73.61	88.74	0	1.06	12.93	0.94	24.97	4,284	0	100	0	0	37	27.17	-14.81			Jul-00
	-0.77	14.29	7.33	14.83	21.60	2.22	1.51	11.16	1	11	147.4	0	100	0	0	91			5.75		Apr-13
	-0.93	13.97	6.63	12.37	16.53	1.68	2.18	11.2	1	10.94	147.4	0	100	0	0	91				5.00	Apr-13
	-0.95	13.85	6.52	11.92	15.81	1.58	2.3	11.17	1	10.93	147.4	0	100	0	0	91				1.00	Apr-13
	-0.57	14.50	7.79	16.00	22.73	2.63	1.05	11.16	1	11.03	147.4	0	100	0	0	91					Apr-13
	-0.63	14.51	7.80	15.81	22.63	2.65	1.05	11.2	1	11.04	147.4	0	100	0	0	91					Jul-17
	-0.78	14.09	7.01	13.59	18.70	1.94	1.81	11.18	1	10.98	147.4	0	100	0	0	91					Apr-13
	-0.72	14.39	7.43	15.01	22.33	2.27	1.46	11.16	1	11.13	147.4	0	100	0	0	91					Apr-13
	1.47	12.40	-3.34	25.06	11.22	1.46	1.35	12.25	1.06	10.33	174.2	2	97	0	0	71	15.95	-24.5	5.75		Apr-07
	1.31	12.20	-4.33	22.19	6.41	0.83	2.26	12.61	1.09	10.02	174.2	2	97	0	0	71	15.57	-25.12		5.00	Apr-07
	1.41	12.27	-4.23	22.56	7.03	0.91	2.14	12.57	1.09	10.06	174.2	2	97	0	0	71	15.74	-25.07		1.00	Apr-07
	1.56	12.43	-3.05	26.08	12.93	1.7	1.02	12.21	1.06	10.4	174.2	2	97	0	0	71	16.06	-24.32			Apr-07
	1.56	12.41	-3.06	26.09	12.94	1.7	1.01	12.21	1.06	10.41	174.2	2	97	0	0	71	16.06	-24.32			Jul-17
	1.38	12.22	-3.58	24.44	10.26	1.34	1.52	12.28	1.06	10.28	174.2	2	97	0	0	71	15.73	-24.48			Dec-12
	1.57	12.39	-3.25	25.50	11.86	1.54	1.24	12.29	1.06	10.34	174.2	2	97	0	0	71	15.99	-24.52			Apr-07
	4.78	28.32	13.98	69.48	67.00	0	1.3	15.44	1.05	26.5	4,525	1	98	1	0	38	25.39	-20.68	5.75		Jun-00
	4.57	27.74	12.99	65.35	60.51	0	2.08	15.42	1.05	20.35	4,525	1	98	1	0	38	24.71	-20.98		5.00	Jul-00
	4.61	27.92	13.17	65.92	61.10	0	2.02	15.43	1.05	21.99	4,525	1	98	1	0	38	24.75	-20.88		1.00	Jul-00
	4.79	28.27	13.88	69.36	66.35	0	1.28	15.42	1.05	25.77	4,525	1	98	1	0	38	25.2	-20.7	2.50		Apr-07
	4.90	28.59	14.41	71.09	69.60	0	0.79	15.42	1.05	28.87	4,525	1	98	1	0	38	25.62	-20.53			Apr-07
	4.93	28.66	14.48	71.64	70.72	0	0.79	15.45	1.06	29.13	4,525	1	98	1	0	38	25.39	-20.68			Jul-14
	4.73	28.15	13.60	67.82	64.46	0	1.63	15.43	1.05	25.67	4,525	1	98	1	0	38	25.18	-20.73			Dec-05

	MARKET			FUND TYPE, CATEGORY & OBJECTIVE	RATINGS				MINIMUMS	
Fund Name	Ticker Symbol	Traded On	Fund Type	Category and (Prospectus Objective)	Overall Rating	Reward Rating	Risk Rating	Recent Up/ Downgrade	Open to New Investors	Min Initial Investment
Ivy Mid Cap Growth Fund Class Y	WMGYX	NAS CM	Open End	US Equity Mid Cap (Growth)	B-	C+	B	Down	Y	0
Ivy Mid Cap Income Opportunities Fund Class A	IVOAX	NAS CM	Open End	US Equity Mid Cap (Income)	B-	C	B		Y	750
Ivy Mid Cap Income Opportunities Fund Class C	IVOCX	NAS CM	Open End	US Equity Mid Cap (Income)	B-	C	B		Y	750
Ivy Mid Cap Income Opportunities Fund Class E	IVOEX	NAS CM	Open End	US Equity Mid Cap (Income)	B-	C	B		Y	250
Ivy Mid Cap Income Opportunities Fund Class I	IVOIX	NAS CM	Open End	US Equity Mid Cap (Income)	B-	C	B		Y	0
Ivy Mid Cap Income Opportunities Fund Class N	IVOSX	NAS CM	Open End	US Equity Mid Cap (Income)	B-	C	B		Y	1,000,000
Ivy Mid Cap Income Opportunities Fund Class R	IVORX	NAS CM	Open End	US Equity Mid Cap (Income)	B-	C	B		Y	0
Ivy Mid Cap Income Opportunities Fund Class Y	IVOYX	NAS CM	Open End	US Equity Mid Cap (Income)	B-	C	B		Y	0
Ivy Natural Resources Fund Class A	IGNAX	NAS CM	Open End	Natl Resources Sec Equity (Natl Res)	D	D	D+	Down	Y	750
Ivy Natural Resources Fund Class B	IGNBX	NAS CM	Open End	Natl Resources Sec Equity (Natl Res)	D	D	D+	Down		750
Ivy Natural Resources Fund Class C	IGNCX	NAS CM	Open End	Natl Resources Sec Equity (Natl Res)	D	D	D+	Down	Y	750
Ivy Natural Resources Fund Class E	IGNEX	NAS CM	Open End	Natl Resources Sec Equity (Natl Res)	D	D	D+	Down	Y	750
Ivy Natural Resources Fund Class I	IGNIX	NAS CM	Open End	Natl Resources Sec Equity (Natl Res)	D	D	D+	Down	Y	0
Ivy Natural Resources Fund Class N	INRSX	NAS CM	Open End	Natl Resources Sec Equity (Natl Res)	D	D	D+	Down	Y	1,000,000
Ivy Natural Resources Fund Class R	IGNRX	NAS CM	Open End	Natl Resources Sec Equity (Natl Res)	D	D	D+	Down	Y	0
Ivy Natural Resources Fund Class Y	IGNYX	NAS CM	Open End	Natl Resources Sec Equity (Natl Res)	D	D	D+	Down	Y	0
Ivy ProShares MSCI ACWI Index Fund Class A	IMWAX	NAS CM	Open End	Global Equity Large Cap (World Stock)	C	C-	B-	Up	Y	750
Ivy ProShares MSCI ACWI Index Fund Class E	IMWEX	NAS CM	Open End	Global Equity Large Cap (World Stock)	C	C-	B-	Up	Y	250
Ivy ProShares MSCI ACWI Index Fund Class I	IMWIX	NAS CM	Open End	Global Equity Large Cap (World Stock)	C	C-	B-	Up	Y	0
Ivy ProShares MSCI ACWI Index Fund Class N	IMCNX	NAS CM	Open End	Global Equity Large Cap (World Stock)	C	C-	B-	Up	Y	1,000,000
Ivy ProShares MSCI ACWI Index Fund Class R	IMCRX	NAS CM	Open End	Global Equity Large Cap (World Stock)	C	C-	B-	Up	Y	0
Ivy ProShares Russell 2000 Dividend Growers Index Cls A	IRUAX	NAS CM	Open End	US Equity Small Cap (Equity-Income)	C	C	B-	Up	Y	750
Ivy ProShares Russell 2000 Dividend Growers Index Cls E	IRUEX	NAS CM	Open End	US Equity Small Cap (Equity-Income)	C	C	B-	Up	Y	250
Ivy ProShares Russell 2000 Dividend Growers Index Cls I	IRUIX	NAS CM	Open End	US Equity Small Cap (Equity-Income)	C	C	B-	Up	Y	0
Ivy ProShares Russell 2000 Dividend Growers Index Cls N	IRUNX	NAS CM	Open End	US Equity Small Cap (Equity-Income)	C	C	B-	Up	Y	1,000,000
Ivy ProShares Russell 2000 Dividend Growers Index Cls R	IRURX	NAS CM	Open End	US Equity Small Cap (Equity-Income)	C	C	B-	Up	Y	0
Ivy ProShares S&P 500 Dividend Aristocrats Index Cls A	IDAAX	NAS CM	Open End	US Equity Large Cap Value (Equity-Income)	C	C	B	Up	Y	750
Ivy ProShares S&P 500 Dividend Aristocrats Index Cls E	IDAEX	NAS CM	Open End	US Equity Large Cap Value (Equity-Income)	C	C	B	Up	Y	250
Ivy ProShares S&P 500 Dividend Aristocrats Index Cls I	IDAIX	NAS CM	Open End	US Equity Large Cap Value (Equity-Income)	C	C	B	Up	Y	0
Ivy ProShares S&P 500 Dividend Aristocrats Index Cls N	IDANX	NAS CM	Open End	US Equity Large Cap Value (Equity-Income)	C	C	B	Up	Y	1,000,000
Ivy ProShares S&P 500 Dividend Aristocrats Index Cls R	IDARX	NAS CM	Open End	US Equity Large Cap Value (Equity-Income)	C	C	B-	Up	Y	0
Ivy Pzena International Value Fund Class A	ICDAX	NAS CM	Open End	Global Equity Large Cap (World Stock)	C-	C-	C	Down	Y	750
Ivy Pzena International Value Fund Class B	ICDBX	NAS CM	Open End	Global Equity Large Cap (World Stock)	D+	D	C-	Down		750
Ivy Pzena International Value Fund Class C	ICDCX	NAS CM	Open End	Global Equity Large Cap (World Stock)	C-	D+	C		Y	750
Ivy Pzena International Value Fund Class I	ICVIX	NAS CM	Open End	Global Equity Large Cap (World Stock)	C	C-	C		Y	0
Ivy Pzena International Value Fund Class N	ICNGX	NAS CM	Open End	Global Equity Large Cap (World Stock)	C	C-	C		Y	1,000,000
Ivy Pzena International Value Fund Class R	IYCUX	NAS CM	Open End	Global Equity Large Cap (World Stock)	C-	C-	C	Down	Y	0
Ivy Pzena International Value Fund Class Y	ICDYX	NAS CM	Open End	Global Equity Large Cap (World Stock)	C	C-	C		Y	0
Ivy Science And Technology Fund Class A	WSTAX	NAS CM	Open End	Technology Sector Equity (Technology)	B-	B	C+		Y	750
Ivy Science And Technology Fund Class B	WSTBX	NAS CM	Open End	Technology Sector Equity (Technology)	B-	B-	C+			750
Ivy Science And Technology Fund Class C	WSTCX	NAS CM	Open End	Technology Sector Equity (Technology)	B-	B-	C+		Y	750
Ivy Science and Technology Fund Class E	ISTEX	NAS CM	Open End	Technology Sector Equity (Technology)	B-	B	C+		Y	250
Ivy Science and Technology Fund Class I	ISTIX	NAS CM	Open End	Technology Sector Equity (Technology)	B-	B	B-		Y	0
Ivy Science and Technology Fund Class N	ISTNX	NAS CM	Open End	Technology Sector Equity (Technology)	B-	B	B-		Y	1,000,000
Ivy Science and Technology Fund Class R	WSTRX	NAS CM	Open End	Technology Sector Equity (Technology)	B-	B-	C+		Y	0
Ivy Science And Technology Fund Class Y	WSTYX	NAS CM	Open End	Technology Sector Equity (Technology)	B-	B	C+		Y	0
Ivy Securian Real Estate Securities Fund Class A	IRSAX	NAS CM	Open End	Real Estate Sector Equity (Real Estate)	C	C	C+	Down	Y	750
Ivy Securian Real Estate Securities Fund Class B	IRSBX	NAS CM	Open End	Real Estate Sector Equity (Real Estate)	C	C	C+	Down		750
Ivy Securian Real Estate Securities Fund Class C	IRSCX	NAS CM	Open End	Real Estate Sector Equity (Real Estate)	C	C	C+	Down	Y	750
Ivy Securian Real Estate Securities Fund Class E	IREEX	NAS CM	Open End	Real Estate Sector Equity (Real Estate)	C	C	C+	Down	Y	250
Ivy Securian Real Estate Securities Fund Class I	IREIX	NAS CM	Open End	Real Estate Sector Equity (Real Estate)	C	C	C+	Down	Y	0
Ivy Securian Real Estate Securities Fund Class N	IRSEX	NAS CM	Open End	Real Estate Sector Equity (Real Estate)	C	C	C+	Down	Y	1,000,000

★ Expanded analysis of this fund is included in Section II.

	TOTAL RETURNS					PERFORMANCE				ASSETS		ASSET ALLOCATION & TURNOVER					BULL & BEAR		FEES		
Min Additional Investment	3-Month Total Return	6-Month Total Return	1-Year Total Return	3-Year Total Return	5-Year Total Return	Dividend Yield (TTM)	Expense Ratio	3-Yr Std Deviation	3-Year Beta	NAV	Total Assets (MIL)	%Cash	%Stocks	%Bonds	%Other	Turnover Ratio	Last Bull Market Total Return	Last Bear Market Total Return	Front End Fee (%)	Back End Fee (%)	Inception Date
	4.78	28.34	13.98	69.63	67.36	0	1.27	15.42	1.05	27.8	4,525	1	98	1	0	38	25.47	-20.6			Jul-00
	4.72	17.33	8.42	37.08		1.38	1.31	13.31	0.94	14.59	679.3	3	96	0	0	17			5.75		Oct-14
	4.55	17.01	7.69	34.18		0.7	2.07	13.28	0.94	14.53	679.3	3	96	0	0	17				1.00	Oct-14
	4.77	17.51	8.60	37.71		1.54	1.09	13.27	0.94	14.6	679.3	3	96	0	0	17			2.50		Oct-14
	4.81	17.50	8.75	38.28		1.68	0.83	13.31	0.94	14.61	679.3	3	96	0	0	17					Oct-14
	4.82	17.62	8.85	38.74		1.78	0.83	13.25	0.94	14.62	679.3	3	96	0	0	17					Oct-14
	4.65	17.19	8.11	35.70		1.09	1.59	13.33	0.94	14.57	679.3	3	96	0	0	17					Oct-14
	4.66	17.35	8.44	37.01		1.4	1.27	13.3	0.94	14.59	679.3	3	96	0	0	17					Oct-14
	-2.37	10.61	-14.23	-3.25	-36.89	0	1.64	17.85	0.91	13.13	337.9	3	97	0	0	21	18.81	-40.1	5.75		Jan-97
	-2.78	9.74	-15.54	-6.97	-40.50	0	2.89	17.87	0.91	10.81	337.9	3	97	0	0	21	18.31	-40.3		5.00	Jan-97
	-2.51	10.37	-14.63	-4.99	-38.80	0	2.31	17.89	0.91	10.85	337.9	3	97	0	0	21	18.4	-40.28		1.00	Jan-97
	-2.24	10.83	-13.89	-2.02	-35.64	0.44	1.27	17.88	0.91	13.5	337.9	3	97	0	0	21	19.02	-40.08	2.50		Apr-07
	-2.20	10.97	-13.76	-1.66	-35.25	0.52	1.11	17.88	0.91	13.75	337.9	3	97	0	0	21	19.06	-39.98			Apr-07
	-2.19	11.01	-13.65	-1.25	-34.77	0.7	0.95	17.88	0.91	13.81	337.9	3	97	0	0	21	18.81	-40.1			Jul-14
	-2.33	10.68	-14.23	-3.43	-37.10	0	1.69	17.85	0.91	12.95	337.9	3	97	0	0	21	18.72	-40.13			Dec-05
	-2.31	10.85	-13.96	-2.40	-36.02	0.26	1.34	17.86	0.91	13.48	337.9	3	97	0	0	21	18.96	-40.02			Jul-03
	3.58	16.89	5.60			1.4	0.9			11.82	105.9	1	99	0	0	39			2.50		Apr-17
	3.53	16.97	5.65			1.53	0.75			11.82	105.9	1	99	0	0	39			2.50		Apr-17
	3.57	17.03	5.77			1.64	0.65			11.82	105.9	1	99	0	0	39					Apr-17
	3.57	17.03	5.76			1.63	0.65			11.82	105.9	1	99	0	0	39					Apr-17
	3.36	16.52	4.99			0.92	1.4			11.81	105.9	1	99	0	0	39					Apr-17
	2.37	11.82	5.47			1.59	0.9			10.96	126.1	3	97	0	0	36			2.50		Apr-17
	2.31	11.91	5.54			1.74	0.73			10.96	126.1	3	97	0	0	36			2.50		Apr-17
	2.34	11.95	5.63			1.83	0.65			10.96	126.1	3	97	0	0	36					Apr-17
	2.43	11.94	5.73			1.83	0.65			10.97	126.1	3	97	0	0	36					Apr-17
	2.24	11.55	4.95			1.1	1.4			10.96	126.1	3	97	0	0	36					Apr-17
	2.92	16.39	13.42			1.76	0.75			12.28	380.1	0	100	0	0	27			2.50		Apr-17
	2.83	16.39	13.42			1.76	0.75			12.28	380.1	0	100	0	0	27			2.50		Apr-17
	2.90	16.52	13.70			2	0.5			12.28	380.1	0	100	0	0	27					Apr-17
	2.90	16.52	13.71			2.01	0.49			12.28	380.1	0	100	0	0	27					Apr-17
	2.70	16.01	12.87			1.29	1.26			12.27	380.1	0	100	0	0	27					Apr-17
	0.26	7.85	-6.14	24.06	-5.82	0.39	1.54	14.27	1.03	14.97	261.2	5	95	0	0	85	15.16	-23.54	5.75		Sep-01
	-0.07	6.91	-7.70	18.79	-12.01	0	2.91	14.28	1.03	13.15	261.2	5	95	0	0	85	14.55	-23.84		5.00	Sep-01
	0.21	7.57	-6.59	21.96	-8.52	0	2.14	14.29	1.03	13.92	261.2	5	95	0	0	85	14.85	-23.73		1.00	Oct-01
	0.45	8.16	-5.71	25.78	-3.65	0.82	1.11	14.33	1.03	15.37	261.2	5	95	0	0	85	15.6	-23.36			Apr-07
	0.45	8.21	-5.59	26.30	-3.01	0.98	0.94	14.31	1.03	15.41	261.2	5	95	0	0	85	15.16	-23.54			Jul-14
	0.26	7.79	-6.23	23.63	-6.43	0.27	1.67	14.31	1.03	14.94	261.2	5	95	0	0	85	14.99	-23.62			Dec-12
	0.39	8.02	-5.92	24.87	-4.81	0.57	1.34	14.31	1.03	15.22	261.2	5	95	0	0	85	15.71	-23.4			Jul-03
	9.30	34.89	15.71	91.86	64.27	0	1.21	17.27	0.99	71.05	7,179	2	97	1	0	14	22.03	-19.83	5.75		Jul-00
	9.06	34.33	14.75	87.28	57.97	0	2.02	17.25	0.99	56.54	7,179	2	97	1	0	14	21.41	-20.11		5.00	Jul-00
	9.10	34.41	14.87	87.68	58.50	0	1.97	17.25	0.99	59.21	7,179	2	97	1	0	14	21.47	-20.06		1.00	Jul-97
	9.27	34.82	15.55	91.34	63.41	0	1.3	17.26	0.99	70.35	7,179	2	97	1	0	14	21.96	-19.85	2.50		Apr-07
	9.36	35.04	15.97	93.25	66.48	0	0.99	17.26	0.99	79.3	7,179	2	97	1	0	14	22.24	-19.72			Apr-07
	9.40	35.16	16.17	94.16	67.59	0	0.85	17.27	0.99	79.91	7,179	2	97	1	0	14	21.47	-20.06			Jul-14
	9.20	34.65	15.31	89.89	61.66	0	1.58	17.26	0.99	68.69	7,179	2	97	1	0	14	21.82	-19.92			Dec-05
	9.31	34.92	15.73	91.93	64.54	0	1.21	17.26	0.99	75.45	7,179	2	97	1	0	14	22.06	-19.8			Jun-98
	0.64	16.11	9.40	8.96	38.38	1.25	1.42	12.25	0.92	24.54	426.1	1	99	0	0	69	31.54	-18.22	5.75		Feb-99
	0.43	15.56	8.39	5.84	31.99	0.4	2.39	12.23	0.91	23.52	426.1	1	99	0	0	69	30.69	-18.6		5.00	Dec-03
	0.48	15.71	8.63	6.51	33.36	0.61	2.19	12.22	0.91	23.93	426.1	1	99	0	0	69	30.95	-18.48		1.00	Dec-03
	0.68	16.14	9.47	8.95	38.07	1.27	1.42	12.26	0.92	24.55	426.1	1	99	0	0	69	31.64	-18.22	2.50		Apr-07
	0.79	16.34	9.86	10.21	41.17	1.58	1.06	12.25	0.92	24.75	426.1	1	99	0	0	69	32.01	-18.03			Apr-07
	0.83	16.41	10.01	10.75	42.25	1.72	0.89	12.26	0.92	24.79	426.1	1	99	0	0	69	31.54	-18.22			Jul-14

Fund Name	MARKET Ticker Symbol	Traded On	FUND TYPE, CATEGORY & OBJECTIVE Fund Type	Category and (Prospectus Objective)	RATINGS Overall Rating	Reward Rating	Risk Rating	Recent Up/ Downgrade	MINIMUMS Open to New Investors	Min Initial Investment
Ivy Securian Real Estate Securities Fund Class R	IRSRX	NAS CM	Open End	Real Estate Sector Equity (Real Estate)	C	C	C+	Down	Y	0
Ivy Securian Real Estate Securities Fund Class Y	IRSYX	NAS CM	Open End	Real Estate Sector Equity (Real Estate)	C	C	C+	Down	Y	0
Ivy Small Cap Core Fund Class A	IYSAX	NAS CM	Open End	US Equity Small Cap (Small Company)	C	C	C+		Y	750
Ivy Small Cap Core Fund Class B	IYSBX	NAS CM	Open End	US Equity Small Cap (Small Company)	C	C	C+			750
Ivy Small Cap Core Fund Class C	IYSCX	NAS CM	Open End	US Equity Small Cap (Small Company)	C	C	C+		Y	750
Ivy Small Cap Core Fund Class I	IVVIX	NAS CM	Open End	US Equity Small Cap (Small Company)	C	C	C+	Down	Y	0
Ivy Small Cap Core Fund Class N	ISPVX	NAS CM	Open End	US Equity Small Cap (Small Company)	C	C	C+	Down	Y	1,000,000
Ivy Small Cap Core Fund Class R	IYSMX	NAS CM	Open End	US Equity Small Cap (Small Company)	C	C	C+		Y	0
Ivy Small Cap Core Fund Class T	IYCTX	NAS CM	Open End	US Equity Small Cap (Small Company)	C	C	C+	Down	Y	0
Ivy Small Cap Core Fund Class Y	IYSYX	NAS CM	Open End	US Equity Small Cap (Small Company)	C	C	C+		Y	0
Ivy Small Cap Growth Fund Class A	WSGAX	NAS CM	Open End	US Equity Small Cap (Small Company)	C+	C	B-	Down	Y	750
Ivy Small Cap Growth Fund Class B	WSGBX	NAS CM	Open End	US Equity Small Cap (Small Company)	C+	C	C+	Down		750
Ivy Small Cap Growth Fund Class C	WRGCX	NAS CM	Open End	US Equity Small Cap (Small Company)	C+	C	C+	Down	Y	750
Ivy Small Cap Growth Fund Class E	ISGEX	NAS CM	Open End	US Equity Small Cap (Small Company)	C+	C	B-	Down	Y	250
Ivy Small Cap Growth Fund Class Institutional	IYSIX	NAS CM	Open End	US Equity Small Cap (Small Company)	C+	C	B-	Down	Y	0
Ivy Small Cap Growth Fund Class N	IRGFX	NAS CM	Open End	US Equity Small Cap (Small Company)	C+	C	B-	Down	Y	1,000,000
Ivy Small Cap Growth Fund Class R	WSGRX	NAS CM	Open End	US Equity Small Cap (Small Company)	C+	C	C+	Down	Y	0
Ivy Small Cap Growth Fund Class T	IYSTX	NAS CM	Open End	US Equity Small Cap (Small Company)	C+	C	B-	Down	Y	0
Ivy Small Cap Growth Fund Class Y	WSCYX	NAS CM	Open End	US Equity Small Cap (Small Company)	C+	C	B-	Down	Y	0
Ivy Value Fund Class A	IYVAX	NAS CM	Open End	US Equity Large Cap Value (Growth)	C+	C	B		Y	750
Ivy Value Fund Class B	IYVBX	NAS CM	Open End	US Equity Large Cap Value (Growth)	C+	C	B			750
Ivy Value Fund Class C	IYVCX	NAS CM	Open End	US Equity Large Cap Value (Growth)	C+	C	B		Y	750
Ivy Value Fund Class I	IYAIX	NAS CM	Open End	US Equity Large Cap Value (Growth)	C+	C	B		Y	0
Ivy Value Fund Class N	IVALX	NAS CM	Open End	US Equity Large Cap Value (Growth)	C+	C	B		Y	1,000,000
Ivy Value Fund Class R	IYVLX	NAS CM	Open End	US Equity Large Cap Value (Growth)	C+	C	B		Y	0
Ivy Value Fund Class Y	IYVYX	NAS CM	Open End	US Equity Large Cap Value (Growth)	C+	C	B		Y	0
Ivy Wilshire Global Allocation Fund Class A	IWGAX	NAS CM	Open End	Moderate Alloc (Growth & Income)	B-	C	B+	Up		750
Ivy Wilshire Global Allocation Fund Class B	IWGBX	NAS CM	Open End	Moderate Alloc (Growth & Income)	C+	C	B+	Up		750
Ivy Wilshire Global Allocation Fund Class C	IWGCX	NAS CM	Open End	Moderate Alloc (Growth & Income)	C+	C	B+	Up		750
Ivy Wilshire Global Allocation Fund Class I	IWGIX	NAS CM	Open End	Moderate Alloc (Growth & Income)	B-	C	B+	Up	Y	0
Ivy Wilshire Global Allocation Fund Class N	IWGNX	NAS CM	Open End	Moderate Alloc (Growth & Income)	B-	C	B+	Up	Y	0
Ivy Wilshire Global Allocation Fund Class R	IWGRX	NAS CM	Open End	Moderate Alloc (Growth & Income)	B-	C	B+	Up	Y	0
Ivy Wilshire Global Allocation Fund Class Y	IWGYX	NAS CM	Open End	Moderate Alloc (Growth & Income)	B-	C	B+	Up	Y	0
Jackson Square All Cap Growth Fund IS Class	JSSSX	NAS CM	Open End	US Equity Large Cap Growth (Growth)	C+	C	B	Down	Y	1,000,000
Jackson Square Global Growth Fund Institutional Class	JSPTX	NAS CM	Open End	Global Equity Large Cap (Growth)	C+	C	B		Y	100,000
Jackson Square Global Growth Fund IS Class	JSPUX	NAS CM	Open End	Global Equity Large Cap (Growth)	C+	C	B		Y	1,000,000
Jackson Square Large-Cap Growth Fund Institutional Class	JSPIX	NAS CM	Open End	US Equity Large Cap Growth (Growth)	B-	C	B		Y	100,000
Jackson Square Large-Cap Growth Fund Investor Class	JSPJX	NAS CM	Open End	US Equity Large Cap Growth (Growth)	B-	C	B		Y	2,500
Jackson Square Large-Cap Growth Fund IS Class	DPLGX	NAS CM	Open End	US Equity Large Cap Growth (Growth)	B-	C	B		Y	1,000,000
Jackson Square Select 20 Growth Fund IS Class	DPCEX	NAS CM	Open End	US Equity Large Cap Growth (Growth)	B-	C	B		Y	1,000,000
Jackson Square SMID-Cap Growth Fund Institutional Class	JSMTX	NAS CM	Open End	US Equity Mid Cap (Growth)	B-	C+	B	Up	Y	100,000
Jackson Square SMID-Cap Growth Fund Investor Class	JSMVX	NAS CM	Open End	US Equity Mid Cap (Growth)	B-	C+	B	Up	Y	2,500
Jackson Square SMID-Cap Growth Fund IS Class	DCGTX	NAS CM	Open End	US Equity Mid Cap (Growth)	B-	C+	B	Up	Y	1,000,000
Jacob Internet Investor Class	JAMFX	NAS CM	Open End	Technology Sector Equity (Technology)	C+	C+	B-	Up	Y	2,500
Jacob Micro Cap Growth Fund Institutional Class shares	JMIGX	NAS CM	Open End	US Equity Small Cap (Growth)	B	B	B-	Up	Y	100,000
Jacob Micro Cap Growth Fund Investor Class shares	JMCGX	NAS CM	Open End	US Equity Small Cap (Growth)	B	B	B-	Up	Y	2,500
Jacob Small Cap Growth Fund Institutional Class shares	JSIGX	NAS CM	Open End	US Equity Small Cap (Small Company)	C	C	B-	Up	Y	1,000,000
Jacob Small Cap Growth Fund Investor Class shares	JSCGX	NAS CM	Open End	US Equity Small Cap (Small Company)	C	C	B-	Up	Y	2,500
JAG Large Cap Growth Fund Class A	JLGAX	NAS CM	Open End	US Equity Large Cap Growth (Growth)	C+	C	B-	Down	Y	2,500
JAG Large Cap Growth Fund Class I	JLGIX	NAS CM	Open End	US Equity Large Cap Growth (Growth)	C+	C+	B	Down	Y	250,000
Jaguar Global Property Fund Institutional Shares	JAGGX	NAS CM	Open End	Real Estate Sector Equity (Real Estate)	C+	C	B	Up	Y	1,000,000
Jaguar International Property Fund Institutional Shares	JAGOX	NAS CM	Open End	Real Estate Sector Equity (Real Estate)	C	C	B		Y	1,000,000

★ Expanded analysis of this fund is included in Section II.

Min Additional Investment	TOTAL RETURNS 3-Month Total Return	6-Month Total Return	1-Year Total Return	3-Year Total Return	5-Year Total Return	PERFORMANCE Dividend Yield (TTM)	Expense Ratio	3-Yr Std Deviation	3-Year Beta	ASSETS NAV	Total Assets (MIL)	ASSET ALLOCATION & TURNOVER %Cash	%Stocks	%Bonds	%Other	Turnover Ratio	BULL & BEAR Last Bull Market Total Return	Last Bear Market Total Return	FEES Front End Fee (%)	Back End Fee (%)	Inception Date
	0.62	16.00	9.24	8.28	36.97	1.06	1.66	12.27	0.92	24.51	426.1	1	99	0	0	69	31.56	-18.22			Dec-05
	0.73	16.22	9.65	9.51	39.61	1.39	1.27	12.24	0.91	24.59	426.1	1	99	0	0	69	31.8	-18.06			Dec-03
	4.38	21.36	-0.70	43.35	47.92	0	1.46	15.76	0.89	17.61	704.0	1	98	1	0	119	22.94	-27.1	5.75		Jan-97
	4.14	20.90	-1.51	39.48	41.25	0	2.39	15.77	0.89	13.82	704.0	1	98	1	0	119	22.08	-27.4		5.00	Dec-03
	4.25	20.98	-1.33	40.48	43.06	0	2.14	15.73	0.88	14.93	704.0	1	98	1	0	119	22.4	-27.3		1.00	Dec-03
	4.56	21.69	-0.19	45.06	51.08	0	0.89	15.75	0.89	19.24	704.0	1	98	1	0	119	23.42	-26.93			Apr-07
	4.52	21.71	-0.19	45.53	51.97	0	0.89	15.78	0.89	19.39	704.0	1	98	1	0	119	22.94	-27.1			Jul-14
	4.35	21.26	-0.95	42.37	46.40	0	1.68	15.76	0.89	17.51	704.0	1	98	1	0	119	22.76	-27.17			Dec-12
	4.50	21.58	-0.41	44.12	48.71	0	1.19	15.81	0.89	17.63	704.0	1	98	1	0	119	22.94	-27.1	2.50		Jul-17
	4.37	21.40	-0.63	43.79	48.87	0	1.36	15.74	0.88	18.6	704.0	1	98	1	0	119	23.15	-27.02			Dec-03
	5.06	24.89	5.66	63.54	65.62	0	1.34	16.72	0.93	18.06	2,538	2	94	4	0	42	24.18	-24.73	5.75		Jul-00
	4.78	24.34	4.72	59.16	58.44	0	2.22	16.74	0.93	12.26	2,538	2	94	4	0	42	23.43	-25.12		5.00	Jul-00
	4.83	24.39	4.87	60.03	60.10	0	2.05	16.71	0.93	13.87	2,538	2	94	4	0	42	23.73	-24.96		1.00	Sep-92
	5.05	24.89	5.61	63.38	65.21	0	1.35	16.71	0.93	17.86	2,538	2	94	4	0	42	24.07	-24.78	2.50		Apr-07
	5.16	25.13	6.10	65.13	68.52	0	0.89	16.75	0.93	24.64	2,538	2	94	4	0	42	24.48	-24.62			Apr-07
	5.17	25.12	6.11	65.71	69.50	0	0.89	16.76	0.93	24.8	2,538	2	94	4	0	42	23.73	-24.96			Jul-14
	5.00	24.69	5.36	62.11	63.42	0	1.66	16.78	0.93	17.62	2,538	2	94	4	0	42	24.06	-24.81			Dec-05
	5.11	24.91	5.86	62.85	62.92	0	1.19	16.71	0.93	18.1	2,538	2	94	4	0	42	23.73	-24.96	2.50		Jul-17
	5.02	24.91	5.70	63.79	66.23	0	1.31	16.74	0.93	23.01	2,538	2	94	4	0	42	24.33	-24.71			Dec-95
	3.28	13.96	5.15	35.05	29.92	0.83	1.21	13.63	1.09	23.33	1,027	3	95	2	0	51	23.9	-22.08	5.75		Sep-94
	3.03	13.34	4.06	30.94	23.62	0.09	2.23	13.64	1.09	21.4	1,027	3	95	2	0	51	23.03	-22.51		5.00	Dec-03
	3.08	13.55	4.38	32.25	25.56	0.23	1.94	13.61	1.09	22.37	1,027	3	95	2	0	51	23.32	-22.3		1.00	Dec-03
	3.40	14.15	5.48	36.26	32.05	1.11	0.92	13.64	1.09	23.44	1,027	3	95	2	0	51	24.12	-21.9			Apr-07
	3.44	14.21	5.63	37.02	33.08	1.26	0.77	13.64	1.09	23.52	1,027	3	95	2	0	51	23.9	-22.08			Jul-14
	3.23	13.77	4.83	33.87	28.17	0.53	1.52	13.64	1.09	23.28	1,027	3	95	2	0	51	23.72	-22.16			Dec-12
	3.29	14.01	5.21	35.16	30.30	0.89	1.21	13.62	1.09	23.37	1,027	3	95	2	0	51	24.01	-22.01			Dec-03
	2.52	11.55	3.52	19.77	1.54	2.01	1.15	7.96		8.11	1,227	4	64	31	0	35	22.29	-22.14	5.75		Mar-95
	2.29	10.98	2.48	16.22	-3.47	1.21	2.1	7.96		7.58	1,227	4	64	31	0	35	21.66	-22.51		5.00	Oct-99
	2.40	11.30	2.91	17.14	-2.39	1.3	1.92	7.95		7.68	1,227	4	64	31	0	35	21.84	-22.45		1.00	Oct-99
	2.62	11.83	3.98	20.95	3.21	2.31	0.83	7.98		8.22	1,227	4	64	31	0	35	22.55	-22.04			Sep-95
	2.65	11.84	3.95	20.41	2.08	2.28	0.83	7.98		8.12	1,227	4	64	31	0	35	22.29	-22.14			Feb-18
	2.40	11.41	3.36	19.08	0.46	1.87	1.56	7.96		8.1	1,227	4	64	31	0	35	22.11	-22.22			Feb-18
	2.52	11.70	3.62	20.03	1.76	2.1	1.15	7.91		8.11	1,227	4	64	31	0	35	22.29	-22.14			Feb-18
	6.14	24.54	11.62			0.02	0.9			23.14	6.1	0	100	0	0						Sep-16
	7.47	23.72	10.57			0	1.15			25.03	11.8	0	100	0	0						Sep-16
	7.46	23.70	10.56			0	1.05			25.05	11.8	0	100	0	0						Sep-16
	7.62	21.39	10.86	54.91	60.65	0.08	0.74	13.53	0.95	11.86	121.1	0	100	0	0	53	28.4	-12.39			Sep-16
100	7.46	21.14	10.52	53.61	58.51	0	0.99	13.54	0.95	11.8	121.1	0	100	0	0	53	28.21	-12.48			Sep-16
	7.63	21.43	10.89	54.94	60.68	0.1	0.64	13.57	0.95	11.84	121.1	0	100	0	0	53	28.4	-12.38			Nov-05
	7.56	22.98	12.59	49.24	50.91	0	0.87	15.16	0.98	6.26	5.6	0	100	0	0	41	27.06	-8.7			Mar-00
	2.69	28.75	13.33	69.37	94.81	0.18	0.97	15.42	0.88	24.76	970.4	0	98	2	0	47	26.17	-16			Sep-16
100	2.63	28.57	12.99	67.91	92.16	0.07	1.22	15.44	0.88	24.57	970.4	0	98	2	0	47	25.99	-16.08			Sep-16
	2.73	28.83	13.27	69.53	94.98	0.22	0.87	15.45	0.88	24.75	970.4	0	98	2	0	47	26.17	-15.99			Dec-03
100	2.97	26.27	8.84	67.04	98.01	0	2.43	16.84	0.95	5.19	50.1	2	98	0	0	46	17.73	-21.82			Dec-99
100	13.44	37.60	29.81	98.06	56.82	0	2.41	22.9	0.99	20.42	14.6	5	95	0	0	63	40.24	-30.71			Dec-97
100	13.34	37.42	29.61	96.73	54.74	0	2.65	22.86	0.98	18.69	14.6	5	95	0	0	63	40.09	-30.82			May-01
100	1.02	20.10	8.07	84.06	40.66	0	1.95	19.55	0.96	26.64	17.7	2	98	0	0	81	18.58	-31.91			Nov-12
100	1.00	20.03	7.87	82.53	38.79	0	2.25	19.52	0.96	26.18	17.7	2	98	0	0	81	18.58	-31.91			Feb-10
50	2.89	19.55	8.31	67.81	82.73	0	1.51	15.69	1.1	17.79	64.9	1	99	0	0	125			5.75		Dec-11
50	2.99	19.67	8.59	69.15	85.01	0	1.26	15.69	1.1	18.25	64.9	1	99	0	0	125					Dec-11
	0.17	15.10	6.10			2.27	0.9			11.2	8.6	4	94	0	2	21					Dec-16
	-1.12	12.16	0.27	27.26		3.72	1	12.19	1.04	8.76	5.6	7	90	0	3	20					Mar-15

	MARKET		FUND TYPE, CATEGORY & OBJECTIVE		RATINGS				MINIMUMS	
Fund Name	Ticker Symbol	Traded On	Fund Type	Category and (Prospectus Objective)	Overall Rating	Reward Rating	Risk Rating	Recent Up/ Downgrade	Open to New Investors	Min Initial Investment
James Aggressive Allocation Fund	JAVAX	NAS CM	Open End	Aggressive Alloc (Growth & Income)	C	C-	C		Y	10,000
James Alpha EHS Portfolio Class A	JAHAX	NAS CM	Open End	Long/Short Equity (Growth)	C-	D	C+	Up	Y	2,500
James Alpha EHS Portfolio Class C	JAHCX	NAS CM	Open End	Long/Short Equity (Growth)	C-	D	C	Up	Y	2,500
James Alpha EHS Portfolio Class I	JEHIX	NAS CM	Open End	Long/Short Equity (Growth)	C-	D	C+	Up	Y	1,000,000
James Alpha EHS Portfolio Class S	JAHSX	NAS CM	Open End	Long/Short Equity (Growth)	C-	D	C+	Up	Y	0
James Alpha Event Driven Portfolio Class A Shares	JAEAX	NAS CM	Open End	Multialternative (Growth)	C-	D+	B-	Up	Y	2,500
James Alpha Event Driven Portfolio Class C Shares	JAECX	NAS CM	Open End	Multialternative (Growth)	C-	D+	B	Up	Y	2,500
James Alpha Event Driven Portfolio Class I Shares	JAEIX	NAS CM	Open End	Multialternative (Growth)	C-	D+	B-	Up	Y	1,000,000
James Alpha Event Driven Portfolio Class S Shares	JAESX	NAS CM	Open End	Multialternative (Growth)	C-	D+	B	Up	Y	0
James Alpha Family Office Portfolio Class A	JFOAX	NAS CM	Open End	Global Macro (Growth & Income)	C-	D	C+	Up	Y	2,500
James Alpha Family Office Portfolio Class C	JFOCX	NAS CM	Open End	Global Macro (Growth & Income)	C-	D	C	Up	Y	2,500
James Alpha Family Office Portfolio Class I	JFOIX	NAS CM	Open End	Global Macro (Growth & Income)	C-	D	C+	Up	Y	1,000,000
James Alpha Family Office Portfolio Class S Shares	JFOSX	NAS CM	Open End	Global Macro (Growth & Income)	C	D+	B-	Up	Y	0
James Alpha Global Real Estate Inv Port Cls A Shares	JAREX	NAS CM	Open End	Real Estate Sector Equity (Real Estate)	B	B-	B		Y	2,500
James Alpha Global Real Estate Inv Port Cls C Shares	JACRX	NAS CM	Open End	Real Estate Sector Equity (Real Estate)	B-	C+	B	Down	Y	2,500
James Alpha Global Real Estate Inv Port Cls I Shares	JARIX	NAS CM	Open End	Real Estate Sector Equity (Real Estate)	B	B-	B		Y	1,000,000
James Alpha Global Real Estate Inv Port Cls S Shares	JARSX	NAS CM	Open End	Real Estate Sector Equity (Real Estate)	B	B-	B		Y	0
James Alpha Hedged High Income Portfolio Class A	INCAX	NAS CM	Open End	Long/Short Credit (Multisector Bond)	B-	C	B	Up	Y	2,500
James Alpha Hedged High Income Portfolio Class C	INCCX	NAS CM	Open End	Long/Short Credit (Multisector Bond)	C+	C	B	Up	Y	2,500
James Alpha Hedged High Income Portfolio Class I	INCIX	NAS CM	Open End	Long/Short Credit (Multisector Bond)	B-	C	B	Up	Y	1,000,000
James Alpha Hedged High Income Portfolio Class S Shares	INCSX	NAS CM	Open End	Long/Short Credit (Multisector Bond)	B-	C+	B+		Y	0
James Alpha Macro Portfolio Class A	GRRAX	NAS CM	Open End	Multialternative (Income)	C	C-	C+	Up	Y	2,500
James Alpha Macro Portfolio Class C	GRRCX	NAS CM	Open End	Multialternative (Income)	C	C-	C	Up	Y	2,500
James Alpha Macro Portfolio Class I	GRRIX	NAS CM	Open End	Multialternative (Income)	C	C-	C+	Up	Y	1,000,000
James Alpha Macro Portfolio Class S Shares	GRRSX	NAS CM	Open End	Multialternative (Income)	C	C-	C+	Up	Y	0
James Alpha Managed Risk Domestic Equity Portfolio Class A	JDAEX	NAS CM	Open End	Long/Short Equity (Growth)	B	C	A	Up	Y	2,500
James Alpha Managed Risk Domestic Equity Portfolio Class C	JDCEX	NAS CM	Open End	Long/Short Equity (Growth)	B-	C	A-		Y	2,500
James Alpha Managed Risk Domestic Equity Portfolio Class I	JDIEX	NAS CM	Open End	Long/Short Equity (Growth)	B	C	A		Y	1,000,000
James Alpha Managed Risk Domestic Eq Port Cls S Shares	JDSEX	NAS CM	Open End	Long/Short Equity (Growth)	B	C+	A		Y	0
James Alpha Managed Risk Emerging Mkts Eq Port Cls A	JEAMX	NAS CM	Open End	Long/Short Equity (Growth)	C	C-	B		Y	2,500
James Alpha Managed Risk Emerging Mkts Eq Port Cls C	JECMX	NAS CM	Open End	Long/Short Equity (Growth)	C	C-	B-		Y	2,500
James Alpha Managed Risk Emerging Mkts Eq Port Cls I	JEIMX	NAS CM	Open End	Long/Short Equity (Growth)	C+	C	B		Y	1,000,000
James Alpha Managed Risk Emerg Mkts Eq Cls S Shares	JESMX	NAS CM	Open End	Long/Short Equity (Growth)	C+	C	B		Y	0
James Alpha MLP Portfolio Class A	JAMLX	NAS CM	Open End	Energy Sector Equity (Growth & Income)	D	D	D	Down	Y	2,500
James Alpha MLP Portfolio Class C	MLPCX	NAS CM	Open End	Energy Sector Equity (Growth & Income)	D	D	D	Down	Y	2,500
James Alpha MLP Portfolio Class I	JMLPX	NAS CM	Open End	Energy Sector Equity (Growth & Income)	D	D	D	Down	Y	1,000,000
James Alpha Momentum Portfolio Class A	MOMAX	NAS CM	Open End	Moderate Alloc (Growth)	C	C-	C		Y	2,500
James Alpha Momentum Portfolio Class C	MOMCX	NAS CM	Open End	Moderate Alloc (Growth)	C	C-	C		Y	2,500
James Alpha Momentum Portfolio Class I	MOMOX	NAS CM	Open End	Moderate Alloc (Growth)	C	C-	C		Y	1,000,000
James Alpha Momentum Portfolio Class S	MOMSX	NAS CM	Open End	Moderate Alloc (Growth)	C	C-	C		Y	0
James Alpha Multi Strat Alternative Income Cls A Shares	JAAMX	NAS CM	Open End	Multialternative (Growth & Income)	B-	C	B+		Y	2,500
James Alpha Multi Strat Alternative Income Cls C Shares	JACMX	NAS CM	Open End	Multialternative (Growth & Income)	B-	C	B	Up	Y	2,500
James Alpha Multi Strat Alternative Income Cls I Shares	JAIMX	NAS CM	Open End	Multialternative (Growth & Income)	B-	C	B+		Y	1,000,000
James Alpha Multi Strat Alternative Income Cls S Shares	JASMX	NAS CM	Open End	Multialternative (Growth & Income)	B-	C	B+		Y	0
James Alpha Relative Value Portfolio A Shares	JRVAX	NAS CM	Open End	Market Neutral (Growth)	C-	D+	B	Up	Y	2,500
James Alpha Relative Value Portfolio C Shares	JRVCX	NAS CM	Open End	Market Neutral (Growth)	C-	D+	B	Up	Y	2,500
James Alpha Relative Value Portfolio Class S Shares	JRSVX	NAS CM	Open End	Market Neutral (Growth)	C-	D+	B	Up	Y	0
James Alpha Relative Value Portfolio I Shares	JRVIX	NAS CM	Open End	Market Neutral (Growth)	C-	D+	B	Up	Y	1,000,000
James Alpha Total Hedge Portfolio A Shares	JTHAX	NAS CM	Open End	Multialternative (Growth)	C	D+	C+	Up	Y	2,500
James Alpha Total Hedge Portfolio C Shares	JTHCX	NAS CM	Open End	Multialternative (Growth)	C-	D	C+	Up	Y	2,500
James Alpha Total Hedge Portfolio Class S Shares	JTHSX	NAS CM	Open End	Multialternative (Growth)	C	D+	B-	Up	Y	0
James Alpha Total Hedge Portfolio I Shares	JTHIX	NAS CM	Open End	Multialternative (Growth)	C	D+	B-	Up	Y	1,000,000

★ Expanded analysis of this fund is included in Section II.

Min Additional Investment	3-Month Total Return	6-Month Total Return	1-Year Total Return	3-Year Total Return	5-Year Total Return	Dividend Yield (TTM)	Expense Ratio	3-Yr Std Deviation	3-Year Beta	NAV	Total Assets (MIL)	%Cash	%Stocks	%Bonds	%Other	Turnover Ratio	Last Bull Market Total Return	Last Bear Market Total Return	Front End Fee (%)	Back End Fee (%)	Inception Date
TOTAL RETURNS						PERFORMANCE				ASSETS		ASSET ALLOCATION & TURNOVER					BULL & BEAR		FEES		
	1.49	9.67	-3.40	11.90		0.87	1.01	10.42		10.2	22.9	8	71	21	0	219					Jul-15
	1.59	10.12	0.78			1.54	2.29			10.22	2.7	7	64	26	1	181			5.75		Aug-17
	1.29	9.58	-0.21			0.52	3.04			10.18	2.7	7	64	26	1	181				1.00	Aug-17
	1.59	10.12	0.78			1.54	2.04			10.22	2.7	7	64	26	1	181					Aug-17
	1.58	10.11	0.88			1.54	2.04			10.23	2.7	7	64	26	1	181					Aug-17
	2.23	10.59	5.29			1.44	2.71			10.54	9.5	-15	25	32	57	221			5.75		Aug-17
	2.23	10.59	5.29			1.44	3.46			10.54	9.5	-15	25	32	57	221				1.00	Aug-17
	2.23	10.59	5.29			1.44	2.46			10.54	9.5	-15	25	32	57	221					Aug-17
	2.12	10.57	5.38			1.43	2.12			10.56	9.5	-15	25	32	57	221					Aug-17
	2.15	12.77	1.10			1.69	2.18			10.42	9.7	0	70	20	9	167			5.75		Jun-17
	1.96	12.35	0.38			1.11	2.93			10.37	9.7	0	70	20	9	167				1.00	Jun-17
	2.15	12.86	1.40			1.88	1.93			10.44	9.7	0	70	20	9	167					Jun-17
	2.13	12.86	1.58			1.86	1.43			10.53	9.7	0	70	20	9	167					Jun-17
	2.42	20.38	6.60	28.70	38.24	3.38	1.62	13.04	1.08	17.86	825.3	6	94	0	1	204	27.39	-21.27	5.75		Oct-09
	2.25	19.95	5.84	25.93	33.43	2.79	2.37	13.06	1.09	18.03	825.3	6	94	0	1	204	26.97	-21.52		1.00	Jan-12
	2.51	20.59	7.06	30.39	41.51	3.5	1.19	13.05	1.09	18.46	825.3	6	94	0	1	204	27.53	-20.45			Aug-11
	2.60	20.81	7.38	30.44	40.11	3.5	0.9	13.01	1.08	18.58	825.3	6	94	0	1	204	27.38	-21.27			Aug-17
	1.02	3.54	1.75	16.47	12.04	4.16	2.68	2.37	-0.08	9.07	56.6	17	2	73	0	171			5.75		Dec-13
	0.81	3.25	1.20	14.38	8.59	3.38	3.27	2.36	-0.08	9.09	56.6	17	2	73	0	171				1.00	Dec-13
	1.08	3.88	2.33	18.10	14.42	4.38	2.13	2.36	-0.07	9.11	56.6	17	2	73	0	171					Dec-13
	1.18	4.07	2.75	19.35	15.64	4.34	1.15	2.34	-0.08	9.21	56.6	17	2	73	0	171					Aug-17
	3.04	6.52	3.61	-0.52	-1.81	0	2.01	4.45	0.36	9.47	11.2	-45	23	62	60	103	3.5	-0.49	5.75		Feb-11
	2.97	6.26	2.97	-2.60	-5.27	0	2.76	4.47	0.36	8.99	11.2	-45	23	62	60	103	3.01	-0.91		1.00	Jan-12
	3.25	6.72	4.04	0.31	-0.53	0	1.76	4.41	0.36	9.52	11.2	-45	23	62	60	103	3.65	-0.49			Feb-11
	3.13	6.59	3.92	0.31	-0.54	0	1.75	4.47	0.36	9.53	11.2	-45	23	62	60	103	3.65	-0.49			Aug-17
	1.28	8.47	5.99	18.63		2.8	2.68	4.22	0.32	10.24	31.8	-27	93	0	35	84			5.75		Jul-15
	1.10	8.12	5.24	15.89		2.1	3.43	4.16	0.31	10.11	31.8	-27	93	0	35	84				1.00	Jul-15
	1.37	8.62	6.51	20.02		3.11	2.22	4.19	0.31	10.33	31.8	-27	93	0	35	84					Jul-15
	1.55	8.97	7.17	21.57		3.08	1.62	4.2	0.31	10.44	31.8	-27	93	0	35	84					Aug-17
	0.00	2.54	0.79	13.08		0.03	2.99	5.6	0.36	8.47	6.6	-38	90	0	49	335			5.75		Jul-15
	-0.24	2.09	0.00	10.60		0	3.74	5.59	0.36	8.29	6.6	-38	90	0	49	335				1.00	Jul-15
	0.23	2.76	1.23	14.67		0.42	2.48	5.6	0.36	8.55	6.6	-38	90	0	49	335					Jul-15
	0.23	2.87	1.45	15.38		0.41	1.88	5.62	0.36	8.59	6.6	-38	90	0	49	335					Aug-17
	-9.04	5.16	-16.08	-13.37		8.05	2.25	18.44	0.92	4.67	7.5	0	100	0	0	48			5.75		Mar-15
	-9.39	4.83	-16.64	-15.42		7.17	3	18.46	0.93	4.66	7.5	0	100	0	0	48				1.00	Mar-15
	-9.18	5.30	-15.90	-12.87		8.37	2	18.42	0.92	4.66	7.5	0	100	0	0	48					Mar-15
100	1.37	3.11	0.63	14.20	32.46	0.27	1.7	9.43	0.55	9.59	27.5	3	96	0	0				5.75		Jun-18
100	1.47	3.22	0.84	12.75	28.83	0.26	2.45	9.44	0.56	9.61	27.5	3	96	0	0					1.00	Jun-18
100	1.47	3.22	0.84	15.02	34.07	0.26	1.45	9.46	0.56	9.6	27.5	3	96	0	0						Apr-14
	1.47	3.22	0.84	15.02	34.07	0.26	0.94	9.46	0.56	9.61	27.5	3	96	0	0						Jun-18
	0.26	12.20	2.91	14.91		3.58	3.17	8.4	0.4	9.13	14.0	22	52	23	0	183			5.75		Sep-14
	0.18	11.88	2.16	12.31		2.87	3.92	8.41	0.4	8.97	14.0	22	52	23	0	183				1.00	Sep-14
	0.32	12.31	3.05	15.73		3.83	2.92	8.42	0.4	9.15	14.0	22	52	23	0	183					Sep-14
	0.32	12.48	3.37	16.71		3.8	2.62	8.4	0.4	9.22	14.0	22	52	23	0	183					Aug-17
	3.54	10.31	8.60			1.6	2.68			10.8	8.2	-34	9	72	51	252			5.75		Aug-17
	3.54	10.31	8.60			1.6	3.43			10.8	8.2	-34	9	72	51	252				1.00	Aug-17
	3.43	10.39	8.79			1.6	2.16			10.83	8.2	-34	9	72	51	252					Aug-17
	3.54	10.31	8.60			1.6	2.43			10.8	8.2	-34	9	72	51	252					Aug-17
	1.87	8.53	2.19			1.37	2.44			10.3	12.3	-4	42	50	10	195			5.75		Jun-17
	1.58	8.12	1.39			0.8	3.19			10.25	12.3	-4	42	50	10	195				1.00	Jun-17
	1.77	8.62	2.58			1.63	2.12			10.33	12.3	-4	42	50	10	195					Jun-17
	1.87	8.63	2.48			1.63	2.19			10.32	12.3	-4	42	50	10	195					Jun-17

	MARKET		FUND TYPE, CATEGORY & OBJECTIVE		RATINGS				MINIMUMS	
Fund Name	Ticker Symbol	Traded On	Fund Type	Category and (Prospectus Objective)	Overall Rating	Reward Rating	Risk Rating	Recent Up/ Downgrade	Open to New Investors	Min Initial Investment
James Balanced Golden Rainbow Fund Retail Class	GLRBX	NAS CM	Open End	Cautious Alloc (Balanced)	C-	D+	C+		Y	2,000
James Balanced: Golden Rainbow Fund Institutional Class	GLRIX	NAS CM	Open End	Cautious Alloc (Balanced)	C	C-	C+	Up	Y	50,000
James Micro Cap Fund	JMCRX	NAS CM	Open End	US Equity Small Cap (Small Company)	C-	D+	C+	Down	Y	10,000
James Small Cap Fund	JASCX	NAS CM	Open End	US Equity Small Cap (Small Company)	D	D	D+	Down	Y	2,000
Jamestown Equity Fund	JAMEX	NAS CM	Open End	US Equity Large Cap Blend (Growth)	B-	C	B	Up	Y	5,000
Janus Henderson Adaptive Global Allocation Fund Class A	JAGAX	NAS CM	Open End	Moderate Alloc (Growth & Income)	B-	C	A-	Up	Y	2,500
Janus Henderson Adaptive Global Allocation Fund Class C	JAVCX	NAS CM	Open End	Moderate Alloc (Growth & Income)	B-	C	A-	Up	Y	2,500
Janus Henderson Adaptive Global Allocation Fund Class D	JAGDX	NAS CM	Open End	Moderate Alloc (Growth & Income)	B-	C	A-	Up	Y	2,500
Janus Henderson Adaptive Global Allocation Fund Class I	JVGIX	NAS CM	Open End	Moderate Alloc (Growth & Income)	B-	C	A-	Up	Y	1,000,000
Janus Henderson Adaptive Global Allocation Fund Class N	JAGNX	NAS CM	Open End	Moderate Alloc (Growth & Income)	B-	C	A-	Up	Y	1,000,000
Janus Henderson Adaptive Global Allocation Fund Class S	JAGSX	NAS CM	Open End	Moderate Alloc (Growth & Income)	B-	C	A-	Up	Y	2,500
Janus Henderson Adaptive Global Allocation Fund Class T	JVGTX	NAS CM	Open End	Moderate Alloc (Growth & Income)	B-	C	A-	Up	Y	2,500
Janus Henderson Asia Equity Fund Class A	JAQAX	NAS CM	Open End	Asia ex-Japan Equity (Pacific Stock)	C	C	B-		Y	2,500
Janus Henderson Asia Equity Fund Class C	JAQCX	NAS CM	Open End	Asia ex-Japan Equity (Pacific Stock)	C	C	C+		Y	2,500
Janus Henderson Asia Equity Fund Class D	JAQDX	NAS CM	Open End	Asia ex-Japan Equity (Pacific Stock)	C	C	B-			2,500
Janus Henderson Asia Equity Fund Class I	JAQIX	NAS CM	Open End	Asia ex-Japan Equity (Pacific Stock)	C	C	B-		Y	1,000,000
Janus Henderson Asia Equity Fund Class N	JAQNX	NAS CM	Open End	Asia ex-Japan Equity (Pacific Stock)	C	C	B-		Y	1,000,000
Janus Henderson Asia Equity Fund Class S	JAQSX	NAS CM	Open End	Asia ex-Japan Equity (Pacific Stock)	C	C	B-		Y	2,500
Janus Henderson Asia Equity Fund Class T	JAQTX	NAS CM	Open End	Asia ex-Japan Equity (Pacific Stock)	C	C	B-		Y	2,500
Janus Henderson Balanced Fund Class A	JDBAX	NAS CM	Open End	Moderate Alloc (Balanced)	B	C+	A		Y	2,500
Janus Henderson Balanced Fund Class C	JABCX	NAS CM	Open End	Moderate Alloc (Balanced)	B	C+	A		Y	2,500
Janus Henderson Balanced Fund Class D	JANBX	NAS CM	Open End	Moderate Alloc (Balanced)	B	C+	A			2,500
Janus Henderson Balanced Fund Class I	JBALX	NAS CM	Open End	Moderate Alloc (Balanced)	B	C+	A		Y	1,000,000
Janus Henderson Balanced Fund Class N	JABNX	NAS CM	Open End	Moderate Alloc (Balanced)	B	C+	A		Y	1,000,000
Janus Henderson Balanced Fund Class R	JDBRX	NAS CM	Open End	Moderate Alloc (Balanced)	B	C+	A		Y	2,500
Janus Henderson Balanced Fund Class S	JABRX	NAS CM	Open End	Moderate Alloc (Balanced)	B	C+	A		Y	2,500
Janus Henderson Balanced Fund Class T	JABAX	NAS CM	Open End	Moderate Alloc (Balanced)	B	C+	A		Y	2,500
Janus Henderson Contrarian Fund Class A	JCNAX	NAS CM	Open End	US Equity Mid Cap (Growth)	C+	C+	B		Y	2,500
Janus Henderson Contrarian Fund Class C	JCNCX	NAS CM	Open End	US Equity Mid Cap (Growth)	C+	C	B		Y	2,500
Janus Henderson Contrarian Fund Class D	JACNX	NAS CM	Open End	US Equity Mid Cap (Growth)	B-	C+	B	Up		2,500
Janus Henderson Contrarian Fund Class I	JCONX	NAS CM	Open End	US Equity Mid Cap (Growth)	B-	C+	B	Up	Y	1,000,000
Janus Henderson Contrarian Fund Class N	JCNNX	NAS CM	Open End	US Equity Mid Cap (Growth)	B-	C+	B	Up	Y	1,000,000
James Henderson Contrarian Fund Class R	JCNRX	NAS CM	Open End	US Equity Mid Cap (Growth)	C+	C	B		Y	2,500
Janus Henderson Contrarian Fund Class S	JCNIX	NAS CM	Open End	US Equity Mid Cap (Growth)	C+	C	B		Y	2,500
Janus Henderson Contrarian Fund Class T	JSVAX	NAS CM	Open End	US Equity Mid Cap (Growth)	B-	C+	B	Up	Y	2,500
Janus Henderson Diversified Alternatives Fund Class A	JDDAX	NAS CM	Open End	Multialternative (Growth & Income)	C-	D	C	Down	Y	2,500
Janus Henderson Diversified Alternatives Fund Class C	JDDCX	NAS CM	Open End	Multialternative (Growth & Income)	D+	D	C	Down	Y	500,000
Janus Henderson Diversified Alternatives Fund Class D	JDADX	NAS CM	Open End	Multialternative (Growth & Income)	C-	D	C	Down	Y	2,500
Janus Henderson Diversified Alternatives Fund Class I	JDAIX	NAS CM	Open End	Multialternative (Growth & Income)	C-	D	C	Down	Y	1,000,000
Janus Henderson Diversified Alternatives Fund Class N	JDANX	NAS CM	Open End	Multialternative (Growth & Income)	C-	D+	C	Down	Y	1,000,000
Janus Henderson Diversified Alternatives Fund Class S	JDASX	NAS CM	Open End	Multialternative (Growth & Income)	C-	D	C		Y	2,500
Janus Henderson Diversified Alternatives Fund Class T	JDATX	NAS CM	Open End	Multialternative (Growth & Income)	C-	D	C	Down	Y	2,500
Janus Henderson Dividend & Income Builder Fund Class A	HDAVX	NAS CM	Open End	Flexible Alloc (Equity-Income)	B-	C	B+	Up	Y	2,500
Janus Henderson Dividend & Income Builder Fund Class C	HDCVX	NAS CM	Open End	Flexible Alloc (Equity-Income)	C+	C	B	Up	Y	2,500
Janus Henderson Dividend & Income Builder Fund Class D	HDDVX	NAS CM	Open End	Flexible Alloc (Equity-Income)	B-	C	B+	Up	Y	2,500
Janus Henderson Dividend & Income Builder Fund Class I	HDIVX	NAS CM	Open End	Flexible Alloc (Equity-Income)	B-	C	B+	Up	Y	1,000,000
Janus Henderson Dividend & Income Builder Fund Class N	HDRVX	NAS CM	Open End	Flexible Alloc (Equity-Income)	B-	C	B+	Up	Y	1,000,000
Janus Henderson Dividend & Income Builder Fund Class S	HDQVX	NAS CM	Open End	Flexible Alloc (Equity-Income)	B-	C	B+	Up	Y	2,500
Janus Henderson Dividend & Income Builder Fund Class T	HDTVX	NAS CM	Open End	Flexible Alloc (Equity-Income)	B-	C	B+	Up	Y	2,500
Janus Henderson Emerging Markets Fund Class A	HEMAX	NAS CM	Open End	Global Emerg Mkts (Div Emerging Mkts)	C	C-	C+		Y	2,500
Janus Henderson Emerging Markets Fund Class C	HEMCX	NAS CM	Open End	Global Emerg Mkts (Div Emerging Mkts)	C-	D+	C	Down	Y	2,500
Janus Henderson Emerging Markets Fund Class D	HEMDX	NAS CM	Open End	Global Emerg Mkts (Div Emerging Mkts)	C	C-	C+		Y	2,500

★ Expanded analysis of this fund is included in Section II.

Min Additional Investment	TOTAL RETURNS: 3-Month Total Return	6-Month Total Return	1-Year Total Return	3-Year Total Return	5-Year Total Return	PERFORMANCE: Dividend Yield (TTM)	Expense Ratio	3-Yr Std Deviation	3-Year Beta	ASSETS: NAV	Total Assets (MIL)	ASSET ALLOCATION & TURNOVER: %Cash	%Stocks	%Bonds	%Other	Turnover Ratio	BULL & BEAR: Last Bull Market Total Return	Last Bear Market Total Return	FEES: Front End Fee (%)	Back End Fee (%)	Inception Date
	1.77	7.91	-1.24	5.37	7.02	1.28	1	6.34		20.69	1,078	7	42	51	0	75	10.82	-5.43			Jul-91
	1.86	8.05	-0.99	6.18	8.37	1.55	0.75	6.36		20.43	1,078	7	42	51	0	75	10.98	-5.33			Mar-09
	1.40	18.62	-5.24	23.16	31.44	0	1.51	18.77	0.99	15.92	26.6	4	93	4	0	37	32.44	-24.27			Jul-10
	-0.38	11.74	-15.62	6.76	-0.84	0	1.5	18.08	1.02	23.22	42.3	4	96	0	0	124	24.21	-16.37			Oct-98
	2.45	16.93	8.08	40.65	38.43	1.03	1.03	12.97	1.05	22.26	37.6	4	96	0	0	18	23.61	-16.48			Dec-92
	2.28	9.78	4.22	25.28		0.86	1.09	7.58	0.65	10.32	75.1	3	79	18	0	440			5.75		Jun-15
	2.58	10.04	3.95	23.10		0.09	1.83	7.47	0.64	10.3	75.1	3	79	18	0	440				1.00	Jun-15
100	2.27	9.89	4.30	25.63		0.85	0.95	7.57	0.65	10.33	75.1	3	79	18	0	440					Jun-15
	2.27	9.87	4.32	26.05		0.96	0.86	7.59	0.65	10.35	75.1	3	79	18	0	440					Jun-15
	2.37	9.97	4.46	26.27		0.99	0.81	7.55	0.65	10.36	75.1	3	79	18	0	440					Jun-15
	2.47	10.10	4.32	25.14		0.6	1.31	7.5	0.64	10.35	75.1	3	79	18	0	440					Jun-15
	2.37	10.00	4.32	25.70		0.78	1.06	7.53	0.64	10.34	75.1	3	79	18	0	440					Jun-15
	0.09	13.39	-0.35	43.74	35.33	0.17	1.51	14.49	0.97	10.58	23.4	0	100	0	0	41	23.68		5.75		Jul-11
	0.09	13.23	-0.83	40.83	30.78	0	2.22	14.5	0.97	10.44	23.4	0	100	0	0	41	23.55			1.00	Jul-11
100	0.09	13.43	-0.11	44.47	36.54	0.22	1.29	14.58	0.98	10.72	23.4	0	100	0	0	41	24.25				Jul-11
	0.18	13.42	0.00	45.04	37.42	0.24	1.16	14.53	0.97	10.73	23.4	0	100	0	0	41	23.82				Jul-11
	0.18	13.57	-0.01	45.04	37.42	0.39	1.13	14.5	0.97	10.71	23.4	0	100	0	0	41	23.82				Jan-18
	0.18	13.49	-0.21	43.73	35.48	0.37	1.63	14.47	0.97	10.6	23.4	0	100	0	0	41	23.68				Jul-11
	0.09	13.36	-0.07	44.45	36.51	0.11	1.38	14.55	0.98	10.6	23.4	0	100	0	0	41	23.68				Jul-11
	3.85	13.35	9.79	41.39	44.62	1.61	0.95	7.43	0.6	34.54	15,961	2	59	39	0	88	17.76	-12.35	5.75		Jul-09
	3.68	13.00	9.05	38.57	39.73	1.02	1.64	7.44	0.6	34.21	15,961	2	59	39	0	88	17.3	-12.67		1.00	Jul-09
100	3.89	13.49	10.05	42.34	46.17	1.8	0.71	7.42	0.6	34.63	15,961	2	59	39	0	88	17.88	-12.28			Sep-92
	3.94	13.56	10.15	42.69	46.74	1.86	0.64	7.44	0.6	34.65	15,961	2	59	39	0	88	17.94	-12.25			Jul-09
	3.89	13.54	10.17	42.95	47.22	1.92	0.57	7.42	0.6	34.6	15,961	2	59	39	0	88	17.88	-12.28			May-12
	3.74	13.16	9.40	39.80	41.86	1.26	1.32	7.42	0.6	34.34	15,961	2	59	39	0	88	17.51	-12.53			Jul-09
	3.84	13.30	9.69	40.87	43.67	1.47	1.07	7.44	0.6	34.54	15,961	2	59	39	0	88	17.68	-12.43			Jul-09
	3.90	13.46	9.95	41.96	45.49	1.71	0.82	7.42	0.6	34.59	15,961	2	59	39	0	88	17.84	-12.33			Sep-92
	7.46	28.57	13.65	53.42	27.91	0.19	0.87	15.8	1.18	21.15	2,574	2	94	4	0	59	24.69	-26.04	5.75		Jul-09
	7.29	28.24	12.92	50.33	23.44	0	1.6	15.79	1.18	19.57	2,574	2	94	4	0	59	24.28	-26.3		1.00	Jul-09
100	7.50	28.77	13.94	54.39	29.20	0.26	0.65	15.79	1.18	21.21	2,574	2	94	4	0	59	25	-26.06			Feb-00
	7.49	28.74	14.01	54.67	29.63	0.31	0.57	15.81	1.18	21.23	2,574	2	94	4	0	59	24.91	-26.06			Jul-09
	7.51	28.83	14.07	54.77	29.52	0.37	0.5	15.8	1.18	21.18	2,574	2	94	4	0	59	25	-26.06			Aug-17
	7.29	28.23	13.04	51.17	25.07	0	1.42	15.77	1.17	20.44	2,574	2	94	4	0	59	24.53	-26.25			Jul-09
	7.33	28.45	13.31	52.48	26.78	0	1.04	15.8	1.18	21.08	2,574	2	94	4	0	59	24.75	-26.19			Jul-09
	7.45	28.65	13.82	53.98	28.65	0.2	0.74	15.8	1.18	21.19	2,574	2	94	4	0	59	24.93	-26.12			Feb-00
	0.10	1.04	-3.02	4.43	6.66	0.56	1.39	4.14	-0.1	9.7	93.0	56	0	44	0	0			5.75		Dec-12
	0.52	1.38	-3.16	2.84	3.35	0.18	2.13	4.08	-0.06	9.54	93.0	56	0	44	0	0				1.00	Dec-12
100	0.10	1.14	-2.86	4.90	7.35	0.61	1.24	4.18	-0.09	9.75	93.0	56	0	44	0	0					Dec-12
	0.10	1.13	-2.81	5.16	7.72	0.66	1.18	4.15	-0.09	9.77	93.0	56	0	44	0	0					Dec-12
	0.10	1.13	-2.76	5.26	8.04	0.69	1.09	4.18	-0.12	9.8	93.0	56	0	44	0	0					Dec-12
	0.20	1.25	-2.90	4.38	6.40	0.6	1.59	4.12	-0.08	9.66	93.0	56	0	44	0	0					Dec-12
	0.20	1.25	-2.86	4.84	7.30	0.63	1.34	4.18	-0.09	9.71	93.0	56	0	44	0	0					Dec-12
	2.28	11.37	3.14	22.54	19.32	2.82	1.14	8.8	0.73	13.09	168.7	0	77	22	0	36			5.75		Aug-12
	2.13	10.99	2.41	19.79	14.88	2.35	1.9	8.79	0.73	12.89	168.7	0	77	22	0	36				1.00	Aug-12
100	2.30	11.41	3.33	23.23	20.62	2.93	0.98	8.81	0.73	13.09	168.7	0	77	22	0	36					Jun-17
	2.39	11.51	3.40	23.42	20.80	2.99	0.94	8.78	0.72	13.11	168.7	0	77	22	0	36					Aug-12
	2.41	11.55	3.47	23.39	20.70	3.05	1	8.78	0.73	13.08	168.7	0	77	22	0	36					Nov-15
	2.46	11.57	3.27	22.55	19.36	3.08	1.35	8.78	0.72	13.06	168.7	0	77	22	0	36					Jun-17
	2.30	11.41	3.28	23.04	20.43	2.88	1.1	8.81	0.73	13.08	168.7	0	77	22	0	36					Jun-17
	2.61	9.40	0.14	17.46	5.84	1.35	1.33	12.08	0.79	9.42	99.1	0	100	0	0	26	29.31	-28.76	5.75		Dec-10
	2.24	8.97	-0.67	14.78	1.82	0.25	2.1	12.07	0.79	9.11	99.1	0	100	0	0	26	28.71	-29.02		1.00	Dec-10
100	2.48	9.34	0.28	17.89	6.78	1.28	1.17	12.07	0.79	9.48	99.1	0	100	0	0	26	29.57	-28.74			Jun-17

Fund Name	MARKET Ticker Symbol	Traded On	FUND TYPE, CATEGORY & OBJECTIVE Fund Type	Category and (Prospectus Objective)	RATINGS Overall Rating	Reward Rating	Risk Rating	Recent Up/ Downgrade	Open to New Investors	MINIMUMS Min Initial Investment
Janus Henderson Emerging Markets Fund Class I	HEMIX	NAS CM	Open End	Global Emerg Mkts (Div Emerging Mkts)	C	C-	C+		Y	1,000,000
Janus Henderson Emerging Markets Fund Class N	HEMRX	NAS CM	Open End	Global Emerg Mkts (Div Emerging Mkts)	C	C-	C+		Y	1,000,000
Janus Henderson Emerging Markets Fund Class S	HEMSX	NAS CM	Open End	Global Emerg Mkts (Div Emerging Mkts)	C	C-	C+		Y	2,500
Janus Henderson Emerging Markets Fund Class T	HEMTX	NAS CM	Open End	Global Emerg Mkts (Div Emerging Mkts)	C	C-	C+		Y	2,500
Janus Henderson Emerging Markets Managed Volatility Cls A	JOLAX	NAS CM	Open End	Global Emerg Mkts (Growth)	C	C	B		Y	2,500
Janus Henderson Emerging Markets Managed Volatility Cls C	JOLCX	NAS CM	Open End	Global Emerg Mkts (Growth)	C	C	B-		Y	2,500
Janus Henderson Emerging Markets Managed Volatility Cls D	JOLDX	NAS CM	Open End	Global Emerg Mkts (Growth)	C	C	B		Y	2,500
Janus Henderson Emerging Markets Managed Volatility Cls I	JOLIX	NAS CM	Open End	Global Emerg Mkts (Growth)	C	C	B		Y	1,000,000
Janus Henderson Emerging Markets Managed Volatility Cls N	JOLNX	NAS CM	Open End	Global Emerg Mkts (Growth)	C	C	B		Y	2,500
Janus Henderson Emerging Markets Managed Volatility Cls S	JOLSX	NAS CM	Open End	Global Emerg Mkts (Growth)	C	C	B		Y	2,500
Janus Henderson Emerging Markets Managed Volatility Cls T	JOLTX	NAS CM	Open End	Global Emerg Mkts (Growth)	C	C	B		Y	2,500
Janus Henderson Enterprise Fund Class A	JDMAX	NAS CM	Open End	US Equity Mid Cap (Growth)	B	B-	B		Y	2,500
Janus Henderson Enterprise Fund Class C	JGRCX	NAS CM	Open End	US Equity Mid Cap (Growth)	B	B-	B		Y	2,500
Janus Henderson Enterprise Fund Class D	JANEX	NAS CM	Open End	US Equity Mid Cap (Growth)	B	B-	B			2,500
Janus Henderson Enterprise Fund Class I	JMGRX	NAS CM	Open End	US Equity Mid Cap (Growth)	B	B-	B		Y	1,000,000
Janus Henderson Enterprise Fund Class N	JDMNX	NAS CM	Open End	US Equity Mid Cap (Growth)	B	B-	B		Y	1,000,000
Janus Henderson Enterprise Fund Class R	JDMRX	NAS CM	Open End	US Equity Mid Cap (Growth)	B	B-	B		Y	2,500
Janus Henderson Enterprise Fund Class S	JGRTX	NAS CM	Open End	US Equity Mid Cap (Growth)	B	B-	B		Y	2,500
Janus Henderson Enterprise Fund Class T	JAENX	NAS CM	Open End	US Equity Mid Cap (Growth)	B	B-	B		Y	2,500
Janus Henderson European Focus Fund Class A	HFEAX	NAS CM	Open End	Europe Equity Large Cap (Europe Stock)	D+	D	C-	Up	Y	2,500
Janus Henderson European Focus Fund Class C	HFECX	NAS CM	Open End	Europe Equity Large Cap (Europe Stock)	D	D	C-		Y	2,500
Janus Henderson European Focus Fund Class D	HFEDX	NAS CM	Open End	Europe Equity Large Cap (Europe Stock)	D+	D	C-	Up	Y	2,500
Janus Henderson European Focus Fund Class I	HFEIX	NAS CM	Open End	Europe Equity Large Cap (Europe Stock)	D+	D	C-	Up	Y	1,000,000
Janus Henderson European Focus Fund Class N	HFERX	NAS CM	Open End	Europe Equity Large Cap (Europe Stock)	D+	D	C-	Up	Y	1,000,000
Janus Henderson European Focus Fund Class S	HFESX	NAS CM	Open End	Europe Equity Large Cap (Europe Stock)	D+	D	C-	Up	Y	2,500
Janus Henderson European Focus Fund Class T	HFETX	NAS CM	Open End	Europe Equity Large Cap (Europe Stock)	D+	D	C-	Up	Y	2,500
Janus Henderson Forty Fund Class A	JDCAX	NAS CM	Open End	US Equity Large Cap Growth (Growth)	B-	C+	B	Down	Y	2,500
Janus Henderson Forty Fund Class C	JACCX	NAS CM	Open End	US Equity Large Cap Growth (Growth)	B-	C+	B	Down	Y	2,500
Janus Henderson Forty Fund Class D	JFRDX	NAS CM	Open End	US Equity Large Cap Growth (Growth)	B-	C+	B	Down	Y	2,500
Janus Henderson Forty Fund Class I	JCAPX	NAS CM	Open End	US Equity Large Cap Growth (Growth)	B-	C+	B	Down	Y	1,000,000
Janus Henderson Forty Fund Class N	JFRNX	NAS CM	Open End	US Equity Large Cap Growth (Growth)	B-	C+	B	Down	Y	1,000,000
Janus Henderson Forty Fund Class R	JDCRX	NAS CM	Open End	US Equity Large Cap Growth (Growth)	B-	C+	B	Down	Y	2,500
Janus Henderson Forty Fund Class S	JARTX	NAS CM	Open End	US Equity Large Cap Growth (Growth)	B-	C+	B	Down	Y	2,500
Janus Henderson Forty Fund Class T	JACTX	NAS CM	Open End	US Equity Large Cap Growth (Growth)	B-	C+	B	Down	Y	2,500
Janus Henderson Global Allocation - Conservative Cls A	JCAAX	NAS CM	Open End	Cautious Alloc (Growth & Income)	B-	C	B+	Up	Y	2,500
Janus Henderson Global Allocation - Conservative Cls C	JCACX	NAS CM	Open End	Cautious Alloc (Growth & Income)	C+	C	B+	Up	Y	2,500
Janus Henderson Global Allocation - Conservative Cls D	JMSCX	NAS CM	Open End	Cautious Alloc (Growth & Income)	B-	C	B+	Up		2,500
Janus Henderson Global Allocation - Conservative Cls I	JCAIX	NAS CM	Open End	Cautious Alloc (Growth & Income)	B-	C	B+	Up	Y	1,000,000
Janus Henderson Global Allocation - Conservative Cls S	JCASX	NAS CM	Open End	Cautious Alloc (Growth & Income)	B-	C	B+	Up	Y	2,500
Janus Henderson Global Allocation - Conservative Cls T	JSPCX	NAS CM	Open End	Cautious Alloc (Growth & Income)	B-	C	B+	Up	Y	2,500
Janus Henderson Global Allocation Fund - Growth Class A	JGCAX	NAS CM	Open End	Flexible Alloc (Growth & Income)	B-	C	B+	Up	Y	2,500
Janus Henderson Global Allocation Fund - Growth Class C	JGCCX	NAS CM	Open End	Flexible Alloc (Growth & Income)	C+	C	B+	Up	Y	2,500
Janus Henderson Global Allocation Fund - Growth Class D	JNSGX	NAS CM	Open End	Flexible Alloc (Growth & Income)	B-	C	B+	Up		2,500
Janus Henderson Global Allocation Fund - Growth Class I	JGCIX	NAS CM	Open End	Flexible Alloc (Growth & Income)	B-	C	B+	Up	Y	1,000,000
Janus Henderson Global Allocation Fund - Growth Class S	JGCSX	NAS CM	Open End	Flexible Alloc (Growth & Income)	B-	C	B+	Up	Y	2,500
Janus Henderson Global Allocation Fund - Growth Class T	JSPGX	NAS CM	Open End	Flexible Alloc (Growth & Income)	B-	C	B+	Up	Y	2,500
Janus Henderson Global Allocation Fund - Moderate Class A	JMOAX	NAS CM	Open End	Moderate Alloc (Growth & Income)	B-	C	B+	Up	Y	2,500
Janus Henderson Global Allocation Fund - Moderate Class C	JMOCX	NAS CM	Open End	Moderate Alloc (Growth & Income)	C+	C	B+	Up	Y	2,500
Janus Henderson Global Allocation Fund - Moderate Class D	JNSMX	NAS CM	Open End	Moderate Alloc (Growth & Income)	B-	C	A-	Up		2,500
Janus Henderson Global Allocation Fund - Moderate Class I	JMOIX	NAS CM	Open End	Moderate Alloc (Growth & Income)	B-	C	A-	Up	Y	1,000,000
Janus Henderson Global Allocation Fund - Moderate Class S	JMOSX	NAS CM	Open End	Moderate Alloc (Growth & Income)	B-	C	B+	Up	Y	2,500
Janus Henderson Global Allocation Fund - Moderate Class T	JSPMX	NAS CM	Open End	Moderate Alloc (Growth & Income)	B-	C	A-	Up	Y	2,500

★ Expanded analysis of this fund is included in Section II.

	TOTAL RETURNS					PERFORMANCE				ASSETS		ASSET ALLOCATION & TURNOVER					BULL & BEAR		FEES		
Min Additional Investment	3-Month Total Return	6-Month Total Return	1-Year Total Return	3-Year Total Return	5-Year Total Return	Dividend Yield (TTM)	Expense Ratio	3-Yr Std Deviation	3-Year Beta	NAV	Total Assets (MIL)	%Cash	%Stocks	%Bonds	%Other	Turnover Ratio	Last Bull Market Total Return	Last Bear Market Total Return	Front End Fee (%)	Back End Fee (%)	Inception Date
	2.59	9.46	0.39	18.27	7.13	1.38	1.1	12.05	0.79	9.48	99.1	0	100	0	0	26	29.57	-28.74			Dec-10
	2.59	9.58	0.43	18.60	7.29	1.42	1.04	12.08	0.79	9.49	99.1	0	100	0	0	26	29.57	-28.74			Nov-15
	2.58	9.67	0.36	17.40	5.81	0.87	1.54	12.09	0.79	9.52	99.1	0	100	0	0	26	29.38	-28.81			Jun-17
	2.59	9.46	0.20	17.76	6.67	1.21	1.29	12.09	0.79	9.48	99.1	0	100	0	0	26	29.57	-28.74			Jun-17
	2.66	6.50	3.40	31.25		1.1	1.25	10.11	0.66	10.8	7.0	0	100	0	0	132			5.75		Dec-14
	3.41	7.06	3.73	29.77		0	1.99	10.11	0.66	10.91	7.0	0	100	0	0	132				1.00	Dec-14
100	2.84	6.79	3.84	32.22		1.16	1.1	10.18	0.67	10.84	7.0	0	100	0	0	132					Dec-14
	2.64	6.56	3.58	32.20		1.28	1.08	10.24	0.68	10.87	7.0	0	100	0	0	132					Dec-14
	2.94	6.89	3.98	32.76		1.36	0.96	10.17	0.67	10.85	7.0	0	100	0	0	132					Aug-17
	3.03	6.88	3.80	31.48		0.95	1.47	10.15	0.67	10.86	7.0	0	100	0	0	132					Dec-14
	2.84	6.79	3.81	32.10		1.22	1.21	10.21	0.67	10.84	7.0	0	100	0	0	132					Dec-14
	7.09	27.52	16.37	68.88	92.86	0	1.16	12.88	0.88	134.72	19,965	6	93	0	0	13	24.26	-19.05	5.75		Jul-09
	6.94	27.16	15.69	65.91	87.02	0	1.74	12.88	0.88	124.34	19,965	6	93	0	0	13	23.74	-19.31		1.00	Jul-09
100	7.17	27.72	16.74	70.45	95.82	0.13	0.81	12.88	0.88	138.39	19,965	6	93	0	0	13	24.41	-19.03			Sep-92
	7.19	27.75	16.80	70.74	96.45	0.18	0.75	12.88	0.88	139.11	19,965	6	93	0	0	13	24.47	-18.97			Jul-09
	7.22	27.81	16.91	71.23	97.37	0.24	0.66	12.88	0.88	139.64	19,965	6	93	0	0	13	24.41	-19.03			Jul-12
	7.01	27.33	16.04	67.41	90.14	0	1.41	12.87	0.87	130.14	19,965	6	93	0	0	13	23.99	-19.22			Jul-09
	7.08	27.50	16.33	68.70	92.54	0	1.16	12.88	0.88	134.02	19,965	6	93	0	0	13	24.18	-19.15			Jul-09
	7.15	27.65	16.62	69.98	94.98	0.05	0.91	12.88	0.88	137.46	19,965	6	93	0	0	13	24.35	-19.05			Sep-92
	3.47	18.76	-8.86	2.02	-14.36	3.62	1.3	15.59	1.19	28.29	432.0	0	100	0	0	82	25.05	-33.19	5.75		Aug-01
	3.28	18.35	-9.54	-0.28	-17.59	2.1	2.03	15.56	1.18	26.76	432.0	0	100	0	0	82	24.46	-33.41		1.00	Aug-01
100	3.53	18.90	-8.67	2.42	-14.02	4.01	1.11	15.59	1.19	28.11	432.0	0	100	0	0	82	25.05	-33.19			Jun-17
	3.53	18.95	-8.61	2.85	-13.22	3.98	1.02	15.58	1.19	28.12	432.0	0	100	0	0	82	25.32	-33.14			Mar-09
	3.56	19.02	-8.54	2.87	-13.51	4.86	0.97	15.59	1.19	27.9	432.0	0	100	0	0	82	25.05	-33.19			Nov-15
	3.57	18.95	-8.80	2.06	-14.32	7.49	1.46	15.6	1.19	26.98	432.0	0	100	0	0	82	25.05	-33.19			Jun-17
	3.49	18.90	-8.74	2.24	-14.17	3.82	1.21	15.59	1.19	28.12	432.0	0	100	0	0	82	25.05	-33.19			Jun-17
	6.00	24.43	12.53	68.42	99.62	0	1.04	13.08	0.95	36.21	12,447	3	97	0	0	37	28.16	-18.49	5.75		Sep-04
	5.82	24.11	11.81	65.31	93.90	0	1.74	13.06	0.95	29.44	12,447	3	97	0	0	37	27.59	-18.84		1.00	Sep-02
100	6.05	24.60	12.83	69.31	100.52	0	0.79	13.07	0.95	35.05	12,447	3	97	0	0	37	28.1	-18.64			Jan-17
	6.08	24.64	12.90	70.03	102.91	0	0.72	13.09	0.95	37.68	12,447	3	97	0	0	37	28.36	-18.49			Nov-05
	6.08	24.68	12.98	70.38	103.65	0	0.66	13.07	0.95	37.83	12,447	3	97	0	0	37	28.1	-18.64			May-12
	5.89	24.21	12.15	66.59	96.17	0	1.4	13.07	0.95	32.16	12,447	3	97	0	0	37	27.88	-18.71			Sep-04
	5.95	24.36	12.41	67.86	98.80	0	1.15	13.07	0.95	34.71	12,447	3	97	0	0	37	28.1	-18.64			May-97
	6.03	24.56	12.73	69.19	101.30	0	0.91	13.07	0.95	35.5	12,447	3	97	0	0	37	28.25	-18.53			Jul-09
	2.87	8.76	3.46	15.44	13.97	0.78	1.14	5.27	0.69	12.53	195.6	14	34	50	2	14	10.69	-7.18	5.75		Jul-09
	2.67	8.39	2.77	13.22	10.74	0.04	1.87	5.29	0.69	12.26	195.6	14	34	50	2	14	10.28	-7.55		1.00	Jul-09
100	2.94	8.90	3.69	16.14	15.06	0.92	0.94	5.26	0.69	12.59	195.6	14	34	50	2	14	10.81	-7.15			Dec-05
	2.86	8.91	3.70	16.23	15.37	0.99	0.89	5.26	0.69	12.58	195.6	14	34	50	2	14	10.9	-7.15			Jul-09
	2.80	8.63	3.32	14.87	13.08	0.71	1.31	5.25	0.68	12.45	195.6	14	34	50	2	14	10.55	-7.26			Jul-09
	2.86	8.83	3.50	15.77	14.64	0.81	1.05	5.24	0.68	12.56	195.6	14	34	50	2	14	10.79	-7.15			Dec-05
	3.23	13.85	3.56	28.12	22.65	1.15	1.18	8.96	0.77	14.05	243.1	12	72	12	4	12	16.9	-17.47	5.75		Jul-09
	3.07	13.43	2.83	25.53	18.86	0.55	1.94	8.92	0.77	13.76	243.1	12	72	12	4	12	16.4	-17.77		1.00	Jul-09
100	3.35	13.99	3.76	28.76	23.68	1.27	0.99	8.99	0.78	14.17	243.1	12	72	12	4	12	17.12	-17.41			Dec-05
	3.35	14.00	3.80	29.02	24.06	1.36	0.92	8.96	0.77	14.16	243.1	12	72	12	4	12	17.22	-17.48			Jul-09
	3.25	13.77	3.40	27.43	21.56	1.06	1.36	8.93	0.77	13.96	243.1	12	72	12	4	12	16.81	-17.53			Jul-09
	3.28	13.92	3.68	28.54	23.30	1.2	1.09	8.95	0.77	14.15	243.1	12	72	12	4	12	17.08	-17.48			Dec-05
	3.03	10.91	3.32	21.48	17.95	0.78	1.16	6.94	0.59	12.9	230.4	10	56	34	0	14	13.8	-12.5	5.75		Jul-09
	2.83	10.53	2.57	19.05	14.29	0.03	1.92	6.95	0.59	12.7	230.4	10	56	34	0	14	13.36	-12.76		1.00	Jul-09
100	3.09	11.03	3.44	22.22	18.99	0.97	0.97	6.91	0.58	12.98	230.4	10	56	34	0	14	14	-12.46			Dec-05
	3.09	11.04	3.53	22.38	19.30	1.04	0.91	6.92	0.59	12.97	230.4	10	56	34	0	14	14.09	-12.47			Jul-09
	2.97	10.83	3.14	20.94	16.99	0.68	1.33	6.92	0.59	12.79	230.4	10	56	34	0	14	13.7	-12.55			Jul-09
	3.02	10.97	3.37	21.91	18.62	0.9	1.08	6.95	0.59	12.94	230.4	10	56	34	0	14	13.95	-12.48			Dec-05

	MARKET			FUND TYPE, CATEGORY & OBJECTIVE	RATINGS				MINIMUMS	
Fund Name	Ticker Symbol	Traded On	Fund Type	Category and (Prospectus Objective)	Overall Rating	Reward Rating	Risk Rating	Recent Up/ Downgrade	Open to New Investors	Min Initial Investment
Janus Henderson Global Equity Income Fund Class A	HFQAX	NAS CM	Open End	Global Equity Large Cap (Equity-Income)	C	C-	B-		Y	2,500
Janus Henderson Global Equity Income Fund Class C	HFQCX	NAS CM	Open End	Global Equity Large Cap (Equity-Income)	C	C-	C+		Y	2,500
Janus Henderson Global Equity Income Fund Class D	HFQDX	NAS CM	Open End	Global Equity Large Cap (Equity-Income)	C	C-	B-		Y	2,500
Janus Henderson Global Equity Income Fund Class I	HFQIX	NAS CM	Open End	Global Equity Large Cap (Equity-Income)	C	C-	B-		Y	1,000,000
Janus Henderson Global Equity Income Fund Class N	HFQRX	NAS CM	Open End	Global Equity Large Cap (Equity-Income)	C	C-	B		Y	1,000,000
Janus Henderson Global Equity Income Fund Class S	HFQSX	NAS CM	Open End	Global Equity Large Cap (Equity-Income)	C	C-	B-		Y	2,500
Janus Henderson Global Equity Income Fund Class T	HFQTX	NAS CM	Open End	Global Equity Large Cap (Equity-Income)	C	C-	B-		Y	2,500
Janus Henderson Global Income Managed Volatility Cls A	JGDAX	NAS CM	Open End	Global Equity Large Cap (Income)	B-	C+	B	Down	Y	2,500
Janus Henderson Global Income Managed Volatility Cls C	JGDCX	NAS CM	Open End	Global Equity Large Cap (Income)	B-	C	B		Y	2,500
Janus Henderson Global Income Managed Volatility Cls D	JGDDX	NAS CM	Open End	Global Equity Large Cap (Income)	B-	C+	B	Down	Y	2,500
Janus Henderson Global Income Managed Volatility Cls I	JGDIX	NAS CM	Open End	Global Equity Large Cap (Income)	B-	C+	B	Down	Y	1,000,000
Janus Henderson Global Income Managed Volatility Cls N	JGGNX	NAS CM	Open End	Global Equity Large Cap (Income)	B-	C+	B	Down	Y	2,500
Janus Henderson Global Income Managed Volatility Cls S	JGDSX	NAS CM	Open End	Global Equity Large Cap (Income)	B-	C+	B	Down	Y	2,500
Janus Henderson Global Income Managed Volatility Cls T	JDGTX	NAS CM	Open End	Global Equity Large Cap (Income)	B-	C+	B	Down	Y	2,500
Janus Henderson Global Life Sciences Fund Class A	JFNAX	NAS CM	Open End	Healthcare Sector Equity (Health)	C+	C	B	Down	Y	2,500
Janus Henderson Global Life Sciences Fund Class C	JFNCX	NAS CM	Open End	Healthcare Sector Equity (Health)	C+	C	B	Down	Y	2,500
Janus Henderson Global Life Sciences Fund Class D	JNGLX	NAS CM	Open End	Healthcare Sector Equity (Health)	B-	C	B			2,500
Janus Henderson Global Life Sciences Fund Class I	JFNIX	NAS CM	Open End	Healthcare Sector Equity (Health)	B-	C	B		Y	1,000,000
Janus Henderson Global Life Sciences Fund Class N	JFNNX	NAS CM	Open End	Healthcare Sector Equity (Health)	B-	C	B		Y	1,000,000
Janus Henderson Global Life Sciences Fund Class S	JFNSX	NAS CM	Open End	Healthcare Sector Equity (Health)	C+	C	B	Down	Y	2,500
Janus Henderson Global Life Sciences Fund Class T	JAGLX	NAS CM	Open End	Healthcare Sector Equity (Health)	B-	C	B		Y	2,500
Janus Henderson Global Real Estate Fund Class A	JERAX	NAS CM	Open End	Real Estate Sector Equity (Real Estate)	B+	B	A-		Y	2,500
Janus Henderson Global Real Estate Fund Class C	JERCX	NAS CM	Open End	Real Estate Sector Equity (Real Estate)	B	B	A-		Y	2,500
Janus Henderson Global Real Estate Fund Class D	JNGSX	NAS CM	Open End	Real Estate Sector Equity (Real Estate)	B+	B	A-			2,500
Janus Henderson Global Real Estate Fund Class I	JERIX	NAS CM	Open End	Real Estate Sector Equity (Real Estate)	B+	B	A-		Y	1,000,000
Janus Henderson Global Real Estate Fund Class N	JERNX	NAS CM	Open End	Real Estate Sector Equity (Real Estate)	B+	B	A-		Y	1,000,000
Janus Henderson Global Real Estate Fund Class S	JERSX	NAS CM	Open End	Real Estate Sector Equity (Real Estate)	B	B	A-		Y	2,500
Janus Henderson Global Real Estate Fund Class T	JERTX	NAS CM	Open End	Real Estate Sector Equity (Real Estate)	B+	B	A-		Y	2,500
Janus Henderson Global Research Fund Class A	JDWAX	NAS CM	Open End	Global Equity Large Cap (World Stock)	C+	C	B		Y	2,500
Janus Henderson Global Research Fund Class C	JWWCX	NAS CM	Open End	Global Equity Large Cap (World Stock)	C+	C	B		Y	2,500
Janus Henderson Global Research Fund Class D	JANWX	NAS CM	Open End	Global Equity Large Cap (World Stock)	C+	C	B			2,500
Janus Henderson Global Research Fund Class I	JWWFX	NAS CM	Open End	Global Equity Large Cap (World Stock)	C+	C	B		Y	1,000,000
Janus Henderson Global Research Fund Class N	JDWNX	NAS CM	Open End	Global Equity Large Cap (World Stock)	B-	C	B	Up	Y	1,000,000
Janus Henderson Global Research Fund Class R	JDWRX	NAS CM	Open End	Global Equity Large Cap (World Stock)	C+	C	B		Y	2,500
Janus Henderson Global Research Fund Class S	JWGRX	NAS CM	Open End	Global Equity Large Cap (World Stock)	C+	C	B	Up	Y	2,500
Janus Henderson Global Research Fund Class T	JAWWX	NAS CM	Open End	Global Equity Large Cap (World Stock)	C+	C	B		Y	2,500
Janus Henderson Global Select Fund Class A	JORAX	NAS CM	Open End	Global Equity Large Cap (Aggr Growth)	C+	C	B	Up	Y	2,500
Janus Henderson Global Select Fund Class C	JORCX	NAS CM	Open End	Global Equity Large Cap (Aggr Growth)	C+	C	B	Up	Y	2,500
Janus Henderson Global Select Fund Class D	JANRX	NAS CM	Open End	Global Equity Large Cap (Aggr Growth)	C+	C	B	Up		2,500
Janus Henderson Global Select Fund Class I	JORFX	NAS CM	Open End	Global Equity Large Cap (Aggr Growth)	C+	C	B	Up	Y	1,000,000
Janus Henderson Global Select Fund Class N	JSLNX	NAS CM	Open End	Global Equity Large Cap (Aggr Growth)	C+	C	B	Up	Y	1,000,000
Janus Henderson Global Select Fund Class R	JORRX	NAS CM	Open End	Global Equity Large Cap (Aggr Growth)	C+	C	B	Up	Y	2,500
Janus Henderson Global Select Fund Class S	JORIX	NAS CM	Open End	Global Equity Large Cap (Aggr Growth)	C+	C	B	Up	Y	2,500
Janus Henderson Global Select Fund Class T	JORNX	NAS CM	Open End	Global Equity Large Cap (Aggr Growth)	C+	C	B	Up	Y	2,500
Janus Henderson Global Technology Fund Class A	JATAX	NAS CM	Open End	Technology Sector Equity (Technology)	B-	B-	B	Down	Y	2,500
Janus Henderson Global Technology Fund Class C	JAGCX	NAS CM	Open End	Technology Sector Equity (Technology)	B-	B-	B-	Down	Y	2,500
Janus Henderson Global Technology Fund Class D	JNGTX	NAS CM	Open End	Technology Sector Equity (Technology)	B	B-	B			2,500
Janus Henderson Global Technology Fund Class I	JATIX	NAS CM	Open End	Technology Sector Equity (Technology)	B	B-	B		Y	1,000,000
Janus Henderson Global Technology Fund Class N	JATNX	NAS CM	Open End	Technology Sector Equity (Technology)	B	B-	B		Y	1,000,000
Janus Henderson Global Technology Fund Class S	JATSX	NAS CM	Open End	Technology Sector Equity (Technology)	B-	B-	B	Down	Y	2,500
Janus Henderson Global Technology Fund Class T	JAGTX	NAS CM	Open End	Technology Sector Equity (Technology)	B-	B-	B	Down	Y	2,500
Janus Henderson Global Value Fund Class A	JPPAX	NAS CM	Open End	Global Equity Large Cap (World Stock)	B-	C	B+	Up	Y	2,500

★ Expanded analysis of this fund is included in Section II.

	TOTAL RETURNS					PERFORMANCE				ASSETS		ASSET ALLOCATION & TURNOVER					BULL & BEAR		FEES		
Min Additional Investment	3-Month Total Return	6-Month Total Return	1-Year Total Return	3-Year Total Return	5-Year Total Return	Dividend Yield (TTM)	Expense Ratio	3-Yr Std Deviation	3-Year Beta	NAV	Total Assets (MIL)	%Cash	%Stocks	%Bonds	%Other	Turnover Ratio	Last Bull Market Total Return	Last Bear Market Total Return	Front End Fee (%)	Back End Fee (%)	Inception Date
	0.77	10.67	-1.26	17.07	8.27	7.22	1.09	10.66	0.84	6.65	4,399	0	100	0	0	137	13.99	-16.12	5.75		Nov-06
	0.76	10.28	-1.89	14.70	4.55	6.63	1.76	10.64	0.84	6.6	4,399	0	100	0	0	137	13.55	-16.45		1.00	Nov-06
100	0.94	10.74	-1.11	17.53	8.70	7.38	0.88	10.67	0.84	6.64	4,399	0	100	0	0	137	13.99	-16.12			Jun-17
	1.00	10.80	-0.80	18.27	9.92	7.53	0.76	10.61	0.84	6.67	4,399	0	100	0	0	137	14.15	-16			Mar-09
	0.86	10.83	-0.89	18.30	9.59	7.6	0.72	10.61	0.84	6.66	4,399	0	100	0	0	137	13.99	-16.12			Nov-15
	0.73	10.45	-1.44	16.76	7.99	7.35	1.35	10.66	0.84	6.62	4,399	0	100	0	0	137	13.99	-16.12			Jun-17
	0.97	10.79	-0.94	17.66	8.82	7.42	0.94	10.59	0.84	6.64	4,399	0	100	0	0	137	13.99	-16.12			Jun-17
	2.81	12.05	11.22	22.05	32.05	2.92	0.87	7.08	0.49	14.1	276.3	1	99	0	0	60			5.75		Dec-11
	2.57	11.59	10.33	19.43	27.19	2.24	1.61	7.05	0.48	13.99	276.3	1	99	0	0	60				1.00	Dec-11
100	2.87	12.13	11.46	22.83	33.29	3.11	0.65	7.1	0.49	14.06	276.3	1	99	0	0	60					Dec-11
	2.86	12.17	11.52	22.99	33.89	3.13	0.59	7.09	0.49	14.14	276.3	1	99	0	0	60					Dec-11
	2.89	12.23	11.63	23.20	34.11	3.22	0.5	7.07	0.48	14.14	276.3	1	99	0	0	60					Aug-17
	2.95	12.25	11.34	22.07	32.01	3.02	1	7.11	0.49	14.08	276.3	1	99	0	0	60					Dec-11
	2.84	12.14	11.34	22.43	32.65	3.01	0.75	7.08	0.49	14.08	276.3	1	99	0	0	60					Dec-11
	2.14	17.87	11.03	43.06	66.35	0	0.99	15.48	1.14	57.7	3,679	1	97	0	2	46	26.76	-13.08	5.75		Jul-09
	1.97	17.45	10.20	39.86	60.19	0	1.77	15.49	1.14	52.55	3,679	1	97	0	2	46	26.19	-13.34		1.00	Jul-09
100	2.19	17.98	11.20	43.83	67.89	0	0.82	15.51	1.14	58.71	3,679	1	97	0	2	46	26.92	-13.06			Dec-98
	2.20	18.01	11.30	44.13	68.30	0	0.76	15.5	1.14	58.82	3,679	1	97	0	2	46	26.97	-13.03			Jul-09
	2.23	18.05	11.36	44.11	68.21	0	0.7	15.51	1.14	58.64	3,679	1	97	0	2	46	26.92	-13.06			Jan-18
	2.10	17.77	10.80	42.34	65.07	0	1.18	15.5	1.14	56.71	3,679	1	97	0	2	46	26.65	-13.14			Jul-09
	2.18	17.94	11.12	43.46	67.14	0	0.92	15.5	1.14	58.44	3,679	1	97	0	2	46	26.82	-13.03			Dec-98
	3.08	19.98	11.94	35.09	38.79	2.68	1.26	10.06	0.87	12.48	358.4	0	99	0	1	78	25.31	-23.84	5.75		Nov-07
	2.84	19.56	11.05	32.02	33.64	2.06	2.02	10.04	0.87	12.3	358.4	0	99	0	1	78	24.88	-24.12		1.00	Nov-07
100	3.11	20.04	12.06	35.69	39.81	2.84	1.07	10.04	0.86	12.56	358.4	0	99	0	1	78	25.48	-23.78			Feb-10
	3.13	20.10	12.28	36.20	40.56	2.93	0.96	10.04	0.86	12.55	358.4	0	99	0	1	78	25.54	-23.72			Nov-07
	3.15	20.15	12.35	36.35	40.71	2.99	0.92	10.03	0.86	12.55	358.4	0	99	0	1	78	25.54	-23.72			Jan-18
	2.96	19.85	11.64	34.24	37.49	2.5	1.43	10.03	0.86	12.45	358.4	0	99	0	1	78	25.37	-23.89			Nov-07
	3.10	20.03	12.02	35.43	39.50	2.79	1.14	10.04	0.86	12.55	358.4	0	99	0	1	78	25.51	-23.77			Jul-09
	4.40	18.90	6.92	45.96	39.53	0.53	1.14	12.09	1.04	81.95	2,680	0	100	0	0	32	23.52	-20.92	5.75		Jul-09
	4.27	18.55	6.27	43.24	34.86	0	1.64	12.06	1.03	79.93	2,680	0	100	0	0	32	22.87	-21.16		1.00	Jul-09
100	4.51	19.11	7.29	47.39	41.41	0.74	0.69	12.07	1.03	81.08	2,680	0	100	0	0	32	23.57	-20.85			Feb-05
	4.53	19.16	7.39	47.77	42.07	0.8	0.6	12.07	1.03	82.31	2,680	0	100	0	0	32	23.63	-20.82			Jul-09
	4.54	19.21	7.45	47.80	41.80	0.86	0.54	12.07	1.03	80.97	2,680	0	100	0	0	32	23.57	-20.85			Aug-17
	4.33	18.72	6.61	44.68	37.24	0.3	1.31	12.06	1.03	81.14	2,680	0	100	0	0	32	23.22	-21.02			Mar-13
	4.41	18.90	6.92	45.86	39.03	0.49	1.04	12.07	1.03	82.15	2,680	0	100	0	0	32	23.34	-20.99			Jul-09
	4.49	19.07	7.20	47.01	40.88	0.68	0.79	12.07	1.03	80.98	2,680	0	100	0	0	32	23.53	-20.87			Feb-05
	3.03	15.08	3.09	48.80	34.04	0.38	1.04	13	1.11	14.95	1,918	1	99	0	0	41	17.88	-26.11	5.75		Jul-09
	2.85	14.66	2.24	45.20	28.57	0	1.84	13	1.11	14.39	1,918	1	99	0	0	41	17.36	-26.32		1.00	Jul-09
100	3.05	15.19	3.32	49.72	35.02	0.51	0.84	12.99	1.11	14.86	1,918	1	99	0	0	41	18.09	-26.04			Jun-00
	3.04	15.22	3.35	50.01	35.73	0.59	0.77	12.95	1.1	14.91	1,918	1	99	0	0	41	18.07	-26.04			Jul-09
	3.11	15.34	3.48	50.12	35.39	0.68	0.68	12.99	1.11	14.88	1,918	1	99	0	0	41	18.09	-26.04			Aug-17
	2.86	14.74	2.46	46.56	30.74	0	1.63	13	1.11	14.71	1,918	1	99	0	0	41	17.66	-26.21			Jul-09
	2.88	14.90	2.74	47.81	32.58	0.64	1.38	12.99	1.1	14.96	1,918	1	99	0	0	41	18.21	-26.1			Jul-09
	2.97	15.17	3.21	49.35	34.56	0.43	0.92	12.99	1.11	14.88	1,918	1	99	0	0	41	18.05	-26.06			Jun-00
	5.02	28.26	12.79	109.79	129.29	0.01	1	15.81	1.11	36.35	3,008	2	98	0	0	20	23.98	-19.08	5.75		Jul-09
	4.86	27.85	12.02	105.44	121.63	0	1.75	15.81	1.1	32.96	3,008	2	98	0	0	20	23.52	-19.35		1.00	Jul-09
100	5.08	28.38	13.00	110.95	131.61	0.1	0.83	15.81	1.11	37.22	3,008	2	98	0	0	20	24.23	-19.03			Dec-98
	5.09	28.43	13.08	111.49	132.52	0.17	0.75	15.8	1.11	37.53	3,008	2	98	0	0	20	24.22	-18.98			Jul-09
	5.12	28.45	13.17	111.58	131.99	0.21	0.69	15.81	1.11	37.11	3,008	2	98	0	0	20	24.12	-19			Jan-17
	4.99	28.15	12.57	108.79	127.82	0	1.2	15.8	1.1	35.73	3,008	2	98	0	0	20	23.94	-19.1			Jul-09
	5.08	28.34	12.93	110.46	130.76	0.04	0.92	15.81	1.11	36.99	3,008	2	98	0	0	20	24.12	-19			Dec-98
	1.92	11.11	6.47	25.73	20.53	1.76	0.98	8.38	0.7	14.29	197.1	7	93	0	0	21	12.56	-10.47	5.75		Jul-09

	MARKET			FUND TYPE, CATEGORY & OBJECTIVE	RATINGS					MINIMUMS
Fund Name	Ticker Symbol	Traded On	Fund Type	Category and (Prospectus Objective)	Overall Rating	Reward Rating	Risk Rating	Recent Up/ Downgrade	Open to New Investors	Min Initial Investment
Janus Henderson Global Value Fund Class C	JPPCX	NAS CM	Open End	Global Equity Large Cap (World Stock)	B-	C	B+	Up	Y	2,500
Janus Henderson Global Value Fund Class D	JNGOX	NAS CM	Open End	Global Equity Large Cap (World Stock)	B-	C	B+			2,500
Janus Henderson Global Value Fund Class I	JPPIX	NAS CM	Open End	Global Equity Large Cap (World Stock)	B-	C	A-		Y	1,000,000
Janus Henderson Global Value Fund Class N	JPPNX	NAS CM	Open End	Global Equity Large Cap (World Stock)	B-	C	A-		Y	1,000,000
Janus Henderson Global Value Fund Class S	JPPSX	NAS CM	Open End	Global Equity Large Cap (World Stock)	B-	C	B	Up	Y	2,500
Janus Henderson Global Value Fund Class T	JGVAX	NAS CM	Open End	Global Equity Large Cap (World Stock)	B-	C	B+		Y	2,500
Janus Henderson Growth And Income Fund Class A	JDNAX	NAS CM	Open End	US Equity Large Cap Blend (Growth & Income)	B-	C	B+	Down	Y	2,500
Janus Henderson Growth And Income Fund Class C	JGICX	NAS CM	Open End	US Equity Large Cap Blend (Growth & Income)	B-	C	B+	Down	Y	2,500
Janus Henderson Growth And Income Fund Class D	JNGIX	NAS CM	Open End	US Equity Large Cap Blend (Growth & Income)	B-	C	B+	Down		2,500
Janus Henderson Growth And Income Fund Class I	JGINX	NAS CM	Open End	US Equity Large Cap Blend (Growth & Income)	B-	C	B+	Down	Y	1,000,000
Janus Henderson Growth And Income Fund Class N	JDNNX	NAS CM	Open End	US Equity Large Cap Blend (Growth & Income)	B-	C	B+	Down	Y	1,000,000
Janus Henderson Growth And Income Fund Class R	JDNRX	NAS CM	Open End	US Equity Large Cap Blend (Growth & Income)	B-	C	B+	Down	Y	2,500
Janus Henderson Growth And Income Fund Class S	JADGX	NAS CM	Open End	US Equity Large Cap Blend (Growth & Income)	B-	C	B+	Down	Y	2,500
Janus Henderson Growth And Income Fund Class T	JAGIX	NAS CM	Open End	US Equity Large Cap Blend (Growth & Income)	B-	C	B+	Down	Y	2,500
Janus Henderson International Managed Volatility Cls A	JMIAX	NAS CM	Open End	Global Equity Large Cap (Growth)	C	C	B-		Y	2,500
Janus Henderson International Managed Volatility Cls C	JMICX	NAS CM	Open End	Global Equity Large Cap (Growth)	C	C-	B-		Y	2,500
Janus Henderson International Managed Volatility Cls D	JIIDX	NAS CM	Open End	Global Equity Large Cap (Growth)	C	C	B		Y	2,500
Janus Henderson International Managed Volatility Cls I	JMIIX	NAS CM	Open End	Global Equity Large Cap (Growth)	C	C	B		Y	1,000,000
Janus Henderson International Managed Volatility Cls N	JMRNX	NAS CM	Open End	Global Equity Large Cap (Growth)	C	C	B		Y	2,500
Janus Henderson International Managed Volatility Cls S	JMISX	NAS CM	Open End	Global Equity Large Cap (Growth)	C	C	B-		Y	2,500
Janus Henderson International Managed Volatility Cls T	JRMTX	NAS CM	Open End	Global Equity Large Cap (Growth)	C	C	B		Y	2,500
Janus Henderson International Opportunities Fund Class A	HFOAX	NAS CM	Open End	Global Equity Large Cap (Foreign Stock)	C	C-	C+	Up	Y	2,500
Janus Henderson International Opportunities Fund Class C	HFOCX	NAS CM	Open End	Global Equity Large Cap (Foreign Stock)	C	C-	C+	Up	Y	2,500
Janus Henderson International Opportunities Fund Class D	HFODX	NAS CM	Open End	Global Equity Large Cap (Foreign Stock)	C	C-	C+	Up	Y	2,500
Janus Henderson International Opportunities Fund Class I	HFOIX	NAS CM	Open End	Global Equity Large Cap (Foreign Stock)	C	C-	C+	Up	Y	1,000,000
Janus Henderson International Opportunities Fund Class N	HFOSX	NAS CM	Open End	Global Equity Large Cap (Foreign Stock)	C	C-	C+	Up	Y	1,000,000
Janus Henderson International Opportunities Fund Class R	HFORX	NAS CM	Open End	Global Equity Large Cap (Foreign Stock)	C	C-	C+	Up	Y	2,500
Janus Henderson International Opportunities Fund Class S	HFOQX	NAS CM	Open End	Global Equity Large Cap (Foreign Stock)	C	C-	C+	Up	Y	2,500
Janus Henderson International Opportunities Fund Class T	HFOTX	NAS CM	Open End	Global Equity Large Cap (Foreign Stock)	C	C-	C+	Up	Y	2,500
Janus Henderson International Small Cap Fund Class A	HIZAX	NAS CM	Open End	Global Equity Mid/Small Cap (Foreign Stock)	D+	D	C-		Y	2,500
Janus Henderson International Small Cap Fund Class C	HIZCX	NAS CM	Open End	Global Equity Mid/Small Cap (Foreign Stock)	D+	D	D+		Y	2,500
Janus Henderson International Small Cap Fund Class D	HIZDX	NAS CM	Open End	Global Equity Mid/Small Cap (Foreign Stock)	D+	D	C-		Y	2,500
Janus Henderson International Small Cap Fund Class I	HIZIX	NAS CM	Open End	Global Equity Mid/Small Cap (Foreign Stock)	D+	D	C-		Y	1,000,000
Janus Henderson International Small Cap Fund Class N	HIZRX	NAS CM	Open End	Global Equity Mid/Small Cap (Foreign Stock)	D+	D	C-			1,000,000
Janus Henderson International Small Cap Fund Class S	HIZSX	NAS CM	Open End	Global Equity Mid/Small Cap (Foreign Stock)	D+	D	C-		Y	2,500
Janus Henderson International Small Cap Fund Class T	HIZTX	NAS CM	Open End	Global Equity Mid/Small Cap (Foreign Stock)	D+	D	C-		Y	2,500
Janus Henderson International Value Fund Class A	JIFAX	NAS CM	Open End	Global Equity Large Cap (Growth & Income)	C	C-	B-		Y	2,500
Janus Henderson International Value Fund Class C	JIFCX	NAS CM	Open End	Global Equity Large Cap (Growth & Income)	C	C-	B-		Y	2,500
Janus Henderson International Value Fund Class D	JIFDX	NAS CM	Open End	Global Equity Large Cap (Growth & Income)	C	C-	B-			2,500
Janus Henderson International Value Fund Class I	JIFIX	NAS CM	Open End	Global Equity Large Cap (Growth & Income)	C	C-	B-		Y	1,000,000
Janus Henderson International Value Fund Class N	JIFNX	NAS CM	Open End	Global Equity Large Cap (Growth & Income)	C	C-	B-		Y	1,000,000
Janus Henderson International Value Fund Class S	JIFSX	NAS CM	Open End	Global Equity Large Cap (Growth & Income)	C	C-	B-		Y	2,500
Janus Henderson International Value Fund Class T	JIFTX	NAS CM	Open End	Global Equity Large Cap (Growth & Income)	C	C-	B-		Y	2,500
Janus Henderson Large Cap Value Fund Class A	JAPAX	NAS CM	Open End	US Equity Large Cap Value (Growth)	B-	C	B	Up	Y	2,500
Janus Henderson Large Cap Value Fund Class C	JAPCX	NAS CM	Open End	US Equity Large Cap Value (Growth)	B-	C	B	Up	Y	2,500
Janus Henderson Large Cap Value Fund Class D	JNPLX	NAS CM	Open End	US Equity Large Cap Value (Growth)	B-	C	B	Up		2,500
Janus Henderson Large Cap Value Fund Class I	JAPIX	NAS CM	Open End	US Equity Large Cap Value (Growth)	B-	C	B	Up	Y	1,000,000
Janus Henderson Large Cap Value Fund Class N	JPLNX	NAS CM	Open End	US Equity Large Cap Value (Growth)	B-	C	B	Up	Y	1,000,000
Janus Henderson Large Cap Value Fund Class S	JAPSX	NAS CM	Open End	US Equity Large Cap Value (Growth)	B-	C	B	Up	Y	2,500
Janus Henderson Large Cap Value Fund Class T	JPLTX	NAS CM	Open End	US Equity Large Cap Value (Growth)	B-	C	B	Up	Y	2,500
Janus Henderson Mid Cap Value Fund Class A	JDPAX	NAS CM	Open End	US Equity Mid Cap (Growth)	C+	C	B	Up	Y	2,500
Janus Henderson Mid Cap Value Fund Class C	JMVCX	NAS CM	Open End	US Equity Mid Cap (Growth)	C+	C	B	Up	Y	2,500

★ Expanded analysis of this fund is included in Section II.

	TOTAL RETURNS					PERFORMANCE				ASSETS		ASSET ALLOCATION & TURNOVER					BULL & BEAR		FEES		
Min Additional Investment	3-Month Total Return	6-Month Total Return	1-Year Total Return	3-Year Total Return	5-Year Total Return	Dividend Yield (TTM)	Expense Ratio	3-Yr Std Deviation	3-Year Beta	NAV	Total Assets (MIL)	%Cash	%Stocks	%Bonds	%Other	Turnover Ratio	Last Bull Market Total Return	Last Bear Market Total Return	Front End Fee (%)	Back End Fee (%)	Inception Date
	1.82	10.79	5.74	22.99	16.24	0.86	1.73	8.35	0.7	13.96	197.1	7	93	0	0	21	12.66	-10.71		1.00	Jul-09
100	2.05	11.27	6.73	26.43	21.58	1.88	0.8	8.4	0.7	14.41	197.1	7	93	0	0	21	12.54	-10.43			Jun-01
	2.02	11.25	6.72	26.60	22.01	1.92	0.96	8.42	0.7	14.14	197.1	7	93	0	0	21	12.7	-10.42			Jul-09
	2.03	11.24	6.72	26.90	22.50	2.09	0.67	8.39	0.7	14.05	197.1	7	93	0	0	21	12.54	-10.43			May-12
	1.36	9.78	3.94	21.28	15.93	1.23	2.94	8.47	0.7	14.14	197.1	7	93	0	0	21	12.35	-10.56			Jul-09
	1.98	11.12	6.62	26.16	21.23	1.78	0.87	8.41	0.7	14.38	197.1	7	93	0	0	21	12.49	-10.44			Jun-01
	3.85	15.94	11.39	54.48	66.61	1.67	0.95	11.6	0.92	56.94	5,718	0	100	0	0	13	29.41	-21.55	5.75		Jul-09
	3.66	15.51	10.55	51.11	60.56	1.04	1.7	11.61	0.92	56.17	5,718	0	100	0	0	13	28.84	-21.81		1.00	Jul-09
100	3.90	16.06	11.60	55.30	68.01	1.8	0.77	11.62	0.92	57.03	5,718	0	100	0	0	13	29.5	-21.48			May-91
	3.92	16.09	11.68	55.65	68.61	1.87	0.69	11.61	0.92	57.06	5,718	0	100	0	0	13	29.58	-21.46			Jul-09
	3.94	16.12	11.71	55.65	68.38	1.92	0.65	11.61	0.92	56.97	5,718	0	100	0	0	13	29.5	-21.48			Aug-17
	3.72	15.66	10.86	52.41	62.89	1.28	1.41	11.6	0.92	56.58	5,718	0	100	0	0	13	29.04	-21.69			Jul-09
	3.80	15.86	11.19	53.67	65.12	1.48	1.13	11.6	0.92	56.93	5,718	0	100	0	0	13	29.27	-21.63			Jul-09
	3.87	15.98	11.47	54.85	67.26	1.72	0.87	11.61	0.92	56.98	5,718	0	100	0	0	13	29.43	-21.53			May-91
	1.36	9.55	-0.18	20.14	14.24	1.3	1.19	9.9	0.76	8.94	112.8	1	99	0	0	86	12.52	-24.79	5.75		May-07
	1.16	9.14	-0.91	17.75	10.48	0.46	1.91	9.89	0.76	8.71	112.8	1	99	0	0	86	12.7	-24.91		1.00	May-07
100	1.38	9.73	0.06	21.15	15.94	1.56	0.97	9.92	0.76	8.79	112.8	1	99	0	0	86	12.54	-24.67			Apr-15
	1.49	9.82	0.24	21.50	16.42	1.71	0.87	9.98	0.76	8.83	112.8	1	99	0	0	86	12.53	-24.67			May-07
	1.49	9.83	0.31	22.01	16.92	1.78	0.78	9.93	0.76	8.82	112.8	1	99	0	0	86	12.53	-24.67			Oct-16
	1.36	9.61	-0.18	19.99	14.04	1.41	1.38	9.93	0.76	8.89	112.8	1	99	0	0	86	12.35	-24.67			May-07
	1.26	9.57	0.00	20.98	15.27	1.39	1.03	9.94	0.76	8.81	112.8	1	99	0	0	86	12.39	-24.82			Jul-09
	4.05	17.49	0.02	20.29	10.40	1.58	1.29	12.98	1.14	24.38	1,996	0	100	0	0	56	15.23	-24.69	5.75		Aug-01
	3.95	17.18	-0.59	17.75	6.42	0	2	12.96	1.14	22.84	1,996	0	100	0	0	56	14.75	-24.96		1.00	Aug-01
100	4.15	17.68	0.24	20.85	10.91	1.85	1.1	12.97	1.14	24.29	1,996	0	100	0	0	56	15.23	-24.69			Jun-17
	4.15	17.72	0.35	21.38	12.05	1.89	0.99	12.98	1.14	24.31	1,996	0	100	0	0	56	15.47	-24.63			Mar-09
	4.16	17.76	0.34	21.45	11.60	2	0.94	12.98	1.14	24.26	1,996	0	100	0	0	56	15.23	-24.69			Nov-15
	3.97	17.39	-0.25	19.09	8.72	1.09	1.69	12.98	1.14	23.82	1,996	0	100	0	0	56	15.07	-24.81			Sep-05
	4.05	17.44	-0.10	20.06	10.18	1.96	1.44	13	1.14	24.1	1,996	0	100	0	0	56	15.23	-24.69			Jun-17
	4.11	17.62	0.18	20.65	10.73	1.72	1.19	13	1.14	24.29	1,996	0	100	0	0	56	15.23	-24.69			Jun-17
	2.40	15.04	-12.03			2.5	1.28			10.63	9.1	0	100	0	0	119			5.75		Jun-17
	2.30	14.91	-12.49			1.6	2.03			10.63	9.1	0	100	0	0	119				1.00	Jun-17
100	2.39	15.07	-12.00			2.46	1.15			10.69	9.1	0	100	0	0	119					Jun-17
	2.40	15.13	-11.84			2.67	1			10.65	9.1	0	100	0	0	119					Jun-17
	2.42	15.04	-11.83			2.73	0.99			10.55	9.1	0	100	0	0	119					Dec-16
	2.40	15.13	-12.03			2.26	1.48			10.65	9.1	0	100	0	0	119					Jun-17
	2.38	14.99	-12.01			1.89	1.24			10.74	9.1	0	100	0	0	119					Jun-17
	1.21	9.69	-1.18	18.03	4.57	2.86	1.18	9.92	0.87	9.96	40.6	7	93	0	0	23			5.75		Apr-13
	1.52	9.79	-1.43	16.12	1.37	1.94	1.88	9.92	0.87	9.98	40.6	7	93	0	0	23				1.00	Apr-13
100	1.11	9.54	-1.30	18.34	5.17	2.42	1.02	9.94	0.87	9.98	40.6	7	93	0	0	23					Apr-13
	1.11	9.54	-1.15	18.67	5.56	2.46	0.97	9.96	0.87	9.98	40.6	7	93	0	0	23					Apr-13
	1.21	9.63	-1.06	18.96	6.09	2.55	0.86	9.99	0.87	10.01	40.6	7	93	0	0	23					Apr-13
	1.31	9.79	-1.24	17.91	4.34	2.8	1.36	9.99	0.87	9.98	40.6	7	93	0	0	23					Apr-13
	1.11	9.45	-1.37	17.99	4.67	2.44	1.11	9.91	0.87	9.96	40.6	7	93	0	0	23					Apr-13
	4.34	18.23	7.30	33.43	36.93	1.48	0.87	11.67	0.94	13.94	95.0	5	95	0	0	33	20.78	-17.46	5.75		Dec-08
	4.27	17.94	6.65	30.84	32.86	0.67	1.63	11.7	0.94	13.67	95.0	5	95	0	0	33	20.23	-17.7		1.00	Dec-08
100	4.47	18.38	7.55	34.26	38.32	1.56	0.67	11.66	0.94	13.78	95.0	5	95	0	0	33	20.92	-17.34			Feb-10
	4.44	18.44	7.61	34.43	38.67	1.57	0.64	11.67	0.94	13.87	95.0	5	95	0	0	33	21.01	-17.31			Dec-08
	4.45	18.40	7.66	34.79	39.26	1.72	0.53	11.67	0.94	13.83	95.0	5	95	0	0	33	21.01	-17.31			May-12
	4.55	18.42	7.39	33.42	36.90	1.55	1.03	11.66	0.94	14.01	95.0	5	95	0	0	33	20.68	-17.46			Dec-08
	4.40	18.31	7.42	33.81	37.63	1.4	0.78	11.71	0.94	13.76	95.0	5	95	0	0	33	20.82	-17.36			Jul-09
	4.64	20.14	3.98	32.03	35.78	0.78	1.15	12.81	0.95	15.33	3,079	4	96	0	0	41	19.52	-19.24	5.75		Jul-09
	4.48	19.85	3.39	29.66	31.98	0	1.78	12.8	0.95	14.91	3,079	4	96	0	0	41	18.97	-19.44		1.00	Jul-09

	MARKET		FUND TYPE, CATEGORY & OBJECTIVE		RATINGS				MINIMUMS	
Fund Name	Ticker Symbol	Traded On	Fund Type	Category and (Prospectus Objective)	Overall Rating	Reward Rating	Risk Rating	Recent Up/ Downgrade	Open to New Investors	Min Initial Investment
Janus Henderson Mid Cap Value Fund Class D	**JNMCX**	NAS CM	Open End	US Equity Mid Cap (Growth)	**C+**	C	B	Up		2,500
Janus Henderson Mid Cap Value Fund Class I	**JMVAX**	NAS CM	Open End	US Equity Mid Cap (Growth)	**C+**	C	B	Up	Y	1,000,000
Janus Henderson Mid Cap Value Fund Class L	**JMIVX**	NAS CM	Open End	US Equity Mid Cap (Growth)	**C+**	C	B	Up		250,000
Janus Henderson Mid Cap Value Fund Class N	**JDPNX**	NAS CM	Open End	US Equity Mid Cap (Growth)	**C+**	C	B	Up	Y	1,000,000
Janus Henderson Mid Cap Value Fund Class R	**JDPRX**	NAS CM	Open End	US Equity Mid Cap (Growth)	**C+**	C	B	Up	Y	2,500
Janus Henderson Mid Cap Value Fund Class S	**JMVIX**	NAS CM	Open End	US Equity Mid Cap (Growth)	**C+**	C	B	Up	Y	2,500
Janus Henderson Mid Cap Value Fund Class T	**JMCVX**	NAS CM	Open End	US Equity Mid Cap (Growth)	**C+**	C	B	Up	Y	2,500
Janus Henderson Overseas Fund Class A	**JDIAX**	NAS CM	Open End	Global Equity Large Cap (Foreign Stock)	**C**	C	C+		Y	2,500
Janus Henderson Overseas Fund Class C	**JIGCX**	NAS CM	Open End	Global Equity Large Cap (Foreign Stock)	**C**	C	C+		Y	2,500
Janus Henderson Overseas Fund Class D	**JNOSX**	NAS CM	Open End	Global Equity Large Cap (Foreign Stock)	**C**	C	B-			2,500
Janus Henderson Overseas Fund Class I	**JIGFX**	NAS CM	Open End	Global Equity Large Cap (Foreign Stock)	**C**	C	B-		Y	1,000,000
Janus Henderson Overseas Fund Class N	**JDINX**	NAS CM	Open End	Global Equity Large Cap (Foreign Stock)	**C**	C	B-		Y	1,000,000
Janus Henderson Overseas Fund Class R	**JDIRX**	NAS CM	Open End	Global Equity Large Cap (Foreign Stock)	**C**	C	C+		Y	2,500
Janus Henderson Overseas Fund Class S	**JIGRX**	NAS CM	Open End	Global Equity Large Cap (Foreign Stock)	**C**	C	C+		Y	2,500
Janus Henderson Overseas Fund Class T	**JAOSX**	NAS CM	Open End	Global Equity Large Cap (Foreign Stock)	**C**	C	B-		Y	2,500
Janus Henderson Research Fund Class A	**JRAAX**	NAS CM	Open End	US Equity Large Cap Growth (Growth)	**B-**	C+	B		Y	2,500
Janus Henderson Research Fund Class C	**JRACX**	NAS CM	Open End	US Equity Large Cap Growth (Growth)	**B-**	C+	B		Y	2,500
Janus Henderson Research Fund Class D	**JNRFX**	NAS CM	Open End	US Equity Large Cap Growth (Growth)	**B-**	C+	B	Down		2,500
Janus Henderson Research Fund Class I	**JRAIX**	NAS CM	Open End	US Equity Large Cap Growth (Growth)	**B-**	C+	B	Down	Y	1,000,000
Janus Henderson Research Fund Class N	**JRANX**	NAS CM	Open End	US Equity Large Cap Growth (Growth)	**B-**	C+	B	Down	Y	1,000,000
Janus Henderson Research Fund Class R	**JRARX**	NAS CM	Open End	US Equity Large Cap Growth (Growth)	**B-**	C+	B		Y	2,500
Janus Henderson Research Fund Class S	**JRASX**	NAS CM	Open End	US Equity Large Cap Growth (Growth)	**B-**	C+	B		Y	2,500
Janus Henderson Research Fund Class T	**JAMRX**	NAS CM	Open End	US Equity Large Cap Growth (Growth)	**B-**	C+	B	Down	Y	2,500
Janus Henderson Select Value Fund Class A	**JVSAX**	NAS CM	Open End	US Equity Mid Cap (Growth)	**B-**	C	B		Y	2,500
Janus Henderson Select Value Fund Class C	**JVSCX**	NAS CM	Open End	US Equity Mid Cap (Growth)	**B-**	C	B		Y	2,500
Janus Henderson Select Value Fund Class D	**JSVDX**	NAS CM	Open End	US Equity Mid Cap (Growth)	**B-**	C	B		Y	2,500
Janus Henderson Select Value Fund Class I	**JVSIX**	NAS CM	Open End	US Equity Mid Cap (Growth)	**B-**	C	B		Y	1,000,000
Janus Henderson Select Value Fund Class N	**JVSNX**	NAS CM	Open End	US Equity Mid Cap (Growth)	**B-**	C	B		Y	1,000,000
Janus Henderson Select Value Fund Class S	**JSVSX**	NAS CM	Open End	US Equity Mid Cap (Growth)	**B-**	C	B		Y	2,500
Janus Henderson Select Value Fund Class T	**JSVTX**	NAS CM	Open End	US Equity Mid Cap (Growth)	**B-**	C	B		Y	2,500
Janus Henderson Small Cap Value Fund Class A	**JDSAX**	NAS CM	Open End	US Equity Small Cap (Small Company)	**C+**	C	B	Up	Y	2,500
Janus Henderson Small Cap Value Fund Class C	**JCSCX**	NAS CM	Open End	US Equity Small Cap (Small Company)	**C+**	C	B-	Up	Y	2,500
Janus Henderson Small Cap Value Fund Class D	**JNPSX**	NAS CM	Open End	US Equity Small Cap (Small Company)	**C+**	C	B	Up		2,500
Janus Henderson Small Cap Value Fund Class I	**JSCOX**	NAS CM	Open End	US Equity Small Cap (Small Company)	**C+**	C	B	Up	Y	1,000,000
Janus Henderson Small Cap Value Fund Class L	**JSIVX**	NAS CM	Open End	US Equity Small Cap (Small Company)	**C+**	C	B	Up		250,000
Janus Henderson Small Cap Value Fund Class N	**JDSNX**	NAS CM	Open End	US Equity Small Cap (Small Company)	**C+**	C	B	Up	Y	1,000,000
Janus Henderson Small Cap Value Fund Class R	**JDSRX**	NAS CM	Open End	US Equity Small Cap (Small Company)	**C+**	C	B	Up	Y	2,500
Janus Henderson Small Cap Value Fund Class S	**JISCX**	NAS CM	Open End	US Equity Small Cap (Small Company)	**C+**	C	B	Up	Y	2,500
Janus Henderson Small Cap Value Fund Class T	**JSCVX**	NAS CM	Open End	US Equity Small Cap (Small Company)	**C+**	C	B	Up	Y	2,500
Janus Henderson Triton Fund Class A	**JGMAX**	NAS CM	Open End	US Equity Small Cap (Growth)	**C+**	C	B-			2,500
Janus Henderson Triton Fund Class C	**JGMCX**	NAS CM	Open End	US Equity Small Cap (Growth)	**C+**	C	B-			2,500
Janus Henderson Triton Fund Class D	**JANIX**	NAS CM	Open End	US Equity Small Cap (Growth)	**C+**	C	B-	Down		2,500
Janus Henderson Triton Fund Class I	**JSMGX**	NAS CM	Open End	US Equity Small Cap (Growth)	**C+**	C	B-	Down		1,000,000
Janus Henderson Triton Fund Class N	**JGMNX**	NAS CM	Open End	US Equity Small Cap (Growth)	**C+**	C	B-	Down		1,000,000
Janus Henderson Triton Fund Class R	**JGMRX**	NAS CM	Open End	US Equity Small Cap (Growth)	**C+**	C	B-			2,500
Janus Henderson Triton Fund Class S	**JGMIX**	NAS CM	Open End	US Equity Small Cap (Growth)	**C+**	C	B-			2,500
Janus Henderson Triton Fund Class T	**JATTX**	NAS CM	Open End	US Equity Small Cap (Growth)	**C+**	C	B-	Down		2,500
Janus Henderson U.S. Growth Opportunities Fund Class A	**HGRAX**	NAS CM	Open End	US Equity Large Cap Growth (Growth)	**B-**	C+	B	Down	Y	2,500
Janus Henderson U.S. Growth Opportunities Fund Class C	**HGRCX**	NAS CM	Open End	US Equity Large Cap Growth (Growth)	**B-**	C+	B	Down	Y	2,500
Janus Henderson U.S. Growth Opportunities Fund Class D	**HGRDX**	NAS CM	Open End	US Equity Large Cap Growth (Growth)	**B-**	C+	B	Down	Y	2,500
Janus Henderson U.S. Growth Opportunities Fund Class I	**HGRIX**	NAS CM	Open End	US Equity Large Cap Growth (Growth)	**B-**	C+	B	Down	Y	1,000,000
Janus Henderson U.S. Growth Opportunities Fund Class N	**HGRRX**	NAS CM	Open End	US Equity Large Cap Growth (Growth)	**B-**	C+	B	Down	Y	1,000,000

★Expanded analysis of this fund is included in Section II.

	TOTAL RETURNS					PERFORMANCE				ASSETS		ASSET ALLOCATION & TURNOVER					BULL & BEAR		FEES		
Min Additional Investment	3-Month Total Return	6-Month Total Return	1-Year Total Return	3-Year Total Return	5-Year Total Return	Dividend Yield (TTM)	Expense Ratio	3-Yr Std Deviation	3-Year Beta	NAV	Total Assets (MIL)	%Cash	%Stocks	%Bonds	%Other	Turnover Ratio	Last Bull Market Total Return	Last Bear Market Total Return	Front End Fee (%)	Back End Fee (%)	Inception Date
100	4.73	20.32	4.26	33.17	37.76	1.11	0.82	12.76	0.95	15.04	3,079	4	96	0	0	41	19.74	-19.09			Aug-98
	4.72	20.36	4.32	33.37	37.94	1.16	0.77	12.8	0.95	15.07	3,079	4	96	0	0	41	19.73	-19.13			Jul-09
	4.78	20.37	4.32	33.87	38.36	1.12	0.93	12.8	0.95	15.54	3,079	4	96	0	0	41	19.61	-19.07			Aug-98
	4.74	20.48	4.47	33.80	38.84	1.26	0.72	12.8	0.95	15	3,079	4	96	0	0	41	19.61	-19.07			May-12
	4.58	20.00	3.70	30.90	33.78	0.47	1.43	12.78	0.95	15.06	3,079	4	96	0	0	41	19.34	-19.34			Jul-09
	4.64	20.14	3.93	31.85	35.45	0.43	1.18	12.79	0.95	15.33	3,079	4	96	0	0	41	19.48	-19.26			Jul-09
	4.70	20.34	4.22	32.86	37.19	0.99	0.92	12.76	0.95	15.14	3,079	4	96	0	0	41	19.64	-19.18			Aug-98
	3.17	14.61	-2.32	37.08	-11.14	0.76	1.01	13.6	1.14	31.52	1,285	1	99	0	0	23	12.64	-33.39	5.75		Jul-09
	2.99	14.19	-3.03	34.07	-14.40	0	1.72	13.58	1.14	30.97	1,285	1	99	0	0	23	12.2	-33.6		1.00	Jul-09
100	3.24	14.78	-2.00	38.40	-9.80	1	0.68	13.59	1.14	31.21	1,285	1	99	0	0	23	12.88	-33.33			May-94
	3.26	14.84	-1.94	38.43	-9.62	1.04	0.64	13.6	1.14	31.34	1,285	1	99	0	0	23	12.89	-33.32			Jul-09
	3.31	14.89	-1.81	38.91	-9.14	1.18	0.53	13.6	1.14	31.16	1,285	1	99	0	0	23	12.88	-33.33			May-12
	3.09	14.47	-2.56	35.93	-12.40	0.28	1.27	13.59	1.14	31	1,285	1	99	0	0	23	12.49	-33.49			Jul-09
	3.17	14.60	-2.31	36.94	-11.29	0.61	1.02	13.6	1.14	31.24	1,285	1	99	0	0	23	12.67	-33.43			Jul-09
	3.23	14.75	-2.05	38.08	-10.13	0.89	0.77	13.6	1.14	31.26	1,285	1	99	0	0	23	12.8	-33.35			May-94
	5.22	24.17	12.74	56.43	72.15	0.1	0.93	13.38	0.98	49.57	13,727	1	99	0	0	43	24.04	-18.55	5.75		Jul-09
	5.05	23.75	11.95	53.26	66.30	0	1.68	13.38	0.98	46.15	13,727	1	99	0	0	43	23.44	-18.82		1.00	Jul-09
100	5.26	24.27	12.97	57.37	73.89	0.27	0.72	13.38	0.98	49.96	13,727	1	99	0	0	43	24.18	-18.51			May-93
	5.29	24.33	13.05	57.71	74.53	0.33	0.65	13.38	0.98	49.87	13,727	1	99	0	0	43	24.24	-18.46			Jul-09
	5.29	24.36	13.13	58.06	75.21	0.4	0.58	13.38	0.98	49.87	13,727	1	99	0	0	43	24.18	-18.51			May-12
	5.07	23.92	12.27	54.58	69.12	0	1.36	13.39	0.98	49.52	13,727	1	99	0	0	43	23.82	-18.68			Jan-17
	5.15	24.05	12.55	55.73	70.92	0	1.08	13.37	0.98	48.74	13,727	1	99	0	0	43	23.9	-18.6			Jul-09
	5.24	24.23	12.85	56.95	73.18	0.18	0.83	13.38	0.98	49.98	13,727	1	99	0	0	43	24.08	-18.53			May-93
	4.02	17.69	7.46	39.43	48.96	1.22	1.31	11.7	0.92	13.17	55.9	5	95	0	0	58			5.75		Dec-11
	3.83	17.09	6.52	36.02	43.13	0.54	2.07	11.64	0.92	12.74	55.9	5	95	0	0	58				1.00	Dec-11
100	4.08	17.68	7.56	40.19	50.53	1.26	1.07	11.71	0.92	13.24	55.9	5	95	0	0	58					Dec-11
	4.13	17.70	7.65	40.41	50.96	0.76	1.02	11.72	0.93	13.36	55.9	5	95	0	0	58					Dec-11
	4.08	17.79	7.72	40.63	51.19	1.44	0.93	11.74	0.93	13.24	55.9	5	95	0	0	58					Aug-17
	4.22	17.85	7.51	39.32	49.08	1.77	1.43	11.71	0.92	13.07	55.9	5	95	0	0	58					Dec-11
	4.09	17.72	7.51	39.77	49.89	1.15	1.17	11.69	0.92	13.22	55.9	5	95	0	0	58					Dec-11
	3.80	17.22	0.55	35.47	41.69	0	1.35	13.74	0.77	21.57	2,992	5	95	0	0	51	20.38	-20.74	5.75		Jul-09
	3.65	16.84	-0.07	32.99	37.68	0	1.91	13.75	0.77	20.12	2,992	5	95	0	0	51	19.92	-21.03		1.00	Jul-09
100	3.83	17.34	0.81	36.63	43.83	0.21	0.96	13.73	0.77	21.38	2,992	5	95	0	0	51	20.64	-20.63			Oct-87
	3.86	17.35	0.88	36.83	44.17	0.31	0.88	13.75	0.77	21.5	2,992	5	95	0	0	51	20.71	-20.66			Jul-09
	3.84	17.40	0.96	37.17	44.76	0.31	1.02	13.75	0.77	22.13	2,992	5	95	0	0	51	20.75	-20.59			Feb-85
	3.87	17.46	0.96	37.28	45.01	0.37	0.81	13.73	0.77	21.46	2,992	5	95	0	0	51	20.75	-20.59			May-12
	3.68	17.01	0.20	34.20	39.63	0	1.56	13.73	0.77	20.84	2,992	5	95	0	0	51	20.24	-20.85			Jul-09
	3.76	17.16	0.51	35.28	41.44	0	1.3	13.72	0.77	21.23	2,992	5	95	0	0	51	20.4	-20.78			Jul-09
	3.82	17.35	0.76	36.27	43.26	0.09	1.05	13.73	0.77	21.44	2,992	5	95	0	0	51	20.6	-20.68			Oct-87
	6.61	26.65	7.85	63.39	78.15	0	1.3	15.35	0.92	30.93	11,318	2	98	0	0	21	27.45	-20.01	5.75		Jul-09
	6.48	26.34	7.24	60.43	72.70	0	1.76	15.36	0.92	28.39	11,318	2	98	0	0	21	26.84	-20.3		1.00	Jul-09
100	6.71	26.86	8.20	64.95	80.97	0	0.8	15.35	0.92	31.78	11,318	2	98	0	0	21	27.56	-19.91			Feb-05
	6.73	26.92	8.24	65.15	81.39	0	0.75	15.35	0.92	32.01	11,318	2	98	0	0	21	27.61	-19.9			Jul-09
	6.77	26.95	8.34	65.71	82.32	0	0.66	15.37	0.92	32.17	11,318	2	98	0	0	21	27.56	-19.91			May-12
	6.55	26.52	7.53	61.99	75.63	0	1.41	15.35	0.92	29.91	11,318	2	98	0	0	21	27.2	-20.15			Jul-09
	6.61	26.67	7.82	63.20	77.82	0	1.16	15.34	0.92	30.63	11,318	2	98	0	0	21	27.32	-20.05			Jul-09
	6.70	26.81	8.09	64.44	80.13	0	0.91	15.36	0.92	31.5	11,318	2	98	0	0	21	27.55	-19.98			Feb-05
	5.26	24.36	15.91	51.81		0	1.17	12.91	0.9	16.18	28.3	0	100	0	0	21			5.75		Dec-14
	5.10	23.91	15.17	48.69		0	1.85	12.88	0.9	15.65	28.3	0	100	0	0	21				1.00	Dec-14
100	5.28	24.42	16.21	52.82		0	0.95	12.9	0.9	16.35	28.3	0	100	0	0	21					Jun-17
	5.34	24.48	16.35	53.01		0	0.87	12.91	0.9	16.37	28.3	0	100	0	0	21					Dec-14
	5.35	24.54	16.39	52.73		0	0.82	12.9	0.9	16.34	28.3	0	100	0	0	21					Nov-15

	MARKET		FUND TYPE, CATEGORY & OBJECTIVE		RATINGS					MINIMUMS
Fund Name	Ticker Symbol	Traded On	Fund Type	Category and (Prospectus Objective)	Overall Rating	Reward Rating	Risk Rating	Recent Up/ Downgrade	Open to New Investors	Min Initial Investment
Janus Henderson U.S. Growth Opportunities Fund Class S	HGRSX	NAS CM	Open End	US Equity Large Cap Growth (Growth)	B-	C+	B	Down	Y	2,500
Janus Henderson U.S. Growth Opportunities Fund Class T	HGRTX	NAS CM	Open End	US Equity Large Cap Growth (Growth)	B-	C+	B	Down	Y	2,500
Janus Henderson U.S. Managed Volatility Fund Class A	JRSAX	NAS CM	Open End	US Equity Large Cap Blend (Growth)	C+	C	B	Down	Y	2,500
Janus Henderson U.S. Managed Volatility Fund Class C	JRSCX	NAS CM	Open End	US Equity Large Cap Blend (Growth)	C+	C	B		Y	2,500
Janus Henderson U.S. Managed Volatility Fund Class S	JRSSX	NAS CM	Open End	US Equity Large Cap Blend (Growth)	C+	C	B	Down	Y	2,500
Janus Henderson Value Plus Income Fund Class A	JPVAX	NAS CM	Open End	Cautious Alloc (Income)	B	C+	A-	Up	Y	2,500
Janus Henderson Value Plus Income Fund Class C	JPVCX	NAS CM	Open End	Cautious Alloc (Income)	B	C+	A-	Up	Y	2,500
Janus Henderson Value Plus Income Fund Class D	JPVDX	NAS CM	Open End	Cautious Alloc (Income)	B	C+	A		Y	2,500
Janus Henderson Value Plus Income Fund Class I	JPVIX	NAS CM	Open End	Cautious Alloc (Income)	B	C+	A		Y	1,000,000
Janus Henderson Value Plus Income Fund Class N	JPVNX	NAS CM	Open End	Cautious Alloc (Income)	B	C+	A		Y	1,000,000
Janus Henderson Value Plus Income Fund Class S	JPVSX	NAS CM	Open End	Cautious Alloc (Income)	B	C+	A-	Up	Y	2,500
Janus Henderson Value Plus Income Fund Class T	JPVTX	NAS CM	Open End	Cautious Alloc (Income)	B	C+	A		Y	2,500
Janus Henderson Venture Fund Class A	JVTAX	NAS CM	Open End	US Equity Small Cap (Growth)	C+	C	C+	Down		2,500
Janus Henderson Venture Fund Class C	JVTCX	NAS CM	Open End	US Equity Small Cap (Growth)	C+	C	C+			2,500
Janus Henderson Venture Fund Class D	JANVX	NAS CM	Open End	US Equity Small Cap (Growth)	C+	C	C+	Down		2,500
Janus Henderson Venture Fund Class I	JVTIX	NAS CM	Open End	US Equity Small Cap (Growth)	C+	C	C+	Down		1,000,000
Janus Henderson Venture Fund Class N	JVTNX	NAS CM	Open End	US Equity Small Cap (Growth)	C+	C	C+	Down		1,000,000
Janus Henderson Venture Fund Class S	JVTSX	NAS CM	Open End	US Equity Small Cap (Growth)	C+	C	C+	Down		2,500
Janus Henderson Venture Fund Class T	JAVTX	NAS CM	Open End	US Equity Small Cap (Growth)	C+	C	C+	Down		2,500
Janus Henderson VIT Balanced Portfolio Institutional Class	JABLX	NAS CM	Open End	Moderate Alloc (Balanced)	B	C+	A		Y	0
Janus Henderson VIT Balanced Portfolio Service Class			Open End	Moderate Alloc (Balanced)	B	C+	A		Y	0
Janus Henderson VIT Enterprise Portfolio Institutional Cls	JAAGX	NAS CM	Open End	US Equity Mid Cap (Growth)	B	B-	B		Y	0
Janus Henderson VIT Enterprise Portfolio Service Class			Open End	US Equity Mid Cap (Growth)	B	B-	B		Y	0
Janus Henderson VIT Forty Portfolio Institutional Class	JACAX	NAS CM	Open End	US Equity Large Cap Growth (Growth)	B-	C+	B	Down	Y	0
Janus Henderson VIT Forty Portfolio Service Class			Open End	US Equity Large Cap Growth (Growth)	B-	C+	B	Down	Y	0
Janus Henderson VIT Global Research Portfolio Inst Cls	JAWGX	NAS CM	Open End	Global Equity Large Cap (World Stock)	C+	C	B		Y	0
Janus Henderson VIT Global Research Portfolio Service Cls			Open End	Global Equity Large Cap (World Stock)	C+	C	B		Y	0
Janus Henderson VIT Global Technology Portfolio Inst Cls	JGLTX	NAS CM	Open End	Technology Sector Equity (Technology)	B	B-	B		Y	0
Janus Henderson VIT Global Technology Port Serv Cls			Open End	Technology Sector Equity (Technology)	B-	B-	B	Down	Y	0
Janus Henderson VIT Mid Cap Value Portfolio Inst Cls	JAMVX	NAS CM	Open End	US Equity Mid Cap (Growth)	C+	C	B	Up	Y	0
Janus Henderson VIT Mid Cap Value Portfolio Service Class			Open End	US Equity Mid Cap (Growth)	C+	C	B	Up	Y	0
Janus Henderson VIT Overseas Portfolio Institutional Class	JAIGX	NAS CM	Open End	Global Equity Large Cap (Foreign Stock)	C	C	B-		Y	0
Janus Henderson VIT Overseas Portfolio Service Class			Open End	Global Equity Large Cap (Foreign Stock)	C	C	B-			0
Janus Henderson VIT Research Portfolio Institutional Class	JAGRX	NAS CM	Open End	US Equity Large Cap Growth (Growth)	B-	C+	B	Down	Y	0
Janus Henderson VIT Research Portfolio Service Class			Open End	US Equity Large Cap Growth (Growth)	B-	C+	B	Down	Y	0
Janus Henderson VIT U.S. Low Vol Port Serv Shares			Open End	US Equity Large Cap Blend (Growth)	B-	C+	B+	Down	Y	0
Japan Smaller Capitalization Fund	JOF	NYSE	Closed End	Japan Equity (Pacific Stock)	C-	C-	C-		Y	
Jensen Quality Growth Fund Class I	JENIX	NAS CM	Open End	US Equity Large Cap Growth (Growth)	B	C+	B+		Y	250,000
Jensen Quality Growth Fund Class J	JENSX	NAS CM	Open End	US Equity Large Cap Growth (Growth)	B	C+	B+		Y	2,500
Jensen Quality Growth Fund Class Y	JENYX	NAS CM	Open End	US Equity Large Cap Growth (Growth)	B	C+	B+		Y	1,000,000
Jensen Quality Growth FundClass R	JENRX	NAS CM	Open End	US Equity Large Cap Growth (Growth)	B	C+	B+		Y	2,500
Jensen Quality Value Fund Class I	JNVIX	NAS CM	Open End	US Equity Mid Cap (Growth)	B-	C	B		Y	250,000
Jensen Quality Value Fund Class J	JNVSX	NAS CM	Open End	US Equity Mid Cap (Growth)	B-	C	B		Y	2,500
JHancock Global Thematic Opportunities Fund Class A	JTKAX	NAS CM	Open End	Global Equity Large Cap (Growth)	U	U	U		Y	1,000
JHancock Global Thematic Opportunities Fund Class C	JTKCX	NAS CM	Open End	Global Equity Large Cap (Growth)	U	U	U		Y	1,000
JHancock Global Thematic Opportunities Fund Class I	JTKIX	NAS CM	Open End	Global Equity Large Cap (Growth)	U	U	U		Y	250,000
JHancock Global Thematic Opportunities Fund Class NAV	JTKNX	NAS CM	Open End	Global Equity Large Cap (Growth)	U	U	U		Y	0
JHancock Global Thematic Opportunities Fund Class R6	JTKRX	NAS CM	Open End	Global Equity Large Cap (Growth)	U	U	U		Y	1,000,000
JHancock Infrastructure Fund Class A	JEEBX	NAS CM	Open End	Infrastructure Sector Equity (Growth & Income)	B	C+	A-		Y	1,000
JHancock Infrastructure Fund Class C	JEEFX	NAS CM	Open End	Infrastructure Sector Equity (Growth & Income)	B-	C+	B+	Down	Y	1,000
JHancock Infrastructure Fund Class I	JEEIX	NAS CM	Open End	Infrastructure Sector Equity (Growth & Income)	B	C+	A-		Y	250,000
JHancock Infrastructure Fund Class NAV	JEEDX	NAS CM	Open End	Infrastructure Sector Equity (Growth & Income)	B	C+	A-		Y	1,000,000

★ Expanded analysis of this fund is included in Section II.

Min Additional Investment	TOTAL RETURNS 3-Month Total Return	6-Month Total Return	1-Year Total Return	3-Year Total Return	5-Year Total Return	PERFORMANCE Dividend Yield (TTM)	Expense Ratio	3-Yr Std Deviation	3-Year Beta	ASSETS NAV	Total Assets (MIL)	ASSET ALLOCATION & TURNOVER %Cash	%Stocks	%Bonds	%Other	Turnover Ratio	BULL & BEAR Last Bull Market Total Return	Last Bear Market Total Return	FEES Front End Fee (%)	Back End Fee (%)	Inception Date
	5.36	24.54	16.03	51.89		0	1.31	12.91	0.9	16.29	28.3	0	100	0	0	21					Jun-17
	5.28	24.37	16.07	52.63		0	1.07	12.9	0.9	16.33	28.3	0	100	0	0	21					Jun-17
	2.98	17.33	5.53	35.75	52.27	1.4	0.94	10.49	0.77	11.37	1,342	1	99	0	0	102	23.53	-18.08	5.75		Dec-05
	2.88	17.07	4.94	33.17	47.29	0.76	1.63	10.53	0.77	11.04	1,342	1	99	0	0	102	23.15	-18.4		1.00	Dec-05
	2.99	17.37	5.45	35.34	51.52	1.25	1.04	10.52	0.77	11.35	1,342	1	99	0	0	102	23.41	-18.1			Dec-05
	3.87	12.49	7.46	26.33	29.63	2.91	0.95	6.46	0.51	11.49	59.2	2	42	56	0	100	13.24	-9.32	5.75		Jul-10
	2.08	10.39	5.06	21.60	22.99	3.54	1.7	6.42	0.5	11.41	59.2	2	42	56	0	100	13.06	-9.6		1.00	Jul-10
100	3.74	12.38	7.51	26.59	30.24	2.69	0.82	6.52	0.51	11.52	59.2	2	42	56	0	100	13.31	-9.27			Jul-10
	3.74	12.39	7.56	26.81	30.64	2.74	0.76	6.52	0.51	11.53	59.2	2	42	56	0	100	13.26	-9.15			Jul-10
	3.86	12.45	7.65	27.08	30.92	2.82	0.68	6.53	0.52	11.53	59.2	2	42	56	0	100	13.26	-9.15			Aug-17
	3.86	12.57	7.44	25.94	29.24	2.64	1.18	6.47	0.51	11.53	59.2	2	42	56	0	100	13.07	-9.41			Jul-10
	3.81	12.42	7.40	26.32	29.86	2.6	0.93	6.48	0.51	11.53	59.2	2	42	56	0	100	13.23	-9.32			Jul-10
	3.43	26.04	4.78	56.18	65.36	0	1.01	15.66	0.87	79.42	3,348	1	99	0	0	28	28.98	-20.37	5.75		May-11
	3.25	25.59	4.01	52.79	59.50	0	1.75	15.64	0.87	73.06	3,348	1	99	0	0	28	28.58	-20.89		1.00	May-11
100	3.48	26.17	5.00	57.20	67.21	0	0.8	15.66	0.87	81.89	3,348	1	99	0	0	28	29.21	-20.31			Apr-85
	3.49	26.21	5.04	57.44	67.68	0	0.75	15.66	0.87	82.28	3,348	1	99	0	0	28	29.26	-20.28			May-11
	3.52	26.26	5.15	57.85	68.36	0	0.67	15.66	0.87	82.87	3,348	1	99	0	0	28	29.21	-20.31			May-12
	3.39	25.95	4.62	55.49	64.24	0	1.17	15.65	0.87	78.52	3,348	1	99	0	0	28	29.04	-20.43			May-11
	3.46	26.12	4.89	56.74	66.37	0	0.91	15.65	0.87	80.71	3,348	1	99	0	0	28	29.1	-20.33			Apr-85
	3.95	13.49	10.17	42.44	46.44	1.63	0.63	7.34	0.59	36.67	4,318	1	59	39	0	97	18.02	-12.25			Sep-93
	3.89	13.34	9.92	41.36	44.62	1.38	0.88	7.33	0.59	38.73	4,318	1	59	39	0	97	17.82	-12.32			Dec-99
	7.31	27.98	17.30	73.71	101.11	0.16	0.72	13.06	0.89	79.89	1,393	6	94	0	0	14	24.98	-19.18			Sep-93
	7.25	27.83	17.02	72.44	98.64	0.03	0.97	13.05	0.89	74.78	1,384	6	94	0	0	14	24.83	-19.27			Dec-99
	5.84	24.88	13.14	71.81	105.03	0.07	0.71	13.48	0.98	39.99	806.9	3	97	0	0	41	28.82	-18.42			May-97
	5.77	24.71	12.83	70.53	102.44	0.01	0.96	13.48	0.98	37.44	806.9	3	97	0	0	41	28.62	-18.51			Dec-99
	4.56	19.23	7.41	47.87	41.82	1.01	0.6	12.11	1.04	52.1	683.5	1	99	0	0	36	18.42	-23.69			Sep-93
	4.51	19.07	7.15	46.78	40.09	0.86	0.85	12.11	1.04	50.92	683.5	1	99	0	0	36	18.25	-23.76			Dec-99
	5.17	28.42	13.18	112.48	134.93	0	0.76	15.93	1.11	13.08	452.4	1	99	0	0	32	24.37	-19.19			Jan-00
	-2.57	18.99	4.75	95.56	115.12	0	1	15.91	1.11	13.22	452.4	1	99	0	0	32	24.23	-19.37			Jan-00
	4.65	20.16	3.74	32.69	37.05	1.06	0.81	12.82	0.95	15.39	103.3	4	96	0	0	42	20.26	-19.71			May-03
	4.65	20.06	3.54	31.76	35.36	0.92	1.06	12.8	0.95	14.84	103.3	4	96	0	0	42	19.95	-19.79			Dec-02
	3.33	14.83	-1.81	39.28	-7.47	1.65	0.6	13.5	1.13	30.2	627.3	1	99	0	0	25	13.01	-31.85			May-94
	3.28	14.64	-2.07	38.21	-8.62	1.57	0.85	13.48	1.13	28.96	627.3	1	99	0	0	25	12.85	-31.91			Dec-99
	5.30	24.39	13.24	58.03	75.08	0.44	0.58	13.34	0.98	37.09	496.8	0	100	0	0	47	25.43	-18.51			Sep-93
	5.25	24.22	12.98	56.88	72.90	0.29	0.83	13.34	0.98	36.06	496.8	0	100	0	0	47	25.24	-18.58			Dec-99
	5.02	18.61	15.01	29.18	60.53	1.59	0.82	9.46	0.69	17.99	1,048	1	99	0	0	20					Sep-12
	-1.48	2.37	-12.54	26.48	46.75	0.8	1.32	12.44	0.91	9.93	281.4	0	96	0	4	24	4.76	2.06			Mar-90
100	2.55	18.50	14.77	56.62	85.75	1.09	0.62	11.17	0.88	50.69	7,522	3	97	0	0	9	19.96	-16.1			Jul-03
100	2.49	18.35	14.47	55.43	83.41	0.85	0.88	11.18	0.88	50.69	7,522	3	97	0	0	9	19.74	-16.22			Aug-92
100	2.57	18.54	14.85	56.80	85.03	1.15	0.56	11.17	0.88	50.68	7,522	3	97	0	0	9	19.74	-16.22			Sep-16
100	2.38	18.13	14.06	53.70	80.11	0.48	1.25	11.17	0.88	50.46	7,522	3	97	0	0	9	19.6	-16.27			Jul-03
100	3.56	20.52	9.05	39.45	39.69	0.98	0.83	13.53	0.81	13	38.9	3	97	0	0	44	16.9	-14.47			Mar-10
100	3.57	20.35	8.84	38.64	38.47	0.77	1.06	13.59	0.81	13.08	38.9	3	97	0	0	44	16.89	-14.53			Mar-10
	5.82	20.26					1.19			11.63	374.7	4	96	0	0				5.00		Dec-18
	5.65	19.75					1.94			11.58	374.7	4	96	0	0					1.00	Dec-18
	5.91	20.37					0.94			11.64	374.7	4	96	0	0						Dec-18
	5.90	20.35					0.84			11.65	374.7	4	96	0	0						Dec-18
	6.00	20.47					0.85			11.65	374.7	4	96	0	0						Dec-18
	3.70	15.03	12.96	25.82	29.46	1.47	1.31	10.04	0.61	12.91	306.4	6	94	0	0	19			5.00		Dec-13
	3.56	14.75	12.27	23.31	24.83	0.95	2.01	10.03	0.61	12.79	306.4	6	94	0	0	19				1.00	May-14
	3.77	15.29	13.30	26.99	31.29	1.75	1	10.02	0.61	12.92	306.4	6	94	0	0	19					Dec-13
	3.87	15.40	13.45	27.46	32.20	1.82	0.92	10.03	0.61	12.95	306.4	6	94	0	0	19					Dec-13

	MARKET		FUND TYPE, CATEGORY & OBJECTIVE		RATINGS				MINIMUMS	
Fund Name	Ticker Symbol	Traded On	Fund Type	Category and (Prospectus Objective)	Overall Rating	Reward Rating	Risk Rating	Recent Up/ Downgrade	Open to New Investors	Min Initial Investment
JHancock Infrastructure Fund Class R6			Open End	Infrastructure Sector Equity (Growth & Income)	B	C+	A-		Y	0
JHancock International Strategic Equity Allocation Cls NAV			Open End	Global Equity Large Cap (Growth)	C	D+	B-	Up	Y	0
JHancock U.S. Strategic Equity Allocation Fund Class NAV			Open End	US Equity Large Cap Blend (Growth)	C+	C	B		Y	0
JNL Aggressive Growth Allocation Fund Class A			Open End	Aggressive Alloc (Asset Alloc)	B-	C	B	Up	Y	0
JNL Aggressive Growth Allocation Fund Class I			Open End	Aggressive Alloc (Asset Alloc)	B-	C	B	Up	Y	0
JNL Conservative Allocation Fund Class A			Open End	Cautious Alloc (Asset Alloc)	B	C+	A-	Up	Y	0
JNL Conservative Allocation Fund Class I			Open End	Cautious Alloc (Asset Alloc)	B	C+	A-		Y	0
JNL Growth Allocation Fund Class A			Open End	Aggressive Alloc (Asset Alloc)	B-	C	B+	Up	Y	0
JNL Growth Allocation Fund Class I			Open End	Aggressive Alloc (Asset Alloc)	B-	C	B+	Up	Y	0
JNL Institutional Alt 100 Fund Class A			Open End	Multialternative (Growth)	C	C	B-		Y	0
JNL Institutional Alt 100 Fund Class I			Open End	Multialternative (Growth)	C	C	B		Y	0
JNL Institutional Alt 25 Fund Class A			Open End	Moderate Alloc (Growth & Income)	B-	C	A-	Up	Y	0
JNL Institutional Alt 25 Fund Class I			Open End	Moderate Alloc (Growth & Income)	B-	C	A-	Up	Y	0
JNL Institutional Alt 50 Fund Class A			Open End	Cautious Alloc (Growth & Income)	B-	C	A-	Up	Y	0
JNL Institutional Alt 50 Fund Class I			Open End	Cautious Alloc (Growth & Income)	B-	C	A-	Up	Y	0
JNL iShares Tactical Growth A			Open End	Aggressive Alloc (Growth)	B-	C	B	Up	Y	0
JNL iShares Tactical Growth I			Open End	Aggressive Alloc (Growth)	B-	C	B	Up	Y	0
JNL iShares Tactical Moderate A			Open End	Cautious Alloc (Growth)	B-	C	B+	Up	Y	0
JNL iShares Tactical Moderate Growth A			Open End	Moderate Alloc (Growth)	B-	C	B+	Up	Y	0
JNL iShares Tactical Moderate Growth I			Open End	Moderate Alloc (Growth)	B-	C	B+	Up	Y	0
JNL iShares Tactical Moderate I			Open End	Cautious Alloc (Growth)	B-	C	A-	Up	Y	0
JNL Moderate Allocation Fund Class A			Open End	Cautious Alloc (Asset Alloc)	B	C+	A-	Up	Y	0
JNL Moderate Allocation Fund Class I			Open End	Cautious Alloc (Asset Alloc)	B	C+	A-	Up	Y	0
JNL Moderate Growth Allocation Fund Class A			Open End	Moderate Alloc (Asset Alloc)	B-	C	A-	Up	Y	0
JNL Moderate Growth Allocation Fund Class I			Open End	Moderate Alloc (Asset Alloc)	B	C	A-	Up	Y	0
JNL Multi-Manager Alternative Fund Class A			Open End	Multialternative (Growth)	B-	C	B+	Up	Y	0
JNL Multi-Manager Alternative Fund Class I			Open End	Multialternative (Growth)	B-	C	A-	Up	Y	0
JNL Multi-Manager International Small Cap Fund Class A			Open End	Global Equity Mid/Small Cap (Small Company)	U	U	U		Y	0
JNL Multi-Manager International Small Cap Fund Class I			Open End	Global Equity Mid/Small Cap (Small Company)	U	U	U		Y	0
JNL Multi-Manager Mid Cap Fund Class A			Open End	US Equity Mid Cap (Growth & Income)	C+	C	B		Y	0
JNL Multi-Manager Mid Cap Fund Class I			Open End	US Equity Mid Cap (Growth & Income)	C+	C	B		Y	0
JNL Multi-Manager Small Cap Growth Fund Class A			Open End	US Equity Small Cap (Small Company)	B-	B-	C+	Down	Y	0
JNL Multi-Manager Small Cap Growth Fund Class I			Open End	US Equity Small Cap (Small Company)	B-	B-	C+	Down	Y	0
JNL Multi-Manager Small Cap Value Fund Class A			Open End	US Equity Small Cap (Small Company)	C	C-	C+		Y	0
JNL Multi-Manager Small Cap Value Fund Class I			Open End	US Equity Small Cap (Small Company)	C	C	C+		Y	0
JNL S&P 500 Index Fund Class I			Open End	US Equity Large Cap Blend (Growth)	C-	C-	B-	Up	Y	0
JNL/American Funds Balanced Fund Class A			Open End	Moderate Alloc (Balanced)	B-	C	B+	Up	Y	0
JNL/American Funds Balanced Fund Class I			Open End	Moderate Alloc (Balanced)	B-	C	A-		Y	0
JNL/American Funds Blue Chip Income & Growth Cls A			Open End	US Equity Large Cap Value (Income)	C+	C	B	Up	Y	0
JNL/American Funds Blue Chip Income & Growth Cls I			Open End	US Equity Large Cap Value (Income)	C+	C	B	Up	Y	0
JNL/American Funds Capital Income Builder Fund Class A			Open End	Alloc Miscellaneous (Growth & Income)	U	U	U		Y	0
JNL/American Funds Capital Income Builder Fund Class I			Open End	Alloc Miscellaneous (Growth & Income)	U	U	U		Y	0
JNL/American Funds Global Growth Fund A			Open End	Global Equity Large Cap (Growth)	C+	C	B	Up	Y	0
JNL/American Funds Global Growth Fund Class I			Open End	Global Equity Large Cap (Growth)	C+	C	B	Up	Y	0
JNL/American Funds Global Small Capitalization Cls A			Open End	Global Equity Mid/Small Cap (Small Company)	C+	C	B-	Up	Y	0
JNL/American Funds Global Small Capitalization Cls I			Open End	Global Equity Mid/Small Cap (Small Company)	C+	C	B-	Up	Y	0
JNL/American Funds Growth Allocation Fund Class A			Open End	Aggressive Alloc (Growth)	B-	C	B+	Up	Y	0
JNL/American Funds Growth Allocation Fund Class I			Open End	Aggressive Alloc (Growth)	B-	C	B+	Up	Y	0
JNL/American Funds Growth Fund A			Open End	US Equity Large Cap Growth (Growth)	B-	C	B	Down	Y	0
JNL/American Funds Growth Fund Class I			Open End	US Equity Large Cap Growth (Growth)	B-	C	B		Y	0
JNL/American Funds Growth-Income Fund Class A			Open End	US Equity Large Cap Blend (Growth & Income)	B-	C	B		Y	0
JNL/American Funds Growth-Income Fund Class I			Open End	US Equity Large Cap Blend (Growth & Income)	B-	C	B+		Y	0

★ Expanded analysis of this fund is included in Section II.

	TOTAL RETURNS					PERFORMANCE				ASSETS		ASSET ALLOCATION & TURNOVER					BULL & BEAR		FEES		
Min Additional Investment	3-Month Total Return	6-Month Total Return	1-Year Total Return	3-Year Total Return	5-Year Total Return	Dividend Yield (TTM)	Expense Ratio	3-Yr Std Deviation	3-Year Beta	NAV	Total Assets (MIL)	%Cash	%Stocks	%Bonds	%Other	Turnover Ratio	Last Bull Market Total Return	Last Bear Market Total Return	Front End Fee (%)	Back End Fee (%)	Inception Date
	3.79	15.31	13.36	27.38	32.19	1.82	0.92	9.99	0.61	12.94	306.4	6	94	0	0	19					Dec-13
	3.17	13.88	0.51			2.37	0.69			9.43	1,693	7	93	0	0	94					Oct-16
	3.74	18.83	7.57			1.52	0.64			9.97	1,595	3	97	0	0	128					Sep-16
	4.21	17.64	5.42	36.54	34.24	0	1.21	10.71	0.98	13.6	1,491	4	84	11	0		18.37	-18.06			Jan-07
	4.27	17.84	5.80	37.24	34.94	0	0.91	10.65	0.97	13.67	1,491	4	84	11	0		18.37	-18.06			Sep-17
	2.95	9.43	7.00	16.34	15.98	0	1.21	3.77	1.13	12.53	409.2	8	19	70	0						Feb-12
	3.02	9.47	7.24	16.89	16.53	0	0.91	3.71	1.12	12.59	409.2	8	19	70	0						Sep-17
	4.00	16.39	6.01	32.74	32.08	0	1.21	9.36	1.03	14.27	2,369	5	71	22	0	156	17.33	-15.46			Jan-07
	4.06	16.58	6.30	33.29	32.63	0	0.91	9.36	1.03	14.34	2,369	5	71	22	0	156	17.33	-15.47			Sep-17
	1.99	6.98	2.19	5.61	0.77	0	1.87	4.18	1.28	10.72	230.0	31	37	24	1						Feb-12
	2.07	7.24	2.75	6.50	1.62	0	1.52	4.17	1.27	10.81	230.0	31	37	24	1						Sep-17
	3.12	12.71	5.13	25.05	21.04	0	1.32	7.24	1.05	17.82	2,729	11	53	33	0		13.33	-13.9			Apr-09
	3.22	12.91	5.47	25.75	21.72	0	1.02	7.22	1.05	17.92	2,729	11	53	33	0		13.33	-13.9			Sep-17
	2.73	10.43	4.30	17.47	13.15	0	1.48	5.83	0.85	17.68	2,302	18	44	34	0		12.09	-15.44			Apr-09
	2.83	10.57	4.64	18.13	13.79	0	1.18	5.85	0.85	17.78	2,302	18	44	34	0		12.09	-15.44			Sep-17
	2.77	13.98	2.86	31.62	34.68	1.32	0.87	9.93	1.09	14.43	239.9	4	82	14	0						Feb-12
	2.76	14.10	3.15	32.35	35.42	1.52	0.57	9.94	1.09	14.48	239.9	4	82	14	0						Sep-17
	2.39	9.53	3.64	18.41	22.78	1.57	0.84	5.71	1.16	12.41	146.1	11	44	45	0						Feb-12
	2.57	11.78	3.45	25.40	29.28	1.57	0.86	7.74	1.12	13.56	282.7	7	61	32	0						Feb-12
	2.63	11.92	3.76	26.14	30.05	1.78	0.56	7.74	1.12	13.61	282.7	7	61	32	0						Sep-17
	2.46	9.67	4.01	19.13	23.52	1.77	0.54	5.72	1.16	12.47	146.1	11	44	45	0						Sep-17
	3.19	11.39	6.60	20.38	19.38	0	1.23	5.36	1.1	13.88	560.8	7	35	56	0						Feb-12
	3.25	11.51	6.89	20.98	19.98	0	0.93	5.37	1.1	13.95	560.8	7	35	56	0						Sep-17
	3.64	13.81	6.61	27.41	28.55	0	1.2	7.19	1.04	14.5	2,342	6	54	39	0		15.14	-11.75			Jan-07
	3.69	13.99	6.89	28.11	29.26	0	0.9	7.22	1.05	14.58	2,342	6	54	39	0		15.14	-11.75			Sep-17
	1.86	6.12	3.17	12.19		0	2.07	3.62	1.02	10.4	1,196	31	27	28	0	181					Apr-15
	1.95	6.31	3.45	12.83		0.18	1.77	3.64	1.03	10.44	1,196	31	27	28	0	181					Sep-17
	3.45	19.60					1.27			9.58	274.9	4	96	0	0	24					Aug-18
	3.44	19.70					0.97			9.6	274.9	4	96	0	0	24					Aug-18
	3.92	21.26	9.57			0	1.09			13.23	1,141	3	97	0	0	39					Sep-16
	3.99	21.42	9.84			0.3	0.79			13.26	1,141	3	97	0	0	39					Sep-17
	7.10	31.17	10.69	83.30	65.04	0	0.97	16.39	0.99	30.59	2,375	2	98	0	0	92	24.74	-22.01			Sep-96
	7.18	31.32	10.99	84.60	66.98	0	0.67	16.38	0.99	32.24	2,375	2	98	0	0	92	24.9	-21.97			Mar-04
	2.82	16.13	-3.85	34.48	17.71	0.31	1.07	17.13	1.06	13.1	1,224	4	96	0	0	74	31.42	-24.85			May-05
	2.89	16.28	-3.55	35.45	19.17	0.63	0.77	17.18	1.06	13.14	1,224	4	96	0	0	74	31.63	-24.76			May-05
	4.29	19.38	10.17			0	0.15			12.13	52.7	2	98	0	0	98					Sep-17
	2.22	12.29	5.37	27.82	25.64	0.61	0.92	7.94	0.67	11.51	1,325	8	63	29	0		13.92	-14.96			May-00
	2.22	12.42	5.73	28.94	27.07	0.68	0.62	7.98	0.68	11.94	1,325	8	63	29	0		14.11	-14.99			Mar-04
	0.13	11.43	0.67	28.73	43.61	0	0.99	12.32	0.96	22.31	3,175	5	95	0	0		22.6	-16.26			May-10
	0.22	11.62	0.98	29.78	45.38	0	0.69	12.31	0.96	22.66	3,175	5	95	0	0		22.64	-16.12			May-10
	1.37	10.36					1.12			10.33	70.8	6	68	25	0						Aug-18
	1.36	10.44					0.82			10.36	70.8	6	68	25	0						Aug-18
	4.67	21.85	6.76	51.27	53.94	0.28	1.1	13.2	1.11	15.67	339.4	3	97	0	0		21.17	-21.98			Sep-13
	4.79	22.01	7.10	51.93	54.11	0.4	0.8	13.18	1.11	15.74	339.4	3	97	0	0		21.38	-21.88			Sep-17
	4.32	21.01	2.66	44.11	30.99	0.1	1.29	12.53	0.92	15.2	716.1	10	90	0	0		18.74	-26.11			May-10
	4.39	21.28	2.94	45.36	32.64	0.2	0.99	12.55	0.92	15.44	716.1	10	90	0	0		18.71	-25.96			May-10
	3.38	15.22	6.11	38.79	39.58	0	1.06	9.08	0.98	17.71	2,631	6	73	20	0						Apr-12
	3.42	15.42	6.45	39.57	40.37	0	0.76	9.02	0.98	17.81	2,631	6	73	20	0						Sep-17
	2.81	17.32	5.56	61.78	76.39	0	0.95	12.67	0.99	24.85	926.4	5	95	0	0		24.12	-19.53			Feb-12
	2.92	17.48	5.93	62.61	77.37	0	0.65	12.69	0.99	25	926.4	5	95	0	0		24.27	-19.43			Sep-17
	3.19	16.67	6.64	50.83	60.06	0	0.92	11.17	0.9	25.19	7,247	8	91	0	0		22.39	-17.24			May-10
	3.22	16.81	6.94	51.93	61.92	0	0.62	11.17	0.9	25.57	7,247	8	91	0	0		22.45	-17.2			May-10

	MARKET		FUND TYPE, CATEGORY & OBJECTIVE		RATINGS				MINIMUMS	
Fund Name	Ticker Symbol	Traded On	Fund Type	Category and (Prospectus Objective)	Overall Rating	Reward Rating	Risk Rating	Recent Up/ Downgrade	Open to New Investors	Min Initial Investment
JNL/American Funds International Fund Class A			Open End	Global Equity Large Cap (Foreign Stock)	C	C	B-		Y	0
JNL/American Funds International Fund Class I			Open End	Global Equity Large Cap (Foreign Stock)	C	C	B		Y	0
JNL/American Funds Moderate Growth Allocation Class A			Open End	Moderate Alloc (Balanced)	B	C	A-	Up	Y	0
JNL/American Funds Moderate Growth Allocation Class I			Open End	Moderate Alloc (Balanced)	B	C	A-	Up	Y	0
JNL/American Funds New World Fund Class A			Open End	Global Emerg Mkts (Growth)	C	C	B-		Y	0
JNL/American Funds New World Fund Class I			Open End	Global Emerg Mkts (Growth)	C+	C	B-	Up	Y	0
JNL/AQR Large Cap Relaxed Constraint Equity Fund Class A			Open End	US Equity Large Cap Blend (Growth)	C	C	B-		Y	0
JNL/AQR Large Cap Relaxed Constraint Equity Fund Class I			Open End	US Equity Large Cap Blend (Growth)	C	C	B-		Y	0
JNL/AQR Managed Futures Strategy Fund Class A			Open End	Alternative Miscellaneous (Growth)	D	D	D+		Y	0
JNL/AQR Managed Futures Strategy Fund Class I			Open End	Alternative Miscellaneous (Growth)	D	D	D+		Y	0
JNL/BlackRock Global Allocation Fund Class A			Open End	Moderate Alloc (Asset Alloc)	B-	C	B+	Up	Y	0
JNL/BlackRock Global Allocation Fund Class I			Open End	Moderate Alloc (Asset Alloc)	B-	C	B+	Up	Y	0
JNL/BlackRock Global Natural Resources Fund Class A			Open End	Natl Resources Sec Equity (Natl Res)	C-	D+	C-		Y	0
JNL/BlackRock Global Natural Resources Fund Class I			Open End	Natl Resources Sec Equity (Natl Res)	C-	C-	C-		Y	0
JNL/BlackRock Large Cap Select Growth Fund Class A			Open End	US Equity Large Cap Growth (Growth)	B-	C+	B	Down	Y	0
JNL/BlackRock Large Cap Select Growth Fund Class I			Open End	US Equity Large Cap Growth (Growth)	B-	C+	B	Down	Y	0
JNL/Boston Partners Global Long Short Equity Fund Class A			Open End	Long/Short Equity (Equity-Income)	D+	D	C		Y	0
JNL/Boston Partners Global Long Short Equity Fund Class I			Open End	Long/Short Equity (Equity-Income)	D+	D	C	Down	Y	0
JNL/Causeway International Value Select Fund Class A			Open End	Global Equity Large Cap (Foreign Stock)	C	C-	C+		Y	0
JNL/Causeway International Value Select Fund Class I			Open End	Global Equity Large Cap (Foreign Stock)	C	C-	C+		Y	0
JNL/ClearBridge Large Cap Growth Fund Class A			Open End	US Equity Large Cap Growth (Growth)	C-	C-	B	Up	Y	0
JNL/ClearBridge Large Cap Growth Fund Class I			Open End	US Equity Large Cap Growth (Growth)	C-	C-	B	Up	Y	0
JNL/DFA Growth Allocation Fund (A)			Open End	Aggressive Alloc (Growth & Income)	C	C-	B-	Up	Y	0
JNL/DFA Growth Allocation Fund Class I			Open End	Aggressive Alloc (Growth & Income)	C	D+	B-	Up	Y	0
JNL/DFA Moderate Growth Allocation Fund Class A			Open End	Moderate Alloc (Growth & Income)	C	C-	B-	Up	Y	0
JNL/DFA Moderate Growth Allocation Fund Class I			Open End	Moderate Alloc (Growth & Income)	C	D+	B	Up	Y	0
JNL/DFA U.S. Core Equity Fund Class A			Open End	US Equity Large Cap Blend (Growth)	C+	C	B		Y	0
JNL/DFA U.S. Core Equity Fund Class I			Open End	US Equity Large Cap Blend (Growth)	C+	C	B		Y	0
JNL/DFA U.S. Small Cap Fund Class A			Open End	US Equity Small Cap (Small Company)	C	C-	C		Y	0
JNL/DFA U.S. Small Cap Fund Class I			Open End	US Equity Small Cap (Small Company)	C	C-	C+		Y	0
JNL/DoubleLine® Shiller Enhanced CAPE® Fund Class A			Open End	US Equity Large Cap Value (Growth & Income)	B-	B-	B		Y	0
JNL/DoubleLine® Shiller Enhanced CAPE® Fund Class I			Open End	US Equity Large Cap Value (Growth & Income)	B-	B-	B	Down	Y	0
JNL/Epoch Global Shareholder Yield Fund			Open End	Global Equity Large Cap (Income)	C+	C	B		Y	0
JNL/Epoch Global Shareholder Yield Fund Class I			Open End	Global Equity Large Cap (Income)	B-	C	A-		Y	0
JNL/FAMCO Flex Core Covered Call Fund			Open End	Long/Short Equity (Growth)	C+	C	B		Y	0
JNL/FAMCO Flex Core Covered Call Fund Class I			Open End	Long/Short Equity (Growth)	C+	C	B		Y	0
JNL/First State Global Infrastructure A			Open End	Infrastructure Sector Equity (Growth & Income)	B-	C+	B	Down	Y	0
JNL/First State Global Infrastructure I			Open End	Infrastructure Sector Equity (Growth & Income)	B-	C+	B	Down	Y	0
JNL/FPA + DoubleLine Flexible Allocation Fund Class A			Open End	Moderate Alloc (Growth & Income)	C+	C	B	Up	Y	0
JNL/FPA + DoubleLine Flexible Allocation Fund Class I			Open End	Moderate Alloc (Growth & Income)	B-	C	B+	Up	Y	0
JNL/Franklin Templeton Global Fund Class A			Open End	Global Equity Large Cap (Growth)	C-	D+	C	Down	Y	0
JNL/Franklin Templeton Global Fund Class I			Open End	Global Equity Large Cap (Growth)	C-	C-	C	Down	Y	0
JNL/Franklin Templeton Growth Allocation Fund Class A			Open End	Aggressive Alloc (Growth)	C	C	B-		Y	0
JNL/Franklin Templeton Growth Allocation Fund Class I			Open End	Aggressive Alloc (Growth)	C+	C	B-	Up	Y	0
JNL/Franklin Templeton Income Fund Class A			Open End	Cautious Alloc (Income)	B	C	A		Y	0
JNL/Franklin Templeton Income Fund Class I			Open End	Cautious Alloc (Income)	B-	C+	B+	Down	Y	0
JNL/Franklin Templeton International Small Cap A			Open End	Global Equity Mid/Small Cap (Foreign Stock)	C	C-	C+		Y	0
JNL/Franklin Templeton International Small Cap I			Open End	Global Equity Mid/Small Cap (Foreign Stock)	C	C-	C+		Y	0
JNL/Franklin Templeton Mutual Shares Fund Class A			Open End	Aggressive Alloc (Growth)	C+	C	B	Up	Y	0
JNL/Franklin Templeton Mutual Shares Fund Class I			Open End	Aggressive Alloc (Growth)	C+	C	B	Up	Y	0
JNL/GQG Emerging Markets Equity Fund Class A			Open End	Global Emerg Mkts (Div Emerging Mkts)	D+	D	C		Y	0
JNL/GQG Emerging Markets Equity Fund Class I			Open End	Global Emerg Mkts (Div Emerging Mkts)	D+	D	C		Y	0

★Expanded analysis of this fund is included in Section II.

Min Additional Investment	TOTAL RETURNS 3-Month Total Return	6-Month Total Return	1-Year Total Return	3-Year Total Return	5-Year Total Return	PERFORMANCE Dividend Yield (TTM)	Expense Ratio	3-Yr Std Deviation	3-Year Beta	ASSETS NAV	Total Assets (MIL)	ASSET ALLOCATION & TURNOVER %Cash	%Stocks	%Bonds	%Other	Turnover Ratio	BULL & BEAR Last Bull Market Total Return	Last Bear Market Total Return	FEES Front End Fee (%)	Back End Fee (%)	Inception Date
	1.75	15.07	-0.55	38.07	20.00	0.87	1.16	12.01	1.01	14.5	1,913	11	88	1	0		16.62	-25.5			May-10
	1.80	15.30	-0.21	39.11	21.41	1.04	0.86	12.01	1.01	14.69	1,913	11	88	1	0		16.57	-25.27			May-10
	2.78	12.29	5.44	29.08	31.47	0	1.05	7.08	1.02	15.89	2,346	7	54	39	0						Apr-12
	2.83	12.53	5.75	29.81	32.22	0	0.75	7.07	1.02	15.98	2,346	7	54	39	0						Sep-17
	3.58	19.28	6.24	36.16	16.66	0.51	1.4	11.61	0.9	13.3	1,407	17	80	3	0		17.05	-21.9			May-10
	3.69	19.43	6.56	37.29	18.13	0.69	1.1	11.62	0.9	13.46	1,407	17	80	3	0		17.01	-21.76			May-10
	2.28	14.67	1.09	33.47	33.76	0.45	1.68	12.16	0.96	12.11	321.0	2	98	0	0	74	24.32	-23.02			Jan-07
	2.41	14.83	1.34	34.48	35.37	0.69	1.37	12.14	0.96	12.31	321.0	2	98	0	0	74	24.21	-22.86			Jan-07
	0.91	0.78	-2.66	-19.03	-2.28	0	1.38	7.91	45.46	7.68	138.8	72	7	32	-11	0	-5.68				Aug-11
	1.04	0.91	-2.26	-18.38	-1.10	0	1.08	7.91	45.74	7.76	138.8	72	7	32	-11	0	-5.58				Aug-11
	2.86	11.15	3.87	21.43	17.66	0.69	1.07	6.98	0.6	12.55	3,603	10	56	32	1	144	11.08	-13.58			Oct-10
	3.00	11.32	4.25	22.39	19.08	0.91	0.77	6.94	0.6	12.68	3,603	10	56	32	1	144	11.04	-13.45			Oct-10
	0.99	15.50	-5.59	0.94	-32.94	2.08	0.99	16.29	0.97	8.12	681.9	1	99	0	0	64	13.82	-24.25			Jan-07
	0.98	15.67	-5.50	1.50	-32.21	2.32	0.69	16.3	0.97	8.19	681.9	1	99	0	0	64	13.9	-24.22			Jan-07
	5.83	24.97	10.25	77.97	94.54	0	0.87	14.38	1.01	42.09	3,738	1	99	0	0	50	25.46	-17.5			May-95
	5.92	25.14	10.61	79.35	96.82	0	0.57	14.4	1.01	44	3,738	1	99	0	0	50	26.78	-17.43			Mar-04
	0.60	3.20	-2.60	2.89		0	2.16	5.3	0.42	9.97	416.2	52	48	0	0	131					Sep-14
	0.70	3.29	-2.30	3.50		0	1.86	5.3	0.42	10.03	416.2	52	48	0	0	131					Sep-17
	0.00	10.48	-4.20	24.73	-0.80	1.7	0.96	12.36	1.02	15.28	1,484	1	99	0	0	33	13.26	-25.14			Mar-98
	0.06	10.64	-3.90	25.69	0.38	2.09	0.66	12.37	1.02	15.7	1,484	1	99	0	0	33	13.49	-25.2			Mar-04
	5.26	22.81	13.70			0	0.96			13.19	803.8	4	96	0	0	15					Sep-17
	5.32	23.02	14.02			0	0.66			13.25	803.8	4	96	0	0	15					Sep-17
	2.79	13.96	2.62			0	0.89			11.02	202.9	-4	78	26	0						Apr-17
	2.88	14.13	2.89			0	0.54			11.06	202.9	-4	78	26	0						Sep-17
	2.99	12.22	3.97			0	0.87			11.02	151.9	-3	59	44	0						Apr-17
	3.06	12.47	4.33			0	0.52			11.09	151.9	-3	59	44	0						Sep-17
	3.71	18.90	5.78	46.52	51.03	0.9	0.8	13.43	1.07	14.53	1,229	0	100	0	0	6	20.69	-16.6			Sep-96
	3.83	19.21	6.24	47.83	52.94	1.06	0.45	13.44	1.07	15.45	1,229	0	100	0	0	6	20.79	-16.48			Mar-04
	1.55	14.92	-6.27	36.10	32.22	0.35	1.06	18	1.1	8.47	119.2	0	100	0	0						Sep-12
	1.67	15.33	-5.89	37.15	33.25	0.67	0.71	17.97	1.1	8.5	119.2	0	100	0	0						Sep-17
	4.84	22.88	13.29	60.28		0.72	1.03	13.34		15.14	1,770	10	0	85	5	88					Sep-15
	4.97	23.07	13.67	61.24		0.91	0.73	13.37		15.2	1,770	10	0	85	5	88					Sep-17
	2.11	15.98	6.21	22.03	18.25	10.16	1.04	9.17	0.73		29.9	3	97	0	0						Feb-12
	2.17	16.13	6.55	27.69	23.74	10.51	0.74	8.56	0.68		29.9	3	97	0	0						Sep-17
	3.31	15.41	4.96	21.08	24.49	1.11	0.96	10.69	1.24	11.83	155.7	1	99	0	0						Feb-12
	3.31	15.48	5.17	21.63	25.05	1.3	0.66	10.66	1.24	11.86	155.7	1	99	0	0						Sep-17
	4.43	19.33	13.48	20.21	4.92	2.92	1.15	9.3	0.84	15.06	1,028	1	99	0	0	155					Dec-11
	4.48	19.47	13.80	21.02	6.10	3.15	0.85	9.25	0.83	15.15	1,028	1	99	0	0	155					Dec-11
	3.52	14.83	6.02	25.31	5.68	1.46	1.39	9.38	0.78	12.62	1,694	5	66	29	0	55	21.4	-21.43			Sep-09
	3.67	15.14	6.38	26.33	7.01	1.72	1.09	9.4	0.78	12.7	1,694	5	66	29	0	55	21.4	-21.3			Sep-09
	-0.49	7.89	-6.18	23.04	3.52	2.08	1.02	12.84	1.07	9.98	439.8	2	98	0	0	31	17.37	-22.27			Jan-07
	-0.29	8.07	-5.83	24.10	4.86	2.48	0.72	12.89	1.07	10.04	439.8	2	98	0	0	31	17.5	-22.22			Jan-07
	1.08	10.72	0.86	24.79	13.86	0	0.99	10.07	1.05	13.94	1,213	5	75	17	0		16.71	-16.9			Jan-07
	1.15	10.92	1.15	25.42	14.43	0	0.69	10.03	1.05	14.01	1,213	5	75	17	0		16.71	-16.9			Sep-17
	1.58	11.27	5.83	26.74	17.60	4.48	0.93	6.88	0.52	12.14	1,869	5	39	47	0	50	13.04	-11.15			May-06
	1.66	11.51	6.14	27.80	19.01	4.97	0.63	6.94	0.53	11.62	1,869	5	39	47	0	50	13.1	-11.05			May-06
	0.31	14.06	-5.94	26.43	8.86	2.61	1.25	12.81	0.98	9.65	600.1	8	91	0	1	26	13.09	-20.52			Dec-07
	0.41	14.25	-5.63	27.40	10.10	2.81	0.95	12.83	0.98	9.78	600.1	8	91	0	1	26	13.18	-20.41			Dec-07
	3.15	14.15	4.29	25.69	22.33	1.18	1	11.22	0.86	11.45	615.6	8	87	4	0	21	19.65	-17.24			Jan-07
	3.29	14.41	4.73	26.72	23.92	1.51	0.7	11.23	0.86	11.59	615.6	8	87	4	0	21	19.82	-17.24			Jan-07
	7.03	19.66	8.34			0	1.37			10.65	519.8	2	89	0	1	115					Sep-17
	7.10	19.79	8.62			0	1.07			10.71	519.8	2	89	0	1	115					Sep-17

	MARKET		FUND TYPE, CATEGORY & OBJECTIVE		RATINGS					MINIMUMS
Fund Name	Ticker Symbol	Traded On	Fund Type	Category and (Prospectus Objective)	Overall Rating	Reward Rating	Risk Rating	Recent Up/ Downgrade	Open to New Investors	Min Initial Investment
JNL/Harris Oakmark Global Equity Fund Class A			Open End	Global Equity Large Cap (World Stock)	C	C	C+		Y	0
JNL/Harris Oakmark Global Equity Fund Class I			Open End	Global Equity Large Cap (World Stock)	C	C	C+		Y	0
JNL/Heitman U.S. Focused Real Estate Fund Class A			Open End	Real Estate Sector Equity (Real Estate)	U	U	U		Y	0
JNL/Heitman U.S. Focused Real Estate Fund Class I			Open End	Real Estate Sector Equity (Real Estate)	U	U	U		Y	0
JNL/Invesco China-India Fund Class A			Open End	Equity Miscellaneous (Foreign Stock)	C	C-	C		Y	0
JNL/Invesco China-India Fund Class I			Open End	Equity Miscellaneous (Foreign Stock)	C	C-	C		Y	0
JNL/Invesco Diversified Dividend Fund Class A			Open End	US Equity Large Cap Value (Equity-Income)	C-	C-	C+	Up	Y	0
JNL/Invesco Diversified Dividend Fund Class I			Open End	US Equity Large Cap Value (Equity-Income)	C-	C-	B-	Up	Y	0
JNL/Invesco Global Real Estate Fund Class A			Open End	Real Estate Sector Equity (Real Estate)	B-	C	B	Up	Y	0
JNL/Invesco Global Real Estate Fund Class I			Open End	Real Estate Sector Equity (Real Estate)	B-	C	B+	Up	Y	0
JNL/Invesco International Growth Fund Class A			Open End	Global Equity Large Cap (Foreign Stock)	C+	C	B	Up	Y	0
JNL/Invesco International Growth Fund Class I			Open End	Global Equity Large Cap (Foreign Stock)	C+	C	B	Up	Y	0
JNL/Invesco Small Cap Growth Fund Class A			Open End	US Equity Small Cap (Small Company)	C	C	C+		Y	0
JNL/Invesco Small Cap Growth Fund Class I			Open End	US Equity Small Cap (Small Company)	C	C	C+		Y	0
JNL/JPMorgan Global Allocation Fund Class A			Open End	Moderate Alloc (Asset Alloc)	B-	C	B+	Up	Y	0
JNL/JPMorgan Global Allocation Fund Class I			Open End	Moderate Alloc (Asset Alloc)	B-	C	B+	Up	Y	0
JNL/JPMorgan Hedged Equity Fund Class A			Open End	Long/Short Equity (Growth)	U	U	U		Y	0
JNL/JPMorgan Hedged Equity Fund Class I			Open End	Long/Short Equity (Growth)	U	U	U		Y	0
JNL/JPMorgan MidCap Growth Fund Class A			Open End	US Equity Mid Cap (Growth)	B-	B-	B-	Down	Y	0
JNL/JPMorgan MidCap Growth Fund Class I			Open End	US Equity Mid Cap (Growth)	B-	B-	B-	Down	Y	0
JNL/Lazard Emerging Markets Fund Class A			Open End	Global Emerg Mkts (Div Emerging Mkts)	C	C	C+			0
JNL/Lazard Emerging Markets Fund Class I			Open End	Global Emerg Mkts (Div Emerging Mkts)	C	C	C+			0
JNL/Lazard International Strategic Equity Fund			Open End	Global Equity Large Cap (Foreign Stock)	C+	C	B	Up	Y	0
JNL/Lazard International Strategic Equity Fund Class I			Open End	Global Equity Large Cap (Foreign Stock)	C+	C	B	Up	Y	0
JNL/Loomis Sayles Global Growth Fund Class A			Open End	Global Equity Large Cap (Growth)	U	U	U		Y	0
JNL/Loomis Sayles Global Growth Fund Class I			Open End	Global Equity Large Cap (Growth)	U	U	U		Y	0
JNL/Mellon Capital Consumer Discretionary Sector Cls A			Open End	Consumer Goods Sec Equity ()	B-	C+	B		Y	0
JNL/Mellon Capital Consumer Discretionary Sector Cls I			Open End	Consumer Goods Sec Equity ()	B-	C+	B		Y	0
JNL/Mellon Capital Dow Index Fund Class A			Open End	US Equity Large Cap Value (Growth & Income)	B-	C	B+	Down		0
JNL/Mellon Capital Dow Index Fund Class I			Open End	US Equity Large Cap Value (Growth & Income)	B-	C	B+	Down	Y	0
JNL/Mellon Capital Energy Sector Fund Class A			Open End	Energy Sector Equity (Natl Res)	D	D	D+	Down	Y	0
JNL/Mellon Capital Energy Sector Fund Class I			Open End	Energy Sector Equity (Natl Res)	D	D	D+	Down	Y	0
JNL/Mellon Capital Financial Sector Fund Class A			Open End	Financials Sector Equity (Financial)	C+	C	B-	Up	Y	0
JNL/Mellon Capital Financial Sector Fund Class I			Open End	Financials Sector Equity (Financial)	C+	C	B-	Up	Y	0
JNL/Mellon Capital Healthcare Sector Fund Class A			Open End	Healthcare Sector Equity (Health)	B-	C	B		Y	0
JNL/Mellon Capital Healthcare Sector Fund Class I			Open End	Healthcare Sector Equity (Health)	B-	C	B		Y	0
JNL/Mellon Capital Information Technology Sector Cls A			Open End	Technology Sector Equity (Technology)	B-	B-	B-	Down	Y	0
JNL/Mellon Capital Information Technology Sector Cls I			Open End	Technology Sector Equity (Technology)	B-	B-	B-	Down	Y	0
JNL/Mellon Capital MSCI World Index Fund Class A			Open End	Global Equity Large Cap (World Stock)	B-	C	B	Up	Y	0
JNL/Mellon Capital MSCI World Index Fund Class I			Open End	Global Equity Large Cap (World Stock)	B-	C	B	Up	Y	0
JNL/Mellon Capital Nasdaq® 100 Index Fund Class A			Open End	US Equity Large Cap Growth (Growth)	B-	C+	B		Y	0
JNL/Mellon Capital Nasdaq® 100 Index Fund Class I			Open End	US Equity Large Cap Growth (Growth)	B-	C+	B	Down	Y	0
JNL/Mellon Capital Telecommunications Sector Fund Class A			Open End	Communications Sector Equity (Comm)	C	C	C	Down	Y	0
JNL/Mellon Capital Telecommunications Sector Fund Class I			Open End	Communications Sector Equity (Comm)	C	C	C+	Down	Y	0
JNL/Mellon Consumers Staples Sector Fund Class A			Open End	Consumer Goods Sec Equity ()	C-	C-	C	Up	Y	0
JNL/Mellon Consumers Staples Sector Fund Class I			Open End	Consumer Goods Sec Equity ()	C-	C-	C	Up	Y	0
JNL/Mellon Emerging Markets Index Fund Class A			Open End	Global Emerg Mkts (Div Emerging Mkts)	C	C	C+		Y	0
JNL/Mellon Emerging Markets Index Fund Class I			Open End	Global Emerg Mkts (Div Emerging Mkts)	C	C	C+		Y	0
JNL/Mellon Index 5 Fund Class A			Open End	Aggressive Alloc (Growth)	B-	C	B	Up	Y	0
JNL/Mellon Index 5 Fund Class I			Open End	Aggressive Alloc (Growth)	B-	C	B	Up	Y	0
JNL/Mellon Industrials Sector Fund Class A			Open End	Industrials Sector Equity ()	C-	D+	C+	Up	Y	0
JNL/Mellon Industrials Sector Fund Class I			Open End	Industrials Sector Equity ()	C-	D+	C+	Up	Y	0

★ Expanded analysis of this fund is included in Section II.

Min Additional Investment	TOTAL RETURNS 3-Month Total Return	6-Month Total Return	1-Year Total Return	3-Year Total Return	5-Year Total Return	PERFORMANCE Dividend Yield (TTM)	Expense Ratio	3-Yr Std Deviation	3-Year Beta	ASSETS NAV	Total Assets (MIL)	ASSET ALLOCATION & TURNOVER %Cash	%Stocks	%Bonds	%Other	Turnover Ratio	BULL & BEAR Last Bull Market Total Return	Last Bear Market Total Return	FEES Front End Fee (%)	Back End Fee (%)	Inception Date
	4.40	16.24	-3.34	36.81		0.72	1.17	15.72	1.26	10.66	874.7	1	99	0	0	42					Apr-15
	4.39	16.32	-3.06	37.45		0.9	0.87	15.66	1.25	10.69	874.7	1	99	0	0	42					Sep-17
	2.29	19.35					1.11			11.16	184.9	0	100	0	0	94					Aug-18
	2.37	19.55					0.81			11.19	184.9	0	100	0	0	94					Aug-18
	-2.79	8.79	-7.38	36.62	31.40	0.42	1.23	15.5	0.63	9.4	556.5	1	99	0	0	30	9.26	-29.2			Dec-07
	-2.76	8.93	-7.05	37.60	32.89	0.65	0.93	15.55	0.64	9.51	556.5	1	99	0	0	30	9.38	-29.12			Dec-07
	3.10	15.52	8.77			0.39	1			10.94	567.2	8	92	0	0	22					Sep-17
	3.18	15.66	9.05			0.39	0.7			11	567.2	8	92	0	0	22					Sep-17
	0.39	15.81	8.50	14.80	24.05	3.73	1.04	11.16	0.99	10.25	1,344	1	98	0	1	57	24.17	-19.73			May-05
	0.48	16.01	8.82	15.74	25.59	3.96	0.74	11.18	0.99	10.43	1,344	1	98	0	1	57	24.37	-19.67			May-05
	4.94	20.27	8.04	26.79	14.66	1.93	0.98	11.76	0.93	14	1,139	5	95	0	0	38	17.1	-20.01			May-95
	5.03	20.42	8.38	27.82	16.00	2.1	0.68	11.75	0.93	14.8	1,139	5	95	0	0	38	17.12	-19.89			Mar-04
	3.64	21.87	0.11	52.18	54.69	0	1.07	16.87	1.03	25.91	1,994	1	99	0	0	23	28.82	-23.79			Oct-01
	3.72	22.09	0.39	53.41	56.48	0	0.77	16.86	1.03	27.02	1,994	1	99	0	0	23	28.91	-23.76			Mar-04
	2.98	11.82	3.35	22.21	19.54	0.9	1.14	7.56	0.65	11.73	53.4	8	88	3	0	43					Apr-14
	3.06	11.88	3.68	22.92	20.23	1.12	0.84	7.52	0.65	11.77	53.4	8	88	3	0	43					Sep-17
	3.43	7.22					1.01			10.24	259.9	4	96	0	0	12					Aug-18
	3.53	7.43					0.71			10.26	259.9	4	96	0	0	12					Aug-18
	6.62	31.06	16.06	67.13	69.67	0	0.92	15.02	0.99	38.31	2,373	2	98	0	0	56	30.6	-23.81			May-95
	6.69	31.21	16.40	68.42	71.67	0	0.62	15.02	0.99	39.51	2,373	2	98	0	0	56	29.67	-23.77			Mar-04
	2.42	10.71	2.32	24.07	-1.45	1.64	1.24	14.31	0.96	10.13	794.5	5	95	0	0	14	18.85	-23.04			May-06
	2.41	10.79	2.51	24.96	-0.36	2.08	0.94	14.27	0.96	10.16	794.5	5	95	0	0	14	19.04	-23.01			May-06
	3.54	16.04	2.13	31.67	24.01	0.18	1.16	11.2	0.93	13.74	180.1	5	95	0	0						Apr-13
	3.68	16.18	2.42	32.34	24.65	0.37	0.86	11.17	0.92	13.78	180.1	5	95	0	0						Sep-17
	5.27	24.80					1			10.97	299.5	1	99	0	0	9					Aug-18
	5.36	25.00					0.7			11	299.5	1	99	0	0	9					Aug-18
	4.43	20.95	7.72	54.52	76.63	0.6	0.64	14.67	1	24.01	1,299	0	100	0	0		28.81	-12.56			Jul-99
	4.51	21.19	8.05	55.86	78.84	0.85	0.29	14.66	1	24.53	1,299	0	100	0	0		28.98	-12.54			Mar-04
	3.03	16.30	11.46	58.43	66.28	0	0.66	12.36	1	30.53	960.3	2	98	0	0		18.19	-5.38			Jul-99
	3.12	16.54	11.83	59.41	67.32	0	0.31	12.35	1	30.72	960.3	2	98	0	0		18.19	-5.38			Sep-17
	-4.17	12.37	-16.91	-3.99	-33.18	3.33	0.64	21.03	1	22.52	1,178	0	100	0	0		21.73	-25.88			Jul-99
	-4.05	12.55	-16.60	-3.19	-32.33	3.56	0.29	21.03	1	22.95	1,178	0	100	0	0		21.89	-25.82			Mar-04
	7.47	18.38	4.30	54.41	60.57	1.2	0.64	16.9	1	13.52	1,289	0	100	0	0		31.65	-25.23			Jul-99
	7.60	18.58	4.67	55.84	62.66	1.4	0.29	16.86	1	13.59	1,289	0	100	0	0		31.73	-25.13			Mar-04
	1.37	11.13	10.88	38.94	63.22	0.87	0.63	14.13	1	28.74	3,224	0	100	0	0		20.39	-10.61			Jul-99
	1.43	11.30	11.23	40.08	65.16	1.12	0.28	14.13	1	28.94	3,224	0	100	0	0		20.54	-10.54			Mar-04
	5.26	28.07	13.66	97.86	123.09	0.36	0.64	15.96	1	18.98	3,007	0	100	0	0		28.72	-13.31			Jul-99
	5.37	28.35	14.09	99.60	126.02	0.5	0.29	15.96	1	19.42	3,007	0	100	0	0		28.72	-13.28			Mar-04
	3.94	17.73	6.15	36.24	37.53	3.54	0.67	11.59	0.99	25.83	351.3	2	98	0	0		19.32	-21.96			Jul-99
	4.04	17.93	6.53	37.20	38.50	3.75	0.32	11.59	0.99	25.97	351.3	2	98	0	0		19.32	-21.96			Sep-17
	4.07	22.37	9.47	78.24	92.59	0.26	0.67	15.13	1	27.35	2,980	1	99	0	0		22.31	-10.98			Oct-04
	4.16	22.54	9.86	79.65	95.03	0.6	0.32	15.1	1	17.99	2,980	1	99	0	0		22.35	-10.84			Dec-07
	3.96	17.50	17.70	20.10	44.41	3.82	0.68	14.19	0.99	13.36	154.2	0	100	0	0		12.03	-12.53			Jul-99
	4.01	17.78	18.13	21.13	46.21	4.33	0.33	14.2	0.99	12.45	154.2	0	100	0	0		11.75	-12.5			Mar-04
	3.24	15.59	13.70			0	0.7			11.12	86.9	1	99	0	0	45					Sep-17
	3.32	15.73	14.08			0	0.35			11.18	86.9	1	99	0	0	45					Sep-17
	0.46	10.86	0.59	33.57	8.84	1.75	0.74	13.97	1	10.82	1,190	1	99	0	0	13	17.81				Aug-11
	0.55	11.10	0.96	34.77	10.26	1.98	0.44	13.99	1.01	10.91	1,190	1	99	0	0	13	17.92				Aug-11
	3.02	14.33	2.75	31.98	33.63	0	0.62	10.35	1.1	15.31	1,371	2	79	19	0		18.33	-17.03			Apr-07
	3.21	14.57	3.14	32.84	34.50	0	0.32	10.35	1.1	15.41	1,371	2	79	19	0		18.33	-17.03			Sep-17
	4.39	23.69	8.97			0	0.71			11.17	63.4	0	100	0	0	135					Sep-17
	4.46	23.81	9.24			0	0.36			11.23	63.4	0	100	0	0	135					Sep-17

	MARKET		FUND TYPE, CATEGORY & OBJECTIVE		RATINGS				MINIMUMS	
Fund Name	Ticker Symbol	Traded On	Fund Type	Category and (Prospectus Objective)	Overall Rating	Reward Rating	Risk Rating	Recent Up/ Downgrade	Open to New Investors	Min Initial Investment
JNL/Mellon International Index Fund Class A			Open End	Global Equity Large Cap (Foreign Stock)	C	C	B		Y	0
JNL/Mellon International Index Fund Class I			Open End	Global Equity Large Cap (Foreign Stock)	C	C	B		Y	0
JNL/Mellon Materials Sector Fund Class A			Open End	Natl Resources Sec Equity ()	D+	D	C-		Y	0
JNL/Mellon Materials Sector Fund Class I			Open End	Natl Resources Sec Equity ()	D+	D	C-		Y	0
JNL/Mellon MSCI KLD 400 Social Index Fund Class A			Open End	US Equity Large Cap Blend (Growth & Income)	C	C	B-	Up	Y	0
JNL/Mellon MSCI KLD 400 Social Index Fund Class I			Open End	US Equity Large Cap Blend (Growth & Income)	C	C-	B	Up	Y	0
JNL/Mellon Real Estate Sector Fund Class A			Open End	Real Estate Sector Equity (Real Estate)	C-	C	C+	Up	Y	0
JNL/Mellon Real Estate Sector Fund Class I			Open End	Real Estate Sector Equity (Real Estate)	C-	C	C+	Up	Y	0
JNL/Mellon S&P 1500 Growth Index Fund Class A			Open End	US Equity Large Cap Growth (Growth)	C-	C-	B-	Up	Y	0
JNL/Mellon S&P 1500 Growth Index Fund Class I			Open End	US Equity Large Cap Growth (Growth)	C-	C-	B	Up	Y	0
JNL/Mellon S&P 1500 Value Index Fund Class A			Open End	US Equity Large Cap Value (Growth)	C-	D+	C+	Up	Y	0
JNL/Mellon S&P 1500 Value Index Fund Class I			Open End	US Equity Large Cap Value (Growth)	C-	D+	C+	Up	Y	0
JNL/Mellon S&P 400 MidCap Index Fund Class A			Open End	US Equity Mid Cap (Growth)	C+	C	B-	Up	Y	0
JNL/Mellon S&P 400 MidCap Index Fund Class I			Open End	US Equity Mid Cap (Growth)	C+	C	B-	Up	Y	0
JNL/Mellon S&P 500 Index Fund Class A			Open End	US Equity Large Cap Blend (Growth)	B-	C	B		Y	0
JNL/Mellon S&P 500 Index Fund Class I			Open End	US Equity Large Cap Blend (Growth)	B-	C	B		Y	0
JNL/Mellon Small Cap Index Fund Class A			Open End	US Equity Small Cap (Small Company)	C	C-	C+		Y	0
JNL/Mellon Small Cap Index Fund Class I			Open End	US Equity Small Cap (Small Company)	C	C-	C+	Down	Y	0
JNL/Mellon Utilities Sector Fund Class A			Open End	Utilities Sector Equity (Utility)	B	B	B		Y	0
JNL/Mellon Utilities Sector Fund Class I			Open End	Utilities Sector Equity (Utility)	B	B	B		Y	0
JNL/MFS Mid Cap Value Fund Class A			Open End	US Equity Mid Cap (Growth)	C+	C	B	Up	Y	0
JNL/MFS Mid Cap Value Fund Class I			Open End	US Equity Mid Cap (Growth)	C+	C	B	Up	Y	0
JNL/Morningstar Wide Moat Index Fund Class A			Open End	US Equity Large Cap Blend (Growth & Income)	U	U	U		Y	0
JNL/Morningstar Wide Moat Index Fund Class I			Open End	US Equity Large Cap Blend (Growth & Income)	U	U	U		Y	0
JNL/Neuberger Berman Commodity Strategy Fund			Open End	Commodities Broad Basket (Income)	C-	C-	C	Down	Y	0
JNL/Neuberger Berman Commodity Strategy Fund Class I			Open End	Commodities Broad Basket (Income)	C-	C-	C	Down	Y	0
JNL/Nicholas Convertible Arbitrage Fund Class A			Open End	Market Neutral (Convertible Bond)	B	C	A		Y	0
JNL/Nicholas Convertible Arbitrage Fund Class I			Open End	Market Neutral (Convertible Bond)	B-	C+	B+		Y	0
JNL/Oppenheimer Emerging Markets Innovator Fund Class A			Open End	Global Emerg Mkts (Div Emerging Mkts)	C	C-	C	Up	Y	0
JNL/Oppenheimer Emerging Markets Innovator Fund Class I			Open End	Global Emerg Mkts (Div Emerging Mkts)	C	C-	C	Up	Y	0
JNL/Oppenheimer Global Growth Fund Class A			Open End	Global Equity Large Cap (World Stock)	C+	C	B-	Up	Y	0
JNL/Oppenheimer Global Growth Fund Class I			Open End	Global Equity Large Cap (World Stock)	C+	C	B-	Up	Y	0
JNL/PPM America Mid Cap Value Fund Class A			Open End	US Equity Mid Cap (Growth)	C-	D+	C	Down	Y	0
JNL/PPM America Mid Cap Value Fund Class I			Open End	US Equity Mid Cap (Growth)	C-	D+	C	Down	Y	0
JNL/PPM America Small Cap Value Fund Class A			Open End	US Equity Small Cap (Small Company)	C	C-	C			0
JNL/PPM America Small Cap Value Fund Class I			Open End	US Equity Small Cap (Small Company)	C	C-	C			0
JNL/PPM America Value Equity Fund Class A			Open End	US Equity Large Cap Value (Growth)	C	C-	C+		Y	0
JNL/PPM America Value Equity Fund Class I			Open End	US Equity Large Cap Value (Growth)	C	C-	C+		Y	0
JNL/RAFI Fundamental US Small Cap Fund Class A			Open End	US Equity Small Cap (Growth)	D	D	D+	Down	Y	0
JNL/RAFI Fundamental US Small Cap Fund Class I			Open End	US Equity Small Cap (Growth)	D	D	D+	Down	Y	0
JNL/RAFI Multi-Factor U.S. Equity Fund Class A			Open End	US Equity Large Cap Value (Growth & Income)	C	C	B-		Y	0
JNL/RAFI Multi-Factor U.S. Equity Fund Class I			Open End	US Equity Large Cap Value (Growth & Income)	C	C	B-		Y	0
JNL/RAFI® Fundamental Asia Developed Fund Class A			Open End	Asia Equity (Growth)	C	C	B		Y	0
JNL/RAFI® Fundamental Asia Developed Fund Class I			Open End	Asia Equity (Growth)	C	C	B		Y	0
JNL/RAFI® Fundamental Europe Fund Class A			Open End	Europe Equity Large Cap (Growth)	C	C-	B-		Y	0
JNL/RAFI® Fundamental Europe Fund Class I			Open End	Europe Equity Large Cap (Growth)	C	C-	B		Y	0
JNL/S&P 4 Fund Class A			Open End	US Equity Large Cap Value (Growth)	B-	C	B	Up	Y	0
JNL/S&P 4 Fund Class I			Open End	US Equity Large Cap Value (Growth)	B-	C	B	Up	Y	0
JNL/S&P Competitive Advantage Fund Class A			Open End	US Equity Large Cap Growth (Growth)	C+	C	B	Down	Y	0
JNL/S&P Competitive Advantage Fund Class I			Open End	US Equity Large Cap Growth (Growth)	C+	C	B	Down	Y	0
JNL/S&P Dividend Income & Growth Fund Class A			Open End	US Equity Large Cap Value (Growth)	B-	C	B+		Y	0
JNL/S&P Dividend Income & Growth Fund Class I			Open End	US Equity Large Cap Value (Growth)	B-	C	B+		Y	0

★ Expanded analysis of this fund is included in Section II.

	TOTAL RETURNS					PERFORMANCE				ASSETS		ASSET ALLOCATION & TURNOVER					BULL & BEAR		FEES		
Min Additional Investment	3-Month Total Return	6-Month Total Return	1-Year Total Return	3-Year Total Return	5-Year Total Return	Dividend Yield (TTM)	Expense Ratio	3-Yr Std Deviation	3-Year Beta	NAV	Total Assets (MIL)	%Cash	%Stocks	%Bonds	%Other	Turnover Ratio	Last Bull Market Total Return	Last Bear Market Total Return	Front End Fee (%)	Back End Fee (%)	Inception Date
	3.58	14.40	0.80	29.60	9.70	3.47	0.63	10.95	0.98	13.58	1,778	0	100	0	0	2	13.11	-23.39			Jan-02
	3.64	14.51	1.10	30.62	10.93	3.62	0.33	10.92	0.98	14.2	1,778	0	100	0	0	2	13.2	-23.25			Mar-04
	4.65	17.53	-1.65			0	0.72			10.12	22.5	0	100	0	0	182					Sep-17
	4.62	17.57	-1.35			0	0.37			10.17	22.5	0	100	0	0	182					Sep-17
	3.91	19.31	9.63			0.01	0.75			12.48	45.4	0	100	0	0	15					Apr-17
	3.98	19.58	9.99			0.02	0.4			12.52	45.4	0	100	0	0	15					Sep-17
	1.49	19.02	11.42			0	0.68			11.51	129.6	2	98	0	0	61					Sep-17
	1.58	19.23	11.29			0	0.33			11.53	129.6	2	98	0	0	61					Sep-17
	4.18	20.85	10.73			0	0.67			12.69	108.0	0	100	0	0	117					Sep-17
	4.33	21.15	11.14			0	0.32			12.77	108.0	0	100	0	0	117					Sep-17
	3.61	17.17	6.67			0	0.67			11.19	59.4	0	100	0	0	100					Sep-17
	3.69	17.32	7.04			0	0.32			11.24	59.4	0	100	0	0	100					Sep-17
	2.93	18.90	0.84	36.85	43.98	0.87	0.56	15.17	1	21.07	3,116	1	99	0	0	16	27.55	-22.7			Jan-02
	3.01	19.07	1.16	37.90	45.29	1.07	0.26	15.13	1	21.54	3,116	1	99	0	0	16	27.65	-22.58			Mar-04
	4.15	19.24	9.84	48.61	61.93	1.3	0.53	12.19	1	23.05	8,414	2	98	0	0	4	24.57	-16.4			Jan-02
	4.27	19.47	10.25	49.74	63.60	1.46	0.23	12.21	1	23.68	8,414	2	98	0	0	4	24.79	-16.35			Mar-04
	1.74	14.04	-5.35	41.30	42.61	0.89	0.56	17.88	1	18.11	2,479	0	100	0	0	34	27.51	-25.14			Jan-02
	1.81	14.18	-5.11	42.40	44.20	1.1	0.26	17.88	1	18.51	2,479	0	100	0	0	34	27.7	-25.07			Mar-04
	3.20	14.42	17.42	28.04	58.03	1.77	0.69	10.53	1	15.15	241.9	4	96	0	0	42					Apr-13
	3.25	14.69	17.88	28.84	59.01	1.92	0.34	10.54	1	15.22	241.9	4	96	0	0	42					Sep-17
	4.59	20.94	5.60	33.12	29.25	0.43	0.96	13.41	1.04	12.07	1,362	1	99	0	0	40	23.65	-22.1			May-05
	4.72	21.19	5.92	34.15	30.88	0.58	0.66	13.4	1.04	12.18	1,362	1	99	0	0	40	23.84	-22.06			May-05
	3.04	17.46					0.77			10.83	543.6	0	100	0	0	40					Aug-18
	3.22	17.76					0.47			10.87	543.6	0	100	0	0	40					Aug-18
	0.46	8.07	-5.83	1.46	-34.36	0.34	0.93	8.99	0.94	10.84	112.1	21	0	67	12						Apr-14
	0.55	8.25	-5.56	2.01	-34.00	0.52	0.63	9.01	0.94	10.88	112.1	21	0	67	12						Sep-17
	1.83	5.83	4.82	13.42	8.10	2.04	1.35	2.1	2.66	10.52	152.0	43	-42	0	0						Feb-12
	1.94	5.95	5.08	14.04	8.69	2.75	1.05	2.09	2.56	10.5	152.0	43	-42	0	0						Sep-17
	-0.49	13.85	-7.58	22.58		0	1.46	14.39	0.95	10.11	499.4	6	94	0	0	34					Apr-15
	-0.49	13.96	-7.34	23.22		0.36	1.16	14.38	0.95	10.12	499.4	6	94	0	0	34					Sep-17
	3.89	22.30	3.24	57.17	45.23	0.63	0.95	14.02	1.21	18.92	2,568	2	98	0	0	19	17.44	-22.68			May-01
	3.98	22.47	3.57	58.39	46.94	0.85	0.65	14.03	1.21	19.29	2,568	2	98	0	0	19	17.59	-22.6			Mar-04
	-0.15	13.56	-7.56	22.74	23.14	1	0.97	18.57	1.42	12.64	580.4	1	99	0	0	29	32.61	-30.13			Mar-08
	-0.07	13.71	-7.27	23.74	24.56	1.28	0.67	18.59	1.42	12.77	580.4	1	99	0	0	29	32.73	-29.99			Mar-08
	0.67	15.95	-7.39	31.18	37.04	0.74	0.95	20.9	1.1	11.99	575.7	0	100	0	0	35	32.57	-31.95			Mar-08
	0.73	16.12	-7.16	32.17	41.29	0.99	0.65	20.9	1.1	12.39	575.7	0	100	0	0	35	32.7	-31.86			Mar-08
	0.85	12.49	-2.82	31.32	27.50	1.73	0.86	15.64	1.17	22.5	194.7	1	99	0	0	24	30.64	-24.19			May-95
	0.93	12.65	-2.55	32.32	29.13	1.97	0.56	15.64	1.17	22.7	194.7	1	99	0	0	24	30.85	-24.1			Mar-04
	-4.71	6.59	-19.60	-1.85	-0.22	3.33	0.67	19.82	1.18	5.76	433.6	0	100	0	0		34.42	-30.42			Apr-07
	-4.78	6.80	-19.32	-1.07	1.03	4.05	0.32	19.79	1.18	5.6	433.6	0	100	0	0		34.46	-30.34			Apr-07
	0.09	11.79	-1.25	27.26	34.37	5.08	0.66	11.79	0.91	13.2	2,803	0	100	0	0		25.66	-20.34			Oct-04
	0.10	11.84	-1.03	28.19	35.88	5.7	0.36	11.73	0.91	13.21	2,803	0	100	0	0		25.84	-20.27			Oct-04
	1.03	9.85	2.24	30.21	25.12	4.77	0.68	9.2		14.6	234.3	0	100	0	0	95	10.02	-6.21			Oct-08
	1.09	9.97	2.49	31.11	26.52	4.97	0.38	9.15		14.78	234.3	0	100	0	0	95	10.15	-6.11			Oct-08
	0.25	8.61	-0.18	18.07	-3.63	3.57	0.68	13.76		11.98	337.2	0	100	0	0	68	8.51	-23.62			Oct-08
	0.33	8.69	0.07	19.05	-2.53	3.78	0.38	13.8		12.12	337.2	0	100	0	0	68	8.63	-23.53			Oct-08
	1.48	15.24	4.04	34.70	40.04	0	0.71	14.02	1.07	21.85	6,353	0	100	0	0		22.83	-13.64			Dec-07
	1.57	15.44	4.37	35.45	40.80	0	0.41	14.02	1.07	21.97	6,353	0	100	0	0		22.83	-13.64			Sep-17
	-0.27	17.16	7.52	48.72	60.06	0.84	0.66	14.54	1.08	17.95	2,557	0	100	0	0	43	28.7	-9.97			Dec-07
	-0.16	17.33	7.85	49.90	61.99	1.31	0.36	14.5	1.08	18.07	2,557	0	100	0	0	43	28.83	-9.96			Dec-07
	4.31	18.10	11.65	31.60	54.42	2.85	0.65	11.49	0.89	15.72	5,049	0	100	0	0	48	22.32	-7.94			Dec-07
	4.44	18.28	12.00	32.60	56.16	3.12	0.35	11.52	0.89	15.98	5,049	0	100	0	0	48	22.5	-7.82			Dec-07

	MARKET		FUND TYPE, CATEGORY & OBJECTIVE		RATINGS				MINIMUMS	
Fund Name	Ticker Symbol	Traded On	Fund Type	Category and (Prospectus Objective)	Overall Rating	Reward Rating	Risk Rating	Recent Up/ Downgrade	Open to New Investors	Min Initial Investment
JNL/S&P International 5 Fund Class A			Open End	Global Equity Large Cap (World Stock)	C	C	B-		Y	0
JNL/S&P International 5 Fund Class I			Open End	Global Equity Large Cap (World Stock)	C	C	B-		Y	0
JNL/S&P Intrinsic Value Fund Class A			Open End	US Equity Large Cap Value (Growth)	C	C	B-	Down	Y	0
JNL/S&P Intrinsic Value Fund Class I			Open End	US Equity Large Cap Value (Growth)	C	C	B-	Down	Y	0
JNL/S&P Managed Aggressive Growth Fund Class A			Open End	Aggressive Alloc (Aggr Growth)	B-	C	B	Up	Y	0
JNL/S&P Managed Aggressive Growth Fund Class I			Open End	Aggressive Alloc (Aggr Growth)	B-	C	B	Up	Y	0
JNL/S&P Managed Conservative Fund Class A			Open End	Cautious Alloc (Income)	B	C	A-	Up	Y	0
JNL/S&P Managed Conservative Fund Class I			Open End	Cautious Alloc (Income)	B	C+	A-		Y	0
JNL/S&P Managed Growth Fund Class A			Open End	Aggressive Alloc (Growth)	B-	C	B+	Up	Y	0
JNL/S&P Managed Growth Fund Class I			Open End	Aggressive Alloc (Growth)	B-	C	B+	Up	Y	0
JNL/S&P Managed Moderate Fund Class A			Open End	Cautious Alloc (Growth & Income)	B	C	A	Up	Y	0
JNL/S&P Managed Moderate Fund Class I			Open End	Cautious Alloc (Growth & Income)	B	C+	A		Y	0
JNL/S&P Managed Moderate Growth Fund Class A			Open End	Moderate Alloc (Growth & Income)	B-	C	A-		Y	0
JNL/S&P Managed Moderate Growth Fund Class I			Open End	Moderate Alloc (Growth & Income)	B	C	A-	Up	Y	0
JNL/S&P Mid 3 Fund Class A			Open End	US Equity Mid Cap (Growth)	C	D+	C		Y	0
JNL/S&P MID 3 Fund Class I			Open End	US Equity Mid Cap (Growth)	C	D+	C		Y	0
JNL/S&P Total Yield Fund Class A			Open End	US Equity Large Cap Value (Growth)	C	C	B-		Y	0
JNL/S&P Total Yield Fund Class I			Open End	US Equity Large Cap Value (Growth)	C	C	B-		Y	0
JNL/T. Rowe Price Capital Appreciation Fund			Open End	Moderate Alloc (Growth)	B	B-	A		Y	0
JNL/T. Rowe Price Capital Appreciation Fund Class I			Open End	Moderate Alloc (Growth)	B	B-	A	Down	Y	0
JNL/T. Rowe Price Established Growth Fund Class A			Open End	US Equity Large Cap Growth (Growth)	B-	C	B	Down	Y	0
JNL/T. Rowe Price Established Growth Fund Class I			Open End	US Equity Large Cap Growth (Growth)	B-	C+	B	Down	Y	0
JNL/T. Rowe Price Managed Volatility Balanced A			Open End	Moderate Alloc (Growth)	B-	C	B+	Up	Y	0
JNL/T. Rowe Price Managed Volatility Balanced I			Open End	Moderate Alloc (Growth)	B-	C	B+	Up	Y	0
JNL/T. Rowe Price Mid-Cap Growth Fund Class A			Open End	US Equity Mid Cap (Growth)	B-	C+	B	Down	Y	0
JNL/T. Rowe Price Mid-Cap Growth Fund Class I			Open End	US Equity Mid Cap (Growth)	B-	C+	B	Down	Y	0
JNL/T. Rowe Price Value Fund Class A			Open End	US Equity Large Cap Value (Growth)	B-	C	B	Up	Y	0
JNL/T. Rowe Price Value Fund Class I			Open End	US Equity Large Cap Value (Growth)	B-	C	B	Up	Y	0
JNL/The London Company Focused U.S. Equity Fund			Open End	US Equity Large Cap Blend (Growth & Income)	C+	C	B	Down	Y	0
JNL/The London Company Focused U.S. Equity Fund Class I			Open End	US Equity Large Cap Blend (Growth & Income)	C+	C	B	Down	Y	0
JNL/The PIMCO Investment Grade Credit Bond Fund Class A			Open End	US Equity Large Cap Value (Growth & Income)	C+	C	B	Up	Y	0
JNL/The PIMCO Investment Grade Credit Bond Fund Class I			Open End	US Equity Large Cap Value (Growth & Income)	C+	C	B	Up	Y	0
JNL/VanEck International Gold Fund Class A			Open End	Precious Metals Sector Equity (Precious Metals)	D+	D	C-	Down	Y	0
JNL/VanEck International Gold Fund Class I			Open End	Precious Metals Sector Equity (Precious Metals)	D+	D	C-	Down	Y	0
JNL/Vanguard Capital Growth Fund Class A			Open End	US Equity Large Cap Growth (Growth)	B-	C	B	Up	Y	0
JNL/Vanguard Capital Growth Fund Class I			Open End	US Equity Large Cap Growth (Growth)	B-	C	B		Y	0
JNL/Vanguard Equity Income Fund Class A			Open End	US Equity Large Cap Value (Equity-Income)	B-	C	B+		Y	0
JNL/Vanguard Equity Income Fund Class I			Open End	US Equity Large Cap Value (Equity-Income)	B-	C	B+		Y	0
JNL/Vanguard Growth ETF Allocation A			Open End	Aggressive Alloc (Multi-Asset Global)	C-	D+	B-	Up	Y	0
JNL/Vanguard Growth ETF Allocation I			Open End	Aggressive Alloc (Multi-Asset Global)	C-	D+	B-	Up	Y	0
JNL/Vanguard International Fund Class A			Open End	Global Equity Large Cap (Foreign Stock)	C	C	C+		Y	0
JNL/Vanguard International Fund Class I			Open End	Global Equity Large Cap (Foreign Stock)	C	C	C+		Y	0
JNL/Vanguard International Stock Market Index Fund Class A			Open End	Global Equity Large Cap (Foreign Stock)	D+	D	C	Up	Y	0
JNL/Vanguard International Stock Market Index Fund Class I			Open End	Global Equity Large Cap (Foreign Stock)	D+	D	C	Up	Y	0
JNL/Vanguard Moderate ETF Allocation A			Open End	Cautious Alloc (Growth)	C-	D+	B-	Up	Y	0
JNL/Vanguard Moderate ETF Allocation I			Open End	Cautious Alloc (Growth)	C-	D+	B-	Up	Y	0
JNL/Vanguard Moderate Growth ETF Allocation A			Open End	Moderate Alloc (Growth)	C-	D+	B-	Up	Y	0
JNL/Vanguard Moderate Growth ETF Allocation I			Open End	Moderate Alloc (Growth)	C-	D+	B-	Up	Y	0
JNL/Vanguard Small Company Growth Fund Class A			Open End	US Equity Small Cap (Small Company)	C+	C	C+			0
JNL/Vanguard Small Company Growth Fund Class I			Open End	US Equity Small Cap (Small Company)	C+	C	C+			0
JNL/Vanguard U.S. Stock Market Index Fund Class A			Open End	US Equity Large Cap Blend (Growth)	C-	C-	B	Up	Y	0
JNL/Vanguard U.S. Stock Market Index Fund Class I			Open End	US Equity Large Cap Blend (Growth)	C-	C-	B	Up	Y	0

★ Expanded analysis of this fund is included in Section II.

	TOTAL RETURNS					PERFORMANCE				ASSETS		ASSET ALLOCATION & TURNOVER					BULL & BEAR		FEES		
Min Additional Investment	3-Month Total Return	6-Month Total Return	1-Year Total Return	3-Year Total Return	5-Year Total Return	Dividend Yield (TTM)	Expense Ratio	3-Yr Std Deviation	3-Year Beta	NAV	Total Assets (MIL)	%Cash	%Stocks	%Bonds	%Other	Turnover Ratio	Last Bull Market Total Return	Last Bear Market Total Return	Front End Fee (%)	Back End Fee (%)	Inception Date
	0.59	10.64	-3.30	37.46		6.02	0.76	12.18	1.01	10.08	53.3	1	99	0	0	72					Sep-14
	0.69	10.86	-2.95	38.09		6.34	0.41	12.11	1	10.1	53.3	1	99	0	0	72					Sep-17
	-0.68	11.11	-2.72	35.75	24.69	1.59	0.66	16.38	1.17	14.49	2,354	0	100	0	0	64	15.69	-12.58			Dec-07
	-0.60	11.22	-2.44	36.69	26.05	2.12	0.36	16.36	1.17	14.76	2,354	0	100	0	0	64	15.75	-12.47			Dec-07
	4.38	19.26	7.44	46.47	45.66	0	1.11	10.98	1	24.52	2,272	4	88	8	0		21.57	-19.51			Apr-98
	4.44	19.42	7.78	47.25	46.44	0	0.81	10.98	1	24.65	2,272	4	88	8	0		21.57	-19.51			Sep-17
	2.68	8.33	5.90	15.39	15.99	0	1.11	3.3	0.97	14.17	1,272	7	19	72	0		8	-3.67			Oct-04
	2.74	8.47	6.28	15.71	16.32	0	0.81	3.31	0.97	14.21	1,272	7	19	72	0		8	-3.67			Sep-17
	4.06	17.59	7.19	42.21	41.38	0	1.11	9.97	1.09	20.72	5,416	4	78	18	0		19.78	-17.18			Apr-98
	4.15	17.81	7.53	42.96	42.13	0	0.81	9.97	1.09	20.83	5,416	4	78	18	0		19.79	-17.19			Sep-17
	3.00	10.91	6.26	23.66	23.45	0	1.11	5.33	1.08	16.46	2,974	7	39	53	0		11.69	-8.18			Oct-04
	3.11	11.07	6.56	24.34	24.13	0	0.81	5.35	1.09	16.55	2,974	7	39	53	0		11.69	-8.18			Sep-17
	3.33	13.86	6.24	31.91	30.85	0	1.1	7.62	1.1	18.89	5,832	6	58	35	0		15.7	-12.71			Apr-98
	3.48	14.04	6.62	32.68	31.61	0	0.8	7.64	1.1	19	5,832	6	58	35	0		15.7	-12.71			Sep-17
	-1.24	11.78	-7.59	20.93	18.93	1.75	0.71	16.66	1.05	11.86	226.0	0	100	0	0	135					Apr-14
	-1.16	11.94	-7.30	21.94	20.42	2.03	0.36	16.67	1.05	11.9	226.0	0	100	0	0	135					Apr-14
	2.46	14.76	0.28	23.72	23.71	1.26	0.66	15.4	1.15	13.29	2,035	1	99	0	0	83	25.11	-23.57			Dec-07
	2.60	14.94	0.62	24.72	25.18	2.07	0.36	15.35	1.14	13.38	2,035	1	99	0	0	83	25.31	-23.5			Dec-07
	4.76	17.91	14.88	39.86	59.43	0.51	1	7.51	0.58	16.26	4,959	10	60	26	0						Sep-13
	4.88	18.08	15.22	40.55	60.22	0.62	0.7	7.52	0.58	16.32	4,959	10	60	26	0						Sep-17
	3.71	21.57	8.16	72.20	88.63	0.07	0.83	14	0.99	45.76	9,825	1	98	0	0	44	30.88	-16.54			May-95
	3.80	21.77	8.50	73.55	90.86	0.22	0.53	14.01	0.99	47.42	9,825	1	98	0	0	44	30.98	-16.46			Mar-04
	3.43	15.00	6.30	27.00	21.75	0	1.01	8.95	1.28	12.65	518.0	11	59	30	0	216					Apr-14
	3.58	15.32	6.62	27.71	22.42	0	0.71	8.99	1.29	12.72	518.0	11	59	30	0	216					Sep-17
	6.83	25.65	15.59	59.93	81.60	0	1	12.93	0.85	52.99	6,233	6	94	0	0	29	25	-20.25			May-95
	6.91	25.82	15.90	61.17	83.70	0	0.7	12.92	0.85	55.69	6,233	6	94	0	0	29	25.1	-20.15			Mar-04
	4.65	18.70	8.83	39.54	42.69	1.15	0.88	11.17	0.94	16.18	4,398	1	98	0	0	141	24.79	-20.6			May-00
	4.75	18.83	9.16	40.53	44.40	1.49	0.58	11.17	0.94	16.97	4,398	1	98	0	0	141	24.92	-20.49			Mar-04
	0.51	12.72	0.75	32.90	35.88	0.07	1.05	12.49	0.95	13.64	64.6	3	97	0	0						Sep-13
	0.59	12.89	1.07	33.67	36.66	1.05	0.75	12.55	0.95	13.57	64.6	3	97	0	0						Sep-17
	5.31	17.52	5.68	42.78	48.77	1.04	0.91	13.8	1.05	16.63	356.3	1	99	0	0						Feb-12
	5.42	17.68	6.04	43.60	49.64	1.2	0.61	13.79	1.04	16.7	356.3	1	99	0	0						Sep-17
	15.47	24.84	9.81	-8.36	-6.46	5	1.16	26.25	1	10	60.4	0	100	0	0						Sep-12
	15.53	25.18	10.36	-7.71	-5.79	5.23	0.86	26.25	1	10.04	60.4	0	100	0	0						Sep-17
	1.88	12.92	5.41	59.29	68.72	0	0.92	13.48	1.06	11.88	348.6	9	91	0	0		19.48	-17.8			Sep-17
	1.87	12.94	5.75	60.83	71.37	0	0.62	13.51	1.06	11.95	348.6	9	91	0	0		19.69	-17.7			Sep-17
	2.89	14.84	8.28	35.21	46.96	0	0.87	10.72	0.98	11.37	282.4	6	94	0	0		22.8	-12.52			Sep-17
	2.97	14.97	8.64	36.55	49.30	0	0.57	10.7	0.98	11.44	282.4	6	94	0	0		23.01	-12.41			Sep-17
	2.97	15.19	5.42			0	0.67			11.07	349.7	2	79	19	0	11					Sep-17
	3.14	15.40	5.98			0	0.25			11.16	349.7	2	79	19	0	11					Sep-17
	3.10	18.79	-0.84	51.71	31.76	0	0.95	15.49	1.27	10.62	586.4	8	92	0	0		19.1	-25.78			Sep-17
	3.19	18.95	-0.55	53.14	33.80	0	0.65	15.46	1.27	10.67	586.4	8	92	0	0		19.31	-25.69			Sep-17
	2.45	13.46	0.00			0	0.68			10.03	301.0	2	98	0	0						Sep-17
	2.64	13.64	0.29			0	0.38			10.08	301.0	2	98	0	0						Sep-17
	2.96	10.79	6.41			0	0.67			10.78	228.4	3	40	57	0	17					Sep-17
	3.03	11.04	6.88			0	0.25			10.86	228.4	3	40	57	0	17					Sep-17
	3.01	13.16	6.01			0	0.66			10.92	321.6	3	59	37	0	9					Sep-17
	3.09	13.28	6.38			0	0.24			11	321.6	3	59	37	0	9					Sep-17
	1.54	20.75	0.76	54.76	54.09	0	1	16.83	1.03	11.81	314.0	4	96	0	0		27.66	-22.07			Sep-17
	1.53	20.87	1.02	56.13	56.38	0	0.7	16.79	1.02	11.87	314.0	4	96	0	0		27.88	-21.97			Sep-17
	3.91	19.50	8.43			0	0.59			11.95	421.0	1	99	0	0						Sep-17
	4.06	19.70	8.77			0	0.29			12.03	421.0	1	99	0	0						Sep-17

	MARKET		FUND TYPE, CATEGORY & OBJECTIVE		RATINGS				MINIMUMS	
Fund Name	Ticker Symbol	Traded On	Fund Type	Category and (Prospectus Objective)	Overall Rating	Reward Rating	Risk Rating	Recent Up/ Downgrade	Open to New Investors	Min Initial Investment
JNL/WCM Focused International Equity Fund			Open End	Global Equity Large Cap (Foreign Stock)	B-	C+	B	Up	Y	0
JNL/WCM Focused International Equity Fund Class I			Open End	Global Equity Large Cap (Foreign Stock)	B-	C+	B	Up	Y	0
JNL/Westchester Capital Event Driven Fund Class A			Open End	Multialternative (Growth)	B	C+	A+		Y	0
JNL/Westchester Capital Event Driven Fund Class I			Open End	Multialternative (Growth)	B	C+	A+		Y	0
JNL/WMC Balanced Fund Class A			Open End	Moderate Alloc (Balanced)	B	C+	A-		Y	0
JNL/WMC Balanced Fund Class I			Open End	Moderate Alloc (Balanced)	B	C+	A-		Y	0
JNL/WMC Value Fund Class A			Open End	US Equity Large Cap Value (Growth)	C+	C	B	Up	Y	0
JNL/WMC Value Fund Class I			Open End	US Equity Large Cap Value (Growth)	C+	C	B	Up	Y	0
JOHCM Asia Ex-Japan Equity Fund Class I	JOAIX	NAS CM	Open End	Asia ex-Japan Equity (Pacific Stock)	C-	D+	C	Down	Y	0
JOHCM Asia Ex-Japan Equity Fund Class II	JOAAX	NAS CM	Open End	Asia ex-Japan Equity (Pacific Stock)	C-	D+	C	Down	Y	0
JOHCM Asia Ex-Japan Equity Fund Institutional Shares	JOAMX	NAS CM	Open End	Asia ex-Japan Equity (Pacific Stock)	C-	D+	C	Down	Y	1,000,000
JOHCM Emerging Markets Opportunities Fund Class I	JOEIX	NAS CM	Open End	Global Emerg Mkts (Div Emerging Mkts)	C	C	B-		Y	0
JOHCM Emerging Markets Opportunities Fund Class II Shares	JOEAX	NAS CM	Open End	Global Emerg Mkts (Div Emerging Mkts)	C	C	B-		Y	0
JOHCM Emerging Markets Opportunities Institutional Shares	JOEMX	NAS CM	Open End	Global Emerg Mkts (Div Emerging Mkts)	C	C	B-		Y	1,000,000
JOHCM Emerging Markets Small Mid Cap Equity Fund Class I	JOMEX	NAS CM	Open End	Global Emerg Mkts (Div Emerging Mkts)	C	C	C	Up	Y	0
JOHCM Emerging Mkts Small Mid Cap Equity Cls Inst Shares	JOMMX	NAS CM	Open End	Global Emerg Mkts (Div Emerging Mkts)	C	C	C		Y	1,000,000
JOHCM Global Equity Fund Class I	JOGEX	NAS CM	Open End	Global Equity Large Cap (World Stock)	C+	C	B	Up	Y	0
JOHCM Global Equity Fund Institutional Shares	JOGIX	NAS CM	Open End	Global Equity Large Cap (World Stock)	C+	C	B	Up	Y	1,000,000
JOHCM Global Income Builder Fund Class I Shares	JOFIX	NAS CM	Open End	Flexible Alloc (Multi-Asset Global)	D+	D+	B-	Up	Y	0
JOHCM Global Income Builder Fund Institutional Shares	JOBIX	NAS CM	Open End	Flexible Alloc (Multi-Asset Global)	D+	D+	B-	Up	Y	1,000,000
JOHCM International Opportunities Institutional Shares	JOPSX	NAS CM	Open End	Global Equity Large Cap (Foreign Stock)	C+	C	B	Up	Y	1,000,000
JOHCM International Select Fund Class I Shares	JOHIX	NAS CM	Open End	Global Equity Large Cap (Foreign Stock)	C	C	B			0
JOHCM International Select Fund Class II Shares	JOHAX	NAS CM	Open End	Global Equity Large Cap (Foreign Stock)	C	C	B			0
JOHCM International Small Cap Equity Fund Class I	JOISX	NAS CM	Open End	Global Equity Mid/Small Cap (Small Company)	C	C	C	Up	Y	0
JOHCM International Small Cap Equity Fund Class II	JOSAX	NAS CM	Open End	Global Equity Mid/Small Cap (Small Company)	C	C-	C	Up	Y	0
JOHCM International Small Cap Equity Institutional Shares	JOSMX	NAS CM	Open End	Global Equity Mid/Small Cap (Small Company)	C	C	C		Y	1,000,000
JOHCM US Small Mid Cap Equity Fund Class I	JODIX	NAS CM	Open End	US Equity Mid Cap (Growth)	C+	C	B	Down	Y	0
JOHCM US Small Mid Cap Equity Fund Institutional Shares	JODMX	NAS CM	Open End	US Equity Mid Cap (Growth)	C+	C	B	Down	Y	1,000,000
John Hancock Balanced Fund Class A	SVBAX	NAS CM	Open End	Moderate Alloc (Balanced)	B	C+	B+	Up	Y	1,000
John Hancock Balanced Fund Class B	SVBBX	NAS CM	Open End	Moderate Alloc (Balanced)	B-	C	B+			1,000
John Hancock Balanced Fund Class C	SVBCX	NAS CM	Open End	Moderate Alloc (Balanced)	B-	C	B+		Y	1,000
John Hancock Balanced Fund Class I	SVBIX	NAS CM	Open End	Moderate Alloc (Balanced)	B	C+	B+		Y	250,000
John Hancock Balanced Fund Class R1	JBAOX	NAS CM	Open End	Moderate Alloc (Balanced)	B-	C	B+		Y	0
John Hancock Balanced Fund Class R2	JBATX	NAS CM	Open End	Moderate Alloc (Balanced)	B-	C+	B+		Y	0
John Hancock Balanced Fund Class R3	JBAHX	NAS CM	Open End	Moderate Alloc (Balanced)	B-	C	B+		Y	0
John Hancock Balanced Fund Class R4	JBAFX	NAS CM	Open End	Moderate Alloc (Balanced)	B	C+	B+	Up	Y	0
John Hancock Balanced Fund Class R5	JBAVX	NAS CM	Open End	Moderate Alloc (Balanced)	B	C+	B+		Y	0
John Hancock Balanced Fund Class R6	JBAWX	NAS CM	Open End	Moderate Alloc (Balanced)	B	C+	B+		Y	1,000,000
John Hancock Capital Series Classic Value Fund Class R3	JCVHX	NAS CM	Open End	US Equity Large Cap Value (Growth)	C	C	C+		Y	0
John Hancock Capital Series Classic Value Fund Class R4	JCVFX	NAS CM	Open End	US Equity Large Cap Value (Growth)	C	C	B-		Y	0
John Hancock Capital Series Classic Value Fund Class R5	JCVVX	NAS CM	Open End	US Equity Large Cap Value (Growth)	C	C	B-		Y	0
John Hancock Classic Value Fund Class A	PZFVX	NAS CM	Open End	US Equity Large Cap Value (Growth)	C	C	C+		Y	1,000
John Hancock Classic Value Fund Class B	JCVBX	NAS CM	Open End	US Equity Large Cap Value (Growth)	C	C	C+			1,000
John Hancock Classic Value Fund Class C	JCVCX	NAS CM	Open End	US Equity Large Cap Value (Growth)	C	C	C+		Y	1,000
John Hancock Classic Value Fund Class I	JCVIX	NAS CM	Open End	US Equity Large Cap Value (Growth)	C	C	B-		Y	250,000
John Hancock Classic Value Fund Class R1	JCVRX	NAS CM	Open End	US Equity Large Cap Value (Growth)	C	C	C+		Y	0
John Hancock Classic Value Fund Class R2	JCVSX	NAS CM	Open End	US Equity Large Cap Value (Growth)	C	C	C+		Y	0
John Hancock Classic Value Fund Class R6	JCVWX	NAS CM	Open End	US Equity Large Cap Value (Growth)	C	C	B-		Y	1,000,000
John Hancock Disciplined Value International Fund Class A	JDIBX	NAS CM	Open End	Global Equity Large Cap (Foreign Stock)	C-	D+	C		Y	1,000
John Hancock Disciplined Value International Fund Class C	JDICX	NAS CM	Open End	Global Equity Large Cap (Foreign Stock)	D+	D+	C-	Down	Y	1,000
John Hancock Disciplined Value International Fund Class I	JDVIX	NAS CM	Open End	Global Equity Large Cap (Foreign Stock)	C-	D+	C		Y	250,000
John Hancock Disciplined Value International Cls NAV	JDIVX	NAS CM	Open End	Global Equity Large Cap (Foreign Stock)	C-	D+	C		Y	0

★ Expanded analysis of this fund is included in Section II.

Min Additional Investment	3-Month Total Return	6-Month Total Return	1-Year Total Return	3-Year Total Return	5-Year Total Return	Dividend Yield (TTM)	Expense Ratio	3-Yr Std Deviation	3-Year Beta	NAV	Total Assets (MIL)	%Cash	%Stocks	%Bonds	%Other	Turnover Ratio	Last Bull Market Total Return	Last Bear Market Total Return	Front End Fee (%)	Back End Fee (%)	Inception Date
	TOTAL RETURNS					PERFORMANCE				ASSETS		ASSET ALLOCATION & TURNOVER					BULL & BEAR		FEES		
	9.98	25.33	11.95	48.77	52.93	0	1.13	11.86	0.89	16.08	1,456	5	95	0	0						Sep-13
	10.06	25.52	12.23	49.54	53.72	0.42	0.83	11.88	0.89	16.08	1,456	5	95	0	0						Sep-17
	1.43	6.76	5.47	21.30		0	1.82	4.31	1.84	10.58	310.7	40	38	19	-2	267					Apr-15
	1.44	6.91	5.70	21.90		1.05	1.6	4.32	1.84	10.52	310.7	40	38	19	-2	267					Sep-17
	3.24	12.93	9.20	30.41	38.52	1.55	0.73	7.6	0.61	24.53	8,240	3	65	31	0	43	15.5	-10.61			May-95
	3.29	13.10	9.56	31.48	40.15	1.69	0.43	7.59	0.61	25.38	8,240	3	65	31	0	43	15.69	-10.62			Mar-04
	3.83	17.31	5.79	33.37	38.54	1.76	0.78	12.59	1.07	21.68	1,351	1	99	0	0	28	26.7	-20.35			Sep-02
	3.90	17.49	6.09	34.39	40.23	2.09	0.48	12.57	1.06	22.36	1,351	1	99	0	0	28	26.8	-20.21			Mar-04
	0.67	11.19	0.47	16.13	9.87	1.03	0.9	15.32	0.99	8.94	43.7	1	96	0	0	51					Jun-14
	0.68	11.12	0.22	15.53	8.82	1	1.05	15.27	0.98	8.89	43.7	1	96	0	0	51					Jun-14
	0.67	11.36	0.47	16.43	10.28	1.27	0.8	15.26	0.98	8.92	43.7	1	96	0	0	51					Mar-14
	1.25	12.59	1.23	37.75	20.35	0.9	1.34	12.64	0.84	11.26	557.4	4	96	0	0	32					Nov-12
	1.16	12.50	1.09	37.07	19.71	0.77	1.49	12.71	0.85	11.25	557.4	4	96	0	0	32					Dec-13
	1.34	12.67	1.33	38.07	20.84	0.98	1.24	12.68	0.85	11.29	557.4	4	96	0	0	32					Nov-12
	-0.08	10.45	-9.08	27.95		0.4	1.64	13.93	1.02	11.83	24.8	2	95	1	0	127					Jan-16
	-0.08	10.44	-9.07	28.16		0.48	1.54	13.91	1.02	11.84	24.8	2	95	1	0	127					Dec-14
	3.81	18.71	3.05	37.26	28.00	1.03	1.17	11.71	0.88	16.62	384.2	14	86	0	0	25					Mar-13
	3.86	18.84	3.15	37.60	28.55	1.12	1.07	11.74	0.88	16.65	384.2	14	86	0	0	25					Mar-13
	4.27	14.22	8.55			3.78	1			10.08	103.4	4	51	44	2	51					Nov-17
	4.30	14.29	8.66			3.88	0.9			10.08	103.4	4	51	44	2	51					Nov-17
	3.16	12.68	4.02			1.63	0.89			10.75	2.3	18	82	0	0	57					Sep-16
	2.57	15.44	0.89	31.87	31.23	1.31	1	10.69	0.84	23.47	8,578	11	89	0	0	26	17.41	-23.54			Jul-09
	2.53	15.31	0.64	30.89	29.57	1.13	1.25	10.69	0.84	23.49	8,578	11	89	0	0	26	17.25	-23.62			Mar-10
	2.62	12.48	-7.70	25.23	16.66	1.13	1.32	11.67	0.91	11.35	219.6	3	97	0	0	18					Dec-13
	2.51	12.30	-7.79	24.67	15.81	0.99	1.47	11.64	0.91	11.41	219.6	3	97	0	0	18					Nov-13
	2.62	12.51	-7.63	25.60	17.27	1.27	1.22	11.68	0.91	11.33	219.6	3	97	0	0	18					Oct-13
	2.10	20.22	3.64	51.17		0	1.09	15.64	0.99	11.65	7.7	4	96	0	0	66					Oct-14
	2.18	20.24	3.79	51.62		0	0.99	15.66	1	11.7	7.7	4	96	0	0	66					Oct-14
	3.13	14.73	8.92	30.19	33.51	1.55	1.06	8.35	0.67	20.42	1,977	0	64	35	0	58	19.28	-14.53	5.00		Oct-92
	2.91	14.31	8.13	27.42	28.91	0.9	1.76	8.34	0.68	20.38	1,977	0	64	35	0	58	18.84	-14.82		5.00	Oct-92
	2.96	14.29	8.18	27.46	28.88	0.9	1.76	8.37	0.68	20.4	1,977	0	64	35	0	58	18.83	-14.81		1.00	May-99
	3.16	14.85	9.21	31.29	35.50	1.84	0.77	8.34	0.67	20.39	1,977	0	64	35	0	58	19.56	-14.39			Mar-02
	2.98	14.46	8.50	28.76	31.21	1.22	1.42	8.32	0.67	20.51	1,977	0	64	35	0	58	19.15	-14.69			Sep-08
	3.11	14.69	8.83	29.79	32.88	1.46	1.17	8.36	0.68	20.39	1,977	0	64	35	0	58	19.28	-14.53			Mar-12
	3.06	14.61	8.66	29.31	31.98	1.33	1.32	8.34	0.67	20.47	1,977	0	64	35	0	58	19.23	-14.65			Sep-08
	3.16	14.80	9.04	30.76	34.53	1.68	0.92	8.37	0.68	20.51	1,977	0	64	35	0	58	19.46	-14.55			Sep-08
	3.16	14.88	9.22	31.46	35.86	1.87	0.72	8.34	0.67	20.47	1,977	0	64	35	0	58	19.64	-14.38			Sep-08
	3.23	14.95	9.30	31.69	36.30	1.92	0.67	8.35	0.67	20.42	1,977	0	64	35	0	58	19.64	-14.53			Sep-11
	3.36	15.51	-2.44	37.95	29.85	0.96	1.46	16.43	1.26	31.35	2,298	2	98	0	0	28	27.22	-23.64			May-09
	3.48	15.78	-2.01	39.96	33.05	1.43	1.06	16.44	1.26	31.47	2,298	2	98	0	0	28	27.5	-23.57			May-09
	3.48	15.80	-1.92	40.36	33.79	1.54	0.86	16.43	1.26	31.5	2,298	2	98	0	0	28	27.57	-23.45			May-09
	3.42	15.64	-2.22	39.05	31.69	1.22	1.16	16.42	1.26	31.42	2,298	2	98	0	0	28	27.32	-23.57	5.00		Jun-96
	3.20	15.20	-2.93	35.99	26.81	0.42	1.91	16.42	1.26	30.92	2,298	2	98	0	0	28	26.81	-23.84		5.00	Nov-02
	3.20	15.21	-2.94	35.97	26.79	0.43	1.91	16.42	1.26	30.9	2,298	2	98	0	0	28	26.73	-23.8		1.00	Nov-02
	3.48	15.77	-1.99	40.11	33.32	1.48	0.92	16.44	1.26	31.48	2,298	2	98	0	0	28	27.58	-23.46			Nov-02
	3.31	15.40	-2.60	37.43	29.12	0.81	1.56	16.42	1.26	31.46	2,298	2	98	0	0	28	27.07	-23.68			Aug-03
	3.36	15.54	-2.36	38.46	30.79	1.07	1.31	16.42	1.26	31.36	2,298	2	98	0	0	28	27.32	-23.57			Mar-12
	3.51	15.84	-1.87	40.56	34.10	1.59	0.81	16.44	1.26	31.51	2,298	2	98	0	0	28	27.59	-23.54			Aug-11
	0.41	8.49	-7.79	16.05	1.08	1.12	1.29	11.6	1.02	12.01	1,770	4	96	0	0	95			5.00		Sep-14
	0.25	8.11	-8.43	13.69	-2.30	0.35	1.99	11.58	1.02	11.99	1,770	4	96	0	0	95				1.00	Sep-14
	0.50	8.67	-7.49	17.28	2.73	1.48	0.98	11.6	1.02	12.03	1,770	4	96	0	0	95					Sep-14
	0.50	8.68	-7.46	17.56	3.18	1.59	0.88	11.57	1.02	12.02	1,770	4	96	0	0	95					Apr-15

Fund Name	MARKET Ticker Symbol	Traded On	Fund Type	FUND TYPE, CATEGORY & OBJECTIVE Category and (Prospectus Objective)	RATINGS Overall Rating	Reward Rating	Risk Rating	Recent Up/ Downgrade	Open to New Investors	MINIMUMS Min Initial Investment
John Hancock Disciplined Value International Fund Class R2	JDISX	NAS CM	Open End	Global Equity Large Cap (Foreign Stock)	C-	D+	C		Y	0
John Hancock Disciplined Value International Fund Class R4	JDITX	NAS CM	Open End	Global Equity Large Cap (Foreign Stock)	C-	D+	C		Y	0
John Hancock Disciplined Value International Fund Class R6	JDIUX	NAS CM	Open End	Global Equity Large Cap (Foreign Stock)	C-	D+	C		Y	1,000,000
John Hancock Diversified Real Assets Fund Class NAV			Open End	Global Equity Large Cap (Real Estate)	D	D	C		Y	0
John Hancock Emerging Markets Equity Fund Class A	JEMQX	NAS CM	Open End	Global Emerg Mkts (Div Emerging Mkts)	C	C	C+		Y	1,000
John Hancock Emerging Markets Equity Fund Class C	JEMZX	NAS CM	Open End	Global Emerg Mkts (Div Emerging Mkts)	C	C	C+		Y	1,000
John Hancock Emerging Markets Equity Fund Class I	JEMMX	NAS CM	Open End	Global Emerg Mkts (Div Emerging Mkts)	C	C	C+		Y	250,000
John Hancock Emerging Markets Equity Fund Class NAV			Open End	Global Emerg Mkts (Div Emerging Mkts)	C	C	C+		Y	0
John Hancock Emerging Markets Equity Fund Class R2	JEMKX	NAS CM	Open End	Global Emerg Mkts (Div Emerging Mkts)	C	C	C+		Y	0
John Hancock Emerging Markets Equity Fund Class R4	JEMNX	NAS CM	Open End	Global Emerg Mkts (Div Emerging Mkts)	C	C	C+		Y	0
John Hancock Emerging Markets Equity Fund Class R6	JEMGX	NAS CM	Open End	Global Emerg Mkts (Div Emerging Mkts)	C	C	C+		Y	1,000,000
John Hancock ESG All Cap Core Fund Class A	JHKAX	NAS CM	Open End	US Equity Large Cap Growth (Growth)	C+	C	B		Y	1,000
John Hancock ESG All Cap Core Fund Class C	JHKCX	NAS CM	Open End	US Equity Large Cap Growth (Growth)	C+	C	B		Y	1,000
John Hancock ESG All Cap Core Fund Class I	JHKIX	NAS CM	Open End	US Equity Large Cap Growth (Growth)	B-	C	B		Y	250,000
John Hancock ESG All Cap Core Fund Class R6	JHKRX	NAS CM	Open End	US Equity Large Cap Growth (Growth)	B-	C	B		Y	1,000,000
John Hancock ESG International Equity Fund Class A	JTQAX	NAS CM	Open End	Global Equity Large Cap (Foreign Stock)	C	C-	B		Y	1,000
John Hancock ESG International Equity Fund Class I	JTQIX	NAS CM	Open End	Global Equity Large Cap (Foreign Stock)	C	C-	B		Y	250,000
John Hancock ESG International Equity Fund Class R6	JTQRX	NAS CM	Open End	Global Equity Large Cap (Foreign Stock)	C	C-	B		Y	1,000,000
John Hancock ESG Large Cap Core Fund Class A	JHJAX	NAS CM	Open End	US Equity Large Cap Blend (Growth)	B-	C	B		Y	1,000
John Hancock ESG Large Cap Core Fund Class C	JHJCX	NAS CM	Open End	US Equity Large Cap Blend (Growth)	B-	C	B		Y	1,000
John Hancock ESG Large Cap Core Fund Class I	JHJIX	NAS CM	Open End	US Equity Large Cap Blend (Growth)	B-	C	B		Y	250,000
John Hancock ESG Large Cap Core Fund Class R6	JHJRX	NAS CM	Open End	US Equity Large Cap Blend (Growth)	B-	C	B		Y	1,000,000
John Hancock Financial Industries Fund Class A	FIDAX	NAS CM	Open End	Financials Sector Equity (Financial)	C	C	B-		Y	1,000
John Hancock Financial Industries Fund Class B	FIDBX	NAS CM	Open End	Financials Sector Equity (Financial)	C	C	B-			1,000
John Hancock Financial Industries Fund Class C	FIDCX	NAS CM	Open End	Financials Sector Equity (Financial)	C	C	B-		Y	1,000
John Hancock Financial Industries Fund Class I	JFIFX	NAS CM	Open End	Financials Sector Equity (Financial)	C	C	B-		Y	250,000
John Hancock Financial Industries Fund Class NAV			Open End	Financials Sector Equity (Financial)	C	C	B-		Y	0
John Hancock Financial Industries Fund Class R6	JFDRX	NAS CM	Open End	Financials Sector Equity (Financial)	C	C	B-		Y	1,000,000
John Hancock Financial Opportunities Fund	BTO	NYSE	Closed End	Financials Sector Equity (Financial)	C-	C	C-	Down	Y	
John Hancock Fundamental Large Cap Core Fund Class A	TAGRX	NAS CM	Open End	US Equity Large Cap Blend (Growth)	C+	C	C+	Up	Y	1,000
John Hancock Fundamental Large Cap Core Fund Class B	TSGWX	NAS CM	Open End	US Equity Large Cap Blend (Growth)	C+	C	C+	Up		1,000
John Hancock Fundamental Large Cap Core Fund Class C	JHLVX	NAS CM	Open End	US Equity Large Cap Blend (Growth)	C+	C	C+	Up	Y	1,000
John Hancock Fundamental Large Cap Core Fund Class I	JLVIX	NAS CM	Open End	US Equity Large Cap Blend (Growth)	C+	C	C+	Up	Y	250,000
John Hancock Fundamental Large Cap Core Fund Class NAV			Open End	US Equity Large Cap Blend (Growth)	C+	C	C+	Up	Y	0
John Hancock Fundamental Large Cap Core Fund Class R1	JLCRX	NAS CM	Open End	US Equity Large Cap Blend (Growth)	C+	C	C+	Up	Y	0
John Hancock Fundamental Large Cap Core Fund Class R2	JLCYX	NAS CM	Open End	US Equity Large Cap Blend (Growth)	C+	C	C+	Up	Y	0
John Hancock Fundamental Large Cap Core Fund Class R3	JLCHX	NAS CM	Open End	US Equity Large Cap Blend (Growth)	C+	C	C+	Up	Y	0
John Hancock Fundamental Large Cap Core Fund Class R4	JLCFX	NAS CM	Open End	US Equity Large Cap Blend (Growth)	C+	C	C+	Up	Y	0
John Hancock Fundamental Large Cap Core Fund Class R5	JLCVX	NAS CM	Open End	US Equity Large Cap Blend (Growth)	C+	C	C+	Up	Y	0
John Hancock Fundamental Large Cap Core Fund Class R6	JLCWX	NAS CM	Open End	US Equity Large Cap Blend (Growth)	C+	C	C+	Up	Y	1,000,000
John Hancock Funds Alternative Asset Allocation Cls A	JAAAX	NAS CM	Open End	Multialternative (Asset Alloc)	C+	C	B	Up	Y	1,000
John Hancock Funds Alternative Asset Allocation Cls C	JAACX	NAS CM	Open End	Multialternative (Asset Alloc)	C	C	B		Y	1,000
John Hancock Funds Alternative Asset Allocation Cls I	JAAIX	NAS CM	Open End	Multialternative (Asset Alloc)	B-	C	B+	Up	Y	250,000
John Hancock Funds Alternative Asset Allocation Cls R2	JAAPX	NAS CM	Open End	Multialternative (Asset Alloc)	C+	C	B	Up	Y	0
John Hancock Funds Alternative Asset Allocation Cls R4	JAASX	NAS CM	Open End	Multialternative (Asset Alloc)	C+	C	B+	Up	Y	0
John Hancock Funds Alternative Asset Allocation Cls R6	JAARX	NAS CM	Open End	Multialternative (Asset Alloc)	B-	C	B+	Up	Y	1,000,000
John Hancock Funds Disciplined Value Fund Class A	JVLAX	NAS CM	Open End	US Equity Large Cap Value (Growth & Income)	C+	C	B	Up	Y	1,000
John Hancock Funds Disciplined Value Fund Class B	JVLBX	NAS CM	Open End	US Equity Large Cap Value (Growth & Income)	C+	C	B-	Up		0
John Hancock Funds Disciplined Value Fund Class C	JVLCX	NAS CM	Open End	US Equity Large Cap Value (Growth & Income)	C+	C	B-	Up	Y	1,000
John Hancock Funds Disciplined Value Fund Class I	JVLIX	NAS CM	Open End	US Equity Large Cap Value (Growth & Income)	C+	C	B	Up	Y	250,000
John Hancock Funds Disciplined Value Fund Class I2	JVLTX	NAS CM	Open End	US Equity Large Cap Value (Growth & Income)	C+	C	B	Up	Y	250,000
John Hancock Funds Disciplined Value Fund Class NAV	JDVNX	NAS CM	Open End	US Equity Large Cap Value (Growth & Income)	C+	C	B	Up	Y	0

★ Expanded analysis of this fund is included in Section II.

	TOTAL RETURNS					PERFORMANCE				ASSETS		ASSET ALLOCATION & TURNOVER					BULL & BEAR		FEES		
Min Additional Investment	3-Month Total Return	6-Month Total Return	1-Year Total Return	3-Year Total Return	5-Year Total Return	Dividend Yield (TTM)	Expense Ratio	3-Yr Std Deviation	3-Year Beta	NAV	Total Assets (MIL)	%Cash	%Stocks	%Bonds	%Other	Turnover Ratio	Last Bull Market Total Return	Last Bear Market Total Return	Front End Fee (%)	Back End Fee (%)	Inception Date
	0.41	8.38	-7.95	15.73	0.79	1.02	1.39	11.63	1.02	12.02	1,770	4	96	0	0	95					Sep-14
	0.50	8.48	-7.68	16.76	2.06	1.3	1.14	11.56	1.02	12.02	1,770	4	96	0	0	95					Sep-14
	0.50	8.58	-7.46	17.45	3.17	1.59	0.88	11.6	1.02	12.02	1,770	4	96	0	0	95					Dec-11
	0.39	15.65	-2.65			1.87	0.88			10.05	1,002	3	97	0	0	73					Feb-18
	0.56	14.71	0.48	34.46		0.36	1.43	14.97	1.05	10.68	2,091	1	99	0	0	50			5.00		Jun-15
	0.47	14.42	-0.20	31.72		0	2.13	15	1.05	10.47	2,091	1	99	0	0	50				1.00	Jun-15
	0.65	14.93	0.73	35.54		0.65	1.14	14.98	1.05	10.7	2,091	1	99	0	0	50					Jun-15
	0.75	15.05	0.89	36.11		0.78	1.03	15.01	1.05	10.7	2,091	1	99	0	0	50					Jun-15
	0.65	14.83	0.57	34.93		0.51	1.54	15	1.05	10.68	2,091	1	99	0	0	50					Jun-15
	0.65	14.94	0.68	35.29		0.61	1.29	15	1.05	10.69	2,091	1	99	0	0	50					Jun-15
	0.75	15.05	0.87	36.08		0.77	1.04	15.07	1.06	10.7	2,091	1	99	0	0	50					Jun-15
	4.00	19.35	9.88	48.72		0.21	1.17	12.12	0.96	13.26	27.1	1	99	0	0	19			5.00		Jun-16
	3.81	18.90	9.13	45.37		0	1.92	12.11	0.95	13.08	27.1	1	99	0	0	19				1.00	Jun-16
	4.07	19.51	10.19	49.91		0.4	0.93	12.12	0.96	13.29	27.1	1	99	0	0	19					Jun-16
	4.07	19.51	10.33	50.37		0.5	0.82	12.1	0.95	13.29	27.1	1	99	0	0	19					Jun-16
	3.34	15.70	2.08			0.84	1.27			12.67	56.7	0	100	0	0	19			5.00		Dec-16
	3.34	15.79	2.30			1.1	1.03			12.68	56.7	0	100	0	0	19					Dec-16
	3.34	15.79	2.33			1.2	0.92			12.68	56.7	0	100	0	0	19					Dec-16
	4.63	19.86	13.89	51.69		0.32	1.17	11.22	0.9	14	61.0	1	99	0	0	22			5.00		Jun-16
	4.45	19.34	13.02	48.25		0	1.92	11.22	0.9	13.82	61.0	1	99	0	0	22				1.00	Jun-16
	4.70	19.93	14.17	52.86		0.55	0.93	11.22	0.9	14.02	61.0	1	99	0	0	22					Jun-16
	4.77	20.01	14.28	53.40		0.64	0.82	11.21	0.9	14.03	61.0	1	99	0	0	22					Jun-16
	7.18	19.33	1.25	52.42	36.68	0.68	1.24	17.66	1	18.64	740.0	2	97	0	0	23	36.02	-28.88	5.00		Mar-96
	7.01	18.93	0.49	49.10	31.74	0	1.94	17.62	1	16.77	740.0	2	97	0	0	23	35.53	-29.15		5.00	Jan-97
	7.00	18.96	0.55	49.18	31.91	0	1.94	17.59	1	16.81	740.0	2	97	0	0	23	35.53	-29.15		1.00	Mar-99
	7.25	19.51	1.50	53.60	37.73	0.93	0.95	17.62	1	18.62	740.0	2	97	0	0	23	36.02	-28.88			Sep-16
	7.32	19.58	1.63	54.20	39.49	1.04	0.83	17.63	1	18.62	740.0	2	97	0	0	23	36.02	-28.88			Jul-13
	7.31	19.65	1.66	53.58	37.73	1.02	0.84	17.64	1	18.63	740.0	2	97	0	0	23	36.02	-28.88			Aug-17
	6.73	18.78	-7.37	57.38	71.82	3.61		22.08	1.22	33.14	618.7	1	93	3	0	11	37.87	-24.89			Aug-94
	4.68	23.24	4.74	44.99	53.03	0.26	1.02	14.77	1.16	45.34	5,059	1	99	0	0	47	25.48	-23.38	5.00		Oct-84
	4.49	22.77	3.96	41.77	47.39	0	1.77	14.76	1.16	39.51	5,059	1	99	0	0	47	24.96	-23.64		5.00	Aug-91
	4.49	22.78	3.96	41.78	47.41	0	1.77	14.76	1.16	39.5	5,059	1	99	0	0	47	24.91	-23.64		1.00	May-98
	4.75	23.43	5.00	46.12	55.03	0.48	0.78	14.78	1.16	47.62	5,059	1	99	0	0	47	25.72	-23.28			Mar-01
	4.76	23.46	5.11	46.19	54.29	0.57	0.66	14.76	1.16	47.72	5,059	1	99	0	0	47	25.48	-23.38			Feb-17
	4.60	23.02	4.34	43.34	50.12	0	1.42	14.76	1.16	46.76	5,059	1	99	0	0	47	25.28	-23.51			May-09
	4.65	23.16	4.58	44.37	51.97	0.11	1.17	14.76	1.16	47.42	5,059	1	99	0	0	47	25.47	-23.38			Mar-12
	4.61	23.09	4.45	43.81	50.91	0.01	1.32	14.76	1.16	46.96	5,059	1	99	0	0	47	25.28	-23.46			May-09
	4.70	23.33	4.83	45.44	53.87	0.34	0.92	14.77	1.16	47.36	5,059	1	99	0	0	47	25.49	-23.36			May-09
	4.76	23.43	5.04	46.30	55.37	0.52	0.72	14.77	1.16	47.72	5,059	1	99	0	0	47	25.76	-23.29			May-09
	4.76	23.45	5.09	46.58	55.89	0.56	0.67	14.77	1.16	47.74	5,059	1	99	0	0	47	25.82	-23.38			Sep-11
	1.60	6.20	3.05	9.78	6.10	1.88	1.7	3.23	0.72	14.54	575.7	25	37	35	1	18	7.21	-9.05	5.00		Jan-09
	1.46	5.88	2.37	7.47	2.47	1.18	2.4	3.24	0.72	14.57	575.7	25	37	35	1	18	6.84	-9.35		1.00	Jun-11
	1.67	6.35	3.32	10.71	7.65	2.19	1.4	3.22	0.71	14.55	575.7	25	37	35	1	18	7.42	-8.9			Dec-10
	1.60	6.21	2.95	9.47	5.52	1.78	1.81	3.23	0.71	14.53	575.7	25	37	35	1	18	7.28	-9.05			Mar-12
	1.67	6.35	3.22	10.27	6.94	2.03	1.55	3.25	0.72	14.57	575.7	25	37	35	1	18	7.21	-9.05			Jun-13
	1.74	6.43	3.49	11.04	8.31	2.28	1.3	3.25	0.72	14.56	575.7	25	37	35	1	18	7.5	-9.05			Sep-11
	2.81	13.32	3.78	37.42	36.87	1.02	1.05	13.17	1.06	20.83	15,039	2	98	0	0	69	28.48	-19.91	5.00		Dec-08
	2.64	12.89	3.03	34.33	31.74	0.3	1.8	13.17	1.06	19.43	15,039	2	98	0	0	69	27.82	-20.14		5.00	Dec-08
	2.68	12.92	3.02	34.36	31.78	0.3	1.8	13.19	1.06	19.49	15,039	2	98	0	0	69	27.91	-20.14		1.00	Dec-08
	2.91	13.45	4.01	38.43	38.61	1.31	0.8	13.18	1.07	20.15	15,039	2	98	0	0	69	28.79	-19.74			Jan-97
	2.91	13.45	4.00	38.43	38.59	1.31	0.8	13.18	1.07	20.15	15,039	2	98	0	0	69	28.73	-19.78			Dec-08
	2.90	13.49	4.13	38.87	39.40	1.42	0.69	13.19	1.07	20.19	15,039	2	98	0	0	69	28.78	-19.71			May-09

	MARKET			FUND TYPE, CATEGORY & OBJECTIVE	RATINGS				MINIMUMS	
Fund Name	Ticker Symbol	Traded On	Fund Type	Category and (Prospectus Objective)	Overall Rating	Reward Rating	Risk Rating	Recent Up/ Downgrade	Open to New Investors	Min Initial Investment
John Hancock Funds Disciplined Value Fund Class R1	JDVOX	NAS CM	Open End	US Equity Large Cap Value (Growth & Income)	C+	C	B	Up	Y	0
John Hancock Funds Disciplined Value Fund Class R2	JDVPX	NAS CM	Open End	US Equity Large Cap Value (Growth & Income)	C+	C	B	Up	Y	0
John Hancock Funds Disciplined Value Fund Class R3	JDVHX	NAS CM	Open End	US Equity Large Cap Value (Growth & Income)	C+	C	B	Up	Y	0
John Hancock Funds Disciplined Value Fund Class R4	JDVFX	NAS CM	Open End	US Equity Large Cap Value (Growth & Income)	C+	C	B	Up	Y	0
John Hancock Funds Disciplined Value Fund Class R5	JDVVX	NAS CM	Open End	US Equity Large Cap Value (Growth & Income)	C+	C	B	Up	Y	0
John Hancock Funds Disciplined Value Fund Class R6	JDVWX	NAS CM	Open End	US Equity Large Cap Value (Growth & Income)	C+	C	B	Up	Y	1,000,000
John Hancock Funds Disciplined Value Mid Cap Fund Class A	JVMAX	NAS CM	Open End	US Equity Mid Cap (Growth)	C	C	B-			1,000
John Hancock Funds Disciplined Value Mid Cap Cls ADV	JVMVX	NAS CM	Open End	US Equity Mid Cap (Growth)	C	C	B-			0
John Hancock Funds Disciplined Value Mid Cap Fund Class C	JVMCX	NAS CM	Open End	US Equity Mid Cap (Growth)	C	C	B-			1,000
John Hancock Funds Disciplined Value Mid Cap Fund Class I	JVMIX	NAS CM	Open End	US Equity Mid Cap (Growth)	C+	C	B-	Up		250,000
John Hancock Funds Disciplined Value Mid Cap Fund Class R2	JVMSX	NAS CM	Open End	US Equity Mid Cap (Growth)	C	C	B-			0
John Hancock Funds Disciplined Value Mid Cap Fund Class R4	JVMTX	NAS CM	Open End	US Equity Mid Cap (Growth)	C	C	B-			0
John Hancock Funds Disciplined Value Mid Cap Fund Class R6	JVMRX	NAS CM	Open End	US Equity Mid Cap (Growth)	C+	C	B-	Up		1,000,000
John Hancock Funds Diversified Strategies Fund Class A	JDSTX	NAS CM	Open End	Moderate Alloc (Growth & Income)	C	C-	B-		Y	1,000
John Hancock Funds Diversified Strategies Fund Class I	JDSIX	NAS CM	Open End	Moderate Alloc (Growth & Income)	C	C-	B-		Y	250,000
John Hancock Funds Fundamental All Cap Core Fund Class A	JFCAX	NAS CM	Open End	US Equity Large Cap Growth (Growth)	C+	C	C+		Y	1,000
John Hancock Funds Fundamental All Cap Core Fund Class C	JFCCX	NAS CM	Open End	US Equity Large Cap Growth (Growth)	C+	C	C+		Y	1,000
John Hancock Funds Fundamental All Cap Core Fund Class I	JFCIX	NAS CM	Open End	US Equity Large Cap Growth (Growth)	C+	C	C+		Y	250,000
John Hancock Funds Fundamental All Cap Core Fund Class R2	JFACX	NAS CM	Open End	US Equity Large Cap Growth (Growth)	C+	C	C+		Y	0
John Hancock Funds Fundamental All Cap Core Fund Class R4	JFARX	NAS CM	Open End	US Equity Large Cap Growth (Growth)	C+	C	C+		Y	0
John Hancock Funds Fundamental All Cap Core Fund Class R6	JFAIX	NAS CM	Open End	US Equity Large Cap Growth (Growth)	C+	C	C+		Y	1,000,000
John Hancock Funds Fundamental Global Franchise Cls A	JFGAX	NAS CM	Open End	Global Equity Large Cap (Growth)	C+	C	B	Up	Y	1,000
John Hancock Funds Fundamental Global Franchise Cls I	JFGIX	NAS CM	Open End	Global Equity Large Cap (Growth)	C+	C	B	Up	Y	250,000
John Hancock Funds Fundamental Global Franchise Cls NAV			Open End	Global Equity Large Cap (Growth)	C+	C	B	Up	Y	0
John Hancock Funds Fundamental Global Franchise Cls R6	JFGFX	NAS CM	Open End	Global Equity Large Cap (Growth)	C+	C	B	Up	Y	1,000,000
John Hancock Funds Fundamental Large Cap Value Cls A	JFVAX	NAS CM	Open End	US Equity Large Cap Value (Growth)	C+	C	B-	Up	Y	1,000
John Hancock Funds Fundamental Large Cap Value Cls C	JFVCX	NAS CM	Open End	US Equity Large Cap Value (Growth)	C+	C	B-	Up	Y	1,000
John Hancock Funds Fundamental Large Cap Value Cls I	JFVIX	NAS CM	Open End	US Equity Large Cap Value (Growth)	C+	C	B-	Up	Y	250,000
John Hancock Funds Fundamental Large Cap Value Cls NAV			Open End	US Equity Large Cap Value (Growth)	C+	C	B-	Up	Y	0
John Hancock Funds Fundamental Large Cap Value Cls R2	JFLCX	NAS CM	Open End	US Equity Large Cap Value (Growth)	C+	C	B-	Up	Y	0
John Hancock Funds Fundamental Large Cap Value Cls R4	JFLRX	NAS CM	Open End	US Equity Large Cap Value (Growth)	C+	C	B-	Up	Y	0
John Hancock Funds Fundamental Large Cap Value Cls R6	JFLVX	NAS CM	Open End	US Equity Large Cap Value (Growth)	C+	C	B-	Up	Y	1,000,000
John Hancock Funds Global Absolute Return Strategies Cls C	JHACX	NAS CM	Open End	Global Macro (Multi-Asset Global)	C	C-	C+	Up	Y	1,000
John Hancock Funds Global Absolute Return Strat Cls R6	JHASX	NAS CM	Open End	Global Macro (Multi-Asset Global)	C	C	B		Y	1,000,000
John Hancock Funds Global Absolute Return Strategies Cls A	JHAAX	NAS CM	Open End	Global Macro (Multi-Asset Global)	C	C	B-		Y	1,000
John Hancock Funds Global Absolute Return Strategies Cls I	JHAIX	NAS CM	Open End	Global Macro (Multi-Asset Global)	C	C	B		Y	250,000
John Hancock Funds Global Absolute Return Strat Cls NAV			Open End	Global Macro (Multi-Asset Global)	C	C	B		Y	0
John Hancock Funds Global Absolute Return Strat Cls R2	JHARX	NAS CM	Open End	Global Macro (Multi-Asset Global)	C	C	B-		Y	0
John Hancock Funds Global Equity Fund Class A	JHGEX	NAS CM	Open End	Global Equity Large Cap (World Stock)	C+	C	B		Y	1,000
John Hancock Funds Global Equity Fund Class C	JGECX	NAS CM	Open End	Global Equity Large Cap (World Stock)	C+	C	B		Y	1,000
John Hancock Funds Global Equity Fund Class I	JGEFX	NAS CM	Open End	Global Equity Large Cap (World Stock)	B-	C	B	Up	Y	250,000
John Hancock Funds Global Equity Fund Class NAV			Open End	Global Equity Large Cap (World Stock)	B-	C	B	Up	Y	0
John Hancock Funds Global Equity Fund Class R2	JGERX	NAS CM	Open End	Global Equity Large Cap (World Stock)	C+	C	B		Y	0
John Hancock Funds Global Equity Fund Class R4	JGETX	NAS CM	Open End	Global Equity Large Cap (World Stock)	B-	C	B	Up	Y	0
John Hancock Funds Global Equity Fund Class R6	JGEMX	NAS CM	Open End	Global Equity Large Cap (World Stock)	B-	C	B	Up	Y	1,000,000
John Hancock Funds II Blue Chip Growth Fund Class 1	JIBCX	NAS CM	Open End	US Equity Large Cap Growth (Growth & Income)	B-	C+	B	Down	Y	0
John Hancock Funds II Blue Chip Growth Fund Class A	JBGAX	NAS CM	Open End	US Equity Large Cap Growth (Growth & Income)	B-	C+	B	Down	Y	1,000
John Hancock Funds II Blue Chip Growth Fund Class C	JBGCX	NAS CM	Open End	US Equity Large Cap Growth (Growth & Income)	B-	C+	B	Down	Y	1,000
John Hancock Funds II Blue Chip Growth Fund Class NAV	JHBCX	NAS CM	Open End	US Equity Large Cap Growth (Growth & Income)	B-	C+	B	Down	Y	0
John Hancock Funds II Capital Appreciation Fund Class 1	JICPX	NAS CM	Open End	US Equity Large Cap Growth (Growth)	C+	C+	B	Down	Y	0
John Hancock Funds II Capital Appreciation Fund Class NAV	JHCPX	NAS CM	Open End	US Equity Large Cap Growth (Growth)	C+	C+	B	Down	Y	0
John Hancock Funds II Capital Appreciation Value Cls NAV	JCAVX	NAS CM	Open End	Moderate Alloc (Growth)	B	B-	A		Y	0

★ Expanded analysis of this fund is included in Section II.

Min Additional Investment	3-Month Total Return	6-Month Total Return	1-Year Total Return	3-Year Total Return	5-Year Total Return	Dividend Yield (TTM)	Expense Ratio	3-Yr Std Deviation	3-Year Beta	NAV	Total Assets (MIL)	%Cash	%Stocks	%Bonds	%Other	Turnover Ratio	Last Bull Market Total Return	Last Bear Market Total Return	Front End Fee (%)	Back End Fee (%)	Inception Date
	TOTAL RETURNS					PERFORMANCE				ASSETS		ASSET ALLOCATION & TURNOVER					BULL & BEAR		FEES		
	2.76	13.11	3.40	35.81	34.08	0.65	1.45	13.2	1.07	20.1	15,039	2	98	0	0	69	28.12	-19.97			Jul-09
	2.81	13.22	3.64	36.77	35.85	0.91	1.2	13.17	1.06	20.12	15,039	2	98	0	0	69	28.54	-19.82			Mar-12
	2.76	13.11	3.46	36.15	34.76	0.75	1.35	13.2	1.07	20.09	15,039	2	98	0	0	69	28.05	-19.95			May-09
	2.85	13.32	3.87	37.80	37.51	1.16	0.95	13.18	1.06	20.15	15,039	2	98	0	0	69	28.53	-19.88			May-09
	2.90	13.49	4.11	38.61	38.96	1.36	0.75	13.19	1.07	20.19	15,039	2	98	0	0	69	28.68	-19.78			May-09
	2.95	13.55	4.17	38.84	39.38	1.41	0.7	13.18	1.06	20.19	15,039	2	98	0	0	69	28.69	-19.74			Sep-11
	5.50	20.82	3.14	33.58	45.51	0.58	1.1	13.98	1.04	20.13	12,869	2	98	0	0	53	28.35	-21.39	5.00		Jun-97
	5.51	20.89	3.15	33.61	45.38	0.58	1.1	14.03	1.04	20.08	12,869	2	98	0	0	53	28.51	-21.41			Jul-10
	5.27	20.38	2.36	30.57	40.11	0	1.85	14	1.04	20.14	12,869	2	98	0	0	53	27.83	-21.6		1.00	Aug-11
	5.57	20.94	3.38	34.56	47.37	0.78	0.85	14.01	1.04	21.02	12,869	2	98	0	0	53	28.58	-21.26			Jun-97
	5.44	20.70	2.97	32.97	44.45	0.4	1.26	13.99	1.04	20.93	12,869	2	98	0	0	53	28.42	-21.34			Mar-12
	5.52	20.89	3.27	33.99	46.28	0.65	1.01	14.02	1.04	21	12,869	2	98	0	0	53	28.39	-21.34			Jul-13
	5.62	21.08	3.53	35.04	48.16	0.9	0.76	14	1.04	21.02	12,869	2	98	0	0	53	28.61	-21.26			Sep-11
	2.05	2.19	0.45	9.27	5.49	0	1.94	2.29	0.13	7.93	10.2	130	17	-47	0	171	8.94		5.00		Sep-11
	2.17	2.43	0.79	10.49	7.38	0	1.64	2.28	0.13	8	10.2	130	17	-47	0	171	9.25				Sep-11
	4.74	24.24	2.49	53.55	57.02	0	1.33	16.19	1.21	18.09	87.0	2	98	0	0	23	26.48		5.00		Jun-11
	4.53	23.84	1.78	50.45	52.01	0	2.03	16.18	1.21	17.5	87.0	2	98	0	0	23	26.18			1.00	Jun-14
	4.78	24.44	2.78	55.04	59.50	0	1.03	16.19	1.21	18.38	87.0	2	98	0	0	23	26.91				Jun-11
	4.71	24.13	2.31	53.65	57.44	0	1.43	16.2	1.21	18.21	87.0	2	98	0	0	23	26.72				Mar-15
	4.74	24.30	2.68	54.44	58.53	0	1.18	16.19	1.21	18.31	87.0	2	98	0	0	23	26.72				Mar-15
	4.83	24.45	2.94	55.49	60.15	0	0.93	16.2	1.21	18.42	87.0	2	98	0	0	23	26.91				Mar-15
	6.80	23.65	8.35	38.46	56.09	0.18	1.29	11.95	0.96	11.92	492.7	10	90	0	0	40			5.00		Jun-12
	6.87	23.65	8.63	39.66	58.52	0.47	1	11.98	0.96	11.97	492.7	10	90	0	0	40					Jun-12
	6.86	23.76	8.77	40.14	59.44	0.58	0.88	11.98	0.96	11.98	492.7	10	90	0	0	40					Jun-12
	6.86	23.75	8.75	40.07	59.37	0.56	0.89	11.92	0.96	11.98	492.7	10	90	0	0	40					Feb-17
	5.25	23.14	5.23	36.72	30.74	1.42	1.1	14.59	1.16	12.61	88.5	0	100	0	0	26	29.96		5.00		Jun-11
	5.09	22.73	4.53	34.04	26.21	0.89	1.8	14.61	1.16	12.58	88.5	0	100	0	0	26	29.46			1.00	Jun-14
	5.38	23.39	5.55	38.07	32.80	1.65	0.8	14.58	1.16	12.71	88.5	0	100	0	0	26	30.21				Jun-11
	5.39	23.42	5.65	38.51	33.63	1.74	0.69	14.54	1.16	12.7	88.5	0	100	0	0	26	30.39				Aug-11
	5.32	23.17	5.13	36.71	30.91	1.34	1.21	14.57	1.16	12.65	88.5	0	100	0	0	26	30.02				Mar-15
	5.31	23.32	5.50	37.92	32.31	1.61	0.96	14.57	1.16	12.69	88.5	0	100	0	0	26	30.02				Mar-15
	5.39	23.42	5.64	38.60	33.44	1.72	0.71	14.6	1.16	12.7	88.5	0	100	0	0	26	30.21				Mar-15
	1.28	5.69	3.44	3.33	1.29	0	2.34	3.55	8.26	10.21	906.7	42	28	30	0	59				1.00	Aug-12
	1.43	6.20	4.53	6.74	7.09	0	1.25	3.62	8.47	10.61	906.7	42	28	30	0	59					Mar-12
	1.35	5.98	4.08	5.44	4.84	0	1.64	3.56	8.32	10.45	906.7	42	28	30	0	59			5.00		Dec-11
	1.53	6.22	4.44	6.43	6.52	0	1.34	3.58	8.29	10.58	906.7	42	28	30	0	59					Dec-11
	1.53	6.31	4.63	6.84	7.18	0	1.23	3.58	8.37	10.61	906.7	42	28	30	0	59					Dec-11
	1.36	5.90	3.99	5.15	4.07	0	1.75	3.53	8.18	10.4	906.7	42	28	30	0	59					Mar-12
	4.28	20.39	11.47	34.24	29.11	1.61	1.28	11	0.94	11.69	733.6	2	98	0	0	43			5.00		May-13
	4.10	19.93	10.61	31.32	24.83	0.96	1.98	10.98	0.93	11.67	733.6	2	98	0	0	43				1.00	Mar-15
	4.37	20.51	11.68	35.37	30.94	1.92	0.98	11.02	0.94	11.69	733.6	2	98	0	0	43					May-13
	4.37	20.64	11.91	35.84	31.90	2.01	0.87	11.02	0.94	11.69	733.6	2	98	0	0	43					May-13
	4.27	20.34	11.24	34.15	29.44	1.53	1.38	11.03	0.94	11.71	733.6	2	98	0	0	43					Mar-15
	4.28	20.51	11.70	35.14	30.72	1.86	1.13	11.03	0.94	11.69	733.6	2	98	0	0	43					Mar-15
	4.37	20.51	11.90	35.79	31.86	2	0.88	11.02	0.94	11.69	733.6	2	98	0	0	43					Mar-15
	4.00	21.81	10.11	80.48	98.79	0	0.83	14.28	1.07	41.27	4,014	0	100	0	0	25	30.88	-14.86			Oct-05
	3.91	21.60	9.76	78.70	95.86	0	1.14	14.29	1.07	40.64	4,014	0	100	0	0	25	30.75	-14.98	5.00		Mar-15
	3.71	21.15	8.94	74.78	88.75	0	1.89	14.28	1.07	39.06	4,014	0	100	0	0	25	30.22	-15.22		1.00	Mar-15
	4.02	21.83	10.17	80.76	99.28	0	0.78	14.29	1.07	41.35	4,014	0	100	0	0	25	30.98	-14.87			Oct-05
	2.99	22.25	7.95	74.23	89.30	0.09	0.78	15.04	1.08	15.82	1,799	1	99	0	0	39	26.87	-13.78			Oct-05
	2.98	22.35	7.99	74.49	89.87	0.14	0.73	15.06	1.08	15.87	1,799	1	99	0	0	39	26.91	-13.77			Oct-05
	4.92	18.14	15.04	41.07	62.35	2.57	0.83	7.54	0.58	11.72	1,654	5	62	28	0	78	19.92	-12.88			Jan-11

Fund Name	MARKET Ticker Symbol	Traded On	FUND TYPE, CATEGORY & OBJECTIVE Fund Type	Category and (Prospectus Objective)	RATINGS Overall Rating	Reward Rating	Risk Rating	Recent Up/ Downgrade	Open to New Investors	MINIMUMS Min Initial Investment
John Hancock Funds II Disciplined alternative Yield Cls A	JTRAX	NAS CM	Open End	Long/Short Equity (Growth)	C+	C	B		Y	1,000
John Hancock Funds II Disciplined alternative Yield Cls C	JTRCX	NAS CM	Open End	Long/Short Equity (Growth)	C	C	B-	Down	Y	1,000
John Hancock Funds II Disciplined alternative Yield Cls I	JTRIX	NAS CM	Open End	Long/Short Equity (Growth)	C+	C	B		Y	250,000
John Hancock Funds II Disciplined alternative Yield Cls NA			Open End	Long/Short Equity (Growth)	C+	C	B		Y	0
John Hancock Funds II Disciplined alternative Yield Cls R6	JTRRX	NAS CM	Open End	Long/Short Equity (Growth)	C+	C	B		Y	1,000,000
John Hancock Funds II Emerging Markets Fund Class A	JEVAX	NAS CM	Open End	Global Emerg Mkts (Div Emerging Mkts)	C	C	C+		Y	1,000
John Hancock Funds II Emerging Markets Fund Class C	JEVCX	NAS CM	Open End	Global Emerg Mkts (Div Emerging Mkts)	C	C	C+		Y	1,000
John Hancock Funds II Emerging Markets Fund Class I	JEVIX	NAS CM	Open End	Global Emerg Mkts (Div Emerging Mkts)	C	C	C+		Y	250,000
John Hancock Funds II Emerging Markets Fund Class NAV	JEVNX	NAS CM	Open End	Global Emerg Mkts (Div Emerging Mkts)	C	C	C+		Y	0
John Hancock Funds II Emerging Markets Fund Class R6	JEVRX	NAS CM	Open End	Global Emerg Mkts (Div Emerging Mkts)	C	C	C+		Y	1,000,000
John Hancock Funds II Equity Income Fund Class 1	JIEMX	NAS CM	Open End	US Equity Large Cap Value (Equity-Income)	B-	C	B	Up	Y	0
John Hancock Funds II Equity Income Fund Class A	JHEIX	NAS CM	Open End	US Equity Large Cap Value (Equity-Income)	C+	C	B	Up	Y	1,000
John Hancock Funds II Equity Income Fund Class C	JHERX	NAS CM	Open End	US Equity Large Cap Value (Equity-Income)	C+	C	B	Up	Y	1,000
John Hancock Funds II Equity Income Fund Class NAV			Open End	US Equity Large Cap Value (Equity-Income)	B-	C	B	Up	Y	0
John Hancock Funds II Health Sciences Fund Class NAV			Open End	Healthcare Sector Equity (Health)	C+	C	B	Down	Y	0
John Hancock Funds II International Growth Stock Cls NAV	JGSNX	NAS CM	Open End	Global Equity Large Cap (Growth)	C+	C	B-	Up	Y	0
John Hancock Funds II International Small Cap Fund Class 1	JIIMX	NAS CM	Open End	Global Equity Mid/Small Cap (Small Company)	C	C	C+		Y	0
John Hancock Funds II International Small Cap Cls NAV	JHISX	NAS CM	Open End	Global Equity Mid/Small Cap (Small Company)	C	C	C+		Y	0
John Hancock Funds II International Small Company Cls A	JISAX	NAS CM	Open End	Global Equity Mid/Small Cap (Small Company)	C	C-	C	Up	Y	1,000
John Hancock Funds II International Small Company Cls C	JISDX	NAS CM	Open End	Global Equity Mid/Small Cap (Small Company)	C-	D+	C		Y	1,000
John Hancock Funds II International Small Company Cls I	JSCIX	NAS CM	Open End	Global Equity Mid/Small Cap (Small Company)	C	C-	C	Up	Y	250,000
John Hancock Funds II International Small Company Cls NAV	JHATX	NAS CM	Open End	Global Equity Mid/Small Cap (Small Company)	C	C-	C	Up	Y	0
John Hancock Funds II International Small Company Cls R6	JHSMX	NAS CM	Open End	Global Equity Mid/Small Cap (Small Company)	C	C-	C	Up	Y	1,000,000
John Hancock Funds II International Value Fund Class 1	JIVIX	NAS CM	Open End	Global Equity Large Cap (Growth)	C-	D	C	Down	Y	0
John Hancock Funds II International Value Fund Class NAV	JHVIX	NAS CM	Open End	Global Equity Large Cap (Growth)	C-	D	C	Down	Y	0
John Hancock Funds II Mid Cap Stock Fund Class 1	JIMSX	NAS CM	Open End	US Equity Mid Cap (Growth)	B-	B-	B-	Down	Y	0
John Hancock Funds II Mid Cap Stock Fund Class NAV	JHMSX	NAS CM	Open End	US Equity Mid Cap (Growth)	B-	B-	B-	Down	Y	0
John Hancock Funds II Mid Value Fund Class NAV	JMVNX	NAS CM	Open End	US Equity Mid Cap (Growth)	C	C	B-		Y	0
John Hancock Funds II Multimanager 2010 Lifetime Cls 1	JLAOX	NAS CM	Open End	Target Date (Asset Alloc)	B	C+	A	Up	Y	0
John Hancock Funds II Multimanager 2010 Lifetime Cls A	JLAAX	NAS CM	Open End	Target Date (Asset Alloc)	B	C+	A-	Up	Y	1,000
John Hancock Funds II Multimanager 2010 Lifetime Cls I	JHRLX	NAS CM	Open End	Target Date (Asset Alloc)	B	C+	A	Up	Y	250,000
John Hancock Funds II Multimanager 2010 Lifetime Cls R1	JLADX	NAS CM	Open End	Target Date (Asset Alloc)	B	C+	A-	Up	Y	0
John Hancock Funds II Multimanager 2010 Lifetime Cls R2	JLAEX	NAS CM	Open End	Target Date (Asset Alloc)	B	C+	A-	Up	Y	0
John Hancock Funds II Multimanager 2010 Lifetime Cls R3	JLAFX	NAS CM	Open End	Target Date (Asset Alloc)	B	C+	A-	Up	Y	0
John Hancock Funds II Multimanager 2010 Lifetime Cls R4	JLAGX	NAS CM	Open End	Target Date (Asset Alloc)	B	C+	A-	Up	Y	0
John Hancock Funds II Multimanager 2010 Lifetime Cls R5	JLAHX	NAS CM	Open End	Target Date (Asset Alloc)	B	C+	A	Up	Y	0
John Hancock Funds II Multimanager 2010 Lifetime Cls R6	JLAIX	NAS CM	Open End	Target Date (Asset Alloc)	B	C+	A	Up	Y	1,000,000
John Hancock Funds II Multimanager 2015 Lifetime Cls 1	JLBOX	NAS CM	Open End	Target Date (Asset Alloc)	B	C+	A	Up	Y	0
John Hancock Funds II Multimanager 2015 Lifetime Cls A	JLBAX	NAS CM	Open End	Target Date (Asset Alloc)	B	C	A-	Up	Y	1,000
John Hancock Funds II Multimanager 2015 Lifetime Cls I	JHREX	NAS CM	Open End	Target Date (Asset Alloc)	B	C+	A	Up	Y	250,000
John Hancock Funds II Multimanager 2015 Lifetime Cls R1	JLBDX	NAS CM	Open End	Target Date (Asset Alloc)	B	C	A-	Up	Y	0
John Hancock Funds II Multimanager 2015 Lifetime Cls R2	JLBKX	NAS CM	Open End	Target Date (Asset Alloc)	B	C	A-	Up	Y	0
John Hancock Funds II Multimanager 2015 Lifetime Cls R3	JLBFX	NAS CM	Open End	Target Date (Asset Alloc)	B	C	A-	Up	Y	0
John Hancock Funds II Multimanager 2015 Lifetime Cls R4	JLBGX	NAS CM	Open End	Target Date (Asset Alloc)	B	C+	A-	Up	Y	0
John Hancock Funds II Multimanager 2015 Lifetime Cls R5	JLBHX	NAS CM	Open End	Target Date (Asset Alloc)	B	C+	A	Up	Y	0
John Hancock Funds II Multimanager 2015 Lifetime Cls R6	JLBJX	NAS CM	Open End	Target Date (Asset Alloc)	B	C+	A	Up	Y	1,000,000
John Hancock Funds II Multimanager 2020 Lifetime Cls 1	JLDOX	NAS CM	Open End	Target Date (Asset Alloc)	B	C	A	Up	Y	0
John Hancock Funds II Multimanager 2020 Lifetime Cls A	JLDAX	NAS CM	Open End	Target Date (Asset Alloc)	B	C	A-	Up	Y	1,000
John Hancock Funds II Multimanager 2020 Lifetime Cls I	JHRVX	NAS CM	Open End	Target Date (Asset Alloc)	B	C	A	Up	Y	250,000
John Hancock Funds II Multimanager 2020 Lifetime Cls R1	JLDDX	NAS CM	Open End	Target Date (Asset Alloc)	B-	C	A-	Up	Y	0
John Hancock Funds II Multimanager 2020 Lifetime Cls R2	JLDEX	NAS CM	Open End	Target Date (Asset Alloc)	B	C	A-	Up	Y	0
John Hancock Funds II Multimanager 2020 Lifetime Cls R3	JLDFX	NAS CM	Open End	Target Date (Asset Alloc)	B-	C	A-	Up	Y	0

★ Expanded analysis of this fund is included in Section II.

Min Additional Investment	TOTAL RETURNS 3-Month Total Return	6-Month Total Return	1-Year Total Return	3-Year Total Return	5-Year Total Return	PERFORMANCE Dividend Yield (TTM)	Expense Ratio	3-Yr Std Deviation	3-Year Beta	ASSETS NAV	Total Assets (MIL)	ASSET ALLOCATION & TURNOVER %Cash	%Stocks	%Bonds	%Other	Turnover Ratio	BULL & BEAR Last Bull Market Total Return	Last Bear Market Total Return	FEES Front End Fee (%)	Back End Fee (%)	Inception Date
	1.57	7.75	3.14	13.18	10.74	0.36	1.83	4.75	7.95	10.97	84.7	15	85	0	0	73	10.72		5.00		Dec-13
	1.42	7.35	2.43	10.84	6.92	0	2.53	4.81	8.21	10.65	84.7	15	85	0	0	73	10.27			1.00	Jun-14
	1.64	7.95	3.41	14.11	12.41	0.64	1.54	4.7	8.22	11.13	84.7	15	85	0	0	73	10.91				Dec-13
	1.63	7.99	3.53	14.50	13.20	0.76	1.42	4.7	7.94	11.21	84.7	15	85	0	0	73	10.91				Sep-11
	1.63	7.99	3.61	14.49	13.19	0.75	1.44	4.78	8.34	11.21	84.7	15	85	0	0	73	10.91				Dec-13
	0.74	8.59	-0.78	26.91	6.78	1.2	1.43	13.19	0.93	10.87	269.5	2	98	0	0	11	16.69	-31.03	5.00		Mar-11
	0.46	8.14	-1.48	24.19	2.79	0.46	2.13	13.19	0.93	10.89	269.5	2	98	0	0	11	16.52	-31.14		1.00	Jun-14
	0.74	8.70	-0.51	28.04	8.31	1.46	1.13	13.17	0.93	10.86	269.5	2	98	0	0	11	17.02	-30.87			Mar-11
	0.83	8.81	-0.40	28.41	8.99	1.64	1.02	13.22	0.93	10.86	269.5	2	98	0	0	11	17.2	-30.85			May-07
	0.74	8.72	-0.42	28.42	8.86	1.63	1.03	13.2	0.93	10.84	269.5	2	98	0	0	11	17.08	-30.85			Sep-11
	4.24	16.58	5.05	37.91	36.43	2.08	0.78	12.28	1	18.62	1,796	2	96	0	0	19	23.72	-18.22			Oct-05
	4.15	16.39	4.72	36.53	34.25	1.74	1.14	12.28	1	18.61	1,796	2	96	0	0	19	23.51	-18.34	5.00		Mar-15
	3.95	16.01	3.96	33.57	29.55	1.08	1.84	12.28	1	18.67	1,796	2	96	0	0	19	23.01	-18.58		1.00	Mar-15
	4.31	16.63	5.16	38.17	36.85	2.13	0.73	12.31	1	18.6	1,796	2	96	0	0	19	23.72	-18.24			Oct-05
	1.50	18.84	9.41	46.51	78.41	0	1.09	17.08	1.16	4.73	286.4	1	98	0	0	46	27.6				Sep-11
	4.90	20.25	8.28	26.05	13.73	1.5	0.86	11.81	0.93	13.89	60.7	4	96	0	0	41	17.01	-20.05			Sep-10
	1.15	14.47	-5.73	29.56	10.87	1.52	1.08	13.44	1.08	17.56	128.1	8	92	0	0	30	15.88	-24.61			Oct-05
	1.21	14.54	-5.62	29.85	11.23	1.57	1.03	13.42	1.08	17.56	128.1	8	92	0	0	30	15.87	-24.61			Oct-05
	2.04	12.43	-8.51	23.68	10.95	1.06	1.39	12.52	1.02	10.49	783.3	4	96	0	0	19	13.89	-23.71	5.00		Jun-13
	1.84	11.92	-9.23	20.81	6.87	0.16	2.15	12.45	1.01	10.51	783.3	4	96	0	0	19	13.43	-23.93		1.00	Jun-14
	2.04	12.56	-8.34	24.43	12.59	1.3	1.15	12.5	1.02	10.48	783.3	4	96	0	0	19	14.09	-23.61			Jun-13
	2.04	12.56	-8.23	24.85	13.15	1.41	1.04	12.49	1.02	10.48	783.3	4	96	0	0	19	14.09	-23.61			Apr-06
	2.14	12.67	-8.15	24.94	13.23	1.4	1.06	12.53	1.02	10.49	783.3	4	96	0	0	19	14.09	-23.61			Aug-17
	-0.52	6.06	-7.12	18.78	-7.42	2.18	0.9	12.16	1.03	15.05	267.0	2	98	0	0	29	10.41	-24.05			Oct-05
	-0.52	6.07	-7.08	19.02	-7.16	2.25	0.85	12.16	1.03	15.01	267.0	2	98	0	0	29	10.42	-24.05			Oct-05
	5.27	32.18	14.97	73.59	76.54	0	0.91	16.9	1.12	22.55	1,643	8	86	0	1	67	24.82	-24.41			Oct-05
	5.25	32.19	15.05	73.82	76.95	0	0.86	16.9	1.12	22.83	1,643	8	86	0	1	67	24.89	-24.44			Oct-05
	1.08	12.51	-3.13	26.43	34.65	0.91	0.98	12.43	0.92	14.92	1,297	8	91	0	0	39	20.45	-19.57			Jan-09
	3.02	10.62	6.52	21.69	23.55	3.32	0.55	5		8.85	194.6	10	34	55	0	20	14.02	-11.15			Oct-06
	2.90	10.48	6.21	20.46	21.37	2.96	0.9	5.03		8.85	194.6	10	34	55	0	20	13.74	-11.35	5.00		Oct-06
	3.02	10.76	6.58	21.61	23.24	3.26	0.61	5		8.85	194.6	10	34	55	0	20	14.02	-11.15			Mar-15
	2.80	10.40	5.85	19.53	19.72	2.74	1.26	4.97		8.81	194.6	10	34	55	0	20	13.61	-11.38			Oct-06
	2.91	10.49	6.11	20.16	20.84	2.86	1.01	4.98		8.84	194.6	10	34	55	0	20	14.02	-11.22			Mar-12
	2.80	10.26	5.83	19.51	19.83	2.72	1.16	5		8.81	194.6	10	34	55	0	20	13.66	-11.37			Oct-06
	2.91	10.63	6.27	20.95	22.41	3.11	0.76	5.04		8.84	194.6	10	34	55	0	20	13.85	-11.25			Oct-06
	3.02	10.76	6.52	21.71	23.68	3.31	0.56	4.98		8.85	194.6	10	34	55	0	20	14.08	-11.15			Oct-06
	3.02	10.74	6.70	22.02	24.01	3.36	0.5	5.01		8.86	194.6	10	34	55	0	20	14.07	-11.15			Sep-11
	3.05	11.35	6.35	23.96	25.39	3.32	0.57	5.64		9.12	306.0	9	40	49	0	17	15.65	-13.11			Oct-06
	3.04	11.20	5.92	22.67	23.13	2.96	0.93	5.64		9.13	306.0	9	40	49	0	17	15.37	-13.21	5.00		Oct-06
	3.04	11.47	6.28	23.84	25.17	3.26	0.64	5.69		9.13	306.0	9	40	49	0	17	15.65	-13.11			Mar-15
	2.82	10.98	5.53	21.34	21.09	2.62	1.28	5.64		9.09	306.0	9	40	49	0	17	15.22	-13.32			Oct-06
	2.94	11.27	5.84	22.21	22.56	2.88	1.04	5.71		9.08	306.0	9	40	49	0	17	15.54	-13.18			Mar-12
	2.82	10.98	5.65	21.72	21.71	2.73	1.19	5.7		9.09	306.0	9	40	49	0	17	15.28	-13.32			Oct-06
	3.05	11.38	6.13	23.27	24.18	3.12	0.79	5.71		9.1	306.0	9	40	49	0	17	15.5	-13.22			Oct-06
	3.05	11.49	6.23	23.95	25.38	3.31	0.59	5.74		9.12	306.0	9	40	49	0	17	15.7	-13.1			Oct-06
	3.16	11.47	6.41	24.15	25.82	3.37	0.52	5.65		9.13	306.0	9	40	49	0	17	15.72	-13.11			Sep-11
	3.11	12.45	6.12	27.36	28.29	3.07	0.59	6.7		9.93	845.5	9	48	41	0	19	17.48	-15.42			Oct-06
	3.11	12.31	5.68	26.03	25.99	2.7	0.95	6.64		9.94	845.5	9	48	41	0	19	17.32	-15.61	5.00		Oct-06
	3.10	12.42	6.04	27.34	28.17	3.01	0.66	6.7		9.95	845.5	9	48	41	0	19	17.48	-15.42			Mar-15
	2.91	12.00	5.32	24.72	23.83	2.4	1.31	6.71		9.89	845.5	9	48	41	0	19	17.05	-15.64			Oct-06
	3.02	12.13	5.58	25.65	25.39	2.62	1.05	6.68		9.89	845.5	9	48	41	0	19	17.24	-15.49			Mar-12
	2.91	12.11	5.40	25.05	24.42	2.47	1.21	6.67		9.9	845.5	9	48	41	0	19	17.1	-15.63			Oct-06

Fund Name	Ticker Symbol	Traded On	Fund Type	Category and (Prospectus Objective)	Overall Rating	Reward Rating	Risk Rating	Recent Up/ Downgrade	Open to New Investors	Min Initial Investment
	MARKET		FUND TYPE, CATEGORY & OBJECTIVE		RATINGS				MINIMUMS	
John Hancock Funds II Multimanager 2020 Lifetime Cls R4	JLDGX	NAS CM	Open End	Target Date (Asset Alloc)	B	C	A	Up	Y	0
John Hancock Funds II Multimanager 2020 Lifetime Cls R5	JLDHX	NAS CM	Open End	Target Date (Asset Alloc)	B	C	A	Up	Y	0
John Hancock Funds II Multimanager 2020 Lifetime Cls R6	JLDIX	NAS CM	Open End	Target Date (Asset Alloc)	B	C	A	Up	Y	1,000,000
John Hancock Funds II Multimanager 2025 Lifetime Cls 1	JLEOX	NAS CM	Open End	Target Date (Asset Alloc)	B-	C	A-	Up	Y	0
John Hancock Funds II Multimanager 2025 Lifetime Cls A	JLEAX	NAS CM	Open End	Target Date (Asset Alloc)	B-	C	A-	Up	Y	1,000
John Hancock Funds II Multimanager 2025 Lifetime Cls I	JHRNX	NAS CM	Open End	Target Date (Asset Alloc)	B-	C	A-	Up	Y	250,000
John Hancock Funds II Multimanager 2025 Lifetime Cls R1	JLEDX	NAS CM	Open End	Target Date (Asset Alloc)	B-	C	A-	Up	Y	0
John Hancock Funds II Multimanager 2025 Lifetime Cls R2	JLEEX	NAS CM	Open End	Target Date (Asset Alloc)	B-	C	A-	Up	Y	0
John Hancock Funds II Multimanager 2025 Lifetime Cls R3	JLEFX	NAS CM	Open End	Target Date (Asset Alloc)	B-	C	A-	Up	Y	0
John Hancock Funds II Multimanager 2025 Lifetime Cls R4	JLEGX	NAS CM	Open End	Target Date (Asset Alloc)	B-	C	A-	Up	Y	0
John Hancock Funds II Multimanager 2025 Lifetime Cls R5	JLEHX	NAS CM	Open End	Target Date (Asset Alloc)	B-	C	A-	Up	Y	0
John Hancock Funds II Multimanager 2025 Lifetime Cls R6	JLEIX	NAS CM	Open End	Target Date (Asset Alloc)	B-	C	A-	Up	Y	1,000,000
John Hancock Funds II Multimanager 2030 Lifetime Cls 1	JLFOX	NAS CM	Open End	Target Date (Asset Alloc)	B-	C	B+	Up	Y	0
John Hancock Funds II Multimanager 2030 Lifetime Cls A	JLFAX	NAS CM	Open End	Target Date (Asset Alloc)	B-	C	B+	Up	Y	1,000
John Hancock Funds II Multimanager 2030 Lifetime Cls I	JHRGX	NAS CM	Open End	Target Date (Asset Alloc)	B-	C	B+	Up	Y	250,000
John Hancock Funds II Multimanager 2030 Lifetime Cls R1	JLFDX	NAS CM	Open End	Target Date (Asset Alloc)	B-	C	B+	Up	Y	0
John Hancock Funds II Multimanager 2030 Lifetime Cls R2	JLFEX	NAS CM	Open End	Target Date (Asset Alloc)	B-	C	B+	Up	Y	0
John Hancock Funds II Multimanager 2030 Lifetime Cls R3	JLFFX	NAS CM	Open End	Target Date (Asset Alloc)	B-	C	B+	Up	Y	0
John Hancock Funds II Multimanager 2030 Lifetime Cls R4	JLFGX	NAS CM	Open End	Target Date (Asset Alloc)	B-	C	B+	Up	Y	0
John Hancock Funds II Multimanager 2030 Lifetime Cls R5	JLFHX	NAS CM	Open End	Target Date (Asset Alloc)	B-	C	B+	Up	Y	0
John Hancock Funds II Multimanager 2030 Lifetime Cls R6	JLFIX	NAS CM	Open End	Target Date (Asset Alloc)	B-	C	B+	Up	Y	1,000,000
John Hancock Funds II Multimanager 2035 Lifetime Cls 1	JLHOX	NAS CM	Open End	Target Date (Asset Alloc)	B-	C	B+	Up	Y	0
John Hancock Funds II Multimanager 2035 Lifetime Cls A	JLHAX	NAS CM	Open End	Target Date (Asset Alloc)	B-	C	B	Up	Y	1,000
John Hancock Funds II Multimanager 2035 Lifetime Cls I	JHRMX	NAS CM	Open End	Target Date (Asset Alloc)	B-	C	B+	Up	Y	250,000
John Hancock Funds II Multimanager 2035 Lifetime Cls R1	JLHDX	NAS CM	Open End	Target Date (Asset Alloc)	B-	C	B	Up	Y	0
John Hancock Funds II Multimanager 2035 Lifetime Cls R2	JLHEX	NAS CM	Open End	Target Date (Asset Alloc)	B-	C	B	Up	Y	0
John Hancock Funds II Multimanager 2035 Lifetime Cls R3	JLHFX	NAS CM	Open End	Target Date (Asset Alloc)	B-	C	B	Up	Y	0
John Hancock Funds II Multimanager 2035 Lifetime Cls R4	JLHGX	NAS CM	Open End	Target Date (Asset Alloc)	B-	C	B+	Up	Y	0
John Hancock Funds II Multimanager 2035 Lifetime Cls R5	JLHHX	NAS CM	Open End	Target Date (Asset Alloc)	B-	C	B+	Up	Y	0
John Hancock Funds II Multimanager 2035 Lifetime Cls R6	JLHIX	NAS CM	Open End	Target Date (Asset Alloc)	B-	C	B+	Up	Y	1,000,000
John Hancock Funds II Multimanager 2040 Lifetime Cls 1	JLIOX	NAS CM	Open End	Target Date (Asset Alloc)	B-	C	B	Up	Y	0
John Hancock Funds II Multimanager 2040 Lifetime Cls A	JLIAX	NAS CM	Open End	Target Date (Asset Alloc)	B-	C	B	Up	Y	1,000
John Hancock Funds II Multimanager 2040 Lifetime Cls I	JHRDX	NAS CM	Open End	Target Date (Asset Alloc)	B-	C	B	Up	Y	250,000
John Hancock Funds II Multimanager 2040 Lifetime Cls R1	JLIDX	NAS CM	Open End	Target Date (Asset Alloc)	B-	C	B	Up	Y	0
John Hancock Funds II Multimanager 2040 Lifetime Cls R2	JLIEX	NAS CM	Open End	Target Date (Asset Alloc)	B-	C	B	Up	Y	0
John Hancock Funds II Multimanager 2040 Lifetime Cls R3	JLIFX	NAS CM	Open End	Target Date (Asset Alloc)	B-	C	B	Up	Y	0
John Hancock Funds II Multimanager 2040 Lifetime Cls R4	JLIGX	NAS CM	Open End	Target Date (Asset Alloc)	B-	C	B	Up	Y	0
John Hancock Funds II Multimanager 2040 Lifetime Cls R5	JLIHX	NAS CM	Open End	Target Date (Asset Alloc)	B-	C	B	Up	Y	0
John Hancock Funds II Multimanager 2040 Lifetime Cls R6	JLIIX	NAS CM	Open End	Target Date (Asset Alloc)	B-	C	B	Up	Y	1,000,000
John Hancock Funds II Multimanager 2045 Lifetime Cls 1	JLJOX	NAS CM	Open End	Target Date (Asset Alloc)	B-	C	B	Up	Y	0
John Hancock Funds II Multimanager 2045 Lifetime Cls A	JLJAX	NAS CM	Open End	Target Date (Asset Alloc)	B-	C	B	Up	Y	1,000
John Hancock Funds II Multimanager 2045 Lifetime Cls I	JHROX	NAS CM	Open End	Target Date (Asset Alloc)	B-	C	B	Up	Y	250,000
John Hancock Funds II Multimanager 2045 Lifetime Cls R1	JLJDX	NAS CM	Open End	Target Date (Asset Alloc)	B-	C	B	Up	Y	0
John Hancock Funds II Multimanager 2045 Lifetime Cls R2	JLJEX	NAS CM	Open End	Target Date (Asset Alloc)	B-	C	B	Up	Y	0
John Hancock Funds II Multimanager 2045 Lifetime Cls R3	JLJFX	NAS CM	Open End	Target Date (Asset Alloc)	B-	C	B	Up	Y	0
John Hancock Funds II Multimanager 2045 Lifetime Cls R4	JLJGX	NAS CM	Open End	Target Date (Asset Alloc)	B-	C	B	Up	Y	0
John Hancock Funds II Multimanager 2045 Lifetime Cls R5	JLJHX	NAS CM	Open End	Target Date (Asset Alloc)	B-	C	B	Up	Y	0
John Hancock Funds II Multimanager 2045 Lifetime Cls R6	JLJIX	NAS CM	Open End	Target Date (Asset Alloc)	B-	C	B	Up	Y	1,000,000
John Hancock Funds II Multimgr Lifest Aggress Cls 1	JILAX	NAS CM	Open End	Aggressive Alloc (Aggr Growth)	C+	C	B	Up	Y	0
John Hancock Funds II Multimgr Lifest Aggress Cls A	JALAX	NAS CM	Open End	Aggressive Alloc (Aggr Growth)	C+	C	B	Up	Y	1,000
John Hancock Funds II Multimgr Lifest Aggress Cls B	JBLAX	NAS CM	Open End	Aggressive Alloc (Aggr Growth)	C+	C	B	Up		1,000
John Hancock Funds II Multimgr Lifest Aggress Cls C	JCLAX	NAS CM	Open End	Aggressive Alloc (Aggr Growth)	C+	C	B	Up	Y	1,000

★ Expanded analysis of this fund is included in Section II.

Min Additional Investment	TOTAL RETURNS 3-Month Total Return	6-Month Total Return	1-Year Total Return	3-Year Total Return	5-Year Total Return	PERFORMANCE Dividend Yield (TTM)	Expense Ratio	3-Yr Std Deviation	3-Year Beta	ASSETS NAV	Total Assets (MIL)	ASSET ALLOCATION & TURNOVER %Cash	%Stocks	%Bonds	%Other	Turnover Ratio	BULL & BEAR Last Bull Market Total Return	Last Bear Market Total Return	FEES Front End Fee (%)	Back End Fee (%)	Inception Date
	3.12	12.37	5.88	26.63	27.04	2.86	0.81	6.71		9.9	845.5	9	48	41	0	19	17.35	-15.63			Oct-06
	3.11	12.45	6.10	27.33	28.26	3.05	0.6	6.67		9.93	845.5	9	48	41	0	19	17.52	-15.4			Oct-06
	3.12	12.48	6.09	27.49	28.55	3.13	0.54	6.64		9.91	845.5	9	48	41	0	19	17.56	-15.42			Sep-11
	3.14	13.65	5.71	30.97	31.29	2.85	0.61	7.84		10.49	1,267	8	59	32	1	21	19.12	-17.47			Oct-06
	3.13	13.45	5.34	29.72	28.94	2.47	0.97	7.89		10.54	1,267	8	59	32	1	21	18.91	-17.63	5.00		Oct-06
	3.24	13.63	5.64	30.95	31.05	2.79	0.68	7.92		10.5	1,267	8	59	32	1	21	19.12	-17.47			Mar-15
	3.05	13.31	5.05	28.56	27.03	2.21	1.33	7.92		10.47	1,267	8	59	32	1	21	18.67	-17.68			Oct-06
	3.15	13.43	5.27	29.34	28.45	2.4	1.08	7.86		10.47	1,267	8	59	32	1	21	19	-17.54			Mar-12
	3.05	13.31	4.99	28.71	27.43	2.25	1.22	7.84		10.47	1,267	8	59	32	1	21	18.71	-17.58			Oct-06
	3.14	13.62	5.56	30.33	30.11	2.64	0.83	7.88		10.51	1,267	8	59	32	1	21	18.92	-17.47			Oct-06
	3.14	13.65	5.70	30.96	31.27	2.84	0.62	7.92		10.49	1,267	8	59	32	1	21	19.18	-17.47			Oct-06
	3.24	13.77	5.78	31.33	31.78	2.9	0.56	7.89		10.49	1,267	8	59	32	1	21	19.18	-17.47			Sep-11
	3.16	14.83	5.39	34.48	33.86	2.64	0.62	9.06		10.76	1,246	7	71	21	1	20	20.36	-18.95			Oct-06
	3.05	14.66	5.02	32.99	31.40	2.27	0.98	9.07		10.79	1,246	7	71	21	1	20	19.88	-19.01	5.00		Oct-06
	3.16	14.83	5.32	34.22	33.50	2.58	0.68	9.12		10.76	1,246	7	71	21	1	20	20.36	-18.95			Mar-15
	2.97	14.40	4.68	31.74	29.27	1.99	1.34	9.09		10.72	1,246	7	71	21	1	20	19.91	-19.16			Oct-06
	3.17	14.65	4.95	32.75	30.93	2.19	1.08	9.13		10.72	1,246	7	71	21	1	20	20.24	-19.02			Mar-12
	3.07	14.49	4.75	32.18	29.97	2.04	1.23	9.07		10.74	1,246	7	71	21	1	20	19.95	-19.07			Oct-06
	3.17	14.74	5.13	33.67	32.51	2.43	0.83	9.08		10.74	1,246	7	71	21	1	20	20.18	-18.97			Oct-06
	3.16	14.85	5.29	34.50	33.77	2.63	0.63	9.14		10.75	1,246	7	71	21	1	20	20.39	-18.93			Oct-06
	3.16	14.85	5.45	34.60	34.23	2.69	0.57	9.11		10.75	1,246	7	71	21	1	20	20.42	-18.95			Sep-11
	3.23	15.76	4.90	36.91	35.71	2.44	0.64	10.09		11.16	1,042	6	79	13	1	19	21.12	-19.67			Oct-06
	3.16	15.64	4.58	35.47	33.26	2.09	1	10.09		11.09	1,042	6	79	13	1	19	20.78	-19.84	5.00		Oct-06
	3.14	15.66	4.74	36.53	35.24	2.38	0.7	10.09		11.15	1,042	6	79	13	1	19	21.12	-19.67			Mar-15
	3.07	15.46	4.24	34.13	31.06	1.81	1.35	10.1		11.05	1,042	6	79	13	1	19	20.62	-19.86			Oct-06
	3.14	15.55	4.44	35.19	32.78	1.99	1.1	10.08		11.14	1,042	6	79	13	1	19	20.99	-19.74			Mar-12
	3.07	15.43	4.28	34.52	31.70	1.85	1.25	10.08		11.07	1,042	6	79	13	1	19	20.66	-19.77			Oct-06
	3.14	15.68	4.65	36.09	34.23	2.23	0.85	10.08		11.14	1,042	6	79	13	1	19	20.82	-19.77			Oct-06
	3.23	15.76	4.88	36.88	35.68	2.42	0.65	10.05		11.16	1,042	6	79	13	1	19	21.04	-19.58			Oct-06
	3.24	15.78	4.88	37.15	35.97	2.49	0.59	10.08		11.15	1,042	6	79	13	1	19	21.18	-19.67			Sep-11
	3.22	16.52	4.70	38.67	37.24	2.33	0.63	10.81		11.21	843.9	5	86	7	1	19	21.05	-19.65			Oct-06
	3.14	16.28	4.31	37.11	34.66	2.01	0.99	10.74		11.14	843.9	5	86	7	1	19	20.7	-19.73	5.00		Oct-06
	3.12	16.40	4.53	38.38	36.84	2.27	0.69	10.79		11.21	843.9	5	86	7	1	19	21.05	-19.65			Mar-15
	3.06	16.09	4.00	35.79	32.58	1.68	1.34	10.78		11.11	843.9	5	86	7	1	19	20.55	-19.84			Oct-06
	3.13	16.21	4.22	36.80	34.15	1.87	1.1	10.81		11.18	843.9	5	86	7	1	19	20.93	-19.72			Mar-12
	3.15	16.23	4.13	36.27	33.21	1.78	1.25	10.82		11.1	843.9	5	86	7	1	19	20.56	-19.76			Oct-06
	3.14	16.38	4.46	37.72	35.74	2.13	0.84	10.81		11.15	843.9	5	86	7	1	19	20.81	-19.71			Oct-06
	3.22	16.51	4.69	38.61	37.17	2.32	0.64	10.74		11.22	843.9	5	86	7	1	19	21.09	-19.63			Oct-06
	3.22	16.54	4.77	38.92	37.51	2.38	0.58	10.8		11.2	843.9	5	86	7	1	19	20.99	-19.65			Sep-11
	3.18	16.73	4.59	38.77	37.35	2.32	0.63	10.97		11.02	762.5	5	88	5	1	19	21.05	-19.65			Oct-06
	3.20	16.48	4.28	37.35	34.92	1.99	0.99	10.97		10.95	762.5	5	88	5	1	19	20.72	-19.82	5.00		Oct-06
	3.18	16.63	4.51	38.52	37.00	2.26	0.7	10.95		11.01	762.5	5	88	5	1	19	21.06	-19.65			Mar-15
	3.02	16.31	3.89	35.94	32.74	1.67	1.34	10.96		10.91	762.5	5	88	5	1	19	20.56	-19.76			Oct-06
	3.09	16.41	4.19	37.04	34.28	1.85	1.1	10.98		10.99	762.5	5	88	5	1	19	20.93	-19.72			Mar-12
	3.11	16.39	4.04	36.37	33.34	1.72	1.25	11		10.93	762.5	5	88	5	1	19	20.69	-19.84			Oct-06
	3.10	16.57	4.34	37.89	35.93	2.12	0.84	10.96		10.97	762.5	5	88	5	1	19	20.93	-19.78			Oct-06
	3.27	16.70	4.64	38.80	37.39	2.29	0.64	11		11.04	762.5	5	88	5	1	19	21.1	-19.63			Oct-06
	3.18	16.75	4.65	39.02	37.62	2.37	0.58	10.94		11.01	762.5	5	88	5	1	19	21	-19.65			Sep-11
	3.12	17.24	3.68	40.04	36.16	2.16	1.02	11.77	0.93	15.16	3,755	5	92	1	1	22	21.46	-20.88			Oct-05
	3.04	17.06	3.35	38.57	33.84	1.79	1.38	11.73	0.93	15.23	3,755	5	92	1	1	22	21.11	-21.04	5.00		Oct-05
	2.83	16.62	2.61	35.64	29.02	1.09	2.09	11.76	0.93	15.22	3,755	5	92	1	1	22	20.67	-21.34		5.00	Oct-05
	2.83	16.61	2.55	35.62	29.04	1.09	2.09	11.74	0.93	15.23	3,755	5	92	1	1	22	20.65	-21.26		1.00	Oct-05

	MARKET		FUND TYPE, CATEGORY & OBJECTIVE		RATINGS				MINIMUMS	
Fund Name	Ticker Symbol	Traded On	Fund Type	Category and (Prospectus Objective)	Overall Rating	Reward Rating	Risk Rating	Recent Up/ Downgrade	Open to New Investors	Min Initial Investment
John Hancock Funds II Multimgr Lifest Aggress Cls I	JTAIX	NAS CM	Open End	Aggressive Alloc (Aggr Growth)	C+	C	B	Up	Y	250,000
John Hancock Funds II Multimgr Lifest Aggress Cls R1	JPLAX	NAS CM	Open End	Aggressive Alloc (Aggr Growth)	C+	C	B	Up	Y	0
John Hancock Funds II Multimgr Lifest Aggress Cls R2	JQLAX	NAS CM	Open End	Aggressive Alloc (Aggr Growth)	C+	C	B	Up	Y	0
John Hancock Funds II Multimgr Lifest Aggress Cls R3	JRLAX	NAS CM	Open End	Aggressive Alloc (Aggr Growth)	C+	C	B	Up	Y	0
John Hancock Funds II Multimgr Lifest Aggress Cls R4	JSLAX	NAS CM	Open End	Aggressive Alloc (Aggr Growth)	C+	C	B	Up	Y	0
John Hancock Funds II Multimgr Lifest Aggress Cls R5	JTLAX	NAS CM	Open End	Aggressive Alloc (Aggr Growth)	C+	C	B	Up	Y	0
John Hancock Funds II Multimgr Lifest Aggress Cls R6	JULAX	NAS CM	Open End	Aggressive Alloc (Aggr Growth)	C+	C	B	Up	Y	1,000,000
John Hancock Funds II Multimgr Lifest Bal Cls 1	JILBX	NAS CM	Open End	Moderate Alloc (Balanced)	B-	C	A-	Up	Y	0
John Hancock Funds II Multimgr Lifest Bal Cls 5	JHLAX	NAS CM	Open End	Moderate Alloc (Balanced)	B-	C	A-	Up	Y	0
John Hancock Funds II Multimgr Lifest Bal Cls A	JALBX	NAS CM	Open End	Moderate Alloc (Balanced)	B-	C	A-	Up	Y	1,000
John Hancock Funds II Multimgr Lifest Bal Cls B	JBLBX	NAS CM	Open End	Moderate Alloc (Balanced)	B-	C	A-	Up		1,000
John Hancock Funds II Multimgr Lifest Bal Cls C	JCLBX	NAS CM	Open End	Moderate Alloc (Balanced)	B-	C	A-	Up	Y	1,000
John Hancock Funds II Multimgr Lifest Bal Cls I	JTBIX	NAS CM	Open End	Moderate Alloc (Balanced)	B-	C	A-	Up	Y	250,000
John Hancock Funds II Multimgr Lifest Bal Cls R1	JPLBX	NAS CM	Open End	Moderate Alloc (Balanced)	B-	C	A-	Up	Y	0
John Hancock Funds II Multimgr Lifest Bal Cls R2	JQLBX	NAS CM	Open End	Moderate Alloc (Balanced)	B-	C	A-	Up	Y	0
John Hancock Funds II Multimgr Lifest Bal Cls R3	JRLBX	NAS CM	Open End	Moderate Alloc (Balanced)	B-	C	A-	Up	Y	0
John Hancock Funds II Multimgr Lifest Bal Cls R4	JSLBX	NAS CM	Open End	Moderate Alloc (Balanced)	B-	C	A-	Up	Y	0
John Hancock Funds II Multimgr Lifest Bal Cls R5	JTSBX	NAS CM	Open End	Moderate Alloc (Balanced)	B-	C	A-	Up	Y	0
John Hancock Funds II Multimgr Lifest Bal Cls R6	JULBX	NAS CM	Open End	Moderate Alloc (Balanced)	B-	C	A-	Up	Y	1,000,000
John Hancock Funds II Multimgr Lifest Cons Cls 1	JILCX	NAS CM	Open End	Cautious Alloc (Income)	B-	C+	B+		Y	0
John Hancock Funds II Multimgr Lifest Cons Cls A	JALRX	NAS CM	Open End	Cautious Alloc (Income)	B-	C	B+		Y	1,000
John Hancock Funds II Multimgr Lifest Cons Cls B	JBLCX	NAS CM	Open End	Cautious Alloc (Income)	B-	C	B	Up		1,000
John Hancock Funds II Multimgr Lifest Cons Cls C	JCLCX	NAS CM	Open End	Cautious Alloc (Income)	B-	C	B	Up	Y	1,000
John Hancock Funds II Multimgr Lifest Cons Cls I	JTOIX	NAS CM	Open End	Cautious Alloc (Income)	B-	C+	B+		Y	250,000
John Hancock Funds II Multimgr Lifest Cons Cls R1	JPLCX	NAS CM	Open End	Cautious Alloc (Income)	B-	C	B	Up	Y	0
John Hancock Funds II Multimgr Lifest Cons Cls R2	JQLCX	NAS CM	Open End	Cautious Alloc (Income)	B-	C	B+		Y	0
John Hancock Funds II Multimgr Lifest Cons Cls R3	JRLCX	NAS CM	Open End	Cautious Alloc (Income)	B-	C	B+	Up	Y	0
John Hancock Funds II Multimgr Lifest Cons Cls R4	JSLCX	NAS CM	Open End	Cautious Alloc (Income)	B-	C	B+		Y	0
John Hancock Funds II Multimgr Lifest Cons Cls R5	JTLRX	NAS CM	Open End	Cautious Alloc (Income)	B-	C+	B+		Y	0
John Hancock Funds II Multimgr Lifest Cons Cls R6	JULCX	NAS CM	Open End	Cautious Alloc (Income)	B-	C+	B+		Y	1,000,000
John Hancock Funds II Multimgr Lifest Growth Cls 1	JILGX	NAS CM	Open End	Aggressive Alloc (Growth)	B-	C	B+	Up	Y	0
John Hancock Funds II Multimgr Lifest Growth Cls 5	JHLGX	NAS CM	Open End	Aggressive Alloc (Growth)	B-	C	B+	Up	Y	0
John Hancock Funds II Multimgr Lifest Growth Cls A	JALGX	NAS CM	Open End	Aggressive Alloc (Growth)	B-	C	B+	Up	Y	1,000
John Hancock Funds II Multimgr Lifest Growth Cls B	JBLGX	NAS CM	Open End	Aggressive Alloc (Growth)	B-	C	B	Up		1,000
John Hancock Funds II Multimgr Lifest Growth Cls C	JCLGX	NAS CM	Open End	Aggressive Alloc (Growth)	B-	C	B	Up	Y	1,000
John Hancock Funds II Multimgr Lifest Growth Cls I	JTGIX	NAS CM	Open End	Aggressive Alloc (Growth)	B-	C	B+	Up	Y	250,000
John Hancock Funds II Multimgr Lifest Growth Cls R1	JPLGX	NAS CM	Open End	Aggressive Alloc (Growth)	B-	C	B+	Up	Y	0
John Hancock Funds II Multimgr Lifest Growth Cls R2	JQLGX	NAS CM	Open End	Aggressive Alloc (Growth)	B-	C	B+	Up	Y	0
John Hancock Funds II Multimgr Lifest Growth Cls R3	JRLGX	NAS CM	Open End	Aggressive Alloc (Growth)	B-	C	B+	Up	Y	0
John Hancock Funds II Multimgr Lifest Growth Cls R4	JSLGX	NAS CM	Open End	Aggressive Alloc (Growth)	B-	C	B+	Up	Y	0
John Hancock Funds II Multimgr Lifest Growth Cls R5	JTLGX	NAS CM	Open End	Aggressive Alloc (Growth)	B-	C	B+	Up	Y	0
John Hancock Funds II Multimgr Lifest Growth Cls R6	JULGX	NAS CM	Open End	Aggressive Alloc (Growth)	B-	C	B+	Up	Y	1,000,000
John Hancock Funds II Multimgr Lifest Mod Cls 1	JILMX	NAS CM	Open End	Cautious Alloc (Growth & Income)	B	C+	A-	Up	Y	0
John Hancock Funds II Multimgr Lifest Mod Cls 5	JHLMX	NAS CM	Open End	Cautious Alloc (Growth & Income)	B	C+	A-	Up	Y	0
John Hancock Funds II Multimgr Lifest Mod Cls A	JALMX	NAS CM	Open End	Cautious Alloc (Growth & Income)	B	C	A-	Up	Y	1,000
John Hancock Funds II Multimgr Lifest Mod Cls B	JBLMX	NAS CM	Open End	Cautious Alloc (Growth & Income)	B-	C	B+	Up		1,000
John Hancock Funds II Multimgr Lifest Mod Cls C	JCLMX	NAS CM	Open End	Cautious Alloc (Growth & Income)	B-	C	B+	Up	Y	1,000
John Hancock Funds II Multimgr Lifest Mod Cls I	JTMIX	NAS CM	Open End	Cautious Alloc (Growth & Income)	B	C+	A-	Up	Y	250,000
John Hancock Funds II Multimgr Lifest Mod Cls R1	JPLMX	NAS CM	Open End	Cautious Alloc (Growth & Income)	B-	C	A-	Up	Y	0
John Hancock Funds II Multimgr Lifest Mod Cls R2	JQLMX	NAS CM	Open End	Cautious Alloc (Growth & Income)	B	C	A-	Up	Y	0
John Hancock Funds II Multimgr Lifest Mod Cls R3	JRLMX	NAS CM	Open End	Cautious Alloc (Growth & Income)	B	C	A-	Up	Y	0
John Hancock Funds II Multimgr Lifest Mod Cls R4	JSLMX	NAS CM	Open End	Cautious Alloc (Growth & Income)	B	C	A-	Up	Y	0

★ Expanded analysis of this fund is included in Section II.

	TOTAL RETURNS					PERFORMANCE				ASSETS		ASSET ALLOCATION & TURNOVER					BULL & BEAR		FEES		
Min Additional Investment	3-Month Total Return	6-Month Total Return	1-Year Total Return	3-Year Total Return	5-Year Total Return	Dividend Yield (TTM)	Expense Ratio	3-Yr Std Deviation	3-Year Beta	NAV	Total Assets (MIL)	%Cash	%Stocks	%Bonds	%Other	Turnover Ratio	Last Bull Market Total Return	Last Bear Market Total Return	Front End Fee (%)	Back End Fee (%)	Inception Date
	3.12	17.20	3.67	39.78	35.84	2.1	1.08	11.81	0.94	15.19	3,755	5	92	1	1	22	21.45	-20.88			May-15
	2.90	16.79	2.92	37.07	31.26	1.45	1.74	11.76	0.93	15.23	3,755	5	92	1	1	22	20.84	-21.2			Sep-06
	2.99	16.95	3.19	38.07	33.00	1.71	1.49	11.74	0.93	15.11	3,755	5	92	1	1	22	21.33	-20.94			Mar-12
	2.91	16.88	3.06	37.47	31.81	1.56	1.64	11.78	0.93	15.16	3,755	5	92	1	1	22	20.97	-21.15			Oct-05
	3.05	17.15	3.49	39.21	34.54	1.95	1.24	11.75	0.93	15.16	3,755	5	92	1	1	22	21.13	-21.07			Oct-05
	3.12	17.28	3.73	40.07	36.00	2.15	1.04	11.76	0.93	15.2	3,755	5	92	1	1	22	21.47	-20.98			Oct-05
	3.12	17.29	3.73	40.34	36.60	2.2	0.99	11.77	0.93	15.19	3,755	5	92	1	1	22	21.46	-20.88			Sep-11
	3.08	13.28	5.38	28.10	27.65	2.66	0.96	7.54	0.59	14.53	10,927	8	55	36	1	18	15.81	-13.92			Oct-05
	3.09	13.30	5.44	28.29	27.98	2.71	0.91	7.53	0.59	14.54	10,927	8	55	36	1	18	15.83	-13.83			Jul-06
	2.97	12.98	4.97	26.69	25.33	2.3	1.31	7.49	0.59	14.63	10,927	8	55	36	1	18	15.46	-14.07	5.00		Oct-05
	2.74	12.55	4.18	24.00	20.91	1.65	2.02	7.55	0.59	14.62	10,927	8	55	36	1	18	14.98	-14.31		5.00	Oct-05
	2.66	12.54	4.18	23.98	20.86	1.65	2.02	7.53	0.59	14.63	10,927	8	55	36	1	18	14.97	-14.29		1.00	Oct-05
	3.06	13.24	5.31	27.83	27.38	2.6	1.01	7.53	0.59	14.54	10,927	8	55	36	1	18	15.81	-13.92			May-15
	2.89	12.86	4.63	25.39	23.15	1.98	1.67	7.51	0.59	14.56	10,927	8	55	36	1	18	15.24	-14.17			Sep-06
	2.96	12.93	4.89	26.27	24.68	2.22	1.42	7.5	0.59	14.54	10,927	8	55	36	1	18	15.61	-14			Mar-12
	2.92	12.90	4.74	25.77	23.80	2.09	1.57	7.54	0.59	14.59	10,927	8	55	36	1	18	15.29	-14.11			Oct-05
	3.01	13.09	5.13	27.26	26.30	2.45	1.17	7.49	0.59	14.6	10,927	8	55	36	1	18	15.48	-14.04			Oct-05
	2.98	13.18	5.33	28.03	27.47	2.63	0.97	7.5	0.59	14.62	10,927	8	55	36	1	18	15.71	-13.96			Oct-05
	3.02	13.21	5.42	28.18	27.87	2.69	0.92	7.52	0.59	14.53	10,927	8	55	36	1	18	15.71	-13.92			Sep-11
	2.80	8.65	6.37	14.48	16.74	2.96	0.94	3.47	0.53	12.96	2,376	11	18	69	0	11	9.18	-4.85			Oct-05
	2.70	8.53	5.97	13.30	14.68	2.6	1.29	3.45	0.53	12.99	2,376	11	18	69	0	11	8.82	-5	5.00		Oct-05
	2.53	8.07	5.15	10.90	10.57	1.93	2	3.43	0.53	12.99	2,376	11	18	69	0	11	8.35	-5.34		5.00	Oct-05
	2.53	8.07	5.24	10.90	10.67	1.93	2	3.45	0.53	12.99	2,376	11	18	69	0	11	8.36	-5.26		1.00	Oct-05
	2.79	8.62	6.22	14.25	16.43	2.9	0.99	3.43	0.53	12.96	2,376	11	18	69	0	11	9.18	-4.85			May-15
	2.62	8.27	5.54	12.05	12.53	2.28	1.65	3.44	0.53	12.97	2,376	11	18	69	0	11	8.44	-5.18			Sep-06
	2.69	8.41	5.80	12.95	14.04	2.52	1.4	3.46	0.52	12.97	2,376	11	18	69	0	11	8.98	-4.93			Mar-12
	2.67	8.37	5.72	12.62	13.39	2.44	1.55	3.46	0.53	12.95	2,376	11	18	69	0	11	8.67	-5.2			Oct-05
	2.75	8.54	6.14	13.77	15.32	2.75	1.15	3.48	0.53	12.96	2,376	11	18	69	0	11	8.75	-4.99			Oct-05
	2.80	8.64	6.28	14.43	16.47	2.95	0.95	3.45	0.53	12.96	2,376	11	18	69	0	11	9.08	-4.9			Oct-05
	2.81	8.68	6.32	14.64	16.93	2.99	0.9	3.44	0.53	12.95	2,376	11	18	69	0	11	9.18	-4.85			Sep-11
	3.07	15.29	4.48	34.02	32.11	2.47	0.98	9.64	0.76	15.08	11,094	6	74	18	1	20	19.32	-18.12			Oct-05
	3.08	15.31	4.55	34.27	32.49	2.53	0.93	9.68	0.76	15.06	11,094	6	74	18	1	20	19.31	-18.07			Jul-06
	3.06	15.12	4.15	32.64	29.79	2.1	1.34	9.69	0.77	15.15	11,094	6	74	18	1	20	18.96	-18.22	5.00		Oct-05
	2.78	14.68	3.37	29.83	25.24	1.41	2.05	9.67	0.76	15.15	11,094	6	74	18	1	20	18.39	-18.44		5.00	Oct-05
	2.78	14.70	3.38	29.87	25.21	1.41	2.05	9.69	0.77	15.13	11,094	6	74	18	1	20	18.43	-18.45		1.00	Oct-05
	3.07	15.30	4.48	33.80	31.88	2.41	1.04	9.67	0.76	15.07	11,094	6	74	18	1	20	19.32	-18.12			May-15
	2.91	14.89	3.80	31.22	27.55	1.76	1.69	9.69	0.77	15.2	11,094	6	74	18	1	20	18.7	-18.36			Sep-06
	2.94	15.00	4.02	32.17	29.07	2.04	1.44	9.68	0.76	15.02	11,094	6	74	18	1	20	19.11	-18.19			Mar-12
	2.93	14.91	3.91	31.69	28.18	1.9	1.59	9.67	0.76	15.1	11,094	6	74	18	1	20	18.85	-18.32			Oct-05
	3.06	15.23	4.27	33.20	30.72	2.25	1.19	9.69	0.77	15.13	11,094	6	74	18	1	20	18.94	-18.22			Oct-05
	3.05	15.27	4.50	34.03	32.01	2.45	0.99	9.68	0.76	15.17	11,094	6	74	18	1	20	19.24	-18.14			Oct-05
	3.07	15.29	4.52	34.18	32.40	2.51	0.94	9.67	0.76	15.08	11,094	6	74	18	1	20	19.34	-18.12			Sep-11
	2.99	11.07	6.09	21.06	22.27	2.79	0.94	5.34	0.39	13.42	3,179	9	36	54	0	14	12.24	-8.7			Oct-05
	3.00	11.03	6.15	21.28	22.53	2.84	0.89	5.3	0.38	13.4	3,179	9	36	54	0	14	12.19	-8.68			Jul-06
	2.89	10.75	5.69	19.77	20.00	2.44	1.3	5.29	0.38	13.46	3,179	9	36	54	0	14	11.96	-8.9	5.00		Oct-05
	2.71	10.39	4.96	17.25	15.80	1.78	2.01	5.32	0.39	13.45	3,179	9	36	54	0	14	11.39	-9.16		5.00	Oct-05
	2.71	10.46	4.96	17.32	15.89	1.77	2.01	5.29	0.38	13.47	3,179	9	36	54	0	14	11.39	-9.15		1.00	Oct-05
	2.98	11.05	6.03	20.93	21.97	2.74	1	5.34	0.39	13.41	3,179	9	36	54	0	14	12.24	-8.7			May-15
	2.81	10.60	5.36	18.61	17.85	2.13	1.66	5.28	0.39	13.44	3,179	9	36	54	0	14	11.64	-9.09			Sep-06
	2.87	10.74	5.61	19.37	19.38	2.35	1.41	5.34	0.4	13.41	3,179	9	36	54	0	14	12.13	-8.77			Mar-12
	2.84	10.74	5.54	18.96	18.51	2.22	1.56	5.32	0.38	13.44	3,179	9	36	54	0	14	11.75	-9.02			Oct-05
	2.86	10.89	5.80	20.26	20.77	2.6	1.16	5.31	0.4	13.4	3,179	9	36	54	0	14	11.92	-8.91			Oct-05

	MARKET		FUND TYPE, CATEGORY & OBJECTIVE		RATINGS				MINIMUMS	
Fund Name	Ticker Symbol	Traded On	Fund Type	Category and (Prospectus Objective)	Overall Rating	Reward Rating	Risk Rating	Recent Up/ Downgrade	Open to New Investors	Min Initial Investment
John Hancock Funds II Multimgr Lifest Mod Cls R5	JTLMX	NAS CM	Open End	Cautious Alloc (Growth & Income)	B	C+	A-	Up	Y	0
John Hancock Funds II Multimgr Lifest Mod Cls R6	JULMX	NAS CM	Open End	Cautious Alloc (Growth & Income)	B	C+	A-	Up	Y	1,000,000
John Hancock Funds II New Opportunities Fund Class 1	JISOX	NAS CM	Open End	US Equity Small Cap (Small Company)	C	C-	C+		Y	0
John Hancock Funds II New Opportunities Fund Class A	JASOX	NAS CM	Open End	US Equity Small Cap (Small Company)	C	C-	C+		Y	1,000
John Hancock Funds II New Opportunities Fund Class C	JBSOX	NAS CM	Open End	US Equity Small Cap (Small Company)	C	C-	C+		Y	1,000
John Hancock Funds II New Opportunities Fund Class I	JHSOX	NAS CM	Open End	US Equity Small Cap (Small Company)	C	C-	C+		Y	250,000
John Hancock Funds II New Opportunities Fund Class NAV			Open End	US Equity Small Cap (Small Company)	C	C-	C+		Y	0
John Hancock Funds II New Opportunities Fund Class R1	JRSOX	NAS CM	Open End	US Equity Small Cap (Small Company)	C	C-	C+		Y	0
John Hancock Funds II New Opportunities Fund Class R2	JSSOX	NAS CM	Open End	US Equity Small Cap (Small Company)	C	C-	C+		Y	0
John Hancock Funds II New Opportunities Fund Class R3	JTSOX	NAS CM	Open End	US Equity Small Cap (Small Company)	C	C-	C+		Y	0
John Hancock Funds II New Opportunities Fund Class R4	JUSOX	NAS CM	Open End	US Equity Small Cap (Small Company)	C	C-	C+		Y	0
John Hancock Funds II New Opportunities Fund Class R5	JVSOX	NAS CM	Open End	US Equity Small Cap (Small Company)	C	C-	C+		Y	0
John Hancock Funds II New Opportunities Fund Class R6	JWSOX	NAS CM	Open End	US Equity Small Cap (Small Company)	C	C-	C+		Y	1,000,000
John Hancock Funds II Real Estate Securities Fund Class 1	JIREX	NAS CM	Open End	Real Estate Sector Equity (Real Estate)	C+	C	B	Down	Y	0
John Hancock Funds II Science & Technology Cls NAV Shares			Open End	Technology Sector Equity (Technology)	C+	C+	B-	Down	Y	0
John Hancock Funds II Small Cap Stock Fund Class NAV			Open End	US Equity Small Cap (Small Company)	C+	C+	C+	Down	Y	0
John Hancock Funds II Small Company Value Fund Class 1	JISVX	NAS CM	Open End	US Equity Small Cap (Small Company)	C	C	C+		Y	0
John Hancock Funds II Strategic Equity Allocation Fund NAV			Open End	Aggressive Alloc (Equity-Income)	B-	C	B	Up	Y	0
John Hancock Funds Income Allocation Fund Class A	JIAFX	NAS CM	Open End	Cautious Alloc (Growth & Income)	B-	C	B		Y	1,000
John Hancock Funds Income Allocation Fund Class C	JIAGX	NAS CM	Open End	Cautious Alloc (Growth & Income)	C+	C	B		Y	1,000
John Hancock Funds Income Allocation Fund Class I	JIAIX	NAS CM	Open End	Cautious Alloc (Growth & Income)	B-	C+	B		Y	250,000
John Hancock Funds Income Allocation Fund Class R6	JIASX	NAS CM	Open End	Cautious Alloc (Growth & Income)	B-	C+	B		Y	1,000,000
John Hancock Funds International Growth Fund Class 1	GOIOX	NAS CM	Open End	Global Equity Large Cap (Foreign Stock)	C	C	B-		Y	0
John Hancock Funds International Growth Fund Class A	GOIGX	NAS CM	Open End	Global Equity Large Cap (Foreign Stock)	C	C	B-		Y	1,000
John Hancock Funds International Growth Fund Class B	GONBX	NAS CM	Open End	Global Equity Large Cap (Foreign Stock)	C	C	C+			1,000
John Hancock Funds International Growth Fund Class C	GONCX	NAS CM	Open End	Global Equity Large Cap (Foreign Stock)	C	C	C+		Y	1,000
John Hancock Funds International Growth Fund Class I	GOGIX	NAS CM	Open End	Global Equity Large Cap (Foreign Stock)	C	C	B-		Y	250,000
John Hancock Funds International Growth Fund Class NAV	JIGHX	NAS CM	Open End	Global Equity Large Cap (Foreign Stock)	C	C	B-		Y	0
John Hancock Funds International Growth Fund Class R2	JHIGX	NAS CM	Open End	Global Equity Large Cap (Foreign Stock)	C	C	B-		Y	0
John Hancock Funds International Growth Fund Class R4	JIGIX	NAS CM	Open End	Global Equity Large Cap (Foreign Stock)	C	C	B-		Y	0
John Hancock Funds International Growth Fund Class R6	JIGTX	NAS CM	Open End	Global Equity Large Cap (Foreign Stock)	C	C	B-		Y	1,000,000
John Hancock Funds Multi-Index 2010 Lifetime Port Cls 1	JRLDX	NAS CM	Open End	Target Date (Asset Alloc)	B	C+	A-		Y	0
John Hancock Funds Multi-Index 2010 Lifetime Port Cls R6	JRLHX	NAS CM	Open End	Target Date (Asset Alloc)	B	C+	A-		Y	1,000,000
John Hancock Funds Multi-Index 2015 Lifetime Port Cls 1	JRLIX	NAS CM	Open End	Target Date (Asset Alloc)	B	C+	A		Y	0
John Hancock Funds Multi-Index 2015 Lifetime Port Cls R6	JRLLX	NAS CM	Open End	Target Date (Asset Alloc)	B	C+	A		Y	1,000,000
John Hancock Funds Multi-Index 2020 Lifetime Port Cls 1	JRLOX	NAS CM	Open End	Target Date (Asset Alloc)	B	C	A	Up	Y	0
John Hancock Funds Multi-Index 2020 Lifetime Port Cls R6	JRTAX	NAS CM	Open End	Target Date (Asset Alloc)	B	C+	A	Up	Y	1,000,000
John Hancock Funds Multi-Ind 2020 Preserv Port Cls 1	JRWOX	NAS CM	Open End	Target Date (Asset Alloc)	B-	C+	B+		Y	0
John Hancock Funds Multi-Ind 2020 Preserv Port Cls R1	JRWQX	NAS CM	Open End	Target Date (Asset Alloc)	B-	C	B+		Y	0
John Hancock Funds Multi-Ind 2020 Preserv Port Cls R2	JRWRX	NAS CM	Open End	Target Date (Asset Alloc)	B-	C+	B+		Y	0
John Hancock Funds Multi-Ind 2020 Preserv Port Cls R4	JRWPX	NAS CM	Open End	Target Date (Asset Alloc)	B-	C+	B+		Y	0
John Hancock Funds Multi-Ind 2020 Preserv Port Cls R6	JRWSX	NAS CM	Open End	Target Date (Asset Alloc)	B-	C+	B+	Down	Y	1,000,000
John Hancock Funds Multi-Index 2025 Lifetime Port Cls 1	JRTBX	NAS CM	Open End	Target Date (Asset Alloc)	B-	C	A-	Up	Y	0
John Hancock Funds Multi-Index 2025 Lifetime Port Cls R6	JRTFX	NAS CM	Open End	Target Date (Asset Alloc)	B-	C	A-		Y	1,000,000
John Hancock Funds Multi-Ind 2025 Preserv Port Cls 1	JREOX	NAS CM	Open End	Target Date (Asset Alloc)	B	C+	A-	Up	Y	0
John Hancock Funds Multi-Ind 2025 Preserv Port Cls R1	JREQX	NAS CM	Open End	Target Date (Asset Alloc)	B	C+	A-	Up	Y	0
John Hancock Funds Multi-Ind 2025 Preserv Port Cls R2	JRERX	NAS CM	Open End	Target Date (Asset Alloc)	B	C+	A-	Up	Y	0
John Hancock Funds Multi-Ind 2025 Preserv Port Cls R4	JREPX	NAS CM	Open End	Target Date (Asset Alloc)	B	C+	A-	Up	Y	0
John Hancock Funds Multi-Ind 2025 Preserv Port Cls R6	JRESX	NAS CM	Open End	Target Date (Asset Alloc)	B	C+	A		Y	1,000,000
John Hancock Funds Multi-Index 2030 Lifetime Port Cls 1	JRTGX	NAS CM	Open End	Target Date (Asset Alloc)	B-	C	B+	Up	Y	0
John Hancock Funds Multi-Index 2030 Lifetime Port Cls R6	JRTJX	NAS CM	Open End	Target Date (Asset Alloc)	B-	C	B+	Up	Y	1,000,000
John Hancock Funds Multi-Ind 2030 Preserv Port Cls 1	JRHOX	NAS CM	Open End	Target Date (Asset Alloc)	B	C	A-	Up	Y	0

★ Expanded analysis of this fund is included in Section II.

Min Additional Investment	TOTAL RETURNS 3-Month Total Return	6-Month Total Return	1-Year Total Return	3-Year Total Return	5-Year Total Return	PERFORMANCE Dividend Yield (TTM)	Expense Ratio	3-Yr Std Deviation	3-Year Beta	ASSETS NAV	Total Assets (MIL)	ASSET ALLOCATION & TURNOVER %Cash	%Stocks	%Bonds	%Other	Turnover Ratio	BULL & BEAR Last Bull Market Total Return	Last Bear Market Total Return	FEES Front End Fee (%)	Back End Fee (%)	Inception Date
	2.99	10.98	6.08	21.00	22.02	2.78	0.96	5.29	0.39	13.42	3,179	9	36	54	0	14	12.09	-8.74			Oct-05
	3.00	11.11	6.14	21.26	22.51	2.83	0.91	5.34	0.39	13.4	3,179	9	36	54	0	14	12.26	-8.7			Sep-11
	2.65	19.79	-3.95	40.16	32.43	0.41	0.85	18.12	1.05	23.97	400.7	4	96	0	0	52	29.47	-25.75			Oct-05
	2.59	19.58	-4.25	38.60	30.21	0.06	1.21	18.12	1.05	23.75	400.7	4	96	0	0	52	29.26	-25.82	5.00		May-15
	2.36	19.13	-4.95	35.69	25.74	0	1.91	18.12	1.05	22.97	400.7	4	96	0	0	52	28.73	-26.04		1.00	May-15
	2.63	19.73	-3.99	39.89	32.20	0.36	0.91	18.14	1.05	23.78	400.7	4	96	0	0	52	29.48	-25.73			May-15
	2.63	19.79	-3.89	40.39	32.80	0.46	0.8	18.14	1.05	23.78	400.7	4	96	0	0	52	29.48	-25.73			Oct-05
	2.47	19.39	-4.60	37.63	28.95	0	1.56	18.12	1.05	23.58	400.7	4	96	0	0	52	29.11	-25.88			May-15
	2.58	19.68	-4.17	39.07	30.88	0.15	1.31	18.11	1.05	23.77	400.7	4	96	0	0	52	29.29	-25.81			May-15
	2.51	19.42	-4.45	38.06	29.35	0	1.46	18.12	1.05	23.67	400.7	4	96	0	0	52	29.11	-25.88			May-15
	2.63	19.68	-4.08	39.62	31.54	0.31	1.07	18.15	1.05	23.77	400.7	4	96	0	0	52	29.29	-25.81			May-15
	2.67	19.82	-3.90	40.34	32.74	0.45	0.86	18.11	1.05	23.81	400.7	4	96	0	0	52	29.48	-25.73			May-15
	2.67	19.79	-3.88	40.26	32.68	0.44	0.81	18.14	1.05	23.78	400.7	4	96	0	0	52	29.48	-25.73			May-15
	2.17	19.29	13.54	16.57	48.83	1.88	0.8	12.62	0.94	13.6	412.2	0	100	0	0	158	32.02	-17.1			Oct-05
	2.94	26.31	7.41	89.80	112.89	0	1.11	16.9	1.19	3.84	293.6	11	88	0	0	108					Feb-13
	4.76	30.18	8.93	69.63	45.91	0	1.06	18.2	1.02	9.23	25.9	5	91	0	4	92	25.5	-25.7			Sep-08
	3.98	18.00	-1.14	40.98	38.83	0.58	1.22	16.21	0.92	25.82	62.0	4	96	0	0	31	28.41	-23.36			Oct-05
	3.44	16.76	4.73	40.54	39.95	1.79	0.66	11.58	0.93	11.42	7,560	4	96	1	0	115					Apr-12
	2.62	9.83	6.45	14.15		3.37	1.19	4.39	0.47	9.86	6.2	7	25	64	0	50			4.00		Nov-14
	2.45	9.48	5.72	11.82		2.7	1.89	4.4	0.47	9.83	6.2	7	25	64	0	50				1.00	Nov-14
	2.70	10.10	6.87	15.19		3.65	0.89	4.37	0.45	9.87	6.2	7	25	64	0	50					Nov-14
	2.72	10.03	6.98	15.53		3.75	0.79	4.41	0.47	9.87	6.2	7	25	64	0	50					Nov-14
	4.32	19.00	2.36	38.90	41.71	0.9	0.92	13.21	1.04	27.99	9,571	3	97	0	0	98	16.15	-20.42			Jun-06
	4.25	18.80	1.98	37.40	39.06	0.54	1.28	13.18	1.04	27.93	9,571	3	97	0	0	98	15.83	-20.55	5.00		Jun-06
	4.06	18.35	1.25	34.51	34.07	0	1.98	13.16	1.04	27.4	9,571	3	97	0	0	98	15.36	-20.81		5.00	Jun-06
	4.07	18.35	1.25	34.55	34.15	0	1.98	13.18	1.04	27.34	9,571	3	97	0	0	98	15.33	-20.8		1.00	Jun-06
	4.35	18.98	2.29	38.69	41.19	0.81	0.98	13.2	1.04	28.01	9,571	3	97	0	0	98	16.02	-20.4			Jun-06
	4.32	19.00	2.38	39.11	41.94	0.95	0.87	13.19	1.04	27.99	9,571	3	97	0	0	98	16.15	-20.42			Jun-15
	4.25	18.77	1.88	37.03	38.58	0.44	1.39	13.19	1.04	27.96	9,571	3	97	0	0	98	16.01	-20.48			Mar-15
	4.28	18.90	2.14	38.07	40.04	0.68	1.14	13.2	1.04	27.99	9,571	3	97	0	0	98	16.01	-20.48			Mar-15
	4.35	19.02	2.39	39.11	41.97	0.93	0.89	13.19	1.04	28.03	9,571	3	97	0	0	98	16.15	-20.42			Mar-15
	3.15	11.02	7.63	20.74	25.12	3.06	0.4	4.95		10.47	26.8	1	36	62	0	49					Nov-13
	3.25	11.13	7.78	20.90	25.53	3.1	0.35	4.97		10.48	26.8	1	36	62	0	49					Nov-13
	3.25	11.70	7.56	23.02	26.87	2.82	0.42	5.63		10.78	41.4	3	42	55	0	28					Nov-13
	3.25	11.70	7.52	23.20	27.18	2.87	0.37	5.65		10.78	41.4	3	42	55	0	28					Nov-13
	3.18	12.46	7.06	26.06	29.50	2.7	0.43	6.52		11.01	139.1	3	51	46	0	30					Nov-13
	3.28	12.56	7.11	26.35	29.93	2.74	0.38	6.52		11.02	139.1	3	51	46	0	30					Nov-13
	2.85	7.75	7.23	14.19	18.76	2.64	0.38	2.92		11.53	646.6	3	13	83	0	11	10.59	-6.25			Apr-10
	2.66	7.43	6.41	11.96	15.21	1.94	1.09	2.88		11.56	646.6	3	13	83	0	11	10.3	-6.43			Sep-12
	2.75	7.53	6.68	12.64	16.08	2.18	0.84	2.92		11.56	646.6	3	13	83	0	11	10.46	-6.33			Sep-12
	2.75	7.62	7.04	13.78	18.03	2.5	0.59	2.87		11.57	646.6	3	13	83	0	11	10.46	-6.33			May-12
	2.85	7.85	7.28	14.35	19.04	2.69	0.33	2.91		11.54	646.6	3	13	83	0	11	10.59	-6.25			Sep-12
	3.22	13.59	6.69	29.85	32.74	2.58	0.44	7.7		11.2	220.4	3	61	35	0	23					Nov-13
	3.31	13.57	6.74	30.15	33.18	2.62	0.39	7.72		11.21	220.4	3	61	35	0	23					Nov-13
	3.04	10.09	6.92	21.17	24.70	2.55	0.4	4.7		12.54	1,272	5	32	63	0	14	14.53	-10.58			Apr-10
	2.86	9.69	6.27	18.65	20.45	1.86	1.11	4.68		12.56	1,272	5	32	63	0	14	14.23	-10.75			Sep-12
	2.95	9.79	6.47	19.77	22.52	2.1	0.86	4.7		12.56	1,272	5	32	63	0	14	14.4	-10.66			Sep-12
	3.02	10.04	6.90	20.80	23.92	2.4	0.61	4.7		12.6	1,272	5	32	63	0	14	14.4	-10.66			May-12
	3.04	10.09	6.98	21.34	24.91	2.6	0.35	4.69		12.54	1,272	5	32	63	0	14	14.53	-10.58			Sep-12
	3.34	14.75	6.42	33.49	35.53	2.41	0.42	8.87		11.43	245.2	3	73	24	0	19					Nov-13
	3.34	14.75	6.48	33.70	35.94	2.46	0.37	8.87		11.43	245.2	3	73	24	0	19					Nov-13
	3.20	12.25	6.66	27.81	30.07	2.6	0.41	6.69		13.19	1,390	6	50	44	0	18	16.76	-13.07			Apr-10

	MARKET			FUND TYPE, CATEGORY & OBJECTIVE	RATINGS				MINIMUMS	
Fund Name	Ticker Symbol	Traded On	Fund Type	Category and (Prospectus Objective)	Overall Rating	Reward Rating	Risk Rating	Recent Up/ Downgrade	Open to New Investors	Min Initial Investment
John Hancock Funds Multi-Ind 2030 Preserv Port Cls R1	JRHQX	NAS CM	Open End	Target Date (Asset Alloc)	B	C	A-	Up	Y	0
John Hancock Funds Multi-Ind 2030 Preserv Port Cls R2	JRHRX	NAS CM	Open End	Target Date (Asset Alloc)	B	C	A-	Up	Y	0
John Hancock Funds Multi-Ind 2030 Preserv Port Cls R4	JRHPX	NAS CM	Open End	Target Date (Asset Alloc)	B	C	A-	Up	Y	0
John Hancock Funds Multi-Ind 2030 Preserv Port Cls R6	JRHSX	NAS CM	Open End	Target Date (Asset Alloc)	B	C	A-	Up	Y	1,000,000
John Hancock Funds Multi-Index 2035 Lifetime Port Cls 1	JRTKX	NAS CM	Open End	Target Date (Asset Alloc)	B-	C	B+	Up	Y	0
John Hancock Funds Multi-Index 2035 Lifetime Port Cls R6	JRTNX	NAS CM	Open End	Target Date (Asset Alloc)	B-	C	B+	Up	Y	1,000,000
John Hancock Funds Multi-Ind 2035 Preserv Port Cls 1	JRYOX	NAS CM	Open End	Target Date (Asset Alloc)	B-	C	B+	Up	Y	0
John Hancock Funds Multi-Ind 2035 Preserv Port Cls R1	JRYQX	NAS CM	Open End	Target Date (Asset Alloc)	B-	C	B+	Up	Y	0
John Hancock Funds Multi-Ind 2035 Preserv Port Cls R2	JRYRX	NAS CM	Open End	Target Date (Asset Alloc)	B-	C	B+	Up	Y	0
John Hancock Funds Multi-Ind 2035 Preserv Port Cls R4	JRYPX	NAS CM	Open End	Target Date (Asset Alloc)	B-	C	B+	Up	Y	0
John Hancock Funds Multi-Ind 2035 Preserv Port Cls R6	JRYSX	NAS CM	Open End	Target Date (Asset Alloc)	B-	C	B+	Up	Y	1,000,000
John Hancock Funds Multi-Index 2040 Lifetime Port Cls 1	JRTTX	NAS CM	Open End	Target Date (Asset Alloc)	B-	C	B	Up	Y	0
John Hancock Funds Multi-Index 2040 Lifetime Port Cls R6	JRTWX	NAS CM	Open End	Target Date (Asset Alloc)	B-	C	B	Up	Y	1,000,000
John Hancock Funds Multi-Ind 2040 Preserv Port Cls 1	JRROX	NAS CM	Open End	Target Date (Asset Alloc)	B-	C	B+	Up	Y	0
John Hancock Funds Multi-Ind 2040 Preserv Port Cls R1	JRRQX	NAS CM	Open End	Target Date (Asset Alloc)	B-	C	B+	Up	Y	0
John Hancock Funds Multi-Ind 2040 Preserv Port Cls R2	JRRRX	NAS CM	Open End	Target Date (Asset Alloc)	B-	C	B+	Up	Y	0
John Hancock Funds Multi-Ind 2040 Preserv Port Cls R4	JRRPX	NAS CM	Open End	Target Date (Asset Alloc)	B-	C	B+	Up	Y	0
John Hancock Funds Multi-Ind 2040 Preserv Port Cls R6	JRRSX	NAS CM	Open End	Target Date (Asset Alloc)	B-	C	B+	Up	Y	1,000,000
John Hancock Funds Multi-Index 2045 Lifetime Port Cls 1	JRLQX	NAS CM	Open End	Target Date (Asset Alloc)	B-	C	B	Up	Y	0
John Hancock Funds Multi-Index 2045 Lifetime Port Cls R6	JRLVX	NAS CM	Open End	Target Date (Asset Alloc)	B-	C	B	Up	Y	1,000,000
John Hancock Funds Multi-Ind 2045 Preserv Port Cls 1	JRVOX	NAS CM	Open End	Target Date (Asset Alloc)	B-	C	B+	Up	Y	0
John Hancock Funds Multi-Ind 2045 Preserv Port Cls R1	JRVQX	NAS CM	Open End	Target Date (Asset Alloc)	B-	C	B+	Up	Y	0
John Hancock Funds Multi-Ind 2045 Preserv Port Cls R2	JRVRX	NAS CM	Open End	Target Date (Asset Alloc)	B-	C	B+	Up	Y	0
John Hancock Funds Multi-Ind 2045 Preserv Port Cls R4	JRVPX	NAS CM	Open End	Target Date (Asset Alloc)	B-	C	B+	Up	Y	0
John Hancock Funds Multi-Ind 2045 Preserv Port Cls R6	JRVSX	NAS CM	Open End	Target Date (Asset Alloc)	B-	C	B+	Up	Y	1,000,000
John Hancock Funds Multi-Index 2050 Lifetime Port Cls 1	JRLWX	NAS CM	Open End	Target Date (Asset Alloc)	B-	C	B	Up	Y	0
John Hancock Funds Multi-Index 2050 Lifetime Port Cls R6	JRLZX	NAS CM	Open End	Target Date (Asset Alloc)	B-	C	B	Up	Y	1,000,000
John Hancock Funds Multi-Ind 2050 Preserv Port Cls 1	JRIOX	NAS CM	Open End	Target Date (Asset Alloc)	B-	C	B+	Up	Y	0
John Hancock Funds Multi-Ind 2050 Preserv Port Cls R1	JRIQX	NAS CM	Open End	Target Date (Asset Alloc)	B-	C	B+	Up	Y	0
John Hancock Funds Multi-Ind 2050 Preserv Port Cls R2	JRINX	NAS CM	Open End	Target Date (Asset Alloc)	B-	C	B+	Up	Y	0
John Hancock Funds Multi-Ind 2050 Preserv Port Cls R4	JRIPX	NAS CM	Open End	Target Date (Asset Alloc)	B-	C	B+	Up	Y	0
John Hancock Funds Multi-Ind 2050 Preserv Port Cls R6	JRISX	NAS CM	Open End	Target Date (Asset Alloc)	B-	C	B+	Up	Y	1,000,000
John Hancock Funds Multi-Index 2055 Lifetime Port Cls 1	JLKZX	NAS CM	Open End	Target Date (Asset Alloc)	B-	C	B	Up	Y	0
John Hancock Funds Multi-Index 2055 Lifetime Port Cls R6	JLKYX	NAS CM	Open End	Target Date (Asset Alloc)	B-	C	B	Up	Y	1,000,000
John Hancock Funds Multi-Ind 2055 Preserv Port Cls 1	JRIYX	NAS CM	Open End	Target Date (Asset Alloc)	B-	C	B+	Up	Y	0
John Hancock Funds Multi-Ind 2055 Preserv Port Cls R1	JRITX	NAS CM	Open End	Target Date (Asset Alloc)	B-	C	B+	Up	Y	0
John Hancock Funds Multi-Ind 2055 Preserv Port Cls R2	JRIUX	NAS CM	Open End	Target Date (Asset Alloc)	B-	C	B+	Up	Y	0
John Hancock Funds Multi-Ind 2055 Preserv Port Cls R4	JRIVX	NAS CM	Open End	Target Date (Asset Alloc)	B-	C	B+	Up	Y	0
John Hancock Funds Multi-Ind 2055 Preserv Port Cls R6	JRIWX	NAS CM	Open End	Target Date (Asset Alloc)	B-	C	B+	Up	Y	1,000,000
John Hancock Funds Multi-Index 2060 Lifetime Port Cls 1	JRODX	NAS CM	Open End	Target Date (Asset Alloc)	B-	C	B	Up	Y	0
John Hancock Funds Multi-Index 2060 Lifetime Port Cls R4	JHIKX	NAS CM	Open End	Target Date (Asset Alloc)	C+	C	B	Up	Y	0
John Hancock Funds Multi-Index 2060 Lifetime Port Cls R6	JIEHX	NAS CM	Open End	Target Date (Asset Alloc)	B-	C	B	Up	Y	1,000,000
John Hancock Funds Multi-Ind 2060 Preserv Port Cls 1	JCHOX	NAS CM	Open End	Target Date (Asset Alloc)	B-	C	B+	Up	Y	0
John Hancock Funds Multi-Ind 2060 Preserv Port Cls R1	JKIMX	NAS CM	Open End	Target Date (Asset Alloc)	B-	C	B+	Up	Y	0
John Hancock Funds Multi-Ind 2060 Preserv Port Cls R2	JSATX	NAS CM	Open End	Target Date (Asset Alloc)	B-	C	B+	Up	Y	0
John Hancock Funds Multi-Ind 2060 Preserv Port Cls R4	JPORX	NAS CM	Open End	Target Date (Asset Alloc)	B-	C	B+	Up	Y	0
John Hancock Funds Multi-Ind 2060 Preserv Port Cls R6	JTFOX	NAS CM	Open End	Target Date (Asset Alloc)	B-	C	B+	Up	Y	1,000,000
John Hancock Funds Multi-Ind Income Preserv Port Cls 1	JRFOX	NAS CM	Open End	Target Date (Asset Alloc)	B-	C	B+		Y	0
John Hancock Funds Multi-Ind Income Preserv Port Cls R1	JRFQX	NAS CM	Open End	Target Date (Asset Alloc)	B-	C	B+	Up	Y	0
John Hancock Funds Multi-Ind Income Preserv Port Cls R2	JRFNX	NAS CM	Open End	Target Date (Asset Alloc)	B-	C	B+	Up	Y	0
John Hancock Funds Multi-Ind Income Preserv Port Cls R4	JRFPX	NAS CM	Open End	Target Date (Asset Alloc)	B-	C	B+		Y	0
John Hancock Funds Multi-Ind Income Preserv Port Cls R6	JRFSX	NAS CM	Open End	Target Date (Asset Alloc)	B-	C+	B+		Y	1,000,000

★ Expanded analysis of this fund is included in Section II.

	TOTAL RETURNS					PERFORMANCE				ASSETS		ASSET ALLOCATION & TURNOVER					BULL & BEAR		FEES		
Min Additional Investment	3-Month Total Return	6-Month Total Return	1-Year Total Return	3-Year Total Return	5-Year Total Return	Dividend Yield (TTM)	Expense Ratio	3-Yr Std Deviation	3-Year Beta	NAV	Total Assets (MIL)	%Cash	%Stocks	%Bonds	%Other	Turnover Ratio	Last Bull Market Total Return	Last Bear Market Total Return	Front End Fee (%)	Back End Fee (%)	Inception Date
	3.03	11.93	6.04	25.47	25.95	1.96	1.12	6.68		13.22	1,390	6	50	44	0	18	16.47	-13.23			Sep-12
	3.12	11.96	6.20	26.13	27.09	2.15	0.87	6.7		13.19	1,390	6	50	44	0	18	16.64	-13.14			Sep-12
	3.11	12.08	6.47	27.37	29.30	2.46	0.62	6.72		13.26	1,390	6	50	44	0	18	16.64	-13.13			May-12
	3.21	12.17	6.65	28.01	30.41	2.65	0.36	6.7		13.18	1,390	6	50	44	0	18	16.77	-13.07			Sep-12
	3.39	15.70	6.11	36.21	37.58	2.31	0.41	9.85		11.57	227.8	5	80	14	0	15					Nov-13
	3.39	15.69	6.17	36.42	38.00	2.35	0.36	9.82		11.57	227.8	5	80	14	0	15					Nov-13
	3.28	13.80	6.37	32.06	33.45	2.6	0.41	8.25		13.52	1,213	6	64	29	0	17	18.2	-14.5			Apr-10
	3.11	13.47	5.66	29.60	29.25	1.97	1.12	8.29		13.56	1,213	6	64	29	0	17	17.89	-14.66			Sep-12
	3.12	13.60	5.88	30.19	30.46	2.14	0.87	8.28		13.53	1,213	6	64	29	0	17	18.07	-14.57			Sep-12
	3.26	13.80	6.25	31.58	32.62	2.45	0.62	8.27		13.6	1,213	6	64	29	0	17	18.07	-14.57			May-12
	3.28	13.88	6.35	32.24	33.75	2.64	0.36	8.24		13.53	1,213	6	64	29	0	17	18.2	-14.5			Sep-12
	3.44	16.40	5.89	38.05	39.45	2.22	0.41	10.5		11.71	194.6	4	88	8	0	15					Nov-13
	3.44	16.40	5.95	38.13	39.80	2.27	0.36	10.5		11.71	194.6	4	88	8	0	15					Nov-13
	3.38	14.79	6.23	34.71	35.55	2.57	0.41	9.19		13.73	961.1	5	72	22	0	16	18.82	-15.17			Apr-10
	3.15	14.40	5.41	32.02	31.36	1.86	1.13	9.18		13.74	961.1	5	72	22	0	16	18.5	-15.33			Sep-12
	3.23	14.59	5.72	33.13	32.86	2.11	0.88	9.18		13.74	961.1	5	72	22	0	16	18.68	-15.24			Sep-12
	3.29	14.71	6.03	34.11	34.61	2.43	0.63	9.15		13.8	961.1	5	72	22	0	16	18.68	-15.24			May-12
	3.39	14.82	6.29	34.85	35.83	2.63	0.36	9.14		13.71	961.1	5	72	22	0	16	18.81	-15.17			Sep-12
	3.44	16.61	5.84	38.13	39.21	2.2	0.41	10.72		11.72	169.5	3	91	5	0	12					Nov-13
	3.43	16.71	5.98	38.32	39.67	2.25	0.36	10.73		11.73	169.5	3	91	5	0	12					Nov-13
	3.35	15.28	6.10	35.72	36.49	2.6	0.42	9.61		13.88	779.6	7	75	18	0	12	18.88	-15.24			Apr-10
	3.19	14.88	5.37	32.86	31.80	1.9	1.13	9.54		13.89	779.6	7	75	18	0	12	18.57	-15.4			Sep-12
	3.26	14.97	5.67	33.96	33.58	2.14	0.88	9.61		13.9	779.6	7	75	18	0	12	18.75	-15.31			Sep-12
	3.33	15.19	6.00	35.25	35.58	2.47	0.63	9.61		13.95	779.6	7	75	18	0	12	18.75	-15.31			May-12
	3.42	15.36	6.24	36.02	36.83	2.65	0.37	9.6		13.89	779.6	7	75	18	0	12	18.88	-15.24			Sep-12
	3.40	16.53	5.81	38.03	39.51	2.18	0.41	10.73		11.84	119.5	7	87	5	0	14					Nov-13
	3.49	16.65	5.96	38.26	39.96	2.23	0.36	10.72		11.84	119.5	7	87	5	0	14					Nov-13
	3.35	15.34	6.12	35.90	36.67	2.56	0.43	9.71		12.33	617.8	7	77	16	0	13	18.84	-15.16			Apr-11
	3.17	14.99	5.40	33.19	32.33	1.85	1.15	9.65		12.35	617.8	7	77	16	0	13	18.53	-15.32			Sep-12
	3.26	15.11	5.62	34.15	34.03	2.1	0.89	9.7		12.34	617.8	7	77	16	0	13	18.7	-15.24			Sep-12
	3.33	15.27	6.04	35.27	35.60	2.43	0.64	9.7		12.38	617.8	7	77	16	0	13	18.7	-15.24			May-12
	3.43	15.44	6.19	36.12	36.92	2.61	0.38	9.71		12.33	617.8	7	77	16	0	13	18.84	-15.16			Sep-12
	3.44	16.63	5.82	38.11	39.57	2.18	0.41	10.73		11.71	82.4	3	92	5	0	17					Mar-14
	3.35	16.53	5.89	38.23	39.88	2.24	0.36	10.71		11.7	82.4	3	92	5	0	17					Mar-14
	3.37	15.36	6.08	35.80	36.80	2.52	0.43	9.67		11.04	270.3	4	79	17	0	10					Mar-14
	3.28	15.15	5.61	33.95	33.59	2.06	1.15	9.68		11.02	270.3	4	79	17	0	10					Mar-14
	3.27	15.13	5.68	34.63	35.00	2.19	0.9	9.68		11.03	270.3	4	79	17	0	10					Mar-14
	3.36	15.34	6.03	35.44	36.21	2.4	0.65	9.7		11.05	270.3	4	79	17	0	10					Mar-14
	3.36	15.34	6.13	35.97	37.23	2.56	0.38	9.71		11.05	270.3	4	79	17	0	10					Mar-14
	3.45	16.60	5.87	38.22		2.03	0.41	10.66		12.29	25.9	8	86	5	0	24					Mar-16
	3.36	16.49	5.72	37.64		1.91	0.62	10.7		12.29	25.9	8	86	5	0	24					Apr-17
	3.45	16.60	5.93	38.41		2.08	0.36	10.66		12.29	25.9	8	86	5	0	24					Mar-16
	3.37	15.36	6.11	35.76		2.35	0.42	9.64		11.94	89.4	4	79	17	0	10					Mar-16
	3.29	15.05	5.64	33.92		1.89	1.13	9.7		11.92	89.4	4	79	17	0	10					Mar-16
	3.29	15.15	5.84	34.81		2.12	0.88	9.67		11.93	89.4	4	79	17	0	10					Mar-16
	3.37	15.25	5.97	35.31		2.23	0.63	9.68		11.94	89.4	4	79	17	0	10					Mar-16
	3.37	15.34	6.16	35.92		2.39	0.37	9.69		11.95	89.4	4	79	17	0	10					Mar-16
	2.44	6.50	6.72	10.34	15.09	2.51	0.39	2.21		11.29	368.7	3	10	86	0	7	6.02	-0.93			Apr-10
	2.26	6.09	6.02	8.37	11.88	1.89	1.1	2.23		11.31	368.7	3	10	86	0	7	5.75	-1.12			Sep-12
	2.35	6.20	6.21	8.97	13.03	2.05	0.85	2.21		11.3	368.7	3	10	86	0	7	5.9	-1.02			Sep-12
	2.44	6.40	6.58	9.92	14.37	2.39	0.6	2.18		11.3	368.7	3	10	86	0	7	5.9	-1.02			May-12
	2.45	6.41	6.78	10.41	15.28	2.56	0.34	2.2		11.28	368.7	3	10	86	0	7	6.02	-0.93			Sep-12

	MARKET			FUND TYPE, CATEGORY & OBJECTIVE	RATINGS				MINIMUMS	
Fund Name	Ticker Symbol	Traded On	Fund Type	Category and (Prospectus Objective)	Overall Rating	Reward Rating	Risk Rating	Recent Up/ Downgrade	Open to New Investors	Min Initial Investment
John Hancock Funds Multi-Ind Lifestyle Aggress Port Cls 1	JIIOX	NAS CM	Open End	Aggressive Alloc (Aggr Growth)	B-	C	B	Up	Y	0
John Hancock Funds Multi-Ind Lifestyle Aggress Port Cls R6	JIIRX	NAS CM	Open End	Aggressive Alloc (Aggr Growth)	B-	C	B	Up	Y	1,000,000
John Hancock Funds Multi-Ind Lifestyle Balanced Port Cls 1	JIBOX	NAS CM	Open End	Moderate Alloc (Balanced)	B	C	A-	Up	Y	0
John Hancock Funds Multi-Ind Lifest Bal Cls R6	JIBRX	NAS CM	Open End	Moderate Alloc (Balanced)	B	C	A-	Up	Y	1,000,000
John Hancock Funds Multi-Ind Lifestyle Cons Port Cls 1	JLCGX	NAS CM	Open End	Cautious Alloc (Asset Alloc)	B-	C+	B+		Y	0
John Hancock Funds Multi-Ind Lifestyle Cons Port Cls R6	JLCSX	NAS CM	Open End	Cautious Alloc (Asset Alloc)	B-	C+	B+		Y	1,000,000
John Hancock Funds Multi-Index Lifestyle Growth Port Cls 1	JLGOX	NAS CM	Open End	Aggressive Alloc (Growth)	B-	C	B+	Up	Y	0
John Hancock Funds Multi-Ind Lifestyle Growth Port Cls R6	JLGSX	NAS CM	Open End	Aggressive Alloc (Growth)	B-	C	B+	Up	Y	1,000,000
John Hancock Funds Multi-Ind Lifestyle Mod Port Cls 1	JLMOX	NAS CM	Open End	Cautious Alloc (Growth)	B	C+	A-	Up	Y	0
John Hancock Funds Multi-Ind Lifestyle Mod Port Cls R6	JLMRX	NAS CM	Open End	Cautious Alloc (Growth)	B	C+	A-		Y	1,000,000
John Hancock Funds Multimanager 2050 Lifetime Port Cls 1	JLKOX	NAS CM	Open End	Target Date (Asset Alloc)	B-	C	B	Up	Y	0
John Hancock Funds Multimanager 2050 Lifetime Port Cls A	JLKAX	NAS CM	Open End	Target Date (Asset Alloc)	B-	C	B	Up	Y	1,000
John Hancock Funds Multimanager 2050 Lifetime Port Cls I	JHRPX	NAS CM	Open End	Target Date (Asset Alloc)	B-	C	B	Up	Y	250,000
John Hancock Funds Multimanager 2050 Lifetime Port Cls R1	JLKDX	NAS CM	Open End	Target Date (Asset Alloc)	B-	C	B	Up	Y	0
John Hancock Funds Multimanager 2050 Lifetime Port Cls R2	JLKEX	NAS CM	Open End	Target Date (Asset Alloc)	B-	C	B	Up	Y	0
John Hancock Funds Multimanager 2050 Lifetime Port Cls R3	JLKFX	NAS CM	Open End	Target Date (Asset Alloc)	B-	C	B	Up	Y	0
John Hancock Funds Multimanager 2050 Lifetime Port Cls R4	JLKGX	NAS CM	Open End	Target Date (Asset Alloc)	B-	C	B	Up	Y	0
John Hancock Funds Multimanager 2050 Lifetime Port Cls R5	JLKHX	NAS CM	Open End	Target Date (Asset Alloc)	B-	C	B	Up	Y	0
John Hancock Funds Multimanager 2050 Lifetime Port Cls R6	JLKRX	NAS CM	Open End	Target Date (Asset Alloc)	B-	C	B	Up	Y	1,000,000
John Hancock Funds Multimanager 2055 Lifetime Port Cls 1	JLKUX	NAS CM	Open End	Target Date (Asset Alloc)	B-	C	B	Up	Y	0
John Hancock Funds Multimanager 2055 Lifetime Port Cls A	JLKLX	NAS CM	Open End	Target Date (Asset Alloc)	B-	C	B	Up	Y	1,000
John Hancock Funds Multimanager 2055 Lifetime Port Cls I	JHRTX	NAS CM	Open End	Target Date (Asset Alloc)	B-	C	B	Up	Y	250,000
John Hancock Funds Multimanager 2055 Lifetime Port Cls R1	JLKMX	NAS CM	Open End	Target Date (Asset Alloc)	B-	C	B	Up	Y	0
John Hancock Funds Multimanager 2055 Lifetime Port Cls R2	JLKNX	NAS CM	Open End	Target Date (Asset Alloc)	B-	C	B	Up	Y	0
John Hancock Funds Multimanager 2055 Lifetime Port Cls R3	JLKPX	NAS CM	Open End	Target Date (Asset Alloc)	B-	C	B	Up	Y	0
John Hancock Funds Multimanager 2055 Lifetime Port Cls R4	JLKQX	NAS CM	Open End	Target Date (Asset Alloc)	B-	C	B	Up	Y	0
John Hancock Funds Multimanager 2055 Lifetime Port Cls R5	JLKSX	NAS CM	Open End	Target Date (Asset Alloc)	B-	C	B	Up	Y	0
John Hancock Funds Multimanager 2055 Lifetime Port Cls R6	JLKTX	NAS CM	Open End	Target Date (Asset Alloc)	B-	C	B	Up	Y	1,000,000
John Hancock Funds Multimanager 2060 Lifetime Port Cls 1	JRETX	NAS CM	Open End	Target Date (Asset Alloc)	B-	C	B	Up	Y	0
John Hancock Funds Multimanager 2060 Lifetime Port Cls A	JJERX	NAS CM	Open End	Target Date (Asset Alloc)	B-	C	B	Up	Y	1,000
John Hancock Funds Multimanager 2060 Lifetime Port Cls I	JMENX	NAS CM	Open End	Target Date (Asset Alloc)	B-	C	B	Up	Y	250,000
John Hancock Funds Multimanager 2060 Lifetime Port Cls R1	JTLOX	NAS CM	Open End	Target Date (Asset Alloc)	B-	C	B	Up	Y	0
John Hancock Funds Multimanager 2060 Lifetime Port Cls R2	JVIMX	NAS CM	Open End	Target Date (Asset Alloc)	B-	C	B	Up	Y	0
John Hancock Funds Multimanager 2060 Lifetime Port Cls R3	JGTHX	NAS CM	Open End	Target Date (Asset Alloc)	B-	C	B	Up	Y	0
John Hancock Funds Multimanager 2060 Lifetime Port Cls R4	JROUX	NAS CM	Open End	Target Date (Asset Alloc)	B-	C	B	Up	Y	0
John Hancock Funds Multimanager 2060 Lifetime Port Cls R5	JGHTX	NAS CM	Open End	Target Date (Asset Alloc)	B-	C	B	Up	Y	0
John Hancock Funds Multimanager 2060 Lifetime Port Cls R6	JESRX	NAS CM	Open End	Target Date (Asset Alloc)	B-	C	B	Up	Y	1,000,000
John Hancock Funds Small Cap Growth Fund Class A	JSJAX	NAS CM	Open End	US Equity Small Cap (Small Company)	C	C	C+		Y	1,000
John Hancock Funds Small Cap Growth Fund Class C	JSJCX	NAS CM	Open End	US Equity Small Cap (Small Company)	C	C	C+		Y	1,000
John Hancock Funds Small Cap Growth Fund Class I	JSJIX	NAS CM	Open End	US Equity Small Cap (Small Company)	C	C	C+		Y	250,000
John Hancock Funds Small Cap Growth Fund Class NAV			Open End	US Equity Small Cap (Small Company)	C	C	C+		Y	0
John Hancock Funds Small Cap Growth Fund Class R6	JSJFX	NAS CM	Open End	US Equity Small Cap (Small Company)	C	C	C+		Y	1,000,000
John Hancock Global Shareholder Yield Fund Class A	JGYAX	NAS CM	Open End	Global Equity Large Cap (Growth & Income)	C+	C	B		Y	1,000
John Hancock Global Shareholder Yield Fund Class B	JGYBX	NAS CM	Open End	Global Equity Large Cap (Growth & Income)	C+	C	B	Up		1,000
John Hancock Global Shareholder Yield Fund Class C	JGYCX	NAS CM	Open End	Global Equity Large Cap (Growth & Income)	C+	C	B-	Up	Y	1,000
John Hancock Global Shareholder Yield Fund Class I	JGYIX	NAS CM	Open End	Global Equity Large Cap (Growth & Income)	C+	C	B		Y	250,000
John Hancock Global Shareholder Yield Fund Class NAV			Open End	Global Equity Large Cap (Growth & Income)	C+	C	B		Y	0
John Hancock Global Shareholder Yield Fund Class R2	JGSRX	NAS CM	Open End	Global Equity Large Cap (Growth & Income)	C+	C	B		Y	0
John Hancock Global Shareholder Yield Fund Class R6	JGRSX	NAS CM	Open End	Global Equity Large Cap (Growth & Income)	C+	C	B		Y	1,000,000
John Hancock Hedged Equity & Income Fund	HEQ	NYSE	Closed End	Global Equity Large Cap (Corporate Bond)	C-	C	C-		Y	
John Hancock II Small Cap Value Fund Class A	JSCAX	NAS CM	Open End	US Equity Small Cap (Small Company)	C	C	C+		Y	1,000
John Hancock II Small Cap Value Fund Class I	JSCBX	NAS CM	Open End	US Equity Small Cap (Small Company)	C	C	C+		Y	250,000

★ Expanded analysis of this fund is included in Section II.

Min Additional Investment	TOTAL RETURNS 3-Month Total Return	6-Month Total Return	1-Year Total Return	3-Year Total Return	5-Year Total Return	PERFORMANCE Dividend Yield (TTM)	Expense Ratio	3-Yr Std Deviation	3-Year Beta	ASSETS NAV	Total Assets (MIL)	ASSET ALLOCATION & TURNOVER %Cash	%Stocks	%Bonds	%Other	Turnover Ratio	BULL & BEAR Last Bull Market Total Return	Last Bear Market Total Return	FEES Front End Fee (%)	Back End Fee (%)	Inception Date
	3.41	17.27	5.39	39.79	40.70	1.86	0.68	11.52	0.93	11.81	348.1	4	95	0	0	15					Dec-13
	3.50	17.26	5.44	40.05	40.96	1.9	0.65	11.52	0.93	11.82	348.1	4	95	0	0	15					Dec-13
	3.22	13.19	6.66	26.56	30.04	2.37	0.71	7.3	0.2	11.29	899.6	3	57	39	0	17					Dec-13
	3.32	13.32	6.79	26.83	30.44	2.4	0.67	7.29	0.21	11.3	899.6	3	57	39	0	17					Dec-13
	2.91	9.10	7.29	13.58	18.96	2.67	0.74	3.55	0.6	10.69	175.3	2	20	78	0	24					Dec-13
	2.92	9.11	7.43	13.81	19.32	2.71	0.7	3.6	0.62	10.7	175.3	2	20	78	0	24					Dec-13
	3.36	15.18	6.04	32.92	35.49	2.07	0.68	9.33	0.06	11.68	837.8	7	74	19	0	16					Dec-13
	3.35	15.17	6.06	33.01	35.50	2.1	0.64	9.32	0.06	11.69	837.8	7	74	19	0	16					Dec-13
	3.12	11.25	7.38	20.10	24.56	2.6	0.74	5.23	0.42	11.01	258.7	2	38	59	0	20					Dec-13
	3.13	11.28	7.42	20.12	24.71	2.63	0.7	5.27	0.43	11.01	258.7	2	38	59	0	20					Dec-13
	3.20	16.73	4.69	38.80	37.33	2.27	0.65	11.01		11.93	413.0	5	88	5	1	18	21.12	-19.64			Apr-11
	3.20	16.51	4.32	37.39	34.79	1.91	1.01	10.98		11.92	413.0	5	88	5	1	18	20.84	-19.72	5.00		Mar-12
	3.20	16.61	4.53	38.51	36.94	2.21	0.71	10.96		11.93	413.0	5	88	5	1	18	21.12	-19.64			Mar-15
	3.03	16.34	3.96	36.02	32.64	1.6	1.36	11		11.89	413.0	5	88	5	1	18	20.72	-19.79			Mar-12
	3.11	16.52	4.21	37.03	34.34	1.81	1.12	11		11.92	413.0	5	88	5	1	18	20.88	-19.7			Mar-12
	3.03	16.34	4.03	36.41	33.47	1.73	1.26	10.98		11.89	413.0	5	88	5	1	18	20.72	-19.79			Mar-12
	3.20	16.63	4.44	38.00	36.05	2.06	0.86	10.97		11.92	413.0	5	88	5	1	18	20.88	-19.7			Mar-12
	3.19	16.71	4.60	38.80	37.33	2.26	0.66	10.97		11.94	413.0	5	88	5	1	18	21	-19.64			Mar-12
	3.28	16.81	4.75	39.09	37.76	2.32	0.6	10.98		11.95	413.0	5	88	5	1	18	21	-19.64			Mar-12
	3.25	16.71	4.66	38.78	37.29	2.29	0.64	10.97		11.1	207.8	5	88	5	1	14					Mar-14
	3.07	16.40	4.21	37.31	34.58	1.92	1	10.97		11.07	207.8	5	88	5	1	14			5.00		Mar-14
	3.25	16.71	4.68	38.54	37.01	2.23	0.7	10.98		11.1	207.8	5	88	5	1	14					Mar-15
	3.16	16.40	4.24	36.97	34.02	1.86	1.35	10.97		11.07	207.8	5	88	5	1	14					Mar-14
	3.07	16.40	4.17	37.35	35.00	1.88	1.1	10.97		11.07	207.8	5	88	5	1	14					Mar-14
	3.07	16.31	4.03	36.50	33.54	1.77	1.25	10.97		11.05	207.8	5	88	5	1	14					Mar-14
	3.25	16.73	4.57	38.38	36.41	2.2	0.85	10.96		11.09	207.8	5	88	5	1	14					Mar-14
	3.25	16.71	4.64	38.82	37.33	2.27	0.65	10.96		11.1	207.8	5	88	5	1	14					Mar-14
	3.25	16.71	4.72	38.99	37.62	2.34	0.59	10.99		11.1	207.8	5	88	5	1	14					Mar-14
	3.22	16.68	4.63	38.53		2.2	0.63	10.98		12.17	80.5	5	89	5	1	21					Mar-16
	3.05	16.50	4.25	36.99		1.89	0.99	11		12.14	80.5	5	89	5	1	21			5.00		Mar-16
	3.13	16.68	4.56	38.29		2.14	0.69	11.02		12.17	80.5	5	89	5	1	21					Mar-16
	3.05	16.39	4.13	36.61		1.79	1.34	10.95		12.14	80.5	5	89	5	1	21					Mar-16
	3.14	16.60	4.36	37.59		1.97	1.09	11		12.15	80.5	5	89	5	1	21					Mar-16
	3.05	16.39	4.13	36.61		1.79	1.24	10.95		12.14	80.5	5	89	5	1	21					Mar-16
	3.22	16.69	4.55	38.07		2.13	0.84	10.99		12.16	80.5	5	89	5	1	21					Mar-16
	3.13	16.69	4.59	38.55		2.24	0.64	11.01		12.16	80.5	5	89	5	1	21					Mar-16
	3.22	16.77	4.69	38.84		2.25	0.58	11.01		12.18	80.5	5	89	5	1	21					Mar-16
	3.36	20.88	0.20	44.45	45.88	0	1.33	16.61	0.92	17.19	562.9	5	95	0	0	165	28.53	-23.65	5.00		Mar-18
	3.14	20.43	-0.53	41.28	40.56	0	2.08	16.59	0.92	17.03	562.9	5	95	0	0	165	27.97	-23.89		1.00	Mar-18
	3.41	20.98	0.38	45.50	47.67	0	1.09	16.59	0.92	17.24	562.9	5	95	0	0	165	28.71	-23.57			Mar-18
	3.41	21.02	0.55	45.65	47.83	0	0.97	16.59	0.92	17.27	562.9	5	95	0	0	165	28.71	-23.57			Oct-05
	3.47	21.10	0.55	45.74	47.92	0	0.98	16.64	0.92	17.27	562.9	5	95	0	0	165	28.71	-23.57			Mar-18
	1.41	12.48	6.21	18.34	16.45	2.95	1.09	9.75	0.78	11.05	2,021	4	96	0	0	16	13.45	-12.26	5.00		Mar-07
	1.13	11.95	5.42	15.72	12.16	2.22	1.84	9.73	0.77	11.06	2,021	4	96	0	0	16	13.05	-12.58		5.00	Mar-07
	1.13	11.95	5.32	15.61	12.25	2.22	1.84	9.7	0.77	11.06	2,021	4	96	0	0	16	12.92	-12.48		1.00	Mar-07
	1.47	12.57	6.45	19.31	18.06	3.18	0.84	9.72	0.77	11.09	2,021	4	96	0	0	16	13.67	-12.03			Mar-07
	1.40	12.64	6.56	19.57	18.72	3.28	0.85	9.73	0.77	11.08	2,021	4	96	0	0	16	13.7	-12			Apr-08
	1.37	12.34	6.03	17.87	15.65	2.8	1.24	9.72	0.77	11.1	2,021	4	96	0	0	16	13.41	-12.12			Mar-12
	1.40	12.54	6.47	19.59	18.74	3.29	0.74	9.68	0.77	11.07	2,021	4	96	0	0	16	13.67	-12.02			Sep-11
	0.81	8.31	0.64	20.28	17.21	4.54	1.2	7.46		14.84	181.3	3	81	15	0	96	19.36				May-11
	4.41	16.24	-2.31	24.16	32.10	0.36	1.52	17.06	0.96	20.32	627.3	2	98	0	0	25	27.36	-21.49	5.00		Dec-13
	4.41	16.35	-2.03	25.24	34.11	0.64	1.22	17.08	0.96	20.35	627.3	2	98	0	0	25	27.58	-21.39			Dec-13

Fund Name	Ticker Symbol	Traded On	Fund Type	Category and (Prospectus Objective)	Overall Rating	Reward Rating	Risk Rating	Recent Up/ Downgrade	Open to New Investors	Min Initial Investment
	MARKET		FUND TYPE, CATEGORY & OBJECTIVE		RATINGS				MINIMUMS	
John Hancock II Small Cap Value Fund Class NAV	JSCNX	NAS CM	Open End	US Equity Small Cap (Small Company)	C	C	C+		Y	0
John Hancock II Small Cap Value Fund Class R6	JSCCX	NAS CM	Open End	US Equity Small Cap (Small Company)	C	C	C+		Y	1,000,000
John Hancock Preferred Income Fund	HPI	NYSE	Closed End	US Fixed Income (Income)	C	C+	C-		Y	
John Hancock Preferred Income Fund II	HPF	NYSE	Closed End	US Fixed Income (Income)	C	C+	C-		Y	
John Hancock Preferred Income Fund III	HPS	NYSE	Closed End	US Fixed Income (Income)	C	C+	C-		Y	
John Hancock Premium Dividend Fund	PDT	NYSE	Closed End	US Fixed Income (Income)	C	B-	C-	Down	Y	
John Hancock Regional Bank Fund Class A	FRBAX	NAS CM	Open End	Financials Sector Equity (Financial)	C-	C-	C	Down	Y	1,000
John Hancock Regional Bank Fund Class B	FRBFX	NAS CM	Open End	Financials Sector Equity (Financial)	C-	C-	C	Down		1,000
John Hancock Regional Bank Fund Class C	FRBCX	NAS CM	Open End	Financials Sector Equity (Financial)	C-	C-	C	Down	Y	1,000
John Hancock Regional Bank Fund Class I	JRBFX	NAS CM	Open End	Financials Sector Equity (Financial)	C-	C-	C	Down	Y	250,000
John Hancock Regional Bank Fund Class R6	JRGRX	NAS CM	Open End	Financials Sector Equity (Financial)	C-	C-	C	Down	Y	1,000,000
John Hancock Seaport Long/Short Fund Class A	JSFBX	NAS CM	Open End	Long/Short Equity (Growth)	B-	C	A-	Up	Y	1,000
John Hancock Seaport Long/Short Fund Class C	JSFTX	NAS CM	Open End	Long/Short Equity (Growth)	B-	C	B+	Up	Y	1,000
John Hancock Seaport Long/Short Fund Class I	JSFDX	NAS CM	Open End	Long/Short Equity (Growth)	B-	C	A-	Up	Y	250,000
John Hancock Seaport Long/Short Fund Class NAV			Open End	Long/Short Equity (Growth)	B-	C	A-	Up	Y	0
John Hancock Seaport Long/Short Fund Class R6	JSFRX	NAS CM	Open End	Long/Short Equity (Growth)	B-	C	A-	Up	Y	1,000,000
John Hancock Small Cap Core Fund Class I	JCCIX	NAS CM	Open End	US Equity Small Cap (Small Company)	C	C	C+		Y	250,000
John Hancock Small Cap Core Fund Class NAV			Open End	US Equity Small Cap (Small Company)	C	C	C+		Y	0
John Hancock Small Cap Core Fund Class R6	JORSX	NAS CM	Open End	US Equity Small Cap (Small Company)	C	C	C+		Y	1,000,000
John Hancock Tax Advantage Global Shareholder Yield Fund	XHTYX	NYSE	Closed End	Global Equity Large Cap (World Stock)	C	C	C-	Up	Y	
John Hancock Tax-Advantaged Dividend Income Fund	HTD	NYSE	Closed End	Moderate Alloc (Equity-Income)	C+	B	C-	Down	Y	
John Hancock U.S. Global Leaders Growth Fund Class A	USGLX	NAS CM	Open End	US Equity Large Cap Growth (Growth)	B	B-	B+		Y	1,000
John Hancock U.S. Global Leaders Growth Fund Class B	USLBX	NAS CM	Open End	US Equity Large Cap Growth (Growth)	B	B-	B+			1,000
John Hancock U.S. Global Leaders Growth Fund Class C	USLCX	NAS CM	Open End	US Equity Large Cap Growth (Growth)	B	B-	B+		Y	1,000
John Hancock U.S. Global Leaders Growth Fund Class I	USLIX	NAS CM	Open End	US Equity Large Cap Growth (Growth)	B	B-	B+		Y	250,000
John Hancock U.S. Global Leaders Growth Fund Class R2	USLYX	NAS CM	Open End	US Equity Large Cap Growth (Growth)	B	B-	B+		Y	0
John Hancock U.S. Global Leaders Growth Fund Class R6	UGLSX	NAS CM	Open End	US Equity Large Cap Growth (Growth)	B	B-	B+		Y	1,000,000
John Hancock U.S. Quality Growth Fund Class A	JSGAX	NAS CM	Open End	US Equity Large Cap Growth (Growth)	B-	B-	B	Down	Y	1,000
John Hancock U.S. Quality Growth Fund Class C	JSGCX	NAS CM	Open End	US Equity Large Cap Growth (Growth)	B-	C+	B	Down	Y	1,000
John Hancock U.S. Quality Growth Fund Class I	JSGIX	NAS CM	Open End	US Equity Large Cap Growth (Growth)	B-	B-	B	Down	Y	250,000
John Hancock U.S. Quality Growth Fund Class NAV			Open End	US Equity Large Cap Growth (Growth)	B-	B-	B	Down	Y	0
John Hancock U.S. Quality Growth Fund Class R2	JSGRX	NAS CM	Open End	US Equity Large Cap Growth (Growth)	B-	B-	B	Down	Y	0
John Hancock U.S. Quality Growth Fund Class R4	JHSGX	NAS CM	Open End	US Equity Large Cap Growth (Growth)	B-	B-	B	Down	Y	0
John Hancock U.S. Quality Growth Fund Class R6	JSGTX	NAS CM	Open End	US Equity Large Cap Growth (Growth)	B-	B-	B	Down	Y	1,000,000
John Hancock Value Equity Fund Class A	JVEAX	NAS CM	Open End	US Equity Large Cap Value (Equity-Income)	C+	C	B	Up	Y	1,000
John Hancock Value Equity Fund Class C	JVECX	NAS CM	Open End	US Equity Large Cap Value (Equity-Income)	C+	C	B	Up	Y	1,000
John Hancock Value Equity Fund Class I	JVEIX	NAS CM	Open End	US Equity Large Cap Value (Equity-Income)	C+	C	B	Up	Y	250,000
John Hancock Value Equity Fund Class NAV			Open End	US Equity Large Cap Value (Equity-Income)	C+	C	B	Up	Y	0
John Hancock Value Equity Fund Class R6	JVERX	NAS CM	Open End	US Equity Large Cap Value (Equity-Income)	C+	C	B	Up	Y	1,000,000
John Hancock Var Ins Trust 500 Index Trust B Series I	JFIVX	NAS CM	Open End	US Equity Large Cap Blend (Growth & Income)	U	U	U		Y	0
John Hancock Var Ins Trust All Cap Core Trust Series I	JEACX	NAS CM	Open End	US Equity Large Cap Blend (Growth)	U	U	U		Y	0
John Hancock Var Ins Trust Financial Ind Trust Series I	JEFSX	NAS CM	Open End	Financials Sector Equity (Financial)	U	U	U		Y	0
John Hancock Var Ins Trust Fundament All Cap Core Trust Se	JEQAX	NAS CM	Open End	US Equity Large Cap Growth (Growth)	U	U	U		Y	0
John Hancock Var Ins Trust Intl Eq Index Trust B Series I	JIEQX	NAS CM	Open End	Global Equity Large Cap (Foreign Stock)	U	U	U		Y	0
John Hancock Var Ins Trust Mid Cap Index Trust Series I	JECIX	NAS CM	Open End	US Equity Mid Cap (Growth)	U	U	U		Y	0
John Hancock Var Ins Trust Mid Value Trust Series I	JEMUX	NAS CM	Open End	US Equity Mid Cap (Growth)	U	U	U		Y	0
John Hancock Var Ins Trust Science & Tech Trust Ser I	JESTX	NAS CM	Open End	Technology Sector Equity (Technology)	U	U	U		Y	0
John Hancock Var Ins Trust Small Cap Growth Trust Series I	JESGX	NAS CM	Open End	US Equity Small Cap (Growth)	U	U	U		Y	0
John Hancock Var Ins Trust Small Cap Index Trust Series I	JESIX	NAS CM	Open End	US Equity Small Cap (Growth)	U	U	U		Y	0
John Hancock Var Ins Trust Small Cap Value Trust Series I	JESVX	NAS CM	Open End	US Equity Small Cap (Growth)	U	U	U		Y	0
John Hancock Var Ins Trust Total Stock Mkt Ind Trust Ser I	JETSX	NAS CM	Open End	US Equity Large Cap Blend (Growth & Income)	U	U	U		Y	0
John Hancock Var Ins Trust Utilities Trust Series I	JEUTX	NAS CM	Open End	Utilities Sector Equity (Utility)	U	U	U		Y	0

★ Expanded analysis of this fund is included in Section II.

	TOTAL RETURNS					PERFORMANCE				ASSETS		ASSET ALLOCATION & TURNOVER					BULL & BEAR		FEES		
Min Additional Investment	3-Month Total Return	6-Month Total Return	1-Year Total Return	3-Year Total Return	5-Year Total Return	Dividend Yield (TTM)	Expense Ratio	3-Yr Std Deviation	3-Year Beta	NAV	Total Assets (MIL)	%Cash	%Stocks	%Bonds	%Other	Turnover Ratio	Last Bull Market Total Return	Last Bear Market Total Return	Front End Fee (%)	Back End Fee (%)	Inception Date
	4.46	16.42	-1.93	25.71	34.92	0.77	1.11	17.06	0.96	20.34	627.3	2	98	0	0	25	27.58	-21.39			Dec-08
	4.46	16.40	-1.94	25.69	34.93	0.76	1.12	17.07	0.96	20.36	627.3	2	98	0	0	25	27.58	-21.39			Dec-13
	2.40	18.15	6.75	18.40	44.42	7.44	0	8.13	1.2	21.1	549.4	0	13	4	1	20	13.75	-3.72			Aug-02
	2.39	17.95	6.64	18.27	42.94	7.29	0	8.14	0.86	20.79	442.8	0	12	4	0	24	12.98	-3.15			Nov-02
	2.34	17.68	6.16	17.90	43.20	7.46	0	8.01	0.85	18.48	583.9	1	12	3	1	23	14.55	-4.61			Jun-03
	2.68	19.70	10.86	20.82	53.69	5.65		9.12	1	15.32	743.5	0	48	-3	3	24	16	-0.66			Dec-89
	5.40	15.40	-8.89	51.00	62.82	1.36	1.21	21.41	0.93	25.45	1,898	0	100	0	0	3	38.35	-25.7	5.00		Jan-92
	5.24	15.00	-9.53	47.87	57.21	0.67	1.91	21.42	0.93	24.12	1,898	0	100	0	0	3	37.8	-25.91		5.00	Oct-85
	5.28	15.02	-9.51	47.90	57.32	0.66	1.91	21.41	0.93	24.17	1,898	0	100	0	0	3	37.73	-25.87		1.00	Mar-99
	5.48	15.58	-8.64	51.93	61.53	1.66	0.92	21.4	0.92	25.44	1,898	0	100	0	0	3	37.8	-25.91			Sep-16
	5.55	15.69	-8.50	50.92	60.45	1.77	0.81	21.38	0.92	25.45	1,898	0	100	0	0	3	37.8	-25.91			Aug-17
	2.19	10.14	3.48	21.62	24.29	0	1.99	6.74	0.5	11.18	742.6	39	60	0	1	169			5.00		Dec-13
	2.08	9.76	2.73	19.11	20.07	0	2.69	6.76	0.5	10.79	742.6	39	60	0	1	169				1.00	May-14
	2.33	10.35	3.69	22.74	26.26	0	1.7	6.77	0.5	11.4	742.6	39	60	0	1	169					Dec-13
	2.31	10.36	3.84	23.13	27.15	0	1.58	6.79	0.51	11.5	742.6	39	60	0	1	169					Dec-13
	2.31	10.36	3.93	23.13	27.15	0	1.59	6.78	0.5	11.5	742.6	39	60	0	1	169					Dec-13
	2.53	20.84	-1.99	37.36	39.48	0.18	1.11	15.59	0.88	11.71	659.4	2	98	0	0	102					Dec-13
	2.62	20.94	-1.85	37.95	40.42	0.31	0.99	15.65	0.89	11.72	659.4	2	98	0	0	102					Dec-13
	2.62	20.92	-1.86	38.01	40.48	0.29	1	15.61	0.88	11.73	659.4	2	98	0	0	102					Aug-17
	0.79	9.50	4.65	11.41	7.36	7.04	1.3	8.82	0.66	7.57	83.6	1	99	0	0	208	11.97	-9.67			Sep-07
	2.53	19.40	12.82	22.85	56.36	4.18	0	9.61	0.68	25.96	918.6	1	62	-3	3	24	18.58	-3.64			Feb-04
	5.10	23.95	18.72	62.31	86.65	0	1.15	12.1	0.85	51.02	1,524	2	98	0	0	42	31.15	-14.43	5.00		Sep-95
	4.92	23.49	17.87	58.71	79.79	0	1.9	12.1	0.85	41.79	1,524	2	98	0	0	42	30.58	-14.72		5.00	May-02
	4.91	23.47	17.86	58.67	79.74	0	1.9	12.09	0.85	41.81	1,524	2	98	0	0	42	30.57	-14.71		1.00	May-02
	5.16	24.10	19.01	63.52	89.06	0	0.91	12.09	0.85	55.34	1,524	2	98	0	0	42	31.48	-14.3			May-02
	5.06	23.88	18.57	61.61	85.32	0	1.3	12.09	0.85	53.95	1,524	2	98	0	0	42	31.14	-14.43			Mar-12
	5.19	24.17	19.15	64.02	90.05	0	0.8	12.1	0.85	55.73	1,524	2	98	0	0	42	31.52	-14.43			Sep-11
	5.60	24.02	12.42	66.06	81.08	0.14	1.01	13.15	0.96	17.14	850.6	0	100	0	0	88			5.00		Dec-11
	5.41	23.54	11.61	62.36	74.56	0	1.76	13.13	0.96	16.74	850.6	0	100	0	0	88				1.00	Aug-14
	5.62	24.13	12.69	67.27	83.47	0.33	0.75	13.16	0.96	17.28	850.6	0	100	0	0	88					Dec-11
	5.67	24.26	12.84	67.86	84.85	0.45	0.65	13.14	0.96	17.31	850.6	0	100	0	0	88					Dec-11
	5.54	23.90	12.32	65.46	80.64	0.01	1.16	13.16	0.96	17.31	850.6	0	100	0	0	88					Mar-15
	5.61	23.99	12.56	66.73	82.45	0.22	0.91	13.19	0.96	17.31	850.6	0	100	0	0	88					Mar-15
	5.67	24.24	12.83	67.89	84.88	0.44	0.66	13.14	0.96	17.32	850.6	0	100	0	0	88					Mar-15
	3.01	15.65	3.24	36.94	36.91	1.15	1.11	13.53	1.09	11.6	65.3	5	95	0	0	32			5.00		Jun-14
	2.84	15.25	2.53	34.14	32.27	0.45	1.81	13.44	1.09	11.56	65.3	5	95	0	0	32				1.00	Jun-14
	3.01	15.75	3.48	38.14	38.88	1.43	0.82	13.49	1.09	11.61	65.3	5	95	0	0	32					Jun-14
	3.10	15.83	3.63	38.67	40.11	1.56	0.7	13.47	1.09	11.63	65.3	5	95	0	0	32					Jun-14
	3.10	15.83	3.62	38.64	40.10	1.55	0.71	13.46	1.09	11.63	65.3	5	95	0	0	32					Jun-14
	2.79	10.79	12.28	36.25	99.50	1.59	0.3	11.1	1		3,913	3	97	0	0	4	24.92	-16.35			Nov-12
	4.87	11.26	8.35	31.07	95.80	0.95	0.87	11.77	1		247.9	8	91	0	1	238	24.64	-19.51			Jul-96
	0.26	12.81	-0.28	17.72	61.44	0.83	1.07	14.68	1.13		143.0	4	92	2	1	27	20.01	-19.65			Apr-01
	5.62	19.09	10.89	34.95	115.56	0	0.76	15	1.24		1,580	4	96	0	0	49	26.97	-20.63			May-03
	4.69	14.50	5.24	4.32	22.48	2.51	0.39	13.03	0.97		598.0	1	98	0	1	4	14.51	-24.49			Nov-12
	5.69	17.62	16.83	32.54	102.80	0.92	0.46	12.19	1		933.0	7	93	0	0	23	27.56	-22.71			May-00
	4.37	19.34	20.87	37.44	106.17	0.95	1.06	11.46	0.97		788.2	10	89	0	0	93	20.66	-19.45			Apr-05
	10.02	19.39	23.94	52.30	111.82	0	1.13	14.81	1.18		511.5	12	86	0	1	118	21.42	-20.58			Dec-96
	8.58	18.45	-3.33	10.90	70.87	0	1.14	16.78	0.99		407.4	13	84	0	3	87	24.97	-25.48			Apr-05
	8.80	20.79	13.53	23.37	94.77	0.96	0.53	15.09	1		442.4	12	88	0	0	19	27.71	-25.26			May-00
	3.75	15.89	17.69	29.59	103.02	0.4	1.17	14.24	0.96		677.5	7	93	0	0	22	28.22	-21.24			Apr-05
	3.21	11.86	10.67	31.87	94.09	1.25	0.58	11.26	1.01		606.5	4	96	0	0	4	25.11	-17.75			May-00
	1.19	13.85	4.16	16.65	55.29	2.98	0.92	11.95	0.82		376.4	8	88	0	1	37	14.73	-12.24			Apr-01

Fund Name	Ticker Symbol	Traded On	Fund Type	Category and (Prospectus Objective)	Overall Rating	Reward Rating	Risk Rating	Recent Up/ Downgrade	Open to New Investors	Min Initial Investment
	MARKET			FUND TYPE, CATEGORY & OBJECTIVE	RATINGS				MINIMUMS	
John Hancock Variable Insurance Trust Value Trust Series I	JEVLX	NAS CM	Open End	US Equity Mid Cap (Growth)	U	U	U		Y	0
John HancockRetirement Income 2040 Fund Class R6	JRIFX	NAS CM	Open End	Cautious Alloc (Asset Alloc)	C	D+	B-	Up	Y	1,000,000
Johnson Enhanced Return Fund	JENHX	NAS CM	Open End	US Equity Large Cap Blend (Growth)	B-	C+	B		Y	1,000,000
Johnson Equity Income Fund	JEQIX	NAS CM	Open End	US Equity Large Cap Blend (Growth & Income)	B	B	B+		Y	2,000
Johnson International Fund	JINTX	NAS CM	Open End	Global Equity Large Cap (Foreign Stock)	C+	C	B	Up	Y	2,000
Johnson Opportunity Fund	JOPPX	NAS CM	Open End	US Equity Mid Cap (Growth)	C	C	C+		Y	2,000
JPMorgan Diversified Fund Class A	JDVAX	NAS CM	Open End	Moderate Alloc (Balanced)	B-	C	B+	Up	Y	1,000
JPMorgan Diversified Fund Class C	JDVCX	NAS CM	Open End	Moderate Alloc (Balanced)	B-	C	B+	Up	Y	1,000
JPMorgan Diversified Fund Class I	JDVSX	NAS CM	Open End	Moderate Alloc (Balanced)	B-	C	B+	Up	Y	1,000,000
JPMorgan Diversified Fund Class L	JPDVX	NAS CM	Open End	Moderate Alloc (Balanced)	B-	C	B+	Up	Y	3,000,000
JPMorgan Diversified Fund Class R6	JDVZX	NAS CM	Open End	Moderate Alloc (Balanced)	B-	C	B+	Up	Y	15,000,000
JPMorgan Emerging Economies Fund Class A Shares	JEEAX	NAS CM	Open End	Global Emerg Mkts (Div Emerging Mkts)	C	C	C+		Y	1,000
JPMorgan Emerging Economies Fund Class C Shares	JEECX	NAS CM	Open End	Global Emerg Mkts (Div Emerging Mkts)	C	C	C		Y	1,000
JPMorgan Emerging Economies Fund Class I Shares	JEESX	NAS CM	Open End	Global Emerg Mkts (Div Emerging Mkts)	C	C	C+		Y	1,000,000
JPMorgan Emerging Economies Fund Class R5 Shares	JEERX	NAS CM	Open End	Global Emerg Mkts (Div Emerging Mkts)	C	C	C+		Y	0
JPMorgan Emerging Economies Fund Class R6	JEEEX	NAS CM	Open End	Global Emerg Mkts (Div Emerging Mkts)	C	C	C+		Y	15,000,000
JPMorgan Emerging Markets Equity Fund Class A	JFAMX	NAS CM	Open End	Global Emerg Mkts (Div Emerging Mkts)	C	C	C+		Y	1,000
JPMorgan Emerging Markets Equity Fund Class C	JEMCX	NAS CM	Open End	Global Emerg Mkts (Div Emerging Mkts)	C	C	C+		Y	1,000
JPMorgan Emerging Markets Equity Fund Class I	JEMSX	NAS CM	Open End	Global Emerg Mkts (Div Emerging Mkts)	C+	C	C+	Up	Y	1,000,000
JPMorgan Emerging Markets Equity Fund Class L	JMIEX	NAS CM	Open End	Global Emerg Mkts (Div Emerging Mkts)	C+	C	C+	Up	Y	3,000,000
JPMorgan Emerging Markets Equity Fund Class R2	JHUJX	NAS CM	Open End	Global Emerg Mkts (Div Emerging Mkts)	C	C	C+		Y	0
JPMorgan Emerging Markets Equity Fund Class R3	JHURX	NAS CM	Open End	Global Emerg Mkts (Div Emerging Mkts)	C	C	C+		Y	0
JPMorgan Emerging Markets Equity Fund Class R4	JHUKX	NAS CM	Open End	Global Emerg Mkts (Div Emerging Mkts)	C+	C	C+	Up	Y	0
JPMorgan Emerging Markets Equity Fund Class R5	JEMOX	NAS CM	Open End	Global Emerg Mkts (Div Emerging Mkts)	C+	C	C+	Up	Y	0
JPMorgan Emerging Markets Equity Fund Class R6	JEMWX	NAS CM	Open End	Global Emerg Mkts (Div Emerging Mkts)	C+	C	C+	Up	Y	15,000,000
JPMorgan Emerging Markets Research Enhanced Equity Cls I	EMREX	NAS CM	Open End	Global Emerg Mkts (Div Emerging Mkts)	U	U	U		Y	1,000,000
JPMorgan Emerging Markets Research Enhanced Equity Cls R6	EMRSX	NAS CM	Open End	Global Emerg Mkts (Div Emerging Mkts)	U	U	U		Y	15,000,000
JPMorgan Equity Focus Fund Class A	JPFAX	NAS CM	Open End	US Equity Large Cap Growth (Growth)	B-	C+	B		Y	1,000
JPMorgan Equity Focus Fund Class C	JPFCX	NAS CM	Open End	US Equity Large Cap Growth (Growth)	B-	C	B		Y	1,000
JPMorgan Equity Focus Fund Class I	JPFSX	NAS CM	Open End	US Equity Large Cap Growth (Growth)	B-	C+	B		Y	1,000,000
JPMorgan Equity Focus Fund Class R6	JPFRX	NAS CM	Open End	US Equity Large Cap Growth (Growth)	B-	C+	B		Y	15,000,000
JPMorgan Equity Income Fund Class A	OIEIX	NAS CM	Open End	US Equity Large Cap Value (Equity-Income)	B-	C	B+	Down	Y	1,000
JPMorgan Equity Income Fund Class C	OINCX	NAS CM	Open End	US Equity Large Cap Value (Equity-Income)	B-	C	B+		Y	1,000
JPMorgan Equity Income Fund Class I	HLIEX	NAS CM	Open End	US Equity Large Cap Value (Equity-Income)	B-	C	B+	Down	Y	1,000,000
JPMorgan Equity Income Fund Class R2	OIEFX	NAS CM	Open End	US Equity Large Cap Value (Equity-Income)	B-	C	B+	Down	Y	0
JPMorgan Equity Income Fund Class R3	OIEPX	NAS CM	Open End	US Equity Large Cap Value (Equity-Income)	B-	C	B+	Down	Y	0
JPMorgan Equity Income Fund Class R4	OIEQX	NAS CM	Open End	US Equity Large Cap Value (Equity-Income)	B-	C	B+	Down	Y	0
JPMorgan Equity Income Fund Class R5	OIERX	NAS CM	Open End	US Equity Large Cap Value (Equity-Income)	B-	C	B+	Down	Y	0
JPMorgan Equity Income Fund Class R6	OIEJX	NAS CM	Open End	US Equity Large Cap Value (Equity-Income)	B-	C	B+	Down	Y	15,000,000
JPMorgan Equity Index Fund Class A	OGEAX	NAS CM	Open End	US Equity Large Cap Blend (Growth)	B-	C	B		Y	1,000
JPMorgan Equity Index Fund Class C	OEICX	NAS CM	Open End	US Equity Large Cap Blend (Growth)	B-	C	B		Y	1,000
JPMorgan Equity Index Fund Class I	HLEIX	NAS CM	Open End	US Equity Large Cap Blend (Growth)	B-	C	B		Y	1,000,000
JPMorgan Equity Index Fund Class R6	OGFAX	NAS CM	Open End	US Equity Large Cap Blend (Growth)	B-	C	B		Y	15,000,000
JPMorgan Equity Premium Income Fund Class A	JEPAX	NAS CM	Open End	Long/Short Equity (Growth & Income)	U	U	U		Y	1,000
JPMorgan Equity Premium Income Fund Class C	JEPCX	NAS CM	Open End	Long/Short Equity (Growth & Income)	U	U	U		Y	1,000
JPMorgan Equity Premium Income Fund Class I	JEPIX	NAS CM	Open End	Long/Short Equity (Growth & Income)	U	U	U		Y	1,000,000
JPMorgan Equity Premium Income Fund Class R5	JEPSX	NAS CM	Open End	Long/Short Equity (Growth & Income)	U	U	U		Y	0
JPMorgan Equity Premium Income Fund Class R6	JEPRX	NAS CM	Open End	Long/Short Equity (Growth & Income)	U	U	U		Y	15,000,000
JPMorgan Europe Dynamic Fund Class A	VEUAX	NAS CM	Open End	Europe Equity Large Cap (Europe Stock)	C	D+	C+	Up	Y	1,000
JPMorgan Europe Dynamic Fund Class C	VEUCX	NAS CM	Open End	Europe Equity Large Cap (Europe Stock)	C-	D+	C+		Y	1,000
JPMorgan Europe Dynamic Fund Class I	JFESX	NAS CM	Open End	Europe Equity Large Cap (Europe Stock)	C	D+	C+	Up	Y	1,000,000
JPMorgan Europe Dynamic Fund Class L	JFEIX	NAS CM	Open End	Europe Equity Large Cap (Europe Stock)	C	D+	C+	Up	Y	3,000,000

★ Expanded analysis of this fund is included in Section II.

	TOTAL RETURNS					PERFORMANCE				ASSETS		ASSET ALLOCATION & TURNOVER					BULL & BEAR		FEES		
Min Additional Investment	3-Month Total Return	6-Month Total Return	1-Year Total Return	3-Year Total Return	5-Year Total Return	Dividend Yield (TTM)	Expense Ratio	3-Yr Std Deviation	3-Year Beta	NAV	Total Assets (MIL)	%Cash	%Stocks	%Bonds	%Other	Turnover Ratio	Last Bull Market Total Return	Last Bear Market Total Return	Front End Fee (%)	Back End Fee (%)	Inception Date
	3.98	18.94	7.49	20.57	96.19	0.5	0.89	13.73	1.12		538.2	4	96	0	0	26	32.8	-21.58			Dec-96
	4.22	11.01	8.97			3.43	0.52			49.84	28.5	1	24	74	0	25					Jul-17
100	4.92	21.54	11.87	49.10	66.52	2.16	0.36	12.33	1.01	16.93	157.4	5	50	46	0	73	26.05	-15.81			Dec-05
100	5.95	22.15	17.54	59.13	55.38	0.97	1	11.35	0.9	27.24	349.0	6	94	0	0	30	22.68	-14.93			Dec-05
100	3.20	13.05	3.58	28.11	9.62	2.22	1.01	10.74	0.93	26.07	20.3	4	96	0	0	7	17.4	-25.04			Dec-08
100	3.84	20.01	0.00	37.96	38.54	0.69	1.01	14.93	0.95	41.02	75.0	1	99	0	0	61	28.8	-30.13			May-94
50	3.79	14.45	6.14	28.58	29.65	1.7	1.09	8.16		16.54	1,101	3	57	35	0	93	18.02	-14.18	4.50		Mar-03
50	3.63	14.13	5.59	26.68	26.41	1.25	1.59	8.15		16.41	1,101	3	57	35	0	93	17.63	-14.37		1.00	Mar-03
	3.83	14.57	6.37	29.50	31.29	1.92	0.84	8.19		16.64	1,101	3	57	35	0	93	18.09	-14.04			Sep-01
	3.88	14.67	6.56	30.33	32.72	2.09	0.66	8.21		16.61	1,101	3	57	35	0	93	18.34	-13.95			Sep-93
	3.90	14.73	6.64	30.52	32.91	2.16	0.59	8.18		16.61	1,101	3	57	35	0	93	18.34	-13.95			Nov-17
50	1.30	10.96	-1.35	29.48	2.16	0	1.14	14.38	1	13.15	1,330	1	99	0	0	82	23.42	-29.24	5.25		Feb-08
50	1.11	10.70	-1.88	27.53	-0.39	1.84	1.64	14.34	1	12.72	1,330	1	99	0	0	82	23.14	-29.46		1.00	Feb-08
	1.32	11.11	-1.18	30.39	3.37	2.41	0.89	14.38	1	13	1,330	1	99	0	0	82	23.61	-29.16			Feb-08
	1.31	11.13	-1.05	30.86	4.22	2.85	0.79	14.34	1	13.08	1,330	1	99	0	0	82	23.72	-29.12			Feb-08
	1.41	11.22	-0.90	31.32	4.68	3.04	0.69	14.36	1	12.88	1,330	1	99	0	0	82	23.72	-29.12			Sep-15
50	4.17	21.67	9.71	50.49	26.43	0.41	1.24	14.96	1.03	29.41	6,117	2	98	0	0	13	18.56	-24.37	5.25		Sep-01
50	4.05	21.34	9.14	48.28	23.30	0.11	1.74	14.96	1.03	28.48	6,117	2	98	0	0	13	18.19	-24.53		1.00	Feb-06
	4.22	21.82	9.98	51.65	27.98	0.72	0.99	14.98	1.03	30.09	6,117	2	98	0	0	13	18.72	-24.29			Sep-01
	4.22	21.87	10.08	52.15	28.85	0.79	0.95	14.97	1.03	30.31	6,117	2	98	0	0	13	18.8	-24.24			Nov-93
	4.07	21.45	9.34	49.42	25.28	0.55	1.54	14.96	1.03	29.15	6,117	2	98	0	0	13	18.45	-24.4			Jul-17
	4.15	21.66	9.67	50.60	26.90	0.44	1.29	14.97	1.03	29.31	6,117	2	98	0	0	13	18.62	-24.32			Jul-17
	4.20	21.77	9.90	51.66	28.44	0.87	1.04	14.97	1.03	29.98	6,117	2	98	0	0	13	18.8	-24.24			Jul-17
	4.27	21.87	10.08	52.21	28.90	0.86	0.89	14.98	1.03	30.25	6,117	2	98	0	0	13	18.8	-24.24			Sep-16
	4.27	21.95	10.20	52.62	29.52	0.87	0.79	14.98	1.03	30.27	6,117	2	98	0	0	13	18.8	-24.24			Dec-13
	1.14	12.51					0.51			16.72	411.2	1	99	0	0						Jan-19
	1.21	12.50					0.41			16.73	411.2	1	99	0	0						Dec-18
50	4.50	19.26	9.22	57.54	62.42	1.2	1.1	12.38	0.97	30.15	106.8	5	95	0	0	34	30.31		5.25		Jul-11
50	4.38	18.99	8.67	55.19	58.40	0.73	1.6	12.37	0.97	29.01	106.8	5	95	0	0	34	29.9			1.00	Jul-11
	4.57	19.43	9.50	58.76	64.50	1.09	0.85	12.37	0.97	30.6	106.8	5	95	0	0	34	30.42				Jul-11
	4.63	19.57	9.68	59.02	64.77		0.6	12.39	0.97	30.48	106.8	5	95	0	0	34	30.42				Oct-18
50	4.20	16.53	11.17	41.87	52.83	1.83	1.01	11.23	0.91	17.83	23,652	4	96	0	0	20	23.88	-13.2	5.25		Feb-92
50	4.06	16.29	10.66	39.76	49.06	1.46	1.5	11.18	0.91	17.47	23,652	4	96	0	0	20	23.42	-13.24		1.00	Nov-97
	4.25	16.65	11.44	42.94	54.75	2.04	0.75	11.17	0.91	18.14	23,652	4	96	0	0	20	24	-13.05			Jul-87
	4.10	16.34	10.89	40.76	50.95	1.61	1.26	11.18	0.91	17.74	23,652	4	96	0	0	20	23.64	-13.16			Feb-11
	4.15	16.49	11.19	41.94	52.90	1.84	0.99	11.18	0.91	17.81	23,652	4	96	0	0	20	23.82	-13.14			Sep-16
	4.19	16.66	11.45	42.91	54.72	2.04	0.75	11.19	0.91	18.13	23,652	4	96	0	0	20	24	-13.05			Sep-16
	4.28	16.79	11.66	43.67	56.29	2.17	0.58	11.2	0.91	18.16	23,652	4	96	0	0	20	24.12	-12.97			Feb-11
	4.31	16.79	11.72	44.02	56.82	2.27	0.5	11.18	0.91	18.14	23,652	4	96	0	0	20	23.95	-13.05			Jan-12
50	4.17	19.27	9.87	48.81	62.52	1.43	0.45	12.2	1	44.9	4,510	2	98	0	0	14	24.78	-16.4	5.25		Feb-92
50	4.04	18.93	9.23	46.09	57.16	0.98	1.15	12.19	1	44.45	4,510	2	98	0	0	14	24.27	-16.68		1.00	Nov-97
	4.26	19.44	10.16	49.94	64.59	1.63	0.2	12.2	1	44.97	4,510	2	98	0	0	14	24.97	-16.32			Jul-91
	4.27	19.53	10.32	50.61	65.34	1.75	0.05	12.19	1	44.98	4,510	2	98	0	0	14	24.97	-16.32			Sep-16
50	3.74	14.59					0.85			14.93	53.8	0	100	0	0				5.25		Aug-18
50	3.60	14.30					1.35			14.92	53.8	0	100	0	0					1.00	Aug-18
	3.46	14.94					0.6			14.92	53.8	0	100	0	0						Aug-18
0	3.82	14.79					0.45			14.92	53.8	0	100	0	0						Aug-18
0	3.85	14.85					0.35			14.92	53.8	0	100	0	0						Aug-18
50	3.17	14.85	-3.82	22.05	-1.06	2.28	1.24	12.77	0.98	24.05	572.3	0	100	0	0	149	19.25	-27.52	5.25		Nov-95
50	2.99	14.56	-4.32	20.23	-3.49	1.95	1.74	12.76	0.98	21.32	572.3	0	100	0	0	149	18.96	-27.66		1.00	Oct-98
	3.19	15.00	-3.57	23.04	0.38	2.5	0.99	12.76	0.98	24.52	572.3	0	100	0	0	149	19.43	-27.42			Sep-01
	3.24	15.02	-3.49	23.56	1.15	2.31	0.88	12.74	0.98	24.81	572.3	0	100	0	0	149	19.59	-27.39			Sep-01

	MARKET		FUND TYPE, CATEGORY & OBJECTIVE		RATINGS				MINIMUMS	
Fund Name	Ticker Symbol	Traded On	Fund Type	Category and (Prospectus Objective)	Overall Rating	Reward Rating	Risk Rating	Recent Up/ Downgrade	Open to New Investors	Min Initial Investment
JPMorgan Europe Dynamic Fund Class R6	VEUVX	NAS CM	Open End	Europe Equity Large Cap (Europe Stock)	C	D+	C+	Up	Y	0
JPMorgan Global Allocation Fund Class A	GAOAX	NAS CM	Open End	Moderate Alloc (Growth & Income)	B-	C	A-	Up	Y	1,000
JPMorgan Global Allocation Fund Class C	GAOCX	NAS CM	Open End	Moderate Alloc (Growth & Income)	B-	C	A-	Up	Y	1,000
JPMorgan Global Allocation Fund Class I	GAOSX	NAS CM	Open End	Moderate Alloc (Growth & Income)	B-	C	A-	Up	Y	1,000,000
JPMorgan Global Allocation Fund Class R2	GAONX	NAS CM	Open End	Moderate Alloc (Growth & Income)	B-	C	A-	Up	Y	0
JPMorgan Global Allocation Fund Class R3	GAOTX	NAS CM	Open End	Moderate Alloc (Growth & Income)	B-	C	A-	Up	Y	0
JPMorgan Global Allocation Fund Class R4	GAOFX	NAS CM	Open End	Moderate Alloc (Growth & Income)	B-	C	A-	Up	Y	0
JPMorgan Global Allocation Fund Class R5	GAORX	NAS CM	Open End	Moderate Alloc (Growth & Income)	B-	C	A-	Up	Y	0
JPMorgan Global Allocation Fund Class R6	GAOZX	NAS CM	Open End	Moderate Alloc (Growth & Income)	B-	C	A-	Up	Y	15,000,000
JPMorgan Global Research Enhanced Index Fund Class I	JEITX	NAS CM	Open End	Global Equity Large Cap (Growth)	B-	C	B	Up	Y	1,000,000
JPMorgan Global Research Enhanced Index Fund Class R6	JEIYX	NAS CM	Open End	Global Equity Large Cap (Growth)	B-	C	B	Up	Y	15,000,000
JPMorgan Growth Advantage Fund Class A	VHIAX	NAS CM	Open End	US Equity Large Cap Growth (Aggr Growth)	C+	C+	B-	Down	Y	1,000
JPMorgan Growth Advantage Fund Class C	JGACX	NAS CM	Open End	US Equity Large Cap Growth (Aggr Growth)	C+	C+	B-	Down	Y	1,000
JPMorgan Growth Advantage Fund Class I	JGASX	NAS CM	Open End	US Equity Large Cap Growth (Aggr Growth)	C+	C+	B-	Down	Y	1,000,000
JPMorgan Growth Advantage Fund Class R2	JGRJX	NAS CM	Open End	US Equity Large Cap Growth (Aggr Growth)	C+	C+	B-	Down	Y	0
JPMorgan Growth Advantage Fund Class R3	JGTTX	NAS CM	Open End	US Equity Large Cap Growth (Aggr Growth)	C+	C+	B-	Down	Y	0
JPMorgan Growth Advantage Fund Class R4	JGTUX	NAS CM	Open End	US Equity Large Cap Growth (Aggr Growth)	C+	C+	B-	Down	Y	0
JPMorgan Growth Advantage Fund Class R5	JGVRX	NAS CM	Open End	US Equity Large Cap Growth (Aggr Growth)	C+	C+	B-	Down	Y	0
JPMorgan Growth Advantage Fund Class R6	JGVVX	NAS CM	Open End	US Equity Large Cap Growth (Aggr Growth)	C+	C+	B-	Down	Y	15,000,000
JPMorgan Growth And Income Fund Class A	VGRIX	NAS CM	Open End	US Equity Large Cap Value (Growth & Income)	B-	C	B	Up	Y	1,000
JPMorgan Growth And Income Fund Class C	VGICX	NAS CM	Open End	US Equity Large Cap Value (Growth & Income)	B-	C	B	Up	Y	1,000
JPMorgan Growth And Income Fund Class I	VGIIX	NAS CM	Open End	US Equity Large Cap Value (Growth & Income)	B-	C	B	Up	Y	1,000,000
JPMorgan Growth And Income Fund Class R2	VGRTX	NAS CM	Open End	US Equity Large Cap Value (Growth & Income)	B-	C	B	Up	Y	0
JPMorgan Growth and Income Fund Class R3	JGAVX	NAS CM	Open End	US Equity Large Cap Value (Growth & Income)	B-	C	B	Up	Y	0
JPMorgan Growth and Income Fund Class R4	JGRUX	NAS CM	Open End	US Equity Large Cap Value (Growth & Income)	B-	C	B	Up	Y	0
JPMorgan Growth And Income Fund Class R5	VGIFX	NAS CM	Open End	US Equity Large Cap Value (Growth & Income)	B-	C	B	Up	Y	0
JPMorgan Growth And Income Fund Class R6	VGINX	NAS CM	Open End	US Equity Large Cap Value (Growth & Income)	B-	C	B	Up	Y	15,000,000
JPMorgan Hedged Equity Fund Class A	JHQAX	NAS CM	Open End	Long/Short Equity (Growth)	B-	C	A-	Down	Y	1,000
JPMorgan Hedged Equity Fund Class C	JHQCX	NAS CM	Open End	Long/Short Equity (Growth)	B-	C	B	Down	Y	1,000
JPMorgan Hedged Equity Fund Class I	JHEQX	NAS CM	Open End	Long/Short Equity (Growth)	B-	C	A-	Down	Y	1,000,000
JPMorgan Hedged Equity Fund Class R5	JHQPX	NAS CM	Open End	Long/Short Equity (Growth)	B-	C	B+		Y	0
JPMorgan Hedged Equity Fund Class R6	JHQRX	NAS CM	Open End	Long/Short Equity (Growth)	B-	C	B+		Y	15,000,000
JPMorgan Income Builder Fund Class A Shares	JNBAX	NAS CM	Open End	Cautious Alloc (Income)	B	C+	A	Up	Y	1,000
JPMorgan Income Builder Fund Class C Shares	JNBCX	NAS CM	Open End	Cautious Alloc (Income)	B	C+	A-	Up	Y	1,000
JPMorgan Income Builder Fund Class I Shares	JNBSX	NAS CM	Open End	Cautious Alloc (Income)	B	C+	A	Up	Y	1,000,000
JPMorgan Income Builder Fund Class R6	JNBZX	NAS CM	Open End	Cautious Alloc (Income)	B	C+	A	Up	Y	15,000,000
JPMorgan Insurance Trust Global Allocation Portfolio Cls 1			Open End	Cautious Alloc (Growth & Income)	B-	C	A-	Up	Y	0
JPMorgan Insurance Trust Global Allocation Portfolio Cls 2			Open End	Cautious Alloc (Growth & Income)	B-	C	A-	Up	Y	0
JPMorgan Insurance Trust Income Builder Portfolio Class 1			Open End	Cautious Alloc (Growth & Income)	B	C+	A-	Up	Y	0
JPMorgan Insurance Trust Income Builder Portfolio Class 2			Open End	Cautious Alloc (Growth & Income)	B	C+	A-	Up	Y	0
JPMorgan Insurance Trust Mid Cap Value Portfolio Class 1			Open End	US Equity Mid Cap (Growth)	C+	C	B	Up	Y	0
JPMorgan Insurance Trust Small Cap Core Port Cls 1 Shares			Open End	US Equity Small Cap (Small Company)	C	C-	C+		Y	0
JPMorgan Insurance Trust Small Cap Core Port Cls 2 Shares			Open End	US Equity Small Cap (Small Company)	C	C-	C+		Y	0
JPMorgan Insurance Trust U.S. Equity Portfolio Class 1			Open End	US Equity Large Cap Blend (Growth & Income)	B-	C	B		Y	0
JPMorgan Insurance Trust U.S. Equity Portfolio Class 2			Open End	US Equity Large Cap Blend (Growth & Income)	B-	C	B		Y	0
JPMorgan International Advantage Fund Class A	JFTAX	NAS CM	Open End	Global Equity Large Cap (Foreign Stock)	C	C-	C		Y	1,000
JPMorgan International Advantage Fund Class C	JIICX	NAS CM	Open End	Global Equity Large Cap (Foreign Stock)	C-	D+	C		Y	1,000
JPMorgan International Advantage Fund Class I	JISIX	NAS CM	Open End	Global Equity Large Cap (Foreign Stock)	C	C-	C		Y	1,000,000
JPMorgan International Advantage Fund Class R2	JIIZX	NAS CM	Open End	Global Equity Large Cap (Foreign Stock)	C	C-	C	Up	Y	0
JPMorgan International Advantage Fund Class R6	JIFFX	NAS CM	Open End	Global Equity Large Cap (Foreign Stock)	C	C-	C		Y	15,000,000
JPMorgan International Equity Fund Class A	JSEAX	NAS CM	Open End	Global Equity Large Cap (Foreign Stock)	C	C	C+		Y	1,000
JPMorgan International Equity Fund Class C	JIECX	NAS CM	Open End	Global Equity Large Cap (Foreign Stock)	C	C	C+		Y	1,000

★ Expanded analysis of this fund is included in Section II.

	TOTAL RETURNS					PERFORMANCE				ASSETS		ASSET ALLOCATION & TURNOVER					BULL & BEAR		FEES		
Min Additional Investment	3-Month Total Return	6-Month Total Return	1-Year Total Return	3-Year Total Return	5-Year Total Return	Dividend Yield (TTM)	Expense Ratio	3-Yr Std Deviation	3-Year Beta	NAV	Total Assets (MIL)	%Cash	%Stocks	%Bonds	%Other	Turnover Ratio	Last Bull Market Total Return	Last Bear Market Total Return	Front End Fee (%)	Back End Fee (%)	Inception Date
	3.25	15.14	-3.54	22.40	-0.77		0.78	12.76	0.98	24.71	572.3	0	100	0	0	149	19.25	-27.52			Oct-18
50	2.92	10.30	4.49	26.18	25.97	2.39	1.07	6.99	0.59	18.63	3,623	9	50	41	0	131	13.94		4.50		May-11
50	2.83	10.09	4.02	24.29	22.88	2.03	1.57	7.03	0.6	18.37	3,623	9	50	41	0	131	13.57			1.00	May-11
	2.96	10.51	4.78	27.15	27.58	2.61	0.82	6.99	0.59	18.72	3,623	9	50	41	0	131	14.13				May-11
	2.85	10.14	4.14	25.09	24.27	2.11	1.44	7.02	0.59	18.55	3,623	9	50	41	0	131	13.84				May-11
	2.89	10.31	4.44	26.11	25.91		1.19	7	0.59	18.72	3,623	9	50	41	0	131	13.96				Oct-18
	2.95	10.39	4.65	26.99	27.42		0.94	7.01	0.59	18.62	3,623	9	50	41	0	131	14.13				Oct-18
	2.97	10.47	4.74	27.11	27.54		0.79	7.02	0.59	18.72	3,623	9	50	41	0	131	14.13				Oct-18
	3.00	10.56	4.91	27.47	27.90	2.74	0.69	7	0.59	18.71	3,623	9	50	41	0	131	14.13				Nov-17
	4.10	18.03	6.63	41.67	37.93	2.48	0.34	11.49	1.01	21.79	4,473	1	99	0	0	45					Feb-13
	4.16	18.10	6.73	41.88	38.14	2.64	0.25	11.49	1.01	21.53	4,473	1	99	0	0	45					Nov-17
50	4.41	24.45	9.63	73.57	88.68	0	1.14	14.67	1.07	21.78	9,391	3	97	0	0	31	32.2	-19.09	5.25		Oct-99
50	4.31	24.07	9.06	70.98	84.07	0	1.64	14.65	1.07	18.86	9,391	3	97	0	0	31	31.92	-19.29		1.00	May-06
	4.49	24.61	9.90	74.94	90.64	0	0.89	14.65	1.07	22.53	9,391	3	97	0	0	31	32.43	-19.06			May-06
	4.38	24.32	9.36	72.28	86.36	0	1.39	14.65	1.07	21.67	9,391	3	97	0	0	31	32.01	-19.17			Jul-17
	4.45	24.44	9.62	73.63	88.76	0	1.14	14.66	1.07	21.79	9,391	3	97	0	0	31	32.2	-19.09			May-17
	4.49	24.61	9.90	74.55	89.75	0	0.89	14.65	1.07	22.53	9,391	3	97	0	0	31	32.2	-19.09			May-17
	4.54	24.66	10.04	75.66	92.28	0	0.74	14.63	1.06	23	9,391	3	97	0	0	31	32.65	-18.98			Jan-09
	4.56	24.73	10.17	76.21	93.39	0	0.64	14.66	1.07	23.15	9,391	3	97	0	0	31	32.2	-19.09			Dec-13
50	3.81	16.22	6.65	41.00	47.69	1.63	0.94	12.44	1.01	49.83	652.5	2	98	0	0	32	26.95	-17.93	5.25		Sep-87
50	3.71	15.94	6.14	38.94	44.06	1.47	1.44	12.46	1.02	44.59	652.5	2	98	0	0	32	26.64	-18.11		1.00	Jan-98
	3.88	16.37	6.94	42.09	49.55	1.72	0.69	12.45	1.02	52.69	652.5	2	98	0	0	32	27.22	-17.84			Jan-96
	3.76	16.07	6.38	39.96	45.86	1.48	1.19	12.44	1.01	50	652.5	2	98	0	0	32	26.77	-18.02			Nov-15
	3.82	16.24	6.66	41.05	47.75	1.52	0.94	12.45	1.01	52.66	652.5	2	98	0	0	32	26.95	-17.93			Jul-17
	3.90	16.39	6.93	41.70	48.43	1.72	0.69	12.45	1.02	52.69	652.5	2	98	0	0	32	26.95	-17.93			Jul-17
	3.93	16.45	7.08	42.82	49.97	1.82	0.54	12.46	1.02	53.06	652.5	2	98	0	0	32	26.95	-17.93			Nov-15
	3.95	16.50	7.18	43.13	50.36	1.9	0.44	12.45	1.02	53.07	652.5	2	98	0	0	32	26.95	-17.93			Nov-15
50	3.38	7.42	5.28	29.91	34.59	0.93	0.85	6.18	0.45	20.24	5,022	2	98	0	0	44			5.25		Dec-13
50	3.29	7.18	4.76	28.00	31.29	0.57	1.35	6.23	0.46	20.12	5,022	2	98	0	0	44				1.00	Dec-13
	3.44	7.54	5.49	30.91	36.30	1.14	0.6	6.22	0.46	20.29	5,022	2	98	0	0	44					Dec-13
	3.47	7.60	5.73	31.63	37.58	1.27	0.45	6.24	0.46	20.33	5,022	2	98	0	0	44					Dec-13
	3.49	7.70	5.79	31.83	37.95	1.33	0.35	6.22	0.46	20.33	5,022	2	98	0	0	44					Dec-13
50	3.07	10.49	7.02	22.92	22.37	3.91	0.75	5.17	0.42	10.63	13,005	4	34	57	0	59	14.56	-11.85	4.50		May-07
50	2.95	10.13	6.50	21.12	19.33	3.43	1.25	5.16	0.42	10.6	13,005	4	34	57	0	59	14.13	-11.96		1.00	May-07
	3.00	10.45	7.17	23.43	23.25	4.05	0.6	5.17	0.42	10.64	13,005	4	34	57	0	59	14.64	-11.8			May-07
	3.02	10.49	7.27	23.61	23.43	4.14	0.52	5.16	0.42	10.64	13,005	4	34	57	0	59	14.64	-11.8			Nov-17
	3.05	11.01	5.08	27.69		2.36	0.94	7.14	0.61	16.7	88.0	6	42	33	19	141					Dec-14
	3.05	10.83	4.82	26.76		2.12	1.19	7.15	0.61	16.66	88.0	6	42	33	19	141					Dec-14
	2.91	10.16	6.77	21.20		3.42	0.67	5.06	0.41	10.7	80.6	4	33	57	5	68					Dec-14
	2.90	10.07	6.47	20.29		3.22	0.92	5.05	0.41	10.68	80.6	4	33	57	5	68					Dec-14
	3.07	19.32	4.59	29.73	41.24	1.6	0.76	12.88	0.96	11.03	488.8	3	97	0	0	13	27.93	-17.87			Sep-01
	1.47	17.68	-4.95	45.46	39.99	0.4	0.82	18.37	1.07	21.56	192.3	3	87	0	11	59	30.22	-27.24			Jan-95
	-0.03	15.60	-6.84	44.99	35.85	0.18	1.09	18.36	1.07	21.35	192.3	3	87	0	11	59	29.97	-27.31			Apr-09
	4.37	19.60	9.21	52.66	62.24	0.85	0.78	13.35	1.09	29.03	111.2	1	99	0	0	95	25.36	-17.81			Mar-95
	4.20	18.64	8.25	53.04	59.17	0.62	1.03	13.35	1.09	28.67	111.2	1	99	0	0	95	25.18	-17.89			Aug-06
50	1.69	11.99	-3.95	21.73	4.14	2.11	0.95	11.29	0.99	19.8	3,445	1	98	0	0	51	15.71	-25.91	5.25		Apr-01
50	1.56	11.74	-4.43	19.90	1.52	1.53	1.45	11.33	1	20.07	3,445	1	98	0	0	51	15.4	-26.05		1.00	Feb-06
	1.72	12.14	-3.77	22.77	5.67	2.35	0.7	11.3	0.99	20.59	3,445	1	98	0	0	51	15.88	-25.8			Feb-06
	1.61	11.81	-4.25	20.68	2.67	2	1.25	11.32	1	19.49	3,445	1	98	0	0	51	15.57	-25.97			Nov-08
	1.80	12.23	-3.53	23.48	6.24	2.57	0.5	11.31	1	20.27	3,445	1	98	0	0	51	15.71	-25.91			May-15
50	6.10	19.67	2.95	35.68	13.98	1.91	0.95	12.56	1.09	17.03	4,629	2	98	0	0	33	18.25	-23.66	5.25		Feb-02
50	5.92	19.36	2.45	33.69	11.18	1.47	1.45	12.56	1.09	16.09	4,629	2	98	0	0	33	17.91	-23.83		1.00	Jan-03

	MARKET			FUND TYPE, CATEGORY & OBJECTIVE	RATINGS				MINIMUMS	
Fund Name	Ticker Symbol	Traded On	Fund Type	Category and (Prospectus Objective)	Overall Rating	Reward Rating	Risk Rating	Recent Up/ Downgrade	Open to New Investors	Min Initial Investment
JPMorgan International Equity Fund Class I	VSIEX	NAS CM	Open End	Global Equity Large Cap (Foreign Stock)	C	C	C+		Y	1,000,000
JPMorgan International Equity Fund Class R2	JIEZX	NAS CM	Open End	Global Equity Large Cap (Foreign Stock)	C	C	C+		Y	0
JPMorgan International Equity Fund Class R5	JIERX	NAS CM	Open End	Global Equity Large Cap (Foreign Stock)	C	C	B-		Y	0
JPMorgan International Equity Fund Class R6	JNEMX	NAS CM	Open End	Global Equity Large Cap (Foreign Stock)	C	C	B-		Y	15,000,000
JPMorgan International Equity Income Fund Class A	JEIAX	NAS CM	Open End	Global Equity Large Cap (Equity-Income)	C+	C	B	Up	Y	1,000
JPMorgan International Equity Income Fund Class C	JEICX	NAS CM	Open End	Global Equity Large Cap (Equity-Income)	C+	C-	B	Up	Y	1,000
JPMorgan International Equity Income Fund Class I	JEISX	NAS CM	Open End	Global Equity Large Cap (Equity-Income)	C+	C	B	Up	Y	1,000,000
JPMorgan International Equity Income Fund Class R2	JGEZX	NAS CM	Open End	Global Equity Large Cap (Equity-Income)	C+	C	B	Up	Y	0
JPMorgan International Equity Income Fund Class R5	JEIRX	NAS CM	Open End	Global Equity Large Cap (Equity-Income)	C+	C	B	Up	Y	0
JPMorgan International Equity Income Fund Class R6	JIEFX	NAS CM	Open End	Global Equity Large Cap (Equity-Income)	C+	C	B	Up	Y	15,000,000
JPMorgan International Hedged Equity Fund Class A	JIHAX	NAS CM	Open End	Alternative Miscellaneous (Growth)	U	U	U		Y	1,000
JPMorgan International Hedged Equity Fund Class C	JIHCX	NAS CM	Open End	Alternative Miscellaneous (Growth)	U	U	U		Y	1,000
JPMorgan International Hedged Equity Fund Class I	JIHIX	NAS CM	Open End	Alternative Miscellaneous (Growth)	U	U	U		Y	1,000,000
JPMorgan International Hedged Equity Fund Class R5	JIHYX	NAS CM	Open End	Alternative Miscellaneous (Growth)	U	U	U		Y	0
JPMorgan International Hedged Equity Fund Class R6	JIHRX	NAS CM	Open End	Alternative Miscellaneous (Growth)	U	U	U		Y	15,000,000
JPMorgan International Research Enhanced Equity Cls A	OEIAX	NAS CM	Open End	Global Equity Large Cap (Foreign Stock)	C	C	B		Y	1,000
JPMorgan International Research Enhanced Equity Cls I	OIEAX	NAS CM	Open End	Global Equity Large Cap (Foreign Stock)	C	C	B		Y	1,000,000
JPMorgan International Research Enhanced Equity Cls R6	JEIQX	NAS CM	Open End	Global Equity Large Cap (Foreign Stock)	C	C	B		Y	15,000,000
JPMorgan International Unconstrained Equity Fund Class A	IUAEX	NAS CM	Open End	Global Equity Large Cap (Foreign Stock)	C	C	C+		Y	1,000
JPMorgan International Unconstrained Equity Fund Class C	IUCEX	NAS CM	Open End	Global Equity Large Cap (Foreign Stock)	C	C	C+		Y	1,000
JPMorgan International Unconstrained Equity Fund Class I	IUESX	NAS CM	Open End	Global Equity Large Cap (Foreign Stock)	C	C	C+		Y	1,000,000
JPMorgan International Unconstrained Equity Fund Class R2	IUERX	NAS CM	Open End	Global Equity Large Cap (Foreign Stock)	C	C	C+		Y	0
JPMorgan International Unconstrained Equity Fund Class R5	IUEFX	NAS CM	Open End	Global Equity Large Cap (Foreign Stock)	C	C	C+		Y	0
JPMorgan International Unconstrained Equity Fund Class R6	IUENX	NAS CM	Open End	Global Equity Large Cap (Foreign Stock)	C	C	C+		Y	15,000,000
JPMorgan International Value Fund Class A	JFEAX	NAS CM	Open End	Global Equity Large Cap (Foreign Stock)	C-	D+	C		Y	1,000
JPMorgan International Value Fund Class C	JIUCX	NAS CM	Open End	Global Equity Large Cap (Foreign Stock)	C-	D+	C		Y	1,000
JPMorgan International Value Fund Class I	JIESX	NAS CM	Open End	Global Equity Large Cap (Foreign Stock)	C-	D+	C		Y	1,000,000
JPMorgan International Value Fund Class L	JNUSX	NAS CM	Open End	Global Equity Large Cap (Foreign Stock)	C-	D+	C		Y	3,000,000
JPMorgan International Value Fund Class R2	JPVZX	NAS CM	Open End	Global Equity Large Cap (Foreign Stock)	C-	D+	C		Y	0
JPMorgan International Value Fund Class R5	JPVRX	NAS CM	Open End	Global Equity Large Cap (Foreign Stock)	C-	D+	C		Y	0
JPMorgan International Value Fund Class R6	JNVMX	NAS CM	Open End	Global Equity Large Cap (Foreign Stock)	C-	D+	C	Down	Y	15,000,000
JPMorgan Intrepid America Fund Class A	JIAAX	NAS CM	Open End	US Equity Large Cap Blend (Growth)	C+	C	B		Y	1,000
JPMorgan Intrepid America Fund Class C	JIACX	NAS CM	Open End	US Equity Large Cap Blend (Growth)	C+	C	B		Y	1,000
JPMorgan Intrepid America Fund Class I	JPIAX	NAS CM	Open End	US Equity Large Cap Blend (Growth)	C+	C	B		Y	1,000,000
JPMorgan Intrepid America Fund Class R2	JIAZX	NAS CM	Open End	US Equity Large Cap Blend (Growth)	C+	C	B		Y	0
JPMorgan Intrepid America Fund Class R5	JIARX	NAS CM	Open End	US Equity Large Cap Blend (Growth)	C+	C	B		Y	0
JPMorgan Intrepid America Fund Class R6	JIAPX	NAS CM	Open End	US Equity Large Cap Blend (Growth)	C+	C	B		Y	15,000,000
JPMorgan Intrepid Growth Fund Class A	JIGAX	NAS CM	Open End	US Equity Large Cap Growth (Growth)	C+	C	B	Down	Y	1,000
JPMorgan Intrepid Growth Fund Class C	JCICX	NAS CM	Open End	US Equity Large Cap Growth (Growth)	C+	C	B	Down	Y	1,000
JPMorgan Intrepid Growth Fund Class I	JPGSX	NAS CM	Open End	US Equity Large Cap Growth (Growth)	C+	C	B	Down	Y	1,000,000
JPMorgan Intrepid Growth Fund Class R2	JIGZX	NAS CM	Open End	US Equity Large Cap Growth (Growth)	C+	C	B	Down	Y	0
JPMorgan Intrepid Growth Fund Class R5	JGIRX	NAS CM	Open End	US Equity Large Cap Growth (Growth)	C+	C	B	Down	Y	0
JPMorgan Intrepid Growth Fund Class R6	JGISX	NAS CM	Open End	US Equity Large Cap Growth (Growth)	C+	C	B	Down	Y	15,000,000
JPMorgan Intrepid Mid Cap Fund Class A	PECAX	NAS CM	Open End	US Equity Mid Cap (Growth)	C+	C	B	Up	Y	1,000
JPMorgan Intrepid Mid Cap Fund Class C	ODMCX	NAS CM	Open End	US Equity Mid Cap (Growth)	C+	C	B	Up	Y	1,000
JPMorgan Intrepid Mid Cap Fund Class I	WOOPX	NAS CM	Open End	US Equity Mid Cap (Growth)	C+	C	B	Up	Y	1,000,000
JPMorgan Intrepid Mid Cap Fund Class R3	WOOOX	NAS CM	Open End	US Equity Mid Cap (Growth)	C+	C	B	Up	Y	0
JPMorgan Intrepid Mid Cap Fund Class R4	WOOQX	NAS CM	Open End	US Equity Mid Cap (Growth)	C+	C	B	Up	Y	0
JPMorgan Intrepid Mid Cap Fund Class R6	WOOSX	NAS CM	Open End	US Equity Mid Cap (Growth)	C+	C	B	Up	Y	15,000,000
JPMorgan Intrepid Sustainable Equity Fund Class A Shares	JICAX	NAS CM	Open End	US Equity Large Cap Blend (Growth)	B-	C	B		Y	1,000
JPMorgan Intrepid Sustainable Equity Fund Class C Shares	JICCX	NAS CM	Open End	US Equity Large Cap Blend (Growth)	B-	C	B		Y	1,000
JPMorgan Intrepid Sustainable Equity Fund I Class	JIISX	NAS CM	Open End	US Equity Large Cap Blend (Growth)	B-	C	B		Y	1,000,000

★ Expanded analysis of this fund is included in Section II.

	TOTAL RETURNS					PERFORMANCE				ASSETS		ASSET ALLOCATION & TURNOVER					BULL & BEAR		FEES		
Min Additional Investment	3-Month Total Return	6-Month Total Return	1-Year Total Return	3-Year Total Return	5-Year Total Return	Dividend Yield (TTM)	Expense Ratio	3-Yr Std Deviation	3-Year Beta	NAV	Total Assets (MIL)	%Cash	%Stocks	%Bonds	%Other	Turnover Ratio	Last Bull Market Total Return	Last Bear Market Total Return	Front End Fee (%)	Back End Fee (%)	Inception Date
	6.13	19.80	3.19	36.63	15.44	2.12	0.7	12.56	1.09	17.3	4,629	2	98	0	0	33	18.42	-23.6			Dec-96
	6.01	19.49	2.67	34.56	12.50	1.63	1.25	12.56	1.09	16.92	4,629	2	98	0	0	33	18.07	-23.73			Nov-08
	6.18	19.84	3.31	37.19	16.30	2.21	0.6	12.6	1.1	17.33	4,629	2	98	0	0	33	18.62	-23.58			May-06
	6.18	19.93	3.37	37.54	16.79	2.31	0.5	12.6	1.1	17.33	4,629	2	98	0	0	33	18.64	-23.51			Nov-10
50	2.81	13.89	3.71	25.53	12.96	2.74	0.95	10.58	0.93	15.56	85.8	0	99	0	1	92	14.85	-19.42	5.25		Feb-11
50	2.61	13.56	3.18	23.63	10.10	2.37	1.45	10.59	0.93	15.42	85.8	0	99	0	1	92	14.53	-19.62		1.00	Feb-11
	2.85	13.97	3.98	26.61	14.69	2.94	0.7	10.58	0.93	15.61	85.8	0	99	0	1	92	15.06	-19.41			Feb-11
	2.70	13.67	3.42	24.47	11.40	2.53	1.25	10.59	0.93	15.51	85.8	0	99	0	1	92	14.72	-19.56			Feb-11
	2.79	14.01	4.07	26.93	15.24	3.02	0.6	10.57	0.93	15.62	85.8	0	99	0	1	92	15.16	-19.3			Feb-11
	2.88	14.07	4.16	27.24	15.53	3.1	0.5	10.58	0.93	15.61	85.8	0	99	0	1	92	15.16	-19.3			Jan-15
50	2.88						0.85			15.36	53.3	2	97	0	1				5.25		Mar-19
50	2.67						1.35			15.33	53.3	2	97	0	1					1.00	Mar-19
	2.94						0.6			15.37	53.3	2	97	0	1						Mar-19
	2.94						0.45			15.37	53.3	2	97	0	1						Mar-19
	3.01						0.35			15.38	53.3	2	97	0	1						Mar-19
50	3.35	14.24	-0.15	29.26	9.19	2.96	0.6	11.18	1	17.56	4,595	3	96	0	1	42	11.16	-25.72	5.25		Apr-93
	3.43	14.41	0.09	30.22	10.54	3.14	0.35	11.17	1	17.78	4,595	3	96	0	1	42	11.3	-25.6			Oct-92
	3.50	14.54	0.24	30.53	10.81	3.34	0.25	11.18	1	17.72	4,595	3	96	0	1	42	11.3	-25.6			Nov-17
50	5.70	20.56	5.65	34.98	22.04	1.75	1	12.7	1.07	20.93	561.6	6	94	0	0	63			5.25		Nov-11
50	5.56	20.16	5.13	32.96	18.91	1.22	1.5	12.7	1.07	20.68	561.6	6	94	0	0	63				1.00	Nov-11
	5.73	20.67	5.89	36.19	23.87	1.94	0.75	12.72	1.07	21.19	561.6	6	94	0	0	63					Nov-11
	5.64	20.31	5.32	33.82	20.31	1.64	1.3	12.7	1.06	20.79	561.6	6	94	0	0	63					Nov-11
	5.79	20.69	6.01	36.54	24.55	2.07	0.65	12.71	1.07	21.17	561.6	6	94	0	0	63					Nov-11
	5.79	20.75	6.14	36.89	24.97	2.18	0.55	12.7	1.06	21.18	561.6	6	94	0	0	63					Nov-11
50	0.91	9.36	-5.78	20.55	-6.25	3.79	1	12.12	1.05	12.14	410.3	2	98	0	0	90	14.11	-25.37	5.25		Sep-01
50	0.77	9.09	-6.26	18.62	-8.62	3.33	1.5	12.13	1.05	11.75	410.3	2	98	0	0	90	13.72	-25.49		1.00	Jul-06
	0.97	9.50	-5.58	21.44	-4.93	3.98	0.75	12.1	1.05	12.44	410.3	2	98	0	0	90	14.27	-25.27			Sep-01
	1.06	9.66	-5.49	21.92	-4.36	4.18	0.86	12.12	1.05	12.37	410.3	2	98	0	0	90	14.25	-25.2			Nov-93
	0.84	9.18	-6.14	19.41	-7.57	3.7	1.3	12.09	1.05	11.89	410.3	2	98	0	0	90	13.86	-25.41			Nov-08
	0.98	9.52	-5.50	21.77	-4.47	4.3	0.65	12.09	1.05	12.3	410.3	2	98	0	0	90	14.26	-25.2			Sep-16
	1.06	9.60	-5.39	22.30	-3.75	4.39	0.55	12.12	1.05	12.32	410.3	2	98	0	0	90	14.38	-25.2			Nov-10
50	2.02	16.01	4.22	44.46	51.31	0.79	0.84	13.06	1.05	36.8	2,599	2	98	0	0	80	24.57	-18.46	5.25		Feb-05
50	1.89	15.75	3.72	42.30	47.60	0.38	1.34	13.05	1.05	36.52	2,599	2	98	0	0	80	24.18	-18.6		1.00	Feb-05
	2.09	16.17	4.50	45.59	53.38	1.07	0.59	13.07	1.05	37.99	2,599	2	98	0	0	80	24.79	-18.37			Feb-03
	1.96	15.86	3.96	43.38	49.47	0.64	1.09	13.06	1.05	35.85	2,599	2	98	0	0	80	24.4	-18.54			Nov-08
	2.10	16.23	4.64	46.28	54.70	1.18	0.44	13.06	1.05	37.88	2,599	2	98	0	0	80	24.88	-18.28			May-06
	2.17	16.33	4.75	46.72	54.80	1.28	0.34	13.07	1.05	37.18	2,599	2	98	0	0	80	24.79	-18.37			Nov-15
50	2.35	18.97	7.06	60.39	74.50	0.48	0.84	13.96	1.03	56.61	1,148	1	99	0	0	69	24.49	-16.89	5.25		Feb-05
50	2.23	18.68	6.53	58.05	70.23	0.07	1.34	13.96	1.03	55.45	1,148	1	99	0	0	69	24.12	-17.05		1.00	Feb-05
	2.41	19.13	7.32	61.63	76.69	0.71	0.59	13.97	1.03	57.6	1,148	1	99	0	0	69	24.63	-16.79			Feb-03
	2.27	18.80	6.77	59.19	72.34	0.44	1.09	13.95	1.03	55.27	1,148	1	99	0	0	69	24.31	-16.94			Nov-08
	2.45	19.21	7.48	62.46	78.32	0.85	0.44	13.97	1.03	56.82	1,148	1	99	0	0	69	24.82	-16.73			May-06
	2.47	19.24	7.58	62.84	78.24	0.94	0.34	13.96	1.03	56.81	1,148	1	99	0	0	69	24.63	-16.79			Nov-15
50	1.22	16.63	0.75	29.80	32.91	0.34	1.14	13.75	1.01	18.23	530.5	2	98	0	0	62	26.75	-23.07	5.25		May-92
50	1.10	16.37	0.28	27.73	29.19	0.15	1.64	13.72	1.01	14.64	530.5	2	98	0	0	62	26.33	-23.3		1.00	Mar-99
	1.30	16.79	1.00	30.78	34.57	0.58	0.89	13.71	1.01	19.47	530.5	2	98	0	0	62	26.85	-23.02			May-91
	1.22	16.67	0.76	29.80	32.90	0.53	1.14	13.76	1.01	18.12	530.5	2	98	0	0	62	26.67	-23.1			Sep-16
	1.30	16.79	1.00	30.72	34.51	0.62	0.89	13.73	1.01	19.4	530.5	2	98	0	0	62	26.85	-23.02			Sep-16
	1.35	16.91	1.27	31.77	35.78	0.83	0.64	13.72	1.01	19.49	530.5	2	98	0	0	62	26.85	-23.02			Nov-15
50	4.02	18.42	9.90	49.07	56.69	0.93	0.84	12.72	1.03	41.85	30.7	2	98	0	0	38	27.98	-19.67	5.25		Feb-05
50	3.87	18.13	9.36	46.84	52.86	0.42	1.34	12.72	1.03	40.98	30.7	2	98	0	0	38	27.54	-19.8		1.00	Feb-05
	4.07	18.56	10.17	50.16	58.69	1.14	0.59	12.73	1.03	42.15	30.7	2	98	0	0	38	28.16	-19.58			Feb-03

	MARKET			FUND TYPE, CATEGORY & OBJECTIVE	RATINGS				MINIMUMS	
Fund Name	Ticker Symbol	Traded On	Fund Type	Category and (Prospectus Objective)	Overall Rating	Reward Rating	Risk Rating	Recent Up/ Downgrade	Open to New Investors	Min Initial Investment
JPMorgan Intrepid Value Fund Class A Shares	JIVAX	NAS CM	Open End	US Equity Large Cap Value (Growth)	C+	C	B		Y	1,000
JPMorgan Intrepid Value Fund Class C Shares	JIVCX	NAS CM	Open End	US Equity Large Cap Value (Growth)	C+	C	B	Up	Y	1,000
JPMorgan Intrepid Value Fund Class I Shares	JPIVX	NAS CM	Open End	US Equity Large Cap Value (Growth)	C+	C	B		Y	1,000,000
JPMorgan Intrepid Value Fund Class R2 Shares	JIVZX	NAS CM	Open End	US Equity Large Cap Value (Growth)	C+	C	B		Y	0
JPMorgan Intrepid Value Fund Class R5 Shares	JIVRX	NAS CM	Open End	US Equity Large Cap Value (Growth)	C+	C	B		Y	0
JPMorgan Intrepid Value Fund Class R6 Shares	JIVMX	NAS CM	Open End	US Equity Large Cap Value (Growth)	C+	C	B		Y	15,000,000
JPMorgan Investor Balanced Fund Class A	OGIAX	NAS CM	Open End	Moderate Alloc (Balanced)	B	C	A-	Up	Y	1,000
JPMorgan Investor Balanced Fund Class C	OGBCX	NAS CM	Open End	Moderate Alloc (Balanced)	B-	C	A-	Up	Y	500
JPMorgan Investor Balanced Fund Class I	OIBFX	NAS CM	Open End	Moderate Alloc (Balanced)	B	C	A-	Up	Y	1,000,000
JPMorgan Investor Balanced Fund Class R6	JFQUX	NAS CM	Open End	Moderate Alloc (Balanced)	B-	C	B+	Up	Y	15,000,000
JPMorgan Investor Conservative Growth Fund Class A	OICAX	NAS CM	Open End	Cautious Alloc (Growth & Income)	B	C+	A-	Up	Y	1,000
JPMorgan Investor Conservative Growth Fund Class C	OCGCX	NAS CM	Open End	Cautious Alloc (Growth & Income)	B-	C	A-		Y	500
JPMorgan Investor Conservative Growth Fund Class I	ONCFX	NAS CM	Open End	Cautious Alloc (Growth & Income)	B	C+	A-	Up	Y	1,000,000
JPMorgan Investor Conservative Growth Fund Class R6	JFLJX	NAS CM	Open End	Cautious Alloc (Growth & Income)	B	C+	A-	Up	Y	15,000,000
JPMorgan Investor Growth & Income Fund Class A	ONGIX	NAS CM	Open End	Aggressive Alloc (Growth & Income)	B-	C	B+	Up	Y	1,000
JPMorgan Investor Growth & Income Fund Class C	ONECX	NAS CM	Open End	Aggressive Alloc (Growth & Income)	B-	C	B+	Up	Y	500
JPMorgan Investor Growth & Income Fund Class I	ONGFX	NAS CM	Open End	Aggressive Alloc (Growth & Income)	B-	C	B+	Up	Y	1,000,000
JPMorgan Investor Growth & Income Fund Class R6	JFBUX	NAS CM	Open End	Aggressive Alloc (Growth & Income)	B-	C	B+	Up	Y	15,000,000
JPMorgan Investor Growth Fund Class A	ONGAX	NAS CM	Open End	Aggressive Alloc (Growth)	B-	C	B	Up	Y	1,000
JPMorgan Investor Growth Fund Class C	OGGCX	NAS CM	Open End	Aggressive Alloc (Growth)	B-	C	B	Up	Y	500
JPMorgan Investor Growth Fund Class I	ONIFX	NAS CM	Open End	Aggressive Alloc (Growth)	B-	C	B	Up	Y	1,000,000
JPMorgan Investor Growth Fund Class R6	JFTUX	NAS CM	Open End	Aggressive Alloc (Growth)	B-	C	B	Up	Y	15,000,000
JPMorgan Large Cap Growth Fund Class A	OLGAX	NAS CM	Open End	US Equity Large Cap Growth (Growth)	B-	B-	B-	Down	Y	1,000
JPMorgan Large Cap Growth Fund Class C	OLGCX	NAS CM	Open End	US Equity Large Cap Growth (Growth)	B-	B-	B-	Down	Y	1,000
JPMorgan Large Cap Growth Fund Class I	SEEGX	NAS CM	Open End	US Equity Large Cap Growth (Growth)	B-	B-	B-	Down	Y	1,000,000
JPMorgan Large Cap Growth Fund Class R2	JLGZX	NAS CM	Open End	US Equity Large Cap Growth (Growth)	B-	B-	B-	Down	Y	0
JPMorgan Large Cap Growth Fund Class R3	JLGPX	NAS CM	Open End	US Equity Large Cap Growth (Growth)	B-	B-	B-	Down	Y	0
JPMorgan Large Cap Growth Fund Class R4	JLGQX	NAS CM	Open End	US Equity Large Cap Growth (Growth)	B-	B-	B-	Down	Y	0
JPMorgan Large Cap Growth Fund Class R5	JLGRX	NAS CM	Open End	US Equity Large Cap Growth (Growth)	B-	B-	B-	Down	Y	0
JPMorgan Large Cap Growth Fund Class R6	JLGMX	NAS CM	Open End	US Equity Large Cap Growth (Growth)	B-	B-	B-	Down	Y	15,000,000
JPMorgan Large Cap Value Fund Class A	OLVAX	NAS CM	Open End	US Equity Large Cap Value (Growth)	C	C	B-		Y	1,000
JPMorgan Large Cap Value Fund Class C	OLVCX	NAS CM	Open End	US Equity Large Cap Value (Growth)	C	C	B-		Y	1,000
JPMorgan Large Cap Value Fund Class I	HLQVX	NAS CM	Open End	US Equity Large Cap Value (Growth)	C+	C	B-	Up	Y	1,000,000
JPMorgan Large Cap Value Fund Class R2	JLVZX	NAS CM	Open End	US Equity Large Cap Value (Growth)	C	C	B-		Y	0
JPMorgan Large Cap Value Fund Class R3	OLVTX	NAS CM	Open End	US Equity Large Cap Value (Growth)	C	C	B-		Y	0
JPMorgan Large Cap Value Fund Class R4	OLVRX	NAS CM	Open End	US Equity Large Cap Value (Growth)	C+	C	B-	Up	Y	0
JPMorgan Large Cap Value Fund Class R5	JLVRX	NAS CM	Open End	US Equity Large Cap Value (Growth)	C+	C	B-	Up	Y	0
JPMorgan Large Cap Value Fund Class R6	JLVMX	NAS CM	Open End	US Equity Large Cap Value (Growth)	C+	C	B	Up	Y	15,000,000
JPMorgan Market Expansion Enhanced Index Fund Class A	OMEAX	NAS CM	Open End	US Equity Mid Cap (Growth)	C	C	C+		Y	1,000
JPMorgan Market Expansion Enhanced Index Fund Class C	OMECX	NAS CM	Open End	US Equity Mid Cap (Growth)	C	C	C+		Y	1,000
JPMorgan Market Expansion Enhanced Index Fund Class I	PGMIX	NAS CM	Open End	US Equity Mid Cap (Growth)	C	C	C+		Y	1,000,000
JPMorgan Market Expansion Enhanced Index Fund Class R2	JMEZX	NAS CM	Open End	US Equity Mid Cap (Growth)	C	C	C+		Y	0
JPMorgan Market Expansion Enhanced Index Fund Class R6	OMYGX	NAS CM	Open End	US Equity Mid Cap (Growth)	C	C	C+		Y	15,000,000
JPMorgan Mid Cap Equity Fund Class A	JCMAX	NAS CM	Open End	US Equity Mid Cap (Growth)	B-	C+	B			1,000
JPMorgan Mid Cap Equity Fund Class C	JMCCX	NAS CM	Open End	US Equity Mid Cap (Growth)	C+	C	B			1,000
JPMorgan Mid Cap Equity Fund Class I	VSNGX	NAS CM	Open End	US Equity Mid Cap (Growth)	B-	C+	B			1,000,000
JPMorgan Mid Cap Equity Fund Class R2	JMCEX	NAS CM	Open End	US Equity Mid Cap (Growth)	C+	C+	B	Down		0
JPMorgan Mid Cap Equity Fund Class R5	JMEEX	NAS CM	Open End	US Equity Mid Cap (Growth)	B-	C+	B			0
JPMorgan Mid Cap Equity Fund Class R6	JPPEX	NAS CM	Open End	US Equity Mid Cap (Growth)	B-	C+	B			15,000,000
JPMorgan Mid Cap Growth Fund Class A	OSGIX	NAS CM	Open End	US Equity Mid Cap (Growth)	B-	B-	B-		Y	1,000
JPMorgan Mid Cap Growth Fund Class C	OMGCX	NAS CM	Open End	US Equity Mid Cap (Growth)	B-	C+	B-		Y	1,000
JPMorgan Mid Cap Growth Fund Class I	HLGEX	NAS CM	Open End	US Equity Mid Cap (Growth)	B-	B-	B-	Down	Y	1,000,000

★ Expanded analysis of this fund is included in Section II.

	TOTAL RETURNS					PERFORMANCE					ASSETS		ASSET ALLOCATION & TURNOVER					BULL & BEAR		FEES		
Min Additional Investment	3-Month Total Return	6-Month Total Return	1-Year Total Return	3-Year Total Return	5-Year Total Return	Dividend Yield (TTM)	Expense Ratio	3-Yr Std Deviation	3-Year Beta	NAV	Total Assets (MIL)	%Cash	%Stocks	%Bonds	%Other	Turnover Ratio	Last Bull Market Total Return	Last Bear Market Total Return	Front End Fee (%)	Back End Fee (%)	Inception Date
50	2.74	15.85	4.08	39.56	35.00	1.45	0.83	13.54	1.09	31.42	976.7	2	98	0	0	68	23.7	-19.26	5.25		Feb-05
50	2.62	15.57	3.56	37.49	31.70	1.09	1.33	13.52	1.09	30.9	976.7	2	98	0	0	68	23.31	-19.38		1.00	Feb-05
	2.81	16.04	4.32	40.41	36.26	1.63	0.59	13.52	1.09	31.62	976.7	2	98	0	0	68	23.82	-19.2			Feb-03
	2.70	15.74	3.83	38.45	33.24	1.27	1.09	13.52	1.09	31.13	976.7	2	98	0	0	68	23.5	-19.31			Nov-08
	2.83	16.09	4.49	41.12	37.49	1.73	0.44	13.52	1.09	31.73	976.7	2	98	0	0	68	23.9	-19.1			May-06
	2.90	16.16	4.62	41.48	37.95	1.81	0.34	13.53	1.09	31.74	976.7	2	98	0	0	68	23.92	-19.08			Nov-10
50	3.02	11.53	5.52	25.59	27.72	2.36	0.99	6.42	-0.03	15	4,768	6	48	46	0	9	13.57	-10.44	4.50		Dec-96
50	2.79	11.12	4.89	23.38	24.24	1.86	1.54	6.42	-0.03	14.74	4,768	6	48	46	0	9	13.25	-10.63		1.00	Jul-97
	3.01	11.56	5.70	26.48	29.29	2.59	0.74	6.42	-0.03	15.02	4,768	6	48	46	0	9	13.68	-10.31			Dec-96
	3.13	11.72	5.96	26.89	29.71	2.75	0.59	6.44	-0.03	15.02	4,768	6	48	46	0	9	13.68	-10.31			Jul-17
50	2.69	8.78	5.80	18.03	20.74	2.43	0.97	4.08	0.33	12.58	3,419	6	28	65	0	6	9.41	-6.09	4.50		Dec-96
50	2.56	8.57	5.23	16.02	17.51	1.9	1.52	4.1	0.32	12.52	3,419	6	28	65	0	6	9.02	-6.3		1.00	Jul-97
	2.73	8.97	6.02	18.88	22.31	2.65	0.72	4.06	0.35	12.66	3,419	6	28	65	0	6	9.52	-5.97			Dec-96
	2.77	9.08	6.18	19.12	22.56	2.8	0.6	4.06	0.34	12.65	3,419	6	28	65	0	6	9.52	-5.97			Jul-17
50	3.28	13.92	5.44	32.80	33.83	2.27	0.99	8.47	0.66	16.94	2,900	6	63	31	0	11	17.87	-14.08	4.50		Dec-96
50	3.11	13.54	4.77	30.52	30.14	1.81	1.55	8.45	0.66	16.41	2,900	6	63	31	0	11	17.5	-14.3		1.00	Jul-97
	3.27	14.03	5.62	33.76	35.54	2.55	0.74	8.44	0.66	16.64	2,900	6	63	31	0	11	17.97	-13.98			Dec-96
	3.32	14.10	5.85	34.15	35.93	2.7	0.61	8.45	0.66	16.64	2,900	6	63	31	0	11	17.97	-13.98			Jul-17
50	3.51	16.66	4.94	40.44	41.39	2.17	0.97	10.96	0.86	20.16	2,783	5	83	12	0	11	22.31	-18.15	4.50		Dec-96
50	3.37	16.28	4.30	38.05	37.50	2.02	1.55	10.93	0.86	18.67	2,783	5	83	12	0	11	22.03	-18.4		1.00	Jul-97
	3.60	16.77	5.18	41.53	43.23	2.35	0.72	10.96	0.86	20.62	2,783	5	83	12	0	11	22.53	-18.1			Dec-96
	3.59	16.86	5.35	41.87	43.57	2.5	0.6	10.93	0.86	20.61	2,783	5	83	12	0	11	22.53	-18.1			Jul-17
50	7.46	29.58	13.66	87.39	101.02	0	0.94	15.01	1.08	41.87	15,920	2	98	0	0	24	27.95	-13.05	5.25		Feb-94
50	7.33	29.26	13.11	84.58	96.07	0	1.44	15.01	1.08	32.33	15,920	2	98	0	0	24	27.6	-13.22		1.00	Nov-97
	7.54	29.72	13.95	88.55	102.97	0	0.69	15.03	1.08	42.46	15,920	2	98	0	0	24	28.05	-12.97			Feb-92
	7.40	29.39	13.38	85.89	98.46	0	1.19	15.02	1.08	40.32	15,920	2	98	0	0	24	27.74	-13.13			Nov-08
	7.45	29.57	13.67	87.16	100.46	0	0.94	15.03	1.08	42.1	15,920	2	98	0	0	24	27.86	-13.06			Sep-16
	7.52	29.73	13.95	88.52	102.93	0	0.69	15.02	1.08	42.45	15,920	2	98	0	0	24	28.05	-12.97			Sep-16
	7.57	29.86	14.14	89.55	104.83	0	0.54	15.02	1.08	43.44	15,920	2	98	0	0	24	28.25	-12.88			Apr-09
	7.59	29.91	14.23	90.08	105.80	0.06	0.44	15.02	1.08	43.78	15,920	2	98	0	0	24	28.29	-12.88			Nov-10
50	2.26	15.59	1.07	39.73	44.90	1.1	0.93	15.52	1.24	14.11	1,412	2	98	0	0	130	25.48	-21.45	5.25		Feb-92
50	2.08	15.25	0.50	37.53	41.17	0.77	1.44	15.48	1.24	13.49	1,412	2	98	0	0	130	25.03	-21.58		1.00	Mar-99
	2.30	15.70	1.24	40.42	46.19	1.34	0.69	15.47	1.24	13.85	1,412	2	98	0	0	130	25.44	-21.31			Mar-91
	2.22	15.44	0.76	38.53	42.89	0.94	1.19	15.52	1.24	13.98	1,412	2	98	0	0	130	25.17	-21.51			Nov-08
	2.16	15.58	0.94	39.31	44.31		0.94	15.44	1.24	13.84	1,412	2	98	0	0	130	25.25	-21.4			Oct-18
	2.26	15.74	1.23	40.40	46.17		0.69	15.46	1.24	14.11	1,412	2	98	0	0	130	25.44	-21.32			Oct-18
	2.39	15.88	1.43	41.23	47.55	1.45	0.54	15.46	1.24	14	1,412	2	98	0	0	130	25.69	-21.32			May-06
	2.36	15.88	1.52	41.53	48.04	1.53	0.44	15.46	1.24	13.9	1,412	2	98	0	0	130	25.61	-21.3			Nov-10
50	2.27	16.50	-3.69	33.72	41.02	0.82	0.6	16.11	1.02	9.88	949.1	1	99	0	0	33	28.24	-23.33	5.25		Jul-98
50	2.03	16.06	-4.20	31.57	36.85	0.65	1.1	16.08	1.01	8.02	949.1	1	99	0	0	33	27.66	-23.49		1.00	Mar-99
	2.23	16.57	-3.56	34.53	42.70	0.8	0.35	16.08	1.01	10.06	949.1	1	99	0	0	33	28.49	-23.22			Jul-98
	2.10	16.18	-4.10	32.56	39.22	0.55	1	16.03	1.01	9.69	949.1	1	99	0	0	33	28.09	-23.43			Nov-08
	2.24	16.55	-3.53	34.57	42.75		0.25	16.06	1.01	10	949.1	1	99	0	0	33	28.49	-23.22			Oct-18
50	4.70	24.67	9.91	46.03	52.28	0.23	1.14	13.51	1	50.52	2,791	3	97	0	0	31	28.82	-20.62	5.25		Nov-09
50	4.56	24.37	9.38	43.86	48.53	0	1.64	13.5	1	48.32	2,791	3	97	0	0	31	28.42	-20.79		1.00	Nov-09
	4.75	24.84	10.19	47.33	54.71	0.41	0.89	13.51	1	51.35	2,791	3	97	0	0	31	29.05	-20.5			Dec-96
	4.62	24.52	9.65	44.95	50.39	0.06	1.39	13.51	1	49.96	2,791	3	97	0	0	31	28.67	-20.67			Mar-14
	4.79	24.92	10.36	47.90	55.64	0.55	0.74	13.5	1	51.37	2,791	3	97	0	0	31	29.05	-20.5			Mar-14
	4.83	24.99	10.47	48.27	56.15	0.64	0.64	13.51	1	51.41	2,791	3	97	0	0	31	29.05	-20.5			Mar-14
50	6.46	30.61	15.37	64.93	65.35	0	1.24	15.01	1.03	32.94	4,565	4	96	0	0	56	30.46	-23.79	5.25		Feb-92
50	6.33	30.28	14.78	62.43	61.20	0	1.74	14.98	1.03	25.34	4,565	4	96	0	0	56	30.05	-23.95		1.00	Nov-97
	6.55	30.77	15.72	66.45	67.91	0	0.93	15.02	1.03	38.37	4,565	4	96	0	0	56	30.67	-23.67			Mar-89

	MARKET			FUND TYPE, CATEGORY & OBJECTIVE	RATINGS				MINIMUMS	
Fund Name	Ticker Symbol	Traded On	Fund Type	Category and (Prospectus Objective)	Overall Rating	Reward Rating	Risk Rating	Recent Up/ Downgrade	Open to New Investors	Min Initial Investment
JPMorgan Mid Cap Growth Fund Class R2	JMGZX	NAS CM	Open End	US Equity Mid Cap (Growth)	B-	C+	B-		Y	0
JPMorgan Mid Cap Growth Fund Class R3	JMGPX	NAS CM	Open End	US Equity Mid Cap (Growth)	B-	B-	B-		Y	0
JPMorgan Mid Cap Growth Fund Class R4	JMGQX	NAS CM	Open End	US Equity Mid Cap (Growth)	B-	B-	B-	Down	Y	0
JPMorgan Mid Cap Growth Fund Class R5	JMGFX	NAS CM	Open End	US Equity Mid Cap (Growth)	B-	B-	B-	Down	Y	0
JPMorgan Mid Cap Growth Fund Class R6	JMGMX	NAS CM	Open End	US Equity Mid Cap (Growth)	B-	B-	B-	Down	Y	15,000,000
JPMorgan Mid Cap Value Fund Class A	JAMCX	NAS CM	Open End	US Equity Mid Cap (Growth)	C+	C	B	Up		1,000
JPMorgan Mid Cap Value Fund Class C	JCMVX	NAS CM	Open End	US Equity Mid Cap (Growth)	C+	C	B	Up		1,000
JPMorgan Mid Cap Value Fund Class I	JMVSX	NAS CM	Open End	US Equity Mid Cap (Growth)	C+	C	B	Up		1,000,000
JPMorgan Mid Cap Value Fund Class L	FLMVX	NAS CM	Open End	US Equity Mid Cap (Growth)	C+	C	B	Up		3,000,000
JPMorgan Mid Cap Value Fund Class R2	JMVZX	NAS CM	Open End	US Equity Mid Cap (Growth)	C+	C	B	Up		0
JPMorgan Mid Cap Value Fund Class R3	JMVPX	NAS CM	Open End	US Equity Mid Cap (Growth)	C+	C	B	Up	Y	0
JPMorgan Mid Cap Value Fund Class R4	JMVQX	NAS CM	Open End	US Equity Mid Cap (Growth)	C+	C	B	Up	Y	0
JPMorgan Mid Cap Value Fund Class R5	JMVRX	NAS CM	Open End	US Equity Mid Cap (Growth)	C+	C	B	Up	Y	0
JPMorgan Mid Cap Value Fund Class R6	JMVYX	NAS CM	Open End	US Equity Mid Cap (Growth)	C+	C	B	Up	Y	15,000,000
JPMorgan Opportunistic Equity Long/Short Fund Class A	JOELX	NAS CM	Open End	Long/Short Equity (Growth)	C	C-	C+	Down	Y	1,000
JPMorgan Opportunistic Equity Long/Short Fund Class C	JOECX	NAS CM	Open End	Long/Short Equity (Growth)	C	C-	C+	Down	Y	1,000
JPMorgan Opportunistic Equity Long/Short Fund Class I	JOEQX	NAS CM	Open End	Long/Short Equity (Growth)	C	C-	B-	Down	Y	1,000,000
JPMorgan Opportunistic Equity Long/Short Fund Class R6	JOERX	NAS CM	Open End	Long/Short Equity (Growth)	C	C-	B-	Down	Y	15,000,000
JPMorgan Realty Income Fund Class A	URTAX	NAS CM	Open End	Real Estate Sector Equity (Real Estate)	C	C	C+	Down	Y	1,000
JPMorgan Realty Income Fund Class C	URTCX	NAS CM	Open End	Real Estate Sector Equity (Real Estate)	C	C	C+	Down	Y	1,000
JPMorgan Realty Income Fund Class I	URTDX	NAS CM	Open End	Real Estate Sector Equity (Real Estate)	C	C	C+	Down	Y	1,000,000
JPMorgan Realty Income Fund Class L	URTLX	NAS CM	Open End	Real Estate Sector Equity (Real Estate)	C	C	C+	Down	Y	3,000,000
JPMorgan Realty Income Fund Class R5	JRIRX	NAS CM	Open End	Real Estate Sector Equity (Real Estate)	C	C	C+	Down	Y	0
JPMorgan Realty Income Fund Class R6	JPINX	NAS CM	Open End	Real Estate Sector Equity (Real Estate)	C	C	C+	Down	Y	15,000,000
JPMorgan Research Market Neutral Fund Class A	JMNAX	NAS CM	Open End	Market Neutral (Growth)	C+	C	B		Y	1,000
JPMorgan Research Market Neutral Fund Class C	JMNCX	NAS CM	Open End	Market Neutral (Growth)	C+	C	B	Up	Y	1,000
JPMorgan Research Market Neutral Fund Class I	JMNSX	NAS CM	Open End	Market Neutral (Growth)	B-	C	B+	Up	Y	1,000,000
JPMorgan Research Market Neutral Fund Class L	JPMNX	NAS CM	Open End	Market Neutral (Growth)	B-	C	B+	Up	Y	3,000,000
JPMorgan Small Cap Blend Fund Class A	VSCOX	NAS CM	Open End	US Equity Small Cap (Small Company)	C+	C+	C+	Down		1,000
JPMorgan Small Cap Blend Fund Class C	VSCCX	NAS CM	Open End	US Equity Small Cap (Small Company)	C+	C+	C+	Down		1,000
JPMorgan Small Cap Blend Fund Class I	JDSCX	NAS CM	Open End	US Equity Small Cap (Small Company)	C+	C+	C+	Down		1,000,000
JPMorgan Small Cap Blend Fund Class R6	JSCHX	NAS CM	Open End	US Equity Small Cap (Small Company)	C+	C+	C+	Down	Y	15,000,000
JPMorgan Small Cap Core Fund Class A	VSSBX	NAS CM	Open End	US Equity Small Cap (Small Company)	C	C-	C+		Y	1,000
JPMorgan Small Cap Core Fund Class C	VSSRX	NAS CM	Open End	US Equity Small Cap (Small Company)	C	C-	C+		Y	1,000
JPMorgan Small Cap Core Fund Class I	VSSWX	NAS CM	Open End	US Equity Small Cap (Small Company)	C	C-	C+		Y	1,000,000
JPMorgan Small Cap Core Fund Class R2	JRJUX	NAS CM	Open End	US Equity Small Cap (Small Company)	C	C-	C+		Y	0
JPMorgan Small Cap Core Fund Class R3	JGAUX	NAS CM	Open End	US Equity Small Cap (Small Company)	C	C-	C+		Y	0
JPMorgan Small Cap Core Fund Class R4	JGREX	NAS CM	Open End	US Equity Small Cap (Small Company)	C	C-	C+		Y	0
JPMorgan Small Cap Core Fund Class R5	VSSCX	NAS CM	Open End	US Equity Small Cap (Small Company)	C	C-	C+		Y	0
JPMorgan Small Cap Core Fund Class R6	VSSLX	NAS CM	Open End	US Equity Small Cap (Small Company)	C	C-	C+		Y	15,000,000
JPMorgan Small Cap Equity Fund Class A	VSEAX	NAS CM	Open End	US Equity Small Cap (Small Company)	C+	C	B-			1,000
JPMorgan Small Cap Equity Fund Class C	JSECX	NAS CM	Open End	US Equity Small Cap (Small Company)	C+	C	B-	Up		1,000
JPMorgan Small Cap Equity Fund Class I	VSEIX	NAS CM	Open End	US Equity Small Cap (Small Company)	C+	C	B-			1,000,000
JPMorgan Small Cap Equity Fund Class R2	JSEZX	NAS CM	Open End	US Equity Small Cap (Small Company)	C+	C	B-	Up		0
JPMorgan Small Cap Equity Fund Class R3	JSEPX	NAS CM	Open End	US Equity Small Cap (Small Company)	C+	C	B-		Y	0
JPMorgan Small Cap Equity Fund Class R4	JSEQX	NAS CM	Open End	US Equity Small Cap (Small Company)	C+	C	B-		Y	0
JPMorgan Small Cap Equity Fund Class R5	JSERX	NAS CM	Open End	US Equity Small Cap (Small Company)	C+	C	B-			0
JPMorgan Small Cap Equity Fund Class R6	VSENX	NAS CM	Open End	US Equity Small Cap (Small Company)	C+	C	B-		Y	15,000,000
JPMorgan Small Cap Growth Fund Class A	PGSGX	NAS CM	Open End	US Equity Small Cap (Small Company)	C+	C+	C+	Down		1,000
JPMorgan Small Cap Growth Fund Class C	OSGCX	NAS CM	Open End	US Equity Small Cap (Small Company)	C+	C+	C+	Down		1,000
JPMorgan Small Cap Growth Fund Class I	OGGFX	NAS CM	Open End	US Equity Small Cap (Small Company)	C+	C+	C+	Down		1,000,000
JPMorgan Small Cap Growth Fund Class L	JISGX	NAS CM	Open End	US Equity Small Cap (Small Company)	C+	C+	C+	Down		3,000,000

★ Expanded analysis of this fund is included in Section II.

	TOTAL RETURNS					PERFORMANCE				ASSETS		ASSET ALLOCATION & TURNOVER					BULL & BEAR		FEES		
Min Additional Investment	3-Month Total Return	6-Month Total Return	1-Year Total Return	3-Year Total Return	5-Year Total Return	Dividend Yield (TTM)	Expense Ratio	3-Yr Std Deviation	3-Year Beta	NAV	Total Assets (MIL)	%Cash	%Stocks	%Bonds	%Other	Turnover Ratio	Last Bull Market Total Return	Last Bear Market Total Return	Front End Fee (%)	Back End Fee (%)	Inception Date
	6.39	30.43	15.09	63.83	63.72	0	1.49	15.01	1.03	35.91	4,565	4	96	0	0	56	30.3	-23.83			Jun-09
	6.47	30.61	15.38	64.97	65.59	0	1.24	14.99	1.03	38.01	4,565	4	96	0	0	56	30.48	-23.75			Sep-16
	6.53	30.76	15.65	66.17	67.63	0	0.99	15	1.03	38.3	4,565	4	96	0	0	56	30.67	-23.67			Sep-16
	6.57	30.88	15.88	67.16	69.10	0	0.79	15.02	1.03	38.9	4,565	4	96	0	0	56	30.72	-23.67			Nov-11
	6.59	30.94	15.96	67.43	69.54	0	0.74	15.02	1.03	39.1	4,565	4	96	0	0	56	30.72	-23.67			Nov-11
50	2.95	18.84	4.11	28.04	38.24	0.93	1.24	12.78	0.96	38.02	17,031	3	97	0	0	13	27.15	-17.71	5.25		Apr-01
50	2.85	18.58	3.59	26.14	34.77	0.45	1.73	12.77	0.96	36.44	17,031	3	97	0	0	13	26.8	-17.91		1.00	Apr-01
	3.02	19.02	4.38	29.03	39.98	1.18	0.98	12.78	0.96	38.48	17,031	3	97	0	0	13	27.35	-17.64			Oct-01
	3.09	19.16	4.62	29.97	41.68	1.4	0.75	12.79	0.96	38.99	17,031	3	97	0	0	13	27.57	-17.57			Nov-97
	2.88	18.71	3.85	27.09	36.46	0.78	1.49	12.78	0.96	36.35	17,031	3	97	0	0	13	27	-17.81			Nov-08
	2.94	18.85	4.11	28.15	39.00	1.02	1.23	12.78	0.96	37.7	17,031	3	97	0	0	13	27.39	-17.66			Sep-16
	3.04	19.02	4.37	29.07	40.71	1.27	0.98	12.78	0.96	38.29	17,031	3	97	0	0	13	27.57	-17.57			Sep-16
	3.07	19.08	4.52	29.63	41.31	1.31	0.83	12.78	0.96	38.93	17,031	3	97	0	0	13	27.57	-17.57			Sep-16
	3.09	19.17	4.63	29.97	41.68	1.41	0.73	12.8	0.96	38.97	17,031	3	97	0	0	13	27.57	-17.57			Sep-16
50	-0.34	0.51	-0.61	18.22		0	2.59	7.75	0.37	17.56	296.6	48	52	0	0	995			5.25		Aug-14
50	-0.46	0.23	-1.14	16.45		0	3.09	7.73	0.37	17.11	296.6	48	52	0	0	995				1.00	Aug-14
	-0.22	0.62	-0.38	19.09		0	2.34	7.74	0.37	17.79	296.6	48	52	0	0	995					Aug-14
	-0.22	0.72	-0.15	20.02		0	2.09	7.72	0.37	18.02	296.6	48	52	0	0	995					Aug-14
50	2.77	20.75	11.62	10.49	36.67	1.46	1.18	13.23	0.98	14.27	2,414	1	99	0	0	50	32.15	-16.48	5.25		Jun-04
50	2.61	20.43	11.09	8.82	33.34	1.13	1.68	13.25	0.98	13.78	2,414	1	99	0	0	50	31.62	-16.59		1.00	Jun-04
	2.87	20.92	11.88	11.52	39.03	1.63	0.93	13.26	0.98	14.43	2,414	1	99	0	0	50	32.37	-16.25			Feb-17
	2.91	21.06	12.07	11.84	39.43	1.75	0.78	13.24	0.98	14.46	2,414	1	99	0	0	50	32.37	-16.25			Dec-97
	2.98	21.15	12.22	12.02	39.80	1.78	0.78	13.24	0.98	14.54	2,414	1	99	0	0	50	32.41	-16.23			May-06
	2.94	21.09	12.24	12.17	40.02	1.82	0.68	13.2	0.98	14.48	2,414	1	99	0	0	50	32.37	-16.25			Nov-15
50	1.38	1.45	3.49	10.67	3.15	0	3.53	3.5	9.51	13.21	68.3	99	1	0	0	252	-0.69	-3.27	5.25		Feb-02
50	1.26	1.26	3.05	9.09	0.63	0	4.03	3.51	9.6	12.18	68.3	99	1	0	0	252	-0.92	-3.44		1.00	Nov-09
	1.46	1.66	3.82	11.58	4.52	0	3.27	3.52	10.18	13.9	68.3	99	1	0	0	252	-0.54	-3.13			Nov-09
	1.50	1.69	3.95	12.02	5.39	0	3.13	3.53	9.21	14.23	68.3	99	1	0	0	252	-0.33	-3.12			Dec-98
50	2.38	21.57	0.73	86.98	78.98	0	1.28	16.97	0.93	19.78	349.4	3	97	0	0	89	30.62	-27.99	5.25		May-97
50	2.22	21.26	0.22	84.23	74.52	0	1.78	16.96	0.93	12.89	349.4	3	97	0	0	89	30.23	-28.13		1.00	Jan-98
	2.37	21.74	0.96	88.36	81.18	0	1.03	16.97	0.93	23.74	349.4	3	97	0	0	89	30.94	-27.92			Apr-99
	2.45	21.91	1.21	87.87	79.83		0.78	16.95	0.93	23.81	349.4	3	97	0	0	89	30.62	-27.99			Jul-18
50	1.21	17.29	-5.42	43.84	37.54	0.03	1.24	18.33	1.06	49.98	449.5	1	99	0	0	39	30.08	-27.27	5.25		May-16
50	1.08	17.02	-5.88	41.73	34.17	0	1.74	18.32	1.06	49.28	449.5	1	99	0	0	39	29.71	-27.43		1.00	May-16
	1.28	17.45	-5.17	45.15	39.48	0.23	0.99	18.34	1.07	50.26	449.5	1	99	0	0	39	30.27	-27.2			Jan-17
	1.15	17.14	-5.64	43.10	36.15	0	1.49	18.33	1.06	50.02	449.5	1	99	0	0	39	29.9	-27.35			Jul-17
	1.21	17.29	-5.43	44.15	37.84	0.04	1.24	18.34	1.07	50.19	449.5	1	99	0	0	39	30.08	-27.27			Jul-17
	1.26	17.44	-5.17	45.27	39.60	0.23	0.99	18.34	1.07	50.29	449.5	1	99	0	0	39	30.27	-27.2			Jul-17
	1.32	17.57	-5.00	45.81	40.12	0.39	0.8	18.34	1.07	50.43	449.5	1	99	0	0	39	30.27	-27.2			Dec-96
	1.34	17.58	-4.94	46.02	40.36	0.45	0.74	18.35	1.07	50.35	449.5	1	99	0	0	39	30.27	-27.2			May-16
50	5.41	20.77	2.81	43.53	53.93	0.12	1.24	15	0.86	50.05	6,279	5	95	0	0	17	30.37	-20.53	5.25		Dec-94
50	5.28	20.47	2.30	41.39	50.15	0	1.74	14.98	0.85	36.25	6,279	5	95	0	0	17	29.97	-20.67		1.00	Feb-05
	5.45	20.91	3.05	44.67	56.06	0.33	0.99	14.99	0.85	58.34	6,279	5	95	0	0	17	30.6	-20.42			May-96
	5.33	20.61	2.56	42.44	52.00	0	1.49	14.99	0.85	48.98	6,279	5	95	0	0	17	30.14	-20.59			Nov-08
	5.40	20.76	2.79	43.56	53.97	0.12	1.24	14.99	0.86	49.73	6,279	5	95	0	0	17	30.37	-20.53			Sep-16
	5.46	20.89	3.04	44.53	55.00	0.29	0.99	15	0.86	58.26	6,279	5	95	0	0	17	30.37	-20.53			Sep-16
	5.51	21.01	3.26	45.52	57.62	0.5	0.8	15	0.86	58.51	6,279	5	95	0	0	17	30.72	-20.35			May-06
	5.53	21.06	3.33	45.77	56.41	0.55	0.74	15	0.86	58.5	6,279	5	95	0	0	17	30.37	-20.53			May-16
50	2.59	28.12	5.07	93.40	85.81	0	1.28	18.54	1.04	16.99	2,949	2	98	0	0	89	30.81	-27.92	5.25		Jul-91
50	2.43	27.79	4.49	90.60	81.18	0	1.78	18.55	1.04	11.77	2,949	2	98	0	0	89	30.51	-28.11		1.00	Nov-97
	2.64	28.23	5.30	94.85	88.14	0	1.03	18.54	1.04	19.03	2,949	2	98	0	0	89	31.07	-27.86			Mar-96
	2.71	28.42	5.50	95.77	89.58	0	0.89	18.54	1.04	19.7	2,949	2	98	0	0	89	31.16	-27.81			Feb-05

Fund Name	MARKET Ticker Symbol	Traded On	FUND TYPE, CATEGORY & OBJECTIVE Fund Type	Category and (Prospectus Objective)	RATINGS Overall Rating	Reward Rating	Risk Rating	Recent Up/ Downgrade	Open to New Investors	MINIMUMS Min Initial Investment
JPMorgan Small Cap Growth Fund Class R2	JSGZX	NAS CM	Open End	US Equity Small Cap (Small Company)	C+	C+	C+	Down		0
JPMorgan Small Cap Growth Fund Class R3	JGRQX	NAS CM	Open End	US Equity Small Cap (Small Company)	C+	C+	C+	Down	Y	0
JPMorgan Small Cap Growth Fund Class R4	JGLYX	NAS CM	Open End	US Equity Small Cap (Small Company)	C+	C+	C+	Down	Y	0
JPMorgan Small Cap Growth Fund Class R5	JGSVX	NAS CM	Open End	US Equity Small Cap (Small Company)	C+	C+	C+	Down	Y	0
JPMorgan Small Cap Growth Fund Class R6	JGSMX	NAS CM	Open End	US Equity Small Cap (Small Company)	C+	C+	C+	Down		15,000,000
JPMorgan Small Cap Value Fund Class A	PSOAX	NAS CM	Open End	US Equity Small Cap (Small Company)	C-	D+	C	Down	Y	1,000
JPMorgan Small Cap Value Fund Class C	OSVCX	NAS CM	Open End	US Equity Small Cap (Small Company)	C-	D+	C	Down	Y	1,000
JPMorgan Small Cap Value Fund Class I	PSOPX	NAS CM	Open End	US Equity Small Cap (Small Company)	C-	D+	C	Down	Y	1,000,000
JPMorgan Small Cap Value Fund Class R2	JSVZX	NAS CM	Open End	US Equity Small Cap (Small Company)	C-	D+	C	Down	Y	0
JPMorgan Small Cap Value Fund Class R3	JSVPX	NAS CM	Open End	US Equity Small Cap (Small Company)	C-	D+	C	Down	Y	0
JPMorgan Small Cap Value Fund Class R4	JSVQX	NAS CM	Open End	US Equity Small Cap (Small Company)	C-	D+	C	Down	Y	0
JPMorgan Small Cap Value Fund Class R5	JSVRX	NAS CM	Open End	US Equity Small Cap (Small Company)	C-	C-	C	Down	Y	0
JPMorgan Small Cap Value Fund Class R6	JSVUX	NAS CM	Open End	US Equity Small Cap (Small Company)	C-	C-	C	Down	Y	15,000,000
JPMorgan SmartRetirement® 2020 Fund Class A	JTTAX	NAS CM	Open End	Target Date (Asset Alloc)	B	C	A-	Up	Y	500
JPMorgan SmartRetirement® 2020 Fund Class C	JTTCX	NAS CM	Open End	Target Date (Asset Alloc)	B-	C	A-	Up	Y	500
JPMorgan SmartRetirement® 2020 Fund Class I	JTTSX	NAS CM	Open End	Target Date (Asset Alloc)	B	C	A-	Up	Y	1,000,000
JPMorgan SmartRetirement® 2020 Fund Class R2	JTTZX	NAS CM	Open End	Target Date (Asset Alloc)	B-	C	A-	Up	Y	0
JPMorgan SmartRetirement® 2020 Fund Class R3	JTTPX	NAS CM	Open End	Target Date (Asset Alloc)	B	C	A-	Up	Y	0
JPMorgan SmartRetirement® 2020 Fund Class R4	JTTQX	NAS CM	Open End	Target Date (Asset Alloc)	B	C	A-	Up	Y	0
JPMorgan SmartRetirement® 2020 Fund Class R5	JTTIX	NAS CM	Open End	Target Date (Asset Alloc)	B	C	A-	Up	Y	0
JPMorgan SmartRetirement® 2020 Fund Class R6	JTTYX	NAS CM	Open End	Target Date (Asset Alloc)	B	C	A-	Up	Y	15,000,000
JPMorgan SmartRetirement® 2025 Fund Class A	JNSAX	NAS CM	Open End	Target Date (Asset Alloc)	B-	C	A-	Up	Y	500
JPMorgan SmartRetirement® 2025 Fund Class C	JNSCX	NAS CM	Open End	Target Date (Asset Alloc)	B-	C	A-	Up	Y	500
JPMorgan SmartRetirement® 2025 Fund Class I	JNSSX	NAS CM	Open End	Target Date (Asset Alloc)	B-	C	A-	Up	Y	1,000,000
JPMorgan SmartRetirement® 2025 Fund Class R2	JNSZX	NAS CM	Open End	Target Date (Asset Alloc)	B-	C	A-	Up	Y	0
JPMorgan SmartRetirement® 2025 Fund Class R3	JNSPX	NAS CM	Open End	Target Date (Asset Alloc)	B-	C	A-	Up	Y	0
JPMorgan SmartRetirement® 2025 Fund Class R4	JNSQX	NAS CM	Open End	Target Date (Asset Alloc)	B-	C	A-	Up	Y	0
JPMorgan SmartRetirement® 2025 Fund Class R5	JNSIX	NAS CM	Open End	Target Date (Asset Alloc)	B-	C	A-	Up	Y	0
JPMorgan SmartRetirement® 2025 Fund Class R6	JNSYX	NAS CM	Open End	Target Date (Asset Alloc)	B-	C	A-	Up	Y	15,000,000
JPMorgan SmartRetirement® 2030 Fund Class A	JSMAX	NAS CM	Open End	Target Date (Asset Alloc)	B-	C	B+	Up	Y	500
JPMorgan SmartRetirement® 2030 Fund Class C	JSMCX	NAS CM	Open End	Target Date (Asset Alloc)	B-	C	B+	Up	Y	500
JPMorgan SmartRetirement® 2030 Fund Class I	JSMSX	NAS CM	Open End	Target Date (Asset Alloc)	B-	C	B+	Up	Y	1,000,000
JPMorgan SmartRetirement® 2030 Fund Class R2	JSMZX	NAS CM	Open End	Target Date (Asset Alloc)	B-	C	B+	Up	Y	0
JPMorgan SmartRetirement® 2030 Fund Class R3	JSMNX	NAS CM	Open End	Target Date (Asset Alloc)	B-	C	B+	Up	Y	0
JPMorgan SmartRetirement® 2030 Fund Class R4	JSMQX	NAS CM	Open End	Target Date (Asset Alloc)	B-	C	B+	Up	Y	0
JPMorgan SmartRetirement® 2030 Fund Class R5	JSMIX	NAS CM	Open End	Target Date (Asset Alloc)	B-	C	B+	Up	Y	0
JPMorgan SmartRetirement® 2030 Fund Class R6	JSMYX	NAS CM	Open End	Target Date (Asset Alloc)	B-	C	B+	Up	Y	15,000,000
JPMorgan SmartRetirement® 2035 Fund Class A	SRJAX	NAS CM	Open End	Target Date (Asset Alloc)	B-	C	B+	Up	Y	500
JPMorgan SmartRetirement® 2035 Fund Class C	SRJCX	NAS CM	Open End	Target Date (Asset Alloc)	B-	C	B+	Up	Y	500
JPMorgan SmartRetirement® 2035 Fund Class I	SRJSX	NAS CM	Open End	Target Date (Asset Alloc)	B-	C	B+	Up	Y	1,000,000
JPMorgan SmartRetirement® 2035 Fund Class R2	SRJZX	NAS CM	Open End	Target Date (Asset Alloc)	B-	C	B+	Up	Y	0
JPMorgan SmartRetirement® 2035 Fund Class R3	SRJPX	NAS CM	Open End	Target Date (Asset Alloc)	B-	C	B+	Up	Y	0
JPMorgan SmartRetirement® 2035 Fund Class R4	SRJQX	NAS CM	Open End	Target Date (Asset Alloc)	B-	C	B+	Up	Y	0
JPMorgan SmartRetirement® 2035 Fund Class R5	SRJIX	NAS CM	Open End	Target Date (Asset Alloc)	B-	C	B+	Up	Y	0
JPMorgan SmartRetirement® 2035 Fund Class R6	SRJYX	NAS CM	Open End	Target Date (Asset Alloc)	B-	C	B+	Up	Y	15,000,000
JPMorgan SmartRetirement® 2040 Fund Class A	SMTAX	NAS CM	Open End	Target Date (Asset Alloc)	B-	C	B	Up	Y	500
JPMorgan SmartRetirement® 2040 Fund Class C	SMTCX	NAS CM	Open End	Target Date (Asset Alloc)	B-	C	B	Up	Y	500
JPMorgan SmartRetirement® 2040 Fund Class I	SMTSX	NAS CM	Open End	Target Date (Asset Alloc)	B-	C	B	Up	Y	1,000,000
JPMorgan SmartRetirement® 2040 Fund Class R2	SMTZX	NAS CM	Open End	Target Date (Asset Alloc)	B-	C	B	Up	Y	0
JPMorgan SmartRetirement® 2040 Fund Class R3	SMTPX	NAS CM	Open End	Target Date (Asset Alloc)	B-	C	B	Up	Y	0
JPMorgan SmartRetirement® 2040 Fund Class R4	SMTQX	NAS CM	Open End	Target Date (Asset Alloc)	B-	C	B	Up	Y	0
JPMorgan SmartRetirement® 2040 Fund Class R5	SMTIX	NAS CM	Open End	Target Date (Asset Alloc)	B-	C	B	Up	Y	0

★ Expanded analysis of this fund is included in Section II.

	TOTAL RETURNS					PERFORMANCE				ASSETS		ASSET ALLOCATION & TURNOVER					BULL & BEAR		FEES		
Min Additional Investment	3-Month Total Return	6-Month Total Return	1-Year Total Return	3-Year Total Return	5-Year Total Return	Dividend Yield (TTM)	Expense Ratio	3-Yr Std Deviation	3-Year Beta	NAV	Total Assets (MIL)	%Cash	%Stocks	%Bonds	%Other	Turnover Ratio	Last Bull Market Total Return	Last Bear Market Total Return	Front End Fee (%)	Back End Fee (%)	Inception Date
	2.58	27.94	4.84	92.08	83.48	0	1.53	18.54	1.04	16.3	2,949	2	98	0	0	89	30.71	-28.01			Nov-08
	2.65	28.12	5.07	93.40	85.81	0	1.28	18.54	1.04	16.99	2,949	2	98	0	0	89	30.81	-27.92			Jul-17
	2.64	28.32	5.35	94.30	86.68	0	1.03	18.58	1.04	17.08	2,949	2	98	0	0	89	30.81	-27.92			Jul-17
	2.71	28.33	5.49	95.54	87.87	0	0.88	18.56	1.04	19.7	2,949	2	98	0	0	89	30.81	-27.92			Sep-16
	2.73	28.41	5.59	96.39	90.48	0	0.78	18.55	1.04	19.93	2,949	2	98	0	0	89	31.13	-27.79			Nov-10
50	-0.48	11.61	-9.72	22.01	18.30	0.9	1.24	17.58	1.01	23.65	1,564	2	98	0	0	39	30.52	-25.42	5.25		Jan-95
50	-0.65	11.29	-10.18	20.05	14.99	0.84	1.74	17.55	1.01	18.9	1,564	2	98	0	0	39	30	-25.59		1.00	Mar-99
	-0.47	11.73	-9.52	22.92	19.78	1.03	0.99	17.59	1.01	25.31	1,564	2	98	0	0	39	30.68	-25.36			Jan-95
	-0.59	11.41	-9.95	21.03	16.76	0.75	1.49	17.57	1.01	23.36	1,564	2	98	0	0	39	30.35	-25.52			Nov-08
	-0.52	11.55	-9.75	21.95	18.24	0.93	1.24	17.58	1.01	23.6	1,564	2	98	0	0	39	30.49	-25.44			Sep-16
	-0.47	11.69	-9.50	22.83	19.70	1.03	0.99	17.57	1.01	25.28	1,564	2	98	0	0	39	30.68	-25.36			Sep-16
	-0.39	11.84	-9.34	23.46	20.51	1.15	0.84	17.59	1.01	25.34	1,564	2	98	0	0	39	30.74	-25.29			May-06
	-0.40	11.84	-9.28	23.84	21.16	1.23	0.74	17.6	1.01	25.37	1,564	2	98	0	0	39	30.75	-25.29			Feb-05
50	3.11	11.02	5.73	22.86	26.21	2.64	0.81	5.76	0.94	19.25	5,793	4	36	59	0	23	16.64	-12.87	4.50		May-06
50	2.97	10.71	5.08	20.53	22.22	2.08	1.41	5.76	0.94	19.16	5,793	4	36	59	0	23	16.25	-13.12		1.00	May-06
	3.19	11.17	5.88	23.34	26.93	2.78	0.66	5.76	0.94	19.32	5,793	4	36	59	0	23	16.73	-12.81			May-06
	3.01	10.84	5.27	21.50	24.17	2.25	1.2	5.76	0.94	19.19	5,793	4	36	59	0	23	16.48	-12.92			Nov-08
	3.08	10.95	5.51	22.19	25.52	2.58	0.95	5.74	0.94	19.17	5,793	4	36	59	0	23	16.71	-12.88			Sep-16
	3.13	11.11	5.86	23.17	27.16	2.75	0.7	5.76	0.94	19.28	5,793	4	36	59	0	23	16.88	-12.79			Sep-16
	3.16	11.18	5.98	23.69	27.70	2.88	0.55	5.78	0.95	19.34	5,793	4	36	59	0	23	16.88	-12.79			May-06
	3.19	11.21	6.04	24.08	28.21	2.98	0.45	5.76	0.94	19.34	5,793	4	36	59	0	23	16.88	-12.79			Nov-14
50	3.32	12.71	5.80	26.50	29.35	2.49	0.85	7.02	0.99	19.22	7,239	4	49	47	0	26	19.03	-15.58	4.50		Jul-07
50	3.18	12.39	5.19	24.21	25.36	1.93	1.44	7.04	0.99	19.15	7,239	4	49	47	0	26	18.51	-15.79		1.00	Jul-07
	3.41	12.81	6.01	27.04	30.13	2.63	0.69	7.02	0.99	19.27	7,239	4	49	47	0	26	19.05	-15.52			Jul-07
	3.24	12.51	5.42	25.14	27.36	2.13	1.22	7.06	1	19.15	7,239	4	49	47	0	26	18.79	-15.64			Nov-08
	3.31	12.67	5.71	26.04	28.82	2.4	0.97	7.03	0.99	19.16	7,239	4	49	47	0	26	18.94	-15.54			Sep-16
	3.36	12.77	5.95	26.87	30.32	2.63	0.72	7.04	0.99	19.22	7,239	4	49	47	0	26	19.12	-15.45			Sep-16
	3.38	12.90	6.13	27.51	30.97	2.74	0.57	7.03	0.99	19.29	7,239	4	49	47	0	26	19.12	-15.45			Jul-07
	3.41	12.92	6.23	27.83	31.49	2.84	0.47	7.04	0.99	19.29	7,239	4	49	47	0	26	19.12	-15.45			Nov-14
50	3.47	14.07	5.82	30.40	32.15	2.31	0.86	8.27	1.01	21	7,977	4	61	35	0	30	20.68	-17.78	4.50		May-06
50	3.30	13.77	5.20	28.03	28.00	1.77	1.45	8.22	1	20.8	7,977	4	61	35	0	30	20.19	-17.95		1.00	May-06
	3.50	14.16	6.02	30.91	32.92	2.46	0.7	8.25	1.01	21.06	7,977	4	61	35	0	30	20.69	-17.71			May-06
	3.33	13.86	5.38	29.00	30.07	1.96	1.23	8.22	1	20.92	7,977	4	61	35	0	30	20.53	-17.88			Nov-08
	3.44	14.07	5.72	29.95	31.58	2.26	0.98	8.24	1	20.94	7,977	4	61	35	0	30	20.64	-17.71			Sep-16
	3.51	14.18	5.97	30.87	33.17	2.45	0.73	8.28	1.01	21.02	7,977	4	61	35	0	30	20.82	-17.62			Sep-16
	3.52	14.23	6.08	31.42	33.73	2.57	0.58	8.25	1.01	21.11	7,977	4	61	35	0	30	20.82	-17.62			May-06
	3.55	14.31	6.24	31.83	34.26	2.66	0.48	8.22	1	21.11	7,977	4	61	35	0	30	20.82	-17.62			Nov-14
50	3.38	14.72	5.26	31.89	32.86	2.21	0.87	9.17	1	20.4	6,229	4	70	26	0	28	22.35	-19.26	4.50		Jul-07
50	3.27	14.43	4.70	29.57	28.76	1.68	1.45	9.19	1	20.23	6,229	4	70	26	0	28	21.9	-19.46		1.00	Jul-07
	3.46	14.84	5.46	32.48	33.71	2.36	0.7	9.17	1	20.51	6,229	4	70	26	0	28	22.41	-19.22			Jul-07
	3.35	14.58	4.89	30.56	30.84	1.86	1.23	9.17	1	20.34	6,229	4	70	26	0	28	22.1	-19.35			Nov-08
	3.38	14.65	5.14	31.35	32.27	2.14	0.98	9.18	1	20.32	6,229	4	70	26	0	28	22.4	-19.3			Sep-16
	3.46	14.80	5.41	32.39	33.99	2.35	0.73	9.21	1	20.47	6,229	4	70	26	0	28	22.57	-19.22			Sep-16
	3.49	14.87	5.59	32.91	34.52	2.47	0.58	9.18	1	20.52	6,229	4	70	26	0	28	22.57	-19.22			Jul-07
	3.56	15.02	5.69	33.40	35.04	2.57	0.48	9.17	1	20.53	6,229	4	70	26	0	28	22.57	-19.22			Nov-14
50	3.46	15.69	5.15	34.32	34.53	2.08	0.88	10.01	1.02	22.03	6,144	3	79	17	0	29	22.45	-19.39	4.50		May-06
50	3.28	15.35	4.54	31.88	30.38	1.58	1.46	10.02	1.02	21.72	6,144	3	79	17	0	29	22	-19.62		1.00	May-06
	3.49	15.78	5.36	34.92	35.38	2.24	0.71	10.04	1.02	22.1	6,144	3	79	17	0	29	22.52	-19.31			May-06
	3.37	15.51	4.78	32.99	32.51	1.74	1.24	10.02	1.02	21.92	6,144	3	79	17	0	29	22.22	-19.45			Nov-08
	3.39	15.59	5.02	33.80	33.96	2.04	0.99	10.02	1.02	21.96	6,144	3	79	17	0	29	22.4	-19.36			Sep-16
	3.54	15.80	5.35	34.83	35.67	2.23	0.74	10.04	1.02	22.06	6,144	3	79	17	0	29	22.57	-19.28			Sep-16
	3.56	15.90	5.47	35.42	36.26	2.35	0.59	10.03	1.02	22.16	6,144	3	79	17	0	29	22.57	-19.28			May-06

	MARKET			FUND TYPE, CATEGORY & OBJECTIVE	RATINGS				MINIMUMS	
Fund Name	Ticker Symbol	Traded On	Fund Type	Category and (Prospectus Objective)	Overall Rating	Reward Rating	Risk Rating	Recent Up/ Downgrade	Open to New Investors	Min Initial Investment
JPMorgan SmartRetirement® 2040 Fund Class R6	SMTYX	NAS CM	Open End	Target Date (Asset Alloc)	B-	C	B	Up	Y	15,000,000
JPMorgan SmartRetirement® 2045 Fund Class A	JSAAX	NAS CM	Open End	Target Date (Asset Alloc)	B-	C	B	Up	Y	500
JPMorgan SmartRetirement® 2045 Fund Class C	JSACX	NAS CM	Open End	Target Date (Asset Alloc)	B-	C	B	Up	Y	500
JPMorgan SmartRetirement® 2045 Fund Class I	JSASX	NAS CM	Open End	Target Date (Asset Alloc)	B-	C	B	Up	Y	1,000,000
JPMorgan SmartRetirement® 2045 Fund Class R2	JSAZX	NAS CM	Open End	Target Date (Asset Alloc)	B-	C	B	Up	Y	0
JPMorgan SmartRetirement® 2045 Fund Class R3	JSAPX	NAS CM	Open End	Target Date (Asset Alloc)	B-	C	B	Up	Y	0
JPMorgan SmartRetirement® 2045 Fund Class R4	JSAQX	NAS CM	Open End	Target Date (Asset Alloc)	B-	C	B	Up	Y	0
JPMorgan SmartRetirement® 2045 Fund Class R5	JSAIX	NAS CM	Open End	Target Date (Asset Alloc)	B-	C	B	Up	Y	0
JPMorgan SmartRetirement® 2045 Fund Class R6	JSAYX	NAS CM	Open End	Target Date (Asset Alloc)	B-	C	B	Up	Y	15,000,000
JPMorgan SmartRetirement® 2050 Fund Class A	JTSAX	NAS CM	Open End	Target Date (Asset Alloc)	B-	C	B	Up	Y	500
JPMorgan SmartRetirement® 2050 Fund Class C	JTSCX	NAS CM	Open End	Target Date (Asset Alloc)	B-	C	B	Up	Y	500
JPMorgan SmartRetirement® 2050 Fund Class I	JTSSX	NAS CM	Open End	Target Date (Asset Alloc)	B-	C	B	Up	Y	1,000,000
JPMorgan SmartRetirement® 2050 Fund Class R2	JTSZX	NAS CM	Open End	Target Date (Asset Alloc)	B-	C	B	Up	Y	0
JPMorgan SmartRetirement® 2050 Fund Class R3	JTSPX	NAS CM	Open End	Target Date (Asset Alloc)	B-	C	B	Up	Y	0
JPMorgan SmartRetirement® 2050 Fund Class R4	JTSQX	NAS CM	Open End	Target Date (Asset Alloc)	B-	C	B	Up	Y	0
JPMorgan SmartRetirement® 2050 Fund Class R5	JTSIX	NAS CM	Open End	Target Date (Asset Alloc)	B-	C	B	Up	Y	0
JPMorgan SmartRetirement® 2050 Fund Class R6	JTSYX	NAS CM	Open End	Target Date (Asset Alloc)	B-	C	B	Up	Y	15,000,000
JPMorgan SmartRetirement® 2055 Fund Class A	JFFAX	NAS CM	Open End	Target Date (Asset Alloc)	B-	C	B	Up	Y	500
JPMorgan SmartRetirement® 2055 Fund Class C	JFFCX	NAS CM	Open End	Target Date (Asset Alloc)	B-	C	B	Up	Y	500
JPMorgan SmartRetirement® 2055 Fund Class I	JFFSX	NAS CM	Open End	Target Date (Asset Alloc)	B-	C	B	Up	Y	1,000,000
JPMorgan SmartRetirement® 2055 Fund Class R2	JFFRX	NAS CM	Open End	Target Date (Asset Alloc)	B-	C	B	Up	Y	0
JPMorgan SmartRetirement® 2055 Fund Class R3	JFFPX	NAS CM	Open End	Target Date (Asset Alloc)	B-	C	B	Up	Y	0
JPMorgan SmartRetirement® 2055 Fund Class R4	JFFQX	NAS CM	Open End	Target Date (Asset Alloc)	B-	C	B	Up	Y	0
JPMorgan SmartRetirement® 2055 Fund Class R5	JFFIX	NAS CM	Open End	Target Date (Asset Alloc)	B-	C	B	Up	Y	0
JPMorgan SmartRetirement® 2055 Fund Class R6	JFFYX	NAS CM	Open End	Target Date (Asset Alloc)	B-	C	B	Up	Y	15,000,000
JPMorgan SmartRetirement® 2060 Fund Class A	JAKAX	NAS CM	Open End	Target Date (Asset Alloc)	C+	C	B	Up	Y	500
JPMorgan SmartRetirement® 2060 Fund Class C	JAKCX	NAS CM	Open End	Target Date (Asset Alloc)	C+	C	B	Up	Y	500
JPMorgan SmartRetirement® 2060 Fund Class I	JAKSX	NAS CM	Open End	Target Date (Asset Alloc)	C+	C	B	Up	Y	1,000,000
JPMorgan SmartRetirement® 2060 Fund Class R2	JAKZX	NAS CM	Open End	Target Date (Asset Alloc)	C+	C	B	Up	Y	0
JPMorgan SmartRetirement® 2060 Fund Class R3	JAKPX	NAS CM	Open End	Target Date (Asset Alloc)	C+	C	B	Up	Y	0
JPMorgan SmartRetirement® 2060 Fund Class R4	JAKQX	NAS CM	Open End	Target Date (Asset Alloc)	C+	C	B	Up	Y	0
JPMorgan SmartRetirement® 2060 Fund Class R5	JAKIX	NAS CM	Open End	Target Date (Asset Alloc)	C+	C	B	Up	Y	0
JPMorgan SmartRetirement® 2060 Fund Class R6	JAKYX	NAS CM	Open End	Target Date (Asset Alloc)	C+	C	B	Up	Y	15,000,000
JPMorgan SmartRetirement® Blend 2020 Fund Class I	JSSRX	NAS CM	Open End	Target Date (Asset Alloc)	B	C	A-	Up	Y	1,000,000
JPMorgan SmartRetirement® Blend 2020 Fund Class R2	JIORX	NAS CM	Open End	Target Date (Asset Alloc)	B-	C	A-	Up	Y	0
JPMorgan SmartRetirement® Blend 2020 Fund Class R3	JSTKX	NAS CM	Open End	Target Date (Asset Alloc)	B	C	A-	Up	Y	0
JPMorgan SmartRetirement® Blend 2020 Fund Class R4	JSTLX	NAS CM	Open End	Target Date (Asset Alloc)	B	C	A-	Up	Y	0
JPMorgan SmartRetirement® Blend 2020 Fund Class R5	JBSRX	NAS CM	Open End	Target Date (Asset Alloc)	B	C+	A-	Up	Y	0
JPMorgan SmartRetirement® Blend 2020 Fund Class R6	JSYRX	NAS CM	Open End	Target Date (Asset Alloc)	B	C+	A-	Up	Y	15,000,000
JPMorgan SmartRetirement® Blend 2025 Fund Class I	JBSSX	NAS CM	Open End	Target Date (Asset Alloc)	B	C	A-	Up	Y	1,000,000
JPMorgan SmartRetirement® Blend 2025 Fund Class R2	JBRSX	NAS CM	Open End	Target Date (Asset Alloc)	B-	C	A-	Up	Y	0
JPMorgan SmartRetirement® Blend 2025 Fund Class R3	JBTUX	NAS CM	Open End	Target Date (Asset Alloc)	B-	C	A-	Up	Y	0
JPMorgan SmartRetirement® Blend 2025 Fund Class R4	JBTBX	NAS CM	Open End	Target Date (Asset Alloc)	B	C	A-	Up	Y	0
JPMorgan SmartRetirement® Blend 2025 Fund Class R5	JBBSX	NAS CM	Open End	Target Date (Asset Alloc)	B	C	A-	Up	Y	0
JPMorgan SmartRetirement® Blend 2025 Fund Class R6	JBYSX	NAS CM	Open End	Target Date (Asset Alloc)	B	C	A-	Up	Y	15,000,000
JPMorgan SmartRetirement® Blend 2030 Fund Class I	JRBEX	NAS CM	Open End	Target Date (Asset Alloc)	B-	C	B+	Up	Y	1,000,000
JPMorgan SmartRetirement® Blend 2030 Fund Class R2	JRBRX	NAS CM	Open End	Target Date (Asset Alloc)	B-	C	B+	Up	Y	0
JPMorgan SmartRetirement® Blend 2030 Fund Class R3	JUTPX	NAS CM	Open End	Target Date (Asset Alloc)	B-	C	B+	Up	Y	0
JPMorgan SmartRetirement® Blend 2030 Fund Class R4	JUTUX	NAS CM	Open End	Target Date (Asset Alloc)	B-	C	B+	Up	Y	0
JPMorgan SmartRetirement® Blend 2030 Fund Class R5	JRBBX	NAS CM	Open End	Target Date (Asset Alloc)	B-	C	A-	Up	Y	0
JPMorgan SmartRetirement® Blend 2030 Fund Class R6	JRBYX	NAS CM	Open End	Target Date (Asset Alloc)	B-	C	A-	Up	Y	15,000,000
JPMorgan SmartRetirement® Blend 2035 Fund Class I	JPSRX	NAS CM	Open End	Target Date (Asset Alloc)	B-	C	B+	Up	Y	1,000,000

★ Expanded analysis of this fund is included in Section II.

	TOTAL RETURNS					PERFORMANCE				ASSETS		ASSET ALLOCATION & TURNOVER					BULL & BEAR		FEES		
Min Additional Investment	3-Month Total Return	6-Month Total Return	1-Year Total Return	3-Year Total Return	5-Year Total Return	Dividend Yield (TTM)	Expense Ratio	3-Yr Std Deviation	3-Year Beta	NAV	Total Assets (MIL)	%Cash	%Stocks	%Bonds	%Other	Turnover Ratio	Last Bull Market Total Return	Last Bear Market Total Return	Front End Fee (%)	Back End Fee (%)	Inception Date
	3.58	15.93	5.58	35.85	36.80	2.44	0.49	10.02	1.02	22.16	6,144	3	79	17	0	29	22.57	-19.27			Nov-14
50	3.46	16.09	5.16	34.61	34.89	2.05	0.89	10.37	1.02	21.1	4,379	4	83	13	0	26	22.44	-19.3	4.50		Jul-07
50	3.31	15.75	4.57	32.18	30.69	1.58	1.47	10.37	1.02	20.91	4,379	4	83	13	0	26	21.96	-19.53		1.00	Jul-07
	3.54	16.17	5.32	35.19	35.73	2.2	0.72	10.37	1.02	21.18	4,379	4	83	13	0	26	22.52	-19.28			Jul-07
	3.38	15.84	4.75	33.23	32.80	1.7	1.25	10.36	1.02	21.02	4,379	4	83	13	0	26	22.28	-19.41			Nov-08
	3.45	16.02	5.05	34.12	34.35	1.98	1	10.35	1.02	21.03	4,379	4	83	13	0	26	22.41	-19.29			Sep-16
	3.50	16.14	5.27	35.12	36.03	2.19	0.75	10.36	1.02	21.13	4,379	4	83	13	0	26	22.58	-19.21			Sep-16
	3.52	16.26	5.44	35.69	36.60	2.31	0.6	10.32	1.02	21.2	4,379	4	83	13	0	26	22.58	-19.21			Jul-07
	3.60	16.35	5.60	36.12	37.14	2.41	0.5	10.37	1.02	21.2	4,379	4	83	13	0	26	22.58	-19.21			Nov-14
50	3.46	16.11	5.17	34.59	34.92	2.04	0.88	10.36	0.99	21.14	3,936	4	83	13	0	25	22.52	-19.37	4.50		Jul-07
50	3.31	15.73	4.53	32.13	30.67	1.57	1.46	10.35	0.99	20.92	3,936	4	83	13	0	25	21.97	-19.55		1.00	Jul-07
	3.54	16.19	5.32	35.16	35.74	2.19	0.71	10.36	0.99	21.22	3,936	4	83	13	0	25	22.6	-19.29			Jul-07
	3.38	15.87	4.76	33.15	32.77	1.7	1.24	10.36	0.99	21.05	3,936	4	83	13	0	25	22.29	-19.43			Nov-08
	3.46	15.98	5.06	34.03	34.31	1.98	0.99	10.36	0.99	21.07	3,936	4	83	13	0	25	22.49	-19.36			Sep-16
	3.49	16.14	5.26	35.04	35.99	2.18	0.74	10.36	0.99	21.18	3,936	4	83	13	0	25	22.66	-19.27			Sep-16
	3.51	16.20	5.44	35.63	36.59	2.31	0.59	10.35	0.99	21.25	3,936	4	83	13	0	25	22.66	-19.27			Jul-07
	3.59	16.28	5.55	36.04	37.18	2.4	0.49	10.34	0.99	21.26	3,936	4	83	13	0	25	22.66	-19.27			Nov-14
50	3.44	16.04	5.17	34.51	34.83	2.04	0.88	10.35	0.98	23.8	1,800	6	81	13	0	21			4.50		Jan-12
50	3.27	15.69	4.55	32.04	30.64	1.55	1.46	10.34	0.98	23.66	1,800	6	81	13	0	21				1.00	Jan-12
	3.48	16.09	5.33	35.00	35.63	2.19	0.71	10.35	0.98	23.84	1,800	6	81	13	0	21					Jan-12
	3.35	15.81	4.80	33.08	32.75	1.7	1.24	10.34	0.98	23.75	1,800	6	81	13	0	21					Jan-12
	3.43	15.97	5.06	33.95	34.26	1.97	0.99	10.35	0.98	23.73	1,800	6	81	13	0	21					Sep-16
	3.48	16.11	5.32	34.99	35.97	2.19	0.74	10.34	0.98	23.81	1,800	6	81	13	0	21					Sep-16
	3.50	16.18	5.45	35.56	36.54	2.31	0.59	10.33	0.98	23.86	1,800	6	81	13	0	21					Jan-12
	3.53	16.26	5.60	35.95	37.05	2.4	0.49	10.34	0.98	23.87	1,800	6	81	13	0	21					Nov-14
50	3.45	16.10	5.26			2.07	0.88			18.17	168.7	10	77	13	0	39			4.50		Aug-16
50	3.27	15.75	4.65			1.6	1.46			18.11	168.7	10	77	13	0	39				1.00	Aug-16
	3.49	16.20	5.47			2.22	0.71			18.2	168.7	10	77	13	0	39					Aug-16
	3.37	15.88	4.90			1.74	1.24			18.16	168.7	10	77	13	0	39					Aug-16
	3.39	16.04	5.18			2	0.99			18.17	168.7	10	77	13	0	39					Sep-16
	3.49	16.20	5.46			2.2	0.74			18.2	168.7	10	77	13	0	39					Sep-16
	3.52	16.30	5.59			2.32	0.59			18.2	168.7	10	77	13	0	39					Aug-16
	3.54	16.29	5.68			2.41	0.49			18.22	168.7	10	77	13	0	39					Aug-16
	2.89	10.38	5.66	22.36	26.13	2.53	0.54	5.55	0.91	19.53	842.3	7	33	59	0	55					Jul-12
	2.78	10.10	5.12	20.54	23.30	2.14	1.04	5.54	0.91	19.52	842.3	7	33	59	0	55					Jul-12
	2.83	10.26	5.42	21.69	25.47	2.35	0.79	5.56	0.91	19.51	842.3	7	33	59	0	55					May-17
	2.89	10.39	5.66	22.58	27.02	2.4	0.54	5.56	0.91	19.55	842.3	7	33	59	0	55					May-17
	2.93	10.45	5.82	22.93	27.26	2.68	0.39	5.56	0.91	19.54	842.3	7	33	59	0	55					Jul-12
	3.00	10.52	5.98	23.26	27.73	2.78	0.29	5.52	0.9	19.55	842.3	7	33	59	0	55					Jul-12
	3.07	12.02	5.88	25.90	29.34	2.4	0.54	6.82	0.96	20.85	1,109	5	48	47	0	57					Jul-12
	2.95	11.75	5.38	24.04	26.38	1.94	1.04	6.81	0.96	20.84	1,109	5	48	47	0	57					Jul-12
	3.01	11.90	5.64	25.31	28.70	2.22	0.79	6.8	0.96	20.82	1,109	5	48	47	0	57					May-17
	3.06	12.03	5.89	26.26	30.33	2.28	0.54	6.78	0.96	20.87	1,109	5	48	47	0	57					May-17
	3.11	12.09	6.04	26.54	30.49	2.55	0.39	6.78	0.96	20.86	1,109	5	48	47	0	57					Jul-12
	3.13	12.17	6.14	26.89	30.98	2.64	0.29	6.8	0.96	20.86	1,109	5	48	47	0	57					Jul-12
	3.05	13.13	5.76	29.34	31.97	2.25	0.54	7.87	0.96	21.85	1,167	4	60	36	0	54					Jul-12
	2.93	12.87	5.24	27.42	29.03	1.78	1.04	7.87	0.96	21.86	1,167	4	60	36	0	54					Jul-12
	3.04	12.98	5.49	28.55	31.10	2.09	0.79	7.88	0.97	21.81	1,167	4	60	36	0	54					May-17
	3.05	13.12	5.75	29.52	32.74	2.08	0.54	7.87	0.96	21.88	1,167	4	60	36	0	54					May-17
	3.14	13.21	5.92	29.94	33.17	2.4	0.39	7.9	0.97	21.86	1,167	4	60	36	0	54					Jul-12
	3.16	13.28	6.03	30.35	33.65	2.49	0.29	7.89	0.97	21.87	1,167	4	60	36	0	54					Jul-12
	3.13	14.15	5.72	31.76	33.96	2.13	0.54	8.83	0.96	22.8	954.0	3	72	25	0	52					Jul-12

Fund Name	Ticker Symbol	Traded On	Fund Type	Category and (Prospectus Objective)	Overall Rating	Reward Rating	Risk Rating	Recent Up/ Downgrade	Open to New Investors	Min Initial Investment
	MARKET			FUND TYPE, CATEGORY & OBJECTIVE	RATINGS				MINIMUMS	
JPMorgan SmartRetirement® Blend 2035 Fund Class R2	JPRRX	NAS CM	Open End	Target Date (Asset Alloc)	B-	C	B+	Up	Y	0
JPMorgan SmartRetirement® Blend 2035 Fund Class R3	JPTLX	NAS CM	Open End	Target Date (Asset Alloc)	B-	C	B+	Up	Y	0
JPMorgan SmartRetirement® Blend 2035 Fund Class R4	JPTKX	NAS CM	Open End	Target Date (Asset Alloc)	B-	C	B+	Up	Y	0
JPMorgan SmartRetirement® Blend 2035 Fund Class R5	JPBRX	NAS CM	Open End	Target Date (Asset Alloc)	B-	C	B+	Up	Y	0
JPMorgan SmartRetirement® Blend 2035 Fund Class R6	JPYRX	NAS CM	Open End	Target Date (Asset Alloc)	B-	C	B+	Up	Y	15,000,000
JPMorgan SmartRetirement® Blend 2040 Fund Class I	JOBEX	NAS CM	Open End	Target Date (Asset Alloc)	B-	C	B+	Up	Y	1,000,000
JPMorgan SmartRetirement® Blend 2040 Fund Class R2	JOBRX	NAS CM	Open End	Target Date (Asset Alloc)	B-	C	B+	Up	Y	0
JPMorgan SmartRetirement® Blend 2040 Fund Class R3	JNTEX	NAS CM	Open End	Target Date (Asset Alloc)	B-	C	B+	Up	Y	0
JPMorgan SmartRetirement® Blend 2040 Fund Class R4	JNTNX	NAS CM	Open End	Target Date (Asset Alloc)	B-	C	B+	Up	Y	0
JPMorgan SmartRetirement® Blend 2040 Fund Class R5	JOBBX	NAS CM	Open End	Target Date (Asset Alloc)	B-	C	B+	Up	Y	0
JPMorgan SmartRetirement® Blend 2040 Fund Class R6	JOBYX	NAS CM	Open End	Target Date (Asset Alloc)	B-	C	B+	Up	Y	15,000,000
JPMorgan SmartRetirement® Blend 2045 Fund Class I	JMSSX	NAS CM	Open End	Target Date (Asset Alloc)	B-	C	B+	Up	Y	1,000,000
JPMorgan SmartRetirement® Blend 2045 Fund Class R2	JNARX	NAS CM	Open End	Target Date (Asset Alloc)	B-	C	B	Up	Y	0
JPMorgan SmartRetirement® Blend 2045 Fund Class R3	JNTOX	NAS CM	Open End	Target Date (Asset Alloc)	B-	C	B	Up	Y	0
JPMorgan SmartRetirement® Blend 2045 Fund Class R4	JNTLX	NAS CM	Open End	Target Date (Asset Alloc)	B-	C	B+	Up	Y	0
JPMorgan SmartRetirement® Blend 2045 Fund Class R5	JMBRX	NAS CM	Open End	Target Date (Asset Alloc)	B-	C	B+	Up	Y	0
JPMorgan SmartRetirement® Blend 2045 Fund Class R6	JMYAX	NAS CM	Open End	Target Date (Asset Alloc)	B-	C	B+	Up	Y	15,000,000
JPMorgan SmartRetirement® Blend 2050 Fund Class I	JNEAX	NAS CM	Open End	Target Date (Asset Alloc)	B-	C	B+	Up	Y	1,000,000
JPMorgan SmartRetirement® Blend 2050 Fund Class R2	JNNRX	NAS CM	Open End	Target Date (Asset Alloc)	B-	C	B	Up	Y	0
JPMorgan SmartRetirement® Blend 2050 Fund Class R3	JNTKX	NAS CM	Open End	Target Date (Asset Alloc)	B-	C	B+	Up	Y	0
JPMorgan SmartRetirement® Blend 2050 Fund Class R4	JNTPX	NAS CM	Open End	Target Date (Asset Alloc)	B-	C	B+	Up	Y	0
JPMorgan SmartRetirement® Blend 2050 Fund Class R5	JNABX	NAS CM	Open End	Target Date (Asset Alloc)	B-	C	B+	Up	Y	0
JPMorgan SmartRetirement® Blend 2050 Fund Class R6	JNYAX	NAS CM	Open End	Target Date (Asset Alloc)	B-	C	B+	Up	Y	15,000,000
JPMorgan SmartRetirement® Blend 2055 Fund Class I	JPTBX	NAS CM	Open End	Target Date (Asset Alloc)	B-	C	B+	Up	Y	1,000,000
JPMorgan SmartRetirement® Blend 2055 Fund Class R2	JTRBX	NAS CM	Open End	Target Date (Asset Alloc)	B-	C	B	Up	Y	0
JPMorgan SmartRetirement® Blend 2055 Fund Class R3	JTTUX	NAS CM	Open End	Target Date (Asset Alloc)	B-	C	B	Up	Y	0
JPMorgan SmartRetirement® Blend 2055 Fund Class R4	JTTLX	NAS CM	Open End	Target Date (Asset Alloc)	B-	C	B+	Up	Y	0
JPMorgan SmartRetirement® Blend 2055 Fund Class R5	JTBBX	NAS CM	Open End	Target Date (Asset Alloc)	B-	C	B+	Up	Y	0
JPMorgan SmartRetirement® Blend 2055 Fund Class R6	JTYBX	NAS CM	Open End	Target Date (Asset Alloc)	B-	C	B+	Up	Y	15,000,000
JPMorgan SmartRetirement® Blend 2060 Fund Class I	JACSX	NAS CM	Open End	Target Date (Asset Alloc)	C+	C	B	Up	Y	1,000,000
JPMorgan SmartRetirement® Blend 2060 Fund Class R2	JATPX	NAS CM	Open End	Target Date (Asset Alloc)	C+	C	B	Up	Y	0
JPMorgan SmartRetirement® Blend 2060 Fund Class R3	JATQX	NAS CM	Open End	Target Date (Asset Alloc)	C+	C	B	Up	Y	0
JPMorgan SmartRetirement® Blend 2060 Fund Class R4	JATUX	NAS CM	Open End	Target Date (Asset Alloc)	C+	C	B	Up	Y	0
JPMorgan SmartRetirement® Blend 2060 Fund Class R5	JAABX	NAS CM	Open End	Target Date (Asset Alloc)	C+	C	B	Up	Y	0
JPMorgan SmartRetirement® Blend 2060 Fund Class R6	JAAYX	NAS CM	Open End	Target Date (Asset Alloc)	C+	C	B	Up	Y	15,000,000
JPMorgan SmartRetirement® Blend Inc Fund Class R3	JITLX	NAS CM	Open End	Target Date (Asset Alloc)	B	C	A-	Up	Y	0
JPMorgan SmartRetirement® Blend Inc Fund Class R4	JITKX	NAS CM	Open End	Target Date (Asset Alloc)	B	C+	A-	Up	Y	0
JPMorgan SmartRetirement® Blend Income Fund Class I	JIJSX	NAS CM	Open End	Target Date (Asset Alloc)	B	C+	A-	Up	Y	1,000,000
JPMorgan SmartRetirement® Blend Income Fund Class R2	JIRBX	NAS CM	Open End	Target Date (Asset Alloc)	B-	C	B+	Up	Y	0
JPMorgan SmartRetirement® Blend Income Fund Class R5	JIBBX	NAS CM	Open End	Target Date (Asset Alloc)	B	C+	A-	Up	Y	0
JPMorgan SmartRetirement® Blend Income Fund Class R6	JIYBX	NAS CM	Open End	Target Date (Asset Alloc)	B	C+	A-	Up	Y	15,000,000
JPMorgan SmartRetirement® Income Fund Class A	JSRAX	NAS CM	Open End	Target Date (Asset Alloc)	B	C+	A-	Up	Y	500
JPMorgan SmartRetirement® Income Fund Class C	JSRCX	NAS CM	Open End	Target Date (Asset Alloc)	B-	C	B+	Up	Y	500
JPMorgan SmartRetirement® Income Fund Class I	JSRSX	NAS CM	Open End	Target Date (Asset Alloc)	B	C+	A-	Up	Y	1,000,000
JPMorgan SmartRetirement® Income Fund Class R2	JSIZX	NAS CM	Open End	Target Date (Asset Alloc)	B-	C	A-	Up	Y	0
JPMorgan SmartRetirement® Income Fund Class R3	JSIPX	NAS CM	Open End	Target Date (Asset Alloc)	B-	C	A-	Up	Y	0
JPMorgan SmartRetirement® Income Fund Class R4	JSIQX	NAS CM	Open End	Target Date (Asset Alloc)	B	C+	A-	Up	Y	0
JPMorgan SmartRetirement® Income Fund Class R5	JSIIX	NAS CM	Open End	Target Date (Asset Alloc)	B	C+	A-	Up	Y	0
JPMorgan SmartRetirement® Income Fund Class R6	JSIYX	NAS CM	Open End	Target Date (Asset Alloc)	B	C+	A-	Up	Y	15,000,000
JPMorgan SmartSpending 2050 Fund Class A	JTQBX	NAS CM	Open End	Cautious Alloc (Asset Alloc)	C+	C	B	Up	Y	1,000
JPMorgan SmartSpending 2050 Fund Class I	JTQDX	NAS CM	Open End	Cautious Alloc (Asset Alloc)	C+	C	B	Up	Y	1,000,000
JPMorgan SmartSpending 2050 Fund Class R2	JTQEX	NAS CM	Open End	Cautious Alloc (Asset Alloc)	C	C	B		Y	0

★ Expanded analysis of this fund is included in Section II.

	TOTAL RETURNS					PERFORMANCE				ASSETS		ASSET ALLOCATION & TURNOVER					BULL & BEAR		FEES		
Min Additional Investment	3-Month Total Return	6-Month Total Return	1-Year Total Return	3-Year Total Return	5-Year Total Return	Dividend Yield (TTM)	Expense Ratio	3-Yr Std Deviation	3-Year Beta	NAV	Total Assets (MIL)	%Cash	%Stocks	%Bonds	%Other	Turnover Ratio	Last Bull Market Total Return	Last Bear Market Total Return	Front End Fee (%)	Back End Fee (%)	Inception Date
	3.01	13.92	5.20	29.81	30.95	1.77	1.04	8.83	0.96	22.78	954.0	3	72	25	0	52					Jul-12
	3.07	14.05	5.47	31.03	33.25	1.97	0.79	8.86	0.97	22.77	954.0	3	72	25	0	52					May-17
	3.13	14.21	5.73	32.06	34.97	2.02	0.54	8.83	0.96	22.83	954.0	3	72	25	0	52					May-17
	3.16	14.27	5.89	32.42	35.14	2.27	0.39	8.83	0.96	22.82	954.0	3	72	25	0	52					Jul-12
	3.19	14.30	5.99	32.72	35.65	2.37	0.29	8.83	0.96	22.82	954.0	3	72	25	0	52					Jul-12
	3.12	15.01	5.62	34.31	35.88	2.01	0.54	9.64	0.99	23.27	868.2	3	81	16	0	52					Jul-12
	3.01	14.74	5.12	32.29	32.80	1.64	1.04	9.62	0.98	23.25	868.2	3	81	16	0	52					Jul-12
	3.10	14.94	5.42	33.48	34.95	1.87	0.79	9.66	0.99	23.24	868.2	3	81	16	0	52					May-17
	3.12	15.03	5.63	34.46	36.62	1.91	0.54	9.68	0.99	23.29	868.2	3	81	16	0	52					May-17
	3.15	15.10	5.78	34.85	37.02	2.17	0.39	9.65	0.99	23.28	868.2	3	81	16	0	52					Jul-12
	3.18	15.18	5.93	35.30	37.61	2.26	0.29	9.64	0.99	23.29	868.2	3	81	16	0	52					Jul-12
	3.14	15.43	5.58	34.35	36.04	1.97	0.54	9.96	0.98	23.43	689.7	3	86	11	0	49					Jul-12
	3.03	15.12	5.07	32.38	32.95	1.6	1.04	9.96	0.98	23.41	689.7	3	86	11	0	49					Jul-12
	3.09	15.27	5.31	33.69	35.40	1.84	0.79	9.97	0.98	23.38	689.7	3	86	11	0	49					May-17
	3.14	15.42	5.61	34.69	37.10	1.93	0.54	9.98	0.98	23.43	689.7	3	86	11	0	49					May-17
	3.18	15.48	5.72	34.99	37.21	2.14	0.39	10	0.99	23.43	689.7	3	86	11	0	49					Jul-12
	3.20	15.54	5.86	35.40	37.82	2.23	0.29	9.97	0.98	23.46	689.7	3	86	11	0	49					Jul-12
	3.10	15.39	5.59	34.46	36.10	1.95	0.54	10.01	0.96	23.37	508.1	4	85	11	0	50					Jul-12
	3.00	15.13	5.11	32.52	33.02	1.63	1.04	9.99	0.96	23.34	508.1	4	85	11	0	50					Jul-12
	3.05	15.30	5.37	33.81	35.40	1.78	0.79	10.01	0.96	23.35	508.1	4	85	11	0	50					May-17
	3.15	15.41	5.61	34.79	37.07	1.89	0.54	10.01	0.96	23.38	508.1	4	85	11	0	50					May-17
	3.15	15.51	5.79	35.12	37.28	2.13	0.39	9.99	0.96	23.37	508.1	4	85	11	0	50					Jul-12
	3.17	15.53	5.85	35.49	37.78	2.22	0.29	9.97	0.96	23.38	508.1	4	85	11	0	50					Jul-12
	3.08	15.40	5.56	34.23	36.17	1.96	0.54	9.96	0.95	23.18	259.1	3	86	11	0	48					Jul-12
	3.02	15.17	5.10	32.24	33.10	1.61	1.04	9.98	0.95	23.16	259.1	3	86	11	0	48					Jul-12
	3.08	15.27	5.37	33.55	35.50	1.86	0.79	9.98	0.95	23.14	259.1	3	86	11	0	48					May-17
	3.13	15.41	5.62	34.54	37.18	1.96	0.54	9.97	0.95	23.17	259.1	3	86	11	0	48					May-17
	3.16	15.47	5.77	34.82	37.34	2.14	0.39	10	0.96	23.18	259.1	3	86	11	0	48					Jul-12
	3.19	15.54	5.87	35.24	37.90	2.23	0.29	9.98	0.95	23.2	259.1	3	86	11	0	48					Jul-12
	3.16	15.49	5.83			1.91	0.54			17.96	39.5	3	88	9	0	79					Aug-16
	3.04	15.17	5.28			1.52	1.04			17.94	39.5	3	88	9	0	79					Aug-16
	3.04	15.28	5.50			1.77	0.79			17.92	39.5	3	88	9	0	79					May-17
	3.15	15.46	5.80			1.79	0.54			17.97	39.5	3	88	9	0	79					May-17
	3.21	15.57	5.95			2.13	0.39			17.94	39.5	3	88	9	0	79					Aug-16
	3.22	15.63	6.09			2.2	0.29			17.95	39.5	3	88	9	0	79					Aug-16
	2.70	9.20	5.37	17.42	20.34	2.27	0.79	4.57	1.12	17.52	421.2	7	29	64	0	51					May-17
	2.83	9.43	5.66	18.36	21.91	2.42	0.54	4.63	1.14	17.52	421.2	7	29	64	0	51					May-17
	2.82	9.44	5.67	18.09	21.06	2.48	0.54	4.59	1.13	17.52	421.2	7	29	64	0	51					Jul-12
	2.64	9.14	5.12	16.28	18.30	2.04	1.04	4.6	1.13	17.51	421.2	7	29	64	0	51					Jul-12
	2.80	9.46	5.79	18.61	22.05	2.65	0.39	4.57	1.12	17.51	421.2	7	29	64	0	51					Jul-12
	2.83	9.54	5.90	18.94	22.51	2.75	0.29	4.59	1.13	17.52	421.2	7	29	64	0	51					Jul-12
50	2.98	9.88	5.65	18.40	20.85	2.74	0.73	4.76	1.16	18.14	3,326	5	30	65	0	23	11.05	-7.51	4.50		May-06
50	2.83	9.54	5.01	16.17	17.06	2.15	1.36	4.77	1.17	18.07	3,326	5	30	65	0	23	10.6	-7.7		1.00	May-06
	3.01	9.96	5.82	18.84	21.59	2.85	0.61	4.78	1.17	18.18	3,326	5	30	65	0	23	11.09	-7.46			May-06
	2.93	9.72	5.24	17.06	18.91	2.31	1.17	4.8	1.18	18.11	3,326	5	30	65	0	23	10.91	-7.63			Nov-08
	2.97	9.85	5.51	17.69	20.15	2.61	0.92	4.79	1.17	18.08	3,326	5	30	65	0	23	11	-7.48			Sep-16
	3.00	9.94	5.78	18.58	21.66	2.81	0.67	4.76	1.16	18.15	3,326	5	30	65	0	23	11.16	-7.38			Sep-16
	3.03	10.02	5.91	19.11	22.21	2.94	0.52	4.78	1.17	18.21	3,326	5	30	65	0	23	11.16	-7.38			May-06
	3.05	10.10	6.02	19.48	22.67	3.04	0.42	4.79	1.17	18.21	3,326	5	30	65	0	23	11.16	-7.38			Nov-14
50	2.76	8.36	5.44			2.42	0.74			15.97	30.7	5	22	72	0	30			4.50		Dec-16
	2.82	8.46	5.68			2.63	0.49			15.99	30.7	5	22	72	0	30					Dec-16
	2.64	8.17	5.04			2.06	1.15			15.94	30.7	5	22	72	0	30					Dec-16

	MARKET		FUND TYPE, CATEGORY & OBJECTIVE		RATINGS				MINIMUMS	
Fund Name	Ticker Symbol	Traded On	Fund Type	Category and (Prospectus Objective)	Overall Rating	Reward Rating	Risk Rating	Recent Up/ Downgrade	Open to New Investors	Min Initial Investment
JPMorgan SmartSpending 2050 Fund Class R3	**JTQFX**	NAS CM	Open End	Cautious Alloc (Asset Alloc)	**C+**	C	B	Up	Y	0
JPMorgan SmartSpending 2050 Fund Class R4	**JTQGX**	NAS CM	Open End	Cautious Alloc (Asset Alloc)	**C+**	C	B	Up	Y	0
JPMorgan SmartSpending 2050 Fund Class R5	**JTQHX**	NAS CM	Open End	Cautious Alloc (Asset Alloc)	**C+**	C	B	Up	Y	0
JPMorgan SmartSpending 2050 Fund Class R6	**JTQJX**	NAS CM	Open End	Cautious Alloc (Asset Alloc)	**C+**	C	B	Up	Y	15,000,000
JPMorgan Systematic Alpha Fund Class A	**JSALX**	NAS CM	Open End	Multialternative (Growth & Income)	**D**	D-	C-		Y	1,000
JPMorgan Systematic Alpha Fund Class C	**JSYAX**	NAS CM	Open End	Multialternative (Growth & Income)	**D**	D-	C-		Y	1,000
JPMorgan Systematic Alpha Fund Class I	**SSALX**	NAS CM	Open End	Multialternative (Growth & Income)	**D**	D-	C-	Down	Y	1,000,000
JPMorgan Systematic Alpha Fund Class R6	**JALPX**	NAS CM	Open End	Multialternative (Growth & Income)	**D**	D	C-	Down	Y	15,000,000
JPMorgan Tax Aware Equity Fund Class A	**JPEAX**	NAS CM	Open End	US Equity Large Cap Growth (Growth & Income)	**B-**	C	B		Y	1,000
JPMorgan Tax Aware Equity Fund Class C	**JPECX**	NAS CM	Open End	US Equity Large Cap Growth (Growth & Income)	**C+**	C	B	Down	Y	1,000
JPMorgan Tax Aware Equity Fund Class R6	**JPELX**	NAS CM	Open End	US Equity Large Cap Growth (Growth & Income)	**B-**	C+	B		Y	15,000,000
JPMorgan U.S. Equity Fund Class A	**JUEAX**	NAS CM	Open End	US Equity Large Cap Blend (Growth)	**C+**	C	B	Down	Y	1,000
JPMorgan U.S. Equity Fund Class C	**JUECX**	NAS CM	Open End	US Equity Large Cap Blend (Growth)	**C+**	C	B	Down	Y	1,000
JPMorgan U.S. Equity Fund Class I	**JUESX**	NAS CM	Open End	US Equity Large Cap Blend (Growth)	**B-**	C	B		Y	1,000,000
JPMorgan U.S. Equity Fund Class L	**JMUEX**	NAS CM	Open End	US Equity Large Cap Blend (Growth)	**B-**	C	B		Y	3,000,000
JPMorgan U.S. Equity Fund Class R2	**JUEZX**	NAS CM	Open End	US Equity Large Cap Blend (Growth)	**C+**	C	B	Down	Y	0
JPMorgan U.S. Equity Fund Class R3	**JUEPX**	NAS CM	Open End	US Equity Large Cap Blend (Growth)	**C+**	C	B	Down	Y	0
JPMorgan U.S. Equity Fund Class R4	**JUEQX**	NAS CM	Open End	US Equity Large Cap Blend (Growth)	**B-**	C	B		Y	0
JPMorgan U.S. Equity Fund Class R5	**JUSRX**	NAS CM	Open End	US Equity Large Cap Blend (Growth)	**B-**	C	B		Y	0
JPMorgan U.S. Equity Fund Class R6	**JUEMX**	NAS CM	Open End	US Equity Large Cap Blend (Growth)	**B-**	C	B		Y	15,000,000
JPMorgan U.S. Large Cap Core Plus Fund Class A Shares	**JLCAX**	NAS CM	Open End	US Equity Large Cap Blend (Growth)	**C+**	C	B			1,000
JPMorgan U.S. Large Cap Core Plus Fund Class C Shares	**JLPCX**	NAS CM	Open End	US Equity Large Cap Blend (Growth)	**C+**	C	B			1,000
JPMorgan U.S. Large Cap Core Plus Fund Class I Shares	**JLPSX**	NAS CM	Open End	US Equity Large Cap Blend (Growth)	**C+**	C	B			1,000,000
JPMorgan U.S. Large Cap Core Plus Fund Class R2 Shares	**JLPZX**	NAS CM	Open End	US Equity Large Cap Blend (Growth)	**C+**	C	B			0
JPMorgan U.S. Large Cap Core Plus Fund Class R5 Shares	**JCPRX**	NAS CM	Open End	US Equity Large Cap Blend (Growth)	**C+**	C	B			0
JPMorgan U.S. Large Cap Core Plus Fund Class R6	**JLPYX**	NAS CM	Open End	US Equity Large Cap Blend (Growth)	**C+**	C	B		Y	15,000,000
JPMorgan U.S. Research Enhanced Equity Fund Class A	**JDEAX**	NAS CM	Open End	US Equity Large Cap Blend (Growth)	**B-**	C	B		Y	1,000
JPMorgan U.S. Research Enhanced Equity Fund Class I	**JDESX**	NAS CM	Open End	US Equity Large Cap Blend (Growth)	**B-**	C	B		Y	1,000,000
JPMorgan U.S. Research Enhanced Equity Fund Class L	**JPIEX**	NAS CM	Open End	US Equity Large Cap Blend (Growth)	**B-**	C	B		Y	3,000,000
JPMorgan U.S. Research Enhanced Equity Fund Class R6	**JDEUX**	NAS CM	Open End	US Equity Large Cap Blend (Growth)	**B-**	C	B		Y	15,000,000
JPMorgan U.S. Small Company Fund Class A	**JTUAX**	NAS CM	Open End	US Equity Small Cap (Small Company)	**C**	C-	C		Y	1,000
JPMorgan U.S. Small Company Fund Class C	**JTUCX**	NAS CM	Open End	US Equity Small Cap (Small Company)	**C-**	C-	C	Down	Y	1,000
JPMorgan U.S. Small Company Fund Class I	**JSCSX**	NAS CM	Open End	US Equity Small Cap (Small Company)	**C**	C-	C		Y	1,000,000
JPMorgan U.S. Small Company Fund Class L	**JUSSX**	NAS CM	Open End	US Equity Small Cap (Small Company)	**C**	C-	C		Y	3,000,000
JPMorgan U.S. Small Company Fund Class R2	**JSCZX**	NAS CM	Open End	US Equity Small Cap (Small Company)	**C-**	C-	C	Down	Y	0
JPMorgan U.S. Small Company Fund Class R3	**JUSPX**	NAS CM	Open End	US Equity Small Cap (Small Company)	**C**	C-	C		Y	0
JPMorgan U.S. Small Company Fund Class R4	**JUSQX**	NAS CM	Open End	US Equity Small Cap (Small Company)	**C**	C-	C		Y	0
JPMorgan U.S. Small Company Fund Class R5	**JUSYX**	NAS CM	Open End	US Equity Small Cap (Small Company)	**C**	C-	C		Y	0
JPMorgan U.S. Small Company Fund Class R6	**JUSMX**	NAS CM	Open End	US Equity Small Cap (Small Company)	**C**	C-	C		Y	15,000,000
JPMorgan Value Advantage Fund Class A	**JVAAX**	NAS CM	Open End	US Equity Large Cap Value (Growth & Income)	**B-**	C	B	Up	Y	1,000
JPMorgan Value Advantage Fund Class C	**JVACX**	NAS CM	Open End	US Equity Large Cap Value (Growth & Income)	**C+**	C	B		Y	1,000
JPMorgan Value Advantage Fund Class I	**JVASX**	NAS CM	Open End	US Equity Large Cap Value (Growth & Income)	**B-**	C	B	Up	Y	1,000,000
JPMorgan Value Advantage Fund Class L	**JVAIX**	NAS CM	Open End	US Equity Large Cap Value (Growth & Income)	**B-**	C	B	Up	Y	3,000,000
JPMorgan Value Advantage Fund Class R2	**JGAQX**	NAS CM	Open End	US Equity Large Cap Value (Growth & Income)	**B-**	C	B	Up	Y	0
JPMorgan Value Advantage Fund Class R3	**JVAPX**	NAS CM	Open End	US Equity Large Cap Value (Growth & Income)	**B-**	C	B	Up	Y	0
JPMorgan Value Advantage Fund Class R4	**JVAQX**	NAS CM	Open End	US Equity Large Cap Value (Growth & Income)	**B-**	C	B	Up	Y	0
JPMorgan Value Advantage Fund Class R5	**JVARX**	NAS CM	Open End	US Equity Large Cap Value (Growth & Income)	**B-**	C	B	Up	Y	0
JPMorgan Value Advantage Fund Class R6	**JVAYX**	NAS CM	Open End	US Equity Large Cap Value (Growth & Income)	**B-**	C	B	Up	Y	15,000,000
Kayne Anderson Midstream/Energy Fund, Inc.	**KMF**	NYSE	Closed End	Energy Sector Equity (Natl Res)	**C**	C	C	Down	Y	
Kayne Anderson MLP/Midstream Investment Company	**KYN**	NYSE	Closed End	Energy Sector Equity (Natl Res)	**C**	C	C	Down	Y	
KBI Global Investors Aquarius Fund Institutional Shares	**KBIWX**	NAS CM	Open End	Natl Resources Sec Equity (Natl Res)	**U**	U	U		Y	100,000
KCM Macro Trends Fund Class R-1	**KCMTX**	NAS CM	Open End	Multialternative (Growth)	**B-**	C	B		Y	5,000

★ Expanded analysis of this fund is included in Section II.

Min Additional Investment	3-Month Total Return	6-Month Total Return	1-Year Total Return	3-Year Total Return	5-Year Total Return	Dividend Yield (TTM)	Expense Ratio	3-Yr Std Deviation	3-Year Beta	NAV	Total Assets (MIL)	%Cash	%Stocks	%Bonds	%Other	Turnover Ratio	Last Bull Market Total Return	Last Bear Market Total Return	Front End Fee (%)	Back End Fee (%)	Inception Date
	TOTAL RETURNS					PERFORMANCE				ASSETS		ASSET ALLOCATION & TURNOVER					BULL & BEAR		FEES		
	2.70	8.27	5.28			2.28	0.9			15.96	30.7	5	22	72	0	30					Dec-16
	2.76	8.44	5.53			2.49	0.65			15.98	30.7	5	22	72	0	30					Dec-16
	2.82	8.52	5.67			2.62	0.5			15.99	30.7	5	22	72	0	30					Dec-16
	2.82	8.55	5.83			2.71	0.4			16	30.7	5	22	72	0	30					Dec-16
50	-1.85	-0.93	-2.86	-5.67	-5.34	0	1.25	2.81	4.5	13.76	376.7	35	54	0	0	154			4.50		Feb-13
50	-1.97	-1.18	-3.36	-7.00	-7.63	0	1.75	2.8	4.46	13.38	376.7	35	54	0	0	154				1.00	Feb-13
	-1.86	-0.83	-2.64	-4.98	-4.18	0	1	2.82	4.35	14.22	376.7	35	54	0	0	154					Feb-13
	-1.73	-0.70	-2.38	-4.21	-2.97	0	0.75	2.8	3.67	14.17	376.7	35	54	0	0	154					Feb-13
50	4.37	19.09	8.90	52.98	62.63	0.68	0.95	12.51	1.01	35.81	1,278	0	100	0	0	38	26.32	-18.64	5.25		Mar-11
50	4.26	18.81	8.36	50.73	58.59	0.32	1.46	12.5	1.01	35.43	1,278	0	100	0	0	38	25.92	-18.82		1.00	Mar-11
	4.50	19.41	9.40	55.07	66.26		0.44	12.51	1.01	36.02	1,278	0	100	0	0	38	26.64	-18.54			Oct-18
50	4.51	19.61	9.17	49.99	59.18	0.7	0.94	13.29	1.08	15.86	14,317	2	98	0	0	97	25.81	-17.78	5.25		Sep-01
50	4.34	19.29	8.62	47.67	55.13	0.34	1.44	13.25	1.08	15.31	14,317	2	98	0	0	97	25.54	-18.02		1.00	Sep-01
	4.56	19.81	9.46	50.93	60.80	0.85	0.69	13.3	1.08	15.91	14,317	2	98	0	0	97	25.9	-17.71			Sep-01
	4.52	19.79	9.59	51.56	61.85	0.96	0.6	13.27	1.08	15.93	14,317	2	98	0	0	97	26.07	-17.72			Sep-93
	4.42	19.49	8.89	48.72	57.09	0.5	1.19	13.31	1.08	15.7	14,317	2	98	0	0	97	25.57	-17.93			Nov-08
	4.47	19.59	9.14	49.81	59.19	0.7	0.94	13.29	1.08	15.8	14,317	2	98	0	0	97	25.89	-17.8			Sep-16
	4.57	19.77	9.43	50.91	61.16	0.87	0.69	13.28	1.08	15.89	14,317	2	98	0	0	97	26.07	-17.72			Sep-16
	4.59	19.87	9.59	51.66	62.13	0.97	0.54	13.28	1.08	15.94	14,317	2	98	0	0	97	26.1	-17.7			May-06
	4.61	19.88	9.73	52.12	62.81	1.04	0.44	13.29	1.08	15.97	14,317	2	98	0	0	97	26.1	-17.66			Nov-10
50	3.96	18.52	6.84	48.78	53.13	0.16	1.95	13.3	1.08	27.51	6,421	1	99	0	0	110	24.55	-18.52	5.25		Nov-05
50	3.85	18.22	6.31	46.61	49.32	0	2.45	13.32	1.08	25.88	6,421	1	99	0	0	110	24.26	-18.7		1.00	Nov-05
	4.05	18.69	7.11	49.97	55.09	0.38	1.7	13.3	1.08	27.94	6,421	1	99	0	0	110	24.77	-18.45			Nov-05
	3.86	18.31	6.45	47.42	50.93	0	2.3	13.31	1.08	26.62	6,421	1	99	0	0	110	24.36	-18.58			Nov-08
	4.03	18.68	7.13	50.41	56.20	0.42	1.65	13.3	1.08	28.08	6,421	1	99	0	0	110	24.93	-18.39			May-06
	4.07	18.78	7.26	50.32	55.45	0.51	1.55	13.32	1.08	28.07	6,421	1	99	0	0	110	24.77	-18.45			Nov-17
50	4.13	19.00	9.39	48.30	52.85	1.18	0.6	12.59	1.03	27.38	5,820	1	99	0	0	45	24.78	-16.25	5.25		Sep-01
	4.19	19.13	9.64	49.40	54.73	1.36	0.35	12.58	1.03	27.65	5,820	1	99	0	0	45	25.02	-16.18			Sep-01
	4.24	19.17	9.66	49.45	55.28	1.36	0.44	12.58	1.03	27.61	5,820	1	99	0	0	45	25.07	-16.09			Jan-97
	4.22	19.22	9.78	49.97	56.08	1.43	0.25	12.58	1.03	27.62	5,820	1	99	0	0	45	25.13	-16.04			Mar-03
50	-0.37	12.23	-8.72	28.51	27.81	0	1.24	17.2	1	15.96	1,395	1	99	0	0	52	30.04	-26.64	5.25		Nov-07
50	-0.52	11.97	-9.16	26.60	24.61	0	1.74	17.21	1	15.06	1,395	1	99	0	0	52	29.67	-26.69		1.00	Nov-07
	-0.30	12.40	-8.44	29.57	29.46	0.11	0.98	17.17	1	16.4	1,395	1	99	0	0	52	30.22	-26.49			Sep-01
	-0.30	12.49	-8.32	30.16	30.54	0.28	0.83	17.21	1	16.38	1,395	1	99	0	0	52	30.29	-26.45			Nov-93
	-0.44	12.16	-8.90	27.53	26.21	0	1.49	17.21	1	15.58	1,395	1	99	0	0	52	29.82	-26.6			Nov-11
	-0.37	12.31	-8.70	28.69	28.42	0.01	1.22	17.21	1	15.87	1,395	1	99	0	0	52	30.1	-26.52			Sep-16
	-0.30	12.47	-8.47	29.56	29.94	0.17	1.01	17.21	1	16.32	1,395	1	99	0	0	52	30.29	-26.45			Sep-16
	-0.30	12.45	-8.34	30.08	30.46	0.33	0.86	17.19	1	16.34	1,395	1	99	0	0	52	30.29	-26.45			Sep-16
	-0.24	12.56	-8.20	30.60	31.16	0.38	0.73	17.19	1	16.4	1,395	1	99	0	0	52	30.37	-26.45			Nov-11
50	3.77	17.68	6.99	37.76	40.13	1.23	1.14	12.62	1.01	35.46	10,840	3	97	0	0	23	26.63	-17.35	5.25		Feb-05
50	3.64	17.35	6.48	35.67	36.63	0.75	1.64	12.62	1.01	35.29	10,840	3	97	0	0	23	26.24	-17.54		1.00	Feb-05
	3.84	17.83	7.28	38.80	41.91	1.51	0.89	12.62	1.01	35.67	10,840	3	97	0	0	23	26.82	-17.26			Feb-05
	3.87	17.90	7.44	39.57	43.41	1.61	0.75	12.62	1.01	35.69	10,840	3	97	0	0	23	27.01	-17.22			Feb-05
	3.70	17.50	6.75	37.06	39.43	1.13	1.39	12.63	1.01	35.24	10,840	3	97	0	0	23	26.64	-17.39			Jul-17
	3.78	17.67	7.00	37.87	40.96	1.46	1.14	12.63	1.01	35.08	10,840	3	97	0	0	23	26.82	-17.31			Sep-16
	3.82	17.81	7.27	38.88	42.70	1.53	0.89	12.64	1.01	35.52	10,840	3	97	0	0	23	27.01	-17.22			Sep-16
	3.84	17.90	7.40	39.43	43.27	1.65	0.74	12.63	1.01	35.62	10,840	3	97	0	0	23	27.01	-17.22			Sep-16
	3.90	17.99	7.56	39.83	43.68	1.73	0.64	12.62	1.01	35.67	10,840	3	97	0	0	23	27.01	-17.22			Sep-16
	-0.39	33.39	3.69	13.33	-52.44	0.82	2.03	24.36		13.44	634.3	-12	129	3	-20	22	39.19	-16.9			Nov-10
	-0.33	27.66	2.87	18.72	-28.34	2.91	5.18	26.06	0.89	17.05	2,154	-13	150	0	-41	26	23.34	-13.34			Sep-04
	0.85	15.15					1.1			10.64	48.4										Oct-18
100	1.97	9.88	4.11	40.17	32.20	0	1.66	11.54	1.54	11.34	94.4	0	100	0	0	534	12.32	-21.7			Aug-08

	MARKET		FUND TYPE, CATEGORY & OBJECTIVE		RATINGS				MINIMUMS	
Fund Name	Ticker Symbol	Traded On	Fund Type	Category and (Prospectus Objective)	Overall Rating	Reward Rating	Risk Rating	Recent Up/ Downgrade	Open to New Investors	Min Initial Investment
KCM Macro Trends Fund Institutional Class	KCMIX	NAS CM	Open End	Multialternative (Growth)	B-	C	B+		Y	250,000
Keeley Mid Cap Dividend Value Fund Class A	KMDVX	NAS CM	Open End	US Equity Mid Cap (Growth)	C+	C	B	Up	Y	2,500
Keeley Mid Cap Dividend Value Fund Class I	KMDIX	NAS CM	Open End	US Equity Mid Cap (Growth)	C+	C	B	Up	Y	1,000,000
Keeley Small Cap Dividend Value Fund Class A	KSDVX	NAS CM	Open End	US Equity Small Cap (Small Company)	C	C	C+		Y	2,500
Keeley Small Cap Dividend Value Fund Class I	KSDIX	NAS CM	Open End	US Equity Small Cap (Small Company)	C	C	C+		Y	1,000,000
Keeley Small-Mid Cap Value Fund Class A	KSMVX	NAS CM	Open End	US Equity Mid Cap (Growth)	C	C-	C+		Y	2,500
Keeley Small-Mid Cap Value Fund Class I	KSMIX	NAS CM	Open End	US Equity Mid Cap (Growth)	C	C-	C+		Y	1,000,000
Kellner Merger Fund Institutional Class	GAKIX	NAS CM	Open End	Market Neutral (World Stock)	B-	C	B+	Up	Y	100,000
Kellner Merger Fund Investor Class	GAKAX	NAS CM	Open End	Market Neutral (World Stock)	C+	C	B		Y	2,000
Kempner Multi-Cap Deep Value Fund Institutional Class	FIKDX	NAS CM	Open End	US Equity Large Cap Value (Growth & Income)	C+	C	B		Y	500,000
Kempner Multi-Cap Deep Value Fund Investor Class	FAKDX	NAS CM	Open End	US Equity Large Cap Value (Growth & Income)	C+	C	B		Y	500
Kinetics Global Fund Class Advisor Class A	KGLAX	NAS CM	Open End	Global Equity Mid/Small Cap (World Stock)	C	C	C		Y	2,500
Kinetics Global Fund Class Advisor Class C	KGLCX	NAS CM	Open End	Global Equity Mid/Small Cap (World Stock)	C	C	C		Y	2,500
Kinetics Global No Load Class	WWWEX	NAS CM	Open End	Global Equity Mid/Small Cap (World Stock)	C	C	C		Y	2,500
Kinetics Internet Advisor Fund Class A	KINAX	NAS CM	Open End	US Equity Large Cap Growth (Technology)	C	C	C		Y	2,500
Kinetics Internet Advisor Fund Class C	KINCX	NAS CM	Open End	US Equity Large Cap Growth (Technology)	C	C	C		Y	2,500
Kinetics Internet Fund No Load Class	WWWFX	NAS CM	Open End	US Equity Large Cap Growth (Technology)	C	C	C		Y	2,500
Kinetics Market Opportunities Fund Advisor Class A	KMKAX	NAS CM	Open End	Financials Sector Equity (Growth)	B-	B-	C+	Up	Y	2,500
Kinetics Market Opportunities Fund Advisor Class C	KMKCX	NAS CM	Open End	Financials Sector Equity (Growth)	B-	B-	C+	Up	Y	2,500
Kinetics Market Opportunities Fund Class Institutional	KMKYX	NAS CM	Open End	Financials Sector Equity (Growth)	B-	B-	C+	Up	Y	1,000,000
Kinetics Market Opportunities Fund No Load Class	KMKNX	NAS CM	Open End	Financials Sector Equity (Growth)	B-	B-	C+	Up	Y	2,500
Kinetics Medical Advisor Fund Class C	KRXCX	NAS CM	Open End	Healthcare Sector Equity (Health)	C	C	C	Down	Y	2,500
Kinetics Medical Fund Class A	KRXAX	NAS CM	Open End	Healthcare Sector Equity (Health)	C	C	C+	Down	Y	2,500
Kinetics Medical Fund No Load Class	MEDRX	NAS CM	Open End	Healthcare Sector Equity (Health)	C	C	C+	Down	Y	2,500
Kinetics Paradigm Fund Advisor Class A	KNPAX	NAS CM	Open End	US Equity Mid Cap (Growth)	B-	B	C+	Down	Y	2,500
Kinetics Paradigm Fund Advisor Class C	KNPCX	NAS CM	Open End	US Equity Mid Cap (Growth)	B-	B	C+	Down	Y	2,500
Kinetics Paradigm Fund Class Institutional	KNPYX	NAS CM	Open End	US Equity Mid Cap (Growth)	B	B	C+		Y	1,000,000
Kinetics Paradigm Fund No Load Class	WWNPX	NAS CM	Open End	US Equity Mid Cap (Growth)	B	B	C+		Y	2,500
Kinetics Small Capital Opportunities Advisor Fund Class A	KSOAX	NAS CM	Open End	US Equity Small Cap (Small Company)	B-	B-	C+	Down	Y	2,500
Kinetics Small Capital Opportunities Fund Advisor Class C	KSOCX	NAS CM	Open End	US Equity Small Cap (Small Company)	C+	C+	C+	Down	Y	2,500
Kinetics Small Capital Opportunities Cls Institutional	KSCYX	NAS CM	Open End	US Equity Small Cap (Small Company)	B-	B-	C+	Down	Y	1,000,000
Kinetics Small Capital Opportunities Fund No Load Class	KSCOX	NAS CM	Open End	US Equity Small Cap (Small Company)	B-	B-	C+	Down	Y	2,500
Kinetics Spin-Off & Corporate Restructuring Advisor Cls A	LSHAX	NAS CM	Open End	US Equity Mid Cap (Growth)	C	C	C+	Down	Y	2,500
Kinetics Spin-Off & Corporate Restructuring Advisor Cls C	LSHCX	NAS CM	Open End	US Equity Mid Cap (Growth)	C	C	C	Down	Y	2,500
Kinetics Spin-Off & Corporate Restructuring Inst Cls	LSHUX	NAS CM	Open End	US Equity Mid Cap (Growth)	C	C	C+	Down	Y	1,000,000
Kinetics Spin-Off & Corporate Restructuring No Load Cls	LSHEX	NAS CM	Open End	US Equity Mid Cap (Growth)	C	C	C+	Down	Y	2,500
Kirr Marbach Partners Value Fund	KMVAX	NAS CM	Open End	US Equity Mid Cap (Growth)	C	C-	C+		Y	1,000
KL Allocation Fund Advisor Class	GAVAX	NAS CM	Open End	Aggressive Alloc (Asset Alloc)	C	C-	B-	Up	Y	2,500
KL Allocation Fund Institutional Class	GAVIX	NAS CM	Open End	Aggressive Alloc (Asset Alloc)	C	C-	B-	Up	Y	500,000
Kopernik Global All-Cap Fund Class A	KGGAX	NAS CM	Open End	Global Equity Mid/Small Cap (World Stock)	C	C-	C+		Y	3,000
Kopernik Global All-Cap Fund Class I	KGGIX	NAS CM	Open End	Global Equity Mid/Small Cap (World Stock)	C	C-	C+		Y	1,000,000
Kopernik International Fund Class A			Open End	Global Equity Large Cap (Foreign Stock)	C+	C-	B	Up	Y	3,000
Kopernik International Fund Class I	KGIIX	NAS CM	Open End	Global Equity Large Cap (Foreign Stock)	C+	C-	B		Y	1,000,000
Korea Fund Inc	KF	NYSE	Closed End	Equity Miscellaneous (Pacific Stock)	D+	D	D+	Down	Y	
KP International Equity Fund Institutional Shares	KPIEX	NAS CM	Open End	Global Equity Large Cap (Foreign Stock)	C	C	B		Y	0
KP Large Cap Equity Fund Institutional Shares	KPLCX	NAS CM	Open End	US Equity Large Cap Blend (Growth)	B-	C	B		Y	0
KP Retirement Path 2015 Fund Institutional Shares	KPRAX	NAS CM	Open End	Target Date (Asset Alloc)	B	C+	A		Y	0
KP Retirement Path 2020 Fund Institutional Shares	KPRBX	NAS CM	Open End	Target Date (Asset Alloc)	B	C+	A		Y	0
KP Retirement Path 2025 Fund Institutional Shares	KPRCX	NAS CM	Open End	Target Date (Asset Alloc)	B	C	A	Up	Y	0
KP Retirement Path 2030 Fund Institutional Shares	KPRDX	NAS CM	Open End	Target Date (Asset Alloc)	B-	C	A-		Y	0
KP Retirement Path 2035 Fund Institutional Shares	KPREX	NAS CM	Open End	Target Date (Asset Alloc)	B-	C	B+	Up	Y	0
KP Retirement Path 2040 Fund Institutional Shares	KPRFX	NAS CM	Open End	Target Date (Asset Alloc)	B-	C	B+	Up	Y	0

★Expanded analysis of this fund is included in Section II.

	TOTAL RETURNS					PERFORMANCE				ASSETS		ASSET ALLOCATION & TURNOVER					BULL & BEAR		FEES		
Min Additional Investment	3-Month Total Return	6-Month Total Return	1-Year Total Return	3-Year Total Return	5-Year Total Return	Dividend Yield (TTM)	Expense Ratio	3-Yr Std Deviation	3-Year Beta	NAV	Total Assets (MIL)	%Cash	%Stocks	%Bonds	%Other	Turnover Ratio	Last Bull Market Total Return	Last Bear Market Total Return	Front End Fee (%)	Back End Fee (%)	Inception Date
100	1.97	9.95	4.35	40.90	32.90	0	1.65	11.49	1.54	11.38	94.4	0	100	0	0	534	12.32	-21.7			Mar-17
50	1.90	16.91	0.46	32.88	43.30	1.15	1.21	14.44	1.07	22.39	173.7	5	95	0	0	19			4.50		Oct-11
10,000	1.96	17.06	0.72	33.87	45.14	1.4	0.96	14.46	1.07	22.39	173.7	5	95	0	0	19					Oct-11
50	4.08	19.17	-5.13	29.89	28.26	1.27	1.41	16.97	0.97	16.3	490.3	1	99	0	0	24	26.63	-19.53	4.50		Dec-09
10,000	4.18	19.41	-4.78	30.96	29.94	1.5	1.16	17	0.97	16.34	490.3	1	99	0	0	24	26.83	-19.42			Dec-09
50	1.74	20.05	-4.37	35.43	20.33	0.25	1.39	16.07	1.04	12.27	79.2	4	96	0	0	27	34.89	-28.05	4.50		Aug-07
10,000	1.86	20.28	-4.13	36.47	21.84	0.5	1.14	16.11	1.04	12.57	79.2	4	96	0	0	27	35.03	-27.98			Aug-07
100	0.45	2.60	1.97	8.84	11.90	0	2.07	3.11	10.26	11.03	164.0	39	28	0	33	285					Jun-12
100	0.37	2.47	1.73	8.08	10.19	0	2.32	3.13	10.4	10.78	164.0	39	28	0	33	285					Jun-12
100	3.05	14.94	2.65	35.82	24.07	2.11	0.96	13.73	1.02	10.58	74.6	10	90	0	0	25	19.24	-18.18			Apr-08
100	2.99	14.82	2.40	34.73	22.50	1.87	1.21	13.66	1.01	10.57	74.6	10	90	0	0	25	19.07	-18.26			Jun-08
	14.28	27.47	4.74	57.96	23.94	0	1.64	16.61	0.49	6.96	14.2	42	52	0	6	28	18.85	-20.37	5.75		May-08
	14.16	27.29	4.23	54.21	19.59	0	2.14	16.78	0.5	6.53	14.2	42	52	0	6	28	18.56	-20.76		1.00	May-08
	14.40	27.78	5.03	57.72	24.11	0	1.39	16.86	0.5	6.99	14.2	42	52	0	6	28	18.85	-20.37			Dec-99
	21.85	37.89	17.87	69.02	56.15	0	2.09	18.63	0.57	34.57	138.7	29	58	0	14	15	21.45	-22.15	5.75		Apr-01
	21.69	37.57	17.31	66.54	52.40	0	2.59	18.63	0.57	29.22	138.7	29	58	0	14	15	21.18	-22.34		1.00	Feb-07
	21.92	38.06	18.16	70.21	58.04	0	1.84	18.65	0.57	37.65	138.7	29	58	0	14	15	21.67	-22.11			Oct-96
	9.18	25.13	9.65	88.58	68.14	0	1.65	15.77	0.58	26.98	89.1	41	53	0	5	8	20.76	-18.66	5.75		Jan-06
	9.04	24.81	9.09	85.78	63.97	0	2.15	15.76	0.58	25.8	89.1	41	53	0	5	8	20.51	-18.9		1.00	Feb-07
	9.29	25.41	10.11	91.27	72.03	0	1.2	15.79	0.58	27.88	89.1	41	53	0	5	8	21.18	-18.55			May-08
	9.23	25.29	9.90	89.98	70.23	0	1.4	15.77	0.58	27.44	89.1	41	53	0	5	8	20.96	-18.6			Jan-06
	-3.17	5.67	9.06	16.24	17.48	0.41	2.14	13.67	0.79	22.55	16.4	1	99	0	0	0	12.64	-15.62		1.00	Feb-07
	-3.05	5.91	9.60	17.98	20.45	0.66	1.64	13.68	0.79	23.45	16.4	1	99	0	0	0	12.96	-15.46	5.75		Apr-01
	-2.97	6.06	9.86	18.90	22.01	1.08	1.39	13.67	0.79	24.49	16.4	1	99	0	0	0	13.1	-15.34			Sep-99
	5.60	28.92	7.26	80.55	62.25	0	1.89	16.61	0.98	51.44	811.6	13	85	0	2	3	23.4	-24.98	5.75		Apr-01
	5.48	28.58	6.73	77.89	58.27	0	2.39	16.59	0.98	47.68	811.6	13	85	0	2	3	23.05	-25.14		1.00	Jun-02
	5.71	29.22	7.75	83.00	65.97	0	1.44	16.62	0.98	53.81	811.6	13	85	0	2	3	23.72	-24.84			May-05
	5.67	29.07	7.52	81.93	64.30	0	1.64	16.62	0.98	53.27	811.6	13	85	0	2	3	23.58	-24.9			Dec-99
	2.47	22.47	3.80	81.32	49.74	0	1.9	14.97	0.57	60.87	313.1	31	66	0	2	3	26.46	-22.13	5.75		Dec-01
	2.34	22.15	3.27	78.66	46.01	0	2.4	14.97	0.57	57.94	313.1	31	66	0	2	3	26.15	-22.33		1.00	Feb-07
	2.59	22.74	4.28	83.81	53.18	0	1.45	14.99	0.57	64.06	313.1	31	66	0	2	3	26.82	-21.99			Aug-05
	2.54	22.63	4.08	82.79	51.71	0	1.65	14.98	0.57	62.9	313.1	31	66	0	2	3	26.7	-22.08			Mar-00
	1.89	27.15	2.18	50.55	22.18	0	1.61	17.7	1.12	11.8	22.2	4	96	0	0	9	23.52	-23.85	5.75		May-07
	1.64	26.59	1.41	47.14	17.63	0	2.36	17.74	1.13	11.09	22.2	4	96	0	0	9	23.12	-24.01		1.00	May-07
	1.97	27.25	2.43	51.59	23.63	0	1.36	17.78	1.13	11.86	22.2	4	96	0	0	9	23.77	-23.84			Jul-07
	1.89	27.16	2.25	50.73	22.32	0	1.56	17.74	1.12	12.36	22.2	4	96	0	0	9	23.52	-23.85			Dec-17
100	1.73	19.41	-3.64	31.57	15.75	0	1.45	16.19	1.23	21.71	67.6	1	99	0	0	14	35.82	-25.77			Dec-98
250	3.06	9.78	-0.47	7.13	20.65	0	1.49	7.29	0.46	13.46	159.0	19	37	44	0	87	14.51	-2.31			Sep-10
25,000	3.16	9.95	-0.17	7.93	22.14	0	1.24	7.3	0.46	13.69	159.0	19	37	44	0	87	14.83	-2.21			Sep-10
250	4.17	9.75	0.49	17.05	5.52	0	1.29	11.32	0.47	10.24	1,079	3	96	2	0	44			5.75		Nov-13
	4.18	9.79	0.64	17.86	6.68	0.23	1.04	11.27	0.46	10.2	1,079	3	96	2	0	44					Nov-13
250	5.75	12.41	3.05	13.93			1.35	9.21	0.5	12.5	163.6	34	66	0	0	34			5.75		Dec-18
	5.74	12.50	3.26	14.73		1.07	1.1	9.22	0.5	12.51	163.6	34	66	0	0	34					Jun-15
	-2.67	1.11	-9.91	16.32	0.00	1.63	0	16.56	0.89	32.78	170.5	1	99	0	0	69	18.08	-26.46			Aug-84
	3.70	15.00	2.01	34.07	16.67	1.75	0.47	11.19	0.97	10.35	1,898	3	97	0	0	32					Jan-14
	3.74	18.94	8.59	52.78	66.05	1.36	0.3	12.4	1	13.31	2,927	2	98	0	0	49					Jan-14
	3.03	9.91	6.66	19.58	24.06	2.33	0.35	4.38	1.08	10.53	469.8	2	34	63	1	23					Jan-14
	3.01	10.75	6.42	23.12	26.68	2.32	0.36	5.23	0.86	10.92	1,053	2	42	55	1	17					Jan-14
	3.21	12.17	6.36	27.81	29.74	2.34	0.38	6.49	0.92	11.24	1,353	2	53	45	1	13					Jan-14
	3.34	13.49	6.12	32.45	32.58	2.36	0.4	7.69	0.95	11.44	1,344	2	63	35	1	12					Jan-14
	3.38	14.49	5.82	35.84	34.89	2.38	0.42	8.68	0.95	11.61	1,504	2	71	26	1	12					Jan-14
	3.53	15.22	5.57	38.03	36.41	2.39	0.43	9.41	0.96	11.73	1,377	2	78	20	0	11					Jan-14

	MARKET		FUND TYPE, CATEGORY & OBJECTIVE		RATINGS				MINIMUMS	
Fund Name	Ticker Symbol	Traded On	Fund Type	Category and (Prospectus Objective)	Overall Rating	Reward Rating	Risk Rating	Recent Up/ Downgrade	Open to New Investors	Min Initial Investment
KP Retirement Path 2045 Fund Institutional Shares	KPRGX	NAS CM	Open End	Target Date (Asset Alloc)	B-	C	B+	Up	Y	0
KP Retirement Path 2050 Fund Institutional Shares	KPRHX	NAS CM	Open End	Target Date (Asset Alloc)	B-	C	B+	Up	Y	0
KP Retirement Path 2055 Fund Institutional Shares	KPRIX	NAS CM	Open End	Target Date (Asset Alloc)	B-	C	B	Up	Y	0
KP Retirement Path 2060 Fund Institutional Shares	KPRJX	NAS CM	Open End	Target Date (Asset Alloc)	B-	C	B	Up	Y	0
KP Small Cap Equity Fund Institutional Shares	KPSCX	NAS CM	Open End	US Equity Small Cap (Small Company)	C+	C	C+		Y	0
Ladenburg Aggressive Growth Fund Class A	LAWAX	NAS CM	Open End	Aggressive Alloc (Aggr Growth)	C+	C	B	Up	Y	1,000
Ladenburg Aggressive Growth Fund Class C	LAWCX	NAS CM	Open End	Aggressive Alloc (Aggr Growth)	C+	C	B	Up	Y	1,000
Ladenburg Aggressive Growth Fund Class I	LAGIX	NAS CM	Open End	Aggressive Alloc (Aggr Growth)	C+	C	B	Up	Y	1,000,000
Ladenburg Growth & Income Fund Class A	LOWAX	NAS CM	Open End	Moderate Alloc (Growth & Income)	B-	C	B+	Up	Y	1,000
Ladenburg Growth & Income Fund Class C	LOWCX	NAS CM	Open End	Moderate Alloc (Growth & Income)	B-	C	B+	Up	Y	1,000
Ladenburg Growth & Income Fund Class I	LOWIX	NAS CM	Open End	Moderate Alloc (Growth & Income)	B-	C	B+	Up	Y	1,000,000
Ladenburg Growth Fund Class A	LGWAX	NAS CM	Open End	Aggressive Alloc (Growth)	B-	C	B	Up	Y	1,000
Ladenburg Growth Fund Class C	LGWCX	NAS CM	Open End	Aggressive Alloc (Growth)	B-	C	B	Up	Y	1,000
Ladenburg Growth Fund Class I	LGWIX	NAS CM	Open End	Aggressive Alloc (Growth)	B-	C	B	Up	Y	1,000,000
Ladenburg Income & Growth Fund Class A	LNOAX	NAS CM	Open End	Cautious Alloc (Growth & Income)	B-	C	A-	Up	Y	1,000
Ladenburg Income & Growth Fund Class C	LNOCX	NAS CM	Open End	Cautious Alloc (Growth & Income)	B-	C	B+	Up	Y	1,000
Ladenburg Income & Growth Fund Class I	LNOIX	NAS CM	Open End	Cautious Alloc (Growth & Income)	B-	C	A-	Up	Y	1,000,000
Ladenburg Income Fund Class A	LNCAX	NAS CM	Open End	Cautious Alloc (Income)	B-	C	B+	Up	Y	1,000
Ladenburg Income Fund Class C	LNCCX	NAS CM	Open End	Cautious Alloc (Income)	C+	C	B	Up	Y	1,000
Ladenburg Income Fund Class I	LNCIX	NAS CM	Open End	Cautious Alloc (Income)	B-	C	B+		Y	1,000,000
Lateef Focused Growth Fund Class A	LIMAX	NAS CM	Open End	US Equity Large Cap Growth (Growth)	C+	C	B-	Down	Y	5,000
Lateef Focused Growth Fund Class C	LIMCX	NAS CM	Open End	US Equity Large Cap Growth (Growth)	C+	C	B-	Down	Y	5,000
Lateef Focused Growth Fund Class I	LIMIX	NAS CM	Open End	US Equity Large Cap Growth (Growth)	C+	C+	B-	Down	Y	100,000
Laudus International MarketMasters Fund™	SWMIX	NAS CM	Open End	Global Equity Large Cap (Foreign Stock)	C	C	C+		Y	0
Laudus U.S. Large Cap Growth Fund	LGILX	NAS CM	Open End	US Equity Large Cap Growth (Growth)	B-	C+	B	Down	Y	0
Lazard Developing Mkts Eq Port Institutiona Shares	LDMIX	NAS CM	Open End	Global Emerg Mkts (Div Emerging Mkts)	C	C	C+		Y	100,000
Lazard Developing Markets Equity Portfolio Open Shares	LDMOX	NAS CM	Open End	Global Emerg Mkts (Div Emerging Mkts)	C	C	C+		Y	2,500
Lazard Emerging Mkts Core Equity Portfolio Inst Shares	ECEIX	NAS CM	Open End	Global Emerg Mkts (Div Emerging Mkts)	C	C	C+		Y	100,000
Lazard Emerging Markets Core Equity Portfolio Open Shares	ECEOX	NAS CM	Open End	Global Emerg Mkts (Div Emerging Mkts)	C	C	C+		Y	2,500
Lazard Emerging Markets Core Equity Portfolio R6 Shares	RLEOX	NAS CM	Open End	Global Emerg Mkts (Div Emerging Mkts)	C	C	C+		Y	1,000,000
Lazard Emerging Mkts Eq Advantage Port Inst Shares	LEAIX	NAS CM	Open End	Global Emerg Mkts (Div Emerging Mkts)	C	C	C+		Y	100,000
Lazard Emerging Mkts Eq Advantage Port Open Shares	LEAOX	NAS CM	Open End	Global Emerg Mkts (Div Emerging Mkts)	C	C	C+		Y	2,500
Lazard Emerging Mkts Equity Blend Portfolio Inst Shares	EMBIX	NAS CM	Open End	Global Emerg Mkts (Div Emerging Mkts)	C	C	C+		Y	100,000
Lazard Emerging Markets Equity Blend Portfolio Open Shares	EMBOX	NAS CM	Open End	Global Emerg Mkts (Div Emerging Mkts)	C	C	C+		Y	2,500
Lazard Emerging Mkts Equity Portfolio Inst Shares	LZEMX	NAS CM	Open End	Global Emerg Mkts (Div Emerging Mkts)	C	C	C+			100,000
Lazard Emerging Markets Equity Portfolio Open Shares	LZOEX	NAS CM	Open End	Global Emerg Mkts (Div Emerging Mkts)	C	C	C+			2,500
Lazard Emerging Markets Equity Portfolio R6 Shares	RLEMX	NAS CM	Open End	Global Emerg Mkts (Div Emerging Mkts)	C	C	C+			1,000,000
Lazard Equity Franchise Portfolio Institutional Shares	LZFIX	NAS CM	Open End	US Equity Large Cap Value (World Stock)	C-	D+	B	Up	Y	100,000
Lazard Equity Franchise Portfolio Open Shares	LZFOX	NAS CM	Open End	US Equity Large Cap Value (World Stock)	C-	D+	B-	Up	Y	2,500
Lazard Global Dynamic Multi-Asset Portfolio Inst Shares	GDMIX	NAS CM	Open End	Flexible Alloc (Asset Alloc)	C+	C	B	Up	Y	100,000
Lazard Global Dynamic Multi-Asset Portfolio Open Shares	GDMOX	NAS CM	Open End	Flexible Alloc (Asset Alloc)	C+	C	B	Up	Y	2,500
Lazard Global Equity Select Portfolio Institutional Shares	GESIX	NAS CM	Open End	Global Equity Large Cap (Growth)	B-	C	B	Up	Y	100,000
Lazard Global Equity Select Portfolio Open Shares	GESOX	NAS CM	Open End	Global Equity Large Cap (Growth)	B-	C	B	Up	Y	2,500
Lazard Global Listed Infrastructure Portfolio Inst Shares	GLIFX	NAS CM	Open End	Infrastructure Sector Equity (Equity-Income)	B	B-	B	Up	Y	100,000
Lazard Global Listed Infrastructure Portfolio Open Shares	GLFOX	NAS CM	Open End	Infrastructure Sector Equity (Equity-Income)	B-	B-	B		Y	2,500
Lazard Global Strategic Equity Portfolio Inst Shares	LSTIX	NAS CM	Open End	Global Equity Large Cap (Growth)	C+	C	B		Y	100,000
Lazard Global Strategic Equity Portfolio Open Shares	LSTOX	NAS CM	Open End	Global Equity Large Cap (Growth)	C+	C	B		Y	2,500
Lazard Global Total Return and Income Fund Inc	LGI	NYSE	Closed End	Global Equity Large Cap (World Stock)	C	C	C-		Y	
Lazard Intl Compounders Portfolio Inst Shares	ICMPX	NAS CM	Open End	Global Equity Large Cap (Growth)	U	U	U		Y	100,000
Lazard International Compounders Portfolio Open Shares	OCMPX	NAS CM	Open End	Global Equity Large Cap (Growth)	U	U	U		Y	100,000
Lazard Intl Equity Advantage Portfolio Inst Shares	IEAIX	NAS CM	Open End	Global Equity Large Cap (Foreign Stock)	C	C-	C+		Y	100,000
Lazard Intl Equity Advantage Portfolio Open Shares	IEAOX	NAS CM	Open End	Global Equity Large Cap (Foreign Stock)	C	C-	C+		Y	2,500

★ Expanded analysis of this fund is included in Section II.

	TOTAL RETURNS					PERFORMANCE				ASSETS		ASSET ALLOCATION & TURNOVER					BULL & BEAR		FEES		
Min Additional Investment	3-Month Total Return	6-Month Total Return	1-Year Total Return	3-Year Total Return	5-Year Total Return	Dividend Yield (TTM)	Expense Ratio	3-Yr Std Deviation	3-Year Beta	NAV	Total Assets (MIL)	%Cash	%Stocks	%Bonds	%Other	Turnover Ratio	Last Bull Market Total Return	Last Bear Market Total Return	Front End Fee (%)	Back End Fee (%)	Inception Date
	3.59	15.57	5.48	39.42	37.25	2.38	0.44	9.83	0.97	11.8	1,071	2	81	17	0	11					Jan-14
	3.55	15.82	5.34	39.82	37.60	2.38	0.44	10.04	0.97	11.93	654.3	2	83	14	0	10					Jan-14
	3.62	16.02	5.33	39.92	37.96	2.38	0.44	10.17	0.97	12.02	228.8	2	85	13	0	12					Jan-14
	3.62	16.02	5.27	40.05	38.04	2.32	0.44	10.19	0.97	11.73	47.6	2	85	13	0	36					Jan-14
	4.04	20.19	0.97	50.90	44.82	0.51	0.52	16.83	0.98	11.07	1,281	4	96	0	0	85					Jan-14
1,000	3.26	17.07	4.56	36.74		0.31	1.18	11.35	0.92	13.3	22.0	3	90	7	0	17			5.00		Aug-15
1,000	3.02	16.59	3.79	32.15		0	1.93	11.22	0.91	12.93	22.0	3	90	7	0	17				1.00	Aug-15
1,000	3.30	17.24	4.86	35.95		0.57	0.93	11.22	0.9	13.12	22.0	3	90	7	0	17				1.00	Aug-15
1,000	2.96	13.41	4.76	24.42		1.01	1.23	8.13	0.65	11.85	114.6	2	64	33	0	25			5.00		Aug-15
1,000	2.73	12.96	3.93	21.68		0.69	1.98	8.1	0.65	11.67	114.6	2	64	33	0	25				1.00	Aug-15
1,000	3.01	13.50	5.03	25.00		1.18	0.98	8.11	0.65	11.87	114.6	2	64	33	0	25				1.00	Aug-15
1,000	3.05	15.44	4.71	30.30		0.69	1.23	9.87	0.8	12.48	59.5	2	78	19	0	16			5.00		Aug-15
1,000	2.92	15.01	3.91	27.35		0	1.98	9.83	0.79	12.33	59.5	2	78	19	0	16				1.00	Aug-15
1,000	3.14	15.66	4.99	30.85		0.92	0.98	9.84	0.79	12.48	59.5	2	78	19	0	16				1.00	Aug-15
1,000	2.72	10.53	5.20	18.32		1.3	1.27	5.62	0.44	11.32	35.4	4	47	49	0	24			5.00		Aug-15
1,000	2.44	10.07	4.29	14.42		0.71	2.02	5.69	0.45	11.23	35.4	4	47	49	0	24				1.00	Aug-15
1,000	2.77	10.69	5.41	18.86		1.52	1.02	5.68	0.45	11.38	35.4	4	47	49	0	24				1.00	Aug-15
1,000	2.55	8.39	5.31	12.31		1.52	1.29	3.79	0.28	10.9	10.5	6	29	65	0	27			5.00		Aug-15
1,000	2.36	8.02	4.51	9.84		0.77	2.04	3.76	0.27	10.83	10.5	6	29	65	0	27				1.00	Aug-15
1,000	2.61	8.54	5.58	6.68		1.77	1.04	3.76	0.27	10.88	10.5	6	29	65	0	27				1.00	Aug-15
250	9.80	35.00	15.02	56.22	52.33	0	1.1	15.25	1.17	8.06	52.3	2	98	0	0	50	29.32	-15.7	5.00		Sep-07
250	9.60	34.52	14.09	52.81	46.72	0	1.85	15.3	1.17	6.39	52.3	2	98	0	0	50	28.7	-15.98			Sep-07
	9.98	35.24	15.40	57.47	54.39	0	0.85	15.33	1.17	8.48	52.3	2	98	0	0	50	29.44	-15.63			Sep-07
	3.89	16.43	-4.76	31.79	15.78	1.2	1.25	13.37	1.16	22.39	1,458	3	97	0	0	69	18.51	-23.67			Apr-04
	5.91	25.04	10.48	78.92	95.11	0	0.76	14.31	1.02	22.57	2,384	1	99	0	0	53	29.41	-15.39			Oct-97
50	1.59	17.01	2.00	38.82	13.17	0.66	1.14	14.63	1	13.34	242.2	2	98	0	0	63	23.21	-32.3			Sep-08
50	1.45	16.75	1.62	37.05	11.07	0.67	1.51	14.63	1	13.24	242.2	2	98	0	0	63	23.11	-32.42			Sep-08
50	1.36	12.67	0.38	33.10	11.86	1.6	1.18	14.21	1	11.11	232.0	1	99	0	0	30					Oct-13
50	1.18	12.39	-0.04	31.52	9.71	1.23	1.55	14.2	1	11.06	232.0	1	99	0	0	30					Oct-13
	1.36	12.66	0.47	33.22	11.96	1.6	1.16	14.26	1	11.12	232.0	1	99	0	0	30					Apr-18
50	0.62	11.86	0.07	38.76		2.02	1.1	14.44	1.02	11.22	10.1	3	97	0	0	61					May-15
50	0.53	11.76	-0.23	37.56		1.75	1.4	14.42	1.02	11.21	10.1	3	97	0	0	61					May-15
50	0.61	15.09	0.74	29.90	6.79	1.61	1.15	14.42	1	11.51	98.8	2	98	0	0	61	21.63	-27.02			May-10
50	0.61	14.96	0.44	28.47	5.28	1.28	1.53	14.43	1	11.52	98.8	2	98	0	0	61	21.4	-27.16			May-10
50	2.66	10.74	2.57	24.01	-1.86	1.9	1.07	14.32	0.96	17.73	8,366	1	99	0	0	16	18.86	-23.09			Jul-94
50	2.64	10.61	2.35	23.12	-3.08	1.63	1.32	14.31	0.96	18.23	8,366	1	99	0	0	16	18.65	-23.21			Jan-97
	2.66	10.74	2.57	24.01	-1.88	1.9	1.07	14.32	0.96	17.73	8,366	1	99	0	0	16	18.86	-23.09			Jan-15
50	5.27	13.40	5.61			1.93	0.95			9.98	37.1	2	98	0	0	97					Sep-17
50	5.17	13.18	5.32			1.71	1.2			9.96	37.1	2	98	0	0	97					Sep-17
50	3.07	12.58	5.41	28.26		1.71	0.9	8.3	0.7	10.38	49.6	5	64	31	0	120					May-16
50	2.97	12.47	5.16	27.25		1.44	1.2	8.3	0.7	10.37	49.6	5	64	31	0	120					May-16
50	4.74	19.50	8.89	46.42	46.57	0.42	1.05	11.02	0.94	13.91	71.6	3	97	0	0	34					Dec-13
50	4.66	19.41	8.64	45.14	44.42	0.17	1.35	11.02	0.94	13.9	71.6	3	97	0	0	34					Dec-13
50	4.47	14.20	9.67	43.12	64.96	5.01	0.96	9.42	0.45	15.27	6,725	4	96	0	0	49	6.99	-9.84			Dec-09
50	4.48	14.13	9.39	42.08	62.95	4.78	1.21	9.44	0.45	15.29	6,725	4	96	0	0	49	6.81	-10.09			Dec-09
50	4.27	19.63	8.01	36.92		0.38	1	11.35	0.96	1.95	3.1	2	98	0	0	46					Aug-14
50	4.30	19.75	7.83	36.04		0.17	1.3	11.23	0.96	1.94	3.1	2	98	0	0	46					Aug-14
	5.88	21.87	9.38	55.37	31.73	3.09	0	12.11	1.02	17.84	171.4	4	87	10	0	35	19.05	-16.93			Apr-04
50	6.46	20.30					0.85			12.03	3.6	6	94	0	0	0					Dec-18
50	6.28	20.00					1.1			12	3.6	6	94	0	0	0					Dec-18
50	1.04	12.00	-2.71	24.12		3.34	0.9	11.54	1.03	9.7	2.4	1	99	0	0	72					May-15
50	1.04	11.89	-2.93	23.17		3.07	1.2	11.52	1.02	9.69	2.4	1	99	0	0	72					May-15

	MARKET		FUND TYPE, CATEGORY & OBJECTIVE		RATINGS				MINIMUMS	
Fund Name	Ticker Symbol	Traded On	Fund Type	Category and (Prospectus Objective)	Overall Rating	Reward Rating	Risk Rating	Recent Up/ Downgrade	Open to New Investors	Min Initial Investment
Lazard Intl Equity Concentrated Portfolio Inst Shares	LCNIX	NAS CM	Open End	Global Equity Large Cap (World Stock)	C	C-	B-		Y	100,000
Lazard Intl Equity Concentrated Portfolio Open Shares	LCNOX	NAS CM	Open End	Global Equity Large Cap (World Stock)	C	C-	B-		Y	2,500
Lazard International Equity Portfolio Institutional Shares	LZIEX	NAS CM	Open End	Global Equity Large Cap (Foreign Stock)	C	C-	B		Y	100,000
Lazard International Equity Portfolio Open Shares	LZIOX	NAS CM	Open End	Global Equity Large Cap (Foreign Stock)	C	C-	B		Y	2,500
Lazard International Equity Portfolio R6 Shares	RLIEX	NAS CM	Open End	Global Equity Large Cap (Foreign Stock)	C	C-	B		Y	1,000,000
Lazard Intl Equity Select Portfolio Inst Shares	LZSIX	NAS CM	Open End	Global Equity Large Cap (Foreign Stock)	C	C	B-		Y	100,000
Lazard International Equity Select Portfolio Open Shares	LZESX	NAS CM	Open End	Global Equity Large Cap (Foreign Stock)	C	C	B-		Y	2,500
Lazard Intl Equity Value Portfolio Inst Shares	IEVIX	NAS CM	Open End	Global Equity Large Cap (Growth)	U	U	U		Y	100,000
Lazard International Equity Value Portfolio Open Shares	IEVOX	NAS CM	Open End	Global Equity Large Cap (Growth)	U	U	U		Y	2,500
Lazard Intl Small Cap Equity Portfolio Inst Shares	LZISX	NAS CM	Open End	Global Equity Mid/Small Cap (Foreign Stock)	C-	C-	C		Y	100,000
Lazard Intl Small Cap Equity Portfolio Open Shares	LZSMX	NAS CM	Open End	Global Equity Mid/Small Cap (Foreign Stock)	C-	C-	C		Y	2,500
Lazard Intl Strategic Equity Portfolio Inst Shares	LISIX	NAS CM	Open End	Global Equity Large Cap (Growth)	C+	C	B	Up	Y	100,000
Lazard Intl Strategic Equity Portfolio Open Shares	LISOX	NAS CM	Open End	Global Equity Large Cap (Growth)	C+	C	B	Up	Y	2,500
Lazard International Strategic Equity Portfolio R6 Shares	RLITX	NAS CM	Open End	Global Equity Large Cap (Growth)	C+	C	B	Up	Y	1,000,000
Lazard Managed Equity Volatility Portfolio Inst Shares	MEVIX	NAS CM	Open End	Global Equity Large Cap (Growth & Income)	B-	C	B+		Y	100,000
Lazard Managed Equity Volatility Portfolio Open Shares	MEVOX	NAS CM	Open End	Global Equity Large Cap (Growth & Income)	B-	C	B+		Y	2,500
Lazard Opportunistic Strategies Portfolio Inst Shares	LCAIX	NAS CM	Open End	Moderate Alloc (Growth)	C	C	B		Y	100,000
Lazard Opportunistic Strategies Portfolio Open Shares	LCAOX	NAS CM	Open End	Moderate Alloc (Growth)	C	C	B		Y	2,500
Lazard Real Assets & Pricing Opp Portfolio Inst Shares	RALIX	NAS CM	Open End	Moderate Alloc (Growth)	C	C	B		Y	100,000
Lazard Real Assets & Pricing Opp Portfolio Open Shares	RALOX	NAS CM	Open End	Moderate Alloc (Growth)	C	C	B		Y	2,500
Lazard US Equity Concentrated Portfolio Inst Shares	LEVIX	NAS CM	Open End	US Equity Large Cap Blend (Growth)	B-	C	B	Down	Y	100,000
Lazard US Equity Concentrated Portfolio Open Shares	LEVOX	NAS CM	Open End	US Equity Large Cap Blend (Growth)	B-	C	B	Down	Y	2,500
Lazard US Equity Concentrated Portfolio R6 Shares	RLUEX	NAS CM	Open End	US Equity Large Cap Blend (Growth)	B-	C	B	Down	Y	1,000,000
Lazard US Equity Select Portfolio Institutional Shares	LZUSX	NAS CM	Open End	US Equity Large Cap Blend (Growth)	B-	C+	B	Down	Y	100,000
Lazard US Equity Select Portfolio Open Shares	LZUOX	NAS CM	Open End	US Equity Large Cap Blend (Growth)	B-	C+	B	Down	Y	2,500
Lazard US Equity Select Portfolio R6 Shares	RLUSX	NAS CM	Open End	US Equity Large Cap Blend (Growth)	B-	C+	B	Down	Y	1,000,000
Lazard US Realty Equity Portfolio Institutional Shares	LREIX	NAS CM	Open End	Real Estate Sector Equity (Real Estate)	C+	C	B-	Down	Y	100,000
Lazard US Realty Equity Portfolio Open Shares	LREOX	NAS CM	Open End	Real Estate Sector Equity (Real Estate)	C+	C	B-	Down	Y	2,500
Lazard US Small-Mid Cap Equity Portfolio Inst Shares	LZSCX	NAS CM	Open End	US Equity Small Cap (Growth)	C	C	C+		Y	100,000
Lazard US Small-Mid Cap Equity Portfolio Open Shares	LZCOX	NAS CM	Open End	US Equity Small Cap (Growth)	C	C	C+		Y	2,500
Lazard World Dividend & Income Fund Inc	LOR	NYSE	Closed End	Global Equity Large Cap (World Stock)	C-	C	C-	Down	Y	
Leigh Baldwin Total Return Fund	LEBOX	NAS CM	Open End	Long/Short Equity (Growth & Income)	C-	C-	C		Y	1,000
Leland Real Asset Opportunities Fund Class A	GHTAX	NAS CM	Open End	Aggressive Alloc (Income)	D+	D+	C-	Down	Y	2,500
Leland Real Asset Opportunities Fund Class C	GHTCX	NAS CM	Open End	Aggressive Alloc (Income)	D+	D	C-	Down	Y	2,500
Leland Real Asset Opportunities Fund Class I	GHTIX	NAS CM	Open End	Aggressive Alloc (Income)	D+	D+	C-	Down	Y	250,000
Leland Thomson Reuters Private Equity Buyout Index Cls A	LDPAX	NAS CM	Open End	US Equity Large Cap Blend (Growth)	C	C	C+		Y	2,500
Leland Thomson Reuters Private Equity Buyout Index Cls C	LDPCX	NAS CM	Open End	US Equity Large Cap Blend (Growth)	C	C	C+		Y	2,500
Leland Thomson Reuters Private Equity Buyout Index Cls I	LDPIX	NAS CM	Open End	US Equity Large Cap Blend (Growth)	C	C	C+		Y	250,000
Leland Thomson Reuters Venture Capital Index Fund Class A	LDVAX	NAS CM	Open End	US Equity Large Cap Growth (Growth)	C+	C+	C+	Down	Y	2,500
Leland Thomson Reuters Venture Capital Index Fund Class C	LDVCX	NAS CM	Open End	US Equity Large Cap Growth (Growth)	C+	C+	C+	Down	Y	2,500
Leland Thomson Reuters Venture Capital Index Fund Class I	LDVIX	NAS CM	Open End	US Equity Large Cap Growth (Growth)	C+	C+	C+	Down	Y	250,000
Leuthold Core Investment Fund Class Institutional	LCRIX	NAS CM	Open End	Moderate Alloc (Growth & Income)	C	C	B		Y	1,000,000
Leuthold Core Investment Fund Retail Class	LCORX	NAS CM	Open End	Moderate Alloc (Growth & Income)	C	C	B		Y	10,000
Leuthold Global Fund Class Institutional	GLBIX	NAS CM	Open End	Moderate Alloc (Growth & Income)	C-	C-	C		Y	1,000,000
Leuthold Global Fund Class Retail	GLBLX	NAS CM	Open End	Moderate Alloc (Growth & Income)	C-	C-	C		Y	10,000
Leuthold Global Industries Fund Institutional Class	LGIIX	NAS CM	Open End	Global Equity Large Cap (World Stock)	C	C-	C		Y	1,000,000
Leuthold Global Industries Fund Retail Class	LGINX	NAS CM	Open End	Global Equity Large Cap (World Stock)	C	C-	C	Up	Y	10,000
Leuthold Select Industries Fund	LSLTX	NAS CM	Open End	US Equity Mid Cap (Growth)	C	C	B-		Y	10,000
Liberty All-Star Equity	USA	NYSE	Closed End	US Equity Large Cap Blend (Growth & Income)	C+	C	C+		Y	
Liberty All-Star Growth	ASG	NYSE	Closed End	US Equity Mid Cap (Growth)	C+	B-	C+	Down	Y	
Linde Hansen Contrarian Value Fund Class A Shares	LHVAX	NAS CM	Open End	US Equity Mid Cap (Growth & Income)	D+	D	C	Down	Y	2,500
Linde Hansen Contrarian Value Fund Class I Shares	LHVIX	NAS CM	Open End	US Equity Mid Cap (Growth & Income)	D+	D	C	Down	Y	10,000

★ Expanded analysis of this fund is included in Section II.

Min Additional Investment	TOTAL RETURNS 3-Month Total Return	6-Month Total Return	1-Year Total Return	3-Year Total Return	5-Year Total Return	PERFORMANCE Dividend Yield (TTM)	Expense Ratio	3-Yr Std Deviation	3-Year Beta	ASSETS NAV	Total Assets (MIL)	ASSET ALLOCATION & TURNOVER %Cash	%Stocks	%Bonds	%Other	Turnover Ratio	BULL & BEAR Last Bull Market Total Return	Last Bear Market Total Return	FEES Front End Fee (%)	Back End Fee (%)	Inception Date
50	4.45	18.69	2.81	22.06		1.67	0.95	12.77	1.05	9.84	87.5	9	91	0	0	76					Aug-14
50	4.34	18.41	2.55	20.88		1.46	1.25	12.74	1.05	9.84	87.5	9	91	0	0	76					Aug-14
50	5.10	16.22	2.60	21.61	9.59	2.22	0.81	10.39	0.89	18.12	2,879	5	95	0	0	36	18.72	-19.62			Oct-91
50	4.98	16.03	2.30	20.62	8.10	1.98	1.06	10.39	0.89	18.31	2,879	5	95	0	0	36	18.47	-19.69			Jan-97
	5.05	16.18	2.56	21.52	9.64	2.23	0.8	10.37	0.89	18.09	2,879	5	95	0	0	36	18.72	-19.62			Apr-15
50	4.78	15.74	1.84	24.34	8.54	2.41	1.06	11.22	0.94	10.51	92.6	5	95	0	0	32	18.7	-19.83			May-01
50	4.66	15.44	1.46	23.14	6.80	1.79	1.36	11.28	0.95	10.54	92.6	5	95	0	0	32	18.64	-20.04			May-01
50	1.32	9.00					0.95			9.93	25.3	9	91	0	0	37					Oct-18
50	1.22	8.90					1.2			9.91	25.3	9	91	0	0	37					Oct-18
50	3.36	15.31	-11.66	15.90	13.30	2.38	1.08	14.04	1.09	11.37	57.6	2	98	0	0	59	16.34	-19.95			Dec-93
50	3.26	15.06	-11.95	15.00	11.78	2.09	1.34	14.06	1.09	11.38	57.6	2	98	0	0	59	16.15	-20.08			Feb-97
50	3.54	15.88	3.29	29.35	14.75	1.3	0.81	11.29	0.95	14.88	6,405	4	96	0	0	40	19.14	-21.78			Oct-05
50	3.51	15.82	3.06	28.37	13.30	1.06	1.06	11.28	0.95	15	6,405	4	96	0	0	40	19	-21.92			Feb-06
	3.54	15.95	3.35	29.40	14.52	1.29	0.81	11.26	0.95	14.9	6,405	4	96	0	0	40	19.14	-21.78			Jan-15
50	2.70	15.74	8.47	31.84		1.35	0.75	9.25	0.78	12.13	25.4	3	96	0	0	122					May-15
50	2.71	15.66	8.15	30.59		1.09	1.05	9.32	0.79	12.11	25.4	3	96	0	0	122					May-15
50	1.78	11.73	-0.49	20.41	17.57	0.44	1.39	9.32	0.79	9.71	88.9	17	63	20	0	227	12.39	-12.74			Mar-08
50	1.79	11.56	-0.71	19.45	15.43	0.18	1.69	9.39	0.8	9.65	88.9	17	63	20	0	227	12.18	-12.97			Mar-08
50	2.05	10.93	3.52			2.38	0.92			10.4	17.9	3	74	22	0	72					Dec-16
50	1.89	10.82	3.17			2.15	1.17			10.38	17.9	3	74	22	0	72					Jan-17
50	5.16	22.69	11.35	40.17	65.52	1.19	0.76	12.54	0.97	15.68	1,292	5	95	0	0	69	25.44	-20.23			Sep-05
50	5.05	22.51	11.02	39.02	63.04	0.96	1.04	12.54	0.97	15.78	1,292	5	95	0	0	69	25.08	-20.32			Sep-05
	5.15	22.71	11.36	40.13	65.47	1.17	0.76	12.57	0.97	15.72	1,292	5	95	0	0	69	25.44	-20.23			Nov-16
50	4.74	19.74	11.63	49.59	51.64	2.15	0.75	11.69	0.95	12.13	78.9	1	99	0	0	62	22.41	-17			Dec-04
50	4.64	19.54	11.24	48.33	49.42	1.89	1.05	11.67	0.94	12.17	78.9	1	99	0	0	62	22.26	-17.18			Dec-04
	4.74	19.72	11.62	49.70	52.03	2.14	0.75	11.69	0.95	12.14	78.9	1	99	0	0	62	22.41	-17			May-14
50	2.28	21.11	11.06	16.75	43.48	1.55	1	12.17	0.9	20.13	65.7	1	99	0	0	52	40.97	-19.31			Sep-11
50	2.22	20.95	10.74	15.82	41.50	1.3	1.29	12.14	0.89	20.2	65.7	1	99	0	0	52	40.73	-19.31			Dec-08
50	6.21	22.76	1.18	42.40	41.14	0.27	0.87	15.39	0.97	13.16	141.3	4	96	0	0	81	28.77	-29.13			Oct-91
50	6.19	22.55	0.91	41.28	39.11	0.02	1.18	15.34	0.96	12.17	141.3	4	96	0	0	81	28.52	-29.21			Jan-97
	2.18	13.96	1.64	23.15	-8.38	6.59	0	13.15	1.08	10.9	75.0	5	87	8	0	56	19.96	-21.36			Jun-05
100	0.57	0.99	1.20	0.34	-5.30	1.19	1.05	1.37	0.04	6.87	2.3	13	79	0	8	687	2.76	-6.26			Aug-08
250	-2.90	11.18	-5.65	6.34	-14.48	3.35	1.86	13.59	0.81	7.83	14.8	8	92	0	0	61			5.75		Sep-13
250	-3.15	10.80	-6.37	3.90	-17.73	2.71	2.61	13.57	0.81	7.8	14.8	8	92	0	0	61				1.00	Sep-13
10,000	-2.91	11.24	-5.53	7.00	-13.53	3.67	1.61	13.57	0.81	7.67	14.8	8	92	0	0	61					Sep-13
250	4.37	22.14	7.03	46.79		0	1.76	18.88	0.98	12.41	20.4	-139	104	0	135	38			5.75		Sep-15
250	4.18	21.75	6.26	43.39		0	2.51	18.86	0.98	12.2	20.4	-139	104	0	135	38				1.00	Sep-15
10,000	4.42	22.28	7.33	47.89		0	1.51	18.85	0.98	12.51	20.4	-139	104	0	135	38					Sep-15
100	4.53	35.21	13.14	144.67		0	1.76	23.57	0.97	19.12	117.9	-164	99	0	165	47			5.75		Oct-14
250	4.32	34.71	12.29	139.33		0	2.51	23.52	0.96	18.59	117.9	-164	99	0	165	47				1.00	Sep-15
10,000	4.56	35.27	13.37	146.06		0	1.51	23.57	0.97	19.25	117.9	-164	99	0	165	47					Oct-14
100	2.25	7.03	1.49	22.07	21.94	0.41	1.32	6.72	0.5	18.57	657.4	32	48	17	3	79	10.31	-15.34			Jan-06
100	2.23	6.99	1.42	21.74	21.32	0.35	1.43	6.71	0.49	18.54	657.4	32	48	17	3	79	10.24	-15.39			Nov-95
100	1.00	6.39	-3.06	12.76	4.40	0.21	1.55	7.29	0.52	8.24	61.3	31	50	16	3	79	9.92	-14.31			Apr-08
100	0.94	6.22	-3.36	11.94	3.23	0.07	1.8	7.28	0.52	8.12	61.3	31	50	16	3	79	9.81	-14.32			Jul-08
100	0.28	13.55	-6.18	20.89	7.25	1.48	1.25	13.8	1.04	13.5811	3.2	1	99	0	0	101	17.63	-24.65			May-10
100	0.20	13.47	-6.42	19.98	5.97	1.12	1.5	13.8	1.03	13.5021	3.2	1	99	0	0	101	17.42	-24.71			May-10
100	3.63	16.57	2.12	38.05	37.18	0	1.5	13.41	1.04	24.55	13.0	1	99	0	0	104	21.41	-25.31			Jun-00
	4.30	19.85	8.92	48.93	48.36	7.51	1.01	12.67	1.02	6.66	1,312	3	97	0	0	22	25.67	-21.97			Oct-86
	4.44	28.43	10.42	67.35	73.33	5.7	0	14.56	1.08	6.04	224.1	2	98	0	0	49	24.13	-18.83			Mar-86
250	-2.71	8.25	-6.27	4.04	0.32	0.45	1.4	13.42	0.96	12.2	34.6	22	78	0	0	38			5.25		Feb-12
1,000	-2.60	8.42	-6.00	4.92	1.63	0.71	1.15	13.44	0.96	12.36	34.6	22	78	0	0	38					Feb-12

Fund Name	Ticker Symbol	Traded On	Fund Type	Category and (Prospectus Objective)	Overall Rating	Reward Rating	Risk Rating	Recent Up/ Downgrade	Open to New Investors	Min Initial Investment
		MARKET		FUND TYPE, CATEGORY & OBJECTIVE	RATINGS				MINIMUMS	
Lisanti Small Cap Growth Fund	ASCGX	NAS CM	Open End	US Equity Small Cap (Small Company)	C+	C+	C+		Y	2,000
Litman Gregory Masters Alternative Strategies Inst Cls	MASFX	NAS CM	Open End	Multialternative (Growth & Income)	B-	C	B	Up	Y	100,000
Litman Gregory Masters Alternative Strategies Investor Cls	MASNX	NAS CM	Open End	Multialternative (Growth & Income)	C+	C	B		Y	1,000
Litman Gregory Masters Equity Fund Institutional Class	MSEFX	NAS CM	Open End	US Equity Large Cap Growth (Growth)	C+	C	B	Up	Y	10,000
Litman Gregory Masters Equity Fund Investor Class	MSENX	NAS CM	Open End	US Equity Large Cap Growth (Growth)	C+	C	B	Up	Y	1,000
Litman Gregory Masters High Income Alternative Inst Cls	MAHIX	NAS CM	Open End	Cautious Alloc (Growth & Income)	U	U	U		Y	100,000
Litman Gregory Masters High Income Alternative Inv Cls	MAHNX	NAS CM	Open End	Cautious Alloc (Growth & Income)	U	U	U		Y	1,000
Litman Gregory Masters International Institutional Cls	MSILX	NAS CM	Open End	Global Equity Large Cap (Foreign Stock)	C	C-	C+	Up	Y	10,000
Litman Gregory Masters International Fund Investor Class	MNILX	NAS CM	Open End	Global Equity Large Cap (Foreign Stock)	C	D+	C+	Up	Y	1,000
Litman Gregory Masters Smaller Companies Institutional Cls	MSSFX	NAS CM	Open End	US Equity Small Cap (Small Company)	C+	C	B	Up	Y	10,000
Live Oak Health Sciences Fund	LOGSX	NAS CM	Open End	Healthcare Sector Equity (Health)	C-	C-	C	Down	Y	2,000
LK Balanced Fund Institutional Class Shares	LKBLX	NAS CM	Open End	Moderate Alloc (Balanced)	B-	C+	B+	Down	Y	50,000
LKCM Aquinas Catholic Equity Fund	AQEIX	NAS CM	Open End	US Equity Large Cap Blend (Growth)	C+	C	B-	Down	Y	2,000
LKCM Balanced Fund	LKBAX	NAS CM	Open End	Moderate Alloc (Balanced)	B	C+	A-		Y	2,000
LKCM Equity Fund Institutional Class	LKEQX	NAS CM	Open End	US Equity Large Cap Growth (Growth)	B-	C	B	Down	Y	2,000
LKCM Small Capital Equity Fund Class Institutional	LKSCX	NAS CM	Open End	US Equity Small Cap (Small Company)	C+	C	C+		Y	2,000
LKCM Small-Mid Cap Equity Fund Institutional Class	LKSMX	NAS CM	Open End	US Equity Mid Cap (Growth)	C+	C	C+		Y	2,000
LMCG Global MultiCap Fund Institutional Shares	GMCIX	NAS CM	Open End	Global Equity Large Cap (Growth)	C+	C	B	Up	Y	100,000
LMCG Global MultiCap Fund Investor Shares	GMCRX	NAS CM	Open End	Global Equity Large Cap (Growth)	C+	C	B	Up	Y	2,500
LMCG International Small Cap Fund Institutional Shares	ISMIX	NAS CM	Open End	Global Equity Mid/Small Cap (Growth)	C	C-	C	Up	Y	100,000
LMCG International Small Cap Fund Investor shares	ISMRX	NAS CM	Open End	Global Equity Mid/Small Cap (Growth)	C	C-	C	Up	Y	2,500
LMP Capital and Income Fund Inc	SCD	NYSE	Closed End	Aggressive Alloc (Growth & Income)	C	C	C-		Y	
LoCorr Dynamic Equity Fund Class A	LEQAX	NAS CM	Open End	Long/Short Equity (Growth)	C+	C	B	Up	Y	2,500
LoCorr Dynamic Equity Fund Class C	LEQCX	NAS CM	Open End	Long/Short Equity (Growth)	C	C-	B-		Y	2,500
LoCorr Dynamic Equity Fund Class I	LEQIX	NAS CM	Open End	Long/Short Equity (Growth)	C+	C	B	Up	Y	100,000
LoCorr Long/Short Commodity Strategies Fund Class A	LCSAX	NAS CM	Open End	Alternative Miscellaneous (Growth)	C+	C+	C+		Y	2,500
LoCorr Long/Short Commodity Strategies Fund Class I	LCSIX	NAS CM	Open End	Alternative Miscellaneous (Growth)	C+	C+	C+		Y	100,000
LoCorr Long/Short Commodity Strategies Fund ClassC	LCSCX	NAS CM	Open End	Alternative Miscellaneous (Growth)	C+	C+	C+	Up	Y	2,500
LoCorr Macro Strategies Fund Class A	LFMAX	NAS CM	Open End	Alternative Miscellaneous (Growth)	C	C	C+	Up	Y	2,500
LoCorr Macro Strategies Fund Class C	LFMCX	NAS CM	Open End	Alternative Miscellaneous (Growth)	C	D+	C	Up	Y	2,500
LoCorr Macro Strategies Fund Class I	LFMIX	NAS CM	Open End	Alternative Miscellaneous (Growth)	C	C	C+	Up	Y	100,000
LoCorr Market Trend Fund Class A	LOTAX	NAS CM	Open End	Alternative Miscellaneous (Growth)	D+	D	C-	Up	Y	2,500
LoCorr Market Trend Fund Class C	LOTCX	NAS CM	Open End	Alternative Miscellaneous (Growth)	D	D	C-		Y	2,500
LoCorr Market Trend Fund Class I	LOTIX	NAS CM	Open End	Alternative Miscellaneous (Growth)	D+	D	C-	Up	Y	100,000
LoCorr Spectrum Income Fund Class A	LSPAX	NAS CM	Open End	Aggressive Alloc (Income)	C	C	C+		Y	2,500
LoCorr Spectrum Income Fund Class C	LSPCX	NAS CM	Open End	Aggressive Alloc (Income)	C	C	C		Y	2,500
LoCorr Spectrum Income Fund Class I	LSPIX	NAS CM	Open End	Aggressive Alloc (Income)	C	C	B-		Y	100,000
Logan Capital Large Cap Growth Fund Institutional Class	LGNGX	NAS CM	Open End	US Equity Large Cap Growth (Growth)	B-	B-	B-		Y	100,000
Logan Capital Large Cap Growth Fund Investor Class	LGNHX	NAS CM	Open End	US Equity Large Cap Growth (Growth)	B-	B-	B-		Y	5,000
Longboard Alternative Growth Fund Class A	LONAX	NAS CM	Open End	Long/Short Equity (Growth)	C	C	C	Up	Y	2,500
Longboard Alternative Growth Fund Class I	LONGX	NAS CM	Open End	Long/Short Equity (Growth)	C	C	C	Up	Y	100,000
Longboard Managed Futures Strategy Fund Class A Shares	WAVEX	NAS CM	Open End	Alternative Miscellaneous (Growth & Income)	D	D	D		Y	2,500
Longboard Managed Futures Strategy Fund Class I Shares	WAVIX	NAS CM	Open End	Alternative Miscellaneous (Growth & Income)	D	D	D		Y	10,000
Longleaf Partners Fund	LLPFX	NAS CM	Open End	US Equity Large Cap Value (Growth)	D+	D	C-	Down	Y	10,000
Longleaf Partners Global Fund	LLGLX	NAS CM	Open End	Global Equity Large Cap (World Stock)	C	C-	C		Y	10,000
Longleaf Partners International Fund	LLINX	NAS CM	Open End	Global Equity Large Cap (Foreign Stock)	B-	C	B+		Y	10,000
Longleaf Partners Small-Cap Fund	LLSCX	NAS CM	Open End	US Equity Mid Cap (Small Company)	C	C-	B-			10,000
Loomis Sayles Global Allocation Fund Class A	LGMAX	NAS CM	Open End	Moderate Alloc (Multi-Asset Global)	B	C+	B+	Up	Y	2,500
Loomis Sayles Global Allocation Fund Class C	LGMCX	NAS CM	Open End	Moderate Alloc (Multi-Asset Global)	B-	C	B+	Up	Y	2,500
Loomis Sayles Global Allocation Fund Class N	LGMNX	NAS CM	Open End	Moderate Alloc (Multi-Asset Global)	B	C+	B+	Up	Y	1,000,000
Loomis Sayles Global Allocation Fund Class Y	LSWWX	NAS CM	Open End	Moderate Alloc (Multi-Asset Global)	B	C+	B+	Up	Y	100,000
Loomis Sayles Global Growth Fund Class A	LSAGX	NAS CM	Open End	Global Equity Large Cap (Growth)	B-	B-	B	Up	Y	2,500

★ Expanded analysis of this fund is included in Section II.

	TOTAL RETURNS					PERFORMANCE				ASSETS		ASSET ALLOCATION & TURNOVER					BULL & BEAR		FEES		
Min Additional Investment	3-Month Total Return	6-Month Total Return	1-Year Total Return	3-Year Total Return	5-Year Total Return	Dividend Yield (TTM)	Expense Ratio	3-Yr Std Deviation	3-Year Beta	NAV	Total Assets (MIL)	%Cash	%Stocks	%Bonds	%Other	Turnover Ratio	Last Bull Market Total Return	Last Bear Market Total Return	Front End Fee (%)	Back End Fee (%)	Inception Date
250	6.24	26.68	7.90	85.49	77.26	0	1.35	17.65	0.96	22.12	45.1	8	92	0	0	220	28.34	-26.35			Feb-04
250	1.83	5.94	3.92	13.30	14.93	3.27	1.54	2.86	11.78	11.59	1,887	8	24	67	0	197	7.91				Sep-11
100	1.76	5.80	3.65	12.44	13.44	3.02	1.79	2.82	11.93	11.6	1,887	8	24	67	0	197	7.84				Sep-11
250	4.43	20.14	4.45	45.30	47.05	0	1.17	14.05	1.08	17.89	296.8	8	92	0	0	42	20.12	-19.88			Dec-96
100	9.62	14.27	7.13	43.00	55.49	0	1.4	12.7	1.08		292.2	8	92	0	0	42	19.84	-19.88			Apr-09
250	1.51	5.81					1.7			10.01	90.5	17	12	68	2	126					Sep-18
100	1.45	5.69					1.96			10.01	90.5	17	12	68	2	126					Sep-18
250	2.10	17.65	-5.04	23.76	-2.54	0.63	1.09	14.41	1.2	16.46	390.0	2	98	0	0	35	13.36	-26.29			Dec-97
100	11.33	11.74	-4.01	18.19	2.76	0.32	1.32	13.13	1.14		406.0	2	98	0	0	35	13.15	-26.36			Apr-09
250	3.58	22.52	3.04	42.15	14.81	0	1.38	15.34	0.85	25.73	30.9	14	86	0	0	75	33.39	-24.67			Jun-03
25	-0.46	5.44	0.89	10.40	33.29	0.69	1.01	14.77	1.02	17.05	49.6	0	100	0	0	23	14.44	-10.35			Jun-01
500	5.57	15.45	9.06	34.24	26.73	1.55	1.01	8.94	0.69	50.19	29.6	5	67	28	0	10	14.66	-16.84			Jun-12
500	6.13	24.23	8.44	50.31	41.81	0.38	1	13.79	1.1	15.74	46.1	1	99	0	0	14	24.27	-19.71			Jul-05
1,000	4.43	15.67	10.56	35.16	42.36	1.05	0.8	8.13	0.66	24.08	100.7	2	68	30	0	17	18.98	-10.62			Dec-97
1,000	4.10	20.63	9.87	51.25	53.24	0.71	0.81	12.62	1.01	27.89	361.1	3	97	0	0	16	25.81	-16.35			Jan-96
1,000	3.93	20.73	1.91	45.81	32.98	0	1	17.55	1	17.18	189.1	3	97	0	0	45	25.79	-20.4			Jul-94
1,000	5.13	25.70	6.73	48.25	34.48	0	1	16.34	1.02	9.83	13.0	3	97	0	0	56	23.02				May-11
	2.31	15.26	0.78	37.01	29.98	1.3	0.71	12.88	1.11	11.5	1.5	2	98	0	0	61					Sep-13
100	2.22	14.99	0.50	36.09	28.72	1.12	0.96	12.86	1.11	11.51	1.5	2	98	0	0	61					Sep-13
	2.28	12.64	-7.16	25.54	26.59	2.65	0.86	12.36	0.98	11.17	45.0	2	98	0	0	90	12.74	-21			Apr-16
100	2.19	12.61	-7.33	24.59	25.05	2.43	1.11	12.34	0.98	11.15	45.0	2	98	0	0	90	12.57	-21.08			Apr-16
	5.05	24.64	14.86	24.04	12.20	2.77	0	14.43		14.86	267.2	0	90	0	2	26	20.34	-13.32			Feb-04
500	5.04	14.17	3.46	20.79	14.27	0	2.46	10.54	0.62	11.25	27.4	37	62	0	1	449			5.75		May-13
500	4.79	13.66	2.66	18.07	10.08	0	3.21	10.5	0.62	10.7	27.4	37	62	0	1	449				1.00	May-13
500	5.04	14.24	3.67	21.73	15.75	0	2.21	10.49	0.62	11.44	27.4	37	62	0	1	449					May-13
500	0.10	0.10	8.14	12.87	58.58	12.35	2.71	8.23	18.59	9.89	319.4	3	0	80	16	92			5.75		Dec-11
500	0.19	0.29	8.43	13.80	60.76	12.36	2.46	8.22	18.55	10.03	319.4	3	0	80	16	92					Dec-11
500	-0.10	-0.31	7.32	10.27	52.58	12.1	3.46	8.18	18.11	9.5	319.4	3	0	80	16	92				1.00	Dec-11
500	4.41	6.77	6.87	-0.42	20.12	1.13	2.25	7.87	52.8	8.51	605.9	6	1	92	1	105	-6.79	-7.17	5.75		Mar-11
500	4.10	6.28	5.95	-2.69	15.75	0.31	3	7.78	52.28	8.12	605.9	6	1	92	1	105	-7.23	-7.46		1.00	Mar-11
500	4.46	6.92	7.11	0.34	21.82	1.41	2	7.86	53.47	8.65	605.9	6	1	92	1	105	-6.57	-7.08			Mar-11
500	7.25	11.16	5.13	-12.20	13.29	0	2	12.16	62.26	10.65	262.2	7	1	92	0	91			5.75		Jun-14
500	7.03	10.82	4.33	-14.15	9.11	0	2.75	12.16	63.02	10.34	262.2	7	1	92	0	91				1.00	Jun-14
500	7.18	11.29	5.29	-11.56	14.64	0	1.75	12.19	62.28	10.74	262.2	7	1	92	0	91					Jun-14
500	0.23	13.90	1.29	11.13	-5.58	8.11	3.54	12.24	0.17	6.86	76.1	17	68	13	0	82			5.75		Dec-13
500	0.03	13.47	0.71	8.79	-8.98	7.02	4.29	12.28	0.16	6.93	76.1	17	68	13	0	82				1.00	Dec-13
500	0.31	13.96	1.63	12.14	-4.19	8.47	3.29	12.23	0.18	6.85	76.1	17	68	13	0	82					Dec-13
50	5.13	29.99	10.06	72.81	82.15	0	1.24	16.08	1.16	25.57	35.8	0	100	0	0	8					Jun-12
50	5.06	29.81	9.78	71.76	80.02	0	1.49	16.07	1.16	25.12	35.8	0	100	0	0	8					Jun-12
250	6.19	7.48	-1.39	22.20		2.69	2.24	12.8	0.46	10.62	11.4	176	0	0	-76	0			5.75		Dec-15
2,500	6.45	7.87	-0.95	23.54		2.87	1.99	12.79	0.46	10.55	11.4	176	0	0	-76	0					Mar-15
250	0.76	-11.37	-14.15	-14.71	2.17	0	3.12	13.83	52.8	9.19	143.2	88	12	0	0	0			5.75		Mar-13
2,500	0.86	-11.19	-13.85	-14.01	3.51	0	2.88	13.84	54.06	9.36	143.2	88	12	0	0	0					Jun-12
0	-2.87	8.96	-11.46	17.96	-0.59	1.99	0.97	15.28	1.11	19.94	1,962	6	94	0	0	37	22.63	-20.66			Apr-87
0	0.15	13.20	-5.11	44.46	11.62	0.93	1.2	15.12	1.14	12.69	287.4	5	95	0	0	29					Dec-12
0	0.75	13.96	5.40	48.74	13.91	0	1.15	12.98	1.01	17.3	1,317	4	96	0	0	46	7.14	-24.47			Oct-98
0	-1.10	9.72	-5.16	23.47	29.83	2.79	0.92	12.62	0.66	24.15	3,419	22	73	4	0	32	18.84	-16.72			Feb-89
50	5.77	18.79	8.71	41.67	42.42	0.66	1.16	9.28	0.79	23.64	2,939	4	67	28	0	22	19.89	-16.57	5.75		Feb-06
50	5.56	18.34	7.90	38.54	37.13	0.01	1.91	9.3	0.79	23.35	2,939	4	67	28	0	22	19.33	-16.81		1.00	Feb-06
	5.87	19.01	9.10	42.92	44.36	0.96	0.83	9.32	0.79	23.78	2,939	4	67	28	0	22	20.04	-16.46			Feb-17
50	5.82	19.00	9.00	42.78	44.22	0.89	0.91	9.31	0.79	23.79	2,939	4	67	28	0	22	20.04	-16.46			May-96
50	5.20	24.55	13.15	57.60		0.34	1.25	13.55	1.14	14.56	66.7	2	98	0	0	24			5.75		Mar-16

	MARKET			FUND TYPE, CATEGORY & OBJECTIVE	RATINGS				MINIMUMS	
Fund Name	Ticker Symbol	Traded On	Fund Type	Category and (Prospectus Objective)	Overall Rating	Reward Rating	Risk Rating	Recent Up/ Downgrade	Open to New Investors	Min Initial Investment
Loomis Sayles Global Growth Fund Class C	**LSCGX**	NAS CM	Open End	Global Equity Large Cap (Growth)	**B-**	B-	B	Up	Y	2,500
Loomis Sayles Global Growth Fund Class N	**LSNGX**	NAS CM	Open End	Global Equity Large Cap (Growth)	**C+**	C	B		Y	1,000,000
Loomis Sayles Global Growth Fund Class Y	**LSGGX**	NAS CM	Open End	Global Equity Large Cap (Growth)	**B-**	B-	B	Up	Y	100,000
Loomis Sayles Growth Fund Class A	**LGRRX**	NAS CM	Open End	US Equity Large Cap Growth (Growth)	**B-**	C+	B	Down	Y	2,500
Loomis Sayles Growth Fund Class C	**LGRCX**	NAS CM	Open End	US Equity Large Cap Growth (Growth)	**B-**	C+	B	Down	Y	2,500
Loomis Sayles Growth Fund Class N	**LGRNX**	NAS CM	Open End	US Equity Large Cap Growth (Growth)	**B-**	C+	B	Down	Y	1,000,000
Loomis Sayles Growth Fund Class Y	**LSGRX**	NAS CM	Open End	US Equity Large Cap Growth (Growth)	**B-**	C+	B	Down	Y	100,000
Loomis Sayles Multi-Asset Income Fund Class A	**IIDPX**	NAS CM	Open End	Moderate Alloc (Growth & Income)	**C**	C	B		Y	2,500
Loomis Sayles Multi-Asset Income Fund Class C	**CIDPX**	NAS CM	Open End	Moderate Alloc (Growth & Income)	**C**	C-	B-		Y	2,500
Loomis Sayles Multi-Asset Income Fund Class N	**LMINX**	NAS CM	Open End	Moderate Alloc (Growth & Income)	**C+**	C	B	Up	Y	1,000,000
Loomis Sayles Multi-Asset Income Fund Class Y	**YIDPX**	NAS CM	Open End	Moderate Alloc (Growth & Income)	**C+**	C	B	Up	Y	100,000
Loomis Sayles Small Cap Growth Fund Class N	**LSSNX**	NAS CM	Open End	US Equity Small Cap (Small Company)	**C+**	C	B-	Down		1,000,000
Loomis Sayles Small Cap Growth Fund Institutional Class	**LSSIX**	NAS CM	Open End	US Equity Small Cap (Small Company)	**C+**	C	B-	Down		100,000
Loomis Sayles Small Cap Growth Fund Retail Class	**LCGRX**	NAS CM	Open End	US Equity Small Cap (Small Company)	**C+**	C	B-			2,500
Loomis Sayles Small Cap Value Fund Class N	**LSCNX**	NAS CM	Open End	US Equity Small Cap (Small Company)	**C**	C	C+			1,000,000
Loomis Sayles Small Capital Value Fund Admin Class	**LSVAX**	NAS CM	Open End	US Equity Small Cap (Small Company)	**C**	C	C+			0
Loomis Sayles Small Capital Value Fund Institutional Class	**LSSCX**	NAS CM	Open End	US Equity Small Cap (Small Company)	**C**	C	C+			100,000
Loomis Sayles Small Capital Value Fund Retail Class	**LSCRX**	NAS CM	Open End	US Equity Small Cap (Small Company)	**C**	C	C+			2,500
Loomis Sayles Small/Mid Cap Growth Institutional Cls	**LSMIX**	NAS CM	Open End	US Equity Mid Cap (Growth)	**C+**	C	C+		Y	1,000,000
Lord Abbett Affiliated Fund Class A	**LAFFX**	NAS CM	Open End	US Equity Large Cap Value (Growth & Income)	**B-**	C	B	Up	Y	1,000
Lord Abbett Affiliated Fund Class C	**LAFCX**	NAS CM	Open End	US Equity Large Cap Value (Growth & Income)	**B-**	C	B	Up	Y	1,000
Lord Abbett Affiliated Fund Class F	**LAAFX**	NAS CM	Open End	US Equity Large Cap Value (Growth & Income)	**B-**	C	B+	Up	Y	0
Lord Abbett Affiliated Fund Class F3	**LTFOX**	NAS CM	Open End	US Equity Large Cap Value (Growth & Income)	**B-**	C	B+		Y	0
Lord Abbett Affiliated Fund Class I	**LAFYX**	NAS CM	Open End	US Equity Large Cap Value (Growth & Income)	**B-**	C	B+	Up	Y	1,000,000
Lord Abbett Affiliated Fund Class P	**LAFPX**	NAS CM	Open End	US Equity Large Cap Value (Growth & Income)	**B-**	C	B	Up		0
Lord Abbett Affiliated Fund Class R2	**LAFQX**	NAS CM	Open End	US Equity Large Cap Value (Growth & Income)	**B-**	C	B	Up	Y	0
Lord Abbett Affiliated Fund Class R3	**LAFRX**	NAS CM	Open End	US Equity Large Cap Value (Growth & Income)	**B-**	C	B	Up	Y	0
Lord Abbett Affiliated Fund Class R4	**LAFSX**	NAS CM	Open End	US Equity Large Cap Value (Growth & Income)	**B-**	C	B	Up	Y	0
Lord Abbett Affiliated Fund Class R5	**LAFTX**	NAS CM	Open End	US Equity Large Cap Value (Growth & Income)	**B-**	C	B+	Up	Y	0
Lord Abbett Affiliated Fund Class R6	**LAFVX**	NAS CM	Open End	US Equity Large Cap Value (Growth & Income)	**B-**	C	B+		Y	0
Lord Abbett Alpha Strategy Fund Class A	**ALFAX**	NAS CM	Open End	US Equity Small Cap (Growth)	**C+**	C	C+		Y	1,500
Lord Abbett Alpha Strategy Fund Class C	**ALFCX**	NAS CM	Open End	US Equity Small Cap (Growth)	**C+**	C	C+	Up	Y	1,500
Lord Abbett Alpha Strategy Fund Class F	**ALFFX**	NAS CM	Open End	US Equity Small Cap (Growth)	**C+**	C	C+		Y	0
Lord Abbett Alpha Strategy Fund Class F3	**ALFOX**	NAS CM	Open End	US Equity Small Cap (Growth)	**C+**	C	C+		Y	0
Lord Abbett Alpha Strategy Fund Class I	**ALFYX**	NAS CM	Open End	US Equity Small Cap (Growth)	**C+**	C	C+		Y	1,000,000
Lord Abbett Alpha Strategy Fund Class R2	**ALFQX**	NAS CM	Open End	US Equity Small Cap (Growth)	**C+**	C	C+	Up	Y	0
Lord Abbett Alpha Strategy Fund Class R3	**ALFRX**	NAS CM	Open End	US Equity Small Cap (Growth)	**C+**	C	C+	Up	Y	0
Lord Abbett Alpha Strategy Fund Class R4	**ALFKX**	NAS CM	Open End	US Equity Small Cap (Growth)	**C+**	C	C+		Y	0
Lord Abbett Alpha Strategy Fund Class R5	**ALFTX**	NAS CM	Open End	US Equity Small Cap (Growth)	**C+**	C	C+		Y	0
Lord Abbett Alpha Strategy Fund Class R6	**ALFVX**	NAS CM	Open End	US Equity Small Cap (Growth)	**C+**	C	C+		Y	0
Lord Abbett Calibrated Dividend Growth Fund Class A	**LAMAX**	NAS CM	Open End	US Equity Large Cap Blend (Growth & Income)	**B-**	C+	B+	Down	Y	1,000
Lord Abbett Calibrated Dividend Growth Fund Class C	**LAMCX**	NAS CM	Open End	US Equity Large Cap Blend (Growth & Income)	**B-**	C+	B		Y	1,000
Lord Abbett Calibrated Dividend Growth Fund Class F	**LAMFX**	NAS CM	Open End	US Equity Large Cap Blend (Growth & Income)	**B-**	C+	B+	Down	Y	0
Lord Abbett Calibrated Dividend Growth Fund Class F3	**LRMAX**	NAS CM	Open End	US Equity Large Cap Blend (Growth & Income)	**B-**	C+	B+	Down	Y	0
Lord Abbett Calibrated Dividend Growth Fund Class I	**LAMYX**	NAS CM	Open End	US Equity Large Cap Blend (Growth & Income)	**B-**	C+	B+	Down	Y	1,000,000
Lord Abbett Calibrated Dividend Growth Fund Class P	**LAMPX**	NAS CM	Open End	US Equity Large Cap Blend (Growth & Income)	**B-**	C+	B+	Down		0
Lord Abbett Calibrated Dividend Growth Fund Class R2	**LAMQX**	NAS CM	Open End	US Equity Large Cap Blend (Growth & Income)	**B-**	C+	B+	Down	Y	0
Lord Abbett Calibrated Dividend Growth Fund Class R3	**LAMRX**	NAS CM	Open End	US Equity Large Cap Blend (Growth & Income)	**B-**	C+	B+	Down	Y	0
Lord Abbett Calibrated Dividend Growth Fund Class R4	**LAMSX**	NAS CM	Open End	US Equity Large Cap Blend (Growth & Income)	**B-**	C+	B+	Down	Y	0
Lord Abbett Calibrated Dividend Growth Fund Class R5	**LAMTX**	NAS CM	Open End	US Equity Large Cap Blend (Growth & Income)	**B-**	C+	B+	Down	Y	0
Lord Abbett Calibrated Dividend Growth Fund Class R6	**LAMHX**	NAS CM	Open End	US Equity Large Cap Blend (Growth & Income)	**B-**	C+	B+	Down	Y	0
Lord Abbett Convertible Fund Class A	**LACFX**	NAS CM	Open End	Convertibles (Convertible Bond)	**B-**	C+	B+	Down	Y	1,500

★Expanded analysis of this fund is included in Section II.

	TOTAL RETURNS					PERFORMANCE				ASSETS		ASSET ALLOCATION & TURNOVER					BULL & BEAR		FEES		
Min Additional Investment	3-Month Total Return	6-Month Total Return	1-Year Total Return	3-Year Total Return	5-Year Total Return	Dividend Yield (TTM)	Expense Ratio	3-Yr Std Deviation	3-Year Beta	NAV	Total Assets (MIL)	%Cash	%Stocks	%Bonds	%Other	Turnover Ratio	Last Bull Market Total Return	Last Bear Market Total Return	Front End Fee (%)	Back End Fee (%)	Inception Date
50	4.98	24.11	12.24	53.85		0.01	2	13.6	1.15	14.31	66.7	2	98	0	0	24				1.00	Mar-16
	5.25	24.76	13.45	58.95		0.59	0.95	13.57	1.15	14.61	66.7	2	98	0	0	24					Mar-17
50	5.33	24.76	13.40	58.83		0.55	1	13.53	1.14	14.61	66.7	2	98	0	0	24					Mar-16
50	5.10	22.68	15.13	63.47	93.66	0.32	0.9	14.09	1	16.28	8,854	1	99	0	0	11	20.4	-12.95	5.75		Dec-96
50	4.89	22.13	14.24	59.81	86.47	0	1.65	14.07	1	14.79	8,854	1	99	0	0	11	19.83	-13.18		1.00	Sep-03
	5.19	22.83	15.48	65.16	96.80	0.6	0.58	14.12	1	17.43	8,854	1	99	0	0	11	20.6	-12.85			Feb-13
50	5.18	22.81	15.43	64.71	95.99	0.52	0.65	14.09	1	17.44	8,854	1	99	0	0	11	20.6	-12.85			May-91
50	1.98	9.85	1.52	16.34	24.16	3.86	1	7.46	-0.02	12.59	106.9	3	45	42	0	282	15.83	-7.45	4.25		Nov-05
50	1.80	9.41	0.76	13.71	19.53	3.13	1.75	7.47	-0.02	12.53	106.9	3	45	42	0	282	15.41	-7.76		1.00	Nov-05
	2.16	10.00	1.85	17.51	25.59	4.19	0.7	7.47	-0.02	12.51	106.9	3	45	42	0	282	15.83	-7.45			Aug-15
50	2.07	9.97	1.80	17.25	25.70	4.14	0.75	7.48	-0.03	12.51	106.9	3	45	42	0	282	15.83	-7.45			Dec-12
	5.62	23.13	6.59	70.76	70.95	0	0.82	16.18	0.9	28	1,610	5	95	0	0	41	26.16	-22.45			Feb-13
50	5.58	23.09	6.45	70.18	69.98	0	0.94	16.15	0.9	27.77	1,610	5	95	0	0	41	26.16	-22.45			Dec-96
50	5.50	22.93	6.15	68.91	67.83	0	1.19	16.16	0.9	25.3	1,610	5	95	0	0	41	25.89	-22.47			Dec-96
	3.72	19.57	-2.02	32.61	34.79	0.33	0.86	16.79	0.95	28.71	770.2	1	99	0	0	19	29.96	-23.86			Feb-13
	3.60	19.25	-2.56	30.40	31.07	0	1.43	16.79	0.95	26.75	770.2	1	99	0	0	19	29.55	-24			Jan-98
50	3.72	19.58	-2.06	32.35	34.39	0.25	0.93	16.78	0.95	28.7	770.2	1	99	0	0	19	29.96	-23.86			May-91
50	3.68	19.42	-2.32	31.38	32.70	0	1.18	16.81	0.95	28.16	770.2	1	99	0	0	19	29.72	-23.91			Dec-96
50,000	7.28	28.18	8.28	68.50		0	0.85	14.37	0.84	10.46	26.6	3	97	0	0	102					Jun-15
	3.81	15.70	8.24	38.89	45.93	2.02	0.71	12.08	0.99	14.95	6,252	0	100	0	0	62	25.6	-24.11	5.75		Jan-50
	3.67	15.28	7.45	35.84	40.65	1.31	1.46	12.12	1	15.01	6,252	0	100	0	0	62	25.09	-24.38		1.00	Aug-96
	3.84	15.78	8.53	39.57	47.14	2.16	0.56	12.08	0.99	14.96	6,252	0	100	0	0	62	25.75	-24.07			Sep-07
	3.85	15.80	8.68	39.95	47.05	2.26	0.39	12.08	0.99	15.07	6,252	0	100	0	0	62	25.6	-24.11			Apr-17
	3.85	15.85	8.53	39.90	47.72	2.24	0.46	12.09	0.99	15.02	6,252	0	100	0	0	62	25.98	-24.11			Mar-98
	3.76	15.53	8.02	38.54	45.64	1.83	0.91	12.1	0.99	14.92	6,252	0	100	0	0	62	25.54	-24.16			Nov-97
	3.72	15.49	7.93	37.55	43.52	1.71	1.06	12.07	0.99	14.97	6,252	0	100	0	0	62	25.38	-24.23			Sep-07
	3.74	15.55	8.10	38.01	44.33	1.79	0.96	12.1	0.99	14.95	6,252	0	100	0	0	62	25.56	-24.24			Sep-07
	3.81	15.72	8.24	38.93	45.98	2.02	0.71	12.09	0.99	14.93	6,252	0	100	0	0	62	25.6	-24.11			Jun-15
	3.85	15.84	8.54	39.99	47.47	2.24	0.46	12.05	0.99	15.03	6,252	0	100	0	0	62	25.6	-24.11			Jun-15
	3.85	15.82	8.62	40.25	47.86	2.26	0.39	12.11	0.99	15.06	6,252	0	100	0	0	62	25.6	-24.11			Jun-15
	3.61	21.09	0.92	45.94	40.52	0.94	1.52	15.17	0.85	24.63	973.7	0	100	0	0	8	26.38	-25.35	5.75		Mar-98
	3.41	20.65	0.17	42.73	35.38	0.14	2.27	15.18	0.85	20.27	973.7	0	100	0	0	8	25.84	-25.55		1.00	Mar-98
	3.63	21.21	1.06	46.62	41.57	1.08	1.37	15.18	0.85	24.8	973.7	0	100	0	0	8	26.52	-25.31			Sep-07
	3.72	21.33	1.28	47.03	41.57	1.18	1.19	15.19	0.85	25.36	973.7	0	100	0	0	8	26.38	-25.35			Apr-17
	3.68	21.27	1.18	47.07	42.30	1.16	1.27	15.17	0.85	25.31	973.7	0	100	0	0	8	26.56	-25.24			Oct-04
	3.53	20.90	0.57	44.43	38.06	0.4	1.87	15.19	0.85	23.71	973.7	0	100	0	0	8	26.17	-25.45			Sep-07
	3.55	20.99	0.69	44.89	38.82	0.7	1.77	15.18	0.85	23.86	973.7	0	100	0	0	8	26.18	-25.42			Sep-07
	3.62	21.14	0.95	46.01	40.58	0.96	1.52	15.18	0.85	24.58	973.7	0	100	0	0	8	26.38	-25.35			Jun-15
	3.68	21.26	1.19	47.12	42.01	1.17	1.27	15.15	0.85	25.32	973.7	0	100	0	0	8	26.38	-25.35			Jun-15
	3.72	21.32	1.28	47.40	42.30	1.18	1.19	15.16	0.85	25.37	973.7	0	100	0	0	8	26.38	-25.35			Jun-15
	3.95	17.40	12.58	38.82	55.75	1.43	0.95	11.39	0.89	15.49	2,400	0	100	0	0	51	20.94	-16.02	5.75		Dec-01
	3.81	16.97	11.77	35.76	50.12	0.76	1.7	11.39	0.89	15.29	2,400	0	100	0	0	51	20.49	-16.24		1.00	Dec-01
	4.05	17.55	12.88	39.79	57.26	1.57	0.7	11.4	0.9	15.51	2,400	0	100	0	0	51	21.11	-15.92			Sep-07
	4.10	17.62	12.91	40.19	58.07	1.65	0.62	11.4	0.9	15.71	2,400	0	100	0	0	51	21.12	-15.86			Apr-17
	4.04	17.60	12.87	39.88	57.71	1.64	0.7	11.39	0.9	15.65	2,400	0	100	0	0	51	21.12	-15.86			Dec-01
	3.92	17.29	12.38	37.96	54.16	1.2	1.15	11.36	0.89	15.59	2,400	0	100	0	0	51	20.91	-16.03			Dec-01
	3.86	17.22	12.17	37.32	52.99	1.07	1.3	11.39	0.89	15.66	2,400	0	100	0	0	51	20.79	-16.12			Sep-07
	3.97	17.26	12.36	37.93	54.00	1.21	1.2	11.41	0.9	15.42	2,400	0	100	0	0	51	20.92	-16.11			Sep-07
	4.02	17.42	12.60	38.86	55.77	1.44	0.95	11.4	0.9	15.48	2,400	0	100	0	0	51	20.94	-15.95			Jun-15
	4.04	17.52	12.87	39.91	57.64	1.64	0.7	11.42	0.9	15.64	2,400	0	100	0	0	51	21.12	-15.86			Jun-15
	4.10	17.62	12.99	40.30	58.32	1.65	0.62	11.39	0.9	15.71	2,400	0	100	0	0	51	21.12	-15.86			Jun-15
	4.69	17.21	8.25	46.00	35.58	3.73	1.04	9.74	1.12	13.64	739.6	0	17	0	0	213	11.4	-17.34	2.25		Jun-03

	MARKET			FUND TYPE, CATEGORY & OBJECTIVE	RATINGS					MINIMUMS
Fund Name	Ticker Symbol	Traded On	Fund Type	Category and (Prospectus Objective)	Overall Rating	Reward Rating	Risk Rating	Recent Up/ Downgrade	Open to New Investors	Min Initial Investment
Lord Abbett Convertible Fund Class C	LACCX	NAS CM	Open End	Convertibles (Convertible Bond)	B-	C	B+		Y	1,500
Lord Abbett Convertible Fund Class F	LBFFX	NAS CM	Open End	Convertibles (Convertible Bond)	B-	C+	B+	Down	Y	0
Lord Abbett Convertible Fund Class F3	LOCFX	NAS CM	Open End	Convertibles (Convertible Bond)	B-	C+	B+	Down	Y	0
Lord Abbett Convertible Fund Class I	LCFYX	NAS CM	Open End	Convertibles (Convertible Bond)	B-	C	B+	Down	Y	1,000,000
Lord Abbett Convertible Fund Class P	LCFPX	NAS CM	Open End	Convertibles (Convertible Bond)	B-	C	B+	Down		0
Lord Abbett Convertible Fund Class R2	LBCQX	NAS CM	Open End	Convertibles (Convertible Bond)	B-	C	B+		Y	0
Lord Abbett Convertible Fund Class R3	LCFRX	NAS CM	Open End	Convertibles (Convertible Bond)	B-	C	B+	Down	Y	0
Lord Abbett Convertible Fund Class R4	LCFSX	NAS CM	Open End	Convertibles (Convertible Bond)	B-	C	B+	Down	Y	0
Lord Abbett Convertible Fund Class R5	LCFTX	NAS CM	Open End	Convertibles (Convertible Bond)	B-	C	B		Y	0
Lord Abbett Convertible Fund Class R6	LCFVX	NAS CM	Open End	Convertibles (Convertible Bond)	B-	C+	B+	Down	Y	0
Lord Abbett Developing Growth Fund Class A	LAGWX	NAS CM	Open End	US Equity Small Cap (Growth)	C+	C+	C+	Down		1,000
Lord Abbett Developing Growth Fund Class C	LADCX	NAS CM	Open End	US Equity Small Cap (Growth)	C+	C+	C+	Down		1,000
Lord Abbett Developing Growth Fund Class F	LADFX	NAS CM	Open End	US Equity Small Cap (Growth)	C+	C+	C+	Down		0
Lord Abbett Developing Growth Fund Class F3	LOGWX	NAS CM	Open End	US Equity Small Cap (Growth)	C+	C+	C+	Down	Y	0
Lord Abbett Developing Growth Fund Class I	LADYX	NAS CM	Open End	US Equity Small Cap (Growth)	C+	C+	C+	Down		1,000,000
Lord Abbett Developing Growth Fund Class P	LADPX	NAS CM	Open End	US Equity Small Cap (Growth)	C+	C+	C+	Down		0
Lord Abbett Developing Growth Fund Class R2	LADQX	NAS CM	Open End	US Equity Small Cap (Growth)	C+	C+	C+	Down		0
Lord Abbett Developing Growth Fund Class R3	LADRX	NAS CM	Open End	US Equity Small Cap (Growth)	C+	C+	C+	Down		0
Lord Abbett Developing Growth Fund Class R4	LADSX	NAS CM	Open End	US Equity Small Cap (Growth)	C+	C+	C+	Down		0
Lord Abbett Developing Growth Fund Class R5	LADTX	NAS CM	Open End	US Equity Small Cap (Growth)	C+	C+	C+	Down		0
Lord Abbett Developing Growth Fund Class R6	LADVX	NAS CM	Open End	US Equity Small Cap (Growth)	C+	C+	C+	Down		0
Lord Abbett Focused Growth Fund Class A	LFGAX	NAS CM	Open End	US Equity Large Cap Growth (Growth)	U	U	U		Y	1,500
Lord Abbett Focused Growth Fund Class C	LFGCX	NAS CM	Open End	US Equity Large Cap Growth (Growth)	U	U	U		Y	1,500
Lord Abbett Focused Growth Fund Class F	LFGFX	NAS CM	Open End	US Equity Large Cap Growth (Growth)	U	U	U		Y	0
Lord Abbett Focused Growth Fund Class F3	LFGOX	NAS CM	Open End	US Equity Large Cap Growth (Growth)	U	U	U		Y	0
Lord Abbett Focused Growth Fund Class I	LFGIX	NAS CM	Open End	US Equity Large Cap Growth (Growth)	U	U	U		Y	1,000,000
Lord Abbett Focused Growth Fund Class R3	LFGQX	NAS CM	Open End	US Equity Large Cap Growth (Growth)	U	U	U		Y	0
Lord Abbett Focused Growth Fund Class R4	LFGSX	NAS CM	Open End	US Equity Large Cap Growth (Growth)	U	U	U		Y	0
Lord Abbett Focused Growth Fund Class R5	LFGTX	NAS CM	Open End	US Equity Large Cap Growth (Growth)	U	U	U		Y	0
Lord Abbett Focused Growth Fund Class R6	LFGVX	NAS CM	Open End	US Equity Large Cap Growth (Growth)	U	U	U		Y	0
Lord Abbett Fundamental Equity Class R4	LAVSX	NAS CM	Open End	US Equity Large Cap Value (Growth)	B-	C	B	Up	Y	0
Lord Abbett Fundamental Equity Class R5	LAVTX	NAS CM	Open End	US Equity Large Cap Value (Growth)	B-	C	B	Up	Y	0
Lord Abbett Fundamental Equity Class R6	LAVVX	NAS CM	Open End	US Equity Large Cap Value (Growth)	B-	C	B	Up	Y	0
Lord Abbett Fundamental Equity Fund Class A	LDFVX	NAS CM	Open End	US Equity Large Cap Value (Growth)	B-	C	B	Up	Y	1,500
Lord Abbett Fundamental Equity Fund Class C	GILAX	NAS CM	Open End	US Equity Large Cap Value (Growth)	B-	C	B	Up	Y	1,500
Lord Abbett Fundamental Equity Fund Class F	LAVFX	NAS CM	Open End	US Equity Large Cap Value (Growth)	B-	C	B	Up	Y	0
Lord Abbett Fundamental Equity Fund Class F3	LDFOX	NAS CM	Open End	US Equity Large Cap Value (Growth)	B-	C	B	Up	Y	0
Lord Abbett Fundamental Equity Fund Class I	LAVYX	NAS CM	Open End	US Equity Large Cap Value (Growth)	B-	C	B	Up	Y	1,000,000
Lord Abbett Fundamental Equity Fund Class P	LAVPX	NAS CM	Open End	US Equity Large Cap Value (Growth)	B-	C	B	Up		0
Lord Abbett Fundamental Equity Fund Class R2	LAVQX	NAS CM	Open End	US Equity Large Cap Value (Growth)	B-	C	B	Up	Y	0
Lord Abbett Fundamental Equity Fund Class R3	LAVRX	NAS CM	Open End	US Equity Large Cap Value (Growth)	B-	C	B	Up	Y	0
Lord Abbett Global Equity Research Fund Class A	LGCAX	NAS CM	Open End	Global Equity Large Cap (World Stock)	C	C	B		Y	1,500
Lord Abbett Global Equity Research Fund Class C	LGCCX	NAS CM	Open End	Global Equity Large Cap (World Stock)	C	C-	B		Y	1,500
Lord Abbett Global Equity Research Fund Class F	LGCFX	NAS CM	Open End	Global Equity Large Cap (World Stock)	C	C	B		Y	0
Lord Abbett Global Equity Research Fund Class F3	LGCOX	NAS CM	Open End	Global Equity Large Cap (World Stock)	C	C	B	Up	Y	0
Lord Abbett Global Equity Research Fund Class I	LGCYX	NAS CM	Open End	Global Equity Large Cap (World Stock)	C	C	B		Y	1,000,000
Lord Abbett Global Equity Research Fund Class R2	LGCQX	NAS CM	Open End	Global Equity Large Cap (World Stock)	C	C	B		Y	0
Lord Abbett Global Equity Research Fund Class R3	LGCRX	NAS CM	Open End	Global Equity Large Cap (World Stock)	C	C	B		Y	0
Lord Abbett Global Equity Research Fund Class R4	LGCSX	NAS CM	Open End	Global Equity Large Cap (World Stock)	C	C	B		Y	0
Lord Abbett Global Equity Research Fund Class R5	LGCVX	NAS CM	Open End	Global Equity Large Cap (World Stock)	C	C	B		Y	0
Lord Abbett Global Equity Research Fund Class R6	LGCWX	NAS CM	Open End	Global Equity Large Cap (World Stock)	C	C	B		Y	0
Lord Abbett Global Select Equity Fund Class A	LGSAX	NAS CM	Open End	Global Equity Large Cap (Growth)	D-	D+	C+		Y	1,500

★ Expanded analysis of this fund is included in Section II.

	TOTAL RETURNS					PERFORMANCE				ASSETS		ASSET ALLOCATION & TURNOVER					BULL & BEAR		FEES		
Min Additional Investment	3-Month Total Return	6-Month Total Return	1-Year Total Return	3-Year Total Return	5-Year Total Return	Dividend Yield (TTM)	Expense Ratio	3-Yr Std Deviation	3-Year Beta	NAV	Total Assets (MIL)	%Cash	%Stocks	%Bonds	%Other	Turnover Ratio	Last Bull Market Total Return	Last Bear Market Total Return	Front End Fee (%)	Back End Fee (%)	Inception Date
	4.47	16.86	7.54	43.20	31.29	3.16	1.69	9.77	1.12	13.56	739.6	0	17	0	0	213	10.98	-17.54		1.00	Jun-03
	4.72	17.26	8.35	46.45	36.27	3.82	0.94	9.74	1.12	13.64	739.6	0	17	0	0	213	11.46	-17.29			Sep-07
	4.79	17.39	8.49	46.84	37.02	3.89	0.81	9.81	1.12	13.73	739.6	0	17	0	0	213	11.58	-17.34			Apr-17
	4.71	17.30	8.49	46.84	37.03	3.89	0.84	9.8	1.12	13.72	739.6	0	17	0	0	213	11.58	-17.34			Jun-03
	4.63	17.04	7.93	44.89	34.32	3.44	1.29	9.77	1.12	13.86	739.6	0	17	0	0	213	11.25	-17.44			Jun-03
	4.58	17.04	7.84	44.30	32.96	3.28	1.44	9.8	1.12	13.86	739.6	0	17	0	0	213	11.08	-17.45			Sep-07
	4.56	17.03	7.91	44.65	33.65	3.49	1.34	9.78	1.12	13.58	739.6	0	17	0	0	213	11.17	-17.43			Sep-07
	4.68	17.18	8.21	45.82	35.30	3.69	1.09	9.79	1.12	13.64	739.6	0	17	0	0	213	11.42	-17.42			Jun-15
	4.72	17.32	8.42	46.73	36.94	3.89	0.84	9.77	1.12	13.71	739.6	0	17	0	0	213	11.58	-17.34			Jun-15
	4.71	17.29	8.49	46.96	37.15	3.89	0.81	9.78	1.12	13.73	739.6	0	17	0	0	213	11.58	-17.34			Jun-15
	9.09	40.53	18.19	103.70	71.39	0	0.93	19.88	1.04	25.55	2,065	0	100	0	0	90	23.66	-23.64	5.75		Oct-73
	8.83	39.93	17.26	98.88	64.91	0	1.68	19.85	1.04	16.75	2,065	0	100	0	0	90	23.16	-23.87		1.00	Aug-96
	9.15	40.63	18.36	104.74	72.73	0	0.78	19.9	1.04	26.82	2,065	0	100	0	0	90	23.85	-23.59			Sep-07
	9.19	40.73	18.57	105.26	72.71	0	0.59	19.89	1.04	30.75	2,065	0	100	0	0	90	23.66	-23.64			Apr-17
	9.17	40.68	18.47	105.32	73.58	0	0.68	19.88	1.04	30.57	2,065	0	100	0	0	90	23.84	-23.53			Dec-97
	9.05	40.33	17.93	103.32	71.01	0	1.13	19.89	1.04	24.46	2,065	0	100	0	0	90	23.62	-23.64			Jan-98
	9.00	40.25	17.80	101.62	68.47	0	1.28	19.86	1.04	23.97	2,065	0	100	0	0	90	23.45	-23.73			Sep-07
	9.07	40.33	17.89	102.26	69.28	0	1.18	19.88	1.04	24.53	2,065	0	100	0	0	90	23.52	-23.69			Sep-07
	9.09	40.48	18.16	103.77	71.35	0	0.93	19.89	1.04	25.54	2,065	0	100	0	0	90	23.66	-23.64			Jun-15
	9.17	40.68	18.47	105.32	73.14	0	0.68	19.9	1.04	30.57	2,065	0	100	0	0	90	23.66	-23.64			Jun-15
	9.19	40.73	18.60	105.97	73.96	0	0.59	19.9	1.04	30.75	2,065	0	100	0	0	90	23.66	-23.64			Jun-15
	4.42						1.05			16.74	7.5	0	100	0	0				5.75		Jan-19
	4.24						1.8			16.69	7.5	0	100	0	0					1.00	Jan-19
	4.48						0.8			16.76	7.5	0	100	0	0						Jan-19
	4.55						0.73			16.77	7.5	0	100	0	0						Jan-19
	4.48						0.8			16.76	7.5	0	100	0	0						Jan-19
	4.36						1.3			16.73	7.5	0	100	0	0						Jan-19
	4.42						1.05			16.74	7.5	0	100	0	0						Jan-19
	4.48						0.8			16.76	7.5	0	100	0	0						Jan-19
	4.55						0.73			16.77	7.5	0	100	0	0						Jan-19
	2.26	14.43	7.00	32.35	35.80	1.36	0.96	12.32	1.01	12.21	2,533	0	100	0	0	92	24.43	-22.18			Jun-15
	2.23	14.44	7.19	33.34	37.10	1.58	0.71	12.23	1	12.36	2,533	0	100	0	0	92	24.43	-22.18			Jun-15
	2.30	14.57	7.35	33.69	37.71	1.58	0.62	12.29	1	12.42	2,533	0	100	0	0	92	24.43	-22.18			Jun-15
	2.16	14.35	6.94	32.24	36.61	1.33	0.96	12.26	1	12.27	2,533	0	100	0	0	92	24.85	-21.99	5.75		Jul-96
	1.97	13.86	6.14	29.29	31.70	0.45	1.71	12.31	1.01	10.84	2,533	0	100	0	0	92	24.44	-22.18		1.00	Jan-94
	2.27	14.42	7.19	32.92	37.76	1.5	0.81	12.29	1	12.14	2,533	0	100	0	0	92	24.97	-21.87			Sep-07
	2.22	14.48	7.35	32.46	34.93	1.59	0.62	12.28	1	12.41	2,533	0	100	0	0	92	24.43	-22.18			Apr-17
	2.23	14.55	7.27	33.30	38.43	1.57	0.71	12.32	1.01	12.36	2,533	0	100	0	0	92	25.07	-21.89			Mar-03
	2.12	14.13	6.69	31.42	35.28	1.1	1.16	12.26	1	12.03	2,533	0	100	0	0	92	24.79	-22.03			Aug-01
	2.12	14.17	6.56	30.87	34.31	0.74	1.31	12.3	1.01	12	2,533	0	100	0	0	92	24.55	-22			Sep-07
	2.12	14.23	6.66	31.25	34.97	1.08	1.21	12.28	1	12.04	2,533	0	100	0	0	92	24.64	-21.96			Sep-07
	2.46	16.49	3.51			0.73	0.9			11.23	7.5	0	100	0	0	108			5.75		Jan-17
	2.20	16.05	2.68			0.1	1.65			11.13	7.5	0	100	0	0	108				1.00	Jan-17
	2.46	16.59	3.63			0.83	0.75			11.24	7.5	0	100	0	0	108					Jan-17
	2.55	16.68	3.79			0.97	0.63			11.26	7.5	0	100	0	0	108					Apr-17
	2.45	16.70	3.75			0.93	0.65			11.25	7.5	0	100	0	0	108					Jan-17
	2.37	16.26	3.14			0.35	1.25			11.22	7.5	0	100	0	0	108					Jan-17
	2.38	16.35	3.19			0.84	1.15			11.17	7.5	0	100	0	0	108					Jan-17
	2.37	16.49	3.46			0.69	0.9			11.23	7.5	0	100	0	0	108					Jan-17
	2.45	16.70	3.75			0.93	0.65			11.25	7.5	0	100	0	0	108					Jan-17
	2.45	16.58	3.78			0.97	0.63			11.25	7.5	0	100	0	0	108					Jan-17
	2.57	13.80					1.05			14.76	2.6	0	100	0	0	23			5.75		Jul-18

	MARKET			FUND TYPE, CATEGORY & OBJECTIVE	RATINGS				MINIMUMS	
Fund Name	Ticker Symbol	Traded On	Fund Type	Category and (Prospectus Objective)	Overall Rating	Reward Rating	Risk Rating	Recent Up/ Downgrade	Open to New Investors	Min Initial Investment
Lord Abbett Global Select Equity Fund Class C	LGECX	NAS CM	Open End	Global Equity Large Cap (Growth)	D-	D+	C+		Y	1,500
Lord Abbett Global Select Equity Fund Class F	LGSFX	NAS CM	Open End	Global Equity Large Cap (Growth)	D-	D+	C+		Y	0
Lord Abbett Global Select Equity Fund Class F3	LGSOX	NAS CM	Open End	Global Equity Large Cap (Growth)	D-	D+	C+		Y	0
Lord Abbett Global Select Equity Fund Class I	LGSIX	NAS CM	Open End	Global Equity Large Cap (Growth)	D-	D+	C+		Y	1,000,000
Lord Abbett Global Select Equity Fund Class R3	LGSRX	NAS CM	Open End	Global Equity Large Cap (Growth)	D-	D+	C+		Y	0
Lord Abbett Global Select Equity Fund Class R4	LGSUX	NAS CM	Open End	Global Equity Large Cap (Growth)	D-	D+	C+		Y	0
Lord Abbett Global Select Equity Fund Class R5	LGSVX	NAS CM	Open End	Global Equity Large Cap (Growth)	D-	D+	C+		Y	0
Lord Abbett Global Select Equity Fund Class R6	LGSWX	NAS CM	Open End	Global Equity Large Cap (Growth)	D-	D+	C+		Y	0
Lord Abbett Growth Leaders Fund Class A	LGLAX	NAS CM	Open End	US Equity Large Cap Growth (Growth)	C+	C+	B-	Down	Y	1,500
Lord Abbett Growth Leaders Fund Class C	LGLCX	NAS CM	Open End	US Equity Large Cap Growth (Growth)	C+	C+	C+	Down	Y	1,500
Lord Abbett Growth Leaders Fund Class F	LGLFX	NAS CM	Open End	US Equity Large Cap Growth (Growth)	C+	C+	B-	Down	Y	0
Lord Abbett Growth Leaders Fund Class F3	LGLOX	NAS CM	Open End	US Equity Large Cap Growth (Growth)	C+	C+	B-	Down	Y	0
Lord Abbett Growth Leaders Fund Class I	LGLIX	NAS CM	Open End	US Equity Large Cap Growth (Growth)	C+	C+	B-	Down	Y	1,000,000
Lord Abbett Growth Leaders Fund Class R2	LGLQX	NAS CM	Open End	US Equity Large Cap Growth (Growth)	C+	C+	B-	Down	Y	0
Lord Abbett Growth Leaders Fund Class R3	LGLRX	NAS CM	Open End	US Equity Large Cap Growth (Growth)	C+	C+	B-	Down	Y	0
Lord Abbett Growth Leaders Fund Class R4	LGLSX	NAS CM	Open End	US Equity Large Cap Growth (Growth)	C+	C+	B-	Down	Y	0
Lord Abbett Growth Leaders Fund Class R5	LGLUX	NAS CM	Open End	US Equity Large Cap Growth (Growth)	C+	C+	B-	Down	Y	0
Lord Abbett Growth Leaders Fund Class R6	LGLVX	NAS CM	Open End	US Equity Large Cap Growth (Growth)	C+	C+	B-	Down	Y	0
Lord Abbett Growth Opportunities Fund Class A	LMGAX	NAS CM	Open End	US Equity Mid Cap (Growth)	B-	B-	B		Y	1,000
Lord Abbett Growth Opportunities Fund Class C	LMGCX	NAS CM	Open End	US Equity Mid Cap (Growth)	B-	C+	B		Y	1,000
Lord Abbett Growth Opportunities Fund Class F	LGOFX	NAS CM	Open End	US Equity Mid Cap (Growth)	B	B-	B	Up	Y	0
Lord Abbett Growth Opportunities Fund Class F3	LOMGX	NAS CM	Open End	US Equity Mid Cap (Growth)	B	B-	B	Up	Y	0
Lord Abbett Growth Opportunities Fund Class I	LMGYX	NAS CM	Open End	US Equity Mid Cap (Growth)	B	B-	B	Up	Y	1,000,000
Lord Abbett Growth Opportunities Fund Class P	LGOPX	NAS CM	Open End	US Equity Mid Cap (Growth)	B-	B-	B			0
Lord Abbett Growth Opportunities Fund Class R2	LGOQX	NAS CM	Open End	US Equity Mid Cap (Growth)	B-	C+	B		Y	0
Lord Abbett Growth Opportunities Fund Class R3	LGORX	NAS CM	Open End	US Equity Mid Cap (Growth)	B-	B-	B		Y	0
Lord Abbett Growth Opportunities Fund Class R4	LGOSX	NAS CM	Open End	US Equity Mid Cap (Growth)	B-	B-	B		Y	0
Lord Abbett Growth Opportunities Fund Class R5	LGOTX	NAS CM	Open End	US Equity Mid Cap (Growth)	B	B-	B	Up	Y	0
Lord Abbett Growth Opportunities Fund Class R6	LGOVX	NAS CM	Open End	US Equity Mid Cap (Growth)	B	B-	B	Up	Y	0
Lord Abbett International Equity Fund Class A	LICAX	NAS CM	Open End	Global Equity Large Cap (Foreign Stock)	C	C-	C+	Up	Y	1,500
Lord Abbett International Equity Fund Class C	LICCX	NAS CM	Open End	Global Equity Large Cap (Foreign Stock)	C	C-	C+	Up	Y	1,500
Lord Abbett International Equity Fund Class F	LICFX	NAS CM	Open End	Global Equity Large Cap (Foreign Stock)	C	C-	C+	Up	Y	0
Lord Abbett International Equity Fund Class F3	LICOX	NAS CM	Open End	Global Equity Large Cap (Foreign Stock)	C	C-	C+	Up	Y	0
Lord Abbett International Equity Fund Class I	LICYX	NAS CM	Open End	Global Equity Large Cap (Foreign Stock)	C	C-	C+	Up	Y	1,000,000
Lord Abbett International Equity Fund Class P	LICPX	NAS CM	Open End	Global Equity Large Cap (Foreign Stock)	C	C-	C+	Up		0
Lord Abbett International Equity Fund Class R2	LICQX	NAS CM	Open End	Global Equity Large Cap (Foreign Stock)	C	C-	C+	Up	Y	0
Lord Abbett International Equity Fund Class R3	LICRX	NAS CM	Open End	Global Equity Large Cap (Foreign Stock)	C	C-	C+	Up	Y	0
Lord Abbett International Equity Fund Class R4	LICSX	NAS CM	Open End	Global Equity Large Cap (Foreign Stock)	C	C-	C+	Up	Y	0
Lord Abbett International Equity Fund Class R5	LICTX	NAS CM	Open End	Global Equity Large Cap (Foreign Stock)	C	C-	C+	Up	Y	0
Lord Abbett International Equity Fund Class R6	LICVX	NAS CM	Open End	Global Equity Large Cap (Foreign Stock)	C	C-	C+	Up	Y	0
Lord Abbett International Opportunities Fund Clas R4	LINSX	NAS CM	Open End	Global Equity Mid/Small Cap (Foreign Stock)	C-	D+	C		Y	0
Lord Abbett International Opportunities Fund Clas R5	LINTX	NAS CM	Open End	Global Equity Mid/Small Cap (Foreign Stock)	C-	C-	C		Y	0
Lord Abbett International Opportunities Fund Clas R6	LINVX	NAS CM	Open End	Global Equity Mid/Small Cap (Foreign Stock)	C	C-	C	Up	Y	0
Lord Abbett International Opportunities Fund Class A	LAIEX	NAS CM	Open End	Global Equity Mid/Small Cap (Foreign Stock)	C-	D+	C		Y	1,500
Lord Abbett International Opportunities Fund Class C	LINCX	NAS CM	Open End	Global Equity Mid/Small Cap (Foreign Stock)	C-	D+	C		Y	1,500
Lord Abbett International Opportunities Fund Class F	LINFX	NAS CM	Open End	Global Equity Mid/Small Cap (Foreign Stock)	C-	D+	C		Y	0
Lord Abbett International Opportunities Fund Class F3	LOIEX	NAS CM	Open End	Global Equity Mid/Small Cap (Foreign Stock)	C	C-	C	Up	Y	0
Lord Abbett International Opportunities Fund Class I	LINYX	NAS CM	Open End	Global Equity Mid/Small Cap (Foreign Stock)	C-	C-	C		Y	1,000,000
Lord Abbett International Opportunities Fund Class P	LINPX	NAS CM	Open End	Global Equity Mid/Small Cap (Foreign Stock)	C-	D+	C			0
Lord Abbett International Opportunities Fund Class R2	LINQX	NAS CM	Open End	Global Equity Mid/Small Cap (Foreign Stock)	C-	D+	C		Y	0
Lord Abbett International Opportunities Fund Class R3	LINRX	NAS CM	Open End	Global Equity Mid/Small Cap (Foreign Stock)	C-	D+	C		Y	0
Lord Abbett International Value Fund Class A	LIDAX	NAS CM	Open End	Global Equity Large Cap (Equity-Income)	C	C-	C		Y	1,500

★ Expanded analysis of this fund is included in Section II.

	TOTAL RETURNS					PERFORMANCE				ASSETS		ASSET ALLOCATION & TURNOVER					BULL & BEAR		FEES		
Min Additional Investment	3-Month Total Return	6-Month Total Return	1-Year Total Return	3-Year Total Return	5-Year Total Return	Dividend Yield (TTM)	Expense Ratio	3-Yr Std Deviation	3-Year Beta	NAV	Total Assets (MIL)	%Cash	%Stocks	%Bonds	%Other	Turnover Ratio	Last Bull Market Total Return	Last Bear Market Total Return	Front End Fee (%)	Back End Fee (%)	Inception Date
	2.43	13.40					1.8			14.72	2.6	0	100	0	0	23				1.00	Jul-18
	2.63	13.94					0.8			14.79	2.6	0	100	0	0	23					Jul-18
	2.70	14.03					0.69			14.79	2.6	0	100	0	0	23					Jul-18
	2.63	13.95					0.8			14.78	2.6	0	100	0	0	23					Jul-18
	2.57	13.72					1.3			14.75	2.6	0	100	0	0	23					Jul-18
	2.64	13.87					1.05			14.77	2.6	0	100	0	0	23					Jul-18
	2.63	13.95					0.8			14.78	2.6	0	100	0	0	23					Jul-18
	2.70	14.03					0.69			14.79	2.6	0	100	0	0	23					Jul-18
	6.31	30.05	13.75	75.30	87.04	0	0.91	15.62	1.1	29.47	3,922	0	100	0	0	161	23.04		5.75		Jun-11
	6.09	29.52	12.83	71.39	80.20	0	1.66	15.61	1.1	27.33	3,922	0	100	0	0	161	22.62			1.00	Jun-11
	6.34	30.17	13.98	76.43	88.86	0	0.66	15.61	1.1	29.98	3,922	0	100	0	0	161	23.29				Jun-11
	6.39	30.18	14.07	76.83	89.68	0	0.6	15.62	1.1	30.28	3,922	0	100	0	0	161	23.41				Apr-17
	6.38	30.15	14.01	76.59	89.42	0	0.66	15.62	1.1	30.17	3,922	0	100	0	0	161	23.41				Jun-11
	6.22	29.77	13.31	73.45	83.78	0	1.26	15.61	1.1	29.03	3,922	0	100	0	0	161	23.29				Jun-11
	6.27	29.86	13.42	73.98	84.64	0	1.16	15.6	1.1	28.96	3,922	0	100	0	0	161	23.29				Jun-11
	6.31	29.99	13.70	75.20	86.99	0	0.91	15.62	1.1	29.47	3,922	0	100	0	0	161	23.23				Jun-15
	6.37	30.14	14.00	76.63	89.47	0	0.66	15.62	1.1	30.18	3,922	0	100	0	0	161	23.41				Jun-15
	6.39	30.23	14.07	76.95	89.98	0	0.6	15.62	1.1	30.28	3,922	0	100	0	0	161	23.41				Jun-15
	6.38	28.88	18.16	54.76	60.74	0	1.18	13.17	0.9	23.65	879.5	0	100	0	0	55	30.68	-27.57	5.75		Aug-95
	6.20	28.45	17.26	51.34	54.89	0	1.93	13.14	0.9	17.11	879.5	0	100	0	0	55	30.14	-27.76		1.00	Oct-98
	6.42	28.99	18.32	55.41	61.96	0	1.03	13.19	0.9	24.69	879.5	0	100	0	0	55	30.81	-27.48			Sep-07
	6.47	29.13	18.50	55.87	61.90	0	0.85	13.2	0.9	27.3	879.5	0	100	0	0	55	30.68	-27.57			Apr-17
	6.43	29.05	18.43	55.87	62.79	0	0.93	13.18	0.9	27.14	879.5	0	100	0	0	55	30.89	-27.46			Dec-98
	6.34	28.75	17.89	53.83	59.16	0	1.38	13.18	0.9	22.97	879.5	0	100	0	0	55	30.6	-27.58			Aug-00
	6.27	28.67	17.73	53.14	57.97	0	1.53	13.14	0.9	22.35	879.5	0	100	0	0	55	30.45	-27.61			Sep-07
	6.32	28.78	17.87	53.54	58.80	0	1.43	13.16	0.9	22.86	879.5	0	100	0	0	55	30.53	-27.61			Sep-07
	6.38	28.88	18.16	54.68	60.74	0	1.18	13.16	0.9	23.65	879.5	0	100	0	0	55	30.68	-27.57			Jun-15
	6.42	29.08	18.41	55.89	62.42	0	0.93	13.18	0.9	27.16	879.5	0	100	0	0	55	30.68	-27.57			Jun-15
	6.47	29.09	18.51	56.32	63.08	0	0.85	13.18	0.9	27.29	879.5	0	100	0	0	55	30.68	-27.57			Jun-15
	4.47	14.93	-0.34	23.49	-0.34	1.9	1.17	11.93	1.02	13.08	478.1	0	100	0	0	124	13.31	-23.48	5.75		Dec-03
	4.25	14.53	-1.07	20.75	-3.92	0.79	1.92	11.92	1.02	13	478.1	0	100	0	0	124	12.89	-23.69		1.00	Dec-03
	4.49	15.13	-0.08	24.42	0.86	2.08	0.96	11.94	1.02	13.01	478.1	0	100	0	0	124	13.5	-23.4			Sep-07
	4.50	15.15	-0.02	24.77	1.43	2.16	0.85	11.93	1.02	13.22	478.1	0	100	0	0	124	13.51	-23.29			Apr-17
	4.51	15.18	-0.03	24.75	1.41	2.15	0.86	11.94	1.02	13.2	478.1	0	100	0	0	124	13.51	-23.29			Dec-03
	4.38	14.82	-0.55	22.78	-1.27	1.65	1.37	11.93	1.02	13.09	478.1	0	100	0	0	124	13.18	-23.43			Dec-03
	4.30	14.74	-0.67	22.19	-1.99	1.41	1.52	11.95	1.02	13.07	478.1	0	100	0	0	124	13.19	-23.5			Sep-07
	4.37	14.79	-0.58	22.65	-1.44	1.65	1.42	11.93	1.02	12.88	478.1	0	100	0	0	124	13.29	-23.54			Sep-07
	4.41	15.01	-0.34	23.48	-0.18	1.97	1.17	11.93	1.02	13.02	478.1	0	100	0	0	124	13.35	-23.37			Jun-15
	4.53	15.14	-0.03	24.39	1.03	2.16	0.92	11.95	1.02	13.15	478.1	0	100	0	0	124	13.51	-23.29			Jun-15
	4.50	15.15	0.05	24.87	1.62	2.16	0.85	11.95	1.02	13.22	478.1	0	100	0	0	124	13.51	-23.29			Jun-15
	2.48	13.21	-9.01	22.01	14.50	1.03	1.2	13.1	1.02	15.68	613.9	0	98	0	2	81	19.37	-24.25			Jun-15
	2.59	13.35	-8.79	22.93	15.65	1.29	0.95	13.1	1.02	16.21	613.9	0	98	0	2	81	19.37	-24.25			Jun-15
	2.58	13.44	-8.65	23.30	16.23	1.29	0.87	13.06	1.02	16.29	613.9	0	98	0	2	81	19.37	-24.25			Jun-15
	2.53	13.22	-8.96	22.00	14.55	1	1.2	13.1	1.02	15.75	613.9	0	98	0	2	81	19.37	-24.25	5.75		Dec-96
	2.31	12.85	-9.63	19.39	10.35	0.03	1.95	13.1	1.02	14.57	613.9	0	98	0	2	81	18.92	-24.45		1.00	Jun-97
	2.50	13.30	-8.89	22.59	15.37	1.16	1.05	13.1	1.02	15.58	613.9	0	98	0	2	81	19.49	-24.2			Sep-07
	2.58	13.44	-8.65	22.84	15.33	1.29	0.87	13.09	1.02	16.29	613.9	0	98	0	2	81	19.37	-24.25			Apr-17
	2.59	13.42	-8.75	22.97	15.97	1.28	0.95	13.08	1.02	16.22	613.9	0	98	0	2	81	19.59	-24.17			Dec-97
	2.47	13.08	-9.17	21.28	13.37	0.55	1.4	13.12	1.02	16.16	613.9	0	98	0	2	81	19.24	-24.3			Mar-99
	2.38	13.00	-9.33	20.75	12.55	0.61	1.55	13.07	1.02	15.47	613.9	0	98	0	2	81	19.18	-24.35			Sep-07
	2.39	13.07	-9.22	21.16	13.21	0.99	1.45	13.09	1.02	15.39	613.9	0	98	0	2	81	19.26	-24.28			Sep-07
	2.17	9.94	-2.17	16.91	-9.30	3.5	1.12	11.18	0.92	6.87	605.3	0	100	0	0	74	12.66	-22.9	5.75		Jun-08

	MARKET			FUND TYPE, CATEGORY & OBJECTIVE	RATINGS				MINIMUMS	
Fund Name	Ticker Symbol	Traded On	Fund Type	Category and (Prospectus Objective)	Overall Rating	Reward Rating	Risk Rating	Recent Up/ Downgrade	Open to New Investors	Min Initial Investment
Lord Abbett International Value Fund Class C	LIDCX	NAS CM	Open End	Global Equity Large Cap (Equity-Income)	C-	D+	C		Y	1,500
Lord Abbett International Value Fund Class F	LIDFX	NAS CM	Open End	Global Equity Large Cap (Equity-Income)	C	C-	C+		Y	0
Lord Abbett International Value Fund Class F3	LIDOX	NAS CM	Open End	Global Equity Large Cap (Equity-Income)	C	C-	C+		Y	0
Lord Abbett International Value Fund Class I	LAIDX	NAS CM	Open End	Global Equity Large Cap (Equity-Income)	C	C-	C+		Y	1,000,000
Lord Abbett International Value Fund Class R2	LIDRX	NAS CM	Open End	Global Equity Large Cap (Equity-Income)	C	C-	C	Up	Y	0
Lord Abbett International Value Fund Class R3	LIRRX	NAS CM	Open End	Global Equity Large Cap (Equity-Income)	C	C-	C	Up	Y	0
Lord Abbett International Value Fund Class R4	LIRSX	NAS CM	Open End	Global Equity Large Cap (Equity-Income)	C	C-	C		Y	0
Lord Abbett International Value Fund Class R5	LIRTX	NAS CM	Open End	Global Equity Large Cap (Equity-Income)	C	C-	C+		Y	0
Lord Abbett International Value Fund Class R6	LIRVX	NAS CM	Open End	Global Equity Large Cap (Equity-Income)	C	C-	C+		Y	0
Lord Abbett Micro Cap Growth Fund Class I	LMIYX	NAS CM	Open End	US Equity Small Cap (Growth)	C+	C+	C+	Down	Y	1,000,000
Lord Abbett Micro Cap Value Fund Class I	LMVYX	NAS CM	Open End	US Equity Small Cap (Growth)	C	C-	C+		Y	1,000,000
Lord Abbett Mid Cap Stock Fund Class A	LAVLX	NAS CM	Open End	US Equity Mid Cap (Growth)	C	C-	B-		Y	1,000
Lord Abbett Mid Cap Stock Fund Class C	LMCCX	NAS CM	Open End	US Equity Mid Cap (Growth)	C	D+	B-		Y	1,000
Lord Abbett Mid Cap Stock Fund Class F	LMCFX	NAS CM	Open End	US Equity Mid Cap (Growth)	C	C-	B-		Y	0
Lord Abbett Mid Cap Stock Fund Class F3	LOVLX	NAS CM	Open End	US Equity Mid Cap (Growth)	C	C-	B-		Y	0
Lord Abbett Mid Cap Stock Fund Class I	LMCYX	NAS CM	Open End	US Equity Mid Cap (Growth)	C	C-	B-		Y	1,000,000
Lord Abbett Mid Cap Stock Fund Class P	LMCPX	NAS CM	Open End	US Equity Mid Cap (Growth)	C	C-	B-			0
Lord Abbett Mid Cap Stock Fund Class R2	LMCQX	NAS CM	Open End	US Equity Mid Cap (Growth)	C	C-	B-		Y	0
Lord Abbett Mid Cap Stock Fund Class R3	LMCRX	NAS CM	Open End	US Equity Mid Cap (Growth)	C	C-	B-		Y	0
Lord Abbett Mid Cap Stock Fund Class R4	LMCSX	NAS CM	Open End	US Equity Mid Cap (Growth)	C	C-	B-		Y	0
Lord Abbett Mid Cap Stock Fund Class R5	LMCTX	NAS CM	Open End	US Equity Mid Cap (Growth)	C	C-	B-		Y	0
Lord Abbett Mid Cap Stock Fund Class R6	LMCHX	NAS CM	Open End	US Equity Mid Cap (Growth)	C	C-	B-		Y	0
Lord Abbett Multi-Asset Balanced Opportunity Fund Class A	LABFX	NAS CM	Open End	Moderate Alloc (Growth & Income)	C+	C	B	Up	Y	1,500
Lord Abbett Multi-Asset Balanced Opportunity Fund Class C	BFLAX	NAS CM	Open End	Moderate Alloc (Growth & Income)	B-	C	B+	Up	Y	1,500
Lord Abbett Multi-Asset Balanced Opportunity Fund Class F	BLAFX	NAS CM	Open End	Moderate Alloc (Growth & Income)	B-	C	B+	Up	Y	0
Lord Abbett Multi-Asset Balanced Opportunity Fund Class F3	LOBFX	NAS CM	Open End	Moderate Alloc (Growth & Income)	B-	C	B	Up	Y	0
Lord Abbett Multi-Asset Balanced Opportunity Fund Class I	LABYX	NAS CM	Open End	Moderate Alloc (Growth & Income)	C+	C	B	Up	Y	1,000,000
Lord Abbett Multi-Asset Balanced Opportunity Fund Class P	LABPX	NAS CM	Open End	Moderate Alloc (Growth & Income)	C+	C	B	Up		0
Lord Abbett Multi-Asset Balanced Opportunity Fund Class R2	BLAQX	NAS CM	Open End	Moderate Alloc (Growth & Income)	B-	C	B+	Up	Y	0
Lord Abbett Multi-Asset Balanced Opportunity Fund Class R3	BLARX	NAS CM	Open End	Moderate Alloc (Growth & Income)	C+	C	B	Up	Y	0
Lord Abbett Multi-Asset Balanced Opportunity Fund Class R4	BLASX	NAS CM	Open End	Moderate Alloc (Growth & Income)	C+	C	B	Up	Y	0
Lord Abbett Multi-Asset Balanced Opportunity Fund Class R5	BLATX	NAS CM	Open End	Moderate Alloc (Growth & Income)	B-	C	B	Up	Y	0
Lord Abbett Multi-Asset Balanced Opportunity Fund Class R6	BLAVX	NAS CM	Open End	Moderate Alloc (Growth & Income)	B-	C	B	Up	Y	0
Lord Abbett Multi-Asset Income Fund Class A	ISFAX	NAS CM	Open End	Cautious Alloc (Equity-Income)	C+	C	B	Up	Y	1,500
Lord Abbett Multi-Asset Income Fund Class C	ISFCX	NAS CM	Open End	Cautious Alloc (Equity-Income)	C+	C	B	Up	Y	1,500
Lord Abbett Multi-Asset Income Fund Class F	LIGFX	NAS CM	Open End	Cautious Alloc (Equity-Income)	C+	C	B	Up	Y	0
Lord Abbett Multi-Asset Income Fund Class F3	ISFOX	NAS CM	Open End	Cautious Alloc (Equity-Income)	C+	C	B	Up	Y	0
Lord Abbett Multi-Asset Income Fund Class I	ISFYX	NAS CM	Open End	Cautious Alloc (Equity-Income)	C+	C	B	Up	Y	1,000,000
Lord Abbett Multi-Asset Income Fund Class R2	LIGQX	NAS CM	Open End	Cautious Alloc (Equity-Income)	C+	C	B	Up	Y	0
Lord Abbett Multi-Asset Income Fund Class R3	LIXRX	NAS CM	Open End	Cautious Alloc (Equity-Income)	C+	C	B	Up	Y	0
Lord Abbett Multi-Asset Income Fund Class R4	LIXSX	NAS CM	Open End	Cautious Alloc (Equity-Income)	C+	C	B	Up	Y	0
Lord Abbett Multi-Asset Income Fund Class R5	LIXTX	NAS CM	Open End	Cautious Alloc (Equity-Income)	C+	C	B	Up	Y	0
Lord Abbett Multi-Asset Income Fund Class R6	LIXVX	NAS CM	Open End	Cautious Alloc (Equity-Income)	C+	C	B	Up	Y	0
Lord Abbett Small Cap Value Fund Class A	LRSCX	NAS CM	Open End	US Equity Small Cap (Small Company)	C	C-	C		Y	1,000
Lord Abbett Small Cap Value Fund Class C	LSRCX	NAS CM	Open End	US Equity Small Cap (Small Company)	C	C-	C		Y	1,000
Lord Abbett Small Cap Value Fund Class F	LRSFX	NAS CM	Open End	US Equity Small Cap (Small Company)	C	C-	C		Y	0
Lord Abbett Small Cap Value Fund Class F3	LRSOX	NAS CM	Open End	US Equity Small Cap (Small Company)	C	C-	C+		Y	0
Lord Abbett Small Cap Value Fund Class I	LRSYX	NAS CM	Open End	US Equity Small Cap (Small Company)	C	C-	C+		Y	1,000,000
Lord Abbett Small Cap Value Fund Class P	LRSPX	NAS CM	Open End	US Equity Small Cap (Small Company)	C	C-	C			0
Lord Abbett Small Cap Value Fund Class R2	LRSQX	NAS CM	Open End	US Equity Small Cap (Small Company)	C	C-	C		Y	0
Lord Abbett Small Cap Value Fund Class R3	LRSRX	NAS CM	Open End	US Equity Small Cap (Small Company)	C	C-	C		Y	0
Lord Abbett Small Cap Value Fund Class R4	LRSSX	NAS CM	Open End	US Equity Small Cap (Small Company)	C	C-	C		Y	0

★ Expanded analysis of this fund is included in Section II.

	TOTAL RETURNS					PERFORMANCE				ASSETS		ASSET ALLOCATION & TURNOVER					BULL & BEAR		FEES		
Min Additional Investment	3-Month Total Return	6-Month Total Return	1-Year Total Return	3-Year Total Return	5-Year Total Return	Dividend Yield (TTM)	Expense Ratio	3-Yr Std Deviation	3-Year Beta	NAV	Total Assets (MIL)	%Cash	%Stocks	%Bonds	%Other	Turnover Ratio	Last Bull Market Total Return	Last Bear Market Total Return	Front End Fee (%)	Back End Fee (%)	Inception Date
	1.99	9.59	-2.83	14.28	-12.55	2.73	1.87	11.16	0.92	6.82	605.3	0	100	0	0	74	12.15	-22.98		1.00	Jun-08
	2.19	9.97	-1.89	17.60	-8.37	3.63	0.92	11.15	0.92	6.9	605.3	0	100	0	0	74	12.77	-22.7			Jun-08
	2.22	10.02	-1.77	17.89	-8.15	3.74	0.81	11.17	0.92	6.91	605.3	0	100	0	0	74	12.77	-22.7			Apr-17
	2.21	10.17	-1.78	17.95	-7.86	3.73	0.82	11.19	0.92	6.92	605.3	0	100	0	0	74	12.79	-22.72			Jun-08
	2.04	9.68	-2.46	15.66	-10.88	3.08	1.47	11.13	0.92	7.03	605.3	0	100	0	0	74	12.44	-22.87			Jun-08
	2.08	9.84	-2.27	16.08	-10.37	3.2	1.37	11.2	0.92	6.95	605.3	0	100	0	0	74	12.46	-22.87			Jun-08
	2.16	9.95	-2.16	16.84	-9.35	3.52	1.12	11.19	0.92	6.86	605.3	0	100	0	0	74	12.67	-22.75			Jun-15
	2.22	10.03	-1.78	17.82	-8.21	3.74	0.87	11.15	0.92	6.9	605.3	0	100	0	0	74	12.77	-22.7			Jun-15
	2.22	10.02	-1.91	17.82	-8.08	3.74	0.81	11.17	0.92	6.91	605.3	0	100	0	0	74	12.77	-22.7			Jun-15
	7.46	33.76	11.13	113.23	98.07	0	1.63	21.47	1.09	17.71	138.0	0	100	0	0	73	30.59	-26.03			Jul-99
	1.70	14.89	-5.60	35.69	42.83	0	1.63	17.79	0.98	27.39	118.8	0	100	0	0	57	30.46	-27.14			Jul-99
	1.43	16.25	-0.96	18.03	22.21	0.89	0.98	13.88	1.03	27.61	1,812	0	100	0	0	47	26.39	-24.17	5.75		Jun-83
	1.26	15.82	-1.69	15.39	17.76	0.01	1.73	13.91	1.04	25.54	1,812	0	100	0	0	47	25.9	-24.34		1.00	May-97
	1.48	16.34	-0.75	18.65	23.27	1.05	0.83	13.89	1.03	27.4	1,812	0	100	0	0	47	26.61	-24.1			Sep-07
	1.51	16.46	-0.57	18.95	23.17	1.17	0.64	13.89	1.03	27.52	1,812	0	100	0	0	47	26.39	-24.17			Apr-17
	1.48	16.39	-0.73	18.90	23.75	1.16	0.73	13.9	1.04	27.4	1,812	0	100	0	0	47	26.64	-24.03			May-99
	1.36	16.13	-1.16	17.30	21.15	0.67	1.18	13.89	1.03	26.71	1,812	0	100	0	0	47	26.43	-24.14			Nov-97
	1.31	16.06	-1.34	16.77	20.11	0.74	1.33	13.87	1.03	27.02	1,812	0	100	0	0	47	26.19	-24.23			Mar-08
	1.37	16.10	-1.12	17.27	20.90	0.61	1.23	13.88	1.03	27.32	1,812	0	100	0	0	47	26.32	-24.21			Mar-08
	1.43	16.30	-0.95	18.04	22.30	0.84	0.98	13.89	1.03	27.53	1,812	0	100	0	0	47	26.39	-24.17			Jun-15
	1.48	16.40	-0.73	18.83	23.42	1.16	0.73	13.88	1.03	27.39	1,812	0	100	0	0	47	26.39	-24.17			Jun-15
	1.51	16.46	-0.64	19.27	23.99	1.17	0.64	13.88	1.03	27.51	1,812	0	100	0	0	47	26.39	-24.17			Jun-15
	2.86	14.95	4.99	25.63	20.80	3.3	1.2	8.74	0.68	11.39	2,637	3	60	30	0	31	17.65	-16.61	2.25		Dec-94
	2.79	14.54	4.27	22.95	16.46	2.62	1.95	8.73	0.68	11.32	2,637	3	60	30	0	31	17.1	-16.84		1.00	Jul-96
	2.98	15.03	5.14	26.34	21.81	3.43	1.05	8.71	0.68	11.39	2,637	3	60	30	0	31	17.76	-16.64			Sep-07
	3.00	15.18	5.35	26.56	21.70	3.54	0.87	8.72	0.68	11.41	2,637	3	60	30	0	31	17.64	-16.61			Apr-17
	3.01	15.08	5.24	26.59	22.39	3.53	0.95	8.73	0.68	11.39	2,637	3	60	30	0	31	17.7	-16.52			Oct-04
	2.92	14.92	4.81	25.00	19.71	3.12	1.4	8.74	0.68	11.34	2,637	3	60	30	0	31	17.56	-16.66			Dec-02
	2.80	14.71	4.62	24.33	18.78	2.9	1.55	8.77	0.68	11.65	2,637	3	60	30	0	31	17.38	-16.76			Sep-07
	2.90	14.84	4.75	24.88	19.43	3.07	1.45	8.76	0.68	11.37	2,637	3	60	30	0	31	17.39	-16.71			Sep-07
	2.95	15.05	5.08	25.81	20.98	3.29	1.2	8.75	0.68	11.4	2,637	3	60	30	0	31	17.65	-16.61			Jun-15
	3.00	15.17	5.33	26.74	22.13	3.52	0.95	8.82	0.69	11.41	2,637	3	60	30	0	31	17.65	-16.61			Jun-15
	3.01	15.08	5.26	26.90	22.20	3.54	0.87	8.74	0.68	11.4	2,637	3	60	30	0	31	17.65	-16.61			Jun-15
	2.61	11.65	3.78	20.91	17.77	3.35	1.17	6.45	0.06	14.85	1,348	7	41	42	0	41	12.54	-9.82	2.25		Jun-05
	2.38	11.12	3.01	18.12	13.40	2.56	1.92	6.44	0.06	15.07	1,348	7	41	42	0	41	12	-10.06		1.00	Jun-05
	2.58	11.66	3.94	21.39	18.65	3.5	1.02	6.45	0.07	14.84	1,348	7	41	42	0	41	12.56	-9.7			Sep-07
	2.62	11.79	4.08	21.92	19.38	3.63	0.86	6.45	0.06	14.77	1,348	7	41	42	0	41	12.67	-9.7			Apr-17
	2.62	11.70	4.07	21.81	19.27	3.62	0.92	6.48	0.06	14.76	1,348	7	41	42	0	41	12.67	-9.7			Jun-05
	2.45	11.35	3.45	19.65	15.72	2.91	1.52	6.47	0.06	15.26	1,348	7	41	42	0	41	12.24	-9.88			Sep-07
	2.55	11.52	3.53	20.01	16.36	3.11	1.42	6.44	0.07	14.85	1,348	7	41	42	0	41	12.3	-9.84			Sep-07
	2.54	11.58	3.78	20.81	17.76	3.35	1.17	6.43	0.06	14.84	1,348	7	41	42	0	41	12.51	-9.79			Jun-15
	2.62	11.70	4.06	21.80	19.26	3.62	0.92	6.45	0.06	14.76	1,348	7	41	42	0	41	12.67	-9.7			Jun-15
	2.62	11.79	4.07	21.95	19.42	3.63	0.86	6.44	0.07	14.77	1,348	7	41	42	0	41	12.67	-9.7			Jun-15
	0.53	14.38	-5.55	23.90	24.55	0	1.18	16.88	0.94	16.94	809.9	0	100	0	0	42	33.42	-28.31	5.75		Dec-95
	0.37	13.96	-6.25	21.22	20.04	0	1.93	16.87	0.94	8	809.9	0	100	0	0	42	32.87	-28.51		1.00	Apr-97
	0.58	14.45	-5.41	24.45	25.49	0	1.03	16.9	0.94	17.1	809.9	0	100	0	0	42	33.56	-28.24			Sep-07
	0.62	14.53	-5.23	24.80	25.45	0	0.84	16.9	0.94	20.88	809.9	0	100	0	0	42	33.42	-28.31			Apr-17
	0.63	14.50	-5.29	24.87	26.12	0	0.93	16.87	0.94	20.76	809.9	0	100	0	0	42	33.6	-28.21			Dec-97
	0.50	14.24	-5.71	23.18	23.33	0	1.38	16.85	0.94	15.88	809.9	0	100	0	0	42	33.26	-28.35			Jun-99
	0.38	14.06	-5.94	22.60	22.37	0	1.53	16.87	0.94	15.65	809.9	0	100	0	0	42	33.14	-28.38			Mar-08
	0.50	14.16	-5.79	23.06	23.15	0	1.43	16.88	0.94	15.96	809.9	0	100	0	0	42	33.22	-28.34			Mar-08
	0.53	14.30	-5.60	23.88	24.53	0	1.18	16.87	0.94	16.94	809.9	0	100	0	0	42	33.42	-28.31			Jun-15

Fund Name	MARKET Ticker Symbol	Traded On	FUND TYPE, CATEGORY & OBJECTIVE Fund Type	Category and (Prospectus Objective)	RATINGS Overall Rating	Reward Rating	Risk Rating	Recent Up/ Downgrade	MINIMUMS Open to New Investors	Min Initial Investment
Lord Abbett Small Cap Value Fund Class R5	**LRSTX**	NAS CM	Open End	US Equity Small Cap (Small Company)	**C**	C-	C+		Y	0
Lord Abbett Small Cap Value Fund Class R6	**LRSVX**	NAS CM	Open End	US Equity Small Cap (Small Company)	**C**	C-	C+		Y	0
Lord Abbett Value Opportunities Fund Class A	**LVOAX**	NAS CM	Open End	US Equity Mid Cap (Growth)	**C**	C	B-		Y	1,500
Lord Abbett Value Opportunities Fund Class C	**LVOCX**	NAS CM	Open End	US Equity Mid Cap (Growth)	**C**	C	C+		Y	1,500
Lord Abbett Value Opportunities Fund Class F	**LVOFX**	NAS CM	Open End	US Equity Mid Cap (Growth)	**C**	C	B-		Y	0
Lord Abbett Value Opportunities Fund Class F3	**LVOOX**	NAS CM	Open End	US Equity Mid Cap (Growth)	**C**	C	B-		Y	0
Lord Abbett Value Opportunities Fund Class I	**LVOYX**	NAS CM	Open End	US Equity Mid Cap (Growth)	**C**	C	B-		Y	1,000,000
Lord Abbett Value Opportunities Fund Class P	**LVOPX**	NAS CM	Open End	US Equity Mid Cap (Growth)	**C**	C	B-			0
Lord Abbett Value Opportunities Fund Class R2	**LVOQX**	NAS CM	Open End	US Equity Mid Cap (Growth)	**C**	C	B-		Y	0
Lord Abbett Value Opportunities Fund Class R3	**LVORX**	NAS CM	Open End	US Equity Mid Cap (Growth)	**C**	C	B-		Y	0
Lord Abbett Value Opportunities Fund Class R4	**LVOSX**	NAS CM	Open End	US Equity Mid Cap (Growth)	**C**	C	B-		Y	0
Lord Abbett Value Opportunities Fund Class R5	**LVOTX**	NAS CM	Open End	US Equity Mid Cap (Growth)	**C**	C	B-		Y	0
Lord Abbett Value Opportunities Fund Class R6	**LVOVX**	NAS CM	Open End	US Equity Mid Cap (Growth)	**C**	C	B-		Y	0
Low Beta Tactical 500 Fund Institutional Class	**LBETX**	NAS CM	Open End	US Equity Large Cap Blend (Growth & Income)	**C**	D+	B	Up	Y	100,000
Low Beta Tactical 500 Fund Investor Class	**LBTTX**	NAS CM	Open End	US Equity Large Cap Blend (Growth & Income)	**C**	D+	B	Up	Y	2,500
LS Opportunity Fund - Institutional Class	**LSOFX**	NAS CM	Open End	Long/Short Equity (Growth)	**B**	C+	A-	Up	Y	5,000
LSV Conservative Value Equity Fund	**LSVVX**	NAS CM	Open End	US Equity Large Cap Value (Growth)	**C+**	C	B	Up	Y	100,000
LSV Conservative Value Equity Fund Investor Class	**LVAVX**	NAS CM	Open End	US Equity Large Cap Value (Growth)	**C+**	C	B	Up	Y	1,000
LSV Emerging Markets Equity Institutional Cls Shares	**LSVZX**	NAS CM	Open End	Global Emerg Mkts (Div Emerging Mkts)	**U**	U	U		Y	100,000
LSV Emerging Markets Equity Fund Investor Class Shares	**LVAZX**	NAS CM	Open End	Global Emerg Mkts (Div Emerging Mkts)	**U**	U	U		Y	1,000
LSV Global Managed Volatility Fund Institutional Class	**LSVFX**	NAS CM	Open End	Global Equity Large Cap (Income)	**B-**	C	A-	Up	Y	100,000
LSV Global Managed Volatility Fund Investor Class	**LVAFX**	NAS CM	Open End	Global Equity Large Cap (Income)	**B-**	C	A-	Up	Y	1,000
LSV Global Value Fund Institutional Class	**LSVGX**	NAS CM	Open End	Global Equity Large Cap (Growth)	**C**	C	C+		Y	100,000
LSV Global Value Fund Investor Class	**LVAGX**	NAS CM	Open End	Global Equity Large Cap (Growth)	**C**	C	C+		Y	1,000
LSV Small Cap Value Fund Institutional Class	**LSVQX**	NAS CM	Open End	US Equity Small Cap (Small Company)	**C-**	D+	C	Down	Y	100,000
LSV Small Cap Value Fund Investor Class	**LVAQX**	NAS CM	Open End	US Equity Small Cap (Small Company)	**C-**	D+	C	Down	Y	1,000
LSV U.S. Managed Volatility Fund Institutional Class	**LSVMX**	NAS CM	Open End	US Equity Large Cap Value (Growth)	**B-**	C	A-	Down	Y	100,000
LSV U.S. Managed Volatility Fund Investor Class	**LVAMX**	NAS CM	Open End	US Equity Large Cap Value (Growth)	**B-**	C	A-	Down	Y	1,000
LSV Value Equity Fund	**LSVEX**	NAS CM	Open End	US Equity Large Cap Value (Growth)	**C**	C	B-		Y	100,000
LSV Value Equity Fund Investor Class	**LVAEX**	NAS CM	Open End	US Equity Large Cap Value (Growth)	**C**	C	B-		Y	1,000
Lyrical U.S. Value Equity Fund Institutional Class	**LYRIX**	NAS CM	Open End	US Equity Large Cap Value (Growth)	**C**	C-	B-	Down	Y	100,000
Lyrical U.S. Value Equity Fund Investor Class	**LYRBX**	NAS CM	Open End	US Equity Large Cap Value (Growth)	**C**	D+	C+	Down	Y	2,500
M.D. Sass Equity Income Plus Fund Institutional Class	**MDEIX**	NAS CM	Open End	Long/Short Equity (Growth & Income)	**C+**	C	B		Y	1,000,000
M.D. Sass Equity Income Plus Fund Investor Class	**MDEPX**	NAS CM	Open End	Long/Short Equity (Growth & Income)	**C+**	C	B		Y	2,500
Macquarie Global Infrastructure Total Return Fund Inc.	**MGU**	NYSE	Closed End	Infrastructure Sector Equity (World Stock)	**C**	C	C-		Y	
Macquarie Pooled Trust Emerging Markets Portfolio	**DPEMX**	NAS CM	Open End	Global Emerg Mkts (Div Emerging Mkts)	**C**	C-	B-			1,000,000
Macquarie Pooled Trust Emerging Markets Portfolio II	**DPEGX**	NAS CM	Open End	Global Emerg Mkts (Div Emerging Mkts)	**C**	C	C+		Y	1,000,000
Macquarie Pooled Trust Labor Select Intl Equity Portfolio	**DELPX**	NAS CM	Open End	Global Equity Large Cap (Foreign Stock)	**C**	C	B		Y	1,000,000
Macquarie Pooled Trust Large Cap Value Portfolio	**DPDEX**	NAS CM	Open End	US Equity Large Cap Value (Growth)	**B-**	C	B+		Y	1,000,000
Macquarie/First Trust Global Infrastr/Util Div & Income	**MFD**	NYSE	Closed End	Utilities Sector Equity (Utility)	**C**	C	C-		Y	
Madison Aggressive Allocation Fund Class A	**MAGSX**	NAS CM	Open End	Aggressive Alloc (Asset Alloc)	**B-**	C	B+	Up	Y	1,000
Madison Aggressive Allocation Fund Class B	**MAGBX**	NAS CM	Open End	Aggressive Alloc (Asset Alloc)	**B-**	C	B+	Up	Y	1,000
Madison Aggressive Allocation Fund Class C	**MAACX**	NAS CM	Open End	Aggressive Alloc (Asset Alloc)	**B-**	C	B+	Up	Y	1,000
Madison Conservative Allocation Fund Class A	**MCNAX**	NAS CM	Open End	Cautious Alloc (Asset Alloc)	**B**	C+	A-	Up	Y	1,000
Madison Conservative Allocation Fund Class B	**MCNBX**	NAS CM	Open End	Cautious Alloc (Asset Alloc)	**B-**	C	B+	Up	Y	1,000
Madison Conservative Allocation Fund Class C	**MCOCX**	NAS CM	Open End	Cautious Alloc (Asset Alloc)	**B-**	C	B+	Up	Y	1,000
Madison Covered Call & Equity Income Fund Class A	**MENAX**	NAS CM	Open End	Long/Short Equity (Equity-Income)	**C**	C-	C+		Y	1,000
Madison Covered Call & Equity Income Fund Class C	**MENCX**	NAS CM	Open End	Long/Short Equity (Equity-Income)	**C**	C-	C		Y	1,000
Madison Covered Call & Equity Income Fund Class R6	**MENRX**	NAS CM	Open End	Long/Short Equity (Equity-Income)	**C**	C-	C+		Y	500,000
Madison Covered Call & Equity Income Fund Class Y	**MENYX**	NAS CM	Open End	Long/Short Equity (Equity-Income)	**C**	C-	C+		Y	0
Madison Covered Call and Equity Strategy Fund	**MCN**	NYSE	Closed End	Alternative Miscellaneous (Equity-Income)	**C-**	C-	C-	Down	Y	
Madison Diversified Income Fund Class A	**MBLAX**	NAS CM	Open End	Moderate Alloc (Growth & Income)	**B**	C+	A		Y	1,000

★ Expanded analysis of this fund is included in Section II.

Min Additional Investment	TOTAL RETURNS 3-Month Total Return	6-Month Total Return	1-Year Total Return	3-Year Total Return	5-Year Total Return	PERFORMANCE Dividend Yield (TTM)	Expense Ratio	3-Yr Std Deviation	3-Year Beta	ASSETS NAV	Total Assets (MIL)	ASSET ALLOCATION & TURNOVER %Cash	%Stocks	%Bonds	%Other	Turnover Ratio	BULL & BEAR Last Bull Market Total Return	Last Bear Market Total Return	FEES Front End Fee (%)	Back End Fee (%)	Inception Date
	0.62	14.49	-5.32	24.87	25.87	0	0.93	16.87	0.94	20.78	809.9	0	100	0	0	42	33.42	-28.31			Jun-15
	0.57	14.48	-5.27	25.17	26.27	0	0.84	16.84	0.93	20.87	809.9	0	100	0	0	42	33.42	-28.31			Jun-15
	1.61	15.05	-0.03	23.91	27.37	0.04	1.11	13.97	0.88	18.27	2,072	0	100	0	0	54	24.33	-23	5.75		Dec-05
	1.39	14.58	-0.75	21.12	22.72	0	1.86	13.96	0.88	15.95	2,072	0	100	0	0	54	23.87	-23.22		1.00	Dec-05
	1.63	15.15	0.16	24.57	28.45	0.18	0.96	13.93	0.88	18.69	2,072	0	100	0	0	54	24.48	-22.91			Sep-07
	1.69	15.27	0.40	25.25	29.42	0.3	0.78	13.97	0.88	19.17	2,072	0	100	0	0	54	24.58	-22.9			Apr-17
	1.70	15.22	0.23	24.89	29.04	0.29	0.86	13.98	0.89	19.07	2,072	0	100	0	0	54	24.58	-22.89			Dec-05
	1.59	14.91	-0.19	23.16	26.11	0	1.31	14	0.89	17.87	2,072	0	100	0	0	54	24.29	-23.04			Dec-05
	1.57	14.88	-0.25	22.79	25.38	0	1.46	13.97	0.88	17.44	2,072	0	100	0	0	54	24.19	-23.09			Sep-07
	1.55	14.90	-0.20	23.09	25.93	0	1.36	13.97	0.88	17.65	2,072	0	100	0	0	54	24.23	-23.02			Sep-07
	1.67	15.06	0.00	23.99	27.47	0.03	1.11	14	0.89	18.25	2,072	0	100	0	0	54	24.4	-22.98			Jun-15
	1.65	15.14	0.23	24.82	29.03	0.28	0.86	13.98	0.89	19.08	2,072	0	100	0	0	54	24.58	-22.9			Jun-15
	1.69	15.28	0.30	25.23	29.60	0.3	0.78	13.99	0.89	19.16	2,072	0	100	0	0	54	24.58	-22.9			Jun-15
1,000	0.09	8.82	2.55			0	1.67			10.6	50.6	2	98	0	0						Jun-17
1,000	0.00	8.66	2.28			0	1.92			10.54	50.6	2	98	0	0						Jun-17
100	4.74	13.13	8.27	29.09	27.26	0	2.97	7.6	0.56	14.56	71.9	44	56	0	0	55	3.65	-11.34			Sep-10
	2.58	15.21	4.51	36.55	37.56	2.25	0.35	13.71	1.12	13.1	124.6	1	99	0	0		25.76	-21.09			Mar-07
	2.51	15.00	4.22	35.49	35.81	2.06	0.6	13.67	1.12	13.03	124.6	1	99	0	0		25.58	-21.17			Jun-14
	0.76						1.2			10.5	6.4	3	97	0	0						Jan-19
	0.86						1.45			10.53	6.4	3	97	0	0						Jan-19
	1.27	10.79	5.51	27.24	30.07	2.29	0.75	8.62	0.73	11.08	22.1	2	98	0	0						Jun-14
	1.18	10.65	5.23	26.25	28.49	2.04	1	8.65	0.74	11.11	22.1	2	98	0	0						Jun-14
	2.22	12.44	-0.99	30.94	20.10	1.85	0.9	13.05	1.11	10.57	5.7	2	98	0	0						Jun-14
	2.22	12.34	-1.30	29.96	18.66	1.66	1.15	12.95	1.1	10.56	5.7	2	98	0	0						Jun-14
	0.82	13.04	-8.87	25.25	26.04	1.13	0.81	19.15	1.09	13.52	395.4	1	99	0	0						Feb-13
	0.74	12.90	-9.13	24.28	24.28	0.74	1.06	19.12	1.09	13.47	395.4	1	99	0	0						Jun-14
	1.88	13.69	11.71	30.32	51.96	2.28	0.55	9.48	0.73	12.95	72.8	0	100	0	0						Jun-14
	1.80	13.47	11.35	29.59	50.40	1.87	0.8	9.48	0.73	12.97	72.8	0	100	0	0						Jun-14
	2.26	14.85	0.34	35.68	36.98	1.82	0.64	15.31	1.24	26.21	3,102	0	100	0	0		27.46	-23.28			Mar-99
	2.19	14.71	0.08	34.68	35.33	1.44	0.89	15.3	1.24	26.11	3,102	0	100	0	0		27.28	-23.36			Jun-14
	0.32	13.90	-4.02	27.19	22.10	0.3	1.37	19.5	1.44	15.48	794.3	0	100	0	0	39					Feb-13
	0.26	13.67	-4.33	25.94	20.24	0	1.72	19.51	1.44	15.38	794.3	0	100	0	0	39					Feb-14
25,000	3.38	12.97	6.19	14.13	11.49	2.63	0.76	8.41	0.92	11.01	35.5	13	87	0	0	94					Jun-13
100	3.32	12.85	5.92	13.16	9.67	2.37	1.11	8.45	0.92	10.99	35.5	13	87	0	0	94			5.75		Jun-13
	4.43	24.40	10.43	29.07	25.21	1.71	0	13.52	0.9	26.97	336.3	5	135	0	-40	99	22.05	-20.05			Aug-05
	-0.24	10.31	4.62	20.51	-0.67	1.97	1.26	12.17	0.83	8.13	80.5	0	99	0	0	40	19.98	-20.61			Apr-97
	-0.42	12.27	1.32	45.49	11.81	0.49	1.2	15.91	1.11	9.33	41.3	1	98	0	1	12	15.73	-28.79			Jun-10
	1.30	10.26	0.11	21.98	2.98	3.03	0.87	11.7	1	13.96	433.8	1	98	0	1	20	7.26	-16.2			Dec-95
	0.59	11.96	6.44	29.27	47.26	1.88	0.7	11.62	0.92	23.86	84.4	1	99	0	0	16	24.35	-13.57			Feb-92
	2.24	17.61	6.14	9.41	-5.51	9.32	0	10.97	0.55	11.42	97.6	8	67	25	0	216	16.52	-14.73			Mar-04
50	2.88	13.63	5.97	31.71	34.99	1.12	1.16	8.41	0.67	11.75	64.1	11	69	20	0	71	14.58	-13.31	5.75		Jun-06
150	2.70	13.22	5.22	28.85	30.08	0.55	1.91	8.37	0.67	11.39	64.1	11	69	20	0	71	14.05	-13.59		4.50	Jun-06
50	2.70	13.20	5.22	28.82	30.05	0.55	1.91	8.38	0.67	11.4	64.1	11	69	20	0	71	14.03	-13.58		1.00	Feb-08
50	2.68	9.07	6.46	16.81	21.54	1.65	1.14	4.11	0.52	10.75	69.1	6	29	64	0	63	8.37	-5.15	5.75		Jun-06
150	2.55	8.64	5.67	14.20	17.12	0.48	1.89	4.07	0.52	10.9	69.1	6	29	64	0	63	7.91	-5.41		4.50	Jun-06
50	2.54	8.63	5.67	14.30	17.11	0.48	1.89	4.08	0.52	10.91	69.1	6	29	64	0	63	7.91	-5.5		1.00	Feb-08
50	0.49	8.06	-1.48	13.08	16.67	5.36	1.3	8.96	0.68	7.9	129.2	21	78	0	0	130	22.06	-11.21	5.75		Oct-09
50	0.39	7.72	-2.13	10.56	12.49	5.53	2.05	9	0.68	7.4	129.2	21	78	0	0	130	21.55	-11.53		1.00	Jul-12
50,000	0.72	8.30	-1.15	14.32	18.95	5.22	0.92	8.96	0.68	8.21	129.2	21	78	0	0	130	22.26	-11.16			Jul-12
	0.60	8.25	-1.27	13.91	18.17	5.28	1.05	8.9	0.67	8.12	129.2	21	78	0	0	130	22.25	-11.16			Oct-09
	0.74	10.13	-1.26	13.22	17.20	0.84	0	9.77	0.74	7.2	150.8	18	81	0	0	114	19.7	-14.79			Jul-04
50	3.87	13.32	13.15	29.89	39.18	1.66	1.1	6.92	0.53	16.06	175.4	3	64	32	0	27	11.51	-5.03	5.75		Dec-97

	MARKET			FUND TYPE, CATEGORY & OBJECTIVE	RATINGS				MINIMUMS	
Fund Name	Ticker Symbol	Traded On	Fund Type	Category and (Prospectus Objective)	Overall Rating	Reward Rating	Risk Rating	Recent Up/ Downgrade	Open to New Investors	Min Initial Investment
Madison Diversified Income Fund Class B	MBLNX	NAS CM	Open End	Moderate Alloc (Growth & Income)	B	C+	A		Y	1,000
Madison Diversified Income Fund Class C	MBLCX	NAS CM	Open End	Moderate Alloc (Growth & Income)	B	C+	A		Y	1,000
Madison Dividend Income Fund Class Y	BHBFX	NAS CM	Open End	US Equity Large Cap Value (Equity-Income)	B	C+	A-		Y	25,000
Madison International Stock Fund Class A	MINAX	NAS CM	Open End	Global Equity Large Cap (Foreign Stock)	C	C-	B-		Y	1,000
Madison International Stock Fund Class B	MINBX	NAS CM	Open End	Global Equity Large Cap (Foreign Stock)	C	C-	B-	Up	Y	1,000
Madison International Stock Fund Class Y	MINYX	NAS CM	Open End	Global Equity Large Cap (Foreign Stock)	C	C-	B		Y	0
Madison Investors Fund Class A	MNVAX	NAS CM	Open End	US Equity Large Cap Growth (Growth)	B	B-	A-		Y	1,000
Madison Investors Fund Class R6	MNVRX	NAS CM	Open End	US Equity Large Cap Growth (Growth)	B	B-	A-		Y	500,000
Madison Investors Fund Class Y	MINVX	NAS CM	Open End	US Equity Large Cap Growth (Growth)	B	B-	A-		Y	25,000
Madison Large Cap Value Fund Class A	MGWAX	NAS CM	Open End	US Equity Large Cap Value (Growth & Income)	C	C	B-	Down	Y	1,000
Madison Large Cap Value Fund Class B	MGWBX	NAS CM	Open End	US Equity Large Cap Value (Growth & Income)	C	C	C+	Down	Y	1,000
Madison Large Cap Value Fund Class Y	MYLVX	NAS CM	Open End	US Equity Large Cap Value (Growth & Income)	C	C	B-	Down	Y	0
Madison Mid Cap Fund Class A	MERAX	NAS CM	Open End	US Equity Mid Cap (Growth)	B	B	B+	Up	Y	1,000
Madison Mid Cap Fund Class B	MERBX	NAS CM	Open End	US Equity Mid Cap (Growth)	B	B-	B+	Up	Y	1,000
Madison Mid Cap Fund Class R6	MMCRX	NAS CM	Open End	US Equity Mid Cap (Growth)	B	B	B+	Up	Y	500,000
Madison Mid Cap Fund Class Y	GTSGX	NAS CM	Open End	US Equity Mid Cap (Growth)	B	B	B+	Up	Y	0
Madison Moderate Allocation Fund Class A	MMDAX	NAS CM	Open End	Moderate Alloc (Asset Alloc)	B	C+	A	Up	Y	1,000
Madison Moderate Allocation Fund Class B	MMDRX	NAS CM	Open End	Moderate Alloc (Asset Alloc)	B	C	A-	Up	Y	1,000
Madison Moderate Allocation Fund Class C	MMDCX	NAS CM	Open End	Moderate Alloc (Asset Alloc)	B	C	A-	Up	Y	1,000
Madison Small Cap Fund Class A	MASVX	NAS CM	Open End	US Equity Small Cap (Small Company)	C	C-	C+		Y	1,000
Madison Small Cap Fund Class B	MBSVX	NAS CM	Open End	US Equity Small Cap (Small Company)	C	C-	C		Y	1,000
Madison Small Cap Fund Class Y	MYSVX	NAS CM	Open End	US Equity Small Cap (Small Company)	C	C	C+		Y	0
MAI Managed Volatility Fund Institutional Class	MAIPX	NAS CM	Open End	Long/Short Equity (Growth)	B-	C	A-		Y	50,000
MAI Managed Volatility Fund Investor Class	DIVPX	NAS CM	Open End	Long/Short Equity (Growth)	B-	C	A-		Y	2,500
Main BuyWrite Fund Class I Shares	BUYWX	NAS CM	Open End	Long/Short Equity (Growth & Income)	C	C-	B-		Y	100,000
MainGate MLP Fund Class A	AMLPX	NAS CM	Open End	Energy Sector Equity (Growth & Income)	D	D	D+	Down	Y	2,500
MainGate MLP Fund Class C	MLCPX	NAS CM	Open End	Energy Sector Equity (Growth & Income)	D	D	D+	Down	Y	2,500
MainGate MLP Fund Class I	IMLPX	NAS CM	Open End	Energy Sector Equity (Growth & Income)	D	D	D+	Down	Y	1,000,000
MainStay Balanced Fund Class A	MBNAX	NAS CM	Open End	Moderate Alloc (Balanced)	B-	C	B+	Up	Y	15,000
MainStay Balanced Fund Class B	MBNBX	NAS CM	Open End	Moderate Alloc (Balanced)	C+	C	B	Up		1,000
MainStay Balanced Fund Class C	MBACX	NAS CM	Open End	Moderate Alloc (Balanced)	C+	C	B	Up	Y	1,000
MainStay Balanced Fund Class I	MBAIX	NAS CM	Open End	Moderate Alloc (Balanced)	B-	C	B+	Up	Y	1,000,000
MainStay Balanced Fund Class R1	MBNRX	NAS CM	Open End	Moderate Alloc (Balanced)	B-	C	B+	Up	Y	0
MainStay Balanced Fund Class R2	MBCRX	NAS CM	Open End	Moderate Alloc (Balanced)	B-	C	B+	Up	Y	0
MainStay Balanced Fund Class R3	MBDRX	NAS CM	Open End	Moderate Alloc (Balanced)	B-	C	B	Up	Y	0
MainStay Balanced Fund Class R6	MBERX	NAS CM	Open End	Moderate Alloc (Balanced)	B-	C	B+	Up	Y	0
MainStay Balanced Fund Investor Class	MBINX	NAS CM	Open End	Moderate Alloc (Balanced)	B-	C	B+	Up	Y	1,000
MainStay Candriam Emerging Markets Equity Fund Class A	MCYAX	NAS CM	Open End	Global Emerg Mkts (Div Emerging Mkts)	D	D	D+		Y	15,000
MainStay Candriam Emerging Markets Equity Fund Class C	MCYCX	NAS CM	Open End	Global Emerg Mkts (Div Emerging Mkts)	D	D	D+		Y	2,500
MainStay Candriam Emerging Markets Equity Fund Class I	MCYIX	NAS CM	Open End	Global Emerg Mkts (Div Emerging Mkts)	D	D	D+		Y	1,000,000
MainStay Candriam Emerging Markets Equity Fund Class R6	MCYSX	NAS CM	Open End	Global Emerg Mkts (Div Emerging Mkts)	D	D	D+		Y	0
MainStay Candriam Emerging Markets Equity Investor Cls	MCYVX	NAS CM	Open End	Global Emerg Mkts (Div Emerging Mkts)	D	D	D+		Y	2,500
MainStay Conservative Allocation Fund Class A	MCKAX	NAS CM	Open End	Cautious Alloc (Asset Alloc)	B-	C	B+	Up	Y	15,000
MainStay Conservative Allocation Fund Class B	MCKBX	NAS CM	Open End	Cautious Alloc (Asset Alloc)	C+	C	B	Up		1,000
MainStay Conservative Allocation Fund Class C	MCKCX	NAS CM	Open End	Cautious Alloc (Asset Alloc)	C+	C	B	Up	Y	1,000
MainStay Conservative Allocation Fund Class I	MCKIX	NAS CM	Open End	Cautious Alloc (Asset Alloc)	B-	C	B+	Up	Y	1,000,000
MainStay Conservative Allocation Fund Class R2	MCKKX	NAS CM	Open End	Cautious Alloc (Asset Alloc)	B-	C	B+			0
MainStay Conservative Allocation Fund Class R3	MCKRX	NAS CM	Open End	Cautious Alloc (Asset Alloc)	B-	C	B+	Up	Y	0
MainStay Conservative Allocation Fund Investor Class	MCKNX	NAS CM	Open End	Cautious Alloc (Asset Alloc)	B-	C	B+	Up	Y	1,000
MainStay Cushing® Energy Income Fund Class A	CURAX	NAS CM	Open End	Energy Sector Equity (Natl Res)	D	D	D	Down	Y	15,000
MainStay Cushing® Energy Income Fund Class C	CURCX	NAS CM	Open End	Energy Sector Equity (Natl Res)	D	D	D	Down	Y	2,500
MainStay Cushing® Energy Income Fund Class I	CURZX	NAS CM	Open End	Energy Sector Equity (Natl Res)	D	D	D	Down	Y	1,000,000

★ Expanded analysis of this fund is included in Section II.

	TOTAL RETURNS					PERFORMANCE				ASSETS		ASSET ALLOCATION & TURNOVER					BULL & BEAR		FEES		
Min. Additional Investment	3-Month Total Return	6-Month Total Return	1-Year Total Return	3-Year Total Return	5-Year Total Return	Dividend Yield (TTM)	Expense Ratio	3-Yr Std Deviation	3-Year Beta	NAV	Total Assets (MIL)	%Cash	%Stocks	%Bonds	%Other	Turnover Ratio	Last Bull Market Total Return	Last Bear Market Total Return	Front End Fee (%)	Back End Fee (%)	Inception Date
150	3.65	12.87	12.30	26.98	34.10	0.97	1.85	6.93	0.53	16.17	175.4	3	64	32	0	27	11.03	-5.3		4.50	Dec-97
50	3.65	12.80	12.30	27.00	34.03	0.97	1.85	6.89	0.53	16.16	175.4	3	64	32	0	27	11.02	-5.33		1.00	Jul-12
50	4.34	17.03	16.68	48.93	60.39	1.53	0.95	10.37	0.8	27	177.9	3	97	0	0	32	15.32	-9.67			Dec-86
50	4.90	15.82	1.65	19.19	6.22	1.39	1.6	10.44	0.89	13.47	19.9	4	96	0	0	29	16.46	-20.39	5.75		Dec-97
150	4.71	15.30	0.91	16.54	2.29	0.77	2.35	10.46	0.89	13.11	19.9	4	96	0	0	29	15.91	-20.63		4.50	Dec-97
	4.97	15.97	1.98	20.14	7.57	1.6	1.35	10.45	0.89	13.5	19.9	4	96	0	0	29	16.63	-20.24			Jun-06
50	5.52	20.83	18.19	54.44	72.17	0.39	1.2	10.64	0.84	22.91	329.3	4	96	0	0	40	21.1	-15.07	5.75		Sep-13
50,000	5.60	21.11	18.72	56.43	75.95	0.58	0.77	10.68	0.84	23.17	329.3	4	96	0	0	40	21.28	-14.98			Sep-13
50	5.56	20.96	18.51	55.52	74.28	0.59	0.95	10.65	0.84	22.96	329.3	4	96	0	0	40	21.28	-14.98			Nov-78
50	2.38	17.16	0.01	25.82	30.97	1.05	1.16	13.05	1.02	12.9	67.4	2	98	0	0	91	22.51	-14.48	5.75		Dec-97
150	2.20	16.69	-0.70	23.09	26.16	0.44	1.91	13.04	1.02	12.51	67.4	2	98	0	0	91	21.95	-14.75		4.50	Dec-97
	2.46	17.27	0.34	26.83	32.64	1.26	0.91	13.07	1.02	12.9	67.4	2	98	0	0	91	22.71	-14.4			Jun-06
50	8.23	24.35	16.70	50.79	65.06	0	1.4	11.3	0.81	10.52	552.8	8	92	0	0	27	26.24	-18.52	5.75		Apr-13
150	7.96	23.89	15.84	47.35	58.85	0	2.15	11.24	0.8	8.4	552.8	8	92	0	0	27	25.69	-18.78		4.50	Apr-13
50,000	8.20	24.75	17.35	53.53	70.17	0.02	0.77	11.28	0.8	11.34	552.8	8	92	0	0	27	26.62	-18.44			Feb-12
	8.20	24.63	17.10	52.57	67.95	0.02	0.98	11.26	0.8	11.08	552.8	8	92	0	0	27	26.42	-18.44			Jul-83
50	2.77	11.54	6.40	25.24	29.30	1.37	1.16	6.31	0.49	11.5	137.4	9	50	40	0	75	12.26	-9.53	5.75		Jun-06
150	2.52	11.03	5.58	22.34	24.46	0.81	1.91	6.31	0.49	11.37	137.4	9	50	40	0	75	11.68	-9.66		4.50	Jun-06
50	2.52	11.02	5.58	22.43	24.54	0.81	1.91	6.32	0.49	11.38	137.4	9	50	40	0	75	11.68	-9.75		1.00	Feb-08
50	4.56	15.65	-3.18	23.30	30.46	0.64	1.55	17.39	0.98	11.23	29.4	5	95	0	0	16	28.06	-21.94	5.75		Dec-06
150	4.29	15.27	-3.95	20.48	25.56	0	2.3	17.36	0.98	10.19	29.4	5	95	0	0	16	27.57	-22.25		4.50	Dec-06
	4.54	15.70	-2.98	24.09	31.95	0.86	1.3	17.45	0.99	11.27	29.4	5	95	0	0	16	28.34	-21.91			Jan-07
5,000	2.60	11.49	6.12	21.52	24.06	1.2	1.01	6.43	0.49	11.79	140.6	25	45	30	0	21	13.15	-7.29			Sep-10
100	2.51	11.34	5.81	20.51	22.49	0.14	1.26	6.41	0.49	12.13	140.6	25	45	30	0	21	12.91	-7.35			Dec-10
	1.76	10.39	-1.30	12.43		0.43	1.5	8.29	1.09	10.94	70.1	3	97	0	0	22					Dec-15
100	-2.08	19.65	-4.93	-5.98	-30.63	8.8	1.66	18.93	1.03	7.16	1,315	0	100	0	0	45	15.49	-6.86	5.75		Feb-11
100	-2.29	19.23	-5.70	-8.04	-33.16	9.1	2.41	18.87	1.02	6.92	1,315	0	100	0	0	45	15	-7.05		1.00	Mar-14
10,000	-2.02	19.94	-4.68	-5.29	-29.78	8.55	1.41	18.93	1.03	7.37	1,315	0	100	0	0	45	15.67	-6.67			Feb-11
	2.50	12.30	3.67	19.62	24.40	1.5	1.11	8.27	0.62	30.63	615.7	1	60	39	0	200	15.19	-11.18	5.50		Jan-04
50	2.23	11.74	2.66	16.28	18.76	0.59	2.06	8.29	0.62	30.5	615.7	1	60	39	0	200	14.55	-11.54		5.00	Jan-04
50	2.23	11.75	2.70	16.33	18.81	0.59	2.06	8.28	0.62	30.49	615.7	1	60	39	0	200	14.52	-11.54		1.00	Dec-02
	2.53	12.40	3.92	20.50	25.94	1.74	0.86	8.28	0.62	30.7	615.7	1	60	39	0	200	15.35	-11.09			May-89
	2.50	12.37	3.82	20.12	25.32	1.64	0.96	8.28	0.62	30.66	615.7	1	60	39	0	200	15.27	-11.14			Jan-04
	2.44	12.19	3.56	19.41	23.92	1.4	1.21	8.27	0.62	30.67	615.7	1	60	39	0	200	15.09	-11.23			Jan-04
	2.42	12.08	3.33	18.34	22.19	1.15	1.46	8.27	0.62	30.61	615.7	1	60	39	0	200	14.95	-11.31			Apr-06
	2.55	12.46	4.02	20.68	26.13	1.83	0.77	8.28	0.62	30.7	615.7	1	60	39	0	200	15.35	-11.09			Dec-17
50	2.41	12.16	3.45	18.97	23.36	1.3	1.31	8.26	0.62	30.66	615.7	1	60	39	0	200	15.08	-11.27	5.50		Feb-08
	0.45	13.26	-3.31			0.44	1.56			8.88	69.1	1	99	0	1	80			5.50		Nov-17
50	0.34	12.82	-4.24			0	2.4			8.8	69.1	1	99	0	1	80				1.00	Nov-17
	0.56	13.51	-3.01			0.71	1.21			8.9	69.1	1	99	0	1	80					Nov-17
	0.67	13.50	-2.87			0.73	1.21			8.91	69.1	1	99	0	1	80					Nov-17
50	0.45	13.28	-3.44			0.32	1.7			8.87	69.1	1	99	0	1	80			5.50		Nov-17
	2.34	10.00	3.46	17.08	16.74	2.16	1.13	5.9	0.46	11.77	453.1	1	40	53	5	59	12.89	-8.44	5.50		Apr-05
50	2.13	9.55	2.61	14.09	11.70	1.53	2.06	5.88	0.46	11.7	453.1	1	40	53	5	59	12.34	-8.87		5.00	Apr-05
50	2.22	9.64	2.61	14.09	11.79	1.53	2.06	5.9	0.46	11.7	453.1	1	40	53	5	59	12.34	-8.79		1.00	Apr-05
	2.55	10.28	3.85	18.15	18.52	2.38	0.88	5.88	0.46	11.89	453.1	1	40	53	5	59	13.15	-8.36			Apr-05
0							1.23	5.87	0.46	11.78	453.1	1	40	53	5	59					Jun-19
	2.35	9.93	3.12	15.94	15.09	1.85	1.48	5.86	0.46	11.75	453.1	1	40	53	5	59	12.82	-8.55			Feb-16
50	2.34	9.99	3.33	16.61	15.99	1.99	1.31	5.91	0.46	11.78	453.1	1	40	53	5	59	12.8	-8.49	5.50		Feb-08
	-6.96	7.48	-20.80	-6.90	-73.88	3.94	1.45	18.97	1.12	3.52	28.8	2	93	5	0	32			5.50		Jul-12
50	-7.49	6.74	-21.73	-9.52	-75.05	3.42	2.35	18.9	1.12	3.36	28.8	2	93	5	0	32				1.00	Jul-12
	-7.07	7.54	-20.76	-6.30	-73.60	4.12	1.2	19.04	1.12	3.56	28.8	2	93	5	0	32					Jul-12

	MARKET		FUND TYPE, CATEGORY & OBJECTIVE		RATINGS					MINIMUMS
Fund Name	Ticker Symbol	Traded On	Fund Type	Category and (Prospectus Objective)	Overall Rating	Reward Rating	Risk Rating	Recent Up/ Downgrade	Open to New Investors	Min Initial Investment
MainStay Cushing® Energy Income Fund Investor Class	CURNX	NAS CM	Open End	Energy Sector Equity (Natl Res)	D	D	D	Down	Y	2,500
MainStay Cushing® MLP Premier Fund Class A	CSHAX	NAS CM	Open End	Energy Sector Equity (Equity-Income)	C-	C-	C	Down	Y	15,000
MainStay Cushing® MLP Premier Fund Class C	CSHCX	NAS CM	Open End	Energy Sector Equity (Equity-Income)	C-	C-	C-	Down	Y	2,500
MainStay Cushing® MLP Premier Fund Class I	CSHZX	NAS CM	Open End	Energy Sector Equity (Equity-Income)	C	C-	C	Down	Y	1,000,000
MainStay Cushing® MLP Premier Fund Investor Class	CSHNX	NAS CM	Open End	Energy Sector Equity (Equity-Income)	C-	C-	C	Down	Y	2,500
MainStay Cushing® Renaissance Advantage Fund Class A	CRZAX	NAS CM	Open End	Natl Resources Sec Equity (Natl Res)	D	D	D+	Down	Y	15,000
MainStay Cushing® Renaissance Advantage Fund Class C	CRZCX	NAS CM	Open End	Natl Resources Sec Equity (Natl Res)	D	D	D+	Down	Y	2,500
MainStay Cushing® Renaissance Advantage Fund Class I	CRZZX	NAS CM	Open End	Natl Resources Sec Equity (Natl Res)	D	D	D+	Down	Y	1,000,000
MainStay Cushing® Renaissance Advantage Investor Cls	CRZNX	NAS CM	Open End	Natl Resources Sec Equity (Natl Res)	D	D	D+	Down	Y	2,500
MainStay Epoch Capital Growth Fund Class A	MECDX	NAS CM	Open End	Global Equity Large Cap (Growth)	C+	C	B	Up	Y	15,000
MainStay Epoch Capital Growth Fund Class C	MECEX	NAS CM	Open End	Global Equity Large Cap (Growth)	C+	C	B	Up	Y	2,500
MainStay Epoch Capital Growth Fund Class I	MECFX	NAS CM	Open End	Global Equity Large Cap (Growth)	C+	C	B	Up	Y	1,000,000
MainStay Epoch Capital Growth Fund Investor Class	MECVX	NAS CM	Open End	Global Equity Large Cap (Growth)	C+	C	B	Up	Y	2,500
MainStay Epoch Global Equity Yield Fund Class A	EPSPX	NAS CM	Open End	Global Equity Large Cap (Equity-Income)	C+	C	B		Y	15,000
MainStay Epoch Global Equity Yield Fund Class C	EPSKX	NAS CM	Open End	Global Equity Large Cap (Equity-Income)	C+	C	B-		Y	2,500
Mainstay Epoch Global Equity Yield Fund Class I	EPSYX	NAS CM	Open End	Global Equity Large Cap (Equity-Income)	C+	C	B		Y	1,000,000
MainStay Epoch Global Equity Yield Fund Class R2	EPSZX	NAS CM	Open End	Global Equity Large Cap (Equity-Income)	C+	C	B		Y	0
MainStay Epoch Global Equity Yield Fund Class R3	EPSHX	NAS CM	Open End	Global Equity Large Cap (Equity-Income)	C+	C	B		Y	0
MainStay Epoch Global Equity Yield Fund Class R6	EPSRX	NAS CM	Open End	Global Equity Large Cap (Equity-Income)	C+	C	B		Y	0
MainStay Epoch Global Equity Yield Fund Investor Class	EPSIX	NAS CM	Open End	Global Equity Large Cap (Equity-Income)	C+	C	B		Y	2,500
MainStay Epoch International Choice Fund Class A	ICEVX	NAS CM	Open End	Global Equity Large Cap (Foreign Stock)	C	C	B		Y	15,000
MainStay Epoch International Choice Fund Class C	ICEWX	NAS CM	Open End	Global Equity Large Cap (Foreign Stock)	C	C	B		Y	1,000
MainStay Epoch International Choice Fund Class I	ICEUX	NAS CM	Open End	Global Equity Large Cap (Foreign Stock)	C	C	B		Y	1,000,000
MainStay Epoch International Choice Fund Class R1	ICETX	NAS CM	Open End	Global Equity Large Cap (Foreign Stock)	C	C	B		Y	0
MainStay Epoch International Choice Fund Class R2	ICEYX	NAS CM	Open End	Global Equity Large Cap (Foreign Stock)	C	C	B		Y	0
MainStay Epoch International Choice Fund Class R3	ICEZX	NAS CM	Open End	Global Equity Large Cap (Foreign Stock)	C	C	B		Y	0
MainStay Epoch International Choice Fund Investor Class	ICELX	NAS CM	Open End	Global Equity Large Cap (Foreign Stock)	C	C	B		Y	1,000
MainStay Epoch U.S. All Cap Fund Class A	MAAAX	NAS CM	Open End	US Equity Large Cap Blend (Growth)	C+	C	B-	Up	Y	15,000
MainStay Epoch U.S. All Cap Fund Class B	MAWBX	NAS CM	Open End	US Equity Large Cap Blend (Growth)	C+	C	B-	Up		1,000
MainStay Epoch U.S. All Cap Fund Class C	MAWCX	NAS CM	Open End	US Equity Large Cap Blend (Growth)	C+	C	B-	Up	Y	1,000
MainStay Epoch U.S. All Cap Fund Class I	MATIX	NAS CM	Open End	US Equity Large Cap Blend (Growth)	C+	C	B		Y	1,000,000
MainStay Epoch U.S. All Cap Fund Class R6	MAWDX	NAS CM	Open End	US Equity Large Cap Blend (Growth)	C+	C	B		Y	0
MainStay Epoch U.S. All Cap Fund Investor Class	MAWNX	NAS CM	Open End	US Equity Large Cap Blend (Growth)	C+	C	B-	Up	Y	1,000
MainStay Epoch U.S. Equity Yield Fund Class A	EPLPX	NAS CM	Open End	US Equity Large Cap Value (Growth & Income)	B-	C	B+	Down	Y	15,000
MainStay Epoch U.S. Equity Yield Fund Class B	EPLBX	NAS CM	Open End	US Equity Large Cap Value (Growth & Income)	B-	C	B		Y	1,000
MainStay Epoch U.S. Equity Yield Fund Class C	EPLKX	NAS CM	Open End	US Equity Large Cap Value (Growth & Income)	B-	C	B		Y	2,500
MainStay Epoch U.S. Equity Yield Fund Class I	EPLCX	NAS CM	Open End	US Equity Large Cap Value (Growth & Income)	B-	C+	B+	Down	Y	1,000,000
MainStay Epoch U.S. Equity Yield Fund Class R1	EPLRX	NAS CM	Open End	US Equity Large Cap Value (Growth & Income)	B-	C	B+	Down	Y	0
MainStay Epoch U.S. Equity Yield Fund Class R2	EPLSX	NAS CM	Open End	US Equity Large Cap Value (Growth & Income)	B-	C	B+	Down	Y	0
MainStay Epoch U.S. Equity Yield Fund Class R3	EPLTX	NAS CM	Open End	US Equity Large Cap Value (Growth & Income)	B-	C	B+	Down	Y	0
MainStay Epoch U.S. Equity Yield Fund Class R6	EPLDX	NAS CM	Open End	US Equity Large Cap Value (Growth & Income)	B-	C+	B+	Down	Y	0
MainStay Epoch U.S. Equity Yield Fund Investor Class	EPLIX	NAS CM	Open End	US Equity Large Cap Value (Growth & Income)	B-	C	B+	Down	Y	2,500
MainStay Growth Allocation Class R3	MGXRX	NAS CM	Open End	Aggressive Alloc (Asset Alloc)	C	C	B		Y	0
MainStay Growth Allocation Fund Class A	MGXAX	NAS CM	Open End	Aggressive Alloc (Asset Alloc)	C	C	B		Y	15,000
MainStay Growth Allocation Fund Class B	MGXBX	NAS CM	Open End	Aggressive Alloc (Asset Alloc)	C	C	B			1,000
MainStay Growth Allocation Fund Class C	MGXCX	NAS CM	Open End	Aggressive Alloc (Asset Alloc)	C	C	B		Y	1,000
MainStay Growth Allocation Fund Class I	MGXIX	NAS CM	Open End	Aggressive Alloc (Asset Alloc)	C	C	B		Y	1,000,000
MainStay Growth Allocation Fund Investor Class	MGXNX	NAS CM	Open End	Aggressive Alloc (Asset Alloc)	C	C	B		Y	1,000
MainStay Income Builder Fund Class A	MTRAX	NAS CM	Open End	Moderate Alloc (Income)	B-	C+	B		Y	15,000
MainStay Income Builder Fund Class B	MKTRX	NAS CM	Open End	Moderate Alloc (Income)	B-	C	B			1,000
MainStay Income Builder Fund Class C	MCTRX	NAS CM	Open End	Moderate Alloc (Income)	B-	C	B		Y	1,000
MainStay Income Builder Fund Class I	MTOIX	NAS CM	Open End	Moderate Alloc (Income)	B-	C+	B	Down	Y	1,000,000

★Expanded analysis of this fund is included in Section II.

	TOTAL RETURNS					PERFORMANCE				ASSETS		ASSET ALLOCATION & TURNOVER					BULL & BEAR		FEES		
Min Additional Investment	3-Month Total Return	6-Month Total Return	1-Year Total Return	3-Year Total Return	5-Year Total Return	Dividend Yield (TTM)	Expense Ratio	3-Yr Std Deviation	3-Year Beta	NAV	Total Assets (MIL)	%Cash	%Stocks	%Bonds	%Other	Turnover Ratio	Last Bull Market Total Return	Last Bear Market Total Return	Front End Fee (%)	Back End Fee (%)	Inception Date
50	-7.28	7.49	-21.00	-7.41	-74.09	3.88	1.6	18.92	1.11	3.5	28.8	2	93	5	0	32			5.50		Jul-14
	-1.36	20.34	2.92	3.29	-28.17	5.81	1.51	18.05	1.06	10.76	1,243	3	97	0	0	50	9.87	-8.16	5.50		Oct-10
50	-1.41	20.02	2.20	1.00	-30.83	6.44	2.28	18.05	1.06	9.71	1,243	3	97	0	0	50	9.36	-8.43		1.00	Oct-10
	-1.32	20.48	3.19	4.09	-27.27	5.63	1.26	18.08	1.06	11.11	1,243	3	97	0	0	50	10.02	-8.06			Oct-10
50	-1.36	20.32	3.00	3.37	-28.14	5.81	1.53	18.08	1.06	10.77	1,243	3	97	0	0	50	9.86	-8.16	5.50		Jul-14
	-2.66	14.87	-14.38	6.00	-26.86	1.62	1.58	21.64	1.4	17.28	60.4	1	99	0	0	137			5.50		Apr-13
50	-2.93	14.34	-15.17	3.20	-30.03	1.71	2.45	21.6	1.4	16.33	60.4	1	99	0	0	137				1.00	Apr-13
	-2.57	15.05	-14.15	6.83	-25.90	1.59	1.33	21.61	1.4	17.56	60.4	1	99	0	0	137					Apr-13
50	-2.68	14.82	-14.50	5.54	-27.27	1.63	1.7	21.58	1.39	17.18	60.4	1	99	0	0	137			5.50		Jul-14
	5.18	20.13	6.64	35.06		0.61	1.09	12.21	1.05	12.77	124.2	1	98	0	1	51			5.50		Jun-16
50	4.91	19.56	5.53	31.39		0	2.08	12.2	1.05	12.59	124.2	1	98	0	1	51				1.00	Jun-16
	5.26	20.20	6.92	36.00		0.83	0.84	12.24	1.05	12.79	124.2	1	98	0	1	51					Jun-16
50	5.11	19.94	6.32	34.38		0.35	1.33	12.24	1.05	12.75	124.2	1	98	0	1	51			5.50		Jun-16
	1.37	12.38	6.26	18.49	17.35	3.01	1.09	9.62	0.76	18.21	1,981	0	99	0	1	15	13.4	-12.23	5.50		Aug-06
50	1.18	11.99	5.47	15.87	13.01	2.27	1.84	9.63	0.76	18.09	1,981	0	99	0	1	15	12.87	-12.49		1.00	Nov-09
	1.43	12.55	6.50	19.39	18.83	3.27	0.84	9.63	0.76	18.17	1,981	0	99	0	1	15	13.54	-12.15			Dec-05
	1.35	12.30	6.05	18.02	16.70	2.82	1.27	9.62	0.76	18.22	1,981	0	99	0	1	15	13.38	-12.24			Feb-14
	1.27	12.16	5.78	17.09	15.39	2.57	1.52	9.61	0.76	18.2	1,981	0	99	0	1	15	13.21	-12.33			Feb-16
	1.46	12.67	6.66	19.86	19.59	3.37	0.74	9.66	0.77	18.18	1,981	0	99	0	1	15	13.54	-12.15			Jun-13
50	1.37	12.34	6.19	18.47	17.30	2.99	1.1	9.58	0.76	18.17	1,981	0	99	0	1	15	13.42	-12.17	5.50		Nov-09
	5.30	16.08	2.79	32.44	5.97	1.41	1.18	11.79	1.03	35.36	431.0	0	97	0	3	44	12.7	-22.92	5.50		Sep-06
50	5.06	15.53	1.80	28.47	0.94	0.43	2.13	11.82	1.03	34.65	431.0	0	97	0	3	44	12.13	-23.19		1.00	Sep-06
	5.39	16.24	3.05	33.52	7.40	1.69	0.93	11.81	1.03	35.35	431.0	0	97	0	3	44	12.92	-22.79			Dec-97
	5.34	16.17	2.95	33.06	6.82	1.58	1.03	11.81	1.03	35.26	431.0	0	97	0	3	44	12.89	-22.86			Sep-06
	5.30	16.05	2.71	32.12	5.56	1.3	1.28	11.8	1.03	35.35	431.0	0	97	0	3	44	12.62	-22.95			Sep-06
	5.23	15.89	2.43	31.07	4.16	1.01	1.53	11.81	1.03	35.15	431.0	0	97	0	3	44	12.48	-23.03			Sep-06
50	5.24	15.99	2.57	31.73	5.07	1.19	1.38	11.79	1.03	35.32	431.0	0	97	0	3	44	12.58	-22.95	5.50		Apr-08
	6.67	22.34	8.26	46.88	52.10	0.37	1.17	13.5	1.06	25.08	697.6	0	98	0	2	41	25.64	-20.89	5.50		Jan-04
50	6.42	21.74	7.18	42.50	44.43	0	2.23	13.52	1.06	20.55	697.6	0	98	0	2	41	24.82	-21.31		5.00	Jan-04
50	6.41	21.72	7.18	42.40	44.33	0	2.23	13.53	1.07	20.56	697.6	0	98	0	2	41	24.8	-21.29		1.00	Jan-04
	6.76	22.51	8.51	47.99	54.03	0.54	0.92	13.5	1.06	28.4	697.6	0	98	0	2	41	25.85	-20.8			Jan-91
	6.80	22.57	8.61	48.14	54.19	0.62	0.87	13.49	1.06	28.4	697.6	0	98	0	2	41	25.85	-20.8			Feb-18
50	6.62	22.16	7.98	45.74	49.86	0.18	1.48	13.51	1.06	24.47	697.6	0	98	0	2	41	25.31	-21.01	5.50		Feb-08
	3.04	15.23	10.52	30.16	48.68	2.12	1.07	9.78	0.75	16.47	1,056	0	98	0	2	17	23.53	-19.01	5.50		Feb-09
50	2.83	14.61	9.46	26.75	42.61	1.24	2.04	9.79	0.75	15.91	1,056	0	98	0	2	17	22.97	-19.26		5.00	May-17
50	2.83	14.61	9.46	26.54	41.97	1.24	2.04	9.77	0.75	15.91	1,056	0	98	0	2	17	23.01	-19.3		1.00	Nov-09
	3.14	15.36	10.75	31.15	50.53	2.33	0.81	9.78	0.75	16.63	1,056	0	98	0	2	17	23.69	-18.93			Dec-08
	3.05	15.23	10.57	30.79	50.12	2.24	0.92	9.78	0.75	16.62	1,056	0	98	0	2	17	23.69	-18.93			May-17
	3.02	15.10	10.34	29.82	48.26	2.02	1.17	9.82	0.76	16.46	1,056	0	98	0	2	17	23.51	-19.01			May-17
	2.89	14.97	10.07	28.92	46.49	1.79	1.42	9.8	0.75	16.46	1,056	0	98	0	2	17	23.33	-19.1			May-17
	3.10	15.41	10.85	31.43	50.84	2.42	0.73	9.78	0.75	16.63	1,056	0	98	0	2	17	23.69	-18.93			May-17
50	3.00	15.03	10.20	29.35	47.29	1.93	1.29	9.8	0.75	16.39	1,056	0	98	0	2	17	23.53	-19.09	5.50		Nov-09
	2.58	15.72	0.40	30.85	23.94	0.87	1.63	12.39	0.99	14.69	375.7	0	98	0	1	48	22.83	-20.25			Feb-16
	2.78	16.00	0.85	32.29	26.08	1.14	1.28	12.37	0.99	14.78	375.7	0	98	0	1	48	22.92	-20.2	5.50		Apr-05
50	2.49	15.43	-0.12	28.75	20.40	0.15	2.2	12.38	0.99	14.37	375.7	0	98	0	1	48	22.25	-20.46		5.00	Apr-05
50	2.49	15.49	-0.13	28.69	20.44	0.15	2.2	12.4	0.99	14.39	375.7	0	98	0	1	48	22.34	-20.44		1.00	Apr-05
	2.80	16.22	1.08	33.36	27.65	1.37	1.03	12.4	0.99	15.04	375.7	0	98	0	1	48	23.19	-20.08			Apr-05
50	2.71	15.96	0.66	31.66	25.07	0.98	1.45	12.37	0.99	14.77	375.7	0	98	0	1	48	22.87	-20.28	5.50		Feb-08
	2.78	11.70	8.26	21.83	23.65	2.76	1.01	6.27	0.51	19.4	1,506	1	48	49	1	44	15.3	-10.94	5.50		Jan-95
50	2.59	11.18	7.30	18.62	18.25	1.89	1.89	6.27	0.51	19.54	1,506	1	48	49	1	44	14.6	-11.34		5.00	Dec-87
50	2.54	11.21	7.32	18.60	18.22	1.89	1.89	6.33	0.51	19.5	1,506	1	48	49	1	44	14.62	-11.31		1.00	Sep-98
	2.87	11.84	8.56	22.72	25.27	2.97	0.76	6.31	0.51	19.59	1,506	1	48	49	1	44	15.49	-10.87			Jan-04

	MARKET			FUND TYPE, CATEGORY & OBJECTIVE	RATINGS				MINIMUMS	
Fund Name	Ticker Symbol	Traded On	Fund Type	Category and (Prospectus Objective)	Overall Rating	Reward Rating	Risk Rating	Recent Up/ Downgrade	Open to New Investors	Min Initial Investment
MainStay Income Builder Fund Class R2	MTXRX	NAS CM	Open End	Moderate Alloc (Income)	B-	C+	B		Y	0
MainStay Income Builder Fund Class R3	MTXVX	NAS CM	Open End	Moderate Alloc (Income)	B-	C+	B		Y	0
MainStay Income Builder Fund Class R6	MTODX	NAS CM	Open End	Moderate Alloc (Income)	B-	C+	B		Y	0
MainStay Income Builder Fund Investor Class	MTINX	NAS CM	Open End	Moderate Alloc (Income)	B-	C+	B		Y	1,000
MainStay Large Cap Growth Fund Class A	MLAAX	NAS CM	Open End	US Equity Large Cap Growth (Growth)	C+	C+	B	Down	Y	15,000
MainStay Large Cap Growth Fund Class B	MLABX	NAS CM	Open End	US Equity Large Cap Growth (Growth)	C+	C+	B	Down		1,000
MainStay Large Cap Growth Fund Class C	MLACX	NAS CM	Open End	US Equity Large Cap Growth (Growth)	C+	C+	B	Down	Y	1,000
MainStay Large Cap Growth Fund Class I	MLAIX	NAS CM	Open End	US Equity Large Cap Growth (Growth)	B-	C+	B	Down	Y	1,000,000
MainStay Large Cap Growth Fund Class R1	MLRRX	NAS CM	Open End	US Equity Large Cap Growth (Growth)	C+	C+	B	Down	Y	0
MainStay Large Cap Growth Fund Class R2	MLRTX	NAS CM	Open End	US Equity Large Cap Growth (Growth)	C+	C+	B	Down	Y	0
MainStay Large Cap Growth Fund Class R3	MLGRX	NAS CM	Open End	US Equity Large Cap Growth (Growth)	C+	C+	B	Down	Y	0
MainStay Large Cap Growth Fund Class R6	MLRSX	NAS CM	Open End	US Equity Large Cap Growth (Growth)	B-	C+	B	Down	Y	0
MainStay Large Cap Growth Fund Investor Class	MLINX	NAS CM	Open End	US Equity Large Cap Growth (Growth)	C+	C+	B	Down	Y	1,000
MainStay MacKay Common Stock Fund Class A	MSOAX	NAS CM	Open End	US Equity Large Cap Blend (Growth)	C+	C	B		Y	15,000
MainStay MacKay Common Stock Fund Class B	MOPBX	NAS CM	Open End	US Equity Large Cap Blend (Growth)	C+	C	B			1,000
MainStay MacKay Common Stock Fund Class C	MGOCX	NAS CM	Open End	US Equity Large Cap Blend (Growth)	C+	C	B		Y	1,000
MainStay MacKay Common Stock Fund Class I	MSOIX	NAS CM	Open End	US Equity Large Cap Blend (Growth)	C+	C	B		Y	1,000,000
MainStay MacKay Common Stock Fund Class R3	MSOSX	NAS CM	Open End	US Equity Large Cap Blend (Growth)	C+	C	B		Y	0
MainStay MacKay Common Stock Fund Investor Class	MCSSX	NAS CM	Open End	US Equity Large Cap Blend (Growth)	C+	C	B		Y	1,000
MainStay MacKay Convertible Fund Class A	MCOAX	NAS CM	Open End	Convertibles (Convertible Bond)	B-	C	B+	Down	Y	15,000
MainStay MacKay Convertible Fund Class B	MCSVX	NAS CM	Open End	Convertibles (Convertible Bond)	B-	C	B+			1,000
MainStay MacKay Convertible Fund Class C	MCCVX	NAS CM	Open End	Convertibles (Convertible Bond)	B-	C	B+		Y	1,000
MainStay MacKay Convertible Fund Class I	MCNVX	NAS CM	Open End	Convertibles (Convertible Bond)	B-	C	B+	Down	Y	1,000,000
MainStay MacKay Convertible Fund Investor Class	MCINX	NAS CM	Open End	Convertibles (Convertible Bond)	B-	C	B+	Down	Y	1,000
MainStay MacKay Emerging Markets Equity Fund Class A	MEOAX	NAS CM	Open End	Global Emerg Mkts (Div Emerging Mkts)	C	C	C+		Y	15,000
MainStay MacKay Emerging Markets Equity Fund Class C	MEOCX	NAS CM	Open End	Global Emerg Mkts (Div Emerging Mkts)	C	C	C		Y	2,500
MainStay MacKay Emerging Markets Equity Fund Class I	MEOIX	NAS CM	Open End	Global Emerg Mkts (Div Emerging Mkts)	C	C	C+		Y	1,000,000
MainStay MacKay Emerging Markets Equity Fund Class R6	MEODX	NAS CM	Open End	Global Emerg Mkts (Div Emerging Mkts)	C	C	C+		Y	0
MainStay MacKay Emerging Markets Equity Investor Cls	MEOVX	NAS CM	Open End	Global Emerg Mkts (Div Emerging Mkts)	C	C	C+		Y	2,500
MainStay MacKay Growth Fund Class A	KLGAX	NAS CM	Open End	US Equity Large Cap Growth (Growth)	C+	C	B-	Down	Y	15,000
MainStay MacKay Growth Fund Class B	KLGBX	NAS CM	Open End	US Equity Large Cap Growth (Growth)	C+	C	B-		Y	1,000
MainStay MacKay Growth Fund Class C	KLGCX	NAS CM	Open End	US Equity Large Cap Growth (Growth)	C+	C	B-		Y	2,500
MainStay MacKay Growth Fund Class I	KLGIX	NAS CM	Open End	US Equity Large Cap Growth (Growth)	C+	C	B-	Down	Y	1,000,000
MainStay MacKay Growth Fund Class R2	KLGRX	NAS CM	Open End	US Equity Large Cap Growth (Growth)	C+	C	B-	Down	Y	0
MainStay MacKay Growth Fund Investor Class	KLGNX	NAS CM	Open End	US Equity Large Cap Growth (Growth)	C+	C	B-		Y	2,500
MainStay MacKay International Equity Fund Class A	MSEAX	NAS CM	Open End	Global Equity Large Cap (Foreign Stock)	C	C	C+		Y	15,000
MainStay MacKay International Equity Fund Class B	MINEX	NAS CM	Open End	Global Equity Large Cap (Foreign Stock)	C	C	C+			1,000
MainStay MacKay International Equity Fund Class C	MIECX	NAS CM	Open End	Global Equity Large Cap (Foreign Stock)	C	C	C+		Y	1,000
MainStay MacKay International Equity Fund Class I	MSIIX	NAS CM	Open End	Global Equity Large Cap (Foreign Stock)	C	C	C+		Y	1,000,000
MainStay MacKay International Equity Fund Class R1	MIERX	NAS CM	Open End	Global Equity Large Cap (Foreign Stock)	C	C	C+		Y	0
MainStay MacKay International Equity Fund Class R2	MIRRX	NAS CM	Open End	Global Equity Large Cap (Foreign Stock)	C	C	C+		Y	0
MainStay MacKay International Equity Fund Class R3	MIFRX	NAS CM	Open End	Global Equity Large Cap (Foreign Stock)	C	C	C+		Y	0
MainStay MacKay International Equity Fund Class R6	MIFDX	NAS CM	Open End	Global Equity Large Cap (Foreign Stock)	C	C	C+		Y	0
MainStay MacKay International Equity Fund Investor Class	MINNX	NAS CM	Open End	Global Equity Large Cap (Foreign Stock)	C	C	C+		Y	1,000
MainStay MacKay International Opportunities Fund Class A	MYITX	NAS CM	Open End	Global Equity Large Cap (Foreign Stock)	D+	D+	C-		Y	15,000
MainStay MacKay International Opportunities Fund Class C	MYICX	NAS CM	Open End	Global Equity Large Cap (Foreign Stock)	D+	D	C-		Y	1,000
MainStay MacKay International Opportunities Fund Class I	MYIIX	NAS CM	Open End	Global Equity Large Cap (Foreign Stock)	D+	D+	C-		Y	1,000,000
MainStay MacKay International Opportunities Investor Cls	MYINX	NAS CM	Open End	Global Equity Large Cap (Foreign Stock)	D+	D+	C-		Y	1,000
MainStay MacKay S&P 500 Index Fund Class A	MSXAX	NAS CM	Open End	US Equity Large Cap Blend (Growth & Income)	B-	C	B		Y	15,000
MainStay MacKay S&P 500 Index Fund Class I	MSPIX	NAS CM	Open End	US Equity Large Cap Blend (Growth & Income)	B-	C	B		Y	1,000,000
MainStay MacKay S&P 500 Index Fund Investor Class	MYSPX	NAS CM	Open End	US Equity Large Cap Blend (Growth & Income)	B-	C	B		Y	1,000
MainStay MacKay Small Cap Core Fund Class A	MOPAX	NAS CM	Open End	US Equity Small Cap (Small Company)	C	D+	C		Y	15,000

★ Expanded analysis of this fund is included in Section II.

	TOTAL RETURNS					PERFORMANCE				ASSETS		ASSET ALLOCATION & TURNOVER					BULL & BEAR		FEES		
Min Additional Investment	3-Month Total Return	6-Month Total Return	1-Year Total Return	3-Year Total Return	5-Year Total Return	Dividend Yield (TTM)	Expense Ratio	3-Yr Std Deviation	3-Year Beta	NAV	Total Assets (MIL)	%Cash	%Stocks	%Bonds	%Other	Turnover Ratio	Last Bull Market Total Return	Last Bear Market Total Return	Front End Fee (%)	Back End Fee (%)	Inception Date
	2.81	11.65	8.21	21.47	22.43	2.66	1.11	6.3	0.51	19.39	1,506	1	48	49	1	44	14.6	-11.34			Feb-15
	2.69	11.46	7.89	20.55	20.36	2.43	1.36	6.29	0.51	19.4	1,506	1	48	49	1	44	14.6	-11.34			Feb-16
	2.90	11.89	8.67	20.57	20.19	3.07	0.66	6.29	0.51	19.59	1,506	1	48	49	1	44	14.6	-11.34			Feb-18
50	2.80	11.61	8.16	21.35	22.80	2.62	1.14	6.33	0.51	19.42	1,506	1	48	49	1	44	15.1	-11.03	5.50		Feb-08
	4.52	24.11	11.54	72.58	85.57	0	0.98	14.37	1.03	9.47	11,931	0	100	0	0	52	26.84	-17.71	5.50		Jul-95
50	4.32	23.63	10.60	68.32	78.20	0	1.82	14.3	1.03	7.48	11,931	0	100	0	0	52	26.14	-18.05		5.00	Apr-05
50	4.32	23.67	10.75	68.43	78.35	0	1.82	14.39	1.04	7.47	11,931	0	100	0	0	52	26.36	-18.08		1.00	Apr-05
	4.64	24.36	11.86	73.98	88.20	0	0.73	14.4	1.04	10.36	11,931	0	100	0	0	52	26.98	-17.7			Apr-05
	4.58	24.25	11.68	73.51	87.13	0	0.83	14.39	1.03	10.04	11,931	0	100	0	0	52	26.96	-17.75			Apr-05
	4.55	24.11	11.48	72.14	84.72	0	1.08	14.33	1.03	9.42	11,931	0	100	0	0	52	26.75	-17.77			Apr-05
	4.49	24.01	11.24	70.83	82.49	0	1.33	14.34	1.03	8.83	11,931	0	100	0	0	52	26.66	-17.87			Apr-06
	4.60	24.43	11.98	74.53	89.14	0	0.64	14.4	1.04	10.44	11,931	0	100	0	0	52	26.84	-17.71			Jun-13
50	4.48	24.13	11.50	72.26	84.93	0	1.07	14.39	1.03	9.31	11,931	0	100	0	0	52	26.81	-17.78	5.50		Feb-08
	2.23	15.51	4.33	43.21	51.97	0.81	0.97	12.75	1.04	24.27	194.0	0	100	0	0	137	24.36	-17.27	5.50		Jun-98
50	1.94	14.89	3.22	38.89	44.48	0	1.98	12.72	1.03	21.98	194.0	0	100	0	0	137	23.44	-17.69		5.00	Jun-98
50	1.99	14.96	3.27	38.92	44.52	0	1.98	12.73	1.03	21.97	194.0	0	100	0	0	137	23.44	-17.69		1.00	Sep-98
	2.26	15.66	4.54	44.26	53.84	1.05	0.71	12.74	1.03	24.37	194.0	0	100	0	0	137	24.52	-17.16			Dec-04
	2.15	15.32	3.95	41.61	49.49	0.51	1.32	12.74	1.03	24.15	194.0	0	100	0	0	137	24.18	-17.35			Feb-16
50	2.18	15.35	4.05	42.07	50.10	0.57	1.23	12.74	1.03	24.27	194.0	0	100	0	0	137	24.03	-17.48	5.50		Feb-08
	3.36	16.64	7.54	37.95	39.23	0.88	0.98	9.6	1.09	17.79	1,433	0	5	0	5	43	16.65	-19.56	5.50		Jan-95
50	3.14	16.10	6.61	34.27	33.03	0.15	1.89	9.59	1.09	17.69	1,433	0	5	0	5	43	15.94	-19.86		5.00	May-86
50	3.15	16.13	6.61	34.23	33.07	0.15	1.89	9.56	1.08	17.67	1,433	0	5	0	5	43	15.95	-19.87		1.00	Sep-98
	3.45	16.81	7.91	39.35	41.35	1.22	0.61	9.6	1.09	17.82	1,433	0	5	0	5	43	16.78	-19.48			Nov-08
50	3.38	16.54	7.43	37.31	38.15	0.73	1.14	9.6	1.09	17.79	1,433	0	5	0	5	43	16.45	-19.59	5.50		Feb-08
	1.88	11.28	-1.88	30.52	6.75	1.25	1.52	14.64	1.04	9.17	80.4	1	99	0	0	167			5.50		Nov-13
50	1.57	10.64	-2.87	26.64	1.59	0.21	2.47	14.58	1.03	9.04	80.4	1	99	0	0	167				1.00	Nov-13
	1.88	11.50	-1.62	31.50	8.11	1.47	1.17	14.6	1.03	9.21	80.4	1	99	0	0	167					Nov-13
	1.88	11.40	-1.54	31.48	8.09	1.74	1.17	14.66	1.04	9.18	80.4	1	99	0	0	167					Feb-18
50	1.89	11.21	-2.14	29.64	5.37	1.12	1.73	14.64	1.04	9.12	80.4	1	99	0	0	167			5.50		Nov-13
	2.25	18.07	4.10	54.99	56.61	0.17	1.06	14.05	1.04	34.89	699.4	0	100	0	0	116	28.62	-18.62	5.50		Aug-06
50	1.98	17.43	3.05	50.44	49.26	0	2.12	14.04	1.04	32.33	699.4	0	100	0	0	116	28.06	-18.87		5.00	Jan-13
50	1.98	17.44	3.05	50.40	49.22	0	2.12	14.05	1.04	32.32	699.4	0	100	0	0	116	28.06	-18.87		1.00	Jan-13
	2.31	18.20	4.37	56.10	58.54	0.4	0.81	14.05	1.04	35.77	699.4	0	100	0	0	116	28.88	-18.52			Nov-09
	2.24	18.01	4.02	54.66	55.81	0.07	1.16	14.06	1.04	34.65	699.4	0	100	0	0	116	28.62	-18.62			Jan-13
50	2.19	17.92	3.85	53.80	54.95	0	1.37	14.04	1.04	34.4	699.4	0	100	0	0	116	28.62	-18.62	5.50		Jan-13
	1.89	13.26	-2.92	26.29	19.75	0	1.15	13.21	1.05	16.65	308.8	3	96	0	0	53	20.73	-25.58	5.50		Jan-95
50	1.60	12.67	-4.02	22.21	13.29	0	2.27	13.18	1.05	14.58	308.8	3	96	0	0	53	20.03	-25.93		5.00	Sep-94
50	1.60	12.67	-4.02	22.21	13.29	0	2.27	13.21	1.05	14.58	308.8	3	96	0	0	53	20.03	-25.93		1.00	Sep-98
	2.00	13.53	-2.62	27.41	21.30	0.05	0.85	13.22	1.05	16.78	308.8	3	96	0	0	53	20.87	-25.5			Jan-04
	1.89	13.40	-2.75	26.91	20.69	0	1	13.19	1.05	16.67	308.8	3	96	0	0	53	20.88	-25.58			Jan-04
	1.83	13.23	-3.03	25.97	19.19	0	1.25	13.19	1.05	16.68	308.8	3	96	0	0	53	20.66	-25.6			Jan-04
	1.78	13.08	-3.23	25.03	17.65	0	1.5	13.22	1.06	16.51	308.8	3	96	0	0	53	20.46	-25.67			Apr-06
	2.00	13.19	-3.58	22.77	13.82		0.83	13.18	1.05	16.78	308.8	3	96	0	0	53	20.03	-25.93			Feb-19
50	1.78	13.09	-3.23	25.00	17.69	0	1.53	13.21	1.05	16.5	308.8	3	96	0	0	53	20.44	-25.64	5.50		Feb-08
	1.98	11.90	-5.10	14.68	-3.35	5.37	1.78	12.5	1.06	7.71	346.0	0	99	0	0	223	15	-24.31	5.50		Sep-07
50	1.77	11.51	-5.98	11.86	-7.35	4.28	2.62	12.44	1.06	7.46	346.0	0	99	0	0	223	14.44	-24.5		1.00	Sep-07
	2.10	12.28	-4.80	15.75	-1.97	5.7	1.53	12.51	1.06	7.77	346.0	0	99	0	0	223	15.26	-24.25			Sep-07
50	1.99	11.95	-5.28	14.45	-3.89	5.24	1.88	12.48	1.06	7.68	346.0	0	99	0	0	223	14.88	-24.21	5.50		Feb-08
	4.18	19.25	9.91	48.52	61.77	1.47	0.54	12.19	1	47.82	1,023	1	98	0	0	3	24.7	-16.45	3.00		Jan-04
	4.23	19.41	10.17	49.62	63.80	1.68	0.29	12.17	1	48.53	1,023	1	98	0	0	3	24.86	-16.34			Jan-91
50	4.12	19.14	9.71	47.88	60.76	1.33	0.87	12.18	1	47.74	1,023	1	98	0	0	3	24.63	-16.48	3.00		Feb-08
	-0.92	12.30	-6.63	22.30	21.77	0.19	1.18	16.44	0.93	24.73	369.9	0	98	0	2	92	26.57	-21.78	5.50		Jan-04

	MARKET		FUND TYPE, CATEGORY & OBJECTIVE		RATINGS				MINIMUMS	
Fund Name	Ticker Symbol	Traded On	Fund Type	Category and (Prospectus Objective)	Overall Rating	Reward Rating	Risk Rating	Recent Up/ Downgrade	Open to New Investors	Min Initial Investment
MainStay MacKay Small Cap Core Fund Class B	MOTBX	NAS CM	Open End	US Equity Small Cap (Small Company)	C-	D+	C	Down	Y	1,000
MainStay MacKay Small Cap Core Fund Class C	MOPCX	NAS CM	Open End	US Equity Small Cap (Small Company)	C-	D+	C	Down	Y	1,000
MainStay MacKay Small Cap Core Fund Class I	MOPIX	NAS CM	Open End	US Equity Small Cap (Small Company)	C	C-	C		Y	1,000,000
MainStay MacKay Small Cap Core Fund Class R1	MOPRX	NAS CM	Open End	US Equity Small Cap (Small Company)	C	C-	C		Y	0
MainStay MacKay Small Cap Core Fund Class R2	MOTRX	NAS CM	Open End	US Equity Small Cap (Small Company)	C	D+	C		Y	0
MainStay MacKay Small Cap Core Fund Class R3	MOVRX	NAS CM	Open End	US Equity Small Cap (Small Company)	C	D+	C		Y	0
MainStay MacKay Small Cap Core Fund Investor Class	MOINX	NAS CM	Open End	US Equity Small Cap (Small Company)	C	D+	C		Y	1,000
MainStay MacKay U.S. Equity Opportunities Fund Class A	MYCTX	NAS CM	Open End	US Equity Large Cap Blend (Growth)	C	C	B-		Y	15,000
MainStay MacKay U.S. Equity Opportunities Fund Class C	MYCCX	NAS CM	Open End	US Equity Large Cap Blend (Growth)	C	C	B-		Y	1,000
MainStay MacKay U.S. Equity Opportunities Fund Class I	MYCIX	NAS CM	Open End	US Equity Large Cap Blend (Growth)	C	C	B-		Y	1,000,000
MainStay MacKay U.S. Equity Opportunities Investor Cls	MYCNX	NAS CM	Open End	US Equity Large Cap Blend (Growth)	C	C	B-		Y	1,000
MainStay MAP Equity Fund Class A	MAPAX	NAS CM	Open End	US Equity Large Cap Blend (Growth)	C+	C	B		Y	15,000
MainStay MAP Equity Fund Class B	MAPBX	NAS CM	Open End	US Equity Large Cap Blend (Growth)	C+	C	B			1,000
MainStay MAP Equity Fund Class C	MMPCX	NAS CM	Open End	US Equity Large Cap Blend (Growth)	C+	C	B		Y	1,000
MainStay MAP Equity Fund Class I	MUBFX	NAS CM	Open End	US Equity Large Cap Blend (Growth)	C+	C	B		Y	1,000,000
MainStay MAP Equity Fund Class R1	MAPRX	NAS CM	Open End	US Equity Large Cap Blend (Growth)	C+	C	B		Y	0
MainStay MAP Equity Fund Class R2	MPRRX	NAS CM	Open End	US Equity Large Cap Blend (Growth)	C+	C	B		Y	0
MainStay MAP Equity Fund Class R3	MMAPX	NAS CM	Open End	US Equity Large Cap Blend (Growth)	C+	C	B		Y	0
MainStay MAP Equity Fund Investor Class	MSMIX	NAS CM	Open End	US Equity Large Cap Blend (Growth)	C+	C	B		Y	1,000
MainStay Moderate Allocation Class R3	MMRHX	NAS CM	Open End	Moderate Alloc (Asset Alloc)	B-	C	B+	Up	Y	0
MainStay Moderate Allocation Fund Class A	MMRAX	NAS CM	Open End	Moderate Alloc (Asset Alloc)	B-	C	B+	Up	Y	15,000
MainStay Moderate Allocation Fund Class B	MMRBX	NAS CM	Open End	Moderate Alloc (Asset Alloc)	C+	C	B	Up		1,000
MainStay Moderate Allocation Fund Class C	MMRCX	NAS CM	Open End	Moderate Alloc (Asset Alloc)	C+	C	B	Up	Y	1,000
MainStay Moderate Allocation Fund Class I	MMRIX	NAS CM	Open End	Moderate Alloc (Asset Alloc)	B-	C	B+	Up	Y	1,000,000
MainStay Moderate Allocation Fund Class R2	MMRKX	NAS CM	Open End	Moderate Alloc (Asset Alloc)	B-	C	B+			0
MainStay Moderate Allocation Fund Investor Class	MMRDX	NAS CM	Open End	Moderate Alloc (Asset Alloc)	B-	C	B+	Up	Y	1,000
MainStay Moderate Growth Allocation Class R3	MGDRX	NAS CM	Open End	Aggressive Alloc (Asset Alloc)	C+	C	B	Up	Y	0
MainStay Moderate Growth Allocation Fund Class A	MGDAX	NAS CM	Open End	Aggressive Alloc (Asset Alloc)	C+	C	B	Up	Y	15,000
MainStay Moderate Growth Allocation Fund Class B	MGDBX	NAS CM	Open End	Aggressive Alloc (Asset Alloc)	C	C	B			1,000
MainStay Moderate Growth Allocation Fund Class C	MGDCX	NAS CM	Open End	Aggressive Alloc (Asset Alloc)	C	C	B		Y	1,000
MainStay Moderate Growth Allocation Fund Class I	MGDIX	NAS CM	Open End	Aggressive Alloc (Asset Alloc)	C+	C	B	Up	Y	1,000,000
MainStay Moderate Growth Allocation Fund Class R1	MGDJX	NAS CM	Open End	Aggressive Alloc (Asset Alloc)	C+	C	B			0
MainStay Moderate Growth Allocation Fund Class R2	MGDKX	NAS CM	Open End	Aggressive Alloc (Asset Alloc)	C+	C	B			0
MainStay Moderate Growth Allocation Fund Investor Class	MGDNX	NAS CM	Open End	Aggressive Alloc (Asset Alloc)	C+	C	B	Up	Y	1,000
Mairs & Power Balanced Fund Investor Class	MAPOX	NAS CM	Open End	Moderate Alloc (Balanced)	B	C+	B+		Y	2,500
Mairs & Power Growth Fund Investor Class	MPGFX	NAS CM	Open End	US Equity Large Cap Blend (Growth)	B-	C	B	Down	Y	2,500
Mairs & Power Small Cap Fund	MSCFX	NAS CM	Open End	US Equity Small Cap (Small Company)	C+	C	B-		Y	2,500
Manning & Napier Blended Asset Conservative Series Cls R6			Open End	Cautious Alloc (Income)	D+	D+	B	Up	Y	0
Manning & Napier Blended Asset Extended Series Class R6			Open End	Moderate Alloc (Growth)	D+	D+	B-	Up	Y	0
Manning & Napier Blended Asset Maximum Series Class R6			Open End	Aggressive Alloc (Growth)	D+	D+	B-	Up	Y	0
Manning & Napier Blended Asset Moderate Series Class R6			Open End	Cautious Alloc (Growth)	D+	D+	B-	Up	Y	0
Manning & Napier Disciplined Value Series Class I	MNDFX	NAS CM	Open End	US Equity Large Cap Value (Equity-Income)	B-	C	B+	Down	Y	1,000,000
Manning & Napier Disciplined Value Series Class S	MDFSX	NAS CM	Open End	US Equity Large Cap Value (Equity-Income)	B-	C	B+	Down	Y	2,000
Manning & Napier Disciplined Value Series Class W	MDVWX	NAS CM	Open End	US Equity Large Cap Value (Equity-Income)	B-	C	B+	Down	Y	0
Manning & Napier Disciplined Value Series Class Z	MDVZX	NAS CM	Open End	US Equity Large Cap Value (Equity-Income)	B-	C	B+	Down	Y	1,000,000
Manning & Napier Equity Income Series Class I	MNEIX	NAS CM	Open End	US Equity Large Cap Value (Equity-Income)	B-	C	B		Y	1,000,000
Manning & Napier Equity Income Series Class S	MNESX	NAS CM	Open End	US Equity Large Cap Value (Equity-Income)	B-	C	B		Y	2,000
Manning & Napier Equity Income Series Class W	MNEWX	NAS CM	Open End	US Equity Large Cap Value (Equity-Income)	B-	C	B		Y	0
Manning & Napier Equity Income Series Class Z	MNEZX	NAS CM	Open End	US Equity Large Cap Value (Equity-Income)	B-	C	B		Y	1,000,000
Manning & Napier Equity Series Class S	EXEYX	NAS CM	Open End	US Equity Large Cap Growth (Growth)	B-	C+	B	Down	Y	2,000
Manning & Napier Equity Series Class W	MEYWX	NAS CM	Open End	US Equity Large Cap Growth (Growth)	B-	C+	B		Y	0
Manning & Napier Income Series Class I	MSMAX	NAS CM	Open End	Moderate Alloc (Income)	B	C+	A		Y	1,000,000

★ Expanded analysis of this fund is included in Section II.

	TOTAL RETURNS					PERFORMANCE				ASSETS		ASSET ALLOCATION & TURNOVER					BULL & BEAR		FEES		
Min Additional Investment	3-Month Total Return	6-Month Total Return	1-Year Total Return	3-Year Total Return	5-Year Total Return	Dividend Yield (TTM)	Expense Ratio	3-Yr Std Deviation	3-Year Beta	NAV	Total Assets (MIL)	%Cash	%Stocks	%Bonds	%Other	Turnover Ratio	Last Bull Market Total Return	Last Bear Market Total Return	Front End Fee (%)	Back End Fee (%)	Inception Date
50	-1.17	11.67	-7.59	18.60	15.72	0	2.26	16.44	0.93	21.05	369.9	0	98	0	2	92	25.86	-22.17		5.00	Jan-04
50	-1.17	11.73	-7.58	18.62	15.74	0	2.26	16.45	0.93	21.04	369.9	0	98	0	2	92	25.88	-22.22		1.00	Dec-02
	-0.85	12.40	-6.40	23.20	23.29	0.44	0.93	16.46	0.93	25.56	369.9	0	98	0	2	92	26.84	-21.76			Jan-87
	-0.89	12.35	-6.49	22.84	22.71	0.35	1.03	16.46	0.93	25.47	369.9	0	98	0	2	92	26.84	-21.76			Jul-12
	-0.92	12.22	-6.73	21.90	21.16	0.09	1.28	16.46	0.93	24.61	369.9	0	98	0	2	92	26.65	-21.84			Jul-12
	-1.01	12.08	-6.96	21.01	19.84	0	1.53	16.44	0.93	24.49	369.9	0	98	0	2	92	26.47	-21.92			Feb-16
50	-0.98	12.11	-6.88	21.33	20.15	0	1.51	16.45	0.93	24.24	369.9	0	98	0	2	92	26.34	-21.9	5.50		Feb-08
	2.46	14.75	-0.12	40.97	53.92	0.64	1.51	13.41	1.05	8.32	588.2	0	96	0	4	167	23.94	-16.5	5.50		Jun-07
50	2.18	14.37	-0.86	37.53	47.57	0	2.32	13.45	1.05	7	588.2	0	96	0	4	167	23.32	-16.88		1.00	Jun-07
	2.42	14.84	0.15	41.83	55.63	0.89	1.26	13.37	1.04	8.43	588.2	0	96	0	4	167	24.16	-16.47			Jun-07
50	2.38	14.78	-0.16	40.62	52.98	0.61	1.56	13.41	1.05	8.15	588.2	0	96	0	4	167	23.88	-16.56	5.50		Feb-08
	4.91	19.08	8.14	47.92	45.28	0.62	1.1	12.85	1.02	40.37	1,035	0	99	0	1	15	23.27	-19.76	5.50		Jun-99
50	4.64	18.49	7.11	43.73	38.64	0	2.06	12.81	1.01	35.36	1,035	0	99	0	1	15	22.6	-20.06		5.00	Jun-99
50	4.61	18.49	7.11	43.73	38.65	0	2.06	12.81	1.01	35.36	1,035	0	99	0	1	15	22.6	-20.08		1.00	Jun-99
	4.95	19.22	8.42	49.01	47.13	0.84	0.85	12.84	1.01	41.74	1,035	0	99	0	1	15	23.45	-19.65			Jan-71
	4.92	19.16	8.30	48.57	46.39	0.69	0.95	12.84	1.02	40.73	1,035	0	99	0	1	15	23.4	-19.71			Jan-04
	4.85	18.98	8.00	47.43	44.51	0.45	1.2	12.83	1.01	40.61	1,035	0	99	0	1	15	23.2	-19.78			Jan-04
	4.79	18.85	7.74	46.35	42.74	0.2	1.45	12.83	1.01	40.41	1,035	0	99	0	1	15	23.01	-19.85			Apr-06
50	4.80	18.93	7.90	46.97	43.90	0.44	1.31	12.84	1.01	40.33	1,035	0	99	0	1	15	23.14	-19.83	5.50		Feb-08
	2.52	12.14	2.79	22.25	19.93	1.58	1.52	8.02	0.64	12.99	751.9	1	60	33	5	52	16.42	-12.8			Feb-16
	2.60	12.30	3.13	23.52	21.83	2	1.17	8.04	0.64	13.01	751.9	1	60	33	5	52	16.54	-12.68	5.50		Apr-05
50	2.30	11.71	2.14	20.09	16.29	1.01	2.16	8.02	0.64	12.86	751.9	1	60	33	5	52	16.01	-13.05		5.00	Apr-05
50	2.38	11.81	2.22	20.10	16.30	1.01	2.16	8.05	0.64	12.86	751.9	1	60	33	5	52	15.9	-12.97		1.00	Apr-05
	2.66	12.35	3.32	24.31	23.23	2.24	0.92	8.01	0.64	13.09	751.9	1	60	33	5	52	16.76	-12.62			Apr-05
0							1.27	8.01	0.64	13.01	751.9	1	60	33	5	52					Jun-19
50	2.52	12.14	2.91	22.80	20.72	1.82	1.41	8.02	0.64	13.02	751.9	1	60	33	5	52	16.5	-12.84	5.50		Feb-08
	2.40	13.92	1.03	26.63	22.28	1.48	1.59	10.55	0.84	14.07	778.7	1	79	13	5	47	19.99	-17.24			Feb-16
	2.46	14.10	1.39	27.86	24.14	1.85	1.24	10.56	0.84	14.12	778.7	1	79	13	5	47	20.2	-17.11	5.50		Apr-05
50	2.20	13.54	0.41	24.35	18.50	0.84	2.25	10.56	0.84	13.93	778.7	1	79	13	5	47	19.63	-17.49		5.00	Apr-05
50	2.27	13.54	0.41	24.35	18.50	0.84	2.25	10.52	0.84	13.93	778.7	1	79	13	5	47	19.62	-17.49		1.00	Apr-05
	2.58	14.27	1.62	28.89	25.71	2.09	0.99	10.53	0.84	14.29	778.7	1	79	13	5	47	20.34	-17.07			Apr-05
0							1.09	10.53	0.84	14.29	778.7	1	79	13	5	47					Jun-19
0							1.34	10.53	0.84	14.12	778.7	1	79	13	5	47					Jun-19
50	2.46	14.02	1.18	27.17	23.03	1.67	1.5	10.52	0.84	14.13	778.7	1	79	13	5	47	20.06	-17.2	5.50		Feb-08
100	3.19	13.17	12.17	27.06	35.34	2.16	0.72	8		96.43	888.4	2	64	34	0	9	19.85	-11.45			Nov-61
100	2.73	17.46	13.68	36.89	50.24	1.29	0.64	12.61	0.98	122.92	4,404	1	99	0	0	9	29.13	-18.05			Nov-58
100	4.11	17.31	2.76	34.80	42.87	0.56	1.04	16.58	0.9	26.08	436.2	2	98	0	0	20	42.81				Aug-11
	2.83	9.26	6.72			2.24	0.45			11.26	78.7	5	26	69	0	71					Oct-17
	3.47	13.04	6.67			1.62	0.55			10.93	160.6	3	47	50	0	99					Oct-17
	4.40	18.91	6.73			1.04	0.55			12.34	119.6	2	84	14	0	85					Oct-17
	3.28	11.29	6.59			1.91	0.5			11.26	92.7	3	36	62	0	91					Oct-17
	1.66	13.45	8.63	46.08	55.84	1.37	0.6	12.76	1.02	13.58	311.8	2	98	0	0	96	17.81	-10.61			Nov-08
	1.62	13.38	8.42	44.99	53.97	2.11	0.84	12.79	1.02	7.41	311.8	2	98	0	0	96	17.67	-10.61			Mar-12
	1.87	13.68	8.86	46.38	56.16		0.15	12.78	1.02	7.42	311.8	2	98	0	0	96	17.81	-10.61			Mar-19
	1.68	13.48	8.66	46.12	55.88		0.45	12.77	1.02	13.58	311.8	2	98	0	0	96	17.81	-10.61			Mar-19
	3.86	19.22	9.56	36.56	41.17	1.69	0.72	11.88	0.96	12.33	77.2	1	99	0	0	40					Dec-13
	3.76	18.98	9.30	35.62	39.59	1.4	0.96	11.9	0.96	12.33	77.2	1	99	0	0	40					Dec-13
	3.97	19.34	9.67	36.71	41.32		0.12	11.86	0.95	12.32	77.2	1	99	0	0	40					Mar-19
	3.94	19.32	9.65	36.68	41.29		0.57	11.88	0.96	12.33	77.2	1	99	0	0	40					Mar-19
	4.13	21.38	9.04	55.27	51.38	0.04	1.05	12.36	0.91	13.34	65.6	2	98	0	0	45	20.06	-19.94			May-98
	4.36	21.65	9.28	55.61	51.72		0.05	12.36	0.91	13.38	65.6	2	98	0	0	45	20.06	-19.94			Mar-19
	2.71	10.88	8.98	24.46	29.94	3.03	0.63	5.44	0.22	11.05	51.7	7	38	54	0	51					Aug-12

	MARKET			FUND TYPE, CATEGORY & OBJECTIVE	RATINGS				MINIMUMS	
Fund Name	Ticker Symbol	Traded On	Fund Type	Category and (Prospectus Objective)	Overall Rating	Reward Rating	Risk Rating	Recent Up/ Downgrade	Open to New Investors	Min Initial Investment
Manning & Napier Income Series Class S	MSMSX	NAS CM	Open End	Moderate Alloc (Income)	B	C+	A		Y	2,000
Manning & Napier International Series Class I	MNIIX	NAS CM	Open End	Global Equity Large Cap (Foreign Stock)	C-	D+	C		Y	1,000,000
Manning & Napier International Series Class S Shares	EXITX	NAS CM	Open End	Global Equity Large Cap (Foreign Stock)	C-	D+	C		Y	2,000
Manning & Napier International Series Class W	MNIWX	NAS CM	Open End	Global Equity Large Cap (Foreign Stock)	C-	D+	C		Y	0
Manning & Napier Overseas Series Class I	EXOSX	NAS CM	Open End	Global Equity Large Cap (Foreign Stock)	C	C	C+		Y	1,000,000
Manning & Napier Overseas Series Class S	MNOSX	NAS CM	Open End	Global Equity Large Cap (Foreign Stock)	C	C-	C+		Y	2,000
Manning & Napier Overseas Series Class W	MNOWX	NAS CM	Open End	Global Equity Large Cap (Foreign Stock)	C	C	C+		Y	0
Manning & Napier Overseas Series Class Z	MNOZX	NAS CM	Open End	Global Equity Large Cap (Foreign Stock)	C	C	C+		Y	1,000,000
Manning & Napier Pro-Blend Conservative Term Series Cls I	MNCIX	NAS CM	Open End	Cautious Alloc (Growth)	B	C+	B+		Y	1,000,000
Manning & Napier Pro-Blend Conservative Term Series Cls L	MNCCX	NAS CM	Open End	Cautious Alloc (Growth)	B-	C	B		Y	2,000
Manning & Napier Pro-Blend Conservative Term Series Cls R	MNCRX	NAS CM	Open End	Cautious Alloc (Growth)	B-	C+	B+		Y	2,000
Manning & Napier Pro-Blend Conservative Term Series Cls S	EXDAX	NAS CM	Open End	Cautious Alloc (Growth)	B	C+	B+	Up	Y	2,000
Manning & Napier Pro-Blend Conservative Term Series Cls W	MNCWX	NAS CM	Open End	Cautious Alloc (Growth)	B	C+	B+		Y	0
Manning & Napier Pro-Blend Extended Term Series Class I	MNBIX	NAS CM	Open End	Moderate Alloc (Growth)	B	C+	A-	Up	Y	1,000,000
Manning & Napier Pro-Blend Extended Term Series Class L	MNECX	NAS CM	Open End	Moderate Alloc (Growth)	B-	C	A-	Up	Y	2,000
Manning & Napier Pro-Blend Extended Term Series Class R	MNBRX	NAS CM	Open End	Moderate Alloc (Growth)	B	C+	A-	Up	Y	2,000
Manning & Napier Pro-Blend Extended Term Series Class S	MNBAX	NAS CM	Open End	Moderate Alloc (Growth)	B	C+	A-	Up	Y	2,000
Manning & Napier Pro-Blend Extended Term Series Class W	MNBWX	NAS CM	Open End	Moderate Alloc (Growth)	B	C+	A-		Y	0
Manning & Napier Pro-Blend Maximum Term Series Class I	MNHIX	NAS CM	Open End	Aggressive Alloc (Growth)	B-	C	B	Up	Y	1,000,000
Manning & Napier Pro-Blend Maximum Term Series Class L	MNHCX	NAS CM	Open End	Aggressive Alloc (Growth)	B-	C	B	Up	Y	2,000
Manning & Napier Pro-Blend Maximum Term Series Class R	MNHRX	NAS CM	Open End	Aggressive Alloc (Growth)	B-	C	B	Up	Y	2,000
Manning & Napier Pro-Blend Maximum Term Series Class S	EXHAX	NAS CM	Open End	Aggressive Alloc (Growth)	B-	C	B	Up	Y	2,000
Manning & Napier Pro-Blend Maximum Term Series Class W	MNHWX	NAS CM	Open End	Aggressive Alloc (Growth)	B-	C	B		Y	0
Manning & Napier Pro-Blend Moderate Term Series Class I	MNMIX	NAS CM	Open End	Cautious Alloc (Growth)	B	C+	A-	Up	Y	1,000,000
Manning & Napier Pro-Blend Moderate Term Series Class L	MNMCX	NAS CM	Open End	Cautious Alloc (Growth)	B-	C	B+	Up	Y	2,000
Manning & Napier Pro-Blend Moderate Term Series Class R	MNMRX	NAS CM	Open End	Cautious Alloc (Growth)	B-	C	B+		Y	2,000
Manning & Napier Pro-Blend Moderate Term Series Class S	EXBAX	NAS CM	Open End	Cautious Alloc (Growth)	B-	C+	B+		Y	2,000
Manning & Napier Pro-Blend Moderate Term Series Class W	MNMWX	NAS CM	Open End	Cautious Alloc (Growth)	B	C+	B+		Y	0
Manning & Napier Rainier Intl Discovery Series Cls I	RAIIX	NAS CM	Open End	Global Equity Mid/Small Cap (World Stock)	C	C	C		Y	1,000,000
Manning & Napier Rainier Intl Discovery Series Cls S	RISAX	NAS CM	Open End	Global Equity Mid/Small Cap (World Stock)	C	C	C		Y	2,000
Manning & Napier Rainier Intl Discovery Series Cls W	RAIWX	NAS CM	Open End	Global Equity Mid/Small Cap (World Stock)	C	C	C		Y	0
Manning & Napier Rainier Intl Discovery Series Cls Z	RAIRX	NAS CM	Open End	Global Equity Mid/Small Cap (World Stock)	C	C	C		Y	1,000,000
Manning & Napier Real Estate Series Class I	MNRIX	NAS CM	Open End	Real Estate Sector Equity (Real Estate)	C+	C+	B-		Y	1,000,000
Manning & Napier Real Estate Series Class S	MNREX	NAS CM	Open End	Real Estate Sector Equity (Real Estate)	C+	C	B-		Y	2,000
Manning & Napier Real Estate Series Class W	MNRWX	NAS CM	Open End	Real Estate Sector Equity (Real Estate)	C+	C	B-		Y	0
Manning & Napier Real Estate Series Class Z	MNRZX	NAS CM	Open End	Real Estate Sector Equity (Real Estate)	C+	C	B-		Y	1,000,000
Manning & Napier Target 2015 Series Class I	MTJIX	NAS CM	Open End	Target Date (Asset Alloc)	B	C+	B+	Up	Y	1,000,000
Manning & Napier Target 2015 Series Class K	MTJKX	NAS CM	Open End	Target Date (Asset Alloc)	B-	C+	B+		Y	2,000
Manning & Napier Target 2015 Series Class R	MTJRX	NAS CM	Open End	Target Date (Asset Alloc)	B-	C	B+		Y	2,000
Manning & Napier Target 2020 Series Class I	MTNIX	NAS CM	Open End	Target Date (Asset Alloc)	B	C+	A-	Up	Y	1,000,000
Manning & Napier Target 2020 Series Class K	MTNKX	NAS CM	Open End	Target Date (Asset Alloc)	B	C+	B+	Up	Y	2,000
Manning & Napier Target 2020 Series Class R	MTNRX	NAS CM	Open End	Target Date (Asset Alloc)	B-	C	B+		Y	2,000
Manning & Napier Target 2025 Series Class I	MTOAX	NAS CM	Open End	Target Date (Asset Alloc)	B	C+	A-	Up	Y	1,000,000
Manning & Napier Target 2025 Series Class K	MTOKX	NAS CM	Open End	Target Date (Asset Alloc)	B	C+	A-	Up	Y	2,000
Manning & Napier Target 2025 Series Class R	MTORX	NAS CM	Open End	Target Date (Asset Alloc)	B	C+	A-	Up	Y	2,000
Manning & Napier Target 2030 Series Class I	MTPIX	NAS CM	Open End	Target Date (Asset Alloc)	B	C+	A-	Up	Y	1,000,000
Manning & Napier Target 2030 Series Class K	MTPKX	NAS CM	Open End	Target Date (Asset Alloc)	B	C+	A-	Up	Y	2,000
Manning & Napier Target 2030 Series Class R	MTPRX	NAS CM	Open End	Target Date (Asset Alloc)	B	C+	A-	Up	Y	2,000
Manning & Napier Target 2035 Series Class I	MTQIX	NAS CM	Open End	Target Date (Asset Alloc)	B	C+	B+	Up	Y	1,000,000
Manning & Napier Target 2035 Series Class K	MTQKX	NAS CM	Open End	Target Date (Asset Alloc)	B-	C+	B+	Up	Y	2,000
Manning & Napier Target 2035 Series Class R	MTQRX	NAS CM	Open End	Target Date (Asset Alloc)	B-	C	B+	Up	Y	2,000
Manning & Napier Target 2040 Series Class I	MTTIX	NAS CM	Open End	Target Date (Asset Alloc)	B-	C+	B+	Up	Y	1,000,000

★ Expanded analysis of this fund is included in Section II.

	TOTAL RETURNS					PERFORMANCE				ASSETS		ASSET ALLOCATION & TURNOVER					BULL & BEAR		FEES		
Min Additional Investment	3-Month Total Return	6-Month Total Return	1-Year Total Return	3-Year Total Return	5-Year Total Return	Dividend Yield (TTM)	Expense Ratio	3-Yr Std Deviation	3-Year Beta	NAV	Total Assets (MIL)	%Cash	%Stocks	%Bonds	%Other	Turnover Ratio	Last Bull Market Total Return	Last Bear Market Total Return	Front End Fee (%)	Back End Fee (%)	Inception Date
	2.64	10.75	8.72	23.55	28.37	2.81	0.88	5.43	0.22	11.05	51.7	7	38	54	0	51					Aug-12
	1.46	11.85	-6.66	13.93	2.13	1.29	0.87	12.18	1.03	9.72	342.8	9	89	0	2	129	7.35	-22.61			Mar-12
	1.36	11.71	-6.91	12.97	0.86	1.35	1.12	12.17	1.03	7.44	342.8	9	89	0	2	129	7.24	-22.61			Aug-92
	1.77	12.16	-6.54	13.43	1.27		0.12	12.17	1.03	7.47	342.8	9	89	0	2	129	7.24	-22.61			Mar-19
	3.65	18.25	0.44	22.97	2.30	0.77	0.72	12.71	1.06	24.1	574.1	5	95	0	0	34	16.5	-27.02			Jul-02
	3.57	18.01	0.10	21.95	0.94		1.05	12.71	1.06	24.04	574.1	5	95	0	0	34	16.33	-27.09			Sep-18
	3.82	18.45	0.61	23.18	2.47		0.05	12.71	1.06	24.13	574.1	5	95	0	0	34	16.5	-27.02			Mar-19
	3.70	18.31	0.52	23.13	2.43	0.88	0.65	12.69	1.06	24.1	574.1	5	95	0	0	34	16.5	-27.02			May-18
	2.86	9.06	6.93	17.01	16.65	2.48	0.63	3.94	0.75	10.4	907.1	3	26	71	0	80	7.8	-4.04			Mar-08
	2.57	8.57	5.82	13.61	10.99	1.61	1.54	3.94	0.74	9.96	907.1	3	26	71	0	80	7.2	-4.48			Jan-10
	2.65	8.77	6.32	15.37	13.76	2.06	1.07	3.96	0.76	9.96	907.1	3	26	71	0	80	7.39	-4.15			Jun-10
	2.77	8.93	6.64	16.37	15.43	1.66	0.87	3.9	0.75	13.9	907.1	3	26	71	0	80	7.66	-4.13			Nov-95
	2.90	9.07	6.77	16.51	15.57		0.08	3.9	0.76	13.91	907.1	3	26	71	0	80	7.66	-4.13			Apr-19
	3.51	13.03	6.60	25.27	20.68	2.02	0.84	6.65	0.88	8.9	534.3	3	47	50	0	75	14.56	-13.15			Mar-08
	3.20	12.44	5.47	21.51	14.77	0.9	1.76	6.64	0.89	9.76	534.3	3	47	50	0	75	13.87	-13.4			Jan-10
	3.33	12.75	5.99	23.36	17.72	1.14	1.35	6.6	0.89	10.59	534.3	3	47	50	0	75	14.21	-13.23			Jun-10
	3.38	12.86	6.29	24.33	19.16	0.82	1.02	6.63	0.88	17.54	534.3	3	47	50	0	75	14.27	-13.17			Oct-93
	3.50	12.99	6.41	24.47	19.29		0.1	6.64	0.89	17.54	534.3	3	47	50	0	75	14.27	-13.17			Apr-19
	4.23	18.78	6.94	40.32	34.31	1.19	0.85	10.69	0.76	9.21	399.2	2	85	13	0	63	18.62	-20.01			Mar-08
	3.97	18.13	5.90	36.16	27.78	0.23	1.79	10.63	0.76	9.86	399.2	2	85	13	0	63	17.96	-20.35			Jan-10
	4.11	18.47	6.47	38.30	31.06	0.43	1.34	10.67	0.76	12.33	399.2	2	85	13	0	63	18.27	-20.21			Jun-10
	4.21	18.61	6.68	39.30	32.69	0.33	1.08	10.68	0.76	20.81	399.2	2	85	13	0	63	18.5	-20.14			Nov-95
	4.41	18.84	6.89	39.56	32.94		0.1	10.68	0.76	20.81	399.2	2	85	13	0	63	18.5	-20.14			Apr-19
	3.19	11.01	6.36	19.91	16.32	1.97	0.84	5.34	0.83	9.88	410.2	4	36	61	0	74	12.32	-9.85			Mar-08
	2.93	10.48	5.40	16.42	10.68	1	1.75	5.31	0.84	10.05	410.2	4	36	61	0	74	11.7	-10.28			Jan-10
	3.04	10.73	5.90	18.18	13.47	1.15	1.35	5.3	0.83	10.51	410.2	4	36	61	0	74	12.01	-10.05			Jun-10
	3.18	10.96	6.21	19.14	15.01	1.2	1.04	5.32	0.85	13.63	410.2	4	36	61	0	74	12.24	-10.02			Sep-93
	3.28	11.07	6.31	19.26	15.13		0.1	5.32	0.85	13.62	410.2	4	36	61	0	74	12.23	-10.02			Apr-19
	7.17	19.85	-4.73	33.61	41.90	0.32	1.13	14.1	1.07	21.07	472.8	8	92	0	0	73					Mar-12
	7.14	19.69	-4.97	32.54	40.07	0.11	1.41	14.11	1.07	20.85	472.8	8	92	0	0	73			5.75		Nov-12
	7.43	20.15	-4.49	33.94	42.25		0.11	14.1	1.07	20.94	472.8	8	92	0	0	73					Mar-19
	7.21	19.89	-4.61	33.95	42.26	0.42	1.01	14.12	1.07	21.09	472.8	8	92	0	0	73					Aug-17
	2.17	20.25	11.80	19.36	52.16	3.78	0.83	12.93	0.97	6.59	296.3	0	100	0	0	44	33.17	-17.18			Aug-12
	2.08	19.99	11.43	18.43	50.22	1.44	1.1	12.89	0.97	15.66	296.3	0	100	0	0	44	33.17	-17.18			Nov-09
	2.41	20.38	11.78	18.81	50.70		0.1	12.89	0.97	15.71	296.3	0	100	0	0	44	33.17	-17.18			Mar-19
	2.32	20.28	11.69	18.71	50.57		0.7	12.89	0.97	6.6	296.3	0	100	0	0	44	33.17	-17.18			Mar-19
	2.81	9.57	6.05	18.03	14.36	1.9	0.67	4.67	0.76	11.62	1.3	8	29	64	0	46					Jun-12
	2.71	9.38	5.81	17.15	12.90	1.67	0.92	4.67	0.76	11.59	1.3	8	29	64	0	46					Jun-12
	2.96	9.57	5.82	16.58	11.83	1.3	1.17	4.63	0.76	11.79	1.3	8	29	64	0	46					Jun-12
	3.21	11.26	6.33	20.64	16.62	1.6	0.71	5.56	0.8	9.95	55.7	4	37	59	0	27	13.53	-11.94			Mar-08
	3.17	11.03	5.95	19.78	15.07	1.44	0.96	5.47	0.78	9.89	55.7	4	37	59	0	27	13.49	-12.08			Mar-08
	3.13	10.98	5.76	18.94	13.73	1.3	1.21	5.52	0.79	9.75	55.7	4	37	59	0	27	13.27	-12.19			Mar-08
	3.32	11.93	6.35	22.90	18.08	1.56	0.73	6.1	0.74	12.59	66.3	4	41	55	0	25					Jun-12
	3.17	11.75	5.96	21.89	16.49	1.45	0.98	6.08	0.74	12.6	66.3	4	41	55	0	25					Jun-12
	3.14	11.60	5.80	21.12	15.11	1.23	1.23	6.08	0.74	12.63	66.3	4	41	55	0	25					Jun-12
	3.40	13.24	6.23	26.79	21.68	1.99	0.75	6.97	0.75	10.2	77.2	3	50	47	0	29	14.95	-14.65			Mar-08
	3.37	13.09	5.99	25.78	20.02	1.83	1	7.04	0.76	10.08	77.2	3	50	47	0	29	14.73	-14.74			Mar-08
	3.30	13.00	5.77	24.97	18.66	1.69	1.25	7.04	0.75	9.98	77.2	3	50	47	0	29	14.46	-14.82			Mar-08
	3.72	14.74	6.37	30.56	25.06	2.83	0.75	8.1	0.8	13.26	44.7	3	59	38	0	32					Jun-12
	3.61	14.58	6.05	29.45	23.45	2.74	1	8.03	0.79	13.18	44.7	3	59	38	0	32					Jun-12
	3.58	14.52	5.83	28.53	21.97	2.55	1.25	8.06	0.79	13.22	44.7	3	59	38	0	32					Jun-12
	3.96	16.21	6.38	34.22	28.31	3.87	0.75	9.1	0.85	10.24	50.5	3	68	30	0	36	18.63	-20.16			Mar-08

	MARKET		FUND TYPE, CATEGORY & OBJECTIVE		RATINGS				MINIMUMS	
Fund Name	Ticker Symbol	Traded On	Fund Type	Category and (Prospectus Objective)	Overall Rating	Reward Rating	Risk Rating	Recent Up/ Downgrade	Open to New Investors	Min Initial Investment
Manning & Napier Target 2040 Series Class K	MTTKX	NAS CM	Open End	Target Date (Asset Alloc)	B-	C	B+	Up	Y	2,000
Manning & Napier Target 2040 Series Class R	MTTRX	NAS CM	Open End	Target Date (Asset Alloc)	B-	C	B+	Up	Y	2,000
Manning & Napier Target 2045 Series Class I	MTUIX	NAS CM	Open End	Target Date (Asset Alloc)	B-	C	B	Up	Y	1,000,000
Manning & Napier Target 2045 Series Class K	MTUKX	NAS CM	Open End	Target Date (Asset Alloc)	B-	C	B	Up	Y	2,000
Manning & Napier Target 2045 Series Class R	MTURX	NAS CM	Open End	Target Date (Asset Alloc)	B-	C	B	Up	Y	2,000
Manning & Napier Target 2050 Series Class I	MTYIX	NAS CM	Open End	Target Date (Asset Alloc)	B-	C	B	Up	Y	1,000,000
Manning & Napier Target 2050 Series Class K	MTYKX	NAS CM	Open End	Target Date (Asset Alloc)	B-	C	B	Up	Y	2,000
Manning & Napier Target 2050 Series Class R	MTYRX	NAS CM	Open End	Target Date (Asset Alloc)	B-	C	B	Up	Y	2,000
Manning & Napier Target 2055 Series Class I	MTZIX	NAS CM	Open End	Target Date (Asset Alloc)	B-	C	B	Up	Y	1,000,000
Manning & Napier Target 2055 Series Class K	MTZKX	NAS CM	Open End	Target Date (Asset Alloc)	B-	C	B	Up	Y	2,000
Manning & Napier Target 2055 Series Class R	MTZRX	NAS CM	Open End	Target Date (Asset Alloc)	B-	C	B	Up	Y	2,000
Manning & Napier Target 2060 Series Class I	MTKIX	NAS CM	Open End	Target Date (Asset Alloc)	B-	C	B	Up	Y	1,000,000
Manning & Napier Target 2060 Series Class K	MTKKX	NAS CM	Open End	Target Date (Asset Alloc)	B-	C	B	Up	Y	2,000
Manning & Napier Target 2060 Series Class R	MTKRX	NAS CM	Open End	Target Date (Asset Alloc)	B-	C	B	Up	Y	2,000
Manning & Napier Target Income Series Class I	MTDIX	NAS CM	Open End	Target Date (Asset Alloc)	B	C+	B+	Up	Y	1,000,000
Manning & Napier Target Income Series Class K	MTDKX	NAS CM	Open End	Target Date (Asset Alloc)	B-	C+	B+		Y	2,000
Manning & Napier Target Income Series Class R	MTDRX	NAS CM	Open End	Target Date (Asset Alloc)	B-	C	B+		Y	2,000
Manor Investment Funds Growth Fund	MNRGX	NAS CM	Open End	US Equity Large Cap Growth (Growth)	C+	C	B	Down	Y	1,000
Manor Investment Funds Manor Fund	MNRMX	NAS CM	Open End	US Equity Large Cap Blend (Growth & Income)	C	C	C+	Down	Y	1,000
Marathon Value Portfolio	MVPFX	NAS CM	Open End	US Equity Large Cap Blend (Growth)	B-	C	B		Y	2,500
Marketfield Fund Class A	MFADX	NAS CM	Open End	Long/Short Equity (Growth)	C	C-	C+	Up	Y	2,500
Marketfield Fund Class C	MFCDX	NAS CM	Open End	Long/Short Equity (Growth)	C	C-	C	Up	Y	2,500
Marketfield Fund Class I	MFLDX	NAS CM	Open End	Long/Short Equity (Growth)	C	C-	C+		Y	25,000
Marketfield Fund Class R6	MFRIX	NAS CM	Open End	Long/Short Equity (Growth)	C	C-	C+		Y	250,000
Marmont Redwood International Equity Institutional Shares	MRILX	NAS CM	Open End	Global Equity Large Cap (Foreign Stock)	D	D	C		Y	100,000
Marmont Redwood International Equity Fund Retail Shares	MRIDX	NAS CM	Open End	Global Equity Large Cap (Foreign Stock)	D	D	C		Y	3,000
Marshfield Concentrated Opportunity Fund	MRFOX	NAS CM	Open End	US Equity Large Cap Blend (Growth)	B+	B+	A-	Up	Y	10,000
Marsico 21st Century Fund	MXXIX	NAS CM	Open End	US Equity Mid Cap (Growth)	B	B	B		Y	2,500
Marsico Focus Fund	MFOCX	NAS CM	Open End	US Equity Large Cap Growth (Growth)	C+	C	B-	Down	Y	2,500
Marsico Global Fund	MGLBX	NAS CM	Open End	Global Equity Large Cap (World Stock)	C+	C	C+		Y	2,500
Marsico Growth Fund	MGRIX	NAS CM	Open End	US Equity Large Cap Growth (Growth)	C+	C	B	Down	Y	2,500
Marsico International Opportunities Fund	MIOFX	NAS CM	Open End	Global Equity Large Cap (Foreign Stock)	C	C	C		Y	2,500
Martin Currie Emerging Markets Fund Class A	MACEX	NAS CM	Open End	Global Emerg Mkts (Div Emerging Mkts)	C	C	C		Y	1,000
Martin Currie Emerging Markets Fund Class C	MCECX	NAS CM	Open End	Global Emerg Mkts (Div Emerging Mkts)	C	C	C		Y	1,000
Martin Currie Emerging Markets Fund Class FI	MEFIX	NAS CM	Open End	Global Emerg Mkts (Div Emerging Mkts)	C	C	C		Y	0
Martin Currie Emerging Markets Fund Class I	MCEIX	NAS CM	Open End	Global Emerg Mkts (Div Emerging Mkts)	C	C	C		Y	1,000,000
Martin Currie Emerging Markets Fund Class IS	MCEMX	NAS CM	Open End	Global Emerg Mkts (Div Emerging Mkts)	C	C	C		Y	1,000,000
Martin Currie International Unconstrained Equity Cls A	LUFIX	NAS CM	Open End	Global Equity Large Cap (Foreign Stock)	C+	C+	B	Up	Y	1,000
Martin Currie International Unconstrained Equity Cls I	LUEIX	NAS CM	Open End	Global Equity Large Cap (Foreign Stock)	B-	C+	B	Up	Y	1,000,000
Martin Currie International Unconstrained Equity Cls IS	LUISX	NAS CM	Open End	Global Equity Large Cap (Foreign Stock)	B-	C+	B	Up	Y	1,000,000
Martin Currie SMA-Shares Series EM Fund	LCSMX	NAS CM	Open End	Global Emerg Mkts (Div Emerging Mkts)	D	D	D+		Y	0
MassMutual Premier Balanced Fund Administrative Class	MMBLX	NAS CM	Open End	Moderate Alloc (Balanced)	B-	C	B+	Up	Y	0
MassMutual Premier Balanced Fund Class A	MMBDX	NAS CM	Open End	Moderate Alloc (Balanced)	B-	C	B+	Up	Y	0
MassMutual Premier Balanced Fund Class I	MBBIX	NAS CM	Open End	Moderate Alloc (Balanced)	B-	C	B+	Up	Y	0
MassMutual Premier Balanced Fund Class R3	MMBRX	NAS CM	Open End	Moderate Alloc (Balanced)	B-	C	B+	Up	Y	0
MassMutual Premier Balanced Fund Class R4	MBBRX	NAS CM	Open End	Moderate Alloc (Balanced)	B-	C	B+	Up	Y	0
MassMutual Premier Balanced Fund Class R5	MBLDX	NAS CM	Open End	Moderate Alloc (Balanced)	B-	C	B+	Up	Y	0
MassMutual Premier Balanced Fund Service Class	MBAYX	NAS CM	Open End	Moderate Alloc (Balanced)	B-	C	B+	Up	Y	0
MassMutual Premier Disciplined Growth Administrative Cls	MPGLX	NAS CM	Open End	US Equity Large Cap Growth (Growth)	C+	C	B		Y	0
MassMutual Premier Disciplined Growth Fund Class A	MPGAX	NAS CM	Open End	US Equity Large Cap Growth (Growth)	C+	C	B	Down	Y	0
MassMutual Premier Disciplined Growth Fund Class I	MPDIX	NAS CM	Open End	US Equity Large Cap Growth (Growth)	C+	C	B	Down	Y	0
MassMutual Premier Disciplined Growth Fund Class R3	MPDRX	NAS CM	Open End	US Equity Large Cap Growth (Growth)	C+	C	B	Down	Y	0

★ Expanded analysis of this fund is included in Section II.

	TOTAL RETURNS					PERFORMANCE				ASSETS		ASSET ALLOCATION & TURNOVER					BULL & BEAR		FEES		
Min Additional Investment	3-Month Total Return	6-Month Total Return	1-Year Total Return	3-Year Total Return	5-Year Total Return	Dividend Yield (TTM)	Expense Ratio	3-Yr Std Deviation	3-Year Beta	NAV	Total Assets (MIL)	%Cash	%Stocks	%Bonds	%Other	Turnover Ratio	Last Bull Market Total Return	Last Bear Market Total Return	Front End Fee (%)	Back End Fee (%)	Inception Date
	3.93	15.93	6.00	33.15	26.55	3.7	1	9.07	0.85	10.13	50.5	3	68	30	0	36	18.41	-20.18			Mar-08
	3.77	15.87	5.80	32.13	24.96	3.6	1.25	9.1	0.85	10.03	50.5	3	68	30	0	36	18.28	-20.29			Mar-08
	4.13	17.67	6.36	37.74	31.68	4.76	0.75	10.19	0.93	13.37	24.9	2	76	22	0	43					Jun-12
	4.08	17.48	6.03	36.67	30.06	4.69	1	10.16	0.93	13.31	24.9	2	76	22	0	43					Jun-12
	4.04	17.37	5.81	35.55	28.39	4.56	1.25	10.19	0.93	13.19	24.9	2	76	22	0	43					Jun-12
	4.31	18.81	6.48	39.48	33.39	5.39	0.75	10.84	0.98	10.58	29.4	2	83	15	0	40	18.52	-20.12			Mar-08
	4.28	18.67	6.32	38.50	31.77	5.26	1	10.86	0.98	10.48	29.4	2	83	15	0	40	18.34	-20.16			Mar-08
	4.16	18.40	5.98	37.31	30.01	5.22	1.25	10.83	0.98	10.31	29.4	2	83	15	0	40	18.27	-20.28			Mar-08
	4.38	18.81	6.58	39.48	33.57	5.38	0.75	10.83	0.97	13.3	12.3	2	83	15	0	23					Jun-12
	4.27	18.66	6.26	38.37	31.86	5.17	1	10.84	0.97	13.15	12.3	2	83	15	0	23					Jun-12
	4.26	18.46	6.02	37.32	30.31	5.1	1.25	10.84	0.97	12.96	12.3	2	83	15	0	23					Jun-12
	4.36	18.78	6.49	39.48		5.47	0.75	10.82	0.96	11.93	11.6	2	83	15	0	5					Sep-15
	4.29	18.60	6.26	38.47		5.2	1	10.83	0.96	11.92	11.6	2	83	15	0	5					Sep-15
	4.22	18.36	5.88	37.38		5.1	1.25	10.82	0.95	11.86	11.6	2	83	15	0	5					Sep-15
	2.77	9.16	6.54	16.43	15.98	1.88	0.65	4.09	0.96	10.33	77.6	7	27	66	0	9	7.8	-4.03			Mar-08
	2.74	9.04	6.31	15.65	14.63	1.74	0.9	4.08	0.96	10.28	77.6	7	27	66	0	9	7.57	-4.14			Mar-08
	2.68	8.84	5.99	14.70	13.12	1.59	1.15	4.1	0.96	10.13	77.6	7	27	66	0	9	7.45	-4.28			Mar-08
25	1.65	17.77	6.98	46.52	52.40	0	0.99	13.52	1.06	25.24	10.5	6	94	0	0	12	21.35	-15.68			Jun-99
25	4.13	17.27	-0.79	28.11	20.43	0.7	1.25	14.36	1.13	23.69	6.7	4	96	0	0	16	19.34	-15.4			Sep-95
100	3.62	19.51	10.70	40.62	48.76	0.57	1.1	12.51	1	29.15	61.8	1	99	0	0	6	21.46	-14.27			Mar-00
0	0.94	7.72	-3.08	17.00	-9.84	0	2.71	9.36	0.56	16.03	214.9	56	43	1	0	40	15.49	-7.12	5.50		Oct-12
50	0.72	7.33	-3.85	14.26	-13.32	0	3.49	9.33	0.56	15.22	214.9	56	43	1	0	40	14.99	-7.41		1.00	Oct-12
0	1.05	7.88	-2.86	17.80	-8.79	0	2.46	9.35	0.56	16.28	214.9	56	43	1	0	40	15.66	-7.03			Jul-07
0	1.10	7.95	-2.66	18.29	-8.11	0	2.35	9.34	0.56	16.42	214.9	56	43	1	0	40	15.66	-7.03			Jun-13
	5.25	17.35	1.93			0	1.02			10.01	9.4	4	96	0	0	53					Feb-18
	5.15	17.25	1.66				1.27			9.99	9.4	4	96	0	0	53					Sep-18
	6.29	26.58	24.74	87.24		0.02	1.11	11.41	0.85	17.38	71.5	17	83	0	0	10					Dec-15
100	7.21	28.08	15.90	71.38	72.20	0	1.42	13.29	0.85	33.89	283.2	5	95	0	0	90	28.52	-25.45			Feb-00
100	4.47	22.10	7.93	60.77	62.55	0	1.14	14.98	1.07	18.67	573.7	3	97	0	0	53	27.67	-17.72			Dec-97
100	6.06	22.65	3.04	62.67	58.39	0	1.45	15.75	1.22	16.62	245.3	2	98	0	0	33	29.69	-24.24			Jun-07
100	4.80	23.20	8.56	58.95	58.23	0	1.44	14.13	1.05	18.74	266.4	8	92	0	0	40	27.99	-17.43			Dec-97
100	5.41	22.53	-4.46	39.63	30.59	0	1.5	15.28	1.2	18.49	56.0	10	90	0	0	33	21.2	-25.17			Jun-00
50	1.08	15.04	-1.38	42.71			1.35	15.71	1.09	12.16	155.5	3	97	0	0	23			5.75		Jul-18
50	0.83	14.66	-2.06	39.63			2.1	15.68	1.09	12.12	155.5	3	97	0	0	23				1.00	Jul-18
	0.99	14.93	-1.54	41.87		0.62	1.35	15.73	1.09	12.16	155.5	3	97	0	0	23					May-15
	1.07	15.17	-1.24	43.13		0.87	1	15.71	1.09	12.22	155.5	3	97	0	0	23					May-15
	1.07	15.24	-1.14	43.78		0.89	0.9	15.71	1.09	12.25	155.5	3	97	0	0	23					May-15
50	7.62	25.34	12.05	38.80		0.96	1.2	12.89	0.99	12.56	5.7	2	98	0	0	15			5.75		Nov-15
	7.86	25.57	12.50	39.95		1.18	0.85	12.86	0.99	12.62	5.7	2	98	0	0	15					Nov-15
	7.77	25.59	12.51	40.12		1.25	0.75	12.87	0.99	12.61	5.7	2	98	0	0	15					Nov-15
	-2.50	9.49	-8.24			1.46	0			8.19	11.7	0	94	0	5	11					Jan-18
	2.92	11.97	5.43	30.23	33.73	1.38	1.03	8.26	0.67	11.97	124.4	8	53	39	0	77	15.47	-10.25			Apr-99
	2.83	11.84	5.18	29.23	32.10	1.14	1.28	8.24	0.67	11.61	124.4	8	53	39	0	77	15.27	-10.35	5.50		Dec-97
	2.93	12.13	5.73	31.46	35.89	1.7	0.73	8.21	0.66	11.92	124.4	8	53	39	0	77	15.64	-10.12			Apr-14
	2.78	11.71	4.97	28.64	31.11	1.15	1.43	8.25	0.67	11.44	124.4	8	53	39	0	77	15.3	-10.3			Apr-14
	2.85	11.96	5.21	29.71	32.73	1.3	1.18	8.22	0.67	11.51	124.4	8	53	39	0	77	15.47	-10.21			Apr-14
	2.93	12.13	5.63	31.05	35.00	1.61	0.83	8.23	0.67	11.92	124.4	8	53	39	0	77	15.64	-10.12			Sep-94
	2.94	12.02	5.53	30.65	34.32	1.41	0.93	8.22	0.67	12.58	124.4	8	53	39	0	77	15.65	-10.23			Dec-97
	3.75	20.10	7.61	59.16	70.56	0.76	0.82	13.5	1	11.05	309.0	1	99	0	0	73	27.02	-15.84			Nov-04
	3.69	20.02	7.32	57.84	68.39	0.54	1.07	13.49	1	10.67	309.0	1	99	0	0	73	26.94	-15.99	5.50		Nov-04
	3.82	20.28	7.94	60.64	73.13	1.08	0.52	13.46	1	10.85	309.0	1	99	0	0	73	27.09	-15.79			Apr-14
	3.63	19.90	7.20	57.05	67.10	0.46	1.22	13.5	1	10.54	309.0	1	99	0	0	73	26.72	-15.97			Apr-14

	MARKET		FUND TYPE, CATEGORY & OBJECTIVE		RATINGS				MINIMUMS	
Fund Name	Ticker Symbol	Traded On	Fund Type	Category and (Prospectus Objective)	Overall Rating	Reward Rating	Risk Rating	Recent Up/ Downgrade	Open to New Investors	Min Initial Investment
MassMutual Premier Disciplined Growth Fund Class R4	MPDGX	NAS CM	Open End	US Equity Large Cap Growth (Growth)	C+	C	B		Y	0
MassMutual Premier Disciplined Growth Fund Class R5	MPGSX	NAS CM	Open End	US Equity Large Cap Growth (Growth)	C+	C	B	Down	Y	0
MassMutual Premier Disciplined Growth Fund Service Class	DEIGX	NAS CM	Open End	US Equity Large Cap Growth (Growth)	C+	C	B	Down	Y	0
MassMutual Premier Disciplined Value Administrative Cls	MPILX	NAS CM	Open End	US Equity Large Cap Value (Growth)	C+	C	B	Up	Y	0
MassMutual Premier Disciplined Value Fund Class A	MEPAX	NAS CM	Open End	US Equity Large Cap Value (Growth)	C+	C	B	Up	Y	0
MassMutual Premier Disciplined Value Fund Class I	MPIVX	NAS CM	Open End	US Equity Large Cap Value (Growth)	C+	C	B	Up	Y	0
MassMutual Premier Disciplined Value Fund Class R3	MPINX	NAS CM	Open End	US Equity Large Cap Value (Growth)	C+	C	B	Up	Y	0
MassMutual Premier Disciplined Value Fund Class R4	MPIRX	NAS CM	Open End	US Equity Large Cap Value (Growth)	C+	C	B	Up	Y	0
MassMutual Premier Disciplined Value Fund Class R5	MEPSX	NAS CM	Open End	US Equity Large Cap Value (Growth)	C+	C	B	Up	Y	0
MassMutual Premier Disciplined Value Fund Service Class	DENVX	NAS CM	Open End	US Equity Large Cap Value (Growth)	C+	C	B	Up	Y	0
MassMutual Premier Global Fund Administrative Class	MGFLX	NAS CM	Open End	Global Equity Large Cap (Foreign Stock)	C+	C	B-	Up	Y	0
MassMutual Premier Global Fund Class A	MGFAX	NAS CM	Open End	Global Equity Large Cap (Foreign Stock)	C+	C	B-	Up	Y	0
MassMutual Premier Global Fund Class I	MGFZX	NAS CM	Open End	Global Equity Large Cap (Foreign Stock)	C+	C	B-	Up	Y	0
MassMutual Premier Global Fund Class R3	MGFNX	NAS CM	Open End	Global Equity Large Cap (Foreign Stock)	C+	C	B-	Up	Y	0
MassMutual Premier Global Fund Class R4	MGFRX	NAS CM	Open End	Global Equity Large Cap (Foreign Stock)	C+	C	B-	Up	Y	0
MassMutual Premier Global Fund Class R5	MGFSX	NAS CM	Open End	Global Equity Large Cap (Foreign Stock)	C+	C	B-	Up	Y	0
MassMutual Premier Global Fund Service Class	MGFYX	NAS CM	Open End	Global Equity Large Cap (Foreign Stock)	C+	C	B-	Up	Y	0
MassMutual Premier International Equity Administrative Cls	MIELX	NAS CM	Open End	Global Equity Large Cap (Foreign Stock)	C	C-	C+	Up	Y	0
MassMutual Premier International Equity Fund Class A	MMIAX	NAS CM	Open End	Global Equity Large Cap (Foreign Stock)	C	C-	C+	Up	Y	0
MassMutual Premier International Equity Fund Class I	MIZIX	NAS CM	Open End	Global Equity Large Cap (Foreign Stock)	C	C-	C+	Up	Y	0
MassMutual Premier International Equity Fund Class R3	MEERX	NAS CM	Open End	Global Equity Large Cap (Foreign Stock)	C	C-	C+	Up	Y	0
MassMutual Premier International Equity Fund Class R4	MEIRX	NAS CM	Open End	Global Equity Large Cap (Foreign Stock)	C	C-	C+	Up	Y	0
MassMutual Premier International Equity Fund Class R5	MIEDX	NAS CM	Open End	Global Equity Large Cap (Foreign Stock)	C	C-	C+	Up	Y	0
MassMutual Premier International Equity Fund Service Class	MYIEX	NAS CM	Open End	Global Equity Large Cap (Foreign Stock)	C	C-	C+	Up	Y	0
MassMutual Premier Main Street Fund Administrative Class	MMSLX	NAS CM	Open End	US Equity Large Cap Blend (Growth)	B-	C	B		Y	0
MassMutual Premier Main Street Fund Class A	MSSAX	NAS CM	Open End	US Equity Large Cap Blend (Growth)	C+	C	B	Down	Y	0
MassMutual Premier Main Street Fund Class I	MSZIX	NAS CM	Open End	US Equity Large Cap Blend (Growth)	B-	C+	B		Y	0
MassMutual Premier Main Street Fund Class R3	MMSNX	NAS CM	Open End	US Equity Large Cap Blend (Growth)	C+	C	B	Down	Y	0
MassMutual Premier Main Street Fund Class R4	MSSRX	NAS CM	Open End	US Equity Large Cap Blend (Growth)	B-	C	B		Y	0
MassMutual Premier Main Street Fund Class R5	MMSSX	NAS CM	Open End	US Equity Large Cap Blend (Growth)	B-	C	B		Y	0
MassMutual Premier Main Street Fund Service Class	MMSYX	NAS CM	Open End	US Equity Large Cap Blend (Growth)	B-	C	B		Y	0
MassMutual Premier Small Cap Opp Admin Cls	MSCLX	NAS CM	Open End	US Equity Small Cap (Growth)	C	C	C+		Y	0
MassMutual Premier Small Cap Opportunities Fund Class A	DLBMX	NAS CM	Open End	US Equity Small Cap (Growth)	C	C	C+		Y	0
MassMutual Premier Small Cap Opportunities Fund Class I	MSOOX	NAS CM	Open End	US Equity Small Cap (Growth)	C	C	C+		Y	0
MassMutual Premier Small Cap Opportunities Fund Class R3	MCCRX	NAS CM	Open End	US Equity Small Cap (Growth)	C	C	C+		Y	0
MassMutual Premier Small Cap Opportunities Fund Class R4	MOORX	NAS CM	Open End	US Equity Small Cap (Growth)	C	C	C+		Y	0
MassMutual Premier Small Cap Opportunities Fund Class R5	MSCDX	NAS CM	Open End	US Equity Small Cap (Growth)	C	C	C+		Y	0
MassMutual Premier Small Cap Opportunities Service Cls	MSVYX	NAS CM	Open End	US Equity Small Cap (Growth)	C	C	C+		Y	0
MassMutual Premier Strategic Emerging Mkts Admin Cls	MPLSX	NAS CM	Open End	Global Emerg Mkts (Div Emerging Mkts)	C	C	B-		Y	0
MassMutual Premier Strategic Emerging Markets Fund Class A	MPASX	NAS CM	Open End	Global Emerg Mkts (Div Emerging Mkts)	C	C	C+		Y	0
MassMutual Premier Strategic Emerging Markets Fund Class I	MPZSX	NAS CM	Open End	Global Emerg Mkts (Div Emerging Mkts)	C	C	B-		Y	0
MassMutual Premier Strategic Emerging Markets Cls R3	MPZRX	NAS CM	Open End	Global Emerg Mkts (Div Emerging Mkts)	C	C	C+		Y	0
MassMutual Premier Strategic Emerging Markets Cls R4	MPRSX	NAS CM	Open End	Global Emerg Mkts (Div Emerging Mkts)	C	C	C+		Y	0
MassMutual Premier Strategic Emerging Markets Cls R5	MPSMX	NAS CM	Open End	Global Emerg Mkts (Div Emerging Mkts)	C	C	B-		Y	0
MassMutual Premier Strategic Emerging Markets Service Cls	MPEYX	NAS CM	Open End	Global Emerg Mkts (Div Emerging Mkts)	C	C	B-		Y	0
MassMutual RetireSMART by JPMorgan 2020 Administrative Cls	MRTYX	NAS CM	Open End	Target Date (Growth & Income)	B	C+	A	Up	Y	0
MassMutual RetireSMART by JPMorgan 2020 Fund Class A	MRTAX	NAS CM	Open End	Target Date (Growth & Income)	B	C+	A	Up	Y	0
MassMutual RetireSMART by JPMorgan 2020 Fund Class I	MRTDX	NAS CM	Open End	Target Date (Growth & Income)	B	C+	A	Up	Y	0
MassMutual RetireSMART by JPMorgan 2020 Fund Class R3	MRTNX	NAS CM	Open End	Target Date (Growth & Income)	B	C	A-	Up	Y	0
MassMutual RetireSMART by JPMorgan 2020 Fund Class R4	MRTHX	NAS CM	Open End	Target Date (Growth & Income)	B	C+	A	Up	Y	0
MassMutual RetireSMART by JPMorgan 2020 Fund Class R5	MRTBX	NAS CM	Open End	Target Date (Growth & Income)	B	C+	A	Up	Y	0
MassMutual RetireSMART by JPMorgan 2020 Fund Service Class	MRTSX	NAS CM	Open End	Target Date (Growth & Income)	B	C+	A	Up	Y	0

★ Expanded analysis of this fund is included in Section II.

	TOTAL RETURNS					PERFORMANCE				ASSETS		ASSET ALLOCATION & TURNOVER					BULL & BEAR		FEES		
Min Additional Investment	3-Month Total Return	6-Month Total Return	1-Year Total Return	3-Year Total Return	5-Year Total Return	Dividend Yield (TTM)	Expense Ratio	3-Yr Std Deviation	3-Year Beta	NAV	Total Assets (MIL)	%Cash	%Stocks	%Bonds	%Other	Turnover Ratio	Last Bull Market Total Return	Last Bear Market Total Return	Front End Fee (%)	Back End Fee (%)	Inception Date
	3.63	20.00	7.37	58.25	69.15	0.66	0.97	13.5	1	10.56	309.0	1	99	0	0	73	26.9	-15.88			Apr-14
	3.82	20.26	7.81	60.06	72.28	0.97	0.62	13.53	1	10.86	309.0	1	99	0	0	73	27.25	-15.82			Nov-04
	3.80	20.17	7.73	59.56	71.28	0.87	0.72	13.49	1	10.9	309.0	1	99	0	0	73	27.09	-15.79			Dec-00
	2.75	14.56	3.28	31.85	33.46	2.18	0.87	12.78	1.05	14.16	136.5	0	100	0	0	80	22.96	-18.37			Nov-04
	2.69	14.35	3.00	30.82	31.82	1.93	1.12	12.74	1.04	13.7	136.5	0	100	0	0	80	22.65	-18.45	5.50		Nov-04
	2.80	14.65	3.54	32.95	35.40	2.5	0.57	12.79	1.05	13.93	136.5	0	100	0	0	80	22.87	-18.32			Apr-14
	2.67	14.21	2.86	30.24	30.86	1.81	1.27	12.74	1.04	13.82	136.5	0	100	0	0	80	22.38	-18.61			Nov-04
	2.64	14.39	3.06	31.20	32.43	1.97	1.02	12.75	1.04	13.59	136.5	0	100	0	0	80	22.69	-18.4			Apr-14
	2.79	14.61	3.47	32.55	34.76	2.39	0.67	12.78	1.05	13.96	136.5	0	100	0	0	80	23	-18.31			Nov-04
	2.74	14.56	3.34	32.21	34.14	2.27	0.77	12.72	1.04	13.84	136.5	0	100	0	0	80	22.87	-18.32			Dec-00
	3.87	22.08	3.19	56.82	43.86	0.37	1.17	14.1	1.22	12.88	315.2	3	97	0	0	42	17.68	-23.12			Dec-04
	3.83	21.97	3.01	55.75	42.12	0.15	1.42	14.09	1.21	12.71	315.2	3	97	0	0	42	17.44	-23.25	5.50		Dec-04
	3.95	22.31	3.56	58.32	46.09	0.7	0.87	14.1	1.22	12.88	315.2	3	97	0	0	42	17.79	-23.08			Apr-14
	3.77	21.88	2.82	55.04	41.09	0	1.57	14.11	1.22	12.64	315.2	3	97	0	0	42	17.46	-23.3			Dec-04
	3.81	22.04	3.11	56.18	42.81	0.37	1.32	14.11	1.22	12.51	315.2	3	97	0	0	42	17.61	-23.17			Apr-14
	3.95	22.29	3.48	57.84	45.35	0.59	0.97	14.15	1.22	12.89	315.2	3	97	0	0	42	17.79	-23.08			Dec-04
	3.90	22.20	3.38	57.41	44.68	0.39	1.07	14.11	1.22	12.77	315.2	3	97	0	0	42	17.8	-23.15			Dec-04
	5.86	17.98	-2.70	20.75	8.58	0.59	1.27	13.29	1.09	12.27	336.3	3	97	0	0	70	18.15	-20.78			May-99
	5.77	17.82	-2.93	19.77	7.16	0.34	1.52	13.29	1.09	11.9	336.3	3	97	0	0	70	17.97	-20.86	5.50		Jan-98
	5.91	18.16	-2.35	21.87	10.20	0.94	0.97	13.3	1.09	12.36	336.3	3	97	0	0	70	18.2	-20.67			Apr-14
	5.76	17.75	-3.09	19.29	6.41	0.31	1.67	13.34	1.09	11.74	336.3	3	97	0	0	70	17.86	-20.84			Apr-14
	5.83	17.91	-2.80	20.17	7.75	0.49	1.42	13.34	1.1	11.78	336.3	3	97	0	0	70	18.03	-20.75			Apr-14
	5.91	18.05	-2.48	21.44	9.59	0.82	1.07	13.31	1.09	12.36	336.3	3	97	0	0	70	18.2	-20.67			Jan-95
	5.92	18.10	-2.59	21.07	9.12	0.67	1.17	13.32	1.09	12.33	336.3	3	97	0	0	70	18.28	-20.73			Jan-98
	5.79	22.32	11.50	40.56	54.71	0.73	1.01	12.37	0.99	10.96	126.1	2	98	0	0	64	26.43	-15.24			Dec-04
	5.68	22.08	11.19	39.46	52.68	0.52	1.26	12.4	1	10.78	126.1	2	98	0	0	64	26.41	-15.45	5.50		Dec-04
	5.88	22.43	11.89	41.75	56.88	1.04	0.71	12.45	1	10.97	126.1	2	98	0	0	64	26.81	-15.22			Apr-14
	5.67	22.03	11.03	38.85	51.62	0.43	1.41	12.44	1	10.8	126.1	2	98	0	0	64	26.15	-15.49			Dec-04
	5.73	22.17	11.31	39.91	53.47	0.63	1.16	12.4	1	10.69	126.1	2	98	0	0	64	26.63	-15.31			Apr-14
	5.88	22.43	11.76	41.44	56.23	0.93	0.81	12.41	1	10.97	126.1	2	98	0	0	64	26.81	-15.22			Dec-04
	5.84	22.31	11.63	40.91	55.34	0.78	0.91	12.41	1	11.4	126.1	2	98	0	0	64	26.75	-15.25			Dec-04
	3.36	16.33	-4.20	37.64	39.91	0.13	0.99	16.63	0.95	13.53	213.4	1	99	0	0	57	30.05	-23.37			Nov-04
	3.29	16.22	-4.44	36.54	38.19	0	1.24	16.59	0.95	13.18	213.4	1	99	0	0	57	29.89	-23.46	5.50		Jul-98
	3.40	16.53	-3.97	38.83	42.18	0.47	0.69	16.61	0.95	13.67	213.4	1	99	0	0	57	29.89	-23.46			Apr-14
	3.26	16.20	-4.58	36.04	37.22	0	1.39	16.61	0.95	12.98	213.4	1	99	0	0	57	29.7	-23.54			Apr-14
	3.31	16.35	-4.37	37.03	38.94	0.03	1.14	16.61	0.95	13.09	213.4	1	99	0	0	57	29.89	-23.46			Apr-14
	3.40	16.46	-4.02	38.45	41.36	0.37	0.79	16.66	0.95	13.65	213.4	1	99	0	0	57	30.19	-23.36			Nov-04
	3.41	16.50	-4.09	38.03	40.68	0.26	0.89	16.65	0.95	13.62	213.4	1	99	0	0	57	30.18	-23.38			Nov-04
	3.03	16.16	2.90	41.26	11.90	0.22	1.45	13.68	0.95	13.58	163.7	2	98	0	0	38	14.51	-27.65			Nov-08
	2.90	16.00	2.63	40.20	10.52	0.3	1.7	13.65	0.95	13.48	163.7	2	98	0	0	38	14.35	-27.81	5.50		Nov-08
	3.05	16.36	3.24	42.43	13.67	0.62	1.15	13.69	0.95	13.51	163.7	2	98	0	0	38	14.8	-27.62			Mar-11
	2.92	15.94	2.52	39.59	9.71	0	1.85	13.72	0.95	13.38	163.7	2	98	0	0	38	14.3	-27.78			Apr-14
	2.91	16.11	2.77	40.59	11.10	0.21	1.6	13.68	0.95	13.4	163.7	2	98	0	0	38	14.46	-27.71			Apr-14
	3.08	16.29	3.08	42.01	12.97	0.52	1.25	13.68	0.95	13.7	163.7	2	98	0	0	38	14.63	-27.63			Nov-08
	3.04	16.22	3.00	41.58	12.39	0.17	1.35	13.64	0.94	13.54	163.7	2	98	0	0	38	14.61	-27.65			Nov-08
	3.17	11.16	6.10	26.38	23.68	2.57	0.84	5.87	0.97	12.35	385.8	9	35	55	0	62	17.84	-15.56			Dec-03
	3.19	11.03	5.94	25.51	22.24	2.35	1.09	5.86	0.97	12.28	385.8	9	35	55	0	62	17.62	-15.73	5.50		Dec-03
	3.34	11.36	6.50	27.57	25.58	2.9	0.54	5.88	0.97	12.35	385.8	9	35	55	0	62	17.94	-15.58			Apr-14
	3.11	11.00	5.76	24.93	21.24	2.26	1.24	5.9	0.97	11.9	385.8	9	35	55	0	62	17.42	-15.82			Dec-03
	3.24	11.11	6.03	25.94	22.88	2.46	0.99	5.9	0.97	12.1	385.8	9	35	55	0	62	17.77	-15.67			Apr-14
	3.26	11.38	6.35	27.20	25.06	2.84	0.64	5.89	0.97	12.33	385.8	9	35	55	0	62	17.94	-15.58			Apr-14
	3.24	11.21	6.22	26.81	24.23	2.54	0.74	5.88	0.97	12.4	385.8	9	35	55	0	62	17.94	-15.58			Dec-03

	MARKET			FUND TYPE, CATEGORY & OBJECTIVE	RATINGS				MINIMUMS	
Fund Name	Ticker Symbol	Traded On	Fund Type	Category and (Prospectus Objective)	Overall Rating	Reward Rating	Risk Rating	Recent Up/ Downgrade	Open to New Investors	Min Initial Investment
MassMutual RetireSMART by JPMorgan 2025 Administrative Cls	MMIYX	NAS CM	Open End	Target Date (Growth & Income)	B	C	A-	Up	Y	0
MassMutual RetireSMART by JPMorgan 2025 Fund Class A	MMSDX	NAS CM	Open End	Target Date (Growth & Income)	B	C	A-	Up	Y	0
MassMutual RetireSMART by JPMorgan 2025 Fund Class I	MMNUX	NAS CM	Open End	Target Date (Growth & Income)	B	C+	A-	Up	Y	0
MassMutual RetireSMART by JPMorgan 2025 Fund Class R3	MMNRX	NAS CM	Open End	Target Date (Growth & Income)	B-	C	A-	Up	Y	0
MassMutual RetireSMART by JPMorgan 2025 Fund Class R4	MMNZX	NAS CM	Open End	Target Date (Growth & Income)	B	C	A-	Up	Y	0
MassMutual RetireSMART by JPMorgan 2025 Fund Class R5	MMNTX	NAS CM	Open End	Target Date (Growth & Income)	B	C+	A-	Up	Y	0
MassMutual RetireSMART by JPMorgan 2025 Fund Service Class	MMISX	NAS CM	Open End	Target Date (Growth & Income)	B	C	A-	Up	Y	0
MassMutual RetireSMART by JPMorgan 2030 Administrative Cls	MRYYX	NAS CM	Open End	Target Date (Growth & Income)	B-	C	B+	Up	Y	0
MassMutual RetireSMART by JPMorgan 2030 Fund Class A	MRYAX	NAS CM	Open End	Target Date (Growth & Income)	B-	C	B+	Up	Y	0
MassMutual RetireSMART by JPMorgan 2030 Fund Class I	MRYUX	NAS CM	Open End	Target Date (Growth & Income)	B-	C	A-	Up	Y	0
MassMutual RetireSMART by JPMorgan 2030 Fund Class R3	MRYNX	NAS CM	Open End	Target Date (Growth & Income)	B-	C	B+	Up	Y	0
MassMutual RetireSMART by JPMorgan 2030 Fund Class R4	MRYZX	NAS CM	Open End	Target Date (Growth & Income)	B-	C	B+	Up	Y	0
MassMutual RetireSMART by JPMorgan 2030 Fund Class R5	MRYTX	NAS CM	Open End	Target Date (Growth & Income)	B-	C	A-	Up	Y	0
MassMutual RetireSMART by JPMorgan 2030 Fund Service Class	MRYSX	NAS CM	Open End	Target Date (Growth & Income)	B-	C	B+	Up	Y	0
MassMutual RetireSMART by JPMorgan 2035 Administrative Cls	MMXYX	NAS CM	Open End	Target Date (Growth & Income)	B-	C	B+	Up	Y	0
MassMutual RetireSMART by JPMorgan 2035 Fund Class A	MMXAX	NAS CM	Open End	Target Date (Growth & Income)	B-	C	B+	Up	Y	0
MassMutual RetireSMART by JPMorgan 2035 Fund Class I	MMXUX	NAS CM	Open End	Target Date (Growth & Income)	B-	C	B+	Up	Y	0
MassMutual RetireSMART by JPMorgan 2035 Fund Class R3	MMXNX	NAS CM	Open End	Target Date (Growth & Income)	B-	C	B+	Up	Y	0
MassMutual RetireSMART by JPMorgan 2035 Fund Class R4	MMXZX	NAS CM	Open End	Target Date (Growth & Income)	B-	C	B+	Up	Y	0
MassMutual RetireSMART by JPMorgan 2035 Fund Class R5	MMXTX	NAS CM	Open End	Target Date (Growth & Income)	B-	C	B+	Up	Y	0
MassMutual RetireSMART by JPMorgan 2035 Fund Service Class	MMXSX	NAS CM	Open End	Target Date (Growth & Income)	B-	C	B+	Up	Y	0
MassMutual RetireSMART by JPMorgan 2040 Administrative Cls	MRFYX	NAS CM	Open End	Target Date (Growth & Income)	B-	C	B+	Up	Y	0
MassMutual RetireSMART by JPMorgan 2040 Fund Class A	MRFAX	NAS CM	Open End	Target Date (Growth & Income)	B-	C	B+	Up	Y	0
MassMutual RetireSMART by JPMorgan 2040 Fund Class I	MRFUX	NAS CM	Open End	Target Date (Growth & Income)	B-	C	B+	Up	Y	0
MassMutual RetireSMART by JPMorgan 2040 Fund Class R3	MFRNX	NAS CM	Open End	Target Date (Growth & Income)	B-	C	B+	Up	Y	0
MassMutual RetireSMART by JPMorgan 2040 Fund Class R4	MRFZX	NAS CM	Open End	Target Date (Growth & Income)	B-	C	B+	Up	Y	0
MassMutual RetireSMART by JPMorgan 2040 Fund Class R5	MRFTX	NAS CM	Open End	Target Date (Growth & Income)	B-	C	B+	Up	Y	0
MassMutual RetireSMART by JPMorgan 2040 Fund Service Class	MFRSX	NAS CM	Open End	Target Date (Growth & Income)	B-	C	B+	Up	Y	0
MassMutual RetireSMART by JPMorgan 2045 Administrative Cls	MMKYX	NAS CM	Open End	Target Date (Growth & Income)	B-	C	B	Up	Y	0
MassMutual RetireSMART by JPMorgan 2045 Fund Class A	MMKAX	NAS CM	Open End	Target Date (Growth & Income)	B-	C	B	Up	Y	0
MassMutual RetireSMART by JPMorgan 2045 Fund Class I	MMKUX	NAS CM	Open End	Target Date (Growth & Income)	B-	C	B+	Up	Y	0
MassMutual RetireSMART by JPMorgan 2045 Fund Class R3	MMKNX	NAS CM	Open End	Target Date (Growth & Income)	B-	C	B	Up	Y	0
MassMutual RetireSMART by JPMorgan 2045 Fund Class R4	MMKZX	NAS CM	Open End	Target Date (Growth & Income)	B-	C	B	Up	Y	0
MassMutual RetireSMART by JPMorgan 2045 Fund Class R5	MMKTX	NAS CM	Open End	Target Date (Growth & Income)	B-	C	B	Up	Y	0
MassMutual RetireSMART by JPMorgan 2045 Fund Service Class	MMKSX	NAS CM	Open End	Target Date (Growth & Income)	B-	C	B+	Up	Y	0
MassMutual RetireSMART by JPMorgan 2050 Administrative Cls	MMRYX	NAS CM	Open End	Target Date (Growth & Income)	B-	C	B	Up	Y	0
MassMutual RetireSMART by JPMorgan 2050 Fund Class A	MMARX	NAS CM	Open End	Target Date (Growth & Income)	B-	C	B	Up	Y	0
MassMutual RetireSMART by JPMorgan 2050 Fund Class I	MMRUX	NAS CM	Open End	Target Date (Growth & Income)	B-	C	B+	Up	Y	0
MassMutual RetireSMART by JPMorgan 2050 Fund Class R3	MMRNX	NAS CM	Open End	Target Date (Growth & Income)	B-	C	B	Up	Y	0
MassMutual RetireSMART by JPMorgan 2050 Fund Class R4	MMRZX	NAS CM	Open End	Target Date (Growth & Income)	B-	C	B	Up	Y	0
MassMutual RetireSMART by JPMorgan 2050 Fund Class R5	MMRTX	NAS CM	Open End	Target Date (Growth & Income)	B-	C	B	Up	Y	0
MassMutual RetireSMART by JPMorgan 2050 Fund Service Class	MMTSX	NAS CM	Open End	Target Date (Growth & Income)	B-	C	B	Up	Y	0
MassMutual RetireSMART by JPMorgan 2055 Administrative Cls	MMWYX	NAS CM	Open End	Target Date (Growth & Income)	B-	C	B	Up	Y	0
MassMutual RetireSMART by JPMorgan 2055 Fund Class A	MMWAX	NAS CM	Open End	Target Date (Growth & Income)	B-	C	B	Up	Y	0
MassMutual RetireSMART by JPMorgan 2055 Fund Class I	MMWZX	NAS CM	Open End	Target Date (Growth & Income)	B-	C	B+	Up	Y	0
MassMutual RetireSMART by JPMorgan 2055 Fund Class R3	MMWTX	NAS CM	Open End	Target Date (Growth & Income)	B-	C	B	Up	Y	0
MassMutual RetireSMART by JPMorgan 2055 Fund Class R4	MMWEX	NAS CM	Open End	Target Date (Growth & Income)	B-	C	B	Up	Y	0
MassMutual RetireSMART by JPMorgan 2055 Fund Class R5	MMWUX	NAS CM	Open End	Target Date (Growth & Income)	B-	C	B	Up	Y	0
MassMutual RetireSMART by JPMorgan 2055 Fund Service Class	MMWSX	NAS CM	Open End	Target Date (Growth & Income)	B-	C	B	Up	Y	0
MassMutual RetireSMART by JPMorgan 2060 Administrative Cls	MMWFX	NAS CM	Open End	Target Date (Growth & Income)	B-	C	B	Up	Y	0
MassMutual RetireSMART by JPMorgan 2060 Fund Class A	MMWDX	NAS CM	Open End	Target Date (Growth & Income)	B-	C	B	Up	Y	0
MassMutual RetireSMART by JPMorgan 2060 Fund Class I	MMWIX	NAS CM	Open End	Target Date (Growth & Income)	B-	C	B	Up	Y	0

★ Expanded analysis of this fund is included in Section II.

Min Additional Investment	TOTAL RETURNS 3-Month Total Return	6-Month Total Return	1-Year Total Return	3-Year Total Return	5-Year Total Return	PERFORMANCE Dividend Yield (TTM)	Expense Ratio	3-Yr Std Deviation	3-Year Beta	ASSETS NAV	Total Assets (MIL)	ASSET ALLOCATION & TURNOVER %Cash	%Stocks	%Bonds	%Other	Turnover Ratio	BULL & BEAR Last Bull Market Total Return	Last Bear Market Total Return	FEES Front End Fee (%)	Back End Fee (%)	Inception Date
	3.52	12.92	6.58	31.46	27.37	2.68	0.82	7.22	1.02	12.32	279.2	7	49	43	0	67	19.76	-17.56			Apr-10
	3.38	12.75	6.26	30.44	25.69	2.47	1.07	7.22	1.02	12.2	279.2	7	49	43	0	67	19.54	-17.67	5.50		Apr-10
	3.52	13.00	6.79	32.59	29.17	3	0.52	7.28	1.03	12.34	279.2	7	49	43	0	67	19.8	-17.54			Apr-14
	3.41	12.65	6.12	29.89	24.77	2.33	1.22	7.22	1.02	12.11	279.2	7	49	43	0	67	19.46	-17.71			Apr-14
	3.49	12.81	6.41	30.90	26.45	2.58	0.97	7.26	1.03	12.15	279.2	7	49	43	0	67	19.63	-17.63			Apr-14
	3.57	13.06	6.76	32.40	28.75	2.31	0.62	7.23	1.02	12.46	279.2	7	49	43	0	67	19.8	-17.54			Apr-14
	3.51	12.97	6.64	31.84	28.02	2.74	0.72	7.25	1.03	12.36	279.2	7	49	43	0	67	19.8	-17.54			Apr-10
	3.60	14.12	6.52	34.43	29.17	2.63	0.85	8.34	1.02	12.36	510.0	7	61	32	0	63	20.39	-18.22			Dec-03
	3.54	14.02	6.28	33.40	27.63	2.37	1.1	8.26	1.01	12.28	510.0	7	61	32	0	63	20.18	-18.41	5.50		Dec-03
	3.68	14.31	6.82	35.73	31.27	2.94	0.55	8.34	1.02	12.38	510.0	7	61	32	0	63	20.48	-18.25			Apr-14
	3.54	13.86	6.12	32.85	26.60	2.3	1.25	8.31	1.02	11.99	510.0	7	61	32	0	63	19.95	-18.44			Dec-03
	3.57	14.04	6.40	33.87	28.23	2.49	1	8.3	1.02	12.18	510.0	7	61	32	0	63	20.31	-18.33			Apr-14
	3.70	14.27	6.70	35.19	30.51	2.89	0.65	8.32	1.02	12.33	510.0	7	61	32	0	63	20.48	-18.25			Apr-14
	3.67	14.18	6.62	34.79	29.81	2.59	0.75	8.33	1.02	12.4	510.0	7	61	32	0	63	20.48	-18.25			Dec-03
	3.67	14.81	5.98	35.62	29.97	2.61	0.87	9.19	1	12.71	219.1	6	70	24	0	62	20.94	-18.77			Apr-10
	3.53	14.64	5.70	34.64	28.30	2.37	1.12	9.11	1	12.6	219.1	6	70	24	0	62	20.74	-18.89	5.50		Apr-10
	3.69	14.93	6.32	36.92	31.90	2.94	0.57	9.2	1.01	12.62	219.1	6	70	24	0	62	20.94	-18.77			Apr-14
	3.56	14.57	5.57	33.97	27.40	2.25	1.27	9.14	1	12.5	219.1	6	70	24	0	62	20.59	-18.94			Apr-14
	3.55	14.63	5.78	34.90	28.94	2.49	1.02	9.16	1	12.53	219.1	6	70	24	0	62	20.76	-18.86			Apr-14
	3.69	14.90	6.23	36.38	31.24	2.61	0.67	9.16	1	12.64	219.1	6	70	24	0	62	20.94	-18.77			Apr-14
	3.65	14.85	6.07	35.96	30.56	2.63	0.77	9.18	1	12.76	219.1	6	70	24	0	62	21	-18.84			Apr-10
	3.68	15.58	5.77	36.00	30.34	2.57	0.86	9.87	1.01	12.09	331.9	6	78	16	0	59	21.26	-19.02			Dec-03
	3.62	15.48	5.57	35.08	28.75	2.26	1.11	9.85	1.01	12.01	331.9	6	78	16	0	59	20.94	-19.06	5.50		Dec-03
	3.77	15.77	6.15	37.30	32.21	2.87	0.56	9.89	1.01	12.11	331.9	6	78	16	0	59	21.21	-18.95			Apr-14
	3.63	15.49	5.43	34.56	27.80	2.24	1.26	9.87	1.01	11.7	331.9	6	78	16	0	59	20.71	-19.16			Dec-03
	3.65	15.64	5.67	35.53	29.43	2.46	1.01	9.86	1.01	11.9	331.9	6	78	16	0	59	21.03	-19.04			Apr-14
	3.68	15.78	5.99	36.98	31.67	2.82	0.66	9.86	1.01	12.1	331.9	6	78	16	0	59	21.21	-18.95			Apr-14
	3.66	15.71	5.86	36.42	30.99	2.52	0.76	9.84	1.01	12.15	331.9	6	78	16	0	59	21.21	-18.95			Dec-03
	3.77	16.17	5.93	36.92	30.92	2.48	0.85	10.27	1.01	12.64	140.5	5	84	11	0	58	22.62	-20.35			Apr-10
	3.72	16.01	5.61	35.80	29.33	2.22	1.1	10.26	1.01	12.53	140.5	5	84	11	0	58	22.33	-20.47	5.50		Apr-10
	3.84	16.31	6.28	38.22	32.97	2.76	0.55	10.24	1.01	12.69	140.5	5	84	11	0	58	22.62	-20.35			Apr-14
	3.67	15.85	5.50	35.29	28.31	2.11	1.25	10.24	1.01	12.42	140.5	5	84	11	0	58	22.26	-20.52			Apr-14
	3.74	16.12	5.78	36.25	29.98	2.33	1	10.28	1.02	12.46	140.5	5	84	11	0	58	22.44	-20.44			Apr-14
	3.84	16.30	6.14	37.78	32.30	2.65	0.65	10.24	1.01	12.7	140.5	5	84	11	0	58	22.62	-20.35			Apr-14
	3.76	16.11	5.96	37.19	31.55	2.52	0.75	10.24	1.01	12.68	140.5	5	84	11	0	58	22.55	-20.27			Apr-10
	3.79	16.20	6.01	39.13	32.46	2.51	0.84	10.37	1	8.75	196.0	5	84	11	0	65	22.35	-20.12			Dec-07
	3.69	16.02	5.75	38.17	30.87	2.2	1.09	10.36	1	8.69	196.0	5	84	11	0	65	22	-20.18	5.50		Dec-07
	3.79	16.20	6.27	40.40	34.35	2.79	0.54	10.32	0.99	8.75	196.0	5	84	11	0	65	22.24	-20.01			Apr-14
	3.62	15.96	5.69	37.52	29.95	2.11	1.24	10.41	1	8.57	196.0	5	84	11	0	65	21.82	-20.35			Dec-07
	3.72	15.97	5.87	38.50	31.46	2.36	0.99	10.37	1	8.64	196.0	5	84	11	0	65	22.06	-20.09			Apr-14
	3.80	16.22	6.22	39.95	33.94	2.74	0.64	10.34	1	8.74	196.0	5	84	11	0	65	22.24	-20.01			Apr-14
	3.78	16.29	6.21	39.62	33.15	2.39	0.74	10.43	1	8.78	196.0	5	84	11	0	65	22.24	-20.01			Dec-07
	3.70	16.15	6.11	39.43	32.78	2.49	0.83	10.42	1	10.64	59.9	5	84	11	0	62					Sep-13
	3.70	15.92	5.87	38.41	31.16	2.23	1.08	10.36	0.99	10.63	59.9	5	84	11	0	62			5.50		Sep-13
	3.79	16.23	6.37	40.70	34.81	2.77	0.53	10.34	0.99	10.67	59.9	5	84	11	0	62					Apr-14
	3.63	15.82	5.69	37.71	30.12	2.14	1.23	10.35	0.99	10.54	59.9	5	84	11	0	62					Apr-14
	3.72	15.99	5.90	38.77	31.83	2.39	0.98	10.38	0.99	10.59	59.9	5	84	11	0	62					Apr-14
	3.78	16.21	6.33	40.25	34.02	2.67	0.63	10.37	0.99	10.68	59.9	5	84	11	0	62					Apr-14
	3.68	16.19	6.20	39.85	33.42	2.58	0.73	10.4	0.99	10.69	59.9	5	84	11	0	62					Sep-13
	3.78	16.14	6.07	39.19		2.45	0.83	10.41	0.98	10.43	15.2	5	84	11	0	58					Nov-15
	3.68	16.03	5.85	38.15		2.28	1.08	10.4	0.98	10.42	15.2	5	84	11	0	58			5.50		Nov-15
	3.76	16.33	6.40	40.33		2.72	0.53	10.4	0.98	10.47	15.2	5	84	11	0	58					Nov-15

Fund Name	MARKET Ticker Symbol	MARKET Traded On	FUND TYPE, CATEGORY & OBJECTIVE Fund Type	Category and (Prospectus Objective)	RATINGS Overall Rating	Reward Rating	Risk Rating	Recent Up/ Downgrade	MINIMUMS Open to New Investors	Min Initial Investment
MassMutual RetireSMART by JPMorgan 2060 Fund Class R3	**MMWBX**	NAS CM	Open End	Target Date (Growth & Income)	**B-**	C	B	Up	Y	0
MassMutual RetireSMART by JPMorgan 2060 Fund Class R4	**MMWCX**	NAS CM	Open End	Target Date (Growth & Income)	**B-**	C	B	Up	Y	0
MassMutual RetireSMART by JPMorgan 2060 Fund Class R5	**MMWHX**	NAS CM	Open End	Target Date (Growth & Income)	**B-**	C	B	Up	Y	0
MassMutual RetireSMART by JPMorgan 2060 Fund Service Class	**MMWGX**	NAS CM	Open End	Target Date (Growth & Income)	**B-**	C	B	Up	Y	0
MassMutual RetireSMART by JPMorgan In Retmnt Admin Cls	**MDRYX**	NAS CM	Open End	Target Date (Growth & Income)	**B**	C	A-	Up	Y	0
MassMutual RetireSMART by JPMorgan In Retirement Cls A	**MRDAX**	NAS CM	Open End	Target Date (Growth & Income)	**B-**	C	A-	Up	Y	0
MassMutual RetireSMART by JPMorgan In Retirement Cls I	**MDRVX**	NAS CM	Open End	Target Date (Growth & Income)	**B**	C+	A-	Up	Y	0
MassMutual RetireSMART by JPMorgan In Retirement Cls R3	**MDRNX**	NAS CM	Open End	Target Date (Growth & Income)	**B-**	C	A-	Up	Y	0
MassMutual RetireSMART by JPMorgan In Retirement Cls R4	**MDRZX**	NAS CM	Open End	Target Date (Growth & Income)	**B-**	C	A-	Up	Y	0
MassMutual RetireSMART by JPMorgan In Retirement Cls R5	**MDRTX**	NAS CM	Open End	Target Date (Growth & Income)	**B**	C+	A-	Up	Y	0
MassMutual RetireSMART by JPMorgan In Retmnt Service Cls	**MDRSX**	NAS CM	Open End	Target Date (Growth & Income)	**B**	C+	A-	Up	Y	0
MassMutual RetireSMART Conservative Administrative Cls	**MRCLX**	NAS CM	Open End	Cautious Alloc (Asset Alloc)	**B**	C+	A-	Up	Y	0
MassMutual RetireSMART Conservative Fund Class A	**MCTAX**	NAS CM	Open End	Cautious Alloc (Asset Alloc)	**B**	C	A-	Up	Y	0
MassMutual RetireSMART Conservative Fund Class I	**MRCUX**	NAS CM	Open End	Cautious Alloc (Asset Alloc)	**B**	C+	A-	Up	Y	0
MassMutual RetireSMART Conservative Fund Class R3	**MRCVX**	NAS CM	Open End	Cautious Alloc (Asset Alloc)	**B-**	C	A-		Y	0
MassMutual RetireSMART Conservative Fund Class R4	**MRCZX**	NAS CM	Open End	Cautious Alloc (Asset Alloc)	**B**	C+	A-	Up	Y	0
MassMutual RetireSMART Conservative Fund Class R5	**MRCSX**	NAS CM	Open End	Cautious Alloc (Asset Alloc)	**B**	C+	A-	Up	Y	0
MassMutual RetireSMART Conservative Fund Service Class	**MRCYX**	NAS CM	Open End	Cautious Alloc (Asset Alloc)	**B**	C+	A-	Up	Y	0
MassMutual RetireSMART Growth Fund Administrative Class	**MRGLX**	NAS CM	Open End	Aggressive Alloc (Asset Alloc)	**B-**	C	B	Up	Y	0
MassMutual RetireSMART Growth Fund Class A	**MRRAX**	NAS CM	Open End	Aggressive Alloc (Asset Alloc)	**B-**	C	B	Up	Y	0
MassMutual RetireSMART Growth Fund Class I	**MRGUX**	NAS CM	Open End	Aggressive Alloc (Asset Alloc)	**B-**	C	B	Up	Y	0
MassMutual RetireSMART Growth Fund Class R3	**MRGVX**	NAS CM	Open End	Aggressive Alloc (Asset Alloc)	**B-**	C	B	Up	Y	0
MassMutual RetireSMART Growth Fund Class R4	**MRGZX**	NAS CM	Open End	Aggressive Alloc (Asset Alloc)	**B-**	C	B	Up	Y	0
MassMutual RetireSMART Growth Fund Class R5	**MRRSX**	NAS CM	Open End	Aggressive Alloc (Asset Alloc)	**B-**	C	B	Up	Y	0
MassMutual RetireSMART Growth Fund Service Class	**MRGYX**	NAS CM	Open End	Aggressive Alloc (Asset Alloc)	**B-**	C	B	Up	Y	0
MassMutual RetireSMART Moderate Fund Administrative Class	**MRMLX**	NAS CM	Open End	Moderate Alloc (Asset Alloc)	**B-**	C	A-	Up	Y	0
MassMutual RetireSMART Moderate Fund Class A	**MRMAX**	NAS CM	Open End	Moderate Alloc (Asset Alloc)	**B-**	C	A-	Up	Y	0
MassMutual RetireSMART Moderate Fund Class I	**MRMUX**	NAS CM	Open End	Moderate Alloc (Asset Alloc)	**B-**	C	A-	Up	Y	0
MassMutual RetireSMART Moderate Fund Class R3	**MRMTX**	NAS CM	Open End	Moderate Alloc (Asset Alloc)	**B-**	C	A-	Up	Y	0
MassMutual RetireSMART Moderate Fund Class R4	**MRMZX**	NAS CM	Open End	Moderate Alloc (Asset Alloc)	**B-**	C	A-	Up	Y	0
MassMutual RetireSMART Moderate Fund Class R5	**MROSX**	NAS CM	Open End	Moderate Alloc (Asset Alloc)	**B-**	C	A-	Up	Y	0
MassMutual RetireSMART Moderate Fund Service Class	**MRMYX**	NAS CM	Open End	Moderate Alloc (Asset Alloc)	**B-**	C	A-	Up	Y	0
MassMutual RetireSMART Moderate Growth Administrative Cls	**MRSLX**	NAS CM	Open End	Aggressive Alloc (Asset Alloc)	**B-**	C	B+	Up	Y	0
MassMutual RetireSMART Moderate Growth Fund Class A	**MOGAX**	NAS CM	Open End	Aggressive Alloc (Asset Alloc)	**B-**	C	B+	Up	Y	0
MassMutual RetireSMART Moderate Growth Fund Class I	**MROUX**	NAS CM	Open End	Aggressive Alloc (Asset Alloc)	**B-**	C	B+	Up	Y	0
MassMutual RetireSMART Moderate Growth Fund Class R3	**MROTX**	NAS CM	Open End	Aggressive Alloc (Asset Alloc)	**B-**	C	B+	Up	Y	0
MassMutual RetireSMART Moderate Growth Fund Class R4	**MROZX**	NAS CM	Open End	Aggressive Alloc (Asset Alloc)	**B-**	C	B+	Up	Y	0
MassMutual RetireSMART Moderate Growth Fund Class R5	**MRSSX**	NAS CM	Open End	Aggressive Alloc (Asset Alloc)	**B-**	C	B+	Up	Y	0
MassMutual RetireSMART Moderate Growth Fund Service Class	**MROYX**	NAS CM	Open End	Aggressive Alloc (Asset Alloc)	**B-**	C	B+	Up	Y	0
MassMutual Select BlackRock Global Allocation Admin Cls	**MGSLX**	NAS CM	Open End	Moderate Alloc (Growth & Income)	**B-**	C	B+	Up	Y	0
MassMutual Select BlackRock Global Allocation Fund Class A	**MGJAX**	NAS CM	Open End	Moderate Alloc (Growth & Income)	**B-**	C	B+	Up	Y	0
MassMutual Select BlackRock Global Allocation Fund Class I	**MGJIX**	NAS CM	Open End	Moderate Alloc (Growth & Income)	**B-**	C	B+	Up	Y	0
MassMutual Select BlackRock Global Allocation Cls R3	**MGJRX**	NAS CM	Open End	Moderate Alloc (Growth & Income)	**B-**	C	B+	Up	Y	0
MassMutual Select BlackRock Global Allocation Cls R4	**MGJFX**	NAS CM	Open End	Moderate Alloc (Growth & Income)	**B-**	C	B+	Up	Y	0
MassMutual Select BlackRock Global Allocation Cls R5	**MGSSX**	NAS CM	Open End	Moderate Alloc (Growth & Income)	**B-**	C	B+	Up	Y	0
MassMutual Select BlackRock Global Allocation Service Cls	**MGSYX**	NAS CM	Open End	Moderate Alloc (Growth & Income)	**B-**	C	B+	Up	Y	0
MassMutual Select Blue Chip Growth Administrative Cls	**MBCLX**	NAS CM	Open End	US Equity Large Cap Growth (Growth)	**B-**	C+	B	Down	Y	0
MassMutual Select Blue Chip Growth Fund Class A	**MBCGX**	NAS CM	Open End	US Equity Large Cap Growth (Growth)	**B-**	C+	B	Down	Y	0
MassMutual Select Blue Chip Growth Fund Class I	**MBCZX**	NAS CM	Open End	US Equity Large Cap Growth (Growth)	**B-**	C+	B	Down	Y	0
MassMutual Select Blue Chip Growth Fund Class R3	**MBCNX**	NAS CM	Open End	US Equity Large Cap Growth (Growth)	**B-**	C+	B	Down	Y	0
MassMutual Select Blue Chip Growth Fund Class R4	**MBGFX**	NAS CM	Open End	US Equity Large Cap Growth (Growth)	**B-**	C+	B	Down	Y	0
MassMutual Select Blue Chip Growth Fund Class R5	**MBCSX**	NAS CM	Open End	US Equity Large Cap Growth (Growth)	**B-**	C+	B	Down	Y	0

★ Expanded analysis of this fund is included in Section II.

	TOTAL RETURNS					PERFORMANCE				ASSETS		ASSET ALLOCATION & TURNOVER					BULL & BEAR		FEES		
Min Additional Investment	3-Month Total Return	6-Month Total Return	1-Year Total Return	3-Year Total Return	5-Year Total Return	Dividend Yield (TTM)	Expense Ratio	3-Yr Std Deviation	3-Year Beta	NAV	Total Assets (MIL)	%Cash	%Stocks	%Bonds	%Other	Turnover Ratio	Last Bull Market Total Return	Last Bear Market Total Return	Front End Fee (%)	Back End Fee (%)	Inception Date
	3.69	15.99	5.77	37.62		2.2	1.23	10.4	0.98	10.37	15.2	5	84	11	0	58					Nov-15
	3.78	16.14	5.96	38.51		2.36	0.98	10.38	0.98	10.43	15.2	5	84	11	0	58					Nov-15
	3.87	16.35	6.40	39.99		2.64	0.63	10.44	0.99	10.46	15.2	5	84	11	0	58					Nov-15
	3.77	16.12	6.13	39.48		2.59	0.73	10.4	0.98	10.44	15.2	5	84	11	0	58					Nov-15
	3.09	10.22	5.61	17.25	17.22	3.06	0.85	4.69	1.15	11.64	200.1	11	29	60	0	80	10.05	-6.34			Dec-03
	3.04	10.02	5.29	16.34	15.67	3.01	1.1	4.65	1.14	11.52	200.1	11	29	60	0	80	9.92	-6.49	5.50		Dec-03
	3.11	10.37	5.90	18.25	18.89	3.38	0.55	4.68	1.15	11.6	200.1	11	29	60	0	80	10.18	-6.34			Apr-14
	2.89	9.86	5.17	15.71	14.81	2.71	1.25	4.69	1.15	11.36	200.1	11	29	60	0	80	9.7	-6.59			Dec-03
	3.05	10.08	5.37	16.65	16.31	2.91	1	4.66	1.15	11.46	200.1	11	29	60	0	80	10.02	-6.44			Apr-14
	3.19	10.34	5.85	17.95	18.25	3.18	0.65	4.68	1.15	11.63	200.1	11	29	60	0	80	10.18	-6.34			Apr-14
	3.10	10.22	5.71	17.63	17.72	3.15	0.75	4.71	1.16	11.64	200.1	11	29	60	0	80	10.18	-6.34			Dec-03
	3.09	9.30	6.37	16.70	17.72	2.81	0.76	4.01	0.53	9.99	217.5	4	21	74	0	62	9.25				Jun-11
	3.07	9.23	6.14	15.96	16.31	2.54	1.01	3.98	0.54	10.05	217.5	4	21	74	0	62	9.23		5.50		Jun-11
	3.30	9.52	6.75	17.83	19.59	3.13	0.46	4.01	0.56	10	217.5	4	21	74	0	62	9.33				Apr-14
	3.02	9.06	5.84	15.35	15.29	2.5	1.16	3.98	0.54	9.87	217.5	4	21	74	0	62	9.01				Apr-14
	3.12	9.27	6.21	16.18	16.90	2.74	0.91	3.94	0.54	9.9	217.5	4	21	74	0	62	9.17				Apr-14
	3.20	9.53	6.63	17.50	18.94	3.03	0.56	3.99	0.56	9.99	217.5	4	21	74	0	62	9.33				Jun-11
	3.09	9.31	6.42	17.08	18.20	2.95	0.66	3.94	0.52	9.98	217.5	4	21	74	0	62	9.34				Jun-11
	3.92	17.68	5.75	39.45	32.27	2.56	0.89	11.42	0.92	10.58	119.0	2	94	4	0	64	22.8				Jun-11
	3.92	17.55	5.55	38.35	30.67	2.26	1.14	11.42	0.92	10.58	119.0	2	94	4	0	64	22.52		5.50		Jun-11
	4.03	17.83	6.15	40.73	34.35	2.88	0.59	11.44	0.92	10.57	119.0	2	94	4	0	64	22.86				Apr-14
	3.88	17.43	5.42	37.78	29.77	2.21	1.29	11.43	0.92	10.44	119.0	2	94	4	0	64	22.5				Apr-14
	3.87	17.66	5.65	38.82	31.29	2.47	1.04	11.44	0.92	10.46	119.0	2	94	4	0	64	22.68				Apr-14
	3.92	17.81	5.99	40.20	33.70	2.75	0.69	11.44	0.92	10.58	119.0	2	94	4	0	64	22.74				Jun-11
	4.02	17.77	5.97	39.84	33.05	2.66	0.79	11.45	0.92	10.6	119.0	2	94	4	0	64	22.86				Jun-11
	3.56	13.69	6.26	26.25	24.29	2.59	0.82	7.46	0.59	9.88	261.4	3	58	38	0	52	15.1				Jun-11
	3.54	13.63	6.10	25.42	22.77	2.3	1.07	7.48	0.59	9.92	261.4	3	58	38	0	52	14.96		5.50		Jun-11
	3.68	13.87	6.66	27.46	26.16	2.91	0.52	7.54	0.6	9.85	261.4	3	58	38	0	52	15.18				Apr-14
	3.48	13.42	5.94	24.91	21.98	2.21	1.22	7.52	0.59	9.8	261.4	3	58	38	0	52	14.84				Apr-14
	3.48	13.54	6.06	25.69	23.31	2.5	0.97	7.48	0.59	9.81	261.4	3	58	38	0	52	15.01				Apr-14
	3.68	13.74	6.53	27.07	25.56	2.79	0.62	7.5	0.59	9.85	261.4	3	58	38	0	52	15.18				Jun-11
	3.66	13.66	6.39	26.75	24.87	2.7	0.72	7.47	0.59	9.9	261.4	3	58	38	0	52	15.31				Jun-11
	3.78	15.96	5.86	35.45	29.86	2.59	0.85	9.82	0.78	9.88	239.7	3	76	21	0	55	20.13				Jun-11
	3.65	15.88	5.64	34.36	28.16	2.27	1.1	9.86	0.79	9.92	239.7	3	76	21	0	55	19.98		5.50		Jun-11
	3.79	16.15	6.25	36.46	31.68	2.9	0.55	9.86	0.79	9.85	239.7	3	76	21	0	55	20.21				Apr-14
	3.60	15.75	5.46	33.77	27.29	2.26	1.25	9.83	0.78	9.77	239.7	3	76	21	0	55	19.86				Apr-14
	3.70	15.97	5.75	34.77	28.83	2.49	1	9.91	0.79	9.8	239.7	3	76	21	0	55	20.03				Apr-14
	3.78	16.13	6.10	36.30	31.17	2.78	0.65	9.88	0.79	9.86	239.7	3	76	21	0	55	20.21				Jun-11
	3.77	16.07	5.97	35.77	30.41	2.68	0.75	9.85	0.79	9.89	239.7	3	76	21	0	55	20.11				Jun-11
	2.82	10.91	3.69	20.69	16.79	0.74	1.09	7	0.61	11.28	574.6	8	55	33	2	145	11.26	-13.63			Dec-09
	2.73	10.77	3.44	19.81	15.34	0.43	1.34	6.97	0.61	10.9	574.6	8	55	33	2	145	11.22	-14.11	5.50		Dec-09
	2.82	11.07	4.01	21.82	18.56	1.1	0.79	6.94	0.6	10.93	574.6	8	55	33	2	145	11.68	-13.96			Apr-14
	2.77	10.72	3.34	19.37	14.52	0.38	1.49	6.98	0.61	10.74	574.6	8	55	33	2	145	11.36	-14.14			Apr-14
	2.76	10.90	3.60	20.13	15.92	0.62	1.24	6.96	0.61	10.78	574.6	8	55	33	2	145	11.52	-14.05			Apr-14
	2.87	11.11	3.98	21.52	17.93	0.95	0.89	7	0.61	11.1	574.6	8	55	33	2	145	11.68	-13.96			Dec-09
	2.82	10.97	3.75	21.14	17.39	0.87	0.99	6.94	0.61	10.92	574.6	8	55	33	2	145	11.5	-13.97			Dec-09
	4.41	22.09	12.24	74.32	95.45	0.16	0.94	14.05	1.01	22.49	3,215	1	99	0	0	47	30.72	-14.79			May-01
	4.37	21.96	12.00	73.01	93.06	0	1.19	14.05	1.01	21.49	3,215	1	99	0	0	47	30.53	-14.91	5.50		Jun-01
	4.52	22.31	12.59	75.90	98.49	0.43	0.64	14.08	1.02	23.08	3,215	1	99	0	0	47	30.85	-14.75			Apr-14
	4.33	21.82	11.83	72.29	91.64	0	1.34	14.06	1.02	19.98	3,215	1	99	0	0	47	30.31	-15.03			Dec-02
	4.38	22.02	12.09	73.58	94.16	0.08	1.09	14.04	1.01	21.44	3,215	1	99	0	0	47	30.66	-14.84			Apr-14
	4.48	22.28	12.53	75.39	97.48	0.33	0.74	14.07	1.02	23.05	3,215	1	99	0	0	47	30.85	-14.75			May-01

Fund Name	MARKET Ticker Symbol	Traded On	Fund Type	FUND TYPE, CATEGORY & OBJECTIVE Category and (Prospectus Objective)	RATINGS Overall Rating	Reward Rating	Risk Rating	Recent Up/ Downgrade	MINIMUMS Open to New Investors	Min Initial Investment
MassMutual Select Blue Chip Growth Fund Service Class	MBCYX	NAS CM	Open End	US Equity Large Cap Growth (Growth)	B-	C+	B	Down	Y	0
MassMutual Select Diversified Value Administrative Cls	MDDLX	NAS CM	Open End	US Equity Large Cap Value (Growth & Income)	B-	C	B	Up	Y	0
MassMutual Select Diversified Value Fund Class A	MDDAX	NAS CM	Open End	US Equity Large Cap Value (Growth & Income)	B-	C	B	Up	Y	0
MassMutual Select Diversified Value Fund Class I	MDDIX	NAS CM	Open End	US Equity Large Cap Value (Growth & Income)	B-	C	B	Up	Y	0
MassMutual Select Diversified Value Fund Class R3	MDVNX	NAS CM	Open End	US Equity Large Cap Value (Growth & Income)	C+	C	B	Up	Y	0
MassMutual Select Diversified Value Fund Class R4	MDDRX	NAS CM	Open End	US Equity Large Cap Value (Growth & Income)	B-	C	B	Up	Y	0
MassMutual Select Diversified Value Fund Class R5	MDVSX	NAS CM	Open End	US Equity Large Cap Value (Growth & Income)	B-	C	B	Up	Y	0
MassMutual Select Diversified Value Fund Service Class	MDVYX	NAS CM	Open End	US Equity Large Cap Value (Growth & Income)	B-	C	B	Up	Y	0
MassMutual Select Equity Opportunities Administrative Cls	MMFVX	NAS CM	Open End	US Equity Large Cap Blend (Growth)	B	B	B+		Y	0
MassMutual Select Equity Opportunities Fund Class A	MFVAX	NAS CM	Open End	US Equity Large Cap Blend (Growth)	B	B	B+		Y	0
MassMutual Select Equity Opportunities Fund Class I	MFVZX	NAS CM	Open End	US Equity Large Cap Blend (Growth)	B	B	B+		Y	0
MassMutual Select Equity Opportunities Fund Class R3	MFVNX	NAS CM	Open End	US Equity Large Cap Blend (Growth)	B	B	B+		Y	0
MassMutual Select Equity Opportunities Fund Class R4	MFVFX	NAS CM	Open End	US Equity Large Cap Blend (Growth)	B	B	B+		Y	0
MassMutual Select Equity Opportunities Fund Class R5	MFVSX	NAS CM	Open End	US Equity Large Cap Blend (Growth)	B	B	B+		Y	0
MassMutual Select Equity Opportunities Fund Service Class	MMFYX	NAS CM	Open End	US Equity Large Cap Blend (Growth)	B	B	B+		Y	0
MassMutual Select Fundamental Growth Administrative Cls	MOTLX	NAS CM	Open End	US Equity Large Cap Growth (Growth)	B-	C+	B	Down	Y	0
MassMutual Select Fundamental Growth Fund Class A	MOTAX	NAS CM	Open End	US Equity Large Cap Growth (Growth)	B-	C+	B	Down	Y	0
MassMutual Select Fundamental Growth Fund Class I	MOTZX	NAS CM	Open End	US Equity Large Cap Growth (Growth)	B-	C+	B	Down	Y	0
MassMutual Select Fundamental Growth Fund Class R3	MOTNX	NAS CM	Open End	US Equity Large Cap Growth (Growth)	B-	C+	B	Down	Y	0
MassMutual Select Fundamental Growth Fund Class R4	MFGFX	NAS CM	Open End	US Equity Large Cap Growth (Growth)	B-	C+	B	Down	Y	0
MassMutual Select Fundamental Growth Fund Class R5	MOTCX	NAS CM	Open End	US Equity Large Cap Growth (Growth)	B-	C+	B	Down	Y	0
MassMutual Select Fundamental Growth Fund Service Class	MOTYX	NAS CM	Open End	US Equity Large Cap Growth (Growth)	B-	C+	B	Down	Y	0
MassMutual Select Fundamental Value Administrative Cls	MFULX	NAS CM	Open End	US Equity Large Cap Value (Growth & Income)	C+	C	B	Up	Y	0
MassMutual Select Fundamental Value Fund Class A	MFUAX	NAS CM	Open End	US Equity Large Cap Value (Growth & Income)	C+	C	B	Up	Y	0
MassMutual Select Fundamental Value Fund Class I	MFUZX	NAS CM	Open End	US Equity Large Cap Value (Growth & Income)	C+	C	B	Up	Y	0
MassMutual Select Fundamental Value Fund Class R3	MFUNX	NAS CM	Open End	US Equity Large Cap Value (Growth & Income)	C+	C	B	Up	Y	0
MassMutual Select Fundamental Value Fund Class R4	MFUFX	NAS CM	Open End	US Equity Large Cap Value (Growth & Income)	C+	C	B	Up	Y	0
MassMutual Select Fundamental Value Fund Class R5	MVUSX	NAS CM	Open End	US Equity Large Cap Value (Growth & Income)	C+	C	B	Up	Y	0
MassMutual Select Fundamental Value Fund Service Class	MFUYX	NAS CM	Open End	US Equity Large Cap Value (Growth & Income)	C+	C	B	Up	Y	0
MassMutual Select Growth Opportunities Administrative Cls	MAGLX	NAS CM	Open End	US Equity Large Cap Growth (Growth)	C+	C+	B	Down	Y	0
MassMutual Select Growth Opportunities Fund Class A	MMAAX	NAS CM	Open End	US Equity Large Cap Growth (Growth)	C+	C+	B	Down	Y	0
MassMutual Select Growth Opportunities Fund Class I	MMAZX	NAS CM	Open End	US Equity Large Cap Growth (Growth)	C+	C+	B	Down	Y	0
MassMutual Select Growth Opportunities Fund Class R3	MMANX	NAS CM	Open End	US Equity Large Cap Growth (Growth)	C+	C+	B	Down	Y	0
MassMutual Select Growth Opportunities Fund Class R4	MMGFX	NAS CM	Open End	US Equity Large Cap Growth (Growth)	C+	C+	B	Down	Y	0
MassMutual Select Growth Opportunities Fund Class R5	MGRSX	NAS CM	Open End	US Equity Large Cap Growth (Growth)	C+	C+	B	Down	Y	0
MassMutual Select Growth Opportunities Fund Service Class	MAGYX	NAS CM	Open End	US Equity Large Cap Growth (Growth)	C+	C+	B	Down	Y	0
MassMutual Select Mid Cap Growth Fund Administrative Class	MMELX	NAS CM	Open End	US Equity Mid Cap (Growth)	B-	C+	B	Down	Y	0
MassMutual Select Mid Cap Growth Fund Class A	MEFAX	NAS CM	Open End	US Equity Mid Cap (Growth)	B-	C+	B	Down	Y	0
MassMutual Select Mid Cap Growth Fund Class I	MEFZX	NAS CM	Open End	US Equity Mid Cap (Growth)	B-	C+	B	Down	Y	0
MassMutual Select Mid Cap Growth Fund Class R3	MEFNX	NAS CM	Open End	US Equity Mid Cap (Growth)	B-	C+	B	Down	Y	0
MassMutual Select Mid Cap Growth Fund Class R4	MEFFX	NAS CM	Open End	US Equity Mid Cap (Growth)	B-	C+	B	Down	Y	0
MassMutual Select Mid Cap Growth Fund Class R5	MGRFX	NAS CM	Open End	US Equity Mid Cap (Growth)	B-	C+	B	Down	Y	0
MassMutual Select Mid Cap Growth Fund Service Class	MEFYX	NAS CM	Open End	US Equity Mid Cap (Growth)	B-	C+	B	Down	Y	0
MassMutual Select Mid Cap Value Fund Administrative Class	MLULX	NAS CM	Open End	US Equity Mid Cap (Growth)	C+	C	B	Up	Y	0
MassMutual Select Mid Cap Value Fund Class A	MLUAX	NAS CM	Open End	US Equity Mid Cap (Growth)	C+	C	B	Up	Y	0
MassMutual Select Mid Cap Value Fund Class R3	MLUNX	NAS CM	Open End	US Equity Mid Cap (Growth)	C+	C	B	Up	Y	0
MassMutual Select Mid Cap Value Fund Class R4	MLUFX	NAS CM	Open End	US Equity Mid Cap (Growth)	C+	C	B	Up	Y	0
MassMutual Select Mid Cap Value Fund Class R5	MLUSX	NAS CM	Open End	US Equity Mid Cap (Growth)	C+	C	B	Up	Y	0
MassMutual Select Mid Cap Value Fund Service Class	MLUYX	NAS CM	Open End	US Equity Mid Cap (Growth)	C+	C	B	Up	Y	0
MassMutual Select Mid-Cap Value Fund Class I	MLUZX	NAS CM	Open End	US Equity Mid Cap (Growth)	C+	C	B	Up	Y	0
MassMutual Select Overseas Fund Administrative Class	MOSLX	NAS CM	Open End	Global Equity Large Cap (Foreign Stock)	C	C	B-		Y	0
MassMutual Select Overseas Fund Class A	MOSAX	NAS CM	Open End	Global Equity Large Cap (Foreign Stock)	C	C	B-		Y	0

★ Expanded analysis of this fund is included in Section II.

	TOTAL RETURNS					PERFORMANCE				ASSETS		ASSET ALLOCATION & TURNOVER					BULL & BEAR		FEES		
Min Additional Investment	3-Month Total Return	6-Month Total Return	1-Year Total Return	3-Year Total Return	5-Year Total Return	Dividend Yield (TTM)	Expense Ratio	3-Yr Std Deviation	3-Year Beta	NAV	Total Assets (MIL)	%Cash	%Stocks	%Bonds	%Other	Turnover Ratio	Last Bull Market Total Return	Last Bear Market Total Return	Front End Fee (%)	Back End Fee (%)	Inception Date
	4.48	22.20	12.41	74.96	96.56	0.2	0.84	14.07	1.02	22.84	3,215	1	99	0	0	47	30.87	-14.8			May-01
	3.44	15.82	6.05	40.88	42.68	1.71	0.87	12.84	1.05	11.42	354.1	2	97	0	0	75	25.24	-18.87			Oct-04
	3.38	15.77	5.83	39.94	41.03	1.52	1.12	12.84	1.05	11.3	354.1	2	97	0	0	75	24.93	-18.93	5.50		Oct-04
	3.47	16.11	6.40	42.25	44.90	2.04	0.57	12.81	1.05	11.31	354.1	2	97	0	0	75	25.21	-18.75			Apr-14
	3.30	15.63	5.66	39.24	39.96	1.36	1.27	12.78	1.04	11.24	354.1	2	97	0	0	75	24.75	-19.05			Oct-04
	3.43	15.78	5.95	40.38	41.69	1.78	1.02	12.86	1.05	11.15	354.1	2	97	0	0	75	25.02	-18.83			Apr-14
	3.47	15.96	6.27	41.79	44.14	1.94	0.67	12.81	1.05	11.33	354.1	2	97	0	0	75	25.21	-18.75			Oct-04
	3.46	15.95	6.19	41.37	43.45	1.74	0.77	12.81	1.05	11.34	354.1	2	97	0	0	75	25.23	-18.77			Oct-04
	6.01	20.19	14.66	73.27	60.69	1.19	1.04	11.66	0.86	17.26	659.5	2	97	0	0	35	33.26	-20.79			Apr-00
	5.95	20.01	14.36	72.05	58.67	0.96	1.29	11.65	0.86	16.37	659.5	2	97	0	0	35	33.09	-20.88	5.50		May-00
	6.12	20.36	14.97	74.88	63.12	1.46	0.74	11.68	0.86	17.85	659.5	2	97	0	0	35	33.58	-20.65			Nov-10
	5.98	20.01	14.25	71.26	57.52	1.04	1.44	11.68	0.86	15.05	659.5	2	97	0	0	35	32.93	-21.01			Dec-02
	6.00	20.10	14.53	72.57	59.47	1.22	1.19	11.7	0.86	16.07	659.5	2	97	0	0	35	33.29	-20.79			Apr-14
	6.09	20.33	14.90	74.38	62.30	1.35	0.84	11.68	0.86	17.93	659.5	2	97	0	0	35	33.49	-20.7			Apr-00
	6.04	20.30	14.76	73.85	61.48	1.27	0.94	11.68	0.86	17.54	659.5	2	97	0	0	35	33.45	-20.79			Apr-00
	3.59	21.59	11.51	61.49	80.22	0.26	1.08	12.7	0.94	7.49	140.2	1	99	0	0	52	23.93	-10.76			Apr-00
	3.66	21.47	11.33	60.35	78.29	0	1.33	12.65	0.93	7.07	140.2	1	99	0	0	52	23.85	-11.03	5.50		Apr-00
	3.66	21.84	11.84	62.92	82.99	0.53	0.78	12.72	0.94	7.92	140.2	1	99	0	0	52	24.24	-10.8			Apr-14
	3.54	21.32	11.06	59.43	76.62	0	1.48	12.76	0.94	6.43	140.2	1	99	0	0	52	23.62	-11.03			Dec-02
	3.56	21.42	11.34	60.94	78.96	0.12	1.23	12.71	0.94	6.97	140.2	1	99	0	0	52	24.05	-10.89			Apr-14
	3.78	21.74	11.82	62.64	82.30	0.43	0.88	12.7	0.94	7.95	140.2	1	99	0	0	52	24.24	-10.8			Apr-00
	3.75	21.69	11.71	62.16	81.43	0.35	0.98	12.72	0.94	7.74	140.2	1	99	0	0	52	24.02	-10.76			Apr-00
	2.81	13.55	2.24	27.64	32.15	1.73	0.93	12.63	1.03	10.22	847.0	2	98	0	0	13	26.62	-20.51			Dec-01
	2.65	13.40	1.97	26.69	30.46	1.41	1.18	12.59	1.03	10.07	847.0	2	98	0	0	13	26.48	-20.68	5.50		Dec-01
	2.84	13.56	2.55	28.78	34.14	2.07	0.63	12.6	1.03	10.13	847.0	2	98	0	0	13	26.98	-20.41			Nov-10
	2.59	13.18	1.83	26.07	29.55	1.38	1.33	12.61	1.03	9.87	847.0	2	98	0	0	13	26.31	-20.73			Dec-02
	2.69	13.37	2.11	27.05	31.19	1.45	1.08	12.57	1.03	9.92	847.0	2	98	0	0	13	26.53	-20.53			Apr-14
	2.82	13.60	2.39	28.42	33.41	1.94	0.73	12.56	1.03	10.19	847.0	2	98	0	0	13	26.71	-20.45			Dec-01
	2.73	13.54	2.36	27.93	32.79	1.84	0.83	12.58	1.03	10.14	847.0	2	98	0	0	13	26.78	-20.49			Dec-01
	5.96	24.76	11.06	70.63	71.81	0	1.04	15.21	1.06	9.42	548.1	3	97	0	0	19	31.49	-12.21			Apr-00
	5.86	24.70	10.87	69.47	69.68	0	1.29	15.23	1.07	8.48	548.1	3	97	0	0	19	31.38	-12.43	5.50		Apr-00
	6.06	25.02	11.42	72.24	74.50	0	0.74	15.27	1.07	10.49	548.1	3	97	0	0	19	31.64	-12.14			Dec-11
	5.89	24.62	10.64	68.62	68.48	0	1.44	15.29	1.07	7.54	548.1	3	97	0	0	19	30.99	-12.42			Dec-02
	5.94	24.78	11.02	69.89	70.63	0	1.19	15.24	1.07	8.56	548.1	3	97	0	0	19	31.45	-12.23			Apr-14
	6.05	25.06	11.39	71.80	73.58	0	0.84	15.23	1.07	10.33	548.1	3	97	0	0	19	31.65	-12.14			Apr-00
	5.97	24.90	11.26	71.24	72.73	0	0.94	15.21	1.07	9.93	548.1	3	97	0	0	19	31.57	-12.15			Apr-00
	5.89	25.59	14.76	57.98	76.47	0	1.01	13.3	0.91	21.54	8,748	5	95	0	0	34	25.46	-20.28			May-00
	5.84	25.41	14.45	56.80	74.24	0	1.26	13.26	0.91	19.74	8,748	5	95	0	0	34	25.29	-20.37	5.50		May-00
	6.00	25.81	15.13	59.42	79.11	0.04	0.71	13.3	0.91	23.49	8,748	5	95	0	0	34	25.76	-20.14			Nov-10
	5.79	25.38	14.31	56.11	73.01	0	1.41	13.28	0.91	18.08	8,748	5	95	0	0	34	25.01	-20.45			Dec-02
	5.85	25.48	14.59	57.29	75.26	0	1.16	13.3	0.91	19.89	8,748	5	95	0	0	34	25.47	-20.29			Apr-14
	5.97	25.68	14.98	58.92	78.19	0	0.81	13.28	0.91	23.24	8,748	5	95	0	0	34	25.65	-20.21			May-00
	5.89	25.66	14.87	58.41	77.28	0	0.91	13.29	0.91	22.62	8,748	5	95	0	0	34	25.51	-20.17			May-00
	3.35	17.87	2.63	31.71	30.98	0.89	1.11	13.83	1.02	12.33	95.4	2	98	0	0	88	27.16	-22.07			Aug-06
	3.32	17.80	2.43	30.81	29.30	0.64	1.36	13.78	1.02	12.11	95.4	2	98	0	0	88	27.01	-22.02	5.50		Aug-06
	3.28	17.76	2.29	30.22	28.37	0.58	1.51	13.81	1.02	11.93	95.4	2	98	0	0	88	26.76	-22.08			Aug-06
	3.37	17.84	2.49	31.08	29.96	1.07	1.26	13.81	1.02	11.95	95.4	2	98	0	0	88	27.08	-21.88			Apr-14
	3.48	18.13	2.88	32.49	32.22	0.94	0.91	13.82	1.02	12.18	95.4	2	98	0	0	88	27.27	-21.8			Aug-06
	3.42	17.95	2.74	32.00	31.59	1.08	1.01	13.82	1.02	12.09	95.4	2	98	0	0	88	27.2	-21.83			Aug-06
	3.52	18.13	3.00	32.93	33.00	1.23	0.81	13.81	1.02	12.05	95.4	2	98	0	0	88	27.52	-21.8			Dec-11
	5.20	16.78	1.28	36.07	12.83	1.29	1.22	12.66	1.11	8.49	583.3	2	98	0	0	29	16.52	-24.04			Apr-01
	5.19	16.57	1.04	35.05	11.44	0.99	1.47	12.71	1.12	8.3	583.3	2	98	0	0	29	16.52	-24.14	5.50		Apr-01

Fund Name	MARKET Ticker Symbol	Traded On	Fund Type	FUND TYPE, CATEGORY & OBJECTIVE Category and (Prospectus Objective)	RATINGS Overall Rating	Reward Rating	Risk Rating	Recent Up/ Downgrade	MINIMUMS Open to New Investors	Min Initial Investment
MassMutual Select Overseas Fund Class I	**MOSZX**	NAS CM	Open End	Global Equity Large Cap (Foreign Stock)	C	C	B-		Y	0
MassMutual Select Overseas Fund Class R3	**MOSNX**	NAS CM	Open End	Global Equity Large Cap (Foreign Stock)	C	C	B-		Y	0
MassMutual Select Overseas Fund Class R4	**MOSFX**	NAS CM	Open End	Global Equity Large Cap (Foreign Stock)	C	C	B-		Y	0
MassMutual Select Overseas Fund Class R5	**MOSSX**	NAS CM	Open End	Global Equity Large Cap (Foreign Stock)	C	C	B-		Y	0
MassMutual Select Overseas Fund Service Class	**MOSYX**	NAS CM	Open End	Global Equity Large Cap (Foreign Stock)	C	C	B-		Y	0
MassMutual Select Small Cap Growth Equity Admin Cls	**MSGLX**	NAS CM	Open End	US Equity Small Cap (Small Company)	C+	C	C+	Down	Y	0
MassMutual Select Small Cap Growth Equity Fund Class A	**MMGEX**	NAS CM	Open End	US Equity Small Cap (Small Company)	C+	C	C+	Down	Y	0
MassMutual Select Small Cap Growth Equity Fund Class I	**MSGZX**	NAS CM	Open End	US Equity Small Cap (Small Company)	C+	C	C+	Down	Y	0
MassMutual Select Small Cap Growth Equity Fund Class R3	**MSGNX**	NAS CM	Open End	US Equity Small Cap (Small Company)	C+	C	C+	Down	Y	0
MassMutual Select Small Cap Growth Equity Fund Class R4	**MSERX**	NAS CM	Open End	US Equity Small Cap (Small Company)	C+	C	C+	Down	Y	0
MassMutual Select Small Cap Growth Equity Fund Class R5	**MSGSX**	NAS CM	Open End	US Equity Small Cap (Small Company)	C+	C	C+	Down	Y	0
MassMutual Select Small Cap Growth Equity Service Cls	**MSCYX**	NAS CM	Open End	US Equity Small Cap (Small Company)	C+	C	C+	Down	Y	0
MassMutual Select Small Cap Val Equity Fund Class I	**MMQIX**	NAS CM	Open End	US Equity Small Cap (Small Company)	C	C-	C+		Y	0
MassMutual Select Small Cap Val Equity Fund Class R3	**MMQTX**	NAS CM	Open End	US Equity Small Cap (Small Company)	C	C-	C		Y	0
MassMutual Select Small Cap Val Equity Fund Class R4	**MMQFX**	NAS CM	Open End	US Equity Small Cap (Small Company)	C	C-	C		Y	0
MassMutual Select Small Cap Value Equity Admin Cls	**MMQLX**	NAS CM	Open End	US Equity Small Cap (Small Company)	C	C-	C		Y	0
MassMutual Select Small Cap Value Equity Fund Class A	**MMQAX**	NAS CM	Open End	US Equity Small Cap (Small Company)	C	C-	C		Y	0
MassMutual Select Small Cap Value Equity Fund Class R5	**MMQSX**	NAS CM	Open End	US Equity Small Cap (Small Company)	C	C-	C+		Y	0
MassMutual Select Small Cap Value Equity Service Cls	**MMQYX**	NAS CM	Open End	US Equity Small Cap (Small Company)	C	C-	C+		Y	0
MassMutual Select Small Company Value Administrative Cls	**MMYLX**	NAS CM	Open End	US Equity Small Cap (Small Company)	C	C-	C		Y	0
MassMutual Select Small Company Value Fund Class A	**MMYAX**	NAS CM	Open End	US Equity Small Cap (Small Company)	C	C-	C		Y	0
MassMutual Select Small Company Value Fund Class I	**MSVZX**	NAS CM	Open End	US Equity Small Cap (Small Company)	C	C-	C		Y	0
MassMutual Select Small Company Value Fund Class R3	**MSVNX**	NAS CM	Open End	US Equity Small Cap (Small Company)	C	C-	C		Y	0
MassMutual Select Small Company Value Fund Class R4	**MMVFX**	NAS CM	Open End	US Equity Small Cap (Small Company)	C	C-	C		Y	0
MassMutual Select Small Company Value Fund Class R5	**MSVSX**	NAS CM	Open End	US Equity Small Cap (Small Company)	C	C-	C		Y	0
MassMutual Select Small Company Value Fund Service Class	**MMVYX**	NAS CM	Open End	US Equity Small Cap (Small Company)	C	C-	C		Y	0
MassMutual Select T. Rowe Price International Equity Cls I	**MMIUX**	NAS CM	Open End	Global Equity Large Cap (Foreign Stock)	D	D	C		Y	0
MassMutual Select T. Rowe Price Large Cap Blend Fund	**MMLRX**	NAS CM	Open End	US Equity Large Cap Blend (Growth)	D	D+	B-		Y	0
MassMutual Select T. Rowe Price Real Assets Fund Class I	**MMRFX**	NAS CM	Open End	Natl Resources Sec Equity (Growth)	D	D+	B-		Y	0
MassMutual Select T. Rowe Price Retirement 2005 Cls I	**MMFBX**	NAS CM	Open End	Target Date (Asset Alloc)	D	D+	B		Y	0
MassMutual Select T. Rowe Price Retirement 2005 Cls M3	**MMFGX**	NAS CM	Open End	Target Date (Asset Alloc)	D	D+	B		Y	0
MassMutual Select T. Rowe Price Retirement 2005 Cls M4	**MMFEX**	NAS CM	Open End	Target Date (Asset Alloc)	D	D+	B		Y	0
MassMutual Select T. Rowe Price Retirement 2005 Cls M5	**MMFDX**	NAS CM	Open End	Target Date (Asset Alloc)	D	D+	B		Y	0
MassMutual Select T. Rowe Price Retirement 2010 Cls I	**MMXBX**	NAS CM	Open End	Target Date (Asset Alloc)	D	D+	B		Y	0
MassMutual Select T. Rowe Price Retirement 2010 Cls M3	**MMXEX**	NAS CM	Open End	Target Date (Asset Alloc)	D	D+	B		Y	0
MassMutual Select T. Rowe Price Retirement 2010 Cls M4	**MMXDX**	NAS CM	Open End	Target Date (Asset Alloc)	D	D+	B		Y	0
MassMutual Select T. Rowe Price Retirement 2010 Cls M5	**MMXCX**	NAS CM	Open End	Target Date (Asset Alloc)	D	D+	B		Y	0
MassMutual Select T. Rowe Price Retirement 2015 Cls I	**MMFHX**	NAS CM	Open End	Target Date (Asset Alloc)	D	D+	B-		Y	0
MassMutual Select T. Rowe Price Retirement 2015 Cls M3	**MMFLX**	NAS CM	Open End	Target Date (Asset Alloc)	D	D+	B-		Y	0
MassMutual Select T. Rowe Price Retirement 2015 Cls M4	**MMFKX**	NAS CM	Open End	Target Date (Asset Alloc)	D	D+	B-		Y	0
MassMutual Select T. Rowe Price Retirement 2015 Cls M5	**MMFJX**	NAS CM	Open End	Target Date (Asset Alloc)	D	D+	B-		Y	0
MassMutual Select T. Rowe Price Retirement 2020 Cls I	**MMTWX**	NAS CM	Open End	Target Date (Asset Alloc)	D	D+	B-		Y	0
MassMutual Select T. Rowe Price Retirement 2020 Cls M3	**MMTVX**	NAS CM	Open End	Target Date (Asset Alloc)	D	D+	B-		Y	0
MassMutual Select T. Rowe Price Retirement 2020 Cls M4	**MMTUX**	NAS CM	Open End	Target Date (Asset Alloc)	D	D+	B-		Y	0
MassMutual Select T. Rowe Price Retirement 2020 Cls M5	**MMTTX**	NAS CM	Open End	Target Date (Asset Alloc)	D	D+	B-		Y	0
MassMutual Select T. Rowe Price Retirement 2025 Cls I	**MMTFX**	NAS CM	Open End	Target Date (Asset Alloc)	D	D+	B-		Y	0
MassMutual Select T. Rowe Price Retirement 2025 Cls M3	**MMTIX**	NAS CM	Open End	Target Date (Asset Alloc)	D	D+	B-		Y	0
MassMutual Select T. Rowe Price Retirement 2025 Cls M4	**MMTHX**	NAS CM	Open End	Target Date (Asset Alloc)	D	D+	B-		Y	0
MassMutual Select T. Rowe Price Retirement 2025 Cls M5	**MMTGX**	NAS CM	Open End	Target Date (Asset Alloc)	D	D+	B-		Y	0
MassMutual Select T. Rowe Price Retirement 2030 Cls I	**MMTRX**	NAS CM	Open End	Target Date (Asset Alloc)	D	D+	B-		Y	0
MassMutual Select T. Rowe Price Retirement 2030 Cls M3	**MMTQX**	NAS CM	Open End	Target Date (Asset Alloc)	D	D+	B-		Y	0
MassMutual Select T. Rowe Price Retirement 2030 Cls M4	**MMTPX**	NAS CM	Open End	Target Date (Asset Alloc)	D	D+	B-		Y	0

★ Expanded analysis of this fund is included in Section II.

	TOTAL RETURNS					PERFORMANCE				ASSETS		ASSET ALLOCATION & TURNOVER					BULL & BEAR		FEES		
Min Additional Investment	3-Month Total Return	6-Month Total Return	1-Year Total Return	3-Year Total Return	5-Year Total Return	Dividend Yield (TTM)	Expense Ratio	3-Yr Std Deviation	3-Year Beta	NAV	Total Assets (MIL)	%Cash	%Stocks	%Bonds	%Other	Turnover Ratio	Last Bull Market Total Return	Last Bear Market Total Return	Front End Fee (%)	Back End Fee (%)	Inception Date
	5.37	16.92	1.62	37.22	14.52	1.65	0.92	12.72	1.12	8.43	583.3	2	98	0	0	29	16.75	-23.94			Nov-10
	5.12	16.61	0.83	34.41	10.44	1.01	1.62	12.68	1.12	8.21	583.3	2	98	0	0	29	16.29	-24.29			Dec-02
	5.18	16.66	1.05	35.36	11.87	1.3	1.37	12.74	1.12	8.12	583.3	2	98	0	0	29	16.35	-24.12			Apr-14
	5.22	16.85	1.45	36.77	13.94	1.53	1.02	12.74	1.12	8.46	583.3	2	98	0	0	29	16.58	-23.95			Apr-01
	5.25	16.80	1.34	36.38	13.36	1.43	1.12	12.74	1.12	8.41	583.3	2	98	0	0	29	16.66	-24.06			Apr-01
	5.96	28.20	8.96	67.71	60.75	0	1.16	16.83	0.95	13.5	540.4	3	97	0	0	86	27.59	-27.24			May-99
	5.86	27.91	8.65	66.47	58.69	0	1.41	16.79	0.95	11.73	540.4	3	97	0	0	86	27.49	-27.36	5.50		May-99
	6.06	28.36	9.27	69.21	63.06	0	0.86	16.82	0.95	15.75	540.4	3	97	0	0	86	27.91	-27.14			Nov-10
	5.87	27.88	8.46	65.76	57.55	0	1.56	16.81	0.95	10.09	540.4	3	97	0	0	86	27.18	-27.42			Dec-02
	5.99	28.13	8.78	67.17	59.70	0	1.31	16.8	0.95	11.84	540.4	3	97	0	0	86	27.59	-27.23			Apr-14
	6.01	28.28	9.14	68.74	62.36	0	0.96	16.81	0.95	15.51	540.4	3	97	0	0	86	27.78	-27.15			May-99
	5.97	28.21	9.07	68.18	61.51	0	1.06	16.8	0.95	14.54	540.4	3	97	0	0	86	27.65	-27.21			May-99
	3.42	16.70	-4.03	31.76	36.17	0.38	0.89	18.05	1.01	11.18	95.6	6	94	0	0	21	36.22	-27.2			Apr-14
	3.22	16.34	-4.68	29.10	31.50	0	1.59	18.01	1.01	10.89	95.6	6	94	0	0	21	35.82	-27.35			Apr-14
	3.30	16.36	-4.45	30.01	33.11	0	1.34	18.06	1.01	10.95	95.6	6	94	0	0	21	36.02	-27.27			Apr-14
	3.32	16.57	-4.25	30.68	34.21	0.04	1.19	18.04	1.01	11.18	95.6	6	94	0	0	21	35.91	-27.42			Mar-06
	3.27	16.45	-4.54	29.63	32.51	0	1.44	18.04	1.01	11.04	95.6	6	94	0	0	21	35.82	-27.37	5.50		Mar-06
	3.41	16.77	-4.01	31.49	35.68	0.27	0.99	18.05	1.01	11.21	95.6	6	94	0	0	21	36.22	-27.2			Mar-06
	3.39	16.56	-4.21	30.99	34.92	0.06	1.09	18.02	1.01	11.26	95.6	6	94	0	0	21	36.23	-27.22			Mar-06
	1.91	14.53	-6.38	30.45	22.53	0.07	1.25	16.56	0.95	9.06	211.1	3	97	0	0	57	26.93	-24.26			Dec-01
	1.75	14.21	-6.72	29.34	20.88	0	1.5	16.55	0.95	8.68	211.1	3	97	0	0	57	26.7	-24.34	5.50		Dec-01
	1.98	14.60	-6.08	31.61	24.38	0.4	0.95	16.59	0.95	9.26	211.1	3	97	0	0	57	27.16	-24.12			Nov-10
	1.80	14.30	-6.78	28.91	20.12	0	1.65	16.57	0.95	7.91	211.1	3	97	0	0	57	26.5	-24.47			Dec-02
	1.78	14.28	-6.62	29.81	21.48	0	1.4	16.61	0.95	8.56	211.1	3	97	0	0	57	26.77	-24.28			Apr-14
	1.85	14.49	-6.26	31.11	23.65	0.28	1.05	16.6	0.95	9.32	211.1	3	97	0	0	57	27.02	-24.24			Dec-01
	1.86	14.58	-6.35	30.76	23.06	0.15	1.15	16.62	0.95	9.27	211.1	3	97	0	0	57	26.96	-24.2			Dec-01
	2.58	14.43	-0.84			1.47	0.68			9.51	1,092	3	97	0	0						Feb-18
	4.25	20.27	8.86			0.72	0.56			11.27	1,251	2	98	0	0						Feb-18
	0.85	14.84	1.26			1.68	0.61			10.6	79.6	3	97	0	0	13					Feb-18
	3.24	10.48	6.77			1.84	0.38			15.6	25.1	4	35	60	1						Feb-18
	3.05	10.14	6.08			1.42	1.03			15.53	25.1	4	35	60	1						Feb-18
	3.11	10.19	6.26			1.52	0.78			15.56	25.1	4	35	60	1						Feb-18
	3.18	10.34	6.53			1.75	0.53			15.57	25.1	4	35	60	1						Feb-18
	3.32	11.09	6.78			2.36	0.38			15.52	131.2	4	40	55	1						Feb-18
	3.13	10.80	6.15			1.82	1.03			15.48	131.2	4	40	55	1						Feb-18
	3.19	10.88	6.38			2.07	0.78			15.49	131.2	4	40	55	1						Feb-18
	3.26	11.02	6.64			2.24	0.53			15.51	131.2	4	40	55	1						Feb-18
	3.40	11.98	6.67			2.17	0.41			15.51	127.5	4	47	48	1						Feb-18
	3.27	11.62	6.05			1.7	1.06			15.46	127.5	4	47	48	1						Feb-18
	3.26	11.76	6.23			1.85	0.81			15.48	127.5	4	47	48	1						Feb-18
	3.40	11.99	6.59			2.1	0.56			15.5	127.5	4	47	48	1						Feb-18
	3.53	13.29	6.63			2.1	0.45			15.51	677.2	4	56	39	1						Feb-18
	3.34	12.92	5.98			1.55	1.1			15.47	677.2	4	56	39	1						Feb-18
	3.47	13.07	6.28			1.81	0.85			15.48	677.2	4	56	39	1						Feb-18
	3.53	13.22	6.49			1.98	0.6			15.5	677.2	4	56	39	1						Feb-18
	3.67	14.45	6.54			1.89	0.48			15.52	481.3	3	65	31	0						Feb-18
	3.48	14.02	5.85			1.49	1.13			15.45	481.3	3	65	31	0						Feb-18
	3.54	14.23	6.18			1.59	0.88			15.49	481.3	3	65	31	0						Feb-18
	3.60	14.30	6.35			1.79	0.63			15.5	481.3	3	65	31	0						Feb-18
	3.74	15.48	6.45			1.79	0.51			15.51	1,110	3	73	24	0						Feb-18
	3.54	15.10	5.76			1.28	1.16			15.47	1,110	3	73	24	0						Feb-18
	3.68	15.26	6.06			1.53	0.91			15.48	1,110	3	73	24	0						Feb-18

Fund Name	MARKET Ticker Symbol	Traded On	FUND TYPE, CATEGORY & OBJECTIVE Fund Type	Category and (Prospectus Objective)	RATINGS Overall Rating	Reward Rating	Risk Rating	Recent Up/ Downgrade	MINIMUMS Open to New Investors	Min Initial Investment
MassMutual Select T. Rowe Price Retirement 2030 Cls M5	MMTOX	NAS CM	Open End	Target Date (Asset Alloc)	D	D+	B-		Y	0
MassMutual Select T. Rowe Price Retirement 2035 Cls I	MMTJX	NAS CM	Open End	Target Date (Asset Alloc)	D	D+	B-		Y	0
MassMutual Select T. Rowe Price Retirement 2035 Cls M3	MMTMX	NAS CM	Open End	Target Date (Asset Alloc)	D	D+	B-		Y	0
MassMutual Select T. Rowe Price Retirement 2035 Cls M4	MMTLX	NAS CM	Open End	Target Date (Asset Alloc)	D	D+	B-		Y	0
MassMutual Select T. Rowe Price Retirement 2035 Cls M5	MMTKX	NAS CM	Open End	Target Date (Asset Alloc)	D	D+	B-		Y	0
MassMutual Select T. Rowe Price Retirement 2040 Cls I	MMFOX	NAS CM	Open End	Target Date (Asset Alloc)	D	D+	B-		Y	0
MassMutual Select T. Rowe Price Retirement 2040 Cls M3	MMFRX	NAS CM	Open End	Target Date (Asset Alloc)	D	D+	B-		Y	0
MassMutual Select T. Rowe Price Retirement 2040 Cls M4	MMFQX	NAS CM	Open End	Target Date (Asset Alloc)	D	D+	B-		Y	0
MassMutual Select T. Rowe Price Retirement 2040 Cls M5	MMFPX	NAS CM	Open End	Target Date (Asset Alloc)	D	D+	B-		Y	0
MassMutual Select T. Rowe Price Retirement 2045 Cls I	MMFTX	NAS CM	Open End	Target Date (Asset Alloc)	D	D+	B-		Y	0
MassMutual Select T. Rowe Price Retirement 2045 Cls M3	MMFZX	NAS CM	Open End	Target Date (Asset Alloc)	D	D+	B-		Y	0
MassMutual Select T. Rowe Price Retirement 2045 Cls M4	MMFWX	NAS CM	Open End	Target Date (Asset Alloc)	D	D+	B-		Y	0
MassMutual Select T. Rowe Price Retirement 2045 Cls M5	MMFUX	NAS CM	Open End	Target Date (Asset Alloc)	D	D+	B-		Y	0
MassMutual Select T. Rowe Price Retirement 2050 Cls I	MMDDX	NAS CM	Open End	Target Date (Asset Alloc)	D	D+	B-		Y	0
MassMutual Select T. Rowe Price Retirement 2050 Cls M3	MMDHX	NAS CM	Open End	Target Date (Asset Alloc)	D	D+	B-		Y	0
MassMutual Select T. Rowe Price Retirement 2050 Cls M4	MMDGX	NAS CM	Open End	Target Date (Asset Alloc)	D	D+	B-		Y	0
MassMutual Select T. Rowe Price Retirement 2050 Cls M5	MMDFX	NAS CM	Open End	Target Date (Asset Alloc)	D	D+	B-		Y	0
MassMutual Select T. Rowe Price Retirement 2055 Cls I	MMDJX	NAS CM	Open End	Target Date (Asset Alloc)	D	D+	B-		Y	0
MassMutual Select T. Rowe Price Retirement 2055 Cls M3	MMDOX	NAS CM	Open End	Target Date (Asset Alloc)	D	D+	B-		Y	0
MassMutual Select T. Rowe Price Retirement 2055 Cls M4	MMDMX	NAS CM	Open End	Target Date (Asset Alloc)	D	D+	B-		Y	0
MassMutual Select T. Rowe Price Retirement 2055 Cls M5	MMDKX	NAS CM	Open End	Target Date (Asset Alloc)	D	D+	B-		Y	0
MassMutual Select T. Rowe Price Retirement 2060 Cls I	MMSKX	NAS CM	Open End	Target Date (Asset Alloc)	D	D+	B-		Y	0
MassMutual Select T. Rowe Price Retirement 2060 Cls M3	MMSVX	NAS CM	Open End	Target Date (Asset Alloc)	D	D+	B-		Y	0
MassMutual Select T. Rowe Price Retirement 2060 Cls M4	MMSGX	NAS CM	Open End	Target Date (Asset Alloc)	D	D+	B-		Y	0
MassMutual Select T. Rowe Price Retirement 2060 Cls M5	MMSOX	NAS CM	Open End	Target Date (Asset Alloc)	D	D+	B-		Y	0
MassMutual Select T. Rowe Price Retirement Balanced Cls I	MMBVX	NAS CM	Open End	Cautious Alloc (Asset Alloc)	D	D+	B		Y	0
MassMutual Select T. Rowe Price Retirement Balanced Cls M3	MMBZX	NAS CM	Open End	Cautious Alloc (Asset Alloc)	D	D+	B		Y	0
MassMutual Select T. Rowe Price Retirement Balanced Cls M4	MMBYX	NAS CM	Open End	Cautious Alloc (Asset Alloc)	D	D+	B		Y	0
MassMutual Select T. Rowe Price Retirement Balanced Cls M5	MMBWX	NAS CM	Open End	Cautious Alloc (Asset Alloc)	D	D+	B		Y	0
MassMutual Select T. Rowe Price Small & Mid Cap Blend Fund	MMBUX	NAS CM	Open End	US Equity Mid Cap (Growth)	D	D+	B-		Y	0
Matisse Discounted Closed-End Strategy Inst Cls Shares	MDCEX	NAS CM	Open End	Moderate Alloc (Growth & Income)	B	C+	A-	Up	Y	1,000
Matrix Advisors Dividend Fund	MADFX	NAS CM	Open End	US Equity Large Cap Value (Equity-Income)	C+	C	B	Down	Y	1,000
Matrix Advisors Value Fund	MAVFX	NAS CM	Open End	US Equity Large Cap Value (Growth & Income)	C+	C	B		Y	1,000
Matthew 25 Fund	MXXVX	NAS CM	Open End	US Equity Large Cap Blend (Growth)	C+	C+	C+		Y	10,000
Matthews Asia Dividend Fund Institutional Class	MIPIX	NAS CM	Open End	Asia Equity (Pacific Stock)	C	C-	C+		Y	100,000
Matthews Asia Dividend Fund Investor Class	MAPIX	NAS CM	Open End	Asia Equity (Pacific Stock)	C	C-	C+		Y	2,500
Matthews Asia ESG Fund Institutional Class	MISFX	NAS CM	Open End	Asia ex-Japan Equity (Pacific Stock)	C	C-	B		Y	100,000
Matthews Asia ESG Fund Investor Class	MASGX	NAS CM	Open End	Asia ex-Japan Equity (Pacific Stock)	C	C-	B		Y	2,500
Matthews Asia Growth Fund Institutional Class	MIAPX	NAS CM	Open End	Asia Equity (Pacific Stock)	C	C	C+		Y	100,000
Matthews Asia Growth Fund Investor Class	MPACX	NAS CM	Open End	Asia Equity (Pacific Stock)	C	C	C+		Y	2,500
Matthews Asia Innovators Fund Institutional Class Shares	MITEX	NAS CM	Open End	Asia ex-Japan Equity (Pacific Stock)	C	C	C		Y	100,000
Matthews Asia Innovators Fund Investor Class Shares	MATFX	NAS CM	Open End	Asia ex-Japan Equity (Pacific Stock)	C	C	C		Y	2,500
Matthews Asia Small Companies Fund Institutional Class	MISMX	NAS CM	Open End	Asia ex-Japan Equity (Pacific Stock)	C	C-	C	Up	Y	100,000
Matthews Asia Small Companies Fund Investor Class Shares	MSMLX	NAS CM	Open End	Asia ex-Japan Equity (Pacific Stock)	C	C-	C	Up	Y	2,500
Matthews Asia Value Fund Institutional Class	MAVAX	NAS CM	Open End	Asia Equity (Growth)	C	C-	B		Y	100,000
Matthews Asia Value Fund Investor Class	MAVRX	NAS CM	Open End	Asia Equity (Growth)	C	C-	B		Y	2,500
Matthews Asian Growth and Income Fund Institutional Class	MICSX	NAS CM	Open End	Asia ex-Japan Equity (Pacific Stock)	C+	C	B	Up	Y	100,000
Matthews Asian Growth and Income Fund Investor Class	MACSX	NAS CM	Open End	Asia ex-Japan Equity (Pacific Stock)	C+	C	B	Up	Y	2,500
Matthews China Dividend Fund Institutional Class	MICDX	NAS CM	Open End	Greater China Equity (Pacific Stock)	C	C	B-		Y	100,000
Matthews China Dividend Fund Investor Class	MCDFX	NAS CM	Open End	Greater China Equity (Pacific Stock)	C	C	B-		Y	2,500
Matthews China Fund Institutional Class	MICFX	NAS CM	Open End	Greater China Equity (Pacific Stock)	C	C-	C		Y	100,000
Matthews China Fund Investor Class	MCHFX	NAS CM	Open End	Greater China Equity (Pacific Stock)	C	C-	C		Y	2,500

★ Expanded analysis of this fund is included in Section II.

Min Additional Investment	TOTAL RETURNS: 3-Month Total Return	6-Month Total Return	1-Year Total Return	3-Year Total Return	5-Year Total Return	PERFORMANCE: Dividend Yield (TTM)	Expense Ratio	3-Yr Std Deviation	3-Year Beta	ASSETS: NAV	Total Assets (MIL)	ASSET ALLOCATION & TURNOVER: %Cash	%Stocks	%Bonds	%Other	Turnover Ratio	BULL & BEAR: Last Bull Market Total Return	Last Bear Market Total Return	FEES: Front End Fee (%)	Back End Fee (%)	Inception Date
	3.67	15.41	6.24			1.68	0.66			15.5	1,110	3	73	24	0						Feb-18
	3.81	16.35	6.27			1.64	0.54			15.51	434.8	3	79	18	0						Feb-18
	3.62	15.90	5.60			1.21	1.19			15.45	434.8	3	79	18	0						Feb-18
	3.68	16.12	5.91			1.35	0.94			15.48	434.8	3	79	18	0						Feb-18
	3.75	16.20	6.08			1.55	0.69			15.49	434.8	3	79	18	0						Feb-18
	3.81	16.98	6.14			1.53	0.56			15.5	822.8	3	84	13	0						Feb-18
	3.68	16.59	5.45			1.03	1.21			15.46	822.8	3	84	13	0						Feb-18
	3.68	16.76	5.71			1.29	0.96			15.46	822.8	3	84	13	0						Feb-18
	3.82	16.90	6.00			1.42	0.71			15.49	822.8	3	84	13	0						Feb-18
	3.88	17.42	6.08			1.47	0.56			15.5	319.4	3	87	9	0						Feb-18
	3.69	17.04	5.37			1.01	1.21			15.45	319.4	3	87	9	0						Feb-18
	3.75	17.19	5.64			1.18	0.96			15.47	319.4	3	87	9	0						Feb-18
	3.82	17.34	5.95			1.37	0.71			15.49	319.4	3	87	9	0						Feb-18
	3.81	17.42	6.05			1.45	0.56			15.5	480.0	3	87	9	0						Feb-18
	3.62	16.95	5.39			0.97	1.21			15.45	480.0	3	87	9	0						Feb-18
	3.75	17.12	5.63			1.22	0.96			15.46	480.0	3	87	9	0						Feb-18
	3.82	17.34	5.92			1.35	0.71			15.49	480.0	3	87	9	0						Feb-18
	3.88	17.42	6.07			1.47	0.56			15.5	155.4	3	87	9	0						Feb-18
	3.69	17.05	5.41			1.05	1.21			15.44	155.4	3	87	9	0						Feb-18
	3.75	17.19	5.63			1.17	0.96			15.47	155.4	3	87	9	0						Feb-18
	3.75	17.27	5.87			1.36	0.71			15.48	155.4	3	87	9	0						Feb-18
	3.89	17.46	6.04			1.47	0.56			15.47	27.2	3	87	9	0						Feb-18
	3.70	17.02	5.32			1.1	1.21			15.4	27.2	3	87	9	0						Feb-18
	3.76	17.24	5.64			1.25	0.96			15.43	27.2	3	87	9	0						Feb-18
	3.76	17.31	5.86			1.38	0.71			15.45	27.2	3	87	9	0						Feb-18
	3.08	10.51	6.30			2.33	0.34			15.35	48.4	4	39	56	1						Feb-18
	2.96	10.15	5.59			1.85	0.99			15.3	48.4	4	39	56	1						Feb-18
	3.02	10.28	5.91			2	0.74			15.33	48.4	4	39	56	1						Feb-18
	3.08	10.40	6.24			2.05	0.49			15.38	48.4	4	39	56	1						Feb-18
	5.47	22.87	7.86			0.32	0.65			11.55	622.3	5	95	0	0	22					Feb-18
100	0.37	16.94	8.36	36.45	34.59	3.4	2.65	10.15	0.72	10	45.3	1	82	9	1	55					Oct-12
100	4.49	15.70	10.86			2.33	0.9			24.28	15.1	0	100	0	0	6					Oct-16
100	3.99	16.97	5.24	36.41	26.30	1.25	0.99	14.65	1.14	68.01	53.6	0	100	0	0	18	25.64	-25.98			Jul-96
100	7.29	30.59	9.13	62.67	47.82	0.37	1.1	17.38	1.09	29.84	350.6	0	81	0	0	25	42.81	-15.96			Oct-95
100	-1.19	6.34	-4.25	22.86	28.47	1.55	0.9	11.74	0.92	16.82	6,074	2	98	0	0	40	13.79	-13.43			Oct-10
100	-1.16	6.34	-4.34	22.46	27.74	1.45	1.01	11.73	0.92	16.83	6,074	2	98	0	0	40	13.75	-13.54			Oct-06
100	-2.06	10.18	1.22	34.54		0.09	1.25	11.56	0.73	10.93	45.5	0	100	0	0	23					Apr-15
100	-2.14	10.06	1.04	33.56		0.18	1.5	11.63	0.73	10.94	45.5	0	100	0	0	23					Apr-15
100	1.35	15.99	-5.64	33.63	35.51	0.32	0.93	15.36	1.11	26.25	1,119	6	94	0	0	12	12.61	-17.27			Oct-10
100	1.28	15.83	-5.83	32.92	34.22	0.11	1.1	15.34	1.1	26.04	1,119	6	94	0	0	12	12.5	-17.34			Oct-03
100	1.81	19.38	-4.10	44.07	45.31	0.5	1.02	17.41	1.08	13.49	292.4	4	96	0	0	86	13.17	-23.49			Apr-13
100	1.66	19.30	-4.36	43.30	43.79	0.29	1.19	17.4	1.08	13.41	292.4	4	96	0	0	86	13.17	-23.49			Dec-99
100	2.95	13.99	-6.53	21.86	9.34	0.66	1.25	12.26	0.84	17.43	191.6	7	93	0	0	70	12.6	-21.73			Apr-13
100	2.88	13.89	-6.70	21.12	8.17	0.37	1.46	12.29	0.85	17.46	191.6	7	93	0	0	70	12.6	-21.73			Sep-08
100	-1.53	7.44	-1.48	37.52		1.53	1.25	11.43	0.72	11.55	25.0	17	83	0	0	48					Nov-15
100	-1.60	7.29	-1.78	36.47		1.31	1.5	11.45	0.72	11.62	25.0	17	83	0	0	48					Nov-15
100	2.07	13.43	7.34	17.99	13.14	1.76	0.93	10.2	0.64	15.51	1,420	2	81	1	2	32	13.45	-14.59			Oct-10
100	2.06	13.40	7.19	17.50	12.34	1.64	1.08	10.18	0.64	15.54	1,420	2	81	1	2	32	13.32	-14.63			Sep-94
100	-0.59	16.63	0.99	55.17	70.84	1.83	1.01	13.64	0.64	16.29	378.6	7	93	0	0	66	19.59	-19.03			Oct-10
100	-0.65	16.56	0.85	54.50	69.40	1.7	1.15	13.64	0.64	16.29	378.6	7	93	0	0	66	19.57	-19.17			Nov-09
100	-1.40	23.76	-3.55	69.31	51.83	1.61	0.91	21.54	1.06	17.55	863.5	7	93	0	0	97	17.16	-26.28			Oct-10
100	-1.45	23.64	-3.79	68.42	50.63	1.4	1.1	21.49	1.06	17.57	863.5	7	93	0	0	97	17.02	-26.33			Feb-98

	MARKET			FUND TYPE, CATEGORY & OBJECTIVE	RATINGS					MINIMUMS
Fund Name	Ticker Symbol	Traded On	Fund Type	Category and (Prospectus Objective)	Overall Rating	Reward Rating	Risk Rating	Recent Up/ Downgrade	Open to New Investors	Min Initial Investment
Matthews China Small Companies Fund	MCSMX	NAS CM	Open End	Greater China Equity (Pacific Stock)	C	C	C		Y	2,500
Matthews China Small Companies Institutional Cls Shares	MICHX	NAS CM	Open End	Greater China Equity (Pacific Stock)	C	C	C		Y	100,000
Matthews Emerging Asia Fund Institutional Class	MIASX	NAS CM	Open End	Asia ex-Japan Equity (Pacific Stock)	D+	D	C-	Down	Y	100,000
Matthews Emerging Asia Fund Investor Class	MEASX	NAS CM	Open End	Asia ex-Japan Equity (Pacific Stock)	D+	D	C-	Down	Y	2,500
Matthews India Fund Institutional Class	MIDNX	NAS CM	Open End	India Equity (Pacific Stock)	C	C-	C+		Y	100,000
Matthews India Fund Investor Class	MINDX	NAS CM	Open End	India Equity (Pacific Stock)	C	C-	C+		Y	2,500
Matthews Japan Fund Institutional Class	MIJFX	NAS CM	Open End	Japan Equity (Pacific Stock)	C	C-	C	Up		100,000
Matthews Japan Fund Investor Class	MJFOX	NAS CM	Open End	Japan Equity (Pacific Stock)	C	C-	C	Up	Y	2,500
Matthews Korea Fund Institutional Class	MIKOX	NAS CM	Open End	Equity Miscellaneous (Pacific Stock)	D	D	D+	Down	Y	100,000
Matthews Korea Fund Investor Class	MAKOX	NAS CM	Open End	Equity Miscellaneous (Pacific Stock)	D	D	D+	Down	Y	2,500
Matthews Pacific Tiger Fund Institutional Class	MIPTX	NAS CM	Open End	Asia ex-Japan Equity (Pacific Stock)	C	C	B-		Y	100,000
Matthews Pacific Tiger Fund Investor Class	MAPTX	NAS CM	Open End	Asia ex-Japan Equity (Pacific Stock)	C	C	B-		Y	2,500
McKee International Equity Fund Class Institutional	MKIEX	NAS CM	Open End	Global Equity Large Cap (Foreign Stock)	C	C-	C		Y	2,500
Measured Risk Strategy Fund Class A	MRPAX	NAS CM	Open End	Long/Short Equity (Growth & Income)	D	D	D		Y	2,500
Measured Risk Strategy Fund Class I	MRPIX	NAS CM	Open End	Long/Short Equity (Growth & Income)	D	D	D		Y	100,000
Meeder Balanced Fund Adviser Class	BLNAX	NAS CM	Open End	Moderate Alloc (Balanced)	C+	C	B		Y	2,500
Meeder Balanced Fund Institutional Class	BLNIX	NAS CM	Open End	Moderate Alloc (Balanced)	B-	C	B	Up	Y	1,000,000
Meeder Balanced Fund Retail Class	FLDFX	NAS CM	Open End	Moderate Alloc (Balanced)	C+	C	B	Up	Y	2,500
Meeder Conservative Allocation Fund Adviser Class	IFAAX	NAS CM	Open End	Cautious Alloc (Utility)	B-	C	A-		Y	2,500
Meeder Conservative Allocation Fund Institutional Class	IFAIX	NAS CM	Open End	Cautious Alloc (Utility)	B-	C	A-		Y	1,000,000
Meeder Conservative Allocation Fund Retail Class	FLRUX	NAS CM	Open End	Cautious Alloc (Utility)	B-	C	B+	Up	Y	2,500
Meeder Dynamic Allocation Fund Adviser Class	DYGAX	NAS CM	Open End	Aggressive Alloc (Growth)	C+	C	B	Up	Y	2,500
Meeder Dynamic Allocation Fund Institutional Class	DYGIX	NAS CM	Open End	Aggressive Alloc (Growth)	C+	C	B	Up	Y	1,000,000
Meeder Dynamic Allocation Fund Retail Class	FLDGX	NAS CM	Open End	Aggressive Alloc (Growth)	C+	C	B	Up	Y	2,500
Meeder Global Allocation Fund Adviser Class	GBPAX	NAS CM	Open End	Flexible Alloc (Growth)	C	C	C+		Y	2,500
Meeder Global Allocation Fund Institutional Class	GBPIX	NAS CM	Open End	Flexible Alloc (Growth)	C	C	C+		Y	1,000,000
Meeder Global Allocation Fund Retail Class	FLFGX	NAS CM	Open End	Flexible Alloc (Growth)	C	C	C+		Y	2,500
Meeder Moderate Allocation Fund Adviser Class	DVOAX	NAS CM	Open End	Cautious Alloc (Growth & Income)	B-	C	B+	Up	Y	2,500
Meeder Moderate Allocation Fund Institutional Class	DVOIX	NAS CM	Open End	Cautious Alloc (Growth & Income)	B-	C	A-	Up	Y	1,000,000
Meeder Moderate Allocation Fund Retail Class	FLDOX	NAS CM	Open End	Cautious Alloc (Growth & Income)	B-	C	B+	Up	Y	2,500
Meeder Muirfield Fund Adviser Class	FLMAX	NAS CM	Open End	Moderate Alloc (Growth)	C+	C	B-	Up	Y	2,500
Meeder Muirfield Fund Institutional Class	FLMIX	NAS CM	Open End	Moderate Alloc (Growth)	C+	C	B-	Up	Y	1,000,000
Meeder Muirfield Fund Retail Class	FLMFX	NAS CM	Open End	Moderate Alloc (Growth)	C	C	B-		Y	2,500
Meeder Quantex Fund Adviser Class	QNTAX	NAS CM	Open End	US Equity Mid Cap (Growth)	C	D+	C+		Y	2,500
Meeder Quantex Fund Institutional Class	QNTIX	NAS CM	Open End	US Equity Mid Cap (Growth)	C	D+	C+		Y	1,000,000
Meeder Quantex Fund Retail Class	FLCGX	NAS CM	Open End	US Equity Mid Cap (Growth)	C	D+	C+		Y	2,500
Meeder Spectrum Fund Adviser Class	SRUAX	NAS CM	Open End	Long/Short Equity (Growth)	C	C	B-		Y	2,500
Meeder Spectrum Fund Institutional Class	SRUIX	NAS CM	Open End	Long/Short Equity (Growth)	C	C	B-		Y	1,000,000
Meeder Spectrum Fund Retail Class	FLSPX	NAS CM	Open End	Long/Short Equity (Growth)	C	C	B-		Y	2,500
Meehan Focus Fund	MEFOX	NAS CM	Open End	US Equity Large Cap Blend (Growth)	C+	C	B		Y	5,000
Mercator International Opportunity Institutional Cls	MOPPX	NAS CM	Open End	Global Equity Large Cap (Growth)	D	D+	C	Up	Y	1,000
Mercer Emerging Markets Equity Fund Class Y3	MEMQX	NAS CM	Open End	Global Emerg Mkts (Div Emerging Mkts)	C	C	C+		Y	0
Mercer Global Low Volatility Equity Fund Class Y-3	MGLVX	NAS CM	Open End	Global Equity Large Cap (Equity-Income)	B	C+	B+		Y	0
Mercer Non-US Core Equity Fund Class Y3	MNCEX	NAS CM	Open End	Global Equity Large Cap (Equity-Income)	C	C	B		Y	0
Mercer US Large Cap Equity Fund Class Y3	MLCGX	NAS CM	Open End	US Equity Large Cap Growth (Equity-Income)	C+	C	B		Y	0
Mercer US Small/Mid Cap Equity Fund Class Y3	MSCGX	NAS CM	Open End	US Equity Mid Cap (Equity-Income)	C	C	C+		Y	0
Meridian Contrarian Fund A Class	MFCAX	NAS CM	Open End	US Equity Mid Cap (Growth)	C+	C	B-		Y	2,500
Meridian Contrarian Fund Class C	MFCCX	NAS CM	Open End	US Equity Mid Cap (Growth)	C+	C	B-		Y	2,500
Meridian Contrarian Fund Investor Class	MFCIX	NAS CM	Open End	US Equity Mid Cap (Growth)	C+	C	B-		Y	99,999
Meridian Contrarian Fund Legacy Class	MVALX	NAS CM	Open End	US Equity Mid Cap (Growth)	C+	C	B-			1,000
Meridian Enhanced Equity Fund® A Class	MRAEX	NAS CM	Open End	US Equity Large Cap Growth (Equity-Income)	B-	B-	C		Y	2,500
Meridian Enhanced Equity Fund® Class C	MRCEX	NAS CM	Open End	US Equity Large Cap Growth (Equity-Income)	B-	B-	C		Y	2,500

★ Expanded analysis of this fund is included in Section II.

	TOTAL RETURNS					PERFORMANCE				ASSETS		ASSET ALLOCATION & TURNOVER					BULL & BEAR		FEES		
Min Additional Investment	3-Month Total Return	6-Month Total Return	1-Year Total Return	3-Year Total Return	5-Year Total Return	Dividend Yield (TTM)	Expense Ratio	3-Yr Std Deviation	3-Year Beta	NAV	Total Assets (MIL)	%Cash	%Stocks	%Bonds	%Other	Turnover Ratio	Last Bull Market Total Return	Last Bear Market Total Return	Front End Fee (%)	Back End Fee (%)	Inception Date
100	0.79	20.31	-10.36	57.77	51.54	0.46	1.5	19.01	1.08	11.37	73.0	9	91	0	0	77	14.68				May-11
100	0.88	20.50	-10.08	58.44	52.18	0.44	1.25	19	1.08	11.4	73.0	9	91	0	0	77	14.68				Nov-17
100	-6.36	-0.80	-8.75	4.63	19.37	1.05	1.25	9.28	0.41	12.35	427.9	4	96	0	0	26					Apr-13
100	-6.46	-1.04	-9.05	3.83	17.95	0.77	1.48	9.31	0.41	12.29	427.9	4	96	0	0	26					Apr-13
100	-3.06	2.75	-3.12	22.95	52.74	0	0.9	15	0.86	27.18	1,481	1	99	0	0	21	-1.68	-19.22			Oct-10
100	-3.06	2.66	-3.27	22.31	51.31	0	1.09	14.98	0.86	26.92	1,481	1	99	0	0	21	-1.74	-19.27			Oct-05
100	0.95	14.10	-9.22	14.48	40.79	0.35	0.85	15.03	1.16	21.12	2,672	7	93	0	0	46	4.09	-5.46			Oct-10
100	0.95	14.13	-9.27	14.20	40.24	0.27	0.91	15.04	1.16	21.08	2,672	7	93	0	0	46	4.01	-5.46			Dec-98
100	-1.92	-0.86	-12.45	6.31	14.34	2.54	1.02	16.31	0.87	4.58	150.5	1	99	0	0	36	18.2	-21.83			Oct-10
100	-2.15	-1.08	-12.65	5.69	13.34	2.46	1.14	16.3	0.87	4.54	150.5	1	99	0	0	36	18	-21.86			Jan-95
100	0.10	8.28	1.30	30.44	36.07	0.87	0.88	11.63	0.76	28.9	9,202	2	98	0	0	11	14.78	-17.44			Oct-10
100	0.03	8.19	1.13	29.83	34.92	0.69	1.04	11.63	0.76	28.91	9,202	2	98	0	0	11	14.68	-17.49			Sep-94
100	1.98	11.39	-6.08	21.61	3.91	2.58	0.98	13.25	1.16	11.83	136.4	6	94	0	0	8	15.75	-25.86			May-94
50	-9.31	-6.88	-21.69			0	2.27			7.3	8.7	46	0	54	0	0			4.75		Dec-16
5,000	-9.27	-6.85	-21.51			0	2.02			7.34	8.7	46	0	54	0	0					Dec-16
100	2.20	6.20	2.75	24.00	21.81	1.16	1.42	7	0.92	11.76	399.7	0	70	30	0	218	14.1	-14.04			Oct-16
100	2.25	6.29	2.98	24.39	22.20	1.38	1.24	6.94	0.92	11.76	399.7	0	70	30	0	218	14.1	-14.04			Oct-16
100	2.26	6.15	2.60	23.07	20.90	0.92	1.62	6.95	0.92	11.69	399.7	0	70	30	0	218	14.1	-14.04			Jan-06
100	2.56	6.78	4.93	17.30	8.61	2.08	1.58	5.18	1.21	22.65	141.5	0	30	69	0	185	15.59	-15.75			Oct-16
100	2.60	6.86	5.10	17.74	9.03	2.21	1.4	5.17	1.21	22.7	141.5	0	30	69	0	185	15.59	-15.75			Oct-16
100	2.50	6.72	4.80	16.60	7.97	1.85	1.74	5.2	1.22	22.38	141.5	0	30	69	0	185	15.59	-15.75			Jun-95
100	2.78	15.59	4.06	37.01	38.08	0.77	1.33	11.61	1.06	11.23	197.6	0	95	5	0	273	23.09	-20.34			Oct-16
100	2.73	15.59	4.22	37.56	38.64	0.92	1.11	11.64	1.06	11.22	197.6	0	95	5	0	273	23.09	-20.34			Oct-16
100	2.65	15.43	3.82	36.17	37.24	0.64	1.55	11.62	1.06	11.19	197.6	0	95	5	0	273	23.09	-20.34			Feb-00
100	2.31	6.06	-0.66	29.04	13.70	0.7	1.58	9.05	1.16	10.8	58.1	-1	90	11	0	163	22.36	-23.33			Oct-16
100	2.36	6.26	-0.39	29.74	14.31	0.95	1.34	9.05	1.16	10.81	58.1	-1	90	11	0	163	22.36	-23.33			Oct-16
100	2.27	5.98	-0.83	27.97	12.75	0.62	1.77	9.04	1.16	10.78	58.1	-1	90	11	0	163	22.36	-23.33			Jan-06
100	2.45	6.47	3.56	33.11		1.58	1.51	7.25	1.09	11.45	179.3	0	50	49	0	213					Oct-16
100	2.49	6.55	3.74	33.63		1.75	1.32	7.18	1.08	11.47	179.3	0	50	49	0	213					Oct-16
100	2.41	6.38	3.33	32.14		1.45	1.71	7.2	1.08	11.43	179.3	0	50	49	0	213					Jun-15
100	1.94	5.63	0.97	31.82	29.00	0.84	1.22	9.67	1.23	7.58	673.9	0	100	0	0	225	19.05	-19.8			Oct-16
100	1.87	5.70	1.13	32.20	29.37	1.01	1.03	9.58	1.22	7.58	673.9	0	100	0	0	225	19.05	-19.8			Oct-16
100	1.75	5.60	0.65	30.84	28.05	0.66	1.37	9.66	1.23	7.53	673.9	0	100	0	0	225	19.04	-19.8			Aug-88
100	-2.55	11.99	-5.44	26.84	26.47	0.12	1.48	16.87	1.07	35.85	68.9	0	100	0	0	116	23.63	-23.07			Oct-16
100	-2.38	12.27	-5.14	27.56	27.19	0.31	1.27	16.87	1.07	35.89	68.9	0	100	0	0	116	23.63	-23.07			Oct-16
100	-2.47	12.08	-5.46	26.33	25.97	0.08	1.63	16.86	1.07	35.77	68.9	0	100	0	0	116	23.63	-23.08			Mar-85
100	2.12	5.68	0.46	31.96		0.22	1.71	9.64	1.22	11.53	208.3	-7	107	0	0	97					Oct-16
100	2.21	5.76	0.64	32.57		0.38	1.51	9.65	1.23	11.56	208.3	-7	107	0	0	97					Oct-16
100	2.13	5.61	0.27	31.08		0.04	1.9	9.66	1.23	11.47	208.3	-7	107	0	0	97					Jan-15
100	4.35	17.19	8.22	45.79	33.47	0.56	1.02	14.01	1.1	26.37	64.7	0	100	0	0	20	20.71	-15.12			Dec-99
1,000	6.34	24.77	-3.18			0	1.2			9.72	7.4	1	99	0	0	56					Apr-18
	2.22	11.53	2.01	32.55	7.79	0.11	0.63	13.36	0.96	9.15	1,018	6	94	0	0	57					May-12
	50.24	68.02	58.18	68.19	55.04	0	0.34	9.43	0.8	13.74	1,019	4	96	0	0	80					Nov-12
0	90.52	109.92	65.75	102.58	52.76	1.81	0.42	11.23	1	10.22	2,357	5	95	0	0	81	10.18	-22.09			Aug-06
	256.55	307.04	173.24	235.30	126.87	1.23	0.34	13.44	0.94	8.96	385.7	4	96	0	0	74	26.53	-16.73			Aug-05
0	164.25	205.45	108.00	162.69	111.87	0.44	0.53	15.5	1	10.5	764.4	4	96	0	0	47	15.77	-22.56			Aug-05
50	-0.17	16.66	-0.42	55.12	52.44	0.87	1.6	15.06	0.94	34.94	601.6	8	92	0	0	49	28.24	-20.63	5.75		Nov-13
50	-0.34	16.34	-1.02	52.56	48.19	0.53	2.14	15.05	0.94	34.38	601.6	8	92	0	0	49	27.68	-20.88	1.00	1.00	Jul-15
	-0.11	16.89	-0.11	56.38	54.47	0.98	1.35	15.06	0.94	35.63	601.6	8	92	0	0	49	28.43	-20.55			Nov-13
50	-0.11	16.89	-0.04	57.20	55.84	1.13	1.12	15.07	0.94	35.91	601.6	8	92	0	0	49	28.43	-20.55			Feb-94
50	8.01	31.42	10.92	81.41	81.05	0	1.84	19.09	0.62	18.32	64.5	0	100	0	0	49	21.08	-15.08	5.75		Nov-13
50	7.83	31.00	10.31	78.92	76.40	0	2.24	19.08	0.62	18.17	64.5	0	100	0	0	49	20.55	-15.35		1.00	Jul-15

	MARKET			FUND TYPE, CATEGORY & OBJECTIVE	RATINGS				MINIMUMS	
Fund Name	Ticker Symbol	Traded On	Fund Type	Category and (Prospectus Objective)	Overall Rating	Reward Rating	Risk Rating	Recent Up/ Downgrade	Open to New Investors	Min Initial Investment
Meridian Enhanced Equity Fund® Investor Class	MRIEX	NAS CM	Open End	US Equity Large Cap Growth (Equity-Income)	B-	B	C		Y	99,999
Meridian Enhanced Equity Fund® Legacy Class	MEIFX	NAS CM	Open End	US Equity Large Cap Growth (Equity-Income)	B-	B	C+			1,000
Meridian Growth Fund® A Class	MRAGX	NAS CM	Open End	US Equity Small Cap (Growth)	C+	C	B-		Y	2,500
Meridian Growth Fund® Class C	MRCGX	NAS CM	Open End	US Equity Small Cap (Growth)	C+	C	B-		Y	2,500
Meridian Growth Fund® Institutional Class	MRRGX	NAS CM	Open End	US Equity Small Cap (Growth)	C+	C	B-		Y	1,000,000
Meridian Growth Fund® Investor Class	MRIGX	NAS CM	Open End	US Equity Small Cap (Growth)	C+	C	B-		Y	99,999
Meridian Growth Fund® Legacy Class	MERDX	NAS CM	Open End	US Equity Small Cap (Growth)	C+	C	B-	Down		1,000
Meridian Small Cap Growth Fund A Class	MSGAX	NAS CM	Open End	US Equity Small Cap (Small Company)	C	C-	C+	Down	Y	2,500
Meridian Small Cap Growth Fund Class C	MSGCX	NAS CM	Open End	US Equity Small Cap (Small Company)	C	C-	C+	Down	Y	2,500
Meridian Small Cap Growth Fund Institutional Class	MSGRX	NAS CM	Open End	US Equity Small Cap (Small Company)	C	C-	C+	Down	Y	1,000,000
Meridian Small Cap Growth Fund Investor Shares	MISGX	NAS CM	Open End	US Equity Small Cap (Small Company)	C	C-	C+	Down	Y	99,999
Meridian Small Cap Growth Fund Legacy Class	MSGGX	NAS CM	Open End	US Equity Small Cap (Small Company)	C	C-	C+	Down		1,000
Meritage Growth Equity Fund Institutional Shares	MPGIX	NAS CM	Open End	US Equity Large Cap Growth (Growth)	C+	C	B	Down	Y	100,000
Meritage Growth Equity Fund Investor Shares	MPGEX	NAS CM	Open End	US Equity Large Cap Growth (Growth)	C+	C	B	Down	Y	2,500
Meritage Value Equity Fund Institutional Shares	MVEBX	NAS CM	Open End	US Equity Large Cap Value (Growth & Income)	C	C	B-		Y	100,000
Meritage Yield-Focus Equity Fund Institutional Shares	MPYIX	NAS CM	Open End	Aggressive Alloc (Growth & Income)	C+	C	B	Down	Y	100,000
Meritage Yield-Focus Equity Fund Investor Shares	MPYEX	NAS CM	Open End	Aggressive Alloc (Growth & Income)	C+	C	B	Down	Y	2,500
Mesirow Financial Small Cap Value Institutional Shares	MSVIX	NAS CM	Open End	US Equity Small Cap (Small Company)	U	U	U		Y	100,000
Mesirow Financial Small Cap Value Fund Investor Shares	MSVVX	NAS CM	Open End	US Equity Small Cap (Small Company)	U	U	U		Y	5,000
Metropolitan West AlphaTrak 500 Fund	MWATX	NAS CM	Open End	US Equity Large Cap Blend (Growth)	B-	C+	B	Down	Y	5,000
Mexico Equity & Income Fund	MXE	NYSE	Closed End	Equity Miscellaneous (Foreign Stock)	D+	D+	D+		Y	
Mexico Fund, Inc	MXF	NYSE	Closed End	Equity Miscellaneous (Foreign Stock)	D	D	D+	Down	Y	
MFAM Emerging Markets Fund Investor Shares	TMFEX	NAS CM	Open End	Global Emerg Mkts (Growth)	C	C	C+		Y	500
MFAM Global Opportunities Fund Institutional Shares	FOIIX	NAS CM	Open End	Global Equity Large Cap (Growth & Income)	B-	B-	B	Up	Y	100,000
MFAM Global Opportunities Fund Investor Shares	FOOLX	NAS CM	Open End	Global Equity Large Cap (Growth & Income)	B-	B-	B	Up	Y	500
MFAM Mid Cap Growth Fund Institutional Shares	FOGIX	NAS CM	Open End	US Equity Mid Cap (Growth)	C+	C	C+		Y	100,000
MFAM Mid Cap Growth Fund Investor Shares	TMFGX	NAS CM	Open End	US Equity Mid Cap (Growth)	C+	C	C+		Y	500
MFS Aggressive Growth Allocation Fund Class 529A	EAGTX	NAS CM	Open End	Aggressive Alloc (Aggr Growth)	B-	C+	B	Up	Y	250
MFS Aggressive Growth Allocation Fund Class 529B	EBAAX	NAS CM	Open End	Aggressive Alloc (Aggr Growth)	B-	C	B	Up	Y	250
MFS Aggressive Growth Allocation Fund Class 529C	ECAAX	NAS CM	Open End	Aggressive Alloc (Aggr Growth)	B-	C	B	Up	Y	250
MFS Aggressive Growth Allocation Fund Class A	MAAGX	NAS CM	Open End	Aggressive Alloc (Aggr Growth)	B-	C+	B	Up	Y	1,000
MFS Aggressive Growth Allocation Fund Class B	MBAGX	NAS CM	Open End	Aggressive Alloc (Aggr Growth)	B-	C	B	Up	Y	1,000
MFS Aggressive Growth Allocation Fund Class C	MCAGX	NAS CM	Open End	Aggressive Alloc (Aggr Growth)	B-	C	B	Up	Y	1,000
MFS Aggressive Growth Allocation Fund Class I	MIAGX	NAS CM	Open End	Aggressive Alloc (Aggr Growth)	B-	C+	B		Y	0
MFS Aggressive Growth Allocation Fund Class R1	MAAFX	NAS CM	Open End	Aggressive Alloc (Aggr Growth)	B-	C	B	Up	Y	0
MFS Aggressive Growth Allocation Fund Class R2	MAWAX	NAS CM	Open End	Aggressive Alloc (Aggr Growth)	B-	C	B	Up	Y	0
MFS Aggressive Growth Allocation Fund Class R3	MAAHX	NAS CM	Open End	Aggressive Alloc (Aggr Growth)	B-	C+	B	Up	Y	0
MFS Aggressive Growth Allocation Fund Class R4	MAALX	NAS CM	Open End	Aggressive Alloc (Aggr Growth)	B-	C+	B		Y	0
MFS Blended Research Core Equity Fund Class A	MUEAX	NAS CM	Open End	US Equity Large Cap Blend (Growth)	C+	C	B		Y	1,000
MFS Blended Research Core Equity Fund Class B	MUSBX	NAS CM	Open End	US Equity Large Cap Blend (Growth)	C+	C	B		Y	1,000
MFS Blended Research Core Equity Fund Class C	MUECX	NAS CM	Open End	US Equity Large Cap Blend (Growth)	C+	C	B		Y	1,000
MFS Blended Research Core Equity Fund Class I	MUSEX	NAS CM	Open End	US Equity Large Cap Blend (Growth)	C+	C	B		Y	0
MFS Blended Research Core Equity Fund Class R1	MUERX	NAS CM	Open End	US Equity Large Cap Blend (Growth)	C+	C	B		Y	0
MFS Blended Research Core Equity Fund Class R2	MUESX	NAS CM	Open End	US Equity Large Cap Blend (Growth)	C+	C	B		Y	0
MFS Blended Research Core Equity Fund Class R3	MUETX	NAS CM	Open End	US Equity Large Cap Blend (Growth)	C+	C	B		Y	0
MFS Blended Research Core Equity Fund Class R4	MUEUX	NAS CM	Open End	US Equity Large Cap Blend (Growth)	C+	C	B		Y	0
MFS Blended Research Core Equity Fund Class R6	MUEVX	NAS CM	Open End	US Equity Large Cap Blend (Growth)	C+	C	B		Y	0
MFS Blended Research Emerging Markets Equity Fund Class A	BRKAX	NAS CM	Open End	Global Emerg Mkts (Div Emerging Mkts)	C	C	C+		Y	1,000
MFS Blended Research Emerging Markets Equity Fund Class B	BRKBX	NAS CM	Open End	Global Emerg Mkts (Div Emerging Mkts)	C	C	C+		Y	1,000
MFS Blended Research Emerging Markets Equity Fund Class C	BRKCX	NAS CM	Open End	Global Emerg Mkts (Div Emerging Mkts)	C	C	C+		Y	1,000
MFS Blended Research Emerging Markets Equity Fund Class I	BRKIX	NAS CM	Open End	Global Emerg Mkts (Div Emerging Mkts)	C	C	C+		Y	0
MFS Blended Research Emerging Markets Equity Fund Class R1	BRKRX	NAS CM	Open End	Global Emerg Mkts (Div Emerging Mkts)	C	C	C+		Y	0

★ Expanded analysis of this fund is included in Section II.

	TOTAL RETURNS					PERFORMANCE				ASSETS		ASSET ALLOCATION & TURNOVER					BULL & BEAR		FEES		
Min Additional Investment	3-Month Total Return	6-Month Total Return	1-Year Total Return	3-Year Total Return	5-Year Total Return	Dividend Yield (TTM)	Expense Ratio	3-Yr Std Deviation	3-Year Beta	NAV	Total Assets (MIL)	%Cash	%Stocks	%Bonds	%Other	Turnover Ratio	Last Bull Market Total Return	Last Bear Market Total Return	Front End Fee (%)	Back End Fee (%)	Inception Date
	8.10	31.61	11.27	82.46	82.92	0.41	1.59	19.04	0.62	18.4	64.5	0	100	0	0	49	21.25	-15			Nov-13
50	8.09	31.54	11.26	83.40	84.04	0.45	1.44	19.08	0.62	18.43	64.5	0	100	0	0	49	21.25	-14.99			Jan-05
50	1.13	21.25	2.67	53.70	62.82	0	1.15	15.2	0.89	38.39	2,043	8	91	0	1	47	29.51	-19.22	5.75		Nov-13
50	0.93	20.78	1.96	50.34	58.05	0	1.9	15.2	0.89	37.77	2,043	8	91	0	1	47	28.95	-19.47		1.00	Jul-15
	1.19	21.42	2.99	55.11	66.27	0.07	0.85	15.2	0.89	39.67	2,043	8	91	0	1	47	29.7	-19.14			Dec-14
	1.21	21.40	2.97	54.85	65.47	0.03	0.95	15.21	0.89	39.3	2,043	8	91	0	1	47	29.7	-19.14			Nov-13
50	1.19	21.40	3.01	55.12	66.36	0.05	0.86	15.21	0.89	39.7	2,043	8	91	0	1	47	29.7	-19.14			Aug-84
50	-2.65	11.57	-1.75	56.85	63.74	0	1.46	14	0.77	15.42	1,676	9	91	0	0	44			5.75		Dec-13
50	-2.78	11.25	-2.45	53.54	58.24	0	2.2	14	0.77	15.02	1,676	9	91	0	0	44				1.00	Jul-15
	-2.52	11.81	-1.36	58.51	67.01	0	1.15	14.05	0.77	15.81	1,676	9	91	0	0	44					Dec-14
	-2.66	11.67	-1.55	57.85	65.89	0	1.21	14.04	0.77	15.69	1,676	9	91	0	0	44					Dec-13
50	-2.59	11.78	-1.48	58.16	66.36	0	1.2	14.02	0.77	15.74	1,676	9	91	0	0	44					Dec-13
1,000	2.34	19.60	8.89	57.34	74.69	0	1.03	13.82	1.02	15.25	30.0	8	92	0	0	74					Dec-13
100	2.30	19.50	8.70	56.22	72.57	0	1.28	13.8	1.02	15.07	30.0	8	92	0	0	74					Dec-13
1,000	1.35	10.23	0.96	22.37	23.73	1.13	1.04	12.36	0.99	11.96	15.3	8	92	0	0	88					Dec-13
1,000	0.11	10.92	2.96	23.55	14.32	3.29	1.16	11.66	0.91	10.73	28.8	6	89	0	0	73					Dec-13
100	0.14	10.88	2.77	23.22	13.40	3.01	1.41	11.76	0.92	10.85	28.8	6	89	0	0	73					Dec-13
	1.54	15.88					0.98			11.16	10.4	4	96	0	0						Dec-18
	1.54	15.88					1.23			11.16	10.4	4	96	0	0						Dec-18
0	4.60	20.51	11.52	60.41	75.50	2.28	0.91	12.41	0.99	11.16	30.4	30	5	66	0		26.72	-18.56			Jun-98
	0.43	4.41	-1.10	-4.61	-22.57	0.31	1.51	21.87	0.93	11.59	59.9	5	82	10	3	187	24.92	-20.85			Aug-90
	1.04	6.42	-5.33	-3.66	-24.50	0.68	1.03	21.56	0.95	15.67	235.1	5	95	0	1	31	26.06	-23.97			Jun-81
50	5.19	18.61	3.65	36.37	17.11	0.53	1.15	13.43	0.86	14.78	34.8	2	98	0	0	7					Nov-11
	6.99	27.09	13.96	65.22	61.46	0	0.95	14.12	1.08	25.38	469.5	2	98	0	0	15	18.04	-16.13			Jun-14
50	6.93	26.97	13.82	64.62	60.33	0	1.06	14.1	1.07	25.28	469.5	2	98	0	0	15	18.04	-16.13			Jun-09
	5.27	22.43	3.67	53.79	54.53	0	0.95	16.33	1.06	24.94	282.2	0	100	0	0	19	25.74	-17.34			Jun-14
50	5.23	22.35	3.57	52.92	53.04	0	1.12	16.33	1.06	24.74	282.2	0	100	0	0	19	25.74	-17.34			Nov-10
	4.95	20.52	8.33	43.05	45.17	1.34	1.13	10.92	0.86	24.13	1,882	3	93	4	0	2	20.94	-19.02	5.75		Jul-02
	4.74	20.02	7.47	39.82	39.69	0.6	1.88	10.91	0.86	23.62	1,882	3	93	4	0	2	20.43	-19.25		4.00	Jul-02
	4.76	20.04	7.49	39.88	39.76	0.62	1.88	10.93	0.86	23.3	1,882	3	93	4	0	2	20.52	-19.29		1.00	Jul-02
	4.92	20.47	8.31	43.19	45.40	1.36	1.08	10.92	0.86	24.3	1,882	3	93	4	0	2	20.98	-18.97	5.75		Jun-02
	4.77	20.07	7.57	40.03	40.09	0.6	1.83	10.93	0.86	23.93	1,882	3	93	4	0	2	20.48	-19.25		4.00	Jun-02
	4.77	20.08	7.55	40.07	40.07	0.6	1.83	10.93	0.86	23.68	1,882	3	93	4	0	2	20.43	-19.23		1.00	Jun-02
	5.01	20.69	8.65	44.30	47.29	1.57	0.83	10.92	0.86	24.73	1,882	3	93	4	0	2	21.15	-18.91			Jun-02
	4.76	20.04	7.54	40.05	40.03	0.69	1.83	10.92	0.86	23.3	1,882	3	93	4	0	2	20.46	-19.23			Apr-05
	4.89	20.35	8.08	42.14	43.59	1.14	1.33	10.92	0.86	23.77	1,882	3	93	4	0	2	20.74	-19.07			Oct-03
	4.91	20.50	8.32	43.16	45.38	1.32	1.08	10.89	0.86	24.1	1,882	3	93	4	0	2	20.98	-18.97			Apr-05
	5.03	20.68	8.63	44.26	47.28	1.59	0.83	10.92	0.86	24.39	1,882	3	93	4	0	2	21.16	-18.89			Apr-05
	2.71	16.46	5.40	37.99	47.30	1.39	0.74	12.61	1.03	26.1	997.2	1	99	0	0	64	25.11	-16.9	5.75		Aug-97
	2.53	16.03	4.61	34.93	41.87	0.68	1.49	12.6	1.03	25.11	997.2	1	99	0	0	64	24.59	-17.12		4.00	Aug-97
	2.53	16.00	4.61	34.92	41.85	0.67	1.49	12.63	1.03	24.71	997.2	1	99	0	0	64	24.56	-17.08		1.00	Aug-97
	2.79	16.58	5.63	39.03	49.14	1.62	0.49	12.63	1.03	26.5	997.2	1	99	0	0	64	25.33	-16.78			Jan-94
	2.56	16.02	4.63	34.93	41.89	0.69	1.49	12.62	1.03	24.83	997.2	1	99	0	0	64	24.6	-17.12			Sep-08
	2.67	16.27	5.10	36.93	45.46	1.24	0.99	12.64	1.03	24.93	997.2	1	99	0	0	64	24.94	-16.96			Sep-08
	2.76	16.47	5.41	38.00	47.28	1.35	0.74	12.63	1.03	26.02	997.2	1	99	0	0	64	25.09	-16.83			Sep-08
	2.82	16.62	5.69	39.04	49.13	1.66	0.49	12.62	1.03	26.23	997.2	1	99	0	0	64	25.29	-16.78			Sep-08
	2.82	16.65	5.81	39.54	50.00	1.76	0.42	12.65	1.03	26.54	997.2	1	99	0	0	64	25.33	-16.78			Jun-12
	1.39	12.67	-0.48	39.07		1.64	1.24	14.76	1.06	13.07	21.5	1	98	0	0	58			5.75		Sep-15
	1.25	12.21	-1.20	36.03		1.08	1.99	14.75	1.05	12.95	21.5	1	98	0	0	58				4.00	Sep-15
	1.25	12.26	-1.17	36.16		1.11	1.99	14.76	1.06	12.91	21.5	1	98	0	0	58				1.00	Sep-15
	1.47	12.72	-0.27	40.13		1.89	0.99	14.75	1.05	13.11	21.5	1	98	0	0	58					Sep-15
	1.24	12.19	-1.24	36.03		1.18	1.99	14.73	1.05	12.97	21.5	1	98	0	0	58					Sep-15

	MARKET			FUND TYPE, CATEGORY & OBJECTIVE	RATINGS				MINIMUMS	
Fund Name	Ticker Symbol	Traded On	Fund Type	Category and (Prospectus Objective)	Overall Rating	Reward Rating	Risk Rating	Recent Up/ Downgrade	Open to New Investors	Min Initial Investment
MFS Blended Research Emerging Markets Equity Fund Class R2	BRKSX	NAS CM	Open End	Global Emerg Mkts (Div Emerging Mkts)	C	C	C+		Y	0
MFS Blended Research Emerging Markets Equity Fund Class R3	BRKTX	NAS CM	Open End	Global Emerg Mkts (Div Emerging Mkts)	C	C	C+		Y	0
MFS Blended Research Emerging Markets Equity Fund Class R4	BRKUX	NAS CM	Open End	Global Emerg Mkts (Div Emerging Mkts)	C	C	C+		Y	0
MFS Blended Research Emerging Markets Equity Fund Class R6	BRKVX	NAS CM	Open End	Global Emerg Mkts (Div Emerging Mkts)	C	C	C+		Y	0
MFS Blended Research Global Equity Fund Class A	BRLAX	NAS CM	Open End	Global Equity Large Cap (World Stock)	C+	C	B	Up	Y	1,000
MFS Blended Research Global Equity Fund Class B	BRLBX	NAS CM	Open End	Global Equity Large Cap (World Stock)	C	C	B-		Y	1,000
MFS Blended Research Global Equity Fund Class C	BRLCX	NAS CM	Open End	Global Equity Large Cap (World Stock)	C	C	B-		Y	1,000
MFS Blended Research Global Equity Fund Class I	BRLJX	NAS CM	Open End	Global Equity Large Cap (World Stock)	C+	C	B	Up	Y	0
MFS Blended Research Global Equity Fund Class R1	BRLRX	NAS CM	Open End	Global Equity Large Cap (World Stock)	C	C	B-		Y	0
MFS Blended Research Global Equity Fund Class R2	BRLSX	NAS CM	Open End	Global Equity Large Cap (World Stock)	C+	C	B	Up	Y	0
MFS Blended Research Global Equity Fund Class R3	BRLTX	NAS CM	Open End	Global Equity Large Cap (World Stock)	C+	C	B	Up	Y	0
MFS Blended Research Global Equity Fund Class R4	BRLUX	NAS CM	Open End	Global Equity Large Cap (World Stock)	C+	C	B	Up	Y	0
MFS Blended Research Global Equity Fund Class R6	BRLYX	NAS CM	Open End	Global Equity Large Cap (World Stock)	C+	C	B	Up	Y	0
MFS Blended Research Growth Equity Fund Class A	BRWAX	NAS CM	Open End	US Equity Large Cap Growth (Growth)	C+	C	B	Down	Y	1,000
MFS Blended Research Growth Equity Fund Class B	BRWBX	NAS CM	Open End	US Equity Large Cap Growth (Growth)	C+	C	B	Down	Y	1,000
MFS Blended Research Growth Equity Fund Class C	BRWCX	NAS CM	Open End	US Equity Large Cap Growth (Growth)	C+	C	B	Down	Y	1,000
MFS Blended Research Growth Equity Fund Class I	BRWJX	NAS CM	Open End	US Equity Large Cap Growth (Growth)	C+	C	B	Down	Y	0
MFS Blended Research Growth Equity Fund Class R1	BRWRX	NAS CM	Open End	US Equity Large Cap Growth (Growth)	C+	C	B	Down	Y	0
MFS Blended Research Growth Equity Fund Class R2	BRWSX	NAS CM	Open End	US Equity Large Cap Growth (Growth)	C+	C	B		Y	0
MFS Blended Research Growth Equity Fund Class R3	BRWTX	NAS CM	Open End	US Equity Large Cap Growth (Growth)	C+	C	B		Y	0
MFS Blended Research Growth Equity Fund Class R4	BRWUX	NAS CM	Open End	US Equity Large Cap Growth (Growth)	C+	C	B	Down	Y	0
MFS Blended Research Growth Equity Fund Class R6	BRWVX	NAS CM	Open End	US Equity Large Cap Growth (Growth)	C+	C	B	Down	Y	0
MFS Blended Research International Equity Fund Class A	BRXAX	NAS CM	Open End	Global Equity Large Cap (Foreign Stock)	C	C	B-		Y	1,000
MFS Blended Research International Equity Fund Class B	BRXBX	NAS CM	Open End	Global Equity Large Cap (Foreign Stock)	C	C	C+		Y	1,000
MFS Blended Research International Equity Fund Class C	BRXCX	NAS CM	Open End	Global Equity Large Cap (Foreign Stock)	C	C	C+		Y	1,000
MFS Blended Research International Equity Fund Class I	BRXIX	NAS CM	Open End	Global Equity Large Cap (Foreign Stock)	C	C	B-		Y	0
MFS Blended Research International Equity Fund Class R1	BRXRX	NAS CM	Open End	Global Equity Large Cap (Foreign Stock)	C	C	C+		Y	0
MFS Blended Research International Equity Fund Class R2	BRXSX	NAS CM	Open End	Global Equity Large Cap (Foreign Stock)	C	C	B-		Y	0
MFS Blended Research International Equity Fund Class R3	BRXTX	NAS CM	Open End	Global Equity Large Cap (Foreign Stock)	C	C	B-		Y	0
MFS Blended Research International Equity Fund Class R4	BRXUX	NAS CM	Open End	Global Equity Large Cap (Foreign Stock)	C	C	B-		Y	0
MFS Blended Research International Equity Fund Class R6	BRXVX	NAS CM	Open End	Global Equity Large Cap (Foreign Stock)	C	C	B-		Y	0
MFS Blended Research Mid Cap Equity Fund A	BMSFX	NAS CM	Open End	US Equity Mid Cap (Growth)	C+	C	B	Up	Y	1,000
MFS Blended Research Mid Cap Equity Fund B	BMSBX	NAS CM	Open End	US Equity Mid Cap (Growth)	C+	C	B	Up	Y	1,000
MFS Blended Research Mid Cap Equity Fund C	BMSDX	NAS CM	Open End	US Equity Mid Cap (Growth)	C+	C	B	Up	Y	1,000
MFS Blended Research Mid Cap Equity Fund I	BMSLX	NAS CM	Open End	US Equity Mid Cap (Growth)	C+	C	B	Up	Y	0
MFS Blended Research Mid Cap Equity Fund R1	BMSRX	NAS CM	Open End	US Equity Mid Cap (Growth)	C+	C	B	Up	Y	0
MFS Blended Research Mid Cap Equity Fund R2	BMSSX	NAS CM	Open End	US Equity Mid Cap (Growth)	C+	C	B	Up	Y	0
MFS Blended Research Mid Cap Equity Fund R3	BMSTX	NAS CM	Open End	US Equity Mid Cap (Growth)	C+	C	B	Up	Y	0
MFS Blended Research Mid Cap Equity Fund R4	BMSVX	NAS CM	Open End	US Equity Mid Cap (Growth)	C+	C	B	Up	Y	0
MFS Blended Research Mid Cap Equity Fund R6	BMSYX	NAS CM	Open End	US Equity Mid Cap (Growth)	C+	C	B	Up	Y	0
MFS Blended Research Small Cap Equity Fund 529A	BRSNX	NAS CM	Open End	US Equity Small Cap (Small Company)	C	C	B-	Down	Y	250
MFS Blended Research Small Cap Equity Fund 529B	BRSQX	NAS CM	Open End	US Equity Small Cap (Small Company)	C	C	B-	Down	Y	250
MFS Blended Research Small Cap Equity Fund 529C	BRSWX	NAS CM	Open End	US Equity Small Cap (Small Company)	C	C	B-	Down	Y	250
MFS Blended Research Small Cap Equity Fund Class A	BRSDX	NAS CM	Open End	US Equity Small Cap (Small Company)	C	C	B-	Down	Y	1,000
MFS Blended Research Small Cap Equity Fund Class B	BRSBX	NAS CM	Open End	US Equity Small Cap (Small Company)	C	C	B-	Down	Y	1,000
MFS Blended Research Small Cap Equity Fund Class C	BRSHX	NAS CM	Open End	US Equity Small Cap (Small Company)	C	C	B-	Down	Y	1,000
MFS Blended Research Small Cap Equity Fund Class I	BRSJX	NAS CM	Open End	US Equity Small Cap (Small Company)	C	C	B-	Down	Y	0
MFS Blended Research Small Cap Equity Fund Class R1	BRSPX	NAS CM	Open End	US Equity Small Cap (Small Company)	C	C	B-	Down	Y	0
MFS Blended Research Small Cap Equity Fund Class R2	BRSSX	NAS CM	Open End	US Equity Small Cap (Small Company)	C	C	B-	Down	Y	0
MFS Blended Research Small Cap Equity Fund Class R3	BRSTX	NAS CM	Open End	US Equity Small Cap (Small Company)	C	C	B-	Down	Y	0
MFS Blended Research Small Cap Equity Fund Class R4	BRSUX	NAS CM	Open End	US Equity Small Cap (Small Company)	C	C	B-	Down	Y	0
MFS Blended Research Small Cap Equity Fund Class R6	BRSYX	NAS CM	Open End	US Equity Small Cap (Small Company)	C	C	B-	Down	Y	0

★ Expanded analysis of this fund is included in Section II.

	TOTAL RETURNS					PERFORMANCE				ASSETS		ASSET ALLOCATION & TURNOVER					BULL & BEAR		FEES		
Min Additional Investment	3-Month Total Return	6-Month Total Return	1-Year Total Return	3-Year Total Return	5-Year Total Return	Dividend Yield (TTM)	Expense Ratio	3-Yr Std Deviation	3-Year Beta	NAV	Total Assets (MIL)	%Cash	%Stocks	%Bonds	%Other	Turnover Ratio	Last Bull Market Total Return	Last Bear Market Total Return	Front End Fee (%)	Back End Fee (%)	Inception Date
	1.31	12.48	-0.75	38.12		1.53	1.49	14.74	1.05	13.06	21.5	1	98	0	0	58					Sep-15
	1.47	12.65	-0.46	39.24		1.72	1.24	14.76	1.06	13.09	21.5	1	98	0	0	58					Sep-15
	1.46	12.81	-0.19	40.19		1.89	0.99	14.74	1.05	13.12	21.5	1	98	0	0	58					Sep-15
	1.46	12.80	-0.12	40.56		1.95	0.95	14.76	1.06	13.13	21.5	1	98	0	0	58					Sep-15
	3.55	15.00	3.63	38.40		1.73	0.89	11.62	1.01	11.65	5.1	2	99	0	0	48			5.75		Sep-15
	3.38	14.59	2.85	35.19		0.93	1.64	11.62	1.01	11.62	5.1	2	99	0	0	48				4.00	Sep-15
	3.38	14.59	2.83	35.17		0.84	1.64	11.63	1.01	11.62	5.1	2	99	0	0	48				1.00	Sep-15
	3.63	15.15	3.90	39.43		1.88	0.64	11.65	1.01	11.7	5.1	2	99	0	0	48					Sep-15
	3.37	14.58	2.84	35.20		0.92	1.64	11.62	1.01	11.63	5.1	2	99	0	0	48					Sep-15
	3.55	14.87	3.35	37.28		1.42	1.14	11.66	1.01	11.66	5.1	2	99	0	0	48					Sep-15
	3.63	15.07	3.65	38.39		1.67	0.89	11.61	1.01	11.68	5.1	2	99	0	0	48					Sep-15
	3.63	15.17	3.86	39.25		1.92	0.64	11.61	1.01	11.69	5.1	2	99	0	0	48					Sep-15
	3.63	15.17	3.88	39.48		2.01	0.6	11.58	1	11.69	5.1	2	99	0	0	48					Sep-15
	4.18	20.57	7.65	54.47		0.47	0.74	13.6	1.01	14.18	193.7	2	98	0	0	73			5.75		Sep-15
	3.93	20.08	6.83	50.99		0	1.49	13.57	1.01	13.99	193.7	2	98	0	0	73				4.00	Sep-15
	4.01	20.08	6.86	51.19		0.02	1.49	13.61	1.01	13.99	193.7	2	98	0	0	73				1.00	Sep-15
	4.23	20.74	8.01	55.79		0.77	0.49	13.61	1.01	14.26	193.7	2	98	0	0	73					Sep-15
	3.93	20.08	6.84	51.15		0	1.49	13.57	1.01	13.99	193.7	2	98	0	0	73					Sep-15
	4.09	20.38	7.42	53.36		0	0.99	13.58	1.01	14.23	193.7	2	98	0	0	73					Sep-15
	4.16	20.57	7.73	54.59		0.48	0.74	13.61	1.01	14.24	193.7	2	98	0	0	73					Sep-15
	4.23	20.74	7.94	55.78		0.72	0.49	13.6	1.01	14.26	193.7	2	98	0	0	73					Sep-15
	4.23	20.72	8.06	56.21		0.81	0.45	13.62	1.01	14.27	193.7	2	98	0	0	73					Sep-15
	3.50	13.95	-0.65	29.73		2.3	0.89	11.51	0.98	10.94	301.1	2	98	0	0	69			5.75		Sep-15
	3.31	13.54	-1.40	26.75		1.49	1.64	11.48	0.98	10.9	301.1	2	98	0	0	69				4.00	Sep-15
	3.32	13.59	-1.39	26.78		1.43	1.64	11.49	0.98	10.86	301.1	2	98	0	0	69				1.00	Sep-15
	3.58	14.12	-0.36	30.71		2.55	0.64	11.55	0.99	10.99	301.1	2	98	0	0	69					Sep-15
	3.34	13.53	-1.39	26.76		2.07	1.64	11.45	0.98	10.82	301.1	2	98	0	0	69					Sep-15
	3.49	13.81	-0.86	28.76		2.11	1.14	11.51	0.98	10.96	301.1	2	98	0	0	69					Sep-15
	3.56	14.06	-0.65	29.89		2.27	0.89	11.52	0.99	11.03	301.1	2	98	0	0	69					Sep-15
	3.58	14.12	-0.45	30.55		2.55	0.64	11.46	0.98	10.99	301.1	2	98	0	0	69					Sep-15
	3.67	14.22	-0.23	30.93		2.65	0.6	11.49	0.98	11	301.1	2	98	0	0	69					Sep-15
	5.21	22.68	6.35			0.75	0.84			11.9	292.5	2	98	0	0	84			5.75		Aug-16
	5.06	22.21	5.59			0.28	1.59			11.83	292.5	2	98	0	0	84				4.00	Aug-16
	5.05	22.29	5.57			0.13	1.59			11.85	292.5	2	98	0	0	84				1.00	Aug-16
	5.29	22.75	6.57			1.07	0.59			11.92	292.5	2	98	0	0	84					Aug-16
	4.96	22.18	5.45			0.17	1.59			11.84	292.5	2	98	0	0	84					Aug-16
	5.12	22.42	6.05			0.52	1.09			11.9	292.5	2	98	0	0	84					Aug-16
	5.20	22.63	6.36			0.76	0.84			11.92	292.5	2	98	0	0	84					Aug-16
	5.29	22.73	6.57			0.99	0.59			11.93	292.5	2	98	0	0	84					Aug-16
	5.29	22.86	6.70			1.1	0.55			11.93	292.5	2	98	0	0	84					Aug-16
	1.34	19.42	3.25	46.81		0.29	1.04	16.36	0.94	13.59	213.1	1	99	0	0	90			5.75		Jul-16
	1.13	19.01	2.49	43.50		0	1.79	16.37	0.94	13.33	213.1	1	99	0	0	90				4.00	Jul-16
	1.13	18.94	2.42	43.43		0	1.79	16.38	0.94	13.31	213.1	1	99	0	0	90				1.00	Jul-16
	1.34	19.43	3.24	47.07		0.28	0.99	16.37	0.94	13.58	213.1	1	99	0	0	90			5.75		Sep-15
	1.13	18.89	2.49	43.77		0	1.74	16.37	0.94	13.34	213.1	1	99	0	0	90				4.00	Sep-15
	1.13	18.91	2.46	43.73		0.03	1.74	16.34	0.94	13.33	213.1	1	99	0	0	90				1.00	Sep-15
	1.41	19.52	3.52	48.05		0.52	0.74	16.33	0.94	13.65	213.1	1	99	0	0	90					Sep-15
	1.21	18.98	2.57	43.87		0	1.74	16.36	0.94	13.35	213.1	1	99	0	0	90					Sep-15
	1.26	19.31	3.00	45.90		0.02	1.24	16.39	0.94	13.59	213.1	1	99	0	0	90					Sep-15
	1.33	19.43	3.27	47.05		0.25	0.99	16.36	0.94	13.64	213.1	1	99	0	0	90					Sep-15
	1.41	19.61	3.56	48.19		0.49	0.74	16.4	0.94	13.66	213.1	1	99	0	0	90					Sep-15
	1.40	19.70	3.66	48.43		0.57	0.7	16.36	0.94	13.67	213.1	1	99	0	0	90					Sep-15

	MARKET		FUND TYPE, CATEGORY & OBJECTIVE		RATINGS				MINIMUMS	
Fund Name	Ticker Symbol	Traded On	Fund Type	Category and (Prospectus Objective)	Overall Rating	Reward Rating	Risk Rating	Recent Up/ Downgrade	Open to New Investors	Min Initial Investment
MFS Blended Research Value Equity Fund Class A	BRUDX	NAS CM	Open End	US Equity Large Cap Value (Growth)	B-	C	B	Up	Y	1,000
MFS Blended Research Value Equity Fund Class B	BRUEX	NAS CM	Open End	US Equity Large Cap Value (Growth)	B-	C	B	Up	Y	1,000
MFS Blended Research Value Equity Fund Class C	BRUGX	NAS CM	Open End	US Equity Large Cap Value (Growth)	B-	C	B	Up	Y	1,000
MFS Blended Research Value Equity Fund Class I	BRUHX	NAS CM	Open End	US Equity Large Cap Value (Growth)	B-	C	B	Up	Y	0
MFS Blended Research Value Equity Fund Class R1	BRUJX	NAS CM	Open End	US Equity Large Cap Value (Growth)	B-	C	B	Up	Y	0
MFS Blended Research Value Equity Fund Class R2	BRUKX	NAS CM	Open End	US Equity Large Cap Value (Growth)	B-	C	B	Up	Y	0
MFS Blended Research Value Equity Fund Class R3	BRULX	NAS CM	Open End	US Equity Large Cap Value (Growth)	B-	C	B	Up	Y	0
MFS Blended Research Value Equity Fund Class R4	BRUMX	NAS CM	Open End	US Equity Large Cap Value (Growth)	B-	C	B	Up	Y	0
MFS Blended Research Value Equity Fund Class R6	BRUNX	NAS CM	Open End	US Equity Large Cap Value (Growth)	B-	C	B	Up	Y	0
MFS Commodity Strategy Fund Class A	MCSAX	NAS CM	Open End	Commodities Broad Basket (Growth)	D+	D	C-		Y	1,000
MFS Commodity Strategy Fund Class B	MCSFX	NAS CM	Open End	Commodities Broad Basket (Growth)	D	D	C-	Down	Y	1,000
MFS Commodity Strategy Fund Class C	MCSHX	NAS CM	Open End	Commodities Broad Basket (Growth)	D	D	C-	Down	Y	1,000
MFS Commodity Strategy Fund Class I	MCSIX	NAS CM	Open End	Commodities Broad Basket (Growth)	D+	D	C-		Y	0
MFS Commodity Strategy Fund Class R1	MCSNX	NAS CM	Open End	Commodities Broad Basket (Growth)	D	D	C-	Down	Y	0
MFS Commodity Strategy Fund Class R2	MCSOX	NAS CM	Open End	Commodities Broad Basket (Growth)	D	D	C-	Down	Y	0
MFS Commodity Strategy Fund Class R3	MCSQX	NAS CM	Open End	Commodities Broad Basket (Growth)	D+	D	C-		Y	0
MFS Commodity Strategy Fund Class R4	MCSTX	NAS CM	Open End	Commodities Broad Basket (Growth)	D+	D	C-		Y	0
MFS Commodity Strategy Fund Class R6	MCSRX	NAS CM	Open End	Commodities Broad Basket (Growth)	D+	D	C-		Y	0
MFS Conservative Allocation Fund Class 529A	ECLAX	NAS CM	Open End	Cautious Alloc (Balanced)	B	C+	A		Y	250
MFS Conservative Allocation Fund Class 529B	EBCAX	NAS CM	Open End	Cautious Alloc (Balanced)	B	C+	A-	Up	Y	250
MFS Conservative Allocation Fund Class 529C	ECACX	NAS CM	Open End	Cautious Alloc (Balanced)	B	C+	A-	Up	Y	250
MFS Conservative Allocation Fund Class A	MACFX	NAS CM	Open End	Cautious Alloc (Balanced)	B	C+	A		Y	1,000
MFS Conservative Allocation Fund Class B	MACBX	NAS CM	Open End	Cautious Alloc (Balanced)	B	C+	A-	Up	Y	1,000
MFS Conservative Allocation Fund Class C	MACVX	NAS CM	Open End	Cautious Alloc (Balanced)	B	C+	A-	Up	Y	1,000
MFS Conservative Allocation Fund Class I	MACIX	NAS CM	Open End	Cautious Alloc (Balanced)	B	C+	A		Y	0
MFS Conservative Allocation Fund Class R1	MACKX	NAS CM	Open End	Cautious Alloc (Balanced)	B	C+	A-	Up	Y	0
MFS Conservative Allocation Fund Class R2	MCARX	NAS CM	Open End	Cautious Alloc (Balanced)	B	C+	A	Up	Y	0
MFS Conservative Allocation Fund Class R3	MACNX	NAS CM	Open End	Cautious Alloc (Balanced)	B	C+	A		Y	0
MFS Conservative Allocation Fund Class R4	MACJX	NAS CM	Open End	Cautious Alloc (Balanced)	B	C+	A		Y	0
MFS Core Equity Fund Class A	MRGAX	NAS CM	Open End	US Equity Large Cap Blend (Growth)	B-	C+	B	Down	Y	1,000
MFS Core Equity Fund Class B	MRGBX	NAS CM	Open End	US Equity Large Cap Blend (Growth)	B-	C+	B	Down	Y	1,000
MFS Core Equity Fund Class C	MRGCX	NAS CM	Open End	US Equity Large Cap Blend (Growth)	B-	C+	B	Down	Y	1,000
MFS Core Equity Fund Class I	MRGRX	NAS CM	Open End	US Equity Large Cap Blend (Growth)	B-	C+	B	Down	Y	0
MFS Core Equity Fund Class R1	MRGGX	NAS CM	Open End	US Equity Large Cap Blend (Growth)	B-	C+	B	Down	Y	0
MFS Core Equity Fund Class R2	MRERX	NAS CM	Open End	US Equity Large Cap Blend (Growth)	B-	C+	B	Down	Y	0
MFS Core Equity Fund Class R3	MRGHX	NAS CM	Open End	US Equity Large Cap Blend (Growth)	B-	C+	B	Down	Y	0
MFS Core Equity Fund Class R4	MRGJX	NAS CM	Open End	US Equity Large Cap Blend (Growth)	B-	C+	B	Down	Y	0
MFS Core Equity Fund Class R6	MRGKX	NAS CM	Open End	US Equity Large Cap Blend (Growth)	B-	C+	B	Down	Y	0
MFS Diversified Income Fund Class A	DIFAX	NAS CM	Open End	Cautious Alloc (Growth & Income)	B-	C+	B	Down	Y	1,000
MFS Diversified Income Fund Class C	DIFCX	NAS CM	Open End	Cautious Alloc (Growth & Income)	B-	C+	B	Down	Y	1,000
MFS Diversified Income Fund Class I	DIFIX	NAS CM	Open End	Cautious Alloc (Growth & Income)	B	C+	B		Y	0
MFS Diversified Income Fund Class R1	DIFDX	NAS CM	Open End	Cautious Alloc (Growth & Income)	B-	C+	B	Down	Y	0
MFS Diversified Income Fund Class R2	DIFEX	NAS CM	Open End	Cautious Alloc (Growth & Income)	B-	C+	B	Down	Y	0
MFS Diversified Income Fund Class R3	DIFFX	NAS CM	Open End	Cautious Alloc (Growth & Income)	B-	C+	B	Down	Y	0
MFS Diversified Income Fund Class R4	DIFGX	NAS CM	Open End	Cautious Alloc (Growth & Income)	B	C+	B		Y	0
MFS Diversified Income Fund Class R6	DIFHX	NAS CM	Open End	Cautious Alloc (Growth & Income)	B	C+	B		Y	0
MFS Emerging Markets Equity Fund Class A	MEMAX	NAS CM	Open End	Global Emerg Mkts (Div Emerging Mkts)	C	C	B-		Y	1,000
MFS Emerging Markets Equity Fund Class B	MEMBX	NAS CM	Open End	Global Emerg Mkts (Div Emerging Mkts)	C	C	C+		Y	1,000
MFS Emerging Markets Equity Fund Class C	MEMCX	NAS CM	Open End	Global Emerg Mkts (Div Emerging Mkts)	C	C	C+		Y	1,000
MFS Emerging Markets Equity Fund Class I	MEMIX	NAS CM	Open End	Global Emerg Mkts (Div Emerging Mkts)	C	C	B-		Y	0
MFS Emerging Markets Equity Fund Class R1	MEMRX	NAS CM	Open End	Global Emerg Mkts (Div Emerging Mkts)	C	C	C+		Y	0
MFS Emerging Markets Equity Fund Class R2	MEMFX	NAS CM	Open End	Global Emerg Mkts (Div Emerging Mkts)	C	C	C+		Y	0

★ Expanded analysis of this fund is included in Section II.

	TOTAL RETURNS					PERFORMANCE				ASSETS		ASSET ALLOCATION & TURNOVER					BULL & BEAR		FEES		
Min Additional Investment	3-Month Total Return	6-Month Total Return	1-Year Total Return	3-Year Total Return	5-Year Total Return	Dividend Yield (TTM)	Expense Ratio	3-Yr Std Deviation	3-Year Beta	NAV	Total Assets (MIL)	%Cash	%Stocks	%Bonds	%Other	Turnover Ratio	Last Bull Market Total Return	Last Bear Market Total Return	Front End Fee (%)	Back End Fee (%)	Inception Date
	1.74	14.33	5.31	34.61		1.68	0.74	12.17	1	12.84	186.2	1	99	0	0	61			5.75		Sep-15
	1.66	13.94	4.62	31.72		0.88	1.49	12.14	0.99	12.83	186.2	1	99	0	0	61				4.00	Sep-15
	1.58	13.86	4.58	31.63		0.63	1.49	12.12	0.99	12.81	186.2	1	99	0	0	61				1.00	Sep-15
	1.89	14.45	5.63	35.71		1.97	0.49	12.17	0.99	12.91	186.2	1	99	0	0	61					Sep-15
	1.58	13.86	4.54	31.68		0.95	1.49	12.15	0.99	12.81	186.2	1	99	0	0	61					Sep-15
	1.73	14.19	5.04	33.72		1.46	0.99	12.16	0.99	12.87	186.2	1	99	0	0	61					Sep-15
	1.81	14.26	5.34	34.76		1.65	0.74	12.16	0.99	12.9	186.2	1	99	0	0	61					Sep-15
	1.89	14.53	5.66	35.73		1.92	0.49	12.18	1	12.92	186.2	1	99	0	0	61					Sep-15
	1.89	14.52	5.77	36.10		2.02	0.45	12.17	0.99	12.93	186.2	1	99	0	0	61					Sep-15
	-1.84	4.71	-7.68	-8.37	-37.67	3.08	1.1	8.84	0.99	5.33	606.1	18	0	85	-5	72	1.29	-20.98	5.75		Jun-10
	-2.21	4.33	-8.50	-10.54	-40.02		1.85	8.82	0.99	5.3	606.1	18	0	85	-5	72	0.82	-21.22		4.00	Aug-18
	-2.21	4.33	-8.51	-10.55	-40.02		1.85	8.82	0.99	5.3	606.1	18	0	85	-5	72	0.82	-21.22		1.00	Aug-18
	-1.84	4.92	-7.47	-7.71	-36.88	3.31	0.85	8.85	1	5.33	606.1	18	0	85	-5	72	1.41	-20.89			Jun-10
	-2.21	4.33	-8.51	-10.55	-40.02		1.85	8.82	0.99	5.3	606.1	18	0	85	-5	72	0.82	-21.22			Aug-18
	-1.84	4.72	-7.91	-9.06	-38.42		1.35	8.86	1	5.32	606.1	18	0	85	-5	72	1.11	-21.06			Aug-18
	-2.02	4.72	-7.77	-8.47	-37.71		1.1	8.82	0.99	5.32	606.1	18	0	85	-5	72	1.26	-20.97			Aug-18
	-1.84	4.92	-7.47	-7.71	-36.88		0.85	8.85	1	5.33	606.1	18	0	85	-5	72	1.41	-20.89			Aug-18
	-1.84	4.71	-7.48	-7.72	-36.89	3.31	0.84	8.76	0.98	5.33	606.1	18	0	85	-5	72	1.41	-20.89			Sep-12
	3.79	12.19	7.86	21.38	25.14	2.16	0.96	5.14	0.53	15.81	2,934	3	37	60	0	6	10.71	-6.4	5.75		Jul-02
	3.67	11.77	7.03	18.65	20.49	1.47	1.71	5.11	0.52	15.56	2,934	3	37	60	0	6	10.18	-6.66		4.00	Jul-02
	3.69	11.84	7.09	18.71	20.47	1.5	1.71	5.17	0.52	15.5	2,934	3	37	60	0	6	10.23	-6.71		1.00	Jul-02
	3.85	12.21	7.85	21.52	25.38	2.17	0.91	5.13	0.52	15.9	2,934	3	37	60	0	6	10.69	-6.33	5.75		Jun-02
	3.68	11.79	7.06	18.86	20.80	1.45	1.66	5.14	0.53	15.82	2,934	3	37	60	0	6	10.26	-6.66		4.00	Jun-02
	3.66	11.79	7.11	18.81	20.74	1.5	1.66	5.13	0.53	15.66	2,934	3	37	60	0	6	10.26	-6.68		1.00	Jun-02
	3.94	12.36	8.18	22.46	26.94	2.38	0.66	5.14	0.52	16.05	2,934	3	37	60	0	6	10.91	-6.25			Jun-02
	3.68	11.84	7.06	18.87	20.82	1.55	1.66	5.14	0.52	15.34	2,934	3	37	60	0	6	10.29	-6.66			Apr-05
	3.84	12.16	7.69	20.65	23.86	2.01	1.16	5.17	0.52	15.44	2,934	3	37	60	0	6	10.65	-6.45			Oct-03
	3.81	12.25	7.85	21.47	25.35	2.19	0.91	5.14	0.52	15.76	2,934	3	37	60	0	6	10.77	-6.38			Apr-05
	3.90	12.41	8.18	22.43	26.94	2.4	0.66	5.15	0.52	15.91	2,934	3	37	60	0	6	10.9	-6.29			Apr-05
	5.46	21.78	11.39	57.04	67.85	0.46	1.01	12.03	0.95	32.42	2,665	2	98	0	0	42	24.33	-17.61	5.75		Jan-96
	5.25	21.30	10.56	53.54	61.64	0	1.76	12.01	0.95	28.24	2,665	2	98	0	0	42	23.83	-17.92		4.00	Jan-97
	5.24	21.33	10.54	53.45	61.64	0	1.76	12.02	0.95	27.87	2,665	2	98	0	0	42	23.78	-17.88		1.00	Jan-97
	5.51	21.91	11.66	58.22	69.97	0.65	0.76	12.04	0.95	34.43	2,665	2	98	0	0	42	24.53	-17.53			Jan-97
	5.25	21.29	10.55	53.50	61.63	0	1.76	12.02	0.95	27.85	2,665	2	98	0	0	42	23.83	-17.91			Apr-05
	5.40	21.63	11.12	55.89	65.81	0.12	1.26	12.03	0.95	31.6	2,665	2	98	0	0	42	24.17	-17.69			Oct-03
	5.44	21.77	11.38	56.98	67.81	0.48	1.01	12.04	0.95	32.33	2,665	2	98	0	0	42	24.37	-17.65			Apr-05
	5.51	21.90	11.66	58.18	69.93	0.66	0.76	12.04	0.95	32.72	2,665	2	98	0	0	42	24.55	-17.55			Apr-05
	5.53	21.95	11.76	58.56	70.67	0.7	0.68	12.04	0.95	34.5	2,665	2	98	0	0	42	24.33	-17.61			Jan-13
	2.83	11.42	8.83	18.49	26.27	3.05	1	5.23	0.31	12.76	3,710	2	40	58	0	36	15.56	-8.2	4.25		May-06
	2.65	10.93	8.04	15.88	21.65	2.34	1.75	5.18	0.31	12.75	3,710	2	40	58	0	36	15.08	-8.59		1.00	May-06
	2.81	11.47	9.01	19.28	27.75	3.29	0.75	5.21	0.31	12.75	3,710	2	40	58	0	36	15.72	-8.11			May-06
	2.65	10.94	7.95	15.89	21.66	2.34	1.75	5.18	0.31	12.74	3,710	2	40	58	0	36	15.2	-8.59			Jul-08
	2.77	11.20	8.57	17.62	24.72	2.82	1.25	5.19	0.31	12.75	3,710	2	40	58	0	36	15.41	-8.31			Jul-08
	2.83	11.42	8.83	18.49	26.27	3.05	1	5.21	0.31	12.76	3,710	2	40	58	0	36	15.68	-8.3			Jul-08
	2.89	11.55	9.10	19.38	27.85	3.29	0.75	5.2	0.31	12.76	3,710	2	40	58	0	36	15.84	-8.2			Jul-08
	2.91	11.60	9.20	19.71	28.57	3.38	0.65	5.23	0.31	12.76	3,710	2	40	58	0	36	15.72	-8.11			Jul-12
	0.53	12.54	-0.22	39.00	12.23	0.42	1.31	13.31	0.93	33.73	3,001	3	97	0	0	24	19.54	-25.58	5.75		Oct-95
	0.35	12.15	-0.96	35.85	8.07	0	2.06	13.31	0.93	30.92	3,001	3	97	0	0	24	19.06	-25.85		4.00	Oct-95
	0.36	12.18	-0.95	35.91	8.08	0	2.06	13.3	0.93	30.2	3,001	3	97	0	0	24	19.04	-25.85		1.00	Jun-96
	0.59	12.73	0.01	40.00	13.61	0.7	1.06	13.32	0.93	35.51	3,001	3	97	0	0	24	19.73	-25.53			Jan-97
	0.37	12.18	-0.97	35.86	8.06	0.38	2.06	13.31	0.93	29.82	3,001	3	97	0	0	24	19.03	-25.82			Oct-08
	0.45	12.41	-0.46	37.89	10.78	0.25	1.56	13.31	0.93	30.78	3,001	3	97	0	0	24	19.36	-25.67			Oct-08

	MARKET			FUND TYPE, CATEGORY & OBJECTIVE	RATINGS				MINIMUMS	
Fund Name	Ticker Symbol	Traded On	Fund Type	Category and (Prospectus Objective)	Overall Rating	Reward Rating	Risk Rating	Recent Up/ Downgrade	Open to New Investors	Min Initial Investment
MFS Emerging Markets Equity Fund Class R3	MEMGX	NAS CM	Open End	Global Emerg Mkts (Div Emerging Mkts)	C	C	B-		Y	0
MFS Emerging Markets Equity Fund Class R4	MEMHX	NAS CM	Open End	Global Emerg Mkts (Div Emerging Mkts)	C	C	B-		Y	0
MFS Emerging Markets Equity Fund Class R6	MEMJX	NAS CM	Open End	Global Emerg Mkts (Div Emerging Mkts)	C	C	B-		Y	0
MFS Equity Income Fund Class A	EQNAX	NAS CM	Open End	US Equity Large Cap Value (Equity-Income)	B-	C	B		Y	1,000
MFS Equity Income Fund Class B	EQNBX	NAS CM	Open End	US Equity Large Cap Value (Equity-Income)	B-	C	B	Up	Y	1,000
MFS Equity Income Fund Class C	EQNCX	NAS CM	Open End	US Equity Large Cap Value (Equity-Income)	B-	C	B	Up	Y	1,000
MFS Equity Income Fund Class I	EQNIX	NAS CM	Open End	US Equity Large Cap Value (Equity-Income)	B-	C	B		Y	0
MFS Equity Income Fund Class R1	EQNRX	NAS CM	Open End	US Equity Large Cap Value (Equity-Income)	B-	C	B	Up	Y	0
MFS Equity Income Fund Class R2	EQNSX	NAS CM	Open End	US Equity Large Cap Value (Equity-Income)	B-	C	B		Y	0
MFS Equity Income Fund Class R3	EQNTX	NAS CM	Open End	US Equity Large Cap Value (Equity-Income)	B-	C	B		Y	0
MFS Equity Income Fund Class R4	EQNUX	NAS CM	Open End	US Equity Large Cap Value (Equity-Income)	B-	C	B		Y	0
MFS Equity Income Fund Class R6	EQNVX	NAS CM	Open End	US Equity Large Cap Value (Equity-Income)	B-	C	B		Y	0
MFS Equity Opportunities Fund Class A	SRFAX	NAS CM	Open End	US Equity Large Cap Blend (Growth)	C+	C	B		Y	1,000
MFS Equity Opportunities Fund Class B	SRFBX	NAS CM	Open End	US Equity Large Cap Blend (Growth)	C	C	B-		Y	1,000
MFS Equity Opportunities Fund Class C	SRFCX	NAS CM	Open End	US Equity Large Cap Blend (Growth)	C	C	B-		Y	1,000
MFS Equity Opportunities Fund Class I	SRFIX	NAS CM	Open End	US Equity Large Cap Blend (Growth)	C+	C	B		Y	0
MFS Equity Opportunities Fund Class R1	SRFDX	NAS CM	Open End	US Equity Large Cap Blend (Growth)	C	C	B-		Y	0
MFS Equity Opportunities Fund Class R2	SRFEX	NAS CM	Open End	US Equity Large Cap Blend (Growth)	C+	C	B		Y	0
MFS Equity Opportunities Fund Class R3	SRFFX	NAS CM	Open End	US Equity Large Cap Blend (Growth)	C+	C	B		Y	0
MFS Equity Opportunities Fund Class R4	SRFGX	NAS CM	Open End	US Equity Large Cap Blend (Growth)	C+	C	B		Y	0
MFS Equity Opportunities Fund Class R6	SRFHX	NAS CM	Open End	US Equity Large Cap Blend (Growth)	C+	C	B		Y	0
MFS Global Alternative Strategy Fund Class A	DVRAX	NAS CM	Open End	Global Macro (Growth & Income)	B-	C	B		Y	1,000
MFS Global Alternative Strategy Fund Class B	DVRBX	NAS CM	Open End	Global Macro (Growth & Income)	C+	C	B		Y	1,000
MFS Global Alternative Strategy Fund Class C	DVRCX	NAS CM	Open End	Global Macro (Growth & Income)	C+	C	B		Y	1,000
MFS Global Alternative Strategy Fund Class I	DVRIX	NAS CM	Open End	Global Macro (Growth & Income)	B-	C	B		Y	0
MFS Global Alternative Strategy Fund Class R1	DVRFX	NAS CM	Open End	Global Macro (Growth & Income)	C+	C	B		Y	0
MFS Global Alternative Strategy Fund Class R2	DVRHX	NAS CM	Open End	Global Macro (Growth & Income)	B-	C	B	Up	Y	0
MFS Global Alternative Strategy Fund Class R3	DVRJX	NAS CM	Open End	Global Macro (Growth & Income)	B-	C	B		Y	0
MFS Global Alternative Strategy Fund Class R4	DVRKX	NAS CM	Open End	Global Macro (Growth & Income)	B-	C	B		Y	0
MFS Global Alternative Strategy Fund Class R6	DVRLX	NAS CM	Open End	Global Macro (Growth & Income)	B-	C+	B		Y	0
MFS Global Equity Fund Class A	MWEFX	NAS CM	Open End	Global Equity Large Cap (World Stock)	B-	C+	B	Up	Y	1,000
MFS Global Equity Fund Class B	MWEBX	NAS CM	Open End	Global Equity Large Cap (World Stock)	B-	C	B	Up	Y	1,000
MFS Global Equity Fund Class C	MWECX	NAS CM	Open End	Global Equity Large Cap (World Stock)	B-	C	B	Up	Y	1,000
MFS Global Equity Fund Class I	MWEIX	NAS CM	Open End	Global Equity Large Cap (World Stock)	B-	C+	B	Up	Y	0
MFS Global Equity Fund Class R1	MWEGX	NAS CM	Open End	Global Equity Large Cap (World Stock)	B-	C	B	Up	Y	0
MFS Global Equity Fund Class R2	MEQRX	NAS CM	Open End	Global Equity Large Cap (World Stock)	B-	C+	B	Up	Y	0
MFS Global Equity Fund Class R3	MWEHX	NAS CM	Open End	Global Equity Large Cap (World Stock)	B-	C+	B	Up	Y	0
MFS Global Equity Fund Class R4	MWELX	NAS CM	Open End	Global Equity Large Cap (World Stock)	B-	C+	B	Up	Y	0
MFS Global Equity Fund Class R6	MWEMX	NAS CM	Open End	Global Equity Large Cap (World Stock)	B-	C+	B	Up	Y	0
MFS Global Growth Fund Class A	MWOFX	NAS CM	Open End	Global Equity Large Cap (World Stock)	B	B-	B	Up	Y	1,000
MFS Global Growth Fund Class B	MWOBX	NAS CM	Open End	Global Equity Large Cap (World Stock)	B-	C+	B		Y	1,000
MFS Global Growth Fund Class C	MWOCX	NAS CM	Open End	Global Equity Large Cap (World Stock)	B-	C+	B		Y	1,000
MFS Global Growth Fund Class I	MWOIX	NAS CM	Open End	Global Equity Large Cap (World Stock)	B	B-	B	Up	Y	0
MFS Global Growth Fund Class R1	MWOGX	NAS CM	Open End	Global Equity Large Cap (World Stock)	B-	C+	B		Y	0
MFS Global Growth Fund Class R2	MGWRX	NAS CM	Open End	Global Equity Large Cap (World Stock)	B-	B-	B		Y	0
MFS Global Growth Fund Class R3	MWOHX	NAS CM	Open End	Global Equity Large Cap (World Stock)	B	B-	B	Up	Y	0
MFS Global Growth Fund Class R4	MWOJX	NAS CM	Open End	Global Equity Large Cap (World Stock)	B	B-	B	Up	Y	0
MFS Global Growth Fund Class R6	MWOKX	NAS CM	Open End	Global Equity Large Cap (World Stock)	B	B-	B		Y	0
MFS Global New Discovery Fund Class A	GLNAX	NAS CM	Open End	Global Equity Mid/Small Cap (World Stock)	C+	C	B	Up	Y	1,000
MFS Global New Discovery Fund Class B	GLNBX	NAS CM	Open End	Global Equity Mid/Small Cap (World Stock)	C+	C	B	Up	Y	1,000
MFS Global New Discovery Fund Class C	GLNCX	NAS CM	Open End	Global Equity Mid/Small Cap (World Stock)	C+	C	B	Up	Y	1,000
MFS Global New Discovery Fund Class I	GLNIX	NAS CM	Open End	Global Equity Mid/Small Cap (World Stock)	C+	C	B	Up	Y	0

★ Expanded analysis of this fund is included in Section II.

Min Additional Investment	3-Month Total Return	6-Month Total Return	1-Year Total Return	3-Year Total Return	5-Year Total Return	Dividend Yield (TTM)	Expense Ratio	3-Yr Std Deviation	3-Year Beta	NAV	Total Assets (MIL)	%Cash	%Stocks	%Bonds	%Other	Turnover Ratio	Last Bull Market Total Return	Last Bear Market Total Return	Front End Fee (%)	Back End Fee (%)	Inception Date
	TOTAL RETURNS					PERFORMANCE				ASSETS		ASSET ALLOCATION & TURNOVER					BULL & BEAR		FEES		
	0.53	12.57	-0.21	38.99	12.24	0.48	1.31	13.32	0.93	33.57	3,001	3	97	0	0	24	19.59	-25.61			Oct-08
	0.59	12.72	0.03	40.01	13.62	0.73	1.06	13.31	0.93	33.57	3,001	3	97	0	0	24	19.74	-25.53			Oct-08
	0.62	12.79	0.14	40.47	14.23	0.8	0.95	13.31	0.93	35.53	3,001	3	97	0	0	24	19.54	-25.58			Jun-12
	2.16	15.25	6.19	36.89	39.24	1.92	0.89	11.47	0.91	15.39	211.4	2	96	0	0	51			5.75		Sep-12
	1.91	14.78	5.34	33.76	34.15	1.22	1.64	11.41	0.91	15.38	211.4	2	96	0	0	51				4.00	Sep-12
	1.98	14.84	5.38	33.82	34.05	1.2	1.64	11.42	0.91	15.39	211.4	2	96	0	0	51				1.00	Sep-12
	2.22	15.46	6.46	38.05	41.07	2.16	0.64	11.44	0.91	15.4	211.4	2	96	0	0	51					Sep-12
	1.91	14.78	5.31	33.76	33.99	1.21	1.64	11.43	0.91	15.46	211.4	2	96	0	0	51					Sep-12
	2.05	15.11	5.86	35.73	37.36	1.7	1.14	11.44	0.91	15.42	211.4	2	96	0	0	51					Sep-12
	2.15	15.23	6.19	36.91	39.23	1.93	0.89	11.44	0.91	15.42	211.4	2	96	0	0	51					Sep-12
	2.15	15.37	6.38	37.89	40.92	2.15	0.64	11.44	0.91	15.4	211.4	2	96	0	0	51					Sep-12
	2.22	15.47	6.58	38.36	41.93	2.23	0.55	11.46	0.91	15.5	211.4	2	96	0	0	51					Sep-12
	3.31	16.82	2.76	25.89	31.32	1.14	1.19	12.84	1.01	27.7	251.6	1	99	0	0	119	26.82	-18.71	5.75		Aug-00
	3.10	16.39	1.95	23.04	26.46	0.37	1.94	12.85	1.01	25.92	251.6	1	99	0	0	119	26.32	-18.99		4.00	Jan-07
	3.13	16.41	1.98	23.05	26.47	0.16	1.94	12.84	1.01	26.03	251.6	1	99	0	0	119	26.23	-18.97		1.00	Mar-04
	3.34	16.97	2.98	26.79	32.92	1.38	0.94	12.82	1.01	27.77	251.6	1	99	0	0	119	27.05	-18.66			Feb-11
	3.13	16.39	2.01	23.08	26.52	0	1.94	12.84	1.01	25.98	251.6	1	99	0	0	119	26.28	-18.94			May-08
	3.19	16.64	2.45	24.89	29.65	0.79	1.44	12.84	1.01	26.77	251.6	1	99	0	0	119	26.66	-18.77			May-08
	3.29	16.80	2.74	25.83	31.28	1.1	1.19	12.85	1.01	27.59	251.6	1	99	0	0	119	26.77	-18.68			May-08
	3.37	16.98	3.02	26.86	33.02	1.31	0.94	12.86	1.01	27.89	251.6	1	99	0	0	119	26.96	-18.61			May-08
	3.38	17.03	3.07	27.17	33.66	1.48	0.85	12.84	1.01	28.37	251.6	1	99	0	0	119	26.95	-18.64			Mar-08
	2.59	9.08	7.64	13.15	10.12	0.74	1.32	4.04	0.62	10.69	181.2	58	31	15	-4	37	5.18	1.2	5.75		Dec-07
	2.44	8.73	6.84	10.58	6.06	0	2.07	4.05	0.61	10.46	181.2	58	31	15	-4	37	4.68	1		4.00	Dec-07
	2.54	8.70	6.93	10.66	6.04	0	2.07	4.07	0.61	10.49	181.2	58	31	15	-4	37	4.68	0.89		1.00	Dec-07
	2.67	9.12	7.93	13.89	11.46	1.02	1.07	4.1	0.59	10.76	181.2	58	31	15	-4	37	5.27	1.41			Dec-07
	2.47	8.60	6.81	10.55	6.01	0	2.07	4.03	0.64	10.35	181.2	58	31	15	-4	37	4.69	1			Dec-07
	2.52	8.86	7.25	12.16	8.69	0.13	1.57	4.04	0.6	10.56	181.2	58	31	15	-4	37	4.99	1.1			Dec-07
	2.68	9.07	7.62	13.07	10.04	0.81	1.32	4.04	0.58	10.7	181.2	58	31	15	-4	37	5.16	1.2			Dec-07
	2.66	9.21	7.91	14.02	10.93	1.02	1.07	4.09	0.61	10.79	181.2	58	31	15	-4	37	5.27	1.41			Dec-07
	2.75	9.19	7.96	14.25	11.95	1.07	0.99	4.04	0.57	10.81	181.2	58	31	15	-4	37	5.27	1.3			Dec-07
	5.44	21.71	11.30	42.67	41.11	0.91	1.16	11.6	1	44.96	3,024	1	99	0	0	12	22.95	-19.73	5.75		Sep-93
	5.25	21.26	10.48	39.53	35.93	0.25	1.91	11.6	1	41.28	3,024	1	99	0	0	12	22.43	-19.99		4.00	Dec-86
	5.23	21.28	10.50	39.51	35.93	0.3	1.91	11.59	0.99	39.38	3,024	1	99	0	0	12	22.47	-20		1.00	Jan-94
	5.52	21.89	11.60	43.77	42.89	1.1	0.91	11.6	1	46.21	3,024	1	99	0	0	12	23.13	-19.63			Jan-97
	5.24	21.28	10.49	39.50	35.92	0.22	1.91	11.61	1	40.34	3,024	1	99	0	0	12	22.52	-19.97			Apr-05
	5.38	21.57	11.05	41.64	39.35	0.66	1.41	11.61	1	43.62	3,024	1	99	0	0	12	22.81	-19.81			Oct-03
	5.45	21.72	11.32	42.69	41.12	0.9	1.16	11.62	1	44.65	3,024	1	99	0	0	12	22.94	-19.72			Apr-05
	5.51	21.88	11.60	43.78	42.89	1.14	0.91	11.61	1	45.12	3,024	1	99	0	0	12	23.12	-19.64			Apr-05
	5.54	21.94	11.71	44.15	43.58	1.21	0.81	11.62	1	46.23	3,024	1	99	0	0	12	22.43	-19.99			Jun-12
	5.58	22.17	11.96	54.13	55.12	0.08	1.4	11.78	0.93	44.8	468.4	2	98	0	0	22	21.18	-19.25	5.75		Nov-93
	5.41	21.72	11.13	50.64	49.37	0	2.15	11.79	0.93	38.55	468.4	2	98	0	0	22	20.66	-19.55		4.00	Nov-93
	5.40	21.71	11.13	50.67	49.38	0	2.15	11.79	0.93	38.06	468.4	2	98	0	0	22	20.68	-19.55		1.00	Jan-94
	5.65	22.29	12.25	55.23	56.98	0.29	1.15	11.8	0.93	45.96	468.4	2	98	0	0	22	21.37	-19.19			Jan-97
	5.41	21.69	11.13	50.67	49.33	0	2.15	11.8	0.93	37.97	468.4	2	98	0	0	22	20.66	-19.54			Apr-05
	5.53	22.03	11.69	52.94	53.13	0	1.65	11.79	0.93	43.26	468.4	2	98	0	0	22	21.04	-19.37			Oct-03
	5.59	22.14	11.95	54.06	55.04	0.04	1.4	11.8	0.93	44.57	468.4	2	98	0	0	22	21.21	-19.32			Apr-05
	5.64	22.31	12.24	55.22	56.97	0.3	1.15	11.8	0.93	44.89	468.4	2	98	0	0	22	21.36	-19.18			Apr-05
	5.68	22.33	12.31	55.58	57.58	0.35	1.08	11.8	0.93	45.95	468.4	2	98	0	0	22	21.18	-19.25			Mar-13
	4.75	21.16	4.54	49.92	46.07	0.09	1.5	12.2	0.95	19.18	48.4	1	98	0	0	36			5.75		Dec-11
	4.58	20.69	3.79	46.56	40.73	0	2.25	12.16	0.95	18.02	48.4	1	98	0	0	36				4.00	Dec-11
	4.58	20.69	3.79	46.56	40.73	0	2.25	12.21	0.95	18.02	48.4	1	98	0	0	36				1.00	Dec-11
	4.84	21.32	4.81	51.06	48.00	0.22	1.25	12.2	0.95	19.46	48.4	1	98	0	0	36					Dec-11

	MARKET			FUND TYPE, CATEGORY & OBJECTIVE	RATINGS					MINIMUMS
Fund Name	Ticker Symbol	Traded On	Fund Type	Category and (Prospectus Objective)	Overall Rating	Reward Rating	Risk Rating	Recent Up/ Downgrade	Open to New Investors	Min Initial Investment
MFS Global New Discovery Fund Class R1	GLNJX	NAS CM	Open End	Global Equity Mid/Small Cap (World Stock)	C+	C	B	Up	Y	0
MFS Global New Discovery Fund Class R2	GLNKX	NAS CM	Open End	Global Equity Mid/Small Cap (World Stock)	C+	C	B	Up	Y	0
MFS Global New Discovery Fund Class R3	GLNLX	NAS CM	Open End	Global Equity Mid/Small Cap (World Stock)	C+	C	B	Up	Y	0
MFS Global New Discovery Fund Class R4	GLNMX	NAS CM	Open End	Global Equity Mid/Small Cap (World Stock)	C+	C	B	Up	Y	0
MFS Global New Discovery Fund Class R6	GLNNX	NAS CM	Open End	Global Equity Mid/Small Cap (World Stock)	C+	C	B	Up	Y	0
MFS Global Real Estate Fund Class A	MGLAX	NAS CM	Open End	Real Estate Sector Equity (Real Estate)	B	B-	B+		Y	1,000
MFS Global Real Estate Fund Class B	MGLDX	NAS CM	Open End	Real Estate Sector Equity (Real Estate)	B	C+	B+		Y	1,000
MFS Global Real Estate Fund Class C	MGLCX	NAS CM	Open End	Real Estate Sector Equity (Real Estate)	B	C+	B+		Y	1,000
MFS Global Real Estate Fund Class I	MGLIX	NAS CM	Open End	Real Estate Sector Equity (Real Estate)	B	B-	B+		Y	0
MFS Global Real Estate Fund Class R1	MGLJX	NAS CM	Open End	Real Estate Sector Equity (Real Estate)	B	C+	B+		Y	0
MFS Global Real Estate Fund Class R2	MGLKX	NAS CM	Open End	Real Estate Sector Equity (Real Estate)	B	B-	B+		Y	0
MFS Global Real Estate Fund Class R3	MGLLX	NAS CM	Open End	Real Estate Sector Equity (Real Estate)	B	B-	B+		Y	0
MFS Global Real Estate Fund Class R4	MGLMX	NAS CM	Open End	Real Estate Sector Equity (Real Estate)	B	B-	B+		Y	0
MFS Global Real Estate Fund Class R6	MGLRX	NAS CM	Open End	Real Estate Sector Equity (Real Estate)	B	B-	B+		Y	0
MFS Global Total Return Fund Class A	MFWTX	NAS CM	Open End	Moderate Alloc (Balanced)	B-	C	B	Up	Y	1,000
MFS Global Total Return Fund Class B	MFWBX	NAS CM	Open End	Moderate Alloc (Balanced)	C+	C	B	Up	Y	1,000
MFS Global Total Return Fund Class C	MFWCX	NAS CM	Open End	Moderate Alloc (Balanced)	C+	C	B	Up	Y	1,000
MFS Global Total Return Fund Class I	MFWIX	NAS CM	Open End	Moderate Alloc (Balanced)	B-	C	B+	Up	Y	0
MFS Global Total Return Fund Class R1	MFWGX	NAS CM	Open End	Moderate Alloc (Balanced)	C+	C	B	Up	Y	0
MFS Global Total Return Fund Class R2	MGBRX	NAS CM	Open End	Moderate Alloc (Balanced)	B-	C	B	Up	Y	0
MFS Global Total Return Fund Class R3	MFWHX	NAS CM	Open End	Moderate Alloc (Balanced)	B-	C	B	Up	Y	0
MFS Global Total Return Fund Class R4	MFWJX	NAS CM	Open End	Moderate Alloc (Balanced)	B-	C	B+	Up	Y	0
MFS Global Total Return Fund Class R6	MFWLX	NAS CM	Open End	Moderate Alloc (Balanced)	B-	C	B+	Up	Y	0
MFS Growth Allocation Fund Class 529A	EAGWX	NAS CM	Open End	Aggressive Alloc (Growth)	B	C+	B+	Up	Y	250
MFS Growth Allocation Fund Class 529B	EBGWX	NAS CM	Open End	Aggressive Alloc (Growth)	B-	C+	B+	Up	Y	250
MFS Growth Allocation Fund Class 529C	ECGWX	NAS CM	Open End	Aggressive Alloc (Growth)	B-	C+	B+	Up	Y	250
MFS Growth Allocation Fund Class A	MAGWX	NAS CM	Open End	Aggressive Alloc (Growth)	B	C+	B+	Up	Y	1,000
MFS Growth Allocation Fund Class B	MBGWX	NAS CM	Open End	Aggressive Alloc (Growth)	B-	C+	B+	Up	Y	1,000
MFS Growth Allocation Fund Class C	MCGWX	NAS CM	Open End	Aggressive Alloc (Growth)	B-	C+	B+	Up	Y	1,000
MFS Growth Allocation Fund Class I	MGWIX	NAS CM	Open End	Aggressive Alloc (Growth)	B	C+	B+	Up	Y	0
MFS Growth Allocation Fund Class R1	MAGMX	NAS CM	Open End	Aggressive Alloc (Growth)	B-	C+	B+	Up	Y	0
MFS Growth Allocation Fund Class R2	MGALX	NAS CM	Open End	Aggressive Alloc (Growth)	B-	C+	B+		Y	0
MFS Growth Allocation Fund Class R3	MAGEX	NAS CM	Open End	Aggressive Alloc (Growth)	B	C+	B+	Up	Y	0
MFS Growth Allocation Fund Class R4	MAGJX	NAS CM	Open End	Aggressive Alloc (Growth)	B	C+	B+	Up	Y	0
MFS Growth Fund Class A	MFEGX	NAS CM	Open End	US Equity Large Cap Growth (Growth)	B	B-	B		Y	1,000
MFS Growth Fund Class B	MEGBX	NAS CM	Open End	US Equity Large Cap Growth (Growth)	B-	B-	B	Down	Y	1,000
MFS Growth Fund Class C	MFECX	NAS CM	Open End	US Equity Large Cap Growth (Growth)	B-	B-	B	Down	Y	1,000
MFS Growth Fund Class I	MFEIX	NAS CM	Open End	US Equity Large Cap Growth (Growth)	B	B-	B		Y	0
MFS Growth Fund Class R1	MFELX	NAS CM	Open End	US Equity Large Cap Growth (Growth)	B-	B-	B	Down	Y	0
MFS Growth Fund Class R2	MEGRX	NAS CM	Open End	US Equity Large Cap Growth (Growth)	B	B-	B		Y	0
MFS Growth Fund Class R3	MFEHX	NAS CM	Open End	US Equity Large Cap Growth (Growth)	B	B-	B		Y	0
MFS Growth Fund Class R4	MFEJX	NAS CM	Open End	US Equity Large Cap Growth (Growth)	B	B-	B		Y	0
MFS Growth Fund Class R6	MFEKX	NAS CM	Open End	US Equity Large Cap Growth (Growth)	B	B-	B		Y	0
MFS Institutional International Equity Fund	MIEIX	NAS CM	Open End	Global Equity Large Cap (Foreign Stock)	C+	C	B	Up	Y	3,000,000
MFS International Diversification Fund Class A	MDIDX	NAS CM	Open End	Global Equity Large Cap (Growth)	C+	C	B	Up	Y	1,000
MFS International Diversification Fund Class B	MDIFX	NAS CM	Open End	Global Equity Large Cap (Growth)	C+	C	B	Up	Y	1,000
MFS International Diversification Fund Class C	MDIGX	NAS CM	Open End	Global Equity Large Cap (Growth)	C+	C	B	Up	Y	1,000
MFS International Diversification Fund Class I	MDIJX	NAS CM	Open End	Global Equity Large Cap (Growth)	C+	C	B	Up	Y	0
MFS International Diversification Fund Class R1	MDIOX	NAS CM	Open End	Global Equity Large Cap (Growth)	C+	C	B	Up	Y	0
MFS International Diversification Fund Class R2	MDIKX	NAS CM	Open End	Global Equity Large Cap (Growth)	C+	C	B	Up	Y	0
MFS International Diversification Fund Class R3	MDIHX	NAS CM	Open End	Global Equity Large Cap (Growth)	C+	C	B	Up	Y	0
MFS International Diversification Fund Class R4	MDITX	NAS CM	Open End	Global Equity Large Cap (Growth)	C+	C	B	Up	Y	0

★ Expanded analysis of this fund is included in Section II.

Min Additional Investment	TOTAL RETURNS 3-Month Total Return	6-Month Total Return	1-Year Total Return	3-Year Total Return	5-Year Total Return	PERFORMANCE Dividend Yield (TTM)	Expense Ratio	3-Yr Std Deviation	3-Year Beta	ASSETS NAV	Total Assets (MIL)	ASSET ALLOCATION & TURNOVER %Cash	%Stocks	%Bonds	%Other	Turnover Ratio	BULL & BEAR Last Bull Market Total Return	Last Bear Market Total Return	FEES Front End Fee (%)	Back End Fee (%)	Inception Date
	4.58	20.71	3.79	46.49	40.66	0	2.25	12.18	0.95	18.01	48.4	1	98	0	0	36					Dec-11
	4.67	20.96	4.29	48.82	44.25	0	1.75	12.18	0.95	18.81	48.4	1	98	0	0	36					Dec-11
	4.80	21.16	4.57	49.98	46.10	0.07	1.5	12.2	0.95	19.18	48.4	1	98	0	0	36					Dec-11
	4.84	21.32	4.80	51.08	47.82	0.3	1.25	12.19	0.95	19.46	48.4	1	98	0	0	36					Dec-11
	4.90	21.37	4.91	51.46	48.70	0.38	1.22	12.21	0.95	19.48	48.4	1	98	0	0	36					Jan-13
	2.68	17.82	11.04	23.14	40.81	1.92	1.33	10.21	0.9	17.19	2,002	1	98	0	0	20	22.57	-19.66	5.75		Mar-09
	2.54	17.35	10.26	20.49	35.63	1.19	2.08	10.21	0.9	17.31	2,002	1	98	0	0	20	22.01	-19.81		4.00	Dec-14
	2.55	17.37	10.24	20.48	35.58	1.29	2.08	10.29	0.91	17.29	2,002	1	98	0	0	20	22.01	-19.81		1.00	Dec-14
	2.80	17.98	11.40	24.09	42.47	2.18	1.08	10.21	0.9	17.25	2,002	1	98	0	0	20	22.72	-19.48			Mar-09
	2.50	17.34	10.20	20.40	35.63	1.82	2.08	10.26	0.9	17.18	2,002	1	98	0	0	20	22.01	-19.81			Dec-14
	2.67	17.64	10.77	22.21	39.10	1.73	1.58	10.23	0.9	17.27	2,002	1	98	0	0	20	22.36	-19.64			Dec-14
	2.73	17.80	11.11	23.18	40.92	1.88	1.33	10.25	0.9	17.27	2,002	1	98	0	0	20	22.54	-19.56			Dec-14
	2.80	17.90	11.28	23.93	42.51	2.14	1.08	10.24	0.9	17.25	2,002	1	98	0	0	20	22.72	-19.48			Dec-14
	2.79	17.93	11.43	24.37	42.98	2.22	0.99	10.25	0.9	17.29	2,002	1	98	0	0	20	22.72	-19.48			Jul-12
	3.69	12.05	6.76	18.92	21.74	1.32	1.09	6.99	0.57	18.08	1,859	10	59	31	0	52	11.88	-9.25	5.75		Sep-90
	3.48	11.66	5.98	16.25	17.22	0.55	1.84	6.97	0.57	18.45	1,859	10	59	31	0	52	11.43	-9.49		4.00	Sep-93
	3.48	11.65	5.96	16.22	17.26	0.58	1.84	6.96	0.57	18.18	1,859	10	59	31	0	52	11.41	-9.52		1.00	Jan-94
	3.79	12.18	7.04	19.83	23.25	1.57	0.84	6.97	0.57	17.89	1,859	10	59	31	0	52	12.04	-9.14			Jan-97
	3.51	11.61	5.94	16.25	17.19	0.64	1.84	6.94	0.56	18.09	1,859	10	59	31	0	52	11.46	-9.54			Apr-05
	3.61	11.92	6.49	18.00	20.16	1.08	1.34	6.95	0.56	17.89	1,859	10	59	31	0	52	11.84	-9.37			Oct-03
	3.70	12.09	6.79	19.00	21.82	1.33	1.09	6.94	0.56	18.03	1,859	10	59	31	0	52	11.92	-9.27			Apr-05
	3.80	12.23	7.08	19.85	23.29	1.55	0.84	6.98	0.57	18.11	1,859	10	59	31	0	52	12.1	-9.14			Apr-05
	3.76	12.24	7.09	20.17	23.84	1.66	0.78	6.95	0.57	17.89	1,859	10	59	31	0	52	11.88	-9.25			Jun-12
	4.75	18.28	8.56	36.74	38.94	1.76	1.07	9.21	0.72	21.15	5,102	3	75	22	0	2	18.03	-15.24	5.75		Jul-02
	4.60	17.87	7.78	33.70	33.83	1	1.82	9.2	0.72	20.9	5,102	3	75	22	0	2	17.53	-15.43		4.00	Jul-02
	4.57	17.85	7.77	33.69	33.78	1	1.82	9.21	0.72	20.59	5,102	3	75	22	0	2	17.61	-15.54		1.00	Jul-02
	4.76	18.30	8.58	36.88	39.19	1.77	1.02	9.22	0.72	21.33	5,102	3	75	22	0	2	18.07	-15.2	5.75		Jun-02
	4.60	17.91	7.80	33.89	34.11	1	1.77	9.19	0.72	21.13	5,102	3	75	22	0	2	17.52	-15.4		4.00	Jun-02
	4.55	17.89	7.75	33.85	34.11	1.01	1.77	9.19	0.72	20.88	5,102	3	75	22	0	2	17.57	-15.44		1.00	Jun-02
	4.86	18.48	8.85	37.98	40.98	1.99	0.77	9.21	0.72	21.54	5,102	3	75	22	0	2	18.22	-15.1			Jun-02
	4.60	17.88	7.77	33.92	34.05	1.08	1.77	9.2	0.72	20.43	5,102	3	75	22	0	2	17.62	-15.48			Apr-05
	4.72	18.21	8.34	35.93	37.50	1.55	1.27	9.21	0.72	20.83	5,102	3	75	22	0	2	17.96	-15.31			Oct-03
	4.80	18.36	8.58	36.93	39.23	1.77	1.02	9.21	0.72	21.14	5,102	3	75	22	0	2	18.07	-15.18			Apr-05
	4.86	18.51	8.89	37.99	40.93	2.01	0.77	9.21	0.72	21.32	5,102	3	75	22	0	2	18.27	-15.08			Apr-05
	6.48	26.49	14.56	72.41	93.83	0	0.92	13.23	0.96	110.16	22,365	2	98	0	0	18	24.12	-14.39	5.75		Sep-93
	6.29	26.02	13.70	68.57	86.66	0	1.67	13.22	0.96	87.63	22,365	2	98	0	0	18	23.6	-14.66		4.00	Dec-86
	6.29	26.03	13.70	68.57	86.62	0	1.67	13.22	0.96	86.92	22,365	2	98	0	0	18	23.57	-14.65		1.00	Apr-96
	6.56	26.65	14.84	73.69	96.22	0	0.67	13.23	0.96	117.53	22,365	2	98	0	0	18	24.31	-14.29			Jan-97
	6.29	26.02	13.70	68.56	86.65	0	1.67	13.22	0.96	87.25	22,365	2	98	0	0	18	23.59	-14.66			Apr-05
	6.43	26.34	14.27	71.10	91.36	0	1.17	13.23	0.96	103.7	22,365	2	98	0	0	18	23.93	-14.47			Oct-03
	6.48	26.49	14.55	72.38	93.75	0	0.92	13.23	0.96	109.59	22,365	2	98	0	0	18	24.11	-14.38			Apr-05
	6.55	26.66	14.84	73.67	96.19	0	0.67	13.23	0.96	114.23	22,365	2	98	0	0	18	24.29	-14.31			Apr-05
	6.57	26.71	14.94	74.17	97.15	0	0.58	13.23	0.96	117.89	22,365	2	98	0	0	18	24.23	-14.58			Aug-11
	6.73	19.43	7.48	43.16	27.11	1.24	0.7	11.06	0.97	26.61	10,579	1	99	0	0	14	19.23	-23.06			Jan-96
	3.99	16.84	3.97	37.26	26.72	1.87	1.12	10.9	0.91	19.77	18,013	3	97	0	0	1	16.32	-20.01	5.75		Sep-04
	3.82	16.44	3.21	34.26	22.08	1.05	1.87	10.91	0.91	19.54	18,013	3	97	0	0	1	15.73	-20.25		4.00	Sep-04
	3.81	16.40	3.19	34.27	22.09	1.1	1.87	10.91	0.91	19.3	18,013	3	97	0	0	1	15.77	-20.23		1.00	Sep-04
	4.06	16.97	4.21	38.33	28.34	2.09	0.87	10.9	0.91	19.98	18,013	3	97	0	0	1	16.4	-19.93			Sep-04
	3.77	16.36	3.14	34.18	22.07	1.22	1.87	10.88	0.91	18.99	18,013	3	97	0	0	1	15.74	-20.21			Apr-05
	3.95	16.69	3.70	36.27	25.13	1.62	1.37	10.92	0.91	19.43	18,013	3	97	0	0	1	16.01	-20.05			Sep-04
	4.02	16.85	3.97	37.25	26.76	1.9	1.12	10.9	0.91	19.62	18,013	3	97	0	0	1	16.22	-19.95			Apr-05
	4.02	16.97	4.21	38.29	28.28	2.08	0.87	10.88	0.91	19.91	18,013	3	97	0	0	1	16.36	-19.86			Apr-05

	MARKET		FUND TYPE, CATEGORY & OBJECTIVE		RATINGS				MINIMUMS	
Fund Name	Ticker Symbol	Traded On	Fund Type	Category and (Prospectus Objective)	Overall Rating	Reward Rating	Risk Rating	Recent Up/ Downgrade	Open to New Investors	Min Initial Investment
MFS International Diversification Fund Class R6	MDIZX	NAS CM	Open End	Global Equity Large Cap (Growth)	C+	C	B	Up	Y	0
MFS International Growth Fund Class A	MGRAX	NAS CM	Open End	Global Equity Large Cap (Foreign Stock)	C+	C	B	Up	Y	1,000
MFS International Growth Fund Class B	MGRBX	NAS CM	Open End	Global Equity Large Cap (Foreign Stock)	C+	C	B	Up	Y	1,000
MFS International Growth Fund Class C	MGRCX	NAS CM	Open End	Global Equity Large Cap (Foreign Stock)	C+	C	B	Up	Y	1,000
MFS International Growth Fund Class I	MQGIX	NAS CM	Open End	Global Equity Large Cap (Foreign Stock)	C+	C	B	Up	Y	0
MFS International Growth Fund Class R1	MGRRX	NAS CM	Open End	Global Equity Large Cap (Foreign Stock)	C+	C	B	Up	Y	0
MFS International Growth Fund Class R2	MGRQX	NAS CM	Open End	Global Equity Large Cap (Foreign Stock)	C+	C	B	Up	Y	0
MFS International Growth Fund Class R3	MGRTX	NAS CM	Open End	Global Equity Large Cap (Foreign Stock)	C+	C	B	Up	Y	0
MFS International Growth Fund Class R4	MGRVX	NAS CM	Open End	Global Equity Large Cap (Foreign Stock)	C+	C	B	Up	Y	0
MFS International Growth Fund Class R6	MGRDX	NAS CM	Open End	Global Equity Large Cap (Foreign Stock)	C+	C	B	Up	Y	0
MFS International Intrinsic Value Fund Class A	MGIAX	NAS CM	Open End	Global Equity Large Cap (Foreign Stock)	B-	C	B	Up		1,000
MFS International Intrinsic Value Fund Class B	MGIBX	NAS CM	Open End	Global Equity Large Cap (Foreign Stock)	C+	C	B	Up		1,000
MFS International Intrinsic Value Fund Class C	MGICX	NAS CM	Open End	Global Equity Large Cap (Foreign Stock)	C+	C	B	Up		1,000
MFS International Intrinsic Value Fund Class I	MINIX	NAS CM	Open End	Global Equity Large Cap (Foreign Stock)	B-	C	B	Up		0
MFS International Intrinsic Value Fund Class R1	MINRX	NAS CM	Open End	Global Equity Large Cap (Foreign Stock)	C+	C	B	Up		0
MFS International Intrinsic Value Fund Class R2	MINFX	NAS CM	Open End	Global Equity Large Cap (Foreign Stock)	C+	C	B	Up		0
MFS International Intrinsic Value Fund Class R3	MINGX	NAS CM	Open End	Global Equity Large Cap (Foreign Stock)	B-	C	B	Up		0
MFS International Intrinsic Value Fund Class R4	MINHX	NAS CM	Open End	Global Equity Large Cap (Foreign Stock)	B-	C	B	Up		0
MFS International Intrinsic Value Fund Class R6	MINJX	NAS CM	Open End	Global Equity Large Cap (Foreign Stock)	B-	C	B	Up		0
MFS International New Discovery Fund Class 529A	EAIDX	NAS CM	Open End	Global Equity Mid/Small Cap (Foreign Stock)	C	C	B		Y	250
MFS International New Discovery Fund Class 529B	EBIDX	NAS CM	Open End	Global Equity Mid/Small Cap (Foreign Stock)	C	C	B		Y	250
MFS International New Discovery Fund Class 529C	ECIDX	NAS CM	Open End	Global Equity Mid/Small Cap (Foreign Stock)	C	C	B		Y	250
MFS International New Discovery Fund Class A	MIDAX	NAS CM	Open End	Global Equity Mid/Small Cap (Foreign Stock)	C	C	B		Y	1,000
MFS International New Discovery Fund Class B	MIDBX	NAS CM	Open End	Global Equity Mid/Small Cap (Foreign Stock)	C	C	B		Y	1,000
MFS International New Discovery Fund Class C	MIDCX	NAS CM	Open End	Global Equity Mid/Small Cap (Foreign Stock)	C	C	B		Y	1,000
MFS International New Discovery Fund Class I	MWNIX	NAS CM	Open End	Global Equity Mid/Small Cap (Foreign Stock)	C	C	B		Y	0
MFS International New Discovery Fund Class R1	MIDGX	NAS CM	Open End	Global Equity Mid/Small Cap (Foreign Stock)	C	C	B		Y	0
MFS International New Discovery Fund Class R2	MIDRX	NAS CM	Open End	Global Equity Mid/Small Cap (Foreign Stock)	C	C	B		Y	0
MFS International New Discovery Fund Class R3	MIDHX	NAS CM	Open End	Global Equity Mid/Small Cap (Foreign Stock)	C	C	B		Y	0
MFS International New Discovery Fund Class R4	MIDJX	NAS CM	Open End	Global Equity Mid/Small Cap (Foreign Stock)	C	C	B		Y	0
MFS International New Discovery Fund Class R6	MIDLX	NAS CM	Open End	Global Equity Mid/Small Cap (Foreign Stock)	C+	C	B	Up	Y	0
MFS Lifetime 2020 Fund Class A	MFLAX	NAS CM	Open End	Target Date (Asset Alloc)	B	C+	A-		Y	1,000
MFS Lifetime 2020 Fund Class B	MFLBX	NAS CM	Open End	Target Date (Asset Alloc)	B	C	A-	Up	Y	1,000
MFS Lifetime 2020 Fund Class C	MFLCX	NAS CM	Open End	Target Date (Asset Alloc)	B	C	A-	Up	Y	1,000
MFS Lifetime 2020 Fund Class I	MFLIX	NAS CM	Open End	Target Date (Asset Alloc)	B	C+	A		Y	0
MFS Lifetime 2020 Fund Class R1	MFLEX	NAS CM	Open End	Target Date (Asset Alloc)	B	C	A-	Up	Y	0
MFS Lifetime 2020 Fund Class R2	MFLGX	NAS CM	Open End	Target Date (Asset Alloc)	B	C+	A-	Up	Y	0
MFS Lifetime 2020 Fund Class R3	MFLHX	NAS CM	Open End	Target Date (Asset Alloc)	B	C+	A-		Y	0
MFS Lifetime 2020 Fund Class R4	MFLJX	NAS CM	Open End	Target Date (Asset Alloc)	B	C+	A		Y	0
MFS Lifetime 2020 Fund Class R6	MFLKX	NAS CM	Open End	Target Date (Asset Alloc)	B	C+	A		Y	0
MFS Lifetime 2025 Fund Class A	LTTAX	NAS CM	Open End	Target Date (Asset Alloc)	B	C+	A	Up	Y	1,000
MFS Lifetime 2025 Fund Class B	LTTBX	NAS CM	Open End	Target Date (Asset Alloc)	B	C+	A-	Up	Y	1,000
MFS Lifetime 2025 Fund Class C	LTTCX	NAS CM	Open End	Target Date (Asset Alloc)	B	C	A-	Up	Y	1,000
MFS Lifetime 2025 Fund Class I	LTTIX	NAS CM	Open End	Target Date (Asset Alloc)	B	C+	A	Up	Y	0
MFS Lifetime 2025 Fund Class R1	LTTRX	NAS CM	Open End	Target Date (Asset Alloc)	B	C	A-	Up	Y	0
MFS Lifetime 2025 Fund Class R2	LTTSX	NAS CM	Open End	Target Date (Asset Alloc)	B	C+	A	Up	Y	0
MFS Lifetime 2025 Fund Class R3	LTTTX	NAS CM	Open End	Target Date (Asset Alloc)	B	C+	A	Up	Y	0
MFS Lifetime 2025 Fund Class R4	LTTUX	NAS CM	Open End	Target Date (Asset Alloc)	B	C+	A	Up	Y	0
MFS Lifetime 2025 Fund Class R6	LTTKX	NAS CM	Open End	Target Date (Asset Alloc)	B	C+	A	Up	Y	0
MFS Lifetime 2030 Fund Class A	MLTAX	NAS CM	Open End	Target Date (Asset Alloc)	B-	C	B+		Y	1,000
MFS Lifetime 2030 Fund Class B	MLTBX	NAS CM	Open End	Target Date (Asset Alloc)	B-	C	B+	Up	Y	1,000
MFS Lifetime 2030 Fund Class C	MLTCX	NAS CM	Open End	Target Date (Asset Alloc)	B-	C	B+	Up	Y	1,000

★ Expanded analysis of this fund is included in Section II.

Min Additional Investment	TOTAL RETURNS 3-Month Total Return	6-Month Total Return	1-Year Total Return	3-Year Total Return	5-Year Total Return	PERFORMANCE Dividend Yield (TTM)	Expense Ratio	3-Yr Std Deviation	3-Year Beta	ASSETS NAV	Total Assets (MIL)	ASSET ALLOCATION & TURNOVER %Cash	%Stocks	%Bonds	%Other	Turnover Ratio	BULL & BEAR Last Bull Market Total Return	Last Bear Market Total Return	FEES Front End Fee (%)	Back End Fee (%)	Inception Date
	4.11	17.03	4.31	38.56	28.55	2.17	0.77	10.91	0.91	19.99	18,013	3	97	0	0	1	16.4	-19.93			Oct-17
	4.83	18.51	6.16	44.28	33.03	0.82	1.15	11.5	0.92	34.89	9,072	2	98	0	0	12	19.97	-21.81	5.75		Oct-95
	4.64	18.08	5.36	41.10	28.12	0	1.9	11.5	0.92	32.64	9,072	2	98	0	0	12	19.44	-22.06		4.00	Oct-95
	4.65	18.07	5.39	41.09	28.14	0.17	1.9	11.5	0.92	31.68	9,072	2	98	0	0	12	19.45	-22.06		1.00	Jul-96
	4.89	18.64	6.42	45.38	34.69	0.94	0.9	11.51	0.92	39	9,072	2	98	0	0	12	20.13	-21.73			Jan-97
	4.65	18.09	5.39	41.10	28.11	0.36	1.9	11.51	0.92	31	9,072	2	98	0	0	12	19.48	-22.06			Oct-08
	4.80	18.39	5.91	43.22	31.39	0.59	1.4	11.5	0.92	31.86	9,072	2	98	0	0	12	19.82	-21.91			Oct-08
	4.81	18.52	6.15	44.26	33.00	0.86	1.15	11.52	0.92	34.62	9,072	2	98	0	0	12	20.02	-21.8			Oct-08
	4.88	18.66	6.43	45.35	34.67	1.05	0.9	11.51	0.92	34.97	9,072	2	98	0	0	12	20.15	-21.75			Oct-08
	4.92	18.70	6.53	45.79	35.40	1.13	0.8	11.51	0.92	34.96	9,072	2	98	0	0	12	20.08	-21.77			May-06
	4.27	17.24	6.58	35.17	43.65	1.14	0.98	10.53	0.68	43.93	28,593	5	95	0	0	14	12.93	-13.24	5.75		Oct-95
	4.06	16.80	5.78	32.17	38.34	0.41	1.73	10.53	0.68	41.71	28,593	5	95	0	0	14	12.45	-13.52		4.00	Oct-95
	4.06	16.80	5.79	32.14	38.37	0.49	1.73	10.54	0.68	39.69	28,593	5	95	0	0	14	12.48	-13.51		1.00	Jul-96
	4.31	17.38	6.83	36.17	45.45	1.33	0.73	10.54	0.68	46.18	28,593	5	95	0	0	14	13.1	-13.16			Jan-97
	4.06	16.80	5.78	32.16	38.37	0.53	1.73	10.53	0.68	40.17	28,593	5	95	0	0	14	12.42	-13.48			Oct-08
	4.19	17.09	6.30	34.15	41.84	0.97	1.23	10.53	0.68	40.96	28,593	5	95	0	0	14	12.77	-13.33			Oct-08
	4.25	17.23	6.55	35.14	43.62	1.16	0.98	10.53	0.68	43.6	28,593	5	95	0	0	14	12.94	-13.24			Oct-08
	4.33	17.40	6.85	36.19	45.43	1.39	0.73	10.53	0.68	44.05	28,593	5	95	0	0	14	13.08	-13.14			Oct-08
	4.35	17.44	6.95	36.59	46.18	1.5	0.63	10.53	0.68	44.1	28,593	5	95	0	0	14	13.03	-13.18			May-06
	2.69	13.79	0.56	34.67	27.34	0.59	1.35	10.22	0.83	32.41	6,978	7	93	0	0	21	20.12	-20.17	5.75		Jul-02
	2.61	13.46	-0.07	33.50	24.80	0.49	2.1	10.19	0.83	30.58	6,978	7	93	0	0	21	19.63	-20.43		4.00	Jul-02
	2.47	13.33	-0.25	31.48	22.41	0	2.1	10.21	0.83	30.17	6,978	7	93	0	0	21	19.58	-20.4		1.00	Jul-02
	2.70	13.79	0.57	34.70	27.37	0.57	1.3	10.23	0.83	33	6,978	7	93	0	0	21	20.17	-20.15	5.75		Oct-97
	2.50	13.36	-0.18	31.71	22.67	0	2.05	10.21	0.83	31.9	6,978	7	93	0	0	21	19.62	-20.39		4.00	Oct-00
	2.52	13.37	-0.18	31.69	22.68	0	2.05	10.21	0.83	31.28	6,978	7	93	0	0	21	19.66	-20.4		1.00	Oct-00
	2.77	13.96	0.82	35.74	28.97	0.81	1.05	10.24	0.84	34.03	6,978	7	93	0	0	21	20.33	-20.06			Oct-97
	2.52	13.39	-0.19	31.67	22.62	0	2.05	10.22	0.83	30.48	6,978	7	93	0	0	21	19.66	-20.42			Apr-05
	2.62	13.63	0.30	33.66	25.75	0.26	1.55	10.22	0.83	32.08	6,978	7	93	0	0	21	19.99	-20.25			Oct-03
	2.70	13.78	0.56	34.66	27.33	0.56	1.3	10.23	0.84	32.69	6,978	7	93	0	0	21	20.17	-20.16			Apr-05
	2.74	13.93	0.78	35.69	28.91	0.83	1.05	10.21	0.83	32.96	6,978	7	93	0	0	21	20.29	-20.05			Apr-05
	2.77	13.98	0.93	36.15	29.72	0.93	0.93	10.22	0.83	34.06	6,978	7	93	0	0	21	20.33	-20.06			Jun-12
	3.19	10.34	6.75	18.98	23.04	2.39	0.81	4.43		13.23	341.2	3	29	67	0	17	13.59	-10.07	5.75		Sep-05
	3.05	10.04	6.02	16.39	18.61	1.53	1.56	4.45		13.15	341.2	3	29	67	0	17	13.03	-10.32		4.00	Sep-05
	3.02	9.94	5.97	16.34	18.50	1.64	1.56	4.41		12.94	341.2	3	29	67	0	17	12.99	-10.32		1.00	Sep-05
	3.33	10.61	7.06	19.95	24.70	2.61	0.56	4.44		13.34	341.2	3	29	67	0	17	13.69	-9.94			Sep-05
	3.05	10.04	5.95	16.37	18.57	1.69	1.56	4.45		13.15	341.2	3	29	67	0	17	13.01	-10.34			Sep-05
	3.22	10.33	6.49	18.15	21.61	2.14	1.06	4.42		13.13	341.2	3	29	67	0	17	13.31	-10.13			Sep-05
	3.27	10.42	6.78	19.03	23.15	2.41	0.81	4.44		13.24	341.2	3	29	67	0	17	13.48	-10.06			Sep-05
	3.33	10.53	7.00	19.93	24.68	2.62	0.56	4.43		13.33	341.2	3	29	67	0	17	13.7	-9.95			Sep-05
	3.33	10.63	7.14	20.35	25.11	2.75	0.42	4.43		13.32	341.2	3	29	67	0	17	13.69	-9.94			Aug-16
	3.66	12.54	7.06	25.01	28.57	2.33	0.83	5.95		13.28	305.8	3	42	55	0	14			5.75		Nov-12
	3.37	12.09	6.24	22.18	23.72	1.61	1.58	5.94		13.16	305.8	3	42	55	0	14				4.00	Nov-12
	3.39	12.07	6.22	22.08	23.76	1.64	1.58	5.95		13.09	305.8	3	42	55	0	14				1.00	Nov-12
	3.73	12.67	7.23	25.87	30.14	2.56	0.58	5.95		13.33	305.8	3	42	55	0	14					Nov-12
	3.37	12.08	6.16	22.18	23.75	1.76	1.58	5.95		13.17	305.8	3	42	55	0	14					Nov-12
	3.52	12.34	6.67	24.00	26.89	1.98	1.08	5.91		13.2	305.8	3	42	55	0	14					Nov-12
	3.59	12.46	6.94	24.85	28.42	2.3	0.83	5.96		13.26	305.8	3	42	55	0	14					Nov-12
	3.72	12.65	7.24	25.86	30.13	2.5	0.58	5.94		13.35	305.8	3	42	55	0	14					Nov-12
	3.72	12.75	7.39	26.27	30.55	2.63	0.44	5.96		13.35	305.8	3	42	55	0	14					Aug-16
	3.93	15.29	6.97	32.17	34.81	2.24	0.85	8.04		15.83	591.8	3	60	36	0	18	18.93	-16.33	5.75		Sep-05
	3.72	14.80	6.18	29.25	29.89	1.54	1.6	7.96		15.59	591.8	3	60	36	0	18	18.37	-16.5		4.00	Sep-05
	3.74	14.90	6.20	29.29	29.92	1.53	1.6	7.95		15.5	591.8	3	60	36	0	18	18.43	-16.63		1.00	Sep-05

	MARKET			FUND TYPE, CATEGORY & OBJECTIVE	RATINGS				MINIMUMS	
Fund Name	Ticker Symbol	Traded On	Fund Type	Category and (Prospectus Objective)	Overall Rating	Reward Rating	Risk Rating	Recent Up/ Downgrade	Open to New Investors	Min Initial Investment
MFS Lifetime 2030 Fund Class I	**MLTIX**	NAS CM	Open End	Target Date (Asset Alloc)	**B**	C+	A-	Up	Y	0
MFS Lifetime 2030 Fund Class R1	**MLTEX**	NAS CM	Open End	Target Date (Asset Alloc)	**B-**	C	B+	Up	Y	0
MFS Lifetime 2030 Fund Class R2	**MLTGX**	NAS CM	Open End	Target Date (Asset Alloc)	**B-**	C	B+	Up	Y	0
MFS Lifetime 2030 Fund Class R3	**MLTHX**	NAS CM	Open End	Target Date (Asset Alloc)	**B-**	C	B+		Y	0
MFS Lifetime 2030 Fund Class R4	**MLTJX**	NAS CM	Open End	Target Date (Asset Alloc)	**B**	C+	A-	Up	Y	0
MFS Lifetime 2030 Fund Class R6	**MLTKX**	NAS CM	Open End	Target Date (Asset Alloc)	**B**	C+	A-	Up	Y	0
MFS Lifetime 2035 Fund Class A	**LFEAX**	NAS CM	Open End	Target Date (Asset Alloc)	**B-**	C	B+	Up	Y	1,000
MFS Lifetime 2035 Fund Class B	**LFEBX**	NAS CM	Open End	Target Date (Asset Alloc)	**B-**	C	B+	Up	Y	1,000
MFS Lifetime 2035 Fund Class C	**LFECX**	NAS CM	Open End	Target Date (Asset Alloc)	**B-**	C	B+	Up	Y	1,000
MFS Lifetime 2035 Fund Class I	**LFEDX**	NAS CM	Open End	Target Date (Asset Alloc)	**B-**	C	B+	Up	Y	0
MFS Lifetime 2035 Fund Class R1	**LFERX**	NAS CM	Open End	Target Date (Asset Alloc)	**B-**	C	B+	Up	Y	0
MFS Lifetime 2035 Fund Class R2	**LFESX**	NAS CM	Open End	Target Date (Asset Alloc)	**B-**	C	B+	Up	Y	0
MFS Lifetime 2035 Fund Class R3	**LFETX**	NAS CM	Open End	Target Date (Asset Alloc)	**B-**	C	B+	Up	Y	0
MFS Lifetime 2035 Fund Class R4	**LFEUX**	NAS CM	Open End	Target Date (Asset Alloc)	**B-**	C	B+	Up	Y	0
MFS Lifetime 2035 Fund Class R6	**LFEKX**	NAS CM	Open End	Target Date (Asset Alloc)	**B-**	C	B+	Up	Y	0
MFS Lifetime 2040 Fund Class A	**MLFAX**	NAS CM	Open End	Target Date (Asset Alloc)	**B-**	C	B	Up	Y	1,000
MFS Lifetime 2040 Fund Class B	**MLFBX**	NAS CM	Open End	Target Date (Asset Alloc)	**B-**	C	B	Up	Y	1,000
MFS Lifetime 2040 Fund Class C	**MLFCX**	NAS CM	Open End	Target Date (Asset Alloc)	**B-**	C	B	Up	Y	1,000
MFS Lifetime 2040 Fund Class I	**MLFIX**	NAS CM	Open End	Target Date (Asset Alloc)	**B-**	C	B	Up	Y	0
MFS Lifetime 2040 Fund Class R1	**MLFEX**	NAS CM	Open End	Target Date (Asset Alloc)	**B-**	C	B	Up	Y	0
MFS Lifetime 2040 Fund Class R2	**MLFGX**	NAS CM	Open End	Target Date (Asset Alloc)	**B-**	C	B	Up	Y	0
MFS Lifetime 2040 Fund Class R3	**MLFHX**	NAS CM	Open End	Target Date (Asset Alloc)	**B-**	C	B	Up	Y	0
MFS Lifetime 2040 Fund Class R4	**MLFJX**	NAS CM	Open End	Target Date (Asset Alloc)	**B-**	C	B	Up	Y	0
MFS Lifetime 2040 Fund Class R6	**MLFKX**	NAS CM	Open End	Target Date (Asset Alloc)	**B-**	C	B	Up	Y	0
MFS Lifetime 2045 Fund Class A	**LTMAX**	NAS CM	Open End	Target Date (Asset Alloc)	**B-**	C	B	Up	Y	1,000
MFS Lifetime 2045 Fund Class B	**LTMBX**	NAS CM	Open End	Target Date (Asset Alloc)	**B-**	C	B	Up	Y	1,000
MFS Lifetime 2045 Fund Class C	**LTMDX**	NAS CM	Open End	Target Date (Asset Alloc)	**B-**	C	B	Up	Y	1,000
MFS Lifetime 2045 Fund Class I	**LTMKX**	NAS CM	Open End	Target Date (Asset Alloc)	**B-**	C	B	Up	Y	0
MFS Lifetime 2045 Fund Class R1	**LTMRX**	NAS CM	Open End	Target Date (Asset Alloc)	**B-**	C	B	Up	Y	0
MFS Lifetime 2045 Fund Class R2	**LTMSX**	NAS CM	Open End	Target Date (Asset Alloc)	**B-**	C	B	Up	Y	0
MFS Lifetime 2045 Fund Class R3	**LTMTX**	NAS CM	Open End	Target Date (Asset Alloc)	**B-**	C	B	Up	Y	0
MFS Lifetime 2045 Fund Class R4	**LTMUX**	NAS CM	Open End	Target Date (Asset Alloc)	**B-**	C	B	Up	Y	0
MFS Lifetime 2045 Fund Class R6	**LTMLX**	NAS CM	Open End	Target Date (Asset Alloc)	**B-**	C	B	Up	Y	0
MFS Lifetime 2050 Fund Class A	**MFFSX**	NAS CM	Open End	Target Date (Asset Alloc)	**B-**	C	B	Up	Y	1,000
MFS Lifetime 2050 Fund Class B	**MFFRX**	NAS CM	Open End	Target Date (Asset Alloc)	**B-**	C	B	Up	Y	1,000
MFS Lifetime 2050 Fund Class C	**MFFDX**	NAS CM	Open End	Target Date (Asset Alloc)	**B-**	C	B	Up	Y	1,000
MFS Lifetime 2050 Fund Class I	**MFFIX**	NAS CM	Open End	Target Date (Asset Alloc)	**B-**	C	B	Up	Y	0
MFS Lifetime 2050 Fund Class R1	**MFFMX**	NAS CM	Open End	Target Date (Asset Alloc)	**B-**	C	B	Up	Y	0
MFS Lifetime 2050 Fund Class R2	**MFFNX**	NAS CM	Open End	Target Date (Asset Alloc)	**B-**	C	B	Up	Y	0
MFS Lifetime 2050 Fund Class R3	**MFFOX**	NAS CM	Open End	Target Date (Asset Alloc)	**B-**	C	B	Up	Y	0
MFS Lifetime 2050 Fund Class R4	**MFFPX**	NAS CM	Open End	Target Date (Asset Alloc)	**B-**	C	B	Up	Y	0
MFS Lifetime 2050 Fund Class R6	**MFFKX**	NAS CM	Open End	Target Date (Asset Alloc)	**B-**	C	B	Up	Y	0
MFS Lifetime 2055 Fund Class A	**LFIAX**	NAS CM	Open End	Target Date (Asset Alloc)	**B-**	C	B	Up	Y	1,000
MFS Lifetime 2055 Fund Class B	**LFIBX**	NAS CM	Open End	Target Date (Asset Alloc)	**B-**	C	B	Up	Y	1,000
MFS Lifetime 2055 Fund Class C	**LFICX**	NAS CM	Open End	Target Date (Asset Alloc)	**B-**	C	B	Up	Y	1,000
MFS Lifetime 2055 Fund Class I	**LFIIX**	NAS CM	Open End	Target Date (Asset Alloc)	**B-**	C	B	Up	Y	0
MFS Lifetime 2055 Fund Class R1	**LFIRX**	NAS CM	Open End	Target Date (Asset Alloc)	**B-**	C	B	Up	Y	0
MFS Lifetime 2055 Fund Class R2	**LFISX**	NAS CM	Open End	Target Date (Asset Alloc)	**B-**	C	B	Up	Y	0
MFS Lifetime 2055 Fund Class R3	**LFITX**	NAS CM	Open End	Target Date (Asset Alloc)	**B-**	C	B	Up	Y	0
MFS Lifetime 2055 Fund Class R4	**LFIUX**	NAS CM	Open End	Target Date (Asset Alloc)	**B-**	C	B	Up	Y	0
MFS Lifetime 2055 Fund Class R6	**LFIKX**	NAS CM	Open End	Target Date (Asset Alloc)	**B-**	C	B	Up	Y	0
MFS Lifetime 2060 Fund Class A	**MFJAX**	NAS CM	Open End	Target Date (Asset Alloc)	**C+**	C	B	Up	Y	1,000

★ Expanded analysis of this fund is included in Section II.

	TOTAL RETURNS					PERFORMANCE				ASSETS		ASSET ALLOCATION & TURNOVER					BULL & BEAR		FEES		
Min Additional Investment	3-Month Total Return	6-Month Total Return	1-Year Total Return	3-Year Total Return	5-Year Total Return	Dividend Yield (TTM)	Expense Ratio	3-Yr Std Deviation	3-Year Beta	NAV	Total Assets (MIL)	%Cash	%Stocks	%Bonds	%Other	Turnover Ratio	Last Bull Market Total Return	Last Bear Market Total Return	Front End Fee (%)	Back End Fee (%)	Inception Date
	3.98	15.37	7.23	32.85	36.22	2.47	0.6	7.97		15.91	591.8	3	60	36	0	18	19.1	-16.18			Sep-05
	3.78	14.90	6.23	29.25	29.90	1.59	1.6	8		15.65	591.8	3	60	36	0	18	18.36	-16.57			Sep-05
	3.91	15.22	6.74	31.29	33.23	2.01	1.1	7.98		15.67	591.8	3	60	36	0	18	18.8	-16.46			Sep-05
	3.95	15.33	7.02	32.22	34.84	2.26	0.85	8.03		15.79	591.8	3	60	36	0	18	18.95	-16.35			Sep-05
	3.98	15.43	7.22	33.22	36.51	2.46	0.6	8.02		15.93	591.8	3	60	36	0	18	19.12	-16.19			Sep-05
	3.98	15.51	7.37	33.70	37.09	2.58	0.46	7.99		15.93	591.8	3	60	36	0	18	19.1	-16.18			Aug-16
	4.06	17.11	6.68	35.59	38.23	2.11	0.87	9.41		15.12	298.6	3	76	21	0	12			5.75		Nov-12
	3.87	16.64	5.89	32.64	33.15	1.33	1.62	9.46		15	298.6	3	76	21	0	12				4.00	Nov-12
	3.89	16.71	5.95	32.60	33.17	1.42	1.62	9.45		14.94	298.6	3	76	21	0	12				1.00	Nov-12
	4.12	17.26	6.94	36.23	39.57	2.33	0.62	9.45		15.15	298.6	3	76	21	0	12					Nov-12
	3.88	16.65	5.90	32.57	33.18	1.46	1.62	9.46		14.99	298.6	3	76	21	0	12					Nov-12
	4.00	16.92	6.41	34.55	36.52	1.77	1.12	9.46		15.06	298.6	3	76	21	0	12					Nov-12
	4.05	17.09	6.71	35.64	38.16	2.09	0.87	9.49		15.14	298.6	3	76	21	0	12					Nov-12
	4.17	17.27	6.99	36.59	39.95	2.32	0.62	9.47		15.21	298.6	3	76	21	0	12					Nov-12
	4.10	17.27	7.08	37.11	40.47	2.45	0.48	9.48		15.21	298.6	3	76	21	0	12					Aug-16
	4.06	17.76	6.44	37.48	39.97	2.08	0.88	10.09		16.64	426.8	3	83	14	0	17	20.21	-17.94	5.75		Sep-05
	3.84	17.28	5.58	34.40	34.71	1.27	1.63	10.06		16.49	426.8	3	83	14	0	17	19.72	-18.22		4.00	Sep-05
	3.89	17.29	5.64	34.40	34.71	1.27	1.63	10.07		16.28	426.8	3	83	14	0	17	19.61	-18.18		1.00	Sep-05
	4.10	17.87	6.68	38.17	41.33	2.25	0.63	10.05		16.75	426.8	3	83	14	0	17	20.36	-17.85			Sep-05
	3.85	17.28	5.63	34.37	34.77	1.29	1.63	10.07		16.42	426.8	3	83	14	0	17	19.59	-18.15			Sep-05
	3.96	17.60	6.09	36.39	38.11	1.78	1.13	10.07		16.5	426.8	3	83	14	0	17	20.06	-18.06			Sep-05
	4.00	17.69	6.37	37.42	39.82	2.03	0.88	10.09		16.63	426.8	3	83	14	0	17	20.2	-17.94			Sep-05
	4.09	17.90	6.66	38.50	41.66	2.24	0.63	10.06		16.79	426.8	3	83	14	0	17	20.38	-17.86			Sep-05
	4.15	17.90	6.75	39.01	42.18	2.37	0.49	10.08		16.79	426.8	3	83	14	0	17	20.36	-17.85			Aug-16
	4.04	18.16	6.22	37.88	40.38	1.92	0.88	10.36		15.68	207.6	3	88	9	0	12			5.75		Nov-12
	3.80	17.62	5.41	34.83	35.15	1.19	1.63	10.37		15.55	207.6	3	88	9	0	12				4.00	Nov-12
	3.82	17.64	5.40	34.71	35.05	1.28	1.63	10.4		15.47	207.6	3	88	9	0	12				1.00	Nov-12
	4.09	18.24	6.44	39.10	42.26	2.17	0.63	10.43		15.75	207.6	3	88	9	0	12					Nov-12
	3.81	17.65	5.40	34.77	35.13	1.46	1.63	10.38		15.53	207.6	3	88	9	0	12					Nov-12
	4.01	17.96	5.91	36.84	38.55	1.65	1.13	10.41		15.56	207.6	3	88	9	0	12					Nov-12
	4.05	18.09	6.18	37.90	40.24	1.95	0.88	10.41		15.66	207.6	3	88	9	0	12					Nov-12
	4.10	18.27	6.43	38.84	41.99	2.16	0.63	10.4		15.73	207.6	3	88	9	0	12					Nov-12
	4.10	18.27	6.60	39.36	42.52	2.3	0.49	10.43		15.73	207.6	3	88	9	0	12					Aug-16
	4.00	18.04	6.15	37.81	40.24	1.92	0.88	10.39		18.97	216.5	3	88	9	0	24	20.15	-17.63	5.75		Sep-10
	3.83	17.62	5.35	34.71	35.06	1.32	1.63	10.38		18.69	216.5	3	88	9	0	24	19.57	-17.91		4.00	Sep-10
	3.85	17.65	5.35	34.70	35.03	1.26	1.63	10.42		18.59	216.5	3	88	9	0	24	19.63	-17.91		1.00	Sep-10
	4.11	18.20	6.43	38.95	42.11	2.14	0.63	10.41		18.96	216.5	3	88	9	0	24	20.43	-17.6			Sep-10
	3.85	17.64	5.39	34.76	35.04	1.24	1.63	10.41		18.6	216.5	3	88	9	0	24	19.61	-17.91			Sep-10
	4.05	18.03	5.97	36.91	38.58	1.73	1.13	10.41		18.72	216.5	3	88	9	0	24	20.09	-17.79			Sep-10
	4.03	18.11	6.22	37.89	40.24	1.95	0.88	10.42		18.84	216.5	3	88	9	0	24	20.11	-17.61			Sep-10
	4.12	18.21	6.45	38.91	42.07	2.15	0.63	10.4		18.95	216.5	3	88	9	0	24	20.43	-17.6			Sep-10
	4.17	18.36	6.62	39.42	42.58	2.29	0.49	10.42		18.95	216.5	3	88	9	0	24	20.43	-17.6			Aug-16
	4.01	18.06	6.15	37.76	40.26	1.9	0.88	10.38		16.08	107.2	3	88	9	0	20			5.75		Nov-12
	3.83	17.66	5.34	34.64	35.02	1.23	1.63	10.4		15.99	107.2	3	88	9	0	20				4.00	Nov-12
	3.79	17.64	5.33	34.60	34.98	1.25	1.63	10.37		15.87	107.2	3	88	9	0	20				1.00	Nov-12
	4.07	18.22	6.43	38.21	41.44	2.13	0.63	10.39		16.09	107.2	3	88	9	0	20					Nov-12
	3.85	17.70	5.41	34.55	34.99	1.44	1.63	10.37		15.89	107.2	3	88	9	0	20					Nov-12
	3.96	17.93	5.88	36.64	38.43	1.67	1.13	10.36		15.98	107.2	3	88	9	0	20					Nov-12
	4.07	18.14	6.22	37.75	40.20	1.91	0.88	10.41		16.08	107.2	3	88	9	0	20					Nov-12
	4.12	18.21	6.47	38.76	42.01	2.12	0.63	10.4		16.16	107.2	3	88	9	0	20					Nov-12
	4.12	18.28	6.57	39.31	42.57	2.26	0.49	10.43		16.17	107.2	3	88	9	0	20					Aug-16
	4.12	18.12	6.25			2.04	0.88			12.38	12.0	2	89	9	0	34			5.75		Dec-16

	MARKET		FUND TYPE, CATEGORY & OBJECTIVE		RATINGS				MINIMUMS	
Fund Name	Ticker Symbol	Traded On	Fund Type	Category and (Prospectus Objective)	Overall Rating	Reward Rating	Risk Rating	Recent Up/ Downgrade	Open to New Investors	Min Initial Investment
MFS Lifetime 2060 Fund Class B	MFJBX	NAS CM	Open End	Target Date (Asset Alloc)	C+	C	B	Up	Y	1,000
MFS Lifetime 2060 Fund Class C	MFJCX	NAS CM	Open End	Target Date (Asset Alloc)	C+	C	B	Up	Y	1,000
MFS Lifetime 2060 Fund Class I	MFJIX	NAS CM	Open End	Target Date (Asset Alloc)	C+	C	B	Up	Y	0
MFS Lifetime 2060 Fund Class R1	MFJEX	NAS CM	Open End	Target Date (Asset Alloc)	C+	C	B	Up	Y	0
MFS Lifetime 2060 Fund Class R2	MFJGX	NAS CM	Open End	Target Date (Asset Alloc)	C+	C	B	Up	Y	0
MFS Lifetime 2060 Fund Class R3	MFJTX	NAS CM	Open End	Target Date (Asset Alloc)	C+	C	B	Up	Y	0
MFS Lifetime 2060 Fund Class R4	MFJUX	NAS CM	Open End	Target Date (Asset Alloc)	C+	C	B	Up	Y	0
MFS Lifetime 2060 Fund Class R6	MFJKX	NAS CM	Open End	Target Date (Asset Alloc)	C+	C	B	Up	Y	0
MFS Lifetime Income Fund Class 529A	MLLQX	NAS CM	Open End	Target Date (Asset Alloc)	B	C+	A-	Up	Y	250
MFS Lifetime Income Fund Class 529B	MLLRX	NAS CM	Open End	Target Date (Asset Alloc)	B-	C	B+		Y	250
MFS Lifetime Income Fund Class 529C	MLLSX	NAS CM	Open End	Target Date (Asset Alloc)	B-	C	B+		Y	250
MFS Lifetime Income Fund Class A	MLLAX	NAS CM	Open End	Target Date (Asset Alloc)	B	C+	A-	Up	Y	1,000
MFS Lifetime Income Fund Class B	MLLBX	NAS CM	Open End	Target Date (Asset Alloc)	B-	C	B+		Y	1,000
MFS Lifetime Income Fund Class C	MLLCX	NAS CM	Open End	Target Date (Asset Alloc)	B-	C	B+		Y	1,000
MFS Lifetime Income Fund Class I	MLLIX	NAS CM	Open End	Target Date (Asset Alloc)	B	C+	A-		Y	0
MFS Lifetime Income Fund Class R1	MLLEX	NAS CM	Open End	Target Date (Asset Alloc)	B-	C	B+		Y	0
MFS Lifetime Income Fund Class R2	MLLGX	NAS CM	Open End	Target Date (Asset Alloc)	B	C+	A-	Up	Y	0
MFS Lifetime Income Fund Class R3	MLLHX	NAS CM	Open End	Target Date (Asset Alloc)	B	C+	A-	Up	Y	0
MFS Lifetime Income Fund Class R4	MLLJX	NAS CM	Open End	Target Date (Asset Alloc)	B	C+	A-		Y	0
MFS Lifetime Income Fund Class R6	MLLKX	NAS CM	Open End	Target Date (Asset Alloc)	B	C+	A-		Y	0
MFS Low Volatility Equity Fund Class A	MLVAX	NAS CM	Open End	US Equity Large Cap Blend (Equity-Income)	B	B-	A-		Y	1,000
MFS Low Volatility Equity Fund Class B	MLVBX	NAS CM	Open End	US Equity Large Cap Blend (Equity-Income)	B	B-	A-		Y	1,000
MFS Low Volatility Equity Fund Class C	MLVGX	NAS CM	Open End	US Equity Large Cap Blend (Equity-Income)	B	B-	A-		Y	1,000
MFS Low Volatility Equity Fund Class I	MLVHX	NAS CM	Open End	US Equity Large Cap Blend (Equity-Income)	B	B-	A-		Y	0
MFS Low Volatility Equity Fund Class R1	MLVMX	NAS CM	Open End	US Equity Large Cap Blend (Equity-Income)	B	B-	A-		Y	0
MFS Low Volatility Equity Fund Class R2	MLVOX	NAS CM	Open End	US Equity Large Cap Blend (Equity-Income)	B	B-	A-		Y	0
MFS Low Volatility Equity Fund Class R3	MLVPX	NAS CM	Open End	US Equity Large Cap Blend (Equity-Income)	B	B-	A-		Y	0
MFS Low Volatility Equity Fund Class R4	MLVRX	NAS CM	Open End	US Equity Large Cap Blend (Equity-Income)	B	B-	A-		Y	0
MFS Low Volatility Equity Fund Class R6	MLVTX	NAS CM	Open End	US Equity Large Cap Blend (Equity-Income)	B	B-	A-		Y	0
MFS Low Volatility Global Equity Fund Class A	MVGAX	NAS CM	Open End	Global Equity Large Cap (World Stock)	B	C+	A-		Y	1,000
MFS Low Volatility Global Equity Fund Class B	MVGBX	NAS CM	Open End	Global Equity Large Cap (World Stock)	B	C+	A-		Y	1,000
MFS Low Volatility Global Equity Fund Class C	MVGCX	NAS CM	Open End	Global Equity Large Cap (World Stock)	B	C+	A-		Y	1,000
MFS Low Volatility Global Equity Fund Class I	MVGIX	NAS CM	Open End	Global Equity Large Cap (World Stock)	B	C+	A-		Y	0
MFS Low Volatility Global Equity Fund Class R1	MVGJX	NAS CM	Open End	Global Equity Large Cap (World Stock)	B	C+	A-		Y	0
MFS Low Volatility Global Equity Fund Class R2	MVGKX	NAS CM	Open End	Global Equity Large Cap (World Stock)	B	C+	A-		Y	0
MFS Low Volatility Global Equity Fund Class R3	MVGLX	NAS CM	Open End	Global Equity Large Cap (World Stock)	B	C+	A-		Y	0
MFS Low Volatility Global Equity Fund Class R4	MVGMX	NAS CM	Open End	Global Equity Large Cap (World Stock)	B	C+	A-		Y	0
MFS Low Volatility Global Equity Fund Class R6	MVGNX	NAS CM	Open End	Global Equity Large Cap (World Stock)	B	C+	A-		Y	0
MFS Managed Wealth Fund Class A	MNWAX	NAS CM	Open End	Long/Short Equity (Growth & Income)	B	C+	B+	Up	Y	1,000
MFS Managed Wealth Fund Class B	MNWBX	NAS CM	Open End	Long/Short Equity (Growth & Income)	B-	C	B	Up	Y	1,000
MFS Managed Wealth Fund Class C	MNWCX	NAS CM	Open End	Long/Short Equity (Growth & Income)	B	C	A-	Up	Y	1,000
MFS Managed Wealth Fund Class I	MNWIX	NAS CM	Open End	Long/Short Equity (Growth & Income)	B	C+	B+	Up	Y	0
MFS Managed Wealth Fund Class R1	MNWRX	NAS CM	Open End	Long/Short Equity (Growth & Income)	B	C	A-	Up	Y	0
MFS Managed Wealth Fund Class R2	MNWSX	NAS CM	Open End	Long/Short Equity (Growth & Income)	B-	C+	B	Up	Y	0
MFS Managed Wealth Fund Class R3	MNWTX	NAS CM	Open End	Long/Short Equity (Growth & Income)	B-	C+	B+		Y	0
MFS Managed Wealth Fund Class R4	MNWUX	NAS CM	Open End	Long/Short Equity (Growth & Income)	B	C+	B+	Up	Y	0
MFS Managed Wealth Fund Class R6	MNWZX	NAS CM	Open End	Long/Short Equity (Growth & Income)	B	C+	A	Up	Y	0
MFS Massachusetts Investors Growth Stock Fund Class 529A	EISTX	NAS CM	Open End	US Equity Large Cap Growth (Growth)	B	B	B+		Y	250
MFS Massachusetts Investors Growth Stock Fund Class 529B	EMIVX	NAS CM	Open End	US Equity Large Cap Growth (Growth)	B	B-	B		Y	250
MFS Massachusetts Investors Growth Stock Fund Class 529C	EMICX	NAS CM	Open End	US Equity Large Cap Growth (Growth)	B	B-	B		Y	250
MFS Massachusetts Investors Growth Stock Fund Class A	MIGFX	NAS CM	Open End	US Equity Large Cap Growth (Growth)	B	B	B+		Y	1,000
MFS Massachusetts Investors Growth Stock Fund Class B	MIGBX	NAS CM	Open End	US Equity Large Cap Growth (Growth)	B	B-	B		Y	1,000

★ Expanded analysis of this fund is included in Section II.

Min Additional Investment	TOTAL RETURNS 3-Month Total Return	6-Month Total Return	1-Year Total Return	3-Year Total Return	5-Year Total Return	PERFORMANCE Dividend Yield (TTM)	Expense Ratio	3-Yr Std Deviation	3-Year Beta	ASSETS NAV	Total Assets (MIL)	ASSET ALLOCATION & TURNOVER %Cash	%Stocks	%Bonds	%Other	Turnover Ratio	BULL & BEAR Last Bull Market Total Return	Last Bear Market Total Return	FEES Front End Fee (%)	Back End Fee (%)	Inception Date
	3.87	17.63	5.39			1.33	1.63			12.34	12.0	2	89	9	0	34				4.00	Dec-16
	3.88	17.68	5.45			1.52	1.63			12.31	12.0	2	89	9	0	34				1.00	Dec-16
	4.10	18.25	6.54			2.07	0.63			12.44	12.0	2	89	9	0	34					Dec-16
	3.85	17.68	5.38			1.12	1.63			12.38	12.0	2	89	9	0	34					Dec-16
	4.04	17.93	5.98			1.89	1.13			12.36	12.0	2	89	9	0	34					Dec-16
	4.11	18.09	6.26			1.91	0.88			12.4	12.0	2	89	9	0	34					Dec-16
	4.10	18.26	6.50			2.11	0.63			12.43	12.0	2	89	9	0	34					Dec-16
	4.18	18.34	6.64			2.15	0.49			12.45	12.0	2	89	9	0	34					Dec-16
	3.16	10.37	6.66	15.88	19.69	2.51	0.85	3.92		10.32	585.6	3	26	70	0	10	8.29	-4.04	4.25		Jan-15
	2.97	9.95	5.87	13.30	15.29	1.79	1.6	3.92		10.32	585.6	3	26	70	0	10	7.83	-4.34		4.00	Jan-15
	2.87	9.84	5.76	13.20	15.19	1.8	1.6	3.95		10.31	585.6	3	26	70	0	10	7.83	-4.34		1.00	Jan-15
	3.10	10.31	6.67	16.00	19.90	2.56	0.8	3.9		12.6	585.6	3	26	70	0	10	8.3	-4.05	4.25		Sep-05
	2.91	9.89	5.87	13.42	15.49	1.84	1.55	3.9		12.6	585.6	3	26	70	0	10	7.93	-4.43		4.00	Sep-05
	2.99	9.98	5.87	13.42	15.49	1.84	1.55	3.92		12.6	585.6	3	26	70	0	10	7.93	-4.35		1.00	Sep-05
	3.16	10.45	6.93	16.87	21.40	2.8	0.55	3.92		12.6	585.6	3	26	70	0	10	8.45	-3.94			Sep-05
	2.99	10.06	5.95	13.50	15.57	1.84	1.55	3.94		12.62	585.6	3	26	70	0	10	7.83	-4.34			Sep-05
	3.12	10.25	6.48	15.12	18.41	2.32	1.05	3.9		12.61	585.6	3	26	70	0	10	8.14	-4.14			Sep-05
	3.10	10.31	6.67	15.99	19.90	2.56	0.8	3.91		12.6	585.6	3	26	70	0	10	8.4	-4.05			Sep-05
	3.16	10.44	6.93	16.87	21.40	2.8	0.55	3.92		12.6	585.6	3	26	70	0	10	8.55	-3.94			Sep-05
	3.26	10.56	7.09	17.53	22.10	2.88	0.45	3.91		12.64	585.6	3	26	70	0	10	8.45	-3.94			Aug-16
	5.79	19.64	16.70	41.48	66.27	1.05	0.89	9.22	0.7	15.9	258.2	1	99	0	0	30			5.75		Dec-13
	5.61	19.24	15.85	38.34	60.14	0.38	1.64	9.21	0.7	15.89	258.2	1	99	0	0	30				4.00	Dec-13
	5.63	19.24	15.85	38.38	60.15	0.4	1.64	9.22	0.7	15.84	258.2	1	99	0	0	30				1.00	Dec-13
	5.92	19.83	17.05	42.68	68.42	1.27	0.64	9.2	0.7	15.92	258.2	1	99	0	0	30					Dec-13
	5.60	19.19	15.81	38.43	60.23	0.38	1.64	9.2	0.7	15.93	258.2	1	99	0	0	30					Dec-13
	5.77	19.47	16.40	40.42	64.38	0.82	1.14	9.2	0.7	15.98	258.2	1	99	0	0	30					Dec-13
	5.84	19.63	16.70	41.58	66.38	1.04	0.89	9.2	0.7	15.96	258.2	1	99	0	0	30					Dec-13
	5.91	19.80	17.02	42.62	68.40	1.26	0.64	9.22	0.7	15.93	258.2	1	99	0	0	30					Dec-13
	5.86	19.85	17.04	43.02	69.09	1.34	0.57	9.22	0.7	15.93	258.2	1	99	0	0	30					Dec-13
	3.03	12.87	10.10	28.40	42.23	1.65	0.99	7.78	0.61	13.81	242.4	1	99	0	0	41			5.75		Dec-13
	2.87	12.47	9.32	25.52	36.73	0.93	1.74	7.81	0.61	13.73	242.4	1	99	0	0	41				4.00	Dec-13
	2.82	12.41	9.29	25.45	36.73	0.97	1.74	7.85	0.61	13.71	242.4	1	99	0	0	41				1.00	Dec-13
	3.16	12.98	10.43	29.35	43.82	1.86	0.74	7.82	0.61	13.81	242.4	1	99	0	0	41					Dec-13
	2.88	12.53	9.31	25.46	36.80	0.96	1.74	7.79	0.6	13.79	242.4	1	99	0	0	41					Dec-13
	3.04	12.72	9.88	27.38	40.24	1.39	1.24	7.8	0.61	13.82	242.4	1	99	0	0	41					Dec-13
	3.10	12.93	10.14	28.31	42.08	1.62	0.99	7.8	0.61	13.83	242.4	1	99	0	0	41					Dec-13
	3.08	12.98	10.34	29.34	43.65	1.86	0.74	7.78	0.6	13.81	242.4	1	99	0	0	41					Dec-13
	3.10	13.03	10.43	29.47	43.86	1.92	0.68	7.81	0.61	13.79	242.4	1	99	0	0	41					Dec-13
	2.79	7.39	6.33	15.22	16.65	0.34	1.43	2.66	2.76	11.04	41.4	80	39	3	-22	18			5.75		Jun-14
	2.56	6.83	5.37	12.26	11.52	0	2.18	2.68	3.2	10.78	41.4	80	39	3	-22	18				4.00	Jun-14
	2.58	6.87	5.40	12.21	11.54	0	2.18	2.66	3.64	10.73	41.4	80	39	3	-22	18				1.00	Jun-14
	2.88	7.47	6.48	15.64	17.30	0.4	1.18	2.67	3.04	11.07	41.4	80	39	3	-22	18					Jun-14
	2.56	6.83	5.37	12.26	11.52	0	2.18	2.66	3.7	10.78	41.4	80	39	3	-22	18					Jun-14
	2.80	7.21	5.97	14.03	14.49	0	1.68	2.68	3.51	10.99	41.4	80	39	3	-22	18					Jun-14
	2.79	7.28	6.23	14.90	15.91	0.17	1.43	2.69	3.66	11.05	41.4	80	39	3	-22	18					Jun-14
	2.88	7.47	6.48	15.79	17.34	0.4	1.18	2.69	3.57	11.07	41.4	80	39	3	-22	18					Jun-14
	2.88	7.47	6.50	15.64	17.30	0.41	1.15	2.67	3.98	11.07	41.4	80	39	3	-22	18					Oct-17
	5.32	24.84	18.29	65.49	81.16	0.81	0.78	12.26	0.88	30.85	7,515	2	98	0	0	18	22.32	-13.19	5.75		Jul-02
	5.06	24.25	17.36	62.06	74.67	0.5	1.53	12.27	0.89	25.92	7,515	2	98	0	0	18	21.84	-13.41		4.00	Jul-02
	5.03	24.26	17.26	61.56	74.13	0.27	1.53	12.27	0.89	25.66	7,515	2	98	0	0	18	21.85	-13.45		1.00	Jul-02
	5.33	24.88	18.34	65.68	81.49	0.81	0.73	12.27	0.89	31.37	7,515	2	98	0	0	18	22.36	-13.13	5.75		Jan-35
	5.09	24.35	17.39	61.94	74.75	0.21	1.48	12.27	0.89	26.81	7,515	2	98	0	0	18	21.87	-13.45		4.00	Sep-93

	MARKET			FUND TYPE, CATEGORY & OBJECTIVE	RATINGS				MINIMUMS	
Fund Name	Ticker Symbol	Traded On	Fund Type	Category and (Prospectus Objective)	Overall Rating	Reward Rating	Risk Rating	Recent Up/ Downgrade	Open to New Investors	Min Initial Investment
MFS Massachusetts Investors Growth Stock Fund Class C	MIGDX	NAS CM	Open End	US Equity Large Cap Growth (Growth)	B	B-	B		Y	1,000
MFS Massachusetts Investors Growth Stock Fund Class I	MGTIX	NAS CM	Open End	US Equity Large Cap Growth (Growth)	B	B	B+		Y	0
MFS Massachusetts Investors Growth Stock Fund Class R1	MIGMX	NAS CM	Open End	US Equity Large Cap Growth (Growth)	B	B-	B		Y	0
MFS Massachusetts Investors Growth Stock Fund Class R2	MIRGX	NAS CM	Open End	US Equity Large Cap Growth (Growth)	B	B	B+		Y	0
MFS Massachusetts Investors Growth Stock Fund Class R3	MIGHX	NAS CM	Open End	US Equity Large Cap Growth (Growth)	B	B	B+		Y	0
MFS Massachusetts Investors Growth Stock Fund Class R4	MIGKX	NAS CM	Open End	US Equity Large Cap Growth (Growth)	B	B	B+		Y	0
MFS Massachusetts Investors Growth Stock Fund Class R6	MIGNX	NAS CM	Open End	US Equity Large Cap Growth (Growth)	B	B	B+		Y	0
MFS Massachusetts Investors Trust Class 529A	EAMTX	NAS CM	Open End	US Equity Large Cap Blend (Growth)	B-	C+	B	Down	Y	250
MFS Massachusetts Investors Trust Class 529B	EBMTX	NAS CM	Open End	US Equity Large Cap Blend (Growth)	B-	C+	B	Down	Y	250
MFS Massachusetts Investors Trust Class 529C	ECITX	NAS CM	Open End	US Equity Large Cap Blend (Growth)	B-	C+	B		Y	250
MFS Massachusetts Investors Trust Class A	MITTX	NAS CM	Open End	US Equity Large Cap Blend (Growth)	B	C+	B		Y	1,000
MFS Massachusetts Investors Trust Class B	MITBX	NAS CM	Open End	US Equity Large Cap Blend (Growth)	B-	C+	B		Y	1,000
MFS Massachusetts Investors Trust Class C	MITCX	NAS CM	Open End	US Equity Large Cap Blend (Growth)	B-	C+	B		Y	1,000
MFS Massachusetts Investors Trust Class I	MITIX	NAS CM	Open End	US Equity Large Cap Blend (Growth)	B	C+	B		Y	0
MFS Massachusetts Investors Trust Class R1	MITGX	NAS CM	Open End	US Equity Large Cap Blend (Growth)	B-	C+	B		Y	0
MFS Massachusetts Investors Trust Class R2	MIRTX	NAS CM	Open End	US Equity Large Cap Blend (Growth)	B-	C+	B	Down	Y	0
MFS Massachusetts Investors Trust Class R3	MITHX	NAS CM	Open End	US Equity Large Cap Blend (Growth)	B-	C+	B	Down	Y	0
MFS Massachusetts Investors Trust Class R4	MITDX	NAS CM	Open End	US Equity Large Cap Blend (Growth)	B	C+	B		Y	0
MFS Massachusetts Investors Trust Class R6	MITJX	NAS CM	Open End	US Equity Large Cap Blend (Growth)	B	C+	B		Y	0
MFS Mid Cap Growth Fund Class 529A	EAMCX	NAS CM	Open End	US Equity Mid Cap (Growth)	B	B	B		Y	250
MFS Mid Cap Growth Fund Class 529B	EBCGX	NAS CM	Open End	US Equity Mid Cap (Growth)	B	B	B		Y	250
MFS Mid Cap Growth Fund Class 529C	ECGRX	NAS CM	Open End	US Equity Mid Cap (Growth)	B	B	B		Y	250
MFS Mid Cap Growth Fund Class A	OTCAX	NAS CM	Open End	US Equity Mid Cap (Growth)	B	B	B		Y	1,000
MFS Mid Cap Growth Fund Class B	OTCBX	NAS CM	Open End	US Equity Mid Cap (Growth)	B	B	B		Y	1,000
MFS Mid Cap Growth Fund Class C	OTCCX	NAS CM	Open End	US Equity Mid Cap (Growth)	B	B	B		Y	1,000
MFS Mid Cap Growth Fund Class I	OTCIX	NAS CM	Open End	US Equity Mid Cap (Growth)	B	B	B		Y	0
MFS Mid Cap Growth Fund Class R1	OTCGX	NAS CM	Open End	US Equity Mid Cap (Growth)	B	B	B		Y	0
MFS Mid Cap Growth Fund Class R2	MCPRX	NAS CM	Open End	US Equity Mid Cap (Growth)	B	B	B		Y	0
MFS Mid Cap Growth Fund Class R3	OTCHX	NAS CM	Open End	US Equity Mid Cap (Growth)	B	B	B		Y	0
MFS Mid Cap Growth Fund Class R4	OTCJX	NAS CM	Open End	US Equity Mid Cap (Growth)	B	B	B		Y	0
MFS Mid Cap Growth Fund Class R6	OTCKX	NAS CM	Open End	US Equity Mid Cap (Growth)	B	B	B		Y	0
MFS Mid Cap Value Fund Class 529A	EACVX	NAS CM	Open End	US Equity Mid Cap (Growth)	C+	C	B	Up		250
MFS Mid Cap Value Fund Class 529B	EBCVX	NAS CM	Open End	US Equity Mid Cap (Growth)	C+	C	B	Up		250
MFS Mid Cap Value Fund Class 529C	ECCVX	NAS CM	Open End	US Equity Mid Cap (Growth)	C+	C	B	Up		250
MFS Mid Cap Value Fund Class A	MVCAX	NAS CM	Open End	US Equity Mid Cap (Growth)	C+	C	B	Up	Y	1,000
MFS Mid Cap Value Fund Class B	MCBVX	NAS CM	Open End	US Equity Mid Cap (Growth)	C+	C	B	Up	Y	1,000
MFS Mid Cap Value Fund Class C	MVCCX	NAS CM	Open End	US Equity Mid Cap (Growth)	C+	C	B	Up	Y	1,000
MFS Mid Cap Value Fund Class I	MCVIX	NAS CM	Open End	US Equity Mid Cap (Growth)	C+	C	B	Up	Y	0
MFS Mid Cap Value Fund Class R1	MVCGX	NAS CM	Open End	US Equity Mid Cap (Growth)	C+	C	B	Up	Y	0
MFS Mid Cap Value Fund Class R2	MCVRX	NAS CM	Open End	US Equity Mid Cap (Growth)	C+	C	B	Up	Y	0
MFS Mid Cap Value Fund Class R3	MVCHX	NAS CM	Open End	US Equity Mid Cap (Growth)	C+	C	B	Up	Y	0
MFS Mid Cap Value Fund Class R4	MVCJX	NAS CM	Open End	US Equity Mid Cap (Growth)	C+	C	B	Up	Y	0
MFS Mid Cap Value Fund Class R6	MVCKX	NAS CM	Open End	US Equity Mid Cap (Growth)	C+	C	B	Up	Y	0
MFS Moderate Allocation Fund Class 529A	EAMDX	NAS CM	Open End	Moderate Alloc (Asset Alloc)	B	C+	A-	Up	Y	250
MFS Moderate Allocation Fund Class 529B	EBMDX	NAS CM	Open End	Moderate Alloc (Asset Alloc)	B	C+	A-	Up	Y	250
MFS Moderate Allocation Fund Class 529C	ECMAX	NAS CM	Open End	Moderate Alloc (Asset Alloc)	B	C+	A-	Up	Y	250
MFS Moderate Allocation Fund Class A	MAMAX	NAS CM	Open End	Moderate Alloc (Asset Alloc)	B	C+	A-	Up	Y	1,000
MFS Moderate Allocation Fund Class B	MMABX	NAS CM	Open End	Moderate Alloc (Asset Alloc)	B	C+	A-	Up	Y	1,000
MFS Moderate Allocation Fund Class C	MMACX	NAS CM	Open End	Moderate Alloc (Asset Alloc)	B	C+	A-	Up	Y	1,000
MFS Moderate Allocation Fund Class I	MMAIX	NAS CM	Open End	Moderate Alloc (Asset Alloc)	B	C+	A-		Y	0
MFS Moderate Allocation Fund Class R1	MAMFX	NAS CM	Open End	Moderate Alloc (Asset Alloc)	B	C+	A-	Up	Y	0
MFS Moderate Allocation Fund Class R2	MARRX	NAS CM	Open End	Moderate Alloc (Asset Alloc)	B	C+	A-	Up	Y	0

★ Expanded analysis of this fund is included in Section II.

	TOTAL RETURNS					PERFORMANCE				ASSETS		ASSET ALLOCATION & TURNOVER					BULL & BEAR		FEES		
Min Additional Investment	3-Month Total Return	6-Month Total Return	1-Year Total Return	3-Year Total Return	5-Year Total Return	Dividend Yield (TTM)	Expense Ratio	3-Yr Std Deviation	3-Year Beta	NAV	Total Assets (MIL)	%Cash	%Stocks	%Bonds	%Other	Turnover Ratio	Last Bull Market Total Return	Last Bear Market Total Return	Front End Fee (%)	Back End Fee (%)	Inception Date
	5.09	24.33	17.36	61.91	74.65	0	1.48	12.27	0.89	26.62	7,515	2	98	0	0	18	21.88	-13.44		1.00	Nov-97
	5.40	25.04	18.63	66.91	83.68	0.98	0.48	12.26	0.88	32.35	7,515	2	98	0	0	18	22.55	-13.04			Jan-97
	5.09	24.32	17.37	61.85	74.64	0.28	1.48	12.27	0.89	26.22	7,515	2	98	0	0	18	21.87	-13.47			Apr-05
	5.25	24.70	18.01	64.40	79.11	0.45	0.98	12.28	0.89	30.44	7,515	2	98	0	0	18	22.22	-13.26			Oct-03
	5.29	24.84	18.28	65.62	81.32	0.78	0.73	12.28	0.89	31	7,515	2	98	0	0	18	22.46	-13.21			Apr-05
	5.40	25.02	18.60	66.86	83.64	1	0.48	12.29	0.89	31.62	7,515	2	98	0	0	18	22.56	-13.06			Apr-05
	5.43	25.06	18.70	67.40	84.61	1.07	0.38	12.29	0.89	32.38	7,515	2	98	0	0	18	22.36	-13.13			Jun-12
	5.32	21.88	12.88	52.65	62.64	0.88	0.76	11.92	0.96	31.1	5,716	1	99	0	0	13	25.03	-17.95	5.75		Jul-02
	5.04	21.31	12.49	50.18	58.02	0.93	1.51	11.85	0.96	29.08	5,716	1	99	0	0	13	24.48	-18.22		4.00	Jul-02
	5.11	21.40	12.03	49.21	56.56	0.26	1.51	11.9	0.96	28.66	5,716	1	99	0	0	13	24.49	-18.19		1.00	Jul-02
	5.34	21.93	12.98	52.95	63.09	0.89	0.71	11.9	0.96	32	5,716	1	99	0	0	13	25.02	-17.89	5.75		Jul-24
	5.11	21.46	12.09	49.45	56.90	0.16	1.46	11.92	0.96	30.93	5,716	1	99	0	0	13	24.51	-18.14		4.00	Sep-93
	5.14	21.47	12.12	49.46	56.93	0.18	1.46	11.91	0.96	30.26	5,716	1	99	0	0	13	24.48	-18.16		1.00	Jul-96
	5.40	22.07	13.23	54.04	65.02	1.12	0.46	11.93	0.96	31.02	5,716	1	99	0	0	13	25.25	-17.82			Jan-97
	5.14	21.45	12.06	49.46	56.90	0.16	1.46	11.9	0.96	30.06	5,716	1	99	0	0	13	24.46	-18.15			Apr-05
	5.25	21.76	12.63	51.72	60.91	0.67	0.96	11.91	0.96	30.32	5,716	1	99	0	0	13	24.85	-17.99			Oct-03
	5.36	21.91	12.94	52.89	62.96	0.88	0.71	11.91	0.96	31.68	5,716	1	99	0	0	13	25.09	-17.93			Apr-05
	5.41	22.05	13.24	53.97	64.95	1.09	0.46	11.92	0.96	32.32	5,716	1	99	0	0	13	25.26	-17.84			Apr-05
	5.45	22.14	13.32	54.41	65.72	1.21	0.38	11.94	0.96	31.02	5,716	1	99	0	0	13	25.02	-17.89			Jun-12
	9.06	30.87	17.24	71.58	90.50	0	1.18	13.35	0.89	19.37	5,405	2	98	0	0	33	23.3	-19.73	5.75		Jul-02
	8.90	30.32	16.32	67.65	83.29	0	1.93	13.36	0.9	15.9	5,405	2	98	0	0	33	22.65	-19.84		4.00	Jul-02
	8.91	30.31	16.34	67.74	83.33	0	1.93	13.37	0.9	15.39	5,405	2	98	0	0	33	22.77	-19.95		1.00	Jul-02
	9.11	30.82	17.23	71.73	90.74	0	1.13	13.37	0.9	19.99	5,405	2	98	0	0	33	23.27	-19.69	5.75		Dec-93
	8.93	30.43	16.40	67.91	83.72	0	1.88	13.39	0.9	16.33	5,405	2	98	0	0	33	22.58	-19.95		4.00	Dec-93
	8.95	30.42	16.42	68.00	83.76	0	1.88	13.38	0.9	15.82	5,405	2	98	0	0	33	22.67	-19.86		1.00	Aug-94
	9.19	31.07	17.57	73.14	93.11	0	0.88	13.4	0.9	21.26	5,405	2	98	0	0	33	23.32	-19.55			Jan-97
	8.91	30.41	16.41	67.94	83.68	0	1.88	13.38	0.9	16.25	5,405	2	98	0	0	33	22.82	-20.02			Apr-05
	9.00	30.71	16.94	70.44	88.29	0	1.38	13.37	0.9	18.77	5,405	2	98	0	0	33	23.06	-19.75			Oct-03
	9.12	30.82	17.23	71.66	90.62	0	1.13	13.36	0.9	19.86	5,405	2	98	0	0	33	23.27	-19.69			Apr-05
	9.20	31.06	17.54	73.03	93.13	0	0.88	13.36	0.9	20.76	5,405	2	98	0	0	33	23.39	-19.6			Apr-05
	9.23	31.10	17.68	73.62	94.15	0	0.77	13.38	0.9	21.41	5,405	2	98	0	0	33	23.27	-19.69			Jan-13
	4.54	20.78	5.49	32.89	36.70	0.74	1.13	13.32	1	22.78	8,561	2	98	0	0	26	25.08	-20.98	5.75		Jul-02
	4.41	20.34	4.71	29.95	31.56	0.11	1.88	13.34	1	21.06	8,561	2	98	0	0	26	24.48	-21.14		4.00	Jul-02
	4.28	20.23	4.61	29.85	31.60	0	1.88	13.33	1	21.15	8,561	2	98	0	0	26	24.37	-21.12		1.00	Jul-02
	4.55	20.73	5.50	33.02	36.87	0.77	1.08	13.37	1	23.17	8,561	2	98	0	0	26	24.96	-20.85	5.75		Aug-01
	4.35	20.30	4.73	30.07	31.84	0.01	1.83	13.33	1	21.8	8,561	2	98	0	0	26	24.54	-21.14		4.00	Nov-01
	4.37	20.34	4.74	30.09	31.86	0	1.83	13.33	1	21.71	8,561	2	98	0	0	26	24.47	-21.16		1.00	Nov-01
	4.61	20.89	5.77	34.01	38.60	0.98	0.83	13.34	1	23.78	8,561	2	98	0	0	26	25.26	-20.81			Nov-01
	4.35	20.32	4.74	30.06	31.86	0.13	1.83	13.34	1	21.31	8,561	2	98	0	0	26	24.49	-21.13			Apr-05
	4.52	20.64	5.25	32.08	35.19	0.39	1.33	13.33	1	22.62	8,561	2	98	0	0	26	24.93	-21.01			Oct-03
	4.52	20.76	5.47	32.98	36.89	0.73	1.08	13.33	1	23.09	8,561	2	98	0	0	26	25.01	-20.85			Apr-05
	4.62	20.91	5.79	34.04	38.61	0.98	0.83	13.36	1	23.3	8,561	2	98	0	0	26	25.22	-20.8			Apr-05
	4.65	21.03	5.92	34.63	39.66	1.1	0.69	13.36	1	23.82	8,561	2	98	0	0	26	24.96	-20.85			Feb-13
	4.43	15.41	8.39	28.85	32.09	1.93	1.01	7.18	0.55	18.18	5,626	3	56	41	0	2	14.3	-10.77	5.75		Jul-02
	4.26	15.01	7.65	26.03	27.21	1.24	1.76	7.16	0.55	17.87	5,626	3	56	41	0	2	13.88	-11.06		4.00	Jul-02
	4.25	15.02	7.61	25.99	27.22	1.28	1.76	7.18	0.55	17.73	5,626	3	56	41	0	2	13.86	-11.07		1.00	Jul-02
	4.42	15.48	8.44	29.05	32.38	1.95	0.96	7.17	0.55	18.28	5,626	3	56	41	0	2	14.35	-10.76	5.75		Jun-02
	4.28	15.05	7.65	26.21	27.53	1.26	1.71	7.19	0.55	18.07	5,626	3	56	41	0	2	13.85	-11.01		4.00	Jun-02
	4.20	14.99	7.62	26.17	27.45	1.29	1.71	7.16	0.55	17.93	5,626	3	56	41	0	2	13.84	-11.02		1.00	Jun-02
	4.47	15.57	8.71	30.02	34.00	2.15	0.71	7.2	0.55	18.54	5,626	3	56	41	0	2	14.57	-10.68			Jun-02
	4.25	15.02	7.64	26.11	27.43	1.35	1.71	7.16	0.55	17.53	5,626	3	56	41	0	2	13.86	-11.08			Apr-05
	4.40	15.31	8.18	28.09	30.71	1.76	1.21	7.18	0.55	17.87	5,626	3	56	41	0	2	14.15	-10.79			Oct-03

	MARKET		FUND TYPE, CATEGORY & OBJECTIVE		RATINGS				MINIMUMS	
Fund Name	Ticker Symbol	Traded On	Fund Type	Category and (Prospectus Objective)	Overall Rating	Reward Rating	Risk Rating	Recent Up/ Downgrade	Open to New Investors	Min Initial Investment
MFS Moderate Allocation Fund Class R3	MAMHX	NAS CM	Open End	Moderate Alloc (Asset Alloc)	B	C+	A-	Up	Y	0
MFS Moderate Allocation Fund Class R4	MAMJX	NAS CM	Open End	Moderate Alloc (Asset Alloc)	B	C+	A-		Y	0
MFS New Discovery Fund Class A	MNDAX	NAS CM	Open End	US Equity Small Cap (Growth)	B-	C+	B-	Down	Y	1,000
MFS New Discovery Fund Class B	MNDBX	NAS CM	Open End	US Equity Small Cap (Growth)	C+	C+	B-	Down	Y	1,000
MFS New Discovery Fund Class C	MNDCX	NAS CM	Open End	US Equity Small Cap (Growth)	C+	C+	B-	Down	Y	1,000
MFS New Discovery Fund Class I	MNDIX	NAS CM	Open End	US Equity Small Cap (Growth)	B-	C+	B-	Down	Y	0
MFS New Discovery Fund Class R1	MNDGX	NAS CM	Open End	US Equity Small Cap (Growth)	C+	C+	B-	Down	Y	0
MFS New Discovery Fund Class R2	MNDRX	NAS CM	Open End	US Equity Small Cap (Growth)	B-	C+	B-	Down	Y	0
MFS New Discovery Fund Class R3	MNDHX	NAS CM	Open End	US Equity Small Cap (Growth)	B-	C+	B-	Down	Y	0
MFS New Discovery Fund Class R4	MNDJX	NAS CM	Open End	US Equity Small Cap (Growth)	B-	C+	B-	Down	Y	0
MFS New Discovery Fund Class R6	MNDKX	NAS CM	Open End	US Equity Small Cap (Growth)	B-	C+	B-	Down	Y	0
MFS New Discovery Value Fund Class A	NDVAX	NAS CM	Open End	US Equity Small Cap (Growth)	C+	C	B-	Down	Y	1,000
MFS New Discovery Value Fund Class B	NDVBX	NAS CM	Open End	US Equity Small Cap (Growth)	C+	C	B-		Y	1,000
MFS New Discovery Value Fund Class C	NDVCX	NAS CM	Open End	US Equity Small Cap (Growth)	C+	C	B-		Y	1,000
MFS New Discovery Value Fund Class I	NDVIX	NAS CM	Open End	US Equity Small Cap (Growth)	C+	C	B-	Down	Y	0
MFS New Discovery Value Fund Class R1	NDVRX	NAS CM	Open End	US Equity Small Cap (Growth)	C+	C	B-		Y	0
MFS New Discovery Value Fund Class R2	NDVSX	NAS CM	Open End	US Equity Small Cap (Growth)	C+	C	B-		Y	0
MFS New Discovery Value Fund Class R3	NDVTX	NAS CM	Open End	US Equity Small Cap (Growth)	C+	C	B-	Down	Y	0
MFS New Discovery Value Fund Class R4	NDVUX	NAS CM	Open End	US Equity Small Cap (Growth)	C+	C	B-	Down	Y	0
MFS New Discovery Value Fund Class R6	NDVVX	NAS CM	Open End	US Equity Small Cap (Growth)	C+	C	B-	Down	Y	0
MFS Prudent Investor Fund Class A	FPPAX	NAS CM	Open End	Global Fixed Income (Growth & Income)	D	D+	B		Y	1,000
MFS Prudent Investor Fund Class B	FPPDX	NAS CM	Open End	Global Fixed Income (Growth & Income)	D	D+	B		Y	1,000
MFS Prudent Investor Fund Class C	FPPEX	NAS CM	Open End	Global Fixed Income (Growth & Income)	D	D+	B		Y	1,000
MFS Prudent Investor Fund Class I	FPPJX	NAS CM	Open End	Global Fixed Income (Growth & Income)	D	D+	B		Y	0
MFS Prudent Investor Fund Class R1	FPPRX	NAS CM	Open End	Global Fixed Income (Growth & Income)	D	D+	B		Y	0
MFS Prudent Investor Fund Class R2	FPPSX	NAS CM	Open End	Global Fixed Income (Growth & Income)	D	D+	B		Y	0
MFS Prudent Investor Fund Class R3	FPPQX	NAS CM	Open End	Global Fixed Income (Growth & Income)	D	D+	B		Y	0
MFS Prudent Investor Fund Class R4	FPPUX	NAS CM	Open End	Global Fixed Income (Growth & Income)	D	D+	B		Y	0
MFS Prudent Investor Fund Class R6	FPPVX	NAS CM	Open End	Global Fixed Income (Growth & Income)	D	D+	B		Y	0
MFS Research Fund Class A	MFRFX	NAS CM	Open End	US Equity Large Cap Blend (Growth & Income)	B-	C+	B	Down	Y	1,000
MFS Research Fund Class B	MFRBX	NAS CM	Open End	US Equity Large Cap Blend (Growth & Income)	B-	C+	B		Y	1,000
MFS Research Fund Class C	MFRCX	NAS CM	Open End	US Equity Large Cap Blend (Growth & Income)	B-	C+	B		Y	1,000
MFS Research Fund Class I	MRFIX	NAS CM	Open End	US Equity Large Cap Blend (Growth & Income)	B-	C+	B	Down	Y	0
MFS Research Fund Class R1	MFRLX	NAS CM	Open End	US Equity Large Cap Blend (Growth & Income)	B-	C+	B		Y	0
MFS Research Fund Class R2	MSRRX	NAS CM	Open End	US Equity Large Cap Blend (Growth & Income)	B-	C+	B	Down	Y	0
MFS Research Fund Class R3	MFRHX	NAS CM	Open End	US Equity Large Cap Blend (Growth & Income)	B-	C+	B	Down	Y	0
MFS Research Fund Class R4	MFRJX	NAS CM	Open End	US Equity Large Cap Blend (Growth & Income)	B-	C+	B	Down	Y	0
MFS Research Fund Class R6	MFRKX	NAS CM	Open End	US Equity Large Cap Blend (Growth & Income)	B-	C+	B	Down	Y	0
MFS Research International Fund Class 529A	EARSX	NAS CM	Open End	Global Equity Large Cap (Foreign Stock)	C	C	B		Y	250
MFS Research International Fund Class 529B	EBRIX	NAS CM	Open End	Global Equity Large Cap (Foreign Stock)	C	C	B-		Y	250
MFS Research International Fund Class 529C	ECRIX	NAS CM	Open End	Global Equity Large Cap (Foreign Stock)	C	C	B-		Y	250
MFS Research International Fund Class A	MRSAX	NAS CM	Open End	Global Equity Large Cap (Foreign Stock)	C	C	B		Y	1,000
MFS Research International Fund Class B	MRIBX	NAS CM	Open End	Global Equity Large Cap (Foreign Stock)	C	C	B-		Y	1,000
MFS Research International Fund Class C	MRICX	NAS CM	Open End	Global Equity Large Cap (Foreign Stock)	C	C	B-		Y	1,000
MFS Research International Fund Class I	MRSIX	NAS CM	Open End	Global Equity Large Cap (Foreign Stock)	C	C	B		Y	0
MFS Research International Fund Class R1	MRSGX	NAS CM	Open End	Global Equity Large Cap (Foreign Stock)	C	C	B-		Y	0
MFS Research International Fund Class R2	MRSRX	NAS CM	Open End	Global Equity Large Cap (Foreign Stock)	C	C	B		Y	0
MFS Research International Fund Class R3	MRSHX	NAS CM	Open End	Global Equity Large Cap (Foreign Stock)	C	C	B		Y	0
MFS Research International Fund Class R4	MRSJX	NAS CM	Open End	Global Equity Large Cap (Foreign Stock)	C	C	B		Y	0
MFS Research International Fund Class R6	MRSKX	NAS CM	Open End	Global Equity Large Cap (Foreign Stock)	C	C	B		Y	0
MFS Special Value Trust	MFV	NYSE	Closed End	Cautious Alloc (Income)	C	C+	C-		Y	
MFS Technology Fund Class A	MTCAX	NAS CM	Open End	Technology Sector Equity (Technology)	B-	B-	B-	Down	Y	1,000

★ Expanded analysis of this fund is included in Section II.

Min Additional Investment	TOTAL RETURNS 3-Month Total Return	6-Month Total Return	1-Year Total Return	3-Year Total Return	5-Year Total Return	PERFORMANCE Dividend Yield (TTM)	Expense Ratio	3-Yr Std Deviation	3-Year Beta	ASSETS NAV	Total Assets (MIL)	ASSET ALLOCATION & TURNOVER %Cash	%Stocks	%Bonds	%Other	Turnover Ratio	BULL & BEAR Last Bull Market Total Return	Last Bear Market Total Return	FEES Front End Fee (%)	Back End Fee (%)	Inception Date
	4.45	15.48	8.45	28.99	32.35	1.97	0.96	7.18	0.55	18.13	5,626	3	56	41	0	2	14.37	-10.76			Apr-05
	4.54	15.63	8.72	29.98	34.01	2.18	0.71	7.18	0.55	18.26	5,626	3	56	41	0	2	14.58	-10.66			Apr-05
	8.94	32.57	13.02	78.26	63.30	0	1.32	15.58	0.86	28.12	1,451	2	98	0	0	67	26.8	-27.35	5.75		Jan-97
	8.73	32.06	12.19	74.28	57.31	0	2.07	15.58	0.86	21.17	1,451	2	98	0	0	67	26.31	-27.56		4.00	Nov-97
	8.76	32.10	12.20	74.22	57.28	0	2.07	15.59	0.86	21.23	1,451	2	98	0	0	67	26.28	-27.6		1.00	Nov-97
	9.01	32.73	13.29	79.59	65.32	0	1.07	15.6	0.86	31.91	1,451	2	98	0	0	67	27.04	-27.29			Jan-97
	8.71	32.07	12.16	74.28	57.28	0	2.07	15.6	0.86	20.96	1,451	2	98	0	0	67	26.24	-27.55			Apr-05
	8.85	32.39	12.72	76.87	61.23	0	1.57	15.6	0.86	25.95	1,451	2	98	0	0	67	26.66	-27.42			Oct-03
	8.92	32.59	12.99	78.17	63.21	0	1.32	15.58	0.86	28.07	1,451	2	98	0	0	67	26.81	-27.33			Apr-05
	9.00	32.75	13.29	79.72	65.48	0	1.07	15.59	0.86	30.03	1,451	2	98	0	0	67	26.99	-27.28			Apr-05
	9.05	32.85	13.42	80.16	66.34	0	0.96	15.6	0.86	32.27	1,451	2	98	0	0	67	27.04	-27.29			Jun-12
	3.54	19.87	2.48	44.43	48.05	0.25	1.28	15.76	0.88	15.5	2,904	2	98	0	0	57	35.56		5.75		May-11
	3.41	19.41	1.79	41.29	42.61	0	2.03	15.75	0.88	14.82	2,904	2	98	0	0	57	34.92			4.00	May-11
	3.36	19.44	1.74	41.25	42.54	0	2.03	15.77	0.89	14.74	2,904	2	98	0	0	57	34.99			1.00	May-11
	3.65	20.07	2.79	45.63	49.84	0.46	1.03	15.74	0.88	15.61	2,904	2	98	0	0	57	35.91				May-11
	3.41	19.50	1.79	41.30	42.61	0	2.03	15.74	0.88	14.83	2,904	2	98	0	0	57	35.05				May-11
	3.48	19.72	2.30	43.47	46.22	0.09	1.53	15.79	0.89	15.42	2,904	2	98	0	0	57	35.41				May-11
	3.53	19.81	2.48	44.51	48.07	0.25	1.28	15.78	0.89	15.54	2,904	2	98	0	0	57	35.57				May-11
	3.64	20.04	2.80	45.60	49.91	0.48	1.03	15.73	0.88	15.63	2,904	2	98	0	0	57	35.74				May-11
	3.71	20.12	2.88	46.15	50.71	0.55	0.92	15.74	0.88	15.64	2,904	2	98	0	0	57	35.91				Jul-12
	2.11	9.61	6.62			1.19	1.24			10.6	16.8	24	46	30	0	6			5.75		Jan-18
	1.83	9.20	5.84			0.49	1.99			10.56	16.8	24	46	30	0	6				4.00	Jan-18
	1.83	9.12	5.82			0.84	1.99			10.52	16.8	24	46	30	0	6				1.00	Jan-18
	2.11	9.72	6.81			1.36	0.99			10.61	16.8	24	46	30	0	6					Jan-18
	1.83	9.09	5.81			0.47	1.99			10.56	16.8	24	46	30	0	6					Jan-18
	2.02	9.40	6.30			0.92	1.49			10.59	16.8	24	46	30	0	6					Jan-18
	2.02	9.50	6.56			1.14	1.24			10.6	16.8	24	46	30	0	6					Jan-18
	2.11	9.60	6.81			1.36	0.99			10.61	16.8	24	46	30	0	6					Jan-18
	2.21	9.71	6.91			1.37	0.95			10.62	16.8	24	46	30	0	6					Jan-18
	5.91	22.44	12.01	51.70	64.41	0.58	0.82	12.02	0.97	43.69	5,837	1	99	0	0	33	25.12	-16.87	5.75		Oct-71
	5.71	21.97	11.14	48.30	58.31	0.11	1.57	12.01	0.97	39.19	5,837	1	99	0	0	33	24.63	-17.16		4.00	Sep-93
	5.70	21.98	11.14	48.27	58.33	0	1.57	12.01	0.97	38.89	5,837	1	99	0	0	33	24.58	-17.14		1.00	Jan-94
	5.97	22.58	12.24	52.78	66.42	0.99	0.57	12.03	0.97	44.88	5,837	1	99	0	0	33	25.28	-16.81			Jan-97
	5.71	21.96	11.13	48.25	58.28	0.17	1.57	12.02	0.97	38.09	5,837	1	99	0	0	33	24.63	-17.16			Apr-05
	5.85	22.27	11.71	50.54	62.33	0.49	1.07	12.01	0.97	42.1	5,837	1	99	0	0	33	24.99	-17.01			Oct-03
	5.91	22.44	11.99	51.68	64.36	0.74	0.82	12.02	0.97	43.32	5,837	1	99	0	0	33	25.11	-16.89			Apr-05
	5.96	22.58	12.24	52.81	66.42	0.99	0.57	12.03	0.97	43.69	5,837	1	99	0	0	33	25.32	-16.84			Apr-05
	5.97	22.60	12.33	53.18	67.13	1.08	0.48	12.02	0.97	43.6	5,837	1	99	0	0	33	25.26	-16.85			May-06
	4.51	17.29	2.11	33.13	12.83	3.95	1.14	11.24	0.99	18.04	8,816	2	98	0	0	25	13.65	-22.03	5.75		Jul-02
	4.29	16.78	1.34	30.13	8.59	3.36	1.89	11.23	0.99	16.98	8,816	2	98	0	0	25	13.12	-22.29		4.00	Jul-02
	4.32	16.85	1.38	30.20	8.65	3.43	1.89	11.25	0.99	16.64	8,816	2	98	0	0	25	13.15	-22.25		1.00	Jul-02
	4.54	17.32	2.20	33.34	13.04	3.89	1.09	11.28	1	18.42	8,816	2	98	0	0	25	13.6	-21.96	5.75		Jan-97
	4.34	16.90	1.46	30.36	8.88	3.12	1.84	11.26	0.99	17.77	8,816	2	98	0	0	25	13.12	-22.24		4.00	Jan-98
	4.34	16.88	1.47	30.41	8.89	3.07	1.84	11.27	0.99	17.31	8,816	2	98	0	0	25	13.2	-22.28		1.00	Jan-98
	4.60	17.47	2.44	34.30	14.47	3.98	0.84	11.24	0.99	19.09	8,816	2	98	0	0	25	13.83	-21.91			Jan-97
	4.30	16.87	1.36	30.33	8.83	3.43	1.84	11.22	0.99	16.97	8,816	2	98	0	0	25	13.17	-22.24			Apr-05
	4.40	17.13	1.91	32.27	11.59	3.71	1.34	11.23	0.99	17.77	8,816	2	98	0	0	25	13.46	-22.06			Oct-03
	4.53	17.32	2.18	33.34	13.01	3.89	1.09	11.24	0.99	18.22	8,816	2	98	0	0	25	13.71	-22.02			Apr-05
	4.53	17.44	2.42	34.23	14.38	4.13	0.84	11.26	0.99	18.45	8,816	2	98	0	0	25	13.87	-21.92			Apr-05
	4.56	17.52	2.51	34.68	14.96	4.27	0.74	11.24	0.99	18.31	8,816	2	98	0	0	25	13.76	-21.95			May-06
	4.19	14.75	9.94	29.10	31.52	2.86		6.92	1.38	5.57	39.7	4	40	56	0	33	14.48	-11.49			Nov-89
	6.05	27.25	9.99	92.65	127.79	0	1.23	15.54	1.04	44.82	1,278	3	97	0	0	30	24.04	-12.5	5.75		Jan-97

	MARKET			FUND TYPE, CATEGORY & OBJECTIVE	RATINGS				MINIMUMS	
Fund Name	Ticker Symbol	Traded On	Fund Type	Category and (Prospectus Objective)	Overall Rating	Reward Rating	Risk Rating	Recent Up/ Downgrade	Open to New Investors	Min Initial Investment
MFS Technology Fund Class B	MTCBX	NAS CM	Open End	Technology Sector Equity (Technology)	C+	C+	B-	Down	Y	1,000
MFS Technology Fund Class C	MTCCX	NAS CM	Open End	Technology Sector Equity (Technology)	C+	C+	B-	Down	Y	1,000
MFS Technology Fund Class I	MTCIX	NAS CM	Open End	Technology Sector Equity (Technology)	B-	B-	B-	Down	Y	0
MFS Technology Fund Class R1	MTCKX	NAS CM	Open End	Technology Sector Equity (Technology)	C+	C+	B-	Down	Y	0
MFS Technology Fund Class R2	MTERX	NAS CM	Open End	Technology Sector Equity (Technology)	B-	C+	B-	Down	Y	0
MFS Technology Fund Class R3	MTCHX	NAS CM	Open End	Technology Sector Equity (Technology)	B-	B-	B-	Down	Y	0
MFS Technology Fund Class R4	MTCJX	NAS CM	Open End	Technology Sector Equity (Technology)	B-	B-	B-	Down	Y	0
MFS Technology Fund Class R6	MTCLX	NAS CM	Open End	Technology Sector Equity (Technology)	B-	B-	B-	Down	Y	0
MFS Total Return Fund Class 529A	EATRX	NAS CM	Open End	Moderate Alloc (Balanced)	B-	C	A-		Y	250
MFS Total Return Fund Class 529B	EBTRX	NAS CM	Open End	Moderate Alloc (Balanced)	B-	C	B+	Up	Y	250
MFS Total Return Fund Class 529C	ECTRX	NAS CM	Open End	Moderate Alloc (Balanced)	B-	C	B+	Up	Y	250
MFS Total Return Fund Class A	MSFRX	NAS CM	Open End	Moderate Alloc (Balanced)	B-	C	A-		Y	1,000
MFS Total Return Fund Class B	MTRBX	NAS CM	Open End	Moderate Alloc (Balanced)	B-	C	B+	Up	Y	1,000
MFS Total Return Fund Class C	MTRCX	NAS CM	Open End	Moderate Alloc (Balanced)	B-	C	B+	Up	Y	1,000
MFS Total Return Fund Class I	MTRIX	NAS CM	Open End	Moderate Alloc (Balanced)	B	C+	A-	Up	Y	0
MFS Total Return Fund Class R1	MSFFX	NAS CM	Open End	Moderate Alloc (Balanced)	B-	C	B+	Up	Y	0
MFS Total Return Fund Class R2	MTRRX	NAS CM	Open End	Moderate Alloc (Balanced)	B-	C	B+	Up	Y	0
MFS Total Return Fund Class R3	MSFHX	NAS CM	Open End	Moderate Alloc (Balanced)	B-	C	A-		Y	0
MFS Total Return Fund Class R4	MSFJX	NAS CM	Open End	Moderate Alloc (Balanced)	B	C+	A-	Up	Y	0
MFS Total Return Fund Class R6	MSFKX	NAS CM	Open End	Moderate Alloc (Balanced)	B	C+	A-	Up	Y	0
MFS Utilities Fund Class A	MMUFX	NAS CM	Open End	Utilities Sector Equity (Utility)	B	B	A-		Y	1,000
MFS Utilities Fund Class B	MMUBX	NAS CM	Open End	Utilities Sector Equity (Utility)	B	B	B+		Y	1,000
MFS Utilities Fund Class C	MMUCX	NAS CM	Open End	Utilities Sector Equity (Utility)	B	B	B+		Y	1,000
MFS Utilities Fund Class I	MMUIX	NAS CM	Open End	Utilities Sector Equity (Utility)	B	B	A-		Y	0
MFS Utilities Fund Class R1	MMUGX	NAS CM	Open End	Utilities Sector Equity (Utility)	B	B	B+		Y	0
MFS Utilities Fund Class R2	MURRX	NAS CM	Open End	Utilities Sector Equity (Utility)	B	B	B+		Y	0
MFS Utilities Fund Class R3	MMUHX	NAS CM	Open End	Utilities Sector Equity (Utility)	B	B	A-		Y	0
MFS Utilities Fund Class R4	MMUJX	NAS CM	Open End	Utilities Sector Equity (Utility)	B	B	A-		Y	0
MFS Utilities Fund Class R6	MMUKX	NAS CM	Open End	Utilities Sector Equity (Utility)	B+	B	A-		Y	0
MFS Value Fund Class 529A	EAVLX	NAS CM	Open End	US Equity Large Cap Value (Growth)	B-	C	B	Up	Y	250
MFS Value Fund Class 529B	EBVLX	NAS CM	Open End	US Equity Large Cap Value (Growth)	B-	C	B	Up	Y	250
MFS Value Fund Class 529C	ECVLX	NAS CM	Open End	US Equity Large Cap Value (Growth)	B-	C	B	Up	Y	250
MFS Value Fund Class A	MEIAX	NAS CM	Open End	US Equity Large Cap Value (Growth)	B-	C	B	Up	Y	1,000
MFS Value Fund Class B	MFEBX	NAS CM	Open End	US Equity Large Cap Value (Growth)	B-	C	B	Up	Y	1,000
MFS Value Fund Class C	MEICX	NAS CM	Open End	US Equity Large Cap Value (Growth)	B-	C	B	Up	Y	1,000
MFS Value Fund Class I	MEIIX	NAS CM	Open End	US Equity Large Cap Value (Growth)	B-	C	B	Up	Y	0
MFS Value Fund Class R1	MEIGX	NAS CM	Open End	US Equity Large Cap Value (Growth)	B-	C	B	Up	Y	0
MFS Value Fund Class R2	MVRRX	NAS CM	Open End	US Equity Large Cap Value (Growth)	B-	C	B	Up	Y	0
MFS Value Fund Class R3	MEIHX	NAS CM	Open End	US Equity Large Cap Value (Growth)	B-	C	B	Up	Y	0
MFS Value Fund Class R4	MEIJX	NAS CM	Open End	US Equity Large Cap Value (Growth)	B-	C	B	Up	Y	0
MFS Value Fund Class R6	MEIKX	NAS CM	Open End	US Equity Large Cap Value (Growth)	B-	C	B	Up	Y	0
MH Elite Fund of Funds Fund	MHEFX	NAS CM	Open End	Aggressive Alloc (Growth)	C+	C	B	Up	Y	10,000
MH Elite Select Portfolio of Funds Fund	MHESX	NAS CM	Open End	Global Equity Large Cap (Growth)	C	C-	B		Y	10,000
MH Elite Small Capital Fund of Funds	MHELX	NAS CM	Open End	Aggressive Alloc (Small Company)	C	C	C+		Y	10,000
Midas Fund	MIDSX	NAS CM	Open End	Precious Metals Sector Equity (Precious Metals)	C-	D+	C-		Y	1,000
Miles Capital Alternatives Advantage Fund Class I	MILIX	NAS CM	Open End	Multialternative (Growth)	C	C-	C+	Up	Y	50,000
Miller Convertible Bond Fund Class A	MCFAX	NAS CM	Open End	Convertibles (Convertible Bond)	B-	C	B+	Up	Y	2,500
Miller Convertible Bond Fund Class C	MCFCX	NAS CM	Open End	Convertibles (Convertible Bond)	C+	C	B	Up	Y	2,500
Miller Convertible Bond Fund Class I	MCIFX	NAS CM	Open End	Convertibles (Convertible Bond)	B-	C	B+	Up	Y	1,000,000
Miller Convertible Plus Fund Class A	MCPAX	NAS CM	Open End	Convertibles (Convertible Bond)	C+	C	B	Up	Y	2,500
Miller Convertible Plus Fund Class C	MCCCX	NAS CM	Open End	Convertibles (Convertible Bond)	C+	C	B	Up	Y	2,500
Miller Convertible Plus Fund Class I	MCPIX	NAS CM	Open End	Convertibles (Convertible Bond)	C+	C	B	Up	Y	1,000,000

★ Expanded analysis of this fund is included in Section II.

	TOTAL RETURNS					PERFORMANCE				ASSETS		ASSET ALLOCATION & TURNOVER					BULL & BEAR		FEES		
Min Additional Investment	3-Month Total Return	6-Month Total Return	1-Year Total Return	3-Year Total Return	5-Year Total Return	Dividend Yield (TTM)	Expense Ratio	3-Yr Std Deviation	3-Year Beta	NAV	Total Assets (MIL)	%Cash	%Stocks	%Bonds	%Other	Turnover Ratio	Last Bull Market Total Return	Last Bear Market Total Return	Front End Fee (%)	Back End Fee (%)	Inception Date
	5.86	26.79	9.18	88.37	119.35	0	1.98	15.53	1.04	38.28	1,278	3	97	0	0	30	23.42	-12.7		4.00	Apr-00
	5.87	26.78	9.17	88.36	119.39	0	1.98	15.54	1.04	38.2	1,278	3	97	0	0	30	23.46	-12.72		1.00	Apr-00
	6.13	27.41	10.27	94.14	130.59	0	0.98	15.57	1.04	48.1	1,278	3	97	0	0	30	24.16	-12.37			Jan-97
	5.85	26.81	9.19	88.42	119.32	0	1.98	15.55	1.04	38.12	1,278	3	97	0	0	30	23.51	-12.74			Apr-05
	6.00	27.12	9.73	91.25	124.93	0	1.48	15.56	1.04	42.56	1,278	3	97	0	0	30	23.81	-12.54			Oct-03
	6.06	27.27	9.99	92.65	127.70	0	1.23	15.56	1.04	44.8	1,278	3	97	0	0	30	24.04	-12.45			Apr-05
	6.14	27.45	10.27	94.14	130.56	0	0.98	15.56	1.04	46.8	1,278	3	97	0	0	30	24.16	-12.36			Apr-05
	6.15	27.50	10.38	94.73	131.72	0	0.89	15.57	1.04	48.45	1,278	3	97	0	0	30	24.04	-12.5			Jan-13
	3.72	13.36	8.57	24.01	32.59	1.93	0.79	7.22	0.58	19.13	7,506	3	59	38	0	33	15.12	-10.36	5.75		Jul-02
	3.61	13.04	7.86	21.36	27.74	1.23	1.54	7.23	0.58	19.22	7,506	3	59	38	0	33	14.57	-10.57		4.00	Jul-02
	3.48	12.92	7.76	21.20	27.65	1.17	1.54	7.21	0.57	19.3	7,506	3	59	38	0	33	14.6	-10.64		1.00	Jul-02
	3.72	13.40	8.64	24.22	32.90	1.96	0.74	7.24	0.58	19.19	7,506	3	59	38	0	33	15.2	-10.38	5.75		Oct-70
	3.52	12.95	7.80	21.40	27.98	1.23	1.49	7.22	0.58	19.22	7,506	3	59	38	0	33	14.69	-10.61		4.00	Aug-93
	3.49	13.00	7.81	21.39	27.97	1.22	1.49	7.24	0.58	19.32	7,506	3	59	38	0	33	14.63	-10.62		1.00	Aug-94
	3.78	13.57	8.91	25.10	34.50	2.19	0.49	7.21	0.57	19.18	7,506	3	59	38	0	33	15.37	-10.23			Jan-97
	3.52	13.00	7.83	21.37	27.92	1.24	1.49	7.24	0.58	19.16	7,506	3	59	38	0	33	14.65	-10.61			Apr-05
	3.64	13.25	8.33	23.22	31.21	1.7	0.99	7.23	0.58	19.25	7,506	3	59	38	0	33	14.91	-10.39			Oct-03
	3.71	13.39	8.63	24.17	32.83	1.95	0.74	7.25	0.58	19.2	7,506	3	59	38	0	33	15.19	-10.31			Apr-05
	3.78	13.55	8.90	25.12	34.59	2.19	0.49	7.23	0.58	19.21	7,506	3	59	38	0	33	15.36	-10.22			Apr-05
	3.80	13.62	9.00	25.41	35.12	2.27	0.4	7.22	0.58	19.19	7,506	3	59	38	0	33	15.2	-10.38			Jun-12
	3.18	16.82	14.12	31.31	22.90	2.22	1	8.62	0.39	22.36	3,322	4	95	0	0	23	14.64	-12.3	5.75		Feb-92
	2.95	16.35	13.22	28.37	18.31	1.53	1.75	8.6	0.39	22.24	3,322	4	95	0	0	23	14.15	-12.56		4.00	Sep-93
	2.95	16.35	13.22	28.38	18.33	1.53	1.75	8.61	0.39	22.24	3,322	4	95	0	0	23	14.22	-12.61		1.00	Jan-94
	3.23	16.97	14.39	32.31	24.42	2.44	0.75	8.64	0.39	22.45	3,322	4	95	0	0	23	14.83	-12.18			Jan-97
	2.96	16.40	13.22	28.36	18.30	1.55	1.75	8.61	0.39	22.19	3,322	4	95	0	0	23	14.17	-12.58			Apr-05
	3.07	16.65	13.76	30.33	21.29	2	1.25	8.6	0.39	22.29	3,322	4	95	0	0	23	14.45	-12.36			Oct-03
	3.18	16.82	14.12	31.32	22.90	2.22	1	8.6	0.39	22.35	3,322	4	95	0	0	23	14.66	-12.31			Apr-05
	3.24	16.97	14.39	32.36	24.38	2.45	0.75	8.62	0.39	22.38	3,322	4	95	0	0	23	14.8	-12.2			Apr-05
	3.20	16.97	14.43	32.67	24.95	2.52	0.66	8.62	0.39	22.45	3,322	4	95	0	0	23	14.64	-12.3			Jun-12
	5.00	19.30	10.52	35.73	48.70	1.88	0.88	12.28	0.99	41	48,073	1	99	0	0	11	25.08	-18.02	5.75		Jul-02
	4.81	18.99	10.28	34.31	45.40	1.66	1.63	12.25	0.99	40.55	48,073	1	99	0	0	11	24.51	-18.21		4.00	Jul-02
	4.79	18.83	9.66	32.58	42.96	1.18	1.63	12.25	0.99	40.35	48,073	1	99	0	0	11	24.51	-18.25		1.00	Jul-02
	5.01	19.32	10.55	35.77	48.77	1.88	0.83	12.27	0.99	41.35	48,073	1	99	0	0	11	25.11	-17.97	5.75		Jan-96
	4.79	18.85	9.71	32.76	43.27	1.15	1.58	12.25	0.99	41.17	48,073	1	99	0	0	11	24.5	-18.22		4.00	Nov-97
	4.80	18.85	9.72	32.74	43.30	1.18	1.58	12.26	0.99	40.88	48,073	1	99	0	0	11	24.57	-18.23		1.00	Nov-97
	5.07	19.47	10.82	36.82	50.65	2.1	0.58	12.26	0.99	41.58	48,073	1	99	0	0	11	25.24	-17.86			Jan-97
	4.80	18.85	9.71	32.76	43.31	1.21	1.58	12.25	0.99	40.55	48,073	1	99	0	0	11	24.53	-18.22			Apr-05
	4.92	19.15	10.27	34.78	46.93	1.65	1.08	12.27	0.99	40.92	48,073	1	99	0	0	11	24.9	-18.06			Oct-03
	5.01	19.31	10.54	35.79	48.76	1.88	0.83	12.27	0.99	41.18	48,073	1	99	0	0	11	25.08	-17.97			Apr-05
	5.07	19.46	10.83	36.84	50.65	2.11	0.58	12.27	0.99	41.34	48,073	1	99	0	0	11	25.26	-17.89			Apr-05
	5.10	19.52	10.92	37.22	51.40	2.21	0.48	12.26	0.99	41.33	48,073	1	99	0	0	11	25.17	-17.89			May-06
1,000	3.29	16.67	4.54	39.42	36.04	0	1.9	12.1	0.97	6.89	13.1	11	87	1	1	37	21.87	-20.14			Jan-04
1,000	2.70	12.92	-1.92	19.21	6.33	0.23	2.11	10.03	0.84	5.71	5.6	15	86	-3	2	35	11.95	-20.76			Apr-06
1,000	3.91	16.65	-2.80	34.63	23.47	0	2	14.34	0.83	7.17	7.1	13	90	-4	1	62	26.74	-25.68			Sep-98
100	12.92	22.42	15.92	-5.75	-18.12	0	4.29	23.74	0.06	1.31	16.9	0	90	0	10	38	-20.98	-26.05			Jan-86
1,000	0.90	4.98	-0.40	2.74		0.11	3.61	4.35	15.45	10.05	13.2	36	24	19	16	10					Mar-16
100	4.32	10.14	2.85	17.52	17.75	1.89	1.45	6.37	-0.07	12.62	803.0	-3	0	7	4	107	12.42	-15.19	5.75		Dec-07
100	4.22	9.99	2.44	15.81	14.90	1.58	1.95	6.36	-0.06	12.52	803.0	-3	0	7	4	107	12.14	-15.33			Dec-09
100	4.45	10.50	3.46	19.33	20.82	2.38	0.95	6.38	-0.06	12.61	803.0	-3	0	7	4	107	12.83	-15.01			Dec-07
100	6.68	14.56	2.87	26.25		0.4	3.73	9.41	-0.14	23.08	120.1	1	0	-38	0	141			5.75		Dec-14
100	6.49	14.19	2.11	23.42		0.04	4.49	9.39	-0.13	22.76	120.1	1	0	-38	0	141					Dec-14
100	6.73	14.73	3.12	27.18		0.64	3.47	9.37	-0.13	23.05	120.1	1	0	-38	0	141					Dec-14

	MARKET			FUND TYPE, CATEGORY & OBJECTIVE	RATINGS				MINIMUMS	
Fund Name	Ticker Symbol	Traded On	Fund Type	Category and (Prospectus Objective)	Overall Rating	Reward Rating	Risk Rating	Recent Up/ Downgrade	Open to New Investors	Min Initial Investment
Miller Income Fund Class A	LMCJX	NAS CM	Open End	Aggressive Alloc (Income)	C	C-	C+		Y	1,000
Miller Income Fund Class C	LCMNX	NAS CM	Open End	Aggressive Alloc (Income)	C	C-	C+		Y	1,000
Miller Income Fund Class FI	LMCKX	NAS CM	Open End	Aggressive Alloc (Income)	C	C-	C+		Y	0
Miller Income Fund Class I	LMCLX	NAS CM	Open End	Aggressive Alloc (Income)	C	C-	C+		Y	1,000,000
Miller Income Fund Class IS	LMCMX	NAS CM	Open End	Aggressive Alloc (Income)	C	C-	C+		Y	1,000,000
Miller Opportunity Trust Class A	LGOAX	NAS CM	Open End	US Equity Mid Cap (Growth)	C	C-	C		Y	1,000
Miller Opportunity Trust Class C	LMOPX	NAS CM	Open End	US Equity Mid Cap (Growth)	C-	D+	C	Down	Y	1,000
Miller Opportunity Trust Class FI	LMOFX	NAS CM	Open End	US Equity Mid Cap (Growth)	C	C-	C		Y	0
Miller Opportunity Trust Class I	LMNOX	NAS CM	Open End	US Equity Mid Cap (Growth)	C	C-	C		Y	1,000,000
Miller Opportunity Trust Class IS	MVISX	NAS CM	Open End	US Equity Mid Cap (Growth)	C	C-	C		Y	1,000,000
Miller Opportunity Trust Class R	LMORX	NAS CM	Open End	US Equity Mid Cap (Growth)	C	D+	C		Y	0
Miller/Howard Drill Bit to Burner Tip® Adviser Cls Shares	DBBDX	NAS CM	Open End	Energy Sector Equity (Growth & Income)	D+	D	C	Down	Y	2,500
Miller/Howard Drill Bit to Burner Tip® Fund Class I Shares	DBBEX	NAS CM	Open End	Energy Sector Equity (Growth & Income)	D+	D	C	Down	Y	100,000
Miller/Howard High Income Equity	HIE	NYSE	Closed End	US Equity Mid Cap (Growth & Income)	C	C	C-		Y	
Miller/Howard Income-Equity Fund Adviser Class Shares	MHIDX	NAS CM	Open End	US Equity Large Cap Value (Equity-Income)	C+	C	B		Y	2,500
Miller/Howard Income-Equity Fund Class I Shares	MHIEX	NAS CM	Open End	US Equity Large Cap Value (Equity-Income)	C+	C	B		Y	100,000
MIP International Tilts Master Portfolio	US5763536019		Open End	Global Equity Large Cap (Foreign Stock)	U	U	U		Y	0
Mirae Asset Asia Fund Class A	MALAX	NAS CM	Open End	Asia ex-Japan Equity (Pacific Stock)	C	C	C	Up	Y	2,000
Mirae Asset Asia Fund Class C	MCLAX	NAS CM	Open End	Asia ex-Japan Equity (Pacific Stock)	C	C	C	Up	Y	2,000
Mirae Asset Asia Fund Class I	MILAX	NAS CM	Open End	Asia ex-Japan Equity (Pacific Stock)	C	C	C	Up	Y	250,000
Mirae Asset Emerging Markets Fund Class A	MALGX	NAS CM	Open End	Global Emerg Mkts (Div Emerging Mkts)	C	C	C+		Y	2,000
Mirae Asset Emerging Markets Fund Class C	MCLGX	NAS CM	Open End	Global Emerg Mkts (Div Emerging Mkts)	C	C	C		Y	2,000
Mirae Asset Emerging Markets Fund Class I	MILGX	NAS CM	Open End	Global Emerg Mkts (Div Emerging Mkts)	C	C	C+		Y	250,000
Mirae Asset Emerging Markets Great Consumer Fund Class A	MECGX	NAS CM	Open End	Global Emerg Mkts (Div Emerging Mkts)	C	C	C+		Y	2,000
Mirae Asset Emerging Markets Great Consumer Fund Class C	MCCGX	NAS CM	Open End	Global Emerg Mkts (Div Emerging Mkts)	C	C	C+		Y	2,000
Mirae Asset Emerging Markets Great Consumer Fund Class I	MICGX	NAS CM	Open End	Global Emerg Mkts (Div Emerging Mkts)	C	C	C+		Y	250,000
Mirova Global Sustainable Equity Fund Class A	ESGMX	NAS CM	Open End	Global Equity Large Cap (Growth)	B-	C+	B	Up	Y	2,500
Mirova Global Sustainable Equity Fund Class C	ESGCX	NAS CM	Open End	Global Equity Large Cap (Growth)	B-	C	B	Up	Y	2,500
Mirova Global Sustainable Equity Fund Class N	ESGNX	NAS CM	Open End	Global Equity Large Cap (Growth)	C+	C	B		Y	1,000,000
Mirova Global Sustainable Equity Fund Class Y	ESGYX	NAS CM	Open End	Global Equity Large Cap (Growth)	B-	C+	B	Up	Y	100,000
Mirova International Sustainable Equity Fund Class A	MRVAX	NAS CM	Open End	Global Equity Large Cap (Foreign Stock)	U	U	U		Y	2,500
Mirova International Sustainable Equity Fund Class N	MRVNX	NAS CM	Open End	Global Equity Large Cap (Foreign Stock)	U	U	U		Y	1,000,000
Mirova International Sustainable Equity Fund Class Y	MRVYX	NAS CM	Open End	Global Equity Large Cap (Foreign Stock)	U	U	U		Y	100,000
Mission-Auour Risk-Managed Global Equity Fund Class A	OURAX	NAS CM	Open End	Global Equity Large Cap (Growth)	D+	D+	D	Up	Y	1,000
Mission-Auour Risk-Managed Global Equity Fund Class Z	OURZX	NAS CM	Open End	Global Equity Large Cap (Growth)	C+	C	B	Up	Y	10,000,000
Mission-Auour Risk-Managed Global Equity Institutional Cls	OURIX	NAS CM	Open End	Global Equity Large Cap (Growth)	C+	C	B	Up	Y	100,000
Mission-Auour Risk-Managed Global Equity Investor Cls	OURLX	NAS CM	Open End	Global Equity Large Cap (Growth)	D+	D+	C+	Up	Y	1,000
MM MSCI EAFE® International Index Administrative Cls	MKRYX	NAS CM	Open End	Global Equity Large Cap (Growth)	C	C	B		Y	0
MM MSCI EAFE® International Index Fund Class A	MKRAX	NAS CM	Open End	Global Equity Large Cap (Growth)	C	C	B		Y	0
MM MSCI EAFE® International Index Fund Class I	MKRZX	NAS CM	Open End	Global Equity Large Cap (Growth)	C	C	B		Y	0
MM MSCI EAFE® International Index Fund Class R3	MKRTX	NAS CM	Open End	Global Equity Large Cap (Growth)	C	C	B		Y	0
MM MSCI EAFE® International Index Fund Class R4	MKRFX	NAS CM	Open End	Global Equity Large Cap (Growth)	C	C	B		Y	0
MM MSCI EAFE® International Index Fund Class R5	MKRIX	NAS CM	Open End	Global Equity Large Cap (Growth)	C	C	B		Y	0
MM MSCI EAFE® International Index Service Cls shares	MKRSX	NAS CM	Open End	Global Equity Large Cap (Growth)	C	C	B		Y	0
MM Russell 2000® Small Cap Index Fund Administrative Class	MCJYX	NAS CM	Open End	US Equity Small Cap (Small Company)	C	C	C+		Y	0
MM Russell 2000® Small Cap Index Fund Class A	MCJAX	NAS CM	Open End	US Equity Small Cap (Small Company)	C	C	C+		Y	0
MM Russell 2000® Small Cap Index Fund Class I	MCJZX	NAS CM	Open End	US Equity Small Cap (Small Company)	C	C	C+		Y	0
MM Russell 2000® Small Cap Index Fund Class R3	MCJTX	NAS CM	Open End	US Equity Small Cap (Small Company)	C	C	C+		Y	0
MM Russell 2000® Small Cap Index Fund Class R4	MCJFX	NAS CM	Open End	US Equity Small Cap (Small Company)	C	C	C+		Y	0
MM Russell 2000® Small Cap Index Fund Class R5	MCJIX	NAS CM	Open End	US Equity Small Cap (Small Company)	C	C	C+		Y	0
MM Russell 2000® Small Cap Index Fund Service Class shares	MCJSX	NAS CM	Open End	US Equity Small Cap (Small Company)	C	C	C+		Y	0
MM S&P 500® Index Fund Class A	MMFFX	NAS CM	Open End	US Equity Large Cap Blend (Growth & Income)	B-	C	B		Y	0

★ Expanded analysis of this fund is included in Section II.

	TOTAL RETURNS					PERFORMANCE				ASSETS		ASSET ALLOCATION & TURNOVER					BULL & BEAR		FEES		
Min Additional Investment	3-Month Total Return	6-Month Total Return	1-Year Total Return	3-Year Total Return	5-Year Total Return	Dividend Yield (TTM)	Expense Ratio	3-Yr Std Deviation	3-Year Beta	NAV	Total Assets (MIL)	%Cash	%Stocks	%Bonds	%Other	Turnover Ratio	Last Bull Market Total Return	Last Bear Market Total Return	Front End Fee (%)	Back End Fee (%)	Inception Date
50	0.48	10.89	-7.87	32.31	9.28	8.34	2.11	14.34	2.31	7.68	196.5	0	77	23	0	37			5.75		Feb-14
50	0.30	10.51	-8.58	29.45	5.38	7.56	2.86	14.34	2.32	7.67	196.5	0	77	23	0	37				1.00	Feb-14
	0.36	10.78	-7.95	32.07	9.01	8.21	2.11	14.31	2.3	7.65	196.5	0	77	23	0	37					Feb-14
	0.56	11.07	-7.63	33.56	10.84	8.64	1.81	14.36	2.32	7.67	196.5	0	77	23	0	37					Feb-14
	0.58	11.12	-7.43	33.97	11.43	8.75	1.71	14.36	2.31	7.67	196.5	0	77	23	0	37					Feb-14
50	1.14	15.15	-6.59	64.03	34.47	0	1.4	25.08	1.8	24.77	1,509	0	99	0	1	30	32.04	-38.54	5.75		Feb-09
50	0.96	14.67	-7.29	60.40	29.50	0	2.14	25.06	1.8	23.13	1,509	0	99	0	1	30	31.37	-38.78		1.00	Dec-99
	1.10	15.05	-6.68	63.86	34.15	0	1.42	25.06	1.8	25.53	1,509	0	99	0	1	30	32.13	-38.65			Feb-04
	1.20	15.25	-6.35	65.31	36.26	0	1.15	25.06	1.8	26.98	1,509	0	99	0	1	30	32.22	-38.44			Jun-00
	-0.22	13.75	-7.99	65.37	28.89		1.06	25.05	1.8	27	1,509	0	99	0	1	30	31.37	-38.78			Aug-18
	1.06	14.94	-6.91	62.57	32.26	0	1.68	25.03	1.79	24.76	1,509	0	99	0	1	30	31.35	-38.63			Dec-06
	-0.27	16.40	-7.63	0.90		0.21	1.2	16.32	0.74	11	6.4	1	99	0	0	131					Dec-15
	-0.18	16.45	-7.43	1.59		0.41	0.95	16.37	0.74	10.98	6.4	1	99	0	0	131					Dec-15
	1.05	16.88	3.77	17.52		12.9	1.7	16.28	1.16	10.79	148.2	3	97	0	0	100					Nov-14
	1.88	12.19	1.73	20.80		2.94	1.03	12.23	0.95	11.02	80.0	3	97	0	0	76					Dec-15
	2.03	12.43	2.05	21.74		3.16	0.78	12.25	0.95	11.04	80.0	3	97	0	0	76					Dec-15
	-9.70	-14.64	-9.17			0	0.45				--	3	96	0	1	120					Oct-13
100	0.88	14.38	-6.02	33.67	24.06	0	1.4	14.78	0.99	10.26	29.3	1	99	0	0	177	25.05	-30.52	5.75		Sep-10
100	0.64	13.92	-6.73	30.58	19.42	0	2.15	14.74	0.98	9.41	29.3	1	99	0	0	177	24.55	-30.72		1.00	Sep-10
25,000	0.95	14.51	-5.79	34.57	25.53	0	1.15	14.74	0.98	10.57	29.3	1	99	0	0	177	25.21	-30.44			Sep-10
100	2.64	14.00	-1.15	40.20	21.73	0	1.4	13.85	0.97	11.64	81.5	4	96	0	0	72	20.6	-28.69	5.75		Sep-10
100	2.45	13.62	-1.84	37.13	17.12	0	2.15	13.81	0.96	10.84	81.5	4	96	0	0	72	19.84	-28.82		1.00	Sep-10
25,000	2.68	14.06	-0.92	41.29	22.98	0.25	1.15	13.78	0.96	11.84	81.5	4	96	0	0	72	20.69	-28.62			Sep-10
100	5.01	20.11	5.73	48.73	24.02	0	1.4	14.3	0.94	15.29	411.8	5	95	0	0		23.86	-24.6	5.75		Nov-10
100	4.83	19.64	4.98	45.42	19.46	0	2.15	14.29	0.94	14.31	411.8	5	95	0	0		23.22	-24.85		1.00	Nov-10
25,000	4.97	20.18	5.97	49.71	25.52	0	1.15	14.31	0.94	15.6	411.8	5	95	0	0		24.03	-24.49			Sep-10
50	5.60	22.32	11.43	49.81		0.03	1.2	12.73	1.06	13.79	108.9	4	96	0	0	19			5.75		Mar-16
50	5.41	21.84	10.60	46.47		0	1.95	12.73	1.06	13.48	108.9	4	96	0	0	19				1.00	Mar-16
	5.65	22.61	11.77	51.13		0.25	0.92	12.73	1.06	13.86	108.9	4	96	0	0	19					May-17
50	5.65	22.51	11.71	50.99		0.21	0.95	12.76	1.06	13.86	108.9	4	96	0	0	19					Mar-16
50	4.29	14.93					1.2			11.48	14.2	8	92	0	0	0			5.75		Dec-18
	4.48	15.14					0.9			11.5	14.2	8	92	0	0	0					Dec-18
50	4.38	15.14					0.95			11.5	14.2	8	92	0	0	0					Dec-18
100	2.75	13.06	3.85	-20.33	-24.04	0	1.61			26.83	18.3	24	76	0	0		5.28	-29.49	5.75		Feb-96
100	2.82	13.27	4.22	14.81	9.47	0	1.28			26.96	18.3	24	76	0	0		5.28	-29.49			Jan-18
100	2.78	13.19	4.11	14.64	9.31	0	1.36			26.94	18.3	24	76	0	0		5.28	-29.49			Jan-18
100	2.71	13.06	3.77			0	1.61			26.83	18.3	24	76	0	0						Feb-18
	3.59	14.39	0.79	29.28	9.73	2.3	0.6	11.01	0.99	12.4	233.6	3	97	0	0	35					Jul-12
	3.51	14.23	0.55	28.28	8.33	2.09	0.85	11.01	0.99	12.36	233.6	3	97	0	0	35			5.50		Jul-12
	3.65	14.61	1.12	30.76	11.71	2.65	0.25	11.03	0.99	12.47	233.6	3	97	0	0	35					Jul-12
	3.45	14.15	0.36	27.72	7.58	1.94	1	11.05	0.99	12.26	233.6	3	97	0	0	35					Apr-14
	3.53	14.31	0.65	28.70	8.86	2.19	0.75	10.98	0.98	12.3	233.6	3	97	0	0	35					Apr-14
	3.65	14.50	1.08	30.36	11.15	2.55	0.35	11.03	0.99	12.47	233.6	3	97	0	0	35					Jul-12
	3.67	14.48	0.89	29.77	10.28	2.45	0.5	11.01	0.99	12.41	233.6	3	97	0	0	35					Jul-12
	1.95	17.63	-3.73	42.33	38.51	0.73	0.55	17.13	1	12.54	307.4	1	99	0	0	38					Jul-12
	1.88	17.54	-3.96	41.19	36.85	0.49	0.8	17.09	1	12.46	307.4	1	99	0	0	38			5.50		Jul-12
	2.02	17.83	-3.37	43.91	41.03	1.09	0.2	17.14	1	12.62	307.4	1	99	0	0	38					Jul-12
	1.89	17.50	-4.09	40.71	35.93	0.34	0.95	17.1	1	12.35	307.4	1	99	0	0	38					Apr-14
	1.97	17.63	-3.86	41.73	37.55	0.59	0.7	17.09	1	12.41	307.4	1	99	0	0	38					Apr-14
	2.10	17.83	-3.42	43.50	40.42	0.98	0.3	17.17	1	12.62	307.4	1	99	0	0	38					Jul-12
	2.03	17.78	-3.60	42.82	39.25	0.78	0.45	17.13	1	12.52	307.4	1	99	0	0	38					Jul-12
	4.10	19.13	9.58	47.62	60.42	1.23	0.72	12.22	1	17	3,372	1	99	0	0	5	24.57	-16.47	5.50		Apr-14

	MARKET		FUND TYPE, CATEGORY & OBJECTIVE		RATINGS				MINIMUMS	
Fund Name	Ticker Symbol	Traded On	Fund Type	Category and (Prospectus Objective)	Overall Rating	Reward Rating	Risk Rating	Recent Up/ Downgrade	Open to New Investors	Min Initial Investment
MM S&P 500® Index Fund Class Administrative Class	MIEYX	NAS CM	Open End	US Equity Large Cap Blend (Growth & Income)	B-	C	B		Y	0
MM S&P 500® Index Fund Class I	MMIZX	NAS CM	Open End	US Equity Large Cap Blend (Growth & Income)	B-	C	B		Y	0
MM S&P 500® Index Fund Class R3	MMINX	NAS CM	Open End	US Equity Large Cap Blend (Growth & Income)	B-	C	B		Y	0
MM S&P 500® Index Fund Class R4	MIEAX	NAS CM	Open End	US Equity Large Cap Blend (Growth & Income)	B-	C	B		Y	0
MM S&P 500® Index Fund Class R5	MIEZX	NAS CM	Open End	US Equity Large Cap Blend (Growth & Income)	B-	C	B		Y	0
MM S&P 500® Index Fund Class Service Class	MMIEX	NAS CM	Open End	US Equity Large Cap Blend (Growth & Income)	B-	C	B		Y	0
MM S&P® Mid Cap Index Fund Administrative Class	MDKYX	NAS CM	Open End	US Equity Mid Cap (Growth)	C+	C	B-	Up	Y	0
MM S&P® Mid Cap Index Fund Class A	MDKAX	NAS CM	Open End	US Equity Mid Cap (Growth)	C+	C	B-	Up	Y	0
MM S&P® Mid Cap Index Fund Class I	MDKZX	NAS CM	Open End	US Equity Mid Cap (Growth)	C+	C	B-	Up	Y	0
MM S&P® Mid Cap Index Fund Class R3	MDKTX	NAS CM	Open End	US Equity Mid Cap (Growth)	C+	C	B-	Up	Y	0
MM S&P® Mid Cap Index Fund Class R4	MDKFX	NAS CM	Open End	US Equity Mid Cap (Growth)	C+	C	B-	Up	Y	0
MM S&P® Mid Cap Index Fund Class R5	MDKIX	NAS CM	Open End	US Equity Mid Cap (Growth)	C+	C	B-	Up	Y	0
MM S&P® Mid Cap Index Fund Service Class shares	MDKSX	NAS CM	Open End	US Equity Mid Cap (Growth)	C+	C	B-	Up	Y	0
MM Select Equity Asset Fund Class I	MSEJX	NAS CM	Open End	US Equity Large Cap Blend (World Stock)	C+	C	B	Up	Y	0
Moerus Worldwide Value Fund Class N	MOWNX	NAS CM	Open End	Global Equity Mid/Small Cap (World Stock)	D+	D	C		Y	2,500
Moerus Worldwide Value Fund Institutional Class	MOWIX	NAS CM	Open End	Global Equity Mid/Small Cap (World Stock)	D+	D	C		Y	100,000
Mondrian Emerging Markets Value Equity Fund	MPEMX	NAS CM	Open End	Global Emerg Mkts (Div Emerging Mkts)	C	C-	B-		Y	50,000
Mondrian Global Listed Infrastructure Fund	MGIFX	NAS CM	Open End	Infrastructure Sector Equity (Income)	U	U	U		Y	50,000
Mondrian International Value Equity Fund	MPIEX	NAS CM	Open End	Global Equity Large Cap (Foreign Stock)	C+	C	B	Up		50,000
Mondrian U.S. Small Cap Equity Fund	MPUSX	NAS CM	Open End	US Equity Small Cap (Income)	U	U	U		Y	50,000
Monetta Core Growth Fund	MYIFX	NAS CM	Open End	US Equity Large Cap Growth (Growth)	B-	C	B		Y	1,000
Monetta Fund	MONTX	NAS CM	Open End	US Equity Large Cap Growth (Growth)	C+	C	B	Down	Y	1,000
Monongahela All Cap Value Fund	MCMVX	NAS CM	Open End	US Equity Mid Cap (Growth)	B-	C	B		Y	5,000
Monteagle Informed Investor Growth Fund Class I	MIIFX	NAS CM	Open End	US Equity Large Cap Growth (Growth)	B-	C	B+		Y	50,000
Monteagle Opportunity Equity Fund Institutional Class	HEQCX	NAS CM	Open End	US Equity Large Cap Blend (Growth)	C+	C	B		Y	1,000,000
Monteagle Opportunity Equity Fund Investor Class	HEQFX	NAS CM	Open End	US Equity Large Cap Blend (Growth)	C+	C	B		Y	2,000
Monteagle Quality Growth Fund Class I	MFGIX	NAS CM	Open End	US Equity Large Cap Growth (Growth)	C+	C	B-		Y	50,000
Monteagle Select Value Fund Class I	MVEIX	NAS CM	Open End	US Equity Large Cap Value (Growth)	C+	C	B-	Up	Y	50,000
Monteagle Value Fund Class I	MVRGX	NAS CM	Open End	US Equity Large Cap Value (Growth)	C	C-	C		Y	50,000
Morgan Dempsey Small/Micro Cap Value Fund	MITYX	NAS CM	Open End	US Equity Small Cap (Growth)	C-	C-	C	Down	Y	2,500
Morgan Stanley China A Share Fund	CAF	NYSE	Closed End	Greater China Equity (Pacific Stock)	C	C-	C		Y	
Morgan Stanley Emerging Mkts Breakout Nations Port Cls A	EMAPX	NAS CM	Open End	Global Emerg Mkts (Div Emerging Mkts)	D+	D	C-	Down	Y	1,000
Morgan Stanley Emerging Mkts Breakout Nations Port Cls C	EMCPX	NAS CM	Open End	Global Emerg Mkts (Div Emerging Mkts)	D+	D	C-		Y	1,000
Morgan Stanley Emerging Mkts Breakout Nations Port Cls I	EMIPX	NAS CM	Open End	Global Emerg Mkts (Div Emerging Mkts)	D+	D	C	Down	Y	5,000,000
Morgan Stanley Emerging Mkts Breakout Nations Port Cls IS	EMSPX	NAS CM	Open End	Global Emerg Mkts (Div Emerging Mkts)	D+	D	C	Down	Y	10,000,000
Morgan Stanley European Equity Fund Inc. Class A	EUGAX	NAS CM	Open End	Europe Equity Large Cap (Europe Stock)	C	C	B-		Y	1,000
Morgan Stanley European Equity Fund Inc. Class B	EUGBX	NAS CM	Open End	Europe Equity Large Cap (Europe Stock)	C	C	B-			1,000
Morgan Stanley European Equity Fund Inc. Class C	MSEEX	NAS CM	Open End	Europe Equity Large Cap (Europe Stock)	C	C-	B-		Y	1,000
Morgan Stanley European Equity Fund Inc. Class I	EUGDX	NAS CM	Open End	Europe Equity Large Cap (Europe Stock)	C	C	B-		Y	5,000,000
Morgan Stanley European Equity Fund Inc. Class L	EUGCX	NAS CM	Open End	Europe Equity Large Cap (Europe Stock)	C	C	B-			1,000
Morgan Stanley Global Conc Real Estate Port Cls A	MCQAX	NAS CM	Open End	Real Estate Sector Equity (Real Estate)	D	D	C		Y	1,000
Morgan Stanley Global Conc Real Estate Port Cls C	MCQCX	NAS CM	Open End	Real Estate Sector Equity (Real Estate)	D	D	C		Y	1,000
Morgan Stanley Global Conc Real Estate Port Cls I	MCQIX	NAS CM	Open End	Real Estate Sector Equity (Real Estate)	D	D	C		Y	5,000,000
Morgan Stanley Global Conc Real Estate Port Cls IS	MCQJX	NAS CM	Open End	Real Estate Sector Equity (Real Estate)	D	D	C		Y	10,000,000
Morgan Stanley Global Counterpoint Portfolio Class A	GLCAX	NAS CM	Open End	Global Equity Large Cap (Growth)	D	D+	C		Y	1,000
Morgan Stanley Global Counterpoint Portfolio Class C	GLCDX	NAS CM	Open End	Global Equity Large Cap (Growth)	D	D+	C		Y	1,000
Morgan Stanley Global Counterpoint Portfolio Class I	GLCIX	NAS CM	Open End	Global Equity Large Cap (Growth)	D	D+	C		Y	5,000,000
Morgan Stanley Global Counterpoint Portfolio Class IS	GLCSX	NAS CM	Open End	Global Equity Large Cap (Growth)	D	D+	C		Y	10,000,000
Morgan Stanley Global Endurance Portfolio Class A	MSJAX	NAS CM	Open End	Global Equity Large Cap (Growth)	U	U	U		Y	1,000
Morgan Stanley Global Endurance Portfolio Class C	MSJCX	NAS CM	Open End	Global Equity Large Cap (Growth)	U	U	U		Y	1,000
Morgan Stanley Global Endurance Portfolio Class I	MSJIX	NAS CM	Open End	Global Equity Large Cap (Growth)	U	U	U		Y	5,000,000
Morgan Stanley Global Endurance Portfolio Class IS	MSJSX	NAS CM	Open End	Global Equity Large Cap (Growth)	U	U	U		Y	10,000,000

★ Expanded analysis of this fund is included in Section II.

Min Additional Investment	TOTAL RETURNS: 3-Month Total Return	6-Month Total Return	1-Year Total Return	3-Year Total Return	5-Year Total Return	PERFORMANCE: Dividend Yield (TTM)	Expense Ratio	3-Yr Std Deviation	3-Year Beta	ASSETS: NAV	Total Assets (MIL)	ASSET ALLOCATION & TURNOVER: %Cash	%Stocks	%Bonds	%Other	Turnover Ratio	BULL & BEAR: Last Bull Market Total Return	Last Bear Market Total Return	FEES: Front End Fee (%)	Back End Fee (%)	Inception Date
	4.14	19.24	9.85	48.71	62.33	1.5	0.47	12.22	1	17.35	3,372	1	99	0	0	5	24.77	-16.47			Feb-98
	4.26	19.53	10.28	50.37	65.25	1.82	0.12	12.21	1	17.62	3,372	1	99	0	0	5	25	-16.38			Dec-11
	4.07	19.05	9.40	46.97	59.21	1.19	0.87	12.2	1	16.62	3,372	1	99	0	0	5	24.38	-16.65			Dec-02
	4.19	19.20	9.76	48.19	61.19	1.35	0.62	12.21	1	17.13	3,372	1	99	0	0	5	24.56	-16.5			Feb-98
	4.24	19.45	10.14	49.91	64.44	1.68	0.22	12.24	1	17.68	3,372	1	99	0	0	5	24.96	-16.38			Apr-01
	4.23	19.40	9.98	49.21	63.27	1.53	0.37	12.22	1	17.72	3,372	1	99	0	0	5	24.76	-16.38			Feb-98
	2.93	18.88	0.81	36.68	43.72	1.14	0.51	15.08	1	13.66	472.7	1	99	0	0	33					Jul-12
	2.86	18.81	0.64	35.75	42.03	0.87	0.76	15.09	1	13.64	472.7	1	99	0	0	33			5.50		Jul-12
	2.99	19.11	1.16	38.16	46.33	1.48	0.16	15.15	1	13.77	472.7	1	99	0	0	33					Jul-12
	2.81	18.62	0.40	35.08	40.99	0.73	0.91	15.15	1	13.5	472.7	1	99	0	0	33					Apr-14
	2.88	18.84	0.70	36.12	42.64	0.98	0.66	15.16	1	13.56	472.7	1	99	0	0	33					Apr-14
	3.00	19.08	1.09	37.74	45.53	1.36	0.26	15.14	1	13.73	472.7	1	99	0	0	33					Jul-12
	2.93	18.98	0.93	37.13	44.52	1.24	0.41	15.12	1	13.66	472.7	1	99	0	0	33					Jul-12
	4.27	19.26	6.26			4.43	0.26			7.8	474.5	1	99	0	0	37					Sep-16
1,000	2.14	12.08	-3.20	15.88		1.43	1.67	12.12	0.91	11.41	52.1	9	91	0	0	14					May-16
200	2.23	12.16	-2.96	16.74		1.73	1.42	12.14	0.91	11.43	52.1	9	91	0	0	14					May-16
100	-0.13	10.49	3.94	19.56	-4.41	8.56	0.92	12.21	0.84	7.37	48.8	1	99	0	0		20.25	-20.86			Nov-07
100	4.81	17.42					0.95			11.32	1.4	2	98	0	0						Dec-18
100	1.20	10.08	0.61	22.06	4.95	2.67	0.79	11.32	0.98	14.3	592.4	0	100	0	0	23	7.83	-17.12			Feb-92
100	3.52	17.35					0.9			11.16	1.4	1	99	0	0						Dec-18
	3.88	20.31	8.11	53.59	62.51	0.25	1.2	12.59	1.02	22.21	90.1	3	97	0	0	28	23.52	-13.44			Dec-06
	3.46	18.59	7.87	51.46	55.44	0	1.39	13.26	1.04	19.71	60.5	12	88	0	0	129	18.92	-24.04			May-86
250	2.25	16.93	7.66	49.81	52.55	1.77	0.87	13.61	1.04	14.06	13.0	11	89	0	0	37					Jul-13
	2.73	9.06	4.10	30.60	41.31	0.03	1.44	10.43	0.55	10.5	10.6	55	45	0	0	650	26.11	-17.51			Apr-08
	3.13	20.25	7.97	31.10	36.85	1.09	1.04	13.54	1.02	6.12	36.4	1	99	0	0	6	21.4	-15.77			Jun-11
200	3.09	19.84	7.48	29.18	33.47	0.61	1.54	13.56	1.03	5.73	36.4	1	99	0	0	6	21	-15.9			Jun-98
	0.59	14.09	1.40	35.26	48.01	0.53	1.3	13.41	1.07	11.81	18.8	3	97	0	0	67	24.3	-15.91			Mar-98
	2.17	23.60	2.47	34.17	29.01	0.53	1.4	18.81	1.33	12.19	12.4	3	97	0	0	173	18.01	-22.94			Mar-98
	0.66	10.10	-5.04	25.50	15.49	1.62	1.34	15.31	1.11	15.2	19.9	4	96	0	0	6	17.95	-18.87			Dec-99
50	-1.43	5.53	-10.73	30.93	13.18	0.59	1.3	15.48	0.85	15.07	19.4	3	97	0	0	14	22.27	-21.71			Dec-10
	-6.92	14.01	-3.26	35.88	106.60	0.48	1.75	16.91	0.79	24.33	532.4	3	97	0	0	113	3.45	-15.03			Sep-06
	3.88	10.89	3.51			0.24	1.59			10.69	5.4	11	89	0	0	36			5.25		Dec-16
	3.75	10.53	2.77			0.24	2.34			10.49	5.4	11	89	0	0	36				1.00	Dec-16
	4.05	11.25	3.98			0.24	1.24			10.77	5.4	11	89	0	0	36					Dec-16
	4.15	11.24	4.08			0.24	1.14			10.78	5.4	11	89	0	0	36					Dec-16
100	5.39	18.06	1.91	28.65	2.39	0.44	1.38	11.6	0.85	19.15	102.3	1	99	0	0	11	16.03	-25.09	5.25		Jul-97
100	5.24	17.87	1.72	28.53	2.28	0.6	1.37	11.58	0.85	18.07	102.3	1	99	0	0	11	16.06	-25.1		5.00	Jun-90
100	5.15	17.62	1.11	25.71	-1.40	0	2.15	11.57	0.85	18.15	102.3	1	99	0	0	11	15.55	-25.33		1.00	Apr-15
	5.45	18.24	2.21	29.99	4.22	0.86	1.05	11.57	0.85	19.9	102.3	1	99	0	0	11	16.15	-25			Jul-97
100	5.24	17.71	1.34	26.66	-0.21	0.01	1.9	11.57	0.85	18.27	102.3	1	99	0	0	11	15.46	-25.33			Jul-97
	-4.87	8.70	-2.43			4.34	1.3			9.37	4.7	4	96	0	0				5.25		Jun-18
	-5.08	8.23	-3.25			3.95	2.05			9.33	4.7	4	96	0	0					1.00	Jun-18
	-4.86	8.81	-2.22			4.54	0.95			9.38	4.7	4	96	0	0						Jun-18
	-4.76	8.93	-2.09			4.56	0.9			9.39	4.7	4	96	0	0						Jun-18
	7.03	30.20	10.61			0.79	1.4			10.95	7.5	5	95	0	0				5.25		Jun-18
	6.84	29.84	9.84			0.46	2.15			10.92	7.5	5	95	0	0					1.00	Jun-18
	7.12	30.59	11.05			0.96	1.05			10.97	7.5	5	95	0	0						Jun-18
	7.12	30.59	11.07			0.97	1			10.97	7.5	5	95	0	0						Jun-18
	2.78	22.00					1.35			12.2	2.6	1	99	0	0				5.25		Dec-18
	2.61	21.50					2.1			12.15	2.6	1	99	0	0					1.00	Dec-18
	2.86	22.20					1			12.22	2.6	1	99	0	0						Dec-18
	2.86	22.20					0.95			12.22	2.6	1	99	0	0						Dec-18

	MARKET			FUND TYPE, CATEGORY & OBJECTIVE	RATINGS					MINIMUMS
Fund Name	Ticker Symbol	Traded On	Fund Type	Category and (Prospectus Objective)	Overall Rating	Reward Rating	Risk Rating	Recent Up/ Downgrade	Open to New Investors	Min Initial Investment
Morgan Stanley Insight Fund Class A	CPOAX	NAS CM	Open End	US Equity Large Cap Growth (Growth)	B-	B-	B	Up	Y	1,000
Morgan Stanley Insight Fund Class C	MSCMX	NAS CM	Open End	US Equity Large Cap Growth (Growth)	B-	B-	B	Up	Y	1,000
Morgan Stanley Insight Fund Class I	CPODX	NAS CM	Open End	US Equity Large Cap Growth (Growth)	B	B-	B	Up	Y	5,000,000
Morgan Stanley Insight Fund Class IS	MCRTX	NAS CM	Open End	US Equity Large Cap Growth (Growth)	B	B-	B	Up	Y	10,000,000
Morgan Stanley Insight Fund Class L	CPOCX	NAS CM	Open End	US Equity Large Cap Growth (Growth)	B-	B-	B	Up		1,000
Morgan Stanley Inst Trust Discovery Portfolio Cls A	MACGX	NAS CM	Open End	US Equity Mid Cap (Growth)	B	B	B-	Up		1,000
Morgan Stanley Inst Trust Discovery Portfolio Cls C	MSMFX	NAS CM	Open End	US Equity Mid Cap (Growth)	B	B	C+	Up	Y	1,000
Morgan Stanley Inst Trust Discovery Portfolio Cls I	MPEGX	NAS CM	Open End	US Equity Mid Cap (Growth)	B	B	B-	Up		5,000,000
Morgan Stanley Inst Trust Discovery Portfolio Cls IS	MMCGX	NAS CM	Open End	US Equity Mid Cap (Growth)	B	B	B-	Up		10,000,000
Morgan Stanley Inst Trust Discovery Portfolio Cls L	MSKLX	NAS CM	Open End	US Equity Mid Cap (Growth)	B	B	B-	Up		1,000
Morgan Stanley Inst Trust Global Strategist Port Cls A	MBAAX	NAS CM	Open End	Moderate Alloc (Growth & Income)	B-	C	A-	Up	Y	1,000
Morgan Stanley Inst Trust Global Strategist Port Cls C	MSSOX	NAS CM	Open End	Moderate Alloc (Growth & Income)	B-	C	A-	Up	Y	1,000
Morgan Stanley Inst Trust Global Strategist Port Cls Inst	MPBAX	NAS CM	Open End	Moderate Alloc (Growth & Income)	B-	C	A-	Up	Y	5,000,000
Morgan Stanley Inst Trust Global Strategist Port Cls IS	MGPOX	NAS CM	Open End	Moderate Alloc (Growth & Income)	B-	C	A-	Up	Y	10,000,000
Morgan Stanley Inst Trust Global Strategist Port Cls L	MSDLX	NAS CM	Open End	Moderate Alloc (Growth & Income)	B-	C	A-	Up		1,000
Morgan Stanley Inst Fund, Inc. Active Intl Alloc Cls A	MSIBX	NAS CM	Open End	Global Equity Large Cap (Foreign Stock)	C	C	B-		Y	1,000
Morgan Stanley Inst Fund, Inc. Active Intl Alloc Cls C	MSAAX	NAS CM	Open End	Global Equity Large Cap (Foreign Stock)	C	C-	B-		Y	1,000
Morgan Stanley Inst Fund, Inc. Active Intl Alloc Cls I	MSACX	NAS CM	Open End	Global Equity Large Cap (Foreign Stock)	C	C	B-		Y	5,000,000
Morgan Stanley Inst Fund, Inc. Active Intl Alloc Cls L	MSLLX	NAS CM	Open End	Global Equity Large Cap (Foreign Stock)	C	C-	B-			1,000
Morgan Stanley Inst Fund, Inc. Advantage Portfolio Cls A	MAPPX	NAS CM	Open End	US Equity Large Cap Growth (Growth)	B	B	B		Y	1,000
Morgan Stanley Inst Fund, Inc. Advantage Portfolio Cls C	MSPRX	NAS CM	Open End	US Equity Large Cap Growth (Growth)	B	B-	B		Y	1,000
Morgan Stanley Inst Fund, Inc. Advantage Portfolio Cls I	MPAIX	NAS CM	Open End	US Equity Large Cap Growth (Growth)	B	B	B			5,000,000
Morgan Stanley Inst Fund, Inc. Advantage Portfolio Cls IS	MADSX	NAS CM	Open End	US Equity Large Cap Growth (Growth)	B	B	B		Y	10,000,000
Morgan Stanley Inst Fund, Inc. Advantage Portfolio Cls L	MAPLX	NAS CM	Open End	US Equity Large Cap Growth (Growth)	B	B	B			1,000
Morgan Stanley Inst Fund, Inc. Asia Opp Portfolio Cls A	MSAUX	NAS CM	Open End	Asia ex-Japan Equity (Growth)	C	C	C		Y	1,000
Morgan Stanley Inst Fund, Inc. Asia Opp Portfolio Cls C	MSAWX	NAS CM	Open End	Asia ex-Japan Equity (Growth)	C	C	C		Y	1,000
Morgan Stanley Inst Fund, Inc. Asia Opp Portfolio Cls I	MSAQX	NAS CM	Open End	Asia ex-Japan Equity (Growth)	C	C	C		Y	5,000,000
Morgan Stanley Inst Fund, Inc. Asia Opp Portfolio Cls IS	MSAYX	NAS CM	Open End	Asia ex-Japan Equity (Growth)	C	C	C		Y	10,000,000
Morgan Stanley Inst Fund, Inc. Emerg Mkts Leaders Cls A	MELAX	NAS CM	Open End	Global Emerg Mkts (Div Emerging Mkts)	C	C-	C+		Y	1,000
Morgan Stanley Inst Fund, Inc. Emerg Mkts Leaders Cls C	MEMLX	NAS CM	Open End	Global Emerg Mkts (Div Emerging Mkts)	C	C-	C+		Y	1,000
Morgan Stanley Inst Fund, Inc. Emerg Mkts Leaders Cls I	MELIX	NAS CM	Open End	Global Emerg Mkts (Div Emerging Mkts)	C	C-	C+		Y	5,000,000
Morgan Stanley Inst Fund, Inc. Emerg Mkts Leaders Cls IS	MELSX	NAS CM	Open End	Global Emerg Mkts (Div Emerging Mkts)	C	C	C+		Y	10,000,000
Morgan Stanley Inst Fund, Inc. Emerging Mkts Port Cls A	MMKBX	NAS CM	Open End	Global Emerg Mkts (Div Emerging Mkts)	C	C-	C+		Y	1,000
Morgan Stanley Inst Fund, Inc. Emerging Mkts Port Cls C	MSEPX	NAS CM	Open End	Global Emerg Mkts (Div Emerging Mkts)	C	C-	C+		Y	1,000
Morgan Stanley Inst Fund, Inc. Emerging Mkts Port Cls I	MGEMX	NAS CM	Open End	Global Emerg Mkts (Div Emerging Mkts)	C	C	C+		Y	5,000,000
Morgan Stanley Inst Fund, Inc. Emerging Mkts Port Cls IR	MRGEX	NAS CM	Open End	Global Emerg Mkts (Div Emerging Mkts)	C	C	C+		Y	10,000,000
Morgan Stanley Inst Fund, Inc. Emerging Mkts Port Cls IS	MMMPX	NAS CM	Open End	Global Emerg Mkts (Div Emerging Mkts)	C	C	C+		Y	10,000,000
Morgan Stanley Inst Fund, Inc. Emerging Mkts Port Cls L	MSELX	NAS CM	Open End	Global Emerg Mkts (Div Emerging Mkts)	C	C-	C+			1,000
Morgan Stanley Inst Fund, Inc. Emerg Mkts Small Cap Cls A	MSEOX	NAS CM	Open End	Global Emerg Mkts (Div Emerging Mkts)	C	C	C		Y	1,000
Morgan Stanley Inst Fund, Inc. Emerg Mkts Small Cap Cls C	MSESX	NAS CM	Open End	Global Emerg Mkts (Div Emerging Mkts)	C	C-	C		Y	1,000
Morgan Stanley Inst Fund, Inc. Emerg Mkts Small Cap Cls I	MSEMX	NAS CM	Open End	Global Emerg Mkts (Div Emerging Mkts)	C	C	C		Y	5,000,000
Morgan Stanley Inst Fund, Inc. Emerg Mkts Small Cap Cls IS	MSETX	NAS CM	Open End	Global Emerg Mkts (Div Emerging Mkts)	C	C	C		Y	10,000,000
Morgan Stanley Inst Fund, Inc. Frontier Mkts Port Cls A	MFMPX	NAS CM	Open End	Global Emerg Mkts (Div Emerging Mkts)	C-	D	C	Up	Y	1,000
Morgan Stanley Inst Fund, Inc. Frontier Mkts Port Cls C	MSFEX	NAS CM	Open End	Global Emerg Mkts (Div Emerging Mkts)	D+	D	C		Y	1,000
Morgan Stanley Inst Fund, Inc. Frontier Mkts Port Cls I	MFMIX	NAS CM	Open End	Global Emerg Mkts (Div Emerging Mkts)	C-	D	C	Up	Y	5,000,000
Morgan Stanley Inst Fund, Inc. Frontier Mkts Port Cls IS	MSRFX	NAS CM	Open End	Global Emerg Mkts (Div Emerging Mkts)	C-	D	C	Up	Y	10,000,000
Morgan Stanley Inst Fund, Inc. Frontier Mkts Port Cls L	MFMLX	NAS CM	Open End	Global Emerg Mkts (Div Emerging Mkts)	D+	D	C			1,000
Morgan Stanley Inst Fund, Inc. Global Advantage Port Cls A	MIGPX	NAS CM	Open End	Global Equity Large Cap (World Stock)	B-	C+	B-	Up	Y	1,000
Morgan Stanley Inst Fund, Inc. Global Advantage Port Cls C	MSPTX	NAS CM	Open End	Global Equity Large Cap (World Stock)	C+	C+	B-		Y	1,000
Morgan Stanley Inst Fund, Inc. Global Advantage Port Cls I	MIGIX	NAS CM	Open End	Global Equity Large Cap (World Stock)	B-	C+	B-	Up	Y	5,000,000
Morgan Stanley Inst Fund, Inc. Global Advantage Port Cls L	MIGLX	NAS CM	Open End	Global Equity Large Cap (World Stock)	C+	C+	B-			1,000
Morgan Stanley Inst Fund, Inc. Global Conc Port Cls A	MLNAX	NAS CM	Open End	Global Equity Large Cap (Growth)	C	C-	B-	Down	Y	1,000

★ Expanded analysis of this fund is included in Section II.

	TOTAL RETURNS					PERFORMANCE				ASSETS		ASSET ALLOCATION & TURNOVER					BULL & BEAR		FEES		
Min Additional Investment	3-Month Total Return	6-Month Total Return	1-Year Total Return	3-Year Total Return	5-Year Total Return	Dividend Yield (TTM)	Expense Ratio	3-Yr Std Deviation	3-Year Beta	NAV	Total Assets (MIL)	%Cash	%Stocks	%Bonds	%Other	Turnover Ratio	Last Bull Market Total Return	Last Bear Market Total Return	Front End Fee (%)	Back End Fee (%)	Inception Date
100	9.05	38.27	25.76	130.63	143.84	0	1.15	17.19	1.08	44.87	2,027	6	93	0	0	73	20.53	-16.8	5.25		Jul-97
100	8.85	37.81	24.88	125.49	134.85	0	1.9	17.18	1.08	31.53	2,027	6	93	0	0	73	20.03	-17.07		1.00	Apr-15
	9.11	38.51	26.12	132.71	147.74	0	0.86	17.2	1.08	49.96	2,027	6	93	0	0	73	20.75	-16.73			Jul-97
	9.11	38.47	26.14	133.01	148.41	0	0.85	17.19	1.08	50.21	2,027	6	93	0	0	73	20.03	-17.07			Sep-13
100	8.93	37.98	25.22	127.18	137.75	0	1.63	17.18	1.08	32.01	2,027	6	93	0	0	73	20.01	-17.06			Jul-97
	12.72	45.06	30.36	107.27	82.41	0	1.02	19.26	1.11	17.8	927.2	4	95	0	0	86	17.97	-21.22	5.25		Jan-97
	12.52	44.37	29.29	102.22	75.32	0	1.9	19.27	1.11	17.34	927.2	4	95	0	0	86	17.44	-21.46		1.00	May-17
	12.77	45.17	30.68	109.12	84.94	0	0.72	19.25	1.11	21.98	927.2	4	95	0	0	86	18.13	-21.13			Mar-90
	12.78	45.29	30.84	109.35	85.80	0	0.66	19.23	1.11	22.23	927.2	4	95	0	0	86	18.13	-21.13			Sep-13
	12.53	44.65	29.74	103.69	77.30	0	1.51	19.24	1.11	15.71	927.2	4	95	0	0	86	17.61	-21.38			Jun-12
	3.35	12.16	5.74	25.59	17.31	3.11	1.04	7.08	0.61	15.4	398.8	10	48	41	0	132	16.49	-9.43	5.25		Nov-96
	3.19	11.79	4.95	22.66	12.99	2.59	1.84	7.1	0.61	15.16	398.8	10	48	41	0	132	16.08	-9.79		1.00	Apr-15
	3.46	12.36	6.08	26.74	19.21	3.41	0.74	7.12	0.61	15.54	398.8	10	48	41	0	132	16.75	-9.42			Dec-92
	3.52	12.42	6.18	26.93	19.47	3.44	0.71	7.08	0.61	15.56	398.8	10	48	41	0	132	16.75	-9.42			May-15
	3.24	11.86	5.19	23.72	14.36	2.57	1.53	7.08	0.6	15.27	398.8	10	48	41	0	132	16.24	-9.7			Apr-12
	4.19	14.93	2.04	26.96	6.05	1.13	1.25	11.38	0.97	14.16	190.9	7	93	0	0	43	10.91	-23.61	5.25		Jan-96
	4.06	14.55	1.28	24.04	2.07	0.47	2	11.37	0.97	14.09	190.9	7	93	0	0	43	10.43	-23.89		1.00	Apr-15
	4.29	15.12	2.32	28.34	7.84	1.48	0.9	11.36	0.97	13.85	190.9	7	93	0	0	43	11.07	-23.57			Jan-92
	4.13	14.64	1.59	24.96	3.33	0.54	1.75	11.36	0.97	14.09	190.9	7	93	0	0	43	10.75	-23.73			Jun-12
	7.18	27.42	16.31	78.58	109.83	0	1.2	12.71	0.9	25.97	397.1	4	96	0	0	79	25.37	-10.66	5.25		May-10
	7.01	26.98	15.43	74.80	102.41	0	1.95	12.71	0.9	25.32	397.1	4	96	0	0	79	24.79	-11.01		1.00	Apr-15
	7.26	27.63	16.65	80.39	113.42	0	0.85	12.71	0.9	26.56	397.1	4	96	0	0	79	25.52	-10.63			Jun-08
	7.29	27.61	16.70	80.61	113.85	0	0.81	12.72	0.9	26.62	397.1	4	96	0	0	79	25.52	-10.63			Sep-13
	7.25	27.56	16.51	79.76	112.32	0	0.99	12.7	0.9	26.47	397.1	4	96	0	0	79	25.54	-10.63			Jun-08
	3.27	28.45	3.28	91.83		0	1.45	18.93	1.11	18.6	69.8	11	89	0	0	63			5.25		Dec-15
	3.10	27.94	2.53	87.52		0	2.2	18.92	1.11	18.27	69.8	11	89	0	0	63				1.00	Dec-15
	3.35	28.62	3.64	93.74		0	1.1	18.94	1.11	18.78	69.8	11	89	0	0	63					Dec-15
	3.41	28.67	3.70	94.03		0	1.05	18.92	1.11	18.8	69.8	11	89	0	0	63					Dec-15
	6.55	15.82	5.94	20.87	10.97	0	1.55	14	0.8	11.86	47.3	3	97	0	0	47	22.66		5.25		Jan-15
	6.24	15.35	5.04	18.11	6.79	0	2.3	14.24	0.8	11.57	47.3	3	97	0	0	47	22.12			1.00	Apr-15
	6.57	16.06	6.29	22.38	13.16	0.11	1.2	13.87	0.8	11.99	47.3	3	97	0	0	47	22.83				Jan-15
	6.57	16.07	6.40	22.53	13.31	0.2	1.1	13.81	0.79	11.99	47.3	3	97	0	0	47	22.83				Jan-15
	2.28	9.88	-0.29	23.28	4.95	0.98	1.35	13.55	0.95	24.12	819.9	0	100	0	0	56	16.01	-22.83	5.25		Jan-96
	2.07	9.52	-1.03	20.36	0.97	0.01	2.15	13.54	0.95	23.58	819.9	0	100	0	0	56	15.52	-23.07		1.00	Apr-15
	2.35	10.09	0.01	24.45	6.61	1.42	1.04	13.54	0.95	24.76	819.9	0	100	0	0	56	16.19	-22.75			Sep-92
	2.35	10.14	0.11	24.56	6.71	1.54	0.95	13.53	0.95	24.76	819.9	0	100	0	0	56	16.19	-22.75			Jun-18
	2.39	10.14	0.15	24.79	7.09	1.54	0.93	13.58	0.95	24.76	819.9	0	100	0	0	56	16.19	-22.75			Sep-13
	2.15	9.63	-0.81	21.23	2.09	0.62	1.9	13.52	0.95	23.67	819.9	0	100	0	0	56	15.69	-22.99			Apr-12
	2.60	12.48	-0.08	18.39		0	1.65	11.98	0.82	11.8	66.2	1	98	1	0	70			5.25		Dec-15
	2.48	12.12	-0.85	15.87		0	2.4	11.96	0.82	11.56	66.2	1	98	1	0	70				1.00	Dec-15
	2.75	12.77	0.25	19.82		0	1.3	11.96	0.82	11.92	66.2	1	98	1	0	70					Dec-15
	2.84	12.75	0.33	19.93		0	1.25	11.96	0.82	11.93	66.2	1	98	1	0	70					Dec-15
	6.11	12.95	-0.57	8.27	-10.17	2.79	2.06	12.16	1.04	17.53	188.5	0	97	2	0	61	8.94	-21.62	5.25		Sep-12
	5.84	12.55	-1.35	5.78	-13.52	1.37	2.82	12.14	1.04	17.21	188.5	0	97	2	0	61	8.47	-21.86		1.00	Apr-15
	6.21	13.19	-0.22	9.38	-8.62	3.71	1.76	12.16	1.04	17.59	188.5	0	97	2	0	61	9.1	-21.54			Aug-08
	6.22	13.19	-0.27	9.38	-8.58	3.65	1.73	12.16	1.04	17.59	188.5	0	97	2	0	61	9.1	-21.54			Feb-15
	5.94	12.64	-1.08	6.42	-12.87	1.43	2.56	12.12	1.03	17.46	188.5	0	97	2	0	61	8.63	-21.78			Sep-12
	6.48	29.35	11.13	76.62	74.88	0	1.42	13.96	1.1	17.58	136.8	3	97	0	0	130	27.91	-15.84	5.25		Dec-10
	6.25	28.89	10.29	72.57	68.34	0	2.2	13.91	1.1	16.64	136.8	3	97	0	0	130	27.44	-16.09		1.00	Apr-15
	6.53	29.55	11.51	78.36	77.85	0	1.1	13.92	1.1	17.93	136.8	3	97	0	0	130	28.19	-15.74			Dec-10
	6.29	29.02	10.55	73.94	70.40	0	1.95	13.92	1.1	16.89	136.8	3	97	0	0	130	27.47	-15.97			Dec-10
	3.58	19.38	2.31	30.60		0.29	1.35	13.39	1.11	12.44	18.2	1	99	0	0	94			5.25		May-16

	MARKET		FUND TYPE, CATEGORY & OBJECTIVE		RATINGS					MINIMUMS
Fund Name	Ticker Symbol	Traded On	Fund Type	Category and (Prospectus Objective)	Overall Rating	Reward Rating	Risk Rating	Recent Up/ Downgrade	Open to New Investors	Min Initial Investment
Morgan Stanley Inst Fund, Inc. Global Conc Port Cls C	MLNCX	NAS CM	Open End	Global Equity Large Cap (Growth)	C	C-	B-	Down	Y	1,000
Morgan Stanley Inst Fund, Inc. Global Conc Port Cls I	MLNIX	NAS CM	Open End	Global Equity Large Cap (Growth)	C	C-	B-	Down	Y	5,000,000
Morgan Stanley Inst Fund, Inc. Global Conc Port Cls IS	MLNSX	NAS CM	Open End	Global Equity Large Cap (Growth)	C	C-	B-	Down	Y	10,000,000
Morgan Stanley Inst Fund, Inc. Global Core Portfolio Cls A	MLMAX	NAS CM	Open End	Global Equity Large Cap (Growth)	C	C-	B-	Down	Y	1,000
Morgan Stanley Inst Fund, Inc. Global Core Portfolio Cls C	MLMCX	NAS CM	Open End	Global Equity Large Cap (Growth)	C	D+	B-	Down	Y	1,000
Morgan Stanley Inst Fund, Inc. Global Core Portfolio Cls I	MLMIX	NAS CM	Open End	Global Equity Large Cap (Growth)	C	C-	B-	Down	Y	5,000,000
Morgan Stanley Inst Fund, Inc. Global Core Port Cls IS	MLMSX	NAS CM	Open End	Global Equity Large Cap (Growth)	C	C-	B-	Down	Y	10,000,000
Morgan Stanley Inst Fund, Inc. Global Franchise Port Cls A	MSFBX	NAS CM	Open End	Global Equity Large Cap (World Stock)	B	B	B+			1,000
Morgan Stanley Inst Fund, Inc. Global Franchise Port Cls C	MSGFX	NAS CM	Open End	Global Equity Large Cap (World Stock)	B	B	B+		Y	1,000
Morgan Stanley Inst Fund, Inc. Global Franchise Port Cls I	MSFAX	NAS CM	Open End	Global Equity Large Cap (World Stock)	B+	B	B+	Up		5,000,000
Morgan Stanley Inst Fund, Inc. Global Franch Port Cls IS	MGISX	NAS CM	Open End	Global Equity Large Cap (World Stock)	B+	B	B+	Up	Y	10,000,000
Morgan Stanley Inst Fund, Inc. Global Franchise Port Cls L	MSFLX	NAS CM	Open End	Global Equity Large Cap (World Stock)	B	B	B+			1,000
Morgan Stanley Inst Fund, Inc. Global Infrastr Port Cls A	MTIPX	NAS CM	Open End	Infrastructure Sector Equity (World Stock)	B-	C+	B		Y	1,000
Morgan Stanley Inst Fund, Inc. Global Infrastr Port Cls C	MSGTX	NAS CM	Open End	Infrastructure Sector Equity (World Stock)	C+	C	B-	Down	Y	1,000
Morgan Stanley Inst Fund, Inc. Global Infrastr Port Cls I	MTIIX	NAS CM	Open End	Infrastructure Sector Equity (World Stock)	B-	C+	B		Y	5,000,000
Morgan Stanley Inst Fund, Inc. Global Infrastr Port Cls IR	MRGOX	NAS CM	Open End	Infrastructure Sector Equity (World Stock)	B-	C+	B		Y	10,000,000
Morgan Stanley Inst Fund, Inc. Global Infrastr Port Cls IS	MSGPX	NAS CM	Open End	Infrastructure Sector Equity (World Stock)	B-	C+	B		Y	10,000,000
Morgan Stanley Inst Fund, Inc. Global Infrastr Port Cls L	MTILX	NAS CM	Open End	Infrastructure Sector Equity (World Stock)	C+	C	B-	Down		1,000
Morgan Stanley Inst Fund, Inc. Global Opp Portfolio Cls A	MGGPX	NAS CM	Open End	Global Equity Large Cap (World Stock)	C+	C+	C+		Y	1,000
Morgan Stanley Inst Fund, Inc. Global Opp Portfolio Cls C	MSOPX	NAS CM	Open End	Global Equity Large Cap (World Stock)	C+	C+	C+		Y	1,000
Morgan Stanley Inst Fund, Inc. Global Opp Portfolio Cls I	MGGIX	NAS CM	Open End	Global Equity Large Cap (World Stock)	C+	C+	C+		Y	5,000,000
Morgan Stanley Inst Fund, Inc. Global Opp Portfolio Cls IR	MGORX	NAS CM	Open End	Global Equity Large Cap (World Stock)	C+	C+	C+		Y	10,000,000
Morgan Stanley Inst Fund, Inc. Global Opp Portfolio Cls IS	MGTSX	NAS CM	Open End	Global Equity Large Cap (World Stock)	C+	C+	C+		Y	10,000,000
Morgan Stanley Inst Fund, Inc. Global Opp Portfolio Cls L	MGGLX	NAS CM	Open End	Global Equity Large Cap (World Stock)	C+	C+	C+			1,000
Morgan Stanley Inst Fund, Inc. Global Real Est Cls A	MRLBX	NAS CM	Open End	Real Estate Sector Equity (Real Estate)	C+	C	B		Y	1,000
Morgan Stanley Inst Fund, Inc. Global Real Est Cls C	MSRDX	NAS CM	Open End	Real Estate Sector Equity (Real Estate)	C+	C	B		Y	1,000
Morgan Stanley Inst Fund, Inc. Global Real Est Cls I	MRLAX	NAS CM	Open End	Real Estate Sector Equity (Real Estate)	C+	C	B		Y	5,000,000
Morgan Stanley Inst Fund, Inc. Global Real Est Cls IR	MRLEX	NAS CM	Open End	Real Estate Sector Equity (Real Estate)	C+	C	B		Y	10,000,000
Morgan Stanley Inst Fund, Inc. Global Real Est Cls IS	MGREX	NAS CM	Open End	Real Estate Sector Equity (Real Estate)	B-	C	B	Up	Y	10,000,000
Morgan Stanley Inst Fund, Inc. Global Real Est Cls L	MGRLX	NAS CM	Open End	Real Estate Sector Equity (Real Estate)	C+	C	B			1,000
Morgan Stanley Inst Fund, Inc. Global Sustain Port Cls A	MGQAX	NAS CM	Open End	Global Equity Large Cap (World Stock)	B	B-	B+		Y	1,000
Morgan Stanley Inst Fund, Inc. Global Sustain Port Cls C	MSGQX	NAS CM	Open End	Global Equity Large Cap (World Stock)	B	B-	B+		Y	1,000
Morgan Stanley Inst Fund, Inc. Global Sustain Port Cls I	MGQIX	NAS CM	Open End	Global Equity Large Cap (World Stock)	B	B-	B+		Y	5,000,000
Morgan Stanley Inst Fund, Inc. Global Sustain Port Cls IS	MGQSX	NAS CM	Open End	Global Equity Large Cap (World Stock)	B	B-	B+		Y	10,000,000
Morgan Stanley Inst Fund, Inc. Global Sustain Port Cls L	MGQLX	NAS CM	Open End	Global Equity Large Cap (World Stock)	B	B-	B+			1,000
Morgan Stanley Inst Fund, Inc. Growth Portfolio Cls A	MSEGX	NAS CM	Open End	US Equity Large Cap Growth (Growth)	B-	C+	B-		Y	1,000
Morgan Stanley Inst Fund, Inc. Growth Portfolio Cls C	MSGUX	NAS CM	Open End	US Equity Large Cap Growth (Growth)	C+	C+	B-	Down	Y	1,000
Morgan Stanley Inst Fund, Inc. Growth Portfolio Cls I	MSEQX	NAS CM	Open End	US Equity Large Cap Growth (Growth)	B-	C+	B-		Y	5,000,000
Morgan Stanley Inst Fund, Inc. Growth Portfolio Cls IR	MGHRX	NAS CM	Open End	US Equity Large Cap Growth (Growth)	B-	C+	B-		Y	10,000,000
Morgan Stanley Inst Fund, Inc. Growth Portfolio Cls IS	MGRPX	NAS CM	Open End	US Equity Large Cap Growth (Growth)	B-	C+	B-		Y	10,000,000
Morgan Stanley Inst Fund, Inc. Growth Portfolio Cls L	MSHLX	NAS CM	Open End	US Equity Large Cap Growth (Growth)	C+	C+	B-	Down		1,000
Morgan Stanley Inst Fund, Inc. Inception Portfolio Cls A	MSSMX	NAS CM	Open End	US Equity Small Cap (Small Company)	C+	C+	C+	Down		1,000
Morgan Stanley Inst Fund, Inc. Inception Portfolio Cls C	MSCOX	NAS CM	Open End	US Equity Small Cap (Small Company)	C+	C+	C+	Down	Y	1,000
Morgan Stanley Inst Fund, Inc. Inception Portfolio Cls I	MSSGX	NAS CM	Open End	US Equity Small Cap (Small Company)	C+	B-	C+	Down	Y	5,000,000
Morgan Stanley Inst Fund, Inc. Inception Portfolio Cls IS	MFLLX	NAS CM	Open End	US Equity Small Cap (Small Company)	C+	B-	C+	Down	Y	10,000,000
Morgan Stanley Inst Fund, Inc. Inception Portfolio Cls L	MSSLX	NAS CM	Open End	US Equity Small Cap (Small Company)	C+	C+	C+	Down		1,000
Morgan Stanley Inst Fund, Inc. Intl Advantage Port Cls A	MFAPX	NAS CM	Open End	Global Equity Large Cap (Foreign Stock)	C+	C	B		Y	1,000
Morgan Stanley Inst Fund, Inc. Intl Advantage Port Cls C	MSIAX	NAS CM	Open End	Global Equity Large Cap (Foreign Stock)	C+	C	B		Y	1,000
Morgan Stanley Inst Fund, Inc. Intl Advantage Port Cls I	MFAIX	NAS CM	Open End	Global Equity Large Cap (Foreign Stock)	C+	C	B		Y	5,000,000
Morgan Stanley Inst Fund, Inc. Intl Advantage Port Cls IS	IDVSX	NAS CM	Open End	Global Equity Large Cap (Foreign Stock)	C+	C	B		Y	10,000,000
Morgan Stanley Inst Fund, Inc. Intl Advantage Port Cls L	MSALX	NAS CM	Open End	Global Equity Large Cap (Foreign Stock)	C+	C	B			1,000
Morgan Stanley Inst Fund, Inc. Intl Equity Portfolio Cls A	MIQBX	NAS CM	Open End	Global Equity Large Cap (Foreign Stock)	C	C	B		Y	1,000

★ Expanded analysis of this fund is included in Section II.

	TOTAL RETURNS					PERFORMANCE				ASSETS		ASSET ALLOCATION & TURNOVER					BULL & BEAR		FEES		
Min Additional Investment	3-Month Total Return	6-Month Total Return	1-Year Total Return	3-Year Total Return	5-Year Total Return	Dividend Yield (TTM)	Expense Ratio	3-Yr Std Deviation	3-Year Beta	NAV	Total Assets (MIL)	%Cash	%Stocks	%Bonds	%Other	Turnover Ratio	Last Bull Market Total Return	Last Bear Market Total Return	Front End Fee (%)	Back End Fee (%)	Inception Date
	3.37	18.94	1.57	27.65		0	2.1	13.37	1.1	12.24	18.2	1	99	0	0	94				1.00	May-16
	3.64	19.59	2.69	31.95		0.61	1	13.41	1.11	12.51	18.2	1	99	0	0	94					May-16
	3.64	19.59	2.76	32.09		0.67	0.95	13.34	1.1	12.51	18.2	1	99	0	0	94					May-16
	4.26	18.85	2.26	25.96		0.26	1.35	13.26	1.13	11.98	10.3	2	98	0	0	50			5.25		May-16
	4.06	18.27	1.46	23.20		0	2.1	13.22	1.13	11.78	10.3	2	98	0	0	50				1.00	May-16
	4.43	19.02	2.66	27.46		0.67	1	13.29	1.13	12.01	10.3	2	98	0	0	50					May-16
	4.43	19.02	2.64	27.59		0.72	0.95	13.26	1.13	12.01	10.3	2	98	0	0	50					May-16
	5.05	21.45	15.01	49.79	65.88	0.69	1.23	10.35	0.74	27.23	1,742	5	95	0	0	27	17.79	-6.53	5.25		Nov-01
	4.87	21.07	14.19	46.47	59.92	0.14	1.96	10.34	0.74	26.66	1,742	5	95	0	0	27	17.37	-6.83		1.00	Sep-15
	5.16	21.68	15.36	51.00	68.20	0.92	0.94	10.39	0.75	27.89	1,742	5	95	0	0	27	18.05	-6.44			Nov-01
	5.16	21.68	15.42	51.28	68.59	0.96	0.88	10.34	0.74	27.89	1,742	5	95	0	0	27	18.05	-6.44			May-15
	4.94	21.15	14.40	47.58	61.98	0.22	1.73	10.37	0.75	27.15	1,742	5	95	0	0	27	17.54	-6.73			Apr-12
	4.89	19.77	12.28	22.83	23.28	2.14	1.21	9.27	0.89	14.78	356.0	2	98	0	0	43	18.14	-6.79	5.25		Sep-10
	4.69	19.25	11.27	19.67	18.38	1.22	2.07	9.27	0.9	14.49	356.0	2	98	0	0	43	17.62	-7.09		1.00	Apr-15
	4.95	19.88	12.55	23.71	24.90	2.37	0.97	9.28	0.9	14.83	356.0	2	98	0	0	43	18.3	-6.7			Sep-10
	5.02	19.98	12.60	23.76	24.95	2.4	0.94	9.28	0.9	14.83	356.0	2	98	0	0	43	18.3	-6.7			Jun-18
	5.02	19.98	12.59	23.81	24.94	2.4	0.94	9.25	0.89	14.83	356.0	2	98	0	0	43	18.3	-6.7			Sep-13
	4.77	19.51	11.65	20.76	19.78	1.56	1.78	9.24	0.89	14.7	356.0	2	98	0	0	43	17.81	-6.98			Sep-10
	6.21	26.25	5.22	81.80	115.98	0	1.27	14.8	1.12	26.16	3,384	7	92	0	1	28	20.92	-21.44	5.25		May-10
	6.07	25.87	4.52	78.15	108.83	0	1.96	14.8	1.12	25.15	3,384	7	92	0	1	28	20.44	-21.76		1.00	Apr-15
	6.32	26.48	5.56	83.70	119.76	0	0.95	14.81	1.12	27.08	3,384	7	92	0	1	28	21.14	-21.43			May-08
	6.34	26.50	5.67	83.88	119.98	0	0.89	14.82	1.12	27.16	3,384	7	92	0	1	28	21.14	-21.43			Jun-18
	6.31	26.49	5.47	83.72	120.05	0	0.89	14.82	1.12	27.12	3,384	7	92	0	1	28	21.14	-21.43			Sep-13
	6.25	26.25	5.20	81.45	115.33	0	1.33	14.78	1.12	25.82	3,384	7	92	0	1	28	21.05	-21.54			May-08
	-1.81	12.56	3.02	10.21	17.73	4.33	1.35	11.55	1.03	10.3	849.7	1	99	0	0	38	25.33	-21.94	5.25		Aug-06
	-2.06	12.13	2.17	7.54	13.15	3.72	2.1	11.49	1.02	9.98	849.7	1	99	0	0	38	24.71	-22.14		1.00	Apr-15
	-1.89	12.75	3.23	11.19	19.37	4.68	1	11.61	1.03	10.34	849.7	1	99	0	0	38	25.43	-21.82			Aug-06
	-1.80	12.75	3.34	11.31	19.50	4.78	0.94	11.56	1.03	10.34	849.7	1	99	0	0	38	25.43	-21.82			Jun-18
	-1.80	12.86	3.43	11.51	19.92	4.77	0.92	11.59	1.03	10.35	849.7	1	99	0	0	38	25.43	-21.82			Sep-13
	-2.02	12.23	2.39	8.41	14.70	3.79	1.85	11.54	1.02	10.18	849.7	1	99	0	0	38	24.89	-22.05			Jun-08
	6.15	19.91	13.57	47.78	55.00	0.13	1.25	10.6	0.81	13.79	23.4	4	96	0	0	76			5.25		Aug-13
	5.99	19.57	12.82	44.55	49.32	0.04	2	10.61	0.81	13.44	23.4	4	96	0	0	76				1.00	Apr-15
	6.29	20.22	14.09	49.44	57.77	0.48	0.9	10.56	0.81	13.85	23.4	4	96	0	0	76					Aug-13
	6.37	20.22	14.16	49.57	57.95	0.52	0.85	10.56	0.81	13.85	23.4	4	96	0	0	76					Sep-13
	6.05	19.61	13.04	45.50	51.10	0.04	1.75	10.56	0.81	13.66	23.4	4	96	0	0	76					Aug-13
	7.16	29.41	15.15	102.15	122.83	0	0.85	16.56	1.07	50.69	7,525	3	95	0	0	41	22.19	-16	5.25		Jan-96
	6.97	28.95	14.33	97.66	114.69	0	1.58	16.56	1.07	47.39	7,525	3	95	0	0	41	21.71	-16.26		1.00	Apr-15
	7.23	29.57	15.45	103.81	125.88	0	0.59	16.56	1.07	53.49	7,525	3	95	0	0	41	22.42	-15.91			Apr-91
	7.26	29.61	15.54	103.98	126.06	0	0.5	16.56	1.07	53.88	7,525	3	95	0	0	41	22.42	-15.91			Jun-18
	7.26	29.61	15.54	104.29	126.91	0	0.5	16.56	1.07	53.88	7,525	3	95	0	0	41	22.42	-15.91			Sep-13
	7.04	29.08	14.61	99.13	117.10	0	1.32	16.56	1.07	47.89	7,525	3	95	0	0	41	21.88	-16.17			Apr-12
	6.08	40.05	19.20	72.14	52.73	0	1.35	18.41	0.88	10.63	247.7	16	80	0	0	79	20.83	-24.69	5.25		Jan-96
	5.79	39.40	18.15	68.23	47.27	0	2.1	18.4	0.88	10.4	247.7	16	80	0	0	79	20.32	-24.91		1.00	May-17
	6.13	40.16	19.55	73.68	55.10	0	1	18.41	0.88	13.33	247.7	16	80	0	0	79	21.02	-24.59			Nov-89
	6.16	40.33	19.59	74.17	55.77	0	0.93	18.42	0.88	13.43	247.7	16	80	0	0	79	21.02	-24.59			Sep-13
	5.83	39.65	18.46	69.27	48.58	0	1.85	18.36	0.88	9.79	247.7	16	80	0	0	79	20.5	-24.83			Nov-11
	4.10	21.17	4.99	69.90	79.50	0	1.35	12.27	0.91	18.77	1,593	9	91	0	0	29	23.49	-15.88	5.25		Dec-10
	3.91	20.73	4.23	66.20	73.04	0	2.1	12.25	0.9	18.05	1,593	9	91	0	0	29	22.93	-16.04		1.00	Apr-15
	4.16	21.37	5.33	71.66	82.39	0	1	12.27	0.9	19.02	1,593	9	91	0	0	29	23.65	-15.69			Dec-10
	4.21	21.44	5.38	71.75	82.49	0	0.95	12.25	0.9	19.03	1,593	9	91	0	0	29	23.65	-15.69			Jun-18
	3.92	20.84	4.42	67.33	74.85	0	1.85	12.28	0.91	18.26	1,593	9	91	0	0	29	23.27	-16.1			Dec-10
	2.48	14.28	-0.37	23.54	7.36	1.22	1.3	11.5	0.97	15.28	2,368	2	98	0	0	34	16.74	-20.13	5.25		Jan-96

	MARKET			FUND TYPE, CATEGORY & OBJECTIVE	RATINGS				MINIMUMS	
Fund Name	Ticker Symbol	Traded On	Fund Type	Category and (Prospectus Objective)	Overall Rating	Reward Rating	Risk Rating	Recent Up/ Downgrade	Open to New Investors	Min Initial Investment
Morgan Stanley Inst Fund, Inc. Intl Equity Portfolio Cls C	MSECX	NAS CM	Open End	Global Equity Large Cap (Foreign Stock)	C	C-	B-		Y	1,000
Morgan Stanley Inst Fund, Inc. Intl Equity Portfolio Cls I	MSIQX	NAS CM	Open End	Global Equity Large Cap (Foreign Stock)	C	C	B		Y	5,000,000
Morgan Stanley Inst Fund, Inc. Intl Eq Port Cls IS	MIQPX	NAS CM	Open End	Global Equity Large Cap (Foreign Stock)	C	C	B		Y	10,000,000
Morgan Stanley Inst Fund, Inc. Intl Equity Portfolio Cls L	MSQLX	NAS CM	Open End	Global Equity Large Cap (Foreign Stock)	C	C-	B			1,000
Morgan Stanley Inst Fund, Inc. Intl Opp Portfolio Cls A	MIOPX	NAS CM	Open End	Global Equity Large Cap (Foreign Stock)	C	C	C+		Y	1,000
Morgan Stanley Inst Fund, Inc. Intl Opp Portfolio Cls C	MSOCX	NAS CM	Open End	Global Equity Large Cap (Foreign Stock)	C	C	C+		Y	1,000
Morgan Stanley Inst Fund, Inc. Intl Opp Portfolio Cls I	MIOIX	NAS CM	Open End	Global Equity Large Cap (Foreign Stock)	C	C	C+		Y	5,000,000
Morgan Stanley Inst Fund, Inc. Intl Opp Portfolio Cls IR	MRNPX	NAS CM	Open End	Global Equity Large Cap (Foreign Stock)	C	C	C+		Y	10,000,000
Morgan Stanley Inst Fund, Inc. Intl Opp Portfolio Cls IS	MNOPX	NAS CM	Open End	Global Equity Large Cap (Foreign Stock)	C	C	C+		Y	10,000,000
Morgan Stanley Inst Fund, Inc. Intl Opp Portfolio Cls L	MIOLX	NAS CM	Open End	Global Equity Large Cap (Foreign Stock)	C	C	C+			1,000
Morgan Stanley Inst Fund, Inc. Intl Real Estate Port Cls A	IERBX	NAS CM	Open End	Real Estate Sector Equity (Real Estate)	C+	C	B		Y	1,000
Morgan Stanley Inst Fund, Inc. Intl Real Estate Port Cls C	MSIJX	NAS CM	Open End	Real Estate Sector Equity (Real Estate)	C+	C	B	Up	Y	1,000
Morgan Stanley Inst Fund, Inc. Intl Real Estate Port Cls I	MSUAX	NAS CM	Open End	Real Estate Sector Equity (Real Estate)	B-	C	B	Up	Y	5,000,000
Morgan Stanley Inst Fund, Inc. Intl Real Est Cls IS	MIREX	NAS CM	Open End	Real Estate Sector Equity (Real Estate)	B-	C	B	Up	Y	10,000,000
Morgan Stanley Inst Fund, Inc. Intl Real Estate Port Cls L	MSOLX	NAS CM	Open End	Real Estate Sector Equity (Real Estate)	C+	C	B			1,000
Morgan Stanley Inst Fund, Inc. Multi-Asset Portfolio Cls A	MMPPX	NAS CM	Open End	Global Macro (Multi-Asset Global)	C-	D	C		Y	1,000
Morgan Stanley Inst Fund, Inc. Multi-Asset Portfolio Cls C	MSMEX	NAS CM	Open End	Global Macro (Multi-Asset Global)	D+	D	C		Y	1,000
Morgan Stanley Inst Fund, Inc. Multi-Asset Portfolio Cls I	MMPIX	NAS CM	Open End	Global Macro (Multi-Asset Global)	C-	D+	C+	Down	Y	5,000,000
Morgan Stanley Inst Fund, Inc. Multi-Asset Port Cls IS	MSPMX	NAS CM	Open End	Global Macro (Multi-Asset Global)	C-	D+	C+	Down	Y	10,000,000
Morgan Stanley Inst Fund, Inc. Multi-Asset Portfolio Cls L	MMPLX	NAS CM	Open End	Global Macro (Multi-Asset Global)	D+	D	C			1,000
Morgan Stanley Inst Fund, Inc. U.S. Real Estate Port Cls A	MUSDX	NAS CM	Open End	Real Estate Sector Equity (Real Estate)	C	C	B-	Down	Y	1,000
Morgan Stanley Inst Fund, Inc. U.S. Real Estate Port Cls C	MSURX	NAS CM	Open End	Real Estate Sector Equity (Real Estate)	C	C	C	Down	Y	1,000
Morgan Stanley Inst Fund, Inc. U.S. Real Estate Port Cls I	MSUSX	NAS CM	Open End	Real Estate Sector Equity (Real Estate)	C	C	B-	Down	Y	5,000,000
Morgan Stanley Inst Fund, Inc. U.S. Real Est Cls IR	MRETX	NAS CM	Open End	Real Estate Sector Equity (Real Estate)	C	C	B-	Down	Y	10,000,000
Morgan Stanley Inst Fund, Inc. U.S. Real Est Cls IS	MURSX	NAS CM	Open End	Real Estate Sector Equity (Real Estate)	C	C	B-	Down	Y	10,000,000
Morgan Stanley Inst Fund, Inc. U.S. Real Estate Port Cls L	MSULX	NAS CM	Open End	Real Estate Sector Equity (Real Estate)	C	C	C+	Down		1,000
Morgan Stanley Inst Fund, Inc. US Core Portfolio Cls A	MUOAX	NAS CM	Open End	US Equity Large Cap Blend (Growth)	C+	C	B-	Down	Y	1,000
Morgan Stanley Inst Fund, Inc. US Core Portfolio Cls C	MUOCX	NAS CM	Open End	US Equity Large Cap Blend (Growth)	C	C	B-	Down	Y	1,000
Morgan Stanley Inst Fund, Inc. US Core Portfolio Cls I	MUOIX	NAS CM	Open End	US Equity Large Cap Blend (Growth)	C+	C	B-	Down	Y	5,000,000
Morgan Stanley Inst Fund, Inc. US Core Portfolio Cls IS	MUOSX	NAS CM	Open End	US Equity Large Cap Blend (Growth)	C+	C	B-	Down	Y	10,000,000
Morgan Stanley Inst Global Multi-Asset Income Port Cls A	MSGOX	NAS CM	Open End	Cautious Alloc (Growth & Income)	C+	C	B+	Up	Y	1,000
Morgan Stanley Inst Global Multi-Asset Income Port Cls C	MSGYX	NAS CM	Open End	Cautious Alloc (Growth & Income)	C+	C	B	Up	Y	1,000
Morgan Stanley Inst Global Multi-Asset Income Port Cls I	MSGMX	NAS CM	Open End	Cautious Alloc (Growth & Income)	B-	C	B+	Up	Y	5,000,000
Morgan Stanley Inst Global Multi-Asset Income Port Cls IS	MSMUX	NAS CM	Open End	Cautious Alloc (Growth & Income)	B-	C	B+	Up	Y	10,000,000
Morgan Stanley Pathway Funds Alternative Strategies Fund	TALTX	NAS CM	Open End	Multialternative (Growth)	D	D+	B-		Y	1,000
Morgan Stanley Pathway Funds Emerging Markets Equity Fund	TEMUX	NAS CM	Open End	Global Emerg Mkts (Div Emerging Mkts)	C	C	C+		Y	1,000
Morgan Stanley Pathway Funds International Equity Fund	TIEUX	NAS CM	Open End	Global Equity Large Cap (Foreign Stock)	C	C	B-		Y	1,000
Morgan Stanley Pathway Funds Large Cap Equity Fund	TLGUX	NAS CM	Open End	US Equity Large Cap Blend (Growth)	B-	C	B		Y	1,000
Morgan Stanley Pathway Funds Small-Mid Cap Equity Fund	TSGUX	NAS CM	Open End	US Equity Mid Cap (Growth)	C+	C	B-		Y	1,000
Morgan Stanley Real Assets Portfolio Class A	MRJAX	NAS CM	Open End	Aggressive Alloc (Growth & Income)	D	D+	B		Y	1,000
Morgan Stanley Real Assets Portfolio Class C	MRJCX	NAS CM	Open End	Aggressive Alloc (Growth & Income)	D	D+	B		Y	1,000
Morgan Stanley Real Assets Portfolio Class I	MRJIX	NAS CM	Open End	Aggressive Alloc (Growth & Income)	D	D+	B		Y	5,000,000
Morgan Stanley Real Assets Portfolio Class IS	MRJSX	NAS CM	Open End	Aggressive Alloc (Growth & Income)	D	D+	B		Y	10,000,000
Morningstar Aggressive Growth ETF Asset Alloc Port Cls I			Open End	Aggressive Alloc (Aggr Growth)	B-	C	B	Up	Y	0
Morningstar Alternatives Fund	MSTVX	NAS CM	Open End	Multialternative (Growth)	U	U	U		Y	0
Morningstar Balanced ETF Asset Allocation Portfolio Cls I			Open End	Moderate Alloc (Balanced)	B-	C	A-	Up	Y	0
Morningstar Conservative ETF Asset Alloc Port Cls I			Open End	Cautious Alloc (Income)	B-	C	B+		Y	0
Morningstar Global Income Fund	MSTGX	NAS CM	Open End	Flexible Alloc (Growth & Income)	U	U	U		Y	0
Morningstar Growth ETF Asset Allocation Portfolio Class I			Open End	Aggressive Alloc (Growth)	B-	C	B+	Up	Y	0
Morningstar Income & Growth ETF Asset Alloc Port Cls I			Open End	Cautious Alloc (Growth & Income)	B	C	A-	Up	Y	0
Morningstar International Equity Fund	MSTFX	NAS CM	Open End	Global Equity Large Cap (Growth)	U	U	U		Y	0
Morningstar U.S. Equity Fund	MSTQX	NAS CM	Open End	US Equity Large Cap Blend (Growth)	U	U	U		Y	0

★ Expanded analysis of this fund is included in Section II.

Min Additional Investment	3-Month Total Return	6-Month Total Return	1-Year Total Return	3-Year Total Return	5-Year Total Return	Dividend Yield (TTM)	Expense Ratio	3-Yr Std Deviation	3-Year Beta	NAV	Total Assets (MIL)	%Cash	%Stocks	%Bonds	%Other	Turnover Ratio	Last Bull Market Total Return	Last Bear Market Total Return	Front End Fee (%)	Back End Fee (%)	Inception Date
	TOTAL RETURNS					PERFORMANCE				ASSETS		ASSET ALLOCATION & TURNOVER					BULL & BEAR		FEES		
	2.27	13.80	-1.15	20.77	3.50	1.35	2.05	11.47	0.97	14.84	2,368	2	98	0	0	34	16.16	-20.36		1.00	Apr-15
	2.53	14.43	-0.05	24.76	9.24	2.27	0.95	11.49	0.97	15.38	2,368	2	98	0	0	34	16.84	-20.03			Aug-89
	2.53	14.43	-0.01	24.92	9.45	2.31	0.9	11.47	0.97	15.38	2,368	2	98	0	0	34	16.83	-20.03			Sep-13
	2.30	13.89	-0.82	21.73	4.75	1.45	1.72	11.45	0.97	15.08	2,368	2	98	0	0	34	16.33	-20.28			Jun-12
	2.10	24.99	0.94	71.14	78.46	0	1.34	15.53	1.15	24.3	1,474	4	95	0	0	36	20.32	-26.17	5.25		Mar-10
	1.93	24.54	0.25	67.49	72.20	0	2.06	15.53	1.15	23.19	1,474	4	95	0	0	36	19.81	-26.37		1.00	Apr-15
	2.19	25.16	1.30	72.78	81.50	0	1	15.5	1.15	24.72	1,474	4	95	0	0	36	20.5	-26.06			Mar-10
	2.18	25.17	1.38	72.92	81.65	0	0.94	15.52	1.15	24.76	1,474	4	95	0	0	36	20.5	-26.06			Jun-18
	2.18	25.18	1.34	72.89	81.76	0	0.94	15.5	1.14	24.75	1,474	4	95	0	0	36	20.5	-26.06			Sep-13
	1.95	24.61	0.46	68.43	73.72	0	1.85	15.52	1.15	23.44	1,474	4	95	0	0	36	20	-26.28			Mar-10
	-1.44	12.35	2.79	19.73	10.28	4.02	1.35	11.53	1.02	19.1	20.6	2	97	0	1	28	20.99	-24.99	5.25		Oct-97
	-1.61	11.95	2.01	17.09	6.31	2.09	2.1	11.54	1.02	18.92	20.6	2	97	0	1	28	20.42	-25.2		1.00	Apr-15
	-1.34	12.60	3.16	21.05	12.27	4.39	1	11.55	1.02	19.12	20.6	2	97	0	1	28	21.12	-24.89			Oct-97
	-1.29	12.61	3.20	21.16	12.40	4.43	0.97	11.55	1.02	19.11	20.6	2	97	0	1	28	21.12	-24.89			Sep-13
	-1.55	12.10	2.30	17.98	7.58	3.59	1.85	11.55	1.02	18.98	20.6	2	97	0	1	28	20.6	-25.12			Apr-12
	0.32	0.21	0.15	1.32	-13.93	2.51	1.45	4.44	-25.06	9.3	25.0	22	50	27	1	187			5.25		Jun-12
	0.11	-0.11	-0.62	-0.94	-17.04	1.92	2.2	4.46	-25.22	8.98	25.0	22	50	27	1	187				1.00	Apr-15
	0.42	0.42	0.62	2.39	-12.38	2.85	1.1	4.4	-24.32	9.4	25.0	22	50	27	1	187					Jun-12
	0.42	0.42	0.56	2.42	-12.36	2.9	1.07	4.35	-23.52	9.39	25.0	22	50	27	1	187					May-15
	0.21	0.00	-0.19	-0.08	-15.86	1.98	1.95	4.38	-23.84	9.17	25.0	22	50	27	1	187					Jun-12
	-2.26	12.66	2.67	3.08	26.81	2.24	1.25	13.82	1.02	11.57	228.5	1	99	0	0	39	30.35	-17.48	5.25		Jan-96
	-2.46	12.23	1.92	0.74	22.18	1.53	2	13.87	1.02	11.48	228.5	1	99	0	0	39	29.89	-17.77		1.00	Apr-15
	-2.17	12.88	2.97	4.12	28.92	2.44	0.9	13.86	1.02	12.08	228.5	1	99	0	0	39	30.65	-17.43			Feb-95
	-2.23	12.90	3.04	4.19	29.01	2.5	0.83	13.86	1.02	12.08	228.5	1	99	0	0	39	30.65	-17.43			Jun-18
	-2.07	13.00	3.14	4.41	29.47	2.5	0.83	13.83	1.02	12.09	228.5	1	99	0	0	39	30.65	-17.43			Sep-13
	-2.39	12.44	2.18	1.52	23.60	1.77	1.75	13.84	1.02	11.55	228.5	1	99	0	0	39	30.01	-17.69			Nov-11
	6.41	21.84	7.44	36.45		0.09	1.15	13.16	1.05	13.11	13.7	1	99	0	0	60			5.25		May-16
	6.18	21.41	6.68	33.33		0	1.9	13.12	1.05	12.87	13.7	1	99	0	0	60				1.00	May-16
	6.47	22.07	7.90	37.89		0.41	0.8	13.07	1.04	13.16	13.7	1	99	0	0	60					May-16
	6.47	22.07	7.95	38.02		0.45	0.75	13.11	1.05	13.16	13.7	1	99	0	0	60					May-16
	2.63	9.14	4.62	12.06		2.7	1.36	5.31	0.74	10.32	15.6	9	31	54	7	132			5.25		Apr-15
	2.50	8.82	3.81	9.53		2.04	2.11	5.24	0.72	10.23	15.6	9	31	54	7	132				1.00	May-15
	2.82	9.45	5.11	13.24		3.06	1.01	5.27	0.72	10.33	15.6	9	31	54	7	132					Apr-15
	2.83	9.45	5.15	13.51		3.1	0.96	5.27	0.72	10.34	15.6	9	31	54	7	132					Apr-15
	2.34	8.07	3.33			0.71	2.06			10.05	24.1	31	27	30	11						Feb-18
	3.05	14.51	2.28	32.92	12.97	1.46	0.8	14.43	1.02	14.83	540.4	2	98	0	0	24	18.84	-27.03			Apr-94
	3.04	13.95	-1.41	27.52	9.91	1.94	0.66	11.87	1.06	12.17	1,435	2	98	0	0	41	17.9	-25.51			Nov-91
	3.54	18.87	8.80	45.90	56.72	1.6	0.48	12.56	1.02	19.27	1,584	2	98	0	0	29	26.95	-18.39			Nov-91
	2.84	21.60	2.37	45.01	36.21	0.47	0.61	15.3	0.98	19.14	403.5	3	97	0	0	34	29.1	-28.08			Nov-91
	1.39	12.49	4.61			2.87	1.15			10.15	10.2	4	70	26	0	26			5.25		Jun-18
	1.27	12.12	3.95			2.26	1.9			10.14	10.2	4	70	26	0	26				1.00	Jun-18
	1.64	12.76	5.08			3.11	0.8			10.17	10.2	4	70	26	0	26					Jun-18
	1.64	12.76	5.10			3.12	0.75			10.17	10.2	4	70	26	0	26					Jun-18
	2.71	14.27	3.94	34.25	33.07	1.57	0.64	10.18		12.09	103.5	1	89	10	0	32	18.33	-19.1			Apr-07
	1.29	2.46					1.36			10.2	119.2	39	7	29	2						Nov-18
	2.66	10.87	5.07	23.42	25.29	2.17	0.67	6.65		10.4	173.9	2	55	43	0	23	13.62	-12.21			Apr-07
	2.56	6.87	5.86	11.80	15.07	2.36	0.69	2.9		11.19	34.8	2	16	81	0	47	5.93	-2.62			Apr-07
	2.45	12.74					0.75			10.57	188.6	6	70	19	0						Nov-18
	2.68	12.90	4.56	29.62	29.98	1.86	0.66	8.74		11.11	218.5	1	73	25	0	28	16.68	-16.76			Apr-07
	2.57	8.84	5.49	17.64	19.86	2.45	0.68	4.63		9.97	75.0	2	36	62	0	35	9.49	-7.44			Apr-07
	2.80	13.86					1			10.64	481.0	4	96	0	0						Nov-18
	3.51	19.45					0.85			10.59	696.0	4	96	0	0						Nov-18

	MARKET		FUND TYPE, CATEGORY & OBJECTIVE		RATINGS				MINIMUMS	
Fund Name	Ticker Symbol	Traded On	Fund Type	Category and (Prospectus Objective)	Overall Rating	Reward Rating	Risk Rating	Recent Up/ Downgrade	Open to New Investors	Min Initial Investment
Morningstar Unconstrained Allocation Fund	MSTSX	NAS CM	Open End	Flexible Alloc (Growth)	U	U	U		Y	0
Mount Lucas U.S. Focused Equity Fund Class I	BMLEX	NAS CM	Open End	US Equity Large Cap Value (Growth)	C-	C-	C	Down	Y	10,000
MProved Systematic Long-Short Fund Institutional Class	MLSQX	NAS CM	Open End	Long/Short Equity (Growth)	D	D	C-		Y	1,000,000
MProved Systematic Long-Short Fund Investor Class	MLSJX	NAS CM	Open End	Long/Short Equity (Growth)	D	D	C-		Y	10,000
MProved Systematic Merger Arbitrage Institutional Cls	MMAQX	NAS CM	Open End	Market Neutral (Growth & Income)	D+	C-	B	Up	Y	1,000,000
MProved Systematic Merger Arbitrage Fund Investor Class	MMAJX	NAS CM	Open End	Market Neutral (Growth & Income)	D+	C-	B	Up	Y	10,000
MProved Systematic Multi-Strategy Fund Institutional Class	MMSQX	NAS CM	Open End	Multialternative (Growth & Income)	D+	D+	C+	Up	Y	1,000,000
MProved Systematic Multi-Strategy Fund Investor Class	MMSJX	NAS CM	Open End	Multialternative (Growth & Income)	D+	D+	C+	Up	Y	10,000
MS India Investment Fund	IIF	NYSE	Closed End	India Equity (Pacific Stock)	D+	D+	C-		Y	
Muhlenkamp Fund	MUHLX	NAS CM	Open End	US Equity Large Cap Blend (Growth & Income)	C	C-	C		Y	1,500
Multimanager Aggressive Equity Portfolio Class IA			Open End	US Equity Large Cap Growth (Growth)	C+	C	B	Down	Y	0
Multimanager Aggressive Equity Portfolio Class IB			Open End	US Equity Large Cap Growth (Growth)	C+	C	B	Down	Y	0
Multimanager Aggressive Equity Portfolio Class K			Open End	US Equity Large Cap Growth (Growth)	C+	C	B	Down	Y	0
Multi-Manager Alternative Strategies Fund Class A	CPASX	NAS CM	Open End	Multialternative (Growth & Income)	C	C-	C	Up	Y	100
Multi-Manager Alternative Strategies Institutional Cls	CZAMX	NAS CM	Open End	Multialternative (Growth & Income)	C	C-	C+	Up	Y	100
Multi-Manager Directional Alternative Strategies Cls A	CDAAX	NAS CM	Open End	Long/Short Equity (Growth)	C-	D+	C		Y	100
Multi-Manager Directional Alternative Strategies Inst Cls	CDAZX	NAS CM	Open End	Long/Short Equity (Growth)	C-	D+	C		Y	100
Multi-Manager Growth Strategies Fund Class A	CSLGX	NAS CM	Open End	US Equity Large Cap Growth (Growth)	C+	C	B	Down	Y	100
Multi-Manager Growth Strategies Fund Institutional Class	CZMGX	NAS CM	Open End	US Equity Large Cap Growth (Growth)	C+	C	B	Down	Y	100
Multi-Manager Intl Equity Strategies Inst Cls	CMIEX	NAS CM	Open End	Global Equity Large Cap (Foreign Stock)	D	D+	C+		Y	100
Multimanager Mid Cap Growth Portfolio Class IA			Open End	US Equity Mid Cap (Growth)	C+	C	C+	Down	Y	0
Multimanager Mid Cap Growth Portfolio Class IB			Open End	US Equity Mid Cap (Growth)	C+	C	C+	Down	Y	0
Multimanager Mid Cap Growth Portfolio Class K			Open End	US Equity Mid Cap (Growth)	C+	C	C+	Down	Y	0
Multimanager Mid Cap Value Portfolio Class IA			Open End	US Equity Mid Cap (Growth)	C	C	B-		Y	0
Multimanager Mid Cap Value Portfolio Class IB			Open End	US Equity Mid Cap (Growth)	C	C	B-		Y	0
Multimanager Mid Cap Value Portfolio Class K			Open End	US Equity Mid Cap (Growth)	C+	C	B-	Up	Y	0
Multi-Manager Small Cap Equity Strategies Fund Class A	CSCEX	NAS CM	Open End	US Equity Small Cap (Small Company)	C	C	C+		Y	100
Multi-Manager Small Cap Equity Strategies Inst Cls	CZMSX	NAS CM	Open End	US Equity Small Cap (Small Company)	C	C	C+		Y	100
Multimanager Technology Portfolio Class IA			Open End	Technology Sector Equity (Technology)	C+	C+	B-	Down	Y	0
Multimanager Technology Portfolio Class IB			Open End	Technology Sector Equity (Technology)	C+	C+	B-	Down	Y	0
Multimanager Technology Portfolio Class K			Open End	Technology Sector Equity (Technology)	C+	C+	B-	Down	Y	0
Multi-Manager Value Strategies Fund Class A	CDEIX	NAS CM	Open End	US Equity Large Cap Value (Growth)	B-	C	B	Up	Y	100
Multi-Manager Value Strategies Fund Institutional Class	CZMVX	NAS CM	Open End	US Equity Large Cap Value (Growth)	B-	C	B	Up	Y	100
Mundoval Fund	MUNDX	NAS CM	Open End	Global Equity Large Cap (Growth)	C+	C	B	Down	Y	10,000
Mutual of America 2010 Retirement Fund			Open End	Target Date 2000-2020 (Growth & Income)	U	U	U		Y	0
Mutual of America 2015 Retirement Fund			Open End	Target Date 2000-2020 (Growth & Income)	U	U	U		Y	0
Mutual of America 2020 Retirement Fund			Open End	Target Date 2000-2020 (Growth & Income)	U	U	U		Y	0
Mutual of America 2025 Retirement Fund			Open End	Target Date 2021-2045 (Growth & Income)	U	U	U		Y	0
Mutual of America 2030 Retirement Fund			Open End	Target Date 2021-2045 (Growth & Income)	U	U	U		Y	0
Mutual of America 2035 Retirement Fund			Open End	Target Date 2021-2045 (Growth & Income)	U	U	U		Y	0
Mutual of America 2040 Retirement Fund			Open End	Target Date 2021-2045 (Growth & Income)	U	U	U		Y	0
Mutual of America 2045 Retirement Fund			Open End	Target Date 2021-2045 (Growth & Income)	U	U	U		Y	0
Mutual of America 2050 Retirement Fund			Open End	Target Date 2046+ (Growth & Income)	U	U	U		Y	0
Mutual of America Institutional Funds Inc All America Fund	MALLX	NAS CM	Open End	US Equity Large Cap Blend (Growth)	C+	C	B		Y	25,000
Mutual of America Inst Funds Inc Equity Index Fund	MAEQX	NAS CM	Open End	US Equity Large Cap Blend (Growth)	B-	C	B		Y	25,000
Mutual of America Inst Funds Inc Mid-Cap Equity Index Fund	MAMQX	NAS CM	Open End	US Equity Mid Cap (Growth)	C+	C	B-	Up	Y	25,000
Mutual of America Inst Funds Inc Small Cap Growth Fund	MASSX	NAS CM	Open End	US Equity Small Cap (Small Company)	C	C	C+		Y	25,000
Mutual of America Inst Funds Inc Small Cap Value Fund	MAVSX	NAS CM	Open End	US Equity Small Cap (Small Company)	C	C-	C+		Y	25,000
Nationwide AllianzGI International Growth Fund Class A	NWAGX	NAS CM	Open End	Global Equity Large Cap (Growth)	C	C	C+		Y	2,000
Nationwide AllianzGI International Growth Fund Class R6	NWAHX	NAS CM	Open End	Global Equity Large Cap (Growth)	C	C	C+		Y	1,000,000
Nationwide AllianzGI International Growth Fund Eagle Class	NWAJX	NAS CM	Open End	Global Equity Large Cap (Growth)	C	C	C+		Y	50,000
Nationwide AllianzGI Intl Growth Inst Service Cls	NWAKX	NAS CM	Open End	Global Equity Large Cap (Growth)	C	C	C+		Y	50,000

★ Expanded analysis of this fund is included in Section II.

Min Additional Investment	TOTAL RETURNS: 3-Month Total Return	6-Month Total Return	1-Year Total Return	3-Year Total Return	5-Year Total Return	PERFORMANCE: Dividend Yield (TTM)	Expense Ratio	3-Yr Std Deviation	3-Year Beta	ASSETS: NAV	Total Assets (MIL)	ASSET ALLOCATION & TURNOVER: %Cash	%Stocks	%Bonds	%Other	Turnover Ratio	BULL & BEAR: Last Bull Market Total Return	Last Bear Market Total Return	FEES: Front End Fee (%)	Back End Fee (%)	Inception Date
	3.86	10.75					0.93			10.47	54.9	10	69	21	0						Nov-18
	-1.10	4.47	-13.23	32.46	22.82	1.84	0.95	14.99	1.03	9.81	8.2	-1	101	0	0	68	26.09	-23.92			Oct-07
100	-2.35	1.78	-4.84			2.4	1.4			9.14	1.9	45	32	16	7	152					Dec-17
100	-2.56	1.55	-5.11			2.14	1.65			9.12	1.9	45	32	16	7	152					Dec-17
100	-0.47	1.06	6.23			0	1.62			10.45	2.2	80	0	9	11	320					Dec-17
100	-0.57	0.96	5.94			0	1.87			10.41	2.2	80	0	9	11	320					Dec-17
100	-1.45	-0.97	5.18			0	2.18			10.19	16.7	46	-41	24	1	192					Dec-17
100	-1.45	-1.07	4.88			0	2.43			10.15	16.7	46	-41	24	1	192					Dec-17
	0.37	1.70	-5.91	14.75	36.63	0	1.29	18.05	0.43	23.8	331.2	3	97	0	0	35	-1.36	-23.64			Feb-94
50	-0.44	7.23	-2.67	16.69	-4.51	0.33	1.13	11.16	0.87	44.49	187.5	19	77	0	4	10	19.31	-18.96			Nov-88
	2.73	12.61	6.11	62.27	80.89	0.12	0.98	13.24	1.06		1,279	1	99	0	0	45	22.56	-19.21			Jan-86
	2.74	12.62	6.12	62.28	80.90	0.12	0.98	13.25	1.06		1,279	1	99	0	0	45	22.47	-19.32			Oct-96
	2.80	12.76	6.39	63.49	82.66	0.35	0.73	13.26	1.06		1,279	1	99	0	0	45	22.64	-19.21			Aug-11
	1.79	4.35	2.69	-2.20	-3.74	1.18	1.59	3.06	44.33	9.1	500.6	-101	17	188	-7	256					Apr-12
	1.89	4.46	2.95	-1.31	-2.86	1.42	1.34	3.03	43.58	9.13	500.6	-101	17	188	-7	256					Jan-17
	0.14	5.73	-2.91			0.47	2.55			6.82	255.1	40	59	0	1	158					Oct-16
	0.29	5.94	-3.10			0.57	2.3			6.77	255.1	40	59	0	1	158					Jan-17
	4.83	24.28	11.47	58.87	73.86	0	1.1	15.32	1.1	14.58	2,161	1	99	0	0	41					Apr-12
	4.90	24.41	11.78	60.09	75.19	0.01	0.85	15.3	1.1	14.42	2,161	1	99	0	0	41					Jan-17
	3.02	15.07	-0.01			0.72	1.01			9.54	2,003	2	98	0	0	17					May-18
	1.28	12.82	3.00	59.63	65.12	0	1.1	16.15	1.04		217.6	1	98	1	0	55	23.41	-24.76			Dec-01
	1.26	12.89	3.00	59.71	65.08	0	1.1	16.09	1.04		217.6	1	98	1	0	55	23.49	-24.9			Dec-01
	1.35	12.95	3.21	60.94	67.15	0	0.85	16.11	1.04		217.6	1	98	1	0	55	23.54	-24.76			Aug-11
	-1.62	3.30	-3.25	25.32	27.23	0.75	1.1	13.13	0.94		176.7	2	98	0	0	34	16.81	-25.63			Dec-01
	-1.59	3.30	-3.26	25.38	27.20	0.77	1.1	13.14	0.94		176.7	2	98	0	0	34	16.64	-25.71			Dec-01
	-1.55	3.45	-3.04	26.27	28.74	1	0.85	13.13	0.94		176.7	2	98	0	0	34	16.81	-25.63			Aug-11
	3.28	18.15	-1.96	44.07	40.87	0.03	1.34	17	0.99	15.1	1,744	1	99	0	0	82					Apr-12
	3.35	18.33	-1.68	45.03	41.80	0.12	1.09	17.04	0.99	15.1	1,744	1	99	0	0	82					Jan-17
	5.55	19.63	8.87	93.10	125.39	0.13	1.25	15.58	1.04		1,265	2	98	0	0	52	24	-17.2			Dec-01
	5.54	19.62	8.86	93.03	125.33	0.13	1.25	15.59	1.04		1,265	2	98	0	0	52	23.89	-17.25			Dec-01
	5.62	19.76	9.11	94.52	128.05	0.34	1	15.58	1.04		1,265	2	98	0	0	52	24	-17.2			Aug-12
	4.64	17.98	8.65	41.66	45.86	1.19	1.03	12.52	1.02	13.84	3,055	2	98	0	0	21					Apr-12
	4.67	18.14	8.85	42.33	46.55	1.43	0.78	12.53	1.03	13.69	3,055	2	98	0	0	21					Jan-17
100	5.22	20.58	7.52	48.12	27.57	0.19	1.51	12.05	1.01	19.33	23.2	3	97	0	0	7	15.36	-17.33			Sep-04
	2.28	5.71	7.18	19.72	43.99	2.04	0.38	4.53	0.39		25.2	7	35	58	0	23	11.8	-7.1			Nov-07
	2.72	6.28	7.71	21.18	50.49	2	0.4	5.56	0.48		146.6	4	44	51	0	18	13.38	-9.4			Nov-07
	3.20	6.76	8.24	22.31	57.15	1.64	0.38	6.63	0.59		400.1	4	55	41	0	8	15.45	-11.5			Nov-07
	3.69	7.39	8.95	23.95	65.63	1.48	0.36	7.88	0.7		461.7	3	67	30	0	4	17.96	-13.92			Nov-07
	4.03	7.86	9.37	25.50	71.87	1.44	0.35	8.67	0.77		377.6	3	74	23	0	5	19.52	-15.54			Nov-07
	4.36	8.18	9.51	25.76	76.09	1.36	0.35	9.43	0.84		317.4	3	82	15	0	5	20.97	-17.26			Nov-07
	4.54	8.41	9.20	25.03	76.77	1.3	0.36	9.92	0.88		258.4	3	85	12	0	5	21.36	-18.15			Nov-07
	4.68	8.48	9.07	24.57	76.51	1.32	0.37	10.14	0.9		303.2	3	87	10	0	4	21.3	-18.38			Nov-07
	4.78	8.60	9.02	24.32		0.72	0.39	10.34	0.91		133.8	3	89	8	0	3					Oct-12
5,000	3.45	18.47	5.46	41.49	51.27	0.46	0.5	12.76	1.03	11.9037	7.3	1	99	0	0	20	24.35	-18.27			May-96
5,000	4.32	19.59	10.35	50.33	65.39	0.82	0.13	12.04	0.99	12.2391	51.8	4	96	0	0	11	25.01	-16.31			Apr-99
5,000	3.01	19.15	1.22	38.28	46.49	1.64	0.13	15.14	1	11.1673	26.6	5	95	0	0	25	27.91	-22.63			Sep-00
5,000	1.33	18.50	-1.12	40.80	40.92	0.11	0.85	16.92	0.96	11.8707	9.1	0	100	0	0	60	23.13	-23.85			May-07
5,000	1.55	12.83	-5.59	21.67	21.78	0.84	0.85	14.96	0.85	11.6562	11.1	4	96	0	0	29	22.83	-21.71			May-07
100	3.60	19.81	1.38	37.32		0.32	1.05	14.92	1.19	17.84	6.5	0	100	0	0	17			5.75		Feb-15
	3.63	19.93	1.61	38.43		0.46	0.72	14.93	1.19	18.27	6.5	0	100	0	0	17					Feb-15
							0.82	14.93	1.19	18.31	6.5	0	100	0	0	17					Jun-19
							0.97	14.93	1.19	18.3	6.5	0	100	0	0	17					Jun-19

	MARKET			FUND TYPE, CATEGORY & OBJECTIVE	RATINGS					MINIMUMS
Fund Name	Ticker Symbol	Traded On	Fund Type	Category and (Prospectus Objective)	Overall Rating	Reward Rating	Risk Rating	Recent Up/ Downgrade	Open to New Investors	Min Initial Investment
Nationwide Bailard Cognitive Value Fund Class A	NWHDX	NAS CM	Open End	US Equity Small Cap (Small Company)	C-	D+	C		Y	2,000
Nationwide Bailard Cognitive Value Fund Class C	NWHEX	NAS CM	Open End	US Equity Small Cap (Small Company)	C-	D	C		Y	2,000
Nationwide Bailard Cognitive Value Fund Class M	NWHFX	NAS CM	Open End	US Equity Small Cap (Small Company)	C	D+	C	Up	Y	5,000
Nationwide Bailard Cognitive Value Fund Class R6	NWHGX	NAS CM	Open End	US Equity Small Cap (Small Company)	C	D+	C	Up	Y	1,000,000
Nationwide Bailard Cognitive Value Inst Service Cls	NWHHX	NAS CM	Open End	US Equity Small Cap (Small Company)	C-	D+	C		Y	50,000
Nationwide Bailard Emerging Markets Equity Fund Class A	NWWAX	NAS CM	Open End	Global Emerg Mkts (Div Emerging Mkts)	C	C-	C		Y	2,000
Nationwide Bailard Emerging Markets Equity Fund Class C	NWWBX	NAS CM	Open End	Global Emerg Mkts (Div Emerging Mkts)	C	C-	C		Y	2,000
Nationwide Bailard Emerging Markets Equity Fund Class M	NWWEX	NAS CM	Open End	Global Emerg Mkts (Div Emerging Mkts)	C	C-	C+		Y	5,000
Nationwide Bailard Emerging Markets Equity Fund Class R6	NWWCX	NAS CM	Open End	Global Emerg Mkts (Div Emerging Mkts)	C	C	C+		Y	1,000,000
Nationwide Bailard Emerging Mkts Equity Inst Service Cls	NWWDX	NAS CM	Open End	Global Emerg Mkts (Div Emerging Mkts)	C	C-	C+		Y	50,000
Nationwide Bailard International Equities Fund Class A	NWHJX	NAS CM	Open End	Global Equity Large Cap (Foreign Stock)	C	D+	C	Up	Y	2,000
Nationwide Bailard International Equities Fund Class C	NWHKX	NAS CM	Open End	Global Equity Large Cap (Foreign Stock)	C-	D+	C		Y	2,000
Nationwide Bailard International Equities Fund Class M	NWHLX	NAS CM	Open End	Global Equity Large Cap (Foreign Stock)	C	C-	C+	Up	Y	5,000
Nationwide Bailard International Equities Fund Class R6	NWHMX	NAS CM	Open End	Global Equity Large Cap (Foreign Stock)	C	C-	C+	Up	Y	1,000,000
Nationwide Bailard Intl Equities Inst Service Cls	NWHNX	NAS CM	Open End	Global Equity Large Cap (Foreign Stock)	C	C-	C+	Up	Y	50,000
Nationwide Bailard Technology and Science Fund Class A	NWHOX	NAS CM	Open End	Technology Sector Equity (Technology)	C+	C+	C+	Down	Y	2,000
Nationwide Bailard Technology and Science Fund Class C	NWHPX	NAS CM	Open End	Technology Sector Equity (Technology)	C+	C+	C+	Down	Y	2,000
Nationwide Bailard Technology and Science Fund Class M	NWHQX	NAS CM	Open End	Technology Sector Equity (Technology)	C+	C+	C+	Down	Y	5,000
Nationwide Bailard Technology and Science Fund Class R6	NWHTX	NAS CM	Open End	Technology Sector Equity (Technology)	C+	C+	C+	Down	Y	1,000,000
Nationwide Bailard Technology & Science Inst Service Cls	NWHUX	NAS CM	Open End	Technology Sector Equity (Technology)	C+	C+	C+	Down	Y	50,000
Nationwide Destination 2010 Fund Class A	NWDAX	NAS CM	Open End	Target Date (Asset Alloc)	B-	C	A-	Up	Y	2,000
Nationwide Destination 2010 Fund Class C	NWDCX	NAS CM	Open End	Target Date (Asset Alloc)	B-	C	B+	Up	Y	2,000
Nationwide Destination 2010 Fund Class R	NWDBX	NAS CM	Open End	Target Date (Asset Alloc)	B-	C	A-	Up	Y	0
Nationwide Destination 2010 Fund Class R6	NWDIX	NAS CM	Open End	Target Date (Asset Alloc)	B	C	A-	Up	Y	1,000,000
Nationwide Destination 2010 Institutional Service Cls	NWDSX	NAS CM	Open End	Target Date (Asset Alloc)	B	C	A-	Up	Y	50,000
Nationwide Destination 2015 Fund Class A	NWEAX	NAS CM	Open End	Target Date (Asset Alloc)	B-	C	A-	Up	Y	2,000
Nationwide Destination 2015 Fund Class C	NWECX	NAS CM	Open End	Target Date (Asset Alloc)	B-	C	B+	Up	Y	2,000
Nationwide Destination 2015 Fund Class R	NWEBX	NAS CM	Open End	Target Date (Asset Alloc)	B-	C	A-	Up	Y	0
Nationwide Destination 2015 Fund Class R6	NWEIX	NAS CM	Open End	Target Date (Asset Alloc)	B	C	A-	Up	Y	1,000,000
Nationwide Destination 2015 Institutional Service Cls	NWESX	NAS CM	Open End	Target Date (Asset Alloc)	B-	C	A-	Up	Y	50,000
Nationwide Destination 2020 Fund Class A	NWAFX	NAS CM	Open End	Target Date (Asset Alloc)	B-	C	A-	Up	Y	2,000
Nationwide Destination 2020 Fund Class C	NWFCX	NAS CM	Open End	Target Date (Asset Alloc)	B-	C	A-	Up	Y	2,000
Nationwide Destination 2020 Fund Class R	NWFTX	NAS CM	Open End	Target Date (Asset Alloc)	B-	C	A-	Up	Y	0
Nationwide Destination 2020 Fund Class R6	NWFIX	NAS CM	Open End	Target Date (Asset Alloc)	B	C	A-	Up	Y	1,000,000
Nationwide Destination 2020 Institutional Service Cls	NWFSX	NAS CM	Open End	Target Date (Asset Alloc)	B-	C	A-	Up	Y	50,000
Nationwide Destination 2025 Fund Class A	NWHAX	NAS CM	Open End	Target Date (Asset Alloc)	B-	C	A-	Up	Y	2,000
Nationwide Destination 2025 Fund Class C	NWHCX	NAS CM	Open End	Target Date (Asset Alloc)	B-	C	B+	Up	Y	2,000
Nationwide Destination 2025 Fund Class R	NWHBX	NAS CM	Open End	Target Date (Asset Alloc)	B-	C	A-	Up	Y	0
Nationwide Destination 2025 Fund Class R6	NWHIX	NAS CM	Open End	Target Date (Asset Alloc)	B-	C	A-	Up	Y	1,000,000
Nationwide Destination 2025 Institutional Service Cls	NWHSX	NAS CM	Open End	Target Date (Asset Alloc)	B-	C	A-	Up	Y	50,000
Nationwide Destination 2030 Fund Class A	NWIAX	NAS CM	Open End	Target Date (Asset Alloc)	B-	C	B+	Up	Y	2,000
Nationwide Destination 2030 Fund Class C	NWICX	NAS CM	Open End	Target Date (Asset Alloc)	B-	C	B+	Up	Y	2,000
Nationwide Destination 2030 Fund Class R	NWBIX	NAS CM	Open End	Target Date (Asset Alloc)	B-	C	B+	Up	Y	0
Nationwide Destination 2030 Fund Class R6	NWIIX	NAS CM	Open End	Target Date (Asset Alloc)	B-	C	B+	Up	Y	1,000,000
Nationwide Destination 2030 Institutional Service Cls	NWISX	NAS CM	Open End	Target Date (Asset Alloc)	B-	C	B+	Up	Y	50,000
Nationwide Destination 2035 Fund Class A	NWLAX	NAS CM	Open End	Target Date (Asset Alloc)	B-	C	B+	Up	Y	2,000
Nationwide Destination 2035 Fund Class C	NWLCX	NAS CM	Open End	Target Date (Asset Alloc)	B-	C	B+	Up	Y	2,000
Nationwide Destination 2035 Fund Class R	NWLBX	NAS CM	Open End	Target Date (Asset Alloc)	B-	C	B+	Up	Y	0
Nationwide Destination 2035 Fund Class R6	NWLIX	NAS CM	Open End	Target Date (Asset Alloc)	B-	C	B+	Up	Y	1,000,000
Nationwide Destination 2035 Institutional Service Cls	NWLSX	NAS CM	Open End	Target Date (Asset Alloc)	B-	C	B+	Up	Y	50,000
Nationwide Destination 2040 Fund Class A	NWMAX	NAS CM	Open End	Target Date (Asset Alloc)	B-	C	B	Up	Y	2,000
Nationwide Destination 2040 Fund Class C	NWMCX	NAS CM	Open End	Target Date (Asset Alloc)	B-	C	B	Up	Y	2,000

★ Expanded analysis of this fund is included in Section II.

	TOTAL RETURNS					PERFORMANCE				ASSETS		ASSET ALLOCATION & TURNOVER					BULL & BEAR		FEES		
Min Additional Investment	3-Month Total Return	6-Month Total Return	1-Year Total Return	3-Year Total Return	5-Year Total Return	Dividend Yield (TTM)	Expense Ratio	3-Yr Std Deviation	3-Year Beta	NAV	Total Assets (MIL)	%Cash	%Stocks	%Bonds	%Other	Turnover Ratio	Last Bull Market Total Return	Last Bear Market Total Return	Front End Fee (%)	Back End Fee (%)	Inception Date
100	0.63	14.84	-8.48	18.87	17.38	0.54	1.42	17.32	0.97	11.14	62.5	1	99	0	0	138	27.95	-23.27	5.75		Apr-06
100	0.39	14.31	-9.17	16.19	12.96	0.4	2.18	17.31	0.97	10.14	62.5	1	99	0	0	138	27.44	-23.44		1.00	Apr-06
100	0.63	14.93	-8.19	20.05	19.34	0.84	1.08	17.3	0.97	11.16	62.5	1	99	0	0	138	28.23	-23.13			May-01
	0.72	15.05	-8.18	20.07	19.45	0.84	1.08	17.38	0.97	11.16	62.5	1	99	0	0	138	28.23	-23.13			Sep-13
	0.62	14.90	-8.33	19.63	19.00	0.59	1.23	17.33	0.97	11.18	62.5	1	99	0	0	138	28.23	-23.21			Apr-06
100	0.54	11.74	-2.93	24.04	-1.14	6.36	1.52	14.37	1	9.23	31.0	1	99	0	0	78			5.75		Mar-14
100	0.33	11.15	-3.83	21.15	-4.84	5.93	2.27	14.3	1	9.07	31.0	1	99	0	0	78				1.00	Mar-14
100	0.65	11.93	-2.58	25.31	0.48	6.55	1.12	14.44	1.01	9.19	31.0	1	99	0	0	78					Mar-14
	0.73	11.95	-2.26	25.73	0.77	18.93	1.12	14.35	1	8.24	31.0	1	99	0	0	78					Mar-14
	0.77	11.97	-2.64	24.98	0.05	6.51	1.27	14.35	1	9.16	31.0	1	99	0	0	78					Mar-14
100	3.07	14.28	-2.79	16.67	4.41	4.97	1.2	11.66	1	7.71	220.5	1	98	0	2	71	15.73	-26.14	5.75		Apr-06
100	2.83	13.86	-3.49	14.16	0.54	4.22	1.95	11.64	1	7.62	220.5	1	98	0	2	71	15.47	-26.41		1.00	Apr-06
100	3.19	14.58	-2.41	18.16	6.39	5.36	0.85	11.68	1	7.71	220.5	1	98	0	2	71	16.09	-26.1			Sep-79
	3.06	14.43	-2.54	18.01	6.25	5.36	0.85	11.59	1	7.7	220.5	1	98	0	2	71	16.09	-26.1			Sep-13
	3.14	14.36	-2.51	17.74	5.75	5.27	0.95	11.6	1	7.7	220.5	1	98	0	2	71	16.02	-26.14			Apr-06
100	4.76	25.33	7.13	88.59	107.91	1.05	1.24	16.36	1	20.68	130.6	1	99	0	0	23	28.49	-17.62	5.75		Apr-06
100	4.60	24.87	6.31	84.29	100.25	1.18	2.03	16.34	1	18.17	130.6	1	99	0	0	23	27.98	-17.86		1.00	Apr-06
100	4.83	25.42	7.47	90.37	111.32	0.04	0.93	16.37	1	21.9	130.6	1	99	0	0	23	28.83	-17.53			May-01
	4.84	25.44	7.44	90.34	111.36	0.04	0.93	16.35	1	21.84	130.6	1	99	0	0	23	28.83	-17.53			Sep-13
	4.79	25.37	7.33	89.80	110.22	1	1.03	16.35	1	21.84	130.6	1	99	0	0	23	28.73	-17.46			Apr-06
100	2.65	9.75	4.82	17.54	19.26	1.86	0.89	5.1	1.04	8.14	17.3	29	28	43	0	38	8.56	-10.12	5.75		Aug-07
100	2.50	9.49	4.22	15.33	15.37	1.18	1.54	5.12	1.05	8.08	17.3	29	28	43	0	38	8.3	-10.37		1.00	Aug-07
	2.47	9.51	4.57	16.57	17.59	1.62	1.14	5.08	1.04	8.11	17.3	29	28	43	0	38	8.36	-10.15			Aug-07
	2.77	10.02	5.35	19.29	22.09	2.33	0.39	5.08	1.04	8.15	17.3	29	28	43	0	38	8.81	-9.98			Aug-07
	2.65	9.88	5.35	19.14	21.65	2.34	0.64	5.12	1.05	8.14	17.3	29	28	43	0	38	8.96	-10			Aug-07
100	2.64	10.31	4.60	20.21	21.06	1.92	0.9	5.71	1.06	8.3	67.0	26	32	41	0	28	10.16	-11.4	5.75		Aug-07
100	2.52	10.04	4.14	18.21	17.60	1.37	1.45	5.8	1.07	8.25	67.0	26	32	41	0	28	9.77	-11.63		1.00	Aug-07
	2.70	10.19	4.44	19.32	19.44	1.64	1.15	5.8	1.07	8.27	67.0	26	32	41	0	28	9.97	-11.44			Aug-07
	2.75	10.67	5.21	21.91	23.98	2.36	0.4	5.73	1.06	8.33	67.0	26	32	41	0	28	10.4	-11.23			Aug-07
	2.70	10.42	4.95	21.03	22.32	2.13	0.65	5.78	1.07	8.31	67.0	26	32	41	0	28	10.27	-11.27			Aug-07
100	2.90	11.54	4.93	23.44	23.09	1.82	0.91	6.69	1.11	9.04	208.3	20	37	42	0	23	11.49	-12.74	5.75		Aug-07
100	2.68	11.13	4.18	21.03	19.09	1.21	1.51	6.62	1.1	8.91	208.3	20	37	42	0	23	11.29	-13.03		1.00	Aug-07
	2.85	11.30	4.57	22.38	21.27	1.58	1.16	6.63	1.1	9.01	208.3	20	37	42	0	23	11.43	-12.87			Aug-07
	3.01	11.73	5.44	25.20	25.89	2.28	0.41	6.64	1.1	9.1	208.3	20	37	42	0	23	11.96	-12.66			Aug-07
	2.96	11.65	5.20	24.24	24.31	2.05	0.66	6.66	1.1	9.06	208.3	20	37	42	0	23	11.74	-12.71			Aug-07
100	2.92	12.44	4.72	26.36	24.89	1.78	0.91	7.55	1.1	9.34	298.2	18	44	37	0	25	13.67	-14.8	5.75		Aug-07
100	2.68	12.00	4.02	24.10	21.05	1.23	1.5	7.62	1.11	9.23	298.2	18	44	37	0	25	13.3	-14.97		1.00	Aug-07
	2.87	12.34	4.46	25.32	23.10	1.55	1.16	7.55	1.1	9.31	298.2	18	44	37	0	25	13.49	-14.83			Aug-07
	3.14	12.75	5.21	28.27	27.86	2.24	0.41	7.58	1.1	9.41	298.2	18	44	37	0	25	13.99	-14.61			Aug-07
	2.98	12.56	4.98	27.23	26.17	2.02	0.66	7.55	1.1	9.35	298.2	18	44	37	0	25	13.85	-14.76			Aug-07
100	3.14	13.72	4.90	29.24	27.11	1.76	0.93	8.67	1.09	8.94	314.9	12	53	35	0	23	16.16	-16.8	5.75		Aug-07
100	2.93	13.47	4.37	27.15	23.65	1.28	1.47	8.62	1.08	8.83	314.9	12	53	35	0	23	15.8	-16.95		1.00	Aug-07
	3.09	13.64	4.75	28.38	25.54	1.51	1.18	8.63	1.09	8.89	314.9	12	53	35	0	23	15.86	-16.74			Aug-07
	3.24	14.00	5.48	31.14	30.32	2.2	0.43	8.68	1.09	9.01	314.9	12	53	35	0	23	16.48	-16.6			Aug-07
	3.20	13.83	5.14	30.09	28.63	1.98	0.68	8.63	1.09	8.95	314.9	12	53	35	0	23	16.2	-16.65			Aug-07
100	3.14	14.72	4.83	31.25	28.66	1.7	0.92	9.51	1.05	9.64	265.4	11	61	27	0	25	17.81	-17.8	5.75		Aug-07
100	2.97	14.42	4.29	28.86	24.74	1.26	1.49	9.51	1.05	9.43	265.4	11	61	27	0	25	17.52	-18.1		1.00	Aug-07
	3.21	14.68	4.69	30.21	27.02	1.47	1.17	9.54	1.05	9.58	265.4	11	61	27	0	25	17.66	-17.89			Aug-07
	3.24	15.01	5.33	33.03	31.65	2.15	0.42	9.5	1.05	9.71	265.4	11	61	27	0	25	18.28	-17.69			Aug-07
	3.20	14.85	5.10	32.13	30.09	1.93	0.67	9.56	1.05	9.65	265.4	11	61	27	0	25	18	-17.7			Aug-07
100	3.18	15.63	4.78	33.08	30.69	1.63	0.92	10.3	1.04	9.41	222.2	10	66	23	0	21	18.56	-18.94	5.75		Aug-07
100	3.19	15.38	4.33	31.15	27.20	1.21	1.45	10.4	1.05	9.35	222.2	10	66	23	0	21	18.15	-19.03		1.00	Aug-07

Fund Name	MARKET Ticker Symbol	Traded On	FUND TYPE, CATEGORY & OBJECTIVE Fund Type	Category and (Prospectus Objective)	RATINGS Overall Rating	Reward Rating	Risk Rating	Recent Up/ Downgrade	MINIMUMS Open to New Investors	Min Initial Investment
Nationwide Destination 2040 Fund Class R	NWMDX	NAS CM	Open End	Target Date (Asset Alloc)	B-	C	B	Up	Y	0
Nationwide Destination 2040 Fund Class R6	NWMHX	NAS CM	Open End	Target Date (Asset Alloc)	B-	C	B	Up	Y	1,000,000
Nationwide Destination 2040 Institutional Service Cls	NWMSX	NAS CM	Open End	Target Date (Asset Alloc)	B-	C	B	Up	Y	50,000
Nationwide Destination 2045 Fund Class A	NWNAX	NAS CM	Open End	Target Date (Asset Alloc)	B-	C	B	Up	Y	2,000
Nationwide Destination 2045 Fund Class C	NWNCX	NAS CM	Open End	Target Date (Asset Alloc)	B-	C	B	Up	Y	2,000
Nationwide Destination 2045 Fund Class R	NWNBX	NAS CM	Open End	Target Date (Asset Alloc)	B-	C	B	Up	Y	0
Nationwide Destination 2045 Fund Class R6	NWNIX	NAS CM	Open End	Target Date (Asset Alloc)	B-	C	B	Up	Y	1,000,000
Nationwide Destination 2045 Institutional Service Cls	NWNSX	NAS CM	Open End	Target Date (Asset Alloc)	B-	C	B	Up	Y	50,000
Nationwide Destination 2050 Fund Class A	NWOAX	NAS CM	Open End	Target Date (Asset Alloc)	B-	C	B	Up	Y	2,000
Nationwide Destination 2050 Fund Class C	NWOCX	NAS CM	Open End	Target Date (Asset Alloc)	B-	C	B	Up	Y	2,000
Nationwide Destination 2050 Fund Class R	NWOBX	NAS CM	Open End	Target Date (Asset Alloc)	B-	C	B	Up	Y	0
Nationwide Destination 2050 Fund Class R6	NWOIX	NAS CM	Open End	Target Date (Asset Alloc)	B-	C	B	Up	Y	1,000,000
Nationwide Destination 2050 Institutional Service Cls	NWOSX	NAS CM	Open End	Target Date (Asset Alloc)	B-	C	B	Up	Y	50,000
Nationwide Destination 2055 Fund Class A	NTDAX	NAS CM	Open End	Target Date (Asset Alloc)	B-	C	B	Up	Y	2,000
Nationwide Destination 2055 Fund Class C	NTDCX	NAS CM	Open End	Target Date (Asset Alloc)	C+	C	B	Up	Y	2,000
Nationwide Destination 2055 Fund Class R	NTDTX	NAS CM	Open End	Target Date (Asset Alloc)	B-	C	B	Up	Y	0
Nationwide Destination 2055 Fund Class R6	NTDIX	NAS CM	Open End	Target Date (Asset Alloc)	B-	C	B	Up	Y	1,000,000
Nationwide Destination 2055 Institutional Service Cls	NTDSX	NAS CM	Open End	Target Date (Asset Alloc)	B-	C	B	Up	Y	50,000
Nationwide Destination 2060 Fund Class A	NWWRX	NAS CM	Open End	Target Date (Asset Alloc)	B-	C	B	Up	Y	2,000
Nationwide Destination 2060 Fund Class C	NWWSX	NAS CM	Open End	Target Date (Asset Alloc)	C+	C	B	Up	Y	2,000
Nationwide Destination 2060 Fund Class R	NWWTX	NAS CM	Open End	Target Date (Asset Alloc)	B-	C	B	Up	Y	0
Nationwide Destination 2060 Fund Class R6	NWWUX	NAS CM	Open End	Target Date (Asset Alloc)	B-	C	B	Up	Y	1,000,000
Nationwide Destination 2060 Institutional Service Cls	NWWVX	NAS CM	Open End	Target Date (Asset Alloc)	B-	C	B	Up	Y	50,000
Nationwide Diamond Hill Large Cap Concentrated Cls A	NWGHX	NAS CM	Open End	US Equity Large Cap Blend (Growth)	B-	C+	B		Y	2,000
Nationwide Diamond Hill Large Cap Concentrated Cls C	NWGIX	NAS CM	Open End	US Equity Large Cap Blend (Growth)	C+	C	B	Down	Y	2,000
Nationwide Diamond Hill Large Cap Concentrated Cls R6	NWGJX	NAS CM	Open End	US Equity Large Cap Blend (Growth)	B-	C+	B		Y	1,000,000
Nationwide Diamond Hill Large Cap Conc Inst Serv Cls	NWGKX	NAS CM	Open End	US Equity Large Cap Blend (Growth)	B-	C+	B		Y	50,000
Nationwide Dynamic U.S. Growth Fund Class A	NMFAX	NAS CM	Open End	US Equity Large Cap Blend (Growth)	B-	C+	B		Y	2,000
Nationwide Dynamic U.S. Growth Fund Class C	GCGRX	NAS CM	Open End	US Equity Large Cap Blend (Growth)	B-	C+	B		Y	2,000
Nationwide Dynamic U.S. Growth Fund Class R	GGFRX	NAS CM	Open End	US Equity Large Cap Blend (Growth)	B-	C+	B		Y	0
Nationwide Dynamic U.S. Growth Fund Class R6	MUIGX	NAS CM	Open End	US Equity Large Cap Blend (Growth)	B-	C+	B		Y	1,000,000
Nationwide Dynamic U.S. Growth Fund Eagle Class	NWAEX	NAS CM	Open End	US Equity Large Cap Blend (Growth)	B-	C+	B		Y	50,000
Nationwide Dynamic U.S. Growth Institutional Service Cls	NGISX	NAS CM	Open End	US Equity Large Cap Blend (Growth)	B-	C+	B		Y	50,000
Nationwide Fund Class A	NWFAX	NAS CM	Open End	US Equity Large Cap Blend (Growth & Income)	C+	C	B	Down	Y	2,000
Nationwide Fund Class C	GTRCX	NAS CM	Open End	US Equity Large Cap Blend (Growth & Income)	C+	C	B		Y	2,000
Nationwide Fund Class R	GNWRX	NAS CM	Open End	US Equity Large Cap Blend (Growth & Income)	C+	C	B	Down	Y	0
Nationwide Fund Class R6	NWABX	NAS CM	Open End	US Equity Large Cap Blend (Growth & Income)	C+	C	B	Down	Y	1,000,000
Nationwide Fund Institutional Service Class	MUIFX	NAS CM	Open End	US Equity Large Cap Blend (Growth & Income)	C+	C	B	Down	Y	50,000
Nationwide Geneva Mid Cap Growth Fund Class A	NWHVX	NAS CM	Open End	US Equity Mid Cap (Growth)	B-	C+	B-		Y	2,000
Nationwide Geneva Mid Cap Growth Fund Class C	NWHWX	NAS CM	Open End	US Equity Mid Cap (Growth)	C+	C+	B-	Down	Y	2,000
Nationwide Geneva Mid Cap Growth Fund Class R6	NWKAX	NAS CM	Open End	US Equity Mid Cap (Growth)	B-	B-	B		Y	1,000,000
Nationwide Geneva Mid Cap Growth Institutional Service Cls	NWHYX	NAS CM	Open End	US Equity Mid Cap (Growth)	B-	B-	B		Y	50,000
Nationwide Geneva Small Cap Growth Fund Class A	NWHZX	NAS CM	Open End	US Equity Small Cap (Small Company)	C+	C	B-	Down	Y	2,000
Nationwide Geneva Small Cap Growth Fund Class C	NWKBX	NAS CM	Open End	US Equity Small Cap (Small Company)	C+	C	B-	Down	Y	2,000
Nationwide Geneva Small Cap Growth Fund Class R6	NWKCX	NAS CM	Open End	US Equity Small Cap (Small Company)	C+	C	B-	Down	Y	1,000,000
Nationwide Geneva Small Cap Growth Inst Service Cls	NWKDX	NAS CM	Open End	US Equity Small Cap (Small Company)	C+	C	B-	Down	Y	50,000
Nationwide Global Sustainable Equity Fund Class A	GGEAX	NAS CM	Open End	Global Equity Large Cap (World Stock)	C+	C	B	Up	Y	2,000
Nationwide Global Sustainable Equity Fund Class C	GGECX	NAS CM	Open End	Global Equity Large Cap (World Stock)	C+	C	B	Up	Y	2,000
Nationwide Global Sustainable Equity Fund Class R6	GGEIX	NAS CM	Open End	Global Equity Large Cap (World Stock)	C+	C	B	Up	Y	1,000,000
Nationwide Global Sustainable Equity Inst Service Cls	GGESX	NAS CM	Open End	Global Equity Large Cap (World Stock)	C+	C	B	Up	Y	50,000
Nationwide International Index Fund Class A	GIIAX	NAS CM	Open End	Global Equity Large Cap (Foreign Stock)	C	C	B		Y	2,000
Nationwide International Index Fund Class C	GIICX	NAS CM	Open End	Global Equity Large Cap (Foreign Stock)	C	C	B		Y	2,000

★Expanded analysis of this fund is included in Section II.

	TOTAL RETURNS					PERFORMANCE				ASSETS		ASSET ALLOCATION & TURNOVER					BULL & BEAR		FEES		
Min Additional Investment	3-Month Total Return	6-Month Total Return	1-Year Total Return	3-Year Total Return	5-Year Total Return	Dividend Yield (TTM)	Expense Ratio	3-Yr Std Deviation	3-Year Beta	NAV	Total Assets (MIL)	%Cash	%Stocks	%Bonds	%Other	Turnover Ratio	Last Bull Market Total Return	Last Bear Market Total Return	Front End Fee (%)	Back End Fee (%)	Inception Date
	3.25	15.57	4.63	32.14	29.02	1.38	1.17	10.32	1.04	9.36	222.2	10	66	23	0	21	18.27	-18.95			Aug-07
	3.39	15.88	5.38	35.24	33.85	2.07	0.42	10.32	1.04	9.5	222.2	10	66	23	0	21	18.74	-18.65			Aug-07
	3.34	15.80	5.14	34.24	32.31	1.84	0.67	10.37	1.04	9.47	222.2	10	66	23	0	21	18.56	-18.72			Aug-07
100	3.27	16.06	4.85	35.20	32.31	1.58	0.92	10.77	1.04	9.84	174.6	9	68	23	0	22	18.58	-19.08	5.75		Aug-07
100	3.19	15.84	4.31	32.77	28.33	1.16	1.49	10.72	1.03	9.7	174.6	9	68	23	0	22	18.24	-19.2		1.00	Aug-07
	3.24	15.96	4.53	34.13	30.53	1.37	1.17	10.77	1.04	9.75	174.6	9	68	23	0	22	18.32	-19.11			Aug-07
	3.48	16.49	5.45	37.28	35.55	2.04	0.42	10.79	1.04	9.91	174.6	9	68	23	0	22	18.95	-18.92			Aug-07
	3.34	16.25	5.13	36.17	33.79	1.83	0.67	10.74	1.03	9.82	174.6	9	68	23	0	22	18.82	-18.95			Aug-07
100	3.30	16.39	4.78	35.66	32.90	1.56	0.92	10.99	1.04	8.63	146.5	9	70	21	0	19	18.55	-19.21	5.75		Aug-07
100	3.24	15.97	4.16	33.54	29.13	1.18	1.47	10.94	1.04	8.44	146.5	9	70	21	0	19	18.27	-19.45		1.00	Aug-07
	3.29	16.08	4.46	34.58	30.99	1.36	1.17	11.02	1.05	8.5	146.5	9	70	21	0	19	18.45	-19.35			Aug-07
	3.42	16.62	5.29	37.62	36.05	2.02	0.42	10.99	1.04	8.65	146.5	9	70	21	0	19	18.94	-19.15			Aug-07
	3.37	16.40	5.04	36.75	34.36	1.8	0.67	10.98	1.04	8.62	146.5	9	70	21	0	19	18.62	-19.14			Aug-07
100	3.30	16.47	4.59	36.16	33.22	1.54	0.92	11.12	1.05	13.24	81.9	9	71	20	0	19	18.8	-19.24	5.75		Dec-10
100	3.26	16.21	4.14	34.06	29.66	1.14	1.67	11.16	1.06	13.21	81.9	9	71	20	0	19	18.35	-19.41		1.00	Dec-10
	3.33	16.39	4.35	35.25	31.50	1.32	1.17	11.18	1.06	13.21	81.9	9	71	20	0	19	18.48	-19.35			Dec-10
	3.49	16.84	5.17	38.30	36.53	2	0.42	11.14	1.06	13.32	81.9	9	71	20	0	19	19	-19.14			Dec-10
	3.43	16.61	4.91	37.23	34.82	1.77	0.67	11.17	1.06	13.31	81.9	9	71	20	0	19	18.97	-19.14			Dec-10
100	3.36	16.52	4.67	36.31		1.53	0.92	11.18	1.06	10.88	22.5	9	71	19	0	17			5.75		Nov-14
100	3.20	16.21	4.17	34.29		1	1.67	11.18	1.06	10.86	22.5	9	71	19	0	17				1.00	Nov-14
	3.21	16.31	4.36	35.29		1.34	1.17	11.18	1.06	10.86	22.5	9	71	19	0	17					Nov-14
	3.48	16.76	5.08	38.21		1.99	0.42	11.21	1.06	10.9	22.5	9	71	19	0	17					Nov-14
	3.41	16.75	4.93	37.25		1.76	0.67	11.2	1.06	10.9	22.5	9	71	19	0	17					Nov-14
100	7.49	21.65	12.46	45.19	51.03	1.14	1.17	13.1	1.02	6.63	24.3	3	97	0	0	177	25.89	-15.05	5.75		Jun-00
100	7.31	21.19	11.56	42.15	46.04	0.66	1.89	13.1	1.02	5.9	24.3	3	97	0	0	177	25.64	-15.39		1.00	Nov-03
	7.58	21.83	12.86	46.69	53.81	1.49	0.82	13.2	1.02	6.65	24.3	3	97	0	0	177	26.33	-15.05			Sep-13
	7.65	21.75	12.69	46.11	52.94	1.25	0.98	13.13	1.02	6.69	24.3	3	97	0	0	177	26.33	-15.05			May-00
100	5.62	23.61	12.07	62.04	72.84	0.76	0.95	13.58	1.08	9.28	245.3	-22	119	3	0	153	26.79	-17.02	5.75		May-98
100	5.34	23.05	11.07	57.96	65.94	0.53	1.76	13.62	1.08	6	245.3	-22	119	3	0	153	26.37	-17.36		1.00	Mar-01
	5.38	23.17	11.52	59.97	70.13	0.5	1.4	13.58	1.08	8.92	245.3	-22	119	3	0	153	26.54	-17.18			Oct-03
	5.70	23.73	12.37	63.43	75.50	1.09	0.65	13.6	1.08	10.03	245.3	-22	119	3	0	153	27.02	-17.04			Feb-61
	5.62	23.59	12.27	63.30	75.36		0.75	13.57	1.08	10.11	245.3	-22	119	3	0	153	27.02	-17.04			Oct-18
	5.62	23.59	12.15	62.50	73.75	0.9	0.8	13.55	1.08	10.1	245.3	-22	119	3	0	153	27.14	-17.04			Nov-11
100	4.22	20.21	9.36	47.30	55.54	0.53	0.94	12.44	1.01	22.07	1,028	0	100	0	0	140	23.58	-18.43	5.75		May-98
100	4.06	19.77	8.60	44.09	49.74	0.18	1.68	12.43	1.01	19.98	1,028	0	100	0	0	140	23.09	-18.66		1.00	Mar-01
	4.08	19.88	8.84	45.41	52.13	0.23	1.37	12.44	1.01	21.42	1,028	0	100	0	0	140	23.39	-18.57			Oct-03
	4.31	20.37	9.75	48.55	57.58	1	0.62	12.44	1.01	21.56	1,028	0	100	0	0	140	23.81	-18.39			Apr-18
	4.33	20.38	9.69	48.43	57.45	0.9	0.69	12.44	1.01	21.57	1,028	0	100	0	0	140	23.81	-18.39			May-33
100	6.31	24.69	11.07	49.22	65.31	0	1.14	13.53	0.9	21.71	606.5	4	96	0	0	14	29.06	-17.05	5.75		Jan-99
100	6.12	24.27	10.25	45.94	59.34	0	1.88	13.55	0.9	15.77	606.5	4	96	0	0	14	28.65	-17.24		1.00	May-00
	6.43	24.97	11.50	50.89	68.44	0	0.78	13.57	0.9	23.17	606.5	4	96	0	0	14	29.06	-17.05			Sep-13
	6.42	24.97	11.46	50.36	67.39	0	0.93	13.55	0.9	22.87	606.5	4	96	0	0	14	29.27	-16.96			Jun-09
100	6.19	23.92	8.37	62.35	84.34	0.01	1.24	16.33	0.89	61.69	1,083	3	97	0	0	20	22.97	-18.3	5.75		Jun-09
100	5.99	23.47	7.60	58.90	77.86	0.01	1.95	16.32	0.89	56.91	1,083	3	97	0	0	20	22.51	-18.5		1.00	Jun-09
	6.27	24.15	8.76	64.17	87.81	0	0.86	16.33	0.89	64.2	1,083	3	97	0	0	20	23.12	-18.18			Sep-13
	6.26	24.09	8.65	63.66	86.86	0	0.96	16.33	0.89	63.76	1,083	3	97	0	0	20	23.12	-18.18			Jun-09
100	5.35	20.87	6.55	52.39	29.78	0.93	1.35	12.87	1.11	18.17	55.0	4	96	0	0	34	24.45	-25.53	5.75		Jun-97
100	5.23	20.44	5.73	48.96	24.80	0.25	2.11	12.85	1.1	17.05	55.0	4	96	0	0	34	23.85	-25.81		1.00	Nov-01
	5.48	21.14	6.96	54.25	32.38	1.23	0.95	12.89	1.11	18.76	55.0	4	96	0	0	34	24.6	-25.41			Jan-94
	5.46	21.03	6.89	53.84	31.80	1.12	1.03	12.86	1.1	18.78	55.0	4	96	0	0	34	24.59	-25.41			Nov-12
100	3.54	14.28	0.66	29.10	9.13	3.3	0.71	10.99	0.99	7.71	1,363	0	100	0	0	9	12.9	-23.58	5.75		Dec-99
100	3.48	13.97	0.07	26.78	5.59	2.95	1.37	10.99	0.99	7.2	1,363	0	100	0	0	9	12.45	-23.67		1.00	Feb-05

Fund Name	MARKET Ticker Symbol	Traded On	FUND TYPE, CATEGORY & OBJECTIVE Fund Type	Category and (Prospectus Objective)	RATINGS Overall Rating	Reward Rating	Risk Rating	Recent Up/ Downgrade	MINIMUMS Open to New Investors	Min Initial Investment
Nationwide International Index Fund Class R	GIIRX	NAS CM	Open End	Global Equity Large Cap (Foreign Stock)	C	C	B		Y	0
Nationwide International Index Fund Class R6	GIXIX	NAS CM	Open End	Global Equity Large Cap (Foreign Stock)	C	C	B		Y	1,000,000
Nationwide International Index Fund Institutional Service	NWXPX	NAS CM	Open End	Global Equity Large Cap (Foreign Stock)	C	C	B		Y	50,000
Nationwide International Small Cap Fund Class A	NWXSX	NAS CM	Open End	Global Equity Mid/Small Cap (Foreign Stock)	C	D+	C+	Up	Y	2,000
Nationwide International Small Cap Fund Class R6	NWXUX	NAS CM	Open End	Global Equity Mid/Small Cap (Foreign Stock)	C	D+	C+	Up	Y	1,000,000
Nationwide Intl Small Cap Inst Service Cls	NWXVX	NAS CM	Open End	Global Equity Mid/Small Cap (Foreign Stock)	C	D+	C+	Up	Y	50,000
Nationwide Investor Destinations Aggressive Fund Class A	NDAAX	NAS CM	Open End	Aggressive Alloc (Growth & Income)	C+	C	B	Up	Y	2,000
Nationwide Investor Destinations Aggressive Fund Class C	NDACX	NAS CM	Open End	Aggressive Alloc (Growth & Income)	C+	C	B	Up	Y	2,000
Nationwide Investor Destinations Aggressive Fund Class R	GAFRX	NAS CM	Open End	Aggressive Alloc (Growth & Income)	C+	C	B	Up	Y	0
Nationwide Investor Destinations Aggressive Fund Class R6	GAIDX	NAS CM	Open End	Aggressive Alloc (Growth & Income)	B-	C	B	Up	Y	1,000,000
Nationwide Inv Destinations Aggressive Inst Service Cls	NWWHX	NAS CM	Open End	Aggressive Alloc (Growth & Income)	C+	C	B	Up	Y	50,000
Nationwide Investor Destinations Aggressive Service Cls	NDASX	NAS CM	Open End	Aggressive Alloc (Growth & Income)	C+	C	B	Up	Y	50,000
Nationwide Investor Destinations Conservative Fund Class A	NDCAX	NAS CM	Open End	Cautious Alloc (Growth & Income)	B-	C	A-		Y	2,000
Nationwide Investor Destinations Conservative Fund Class C	NDCCX	NAS CM	Open End	Cautious Alloc (Growth & Income)	B-	C	B+	Up	Y	2,000
Nationwide Investor Destinations Conservative Fund Class R	GCFRX	NAS CM	Open End	Cautious Alloc (Growth & Income)	B-	C	B+	Up	Y	0
Nationwide Investor Destinations Conservative Cls R6	GIMCX	NAS CM	Open End	Cautious Alloc (Growth & Income)	B-	C	A-		Y	1,000,000
Nationwide Inv Destinations Conservative Inst Service Cls	NWWLX	NAS CM	Open End	Cautious Alloc (Growth & Income)	B-	C	A-		Y	50,000
Nationwide Investor Destinations Conservative Service Cls	NDCSX	NAS CM	Open End	Cautious Alloc (Growth & Income)	B-	C	A-		Y	50,000
Nationwide Investor Destinations Moderate Fund Class A	NADMX	NAS CM	Open End	Moderate Alloc (Growth & Income)	B-	C	A-	Up	Y	2,000
Nationwide Investor Destinations Moderate Fund Class C	NCDMX	NAS CM	Open End	Moderate Alloc (Growth & Income)	B-	C	B+	Up	Y	2,000
Nationwide Investor Destinations Moderate Fund Class R	GMDRX	NAS CM	Open End	Moderate Alloc (Growth & Income)	B-	C	A-	Up	Y	0
Nationwide Investor Destinations Moderate Fund Class R6	GMDIX	NAS CM	Open End	Moderate Alloc (Growth & Income)	B-	C	A-	Up	Y	1,000,000
Nationwide Investor Destinations Moderate Cls Service	NSDMX	NAS CM	Open End	Moderate Alloc (Growth & Income)	B-	C	A-	Up	Y	50,000
Nationwide Inv Destinations Moderate Inst Service Cls	NWWJX	NAS CM	Open End	Moderate Alloc (Growth & Income)	B-	C	A-	Up	Y	50,000
Nationwide Inv Destinations Moderately Aggressive Cls A	NDMAX	NAS CM	Open End	Aggressive Alloc (Growth & Income)	B-	C	B	Up	Y	2,000
Nationwide Inv Destinations Moderately Aggressive Cls C	NDMCX	NAS CM	Open End	Aggressive Alloc (Growth & Income)	B-	C	B	Up	Y	2,000
Nationwide Inv Destinations Moderately Aggressive Cls R	GMARX	NAS CM	Open End	Aggressive Alloc (Growth & Income)	B-	C	B	Up	Y	0
Nationwide Inv Destinations Moderately Aggressive Cls R6	GMIAX	NAS CM	Open End	Aggressive Alloc (Growth & Income)	B-	C	B+	Up	Y	1,000,000
Nationwide Inv Destinations Mod Aggress Inst Serv Cls	NWWIX	NAS CM	Open End	Aggressive Alloc (Growth & Income)	B-	C	B+	Up	Y	50,000
Nationwide Inv Destinations Moderately Aggressive Serv Cls	NDMSX	NAS CM	Open End	Aggressive Alloc (Growth & Income)	B-	C	B	Up	Y	50,000
Nationwide Inv Destinations Moderately Conservative Cls A	NADCX	NAS CM	Open End	Cautious Alloc (Growth & Income)	B	C	A-	Up	Y	2,000
Nationwide Inv Destinations Moderately Conservative Cls C	NCDCX	NAS CM	Open End	Cautious Alloc (Growth & Income)	B-	C	A-	Up	Y	2,000
Nationwide Inv Destinations Moderately Conservative Cls R	GMMRX	NAS CM	Open End	Cautious Alloc (Growth & Income)	B-	C	A-	Up	Y	0
Nationwide Inv Destinations Moderately Conservative Cls R6	GMIMX	NAS CM	Open End	Cautious Alloc (Growth & Income)	B	C	A-	Up	Y	1,000,000
Nationwide Inv Destinations Mod Cons Inst Serv Cls	NWWKX	NAS CM	Open End	Cautious Alloc (Growth & Income)	B	C	A-	Up	Y	50,000
Nationwide Inv Destinations Mod Cons Serv Cls	NSDCX	NAS CM	Open End	Cautious Alloc (Growth & Income)	B-	C	A-	Up	Y	50,000
Nationwide Long/Short Equity Fund Class A	NWLEX	NAS CM	Open End	Long/Short Equity (Growth)	C+	C	B	Up	Y	2,000
Nationwide Long/Short Equity Fund Class R6	NWLFX	NAS CM	Open End	Long/Short Equity (Growth)	B-	C	B	Up	Y	1,000,000
Nationwide Long/Short Equity Institutional Service Cls	NWLGX	NAS CM	Open End	Long/Short Equity (Growth)	C+	C	B	Up	Y	50,000
Nationwide Loomis All Cap Growth Fund Class A	NWZLX	NAS CM	Open End	US Equity Large Cap Growth (Growth)	C	C-	B	Up	Y	2,000
Nationwide Loomis All Cap Growth Fund Class R6	NWZMX	NAS CM	Open End	US Equity Large Cap Growth (Growth)	C	C-	B	Up	Y	1,000,000
Nationwide Loomis All Cap Growth Fund Eagle Class	NWADX	NAS CM	Open End	US Equity Large Cap Growth (Growth)	C	C-	B	Up	Y	50,000
Nationwide Loomis All Cap Growth Institutional Service Cls	NWZNX	NAS CM	Open End	US Equity Large Cap Growth (Growth)	C	C-	B	Up	Y	50,000
Nationwide Mid Cap Market Index Fund Class A	GMXAX	NAS CM	Open End	US Equity Mid Cap (Growth)	C+	C	B-	Up	Y	2,000
Nationwide Mid Cap Market Index Fund Class C	GMCCX	NAS CM	Open End	US Equity Mid Cap (Growth)	C+	C	B-	Up	Y	2,000
Nationwide Mid Cap Market Index Fund Class R	GMXRX	NAS CM	Open End	US Equity Mid Cap (Growth)	C+	C	B-	Up	Y	0
Nationwide Mid Cap Market Index Fund Class R6	GMXIX	NAS CM	Open End	US Equity Mid Cap (Growth)	C+	C	B-	Up	Y	1,000,000
Nationwide Mid Cap Market Index Institutional Service Cls	NWXQX	NAS CM	Open End	US Equity Mid Cap (Growth)	C+	C	B-	Up	Y	50,000
Nationwide Multi-Cap Portfolio Class R6			Open End	US Equity Large Cap Blend (Growth & Income)	U	U	U		Y	0
Nationwide S&P 500 Index Fund Class A	GRMAX	NAS CM	Open End	US Equity Large Cap Blend (Growth & Income)	B-	C	B		Y	2,000
Nationwide S&P 500 Index Fund Class C	GRMCX	NAS CM	Open End	US Equity Large Cap Blend (Growth & Income)	B-	C	B		Y	2,000
Nationwide S&P 500 Index Fund Class R	GRMRX	NAS CM	Open End	US Equity Large Cap Blend (Growth & Income)	B-	C	B		Y	0

★ Expanded analysis of this fund is included in Section II.

Min Additional Investment	TOTAL RETURNS: 3-Month Total Return	6-Month Total Return	1-Year Total Return	3-Year Total Return	5-Year Total Return	PERFORMANCE: Dividend Yield (TTM)	Expense Ratio	3-Yr Std Deviation	3-Year Beta	ASSETS: NAV	Total Assets (MIL)	ASSET ALLOCATION & TURNOVER: %Cash	%Stocks	%Bonds	%Other	Turnover Ratio	BULL & BEAR: Last Bull Market Total Return	Last Bear Market Total Return	FEES: Front End Fee (%)	Back End Fee (%)	Inception Date
	3.46	14.03	0.30	28.14	7.73	3.09	1.01	11	0.99	7.7	1,363	0	100	0	0	9	12.84	-23.53			Mar-07
	3.62	14.58	1.11	30.83	11.44	3.7	0.3	11.03	0.99	7.76	1,363	0	100	0	0	9	13.12	-23.34			Dec-99
	3.59	14.35	0.93	30.31	11.00	3.54	0.46	11.02	0.99	7.75	1,363	0	100	0	0	9	13.13	-23.34			Dec-16
100	3.89	17.80	-4.49			2.67	1.5			9.58	486.3	3	97	0	0	70			5.75		Dec-16
	4.01	17.88	-4.29			2.93	1			9.61	486.3	3	97	0	0	70					Dec-16
	3.98	17.85	-4.24			2.91	1.25			9.61	486.3	3	97	0	0	70					Dec-16
100	3.43	17.00	4.18	36.53	33.29	2.05	0.89	11.46	1.05	9.28	998.2	8	77	15	0	24	20.59	-19.58	5.75		Mar-00
100	3.28	16.69	3.45	33.68	28.51	1.54	1.63	11.41	1.05	8.88	998.2	8	77	15	0	24	19.97	-19.79		1.00	Mar-01
	3.33	16.78	3.86	35.29	31.37	1.83	1.19	11.45	1.05	9.03	998.2	8	77	15	0	24	20.22	-19.6			Oct-03
	3.58	17.31	4.59	38.09	35.72	2.34	0.54	11.48	1.05	9.43	998.2	8	77	15	0	24	20.75	-19.41			Dec-04
	3.49	17.27	4.45	37.65	34.99	2.28	0.64	11.45	1.05	9.29	998.2	8	77	15	0	24	20.53	-19.62			Mar-14
	3.52	17.05	4.21	36.49	33.13	1.99	0.94	11.43	1.05	9.31	998.2	8	77	15	0	24	20.53	-19.62			Mar-00
100	2.27	6.96	4.80	11.90	15.83	2.2	0.81	3.02	0.9	10.12	659.9	7	16	76	0	22	5.45	-2.3	5.75		Mar-00
100	2.09	6.61	4.05	9.43	11.68	1.5	1.55	2.97	0.88	10.07	659.9	7	16	76	0	22	5	-2.59		1.00	Mar-01
	2.19	6.80	4.48	10.76	14.11	1.9	1.13	2.97	0.89	10.1	659.9	7	16	76	0	22	5.17	-2.41			Oct-03
	2.24	7.10	5.14	12.95	17.81	2.52	0.48	2.96	0.89	10.17	659.9	7	16	76	0	22	5.57	-2.18			Dec-04
	2.33	7.19	5.17	12.71	17.38	2.45	0.56	3.05	0.92	10.15	659.9	7	16	76	0	22	5.37	-2.38			Mar-14
	2.24	7.01	4.82	11.64	15.50	2.13	0.88	3.02	0.9	10.16	659.9	7	16	76	0	22	5.37	-2.38			Mar-00
100	3.08	13.05	5.17	26.09	26.11	2.13	0.86	7.89	1.14	9.47	1,274	19	49	31	0	22	13.58	-11.58	5.75		Mar-00
100	2.85	12.59	4.41	23.40	21.64	1.5	1.58	7.86	1.13	9.25	1,274	19	49	31	0	22	13.18	-11.84		1.00	Mar-01
	2.99	12.81	4.90	24.99	24.31	1.92	1.16	7.85	1.13	9.17	1,274	19	49	31	0	22	13.38	-11.73			Oct-03
	3.19	13.20	5.57	27.44	28.45	2.48	0.51	7.86	1.14	9.41	1,274	19	49	31	0	22	13.89	-11.47			Dec-04
	2.97	12.98	5.04	25.92	25.86	2.1	0.91	7.84	1.13	9.41	1,274	19	49	31	0	22	13.55	-11.65			Mar-00
	3.16	13.16	5.47	27.14	27.89	2.38	0.61	7.87	1.14	9.4	1,274	19	49	31	0	22	13.55	-11.65			Mar-14
100	3.45	15.72	4.90	33.13	31.15	2.17	0.9	9.94	1.09	9.6	1,563	8	64	28	0	22	17.43	-16.16	5.75		Mar-00
100	3.29	15.35	4.18	30.27	26.50	1.65	1.62	9.94	1.09	9.26	1,563	8	64	28	0	22	17.04	-16.41		1.00	Mar-01
	3.38	15.57	4.62	31.93	29.29	1.95	1.2	10.01	1.1	9.29	1,563	8	64	28	0	22	17.28	-16.32			Oct-03
	3.55	15.81	5.28	34.44	33.45	2.5	0.55	9.97	1.09	9.58	1,563	8	64	28	0	22	17.66	-16.06			Dec-04
	3.53	15.79	5.19	34.16	32.87	2.41	0.65	9.97	1.09	9.56	1,563	8	64	28	0	22	17.43	-16.16			Mar-14
	3.45	15.60	4.86	32.88	30.81	2.13	0.95	9.95	1.09	9.57	1,563	8	64	28	0	22	17.44	-16.25			Mar-00
100	2.71	10.06	4.99	18.66	21.35	2.1	0.84	5.4	1.1	9.83	445.7	24	33	42	0	23	9.8	-6.72	5.75		Mar-00
100	2.54	9.72	4.26	16.19	17.00	1.42	1.57	5.41	1.1	9.78	445.7	24	33	42	0	23	9.35	-7		1.00	Mar-01
	2.62	9.97	4.75	17.63	19.55	1.79	1.15	5.44	1.1	9.86	445.7	24	33	42	0	23	9.6	-6.98			Oct-03
	2.76	10.22	5.29	19.86	23.44	2.4	0.5	5.4	1.1	9.95	445.7	24	33	42	0	23	9.99	-6.63			Dec-04
	2.74	10.20	5.30	19.62	22.96	2.31	0.59	5.4	1.1	9.91	445.7	24	33	42	0	23	9.81	-6.85			Mar-14
	2.56	9.93	4.88	18.42	20.96	2.02	0.9	5.36	1.09	9.9	445.7	24	33	42	0	23	9.81	-6.86			Mar-00
100	1.38	11.40	0.72	16.47	24.90	0	3.43	9.69	0.74	13.87	22.5	33	67	0	0	13			5.75		Dec-17
	1.44	11.46	1.00	17.77	27.24	0	2.93	9.66	0.73	14	22.5	33	67	0	0	13					Aug-15
	1.45	11.44	0.94	17.49	26.62	0	3.03	9.68	0.73	13.93	22.5	33	67	0	0	13					Sep-12
100	5.37	23.25	12.71			0.04	1.35			12.35	340.6	1	99	0	0	22			5.75		May-17
	5.52	23.58	13.16			0.21	0.85			12.42	340.6	1	99	0	0	22					May-17
	5.43	23.35	13.02			0.1	0.95			12.41	340.6	1	99	0	0	22					Jun-18
	5.44	23.40	12.99			0.21	1.1			12.39	340.6	1	99	0	0	22					May-17
100	2.89	18.78	0.73	36.29	42.95	1.17	0.67	15.12	1	15.13	878.3	0	100	0	0	22	27.3	-23.02	5.75		Dec-99
100	2.73	18.39	0.02	33.52	38.16	0.81	1.35	15.08	1	13.67	878.3	0	100	0	0	22	26.96	-23.2		1.00	Oct-03
	2.79	18.59	0.42	35.11	40.96	0.96	0.97	15.14	1	14.88	878.3	0	100	0	0	22	27.39	-23.09			Mar-07
	3.00	19.00	1.13	38.03	45.96	1.51	0.26	15.14	1	15.44	878.3	0	100	0	0	22	27.71	-22.89			Dec-99
	2.95	18.87	0.88	37.10	43.79	1.29	0.51	15.14	1	15.44	878.3	0	100	0	0	22	27.3	-23.02			Dec-16
	4.26	20.31					0.27			11.23	2,526	12	60	29	-2						Dec-18
100	4.11	19.19	9.75	48.26	61.36	1.58	0.59	12.23	1	15.27	1,069	0	100	0	0	10	24.79	-16.54	5.75		Dec-99
100	3.99	18.86	9.03	45.35	56.28	1.06	1.23	12.21	1	14.88	1,069	0	100	0	0	10	24.22	-16.71		1.00	Oct-03
	4.10	19.11	9.57	47.30	59.52	1.47	0.76	12.2	1	15.21	1,069	0	100	0	0	10	24.39	-16.6			Jan-07

	MARKET		FUND TYPE, CATEGORY & OBJECTIVE		RATINGS				MINIMUMS	
Fund Name	Ticker Symbol	Traded On	Fund Type	Category and (Prospectus Objective)	Overall Rating	Reward Rating	Risk Rating	Recent Up/ Downgrade	Open to New Investors	Min Initial Investment
Nationwide S&P 500 Index Fund Class R6	GRMIX	NAS CM	Open End	US Equity Large Cap Blend (Growth & Income)	B-	C	B		Y	1,000,000
Nationwide S&P 500 Index Fund Institutional Service Class	GRISX	NAS CM	Open End	US Equity Large Cap Blend (Growth & Income)	B-	C	B		Y	50,000
Nationwide S&P 500 Index Fund Service Class	GRMSX	NAS CM	Open End	US Equity Large Cap Blend (Growth & Income)	B-	C	B		Y	25,000
Nationwide Small Cap Index Fund Class A	GMRAX	NAS CM	Open End	US Equity Small Cap (Small Company)	C	C	C+		Y	2,000
Nationwide Small Cap Index Fund Class C	GMRCX	NAS CM	Open End	US Equity Small Cap (Small Company)	C	C-	C+		Y	2,000
Nationwide Small Cap Index Fund Class R	GMSRX	NAS CM	Open End	US Equity Small Cap (Small Company)	C	C	C+		Y	0
Nationwide Small Cap Index Fund Class R6	GMRIX	NAS CM	Open End	US Equity Small Cap (Small Company)	C	C	C+		Y	1,000,000
Nationwide Small Cap Index Institutional Service Cls	NWXRX	NAS CM	Open End	US Equity Small Cap (Small Company)	C	C	C+		Y	50,000
Nationwide Small Company Growth Fund Class A	NWSAX	NAS CM	Open End	US Equity Small Cap (Small Company)	C+	C+	C+		Y	2,000
Nationwide Small Company Growth Institutional Service Cls	NWSIX	NAS CM	Open End	US Equity Small Cap (Small Company)	C+	C+	C+		Y	50,000
Nationwide U.S. Small Cap Value Fund Class A	NWUAX	NAS CM	Open End	US Equity Small Cap (Small Company)	C-	D+	C	Down	Y	2,000
Nationwide U.S. Small Cap Value Fund Class C	NWUCX	NAS CM	Open End	US Equity Small Cap (Small Company)	C-	D+	C		Y	2,000
Nationwide U.S. Small Cap Value Fund Class R6	NWUIX	NAS CM	Open End	US Equity Small Cap (Small Company)	C-	C-	C	Down	Y	1,000,000
Nationwide U.S. Small Cap Value Institutional Service Cls	NWUSX	NAS CM	Open End	US Equity Small Cap (Small Company)	C-	D+	C	Down	Y	50,000
Nationwide WCM Focused Small Cap Fund Class A	NWGPX	NAS CM	Open End	US Equity Small Cap (Small Company)	C+	C	B-		Y	2,000
Nationwide WCM Focused Small Cap Fund Class C	NWGQX	NAS CM	Open End	US Equity Small Cap (Small Company)	C+	C	B-		Y	2,000
Nationwide WCM Focused Small Cap Fund Class R6	NWKEX	NAS CM	Open End	US Equity Small Cap (Small Company)	C+	C	B-		Y	1,000,000
Nationwide WCM Focused Small Cap Institutional Service Cls	NWGSX	NAS CM	Open End	US Equity Small Cap (Small Company)	C+	C	B-		Y	50,000
Nationwide Ziegler Equity Income Fund Class A	NWGYX	NAS CM	Open End	US Equity Large Cap Value (Equity-Income)	B-	C	B+	Up	Y	2,000
Nationwide Ziegler Equity Income Fund Class C	NWGZX	NAS CM	Open End	US Equity Large Cap Value (Equity-Income)	B-	C	B	Up	Y	2,000
Nationwide Ziegler Equity Income Fund Class R6	NWJAX	NAS CM	Open End	US Equity Large Cap Value (Equity-Income)	B-	C	B+	Up	Y	1,000,000
Nationwide Ziegler Equity Income Institutional Service Cls	NWJBX	NAS CM	Open End	US Equity Large Cap Value (Equity-Income)	B-	C	B+	Up	Y	50,000
Nationwide Ziegler NYSE Arca Tech 100 Index Fund Class A	NWJCX	NAS CM	Open End	Technology Sector Equity (Technology)	B-	C+	B	Down	Y	2,000
Nationwide Ziegler NYSE Arca Tech 100 Index Fund Class C	NWJDX	NAS CM	Open End	Technology Sector Equity (Technology)	B-	C+	B	Down	Y	2,000
Nationwide Ziegler NYSE Arca Tech 100 Index Fund Class R6	NWJEX	NAS CM	Open End	Technology Sector Equity (Technology)	B-	C+	B	Down	Y	1,000,000
Nationwide Ziegler NYSE Arca Tech 100 Index Inst Serv Cls	NWJFX	NAS CM	Open End	Technology Sector Equity (Technology)	B-	C+	B	Down	Y	50,000
Natixis ASG Dynamic Allocation Fund Class A	DAAFX	NAS CM	Open End	Cautious Alloc (Asset Alloc)	C	C-	B-		Y	2,500
Natixis ASG Dynamic Allocation Fund Class C	DACFX	NAS CM	Open End	Cautious Alloc (Asset Alloc)	C	C-	C+		Y	2,500
Natixis ASG Dynamic Allocation Fund Class Y	DAYFX	NAS CM	Open End	Cautious Alloc (Asset Alloc)	C	C	B-		Y	100,000
Natixis ASG Managed Futures Strategy Fund Class A	AMFAX	NAS CM	Open End	Alternative Miscellaneous (Growth)	D	D	C-		Y	2,500
Natixis ASG Managed Futures Strategy Fund Class C	ASFCX	NAS CM	Open End	Alternative Miscellaneous (Growth)	D	D	D+		Y	2,500
Natixis ASG Managed Futures Strategy Fund Class N	AMFNX	NAS CM	Open End	Alternative Miscellaneous (Growth)	D+	D	C-	Up	Y	1,000,000
Natixis ASG Managed Futures Strategy Fund Class Y	ASFYX	NAS CM	Open End	Alternative Miscellaneous (Growth)	D+	D	C-	Up	Y	100,000
Natixis ASG Tactical U.S. Market Fund Class A	USMAX	NAS CM	Open End	Long/Short Equity (Growth)	C+	C	B		Y	2,500
Natixis ASG Tactical U.S. Market Fund Class C	USMCX	NAS CM	Open End	Long/Short Equity (Growth)	C+	C	B	Up	Y	2,500
Natixis ASG Tactical U.S. Market Fund Class Y	USMYX	NAS CM	Open End	Long/Short Equity (Growth)	C+	C	B		Y	100,000
Natixis Funds Trust I Oakmark International Fund Class A	NOIAX	NAS CM	Open End	Global Equity Large Cap (Foreign Stock)	C-	D+	C		Y	2,500
Natixis Funds Trust I Oakmark International Fund Class C	NOICX	NAS CM	Open End	Global Equity Large Cap (Foreign Stock)	C-	D+	C		Y	2,500
Natixis Funds Trust I Oakmark International Fund Class N	NIONX	NAS CM	Open End	Global Equity Large Cap (Foreign Stock)	C-	D+	C		Y	1,000,000
Natixis Funds Trust I Oakmark International Fund Class Y	NOIYX	NAS CM	Open End	Global Equity Large Cap (Foreign Stock)	C-	D+	C		Y	100,000
Natixis Funds Trust I U.S. Equity Opportunities Cls A	NEFSX	NAS CM	Open End	US Equity Large Cap Growth (Growth)	B-	C	B		Y	2,500
Natixis Funds Trust I U.S. Equity Opportunities Cls C	NECCX	NAS CM	Open End	US Equity Large Cap Growth (Growth)	C+	C	B		Y	2,500
Natixis Funds Trust I U.S. Equity Opportunities Cls N	NESNX	NAS CM	Open End	US Equity Large Cap Growth (Growth)	B-	C	B		Y	1,000,000
Natixis Funds Trust I U.S. Equity Opportunities Cls Y	NESYX	NAS CM	Open End	US Equity Large Cap Growth (Growth)	B-	C	B		Y	100,000
Natixis Funds Trust I Vaughan Nelson Small Cap Value Cls A	NEFJX	NAS CM	Open End	US Equity Small Cap (Small Company)	C	C	C+			2,500
Natixis Funds Trust I Vaughan Nelson Small Cap Value Cls C	NEJCX	NAS CM	Open End	US Equity Small Cap (Small Company)	C	C	C+			2,500
Natixis Funds Trust I Vaughan Nelson Small Cap Value Cls N	VSCNX	NAS CM	Open End	US Equity Small Cap (Small Company)	C	C	C+		Y	1,000,000
Natixis Funds Trust I Vaughan Nelson Small Cap Value Cls Y	NEJYX	NAS CM	Open End	US Equity Small Cap (Small Company)	C	C	C+			100,000
Natixis Funds Trust II ASG Global Alternatives Cls A	GAFAX	NAS CM	Open End	Multialternative (Growth)	C+	C	B	Up	Y	2,500
Natixis Funds Trust II ASG Global Alternatives Cls C	GAFCX	NAS CM	Open End	Multialternative (Growth)	C	C-	B		Y	2,500
Natixis Funds Trust II ASG Global Alternatives Cls N	GAFNX	NAS CM	Open End	Multialternative (Growth)	B-	C	B+	Up	Y	1,000,000
Natixis Funds Trust II ASG Global Alternatives Cls Y	GAFYX	NAS CM	Open End	Multialternative (Growth)	B-	C	B+	Up	Y	100,000

★ Expanded analysis of this fund is included in Section II.

	TOTAL RETURNS					PERFORMANCE				ASSETS		ASSET ALLOCATION & TURNOVER					BULL & BEAR		FEES		
Min Additional Investment	3-Month Total Return	6-Month Total Return	1-Year Total Return	3-Year Total Return	5-Year Total Return	Dividend Yield (TTM)	Expense Ratio	3-Yr Std Deviation	3-Year Beta	NAV	Total Assets (MIL)	%Cash	%Stocks	%Bonds	%Other	Turnover Ratio	Last Bull Market Total Return	Last Bear Market Total Return	Front End Fee (%)	Back End Fee (%)	Inception Date
	4.26	19.50	10.21	50.14	64.85	1.96	0.16	12.19	1	15.42	1,069	0	100	0	0	10	25	-16.35			Dec-99
	4.20	19.32	9.96	48.97	62.90	1.74	0.41	12.2	1	15.38	1,069	0	100	0	0	10	24.84	-16.47			Nov-98
	4.19	19.27	9.78	48.40	61.72	1.61	0.56	12.2	1	15.29	1,069	0	100	0	0	10	24.68	-16.45			Nov-98
100	1.88	17.54	-3.88	41.80	37.78	0.78	0.69	17.13	1	9.78	259.3	0	100	0	0	27	27.29	-25.17	5.75		Dec-99
100	1.80	17.14	-4.45	39.05	33.18	0.39	1.38	17.09	1	9.02	259.3	0	100	0	0	27	26.89	-25.36		1.00	Oct-03
	1.88	17.43	-4.11	40.92	36.53	0.63	1	17.12	1	9.61	259.3	0	100	0	0	27	27.21	-25.23			Mar-07
	2.07	17.78	-3.41	43.71	40.73	1.15	0.28	17.16	1	10.07	259.3	0	100	0	0	27	27.56	-25.01			Dec-99
	1.97	17.61	-3.69	42.94	39.97	0.91	0.53	17.16	1	10.06	259.3	0	100	0	0	27	27.56	-25.01			Dec-16
100	7.83	30.23	10.06	85.39	102.14	0	1.32	18.88	1	21.19	332.5	4	96	0	0	16			5.75		Jan-12
	7.84	30.25	10.15	86.06	103.54	0	1.19	18.86	1	21.44	332.5	4	96	0	0	16					Jan-12
100	0.82	13.59	-9.40	24.85	15.79	0.33	1.32	18.56	1.06	11.48	126.2	0	100	0	0	27	29.55	-26.62	5.75		Dec-07
100	0.67	13.13	-10.15	21.97	11.44	0	2.08	18.55	1.06	10.51	126.2	0	100	0	0	27	29.08	-26.88		1.00	Dec-07
	0.93	13.76	-9.14	26.09	17.82	0.9	0.98	18.57	1.06	11.78	126.2	0	100	0	0	27	29.77	-26.53			Dec-07
	0.85	13.61	-9.36	25.25	16.40	0.5	1.23	18.54	1.06	11.57	126.2	0	100	0	0	27	29.56	-26.55			Dec-07
100	4.34	17.00	2.80	47.39	49.12	0	1.4	16.29	0.9	23.32	56.1	6	94	0	0	172	29.31	-25.94	5.75		Mar-07
100	4.22	16.64	2.08	44.16	43.73	0	2.15	16.31	0.9	20.25	56.1	6	94	0	0	172	28.87	-26.12		1.00	Mar-07
	4.42	17.18	3.15	48.99	51.82	0	1.05	16.29	0.9	24.55	56.1	6	94	0	0	172	29.6	-25.86			Sep-13
	4.40	17.13	3.04	48.53	51.24	0	1.15	16.29	0.9	24.4	56.1	6	94	0	0	172	29.61	-25.86			Mar-07
100	3.23	14.82	6.91	35.56	43.08	2.18	1.08	11.78	0.95	12.76	37.0	0	100	0	0	33	23.22	-14.12	5.75		Apr-05
100	3.03	14.44	6.05	32.47	37.84	1.8	1.83	11.78	0.95	12.57	37.0	0	100	0	0	33	22.85	-14.35		1.00	Apr-05
	3.22	14.93	7.06	36.72	45.34	2.39	0.75	11.78	0.95	12.82	37.0	0	100	0	0	33	23.22	-14.12			Sep-13
	3.30	14.99	7.13	36.40	44.69	2.31	0.87	11.79	0.95	12.83	37.0	0	100	0	0	33	23.46	-14.07			Jul-09
100	3.67	22.76	12.37	80.68	88.50	0.59	0.75	15.14	0.99	90.81	678.0	1	99	0	0	17	27.12	-16.45	5.75		Jun-96
100	3.48	22.30	11.55	76.75	81.67	0.2	1.47	15.14	0.99	80.39	678.0	1	99	0	0	17	26.66	-16.66		1.00	May-00
	3.75	22.97	12.76	82.60	91.84	0.9	0.4	15.16	0.99	91.72	678.0	1	99	0	0	17	27.12	-16.45			Sep-13
	3.74	22.91	12.64	81.92	90.65	0.81	0.51	15.15	0.99	91.75	678.0	1	99	0	0	17	27.34	-16.34			Jul-09
50	4.15	9.00	1.18	21.63		1.27	1.21	8.32	1.04	10.52	41.7	10	34	56	0	46			5.75		Nov-15
50	3.88	8.52	0.38	18.99		0.1	1.96	8.32	1.04	10.43	41.7	10	34	56	0	46				1.00	Nov-15
50	4.24	9.19	1.40	22.59		1.47	0.96	8.34	1.04	10.56	41.7	10	34	56	0	46					Nov-15
50	4.37	6.11	-0.52	-11.58	7.07	0	1.7	11.52	0.97	9.54	1,737	70	0	27	3		-5	-6.32	5.75		Jul-10
50	4.15	5.74	-1.31	-13.50	3.07	0	2.45	11.55	0.97	9.02	1,737	70	0	27	3		-5.34	-6.62		1.00	Jul-10
	4.54	6.38	-0.10	-10.59	8.73	0	1.36	11.48	0.97	9.67	1,737	70	0	27	3		-4.78	-6.23			May-17
50	4.43	6.39	-0.20	-10.83	8.44	0	1.45	11.48	0.97	9.65	1,737	70	0	27	3		-4.78	-6.23			Jul-10
50	3.24	11.57	4.61	39.72	43.51	0.56	1.25	11.92	0.94	14.66	181.0	22	71	7	0	88			5.75		Sep-13
50	3.12	11.13	3.86	36.64	38.27	0.24	2	11.95	0.94	14.18	181.0	22	71	7	0	88				1.00	Sep-13
50	3.37	11.77	4.89	40.81	45.33	0.94	1	11.94	0.94	14.72	181.0	22	71	7	0	88					Sep-13
50	3.32	13.35	-7.20	35.57	4.83	2.23	1.21	16.63	1.38	12.73	655.6	1	99	0	0	50	15.22	-22.81	5.75		Dec-10
50	3.13	13.03	-7.92	32.59	0.99	1.33	1.97	16.65	1.38	12.49	655.6	1	99	0	0	50	14.81	-23.06		1.00	Dec-10
	3.41	13.58	-6.96	36.54	5.59	2.78	0.89	16.59	1.38	12.71	655.6	1	99	0	0	50	15.22	-22.81			May-17
50	3.42	13.49	-7.01	36.35	5.43	2.68	0.97	16.6	1.38	12.7	655.6	1	99	0	0	50	15.22	-22.81			May-17
50	4.94	21.26	8.17	58.76	76.64	0.13	1.16	14.45	1.15	36.26	998.7	1	99	0	0	23	25.61	-20.08	5.75		Jul-94
50	4.73	20.81	7.36	55.20	70.13	0.01	1.91	14.44	1.15	23.45	998.7	1	99	0	0	23	25.02	-20.34		1.00	Jul-94
	5.05	21.50	8.57	60.03	78.05	0.38	0.76	14.43	1.15	42.81	998.7	1	99	0	0	23	25.61	-20.08			May-17
50	5.01	21.41	8.46	59.97	78.89	0.31	0.91	14.44	1.15	42.74	998.7	1	99	0	0	23	25.76	-19.99			Nov-94
100	2.79	19.43	-0.52	26.24	31.67	0.07	1.46	15.83	0.89	14.75	125.1	6	94	0	0	70	24.87	-23.31	5.75		Dec-96
100	2.60	18.92	-1.35	23.33	26.75	0.11	2.21	15.85	0.89	7.54	125.1	6	94	0	0	70	24.24	-23.56		1.00	Dec-96
	2.93	19.70	-0.11	27.33	32.81	0.23	1.08	15.81	0.89	15.49	125.1	6	94	0	0	70	24.87	-23.31			May-17
100	2.86	19.54	-0.30	27.20	33.29	0.09	1.21	15.79	0.88	15.47	125.1	6	94	0	0	70	24.98	-23.22			Aug-06
50	1.96	6.74	1.17	17.67	4.84	0.93	1.56	5.7		10.92	1,125	22	18	60	0	59	3.93	-9.76	5.75		Sep-08
50	1.69	6.36	0.40	14.96	0.98	0.1	2.31	5.71		10.19	1,125	22	18	60	0	59	3.41	-10.01		1.00	Sep-08
	2.01	6.92	1.44	18.67	6.31	1.26	1.26	5.73		11.11	1,125	22	18	60	0	59	4	-9.62			May-13
50	2.02	6.82	1.38	18.55	6.19	1.21	1.31	5.69		11.11	1,125	22	18	60	0	59	4	-9.62			Sep-08

	MARKET			FUND TYPE, CATEGORY & OBJECTIVE	RATINGS				MINIMUMS	
Fund Name	Ticker Symbol	Traded On	Fund Type	Category and (Prospectus Objective)	Overall Rating	Reward Rating	Risk Rating	Recent Up/ Downgrade	Open to New Investors	Min Initial Investment
Natixis Funds Trust II Oakmark Fund Class A	NEFOX	NAS CM	Open End	US Equity Large Cap Blend (Growth)	C+	C	B-	Up	Y	2,500
Natixis Funds Trust II Oakmark Fund Class C	NECOX	NAS CM	Open End	US Equity Large Cap Blend (Growth)	C	C	B-		Y	2,500
Natixis Funds Trust II Oakmark Fund Class N	NOANX	NAS CM	Open End	US Equity Large Cap Blend (Growth)	C+	C	B-	Up	Y	1,000,000
Natixis Funds Trust II Oakmark Fund Class Y	NEOYX	NAS CM	Open End	US Equity Large Cap Blend (Growth)	C+	C	B-	Up	Y	100,000
Natixis Funds Trust II Vaughan Nelson Value Opp Cls A	VNVAX	NAS CM	Open End	US Equity Mid Cap (Growth)	C	C	C+		Y	2,500
Natixis Funds Trust II Vaughan Nelson Value Opp Cls C	VNVCX	NAS CM	Open End	US Equity Mid Cap (Growth)	C	C-	C+		Y	2,500
Natixis Funds Trust II Vaughan Nelson Value Opp Cls N	VNVNX	NAS CM	Open End	US Equity Mid Cap (Growth)	C	C	B-		Y	1,000,000
Natixis Funds Trust II Vaughan Nelson Value Opp Cls Y	VNVYX	NAS CM	Open End	US Equity Mid Cap (Growth)	C	C	B-		Y	100,000
Natixis Funds Trust IV AEW Global Focused Real Est Cls A	NRFAX	NAS CM	Open End	Real Estate Sector Equity (Real Estate)	C+	C	C+	Down	Y	2,500
Natixis Funds Trust IV AEW Global Focused Real Est Cls C	NRCFX	NAS CM	Open End	Real Estate Sector Equity (Real Estate)	C	C	C+	Down	Y	2,500
Natixis Funds Trust IV AEW Global Focused Real Est Cls N	NRFNX	NAS CM	Open End	Real Estate Sector Equity (Real Estate)	C+	C	B-	Down	Y	1,000,000
Natixis Funds Trust IV AEW Global Focused Real Est Cls Y	NRFYX	NAS CM	Open End	Real Estate Sector Equity (Real Estate)	C+	C	B-	Down	Y	100,000
Natixis Sustainable Future 2015 Fund Class N	NSFBX	NAS CM	Open End	Target Date (Asset Alloc)	C	C	B		Y	1,000,000
Natixis Sustainable Future 2020 Fund Class N	NSFDX	NAS CM	Open End	Target Date (Asset Alloc)	C	C	B		Y	1,000,000
Natixis Sustainable Future 2025 Fund Class N	NSFEX	NAS CM	Open End	Target Date (Asset Alloc)	C	C	B		Y	1,000,000
Natixis Sustainable Future 2030 Fund Class N	NSFFX	NAS CM	Open End	Target Date (Asset Alloc)	C	C	B		Y	1,000,000
Natixis Sustainable Future 2035 Fund Class N	NSFGX	NAS CM	Open End	Target Date (Asset Alloc)	C	C	B		Y	1,000,000
Natixis Sustainable Future 2040 Fund Class N	NSFHX	NAS CM	Open End	Target Date (Asset Alloc)	C	C	B		Y	1,000,000
Natixis Sustainable Future 2045 Fund Class N	NSFJX	NAS CM	Open End	Target Date (Asset Alloc)	C	C	B	Up	Y	1,000,000
Natixis Sustainable Future 2050 Fund Class N	NSFKX	NAS CM	Open End	Target Date (Asset Alloc)	C	C	B	Up	Y	1,000,000
Natixis Sustainable Future 2055 Fund Class N	NSFLX	NAS CM	Open End	Target Date (Asset Alloc)	C	C	B	Up	Y	1,000,000
Natixis Sustainable Future 2060 Fund Class N	NSFMX	NAS CM	Open End	Target Date (Asset Alloc)	C	C	B	Up	Y	1,000,000
Natixis Vaughan Nelson Select Fund Class A	VNSAX	NAS CM	Open End	US Equity Large Cap Blend (Growth)	C+	C	B	Down	Y	2,500
Natixis Vaughan Nelson Select Fund Class C	VNSCX	NAS CM	Open End	US Equity Large Cap Blend (Growth)	C+	C	B	Down	Y	2,500
Natixis Vaughan Nelson Select Fund Class N	VNSNX	NAS CM	Open End	US Equity Large Cap Blend (Growth)	C+	C	B	Down	Y	1,000,000
Natixis Vaughan Nelson Select Fund Class Y	VNSYX	NAS CM	Open End	US Equity Large Cap Blend (Growth)	C+	C	B	Down	Y	100,000
Navigator Equity Hedged Fund Class A	NAVAX	NAS CM	Open End	Long/Short Equity (Growth)	C	C-	C	Up	Y	5,000
Navigator Equity Hedged Fund Class C	NAVCX	NAS CM	Open End	Long/Short Equity (Growth)	C-	C-	C		Y	5,000
Navigator Equity Hedged Fund Class I	NAVIX	NAS CM	Open End	Long/Short Equity (Growth)	C	C-	C	Up	Y	25,000
Navigator Sentry Managed Volatility Fund Class A	NVXAX	NAS CM	Open End	Alternative Miscellaneous (Equity-Income)	D-	E+	D	Down	Y	5,000
Navigator Sentry Managed Volatility Fund Class C	NVXCX	NAS CM	Open End	Alternative Miscellaneous (Equity-Income)	D-	E+	D	Down	Y	5,000
Navigator Sentry Managed Volatility Fund Class I	NVXIX	NAS CM	Open End	Alternative Miscellaneous (Equity-Income)	D-	E+	D	Down	Y	25,000
Needham Aggressive Growth Fund Institutional Class	NEAIX	NAS CM	Open End	US Equity Small Cap (Aggr Growth)	C	C	C		Y	100,000
Needham Aggressive Growth Fund Retail Class	NEAGX	NAS CM	Open End	US Equity Small Cap (Aggr Growth)	C	C	C		Y	2,000
Needham Growth Fund Institutional Class	NEEIX	NAS CM	Open End	US Equity Mid Cap (Growth)	C+	C	B-	Up	Y	100,000
Needham Growth Fund Retail Class	NEEGX	NAS CM	Open End	US Equity Mid Cap (Growth)	C+	C	B-	Up	Y	2,000
Needham Small Cap Growth Fund Institutional Class	NESIX	NAS CM	Open End	US Equity Small Cap (Small Company)	B	B	B	Up	Y	100,000
Needham Small Cap Growth Fund Retail Class	NESGX	NAS CM	Open End	US Equity Small Cap (Small Company)	B	B	B	Up	Y	2,000
Neiman Large Cap Value Fund A Shares	NEAMX	NAS CM	Open End	US Equity Large Cap Value (Growth)	B-	C	B+	Up	Y	2,500
Neiman Large Cap Value Fund No-Load Shares	NEIMX	NAS CM	Open End	US Equity Large Cap Value (Growth)	B-	C	B+	Up	Y	2,500
Neiman Opportunities Fund Class A	NEOMX	NAS CM	Open End	US Equity Mid Cap (Growth)	C	C	B		Y	2,500
Neuberger Berman Absolute Return Multi-Manager Cls A	NABAX	NAS CM	Open End	Multialternative (Growth)	C	C	B-		Y	1,000
Neuberger Berman Absolute Return Multi-Manager Cls C	NABCX	NAS CM	Open End	Multialternative (Growth)	C	C-	B-	Up	Y	1,000
Neuberger Berman Absolute Return Multi-Manager Cls R6	NRABX	NAS CM	Open End	Multialternative (Growth)	C	C	B-		Y	0
Neuberger Berman Absolute Return Multi-Manager Inst Cls	NABIX	NAS CM	Open End	Multialternative (Growth)	C	C	B-		Y	1,000,000
Neuberger Berman Advisers Mgmt Trust Intl Eq Port Cls I			Open End	Global Equity Large Cap (Foreign Stock)	C	C	B-		Y	0
Neuberger Berman Advisers Mgmt Trust Intl Portfolio Cls S			Open End	Global Equity Large Cap (Foreign Stock)	C	C	C+		Y	0
Neuberger Berman Advisers Mgmt Trust Mid-Cap Growth Cls I			Open End	US Equity Mid Cap (Growth)	C+	C	B-	Down	Y	0
Neuberger Berman Advisers Mgmt Trust Mid-Cap Growth Cls S			Open End	US Equity Mid Cap (Growth)	C+	C	B-	Down	Y	0
Neuberger Berman Advisers Mgmt Trust Sustainable Eq Cls I			Open End	US Equity Large Cap Blend (Growth)	B-	C	B		Y	0
Neuberger Berman Advisers Mgmt Trust Sustainable Eq Cls S			Open End	US Equity Large Cap Blend (Growth)	B-	C	B		Y	0
Neuberger Berman Advisers Mgmt Trust U.S. Eq Ind PutWrite			Open End	Multialternative (Multi-Asset Global)	C	C	B-		Y	0

★ Expanded analysis of this fund is included in Section II.

Min Additional Investment	TOTAL RETURNS 3-Month Total Return	6-Month Total Return	1-Year Total Return	3-Year Total Return	5-Year Total Return	PERFORMANCE Dividend Yield (TTM)	Expense Ratio	3-Yr Std Deviation	3-Year Beta	ASSETS NAV	Total Assets (MIL)	ASSET ALLOCATION & TURNOVER %Cash	%Stocks	%Bonds	%Other	Turnover Ratio	BULL & BEAR Last Bull Market Total Return	Last Bear Market Total Return	FEES Front End Fee (%)	Back End Fee (%)	Inception Date
50	3.27	17.41	0.47	46.30	43.58	0.35	1.13	15.51	1.22	21.6	308.5	5	95	0	0	39	27.84	-19.1	5.75		May-31
50	3.07	16.98	-0.27	43.05	38.36	0	1.88	15.49	1.21	18.29	308.5	5	95	0	0	39	27.24	-19.34		1.00	May-95
	3.37	17.66	0.84	47.57	44.83	0.68	0.75	15.49	1.21	22.86	308.5	5	95	0	0	39	27.84	-19.1			May-17
50	3.28	17.53	0.73	47.39	45.38	0.6	0.88	15.49	1.21	22.81	308.5	5	95	0	0	39	28	-19.03			Nov-98
50	4.68	21.11	1.28	24.81	19.68	0.7	1.41	14.31	1.04	20.83	404.5	4	96	0	0	44	24.48	-23.92	5.75		Oct-08
50	4.47	20.66	0.54	22.09	15.31	0.01	2.16	14.3	1.04	19.63	404.5	4	96	0	0	44	23.96	-24.18		1.00	Oct-08
	4.78	21.31	1.65	26.17	21.79	1.08	1.09	14.33	1.04	21.07	404.5	4	96	0	0	44	24.73	-23.88			May-13
50	4.72	21.28	1.54	25.76	21.20	0.95	1.16	14.29	1.04	21.09	404.5	4	96	0	0	44	24.73	-23.88			Oct-08
50	0.40	15.94	9.10	10.64	39.64	1.34	1.15	13	0.98	14.97	117.0	3	97	0	0	20	30.57	-14.95	5.75		Dec-00
50	0.20	15.44	8.29	8.14	34.44	0.63	1.9	12.99	0.98	15.06	117.0	3	97	0	0	20	30	-15.19		1.00	Dec-00
	0.52	16.08	9.41	11.69	42.35	1.76	0.85	13.02	0.98	13.84	117.0	3	97	0	0	20	30.77	-14.83			May-13
50	0.44	16.01	9.38	11.43	41.39	1.72	0.9	12.98	0.97	13.8	117.0	3	97	0	0	20	30.77	-14.83			Aug-00
	3.21	10.89	6.81			2.06	0.55			10.66	4.8	54	17	28	0	41					Feb-17
	3.32	11.70	7.07			1.99	0.55			10.54	4.9	42	27	31	0	65					Feb-17
	3.26	12.20	6.74			1.76	0.56			10.76	4.2	43	32	25	0	59					Feb-17
	3.54	13.82	7.37			1.55	0.57			10.99	3.5	44	37	19	0	65					Feb-17
	3.55	14.55	7.17			1.37	0.58			11.08	4.7	46	41	13	0	74					Feb-17
	3.50	15.24	7.07			1.34	0.59			10.96	3.8	45	45	10	0	90					Feb-17
	3.64	15.91	7.17			1.35	0.59			11.02	2.8	47	48	5	0	77					Feb-17
	3.50	15.59	6.83			1.33	0.6			10.99	3.2	47	48	4	0	83					Feb-17
	3.62	15.93	7.05			1.28	0.6			11.02	2.9	46	49	4	0	85					Feb-17
	3.64	16.14	7.09			1.33	0.6			11.03	2.7	46	50	4	0	80					Feb-17
50	4.54	18.88	4.92	47.68	57.23	0	1.24	12.65	1	17.5	217.4	3	97	0	0	54			5.75		Jun-12
50	4.35	18.39	4.13	44.37	51.40	0	1.99	12.63	1	16.54	217.4	3	97	0	0	54				1.00	Jun-12
	4.57	18.99	5.16	48.96	59.40	0.29	0.94	12.7	1	17.6	217.4	3	97	0	0	54					Mar-17
50	4.57	18.93	5.15	48.74	59.17	0.25	0.99	12.67	1	17.59	217.4	3	97	0	0	54					Jun-12
500	0.74	5.89	-4.91	13.69	5.22	1.23	1.66	8.43	0.67	8.26	38.7	11	89	0	0	33	7.11	-15.43	5.50		Dec-10
500	0.47	5.37	-5.68	11.15	1.38	0.94	2.41	8.42	0.66	7.77	38.7	11	89	0	0	33	6.66	-15.76			Dec-10
	0.81	6.00	-4.71	14.53	6.62	1.37	1.41	8.45	0.67	8.2	38.7	11	89	0	0	33	7.24	-15.4			Dec-10
500	-12.92	-36.00	-22.42	-74.29	-84.29	0	1.58	34.44		1.28	10.6	94	6	0	0	0			3.75		Mar-14
500	-12.83	-36.13	-22.75	-74.25	-84.17	0	2.33	34.26		1.29	10.6	94	6	0	0	0					Mar-14
	-12.83	-36.13	-22.75	-74.25	-84.17	0	1.33	34.26		1.29	10.6	94	6	0	0	0					Mar-14
	4.85	23.09	-2.63	38.94	35.75	0	2.35	16.81	1.08	20.95	45.7	0	100	0	0	8	29.89	-30.25			Dec-16
100	4.72	22.73	-3.15	37.01	33.86	0	2.91	16.8	1.08	20.62	45.7	0	100	0	0	8	29.89	-30.25			Sep-01
	9.92	26.51	9.38	37.84	36.47	0	2.21	14.66	1.06	42.09	96.6	0	100	0	0	8	30.11	-28.5			Dec-16
100	9.76	26.17	8.76	36.06	34.70	0	2.76	14.64	1.06	41.46	96.6	0	100	0	0	8	30.11	-28.5			Jan-96
	11.06	30.81	17.40	70.71	71.39	0	1.26	17.02	0.87	16.26	37.4	4	96	0	0	103	22.44	-29.04			Dec-16
100	10.88	30.39	16.75	68.39	69.07	0	1.93	17.01	0.87	16	37.4	4	96	0	0	103	22.44	-29.04			May-02
100	3.41	15.90	6.91	36.53	42.91	1.18	1.46	9.94	0.78	28.54	33.6	10	90	0	0	19	18.12	-14.65	5.75		Aug-12
100	3.41	15.90	6.91	36.53	42.91	1.18	1.46	9.94	0.78	28.54	33.6	10	90	0	0	19	18.29	-14.56			Apr-03
100	5.81	16.07	1.91	34.04		0	1.53	10.04	0.64	13.29	10.3	13	82	0	6	97			5.75		Apr-16
100	1.41	5.79	0.09	9.22	0.17	0	2.66	3.52	0.83	10.77	184.7	31	40	28	0	194			5.75		May-12
100	1.18	5.36	-0.68	6.79	-3.60	0	3.5	3.52	0.83	10.22	184.7	31	40	28	0	194				1.00	May-12
	1.47	6.09	0.54	10.58	2.12	0	2.29	3.56	0.84	10.97	184.7	31	40	28	0	194					Dec-13
	1.38	5.89	0.45	10.38	1.89	0	2.39	3.48	0.82	10.95	184.7	31	40	28	0	194					May-12
	3.39	16.63	-1.31	26.86	16.10	0.52	1.01	12.72	1.1	13.11	77.8	3	97	0	0	31	13.86	-23.21			Jan-18
	3.23	16.38	-1.85	25.99	15.30	0.16	1.51	12.74	1.1	13.07	77.8	3	97	0	0	31	13.86	-23.21			Apr-05
	6.70	27.93	10.81	60.09	65.35	0	0.93	15.1	1.04	30.41	485.4	4	96	0	0	50	25.43	-16.51			Nov-97
	6.67	27.80	10.64	58.55	62.95	0	1.11	15.09	1.04	27.95	485.4	4	96	0	0	50	25.31	-16.62			Feb-03
	1.81	14.49	3.01	39.89	46.53	0.47	0.95	12.28	0.98	25.83	575.1	8	92	0	0	13	20.19	-20.76			Feb-99
	1.72	14.34	2.78	38.93	44.98	0.2	1.18	12.29	0.98	25.91	575.1	8	92	0	0	13	20.13	-20.79			May-06
	1.78	9.10	2.47	9.40	0.56	0	1.06	7.04		9.71	32.1	15	0	85	0	23					May-14

Fund Name	MARKET Ticker Symbol	MARKET Traded On	FUND TYPE, CATEGORY & OBJECTIVE Fund Type	Category and (Prospectus Objective)	RATINGS Overall Rating	Reward Rating	Risk Rating	Recent Up/ Downgrade	MINIMUMS Open to New Investors	Min Initial Investment
Neuberger Berman AMT Mid-Cap Intrinsic Value Port Cls I			Open End	US Equity Mid Cap (Growth)	C	C-	C+		Y	0
Neuberger Berman AMT Mid-Cap Intrinsic Value Port Cls S			Open End	US Equity Mid Cap (Growth)	C	C-	C+		Y	0
Neuberger Berman Commodity Strategy Fund Class A	NRBAX	NAS CM	Open End	Commodities Broad Basket (Balanced)	C-	C-	C		Y	1,000
Neuberger Berman Commodity Strategy Fund Class C	NRBCX	NAS CM	Open End	Commodities Broad Basket (Balanced)	C-	C-	C-	Up	Y	1,000
Neuberger Berman Commodity Strategy Institutional Cls	NRBIX	NAS CM	Open End	Commodities Broad Basket (Balanced)	C-	C-	C	Down	Y	1,000,000
Neuberger Berman Dividend Growth Fund Class A	NDGAX	NAS CM	Open End	US Equity Large Cap Value (Equity-Income)	C+	C	B	Up	Y	1,000
Neuberger Berman Dividend Growth Fund Class C	NDGCX	NAS CM	Open End	US Equity Large Cap Value (Equity-Income)	C+	C	B	Up	Y	1,000
Neuberger Berman Dividend Growth Fund Class Institutional	NDGIX	NAS CM	Open End	US Equity Large Cap Value (Equity-Income)	C+	C	B	Up	Y	1,000,000
Neuberger Berman Dividend Growth Fund Class R6	NRDGX	NAS CM	Open End	US Equity Large Cap Value (Equity-Income)	C+	C	B	Up	Y	0
Neuberger Berman Emerging Markets Equity Fund Class A	NEMAX	NAS CM	Open End	Global Emerg Mkts (Div Emerging Mkts)	C	C	C+		Y	1,000
Neuberger Berman Emerging Markets Equity Fund Class C	NEMCX	NAS CM	Open End	Global Emerg Mkts (Div Emerging Mkts)	C	C	C+		Y	1,000
Neuberger Berman Emerging Markets Equity Fund Class R3	NEMRX	NAS CM	Open End	Global Emerg Mkts (Div Emerging Mkts)	C	C	C+		Y	0
Neuberger Berman Emerging Markets Equity Fund Class R6	NREMX	NAS CM	Open End	Global Emerg Mkts (Div Emerging Mkts)	C	C	C+		Y	0
Neuberger Berman Emerging Markets Equity Institutional Cls	NEMIX	NAS CM	Open End	Global Emerg Mkts (Div Emerging Mkts)	C	C	C+		Y	1,000,000
Neuberger Berman Equity Income Fund Class A	NBHAX	NAS CM	Open End	US Equity Large Cap Value (Equity-Income)	B	C+	B+	Up	Y	1,000
Neuberger Berman Equity Income Fund Class C	NBHCX	NAS CM	Open End	US Equity Large Cap Value (Equity-Income)	B-	C	B+		Y	1,000
Neuberger Berman Equity Income Fund Class R3	NBHRX	NAS CM	Open End	US Equity Large Cap Value (Equity-Income)	B	C+	B+	Up	Y	0
Neuberger Berman Equity Income Fund Institutional Class	NBHIX	NAS CM	Open End	US Equity Large Cap Value (Equity-Income)	B	C+	A-	Up	Y	1,000,000
Neuberger Berman Focus Fund Advisor Class	NBFAX	NAS CM	Open End	US Equity Large Cap Blend (Growth)	C+	C	B	Down		0
Neuberger Berman Focus Fund Class A	NFAAX	NAS CM	Open End	US Equity Large Cap Blend (Growth)	C+	C	B	Down	Y	1,000
Neuberger Berman Focus Fund Class C	NFACX	NAS CM	Open End	US Equity Large Cap Blend (Growth)	C+	C	B	Down	Y	1,000
Neuberger Berman Focus Fund Institutional Class	NFALX	NAS CM	Open End	US Equity Large Cap Blend (Growth)	C+	C	B	Down	Y	1,000,000
Neuberger Berman Focus Fund Investor Class	NBSSX	NAS CM	Open End	US Equity Large Cap Blend (Growth)	C+	C	B	Down		1,000
Neuberger Berman Focus Fund Trust Class	NBFCX	NAS CM	Open End	US Equity Large Cap Blend (Growth)	C+	C	B	Down		0
Neuberger Berman Genesis Fund Advisor Class	NBGAX	NAS CM	Open End	US Equity Small Cap (Small Company)	C+	C	B	Down	Y	0
Neuberger Berman Genesis Fund Class R6	NRGSX	NAS CM	Open End	US Equity Small Cap (Small Company)	C+	C	B	Down	Y	0
Neuberger Berman Genesis Fund Investor Class	NBGNX	NAS CM	Open End	US Equity Small Cap (Small Company)	C+	C	B	Down	Y	1,000
Neuberger Berman Genesis Fund Trust Class	NBGEX	NAS CM	Open End	US Equity Small Cap (Small Company)	C+	C	B	Down	Y	0
Neuberger Berman Global Allocation Fund Class A	NGLAX	NAS CM	Open End	Cautious Alloc (Multi-Asset Global)	B-	C	B+	Up	Y	1,000
Neuberger Berman Global Allocation Fund Class C	NGLCX	NAS CM	Open End	Cautious Alloc (Multi-Asset Global)	C+	C	B+	Up	Y	1,000
Neuberger Berman Global Allocation Fund Class R6	NRGLX	NAS CM	Open End	Cautious Alloc (Multi-Asset Global)	B-	C	B+	Up	Y	0
Neuberger Berman Global Allocation Institutional Cls	NGLIX	NAS CM	Open End	Cautious Alloc (Multi-Asset Global)	B-	C	B+	Up	Y	1,000,000
Neuberger Berman Global Equity Fund Class A	NGQAX	NAS CM	Open End	Global Equity Large Cap (World Stock)	C+	C	B	Up	Y	1,000
Neuberger Berman Global Equity Fund Class C	NGQCX	NAS CM	Open End	Global Equity Large Cap (World Stock)	C	C	B-		Y	1,000
Neuberger Berman Global Equity Fund Institutional Class	NGQIX	NAS CM	Open End	Global Equity Large Cap (World Stock)	C+	C	B	Up	Y	1,000,000
Neuberger Berman Global Real Estate Fund Class A	NGRAX	NAS CM	Open End	Real Estate Sector Equity (Real Estate)	B-	C+	B+	Down	Y	1,000
Neuberger Berman Global Real Estate Fund Class C	NGRCX	NAS CM	Open End	Real Estate Sector Equity (Real Estate)	B-	C	B		Y	1,000
Neuberger Berman Global Real Estate Institutional Cls	NGRIX	NAS CM	Open End	Real Estate Sector Equity (Real Estate)	B	C+	B+		Y	1,000,000
Neuberger Berman Greater China Equity Fund Class A	NCEAX	NAS CM	Open End	Greater China Equity (Pacific Stock)	C	C	C		Y	1,000
Neuberger Berman Greater China Equity Fund Class C	NCECX	NAS CM	Open End	Greater China Equity (Pacific Stock)	C	C	C		Y	1,000
Neuberger Berman Greater China Equity Institutional Cls	NCEIX	NAS CM	Open End	Greater China Equity (Pacific Stock)	C	C	C		Y	1,000,000
Neuberger Berman Guardian Fund Class A	NGDAX	NAS CM	Open End	US Equity Large Cap Growth (Growth)	C+	C	B		Y	1,000
Neuberger Berman Guardian Fund Class Advisor	NBGUX	NAS CM	Open End	US Equity Large Cap Growth (Growth)	C+	C	B			0
Neuberger Berman Guardian Fund Class C	NGDCX	NAS CM	Open End	US Equity Large Cap Growth (Growth)	C+	C	B-		Y	2,500
Neuberger Berman Guardian Fund Class Institutional	NGDLX	NAS CM	Open End	US Equity Large Cap Growth (Growth)	B-	C+	B	Up	Y	1,000,000
Neuberger Berman Guardian Fund Class Investor	NGUAX	NAS CM	Open End	US Equity Large Cap Growth (Growth)	C+	C+	B			1,000
Neuberger Berman Guardian Fund Class R3	NGDRX	NAS CM	Open End	US Equity Large Cap Growth (Growth)	C+	C	B		Y	0
Neuberger Berman Guardian Fund Class R6	NGRDX	NAS CM	Open End	US Equity Large Cap Growth (Growth)	C+	C+	B		Y	0
Neuberger Berman Guardian Fund Class Trust	NBGTX	NAS CM	Open End	US Equity Large Cap Growth (Growth)	C+	C	B			0
Neuberger Berman Hedged Option Premium Fund Class A	NHOAX	NAS CM	Open End	Long/Short Equity (Growth & Income)	D+	D+	C-	Up	Y	1,000
Neuberger Berman Hedged Option Premium Fund Class C	NHOCX	NAS CM	Open End	Long/Short Equity (Growth & Income)	D+	D+	C-	Up	Y	1,000
Neuberger Berman Hedged Option Premium Fund Class R6	NHORX	NAS CM	Open End	Long/Short Equity (Growth & Income)	D+	D	C-	Up	Y	0

★ Expanded analysis of this fund is included in Section II.

	TOTAL RETURNS					PERFORMANCE				ASSETS		ASSET ALLOCATION & TURNOVER					BULL & BEAR		FEES		
Min Additional Investment	3-Month Total Return	6-Month Total Return	1-Year Total Return	3-Year Total Return	5-Year Total Return	Dividend Yield (TTM)	Expense Ratio	3-Yr Std Deviation	3-Year Beta	NAV	Total Assets (MIL)	%Cash	%Stocks	%Bonds	%Other	Turnover Ratio	Last Bull Market Total Return	Last Bear Market Total Return	Front End Fee (%)	Back End Fee (%)	Inception Date
	-0.72	14.22	-5.41	26.10	25.65	0.7	1	16.25	1.18	17.83	147.0	4	96	0	0	34	27.39	-25.53			Aug-01
	-0.73	14.10	-5.60	25.20	24.15	0.25	1.26	16.26	1.18	20.38	147.0	4	96	0	0	34	27.25	-25.57			Apr-05
100	0.34	7.96	-6.27	0.59	-35.74	2.26	1.1	9	0.94	5.83	159.0	8	0	74	17	107			5.75		Aug-12
100	0.17	7.45	-6.99	-2.38	-38.65	1.36	1.85	8.95	0.93	5.62	159.0	8	0	74	17	107				1.00	Aug-12
	0.50	8.19	-5.96	1.68	-34.57	2.58	0.74	9.04	0.94	5.94	159.0	8	0	74	17	107					Aug-12
100	4.04	19.25	3.07	37.52		0.74	1.06	12.91	1.01	13.13	57.1	4	96	0	0	43			5.75		Dec-15
100	3.90	18.87	2.35	34.44		0.25	1.81	12.89	1.01	13.04	57.1	4	96	0	0	43				1.00	Dec-15
	4.12	19.48	3.47	39.05		1	0.7	12.9	1.01	13.12	57.1	4	96	0	0	43					Dec-15
	4.20	19.58	3.60	39.26		1.04	0.6	12.94	1.01	13.13	57.1	4	96	0	0	43					Dec-15
100	0.71	11.40	-1.00	34.04	14.17	0.45	1.51	13.38	0.93	19.63	1,512	8	92	0	0	23	16.42	-27.95	5.75		Oct-08
100	0.56	10.97	-1.74	31.09	9.98	0	2.26	13.39	0.93	19.61	1,512	8	92	0	0	23	15.96	-28.22		1.00	Oct-08
	0.66	11.19	-1.41	32.43	11.93	0.04	1.92	13.37	0.93	19.66	1,512	8	92	0	0	23	16.19	-28.08			Jun-10
	0.82	11.57	-0.69	35.40	16.03	0.97	1.16	13.37	0.93	19.57	1,512	8	92	0	0	23	16.63	-27.92			Mar-13
	0.82	11.57	-0.76	35.13	15.68	0.9	1.26	13.38	0.93	19.57	1,512	8	92	0	0	23	16.63	-27.92			Oct-08
100	2.95	14.78	5.50	30.37	36.35	2	1.05	8.58	0.67	13	1,490	1	89	0	0	41	12.43	-9.84	5.75		Jun-08
100	2.77	14.37	4.73	27.56	31.39	1.28	1.8	8.62	0.67	12.92	1,490	1	89	0	0	41	12.01	-10.11		1.00	Jun-08
	2.90	14.68	5.22	29.36	34.56	1.74	1.33	8.59	0.67	12.97	1,490	1	89	0	0	41	12.31	-9.95			Jun-10
	3.03	14.94	5.79	31.84	38.88	2.34	0.69	8.56	0.67	13.04	1,490	1	89	0	0	41	12.72	-9.66			Nov-06
	2.98	17.23	4.00	35.57	38.32	0	1.26	13.24	1.04	25.91	694.0	1	99	0	0	59	24.85	-20.48			Sep-96
100	3.02	17.30	4.17	36.04	39.22	0.24	1.12	13.29	1.04	25.9	694.0	1	99	0	0	59	25	-20.47	5.75		Jun-10
100	2.80	16.90	3.39	32.99	34.19	0	1.87	13.23	1.04	25.66	694.0	1	99	0	0	59	24.33	-20.64		1.00	Jun-10
	3.09	17.55	4.54	37.55	41.78	0.45	0.76	13.26	1.04	25.98	694.0	1	99	0	0	59	25.27	-20.34			Jun-10
100	3.05	17.47	4.37	36.90	40.65	0.34	0.92	13.27	1.04	25.95	694.0	1	99	0	0	59	25.09	-20.38			Oct-55
	3.02	17.33	4.19	36.18	39.34	0.2	1.1	13.26	1.04	25.92	694.0	1	99	0	0	59	24.92	-20.43			Aug-93
	6.34	23.48	8.97	48.75	52.89	0	1.35	15.15	0.84	58.53	10,430	1	99	0	0	13	19.91	-17.72			Apr-97
	6.48	23.84	9.62	51.37	57.50	0.31	0.75	15.16	0.84	58.59	10,430	1	99	0	0	13	20.17	-17.62			Mar-13
100	6.43	23.67	9.32	50.25	55.58	0.04	1.02	15.16	0.84	58.71	10,430	1	99	0	0	13	20.17	-17.62			Sep-88
	6.39	23.62	9.24	49.88	54.94	0	1.1	15.16	0.84	58.72	10,430	1	99	0	0	13	20.08	-17.64			Aug-93
100	3.26	12.79	3.13	24.49	17.02	1.81	1.24	8.03		11.37	16.9	7	52	39	1	59	10.21	-5.91	5.75		Dec-10
100	2.98	12.30	2.25	21.63	12.59	1.04	1.99	7.99		11.04	16.9	7	52	39	1	59	9.85	-6.21		1.00	Dec-10
	3.33	12.91	3.41	25.82	19.12		0.78	8.01		11.45	16.9	7	52	39	1	59	10.46	-5.72			Jan-19
	3.33	12.91	3.41	25.82	19.12	2.2	0.88	8.01		11.45	16.9	7	52	39	1	59	10.46	-5.72			Dec-10
100	3.66	16.98	1.37	37.60	29.99	0.1	1.12	12.96	1.12	7.92	4.8	1	98	0	0	33	15.47		5.75		Jun-11
100	3.41	16.56	0.63	34.32	25.19	0	1.87	12.9	1.11	7.88	4.8	1	98	0	0	33	14.92			1.00	Jun-11
	3.68	17.28	1.68	38.97	32.22	0.82	0.76	12.97	1.12	7.87	4.8	1	98	0	0	33	15.66				Jun-11
100	1.34	17.08	11.21	21.94		1.88	1.37	10.86	0.96	11.48	4.0	1	99	0	0	48			5.75		Dec-14
100	1.15	16.69	10.41	19.31		1.18	2.12	10.86	0.96	11.46	4.0	1	99	0	0	48				1.00	Dec-14
	1.42	17.35	11.66	23.40		2.19	1.01	10.92	0.97	11.49	4.0	1	99	0	0	48					Dec-14
100	0.42	21.61	-5.00	64.05	81.11	0	1.87	20.49	1.01	9.51	56.0	6	94	0	0	60			5.75		Jul-13
100	0.33	21.18	-5.67	60.51	74.00	0	2.62	20.49	1.01	8.98	56.0	6	94	0	0	60				1.00	Jul-13
	0.52	21.88	-4.60	65.97	83.85	0	1.51	20.46	1.01	9.58	56.0	6	94	0	0	60					Jul-13
100	5.70	22.03	8.16	50.59	53.55	0.38	1.09	13.05	1.05	17.78	1,242	3	96	0	0	41	19.81	-20.09	5.75		May-09
	5.60	21.87	7.82	49.70	51.42	0.25	1.4	13.08	1.06	17.72	1,242	3	96	0	0	41	19.57	-20.22			Sep-96
100	5.56	21.65	7.41	47.46	47.95	0.1	1.83	13.05	1.05	17.64	1,242	3	96	0	0	41	19.3	-20.32		1.00	May-09
	5.82	22.32	8.56	52.39	56.39	0.74	0.71	13.06	1.05	17.81	1,242	3	96	0	0	41	20.11	-19.96			May-09
100	5.76	22.18	8.34	51.55	54.98	0.57	0.89	13.08	1.06	17.79	1,242	3	96	0	0	41	19.92	-20			Jun-50
	5.59	21.85	7.81	49.35	51.41	0.25	1.37	13.06	1.05	17.73	1,242	3	96	0	0	41	19.65	-20.16			May-09
	5.82	22.24	8.40	51.64	55.07		0.62	13.07	1.06	17.81	1,242	3	96	0	0	41	19.92	-20			Mar-19
	5.76	22.10	8.19	50.91	53.80	0.41	1.06	13.07	1.05	17.79	1,242	3	96	0	0	41	19.85	-20.1			Aug-93
100	1.01	0.98	-2.77			0.94	1.02			23.53	18.3	12	-1	89	0	13			5.75		Apr-17
100	0.84	0.60	-3.50			0.25	1.77			23.39	18.3	12	-1	89	0	13				1.00	Apr-17
	1.13	1.24	-2.35			1.42	0.56			23.52	18.3	12	-1	89	0	13					Apr-17

Fund Name	MARKET Ticker Symbol	MARKET Traded On	FUND TYPE Fund Type	Category and (Prospectus Objective)	RATINGS Overall Rating	RATINGS Reward Rating	RATINGS Risk Rating	RATINGS Recent Up/ Downgrade	MINIMUMS Open to New Investors	MINIMUMS Min Initial Investment
Neuberger Berman Hedged Option Premium Institutional Cls	NHOIX	NAS CM	Open End	Long/Short Equity (Growth & Income)	D+	D	C-	Up	Y	1,000,000
Neuberger Berman International Equity Fund Class A	NIQAX	NAS CM	Open End	Global Equity Large Cap (Foreign Stock)	C	C	B-		Y	1,000
Neuberger Berman International Equity Fund Class C	NIQCX	NAS CM	Open End	Global Equity Large Cap (Foreign Stock)	C	C-	C+		Y	1,000
Neuberger Berman International Equity Fund Class R6	NRIQX	NAS CM	Open End	Global Equity Large Cap (Foreign Stock)	C	C	B-		Y	0
Neuberger Berman International Equity Institutional Cls	NBIIX	NAS CM	Open End	Global Equity Large Cap (Foreign Stock)	C	C	B-		Y	1,000,000
Neuberger Berman International Equity Fund Investor Class	NIQVX	NAS CM	Open End	Global Equity Large Cap (Foreign Stock)	C	C	B-		Y	1,000
Neuberger Berman International Equity Fund Trust Class	NIQTX	NAS CM	Open End	Global Equity Large Cap (Foreign Stock)	C	C	B-			0
Neuberger Berman International Select Fund Class A	NBNAX	NAS CM	Open End	Global Equity Large Cap (Foreign Stock)	C	C	B-		Y	1,000
Neuberger Berman International Select Fund Class C	NBNCX	NAS CM	Open End	Global Equity Large Cap (Foreign Stock)	C	C-	B-		Y	1,000
Neuberger Berman International Select Cls Institutional	NILIX	NAS CM	Open End	Global Equity Large Cap (Foreign Stock)	C	C	B-		Y	1,000,000
Neuberger Berman International Select Fund Class R3	NBNRX	NAS CM	Open End	Global Equity Large Cap (Foreign Stock)	C	C	B-		Y	0
Neuberger Berman International Select Fund Class R6	NRILX	NAS CM	Open End	Global Equity Large Cap (Foreign Stock)	C	C	B-		Y	0
Neuberger Berman International Select Fund Class Trust	NILTX	NAS CM	Open End	Global Equity Large Cap (Foreign Stock)	C	C	B-			1,000
Neuberger Berman International Small Cap Fund Class A	NIOAX	NAS CM	Open End	Global Equity Mid/Small Cap (Small Company)	C-	D+	C	Up	Y	1,000
Neuberger Berman International Small Cap Fund Class C	NIOCX	NAS CM	Open End	Global Equity Mid/Small Cap (Small Company)	C-	D+	C	Up	Y	1,000
Neuberger Berman International Small Cap Fund Class R6	NIORX	NAS CM	Open End	Global Equity Mid/Small Cap (Small Company)	C-	D+	C	Up	Y	0
Neuberger Berman International Small Cap Institutional Cls	NIOIX	NAS CM	Open End	Global Equity Mid/Small Cap (Small Company)	C-	D+	C	Up	Y	1,000,000
Neuberger Berman Intrinsic Value Fund Class A	NINAX	NAS CM	Open End	US Equity Small Cap (Growth)	C	C-	B-	Down	Y	1,000
Neuberger Berman Intrinsic Value Fund Class C	NINCX	NAS CM	Open End	US Equity Small Cap (Growth)	C	C-	B-	Down	Y	1,000
Neuberger Berman Intrinsic Value Fund Class R6	NRINX	NAS CM	Open End	US Equity Small Cap (Growth)	C	C-	B-	Down	Y	0
Neuberger Berman Intrinsic Value Fund Institutional Class	NINLX	NAS CM	Open End	US Equity Small Cap (Growth)	C	C-	B-	Down	Y	1,000,000
Neuberger Berman Large Cap Value Fund Advisor Class	NBPBX	NAS CM	Open End	US Equity Large Cap Value (Growth)	B	C+	A-			0
Neuberger Berman Large Cap Value Fund Class A	NPNAX	NAS CM	Open End	US Equity Large Cap Value (Growth)	B	C+	A-		Y	1,000
Neuberger Berman Large Cap Value Fund Class C	NPNCX	NAS CM	Open End	US Equity Large Cap Value (Growth)	B	C+	A-		Y	1,000
Neuberger Berman Large Cap Value Fund Class R3	NPNRX	NAS CM	Open End	US Equity Large Cap Value (Growth)	B	C+	A-		Y	0
Neuberger Berman Large Cap Value Fund Class R6	NRLCX	NAS CM	Open End	US Equity Large Cap Value (Growth)	B	C+	A-		Y	0
Neuberger Berman Large Cap Value Fund Institutional Class	NBPIX	NAS CM	Open End	US Equity Large Cap Value (Growth)	B	C+	A-		Y	1,000,000
Neuberger Berman Large Cap Value Fund Investor Class	NPRTX	NAS CM	Open End	US Equity Large Cap Value (Growth)	B	C+	A-			1,000
Neuberger Berman Large Cap Value Fund Trust Class	NBPTX	NAS CM	Open End	US Equity Large Cap Value (Growth)	B	C+	A-			0
Neuberger Berman Long Short Fund Class A	NLSAX	NAS CM	Open End	Long/Short Equity (Growth)	B-	C	B+	Up	Y	1,000
Neuberger Berman Long Short Fund Class C	NLSCX	NAS CM	Open End	Long/Short Equity (Growth)	C+	C	B	Up	Y	1,000
Neuberger Berman Long Short Fund Institutional Class	NLSIX	NAS CM	Open End	Long/Short Equity (Growth)	B-	C	B+	Up	Y	1,000,000
Neuberger Berman Mid Cap Growth Fund Advisor Class	NBMBX	NAS CM	Open End	US Equity Mid Cap (Growth)	C+	C	B-	Down		0
Neuberger Berman Mid Cap Growth Fund Class A	NMGAX	NAS CM	Open End	US Equity Mid Cap (Growth)	C+	C	B-	Down	Y	1,000
Neuberger Berman Mid Cap Growth Fund Class C	NMGCX	NAS CM	Open End	US Equity Mid Cap (Growth)	C+	C	B-		Y	2,500
Neuberger Berman Mid Cap Growth Fund Class R3	NMGRX	NAS CM	Open End	US Equity Mid Cap (Growth)	C+	C	B-	Down	Y	0
Neuberger Berman Mid Cap Growth Fund Class R6	NRMGX	NAS CM	Open End	US Equity Mid Cap (Growth)	C+	C+	B-	Down	Y	0
Neuberger Berman Mid Cap Growth Fund Institutional Class	NBMLX	NAS CM	Open End	US Equity Mid Cap (Growth)	C+	C+	B-	Down	Y	1,000,000
Neuberger Berman Mid Cap Growth Fund Investor Class	NMANX	NAS CM	Open End	US Equity Mid Cap (Growth)	C+	C+	B-	Down		1,000
Neuberger Berman Mid Cap Growth Fund Trust Class	NBMTX	NAS CM	Open End	US Equity Mid Cap (Growth)	C+	C+	B-	Down		0
Neuberger Berman Mid Cap Intrinsic Value Fund Class A	NBRAX	NAS CM	Open End	US Equity Mid Cap (Growth)	C	C-	C+		Y	1,000
Neuberger Berman Mid Cap Intrinsic Value Fund Class C	NBRCX	NAS CM	Open End	US Equity Mid Cap (Growth)	C	C-	C+		Y	1,000
Neuberger Berman Mid Cap Intrinsic Value Fund Class R3	NBRRX	NAS CM	Open End	US Equity Mid Cap (Growth)	C	C-	C+		Y	0
Neuberger Berman Mid Cap Intrinsic Value Fund Class R6	NBMRX	NAS CM	Open End	US Equity Mid Cap (Growth)	C	C-	C+		Y	0
Neuberger Berman Mid Cap Intrinsic Value Fund Class Trust	NBREX	NAS CM	Open End	US Equity Mid Cap (Growth)	C	C-	C+			0
Neuberger Berman Mid Cap Intrinsic Value Institutional Cls	NBRTX	NAS CM	Open End	US Equity Mid Cap (Growth)	C	C-	C+		Y	1,000,000
Neuberger Berman Mid Cap Intrinsic Value Investor Cls	NBRVX	NAS CM	Open End	US Equity Mid Cap (Growth)	C	C-	C+			1,000
Neuberger Berman MLP Income Fund Inc.	NML	AMEX	Closed End	Energy Sector Equity (Natl Res)	C-	D+	C	Down	Y	
Neuberger Berman Multi-Asset Income Fund Class A	NANAX	NAS CM	Open End	Cautious Alloc (Growth & Income)	B-	C	B+	Up	Y	1,000
Neuberger Berman Multi-Asset Income Fund Class C	NANCX	NAS CM	Open End	Cautious Alloc (Growth & Income)	C+	C	B	Up	Y	1,000
Neuberger Berman Multi-Asset Income Fund Class R6	NRANX	NAS CM	Open End	Cautious Alloc (Growth & Income)	B-	C	B+	Up	Y	0
Neuberger Berman Multi-Asset Income Institutional Cls	NANIX	NAS CM	Open End	Cautious Alloc (Growth & Income)	B-	C	B+	Up	Y	1,000,000

★ Expanded analysis of this fund is included in Section II.

	TOTAL RETURNS					PERFORMANCE				ASSETS		ASSET ALLOCATION & TURNOVER					BULL & BEAR		FEES		
Min Additional Investment	3-Month Total Return	6-Month Total Return	1-Year Total Return	3-Year Total Return	5-Year Total Return	Dividend Yield (TTM)	Expense Ratio	3-Yr Std Deviation	3-Year Beta	NAV	Total Assets (MIL)	%Cash	%Stocks	%Bonds	%Other	Turnover Ratio	Last Bull Market Total Return	Last Bear Market Total Return	Front End Fee (%)	Back End Fee (%)	Inception Date
	1.11	1.19	-2.43			1.34	0.66			23.52	18.3	12	-1	89	0	13					Apr-17
100	2.82	16.01	-2.06	26.13	16.31	0.62	1.22	12.69	1.09	12.75	1,856	1	99	0	0	32	13.75	-23.06	5.75		Jan-13
100	2.75	15.66	-2.74	23.41	12.11	0.03	1.97	12.65	1.09	12.7	1,856	1	99	0	0	32	13.26	-23.3		1.00	Jan-13
	2.98	16.39	-1.56	27.96	18.97	1.06	0.76	12.7	1.1	12.78	1,856	1	99	0	0	32	13.99	-22.94			Sep-13
	2.98	16.30	-1.64	27.59	18.46	0.99	0.86	12.67	1.09	12.77	1,856	1	99	0	0	32	13.99	-22.94			Jun-05
100	2.90	16.21	-2.00	27.09	17.55	0.68	1.2	12.68	1.09	12.76	1,856	1	99	0	0	32	13.92	-22.98			Jan-13
	2.90	16.21	-1.96	26.99	17.27	0.64	1.24	12.68	1.09	12.76	1,856	1	99	0	0	32	13.83	-23.02			Jan-13
100	3.46	15.98	-0.27	28.02	15.78	0.4	1.17	12.53	1.08	12.55	180.3	3	96	0	0	44	13.6	-24.56	5.75		Dec-07
100	3.26	15.54	-1.06	25.17	11.48	0	1.92	12.45	1.07	12.34	180.3	3	96	0	0	44	13.02	-24.74		1.00	Dec-07
	3.52	16.20	0.08	29.42	17.94	0.78	0.81	12.5	1.07	12.62	180.3	3	96	0	0	44	13.85	-24.42			Oct-06
	3.40	15.82	-0.56	27.07	14.34	0.16	1.42	12.5	1.07	12.44	180.3	3	96	0	0	44	13.32	-24.6			May-09
	3.52	16.20	0.11	29.35	16.98	0.87	0.71	12.48	1.07	12.62	180.3	3	96	0	0	44	13.54	-24.51			Apr-17
100	3.51	16.05	-0.21	28.19	15.94	0.44	1.16	12.54	1.08	12.65	180.3	3	96	0	0	44	13.54	-24.51			Aug-06
100	5.98	17.65	-6.24			0	1.42			11.86	6.2	3	97	0	0	48			5.75		Dec-16
100	5.79	17.25	-6.99			0	2.17			11.69	6.2	3	97	0	0	48				1.00	Dec-16
	6.14	17.92	-5.89			0.3	0.96			11.91	6.2	3	97	0	0	48					Dec-16
	6.15	17.93	-5.95			0.25	1.06			11.9	6.2	3	97	0	0	48					Dec-16
100	-0.89	20.90	2.32	43.33	36.05	0	1.37	17.29	0.92	15.44	658.5	3	96	0	0	25	24.08	-29.4	5.75		May-10
100	-1.09	20.58	1.61	40.15	31.06	0	2.12	17.25	0.92	15.35	658.5	3	96	0	0	25	23.47	-29.61		1.00	May-10
	-0.76	21.18	2.73	44.92	38.60		0.91	17.28	0.92	15.51	658.5	3	96	0	0	25	24.31	-29.28			Jan-19
	-0.83	21.11	2.67	44.83	38.51	0	1.01	17.28	0.92	15.49	658.5	3	96	0	0	25	24.31	-29.29			May-10
	4.18	15.35	14.26	52.37	48.01	1.23	1.21	10.17	0.79	31.1	1,707	7	93	0	0	153	19.79	-26.46			Aug-96
100	4.18	15.40	14.40	52.86	48.86	1.33	1.09	10.16	0.79	31.09	1,707	7	93	0	0	153	19.9	-26.42	5.75		Jun-10
100	4.04	15.02	13.59	49.51	43.51	0.66	1.83	10.18	0.79	31.15	1,707	7	93	0	0	153	19.31	-26.65		1.00	Jun-10
	4.14	15.25	14.12	51.56	46.82	1.07	1.36	10.19	0.79	31.13	1,707	7	93	0	0	153	19.73	-26.49			Jun-10
	4.33	15.66	14.80	54.02	50.65		0.61	10.17	0.79	31.07	1,707	7	93	0	0	153	20.02	-26.36			Jan-19
	4.29	15.64	14.86	54.62	51.76	1.69	0.71	10.17	0.79	31.05	1,707	7	93	0	0	153	20.11	-26.29			Jun-06
100	4.26	15.54	14.68	53.86	50.50	1.53	0.88	10.18	0.79	31.07	1,707	7	93	0	0	153	20.02	-26.36			Jan-75
	4.22	15.44	14.45	53.08	49.19	1.36	1.06	10.17	0.79	31.09	1,707	7	93	0	0	153	19.87	-26.39			Aug-93
100	3.91	11.86	3.32	18.93	16.12	0	1.98	6.63	1	14.33	2,606	29	62	7	0	83			5.75		Dec-11
100	3.71	11.42	2.52	16.22	11.76	0	2.73	6.61	0.99	14.24	2,606	29	62	7	0	83				1.00	Dec-11
	4.05	12.09	3.72	20.26	18.24	0	1.61	6.66	1	14.37	2,606	29	62	7	0	83					Dec-11
	6.83	28.40	11.21	60.55	65.07	0	1.22	15.18	1.05	15.64	1,441	1	99	0	0	50	24.32	-15.2			Sep-96
100	6.81	28.44	11.34	61.06	66.07	0	1.08	15.19	1.05	15.67	1,441	1	99	0	0	50	24.58	-15.07	5.75		May-09
100	6.62	27.98	10.52	57.47	59.92	0	1.86	15.16	1.04	15.46	1,441	1	99	0	0	50	23.99	-15.3		1.00	May-09
	6.77	28.28	11.10	59.89	64.02	0	1.37	15.21	1.05	15.6	1,441	1	99	0	0	50	24.43	-15.16			May-09
	6.90	28.76	11.84	63.34	69.89	0	0.61	15.19	1.05	15.8	1,441	1	99	0	0	50	24.64	-15.03			Mar-13
	6.91	28.71	11.79	62.93	69.23	0	0.71	15.19	1.05	15.78	1,441	1	99	0	0	50	24.91	-14.99			Apr-07
100	6.93	28.61	11.60	62.10	67.72	0	0.91	15.22	1.05	15.73	1,441	1	99	0	0	50	24.64	-15.03			Mar-79
	6.87	28.55	11.54	61.75	67.24	0	0.96	15.19	1.05	15.71	1,441	1	99	0	0	50	24.63	-15.03			Aug-93
100	-0.67	14.92	-4.12	28.19	28.46	0.54	1.22	16.42	1.19	20.48	104.2	0	100	0	0	36	27.06	-25.68	5.75		Jun-10
100	-0.87	14.47	-4.84	25.41	23.74	0.02	1.97	16.4	1.19	20.48	104.2	0	100	0	0	36	26.55	-25.99		1.00	Jun-10
	-0.72	14.78	-4.36	27.28	26.89	0.29	1.46	16.44	1.19	20.5	104.2	0	100	0	0	36	27.03	-25.89			Jun-10
	-0.58	15.03	-3.99	28.72	29.30		0.75	16.42	1.19	20.46	104.2	0	100	0	0	36	27.37	-25.76			Mar-19
	-0.72	14.86	-4.18	28.07	28.25	0.5	1.26	16.42	1.19	20.48	104.2	0	100	0	0	36	27.09	-25.73			Jun-99
	-0.63	15.08	-3.80	29.63	30.81	0.91	0.85	16.41	1.19	20.45	104.2	0	100	0	0	36	27.42	-25.64			Mar-10
100	-0.67	14.92	-4.09	28.59	29.18	0.56	1.21	16.43	1.19	20.48	104.2	0	100	0	0	36	27.37	-25.76			Jun-99
	-3.72	20.80	-2.73	14.32	-44.22	0	1.98	21.74		8.56	485.0	3	129	0	-32	35					Mar-13
100	2.13	10.53	3.94	16.24		3.51	1.1	6.12		9.95	22.2	8	39	50	0	74			4.25		Mar-15
100	1.84	10.02	3.07	13.56		2.78	1.85	6.07		9.94	22.2	8	39	50	0	74				1.00	Mar-15
	2.25	10.78	4.41	17.80		3.96	0.63	6.11		9.95	22.2	8	39	50	0	74					Mar-15
	2.22	10.73	4.32	17.53		3.88	0.73	6.1		9.95	22.2	8	39	50	0	74					Mar-15

	MARKET			FUND TYPE, CATEGORY & OBJECTIVE	RATINGS					MINIMUMS
Fund Name	Ticker Symbol	Traded On	Fund Type	Category and (Prospectus Objective)	Overall Rating	Reward Rating	Risk Rating	Recent Up/ Downgrade	Open to New Investors	Min Initial Investment
Neuberger Berman Multi-Cap Opportunities Fund Class A	NMUAX	NAS CM	Open End	US Equity Large Cap Blend (Growth & Income)	B-	C	B	Down	Y	1,000
Neuberger Berman Multi-Cap Opportunities Fund Class C	NMUCX	NAS CM	Open End	US Equity Large Cap Blend (Growth & Income)	B-	C	B		Y	2,500
Neuberger Berman Multi-Cap Opportunities Institutional Cls	NMULX	NAS CM	Open End	US Equity Large Cap Blend (Growth & Income)	B-	C	B	Down	Y	1,000,000
Neuberger Berman Multi-Style Premia Fund Class A	NMLAX	NAS CM	Open End	Multialternative (Growth)	D	D+	C		Y	1,000
Neuberger Berman Multi-Style Premia Fund Class C	NMLCX	NAS CM	Open End	Multialternative (Growth)	D	D+	C		Y	1,000
Neuberger Berman Multi-Style Premia Fund Class R6	NMLRX	NAS CM	Open End	Multialternative (Growth)	D	D+	C		Y	0
Neuberger Berman Multi-Style Premia Institutional Cls	NMLIX	NAS CM	Open End	Multialternative (Growth)	D	D+	C		Y	1,000,000
Neuberger Berman Real Estate Fund Class A	NREAX	NAS CM	Open End	Real Estate Sector Equity (Real Estate)	B-	C+	B	Down	Y	1,000
Neuberger Berman Real Estate Fund Class C	NRECX	NAS CM	Open End	Real Estate Sector Equity (Real Estate)	C+	C	B	Down	Y	1,000
Neuberger Berman Real Estate Fund Class R3	NRERX	NAS CM	Open End	Real Estate Sector Equity (Real Estate)	B-	C+	B		Y	0
Neuberger Berman Real Estate Fund Class R6	NRREX	NAS CM	Open End	Real Estate Sector Equity (Real Estate)	B-	C+	B	Down	Y	0
Neuberger Berman Real Estate Fund Institutional Class	NBRIX	NAS CM	Open End	Real Estate Sector Equity (Real Estate)	B-	C+	B	Down	Y	1,000,000
Neuberger Berman Real Estate Fund Trust Class	NBRFX	NAS CM	Open End	Real Estate Sector Equity (Real Estate)	B-	C+	B	Down		1,000
Neuberger Berman Real Estate Securities Income Fund Inc	NRO	AMEX	Closed End	Real Estate Sector Equity (Real Estate)	C	C	C	Down	Y	
Neuberger Berman Small Cap Growth Fund Advisor Class	NBMVX	NAS CM	Open End	US Equity Small Cap (Small Company)	B-	B-	B	Down		0
Neuberger Berman Small Cap Growth Fund Class A	NSNAX	NAS CM	Open End	US Equity Small Cap (Small Company)	B-	B-	B	Down	Y	1,000
Neuberger Berman Small Cap Growth Fund Class C	NSNCX	NAS CM	Open End	US Equity Small Cap (Small Company)	B-	B-	B	Down	Y	2,500
Neuberger Berman Small Cap Growth Fund Class R3	NSNRX	NAS CM	Open End	US Equity Small Cap (Small Company)	B-	B-	B	Down	Y	0
Neuberger Berman Small Cap Growth Fund Class R6	NSRSX	NAS CM	Open End	US Equity Small Cap (Small Company)	B-	B-	B	Down	Y	0
Neuberger Berman Small Cap Growth Fund Institutional Class	NBSMX	NAS CM	Open End	US Equity Small Cap (Small Company)	B-	B-	B	Down	Y	1,000,000
Neuberger Berman Small Cap Growth Fund Investor Class	NBMIX	NAS CM	Open End	US Equity Small Cap (Small Company)	B-	B-	B	Down		1,000
Neuberger Berman Small Cap Growth Fund Trust Class	NBMOX	NAS CM	Open End	US Equity Small Cap (Small Company)	B-	B-	B	Down		0
Neuberger Berman Sustainable Equity Fund Class A	NRAAX	NAS CM	Open End	US Equity Large Cap Blend (Growth)	B-	C	B		Y	1,000
Neuberger Berman Sustainable Equity Fund Class C	NRACX	NAS CM	Open End	US Equity Large Cap Blend (Growth)	C+	C	B	Down	Y	2,500
Neuberger Berman Sustainable Equity Fund Class R3	NRARX	NAS CM	Open End	US Equity Large Cap Blend (Growth)	C+	C	B	Down	Y	0
Neuberger Berman Sustainable Equity Fund Class R6	NRSRX	NAS CM	Open End	US Equity Large Cap Blend (Growth)	B-	C	B		Y	0
Neuberger Berman Sustainable Equity Institutional Cls	NBSLX	NAS CM	Open End	US Equity Large Cap Blend (Growth)	B-	C	B		Y	1,000,000
Neuberger Berman Sustainable Equity Fund Investor Class	NBSRX	NAS CM	Open End	US Equity Large Cap Blend (Growth)	B-	C	B			1,000
Neuberger Berman Sustainable Equity Fund Trust Class	NBSTX	NAS CM	Open End	US Equity Large Cap Blend (Growth)	B-	C	B			0
Neuberger Berman U.S. Equity Index PutWrite Strategy Cls A	NUPAX	NAS CM	Open End	Long/Short Equity (Growth & Income)	C	C	B-		Y	1,000
Neuberger Berman U.S. Equity Index PutWrite Strategy Cls C	NUPCX	NAS CM	Open End	Long/Short Equity (Growth & Income)	C	C	C+	Up	Y	1,000
Neuberger Berman U.S. Eq Index PutWrite Strategy Cls R6	NUPRX	NAS CM	Open End	Long/Short Equity (Growth & Income)	C	C	B		Y	0
Neuberger Berman U.S. Eq Index PutWrite Strategy Inst Cls	NUPIX	NAS CM	Open End	Long/Short Equity (Growth & Income)	C	C	B		Y	1,000,000
Neuberger Berman Value Fund Class A	NVAAX	NAS CM	Open End	US Equity Large Cap Value (Growth)	B	C+	A-		Y	1,000
Neuberger Berman Value Fund Class C	NVACX	NAS CM	Open End	US Equity Large Cap Value (Growth)	B	C+	A-		Y	2,500
Neuberger Berman Value Fund Institutional Class	NLRLX	NAS CM	Open End	US Equity Large Cap Value (Growth)	B	C+	A		Y	1,000,000
New Alternatives Fund Class A	NALFX	NAS CM	Open End	Global Equity Mid/Small Cap (Growth & Income)	B	B	B		Y	2,500
New Alternatives Fund Investor Shares	NAEFX	NAS CM	Open End	Global Equity Mid/Small Cap (Growth & Income)	B	B	B		Y	3,500
New Covenant Balanced Growth Fund	NCBGX	NAS CM	Open End	Moderate Alloc (Balanced)	B	C	A-	Up	Y	500
New Covenant Balanced Income Fund	NCBIX	NAS CM	Open End	Cautious Alloc (Balanced)	B	C+	A-		Y	500
New Covenant Growth Fund	NCGFX	NAS CM	Open End	US Equity Large Cap Blend (Growth)	B-	C	B		Y	500
New Germany Fund Inc.	GF	NYSE	Closed End	Equity Miscellaneous (Europe Stock)	C-	C	C-	Down	Y	
New Ireland Fund	IRL	NYSE	Closed End	Equity Miscellaneous (Europe Stock)	D	D	D+		Y	
Newfound Multi-Asset Income Fund Class A	NFMAX	NAS CM	Open End	Moderate Alloc (Growth & Income)	C-	D+	C	Up	Y	2,500
Newfound Multi-Asset Income Fund Class I	NFMIX	NAS CM	Open End	Moderate Alloc (Growth & Income)	C-	D+	C	Up	Y	100,000
Newfound Risk Managed Global Sectors Fund Class A	NFGAX	NAS CM	Open End	Moderate Alloc (Growth)	C	C	B		Y	2,500
Newfound Risk Managed Global Sectors Fund Class I	NFGIX	NAS CM	Open End	Moderate Alloc (Growth)	C	C	B		Y	100,000
Newfound Risk Managed U.S. Sectors Fund Class A	NFDAX	NAS CM	Open End	Moderate Alloc (Growth & Income)	C+	C	B-	Up	Y	2,500
Newfound Risk Managed U.S. Sectors Fund Class I	NFDIX	NAS CM	Open End	Moderate Alloc (Growth & Income)	C+	C	B	Up	Y	100,000
Nexpoint Healthcare Opportunities Fund Class A	NXHAX	NAS CM	Closed End	Healthcare Sector Equity (Health)	D	D	D		Y	500
Nexpoint Healthcare Opportunities Fund Class C	NXHCX	NAS CM	Closed End	Healthcare Sector Equity (Health)	D	D	D		Y	500
NexPoint Real Estate Strategies Fund Class A	NRSAX	NAS CM	Closed End	Real Estate Sector Equity (Real Estate)	C+	C	B	Up	Y	500

★Expanded analysis of this fund is included in Section II.

	TOTAL RETURNS					PERFORMANCE				ASSETS		ASSET ALLOCATION & TURNOVER					BULL & BEAR		FEES		
Min Additional Investment	3-Month Total Return	6-Month Total Return	1-Year Total Return	3-Year Total Return	5-Year Total Return	Dividend Yield (TTM)	Expense Ratio	3-Yr Std Deviation	3-Year Beta	NAV	Total Assets (MIL)	%Cash	%Stocks	%Bonds	%Other	Turnover Ratio	Last Bull Market Total Return	Last Bear Market Total Return	Front End Fee (%)	Back End Fee (%)	Inception Date
100	3.45	17.24	8.92	56.69	56.50	0.34	1.1	12.34	0.99	18.56	1,208	2	98	0	0	23	27.04	-17.64	5.75		Dec-09
100	3.28	16.90	8.15	53.32	50.94	0	1.83	12.33	0.99	18.53	1,208	2	98	0	0	23	26.54	-17.97		1.00	Dec-09
	3.57	17.49	9.37	58.40	59.46	0.68	0.72	12.35	0.99	18.54	1,208	2	98	0	0	23	27.38	-17.61			Nov-06
100	-0.38	2.37	-0.94			5.57	1.35			23.28	14.8	43	35	18	4	31			5.75		May-18
100	-0.51	2.02	-1.62			5.03	2.1			23.22	14.8	43	35	18	4	31				1.00	May-18
	-0.25	2.63	-0.47			5.65	0.89			23.38	14.8	43	35	18	4	31					May-18
	-0.25	2.58	-0.55			5.57	0.99			23.38	14.8	43	35	18	4	31					May-18
100	3.41	21.67	15.07	21.27	47.93	1.4	1.22	11.72	0.91	14.01	476.9	1	99	0	0	47	31.02	-16.78	5.75		Jun-10
100	3.20	21.24	14.22	18.59	42.48	0.68	1.97	11.73	0.91	14.05	476.9	1	99	0	0	47	30.45	-17.12		1.00	Jun-10
	3.27	21.47	14.73	20.34	46.04	1.17	1.47	11.72	0.91	13.98	476.9	1	99	0	0	47	30.87	-16.93			Jun-10
	3.51	21.96	15.62	22.92	51.22	1.79	0.76	11.75	0.91	14.05	476.9	1	99	0	0	47	31.12	-16.7			Mar-13
	3.41	21.80	15.43	22.54	50.62	1.72	0.86	11.75	0.91	14.05	476.9	1	99	0	0	47	31.27	-16.67			Jun-08
100	3.44	21.76	15.26	21.91	49.25	1.54	1.42	11.75	0.91	14.01	476.9	1	99	0	0	47	31.13	-16.7			May-02
	0.90	23.36	12.53	14.88	37.09	3.32		14.15	1.06	5.51	261.3	2	62	0	0	12	30.85	-16.4			Oct-03
	2.93	33.10	18.06	101.03	87.50	0	1.61	16.82	0.9	39.24	232.9	8	93	0	0	217	21.79	-21.19			May-02
100	2.98	33.25	18.27	102.42	89.72	0	1.27	16.83	0.9	39.39	232.9	8	93	0	0	217	22.08	-21.08	5.75		May-09
100	2.80	32.74	17.40	97.92	82.81	0	2.02	16.82	0.9	38.88	232.9	8	93	0	0	217	21.59	-21.32		1.00	May-09
	2.88	33.05	17.98	100.87	87.38	0	1.52	16.82	0.9	39.21	232.9	8	93	0	0	217	21.84	-21.11			May-09
	3.09	33.52	18.68	103.35	90.83		0.81	16.84	0.9	39.67	232.9	8	93	0	0	217	22.11	-21.05			Sep-18
	3.06	33.46	18.69	104.58	93.24	0	0.91	16.84	0.9	39.64	232.9	8	93	0	0	217	22.36	-20.96			Apr-08
100	2.97	33.26	18.32	102.73	90.26	0	1.31	16.84	0.9	39.42	232.9	8	93	0	0	217	22.11	-21.05			Oct-98
	2.95	33.22	18.23	101.91	88.82	0	1.41	16.83	0.9	39.34	232.9	8	93	0	0	217	22.03	-21.13			Nov-98
100	1.74	14.41	2.76	39.45	45.60	0.27	1.04	12.35	0.99	37.22	1,912	1	99	0	0	12	20	-20.64	5.75		May-09
100	1.56	13.96	2.02	36.33	40.28	0	1.78	12.35	0.99	37.04	1,912	1	99	0	0	12	19.49	-20.9		1.00	May-09
	1.69	14.29	2.53	38.43	43.85	0.07	1.28	12.35	0.99	37.26	1,912	1	99	0	0	12	19.86	-20.73			May-09
	1.86	14.70	3.26	41.32	48.89	0.72	0.57	12.35	0.99	37.13	1,912	1	99	0	0	12	20.15	-20.58			Mar-13
	1.83	14.62	3.17	41.02	48.36	0.65	0.67	12.36	0.99	37.14	1,912	1	99	0	0	12	20.29	-20.53			Nov-07
100	1.80	14.52	2.98	40.23	46.99	0.4	0.86	12.38	0.99	37.21	1,912	1	99	0	0	12	20.15	-20.58			Mar-94
	1.74	14.40	2.80	39.53	45.74	0.25	1.02	12.36	0.99	37.24	1,912	1	99	0	0	12	20.05	-20.65			Mar-97
100	2.02	9.67	3.04			1.48	1.02			10.95	264.7	11	-1	90	0	56			5.75		Sep-16
100	1.85	9.24	2.23			0.69	1.77			10.83	264.7	11	-1	90	0	56				1.00	Sep-16
	2.13	10.00	3.45			1.88	0.56			10.97	264.7	11	-1	90	0	56					Sep-16
	2.11	9.85	3.36			1.79	0.66			10.96	264.7	11	-1	90	0	56					Sep-16
100	4.03	15.33	15.16	53.84	48.73	0.79	1.12	9.94	0.77	18.58	28.7	10	90	0	0	151	20.51	-15.81	5.75		Mar-11
100	3.87	14.97	14.42	50.58	43.33	0.15	1.87	9.98	0.77	17.97	28.7	10	90	0	0	151	19.99	-16.1		1.00	Mar-11
	4.13	15.63	15.70	55.70	51.55	1.13	0.76	10.01	0.78	18.64	28.7	10	90	0	0	151	20.9	-15.79			Nov-06
250	6.42	21.91	15.19	35.83	27.09	0.54	1.12	11.76	0.6	58.6	208.9	8	92	0	0	18	2.53	-24.72	3.50		Sep-82
250	6.35	21.78	14.93	34.83	25.55	0.35	1.37	11.77	0.6	58.39	208.9	8	92	0	0	18	2.38	-24.8			Jan-15
100	3.10	13.07	7.10	29.30	33.69	1.69	1.05	7.66	0.62	103.44	293.8	6	58	36	0	11	16.11	-11.39			Jul-99
100	2.79	9.71	6.76	18.93	24.05	1.89	1.03	4.65	0.36	21.41	78.4	7	34	59	0	10	10.67	-6.14			Jul-99
100	3.57	18.64	7.20	46.84	49.01	1.11	1.12	12.74	1.03	42.86	448.8	5	95	0	0	24	24.68	-18.95			Jul-99
	4.20	21.99	-2.23	52.87	44.34	0.53		16.88		16.19	251.9	11	98	0	-9	37	25	-32.53			Jan-90
	0.84	11.94	-15.65	11.94	12.94	0	0	13.62	1	10.76	53.6	0	98	0	2	18	20.17	-19.77			Mar-90
250	2.10	5.53	-1.11	3.49		4.33	1.79	5.68	0.39	8.93	21.7	1	20	59	3	347			5.75		Sep-14
10,000	2.10	5.59	-0.91	4.20		4.65	1.54	5.73	0.39	8.92	21.7	1	20	59	3	347					Sep-14
250	2.82	7.72	0.27	22.74	10.76	0.01	2.1	9.52	0.77	11.29	45.3	0	100	0	0	318			5.75		May-14
10,000	2.82	7.82	0.54	23.64	12.13	0.34	1.85	9.51	0.77	11.3	45.3	0	100	0	0	318					May-14
250	4.04	7.87	2.25	26.70		0.74	1.61	10.13	0.76	10.29	48.8	0	79	21	0	360			5.75		Jun-15
10,000	4.07	8.06	2.50	28.11		0.98	1.36	10.2	0.76	10.35	48.8	0	79	21	0	360					Jun-15
50	-3.60	13.79	-14.48			0	5.92			16.83	--	0	100	0	0				5.75		May-18
50	-3.80	13.38	-15.14			0	6.38			16.69	--	0	100	0	0					1.00	May-18
50	4.66	13.26	7.19	24.77		6.51	2.38			20.72	--	0	49	39	0				5.75		Jul-16

Fund Name	MARKET Ticker Symbol	MARKET Traded On	FUND TYPE, CATEGORY & OBJECTIVE Fund Type	Category and (Prospectus Objective)	RATINGS Overall Rating	Reward Rating	Risk Rating	Recent Up/ Downgrade	MINIMUMS Open to New Investors	Min Initial Investment
NexPoint Real Estate Strategies Fund Class C	NRSCX	NAS CM	Closed End	Real Estate Sector Equity (Real Estate)	C+	C	B	Up	Y	500
NexPoint Real Estate Strategies Fund Class Z	NRSZX	NAS CM	Closed End	Real Estate Sector Equity (Real Estate)	C+	C	B	Up	Y	0
NexPoint Strategic Opportunities Fund	NHF	NYSE	Closed End	Moderate Alloc (Multisector Bond)	C	C-	C+		Y	
Nicholas Equity Income Fund Class I	NSEIX	NAS CM	Open End	US Equity Large Cap Value (Equity-Income)	B-	C	B		Y	500
Nicholas Fund	NICSX	NAS CM	Open End	US Equity Large Cap Growth (Growth)	B-	C	B		Y	500
Nicholas II Fund Class I	NCTWX	NAS CM	Open End	US Equity Mid Cap (Growth)	B	B-	B		Y	100,000
Nicholas II Fund Class N	NNTWX	NAS CM	Open End	US Equity Mid Cap (Growth)	B	B-	B		Y	500
Nicholas Limited Edition Fund Class Institutional	NCLEX	NAS CM	Open End	US Equity Small Cap (Growth)	B-	C+	B		Y	100,000
Nicholas Limited Edition Fund Class N	NNLEX	NAS CM	Open End	US Equity Small Cap (Growth)	B-	C+	B		Y	500
Nicholas Partners Small Cap Growth Institutional Shares	NPSGX	NAS CM	Open End	US Equity Small Cap (Small Company)	U	U	U		Y	100,000
North Country Equity Growth Fund	NCEGX	NAS CM	Open End	US Equity Large Cap Growth (Growth)	C+	C	B	Down	Y	500
North Square Oak Ridge Disciplined Growth Fund Class I	ODGIX	NAS CM	Open End	US Equity Large Cap Growth (Growth)	C+	C	B	Down	Y	1,000,000
North Square Oak Ridge Dividend Growth Fund Class A	ORDAX	NAS CM	Open End	US Equity Large Cap Blend (Equity-Income)	B	C+	B+		Y	1,000
North Square Oak Ridge Dividend Growth Fund Class I	ORDNX	NAS CM	Open End	US Equity Large Cap Blend (Equity-Income)	B	C+	B+		Y	1,000,000
North Square Oak Ridge Dynamic Small Cap Fund Class A	ORSAX	NAS CM	Open End	US Equity Small Cap (Small Company)	C	C	C+	Down	Y	1,000
North Square Oak Ridge Dynamic Small Cap Fund Class I	ORSIX	NAS CM	Open End	US Equity Small Cap (Small Company)	C	C	C+	Down	Y	1,000,000
North Square Oak Ridge Global Res & Infrastr Cls A Shares	INNAX	NAS CM	Open End	Natl Resources Sec Equity (Natl Res)	C-	C-	C	Down	Y	1,000
North Square Oak Ridge Global Res & Infrastr Cls I Shares	INNNX	NAS CM	Open End	Natl Resources Sec Equity (Natl Res)	C-	C-	C	Down	Y	1,000,000
North Square Oak Ridge International Small Cap Cls A	ORIAX	NAS CM	Open End	Global Equity Mid/Small Cap (Small Company)	C-	D+	C		Y	1,000
North Square Oak Ridge International Small Cap Cls I	ORIIX	NAS CM	Open End	Global Equity Mid/Small Cap (Small Company)	C-	D+	C		Y	1,000,000
North Square Oak Ridge Multi Strategy Fund Class A	ORILX	NAS CM	Open End	Aggressive Alloc (Growth)	C+	C	B	Up	Y	1,000
North Square Oak Ridge Multi Strategy Fund Class C	ORLCX	NAS CM	Open End	Aggressive Alloc (Growth)	C+	C	B-	Up	Y	1,000
North Square Oak Ridge Multi Strategy Fund Class I	PORYX	NAS CM	Open End	Aggressive Alloc (Growth)	C+	C	B		Y	1,000,000
North Square Oak Ridge Small Cap Growth Fund Class A	ORIGX	NAS CM	Open End	US Equity Small Cap (Small Company)	C	C	C+	Down	Y	1,000
North Square Oak Ridge Small Cap Growth Fund Class C	ORICX	NAS CM	Open End	US Equity Small Cap (Small Company)	C	C	C+	Down	Y	1,000
North Square Oak Ridge Small Cap Growth Fund Class I	ORIYX	NAS CM	Open End	US Equity Small Cap (Small Company)	C	C	C+	Down	Y	1,000,000
North Square Oak Ridge Small Cap Growth Fund Class K	ORIKX	NAS CM	Open End	US Equity Small Cap (Small Company)	C	C	C+	Down	Y	1,000,000
North Star Dividend Fund Class I	NSDVX	NAS CM	Open End	US Equity Small Cap (Equity-Income)	C-	C-	C	Down	Y	5,000
North Star Micro Cap Fund Class I	NSMVX	NAS CM	Open End	US Equity Small Cap (Growth)	C	C	C		Y	5,000
North Star Opportunity Fund Class A Shares	NSOPX	NAS CM	Open End	Aggressive Alloc (Growth)	C+	C	B		Y	2,500
North Star Opportunity Fund Class I Shares	NSOIX	NAS CM	Open End	Aggressive Alloc (Growth)	C+	C	B		Y	5,000
Northern Active M Emerging Market Equity Fund	NMMEX	NAS CM	Open End	Global Emerg Mkts (Div Emerging Mkts)	C	C	C+		Y	2,500
Northern Active M International Equity Fund	NMIEX	NAS CM	Open End	Global Equity Large Cap (Foreign Stock)	C	C	B		Y	2,500
Northern Emerging Markets Equity Index Fund	NOEMX	NAS CM	Open End	Global Emerg Mkts (Div Emerging Mkts)	C	C	C+		Y	2,500
Northern Engage360™ Fund	NENGX	NAS CM	Open End	Global Equity Large Cap (Growth & Income)	D+	D	C+	Up	Y	1,000,000
Northern Global Real Estate Index Fund	NGREX	NAS CM	Open End	Real Estate Sector Equity (Real Estate)	B-	C	B		Y	2,500
Northern Global Sustainability Index Fund	NSRIX	NAS CM	Open End	Global Equity Large Cap (World Stock)	B-	C	B	Up	Y	2,500
Northern Global Tactical Asset Allocation Fund	BBALX	NAS CM	Open End	Moderate Alloc (Asset Alloc)	B-	C	A-	Up	Y	2,500
Northern Income Equity Fund	NOIEX	NAS CM	Open End	US Equity Large Cap Value (Equity-Income)	C+	C	B	Down	Y	2,500
Northern International Equity Fund	NOIGX	NAS CM	Open End	Global Equity Large Cap (Foreign Stock)	C	C	B-		Y	2,500
Northern International Equity Index Fund	NOINX	NAS CM	Open End	Global Equity Large Cap (Foreign Stock)	C	C	B		Y	2,500
Northern Large Cap Core Fund	NOLCX	NAS CM	Open End	US Equity Large Cap Value (Growth & Income)	B-	C	B	Up	Y	2,500
Northern Large Cap Value Fund	NOLVX	NAS CM	Open End	US Equity Large Cap Value (Growth)	B-	C	B		Y	2,500
Northern Mid Cap Index Fund	NOMIX	NAS CM	Open End	US Equity Mid Cap (Growth)	C+	C	B-	Up	Y	2,500
Northern Multi-Manager Global Listed Infrastructure Fund	NMFIX	NAS CM	Open End	Infrastructure Sector Equity (Utility)	B-	C+	B-		Y	2,500
Northern Multi-Manager Global Real Estate Fund	NMMGX	NAS CM	Open End	Real Estate Sector Equity (Real Estate)	B-	C+	B+		Y	2,500
Northern Small Cap Core Fund	NSGRX	NAS CM	Open End	US Equity Small Cap (Small Company)	C	C	B-		Y	2,500
Northern Small Cap Index Fund	NSIDX	NAS CM	Open End	US Equity Small Cap (Small Company)	C	C	C+		Y	2,500
Northern Small Cap Value Fund	NOSGX	NAS CM	Open End	US Equity Small Cap (Small Company)	C	C-	C+		Y	2,500
Northern Stock Index Fund	NOSIX	NAS CM	Open End	US Equity Large Cap Blend (Growth)	B-	C	B		Y	2,500
Northern U.S. Quality ESG Fund	NUESX	NAS CM	Open End	US Equity Large Cap Blend (Growth)	C-	C-	B-	Up	Y	2,500
NorthPointe Large Cap Value Fund Institutional Shares	NPILX	NAS CM	Open End	US Equity Large Cap Value (Growth)	C+	C	B	Up	Y	100,000

★ Expanded analysis of this fund is included in Section II.

Min Additional Investment	3-Month Total Return	6-Month Total Return	1-Year Total Return	3-Year Total Return	5-Year Total Return	Dividend Yield (TTM)	Expense Ratio	3-Yr Std Deviation	3-Year Beta	NAV	Total Assets (MIL)	%Cash	%Stocks	%Bonds	%Other	Turnover Ratio	Last Bull Market Total Return	Last Bear Market Total Return	Front End Fee (%)	Back End Fee (%)	Inception Date
	TOTAL RETURNS					PERFORMANCE				ASSETS		ASSET ALLOCATION & TURNOVER					BULL & BEAR		FEES		
50	4.49	12.87	6.62	23.15		5.76	3.12			20.85	--	0	49	39	0					1.00	Jul-16
	4.70	13.43	7.51	26.59		6.71	2.13			20.83	--	0	49	39	0						Jul-16
	-5.88	-1.68	-1.28	28.05	7.67	10.13	1.94	8.82	-0.74	21.86	707.0	-12	63	22	0	48	7.73	-8.19			Jun-06
100	5.32	19.15	9.87	36.07	40.91	1.55	0.72	11.43	0.9	19.11	394.3	7	93	0	0	37	19.28	-15.06			Nov-93
100	5.33	22.64	16.19	43.00	49.94	0.55	0.72	11.74	0.93	66.58	2,826	7	93	0	0	13	25.44	-15.66			Jul-69
100	6.70	25.90	14.12	58.34	68.34	0.57	0.6	12.49	0.84	29.11	919.5	6	94	0	0	27	27.62	-19.58			Oct-83
100	6.63	25.66	13.73	56.79	65.49	0.26	0.93	12.48	0.84	28.45	919.5	6	94	0	0	27	27.35	-19.67			Feb-05
100	5.06	20.51	9.97	57.45	63.35	0.02	0.86	13.28	0.73	28.02	448.5	5	95	0	0	23	24.19	-19.03			May-87
100	4.95	20.34	9.64	55.92	60.68	0	1.17	13.29	0.73	26.03	448.5	5	95	0	0	23	23.92	-19.13			Feb-05
2,500	7.25						0.99			11.82	54.4	6	94	0	0						Jan-19
100	4.77	18.89	6.25	53.31	63.59	0.22	1.03	12.86	1.03	18.88	130.0	2	98	0	0	22	23.14	-16.26			Mar-01
	3.48	22.00	11.80	48.54		0	0.95			14.7256	14.6	7	93	0	0	74					Jul-16
100	6.46	18.40	13.66	53.83	62.70	1.03	1.25	10.96	0.88	17.1271	13.3	4	96	0	0	30			5.75		Jun-13
	6.48	18.49	13.85	54.98	64.64	1.19	1	10.94	0.87	17.2473	13.3	4	96	0	0	30					Jun-13
100	2.94	19.80	-0.70	56.49	58.60	0	1.4	18.57	1.06	12.4355	22.6	1	99	0	0	170	26.75	-21.43	5.75		Dec-15
	3.05	19.98	-0.43	57.69	60.61	0	1.15	18.55	1.05	12.5627	22.6	1	99	0	0	170	26.94	-21.35			Sep-15
100	-1.06	11.66	-10.98	22.20	-0.74	1.59	1.4	17.01	1.16	11.2784	13.6	0	100	0	0	59			5.75		Sep-12
	-1.04	11.81	-10.71	23.17	0.56	1.73	1.15	17.02	1.16	11.3496	13.6	0	100	0	0	59					Sep-12
100	1.60	13.09	-10.33	18.18		1.27	1.51	13.26	1.04	10.0996	45.2	1	98	0	1	234			5.75		Dec-15
	1.64	13.37	-9.98	19.09		1.56	1.26	13.28	1.05	10.1243	45.2	1	98	0	1	234					Sep-15
100	3.00	17.54	1.83	42.56	50.81	0	1.78	12.96	0.92	18.0671	58.6	4	91	4	0	117	28.3	-16.39	5.75		Mar-99
100	2.67	16.99	1.01	39.21	44.64	0	2.53	12.93	0.92	14.8469	58.6	4	91	4	0	117	27.6	-16.69		1.00	Feb-04
	3.08	17.96	2.54	43.96	52.46	0	1.53	12.94	0.92	18.7921	58.6	4	91	4	0	117	28.41	-16.37			Aug-04
100	3.44	20.50	0.05	39.17	33.03	0	1.42	16.16	0.88	14.5449	209.6	3	95	0	1	39	19.95	-21.49	5.75		Jan-94
100	3.14	20.02	-0.73	36.15	28.21	0	2.17	16.21	0.88	4.693	209.6	3	95	0	1	39	19.47	-21.76		1.00	Mar-97
	3.48	20.65	0.31	40.38	35.12	0	1.17	16.18	0.88	16.0707	209.6	3	95	0	1	39	20.25	-21.43			Dec-09
	3.53	20.72	0.44	40.95	36.03	0	1.02	16.19	0.88	15.8507	209.6	3	95	0	1	39	19.95	-21.5			Dec-12
500	3.94	10.02	-11.02	18.85	30.28	2.68	1.43	12.6	0.61	19.16	77.2	7	93	0	0	20	16.36	-12.22			May-13
500	5.03	16.21	-4.89	29.67	24.61	0.14	1.42	14.29	0.73	26.3	78.0	7	93	0	0	32	22.73	-14.47			May-13
500	3.60	16.08	3.88	34.35	23.90	1.71	1.56	14.46	1.06	13.39	125.9	19	74	5	0	44			5.75		Dec-11
500	3.76	16.22	4.21	35.37	24.94	1.93	1.31	14.5	1.07	13.35	125.9	19	74	5	0	44					Dec-11
50	1.07	7.88	-2.17	31.82	7.01	0.92	1.1	13.82	0.98	19.7	742.5	0	100	0	0	81	20.28	-25.52			Nov-08
50	3.66	13.86	-0.66	30.68	7.53	2.62	0.85	11.41	1	10.76	906.2	0	99	1	0	35	14.15	-23.3			Jun-06
50	0.68	10.81	1.32	35.49	11.59	2.49	0.31	14.3	1.03	11.78	2,773	0	100	0	0	55	18.51	-27.2			Apr-06
	3.78	17.36	3.71			0.86	0.7			10.41	287.9	0	100	0	0	49					Nov-17
50	0.27	15.29	7.71	18.97	29.29	3.13	0.5	11.27	1.01	10.98	2,123	0	100	0	0	27	23.8	-20.74			Jul-06
50	4.08	17.54	7.65	39.75	36.95	1.78	0.3	11.11	1	14.54	742.4	0	100	0	0	9	18.14	-19.3			Mar-08
50	2.09	11.64	4.61	23.08	21.71	3.01	0.63	7.23	0.62	12.9	90.8	1	59	40	0	88	14.45	-11.19			Jul-93
50	3.29	16.74	7.29	37.95	50.23	1.85	1.01	11.87	0.95	13.31	188.4	0	100	0	0	41	17.27	-15.26			Mar-94
50	1.17	12.07	-1.43	24.68	1.73	2.42	0.51	11.36	1	9.47	196.3	0	100	0	0	59	16.72	-26.14			Mar-94
50	3.62	14.53	1.10	30.46	11.32	3.04	0.25	11.03	0.99	12.29	5,495	0	100	0	0	27	13.41	-23.59			Mar-05
50	2.41	15.29	5.90	42.57	49.81	1.74	0.46	12.37	1	19.74	246.4	0	100	0	0	46	25.04	-15.51			Dec-05
50	2.80	15.85	6.65	36.46	37.50	1.48	0.58	13.25	1.08	16.88	69.0	0	100	0	0	96	26.97	-25.5			Aug-00
50	3.00	19.05	1.18	38.34	46.52	1.41	0.15	15.12	1	18.49	2,348	0	100	0	0	21	27.72	-22.71			Mar-05
50	4.81	16.90	7.81	29.11	20.45	2.55	1.01	10.26	0.93	12.54	1,027	0	100	0	0	39					Sep-12
50	1.68	16.59	9.29	19.18	27.90	3.79	0.93	10.46	0.93	11.23	102.1	0	99	0	1	66	23.66	-20.01			Nov-08
50	2.77	16.80	-2.18	40.88	40.87	0.6	0.65	16.07	0.94	26.28	470.1	0	100	0	0	21	27.13	-23.81			Sep-99
50	2.02	17.88	-3.42	43.69	40.21	1.07	0.15	17.12	1	12.59	1,200	0	100	0	0	21	27.48	-25.1			Sep-99
50	2.18	15.00	-4.34	29.05	31.80	0.69	1	16.74	0.96	20.62	3,064	0	100	0	0	16	26.9	-21.39			Mar-94
50	4.29	19.53	10.32	50.46	65.47	1.77	0.1	12.19	1	33.99	8,781	0	100	0	0	7	24.99	-16.33			Oct-96
50	3.53	18.89	9.06			1.43	0.43			11.49	98.1	0	100	0	0	51					Oct-17
10,000	2.69	14.98	3.79	27.98	34.20	1.57	0.65	12.11	0.98	11.82	44.4	1	99	0	0	119					Mar-14

	MARKET		FUND TYPE, CATEGORY & OBJECTIVE		RATINGS				MINIMUMS	
Fund Name	Ticker Symbol	Traded On	Fund Type	Category and (Prospectus Objective)	Overall Rating	Reward Rating	Risk Rating	Recent Up/ Downgrade	Open to New Investors	Min Initial Investment
NorthPointe Large Cap Value Fund Investor Shares	NPLVX	NAS CM	Open End	US Equity Large Cap Value (Growth)	C+	C	B	Up	Y	1,000
NorthQuest Capital Fund	NQCFX	NAS CM	Open End	US Equity Large Cap Growth (Growth & Income)	B-	C+	B	Down	Y	1,000
NorthStar Real Estate Capital Income Fund Class ADV	XNVFX	NAS CM	Closed End	Real Estate Sector Equity (Real Estate)	D+	D+	C	Up	Y	4,000
NorthStar Real Estate Capital Income Fund Class D	US66707F2020		Closed End	Real Estate Sector Equity (Real Estate)	U	U	U		Y	4,000
Nuance Concentrated Value Fund Institutional Class	NCVLX	NAS CM	Open End	US Equity Large Cap Value (Growth)	B	B-	A	Up	Y	10,000
Nuance Concentrated Value Fund Investor Class	NCAVX	NAS CM	Open End	US Equity Large Cap Value (Growth)	B	C+	A-	Up	Y	2,500
Nuance Concentrated Value Long-Short Inst Cls Shares	NCLSX	NAS CM	Open End	Long/Short Equity (Growth)	C+	C-	B+	Up	Y	10,000
Nuance Concentrated Value Long-Short Investor Cls Shares	NCLIX	NAS CM	Open End	Long/Short Equity (Growth)	C+	C-	B+	Up	Y	2,500
Nuance Mid Cap Value Fund Institutional Class	NMVLX	NAS CM	Open End	US Equity Mid Cap (Growth)	B	B-	A-		Y	10,000
Nuance Mid Cap Value Fund Investor Class	NMAVX	NAS CM	Open End	US Equity Mid Cap (Growth)	B	B-	A-		Y	2,500
Nuance Mid Cap Value Fund Z Class Shares	NMVZX	NAS CM	Open End	US Equity Mid Cap (Growth)	B	B-	A-		Y	2,500
Nuveen All Cap Energy MLP Opportunities Fund	JMLP	NYSE	Closed End	Energy Sector Equity (Income)	D+	D+	C-	Down	Y	
Nuveen Core Equity Alpha Fund	JCE	NYSE	Closed End	US Equity Large Cap Growth (Growth & Income)	C	C	C-		Y	
Nuveen Diversified Dividend and Income Fund	JDD	NYSE	Closed End	Alloc Miscellaneous (Multi-Asset Global)	C	C	C-		Y	
Nuveen Dividend Value Fund Class A	FFEIX	NAS CM	Open End	US Equity Large Cap Value (Equity-Income)	C+	C	B	Up	Y	3,000
Nuveen Dividend Value Fund Class C	FFECX	NAS CM	Open End	US Equity Large Cap Value (Equity-Income)	C+	C	B	Up	Y	3,000
Nuveen Dividend Value Fund Class I	FAQIX	NAS CM	Open End	US Equity Large Cap Value (Equity-Income)	C+	C	B	Up	Y	100,000
Nuveen Dividend Value Fund Class R3	FEISX	NAS CM	Open End	US Equity Large Cap Value (Equity-Income)	C+	C	B	Up	Y	0
Nuveen Dividend Value Fund Class R6	FFEFX	NAS CM	Open End	US Equity Large Cap Value (Equity-Income)	C+	C	B		Y	1,000,000
Nuveen Dow 30 Dynamic Overwrite Fund	DIAX	NYSE	Closed End	Long/Short Equity (Equity-Income)	C	C	C-	Down	Y	
Nuveen Emerging Markets Equity Fund Class A	NEKAX	NAS CM	Open End	Global Emerg Mkts (Div Emerging Mkts)	U	U	U		Y	3,000
Nuveen Emerging Markets Equity Fund Class C	NEKCX	NAS CM	Open End	Global Emerg Mkts (Div Emerging Mkts)	U	U	U		Y	3,000
Nuveen Emerging Markets Equity Fund Class I	NEKIX	NAS CM	Open End	Global Emerg Mkts (Div Emerging Mkts)	U	U	U		Y	100,000
Nuveen Emerging Markets Equity Fund Class R6	NEKFX	NAS CM	Open End	Global Emerg Mkts (Div Emerging Mkts)	U	U	U		Y	1,000,000
Nuveen Energy MLP Total Return Fund	JMF	NYSE	Closed End	Energy Sector Equity (Growth & Income)	C-	D+	C-	Down	Y	
Nuveen Equity Long/Short Fund Class A	NELAX	NAS CM	Open End	Long/Short Equity (Growth)	C	C-	C		Y	3,000
Nuveen Equity Long/Short Fund Class C	NELCX	NAS CM	Open End	Long/Short Equity (Growth)	C	C-	C		Y	3,000
Nuveen Equity Long/Short Fund Class I	NELIX	NAS CM	Open End	Long/Short Equity (Growth)	C	C	C		Y	100,000
Nuveen Equity Market Neutral Fund Class A	NMAEX	NAS CM	Open End	Market Neutral (Growth)	C-	D+	C	Down	Y	3,000
Nuveen Equity Market Neutral Fund Class C	NMECX	NAS CM	Open End	Market Neutral (Growth)	C-	D+	C-	Down	Y	3,000
Nuveen Equity Market Neutral Fund Class I	NIMEX	NAS CM	Open End	Market Neutral (Growth)	C-	D+	C	Down	Y	100,000
Nuveen Global Infrastructure Fund Class A	FGIAX	NAS CM	Open End	Infrastructure Sector Equity (Utility)	B-	C+	B	Down	Y	3,000
Nuveen Global Infrastructure Fund Class C	FGNCX	NAS CM	Open End	Infrastructure Sector Equity (Utility)	B-	C+	B		Y	3,000
Nuveen Global Infrastructure Fund Class I	FGIYX	NAS CM	Open End	Infrastructure Sector Equity (Utility)	B-	B-	B	Down	Y	100,000
Nuveen Global Infrastructure Fund Class R3	FGNRX	NAS CM	Open End	Infrastructure Sector Equity (Utility)	B-	C+	B	Down	Y	0
Nuveen Global Infrastructure Fund Class R6	FGIWX	NAS CM	Open End	Infrastructure Sector Equity (Utility)	B-	B-	B	Down	Y	1,000,000
Nuveen Global Real Estate Securities Fund Class A	NGJAX	NAS CM	Open End	Real Estate Sector Equity (Real Estate)	D	C-	B-		Y	3,000
Nuveen Global Real Estate Securities Fund Class C	NGJCX	NAS CM	Open End	Real Estate Sector Equity (Real Estate)	D	C-	B-		Y	3,000
Nuveen Global Real Estate Securities Fund Class I	NGJIX	NAS CM	Open End	Real Estate Sector Equity (Real Estate)	D	C-	B-		Y	100,000
Nuveen Global Real Estate Securities Fund Class R6	NGJFX	NAS CM	Open End	Real Estate Sector Equity (Real Estate)	D	C-	B-		Y	1,000,000
Nuveen Gresham Diversified Commodity Strategy Fund Class A	NGVAX	NAS CM	Open End	Commodities Broad Basket (Growth & Income)	C-	D+	C-	Up	Y	3,000
Nuveen Gresham Diversified Commodity Strategy Fund Class C	NGVCX	NAS CM	Open End	Commodities Broad Basket (Growth & Income)	D+	D	C-		Y	3,000
Nuveen Gresham Diversified Commodity Strategy Fund Class I	NGVIX	NAS CM	Open End	Commodities Broad Basket (Growth & Income)	C-	D+	C-	Up	Y	100,000
Nuveen Gresham Managed Futures Strategy Fund Class A	NGAFX	NAS CM	Open End	Alternative Miscellaneous (Growth)	U	U	U		Y	3,000
Nuveen Gresham Managed Futures Strategy Fund Class C	NGCFX	NAS CM	Open End	Alternative Miscellaneous (Growth)	U	U	U		Y	3,000
Nuveen Gresham Managed Futures Strategy Fund Class I	NGIFX	NAS CM	Open End	Alternative Miscellaneous (Growth)	U	U	U		Y	100,000
Nuveen Gresham Managed Futures Strategy Fund Class R6	NGFFX	NAS CM	Open End	Alternative Miscellaneous (Growth)	U	U	U		Y	1,000,000
Nuveen International Growth Fund Class A	NBQAX	NAS CM	Open End	Global Equity Large Cap (Foreign Stock)	C	C	C		Y	3,000
Nuveen International Growth Fund Class C	NBQCX	NAS CM	Open End	Global Equity Large Cap (Foreign Stock)	C	C	C	Up	Y	3,000
Nuveen International Growth Fund Class I	NBQIX	NAS CM	Open End	Global Equity Large Cap (Foreign Stock)	C	C	C		Y	100,000
Nuveen International Growth Fund Class R3	NBQBX	NAS CM	Open End	Global Equity Large Cap (Foreign Stock)	C	C	C	Up	Y	0
Nuveen International Growth Fund Class R6	NBQFX	NAS CM	Open End	Global Equity Large Cap (Foreign Stock)	C	C	C		Y	1,000,000

★ Expanded analysis of this fund is included in Section II.

	TOTAL RETURNS					PERFORMANCE				ASSETS		ASSET ALLOCATION & TURNOVER					BULL & BEAR		FEES		
Min Additional Investment	3-Month Total Return	6-Month Total Return	1-Year Total Return	3-Year Total Return	5-Year Total Return	Dividend Yield (TTM)	Expense Ratio	3-Yr Std Deviation	3-Year Beta	NAV	Total Assets (MIL)	%Cash	%Stocks	%Bonds	%Other	Turnover Ratio	Last Bull Market Total Return	Last Bear Market Total Return	Front End Fee (%)	Back End Fee (%)	Inception Date
500	2.52	14.82	3.46	26.93	32.76	1.37	0.9	12.1	0.98	11.77	44.4	1	99	0	0	119					Mar-14
100	2.35	22.22	12.10	48.78	58.42	0	1.65	13.14	1	18.26	4.6	1	99	0	0	13	21.01	-16.93			Jan-02
100	-8.78	-3.79	-4.51			4.78	2.57			8.25	--										Nov-17
100	0.00	-0.11	7.87			0	3.03				--								2.00		Jan-17
100	5.10	17.49	14.47	35.93	39.66	1.21	1.07	9.2	0.69	14.27	437.7	15	85	0	0	151	19.45				May-11
100	5.03	17.27	14.11	34.59	37.56	0.9	1.32	9.18	0.69	14.23	437.7	15	85	0	0	151	19.27		5.00		Jul-12
100	0.00	0.85	4.78	15.48		0	2.59	5.33	-0.1	10.66	42.2	118	-18	0	0	177					Dec-15
100	0.00	0.86	4.64	14.41		0	2.84	5.33	-0.1	10.54	42.2	118	-18	0	0	177					Dec-15
100	5.67	19.18	13.32	46.97	56.34	1.36	0.94	10.06	0.71	12.93	1,211	12	84	0	0	152					Dec-13
100	5.69	19.02	13.13	45.95	54.45	1.05	1.19	10.08	0.71	12.93	1,211	12	84	0	0	152			5.00		Dec-13
100	5.76	19.28	13.56	47.54	56.95	1.42	0.79	10.09	0.71	12.96	1,211	12	84	0	0	152					May-17
	-5.02	22.59	-7.73	4.20	-42.62	2.73	1.99	24.66	1.38	6.88	92.9	0	100	0	0	24					Mar-14
	4.18	19.74	6.77	36.81	46.70	0.56	1.07	11.58		14.51	232.6	1	100	0	0	121	25.11	-14.46			Mar-07
	2.70	15.95	5.26	18.92	29.20	3.51	0	9.8	0.67	11.49	226.8	2	52	44	2	45	23.6	-15.56			Sep-03
100	4.39	15.20	3.98	38.43	39.46	1.75	1.08	13.19	1.07	13.78	1,122	1	99	0	0	68	24.99	-16.96	5.75		Dec-92
100	4.28	14.80	3.23	35.46	34.42	1.04	1.83	13.17	1.07	13.52	1,122	1	99	0	0	68	24.42	-17.19		1.00	Feb-99
	4.47	15.31	4.21	39.50	41.23	1.99	0.83	13.2	1.07	13.97	1,122	1	99	0	0	68	25.13	-16.85			Aug-94
	4.42	15.13	3.73	37.44	37.84	1.51	1.33	13.19	1.07	13.72	1,122	1	99	0	0	68	24.88	-17.09			Sep-01
	4.62	15.48	4.44	40.03	42.13	2.01	0.72	13.24	1.07	14.09	1,122	1	99	0	0	68	24.99	-16.96			Feb-13
	1.94	11.08	6.32	39.48	49.86	1.71	0	9.78	0.78	17.95	650.7	0	100	0	0	9	20.92	-12.8			Apr-05
100	3.91	18.08					1.24			23.11	11.7	7	93	0	1				5.75		Nov-18
100	3.69	17.85					1.99			23.04	11.7	7	93	0	1					1.00	Nov-18
	3.91	18.20					0.99			23.11	11.7	7	93	0	1						Nov-18
	4.17	18.67					0.89			23.2	11.7	7	93	0	1						Nov-18
	-4.66	17.85	-3.53	-0.25	-33.01	2.54	2.09	20.21		9.86	402.2	0	103	0	-4	23	22.08	-16.58			Feb-11
100	1.44	2.00	-4.48	35.34	33.87	0	2.63	10.51	0.66	40.14	345.2	0	67	0	33	213	27.07	-17.53	5.75		Dec-08
100	1.21	1.60	-5.21	32.32	28.93	0	3.37	10.49	0.66	36.74	345.2	0	67	0	33	213	26.48	-17.77		1.00	Dec-08
	1.47	2.12	-4.25	36.37	35.57	0	2.37	10.51	0.66	41.27	345.2	0	67	0	33	213	27.27	-17.46			Dec-08
100	0.43	-7.57	-3.98	12.94	18.41	0	2.55	5.96	-4.57	23.31	701.6	0	7	0	93	156			5.75		Jun-13
100	0.22	-7.94	-4.70	10.41	14.00	0	3.3	5.96	-4.92	22.25	701.6	0	7	0	93	156				1.00	Jun-13
	0.46	-7.46	-3.77	13.74	19.83	0	2.29	5.98	-4.74	23.67	701.6	0	7	0	93	156					Jun-13
100	6.16	22.11	14.86	28.96	33.11	1.84	1.22	9.96	0.93	11.54	533.0	0	94	0	6	174	16.38	-15.51	5.75		Dec-07
100	5.94	21.64	13.98	26.14	28.17	1.23	1.97	9.95	0.93	11.41	533.0	0	94	0	6	174	15.79	-15.68		1.00	Nov-08
	6.18	22.31	15.10	29.93	34.77	2.04	0.97	9.98	0.93	11.51	533.0	0	94	0	6	174	16.61	-15.45			Dec-07
	6.06	21.95	14.56	27.98	31.40	1.63	1.47	9.97	0.93	11.72	533.0	0	94	0	6	174	16.2	-16			Nov-08
	6.35	22.48	15.28	30.49	35.35	2.03	0.89	9.94	0.93	11.55	533.0	0	94	0	6	174	16.61	-15.45			Jun-16
100	1.93	18.76	12.24			2.55	1.3			22.28	27.9	1	98	0	0	161			5.75		Mar-18
100	1.74	18.28	11.41			1.84	2.05			22.27	27.9	1	98	0	0	161				1.00	Mar-18
	2.04	18.90	12.52			2.78	1.05			22.28	27.9	1	98	0	0	161					Mar-18
	2.05	18.91	12.58			2.79	1.02			22.29	27.9	1	98	0	0	161					Mar-18
100	-2.33	3.88	-9.34	-4.90	-39.68	7.48	1.26	9.53	1.06	10.44	88.5	23	0	71	5	0			5.75		Jul-12
100	-2.50	3.37	-10.07	-7.12	-41.90	6.6	2.01	9.53	1.06	10.11	88.5	23	0	71	5	0				1.00	Jul-12
	-2.31	3.93	-9.11	-4.24	-38.87	7.77	1.01	9.52	1.06	10.57	88.5	23	0	71	5	0					Jul-12
100	7.49	9.41					1.56			22.09	27.7	45	0	37	18				5.75		Oct-18
100	7.27	9.03					2.31			21.97	27.7	45	0	37	18					1.00	Oct-18
	7.54	9.56					1.31			22.1	27.7	45	0	37	18						Oct-18
	7.53	9.61					1.3			22.11	27.7	45	0	37	18						Oct-18
100	5.61	22.48	-2.80	31.40	17.41	1.02	1.13	15.28	1.24	44.61	393.1	0	96	0	4	81	15.83	-25.37	5.75		Apr-09
100	5.42	22.03	-3.54	28.47	13.10	0.25	1.88	15.27	1.24	42.36	393.1	0	96	0	4	81	15.37	-25.61		1.00	Apr-09
	5.68	22.64	-2.56	32.37	18.91	1.28	0.88	15.27	1.24	45	393.1	0	96	0	4	81	15.99	-25.27			Apr-09
	5.53	22.31	-3.05	30.40	15.96	0.77	1.38	15.27	1.24	44.02	393.1	0	96	0	4	81	15.68	-25.45			Apr-09
	5.71	22.69	-2.46	32.76	19.27	1.28	0.79	15.28	1.24	45.14	393.1	0	96	0	4	81	15.99	-25.27			Jun-16

	MARKET			FUND TYPE, CATEGORY & OBJECTIVE	RATINGS				MINIMUMS	
Fund Name	Ticker Symbol	Traded On	Fund Type	Category and (Prospectus Objective)	Overall Rating	Reward Rating	Risk Rating	Recent Up/ Downgrade	Open to New Investors	Min Initial Investment
Nuveen Large Cap Core Fund Class A	NLACX	NAS CM	Open End	US Equity Large Cap Blend (Growth)	C	C	C+		Y	3,000
Nuveen Large Cap Core Fund Class C	NLCDX	NAS CM	Open End	US Equity Large Cap Blend (Growth)	C	C	C+		Y	3,000
Nuveen Large Cap Core Fund Class I	NLCIX	NAS CM	Open End	US Equity Large Cap Blend (Growth)	C	C	C+		Y	100,000
Nuveen Large Cap Core Fund Class R6	NLCFX	NAS CM	Open End	US Equity Large Cap Blend (Growth)	C	C	C+		Y	1,000,000
Nuveen Large Cap Growth Fund Class A	NLAGX	NAS CM	Open End	US Equity Large Cap Growth (Growth)	C+	C	B-		Y	3,000
Nuveen Large Cap Growth Fund Class C	NLCGX	NAS CM	Open End	US Equity Large Cap Growth (Growth)	C+	C	B-		Y	3,000
Nuveen Large Cap Growth Fund Class I	NLIGX	NAS CM	Open End	US Equity Large Cap Growth (Growth)	C+	C	B-		Y	100,000
Nuveen Large Cap Growth Fund Class R6	NLAFX	NAS CM	Open End	US Equity Large Cap Growth (Growth)	C+	C	B-		Y	1,000,000
Nuveen Large Cap Select Fund Class A	FLRAX	NAS CM	Open End	US Equity Large Cap Blend (Growth & Income)	C+	C	B		Y	3,000
Nuveen Large Cap Select Fund Class C	FLYCX	NAS CM	Open End	US Equity Large Cap Blend (Growth & Income)	C+	C	B		Y	3,000
Nuveen Large Cap Select Fund Class I	FLRYX	NAS CM	Open End	US Equity Large Cap Blend (Growth & Income)	C+	C	B		Y	100,000
Nuveen Large-Cap Value Fund Class A	NNGAX	NAS CM	Open End	US Equity Large Cap Value (Growth)	C	C	C		Y	3,000
Nuveen Large-Cap Value Fund Class C	NNGCX	NAS CM	Open End	US Equity Large Cap Value (Growth)	C	C-	C		Y	3,000
Nuveen Large-Cap Value Fund Class I	NNGRX	NAS CM	Open End	US Equity Large Cap Value (Growth)	C	C	C		Y	100,000
Nuveen Large-Cap Value Fund Class R3	NMMTX	NAS CM	Open End	US Equity Large Cap Value (Growth)	C	C	C		Y	0
Nuveen Large-Cap Value Fund Class R6	NNGFX	NAS CM	Open End	US Equity Large Cap Value (Growth)	C	C	C		Y	1,000,000
Nuveen Mid Cap Growth Opportunities Fund Class A	FRSLX	NAS CM	Open End	US Equity Mid Cap (Growth)	C+	C	B-		Y	3,000
Nuveen Mid Cap Growth Opportunities Fund Class C	FMECX	NAS CM	Open End	US Equity Mid Cap (Growth)	C+	C	B-		Y	3,000
Nuveen Mid Cap Growth Opportunities Fund Class I	FISGX	NAS CM	Open End	US Equity Mid Cap (Growth)	C+	C	B-		Y	100,000
Nuveen Mid Cap Growth Opportunities Fund Class R3	FMEYX	NAS CM	Open End	US Equity Mid Cap (Growth)	C+	C	B-		Y	0
Nuveen Mid Cap Growth Opportunities Fund Class R6	FMEFX	NAS CM	Open End	US Equity Mid Cap (Growth)	C+	C	B-		Y	1,000,000
Nuveen Mid Cap Value Fund Class A	FASEX	NAS CM	Open End	US Equity Mid Cap (Growth)	C	C	B-		Y	3,000
Nuveen Mid Cap Value Fund Class C	FACSX	NAS CM	Open End	US Equity Mid Cap (Growth)	C	C	B-		Y	3,000
Nuveen Mid Cap Value Fund Class I	FSEIX	NAS CM	Open End	US Equity Mid Cap (Growth)	C	C	B-		Y	100,000
Nuveen Mid Cap Value Fund Class R3	FMVSX	NAS CM	Open End	US Equity Mid Cap (Growth)	C	C	B-		Y	0
Nuveen Mid Cap Value Fund Class R6	FMVQX	NAS CM	Open End	US Equity Mid Cap (Growth)	C	C	B-		Y	1,000,000
Nuveen NASDAQ 100 Dynamic Overwrite Fund	QQQX	NAS CM	Closed End	Long/Short Equity (Equity-Income)	C+	C	C+	Down	Y	
Nuveen NWQ Flexible Income Fund Class A	NWQAX	NAS CM	Open End	Cautious Alloc (Growth & Income)	B	B-	B+	Up	Y	3,000
Nuveen NWQ Flexible Income Fund Class C	NWQCX	NAS CM	Open End	Cautious Alloc (Growth & Income)	B	C+	B	Up	Y	3,000
Nuveen NWQ Flexible Income Fund Class I	NWQIX	NAS CM	Open End	Cautious Alloc (Growth & Income)	B	B-	A-	Up	Y	100,000
Nuveen NWQ Flexible Income Fund Class R6	NQWFX	NAS CM	Open End	Cautious Alloc (Growth & Income)	B	B-	A-	Up	Y	1,000,000
Nuveen NWQ Global Equity Income Fund Class A	NQGAX	NAS CM	Open End	Global Equity Large Cap (Equity-Income)	C	C	B		Y	3,000
Nuveen NWQ Global Equity Income Fund Class C	NQGCX	NAS CM	Open End	Global Equity Large Cap (Equity-Income)	C	C-	B		Y	3,000
Nuveen NWQ Global Equity Income Fund Class I	NQGIX	NAS CM	Open End	Global Equity Large Cap (Equity-Income)	C	C	B		Y	100,000
Nuveen NWQ Global Equity Income Fund Class R3	NQGRX	NAS CM	Open End	Global Equity Large Cap (Equity-Income)	C	C-	B		Y	0
Nuveen NWQ International Value Fund Class A	NAIGX	NAS CM	Open End	Global Equity Large Cap (Foreign Stock)	C-	D+	C		Y	3,000
Nuveen NWQ International Value Fund Class C	NCIGX	NAS CM	Open End	Global Equity Large Cap (Foreign Stock)	C-	D+	C		Y	3,000
Nuveen NWQ International Value Fund Class I	NGRRX	NAS CM	Open End	Global Equity Large Cap (Foreign Stock)	C-	D+	C		Y	100,000
Nuveen NWQ International Value Fund Class R3	NTITX	NAS CM	Open End	Global Equity Large Cap (Foreign Stock)	C-	D+	C		Y	0
Nuveen NWQ Large Cap Value Fund Class A	NQCAX	NAS CM	Open End	US Equity Large Cap Value (Growth)	C+	C	B-	Up	Y	3,000
Nuveen NWQ Large Cap Value Fund Class C	NQCCX	NAS CM	Open End	US Equity Large Cap Value (Growth)	C+	C	B-	Up	Y	3,000
Nuveen NWQ Large Cap Value Fund Class I	NQCRX	NAS CM	Open End	US Equity Large Cap Value (Growth)	C+	C	B-	Up	Y	100,000
Nuveen NWQ Large Cap Value Fund Class R3	NQCQX	NAS CM	Open End	US Equity Large Cap Value (Growth)	C+	C	B-	Up	Y	0
Nuveen NWQ Multi Cap Value Fund Class A	NQVAX	NAS CM	Open End	US Equity Large Cap Value (Growth)	C+	C	C+	Up	Y	3,000
Nuveen NWQ Multi Cap Value Fund Class C	NQVCX	NAS CM	Open End	US Equity Large Cap Value (Growth)	C+	C	C+	Up	Y	3,000
Nuveen NWQ Multi Cap Value Fund Class I	NQVRX	NAS CM	Open End	US Equity Large Cap Value (Growth)	C+	C	C+	Up	Y	100,000
Nuveen NWQ Multi-Cap Value Fund Class R3	NMCTX	NAS CM	Open End	US Equity Large Cap Value (Growth)	C+	C	C+	Up	Y	0
Nuveen NWQ Small Mid/Cap Value Fund Class R3	NWQRX	NAS CM	Open End	US Equity Small Cap (Growth)	C	C	C		Y	0
Nuveen NWQ Small/Mid Cap Value Fund Class A	NSMAX	NAS CM	Open End	US Equity Small Cap (Growth)	C	C	C		Y	3,000
Nuveen NWQ Small/Mid Cap Value Fund Class C	NSMCX	NAS CM	Open End	US Equity Small Cap (Growth)	C	C	C		Y	3,000
Nuveen NWQ Small/Mid Cap Value Fund Class I	NSMRX	NAS CM	Open End	US Equity Small Cap (Growth)	C	C	C		Y	100,000
Nuveen NWQ Small/Mid Cap Value Fund Class R6	NWQFX	NAS CM	Open End	US Equity Small Cap (Growth)	C	C	C		Y	5,000,000

★ Expanded analysis of this fund is included in Section II.

	TOTAL RETURNS					PERFORMANCE				ASSETS		ASSET ALLOCATION & TURNOVER					BULL & BEAR		FEES		
Min Additional Investment	3-Month Total Return	6-Month Total Return	1-Year Total Return	3-Year Total Return	5-Year Total Return	Dividend Yield (TTM)	Expense Ratio	3-Yr Std Deviation	3-Year Beta	NAV	Total Assets (MIL)	%Cash	%Stocks	%Bonds	%Other	Turnover Ratio	Last Bull Market Total Return	Last Bear Market Total Return	Front End Fee (%)	Back End Fee (%)	Inception Date
100	1.95	12.17	-3.04	42.21	47.24	0.49	0.98	14.83	1.14	31.24	956.5	0	100	0	0	117			5.75		Jun-13
100	1.72	11.71	-3.78	39.02	41.78	0	1.73	14.82	1.14	30.6	956.5	0	100	0	0	117				1.00	Jun-13
	1.99	12.28	-2.82	43.25	49.09	0.89	0.73	14.8	1.14	31.17	956.5	0	100	0	0	117					Jun-13
	2.02	12.34	-2.76	43.52	49.38	0.89	0.68	14.82	1.14	31.22	956.5	0	100	0	0	117					Jun-16
100	2.33	16.03	1.22	51.82	57.69	0.15	0.99	13.91	0.99	26.34	341.3	0	99	0	1	128			5.75		Jun-13
100	2.12	15.59	0.50	48.45	51.89	0	1.74	13.91	0.98	25.42	341.3	0	99	0	1	128				1.00	Jun-13
	2.40	16.19	1.50	53.02	59.71	0.38	0.74	13.92	0.99	26.41	341.3	0	99	0	1	128					Jun-13
	2.40	16.21	1.57	53.28	59.98	0.38	0.65	13.9	0.99	26.45	341.3	0	99	0	1	128					Jun-16
100	4.67	17.50	4.50	56.15	60.57	0.31	1.14	15.08	1.2	29.53	65.1	0	100	0	0	101	29.93	-23.26	5.75		Jan-03
100	4.44	17.09	3.72	52.63	54.63	0	1.89	15.05	1.2	27.26	65.1	0	100	0	0	101	29.27	-23.47		1.00	Jan-03
	4.71	17.67	4.77	57.29	62.59	0.56	0.89	15.08	1.2	29.76	65.1	0	100	0	0	101	30.09	-23.21			Jan-03
100	1.73	12.46	-3.64	36.12	32.56	0.96	1	15.3	1.21	22.29	422.1	0	99	0	1	169	24.16	-19.55	5.75		Aug-96
100	1.53	12.02	-4.36	33.03	27.64	0.17	1.75	15.29	1.21	21.15	422.1	0	99	0	1	169	23.63	-19.78		1.00	Aug-96
	1.77	12.61	-3.39	37.09	34.19	1.22	0.75	15.28	1.21	22.4	422.1	0	99	0	1	169	24.37	-19.48			Aug-96
	1.66	12.30	-3.86	35.06	30.88	0.7	1.25	15.29	1.21	22.54	422.1	0	99	0	1	169	23.99	-19.64			Aug-08
	1.81	12.65	-3.31	37.38	34.47	1.22	0.71	15.29	1.21	22.43	422.1	0	99	0	1	169	24.37	-19.48			Jun-16
100	6.35	28.76	9.80	52.48	49.91	0	1.18	15.74	1.08	34.33	458.5	1	99	0	0	106	26.24	-20.49	5.75		Jan-95
100	6.17	28.30	8.99	49.10	44.39	0	1.93	15.74	1.08	22.71	458.5	1	99	0	0	106	25.66	-20.73		1.00	Sep-01
	6.41	28.93	10.08	53.64	51.79	0	0.93	15.74	1.08	43.31	458.5	1	99	0	0	106	26.42	-20.4			Dec-89
	6.27	28.60	9.54	51.36	48.06	0	1.43	15.72	1.08	31.16	458.5	1	99	0	0	106	26.07	-20.57			Dec-00
	6.42	29.02	10.23	54.28	52.84	0	0.79	15.74	1.08	43.88	458.5	1	99	0	0	106	26.42	-20.4			Feb-13
100	3.34	16.96	-0.98	35.05	38.92	0.22	1.17	14.31	1.05	39.58	339.2	1	99	0	0	49	24.18	-24.2	5.75		Dec-87
100	3.16	16.51	-1.74	32.03	33.79	0	1.92	14.29	1.05	37.18	339.2	1	99	0	0	49	23.64	-24.44		1.00	Feb-99
	3.43	17.13	-0.73	36.07	40.66	0.47	0.92	14.32	1.06	39.71	339.2	1	99	0	0	49	24.28	-24.1			Feb-94
	3.29	16.82	-1.22	34.03	37.19	0	1.42	14.3	1.05	39.23	339.2	1	99	0	0	49	23.94	-24.25			Sep-01
	3.46	17.18	-0.60	35.56	39.44	0.47	0.83	14.3	1.05	39.76	339.2	1	99	0	0	49	24.18	-24.2			Jun-18
	2.82	15.25	4.45	48.20	67.88	0.38	1.07	12.19	0.79	22.4	877.7	0	101	0	-1	23	26.89	-9.14			Jan-07
100	3.61	11.94	7.06	20.99	26.41	5.36	0.96	5.18	0.62	21.62	1,248	2	13	66	0	29	11.65	-3.39	4.75		Dec-09
100	3.37	11.43	6.22	18.22	21.70	4.64	1.71	5.18	0.61	21.57	1,248	2	13	66	0	29	11.13	-3.66		1.00	Dec-09
	3.67	12.03	7.33	21.87	27.97	5.61	0.71	5.19	0.62	21.64	1,248	2	13	66	0	29	11.81	-3.28			Dec-09
	3.62	11.99	7.29	22.14	28.25	5.62	0.64	5.18	0.62	21.75	1,248	2	13	66	0	29	11.81	-3.28			Jun-16
100	4.76	15.83	2.22	23.85	18.05	2.65	1.11	11.77	0.99	26.6	204.0	0	99	0	0	31	20.23	-20.32	5.75		Sep-09
100	4.54	15.39	1.45	21.07	13.69	1.92	1.86	11.76	0.99	26.54	204.0	0	99	0	0	31	19.68	-20.61		1.00	Sep-09
	4.78	15.92	2.44	24.76	19.53	2.89	0.86	11.77	0.99	26.6	204.0	0	99	0	0	31	20.37	-20.25			Sep-09
	4.70	15.67	1.96	22.96	16.64	2.41	1.36	11.76	0.99	26.55	204.0	0	99	0	0	31	20.02	-20.41			Jul-16
100	2.58	11.28	-5.90	16.47	0.35	1.13	1.15	11.73	1.02	23.38	245.7	1	99	0	0	17	-1.65	-18.44	5.75		Dec-99
100	2.34	10.85	-6.68	13.79	-3.40	0.33	1.9	11.7	1.02	22.26	245.7	1	99	0	0	17	-2.07	-18.71		1.00	Dec-99
	2.66	11.43	-5.66	17.33	1.60	1.4	0.9	11.72	1.02	23.49	245.7	1	99	0	0	17	-1.52	-18.34			Dec-99
	2.52	11.13	-6.17	15.60	-0.91	0.86	1.4	11.71	1.02	23.55	245.7	1	99	0	0	17	-1.77	-18.52			Aug-08
100	3.83	21.17	1.96	34.64	25.92	0.44	1	16.02	1.28	5.15	45.9	2	98	0	0	46	21.02	-22.77	5.75		Dec-06
100	3.56	20.44	1.21	31.47	21.22	0	1.75	15.9	1.27	4.36	45.9	2	98	0	0	46	20.47	-23		1.00	Dec-06
	3.81	21.07	2.13	35.41	27.37	0.69	0.75	15.95	1.27	5.17	45.9	2	98	0	0	46	21.16	-22.64			Dec-06
	3.68	20.71	1.65	33.52	24.23	0.18	1.25	16	1.28	5.07	45.9	2	98	0	0	46	20.83	-22.8			Sep-09
100	4.25	23.38	2.22	42.22	25.66	0	1.15	16.47	1.29	32.55	83.7	2	98	0	0	118	25.19	-23.79	5.75		Dec-02
100	4.07	22.92	1.43	39.02	20.97	0	1.9	16.46	1.28	30.4	83.7	2	98	0	0	118	24.61	-24		1.00	Dec-02
	4.32	23.51	2.49	43.30	27.23	0	0.9	16.48	1.29	32.83	83.7	2	98	0	0	118	25.29	-23.68			Nov-97
	4.21	23.21	2.00	41.16	24.06	0	1.4	16.47	1.29	32.11	83.7	2	98	0	0	118	25.01	-23.86			Aug-08
	4.18	21.15	-6.64	29.56	17.01	0	1.56	18.2	1.16	22.39	23.7	4	96	0	0	49	26.34	-23.11			Sep-09
100	4.21	21.29	-6.42	30.53	18.49	0	1.31	18.2	1.16	23.47	23.7	4	96	0	0	49	26.51	-23.04	5.75		Dec-06
100	4.04	20.79	-7.12	27.59	14.13	0	2.06	18.23	1.17	20.33	23.7	4	96	0	0	49	25.98	-23.25		1.00	Dec-06
	4.30	21.46	-6.18	31.53	20.02	0	1.06	18.22	1.17	23.99	23.7	4	96	0	0	49	26.7	-22.97			Dec-06
	4.27	21.53	-6.03	32.16	20.60	0	0.89	18.2	1.16	24.15	23.7	4	96	0	0	49	26.7	-22.97			Jun-16

	MARKET		FUND TYPE, CATEGORY & OBJECTIVE		RATINGS					MINIMUMS
Fund Name	Ticker Symbol	Traded On	Fund Type	Category and (Prospectus Objective)	Overall Rating	Reward Rating	Risk Rating	Recent Up/ Downgrade	Open to New Investors	Min Initial Investment
Nuveen NWQ Small-Cap Value Fund Class A	NSCAX	NAS CM	Open End	US Equity Small Cap (Small Company)	C-	C-	C	Down	Y	3,000
Nuveen NWQ Small-Cap Value Fund Class C	NSCCX	NAS CM	Open End	US Equity Small Cap (Small Company)	C-	C-	C		Y	3,000
Nuveen NWQ Small-Cap Value Fund Class I	NSCRX	NAS CM	Open End	US Equity Small Cap (Small Company)	C-	C-	C	Down	Y	100,000
Nuveen NWQ Small-Cap Value Fund Class R3	NSCQX	NAS CM	Open End	US Equity Small Cap (Small Company)	C-	C-	C	Down	Y	0
Nuveen NWQ Small-Cap Value Fund Class R6	NSCFX	NAS CM	Open End	US Equity Small Cap (Small Company)	C-	C-	C	Down	Y	5,000,000
Nuveen Preferred & Income Opportunities Fund	JPC	NYSE	Closed End	US Fixed Income (Income)	B-	B-	C+	Up	Y	
Nuveen Preferred & Income Securities Fund	JPS	NYSE	Closed End	US Fixed Income (Income)	B-	B-	C+	Up	Y	
Nuveen Preferred & Income Term Fund	JPI	NYSE	Closed End	US Fixed Income (Growth & Income)	C	B-	C-	Up	Y	
Nuveen Preferred Securities & Income Fund Class A	NPSAX	NAS CM	Open End	US Fixed Income (Growth & Income)	B	B-	B+	Up	Y	3,000
Nuveen Preferred Securities & Income Fund Class C	NPSCX	NAS CM	Open End	US Fixed Income (Growth & Income)	B-	C+	B	Up	Y	3,000
Nuveen Preferred Securities & Income Fund Class I	NPSRX	NAS CM	Open End	US Fixed Income (Growth & Income)	B	B-	B+	Up	Y	100,000
Nuveen Preferred Securities & Income Fund Class R3	NPSTX	NAS CM	Open End	US Fixed Income (Growth & Income)	B	C+	B	Up	Y	0
Nuveen Preferred Securities & Income Fund Class R6	NPSFX	NAS CM	Open End	US Fixed Income (Growth & Income)	B	B-	B+	Up	Y	1,000,000
Nuveen Real Asset Income and Growth Fund	JRI	NYSE	Closed End	Alloc Miscellaneous (Growth & Income)	C	B-	C-		Y	
Nuveen Real Asset Income Fund Class A	NRIAX	NAS CM	Open End	Cautious Alloc (Income)	B	B-	B		Y	3,000
Nuveen Real Asset Income Fund Class C	NRICX	NAS CM	Open End	Cautious Alloc (Income)	B-	C+	B		Y	3,000
Nuveen Real Asset Income Fund Class I	NRIIX	NAS CM	Open End	Cautious Alloc (Income)	B	B-	B		Y	100,000
Nuveen Real Asset Income Fund Class R6	NRIFX	NAS CM	Open End	Cautious Alloc (Income)	B	B-	B		Y	1,000,000
Nuveen Real Estate Income Fund	JRS	NYSE	Closed End	Real Estate Sector Equity (Real Estate)	C	C	C-		Y	
Nuveen Real Estate Securities Fund Class A	FREAX	NAS CM	Open End	Real Estate Sector Equity (Real Estate)	C+	C	B-			3,000
Nuveen Real Estate Securities Fund Class C	FRLCX	NAS CM	Open End	Real Estate Sector Equity (Real Estate)	C+	C	C+			3,000
Nuveen Real Estate Securities Fund Class I	FARCX	NAS CM	Open End	Real Estate Sector Equity (Real Estate)	C+	C	B-			100,000
Nuveen Real Estate Securities Fund Class R3	FRSSX	NAS CM	Open End	Real Estate Sector Equity (Real Estate)	C+	C	B-			0
Nuveen Real Estate Securities Fund Class R6	FREGX	NAS CM	Open End	Real Estate Sector Equity (Real Estate)	C+	C	B-			1,000,000
Nuveen S&P 500 Buy-Write Income Fund	BXMX	NYSE	Closed End	Long/Short Equity (Equity-Income)	C	C	C+	Down	Y	
Nuveen S&P 500 Dynamic Overwrite Fund	SPXX	NYSE	Closed End	Long/Short Equity (Equity-Income)	C	C	C-		Y	
Nuveen Santa Barbara Dividend Growth Fund Class A	NSBAX	NAS CM	Open End	US Equity Large Cap Blend (Equity-Income)	B	C+	B		Y	3,000
Nuveen Santa Barbara Dividend Growth Fund Class C	NSBCX	NAS CM	Open End	US Equity Large Cap Blend (Equity-Income)	B-	C+	B		Y	3,000
Nuveen Santa Barbara Dividend Growth Fund Class I	NSBRX	NAS CM	Open End	US Equity Large Cap Blend (Equity-Income)	B	B-	B		Y	100,000
Nuveen Santa Barbara Dividend Growth Fund Class R3	NBDRX	NAS CM	Open End	US Equity Large Cap Blend (Equity-Income)	B-	C+	B		Y	0
Nuveen Santa Barbara Dividend Growth Fund Class R6	NSBFX	NAS CM	Open End	US Equity Large Cap Blend (Equity-Income)	B	B-	B		Y	1,000,000
Nuveen Santa Barbara Global Dividend Growth Fund Class A	NUGAX	NAS CM	Open End	Global Equity Large Cap (Equity-Income)	C+	C	B	Up	Y	3,000
Nuveen Santa Barbara Global Dividend Growth Fund Class C	NUGCX	NAS CM	Open End	Global Equity Large Cap (Equity-Income)	C+	C	B	Up	Y	3,000
Nuveen Santa Barbara Global Dividend Growth Fund Class I	NUGIX	NAS CM	Open End	Global Equity Large Cap (Equity-Income)	C+	C	B		Y	100,000
Nuveen Santa Barbara Global Dividend Growth Fund Class R3	NUGRX	NAS CM	Open End	Global Equity Large Cap (Equity-Income)	C+	C	B	Up	Y	0
Nuveen Santa Barbara International Dividend Growth Cls A	NUIAX	NAS CM	Open End	Global Equity Large Cap (Equity-Income)	C+	C	B	Up	Y	3,000
Nuveen Santa Barbara International Dividend Growth Cls C	NUICX	NAS CM	Open End	Global Equity Large Cap (Equity-Income)	C	C-	B		Y	3,000
Nuveen Santa Barbara International Dividend Growth Cls I	NUIIX	NAS CM	Open End	Global Equity Large Cap (Equity-Income)	C+	C	B	Up	Y	100,000
Nuveen Santa Barbara International Dividend Growth Cls R3	NUIRX	NAS CM	Open End	Global Equity Large Cap (Equity-Income)	C+	C	B	Up	Y	0
Nuveen Small Cap Growth Opportunities Fund Class A	FRMPX	NAS CM	Open End	US Equity Small Cap (Small Company)	C+	C	C+		Y	3,000
Nuveen Small Cap Growth Opportunities Fund Class C	FMPCX	NAS CM	Open End	US Equity Small Cap (Small Company)	C+	C	C+		Y	3,000
Nuveen Small Cap Growth Opportunities Fund Class I	FIMPX	NAS CM	Open End	US Equity Small Cap (Small Company)	C+	C	C+		Y	100,000
Nuveen Small Cap Growth Opportunities Fund Class R3	FMPYX	NAS CM	Open End	US Equity Small Cap (Small Company)	C+	C	C+		Y	0
Nuveen Small Cap Growth Opportunities Fund Class R6	FMPFX	NAS CM	Open End	US Equity Small Cap (Small Company)	C+	C	C+		Y	1,000,000
Nuveen Small Cap Select Fund Class A	EMGRX	NAS CM	Open End	US Equity Small Cap (Small Company)	C	C	C+		Y	3,000
Nuveen Small Cap Select Fund Class C	FHMCX	NAS CM	Open End	US Equity Small Cap (Small Company)	C	C	C+		Y	3,000
Nuveen Small Cap Select Fund Class I	ARSTX	NAS CM	Open End	US Equity Small Cap (Small Company)	C	C	C+		Y	100,000
Nuveen Small Cap Select Fund Class R3	ASEIX	NAS CM	Open End	US Equity Small Cap (Small Company)	C	C	C+		Y	0
Nuveen Small Cap Select Fund Class R6	ASEFX	NAS CM	Open End	US Equity Small Cap (Small Company)	C	C	C+		Y	1,000,000
Nuveen Small Cap Value Fund Class A	FSCAX	NAS CM	Open End	US Equity Small Cap (Small Company)	D+	D	C-	Down	Y	3,000
Nuveen Small Cap Value Fund Class C	FSCVX	NAS CM	Open End	US Equity Small Cap (Small Company)	D+	D	C-	Down	Y	3,000
Nuveen Small Cap Value Fund Class I	FSCCX	NAS CM	Open End	US Equity Small Cap (Small Company)	D+	D	C	Down	Y	100,000

★ Expanded analysis of this fund is included in Section II.

	TOTAL RETURNS					PERFORMANCE				ASSETS		ASSET ALLOCATION & TURNOVER					BULL & BEAR		FEES		
Min Additional Investment	3-Month Total Return	6-Month Total Return	1-Year Total Return	3-Year Total Return	5-Year Total Return	Dividend Yield (TTM)	Expense Ratio	3-Yr Std Deviation	3-Year Beta	NAV	Total Assets (MIL)	%Cash	%Stocks	%Bonds	%Other	Turnover Ratio	Last Bull Market Total Return	Last Bear Market Total Return	Front End Fee (%)	Back End Fee (%)	Inception Date
100	1.89	15.88	-11.47	27.00	23.45	0	1.27	18	1	42.97	552.1	8	92	0	0	67	27.22	-21.3	5.75		Dec-04
100	1.71	15.47	-12.13	24.16	18.90	0	2.01	17.99	1	37.99	552.1	8	92	0	0	67	26.66	-21.58		1.00	Dec-04
	1.95	16.03	-11.26	27.96	25.00	0	1.01	18.02	1	44.43	552.1	8	92	0	0	67	27.42	-21.22			Dec-04
	1.84	15.74	-11.68	26.04	21.93	0	1.51	17.99	1	42.06	552.1	8	92	0	0	67	27.05	-21.41			Sep-09
	1.99	16.12	-11.12	28.57	25.99	0	0.85	18.01	1	44.93	552.1	8	92	0	0	67	27.42	-21.22			Feb-13
	3.72	14.05	7.07	22.48	35.45	7.31	0	6.51	0.84	10.01	1,034	-7	1	47	9	29	16.17	-13.07			Mar-03
	4.66	13.65	8.91	29.78	41.00	6.9	1.76	6.32	0.49	9.74	1,985	-7	1	51	12	13	14.02	-7.01			Sep-02
	4.44	13.91	8.29	25.88	39.10	6.67		6.29	0.96	24.38	554.8	-7	0	42	10	26					Jul-12
100	3.48	10.56	7.16	18.58	27.43	5.31	1.03	4.49	0.86	16.94	3,523	1	0	46	3	30	13.94	-8.2	4.75		Dec-06
100	3.29	10.10	6.31	15.98	22.68	4.6	1.78	4.5	0.87	16.95	3,523	1	0	46	3	30	13.43	-8.48		1.00	Dec-06
	3.60	10.71	7.49	19.59	29.06	5.55	0.78	4.5	0.87	16.96	3,523	1	0	46	3	30	14.04	-8.09			Dec-06
	3.46	10.38	6.94	17.70	25.82	5.06	1.27	4.54	0.87	17.06	3,523	1	0	46	3	30	13.7	-8.28			Sep-09
	3.56	10.66	7.47	19.79	29.28	5.58	0.71	4.52	0.87	16.99	3,523	1	0	46	3	30	14.04	-8.09			Jun-16
	3.47	19.30	9.87	25.23	34.97	5.36	0	9.27		18.92	519.7	0	45	29	4	92					Apr-12
100	3.21	14.77	9.14	20.34	29.49	4.97	1.14	6.56	1.2	23.93	1,943	0	45	30	3	94	12.96		5.75		Sep-11
100	2.98	14.29	8.33	17.68	24.75	4.26	1.89	6.56	1.19	23.94	1,943	0	45	30	3	94	12.43			1.00	Sep-11
	3.27	14.87	9.42	21.25	31.13	5.22	0.89	6.57	1.19	23.93	1,943	0	45	30	3	94	13.09				Sep-11
	3.27	14.92	9.56	21.56	31.46	5.23	0.81	6.57	1.19	24.05	1,943	0	45	30	3	94	13.09				Jun-16
	1.15	21.25	9.19	14.74	47.08	2.56	0	13.47	0.94	11.03	318.7	3	62	0	0	67	29.89	-14.56			Nov-01
100	1.40	18.60	10.98	13.26	42.35	2.16	1.26	12.56	0.94	21.04	3,386	2	99	0	-1	131	30.87	-16.39	5.75		Sep-95
100	1.24	18.18	10.14	10.77	37.17	1.46	2.02	12.54	0.94	20.41	3,386	2	99	0	-1	131	30.39	-16.67		1.00	Feb-00
	1.50	18.79	11.27	14.11	44.16	2.39	1.02	12.57	0.94	21.4	3,386	2	99	0	-1	131	31.13	-16.29			Jun-95
	1.37	18.44	10.71	12.42	40.60	1.93	1.52	12.54	0.94	21.4	3,386	2	99	0	-1	131	30.73	-16.49			Sep-01
	1.58	18.86	11.43	14.71	45.35	2.43	0.88	12.57	0.94	21.65	3,386	2	99	0	-1	131	31.13	-16.29			Apr-13
	1.92	9.78	3.04	24.36	35.64	1.29	0	7.41	0.9	13.25	1,374	2	100	0	-2	5	16.72	-8.67			Oct-04
	2.95	13.46	4.18	31.79	38.71	1.32	0	9.92	0.8	15.66	259.9	0	100	0	0	16	17.38	-9.51			Nov-05
100	5.70	19.11	12.52	43.63	55.28	1.32	0.96	11.38	0.91	43.38	3,357	2	98	0	0	28	23.37	-13.94	5.75		Mar-06
100	5.50	18.69	11.68	40.44	49.55	0.57	1.71	11.37	0.91	43.36	3,357	2	98	0	0	28	22.85	-14.25		1.00	Mar-06
	5.77	19.28	12.80	44.70	57.26	1.71	0.71	11.37	0.91	43.33	3,357	2	98	0	0	28	23.56	-13.9			Mar-06
	5.64	18.96	12.22	42.53	53.36	1.02	1.21	11.39	0.91	43.72	3,357	2	98	0	0	28	23.2	-14.06			Mar-09
	5.78	19.30	12.87	45.03	57.79	1.72	0.64	11.38	0.91	43.77	3,357	2	98	0	0	28	23.56	-13.9			Mar-13
100	3.93	16.97	5.74	32.08	33.63	2.01	1.15	10.68	0.92	27.25	22.7	6	95	0	0	48			5.75		Jun-12
100	3.75	16.54	4.91	29.12	28.75	1.29	1.9	10.66	0.92	27.18	22.7	6	95	0	0	48				1.00	Jun-12
	3.99	17.12	6.00	33.06	35.29	2.25	0.9	10.68	0.92	27.24	22.7	6	95	0	0	48					Jun-12
	3.87	16.87	5.48	31.13	32.02	1.77	1.4	10.67	0.92	27.19	22.7	6	95	0	0	48					Jun-12
100	3.81	14.37	2.75	22.16	10.38	3.88	1.15	9.7	0.84	26.43	5.2	5	95	0	0	31			5.75		Jun-12
100	3.59	13.97	2.01	19.41	6.32	3.14	1.9	9.69	0.84	26.18	5.2	5	95	0	0	31				1.00	Jun-12
	3.79	14.46	2.94	23.00	11.66	4.13	0.9	9.7	0.84	26.44	5.2	5	95	0	0	31					Jun-12
	3.71	14.18	2.49	21.21	8.99	3.63	1.4	9.7	0.84	26.33	5.2	5	95	0	0	31					Jun-12
100	3.74	22.13	1.65	55.84	48.55	0	1.25	18.5	1.04	21.35	198.1	1	98	0	1	139	30.67	-25.27	5.75		Aug-95
100	3.58	21.76	0.92	52.42	43.14	0	2	18.49	1.04	15.33	198.1	1	98	0	1	139	30.07	-25.53		1.00	Sep-01
	3.79	22.32	1.89	57.06	50.43	0	1	18.5	1.04	25.97	198.1	1	98	0	1	139	30.82	-25.19			Aug-95
	3.71	22.01	1.43	54.78	46.73	0	1.5	18.5	1.04	19.84	198.1	1	98	0	1	139	30.49	-25.36			Dec-00
	3.86	22.43	2.03	57.68	51.01	0	0.89	18.49	1.04	26.09	198.1	1	98	0	1	139	30.82	-25.19			Jun-16
100	2.85	20.15	-2.27	39.91	42.99	0.02	1.24	18.06	1.04	7.57	100.5	0	99	0	1	95	32.24	-27.06	5.75		May-92
100	2.73	19.71	-2.87	36.93	37.88	0	1.99	18.08	1.04	4.13	100.5	0	99	0	1	95	31.67	-27.26		1.00	Sep-01
	2.90	20.39	-2.00	40.84	44.75	0.28	0.99	18.12	1.05	10.27	100.5	0	99	0	1	95	32.48	-27.02			May-92
	2.63	19.92	-2.58	38.72	41.05	0	1.49	18.14	1.05	6.62	100.5	0	99	0	1	95	32.21	-27.22			Jan-94
	2.89	20.46	-1.83	41.20	45.12	0.28	0.85	18.1	1.05	10.3	100.5	0	99	0	1	95	32.48	-27.02			Feb-18
100	0.31	13.80	-10.96	19.21	27.97	0.58	1.2	18.38	1.05	22.17	1,777	1	99	0	0	35	32.39	-24.17	5.75		Aug-94
100	0.10	13.38	-11.65	16.54	23.26	0	1.95	18.39	1.05	18.64	1,777	1	99	0	0	35	31.91	-24.46		1.00	Feb-99
	0.39	14.00	-10.74	20.07	29.57	0.86	0.95	18.4	1.05	22.96	1,777	1	99	0	0	35	32.66	-24.15			Aug-94

	MARKET			FUND TYPE, CATEGORY & OBJECTIVE	RATINGS				MINIMUMS	
Fund Name	Ticker Symbol	Traded On	Fund Type	Category and (Prospectus Objective)	Overall Rating	Reward Rating	Risk Rating	Recent Up/ Downgrade	Open to New Investors	Min Initial Investment
Nuveen Small Cap Value Fund Class R3	FSVSX	NAS CM	Open End	US Equity Small Cap (Small Company)	D+	D	C-	Down	Y	0
Nuveen Small Cap Value Fund Class R6	FSCWX	NAS CM	Open End	US Equity Small Cap (Small Company)	D+	D+	C	Down	Y	1,000,000
Nuveen Strategy Aggressive Growth Allocation Fund Class A	FAAGX	NAS CM	Open End	Aggressive Alloc (Aggr Growth)	C	C	B		Y	3,000
Nuveen Strategy Aggressive Growth Allocation Fund Class C	FSACX	NAS CM	Open End	Aggressive Alloc (Aggr Growth)	C	C	B		Y	3,000
Nuveen Strategy Aggressive Growth Allocation Fund Class I	FSAYX	NAS CM	Open End	Aggressive Alloc (Aggr Growth)	C	C	B		Y	100,000
Nuveen Strategy Aggressive Growth Allocation Fund Class R3	FSASX	NAS CM	Open End	Aggressive Alloc (Aggr Growth)	C	C	B		Y	0
Nuveen Strategy Balanced Allocation Fund Class A	FSGNX	NAS CM	Open End	Moderate Alloc (Balanced)	C+	C	B+	Up	Y	3,000
Nuveen Strategy Balanced Allocation Fund Class C	FSKCX	NAS CM	Open End	Moderate Alloc (Balanced)	C+	C-	B	Up	Y	3,000
Nuveen Strategy Balanced Allocation Fund Class I	FSKYX	NAS CM	Open End	Moderate Alloc (Balanced)	C+	C	B+	Up	Y	100,000
Nuveen Strategy Balanced Allocation Fund Class R3	FSKSX	NAS CM	Open End	Moderate Alloc (Balanced)	C+	C	B+	Up	Y	0
Nuveen Strategy Conservative Allocation Fund Class A	FSFIX	NAS CM	Open End	Cautious Alloc (Asset Alloc)	C+	C	B	Up	Y	3,000
Nuveen Strategy Conservative Allocation Fund Class C	FSJCX	NAS CM	Open End	Cautious Alloc (Asset Alloc)	C+	C	B	Up	Y	3,000
Nuveen Strategy Conservative Allocation Fund Class I	FSFYX	NAS CM	Open End	Cautious Alloc (Asset Alloc)	C+	C	B+	Up	Y	100,000
Nuveen Strategy Conservative Allocation Fund Class R3	FSJSX	NAS CM	Open End	Cautious Alloc (Asset Alloc)	C+	C	B	Up	Y	0
Nuveen Strategy Growth Allocation Fund Class A	FSNAX	NAS CM	Open End	Moderate Alloc (Growth)	C+	C	B	Up	Y	3,000
Nuveen Strategy Growth Allocation Fund Class C	FSNCX	NAS CM	Open End	Moderate Alloc (Growth)	C+	C	B	Up	Y	3,000
Nuveen Strategy Growth Allocation Fund Class I	FSGYX	NAS CM	Open End	Moderate Alloc (Growth)	C+	C	B	Up	Y	100,000
Nuveen Strategy Growth Allocation Fund Class R3	FSNSX	NAS CM	Open End	Moderate Alloc (Growth)	C+	C	B	Up	Y	0
Nuveen Tax-Advantaged Dividend Growth Fund	JTD	NYSE	Closed End	Aggressive Alloc (Equity-Income)	C	C	C-		Y	
Nuveen Tax-Advantaged Total Return Strategy Fund	JTA	NYSE	Closed End	Alloc Miscellaneous (Equity-Income)	C-	C	C-		Y	
Nuveen Winslow International Large Cap Fund Class A	NVBAX	NAS CM	Open End	Global Equity Large Cap (Foreign Stock)	U	U	U		Y	3,000
Nuveen Winslow International Large Cap Fund Class C	NVBCX	NAS CM	Open End	Global Equity Large Cap (Foreign Stock)	U	U	U		Y	3,000
Nuveen Winslow International Large Cap Fund Class I	NVBIX	NAS CM	Open End	Global Equity Large Cap (Foreign Stock)	U	U	U		Y	100,000
Nuveen Winslow International Large Cap Fund Class R6	NVBFX	NAS CM	Open End	Global Equity Large Cap (Foreign Stock)	U	U	U		Y	1,000,000
Nuveen Winslow International Small Cap Fund Class A	NWAIX	NAS CM	Open End	Global Equity Mid/Small Cap (Small Company)	D+	D+	C+	Up	Y	3,000
Nuveen Winslow International Small Cap Fund Class C	NWSCX	NAS CM	Open End	Global Equity Mid/Small Cap (Small Company)	D+	D	C+	Up	Y	3,000
Nuveen Winslow International Small Cap Fund Class I	NWPIX	NAS CM	Open End	Global Equity Mid/Small Cap (Small Company)	D+	D+	C+	Up	Y	100,000
Nuveen Winslow International Small Cap Fund Class R6	NWIFX	NAS CM	Open End	Global Equity Mid/Small Cap (Small Company)	D+	D+	C+	Up	Y	1,000,000
Nuveen Winslow Large-Cap Growth Fund Class A	NWCAX	NAS CM	Open End	US Equity Large Cap Growth (Growth)	C+	C+	B	Down	Y	3,000
Nuveen Winslow Large-Cap Growth Fund Class C	NWCCX	NAS CM	Open End	US Equity Large Cap Growth (Growth)	C+	C+	B	Down	Y	3,000
Nuveen Winslow Large-Cap Growth Fund Class I	NVLIX	NAS CM	Open End	US Equity Large Cap Growth (Growth)	C+	C+	B	Down	Y	100,000
Nuveen Winslow Large-Cap Growth Fund Class R3	NWCRX	NAS CM	Open End	US Equity Large Cap Growth (Growth)	C+	C+	B	Down	Y	0
Nuveen Winslow Large-Cap Growth Fund Class R6	NWCFX	NAS CM	Open End	US Equity Large Cap Growth (Growth)	B-	C+	B	Down	Y	0
Nysa Fund	NYSAX	NAS CM	Open End	US Equity Small Cap (Growth)	D+	D+	D		Y	1,000
O'Shaughnessy Market Leaders Value Fund Class I	OFVIX	NAS CM	Open End	US Equity Large Cap Value (Growth & Income)	C	C	B-		Y	10,000
O'Shaughnessy Small Cap Value Fund Class I	OFSIX	NAS CM	Open End	US Equity Small Cap (Small Company)	C-	D+	C-		Y	10,000
Oakhurst Strategic Defined Risk Fund Insitutional Class	OASDX	NAS CM	Open End	Multialternative (Growth)	D+	D	C		Y	25,000
Oakmark Equity and Income Fund Class Advisor	OAYBX	NAS CM	Open End	Moderate Alloc (Balanced)	B-	C	B+	Up	Y	100,000
Oakmark Equity and Income Fund Class Institutional	OANBX	NAS CM	Open End	Moderate Alloc (Balanced)	B-	C	B+	Up	Y	1,000,000
Oakmark Equity And Income Fund Investor Class	OAKBX	NAS CM	Open End	Moderate Alloc (Balanced)	B-	C	B+	Up	Y	1,000
Oakmark Equity And Income Fund Service Class	OARBX	NAS CM	Open End	Moderate Alloc (Balanced)	B-	C	B+	Up	Y	0
Oakmark Fund Advisor Class	OAYMX	NAS CM	Open End	US Equity Large Cap Blend (Growth)	C+	C	B-	Up	Y	100,000
Oakmark Fund Institutional Class	OANMX	NAS CM	Open End	US Equity Large Cap Blend (Growth)	C+	C	B-	Up	Y	1,000,000
Oakmark Fund Investor Class	OAKMX	NAS CM	Open End	US Equity Large Cap Blend (Growth)	C+	C	B-	Up	Y	1,000
Oakmark Fund Service Class	OARMX	NAS CM	Open End	US Equity Large Cap Blend (Growth)	C	C	B-		Y	0
Oakmark Global Fund Class Advisor	OAYGX	NAS CM	Open End	Global Equity Large Cap (World Stock)	C	C	C+		Y	100,000
Oakmark Global Fund Class Institutional	OANGX	NAS CM	Open End	Global Equity Large Cap (World Stock)	C	C	C+		Y	1,000,000
Oakmark Global Fund Investor Class	OAKGX	NAS CM	Open End	Global Equity Large Cap (World Stock)	C	C	C+			1,000
Oakmark Global Fund Service Class	OARGX	NAS CM	Open End	Global Equity Large Cap (World Stock)	C	C	C+		Y	0
Oakmark Global Select Fund Class Advisor	OAYWX	NAS CM	Open End	Global Equity Large Cap (World Stock)	C	C	C+		Y	100,000
Oakmark Global Select Fund Class Institutional	OANWX	NAS CM	Open End	Global Equity Large Cap (World Stock)	C	C	C+		Y	1,000,000
Oakmark Global Select Fund Investor Class	OAKWX	NAS CM	Open End	Global Equity Large Cap (World Stock)	C	C	C+		Y	1,000

★ Expanded analysis of this fund is included in Section II.

	TOTAL RETURNS					PERFORMANCE				ASSETS		ASSET ALLOCATION & TURNOVER					BULL & BEAR		FEES		
Min Additional Investment	3-Month Total Return	6-Month Total Return	1-Year Total Return	3-Year Total Return	5-Year Total Return	Dividend Yield (TTM)	Expense Ratio	3-Yr Std Deviation	3-Year Beta	NAV	Total Assets (MIL)	%Cash	%Stocks	%Bonds	%Other	Turnover Ratio	Last Bull Market Total Return	Last Bear Market Total Return	Front End Fee (%)	Back End Fee (%)	Inception Date
	0.27	13.69	-11.19	18.28	26.32	0.3	1.45	18.39	1.05	21.67	1,777	1	99	0	0	35	32.2	-24.24			Sep-01
	0.47	14.11	-10.53	20.53	30.07	0.85	0.78	18.4	1.05	23.04	1,777	1	99	0	0	35	32.66	-24.15			Jun-16
100	3.43	16.70	-0.28	26.12	23.03	2.08	1.2	12.39	1.13	14.74	51.5	11	76	12	0	17	20.15	-19.38	5.75		Sep-01
100	3.22	16.26	-1.11	23.30	18.44	1.3	1.95	12.41	1.13	14.08	51.5	11	76	12	0	17	19.67	-19.62		1.00	Sep-01
	3.57	16.82	-0.04	27.03	24.59	2.33	0.95	12.41	1.13	14.79	51.5	11	76	12	0	17	20.41	-19.34			Sep-01
	3.41	16.51	-0.56	25.19	21.47	1.82	1.45	12.4	1.13	14.53	51.5	11	76	12	0	17	19.99	-19.52			Oct-96
100	3.31	12.80	2.36	17.28	17.72	1.43	1.14	7.75	1.11	10.15	164.6	7	46	46	0	12	15.47	-13.29	5.75		Sep-01
100	3.08	12.42	1.61	14.69	13.26	0.71	1.89	7.77	1.11	9.95	164.6	7	46	46	0	12	15.02	-13.62		1.00	Sep-01
	3.38	13.00	2.62	18.17	19.21	1.66	0.89	7.83	1.12	10.11	164.6	7	46	46	0	12	15.66	-13.29			Sep-01
	3.19	12.62	2.11	16.42	16.17	1.19	1.39	7.76	1.11	10	164.6	7	46	46	0	12	15.49	-13.53			Oct-96
100	3.27	11.01	3.68	11.92	12.35	1.32	1.07	5.74	1.16	11.7	63.7	5	26	69	-1	16	10.23	-6.44	5.75		Sep-01
100	3.03	10.50	2.87	9.38	8.14	0.62	1.82	5.73	1.15	11.61	63.7	5	26	69	-1	16	9.7	-6.68		1.00	Sep-01
	3.25	11.06	3.87	12.77	13.77	1.58	0.82	5.66	1.14	11.69	63.7	5	26	69	-1	16	10.3	-6.33			Sep-01
	3.14	10.81	3.44	11.07	10.99	1.09	1.32	5.76	1.16	11.67	63.7	5	26	69	-1	16	10.01	-6.53			Oct-96
100	3.33	14.39	1.12	23.81	23.08	0.97	1.19	10.09	1.1	12.4	106.0	11	64	24	0	15	17.74	-16.08	5.75		Sep-01
100	3.08	14.02	0.33	21.06	18.51	0.22	1.94	10.08	1.1	12.03	106.0	11	64	24	0	15	17.25	-16.36		1.00	Sep-01
	3.39	14.61	1.34	24.76	24.60	1.22	0.94	10.11	1.1	12.47	106.0	11	64	24	0	15	17.86	-16.01			Sep-01
	3.21	14.21	0.83	22.85	21.50	0.72	1.44	10.1	1.1	12.21	106.0	11	64	24	0	15	17.54	-16.18			Oct-96
	5.16	21.53	7.27	34.91	38.75	2.55	0	12.72		16.94	245.4	2	75	10	0	14	26.66	-15.4			Jun-07
	4.45	17.50	0.04	24.88	18.72	5.03	0	13.81	0.98	12.09	167.5	2	73	22	-2	28	24.04	-21.27			Jan-04
100	3.75	16.57					1.19			22.65	5.7	3	97	0	0				5.75		Dec-18
100	3.53	16.16					1.94			22.56	5.7	3	97	0	0					1.00	Dec-18
	3.79	16.72					0.94			22.68	5.7	3	97	0	0						Dec-18
	3.79	16.72					0.85			22.68	5.7	3	97	0	0						Dec-18
100	3.87	19.07	4.22			0.24	1.2			20.91	44.6	4	94	0	2	44			5.75		Dec-17
100	3.70	18.66	3.49			0	1.95			20.73	44.6	4	94	0	2	44				1.00	Dec-17
	3.97	19.25	4.51			0.48	0.95			20.93	44.6	4	94	0	2	44					Dec-17
	3.97	19.25	4.51			0.48	0.94			20.93	44.6	4	94	0	2	44					Dec-17
100	4.54	23.93	11.27	72.72	86.86	0	0.98	14.37	1.03	39.35	725.9	2	99	0	0	56	26.31	-17.69	5.75		May-09
100	4.35	23.49	10.45	68.90	80.00	0	1.73	14.38	1.03	34.01	725.9	2	99	0	0	56	25.79	-17.99		1.00	May-09
	4.60	24.11	11.55	74.03	89.24	0.05	0.73	14.4	1.04	40.86	725.9	2	99	0	0	56	26.52	-17.61			May-09
	4.47	23.78	11.00	71.39	84.53	0	1.23	14.37	1.03	37.58	725.9	2	99	0	0	56	26.14	-17.78			May-09
	4.63	24.20	11.76	74.92	90.83	0.05	0.55	14.38	1.03	41.51	725.9	2	99	0	0	56	26.52	-17.61			Mar-13
250	-5.54	-9.77	-24.53	-0.67	-40.37	0	5.27	23.29	1.06	4.43	1.7	-1	92	8	0	44	5.25	-21.4	2.50		May-97
	4.50	17.96	1.56	47.29		0.85	0.65	15.15	1.2	13.46	191.3	0	100	0	0	51					Feb-16
	-3.70	5.60	-14.67	26.08		0.53	0.99	18.85	1.07	11.69	19.4	0	100	0	0	67					Feb-16
250	0.00	5.76	-0.51			0	2.94			10.09	20.6	29	53	11	7	1					May-17
	3.45	13.07	4.74	32.25	27.89	1.72	0.64	9.78	0.76	30.26	12,521	9	61	29	0	23	17.1	-13.65			Nov-16
	3.48	13.11	4.83	32.37	28.02	1.76	0.59	9.79	0.76	30.27	12,521	9	61	29	0	23	17.1	-13.65			Nov-16
	3.45	12.99	4.62	31.72	27.39	1.56	0.78	9.78	0.76	30.25	12,521	9	61	29	0	23	17.1	-13.65			Nov-95
	3.36	12.83	4.30	30.66	25.52	1.23	1.05	9.76	0.76	30.07	12,521	9	61	29	0	23	16.85	-13.75			Jul-00
	3.23	17.44	0.50	47.27	45.85	0.76	0.73	15.52	1.22	79.51	17,773	8	92	0	0	29	26.73	-16.29			Nov-16
	3.25	17.50	0.57	47.43	46.00	0.78	0.7	15.54	1.22	79.56	17,773	8	92	0	0	29	26.73	-16.29			Nov-16
	3.21	17.38	0.39	46.79	45.37	0.59	0.85	15.53	1.22	79.53	17,773	8	92	0	0	29	26.73	-16.29			Aug-91
	3.13	17.22	0.11	45.54	43.16	0.27	1.13	15.52	1.22	79.22	17,773	8	92	0	0	29	26.54	-16.5			Apr-01
	4.30	17.93	-1.93	43.85	20.11	1.06	1.06	15.53	1.28	27.62	1,713	1	99	0	0	25	19.13	-21.09			Nov-16
	4.34	17.97	-1.85	44.12	20.34	1.16	0.98	15.52	1.28	27.63	1,713	1	99	0	0	25	19.13	-21.09			Nov-16
	4.30	17.83	-2.03	43.43	19.76	0.95	1.15	15.54	1.28	27.62	1,713	1	99	0	0	25	19.13	-21.09			Aug-99
	4.20	17.66	-2.31	42.15	17.83	0.54	1.44	15.52	1.28	26.78	1,713	1	99	0	0	25	18.89	-21.24			Oct-01
	3.80	17.50	-2.38	34.82	23.28	1.45	1.02	15.31	1.25	16.92	1,897	3	97	0	0	26	20.88	-18.36			Nov-16
	3.86	17.56	-2.33	35.02	23.45	1.49	0.96	15.3	1.25	16.93	1,897	3	97	0	0	26	20.88	-18.36			Nov-16
	3.86	17.47	-2.43	34.47	22.96	1.25	1.12	15.31	1.25	16.94	1,897	3	97	0	0	26	20.88	-18.36			Oct-06

Fund Name	Ticker Symbol	Traded On (MARKET)	Fund Type	Category and (Prospectus Objective)	Overall Rating	Reward Rating	Risk Rating	Recent Up/ Downgrade	Open to New Investors	Min Initial Investment
Oakmark International Fund Class Advisor	OAYIX	NAS CM	Open End	Global Equity Large Cap (Foreign Stock)	C-	D+	C		Y	100,000
Oakmark International Fund Class Institutional	OANIX	NAS CM	Open End	Global Equity Large Cap (Foreign Stock)	C-	D+	C		Y	1,000,000
Oakmark International Fund Investor Class	OAKIX	NAS CM	Open End	Global Equity Large Cap (Foreign Stock)	C-	D+	C			1,000
Oakmark International Fund Service Class	OARIX	NAS CM	Open End	Global Equity Large Cap (Foreign Stock)	C-	D+	C			0
Oakmark International Small Cap Fund Class Advisor	OAYEX	NAS CM	Open End	Global Equity Mid/Small Cap (Small Company)	C	D+	C+	Up	Y	100,000
Oakmark International Small Cap Fund Class Institutional	OANEX	NAS CM	Open End	Global Equity Mid/Small Cap (Small Company)	C	D+	C+	Up	Y	1,000,000
Oakmark International Small Cap Fund Investor Class	OAKEX	NAS CM	Open End	Global Equity Mid/Small Cap (Small Company)	C	D+	C+	Up		1,000
Oakmark International Small Cap Service Class	OAREX	NAS CM	Open End	Global Equity Mid/Small Cap (Small Company)	C	D+	C+	Up	Y	0
Oakmark Select Fund Class Advisor	OAYLX	NAS CM	Open End	US Equity Large Cap Blend (Growth)	C	C-	C	Down	Y	100,000
Oakmark Select Fund Class Institutional	OANLX	NAS CM	Open End	US Equity Large Cap Blend (Growth)	C	C-	C	Down	Y	1,000,000
Oakmark Select Fund Investor Class	OAKLX	NAS CM	Open End	US Equity Large Cap Blend (Growth)	C	D+	C	Down	Y	1,000
Oakmark Select Fund Service Class	OARLX	NAS CM	Open End	US Equity Large Cap Blend (Growth)	C	D+	C	Down	Y	0
Oberweis China Opportunities Fund	OBCHX	NAS CM	Open End	Greater China Equity (Foreign Stock)	C-	C-	C-		Y	1,000
Oberweis China Opportunities Fund Institutional Class	OCHIX	NAS CM	Open End	Greater China Equity (Foreign Stock)	C-	C-	C-		Y	1,000,000
Oberweis Emerging Markets Fund Institutional Class	OIEMX	NAS CM	Open End	Global Emerg Mkts (Div Emerging Mkts)	D	D+	C-		Y	1,000,000
Oberweis Emerging Markets Fund Investor Class	OBEMX	NAS CM	Open End	Global Emerg Mkts (Div Emerging Mkts)	D	D+	C-		Y	1,000
Oberweis Global Opportunities Fund Institutional Class	OBGIX	NAS CM	Open End	Global Equity Mid/Small Cap (Small Company)	C	C-	C	Up	Y	1,000,000
Oberweis Global Opportunities Fund Investor Class	OBEGX	NAS CM	Open End	Global Equity Mid/Small Cap (Small Company)	C	C-	C	Up	Y	1,000
Oberweis International Opportunities Fund	OBIOX	NAS CM	Open End	Global Equity Mid/Small Cap (Foreign Stock)	C	C	C	Up	Y	1,000
Oberweis International Opportunities Institutional Fund	OBIIX	NAS CM	Open End	Global Equity Mid/Small Cap (Foreign Stock)	C	C	C	Up	Y	1,000,000
Oberweis Micro Cap Fund Institutional Class	OMCIX	NAS CM	Open End	US Equity Small Cap (Small Company)	C	C	C	Down	Y	1,000,000
Oberweis Micro-Cap Fund	OBMCX	NAS CM	Open End	US Equity Small Cap (Small Company)	C	C	C	Down	Y	1,000
Oberweis Small-Cap Opportunities Fund	OBSOX	NAS CM	Open End	US Equity Small Cap (Small Company)	C+	C	C+		Y	1,000
Oberweis Small-Cap Opportunities Fund Institutional Class	OBSIX	NAS CM	Open End	US Equity Small Cap (Small Company)	C+	C	C+		Y	1,000,000
Oberweis Small-Cap Value Fund Institutional Class	OBVLX	NAS CM	Open End	US Equity Small Cap (Small Company)	C-	C-	C	Down	Y	1,000,000
Oberweis Small-Cap Value Fund Investor Class	OBIVX	NAS CM	Open End	US Equity Small Cap (Small Company)	C-	C-	C	Down	Y	1,000
OCM Gold Fund Advisors Class	OCMAX	NAS CM	Open End	Precious Metals Sector Equity (Precious Metals)	D+	D	C	Down	Y	1,000
OCM Gold Fund Investor Class	OCMGX	NAS CM	Open End	Precious Metals Sector Equity (Precious Metals)	D+	D	C-	Down	Y	1,000
Old Westbury All Cap Core Fund	OWACX	NAS CM	Open End	US Equity Large Cap Growth (Growth)	B-	B-	B		Y	1,000
Old Westbury All Cap ESG Fund	OWSIX	NAS CM	Open End	Global Equity Large Cap (Growth)	D	D+	B-		Y	1,000
Old Westbury Large Cap Strategies Fund	OWLSX	NAS CM	Open End	Global Equity Large Cap (World Stock)	C+	C	B	Up	Y	1,000
Old Westbury Small & Mid Cap Strategies Fund	OWSMX	NAS CM	Open End	Global Equity Mid/Small Cap (World Stock)	C	C	B		Y	1,000
Old Westbury Strategic Opportunities Fund	OWSOX	NAS CM	Open End	Cautious Alloc (World Stock)	B-	C	B+	Up	Y	1,000
Olstein All Cap Value Fund Class A	OFAVX	NAS CM	Open End	US Equity Large Cap Value (Growth)	C+	C	B	Up	Y	1,000
Olstein All Cap Value Fund Class Advisor	OFAFX	NAS CM	Open End	US Equity Large Cap Value (Growth)	C+	C	B	Up	Y	1,000
Olstein All Cap Value Fund Class C	OFALX	NAS CM	Open End	US Equity Large Cap Value (Growth)	C+	C	B	Up	Y	1,000
Olstein Strategic Opportunities Fund Adviser Class	OFSFX	NAS CM	Open End	US Equity Small Cap (Growth)	C	C	C+		Y	1,000
Olstein Strategic Opportunities Fund Class A	OFSAX	NAS CM	Open End	US Equity Small Cap (Growth)	C	C-	C+		Y	1,000
Olstein Strategic Opportunities Fund Class C	OFSCX	NAS CM	Open End	US Equity Small Cap (Growth)	C	C-	C+		Y	1,000
OnTrack Core Fund Advisor Class	OTRGX	NAS CM	Open End	Multialternative (Growth & Income)	C	C-	B-	Up	Y	1,000
OnTrack Core Fund Investor Class	OTRFX	NAS CM	Open End	Multialternative (Growth & Income)	C	C-	B-	Up	Y	1,000
Optimum International Fund Class A	OAIEX	NAS CM	Open End	Global Equity Large Cap (Foreign Stock)	C	C	B-		Y	1,000
Optimum International Fund Class C	OCIEX	NAS CM	Open End	Global Equity Large Cap (Foreign Stock)	C	C	B-		Y	1,000
Optimum International Fund Institutional Class	OIIEX	NAS CM	Open End	Global Equity Large Cap (Foreign Stock)	C	C	B-		Y	0
Optimum Large Cap Growth Fund Class A	OALGX	NAS CM	Open End	US Equity Large Cap Growth (Growth)	B-	C	B	Down	Y	1,000
Optimum Large Cap Growth Fund Class C	OCLGX	NAS CM	Open End	US Equity Large Cap Growth (Growth)	B-	C	B	Down	Y	1,000
Optimum Large Cap Growth Fund Institutional Class	OILGX	NAS CM	Open End	US Equity Large Cap Growth (Growth)	B-	C	B	Down	Y	0
Optimum Large Cap Value Fund Class A	OALVX	NAS CM	Open End	US Equity Large Cap Blend (Growth)	B-	C	B	Up	Y	1,000
Optimum Large Cap Value Fund Class C	OCLVX	NAS CM	Open End	US Equity Large Cap Blend (Growth)	B-	C	B	Up	Y	1,000
Optimum Large Cap Value Fund Institutional Class	OILVX	NAS CM	Open End	US Equity Large Cap Blend (Growth)	B-	C	B	Up	Y	0
Optimum Small-Mid Cap Growth Fund Class A	OASGX	NAS CM	Open End	US Equity Small Cap (Growth)	C+	C	C+	Down	Y	1,000
Optimum Small-Mid Cap Growth Fund Class C	OCSGX	NAS CM	Open End	US Equity Small Cap (Growth)	C+	C	C+	Down	Y	1,000

★ Expanded analysis of this fund is included in Section II.

	TOTAL RETURNS					PERFORMANCE				ASSETS		ASSET ALLOCATION & TURNOVER					BULL & BEAR		FEES		
Min Additional Investment	3-Month Total Return	6-Month Total Return	1-Year Total Return	3-Year Total Return	5-Year Total Return	Dividend Yield (TTM)	Expense Ratio	3-Yr Std Deviation	3-Year Beta	NAV	Total Assets (MIL)	%Cash	%Stocks	%Bonds	%Other	Turnover Ratio	Last Bull Market Total Return	Last Bear Market Total Return	Front End Fee (%)	Back End Fee (%)	Inception Date
	3.36	13.33	-6.42	37.61	8.32	2.07	0.83	16.21	1.35	23.04	33,013	4	96	0	0	36	15.09	-22.78			Nov-16
	3.45	13.42	-6.35	37.84	8.51	2.09	0.79	16.21	1.35	23.07	33,013	4	96	0	0	36	15.09	-22.78			Nov-16
	3.36	13.26	-6.52	37.15	7.96	1.81	0.96	16.19	1.35	23.06	33,013	4	96	0	0	36	15.08	-22.78			Sep-92
	3.29	13.11	-6.77	35.94	6.26	1.49	1.24	16.18	1.35	23.2	33,013	4	96	0	0	36	14.88	-22.91			Nov-99
	4.61	18.87	-6.13	27.68	8.08	1.2	1.32	14.72	1.11	14.74	1,488	4	96	0	0	45	21.02	-23.79			Nov-16
	4.62	18.83	-5.98	28.01	8.36	1.63	1.17	14.74	1.11	14.7	1,488	4	96	0	0	45	21.02	-23.79			Nov-16
	4.61	18.79	-6.13	27.40	7.84	1.26	1.36	14.75	1.12	14.73	1,488	4	96	0	0	45	21.02	-23.79			Nov-95
	4.50	18.65	-6.30	26.30	6.25	0.94	1.71	14.73	1.11	14.63	1,488	4	96	0	0	45	20.89	-23.94			Jan-01
	4.55	20.01	-6.77	24.33	19.56	0.34	0.82	17.6	1.31	40.59	4,818	4	97	0	0	41	27.64	-16.88			Nov-16
	4.55	20.04	-6.73	24.42	19.65	0.37	0.79	17.6	1.31	40.6	4,818	4	97	0	0	41	27.64	-16.88			Nov-16
	4.53	19.94	-6.89	23.86	19.12	0.15	0.97	17.61	1.31	40.59	4,818	4	97	0	0	41	27.64	-16.88			Nov-96
	4.46	19.76	-7.06	22.87	17.37	0	1.23	17.61	1.31	40	4,818	4	97	0	0	41	27.4	-16.97			Dec-99
100	-1.89	22.01	-11.27	46.27	17.87	0	1.91	20.29	1.13	11.36	86.1	0	93	0	7	85	24.85	-41.64			Oct-05
	-2.73	22.31	-10.97	47.10	18.54	0	1.65	20.37	1.13	11.4	86.1	0	93	0	7	85	24.85	-41.64			May-17
	0.22	15.92	-4.21			0	1.5			9.1	8.0	0	92	0	8						May-18
100	0.11	15.68	-4.52			0	1.75			9.07	8.0	0	92	0	8						May-18
	4.60	21.27	-10.30	23.24	21.43	0	1.28	17.07	1.18	23.83	43.6	0	99	0	1	155	25.59	-32.93			May-17
100	4.54	21.10	-10.48	22.62	20.82	0	1.52	17.09	1.18	23.7	43.6	0	99	0	1	155	25.59	-32.93			Jan-87
100	3.13	20.51	-10.39	21.88	26.03	0.19	1.6	15.67	1.14	19.09	441.1	0	90	0	10	145	24.61	-25.39			Feb-07
	3.23	20.70	-9.33	23.92	28.57	0.1	1.11	15.5	1.13	10.2	941.3	0	90	0	10	145					Mar-14
	2.18	25.52	-1.20	69.44	74.41	0	1.32	19.44	1.06	22.87	78.8	0	98	0	2	119	29.46	-28.95			May-17
100	2.11	25.42	-1.47	68.72	73.67	0	1.57	19.49	1.06	22.74	78.8	0	98	0	2	119	29.46	-28.95			Dec-95
100	3.03	22.19	3.09	58.38	52.60	0	1.55	18.32	1.01	14.26	11.6	0	98	0	2	160	24.28	-23.38			Sep-96
	3.15	22.29	3.32	59.23	53.43	0	1.3	18.34	1.01	14.37	11.6	0	98	0	2	160	24.28	-23.38			May-17
	-0.32	12.57	-9.09	25.14	22.13	0.26	1.29	18.31	1.04	18.62	26.6	0	99	0	1	54	25.12	-20.74			Jul-14
100	-0.37	12.45	-9.28	24.22	14.32	0.12	1.55	18.29	1.04	18.6	26.6	0	99	0	1	54					May-18
50	16.68	26.83	12.65	-7.08	2.61	0	2.36	26.98	0.04	8.46	28.1	2	98	0	0	6	-13.67	-11.56			Mar-10
50	16.23	26.19	11.77	-9.33	-1.27	0	2.86	26.97	0.04	7.66	28.1	2	98	0	0	6	-13.91	-11.77	4.50		Feb-88
100	5.95	22.33	11.46	52.26	44.22	0.43	0.99	11.71	0.98	18.51	1,989	2	98	0	0	38	6.4	-18.31			Mar-98
100	1.68	14.01	6.12			1.33	1.01			10.25	37.8	1	99	0	0	33					Mar-18
100	4.54	17.19	5.05	32.56	33.76	0.91	1.13	11.02	0.96	14.72	16,969	2	98	0	0	38	15.04	-25.49			Oct-93
100	3.66	17.70	0.60	30.00	32.12	0.51	1.13	11.72	0.93	15.29	6,233	4	96	0	0	62	20.83	-21.96			Apr-05
100	2.17	11.92	2.68	23.67	19.81	3.37	1.32	7.59	0.65	7.51	5,193	58	8	33	0	92	9.18	-15.41			Nov-07
100	4.91	18.42	5.62	34.94	32.56		1.43	14.26	1.12	24.1	608.2	11	90	0	0	54	28.18	-19.35	5.50		Sep-18
100	4.95	18.55	6.05	38.31	38.60	0	1.18	14.27	1.12	24.15	608.2	11	90	0	0	54	28.73	-19.1			Sep-99
100	4.73	17.99	5.06	34.23	31.87	0	2.18	14.28	1.12	18.82	608.2	11	90	0	0	54	28.18	-19.35		1.00	Sep-95
100	5.25	16.99	-0.14	30.66	17.34	0	1.32	17.44	1.07	17.42	78.6	6	94	0	0	53	32.25	-23.95			May-15
100	5.18	16.88	-0.37	29.70	16.15	0	1.57	17.45	1.07	17.24	78.6	6	94	0	0	53	32.25	-23.95	5.50		Nov-06
100	4.95	16.42	-1.11	26.85	11.90	0	2.32	17.43	1.07	15.45	78.6	6	94	0	0	53	31.66	-24.17		1.00	Nov-06
500	1.86	4.57	0.78	10.77	7.85	6.31	3.57	4.44	41.97	45.9	25.6	-27	0	96	29	604					Jun-13
500	1.85	4.64	0.93	11.42	8.94	6.84	3.35	4.43	41.99	45.55	25.6	-27	0	96	29	604					Jan-13
100	1.42	12.41	-1.58	31.20	13.74	1.3	1.36	11.28	0.96	12.77	557.4	0	100	0	0	63	10.56	-20.98	5.75		Aug-03
100	1.30	12.08	-2.27	28.42	9.58	0.46	2.11	11.32	0.97	12.43	557.4	0	100	0	0	63	10.2	-21.18		1.00	Aug-03
	1.49	12.59	-1.35	32.29	15.21	1.56	1.11	11.27	0.96	12.87	557.4	0	100	0	0	63	10.81	-20.86			Aug-03
100	4.31	21.90	10.32	68.40	82.31	0	1.26	13.69	0.99	17.42	1,728	3	97	0	0	25	28.12	-18.17	5.75		Aug-03
100	4.16	21.48	9.58	64.73	75.65	0	2.01	13.7	0.99	14.25	1,728	3	97	0	0	25	27.69	-18.47		1.00	Aug-03
	4.41	22.12	10.67	69.73	84.68	0	1.01	13.69	0.99	18.93	1,728	3	97	0	0	25	28.38	-18.08			Aug-03
100	4.48	17.80	8.99	34.97	32.31	1.05	1.21	12.06	0.99	16.54	1,637	2	98	0	0	22	24.78	-17	5.75		Aug-03
100	4.28	17.41	8.21	31.96	27.45	0.26	1.96	12.01	0.98	16.32	1,637	2	98	0	0	22	24.38	-17.18		1.00	Aug-03
	4.53	17.99	9.27	35.98	33.99	1.31	0.96	12.02	0.98	16.59	1,637	2	98	0	0	22	25.16	-16.86			Aug-03
100	3.27	23.28	4.00	64.19	46.69	0	1.54	17.35	1.03	13.87	528.8	2	97	0	0	82	26.05	-24.5	5.75		Aug-03
100	3.10	22.87	3.25	60.62	41.31	0	2.29	17.36	1.03	11.28	528.8	2	97	0	0	82	25.68	-24.68		1.00	Aug-03

		MARKET		FUND TYPE, CATEGORY & OBJECTIVE	RATINGS					MINIMUMS
Fund Name	Ticker Symbol	Traded On	Fund Type	Category and (Prospectus Objective)	Overall Rating	Reward Rating	Risk Rating	Recent Up/ Downgrade	Open to New Investors	Min Initial Investment
Optimum Small-Mid Cap Growth Fund Institutional Class	OISGX	NAS CM	Open End	US Equity Small Cap (Growth)	C+	C	C+	Down	Y	0
Optimum Small-Mid Cap Value Fund Class A	OASVX	NAS CM	Open End	US Equity Small Cap (Growth)	C	C-	C+		Y	1,000
Optimum Small-Mid Cap Value Fund Class C	OCSVX	NAS CM	Open End	US Equity Small Cap (Growth)	C	C-	C	Up	Y	1,000
Optimum Small-Mid Cap Value Fund Institutional Class	OISVX	NAS CM	Open End	US Equity Small Cap (Growth)	C	C-	C+		Y	0
Orchard Small Cap Value Fund Class I	OCSIX	NAS CM	Open End	US Equity Small Cap (Small Company)	C-	D+	C-		Y	1,000,000
Orchard Small Cap Value Fund Class N	OCSNX	NAS CM	Open End	US Equity Small Cap (Small Company)	C-	D+	C-		Y	1,000
Orinda Income Opportunities Fund Class A	OIOAX	NAS CM	Open End	US Fixed Income (Income)	B-	B-	B-		Y	5,000
Orinda Income Opportunities Fund Class D	OIODX	NAS CM	Open End	US Fixed Income (Income)	C+	C+	B-	Down	Y	5,000
Orinda Income Opportunities Fund Class I	OIOIX	NAS CM	Open End	US Fixed Income (Income)	B-	B-	B		Y	100,000
O'Shaughnessy All Cap Core Fund Class A	OFAAX	NAS CM	Open End	US Equity Large Cap Blend (Growth)	C	C	C+		Y	2,500
O'Shaughnessy All Cap Core Fund Class C	OFACX	NAS CM	Open End	US Equity Large Cap Blend (Growth)	C	C	C+		Y	2,500
O'Shaughnessy All Cap Core Fund Class I	OFAIX	NAS CM	Open End	US Equity Large Cap Blend (Growth)	C	C	C+		Y	10,000
O'Shaughnessy Enhanced Dividend Fund Class I	OFDIX	NAS CM	Open End	Global Equity Large Cap (Equity-Income)	C	C-	C		Y	10,000
O'Shaughnessy Small/Mid Cap Growth Fund Class I	OFMIX	NAS CM	Open End	US Equity Small Cap (Growth)	C	C	C+		Y	10,000
Osterweis Emerging Opportunity Fund	OSTGX	NAS CM	Open End	US Equity Small Cap (Growth)	C+	C+	C	Down	Y	5,000
Osterweis Fund	OSTFX	NAS CM	Open End	US Equity Large Cap Blend (Growth)	B-	C	B		Y	5,000
Osterweis Strategic Investment Investment	OSTVX	NAS CM	Open End	Moderate Alloc (Growth & Income)	B-	C+	B+		Y	5,000
Otter Creek Long/Short Opportunity Institutional Cls	OTTRX	NAS CM	Open End	Long/Short Equity (Growth)	C-	C-	C	Down	Y	100,000
Otter Creek Long/Short Opportunity Fund Investor Class	OTCRX	NAS CM	Open End	Long/Short Equity (Growth)	C-	C-	C	Down	Y	2,500
PACE Alternative Strategies Investments Class A	PASIX	NAS CM	Open End	Multialternative (Growth)	C	C-	B-	Up	Y	1,000
PACE Alternative Strategies Investments Class P	PASPX	NAS CM	Open End	Multialternative (Growth)	C	C-	B-		Y	10,000
PACE Alternative Strategies Investments Class Y	PASYX	NAS CM	Open End	Multialternative (Growth)	C	C-	B-		Y	2,000,000
PACE Global Real Estate Securities Investments Class A	PREAX	NAS CM	Open End	Real Estate Sector Equity (Real Estate)	B-	C	B		Y	1,000
PACE Global Real Estate Securities Investments Class P	PREQX	NAS CM	Open End	Real Estate Sector Equity (Real Estate)	B-	C	B		Y	10,000
PACE Intl Emerging Mkts Equity Investments Cls A	PWEAX	NAS CM	Open End	Global Emerg Mkts (Div Emerging Mkts)	C	C	C+		Y	1,000
PACE Intl Emerging Mkts Equity Investments Cls P	PCEMX	NAS CM	Open End	Global Emerg Mkts (Div Emerging Mkts)	C	C	C+		Y	10,000
PACE Intl Emerging Mkts Equity Investments Cls Y	PWEYX	NAS CM	Open End	Global Emerg Mkts (Div Emerging Mkts)	C	C	C+		Y	2,000,000
PACE International Equity Investments Class A	PWGAX	NAS CM	Open End	Global Equity Large Cap (Growth)	C	C	B		Y	1,000
PACE International Equity Investments Class P	PCIEX	NAS CM	Open End	Global Equity Large Cap (Growth)	C	C	B		Y	10,000
PACE International Equity Investments Class Y	PWIYX	NAS CM	Open End	Global Equity Large Cap (Growth)	C	C	B		Y	2,000,000
PACE Large Co Growth Equity Investments Class A	PLAAX	NAS CM	Open End	US Equity Large Cap Growth (Growth)	B-	C+	B		Y	1,000
PACE Large Co Growth Equity Investments Class P	PCLCX	NAS CM	Open End	US Equity Large Cap Growth (Growth)	B-	C+	B		Y	10,000
PACE Large Co Growth Equity Investments Class Y	PLAYX	NAS CM	Open End	US Equity Large Cap Growth (Growth)	B-	C+	B		Y	2,000,000
PACE Large Co Value Equity Investments Class A	PCPAX	NAS CM	Open End	US Equity Large Cap Value (Growth & Income)	C+	C	B	Up	Y	1,000
PACE Large Co Value Equity Investments Class P	PCLVX	NAS CM	Open End	US Equity Large Cap Value (Growth & Income)	C+	C	B	Up	Y	10,000
PACE Large Co Value Equity Investments Class Y	PLVYX	NAS CM	Open End	US Equity Large Cap Value (Growth & Income)	C+	C	B	Up	Y	2,000,000
PACE Small/Medium Co Growth Equity Investments Class A	PQUAX	NAS CM	Open End	US Equity Small Cap (Growth)	C+	C	C+	Down	Y	1,000
PACE Small/Medium Co Growth Equity Investments Class P	PCSGX	NAS CM	Open End	US Equity Small Cap (Growth)	C+	C	C+	Down	Y	10,000
PACE Small/Medium Co Growth Equity Investments Class Y	PUMYX	NAS CM	Open End	US Equity Small Cap (Growth)	C+	C	C+	Down	Y	2,000,000
PACE Small/Medium Co Value Equity Investments Class A	PEVAX	NAS CM	Open End	US Equity Small Cap (Growth)	C	C-	C+		Y	1,000
PACE Small/Medium Co Value Equity Investments Class P	PCSVX	NAS CM	Open End	US Equity Small Cap (Growth)	C	C-	C+		Y	10,000
PACE Small/Medium Co Value Equity Investments Class Y	PVEYX	NAS CM	Open End	US Equity Small Cap (Growth)	C	C-	C+		Y	2,000,000
Pacific Advisors Balanced Fund Class A	PAABX	NAS CM	Open End	Aggressive Alloc (Balanced)	C	C-	C+		Y	1,000
Pacific Advisors Balanced Fund Class C	PGBCX	NAS CM	Open End	Aggressive Alloc (Balanced)	C	C-	C		Y	10,000
Pacific Advisors Income and Equity Fund Class A	PADIX	NAS CM	Open End	Cautious Alloc (Equity-Income)	C+	C	B	Up	Y	1,000
Pacific Advisors Income and Equity Fund Class C	PIECX	NAS CM	Open End	Cautious Alloc (Equity-Income)	C	C	B-		Y	10,000
Pacific Advisors Large Cap Value Fund Class A	PAGTX	NAS CM	Open End	US Equity Large Cap Blend (Growth)	C+	C	B	Down	Y	1,000
Pacific Advisors Large Cap Value Fund Class C	PGCCX	NAS CM	Open End	US Equity Large Cap Blend (Growth)	C+	C	B	Down	Y	10,000
Pacific Advisors Mid Cap Value Fund Class A	PAMVX	NAS CM	Open End	US Equity Mid Cap (Growth)	C-	D+	C	Down	Y	1,000
Pacific Advisors Mid Cap Value Fund Class C	PMVCX	NAS CM	Open End	US Equity Mid Cap (Growth)	C-	D+	C-	Down	Y	10,000
Pacific Advisors Small Cap Value Fund Class A	PASMX	NAS CM	Open End	US Equity Small Cap (Small Company)	C-	C-	C-	Down	Y	1,000
Pacific Advisors Small Cap Value Fund Class C	PGSCX	NAS CM	Open End	US Equity Small Cap (Small Company)	C-	C-	C-	Down	Y	10,000

★ Expanded analysis of this fund is included in Section II.

	TOTAL RETURNS					PERFORMANCE				ASSETS		ASSET ALLOCATION & TURNOVER					BULL & BEAR		FEES		
Min Additional Investment	3-Month Total Return	6-Month Total Return	1-Year Total Return	3-Year Total Return	5-Year Total Return	Dividend Yield (TTM)	Expense Ratio	3-Yr Std Deviation	3-Year Beta	NAV	Total Assets (MIL)	%Cash	%Stocks	%Bonds	%Other	Turnover Ratio	Last Bull Market Total Return	Last Bear Market Total Return	Front End Fee (%)	Back End Fee (%)	Inception Date
	3.26	23.43	4.19	65.38	48.39	0	1.29	17.33	1.03	15.17	528.8	2	97	0	0	82	26.41	-24.4			Aug-03
100	1.97	15.48	-4.24	23.13	5.32	0.47	1.46	15.4	1	12.38	537.1	1	99	0	0	32	30.75	-25.7	5.75		Aug-03
100	1.70	15.02	-5.00	20.39	1.38	0	2.21	15.32	1	10.72	537.1	1	99	0	0	32	30.26	-25.92		1.00	Aug-03
	2.01	15.54	-4.00	24.07	6.60	0.71	1.21	15.37	1	13.16	537.1	1	99	0	0	32	31	-25.6			Aug-03
1,000	-1.31	11.34	-19.41	27.15		0	1.27	19.99	1.1	10.5	5.4	9	91	0	0	37					Dec-15
100	-1.42	11.13	-19.64	26.18		0	1.52	20.03	1.1	10.38	5.4	9	91	0	0	37					Dec-15
0	0.64	14.55	5.15	14.95	15.98	6.75	2.1	7.77	0.56	21.43	276.0	1	14	1	0	102			5.00		Jun-13
0	0.46	14.17	4.40	12.52	12.20	6.21	2.95	7.76	0.56	21.21	276.0	1	14	1	0	102					Sep-13
	0.72	14.74	5.50	16.02	17.81	6.98	1.95	7.77	0.56	21.48	276.0	1	14	1	0	102					Jun-13
100	1.84	13.63	-2.48	41.01	46.64	1.36	0.85	14.38	1.1	9.92	8.3	0	100	0	0	86	26.11	-19.73	5.25		Aug-10
100	1.64	13.21	-2.69	38.42	41.61	1.06	1.6	14.4	1.1	9.25	8.3	0	100	0	0	86	25.63	-20.03		1.00	Aug-10
	1.88	13.76	-2.25	41.90	48.14	1.61	0.6	14.34	1.1	9.75	8.3	0	100	0	0	86	26.23	-19.65			Aug-10
	1.40	8.86	-5.76	26.88	-1.63	3.46	0.99	14.04	1.13	10.79	4.0	0	100	0	0	64	13.24	-16.65			Aug-10
	3.54	16.25	-4.31	37.49	36.09	0	1.19	14.8	0.86	13.73	16.1	0	100	0	0	85	25.92	-28.36			Aug-10
100	9.78	32.79	10.66	94.17	108.83	0	1.13			13.24	108.6	17	83	0	0	215					Nov-16
100	3.50	20.05	9.59	32.73	22.22	3.73	0.96	11.16	0.87	16.82	128.5	3	95	2	0	43	19.97	-20.58			Oct-93
100	3.28	15.75	6.79	29.10	22.09	2.34	1.2	8.45	0.12	14.77	134.1	4	66	25	0	47	16.75	-13.93			Aug-10
	2.27	-0.08	2.96	-2.49	5.90	0	2.32	5.74	-0.13	11.7	132.5	67	33	0	0	163					Dec-13
	2.12	-0.25	2.72	-3.26	4.64	0	2.55	5.8	-0.13	11.55	132.5	67	33	0	0	163					Dec-13
100	1.24	5.29	1.15	4.77	3.70	0	2.41	3.96	30.34	10.54	532.4	42	53	4	0	346	7.57	-8.38	5.50		Apr-06
500	1.25	5.32	1.35	5.41	5.07	0	2.18	3.98	30.98	10.49	532.4	42	53	4	0	346	7.77	-8.35			Apr-06
0	1.24	5.29	1.35	5.39	5.14	0	2.16	3.92	29.7	10.53	532.4	42	53	4	0	346	7.74	-8.33			Jul-08
100	-0.25	15.08	5.20	15.94	22.72	2.98	1.45	11.39	1	7.78	123.1	2	98	0	0	73	24.88	-20.13	5.50		Dec-06
500	-0.13	15.23	5.48	16.95	24.13	3.28	1.2	11.3	0.99	7.49	123.1	2	98	0	0	73	25.05	-19.96			Jan-07
100	0.83	11.64	0.21	27.14	2.84	1.48	1.7	12.97	0.93	13.23	396.7	1	99	0	0	65	18.47	-25.37	5.50		Dec-00
500	0.91	11.78	0.48	28.01	4.03	1.66	1.45	12.97	0.93	13.28	396.7	1	99	0	0	65	18.47	-25.3			Aug-95
0	0.83	11.72	0.42	28.04	4.12	1.66	1.45	12.98	0.93	13.34	396.7	1	99	0	0	65	18.6	-25.26			Feb-01
100	2.67	13.30	-0.17	28.07	11.74	1.6	1.86	11.54	1.02	15.33	1,019	1	99	0	0	78	13.97	-22.31	5.50		Nov-00
500	2.69	13.41	0.08	29.14	13.27	1.9	1.59	11.52	1.02	15.22	1,019	1	99	0	0	78	14.17	-22.23			Aug-95
0	2.69	13.45	0.08	29.15	13.31	1.89	1.59	11.55	1.02	15.26	1,019	1	99	0	0	78	14.15	-22.26			Jan-01
100	6.99	23.87	11.68	58.74	70.98	0	1.13	13.23	0.97	23.87	1,217	2	98	0	0	41	26.62	-17.43	5.50		Nov-00
500	7.08	24.00	11.99	59.96	73.13	0.03	0.88	13.24	0.97	24.95	1,217	2	98	0	0	41	26.81	-17.32			Aug-95
0	7.10	24.02	12.02	60.03	73.28	0.05	0.88	13.26	0.97	25.19	1,217	2	98	0	0	41	26.78	-17.3			Feb-01
100	2.89	14.11	3.82	32.11	36.38	1.5	1.46	12.99	1.06	21.35	1,131	2	98	0	0	68	25.3	-20.63	5.50		Nov-00
500	2.90	14.22	4.01	32.96	37.97	1.74	1.23	12.98	1.06	21.28	1,131	2	98	0	0	68	25.43	-20.53			Aug-95
0	2.98	14.30	4.11	33.11	38.11	1.75	1.21	12.99	1.06	21.41	1,131	2	98	0	0	68	25.49	-20.58			Jan-01
100	2.21	20.15	3.59	59.27	52.39	0	1.2	17.11	1	16.63	459.1	2	98	0	0	41	27.94	-22.94	5.50		Nov-00
500	2.27	20.30	3.77	59.95	53.35	0	1.06	17.09	1	18.01	459.1	2	98	0	0	41	28.05	-22.89			Aug-95
0	2.21	20.33	3.99	60.69	54.05	0	0.7	17.08	1	18.46	459.1	2	98	0	0	41	28.07	-22.89			Feb-01
100	1.94	18.43	-4.78	27.78	26.73	0.68	1.21	16.64	1.09	18.31	432.6	2	98	0	0	60	31.19	-27.71	5.50		Nov-00
500	1.94	18.48	-4.64	28.37	27.67	0.79	1.04	16.63	1.09	18.91	432.6	2	98	0	0	60	31.29	-27.68			Aug-95
0	2.02	18.54	-4.50	28.69	28.00	0.94	0.89	16.64	1.09	19.18	432.6	2	98	0	0	60	31.34	-27.68			Dec-00
25	0.53	9.88	-4.24	14.52	-15.98	0	5.16	11.98	0.89	11.34	3.8	2	72	26	0	23	16.93	-14.57	5.75		Feb-93
500	0.31	9.50	-5.00	11.97	-19.12	0	5.91	11.97	0.89	9.68	3.8	2	72	26	0	23	16.46	-14.88		1.00	Apr-98
25	1.24	6.74	2.81	9.62	13.91	0.11	4	5.82	0.21	12.2	9.5	3	51	44	0	16	8.32	-5.03	4.75		Feb-93
500	1.14	6.40	2.08	7.27	9.73	0	4.75	5.82	0.2	11.47	9.5	3	51	44	0	16	7.84	-5.37		1.00	Apr-98
25	4.48	16.54	9.57	37.14	40.60	0	4.87	12.16	0.96	16.55	5.7	0	100	0	0	0	21.57	-10.93	5.75		May-99
500	4.28	16.11	8.80	34.06	35.43	0	5.62	12.16	0.96	13.62	5.7	0	100	0	0	0	21.08	-11.18		1.00	May-99
25	0.37	15.83	-11.04	21.94	-18.99	0	5.33	21.82	1.46	10.61	3.9	0	100	0	0	2	30.81	-33.48	5.75		Apr-02
500	0.11	15.23	-11.77	19.11	-22.07	0	6.08	21.81	1.46	9	3.9	0	100	0	0	2	30.08	-33.73		1.00	Apr-02
25	-5.38	8.38	-19.07	33.47	-31.65	0	4.4	26.75	1.42	22.48	13.9	0	100	0	0	8	47.32	-29.97	5.75		Feb-93
500	-5.54	8.01	-19.68	30.51	-34.16	0	5.15	26.7	1.42	14.82	13.9	0	100	0	0	8	46.61	-30.19		1.00	Apr-98

	MARKET		FUND TYPE, CATEGORY & OBJECTIVE		RATINGS				MINIMUMS	
Fund Name	Ticker Symbol	Traded On	Fund Type	Category and (Prospectus Objective)	Overall Rating	Reward Rating	Risk Rating	Recent Up/ Downgrade	Open to New Investors	Min Initial Investment
Pacific Advisors Small Cap Value Fund Class I	PGISX	NAS CM	Open End	US Equity Small Cap (Small Company)	C-	C-	C	Down	Y	1,000
Pacific Funds Diversified Alternatives Fund Advisor Class	PLDLX	NAS CM	Open End	Multialternative (Growth & Income)	C	C-	B		Y	0
Pacific Funds Diversified Alternatives Fund Class A	PLALX	NAS CM	Open End	Multialternative (Growth & Income)	C	C-	B-		Y	1,000
Pacific Funds Diversified Alternatives Fund Class C	PLCLX	NAS CM	Open End	Multialternative (Growth & Income)	C	D+	C+	Up	Y	1,000
Pacific Funds Large-Cap Advisor Class	PFCDX	NAS CM	Open End	US Equity Large Cap Blend (Growth)	B-	C	B	Up	Y	0
Pacific Funds Large-Cap Class A	PFLAX	NAS CM	Open End	US Equity Large Cap Blend (Growth)	B-	C	B	Up	Y	1,000
Pacific Funds Large-Cap Class C	PFCCX	NAS CM	Open End	US Equity Large Cap Blend (Growth)	C+	C	B		Y	1,000
Pacific Funds Large-Cap S Class	PFKIX	NAS CM	Open End	US Equity Large Cap Blend (Growth)	B-	C	B		Y	0
Pacific Funds Large-Cap Value Advisor Class	PFVDX	NAS CM	Open End	US Equity Large Cap Value (Growth)	B-	C	B	Up	Y	0
Pacific Funds Large-Cap Value Class A	PFAAX	NAS CM	Open End	US Equity Large Cap Value (Growth)	B-	C	B	Up	Y	1,000
Pacific Funds Large-Cap Value Class C	PFVCX	NAS CM	Open End	US Equity Large Cap Value (Growth)	B-	C	B	Up	Y	1,000
Pacific Funds Large-Cap Value S Class	PFVIX	NAS CM	Open End	US Equity Large Cap Value (Growth)	B-	C	B	Up	Y	0
Pacific Funds Port Optimization Aggressive-Growth Adv Cls	POEDX	NAS CM	Open End	Aggressive Alloc (Asset Alloc)	B-	C	B	Up	Y	0
Pacific Funds Port Optimization Aggressive-Growth Cls A	POEAX	NAS CM	Open End	Aggressive Alloc (Asset Alloc)	B-	C	B	Up	Y	1,000
Pacific Funds Port Optimization Aggressive-Growth Cls B	POEBX	NAS CM	Open End	Aggressive Alloc (Asset Alloc)	C+	C	B	Up	Y	1,000
Pacific Funds Port Optimization Aggressive-Growth Cls C	POCEX	NAS CM	Open End	Aggressive Alloc (Asset Alloc)	C+	C	B	Up	Y	1,000
Pacific Funds Portfolio Optimization Conservative Adv Cls	PLCDX	NAS CM	Open End	Cautious Alloc (Asset Alloc)	B-	C	B+	Up	Y	0
Pacific Funds Portfolio Optimization Conservative Cls A	POAAX	NAS CM	Open End	Cautious Alloc (Asset Alloc)	B-	C	B+	Up	Y	1,000
Pacific Funds Portfolio Optimization Conservative Cls B	POABX	NAS CM	Open End	Cautious Alloc (Asset Alloc)	B-	C	B	Up	Y	1,000
Pacific Funds Portfolio Optimization Conservative Cls C	POACX	NAS CM	Open End	Cautious Alloc (Asset Alloc)	B-	C	B	Up	Y	1,000
Pacific Funds Portfolio Optimization Growth Advisor Cls	PMADX	NAS CM	Open End	Aggressive Alloc (Asset Alloc)	B-	C	B+	Up	Y	0
Pacific Funds Portfolio Optimization Growth Fund Class A	PODAX	NAS CM	Open End	Aggressive Alloc (Asset Alloc)	B-	C	B	Up	Y	1,000
Pacific Funds Portfolio Optimization Growth Fund Class B	PODBX	NAS CM	Open End	Aggressive Alloc (Asset Alloc)	B-	C	B	Up	Y	1,000
Pacific Funds Portfolio Optimization Growth Fund Class C	PODCX	NAS CM	Open End	Aggressive Alloc (Asset Alloc)	B-	C	B	Up	Y	1,000
Pacific Funds Portfolio Optimization Moderate Advisor Cls	POMDX	NAS CM	Open End	Moderate Alloc (Asset Alloc)	B-	C	B+	Up	Y	0
Pacific Funds Portfolio Optimization Moderate Fund Class A	POCAX	NAS CM	Open End	Moderate Alloc (Asset Alloc)	B-	C	B+	Up	Y	1,000
Pacific Funds Portfolio Optimization Moderate Fund Class B	POMBX	NAS CM	Open End	Moderate Alloc (Asset Alloc)	B-	C	B+	Up	Y	1,000
Pacific Funds Portfolio Optimization Moderate Fund Class C	POMCX	NAS CM	Open End	Moderate Alloc (Asset Alloc)	B-	C	B+	Up	Y	1,000
Pacific Funds Port Optimization Mod-Cons Adv Cls	PMCDX	NAS CM	Open End	Cautious Alloc (Asset Alloc)	B	C	A-	Up	Y	0
Pacific Funds Port Optimization Mod-Cons Cls A	POBAX	NAS CM	Open End	Cautious Alloc (Asset Alloc)	B	C	A-	Up	Y	1,000
Pacific Funds Port Optimization Mod-Cons Cls B	POBBX	NAS CM	Open End	Cautious Alloc (Asset Alloc)	B-	C	B+	Up	Y	1,000
Pacific Funds Port Optimization Mod-Cons Cls C	POBCX	NAS CM	Open End	Cautious Alloc (Asset Alloc)	B-	C	B+	Up	Y	1,000
Pacific Funds Small/Mid-Cap Advisor Class	PFMDX	NAS CM	Open End	US Equity Small Cap (Growth)	C	C	B-		Y	0
Pacific Funds Small/Mid-Cap Class A	PFDAX	NAS CM	Open End	US Equity Small Cap (Growth)	C	C	C+		Y	1,000
Pacific Funds Small/Mid-Cap Class C	PFPCX	NAS CM	Open End	US Equity Small Cap (Growth)	C	C	C+		Y	1,000
Pacific Funds Small/Mid-Cap S Class	PFOIX	NAS CM	Open End	US Equity Small Cap (Growth)	C	C	B-		Y	0
Pacific Funds Small-Cap Advisor Class	PFQDX	NAS CM	Open End	US Equity Small Cap (Small Company)	C	C-	C+		Y	0
Pacific Funds Small-Cap Class A	PFKAX	NAS CM	Open End	US Equity Small Cap (Small Company)	C	C-	C+		Y	1,000
Pacific Funds Small-Cap Class C	PFACX	NAS CM	Open End	US Equity Small Cap (Small Company)	C	C-	C+		Y	1,000
Pacific Funds Small-Cap Growth Advisor Class	PFWDX	NAS CM	Open End	US Equity Small Cap (Small Company)	C	C-	B-	Down	Y	0
Pacific Funds Small-Cap Growth Class A	PFMAX	NAS CM	Open End	US Equity Small Cap (Small Company)	C	C-	B-	Down	Y	1,000
Pacific Funds Small-Cap Growth Class C	PFMCX	NAS CM	Open End	US Equity Small Cap (Small Company)	C	D+	C+	Down	Y	1,000
Pacific Funds Small-Cap Growth Class P			Open End	US Equity Small Cap (Small Company)	C	C-	B-	Down	Y	0
Pacific Funds Small-Cap Growth S Class	PFYIX	NAS CM	Open End	US Equity Small Cap (Small Company)	C	C-	B-	Down	Y	0
Pacific Funds Small-Cap S Class	PFJIX	NAS CM	Open End	US Equity Small Cap (Small Company)	C	C-	C+		Y	0
Pacific Funds Small-Cap Value Advisor Class	PFFDX	NAS CM	Open End	US Equity Small Cap (Small Company)	C	C	C		Y	0
Pacific Funds Small-Cap Value Class A	PFEAX	NAS CM	Open End	US Equity Small Cap (Small Company)	C	C	C		Y	1,000
Pacific Funds Small-Cap Value Class C	PFHCX	NAS CM	Open End	US Equity Small Cap (Small Company)	C	C	C		Y	1,000
Pacific Funds Small-Cap Value S Class	PFEIX	NAS CM	Open End	US Equity Small Cap (Small Company)	C	C	C		Y	0
Palmer Square Strategic Credit Fund Class A	PSQAX	NAS CM	Open End	Multialternative (Growth)	B-	C	B	Down	Y	2,500
Palmer Square Strategic Credit Fund Class I	PSQIX	NAS CM	Open End	Multialternative (Growth)	B-	C	B+	Down	Y	1,000,000
Papp Small & Mid-Cap Growth Fund	PAPPX	NAS CM	Open End	US Equity Mid Cap (Growth)	B	B-	B		Y	5,000

★ Expanded analysis of this fund is included in Section II.

	TOTAL RETURNS					PERFORMANCE				ASSETS		ASSET ALLOCATION & TURNOVER					BULL & BEAR		FEES		
Min Additional Investment	3-Month Total Return	6-Month Total Return	1-Year Total Return	3-Year Total Return	5-Year Total Return	Dividend Yield (TTM)	Expense Ratio	3-Yr Std Deviation	3-Year Beta	NAV	Total Assets (MIL)	%Cash	%Stocks	%Bonds	%Other	Turnover Ratio	Last Bull Market Total Return	Last Bear Market Total Return	Front End Fee (%)	Back End Fee (%)	Inception Date
500	-5.32	8.53	-18.86	34.19	-30.76	0	4.41	26.68	1.41	30.38	13.9	0	100	0	0	8	47.49	-29.9			Oct-06
	1.79	6.05	0.74	9.11	11.60	0.7	1.59	3.96	39.76	9.64	16.3	29	23	49	0	58					Dec-13
50	1.69	5.85	0.40	8.25	10.31	0.48	1.84	3.96	39.89	9.59	16.3	29	23	49	0	58			5.50		Dec-13
50	1.51	5.50	-0.31	5.88	6.26	0	2.59	3.98	42.17	9.39	16.3	29	23	49	0	58				1.00	Dec-13
	3.97	17.43	7.49	45.58		0.91	0.75	12.52	1.02	13.07	21.4	2	98	0	0	79					Jan-16
50	3.84	17.28	7.18	44.48		0.69	1	12.48	1.02	12.96	21.4	2	98	0	0	79			4.25		Jan-16
50	3.70	16.87	6.41	41.31		0.05	1.75	12.49	1.02	12.88	21.4	2	98	0	0	79				1.00	Jan-16
	3.97	17.50	7.59	45.95		1.03	0.65	12.5	1.02	12.82	21.4	2	98	0	0	79					Mar-15
	4.20	16.46	8.11	34.26		1.29	0.85	11.87	0.97	11.39	19.5	3	97	0	0	39					Jan-16
50	4.22	16.29	7.77	33.27		1.08	1.1	11.87	0.97	11.35	19.5	3	97	0	0	39			4.25		Jan-16
50	3.97	15.84	6.94	30.20		0.23	1.85	11.88	0.97	11.26	19.5	3	97	0	0	39				1.00	Jan-16
	4.33	16.59	8.15	34.51		1.67	0.75	11.86	0.97	11.31	19.5	3	97	0	0	39					Jan-16
	4.12	18.66	6.11	39.99	37.34	1.55	1.05	11.26	0.9	14.88	316.0	7	37	58	-2	55	21.83	-19.37			Dec-12
50	4.07	18.54	5.91	39.05	35.66	1.39	1.3	11.24	0.9	14.83	316.0	7	37	58	-2	55	21.83	-19.37	5.50		Dec-03
50	3.84	18.03	5.07	35.87	30.58	0.93	2.05	11.23	0.9	14.33	316.0	7	37	58	-2	55	21.94	-20.03		5.00	Dec-03
50	3.92	18.18	5.13	36.03	30.66	0.96	2.05	11.24	0.9	14.3	316.0	7	37	58	-2	55	21.94	-20.03		1.00	Dec-03
	2.92	9.08	5.80	15.49	17.79	2	1.01	3.81	0.49	10.57	248.4	7	8	85	0	30	8.55	-4.6			Dec-12
50	2.93	9.00	5.61	14.66	16.38	1.83	1.26	3.78	0.49	10.53	248.4	7	8	85	0	30	8.55	-4.6	5.50		Dec-03
50	2.70	8.46	4.74	12.12	12.12	1.26	2.01	3.8	0.49	10.25	248.4	7	8	85	0	30	8.2	-4.92		5.00	Dec-03
50	2.70	8.58	4.81	12.20	12.09	1.33	2.01	3.8	0.48	10.24	248.4	7	8	85	0	30	8.25	-4.92		1.00	Dec-03
	3.90	16.73	5.98	33.50	33.36	1.46	1.04	9.76	0.78	13.32	872.6	7	31	63	-1	53	19.47	-15.98			Dec-12
50	3.83	16.62	5.77	32.47	31.69	1.31	1.29	9.78	0.78	13.26	872.6	7	31	63	-1	53	19.47	-15.98	5.50		Dec-03
50	3.59	16.12	4.92	29.54	26.85	0.83	2.04	9.71	0.78	12.96	872.6	7	31	63	-1	53	19.19	-16.46		5.00	Dec-03
50	3.69	16.20	4.99	29.61	26.90	0.87	2.04	9.76	0.78	12.91	872.6	7	31	63	-1	53	19.2	-16.42		1.00	Dec-03
	3.73	14.46	6.06	27.58	28.44	1.72	1.02	7.77	0.61	12.5	1,129	7	26	67	-1	41	16.16	-12.2			Dec-12
50	3.66	14.32	5.80	26.64	26.86	1.56	1.27	7.76	0.61	12.45	1,129	7	26	67	-1	41	16.16	-12.2	5.50		Dec-03
50	3.38	13.91	4.97	23.77	22.17	1.06	2.02	7.76	0.61	12.2	1,129	7	26	67	-1	41	15.72	-12.54		5.00	Dec-03
50	3.39	13.84	4.93	23.85	22.09	1.1	2.02	7.73	0.61	12.17	1,129	7	26	67	-1	41	15.8	-12.56		1.00	Dec-03
	3.34	11.43	5.93	20.63	22.67	1.7	1.01	5.55	0.36	11.11	363.1	7	19	74	-1	45	12.11	-8.34			Dec-12
50	3.26	11.26	5.65	19.79	21.16	1.54	1.26	5.52	0.36	11.06	363.1	7	19	74	-1	45	12.11	-8.34	5.50		Dec-03
50	3.06	10.80	4.84	17.07	16.69	1.04	2.01	5.49	0.36	10.77	363.1	7	19	74	-1	45	11.75	-8.83		5.00	Dec-03
50	3.06	10.81	4.79	17.12	16.77	1.07	2.01	5.5	0.36	10.76	363.1	7	19	74	-1	45	11.79	-8.75		1.00	Dec-03
	1.06	16.73	-1.35	39.15		0.01	1.05	15.03	0.96	13.25	364.1	2	98	0	0	33					Jan-16
50	1.07	16.66	-1.59	38.13		0	1.3	15.09	0.97	13.16	364.1	2	98	0	0	33			4.25		Jan-16
50	0.86	16.13	-2.30	35.10		0	2.05	15.06	0.96	12.81	364.1	2	98	0	0	33				1.00	Jan-16
	1.06	16.82	-1.26	39.34		0.03	1	15.02	0.96	13.26	364.1	2	98	0	0	33					Dec-14
	0.97	14.97	-4.55	38.95		0.09	1.05	16.27	0.94	12.44	19.0	2	98	0	0	56					Jan-16
50	0.90	14.83	-4.87	37.91		0	1.3	16.31	0.95	12.23	19.0	2	98	0	0	56			4.25		Jan-16
50	0.66	14.36	-5.54	34.86		0	2.05	16.26	0.94	12.02	19.0	2	98	0	0	56				1.00	Jan-16
	-2.06	13.96	-2.93	43.23		0	1.05	16.95	0.96	11.83	34.0	2	98	0	0	72					Jan-16
50	-2.17	13.81	-3.12	42.10		0	1.25	16.94	0.96	11.7	34.0	2	98	0	0	72			4.25		Jan-16
50	-2.40	13.36	-3.91	38.89		0	2.05	16.92	0.95	11.37	34.0	2	98	0	0	72				1.00	Jan-16
	-2.50	12.63	-4.16	44.31		0	1.05	16.97	0.96	11.82	34.0	2	98	0	0	72					Jun-16
	-2.14	13.81	-2.93	43.55		0	0.9	16.92	0.95	11.86	34.0	2	98	0	0	72					Jan-16
	0.88	14.93	-4.62	39.05		0.11	1	16.33	0.95	11.39	19.0	2	98	0	0	56					Dec-14
	3.38	17.20	-5.30	29.30		0.45	1.05	17.07	0.98	9.47	17.6	2	98	0	0	51					Jan-16
50	3.29	17.06	-5.49	28.36		0.25	1.3	17.05	0.98	9.4	17.6	2	98	0	0	51			4.25		Jan-16
50	3.01	16.58	-6.24	25.40		0	2.05	17.04	0.98	9.21	17.6	2	98	0	0	51				1.00	Jan-16
	3.39	17.14	-5.30	29.41		0.54	1	17.07	0.98	9.43	17.6	2	98	0	0	51					Dec-14
100	0.41	1.82	1.90	14.75	2.49	2.73	3.33	2.64	4.16	8.56	7.2	30	0	43	27	204	2		5.75		May-11
5,000	0.55	1.96	2.18	15.58	3.97	3	3.08	2.62	3.82	8.59	7.2	30	0	43	27	204	2.21				May-11
1,000	7.67	28.55	17.18	59.26	67.53	0	1.27	14.36	0.93	24.83	37.8	3	97	0	0	5	25.43	-19.21			Mar-10

	MARKET			FUND TYPE, CATEGORY & OBJECTIVE	RATINGS				MINIMUMS	
Fund Name	Ticker Symbol	Traded On	Fund Type	Category and (Prospectus Objective)	Overall Rating	Reward Rating	Risk Rating	Recent Up/ Downgrade	Open to New Investors	Min Initial Investment
Paradigm Micro-Cap Fund	PVIVX	NAS CM	Open End	US Equity Small Cap (Growth)	C	C-	C		Y	2,500
Paradigm Opportunity Fund	PFOPX	NAS CM	Open End	US Equity Small Cap (Growth)	C	C	B-	Down	Y	2,500
Paradigm Select Fund	PFSLX	NAS CM	Open End	US Equity Small Cap (Growth)	C	C	B-	Down	Y	2,500
Paradigm Value Fund	PVFAX	NAS CM	Open End	US Equity Small Cap (Growth)	C	C	B-	Down	Y	2,500
Parametric Commodity Strategy Fund Institutional Class	EIPCX	NAS CM	Open End	Commodities Broad Basket (Growth)	C-	D+	C	Down	Y	50,000
Parametric Commodity Strategy Fund Investor Class	EAPCX	NAS CM	Open End	Commodities Broad Basket (Growth)	C-	D+	C	Down	Y	1,000
Parametric Dividend Income Fund Institutional Class	EIPDX	NAS CM	Open End	US Equity Large Cap Value (Equity-Income)	B-	C	B		Y	50,000
Parametric Dividend Income Fund Investor Class	EAPDX	NAS CM	Open End	US Equity Large Cap Value (Equity-Income)	B-	C	B		Y	1,000
Parametric Emerging Markets Fund Class C	ECEMX	NAS CM	Open End	Global Emerg Mkts (Div Emerging Mkts)	C	C-	B-			1,000
Parametric Emerging Markets Fund Class R6	EREMX	NAS CM	Open End	Global Emerg Mkts (Div Emerging Mkts)	C	C	B-		Y	1,000,000
Parametric Emerging Markets Fund Institutional Class	EIEMX	NAS CM	Open End	Global Emerg Mkts (Div Emerging Mkts)	C	C	B-		Y	50,000
Parametric Emerging Markets Fund Investor Class	EAEMX	NAS CM	Open End	Global Emerg Mkts (Div Emerging Mkts)	C	C	B-		Y	1,000
Parametric International Equity Fund Class R	ERISX	NAS CM	Open End	Global Equity Large Cap (Foreign Stock)	C+	C	B	Up	Y	1,000
Parametric International Equity Fund Class R6	ESISX	NAS CM	Open End	Global Equity Large Cap (Foreign Stock)	C+	C	B	Up	Y	1,000,000
Parametric International Equity Fund Institutional Class	EIISX	NAS CM	Open End	Global Equity Large Cap (Foreign Stock)	C+	C	B	Up	Y	50,000
Parametric International Equity Fund Investor Class	EAISX	NAS CM	Open End	Global Equity Large Cap (Foreign Stock)	C+	C	B	Up	Y	1,000
Parametric Research Affiliates Systematic Alternative Risk	ESATX	NAS CM	Open End	Multialternative (Growth & Income)	D-	D	C		Y	50,000
Parametric Tax-Managed Emerging Markets Institutional Cls	EITEX	NAS CM	Open End	Global Emerg Mkts (Div Emerging Mkts)	C	C	B-		Y	50,000
Parametric Tax-Managed International Equity Fund Class C	ECIGX	NAS CM	Open End	Global Equity Large Cap (Foreign Stock)	C	C	B			1,000
Parametric Tax-Managed Intl Equity Inst Cls	EITIX	NAS CM	Open End	Global Equity Large Cap (Foreign Stock)	C+	C	B	Up	Y	50,000
Parametric Tax-Managed International Equity Investor Cls	ETIGX	NAS CM	Open End	Global Equity Large Cap (Foreign Stock)	C+	C	B	Up	Y	1,000
Parametric Volatility Risk Premium - Defensive Inst Cls	EIVPX	NAS CM	Open End	Long/Short Equity (Growth & Income)	C	C	B		Y	50,000
Parnassus Core Equity Fund - Institutional Shares	PRILX	NAS CM	Open End	US Equity Large Cap Blend (Equity-Income)	B	B-	B+		Y	100,000
Parnassus Core Equity Fund - Investor Shares	PRBLX	NAS CM	Open End	US Equity Large Cap Blend (Equity-Income)	B	B-	B+		Y	2,000
Parnassus Endeavor Fund Institutional Shares	PFPWX	NAS CM	Open End	US Equity Large Cap Growth (Growth)	C	C-	B-	Down	Y	100,000
Parnassus Endeavor Fund Investor Shares	PARWX	NAS CM	Open End	US Equity Large Cap Growth (Growth)	C	C-	B-	Down	Y	2,000
Parnassus Fund	PARNX	NAS CM	Open End	US Equity Large Cap Growth (Growth)	B-	C	B		Y	2,000
Parnassus Fund Institutional Shares	PFPRX	NAS CM	Open End	US Equity Large Cap Growth (Growth)	B-	C	B		Y	100,000
Parnassus Mid Cap Fund	PARMX	NAS CM	Open End	US Equity Mid Cap (Growth)	B	C+	B+		Y	2,000
Parnassus Mid Cap Fund Institutional Shares	PFPMX	NAS CM	Open End	US Equity Mid Cap (Growth)	B	B-	B+		Y	100,000
Parnassus Mid Cap Fund Institutional Shares	TRFAX	NAS CM	Open End	US Equity Large Cap Blend (Growth)	B-	C	B		Y	1,000
Parnassus Mid Cap Fund Institutional Shares	TRFCX	NAS CM	Open End	US Equity Large Cap Blend (Growth)	C+	C	B		Y	1,000
Parnassus Mid Cap Fund Institutional Shares	TRFTX	NAS CM	Open End	US Equity Large Cap Blend (Growth)	B-	C	B		Y	1,000,000
Pax Balanced Fund Class Institutional	PAXIX	NAS CM	Open End	Moderate Alloc (Balanced)	B	C+	A-	Up	Y	250,000
Pax Balanced Fund Individual Investor Class	PAXWX	NAS CM	Open End	Moderate Alloc (Balanced)	B	C	A-	Up	Y	1,000
Pax Ellevate Global Women's Leadership Individual Inv Cls	PXWEX	NAS CM	Open End	Global Equity Large Cap (Growth)	B-	C	B	Up	Y	1,000
Pax Ellevate Global Women's Leadership Institutional Cls	PXWIX	NAS CM	Open End	Global Equity Large Cap (Growth)	B-	C+	B	Up	Y	250,000
Pax ESG Beta Dividend Fund Individual Investor Class	PAXDX	NAS CM	Open End	US Equity Large Cap Blend (Equity-Income)	C+	C	B	Up	Y	1,000
Pax ESG Beta Dividend Fund Institutional Class	PXDIX	NAS CM	Open End	US Equity Large Cap Blend (Equity-Income)	C+	C	B	Up	Y	250,000
Pax ESG Beta Quality Fund Class A	PXGAX	NAS CM	Open End	US Equity Large Cap Growth (Growth)	B-	C	B+	Down	Y	1,000
Pax ESG Beta Quality Fund Individual Investor Class	PXWGX	NAS CM	Open End	US Equity Large Cap Growth (Growth)	B-	C	B+	Down	Y	1,000
Pax ESG Beta Quality Fund Institutional Class	PWGIX	NAS CM	Open End	US Equity Large Cap Growth (Growth)	B-	C	B+	Down	Y	250,000
Pax Global Environmental Markets Fund Class A	PXEAX	NAS CM	Open End	Global Equity Large Cap (Growth)	C+	C	B		Y	1,000
Pax Global Environmental Markets Individual Investor Cls	PGRNX	NAS CM	Open End	Global Equity Large Cap (Growth)	C+	C	B		Y	1,000
Pax Global Environmental Markets Fund Institutional Class	PGINX	NAS CM	Open End	Global Equity Large Cap (Growth)	C+	C	B		Y	250,000
Pax Global Opportunities Fund Institutional Class	PXGOX	NAS CM	Open End	Global Equity Large Cap (Growth)	D	D+	C+		Y	250,000
Pax Global Opportunities Fund Investor Class	PAXGX	NAS CM	Open End	Global Equity Large Cap (Growth)	D	D+	C+		Y	1,000
Pax Large Cap Fund Individual Investor Class	PAXLX	NAS CM	Open End	US Equity Large Cap Blend (Growth)	C+	C	B	Up	Y	1,000
Pax Large Cap Fund Institutional Class	PXLIX	NAS CM	Open End	US Equity Large Cap Blend (Growth)	C+	C	B	Up	Y	250,000
Pax Mid Cap Fund Individual Investor Class	PWMDX	NAS CM	Open End	US Equity Mid Cap (Growth)	C+	C	B	Up	Y	1,000
Pax Mid Cap Fund Institutional Class	PMIDX	NAS CM	Open End	US Equity Mid Cap (Growth)	C+	C	B	Up	Y	250,000
Pax MSCI EAFE ESG Leaders Index Individual Investor Cls	PXINX	NAS CM	Open End	Global Equity Large Cap (Pacific Stock)	C	C	B		Y	1,000

★ Expanded analysis of this fund is included in Section II.

	TOTAL RETURNS					PERFORMANCE				ASSETS		ASSET ALLOCATION & TURNOVER					BULL & BEAR		FEES		
Min Additional Investment	3-Month Total Return	6-Month Total Return	1-Year Total Return	3-Year Total Return	5-Year Total Return	Dividend Yield (TTM)	Expense Ratio	3-Yr Std Deviation	3-Year Beta	NAV	Total Assets (MIL)	%Cash	%Stocks	%Bonds	%Other	Turnover Ratio	Last Bull Market Total Return	Last Bear Market Total Return	Front End Fee (%)	Back End Fee (%)	Inception Date
100	-6.82	10.13	-14.65	46.15	42.54	0	1.26	20.09	1.02	27.59	48.3	5	95	0	0	111	22.4	-21.21			Dec-07
100	2.00	13.14	-3.22	47.12	35.75	0	1.26	15.65	0.82	42.27	9.3	2	98	0	0	19	20.11	-19.05			Jan-05
100	2.33	20.51	2.38	48.68	44.62	0	1.16	16.34	0.98	39.07	28.3	6	94	0	0	20	24.25	-18.82			Jan-05
100	1.62	13.26	-0.52	53.61	41.77	0	1.51	16.22	0.88	47.04	52.8	4	96	0	0	21	21.04	-21.56			Dec-02
	-1.33	4.45	-3.97	2.53	-28.72	0.83	0.65	7.56	0.78	5.16	317.9	14	0	84	2	0	1.77				May-11
	-1.35	4.49	-4.27	1.70	-29.57	0.39	0.9	7.56	0.79	5.11	317.9	14	0	84	2	0	1.68				Jan-12
	1.90	15.19	4.66	33.01	51.62	2.66	0.4	12.16	0.99	13	54.6	0	100	0	0	77					Mar-14
	1.83	14.97	4.40	32.08	49.74	2.42	0.65	12.16	0.99	12.98	54.6	0	100	0	0	77					Mar-14
	1.65	9.11	0.62	20.95	-3.84	1.29	2.19	11.62	0.81	14.12	1,345	0	99	0	0	2	15.55	-24.93		1.00	Jun-06
	1.82	9.62	1.60	24.72	1.21	2.42	1.13	11.61	0.81	14.47	1,345	0	99	0	0	2	16.15	-24.57			Jul-14
	1.82	9.61	1.65	24.58	1.05	2.34	1.19	11.59	0.81	14.48	1,345	0	99	0	0	2	16.15	-24.57			Jun-06
	1.76	9.48	1.38	23.61	-0.22	1.96	1.44	11.59	0.81	14.43	1,345	0	99	0	0	2	16.01	-24.69			Jun-06
	3.57	14.32	1.64	29.50	17.33	1.44	1	10.5	0.92	13.33	438.9	1	99	0	0	30	12.05	-21.32			Aug-15
	3.77	14.62	2.14	31.54	20.34	1.81	0.47	10.53	0.93	13.48	438.9	1	99	0	0	30	12.37	-21.16			Aug-15
	3.76	14.71	2.17	31.47	20.26	1.76	0.5	10.58	0.93	13.49	438.9	1	99	0	0	30	12.37	-21.16			Apr-10
	3.70	14.50	1.92	30.59	18.78	1.55	0.75	10.51	0.93	13.42	438.9	1	99	0	0	30	12.11	-21.28			Apr-10
	-1.05	5.52					0.99			9.35	23.5										Aug-18
	2.06	9.79	2.12	25.43	2.41	2.07	0.95	11.48	0.8	48.52	2,343	1	99	0	0	6	16.56	-24.15			Jun-98
	3.64	13.83	1.11	25.70	11.97	0.81	1.8	10.48	0.92	10.53	37.0	1	99	0	0	30	17.86	-28.11		1.00	Apr-98
	3.83	14.31	2.05	29.45	17.64	1.8	0.8	10.47	0.92	11.1	37.0	1	99	0	0	30	18.66	-27.75			Sep-08
	3.72	14.15	1.74	28.45	16.10	1.52	1.05	10.47	0.92	11.13	37.0	1	99	0	0	30	18.37	-27.82			Apr-98
	1.79	9.55	4.60			1.14	0.52			11.35	584.2	15	52	34	0	55					Feb-17
50	6.12	21.30	17.43	52.37	63.97	0.93	0.63	10.97	0.86	46.76	17,021	3	97	0	0	31	20.6	-14.65			Apr-06
50	6.07	21.20	17.21	51.44	62.31	0.72	0.87	10.98	0.86	46.7	17,021	3	97	0	0	31	20.51	-14.79			Aug-92
50	-0.02	19.52	3.56	48.95	68.79	1.64	0.72	17.64	1.36	34.22	4,002	17	83	0	0	71	29.6	-19.94			Apr-15
50	-0.08	19.39	3.28	47.98	67.27	1.4	0.95	17.65	1.36	34.16	4,002	17	83	0	0	71	29.6	-19.94			Apr-05
50	4.26	21.15	11.08	47.26	52.30	1.04	0.85	13.14	0.99	48.68	951.8	2	98	0	0	47	35.21	-25.88			Dec-84
50	4.28	21.24	11.27	47.94	53.25	1.2	0.69	13.13	0.99	48.69	951.8	2	98	0	0	47	35.21	-25.88			Apr-15
50	4.95	23.03	12.00	42.84	57.84	0.61	0.99	11.27	0.8	35.15	3,771	5	95	0	0	32	26.64	-20.42			Apr-05
50	4.97	23.10	12.22	43.74	59.32	0.81	0.75	11.24	0.8	35.22	3,771	5	95	0	0	32	26.64	-20.42			Apr-15
100	2.24	15.88	5.27	35.45	50.33	0	2.46	12.3	0.99	16.85	3,771	1	99	0	0	45			5.75		Mar-12
100	2.06	15.53	4.49	32.45	44.86	0	3.21	12.3	0.99	15.84	3,771	1	99	0	0	45					Mar-12
25,000	2.31	16.08	5.52	36.56	52.37	0	2.21	12.28	0.99	17.25	3,771	1	99	0	0	45					Mar-12
	3.78	13.16	7.60	27.81	33.93	1.74	0.66	7.34	0.58	23.84	1,810	2	59	38	0	12	17.64	-15.77			Apr-07
50	3.72	13.00	7.35	26.75	32.22	1.52	0.91	7.35	0.58	23.46	1,810	2	59	38	0	12	17.51	-15.86			Aug-71
50	4.91	19.25	8.59	43.25	42.87	1.77	0.81	11.18		25.71	356.4	0	100	0	0	67	19.47	-22.24			Oct-93
	5.00	19.37	8.86	44.39	44.65	1.99	0.56	11.2		25.84	356.4	0	100	0	0	67	19.64	-22.18			Apr-06
50	2.03	15.67	8.94			1.96	0.9			12.09	130.0	1	99	0	0	52					Dec-16
	2.14	15.86	9.26			2.17	0.65			12.12	130.0	1	99	0	0	52					Dec-16
50	2.83	16.33	9.08	44.97	55.29	1.57	0.9	11.4	0.92	19.88	224.1	1	99	0	0	55	24.02	-20.08	5.50		May-13
50	2.82	16.28	9.05	44.95	55.25	1.56	0.9	11.44	0.92	19.93	224.1	1	99	0	0	55	24.02	-20.08			Jun-97
	2.90	16.45	9.33	46.09	57.24	1.75	0.65	11.4	0.92	20.53	224.1	1	99	0	0	55	24.22	-20.02			Apr-07
50	4.75	21.10	8.41	40.50	33.89	0.65	1.24	13.49	1.12	15.83	840.4	3	97	0	0	26	22.48	-23.73	5.50		May-13
50	4.75	21.15	8.48	40.55	33.91	0.66	1.24	13.5	1.12	15.86	840.4	3	97	0	0	26	22.46	-23.7			Mar-08
	4.77	21.31	8.70	41.63	35.61	0.89	0.99	13.51	1.12	15.96	840.4	3	97	0	0	26	22.66	-23.65			Mar-08
	7.94	26.70	15.51			0.32	0.92			11.48	32.1	3	97	0	0	17					Jun-18
50	7.87	26.62	15.45			0.27	1.16			11.48	32.1	3	97	0	0	17					Jun-18
50	4.94	19.69	9.28			0.69	0.96			9.42	673.9	2	98	0	0	54					Dec-16
	4.94	19.80	9.52			0.88	0.7			9.43	673.9	2	98	0	0	54					Dec-16
50	4.23	18.71	3.04	23.35		0.3	1.18	11.17	0.81	10.4	89.0	5	95	0	0	50					Mar-16
	4.43	18.94	3.30	24.31		0.43	0.93	11.17	0.81	10.42	89.0	5	95	0	0	50					Mar-16
50	4.15	14.02	1.66	26.15	8.93	2.17	0.8	10.85	0.98	8.88	591.4	0	100	0	0	30	12.41	-21.2			Mar-14

	MARKET			FUND TYPE, CATEGORY & OBJECTIVE	RATINGS				MINIMUMS	
Fund Name	Ticker Symbol	Traded On	Fund Type	Category and (Prospectus Objective)	Overall Rating	Reward Rating	Risk Rating	Recent Up/ Downgrade	Open to New Investors	Min Initial Investment
Pax MSCI EAFE ESG Leaders Index Fund Institutional Class	PXNIX	NAS CM	Open End	Global Equity Large Cap (Pacific Stock)	C	C	B		Y	250,000
Pax Small Cap Fund Class A	PXSAX	NAS CM	Open End	US Equity Small Cap (Small Company)	C	C	B-		Y	1,000
Pax Small Cap Fund Individual Investor Class	PXSCX	NAS CM	Open End	US Equity Small Cap (Small Company)	C	C	B-		Y	1,000
Pax Small Cap Fund Institutional Class	PXSIX	NAS CM	Open End	US Equity Small Cap (Small Company)	C	C	B-		Y	250,000
Payden Equity Income Fund	PYVLX	NAS CM	Open End	US Equity Large Cap Value (Growth & Income)	B-	C+	B+		Y	100,000
Payden Equity Income Fund Adviser Class	PYVAX	NAS CM	Open End	US Equity Large Cap Value (Growth & Income)	B-	C+	B		Y	5,000
Payden Equity Income Fund SI Class	PYVSX	NAS CM	Open End	US Equity Large Cap Value (Growth & Income)	B-	C+	B+		Y	50,000,000
Payson Total Return Fund	PBFDX	NAS CM	Open End	US Equity Large Cap Blend (Growth & Income)	B-	C	B	Down	Y	2,000
PCS Commodity Strategy Fund Class A	PCYAX	NAS CM	Open End	Commodities Broad Basket (Growth)	C-	D+	C		Y	5,000
PCS Commodity Strategy Fund Class C	PCYCX	NAS CM	Open End	Commodities Broad Basket (Growth)	C-	D+	C-	Up	Y	5,000
PCS Commodity Strategy Fund Class I	PCYIX	NAS CM	Open End	Commodities Broad Basket (Growth)	C-	D+	C		Y	5,000,000
Pear Tree Axiom Emerging Mkts World Equity Inst Cls	QEMAX	NAS CM	Open End	Global Emerg Mkts (Div Emerging Mkts)	C	C	C+		Y	1,000,000
Pear Tree Axiom Emerging Markets World Equity Ordinary Cls	QFFOX	NAS CM	Open End	Global Emerg Mkts (Div Emerging Mkts)	C	C-	C+		Y	2,500
Pear Tree Axiom Emerging Markets World Equity R6 Shares	QFFRX	NAS CM	Open End	Global Emerg Mkts (Div Emerging Mkts)	C	C-	C+		Y	100,000
Pear Tree PNC International Small Cap Institutional Shares	QISIX	NAS CM	Open End	Global Equity Mid/Small Cap (Small Company)	U	U	U		Y	1,000,000
Pear Tree PNC International Small Cap Fund Ordinary Shares	QISOX	NAS CM	Open End	Global Equity Mid/Small Cap (Small Company)	U	U	U		Y	2,500
Pear Tree PNC International Small Cap Fund R6 Shares	QISRX	NAS CM	Open End	Global Equity Mid/Small Cap (Small Company)	U	U	U		Y	100,000
Pear Tree Polaris Foreign Value Fund Class Institutional	QFVIX	NAS CM	Open End	Global Equity Large Cap (Foreign Stock)	C	C	B-		Y	1,000,000
Pear Tree Polaris Foreign Value Fund Class Ordinary	QFVOX	NAS CM	Open End	Global Equity Large Cap (Foreign Stock)	C	C-	B-		Y	2,500
Pear Tree Polaris Foreign Value Fund Class R6	QFVRX	NAS CM	Open End	Global Equity Large Cap (Foreign Stock)	C	C	B-		Y	100,000
Pear Tree Polaris Foreign Value Small Cap Fund Class R6	QUSRX	NAS CM	Open End	Global Equity Mid/Small Cap (Foreign Stock)	C	C-	C		Y	100,000
Pear Tree Polaris Foreign Value Small Cap Inst Cls	QUSIX	NAS CM	Open End	Global Equity Mid/Small Cap (Foreign Stock)	C	C-	C		Y	1,000,000
Pear Tree Polaris Foreign Value Small Cap Ordinary Cls	QUSOX	NAS CM	Open End	Global Equity Mid/Small Cap (Foreign Stock)	C	C-	C	Up	Y	2,500
Pear Tree Polaris Small Cap Fund Institutional Class	QBNAX	NAS CM	Open End	US Equity Small Cap (Small Company)	C	C-	C+		Y	1,000,000
Pear Tree Polaris Small Cap Fund Ordinary Class	USBNX	NAS CM	Open End	US Equity Small Cap (Small Company)	C	C-	C+		Y	2,500
Pear Tree Quality Fund Institutional Shares	QGIAX	NAS CM	Open End	US Equity Large Cap Blend (Growth)	B-	C+	B	Down	Y	1,000,000
Pear Tree Quality Fund Ordinary Shares	USBOX	NAS CM	Open End	US Equity Large Cap Blend (Growth)	B-	C+	B	Down	Y	2,500
Penn Capital Managed Alpha SMID Cap Equity Inst Cls	PSMPX	NAS CM	Open End	US Equity Mid Cap (Growth & Income)	C+	C	B-		Y	2,500
Penn Capital Special Situations Small Cap Equity Inst Cls	PSCNX	NAS CM	Open End	US Equity Small Cap (Small Company)	C	D+	C+		Y	2,500
Perkins Discovery Fund	PDFDX	NAS CM	Open End	US Equity Small Cap (Aggr Growth)	C+	C	B-	Down	Y	2,500
Permanent Portfolio Aggressive Growth Portfolio Class A	PAGDX	NAS CM	Open End	US Equity Large Cap Growth (Aggr Growth)	C	C	B-	Down	Y	1,000
Permanent Portfolio Aggressive Growth Portfolio Class C	PAGHX	NAS CM	Open End	US Equity Large Cap Growth (Aggr Growth)	C	C-	C+	Down	Y	1,000
Permanent Portfolio Aggressive Growth Portfolio Class I	PAGRX	NAS CM	Open End	US Equity Large Cap Growth (Aggr Growth)	C	C	B-	Down	Y	1,000
Permanent Portfolio Permanent Portfolio Class A	PRPDX	NAS CM	Open End	Cautious Alloc (Multi-Asset Global)	B-	C	B+	Up	Y	1,000
Permanent Portfolio Permanent Portfolio Class C	PRPHX	NAS CM	Open End	Cautious Alloc (Multi-Asset Global)	C+	C	B		Y	1,000
Permanent Portfolio Permanent Portfolio Class I	PRPFX	NAS CM	Open End	Cautious Alloc (Multi-Asset Global)	B-	C	B+	Up	Y	1,000
Perritt MicroCap Opportunities Fund Investor Class	PRCGX	NAS CM	Open End	US Equity Small Cap (Growth)	D+	D	D+	Down	Y	1,000
Perritt Ultra MicroCap Fund	PREOX	NAS CM	Open End	US Equity Small Cap (Growth)	C-	D+	C	Down	Y	1,000
Persimmon Long/Short Fund Class A Shares	LSEAX	NAS CM	Open End	Long/Short Equity (Growth)	U	U	U		Y	2,500
Persimmon Long/Short Fund Class I Shares	LSEIX	NAS CM	Open End	Long/Short Equity (Growth)	C	C-	C	Up	Y	100,000
PF Developing Growth Fund Class P			Open End	US Equity Small Cap (Small Company)	C+	C+	C+	Down	Y	0
PF Emerging Markets Fund Class P			Open End	Global Emerg Mkts (Div Emerging Mkts)	C	C	B-		Y	0
PF Growth Fund Class P			Open End	US Equity Large Cap Growth (Growth)	B	B-	B		Y	0
PF International Large-Cap Fund Class P			Open End	Global Equity Large Cap (Foreign Stock)	C+	C	B	Up	Y	0
PF International Small-Cap Fund Class P			Open End	Global Equity Mid/Small Cap (Small Company)	C	C-	C	Up	Y	0
PF International Value Fund Class P			Open End	Global Equity Large Cap (Foreign Stock)	C	C-	C		Y	0
PF Large-Cap Value Fund Class P			Open End	US Equity Large Cap Value (Growth)	B-	C	B	Up	Y	0
PF Mid-Cap Equity Fund Class P			Open End	US Equity Mid Cap (Growth)	C+	C	B		Y	0
PF Multi-Asset Fund Class P			Open End	US Equity Large Cap Blend (Growth)	D	D+	C+		Y	0
PF Real Estate Fund Class P			Open End	Real Estate Sector Equity (Real Estate)	C+	C	C+	Down	Y	0
PF Small-Cap Value Fund Class P			Open End	US Equity Small Cap (Small Company)	C	C-	C		Y	0
PFM Multi-Manager Domestic Equity Fund Institutional Class			Open End	US Equity Large Cap Blend (Growth)	D+	D+	B-		Y	1,000,000

★ Expanded analysis of this fund is included in Section II.

Min Additional Investment	TOTAL RETURNS: 3-Month Total Return	6-Month Total Return	1-Year Total Return	3-Year Total Return	5-Year Total Return	PERFORMANCE: Dividend Yield (TTM)	Expense Ratio	3-Yr Std Deviation	3-Year Beta	ASSETS: NAV	Total Assets (MIL)	ASSET ALLOCATION & TURNOVER: %Cash	%Stocks	%Bonds	%Other	Turnover Ratio	BULL & BEAR: Last Bull Market Total Return	Last Bear Market Total Return	FEES: Front End Fee (%)	Back End Fee (%)	Inception Date
	4.36	14.17	1.98	27.10	10.38	2.47	0.55	10.9	0.98	8.71	591.4	0	100	0	0	30	12.58	-21.12			Jan-11
50	4.31	18.65	-2.67	22.98	23.31	0.87	1.18	13.02	0.71	13.93	447.7	3	97	0	0	57	23.74	-23.91	5.50		May-13
50	4.29	18.69	-2.62	23.07	23.40	0.85	1.18	13.03	0.71	13.97	447.7	3	97	0	0	57	23.74	-23.91			Mar-08
	4.37	18.82	-2.36	24.04	24.96	1.11	0.93	13	0.71	14.1	447.7	3	97	0	0	57	23.92	-23.83			Mar-08
250	4.27	18.94	10.33	35.50	51.91	1.97	0.74	10.84	0.87	17.51	1,358	3	92	3	0	42	19.63	-5.55			Nov-96
250	4.22	18.81	10.09	34.48	50.05	1.76	0.99	10.83	0.86	17.5	1,358	3	92	3	0	42	19.47	-5.65			Dec-11
250	4.29	19.06	10.48	35.98	52.86	2.04	0.65	10.82	0.86	17.52	1,358	3	92	3	0	42	19.63	-5.55			Aug-14
250	3.43	18.61	10.33	55.13	51.14	0.65	0.94	11.89	0.95	20	112.9	2	99	0	0	27	24.54	-14.51			Nov-91
500	-1.62	6.77	-9.12	-0.80		4.77	1.35	9.84	1.06	7.25	45.6	81	0	19	0	0			5.50		Dec-14
500	-1.66	6.45	-9.72	-2.96		4.15	2.1	9.88	1.06	7.09	45.6	81	0	19	0	0				1.00	Dec-14
10,000	-1.48	7.03	-8.90	-0.05		5.05	1.1	9.93	1.07	7.3	45.6	81	0	19	0	0					Dec-14
50	2.22	13.60	3.95	21.05	-0.58	2.47	1.06	13.38	0.93	21.63	92.3	0	99	0	0	172	17.42	-24.95			Apr-96
50	2.10	13.41	3.58	19.75	-2.16	2.1	1.44	13.39	0.93	21.3	92.3	0	99	0	0	172	17.27	-25.03			Sep-94
	2.19	13.62	3.77	19.96	-1.98		0.99	13.38	0.93	10.69	92.3	0	99	0	0	172	17.27	-25.03			Jan-19
50	3.86						1.45			11.01	11.1	2	98	0	0	22					Jan-19
50	3.67						1.82			10.99	11.1	2	98	0	0	22					Jan-19
	3.86						1.42			11.01	11.1	2	98	0	0	22					Jan-19
50	1.78	11.59	-2.41	38.20	15.09	0.96	1.04	12.66	1.08	21.08	3,661	3	97	0	0	12	15.88	-23.58			Dec-98
50	1.68	11.33	-2.78	36.76	13.31	0.52	1.41	12.68	1.09	21.12	3,661	3	97	0	0	12	15.72	-23.65			May-98
	1.82	11.69	-2.31	38.15	14.47	1.85	0.94	12.67	1.09	11.17	3,661	3	97	0	0	12	15.72	-23.65			Feb-17
	-0.09	9.98	-7.26	27.58	14.81	2.96	1.02	11.7	0.94	10.24	1,079	2	98	0	0	52	13.73	-22.06			Feb-17
50	-0.07	10.06	-7.24	27.59	14.82	2.22	1.05	11.69	0.94	13.56	1,079	2	98	0	0	52	13.72	-22.06			May-08
50	-0.14	9.81	-7.62	26.31	13.04	1.72	1.42	11.69	0.94	13.54	1,079	2	98	0	0	52	13.63	-22.18			May-08
50	1.60	14.01	-3.59	31.46	27.77	0.34	1.18	16.95	0.97	29.13	118.2	1	99	0	0	24	30.77	-21.6			Jan-93
50	1.54	13.79	-3.94	30.15	25.85	0.05	1.55	16.99	0.98	24.34	118.2	1	99	0	0	24	30.63	-21.69			Aug-92
50	3.41	18.37	14.04	54.26	75.00	0.78	0.92	11.58	0.88	20.87	140.5	3	97	0	0	57	20.5	-7.76			Mar-91
50	3.32	18.13	13.66	52.68	72.36	0.55	1.29	11.58	0.88	19.28	140.5	3	97	0	0	57	20.12	-7.85			May-85
100	4.01	20.53	3.64	49.94		0	1.07	15.47	0.97	12.68	14.4	4	96	0	0	64					Nov-15
100	-1.29	18.86	-7.68	36.22		0	1.09	19.85	1.13	10.65	10.2	1	99	0	0	105					Dec-15
100	0.94	25.94	12.89	91.97	48.96	0	2.5	19.77	0.93	57.71	26.9	8	92	0	0	26	11.63	-26.71			Apr-98
100	-0.20	20.21	1.17	43.54	27.75	0.08	1.48	18.74	1.33	59.28	27.7	-1	101	0	0	10	25.72	-25.33	5.00		May-16
100	-0.37	19.78	0.42	40.39	23.09	0	2.23	18.73	1.33	58.18	27.7	-1	101	0	0	10	25.17	-25.56		1.00	May-16
100	-0.13	20.39	1.43	44.66	29.39	0.17	1.23	18.73	1.33	59.51	27.7	-1	101	0	0	10	25.9	-25.25			Jan-90
100	2.50	10.85	4.10	13.54	11.08	0.56	1.09	7.19	58.29	39.63	1,946	1	38	34	27	19	8.05	-8.4	5.00		May-16
100	2.29	10.40	3.31	10.97	6.97	0.03	1.84	7.19	57.99	39.17	1,946	1	38	34	27	19	7.58	-8.68		1.00	May-16
100	2.55	10.97	4.34	14.35	12.44	0.75	0.84	7.19	58.34	39.75	1,946	1	38	34	27	19	8.21	-8.3			Dec-82
50	-3.57	5.15	-19.66	18.01	7.97	0	1.28	18.02	0.97	22.65	126.4	4	96	0	0	14	30.85	-28.97			May-88
50	-0.35	12.98	-9.14	24.38	17.97	0	1.72	14.67	0.73	14.1	44.9	5	95	0	0	28	16.44	-22.66			Aug-04
100	1.88	-4.53	-2.28	8.41		0	3.27	5.63	0.41		28.3	81	19	0	0	214			5.00		Dec-12
100	1.39	3.77	-2.57	10.37	9.84	0	3.48	7.01	0.42	10.18	28.8	6	94	0	0	263					Dec-12
	9.12	40.65	18.70	106.42	73.99	0	0.75	19.88	1.04	20.1	16.5	1	99	0	0	127	28.97	-26.08			Sep-01
	3.33	16.56	3.86	45.09	15.43	0.52	0.95	13.64	0.95	15.2	85.1	4	96	0	0	46	18.34	-23.22			Sep-05
	6.69	27.24	15.02	75.02	97.88	0.02	0.7	13.49	0.98	29	185.9	1	99	0	0	28	24.39	-18.38			Sep-01
	6.62	19.24	7.39	42.41	24.22	1.18	1	11.22	0.98	12.39	58.9	1	99	0	0	41	19.09	-23.45			Sep-01
	0.10	10.72	-9.38	22.80		0.48	1.1	12.86	1.02	9.6	29.9	0	100	0	0	50					Jan-15
	1.99	9.11	-2.06	28.02	1.22	3.77	0.8	12.24	1.04	7.66	63.7	3	97	0	0	54	14.64	-24.75			Sep-01
	5.43	19.65	9.81	36.62	40.39	0.92	0.8	12.4	1	12.6	172.3	1	99	0	0	43	25.81	-16.37			Sep-01
	3.45	22.19	6.14	52.78	59.30	0.19	0.8	14.25	1.04	11.67	10.3	2	98	0	0	119	22.5	-21.46			Dec-04
	4.48	20.30	7.82			1.25	0.51			10.25	1,118	9	0	93	-3	75					Jan-18
	3.01	21.79	14.52	13.08	39.16	1.48	1.05	13.05	0.61	12.63	78.1	1	99	0	0	104	31.67	-18			Dec-04
	2.80	15.77	-7.17	32.13	36.60	0.27	0.9	18.12	1.03	8.44	69.8	2	98	0	0	56	21.9	-18.45			Jun-07
0	3.91	19.18	7.83			0	0.39			10.87	693.1					13					Dec-17

	MARKET		FUND TYPE, CATEGORY & OBJECTIVE		RATINGS				MINIMUMS	
Fund Name	Ticker Symbol	Traded On	Fund Type	Category and (Prospectus Objective)	Overall Rating	Reward Rating	Risk Rating	Recent Up/ Downgrade	Open to New Investors	Min Initial Investment
PFM Multi-Manager International Equity Institutional Cls			Open End	Global Equity Large Cap (Growth)	D+	D	C		Y	1,000,000
PGIM 60/40 Allocation Fund-Class R6	PALDX	NAS CM	Open End	Moderate Alloc (Balanced)	C-	D+	B	Up	Y	0
PGIM Balanced Fund- Class A	PIBAX	NAS CM	Open End	Moderate Alloc (Balanced)	B-	C	B+	Up	Y	2,500
PGIM Balanced Fund- Class B	PBFBX	NAS CM	Open End	Moderate Alloc (Balanced)	B-	C	B+	Up		2,500
PGIM Balanced Fund- Class C	PABCX	NAS CM	Open End	Moderate Alloc (Balanced)	B-	C	B+	Up	Y	2,500
PGIM Balanced Fund- Class R	PALRX	NAS CM	Open End	Moderate Alloc (Balanced)	B-	C	B+	Up	Y	0
PGIM Balanced Fund- Class R6	PIBQX	NAS CM	Open End	Moderate Alloc (Balanced)	B-	C	A-	Up	Y	0
PGIM Balanced Fund- Class Z	PABFX	NAS CM	Open End	Moderate Alloc (Balanced)	B-	C	B+	Up	Y	0
PGIM Global Real Estate Fund- Class A	PURAX	NAS CM	Open End	Real Estate Sector Equity (Real Estate)	B-	C	B+		Y	2,500
PGIM Global Real Estate Fund- Class B	PURBX	NAS CM	Open End	Real Estate Sector Equity (Real Estate)	B-	C	B	Up		2,500
PGIM Global Real Estate Fund- Class C	PURCX	NAS CM	Open End	Real Estate Sector Equity (Real Estate)	B-	C	B	Up	Y	2,500
PGIM Global Real Estate Fund- Class R	PURRX	NAS CM	Open End	Real Estate Sector Equity (Real Estate)	B-	C	B	Up	Y	0
PGIM Global Real Estate Fund- Class R2	PUREX	NAS CM	Open End	Real Estate Sector Equity (Real Estate)	B-	C	B+		Y	0
PGIM Global Real Estate Fund- Class R4	PURGX	NAS CM	Open End	Real Estate Sector Equity (Real Estate)	B-	C	B+		Y	0
PGIM Global Real Estate Fund- Class R6	PGRQX	NAS CM	Open End	Real Estate Sector Equity (Real Estate)	B-	C+	B+		Y	0
PGIM Global Real Estate Fund- Class Z	PURZX	NAS CM	Open End	Real Estate Sector Equity (Real Estate)	B-	C	B+		Y	0
PGIM Income Builder Fund-Class A	PCGAX	NAS CM	Open End	Moderate Alloc (Growth & Income)	B-	C	B		Y	2,500
PGIM Income Builder Fund-Class B	PBCFX	NAS CM	Open End	Moderate Alloc (Growth & Income)	C+	C	B	Down		2,500
PGIM Income Builder Fund-Class C	PCCFX	NAS CM	Open End	Moderate Alloc (Growth & Income)	C+	C	B	Down	Y	2,500
PGIM Income Builder Fund-Class R	PCLRX	NAS CM	Open End	Moderate Alloc (Growth & Income)	B-	C	B		Y	0
PGIM Income Builder Fund-Class R6	PCGQX	NAS CM	Open End	Moderate Alloc (Growth & Income)	B-	C	B+		Y	0
PGIM Income Builder Fund-Class Z	PDCZX	NAS CM	Open End	Moderate Alloc (Growth & Income)	B-	C	B+		Y	0
PGIM Jennison 20/20 Focus Fund- Class A	PTWAX	NAS CM	Open End	US Equity Large Cap Growth (Growth)	C+	C	B	Down	Y	2,500
PGIM Jennison 20/20 Focus Fund- Class B	PTWBX	NAS CM	Open End	US Equity Large Cap Growth (Growth)	C+	C	B			2,500
PGIM Jennison 20/20 Focus Fund- Class C	PTWCX	NAS CM	Open End	US Equity Large Cap Growth (Growth)	C+	C	B		Y	2,500
PGIM Jennison 20/20 Focus Fund- Class R	JTWRX	NAS CM	Open End	US Equity Large Cap Growth (Growth)	C+	C	B	Down	Y	0
PGIM Jennison 20/20 Focus Fund- Class R6	PJTQX	NAS CM	Open End	US Equity Large Cap Growth (Growth)	C+	C	B	Down	Y	0
PGIM Jennison 20/20 Focus Fund- Class Z	PTWZX	NAS CM	Open End	US Equity Large Cap Growth (Growth)	C+	C	B	Down	Y	0
PGIM Jennison Blend Fund- Class A	PBQAX	NAS CM	Open End	US Equity Large Cap Growth (Growth)	C+	C	B-		Y	2,500
PGIM Jennison Blend Fund- Class B	PBQFX	NAS CM	Open End	US Equity Large Cap Growth (Growth)	C+	C	B-	Up		2,500
PGIM Jennison Blend Fund- Class C	PRECX	NAS CM	Open End	US Equity Large Cap Growth (Growth)	C+	C	B-	Up	Y	2,500
PGIM Jennison Blend Fund- Class R6	PBQQX	NAS CM	Open End	US Equity Large Cap Growth (Growth)	C+	C	B-	Up	Y	0
PGIM Jennison Blend Fund- Class Z	PEQZX	NAS CM	Open End	US Equity Large Cap Growth (Growth)	C+	C	B-		Y	0
PGIM Jennison Diversified Growth Fund-Class A	TBDAX	NAS CM	Open End	US Equity Large Cap Growth (Growth)	B-	C	B		Y	2,500
PGIM Jennison Diversified Growth Fund-Class B	TBDBX	NAS CM	Open End	US Equity Large Cap Growth (Growth)	C+	C	B	Down		2,500
PGIM Jennison Diversified Growth Fund-Class C	TBDCX	NAS CM	Open End	US Equity Large Cap Growth (Growth)	C+	C	B	Down	Y	2,500
PGIM Jennison Diversified Growth Fund-Class R6	TBDQX	NAS CM	Open End	US Equity Large Cap Growth (Growth)	B-	C	B		Y	0
PGIM Jennison Diversified Growth Fund-Class Z	TBDZX	NAS CM	Open End	US Equity Large Cap Growth (Growth)	B-	C	B		Y	0
PGIM Jennison Emerging Mkts Equity Opp Fund- Cls A	PDEAX	NAS CM	Open End	Global Emerg Mkts (Div Emerging Mkts)	C	C	C		Y	2,500
PGIM Jennison Emerging Mkts Equity Opp Fund- Cls C	PDECX	NAS CM	Open End	Global Emerg Mkts (Div Emerging Mkts)	C	C	C		Y	2,500
PGIM Jennison Emerging Mkts Equity Opp Fund- Cls R6	PDEQX	NAS CM	Open End	Global Emerg Mkts (Div Emerging Mkts)	C	C	C		Y	0
PGIM Jennison Emerging Mkts Equity Opp Fund- Cls Z	PDEZX	NAS CM	Open End	Global Emerg Mkts (Div Emerging Mkts)	C	C	C		Y	0
PGIM Jennison Equity Income Fund- Class A	SPQAX	NAS CM	Open End	US Equity Large Cap Blend (Equity-Income)	B-	C	B	Up	Y	2,500
PGIM Jennison Equity Income Fund- Class B	JEIBX	NAS CM	Open End	US Equity Large Cap Blend (Equity-Income)	C+	C	B			2,500
PGIM Jennison Equity Income Fund- Class C	AGOCX	NAS CM	Open End	US Equity Large Cap Blend (Equity-Income)	C+	C	B		Y	2,500
PGIM Jennison Equity Income Fund- Class R	PJERX	NAS CM	Open End	US Equity Large Cap Blend (Equity-Income)	C+	C	B		Y	0
PGIM Jennison Equity Income Fund- Class R6	PJIQX	NAS CM	Open End	US Equity Large Cap Blend (Equity-Income)	B-	C	B	Up	Y	0
PGIM Jennison Equity Income Fund- Class Z	JDEZX	NAS CM	Open End	US Equity Large Cap Blend (Equity-Income)	B-	C	B	Up	Y	0
PGIM Jennison Equity Opportunity Fund- Class A	PJIAX	NAS CM	Open End	US Equity Large Cap Blend (Growth)	C	C	C+		Y	2,500
PGIM Jennison Equity Opportunity Fund- Class B	PJIBX	NAS CM	Open End	US Equity Large Cap Blend (Growth)	C	C-	C+			2,500
PGIM Jennison Equity Opportunity Fund- Class C	PJGCX	NAS CM	Open End	US Equity Large Cap Blend (Growth)	C	C-	C+		Y	2,500
PGIM Jennison Equity Opportunity Fund- Class R	PJORX	NAS CM	Open End	US Equity Large Cap Blend (Growth)	C	C-	C+		Y	0

★Expanded analysis of this fund is included in Section II.

	TOTAL RETURNS					PERFORMANCE				ASSETS		ASSET ALLOCATION & TURNOVER					BULL & BEAR		FEES		
Min Additional Investment	3-Month Total Return	6-Month Total Return	1-Year Total Return	3-Year Total Return	5-Year Total Return	Dividend Yield (TTM)	Expense Ratio	3-Yr Std Deviation	3-Year Beta	NAV	Total Assets (MIL)	%Cash	%Stocks	%Bonds	%Other	Turnover Ratio	Last Bull Market Total Return	Last Bear Market Total Return	Front End Fee (%)	Back End Fee (%)	Inception Date
0	3.78	14.57	-0.31			0	0.67			9.59	376.6					21					Dec-17
	3.87	14.47	8.17			3.14	0.4			10.99	16.0	3	57	40	0						Sep-17
100	2.84	12.40	5.23	27.04	34.74	1.52	1	8.02		15.51	924.4	2	59	39	0	145	16.09	-10.51	5.50		Nov-96
100	2.50	11.76	4.09	23.72	29.39	0.46	1.97	8.01		15.61	924.4	2	59	39	0	145	15.63	-10.79		5.00	Nov-96
100	2.62	11.95	4.41	24.35	30.06	0.8	1.79	7.99		15.61	924.4	2	59	39	0	145	15.63	-10.79		1.00	Nov-96
	2.67	12.09	4.56	25.50	32.63	0.93	1.47	8.04		15.52	924.4	2	59	39	0	145	15.96	-10.59			Dec-04
	2.98	12.62	5.64	28.38	37.00	1.85	0.65	8.02		15.64	924.4	2	59	39	0	145	16.24	-10.45			Nov-17
	2.87	12.55	5.52	28.15	36.76	1.74	0.79	8.02		15.63	924.4	2	59	39	0	145	16.24	-10.45			Jan-93
100	0.83	17.43	10.88	17.99	25.82	2.05	1.46	11.06	0.99	25.62	1,922	0	98	0	2	57	24.51	-18.99	5.50		May-98
100	0.61	16.94	9.96	15.41	21.35	1.42	2.21	11.04	0.98	25	1,922	0	98	0	2	57	23.97	-19.22		5.00	May-98
100	0.72	17.16	10.38	16.04	22.02	1.73	1.92	11.08	0.99	25.02	1,922	0	98	0	2	57	23.91	-19.22		1.00	May-98
	0.81	17.37	10.78	17.43	24.73	1.99	1.6	11.05	0.98	25.54	1,922	0	98	0	2	57	24.35	-19.04			Jun-08
	0.88	17.56	11.11	18.46	26.47	2.28	1.3	11.06	0.99	25.73	1,922	0	98	0	2	57	24.57	-18.99			Dec-17
	0.98	17.73	11.41	19.39	28.11	2.52	1.05	11.06	0.99	25.75	1,922	0	98	0	2	57	24.75	-18.91			Dec-17
	1.02	17.86	11.63	20.09	29.30	2.68	0.8	11.08	0.99	25.77	1,922	0	98	0	2	57	24.75	-18.91			Aug-13
	1.02	17.81	11.56	19.62	28.35	2.58	0.93	11.07	0.99	25.78	1,922	0	98	0	2	57	24.75	-18.91			May-98
100	2.49	14.36	7.33	17.89	19.48	4.32	0.95	7.18	0.52	9.67	406.2	4	39	45	0	114	11.73	-6.63	4.50		Nov-98
100	2.35	13.81	6.47	15.22	15.03	3.7	1.7	7.14	0.51	9.47	406.2	4	39	45	0	114	11.22	-7		5.00	Nov-98
100	2.35	13.94	6.47	15.35	15.03	3.7	1.7	7.14	0.52	9.47	406.2	4	39	45	0	114	11.22	-7		1.00	Nov-98
	2.53	14.21	7.08	17.14	18.10	4.09	1.2	7.15	0.51	9.66	406.2	4	39	45	0	114	11.48	-6.73			Oct-04
	2.64	14.53	7.55	18.83	21.04	4.53	0.7	7.11	0.51	9.74	406.2	4	39	45	0	114	11.82	-6.5			Dec-16
	2.64	14.53	7.54	18.78	20.99	4.53	0.7	7.15	0.51	9.74	406.2	4	39	45	0	114	11.82	-6.5			Nov-98
100	3.15	18.21	5.18	53.03	51.19	0.32	1.19	13.23	1.04	14.73	982.7	2	98	0	0	43	20.7	-18.56	5.50		Jul-98
100	2.82	17.42	4.06	49.10	45.24	0	2.15	13.22	1.04	9.84	982.7	2	98	0	0	43	20.2	-18.83		5.00	Jul-98
100	3.01	17.81	4.55	50.01	46.14	0	1.87	13.21	1.04	9.92	982.7	2	98	0	0	43	20.19	-18.76		1.00	Jul-98
	3.11	18.09	4.98	51.97	49.62	0.12	1.45	13.28	1.04	13.9	982.7	2	98	0	0	43	20.55	-18.63			Jun-04
	3.28	18.46	5.65	54.90	54.35	0.57	0.84	13.25	1.04	16.68	982.7	2	98	0	0	43	21	-18.44			Mar-11
	3.25	18.42	5.55	54.49	53.59	0.56	0.87	13.22	1.04	16.52	982.7	2	98	0	0	43	20.86	-18.43			Jul-98
100	3.15	19.38	2.34	47.63	43.41	0.41	0.93	13.58	1.06	20.26	946.3	1	97	2	1	50	23.13	-20.98	5.50		Jan-90
100	2.91	18.81	1.33	43.75	37.71	0	1.91	13.56	1.06	17.68	946.3	1	97	2	1	50	22.62	-21.21		5.00	Mar-82
100	2.89	18.80	1.48	44.23	38.15	0	1.7	13.59	1.07	17.75	946.3	1	97	2	1	50	22.69	-21.21		1.00	Aug-94
	3.20	19.55	2.60	46.78	40.62	0.68	0.66	13.55	1.06	20.3	946.3	1	97	2	1	50	22.62	-21.21			Oct-17
	3.25	19.54	2.65	48.90	45.49	0.68	0.66	13.58	1.07	20.31	946.3	1	97	2	1	50	23.29	-20.81			Mar-96
100	3.74	20.81	7.30	60.61	66.55	0.08	1.2	13.84	1	13.29	243.8	0	100	0	0	185	21.64	-15.44	5.50		Nov-99
100	3.37	20.20	6.21	56.04	59.36	0	2.26	13.82	1	10.71	243.8	0	100	0	0	185	21.33	-15.81		5.00	Nov-99
100	3.26	20.20	6.37	56.79	60.13	0	1.92	13.85	1	10.77	243.8	0	100	0	0	185	21.17	-15.81		1.00	Nov-99
	3.74	21.01	7.56	61.12	67.08	0.3	1	13.84	1	13.3	243.8	0	100	0	0	185	21.64	-15.45			Sep-17
	3.74	21.01	7.56	61.12	67.08	0.3	1	13.84	1	13.3	243.8	0	100	0	0	185	21.64	-15.45			Sep-17
100	2.34	22.53	-0.08	36.25		0	1.45	16.3	1.02	11.8	19.1	2	94	3	1	23			5.50		Sep-14
100	2.24	22.07	-0.78	33.21		0	2.2	16.31	1.03	11.39	19.1	2	94	3	1	23				1.00	Sep-14
	2.48	22.71	0.25	37.39		0	1.2	16.28	1.03	11.94	19.1	2	94	3	1	23					Sep-14
	2.48	22.71	0.25	37.55		0	1.2	16.3	1.03	11.94	19.1	2	94	3	1	23					Sep-14
100	2.64	14.86	7.12	25.76	26.87	2.72	1.13	10.74	0.85	14.28	1,381	2	95	0	0	88	20.01	-17.15	5.50		Apr-04
100	2.48	14.42	6.26	22.76	21.99	2.25	1.93	10.72	0.85	12.9	1,381	2	95	0	0	88	19.49	-17.44		5.00	Apr-04
100	2.45	14.47	6.34	22.96	22.19	2.36	1.85	10.74	0.85	12.85	1,381	2	95	0	0	88	19.63	-17.48		1.00	Dec-97
	2.56	14.70	6.77	24.66	25.13	2.43	1.45	10.72	0.85	14.28	1,381	2	95	0	0	88	19.86	-17.25			Jan-11
	2.73	15.13	7.48	27.08	29.12	3.03	0.8	10.76	0.85	14.29	1,381	2	95	0	0	88	20.31	-17.02			Jan-11
	2.72	15.02	7.42	26.69	28.44	2.98	0.86	10.74	0.85	14.26	1,381	2	95	0	0	88	20.26	-17.11			Aug-08
100	2.14	15.38	-2.50	32.68	26.99	0.44	1.06	15.19	1.19	16.2	288.6	6	94	0	0	59	24.91	-19.94	5.50		Nov-96
100	1.94	14.89	-3.36	29.43	22.10	0	2.03	15.17	1.18	12.57	288.6	6	94	0	0	59	24.44	-20.17		5.00	Nov-96
100	2.02	15.04	-3.16	29.93	22.57	0	1.78	15.19	1.19	12.62	288.6	6	94	0	0	59	24.44	-20.17		1.00	Nov-96
	2.14	15.17	-2.89	31.34	25.19	0.07	1.53	15.25	1.19	13.81	288.6	6	94	0	0	59	24.79	-19.98			Dec-04

	MARKET			FUND TYPE, CATEGORY & OBJECTIVE	RATINGS				MINIMUMS	
Fund Name	Ticker Symbol	Traded On	Fund Type	Category and (Prospectus Objective)	Overall Rating	Reward Rating	Risk Rating	Recent Up/ Downgrade	Open to New Investors	Min Initial Investment
PGIM Jennison Equity Opportunity Fund- Class R6	PJOQX	NAS CM	Open End	US Equity Large Cap Blend (Growth)	C	C	B-		Y	0
PGIM Jennison Equity Opportunity Fund- Class Z	PJGZX	NAS CM	Open End	US Equity Large Cap Blend (Growth)	C	C	B-		Y	0
PGIM Jennison Financial Services Fund- Class A	PFSAX	NAS CM	Open End	Financials Sector Equity (Financial)	C	C	C+	Down	Y	2,500
PGIM Jennison Financial Services Fund- Class B	PUFBX	NAS CM	Open End	Financials Sector Equity (Financial)	C	C	C+	Down		2,500
PGIM Jennison Financial Services Fund- Class C	PUFCX	NAS CM	Open End	Financials Sector Equity (Financial)	C	C	C+	Down	Y	2,500
PGIM Jennison Financial Services Fund- Class R	PSSRX	NAS CM	Open End	Financials Sector Equity (Financial)	C	C	C+	Down	Y	0
PGIM Jennison Financial Services Fund- Class R6	PFSQX	NAS CM	Open End	Financials Sector Equity (Financial)	C	C	C+	Down	Y	0
PGIM Jennison Financial Services Fund- Class Z	PFSZX	NAS CM	Open End	Financials Sector Equity (Financial)	C	C	C+	Down	Y	0
PGIM Jennison Focused Growth Fund-Class A	SPFAX	NAS CM	Open End	US Equity Large Cap Growth (Aggr Growth)	C+	C+	B	Down	Y	2,500
PGIM Jennison Focused Growth Fund-Class B	SPFBX	NAS CM	Open End	US Equity Large Cap Growth (Aggr Growth)	C+	C+	B-	Down		2,500
PGIM Jennison Focused Growth Fund-Class C	SPFCX	NAS CM	Open End	US Equity Large Cap Growth (Aggr Growth)	C+	C+	B-	Down	Y	2,500
PGIM Jennison Focused Growth Fund-Class R6	PSGQX	NAS CM	Open End	US Equity Large Cap Growth (Aggr Growth)	C+	C+	B	Down	Y	0
PGIM Jennison Focused Growth Fund-Class Z	SPFZX	NAS CM	Open End	US Equity Large Cap Growth (Aggr Growth)	C+	C+	B	Down	Y	0
PGIM Jennison Global Infrastructure Fund- Class A	PGJAX	NAS CM	Open End	Infrastructure Sector Equity (Growth & Income)	B-	C+	B		Y	2,500
PGIM Jennison Global Infrastructure Fund- Class C	PGJCX	NAS CM	Open End	Infrastructure Sector Equity (Growth & Income)	B-	C	B		Y	2,500
PGIM Jennison Global Infrastructure Fund- Class R6	PGJQX	NAS CM	Open End	Infrastructure Sector Equity (Growth & Income)	B-	C+	B	Down	Y	0
PGIM Jennison Global Infrastructure Fund- Class Z	PGJZX	NAS CM	Open End	Infrastructure Sector Equity (Growth & Income)	B-	C+	B+	Down	Y	0
PGIM Jennison Global Opportunities Fund-Class A	PRJAX	NAS CM	Open End	Global Equity Large Cap (World Stock)	C+	C+	B-	Down	Y	2,500
PGIM Jennison Global Opportunities Fund-Class C	PRJCX	NAS CM	Open End	Global Equity Large Cap (World Stock)	C+	C	B-	Down	Y	2,500
PGIM Jennison Global Opportunities Fund-Class R2	PRJBX	NAS CM	Open End	Global Equity Large Cap (World Stock)	C+	C+	B-	Down	Y	0
PGIM Jennison Global Opportunities Fund-Class R4	PRJDX	NAS CM	Open End	Global Equity Large Cap (World Stock)	C+	C+	B-	Down	Y	0
PGIM Jennison Global Opportunities Fund-Class R6	PRJQX	NAS CM	Open End	Global Equity Large Cap (World Stock)	C+	C+	B-	Down	Y	0
PGIM Jennison Global Opportunities Fund-Class Z	PRJZX	NAS CM	Open End	Global Equity Large Cap (World Stock)	C+	C+	B-	Down	Y	0
PGIM Jennison Growth Fund- Class A	PJFAX	NAS CM	Open End	US Equity Large Cap Growth (Growth)	C+	C+	B	Down	Y	2,500
PGIM Jennison Growth Fund- Class B	PJFBX	NAS CM	Open End	US Equity Large Cap Growth (Growth)	C+	C	B	Down		2,500
PGIM Jennison Growth Fund- Class C	PJFCX	NAS CM	Open End	US Equity Large Cap Growth (Growth)	C+	C	B	Down	Y	2,500
PGIM Jennison Growth Fund- Class R	PJGRX	NAS CM	Open End	US Equity Large Cap Growth (Growth)	C+	C+	B	Down	Y	0
PGIM Jennison Growth Fund- Class R2	PJFOX	NAS CM	Open End	US Equity Large Cap Growth (Growth)	C+	C+	B	Down	Y	0
PGIM Jennison Growth Fund- Class R4	PJFPX	NAS CM	Open End	US Equity Large Cap Growth (Growth)	C+	C+	B	Down	Y	0
PGIM Jennison Growth Fund- Class R6	PJFQX	NAS CM	Open End	US Equity Large Cap Growth (Growth)	C+	C+	B	Down	Y	0
PGIM Jennison Growth Fund- Class Z	PJFZX	NAS CM	Open End	US Equity Large Cap Growth (Growth)	C+	C+	B	Down	Y	0
PGIM Jennison Health Sciences Fund- Class A	PHLAX	NAS CM	Open End	Healthcare Sector Equity (Health)	C+	C	C+			2,500
PGIM Jennison Health Sciences Fund- Class B	PHLBX	NAS CM	Open End	Healthcare Sector Equity (Health)	C	C	C+	Down		2,500
PGIM Jennison Health Sciences Fund- Class C	PHLCX	NAS CM	Open End	Healthcare Sector Equity (Health)	C	C	C+	Down		2,500
PGIM Jennison Health Sciences Fund- Class R	PJHRX	NAS CM	Open End	Healthcare Sector Equity (Health)	C+	C	C+			0
PGIM Jennison Health Sciences Fund- Class R6	PHLQX	NAS CM	Open End	Healthcare Sector Equity (Health)	C+	C	C+		Y	0
PGIM Jennison Health Sciences Fund- Class Z	PHSZX	NAS CM	Open End	Healthcare Sector Equity (Health)	C+	C	C+			5,000,000
PGIM Jennison International Opportunities Fund- Class A	PWJAX	NAS CM	Open End	Global Equity Large Cap (Foreign Stock)	C	C	C+		Y	2,500
PGIM Jennison International Opportunities Fund- Class C	PWJCX	NAS CM	Open End	Global Equity Large Cap (Foreign Stock)	C	C	C		Y	2,500
PGIM Jennison International Opportunities Fund- Class R	PWJRX	NAS CM	Open End	Global Equity Large Cap (Foreign Stock)	C	C	C		Y	0
PGIM Jennison International Opportunities Fund- Class R6	PWJQX	NAS CM	Open End	Global Equity Large Cap (Foreign Stock)	C	C	C+		Y	0
PGIM Jennison International Opportunities Fund- Class Z	PWJZX	NAS CM	Open End	Global Equity Large Cap (Foreign Stock)	C	C	C+		Y	0
PGIM Jennison International Opportunities Fund-Class R2	PWJBX	NAS CM	Open End	Global Equity Large Cap (Foreign Stock)	C	C	C+		Y	0
PGIM Jennison International Opportunities Fund-Class R4	PWJDX	NAS CM	Open End	Global Equity Large Cap (Foreign Stock)	C	C	C+		Y	0
PGIM Jennison Mid-Cap Growth Fund- Class A	PEEAX	NAS CM	Open End	US Equity Mid Cap (Growth)	B-	C+	B			2,500
PGIM Jennison Mid-Cap Growth Fund- Class B	PEEBX	NAS CM	Open End	US Equity Mid Cap (Growth)	C+	C	B			2,500
PGIM Jennison Mid-Cap Growth Fund- Class C	PEGCX	NAS CM	Open End	US Equity Mid Cap (Growth)	C+	C	B			2,500
PGIM Jennison Mid-Cap Growth Fund- Class R	JDERX	NAS CM	Open End	US Equity Mid Cap (Growth)	B-	C+	B	Up		0
PGIM Jennison Mid-Cap Growth Fund- Class R2	PEGEX	NAS CM	Open End	US Equity Mid Cap (Growth)	B-	C+	B		Y	0
PGIM Jennison Mid-Cap Growth Fund- Class R4	PEGGX	NAS CM	Open End	US Equity Mid Cap (Growth)	B-	C+	B		Y	0
PGIM Jennison Mid-Cap Growth Fund- Class R6	PJGQX	NAS CM	Open End	US Equity Mid Cap (Growth)	B-	C+	B			0
PGIM Jennison Mid-Cap Growth Fund- Class Z	PEGZX	NAS CM	Open End	US Equity Mid Cap (Growth)	B-	C+	B			0

★ Expanded analysis of this fund is included in Section II.

	TOTAL RETURNS					PERFORMANCE				ASSETS		ASSET ALLOCATION & TURNOVER					BULL & BEAR		FEES		
Min Additional Investment	3-Month Total Return	6-Month Total Return	1-Year Total Return	3-Year Total Return	5-Year Total Return	Dividend Yield (TTM)	Expense Ratio	3-Yr Std Deviation	3-Year Beta	NAV	Total Assets (MIL)	%Cash	%Stocks	%Bonds	%Other	Turnover Ratio	Last Bull Market Total Return	Last Bear Market Total Return	Front End Fee (%)	Back End Fee (%)	Inception Date
	2.28	15.61	-2.16	34.22	29.50	0.76	0.72	15.21	1.19	17.03	288.6	6	94	0	0	59	25.2	-19.83			Nov-14
	2.28	15.62	-2.21	33.91	28.90	0.71	0.76	15.19	1.19	17.02	288.6	6	94	0	0	59	25.2	-19.83			Nov-96
100	7.03	22.71	2.93	56.02	9.73	0.21	1.33	15	0.78	14.91	155.1	0	100	0	0	23	27.52	-30.1	5.50		Jun-99
100	6.78	22.18	1.97	52.30	5.60	0	2.31	14.95	0.78	13.22	155.1	0	100	0	0	23	27.04	-30.24		5.00	Jun-99
100	6.84	22.30	2.20	52.87	6.00	0	2.02	14.95	0.78	13.27	155.1	0	100	0	0	23	26.93	-30.24		1.00	Jun-99
	7.04	22.53	2.73	55.13	8.67	0	1.59	14.95	0.78	14.9	155.1	0	100	0	0	23	27.23	-30.19			Feb-12
	7.16	22.90	3.30	57.63	11.55	0.51	1	14.98	0.78	15.4	155.1	0	100	0	0	23	27.71	-29.97			Jan-18
	7.16	22.90	3.30	57.63	11.55	0.51	1.01	14.98	0.78	15.4	155.1	0	100	0	0	23	27.71	-29.97			Jun-99
100	3.67	24.29	8.81	81.15	95.41	0	1.11	15.99	1.12	15.81	666.6	1	99	0	0	52	26.1	-12.95	5.50		Jun-00
100	3.38	23.71	7.86	76.88	87.92	0	1.99	16.01	1.12	12.52	666.6	1	99	0	0	52	25.51	-13.21		5.00	Jun-00
100	3.46	23.81	8.13	77.25	88.32	0	1.83	16.02	1.12	12.53	666.6	1	99	0	0	52	25.51	-13.11		1.00	Jun-00
	3.77	24.52	9.35	82.75	98.18	0	0.67	16.02	1.12	17.06	666.6	1	99	0	0	52	26.31	-12.8			May-12
	3.76	24.56	9.27	82.82	98.07	0	0.75	16.04	1.12	17.09	666.6	1	99	0	0	52	26.31	-12.8			Jun-00
100	4.88	20.63	11.52	26.40	18.04	1.67	1.5	10.27	0.58	14.33	49.0	1	99	0	0	75			5.50		Sep-13
100	4.68	20.12	10.72	23.56	13.71	1.01	2.25	10.26	0.58	14.2	49.0	1	99	0	0	75				1.00	Sep-13
	4.95	20.81	11.92	27.44	19.54	1.93	1.17	10.26	0.58	14.34	49.0	1	99	0	0	75					Dec-16
	5.03	20.80	11.91	27.50	19.59	1.92	1.17	10.25	0.58	14.35	49.0	1	99	0	0	75					Sep-13
100	3.94	24.54	7.16	77.33	85.80	0	1.08	15.78	1.22	25.27	2,417	1	99	0	0	62			5.50		Mar-12
100	3.77	24.03	6.27	73.24	78.81	0	1.94	15.79	1.22	23.89	2,417	1	99	0	0	62				1.00	Mar-12
	3.91	24.39	7.02	77.11	85.64		1.34	15.77	1.22	25.75	2,417	1	99	0	0	62					Dec-18
	3.99	24.54	7.28	78.43	87.95		1.09	15.78	1.22	25.78	2,417	1	99	0	0	62					Dec-18
	4.07	24.73	7.44	79.18	89.01	0	0.84	15.78	1.22	25.82	2,417	1	99	0	0	62					Dec-14
	4.04	24.62	7.34	78.54	88.07	0	0.92	15.78	1.22	25.71	2,417	1	99	0	0	62					Mar-12
100	2.92	22.11	7.71	73.11	87.08	0	1.02	15	1.08	40.86	5,415	1	99	0	0	40	27.01	-14	5.50		Nov-95
100	2.70	21.54	6.70	68.80	79.94	0	1.95	15	1.08	31.93	5,415	1	99	0	0	40	26.57	-14.26		5.00	Nov-95
100	2.78	21.72	7.00	69.60	80.78	0	1.69	14.98	1.08	32.16	5,415	1	99	0	0	40	26.52	-14.24		1.00	Nov-95
	2.86	21.97	7.47	72.00	85.19	0	1.23	15	1.08	35.52	5,415	1	99	0	0	40	26.97	-14.11			Dec-04
	2.89	22.02	7.61	72.90	86.86	0	1.1	14.99	1.08	44.05	5,415	1	99	0	0	40	27.01	-14			Nov-17
	2.97	22.20	7.89	73.58	87.59	0	0.85	15	1.08	44.24	5,415	1	99	0	0	40	27.01	-14			Nov-17
	3.04	22.37	8.17	74.48	88.57	0.14	0.6	14.99	1.08	44.36	5,415	1	99	0	0	40	27.01	-14			Sep-17
	3.02	22.30	8.05	74.73	89.95	0.04	0.71	15	1.08	44.31	5,415	1	99	0	0	40	27.29	-13.92			Apr-96
100	2.05	18.07	0.58	52.32	59.68	0	1.14	20.36	1.28	44.28	2,130	1	99	0	0	36	32.14	-14.36	5.50		Jun-99
100	1.77	17.46	-0.34	48.73	53.72	0	1.96	20.32	1.28	32.08	2,130	1	99	0	0	36	31.59	-14.59		5.00	Jun-99
100	1.86	17.65	-0.11	49.22	54.24	0	1.8	20.34	1.28	32.18	2,130	1	99	0	0	36	31.65	-14.63		1.00	Jun-99
	1.95	17.84	0.24	51.06	57.75	0	1.47	20.35	1.28	43.25	2,130	1	99	0	0	36	31.8	-14.52			Feb-12
	2.14	18.27	0.91	54.00	62.48	0	0.82	20.36	1.28	49.63	2,130	1	99	0	0	36	32.36	-14.25			Jan-16
	2.14	18.25	0.87	53.70	62.08	0	0.85	20.36	1.28	49.49	2,130	1	99	0	0	36	32.36	-14.25			Jun-99
100	7.32	28.31	4.76	60.18	44.83	0	1.09	15.61	1.17	19.35	518.6	3	97	0	0	59			5.50		Jun-12
100	7.06	27.73	3.85	56.39	39.39	0	1.91	15.57	1.17	18.33	518.6	3	97	0	0	59				1.00	Jun-12
	7.20	28.07	4.37	58.03	41.53	0	1.47	15.6	1.17	19.34	518.6	3	97	0	0	59					Nov-17
	7.39	28.44	5.06	61.70	47.12	0.11	0.84	15.64	1.17	19.6	518.6	3	97	0	0	59					Dec-15
	7.40	28.37	4.99	61.33	46.66	0.05	0.9	15.62	1.17	19.59	518.6	3	97	0	0	59					Jun-12
	7.24	28.13	4.59	59.91	44.65		1.34	15.61	1.17	19.54	518.6	3	97	0	0	59					Dec-18
	7.35	28.32	4.88	61.16	46.51		1.09	15.62	1.17	19.57	518.6	3	97	0	0	59					Dec-18
100	6.88	29.15	13.78	49.69	52.94	0	1.06	13.2	0.9	28.88	3,442	2	98	0	0	36	27.24	-17.26	5.50		Dec-96
100	6.67	28.59	12.84	46.10	47.16	0	1.94	13.2	0.9	19.34	3,442	2	98	0	0	36	26.75	-17.52		5.00	Dec-96
100	6.68	28.68	13.00	46.70	47.76	0	1.69	13.16	0.89	19.47	3,442	2	98	0	0	36	26.7	-17.51		1.00	Dec-96
	6.82	29.07	13.56	48.85	51.47	0	1.24	13.19	0.9	27.39	3,442	2	98	0	0	36	27.05	-17.32			Jun-05
	6.87	29.17	13.75	49.78	53.18	0	1.08	13.19	0.9	32.63	3,442	2	98	0	0	36	27.27	-17.26			Dec-17
	6.98	29.34	14.08	50.94	55.14	0	0.83	13.21	0.9	32.79	3,442	2	98	0	0	36	27.45	-17.17			Dec-17
	7.01	29.48	14.33	51.87	56.63	0	0.58	13.22	0.9	32.94	3,442	2	98	0	0	36	27.58	-17.1			Jan-11
	6.98	29.35	14.08	50.95	55.15	0	0.8	13.21	0.9	32.3	3,442	2	98	0	0	36	27.45	-17.17			Dec-96

	MARKET		FUND TYPE, CATEGORY & OBJECTIVE		RATINGS				MINIMUMS	
Fund Name	Ticker Symbol	Traded On	Fund Type	Category and (Prospectus Objective)	Overall Rating	Reward Rating	Risk Rating	Recent Up/ Downgrade	Open to New Investors	Min Initial Investment
PGIM Jennison MLP Fund-Class A	PRPAX	NAS CM	Open End	Energy Sector Equity (Growth & Income)	C-	C-	C	Down	Y	2,500
PGIM Jennison MLP Fund-Class C	PRPCX	NAS CM	Open End	Energy Sector Equity (Growth & Income)	C-	C-	C	Down	Y	2,500
PGIM Jennison MLP Fund-Class R6	PRPQX	NAS CM	Open End	Energy Sector Equity (Growth & Income)	C	C-	C	Down	Y	0
PGIM Jennison MLP Fund-Class Z	PRPZX	NAS CM	Open End	Energy Sector Equity (Growth & Income)	C-	C-	C	Down	Y	0
PGIM Jennison Natural Resources Fund - Class A	PGNAX	NAS CM	Open End	Natl Resources Sec Equity (Natl Res)	D	D	D+	Down	Y	2,500
PGIM Jennison Natural Resources Fund - Class B	PRGNX	NAS CM	Open End	Natl Resources Sec Equity (Natl Res)	D	D	D+	Down		2,500
PGIM Jennison Natural Resources Fund - Class C	PNRCX	NAS CM	Open End	Natl Resources Sec Equity (Natl Res)	D	D	D+	Down	Y	2,500
PGIM Jennison Natural Resources Fund - Class R	JNRRX	NAS CM	Open End	Natl Resources Sec Equity (Natl Res)	D	D	D+	Down	Y	0
PGIM Jennison Natural Resources Fund - Class R6	PJNQX	NAS CM	Open End	Natl Resources Sec Equity (Natl Res)	D+	D	D+	Down	Y	0
PGIM Jennison Natural Resources Fund - Class Z	PNRZX	NAS CM	Open End	Natl Resources Sec Equity (Natl Res)	D+	D	D+	Down	Y	0
PGIM Jennison Rising Dividend Fund- Class A	PJDAX	NAS CM	Open End	US Equity Large Cap Blend (Equity-Income)	C+	C	B		Y	2,500
PGIM Jennison Rising Dividend Fund- Class C	PJDCX	NAS CM	Open End	US Equity Large Cap Blend (Equity-Income)	C+	C	B		Y	2,500
PGIM Jennison Rising Dividend Fund- Class R6	PJDQX	NAS CM	Open End	US Equity Large Cap Blend (Equity-Income)	B-	C	B	Up	Y	0
PGIM Jennison Rising Dividend Fund- Class Z	PJDZX	NAS CM	Open End	US Equity Large Cap Blend (Equity-Income)	B-	C	B	Up	Y	0
PGIM Jennison Small Company Fund- Class A	PGOAX	NAS CM	Open End	US Equity Small Cap (Small Company)	C	C	C+		Y	2,500
PGIM Jennison Small Company Fund- Class B	CHNDX	NAS CM	Open End	US Equity Small Cap (Small Company)	C	C	C+			2,500
PGIM Jennison Small Company Fund- Class C	PSCCX	NAS CM	Open End	US Equity Small Cap (Small Company)	C	C	C+		Y	2,500
PGIM Jennison Small Company Fund- Class R	JSCRX	NAS CM	Open End	US Equity Small Cap (Small Company)	C	C	C+		Y	0
PGIM Jennison Small Company Fund- Class R2	PSCHX	NAS CM	Open End	US Equity Small Cap (Small Company)	C	C	C+		Y	0
PGIM Jennison Small Company Fund- Class R4	PSCJX	NAS CM	Open End	US Equity Small Cap (Small Company)	C	C	C+		Y	0
PGIM Jennison Small Company Fund- Class R6	PJSQX	NAS CM	Open End	US Equity Small Cap (Small Company)	C	C	C+		Y	0
PGIM Jennison Small Company Fund- Class Z	PSCZX	NAS CM	Open End	US Equity Small Cap (Small Company)	C	C	C+		Y	0
PGIM Jennison Small-Cap Core Equity Fund-Class R6	PQJCX	NAS CM	Open End	US Equity Small Cap (Small Company)	C	C-	C+	Up	Y	0
PGIM Jennison Technology Fund Class A	PGKAX	NAS CM	Open End	Technology Sector Equity (Growth)	D	D+	C+		Y	2,500
PGIM Jennison Technology Fund Class C	PGKCX	NAS CM	Open End	Technology Sector Equity (Growth)	D	D+	C+		Y	2,500
PGIM Jennison Technology Fund Class R6	PGKRX	NAS CM	Open End	Technology Sector Equity (Growth)	D	D+	C+		Y	0
PGIM Jennison Technology Fund Class Z	PGKZX	NAS CM	Open End	Technology Sector Equity (Growth)	D	D+	C+		Y	0
PGIM Jennison Utility Fund- Class A	PRUAX	NAS CM	Open End	Utilities Sector Equity (Utility)	B	B	B		Y	2,500
PGIM Jennison Utility Fund- Class B	PRUTX	NAS CM	Open End	Utilities Sector Equity (Utility)	B	B	B			2,500
PGIM Jennison Utility Fund- Class C	PCUFX	NAS CM	Open End	Utilities Sector Equity (Utility)	B	B	B		Y	2,500
PGIM Jennison Utility Fund- Class R	JDURX	NAS CM	Open End	Utilities Sector Equity (Utility)	B	B	B		Y	0
PGIM Jennison Utility Fund- Class R6	PRUQX	NAS CM	Open End	Utilities Sector Equity (Utility)	B	B	B		Y	0
PGIM Jennison Utility Fund- Class Z	PRUZX	NAS CM	Open End	Utilities Sector Equity (Utility)	B	B	B		Y	0
PGIM Jennison Value Fund- Class A	PBEAX	NAS CM	Open End	US Equity Large Cap Value (Growth)	C+	C	B	Up	Y	2,500
PGIM Jennison Value Fund- Class B	PBQIX	NAS CM	Open End	US Equity Large Cap Value (Growth)	C+	C	B	Up		2,500
PGIM Jennison Value Fund- Class C	PEICX	NAS CM	Open End	US Equity Large Cap Value (Growth)	C+	C	B	Up	Y	2,500
PGIM Jennison Value Fund- Class R	JDVRX	NAS CM	Open End	US Equity Large Cap Value (Growth)	C+	C	B	Up	Y	0
PGIM Jennison Value Fund- Class R6	PJVQX	NAS CM	Open End	US Equity Large Cap Value (Growth)	B-	C	B	Up	Y	0
PGIM Jennison Value Fund- Class Z	PEIZX	NAS CM	Open End	US Equity Large Cap Value (Growth)	B-	C	B	Up	Y	0
PGIM QMA Commodity Strategies Fund- Class R6	PQCMX	NAS CM	Open End	Commodities Broad Basket (Growth & Income)	D+	D	C-		Y	0
PGIM QMA Emerging Markets Equity Fund-Class R6	PQEMX	NAS CM	Open End	Global Emerg Mkts (Div Emerging Mkts)	C-	D+	C		Y	0
PGIM QMA Global Tactical Allocation Fund- Class A	PTALX	NAS CM	Open End	Global Macro (Asset Alloc)	B-	C	A-	Up	Y	2,500
PGIM QMA Global Tactical Allocation Fund- Class C	PTCLX	NAS CM	Open End	Global Macro (Asset Alloc)	B-	C	B+	Up	Y	2,500
PGIM QMA Global Tactical Allocation Fund- Class R6	PTQLX	NAS CM	Open End	Global Macro (Asset Alloc)	B-	C	A-	Up	Y	0
PGIM QMA Global Tactical Allocation Fund- Class Z	PTZLX	NAS CM	Open End	Global Macro (Asset Alloc)	B-	C	A-	Up	Y	0
PGIM QMA International Developed Markets Index Fund-Cls R6	PQDMX	NAS CM	Open End	Global Equity Large Cap (Growth & Income)	C	D+	B-	Up	Y	0
PGIM QMA International Equity Fund- Class A	PJRAX	NAS CM	Open End	Global Equity Large Cap (Foreign Stock)	C	C	B-		Y	2,500
PGIM QMA International Equity Fund- Class B	PJRBX	NAS CM	Open End	Global Equity Large Cap (Foreign Stock)	C	C-	C+			2,500
PGIM QMA International Equity Fund- Class C	PJRCX	NAS CM	Open End	Global Equity Large Cap (Foreign Stock)	C	C-	C+		Y	2,500
PGIM QMA International Equity Fund- Class R6	PJRQX	NAS CM	Open End	Global Equity Large Cap (Foreign Stock)	C	C	B-		Y	0
PGIM QMA International Equity Fund- Class Z	PJIZX	NAS CM	Open End	Global Equity Large Cap (Foreign Stock)	C	C	B-		Y	0
PGIM QMA Large-Cap Core Equity Fund- Class A	PTMAX	NAS CM	Open End	US Equity Large Cap Blend (Growth)	C+	C	B		Y	2,500

★ Expanded analysis of this fund is included in Section II.

Min Additional Investment	TOTAL RETURNS 3-Month Total Return	6-Month Total Return	1-Year Total Return	3-Year Total Return	5-Year Total Return	PERFORMANCE Dividend Yield (TTM)	Expense Ratio	3-Yr Std Deviation	3-Year Beta	ASSETS NAV	Total Assets (ML)	ASSET ALLOCATION & TURNOVER %Cash	%Stocks	%Bonds	%Other	Turnover Ratio	BULL & BEAR Last Bull Market Total Return	Last Bear Market Total Return	FEES Front End Fee (%)	Back End Fee (%)	Inception Date
100	-1.14	20.71	1.02	3.67	-23.21	6.51	2	15.7	0.89	6.77	516.4	2	98	0	0	41			5.50		Dec-13
100	-1.20	20.37	0.31	1.49	-25.94	6.84	2.73	15.74	0.9	6.45	516.4	2	98	0	0	41				1.00	Dec-13
	-0.98	20.90	1.29	4.34	-22.22	6.4	1.7	15.67	0.89	6.89	516.4	2	98	0	0	41					Jan-18
	-0.98	20.90	1.29	4.48	-22.12	6.4	1.7	15.7	0.89	6.89	516.4	2	98	0	0	41					Dec-13
100	-0.40	17.11	-17.47	-2.73	-43.06	1.37	1.24	20.7	1.22	32.16	817.6	2	98	0	0	27	17.35	-32.96	5.50		Jan-90
100	-0.61	16.61	-18.23	-5.09	-45.23	0.72	2.19	20.68	1.21	25.69	817.6	2	98	0	0	27	16.88	-33.15		5.00	Sep-87
100	-0.58	16.70	-18.02	-4.71	-45.00	1.06	1.9	20.69	1.22	25.71	817.6	2	98	0	0	27	16.85	-33.14		1.00	Aug-94
	-0.47	16.95	-17.68	-3.40	-43.69	1.1	1.5	20.7	1.22	31.6	817.6	2	98	0	0	27	17.21	-33.01			Aug-06
	-0.26	17.41	-17.06	-1.33	-41.69	1.83	0.78	20.72	1.22	33.84	817.6	2	98	0	0	27	17.65	-32.83			Dec-10
	-0.29	17.33	-17.18	-1.70	-42.12	1.73	0.87	20.69	1.21	33.58	817.6	2	98	0	0	27	17.55	-32.86			Sep-96
100	6.07	21.17	11.09	38.04	48.53	0.88	1.24	11.12	0.88	13.39	15.9	1	97	2	1	104			5.50		Mar-14
100	5.85	20.76	10.28	35.08	43.19	0.36	1.99	11.12	0.88	13.37	15.9	1	97	2	1	104				1.00	Mar-14
	6.05	21.30	11.29	38.96	50.24	1.11	0.99	11.1	0.88	13.39	15.9	1	97	2	1	104					Sep-17
	6.04	21.29	11.37	39.06	50.34	1.11	0.99	11.11	0.88	13.4	15.9	1	97	2	1	104					Mar-14
100	4.16	21.84	-1.74	39.78	38.79	0.21	1.13	15.24	0.96	21.75	2,671	1	97	2	1	43	25.94	-23.87	5.50		Jan-90
100	3.94	21.59	-2.54	36.36	33.29	0	2.04	15.29	0.97	9.74	2,671	1	97	2	1	43	25.19	-24		5.00	Nov-80
100	4.03	21.52	-2.08	37.18	34.20	0.07	1.81	15.23	0.96	10.05	2,671	1	97	2	1	43	25.4	-24.05		1.00	Aug-94
	4.15	21.86	-1.85	38.98	37.45	0.02	1.33	15.24	0.96	21.07	2,671	1	97	2	1	43	25.74	-23.85			May-04
	4.17	21.90	-2.00	37.93	34.82	0.14	1.18	15.18	0.96	23.21	2,671	1	97	2	1	43	25.19	-24			Nov-17
	4.25	22.02	-1.65	38.65	35.52	0.38	0.93	15.25	0.96	23.27	2,671	1	97	2	1	43	25.19	-24			Nov-17
	4.28	22.19	-1.19	41.77	42.06	0.62	0.68	15.26	0.97	23.34	2,671	1	97	2	1	43	26.51	-25.37			Nov-10
	4.25	22.14	-1.36	40.99	40.75	0.48	0.81	15.25	0.96	23.77	2,671	1	97	2	1	43	26	-23.63			Mar-96
	2.44	19.85	-4.44			0.37	0.95			11.71	17.3	1	97	1	0	39					Nov-16
100	4.20	22.95	14.37			0	1.1			11.14	11.1	1	99	0	0	19			5.50		Jun-18
100	3.94	22.48	13.66			0	1.85			11.06	11.1	1	99	0	0	19				1.00	Jun-18
	4.29	23.15	14.81			0.09	0.8			11.17	11.1	1	99	0	0	19					Jun-18
	4.19	23.15	14.78			0.07	0.85			11.17	11.1	1	99	0	0	19					Jun-18
100	3.09	16.65	16.85	29.80	34.95	1.79	0.83	9.79	0.8	14.99	3,277	1	99	0	0	39	19.6	-12.16	5.50		Jan-90
100	2.87	16.05	15.80	26.61	29.90	0.94	1.78	9.79	0.8	14.95	3,277	1	99	0	0	39	19.11	-12.49		5.00	Aug-81
100	2.85	16.18	15.98	26.97	30.19	1.13	1.57	9.83	0.8	14.92	3,277	1	99	0	0	39	19.23	-12.5		1.00	Aug-94
	3.03	16.44	16.54	28.87	33.45	1.54	1.11	9.79	0.8	14.98	3,277	1	99	0	0	39	19.5	-12.26			Aug-06
	3.10	16.80	17.20	28.83	32.18	2.07	0.52	9.82	0.8	15	3,277	1	99	0	0	39	19.11	-12.49			Jan-18
	3.16	16.78	17.16	30.89	36.97	2.04	0.56	9.81	0.8	15	3,277	1	99	0	0	39	19.78	-12.1			Mar-96
100	3.71	17.16	6.18	38.67	23.51	1.08	1.06	12.01	0.98	19.25	446.9	1	99	0	0	21	19.96	-23.22	5.50		Jan-90
100	3.46	16.58	5.19	35.05	18.67	0.15	2.06	12	0.98	18.49	446.9	1	99	0	0	21	19.49	-23.47		5.00	Jan-87
100	3.41	16.60	5.24	35.33	18.91	0.33	1.87	11.99	0.98	18.47	446.9	1	99	0	0	21	19.41	-23.42		1.00	Aug-94
	3.62	16.89	5.76	37.29	21.84	0.68	1.46	12	0.98	19.17	446.9	1	99	0	0	21	19.74	-23.21			Jun-05
	3.82	17.35	6.60	40.31	26.09	1.43	0.7	12	0.98	19.27	446.9	1	99	0	0	21	20.19	-23.47			Oct-11
	3.82	17.33	6.49	39.79	25.35	1.35	0.77	12	0.98	19.29	446.9	1	99	0	0	21	20.05	-23.07			Mar-96
	-1.34	4.39	-7.68			2.87	0.84			9.51	20.9	89	0	0	11	0					Nov-16
	0.97	10.42	-2.15			1.83	1.2			11.44	30.1	0	100	0	0	118					Nov-16
100	2.48	10.75	2.38	23.07		0	1.45	7.27		9.89	39.6	94	6	1	0	0			5.50		Apr-15
100	2.33	10.30	1.58	20.32		0	2.2	7.27		9.63	39.6	94	6	1	0	0				1.00	Apr-15
	2.57	10.80	2.57	23.87		0	1.2	7.3		9.95	39.6	94	6	1	0	0					Apr-15
	2.57	10.91	2.68	24.12		0	1.2	7.33		9.96	39.6	94	6	1	0	0					Apr-15
	3.12	13.67	0.12			2.29	0.3			11.89	48.1	5	95	0	0	9					Nov-16
100	2.41	13.70	-1.25	27.48	3.01	2.4	1.34	11.98	1.03	7.22	201.6	0	99	0	1	114	15.61	-24.12	5.50		Mar-00
100	2.06	13.09	-2.37	24.06	-1.23	1.28	2.53	11.92	1.03	6.91	201.6	0	99	0	1	114	15.15	-24.27		5.00	Mar-00
100	1.92	12.97	-2.44	24.30	-1.03	1.74	2.1	11.81	1.02	6.88	201.6	0	99	0	1	114	15.15	-24.27		1.00	Mar-00
	2.67	14.08	-0.70	29.77	5.41	2.99	0.78	11.86	1.02	7.29	201.6	0	99	0	1	114	15.87	-23.98			Dec-16
	2.53	13.92	-0.97	28.89	4.69	2.75	1	11.9	1.02	7.28	201.6	0	99	0	1	114	15.87	-23.98			Mar-00
100	3.66	18.23	6.12	46.08	57.65	1.25	0.72	13.2	1.08	14.72	591.0	2	98	0	0	95	26.67	-17.7	5.50		Mar-99

	MARKET			FUND TYPE, CATEGORY & OBJECTIVE	RATINGS				MINIMUMS	
Fund Name	Ticker Symbol	Traded On	Fund Type	Category and (Prospectus Objective)	Overall Rating	Reward Rating	Risk Rating	Recent Up/ Downgrade	Open to New Investors	Min Initial Investment
PGIM QMA Large-Cap Core Equity Fund- Class B	PTMBX	NAS CM	Open End	US Equity Large Cap Blend (Growth)	C+	C	B			2,500
PGIM QMA Large-Cap Core Equity Fund- Class C	PTMCX	NAS CM	Open End	US Equity Large Cap Blend (Growth)	C+	C	B		Y	2,500
PGIM QMA Large-Cap Core Equity Fund- Class R6	PTMQX	NAS CM	Open End	US Equity Large Cap Blend (Growth)	C+	C	B		Y	0
PGIM QMA Large-Cap Core Equity Fund- Class Z	PTEZX	NAS CM	Open End	US Equity Large Cap Blend (Growth)	C+	C	B		Y	0
PGIM QMA Large-Cap Core Equity PLUS Fund-Class A	PQMAX	NAS CM	Open End	US Equity Large Cap Blend (Growth)	C-	D+	C	Up	Y	2,500
PGIM QMA Large-Cap Core Equity PLUS Fund-Class C	PQMCX	NAS CM	Open End	US Equity Large Cap Blend (Growth)	C-	D+	C	Up	Y	2,500
PGIM QMA Large-Cap Core Equity PLUS Fund-Class R6	PQMQX	NAS CM	Open End	US Equity Large Cap Blend (Growth)	C-	D+	C	Up	Y	0
PGIM QMA Large-Cap Core Equity PLUS Fund-Class Z	PQMZX	NAS CM	Open End	US Equity Large Cap Blend (Growth)	C-	D+	C	Up	Y	0
PGIM QMA Large-Cap Value Fund- Class A	SUVAX	NAS CM	Open End	US Equity Large Cap Value (Growth)	C	C-	C+		Y	2,500
PGIM QMA Large-Cap Value Fund- Class B	SUVBX	NAS CM	Open End	US Equity Large Cap Value (Growth)	C	C-	C			2,500
PGIM QMA Large-Cap Value Fund- Class C	SUVCX	NAS CM	Open End	US Equity Large Cap Value (Growth)	C	C-	C		Y	2,500
PGIM QMA Large-Cap Value Fund- Class R	PRVRX	NAS CM	Open End	US Equity Large Cap Value (Growth)	C	C-	C+		Y	0
PGIM QMA Large-Cap Value Fund- Class R6	SUVQX	NAS CM	Open End	US Equity Large Cap Value (Growth)	C	C-	C+		Y	0
PGIM QMA Large-Cap Value Fund- Class Z	SUVZX	NAS CM	Open End	US Equity Large Cap Value (Growth)	C	C-	C+		Y	0
PGIM QMA Long-Short Equity Fund-Class A	PLHAX	NAS CM	Open End	Long/Short Equity (Growth)	C-	D+	C	Down	Y	2,500
PGIM QMA Long-Short Equity Fund-Class C	PLHCX	NAS CM	Open End	Long/Short Equity (Growth)	C-	D+	C	Down	Y	2,500
PGIM QMA Long-Short Equity Fund-Class R6	PLHQX	NAS CM	Open End	Long/Short Equity (Growth)	C-	D+	C+	Down	Y	0
PGIM QMA Long-Short Equity Fund-Class Z	PLHZX	NAS CM	Open End	Long/Short Equity (Growth)	C-	D+	C+	Down	Y	0
PGIM QMA Mid-Cap Core Equity Fund- Class R6	PQCCX	NAS CM	Open End	US Equity Mid Cap (Growth & Income)	C-	D+	C+		Y	0
PGIM QMA Mid-Cap Value Fund- Class A	SPRAX	NAS CM	Open End	US Equity Mid Cap (Growth)	C-	D+	C		Y	2,500
PGIM QMA Mid-Cap Value Fund- Class B	SVUBX	NAS CM	Open End	US Equity Mid Cap (Growth)	D+	D+	C-	Down		2,500
PGIM QMA Mid-Cap Value Fund- Class C	NCBVX	NAS CM	Open End	US Equity Mid Cap (Growth)	D+	D+	C-	Down	Y	2,500
PGIM QMA Mid-Cap Value Fund- Class R	SDVRX	NAS CM	Open End	US Equity Mid Cap (Growth)	C-	D+	C			0
PGIM QMA Mid-Cap Value Fund- Class R2	PMVEX	NAS CM	Open End	US Equity Mid Cap (Growth)	C-	D+	C		Y	0
PGIM QMA Mid-Cap Value Fund- Class R4	PMVFX	NAS CM	Open End	US Equity Mid Cap (Growth)	C-	D+	C		Y	0
PGIM QMA Mid-Cap Value Fund- Class R6	PMVQX	NAS CM	Open End	US Equity Mid Cap (Growth)	C	C-	C	Up	Y	0
PGIM QMA Mid-Cap Value Fund- Class Z	SPVZX	NAS CM	Open End	US Equity Mid Cap (Growth)	C-	C-	C		Y	0
PGIM QMA Small-Cap Value Fund- Class A	TSVAX	NAS CM	Open End	US Equity Small Cap (Small Company)	D+	D	C-	Down	Y	2,500
PGIM QMA Small-Cap Value Fund- Class C	TRACX	NAS CM	Open End	US Equity Small Cap (Small Company)	D+	D	C-	Down	Y	2,500
PGIM QMA Small-Cap Value Fund- Class R	TSVRX	NAS CM	Open End	US Equity Small Cap (Small Company)	D+	D	C-	Down	Y	0
PGIM QMA Small-Cap Value Fund- Class R2	PSVDX	NAS CM	Open End	US Equity Small Cap (Small Company)	D+	D	C-	Down	Y	0
PGIM QMA Small-Cap Value Fund- Class R4	PSVKX	NAS CM	Open End	US Equity Small Cap (Small Company)	D+	D	C-	Down	Y	0
PGIM QMA Small-Cap Value Fund- Class R6	TSVQX	NAS CM	Open End	US Equity Small Cap (Small Company)	D+	D+	C-	Down	Y	0
PGIM QMA Small-Cap Value Fund- Class Z	TASVX	NAS CM	Open End	US Equity Small Cap (Small Company)	D+	D+	C-	Down	Y	0
PGIM QMA Stock Index Fund- Class A	PSIAX	NAS CM	Open End	US Equity Large Cap Blend (Growth)	B-	C	B		Y	2,500
PGIM QMA Stock Index Fund- Class C	PSICX	NAS CM	Open End	US Equity Large Cap Blend (Growth)	B-	C	B		Y	2,500
PGIM QMA Stock Index Fund- Class I	PDSIX	NAS CM	Open End	US Equity Large Cap Blend (Growth)	B-	C	B		Y	0
PGIM QMA Stock Index Fund- Class R6	PQSIX	NAS CM	Open End	US Equity Large Cap Blend (Growth)	B-	C	B		Y	0
PGIM QMA Stock Index Fund- Class Z	PSIFX	NAS CM	Open End	US Equity Large Cap Blend (Growth)	B-	C	B		Y	0
PGIM QMA US Broad Market Index Fund- Class R6	PQBMX	NAS CM	Open End	US Equity Large Cap Blend (Growth & Income)	C+	C	B	Up	Y	0
PGIM Real Assets Fund- Class A	PUDAX	NAS CM	Open End	Moderate Alloc (Growth & Income)	C+	C	B	Up	Y	2,500
PGIM Real Assets Fund- Class B	PUDBX	NAS CM	Open End	Moderate Alloc (Growth & Income)	C	C	B-			2,500
PGIM Real Assets Fund- Class C	PUDCX	NAS CM	Open End	Moderate Alloc (Growth & Income)	C	C	B-		Y	2,500
PGIM Real Assets Fund- Class R6	PUDQX	NAS CM	Open End	Moderate Alloc (Growth & Income)	C+	C	B	Up	Y	0
PGIM Real Assets Fund- Class Z	PUDZX	NAS CM	Open End	Moderate Alloc (Growth & Income)	C+	C	B	Up	Y	0
PGIM Real Estate Income Fund- Class A	PRKAX	NAS CM	Open End	Real Estate Sector Equity (Real Estate)	C+	C+	C+		Y	2,500
PGIM Real Estate Income Fund- Class C	PRKCX	NAS CM	Open End	Real Estate Sector Equity (Real Estate)	C+	C+	C+		Y	2,500
PGIM Real Estate Income Fund- Class R6	PRKQX	NAS CM	Open End	Real Estate Sector Equity (Real Estate)	C+	C+	B-	Down	Y	0
PGIM Real Estate Income Fund- Class Z	PRKZX	NAS CM	Open End	Real Estate Sector Equity (Real Estate)	C+	C+	B-	Down	Y	0
PGIM Select Real Estate Fund- Class A	SREAX	NAS CM	Open End	Real Estate Sector Equity (Real Estate)	B	B	B+		Y	2,500
PGIM Select Real Estate Fund- Class C	SRECX	NAS CM	Open End	Real Estate Sector Equity (Real Estate)	B	B-	B	Up	Y	2,500
PGIM Select Real Estate Fund- Class R6	SREQX	NAS CM	Open End	Real Estate Sector Equity (Real Estate)	B	B	B+		Y	0

★ Expanded analysis of this fund is included in Section II.

	TOTAL RETURNS					PERFORMANCE				ASSETS		ASSET ALLOCATION & TURNOVER					BULL & BEAR		FEES		
Min Additional Investment	3-Month Total Return	6-Month Total Return	1-Year Total Return	3-Year Total Return	5-Year Total Return	Dividend Yield (TTM)	Expense Ratio	3-Yr Std Deviation	3-Year Beta	NAV	Total Assets (MIL)	%Cash	%Stocks	%Bonds	%Other	Turnover Ratio	Last Bull Market Total Return	Last Bear Market Total Return	Front End Fee (%)	Back End Fee (%)	Inception Date
100	3.48	17.83	5.26	42.61	51.57	0.47	1.58	13.15	1.07	13.08	591.0	2	98	0	0	95	26.05	-17.98		5.00	Mar-99
100	3.47	17.80	5.38	42.95	52.03	0.7	1.44	13.2	1.08	13.1	591.0	2	98	0	0	95	26.02	-17.9		1.00	Mar-99
	3.75	18.47	6.59	47.68	60.21	1.57	0.35	13.18	1.07	15.2	591.0	2	98	0	0	95	26.82	-17.67			Dec-16
	3.75	18.50	6.46	47.27	59.77	1.46	0.48	13.17	1.07	15.18	591.0	2	98	0	0	95	26.82	-17.67			Mar-99
100	0.55	12.75	0.99			0.63	2.1			10.87	22.2	0	100	0	0	88			5.50		Sep-17
100	0.46	12.35	0.20			0	2.85			10.82	22.2	0	100	0	0	88				1.00	Sep-17
	0.64	12.75	1.18			0.88	1.85			10.87	22.2	0	100	0	0	88					Sep-17
	0.64	12.78	1.18			0.89	1.85			10.85	22.2	0	100	0	0	88					Sep-17
100	1.58	12.36	-2.61	30.91	30.77	1.81	1.13	15.34	1.23	12.18	302.7	1	99	0	0	76	20.65	-18.34	5.50		Mar-01
100	1.36	11.82	-3.55	27.51	25.53	1.13	2.07	15.33	1.23	11.16	302.7	1	99	0	0	76	20.16	-18.59		5.00	Mar-01
100	1.18	11.73	-3.56	27.68	25.68	1.28	1.91	15.33	1.23	11.14	302.7	1	99	0	0	76	20.16	-18.59		1.00	Mar-01
	1.45	12.19	-2.83	30.06	28.92	1.57	1.33	15.33	1.23	12.51	302.7	1	99	0	0	76	20.27	-18.42			Jun-15
	1.62	12.57	-2.32	32.16	32.69	2.04	0.8	15.33	1.23	12.53	302.7	1	99	0	0	76	20.79	-18.16			Apr-17
	1.62	12.48	-2.32	32.08	32.60	2.04	0.8	15.32	1.23	12.52	302.7	1	99	0	0	76	20.79	-18.16			Mar-01
100	-2.42	2.55	-3.44	13.46	25.13	0	2.15	7.29	0.5	12.05	386.4	57	43	0	0	160			5.50		May-14
100	-2.60	2.20	-4.13	10.95	20.59	0	2.9	7.29	0.5	11.59	386.4	57	43	0	0	160				1.00	May-14
	-2.39	2.69	-3.24	14.40	26.85	0	1.9	7.27	0.5	12.21	386.4	57	43	0	0	160					May-17
	-2.39	2.69	-3.24	14.31	26.75	0	1.9	7.28	0.5	12.21	386.4	57	43	0	0	160					May-14
	1.69	17.53	-2.42			0.84	0.85			10.79	15.4	1	99	0	0	113					Nov-16
100	0.94	13.62	-6.66	20.98	19.66	2.05	1.13	16.36	1.2	18.1	660.5	0	100	0	0	78	21.78	-21.15	5.50		Apr-04
100	0.72	13.17	-7.41	18.21	15.21	1.59	1.95	16.35	1.2	15.29	660.5	0	100	0	0	78	21.21	-21.42		5.00	Apr-04
100	0.72	13.16	-7.40	18.30	15.27	1.64	1.88	16.34	1.2	15.21	660.5	0	100	0	0	78	21.18	-21.36		1.00	Aug-98
	0.88	13.41	-6.92	20.10	17.88	1.74	1.45	16.33	1.2	18.26	660.5	0	100	0	0	78	21.18	-21.36			Dec-14
	0.94	13.57	-6.68	19.52	16.46	1.93	1.23	16.32	1.2	18.24	660.5	0	100	0	0	78	21.18	-21.36			Dec-17
	0.99	13.69	-6.47	19.96	16.89	2.17	0.98	16.32	1.2	18.26	660.5	0	100	0	0	78	21.18	-21.36			Dec-17
	1.05	13.83	-6.28	22.48	22.14	2.47	0.73	16.34	1.2	18.27	660.5	0	100	0	0	78	22.08	-21			Jan-11
	0.99	13.79	-6.42	21.90	21.22	2.28	0.89	16.33	1.2	18.31	660.5	0	100	0	0	78	21.93	-21.06			Nov-05
100	-2.22	9.36	-13.43	21.66	17.44	1.6	1.02	19.55	1.12	16.24	1,245	1	99	0	0		25.44	-21.88	5.50		Feb-14
100	-2.45	8.90	-14.12	18.80	12.94	0.7	1.81	19.55	1.12	16.27	1,245	1	99	0	0		24.94	-22.11		1.00	Jun-15
	-2.31	9.28	-13.58	20.80	16.07	1.34	1.26	19.54	1.11	16.01	1,245	1	99	0	0		25.32	-21.95			Aug-06
	-2.29	9.30	-13.49	21.52	17.30	1.51	1.14	19.56	1.12	16.21	1,245	1	99	0	0		25.48	-21.86			Dec-17
	-2.16	9.50	-13.22	22.48	18.81	1.72	0.89	19.58	1.12	16.24	1,245	1	99	0	0		25.66	-21.78			Dec-17
	-2.16	9.58	-13.05	23.00	19.57	2.04	0.63	19.55	1.12	16.24	1,245	1	99	0	0		25.66	-21.78			Sep-14
	-2.11	9.58	-13.08	22.86	19.19	1.98	0.69	19.57	1.12	16.23	1,245	1	99	0	0		25.66	-21.78			Jan-93
100	4.19	19.27	9.88	48.63	62.18	1.85	0.52	12.19	1	47.71	923.4	2	98	0	0	2	24.79	-16.46	3.25		Nov-99
100	4.00	18.86	9.15	45.73	57.04	1.09	1.18	12.2	1	47.25	923.4	2	98	0	0	2	24.29	-16.64		1.00	Nov-99
	4.26	19.48	10.25	50.15	64.96	2.25	0.18	12.2	1	47.9	923.4	2	98	0	0	2	25	-16.33			Aug-97
	4.28	19.47	10.27	50.03	64.68	2.25	0.18	12.2	1	47.92	923.4	2	98	0	0	2	24.98	-16.34			Nov-17
	4.26	19.44	10.20	49.88	64.51	2.18	0.24	12.2	1	47.91	923.4	2	98	0	0	2	24.98	-16.34			Nov-92
	4.11	19.20	9.24			1.4	0.2			13.41	45.1	4	96	0	0	15					Nov-16
100	1.88	12.21	2.77	4.93	-3.64	1.5	1.27	7.12		9.63	107.3	2	48	33	17	77	8.11	-7.94	5.50		Dec-10
100	1.70	11.68	1.77	2.27	-7.44	0.66	2.2	7.14		9.56	107.3	2	48	33	17	77	7.56	-8.17		5.00	Dec-10
100	1.72	11.70	1.96	2.54	-7.11	0.84	1.99	7.08		9.56	107.3	2	48	33	17	77	7.57	-8.18		1.00	Dec-10
	1.97	12.34	3.08	6.00	-2.03	1.89	0.85	7.07		9.64	107.3	2	48	33	17	77	8.22	-7.8			Jan-15
	1.95	12.30	3.01	5.87	-2.26	1.83	0.92	7.08		9.65	107.3	2	48	33	17	77	8.22	-7.8			Dec-10
100	2.54	22.96	11.12	19.65		4.14	1.35	12.05		9.93	16.3	1	79	0	1	153			5.50		Jun-15
100	2.27	22.48	10.31	16.81		3.47	2.1	11.98		9.91	16.3	1	79	0	1	153				1.00	Jun-15
	2.59	23.16	11.39	20.51		4.37	1.1	12.01		9.94	16.3	1	79	0	1	153					Dec-16
	2.69	23.11	11.61	20.75		4.36	1.1	11.98		9.96	16.3	1	79	0	1	153					Jun-15
100	3.57	23.19	18.47	30.20		1.81	1.3	11.55	1.01	12.12	12.6	2	97	0	1	202			5.50		Aug-14
100	3.42	22.66	17.61	27.23		1.18	2.05	11.49	1.01	11.98	12.6	2	97	0	1	202				1.00	Aug-14
	3.68	23.27	18.82	31.12		2.05	1.05	11.54	1.01	11.96	12.6	2	97	0	1	202					Aug-14

Fund Name	MARKET Ticker Symbol	Traded On	FUND TYPE, CATEGORY & OBJECTIVE Fund Type	Category and (Prospectus Objective)	RATINGS Overall Rating	Reward Rating	Risk Rating	Recent Up/ Downgrade	MINIMUMS Open to New Investors	Min Initial Investment
PGIM Select Real Estate Fund- Class Z	SREZX	NAS CM	Open End	Real Estate Sector Equity (Real Estate)	B	B	B+		Y	0
PGIM US Real Estate Fund- Class A	PJEAX	NAS CM	Open End	Real Estate Sector Equity (Real Estate)	B-	C+	B-	Down	Y	2,500
PGIM US Real Estate Fund- Class B	PJEBX	NAS CM	Open End	Real Estate Sector Equity (Real Estate)	C+	C	B-	Down		2,500
PGIM US Real Estate Fund- Class C	PJECX	NAS CM	Open End	Real Estate Sector Equity (Real Estate)	C+	C	B-	Down	Y	2,500
PGIM US Real Estate Fund- Class R6	PJEQX	NAS CM	Open End	Real Estate Sector Equity (Real Estate)	B-	C+	B-	Down	Y	0
PGIM US Real Estate Fund- Class Z	PJEZX	NAS CM	Open End	Real Estate Sector Equity (Real Estate)	B-	C+	B-	Down	Y	0
PIMCO All Asset All Authority Fund Class A	PAUAX	NAS CM	Open End	Moderate Alloc (Asset Alloc)	C	C-	B		Y	1,000
PIMCO All Asset All Authority Fund Class C	PAUCX	NAS CM	Open End	Moderate Alloc (Asset Alloc)	C	C-	B-		Y	1,000
PIMCO All Asset All Authority Fund Class I-2	PAUPX	NAS CM	Open End	Moderate Alloc (Asset Alloc)	C+	C-	B	Up	Y	1,000,000
PIMCO All Asset All Authority Fund I-3	PAUNX	NAS CM	Open End	Moderate Alloc (Asset Alloc)	C+	C-	B	Up	Y	1,000,000
PIMCO All Asset All Authority Fund Institutional Class	PAUIX	NAS CM	Open End	Moderate Alloc (Asset Alloc)	C+	C	B	Up	Y	1,000,000
PIMCO All Asset Fund Administrative Class	PAALX	NAS CM	Open End	Moderate Alloc (Asset Alloc)	B-	C	A-	Up	Y	1,000,000
PIMCO All Asset Fund Class A	PASAX	NAS CM	Open End	Moderate Alloc (Asset Alloc)	B-	C	A-	Up	Y	1,000
PIMCO All Asset Fund Class C	PASCX	NAS CM	Open End	Moderate Alloc (Asset Alloc)	B-	C	B+	Up	Y	1,000
PIMCO All Asset Fund Class I-2	PALPX	NAS CM	Open End	Moderate Alloc (Asset Alloc)	B-	C	A-	Up	Y	1,000,000
PIMCO All Asset Fund Class R	PATRX	NAS CM	Open End	Moderate Alloc (Asset Alloc)	B-	C	B+	Up	Y	0
PIMCO All Asset Fund I-3	PAANX	NAS CM	Open End	Moderate Alloc (Asset Alloc)	B-	C	A-	Up	Y	1,000,000
PIMCO All Asset Fund Institutional Class	PAAIX	NAS CM	Open End	Moderate Alloc (Asset Alloc)	B-	C	A-	Up	Y	1,000,000
PIMCO CommoditiesPLUS® Strategy Fund Administrative Class	PCPSX	NAS CM	Open End	Commodities Broad Basket (Growth & Income)	C	C-	C+		Y	1,000,000
PIMCO CommoditiesPLUS® Strategy Fund Class A	PCLAX	NAS CM	Open End	Commodities Broad Basket (Growth & Income)	C	C-	C+		Y	1,000
PIMCO CommoditiesPLUS® Strategy Fund Class C	PCPCX	NAS CM	Open End	Commodities Broad Basket (Growth & Income)	C	C-	C+		Y	1,000
PIMCO CommoditiesPLUS® Strategy Fund Class I-2	PCLPX	NAS CM	Open End	Commodities Broad Basket (Growth & Income)	C	C-	C+		Y	1,000,000
PIMCO CommoditiesPLUS® Strategy Fund Class I-3	PCLNX	NAS CM	Open End	Commodities Broad Basket (Growth & Income)	C	C-	C+		Y	1,000,000
PIMCO CommoditiesPLUS® Strategy Fund Institutional Class	PCLIX	NAS CM	Open End	Commodities Broad Basket (Growth & Income)	C	C-	C+		Y	1,000,000
PIMCO Commodity Real Return Strategy Fund Class I-3	PCRNX	NAS CM	Open End	Commodities Broad Basket (Growth & Income)	D+	D+	C-		Y	1,000,000
PIMCO CommodityRealReturn Strategy Administrative Cls	PCRRX	NAS CM	Open End	Commodities Broad Basket (Growth & Income)	D+	D	C-		Y	1,000,000
PIMCO CommodityRealReturn Strategy Fund Class A	PCRAX	NAS CM	Open End	Commodities Broad Basket (Growth & Income)	D+	D	C-		Y	1,000
PIMCO CommodityRealReturn Strategy Fund Class C	PCRCX	NAS CM	Open End	Commodities Broad Basket (Growth & Income)	D	D	C-	Down	Y	1,000
PIMCO CommodityRealReturn Strategy Fund Class I-2	PCRPX	NAS CM	Open End	Commodities Broad Basket (Growth & Income)	D+	D+	C-		Y	1,000,000
PIMCO CommodityRealReturn Strategy Fund Class R	PCSRX	NAS CM	Open End	Commodities Broad Basket (Growth & Income)	D+	D	C-		Y	0
PIMCO CommodityRealReturn Strategy Institutional Cls	PCRIX	NAS CM	Open End	Commodities Broad Basket (Growth & Income)	C-	D+	C-	Up	Y	1,000,000
PIMCO Credit Opportunities Bond Fund Class A	PZCRX	NAS CM	Open End	Long/Short Credit (Income)	B-	C+	B+		Y	1,000
PIMCO Credit Opportunities Bond Fund Class C	PCCRX	NAS CM	Open End	Long/Short Credit (Income)	B-	C+	B	Up	Y	1,000
PIMCO Credit Opportunities Bond Fund Class I-2	PPCRX	NAS CM	Open End	Long/Short Credit (Income)	B	C+	B+	Up	Y	1,000,000
PIMCO Credit Opportunities Bond Fund Institutional Class	PCARX	NAS CM	Open End	Long/Short Credit (Income)	B	C+	B+	Up	Y	1,000,000
PIMCO Dividend and Income Fund Class A	PQIZX	NAS CM	Open End	Flexible Alloc (Income)	C+	C	B	Up	Y	1,000
PIMCO Dividend and Income Fund Class C	PQICX	NAS CM	Open End	Flexible Alloc (Income)	C	C	B		Y	1,000
PIMCO Dividend and Income Fund Class I2	PQIPX	NAS CM	Open End	Flexible Alloc (Income)	C	C	B		Y	1,000,000
PIMCO Dividend and Income Fund Institutional Class	PQIIX	NAS CM	Open End	Flexible Alloc (Income)	C+	C	B	Up	Y	1,000,000
PIMCO Energy & Tactical Credit Opps	NRGX	NYSE	Closed End	Alloc Miscellaneous (Utility)	U	U	U		Y	
PIMCO EqS® Long/Short Fund Class A	PMHAX	NAS CM	Open End	Long/Short Equity (Growth)	C	C-	B-	Down	Y	1,000
PIMCO EqS® Long/Short Fund Class C	PMHCX	NAS CM	Open End	Long/Short Equity (Growth)	C	C-	C+		Y	1,000
PIMCO EqS® Long/Short Fund Class I2	PMHBX	NAS CM	Open End	Long/Short Equity (Growth)	C	C-	B	Down	Y	1,000,000
PIMCO EqS® Long/Short Fund Class I-3	PMHNX	NAS CM	Open End	Long/Short Equity (Growth)	C	C-	B-	Down	Y	1,000,000
PIMCO EqS® Long/Short Fund Institutional Class	PMHIX	NAS CM	Open End	Long/Short Equity (Growth)	C	C-	B	Down	Y	1,000,000
PIMCO Global Multi-Asset Fund Class A	PGMAX	NAS CM	Open End	Moderate Alloc (Growth & Income)	B-	C	A-	Up	Y	1,000
PIMCO Global Multi-Asset Fund Class C	PGMCX	NAS CM	Open End	Moderate Alloc (Growth & Income)	B-	C	A-	Up	Y	1,000
PIMCO Global Multi-Asset Fund Class I-2	PGAPX	NAS CM	Open End	Moderate Alloc (Growth & Income)	B	C	A-	Up	Y	1,000,000
PIMCO Global Multi-Asset Fund Institutional Class	PGAIX	NAS CM	Open End	Moderate Alloc (Growth & Income)	B	C	A-	Up	Y	1,000,000
PIMCO Global StocksPLUS and Income Fund	PGP	NYSE	Closed End	Global Equity Large Cap (Multi-Asset Global)	C	C	C-		Y	
PIMCO Inflation Response Multi-Asset Fund Class A	PZRMX	NAS CM	Open End	Cautious Alloc (Growth & Income)	B-	C	A-		Y	1,000
PIMCO Inflation Response Multi-Asset Fund Class I-2	PPRMX	NAS CM	Open End	Cautious Alloc (Growth & Income)	B-	C	A-		Y	1,000,000

★ Expanded analysis of this fund is included in Section II.

Min Additional Investment	3-Month Total Return	6-Month Total Return	1-Year Total Return	3-Year Total Return	5-Year Total Return	Dividend Yield (TTM)	Expense Ratio	3-Yr Std Deviation	3-Year Beta	NAV	Total Assets (MIL)	%Cash	%Stocks	%Bonds	%Other	Turnover Ratio	Last Bull Market Total Return	Last Bear Market Total Return	Front End Fee (%)	Back End Fee (%)	Inception Date
	TOTAL RETURNS					PERFORMANCE				ASSETS		ASSET ALLOCATION & TURNOVER					BULL & BEAR		FEES		
	3.63	23.22	18.73	31.08		2.02	1.05	11.57	1.01	12.14	12.6	2	97	0	1	202					Aug-14
100	2.35	23.28	16.33	21.40	46.50	1.4	1.25	13.32	1	13.41	30.9	5	95	0	0	154	31	-18.24	5.50		Dec-10
100	2.21	22.83	15.46	18.81	41.19	0.78	2	13.36	1	13.14	30.9	5	95	0	0	154	30.37	-18.46		5.00	Dec-10
100	2.22	22.78	15.50	18.76	41.17	0.78	2	13.32	1	13.11	30.9	5	95	0	0	154	30.44	-18.56		1.00	Dec-10
	2.41	23.42	16.59	22.40	48.49	1.62	1	13.36	1	13.43	30.9	5	95	0	0	154	31.16	-18.14			May-17
	2.41	23.42	16.59	22.30	48.36	1.62	1	13.37	1	13.43	30.9	5	95	0	0	154	31.16	-18.14			Dec-10
50	1.79	5.72	1.95	13.81	0.15	4.88	2.74	5.47	0.16	8.3	5,303	-23	28	79	13	39	13.04	-7.39	5.50		Jul-05
50	1.52	5.26	1.17	11.27	-3.57	4.13	3.49	5.47	0.16	8.3	5,303	-23	28	79	13	39	12.47	-7.66		1.00	Jul-05
	1.85	5.86	2.30	15.11	1.94	5.22	2.39	5.47	0.16	8.3	5,303	-23	28	79	13	39	13.15	-7.2			Jul-08
	1.88	5.75	2.19	14.80	1.48	5.11	2.44	5.48	0.16	8.3	5,303	-23	28	79	13	39	13.17	-7.32			Apr-18
	1.87	5.78	2.29	15.32	2.35	5.32	2.29	5.46	0.17	8.3	5,303	-23	28	79	13	39	13.3	-7.24			Oct-03
	2.62	8.38	4.67	21.28	12.90	4.62	1.26	5.46	1.07	11.74	18,004	-35	38	88	8	42	11.38	-7.4			Dec-02
50	2.59	8.30	4.56	20.61	11.69	4.44	1.46	5.49	1.08	11.73	18,004	-35	38	88	8	42	11.21	-7.47	3.75		Apr-03
50	2.37	7.91	3.70	17.86	7.50	3.72	2.21	5.49	1.09	11.67	18,004	-35	38	88	8	42	10.77	-7.79		1.00	Apr-03
	2.65	8.44	4.82	21.82	13.74	4.76	1.11	5.47	1.09	11.75	18,004	-35	38	88	8	42	11.43	-7.32			Apr-08
	2.47	8.15	4.25	19.68	10.28	4.23	1.71	5.46	1.08	11.65	18,004	-35	38	88	8	42	11.07	-7.62			Jan-06
	2.61	8.48	4.76	21.56	13.27	4.62	1.16	5.43	1.09	11.75	18,004	-35	38	88	8	42	11.45	-7.43			Apr-18
	2.68	8.60	5.03	22.22	14.33	4.87	1.01	5.47	1.08	11.72	18,004	-35	38	88	8	42	11.58	-7.36			Jul-02
	-1.49	14.36	-8.32	15.42	-35.62	11.77	1.02	14.46	1.06	5.3	2,705	19	0	32	49	322	10.35	-21.63			Jul-14
50	-1.36	14.25	-8.52	14.78	-36.27	11.65	1.22	14.52	1.06	5.23	2,705	19	0	32	49	322	10.21	-21.75	5.50		May-10
50	-1.57	13.65	-9.23	12.22	-38.69	11.5	1.97	14.42	1.05	4.98	2,705	19	0	32	49	322	9.76	-22.04		1.00	May-10
	-1.27	14.47	-8.22	15.99	-35.06	11.91	0.87	14.53	1.06	5.29	2,705	19	0	32	49	322	10.45	-21.57			May-10
	-1.29	14.46	-8.12	15.68	-35.39	11.92	0.92	14.48	1.06	5.28	2,705	19	0	32	49	322	10.38	-21.61			Apr-18
	-1.43	14.44	-8.27	16.21	-34.83	11.95	0.77	14.4	1.05	5.31	2,705	19	0	32	49	322	10.51	-21.55			May-10
	-0.42	7.92	-6.47	-4.97	-40.10	5.11	1.39	9.59	1.1	5.9	4,994	-14	0	85	29	226	6.01	-19.91			Apr-18
	-0.44	7.86	-6.52	-5.22	-40.37	5.12	1.49	9.59	1.09	5.79	4,994	-14	0	85	29	226	6.04	-20.06			Feb-03
50	-0.48	7.81	-6.74	-5.75	-40.97	4.95	1.69	9.51	1.08	5.76	4,994	-14	0	85	29	226	5.83	-20.03	5.50		Nov-02
50	-0.83	7.33	-7.48	-8.03	-43.17	4.49	2.44	9.57	1.09	5.44	4,994	-14	0	85	29	226	5.58	-20.32		1.00	Nov-02
	-0.58	7.77	-6.45	-4.93	-39.87	5.16	1.34	9.52	1.09	5.89	4,994	-14	0	85	29	226	6.07	-19.9			Apr-08
	-0.54	7.71	-6.95	-6.58	-41.65	4.84	1.94	9.53	1.09	5.62	4,994	-14	0	85	29	226	5.66	-20.11			Mar-10
	-0.55	7.98	-6.46	-4.65	-39.65	5.26	1.24	9.51	1.08	5.91	4,994	-14	0	85	29	226	6.13	-19.84			Jun-02
50	2.20	5.97	5.18	17.69	15.04	3.68	1.31	2.28	10.47	10.06	424.8	28	-1	73	0	110	5.17		3.75		Aug-11
50	1.90	5.55	4.29	14.99	10.74	3.03	2.06	2.27	10.31	9.91	424.8	28	-1	73	0	110	4.8			1.00	Aug-11
	2.18	6.05	5.34	18.65	16.67	4.02	1.01	2.26	10.17	10	424.8	28	-1	73	0	110	5.43				Aug-11
	2.19	6.18	5.52	19.05	17.33	4.09	0.91	2.27	10.67	10.04	424.8	28	-1	73	0	110	5.49				Aug-11
50	1.77	9.77	1.60	24.58	10.76	3.74	1.2	8.6	0.73	11.27	252.0	-8	75	33	0	80			5.50		Dec-11
50	1.57	9.33	0.87	21.76	6.68	2.41	1.95	8.63	0.73	11.29	252.0	-8	75	33	0	80				1.00	Dec-11
	1.84	9.93	1.90	25.67	12.31	4.12	0.95	8.63	0.73	11.29	252.0	-8	75	33	0	80					Dec-11
	1.84	9.95	2.05	25.99	12.80	4.27	0.85	8.7	0.74	11.27	252.0	-8	75	33	0	80					Dec-11
	-0.87						2.96			20	800.0	-40	54	30	55						Jan-19
50	-1.01	0.74	0.00	12.44	10.92	0	2.4	4.56	15.64	10.76	364.0	81	12	-9	17	276	2.89	-7.7	5.50		Apr-12
50	-1.25	0.39	-0.85	9.89	6.77	0	3.15	4.52	15.58	10.19	364.0	81	12	-9	17	276	2.45	-7.98		1.00	Apr-12
	-0.99	0.92	0.17	13.31	12.36	0	2.15	4.58	15.86	10.96	364.0	81	12	-9	17	276	3.04	-7.6			Apr-12
	-0.99	0.82	0.08	12.97	11.78	0	2.2	4.55	15.68	10.95	364.0	81	12	-9	17	276					Apr-18
	-0.98	0.91	0.25	13.59	12.83	0	2.05	4.57	15.62	11.05	364.0	81	12	-9	17	276	3.1	-7.56			Apr-12
50	1.12	9.77	3.98	24.20	22.14	1.76	1.67	6.89		12.65	397.2	-36	55	74	5	551	7.42	-10.13	5.50		Oct-08
50	0.90	9.31	3.21	21.36	17.63	1.22	2.42	6.91		12.28	397.2	-36	55	74	5	551	6.9	-10.44		1.00	Oct-08
	1.19	9.95	4.33	25.57	24.69	2.01	1.32	6.88		12.75	397.2	-36	55	74	5	551	7.73	-9.96			Oct-08
	1.27	10.05	4.48	25.96	25.35	2.08	1.22	6.87		12.78	397.2	-36	55	74	5	551	7.85	-9.99			Oct-08
	6.17	19.78	8.43	63.81	51.51	10.74	0	11.07	0.81	9.89	107.4	-216	57	198	50	63	25.4	-24.33			May-05
50	1.14	6.40	2.48	10.65	4.35	8.78	1.67	4.08		7.96	1,068	33	10	50	7	373	6.82		5.50		Aug-11
	1.19	6.67	2.86	11.91	6.18	8.95	1.32	4.11		8.05	1,068	33	10	50	7	373	6.95				Aug-11

	MARKET		FUND TYPE, CATEGORY & OBJECTIVE		RATINGS				MINIMUMS	
Fund Name	Ticker Symbol	Traded On	Fund Type	Category and (Prospectus Objective)	Overall Rating	Reward Rating	Risk Rating	Recent Up/ Downgrade	Open to New Investors	Min Initial Investment
PIMCO Inflation Response Multi-Asset Fund Institutional	PIRMX	NAS CM	Open End	Cautious Alloc (Growth & Income)	B-	C	B		Y	1,000,000
PIMCO Multi-Strategy Alternative Fund Class A	PXAAX	NAS CM	Open End	Multialternative (Growth & Income)	C+	C	B		Y	1,000
PIMCO Multi-Strategy Alternative Fund Class I-2	PXAPX	NAS CM	Open End	Multialternative (Growth & Income)	B-	C	B+	Up	Y	1,000,000
PIMCO Multi-Strategy Alternative Fund Institutional Class	PXAIX	NAS CM	Open End	Multialternative (Growth & Income)	B-	C	B+		Y	1,000,000
PIMCO Preferred and Capital Securities Fund Class A	PFANX	NAS CM	Open End	US Fixed Income (Growth & Income)	B	B-	A-	Up	Y	1,000
PIMCO Preferred and Capital Securities Fund Class I-2	PFPNX	NAS CM	Open End	US Fixed Income (Growth & Income)	B	B-	A-	Up	Y	1,000,000
PIMCO Preferred and Capital Securities Fund Class I-3	PFNNX	NAS CM	Open End	US Fixed Income (Growth & Income)	B	B-	B	Up	Y	1,000,000
PIMCO Preferred & Capital Securities Institutional Cls	PFINX	NAS CM	Open End	US Fixed Income (Growth & Income)	B	B-	B	Up	Y	1,000,000
PIMCO RAE Emerging Markets Fund Class A	PEAFX	NAS CM	Open End	Global Emerg Mkts (Div Emerging Mkts)	C	C	B-		Y	1,000
PIMCO RAE Emerging Markets Fund Class I-2	PEPFX	NAS CM	Open End	Global Emerg Mkts (Div Emerging Mkts)	C	C	B-		Y	1,000,000
PIMCO RAE Emerging Markets Fund Institutional Class	PEIFX	NAS CM	Open End	Global Emerg Mkts (Div Emerging Mkts)	C	C	B-		Y	1,000,000
PIMCO RAE Fundamental Advantage PLUS Fund Class A	PTFAX	NAS CM	Open End	Market Neutral (Growth & Income)	D+	D	C		Y	1,000
PIMCO RAE Fundamental Advantage PLUS Fund Class I-2	PFAPX	NAS CM	Open End	Market Neutral (Growth & Income)	D+	D	C		Y	1,000,000
PIMCO RAE Fundamental Advantage PLUS Institutional Cls	PFATX	NAS CM	Open End	Market Neutral (Growth & Income)	D+	D	C	Down	Y	1,000,000
PIMCO RAE Global ex-US Fund Class A	PZRAX	NAS CM	Open End	Global Equity Large Cap (Growth)	C	C	C+		Y	1,000
PIMCO RAE Global ex-US Fund Class I-2	PZRPX	NAS CM	Open End	Global Equity Large Cap (Growth)	C	C	C+		Y	1,000,000
PIMCO RAE Global ex-US Fund Institutional Class	PZRIX	NAS CM	Open End	Global Equity Large Cap (Growth)	C	C	C+		Y	1,000,000
PIMCO RAE Global Fund Class A	PFQAX	NAS CM	Open End	Global Equity Large Cap (Growth)	C	C	B		Y	1,000
PIMCO RAE Global Fund Class I-2	PFQPX	NAS CM	Open End	Global Equity Large Cap (Growth)	C	C	B-		Y	1,000,000
PIMCO RAE Global Fund Institutional Class	PFQIX	NAS CM	Open End	Global Equity Large Cap (Growth)	C	C	B-		Y	1,000,000
PIMCO RAE International Fund Class A	PPYAX	NAS CM	Open End	Global Equity Large Cap (Growth)	C	C	C		Y	1,000
PIMCO RAE International Fund Class I-2	PPYPX	NAS CM	Open End	Global Equity Large Cap (Growth)	C	C	C+		Y	1,000,000
PIMCO RAE International Fund Institutional Class	PPYIX	NAS CM	Open End	Global Equity Large Cap (Growth)	C	C	C+		Y	1,000,000
PIMCO RAE Low Volatility PLUS EMG Fund Institutional Class	PLVLX	NAS CM	Open End	Global Emerg Mkts (Div Emerging Mkts)	C	C-	B-		Y	1,000,000
PIMCO RAE Low Volatility PLUS Fund Class A	PXLVX	NAS CM	Open End	US Equity Large Cap Value (Growth & Income)	B-	C+	B+		Y	1,000
PIMCO RAE Low Volatility PLUS Fund Institutional Class	PILVX	NAS CM	Open End	US Equity Large Cap Value (Growth & Income)	B-	C+	B+		Y	1,000,000
PIMCO RAE Low Volatility PLUS International Fund Class I-2	PLVZX	NAS CM	Open End	Global Equity Large Cap (Growth & Income)	C+	C	B	Up	Y	1,000,000
PIMCO RAE Low Volatility PLUS Intl Inst Cls	PLVTX	NAS CM	Open End	Global Equity Large Cap (Growth & Income)	C+	C	B	Up	Y	1,000,000
PIMCO RAE PLUS EMG Fund Class A	PEFFX	NAS CM	Open End	Global Emerg Mkts (Growth & Income)	C	C	B-		Y	1,000
PIMCO RAE PLUS EMG Fund Class C	PEFCX	NAS CM	Open End	Global Emerg Mkts (Growth & Income)	C	C	C+		Y	1,000
PIMCO RAE PLUS EMG Fund Class I-2	PEFPX	NAS CM	Open End	Global Emerg Mkts (Growth & Income)	C	C	B-		Y	1,000,000
PIMCO RAE PLUS EMG Fund Institutional Class	PEFIX	NAS CM	Open End	Global Emerg Mkts (Growth & Income)	C	C	B-		Y	1,000,000
PIMCO RAE PLUS Fund Administrative Class	PXTAX	NAS CM	Open End	US Equity Large Cap Value (Growth & Income)	C+	C	B	Up	Y	1,000,000
PIMCO RAE PLUS Fund Class A	PIXAX	NAS CM	Open End	US Equity Large Cap Value (Growth & Income)	C+	C	B	Up	Y	1,000
PIMCO RAE PLUS Fund Class C	PIXCX	NAS CM	Open End	US Equity Large Cap Value (Growth & Income)	C+	C	B	Up	Y	1,000
PIMCO RAE PLUS Fund Class I-2	PIXPX	NAS CM	Open End	US Equity Large Cap Value (Growth & Income)	C+	C	B		Y	1,000,000
PIMCO RAE PLUS Fund Class I-3	PXTNX	NAS CM	Open End	US Equity Large Cap Value (Growth & Income)	C+	C	B	Up	Y	1,000,000
PIMCO RAE PLUS Fund Institutional Class	PXTIX	NAS CM	Open End	US Equity Large Cap Value (Growth & Income)	C+	C	B		Y	1,000,000
PIMCO RAE PLUS International Fund Class A	PTSOX	NAS CM	Open End	Global Equity Large Cap (Growth & Income)	C	C	C		Y	1,000
PIMCO RAE PLUS International Fund Class I-2	PTIPX	NAS CM	Open End	Global Equity Large Cap (Growth & Income)	C	C	C		Y	1,000,000
PIMCO RAE PLUS International Fund Institutional Class	PTSIX	NAS CM	Open End	Global Equity Large Cap (Growth & Income)	C	C	C		Y	1,000,000
PIMCO RAE PLUS Small Fund Class A	PCFAX	NAS CM	Open End	US Equity Small Cap (Small Company)	C	C-	C		Y	1,000
PIMCO RAE PLUS Small Fund Class C	PCFEX	NAS CM	Open End	US Equity Small Cap (Small Company)	C-	C-	C	Down	Y	1,000
PIMCO RAE PLUS Small Fund Class I-2	PCCPX	NAS CM	Open End	US Equity Small Cap (Small Company)	C	C-	C		Y	1,000,000
PIMCO RAE PLUS Small Fund Institutional Class	PCFIX	NAS CM	Open End	US Equity Small Cap (Small Company)	C	C-	C		Y	1,000,000
PIMCO RAE US Fund Class A	PKAAX	NAS CM	Open End	US Equity Large Cap Value (Growth)	C+	C	B		Y	1,000
PIMCO RAE US Fund Class I-2	PKAPX	NAS CM	Open End	US Equity Large Cap Value (Growth)	C+	C	B		Y	1,000,000
PIMCO RAE US Fund Institutional Class	PKAIX	NAS CM	Open End	US Equity Large Cap Value (Growth)	C+	C	B		Y	1,000,000
PIMCO RAE US Small Fund Class A	PMJAX	NAS CM	Open End	US Equity Small Cap (Small Company)	C	C-	C		Y	1,000
PIMCO RAE US Small Fund Class I-2	PMJPX	NAS CM	Open End	US Equity Small Cap (Small Company)	C	C-	C		Y	1,000,000
PIMCO RAE US Small Fund Institutional Class	PMJIX	NAS CM	Open End	US Equity Small Cap (Small Company)	C	C-	C		Y	1,000,000
PIMCO RAE Worldwide Long/Short PLUS Institutional Cls	PWLIX	NAS CM	Open End	Long/Short Equity (Growth)	B	C	A-		Y	1,000,000

★ Expanded analysis of this fund is included in Section II.

	TOTAL RETURNS					PERFORMANCE				ASSETS		ASSET ALLOCATION & TURNOVER					BULL & BEAR		FEES		
Min Additional Investment	3-Month Total Return	6-Month Total Return	1-Year Total Return	3-Year Total Return	5-Year Total Return	Dividend Yield (TTM)	Expense Ratio	3-Yr Std Deviation	3-Year Beta	NAV	Total Assets (MIL)	%Cash	%Stocks	%Bonds	%Other	Turnover Ratio	Last Bull Market Total Return	Last Bear Market Total Return	Front End Fee (%)	Back End Fee (%)	Inception Date
	1.21	6.69	2.92	12.24	6.68	9.01	1.22	4.14		8.05	1,068	33	10	50	7	373	6.97				Aug-11
50	0.28	3.36	2.79	9.60		1.72	1.74	2.59	10.76	10.05	136.1	4	17	49	30	148			3.75		Dec-14
	0.43	3.60	3.22	10.69		2.12	1.44	2.58	11.3	10	136.1	4	17	49	30	148					Dec-14
	0.45	3.64	3.28	11.06		2.19	1.34	2.6	10.92	10.01	136.1	4	17	49	30	148					Dec-14
50	4.40	11.42	8.29	29.44		5.56	1.15	5.05		10.24	771.6	11	2	49	13	57			3.75		Apr-15
	4.44	11.62	8.57	30.44		5.71	0.9	5		10.26	771.6	11	2	49	13	57					Apr-15
	4.54	11.61	8.56	30.17		5.8	0.95	5.05		10.25	771.6	11	2	49	13	57					Apr-18
	4.55	11.75	8.76	30.84		5.79	0.8	5.04		10.28	771.6	11	2	49	13	57					Apr-15
50	2.71	9.45	2.21	40.84	15.25	2.43	1.11	14.61	1.08	9.84	2,665	0	100	0	0	28	17.38	-26.83	3.75		Jun-15
	2.81	9.67	2.41	41.97	16.44	2.43	0.86	14.66	1.08	9.86	2,665	0	100	0	0	28	17.55	-26.75			Jun-15
	2.79	9.61	2.40	42.33	17.16	2.41	0.76	14.64	1.08	9.92	2,665	0	100	0	0	28	17.61	-26.72			Jun-15
50	-1.04	-1.65	-3.69	-0.08	-8.31	0.15	1.36	3.07	-1.08	9.51	1,812	132	0	-48	13	408	4.37	-5.31	3.75		Jul-08
	-1.01	-1.62	-3.47	0.65	-6.85	0.31	1.06	3.11	-0.93	9.72	1,812	132	0	-48	13	408	4.42	-5.09			Jun-10
	-1.01	-1.61	-3.30	1.05	-6.50	0.37	0.96	3.05	-1.13	9.75	1,812	132	0	-48	13	408	4.7	-5.11			Feb-08
50	1.50	9.62	-1.89	30.00		2.4	0.9	11.62	1.01	10.14	78.1	1	99	0	0	9			3.75		Jun-15
	1.59	9.79	-1.59	30.87		2.48	0.65	11.68	1.02	10.2	78.1	1	99	0	0	9					Jun-15
	1.58	9.88	-1.50	31.26		2.56	0.55	11.67	1.02	10.23	78.1	1	99	0	0	9					Jun-15
50	1.79	11.84	0.82	32.39		2.63	0.86	11.33	1.03	10.2	294.3	0	100	0	0	19			3.75		Jun-15
	1.88	11.87	0.99	33.31		2.68	0.61	11.36	1.04	10.27	294.3	0	100	0	0	19					Jun-15
	1.87	11.95	1.07	33.68		2.75	0.51	11.35	1.04	10.3	294.3	0	100	0	0	19					Jun-15
50	1.26	9.79	-3.03	26.96		2.56	0.86	11.35	0.97	9.64	553.0	0	100	0	0	47			3.75		Jun-15
	1.35	9.96	-2.72	28.08		2.55	0.61	11.4	0.98	9.71	553.0	0	100	0	0	47					Jun-15
	1.35	9.93	-2.72	28.23		2.54	0.51	11.45	0.98	9.74	553.0	0	100	0	0	47					Jun-15
	0.53	4.82	1.31	31.32	5.13	10.97	1.27	11.64	0.8	8.55	742.4	54	100	-72	15	307					Dec-13
50	2.49	15.64	9.81	34.19	53.25	7.24	1.27	10.74	0.8	8.8	68.0	48	100	-50	0	431			3.75		Dec-13
	2.74	15.94	10.39	35.98	56.55	7.28	0.87	10.72	0.81	8.98	68.0	48	100	-50	0	431					Dec-13
	1.89	11.59	0.48	30.26	22.25	2.38	1.02	9.88	0.83	7.94	510.7	29	100	-41	10	339					Dec-13
	1.90	11.59	0.54	30.62	22.84	2.43	0.92	9.83	0.83	7.97	510.7	29	100	-41	10	339					Dec-13
50	3.77	11.25	2.61	48.32	13.30	1.38	1.58	15.18	1.12	10.18	3,120	23	100	-35	9	339	24.37	-29.13	3.75		May-13
50	3.68	10.79	1.89	44.92	9.13	1.07	2.33	15.09	1.12	9.85	3,120	23	100	-35	9	339	23.83	-29.35		1.00	May-13
	3.82	11.44	2.91	49.58	15.08	1.57	1.28	15.12	1.12	10.32	3,120	23	100	-35	9	339	24.69	-29.14			Jan-11
	3.92	11.55	3.08	50.13	15.60	1.63	1.18	15.12	1.12	10.33	3,120	23	100	-35	9	339	24.66	-29.01			Nov-08
	2.32	15.73	3.86	43.69	43.15	0.88	1.1	13.28	1.08	6.96	1,722	15	100	-33	16	399	31.56	-18.59			Jun-05
50	2.21	15.84	3.72	42.83	42.04	0.82	1.25	13.2	1.07	6.76	1,722	15	100	-33	16	399	31.13	-18.41	3.75		Jun-05
50	1.97	15.34	2.87	39.60	36.70	0.54	2	13.26	1.08	6.16	1,722	15	100	-33	16	399	30.98	-18.79		1.00	Jun-05
	2.31	16.00	3.91	44.32	44.16	0.97	0.95	13.15	1.07	7.09	1,722	15	100	-33	16	399	31.5	-18.37			Apr-08
	2.30	15.82	3.95	43.79	43.49	1.02	1	13.32	1.08	7.09	1,722	15	100	-33	16	399	31.52	-18.4			Apr-18
	2.45	16.04	4.06	44.60	44.88	1.01	0.85	13.28	1.08	7.15	1,722	15	100	-33	16	399	31.67	-18.33			Jun-05
50	1.48	10.94	-3.74	35.88	2.65	19.38	1.29	12.24	1.06	7.15	482.6	15	100	-19	0	366	13.43		3.75		Feb-14
	1.67	11.02	-3.48	37.10	4.14	19.58	1.04	12.27	1.06	7.17	482.6	15	100	-19	0	366	13.59				May-14
	1.70	11.05	-3.38	37.38	4.64	19.68	0.94	12.29	1.07	7.18	482.6	15	100	-19	0	366	13.66				Sep-11
50	0.70	13.25	-8.14	42.02	35.47	2.48	1.24	17.69	1.01	10.34	163.7	5	101	-18	9	405	31.54		3.75		Feb-14
50	0.49	12.74	-8.80	38.88	30.46	1.89	1.99	17.64	1.01	10.13	163.7	5	101	-18	9	405	30.97			1.00	Feb-14
	0.74	13.37	-7.87	43.04	37.23	2.7	0.99	17.65	1.01	10.41	163.7	5	101	-18	9	405	31.73				May-14
	0.77	13.39	-7.82	43.48	37.82	2.79	0.89	17.67	1.01	10.44	163.7	5	101	-18	9	405	31.81				Sep-11
50	2.05	14.57	4.24	34.51	43.73	1.87	0.81	12.67	1.03	10.93	764.3	1	99	0	0	44	23.38	-17.48	3.75		Jun-15
	2.12	14.76	4.58	35.77	46.15	1.85	0.51	12.62	1.02	11.04	764.3	1	99	0	0	44	23.59	-17.37			Jun-15
	2.21	14.80	4.66	36.22	46.90	1.84	0.41	12.68	1.03	11.09	764.3	1	99	0	0	44	23.67	-17.34			Jun-15
50	0.47	12.28	-7.04	31.95	34.57	0.78	0.91	17.21	0.99	10.6	125.8	1	99	0	0	30	27.69	-25.63	3.75		Jun-15
	0.56	12.43	-6.84	33.19	36.58	0.78	0.61	17.16	0.98	10.67	125.8	1	99	0	0	30	27.91	-25.53			Jun-15
	0.56	12.48	-6.74	33.56	37.27	0.77	0.51	17.21	0.99	10.72	125.8	1	99	0	0	30	27.98	-25.5			Jun-15
	0.68	6.35	6.00	23.35		3.14	1.23	6.83	17.54	10.12	1,629	24	85	-21	9	337					Dec-14

	MARKET			FUND TYPE, CATEGORY & OBJECTIVE	RATINGS				MINIMUMS	
Fund Name	Ticker Symbol	Traded On	Fund Type	Category and (Prospectus Objective)	Overall Rating	Reward Rating	Risk Rating	Recent Up/ Downgrade	Open to New Investors	Min Initial Investment
PIMCO RealEstateRealReturn Strategy Fund Class A	PETAX	NAS CM	Open End	Real Estate Sector Equity (Real Estate)	C	C	C+		Y	1,000
PIMCO RealEstateRealReturn Strategy Fund Class C	PETCX	NAS CM	Open End	Real Estate Sector Equity (Real Estate)	C	C	C+		Y	1,000
PIMCO RealEstateRealReturn Strategy Fund Class I-2	PETPX	NAS CM	Open End	Real Estate Sector Equity (Real Estate)	C+	C	C+	Up	Y	1,000,000
PIMCO RealEstateRealReturn Strategy Fund I-3	PNRNX	NAS CM	Open End	Real Estate Sector Equity (Real Estate)	C	C	C+		Y	1,000,000
PIMCO RealEstateRealReturn Strategy Institutional Cls	PRRSX	NAS CM	Open End	Real Estate Sector Equity (Real Estate)	C+	C	C+	Up	Y	1,000,000
PIMCO RealPath Blend 2020 Fund Administrative Class	PBZDX	NAS CM	Open End	Target Date (Asset Alloc)	B	C+	A	Up	Y	1,000,000
PIMCO RealPath Blend 2020 Fund Class A	PBZAX	NAS CM	Open End	Target Date (Asset Alloc)	B	C+	A-	Up	Y	1,000
PIMCO RealPath Blend 2020 Fund Institutional Class	PBZNX	NAS CM	Open End	Target Date (Asset Alloc)	B	C+	A	Up	Y	1,000,000
PIMCO RealPath Blend 2025 Fund Administrative Class	PPZDX	NAS CM	Open End	Target Date (Asset Alloc)	B	C+	A	Up	Y	1,000,000
PIMCO RealPath Blend 2025 Fund Class A	PPZAX	NAS CM	Open End	Target Date (Asset Alloc)	B	C	A-	Up	Y	1,000
PIMCO RealPath Blend 2025 Fund Institutional Class	PPZRX	NAS CM	Open End	Target Date (Asset Alloc)	B	C+	A	Up	Y	1,000,000
PIMCO RealPath Blend 2030 Fund Administrative Class	PBPRX	NAS CM	Open End	Target Date (Asset Alloc)	B	C	A-	Up	Y	1,000,000
PIMCO RealPath Blend 2030 Fund Class A	PBPAX	NAS CM	Open End	Target Date (Asset Alloc)	B-	C	A-	Up	Y	1,000
PIMCO RealPath Blend 2030 Fund Institutional Class	PBPNX	NAS CM	Open End	Target Date (Asset Alloc)	B	C	A-	Up	Y	1,000,000
PIMCO RealPath Blend 2035 Fund Administrative Class	PDGDX	NAS CM	Open End	Target Date (Asset Alloc)	B-	C	B+	Up	Y	1,000,000
PIMCO RealPath Blend 2035 Fund Class A	PDGAX	NAS CM	Open End	Target Date (Asset Alloc)	B-	C	B+	Up	Y	1,000
PIMCO RealPath Blend 2035 Fund Institutional Class	PDGZX	NAS CM	Open End	Target Date (Asset Alloc)	B-	C	B+	Up	Y	1,000,000
PIMCO RealPath Blend 2040 Fund Administrative Class	PVPRX	NAS CM	Open End	Target Date (Asset Alloc)	B-	C	B+	Up	Y	1,000,000
PIMCO RealPath Blend 2040 Fund Class A	PVPAX	NAS CM	Open End	Target Date (Asset Alloc)	B-	C	B+	Up	Y	1,000
PIMCO RealPath Blend 2040 Fund Institutional Class	PVPNX	NAS CM	Open End	Target Date (Asset Alloc)	B-	C	B+	Up	Y	1,000,000
PIMCO RealPath Blend 2045 Fund Administrative Class	PVQDX	NAS CM	Open End	Target Date (Asset Alloc)	B-	C	B+	Up	Y	1,000,000
PIMCO RealPath Blend 2045 Fund Class A	PVQAX	NAS CM	Open End	Target Date (Asset Alloc)	B-	C	B+	Up	Y	1,000
PIMCO RealPath Blend 2045 Fund Institutional Class	PVQNX	NAS CM	Open End	Target Date (Asset Alloc)	B-	C	B+	Up	Y	1,000,000
PIMCO RealPath Blend 2050 Fund Administrative Class	PPQDX	NAS CM	Open End	Target Date (Asset Alloc)	B-	C	B+	Up	Y	1,000,000
PIMCO RealPath Blend 2050 Fund Class A	PPQAX	NAS CM	Open End	Target Date (Asset Alloc)	B-	C	B+	Up	Y	1,000
PIMCO RealPath Blend 2050 Fund Institutional Class	PPQZX	NAS CM	Open End	Target Date (Asset Alloc)	B-	C	B+	Up	Y	1,000,000
PIMCO RealPath Blend 2055 Fund Administrative Class	PRQDX	NAS CM	Open End	Target Date (Asset Alloc)	B-	C	B+	Up	Y	1,000,000
PIMCO RealPath Blend 2055 Fund Class A	PRQAX	NAS CM	Open End	Target Date (Asset Alloc)	B-	C	B+	Up	Y	1,000
PIMCO RealPath Blend 2055 Fund Institutional Class	PRQZX	NAS CM	Open End	Target Date (Asset Alloc)	B-	C	B+	Up	Y	1,000,000
PIMCO RealPath Blend Income Fund Administrative Class	PBRDX	NAS CM	Open End	Target Date (Asset Alloc)	B	C+	A	Up	Y	1,000,000
PIMCO RealPath Blend Income Fund Class A	PBRAX	NAS CM	Open End	Target Date (Asset Alloc)	B	C+	A-	Up	Y	1,000
PIMCO RealPath Blend Income Fund Institutional Class	PBRNX	NAS CM	Open End	Target Date (Asset Alloc)	B	C+	A	Up	Y	1,000,000
PIMCO StocksPLUS® Absolute Return Fund Class A	PTOAX	NAS CM	Open End	US Equity Large Cap Blend (Growth & Income)	B-	C	B		Y	1,000
PIMCO StocksPLUS® Absolute Return Fund Class C	PSOCX	NAS CM	Open End	US Equity Large Cap Blend (Growth & Income)	B-	C	B	Up	Y	1,000
PIMCO StocksPLUS® Absolute Return Fund Class I-2	PTOPX	NAS CM	Open End	US Equity Large Cap Blend (Growth & Income)	B-	C	B		Y	1,000,000
PIMCO StocksPLUS® Absolute Return Fund I-3	PSPNX	NAS CM	Open End	US Equity Large Cap Blend (Growth & Income)	B-	C	B		Y	1,000,000
PIMCO StocksPLUS® Absolute Return Fund Institutional Class	PSPTX	NAS CM	Open End	US Equity Large Cap Blend (Growth & Income)	B-	C+	B		Y	1,000,000
PIMCO StocksPLUS® Fund Administrative Class	PPLAX	NAS CM	Open End	US Equity Large Cap Blend (Growth & Income)	B-	C+	B		Y	1,000,000
PIMCO StocksPLUS® Fund Class A	PSPAX	NAS CM	Open End	US Equity Large Cap Blend (Growth & Income)	B-	C+	B		Y	1,000
PIMCO StocksPLUS® Fund Class C	PSPCX	NAS CM	Open End	US Equity Large Cap Blend (Growth & Income)	B-	C	B		Y	1,000
PIMCO StocksPLUS® Fund Class I-2	PSKPX	NAS CM	Open End	US Equity Large Cap Blend (Growth & Income)	B-	C+	B		Y	1,000,000
PIMCO StocksPLUS® Fund Class R	PSPRX	NAS CM	Open End	US Equity Large Cap Blend (Growth & Income)	B-	C+	B		Y	0
PIMCO StocksPLUS® Fund I-3	PSTNX	NAS CM	Open End	US Equity Large Cap Blend (Growth & Income)	B-	C+	B		Y	1,000,000
PIMCO StocksPLUS® Fund Institutional Class	PSTKX	NAS CM	Open End	US Equity Large Cap Blend (Growth & Income)	B-	C+	B		Y	1,000,000
PIMCO StocksPLUS® International (U.S. Dollar-Hedged) Cls A	PIPAX	NAS CM	Open End	Global Equity Large Cap (Growth & Income)	B-	C	B	Up	Y	1,000
PIMCO StocksPLUS® International (U.S. Dollar-Hedged) Cls C	PIPCX	NAS CM	Open End	Global Equity Large Cap (Growth & Income)	B-	C	B	Up	Y	1,000
PIMCO StocksPLUS® Intl (U.S. Dollar-Hedged) Cls I-2	PIUHX	NAS CM	Open End	Global Equity Large Cap (Growth & Income)	B-	C	B	Up	Y	1,000,000
PIMCO StocksPLUS® International (U.S. Dollar-Hedged) I-3	PISNX	NAS CM	Open End	Global Equity Large Cap (Growth & Income)	B-	C	B	Up	Y	1,000,000
PIMCO StocksPLUS® Intl (U.S. Dollar-Hedged) Inst Cls	PISIX	NAS CM	Open End	Global Equity Large Cap (Growth & Income)	B-	C	B	Up	Y	1,000,000
PIMCO StocksPLUS® International Fund (Unhedged) Class A	PPUAX	NAS CM	Open End	Global Equity Large Cap (Growth & Income)	C	C	B		Y	1,000
PIMCO StocksPLUS® International Fund (Unhedged) Class C	PPUCX	NAS CM	Open End	Global Equity Large Cap (Growth & Income)	C	C	B-		Y	1,000
PIMCO StocksPLUS® International Fund (Unhedged) Class I-2	PPLPX	NAS CM	Open End	Global Equity Large Cap (Growth & Income)	C	C	B		Y	1,000,000

★Expanded analysis of this fund is included in Section II.

Min Additional Investment	TOTAL RETURNS: 3-Month Total Return	6-Month Total Return	1-Year Total Return	3-Year Total Return	5-Year Total Return	PERFORMANCE: Dividend Yield (TTM)	Expense Ratio	3-Yr Std Deviation	3-Year Beta	ASSETS: NAV	Total Assets (MIL)	ASSET ALLOCATION & TURNOVER: %Cash	%Stocks	%Bonds	%Other	Turnover Ratio	BULL & BEAR: Last Bull Market Total Return	Last Bear Market Total Return	FEES: Front End Fee (%)	Back End Fee (%)	Inception Date
50	2.66	21.31	12.36	14.01	42.96	5.15	1.66	13.44	1.01	8.14	1,371	-108	99	108	0	200	39.86	-10.33	5.50		Oct-03
50	2.56	21.06	11.57	11.59	37.86	6.51	2.41	13.45	1.02	6.93	1,371	-108	99	108	0	200	39.11	-10.55		1.00	Oct-03
	2.84	21.59	12.84	15.09	45.36	5.02	1.36	13.42	1.01	8.88	1,371	-108	99	108	0	200	40.08	-10.11			Apr-08
	2.82	21.65	12.67	14.81	44.44	4.66	1.41	13.4	1.01	8.9	1,371	-108	99	108	0	200	40.07	-10.3			Apr-18
	2.78	21.56	12.76	15.45	45.83	4.75	1.26	13.48	1.02	9.07	1,371	-108	99	108	0	200	40.24	-10.23			Oct-03
	3.10	10.94	6.24	23.40		2.8	0.73	5.38	0.86	11.13	48.6	-15	40	69	6	71					Dec-14
50	3.14	10.92	5.99	22.66		2.57	0.98	5.41	0.87	11.13	48.6	-15	40	69	6	71			5.50		Dec-14
	3.16	11.06	6.49	24.32		3.03	0.48	5.38	0.86	11.14	48.6	-15	40	69	6	71					Dec-14
	3.14	12.19	6.19	25.70		2.58	0.68	6.4	0.89	11.31	58.4	-8	49	53	5	75					Dec-14
50	3.17	12.16	6.03	24.89		2.36	0.93	6.42	0.89	11.31	58.4	-8	49	53	5	75			5.50		Dec-14
	3.20	12.40	6.43	26.71		2.8	0.43	6.43	0.89	11.33	58.4	-8	49	53	5	75					Dec-14
	3.28	13.71	6.49	29.41		2.46	0.63	7.51	0.91	11.52	79.9	-6	57	42	5	98					Dec-14
50	3.22	13.61	6.27	28.54		2.26	0.88	7.56	0.92	11.5	79.9	-6	57	42	5	98			5.50		Dec-14
	3.43	13.93	6.83	30.41		2.68	0.38	7.54	0.91	11.54	79.9	-6	57	42	5	98					Dec-14
	3.38	14.48	6.42	31.57		2.43	0.57	8.36	0.91	11.57	65.7	-4	65	33	5	101					Dec-14
50	3.30	14.28	6.15	30.55		2.2	0.82	8.36	0.91	11.61	65.7	-4	65	33	5	101			5.50		Dec-14
	3.35	14.59	6.67	32.53		2.65	0.32	8.37	0.91	11.58	65.7	-4	65	33	5	101					Dec-14
	3.31	15.07	6.20	32.60		2.31	0.52	9.07	0.92	11.69	84.8	-3	72	25	5	95					Dec-14
50	3.27	14.87	5.98	31.57		2.11	0.77	9.08	0.92	11.67	84.8	-3	72	25	5	95			5.50		Dec-14
	3.37	15.17	6.44	33.65		2.53	0.27	9.08	0.92	11.71	84.8	-3	72	25	5	95					Dec-14
	3.28	15.55	6.21	33.59		2.44	0.49	9.58	0.94	11.65	84.7	-2	77	20	5	105					Dec-14
50	3.22	15.44	5.87	32.49		2.23	0.74	9.57	0.94	11.64	84.7	-2	77	20	5	105			5.50		Dec-14
	3.33	15.65	6.44	34.46		2.65	0.24	9.55	0.94	11.67	84.7	-2	77	20	5	105					Dec-14
	3.27	15.99	6.21	34.08		2.35	0.47	9.86	0.94	11.71	105.8	-1	80	16	5	108					Dec-14
50	3.22	15.81	5.99	33.14		2.14	0.72	9.88	0.94	11.67	105.8	-1	80	16	5	108			5.50		Dec-14
	3.41	16.18	6.53	35.21		2.56	0.22	9.91	0.95	11.74	105.8	-1	80	16	5	108					Dec-14
	3.18	15.74	6.01	33.68		1.57	0.47	9.86	0.94	11.78	35.4	-1	81	15	5	67					Dec-14
50	3.21	15.68	5.86	32.65		1.33	0.72	9.83	0.93	11.73	35.4	-1	81	15	5	67			5.50		Dec-14
	3.32	15.95	6.40	34.81		1.75	0.22	9.9	0.94	11.79	35.4	-1	81	15	5	67					Dec-14
	3.10	10.73	6.43	22.54		2.85	0.75	5.03	1.22	11.28	40.2	-12	38	68	6	34					Dec-14
50	3.16	10.67	6.25	21.67		2.67	1	5.01	1.22	11.24	40.2	-12	38	68	6	34			5.50		Dec-14
	3.26	10.86	6.69	23.42		3.08	0.5	4.96	1.21	11.28	40.2	-12	38	68	6	34					Dec-14
50	4.47	20.52	9.19	54.56	62.59	2.93	1.11	12.65	1.03	10.41	2,030	30	100	-45	13	412	32.47	-19.02	3.75		Jul-03
50	4.18	20.06	8.36	51.02	56.49	2.67	1.86	12.67	1.04	9.35	2,030	30	100	-45	13	412	31.94	-19.32		1.00	Jul-03
	4.51	20.67	9.46	55.99	65.01	3.19	0.81	12.6	1.03	10.47	2,030	30	100	-45	13	412	32.64	-18.86			Apr-08
	4.50	20.66	9.46	55.58	64.37	3.19	0.86	12.68	1.04	10.46	2,030	30	100	-45	13	412	32.64	-18.94			Apr-18
	4.56	20.76	9.63	56.42	65.93	3.23	0.71	12.68	1.04	10.62	2,030	30	100	-45	13	412	32.79	-18.87			Jun-02
	4.50	20.45	10.20	50.89	63.11	3.71	0.82	12.53	1.03	9.65	845.6	-12	100	1	10	281	28.63	-18.71			Jan-97
50	4.42	20.51	10.06	50.38	61.80	3.62	0.97	12.47	1.02	9.54	845.6	-12	100	1	10	281	28.19	-18.81	3.75		Jan-97
50	4.28	20.04	9.41	47.95	57.71	3.46	1.47	12.43	1.02	8.93	845.6	-12	100	1	10	281	27.78	-18.93		1.00	Jan-97
	4.50	20.63	10.38	51.63	64.24	3.54	0.67	12.51	1.02	10.42	845.6	-12	100	1	10	281	28.51	-18.86			Apr-08
	4.33	20.32	9.82	49.11	59.79	3.34	1.22	12.5	1.02	9.87	845.6	-12	100	1	10	281	28.1	-18.89			Dec-02
	4.45	20.62	10.33	51.13	63.36	3.48	0.72	12.53	1.03	10.41	845.6	-12	100	1	10	281	28.26	-18.67			Apr-18
	4.50	20.60	10.48	52.01	64.97	3.64	0.57	12.54	1.03	10.45	845.6	-12	100	1	10	281	28.4	-18.6			May-93
50	3.91	16.76	4.10	46.04	37.19	4.9	1.24	10.81	1.11	7.49	3,084	19	100	-37	16	301	16.99	-19.47	3.75		Oct-03
50	3.72	16.30	3.35	42.91	32.03	4.71	1.99	10.86	1.11	6.82	3,084	19	100	-37	16	301	16.51	-19.75		1.00	Oct-03
	3.93	16.84	4.35	47.38	39.20	4.97	0.94	10.79	1.1	7.84	3,084	19	100	-37	16	301	17.42	-19.49			Mar-12
	3.92	16.91	4.34	47.09	38.58	5.09	0.99	10.74	1.1	7.83	3,084	19	100	-37	16	301	17.17	-19.52			Apr-18
	3.90	16.87	4.51	47.81	39.82	4.99	0.84	10.77	1.1	7.92	3,084	19	100	-37	16	301	17.31	-19.46			Oct-03
50	3.76	15.51	-0.26	34.63	9.31	2.65	1.12	11.8	1.06	5.6	341.7	33	100	-38	0	325	19.27	-24.64	3.75		Nov-06
50	3.65	15.14	-1.03	31.76	5.28	2.26	1.87	11.82	1.06	5.29	341.7	33	100	-38	0	325	18.88	-24.73		1.00	Nov-06
	3.69	15.42	-0.05	35.83	10.96	2.77	0.82	11.8	1.06	5.8	341.7	33	100	-38	0	325	19.65	-24.45			Apr-08

	MARKET			FUND TYPE, CATEGORY & OBJECTIVE	RATINGS				MINIMUMS	
Fund Name	Ticker Symbol	Traded On	Fund Type	Category and (Prospectus Objective)	Overall Rating	Reward Rating	Risk Rating	Recent Up/ Downgrade	Open to New Investors	Min Initial Investment
PIMCO StocksPLUS® International Fund (Unhedged) Class I-3	PSKNX	NAS CM	Open End	Global Equity Large Cap (Growth & Income)	C	C	B		Y	1,000,000
PIMCO StocksPLUS® Intl (Unhedged) Inst Cls	PSKIX	NAS CM	Open End	Global Equity Large Cap (Growth & Income)	C	C	B		Y	1,000,000
PIMCO StocksPLUS® Long Duration Fund Institutional Class	PSLDX	NAS CM	Open End	Aggressive Alloc (Growth & Income)	B	B	B-	Up	Y	1,000,000
PIMCO StocksPLUS® Short Fund Class A	PSSAX	NAS CM	Open End	Alternative Miscellaneous (Growth & Income)	D	D	D		Y	1,000
PIMCO StocksPLUS® Short Fund Class C	PSSCX	NAS CM	Open End	Alternative Miscellaneous (Growth & Income)	D	D	D		Y	1,000
PIMCO StocksPLUS® Short Fund Class I-2	PSPLX	NAS CM	Open End	Alternative Miscellaneous (Growth & Income)	D	D	D		Y	1,000,000
PIMCO StocksPLUS® Short Fund I-3	PSNNX	NAS CM	Open End	Alternative Miscellaneous (Growth & Income)	D	D	D		Y	1,000,000
PIMCO StocksPLUS® Short Fund Institutional Class	PSTIX	NAS CM	Open End	Alternative Miscellaneous (Growth & Income)	D	D	D		Y	1,000,000
PIMCO StocksPLUS® Small Fund Administrative Class	PCKTX	NAS CM	Open End	US Equity Small Cap (Growth & Income)	C	C	C+		Y	1,000,000
PIMCO StocksPLUS® Small Fund Class A	PCKAX	NAS CM	Open End	US Equity Small Cap (Growth & Income)	C	C	C+		Y	1,000
PIMCO StocksPLUS® Small Fund Class C	PCKCX	NAS CM	Open End	US Equity Small Cap (Growth & Income)	C	C	C+		Y	1,000
PIMCO StocksPLUS® Small Fund Class I-2	PCKPX	NAS CM	Open End	US Equity Small Cap (Growth & Income)	C	C	C+		Y	1,000,000
PIMCO StocksPLUS® Small Fund Class I-3	PSNSX	NAS CM	Open End	US Equity Small Cap (Growth & Income)	C	C	C+		Y	1,000,000
PIMCO StocksPLUS® Small Fund Institutional Class	PSCSX	NAS CM	Open End	US Equity Small Cap (Growth & Income)	C	C	C+		Y	1,000,000
PIMCO TRENDS Managed Futures Strategy Fund Class A	PQTAX	NAS CM	Open End	Alternative Miscellaneous (Income)	C	C	B-		Y	1,000
PIMCO TRENDS Managed Futures Strategy Fund Class C	PQTCX	NAS CM	Open End	Alternative Miscellaneous (Income)	C	C	C+	Up	Y	1,000
PIMCO TRENDS Managed Futures Strategy Fund Class I-2	PQTPX	NAS CM	Open End	Alternative Miscellaneous (Income)	C	C	B-		Y	1,000,000
PIMCO TRENDS Managed Futures Strategy Fund Class I-3	PQTNX	NAS CM	Open End	Alternative Miscellaneous (Income)	C	C	B-		Y	1,000,000
PIMCO TRENDS Managed Futures Strategy Institutional Cls	PQTIX	NAS CM	Open End	Alternative Miscellaneous (Income)	C+	C	B-	Up	Y	1,000,000
Pin Oak Equity Fund	POGSX	NAS CM	Open End	US Equity Large Cap Blend (Aggr Growth)	B-	C	B		Y	2,000
PineBridge Dynamic Asset Allocation Institutional Shares	PDAIX	NAS CM	Open End	Moderate Alloc (Asset Alloc)	C+	C-	B	Up	Y	1,000,000
PineBridge Dynamic Asset Allocation Inv Servicing Shares	PDAVX	NAS CM	Open End	Moderate Alloc (Asset Alloc)	C+	C-	B	Up	Y	100,000
Pinnacle Dynamic Growth Fund Class C	PCDGX	NAS CM	Open End	Flexible Alloc (Growth)	U	U	U		Y	2,000
Pinnacle Dynamic Growth Fund Class I	PIDGX	NAS CM	Open End	Flexible Alloc (Growth)	U	U	U		Y	1,000,000
Pinnacle Sherman Multi-Strategy Core Fund Class A	APSHX	NAS CM	Open End	Moderate Alloc (Growth & Income)	C-	C-	C-	Up	Y	2,000
Pinnacle Sherman Multi-Strategy Core Fund Class C	CPSHX	NAS CM	Open End	Moderate Alloc (Growth & Income)	D+	D+	C-		Y	2,000
Pinnacle Sherman Multi-Strategy Core Fund Class I	IPSHX	NAS CM	Open End	Moderate Alloc (Growth & Income)	C-	C-	C-	Up	Y	1,000,000
Pinnacle Sherman Tactical Allocation Fund Class A Shares	PTAFX	NAS CM	Open End	Moderate Alloc (Growth & Income)	D+	D+	C	Up	Y	2,000
Pinnacle Sherman Tactical Allocation Fund Class C Shares	PTCFX	NAS CM	Open End	Moderate Alloc (Growth & Income)	D+	D	C-	Up	Y	2,000
Pinnacle Sherman Tactical Allocation Fund Class I Shares	PTIFX	NAS CM	Open End	Moderate Alloc (Growth & Income)	D+	D+	C		Y	1,000,000
Pinnacle TrendRating Innovative Equity Fund Class A	APTRX	NAS CM	Open End	US Equity Large Cap Blend (Income)	U	U	U		Y	2,000
Pinnacle TrendRating Innovative Equity Fund Class C	CPTRX	NAS CM	Open End	US Equity Large Cap Blend (Income)	U	U	U		Y	2,000
Pinnacle TrendRating Innovative Equity Fund Class I	IPTRX	NAS CM	Open End	US Equity Large Cap Blend (Income)	U	U	U		Y	1,000,000
Pinnacle Value Fund	PVFIX	NAS CM	Open End	US Equity Small Cap (Small Company)	D+	D	C-	Down	Y	2,500
Pioneer Classic Balanced Fund Class A	AOBLX	NAS CM	Open End	Moderate Alloc (Balanced)	B	C+	A-	Up	Y	1,000
Pioneer Classic Balanced Fund Class C	PCBCX	NAS CM	Open End	Moderate Alloc (Balanced)	B	C	A-	Up	Y	1,000
Pioneer Classic Balanced Fund Class K	PCBKX	NAS CM	Open End	Moderate Alloc (Balanced)	B	C+	A-	Up	Y	5,000,000
Pioneer Classic Balanced Fund Class R	CBPRX	NAS CM	Open End	Moderate Alloc (Balanced)	B	C+	A-	Up	Y	0
Pioneer Classic Balanced Fund Class Y	AYBLX	NAS CM	Open End	Moderate Alloc (Balanced)	B	C+	A-	Up	Y	5,000,000
Pioneer Core Equity Fund Class A	PIOTX	NAS CM	Open End	US Equity Large Cap Blend (Growth)	C+	C	B		Y	1,000
Pioneer Core Equity Fund Class C	PCOTX	NAS CM	Open End	US Equity Large Cap Blend (Growth)	C+	C	B		Y	1,000
Pioneer Core Equity Fund Class K	PCEKX	NAS CM	Open End	US Equity Large Cap Blend (Growth)	C+	C	B		Y	5,000,000
Pioneer Core Equity Fund Class R	CERPX	NAS CM	Open End	US Equity Large Cap Blend (Growth)	D-	D+	C+		Y	0
Pioneer Core Equity Fund Class Y	PVFYX	NAS CM	Open End	US Equity Large Cap Blend (Growth)	C+	C	B		Y	5,000,000
Pioneer Disciplined Growth Fund Class A	PINDX	NAS CM	Open End	US Equity Large Cap Growth (Growth)	B-	C+	B	Down	Y	1,000
Pioneer Disciplined Growth Fund Class C	INDCX	NAS CM	Open End	US Equity Large Cap Growth (Growth)	B-	C+	B		Y	1,000
Pioneer Disciplined Growth Fund Class Y	INYDX	NAS CM	Open End	US Equity Large Cap Growth (Growth)	B-	C+	B	Down	Y	5,000,000
Pioneer Disciplined Value Fund Class A	CVFCX	NAS CM	Open End	US Equity Large Cap Value (Growth)	C+	C	B		Y	1,000
Pioneer Disciplined Value Fund Class C	CVCFX	NAS CM	Open End	US Equity Large Cap Value (Growth)	C+	C	B		Y	1,000
Pioneer Disciplined Value Fund Class R	CVRFX	NAS CM	Open End	US Equity Large Cap Value (Growth)	C+	C	B		Y	5,000,000
Pioneer Disciplined Value Fund Class Y	CVFYX	NAS CM	Open End	US Equity Large Cap Value (Growth)	C+	C	B		Y	5,000,000
Pioneer Equity Income Fund Class A	PEQIX	NAS CM	Open End	US Equity Large Cap Value (Equity-Income)	B-	C	B	Up	Y	1,000

★Expanded analysis of this fund is included in Section II.

	TOTAL RETURNS					PERFORMANCE				ASSETS		ASSET ALLOCATION & TURNOVER					BULL & BEAR		FEES		
Min Additional Investment	3-Month Total Return	6-Month Total Return	1-Year Total Return	3-Year Total Return	5-Year Total Return	Dividend Yield (TTM)	Expense Ratio	3-Yr Std Deviation	3-Year Beta	NAV	Total Assets (MIL)	%Cash	%Stocks	%Bonds	%Other	Turnover Ratio	Last Bull Market Total Return	Last Bear Market Total Return	Front End Fee (%)	Back End Fee (%)	Inception Date
	3.71	15.46	-0.16	35.37	10.41	2.8	0.87	11.89	1.07	5.79	341.7	33	100	-38	0	325	19.62	-24.53			Apr-18
	3.71	15.70	0.03	36.13	11.48	2.84	0.72	11.77	1.06	5.79	341.7	33	100	-38	0	325	19.76	-24.47			Nov-06
	10.05	33.65	22.35	63.68	107.98	10.2	0.85	14.02	0.99	7.29	430.9	-113	100	111	0	144	30.79	-5.9			Aug-07
50	-2.93	-13.83	-7.60	-26.77	-36.85	1.83	1.06	11.59	-0.94	7.28	1,448	233	-99	-57	21	325	-17.01	12.88	3.75		Jul-06
50	-3.21	-14.22	-8.40	-28.51	-39.26	1.21	1.81	11.54	-0.94	6.93	1,448	233	-99	-57	21	325	-17.27	12.5		1.00	Jul-06
	-2.97	-13.86	-7.36	-26.19	-35.90	1.94	0.76	11.68	-0.95	7.51	1,448	233	-99	-57	21	325	-16.8	12.91			Jan-10
	-2.97	-13.90	-7.53	-26.44	-36.23	1.88	0.81	11.62	-0.94	7.5	1,448	233	-99	-57	21	325	-16.83	13.02			Apr-18
	-2.96	-13.72	-7.32	-25.94	-35.54	1.96	0.66	11.62	-0.94	7.53	1,448	233	-99	-57	21	325	-16.73	13.12			Jul-03
	2.17	18.82	-4.34	50.98	43.47	2.38	1.04	17.44	1.02	9.61	1,617	27	99	-41	13	436	34.96	-27.89			Jun-14
50	2.18	18.82	-4.40	50.37	42.43	2.29	1.19	17.46	1.02	9.39	1,617	27	99	-41	13	436	35.14	-28.07	3.75		Jul-06
50	2.03	18.34	-5.10	47.11	37.18	1.86	1.94	17.45	1.02	8.57	1,617	27	99	-41	13	436	34.34	-28.22		1.00	Jul-06
	2.32	18.91	-4.13	51.84	44.55	2.53	0.89	17.46	1.02	9.54	1,617	27	99	-41	13	436	35.25	-27.96			Apr-08
	2.32	18.93	-4.09	51.38	43.92	2.58	0.94	17.51	1.02	9.53	1,617	27	99	-41	13	436	35	-27.88			Apr-18
	2.31	19.03	-4.01	52.23	45.30	2.59	0.79	17.43	1.02	9.63	1,617	27	99	-41	13	436	35.16	-27.82			Mar-06
50	1.17	1.07	4.75	3.45	9.54	0.71	1.67	7.49	6.06	9.85	519.1	-210	34	238	37	30			5.50		Dec-13
50	0.99	0.72	3.88	1.15	5.52	0.41	2.42	7.49	6.32	9.57	519.1	-210	34	238	37	30				1.00	Dec-13
	1.23	1.19	5.00	4.37	10.93	0.97	1.37	7.49	6.31	9.93	519.1	-210	34	238	37	30					Dec-13
	1.21	1.18	5.08	4.24	10.78	0.95	1.42	7.46	6.21	9.94	519.1	-210	34	238	37	30					Apr-18
	1.34	1.32	5.20	4.73	11.75	1.06	1.27	7.49	6.19	9.95	519.1	-210	34	238	37	30					Dec-13
25	2.58	16.93	3.85	53.70	58.54	0.88	0.95	13.35	1	69.73	247.2	6	94	0	0	12	30.87	-20.79			Aug-92
	1.40	9.81	1.06	19.93		0.25	0.79	8.32	0.69	10.85	224.4	19	54	26	1	109					Mar-16
	1.40	9.70	0.89	19.65		0.18	0.94	8.35	0.69	10.85	224.4	19	54	26	1	109					Mar-16
500	-0.57	11.18					2.91			10.44	1.6	3	97	0	0						Dec-18
5,000	-0.57	11.18					1.91			10.44	1.6	3	97	0	0						Dec-18
500	0.49	8.59	-4.05	10.87		0	1.76	10.96	1.02	10.23	37.7	34	35	31	0	402			5.75	1.00	Oct-15
500	0.30	8.15	-4.79	8.33		0	2.51	10.96	1.02	9.95	37.7	34	35	31	0	402				1.00	Oct-15
5,000	0.48	8.75	-3.76	11.63		0	1.51	11.01	1.03	10.31	37.7	34	35	31	0	402					Oct-15
500	0.81	6.78	-3.24	-0.10	-6.83	0.26	1.96	7.23	0.88	9.92	13.0	36	21	43	0	419			5.75		Jun-13
500	0.63	6.34	-3.91	-2.33	-10.31	0	2.71	7.24	0.89	9.56	13.0	36	21	43	0	419				1.00	Jun-13
5,000	0.91	6.86	-2.97	0.59	-5.68	0.6	1.71	7.19	0.88	9.96	13.0	36	21	43	0	419					Jun-13
500	6.48	19.23					1.24			11.16	1.4	3	97	0	0				5.75		Dec-18
500	6.58	19.33					1.99			11.17	1.4	3	97	0	0						Dec-18
5,000	6.92	18.69					0.99			11.17	1.4	3	97	0	0						Dec-18
100	-2.13	3.77	-8.31	1.40	2.55	0.39	1.33	9.44	0.46	13.75	32.7	35	64	0	0	32	11.79	-7.64			Apr-03
100	4.19	14.92	8.95	31.43	35.13	1.75	1.03	7.37	0.59	9.4	295.5	2	63	34	0	65	16.41	-12.04	4.50		Dec-91
500	3.99	14.53	8.12	28.60	30.12	1.01	1.8	7.32	0.59	9.34	295.5	2	63	34	0	65	15.84	-12.36		1.00	Sep-05
	4.19	14.94	9.16	32.45	36.78	1.92	0.75	7.41	0.6	9.39	295.5	2	63	34	0	65	16.59	-11.94			Dec-15
	4.07	14.64	8.68	30.58	33.70	1.34	1.34	7.36	0.59	9.42	295.5	2	63	34	0	65	16.25	-12.12			Jul-15
	4.27	15.06	9.32	32.39	36.70	2.01	0.69	7.4	0.59	9.47	295.5	2	63	34	0	65	16.59	-11.94			Dec-91
100	3.89	19.82	5.87	50.14	51.37	0.65	0.9	12.89	1.04	18.92	1,619	3	97	0	0	114	25.31	-16.3	5.75		Nov-99
500	3.67	19.34	5.05	46.58	45.26	0	1.69	12.89	1.04	16.35	1,619	3	97	0	0	114	24.81	-16.66		1.00	Nov-99
	4.01	20.03	6.26	50.78	52.00	0.93	0.57	12.89	1.04	18.93	1,619	3	97	0	0	114	25.31	-16.3			May-18
	3.74	19.53	5.20			0.73	1.06			18.85	1,619	3	97	0	0	114					Jun-18
	3.95	19.92	6.11	51.32	53.41	0.75	0.64	12.91	1.04	19.2	1,619	3	97	0	0	114	25.58	-16.24			Aug-04
100	4.72	23.47	11.23	54.25	67.53	0.01	1.05	12.48	0.9	16.83	1,318	0	100	0	0	98	27.16	-17.54	5.75		Dec-05
500	4.51	22.94	10.32	50.50	60.79	0	1.87	12.42	0.89	14.36	1,318	0	100	0	0	98	26.61	-17.94		1.00	Jul-08
	4.78	23.57	11.38	55.22	69.55	0.13	0.87	12.43	0.89	17.3	1,318	0	100	0	0	98	27.43	-17.45			Jul-08
100	3.29	18.18	4.38	40.25	37.77	0.85	1.13	13.28	1.07	13.78	421.1	5	95	0	0	112	24.23	-18.51	5.75		Dec-05
500	3.12	17.78	3.60	37.20	32.86	0	1.84	13.32	1.07	13.51	421.1	5	95	0	0	112	23.68	-18.89		1.00	Jul-08
	3.12	17.93	4.02	39.10	36.02	0.65	1.52	13.3	1.07	13.22	421.1	5	95	0	0	112	24.24	-18.51			Dec-05
	3.35	18.24	4.65	41.51	39.93	1.07	0.83	13.26	1.07	13.87	421.1	5	95	0	0	112	24.53	-18.47			Jul-08
100	1.70	15.16	4.44	34.41	49.20	2.16	1	11.91	0.97	34.42	2,634	0	100	0	0	27	19.42	-14.37	5.75		Jul-90

Fund Name	MARKET Ticker Symbol	Traded On	FUND TYPE, CATEGORY & OBJECTIVE Fund Type	Category and (Prospectus Objective)	RATINGS Overall Rating	Reward Rating	Risk Rating	Recent Up/ Downgrade	MINIMUMS Open to New Investors	Min Initial Investment
Pioneer Equity Income Fund Class C	PCEQX	NAS CM	Open End	US Equity Large Cap Value (Equity-Income)	B-	C	B	Up	Y	1,000
Pioneer Equity Income Fund Class K	PEQKX	NAS CM	Open End	US Equity Large Cap Value (Equity-Income)	B-	C	B	Up	Y	5,000,000
Pioneer Equity Income Fund Class R	PQIRX	NAS CM	Open End	US Equity Large Cap Value (Equity-Income)	B-	C	B	Up	Y	0
Pioneer Equity Income Fund Class Y	PYEQX	NAS CM	Open End	US Equity Large Cap Value (Equity-Income)	B-	C	B	Up	Y	5,000,000
Pioneer Flexible Opportunities Fund Class A	PMARX	NAS CM	Open End	Moderate Alloc (Growth & Income)	C	C	B-		Y	1,000
Pioneer Flexible Opportunities Fund Class C	PRRCX	NAS CM	Open End	Moderate Alloc (Growth & Income)	C	C	B-		Y	1,000
Pioneer Flexible Opportunities Fund Class K	FLEKX	NAS CM	Open End	Moderate Alloc (Growth & Income)	C	C	B		Y	5,000,000
Pioneer Flexible Opportunities Fund Class R	MUARX	NAS CM	Open End	Moderate Alloc (Growth & Income)	C	C	B-		Y	0
Pioneer Flexible Opportunities Fund Class Y	PMYRX	NAS CM	Open End	Moderate Alloc (Growth & Income)	C	C	B		Y	5,000,000
Pioneer Fund Class A	PIODX	NAS CM	Open End	US Equity Large Cap Blend (Growth & Income)	B	B-	B+		Y	1,000
Pioneer Fund Class C	PCODX	NAS CM	Open End	US Equity Large Cap Blend (Growth & Income)	B	C+	B+		Y	1,000
Pioneer Fund Class R	PIORX	NAS CM	Open End	US Equity Large Cap Blend (Growth & Income)	B	B-	B+		Y	0
Pioneer Fund Class Y	PYODX	NAS CM	Open End	US Equity Large Cap Blend (Growth & Income)	B	B-	B+		Y	5,000,000
Pioneer Fundamental Growth Fund Class A	PIGFX	NAS CM	Open End	US Equity Large Cap Growth (Growth)	B	C+	B		Y	1,000
Pioneer Fundamental Growth Fund Class C	FUNCX	NAS CM	Open End	US Equity Large Cap Growth (Growth)	B	C+	B		Y	1,000
Pioneer Fundamental Growth Fund Class K Shares	PFGKX	NAS CM	Open End	US Equity Large Cap Growth (Growth)	B	B-	B		Y	5,000,000
Pioneer Fundamental Growth Fund Class R	PFGRX	NAS CM	Open End	US Equity Large Cap Growth (Growth)	B	C+	B		Y	0
Pioneer Fundamental Growth Fund Class Y	FUNYX	NAS CM	Open End	US Equity Large Cap Growth (Growth)	B	B-	B		Y	5,000,000
Pioneer Global Equity Fund Class A	GLOSX	NAS CM	Open End	Global Equity Large Cap (World Stock)	C	C-	C+		Y	1,000
Pioneer Global Equity Fund Class C	GCSLX	NAS CM	Open End	Global Equity Large Cap (World Stock)	C	C-	C+		Y	1,000
Pioneer Global Equity Fund Class K	PGEKX	NAS CM	Open End	Global Equity Large Cap (World Stock)	C	C	C+		Y	5,000,000
Pioneer Global Equity Fund Class R	PRGEX	NAS CM	Open End	Global Equity Large Cap (World Stock)	C	C-	C+		Y	0
Pioneer Global Equity Fund Class Y	PGSYX	NAS CM	Open End	Global Equity Large Cap (World Stock)	C	C	C+		Y	5,000,000
Pioneer International Equity Fund Class A	PIIFX	NAS CM	Open End	Global Equity Large Cap (Foreign Stock)	C	C-	C	Up	Y	1,000
Pioneer International Equity Fund Class C	PCITX	NAS CM	Open End	Global Equity Large Cap (Foreign Stock)	C-	D+	C		Y	1,000
Pioneer International Equity Fund Class Y	INVYX	NAS CM	Open End	Global Equity Large Cap (Foreign Stock)	C	C-	C	Up	Y	5,000,000
Pioneer Mid Cap Value Fund Class A	PCGRX	NAS CM	Open End	US Equity Mid Cap (Growth)	C	C	C+		Y	1,000
Pioneer Mid Cap Value Fund Class C	PCCGX	NAS CM	Open End	US Equity Mid Cap (Growth)	C	C-	C+		Y	1,000
Pioneer Mid Cap Value Fund Class K	PMCKX	NAS CM	Open End	US Equity Mid Cap (Growth)	C	C	C+		Y	5,000,000
Pioneer Mid Cap Value Fund Class R	PCMRX	NAS CM	Open End	US Equity Mid Cap (Growth)	C	C	C+		Y	0
Pioneer Mid Cap Value Fund Class Y	PYCGX	NAS CM	Open End	US Equity Mid Cap (Growth)	C	C	C+		Y	5,000,000
Pioneer Multi-Asset Income Fund A	PMAIX	NAS CM	Open End	Cautious Alloc (Multi-Asset Global)	C+	C	B	Up	Y	1,000
Pioneer Multi-Asset Income Fund C	PMACX	NAS CM	Open End	Cautious Alloc (Multi-Asset Global)	C	C-	B		Y	1,000
Pioneer Multi-Asset Income Fund Class K	PMFKX	NAS CM	Open End	Cautious Alloc (Multi-Asset Global)	C+	C	B	Up	Y	5,000,000
Pioneer Multi-Asset Income Fund Class R	PMFRX	NAS CM	Open End	Cautious Alloc (Multi-Asset Global)	C	C	B		Y	0
Pioneer Multi-Asset Income Fund Y	PMFYX	NAS CM	Open End	Cautious Alloc (Multi-Asset Global)	C+	C	B	Up	Y	5,000,000
Pioneer Real Estate Fund Class A	PWREX	NAS CM	Open End	Real Estate Sector Equity (Real Estate)	C	C	C+	Down	Y	1,000
Pioneer Real Estate Fund Class C	PCREX	NAS CM	Open End	Real Estate Sector Equity (Real Estate)	C	C	C+	Down	Y	1,000
Pioneer Real Estate Fund Class Y	PYREX	NAS CM	Open End	Real Estate Sector Equity (Real Estate)	C	C	C+	Down	Y	5,000,000
Pioneer Select Mid Cap Growth Fund Class A	PGOFX	NAS CM	Open End	US Equity Mid Cap (Growth)	C+	C+	B-	Down	Y	1,000
Pioneer Select Mid Cap Growth Fund Class C	GOFCX	NAS CM	Open End	US Equity Mid Cap (Growth)	C+	C	B-	Down	Y	1,000
Pioneer Select Mid Cap Growth Fund Class K	PSMKX	NAS CM	Open End	US Equity Mid Cap (Growth)	C+	C+	B-	Down	Y	5,000,000
Pioneer Select Mid Cap Growth Fund Class R	PGRRX	NAS CM	Open End	US Equity Mid Cap (Growth)	C+	C+	B-	Down	Y	0
Pioneer Select Mid Cap Growth Fund Class Y	GROYX	NAS CM	Open End	US Equity Mid Cap (Growth)	C+	C+	B-	Down	Y	5,000,000
Pioneer Solutions - Balanced Fund Class A	PIALX	NAS CM	Open End	Moderate Alloc (Asset Alloc)	C	C-	B		Y	1,000
Pioneer Solutions - Balanced Fund Class C	PIDCX	NAS CM	Open End	Moderate Alloc (Asset Alloc)	C	C-	B-		Y	1,000
Pioneer Solutions - Balanced Fund Class R	BALRX	NAS CM	Open End	Moderate Alloc (Asset Alloc)	C	C-	B-		Y	0
Pioneer Solutions - Balanced Fund Class Y	IMOYX	NAS CM	Open End	Moderate Alloc (Asset Alloc)	C	C-	B		Y	5,000,000
Plumb Balanced Fund	PLBBX	NAS CM	Open End	Moderate Alloc (Balanced)	B-	C+	B	Down	Y	2,500
Plumb Equity Fund	PLBEX	NAS CM	Open End	US Equity Large Cap Growth (Growth)	C+	C+	C+	Down	Y	2,500
PMC Diversified Equity Fund	PMDEX	NAS CM	Open End	Global Equity Large Cap (Growth)	C+	C	B	Up	Y	1,000
PNC Balanced Allocation Fund Class A	PBAAX	NAS CM	Open End	Moderate Alloc (Balanced)	B-	C	A-	Up	Y	1,000

★ Expanded analysis of this fund is included in Section II.

	TOTAL RETURNS					PERFORMANCE				ASSETS		ASSET ALLOCATION & TURNOVER					BULL & BEAR		FEES		
Min Additional Investment	3-Month Total Return	6-Month Total Return	1-Year Total Return	3-Year Total Return	5-Year Total Return	Dividend Yield (TTM)	Expense Ratio	3-Yr Std Deviation	3-Year Beta	NAV	Total Assets (MIL)	%Cash	%Stocks	%Bonds	%Other	Turnover Ratio	Last Bull Market Total Return	Last Bear Market Total Return	Front End Fee (%)	Back End Fee (%)	Inception Date
500	1.52	14.72	3.66	31.47	43.83	1.24	1.72	11.92	0.97	33.88	2,634	0	100	0	0	27	18.91	-14.65		1.00	Jan-96
	1.82	15.37	4.79	35.85	51.97	2.53	0.66	11.92	0.97	34.47	2,634	0	100	0	0	27	19.42	-14.37			Dec-12
	1.67	14.98	4.00	32.82	46.35	1.66	1.44	11.92	0.97	35.13	2,634	0	100	0	0	27	19.29	-14.55			Apr-03
	1.77	15.30	4.70	35.40	51.16	2.39	0.76	11.92	0.97	34.86	2,634	0	100	0	0	27	19.69	-14.24			Jul-98
100	1.98	13.13	0.26	24.82	26.68	1.05	1.16	10.46	0.78	12	528.4	14	79	6	1		11.37	-5.73	4.50		May-10
500	1.85	12.76	-0.44	22.08	21.94	0.49	1.93	10.53	0.78	11.75	528.4	14	79	6	1		10.88	-6.03		1.00	May-10
	2.16	13.31	0.60	26.02	28.54	1.35	0.9	10.53	0.8	12	528.4	14	79	6	1		11.51	-5.55			Jun-18
	2.03	12.99	-0.30	22.90	22.93	0.53	1.84	10.46	0.78	11.92	528.4	14	79	6	1		11.18	-5.74			Sep-13
	2.15	13.34	0.56	25.97	28.49	1.32	0.92	10.51	0.79	12.06	528.4	14	79	6	1		11.51	-5.55			May-10
100	6.68	19.88	14.76	53.47	61.06	0.81	0.96	11.09	0.89	29.33	5,068	1	99	0	0	60	21.1	-20.2	5.75		Feb-28
500	6.48	19.38	13.86	49.81	54.81	0.17	1.76	11.1	0.89	25.1	5,068	1	99	0	0	60	20.51	-20.43		1.00	Jul-96
	6.61	19.65	14.31	51.53	57.91	0.47	1.37	11.11	0.9	29.48	5,068	1	99	0	0	60	20.93	-20.31			Apr-03
	6.76	20.04	15.06	54.48	63.14	1	0.77	11.08	0.89	29.75	5,068	1	99	0	0	60	21.37	-20.07			May-99
100	4.58	20.74	14.39	53.58	73.73	0.19	1.09	11	0.8	25.32	6,012	1	99	0	0	26	24.31	-11.31	5.75		Aug-02
500	4.46	20.38	13.72	50.56	68.07	0	1.74	10.95	0.79	22.91	6,012	1	99	0	0	26	23.72	-11.58		1.00	Dec-05
	4.70	21.00	14.92	55.60	77.59	0.62	0.66	10.98	0.8	25.35	6,012	1	99	0	0	26	24.31	-11.31			Dec-12
	4.53	20.61	14.10	52.22	71.13	0	1.4	10.99	0.8	24.87	6,012	1	99	0	0	26	24.13	-11.41			Apr-12
	4.70	20.95	14.79	55.15	76.57	0.51	0.77	10.99	0.8	25.57	6,012	1	99	0	0	26	24.52	-11.11			Apr-09
100	0.87	12.10	-2.68	30.37	23.28	0.56	1.15	13.49	1.16	13.89	230.0	0	100	0	0	98	17.93	-21.3	5.75		Dec-05
500	0.66	11.62	-3.41	27.44	18.69	0	2.03	13.48	1.16	13.54	230.0	0	100	0	0	98	17.23	-21.63		1.00	Dec-05
	1.09	12.37	-2.15	32.16	25.89	1.03	0.8	13.5	1.16	13.89	230.0	0	100	0	0	98	17.93	-21.3			Dec-14
	0.80	11.99	-2.94	29.17	21.70	0.17	1.55	13.48	1.16	13.82	230.0	0	100	0	0	98	17.76	-21.38			Jul-15
	1.01	12.33	-2.19	32.26	26.22	1.04	0.7	13.5	1.16	13.93	230.0	0	100	0	0	98	18.12	-21.11			Dec-08
100	4.06	11.78	-5.54	22.62	6.67	2.25	1.15	11.74	1.03	21.25	131.7	3	97	0	0	41	10.33	-22.05	5.75		Mar-93
500	3.82	11.28	-6.35	19.32	2.01	1.27	2.1	11.72	1.02	18.44	131.7	3	97	0	0	41	9.83	-22.38		1.00	Jan-96
	4.21	12.07	-5.16	23.97	8.73	2.68	0.7	11.75	1.03	21.26	131.7	3	97	0	0	41	10.62	-21.91			Apr-09
100	4.44	20.45	1.06	23.00	22.10	0.73	1.02	15.03	1.12	21.85	759.9	2	98	0	0	78	23.83	-22.94	5.75		Jul-90
500	4.18	19.93	0.13	19.97	17.07	0	1.83	14.98	1.11	14.44	759.9	2	98	0	0	78	23.2	-23.23		1.00	Jan-96
	4.53	20.75	1.44	24.38	24.05	1.06	0.68	15.01	1.11	21.88	759.9	2	98	0	0	78	23.83	-22.94			Mar-15
	4.35	20.25	0.65	21.45	19.59	0.3	1.48	14.99	1.11	21.31	759.9	2	98	0	0	78	23.56	-23.06			Apr-03
	4.53	20.64	1.32	23.94	23.74	0.88	0.78	15.01	1.11	23.73	759.9	2	98	0	0	78	24.16	-22.82			Jul-98
100	0.35	6.31	0.69	25.85	19.23	5.65	0.9	6.61	-0.16	10.89	1,779	2	49	33	0	126			4.50		Dec-11
500	0.16	5.91	0.00	22.96	14.56	4.88	1.7	6.62	-0.17	10.86	1,779	2	49	33	0	126				1.00	Dec-11
	0.37	6.36	0.95	29.27	24.28	5.95	0.64	6.56	-0.25	11.22	1,779	2	49	33	0	126					Dec-14
	0.17	5.75	0.19	23.75	16.73	5.05	1.45	6.67	-0.17	10.92	1,779	2	49	33	0	126					Dec-14
	0.40	6.32	0.89	26.51	20.35	5.87	0.7	6.61	-0.17	10.87	1,779	2	49	33	0	126					Dec-11
100	2.43	19.05	9.92	9.76	38.35	2.14	1.68	12.56	0.94	16.38	88.6	0	100	0	0	155	30.47	-15.64	5.75		Oct-93
500	2.26	18.61	9.16	7.39	33.10	1.74	2.35	12.58	0.94	15.8	88.6	0	100	0	0	155	29.84	-15.96		1.00	Jan-96
	2.56	19.34	10.35	11.01	41.05	2.41	1.23	12.58	0.94	16.33	88.6	0	100	0	0	155	30.85	-15.4			Apr-98
100	5.71	28.15	10.92	61.01	65.10	0	1.02	15.31	1.05	43.47	2,111	2	98	0	0	82	28.59	-21.01	5.75		Jun-93
500	5.49	27.62	10.04	57.24	58.63	0	1.78	15.31	1.05	29.94	2,111	2	98	0	0	82	27.84	-21.26		1.00	Jan-02
	5.81	28.38	11.32	62.78	67.89	0	0.66	15.32	1.05	44.37	2,111	2	98	0	0	82	28.59	-21.01			Dec-14
	5.59	27.82	10.36	59.00	61.79	0	1.44	15.32	1.05	41.35	2,111	2	98	0	0	82	28.59	-21.01			Jun-93
	5.79	28.27	11.14	62.21	67.28	0	0.78	15.32	1.05	47.63	2,111	2	98	0	0	82	28.93	-20.86			Jun-04
100	1.80	9.38	0.76	13.51	9.61	2.94	1.24	7.33		11.31	434.9	5	61	29	0	146	13.58	-13.34	5.75		Aug-04
500	1.57	8.94	0.03	11.13	5.73	2.29	1.94	7.3		10.35	434.9	5	61	29	0	146	13.06	-13.54		1.00	Aug-04
	1.63	9.15	0.45	12.58	8.24	2.83	1.48	7.29		11.21	434.9	5	61	29	0	146	13.41	-13.43			Jul-15
	1.77	9.34	0.83	14.14	10.71	3.05	1.07	7.3		11.47	434.9	5	61	29	0	146	13.93	-13.27			Sep-05
100	4.22	18.75	8.16	50.40	54.63	0.02	1.19	10.7	0.82	32.29	110.2	3	63	31	0	58	15.18	-13.12			May-07
100	4.86	28.20	8.81	88.51	93.40	0	1.2	17.31	1.31	29.73	40.2	5	95	0	0	64	19.43	-18.8			May-07
50	2.63	14.04	1.33	32.40	26.32	0.63	0.99	11.25	0.98	24.52	834.0	1	99	0	0	104	22.24	-20.82			Aug-09
50	3.54	12.78	5.90	24.64	26.73	1.66	1.33	6.99	0.55	12.26	17.9	3	60	37	0	57	17.8	-12.41	4.75		Jul-98

	MARKET			FUND TYPE, CATEGORY & OBJECTIVE	RATINGS				MINIMUMS	
Fund Name	Ticker Symbol	Traded On	Fund Type	Category and (Prospectus Objective)	Overall Rating	Reward Rating	Risk Rating	Recent Up/ Downgrade	Open to New Investors	Min Initial Investment
PNC Balanced Allocation Fund Class C	PBCCX	NAS CM	Open End	Moderate Alloc (Balanced)	B-	C	B+	Up	Y	1,000
PNC Balanced Allocation Fund Class I	PBLIX	NAS CM	Open End	Moderate Alloc (Balanced)	B-	C	A-	Up	Y	0
PNC Emerging Markets Equity Fund Class A	PAEFX	NAS CM	Open End	Global Emerg Mkts (Div Emerging Mkts)	C-	D+	C	Up	Y	1,000
PNC Emerging Markets Equity Fund Class I	PIEFX	NAS CM	Open End	Global Emerg Mkts (Div Emerging Mkts)	C	C-	C	Up	Y	1,000
PNC Emerging Markets Equity Fund Class R6	PEREX	NAS CM	Open End	Global Emerg Mkts (Div Emerging Mkts)	C-	D+	C	Up	Y	0
PNC International Equity Class R6	PEIRX	NAS CM	Open End	Global Equity Large Cap (Foreign Stock)	C	C	B		Y	0
PNC International Equity Fund Class A	PMIEX	NAS CM	Open End	Global Equity Large Cap (Foreign Stock)	C	C	B		Y	1,000
PNC International Equity Fund Class C	PIUCX	NAS CM	Open End	Global Equity Large Cap (Foreign Stock)	C	C	B-		Y	1,000
PNC International Equity Fund Class Institutional	PIUIX	NAS CM	Open End	Global Equity Large Cap (Foreign Stock)	C	C	B		Y	0
PNC International Growth Fund Class A	PIGAX	NAS CM	Open End	Global Equity Large Cap (Growth)	C	C	C+		Y	1,000
PNC International Growth Fund Class I	PIGDX	NAS CM	Open End	Global Equity Large Cap (Growth)	C	C	C+		Y	0
PNC International Growth Fund Class R6	PIRSX	NAS CM	Open End	Global Equity Large Cap (Growth)	C	C	C+		Y	0
PNC Multi Factor Small Cap Core Class R6	PSORX	NAS CM	Open End	US Equity Small Cap (Small Company)	C	C	C		Y	0
PNC Multi Factor Small Cap Growth Class R6	PSWRX	NAS CM	Open End	US Equity Small Cap (Small Company)	C	C	C+	Down	Y	0
PNC Multi Factor Small Cap Growth Fund Class A	PLWAX	NAS CM	Open End	US Equity Small Cap (Small Company)	C	C	C+	Down	Y	1,000
PNC Multi Factor Small Cap Growth Fund Class C	PLWCX	NAS CM	Open End	US Equity Small Cap (Small Company)	C	C	C+	Down	Y	1,000
PNC Multi Factor Small Cap Growth Fund Class I	PLTIX	NAS CM	Open End	US Equity Small Cap (Small Company)	C	C	C+	Down	Y	0
PNC Multi-Factor All Cap Fund Class A	PLEAX	NAS CM	Open End	US Equity Large Cap Blend (Growth)	C	C-	C+		Y	1,000
PNC Multi-Factor All Cap Fund Class C	PLECX	NAS CM	Open End	US Equity Large Cap Blend (Growth)	C	C-	C+		Y	1,000
PNC Multi-Factor All Cap Fund Class I	PLEIX	NAS CM	Open End	US Equity Large Cap Blend (Growth)	C	C-	C+		Y	0
PNC Multi-Factor Large Cap Growth Fund Class A	PEWAX	NAS CM	Open End	US Equity Large Cap Growth (Growth)	C+	C	B		Y	1,000
PNC Multi-Factor Large Cap Growth Fund Class C	PEWCX	NAS CM	Open End	US Equity Large Cap Growth (Growth)	C+	C	B		Y	1,000
PNC Multi-Factor Large Cap Growth Fund Class I	PEWIX	NAS CM	Open End	US Equity Large Cap Growth (Growth)	C+	C	B		Y	0
PNC Multi-Factor Large Cap Value Fund Class A	PLVAX	NAS CM	Open End	US Equity Large Cap Value (Growth)	C+	C	B	Up	Y	1,000
PNC Multi-Factor Large Cap Value Fund Class C	PALVX	NAS CM	Open End	US Equity Large Cap Value (Growth)	C	C	B		Y	1,000
PNC Multi-Factor Large Cap Value Fund Class I	PLIVX	NAS CM	Open End	US Equity Large Cap Value (Growth)	C+	C	B	Up	Y	0
PNC Multiple Factor Small Cap Core Fund Class A	PLOAX	NAS CM	Open End	US Equity Small Cap (Small Company)	C	C	C		Y	1,000
PNC Multiple Factor Small Cap Core Fund Class C	PLOCX	NAS CM	Open End	US Equity Small Cap (Small Company)	C	C	C		Y	1,000
PNC Multiple Factor Small Cap Core Fund Class I	PLOIX	NAS CM	Open End	US Equity Small Cap (Small Company)	C	C	C		Y	0
PNC Multiple Factor Small Cap Value Fund Class A	PMRRX	NAS CM	Open End	US Equity Small Cap (Small Company)	C-	C-	C-		Y	1,000
PNC Multiple Factor Small Cap Value Fund Class C	PSVCX	NAS CM	Open End	US Equity Small Cap (Small Company)	D+	D+	C-	Down	Y	1,000
PNC Multiple Factor Small Cap Value Fund Class I	PMUIX	NAS CM	Open End	US Equity Small Cap (Small Company)	C-	C-	C		Y	0
PNC Small Cap Fund Class A	PPCAX	NAS CM	Open End	US Equity Small Cap (Small Company)	C	C	C+		Y	1,000
PNC Small Cap Fund Class C	PPCCX	NAS CM	Open End	US Equity Small Cap (Small Company)	C	C	C+		Y	1,000
PNC Small Cap Fund Class I	PPCIX	NAS CM	Open End	US Equity Small Cap (Small Company)	C	C	C+		Y	0
Polaris Global Value Fund	PGVFX	NAS CM	Open End	Global Equity Mid/Small Cap (Growth)	C+	C	B	Up	Y	2,500
Polen Global Growth Fund Institutional Class	PGIIX	NAS CM	Open End	Global Equity Large Cap (Growth)	B	B-	B		Y	100,000
Polen Global Growth Fund Investor Class	PGIRX	NAS CM	Open End	Global Equity Large Cap (Growth)	B	B-	B		Y	3,000
Polen Growth Fund Institutional Class	POLIX	NAS CM	Open End	US Equity Large Cap Growth (Growth)	B	B	B+		Y	100,000
Polen Growth Fund Investor Class	POLRX	NAS CM	Open End	US Equity Large Cap Growth (Growth)	B	B	B		Y	3,000
Polen International Growth Fund Institutional Class	POIIX	NAS CM	Open End	Global Equity Large Cap (Foreign Stock)	C+	C	B	Up	Y	100,000
Polen International Growth Fund Investor Class	POIRX	NAS CM	Open End	Global Equity Large Cap (Foreign Stock)	C+	C	B	Up	Y	3,000
Polen International Small Company Growth Institutional Cls	PBIIX	NAS CM	Open End	Global Equity Mid/Small Cap (Small Company)	U	U	U		Y	100,000
Polen International Small Company Growth Investor Cls	PBIRX	NAS CM	Open End	Global Equity Mid/Small Cap (Small Company)	U	U	U		Y	3,000
Polen U.S. Small Company Growth Fund Institutional Class	PBSIX	NAS CM	Open End	US Equity Small Cap (Small Company)	D+	C-	C+	Up	Y	100,000
Poplar Forest Cornerstone Fund Class A	PFCFX	NAS CM	Open End	Moderate Alloc (Balanced)	C	C-	C+		Y	25,000
Poplar Forest Cornerstone Fund Institutional Class	IPFCX	NAS CM	Open End	Moderate Alloc (Balanced)	C	C	C+		Y	100,000
Poplar Forest Partners Fund Class A	PFPFX	NAS CM	Open End	US Equity Large Cap Value (Growth)	C-	C-	C	Down	Y	25,000
Poplar Forest Partners Fund Institutional Class	IPFPX	NAS CM	Open End	US Equity Large Cap Value (Growth)	C-	C-	C	Down	Y	100,000
Port Street Quality Growth Fund Institutional Class	PSQGX	NAS CM	Open End	US Equity Large Cap Blend (Growth)	B	C	A		Y	2,000
Powell Alternative Income Strategies Investor Cls Shares	PAISX	NAS CM	Open End	Moderate Alloc (Growth & Income)	D	D	C-	Up	Y	1,000
Power Dividend Index Fund Class A	PWDAX	NAS CM	Open End	US Equity Large Cap Value (Equity-Income)	D+	D	C-	Down	Y	1,000

★Expanded analysis of this fund is included in Section II.

	TOTAL RETURNS					PERFORMANCE				ASSETS		ASSET ALLOCATION & TURNOVER					BULL & BEAR		FEES		
Min Additional Investment	3-Month Total Return	6-Month Total Return	1-Year Total Return	3-Year Total Return	5-Year Total Return	Dividend Yield (TTM)	Expense Ratio	3-Yr Std Deviation	3-Year Beta	NAV	Total Assets (MIL)	%Cash	%Stocks	%Bonds	%Other	Turnover Ratio	Last Bull Market Total Return	Last Bear Market Total Return	Front End Fee (%)	Back End Fee (%)	Inception Date
50	3.36	12.37	5.13	21.86	22.32	0.92	2.07	6.97	0.54	11.99	17.9	3	60	37	0	57	17.1	-12.62		1.00	Apr-00
	3.56	12.85	6.16	25.45	28.33	1.86	1.07	6.92	0.54	12.2	17.9	3	60	37	0	57	17.77	-12.27			Jul-98
50	1.01	15.04	-4.11				1.52			11.93	12.3	2	98	0	0	36			5.50		Aug-18
	1.18	15.23	-3.68			0.15	1.26			11.95	12.3	2	98	0	0	36					Mar-17
	1.10	15.13	-3.76				1.25			11.94	12.3	2	98	0	0	36					Jan-19
	3.03	15.02	-0.78	40.33	24.91	0.99	0.91	12.74	1.06	23.73	1,660	1	99	0	0	33	17.54	-25.31			Jun-18
50	2.93	14.80	-1.17	39.08	22.92	0.7	1.27	12.73	1.06	23.49	1,660	1	99	0	0	33	17.51	-25.41	5.50		Aug-97
50	2.75	14.39	-1.86	36.11	18.87	0.17	1.99	12.72	1.06	22.41	1,660	1	99	0	0	33	16.83	-25.63		1.00	Jan-00
	2.99	14.97	-0.86	40.22	24.81	0.95	0.95	12.74	1.06	23.72	1,660	1	99	0	0	33	17.54	-25.31			Aug-97
50	4.11	18.68	-0.63	39.65		0.09	1.13	14.3	1.12	12.64	5.8	2	98	0	0	64			5.50		Feb-16
	4.21	18.83	-0.36	40.30		0.42	0.87	14.29	1.12	12.62	5.8	2	98	0	0	64					Feb-16
	4.29	18.93	-0.28	40.42			0.86	14.3	1.12	12.62	5.8	2	98	0	0	64					Jan-19
	2.20	13.49	-6.31	30.67	35.09	0.76	0.84	15.05	0.86	23.63	308.7	2	98	0	0	68	23.5	-19.83			Jun-18
	4.11	18.03	0.73	46.11	52.14	0	0.84	16.59	0.92	22.25	137.9	0	100	0	0	92	21.39	-19.95			Jun-18
50	4.09	17.88	0.46	45.72	51.74	0	1.13	16.6	0.92	21.62	137.9	0	100	0	0	92	21.39	-19.95	5.50		Sep-05
50	3.86	17.43	-0.23	42.51	46.45	0	1.85	16.57	0.92	20.41	137.9	0	100	0	0	92	20.77	-20.23		1.00	Sep-05
	4.11	18.03	0.73	46.85	53.75	0	0.85	16.58	0.92	22.25	137.9	0	100	0	0	92	21.51	-19.87			Sep-05
50	2.88	19.52	-2.87	24.61	37.92	0.82	0.93	16.09	1.22	20.32	6.1	0	100	0	0	220	24.49	-15.28	5.50		Aug-97
50	2.70	19.16	-3.00	21.98	33.22	0.07	1.65	16.11	1.22	18.59	6.1	0	100	0	0	220	23.95	-15.56		1.00	Jan-00
	2.96	19.73	-2.64	25.60	39.76	0.98	0.65	16.09	1.22	20.81	6.1	0	100	0	0	220	24.56	-15.17			Aug-97
50	4.12	20.95	8.20	54.40	68.63	0.39	0.94	13.35	0.98	33.6	100.6	1	99	0	0	169	27.78	-15.37	5.50		Apr-91
50	3.93	20.48	7.44	51.09	63.19	0	1.66	13.33	0.98	29.35	100.6	1	99	0	0	169	27.1	-15.58		1.00	Jan-00
	4.21	21.11	8.51	55.55	70.87	0.54	0.66	13.34	0.98	34.36	100.6	1	99	0	0	169	27.86	-15.27			Dec-89
50	2.70	16.17	3.11	21.46	26.84	1.24	0.94	14.56	1.17	25.07	104.4	1	99	0	0	122	23.11	-17.52	5.50		Aug-94
50	2.51	15.78	2.39	18.92	22.88	0.79	1.66	14.56	1.17	24.42	104.4	1	99	0	0	122	22.45	-17.77		1.00	Jan-00
	2.81	16.36	3.45	22.30	28.45	1.25	0.66	14.57	1.17	25.17	104.4	1	99	0	0	122	23.21	-17.45			Jul-94
50	2.18	13.29	-6.59	29.65	33.28	0.5	1.13	15.04	0.86	23.43	308.7	2	98	0	0	68	23.33	-19.88	5.50		Sep-05
	1.96	12.91	-7.23	27.52	29.88	0	1.85	15	0.86	23.34	308.7	2	98	0	0	68	22.97	-20.08		1.00	Sep-16
	2.20	13.44	-6.32	30.66	35.08	0.75	0.85	15.04	0.86	23.63	308.7	2	98	0	0	68	23.5	-19.83			Sep-05
50	2.31	14.44	-9.85	19.35	20.30	1.82	1.14	16.24	0.91	20.36	18.2	1	99	0	0	93	20.14	-19.61	5.50		Aug-94
50	2.15	14.02	-10.48	16.77	16.39	1.14	1.86	16.19	0.9	18.05	18.2	1	99	0	0	93	19.54	-19.89		1.00	Jan-00
	2.39	14.64	-9.55	20.28	21.87	1.87	0.86	16.25	0.91	22.23	18.2	1	99	0	0	93	20.19	-19.47			Jul-94
50	6.85	22.81	0.69	36.34	36.27	0	1.27	16.72	0.93	14.79	248.9	4	96	0	0	24	33.56	-20.97	5.50		Apr-04
50	6.69	22.42	0.03	33.32	31.59	0	1.99	16.71	0.93	11.99	248.9	4	96	0	0	24	32.77	-21.21		1.00	Apr-04
	6.93	22.96	0.98	37.35	38.10	0	0.99	16.73	0.93	15.82	248.9	4	96	0	0	24	33.62	-20.9			Apr-04
250	3.17	14.53	0.66	39.22	32.44	2.88	0.99	11.84	1.01	26.66	461.3	2	98	0	0	22	22.03	-22.51			Jun-98
0	5.72	23.10	13.96	69.83		0	1.1	12.28	0.98	17.53	87.2	5	95	0	0	14					Dec-14
100	5.66	22.89	13.69	68.50		0	1.35	12.28	0.98	17.34	87.2	5	95	0	0	14					Jul-15
0	5.82	24.43	18.75	75.80	116.68	0	1	12.54	0.95	31.42	3,924	7	93	0	0	20	25.02	-8.84			Sep-10
100	5.77	24.30	18.44	74.45	113.87	0	1.25	12.52	0.95	30.79	3,924	7	93	0	0	20	24.8	-8.93			Dec-10
0	4.57	17.51	6.66			0.03	1.1			14.63	91.1	4	96	0	0	6					Dec-16
100	4.52	17.32	6.42			0	1.35			14.56	91.1	4	96	0	0	6					Mar-17
	8.15	23.30					1.25			12.42	4.0	3	97	0	0						Jan-19
100	8.00	24.15					1.5			12.41	4.0	3	97	0	0						Feb-19
0	6.18	22.37	11.52			0	1.25			12.36	9.1	6	94	0	0	8					Nov-17
1,000	0.67	10.71	-0.94	16.91		1.31	1.16	11.25	0.83	25.42	27.7	7	66	26	0	30			5.00		Dec-14
1,000	0.75	10.84	-0.79	17.71		1.59	0.91	11.24	0.83	25.45	27.7	7	66	26	0	30					Dec-14
1,000	-0.33	14.04	-5.40	18.42	14.37	1.08	1.25	17.03	1.21	42.13	441.0	3	97	0	0	32	24.1	-21.73	5.00		Dec-09
1,000	-0.26	14.21	-5.13	19.32	15.83	1.4	1	17.04	1.21	42.18	441.0	3	97	0	0	32	24.28	-21.63			Dec-09
100	2.16	10.85	8.70	29.10	39.10	0.53	1.05	7.39	0.52	13.69	114.1	37	63	0	0	6					Mar-14
100	0.11	1.82	-2.74			0	2.61			8.92	10.1	47	50	3	0	995					Apr-18
100	-4.17	-3.57	-5.82	6.91	8.41	1.69	1.44	10.42	0.58	8.43	296.9	0	100	0	0	265			5.00		Nov-13

	MARKET			FUND TYPE, CATEGORY & OBJECTIVE	RATINGS				MINIMUMS	
Fund Name	Ticker Symbol	Traded On	Fund Type	Category and (Prospectus Objective)	Overall Rating	Reward Rating	Risk Rating	Recent Up/ Downgrade	Open to New Investors	Min Initial Investment
Power Dividend Index Fund Class C	PWDCX	NAS CM	Open End	US Equity Large Cap Value (Equity-Income)	D+	D	C-	Down	Y	2,500
Power Dividend Index Fund Class I	PWDIX	NAS CM	Open End	US Equity Large Cap Value (Equity-Income)	D+	D	C-	Down	Y	100,000
Power Dividend Index VIT Fund Class 1 shares			Open End	US Equity Large Cap Value (Growth & Income)	D+	D	C-	Down	Y	0
Power Dividend Mid-Cap Index Fund Class A	DMCAX	NAS CM	Open End	US Equity Mid Cap (Growth & Income)	D+	D	C-	Up	Y	1,000
Power Dividend Mid-Cap Index Fund Class C	DMCCX	NAS CM	Open End	US Equity Mid Cap (Growth & Income)	D	D	C-		Y	1,000
Power Dividend Mid-Cap Index Fund Class I	DMCIX	NAS CM	Open End	US Equity Mid Cap (Growth & Income)	D+	D	C-	Up	Y	100,000
Power Global Tactical Allocation/JAForlines Fund Class A	GTAAX	NAS CM	Open End	Flexible Alloc (Growth)	D	D+	C	Up	Y	1,000
Power Global Tactical Allocation/JAForlines Fund Class C	GLACX	NAS CM	Open End	Flexible Alloc (Growth)	D	D+	C	Up	Y	1,000
Power Global Tactical Allocation/JAForlines Fund Class I	GTAIX	NAS CM	Open End	Flexible Alloc (Growth)	D	D+	C	Up	Y	100,000
Power Momentum Index Fund Classs A Shares	MOJAX	NAS CM	Open End	Moderate Alloc (Growth & Income)	C	C	B-		Y	1,000
Power Momentum Index Fund Classs C Shares	MOJCX	NAS CM	Open End	Moderate Alloc (Growth & Income)	C	C	C+		Y	1,000
Power Momentum Index Fund Classs I Shares	MOJOX	NAS CM	Open End	Moderate Alloc (Growth & Income)	C	C	B-		Y	100,000
Power Momentum Index VIT Fund Class 1 shares			Open End	Flexible Alloc (Growth & Income)	B-	C	B	Up	Y	0
PPM Large Cap Value Fund Institutional Shares	PZLIX	NAS CM	Open End	US Equity Large Cap Value (Growth)	D	D+	D+	Up	Y	500,000
PPM Long Short Credit Fund Institutional Shares	PKLIX	NAS CM	Open End	Long/Short Credit (Growth)	D-	D+	C+		Y	1,000,000
PPM Mid Cap Value Fund Institutional Shares	PZMIX	NAS CM	Open End	US Equity Mid Cap (Growth)	D	D	D	Up	Y	500,000
PPM Small Cap Value Fund Institutional Shares	PZSIX	NAS CM	Open End	US Equity Small Cap (Growth)	D	D	D	Up	Y	500,000
Praxis Genesis Balanced Portfolio Class A	MBAPX	NAS CM	Open End	Moderate Alloc (Balanced)	B	C	A-	Up	Y	1,000
Praxis Genesis Conservative Portfolio Class A	MCONX	NAS CM	Open End	Cautious Alloc (Growth & Income)	B	C+	B+	Up	Y	1,000
Praxis Genesis Growth Portfolio Class A	MGAFX	NAS CM	Open End	Aggressive Alloc (Growth)	B-	C	B+	Up	Y	1,000
Praxis Growth Index Fund Class A	MGNDX	NAS CM	Open End	US Equity Large Cap Growth (Growth)	B-	C+	B	Down	Y	2,500
Praxis Growth Index Fund Class I	MMDEX	NAS CM	Open End	US Equity Large Cap Growth (Growth)	B-	B-	B	Down	Y	100,000
Praxis International Index Fund Class A	MPLAX	NAS CM	Open End	Global Equity Large Cap (Foreign Stock)	C	C	B		Y	2,500
Praxis International Index Fund Class I	MPLIX	NAS CM	Open End	Global Equity Large Cap (Foreign Stock)	C	C	B		Y	100,000
Praxis Small Cap Index Fund Class A	MMSCX	NAS CM	Open End	US Equity Small Cap (Small Company)	C	C-	C		Y	2,500
Praxis Small Cap Index Fund Class I	MMSIX	NAS CM	Open End	US Equity Small Cap (Small Company)	C	C-	C+		Y	100,000
Praxis Value Index Fund Class A	MVIAX	NAS CM	Open End	US Equity Large Cap Value (Growth)	B-	C	B	Up	Y	2,500
Praxis Value Index Fund Class I	MVIIX	NAS CM	Open End	US Equity Large Cap Value (Growth)	B-	C	B		Y	100,000
PREDEX Fund	PRDEX	NAS CM	Closed End	Real Estate Sector Equity (Growth)	B-	C	A-	Up	Y	1,000,000
Preserver Alternative Opportunities Institutional Shares	PAOIX	NAS CM	Open End	Moderate Alloc (Growth & Income)	B-	C	B+	Up	Y	2,000
PRIMECAP Odyssey Aggressive Growth Fund	POAGX	NAS CM	Open End	US Equity Mid Cap (Aggr Growth)	C	C	C+			2,000
PRIMECAP Odyssey Growth Fund	POGRX	NAS CM	Open End	US Equity Large Cap Growth (Growth)	C	C	B-		Y	2,000
PRIMECAP Odyssey Stock Fund	POSKX	NAS CM	Open End	US Equity Large Cap Blend (Growth)	B-	C	B	Up	Y	2,000
Princeton Long/Short Treasury Fund Class A shares	PTAAX	NAS CM	Open End	Long/Short Credit (Growth & Income)	C	C-	C	Up	Y	2,500
Princeton Long/Short Treasury Fund Class I shares	PTAIX	NAS CM	Open End	Long/Short Credit (Growth & Income)	C	C	C+	Up	Y	100,000
Princeton Premium Fund Class A	PPFAX	NAS CM	Open End	Long/Short Equity (Growth & Income)	C	C	C+		Y	2,500
Princeton Premium Fund Class I	PPFIX	NAS CM	Open End	Long/Short Equity (Growth & Income)	C	C	C+		Y	100,000
Principal Blue Chip Fund Class A	PBLAX	NAS CM	Open End	US Equity Large Cap Growth (Growth)	B	B	B		Y	1,000
Principal Blue Chip Fund Class C	PBLCX	NAS CM	Open End	US Equity Large Cap Growth (Growth)	B	B	B		Y	1,000
Principal Blue Chip Fund Class J	PBCJX	NAS CM	Open End	US Equity Large Cap Growth (Growth)	B	B	B		Y	1,000
Principal Blue Chip Fund Class R-3	PGBEX	NAS CM	Open End	US Equity Large Cap Growth (Growth)	B	B	B		Y	0
Principal Blue Chip Fund Class R-4	PGBFX	NAS CM	Open End	US Equity Large Cap Growth (Growth)	B	B	B		Y	0
Principal Blue Chip Fund Class R-5	PGBGX	NAS CM	Open End	US Equity Large Cap Growth (Growth)	B	B	B		Y	0
Principal Blue Chip Fund Class R-6	PGBHX	NAS CM	Open End	US Equity Large Cap Growth (Growth)	B	B	B		Y	0
Principal Blue Chip Fund Institutional Class	PBCKX	NAS CM	Open End	US Equity Large Cap Growth (Growth)	B	B	B		Y	0
Principal Capital Appreciation Fund Class A	CMNWX	NAS CM	Open End	US Equity Large Cap Blend (Growth)	B-	C+	B	Down	Y	1,000
Principal Capital Appreciation Fund Class C	CMNCX	NAS CM	Open End	US Equity Large Cap Blend (Growth)	B-	C+	B		Y	1,000
Principal Capital Appreciation Fund Institutional Class	PWCIX	NAS CM	Open End	US Equity Large Cap Blend (Growth)	B-	C+	B	Down	Y	0
Principal Capital Appreciation Fund R-1 Class	PCAMX	NAS CM	Open End	US Equity Large Cap Blend (Growth)	B-	C+	B		Y	0
Principal Capital Appreciation Fund R-2 Class	PCANX	NAS CM	Open End	US Equity Large Cap Blend (Growth)	B-	C+	B	Down	Y	0
Principal Capital Appreciation Fund R-3 Class	PCAOX	NAS CM	Open End	US Equity Large Cap Blend (Growth)	B-	C+	B	Down	Y	0
Principal Capital Appreciation Fund R-4 Class	PCAPX	NAS CM	Open End	US Equity Large Cap Blend (Growth)	B-	C+	B	Down	Y	0

★ Expanded analysis of this fund is included in Section II.

	TOTAL RETURNS					PERFORMANCE				ASSETS		ASSET ALLOCATION & TURNOVER					BULL & BEAR		FEES		
Min Additional Investment	3-Month Total Return	6-Month Total Return	1-Year Total Return	3-Year Total Return	5-Year Total Return	Dividend Yield (TTM)	Expense Ratio	3-Yr Std Deviation	3-Year Beta	NAV	Total Assets (MIL)	%Cash	%Stocks	%Bonds	%Other	Turnover Ratio	Last Bull Market Total Return	Last Bear Market Total Return	Front End Fee (%)	Back End Fee (%)	Inception Date
500	-4.22	-3.89	-6.51	4.55	4.54	0.78	2.19	10.42	0.58	8.38	296.9	0	100	0	0	265					Nov-14
	-4.03	-3.41	-5.61	7.77	9.74	2.35	1.19	10.43	0.58	8.39	296.9	0	100	0	0	265					Nov-13
	-4.60	-3.89	-6.08	-1.29	-4.26	1.58	1.27	9.5	0.51	14.93	31.9	1	99	0	0	322	18.21	-9.22			May-07
100	4.73	1.77	-2.57			1.56	2.26			9.33	33.7	1	99	0	0				5.00		Dec-17
100	4.46	1.45	-3.15			0.56	3.01			9.35	33.7	1	99	0	0						Dec-17
	4.79	1.94	-2.20			1.94	1.92			9.34	33.7	1	99	0	0						Dec-17
100	2.35	10.71	0.95			1.68	1.58			9.8	117.9	6	42	35	9				5.00		Apr-18
100	2.08	10.24	0.15			0.91	2.33			9.79	117.9	6	42	35	9					1.00	Apr-18
	2.38	10.93	1.27			2.2	1.33			9.78	117.9	6	42	35	9					1.00	Apr-18
100	2.87	4.93	3.36			0.07	1.95			10.38	51.9	1	90	10	0	484			5.00		Dec-16
100	2.72	4.51	2.54			0	2.7			10.19	51.9	1	90	10	0	484					Dec-16
	2.86	4.95	3.53			0.24	1.7			10.42	51.9	1	90	10	0	484					Dec-16
	2.94	5.13	3.97	32.86	31.01	0.31	1.29	8.23	0.91	27.63	77.2	1	89	9	0	458	27.95	-21			May-07
	0.73	12.38	-2.58			1.32	0.75			9.53	7.4	1	99	0	0	17					May-18
	1.23	5.20					0.97			9.8	51.3	8	0	91	0	38					Jul-18
	-0.11	13.54	-7.49			0.96	0.9			9.05	5.5	0	100	0	0	24					May-18
	0.76	16.20	-7.51			0.42	1			9.25	9.9	1	99	0	0	22					May-18
50	3.13	12.09	5.79	25.37	27.17	1.94	1.03	7.1	0.99	13.79	78.1	2	58	40	0	13	13.29	-10.9	5.25		Dec-09
50	2.92	9.02	6.79	15.59	20.29	2.01	1.12	3.86	0.92	11.9	24.5	3	28	68	0	15	7.77	-3.75	5.25		Dec-09
50	3.21	14.11	4.81	31.63	30.94	1.78	1.1	9.49	1.02	15.09	69.2	1	78	21	0	13	17.08	-15.36	5.25		Dec-09
100	4.66	21.15	12.28	61.68	80.67	0.76	0.82	12.26	0.98	26.48	301.1	1	99	1	0	27	26.17	-13.82	5.25		May-07
	4.74	21.37	12.66	63.61	84.25	1.12	0.43	12.26	0.98	26.71	301.1	1	99	1	0	27	26.46	-13.51			May-07
100	2.32	12.62	-0.62	26.78	7.25	1.38	1.31	11.58	1.01	10.98	277.5	1	99	1	0	21	14.43	-25.32	5.25		Dec-10
	2.59	13.11	0.22	29.40	10.61	2.21	0.65	11.59	1.01	11.07	277.5	1	99	1	0	21	15.02	-25.25			Dec-10
100	1.58	12.83	-6.08	24.34	13.83	0	1.11	17.02	0.94	8.35	113.1	2	98	1	0	25	25.37	-19.61	5.25		May-07
	1.77	13.18	-5.54	26.82	17.44	0.48	0.46	16.96	0.94	9.15	113.1	2	98	1	0	25	25.87	-19.53			May-07
100	4.52	18.19	8.91	39.48	41.62	1.61	0.89	12.88	0.99	13.85	224.0	1	99	1	0	32	22.5	-19.46	5.25		May-01
	4.63	18.43	9.37	41.44	44.93	2.13	0.42	12.91	0.99	13.77	224.0	1	99	1	0	32	22.92	-19.15			May-06
	1.13	1.65	4.57	13.45		4.22	1.17	0.86		26.16	--	10	8	0	82				4.25		Jun-16
500	3.20	14.41	4.18	22.56		0.5	1.53	7.81	2.28	11.59	21.1	1	49	41	0	68					Mar-16
100	2.32	18.04	0.20	70.72	82.82	0.05	0.64	19.16	1.31	44.82	10,665	5	94	0	0	12	24.35	-20.48			Nov-04
100	0.69	14.36	0.78	65.75	75.53	0.31	0.65	17.13	1.26	39.33	13,117	4	96	0	0	4	21.42	-20.12			Nov-04
100	3.28	15.70	6.40	54.14	64.64	1.02	0.66	14.42	1.14	33	10,114	5	95	0	0	5	20.21	-16.02			Nov-04
100	-1.39	2.58	2.37			0	1.76			9.93	13.0	74	26	0	0	0			5.75		Feb-17
100	-1.28	2.87	2.81			0.14	1.51			10.01	13.0	74	26	0	0	0					Feb-17
100	3.32	6.54	4.41			0	3.07			10.58	50.4	100	0	0	0	0			5.75		Nov-16
100	3.39	6.71	4.68			0	2.82			10.65	50.4	100	0	0	0	0					Nov-16
100	7.01	26.79	18.23	77.45	95.92	0	0.99	12.6	0.91	25.03	4,088	1	99	0	0	34			5.50		Sep-13
100	6.83	26.36	17.40	73.48	88.60	0	1.74	12.59	0.91	23.92	4,088	1	99	0	0	34				1.00	Sep-13
100	7.01	26.84	18.35	78.46	98.81	0	0.94	12.61	0.91	25.33	4,088	1	99	0	0	34				1.00	Sep-17
	6.99	26.68	18.08	76.86	96.38	0	1.14	12.58	0.91	25.07	4,088	1	99	0	0	34					Mar-16
	7.04	26.84	18.28	77.93	98.21	0	0.95	12.56	0.91	25.23	4,088	1	99	0	0	34					Mar-16
	7.06	26.91	18.42	78.47	99.29	0	0.83	12.58	0.91	25.32	4,088	1	99	0	0	34					Mar-16
	7.10	27.01	18.72	79.67	100.75	0.01	0.57	12.57	0.91	25.48	4,088	1	99	0	0	34					Jan-17
	7.11	26.99	18.63	79.54	100.61	0	0.65	12.6	0.91	25.45	4,088	1	99	0	0	34					Jun-12
100	5.23	20.29	12.06	49.59	61.78	0.99	0.83	11.88	0.94	48.24	1,758	3	97	0	0	36	23.92	-17.59	5.50		Nov-86
100	5.00	19.77	11.14	45.93	55.23	0.89	1.65	11.87	0.94	32.28	1,758	3	97	0	0	36	23.34	-17.9		1.00	Mar-02
	5.34	20.51	12.50	51.24	64.77	1.22	0.47	11.88	0.94	49.63	1,758	3	97	0	0	36	24.27	-17.45			Jun-99
	5.10	19.97	11.49	47.30	57.70	0.61	1.35	11.89	0.94	48.18	1,758	3	97	0	0	36	23.62	-17.74			Mar-10
	5.15	20.08	11.64	47.90	58.77	0.57	1.22	11.89	0.94	48.37	1,758	3	97	0	0	36	23.69	-17.7			Mar-10
	5.20	20.19	11.84	48.68	60.19	0.77	1.04	11.89	0.94	48.33	1,758	3	97	0	0	36	23.82	-17.64			Mar-10
	5.23	20.30	12.06	49.55	61.72	0.95	0.85	11.89	0.94	48.88	1,758	3	97	0	0	36	23.95	-17.57			Mar-10

Fund Name	MARKET Ticker Symbol	Traded On	FUND TYPE, CATEGORY & OBJECTIVE Fund Type	Category and (Prospectus Objective)	RATINGS Overall Rating	Reward Rating	Risk Rating	Recent Up/ Downgrade	MINIMUMS Open to New Investors	Min Initial Investment
Principal Capital Appreciation Fund R-5 Class	PCAQX	NAS CM	Open End	US Equity Large Cap Blend (Growth)	B-	C+	B	Down	Y	0
Principal Capital Securities Fund Class S	PCSFX	NAS CM	Open End	US Fixed Income (Income)	B	B-	B+	Up	Y	0
Principal Diversified International Fund Class A	PRWLX	NAS CM	Open End	Global Equity Large Cap (Foreign Stock)	C	C	C+		Y	1,000
Principal Diversified International Fund Class C	PDNCX	NAS CM	Open End	Global Equity Large Cap (Foreign Stock)	C	C-	C+		Y	1,000
Principal Diversified International Fund Class J	PIIJX	NAS CM	Open End	Global Equity Large Cap (Foreign Stock)	C	C	C+		Y	1,000
Principal Diversified International Fund Class R-6	PDIFX	NAS CM	Open End	Global Equity Large Cap (Foreign Stock)	C	C	C+		Y	0
Principal Diversified International Institutional Cls	PIIIX	NAS CM	Open End	Global Equity Large Cap (Foreign Stock)	C	C	C+		Y	0
Principal Diversified International Fund R-1 Class	PDVIX	NAS CM	Open End	Global Equity Large Cap (Foreign Stock)	C	C-	C+		Y	0
Principal Diversified International Fund R-2 Class	PINNX	NAS CM	Open End	Global Equity Large Cap (Foreign Stock)	C	C	C+		Y	0
Principal Diversified International Fund R-3 Class	PINRX	NAS CM	Open End	Global Equity Large Cap (Foreign Stock)	C	C	C+		Y	0
Principal Diversified International Fund R-4 Class	PINLX	NAS CM	Open End	Global Equity Large Cap (Foreign Stock)	C	C	C+		Y	0
Principal Diversified International Fund R-5 Class	PINPX	NAS CM	Open End	Global Equity Large Cap (Foreign Stock)	C	C	C+		Y	0
Principal Diversified Real Asset Fund Class A	PRDAX	NAS CM	Open End	Flexible Alloc (Growth & Income)	C+	C-	B	Up	Y	1,000
Principal Diversified Real Asset Fund Class C	PRDCX	NAS CM	Open End	Flexible Alloc (Growth & Income)	C	C-	B		Y	1,000
Principal Diversified Real Asset Fund Class R-3	PGDRX	NAS CM	Open End	Flexible Alloc (Growth & Income)	C+	C-	B	Up	Y	0
Principal Diversified Real Asset Fund Class R-4	PGDSX	NAS CM	Open End	Flexible Alloc (Growth & Income)	C+	C-	B	Up	Y	0
Principal Diversified Real Asset Fund Class R-5	PGDTX	NAS CM	Open End	Flexible Alloc (Growth & Income)	C+	C	B	Up	Y	0
Principal Diversified Real Asset Fund Class R-6	PDARX	NAS CM	Open End	Flexible Alloc (Growth & Income)	C+	C	B+	Up	Y	0
Principal Diversified Real Asset Fund Institutional Class	PDRDX	NAS CM	Open End	Flexible Alloc (Growth & Income)	C+	C	B	Up	Y	0
Principal EDGE MidCap Fund Class A	PEMCX	NAS CM	Open End	US Equity Mid Cap (Growth)	C+	C	B	Down	Y	1,000
Principal EDGE MidCap Fund Class Institutional	PEDGX	NAS CM	Open End	US Equity Mid Cap (Growth)	C+	C	B	Down	Y	0
Principal EDGE MidCap Fund R-6	PEDMX	NAS CM	Open End	US Equity Mid Cap (Growth)	C+	C	B	Down	Y	0
Principal Equity Income Fund Class A	PQIAX	NAS CM	Open End	US Equity Large Cap Value (Equity-Income)	B-	C	B+		Y	1,000
Principal Equity Income Fund Class C	PEUCX	NAS CM	Open End	US Equity Large Cap Value (Equity-Income)	B-	C	B+		Y	1,000
Principal Equity Income Fund Class J	PEIJX	NAS CM	Open End	US Equity Large Cap Value (Equity-Income)	B-	C	B+		Y	1,000
Principal Equity Income Fund Institutional Class	PEIIX	NAS CM	Open End	US Equity Large Cap Value (Equity-Income)	B-	C+	B+	Down	Y	0
Principal Equity Income Fund R-1 Class	PIEMX	NAS CM	Open End	US Equity Large Cap Value (Equity-Income)	B-	C	B+		Y	0
Principal Equity Income Fund R-2 Class	PEINX	NAS CM	Open End	US Equity Large Cap Value (Equity-Income)	B-	C	B+		Y	0
Principal Equity Income Fund R-3 Class	PEIOX	NAS CM	Open End	US Equity Large Cap Value (Equity-Income)	B-	C	B+		Y	0
Principal Equity Income Fund R-4 Class	PEIPX	NAS CM	Open End	US Equity Large Cap Value (Equity-Income)	B-	C	B+		Y	0
Principal Equity Income Fund R-5 Class	PEIQX	NAS CM	Open End	US Equity Large Cap Value (Equity-Income)	B-	C	B+		Y	0
Principal Global Diversified Income Fund Class A	PGBAX	NAS CM	Open End	Cautious Alloc (Income)	B	C+	B+	Up	Y	1,000
Principal Global Diversified Income Fund Class C	PGDCX	NAS CM	Open End	Cautious Alloc (Income)	B-	C	B+	Up	Y	1,000
Principal Global Diversified Income Fund Class R-6	PGBLX	NAS CM	Open End	Cautious Alloc (Income)	B	C+	A-	Up	Y	0
Principal Global Diversified Income Institutional Cls	PGDIX	NAS CM	Open End	Cautious Alloc (Income)	B	C+	A-	Up	Y	0
Principal Global Investors Funds Preferred Securities R-6	PPREX	NAS CM	Open End	US Fixed Income (Income)	B	B-	B+	Up	Y	0
Principal Global Multi-Strategy Fund Class A Shares	PMSAX	NAS CM	Open End	Multialternative (Growth)	C+	C	B	Up	Y	1,000
Principal Global Multi-Strategy Fund Class C	PMSCX	NAS CM	Open End	Multialternative (Growth)	C	C-	B-		Y	1,000
Principal Global Multi-Strategy Institutional Cls Shares	PSMIX	NAS CM	Open End	Multialternative (Growth)	C+	C	B	Up	Y	0
Principal Global Multi-Strategy Fund R-6	PGLSX	NAS CM	Open End	Multialternative (Growth)	C+	C	B	Up	Y	0
Principal Global Opportunities Fund Class A	PGLAX	NAS CM	Open End	Global Equity Large Cap (Growth)	B-	C	B	Up	Y	1,000
Principal Global Opportunities Fund Institutional Class	PGOIX	NAS CM	Open End	Global Equity Large Cap (Growth)	B-	C	B	Up	Y	0
Principal Global Real Estate Securities Fund Class A	POSAX	NAS CM	Open End	Real Estate Sector Equity (Real Estate)	B	C+	B+	Up	Y	1,000
Principal Global Real Estate Securities Fund Class C	POSCX	NAS CM	Open End	Real Estate Sector Equity (Real Estate)	B-	C	B+		Y	1,000
Principal Global Real Estate Securities Fund Class R-6	PGRSX	NAS CM	Open End	Real Estate Sector Equity (Real Estate)	B	C+	B+	Up	Y	0
Principal Global Real Estate Securities Institutional Cls	POSIX	NAS CM	Open End	Real Estate Sector Equity (Real Estate)	B	C+	B+	Up	Y	0
Principal Global Real Estate Securities Fund R-3	PGRKX	NAS CM	Open End	Real Estate Sector Equity (Real Estate)	B-	C+	B+		Y	0
Principal Global Real Estate Securities Fund R-4	PGRVX	NAS CM	Open End	Real Estate Sector Equity (Real Estate)	B	C+	B+	Up	Y	0
Principal Global Real Estate Securities Fund R-5	PGRUX	NAS CM	Open End	Real Estate Sector Equity (Real Estate)	B	C+	B+	Up	Y	0
Principal International Emerging Markets Fund Class A	PRIAX	NAS CM	Open End	Global Emerg Mkts (Div Emerging Mkts)	C	C	C	Up	Y	1,000
Principal International Emerging Markets Fund Class C	PMKCX	NAS CM	Open End	Global Emerg Mkts (Div Emerging Mkts)	C	C-	C	Up	Y	1,000
Principal International Emerging Markets Fund Class J	PIEJX	NAS CM	Open End	Global Emerg Mkts (Div Emerging Mkts)	C	C	C	Up	Y	1,000

★Expanded analysis of this fund is included in Section II.

Min Additional Investment	TOTAL RETURNS 3-Month Total Return	6-Month Total Return	1-Year Total Return	3-Year Total Return	5-Year Total Return	PERFORMANCE Dividend Yield (TTM)	Expense Ratio	3-Yr Std Deviation	3-Year Beta	ASSETS NAV	Total Assets (MIL)	ASSET ALLOCATION & TURNOVER %Cash	%Stocks	%Bonds	%Other	Turnover Ratio	BULL & BEAR Last Bull Market Total Return	Last Bear Market Total Return	FEES Front End Fee (%)	Back End Fee (%)	Inception Date
	5.27	20.35	12.20	50.08	62.69	1.04	0.73	11.89	0.94	49.13	1,758	3	97	0	0	36	24.08	-17.54			Mar-10
	3.94	10.43	7.79	22.34	30.34	5.63	0	4.05	0.76	10.04	612.4	1	1	73	0	9					Mar-14
100	3.42	14.96	-1.75	25.24	10.25	1.18	1.21	12.04	1.03	12.37	12,066	3	96	0	1	51	16.58	-22.36	5.50		Jun-05
100	3.25	14.64	-2.41	22.55	6.31	0.41	1.98	12.05	1.03	12.37	12,066	3	96	0	1	51	16.09	-22.52		1.00	Jan-07
100	3.38	14.97	-1.70	25.80	11.00	1.33	1.1	12.01	1.03	12.21	12,066	3	96	0	1	51	16.54	-22.38		1.00	Mar-01
	3.72	14.82	-0.89	28.38	11.34		0.73	12.03	1.03	12.3	12,066	3	96	0	1	51	16.66	-22.22			Mar-19
	3.53	15.27	-1.26	27.05	12.96	1.68	0.73	12.05	1.03	12.3	12,066	3	96	0	1	51	16.93	-22.24			Mar-01
	3.26	14.71	-2.11	23.79	8.11	0.82	1.61	12	1.03	12.32	12,066	3	96	0	1	51	16.17	-22.48			Nov-04
	3.36	14.85	-1.94	24.36	8.87	0.83	1.48	12.01	1.03	12.29	12,066	3	96	0	1	51	16.33	-22.4			Dec-00
	3.43	15.00	-1.76	24.99	9.89	0.98	1.3	12.03	1.03	12.34	12,066	3	96	0	1	51	16.5	-22.37			Dec-00
	3.39	15.10	-1.58	25.70	10.91	1.24	1.11	12.01	1.03	12.5	12,066	3	96	0	1	51	16.61	-22.34			Dec-00
	3.48	15.14	-1.49	26.13	11.65	1.38	0.99	12.04	1.03	12.47	12,066	3	96	0	1	51	16.66	-22.22			Dec-00
100	1.42	10.45	0.21	12.26	-4.76	2.74	1.22	7.17		11.41	3,975	21	61	18	0	84	12	-12.8	3.75		Mar-10
100	1.26	10.02	-0.51	9.83	-8.25	1.96	1.97	7.14		11.19	3,975	21	61	18	0	84	11.57	-13.12		1.00	Mar-10
	1.33	10.37	0.06	11.71	-4.97	2.76	1.35	7.16		11.38	3,975	21	61	18	0	84	12.15	-12.77			Mar-16
	1.51	10.55	0.37	12.58	-3.98	2.88	1.16	7.14		11.42	3,975	21	61	18	0	84	12.25	-12.71			Mar-16
	1.51	10.56	0.49	12.97	-3.39	3.15	1.04	7.11		11.41	3,975	21	61	18	0	84	12.31	-12.68			Mar-16
	1.50	10.64	0.64	13.67	-2.76	3.21	0.79	7.12		11.43	3,975	21	61	18	0	84	12.31	-12.68			Dec-14
	1.50	10.64	0.58	13.52	-2.92	3.15	0.85	7.15		11.43	3,975	21	61	18	0	84	12.31	-12.68			Mar-10
100	2.98	18.92	5.02	38.26			1.1	13.81	0.99	14.3	668.9	3	97	0	0	17			5.50	1.00	Dec-18
	3.99	20.35	6.20	38.75		1.03	0.77	13.82	0.99	14.31	668.9	3	97	0	0	17					Sep-15
	3.98	20.38	6.35	39.86		1.1	0.66	13.84	1	14.35	668.9	3	97	0	0	17					Jan-17
100	5.35	17.81	10.96	44.94	51.99	1.85	0.89	11.46	0.92	32.07	7,444	2	98	0	0	13	21.74	-14.18	5.50		May-39
100	5.16	17.38	10.19	41.75	46.48	1.21	1.62	11.45	0.92	31.21	7,444	2	98	0	0	13	21.24	-14.45		1.00	Mar-02
100	5.34	17.84	10.99	44.99	52.04		0.84	11.46	0.92	32.11	7,444	2	98	0	0	13	21.74	-14.17		1.00	Oct-18
	5.44	18.00	11.39	46.53	54.92	2.19	0.52	11.48	0.92	32.11	7,444	2	98	0	0	13	22.06	-14.08			Aug-00
	5.22	17.51	10.44	42.76	48.26	1.41	1.39	11.47	0.92	31.93	7,444	2	98	0	0	13	21.5	-14.39			Mar-10
	5.25	17.61	10.58	43.38	49.30	1.51	1.26	11.45	0.92	32.08	7,444	2	98	0	0	13	21.53	-14.3			Mar-10
	5.28	17.68	10.77	44.13	50.61	1.67	1.08	11.46	0.92	31.97	7,444	2	98	0	0	13	21.68	-14.26			Mar-10
	5.32	17.80	10.97	44.91	52.08	1.85	0.89	11.48	0.92	32.03	7,444	2	98	0	0	13	21.76	-14.15			Mar-10
	5.38	17.89	11.13	45.49	53.04	1.97	0.77	11.47	0.92	32.08	7,444	2	98	0	0	13	21.86	-14.13			Mar-10
100	2.59	9.47	5.60	17.05	17.75	4.69	1	4.82	0.48	13.66	7,703	4	15	77	0	107	13.82	-8.86	3.75		Dec-08
100	2.41	9.04	4.84	14.38	13.42	3.98	1.75	4.81	0.48	13.57	7,703	4	15	77	0	107	13.42	-9.15		1.00	Dec-08
	2.77	9.71	6.00	18.18	19.64	5.06	0.66	4.83	0.48	13.59	7,703	4	15	77	0	107	14.1	-8.72			Jun-17
	2.77	9.70	5.98	18.21	19.66	5.04	0.69	4.87	0.49	13.6	7,703	4	15	77	0	107	14.1	-8.73			Dec-08
	3.55	10.45	7.22	17.93	29.22	5.42	0.71	3.9	0.8	10.09	5,513	1	1	56	0	12	10.53	-5.77			Jan-17
100	2.11	5.46	2.54	9.21	10.11	1.01	2.49	3.23	0.77	10.61	1,866	-23	16	102	2	378			3.75		Oct-11
100	1.98	5.10	1.75	6.70	5.96	0.25	3.27	3.22	0.77	10.29	1,866	-23	16	102	2	378				1.00	Jun-12
	2.29	5.71	2.86	10.39	12.09	1.4	2.18	3.23	0.77	10.72	1,866	-23	16	102	2	378					Oct-11
	2.29	5.72	3.00	10.41	12.10	1.52	2.09	3.25	0.77	10.71	1,866	-23	16	102	2	378					Jun-17
100	1.65	13.19	3.84	28.45	22.76	29.96	1.5	11.59	1	3.69	17.5	7	92	0	1	93			5.50		Sep-13
	1.83	13.45	4.79	31.31	27.22	29.71	0.85	11.54	0.99	3.88	17.5	7	92	0	1	93					Dec-12
100	1.33	16.91	10.44	22.73	35.48	2.85	1.31	10.92	0.97	9.53	3,881	2	98	0	0	24	25.51	-20.96	5.50		Oct-07
100	1.19	16.47	9.61	19.96	30.25	2.23	2.07	10.95	0.97	9.2	3,881	2	98	0	0	24	24.95	-21.23		1.00	Oct-07
	1.45	17.08	10.88	24.12	38.23	3.02	0.88	10.94	0.97	10.25	3,881	2	98	0	0	24	25.8	-20.73			Nov-14
	1.43	17.05	10.71	24.14	38.16	2.96	0.94	10.88	0.96	10.25	3,881	2	98	0	0	24	25.81	-20.73			Oct-07
	1.30	16.77	10.28	22.30	35.37	2.49	1.44	10.91	0.96	10.24	3,881	2	98	0	0	24	25.62	-20.81			Mar-16
	1.35	16.89	10.49	22.83	36.46	2.67	1.25	10.87	0.96	10.24	3,881	2	98	0	0	24	25.73	-20.76			Mar-16
	1.41	17.10	10.65	23.54	37.49	2.83	1.13	10.86	0.96	10.26	3,881	2	98	0	0	24	25.81	-20.73			Mar-16
100	0.55	10.05	-6.52	28.34	5.06	0.65	1.55	15.05	1.06	25.17	357.5	3	97	0	0	118	20.44	-26.19	5.50		Jun-05
100	0.33	9.51	-7.49	24.42	-0.20	0	2.51	15.04	1.06	23.83	357.5	3	97	0	0	118	19.8	-26.48		1.00	Jan-07
100	0.58	10.14	-6.40	28.79	5.63	0.78	1.37	15.06	1.06	24.21	357.5	3	97	0	0	118	20.49	-26.16		1.00	Mar-01

	MARKET			FUND TYPE, CATEGORY & OBJECTIVE	RATINGS				MINIMUMS	
Fund Name	Ticker Symbol	Traded On	Fund Type	Category and (Prospectus Objective)	Overall Rating	Reward Rating	Risk Rating	Recent Up/ Downgrade	Open to New Investors	Min Initial Investment
Principal International Emerging Markets Fund Class R-6	PIIMX	NAS CM	Open End	Global Emerg Mkts (Div Emerging Mkts)	C	C	C	Up	Y	0
Principal International Emerging Markets Institutional Cls	PIEIX	NAS CM	Open End	Global Emerg Mkts (Div Emerging Mkts)	C	C	C	Up	Y	0
Principal International Emerging Markets Fund R-1 Class	PIXEX	NAS CM	Open End	Global Emerg Mkts (Div Emerging Mkts)	C	C-	C	Up	Y	0
Principal International Emerging Markets Fund R-2 Class	PEASX	NAS CM	Open End	Global Emerg Mkts (Div Emerging Mkts)	C	C	C	Up	Y	0
Principal International Emerging Markets Fund R-3 Class	PEAPX	NAS CM	Open End	Global Emerg Mkts (Div Emerging Mkts)	C	C	C	Up	Y	0
Principal International Emerging Markets Fund R-4 Class	PESSX	NAS CM	Open End	Global Emerg Mkts (Div Emerging Mkts)	C	C	C	Up	Y	0
Principal International Emerging Markets Fund R-5 Class	PEPSX	NAS CM	Open End	Global Emerg Mkts (Div Emerging Mkts)	C	C	C	Up	Y	0
Principal International Equity Index Institutional Cls	PIDIX	NAS CM	Open End	Global Equity Large Cap (Foreign Stock)	C	C	B		Y	0
Principal International Equity Index Fund R-1 Class	PILIX	NAS CM	Open End	Global Equity Large Cap (Foreign Stock)	C	C	B		Y	0
Principal International Equity Index Fund R-2 Class	PINEX	NAS CM	Open End	Global Equity Large Cap (Foreign Stock)	C	C	B		Y	0
Principal International Equity Index Fund R-3 Class	PIIOX	NAS CM	Open End	Global Equity Large Cap (Foreign Stock)	C	C	B		Y	0
Principal International Equity Index Fund R-4 Class	PIIPX	NAS CM	Open End	Global Equity Large Cap (Foreign Stock)	C	C	B		Y	0
Principal International Equity Index Fund R-5 Class	PIIQX	NAS CM	Open End	Global Equity Large Cap (Foreign Stock)	C	C	B		Y	0
Principal International Equity Index Fund R-6	PFIEX	NAS CM	Open End	Global Equity Large Cap (Foreign Stock)	C	C	B		Y	0
Principal International Fund I Class A	PFAFX	NAS CM	Open End	Global Equity Large Cap (Foreign Stock)	C	C	C	Up	Y	1,000
Principal International Fund I Class R-6	PIIDX	NAS CM	Open End	Global Equity Large Cap (Foreign Stock)	C	C	C	Up	Y	0
Principal International Fund I Institutional Class	PINIX	NAS CM	Open End	Global Equity Large Cap (Foreign Stock)	C	C	C	Up	Y	0
Principal International Fund I R-1 Class	PPISX	NAS CM	Open End	Global Equity Large Cap (Foreign Stock)	C	C-	C	Up	Y	0
Principal International Fund I R-2 Class	PSPPX	NAS CM	Open End	Global Equity Large Cap (Foreign Stock)	C	C	C	Up	Y	0
Principal International Fund I R-3 Class	PRPPX	NAS CM	Open End	Global Equity Large Cap (Foreign Stock)	C	C	C	Up	Y	0
Principal International Fund I R-4 Class	PUPPX	NAS CM	Open End	Global Equity Large Cap (Foreign Stock)	C	C	C	Up	Y	0
Principal International Fund I R-5 Class	PTPPX	NAS CM	Open End	Global Equity Large Cap (Foreign Stock)	C	C	C	Up	Y	0
Principal International Small Company Fund Class A	PICAX	NAS CM	Open End	Global Equity Mid/Small Cap (Small Company)	C	C	C		Y	1,000
Principal International Small Company Institutional Cls	PISMX	NAS CM	Open End	Global Equity Mid/Small Cap (Small Company)	C	C	C+		Y	0
Principal International Small Company Fund R-6	PFISX	NAS CM	Open End	Global Equity Mid/Small Cap (Small Company)	C	C	C+		Y	0
Principal LargeCap Growth Fund Class A	PRGWX	NAS CM	Open End	US Equity Large Cap Growth (Growth)	C+	C	C+		Y	1,000
Principal LargeCap Growth Fund Class J	PGLJX	NAS CM	Open End	US Equity Large Cap Growth (Growth)	C+	C	C+		Y	1,000
Principal LargeCap Growth Fund I Class A	PLGAX	NAS CM	Open End	US Equity Large Cap Growth (Growth)	B-	C+	B	Down	Y	1,000
Principal LargeCap Growth Fund I Class J	PLGJX	NAS CM	Open End	US Equity Large Cap Growth (Growth)	B-	C+	B	Down	Y	1,000
Principal LargeCap Growth Fund I Class R-6	PLCGX	NAS CM	Open End	US Equity Large Cap Growth (Growth)	B-	C+	B	Down	Y	0
Principal LargeCap Growth Fund I Institutional Class	PLGIX	NAS CM	Open End	US Equity Large Cap Growth (Growth)	B-	C+	B	Down	Y	0
Principal LargeCap Growth Fund I R-1 Class	PCRSX	NAS CM	Open End	US Equity Large Cap Growth (Growth)	B-	C+	B	Down	Y	0
Principal LargeCap Growth Fund I R-2 Class	PPUNX	NAS CM	Open End	US Equity Large Cap Growth (Growth)	B-	C+	B	Down	Y	0
Principal LargeCap Growth Fund I R-3 Class	PPUMX	NAS CM	Open End	US Equity Large Cap Growth (Growth)	B-	C+	B	Down	Y	0
Principal LargeCap Growth Fund I R-4 Class	PPUSX	NAS CM	Open End	US Equity Large Cap Growth (Growth)	B-	C+	B	Down	Y	0
Principal LargeCap Growth Fund I R-5 Class	PPUPX	NAS CM	Open End	US Equity Large Cap Growth (Growth)	B-	C+	B	Down	Y	0
Principal LargeCap Growth Fund Institutional Class	PGLIX	NAS CM	Open End	US Equity Large Cap Growth (Growth)	C+	C	C+		Y	0
Principal LargeCap Growth Fund R-1 Class	PLSGX	NAS CM	Open End	US Equity Large Cap Growth (Growth)	C	C	C+	Down	Y	0
Principal LargeCap Growth Fund R-2 Class	PCPPX	NAS CM	Open End	US Equity Large Cap Growth (Growth)	C+	C	C+		Y	0
Principal LargeCap Growth Fund R-3 Class	PLGPX	NAS CM	Open End	US Equity Large Cap Growth (Growth)	C+	C	C+		Y	0
Principal LargeCap Growth Fund R-4 Class	PEPPX	NAS CM	Open End	US Equity Large Cap Growth (Growth)	C+	C	C+		Y	0
Principal LargeCap Growth Fund R-5 Class	PDPPX	NAS CM	Open End	US Equity Large Cap Growth (Growth)	C+	C	C+		Y	0
Principal LargeCap S&P 500 Index Fund Class A	PLSAX	NAS CM	Open End	US Equity Large Cap Blend (Growth)	B-	C	B		Y	1,000
Principal LargeCap S&P 500 Index Fund Class C	PLICX	NAS CM	Open End	US Equity Large Cap Blend (Growth)	B-	C	B		Y	1,000
Principal LargeCap S&P 500 Index Fund Class J	PSPJX	NAS CM	Open End	US Equity Large Cap Blend (Growth)	B-	C	B		Y	1,000
Principal LargeCap S&P 500 Index Fund Institutional Class	PLFIX	NAS CM	Open End	US Equity Large Cap Blend (Growth)	B-	C	B		Y	0
Principal LargeCap S&P 500 Index Fund R-1 Class	PLPIX	NAS CM	Open End	US Equity Large Cap Blend (Growth)	B-	C	B		Y	0
Principal LargeCap S&P 500 Index Fund R-2 Class	PLFNX	NAS CM	Open End	US Equity Large Cap Blend (Growth)	B-	C	B		Y	0
Principal LargeCap S&P 500 Index Fund R-3 Class	PLFMX	NAS CM	Open End	US Equity Large Cap Blend (Growth)	B-	C	B		Y	0
Principal LargeCap S&P 500 Index Fund R-4 Class	PLFSX	NAS CM	Open End	US Equity Large Cap Blend (Growth)	B-	C	B		Y	0
Principal LargeCap S&P 500 Index Fund R-5 Class	PLFPX	NAS CM	Open End	US Equity Large Cap Blend (Growth)	B-	C	B		Y	0
Principal LargeCap Value Fund III Class J	PLVJX	NAS CM	Open End	US Equity Large Cap Value (Growth)	B-	C	B		Y	1,000

★ Expanded analysis of this fund is included in Section II.

Min Additional Investment	3-Month Total Return	6-Month Total Return	1-Year Total Return	3-Year Total Return	5-Year Total Return	Dividend Yield (TTM)	Expense Ratio	3-Yr Std Deviation	3-Year Beta	NAV	Total Assets (MIL)	%Cash	%Stocks	%Bonds	%Other	Turnover Ratio	Last Bull Market Total Return	Last Bear Market Total Return	Front End Fee (%)	Back End Fee (%)	Inception Date
	TOTAL RETURNS					PERFORMANCE				ASSETS		ASSET ALLOCATION & TURNOVER					BULL & BEAR		FEES		
	0.60	10.17	-6.22	29.67	6.64	1.08	1.08	15.06	1.06	24.9	357.5	3	97	0	0	118	20.67	-26.11			Nov-16
	0.64	10.22	-6.20	29.66	7.16	1.03	1.2	15.05	1.06	24.9	357.5	3	97	0	0	118	20.83	-26.03			Mar-01
	0.48	9.80	-6.93	26.54	2.82	0.1	1.97	15.04	1.06	24.85	357.5	3	97	0	0	118	20.21	-26.31			Nov-04
	0.52	9.90	-6.84	27.01	3.49	0.09	1.84	15.06	1.06	24.74	357.5	3	97	0	0	118	20.33	-26.27			Dec-00
	0.52	9.94	-6.70	27.66	4.41	0.32	1.66	15.06	1.06	24.88	357.5	3	97	0	0	118	20.43	-26.23			Dec-00
	0.60	10.08	-6.51	28.45	5.39	0.54	1.47	15.04	1.06	24.99	357.5	3	97	0	0	118	20.58	-26.17			Dec-00
	0.60	10.14	-6.42	28.87	5.98	0.79	1.35	15.05	1.06	24.98	357.5	3	97	0	0	118	20.67	-26.11			Dec-00
	3.54	14.30	1.07	30.09	10.31	2.53	0.32	11.03	0.99	10.23	1,104	1	99	0	0	27	13.07	-23.38			Dec-09
	3.33	13.90	0.24	26.84	5.70	1.59	1.2	11.02	0.99	9.91	1,104	1	99	0	0	27	12.34	-23.51			Dec-09
	3.34	13.95	0.40	27.29	6.44	1.69	1.07	11.09	0.99	10.21	1,104	1	99	0	0	27	12.35	-23.57			Dec-09
	3.39	14.07	0.55	27.96	7.34	1.93	0.89	11.05	0.99	10.05	1,104	1	99	0	0	27	12.7	-23.48			Dec-09
	3.46	14.15	0.71	28.70	8.38	2.14	0.7	11.1	0.99	10.16	1,104	1	99	0	0	27	12.74	-23.37			Dec-09
	3.45	14.25	0.82	29.18	8.97	2.23	0.58	11.01	0.99	10.18	1,104	1	99	0	0	27	12.75	-23.35			Dec-09
	3.64	14.41	1.17	30.23	10.43	2.53	0.3	11.07	0.99	10.24	1,104	1	99	0	0	27	13.07	-23.38			Jan-17
100	4.27	20.20	-4.39	26.37	14.80	1.71	1.3	14.31	1.16	14.4	349.0	1	98	0	1	70	16.34	-26.02	5.50		Jun-14
	4.39	20.46	-3.90	28.20	17.57	2.2	0.79	14.33	1.16	14.48	349.0	1	98	0	1	70	16.51	-25.95			Nov-16
	4.32	20.36	-4.04	27.99	17.37	2.13	0.88	14.34	1.16	14.48	349.0	1	98	0	1	70	16.51	-25.95			Dec-03
	4.10	19.93	-4.81	24.85	12.62	1.28	1.67	14.3	1.16	14.44	349.0	1	98	0	1	70	15.93	-26.19			Nov-04
	4.16	20.01	-4.67	25.45	13.38	1.27	1.54	14.31	1.16	14.51	349.0	1	98	0	1	70	16	-26.17			Jun-04
	4.25	20.18	-4.45	26.11	14.47	1.58	1.36	14.3	1.15	14.47	349.0	1	98	0	1	70	16.08	-26.09			Jun-04
	4.25	20.19	-4.33	26.75	15.52	1.9	1.17	14.34	1.16	14.46	349.0	1	98	0	1	70	16.16	-26.03			Jun-04
	4.25	20.29	-4.24	27.22	16.12	1.86	1.05	14.31	1.16	14.46	349.0	1	98	0	1	70	16.37	-26.07			Jun-04
100	3.58	16.97	-5.53	31.33	23.92	0.79	1.6	13.26	1.06	10.68	902.2	2	98	0	0	46			5.50		Jun-14
	3.67	17.26	-5.14	32.63	25.95	1.25	1.2	13.2	1.06	10.73	902.2	2	98	0	0	46					Dec-14
	3.65	17.30	-5.06	32.94	25.44	1.3	1.07	13.23	1.06	10.78	902.2	2	98	0	0	46					Jan-17
100	3.71	22.80	2.36	51.73	56.21	0	1.1	15.26	1.09	5.87	558.2	1	99	0	0	77	26.52	-16.66	5.50		Jun-05
100	3.66	22.94	2.48	52.45	57.07	0.04	0.98	15.3	1.1	5.09	558.2	1	99	0	0	77	26.7	-16.68		1.00	Mar-01
100	4.25	23.17	12.76	76.12	90.10	0	1.04	13.58	0.99	15.2	9,006	1	99	0	0	35	29.8	-17.49	5.50		Mar-13
100	4.28	23.39	12.99	77.74	92.62	0.04	0.84	13.58	0.99	12.66	9,006	1	99	0	0	35	29.58	-17.61		1.00	Mar-01
	4.37	23.45	13.23	78.74	95.05	0.17	0.59	13.57	0.99	15.74	9,006	1	99	0	0	35	29.99	-17.4			Nov-14
	4.30	23.43	13.12	78.46	94.84	0.1	0.67	13.58	0.99	15.75	9,006	1	99	0	0	35	29.99	-17.4			Dec-00
	4.11	22.85	12.22	74.10	86.84	0	1.47	13.56	0.99	13.17	9,006	1	99	0	0	35	29.29	-17.69			Nov-04
	4.22	23.01	12.38	74.98	88.22	0	1.34	13.58	0.99	12.83	9,006	1	99	0	0	35	29.42	-17.66			Dec-00
	4.20	23.10	12.61	75.84	89.87	0	1.16	13.6	0.99	14.12	9,006	1	99	0	0	35	29.53	-17.52			Dec-00
	4.25	23.18	12.80	76.88	91.67	0	0.97	13.61	0.99	14.45	9,006	1	99	0	0	35	29.58	-17.48			Dec-00
	4.28	23.28	12.93	77.43	92.84	0	0.85	13.59	0.99	15.09	9,006	1	99	0	0	35	29.85	-17.5			Dec-00
	3.80	23.12	2.88	53.79	59.74	0.17	0.67	15.32	1.1	6.55	558.2	1	99	0	0	77	27.14	-16.62			Mar-01
	3.43	22.48	1.87	49.60	52.78	0	1.56	15.3	1.1	5.12	558.2	1	99	0	0	77	26.48	-16.84			Nov-04
	3.63	22.67	2.10	50.35	53.97	0	1.43	15.36	1.1	5.41	558.2	1	99	0	0	77	26.58	-16.84			Dec-00
	3.51	22.82	2.19	51.09	55.15	0	1.25	15.32	1.1	6.78	558.2	1	99	0	0	77	26.62	-16.66			Dec-00
	3.67	22.86	2.37	52.03	56.73	0	1.06	15.29	1.1	6.77	558.2	1	99	0	0	77	26.87	-16.7			Dec-00
	3.75	22.96	2.53	52.49	57.72	0	0.94	15.31	1.1	6.64	558.2	1	99	0	0	77	27.04	-16.64			Dec-00
100	4.18	19.31	9.90	48.86	62.38	1.47	0.44	12.2	1	18.41	5,904	0	100	0	0	6	24.55	-16.38	1.50		Jun-05
100	3.99	18.79	9.01	45.15	55.84	0.78	1.3	12.15	1	17.95	5,904	0	100	0	0	6	24.14	-16.71		1.00	Jan-07
100	4.23	19.39	10.04	49.24	62.96	1.55	0.4	12.21	1	18.22	5,904	0	100	0	0	6	24.73	-16.5		1.00	Mar-01
	4.24	19.46	10.24	50.15	64.91	1.72	0.16	12.19	1	18.41	5,904	0	100	0	0	6	24.89	-16.28			Mar-01
	4.02	19.00	9.33	46.25	57.89	0.87	1.03	12.16	1	18.35	5,904	0	100	0	0	6	24.25	-16.54			Nov-04
	4.04	19.03	9.45	46.86	58.88	0.97	0.9	12.18	1	18.51	5,904	0	100	0	0	6	24.49	-16.56			Dec-00
	4.12	19.19	9.67	47.66	60.37	1.16	0.72	12.16	1	18.44	5,904	0	100	0	0	6	24.47	-16.45			Dec-00
	4.11	19.21	9.83	48.44	61.80	1.34	0.53	12.17	1	18.49	5,904	0	100	0	0	6	24.76	-16.51			Dec-00
	4.18	19.29	9.95	49.01	62.90	1.45	0.41	12.19	1	18.67	5,904	0	100	0	0	6	24.81	-16.4			Dec-00
100	4.41	16.25	8.62	38.82	45.45	1.31	1.06	11.75	0.96	16.31	2,138	1	99	0	0	44	23.78	-21.32		1.00	Mar-01

Fund Name	MARKET Ticker Symbol	Traded On	FUND TYPE, CATEGORY & OBJECTIVE Fund Type	Category and (Prospectus Objective)	RATINGS Overall Rating	Reward Rating	Risk Rating	Recent Up/ Downgrade	Open to New Investors	MINIMUMS Min Initial Investment
Principal LargeCap Value Fund III Institutional Class	PLVIX	NAS CM	Open End	US Equity Large Cap Value (Growth)	B-	C	B		Y	0
Principal LargeCap Value Fund III R-1 Class	PESAX	NAS CM	Open End	US Equity Large Cap Value (Growth)	B-	C	B	Up	Y	0
Principal LargeCap Value Fund III R-2 Class	PPSNX	NAS CM	Open End	US Equity Large Cap Value (Growth)	B-	C	B	Up	Y	0
Principal LargeCap Value Fund III R-3 Class	PPSFX	NAS CM	Open End	US Equity Large Cap Value (Growth)	B-	C	B	Up	Y	0
Principal LargeCap Value Fund III R-4 Class	PPSSX	NAS CM	Open End	US Equity Large Cap Value (Growth)	B-	C	B	Up	Y	0
Principal LargeCap Value Fund III R-5 Class	PPSRX	NAS CM	Open End	US Equity Large Cap Value (Growth)	B-	C	B		Y	0
Principal LifeTime 2010 Fund Class A	PENAX	NAS CM	Open End	Target Date (Asset Alloc)	B	C+	A-	Up	Y	1,000
Principal LifeTime 2010 Fund Class J	PTAJX	NAS CM	Open End	Target Date (Asset Alloc)	B	C+	A-	Up	Y	1,000
Principal LifeTime 2010 Fund Institutional Class	PTTIX	NAS CM	Open End	Target Date (Asset Alloc)	B	C+	A-	Up	Y	0
Principal LifeTime 2010 Fund R-1 Class	PVASX	NAS CM	Open End	Target Date (Asset Alloc)	B-	C	A-	Up	Y	0
Principal LifeTime 2010 Fund R-2 Class	PTANX	NAS CM	Open End	Target Date (Asset Alloc)	B	C	A-	Up	Y	0
Principal LifeTime 2010 Fund R-3 Class	PTAMX	NAS CM	Open End	Target Date (Asset Alloc)	B	C+	A-	Up	Y	0
Principal LifeTime 2010 Fund R-4 Class	PTASX	NAS CM	Open End	Target Date (Asset Alloc)	B	C+	A-	Up	Y	0
Principal LifeTime 2010 Fund R-5 Class	PTAPX	NAS CM	Open End	Target Date (Asset Alloc)	B	C+	A-	Up	Y	0
Principal LifeTime 2015 Fund Institutional Class	LTINX	NAS CM	Open End	Target Date (Asset Alloc)	B	C+	A-	Up	Y	0
Principal LifeTime 2015 Fund R-1 Class	LTSGX	NAS CM	Open End	Target Date (Asset Alloc)	B-	C	A-	Up	Y	0
Principal LifeTime 2015 Fund R-2 Class	LTASX	NAS CM	Open End	Target Date (Asset Alloc)	B	C	A-	Up	Y	0
Principal LifeTime 2015 Fund R-3 Class	LTAPX	NAS CM	Open End	Target Date (Asset Alloc)	B	C	A-	Up	Y	0
Principal LifeTime 2015 Fund R-4 Class	LTSLX	NAS CM	Open End	Target Date (Asset Alloc)	B	C	A-	Up	Y	0
Principal LifeTime 2015 Fund R-5 Class	LTPFX	NAS CM	Open End	Target Date (Asset Alloc)	B	C	A-	Up	Y	0
Principal LifeTime 2020 Fund Class A	PTBAX	NAS CM	Open End	Target Date (Asset Alloc)	B-	C	A-	Up	Y	1,000
Principal LifeTime 2020 Fund Class J	PLFJX	NAS CM	Open End	Target Date (Asset Alloc)	B-	C	A-	Up	Y	1,000
Principal LifeTime 2020 Fund Institutional Class	PLWIX	NAS CM	Open End	Target Date (Asset Alloc)	B	C	A-	Up	Y	0
Principal LifeTime 2020 Fund R-1 Class	PWASX	NAS CM	Open End	Target Date (Asset Alloc)	B-	C	A-	Up	Y	0
Principal LifeTime 2020 Fund R-2 Class	PTBNX	NAS CM	Open End	Target Date (Asset Alloc)	B-	C	A-	Up	Y	0
Principal LifeTime 2020 Fund R-3 Class	PTBMX	NAS CM	Open End	Target Date (Asset Alloc)	B-	C	A-	Up	Y	0
Principal LifeTime 2020 Fund R-4 Class	PTBSX	NAS CM	Open End	Target Date (Asset Alloc)	B-	C	A-	Up	Y	0
Principal LifeTime 2020 Fund R-5 Class	PTBPX	NAS CM	Open End	Target Date (Asset Alloc)	B-	C	A-	Up	Y	0
Principal LifeTime 2025 Fund Institutional Class	LTSTX	NAS CM	Open End	Target Date (Asset Alloc)	B-	C	B+	Up	Y	0
Principal LifeTime 2025 Fund R-1 Class	LTSNX	NAS CM	Open End	Target Date (Asset Alloc)	B-	C	B+	Up	Y	0
Principal LifeTime 2025 Fund R-2 Class	LTADX	NAS CM	Open End	Target Date (Asset Alloc)	B-	C	B+	Up	Y	0
Principal LifeTime 2025 Fund R-3 Class	LTVPX	NAS CM	Open End	Target Date (Asset Alloc)	B-	C	B+	Up	Y	0
Principal LifeTime 2025 Fund R-4 Class	LTEEX	NAS CM	Open End	Target Date (Asset Alloc)	B-	C	B+	Up	Y	0
Principal LifeTime 2025 Fund R-5 Class	LTPDX	NAS CM	Open End	Target Date (Asset Alloc)	B-	C	B+	Up	Y	0
Principal LifeTime 2030 Fund Class A	PTCAX	NAS CM	Open End	Target Date (Asset Alloc)	B-	C	B+	Up	Y	1,000
Principal LifeTime 2030 Fund Class J	PLTJX	NAS CM	Open End	Target Date (Asset Alloc)	B-	C	B+	Up	Y	1,000
Principal LifeTime 2030 Fund Institutional Class	PMTIX	NAS CM	Open End	Target Date (Asset Alloc)	B-	C	B+	Up	Y	0
Principal LifeTime 2030 Fund R-1 Class	PXASX	NAS CM	Open End	Target Date (Asset Alloc)	B-	C	B+	Up	Y	0
Principal LifeTime 2030 Fund R-2 Class	PTCNX	NAS CM	Open End	Target Date (Asset Alloc)	B-	C	B+	Up	Y	0
Principal LifeTime 2030 Fund R-3 Class	PTCMX	NAS CM	Open End	Target Date (Asset Alloc)	B-	C	B+	Up	Y	0
Principal LifeTime 2030 Fund R-4 Class	PTCSX	NAS CM	Open End	Target Date (Asset Alloc)	B-	C	B+	Up	Y	0
Principal LifeTime 2030 Fund R-5 Class	PTCPX	NAS CM	Open End	Target Date (Asset Alloc)	B-	C	B+	Up	Y	0
Principal LifeTime 2035 Fund Institutional Class	LTIUX	NAS CM	Open End	Target Date (Asset Alloc)	B-	C	B+	Up	Y	0
Principal LifeTime 2035 Fund R-1 Class	LTANX	NAS CM	Open End	Target Date (Asset Alloc)	B-	C	B+	Up	Y	0
Principal LifeTime 2035 Fund R-2 Class	LTVIX	NAS CM	Open End	Target Date (Asset Alloc)	B-	C	B+	Up	Y	0
Principal LifeTime 2035 Fund R-3 Class	LTAOX	NAS CM	Open End	Target Date (Asset Alloc)	B-	C	B+	Up	Y	0
Principal LifeTime 2035 Fund R-4 Class	LTSEX	NAS CM	Open End	Target Date (Asset Alloc)	B-	C	B+	Up	Y	0
Principal LifeTime 2035 Fund R-5 Class	LTPEX	NAS CM	Open End	Target Date (Asset Alloc)	B-	C	B+	Up	Y	0
Principal LifeTime 2040 Fund Class A	PTDAX	NAS CM	Open End	Target Date (Asset Alloc)	B-	C	B	Up	Y	1,000
Principal LifeTime 2040 Fund Class J	PTDJX	NAS CM	Open End	Target Date (Asset Alloc)	B-	C	B	Up	Y	1,000
Principal LifeTime 2040 Fund Institutional Class	PTDIX	NAS CM	Open End	Target Date (Asset Alloc)	B-	C	B	Up	Y	0
Principal LifeTime 2040 Fund R-1 Class	PYASX	NAS CM	Open End	Target Date (Asset Alloc)	B-	C	B	Up	Y	0

★ Expanded analysis of this fund is included in Section II.

Min Additional Investment	TOTAL RETURNS 3-Month Total Return	6-Month Total Return	1-Year Total Return	3-Year Total Return	5-Year Total Return	PERFORMANCE Dividend Yield (TTM)	Expense Ratio	3-Yr Std Deviation	3-Year Beta	ASSETS NAV	Total Assets (MIL)	ASSET ALLOCATION & TURNOVER %Cash	%Stocks	%Bonds	%Other	Turnover Ratio	BULL & BEAR Last Bull Market Total Return	Last Bear Market Total Return	FEES Front End Fee (%)	Back End Fee (%)	Inception Date
	4.47	16.37	8.92	40.09	47.84	1.58	0.71	11.74	0.96	16.56	2,138	1	99	0	0	44	24.12	-21.16			Dec-00
	4.30	15.88	8.07	36.56	41.50	0.79	1.59	11.78	0.96	16.49	2,138	1	99	0	0	44	23.49	-21.49			Nov-04
	4.28	15.96	8.13	36.96	42.35	0.87	1.46	11.75	0.96	16.56	2,138	1	99	0	0	44	23.64	-21.4			Dec-00
	4.38	16.10	8.35	37.81	43.71	0.85	1.28	11.76	0.96	17.37	2,138	1	99	0	0	44	23.67	-21.34			Dec-00
	4.41	16.22	8.56	38.59	45.10	1.24	1.09	11.76	0.96	16.55	2,138	1	99	0	0	44	23.91	-21.31			Dec-00
	4.38	16.23	8.65	39.02	45.87	1.36	0.97	11.74	0.96	16.68	2,138	1	99	0	0	44	23.93	-21.28			Dec-00
100	3.03	9.97	5.65	19.09	20.39	2.23	1.01	4.83	1.03	13.23	764.1	4	32	63	0	22	12.82	-10.1	3.75		Jun-05
100	3.07	10.07	5.88	19.73	21.40	2.46	0.84	4.84	1.03	13.08	764.1	4	32	63	0	22	12.88	-10.17		1.00	Jun-01
	3.13	10.23	6.04	20.36	22.62	2.61	0.64	4.82	1.02	13.14	764.1	4	32	63	0	22	13.05	-9.98			Mar-01
	2.90	9.72	5.12	17.21	17.32	1.69	1.52	4.83	1.03	13.11	764.1	4	32	63	0	22	12.46	-10.3			Nov-04
	2.90	9.77	5.26	17.73	18.19	1.87	1.39	4.82	1.02	13.11	764.1	4	32	63	0	22	12.63	-10.32			Mar-01
	3.00	9.89	5.52	18.44	19.26	2.01	1.21	4.84	1.03	13.04	764.1	4	32	63	0	22	12.61	-10.15			Mar-01
	3.07	9.97	5.69	19.07	20.39	2.23	1.02	4.84	1.03	13.07	764.1	4	32	63	0	22	12.89	-10.13			Mar-01
	3.07	10.05	5.77	19.44	21.01	2.37	0.9	4.84	1.03	13.08	764.1	4	32	63	0	22	12.87	-10.02			Mar-01
	3.39	11.42	6.13	23.63	25.24	2.64	0.66	5.75	1.06	10.05	416.8	4	40	55	0	24	15.63	-12.58			Feb-08
	3.05	10.86	5.23	20.31	19.85	1.73	1.53	5.75	1.06	9.79	416.8	4	40	55	0	24	14.99	-12.82			Feb-08
	3.13	11.02	5.42	20.95	20.69	1.82	1.4	5.76	1.06	9.87	416.8	4	40	55	0	24	15.17	-12.79			Feb-08
	3.15	11.06	5.56	21.45	21.82	2.1	1.22	5.72	1.05	9.81	416.8	4	40	55	0	24	15.17	-12.75			Feb-08
	3.23	11.17	5.81	22.23	22.97	2.25	1.03	5.72	1.06	9.9	416.8	4	40	55	0	24	15.29	-12.62			Feb-08
	3.33	11.27	5.92	22.72	23.68	2.43	0.91	5.68	1.05	9.91	416.8	4	40	55	0	24	15.49	-12.59			Feb-08
100	3.44	12.71	5.73	25.07	25.72	2.01	1.04	6.9	1.14	14.13	4,126	3	51	46	0	20	17.71	-14.65	5.50		Jun-05
100	3.56	12.81	5.99	25.84	26.85	2.25	0.86	6.87	1.14	13.96	4,126	3	51	46	0	20	17.61	-14.62		1.00	Jun-01
	3.61	12.92	6.14	26.50	28.11	2.39	0.67	6.82	1.13	14.04	4,126	3	51	46	0	20	17.95	-14.56			Mar-01
	3.33	12.41	5.20	23.21	22.61	1.46	1.54	6.86	1.13	13.95	4,126	3	51	46	0	20	17.23	-14.82			Nov-04
	3.40	12.56	5.41	23.73	23.45	1.44	1.41	6.86	1.13	13.96	4,126	3	51	46	0	20	17.39	-14.79			Mar-01
	3.42	12.63	5.54	24.34	24.57	1.8	1.23	6.84	1.13	13.9	4,126	3	51	46	0	20	17.51	-14.75			Mar-01
	3.49	12.69	5.78	25.07	25.72	2	1.04	6.88	1.14	13.93	4,126	3	51	46	0	20	17.62	-14.66			Mar-01
	3.48	12.77	5.87	25.40	26.43	2.15	0.92	6.84	1.13	13.96	4,126	3	51	46	0	20	17.71	-14.62			Mar-01
	3.79	14.22	6.39	29.50	30.96	2.29	0.68	7.8	1.1	11.48	1,573	2	59	38	0	26	19.01	-15.74			Feb-08
	3.50	13.75	5.45	26.22	25.32	1.43	1.55	7.72	1.09	11.21	1,573	2	59	38	0	26	18.43	-16.05			Feb-08
	3.59	13.83	5.66	26.73	26.26	1.62	1.42	7.79	1.1	11.25	1,573	2	59	38	0	26	18.4	-15.94			Feb-08
	3.59	13.82	5.84	27.34	27.32	1.77	1.24	7.78	1.1	11.24	1,573	2	59	38	0	26	18.54	-15.91			Feb-08
	3.64	14.00	5.99	28.08	28.55	1.93	1.05	7.78	1.1	11.36	1,573	2	59	38	0	26	18.61	-15.75			Feb-08
	3.73	14.12	6.13	28.63	29.29	2.06	0.93	7.73	1.09	11.4	1,573	2	59	38	0	26	18.81	-15.8			Feb-08
100	3.71	15.05	5.63	30.41	30.30	1.77	1.08	8.76	1.07	14.5	5,552	2	68	29	0	24	19.39	-16.62	5.50		Jun-05
100	3.81	15.24	5.84	31.21	31.42	1.98	0.9	8.81	1.08	14.42	5,552	2	68	29	0	24	19.39	-16.62		1.00	Jun-01
	3.80	15.32	6.01	31.79	32.74	2.13	0.71	8.81	1.08	14.46	5,552	2	68	29	0	24	19.69	-16.52			Mar-01
	3.60	14.86	5.11	28.44	27.04	1.19	1.58	8.81	1.08	14.36	5,552	2	68	29	0	24	19.07	-16.86			Nov-04
	3.59	14.82	5.19	28.95	27.86	1.21	1.45	8.78	1.08	14.42	5,552	2	68	29	0	24	19.13	-16.78			Mar-01
	3.74	15.04	5.47	29.67	29.11	1.55	1.27	8.78	1.08	14.4	5,552	2	68	29	0	24	19.26	-16.73			Mar-01
	3.75	15.10	5.62	30.36	30.25	1.67	1.08	8.78	1.08	14.93	5,552	2	68	29	0	24	19.41	-16.71			Mar-01
	3.73	15.11	5.72	30.76	31.01	1.89	0.96	8.79	1.08	14.44	5,552	2	68	29	0	24	19.49	-16.61			Mar-01
	3.83	16.06	6.17	34.49	34.75	2.1	0.66	9.38	1.02	12.18	1,256	1	74	25	0	20	20.58	-17.52			Feb-08
	3.64	15.54	5.22	31.12	29.07	1.26	1.53	9.37	1.02	11.94	1,256	1	74	25	0	20	19.98	-17.75			Feb-08
	3.64	15.65	5.40	31.71	29.91	1.41	1.4	9.43	1.03	11.93	1,256	1	74	25	0	20	20.07	-17.75			Feb-08
	3.63	15.70	5.59	32.34	31.04	1.57	1.22	9.36	1.02	11.98	1,256	1	74	25	0	20	20.18	-17.68			Feb-08
	3.78	15.91	5.76	33.10	32.37	1.74	1.03	9.43	1.03	12.08	1,256	1	74	25	0	20	20.27	-17.61			Feb-08
	3.68	15.84	5.83	33.46	33.04	1.88	0.91	9.37	1.02	12.11	1,256	1	74	25	0	20	20.49	-17.57			Feb-08
100	3.79	16.67	5.73	34.90	33.70	1.65	1.05	10.04	1.02	15.06	3,821	1	81	18	0	16	20.93	-18.34	5.50		Jun-05
100	3.81	16.72	5.88	35.59	34.62	1.81	0.89	10.03	1.02	15.22	3,821	1	81	18	0	16	20.95	-18.38		1.00	Jun-01
	3.85	16.87	6.04	36.28	36.14	1.97	0.68	10.03	1.02	15.36	3,821	1	81	18	0	16	21.1	-18.13			Mar-01
	3.68	16.39	5.18	32.81	30.26	1.13	1.55	10.06	1.03	15.2	3,821	1	81	18	0	16	20.53	-18.51			Nov-04

Fund Name	MARKET Ticker Symbol	MARKET Traded On	FUND TYPE, CATEGORY & OBJECTIVE Fund Type	Category and (Prospectus Objective)	RATINGS Overall Rating	Reward Rating	Risk Rating	Recent Up/ Downgrade	Open to New Investors	MINIMUMS Min Initial Investment
Principal LifeTime 2040 Fund R-2 Class	PTDNX	NAS CM	Open End	Target Date (Asset Alloc)	B-	C	B	Up	Y	0
Principal LifeTime 2040 Fund R-3 Class	PTDMX	NAS CM	Open End	Target Date (Asset Alloc)	B-	C	B	Up	Y	0
Principal LifeTime 2040 Fund R-4 Class	PTDSX	NAS CM	Open End	Target Date (Asset Alloc)	B-	C	B	Up	Y	0
Principal LifeTime 2040 Fund R-5 Class	PTDPX	NAS CM	Open End	Target Date (Asset Alloc)	B-	C	B	Up	Y	0
Principal LifeTime 2045 Fund Institutional Class	LTRIX	NAS CM	Open End	Target Date (Asset Alloc)	B-	C	B	Up	Y	0
Principal LifeTime 2045 Fund R-1 Class	LTRGX	NAS CM	Open End	Target Date (Asset Alloc)	B-	C	B	Up	Y	0
Principal LifeTime 2045 Fund R-2 Class	LTRSX	NAS CM	Open End	Target Date (Asset Alloc)	B-	C	B	Up	Y	0
Principal LifeTime 2045 Fund R-3 Class	LTRVX	NAS CM	Open End	Target Date (Asset Alloc)	B-	C	B	Up	Y	0
Principal LifeTime 2045 Fund R-4 Class	LTRLX	NAS CM	Open End	Target Date (Asset Alloc)	B-	C	B	Up	Y	0
Principal LifeTime 2045 Fund R-5 Class	LTRDX	NAS CM	Open End	Target Date (Asset Alloc)	B-	C	B	Up	Y	0
Principal LifeTime 2050 Fund Class A	PPEAX	NAS CM	Open End	Target Date (Asset Alloc)	B-	C	B	Up	Y	1,000
Principal LifeTime 2050 Fund Class J	PFLJX	NAS CM	Open End	Target Date (Asset Alloc)	B-	C	B	Up	Y	1,000
Principal LifeTime 2050 Fund Institutional Class	PPLIX	NAS CM	Open End	Target Date (Asset Alloc)	B-	C	B	Up	Y	0
Principal LifeTime 2050 Fund R-1 Class	PZASX	NAS CM	Open End	Target Date (Asset Alloc)	C+	C	B	Up	Y	0
Principal LifeTime 2050 Fund R-2 Class	PTENX	NAS CM	Open End	Target Date (Asset Alloc)	C+	C	B	Up	Y	0
Principal LifeTime 2050 Fund R-3 Class	PTERX	NAS CM	Open End	Target Date (Asset Alloc)	B-	C	B	Up	Y	0
Principal LifeTime 2050 Fund R-4 Class	PTESX	NAS CM	Open End	Target Date (Asset Alloc)	B-	C	B	Up	Y	0
Principal LifeTime 2050 Fund R-5 Class	PTEFX	NAS CM	Open End	Target Date (Asset Alloc)	B-	C	B	Up	Y	0
Principal LifeTime 2055 Fund Institutional Class	LTFIX	NAS CM	Open End	Target Date (Asset Alloc)	B-	C	B	Up	Y	0
Principal LifeTime 2055 Fund R-1 Class	LTFGX	NAS CM	Open End	Target Date (Asset Alloc)	C+	C	B	Up	Y	0
Principal LifeTime 2055 Fund R-2 Class	LTFSX	NAS CM	Open End	Target Date (Asset Alloc)	C+	C	B	Up	Y	0
Principal LifeTime 2055 Fund R-3 Class	LTFDX	NAS CM	Open End	Target Date (Asset Alloc)	C+	C	B	Up	Y	0
Principal LifeTime 2055 Fund R-4 Class	LTFLX	NAS CM	Open End	Target Date (Asset Alloc)	C+	C	B	Up	Y	0
Principal LifeTime 2055 Fund R-5 Class	LTFPX	NAS CM	Open End	Target Date (Asset Alloc)	C+	C	B	Up	Y	0
Principal LifeTime 2060 Fund Class J	PLTAX	NAS CM	Open End	Target Date (Asset Alloc)	C+	C	B	Up	Y	1,000
Principal LifeTime 2060 Fund Class R-1	PLTRX	NAS CM	Open End	Target Date (Asset Alloc)	C+	C	B	Up	Y	0
Principal LifeTime 2060 Fund Class R-2	PLTBX	NAS CM	Open End	Target Date (Asset Alloc)	C+	C	B	Up	Y	0
Principal LifeTime 2060 Fund Class R-3	PLTCX	NAS CM	Open End	Target Date (Asset Alloc)	C+	C	B	Up	Y	0
Principal LifeTime 2060 Fund Class R-4	PLTMX	NAS CM	Open End	Target Date (Asset Alloc)	C+	C	B	Up	Y	0
Principal LifeTime 2060 Fund Class R-5	PLTOX	NAS CM	Open End	Target Date (Asset Alloc)	C+	C	B	Up	Y	0
Principal LifeTime 2060 Fund Institutional Class	PLTZX	NAS CM	Open End	Target Date (Asset Alloc)	C+	C	B	Up	Y	0
Principal LifeTime 2065 Class R-1 Shares	PLJAX	NAS CM	Open End	Target Date (Asset Alloc)	C-	D+	B-	Up	Y	0
Principal LifeTime 2065 Class R-2 Shares	PLJBX	NAS CM	Open End	Target Date (Asset Alloc)	C-	D+	B-	Up	Y	0
Principal LifeTime 2065 Class R-3 Shares	PLJCX	NAS CM	Open End	Target Date (Asset Alloc)	C-	D+	B-	Up	Y	0
Principal LifeTime 2065 Class R-4 Shares	PLJDX	NAS CM	Open End	Target Date (Asset Alloc)	C-	D+	B-	Up	Y	0
Principal LifeTime 2065 Class R-5 Shares	PLJEX	NAS CM	Open End	Target Date (Asset Alloc)	C-	D+	B-	Up	Y	0
Principal LifeTime 2065 Institutional Class Shares	PLJIX	NAS CM	Open End	Target Date (Asset Alloc)	C-	D+	B-	Up	Y	0
Principal LifeTime Hybrid 2015 Fund Class J	PHJMX	NAS CM	Open End	Target Date (Asset Alloc)	B	C	A-	Up	Y	1,000
Principal LifeTime Hybrid 2015 Fund Class R-3	PHTCX	NAS CM	Open End	Target Date (Asset Alloc)	B	C	A-	Up	Y	0
Principal LifeTime Hybrid 2015 Fund Class R-5	PHTRX	NAS CM	Open End	Target Date (Asset Alloc)	B	C	A-	Up	Y	0
Principal LifeTime Hybrid 2015 Fund Institutional Class	PHTMX	NAS CM	Open End	Target Date (Asset Alloc)	B	C	A-	Up	Y	0
Principal LifeTime Hybrid 2015 Fund R-6	PLRRX	NAS CM	Open End	Target Date (Asset Alloc)	B	C	A-	Up	Y	0
Principal LifeTime Hybrid 2020 Fund Class J	PHJTX	NAS CM	Open End	Target Date (Asset Alloc)	B-	C	A-	Up	Y	1,000
Principal LifeTime Hybrid 2020 Fund Class R-3	PHWIX	NAS CM	Open End	Target Date (Asset Alloc)	B-	C	A-	Up	Y	0
Principal LifeTime Hybrid 2020 Fund Class R-5	PHTIX	NAS CM	Open End	Target Date (Asset Alloc)	B-	C	A-	Up	Y	0
Principal LifeTime Hybrid 2020 Fund Institutional Class	PHTTX	NAS CM	Open End	Target Date (Asset Alloc)	B-	C	A-	Up	Y	0
Principal LifeTime Hybrid 2020 Fund R-6	PLTTX	NAS CM	Open End	Target Date (Asset Alloc)	B-	C	A-	Up	Y	0
Principal LifeTime Hybrid 2025 Fund Class J	PHJQX	NAS CM	Open End	Target Date (Asset Alloc)	B-	C	B+	Up	Y	1,000
Principal LifeTime Hybrid 2025 Fund Class R-3	PHTPX	NAS CM	Open End	Target Date (Asset Alloc)	B-	C	B+	Up	Y	0
Principal LifeTime Hybrid 2025 Fund Class R-5	PHTOX	NAS CM	Open End	Target Date (Asset Alloc)	B-	C	B+	Up	Y	0
Principal LifeTime Hybrid 2025 Fund Institutional Class	PHTQX	NAS CM	Open End	Target Date (Asset Alloc)	B-	C	B+	Up	Y	0
Principal LifeTime Hybrid 2025 Fund R-6	PLFTX	NAS CM	Open End	Target Date (Asset Alloc)	B-	C	B+	Up	Y	0

★Expanded analysis of this fund is included in Section II.

	TOTAL RETURNS					PERFORMANCE				ASSETS		ASSET ALLOCATION & TURNOVER					BULL & BEAR		FEES		
Min Additional Investment	3-Month Total Return	6-Month Total Return	1-Year Total Return	3-Year Total Return	5-Year Total Return	Dividend Yield (TTM)	Expense Ratio	3-Yr Std Deviation	3-Year Beta	NAV	Total Assets (MIL)	%Cash	%Stocks	%Bonds	%Other	Turnover Ratio	Last Bull Market Total Return	Last Bear Market Total Return	Front End Fee (%)	Back End Fee (%)	Inception Date
	3.74	16.47	5.33	33.29	31.13	1.03	1.42	10.03	1.02	15.24	3,821	1	81	18	0	16	20.6	-18.43			Mar-01
	3.76	16.50	5.48	34.04	32.31	1.41	1.24	10.03	1.02	15.15	3,821	1	81	18	0	16	20.81	-18.37			Mar-01
	3.83	16.65	5.71	34.85	33.64	1.61	1.05	10.06	1.03	15.18	3,821	1	81	18	0	16	20.83	-18.28			Mar-01
	3.80	16.71	5.77	35.28	34.36	1.73	0.93	10.01	1.02	15.28	3,821	1	81	18	0	16	20.97	-18.27			Mar-01
	3.90	17.39	5.93	37.53	37.05	1.91	0.69	10.5	1.04	12.78	910.1	1	85	13	0	21	21.53	-18.51			Feb-08
	3.68	16.85	4.99	33.95	31.12	1.13	1.57	10.54	1.04	12.38	910.1	1	85	13	0	21	20.9	-18.86			Feb-08
	3.68	17.03	5.15	34.47	32.06	1.26	1.44	10.53	1.04	12.38	910.1	1	85	13	0	21	21.03	-18.75			Feb-08
	3.83	17.15	5.42	35.27	33.28	1.42	1.26	10.52	1.04	12.46	910.1	1	85	13	0	21	21.3	-18.77			Feb-08
	3.79	17.18	5.55	36.01	34.47	1.56	1.07	10.52	1.04	12.57	910.1	1	85	13	0	21	21.37	-18.7			Feb-08
	3.87	17.35	5.73	36.57	35.30	1.71	0.95	10.56	1.04	12.6	910.1	1	85	13	0	21	21.48	-18.66			Feb-08
100	3.88	17.71	5.50	37.16	35.43	1.5	1.07	10.93	1.05	15.5	2,274	1	89	9	0	17	21.8	-19.32	5.50		Jun-05
100	3.95	17.84	5.60	37.72	35.83	1.7	0.95	10.96	1.05	14.97	2,274	1	89	9	0	17	21.76	-19.43		1.00	Jun-01
	3.97	17.96	5.90	38.76	37.97	1.86	0.7	10.95	1.05	15.43	2,274	1	89	9	0	17	22.15	-19.25			Mar-01
	3.74	17.48	4.94	35.10	32.04	1	1.57	10.93	1.05	15.25	2,274	1	89	9	0	17	21.49	-19.49			Nov-04
	3.80	17.53	5.12	35.70	32.87	0.93	1.44	10.94	1.05	15.27	2,274	1	89	9	0	17	21.55	-19.47			Mar-01
	3.88	17.64	5.30	36.40	34.14	1.34	1.26	10.96	1.05	15.23	2,274	1	89	9	0	17	21.75	-19.45			Mar-01
	3.86	17.65	5.46	37.13	35.29	1.49	1.07	10.91	1.05	15.32	2,274	1	89	9	0	17	21.8	-19.33			Mar-01
	3.92	17.72	5.56	37.59	36.13	1.63	0.95	10.92	1.05	15.36	2,274	1	89	9	0	17	21.99	-19.29			Mar-01
	3.96	18.27	5.74	39.34	38.49	1.84	0.72	11.27	1.08	13.64	458.4	1	92	6	0	20	22.14	-19.43			Feb-08
	3.78	17.77	4.85	35.82	32.66	1.08	1.59	11.22	1.07	13.16	458.4	1	92	6	0	20	21.6	-19.78			Feb-08
	3.77	17.88	4.90	36.37	33.48	1.26	1.46	11.22	1.07	13.19	458.4	1	92	6	0	20	21.54	-19.68			Feb-08
	3.91	18.01	5.18	37.14	34.79	1.37	1.28	11.23	1.07	13.28	458.4	1	92	6	0	20	21.77	-19.66			Feb-08
	3.87	18.08	5.36	37.87	35.92	1.47	1.09	11.26	1.08	13.41	458.4	1	92	6	0	20	21.81	-19.58			Feb-08
	3.93	18.17	5.49	38.35	36.78	1.66	0.97	11.22	1.07	13.46	458.4	1	92	6	0	20	21.93	-19.47			Feb-08
100	3.93	18.24	5.29	38.02	35.95	1.5	1.08	11.36	1.07	14.25	348.1	2	93	5	0	24				1.00	Mar-13
	3.78	17.95	4.73	36.00	32.39	1.12	1.59	11.32	1.07	13.99	348.1	2	93	5	0	24					Mar-13
	3.76	18.04	4.85	36.48	33.34	1.17	1.46	11.36	1.07	14.05	348.1	2	93	5	0	24					Mar-13
	3.80	18.07	5.08	37.20	34.38	1.38	1.28	11.38	1.07	14.17	348.1	2	93	5	0	24					Mar-13
	3.87	18.26	5.26	38.00	35.79	1.47	1.09	11.36	1.07	14.21	348.1	2	93	5	0	24					Mar-13
	3.93	18.33	5.45	38.47	36.59	1.63	0.97	11.36	1.07	14.25	348.1	2	93	5	0	24					Mar-13
	3.98	18.39	5.67	39.43	38.16	1.83	0.73	11.37	1.07	14.34	348.1	2	93	5	0	24					Mar-13
	3.74	17.73	4.65			1.34	1.62			10.79	16.3	1	93	5	0	196					Sep-17
	3.84	17.98	4.88			1.44	1.49			10.8	16.3	1	93	5	0	196					Sep-17
	3.73	18.00	4.93			1.49	1.31			10.83	16.3	1	93	5	0	196					Sep-17
	3.92	18.17	5.22			1.65	1.12			10.86	16.3	1	93	5	0	196					Sep-17
	3.91	18.18	5.35			1.68	1			10.88	16.3	1	93	5	0	196					Sep-17
	4.00	18.41	5.56			1.7	0.79			10.91	16.3	1	93	5	0	196					Sep-17
100	2.85	10.36	5.14	20.45		1.24	0.66	5.44	1.01	11.17	101.1	6	39	54	0	41				1.00	Mar-18
	2.85	10.29	5.06	20.17			0.95	5.39	1	11.17	101.1	6	39	54	0	41					Mar-19
	2.94	10.46	5.35	21.11			0.64	5.42	1.01	11.18	101.1	6	39	54	0	41					Mar-19
	2.94	10.46	5.34	21.11		1.34	0.41	5.42	1.01	11.19	101.1	6	39	54	0	41					Sep-14
	2.93	10.45	5.44	21.20		1.34	0.38	5.46	1.01	11.21	101.1	6	39	54	0	41					Aug-15
100	3.00	11.52	5.09	23.26		1.56	0.66	6.54	1.09	11.3	315.9	5	49	46	0	34				1.00	Mar-18
	2.90	11.48	4.93	22.89			0.95	6.46	1.07	11.32	315.9	5	49	46	0	34					Mar-19
	3.00	11.65	5.22	23.85			0.64	6.46	1.07	11.33	315.9	5	49	46	0	34					Mar-19
	3.09	11.75	5.31	23.96		1.6	0.41	6.48	1.08	11.34	315.9	5	49	46	0	34					Sep-14
	3.09	11.69	5.36	24.17		1.64	0.38	6.52	1.08	11.34	315.9	5	49	46	0	34					Aug-15
100	3.20	12.76	4.80	25.84		1.63	0.66	7.54	1.07	11.58	220.4	4	58	38	0	23				1.00	Mar-18
	3.11	12.63	4.75	25.49			0.95	7.57	1.08	11.59	220.4	4	58	38	0	23					Mar-19
	3.20	12.80	5.04	26.46			0.64	7.55	1.07	11.6	220.4	4	58	38	0	23					Mar-19
	3.29	12.90	5.13	26.57		1.68	0.41	7.59	1.08	11.61	220.4	4	58	38	0	23					Sep-14
	3.28	12.94	5.17	26.61		1.72	0.38	7.51	1.07	11.62	220.4	4	58	38	0	23					Aug-15

	MARKET		FUND TYPE, CATEGORY & OBJECTIVE		RATINGS					MINIMUMS
Fund Name	Ticker Symbol	Traded On	Fund Type	Category and (Prospectus Objective)	Overall Rating	Reward Rating	Risk Rating	Recent Up/ Downgrade	Open to New Investors	Min Initial Investment
Principal LifeTime Hybrid 2030 Fund Class J	PHJNX	NAS CM	Open End	Target Date (Asset Alloc)	B-	C	B+	Up	Y	1,000
Principal LifeTime Hybrid 2030 Fund Class R-3	PHTLX	NAS CM	Open End	Target Date (Asset Alloc)	B-	C	B+	Up	Y	0
Principal LifeTime Hybrid 2030 Fund Class R-5	PHTKX	NAS CM	Open End	Target Date (Asset Alloc)	B-	C	B+	Up	Y	0
Principal LifeTime Hybrid 2030 Fund Institutional Class	PHTNX	NAS CM	Open End	Target Date (Asset Alloc)	B-	C	B+	Up	Y	0
Principal LifeTime Hybrid 2030 Fund R-6	PLZTX	NAS CM	Open End	Target Date (Asset Alloc)	B-	C	B+	Up	Y	0
Principal LifeTime Hybrid 2035 Fund Class J	PHJJX	NAS CM	Open End	Target Date (Asset Alloc)	B-	C	B+	Up	Y	1,000
Principal LifeTime Hybrid 2035 Fund Class R-3	PHTHX	NAS CM	Open End	Target Date (Asset Alloc)	B-	C	B+	Up	Y	0
Principal LifeTime Hybrid 2035 Fund Class R-5	PHTGX	NAS CM	Open End	Target Date (Asset Alloc)	B-	C	B+	Up	Y	0
Principal LifeTime Hybrid 2035 Fund Institutional Class	PHTJX	NAS CM	Open End	Target Date (Asset Alloc)	B-	C	B+	Up	Y	0
Principal LifeTime Hybrid 2035 Fund R-6	PLRTX	NAS CM	Open End	Target Date (Asset Alloc)	B-	C	B+	Up	Y	0
Principal LifeTime Hybrid 2040 Fund Class J	PHJEX	NAS CM	Open End	Target Date (Asset Alloc)	B-	C	B	Up	Y	1,000
Principal LifeTime Hybrid 2040 Fund Class R-3	PLHBX	NAS CM	Open End	Target Date (Asset Alloc)	B-	C	B	Up	Y	0
Principal LifeTime Hybrid 2040 Fund Class R-5	PHTZX	NAS CM	Open End	Target Date (Asset Alloc)	B-	C	B	Up	Y	0
Principal LifeTime Hybrid 2040 Fund Institutional Class	PLTQX	NAS CM	Open End	Target Date (Asset Alloc)	B-	C	B	Up	Y	0
Principal LifeTime Hybrid 2040 Fund R-6	PLMTX	NAS CM	Open End	Target Date (Asset Alloc)	B-	C	B	Up	Y	0
Principal LifeTime Hybrid 2045 Fund Class J	PHJYX	NAS CM	Open End	Target Date (Asset Alloc)	B-	C	B	Up	Y	1,000
Principal LifeTime Hybrid 2045 Fund Class R-3	PHTWX	NAS CM	Open End	Target Date (Asset Alloc)	B-	C	B	Up	Y	0
Principal LifeTime Hybrid 2045 Fund Class R-5	PHTVX	NAS CM	Open End	Target Date (Asset Alloc)	B-	C	B	Up	Y	0
Principal LifeTime Hybrid 2045 Fund Institutional Class	PHTYX	NAS CM	Open End	Target Date (Asset Alloc)	B-	C	B	Up	Y	0
Principal LifeTime Hybrid 2045 Fund R-6	PLNTX	NAS CM	Open End	Target Date (Asset Alloc)	B-	C	B	Up	Y	0
Principal LifeTime Hybrid 2050 Fund Class J	PHJUX	NAS CM	Open End	Target Date (Asset Alloc)	C+	C	B	Up	Y	1,000
Principal LifeTime Hybrid 2050 Fund Class R-3	PHTSX	NAS CM	Open End	Target Date (Asset Alloc)	C+	C	B	Up	Y	0
Principal LifeTime Hybrid 2050 Fund Class R-5	PLRJX	NAS CM	Open End	Target Date (Asset Alloc)	C+	C	B	Up	Y	0
Principal LifeTime Hybrid 2050 Fund Institutional Class	PHTUX	NAS CM	Open End	Target Date (Asset Alloc)	C+	C	B	Up	Y	0
Principal LifeTime Hybrid 2050 Fund R-6	PLJTX	NAS CM	Open End	Target Date (Asset Alloc)	C+	C	B	Up	Y	0
Principal LifeTime Hybrid 2055 Fund Class J	PHJBX	NAS CM	Open End	Target Date (Asset Alloc)	C+	C	B	Up	Y	1,000
Principal LifeTime Hybrid 2055 Fund Class R-3	PLTLX	NAS CM	Open End	Target Date (Asset Alloc)	C+	C	B	Up	Y	0
Principal LifeTime Hybrid 2055 Fund Class R-5	PLTKX	NAS CM	Open End	Target Date (Asset Alloc)	C+	C	B	Up	Y	0
Principal LifeTime Hybrid 2055 Fund Institutional Class	PLTNX	NAS CM	Open End	Target Date (Asset Alloc)	C+	C	B	Up	Y	0
Principal LifeTime Hybrid 2055 Fund R-6	PLHTX	NAS CM	Open End	Target Date (Asset Alloc)	C+	C	B	Up	Y	0
Principal LifeTime Hybrid 2060 Fund Class J	PHJGX	NAS CM	Open End	Target Date (Asset Alloc)	C+	C	B	Up	Y	1,000
Principal LifeTime Hybrid 2060 Fund Class R-3	PLTEX	NAS CM	Open End	Target Date (Asset Alloc)	C+	C	B	Up	Y	0
Principal LifeTime Hybrid 2060 Fund Class R-5	PLTDX	NAS CM	Open End	Target Date (Asset Alloc)	C+	C	B	Up	Y	0
Principal LifeTime Hybrid 2060 Fund Institutional Class	PLTHX	NAS CM	Open End	Target Date (Asset Alloc)	C+	C	B	Up	Y	0
Principal LifeTime Hybrid 2060 Fund R-6	PLKTX	NAS CM	Open End	Target Date (Asset Alloc)	C+	C	B	Up	Y	0
Principal LifeTime Hybrid 2065 Class R-6 Shares	PLHRX	NAS CM	Open End	Target Date (Asset Alloc)	C-	D	C+	Up	Y	0
Principal LifeTime Hybrid 2065 Fund Class J	PHJDX	NAS CM	Open End	Target Date (Asset Alloc)	C-	D+	B-	Up	Y	1,000
Principal LifeTime Hybrid 2065 Fund Class R-3	PLTFX	NAS CM	Open End	Target Date (Asset Alloc)	D+	D	C	Up	Y	0
Principal LifeTime Hybrid 2065 Fund Class R-5	PLHKX	NAS CM	Open End	Target Date (Asset Alloc)	D+	D	C	Up	Y	0
Principal LifeTime Hybrid 2065 Institutional Class Shares	PLHHX	NAS CM	Open End	Target Date (Asset Alloc)	C-	D+	B-	Up	Y	0
Principal LifeTime Hybrid Income Fund Class J	PHJFX	NAS CM	Open End	Target Date (Asset Alloc)	B-	C	B+		Y	1,000
Principal LifeTime Hybrid Income Fund Class R-3	PHTEX	NAS CM	Open End	Target Date (Asset Alloc)	B-	C	B+		Y	0
Principal LifeTime Hybrid Income Fund Class R-5	PHTDX	NAS CM	Open End	Target Date (Asset Alloc)	B-	C	A-		Y	0
Principal LifeTime Hybrid Income Fund Institutional Class	PHTFX	NAS CM	Open End	Target Date (Asset Alloc)	B-	C	A-		Y	0
Principal LifeTime Hybrid Income Fund R-6	PLTYX	NAS CM	Open End	Target Date (Asset Alloc)	B-	C	A-		Y	0
Principal LifeTime Strategic Income Fund Class A	PALTX	NAS CM	Open End	Target Date (Asset Alloc)	B-	C	A-		Y	1,000
Principal LifeTime Strategic Income Fund Class J	PLSJX	NAS CM	Open End	Target Date (Asset Alloc)	B	C+	A-	Up	Y	1,000
Principal LifeTime Strategic Income Institutional Cls	PLSIX	NAS CM	Open End	Target Date (Asset Alloc)	B	C+	A-	Up	Y	0
Principal LifeTime Strategic Income Fund R-1 Class	PLAIX	NAS CM	Open End	Target Date (Asset Alloc)	B-	C	B+	Up	Y	0
Principal LifeTime Strategic Income Fund R-2 Class	PLSNX	NAS CM	Open End	Target Date (Asset Alloc)	B-	C	B+	Up	Y	0
Principal LifeTime Strategic Income Fund R-3 Class	PLSMX	NAS CM	Open End	Target Date (Asset Alloc)	B-	C	B+	Up	Y	0
Principal LifeTime Strategic Income Fund R-4 Class	PLSSX	NAS CM	Open End	Target Date (Asset Alloc)	B-	C	A-		Y	0

★ Expanded analysis of this fund is included in Section II.

Min Additional Investment	TOTAL RETURNS 3-Month Total Return	6-Month Total Return	1-Year Total Return	3-Year Total Return	5-Year Total Return	PERFORMANCE Dividend Yield (TTM)	Expense Ratio	3-Yr Std Deviation	3-Year Beta	ASSETS NAV	Total Assets (MIL)	ASSET ALLOCATION & TURNOVER %Cash	%Stocks	%Bonds	%Other	Turnover Ratio	BULL & BEAR Last Bull Market Total Return	Last Bear Market Total Return	FEES Front End Fee (%)	Back End Fee (%)	Inception Date
100	3.35	13.85	4.71	28.54		1.74	0.67	8.46	1.04	11.72	266.4	3	66	30	0	26				1.00	Mar-18
	3.25	13.71	4.66	28.17			0.96	8.48	1.04	11.73	266.4	3	66	30	0	26					Mar-19
	3.34	13.88	4.94	29.16			0.65	8.49	1.04	11.75	266.4	3	66	30	0	26					Mar-19
	3.42	13.98	5.03	29.27		1.79	0.42	8.5	1.04	11.76	266.4	3	66	30	0	26					Sep-14
	3.34	14.04	4.99	29.24		1.83	0.39	8.48	1.04	11.75	266.4	3	66	30	0	26					Aug-15
100	3.36	14.91	4.67	30.94		1.68	0.68	9.26	1.02	11.97	160.9	1	74	24	0	14				1.00	Mar-18
	3.36	14.86	4.69	30.65			0.97	9.28	1.02	11.99	160.9	1	74	24	0	14					Mar-19
	3.35	14.93	4.88	31.55			0.66	9.26	1.01	12	160.9	1	74	24	0	14					Mar-19
	3.44	15.02	4.97	31.66		1.72	0.43	9.26	1.01	12.01	160.9	1	74	24	0	14					Sep-14
	3.52	15.15	5.09	31.92		1.75	0.4	9.27	1.02	12.03	160.9	1	74	24	0	14					Aug-15
100	3.52	15.68	4.50	32.58		1.73	0.69	9.95	1.02	12.03	185.6	1	80	18	0	15				1.00	Mar-18
	3.43	15.64	4.45	32.42			0.98	9.95	1.02	12.05	185.6	1	80	18	0	15					Mar-19
	3.43	15.71	4.64	33.33			0.67	9.95	1.02	12.06	185.6	1	80	18	0	15					Mar-19
	3.51	15.81	4.73	33.43		1.78	0.44	9.96	1.02	12.07	185.6	1	80	18	0	15					Sep-14
	3.51	15.82	4.85	33.56		1.81	0.41	9.98	1.02	12.09	185.6	1	80	18	0	15					Aug-15
100	3.49	16.18	4.33	33.92		1.71	0.7	10.52	1.04	12.14	99.3	1	85	13	0	12				1.00	Mar-18
	3.40	16.06	4.21	33.55			0.99	10.51	1.04	12.16	99.3	1	85	13	0	12					Mar-19
	3.48	16.22	4.49	34.58			0.68	10.49	1.04	12.17	99.3	1	85	13	0	12					Mar-19
	3.57	16.32	4.57	34.69		1.77	0.45	10.5	1.04	12.18	99.3	1	85	13	0	12					Sep-14
	3.56	16.32	4.58	34.81		1.78	0.42	10.48	1.04	12.19	99.3	1	85	13	0	12					Aug-15
100	3.46	16.59	4.17	35.10		1.78	0.7	10.89	1.05	12.23	88.6	1	89	10	0	12				1.00	Mar-18
	3.46	16.60	4.14	34.75			0.99	10.88	1.05	12.23	88.6	1	89	10	0	12					Mar-19
	3.55	16.77	4.42	35.79			0.68	10.87	1.05	12.24	88.6	1	89	10	0	12					Mar-19
	3.55	16.77	4.42	35.78		1.85	0.45	10.9	1.05	12.25	88.6	1	89	10	0	12					Sep-14
	3.54	16.78	4.43	35.80		1.86	0.42	10.86	1.05	12.25	88.6	1	89	10	0	12					Aug-15
100	3.61	17.04	4.02	35.81		1.81	0.71	11.26	1.08	12.34	29.9	1	92	7	0	14				1.00	Mar-18
	3.43	16.92	3.98	35.32			1	11.21	1.07	12.35	29.9	1	92	7	0	14					Mar-19
	3.51	17.09	4.26	36.37			0.69	11.19	1.07	12.36	29.9	1	92	7	0	14					Mar-19
	3.60	17.19	4.34	36.48		1.87	0.46	11.17	1.07	12.37	29.9	1	92	7	0	14					Sep-14
	3.59	17.17	4.34	36.58		1.87	0.43	11.21	1.07	12.38	29.9	1	92	7	0	14					Aug-15
100	3.57	17.14	3.90	36.25		1.87	0.71	11.4	1.08	12.47	10.0	1	93	6	0	23				1.00	Mar-18
	3.47	17.11	3.86	35.99			1	11.4	1.08	12.5	10.0	1	93	6	0	23					Mar-19
	3.55	17.27	4.13	37.03			0.69	11.39	1.08	12.52	10.0	1	93	6	0	23					Mar-19
	3.55	17.27	4.13	37.03		1.87	0.46	11.39	1.08	12.52	10.0	1	93	6	0	23					Sep-14
	3.63	17.35	4.21	37.10		1.86	0.43	11.44	1.08	12.54	10.0	1	93	6	0	23					Aug-15
	7.30	21.72	4.29			2.46	0.42			10.72	1.2	0	94	6	0	14					Sep-17
100	3.58	17.40	3.89			2.47	0.7			10.68	1.2	0	94	6	0	14				1.00	Mar-18
	3.40	16.65	0.20				0.99			10.7	1.2	0	94	6	0	14					Mar-19
	3.57	17.49	0.67				0.68			10.71	1.2	0	94	6	0	14					Mar-19
	3.67	17.58	4.17			2.46	0.45			10.72	1.2	0	94	6	0	14					Sep-17
100	2.60	8.12	5.35	13.21		1.5	0.65	3.51	0.85	10.64	54.8	6	22	72	0	59				1.00	Mar-18
	2.60	8.12	5.44	13.04			0.94	3.55	0.86	10.65	54.8	6	22	72	0	59					Mar-19
	2.59	8.19	5.63	13.81			0.63	3.55	0.86	10.66	54.8	6	22	72	0	59					Mar-19
	2.69	8.29	5.73	13.92		1.57	0.4	3.54	0.86	10.67	54.8	6	22	72	0	59					Sep-14
	2.69	8.28	5.73	13.90		1.57	0.37	3.55	0.86	10.68	54.8	6	22	72	0	59					Aug-15
100	2.95	8.96	5.80	14.91	16.99	2.4	1	3.87	0.94	12.2	426.8	3	24	72	0	23	8.65	-4.66	3.75		Jun-05
100	2.99	8.98	5.97	15.44	17.71	2.57	0.87	3.9	0.95	12.03	426.8	3	24	72	0	23	8.63	-4.71		1.00	Jun-01
	3.06	9.17	6.25	16.19	19.20	2.76	0.64	3.9	0.95	12.1	426.8	3	24	72	0	23	8.9	-4.59			Mar-01
	2.88	8.66	5.32	13.17	14.08	1.88	1.51	3.91	0.95	12.12	426.8	3	24	72	0	23	8.32	-4.88			Nov-04
	2.88	8.78	5.43	13.66	14.87	2.05	1.38	3.91	0.95	12.12	426.8	3	24	72	0	23	8.4	-4.79			Mar-01
	3.00	8.86	5.66	14.28	15.92	2.22	1.2	3.89	0.94	11.99	426.8	3	24	72	0	23	8.65	-4.82			Mar-01
	2.91	8.95	5.84	14.80	16.93	2.38	1.01	3.9	0.94	12.01	426.8	3	24	72	0	23	8.69	-4.72			Mar-01

	MARKET			FUND TYPE, CATEGORY & OBJECTIVE	RATINGS				MINIMUMS	
Fund Name	Ticker Symbol	Traded On	Fund Type	Category and (Prospectus Objective)	Overall Rating	Reward Rating	Risk Rating	Recent Up/ Downgrade	Open to New Investors	Min Initial Investment
Principal LifeTime Strategic Income Fund R-5 Class	PLSPX	NAS CM	Open End	Target Date (Asset Alloc)	B	C+	A-	Up	Y	0
Principal MidCap Fund Class A	PEMGX	NAS CM	Open End	US Equity Mid Cap (Growth)	B	B	B			1,000
Principal MidCap Fund Class C	PMBCX	NAS CM	Open End	US Equity Mid Cap (Growth)	B	B	B	Up		1,000
Principal MidCap Fund Class J	PMBJX	NAS CM	Open End	US Equity Mid Cap (Growth)	B	B	B			1,000
PRINCIPAL MIDCAP FUND Class R-6	PMAQX	NAS CM	Open End	US Equity Mid Cap (Growth)	B	B	B		Y	0
Principal MidCap Fund Institutional Class	PCBIX	NAS CM	Open End	US Equity Mid Cap (Growth)	B	B	B			0
Principal MidCap Fund R-1 Class	PMSBX	NAS CM	Open End	US Equity Mid Cap (Growth)	B	B	B			0
Principal MidCap Fund R-2 Class	PMBNX	NAS CM	Open End	US Equity Mid Cap (Growth)	B	B	B			0
Principal MidCap Fund R-3 Class	PMBMX	NAS CM	Open End	US Equity Mid Cap (Growth)	B	B	B			0
Principal MidCap Fund R-4 Class	PMBSX	NAS CM	Open End	US Equity Mid Cap (Growth)	B	B	B			0
Principal MidCap Fund R-5 Class	PMBPX	NAS CM	Open End	US Equity Mid Cap (Growth)	B	B	B			0
Principal MidCap Growth Fund Class J	PMGJX	NAS CM	Open End	US Equity Mid Cap (Growth)	C+	C	C+		Y	1,000
Principal MidCap Growth Fund III Class J	PPQJX	NAS CM	Open End	US Equity Mid Cap (Growth)	B-	C+	B-		Y	1,000
Principal MidCap Growth Fund III Institutional Class	PPIMX	NAS CM	Open End	US Equity Mid Cap (Growth)	B-	C+	B-		Y	0
Principal MidCap Growth Fund III R-1 Class	PHASX	NAS CM	Open End	US Equity Mid Cap (Growth)	C+	C+	B-	Down	Y	0
Principal MidCap Growth Fund III R-2 Class	PPQNX	NAS CM	Open End	US Equity Mid Cap (Growth)	C+	C+	B-	Down	Y	0
Principal MidCap Growth Fund III R-3 Class	PPQMX	NAS CM	Open End	US Equity Mid Cap (Growth)	B-	C+	B-		Y	0
Principal MidCap Growth Fund III R-4 Class	PPQSX	NAS CM	Open End	US Equity Mid Cap (Growth)	B-	C+	B-		Y	0
Principal MidCap Growth Fund III R-5 Class	PPQPX	NAS CM	Open End	US Equity Mid Cap (Growth)	B-	C+	B-		Y	0
Principal MidCap Growth Fund Institutional Class	PGWIX	NAS CM	Open End	US Equity Mid Cap (Growth)	C+	C	C+		Y	0
Principal MidCap Growth Fund R-1 Class	PMSGX	NAS CM	Open End	US Equity Mid Cap (Growth)	C+	C	C+		Y	0
Principal MidCap Growth Fund R-2 Class	PGPPX	NAS CM	Open End	US Equity Mid Cap (Growth)	C+	C	C+		Y	0
Principal MidCap Growth Fund R-3 Class	PFPPX	NAS CM	Open End	US Equity Mid Cap (Growth)	C+	C	C+		Y	0
Principal MidCap Growth Fund R-4 Class	PIPPX	NAS CM	Open End	US Equity Mid Cap (Growth)	C+	C	C+		Y	0
Principal MidCap Growth Fund R-5 Class	PHPPX	NAS CM	Open End	US Equity Mid Cap (Growth)	C+	C	C+		Y	0
Principal MidCap S&P 400 Index Fund Class J	PMFJX	NAS CM	Open End	US Equity Mid Cap (Growth)	C+	C	B-	Up	Y	1,000
Principal MidCap S&P 400 Index Fund Class R-6	PMAPX	NAS CM	Open End	US Equity Mid Cap (Growth)	C+	C	B-	Up	Y	0
Principal MidCap S&P 400 Index Fund Institutional Class	MPSIX	NAS CM	Open End	US Equity Mid Cap (Growth)	C+	C	B-	Up	Y	0
Principal MidCap S&P 400 Index Fund R-1 Class	PMSSX	NAS CM	Open End	US Equity Mid Cap (Growth)	C+	C	B-	Up	Y	0
Principal MidCap S&P 400 Index Fund R-2 Class	PMFNX	NAS CM	Open End	US Equity Mid Cap (Growth)	C+	C	B-	Up	Y	0
Principal MidCap S&P 400 Index Fund R-3 Class	PMFMX	NAS CM	Open End	US Equity Mid Cap (Growth)	C+	C	B-	Up	Y	0
Principal MidCap S&P 400 Index Fund R-4 Class	PMFSX	NAS CM	Open End	US Equity Mid Cap (Growth)	C+	C	B-	Up	Y	0
Principal MidCap S&P 400 Index Fund R-5 Class	PMFPX	NAS CM	Open End	US Equity Mid Cap (Growth)	C+	C	B-	Up	Y	0
Principal MidCap Value Fund I Class A	PCMVX	NAS CM	Open End	US Equity Mid Cap (Growth)	C+	C	B		Y	1,000
Principal MidCap Value Fund I Class J	PVEJX	NAS CM	Open End	US Equity Mid Cap (Growth)	C+	C	B	Up	Y	1,000
Principal MidCap Value Fund I Class R-6	PCMSX	NAS CM	Open End	US Equity Mid Cap (Growth)	C+	C	B		Y	0
Principal MidCap Value Fund I Institutional Class	PVMIX	NAS CM	Open End	US Equity Mid Cap (Growth)	C+	C	B	Up	Y	0
Principal MidCap Value Fund I R-1 Class	PLASX	NAS CM	Open End	US Equity Mid Cap (Growth)	C+	C	B	Up	Y	0
Principal MidCap Value Fund I R-2 Class	PABUX	NAS CM	Open End	US Equity Mid Cap (Growth)	C+	C	B	Up	Y	0
Principal MidCap Value Fund I R-3 Class	PMPRX	NAS CM	Open End	US Equity Mid Cap (Growth)	C+	C	B	Up	Y	0
Principal MidCap Value Fund I R-4 Class	PABWX	NAS CM	Open End	US Equity Mid Cap (Growth)	C+	C	B	Up	Y	0
Principal MidCap Value Fund I R-5 Class	PABVX	NAS CM	Open End	US Equity Mid Cap (Growth)	C+	C	B	Up	Y	0
Principal Multi-Manager Equity Long/Short Fund Class A	PGMMX	NAS CM	Open End	Long/Short Equity (Growth)	C	C-	B-		Y	1,000
Principal Multi-Manager Equity Long/Short Fund Class R-6	PGPMX	NAS CM	Open End	Long/Short Equity (Growth)	C	C-	B-		Y	0
Principal Multi-Manager Equity Long/Short Inst Cls	PGPIX	NAS CM	Open End	Long/Short Equity (Growth)	C	C-	B-		Y	0
Principal Origin Emerging Markets Fund Class A	POEYX	NAS CM	Open End	Global Emerg Mkts (Div Emerging Mkts)	C	C	C	Up	Y	1,000
Principal Origin Emerging Markets Fund Class R-6	POEFX	NAS CM	Open End	Global Emerg Mkts (Div Emerging Mkts)	C	C	C	Up	Y	0
Principal Origin Emerging Markets Fund Institutional Class	POEIX	NAS CM	Open End	Global Emerg Mkts (Div Emerging Mkts)	C	C	C	Up	Y	0
Principal Overseas Fund Institutional Class	PINZX	NAS CM	Open End	Global Equity Large Cap (World Stock)	C	C-	C+		Y	0
Principal Overseas Fund R-1 Class	PINQX	NAS CM	Open End	Global Equity Large Cap (World Stock)	C	C-	C		Y	0
Principal Overseas Fund R-2 Class	PINSX	NAS CM	Open End	Global Equity Large Cap (World Stock)	C	C-	C		Y	0
Principal Overseas Fund R-3 Class	PINTX	NAS CM	Open End	Global Equity Large Cap (World Stock)	C	C-	C+		Y	0

★ Expanded analysis of this fund is included in Section II.

	TOTAL RETURNS					PERFORMANCE				ASSETS		ASSET ALLOCATION & TURNOVER					BULL & BEAR		FEES		
Min Additional Investment	3-Month Total Return	6-Month Total Return	1-Year Total Return	3-Year Total Return	5-Year Total Return	Dividend Yield (TTM)	Expense Ratio	3-Yr Std Deviation	3-Year Beta	NAV	Total Assets (MIL)	%Cash	%Stocks	%Bonds	%Other	Turnover Ratio	Last Bull Market Total Return	Last Bear Market Total Return	Front End Fee (%)	Back End Fee (%)	Inception Date
	2.98	8.97	5.97	15.32	17.68	2.51	0.89	3.88	0.94	12.09	426.8	3	24	72	0	23	8.74	-4.69			Mar-01
100	9.18	31.36	17.80	62.13	78.43	0	0.96	12.88	0.91	28.77	16,562	0	100	0	0	26	26.67	-15.86	5.50		Jun-05
100	8.98	30.87	16.94	58.59	72.02	0	1.69	12.88	0.91	25.6	16,562	0	100	0	0	26	26.05	-16.05		1.00	Jan-07
100	9.20	31.43	17.95	62.92	79.72	0	0.85	12.89	0.91	27.64	16,562	0	100	0	0	26	26.65	-15.82		1.00	Mar-01
	9.25	31.62	18.20	63.73	80.76	0.14	0.59	12.9	0.91	29.51	16,562	0	100	0	0	26	26.84	-15.8			Nov-16
	9.28	31.56	18.12	63.58	81.19	0.05	0.69	12.9	0.91	29.55	16,562	0	100	0	0	26	26.97	-15.69			Mar-01
	9.04	31.06	17.25	59.78	74.13	0	1.47	12.88	0.91	26.41	16,562	0	100	0	0	26	26.34	-15.99			Nov-04
	9.07	31.14	17.37	60.39	75.24	0	1.34	12.9	0.91	26.91	16,562	0	100	0	0	26	26.51	-15.94			Dec-00
	9.14	31.25	17.57	61.22	76.92	0	1.16	12.87	0.91	28.05	16,562	0	100	0	0	26	26.53	-15.87			Dec-00
	9.20	31.39	17.80	62.21	78.55	0	0.97	12.89	0.91	29.3	16,562	0	100	0	0	26	26.7	-15.8			Dec-00
	9.22	31.46	17.92	62.76	79.69	0	0.85	12.88	0.91	29.12	16,562	0	100	0	0	26	26.84	-15.8			Dec-00
100	5.19	29.96	9.06	56.31	60.97	0	0.96	16.77	1.14	6.68	181.1	2	98	0	0	114	22.92	-22.44		1.00	Mar-01
100	7.12	27.80	12.88	55.66	58.56	0	1.27	14.44	1	9.47	1,126	1	99	0	0	44	23.65	-22.43		1.00	Mar-01
	7.32	28.14	13.30	57.57	61.60	0.01	0.91	14.5	1	12.02	1,126	1	99	0	0	44	24.16	-22.35			Mar-01
	7.11	27.55	12.36	53.46	54.73	0	1.78	14.46	1	9.49	1,126	1	99	0	0	44	23.54	-22.63			Nov-04
	7.05	27.67	12.50	54.01	55.61	0	1.65	14.44	1	10.01	1,126	1	99	0	0	44	23.48	-22.54			Dec-00
	7.06	27.71	12.64	54.75	56.88	0	1.47	14.44	1	11.06	1,126	1	99	0	0	44	23.64	-22.52			Dec-00
	7.19	27.87	12.90	55.57	58.42	0	1.28	14.47	1	11.47	1,126	1	99	0	0	44	23.81	-22.4			Dec-00
	7.19	27.99	13.02	56.35	59.54	0	1.16	14.43	0.99	12.07	1,126	1	99	0	0	44	23.94	-22.43			Dec-00
	5.23	29.99	9.19	57.19	63.24	0	0.75	16.78	1.14	8.84	181.1	2	98	0	0	114	23.16	-22.24			Mar-01
	5.00	29.53	8.28	53.45	56.78	0	1.55	16.75	1.14	6.93	181.1	2	98	0	0	114	22.6	-22.52			Nov-04
	4.97	29.52	8.41	53.97	57.61	0	1.42	16.76	1.14	7.59	181.1	2	98	0	0	114	22.68	-22.45			Dec-00
	5.00	29.63	8.60	54.80	59.16	0	1.24	16.76	1.14	8.18	181.1	2	98	0	0	114	22.78	-22.42			Dec-00
	5.04	29.67	8.79	55.64	60.54	0	1.05	16.68	1.13	8.74	181.1	2	98	0	0	114	22.94	-22.35			Dec-00
	5.05	29.82	8.89	56.18	61.59	0	0.93	16.69	1.13	9.14	181.1	2	98	0	0	114	23.04	-22.36			Dec-00
100	2.90	18.93	0.95	37.20	44.12	1.03	0.42	15.14	1	19.47	1,304	0	100	0	0	14	27.34	-22.72		1.00	Mar-01
	2.97	19.12	1.24	38.06	45.31	1.22	0.16	15.14	1	20.06	1,304	0	100	0	0	14	27.57	-22.66			Nov-16
	3.02	19.09	1.20	38.10	46.05	1.18	0.2	15.12	1	20.08	1,304	0	100	0	0	14	27.68	-22.58			Mar-01
	2.79	18.57	0.33	34.69	40.05	0.37	1.04	15.1	1	19.85	1,304	0	100	0	0	14	27.07	-22.83			Nov-04
	2.80	18.63	0.47	35.25	40.97	0.4	0.91	15.12	1	20.56	1,304	0	100	0	0	14	27.25	-22.82			Dec-00
	2.86	18.81	0.69	35.98	42.29	0.65	0.73	15.11	1	20.46	1,304	0	100	0	0	14	27.33	-22.79			Dec-00
	2.90	18.86	0.86	36.70	43.59	0.79	0.54	15.14	1	20.54	1,304	0	100	0	0	14	27.46	-22.7			Dec-00
	2.93	18.94	0.98	37.24	44.45	0.93	0.42	15.14	1	20.72	1,304	0	100	0	0	14	27.57	-22.66			Dec-00
100	3.68	18.69	4.10	33.87	32.61		1.19	13	0.98	13.99	2,552	1	99	0	0	61	25.26	-22.11	5.50	1.00	Apr-19
100	3.90	19.00	4.30	34.06	32.45	0.59	0.98	12.97	0.97	13.84	2,552	1	99	0	0	61	25	-22.2		1.00	Mar-09
	3.93	19.04	4.54	35.11	34.51		0.63	12.98	0.98	14.02	2,552	1	99	0	0	61	25.44	-22.02			Apr-19
	3.86	18.96	4.47	35.02	34.41	0.86	0.72	13	0.98	13.99	2,552	1	99	0	0	61	25.44	-22.02			Dec-03
	3.80	18.63	3.78	31.85	28.93	0.03	1.51	12.99	0.97	13.37	2,552	1	99	0	0	61	24.77	-22.3			Nov-04
	3.84	18.70	3.85	32.25	29.72	0.12	1.38	12.99	0.98	13.52	2,552	1	99	0	0	61	24.93	-22.28			Jun-04
	3.91	18.86	4.07	33.03	30.97	0.29	1.2	12.99	0.98	13.8	2,552	1	99	0	0	61	25.05	-22.21			Jun-04
	3.90	18.91	4.24	33.81	32.13	0.48	1.01	12.96	0.97	13.83	2,552	1	99	0	0	61	25.22	-22.16			Jun-04
	3.96	19.09	4.40	34.31	33.03	0.62	0.89	12.96	0.97	13.91	2,552	1	99	0	0	61	25.23	-22.09			Jun-04
100	1.20	6.92	0.41	12.76		0	2.77	6.91	1.1	9.27	255.2	51	45	5	0	268			5.50		Mar-16
	1.40	7.20	0.88	14.23		0.07	2.34	6.93	1.1	9.37	255.2	51	45	5	0	268					Mar-16
	1.30	7.10	0.76	13.93		0.04	2.42	6.92	1.1	9.35	255.2	51	45	5	0	268					Mar-16
100	1.77	15.69	-4.71	32.87		0.76	1.6	16.09	1.07	10.91	1,113	1	99	0	0	52			5.50		Jan-15
	1.89	16.09	-4.18	34.85		1.54	1.08	16.1	1.07	10.75	1,113	1	99	0	0	52					Jan-15
	1.89	15.98	-4.31	34.70		1.5	1.18	16.09	1.07	10.74	1,113	1	99	0	0	52					Jan-15
	1.27	12.01	-4.15	25.22	0.94	2.41	1.02	12.53	1.06	9.51	2,911	2	98	0	0	46	15.2	-24.87			Sep-08
	1.07	11.46	-4.93	21.89	-3.47	1.58	1.89	12.53	1.06	9.43	2,911	2	98	0	0	46	14.99	-24.98			Mar-12
	1.17	11.55	-4.80	22.46	-2.69	1.67	1.76	12.51	1.06	9.46	2,911	2	98	0	0	46	14.91	-24.96			Mar-12
	1.18	11.61	-4.65	23.07	-1.87	1.84	1.58	12.5	1.06	9.42	2,911	2	98	0	0	46	14.93	-24.95			Mar-12

	MARKET			FUND TYPE, CATEGORY & OBJECTIVE	RATINGS				MINIMUMS	
Fund Name	Ticker Symbol	Traded On	Fund Type	Category and (Prospectus Objective)	Overall Rating	Reward Rating	Risk Rating	Recent Up/ Downgrade	Open to New Investors	Min Initial Investment
Principal Overseas Fund R-4 Class	PINUX	NAS CM	Open End	Global Equity Large Cap (World Stock)	C	C-	C+		Y	0
Principal Overseas Fund R-5 Class	PINGX	NAS CM	Open End	Global Equity Large Cap (World Stock)	C	C-	C+		Y	0
Principal Preferred Securities Fund Class A	PPSAX	NAS CM	Open End	US Fixed Income (Income)	B	B-	B+	Up	Y	1,000
Principal Preferred Securities Fund Class C	PRFCX	NAS CM	Open End	US Fixed Income (Income)	B-	C+	B	Up	Y	1,000
Principal Preferred Securities Fund Class J	PPSJX	NAS CM	Open End	US Fixed Income (Income)	B	B-	B+	Up	Y	1,000
Principal Preferred Securities Fund Institutional Class	PPSIX	NAS CM	Open End	US Fixed Income (Income)	B	B-	B+	Up	Y	0
Principal Preferred Securities Fund R-1 Class	PUSAX	NAS CM	Open End	US Fixed Income (Income)	B-	C+	B	Up	Y	0
Principal Preferred Securities Fund R-2 Class	PPRSX	NAS CM	Open End	US Fixed Income (Income)	B	C+	B	Up	Y	0
Principal Preferred Securities Fund R-3 Class	PNARX	NAS CM	Open End	US Fixed Income (Income)	B	C+	B	Up	Y	0
Principal Preferred Securities Fund R-4 Class	PQARX	NAS CM	Open End	US Fixed Income (Income)	B	B-	B	Up	Y	0
Principal Preferred Securities Fund R-5 Class	PPARX	NAS CM	Open End	US Fixed Income (Income)	B	B-	B+	Up	Y	0
Principal Real Estate Income Fund	PGZ	NYSE	Closed End	Real Estate Sector Equity (Real Estate)	B-	B	C-		Y	
Principal Real Estate Securities Fund Class A	PRRAX	NAS CM	Open End	Real Estate Sector Equity (Real Estate)	B-	C+	B		Y	1,000
Principal Real Estate Securities Fund Class C	PRCEX	NAS CM	Open End	Real Estate Sector Equity (Real Estate)	C+	C	B	Down	Y	1,000
Principal Real Estate Securities Fund Class J	PREJX	NAS CM	Open End	Real Estate Sector Equity (Real Estate)	B-	C+	B		Y	1,000
Principal Real Estate Securities Fund Class R-6	PFRSX	NAS CM	Open End	Real Estate Sector Equity (Real Estate)	B-	C+	B		Y	0
Principal Real Estate Securities Fund Institutional Class	PIREX	NAS CM	Open End	Real Estate Sector Equity (Real Estate)	B-	C+	B		Y	0
Principal Real Estate Securities Fund R-1 Class	PRAEX	NAS CM	Open End	Real Estate Sector Equity (Real Estate)	C+	C	B	Down	Y	0
Principal Real Estate Securities Fund R-2 Class	PRENX	NAS CM	Open End	Real Estate Sector Equity (Real Estate)	B-	C+	B		Y	0
Principal Real Estate Securities Fund R-3 Class	PRERX	NAS CM	Open End	Real Estate Sector Equity (Real Estate)	B-	C+	B		Y	0
Principal Real Estate Securities Fund R-4 Class	PRETX	NAS CM	Open End	Real Estate Sector Equity (Real Estate)	B-	C+	B		Y	0
Principal Real Estate Securities Fund R-5 Class	PREPX	NAS CM	Open End	Real Estate Sector Equity (Real Estate)	B-	C+	B		Y	0
Principal SmallCap Fund Class A	PLLAX	NAS CM	Open End	US Equity Small Cap (Small Company)	C	C	C+		Y	1,000
Principal SmallCap Fund Class C	PSMCX	NAS CM	Open End	US Equity Small Cap (Small Company)	C	C	C+		Y	1,000
Principal SmallCap Fund Class J	PSBJX	NAS CM	Open End	US Equity Small Cap (Small Company)	C	C	C+		Y	1,000
Principal SmallCap Fund Class R-6	PSMLX	NAS CM	Open End	US Equity Small Cap (Small Company)	C	C	C+		Y	0
Principal SmallCap Fund Institutional Class	PSLIX	NAS CM	Open End	US Equity Small Cap (Small Company)	C	C	C+		Y	0
Principal SmallCap Fund R-1 Class	PSABX	NAS CM	Open End	US Equity Small Cap (Small Company)	C	C	C+		Y	0
Principal SmallCap Fund R-2 Class	PSBNX	NAS CM	Open End	US Equity Small Cap (Small Company)	C	C	C+		Y	0
Principal SmallCap Fund R-3 Class	PSBMX	NAS CM	Open End	US Equity Small Cap (Small Company)	C	C	C+		Y	0
Principal SmallCap Fund R-4 Class	PSBSX	NAS CM	Open End	US Equity Small Cap (Small Company)	C	C	C+		Y	0
Principal SmallCap Fund R-5 Class	PSBPX	NAS CM	Open End	US Equity Small Cap (Small Company)	C	C	C+		Y	0
Principal SmallCap Growth Fund I Class J	PSIJX	NAS CM	Open End	US Equity Small Cap (Growth)	C+	C+	C+	Down	Y	1,000
Principal SmallCap Growth Fund I Class R-6	PCSMX	NAS CM	Open End	US Equity Small Cap (Growth)	C+	C+	C+	Down	Y	0
Principal SmallCap Growth Fund I Institutional Class	PGRTX	NAS CM	Open End	US Equity Small Cap (Growth)	C+	C+	C+	Down	Y	0
Principal SmallCap Growth Fund I R-1 Class	PNASX	NAS CM	Open End	US Equity Small Cap (Growth)	C+	C+	C+	Down	Y	0
Principal SmallCap Growth Fund I R-2 Class	PPNNX	NAS CM	Open End	US Equity Small Cap (Growth)	C+	C+	C+	Down	Y	0
Principal SmallCap Growth Fund I R-3 Class	PPNMX	NAS CM	Open End	US Equity Small Cap (Growth)	C+	C+	C+	Down	Y	0
Principal SmallCap Growth Fund I R-4 Class	PPNSX	NAS CM	Open End	US Equity Small Cap (Growth)	C+	C+	C+	Down	Y	0
Principal SmallCap Growth Fund I R-5 Class	PPNPX	NAS CM	Open End	US Equity Small Cap (Growth)	C+	C+	C+	Down	Y	0
Principal SmallCap S&P 600 Index Fund Class J	PSSJX	NAS CM	Open End	US Equity Small Cap (Small Company)	C	C-	C+	Down	Y	1,000
Principal SmallCap S&P 600 Index Fund Class R-6	PSPIX	NAS CM	Open End	US Equity Small Cap (Small Company)	C	C-	C+	Down	Y	0
Principal SmallCap S&P 600 Index Fund Institutional Class	PSSIX	NAS CM	Open End	US Equity Small Cap (Small Company)	C	C-	C+	Down	Y	0
Principal SmallCap S&P 600 Index Fund R-1 Class	PSAPX	NAS CM	Open End	US Equity Small Cap (Small Company)	C	C-	C+		Y	0
Principal SmallCap S&P 600 Index Fund R-2 Class	PSSNX	NAS CM	Open End	US Equity Small Cap (Small Company)	C	C-	C+		Y	0
Principal SmallCap S&P 600 Index Fund R-3 Class	PSSMX	NAS CM	Open End	US Equity Small Cap (Small Company)	C	C-	C+		Y	0
Principal SmallCap S&P 600 Index Fund R-4 Class	PSSSX	NAS CM	Open End	US Equity Small Cap (Small Company)	C	C-	C+		Y	0
Principal SmallCap S&P 600 Index Fund R-5 Class	PSSPX	NAS CM	Open End	US Equity Small Cap (Small Company)	C	C-	C+	Down	Y	0
Principal SmallCap Value Fund II Class A	PSVAX	NAS CM	Open End	US Equity Small Cap (Small Company)	C	C-	C+		Y	1,000
Principal SmallCap Value Fund II Class J	PSMJX	NAS CM	Open End	US Equity Small Cap (Small Company)	C	C-	C+		Y	1,000
Principal SmallCap Value Fund II Class R-6	PSMVX	NAS CM	Open End	US Equity Small Cap (Small Company)	C	C-	C+		Y	0
Principal SmallCap Value Fund II Institutional Class	PPVIX	NAS CM	Open End	US Equity Small Cap (Small Company)	C	C-	C+		Y	0

★Expanded analysis of this fund is included in Section II.

	TOTAL RETURNS					PERFORMANCE				ASSETS		ASSET ALLOCATION & TURNOVER					BULL & BEAR		FEES		
Min Additional Investment	3-Month Total Return	6-Month Total Return	1-Year Total Return	3-Year Total Return	5-Year Total Return	Dividend Yield (TTM)	Expense Ratio	3-Yr Std Deviation	3-Year Beta	NAV	Total Assets (MIL)	%Cash	%Stocks	%Bonds	%Other	Turnover Ratio	Last Bull Market Total Return	Last Bear Market Total Return	Front End Fee (%)	Back End Fee (%)	Inception Date
	1.17	11.80	-4.49	23.85	-0.94	2.04	1.39	12.46	1.05	9.47	2,911	2	98	0	0	46	15.14	-24.9			Mar-12
	1.28	11.80	-4.36	24.21	-0.37	2.15	1.27	12.58	1.06	9.47	2,911	2	98	0	0	46	15.2	-24.87			Mar-12
100	3.43	10.30	6.89	16.84	27.31	5.04	1.06	3.9	0.8	10.17	5,513	1	1	56	0	12	10.28	-5.91	3.75		Jun-05
100	3.34	9.89	6.09	14.30	22.59	4.3	1.81	3.93	0.8	10.16	5,513	1	1	56	0	12	9.71	-6.19		1.00	Jan-07
100	3.43	10.26	6.87	16.90	27.27	5.18	1.05	3.89	0.8	9.88	5,513	1	1	56	0	12	10.1	-5.98		1.00	Dec-03
	3.52	10.40	7.10	17.72	29.00	5.32	0.8	3.91	0.8	10.09	5,513	1	1	56	0	12	10.53	-5.77			May-02
	3.34	10.04	6.33	14.97	23.97	4.6	1.58	3.87	0.79	10.04	5,513	1	1	56	0	12	9.93	-6.13			Nov-04
	3.40	10.06	6.50	15.45	24.78	4.76	1.45	3.9	0.8	9.98	5,513	1	1	56	0	12	10.04	-6			Jun-04
	3.43	10.23	6.67	16.11	25.88	4.91	1.27	3.88	0.79	10.02	5,513	1	1	56	0	12	10.13	-5.91			Jun-04
	3.49	10.36	6.89	16.71	27.03	5.11	1.08	3.89	0.79	10	5,513	1	1	56	0	12	10.25	-5.94			Jun-04
	3.50	10.36	6.97	17.18	27.92	5.2	0.96	3.94	0.8	10.05	5,513	1	1	56	0	12	10.31	-5.88			Jun-04
	4.61	16.62	16.02	42.24	52.78	4.93	2.62	7.12		21.61	149.1	-39	48	91	0	37					Jun-13
100	3.02	21.34	14.15	20.17	53.70	1.68	1.25	12.3	0.91	26.18	4,636	2	98	0	0	23	31.59	-16.32	5.50		Jun-05
100	2.84	20.92	13.27	17.38	47.80	1	2.03	12.3	0.91	25.7	4,636	2	98	0	0	23	30.99	-16.6		1.00	Jan-07
100	3.07	21.46	14.27	20.64	54.67	1.84	1.15	12.32	0.91	25.39	4,636	2	98	0	0	23	31.65	-16.29		1.00	Mar-01
	3.14	21.63	14.63	21.51	56.09	2.08	0.83	12.29	0.91	26.19	4,636	2	98	0	0	23	31.86	-16.28			Nov-16
	3.11	21.57	14.51	21.46	56.66	1.98	0.91	12.31	0.91	26.2	4,636	2	98	0	0	23	32.06	-16.19			Mar-01
	2.92	21.09	13.64	18.60	50.46	1.29	1.69	12.29	0.91	25.85	4,636	2	98	0	0	23	31.3	-16.44			Nov-04
	2.94	21.19	13.80	19.05	51.46	1.48	1.56	12.33	0.91	24.86	4,636	2	98	0	0	23	31.38	-16.39			Dec-00
	3.00	21.27	13.98	19.71	52.83	1.62	1.38	12.3	0.91	25.51	4,636	2	98	0	0	23	31.58	-16.33			Dec-00
	3.04	21.38	14.17	20.36	54.22	1.8	1.19	12.32	0.91	25.21	4,636	2	98	0	0	23	31.76	-16.3			Dec-00
	3.10	21.51	14.38	20.84	55.24	1.92	1.07	12.31	0.91	25.27	4,636	2	98	0	0	23	31.85	-16.28			Dec-00
100	3.22	20.71	-3.53	40.32	38.20	0.04	1.18	17.48	1.01	20.8	683.2	4	96	0	0	52	31.89	-24.8	5.50		Jun-05
100	2.98	20.21	-4.31	36.98	32.60	0	1.98	17.45	1.01	18.26	683.2	4	96	0	0	52	31.38	-25.08		1.00	Jan-07
100	3.23	20.76	-3.38	41.10	39.31	0.2	1.05	17.46	1.01	19.77	683.2	4	96	0	0	52	32.1	-24.8		1.00	Mar-01
	3.30	20.93	-3.13	42.01	40.36	0.39	0.77	17.47	1.01	22.53	683.2	4	96	0	0	52	32.27	-24.72			Nov-16
	3.25	20.85	-3.22	41.95	40.97	0.34	0.85	17.45	1.01	22.54	683.2	4	96	0	0	52	32.38	-24.64			Mar-01
	3.11	20.48	-3.97	38.53	35.28	0	1.63	17.48	1.01	19.53	683.2	4	96	0	0	52	31.72	-24.87			Nov-04
	3.12	20.51	-3.88	39.07	36.10	0	1.5	17.47	1.01	19.8	683.2	4	96	0	0	52	31.84	-24.83			Dec-00
	3.18	20.58	-3.68	39.82	37.38	0	1.32	17.5	1.01	20.74	683.2	4	96	0	0	52	31.98	-24.76			Dec-00
	3.23	20.75	-3.47	40.61	38.69	0.14	1.13	17.47	1.01	21.7	683.2	4	96	0	0	52	32.23	-24.75			Dec-00
	3.24	20.82	-3.36	41.18	39.54	0.2	1.01	17.47	1.01	22.28	683.2	4	96	0	0	52	32.27	-24.72			Dec-00
100	6.33	30.56	9.04	72.23	70.58	0	1.33	16.9	0.95	9.74	1,930	4	96	0	0	69	32.45	-25.33		1.00	Mar-01
	6.43	30.79	9.38	73.97	73.60	0	1	16.86	0.95	14.06	1,930	4	96	0	0	69	32.9	-25.12			Nov-14
	6.42	30.73	9.36	73.82	73.73	0	1.03	16.9	0.95	14.08	1,930	4	96	0	0	69	32.9	-25.11			Dec-00
	6.22	30.15	8.40	69.40	66.42	0	1.88	16.9	0.95	10.92	1,930	4	96	0	0	69	32.16	-25.38			Nov-04
	6.24	30.24	8.57	70.06	67.48	0	1.75	16.85	0.95	10.55	1,930	4	96	0	0	69	32.26	-25.32			Dec-00
	6.33	30.39	8.79	71.19	69.02	0	1.57	16.89	0.95	11.41	1,930	4	96	0	0	69	32.47	-25.29			Dec-00
	6.30	30.54	8.94	72.06	70.58	0	1.38	16.87	0.95	12.31	1,930	4	96	0	0	69	32.53	-25.18			Dec-00
	6.37	30.62	9.05	72.58	71.61	0	1.26	16.87	0.95	13.01	1,930	4	96	0	0	69	32.63	-25.16			Dec-00
100	1.75	14.13	-5.23	41.52	46.71	1.04	0.44	17.86	1	23.18	1,299	1	99	0	0	17	28.91	-22.22		1.00	Mar-01
	1.82	14.30	-4.98	42.45	47.85	1.21	0.16	17.85	1	24.61	1,299	1	99	0	0	17	29.09	-22.09			Nov-16
	1.81	14.29	-5.00	42.44	48.52	1.16	0.22	17.87	1	24.63	1,299	1	99	0	0	17	29.31	-22.06			Mar-01
	1.59	13.79	-5.79	38.99	42.52	0.38	1.04	17.85	1	24.17	1,299	1	99	0	0	17	28.71	-22.35			Nov-04
	1.63	13.88	-5.68	39.51	43.42	0.45	0.91	17.86	1	24.93	1,299	1	99	0	0	17	28.72	-22.27			Dec-00
	1.69	14.00	-5.49	40.30	44.71	0.65	0.73	17.86	1	25.15	1,299	1	99	0	0	17	28.9	-22.27			Dec-00
	1.71	14.08	-5.31	41.05	46.12	0.79	0.54	17.86	1	25.44	1,299	1	99	0	0	17	29.03	-22.19			Dec-00
	1.74	14.19	-5.20	41.61	46.98	0.91	0.42	17.86	1	25.59	1,299	1	99	0	0	17	29.09	-22.09			Dec-00
100	1.88	16.08	-5.07	28.18	25.94	0.31	1.5	17.02	0.98	10.25	1,043	4	96	0	0	84	27.18	-25.94	5.50		Jun-14
100	1.92	16.16	-4.99	28.47	26.19	0.38	1.44	17.12	0.98	10.06	1,043	4	96	0	0	84	26.73	-26.04		1.00	Mar-09
	2.06	16.47	-4.51	30.14	29.00	0.71	1.01	17.06	0.98	10.39	1,043	4	96	0	0	84	27.37	-25.87			Nov-14
	2.06	16.34	-4.64	29.92	28.77	0.68	1.04	17.06	0.98	10.39	1,043	4	96	0	0	84	27.37	-25.87			Jun-04

	MARKET			FUND TYPE, CATEGORY & OBJECTIVE	RATINGS				MINIMUMS	
Fund Name	Ticker Symbol	Traded On	Fund Type	Category and (Prospectus Objective)	Overall Rating	Reward Rating	Risk Rating	Recent Up/ Downgrade	Open to New Investors	Min Initial Investment
Principal SmallCap Value Fund II R-1 Class	PCPTX	NAS CM	Open End	US Equity Small Cap (Small Company)	C	C-	C+		Y	0
Principal SmallCap Value Fund II R-2 Class	PKARX	NAS CM	Open End	US Equity Small Cap (Small Company)	C	C-	C+		Y	0
Principal SmallCap Value Fund II R-3 Class	PJARX	NAS CM	Open End	US Equity Small Cap (Small Company)	C	C-	C+		Y	0
Principal SmallCap Value Fund II R-4 Class	PSTWX	NAS CM	Open End	US Equity Small Cap (Small Company)	C	C-	C+		Y	0
Principal SmallCap Value Fund II R-5 Class	PLARX	NAS CM	Open End	US Equity Small Cap (Small Company)	C	C-	C+		Y	0
Principal Small-MidCap Dividend Income Fund Class A	PMDAX	NAS CM	Open End	US Equity Small Cap (Equity-Income)	C	C	B-			1,000
Principal Small-MidCap Dividend Income Fund Class C	PMDDX	NAS CM	Open End	US Equity Small Cap (Equity-Income)	C	C	C+			1,000
Principal Small-MidCap Dividend Income Institutional Cls	PMDIX	NAS CM	Open End	US Equity Small Cap (Equity-Income)	C	C	B-			0
Principal Small-MidCap Dividend Income Fund R-6	PMDHX	NAS CM	Open End	US Equity Small Cap (Equity-Income)	C	C	B-		Y	0
Principal Strategic Asset Mgmt Balanced Portfolio Cls A	SABPX	NAS CM	Open End	Moderate Alloc (Balanced)	B	C	A-	Up	Y	1,000
Principal Strategic Asset Mgmt Balanced Portfolio Cls C	SCBPX	NAS CM	Open End	Moderate Alloc (Balanced)	B-	C	A-	Up	Y	1,000
Principal Strategic Asset Mgmt Balanced Portfolio Cls J	PSAJX	NAS CM	Open End	Moderate Alloc (Balanced)	B	C+	A-	Up	Y	1,000
Principal Strategic Asset Mgmt Balanced Portfolio Inst Cls	PSBIX	NAS CM	Open End	Moderate Alloc (Balanced)	B	C+	A-	Up	Y	0
Principal Strategic Asset Mgmt Balanced Portfolio R-1 Cls	PSBGX	NAS CM	Open End	Moderate Alloc (Balanced)	B-	C	A-	Up	Y	0
Principal Strategic Asset Mgmt Balanced Portfolio R-2 Cls	PSBVX	NAS CM	Open End	Moderate Alloc (Balanced)	B	C	A-	Up	Y	0
Principal Strategic Asset Mgmt Balanced Portfolio R-3 Cls	PBAPX	NAS CM	Open End	Moderate Alloc (Balanced)	B	C	A-	Up	Y	0
Principal Strategic Asset Mgmt Balanced Portfolio R-4 Cls	PSBLX	NAS CM	Open End	Moderate Alloc (Balanced)	B	C	A-	Up	Y	0
Principal Strategic Asset Mgmt Balanced Portfolio R-5 Cls	PSBFX	NAS CM	Open End	Moderate Alloc (Balanced)	B	C	A-	Up	Y	0
Principal Strategic Asset Mgmt Conservative Balanced Cls A	SAIPX	NAS CM	Open End	Cautious Alloc (Corporate Bond)	B	C+	A-	Up	Y	1,000
Principal Strategic Asset Mgmt Conservative Balanced Cls C	SCIPX	NAS CM	Open End	Cautious Alloc (Corporate Bond)	B-	C	A-	Up	Y	1,000
Principal Strategic Asset Mgmt Conservative Balanced Cls J	PCBJX	NAS CM	Open End	Cautious Alloc (Corporate Bond)	B	C+	A-	Up	Y	1,000
Principal Strat Asset Mgmt Cons Balanced Inst Cls	PCCIX	NAS CM	Open End	Cautious Alloc (Corporate Bond)	B	C+	A-	Up	Y	0
Principal Strat Asset Mgmt Cons Balanced R-1 Cls	PCSSX	NAS CM	Open End	Cautious Alloc (Corporate Bond)	B	C+	A-	Up	Y	0
Principal Strat Asset Mgmt Cons Balanced R-2 Cls	PCNSX	NAS CM	Open End	Cautious Alloc (Corporate Bond)	B	C+	A-	Up	Y	0
Principal Strat Asset Mgmt Cons Balanced R-3 Cls	PCBPX	NAS CM	Open End	Cautious Alloc (Corporate Bond)	B	C+	A-	Up	Y	0
Principal Strat Asset Mgmt Cons Balanced R-4 Cls	PCBLX	NAS CM	Open End	Cautious Alloc (Corporate Bond)	B	C+	A-	Up	Y	0
Principal Strat Asset Mgmt Cons Balanced R-5 Cls	PCBFX	NAS CM	Open End	Cautious Alloc (Corporate Bond)	B	C+	A-	Up	Y	0
Principal Strategic Asset Mgmt Conservative Growth Cls A	SAGPX	NAS CM	Open End	Aggressive Alloc (Growth)	B-	C	B+	Up	Y	1,000
Principal Strategic Asset Mgmt Conservative Growth Cls C	SCGPX	NAS CM	Open End	Aggressive Alloc (Growth)	B-	C	B+	Up	Y	1,000
Principal Strategic Asset Mgmt Conservative Growth Cls J	PCGJX	NAS CM	Open End	Aggressive Alloc (Growth)	B-	C	B+	Up	Y	1,000
Principal Strat Asset Mgmt Cons Growth Inst Cls	PCWIX	NAS CM	Open End	Aggressive Alloc (Growth)	B-	C	B+	Up	Y	0
Principal Strategic Asset Mgmt Conservative Growth R-1 Cls	PCGGX	NAS CM	Open End	Aggressive Alloc (Growth)	B-	C	B+	Up	Y	0
Principal Strategic Asset Mgmt Conservative Growth R-2 Cls	PCGVX	NAS CM	Open End	Aggressive Alloc (Growth)	B-	C	B+	Up	Y	0
Principal Strategic Asset Mgmt Conservative Growth R-3 Cls	PCGPX	NAS CM	Open End	Aggressive Alloc (Growth)	B-	C	B+	Up	Y	0
Principal Strategic Asset Mgmt Conservative Growth R-4 Cls	PCWSX	NAS CM	Open End	Aggressive Alloc (Growth)	B-	C	B+	Up	Y	0
Principal Strategic Asset Mgmt Conservative Growth R-5 Cls	PCWPX	NAS CM	Open End	Aggressive Alloc (Growth)	B-	C	B+	Up	Y	0
Principal Strategic Asset Management Flexible Income Cls A	SAUPX	NAS CM	Open End	Cautious Alloc (Corporate Bond)	B	C+	A-		Y	1,000
Principal Strategic Asset Management Flexible Income Cls C	SCUPX	NAS CM	Open End	Cautious Alloc (Corporate Bond)	B-	C	B+		Y	1,000
Principal Strategic Asset Management Flexible Income Cls J	PFIJX	NAS CM	Open End	Cautious Alloc (Corporate Bond)	B	C+	A-		Y	1,000
Principal Strategic Asset Mgmt Flexible Income Inst Cls	PIFIX	NAS CM	Open End	Cautious Alloc (Corporate Bond)	B	C+	A-		Y	0
Principal Strategic Asset Mgmt Flexible Income R-1 Cls	PFIGX	NAS CM	Open End	Cautious Alloc (Corporate Bond)	B-	C+	B+		Y	0
Principal Strategic Asset Mgmt Flexible Income R-2 Cls	PFIVX	NAS CM	Open End	Cautious Alloc (Corporate Bond)	B	C+	B+	Up	Y	0
Principal Strategic Asset Mgmt Flexible Income R-3 Cls	PFIPX	NAS CM	Open End	Cautious Alloc (Corporate Bond)	B	C+	A-	Up	Y	0
Principal Strategic Asset Mgmt Flexible Income R-4 Cls	PFILX	NAS CM	Open End	Cautious Alloc (Corporate Bond)	B	C+	A-		Y	0
Principal Strategic Asset Mgmt Flexible Income R-5 Cls	PFIFX	NAS CM	Open End	Cautious Alloc (Corporate Bond)	B	C+	A-		Y	0
Principal Strategic Asset Mgmt Strategic Growth Cls A	SACAX	NAS CM	Open End	Aggressive Alloc (Growth)	B-	C	B	Up	Y	1,000
Principal Strategic Asset Mgmt Strategic Growth Cls C	SWHCX	NAS CM	Open End	Aggressive Alloc (Growth)	B-	C	B	Up	Y	1,000
Principal Strategic Asset Mgmt Strategic Growth Cls J	PSWJX	NAS CM	Open End	Aggressive Alloc (Growth)	B-	C	B	Up	Y	1,000
Principal Strategic Asset Mgmt Strategic Growth Inst Cls	PSWIX	NAS CM	Open End	Aggressive Alloc (Growth)	B-	C	B	Up	Y	0
Principal Strategic Asset Mgmt Strategic Growth R-1 Cls	PSGGX	NAS CM	Open End	Aggressive Alloc (Growth)	B-	C	B	Up	Y	0
Principal Strategic Asset Mgmt Strategic Growth R-2 Cls	PSGVX	NAS CM	Open End	Aggressive Alloc (Growth)	B-	C	B	Up	Y	0
Principal Strategic Asset Mgmt Strategic Growth R-3 Cls	PSGPX	NAS CM	Open End	Aggressive Alloc (Growth)	B-	C	B	Up	Y	0

★Expanded analysis of this fund is included in Section II.

	TOTAL RETURNS					PERFORMANCE				ASSETS		ASSET ALLOCATION & TURNOVER					BULL & BEAR		FEES		
Min Additional Investment	3-Month Total Return	6-Month Total Return	1-Year Total Return	3-Year Total Return	5-Year Total Return	Dividend Yield (TTM)	Expense Ratio	3-Yr Std Deviation	3-Year Beta	NAV	Total Assets (ML)	%Cash	%Stocks	%Bonds	%Other	Turnover Ratio	Last Bull Market Total Return	Last Bear Market Total Return	Front End Fee (%)	Back End Fee (%)	Inception Date
	1.88	15.84	-5.44	26.71	23.43	0	1.89	17.08	0.98	9.21	1,043	4	96	0	0	84	26.69	-26.1			Nov-04
	1.83	16.00	-5.34	27.19	24.24	0	1.76	17.05	0.98	9.42	1,043	4	96	0	0	84	26.85	-26.09			Jun-04
	1.96	16.09	-5.14	27.93	25.35	0.2	1.58	17.06	0.98	9.88	1,043	4	96	0	0	84	26.75	-25.96			Jun-04
	2.02	16.16	-4.93	28.71	26.61	0.35	1.39	17.09	0.98	10.06	1,043	4	96	0	0	84	26.93	-25.97			Jun-04
	2.00	16.32	-4.81	29.14	27.43	0.48	1.27	17.04	0.98	10.19	1,043	4	96	0	0	84	27.14	-25.92			Jun-04
100	2.51	15.21	-1.61	32.07	37.28	2.19	1.25	14.54	0.95	14.25	2,263	1	99	0	0	32	26.46		5.50		Jun-11
100	2.33	14.76	-2.37	29.08	32.09	1.5	2	14.55	0.95	14.12	2,263	1	99	0	0	32	26.07			1.00	Jun-12
	2.64	15.44	-1.27	33.20	39.50	2.44	0.98	14.58	0.95	14.33	2,263	1	99	0	0	32	26.8				Jun-11
	2.65	15.41	-1.36	33.50	39.81	2.39	0.9	14.53	0.95	14.39	2,263	1	99	0	0	32	26.8				Jan-17
100	3.39	12.86	6.26	27.15	29.39	1.82	1.25	7.14	0.55	15.38	4,529	3	61	34	0	27	16.19	-12.18	5.50		Jul-96
100	3.24	12.43	5.48	24.29	24.67	1.13	2	7.14	0.55	15.13	4,529	3	61	34	0	27	15.67	-12.42		1.00	Mar-02
100	3.42	12.97	6.47	27.79	30.34	2.06	1.1	7.14	0.55	14.82	4,529	3	61	34	0	27	16.27	-12.25		1.00	Jan-07
	3.46	13.07	6.58	28.41	31.59	2.16	0.93	7.14	0.54	15.11	4,529	3	61	34	0	27	16.42	-12.08			Jan-07
	3.29	12.67	5.75	25.16	26.02	1.36	1.8	7.15	0.55	15.09	4,529	3	61	34	0	27	15.87	-12.42			Jan-07
	3.36	12.67	5.95	25.67	26.87	1.46	1.67	7.15	0.55	15.04	4,529	3	61	34	0	27	16.01	-12.35			Jan-07
	3.33	12.79	6.07	26.25	27.93	1.64	1.49	7.15	0.55	15.07	4,529	3	61	34	0	27	16.06	-12.26			Jan-07
	3.44	12.92	6.25	26.97	29.19	1.8	1.3	7.16	0.55	15.1	4,529	3	61	34	0	27	16.24	-12.24			Jan-07
	3.40	12.96	6.33	27.43	29.91	1.93	1.18	7.15	0.55	15.09	4,529	3	61	34	0	27	16.3	-12.2			Jan-07
100	3.01	10.35	5.88	20.58	23.54	2.22	1.24	5.12	0.36	11.94	1,676	4	40	53	0	22	12.29	-8.41	5.50		Jul-96
100	2.75	9.90	5.12	17.87	18.91	1.5	1.99	5.1	0.35	11.81	1,676	4	40	53	0	22	11.86	-8.64		1.00	Mar-02
100	3.01	10.46	6.08	21.25	24.31	2.44	1.08	5.12	0.34	11.77	1,676	4	40	53	0	22	12.42	-8.4		1.00	Jan-07
	3.04	10.55	6.31	21.79	25.49	2.57	0.92	5.15	0.35	11.81	1,676	4	40	53	0	22	12.57	-8.31			Jan-07
	2.83	10.09	5.33	18.69	20.17	1.76	1.77	5.08	0.36	11.77	1,676	4	40	53	0	22	12.04	-8.64			Jan-07
	2.84	10.09	5.49	19.10	20.97	1.86	1.64	5.09	0.35	11.87	1,676	4	40	53	0	22	12.12	-8.59			Jan-07
	2.90	10.22	5.65	19.74	22.09	2.06	1.46	5.11	0.35	11.79	1,676	4	40	53	0	22	12.29	-8.55			Jan-07
	2.90	10.31	5.79	20.42	23.15	2.19	1.27	5.15	0.35	11.8	1,676	4	40	53	0	22	12.4	-8.39			Jan-07
	2.98	10.35	5.96	20.83	23.96	2.34	1.15	5.17	0.35	11.8	1,676	4	40	53	0	22	12.45	-8.33			Jan-07
100	3.77	15.37	6.46	34.38	35.26	1.4	1.28	9.26	0.72	17.05	3,032	4	80	15	0	34	20.1	-16.17	5.50		Jul-96
100	3.57	14.87	5.59	31.30	30.20	0.85	2.03	9.23	0.71	15.66	3,032	4	80	15	0	34	19.46	-16.36		1.00	Mar-02
100	3.80	15.46	6.62	35.05	36.17	1.62	1.14	9.25	0.72	16.37	3,032	4	80	15	0	34	20.06	-16.09		1.00	Jan-07
	3.87	15.55	6.82	35.73	37.57	1.73	0.96	9.24	0.71	16.63	3,032	4	80	15	0	34	20.28	-16.01			Jan-07
	3.59	15.03	5.88	32.26	31.67	0.64	1.83	9.24	0.71	16.43	3,032	4	80	15	0	34	19.78	-16.35			Jan-07
	3.65	15.13	6.00	32.74	32.55	0.89	1.7	9.26	0.72	16.44	3,032	4	80	15	0	34	19.84	-16.28			Jan-07
	3.74	15.23	6.20	33.45	33.77	1.28	1.52	9.27	0.72	16.35	3,032	4	80	15	0	34	19.95	-16.21			Jan-07
	3.75	15.40	6.44	34.26	35.03	1.37	1.33	9.25	0.72	16.56	3,032	4	80	15	0	34	20.02	-16.12			Jan-07
	3.76	15.44	6.53	34.70	35.82	1.48	1.21	9.26	0.72	16.52	3,032	4	80	15	0	34	20.2	-16.09			Jan-07
100	2.77	8.73	6.33	16.45	19.86	2.69	1.11	3.59	0.46	12.21	2,643	8	25	64	0	23	10.18	-5.55	3.75		Jul-96
100	2.60	8.33	5.49	13.90	15.40	1.97	1.88	3.58	0.46	12.08	2,643	8	25	64	0	23	9.69	-5.81		1.00	Mar-02
100	2.84	8.83	6.50	17.09	20.61	2.88	0.97	3.59	0.45	12.1	2,643	8	25	64	0	23	10.14	-5.51		1.00	Jan-07
	2.85	8.94	6.67	17.59	21.69	2.98	0.81	3.59	0.44	12.17	2,643	8	25	64	0	23	10.4	-5.44			Jan-07
	2.59	8.40	5.67	14.47	16.55	2.22	1.67	3.56	0.45	12.1	2,643	8	25	64	0	23	9.8	-5.7			Jan-07
	2.68	8.51	5.93	15.01	17.37	2.31	1.54	3.59	0.44	12.15	2,643	8	25	64	0	23	9.86	-5.64			Jan-07
	2.72	8.63	6.03	15.65	18.36	2.47	1.36	3.58	0.44	12.14	2,643	8	25	64	0	23	10.09	-5.65			Jan-07
	2.77	8.74	6.23	16.33	19.49	2.66	1.17	3.57	0.44	12.15	2,643	8	25	64	0	23	10.11	-5.5			Jan-07
	2.80	8.72	6.35	16.66	20.25	2.77	1.05	3.57	0.45	12.14	2,643	8	25	64	0	23	10.18	-5.45			Jan-07
100	4.08	17.38	6.12	36.72	36.55	1.59	1.31	10.56	0.82	18.1	1,875	2	93	4	0	34	23.25	-18.91	5.50		Jul-96
100	3.92	16.95	5.36	33.65	31.53	1.11	2.06	10.62	0.82	16.14	1,875	2	93	4	0	34	22.73	-19.15		1.00	Mar-02
100	4.13	17.54	6.35	37.42	37.61	1.81	1.16	10.6	0.82	17.38	1,875	2	93	4	0	34	23.24	-18.91		1.00	Jan-07
	4.20	17.65	6.50	38.10	39.00	1.93	0.97	10.56	0.82	17.61	1,875	2	93	4	0	34	23.59	-18.79			Jan-07
	3.92	17.08	5.57	34.54	33.07	0.78	1.84	10.59	0.82	17.47	1,875	2	93	4	0	34	22.86	-19.05			Jan-07
	4.01	17.24	5.74	35.16	33.97	1.34	1.71	10.6	0.82	17.34	1,875	2	93	4	0	34	22.99	-19.02			Jan-07
	4.02	17.30	5.93	35.84	35.20	1.48	1.53	10.6	0.82	17.33	1,875	2	93	4	0	34	23.16	-18.98			Jan-07

	MARKET			FUND TYPE, CATEGORY & OBJECTIVE	RATINGS				MINIMUMS	
Fund Name	Ticker Symbol	Traded On	Fund Type	Category and (Prospectus Objective)	Overall Rating	Reward Rating	Risk Rating	Recent Up/ Downgrade	Open to New Investors	Min Initial Investment
Principal Strategic Asset Mgmt Strategic Growth R-4 Cls	PSGLX	NAS CM	Open End	Aggressive Alloc (Growth)	B-	C	B	Up	Y	0
Principal Strategic Asset Mgmt Strategic Growth R-5 Cls	PSGFX	NAS CM	Open End	Aggressive Alloc (Growth)	B-	C	B	Up	Y	0
Principal SystematEx International Fund Class R-6	PSTMX	NAS CM	Open End	Global Equity Large Cap (Growth)	C	C	B		Y	0
Principal SystematEx International Institutional Cls	PSOMX	NAS CM	Open End	Global Equity Large Cap (Growth)	C	C	B		Y	0
Private Capital Management Value Fund Class A	VFPAX	NAS CM	Open End	US Equity Small Cap (Growth)	C	D+	C+		Y	5,000
Private Capital Management Value Fund Class I	VFPIX	NAS CM	Open End	US Equity Small Cap (Growth)	C	D+	C+		Y	750,000
Private Capital Management Value Fund Class I	PROAX	NAS CM	Open End	Long/Short Equity (Growth)	C	C	B-		Y	2,500
Private Capital Management Value Fund Class I	PROCX	NAS CM	Open End	Long/Short Equity (Growth)	C	C	C+	Up	Y	2,500
Private Capital Management Value Fund Class I	PROTX	NAS CM	Open End	Long/Short Equity (Growth)	C	C	B-		Y	2,500
ProFunds Banks UltraSector Fund Investor Class	BKPIX	NAS CM	Open End	Trading Tools (Financial)	C	C	C		Y	15,000
ProFunds Banks UltraSector Fund Service Class	BKPSX	NAS CM	Open End	Trading Tools (Financial)	C-	C-	C	Down	Y	15,000
ProFunds Basic Materials UltraSector Fund Investor Class	BMPIX	NAS CM	Open End	Trading Tools ()	C	C	C		Y	15,000
ProFunds Basic Materials UltraSector Fund Service Class	BMPSX	NAS CM	Open End	Trading Tools ()	C	C-	C		Y	15,000
ProFunds Bear Fund Investor Class	BRPIX	NAS CM	Open End	Alternative Miscellaneous (Growth)	D	D-	D		Y	15,000
ProFunds Bear Fund Service Class	BRPSX	NAS CM	Open End	Alternative Miscellaneous (Growth)	D	D-	D		Y	15,000
ProFunds Biotechnology UltraSector Fund Investor Class	BIPIX	NAS CM	Open End	Trading Tools ()	D+	D+	D+	Down	Y	15,000
ProFunds Biotechnology UltraSector Fund Service Class	BIPSX	NAS CM	Open End	Trading Tools ()	D+	D+	D+	Down	Y	15,000
ProFunds Bull Fund Investor Class	BLPIX	NAS CM	Open End	Trading Tools (Growth & Income)	B-	C	B	Up	Y	15,000
ProFunds Bull Fund Service Class	BLPSX	NAS CM	Open End	Trading Tools (Growth & Income)	C+	C	B		Y	15,000
ProFunds Consumer Goods Ultra Sector Fund Investor Class	CNPIX	NAS CM	Open End	Trading Tools ()	C	C	C		Y	15,000
ProFunds Consumer Goods Ultra Sector Fund Service Class	CNPSX	NAS CM	Open End	Trading Tools ()	C	C-	C	Up	Y	15,000
ProFunds Consumer Services UltraSector Fund Investor Class	CYPIX	NAS CM	Open End	Trading Tools ()	B-	B-	C+		Y	15,000
ProFunds Consumer Services UltraSector Fund Service Class	CYPSX	NAS CM	Open End	Trading Tools ()	B-	B-	C+	Up	Y	15,000
ProFunds Europe 30 Fund Investor Class	UEPIX	NAS CM	Open End	Europe Equity Large Cap (Europe Stock)	C	C	B	Down	Y	15,000
ProFunds Europe 30 Fund Service Class	UEPSX	NAS CM	Open End	Europe Equity Large Cap (Europe Stock)	C	C	B	Down	Y	15,000
ProFunds Financials UltraSector Fund Investor Class	FNPIX	NAS CM	Open End	Trading Tools (Financial)	C+	C	C+	Up	Y	15,000
ProFunds Financials UltraSector Fund Service Class	FNPSX	NAS CM	Open End	Trading Tools (Financial)	C+	C	C+	Up	Y	15,000
ProFunds Industrial Ultra Sector Fund Investor Class	IDPIX	NAS CM	Open End	Trading Tools (Growth)	C	C	C		Y	15,000
ProFunds Industrial Ultra Sector Fund Service Class	IDPSX	NAS CM	Open End	Trading Tools (Growth)	C	C	C		Y	15,000
ProFunds Internet UltraSector Fund Investor Class	INPIX	NAS CM	Open End	Trading Tools (Technology)	C+	B-	C	Down	Y	15,000
ProFunds Internet UltraSector Fund Service Class	INPSX	NAS CM	Open End	Trading Tools (Technology)	C+	B-	C	Down	Y	15,000
ProFunds Large Cap Growth Fund Investor Class	LGPIX	NAS CM	Open End	US Equity Large Cap Growth (Growth)	B-	C+	B		Y	15,000
ProFunds Large Cap Growth Fund Service Class	LGPSX	NAS CM	Open End	US Equity Large Cap Growth (Growth)	B-	C+	B		Y	15,000
ProFunds Large Cap Value Fund Investor Class	LVPIX	NAS CM	Open End	US Equity Large Cap Value (Growth & Income)	C+	C	B	Up	Y	15,000
ProFunds Large Cap Value Fund Service Class	LVPSX	NAS CM	Open End	US Equity Large Cap Value (Growth & Income)	C+	C	B	Up	Y	15,000
ProFunds Mid Cap Fund Investor Class	MDPIX	NAS CM	Open End	US Equity Mid Cap (Growth)	C	C	B-		Y	15,000
ProFunds Mid Cap Fund Service Class	MDPSX	NAS CM	Open End	US Equity Mid Cap (Growth)	C	C	B-		Y	15,000
ProFunds Mid Cap Growth Fund Investor Class	MGPIX	NAS CM	Open End	US Equity Mid Cap (Growth)	C	C	B-		Y	15,000
ProFunds Mid Cap Growth Fund Service Class	MGPSX	NAS CM	Open End	US Equity Mid Cap (Growth)	C	C	B-		Y	15,000
ProFunds Mid Cap Value Fund Investor Class	MLPIX	NAS CM	Open End	US Equity Mid Cap (Growth)	C	C	B-		Y	15,000
ProFunds Mid Cap Value Fund Service Class	MLPSX	NAS CM	Open End	US Equity Mid Cap (Growth)	C	C-	B-		Y	15,000
ProFunds NASDAQ-100 Fund Investor Class	OTPIX	NAS CM	Open End	US Equity Large Cap Growth (Growth)	C+	C	B	Down	Y	15,000
ProFunds NASDAQ-100 Fund Service Class	OTPSX	NAS CM	Open End	US Equity Large Cap Growth (Growth)	C+	C	B-	Down	Y	15,000
ProFunds Oil Equipment Service & Distribution Investor Cls	OEPIX	NAS CM	Open End	Energy Sector Equity (Utility)	D-	E+	D	Down	Y	15,000
ProFunds Oil Equipment Service & Distribution Service Cls	OEPSX	NAS CM	Open End	Energy Sector Equity (Utility)	D-	E+	D	Down	Y	15,000
ProFunds Pharmaceuticals UltraSector Fund Investor Class	PHPIX	NAS CM	Open End	Trading Tools (Health)	D+	D	D+	Down	Y	15,000
ProFunds Pharmaceuticals UltraSector Fund Service Class	PHPSX	NAS CM	Open End	Trading Tools (Health)	D	D	D+	Down	Y	15,000
ProFunds Precious Metals UltraSector Fund Investor Class	PMPIX	NAS CM	Open End	Trading Tools (Precious Metals)	D	D	D+	Down	Y	15,000
ProFunds Precious Metals UltraSector Fund Service Class	PMPSX	NAS CM	Open End	Trading Tools (Precious Metals)	D	D	D	Down	Y	15,000
ProFunds Real Estate UltraSector Fund Investor Class	REPIX	NAS CM	Open End	Trading Tools (Real Estate)	C	C	C		Y	15,000
ProFunds Real Estate UltraSector Fund Service Class	REPSX	NAS CM	Open End	Trading Tools (Real Estate)	C	C	C		Y	15,000
ProFunds Rising Rates Opportunity 10 Fund Investor Class	RTPIX	NAS CM	Open End	Trading Tools (Govt Bond - Treasury)	D+	D	C-	Down	Y	15,000

★ Expanded analysis of this fund is included in Section II.

	TOTAL RETURNS					PERFORMANCE				ASSETS		ASSET ALLOCATION & TURNOVER					BULL & BEAR		FEES		
Min Additional Investment	3-Month Total Return	6-Month Total Return	1-Year Total Return	3-Year Total Return	5-Year Total Return	Dividend Yield (TTM)	Expense Ratio	3-Yr Std Deviation	3-Year Beta	NAV	Total Assets (MIL)	%Cash	%Stocks	%Bonds	%Other	Turnover Ratio	Last Bull Market Total Return	Last Bear Market Total Return	Front End Fee (%)	Back End Fee (%)	Inception Date
	4.10	17.41	6.16	36.64	36.50	1.59	1.34	10.6	0.82	17.48	1,875	2	93	4	0	34	23.26	-18.9			Jan-07
	4.12	17.46	6.24	37.08	37.24	1.73	1.22	10.59	0.82	17.42	1,875	2	93	4	0	34	23.36	-18.88			Jan-07
	1.88	12.98	-0.48	29.40		3.21	0.64	11.15	0.99	10.27	51.7	2	97	0	1	46					Sep-15
	1.80	12.88	-0.60	28.34		3.22	0.75	11.17	0.99	10.16	51.7	2	97	0	1	46					Sep-15
50	1.76	17.42	-5.64	41.09	28.39	0	1.35	16.95	1.17	15.03	45.6	3	97	0	0	20	24.02	-20.3	5.00		Oct-10
	1.79	17.56	-5.44	42.08	30.01	0	1.1	16.92	1.17	15.33	45.6	3	97	0	0	20	24.21	-20.22			May-10
100	6.33	19.31	6.87	16.13	18.48	0	2.26	12.46	0.84	10.75	45.6	-17	107	0	10	2,238	32.73	-17.53	5.75		Jan-14
100	5.98	18.72	5.99	13.54	13.96	0	3.06	12.48	0.84	10.27	45.6	-17	107	0	10	2,238	32.16	-17.79			Jan-14
100	6.23	19.38	6.98	16.94	19.76	0	2.07	12.48	0.84	10.9	45.6	-17	107	0	10	2,238	32.93	-17.45			Dec-13
	9.53	25.34	-3.48	90.14	65.86	1.23	1.54	33.39		47.58	9.0	22	76	0	1	293	56.57	-46.07			Sep-01
	9.27	24.71	-4.43	84.53	57.67	0	2.54	33.37		44.4	9.0	22	76	0	1	293	55.17	-46.21			Sep-01
	5.63	20.79	-7.60	38.98	9.90	0	1.63	23.26		65.47	4.2	25	75	0	0	460	36.28	-45.73			Sep-01
	5.37	20.21	-8.51	34.92	4.60	0	2.63	23.26		58.41	4.2	25	75	0	0	460	35.5	-45.98			Sep-01
	-3.75	-15.80	-8.94	-34.37	-44.57	0	1.59	12.1		28.71	21.2	100	0	0	0	1,297	-22.61	14.81			Dec-97
	-3.97	-16.20	-9.83	-36.33	-47.31	0	2.59	12.09		26.58	21.2	100	0	0	0	1,297	-23.03	14.37			Dec-97
	-4.09	9.86	-2.19	30.69	29.13	0	1.43	30.5		55.48	169.9	19	81	0	0	11	45.79	-16.7			Jun-00
	-4.34	9.30	-3.15	26.85	22.84	0	2.43	30.49		43.11	169.9	19	81	0	0	11	44.93	-17.04			Jun-00
	3.81	18.45	8.40	42.61	51.39	0	1.44	12.18	1	134.28	75.4	47	53	0	0	26	23.65	-17.06			Dec-97
	3.55	17.87	7.32	38.42	44.02	0	2.44	12.17	1	111.18	75.4	47	53	0	0	26	22.91	-17.37			Dec-97
	2.80	22.54	4.47	13.86	39.93	1.34	1.78	17.5		103.02	4.4	25	74	0	1	155	27.87	-13.61			Jan-04
	2.55	21.93	3.46	10.54	33.16	0.3	2.78	17.49		93.79	4.4	25	74	0	1	155	27.12	-14			Jan-04
	9.74	33.59	16.61	81.41	120.38	0	1.52	21.55		138.32	48.0	24	75	0	0	35	44.32	-19.69			Jan-04
	9.47	32.92	15.46	76.07	109.64	0	2.52	21.54		118.93	48.0	24	75	0	0	35	43.46	-20.02			Jan-04
	0.70	14.27	0.30	30.85	1.22	11.02	1.78	12.1		12.81	5.4	1	99	0	0	540	14.34	-27.69			Mar-99
	0.42	13.70	-0.65	26.84	-3.67	6.11	2.78	12.04		14.02	5.4	1	99	0	0	540	13.76	-28.02			Mar-99
	9.52	29.47	9.52	76.30	81.22	0	1.66	20.62		24.03	36.3	23	76	0	1	360	47.67	-37.37			Jun-00
	9.29	28.84	8.42	71.21	72.51	0	2.66	20.62		20.46	36.3	23	76	0	1	360	47.25	-37.79			Jun-00
	6.08	37.87	13.50	72.65	81.01	0	1.63	23.48		116.31	10.4	26	74	0	0	240	45.36	-35.63			Jan-04
	5.81	37.17	12.37	67.53	72.19	0	2.63	23.46		101.62	10.4	26	74	0	0	240	44.55	-35.91			Jan-04
	4.23	36.02	2.17	159.59	222.73	0	1.42	25.34		97.23	236.3	25	74	0	0	69	37.54	-32.94			Jun-00
	3.97	35.33	1.14	151.94	206.98	0	2.42	25.32		75.34	236.3	25	74	0	0	69	36.75	-33.23			Jun-00
	4.07	20.29	10.01	54.53	68.51	0	1.57	12.46	1	95.02	36.0	0	100	0	0	380	22.78	-13.7			Oct-02
	3.81	19.70	8.93	49.97	60.35	0	2.57	12.45	1	79.77	36.0	0	100	0	0	380	22.08	-14.08			Oct-02
	3.55	16.70	7.06	30.60	34.37	0	1.78	12.96	1	65.46	11.8	0	100	0	0	788	24.44	-20.07			Oct-02
	3.30	16.13	6.03	26.76	27.83	0	2.78	12.94	1	58.53	11.8	0	100	0	0	788	23.69	-20.38			Oct-02
	2.46	17.95	-0.66	31.27	34.67	0.06	1.54	15.12	1	86.53	12.3	41	59	0	0	21	26.27	-23.26			Sep-01
	2.20	17.36	-1.63	27.40	28.09	0	2.54	15.1	1	71.7	12.3	41	59	0	0	21	25.58	-23.62			Sep-01
	3.10	19.40	0.29	34.30	40.91	0	1.57	14.5	1	92.99	16.4	0	100	0	0	384	24.25	-21.6			Sep-01
	2.85	18.82	-0.69	30.34	34.00	0	2.57	14.48	1	77.44	16.4	0	100	0	0	384	23.57	-21.92			Sep-01
	2.05	16.75	-0.96	28.79	28.15	0.14	1.78	16.1	0.99	72.94	5.7	0	100	0	0	312	28.72	-24.71			Sep-01
	1.80	16.21	-1.93	25.00	21.77	0	2.78	16.08	0.99	59.71	5.7	0	100	0	0	312	27.95	-25.01			Sep-01
	3.65	21.41	8.07	71.50	91.28	0	1.44	15.08	1	75.18	91.2	45	55	0	0	3	26.44	-11.43			Aug-00
	3.41	20.80	7.00	66.40	81.87	0	2.44	15.07	1	61.54	91.2	45	55	0	0	3	25.69	-11.79			Aug-00
	-20.97	7.21	-56.00	-57.27	-83.44	2.37	1.6	44.33		5.35	5.2	29	71	0	0	316	38.36	-47.08			Jun-06
	-21.13	7.00	-56.35	-58.43	-84.23	0.05	2.6	44.43		4.89	5.2	29	71	0	0	316	37.6	-47.32			Jun-06
	-3.22	12.41	0.00	-1.18	17.32	0.18	1.78	22.4		22.19	5.1	20	79	0	1	192	26.72	-8.43			Jun-00
	-3.50	11.81	-1.03	-4.15	11.54	0	2.78	22.38		19.3	5.1	20	79	0	1	192	25.91	-8.84			Jun-00
	19.73	35.02	15.26	-28.15	-43.38	0	1.52	39.31		40.17	17.9	29	71	0	0	192	-16.97	-26.62			Jun-02
	19.39	34.29	14.07	-30.28	-46.13	0	2.52	39.3		34.85	17.9	29	71	0	0	192	-17.45	-26.94			Jun-02
	1.81	28.02	14.95	19.84	55.63	1.62	1.78	18.65		50.41	57.5	21	73	0	6	374	44	-26.39			Jun-00
	1.54	27.36	13.78	16.31	48.00	0.13	2.78	18.62		48.18	57.5	21	73	0	6	374	43.19	-26.71			Jun-00
	-3.47	-6.22	-7.75	-1.53	-17.29	0	1.73	5.37		14.15	3.1	100	0	0	0	1,297	-3.03	-13.83			Jan-05

	MARKET		FUND TYPE, CATEGORY & OBJECTIVE		RATINGS				MINIMUMS	
Fund Name	Ticker Symbol	Traded On	Fund Type	Category and (Prospectus Objective)	Overall Rating	Reward Rating	Risk Rating	Recent Up/ Downgrade	Open to New Investors	Min Initial Investment
ProFunds Rising Rates Opportunity 10 Fund Service Class	RTPSX	NAS CM	Open End	Trading Tools (Govt Bond - Treasury)	D+	D	C-		Y	15,000
ProFunds Rising Rates Opportunity Fund Investor Class	RRPIX	NAS CM	Open End	Trading Tools (Govt Bond - Treasury)	D	D	D	Down	Y	15,000
ProFunds Rising Rates Opportunity Fund Service Class	RRPSX	NAS CM	Open End	Trading Tools (Govt Bond - Treasury)	D	D	D	Down	Y	15,000
ProFunds Semiconductor UltraSector Fund Investor Class	SMPIX	NAS CM	Open End	Trading Tools (Technology)	C	C	C		Y	15,000
ProFunds Semiconductor UltraSector Fund Service Class	SMPSX	NAS CM	Open End	Trading Tools (Technology)	C	C	C		Y	15,000
ProFunds Short NASDAQ-100 Fund Investor Class	SOPIX	NAS CM	Open End	Alternative Miscellaneous (Growth)	D	D-	D		Y	15,000
ProFunds Short NASDAQ-100 Fund Service Class	SOPSX	NAS CM	Open End	Alternative Miscellaneous (Growth)	D	D-	D		Y	15,000
ProFunds Short Oil & Gas Fund Investor Class	SNPIX	NAS CM	Open End	Trading Tools (Natl Res)	C-	D+	D+		Y	15,000
ProFunds Short Oil & Gas Fund Service Class	SNPSX	NAS CM	Open End	Trading Tools (Natl Res)	C-	D+	D+		Y	15,000
ProFunds Short Precious Metals Fund Investor Class	SPPIX	NAS CM	Open End	Trading Tools (Precious Metals)	D	D	D		Y	15,000
ProFunds Short Precious Metals Fund Service Class	SPPSX	NAS CM	Open End	Trading Tools (Precious Metals)	D	D	D		Y	15,000
ProFunds Short Real Estate Fund Investor Class	SRPIX	NAS CM	Open End	Trading Tools (Real Estate)	D	D	D		Y	15,000
ProFunds Short Real Estate Fund Service Class	SRPSX	NAS CM	Open End	Trading Tools (Real Estate)	D	D	D		Y	15,000
ProFunds Short Small Cap Fund Investor Class	SHPIX	NAS CM	Open End	Alternative Miscellaneous (Small Company)	D+	D	D	Up	Y	15,000
ProFunds Short Small Cap Fund Service Class	SHPSX	NAS CM	Open End	Alternative Miscellaneous (Small Company)	D	D	D		Y	15,000
ProFunds Small Cap Fund Investor Class	SLPIX	NAS CM	Open End	US Equity Small Cap (Small Company)	C	C-	C+		Y	15,000
ProFunds Small Cap Fund Service Class	SLPSX	NAS CM	Open End	US Equity Small Cap (Small Company)	C	C-	C+		Y	15,000
ProFunds Small Cap Growth Fund Investor Class	SGPIX	NAS CM	Open End	US Equity Small Cap (Small Company)	C	C	C+	Down	Y	15,000
ProFunds Small Cap Growth Fund Service Class	SGPSX	NAS CM	Open End	US Equity Small Cap (Small Company)	C	C	C+		Y	15,000
ProFunds Small Cap Value Fund Investor Class	SVPIX	NAS CM	Open End	US Equity Small Cap (Small Company)	C-	C-	C	Down	Y	15,000
ProFunds Small Cap Value Fund Services Class	SVPSX	NAS CM	Open End	US Equity Small Cap (Small Company)	C-	C-	C	Down	Y	15,000
ProFunds Technology UltraSector Fund Investor Class	TEPIX	NAS CM	Open End	Trading Tools (Technology)	C+	C+	C	Down	Y	15,000
ProFunds Technology UltraSector Fund Service Class	TEPSX	NAS CM	Open End	Trading Tools (Technology)	C+	C+	C	Down	Y	15,000
ProFunds Telecommunications UltraSector Investor Cls	TCPIX	NAS CM	Open End	Trading Tools (Comm)	C-	D+	C-	Down	Y	15,000
ProFunds Telecommunications UltraSector Fund Service Class	TCPSX	NAS CM	Open End	Trading Tools (Comm)	D+	D+	C-	Down	Y	15,000
ProFunds U.S. Government Plus Fund Investor Class	GVPIX	NAS CM	Open End	Trading Tools (Govt Bond - Treasury)	C	C	C	Up	Y	15,000
ProFunds U.S. Government Plus Fund Service Class	GVPSX	NAS CM	Open End	Trading Tools (Govt Bond - Treasury)	C	C	C	Up	Y	15,000
ProFunds Ultra Dow 30 Fund Investor Class	UDPIX	NAS CM	Open End	Trading Tools (Growth)	C+	C+	C		Y	15,000
ProFunds Ultra Dow 30 Fund Service Class	UDPSX	NAS CM	Open End	Trading Tools (Growth)	C+	C+	C	Up	Y	15,000
ProFunds Ultra International Fund Investor Class	UNPIX	NAS CM	Open End	Trading Tools (Growth)	C-	C-	C-		Y	15,000
ProFunds Ultra International Fund Service Class	UNPSX	NAS CM	Open End	Trading Tools (Growth)	C-	C-	C-		Y	15,000
ProFunds UltraBear Fund Investor Class	URPIX	NAS CM	Open End	Alternative Miscellaneous (Growth)	D	D-	D		Y	15,000
ProFunds UltraBear Fund Service Class	URPSX	NAS CM	Open End	Alternative Miscellaneous (Growth)	D	D-	D		Y	15,000
ProFunds UltraBull Fund Investor Class	ULPIX	NAS CM	Open End	Trading Tools (Growth & Income)	C	C+	C		Y	15,000
ProFunds UltraBull Fund Service Class	ULPSX	NAS CM	Open End	Trading Tools (Growth & Income)	C	C+	C		Y	15,000
ProFunds UltraChina Fund Investor Class	UGPIX	NAS CM	Open End	Trading Tools (Foreign Stock)	D+	D+	D+	Down	Y	15,000
ProFunds UltraChina Fund Service Class	UGPSX	NAS CM	Open End	Trading Tools (Foreign Stock)	D+	D+	D+	Down	Y	15,000
ProFunds UltraEmerging Markets Fund Investor Class	UUPIX	NAS CM	Open End	Trading Tools (Growth)	C-	C-	D+	Down	Y	15,000
ProFunds UltraEmerging Markets Fund Service Class	UUPSX	NAS CM	Open End	Trading Tools (Growth)	C-	C-	D+	Down	Y	15,000
ProFunds UltraJapan Fund Investor Class	UJPIX	NAS CM	Open End	Trading Tools (Pacific Stock)	C-	C-	C-		Y	15,000
ProFunds UltraJapan Fund Service Class	UJPSX	NAS CM	Open End	Trading Tools (Pacific Stock)	C-	C-	C-		Y	15,000
ProFunds UltraLatin America Fund Investor Class	UBPIX	NAS CM	Open End	Trading Tools (Growth)	D+	D+	D+	Down	Y	15,000
ProFunds UltraLatin America Fund Service Class	UBPSX	NAS CM	Open End	Trading Tools (Growth)	D+	D+	D+	Down	Y	15,000
ProFunds UltraMid Cap Fund Investor Class	UMPIX	NAS CM	Open End	Trading Tools (Growth)	C	C	C-		Y	15,000
ProFunds UltraMid Cap Fund Service Class	UMPSX	NAS CM	Open End	Trading Tools (Growth)	C	C	C-		Y	15,000
ProFunds UltraNASDAQ-100 Fund Investor Class	UOPIX	NAS CM	Open End	Trading Tools (Growth)	C	B-	C	Down	Y	15,000
ProFunds UltraNASDAQ-100 Fund Service Class	UOPSX	NAS CM	Open End	Trading Tools (Growth)	C	C+	C-		Y	15,000
ProFunds UltraSector Health Care Fund Investor Class	HCPIX	NAS CM	Open End	Trading Tools (Health)	C+	C	B-	Down	Y	15,000
ProFunds UltraSector Health Care Fund Service Class	HCPSX	NAS CM	Open End	Trading Tools (Health)	C	C	C+	Down	Y	15,000
ProFunds UltraSector Oil & Gas Fund Investor Class	ENPIX	NAS CM	Open End	Trading Tools (Natl Res)	D	D	D	Down	Y	15,000
ProFunds UltraSector Oil & Gas Fund Service Class	ENPSX	NAS CM	Open End	Trading Tools (Natl Res)	D	D	D	Down	Y	15,000
ProFunds UltraShort China Fund Investor Class	UHPIX	NAS CM	Open End	Alternative Miscellaneous (Foreign Stock)	D+	D	D	Up	Y	15,000

★ Expanded analysis of this fund is included in Section II.

Min Additional Investment	TOTAL RETURNS 3-Month Total Return	6-Month Total Return	1-Year Total Return	3-Year Total Return	5-Year Total Return	PERFORMANCE Dividend Yield (TTM)	Expense Ratio	3-Yr Std Deviation	3-Year Beta	ASSETS NAV	Total Assets (MIL)	ASSET ALLOCATION & TURNOVER %Cash	%Stocks	%Bonds	%Other	Turnover Ratio	BULL & BEAR Last Bull Market Total Return	Last Bear Market Total Return	FEES Front End Fee (%)	Back End Fee (%)	Inception Date
	-3.71	-6.70	-8.63	-4.41	-21.30	0	2.73	5.43		13.22	3.1	100	0	0	0	1,297	-3.64	-14.14			Jan-05
	-7.15	-12.61	-12.73	-5.25	-37.67	0	1.5	13.91		35.55	20.7	100	0	0	0	1,297	-2.32	-33.22			May-02
	-7.40	-13.00	-13.60	-7.97	-40.68	0	2.5	13.85		31.51	20.7	100	0	0	0	1,297	-2.67	-33.5			May-02
	0.44	31.43	0.67	139.23	170.20	0.96	1.44	32.94		42.94	36.7	29	71	0	0	56	34.05	-29.9			Jun-00
	0.18	30.79	-0.33	132.16	156.93	0	2.44	32.9		33.34	36.7	29	71	0	0	56	33.48	-30.17			Jun-00
	-3.93	-18.49	-10.75	-47.57	-59.74	0	1.78	14.71		8.55	4.2	99	0	0	1	1,297	-24.75	7.15			May-02
	-4.22	-18.92	-11.68	-49.07	-61.56	0	2.78	14.67		7.71	4.2	99	0	0	1	1,297	-25.3	6.59			May-02
	3.50	-11.80	15.39	-7.83	10.28	0	1.78	20.93		45.79	1.8	97	0	0	3	166	-22.43	26.76			Sep-05
	3.26	-12.22	14.31	-10.55	4.66	0	2.78	20.95		43.29	1.8	97	0	0	3	166	-22.79	26.19			Sep-05
	-12.89	-20.76	-17.41	-14.86	-43.88	0	1.78	26.13		33.85	7.4	100	0	0	0		3.2	15.31			Jan-06
	-13.13	-21.16	-18.24	-17.50	-46.79	0	2.78	26.19		33.33	7.4	100	0	0	0		2.72	14.85			Jan-06
	-1.57	-15.74	-10.99	-20.30	-40.97	0	1.78	11.92		13.11	0.70	100	0	0	0	1,298	-26.19	13.86			Sep-05
	-1.83	-16.08	-11.86	-22.66	-43.74	0	2.78	11.92		11.74	0.70	100	0	0	0	1,298	-26.62	13.43			Sep-05
	-2.00	-15.35	2.09	-35.05	-40.48	0	1.78	17.14		13.17	4.1	100	0	0	0		-26.94	24.17			May-02
	-2.31	-15.81	1.03	-37.05	-43.41	0	2.78	17.13		12.67	4.1	100	0	0	0		-27.32	23.85			May-02
	1.26	16.88	-5.25	35.09	27.70	0	1.56	17.26	1.01	84.72	10.0	43	57	0	0	63	26.62	-25.23			Sep-01
	1.01	16.33	-6.18	31.23	21.61	0	2.56	17.25	1.01	70.88	10.0	43	57	0	0	63	25.94	-25.56			Sep-01
	2.01	13.36	-4.08	42.22	46.45	0	1.55	17.48	1	88.41	11.3	0	100	0	0	629	26.57	-21.98			Sep-01
	1.76	12.78	-5.03	37.97	39.23	0	2.55	17.48	1	72.15	11.3	0	100	0	0	629	25.8	-22.31			Sep-01
	0.80	13.37	-8.64	29.86	27.15	0	1.57	18.57	1	77.55	8.2	0	100	0	0	447	30.03	-23.22			Sep-01
	0.58	12.85	-9.52	26.07	21.03	0	2.57	18.56	1	63.83	8.2	0	100	0	0	447	29.22	-23.53			Sep-01
	5.19	37.42	13.04	148.01	170.93	0	1.49	24.51		139.38	75.7	20	77	0	3	174	42.92	-20.66			Jun-00
	4.92	36.74	11.92	140.67	157.74	0	2.49	24.48		116.7	75.7	20	77	0	3	174	42.12	-20.99			Jun-00
	-1.48	19.73	5.79	-13.82	10.88	2.44	1.78	23.54		21.3	9.8	32	68	0	0	818	23.04	-15.32			Jun-00
	-1.72	19.15	4.78	-16.36	5.42	0.38	2.78	23.55		20.53	9.8	32	68	0	0	818	22.32	-15.69			Jun-00
	7.59	14.20	14.08	-1.59	31.77	1	1.35	14.04		60.06	30.4	64	0	36	0	714	-3.15	41.98			May-02
	7.31	13.60	12.91	-4.57	25.40	0.14	2.35	14.02		55.35	30.4	64	0	36	0	714	-3.68	41.44			May-02
	4.84	31.85	17.20	120.35	143.80	0.72	1.48	25.01		139.29	29.7	24	76	0	0	59	46.18	-28.5			Jun-02
	4.58	31.19	16.03	113.91	132.02	0	2.48	25		121.95	29.7	24	76	0	0	59	45.27	-28.82			Jun-02
	4.77	25.79	-5.36	39.63	-12.35	0	1.62	22.05		16.24	3.0	100	0	0	0	1,297	22.83	-46.54			Apr-06
	4.46	25.17	-6.26	35.44	-16.64	0	2.62	22.04		14.52	3.0	100	0	0	0	1,297	22	-46.74			Apr-06
	-7.60	-29.68	-19.60	-58.65	-70.67	0	1.78	23.91		19.68	12.7	100	0	0	0	1,297	-41.15	28.05			Dec-97
	-7.86	-30.04	-20.41	-59.79	-72.02	0	2.78	23.88		17.93	12.7	100	0	0	0	1,297	-41.51	27.68			Dec-97
	7.03	38.28	13.47	93.71	114.20	0.09	1.4	24.43		66.31	93.2	37	63	0	0	174	50.57	-33.14			Nov-97
	6.78	37.60	12.36	88.02	103.82	0	2.4	24.44		55.07	93.2	37	63	0	0	174	49.75	-33.41			Nov-97
	-16.81	20.11	-34.76	46.79	-1.66	0	1.51	42.7		12.12	24.3	10	90	0	0	312	27.07	-54.07			Feb-08
	-17.02	19.58	-35.45	42.35	-6.43	0	2.51	42.65		10.87	24.3	10	90	0	0	312	26.33	-54.23			Feb-08
	-6.50	18.09	-8.22	54.09	-7.90	0.54	1.52	34.1		53.2	9.3	14	86	0	0	125	26.53	-45.74			Apr-06
	-6.74	17.47	-9.15	49.31	-12.45	0	2.52	34.06		49.2	9.3	14	86	0	0	125	25.87	-45.99			Apr-06
	-0.45	14.23	-8.85	72.11	56.58	0	1.66	30.22		21.67	14.4	31	69	0	0	1,297	17.8	-27.36			Feb-00
	-0.69	13.71	-9.73	67.09	49.36	0	2.66	30.19		18.49	14.4	31	69	0	0	1,297	16.88	-27.65			Feb-00
	2.81	14.03	23.59	48.55	-50.16	1.41	1.53	46.24		33.55	29.3	13	87	0	0	315	41.19	-47.46			Oct-07
	2.56	13.45	22.37	44.16	-52.59	0	2.53	46.2		32.38	29.3	13	87	0	0	315	40.3	-47.66			Oct-07
	4.34	37.21	-4.34	63.33	67.42	0.02	1.43	30.19		43.51	71.1	37	63	0	0	28	55.63	-43.32			Feb-00
	4.05	36.40	-5.35	58.47	59.21	0	2.43	30.17		35.67	71.1	37	63	0	0	28	54.7	-43.57			Feb-00
	6.59	44.87	10.27	168.74	225.14	0	1.41	30.66		75.48	450.9	42	58	0	0	3	58.29	-23.31			Dec-97
	6.33	44.13	9.18	160.79	209.25	0	2.41	30.63		61.27	450.9	42	58	0	0	3	57.45	-23.63			Dec-97
	0.70	13.67	13.93	49.30	81.90	0.03	1.56	20.85		63.03	20.5	24	75	0	1	151	30.76	-16.67			Jun-00
	0.45	13.09	12.85	44.95	73.13	0	2.56	20.84		52.51	20.5	24	75	0	1	151	30.06	-17.02			Jun-00
	-6.44	17.21	-25.72	-12.82	-52.28	1.51	1.56	30.76		30.36	12.7	29	71	0	0	152	31.39	-37.72			Jun-00
	-6.67	16.62	-26.47	-15.36	-54.59	0.32	2.56	30.75		26.02	12.7	29	71	0	0	152	30.64	-37.99			Jun-00
	13.07	-26.90	13.13	-64.47	-71.56	0	1.78	43.6		44.88	5.5	100	0	0	0		-38.28	72.51			Feb-08

	MARKET			FUND TYPE, CATEGORY & OBJECTIVE	RATINGS				MINIMUMS	
Fund Name	Ticker Symbol	Traded On	Fund Type	Category and (Prospectus Objective)	Overall Rating	Reward Rating	Risk Rating	Recent Up/ Downgrade	Open to New Investors	Min Initial Investment
ProFunds UltraShort China Fund Service Class	UHPSX	NAS CM	Open End	Alternative Miscellaneous (Foreign Stock)	D+	D	D	Up	Y	15,000
ProFunds UltraShort Dow 30 Fund Investor Class	UWPIX	NAS CM	Open End	Alternative Miscellaneous (Growth)	D	D-	D-		Y	15,000
ProFunds UltraShort Dow 30 Fund Service Class	UWPSX	NAS CM	Open End	Alternative Miscellaneous (Growth)	D	D-	D-		Y	15,000
ProFunds UltraShort Emerging Market Fund Investor Class	UVPIX	NAS CM	Open End	Alternative Miscellaneous (Growth)	D	D	D		Y	15,000
ProFunds UltraShort Emerging Market Fund Service Class	UVPSX	NAS CM	Open End	Alternative Miscellaneous (Growth)	D	D	D		Y	15,000
ProFunds UltraShort International Fund Investor Class	UXPIX	NAS CM	Open End	Alternative Miscellaneous (Growth)	D+	D	D		Y	15,000
ProFunds UltraShort International Fund Service Class	UXPSX	NAS CM	Open End	Alternative Miscellaneous (Growth)	D+	D	D		Y	15,000
ProFunds UltraShort Japan Fund Investor Class	UKPIX	NAS CM	Open End	Alternative Miscellaneous (Growth)	D	D-	D		Y	15,000
ProFunds UltraShort Japan Fund Service Class	UKPSX	NAS CM	Open End	Alternative Miscellaneous (Growth)	D	D-	D		Y	15,000
ProFunds UltraShort Latin America Fund Investor Class	UFPIX	NAS CM	Open End	Alternative Miscellaneous (Growth)	D	D-	D		Y	15,000
ProFunds UltraShort Latin America Fund Service Class	UFPSX	NAS CM	Open End	Alternative Miscellaneous (Growth)	D	D-	D		Y	15,000
ProFunds UltraShort Mid-Cap Fund Investor Class	UIPIX	NAS CM	Open End	Alternative Miscellaneous (Growth)	D	D-	D		Y	15,000
ProFunds UltraShort Mid-Cap Fund Service Class	UIPSX	NAS CM	Open End	Alternative Miscellaneous (Growth)	D	D-	D		Y	15,000
ProFunds UltraShort NASDAQ-100 Fund Investor Class	USPIX	NAS CM	Open End	Alternative Miscellaneous (Growth)	D	E+	D		Y	15,000
ProFunds UltraShort NASDAQ-100 Fund Service Class	USPSX	NAS CM	Open End	Alternative Miscellaneous (Growth)	D	E+	D		Y	15,000
ProFunds UltraShort Small-Cap Fund Investor Class	UCPIX	NAS CM	Open End	Alternative Miscellaneous (Small Company)	D	D-	D		Y	15,000
ProFunds UltraShort Small-Cap Fund Service Class	UCPSX	NAS CM	Open End	Alternative Miscellaneous (Small Company)	D	D-	D		Y	15,000
ProFunds UltraSmall Cap Fund Investor Class	UAPIX	NAS CM	Open End	Trading Tools (Small Company)	C-	C-	D+		Y	15,000
ProFunds UltraSmall Cap Fund Service Class	UAPSX	NAS CM	Open End	Trading Tools (Small Company)	C-	C-	D+		Y	15,000
ProFunds Utilities UltraSector Fund Investor Class	UTPIX	NAS CM	Open End	Trading Tools (Utility)	B	B	C+	Up	Y	15,000
ProFunds Utilities UltraSector Fund Service Class	UTPSX	NAS CM	Open End	Trading Tools (Utility)	B	B	C+	Up	Y	15,000
Prospector Capital Appreciation Fund	PCAFX	NAS CM	Open End	Aggressive Alloc (Growth)	B	C+	B+		Y	10,000
Prospector Opportunity Fund	POPFX	NAS CM	Open End	US Equity Mid Cap (Growth)	B	C+	B+	Up	Y	10,000
Provident Trust Strategy Fund	PROVX	NAS CM	Open End	US Equity Large Cap Growth (Growth)	B-	C+	B	Down	Y	1,000
Prudential Day One 2010 Fund Class R1	PDBDX	NAS CM	Open End	Target Date (Asset Alloc)	C+	C	B	Up	Y	0
Prudential Day One 2010 Fund Class R2	PDBEX	NAS CM	Open End	Target Date (Asset Alloc)	C+	C	B	Up	Y	2,500
Prudential Day One 2010 Fund Class R3	PDBFX	NAS CM	Open End	Target Date (Asset Alloc)	C+	C	B	Up	Y	0
Prudential Day One 2010 Fund Class R4	PDBGX	NAS CM	Open End	Target Date (Asset Alloc)	C+	C	B	Up	Y	0
Prudential Day One 2010 Fund Class R5	PDBHX	NAS CM	Open End	Target Date (Asset Alloc)	C+	C	B	Up	Y	2,500
Prudential Day One 2010 Fund Class R6	PDBJX	NAS CM	Open End	Target Date (Asset Alloc)	C+	C	B	Up	Y	0
Prudential Day One 2015 Fund Class R1	PDCDX	NAS CM	Open End	Target Date (Asset Alloc)	C+	C	B	Up	Y	0
Prudential Day One 2015 Fund Class R2	PDCEX	NAS CM	Open End	Target Date (Asset Alloc)	C+	C	B	Up	Y	2,500
Prudential Day One 2015 Fund Class R3	PDCFX	NAS CM	Open End	Target Date (Asset Alloc)	C+	C	B	Up	Y	0
Prudential Day One 2015 Fund Class R4	PDCGX	NAS CM	Open End	Target Date (Asset Alloc)	C+	C	B	Up	Y	0
Prudential Day One 2015 Fund Class R5	PDCHX	NAS CM	Open End	Target Date (Asset Alloc)	C+	C	B	Up	Y	2,500
Prudential Day One 2015 Fund Class R6	PDCJX	NAS CM	Open End	Target Date (Asset Alloc)	C+	C	B	Up	Y	0
Prudential Day One 2020 Fund Class R1	PDDDX	NAS CM	Open End	Target Date (Asset Alloc)	C+	C	B	Up	Y	0
Prudential Day One 2020 Fund Class R2	PDDEX	NAS CM	Open End	Target Date (Asset Alloc)	C+	C	B	Up	Y	2,500
Prudential Day One 2020 Fund Class R3	PDDFX	NAS CM	Open End	Target Date (Asset Alloc)	C+	C	B	Up	Y	0
Prudential Day One 2020 Fund Class R4	PDDGX	NAS CM	Open End	Target Date (Asset Alloc)	C+	C	B	Up	Y	0
Prudential Day One 2020 Fund Class R5	PDDHX	NAS CM	Open End	Target Date (Asset Alloc)	C+	C	B	Up	Y	2,500
Prudential Day One 2020 Fund Class R6	PDDJX	NAS CM	Open End	Target Date (Asset Alloc)	C+	C	B	Up	Y	0
Prudential Day One 2025 Fund Class R1	PDEDX	NAS CM	Open End	Target Date (Asset Alloc)	C+	C	B	Up	Y	0
Prudential Day One 2025 Fund Class R2	PDEEX	NAS CM	Open End	Target Date (Asset Alloc)	C+	C	B	Up	Y	2,500
Prudential Day One 2025 Fund Class R3	PDEFX	NAS CM	Open End	Target Date (Asset Alloc)	C+	C	B	Up	Y	0
Prudential Day One 2025 Fund Class R4	PDEGX	NAS CM	Open End	Target Date (Asset Alloc)	C+	C	B	Up	Y	0
Prudential Day One 2025 Fund Class R5	PDEHX	NAS CM	Open End	Target Date (Asset Alloc)	C+	C	B	Up	Y	2,500
Prudential Day One 2025 Fund Class R6	PDEJX	NAS CM	Open End	Target Date (Asset Alloc)	C+	C	B	Up	Y	0
Prudential Day One 2030 Fund Class R1	PDFCX	NAS CM	Open End	Target Date (Asset Alloc)	C+	C	B	Up	Y	0
Prudential Day One 2030 Fund Class R2	PDFEX	NAS CM	Open End	Target Date (Asset Alloc)	C+	C	B	Up	Y	2,500
Prudential Day One 2030 Fund Class R3	PDFFX	NAS CM	Open End	Target Date (Asset Alloc)	C+	C	B	Up	Y	0
Prudential Day One 2030 Fund Class R4	PDFGX	NAS CM	Open End	Target Date (Asset Alloc)	C+	C	B	Up	Y	0

★ Expanded analysis of this fund is included in Section II.

Min Additional Investment	3-Month Total Return	6-Month Total Return	1-Year Total Return	3-Year Total Return	5-Year Total Return	Dividend Yield (TTM)	Expense Ratio	3-Yr Std Deviation	3-Year Beta	NAV	Total Assets (MIL)	%Cash	%Stocks	%Bonds	%Other	Turnover Ratio	Last Bull Market Total Return	Last Bear Market Total Return	Front End Fee (%)	Back End Fee (%)	Inception Date
	TOTAL RETURNS					PERFORMANCE				ASSETS		ASSET ALLOCATION & TURNOVER					BULL & BEAR		FEES		
	12.81	-27.27	12.06	-65.52	-72.94	0	2.78	43.53		40.13	5.5	100	0	0	0		-38.81	71.97			Feb-08
	-5.78	-26.34	-22.11	-64.20	-74.73	0	1.78	23.93		15.32	4.1	100	0	0	0	181	-37.85	23.52			Jul-04
	-6.00	-26.73	-22.92	-65.25	-76.02	0	2.78	23.94		13.62	4.1	100	0	0	0	181	-38.27	23.1			Jul-04
	3.53	-21.00	-8.06	-58.44	-56.54	0	1.78	32.39		18.47	3.3	100	0	0	1	125	-35.05	51.78			Apr-06
	3.29	-21.40	-8.92	-59.64	-58.60	0	2.78	32.35		16.93	3.3	100	0	0	1	125	-35.41	51.35			Apr-06
	-6.11	-23.46	-4.18	-46.27	-42.23	0	1.78	22.04		13.05	2.5	100	0	0	0		-33.46	47.18			Apr-06
	-6.32	-23.85	-5.05	-47.81	-45.00	0	2.78	22.03		11.84	2.5	100	0	0	0		-33.81	46.53			Apr-06
	-1.76	-16.91	-3.61	-60.14	-75.23	0	1.78	30.64		32.76	1.0	100	0	0	0		-24.42	21.65			Mar-06
	-2.07	-17.34	-4.58	-61.32	-76.43	0	2.78	30.63		29.78	1.0	100	0	0	0		-24.83	21.2			Mar-06
	-6.59	-21.71	-38.77	-69.79	-59.71	0	1.78	43.39		26.49	3.3	100	0	0	0		-42.23	55.55			Oct-07
	-6.74	-22.06	-39.39	-70.71	-61.67	0	2.78	43.37		23.63	3.3	100	0	0	0		-42.59	55.39			Oct-07
	-6.11	-30.08	-5.54	-52.88	-65.48	0	1.78	30.62		20.26	1.9	100	0	0	0		-45.83	43.66			Jan-04
	-6.35	-30.45	-6.49	-54.33	-67.27	0	2.78	30.67		18.13	1.9	100	0	0	0		-46.07	43.63			Jan-04
	-8.47	-34.67	-23.28	-74.23	-84.52	0	1.61	29.11		13.28	16.8	99	0	0	1	1,297	-43.86	12.96			Jun-98
	-8.58	-34.92	-23.92	-74.94	-85.23	0	2.61	29.12		12.78	16.8	99	0	0	1	1,297	-44.17	12.45			Jun-98
	-4.94	-29.41	0.74	-59.88	-67.17	0	1.78	34.31		31.13	14.6	99	0	0	1	1,297	-49.27	47.55			Jan-04
	-5.19	-29.78	-0.27	-61.07	-68.84	0	2.78	34.24		29.21	14.6	99	0	0	1	1,297	-49.43	46.52			Jan-04
	2.07	33.86	-13.98	72.05	47.67	0.08	1.49	34.41		57.44	52.4	75	25	0	0	29	53.14	-47.47			Feb-00
	1.86	33.23	-14.84	66.86	40.37	0	2.49	34.38		47.5	52.4	75	25	0	0	29	52.34	-47.71			Feb-00
	3.92	20.32	23.09	32.67	76.09	0.55	1.69	16.01		54.53	27.6	25	74	0	2	314	12.43	0.1			Jul-00
	3.66	19.77	21.96	28.78	67.51	0	2.69	16.02		51.25	27.6	25	74	0	2	314	11.83	-0.31			Jul-00
1,000	4.79	17.26	11.06	37.27	36.83	0.59	1.31	9.59	0.74	19.02	28.5	5	76	2	0	28	9.41	-16.13			Sep-07
1,000	8.10	20.19	11.32	45.31	60.21	0.81	1.31	11.56	0.6	22.02	132.3	4	96	0	0	39	18.32	-15.58			Sep-07
100	2.55	14.46	6.27	57.58	71.53	0.28	1.01	10.69	0.83	15.67	179.4	22	78	0	0	2	19.29	-15.63			Dec-86
	2.49	9.07	4.87			2.35	1.15			10.7	5.7	15	29	55	1	53					Dec-16
100	2.48	9.17	5.04			2.6	0.9			10.71	5.7	15	29	55	1	53					Dec-16
	2.58	9.27	5.30			2.74	0.75			10.72	5.7	15	29	55	1	53					Dec-16
	2.58	9.27	5.31			2.84	0.65			10.72	5.7	15	29	55	1	53					Dec-16
100	2.58	9.37	5.42			2.93	0.55			10.73	5.7	15	29	55	1	53					Dec-16
	2.67	9.47	5.59			3.08	0.4			10.74	5.7	15	29	55	1	53					Dec-16
	2.54	9.56	4.64			2.08	1.15			10.88	11.1	15	33	51	1	57					Dec-16
100	2.54	9.66	4.82			2.32	0.9			10.89	11.1	15	33	51	1	57					Dec-16
	2.63	9.76	5.08			2.46	0.75			10.9	11.1	15	33	51	1	57					Dec-16
	2.63	9.87	5.19			2.56	0.65			10.9	11.1	15	33	51	1	57					Dec-16
100	2.63	9.86	5.20			2.66	0.55			10.91	11.1	15	33	51	1	57					Dec-16
	2.73	9.86	5.37			2.8	0.4			10.91	11.1	15	33	51	1	57					Dec-16
	2.59	10.15	4.77			1.82	1.15			11.06	41.3	14	39	46	1	41					Dec-16
100	2.59	10.36	5.04			2.06	0.9			11.07	41.3	14	39	46	1	41					Dec-16
	2.68	10.45	5.20			2.2	0.75			11.09	41.3	14	39	46	1	41					Dec-16
	2.68	10.44	5.40			2.29	0.65			11.1	41.3	14	39	46	1	41					Dec-16
100	2.68	10.55	5.42			2.39	0.55			11.1	41.3	14	39	46	1	41					Dec-16
	2.78	10.69	5.60			2.54	0.4			11.07	41.3	14	39	46	1	41					Dec-16
	2.68	10.87	4.66			1.82	1.15			11.11	49.3	7	44	48	1	37					Dec-16
100	2.67	10.97	4.94			2.06	0.9			11.12	49.3	7	44	48	1	37					Dec-16
	2.77	11.07	5.01			2.21	0.75			11.13	49.3	7	44	48	1	37					Dec-16
	2.77	11.07	5.12			2.3	0.65			11.13	49.3	7	44	48	1	37					Dec-16
100	2.86	11.17	5.23			2.4	0.55			11.14	49.3	7	44	48	1	37					Dec-16
	2.85	11.26	5.49			2.54	0.4			11.16	49.3	7	44	48	1	37					Dec-16
	2.79	12.41	4.63			1.94	1.15			11.41	44.5	11	58	30	1	36					Dec-16
100	2.88	12.61	4.91			2.18	0.9			11.43	44.5	11	58	30	1	36					Dec-16
	2.97	12.72	5.08			2.33	0.75			11.43	44.5	11	58	30	1	36					Dec-16
	2.97	12.62	5.10			2.42	0.65			11.42	44.5	11	58	30	1	36					Dec-16

	MARKET			FUND TYPE, CATEGORY & OBJECTIVE	RATINGS				MINIMUMS	
Fund Name	Ticker Symbol	Traded On	Fund Type	Category and (Prospectus Objective)	Overall Rating	Reward Rating	Risk Rating	Recent Up/ Downgrade	Open to New Investors	Min Initial Investment
Prudential Day One 2030 Fund Class R5	PDFHX	NAS CM	Open End	Target Date (Asset Alloc)	C+	C	B	Up	Y	2,500
Prudential Day One 2030 Fund Class R6	PDFJX	NAS CM	Open End	Target Date (Asset Alloc)	C+	C	B	Up	Y	0
Prudential Day One 2035 Fund Class R1	PDGCX	NAS CM	Open End	Target Date (Asset Alloc)	C+	C	B	Up	Y	0
Prudential Day One 2035 Fund Class R2	PDGEX	NAS CM	Open End	Target Date (Asset Alloc)	C+	C	B	Up	Y	2,500
Prudential Day One 2035 Fund Class R3	PDGFX	NAS CM	Open End	Target Date (Asset Alloc)	C+	C	B	Up	Y	0
Prudential Day One 2035 Fund Class R4	PDGGX	NAS CM	Open End	Target Date (Asset Alloc)	C+	C	B	Up	Y	0
Prudential Day One 2035 Fund Class R5	PDGHX	NAS CM	Open End	Target Date (Asset Alloc)	C+	C	B	Up	Y	2,500
Prudential Day One 2035 Fund Class R6	PDGJX	NAS CM	Open End	Target Date (Asset Alloc)	C+	C	B	Up	Y	0
Prudential Day One 2040 Fund Class R1	PDHDX	NAS CM	Open End	Target Date (Asset Alloc)	C+	C	B	Up	Y	0
Prudential Day One 2040 Fund Class R2	PDHEX	NAS CM	Open End	Target Date (Asset Alloc)	C+	C	B	Up	Y	2,500
Prudential Day One 2040 Fund Class R3	PDHFX	NAS CM	Open End	Target Date (Asset Alloc)	C+	C	B	Up	Y	0
Prudential Day One 2040 Fund Class R4	PDHGX	NAS CM	Open End	Target Date (Asset Alloc)	C+	C	B	Up	Y	0
Prudential Day One 2040 Fund Class R5	PDHHX	NAS CM	Open End	Target Date (Asset Alloc)	C+	C	B	Up	Y	2,500
Prudential Day One 2040 Fund Class R6	PDHJX	NAS CM	Open End	Target Date (Asset Alloc)	C+	C	B	Up	Y	0
Prudential Day One 2045 Fund Class R1	PDIDX	NAS CM	Open End	Target Date (Asset Alloc)	C+	C	B	Up	Y	0
Prudential Day One 2045 Fund Class R2	PDIEX	NAS CM	Open End	Target Date (Asset Alloc)	C+	C	B	Up	Y	2,500
Prudential Day One 2045 Fund Class R3	PDIKX	NAS CM	Open End	Target Date (Asset Alloc)	C+	C	B	Up	Y	0
Prudential Day One 2045 Fund Class R4	PDIGX	NAS CM	Open End	Target Date (Asset Alloc)	C+	C	B	Up	Y	0
Prudential Day One 2045 Fund Class R5	PDIHX	NAS CM	Open End	Target Date (Asset Alloc)	C+	C	B	Up	Y	2,500
Prudential Day One 2045 Fund Class R6	PDIJX	NAS CM	Open End	Target Date (Asset Alloc)	C+	C	B	Up	Y	0
Prudential Day One 2050 Fund Class R1	PDJDX	NAS CM	Open End	Target Date (Asset Alloc)	C+	C	B	Up	Y	0
Prudential Day One 2050 Fund Class R2	PDJEX	NAS CM	Open End	Target Date (Asset Alloc)	C+	C	B	Up	Y	2,500
Prudential Day One 2050 Fund Class R3	PDJFX	NAS CM	Open End	Target Date (Asset Alloc)	C+	C	B	Up	Y	0
Prudential Day One 2050 Fund Class R4	PDJGX	NAS CM	Open End	Target Date (Asset Alloc)	C+	C	B	Up	Y	0
Prudential Day One 2050 Fund Class R5	PDJHX	NAS CM	Open End	Target Date (Asset Alloc)	C+	C	B	Up	Y	2,500
Prudential Day One 2050 Fund Class R6	PDJJX	NAS CM	Open End	Target Date (Asset Alloc)	C+	C	B	Up	Y	0
Prudential Day One 2055 Fund Class R1	PDKDX	NAS CM	Open End	Target Date (Asset Alloc)	C+	C	B	Up	Y	0
Prudential Day One 2055 Fund Class R2	PDKEX	NAS CM	Open End	Target Date (Asset Alloc)	C+	C	B	Up	Y	2,500
Prudential Day One 2055 Fund Class R3	PDKFX	NAS CM	Open End	Target Date (Asset Alloc)	C+	C	B	Up	Y	0
Prudential Day One 2055 Fund Class R4	PDKGX	NAS CM	Open End	Target Date (Asset Alloc)	C+	C	B	Up	Y	0
Prudential Day One 2055 Fund Class R5	PDKHX	NAS CM	Open End	Target Date (Asset Alloc)	C+	C	B	Up	Y	2,500
Prudential Day One 2055 Fund Class R6	PDKJX	NAS CM	Open End	Target Date (Asset Alloc)	C+	C	B	Up	Y	0
Prudential Day One 2060 Fund Class R1	PDLDX	NAS CM	Open End	Target Date (Asset Alloc)	C+	C	B	Up	Y	0
Prudential Day One 2060 Fund Class R2	PDLEX	NAS CM	Open End	Target Date (Asset Alloc)	C+	C	B	Up	Y	2,500
Prudential Day One 2060 Fund Class R3	PDLFX	NAS CM	Open End	Target Date (Asset Alloc)	C+	C	B	Up	Y	0
Prudential Day One 2060 Fund Class R4	PDLGX	NAS CM	Open End	Target Date (Asset Alloc)	C+	C	B	Up	Y	0
Prudential Day One 2060 Fund Class R5	PDLHX	NAS CM	Open End	Target Date (Asset Alloc)	C+	C	B	Up	Y	2,500
Prudential Day One 2060 Fund Class R6	PDLJX	NAS CM	Open End	Target Date (Asset Alloc)	C+	C	B	Up	Y	0
Prudential Day One Income Fund Class R1	PDADX	NAS CM	Open End	Target Date (Asset Alloc)	C+	C	B	Up	Y	0
Prudential Day One Income Fund Class R2	PDAEX	NAS CM	Open End	Target Date (Asset Alloc)	C+	C	B	Up	Y	2,500
Prudential Day One Income Fund Class R3	PDAFX	NAS CM	Open End	Target Date (Asset Alloc)	C+	C	B	Up	Y	0
Prudential Day One Income Fund Class R4	PDAGX	NAS CM	Open End	Target Date (Asset Alloc)	C+	C	B	Up	Y	0
Prudential Day One Income Fund Class R5	PDAHX	NAS CM	Open End	Target Date (Asset Alloc)	C+	C	B	Up	Y	2,500
Prudential Day One Income Fund Class R6	PDAJX	NAS CM	Open End	Target Date (Asset Alloc)	C+	C	B	Up	Y	0
PSG Tactical Growth Fund	PSGTX	NAS CM	Open End	Moderate Alloc (Growth & Income)	C+	C	B	Up	Y	2,500
PSI All Asset Fund Class A Shares	FXMAX	NAS CM	Open End	Long/Short Equity (Growth & Income)	D+	D	D+	Up	Y	2,500
PSI Strategic Growth Fund Class A Shares	FXSAX	NAS CM	Open End	Moderate Alloc (Growth)	C	C	C+	Up	Y	2,500
PSI Tactical Growth Fund Class A Shares	FXTAX	NAS CM	Open End	Moderate Alloc (Growth & Income)	C+	C	B	Up	Y	2,500
Putnam Capital Spectrum Fund Class A	PVSAX	NAS CM	Open End	Aggressive Alloc (Growth & Income)	D	D	D+	Down	Y	0
Putnam Capital Spectrum Fund Class B	PVSBX	NAS CM	Open End	Aggressive Alloc (Growth & Income)	D	D	D+		Y	0
Putnam Capital Spectrum Fund Class C	PVSCX	NAS CM	Open End	Aggressive Alloc (Growth & Income)	D	D	D+		Y	0
Putnam Capital Spectrum Fund Class M	PVSMX	NAS CM	Open End	Aggressive Alloc (Growth & Income)	D	D	D+		Y	0

★ Expanded analysis of this fund is included in Section II.

	TOTAL RETURNS					PERFORMANCE				ASSETS		ASSET ALLOCATION & TURNOVER					BULL & BEAR		FEES		
Min Additional Investment	3-Month Total Return	6-Month Total Return	1-Year Total Return	3-Year Total Return	5-Year Total Return	Dividend Yield (TTM)	Expense Ratio	3-Yr Std Deviation	3-Year Beta	NAV	Total Assets (MIL)	%Cash	%Stocks	%Bonds	%Other	Turnover Ratio	Last Bull Market Total Return	Last Bear Market Total Return	Front End Fee (%)	Back End Fee (%)	Inception Date
100	2.97	12.81	5.31			2.52	0.55			11.44	44.5	11	58	30	1	36					Dec-16
	3.05	12.90	5.47			2.66	0.4			11.46	44.5	11	58	30	1	36					Dec-16
	2.89	13.80	4.24			1.99	1.15			11.38	31.4	8	69	22	1	28					Dec-16
100	2.98	14.01	4.53			2.23	0.9			11.39	31.4	8	69	22	1	28					Dec-16
	2.97	14.09	4.70			2.37	0.75			11.41	31.4	8	69	22	1	28					Dec-16
	3.06	14.19	4.91			2.47	0.65			11.42	31.4	8	69	22	1	28					Dec-16
100	3.07	14.21	4.93			2.57	0.55			11.41	31.4	8	69	22	1	28					Dec-16
	3.06	14.31	5.01			2.72	0.4			11.42	31.4	8	69	22	1	28					Dec-16
	2.93	14.52	4.39			2.08	1.15			11.59	27.4	7	75	17	1	27					Dec-16
100	3.01	14.62	4.59			2.32	0.9			11.6	27.4	7	75	17	1	27					Dec-16
	3.01	14.72	4.76			2.46	0.75			11.61	27.4	7	75	17	1	27					Dec-16
	3.01	14.70	4.87			2.56	0.65			11.62	27.4	7	75	17	1	27					Dec-16
100	3.01	14.82	4.90			2.66	0.55			11.62	27.4	7	75	17	1	27					Dec-16
	3.10	14.92	5.07			2.8	0.4			11.63	27.4	7	75	17	1	27					Dec-16
	2.96	15.06	4.04			2.07	1.15			11.46	17.4	5	81	13	1	33					Dec-16
100	2.96	15.16	4.25			2.32	0.9			11.47	17.4	5	81	13	1	33					Dec-16
	3.05	15.37	4.44			2.47	0.75			11.48	17.4	5	81	13	1	33					Dec-16
	3.05	15.37	4.56			2.56	0.65			11.48	17.4	5	81	13	1	33					Dec-16
100	3.04	15.36	4.67			2.66	0.55			11.49	17.4	5	81	13	1	33					Dec-16
	3.13	15.44	4.76			2.8	0.4			11.51	17.4	5	81	13	1	33					Dec-16
	2.93	15.33	3.96			2.06	1.15			11.58	10.4	5	84	10	1	56					Dec-16
100	2.93	15.45	4.18			2.31	0.9			11.58	10.4	5	84	10	1	56					Dec-16
	2.93	15.55	4.27			2.45	0.75			11.59	10.4	5	84	10	1	56					Dec-16
	3.02	15.56	4.30			2.55	0.65			11.58	10.4	5	84	10	1	56					Dec-16
100	3.01	15.65	4.51			2.65	0.55			11.6	10.4	5	84	10	1	56					Dec-16
	3.01	15.73	4.59			2.79	0.4			11.62	10.4	5	84	10	1	56					Dec-16
	2.85	15.53	3.45			2.04	1.15			11.53	7.5	6	88	6	1	29					Dec-16
100	2.85	15.63	3.67			2.29	0.9			11.54	7.5	6	88	6	1	29					Dec-16
	2.94	15.73	3.94			2.43	0.75			11.55	7.5	6	88	6	1	29					Dec-16
	2.84	15.73	3.88			2.53	0.65			11.55	7.5	6	88	6	1	29					Dec-16
100	2.93	15.83	4.09			2.63	0.55			11.56	7.5	6	88	6	1	29					Dec-16
	2.93	15.94	4.19			2.78	0.4			11.56	7.5	6	88	6	1	29					Dec-16
	2.83	15.72	3.22			2.14	1.15			11.63	2.1	6	89	4	1	90					Dec-16
100	2.82	15.93	3.44			2.39	0.9			11.64	2.1	6	89	4	1	90					Dec-16
	2.82	15.92	3.62			2.54	0.75			11.65	2.1	6	89	4	1	90					Dec-16
	2.82	15.91	3.74			2.64	0.65			11.65	2.1	6	89	4	1	90					Dec-16
100	2.91	16.02	3.86			2.74	0.55			11.66	2.1	6	89	4	1	90					Dec-16
	3.00	16.13	4.05			2.88	0.4			11.66	2.1	6	89	4	1	90					Dec-16
	2.42	8.84	4.76			2.25	1.15			10.7	10.1	16	28	55	1	22					Dec-16
100	2.49	8.96	5.02			2.5	0.9			10.7	10.1	16	28	55	1	22					Dec-16
	2.53	9.14	5.17			2.64	0.75			10.71	10.1	16	28	55	1	22					Dec-16
	2.55	9.18	5.27			2.73	0.65			10.71	10.1	16	28	55	1	22					Dec-16
100	2.68	9.23	5.39			2.84	0.55			10.71	10.1	16	28	55	1	22					Dec-16
	2.61	9.30	5.53			2.97	0.4			10.72	10.1	16	28	55	1	22					Dec-16
250	2.77	12.72	4.12	10.89	-7.91	0.79	2.33	7.68	2.75	10.01	21.1	44	35	9	0	44					Apr-12
500	1.22	9.39	-10.24	-5.21	-14.26	0	2.21	9.85	0.57	7.45	12.9	-10	101	8	0		-2.22	-7.58	5.75		Aug-10
500	2.76	13.28	10.40	11.54	0.85	0	2.41	14.25	0.95	10.4	21.3	-7	107	0	0	6,067	11.34	-18.58	5.75		Aug-10
500	-0.95	8.13	0.87	12.03	0.56	3.42	2.46	7.91	0.54	9.3	13.6	33	27	29	10	5,702	6.17	-13.73	5.75		Aug-10
	6.00	18.05	-7.17	1.02	-8.44	0	0.66	14.36		30.53	752.4	9	71	11	0	35	26.04	-14.18	5.75	1.00	May-09
	5.76	17.60	-7.87	-1.25	-11.84	0	1.41	14.36		28.79	752.4	9	71	11	0	35	25.48	-14.43		5.00	May-09
	5.81	17.64	-7.85	-1.22	-11.81	0	1.41	14.36		28.73	752.4	9	71	11	0	35	25.47	-14.43		1.00	May-09
	5.83	17.75	-7.66	-0.50	-10.71	0	1.16	14.36		29.38	752.4	9	71	11	0	35	25.66	-14.35	3.50		May-09

Fund Name	MARKET Ticker Symbol	Traded On	FUND TYPE, CATEGORY & OBJECTIVE Fund Type	Category and (Prospectus Objective)	RATINGS Overall Rating	Reward Rating	Risk Rating	Recent Up/ Downgrade	MINIMUMS Open to New Investors	Min Initial Investment
Putnam Capital Spectrum Fund Class R	PVSRX	NAS CM	Open End	Aggressive Alloc (Growth & Income)	D	D	D+		Y	0
Putnam Capital Spectrum Fund Class Y	PVSYX	NAS CM	Open End	Aggressive Alloc (Growth & Income)	D	D	D+	Down	Y	0
Putnam Convertible Securities Fund Class A	PCONX	NAS CM	Open End	Convertibles (Growth & Income)	B	C+	B+		Y	0
Putnam Convertible Securities Fund Class B	PCNBX	NAS CM	Open End	Convertibles (Growth & Income)	B-	C	B+	Down	Y	0
Putnam Convertible Securities Fund Class C	PRCCX	NAS CM	Open End	Convertibles (Growth & Income)	B-	C	B+	Down	Y	0
Putnam Convertible Securities Fund Class M	PCNMX	NAS CM	Open End	Convertibles (Growth & Income)	B-	C+	B+	Down	Y	0
Putnam Convertible Securities Fund Class R	PCVRX	NAS CM	Open End	Convertibles (Growth & Income)	B-	C+	B+	Down	Y	0
Putnam Convertible Securities Fund Class R6 Shares	PCNTX	NAS CM	Open End	Convertibles (Growth & Income)	B	C+	B+		Y	0
Putnam Convertible Securities Fund Class Y	PCGYX	NAS CM	Open End	Convertibles (Growth & Income)	B	C+	B+		Y	0
Putnam Dynamic Asset Allocation Balanced Fund Class A	PABAX	NAS CM	Open End	Moderate Alloc (Asset Alloc)	B-	C	B+	Up	Y	0
Putnam Dynamic Asset Allocation Balanced Fund Class B	PABBX	NAS CM	Open End	Moderate Alloc (Asset Alloc)	B-	C	B+	Up	Y	0
Putnam Dynamic Asset Allocation Balanced Fund Class C	AABCX	NAS CM	Open End	Moderate Alloc (Asset Alloc)	B-	C	B+	Up	Y	0
Putnam Dynamic Asset Allocation Balanced Fund Class M	PABMX	NAS CM	Open End	Moderate Alloc (Asset Alloc)	B-	C	B+	Up	Y	0
Putnam Dynamic Asset Allocation Balanced Fund Class P			Open End	Moderate Alloc (Asset Alloc)	B-	C	B+	Up		0
Putnam Dynamic Asset Allocation Balanced Fund Class R	PAARX	NAS CM	Open End	Moderate Alloc (Asset Alloc)	B-	C	B+	Up	Y	0
Putnam Dynamic Asset Allocation Balanced Fund Class R5	PAADX	NAS CM	Open End	Moderate Alloc (Asset Alloc)	B-	C	B+	Up	Y	0
Putnam Dynamic Asset Allocation Balanced Fund Class R6	PAAEX	NAS CM	Open End	Moderate Alloc (Asset Alloc)	B-	C	B+	Up	Y	0
Putnam Dynamic Asset Allocation Balanced Fund Class Y	PABYX	NAS CM	Open End	Moderate Alloc (Asset Alloc)	B-	C	B+	Up	Y	0
Putnam Dynamic Asset Allocation Conservative Fund Class A	PACAX	NAS CM	Open End	Cautious Alloc (Asset Alloc)	B-	C	B+		Y	0
Putnam Dynamic Asset Allocation Conservative Fund Class B	PACBX	NAS CM	Open End	Cautious Alloc (Asset Alloc)	B-	C	B+	Up	Y	0
Putnam Dynamic Asset Allocation Conservative Fund Class C	PACCX	NAS CM	Open End	Cautious Alloc (Asset Alloc)	B-	C	B+	Up	Y	0
Putnam Dynamic Asset Allocation Conservative Fund Class M	PACMX	NAS CM	Open End	Cautious Alloc (Asset Alloc)	B-	C	B+	Up	Y	0
Putnam Dynamic Asset Allocation Conservative Fund Class P			Open End	Cautious Alloc (Asset Alloc)	B-	C	B+			0
Putnam Dynamic Asset Allocation Conservative Fund Class R	PACRX	NAS CM	Open End	Cautious Alloc (Asset Alloc)	B-	C	B+	Up	Y	0
Putnam Dynamic Asset Allocation Conservative Fund Class R5	PACDX	NAS CM	Open End	Cautious Alloc (Asset Alloc)	B	C	A-	Up	Y	0
Putnam Dynamic Asset Allocation Conservative Fund Class R6	PCCEX	NAS CM	Open End	Cautious Alloc (Asset Alloc)	B	C+	A-	Up	Y	0
Putnam Dynamic Asset Allocation Conservative Fund Class Y	PACYX	NAS CM	Open End	Cautious Alloc (Asset Alloc)	B-	C	A-		Y	0
Putnam Dynamic Asset Allocation Equity Fund Class A			Open End	US Equity Large Cap Blend (Asset Alloc)	C+	C	B	Up	Y	0
Putnam Dynamic Asset Allocation Equity Fund Class P			Open End	US Equity Large Cap Blend (Asset Alloc)	C+	C	B	Up		0
Putnam Dynamic Asset Allocation Growth Fund Class A	PAEAX	NAS CM	Open End	Aggressive Alloc (Asset Alloc)	B-	C	B	Up	Y	0
Putnam Dynamic Asset Allocation Growth Fund Class B	PAEBX	NAS CM	Open End	Aggressive Alloc (Asset Alloc)	C+	C	B	Up	Y	0
Putnam Dynamic Asset Allocation Growth Fund Class C	PAECX	NAS CM	Open End	Aggressive Alloc (Asset Alloc)	C+	C	B	Up	Y	0
Putnam Dynamic Asset Allocation Growth Fund Class M	PAGMX	NAS CM	Open End	Aggressive Alloc (Asset Alloc)	C+	C	B	Up	Y	0
Putnam Dynamic Asset Allocation Growth Fund Class P			Open End	Aggressive Alloc (Asset Alloc)	B-	C	B	Up		0
Putnam Dynamic Asset Allocation Growth Fund Class R	PASRX	NAS CM	Open End	Aggressive Alloc (Asset Alloc)	B-	C	B	Up	Y	0
Putnam Dynamic Asset Allocation Growth Fund Class R5	PADEX	NAS CM	Open End	Aggressive Alloc (Asset Alloc)	B-	C	B	Up	Y	0
Putnam Dynamic Asset Allocation Growth Fund Class R6	PAEEX	NAS CM	Open End	Aggressive Alloc (Asset Alloc)	B-	C	B	Up	Y	0
Putnam Dynamic Asset Allocation Growth Fund Class Y	PAGYX	NAS CM	Open End	Aggressive Alloc (Asset Alloc)	B-	C	B	Up	Y	0
Putnam Dynamic Risk Allocation Fund Class A	PDREX	NAS CM	Open End	Cautious Alloc (Growth & Income)	C+	C	B	Up	Y	0
Putnam Dynamic Risk Allocation Fund Class B	PDRBX	NAS CM	Open End	Cautious Alloc (Growth & Income)	C	C-	B		Y	0
Putnam Dynamic Risk Allocation Fund Class C	PDRFX	NAS CM	Open End	Cautious Alloc (Growth & Income)	C	C-	B		Y	0
Putnam Dynamic Risk Allocation Fund Class M	PDRTX	NAS CM	Open End	Cautious Alloc (Growth & Income)	C	C-	B		Y	0
Putnam Dynamic Risk Allocation Fund Class R	PDRRX	NAS CM	Open End	Cautious Alloc (Growth & Income)	C+	C-	B	Up	Y	0
Putnam Dynamic Risk Allocation Fund Class R6	PDRGX	NAS CM	Open End	Cautious Alloc (Growth & Income)	C+	C	B+	Up	Y	0
Putnam Dynamic Risk Allocation Fund Class Y	PDRYX	NAS CM	Open End	Cautious Alloc (Growth & Income)	C+	C	B	Up	Y	0
Putnam Emerging Markets Equity Fund Class A	PEMMX	NAS CM	Open End	Global Emerg Mkts (Div Emerging Mkts)	C	C	C+		Y	0
Putnam Emerging Markets Equity Fund Class B	PEMBX	NAS CM	Open End	Global Emerg Mkts (Div Emerging Mkts)	C	C	C+		Y	0
Putnam Emerging Markets Equity Fund Class C	PEMZX	NAS CM	Open End	Global Emerg Mkts (Div Emerging Mkts)	C	C	C+		Y	0
Putnam Emerging Markets Equity Fund Class M	PEMAX	NAS CM	Open End	Global Emerg Mkts (Div Emerging Mkts)	C	C	C+		Y	0
Putnam Emerging Markets Equity Fund Class R	PEMLX	NAS CM	Open End	Global Emerg Mkts (Div Emerging Mkts)	C	C	C+		Y	0
Putnam Emerging Markets Equity Fund Class R6 Shares	PEMQX	NAS CM	Open End	Global Emerg Mkts (Div Emerging Mkts)	C	C	C+		Y	0
Putnam Emerging Markets Equity Fund Class Y	PEMYX	NAS CM	Open End	Global Emerg Mkts (Div Emerging Mkts)	C	C	C+		Y	0

★ Expanded analysis of this fund is included in Section II.

	TOTAL RETURNS					PERFORMANCE				ASSETS		ASSET ALLOCATION & TURNOVER					BULL & BEAR		FEES		
Min Additional Investment	3-Month Total Return	6-Month Total Return	1-Year Total Return	3-Year Total Return	5-Year Total Return	Dividend Yield (TTM)	Expense Ratio	3-Yr Std Deviation	3-Year Beta	NAV	Total Assets (MIL)	%Cash	%Stocks	%Bonds	%Other	Turnover Ratio	Last Bull Market Total Return	Last Bear Market Total Return	Front End Fee (%)	Back End Fee (%)	Inception Date
	5.90	17.91	-7.41	0.23	-9.60	0	0.91	14.36		29.95	752.4	9	71	11	0	35	25.81	-14.23			May-09
	6.05	18.19	-6.96	1.76	-7.28	0	0.41	14.37		30.99	752.4	9	71	11	0	35	26.21	-14.09			May-09
	4.82	17.87	9.11	41.69	33.50	1.74	1.05	8.97	1.03	25.13	732.1	3	7	0	0	68	12.34	-16	5.75	1.00	Jun-72
	4.59	17.42	8.26	38.50	28.59	1.04	1.8	8.95	1.03	24.56	732.1	3	7	0	0	68	11.77	-16.26		5.00	Jul-93
	4.60	17.42	8.31	38.51	28.57	1.07	1.8	8.94	1.03	24.81	732.1	3	7	0	0	68	11.84	-16.27		1.00	Jul-99
	4.66	17.56	8.57	39.56	30.21	1.3	1.55	8.95	1.03	24.83	732.1	3	7	0	0	68	11.93	-16.14	3.50		Mar-95
	4.77	17.77	8.83	40.66	31.84	1.51	1.3	8.95	1.03	25.01	732.1	3	7	0	0	68	12.19	-16.12			Dec-03
	4.90	18.07	9.47	42.23	34.00	2.04	0.72	8.96	1.03	25.12	732.1	3	7	0	0	68	12.34	-16			May-18
	4.88	18.03	9.39	42.76	35.20	1.96	0.8	8.97	1.03	25.11	732.1	3	7	0	0	68	12.49	-15.93			Dec-98
	2.73	12.89	4.34	27.59	32.57	1.71	0.97	8.2	0.64	14.54	2,787	-4	62	42	0	129	16.93	-13.77	5.75		Feb-94
	2.54	12.43	3.53	24.81	27.75	0.97	1.72	8.21	0.64	14.48	2,787	-4	62	42	0	129	16.36	-14.02		5.00	Feb-94
	2.55	12.39	3.54	24.75	27.67	1.05	1.72	8.19	0.64	14.1	2,787	-4	62	42	0	129	16.32	-13.96		1.00	Sep-94
	2.61	12.55	3.81	25.74	29.34	1.23	1.47	8.21	0.64	14.51	2,787	-4	62	42	0	129	16.48	-13.94	3.50		Feb-95
	2.83	13.07	4.74	28.50	33.51	2.09	0.58	8.17	0.64	14.58	2,787	-4	62	42	0	129	16.93	-13.77			Aug-16
	2.62	12.63	4.05	26.61	30.87	1.49	1.22	8.2	0.64	14.4	2,787	-4	62	42	0	129	16.69	-13.81			Jan-03
	2.79	13.00	4.59	28.58	34.30	1.95	0.72	8.21	0.64	14.57	2,787	-4	62	42	0	129	16.93	-13.77			Jul-12
	2.82	13.06	4.70	28.89	34.98	2.04	0.62	8.18	0.64	14.57	2,787	-4	62	42	0	129	16.93	-13.77			Jul-12
	2.80	13.00	4.59	28.58	34.26	1.95	0.72	8.19	0.64	14.57	2,787	-4	62	42	0	129	17.06	-13.65			Jul-94
	2.64	9.23	4.98	16.57	22.43	1.95	0.99	4.69	0.46	10.71	1,088	-7	32	75	0	166	9.9	-7.04	5.75		Feb-94
	2.47	8.92	4.23	14.02	18.02	1.24	1.74	4.74	0.46	10.62	1,088	-7	32	75	0	166	9.47	-7.28		5.00	Feb-94
	2.39	8.86	4.17	13.90	17.98	1.25	1.74	4.65	0.47	10.56	1,088	-7	32	75	0	166	9.4	-7.29		1.00	Sep-94
	2.55	8.98	4.52	14.81	19.50	1.49	1.49	4.72	0.46	10.58	1,088	-7	32	75	0	166	9.54	-7.19	3.50		Feb-95
	2.74	9.51	5.48	17.30	23.20	2.32	0.6	4.75	0.48	10.75	1,088	-7	32	75	0	166	9.9	-7.04			Aug-16
	2.59	9.12	4.75	15.64	20.94	1.65	1.24	4.7	0.45	11.03	1,088	-7	32	75	0	166	9.74	-7.09			Jan-03
	2.71	9.45	5.26	17.60	24.28	2.21	0.71	4.73	0.46	10.75	1,088	-7	32	75	0	166	9.9	-7.04			Jul-12
	2.72	9.48	5.41	17.82	24.76	2.27	0.64	4.72	0.45	10.76	1,088	-7	32	75	0	166	9.9	-7.04			Jul-12
	2.69	9.32	5.20	17.32	23.93	2.16	0.74	4.69	0.46	10.75	1,088	-7	32	75	0	166	10.03	-6.82			Jul-94
	2.86	16.07	3.67	40.18	41.22	1.15	0.87	12.17	0.95	11.84	85.0	10	90	0	0	50	25.04	-21.59	5.75	1.00	Jan-09
	2.86	16.17	3.88	39.21	40.25	1.39	0.63	12.09	0.95	11.85	85.0	10	90	0	0	50	25.04	-21.59			Aug-16
	2.57	14.86	3.04	34.08	36.32	1.05	1.07	10.59	0.83	15.92	2,872	1	82	16	0	109	21.42	-19.23	5.75		Feb-94
	2.44	14.44	2.29	31.13	31.38	0.17	1.82	10.56	0.83	15.53	2,872	1	82	16	0	109	20.94	-19.57		5.00	Feb-94
	2.41	14.42	2.27	31.12	31.28	0.3	1.82	10.58	0.83	14.83	2,872	1	82	16	0	109	20.9	-19.53		1.00	Sep-94
	2.51	14.64	2.58	32.19	33.07	0.57	1.57	10.58	0.83	15.5	2,872	1	82	16	0	109	21.15	-19.46	3.50		Feb-95
	2.73	15.09	3.48	35.74	38.01	1.44	0.66	10.57	0.83	16.16	2,872	1	82	16	0	109	21.42	-19.23			Aug-16
	2.51	14.71	2.81	33.03	34.65	0.82	1.32	10.55	0.82	15.51	2,872	1	82	16	0	109	21.31	-19.39			Jan-03
	2.67	14.98	3.32	35.21	38.13	1.31	0.8	10.58	0.83	16.11	2,872	1	82	16	0	109	21.42	-19.23			Jul-12
	2.73	15.09	3.50	35.65	38.90	1.41	0.7	10.6	0.83	16.16	2,872	1	82	16	0	109	21.42	-19.23			Jul-12
	2.67	14.97	3.31	35.12	38.05	1.29	0.82	10.57	0.83	16.12	2,872	1	82	16	0	109	21.59	-19.22			Jul-94
	1.98	12.19	-0.35	16.22	10.89	1.43	1.15	7.87		11.32	89.8	-41	46	94	0	312	12.1		5.75		Sep-11
	1.83	11.85	-1.03	13.76	6.82	0.59	1.9	7.83		11.13	89.8	-41	46	94	0	312	11.49			5.00	Sep-11
	1.82	11.83	-1.13	13.68	6.73	0.58	1.9	7.84		11.15	89.8	-41	46	94	0	312	11.51			1.00	Sep-11
	1.89	11.98	-0.81	14.62	8.14	0.94	1.65	7.9		11.31	89.8	-41	46	94	0	312	11.7		3.50		Sep-11
	1.97	12.15	-0.50	15.39	9.50	0.65	1.4	7.84		11.35	89.8	-41	46	94	0	312	11.91				Sep-11
	2.16	12.54	0.13	17.75	13.02	1.89	0.76	7.88		11.29	89.8	-41	46	94	0	312	12.26				Jul-12
	2.07	12.38	-0.13	17.17	12.22	1.71	0.9	7.85		11.34	89.8	-41	46	94	0	312	12.26				Sep-11
	1.91	13.39	-2.07	36.29	16.04	0.08	1.32	14.11	0.98	11.68	151.0	5	95	0	0	172	21.98	-34.33	5.75	1.00	Sep-08
	1.73	12.99	-2.76	33.27	11.71	0	2.07	14.11	0.98	11.13	151.0	5	95	0	0	172	21.58	-34.58		5.00	Sep-08
	1.65	12.94	-2.86	33.19	11.66	0	2.07	14.07	0.98	11.08	151.0	5	95	0	0	172	21.47	-34.56		1.00	Sep-08
	1.79	13.16	-2.55	34.22	13.18	0	1.82	14.06	0.98	11.35	151.0	5	95	0	0	172	21.66	-34.47	3.50		Sep-08
	1.84	13.29	-2.33	35.22	14.47	0	1.57	14.1	0.98	11.59	151.0	5	95	0	0	172	21.85	-34.39			Sep-08
	2.06	13.72	-1.60	37.59	17.74	0.17	0.9	14.07	0.98	11.85	151.0	5	95	0	0	172	22.18	-34.2			May-18
	1.98	13.54	-1.87	37.22	17.42	0.16	1.07	14.07	0.98	11.82	151.0	5	95	0	0	172	22.18	-34.2			Sep-08

	MARKET		FUND TYPE, CATEGORY & OBJECTIVE		RATINGS				MINIMUMS	
Fund Name	Ticker Symbol	Traded On	Fund Type	Category and (Prospectus Objective)	Overall Rating	Reward Rating	Risk Rating	Recent Up/ Downgrade	Open to New Investors	Min Initial Investment
Putnam Equity Income Fund Class A	PEYAX	NAS CM	Open End	US Equity Large Cap Value (Equity-Income)	C+	C	B		Y	0
Putnam Equity Income Fund Class B	PEQNX	NAS CM	Open End	US Equity Large Cap Value (Equity-Income)	C+	C	B	Up	Y	0
Putnam Equity Income Fund Class C	PEQCX	NAS CM	Open End	US Equity Large Cap Value (Equity-Income)	C+	C	B	Up	Y	0
Putnam Equity Income Fund Class M	PEIMX	NAS CM	Open End	US Equity Large Cap Value (Equity-Income)	C+	C	B		Y	0
Putnam Equity Income Fund Class R	PEQRX	NAS CM	Open End	US Equity Large Cap Value (Equity-Income)	C+	C	B		Y	0
Putnam Equity Income Fund Class R5	PEQLX	NAS CM	Open End	US Equity Large Cap Value (Equity-Income)	B-	C	B	Up	Y	0
Putnam Equity Income Fund Class R6	PEQSX	NAS CM	Open End	US Equity Large Cap Value (Equity-Income)	B-	C	B	Up	Y	0
Putnam Equity Income Fund Class Y	PEIYX	NAS CM	Open End	US Equity Large Cap Value (Equity-Income)	B-	C	B	Up	Y	0
Putnam Equity Spectrum Fund Class A	PYSAX	NAS CM	Open End	US Equity Mid Cap (Growth)	D+	D+	C		Y	0
Putnam Equity Spectrum Fund Class B	PYSOX	NAS CM	Open End	US Equity Mid Cap (Growth)	D+	D+	C-		Y	0
Putnam Equity Spectrum Fund Class C	PYSCX	NAS CM	Open End	US Equity Mid Cap (Growth)	D+	D+	C-		Y	0
Putnam Equity Spectrum Fund Class M	PYSMX	NAS CM	Open End	US Equity Mid Cap (Growth)	D+	D+	C-		Y	0
Putnam Equity Spectrum Fund Class R	PYSRX	NAS CM	Open End	US Equity Mid Cap (Growth)	D+	D+	C-		Y	0
Putnam Equity Spectrum Fund Class Y	PYSYX	NAS CM	Open End	US Equity Mid Cap (Growth)	C-	D+	C	Up	Y	0
Putnam Focused Equity Fund Class A	PGIAX	NAS CM	Open End	Industrials Sector Equity (Growth & Income)	C+	C	B-	Down	Y	0
Putnam Focused Equity Fund Class B	PGIVX	NAS CM	Open End	Industrials Sector Equity (Growth & Income)	C+	C	B-	Down	Y	0
Putnam Focused Equity Fund Class C	PGIEX	NAS CM	Open End	Industrials Sector Equity (Growth & Income)	C+	C	B-	Down	Y	0
Putnam Focused Equity Fund Class M	PGIHX	NAS CM	Open End	Industrials Sector Equity (Growth & Income)	C+	C	B-	Down	Y	0
Putnam Focused Equity Fund Class R	PGIOX	NAS CM	Open End	Industrials Sector Equity (Growth & Income)	C+	C	B-	Down	Y	0
Putnam Focused Equity Fund Class R6 Shares	PGWTX	NAS CM	Open End	Industrials Sector Equity (Growth & Income)	C+	C	B-	Down	Y	0
Putnam Focused Equity Fund Class Y	PGILX	NAS CM	Open End	Industrials Sector Equity (Growth & Income)	C+	C	B-	Down	Y	0
Putnam Global Equity Fund Class A	PEQUX	NAS CM	Open End	Global Equity Large Cap (World Stock)	C	C	B-		Y	0
Putnam Global Equity Fund Class B	PEQBX	NAS CM	Open End	Global Equity Large Cap (World Stock)	C	C	B-		Y	0
Putnam Global Equity Fund Class C	PUGCX	NAS CM	Open End	Global Equity Large Cap (World Stock)	C	C	B-		Y	0
Putnam Global Equity Fund Class M	PEQMX	NAS CM	Open End	Global Equity Large Cap (World Stock)	C	C	B-		Y	0
Putnam Global Equity Fund Class R	PGLRX	NAS CM	Open End	Global Equity Large Cap (World Stock)	C	C	B-		Y	0
Putnam Global Equity Fund Class R6	PGLEX	NAS CM	Open End	Global Equity Large Cap (World Stock)	C+	C	B	Up	Y	0
Putnam Global Equity Fund Class Y	PEQYX	NAS CM	Open End	Global Equity Large Cap (World Stock)	C	C	B		Y	0
Putnam Global Health Care Fund Class A	PHSTX	NAS CM	Open End	Healthcare Sector Equity (Health)	B-	C	B		Y	0
Putnam Global Health Care Fund Class B	PHSBX	NAS CM	Open End	Healthcare Sector Equity (Health)	C+	C	B	Down	Y	0
Putnam Global Health Care Fund Class C	PCHSX	NAS CM	Open End	Healthcare Sector Equity (Health)	C+	C	B	Down	Y	0
Putnam Global Health Care Fund Class M	PHLMX	NAS CM	Open End	Healthcare Sector Equity (Health)	C+	C	B	Down	Y	0
Putnam Global Health Care Fund Class R	PHSRX	NAS CM	Open End	Healthcare Sector Equity (Health)	C+	C	B	Down	Y	0
Putnam Global Health Care Fund Class Y	PHSYX	NAS CM	Open End	Healthcare Sector Equity (Health)	B-	C	B		Y	0
Putnam Global Technology Fund Class A	PGTAX	NAS CM	Open End	Technology Sector Equity (Technology)	C+	C+	C+		Y	0
Putnam Global Technology Fund Class B	PGTPX	NAS CM	Open End	Technology Sector Equity (Technology)	C+	C+	C+		Y	0
Putnam Global Technology Fund Class C	PGTDX	NAS CM	Open End	Technology Sector Equity (Technology)	C+	C+	C+		Y	0
Putnam Global Technology Fund Class M	PGTMX	NAS CM	Open End	Technology Sector Equity (Technology)	C+	C+	C+		Y	0
Putnam Global Technology Fund Class R	PGTRX	NAS CM	Open End	Technology Sector Equity (Technology)	C+	C+	C+		Y	0
Putnam Global Technology Fund Class R6 Shares	PTTEX	NAS CM	Open End	Technology Sector Equity (Technology)	C+	C+	C+		Y	0
Putnam Global Technology Fund Class Y	PGTYX	NAS CM	Open End	Technology Sector Equity (Technology)	C+	C+	C+		Y	0
Putnam Growth Opportunities Fund Class A	POGAX	NAS CM	Open End	US Equity Large Cap Growth (Growth)	B	B-	B		Y	0
Putnam Growth Opportunities Fund Class B	POGBX	NAS CM	Open End	US Equity Large Cap Growth (Growth)	B	B-	B		Y	0
Putnam Growth Opportunities Fund Class C	POGCX	NAS CM	Open End	US Equity Large Cap Growth (Growth)	B	B-	B		Y	0
Putnam Growth Opportunities Fund Class M	PGOMX	NAS CM	Open End	US Equity Large Cap Growth (Growth)	B	B-	B		Y	0
Putnam Growth Opportunities Fund Class R	PGORX	NAS CM	Open End	US Equity Large Cap Growth (Growth)	B	B-	B		Y	0
Putnam Growth Opportunities Fund Class R5	PGODX	NAS CM	Open End	US Equity Large Cap Growth (Growth)	B	B-	B		Y	0
Putnam Growth Opportunities Fund Class R6	PGOEX	NAS CM	Open End	US Equity Large Cap Growth (Growth)	B	B-	B		Y	0
Putnam Growth Opportunities Fund Class Y	PGOYX	NAS CM	Open End	US Equity Large Cap Growth (Growth)	B	B-	B		Y	0
Putnam International Capital Opportunities Fund Class A	PNVAX	NAS CM	Open End	Global Equity Mid/Small Cap (Foreign Stock)	C	C	C+		Y	0
Putnam International Capital Opportunities Fund Class B	PVNBX	NAS CM	Open End	Global Equity Mid/Small Cap (Foreign Stock)	C	C	C+		Y	0
Putnam International Capital Opportunities Fund Class C	PUVCX	NAS CM	Open End	Global Equity Mid/Small Cap (Foreign Stock)	C	C	C+		Y	0

★ Expanded analysis of this fund is included in Section II.

Min Additional Investment	TOTAL RETURNS 3-Month Total Return	6-Month Total Return	1-Year Total Return	3-Year Total Return	5-Year Total Return	PERFORMANCE Dividend Yield (TTM)	Expense Ratio	3-Yr Std Deviation	3-Year Beta	ASSETS NAV	Total Assets (MIL)	ASSET ALLOCATION & TURNOVER %Cash	%Stocks	%Bonds	%Other	Turnover Ratio	BULL & BEAR Last Bull Market Total Return	Last Bear Market Total Return	FEES Front End Fee (%)	Back End Fee (%)	Inception Date
	4.15	17.29	6.54	41.11	44.97	1.67	0.91	12.06	0.98	24.48	12,785	3	96	0	0	16	25.6	-19.66	5.75		Jun-77
	3.96	16.80	5.74	37.93	39.59	0.95	1.66	12.04	0.97	24.18	12,785	3	96	0	0	16	25.12	-19.93		5.00	Sep-93
	3.96	16.87	5.77	37.95	39.64	0.98	1.66	12.05	0.98	24.18	12,785	3	96	0	0	16	25.11	-19.93		1.00	Feb-99
	4.04	17.00	6.00	38.97	41.40	1.22	1.41	12.06	0.98	24.14	12,785	3	96	0	0	16	25.21	-19.81	3.50		Dec-94
	4.08	17.13	6.27	39.98	43.12	1.44	1.16	12.06	0.98	24.28	12,785	3	96	0	0	16	25.44	-19.73			Jan-03
	4.22	17.45	6.84	42.23	47.06	1.94	0.65	12.06	0.98	24.49	12,785	3	96	0	0	16	25.6	-19.66			Jul-12
	4.24	17.49	6.92	42.64	47.77	2.02	0.55	12.05	0.97	24.48	12,785	3	96	0	0	16	25.6	-19.66			Jul-12
	4.21	17.43	6.81	42.14	46.77	1.91	0.66	12.05	0.98	24.48	12,785	3	96	0	0	16	25.76	-19.55			Oct-98
	4.78	15.92	-5.84	14.76	-7.43	0	0.39	15.16	0.99	36.54	419.1	18	73	0	0	34	28.73	-14.43	5.75	1.00	May-09
	4.61	15.51	-6.53	12.23	-10.84	0	1.14	15.14	0.99	34.03	419.1	18	73	0	0	34	28.15	-14.68		5.00	May-09
	4.58	15.47	-6.54	12.22	-10.86	0	1.14	15.16	0.99	33.96	419.1	18	73	0	0	34	28.11	-14.65		1.00	May-09
	4.67	15.63	-6.30	13.09	-9.73	0	0.89	15.16	0.99	34.9	419.1	18	73	0	0	34	28.31	-14.58	3.50		May-09
	4.71	15.77	-6.07	13.93	-8.59	0	0.64	15.15	0.99	35.74	419.1	18	73	0	0	34	28.52	-14.51			May-09
	4.86	16.04	-5.61	15.61	-6.27	0	0.14	15.16	0.99	37.32	419.1	18	73	0	0	34	28.92	-14.33			May-09
	3.22	24.45	8.14	44.86	53.19	0.31	1.27	15.26	1.1	21.78	187.3	2	98	0	0	293	27.83	-30.67	5.75	1.00	Dec-08
	3.03	24.00	7.36	41.65	47.57	0.09	2.02	15.23	1.1	20.35	187.3	2	98	0	0	293	27.29	-30.9		5.00	Dec-08
	3.03	23.96	7.35	41.59	47.50	0.1	2.02	15.22	1.1	20.38	187.3	2	98	0	0	293	27.37	-30.94		1.00	Dec-08
	3.11	24.16	7.60	42.70	49.43	0.17	1.77	15.2	1.1	21.17	187.3	2	98	0	0	293	27.56	-30.88	3.50		Dec-08
	3.16	24.33	7.88	43.77	51.27	0.23	1.52	15.23	1.1	21.51	187.3	2	98	0	0	293	27.71	-30.77			Dec-08
	3.31	24.76	8.57	46.20	55.30	0	0.88	15.22	1.1	22.12	187.3	2	98	0	0	293	28.05	-30.58			May-18
	3.27	24.60	8.39	45.95	55.04	0.39	1.02	15.24	1.1	22.08	187.3	2	98	0	0	293	28.05	-30.58			Dec-08
	2.68	17.68	0.88	37.17	24.81	0	1.15	12.09	1.03	16.04	1,005	2	97	0	0	60	23.85	-23.36	5.75		Jul-94
	2.45	17.18	0.14	34.14	20.27	0	1.9	12.08	1.03	14.18	1,005	2	97	0	0	60	23.37	-23.63		5.00	Jul-94
	2.47	17.20	0.13	34.06	20.22	0	1.9	12.04	1.02	14.92	1,005	2	97	0	0	60	23.43	-23.62		1.00	Feb-99
	2.55	17.41	0.39	35.12	21.77	0	1.65	12.05	1.02	15.24	1,005	2	97	0	0	60	23.52	-23.5	3.50		Jul-95
	2.58	17.45	0.63	36.15	23.31	0	1.4	12.08	1.03	15.88	1,005	2	97	0	0	60	23.74	-23.49			Jan-03
	2.76	17.85	1.27	38.82	27.37	0	0.76	12.06	1.03	16.7	1,005	2	97	0	0	60	23.85	-23.36			Jul-12
	2.78	17.85	1.15	38.18	26.46	0	0.9	12.1	1.03	16.63	1,005	2	97	0	0	60	23.96	-23.24			Sep-02
	1.36	13.33	7.50	24.04	38.12	0.06	1.08	13.36	1.03	51.24	1,287	3	97	0	0	49	18.21	-19.36	5.75	1.00	May-82
	1.16	12.89	6.67	21.26	33.01	0	1.83	13.36	1.03	28.63	1,287	3	97	0	0	49	17.67	-19.6		5.00	Mar-93
	1.17	12.90	6.70	21.26	33.01	0	1.83	13.36	1.03	37.1	1,287	3	97	0	0	49	17.67	-19.6		1.00	Jul-99
	1.22	13.04	6.96	22.20	34.71	0	1.58	13.36	1.03	38.92	1,287	3	97	0	0	49	17.84	-19.49	3.50		Jul-95
	1.32	13.22	7.24	23.13	36.42	0	1.33	13.37	1.03	47.53	1,287	3	97	0	0	49	18	-19.42			Jan-03
	1.43	13.49	7.77	25.00	39.88	0.29	0.83	13.37	1.03	55.25	1,287	3	97	0	0	49	18.35	-19.25			Apr-00
	7.41	29.49	3.53	101.19	130.63	0.15	1.15	16.48	0.98	37.54	411.0	1	99	0	0	93	24.54	-15.48	5.75	1.00	Dec-08
	7.17	29.00	2.73	96.63	122.10	0	1.9	16.46	0.98	34.34	411.0	1	99	0	0	93	23.97	-15.73		5.00	Dec-08
	7.18	28.97	2.73	96.70	122.07	0	1.9	16.45	0.98	34.32	411.0	1	99	0	0	93	23.97	-15.67		1.00	Dec-08
	7.26	29.15	2.99	98.16	124.94	0	1.65	16.45	0.98	35.44	411.0	1	99	0	0	93	24.16	-15.63	3.50		Dec-08
	7.34	29.30	3.27	99.70	127.78	0.06	1.4	16.46	0.98	36.53	411.0	1	99	0	0	93	24.35	-15.53			Dec-08
	7.49	29.71	3.91	103.01	133.81	0.31	0.77	16.48	0.98	38.59	411.0	1	99	0	0	93	24.69	-15.35			May-18
	7.47	29.66	3.80	102.74	133.50	0.36	0.9	16.47	0.98	38.51	411.0	1	99	0	0	93	24.69	-15.35			Dec-08
	6.43	25.50	15.78	80.39	89.48	0	0.91	13.23	0.97	37.05	5,747	4	96	0	0	73	28.75	-20.3	5.75		Oct-95
	6.23	25.07	14.94	76.41	82.52	0	1.66	13.24	0.97	30.83	5,747	4	96	0	0	73	28.22	-20.58		5.00	Aug-97
	6.25	25.06	14.95	76.41	82.51	0	1.66	13.22	0.97	31.43	5,747	4	96	0	0	73	28.21	-20.55		1.00	Feb-99
	6.27	25.22	15.20	77.70	84.78	0	1.41	13.24	0.97	33.01	5,747	4	96	0	0	73	28.35	-20.48	3.50		Aug-97
	6.36	25.39	15.52	79.10	87.10	0	1.16	13.23	0.97	35.6	5,747	4	96	0	0	73	28.61	-20.44			Jan-03
	6.50	25.71	16.12	82.01	92.29	0.1	0.63	13.25	0.97	39.11	5,747	4	96	0	0	73	28.75	-20.3			Jul-12
	6.52	25.76	16.24	82.59	93.24	0.32	0.53	13.24	0.97	39	5,747	4	96	0	0	73	28.75	-20.3			Jul-12
	6.50	25.70	16.10	81.78	91.88	0.22	0.66	13.23	0.97	38.78	5,747	4	96	0	0	73	28.94	-20.22			Jul-99
	2.10	12.98	-4.02	29.76	6.88	0	1.37	12.36	0.96	35.94	365.4	3	97	0	0	44	17.42	-27.79	5.75	1.00	Dec-95
	1.91	12.54	-4.73	26.87	2.94	0	2.12	12.34	0.96	35.7	365.4	3	97	0	0	44	16.94	-28.01		5.00	Oct-96
	1.92	12.57	-4.73	26.87	2.94	0	2.12	12.34	0.96	35.46	365.4	3	97	0	0	44	16.93	-28.03		1.00	Jul-99

	MARKET		FUND TYPE, CATEGORY & OBJECTIVE		RATINGS				MINIMUMS	
Fund Name	Ticker Symbol	Traded On	Fund Type	Category and (Prospectus Objective)	Overall Rating	Reward Rating	Risk Rating	Recent Up/ Downgrade	Open to New Investors	Min Initial Investment
Putnam International Capital Opportunities Fund Class M	PIVMX	NAS CM	Open End	Global Equity Mid/Small Cap (Foreign Stock)	C	C	C+		Y	0
Putnam International Capital Opportunities Fund Class R	PICRX	NAS CM	Open End	Global Equity Mid/Small Cap (Foreign Stock)	C	C	C+		Y	0
Putnam International Capital Opportunities Cls R6 Shares	PICOX	NAS CM	Open End	Global Equity Mid/Small Cap (Foreign Stock)	C	C	B-		Y	0
Putnam International Capital Opportunities Fund Class Y	PIVYX	NAS CM	Open End	Global Equity Mid/Small Cap (Foreign Stock)	C	C	B-		Y	0
Putnam International Equity Fund Class A	POVSX	NAS CM	Open End	Global Equity Large Cap (Foreign Stock)	C	C-	C+	Up	Y	0
Putnam International Equity Fund Class B	POVBX	NAS CM	Open End	Global Equity Large Cap (Foreign Stock)	C	C-	C+	Up	Y	0
Putnam International Equity Fund Class C	PIGCX	NAS CM	Open End	Global Equity Large Cap (Foreign Stock)	C	C-	C+	Up	Y	0
Putnam International Equity Fund Class M	POVMX	NAS CM	Open End	Global Equity Large Cap (Foreign Stock)	C	C-	C+	Up	Y	0
Putnam International Equity Fund Class R	PIERX	NAS CM	Open End	Global Equity Large Cap (Foreign Stock)	C	C-	C+	Up	Y	0
Putnam International Equity Fund Class R5	POVDX	NAS CM	Open End	Global Equity Large Cap (Foreign Stock)	C	C-	C+	Up	Y	0
Putnam International Equity Fund Class R6	POVEX	NAS CM	Open End	Global Equity Large Cap (Foreign Stock)	C	C-	C+	Up	Y	0
Putnam International Equity Fund Class Y	POVYX	NAS CM	Open End	Global Equity Large Cap (Foreign Stock)	C	C-	C+	Up	Y	0
Putnam International Growth Fund Class A	PINOX	NAS CM	Open End	Global Equity Large Cap (Growth)	C	C	C+	Up	Y	0
Putnam International Growth Fund Class B	PINWX	NAS CM	Open End	Global Equity Large Cap (Growth)	C	C	C+	Up	Y	0
Putnam International Growth Fund Class C	PIOCX	NAS CM	Open End	Global Equity Large Cap (Growth)	C	C	C+	Up	Y	0
Putnam International Growth Fund Class M	PINMX	NAS CM	Open End	Global Equity Large Cap (Growth)	C	C	C+	Up	Y	0
Putnam International Growth Fund Class R	PNPRX	NAS CM	Open End	Global Equity Large Cap (Growth)	C	C	C+	Up	Y	0
Putnam International Growth Fund Class R6 Shares	PIDRX	NAS CM	Open End	Global Equity Large Cap (Growth)	C	C	C+		Y	0
Putnam International Growth Fund Class Y	PINYX	NAS CM	Open End	Global Equity Large Cap (Growth)	C	C	C+		Y	0
Putnam International Value Fund Class A	PNGAX	NAS CM	Open End	Global Equity Large Cap (Growth)	C	C-	C	Up	Y	0
Putnam International Value Fund Class B	PGNBX	NAS CM	Open End	Global Equity Large Cap (Growth)	C-	D+	C		Y	0
Putnam International Value Fund Class C	PIGRX	NAS CM	Open End	Global Equity Large Cap (Growth)	C-	D+	C		Y	0
Putnam International Value Fund Class M	PIGMX	NAS CM	Open End	Global Equity Large Cap (Growth)	C-	D+	C		Y	0
Putnam International Value Fund Class R	PIIRX	NAS CM	Open End	Global Equity Large Cap (Growth)	C-	D+	C		Y	0
Putnam International Value Fund Class R6	PIGWX	NAS CM	Open End	Global Equity Large Cap (Growth)	C	C-	C	Up	Y	0
Putnam International Value Fund Class Y	PNGYX	NAS CM	Open End	Global Equity Large Cap (Growth)	C	C-	C	Up	Y	0
Putnam Multi-Asset Absolute Return Fund Class A	PDMAX	NAS CM	Open End	Global Macro (Income)	C	C-	B		Y	0
Putnam Multi-Asset Absolute Return Fund Class B	PDMBX	NAS CM	Open End	Global Macro (Income)	C	C-	B-	Up	Y	0
Putnam Multi-Asset Absolute Return Fund Class C	PDMCX	NAS CM	Open End	Global Macro (Income)	C	C-	B-	Up	Y	0
Putnam Multi-Asset Absolute Return Fund Class M	PDMMX	NAS CM	Open End	Global Macro (Income)	C	C-	B-	Up	Y	0
Putnam Multi-Asset Absolute Return Fund Class P			Open End	Global Macro (Income)	C	C-	B			0
Putnam Multi-Asset Absolute Return Fund Class R	PDMRX	NAS CM	Open End	Global Macro (Income)	C	C-	B-		Y	0
Putnam Multi-Asset Absolute Return Fund Class R6	PDMEX	NAS CM	Open End	Global Macro (Income)	C	C-	B		Y	0
Putnam Multi-Asset Absolute Return Fund Class Y	PDMYX	NAS CM	Open End	Global Macro (Income)	C	C-	B		Y	0
Putnam Multi-Cap Core Fund Class A	PMYAX	NAS CM	Open End	US Equity Large Cap Blend (Growth)	C+	C	B		Y	0
Putnam Multi-Cap Core Fund Class B	PMYBX	NAS CM	Open End	US Equity Large Cap Blend (Growth)	C+	C	B	Up	Y	0
Putnam Multi-Cap Core Fund Class C	PMYCX	NAS CM	Open End	US Equity Large Cap Blend (Growth)	C+	C	B	Up	Y	0
Putnam Multi-Cap Core Fund Class M	PMYMX	NAS CM	Open End	US Equity Large Cap Blend (Growth)	C+	C	B	Up	Y	0
Putnam Multi-Cap Core Fund Class R	PMYZX	NAS CM	Open End	US Equity Large Cap Blend (Growth)	C+	C	B	Up	Y	0
Putnam Multi-Cap Core Fund Class R6 Shares	PMYTX	NAS CM	Open End	US Equity Large Cap Blend (Growth)	C+	C	B		Y	0
Putnam Multi-Cap Core Fund Class Y	PMYYX	NAS CM	Open End	US Equity Large Cap Blend (Growth)	C+	C	B		Y	0
Putnam PanAgora Managed Futures Strategy Class A	PPMFX	NAS CM	Open End	Alternative Miscellaneous (Income)	D+	D	C	Up	Y	0
Putnam PanAgora Managed Futures Strategy Class B	PPFMX	NAS CM	Open End	Alternative Miscellaneous (Income)	D+	D	C-	Up	Y	0
Putnam PanAgora Managed Futures Strategy Class C	PPFLX	NAS CM	Open End	Alternative Miscellaneous (Income)	D+	D	C-	Up	Y	0
Putnam PanAgora Managed Futures Strategy Class M	PPFVX	NAS CM	Open End	Alternative Miscellaneous (Income)	D+	D	C	Up	Y	0
Putnam PanAgora Managed Futures Strategy Class R	PPFWX	NAS CM	Open End	Alternative Miscellaneous (Income)	D+	D	C	Up	Y	0
Putnam PanAgora Managed Futures Strategy Class R6	PPFRX	NAS CM	Open End	Alternative Miscellaneous (Income)	D+	D	C	Up	Y	0
Putnam PanAgora Managed Futures Strategy Class Y	PPFYX	NAS CM	Open End	Alternative Miscellaneous (Income)	D+	D	C	Up	Y	0
Putnam PanAgora Market Neutral Fund Class A	PPMAX	NAS CM	Open End	Market Neutral (Income)	D	D	D+		Y	0
Putnam PanAgora Market Neutral Fund Class B	PPMBX	NAS CM	Open End	Market Neutral (Income)	D	D	D		Y	0
Putnam PanAgora Market Neutral Fund Class C	PPMDX	NAS CM	Open End	Market Neutral (Income)	D	D	D		Y	0
Putnam PanAgora Market Neutral Fund Class M	PPMVX	NAS CM	Open End	Market Neutral (Income)	D	D	D		Y	0

★ Expanded analysis of this fund is included in Section II.

	TOTAL RETURNS					PERFORMANCE				ASSETS		ASSET ALLOCATION & TURNOVER					BULL & BEAR		FEES		
Min Additional Investment	3-Month Total Return	6-Month Total Return	1-Year Total Return	3-Year Total Return	5-Year Total Return	Dividend Yield (TTM)	Expense Ratio	3-Yr Std Deviation	3-Year Beta	NAV	Total Assets (MIL)	%Cash	%Stocks	%Bonds	%Other	Turnover Ratio	Last Bull Market Total Return	Last Bear Market Total Return	Front End Fee (%)	Back End Fee (%)	Inception Date
	2.00	12.73	-4.48	27.86	4.26	0	1.87	12.35	0.96	35.58	365.4	3	97	0	0	44	17.12	-27.94	3.50		Oct-96
	2.07	12.87	-4.23	28.83	5.57	0	1.62	12.36	0.96	35.34	365.4	3	97	0	0	44	17.27	-27.87			Jan-03
	2.23	13.23	-3.59	30.40	7.41	0	0.95	12.35	0.96	36.1	365.4	3	97	0	0	44	17.42	-27.79			May-18
	2.18	13.12	-3.77	30.76	8.23	0	1.12	12.36	0.96	36.02	365.4	3	97	0	0	44	17.64	-27.73			Feb-00
	5.92	16.98	-3.04	25.54	4.19	1.82	1.22	12.47	1.09	23.07	932.6	7	93	0	0	61	18.49	-26.16	5.75		Feb-91
	5.69	16.56	-3.78	22.73	0.35	0.94	1.97	12.45	1.09	21.89	932.6	7	93	0	0	61	17.98	-26.39		5.00	Jun-94
	5.71	16.54	-3.78	22.75	0.33	0.12	1.97	12.45	1.09	22.4	932.6	7	93	0	0	61	17.88	-26.38		1.00	Jul-99
	5.76	16.72	-3.52	23.64	1.60	1.28	1.72	12.46	1.09	22.4	932.6	7	93	0	0	61	18.13	-26.3	3.50		Dec-94
	5.79	16.81	-3.30	24.55	2.85	1.46	1.47	12.44	1.09	22.65	932.6	7	93	0	0	61	18.23	-26.19			Jan-03
	5.95	17.17	-2.77	26.73	5.84	2.15	0.89	12.46	1.09	23.47	932.6	7	93	0	0	61	18.49	-26.16			Jul-12
	5.96	17.25	-2.64	27.13	6.40	2.26	0.79	12.46	1.09	23.44	932.6	7	93	0	0	61	18.49	-26.16			Jul-12
	5.94	17.10	-2.85	26.43	5.46	2.07	0.97	12.45	1.09	23.34	932.6	7	93	0	0	61	18.62	-26.07			Jul-96
	4.77	17.32	-5.68	28.19	9.01	0	1.4	13.16	1.08	21.74	266.0	1	99	0	0	96	19.29	-27.82	5.75	1.00	Jan-95
	4.55	16.85	-6.41	25.34	4.96	0	2.15	13.13	1.08	19.27	266.0	1	99	0	0	96	18.75	-28.07		5.00	Jul-95
	4.55	16.88	-6.40	25.37	4.95	0	2.15	13.15	1.08	19.73	266.0	1	99	0	0	96	18.73	-28.07		1.00	Feb-99
	4.63	17.06	-6.16	26.32	6.31	0	1.9	13.16	1.08	20.1	266.0	1	99	0	0	96	18.88	-27.99	3.50		Jul-95
	4.69	17.21	-5.90	27.25	7.66	0	1.65	13.15	1.08	21.18	266.0	1	99	0	0	96	19.1	-27.93			Dec-03
	4.83	17.55	-5.31	28.78	9.51	0	0.97	13.14	1.08	22.1	266.0	1	99	0	0	96	19.29	-27.82			May-18
	4.79	17.46	-5.48	29.21	10.35	0	1.15	13.13	1.08	22.06	266.0	1	99	0	0	96	19.48	-27.75			Oct-05
	2.60	11.20	-5.27	20.83	-1.41	2.05	1.38	11.33	0.95	10.62	126.1	3	97	0	0	15	16.55	-24.83	5.75		Aug-96
	2.40	10.69	-6.00	18.16	-5.00	0.96	2.13	11.33	0.95	10.66	126.1	3	97	0	0	15	16.1	-25.04		5.00	Aug-96
	2.50	10.84	-5.91	18.27	-4.93	0.67	2.13	11.33	0.95	10.63	126.1	3	97	0	0	15	16.11	-25.06		1.00	Feb-99
	2.50	10.93	-5.74	19.06	-3.78	1.51	1.88	11.34	0.95	10.65	126.1	3	97	0	0	15	16.25	-25.02	3.50		Aug-96
	2.53	10.98	-5.46	20.01	-2.65	1.63	1.63	11.34	0.95	10.51	126.1	3	97	0	0	15	16.48	-24.9			Dec-03
	2.69	11.50	-4.85	22.52	0.67	2.57	0.93	11.36	0.96	10.66	126.1	3	97	0	0	15	16.55	-24.83			Dec-13
	2.70	11.30	-5.03	21.77	-0.10	2.26	1.13	11.3	0.95	10.63	126.1	3	97	0	0	15	16.74	-24.7			Oct-00
	2.31	8.19	0.62	9.58	11.05	3.25	1.01	4.67	17.44	11.49	1,179	-6	20	84	2	479	9.88	-7.85	5.75		Dec-08
	2.19	7.81	-0.12	7.19	6.99	2.54	1.76	4.69	17.59	11.17	1,179	-6	20	84	2	479	9.32	-8.1		5.00	Dec-08
	2.11	7.84	-0.05	7.17	6.98	2.61	1.76	4.67	17.94	11.13	1,179	-6	20	84	2	479	9.35	-8.1		1.00	Dec-08
	2.18	7.98	0.13	8.06	8.36	2.94	1.51	4.71	17.54	11.23	1,179	-6	20	84	2	479	9.5	-8	3.50		Dec-08
	2.39	8.45	1.05	10.92	12.90	3.64	0.62	4.66	17.67	11.55	1,179	-6	20	84	2	479	10.03	-7.76			Aug-16
	2.25	8.12	0.44	8.87	9.76	3.04	1.26	4.71	17.07	11.31	1,179	-6	20	84	2	479	9.69	-7.99			Dec-08
	2.65	8.60	1.18	10.97	13.20	3.58	0.66	4.67	17.24	11.59	1,179	-6	20	84	2	479	10.03	-7.76			Jul-12
	2.39	8.35	0.95	10.49	12.47	3.47	0.76	4.69	17.72	11.54	1,179	-6	20	84	2	479	10.03	-7.76			Dec-08
	4.34	17.88	5.87	53.54	52.41	0	1.02	13.17	1.03	23.99	2,510	1	99	0	0	41	28.49	-20.09	5.75	1.00	Sep-10
	4.18	17.44	5.08	50.16	46.76	0	1.77	13.16	1.03	23.16	2,510	1	99	0	0	41	27.85	-20.33		5.00	Sep-10
	4.18	17.41	5.09	50.13	46.78	0	1.77	13.15	1.03	23.13	2,510	1	99	0	0	41	27.79	-20.31		1.00	Sep-10
	4.24	17.62	5.36	51.35	48.71	0	1.52	13.16	1.03	23.56	2,510	1	99	0	0	41	28.04	-20.28	3.50		Sep-10
	4.28	17.73	5.63	52.47	50.54	0	1.27	13.19	1.04	23.83	2,510	1	99	0	0	41	28.3	-20.18			Sep-10
	4.49	18.06	6.24	54.92	54.48	0	0.67	13.16	1.03	24.18	2,510	1	99	0	0	41	28.66	-20.06			May-18
	4.45	18.02	6.15	54.79	54.35	0	0.77	13.17	1.03	24.16	2,510	1	99	0	0	41	28.66	-20.06			Sep-10
	-0.85	0.32	-3.22			2.51	1.63			9.27	12.0	23	-14	97	-5				5.75		Sep-17
	-0.96	0.00	-4.00			1.72	2.38			9.22	12.0	23	-14	97	-5					5.00	Sep-17
	-1.08	-0.10	-4.06			2.55	2.38			9.14	12.0	23	-14	97	-5					1.00	Sep-17
	-0.85	0.10	-3.74			1.98	2.13			9.24	12.0	23	-14	97	-5				3.50		Sep-17
	-0.85	0.21	-3.47			2.26	1.88			9.25	12.0	23	-14	97	-5						Sep-17
	-0.85	0.43	-3.06			2.77	1.38			9.28	12.0	23	-14	97	-5						Sep-17
	-0.74	0.54	-2.96			2.77	1.38			9.29	12.0	23	-14	97	-5						Sep-17
	-2.22	-4.46	-6.39			0	1.82			8.78	10.6	92	0	-1	8				5.75		Sep-17
	-2.36	-4.82	-7.07			0	2.57			8.67	10.6	92	0	-1	8					5.00	Sep-17
	-2.36	-4.82	-7.07			0	2.57			8.67	10.6	92	0	-1	8					1.00	Sep-17
	-2.35	-4.70	-6.84			0	2.32			8.71	10.6	92	0	-1	8				3.50		Sep-17

	MARKET		FUND TYPE, CATEGORY & OBJECTIVE		RATINGS				MINIMUMS	
Fund Name	Ticker Symbol	Traded On	Fund Type	Category and (Prospectus Objective)	Overall Rating	Reward Rating	Risk Rating	Recent Up/ Downgrade	Open to New Investors	Min Initial Investment
Putnam PanAgora Market Neutral Fund Class R	PPMLX	NAS CM	Open End	Market Neutral (Income)	D	D	D+		Y	0
Putnam PanAgora Market Neutral Fund Class R6	PPMRX	NAS CM	Open End	Market Neutral (Income)	D	D	D+		Y	0
Putnam PanAgora Market Neutral Fund Class Y	PPMYX	NAS CM	Open End	Market Neutral (Income)	D	D	D+		Y	0
Putnam PanAgora Risk Parity Fund Class A	PPRPX	NAS CM	Open End	Moderate Alloc (Growth & Income)	C-	D+	B-	Up	Y	0
Putnam PanAgora Risk Parity Fund Class B	PPRLX	NAS CM	Open End	Moderate Alloc (Growth & Income)	C-	D+	B-	Up	Y	0
Putnam PanAgora Risk Parity Fund Class C	PPRNX	NAS CM	Open End	Moderate Alloc (Growth & Income)	C-	D+	B-	Up	Y	0
Putnam PanAgora Risk Parity Fund Class M	PPRVX	NAS CM	Open End	Moderate Alloc (Growth & Income)	C-	D+	B-	Up	Y	0
Putnam PanAgora Risk Parity Fund Class R	PPROX	NAS CM	Open End	Moderate Alloc (Growth & Income)	C-	D+	B-	Up	Y	0
Putnam PanAgora Risk Parity Fund Class R6	PPRWX	NAS CM	Open End	Moderate Alloc (Growth & Income)	C-	D+	B-	Up	Y	0
Putnam PanAgora Risk Parity Fund Class Y	PPRYX	NAS CM	Open End	Moderate Alloc (Growth & Income)	C-	D+	B-	Up	Y	0
Putnam Research Fund Class A	PNRAX	NAS CM	Open End	US Equity Large Cap Blend (Growth)	B-	C+	B		Y	0
Putnam Research Fund Class B	PRFBX	NAS CM	Open End	US Equity Large Cap Blend (Growth)	B-	C+	B		Y	0
Putnam Research Fund Class C	PRACX	NAS CM	Open End	US Equity Large Cap Blend (Growth)	B-	C+	B		Y	0
Putnam Research Fund Class M	PRFMX	NAS CM	Open End	US Equity Large Cap Blend (Growth)	B-	C+	B		Y	0
Putnam Research Fund Class R	PRSRX	NAS CM	Open End	US Equity Large Cap Blend (Growth)	B-	C+	B		Y	0
Putnam Research Fund Class R6 Shares	PLJMX	NAS CM	Open End	US Equity Large Cap Blend (Growth)	B-	C+	B	Down	Y	0
Putnam Research Fund Class Y	PURYX	NAS CM	Open End	US Equity Large Cap Blend (Growth)	B-	C+	B		Y	0
Putnam Retirement Income Fund Lifestyle 1 Class A	PRMAX	NAS CM	Open End	Target Date (Asset Alloc)	B-	C	B+	Up	Y	0
Putnam Retirement Income Fund Lifestyle 1 Class B	PRMLX	NAS CM	Open End	Target Date (Asset Alloc)	C+	C	B	Up	Y	0
Putnam Retirement Income Fund Lifestyle 1 Class C	PRMCX	NAS CM	Open End	Target Date (Asset Alloc)	C+	C	B	Up	Y	0
Putnam Retirement Income Fund Lifestyle 1 Class M	PRMMX	NAS CM	Open End	Target Date (Asset Alloc)	B-	C	B+	Up	Y	0
Putnam Retirement Income Fund Lifestyle 1 Class R	PRMKX	NAS CM	Open End	Target Date (Asset Alloc)	B-	C	B+	Up	Y	0
Putnam Retirement Income Fund Lifestyle 1 Class R6	PREWX	NAS CM	Open End	Target Date (Asset Alloc)	C+	C	B	Up	Y	0
Putnam Retirement Income Fund Lifestyle 1 Class Y	PRMYX	NAS CM	Open End	Target Date (Asset Alloc)	B-	C	A-	Up	Y	0
Putnam RetirementReady 2020 Fund Class A	PRRMX	NAS CM	Open End	Target Date (Asset Alloc)	B-	C	B+	Up	Y	0
Putnam RetirementReady 2020 Fund Class B			Open End	Target Date (Asset Alloc)	C+	C	B+	Up	Y	0
Putnam RetirementReady 2020 Fund Class C			Open End	Target Date (Asset Alloc)	C+	C	B+	Up	Y	0
Putnam RetirementReady 2020 Fund Class M			Open End	Target Date (Asset Alloc)	B-	C	B+	Up	Y	0
Putnam RetirementReady 2020 Fund Class R			Open End	Target Date (Asset Alloc)	B-	C	B+	Up	Y	0
Putnam RetirementReady 2020 Fund Class R6	PMRGX	NAS CM	Open End	Target Date (Asset Alloc)	B-	C	A-	Up	Y	0
Putnam RetirementReady 2020 Fund Class Y	PRRNX	NAS CM	Open End	Target Date (Asset Alloc)	B-	C	A-	Up	Y	0
Putnam RetirementReady 2025 Fund Class A	PRROX	NAS CM	Open End	Target Date (Asset Alloc)	B-	C	B+	Up	Y	0
Putnam RetirementReady 2025 Fund Class B			Open End	Target Date (Asset Alloc)	B-	C	B+	Up	Y	0
Putnam RetirementReady 2025 Fund Class C			Open End	Target Date (Asset Alloc)	B-	C	B+	Up	Y	0
Putnam RetirementReady 2025 Fund Class M			Open End	Target Date (Asset Alloc)	B-	C	B+	Up	Y	0
Putnam RetirementReady 2025 Fund Class R			Open End	Target Date (Asset Alloc)	B-	C	B+	Up	Y	0
Putnam RetirementReady 2025 Fund Class R6	PRMFX	NAS CM	Open End	Target Date (Asset Alloc)	B-	C	A-	Up	Y	0
Putnam RetirementReady 2025 Fund Class Y	PRRPX	NAS CM	Open End	Target Date (Asset Alloc)	B-	C	A-	Up	Y	0
Putnam RetirementReady 2030 Fund Class A	PRRQX	NAS CM	Open End	Target Date (Asset Alloc)	B-	C	B+	Up	Y	0
Putnam RetirementReady 2030 Fund Class B			Open End	Target Date (Asset Alloc)	B-	C	B+	Up	Y	0
Putnam RetirementReady 2030 Fund Class C			Open End	Target Date (Asset Alloc)	B-	C	B+	Up	Y	0
Putnam RetirementReady 2030 Fund Class M			Open End	Target Date (Asset Alloc)	B-	C	B+	Up	Y	0
Putnam RetirementReady 2030 Fund Class R			Open End	Target Date (Asset Alloc)	B-	C	B+	Up	Y	0
Putnam RetirementReady 2030 Fund Class R6	PREZX	NAS CM	Open End	Target Date (Asset Alloc)	B-	C	A-	Up	Y	0
Putnam RetirementReady 2030 Fund Class Y	PRRTX	NAS CM	Open End	Target Date (Asset Alloc)	B-	C	A-	Up	Y	0
Putnam RetirementReady 2035 Fund Class A	PRRWX	NAS CM	Open End	Target Date (Asset Alloc)	B-	C	B+	Up	Y	0
Putnam RetirementReady 2035 Fund Class B			Open End	Target Date (Asset Alloc)	B-	C	B+	Up	Y	0
Putnam RetirementReady 2035 Fund Class C			Open End	Target Date (Asset Alloc)	B-	C	B+	Up	Y	0
Putnam RetirementReady 2035 Fund Class M			Open End	Target Date (Asset Alloc)	B-	C	B+	Up	Y	0
Putnam RetirementReady 2035 Fund Class R			Open End	Target Date (Asset Alloc)	B-	C	B+	Up	Y	0
Putnam RetirementReady 2035 Fund Class R6	PREGX	NAS CM	Open End	Target Date (Asset Alloc)	B-	C	B+	Up	Y	0
Putnam RetirementReady 2035 Fund Class Y	PRRYX	NAS CM	Open End	Target Date (Asset Alloc)	B-	C	B+	Up	Y	0

★ Expanded analysis of this fund is included in Section II.

	TOTAL RETURNS					PERFORMANCE				ASSETS		ASSET ALLOCATION & TURNOVER					BULL & BEAR		FEES		
Min Additional Investment	3-Month Total Return	6-Month Total Return	1-Year Total Return	3-Year Total Return	5-Year Total Return	Dividend Yield (TTM)	Expense Ratio	3-Yr Std Deviation	3-Year Beta	NAV	Total Assets (MIL)	%Cash	%Stocks	%Bonds	%Other	Turnover Ratio	Last Bull Market Total Return	Last Bear Market Total Return	Front End Fee (%)	Back End Fee (%)	Inception Date
	-2.23	-4.58	-6.51			0	2.07			8.75	10.6	92	0	-1	8						Sep-17
	-2.21	-4.33	-6.17			0	1.58			8.82	10.6	92	0	-1	8						Sep-17
	-2.10	-4.33	-6.17			0	1.57			8.82	10.6	92	0	-1	8						Sep-17
	5.17	16.33	10.64			0.64	1.37			10.97	34.4	-201	62	239	0				5.75		Sep-17
	5.00	15.81	9.86			0	2.12			10.91	34.4	-201	62	239	0					5.00	Sep-17
	5.00	15.83	9.87			0.08	2.12			10.9	34.4	-201	62	239	0					1.00	Sep-17
	4.99	15.90	10.08			0.18	1.87			10.93	34.4	-201	62	239	0				3.50		Sep-17
	5.08	16.11	10.37			0.42	1.62			10.95	34.4	-201	62	239	0						Sep-17
	5.26	16.42	10.90			0.86	1.13			10.99	34.4	-201	62	239	0						Sep-17
	5.26	16.42	10.90			0.86	1.12			10.99	34.4	-201	62	239	0						Sep-17
	5.66	20.64	10.52	53.31	60.36	0.31	1.11	11.98	0.97	33.02	329.9	1	99	0	0	97	26.72	-19.01	5.75		Oct-95
	5.44	20.22	9.66	49.88	54.43	0	1.86	11.98	0.97	30.2	329.9	1	99	0	0	97	26.12	-19.27		5.00	Jun-98
	5.45	20.19	9.67	49.87	54.46	0	1.86	12	0.97	30.18	329.9	1	99	0	0	97	26.14	-19.26		1.00	Feb-99
	5.50	20.32	9.94	51.03	56.37	0	1.61	11.98	0.97	31.26	329.9	1	99	0	0	97	26.4	-19.21	3.50		Jun-98
	5.57	20.50	10.23	52.18	58.37	0.03	1.36	12	0.97	32.56	329.9	1	99	0	0	97	26.53	-19.09			Jan-03
	5.73	20.91	10.93	55.26	62.96	0.69	0.7	11.99	0.97	33.53	329.9	1	99	0	0	97	26.72	-19.01			Jun-15
	5.70	20.78	10.75	54.42	62.36	0.59	0.86	11.99	0.97	33.36	329.9	1	99	0	0	97	26.94	-18.95			Apr-00
	2.18	7.19	3.03	11.84	13.06	3.02	0.97	3.1	0.28	17.51	114.2	1	18	81	0	68	6.38	-5.8	4.00		Nov-04
	1.99	6.78	2.27	9.34	8.87	2.35	1.72	3.14	0.29	17.08	114.2	1	18	81	0	68	5.9	-6.09		5.00	Nov-04
	1.93	6.76	2.22	9.32	8.86	2.36	1.72	3.12	0.28	17.12	114.2	1	18	81	0	68	5.88	-6.07		1.00	Nov-04
	2.07	7.04	2.76	11.04	11.61	2.76	1.22	3.11	0.29	17.56	114.2	1	18	81	0	68	6.21	-5.91	3.25		Nov-04
	2.12	7.06	2.76	11.01	11.58	2.76	1.22	3.12	0.28	17.5	114.2	1	18	81	0	68	6.17	-5.84			Nov-04
	2.26	7.35	3.36	12.98	14.73	3.34	0.63	3.11	0.28	17.57	114.2	1	18	81	0	68	6.51	-5.68			Sep-16
	2.24	7.36	3.33	12.76	14.50	3.25	0.72	3.11	0.28	17.58	114.2	1	18	81	0	68	6.51	-5.68			Nov-04
	2.24	7.78	3.25	14.60	16.64	3.26	0.96	3.67	0.26	19.1	208.5	1	23	77	0	69	11.36	-10.11	5.75		Nov-04
	1.99	7.33	2.41	12.02	12.33	2.56	1.71	3.67	0.26	18.37	208.5	1	23	77	0	69	10.87	-10.37		5.00	Nov-04
	2.00	7.29	2.43	11.99	12.31	2.63	1.71	3.64	0.26	18.33	208.5	1	23	77	0	69	10.86	-10.34		1.00	Nov-04
	2.11	7.49	2.73	12.86	13.73	2.64	1.46	3.65	0.26	18.82	208.5	1	23	77	0	69	11.06	-10.29	3.50		Nov-04
	2.16	7.58	2.94	13.77	15.16	3.04	1.21	3.65	0.26	18.37	208.5	1	23	77	0	69	11.18	-10.21			Nov-04
	2.31	7.92	3.60	15.70	18.37	3.16	0.63	3.65	0.26	21.68	208.5	1	23	77	0	69	11.5	-10			Sep-16
	2.26	7.84	3.47	15.43	18.08	3.13	0.71	3.67	0.26	21.64	208.5	1	23	77	0	69	11.5	-10			Nov-04
	2.34	9.09	3.37	18.43	20.83	3.53	0.99	4.88	0.37	21.83	147.8	0	34	66	0	52	14.42	-13.05	5.75		Nov-04
	2.16	8.70	2.62	15.83	16.40	2.94	1.74	4.88	0.37	20.25	147.8	0	34	66	0	52	13.92	-13.33		5.00	Nov-04
	2.12	8.71	2.61	15.78	16.40	3.16	1.74	4.89	0.37	20.14	147.8	0	34	66	0	52	13.87	-13.3		1.00	Nov-04
	2.23	8.85	2.87	16.67	17.90	3.15	1.49	4.89	0.37	20.61	147.8	0	34	66	0	52	14.09	-13.22	3.50		Nov-04
	2.30	9.02	3.11	17.54	19.35	3.06	1.24	4.88	0.37	20.44	147.8	0	34	66	0	52	14.25	-13.16			Nov-04
	2.41	9.27	3.73	19.65	22.70	3.85	0.63	4.89	0.37	22.02	147.8	0	34	66	0	52	14.55	-12.94			Sep-16
	2.42	9.26	3.66	19.33	22.37	3.75	0.74	4.88	0.37	21.98	147.8	0	34	66	0	52	14.55	-12.94			Nov-04
	2.44	10.64	3.43	23.00	25.30	3.1	0.98	6.3	0.49	21.8	213.9	1	46	53	0	46	17.33	-15.97	5.75		Nov-04
	2.27	10.27	2.70	20.35	20.77	2.37	1.73	6.3	0.49	20.64	213.9	1	46	53	0	46	16.75	-16.22		5.00	Nov-04
	2.24	10.26	2.71	20.32	20.76	2.47	1.73	6.33	0.49	20.54	213.9	1	46	53	0	46	16.81	-16.19		1.00	Nov-04
	2.32	10.40	2.95	21.23	22.25	2.76	1.48	6.33	0.49	21.12	213.9	1	46	53	0	46	16.94	-16.12	3.50		Nov-04
	2.37	10.55	3.21	22.17	23.83	2.73	1.23	6.32	0.49	20.66	213.9	1	46	53	0	46	17.15	-16.03			Nov-04
	2.54	10.86	3.84	24.27	27.26	2.96	0.64	6.35	0.5	25.43	213.9	1	46	53	0	46	17.44	-15.83			Sep-16
	2.50	10.80	3.73	23.94	26.92	2.87	0.73	6.33	0.49	25.39	213.9	1	46	53	0	46	17.44	-15.83			Nov-04
	2.46	12.08	3.21	27.06	29.07	3.31	1.03	7.79	0.62	22.04	137.8	2	59	40	0	43	19.6	-17.81	5.75		Nov-04
	2.29	11.64	2.43	24.25	24.28	2.8	1.78	7.77	0.61	20.06	137.8	2	59	40	0	43	18.98	-18.03		5.00	Nov-04
	2.25	11.64	2.43	24.22	24.25	2.94	1.78	7.77	0.61	19.91	137.8	2	59	40	0	43	19.09	-18.07		1.00	Nov-04
	2.37	11.78	2.68	25.18	25.87	2.74	1.53	7.79	0.62	21.16	137.8	2	59	40	0	43	19.18	-17.99	3.50		Nov-04
	2.41	11.91	2.94	26.12	27.45	2.93	1.28	7.78	0.61	21.18	137.8	2	59	40	0	43	19.42	-17.89			Nov-04
	2.60	12.27	3.59	28.43	31.08	3.07	0.67	7.78	0.62	26.36	137.8	2	59	40	0	43	19.78	-17.72			Sep-16
	2.53	12.18	3.45	27.99	30.63	2.98	0.78	7.79	0.62	26.31	137.8	2	59	40	0	43	19.77	-17.72			Nov-04

	MARKET		FUND TYPE, CATEGORY & OBJECTIVE		RATINGS				MINIMUMS	
Fund Name	Ticker Symbol	Traded On	Fund Type	Category and (Prospectus Objective)	Overall Rating	Reward Rating	Risk Rating	Recent Up/ Downgrade	Open to New Investors	Min Initial Investment
Putnam RetirementReady 2040 Fund Class A	PRRZX	NAS CM	Open End	Target Date (Asset Alloc)	B-	C	B+	Up	Y	0
Putnam RetirementReady 2040 Fund Class B			Open End	Target Date (Asset Alloc)	B-	C	B+	Up	Y	0
Putnam RetirementReady 2040 Fund Class C			Open End	Target Date (Asset Alloc)	B-	C	B+	Up	Y	0
Putnam RetirementReady 2040 Fund Class M			Open End	Target Date (Asset Alloc)	B-	C	B+	Up	Y	0
Putnam RetirementReady 2040 Fund Class R			Open End	Target Date (Asset Alloc)	B-	C	B+	Up	Y	0
Putnam RetirementReady 2040 Fund Class R6	PREHX	NAS CM	Open End	Target Date (Asset Alloc)	B-	C	B+	Up	Y	0
Putnam RetirementReady 2040 Fund Class Y	PRZZX	NAS CM	Open End	Target Date (Asset Alloc)	B-	C	B+	Up	Y	0
Putnam RetirementReady 2045 Fund Class A	PRVLX	NAS CM	Open End	Target Date (Asset Alloc)	B-	C	B	Up	Y	0
Putnam RetirementReady 2045 Fund Class B			Open End	Target Date (Asset Alloc)	B-	C	B	Up	Y	0
Putnam RetirementReady 2045 Fund Class C			Open End	Target Date (Asset Alloc)	B-	C	B	Up	Y	0
Putnam RetirementReady 2045 Fund Class M			Open End	Target Date (Asset Alloc)	B-	C	B	Up	Y	0
Putnam RetirementReady 2045 Fund Class R			Open End	Target Date (Asset Alloc)	B-	C	B	Up	Y	0
Putnam RetirementReady 2045 Fund Class R6	PREKX	NAS CM	Open End	Target Date (Asset Alloc)	B-	C	B	Up	Y	0
Putnam RetirementReady 2045 Fund Class Y	PRVYX	NAS CM	Open End	Target Date (Asset Alloc)	B-	C	B	Up	Y	0
Putnam RetirementReady 2050 Fund Class A	PRRJX	NAS CM	Open End	Target Date (Asset Alloc)	B-	C	B	Up	Y	0
Putnam RetirementReady 2050 Fund Class B			Open End	Target Date (Asset Alloc)	C+	C	B	Up	Y	0
Putnam RetirementReady 2050 Fund Class C			Open End	Target Date (Asset Alloc)	C+	C	B	Up	Y	0
Putnam RetirementReady 2050 Fund Class M			Open End	Target Date (Asset Alloc)	B-	C	B	Up	Y	0
Putnam RetirementReady 2050 Fund Class R	PRRKX	NAS CM	Open End	Target Date (Asset Alloc)	B-	C	B	Up	Y	0
Putnam RetirementReady 2050 Fund Class R6	PREUX	NAS CM	Open End	Target Date (Asset Alloc)	B-	C	B	Up	Y	0
Putnam RetirementReady 2050 Fund Class Y	PRRUX	NAS CM	Open End	Target Date (Asset Alloc)	B-	C	B	Up	Y	0
Putnam RetirementReady 2055 Fund Class A	PRRFX	NAS CM	Open End	Target Date (Asset Alloc)	B-	C	B	Up	Y	0
Putnam RetirementReady 2055 Fund Class B			Open End	Target Date (Asset Alloc)	C+	C	B	Up	Y	0
Putnam RetirementReady 2055 Fund Class C			Open End	Target Date (Asset Alloc)	C+	C	B	Up	Y	0
Putnam RetirementReady 2055 Fund Class M			Open End	Target Date (Asset Alloc)	C+	C	B	Up	Y	0
Putnam RetirementReady 2055 Fund Class R	PRRVX	NAS CM	Open End	Target Date (Asset Alloc)	C+	C	B	Up	Y	0
Putnam RetirementReady 2055 Fund Class R6	PREVX	NAS CM	Open End	Target Date (Asset Alloc)	B-	C	B	Up	Y	0
Putnam RetirementReady 2055 Fund Class Y	PRTLX	NAS CM	Open End	Target Date (Asset Alloc)	B-	C	B	Up	Y	0
Putnam RetirementReady 2060 Fund Class A	PRTFX	NAS CM	Open End	Target Date (Asset Alloc)	C+	C	B	Up	Y	0
Putnam RetirementReady 2060 Fund Class B			Open End	Target Date (Asset Alloc)	C+	C	B	Up		0
Putnam RetirementReady 2060 Fund Class C			Open End	Target Date (Asset Alloc)	C+	C	B	Up	Y	0
Putnam RetirementReady 2060 Fund Class M			Open End	Target Date (Asset Alloc)	C+	C	B	Up	Y	0
Putnam RetirementReady 2060 Fund Class R	PRTRX	NAS CM	Open End	Target Date (Asset Alloc)	C+	C	B	Up	Y	0
Putnam RetirementReady 2060 Fund Class R6	PEFGX	NAS CM	Open End	Target Date (Asset Alloc)	B-	C	B	Up	Y	0
Putnam RetirementReady 2060 Fund Class Y	PRTYX	NAS CM	Open End	Target Date (Asset Alloc)	B-	C	B	Up	Y	0
Putnam Small Cap Growth Fund Class A	PNSAX	NAS CM	Open End	US Equity Small Cap (Small Company)	C+	C+	C+	Down	Y	0
Putnam Small Cap Growth Fund Class B	PNSBX	NAS CM	Open End	US Equity Small Cap (Small Company)	C+	C+	C+	Down	Y	0
Putnam Small Cap Growth Fund Class C	PNSCX	NAS CM	Open End	US Equity Small Cap (Small Company)	C+	C+	C+	Down	Y	0
Putnam Small Cap Growth Fund Class M	PSGMX	NAS CM	Open End	US Equity Small Cap (Small Company)	C+	C+	C+	Down	Y	0
Putnam Small Cap Growth Fund Class R	PSGRX	NAS CM	Open End	US Equity Small Cap (Small Company)	C+	C+	C+	Down	Y	0
Putnam Small Cap Growth Fund Class R6	PLKGX	NAS CM	Open End	US Equity Small Cap (Small Company)	C+	C+	C+	Down	Y	0
Putnam Small Cap Growth Fund Class Y	PSYGX	NAS CM	Open End	US Equity Small Cap (Small Company)	C+	C+	C+	Down	Y	0
Putnam Small Cap Value Fund Class A	PSLAX	NAS CM	Open End	US Equity Small Cap (Small Company)	C-	D+	C		Y	0
Putnam Small Cap Value Fund Class B	PSLBX	NAS CM	Open End	US Equity Small Cap (Small Company)	C-	D+	C		Y	0
Putnam Small Cap Value Fund Class C	PSLCX	NAS CM	Open End	US Equity Small Cap (Small Company)	C-	D+	C		Y	0
Putnam Small Cap Value Fund Class M	PSLMX	NAS CM	Open End	US Equity Small Cap (Small Company)	C-	D+	C		Y	0
Putnam Small Cap Value Fund Class R	PSCRX	NAS CM	Open End	US Equity Small Cap (Small Company)	C-	D+	C		Y	0
Putnam Small Cap Value Fund Class R5	PSLRX	NAS CM	Open End	US Equity Small Cap (Small Company)	C-	C-	C		Y	0
Putnam Small Cap Value Fund Class R6	PSCMX	NAS CM	Open End	US Equity Small Cap (Small Company)	C-	C-	C		Y	0
Putnam Small Cap Value Fund Class Y	PYSVX	NAS CM	Open End	US Equity Small Cap (Small Company)	C-	C-	C		Y	0
Putnam Sustainable Future Fund Class A	PMVAX	NAS CM	Open End	US Equity Mid Cap (Growth & Income)	C+	C	B	Down	Y	0
Putnam Sustainable Future Fund Class B	PMVBX	NAS CM	Open End	US Equity Mid Cap (Growth & Income)	C+	C	B		Y	0

★ Expanded analysis of this fund is included in Section II.

	TOTAL RETURNS					PERFORMANCE				ASSETS		ASSET ALLOCATION & TURNOVER					BULL & BEAR		FEES		
Min Additional Investment	3-Month Total Return	6-Month Total Return	1-Year Total Return	3-Year Total Return	5-Year Total Return	Dividend Yield (TTM)	Expense Ratio	3-Yr Std Deviation	3-Year Beta	NAV	Total Assets (MIL)	%Cash	%Stocks	%Bonds	%Other	Turnover Ratio	Last Bull Market Total Return	Last Bear Market Total Return	Front End Fee (%)	Back End Fee (%)	Inception Date
	2.53	13.29	3.06	30.44	32.08	2.73	1.03	9.05	0.72	21.88	163.9	2	70	28	0	39	21.16	-18.84	5.75		Nov-04
	2.31	12.87	2.32	27.52	27.24	2.14	1.78	9.05	0.72	19.89	163.9	2	70	28	0	39	20.54	-19.09		5.00	Nov-04
	2.35	12.90	2.35	27.60	27.24	2.29	1.78	9.06	0.72	19.54	163.9	2	70	28	0	39	20.61	-19.06		1.00	Nov-04
	2.42	13.06	2.57	28.54	28.85	2.43	1.53	9.08	0.72	20.25	163.9	2	70	28	0	39	20.77	-18.97	3.50		Nov-04
	2.50	13.22	2.84	29.51	30.48	1.71	1.28	9.06	0.72	22.94	163.9	2	70	28	0	39	20.93	-18.93			Nov-04
	2.60	13.50	3.40	31.79	34.10	2.55	0.69	9.08	0.72	26.41	163.9	2	70	28	0	39	21.39	-18.79			Sep-16
	2.60	13.46	3.34	31.48	33.78	2.41	0.78	9.06	0.72	26.39	163.9	2	70	28	0	39	21.39	-18.79			Nov-04
	2.59	14.08	3.04	32.71	34.06	3.18	1.07	9.94	0.8	19.79	75.1	4	76	20	0	43	21.9	-19.35	5.75		Nov-04
	2.43	13.68	2.31	29.85	29.16	2.71	1.82	9.94	0.8	17.67	75.1	4	76	20	0	43	21.43	-19.63		5.00	Nov-04
	2.43	13.65	2.30	29.82	29.10	2.89	1.82	9.94	0.8	17.65	75.1	4	76	20	0	43	21.46	-19.69		1.00	Nov-04
	2.46	13.76	2.52	30.72	30.76	2.76	1.57	9.95	0.8	19.16	75.1	4	76	20	0	43	21.6	-19.58	3.50		Nov-04
	2.54	13.91	2.79	31.77	32.41	2.55	1.32	9.94	0.8	20.53	75.1	4	76	20	0	43	21.84	-19.51			Nov-04
	2.29	13.80	2.99	33.62	35.64	2.89	0.7	9.95	0.8	24.58	75.1	4	76	20	0	43	22.12	-19.3			Sep-16
	2.67	14.20	3.29	33.72	35.74	2.79	0.82	9.94	0.8	24.53	75.1	4	76	20	0	43	22.12	-19.3			Nov-04
	2.64	14.53	3.17	33.96	35.00	2.6	1.05	10.42	0.83	17.87	68.9	5	79	16	0	38	22.59	-19.82	5.75		May-05
	2.44	14.09	2.42	31.05	30.07	1.83	1.8	10.39	0.83	17.6	68.9	5	79	16	0	38	22.04	-20.02		5.00	May-05
	2.47	14.14	2.43	31.06	30.03	1.93	1.8	10.39	0.83	17.41	68.9	5	79	16	0	38	22.1	-20.13		1.00	May-05
	2.49	14.23	2.65	31.98	31.65	2.16	1.55	10.41	0.83	18.04	68.9	5	79	16	0	38	22.28	-19.98	3.50		May-05
	2.55	14.39	2.91	33.04	33.34	2.42	1.3	10.4	0.83	17.63	68.9	5	79	16	0	38	22.47	-19.95			May-05
	2.27	14.24	3.07	34.78	36.52	2.94	0.69	10.39	0.83	18.03	68.9	5	79	16	0	38	22.89	-19.82			Sep-16
	2.67	14.65	3.41	34.94	36.68	2.66	0.8	10.4	0.83	18.04	68.9	5	79	16	0	38	22.89	-19.82			May-05
	2.71	14.79	3.22	34.71	35.54	2.55	1.08	10.73	0.86	10.96	25.5	7	80	13	0	34	22.31	-20.58	5.75		Nov-10
	2.45	14.29	2.40	31.73	30.59	1.79	1.83	10.66	0.86	10.87	25.5	7	80	13	0	34	21.72	-20.82		5.00	Nov-10
	2.49	14.26	2.39	31.80	30.58	1.93	1.83	10.7	0.86	10.68	25.5	7	80	13	0	34	21.84	-20.82		1.00	Nov-10
	2.53	14.45	2.64	32.72	32.15	2.22	1.58	10.72	0.86	10.94	25.5	7	80	13	0	34	21.99	-20.8	3.50		Nov-10
	2.60	14.64	2.86	33.80	33.87	1.51	1.33	10.72	0.86	11.02	25.5	7	80	13	0	34	22.19	-20.69			Nov-10
	2.31	14.51	3.19	35.73	37.27	2.91	0.69	10.72	0.86	11.09	25.5	7	80	13	0	34	22.62	-20.56			Sep-16
	2.69	14.86	3.39	35.74	37.28	2.77	0.83	10.66	0.85	11.06	25.5	7	80	13	0	34	22.61	-20.56			Nov-10
	2.62	14.90	3.16	34.99		2.99	1.04	10.82	0.87	10.93	2.2	7	82	11	0	63			5.75		Nov-15
	2.44	14.38	2.37	32.07		2.38	1.79	10.81	0.87	10.89	2.2	7	82	11	0	63				5.00	Nov-15
	2.54	14.48	2.49	32.17		2.25	1.79	10.88	0.87	10.86	2.2	7	82	11	0	63				1.00	Nov-15
	2.61	14.60	2.68	33.16		1.94	1.54	10.84	0.87	11	2.2	7	82	11	0	63			3.50		Nov-15
	2.62	14.79	2.96	34.20		2.57	1.29	10.86	0.87	10.96	2.2	7	82	11	0	63					Nov-15
	2.23	14.51	2.99	35.72		3.07	0.69	10.87	0.87	11.03	2.2	7	82	11	0	63					Sep-16
	2.80	15.05	3.46	36.12		2.99	0.79	10.89	0.87	11.01	2.2	7	82	11	0	63					Nov-15
	9.42	32.82	12.37	78.92	65.99	0	1.2	17.2	0.96	47.5	498.0	2	98	0	0	68	29.92	-27.54	5.75		Dec-97
	9.21	32.32	11.53	74.89	59.84	0	1.95	17.17	0.96	41.47	498.0	2	98	0	0	68	29.75	-27.77		5.00	Mar-02
	9.22	32.35	11.52	74.92	59.88	0	1.95	17.19	0.96	41.32	498.0	2	98	0	0	68	29.33	-27.79		1.00	Mar-02
	9.28	32.49	11.79	76.26	61.84	0	1.7	17.2	0.96	43.42	498.0	2	98	0	0	68	29.54	-27.72	3.50		Mar-02
	9.33	32.65	12.09	77.57	63.90	0	1.45	17.19	0.96	45.7	498.0	2	98	0	0	68	29.74	-27.64			Dec-03
	9.50	33.10	12.81	81.19	68.80	0	0.77	17.19	0.96	49.54	498.0	2	98	0	0	68	29.92	-27.54			Jun-15
	9.48	32.99	12.65	80.28	68.07	0	0.95	17.19	0.96	49.3	498.0	2	98	0	0	68	30.04	-27.47			Nov-03
	2.23	16.61	-9.64	26.70	21.95	1.77	1.44	17.96	1.01	10.53	239.4	2	98	0	1	534	28.51	-24.84	5.75		Apr-99
	1.96	16.14	-10.40	23.83	17.39	1.42	2.19	17.98	1.01	7.77	239.4	2	98	0	1	534	27.86	-25.02		5.00	May-99
	2.11	16.21	-10.35	23.97	17.44	1.3	2.19	17.98	1.01	7.74	239.4	2	98	0	1	534	28.09	-25.15		1.00	Jul-99
	2.05	16.23	-10.17	24.71	18.80	1.52	1.94	17.94	1.01	8.95	239.4	2	98	0	1	534	28.23	-25.04	3.50		Mar-00
	2.19	16.62	-9.87	25.84	20.42	1.51	1.69	17.98	1.01	10.24	239.4	2	98	0	1	534	28.36	-24.93			Mar-07
	2.27	16.73	-9.40	27.95	23.90	2.01	1.11	17.96	1.01	11.23	239.4	2	98	0	1	534	28.51	-24.84			Nov-13
	2.37	16.85	-9.29	28.42	24.53	2.12	1.01	17.97	1.01	11.23	239.4	2	98	0	1	534	28.51	-24.84			Nov-13
	2.28	16.80	-9.43	27.75	23.46	1.9	1.19	17.92	1.01	11.19	239.4	2	98	0	1	534	28.75	-24.76			Jan-01
	4.62	24.03	11.29	38.31	40.68	0.98	1.07	12.99	0.85	17.65	413.2	3	97	0	0	31	26.95	-22.23	5.75		Nov-99
	4.46	23.64	10.50	35.24	35.53	0.52	1.82	13.04	0.86	15.69	413.2	3	97	0	0	31	26.31	-22.44		5.00	Jan-01

		MARKET	FUND TYPE, CATEGORY & OBJECTIVE		RATINGS				MINIMUMS	
Fund Name	Ticker Symbol	Traded On	Fund Type	Category and (Prospectus Objective)	Overall Rating	Reward Rating	Risk Rating	Recent Up/ Downgrade	Open to New Investors	Min Initial Investment
Putnam Sustainable Future Fund Class C	PMPCX	NAS CM	Open End	US Equity Mid Cap (Growth & Income)	C+	C	B		Y	0
Putnam Sustainable Future Fund Class M	PMCVX	NAS CM	Open End	US Equity Mid Cap (Growth & Income)	C+	C	B	Down	Y	0
Putnam Sustainable Future Fund Class R	PMVRX	NAS CM	Open End	US Equity Mid Cap (Growth & Income)	C+	C	B	Down	Y	0
Putnam Sustainable Future Fund Class R6 Shares	PNOTX	NAS CM	Open End	US Equity Mid Cap (Growth & Income)	C+	C	B	Down	Y	0
Putnam Sustainable Future Fund Class Y	PMVYX	NAS CM	Open End	US Equity Mid Cap (Growth & Income)	C+	C	B	Down	Y	0
Putnam Sustainable Leaders Fund Class A	PNOPX	NAS CM	Open End	US Equity Large Cap Growth (Aggr Growth)	B	B-	B		Y	0
Putnam Sustainable Leaders Fund Class B	PNOBX	NAS CM	Open End	US Equity Large Cap Growth (Aggr Growth)	B	B-	B		Y	0
Putnam Sustainable Leaders Fund Class C	PNOCX	NAS CM	Open End	US Equity Large Cap Growth (Aggr Growth)	B	B-	B		Y	0
Putnam Sustainable Leaders Fund Class M	PNOMX	NAS CM	Open End	US Equity Large Cap Growth (Aggr Growth)	B	B-	B		Y	0
Putnam Sustainable Leaders Fund Class R	PNORX	NAS CM	Open End	US Equity Large Cap Growth (Aggr Growth)	B	B-	B		Y	0
Putnam Sustainable Leaders Fund Class R6 Shares	PSLGX	NAS CM	Open End	US Equity Large Cap Growth (Aggr Growth)	B	B-	B		Y	0
Putnam Sustainable Leaders Fund Class Y	PNOYX	NAS CM	Open End	US Equity Large Cap Growth (Aggr Growth)	B	B-	B		Y	0
Pzena Emerging Markets Value Fund Institutional	PZIEX	NAS CM	Open End	Global Emerg Mkts (Div Emerging Mkts)	C	C-	B		Y	1,000,000
Pzena Emerging Markets Value Fund Investor	PZVEX	NAS CM	Open End	Global Emerg Mkts (Div Emerging Mkts)	C	C-	B		Y	5,000
Pzena International Small Cap Value Institutional Cls	PZIIX	NAS CM	Open End	Global Equity Mid/Small Cap (Small Company)	D-	D	D		Y	1,000,000
Pzena International Small Cap Value Fund Investor Class	PZVIX	NAS CM	Open End	Global Equity Mid/Small Cap (Small Company)	D-	D	D		Y	5,000
Pzena Long/Short Value Fund Institutional Class	PZILX	NAS CM	Open End	Long/Short Equity (Growth)	D+	D	C	Down	Y	1,000,000
Pzena Long/Short Value Fund Investor Class	PZVLX	NAS CM	Open End	Long/Short Equity (Growth)	D+	D	C	Down	Y	5,000
Pzena Mid Cap Value Fund Institutional Class	PZIMX	NAS CM	Open End	US Equity Mid Cap (Growth)	C	C	C		Y	1,000,000
Pzena Mid Cap Value Fund Investor Class	PZVMX	NAS CM	Open End	US Equity Mid Cap (Growth)	C	C	C		Y	5,000
Pzena Small Cap Value Fund Institutional Class	PZISX	NAS CM	Open End	US Equity Small Cap (Small Company)	C-	D+	C		Y	1,000,000
Pzena Small Cap Value Fund Investor Class	PZVSX	NAS CM	Open End	US Equity Small Cap (Small Company)	C-	D+	C		Y	5,000
QCI Balanced Fund Institutional Class	QCIBX	NAS CM	Open End	Cautious Alloc (Balanced)	B	C	A		Y	25,000
QS Conservative Growth Fund Class A	SBBAX	NAS CM	Open End	Moderate Alloc (Balanced)	B-	C	A-	Up	Y	1,000
QS Conservative Growth Fund Class C	SCBCX	NAS CM	Open End	Moderate Alloc (Balanced)	B-	C	A-	Up	Y	1,000
QS Conservative Growth Fund Class I	LMEIX	NAS CM	Open End	Moderate Alloc (Balanced)	B-	C	A-		Y	1,000,000
QS Conservative Growth Fund Class R	LLARX	NAS CM	Open End	Moderate Alloc (Balanced)	B-	C	A-	Up	Y	0
QS Defensive Growth Fund Class A	SBCPX	NAS CM	Open End	Cautious Alloc (Growth & Income)	B	C+	A-	Up	Y	1,000
QS Defensive Growth Fund Class C	LWLAX	NAS CM	Open End	Cautious Alloc (Growth & Income)	B-	C	B+	Up	Y	1,000
QS Defensive Growth Fund Class C1	SBCLX	NAS CM	Open End	Cautious Alloc (Growth & Income)	B-	C	B+			1,000
QS Defensive Growth Fund Class I	LMGIX	NAS CM	Open End	Cautious Alloc (Growth & Income)	B	C+	A-		Y	1,000,000
QS Defensive Growth Fund Class R	LMLRX	NAS CM	Open End	Cautious Alloc (Growth & Income)	B	C	A-	Up	Y	0
QS Global Dividend Fund Class A	LGDAX	NAS CM	Open End	Global Equity Large Cap (Equity-Income)	B-	C	B+		Y	1,000
QS Global Dividend Fund Class A2	LMQSX	NAS CM	Open End	Global Equity Large Cap (Equity-Income)	B-	C	B+		Y	1,000
QS Global Dividend Fund Class C	LGDCX	NAS CM	Open End	Global Equity Large Cap (Equity-Income)	B-	C	B	Up	Y	1,000
QS Global Dividend Fund Class FI	LDIGX	NAS CM	Open End	Global Equity Large Cap (Equity-Income)	B-	C	B+		Y	0
QS Global Dividend Fund Class I	LTTMX	NAS CM	Open End	Global Equity Large Cap (Equity-Income)	B-	C	B+		Y	1,000,000
QS Global Dividend Fund Class IS	LDIFX	NAS CM	Open End	Global Equity Large Cap (Equity-Income)	B-	C	B+		Y	1,000,000
QS Global Equity Fund Class 1	LMPEX	NAS CM	Open End	Global Equity Large Cap (World Stock)	C	C	B			0
QS Global Equity Fund Class A	CFIPX	NAS CM	Open End	Global Equity Large Cap (World Stock)	C	C	B		Y	1,000
QS Global Equity Fund Class C	SILLX	NAS CM	Open End	Global Equity Large Cap (World Stock)	C	C	B-		Y	1,000
QS Global Equity Fund Class I	SMYIX	NAS CM	Open End	Global Equity Large Cap (World Stock)	C+	C	B	Up	Y	1,000,000
QS Global Market Neutral Fund Class A	LNFIX	NAS CM	Open End	Market Neutral (Growth & Income)	C-	D+	C	Down	Y	1,000
QS Global Market Neutral Fund Class C	LQNCX	NAS CM	Open End	Market Neutral (Growth & Income)	D+	D	C	Down	Y	1,000
QS Global Market Neutral Fund Class I	LQNIX	NAS CM	Open End	Market Neutral (Growth & Income)	C-	D+	C	Down	Y	1,000,000
QS Global Market Neutral Fund Class IS	LQISX	NAS CM	Open End	Market Neutral (Growth & Income)	C-	D+	C	Down	Y	1,000,000
QS Growth Fund Class A	SCHAX	NAS CM	Open End	Aggressive Alloc (Growth)	B-	C	B	Up	Y	1,000
QS Growth Fund Class C	SCHCX	NAS CM	Open End	Aggressive Alloc (Growth)	B-	C	B	Up	Y	1,000
QS Growth Fund Class I	LANIX	NAS CM	Open End	Aggressive Alloc (Growth)	B-	C	B	Up	Y	1,000,000
QS Growth Fund Class R	LLLRX	NAS CM	Open End	Aggressive Alloc (Growth)	B-	C	B	Up	Y	0
QS International Equity Fund Class A	LMEAX	NAS CM	Open End	Global Equity Large Cap (Foreign Stock)	C	C-	C+		Y	1,000
QS International Equity Fund Class A2	LIATX	NAS CM	Open End	Global Equity Large Cap (Foreign Stock)	C	C-	C+		Y	1,000

★ Expanded analysis of this fund is included in Section II.

	TOTAL RETURNS					PERFORMANCE				ASSETS		ASSET ALLOCATION & TURNOVER					BULL & BEAR		FEES		
Min Additional Investment	3-Month Total Return	6-Month Total Return	1-Year Total Return	3-Year Total Return	5-Year Total Return	Dividend Yield (TTM)	Expense Ratio	3-Yr Std Deviation	3-Year Beta	NAV	Total Assets (MIL)	%Cash	%Stocks	%Bonds	%Other	Turnover Ratio	Last Bull Market Total Return	Last Bear Market Total Return	Front End Fee (%)	Back End Fee (%)	Inception Date
	4.40	23.53	10.44	35.19	35.47	0.12	1.82	13.02	0.85	15.64	413.2	3	97	0	0	31	26.36	-22.48		1.00	Jan-01
	4.44	23.75	10.78	36.27	37.20	0.58	1.57	13.01	0.85	16.46	413.2	3	97	0	0	31	26.6	-22.46	3.50		Jan-01
	4.53	23.89	11.03	37.31	38.96	0.73	1.32	13.02	0.85	17.06	413.2	3	97	0	0	31	26.75	-22.38			Apr-03
	4.70	24.31	11.75	38.88	41.26	1.15	0.67	13.02	0.85	17.79	413.2	3	97	0	0	31	26.95	-22.23			May-18
	4.66	24.14	11.55	39.32	42.43	1.2	0.82	13.05	0.86	17.74	413.2	3	97	0	0	31	27.1	-22.17			Apr-02
	6.52	26.07	15.45	74.46	81.30	0.04	0.99	13.08	0.94	92.99	4,727	4	96	0	0	87	29.81	-22.16	5.75		Aug-90
	6.33	25.58	14.59	70.57	74.63	0	1.74	13.06	0.94	68.68	4,727	4	96	0	0	87	29.21	-22.38		5.00	Mar-93
	6.34	25.59	14.61	70.59	74.62	0	1.74	13.07	0.94	76.06	4,727	4	96	0	0	87	29.23	-22.39		1.00	Jul-99
	6.39	25.75	14.88	71.86	76.81	0	1.49	13.07	0.94	78.02	4,727	4	96	0	0	87	29.43	-22.31	3.50		Dec-94
	6.47	25.90	15.17	73.15	79.05	0	1.24	13.07	0.94	89.28	4,727	4	96	0	0	87	29.6	-22.23			Jan-03
	6.63	26.30	15.89	75.18	82.04	0.18	0.61	13.07	0.94	100.88	4,727	4	96	0	0	87	29.81	-22.16			May-18
	6.60	26.23	15.76	75.78	83.59	0.24	0.74	13.08	0.94	100.65	4,727	4	96	0	0	87	29.98	-22.05			Jul-94
	-0.66	6.38	1.39	40.44	5.19	1.21	1.26	13.17	0.9	10.41	310.7	1	99	0	0	21					Mar-14
100	-0.76	6.16	1.07	39.14	3.71	0.92	1.61	13.15	0.9	10.39	310.7	1	99	0	0	21					Mar-14
	-4.61	3.03	-13.35				1.18			8.48	1.8	4	96	0	0	32					Jul-18
100	-4.61	2.91	-13.60				1.53			8.47	1.8	4	96	0	0	32					Jul-18
	1.21	4.72	-4.27	10.52	6.26	0.33	2.7	10.06	0.65	9.95	23.5	53	47	0	0	58					Mar-14
100	1.23	4.54	-4.49	9.51	4.84	0.07	3.05	10.05	0.64	9.83	23.5	53	47	0	0	58					Mar-14
	4.41	17.90	-5.07	34.76	30.18	1.55	0.91	18.94	1.37	11.59	42.7	2	98	0	0	34					Mar-14
100	4.27	17.67	-5.40	33.43	28.23	0	1.26	18.92	1.37	11.72	42.7	2	98	0	0	34					Mar-14
	2.20	14.04	-11.25	30.73		0.24	1.11	19.98	1.11	10.64	26.4	3	97	0	0	52					Apr-16
100	2.13	13.80	-11.56	29.52		0	1.46	19.95	1.11	10.55	26.4	3	97	0	0	52					Apr-16
250	2.23	12.61	9.91	27.33	31.75	1.15	0.99	6.87		12.03	64.4	4	51	44	0	44					Jan-14
50	2.52	10.99	5.46	23.97	24.10	2.39	1.17	6.72	0.22	13.85	281.4	4	47	48	0	12	15.3	-11.43	5.75		Feb-96
50	2.30	10.56	4.72	21.32	19.65	1.5	1.9	6.69	0.23	14.51	281.4	4	47	48	0	12	14.77	-11.72		1.00	Feb-96
	2.59	11.10	5.76	24.97	25.66	2.6	0.94	6.72	0.22	13.84	281.4	4	47	48	0	12	15.3	-11.43			Jul-14
	2.50	10.79	5.17	22.90	22.24	1.92	1.5	6.74	0.22	13.89	281.4	4	47	48	0	12	15.13	-11.53			Jun-14
50	2.78	9.52	6.43	18.27	20.59	2.7	1.21	4.63	0.53	13.05	121.9	4	29	67	0	9	11.18	-7.33	4.25		Feb-96
50	2.67	9.15	5.74	15.82	16.39	1.97	1.93	4.63	0.52	13	121.9	4	29	67	0	9	10.7	-7.62		1.00	Aug-12
50	2.68	9.20	5.92	16.56	17.64	2.01	1.68	4.65	0.51	13.39	121.9	4	29	67	0	9	10.81	-7.55		1.00	Feb-96
	2.87	9.71	6.77	19.34	22.25	3	0.9	4.66	0.52	13.02	121.9	4	29	67	0	9	11.18	-7.32			Mar-12
	2.73	9.32	6.17	17.36	18.98	2.45	1.45	4.62	0.52	13.04	121.9	4	29	67	0	9	11.02	-7.42			Jun-14
50	0.48	9.86	4.27	19.63	36.84	2.43	1.12	8.66	0.72	12.71	340.3	1	99	0	0	14			5.75		Sep-15
50	0.43	9.75	4.09	19.08	36.14	2.26	1.28	8.67	0.72	12.71	340.3	1	99	0	0	14			5.75		Apr-15
50	0.26	9.36	3.54	17.12	31.90	1.67	1.82	8.7	0.72	12.74	340.3	1	99	0	0	14				1.00	Sep-15
	0.54	9.81	4.24	19.34	36.18	2.33	1.18	8.72	0.73	12.71	340.3	1	99	0	0	14					Sep-14
	0.54	9.96	4.49	20.35	38.38	2.63	0.9	8.7	0.72	12.63	340.3	1	99	0	0	14					Mar-15
	0.56	9.98	4.66	20.97	39.14	2.8	0.76	8.7	0.72	12.66	340.3	1	99	0	0	14					Feb-13
	0.82	13.12	0.66	36.32	41.91	1.4	1.19	12.52	1.07	15.94	161.1	1	99	0	0	25	19.83	-20.36			Dec-06
50	0.81	13.12	0.57	36.03	41.57	1.2	1.3	12.53	1.07	16.03	161.1	1	99	0	0	25	19.71	-20.4	5.75		Mar-91
50	0.55	12.69	-0.22	32.93	36.30	0.35	2.05	12.48	1.07	16.25	161.1	1	99	0	0	25	19.04	-20.62		1.00	Sep-00
	0.88	13.33	0.92	37.48	44.14	1.64	0.95	12.55	1.08	15.98	161.1	1	99	0	0	25	19.81	-20.14			May-03
50	-2.73	-2.92	-3.55	4.12		1.81	3.16	5.33	26.93	9.62	41.5	101	-1	0	0	64			5.75		Nov-15
50	-2.95	-3.24	-4.17	2.21			3.91	5.28	27	9.53	41.5	101	-1	0	0	64				1.00	Jul-18
	-2.62	-2.82	-3.22	5.20		2.56	2.81	5.27	26.17	9.64	41.5	101	-1	0	0	64					Nov-15
	-2.62	-2.71	-3.10	5.43		2.57	2.71	5.27	27.84	9.66	41.5	101	-1	0	0	64					Nov-15
50	2.13	13.55	3.13	30.26	24.57	1.74	1.28	10.52	-0.26	15.33	730.9	4	81	14	0	15	21.16	-18.57	5.75		Feb-96
50	1.95	13.17	2.46	27.65	20.44	1.21	1.96	10.53	-0.26	14.19	730.9	4	81	14	0	15	20.86	-18.82		1.00	Feb-96
	2.20	13.69	3.41	31.34	26.38	2.04	0.99	10.51	-0.26	15.27	730.9	4	81	14	0	15	21.42	-18.58			Dec-08
	2.01	13.33	2.76	28.97	22.85	1.37	1.61	10.49	-0.26	15.22	730.9	4	81	14	0	15	20.98	-18.66			Jun-14
50	1.14	11.54	-3.35	24.14	11.67	2.3	1.3	11.36	1.01	15.07	215.7	2	98	0	0	27	12.94	-23.72	5.75		Feb-09
50	1.14	11.54	-3.55	23.78	9.65	2.25	1.5	11.38	1.01	14.98	215.7	2	98	0	0	27	12.46	-23.96	5.75		May-16

	MARKET			FUND TYPE, CATEGORY & OBJECTIVE	RATINGS					MINIMUMS
Fund Name	Ticker Symbol	Traded On	Fund Type	Category and (Prospectus Objective)	Overall Rating	Reward Rating	Risk Rating	Recent Up/ Downgrade	Open to New Investors	Min Initial Investment
QS International Equity Fund Class C	LMGEX	NAS CM	Open End	Global Equity Large Cap (Foreign Stock)	C	C-	C+		Y	1,000
QS International Equity Fund Class FI	LGFEX	NAS CM	Open End	Global Equity Large Cap (Foreign Stock)	C	C-	C+		Y	0
QS International Equity Fund Class I	LGIEX	NAS CM	Open End	Global Equity Large Cap (Foreign Stock)	C	C	B-		Y	1,000,000
QS International Equity Fund Class IS	LIESX	NAS CM	Open End	Global Equity Large Cap (Foreign Stock)	C	C	B-		Y	1,000,000
QS International Equity Fund Class R	LMIRX	NAS CM	Open End	Global Equity Large Cap (Foreign Stock)	C	C-	C+		Y	0
QS Moderate Growth Fund Class A	SCGRX	NAS CM	Open End	Aggressive Alloc (Balanced)	B-	C	B+	Up	Y	1,000
QS Moderate Growth Fund Class C	SCGCX	NAS CM	Open End	Aggressive Alloc (Balanced)	B-	C	B+	Up	Y	1,000
QS Moderate Growth Fund Class I	LLAIX	NAS CM	Open End	Aggressive Alloc (Balanced)	B-	C	B+	Up	Y	1,000,000
QS Moderate Growth Fund Class R	LLMRX	NAS CM	Open End	Aggressive Alloc (Balanced)	B-	C	B+	Up	Y	0
QS S&P 500 Index Fund Class A	SBSPX	NAS CM	Open End	US Equity Large Cap Blend (Growth)	B-	C	B		Y	0
QS S&P 500 Index Fund Class D	SBSDX	NAS CM	Open End	US Equity Large Cap Blend (Growth)	B-	C	B		Y	0
QS Strategic Real Return Fund Class A	LRRAX	NAS CM	Open End	Moderate Alloc (Asset Alloc)	C+	C	B	Up	Y	1,000
QS Strategic Real Return Fund Class A2	LSRAX	NAS CM	Open End	Moderate Alloc (Asset Alloc)	C+	C	B	Up	Y	1,000
QS Strategic Real Return Fund Class C	LRRCX	NAS CM	Open End	Moderate Alloc (Asset Alloc)	C+	C-	B	Up	Y	1,000
QS Strategic Real Return Fund Class I	LRRIX	NAS CM	Open End	Moderate Alloc (Asset Alloc)	B-	C	B+	Up	Y	1,000,000
QS Strategic Real Return Fund Class IS	LRRSX	NAS CM	Open End	Moderate Alloc (Asset Alloc)	B-	C	B+	Up	Y	1,000,000
QS U.S. Large Cap Equity Fund Class FI	LMUSX	NAS CM	Open End	US Equity Large Cap Blend (Growth)	C+	C	B			0
QS U.S. Large Cap Equity Fund Class I	LMTIX	NAS CM	Open End	US Equity Large Cap Blend (Growth)	C+	C	B			1,000,000
QS U.S. Large Cap Equity Fund Class IS	LMISX	NAS CM	Open End	US Equity Large Cap Blend (Growth)	C+	C	B		Y	1,000,000
QS U.S. Small Capitalization Equity Fund Class A	LMBAX	NAS CM	Open End	US Equity Small Cap (Small Company)	C	C-	C		Y	1,000
QS U.S. Small Capitalization Equity Fund Class A2	LUSAX	NAS CM	Open End	US Equity Small Cap (Small Company)	C	C-	C		Y	1,000
QS U.S. Small Capitalization Equity Fund Class C	LMBCX	NAS CM	Open End	US Equity Small Cap (Small Company)	C	C-	C		Y	1,000
QS U.S. Small Capitalization Equity Fund Class FI	LGSCX	NAS CM	Open End	US Equity Small Cap (Small Company)	C	C-	C		Y	0
QS U.S. Small Capitalization Equity Fund Class I	LMSIX	NAS CM	Open End	US Equity Small Cap (Small Company)	C	C-	C		Y	1,000,000
QS U.S. Small Capitalization Equity Fund Class IS	LMBMX	NAS CM	Open End	US Equity Small Cap (Small Company)	C	C-	C+		Y	1,000,000
Quaker Impact Growth Fund Advisor Class	QUAGX	NAS CM	Open End	US Equity Large Cap Growth (Aggr Growth)	C+	C	B		Y	2,000
Quaker Impact Growth Fund Class Institutional	QAGIX	NAS CM	Open End	US Equity Large Cap Growth (Aggr Growth)	C+	C	B		Y	1,000,000
Quaker Small/Mid-Cap Impact Value Fund Advisor Class	QUSVX	NAS CM	Open End	US Equity Small Cap (Small Company)	B-	C	B		Y	2,000
Quaker Small/Mid-Cap Impact Value Fund Class Institutional	QSVIX	NAS CM	Open End	US Equity Small Cap (Small Company)	B-	C	B		Y	1,000,000
Quantified All-Cap Equity Fund Advisor Class	QACAX	NAS CM	Open End	US Equity Mid Cap (Equity-Income)	C-	C-	C		Y	10,000
Quantified All-Cap Equity Fund Investor Class	QACFX	NAS CM	Open End	US Equity Mid Cap (Equity-Income)	C	C-	C		Y	10,000
Quantified Alternative Investment Fund Advisor Class	QALAX	NAS CM	Open End	Multialternative (Growth)	C-	C-	C		Y	10,000
Quantified Alternative Investment Fund Investor Class	QALTX	NAS CM	Open End	Multialternative (Growth)	C-	C-	C		Y	10,000
Quantified Market Leaders Fund Advisor Class	QMLAX	NAS CM	Open End	US Equity Mid Cap (Growth & Income)	C	C	C	Up	Y	10,000
Quantified Market Leaders Fund Investor Class	QMLFX	NAS CM	Open End	US Equity Mid Cap (Growth & Income)	C	C	C		Y	10,000
Quantified STF Fund Advisor Class	QSTAX	NAS CM	Open End	US Equity Large Cap Growth (Growth & Income)	C	C	C		Y	10,000
Quantified STF Fund Investor Class	QSTFX	NAS CM	Open End	US Equity Large Cap Growth (Growth & Income)	C	C	C		Y	10,000
Queens Road Small Cap Value Fund	QRSVX	NAS CM	Open End	US Equity Small Cap (Small Company)	C	C-	B	Down	Y	2,500
Queens Road Value Fund	QRVLX	NAS CM	Open End	US Equity Large Cap Value (Growth)	B-	C	B+	Down	Y	2,500
Ranger Micro Cap Fund Institutional Class	RFIMX	NAS CM	Open End	US Equity Small Cap (Small Company)	D	D+	C		Y	250,000
Ranger Quest For Income & Growth Institutional Cls	RFIDX	NAS CM	Open End	Global Equity Large Cap (Growth & Income)	B-	C	B+	Up	Y	250,000
Ranger Quest for Income and Growth Investor	RFTDX	NAS CM	Open End	Global Equity Large Cap (Growth & Income)	B-	C	B+	Up	Y	25,000
Ranger Small Cap Fund Institutional Class	RFISX	NAS CM	Open End	US Equity Small Cap (Small Company)	C+	C	C+		Y	250,000
RARE Global Infrastructure Value Fund Class A	RGAVX	NAS CM	Open End	Infrastructure Sector Equity (Utility)	C+	C+	B-	Up	Y	1,000
RARE Global Infrastructure Value Fund Class I	RGIVX	NAS CM	Open End	Infrastructure Sector Equity (Utility)	C+	C+	B-	Up	Y	1,000,000
RARE Global Infrastructure Value Fund Class IS	RGSVX	NAS CM	Open End	Infrastructure Sector Equity (Utility)	B-	C+	B-	Up	Y	1,000,000
Rareview Longevity Income Generation Institutional Cls	RVIGX	NAS CM	Open End	Moderate Alloc (Growth & Income)	C	C	B		Y	1,000,000
Rareview Longevity Income Generation Fund Retail Class	RLIGX	NAS CM	Open End	Moderate Alloc (Growth & Income)	C	C	B		Y	2,500
Rational Dividend Capture Fund Class A	HDCAX	NAS CM	Open End	US Equity Large Cap Value (Equity-Income)	D	D	D+	Down	Y	1,000
Rational Dividend Capture Fund Class C	HDCEX	NAS CM	Open End	US Equity Large Cap Value (Equity-Income)	D	D	D+		Y	1,000
Rational Dividend Capture Fund Class Institutional	HDCTX	NAS CM	Open End	US Equity Large Cap Value (Equity-Income)	D	D	D+	Down	Y	1,000
Rational Dynamic Brands Fund Class A	HSUAX	NAS CM	Open End	US Equity Large Cap Growth (Growth)	B-	C	B		Y	1,000

★ Expanded analysis of this fund is included in Section II.

	TOTAL RETURNS					PERFORMANCE				ASSETS		ASSET ALLOCATION & TURNOVER					BULL & BEAR		FEES		
Min Additional Investment	3-Month Total Return	6-Month Total Return	1-Year Total Return	3-Year Total Return	5-Year Total Return	Dividend Yield (TTM)	Expense Ratio	3-Yr Std Deviation	3-Year Beta	NAV	Total Assets (MIL)	%Cash	%Stocks	%Bonds	%Other	Turnover Ratio	Last Bull Market Total Return	Last Bear Market Total Return	Front End Fee (%)	Back End Fee (%)	Inception Date
50	1.00	11.17	-4.07	21.34	7.41	1.46	1.98	11.35	1.01	15.12	215.7	2	98	0	0	27	12.46	-23.96		1.00	Feb-95
	1.16	11.59	-3.39	24.08	11.47	2.04	1.3	11.39	1.01	15.69	215.7	2	98	0	0	27	12.93	-23.68			May-03
	1.22	11.75	-3.04	25.37	13.42	2.49	0.95	11.38	1.01	15.69	215.7	2	98	0	0	27	13.21	-23.62			May-98
	1.22	11.85	-2.93	25.73	14.03	2.62	0.85	11.39	1.01	15.66	215.7	2	98	0	0	27	13.24	-23.57			Aug-08
	1.03	11.42	-3.64	23.06	10.02	1.95	1.55	11.35	1.01	15.6	215.7	2	98	0	0	27	12.83	-23.89			Dec-06
50	2.24	12.34	4.14	28.20	25.41	2.11	1.23	8.85	-0.06	15.31	463.3	4	66	29	0	15	18.77	-15.41	5.75		Feb-96
50	2.07	12.00	3.44	25.46	21.16	1.36	1.91	8.86	-0.06	15.61	463.3	4	66	29	0	15	18.3	-15.65		1.00	Feb-96
	2.39	12.54	4.49	29.36	27.26	2.4	0.95	8.85	-0.06	15.18	463.3	4	66	29	0	15	18.96	-15.37			Oct-07
	2.20	12.19	3.84	26.89	23.42	1.78	1.57	8.87	-0.07	15.11	463.3	4	66	29	0	15	18.6	-15.5			Jun-14
	4.15	19.21	9.76	48.27	61.57	1.22	0.59	12.18	1	26.8	272.2	1	99	0	0	2	24.69	-16.47			Jan-98
	4.20	19.34	9.99	49.23	63.17	1.4	0.39	12.2	1	27.02	272.2	1	99	0	0	2	24.86	-16.37			Aug-98
50	1.63	11.24	0.60	11.81	-8.51	4.19	1.35	7.79	0.92	11.18	100.1	3	58	39	0	61	13.7	-13.05	5.75		Feb-10
50	1.57	11.03	0.40	11.06	-9.48	4.24	1.55	7.75	0.92	10.97	100.1	3	58	39	0	61	13.72	-13.07	5.75		Oct-12
50	1.40	10.83	-0.12	9.22	-11.88	3.16	2.1	7.83	0.92	10.84	100.1	3	58	39	0	61	13.29	-13.34		1.00	Feb-10
	1.69	11.30	0.77	12.59	-7.35	4.51	1.1	7.79	0.91	11.42	100.1	3	58	39	0	61	13.89	-12.98			Feb-10
	1.71	11.47	0.96	12.96	-6.91	4.65	1	7.71	0.92	11.27	100.1	3	58	39	0	61	13.89	-12.98			Dec-11
	2.45	16.66	4.44	46.13	48.97	1.16	1.05	13.12	1.06	17.86	675.5	1	99	0	0	40	25.32	-17.57			Apr-08
	2.52	16.85	4.52	47.19	51.05	1.24	0.74	13.12	1.06	17.76	675.5	1	99	0	0	40	25.61	-17.48			May-15
	2.57	16.90	4.57	47.34	51.19	1.24	0.7	13.12	1.06	17.78	675.5	1	99	0	0	40	25.61	-17.48			Apr-08
50	0.00	15.22	-8.47	26.39	25.50	0.05	1.22	18.05	1.05	11.6	199.6	1	99	0	0	26	26.97	-25.4	5.75		Feb-09
50	-0.07	15.16	-8.71	25.62	24.22	0	1.45	18.01	1.04	11.41	199.6	1	99	0	0	26	26.97	-25.32	5.75		Oct-12
50	-0.26	14.72	-9.19	23.59	20.86	0	1.92	18.01	1.04	10.62	199.6	1	99	0	0	26	26.23	-25.61		1.00	Feb-09
	0.00	15.18	-8.55	26.22	25.30	0	1.3	18.08	1.05	11.02	199.6	1	99	0	0	26	26.89	-25.46			Jan-03
	0.00	15.34	-8.31	27.39	27.50	0.26	1	18.05	1.05	11.89	199.6	1	99	0	0	26	27.16	-25.24			Mar-00
	0.09	15.46	-8.13	27.99	28.16	0.48	0.75	18.06	1.05	11.59	199.6	1	99	0	0	26	27.15	-25.24			Mar-12
100	3.75	21.21	7.37	44.93	41.52	0	2.28	13.16	1.06	34.22	62.1	4	96	0	0	119	21.78	-19.31	5.50		Nov-96
	3.84	21.40	7.66	46.06	43.32	0	2.03	13.18	1.06	35.96	62.1	4	96	0	0	119	21.96	-19.3			Jul-00
100	-0.22	15.58	3.17	41.06	31.66	0	1.61	13.76	0.84	17.65	20.0	6	94	0	0	122	28.41	-24.14	5.50		Nov-96
	-0.10	15.78	3.46	42.23	33.40	0	1.36	13.8	0.84	19.36	20.0	6	94	0	0	122	28.62	-24.1			Sep-00
1,000	-0.77	3.00	-9.44	17.36	13.62	0	2.15	12.91	0.93	8.92	13.4	-4	96	5	2	942					Mar-16
1,000	-0.54	3.42	-8.74	19.70	17.54	0.39	1.55	12.99	0.94	9.07	13.4	-4	96	5	2	942					Aug-13
1,000	0.00	3.54	-0.42	6.46	-2.23	0	2.67	8.32	0.53	9.35	8.7	21	47	26	3	553					Mar-16
1,000	0.21	3.83	0.17	8.61	1.05	0.07	2.07	8.37	0.54	9.48	8.7	21	47	26	3	553					Aug-13
1,000	0.00	11.91	-6.76	30.45	18.30	0	2.36	17.54	1.26	9.3	157.9	-49	78	0	71	495					Mar-16
1,000	0.21	12.33	-6.17	32.98	22.32	1.11	1.76	17.48	1.25	9.38	157.9	-49	78	0	71	495					Aug-13
1,000	-1.58	1.52	-3.65	60.76		0	2.31	25.35	1.26	9.31	70.4	29	0	69	0	72					Nov-15
1,000	-1.45	1.81	-3.11	63.67		0.18	1.71	25.36	1.26	9.51	70.4	29	0	69	0	72					Nov-15
1,000	0.59	9.53	1.06	21.04	27.34	0.11	1.18	12.62	0.67	25.15	124.8	18	82	0	0	6	10.01	-14.63			Jun-02
1,000	4.00	17.55	12.65	44.31	54.00	1.34	0.95	11.76	0.87	24.17	41.7	1	98	0	0	8	14.54	-10.33			Jun-02
	1.82	20.59	-0.51			0	1.5			10.07	17.0	3	97	0	0	3					Jun-18
	5.69	17.37	8.18	28.92	18.35	4.17	1.53	9.54	0.73	12.82	14.4	1	98	0	0	51	15.95				Sep-11
5,000	5.59	17.21	8.00	27.80	16.65	4.23	1.78	9.53	0.73	12.65	14.4	1	98	0	0	51	15.78				Jun-13
	7.45	24.54	4.01	51.40	65.63	0	1.1	16.51	0.92	17.3	24.8	4	96	0	0	49	39.46				Sep-11
50	2.97	17.31	9.86	24.59		2.2	1.35	10.36	0.96	11.65	24.8	2	98	0	0	58			5.75		Mar-16
	3.10	17.54	10.36	25.69		2.56	1	10.32	0.96	11.66	24.8	2	98	0	0	58					Mar-16
	3.13	17.57	10.46	26.11		2.65	0.9	10.34	0.96	11.68	24.8	2	98	0	0	58					Mar-16
1,000	1.44	10.94	7.28			6.13	3.79			10.06	17.4	10	32	62	-6						Nov-16
500	1.31	10.74	6.96			5.83	4.04			10.06	17.4	10	32	62	-6						Nov-16
50	-1.48	4.86	-7.85	-10.72	-7.10	7.21	2.39	11.91	0.77	6.76	17.8	1	85	0	0	307	17.64	-11.85	4.75		Feb-01
50	-1.83	4.18	-8.69	-12.37	-9.77	6.43	3.14	11.83	0.77	6.74	17.8	1	85	0	0	307	17.24	-12.13		1.00	Jan-14
500	-1.59	4.82	-7.74	-10.05	-6.04	7.49	2.14	11.95	0.77	6.76	17.8	1	85	0	0	307	17.93	-11.76			Feb-01
50	3.22	13.91	5.42	39.61	23.66	0	1.51	11.58	0.84	27.18	31.6	1	99	0	0	411	30.28	-23.06	4.75		Sep-02

	MARKET			FUND TYPE, CATEGORY & OBJECTIVE	RATINGS				MINIMUMS	
Fund Name	Ticker Symbol	Traded On	Fund Type	Category and (Prospectus Objective)	Overall Rating	Reward Rating	Risk Rating	Recent Up/ Downgrade	Open to New Investors	Min Initial Investment
Rational Dynamic Brands Fund Class C	HSUCX	NAS CM	Open End	US Equity Large Cap Growth (Growth)	B-	C	B		Y	1,000
Rational Dynamic Brands Fund Institutional Class	HSUTX	NAS CM	Open End	US Equity Large Cap Growth (Growth)	B-	C	B		Y	1,000
Rational Iron Horse Fund Class A	IRHAX	NAS CM	Open End	Long/Short Equity (Growth & Income)	C	C	C+	Down	Y	1,000
Rational Iron Horse Fund Class C	IRHCX	NAS CM	Open End	Long/Short Equity (Growth & Income)	C	C-	C	Down	Y	1,000
Rational Iron Horse Fund Class I	IRHIX	NAS CM	Open End	Long/Short Equity (Growth & Income)	C	C	C+	Down	Y	1,000
Rational NuWave Enhanced Market Opportunity Cls A Shares	NUXAX	NAS CM	Open End	Aggressive Alloc (Growth)	D	C	B		Y	1,000
Rational NuWave Enhanced Market Opportunity Cls C Shares	NUXCX	NAS CM	Open End	Aggressive Alloc (Growth)	D	C	B		Y	1,000
Rational NuWave Enhanced Mkt Opp Inst Shares	NUXIX	NAS CM	Open End	Aggressive Alloc (Growth)	D	C	B		Y	1,000
Rational Strategic Allocation Fund Class A	HBAFX	NAS CM	Open End	Moderate Alloc (Growth & Income)	B-	C	A-	Up	Y	1,000
Rational Strategic Allocation Fund Class C	RHSCX	NAS CM	Open End	Moderate Alloc (Growth & Income)	B-	C	B+	Up	Y	1,000
Rational Strategic Allocation Fund Class Institutional	RHSIX	NAS CM	Open End	Moderate Alloc (Growth & Income)	B-	C	A-		Y	1,000
Rational Tactical Return Fund Class A	HRSAX	NAS CM	Open End	Flexible Alloc (Growth & Income)	C+	C+	C+		Y	1,000
Rational Tactical Return Fund Class C	HRSFX	NAS CM	Open End	Flexible Alloc (Growth & Income)	C+	C+	C+		Y	1,000
Rational Tactical Return Fund Class Institutional	HRSTX	NAS CM	Open End	Flexible Alloc (Growth & Income)	C+	C+	C+		Y	1,000
Rational/ReSolve Adaptive Asset Allocation Fund Class A	RDMAX	NAS CM	Open End	Alternative Miscellaneous (Growth)	C	C-	B-	Up	Y	1,000
Rational/ReSolve Adaptive Asset Allocation Fund Class C	RDMCX	NAS CM	Open End	Alternative Miscellaneous (Growth)	C	C-	C+	Up	Y	1,000
Rational/ReSolve Adaptive Asset Allocation Fund Class I	RDMIX	NAS CM	Open End	Alternative Miscellaneous (Growth)	C	C-	B-	Up	Y	1,000
RBB Free Market U.S. Equity Fund Institutional Class	FMUEX	NAS CM	Open End	US Equity Mid Cap (Growth)	C	C-	C+		Y	0
RBC Emerging Markets Equity Fund Class A	REEAX	NAS CM	Open End	Global Emerg Mkts (Div Emerging Mkts)	C+	C	B	Up	Y	1,000
RBC Emerging Markets Equity Fund Class I	REEIX	NAS CM	Open End	Global Emerg Mkts (Div Emerging Mkts)	C+	C	B	Up	Y	250,000
RBC Emerging Markets Equity Fund Class R6	RREMX	NAS CM	Open End	Global Emerg Mkts (Div Emerging Mkts)	C+	C	B	Up	Y	250,000
RBC Emerging Markets Small Cap Equity Fund Class A	RSMAX	NAS CM	Open End	Global Emerg Mkts (Small Company)	C	C-	C+		Y	1,000
RBC Emerging Markets Small Cap Equity Fund Class I	RESIX	NAS CM	Open End	Global Emerg Mkts (Small Company)	C	C-	C+		Y	250,000
RBC Emerging Markets Value Equity Fund Class I	REMVX	NAS CM	Open End	Global Emerg Mkts (Div Emerging Mkts)	D	D	D+		Y	250,000
RBC Emerging Markets Value Equity Fund Class R6	RMVRX	NAS CM	Open End	Global Emerg Mkts (Div Emerging Mkts)	D	D	D+		Y	250,000
RBC Enterprise Fund Class A	TETAX	NAS CM	Open End	US Equity Small Cap (Small Company)	C	C-	C		Y	1,000
RBC Enterprise Fund Class I	TETIX	NAS CM	Open End	US Equity Small Cap (Small Company)	C	C-	C		Y	250,000
RBC Global Opportunities Fund Class I	RGOIX	NAS CM	Open End	Global Equity Large Cap (Growth)	B-	C+	B	Up	Y	250,000
RBC Global Opportunities Fund Class R6	RGORX	NAS CM	Open End	Global Equity Large Cap (Growth)	B-	C+	B	Up	Y	250,000
RBC International Opportunities Fund Class I	RIOIX	NAS CM	Open End	Global Equity Large Cap (Growth)	C	C	B-		Y	250,000
RBC International Opportunities Fund Class R6	RIORX	NAS CM	Open End	Global Equity Large Cap (Growth)	C	C	B-		Y	250,000
RBC Microcap Value Fund Class A	TMVAX	NAS CM	Open End	US Equity Small Cap (Small Company)	C	C-	C		Y	1,000
RBC Microcap Value Fund Class I	RMVIX	NAS CM	Open End	US Equity Small Cap (Small Company)	C	C-	C		Y	250,000
RBC Small Cap Core Fund Class A	TEEAX	NAS CM	Open End	US Equity Small Cap (Small Company)	D+	D+	C-	Down	Y	1,000
RBC Small Cap Core Fund Class I	RCSIX	NAS CM	Open End	US Equity Small Cap (Small Company)	D+	D+	C-	Down	Y	250,000
RBC Small Cap Core Fund Class R6	RBRCX	NAS CM	Open End	US Equity Small Cap (Small Company)	D+	D+	C-	Down	Y	250,000
RBC Small Cap Value Fund Class I	RSVIX	NAS CM	Open End	US Equity Small Cap (Small Company)	C	C-	C	Up	Y	250,000
RBC Small Cap Value Fund Class R6	RRSVX	NAS CM	Open End	US Equity Small Cap (Small Company)	C	C-	C	Up	Y	250,000
RBC SMID Cap Growth Fund Class A	TMCAX	NAS CM	Open End	US Equity Mid Cap (Growth)	C+	C+	B-	Down	Y	1,000
RBC SMID Cap Growth Fund Class I	TMCIX	NAS CM	Open End	US Equity Mid Cap (Growth)	B-	C+	B-		Y	250,000
RBC SMID Cap Growth Fund Class R6	RSMRX	NAS CM	Open End	US Equity Mid Cap (Growth)	B-	C+	B-		Y	250,000
Reaves Utilities & Energy Infrastructure Cls Institutional	RSRFX	NAS CM	Open End	Infrastructure Sector Equity (Growth & Income)	B-	C+	B		Y	1,000
Reaves Utility Income Trust	UTG	AMEX	Closed End	Utilities Sector Equity (Utility)	B-	B-	C+	Down	Y	
Recurrent MLP & Infrastructure Fund Class I	RMLPX	NAS CM	Open End	Energy Sector Equity ()	D+	D+	C	Up	Y	2,500
Red Oak Technology Select Fund	ROGSX	NAS CM	Open End	Technology Sector Equity (Technology)	B-	C+	B	Down	Y	2,000
Redwood Activist Leaders Fund Class I	RWLIX	NAS CM	Open End	US Equity Mid Cap (Growth)	D	D	C-		Y	10,000
Redwood Activist Leaders Fund Class N	RWLNX	NAS CM	Open End	US Equity Mid Cap (Growth)	D	D	D+		Y	10,000
Redwood AlphaFactor Tactical Core Fund Class I	RWTIX	NAS CM	Open End	US Equity Mid Cap (Growth & Income)	C	D+	C		Y	250,000
Redwood AlphaFactor Tactical Core Fund Class N	RWTNX	NAS CM	Open End	US Equity Mid Cap (Growth & Income)	C-	D+	C	Down	Y	10,000
Redwood AlphaFactor Tactical International Fund Class I	RWIIX	NAS CM	Open End	Global Equity Large Cap (Growth)	D+	D+	C+	Up	Y	10,000
Redwood AlphaFactor Tactical International Fund Class N	RWINX	NAS CM	Open End	Global Equity Large Cap (Growth)	D+	D+	C+	Up	Y	10,000
Redwood Systematic Macro Trend ("SMarT") Fund Class I	RWSIX	NAS CM	Open End	Cautious Alloc (Growth)	D+	D	C	Up	Y	10,000

★ Expanded analysis of this fund is included in Section II.

Min Additional Investment	TOTAL RETURNS: 3-Month Total Return	6-Month Total Return	1-Year Total Return	3-Year Total Return	5-Year Total Return	PERFORMANCE: Dividend Yield (TTM)	Expense Ratio	3-Yr Std Deviation	3-Year Beta	ASSETS: NAV	Total Assets (MIL)	ASSET ALLOCATION & TURNOVER: %Cash	%Stocks	%Bonds	%Other	Turnover Ratio	BULL & BEAR: Last Bull Market Total Return	Last Bear Market Total Return	FEES: Front End Fee (%)	Back End Fee (%)	Inception Date
50	2.98	13.28	4.70	37.05	20.17	0	2.26	11.51	0.84	24.48	31.6	1	99	0	0	411	29.72	-23.31		1.00	Jan-14
500	3.24	14.06	5.69	40.65	25.24	0.24	1.26	11.5	0.84	38.77	31.6	1	99	0	0	411	30.51	-23			Sep-02
50	-0.62	0.02	1.06	7.31	10.24	1.06	1.98	3.08	0.12	9.34	8.1	11	89	0	0	162	16.37		5.75		Jul-11
50	-0.78	-0.18	0.69	5.39	6.66	0.7	2.73	3.07	0.12	9.29	8.1	11	89	0	0	162	15.86			1.00	Apr-17
500	-0.55	0.16	1.36	8.03	11.74	1.25	1.74	3.13	0.12	9.35	8.1	11	89	0	0	162	16.38				Nov-11
50	2.65	11.70	19.26			8.32	2.26			16.23	26.9	17	83	0	0				5.75		Feb-18
50	2.48	11.27	18.37			8.25	3.01			16.08	26.9	17	83	0	0					1.00	Feb-18
500	2.77	11.88	19.58			8.34	2.01			16.28	26.9	17	83	0	0						Feb-18
50	1.16	7.92	3.76	21.73	22.45	3.9	1.94	5.93	0.46	9.72	9.8	9	41	47	0	53	13.18	-11.08	4.75		Jul-09
50	0.98	7.45	2.98	18.92	17.98	3.26	2.69	5.98	0.46	9.68	9.8	9	41	47	0	53	12.69	-11.36		1.00	May-16
500	1.23	8.00	3.95	22.53	23.34	4.19	1.69	5.95	0.46	9.68	9.8	9	41	47	0	53	13.18	-11.08			May-16
50	2.32	4.77	10.50	26.00	-16.97	0	2.32	10.25	0.12	5.71	92.2	68	0	32	0	0	15.36	-24.34	4.75		May-07
50	2.16	4.42	9.54	23.29	-20.32	0	3.07	10.21	0.13	5.66	92.2	68	0	32	0	0	14.69	-24.54		1.00	May-16
500	2.35	4.81	10.50	26.56	-16.79	0.1	2.07	10.26	0.12	5.66	92.2	68	0	32	0	0	15.35	-24.22			May-07
50	4.47	13.54	5.18	9.13	22.53	0	2.35			25.9	36.6	96	4	0	0	0	3.68	-22.82	5.75		Sep-16
50	4.35	13.17	4.42	6.79	18.13	0	3.1			25.42	36.6	96	4	0	0	0	3.23	-23.06		1.00	Sep-16
500	4.56	13.68	5.43	10.00	24.11	0	2.1			26.09	36.6	96	4	0	0	0	3.84	-22.74			Sep-16
	1.66	14.24	-2.71	35.47	33.71	0.84	0.86	15.49	0.98	17.72	3,067	1	97	0	2		26.99	-24.07			Dec-07
	3.13	12.97	8.49	34.49	29.69	0.8	1.13	12.48	0.86	12.19	1,208	4	96	0	0	19			5.75		Dec-13
	3.24	13.13	8.79	35.41	31.22	1.07	0.88	12.45	0.86	12.4	1,208	4	96	0	0	19					Dec-13
	3.14	13.07	8.76	35.19	31.01	1.07	0.88	12.47	0.86	12.45	1,208	4	96	0	0	19					Nov-16
100	-2.12	3.47	-3.07	13.40	3.03	0	1.7	10.74	0.76	10.11	9.1	4	95	0	1	33			5.75		Dec-13
	-2.12	3.47	-2.87	14.16	4.23	0.2	1.45	10.78	0.76	10.12	9.1	4	95	0	1	33					Dec-13
	-1.14	9.50	-2.31			2.1	0.95			8.64	4.4	1	99	0	0	75					Feb-18
	-1.14	9.50	-2.24			2.17	0.88			8.64	4.4	1	99	0	0	75					Feb-18
	2.20	19.01	-9.35	33.10	14.49	0	1.33	20.15	1.11	17.65	70.8	2	98	0	0	15	28.45	-21.97	5.75		Apr-04
	2.25	19.11	-9.13	34.08	15.89	0	1.08	20.13	1.11	18.57	70.8	2	98	0	0	15	28.63	-21.96			Sep-04
	4.84	22.36	8.48	56.93		0.12	0.86	12.92	1.1	14.72	28.3	1	99	0	0	28					Dec-14
	4.82	22.38	8.53	57.20		0.41	0.81	12.92	1.1	14.76	28.3	1	99	0	0	28					Nov-16
	4.86	20.47	3.84	32.42		0.9	0.89	12.97	1.07	10.77	74.8	1	99	0	0	49					Dec-14
	4.74	20.35	3.82	32.50		0.9	0.84	12.96	1.07	10.82	74.8	1	99	0	0	49					Nov-16
	-0.49	10.74	-8.61	27.43	25.48	0.72	1.32	16.72	0.92	26.08	115.7	2	98	0	0	5	27.5	-20.42	5.75		Apr-04
	-0.41	10.87	-8.35	28.41	27.10	1.01	1.07	16.74	0.93	26.09	115.7	2	98	0	0	5	27.69	-20.3			Sep-87
	2.25	16.86	-12.37	17.58	13.99	0	1.15	20.63	1.18	29.45	164.1	1	99	0	0	24	28.22	-23.98	5.75		Apr-04
	2.31	16.98	-12.14	18.48	15.39	0	0.9	20.62	1.18	31	164.1	1	99	0	0	24	28.47	-23.91			Aug-91
0	2.27	16.79	-12.28	18.35	15.27	0	0.87	20.67	1.18	31.01	164.1	1	99	0	0	24	28.47	-23.91			Nov-16
	3.15	17.50	-7.44	26.72		0.75	0.86	17.76	1.01	12.08	104.4	2	98	0	0	29					Dec-14
0	3.14	17.50	-7.42	26.94		0.79	0.81	17.76	1.01	12.15	104.4	2	98	0	0	29					Nov-16
	6.14	28.72	12.06	51.25	64.36	0	1.07	15.87	0.93	13.31	97.8	2	98	0	0	22	27.8	-17.8	5.75		Jun-94
	6.16	28.84	12.33	52.25	66.35	0	0.82	15.82	0.93	15.32	97.8	2	98	0	0	22	27.94	-17.69			Jun-94
0	6.22	28.88	12.38	52.40	66.52	0	0.77	15.82	0.93	15.35	97.8	2	98	0	0	22	27.95	-17.7			Nov-16
	5.43	22.88	14.02	26.53	38.70	1.18	1.47	10.42	0.67	10.45	40.0	0	100	0	0	66	14.73	-10			Dec-04
	3.90	22.60	17.80	30.29	56.75	2.77		12.36	0.72	35.11	1,709	-26	126	0	0	24	16.55	-6.7			Feb-04
500	-1.97	20.06	3.23			6.81	1.25			19.1	35.0	1	99	0	0	116					Nov-17
25	1.69	21.87	12.86	92.44	118.24	0.73	0.94	14.06	0.85	28.75	629.2	7	93	0	0	9	25	-15.58			Dec-98
1,000	-0.39	16.46	-6.82			0.47	0.9			14.59	37.6	0	100	0	0						Nov-17
1,000	-0.68	15.94	-7.27			0.28	1.15			14.53	37.6	0	100	0	0						Nov-17
1,000	3.04	3.11	-0.87			0.55	1.2			15.22	99.1	2	98	0	0						Mar-17
1,000	2.98	2.91	-1.14			0.35	1.45			15.19	99.1	2	98	0	0						Mar-17
1,000	1.76	4.55	5.28			1.7	1.33			15.18	104.1	2	40	0	58						Nov-17
1,000	1.66	4.42	5.02			0.61	1.58			15.3	104.1	2	40	0	58						Nov-17
1,000	1.68	3.15	-2.18			1.95	1.58			14.5	69.5	1	42	0	57						Nov-17

	MARKET		FUND TYPE, CATEGORY & OBJECTIVE		RATINGS				MINIMUMS	
Fund Name	Ticker Symbol	Traded On	Fund Type	Category and (Prospectus Objective)	Overall Rating	Reward Rating	Risk Rating	Recent Up/ Downgrade	Open to New Investors	Min Initial Investment
Redwood Systematic Macro Trend ("SMarT") Fund Class N	RWSNX	NAS CM	Open End	Cautious Alloc (Growth)	D+	D	C	Up	Y	10,000
Reinhart Genesis PMV Fund Advisor Class	RPMFX	NAS CM	Open End	US Equity Small Cap (Growth)	D	D+	C+		Y	5,000
Reinhart Genesis PMV Fund Investor Class	RPMAX	NAS CM	Open End	US Equity Small Cap (Growth)	D	D+	C+		Y	5,000
Reinhart Mid Cap PMV Fund Advisor Class	RPMVX	NAS CM	Open End	US Equity Mid Cap (Growth)	C	C	B-		Y	5,000
Reinhart Mid Cap PMV Fund Institutional Class	RPMNX	NAS CM	Open End	US Equity Mid Cap (Growth)	C	C	B-		Y	1,000,000
Reinhart Mid Cap PMV Fund Investor Class	RPMMX	NAS CM	Open End	US Equity Mid Cap (Growth)	C	C	B-		Y	5,000
Relative Value Fund CIA Class Shares	VFLEX	NAS CM	Closed End	Multialternative (Growth & Income)	C	D+	C+	Up	Y	1,000
REMS Intl Real Estate Value-Opp Founders Shares	REIFX	NAS CM	Open End	Real Estate Sector Equity (Real Estate)	B-	C	B+		Y	50,000
REMS International Real Estate Value-Opportunity Z Shares	REIZX	NAS CM	Open End	Real Estate Sector Equity (Real Estate)	B-	C	B+		Y	100,000
REMS Real Estate Income 50/50 Fund Class Platform Shares	RREFX	NAS CM	Open End	Real Estate Sector Equity (Real Estate)	C	C	C+		Y	2,500
REMS Real Estate Income 50/50 Fund Institutional Shares	RREIX	NAS CM	Open End	Real Estate Sector Equity (Real Estate)	C	C	C+	Down	Y	50,000
REMS Real Estate Value Opportunity Institutional Cls	HLRRX	NAS CM	Open End	Real Estate Sector Equity (Real Estate)	C	C	C		Y	50,000
REMS Real Estate Value-Opportunity Fund, P Class	HLPPX	NAS CM	Open End	Real Estate Sector Equity (Real Estate)	C	C	C		Y	2,500
RENN Global Entrepreneurs Fund, Inc.	RCG	AMEX	Closed End	Moderate Alloc (Growth & Income)	C-	C-	C-	Down	Y	
Resource Real Estate Diversified Income Fund Class A	RREDX	NAS CM	Closed End	Real Estate Sector Equity (Real Estate)	B	C+	A		Y	2,500
Resource Real Estate Diversified Income Fund Class C	CRREX	NAS CM	Closed End	Real Estate Sector Equity (Real Estate)	B	C+	A		Y	2,500
Resource Real Estate Diversified Income Fund Class D	DRREX	NAS CM	Closed End	Real Estate Sector Equity (Real Estate)	B	C+	A		Y	2,500
Resource Real Estate Diversified Income Fund Class I	IRREX	NAS CM	Closed End	Real Estate Sector Equity (Real Estate)	B	C+	A		Y	2,500
Resource Real Estate Diversified Income Fund Class L	LRREX	NAS CM	Closed End	Real Estate Sector Equity (Real Estate)	B	C+	A		Y	2,500
Resource Real Estate Diversified Income Fund Class T	RRETX	NAS CM	Closed End	Real Estate Sector Equity (Real Estate)	B	C+	A		Y	2,500
Resource Real Estate Diversified Income Fund Class U	URREX	NAS CM	Closed End	Real Estate Sector Equity (Real Estate)	B	C+	A		Y	2,500
Resource Real Estate Diversified Income Cls W Shares	WRREX	NAS CM	Closed End	Real Estate Sector Equity (Real Estate)	B	C+	A		Y	2,500
RESQ Dynamic Allocation Fund Class A	RQEAX	NAS CM	Open End	Moderate Alloc (Growth)	D+	D	C-	Down	Y	1,000
RESQ Dynamic Allocation Fund Class C	RQECX	NAS CM	Open End	Moderate Alloc (Growth)	D+	D	C-		Y	1,000
RESQ Dynamic Allocation Fund Class I	RQEIX	NAS CM	Open End	Moderate Alloc (Growth)	D+	D+	C-	Down	Y	100,000
RESQ Strategic Income Fund Class A	RQIAX	NAS CM	Open End	Cautious Alloc (Income)	D	D	D+		Y	1,000
RESQ Strategic Income Fund Class C	RQICX	NAS CM	Open End	Cautious Alloc (Income)	D	D	D+		Y	1,000
RESQ Strategic Income Fund Class I	RQIIX	NAS CM	Open End	Cautious Alloc (Income)	D	D	C-		Y	100,000
Reynders McVeigh Core Equity Fund Institutional Shares	ESGEX	NAS CM	Open End	US Equity Large Cap Growth (Growth)	U	U	U		Y	1,000
Reynolds Blue Chip Growth Fund	RBCGX	NAS CM	Open End	US Equity Large Cap Growth (Growth)	C+	C	B-		Y	1,000
Rice Hall James Micro Cap Portfolio Institutional Class	RHJSX	NAS CM	Open End	US Equity Small Cap (Small Company)	C	C-	B-	Down	Y	2,500
Rice Hall James Small Cap Portfolio Institutional Class	RHJMX	NAS CM	Open End	US Equity Small Cap (Small Company)	C	C	C		Y	2,500
Rice Hall James Smid Cap Portfolio Investor	RHJVX	NAS CM	Open End	US Equity Mid Cap (Growth)	C+	C	B		Y	2,500
RiskPro® 30+ Fund Class R	PFSEX	NAS CM	Open End	US Equity Large Cap Growth (Aggr Growth)	D+	D	C	Up	Y	1,000
RiskPro® Aggressive 30+ Fund Class R	PFLWX	NAS CM	Open End	Global Equity Large Cap (Aggr Growth)	D+	D	C-	Up	Y	1,000
RiskPro® Alternative 0-15 Fund Class R	PFAOX	NAS CM	Open End	Multialternative (Growth & Income)	D+	D+	C+	Up	Y	1,000
RiskPro® Dynamic 15-25 Fund Class R	PFDPX	NAS CM	Open End	Moderate Alloc (Growth & Income)	D+	D+	C+	Up	Y	1,000
RiskPro® Dynamic 20-30 Fund Class R	PFJDX	NAS CM	Open End	Moderate Alloc (Growth & Income)	D	D+	C		Y	1,000
RiskPro® PFG 30+ Fund Class R	PFSMX	NAS CM	Open End	Global Equity Large Cap (Aggr Growth)	D+	D+	C+	Up	Y	1,000
RiskPro® PFG Aggressive 30+ Fund Class R	PFSUX	NAS CM	Open End	Global Equity Large Cap (Aggr Growth)	D+	D	C	Up	Y	1,000
RiskPro® PFG Balanced 20-30 Fund Class R	PFDBX	NAS CM	Open End	Moderate Alloc (Balanced)	D+	D+	C+	Up	Y	1,000
RiskPro® PFG Equity 30+ Fund Class R	PFDEX	NAS CM	Open End	US Equity Large Cap Blend (Aggr Growth)	D+	D+	C+	Up	Y	1,000
RiskPro® PFG Global 30+ Fund Class R	PFDGX	NAS CM	Open End	Global Equity Large Cap (World Stock)	D+	D	C	Up	Y	1,000
RiskPro® Tactical 0-30 Fund Class R	PFTEX	NAS CM	Open End	Moderate Alloc (Growth & Income)	D+	D	C	Up	Y	1,000
RiskPro®PFG 0-15 Fund Class R	PFADX	NAS CM	Open End	Cautious Alloc (Growth & Income)	D+	D+	C+	Up	Y	1,000
River Oak Discovery Fund	RIVSX	NAS CM	Open End	US Equity Small Cap (Growth)	C	C	C	Down	Y	2,000
Riverbridge Eco Leaders® Fund Institutional Class	RIVEX	NAS CM	Open End	US Equity Mid Cap (Growth)	B-	C+	B	Down		2,500
Riverbridge Eco Leaders® Fund Investor Class	ECOLX	NAS CM	Open End	US Equity Mid Cap (Growth)	B-	C+	B	Down		2,500
Riverbridge Growth Fund Institutional Class	RIVBX	NAS CM	Open End	US Equity Mid Cap (Growth)	B-	C+	B	Down	Y	2,500
Riverbridge Growth Fund Investor Class	RIVRX	NAS CM	Open End	US Equity Mid Cap (Growth)	B-	C+	B	Down	Y	2,500
RiverFront Asset Allocation Aggressive Class A	RLAAX	NAS CM	Open End	Global Equity Large Cap (Growth)	C	C	C+		Y	2,500
RiverFront Asset Allocation Aggressive Class C	RLTCX	NAS CM	Open End	Global Equity Large Cap (Growth)	C	C-	C+		Y	2,500

★ Expanded analysis of this fund is included in Section II.

	TOTAL RETURNS					PERFORMANCE				ASSETS		ASSET ALLOCATION & TURNOVER					BULL & BEAR		FEES		
Min Additional Investment	3-Month Total Return	6-Month Total Return	1-Year Total Return	3-Year Total Return	5-Year Total Return	Dividend Yield (TTM)	Expense Ratio	3-Yr Std Deviation	3-Year Beta	NAV	Total Assets (MIL)	%Cash	%Stocks	%Bonds	%Other	Turnover Ratio	Last Bull Market Total Return	Last Bear Market Total Return	Front End Fee (%)	Back End Fee (%)	Inception Date
1,000	1.60	2.98	-2.39			1.05	1.83			14.59	69.5	1	42	0	57						Nov-17
100	4.62	18.88	6.97			0.31	0.95			10.64	18.8	6	94	0	0						May-18
100	4.42	18.67	6.62			0.19	1.2			10.61	18.8	6	94	0	0						May-18
100	3.24	18.33	-1.66	28.22	32.18	0.52	1.06	14.83	1.09	14.65	229.3	4	96	0	0						Jun-12
	3.23	18.40	-1.54	28.49	32.46	0.56	0.91	14.81	1.08	14.67	229.3	4	96	0	0						Sep-17
100	3.16	18.14	-1.94	27.26	30.51	0.12	1.31	14.84	1.09	14.65	229.3	4	96	0	0						Jun-12
1,000	1.82	5.34	3.41			1.09	3.1			25.6	--	23	15	33	27						Jun-17
5,000	-1.53	11.31	2.63	37.79	30.91	1.91	1	10.67	0.82	10.92	77.1	5	95	0	0	53					May-14
5,000	-1.51	11.29	2.58	37.73	30.84	0.95	1	10.66	0.82	11.04	77.1	5	95	0	0	53					Apr-18
100	2.22	17.85	7.31	10.89	32.00	4.35	0.87	9.9	0.68	12.19	37.4	2	45	0	0	20	16.47	-9.38			Mar-06
5,000	2.25	17.98	7.52	11.69	33.63	4.57	0.61	9.89	0.68	12.34	37.4	2	45	0	0	20	16.74	-9.26			Apr-11
5,000	4.20	20.46	3.71	9.21	18.89	2.5	1.09	12.35	0.85	12.73	65.9	3	90	0	0	38	37.37	-24.05			Dec-02
100	4.14	20.29	3.50	8.43	17.40	2.22	1.34	12.32	0.85	12.59	65.9	3	90	0	0	38	37.12	-24.14			Dec-09
	3.27	0.00	11.83	58.82	-20.92	0	1	34.29	0.32	1.89	11.2	52	48	0	0	12	15.38	-16.42			Jan-94
1,000	1.92	8.17	7.93	26.77	40.04	5.73	2.76	5.28		10.47	--	-18	45	0	54				5.75		Mar-13
1,000	1.82	7.76	7.21	24.03	35.16	4.97	3.51	5.3		10.47	--	-18	45	0	54				1.50		Aug-14
2,500	1.78	7.81	7.35	24.85	36.99	5.23	3.27	5.32		10.63	--	-18	45	0	54						Feb-15
	2.05	8.29	8.22	26.23	38.44	5.98	2.49	5.31		10.91	--	-18	45	0	54						Aug-14
1,000	1.95	8.03	7.76	26.24	39.46	5.47	2.99			10.48	--	-18	45	0	54				4.25		Jul-17
2,500	1.72	7.66	7.11	23.92	35.35	4.97	3.51	5.31		10.45	--	-18	45	0	54				1.50	1.00	Feb-15
2,500	2.01	8.16	8.02	26.87	40.15	5.73	2.76	5.27		10.48	--	-18	45	0	54				6.50		Feb-15
1,000	2.00	8.09	8.00	26.45	38.65	5.73	2.76	5.29		10.63	--	-18	45	0	54						Nov-14
	0.68	1.95	-6.54	4.48	-11.54	0	2.58	6.71	0.39	8.86	37.6	21	58	9	11	448			5.75		Dec-13
	0.46	1.65	-7.11	2.61	-14.05	0	3.18	6.75	0.39	8.62	37.6	21	58	9	11	448				1.00	Oct-14
	0.77	2.13	-6.10	5.95	-9.63	0	2.18	6.74	0.4	9.07	37.6	21	58	9	11	448					Dec-13
	1.43	3.53	-6.37	-8.92	-13.22	0.47	2.58	5.4	0.72	8.51	33.5	5	0	86	8	738			4.75		Dec-13
	1.32	3.32	-6.89	-10.54	-15.71	0.1	3.18	5.44	0.72	8.39	33.5	5	0	86	8	738				1.00	Oct-14
	1.50	3.84	-5.96	-7.70	-11.34	0.88	2.18	5.42	0.71	8.54	33.5	5	0	86	8	738					Dec-13
100	4.30						1.01			10.43	18.9	4	96	0	0						Mar-19
100	1.42	18.06	1.19	47.93	38.26	0	1.96	15.22	1.14	52.54	63.1	1	99	0	0	476	26.64	-22.87			Aug-88
100	0.61	16.52	0.28	56.60	46.85	0	1.26	16.35	0.88	29.27	47.0	2	98	0	0	64	35.87	-23.73			Jul-94
100	3.12	17.16	-4.63	27.77	23.72	0	1.01	16.73	0.93	8.26	43.6	5	95	0	0	103	21.14	-18.97			Nov-96
100	4.47	21.11	5.42	38.28	26.32	0	1.01	14.74	0.92	20.76	3.6	2	98	0	0	48	24.12	-25.49			Jul-04
250	2.35	14.97	1.66			0	2.43			9.98	89.6	6	94	0	0						Dec-17
250	1.95	13.26	-0.85			0	2.75			9.39	127.4	1	99	0	0						Dec-17
250	0.30	1.88	1.57			0.7	3.09			9.71	71.9	62	19	11	7						Dec-17
250	2.16	10.13	3.38			0.6	2.6			9.89	195.0	-12	60	48	3						Dec-17
250	2.23	11.65	2.28			0	2.44			10.06	148.0	3	57	40	0						Mar-18
250	4.42	19.32	6.44			0	2.8			10.62	119.0	5	95	0	0						Dec-17
250	3.12	15.13	2.13			0.12	2.95			9.89	215.8	2	98	0	0						Dec-17
250	2.41	12.87	3.88			0.5	2.61			10.17	371.3	4	70	24	0						Dec-17
250	3.05	17.90	5.77			0	2.4			10.8	401.1	2	93	5	0						Dec-17
250	2.55	18.03	0.71			0	3.04			9.62	127.5	3	99	-4	1						Dec-17
250	1.63	5.07	0.58			0.17	2.97			9.93	108.4	9	62	29	0						Dec-17
250	2.59	6.35	3.75			0.82	2.9			9.87	63.4	4	19	75	1						Dec-17
25	4.92	16.58	-5.94	29.67	24.78	0	1.35	15.12	0.78	14.27	12.3	11	89	0	0	43	27.99	-26			Jun-05
	6.89	25.59	18.18	70.62		0	0.97	13.76	0.94	14.72	7.0	2	98	0	0	67					Dec-14
100	6.90	25.53	17.97	69.41		0	1.22	13.72	0.94	14.55	7.0	2	98	0	0	67					Dec-14
	6.22	23.52	16.88	69.85	82.98	0	0.96	13.59	0.94	21.32	111.3	1	99	0	0	25					Dec-12
100	6.12	23.43	16.64	68.68	80.88	0	1.21	13.59	0.94	20.96	111.3	1	99	0	0	25					Dec-12
	1.15	13.59	-3.89	23.33	16.29	1.31	1.05	12.51	1.09	11.36	39.1	2	98	0	0	200	18.73	-22.12	5.50		Jun-18
	1.02	13.20	-4.66	20.56	12.03	1.23	1.8	12.55	1.09	10.8	39.1	2	98	0	0	200	18.23	-22.37		1.00	Sep-10

Fund Name	MARKET Ticker Symbol	Traded On	Fund Type	FUND TYPE, CATEGORY & OBJECTIVE Category and (Prospectus Objective)	RATINGS Overall Rating	Reward Rating	Risk Rating	Recent Up/ Downgrade	Open to New Investors	MINIMUMS Min Initial Investment
RiverFront Asset Allocation Aggressive Class I	RLFIX	NAS CM	Open End	Global Equity Large Cap (Growth)	C	C	C+		Y	100,000
RiverFront Asset Allocation Aggressive Class Investor	RLTAX	NAS CM	Open End	Global Equity Large Cap (Growth)	C	C	C+		Y	2,500
RiverFront Asset Allocation Aggressive Class Investor II	RLTSX	NAS CM	Open End	Global Equity Large Cap (Growth)	C	C	C+		Y	2,500
RiverFront Asset Allocation Aggressive Class L	RLTIX	NAS CM	Open End	Global Equity Large Cap (Growth)	C	C	C+		Y	1,000,000
RiverFront Asset Allocation Growth & Income Class A	RAGIX	NAS CM	Open End	Flexible Alloc (Growth & Income)	C	C	B		Y	2,500
RiverFront Asset Allocation Growth & Income Class C	RLGCX	NAS CM	Open End	Flexible Alloc (Growth & Income)	C	C	B		Y	2,500
RiverFront Asset Allocation Growth & Income Class I	RLIIX	NAS CM	Open End	Flexible Alloc (Growth & Income)	C	C	B		Y	100,000
RiverFront Asset Allocation Growth & Income Class Investor	RLGAX	NAS CM	Open End	Flexible Alloc (Growth & Income)	C	C	B		Y	2,500
RiverFront Asset Allocation Growth Class A	RMBAX	NAS CM	Open End	Global Equity Large Cap (Growth)	C	C	B-		Y	2,500
RiverFront Asset Allocation Growth Class C	RMGCX	NAS CM	Open End	Global Equity Large Cap (Growth)	C	C-	B-		Y	2,500
RiverFront Asset Allocation Growth Class I	RMGIX	NAS CM	Open End	Global Equity Large Cap (Growth)	C	C	B-		Y	100,000
RiverFront Asset Allocation Growth Class Investor	RMGAX	NAS CM	Open End	Global Equity Large Cap (Growth)	C	C	B-		Y	2,500
RiverFront Asset Allocation Income & Growth Class A	RCCAX	NAS CM	Open End	Cautious Alloc (Income)	B-	C	B+	Up	Y	2,500
RiverFront Asset Allocation Income & Growth Class C	RCCBX	NAS CM	Open End	Cautious Alloc (Income)	C+	C	B+	Up	Y	2,500
RiverFront Asset Allocation Income & Growth Class I	RCIBX	NAS CM	Open End	Cautious Alloc (Income)	B-	C	B+	Up	Y	100,000
RiverFront Asset Allocation Income & Growth Class Investor	RCABX	NAS CM	Open End	Cautious Alloc (Income)	B-	C	B+	Up	Y	2,500
RiverFront Asset Allocation Moderate Class A	RMOAX	NAS CM	Open End	Moderate Alloc (Growth & Income)	B-	C	B+	Up	Y	2,500
RiverFront Asset Allocation Moderate Class C	RMICX	NAS CM	Open End	Moderate Alloc (Growth & Income)	C+	C	B	Up	Y	2,500
RiverFront Asset Allocation Moderate Class I	RMIIX	NAS CM	Open End	Moderate Alloc (Growth & Income)	B-	C	B+	Up	Y	100,000
RiverFront Asset Allocation Moderate Class Investor	RMIAX	NAS CM	Open End	Moderate Alloc (Growth & Income)	B-	C	B+	Up	Y	2,500
RiverNorth Core Opportunity Fund Class I	RNCIX	NAS CM	Open End	Moderate Alloc (Growth & Income)	B-	C	B+	Up	Y	5,000,000
RiverNorth Core Opportunity Fund Class R	RNCOX	NAS CM	Open End	Moderate Alloc (Growth & Income)	B-	C	B+	Up	Y	5,000
RiverNorth Opportunities	RIV	NYSE	Closed End	Moderate Alloc (Growth & Income)	C	C+	C-		Y	
RiverNorth/DoubleLine Strategic Opportunity Fund	OPP	NYSE	Closed End	Moderate Alloc (Growth & Income)	C	C	C-	Up	Y	
RiverPark Large Growth Fund Class Institutional	RPXIX	NAS CM	Open End	US Equity Large Cap Growth (Growth)	B-	C+	B		Y	100,000
RiverPark Large Growth Fund Class Retail	RPXFX	NAS CM	Open End	US Equity Large Cap Growth (Growth)	C+	C+	B	Down	Y	1,000
RiverPark Long/Short Opportunity Fund Institutional Class	RLSIX	NAS CM	Open End	Long/Short Equity (Growth)	B-	C	B		Y	100,000
RiverPark Long/Short Opportunity Fund Retail Class	RLSFX	NAS CM	Open End	Long/Short Equity (Growth)	B-	C	B		Y	1,000
RiverPark/Wedgewood Fund Class Institutional	RWGIX	NAS CM	Open End	US Equity Large Cap Growth (Growth)	C+	C	B	Down	Y	100,000
RiverPark/Wedgewood Fund Class Retail	RWGFX	NAS CM	Open End	US Equity Large Cap Growth (Growth)	C+	C	B	Down	Y	1,000
RMB Dividend Growth Fund Class I	RMBDX	NAS CM	Open End	US Equity Large Cap Growth (Growth)	B	C+	B+		Y	100,000
RMB Fund Class A	RMBHX	NAS CM	Open End	US Equity Large Cap Growth (Growth)	B	B-	B		Y	2,500
RMB Fund Class C	RMBJX	NAS CM	Open End	US Equity Large Cap Growth (Growth)	B	B-	B		Y	2,500
RMB Fund Class I	RMBGX	NAS CM	Open End	US Equity Large Cap Growth (Growth)	B	B-	B		Y	100,000
RMB International Fund Class I	RMBTX	NAS CM	Open End	Global Equity Mid/Small Cap (Foreign Stock)	D	D	D+		Y	100,000
RMB International Small Cap Fund Class I	RMBSX	NAS CM	Open End	Global Equity Mid/Small Cap (Small Company)	D	D	D+		Y	100,000
RMB Japan Fund Class I	RMBPX	NAS CM	Open End	Japan Equity (Pacific Stock)	D	D	D+		Y	100,000
RMB Mendon Financial Long/Short Fund Class A	RMBFX	NAS CM	Open End	Long/Short Equity (Financial)	D	D	D	Down	Y	2,500
RMB Mendon Financial Long/Short Fund Class C	RMBCX	NAS CM	Open End	Long/Short Equity (Financial)	D	D	D	Down	Y	2,500
RMB Mendon Financial Long/Short Fund Class I	RMBIX	NAS CM	Open End	Long/Short Equity (Financial)	D	D	D	Down		100,000
RMB Mendon Financial Services Fund Class A	RMBKX	NAS CM	Open End	Financials Sector Equity (Financial)	C-	D+	C-	Down	Y	2,500
RMB Mendon Financial Services Fund Class C	RMBNX	NAS CM	Open End	Financials Sector Equity (Financial)	C-	D+	C-	Down	Y	2,500
RMB Mendon Financial Services Fund Class I	RMBLX	NAS CM	Open End	Financials Sector Equity (Financial)	C-	C-	C-	Down	Y	100,000
RMB Small Cap Fund Class I	RMBBX	NAS CM	Open End	US Equity Small Cap (Growth)	C+	C	B-	Down	Y	100,000
RMB SMID Cap Fund Class I	RMBMX	NAS CM	Open End	US Equity Mid Cap (Growth)	C+	C	B-		Y	100,000
RMR Real Estate Income Fund	RIF	AMEX	Closed End	Real Estate Sector Equity (Real Estate)	C	C	C-		Y	
RNC Genter Dividend Income Fund	GDIIX	NAS CM	Open End	US Equity Large Cap Value (Equity-Income)	C+	C	B		Y	2,500
Rock Oak Core Growth Fund	RCKSX	NAS CM	Open End	US Equity Large Cap Blend (Growth)	C	C-	C		Y	2,000
Rockefeller Equity Allocation Fund Institutional Class	ROCKX	NAS CM	Open End	Global Equity Large Cap (Growth & Income)	C+	C	B	Up	Y	1,000,000
Rondure New World Fund Institutional Class	RNWIX	NAS CM	Open End	Global Equity Large Cap (Foreign Stock)	C	D+	C+	Up	Y	2,000
Rondure New World Fund Investor Class	RNWOX	NAS CM	Open End	Global Equity Large Cap (Foreign Stock)	C	D+	C+	Up	Y	2,000
Rondure Overseas Fund Institutional Class	ROSIX	NAS CM	Open End	Global Equity Large Cap (Foreign Stock)	C	D+	B-	Up	Y	2,000

★ Expanded analysis of this fund is included in Section II.

	TOTAL RETURNS					PERFORMANCE				ASSETS		ASSET ALLOCATION & TURNOVER					BULL & BEAR		FEES		
Min Additional Investment	3-Month Total Return	6-Month Total Return	1-Year Total Return	3-Year Total Return	5-Year Total Return	Dividend Yield (TTM)	Expense Ratio	3-Yr Std Deviation	3-Year Beta	NAV	Total Assets (MIL)	%Cash	%Stocks	%Bonds	%Other	Turnover Ratio	Last Bull Market Total Return	Last Bear Market Total Return	Front End Fee (%)	Back End Fee (%)	Inception Date
	1.21	13.76	-3.71	24.22	17.63	1.32	0.8	12.52	1.09	11.65	39.1	2	98	0	0	200	18.86	-22.01			Sep-10
	1.14	13.60	-3.96	23.23	16.25	1.3	1.05	12.51	1.09	11.44	39.1	2	98	0	0	200	18.74	-22.1	5.50		Sep-10
	1.15	13.51	-4.04	23.13	16.11	1.31	1.05	12.51	1.09	11.34	39.1	2	98	0	0	200	18.74	-22.07			Oct-08
	1.21	13.68	-3.65	24.26	17.76	1.32	0.8	12.52	1.09	11.63	39.1	2	98	0	0	200	18.9	-22.04			Oct-08
	1.36	11.80	-0.46	23.18	21.79	1.78	1.01	9.5	0.83	11.84	69.7	5	71	24	0	224	15.83	-16.11	5.50		Jun-18
	1.09	11.34	-1.18	20.36	17.27	1.09	1.76	9.5	0.83	11.5	69.7	5	71	24	0	224	15.16	-16.28		1.00	Aug-10
	1.41	11.91	-0.21	24.10	23.32	1.94	0.76	9.53	0.83	11.8	69.7	5	71	24	0	224	16	-16.02			Aug-10
	1.34	11.81	-0.46	23.16	21.72	1.7	1.01	9.48	0.83	11.85	69.7	5	71	24	0	224	15.76	-16.03	5.50		Aug-10
	1.38	12.80	-2.06	23.44	17.41	1.29	1.03	10.95	0.96	11.01	23.0	4	83	13	0	210	15.93	-18.99	5.50		Jun-18
	1.16	12.35	-2.87	20.68	13.06	1.21	1.78	10.94	0.96	10.46	23.0	4	83	13	0	210	15.46	-19.32		1.00	Aug-10
	1.40	12.88	-1.88	24.28	18.80	1.34	0.78	10.93	0.96	10.86	23.0	4	83	13	0	210	16.1	-18.91			Aug-10
	1.38	12.70	-2.13	23.36	17.39	1.29	1.03	10.94	0.96	11	23.0	4	83	13	0	210	15.87	-19.03	5.50		Aug-10
	1.99	8.81	3.95	14.18	15.75	1.95	0.9	4.74	0.39	10.42	8.5	8	28	64	0	219			5.50		Jun-18
	1.69	8.33	3.10	11.56	11.43	1.24	1.65	4.66	0.39	10.28	8.5	8	28	64	0	219				1.00	Sep-12
	1.95	8.91	4.19	15.01	17.18	2.14	0.65	4.68	0.38	10.25	8.5	8	28	64	0	219					Sep-12
	1.96	8.83	3.97	14.17	15.81	1.79	0.9	4.72	0.39	10.44	8.5	8	28	64	0	219			5.50		Sep-12
	1.75	10.78	2.11	19.32	20.60	1.82	0.93	7.22	0.57	10.26	60.3	6	49	44	0	209	12.45	-10.66	5.50		Jun-18
	1.64	10.40	1.34	16.71	16.22	1.1	1.68	7.23	0.57	10.13	60.3	6	49	44	0	209	11.88	-10.95		1.00	Aug-10
	1.79	10.83	2.30	20.14	22.03	1.97	0.68	7.23	0.58	10.27	60.3	6	49	44	0	209	12.61	-10.57			Aug-10
	1.73	10.80	2.13	19.33	20.61	1.75	0.93	7.25	0.58	10.27	60.3	6	49	44	0	209	12.46	-10.59	5.50		Aug-10
100	2.86	14.25	5.63	33.38	29.92	4.12	2.3	8.88	0.67	8.12	131.4	8	54	35	-1	58	17.13	-13.93			Aug-14
100	3.17	14.65	5.55	31.27	29.04	3.87	2.54	8.93	0.67	8.13	131.4	8	54	35	-1	58	17.13	-13.93			Dec-06
	2.66	14.19	5.99	29.82		6.77	3.72	7.73	0.73	17.46	125.1	-2	46	48	0	74					Dec-15
	3.91	8.92	7.77			5.94	2.94			18.09	199.2	5	0	90	-1	23					Sep-16
100	7.38	25.15	9.87	70.12	61.47	0	0.95	13.86	1	22.84	53.9	1	99	0	0	35	30.12	-13.39			Sep-10
100	7.27	24.91	9.60	68.93	59.42	0	1.23	13.86	1	22.41	53.9	1	99	0	0	35	29.98	-13.48			Sep-10
100	5.79	17.24	6.86	48.46	34.75	0.76	1.8	10.08	0.68	12.78	88.1	10	89	0	1	59	29.8	-6.2			Mar-12
100	5.76	17.22	6.66	47.57	33.35	0.56	2	10.12	0.68	12.66	88.1	10	89	0	1	59	29.8	-6.2			Mar-12
100	4.72	21.52	11.04	47.41	42.40	0	0.92	12.73	0.89	9.09	101.8	2	98	0	0	21	29.35	-10.41			Sep-10
100	4.72	21.34	10.70	46.50	41.30	0	1.15	12.7	0.89	8.87	101.8	2	98	0	0	21	29.12	-10.51			Sep-10
25,000	4.56	19.28	13.12	47.24	61.72	1.6	0.81	11.11	0.89	14.13	35.6	3	97	0	0	58					Mar-12
500	5.20	24.92	14.71	59.37	55.95	0	1.25	12.55	0.99	25.86	101.6	3	97	0	0	23	28.05	-13.35	5.00		Jun-75
500	5.00	24.45	13.90	55.86	50.18	0	2	12.55	0.99	21.17	101.6	3	97	0	0	23	27.49	-13.64		1.00	Apr-04
25,000	5.27	25.04	15.04	60.37	56.92	0	1.02	12.57	0.99	25.96	101.6	3	97	0	0	23	28.05	-13.35			Feb-17
25,000	0.34	13.64	-10.16			0.2	1.16			8.83	172.0	10	90	0	0	27					Dec-17
25,000	1.99	20.07	-6.19			0.19	1.26			9.21	33.8	8	92	0	0	69					Dec-17
25,000	0.43	6.64	-5.54			0.33	1.31			9.15	66.2	2	98	0	0	135					Dec-17
500	1.58	4.18	-18.82	-3.16	8.24	0	1.74	15.42	0.59	14.7	106.6	17	83	0	0	67	23.48	-24	5.00		Apr-04
500	1.35	3.76	-19.41	-5.19	4.46	0	2.43	15.38	0.59	13.49	106.6	17	83	0	0	67	22.89	-24.22		1.00	Apr-04
25,000	1.63	4.27	-18.58	-2.29	9.57	0	1.44	15.42	0.59	14.89	106.6	17	83	0	0	67	23.48	-24			Aug-15
500	5.48	9.72	-15.42	38.95	68.20	0	1.27	19.32		37.47	461.3	1	99	0	0	58	19.63	-20.1	5.00		Jun-99
500	5.26	9.29	-16.06	35.86	61.95	0	2.02	19.3		33.76	461.3	1	99	0	0	58	19.15	-20.41		1.00	Apr-05
25,000	5.55	9.84	-15.23	39.72	69.14	0	1.02	19.32		38.03	461.3	1	99	0	0	58	19.63	-20.1			Feb-17
25,000	4.28	21.15	3.96	39.47	44.45	0	1.1	14.87	0.84	13.63	118.4	4	96	0	0	20	26.25	-23.22			Aug-02
25,000	5.72	23.25	5.71	41.23	46.04	0	0.96	14.4	0.9	11.45	181.6	4	96	0	0	14	24.49	-22.95			Dec-04
	0.53	23.08	8.97	12.54	42.79	5.4		17.67	1.31	23.27	237.4	1	79	0	1	22	29.85	-15.58			Dec-03
500	3.40	13.56	5.58	33.43	35.57	2.11	1.25	11.67	0.93	16.52	16.6	6	96	0	-2	27	20.52	-12.2			Dec-08
25	-2.69	10.07	-7.88	51.73	38.23	0.01	1.25	16.18	1.24	16.6	13.6	0	100	0	0	14	24.58	-21.58			Dec-04
10,000	3.66	13.96	3.23	36.91		0.8	1.15	12.46	1.07	11.8837	112.6	2	98	0	0						Feb-15
	2.54	12.86	2.45			0.83	1.1			10.88	134.4	5	94	0	0						May-17
	2.45	12.77	2.26			0.66	1.35			10.86	134.4	5	94	0	0						May-17
	3.17	11.35	0.98			0.94	0.85			11.38	22.5	5	95	0	0						May-17

	MARKET		FUND TYPE, CATEGORY & OBJECTIVE		RATINGS					MINIMUMS
Fund Name	Ticker Symbol	Traded On	Fund Type	Category and (Prospectus Objective)	Overall Rating	Reward Rating	Risk Rating	Recent Up/ Downgrade	Open to New Investors	Min Initial Investment
Rondure Overseas Fund Investor Class	ROSOX	NAS CM	Open End	Global Equity Large Cap (Foreign Stock)	C	D+	B-	Up	Y	2,000
Rothko Emerging Markets Equity Fund	RKEMX	NAS CM	Open End	Global Emerg Mkts (Div Emerging Mkts)	U	U	U		Y	50,000
Roumell Opportunistic Value Fund Institutional Class	RAMSX	NAS CM	Open End	Moderate Alloc (Growth)	C	C-	B	Down	Y	2,500
Royce Dividend Value Fund Consultant Class	RDVCX	NAS CM	Open End	US Equity Mid Cap (Growth & Income)	C	C	B-		Y	2,000
Royce Dividend Value Fund Institutional Shares	RDIIX	NAS CM	Open End	US Equity Mid Cap (Growth & Income)	C	C	B-		Y	1,000,000
Royce Dividend Value Fund Investment Class	RDVIX	NAS CM	Open End	US Equity Mid Cap (Growth & Income)	C	C	B-		Y	2,000
Royce Dividend Value Fund Service Class	RYDVX	NAS CM	Open End	US Equity Mid Cap (Growth & Income)	C	C	B-		Y	2,000
Royce Global Financial Services Fund Institutional Class	RGFIX	NAS CM	Open End	Financials Sector Equity (Financial)	C	C	B-		Y	1,000,000
Royce Global Financial Services Fund Service Class	RYFSX	NAS CM	Open End	Financials Sector Equity (Financial)	C	C	C+		Y	2,000
Royce Global Value Trust	RGT	NYSE	Closed End	Global Equity Mid/Small Cap (World Stock)	C-	C	C-	Down	Y	
Royce International Premier Fund Consultant Class	RINPX	NAS CM	Open End	Global Equity Mid/Small Cap (Foreign Stock)	C+	C	B-	Up	Y	2,000
Royce International Premier Fund Institutional Class	RIPIX	NAS CM	Open End	Global Equity Mid/Small Cap (Foreign Stock)	C+	C	B	Up	Y	1,000,000
Royce International Premier Fund Investment Class	RIPNX	NAS CM	Open End	Global Equity Mid/Small Cap (Foreign Stock)	C+	C	B	Up	Y	2,000
Royce International Premier Fund Service Class	RYIPX	NAS CM	Open End	Global Equity Mid/Small Cap (Foreign Stock)	C+	C	B	Up	Y	2,000
Royce Low-Priced Stock Fund Investment Class	RLPHX	NAS CM	Open End	US Equity Small Cap (Small Company)	C	C-	C+		Y	2,000
Royce Low-Priced Stock Fund Service Class	RYLPX	NAS CM	Open End	US Equity Small Cap (Small Company)	C	C-	C+		Y	2,000
Royce Micro Cap Trust	RMT	NYSE	Closed End	US Equity Small Cap (Small Company)	C	C-	C			
Royce Micro-Cap Fund Consultant Class	RYMCX	NAS CM	Open End	US Equity Small Cap (Small Company)	C-	C-	C	Down	Y	2,000
Royce Micro-Cap Fund Investment Class	RYOTX	NAS CM	Open End	US Equity Small Cap (Small Company)	C	C-	C		Y	2,000
Royce Micro-Cap Fund Service Class	RMCFX	NAS CM	Open End	US Equity Small Cap (Small Company)	C	C-	C		Y	2,000
Royce Opportunity Fund Consultant Class	ROFCX	NAS CM	Open End	US Equity Small Cap (Small Company)	C-	C-	C	Down	Y	2,000
Royce Opportunity Fund Institutional Class	ROFIX	NAS CM	Open End	US Equity Small Cap (Small Company)	C-	C-	C	Down	Y	1,000,000
Royce Opportunity Fund Investment Class	RYPNX	NAS CM	Open End	US Equity Small Cap (Small Company)	C-	C-	C	Down	Y	2,000
Royce Opportunity Fund Retirement Class	ROFRX	NAS CM	Open End	US Equity Small Cap (Small Company)	C-	C-	C	Down	Y	0
Royce Opportunity Fund Service Class	RYOFX	NAS CM	Open End	US Equity Small Cap (Small Company)	C-	C-	C	Down	Y	2,000
Royce Pennsylvania Mutual Fund Consultant Class	RYPCX	NAS CM	Open End	US Equity Small Cap (Small Company)	C	C	B-		Y	2,000
Royce Pennsylvania Mutual Fund Institutional Class	RPMIX	NAS CM	Open End	US Equity Small Cap (Small Company)	C+	C	B-		Y	1,000,000
Royce Pennsylvania Mutual Fund Investment Class	PENNX	NAS CM	Open End	US Equity Small Cap (Small Company)	C+	C	B-		Y	2,000
Royce Pennsylvania Mutual Fund Retirement Class	RPMRX	NAS CM	Open End	US Equity Small Cap (Small Company)	C	C	B-		Y	0
Royce Pennsylvania Mutual Fund Service Class	RYPFX	NAS CM	Open End	US Equity Small Cap (Small Company)	C+	C	B-	Up	Y	2,000
Royce Premier Fund Consultant Class	RPRCX	NAS CM	Open End	US Equity Small Cap (Small Company)	C+	C	B-	Up		2,000
Royce Premier Fund Institutional Class	RPFIX	NAS CM	Open End	US Equity Small Cap (Small Company)	C+	C	B			1,000,000
Royce Premier Fund Investment Class	RYPRX	NAS CM	Open End	US Equity Small Cap (Small Company)	C+	C	B			2,000
Royce Premier Fund Retirement Class	RPRRX	NAS CM	Open End	US Equity Small Cap (Small Company)	C+	C	B-	Up		0
Royce Premier Fund Service Class	RPFFX	NAS CM	Open End	US Equity Small Cap (Small Company)	C+	C	B	Up		2,000
Royce Small-Cap Value Fund Class R	RVVRX	NAS CM	Open End	US Equity Small Cap (Small Company)	C	D+	C+	Down	Y	0
Royce Small-Cap Value Fund Consultant Class	RVFCX	NAS CM	Open End	US Equity Small Cap (Small Company)	C	D+	C+	Down	Y	2,000
Royce Small-Cap Value Fund Investment Class	RVVHX	NAS CM	Open End	US Equity Small Cap (Small Company)	C	D+	C+	Down	Y	2,000
Royce Small-Cap Value Fund Service Class	RYVFX	NAS CM	Open End	US Equity Small Cap (Small Company)	C	D+	C+	Down	Y	2,000
Royce Smaller-Companies Growth Fund Consultant Class	RVPCX	NAS CM	Open End	US Equity Small Cap (Small Company)	C	C	C+		Y	2,000
Royce Smaller-Companies Growth Fund Institutional Class	RVPIX	NAS CM	Open End	US Equity Small Cap (Small Company)	C	C	C+		Y	1,000,000
Royce Smaller-Companies Growth Fund Investment Class	RVPHX	NAS CM	Open End	US Equity Small Cap (Small Company)	C	C	C+		Y	2,000
Royce Smaller-Companies Growth Fund Service Class	RYVPX	NAS CM	Open End	US Equity Small Cap (Small Company)	C	C	C+		Y	2,000
Royce Special Equity Fund Consultant Class	RSQCX	NAS CM	Open End	US Equity Small Cap (Small Company)	C	D+	C	Down		2,000
Royce Special Equity Fund Institutional Class	RSEIX	NAS CM	Open End	US Equity Small Cap (Small Company)	C	C-	C+	Down		1,000,000
Royce Special Equity Fund Investment Class	RYSEX	NAS CM	Open End	US Equity Small Cap (Small Company)	C	C-	C+	Down		2,000
Royce Special Equity Fund Service Class	RSEFX	NAS CM	Open End	US Equity Small Cap (Small Company)	C	C-	C+	Down		2,000
Royce Total Return Fund Consultant Class	RYTCX	NAS CM	Open End	US Equity Small Cap (Growth & Income)	C	C	B-		Y	2,000
Royce Total Return Fund Institutional Class	RTRIX	NAS CM	Open End	US Equity Small Cap (Growth & Income)	C+	C	B	Up	Y	1,000,000
Royce Total Return Fund Investment Class	RYTRX	NAS CM	Open End	US Equity Small Cap (Growth & Income)	C+	C	B	Up	Y	2,000
Royce Total Return Fund Retirement Class	RTRRX	NAS CM	Open End	US Equity Small Cap (Growth & Income)	C	C	B-		Y	0
Royce Total Return Fund Service Class	RYTFX	NAS CM	Open End	US Equity Small Cap (Growth & Income)	C+	C	B	Up	Y	2,000

★ Expanded analysis of this fund is included in Section II.

Min Additional Investment	TOTAL RETURNS 3-Month Total Return	6-Month Total Return	1-Year Total Return	3-Year Total Return	5-Year Total Return	PERFORMANCE Dividend Yield (TTM)	Expense Ratio	3-Yr Std Deviation	3-Year Beta	ASSETS NAV	Total Assets (MIL)	ASSET ALLOCATION & TURNOVER %Cash	%Stocks	%Bonds	%Other	Turnover Ratio	BULL & BEAR Last Bull Market Total Return	Last Bear Market Total Return	FEES Front End Fee (%)	Back End Fee (%)	Inception Date
	3.17	11.33	0.74			0.81	1.1			11.39	22.5	5	95	0	0						May-17
1,000	1.29	10.27					0.92			10.95	5.5	1	99	0	0						Dec-18
100	-1.60	14.22	2.62	41.11	4.87	1.74	1.25	13.73		9.19	80.0	34	50	5	0	63	1.82	-13.09			Dec-10
50	5.50	21.30	2.49	36.75	23.61	0.11	2.09	15.28	0.83	7.85	109.6	5	95	0	0	13	24.38	-22.33	0.00	1.00	Mar-14
	5.53	21.73	3.48	41.45	30.50	1.23	1.09	15.41	0.84	6.58	109.6	5	95	0	0	13	24.92	-22.09			Aug-12
50	5.77	21.78	3.56	41.15	30.02	1.06	1.09	15.32	0.83	6.68	109.6	5	95	0	0	13	25.08	-21.92			Sep-07
50	5.75	21.76	3.19	40.02	28.46	0.39	1.34	15.32	0.83	6.89	109.6	5	95	0	0	13	24.92	-22.09			May-04
	5.49	16.95	-1.41	43.12	35.04	1.03	1.52	12.56	0.66	12.28	39.4	1	99	0	0	8	22.95	-23.52			Jan-16
50	5.54	16.83	-1.92	41.16	32.85	0.84	1.58	12.59	0.66	9.51	39.4	1	99	0	0	8	22.95	-23.52			Dec-03
	5.34	20.11	0.77	41.32	24.56	0.32	1.58	12.95		12.42	130.2	-3	103	0	0	57					Oct-13
50	6.84	21.76	8.54	43.50	46.60	0	2.19	11.68	0.92	17.79	604.8	5	93	0	0	65	16.44	-22.03		1.00	Feb-16
	7.11	22.45	9.72	47.49	52.73	0.45	1.04	11.65	0.91	13.85	604.8	5	93	0	0	65	16.95	-21.79			May-18
50	7.12	22.36	9.65	47.99	54.06	0.39	1.19	11.66	0.91	13.84	604.8	5	93	0	0	65	16.95	-21.79	0.00	0.00	Jan-14
50	6.99	22.18	9.25	46.86	52.09	0	1.44	11.65	0.91	16.52	604.8	5	93	0	0	65	16.95	-21.79			Dec-10
50	2.81	15.68	-4.83	38.86	7.11	0	1.24	16.42	0.94	7.3	213.5	3	97	0	0	58	18.43	-27.31			Mar-07
50	2.83	15.63	-5.00	37.93	5.84	0	1.49	16.44	0.94	7.25	213.5	3	97	0	0	58	18.26	-27.4			Dec-93
	1.46	14.29	-7.64	35.63	19.81	0.28		15.86		9.32	377.5	-2	101	0	0	21	24.22	-24.41			Dec-93
50	0.50	10.73	-9.71	25.76	-0.22	0	2.56	16.59	0.92	7.94	135.4	3	97	0	0	24	19.36	-27.32	0.00	1.00	May-98
50	0.97	11.54	-8.63	29.93	5.27	0	1.49	16.63	0.92	10.34	135.4	3	97	0	0	24	20.01	-27.04			Dec-91
50	0.89	11.34	-8.74	29.48	4.62	0	1.61	16.6	0.92	10.11	135.4	3	97	0	0	24	19.94	-27.07			Aug-02
50	0.86	15.38	-12.02	40.44	16.34	0	2.29	20.6	1.18	9.3	939.5	5	95	0	0	47	35.29	-31.81	0.00	1.00	Mar-06
	1.20	16.03	-10.91	45.58	23.60	0	1.08	20.65	1.18	11.72	939.5	5	95	0	0	47	36.21	-31.42			Dec-01
50	1.14	15.97	-11.06	45.09	22.90	0	1.2	20.62	1.18	11.47	939.5	5	95	0	0	47	36.16	-31.54			Nov-96
	0.98	15.55	-11.59	42.33	18.99	0	1.84	20.58	1.18	10.25	939.5	5	95	0	0	47	35.62	-31.64			May-07
50	1.13	15.76	-11.28	43.76	21.12	0	1.49	20.63	1.18	10.65	939.5	5	95	0	0	47	36.01	-31.59			May-00
50	3.57	18.07	-0.26	44.39	28.97	0	1.93	16.94	0.98	7.25	1,964	1	99	0	0	35	23.92	-24.49	0.00	1.00	Jun-97
	3.73	18.78	0.85	49.20	36.34	0.19	0.88	16.93	0.98	9.17	1,964	1	99	0	0	35	24.67	-24.21			Jun-11
50	3.63	18.57	0.68	48.64	35.57	0.14	0.92	16.97	0.98	9.13	1,964	1	99	0	0	35	24.72	-24.23			Oct-72
	3.50	18.23	0.02	45.35	30.72	0	1.57	16.89	0.97	8.56	1,964	1	99	0	0	35	24.13	-24.37			May-07
50	3.51	18.28	0.18	46.92	33.22	0	1.3	16.89	0.97	9.12	1,964	1	99	0	0	35	24.44	-24.26			Nov-05
50	4.71	22.35	5.26	54.07	31.92	0	2.21	16.28	0.91	11.11	1,863	1	99	0	0	23	22.87	-21.89	0.00	1.00	Jun-03
	4.97	23.05	6.34	59.32	39.57	0.1	1.12	16.3	0.91	14.36	1,863	1	99	0	0	23	23.67	-21.53			Sep-02
50	4.97	22.95	6.28	58.98	38.97	0.05	1.17	16.28	0.91	14.14	1,863	1	99	0	0	23	23.58	-21.56			Dec-91
	4.83	22.59	5.64	55.76	34.47	0	1.8	16.29	0.91	13.02	1,863	1	99	0	0	23	23.14	-21.73			May-07
50	4.88	22.78	5.97	57.48	36.94	0	1.49	16.24	0.91	13.74	1,863	1	99	0	0	23	23.42	-21.66			Sep-02
	-0.79	9.17	-6.10	25.19	8.47	0	1.92	18.82	1.03	8.69	179.5	9	91	0	0	64	21.39	-26.05			Sep-07
50	-0.86	8.95	-6.44	23.56	6.16	0	2.34	18.86	1.03	8.03	179.5	9	91	0	0	64	21.13	-26.21	0.00	1.00	Mar-06
50	-0.65	9.49	-5.38	27.64	11.98	0.41	1.24	18.84	1.03	9.11	179.5	9	91	0	0	64	21.84	-25.82			Mar-07
50	-0.65	9.40	-5.64	26.76	10.67	0.16	1.49	18.82	1.03	9.07	179.5	9	91	0	0	64	21.66	-25.93			Jun-01
50	4.21	22.04	-2.32	43.90	32.47	0	2.24	16.74	0.92	6.92	287.2	7	93	0	0	61	25.5	-26.6	0.00	1.00	Mar-06
	4.59	22.70	-1.21	48.60	40.10	0	1.21	16.79	0.92	8.43	287.2	7	93	0	0	61	26.41	-26.28			May-06
50	4.52	22.74	-1.36	48.63	39.55	0	1.21	16.73	0.92	8.31	287.2	7	93	0	0	61	26.29	-26.28			Mar-07
50	4.51	22.54	-1.52	47.28	37.88	0	1.49	16.74	0.92	8.1	287.2	7	93	0	0	61	26.11	-26.35			Jun-01
50	-3.10	4.54	-6.33	22.69	13.42	0.08	2.19	14.78	0.76	16.55	1,210	21	79	0	0	21	24.35	-18.36	0.00	1.00	Jun-03
	-2.84	5.11	-5.32	26.79	19.93	1.2	1.11	14.8	0.76	18.08	1,210	21	79	0	0	21	25.26	-18.01			Jul-03
50	-2.87	5.07	-5.42	26.55	19.41	1.12	1.18	14.78	0.76	18.23	1,210	21	79	0	0	21	25.15	-18.04			May-98
50	-2.93	4.95	-5.57	25.71	18.04	0.89	1.39	14.8	0.76	18.2	1,210	21	79	0	0	21	25.03	-18.12			Oct-03
50	3.23	15.41	-0.59	32.00	26.40	0.18	2.19	15.19	0.86	11.48	1,559	1	99	0	0	22	20.56	-19.81	0.00	1.00	Oct-01
	3.49	16.03	0.49	36.34	33.59	1.57	1.11	15.23	0.87	10.97	1,559	1	99	0	0	22	21.25	-19.41			Mar-03
50	3.39	15.91	0.36	35.78	32.73	1.38	1.2	15.19	0.86	11.12	1,559	1	99	0	0	22	21.26	-19.44			Dec-93
	3.22	15.56	-0.29	33.30	28.67	0.44	1.83	15.15	0.86	11.52	1,559	1	99	0	0	22	20.86	-19.65			May-07
50	3.39	15.74	0.09	34.69	30.94	0.8	1.51	15.2	0.87	11.42	1,559	1	99	0	0	22	20.99	-19.54			Jan-02

	MARKET			FUND TYPE, CATEGORY & OBJECTIVE	RATINGS				MINIMUMS	
Fund Name	Ticker Symbol	Traded On	Fund Type	Category and (Prospectus Objective)	Overall Rating	Reward Rating	Risk Rating	Recent Up/ Downgrade	Open to New Investors	Min Initial Investment
Royce Value Trust	RVT	NYSE	Closed End	US Equity Small Cap (Growth)	C	C	C+		Y	
RQSI GAA Systematic Global Macro Fund Institutional Shares	RQSGX	NAS CM	Open End	Alloc Miscellaneous (Multi-Asset Global)	D	D+	B-		Y	100,000
RQSI GAA Systematic Global Macro Fund Retail Shares	RQSRX	NAS CM	Open End	Alloc Miscellaneous (Multi-Asset Global)	D	D+	B-		Y	10,000
Russell Investments Commodity Strategies Fund Class A	RCSAX	NAS CM	Open End	Commodities Broad Basket (Growth & Income)	D	D	C-	Down	Y	0
Russell Investments Commodity Strategies Fund Class C	RCSCX	NAS CM	Open End	Commodities Broad Basket (Growth & Income)	D	D	C-	Down	Y	0
Russell Investments Commodity Strategies Fund Class E	RCSEX	NAS CM	Open End	Commodities Broad Basket (Growth & Income)	D	D	C-	Down	Y	0
Russell Investments Commodity Strategies Fund Class M	RCOTX	NAS CM	Open End	Commodities Broad Basket (Growth & Income)	D+	D	C-		Y	0
Russell Investments Commodity Strategies Fund Class S	RCCSX	NAS CM	Open End	Commodities Broad Basket (Growth & Income)	D	D	C-	Down	Y	0
Russell Investments Commodity Strategies Fund Class Y	RCSYX	NAS CM	Open End	Commodities Broad Basket (Growth & Income)	D+	D	C-		Y	10,000,000
Russell Investments Emerging Markets Fund Class A	REMAX	NAS CM	Open End	Global Emerg Mkts (Div Emerging Mkts)	C	C	C+		Y	0
Russell Investments Emerging Markets Fund Class C	REMCX	NAS CM	Open End	Global Emerg Mkts (Div Emerging Mkts)	C	C	C+		Y	0
Russell Investments Emerging Markets Fund Class E	REMEX	NAS CM	Open End	Global Emerg Mkts (Div Emerging Mkts)	C	C	C+		Y	0
Russell Investments Emerging Markets Fund Class M	RMMTX	NAS CM	Open End	Global Emerg Mkts (Div Emerging Mkts)	C	C	C+		Y	0
Russell Investments Emerging Markets Fund Class R6	REGRX	NAS CM	Open End	Global Emerg Mkts (Div Emerging Mkts)	C	C	C+		Y	0
Russell Investments Emerging Markets Fund Class S	REMSX	NAS CM	Open End	Global Emerg Mkts (Div Emerging Mkts)	C	C	C+		Y	0
Russell Investments Emerging Markets Fund Class Y	REMYX	NAS CM	Open End	Global Emerg Mkts (Div Emerging Mkts)	C	C	C+		Y	10,000,000
Russell Investments Equity Income Fund Class A	RSQAX	NAS CM	Open End	US Equity Large Cap Blend (Growth & Income)	C+	C	B		Y	0
Russell Investments Equity Income Fund Class C	REQSX	NAS CM	Open End	US Equity Large Cap Blend (Growth & Income)	C+	C	B	Up	Y	0
Russell Investments Equity Income Fund Class E	REAEX	NAS CM	Open End	US Equity Large Cap Blend (Growth & Income)	C+	C	B		Y	0
Russell Investments Equity Income Fund Class S	RLISX	NAS CM	Open End	US Equity Large Cap Blend (Growth & Income)	C+	C	B		Y	0
Russell Investments Equity Income Fund Class Y	REAYX	NAS CM	Open End	US Equity Large Cap Blend (Growth & Income)	C+	C	B		Y	10,000,000
Russell Investments Global Equity Fund Class C	RGECX	NAS CM	Open End	Global Equity Large Cap (World Stock)	B-	C	B	Up	Y	0
Russell Investments Global Equity Fund Class E	RGEEX	NAS CM	Open End	Global Equity Large Cap (World Stock)	B-	C	B	Up	Y	0
Russell Investments Global Equity Fund Class M	RGDTX	NAS CM	Open End	Global Equity Large Cap (World Stock)	B-	C	B	Up	Y	0
Russell Investments Global Equity Fund Class S	RGESX	NAS CM	Open End	Global Equity Large Cap (World Stock)	B-	C	B	Up	Y	0
Russell Investments Global Equity Fund Class Y	RLGYX	NAS CM	Open End	Global Equity Large Cap (World Stock)	B-	C	B	Up	Y	10,000,000
Russell Investments Global Infrastructure Fund Class A	RGIAX	NAS CM	Open End	Infrastructure Sector Equity (World Stock)	C+	C+	B-	Down	Y	0
Russell Investments Global Infrastructure Fund Class C	RGCIX	NAS CM	Open End	Infrastructure Sector Equity (World Stock)	C+	C	B-		Y	0
Russell Investments Global Infrastructure Fund Class E	RGIEX	NAS CM	Open End	Infrastructure Sector Equity (World Stock)	C+	C+	B-	Down	Y	0
Russell Investments Global Infrastructure Fund Class M	RGFTX	NAS CM	Open End	Infrastructure Sector Equity (World Stock)	B-	C+	B-		Y	0
Russell Investments Global Infrastructure Fund Class S	RGISX	NAS CM	Open End	Infrastructure Sector Equity (World Stock)	B-	C+	B-		Y	0
Russell Investments Global Infrastructure Fund Class Y	RGIYX	NAS CM	Open End	Infrastructure Sector Equity (World Stock)	B-	C+	B-		Y	10,000,000
Russell Investments Global Real Estate Securities Cls A	RREAX	NAS CM	Open End	Real Estate Sector Equity (Real Estate)	B-	C	B+		Y	0
Russell Investments Global Real Estate Securities Cls C	RRSCX	NAS CM	Open End	Real Estate Sector Equity (Real Estate)	B-	C	B+	Up	Y	0
Russell Investments Global Real Estate Securities Cls E	RREEX	NAS CM	Open End	Real Estate Sector Equity (Real Estate)	B-	C	B+		Y	0
Russell Investments Global Real Estate Securities Cls M	RETTX	NAS CM	Open End	Real Estate Sector Equity (Real Estate)	B-	C	B+		Y	0
Russell Investments Global Real Estate Securities Cls R6	RRSRX	NAS CM	Open End	Real Estate Sector Equity (Real Estate)	B-	C	B+		Y	0
Russell Investments Global Real Estate Securities Cls S	RRESX	NAS CM	Open End	Real Estate Sector Equity (Real Estate)	B-	C	B+		Y	0
Russell Investments Global Real Estate Securities Cls Y	RREYX	NAS CM	Open End	Real Estate Sector Equity (Real Estate)	B-	C	B+		Y	10,000,000
Russell Investments International Developed Markets Cls A	RLNAX	NAS CM	Open End	Global Equity Large Cap (Foreign Stock)	C	C	C+		Y	0
Russell Investments International Developed Markets Cls C	RLNCX	NAS CM	Open End	Global Equity Large Cap (Foreign Stock)	C	C-	C+		Y	0
Russell Investments International Developed Markets Cls E	RIFEX	NAS CM	Open End	Global Equity Large Cap (Foreign Stock)	C	C	B-		Y	0
Russell Investments International Developed Markets Cls M	RNTTX	NAS CM	Open End	Global Equity Large Cap (Foreign Stock)	C	C	B-		Y	0
Russell Investments International Developed Markets Cls S	RINTX	NAS CM	Open End	Global Equity Large Cap (Foreign Stock)	C	C	B-		Y	0
Russell Investments International Developed Markets Cls Y	RINYX	NAS CM	Open End	Global Equity Large Cap (Foreign Stock)	C	C	B-		Y	10,000,000
Russell Investments LifePoints Balanced Strategy Cls A	RBLAX	NAS CM	Open End	Moderate Alloc (Balanced)	B-	C	A-	Up	Y	0
Russell Investments LifePoints Balanced Strategy Cls C	RBLCX	NAS CM	Open End	Moderate Alloc (Balanced)	C+	C	B+	Up	Y	0
Russell Investments LifePoints Balanced Strategy Cls E	RBLEX	NAS CM	Open End	Moderate Alloc (Balanced)	B-	C	B+	Up	Y	0
Russell Investments LifePoints Balanced Strategy Cls R1	RBLRX	NAS CM	Open End	Moderate Alloc (Balanced)	B-	C	A-	Up	Y	0
Russell Investments LifePoints Balanced Strategy Cls R4	RBLUX	NAS CM	Open End	Moderate Alloc (Balanced)	B-	C	A-	Up	Y	0
Russell Investments LifePoints Balanced Strategy Cls R5	RBLVX	NAS CM	Open End	Moderate Alloc (Balanced)	B-	C	B+	Up	Y	0
Russell Investments LifePoints Balanced Strategy Cls S	RBLSX	NAS CM	Open End	Moderate Alloc (Balanced)	B-	C	A-	Up	Y	0

★ Expanded analysis of this fund is included in Section II.

Min Additional Investment	TOTAL RETURNS 3-Month Total Return	6-Month Total Return	1-Year Total Return	3-Year Total Return	5-Year Total Return	PERFORMANCE Dividend Yield (TTM)	Expense Ratio	3-Yr Std Deviation	3-Year Beta	ASSETS NAV	Total Assets (MIL)	ASSET ALLOCATION & TURNOVER %Cash	%Stocks	%Bonds	%Other	Turnover Ratio	BULL & BEAR Last Bull Market Total Return	Last Bear Market Total Return	FEES Front End Fee (%)	Back End Fee (%)	Inception Date
	4.08	19.98	-1.66	41.93	32.30	0.82	0	16.74	0.97	15.76	1,497	-1	101	0	0	28	27.89	-29.67			Nov-86
10,000	8.22	12.80	14.46			0	2.5			10.92	40.0	136	-58	22	0	0					Mar-18
5,000	8.05	12.64	14.06			0	2.85			10.87	40.0	136	-58	22	0	0					Mar-18
	-2.31	3.26	-8.84	-8.79	-41.99	0.88	1.35	8.96	1.01	5.06	523.1	71	16	13	0		-0.42	-19.53	5.75		Jun-10
	-2.41	2.97	-9.51	-10.65	-44.07	0	2.1	8.97	1.01	4.85	523.1	71	16	13	0		-0.82	-19.8			Jun-10
	-2.28	3.22	-8.88	-8.72	-41.95	0.9	1.35	8.94	1.01	5.12	523.1	71	16	13	0		-0.37	-19.54			Jun-10
	-2.29	3.43	-8.51	-7.70	-40.82	1.3	1	8.91	1.01	5.12	523.1	71	16	13	0		-0.07	-19.41			Mar-17
	-2.28	3.22	-8.62	-8.15	-41.26	1.17	1.1	9.03	1.02	5.13	523.1	71	16	13	0		-0.26	-19.49			Jun-10
	-2.26	3.39	-8.50	-7.54	-40.72	1.38	0.91	8.91	1.01	5.18	523.1	71	16	13	0		-0.07	-19.41			Jun-10
	1.13	11.74	0.11	33.28	6.69	1.3	1.6	14.04	1	18.65	1,766	-4	102	1	1		19.66	-26.46	5.75		Mar-07
	0.93	11.33	-0.61	30.25	2.70	0.54	2.35	14.05	1	17.29	1,766	-4	102	1	1		19.16	-26.71			Jan-99
	1.07	11.72	0.14	33.28	6.68	1.23	1.6	14.05	1	18.77	1,766	-4	102	1	1		19.62	-26.48			Sep-98
	1.18	11.92	0.46	34.53	8.23	1.7	1.25	14.06	1	18.77	1,766	-4	102	1	1		19.81	-26.4			Mar-17
	1.23	12.01	0.58	35.03	8.64	1.71	1.2	14.07	1	18.83	1,766	-4	102	1	1		19.81	-26.4			Mar-16
	1.18	11.91	0.37	34.28	8.03	1.57	1.35	14.05	1	18.79	1,766	-4	102	1	1		19.81	-26.4			Jan-93
	1.23	11.96	0.55	35.03	9.04	1.78	1.17	14.07	1	18.81	1,766	-4	102	1	1		20	-26.36			Sep-08
	3.49	17.48	5.18	43.04	51.35	1.12	1.06	12.9	1.04	24.02	320.1	3	97	0	0		25.36	-19.62	5.75		Sep-08
	3.31	17.06	4.38	39.86	45.80	0.46	1.81	12.89	1.04	23.13	320.1	3	97	0	0		24.83	-19.9			Sep-08
	3.53	17.54	5.20	43.07	51.38	1.14	1.06	12.92	1.04	24.09	320.1	3	97	0	0		25.39	-19.59			May-99
	3.57	17.63	5.48	44.24	53.39	1.41	0.77	12.91	1.04	23.93	320.1	3	97	0	0		25.54	-19.53			Sep-08
	3.61	17.76	5.65	44.49	52.90	1.57	0.61	12.92	1.04	23.9	320.1	3	97	0	0		25.39	-19.59			Mar-00
	2.91	14.97	3.15	37.51	32.24	0.05	2.15	10.86	0.95	9.52	1,574	5	94	1	0		17.31	-22.31			Feb-07
	3.17	15.40	3.84	40.49	37.21	0.9	1.4	10.87	0.95	9.74	1,574	5	94	1	0		17.66	-21.96			Feb-07
	3.29	15.59	4.28	42.06	39.44	1.25	1.05	10.93	0.96	9.71	1,574	5	94	1	0		17.9	-21.92			Mar-17
	3.18	15.43	4.12	41.59	38.99	1.13	1.15	10.88	0.96	9.72	1,574	5	94	1	0		17.9	-21.92			Feb-07
	3.18	15.57	4.31	42.34	40.32	1.37	0.95	10.89	0.96	9.72	1,574	5	94	1	0		18.09	-21.9			Sep-08
	5.33	20.73	11.65	25.34	25.19	3.12	1.35	10.1	0.96	11.37	469.3	3	96	0	0		16.18	-16.06	5.75		Sep-10
	5.20	20.26	10.79	22.51	20.57	2.45	2.1	10.1	0.96	11.25	469.3	3	96	0	0		15.73	-16.39			Sep-10
	5.33	20.58	11.55	25.33	25.15	3.13	1.35	10.12	0.96	11.38	469.3	3	96	0	0		16.18	-16.07			Sep-10
	5.42	20.94	12.05	26.76	27.61	3.45	1	10.12	0.96	11.38	469.3	3	96	0	0		16.5	-15.89			Mar-17
	5.38	20.75	11.91	26.20	26.70	3.34	1.1	10.09	0.96	11.39	469.3	3	96	0	0		16.38	-16.01			Sep-10
	5.52	20.91	12.13	27.02	27.88	3.52	0.92	10.14	0.97	11.4	469.3	3	96	0	0		16.5	-15.89			Sep-10
	-0.54	14.50	7.09	15.98	24.85	2.57	1.34	11.15	1	33.76	879.3	1	99	0	0		24.27	-20.69	5.75		Mar-07
	-0.72	14.05	6.26	13.38	20.23	1.97	2.09	11.14	1	32.38	879.3	1	99	0	0		23.73	-20.97			Jan-99
	-0.53	14.49	7.09	15.95	24.85	2.56	1.34	11.16	1	33.86	879.3	1	99	0	0		24.29	-20.7			Nov-96
	-0.44	14.68	7.45	17.11	26.71	2.85	0.99	11.14	1	34.69	879.3	1	99	0	0		24.44	-20.61			Mar-17
	-0.43	14.70	7.53	17.46	27.11	2.9	0.92	11.14	1	34.73	879.3	1	99	0	0		24.44	-20.61			Mar-16
	-0.44	14.62	7.38	16.87	26.46	2.74	1.09	11.14	1	34.73	879.3	1	99	0	0		24.44	-20.61			Jul-89
	-0.42	14.72	7.53	17.52	27.64	2.92	0.89	11.16	1	34.72	879.3	1	99	0	0		24.58	-20.56			Sep-08
	2.45	12.05	-2.04	26.28	8.30	1.81	1.22	11.25	1.01	35.87	2,345	-24	122	2	0		13.64	-24.6	5.75		Sep-08
	2.24	11.60	-2.80	23.44	4.24	0.92	1.97	11.23	1	36.05	2,345	-24	122	2	0		13.31	-24.87			Sep-08
	2.43	12.04	-2.03	26.27	8.28	1.79	1.22	11.24	1	36.19	2,345	-24	122	2	0		13.75	-24.58			May-99
	2.51	12.26	-1.67	27.35	9.20	2.28	0.83	11.23	1	35.88	2,345	-24	122	2	0		13.75	-24.58			Mar-17
	2.51	12.22	-1.75	27.36	9.73	2.16	0.93	11.26	1.01	35.9	2,345	-24	122	2	0		13.95	-24.54			Sep-08
	2.57	12.32	-1.59	27.98	10.72	2.33	0.77	11.25	1.01	35.92	2,345	-24	122	2	0		13.85	-24.47			Mar-00
	1.97	9.36	2.96	19.46	19.19	5.75	1.21	5.48	0.15	10.86	1,516	7	53	40	0	11	13.41	-13.55	5.75		Mar-03
	1.73	8.98	2.13	16.80	14.76	5.31	1.96	5.54	0.15	10.55	1,516	7	53	40	0	11	12.85	-13.82			Jan-99
	1.96	9.30	2.86	19.12	18.63	5.64	1.31	5.49	0.15	10.92	1,516	7	53	40	0	11	13.47	-13.57			Sep-97
	2.03	9.42	3.18	20.14	20.52	5.82	1	5.52	0.16	11.03	1,516	7	53	40	0	11	13.67	-13.35			Jun-06
	2.05	9.43	2.92	19.32	19.04	5.7	1.25	5.56	0.15	10.9	1,516	7	53	40	0	11	13.54	-13.47			Mar-06
	1.96	9.32	2.71	18.45	17.64	5.49	1.5	5.53	0.16	10.9	1,516	7	53	40	0	11	13.3	-13.53			Mar-98
	2.03	9.43	3.13	20.01	20.09	5.78	1.06	5.54	0.16	11.02	1,516	7	53	40	0	11	13.51	-13.39			Jan-00

	MARKET			FUND TYPE, CATEGORY & OBJECTIVE	RATINGS					MINIMUMS
Fund Name	Ticker Symbol	Traded On	Fund Type	Category and (Prospectus Objective)	Overall Rating	Reward Rating	Risk Rating	Recent Up/ Downgrade	Open to New Investors	Min Initial Investment
Russell Investments LifePoints Conservative Strategy Cls A	RCLAX	NAS CM	Open End	Cautious Alloc (Growth & Income)	B-	C	B+	Up	Y	0
Russell Investments LifePoints Conservative Strategy Cls C	RCLCX	NAS CM	Open End	Cautious Alloc (Growth & Income)	C+	C	B	Up	Y	0
Russell Investments LifePoints Conservative Strategy Cls E	RCLEX	NAS CM	Open End	Cautious Alloc (Growth & Income)	B-	C	B+	Up	Y	0
Russell Inv LifePoints Conservative Strategy Cls R1	RCLRX	NAS CM	Open End	Cautious Alloc (Growth & Income)	B-	C	A-		Y	0
Russell Inv LifePoints Conservative Strategy Cls R4	RCLUX	NAS CM	Open End	Cautious Alloc (Growth & Income)	B-	C	B+		Y	0
Russell Inv LifePoints Conservative Strategy Cls R5	RCLVX	NAS CM	Open End	Cautious Alloc (Growth & Income)	B-	C	B+	Up	Y	0
Russell Investments LifePoints Conservative Strategy Cls S	RCLSX	NAS CM	Open End	Cautious Alloc (Growth & Income)	B-	C	B+		Y	0
Russell Inv LifePoints Eq Growth Strategy Cls A	REAAX	NAS CM	Open End	Aggressive Alloc (Growth & Income)	C+	C	B	Up	Y	0
Russell Inv LifePoints Eq Growth Strategy Cls C	RELCX	NAS CM	Open End	Aggressive Alloc (Growth & Income)	C+	C	B	Up	Y	0
Russell Inv LifePoints Eq Growth Strategy Cls E	RELEX	NAS CM	Open End	Aggressive Alloc (Growth & Income)	C+	C	B+	Up	Y	0
Russell Inv LifePoints Eq Growth Strategy Cls R1	RELRX	NAS CM	Open End	Aggressive Alloc (Growth & Income)	C+	C	B	Up	Y	0
Russell Inv LifePoints Eq Growth Strategy Cls R4	RELUX	NAS CM	Open End	Aggressive Alloc (Growth & Income)	C+	C	B	Up	Y	0
Russell Inv LifePoints Eq Growth Strategy Cls R5	RELVX	NAS CM	Open End	Aggressive Alloc (Growth & Income)	C+	C	B+	Up	Y	0
Russell Inv LifePoints Eq Growth Strategy Cls S	RELSX	NAS CM	Open End	Aggressive Alloc (Growth & Income)	B-	C	B+	Up	Y	0
Russell Investments LifePoints Growth Strategy Cls A	RALAX	NAS CM	Open End	Aggressive Alloc (Growth)	B-	C	B+	Up	Y	0
Russell Investments LifePoints Growth Strategy Cls C	RALCX	NAS CM	Open End	Aggressive Alloc (Growth)	C+	C	B+	Up	Y	0
Russell Investments LifePoints Growth Strategy Cls E	RALEX	NAS CM	Open End	Aggressive Alloc (Growth)	B-	C	B+	Up	Y	0
Russell Investments LifePoints Growth Strategy Cls R1	RALRX	NAS CM	Open End	Aggressive Alloc (Growth)	B-	C	A-	Up	Y	0
Russell Investments LifePoints Growth Strategy Cls R4	RALUX	NAS CM	Open End	Aggressive Alloc (Growth)	B-	C	B+	Up	Y	0
Russell Investments LifePoints Growth Strategy Cls R5	RALVX	NAS CM	Open End	Aggressive Alloc (Growth)	B-	C	B+	Up	Y	0
Russell Investments LifePoints Growth Strategy Cls S	RALSX	NAS CM	Open End	Aggressive Alloc (Growth)	C+	C	B	Up	Y	0
Russell Investments LifePoints Moderate Strategy Cls A	RMLAX	NAS CM	Open End	Cautious Alloc (Growth & Income)	B-	C	A-	Up	Y	0
Russell Investments LifePoints Moderate Strategy Cls C	RMLCX	NAS CM	Open End	Cautious Alloc (Growth & Income)	B-	C	B+	Up	Y	0
Russell Investments LifePoints Moderate Strategy Cls E	RMLEX	NAS CM	Open End	Cautious Alloc (Growth & Income)	B-	C	A-	Up	Y	0
Russell Investments LifePoints Moderate Strategy Cls R1	RMLRX	NAS CM	Open End	Cautious Alloc (Growth & Income)	B-	C	A-	Up	Y	0
Russell Investments LifePoints Moderate Strategy Cls R4	RMLUX	NAS CM	Open End	Cautious Alloc (Growth & Income)	B-	C	A-	Up	Y	0
Russell Investments LifePoints Moderate Strategy Cls R5	RMLVX	NAS CM	Open End	Cautious Alloc (Growth & Income)	B-	C	A-	Up	Y	0
Russell Investments LifePoints Moderate Strategy Cls S	RMLSX	NAS CM	Open End	Cautious Alloc (Growth & Income)	B-	C	A-	Up	Y	0
Russell Investments Multi-Asset Growth Strategy Cls A	RAZAX	NAS CM	Open End	Cautious Alloc (Multi-Asset Global)	C	C	B-	Up		0
Russell Investments Multi-Asset Growth Strategy Cls C	RAZCX	NAS CM	Open End	Cautious Alloc (Multi-Asset Global)	C	C-	C+	Up	Y	0
Russell Investments Multi-Asset Growth Strategy Cls M	RMATX	NAS CM	Open End	Cautious Alloc (Multi-Asset Global)	C	C	B	Up	Y	0
Russell Investments Multi-Asset Growth Strategy Cls S	RMGSX	NAS CM	Open End	Cautious Alloc (Multi-Asset Global)	C	C	B-	Up	Y	0
Russell Investments Multi-Asset Growth Strategy Cls Y	RMGYX	NAS CM	Open End	Cautious Alloc (Multi-Asset Global)	C	C	B	Up	Y	0
Russell Investments Multifactor International Equity Cls M	RTITX	NAS CM	Open End	Global Equity Large Cap (Growth)	C	C	B-		Y	0
Russell Investments Multifactor Intl Equity Cls R6	RTIRX	NAS CM	Open End	Global Equity Large Cap (Growth)	C	C	B-		Y	0
Russell Investments Multifactor International Equity Cls S	RTISX	NAS CM	Open End	Global Equity Large Cap (Growth)	C	C	B-		Y	0
Russell Investments Multifactor International Equity Cls Y	RTIYX	NAS CM	Open End	Global Equity Large Cap (Growth)	C	C	B-		Y	10,000,000
Russell Investments Multifactor U.S. Equity Fund Class A	RTDAX	NAS CM	Open End	US Equity Large Cap Blend (Growth)	C+	C	B		Y	0
Russell Investments Multifactor U.S. Equity Fund Class C	RTDCX	NAS CM	Open End	US Equity Large Cap Blend (Growth)	C+	C	B		Y	0
Russell Investments Multifactor U.S. Equity Fund Class M	RTDTX	NAS CM	Open End	US Equity Large Cap Blend (Growth)	C+	C	B		Y	0
Russell Investments Multifactor U.S. Equity Fund Class R6	RTDRX	NAS CM	Open End	US Equity Large Cap Blend (Growth)	C+	C	B		Y	0
Russell Investments Multifactor U.S. Equity Fund Class S	RTDSX	NAS CM	Open End	US Equity Large Cap Blend (Growth)	C+	C	B		Y	0
Russell Investments Multifactor U.S. Equity Fund Class Y	RTDYX	NAS CM	Open End	US Equity Large Cap Blend (Growth)	C+	C	B		Y	10,000,000
Russell Investments Multi-Strategy Income Fund Class A	RMYAX	NAS CM	Open End	Cautious Alloc (Income)	B-	C	A-	Up	Y	0
Russell Investments Multi-Strategy Income Fund Class C	RMYCX	NAS CM	Open End	Cautious Alloc (Income)	B-	C	B+	Up	Y	0
Russell Investments Multi-Strategy Income Fund Class E	RMYEX	NAS CM	Open End	Cautious Alloc (Income)	B-	C	A-	Up	Y	0
Russell Investments Multi-Strategy Income Fund Class M	RGYTX	NAS CM	Open End	Cautious Alloc (Income)	B-	C	A-	Up	Y	0
Russell Investments Multi-Strategy Income Fund Class S	RMYSX	NAS CM	Open End	Cautious Alloc (Income)	B-	C	A-	Up	Y	0
Russell Investments Multi-Strategy Income Fund Class Y	RMYYX	NAS CM	Open End	Cautious Alloc (Income)	B	C	A-	Up	Y	10,000,000
Russell Investments Strategic Call Overwriting Cls S	ROWSX	NAS CM	Open End	Long/Short Equity (Growth)	C+	C	B		Y	0
Russell Investments Sustainable Equity Fund Class A	REQAX	NAS CM	Open End	US Equity Large Cap Blend (Growth & Income)	B-	C	B+	Down	Y	0
Russell Investments Sustainable Equity Fund Class C	REQCX	NAS CM	Open End	US Equity Large Cap Blend (Growth & Income)	B-	C	B+	Down	Y	0

★ Expanded analysis of this fund is included in Section II.

Min Additional Investment	TOTAL RETURNS: 3-Month Total Return	6-Month Total Return	1-Year Total Return	3-Year Total Return	5-Year Total Return	PERFORMANCE: Dividend Yield (TTM)	Expense Ratio	3-Yr Std Deviation	3-Year Beta	ASSETS: NAV	Total Assets (MIL)	ASSET ALLOCATION & TURNOVER: %Cash	%Stocks	%Bonds	%Other	Turnover Ratio	BULL & BEAR: Last Bull Market Total Return	Last Bear Market Total Return	FEES: Front End Fee (%)	Back End Fee (%)	Inception Date
	2.01	6.58	4.39	10.47	13.14	2.57	1.04	2.78	0.38	9.76	209.6	5	19	74	0	7	6.94	-4.23	5.75		Mar-03
	1.80	6.18	3.58	7.99	8.99	2	1.79	2.76	0.38	9.61	209.6	5	19	74	0	7	6.51	-4.53			Feb-99
	1.99	6.53	4.33	10.48	13.13	2.51	1.1	2.78	0.38	9.81	209.6	5	19	74	0	7	6.91	-4.27			Nov-97
	2.07	6.83	4.74	11.77	15.35	2.9	0.72	2.76	0.38	9.85	209.6	5	19	74	0	7	7.14	-4.11			Dec-06
	2.03	6.70	4.50	10.83	13.96	2.67	0.97	2.79	0.38	9.78	209.6	5	19	74	0	7	6.97	-4.17			Mar-06
	1.85	6.47	4.18	10.04	12.45	2.39	1.22	2.77	0.4	9.86	209.6	5	19	74	0	7	6.92	-4.32			Mar-98
	2.04	6.79	4.69	11.35	14.70	2.76	0.85	2.76	0.39	9.86	209.6	5	19	74	0	7	7.09	-4.15			Feb-00
	2.22	12.67	1.61	28.83	22.49	4.59	1.42	8.82	0.67	12.89	512.3	12	116	-28	0	15	18.85	-20.82	5.75		Mar-03
	1.97	12.24	0.80	25.94	18.01	4.81	2.17	8.88	0.68	11.37	512.3	12	116	-28	0	15	18.26	-20.97			Feb-99
	2.27	12.62	1.62	28.77	22.57	4.68	1.42	8.81	0.67	12.58	512.3	12	116	-28	0	15	18.88	-20.86			Sep-97
	2.27	12.82	1.93	30.10	24.60	4.71	1.09	8.83	0.68	13.02	512.3	12	116	-28	0	15	19.14	-20.62			May-06
	2.18	12.66	1.68	29.11	22.98	4.72	1.34	8.83	0.67	12.63	512.3	12	116	-28	0	15	18.93	-20.74			Mar-06
	2.22	12.59	1.50	28.11	21.56	4.68	1.59	8.84	0.68	12.43	512.3	12	116	-28	0	15	18.71	-20.8			Mar-98
	2.28	12.77	1.89	29.77	24.03	4.68	1.17	8.81	0.67	12.98	512.3	12	116	-28	0	15	19.08	-20.72			Jan-00
	2.22	10.84	2.25	25.10	20.35	5.41	1.35	7.14	0.54	11.96	1,109	24	66	10	0	14	16.36	-17.96	5.75		Mar-03
	1.95	10.41	1.55	22.36	15.88	5.04	2.1	7.13	0.54	11.45	1,109	24	66	10	0	14	15.79	-18.19			Jan-99
	2.12	10.78	2.24	25.07	20.39	5.37	1.35	7.08	0.53	12.02	1,109	24	66	10	0	14	16.3	-17.89			Sep-97
	2.27	10.94	2.55	26.23	22.21	5.55	1.05	7.08	0.54	12.16	1,109	24	66	10	0	14	16.65	-17.81			May-06
	2.12	10.79	2.28	25.21	20.66	5.42	1.3	7.07	0.53	12.01	1,109	24	66	10	0	14	16.39	-17.78			Mar-06
	2.04	10.61	1.99	24.27	19.12	5.23	1.55	7.09	0.54	11.98	1,109	24	66	10	0	14	16.26	-18			Mar-98
	2.18	10.95	2.51	26.02	21.79	5.52	1.1	7.09	0.54	12.15	1,109	24	66	10	0	14	16.56	-17.85			Feb-00
	2.09	7.91	3.68	15.03	17.55	4.04	1.13	3.99	0.39	10.23	357.9	5	35	58	0	15	10.05	-8.64	5.75		Mar-03
	1.93	7.50	3.01	12.53	13.18	3.53	1.88	4.03	0.41	10.03	357.9	5	35	58	0	15	9.51	-8.87			Feb-99
	2.08	7.88	3.60	14.75	17.18	3.96	1.21	4.03	0.4	10.26	357.9	5	35	58	0	15	10.04	-8.67			Oct-97
	2.07	7.95	3.96	15.94	19.10	4.2	0.88	4.04	0.4	10.31	357.9	5	35	58	0	15	10.26	-8.41			Oct-06
	2.09	7.89	3.67	14.98	17.61	4.03	1.13	3.97	0.38	10.25	357.9	5	35	58	0	15	10.08	-8.57			Mar-06
	1.98	7.74	3.45	14.23	16.19	3.82	1.38	4.01	0.4	10.29	357.9	5	35	58	0	15	10.04	-8.71			Mar-98
	2.18	7.96	3.90	15.63	18.65	4.15	0.96	3.97	0.38	10.3	357.9	5	35	58	0	15	10.12	-8.47			Jan-00
	0.90	7.52	1.78			1.48	1.2			10.46	2,119	11	56	23	5				5.75		Sep-17
	0.77	7.18	1.01			0.64	1.95			10.44	2,119	11	56	23	5						Sep-17
	1.08	7.72	2.20			1.8	0.85			10.46	2,119	11	56	23	5						Mar-17
	0.95	7.69	1.99			1.69	0.95			10.45	2,119	11	56	23	5						Mar-17
	0.99	7.73	2.18			1.87	0.75			10.46	2,119	11	56	23	5						Aug-17
	2.25	11.75	-1.82	26.46		3.1	0.49	11.26	1.01	9.51	761.2	6	94	0	0						Jan-15
	2.36	11.88	-1.80	26.56		3.11	0.47	11.24	1.01	9.51	761.2	6	94	0	0						Mar-16
	2.15	11.64	-2.07	25.80		2.96	0.64	11.22	1.01	9.49	761.2	6	94	0	0						Jan-15
	2.25	11.76	-1.88	26.51		3.14	0.44	11.23	1.01	9.5	761.2	6	94	0	0						Jul-14
	3.60	18.44	6.22	45.94		1.21	0.8	12.78	1.03	12.77	617.5	4	96	0	0				5.75		Apr-18
	3.47	18.06	5.49	43.40		0.15	1.55	12.76	1.03	12.81	617.5	4	96	0	0						Apr-18
	3.79	18.72	6.68	47.33		1.38	0.4	12.76	1.03	12.83	617.5	4	96	0	0						Jan-15
	3.80	18.83	6.78	47.40		1.4	0.38	12.74	1.03	12.83	617.5	4	96	0	0						Mar-16
	3.68	18.61	6.51	46.56		1.24	0.55	12.71	1.03	12.8	617.5	4	96	0	0						Jan-15
	3.81	18.75	6.72	47.40		1.42	0.35	12.77	1.03	12.82	617.5	4	96	0	0						Jul-14
	1.81	6.99	3.46	17.17		3.14	1.03	4		10.03	1,201	16	33	42	0				5.75		May-15
	1.65	6.62	2.71	14.50		2.43	1.78	4.04		9.98	1,201	16	33	42	0						May-15
	1.85	7.08	3.58	17.23		3.06	1.03	4.06		10.16	1,201	16	33	42	0						May-15
	1.90	7.08	3.77	18.46		3.43	0.68	4.07		10.04	1,201	16	33	42	0						Mar-17
	1.97	7.15	3.83	18.05		3.39	0.78	4.05		10.05	1,201	16	33	42	0						May-15
	1.91	7.19	3.93	18.82		3.58	0.58	4.06		10.06	1,201	16	33	42	0						May-15
	1.87	10.53	3.55	28.33	34.93	1.01	0.77	8.74	1.03	14.01	96.3	5	95	0	0						Aug-12
	3.50	16.09	10.25	39.32	57.36	0.62	1.44	10.21	0.93	52.51	452.3	9	90	1	0	67	26.02	-16.68	5.75		Sep-08
	3.33	15.65	9.39	36.20	51.55	0.14	2.19	10.2	0.93	51.8	452.3	9	90	1	0	67	25.51	-16.97			Sep-08

	MARKET			FUND TYPE, CATEGORY & OBJECTIVE	RATINGS					MINIMUMS
Fund Name	Ticker Symbol	Traded On	Fund Type	Category and (Prospectus Objective)	Overall Rating	Reward Rating	Risk Rating	Recent Up/ Downgrade	Open to New Investors	Min Initial Investment
Russell Investments Sustainable Equity Fund Class E	REQEX	NAS CM	Open End	US Equity Large Cap Blend (Growth & Income)	B-	C	B+	Down	Y	0
Russell Investments Sustainable Equity Fund Class S	REQTX	NAS CM	Open End	US Equity Large Cap Blend (Growth & Income)	B-	C+	B+	Down	Y	0
Russell Investments Sustainable Equity Fund Class Y	REUYX	NAS CM	Open End	US Equity Large Cap Blend (Growth & Income)	B-	C+	B+	Down	Y	10,000,000
Russell Investments Tax-Managed International Equity Cls A	RTNAX	NAS CM	Open End	Global Equity Large Cap (Foreign Stock)	C	C	B-		Y	0
Russell Investments Tax-Managed International Equity Cls C	RTNCX	NAS CM	Open End	Global Equity Large Cap (Foreign Stock)	C	C-	C+		Y	0
Russell Investments Tax-Managed International Equity Cls E	RTNEX	NAS CM	Open End	Global Equity Large Cap (Foreign Stock)	C	C	B-		Y	0
Russell Investments Tax-Managed International Equity Cls M	RTIUX	NAS CM	Open End	Global Equity Large Cap (Foreign Stock)	C	C	B-		Y	0
Russell Investments Tax-Managed International Equity Cls S	RTNSX	NAS CM	Open End	Global Equity Large Cap (Foreign Stock)	C	C	B-		Y	0
Russell Investments Tax-Managed U.S. Large Cap Cls A	RTLAX	NAS CM	Open End	US Equity Large Cap Growth (Growth & Income)	B-	C	B	Up	Y	0
Russell Investments Tax-Managed U.S. Large Cap Cls C	RTLCX	NAS CM	Open End	US Equity Large Cap Growth (Growth & Income)	C+	C	B		Y	0
Russell Investments Tax-Managed U.S. Large Cap Cls E	RTLEX	NAS CM	Open End	US Equity Large Cap Growth (Growth & Income)	B-	C	B	Up	Y	0
Russell Investments Tax-Managed U.S. Large Cap Cls M	RTMTX	NAS CM	Open End	US Equity Large Cap Growth (Growth & Income)	B-	C	B	Up	Y	0
Russell Investments Tax-Managed U.S. Large Cap Cls S	RETSX	NAS CM	Open End	US Equity Large Cap Growth (Growth & Income)	B-	C	B	Up	Y	0
Russell Investments Tax-Managed U.S. Mid & Small Cap Cls A	RTSAX	NAS CM	Open End	US Equity Small Cap (Growth)	C+	C	B-		Y	0
Russell Investments Tax-Managed U.S. Mid & Small Cap Cls C	RTSCX	NAS CM	Open End	US Equity Small Cap (Growth)	C+	C	B-	Up	Y	0
Russell Investments Tax-Managed U.S. Mid & Small Cap Cls E	RTSEX	NAS CM	Open End	US Equity Small Cap (Growth)	C+	C	B-		Y	0
Russell Investments Tax-Managed U.S. Mid & Small Cap Cls M	RTOUX	NAS CM	Open End	US Equity Small Cap (Growth)	C+	C	B-		Y	0
Russell Investments Tax-Managed U.S. Mid & Small Cap Cls S	RTSSX	NAS CM	Open End	US Equity Small Cap (Growth)	C+	C	B-		Y	0
Russell Investments U.S. Dynamic Equity Fund Class A	RSGAX	NAS CM	Open End	US Equity Large Cap Blend (Asset Alloc)	C+	C	B-	Up	Y	0
Russell Investments U.S. Dynamic Equity Fund Class C	RSGCX	NAS CM	Open End	US Equity Large Cap Blend (Asset Alloc)	C	C	B-		Y	0
Russell Investments U.S. Dynamic Equity Fund Class E	RSGEX	NAS CM	Open End	US Equity Large Cap Blend (Asset Alloc)	C+	C	B-	Up	Y	0
Russell Investments U.S. Dynamic Equity Fund Class S	RSGSX	NAS CM	Open End	US Equity Large Cap Blend (Asset Alloc)	C+	C	B-	Up	Y	0
Russell Investments U.S. Dynamic Equity Fund Class Y	RSGTX	NAS CM	Open End	US Equity Large Cap Blend (Asset Alloc)	C+	C	B-	Up	Y	10,000,000
Russell Investments U.S. Small Cap Equity Fund Class A	RLACX	NAS CM	Open End	US Equity Small Cap (Small Company)	C	C	C+		Y	0
Russell Investments U.S. Small Cap Equity Fund Class C	RLECX	NAS CM	Open End	US Equity Small Cap (Small Company)	C	C-	C+		Y	0
Russell Investments U.S. Small Cap Equity Fund Class E	REBEX	NAS CM	Open End	US Equity Small Cap (Small Company)	C	C	C+		Y	0
Russell Investments U.S. Small Cap Equity Fund Class M	RUNTX	NAS CM	Open End	US Equity Small Cap (Small Company)	C	C	C+		Y	0
Russell Investments U.S. Small Cap Equity Fund Class R6	RSCRX	NAS CM	Open End	US Equity Small Cap (Small Company)	C	C	C+		Y	0
Russell Investments U.S. Small Cap Equity Fund Class S	RLESX	NAS CM	Open End	US Equity Small Cap (Small Company)	C	C	C+		Y	0
Russell Investments U.S. Small Cap Equity Fund Class Y	REBYX	NAS CM	Open End	US Equity Small Cap (Small Company)	C	C	C+		Y	10,000,000
Russell Investments U.S. Strategic Equity Fund Class A	RSEAX	NAS CM	Open End	US Equity Large Cap Blend (Growth)	C+	C	B	Up	Y	0
Russell Investments U.S. Strategic Equity Fund Class C	RSECX	NAS CM	Open End	US Equity Large Cap Blend (Growth)	C+	C	B	Up	Y	0
Russell Investments U.S. Strategic Equity Fund Class E	RSEEX	NAS CM	Open End	US Equity Large Cap Blend (Growth)	C+	C	B	Up	Y	0
Russell Investments U.S. Strategic Equity Fund Class M	RUSTX	NAS CM	Open End	US Equity Large Cap Blend (Growth)	C+	C	B	Up	Y	0
Russell Investments U.S. Strategic Equity Fund Class S	RSESX	NAS CM	Open End	US Equity Large Cap Blend (Growth)	C+	C	B	Up	Y	0
RVX Emerging Markets Equity Fund Institutional Shares	RVEMX	NAS CM	Open End	Global Emerg Mkts (Div Emerging Mkts)	D	D+	C	Up	Y	1,000
RWC Global Emerging Equity Fund Class I	RWCIX	NAS CM	Open End	Global Emerg Mkts (Div Emerging Mkts)	C-	D+	C	Up	Y	250,000
RWC Global Emerging Equity Fund Institutional Class	RWCEX	NAS CM	Open End	Global Emerg Mkts (Div Emerging Mkts)	C-	D+	C	Up	Y	10,000,000
Rydex Banking Fund Class A	RYBKX	NAS CM	Open End	Financials Sector Equity (Financial)	C	C-	C		Y	2,500
Rydex Banking Fund Class C	RYKCX	NAS CM	Open End	Financials Sector Equity (Financial)	C-	C-	C	Down	Y	2,500
Rydex Banking Fund Class H	RYKAX	NAS CM	Open End	Financials Sector Equity (Financial)	C	C-	C		Y	2,500
Rydex Banking Fund Class Investor	RYKIX	NAS CM	Open End	Financials Sector Equity (Financial)	C	C-	C		Y	2,500
Rydex Basic Materials Fund Class A	RYBMX	NAS CM	Open End	Natl Resources Sec Equity ()	C	C	C+		Y	2,500
Rydex Basic Materials Fund Class C	RYBCX	NAS CM	Open End	Natl Resources Sec Equity ()	C	C	C+		Y	2,500
Rydex Basic Materials Fund Class H	RYBAX	NAS CM	Open End	Natl Resources Sec Equity ()	C	C	C+		Y	2,500
Rydex Basic Materials Fund Class Investor	RYBIX	NAS CM	Open End	Natl Resources Sec Equity ()	C	C	C+		Y	2,500
Rydex Biotechnology Fund Class A	RYBOX	NAS CM	Open End	Healthcare Sector Equity (Technology)	C	C	C+		Y	2,500
Rydex Biotechnology Fund Class C	RYCFX	NAS CM	Open End	Healthcare Sector Equity (Technology)	C	C	C+		Y	2,500
Rydex Biotechnology Fund Class H	RYOAX	NAS CM	Open End	Healthcare Sector Equity (Technology)	C	C	C+		Y	2,500
Rydex Biotechnology Fund Class Investor	RYOIX	NAS CM	Open End	Healthcare Sector Equity (Technology)	C	C	C+		Y	2,500
Rydex Commodities Fund Class A	RYMEX	NAS CM	Open End	Commodities Broad Basket (Growth)	C-	D+	C		Y	2,500
Rydex Commodities Fund Class C	RYMJX	NAS CM	Open End	Commodities Broad Basket (Growth)	C-	D+	C-	Up	Y	2,500

★ Expanded analysis of this fund is included in Section II.

Min Additional Investment	3-Month Total Return	6-Month Total Return	1-Year Total Return	3-Year Total Return	5-Year Total Return	Dividend Yield (TTM)	Expense Ratio	3-Yr Std Deviation	3-Year Beta	NAV	Total Assets (MIL)	%Cash	%Stocks	%Bonds	%Other	Turnover Ratio	Last Bull Market Total Return	Last Bear Market Total Return	Front End Fee (%)	Back End Fee (%)	Inception Date
	TOTAL RETURNS					PERFORMANCE				ASSETS		ASSET ALLOCATION & TURNOVER					BULL & BEAR		FEES		
	3.49	16.07	10.25	39.32	57.36	0.62	1.44	10.21	0.93	52.65	452.3	9	90	1	0	67	26.1	-16.67			May-99
	3.57	16.23	10.55	40.50	59.49	0.88	1.15	10.21	0.93	52.62	452.3	9	90	1	0	67	26.24	-16.61			Sep-08
	3.61	16.33	10.72	41.19	60.91	1.02	0.99	10.21	0.93	52.53	452.3	9	90	1	0	67	26.36	-16.55			Mar-00
	1.85	11.93	-1.24	27.03		1.09	1.29	11.59	1.01	10.41	1,638	9	91	0	0				5.75		Jun-15
	1.67	11.45	-2.02	24.22		0.48	2.04	11.56	1	10.31	1,638	9	91	0	0						Jun-15
	1.83	11.90	-1.30	27.04		1.1	1.29	11.6	1.01	10.53	1,638	9	91	0	0						Jun-15
	1.95	12.12	-0.88	28.35		1.5	0.94	11.67	1.01	10.45	1,638	9	91	0	0						Mar-17
	1.85	12.01	-1.08	27.92		1.41	1.04	11.63	1.01	10.44	1,638	9	91	0	0						Jun-15
	4.36	18.71	8.27	43.76	52.02	0.55	1.17	12.05	0.98	44.02	3,396	3	97	0	0		28.1	-18.34	5.75		May-10
	4.14	18.28	7.45	40.53	46.40	0	1.92	12.05	0.98	41.66	3,396	3	97	0	0		27.62	-18.61			Dec-99
	4.36	18.73	8.28	43.75	52.04	0.5	1.17	12.06	0.99	44.48	3,396	3	97	0	0		28.17	-18.35			Nov-99
	4.46	18.96	8.68	45.15	54.24	0.86	0.82	12.06	0.99	44.48	3,396	3	97	0	0		28.3	-18.24			Mar-17
	4.43	18.89	8.56	44.85	53.92	0.77	0.92	12.06	0.99	44.49	3,396	3	97	0	0		28.3	-18.24			Oct-96
	3.68	18.47	1.45	38.74	34.08	0	1.48	14.87	0.95	27.26	735.9	3	97	0	0		28.39	-22.96	5.75		May-10
	3.48	18.00	0.74	35.77	29.34	0	2.2	14.89	0.95	23.13	735.9	3	97	0	0		27.84	-23.23			Dec-99
	3.67	18.46	1.48	38.82	34.22	0	1.45	14.86	0.95	27.33	735.9	3	97	0	0		28.46	-23.01			Nov-99
	3.76	18.65	1.81	40.26	36.28	0	1.1	14.88	0.95	28.68	735.9	3	97	0	0		28.58	-22.92			Mar-17
	3.77	18.61	1.74	39.91	35.95	0	1.2	14.88	0.95	28.61	735.9	3	97	0	0		28.58	-22.92			Nov-99
	4.87	20.89	2.75	48.37	49.15	0.47	1.61	14.25	0.96	6.24	114.0	6	94	0	0	137	28.1	-17.4	5.75		Aug-12
	4.77	20.33	2.09	45.21	43.73	0.13	2.36	14.3	0.96	3.97	114.0	6	94	0	0	137	28.1	-17.4			Jan-01
	4.67	20.57	2.58	48.15	48.86	0.38	1.61	14.27	0.96	6.27	114.0	6	94	0	0	137	28.82	-17.19			Jan-01
	4.98	20.95	3.03	49.63	51.18	0.75	1.32	14.3	0.96	6.9	114.0	6	94	0	0	137	28.89	-17.1			Jan-01
	5.04	20.94	3.22	50.32	52.43	0.87	1.21	14.28	0.96	7.09	114.0	6	94	0	0	137	28.1	-17.4			Aug-12
	2.09	17.62	-3.47	39.75	34.09	0.26	1.41	16.37	0.95	27.29	1,590	5	95	0	0		29.49	-24.62	5.75		Sep-08
	1.90	17.17	-4.21	36.61	29.13	0	2.16	16.35	0.95	25.11	1,590	5	95	0	0		28.95	-24.91			Sep-08
	2.07	17.61	-3.50	39.68	34.04	0	1.41	16.36	0.95	27.57	1,590	5	95	0	0		29.54	-24.62			May-99
	2.18	17.88	-3.10	40.98	35.29	0.69	1.02	16.37	0.95	27.62	1,590	5	95	0	0		29.54	-24.62			Mar-17
	2.18	17.87	-3.07	41.53	35.96	0.75	0.99	16.38	0.95	27.63	1,590	5	95	0	0		29.54	-24.62			Mar-16
	2.18	17.81	-3.18	40.96	35.92	0.57	1.12	16.38	0.95	27.64	1,590	5	95	0	0		29.71	-24.58			Sep-08
	2.21	17.91	-3.03	41.66	37.12	0.75	0.96	16.37	0.95	27.65	1,590	5	95	0	0		29.77	-24.5			Mar-00
	5.23	20.61	5.78	45.23	51.76	0.79	0.99	13.21	1.06	11.94	2,583	4	96	0	0				5.75		Aug-12
	5.02	20.10	4.95	41.93	46.02	0.08	1.74	13.21	1.06	11.87	2,583	4	96	0	0						Aug-12
	5.20	20.52	5.75	45.09	51.67	0.79	0.99	13.19	1.06	11.98	2,583	4	96	0	0						Aug-12
	5.31	20.79	6.10	46.70	54.02	1.12	0.64	13.18	1.06	11.96	2,583	4	96	0	0						Mar-17
	5.27	20.73	6.04	46.37	53.67	1.02	0.74	13.19	1.06	11.97	2,583	4	96	0	0						Aug-12
100	-0.55	12.46	-3.10			1	1.28			8.93	6.6	0	97	0	3						Apr-18
	-1.09	16.88	-7.95			0.06	1.33			11.7	153.2	2	98	0	0	91					Sep-17
	-1.09	16.86	-7.95			0.12	1.25			11.71	153.2	2	98	0	0	91					Dec-16
	4.80	15.54	-5.46	43.67	26.29	2.22	1.63	20.29	1.29	71.07	11.9	3	98	0	-1	633	30.77	-30.07	4.75		Sep-04
	4.61	15.11	-6.17	40.47	21.63	2.5	2.38	20.29	1.29	63.3	11.9	3	98	0	-1	633	30.19	-30.3		1.00	Mar-01
	4.81	15.53	-5.47	43.65	26.04	2.29	1.62	20.29	1.29	69.18	11.9	3	98	0	-1	633	30.56	-30.15			Apr-98
	4.88	15.69	-5.22	44.73	27.85	2.02	1.38	20.3	1.29	78.22	11.9	3	98	0	-1	633	30.95	-29.98			Apr-98
	3.42	17.13	-1.55	28.42	14.71	0.42	1.63	15.71	1.08	56.13	38.8	3	100	0	-3	247	16.21	-27.24	4.75		Sep-04
	3.24	16.69	-2.28	25.55	10.50	0.48	2.38	15.7	1.08	49.28	38.8	3	100	0	-3	247	15.73	-27.48		1.00	May-01
	3.42	17.13	-1.55	28.48	14.46	0.43	1.62	15.71	1.08	54.42	38.8	3	100	0	-3	247	16.05	-27.32			Apr-98
	3.48	17.28	-1.31	29.37	16.17	0.39	1.38	15.7	1.08	60.06	38.8	3	100	0	-3	247	16.39	-27.18			Apr-98
	-3.70	16.52	-0.17	38.35	37.25	0	1.62	22.27	1.38	72.86	203.7	4	99	0	-4	100	36	-14.54	4.75		Sep-04
	-3.89	16.09	-0.92	35.26	32.17	0	2.37	22.25	1.38	63.48	203.7	4	99	0	-4	100	35.38	-14.79		1.00	Mar-01
	-3.70	16.51	-0.19	38.33	36.86	0	1.62	22.27	1.38	70.47	203.7	4	99	0	-4	100	35.81	-14.63			Apr-98
	-3.64	16.67	0.06	39.39	38.97	0	1.37	22.27	1.38	79.99	203.7	4	99	0	-4	100	36.18	-14.46			Apr-98
	-2.43	11.36	-13.93	-1.61	-55.33	39.74	1.69	16.09	1.01	59.29	5.0	83	0	6	11	65	14.35	-23.99	4.75		May-05
	-2.61	10.94	-14.56	-3.81	-56.96	46.58	2.43	16.1	1.01	50.59	5.0	83	0	6	11	65	13.83	-24.2		1.00	May-05

	MARKET		FUND TYPE, CATEGORY & OBJECTIVE		RATINGS				MINIMUMS	
Fund Name	Ticker Symbol	Traded On	Fund Type	Category and (Prospectus Objective)	Overall Rating	Reward Rating	Risk Rating	Recent Up/ Downgrade	Open to New Investors	Min Initial Investment
Rydex Commodities Fund Class H	RYMBX	NAS CM	Open End	Commodities Broad Basket (Growth)	C-	D+	C		Y	2,500
Rydex Consumer Products Fund Class A	RYPDX	NAS CM	Open End	Consumer Goods Sec Equity ()	C	C	C+		Y	2,500
Rydex Consumer Products Fund Class C	RYCPX	NAS CM	Open End	Consumer Goods Sec Equity ()	C	C	C+		Y	2,500
Rydex Consumer Products Fund Class H	RYCAX	NAS CM	Open End	Consumer Goods Sec Equity ()	C	C	C+		Y	2,500
Rydex Consumer Products Fund Class Investor	RYCIX	NAS CM	Open End	Consumer Goods Sec Equity ()	C	C	C+		Y	2,500
Rydex Dow 2x Strategy Fund Class A	RYLDX	NAS CM	Open End	Trading Tools (Growth)	C+	C+	C		Y	2,500
Rydex Dow 2x Strategy Fund Class C	RYCYX	NAS CM	Open End	Trading Tools (Growth)	C+	C+	C		Y	2,500
Rydex Dow 2x Strategy Fund Class H	RYCVX	NAS CM	Open End	Trading Tools (Growth)	C+	C+	C		Y	2,500
Rydex Dow Jones Industrial Average® Fund Class A	RYDAX	NAS CM	Open End	US Equity Large Cap Value (Growth)	B-	C	B	Down	Y	2,500
Rydex Dow Jones Industrial Average® Fund Class C	RYDKX	NAS CM	Open End	US Equity Large Cap Value (Growth)	B-	C	B		Y	2,500
Rydex Dow Jones Industrial Average® Fund Class H	RYDHX	NAS CM	Open End	US Equity Large Cap Value (Growth)	B-	C	B	Down	Y	2,500
Rydex Electronics Fund Class A	RYELX	NAS CM	Open End	Technology Sector Equity (Technology)	C+	C	C+	Down	Y	2,500
Rydex Electronics Fund Class C	RYSCX	NAS CM	Open End	Technology Sector Equity (Technology)	C+	C	C+	Down	Y	2,500
Rydex Electronics Fund Class H	RYSAX	NAS CM	Open End	Technology Sector Equity (Technology)	C+	C	C+	Down	Y	2,500
Rydex Electronics Fund Class Investor	RYSIX	NAS CM	Open End	Technology Sector Equity (Technology)	C+	C	C+	Down	Y	2,500
Rydex Emerging Markets 2x Strategy Fund A Class	RYWTX	NAS CM	Open End	Trading Tools (Div Emerging Mkts)	C-	C-	D+		Y	2,500
Rydex Emerging Markets 2x Strategy Fund C Class	RYWUX	NAS CM	Open End	Trading Tools (Div Emerging Mkts)	C-	C-	D+		Y	2,500
Rydex Emerging Markets 2x Strategy Fund H Class	RYWVX	NAS CM	Open End	Trading Tools (Div Emerging Mkts)	C-	C-	D+		Y	2,500
Rydex Energy Fund Class A	RYENX	NAS CM	Open End	Energy Sector Equity (Natl Res)	D	D	D	Down	Y	2,500
Rydex Energy Fund Class C	RYECX	NAS CM	Open End	Energy Sector Equity (Natl Res)	D	D	D	Down	Y	2,500
Rydex Energy Fund Class H	RYEAX	NAS CM	Open End	Energy Sector Equity (Natl Res)	D	D	D	Down	Y	2,500
Rydex Energy Fund Class Investor	RYEIX	NAS CM	Open End	Energy Sector Equity (Natl Res)	D	D	D	Down	Y	2,500
Rydex Energy Services Fund Class A	RYESX	NAS CM	Open End	Energy Sector Equity (Natl Res)	D	D-	D	Down	Y	2,500
Rydex Energy Services Fund Class C	RYVCX	NAS CM	Open End	Energy Sector Equity (Natl Res)	D	D-	D	Down	Y	2,500
Rydex Energy Services Fund Class H	RYVAX	NAS CM	Open End	Energy Sector Equity (Natl Res)	D	D-	D	Down	Y	2,500
Rydex Energy Services Fund Class Investor	RYVIX	NAS CM	Open End	Energy Sector Equity (Natl Res)	D	D-	D	Down	Y	2,500
Rydex Europe Advantage Fund Class A	RYAEX	NAS CM	Open End	Trading Tools (Europe Stock)	C	C	C+		Y	2,500
Rydex Europe Advantage Fund Class C	RYCEX	NAS CM	Open End	Trading Tools (Europe Stock)	C	C-	C+		Y	2,500
Rydex Europe Advantage Fund Class H	RYEUX	NAS CM	Open End	Trading Tools (Europe Stock)	C	C	C+		Y	2,500
Rydex Financial Services Fund Class A	RYFNX	NAS CM	Open End	Financials Sector Equity (Financial)	C+	C	B	Up	Y	2,500
Rydex Financial Services Fund Class C	RYFCX	NAS CM	Open End	Financials Sector Equity (Financial)	C+	C	B	Up	Y	2,500
Rydex Financial Services Fund Class H	RYFAX	NAS CM	Open End	Financials Sector Equity (Financial)	C+	C	B	Up	Y	2,500
Rydex Financial Services Fund Class Investor	RYFIX	NAS CM	Open End	Financials Sector Equity (Financial)	C+	C	B	Up	Y	2,500
Rydex Government Long Bond 1.2x Strategy Fund Class A	RYABX	NAS CM	Open End	Trading Tools (Govt Bond - Treasury)	C	C	C	Up	Y	2,500
Rydex Government Long Bond 1.2x Strategy Fund Class C	RYCGX	NAS CM	Open End	Trading Tools (Govt Bond - Treasury)	C	C	C	Up	Y	2,500
Rydex Government Long Bond 1.2x Strategy Fund Class H	RYHBX	NAS CM	Open End	Trading Tools (Govt Bond - Treasury)	C	C	C	Up	Y	2,500
Rydex Government Long Bond 1.2x Strategy Investor Cls	RYGBX	NAS CM	Open End	Trading Tools (Govt Bond - Treasury)	C	C	C	Up	Y	2,500
Rydex Health Care Fund Class A	RYHEX	NAS CM	Open End	Healthcare Sector Equity (Health)	C+	C	B	Down	Y	2,500
Rydex Health Care Fund Class C	RYHCX	NAS CM	Open End	Healthcare Sector Equity (Health)	C+	C	B	Down	Y	2,500
Rydex Health Care Fund Class H	RYHAX	NAS CM	Open End	Healthcare Sector Equity (Health)	C+	C	B	Down	Y	2,500
Rydex Health Care Fund Class Investor	RYHIX	NAS CM	Open End	Healthcare Sector Equity (Health)	C+	C	B	Down	Y	2,500
Rydex Internet Fund Class A	RYINX	NAS CM	Open End	Technology Sector Equity (Technology)	C+	C+	C+	Down	Y	2,500
Rydex Internet Fund Class C	RYICX	NAS CM	Open End	Technology Sector Equity (Technology)	C+	C+	C+	Down	Y	2,500
Rydex Internet Fund Class H	RYIAX	NAS CM	Open End	Technology Sector Equity (Technology)	C+	C+	C+	Down	Y	2,500
Rydex Internet Fund Class Investor	RYIIX	NAS CM	Open End	Technology Sector Equity (Technology)	C+	C+	C+	Down	Y	2,500
Rydex Inverse Dow 2x Strategy Fund Class A	RYIDX	NAS CM	Open End	Trading Tools (Growth)	D	D-	D-		Y	2,500
Rydex Inverse Dow 2x Strategy Fund Class C	RYCZX	NAS CM	Open End	Trading Tools (Growth)	D	D-	D-		Y	2,500
Rydex Inverse Dow 2x Strategy Fund Class H	RYCWX	NAS CM	Open End	Trading Tools (Growth)	D	D-	D-		Y	2,500
Rydex Inverse Emerging Markets 2x Strategy Fund A Class	RYWWX	NAS CM	Open End	Trading Tools (Div Emerging Mkts)	D	D	D		Y	2,500
Rydex Inverse Emerging Markets 2x Strategy Fund C Class	RYWZX	NAS CM	Open End	Trading Tools (Div Emerging Mkts)	D	D	D		Y	2,500
Rydex Inverse Emerging Markets 2x Strategy Fund H Class	RYWYX	NAS CM	Open End	Trading Tools (Div Emerging Mkts)	D	D	D		Y	2,500
Rydex Inverse Government Long Bond Strategy Fund Class A	RYAQX	NAS CM	Open End	Trading Tools (Govt Bond - Treasury)	D+	D	D+	Down	Y	2,500

★Expanded analysis of this fund is included in Section II.

Min Additional Investment	3-Month Total Return	6-Month Total Return	1-Year Total Return	3-Year Total Return	5-Year Total Return	Dividend Yield (TTM)	Expense Ratio	3-Yr Std Deviation	3-Year Beta	NAV	Total Assets (MIL)	%Cash	%Stocks	%Bonds	%Other	Turnover Ratio	Last Bull Market Total Return	Last Bear Market Total Return	Front End Fee (%)	Back End Fee (%)	Inception Date
TOTAL RETURNS						PERFORMANCE				ASSETS		ASSET ALLOCATION & TURNOVER					BULL & BEAR		FEES		
	-2.45	11.33	-13.96	-1.58	-55.35	39.72	1.69	16.1	1.01	59.32	5.0	83	0	6	11	65	14.28	-24.03			May-05
	1.42	13.59	6.08	8.13	31.97	1.38	1.63	11.19	0.63	54.98	170.9	1	99	0	0	84	14.94	-4.68	4.75		Sep-04
	1.21	13.18	5.31	5.72	27.08	1.62	2.38	11.18	0.63	46.54	170.9	1	99	0	0	84	14.47	-5.03		1.00	Jul-01
	1.42	13.59	6.09	8.12	31.58	1.44	1.63	11.18	0.63	52.81	170.9	1	99	0	0	84	14.77	-4.8			Aug-98
	1.47	13.73	6.35	8.95	33.61	1.26	1.38	11.18	0.63	60.44	170.9	1	99	0	0	84	15.12	-4.62			Jul-98
	4.82	31.77	16.94	120.34	143.58	0	1.8	25.06		98.21	41.6	5	90	6	-1	239	45.6	-28.71	4.75		Sep-04
	4.62	31.28	16.08	115.56	134.75	0	2.54	25.05		86.41	41.6	5	90	6	-1	239	44.78	-28.93		1.00	Feb-04
	4.81	31.78	16.93	120.36	143.46	0	1.8	25.06		97.89	41.6	5	90	6	-1	239	45.4	-28.74			Feb-04
	2.77	15.70	10.22	53.75		0.87	1.56	12.38	1	72.5	42.6	13	71	6	10	465			4.75		Dec-15
	2.58	15.30	9.41	50.38		0.9	2.3	12.38	1	70.52	42.6	13	71	6	10	465				1.00	Dec-15
	2.77	15.72	10.21	53.88		0.87	1.55	12.38	1	72.55	42.6	13	71	6	10	465					Dec-15
	5.12	27.57	7.45	83.05	94.77	0	1.63	22.08	1.45	122.87	16.4	0	100	0	0	521	16.5	-28.38	4.75		Sep-04
	4.93	27.10	6.65	79.00	87.63	0	2.38	22.07	1.45	108.8	16.4	0	100	0	0	521	15.95	-28.64		1.00	Mar-01
	5.12	27.58	7.43	83.05	94.07	0	1.63	22.08	1.45	119.28	16.4	0	100	0	0	521	16.39	-28.43			Apr-98
	5.18	27.73	7.71	84.41	97.13	0	1.38	22.08	1.45	132.86	16.4	0	100	0	0	521	16.7	-28.31			Apr-98
	-6.35	18.36	-8.81	51.50	-11.87	0	1.76	34.26		66.51	7.2	30	51	0	19	1,978	28.03	-47.85	4.75		Oct-10
	-6.51	17.91	-9.50	48.15	-15.12	0	2.56	34.25		63.13	7.2	30	51	0	19	1,978	27.65	-47.5		1.00	Oct-10
	-6.32	18.40	-8.81	51.37	-11.99	0	1.77	34.26		66.53	7.2	30	51	0	19	1,978	28.19	-47.72			Oct-10
	-5.21	11.02	-23.89	-12.08	-50.18	0.79	1.63	23.66	1.32	60.12	19.7	0	99	0	0	525	22.97	-31.23	4.75		Sep-04
	-5.41	10.60	-24.46	-14.04	-52.09	0.9	2.38	23.67	1.33	52.78	19.7	0	99	0	0	525	22.53	-31.46		1.00	Apr-01
	-5.26	10.97	-23.93	-12.18	-50.43	0.81	1.63	23.69	1.33	58.26	19.7	0	99	0	0	525	22.92	-31.33			May-98
	-5.16	11.17	-23.71	-11.45	-49.64	0.74	1.37	23.67	1.33	64.49	19.7	0	99	0	0	525	23.22	-31.16			Apr-98
	-11.59	8.73	-38.80	-44.04	-75.22	1.45	1.63	34.06	1.88	15.56	8.5	4	100	0	-3	1,453	24.57	-34.83	4.75		Sep-04
	-11.77	8.33	-39.26	-45.28	-76.13	1.63	2.38	34.05	1.88	13.78	8.5	4	100	0	-3	1,453	24.06	-35.07		1.00	Mar-01
	-11.56	8.81	-38.85	-44.13	-75.36	1.49	1.63	34.13	1.88	15.06	8.5	4	100	0	-3	1,453	24.4	-34.92			Apr-98
	-11.54	8.90	-38.63	-43.60	-74.90	1.35	1.38	34.04	1.88	16.63	8.5	4	100	0	-3	1,453	24.74	-34.78			Apr-98
	5.69	22.72	6.27	29.23	-8.03	7	1.72	15.41		90.03	2.8	22	44	31	3	1,411	18.21	-31.91	4.75		Mar-04
	5.49	22.25	5.49	26.39	-11.18	8.28	2.47	15.4		76.08	2.8	22	44	31	3	1,411	17.97	-32.27		1.00	May-01
	5.68	22.70	6.28	29.82	-7.90	7.05	1.72	15.37		89.39	2.8	22	44	31	3	1,411	18.31	-31.91			May-00
	5.59	18.98	5.68	40.59	41.18	1.27	1.66	13.17	0.94	67.81	27.7	1	100	0	0	410	27.75	-26.56	4.75		Sep-04
	5.39	18.55	4.90	37.51	36.02	1.44	2.41	13.15	0.94	59.54	27.7	1	100	0	0	410	27.25	-26.8		1.00	Apr-01
	5.60	18.98	5.67	40.65	40.87	1.31	1.66	13.17	0.94	65.75	27.7	1	100	0	0	410	27.55	-26.62			Apr-98
	5.64	19.12	5.95	41.68	42.97	1.19	1.41	13.17	0.94	72.56	27.7	1	100	0	0	410	27.94	-26.47			Apr-98
	7.22	13.37	13.36	-2.15	31.61	1.46	1.23	13.66		57.3	161.0	6	0	65	29	1,182	-1.73	40.2	4.75		Mar-04
	7.03	12.94	12.57	-4.31	26.75	0.79	1.98	13.64		56.91	161.0	6	0	65	29	1,182	-2.22	39.78		1.00	May-01
	7.24	13.38	13.37	-2.20	31.67	1.46	1.23	13.67		57.33	161.0	6	0	65	29	1,182	-1.74	40.18			Sep-14
	7.26	13.48	13.63	-1.53	32.98	1.68	0.98	13.67		56.85	161.0	6	0	65	29	1,182	-1.59	40.33			Jan-94
	0.68	14.24	7.23	36.93	49.50	0	1.63	15.84	1.09	29.2	50.6	2	100	0	-1	341	20.32	-14.57	4.75		Sep-04
	0.52	13.88	6.49	33.98	44.09	0	2.38	15.85	1.09	24.94	50.6	2	100	0	-1	341	19.81	-14.85		1.00	Mar-01
	0.71	14.31	7.28	36.89	49.11	0	1.64	15.86	1.09	28.11	50.6	2	100	0	-1	341	20.19	-14.69			May-98
	0.78	14.42	7.55	38.06	51.48	0	1.38	15.84	1.09	32.28	50.6	2	100	0	-1	341	20.46	-14.51			Apr-98
	1.95	24.34	2.69	78.78	83.73	0	1.63	16.93	1.17	112.33	25.4	3	100	0	-3	349	25.36	-25.04	4.75		Sep-04
	1.77	23.88	1.93	74.85	77.02	0	2.38	16.91	1.17	97.09	25.4	3	100	0	-3	349	24.84	-25.28		1.00	Apr-01
	1.94	24.34	2.68	78.83	83.26	0	1.63	16.92	1.17	108.58	25.4	3	100	0	-3	349	25.22	-25.14			Apr-00
	2.02	24.49	2.95	80.18	86.09	0	1.38	16.92	1.17	121.2	25.4	3	100	0	-3	349	25.57	-24.96			Apr-00
	-5.76	-26.38	-22.19	-64.27	-75.07	0	1.8	24.01		9.15	6.0	38	-2	65	0	0	-38.43	23.34	4.75		Sep-04
	-5.93	-26.72	-22.87	-65.11	-76.02	0	2.55	24		8.09	6.0	38	-2	65	0	0	-38.69	22.91		1.00	Feb-04
	-5.75	-26.40	-22.28	-64.27	-75.08	0	1.8	24		9.17	6.0	38	-2	65	0	0	-38.62	23.31			Feb-04
	3.32	-21.05	-7.31	-57.42	-55.61	0	1.76	32.19		41.92	1.2	105	-2	0	-3	1,085	-35.74	51.9	4.75		Oct-10
	3.01	-21.48	-8.15	-58.46	-57.36	0	2.49	32.19		41.67	1.2	105	-2	0	-3	1,085	-34.16	54.85		1.00	Oct-10
	3.30	-20.97	-7.26	-57.46	-55.92	0	1.76	32.18		41.6	1.2	105	-2	0	-3	1,085	-35.74	51.98			Oct-10
	-5.45	-9.75	-9.75	-2.24	-29.30	0	3.98	11.31		29.99	64.9	97	0	4	-1	603	-1.43	-27.18	4.75		Mar-04

	MARKET			FUND TYPE, CATEGORY & OBJECTIVE	RATINGS				MINIMUMS	
Fund Name	Ticker Symbol	Traded On	Fund Type	Category and (Prospectus Objective)	Overall Rating	Reward Rating	Risk Rating	Recent Up/ Downgrade	Open to New Investors	Min Initial Investment
Rydex Inverse Government Long Bond Strategy Fund Class C	RYJCX	NAS CM	Open End	Trading Tools (Govt Bond - Treasury)	D+	D	D+		Y	2,500
Rydex Inverse Government Long Bond Strategy Fund Class H	RYHJX	NAS CM	Open End	Trading Tools (Govt Bond - Treasury)	D+	D	D+	Down	Y	2,500
Rydex Inverse Government Long Bond Strategy Investor Cls	RYJUX	NAS CM	Open End	Trading Tools (Govt Bond - Treasury)	D+	D	D+	Down	Y	2,500
Rydex Inverse High Yield Strategy Fund Class A	RYILX	NAS CM	Open End	Trading Tools (Corporate Bond - High Yield)	D	D-	D+		Y	2,500
Rydex Inverse High Yield Strategy Fund Class C	RYIYX	NAS CM	Open End	Trading Tools (Corporate Bond - High Yield)	D	D-	D		Y	2,500
Rydex Inverse High Yield Strategy Fund Class H	RYIHX	NAS CM	Open End	Trading Tools (Corporate Bond - High Yield)	D	D-	D+		Y	2,500
Rydex Inverse Mid-Cap Strategy Fund Class A	RYAGX	NAS CM	Open End	Alternative Miscellaneous (Growth)	D	D	D	Down	Y	2,500
Rydex Inverse Mid-Cap Strategy Fund Class C	RYCLX	NAS CM	Open End	Alternative Miscellaneous (Growth)	D	D	D	Down	Y	2,500
Rydex Inverse Mid-Cap Strategy Fund Class H	RYMHX	NAS CM	Open End	Alternative Miscellaneous (Growth)	D	D	D	Down	Y	2,500
Rydex Inverse NASDAQ-100® 2x Strategy Fund Class A	RYVTX	NAS CM	Open End	Trading Tools (Growth)	D	E+	D		Y	2,500
Rydex Inverse NASDAQ-100® 2x Strategy Fund Class C	RYCDX	NAS CM	Open End	Trading Tools (Growth)	D	E+	D		Y	2,500
Rydex Inverse NASDAQ-100® 2x Strategy Fund Class H	RYVNX	NAS CM	Open End	Trading Tools (Growth)	D	E+	D		Y	2,500
Rydex Inverse NASDAQ-100® Strategy Fund Class A	RYAPX	NAS CM	Open End	Alternative Miscellaneous (Growth)	D	D-	D		Y	2,500
Rydex Inverse NASDAQ-100® Strategy Fund Class C	RYACX	NAS CM	Open End	Alternative Miscellaneous (Growth)	D	D-	D		Y	2,500
Rydex Inverse NASDAQ-100® Strategy Fund Class H	RYALX	NAS CM	Open End	Alternative Miscellaneous (Growth)	D	D-	D		Y	2,500
Rydex Inverse NASDAQ-100® Strategy Fund Investor Class	RYAIX	NAS CM	Open End	Alternative Miscellaneous (Growth)	D	D-	D		Y	2,500
Rydex Inverse Russell 2000 2x Strategy Fund Class A	RYIUX	NAS CM	Open End	Trading Tools (Growth)	D	D-	D		Y	2,500
Rydex Inverse Russell 2000 2x Strategy Fund Class C	RYIZX	NAS CM	Open End	Trading Tools (Growth)	D	D-	D		Y	2,500
Rydex Inverse Russell 2000 2x Strategy Fund Class H	RYIRX	NAS CM	Open End	Trading Tools (Growth)	D	D-	D		Y	2,500
Rydex Inverse Russell 2000® Strategy Fund Class A	RYAFX	NAS CM	Open End	Alternative Miscellaneous (Growth)	D+	D	D		Y	2,500
Rydex Inverse Russell 2000® Strategy Fund Class C	RYCQX	NAS CM	Open End	Alternative Miscellaneous (Growth)	D+	D	D	Up	Y	2,500
Rydex Inverse Russell 2000® Strategy Fund Class H	RYSHX	NAS CM	Open End	Alternative Miscellaneous (Growth)	D+	D	D		Y	2,500
Rydex Inverse S&P 500 2x Strategy Fund Class A	RYTMX	NAS CM	Open End	Trading Tools (Growth)	D	D-	D		Y	2,500
Rydex Inverse S&P 500 2x Strategy Fund Class C	RYCBX	NAS CM	Open End	Trading Tools (Growth)	D	D-	D		Y	2,500
Rydex Inverse S&P 500 2x Strategy Fund Class H	RYTPX	NAS CM	Open End	Trading Tools (Growth)	D	D-	D		Y	2,500
Rydex Inverse S&P 500® Strategy Fund Class A	RYARX	NAS CM	Open End	Alternative Miscellaneous (Growth)	D	D-	D		Y	2,500
Rydex Inverse S&P 500® Strategy Fund Class C	RYUCX	NAS CM	Open End	Alternative Miscellaneous (Growth)	D	D-	D		Y	2,500
Rydex Inverse S&P 500® Strategy Fund Class H	RYUHX	NAS CM	Open End	Alternative Miscellaneous (Growth)	D	D-	D		Y	2,500
Rydex Inverse S&P 500® Strategy Fund Investor Class	RYURX	NAS CM	Open End	Alternative Miscellaneous (Growth)	D	D	D		Y	2,500
Rydex Japan 2x Strategy Fund Class A	RYJSX	NAS CM	Open End	Trading Tools (Pacific Stock)	C	C	C	Up	Y	2,500
Rydex Japan 2x Strategy Fund Class C	RYJTX	NAS CM	Open End	Trading Tools (Pacific Stock)	C	C	C	Up	Y	2,500
Rydex Japan 2x Strategy Fund Class H	RYJHX	NAS CM	Open End	Trading Tools (Pacific Stock)	C	C	C	Up	Y	2,500
Rydex Leisure Fund Class A	RYLSX	NAS CM	Open End	Consumer Goods Sec Equity ()	C+	C	B	Up	Y	2,500
Rydex Leisure Fund Class C	RYLCX	NAS CM	Open End	Consumer Goods Sec Equity ()	C+	C	B	Up	Y	2,500
Rydex Leisure Fund Class Investor	RYLIX	NAS CM	Open End	Consumer Goods Sec Equity ()	C+	C	B	Up	Y	2,500
Rydex Leisure Fund H Class	RYLAX	NAS CM	Open End	Consumer Goods Sec Equity ()	C+	C	B	Up	Y	2,500
Rydex Mid-Cap 1.5x Strategy Fund Class A	RYAHX	NAS CM	Open End	Trading Tools (Growth)	C	C	C		Y	2,500
Rydex Mid-Cap 1.5x Strategy Fund Class C	RYDCX	NAS CM	Open End	Trading Tools (Growth)	C	C	C		Y	2,500
Rydex Mid-Cap 1.5x Strategy Fund Class H	RYMDX	NAS CM	Open End	Trading Tools (Growth)	C	C	C		Y	2,500
Rydex Monthly Rebalance NASDAQ-100® 2x Strategy Cls A	RMQAX	NAS CM	Open End	Trading Tools (Aggr Growth)	C	B-	C	Down	Y	2,500
Rydex Monthly Rebalance NASDAQ-100® 2x Strategy Cls C	RMQCX	NAS CM	Open End	Trading Tools (Aggr Growth)	C	B-	C	Down	Y	2,500
Rydex Monthly Rebalance NASDAQ-100® 2x Strategy Cls H	RMQHX	NAS CM	Open End	Trading Tools (Aggr Growth)	C	B-	C	Down	Y	2,500
Rydex NASDAQ-100® 2x Strategy Fund Class A	RYVLX	NAS CM	Open End	Trading Tools (Growth)	C	B-	C	Down	Y	2,500
Rydex NASDAQ-100® 2x Strategy Fund Class C	RYCCX	NAS CM	Open End	Trading Tools (Growth)	C	C+	C	Down	Y	2,500
Rydex NASDAQ-100® 2x Strategy Fund Class H	RYVYX	NAS CM	Open End	Trading Tools (Growth)	C	B-	C	Down	Y	2,500
Rydex NASDAQ-100® Fund Class A	RYATX	NAS CM	Open End	US Equity Large Cap Growth (Growth)	C+	C+	B	Down	Y	2,500
Rydex NASDAQ-100® Fund Class C	RYCOX	NAS CM	Open End	US Equity Large Cap Growth (Growth)	C+	C	B-	Down	Y	2,500
Rydex NASDAQ-100® Fund Class H	RYHOX	NAS CM	Open End	US Equity Large Cap Growth (Growth)	C+	C+	B	Down	Y	2,500
Rydex NASDAQ-100® Fund Investor Class	RYOCX	NAS CM	Open End	US Equity Large Cap Growth (Growth)	C+	C+	B	Down	Y	2,500
Rydex Nova Fund Class A	RYANX	NAS CM	Open End	Trading Tools (Aggr Growth)	C+	C	C+	Down	Y	2,500
Rydex Nova Fund Class C	RYNCX	NAS CM	Open End	Trading Tools (Aggr Growth)	C+	C	C+	Down	Y	2,500
Rydex Nova Fund Class H	RYNHX	NAS CM	Open End	Trading Tools (Aggr Growth)	C+	C	C+	Down	Y	2,500

★ Expanded analysis of this fund is included in Section II.

Min Additional Investment	TOTAL RETURNS 3-Month Total Return	6-Month Total Return	1-Year Total Return	3-Year Total Return	5-Year Total Return	PERFORMANCE Dividend Yield (TTM)	Expense Ratio	3-Yr Std Deviation	3-Year Beta	ASSETS NAV	Total Assets (MIL)	ASSET ALLOCATION & TURNOVER %Cash	%Stocks	%Bonds	%Other	Turnover Ratio	BULL & BEAR Last Bull Market Total Return	Last Bear Market Total Return	FEES Front End Fee (%)	Back End Fee (%)	Inception Date
	-5.65	-10.08	-10.42	-4.44	-31.90	0	4.72	11.29		26.04	64.9	97	0	4	-1	603	-1.79	-27.45		1.00	Mar-01
	-5.50	-9.75	-9.78	-2.08	-29.10	0	4.01	11.28		30.06	64.9	97	0	4	-1	603	-1.43	-27.21			Sep-14
	-5.43	-9.67	-9.54	-1.51	-28.41	0	3.72	11.32		31.29	64.9	97	0	4	-1	603	-1.29	-27.13			Mar-95
	-3.29	-8.76	-8.73	-16.31	-29.16	0	1.54	4		58.48	1.6	72	0	17	11	480	-15.3	5.78	4.75		Apr-07
	-3.64	-9.27	-9.59	-18.44	-31.39	0	2.29	4		53.73	1.6	72	0	17	11	480	-15.54	5.41		1.00	Apr-07
	-3.45	-8.93	-8.90	-15.63	-27.81	0	1.53	4.15		59.83	1.6	72	0	17	11	480	-15.25	5.77			Apr-07
	-2.65	-15.64	-0.84	-28.91	-37.54	0	1.7	15.27		21.24	0.92	49	-1	19	33	48	-24.99	22.48	4.75		Mar-04
	-2.88	-16.00	-1.41	-30.42	-39.80	0	2.46	15.29		18.84	0.92	49	-1	19	33	48	-25.31	22		1.00	Feb-04
	-2.65	-15.46	-0.65	-28.80	-37.36	0	1.7	15.22		21.26	0.92	49	-1	19	33	48	-24.98	22.45			Feb-04
	-8.47	-34.78	-23.38	-74.09	-84.31	0	1.81	29.24		24.73	10.8	66	-2	36	1	0	-43.94	12.53	4.75		Sep-04
	-8.62	-34.99	-23.95	-74.53	-84.74	0	2.49	29.24		21.62	10.8	66	-2	36	1	0	-44.58	12.64		1.00	Mar-01
	-8.43	-34.73	-23.44	-74.05	-84.29	0	1.8	29.23		24.75	10.8	66	-2	36	1	0	-43.82	12.84			May-00
	-3.82	-18.34	-10.59	-46.67	-56.95	0	1.76	14.68		50.98	7.2	23	-1	39	39	38	-24.34	7.77	4.75		Mar-04
	-4.01	-18.65	-11.30	-47.92	-59.14	0	2.5	14.67		43.22	7.2	23	-1	39	39	38	-24.64	7.43		1.00	Mar-01
	-3.82	-18.34	-10.60	-46.73	-57.57	0	1.75	14.68		50.24	7.2	23	-1	39	39	38	-24.28	7.83			Sep-14
	-3.78	-18.23	-10.36	-46.31	-57.04	0	1.5	14.68		52.65	7.2	23	-1	39	39	38	-24.17	7.95			Sep-98
	-4.74	-29.29	1.40	-58.73	-66.00	0	1.78	34.28		41.73	13.7	67	-2	33	1	0	-48.94	49.38	4.75		May-06
	-4.92	-29.55	0.66	-59.62	-67.24	0	2.55	34.27		37.68	13.7	67	-2	33	1	0	-49.05	49.45		1.00	May-06
	-4.81	-29.36	1.34	-58.77	-66.07	0	1.8	34.3		41.52	13.7	67	-2	33	1	0	-49.11	49.56			May-06
	-2.00	-15.03	3.14	-33.05	-37.64	0	1.75	17.26		20.01	6.4	82	-1	7	12	40	-26.44	25.05	4.75		Mar-04
	-2.14	-15.34	2.29	-34.55	-39.93	0	2.49	17.24		17.82	6.4	82	-1	7	12	40	-26.76	24.66		1.00	Feb-04
	-2.00	-14.98	3.23	-32.99	-37.60	0	1.73	17.27		20.08	6.4	82	-1	7	12	40	-26.43	25.03			Feb-04
	-7.59	-29.64	-19.53	-58.45	-70.51	0	1.76	23.97		33.7	19.9	32	-2	68	3	78	-40.71	28.42	4.75		Sep-04
	-7.74	-29.89	-20.09	-59.38	-71.62	0	2.52	23.93		29.31	19.9	32	-2	68	3	78	-40.97	28.05		1.00	Mar-01
	-7.54	-29.62	-19.50	-58.44	-70.50	0	1.76	23.96		33.81	19.9	32	-2	68	3	78	-40.65	28.61			May-00
	-3.55	-15.59	-8.72	-33.62	-43.28	0	1.7	12.12		50.5	51.1	31	-1	57	13	114	-22.38	14.92	4.75		Mar-04
	-3.72	-15.90	-9.40	-35.10	-45.36	0	2.45	12.1		45.17	51.1	31	-1	57	13	114	-22.72	14.55		1.00	Mar-01
	-3.55	-15.61	-8.73	-33.58	-43.31	0	1.71	12.12		50.49	51.1	31	-1	57	13	114	-22.38	14.89			Sep-14
	-3.48	-15.48	-8.48	-33.10	-42.53	0	1.45	12.13		54.79	51.1	31	-1	57	13	114	-22.27	15.01			Jan-94
	3.90	17.22	-6.30	55.19	57.00	0.41	1.53	24.53		124.63	1.8	57	-1	18	26	1,225	10.86	-20.48	4.75		Feb-08
	3.70	16.80	-6.98	51.76	51.45	0.44	2.28	24.51		114.9	1.8	57	-1	18	26	1,225	10.44	-20.78		1.00	Feb-08
	3.89	17.20	-6.28	55.24	57.64	0.41	1.52	24.52		125.6	1.8	57	-1	18	26	1,225	10.83	-20.49			Feb-08
	4.43	22.55	5.40	36.10	44.90	0.74	1.63	13.49	1.02	65.97	24.1	1	100	0	-1	323	30.93	-18.67	4.75		Sep-04
	4.22	22.07	4.62	33.07	39.55	0.83	2.38	13.48	1.02	58.18	24.1	1	100	0	-1	323	30.41	-18.9		1.00	May-01
	4.47	22.69	5.65	37.11	46.74	0.68	1.38	13.48	1.02	72.07	24.1	1	100	0	-1	323	31.15	-18.58			Apr-98
	4.43	22.54	5.41	36.12	44.72	0.76	1.63	13.48	1.02	64.08	24.1	1	100	0	-1	323	30.77	-18.74			Jun-98
	3.52	27.44	-2.07	49.30	54.45	0.12	1.69	22.71		93	19.2	63	4	11	22	721	40.92	-33.74	4.75		Mar-04
	3.33	26.96	-2.80	46.00	48.79	0.14	2.45	22.69		80.46	19.2	63	4	11	22	721	40.31	-33.94		1.00	Aug-01
	3.52	27.31	-2.18	49.35	54.81	0.12	1.68	22.68		93.36	19.2	63	4	11	22	721	41.13	-33.72			Aug-01
	5.70	43.88	10.44	176.20		0	1.35	30.25		142.22	158.9	32	70	3	-5	467			4.75		Nov-14
	5.51	43.35	9.62	170.03		0	2.1	30.23		137.18	158.9	32	70	3	-5	467				1.00	Nov-14
	5.64	43.81	10.37	175.98		0	1.35	30.26		145.58	158.9	32	70	3	-5	467					Nov-14
	6.63	44.89	10.47	169.80	226.58	0	1.79	30.67		160.23	462.0	18	83	2	-3	113	58.36	-23.43	4.75		Sep-04
	6.43	44.34	9.64	163.69	214.34	0	2.54	30.66		127.59	462.0	18	83	2	-3	113	57.69	-23.69		1.00	Nov-00
	6.63	44.89	10.47	169.73	226.48	0	1.79	30.67		160.17	462.0	18	83	2	-3	113	58.35	-23.43			May-00
	3.82	21.74	8.34	73.07	95.66	0	1.53	15.12	1	36.61	1,172	4	91	4	1	32	26.94	-11.07	4.75		Mar-04
	3.62	21.32	7.52	69.33	88.69	0	2.28	15.12	1	31.75	1,172	4	91	4	1	32	26.46	-11.37		1.00	Mar-01
	3.80	21.75	8.34	73.18	95.63	0	1.53	15.12	1	36.6	1,172	4	91	4	1	32	26.96	-11.09			Sep-14
	3.88	21.88	8.60	74.44	98.38	0	1.28	15.14	1	39.88	1,172	4	91	4	1	32	27.15	-10.99			Feb-94
	5.59	28.40	11.49	67.44	83.23	0	1.52	18.34		75.27	296.5	17	69	16	-2	1,078	37.76	-25.08	4.75		Mar-04
	5.38	27.93	10.64	63.95	76.55	0	2.29	18.35		66.55	296.5	17	69	16	-2	1,078	37.12	-25.29		1.00	Mar-01
	5.59	28.36	11.44	67.70	83.41	0	1.53	18.35		75.34	296.5	17	69	16	-2	1,078	37.68	-25.03			Sep-14

	MARKET			FUND TYPE, CATEGORY & OBJECTIVE	RATINGS					MINIMUMS
Fund Name	Ticker Symbol	Traded On	Fund Type	Category and (Prospectus Objective)	Overall Rating	Reward Rating	Risk Rating	Recent Up/ Downgrade	Open to New Investors	Min Initial Investment
Rydex Nova Fund Investor Class	RYNVX	NAS CM	Open End	Trading Tools (Aggr Growth)	C+	C	C+	Down	Y	2,500
Rydex Precious Metals Fund Class A	RYMNX	NAS CM	Open End	Precious Metals Sector Equity (Precious Metals)	D	D	D+	Down	Y	2,500
Rydex Precious Metals Fund Class C	RYZCX	NAS CM	Open End	Precious Metals Sector Equity (Precious Metals)	D	D	D+	Down	Y	2,500
Rydex Precious Metals Fund Class H	RYMPX	NAS CM	Open End	Precious Metals Sector Equity (Precious Metals)	D	D	D+	Down	Y	2,500
Rydex Precious Metals Fund Class Investor	RYPMX	NAS CM	Open End	Precious Metals Sector Equity (Precious Metals)	D	D	D+	Down	Y	2,500
Rydex Real Estate Fund Class A	RYREX	NAS CM	Open End	Real Estate Sector Equity (Real Estate)	C+	C	B-		Y	2,500
Rydex Real Estate Fund Class C	RYCRX	NAS CM	Open End	Real Estate Sector Equity (Real Estate)	C	C	C+		Y	2,500
Rydex Real Estate Fund Class H	RYHRX	NAS CM	Open End	Real Estate Sector Equity (Real Estate)	C+	C	B-		Y	2,500
Rydex Retailing Fund Class A	RYRTX	NAS CM	Open End	Consumer Goods Sec Equity ()	C+	C	B-		Y	2,500
Rydex Retailing Fund Class C	RYRCX	NAS CM	Open End	Consumer Goods Sec Equity ()	C+	C	B-		Y	2,500
Rydex Retailing Fund Class H	RYRAX	NAS CM	Open End	Consumer Goods Sec Equity ()	C+	C	B-		Y	2,500
Rydex Retailing Fund Class Investor	RYRIX	NAS CM	Open End	Consumer Goods Sec Equity ()	C+	C	B-		Y	2,500
Rydex Russell 2000 1.5x Strategy Fund Class A	RYAKX	NAS CM	Open End	Trading Tools (Growth)	C	C-	C		Y	2,500
Rydex Russell 2000 1.5x Strategy Fund Class C	RYCMX	NAS CM	Open End	Trading Tools (Growth)	C	C-	C		Y	2,500
Rydex Russell 2000 1.5x Strategy Fund Class H	RYMKX	NAS CM	Open End	Trading Tools (Growth)	C	C-	C		Y	2,500
Rydex Russell 2000 2x Strategy Fund Class A	RYRUX	NAS CM	Open End	Trading Tools (Growth)	C-	C-	D+		Y	2,500
Rydex Russell 2000 2x Strategy Fund Class C	RYRLX	NAS CM	Open End	Trading Tools (Growth)	C-	C-	D+		Y	2,500
Rydex Russell 2000 2x Strategy Fund Class H	RYRSX	NAS CM	Open End	Trading Tools (Growth)	C-	C-	D+		Y	2,500
Rydex Russell 2000 Fund Class A	RYRRX	NAS CM	Open End	US Equity Small Cap (Growth)	C	C-	C+		Y	2,500
Rydex Russell 2000 Fund Class C	RYROX	NAS CM	Open End	US Equity Small Cap (Growth)	C	C-	C+		Y	2,500
Rydex Russell 2000 Fund Class H	RYRHX	NAS CM	Open End	US Equity Small Cap (Growth)	C	C-	C+		Y	2,500
Rydex S&P 500 2x Strategy Fund Class A	RYTTX	NAS CM	Open End	Trading Tools (Growth)	C	C+	C		Y	2,500
Rydex S&P 500 2x Strategy Fund Class C	RYCTX	NAS CM	Open End	Trading Tools (Growth)	C	C+	C		Y	2,500
Rydex S&P 500 2x Strategy Fund Class H	RYTNX	NAS CM	Open End	Trading Tools (Growth)	C	C+	C		Y	2,500
Rydex S&P 500 Fund Class A	RYSOX	NAS CM	Open End	US Equity Large Cap Blend (Growth)	B-	C	B		Y	2,500
Rydex S&P 500 Fund Class C	RYSYX	NAS CM	Open End	US Equity Large Cap Blend (Growth)	C+	C	B		Y	2,500
Rydex S&P 500 Fund Class H	RYSPX	NAS CM	Open End	US Equity Large Cap Blend (Growth)	B-	C	B		Y	2,500
Rydex S&P 500 Pure Growth Fund Class A	RYLGX	NAS CM	Open End	US Equity Large Cap Growth (Growth)	C+	C	B-	Up	Y	2,500
Rydex S&P 500 Pure Growth Fund Class C	RYGRX	NAS CM	Open End	US Equity Large Cap Growth (Growth)	C+	C	B-	Up	Y	2,500
Rydex S&P 500 Pure Growth Fund Class H	RYAWX	NAS CM	Open End	US Equity Large Cap Growth (Growth)	C+	C	B-	Up	Y	2,500
Rydex S&P 500 Pure Value Fund Class A	RYLVX	NAS CM	Open End	US Equity Large Cap Value (Growth)	C	C	B-		Y	2,500
Rydex S&P 500 Pure Value Fund Class C	RYVVX	NAS CM	Open End	US Equity Large Cap Value (Growth)	C	C	C+		Y	2,500
Rydex S&P 500 Pure Value Fund Class H	RYZAX	NAS CM	Open End	US Equity Large Cap Value (Growth)	C	C	B-		Y	2,500
Rydex S&P MidCap 400 Pure Growth Fund Class A	RYMGX	NAS CM	Open End	US Equity Mid Cap (Growth)	C	C-	C		Y	2,500
Rydex S&P MidCap 400 Pure Growth Fund Class C	RYCKX	NAS CM	Open End	US Equity Mid Cap (Growth)	C-	D+	C	Down	Y	2,500
Rydex S&P MidCap 400 Pure Growth Fund Class H	RYBHX	NAS CM	Open End	US Equity Mid Cap (Growth)	C	C-	C		Y	2,500
Rydex S&P MidCap 400 Pure Value Fund Class A	RYMVX	NAS CM	Open End	US Equity Small Cap (Growth)	C	C-	C+		Y	2,500
Rydex S&P MidCap 400 Pure Value Fund Class C	RYMMX	NAS CM	Open End	US Equity Small Cap (Growth)	C	C-	C+		Y	2,500
Rydex S&P MidCap 400 Pure Value Fund Class H	RYAVX	NAS CM	Open End	US Equity Small Cap (Growth)	C	C-	C+		Y	2,500
Rydex S&P SmallCap 600 Pure Growth Fund Class A	RYSGX	NAS CM	Open End	US Equity Small Cap (Small Company)	C	C-	C		Y	2,500
Rydex S&P SmallCap 600 Pure Growth Fund Class C	RYWCX	NAS CM	Open End	US Equity Small Cap (Small Company)	C-	C-	C	Down	Y	2,500
Rydex S&P SmallCap 600 Pure Growth Fund Class H	RYWAX	NAS CM	Open End	US Equity Small Cap (Small Company)	C	C-	C		Y	2,500
Rydex S&P SmallCap 600 Pure Value Fund Class A	RYSVX	NAS CM	Open End	US Equity Small Cap (Small Company)	D	D	D+	Down	Y	2,500
Rydex S&P SmallCap 600 Pure Value Fund Class C	RYYCX	NAS CM	Open End	US Equity Small Cap (Small Company)	D	D	D+	Down	Y	2,500
Rydex S&P SmallCap 600 Pure Value Fund Class H	RYAZX	NAS CM	Open End	US Equity Small Cap (Small Company)	D	D	D+	Down	Y	2,500
Rydex Strengthening Dollar 2x Strategy Fund Class A	RYSDX	NAS CM	Open End	Trading Tools (Growth)	C+	C+	B-	Up	Y	2,500
Rydex Strengthening Dollar 2x Strategy Fund Class C	RYSJX	NAS CM	Open End	Trading Tools (Growth)	C+	C	C+	Up	Y	2,500
Rydex Strengthening Dollar 2x Strategy Fund Class H	RYSBX	NAS CM	Open End	Trading Tools (Growth)	C+	C+	B-	Up	Y	2,500
Rydex Technology Fund Class A	RYTHX	NAS CM	Open End	Technology Sector Equity (Technology)	B-	C+	B-	Down	Y	2,500
Rydex Technology Fund Class C	RYCHX	NAS CM	Open End	Technology Sector Equity (Technology)	C+	C+	B-	Down	Y	2,500
Rydex Technology Fund Class H	RYTAX	NAS CM	Open End	Technology Sector Equity (Technology)	B-	C+	B-	Down	Y	2,500
Rydex Technology Fund Class Investor	RYTIX	NAS CM	Open End	Technology Sector Equity (Technology)	B-	C+	B	Down	Y	2,500

★ Expanded analysis of this fund is included in Section II.

Min Additional Investment	3-Month Total Return	6-Month Total Return	1-Year Total Return	3-Year Total Return	5-Year Total Return	Dividend Yield (TTM)	Expense Ratio	3-Yr Std Deviation	3-Year Beta	NAV	Total Assets (MIL)	%Cash	%Stocks	%Bonds	%Other	Turnover Ratio	Last Bull Market Total Return	Last Bear Market Total Return	Front End Fee (%)	Back End Fee (%)	Inception Date
	TOTAL RETURNS					PERFORMANCE				ASSETS		ASSET ALLOCATION & TURNOVER					BULL & BEAR		FEES		
	5.63	28.51	11.66	68.74	85.38	0	1.27	18.35		81.16	296.5	17	69	16	-2	1,078	37.88	-24.96			Jul-93
	10.84	22.24	6.56	-14.99	-15.44	1.18	1.53	26.87	0.17	27.59	89.3	4	99	0	-3	571	-8.65	-22.58	4.75		Sep-04
	10.66	21.75	5.73	-16.90	-18.48	1.39	2.28	26.84	0.17	23.45	89.3	4	99	0	-3	571	-9.03	-22.82		1.00	Apr-01
	10.93	22.26	6.55	-15.11	-15.76	1.22	1.53	26.86	0.17	26.69	89.3	4	99	0	-3	571	-8.77	-22.66			Aug-03
	10.94	22.41	6.85	-14.32	-14.25	1.12	1.28	26.85	0.17	29	89.3	4	99	0	-3	571	-8.51	-22.48			Dec-93
	0.07	16.12	6.50	12.88	28.21	0.62	1.63	12.79	0.66	41.27	54.4	1	100	0	-1	877	28.76	-19.69	4.75		Sep-04
	-0.13	15.66	5.68	10.34	23.41	0.71	2.38	12.78	0.66	35.89	54.4	1	100	0	-1	877	28.13	-19.98		1.00	Feb-04
	0.07	16.10	6.52	12.91	28.19	0.62	1.63	12.79	0.66	41.17	54.4	1	100	0	-1	877	28.76	-19.71			Feb-04
	0.09	17.42	1.79	31.44	39.04	0.1	1.63	16.15	1.16	31.67	18.3	3	100	0	-3	314	27.86	-11.08	4.75		Sep-04
	-0.10	16.96	1.00	28.46	33.74	0.12	2.38	16.13	1.15	27.92	18.3	3	100	0	-3	314	27.27	-11.31		1.00	May-01
	0.06	17.44	1.80	31.46	38.70	0.11	1.62	16.14	1.16	30.9	18.3	3	100	0	-3	314	27.56	-11.13			Apr-98
	0.14	17.53	2.03	32.43	40.63	0.1	1.37	16.13	1.15	33.51	18.3	3	100	0	-3	314	28.04	-10.94			Apr-98
	2.21	25.58	-9.20	56.79	43.53	0	1.75	25.69		65.03	13.4	38	9	24	29	258	40.25	-37.27	4.75		Mar-04
	2.01	25.11	-9.86	53.31	38.25	0	2.51	25.67		55.09	13.4	38	9	24	29	258	39.66	-37.46		1.00	Jan-01
	2.20	25.52	-9.18	56.32	43.27	0	1.75	25.65		64.77	13.4	38	9	24	29	258	40.3	-37.27			Nov-00
	2.45	34.20	-13.61	73.01	48.51	0	1.78	34.3		141.71	38.0	36	23	31	10	507	52.36	-47.76	4.75		May-06
	2.26	33.70	-14.26	69.20	43.10	0	2.52	34.28		127.07	38.0	36	23	31	10	507	51.73	-47.89		1.00	May-06
	2.39	34.04	-13.77	72.41	48.02	0	1.81	34.29		140.99	38.0	36	23	31	10	507	52.3	-47.77			May-06
	1.73	17.07	-4.86	37.19	29.58	0	1.63	17.08	1	44.57	36.2	9	55	36	0	112	27.33	-25.54	4.75		May-06
	1.56	16.62	-5.54	34.17	24.82	0	2.38	17.08	1	39.7	36.2	9	55	36	0	112	26.71	-25.82		1.00	May-06
	1.73	17.06	-4.85	37.23	29.50	0	1.63	17.1	1	44.46	36.2	9	55	36	0	112	27.31	-25.56			May-06
	7.08	38.39	13.49	93.68	114.36	0	1.77	24.49		125.52	154.4	19	81	0	0	367	50.93	-33.02	4.75		Sep-04
	6.88	37.87	12.63	89.38	106.48	0	2.52	24.48		107.24	154.4	19	81	0	0	367	50.4	-33.19		1.00	Nov-00
	7.09	38.37	13.47	93.64	114.28	0	1.75	24.49		125.34	154.4	19	81	0	0	367	50.98	-33.06			May-00
	3.84	18.50	8.49	43.41	52.74	0.1	1.58	12.19	1	53.53	163.5	10	90	0	0	157	23.95	-16.83	4.75		May-06
	3.66	18.04	7.68	40.20	47.11	0.11	2.33	12.19	1	47.81	163.5	10	90	0	0	157	23.39	-17.15		1.00	May-06
	3.86	18.50	8.51	43.42	52.74	0.1	1.58	12.2	1	53.53	163.5	10	90	0	0	157	24.01	-16.8			May-06
	2.97	20.74	3.54	46.08	49.13	0	1.53	13.66	0.99	67.82	104.2	1	99	0	0	177	23.27	-17.95	4.75		Sep-04
	2.79	20.30	2.78	42.85	43.64	0	2.28	13.66	0.99	59.26	104.2	1	99	0	0	177	22.76	-18.21		1.00	Feb-04
	2.97	20.72	3.53	46.07	49.12	0	1.53	13.66	0.99	67.8	104.2	1	99	0	0	177	23.28	-17.93			Feb-04
	3.37	15.64	0.11	32.99	24.57	1.37	1.53	15.7	0.99	78.64	52.0	0	99	0	0	190	22.91	-22.15	4.75		Sep-04
	3.17	15.21	-0.64	30.02	19.96	1.59	2.28	15.69	0.99	66.93	52.0	0	99	0	0	190	22.39	-22.39		1.00	Feb-04
	3.37	15.65	0.12	33.00	24.57	1.36	1.53	15.7	0.99	78.97	52.0	0	99	0	0	190	22.91	-22.15			Feb-04
	-2.11	12.98	-8.49	21.82	15.78	0	1.53	15.96	1	44.91	58.7	2	100	0	-2	165	22.48	-18.48	4.75		Sep-04
	-2.28	12.57	-9.15	19.13	11.54	0	2.28	15.95	1	37.68	58.7	2	100	0	-2	165	21.93	-18.73		1.00	Feb-04
	-2.11	12.96	-8.48	21.82	15.78	0	1.53	15.95	1	44.97	58.7	2	100	0	-2	165	22.45	-18.48			Feb-04
	1.35	18.45	-5.05	31.72	23.24	0.05	1.54	21.15	0.99	52.32	20.5	3	99	0	-2	558	28.11	-24.86	4.75		Sep-04
	1.16	18.02	-5.75	28.80	18.73	0.05	2.28	21.13	0.99	45.84	20.5	3	99	0	-2	558	27.51	-25.1		1.00	Feb-04
	1.33	18.43	-5.06	31.63	23.20	0.05	1.53	21.16	0.99	52.23	20.5	3	99	0	-2	558	28.08	-24.84			Feb-04
	-1.85	6.73	-12.88	33.83	31.24	0	1.53	19.28	1	64.01	10.8	4	100	0	-3	421	25.65	-20.41	4.75		Sep-04
	-2.03	6.35	-13.51	30.83	26.41	0	2.28	19.26	1	56.4	10.8	4	100	0	-3	421	25.14	-20.69		1.00	Feb-04
	-1.85	6.73	-12.88	33.84	31.23	0	1.53	19.28	1	64	10.8	4	100	0	-3	421	25.69	-20.46			Feb-04
	-4.83	8.08	-19.33	10.40	-4.68	0	1.53	23.23	1	24.61	4.7	1	100	0	0	534	27.54	-26.21	4.75		Sep-04
	-5.01	7.68	-19.94	7.90	-8.24	0	2.28	23.22	1	21.03	4.7	1	100	0	0	534	26.88	-26.49		1.00	Feb-04
	-4.84	8.10	-19.32	10.63	-4.54	0	1.53	23.21	0.99	24.55	4.7	1	100	0	0	534	27.39	-26.27			Feb-04
	-1.20	1.80	7.39	6.23	42.25	0	1.74	11.19		51.83	5.7	54	0	29	17	9	-5.04	13.38	4.75		May-05
	-1.36	1.44	6.61	3.88	37.02	0	2.49	11.19		46.27	5.7	54	0	29	17	9	-5.4	12.87		1.00	May-05
	-1.16	1.83	7.42	6.25	42.31	0	1.74	11.2		51.64	5.7	54	0	29	17	9	-5	13.37			May-05
	3.89	26.77	12.33	87.76	94.14	0	1.63	16.08	1.17	98.19	76.2	1	99	0	-1	255	23.38	-22.02	4.75		Sep-04
	3.69	26.29	11.49	83.58	87.11	0	2.38	16.08	1.17	87.56	76.2	1	99	0	-1	255	22.79	-22.29		1.00	Apr-01
	3.90	26.77	12.34	87.79	93.58	0	1.63	16.08	1.17	96.01	76.2	1	99	0	-1	255	23.08	-22.05			Apr-98
	3.95	26.93	12.60	89.17	96.53	0	1.37	16.08	1.17	105.8	76.2	1	99	0	-1	255	23.66	-21.94			Apr-98

Fund Name	MARKET Ticker Symbol	Traded On	Fund Type	FUND TYPE, CATEGORY & OBJECTIVE Category and (Prospectus Objective)	RATINGS Overall Rating	Reward Rating	Risk Rating	Recent Up/ Downgrade	Open to New Investors	MINIMUMS Min Initial Investment
Rydex Telecommunications Fund Class A	RYTLX	NAS CM	Open End	Communications Sector Equity (Comm)	B-	C	B+	Up	Y	2,500
Rydex Telecommunications Fund Class C	RYCSX	NAS CM	Open End	Communications Sector Equity (Comm)	C+	C	B		Y	2,500
Rydex Telecommunications Fund Class H	RYMAX	NAS CM	Open End	Communications Sector Equity (Comm)	B-	C	B+		Y	2,500
Rydex Telecommunications Fund Class Investor	RYMIX	NAS CM	Open End	Communications Sector Equity (Comm)	B-	C	B+		Y	2,500
Rydex Transportation Fund Class A	RYTSX	NAS CM	Open End	Industrials Sector Equity ()	C	C-	C+		Y	2,500
Rydex Transportation Fund Class C	RYCNX	NAS CM	Open End	Industrials Sector Equity ()	C	C-	C+		Y	2,500
Rydex Transportation Fund Class H	RYPAX	NAS CM	Open End	Industrials Sector Equity ()	C	C-	C+		Y	2,500
Rydex Transportation Fund Class Investor	RYPIX	NAS CM	Open End	Industrials Sector Equity ()	C	C-	C+		Y	2,500
Rydex Utilities Fund Class A	RYUTX	NAS CM	Open End	Utilities Sector Equity (Utility)	B	B	B	Up	Y	2,500
Rydex Utilities Fund Class C	RYCUX	NAS CM	Open End	Utilities Sector Equity (Utility)	B	B	B	Up	Y	2,500
Rydex Utilities Fund Class H	RYAUX	NAS CM	Open End	Utilities Sector Equity (Utility)	B	B	B	Up	Y	2,500
Rydex Utilities Fund Class Investor	RYUIX	NAS CM	Open End	Utilities Sector Equity (Utility)	B	B	B	Up	Y	2,500
Rydex Weakening Dollar 2x Strategy Fund Class A	RYWDX	NAS CM	Open End	Trading Tools (Growth)	D	D-	D	Down	Y	2,500
Rydex Weakening Dollar 2x Strategy Fund Class C	RYWJX	NAS CM	Open End	Trading Tools (Growth)	D	D-	D		Y	2,500
Rydex Weakening Dollar 2x Strategy Fund Class H	RYWBX	NAS CM	Open End	Trading Tools (Growth)	D	D-	D	Down	Y	2,500
SA Emerging Markets Value Fund Investor Class	SAEMX	NAS CM	Open End	Global Emerg Mkts (Div Emerging Mkts)	C	C	C+		Y	0
SA Emerging Markets Value Fund Select Class	SAELX	NAS CM	Open End	Global Emerg Mkts (Div Emerging Mkts)	C	C	C+		Y	100,000
SA International Small Company Fund Investor Class	SAISX	NAS CM	Open End	Global Equity Mid/Small Cap (Foreign Stock)	C	C-	C	Up	Y	0
SA International Small Company Fund Select Class	SACLX	NAS CM	Open End	Global Equity Mid/Small Cap (Foreign Stock)	C	C-	C		Y	100,000
SA International Value Fund Investor Class	SAHMX	NAS CM	Open End	Global Equity Large Cap (Foreign Stock)	C	C-	C		Y	0
SA International Value Fund Select Class	SATLX	NAS CM	Open End	Global Equity Large Cap (Foreign Stock)	C	C-	C		Y	100,000
SA Real Estate Securities Fund Investor Class	SAREX	NAS CM	Open End	Real Estate Sector Equity (Real Estate)	C+	C	C+		Y	0
SA Real Estate Securities Fund Select Class	SARLX	NAS CM	Open End	Real Estate Sector Equity (Real Estate)	C+	C	C+		Y	100,000
SA U.S. Core Market Fund Investor Class	SAMKX	NAS CM	Open End	US Equity Large Cap Blend (Growth)	B-	C	B		Y	0
SA U.S. Core Market Fund Select Class	SAALX	NAS CM	Open End	US Equity Large Cap Blend (Growth)	B-	C	B		Y	100,000
SA U.S. Small Company Fund Investor Class	SAUMX	NAS CM	Open End	US Equity Small Cap (Small Company)	C	C	C+		Y	0
SA U.S. Small Company Fund Select Class	SASLX	NAS CM	Open End	US Equity Small Cap (Small Company)	C	C	C+		Y	100,000
SA U.S. Value Fund Investor Class	SABTX	NAS CM	Open End	US Equity Large Cap Value (Growth)	C+	C	B-	Up	Y	0
SA U.S. Value Fund Select Class	SAVLX	NAS CM	Open End	US Equity Large Cap Value (Growth)	C+	C	B	Up	Y	100,000
SA Worldwide Moderate Growth Fund	SAWMX	NAS CM	Open End	Aggressive Alloc (Growth & Income)	C+	C	B	Up	Y	5,000
Salient Global Real Estate Fund Class A	KIRAX	NAS CM	Open End	Real Estate Sector Equity (Real Estate)	C+	C	B	Up	Y	2,500
Salient Global Real Estate Fund Class C	KIRCX	NAS CM	Open End	Real Estate Sector Equity (Real Estate)	C+	C	B	Up	Y	2,500
Salient Global Real Estate Fund Institutional Class	KIRYX	NAS CM	Open End	Real Estate Sector Equity (Real Estate)	B-	C	B	Up	Y	100,000
Salient Global Real Estate Fund Investor Class	FFIRX	NAS CM	Open End	Real Estate Sector Equity (Real Estate)	C+	C	B	Up	Y	2,500
Salient International Small Cap Fund Class Investor	PISRX	NAS CM	Open End	Global Equity Mid/Small Cap (Foreign Stock)	C	C	C+		Y	2,500
Salient International Small Cap Fund Institutional Class	PTSCX	NAS CM	Open End	Global Equity Mid/Small Cap (Foreign Stock)	C	C	C+		Y	100,000
Salient Midstream & MLP Fund	SMM	NYSE	Closed End	Energy Sector Equity (Natl Res)	D+	D+	D+	Down	Y	
Salient MLP & Energy Infrastructure Fund Class A	SMAPX	NAS CM	Open End	Energy Sector Equity (Utility)	C-	C-	C-	Down	Y	2,500
Salient MLP & Energy Infrastructure Fund Class C	SMFPX	NAS CM	Open End	Energy Sector Equity (Utility)	C-	C-	D+	Down	Y	2,500
Salient MLP & Energy Infrastructure Fund Class I	SMLPX	NAS CM	Open End	Energy Sector Equity (Utility)	C-	C-	C-	Down	Y	1,000,000
Salient MLP & Energy Infrastructure Fund R6 Shares	SMRPX	NAS CM	Open End	Energy Sector Equity (Utility)	C-	C-	C-	Down	Y	1,000,000
Salient Select Income Fund Class A	KIFAX	NAS CM	Open End	US Fixed Income (Real Estate)	C+	C	C+	Up	Y	2,500
Salient Select Income Fund Class C	KIFCX	NAS CM	Open End	US Fixed Income (Real Estate)	C	C	C		Y	2,500
Salient Select Income Fund Institutional Class	KIFYX	NAS CM	Open End	US Fixed Income (Real Estate)	C+	C+	C+		Y	100,000
Salient Select Income Fund Investor Class	FFSLX	NAS CM	Open End	US Fixed Income (Real Estate)	C+	C+	C+	Up	Y	2,500
Salient Tactical Growth Fund Class A	FTAGX	NAS CM	Open End	Long/Short Equity (Growth)	C+	C	B	Up	Y	2,500
Salient Tactical Growth Fund Class C	FTGOX	NAS CM	Open End	Long/Short Equity (Growth)	C	C	B		Y	2,500
Salient Tactical Growth Fund Institutional Class	FTGWX	NAS CM	Open End	Long/Short Equity (Growth)	B-	C	B	Up	Y	100,000
Salient Tactical Growth Fund Investor Class	FFTGX	NAS CM	Open End	Long/Short Equity (Growth)	C+	C	B	Up	Y	2,500
Salient Tactical Plus Fund Class A	SBTAX	NAS CM	Open End	Long/Short Equity (Growth & Income)	B-	C	A-		Y	2,500
Salient Tactical Plus Fund Class C	SBTCX	NAS CM	Open End	Long/Short Equity (Growth & Income)	B-	C	A-	Up	Y	2,500
Salient Tactical Plus Fund Class F	BTPIX	NAS CM	Open End	Long/Short Equity (Growth & Income)	B	C	A-	Up	Y	0

★ Expanded analysis of this fund is included in Section II.

	TOTAL RETURNS					PERFORMANCE				ASSETS		ASSET ALLOCATION & TURNOVER					BULL & BEAR		FEES		
Min Additional Investment	3-Month Total Return	6-Month Total Return	1-Year Total Return	3-Year Total Return	5-Year Total Return	Dividend Yield (TTM)	Expense Ratio	3-Yr Std Deviation	3-Year Beta	NAV	Total Assets (ML)	%Cash	%Stocks	%Bonds	%Other	Turnover Ratio	Last Bull Market Total Return	Last Bear Market Total Return	Front End Fee (%)	Back End Fee (%)	Inception Date
	0.00	11.94	4.22	22.50	19.48	0.03	1.63	12.01	0.86	46.03	4.5	1	99	0	0	2,115	12.54	-23.1	4.75		Sep-04
	-0.19	11.52	3.44	19.78	15.09	0.03	2.38	12	0.86	40.73	4.5	1	99	0	0	2,115	12.23	-23.44		1.00	Apr-01
	-0.02	11.97	4.43	22.84	19.43	0.03	1.63	11.96	0.85	44.87	4.5	1	99	0	0	2,115	12.35	-23.23			Apr-98
	0.05	12.07	4.46	23.45	21.15	0.02	1.38	12.02	0.86	50.2	4.5	1	99	0	0	2,115	12.62	-23.04			Apr-98
	1.99	13.91	-4.61	35.67	19.69	0	1.63	19.04	1.4	46.49	11.5	2	100	0	-2	476	24.43	-25.98	4.75		Sep-04
	1.82	13.52	-5.31	32.67	15.28	0	2.38	19.05	1.4	41.89	11.5	2	100	0	-2	476	23.82	-26.13		1.00	May-01
	2.01	13.91	-4.63	35.59	19.34	0	1.63	19.06	1.4	45.02	11.5	2	100	0	-2	476	24.25	-26.02			Jun-98
	2.05	14.05	-4.37	36.68	21.20	0	1.37	19.05	1.4	51.11	11.5	2	100	0	-2	476	24.61	-25.92			Apr-98
	2.37	13.10	15.19	25.02	47.87	0	1.63	10.31	0.28	43.51	118.4	0	99	0	0	390	9.47	-2.13	4.75		Sep-04
	2.16	12.65	14.32	22.26	42.49	0	2.38	10.31	0.28	36.4	118.4	0	99	0	0	390	9.01	-2.51		1.00	Apr-01
	2.34	13.06	15.14	24.97	47.50	0	1.63	10.32	0.28	41.88	118.4	0	99	0	0	390	9.35	-2.21			Apr-00
	2.40	13.22	15.49	25.94	49.75	0	1.38	10.32	0.28	47.34	118.4	0	99	0	0	390	9.68	-2.03			Apr-00
	1.27	-1.79	-7.41	-11.52	-39.86	0	1.73	11.1		64.55	2.3	60	0	20	20	77	1.17	-14.55	4.75		May-05
	1.05	-2.18	-8.12	-13.51	-42.11	0	2.48	11.09		57.34	2.3	60	0	20	20	77	0.84	-14.82		1.00	May-05
	1.25	-1.81	-7.45	-11.56	-39.87	0	1.73	11.1		64.47	2.3	60	0	20	20	77	1.22	-14.56			May-05
	0.20	7.06	0.96	33.91	1.03	1.67	1.35	13.49	1.03	9.85	216.8	0	100	0	0	18	13.89	-30.15			Apr-07
	0.20	7.18	1.09	34.32	1.34	1.98	1.15	13.46	1.02	9.84	216.8	0	100	0	0	18	13.89	-30.15			Jul-17
	2.01	12.72	-8.04	23.67	11.06	1.4	1.27	12.4	1.01	19.75	324.5	1	99	0	0	6	13.75	-23.71			Aug-99
	2.07	12.85	-7.80	25.54	15.13	2.06	0.98	12.47	1.01	19.67	324.5	1	99	0	0	6	14.45	-23.33			Jul-17
	1.29	9.70	-5.87	29.59	-0.96	1.77	1.1	12.66	1.1	10.96	692.4	0	100	0	0	21	10.05	-26.29			Aug-99
	1.39	9.84	-5.66	30.16	-0.52	2.39	0.9	12.67	1.1	10.93	692.4	0	100	0	0	21	10.05	-26.29			Jul-17
	1.46	18.72	13.31	14.52	44.32	2.8	0.95	12.78	0.96	12.43	189.6	0	100	0	0	6	30.61	-16.56			Apr-07
	1.55	18.88	13.54	15.01	44.94	3.27	0.75	12.79	0.96	12.4	189.6	0	100	0	0	6	30.61	-16.56			Jul-17
	4.11	19.46	9.29	51.33	60.68	0.64	0.9	12.62	1	24.8	755.5	0	100	0	0	6	24.68	-17.73			Aug-99
	4.17	19.59	9.51	51.94	61.33	1.13	0.68	12.64	1.01	24.72	755.5	0	100	0	0	6	24.68	-17.73			Jul-17
	2.74	16.30	-3.93	35.80	32.65	0	1.15	17.02	0.99	25.46	411.2	0	100	0	0	16	27.75	-24.55			Aug-99
	2.78	16.38	-3.73	36.39	33.23	0.4	0.93	17.02	0.99	25.43	411.2	0	100	0	0	16	27.75	-24.55			Jul-17
	2.94	14.81	2.43	37.59	37.17	1.04	0.95	13.88	1.13	17.13	592.9	0	100	0	0	19	25.41	-24.32			Aug-99
	2.95	14.94	2.62	38.18	37.75	1.58	0.74	13.89	1.14	17.07	592.9	0	100	0	0	19	25.41	-24.32			Jul-17
2,500	2.07	11.07	2.52	28.73		1.84	0.87	8.74		10.83	38.2	1	74	25	0	20					Jul-15
100	-0.89	14.50	1.91	24.12	17.87	0.89	1.55	11.68	0.9	13.99	41.5	1	99	0	0	101	40.33	-26.54	5.75		Apr-06
100	-1.03	14.18	1.14	21.86	14.41	0.42	2.1	11.72	0.9	13.94	41.5	1	99	0	0	101	39.78	-26.79		1.00	Apr-06
	-0.79	14.78	2.24	25.58	20.17	1.14	1.15	11.72	0.9	13.94	41.5	1	99	0	0	101	40.73	-26.49			Apr-06
100	-0.88	14.54	1.93	24.27	18.21	0.92	1.5	11.7	0.9	14.05	41.5	1	99	0	0	101	40.22	-26.58			May-11
100	1.85	14.94	-5.90	28.56	21.83	5.25	1.55	12.77	1.01	15.92	44.3	1	99	0	0	47	16.17	-26.76			Mar-02
	1.86	15.11	-5.59	29.91	23.92	5.87	1.2	12.75	1	15.84	44.3	1	99	0	0	47	16.39	-26.65			Feb-96
	-5.89	20.31	-6.13	0.03	-53.44	0.19	2.59	24.44		10.19	180.6	-40	140	0	0	45					May-12
100	-1.53	19.31	-0.94	5.94	-37.80	4.36	1.46	18.18	1.08	7.33	947.0	1	99	0	0	48			5.50		Dec-12
100	-1.86	18.93	-1.78	3.38	-40.24	3.66	2.21	18.16	1.08	7.27	947.0	1	99	0	0	48				1.00	Jan-13
	-1.48	19.48	-0.74	6.54	-37.13	4.58	1.23	18.2	1.08	7.31	947.0	1	99	0	0	48					Sep-12
	-1.45	19.52	-0.66	6.78	-36.98	4.66	1.15	18.19	1.08	7.31	947.0	1	99	0	0	48					Jan-16
100	0.71	13.30	5.54	9.36	21.73	5.43	1.55	7.84	1.06	21.05	472.4	4	29	2	5	24	13.6	-5.4	5.75		Mar-01
100	0.55	12.96	4.72	7.28	18.14	4.7	2.1	7.85	1.06	20.43	472.4	4	29	2	5	24	13.13	-5.67		1.00	Mar-01
	0.85	13.54	5.91	10.61	24.16	5.77	1.15	7.87	1.06	21	472.4	4	29	2	5	24	13.81	-5.28			Apr-06
100	0.76	13.36	5.58	9.50	22.00	5.46	1.5	7.84	1.05	20.98	472.4	4	29	2	5	24	13.52	-5.4			Oct-11
100	1.58	5.48	1.03	17.55	12.75	0	1.96	6.24	0.83	25.56	296.4	52	48	0	0	531	3.25	-6.97	5.75		Mar-10
100	1.46	5.26	0.35	15.63	9.90	0	2.51	6.24	0.84	24.21	296.4	52	48	0	0	531	3	-7.16		1.00	Sep-09
	1.70	5.74	1.48	19.17	15.46	0.39	1.56	6.27	0.84	26.88	296.4	52	48	0	0	531	3.57	-6.77			Sep-09
100	1.60	5.56	1.16	18.01	13.52	0.06	1.91	6.27	0.84	25.99	296.4	52	48	0	0	531	3.36	-6.95			Sep-09
100	2.09	3.62	6.18	28.25	24.39	0.04	1.82	9.6	0.81	11.71	55.6	100	0	0	0	5,067			5.50		Dec-14
100	1.80	3.20	5.41	25.28	19.60	0	2.57	9.56	0.8	11.26	55.6	100	0	0	0	5,067				1.00	Dec-14
	2.12	3.89	6.72	30.30	27.47	0.09	1.26	9.54	0.8	12.01	55.6	100	0	0	0	5,067					Dec-12

	MARKET			FUND TYPE, CATEGORY & OBJECTIVE	RATINGS				MINIMUMS	
Fund Name	Ticker Symbol	Traded On	Fund Type	Category and (Prospectus Objective)	Overall Rating	Reward Rating	Risk Rating	Recent Up/ Downgrade	Open to New Investors	Min Initial Investment
Salient Tactical Plus Fund Class I	SBTIX	NAS CM	Open End	Long/Short Equity (Growth & Income)	B-	C	A-		Y	1,000,000
Sands Capital Global Growth Fund Institutional Shares	SCMGX	NAS CM	Open End	Global Equity Large Cap (World Stock)	C+	C	B-	Down	Y	1,000,000
Sands Capital Global Growth Fund Investor Shares	SCGVX	NAS CM	Open End	Global Equity Large Cap (World Stock)	C+	C	B-	Down	Y	100,000
Saratoga Aggressive Balanced Allocation Portfolio Class A	SABAX	NAS CM	Open End	Aggressive Alloc (Balanced)	D+	D+	C	Up	Y	2,500
Saratoga Aggressive Balanced Allocation Portfolio Class C	SABCX	NAS CM	Open End	Aggressive Alloc (Balanced)	D+	D+	C	Up	Y	2,500
Saratoga Aggressive Balanced Allocation Portfolio Class I	SABIX	NAS CM	Open End	Aggressive Alloc (Balanced)	D+	D+	C	Up	Y	2,500
Saratoga Conservative Balanced Allocation Portfolio Cls A	SCAAX	NAS CM	Open End	Cautious Alloc (Balanced)	D+	D+	C+	Up	Y	2,500
Saratoga Conservative Balanced Allocation Portfolio Cls C	SUMCX	NAS CM	Open End	Cautious Alloc (Balanced)	D+	D+	C+	Up	Y	2,500
Saratoga Conservative Balanced Allocation Portfolio Cls I	LUNAX	NAS CM	Open End	Cautious Alloc (Balanced)	D+	D+	C+	Up	Y	2,500
Saratoga Energy & Basic Materials Portfolio Fund Class A	SBMBX	NAS CM	Open End	Natl Resources Sec Equity (Natl Res)	D+	D	D+	Down	Y	250
Saratoga Energy & Basic Materials Portfolio Fund Class C	SEPCX	NAS CM	Open End	Natl Resources Sec Equity (Natl Res)	D+	D+	D+	Down	Y	250
Saratoga Energy & Basic Materials Portfolio Cls Inst	SEPIX	NAS CM	Open End	Natl Resources Sec Equity (Natl Res)	D+	D+	D+	Down	Y	250
Saratoga Financial Service Portfolio Fund Class A	SFPAX	NAS CM	Open End	Financials Sector Equity (Financial)	C	C	C+		Y	250
Saratoga Financial Service Portfolio Fund Class C	SFPCX	NAS CM	Open End	Financials Sector Equity (Financial)	C	C	C+		Y	250
Saratoga Financial Service Portfolio Cls Institutional	SFPIX	NAS CM	Open End	Financials Sector Equity (Financial)	C	C	C+		Y	250
Saratoga Health & Biotechnology Portfolio Fund Class A	SHPAX	NAS CM	Open End	Healthcare Sector Equity (Health)	D+	D	C-	Down	Y	250
Saratoga Health & Biotechnology Portfolio Fund Class C	SHPCX	NAS CM	Open End	Healthcare Sector Equity (Health)	D+	D	D+	Down	Y	250
Saratoga Health & Biotechnology Portfolio Cls Inst	SBHIX	NAS CM	Open End	Healthcare Sector Equity (Health)	D+	D	C-	Down	Y	250
Saratoga International Equity Fund Class A	SIEYX	NAS CM	Open End	Global Equity Large Cap (Foreign Stock)	D+	D+	C-		Y	250
Saratoga International Equity Fund Class C	SIECX	NAS CM	Open End	Global Equity Large Cap (Foreign Stock)	D+	D	C-		Y	250
Saratoga International Equity Fund Class Institutional	SIEPX	NAS CM	Open End	Global Equity Large Cap (Foreign Stock)	D+	D+	C		Y	250
Saratoga Large Capitalization Growth Portfolio Cls A	SLGYX	NAS CM	Open End	US Equity Large Cap Growth (Growth)	C+	C	B	Down	Y	250
Saratoga Large Capitalization Growth Portfolio Cls C	SLGCX	NAS CM	Open End	US Equity Large Cap Growth (Growth)	C+	C	B	Down	Y	250
Saratoga Large Capitalization Growth Portfolio Cls Inst	SLCGX	NAS CM	Open End	US Equity Large Cap Growth (Growth)	C+	C	B	Down	Y	250
Saratoga Large Capitalization Value Fund Class A	SLVYX	NAS CM	Open End	US Equity Mid Cap (Growth & Income)	C	C	B-		Y	250
Saratoga Large Capitalization Value Fund Class C	SLVCX	NAS CM	Open End	US Equity Mid Cap (Growth & Income)	C	C	C+		Y	250
Saratoga Large Capitalization Value Cls Institutional	SLCVX	NAS CM	Open End	US Equity Mid Cap (Growth & Income)	C+	C	B-	Up	Y	250
Saratoga Mid Capitalization Portfolio Fund Class A	SPMAX	NAS CM	Open End	US Equity Mid Cap (Growth)	C	C-	C+		Y	250
Saratoga Mid Capitalization Portfolio Fund Class C	SPMCX	NAS CM	Open End	US Equity Mid Cap (Growth)	C	C-	C+		Y	250
Saratoga Mid Capitalization Portfolio Cls Institutional	SMIPX	NAS CM	Open End	US Equity Mid Cap (Growth)	C	C	C+		Y	250
Saratoga Moderate Balanced Allocation Portfolio Class A	SMPAX	NAS CM	Open End	Moderate Alloc (Balanced)	D+	D+	C+	Up	Y	2,500
Saratoga Moderate Balanced Allocation Portfolio Class C	SBMCX	NAS CM	Open End	Moderate Alloc (Balanced)	D+	D+	C+	Up	Y	2,500
Saratoga Moderate Balanced Allocation Portfolio Class I	SBMIX	NAS CM	Open End	Moderate Alloc (Balanced)	D+	D+	C+	Up	Y	2,500
Saratoga Moderately Aggressive Balanced Alloc Port Cls A	SAMAX	NAS CM	Open End	Moderate Alloc (Balanced)	D+	D+	C	Up	Y	2,500
Saratoga Moderately Aggressive Balanced Alloc Port Cls C	SAMCX	NAS CM	Open End	Moderate Alloc (Balanced)	D+	D+	C	Up	Y	2,500
Saratoga Moderately Aggressive Balanced Alloc Port Cls I	SAMIX	NAS CM	Open End	Moderate Alloc (Balanced)	D+	D+	C	Up	Y	2,500
Saratoga Moderately Conservative Balanced Alloc Port Cls A	SMACX	NAS CM	Open End	Moderate Alloc (Balanced)	D+	D+	C+	Up	Y	2,500
Saratoga Moderately Conservative Balanced Alloc Port Cls C	SBCCX	NAS CM	Open End	Moderate Alloc (Balanced)	D+	D+	C+	Up	Y	2,500
Saratoga Moderately Conservative Balanced Alloc Port Cls I	SMICX	NAS CM	Open End	Moderate Alloc (Balanced)	D+	D+	C+	Up	Y	2,500
Saratoga Small Capitalization Portfolio Fund Class A	SSCYX	NAS CM	Open End	US Equity Small Cap (Small Company)	C-	C-	C	Down	Y	250
Saratoga Small Capitalization Portfolio Fund Class C	SSCCX	NAS CM	Open End	US Equity Small Cap (Small Company)	C-	C-	C	Down	Y	250
Saratoga Small Capitalization Portfolio Cls Institutional	SSCPX	NAS CM	Open End	US Equity Small Cap (Small Company)	C	C-	C		Y	250
Saratoga Technology & Communications Portfolio Class A	STPAX	NAS CM	Open End	Technology Sector Equity (Technology)	B-	C+	B	Down	Y	250
Saratoga Technology & Communications Portfolio Class C	STPCX	NAS CM	Open End	Technology Sector Equity (Technology)	B-	C+	B	Down	Y	250
Saratoga Technology & Communications Portfolio Cls Inst	STPIX	NAS CM	Open End	Technology Sector Equity (Technology)	B-	C+	B	Down	Y	250
Sarofim Equity Fund	SRFMX	NAS CM	Open End	US Equity Large Cap Blend (Growth & Income)	B-	B-	B		Y	2,500
Saturna Sustainable Equity Fund	SEEFX	NAS CM	Open End	Global Equity Large Cap (Growth)	B-	C+	B	Up	Y	10,000
Savos Dynamic Hedging Fund	SVDHX	NAS CM	Open End	Moderate Alloc (Growth & Income)	C+	C	B	Up	Y	0
Scharf Alpha Opportunity Fund Retail Class	HEDJX	NAS CM	Open End	Long/Short Equity (Growth)	C	C	C	Down	Y	10,000
Scharf Fund Institutional Class	LOGIX	NAS CM	Open End	US Equity Large Cap Blend (Growth)	C+	C	B	Down	Y	5,000,000
Scharf Fund Retail Class	LOGRX	NAS CM	Open End	US Equity Large Cap Blend (Growth)	C+	C	B	Down	Y	10,000
Scharf Global Opportunity Fund Retail Class	WRLDX	NAS CM	Open End	Global Equity Large Cap (Growth)	B-	C	B+	Up	Y	10,000

★Expanded analysis of this fund is included in Section II.

Min Additional Investment	TOTAL RETURNS: 3-Month Total Return	6-Month Total Return	1-Year Total Return	3-Year Total Return	5-Year Total Return	PERFORMANCE: Dividend Yield (TTM)	Expense Ratio	3-Yr Std Deviation	3-Year Beta	ASSETS: NAV	Total Assets (MIL)	ASSET ALLOCATION & TURNOVER: %Cash	%Stocks	%Bonds	%Other	Turnover Ratio	BULL & BEAR: Last Bull Market Total Return	Last Bear Market Total Return	FEES: Front End Fee (%)	Back End Fee (%)	Inception Date
	2.07	3.68	6.43	29.13	25.63	0.06	1.57	9.6	0.81	11.82	55.6	100	0	0	0	5,067					Dec-14
	5.40	23.39	9.33	71.89	69.33	0.05	0.97	15.02	1.17	26.9	1,410	2	98	0	0	25	26.32	-17.36			Mar-10
	5.32	23.25	9.15	70.72	67.39	0	1.17	14.98	1.17	26.5	1,410	2	98	0	0	25	26.12	-17.47			Mar-10
100	2.24	11.35	2.82			2.7	1.68			10	0.60	13	74	9	4				5.75		Dec-17
100	2.24	11.46	2.92			2.7	2.43			10.01	0.60	13	74	9	4					1.00	Dec-17
100	2.24	11.46	2.92			2.7	1.43			10.01	0.60	13	74	9	4						Dec-17
100	2.11	8.66	3.80			1.91	1.54			10.16	1.6	31	48	19	2				5.75		Dec-17
100	2.21	8.88	3.90			1.91	2.29			10.17	1.6	31	48	19	2					1.00	Dec-17
100	2.21	8.88	3.96			1.96	1.29			10.17	1.6	31	48	19	2						Dec-17
	-6.64	4.33	-18.64	4.33	-39.38	0	3.93	17.73	1.15	10.82	1.6	2	98	0	0	61	24.86	-34.9	5.75		Oct-97
	-6.74	5.64	-17.89	4.05	-40.26	0	4.54	17.78	1.16	8.99	1.6	2	98	0	0	61	24.47	-35.12		1.00	Jan-03
	-6.53	4.58	-18.30	5.60	-38.14	0	3.51	17.78	1.15	11.87	1.6	2	98	0	0	61	25.17	-34.81			Jan-03
	6.26	17.05	-1.81	36.99	26.77	0	3.83	17.05	1.16	8.65	1.4	3	97	0	0	52	25.97	-26.73	5.75		Aug-00
	6.06	16.48	-2.47	34.28	22.84	0	4.42	17.1	1.16	7.35	1.4	3	97	0	0	52	25.61	-26.92		1.00	Aug-00
	6.32	17.16	-1.42	38.56	29.36	0	3.42	17.08	1.16	9.42	1.4	3	97	0	0	52	26.33	-26.59			Jan-03
	-0.93	3.93	-0.52	4.92	23.49	0	2.3	14.94	1.01	19.02	13.8	1	99	0	0	13	14.61	-10.18	5.75		Jul-99
	-1.05	3.67	-1.11	3.01	19.79	0	2.9	14.93	1.01	14.97	13.8	1	99	0	0	13	14.17	-10.42		1.00	Jan-00
	-0.83	4.14	-0.16	6.12	25.92	0	1.9	14.96	1.01	21.35	13.8	1	99	0	0	13	14.87	-10.02			Jan-03
	2.55	15.46	-5.66	12.15	-15.52	0.45	1.66	13.52	1.14	9.63	9.5	3	97	0	0	130	11.73	-28.04	5.75		Feb-06
	2.37	15.10	-6.31	9.96	-18.23	0	2.26	13.47	1.14	8.61	9.5	3	97	0	0	130	11.27	-28.2		1.00	Jan-99
	2.54	15.68	-5.41	13.44	-13.97	0.51	1.26	13.48	1.14	9.66	9.5	3	97	0	0	130	11.81	-27.9			Sep-94
	2.31	15.93	5.09	51.81	73.62	0	1.54	13.57	1.06	22.56	33.8	2	98	0	0	74	20.36	-13.35	5.75		Feb-06
	2.16	15.58	4.43	49.06	68.52	0	2.14	13.58	1.06	16.02	33.8	2	98	0	0	74	19.91	-13.52		1.00	Jan-99
	2.37	16.13	5.46	53.54	77.07	0	1.14	13.56	1.06	24.62	33.8	2	98	0	0	74	20.6	-13.2			Sep-94
	6.25	25.13	6.70	25.54	9.32	0	1.61	16.49	1.2	20.56	14.7	2	98	0	0	100	26.31	-25.33	5.75		Feb-06
	6.11	24.74	6.07	23.34	6.16	0	2.22	16.48	1.2	17.19	14.7	2	98	0	0	100	25.76	-25.43		1.00	Jan-99
	6.38	25.32	7.15	27.07	11.51	0.31	1.22	16.48	1.2	21.48	14.7	2	98	0	0	100	26.64	-25.19			Sep-94
	4.67	21.05	0.29	22.51	16.18	0.12	2.08	14.53	1.05	10.29	10.7	5	95	0	0	39	24.12	-25.24	5.75		Jun-02
	4.48	20.57	-0.37	20.27	12.93	0	2.7	14.46	1.05	8.38	10.7	5	95	0	0	39	23.66	-25.41		1.00	Jun-02
	4.80	21.27	0.65	24.02	18.52	0.51	1.68	14.5	1.05	11.57	10.7	5	95	0	0	39	24.39	-25.15			Jan-03
100	2.32	10.82	4.31			2.78	1.67			10.14	0.65	19	60	17	4				5.75		Dec-17
100	2.32	10.82	4.31			2.78	2.42			10.14	0.65	19	60	17	4					1.00	Dec-17
100	2.32	10.82	4.31			2.78	1.42			10.14	0.65	19	60	17	4						Dec-17
100	2.36	11.31	3.09			2.73	1.71			9.94	0.38	14	65	17	4				5.75		Dec-17
100	2.36	11.31	3.09			2.73	2.46			9.94	0.38	14	65	17	4					1.00	Dec-17
100	2.36	11.31	3.09			2.73	1.46			9.94	0.38	14	65	17	4						Dec-17
100	2.48	10.85	3.44			2.67	1.62			9.91	0.74	21	55	19	5				5.75		Dec-17
100	2.48	10.85	3.44			2.67	2.37			9.91	0.74	21	55	19	5					1.00	Dec-17
100	2.48	10.85	3.44			2.67	1.37			9.91	0.74	21	55	19	5						Dec-17
	0.55	14.16	-9.79	27.37	8.70	0	1.94	17.11	0.97	5.4	5.7	4	96	0	0	115	24.25	-23	5.75		Feb-06
	0.43	13.86	-10.28	25.12	5.40	0	2.54	17	0.96	2.3	5.7	4	96	0	0	115	23.75	-23.17		1.00	Jan-99
	0.67	14.45	-9.43	28.91	10.77	0	1.55	17.13	0.97	5.94	5.7	4	96	0	0	115	24.55	-22.85			Sep-94
	1.84	22.27	11.69	79.25	102.46	0	2.15	14.38	1.07	22.12	56.2	1	99	0	0	1	27.35	-24.17	5.75		Oct-97
	1.72	21.90	11.03	76.11	96.43	0	2.75	14.37	1.07	17.7	56.2	1	99	0	0	1	26.84	-24.38		1.00	Jan-00
	1.99	22.55	12.16	81.45	106.54	0	1.75	14.37	1.07	24.56	56.2	1	99	0	0	1	27.64	-24.06			Jan-03
100	5.51	21.73	11.37	49.64	50.11	1.29	0.7	11.56	0.92	12.43	94.3	0	100	0	0	9					Jan-14
25	6.16	20.87	10.76	45.07		0.74	0.75	10.97	0.92	12.91	6.3	8	92	0	0	8					Mar-15
	3.58	14.60	6.91	27.86		0	1.51	12.65	1	12.186	86.7	28	54	18	0	24					Jul-15
500	2.42	5.78	9.16	5.75		0	1.97	6.1	0.34	24.89	18.7	59	41	0	0	60					Dec-15
	3.95	15.50	14.23	29.50	39.40	0.81	1	10.99	0.84	44.99	381.5	12	88	0	0	40					Dec-11
500	3.87	15.32	13.85	28.37	37.59	0.47	1.25	10.98	0.84	44.77	381.5	12	88	0	0	40					Jan-15
500	4.30	14.96	13.80	38.34		0.88	0.7	13.19	1.06	29.58	19.4	3	97	0	0	66					Oct-14

Fund Name	Ticker Symbol	Traded On	Fund Type	Category and (Prospectus Objective)	Overall Rating	Reward Rating	Risk Rating	Recent Up/ Downgrade	Open to New Investors	Min Initial Investment
	MARKET		FUND TYPE, CATEGORY & OBJECTIVE		RATINGS				MINIMUMS	
Scharf Multi-Asset Opportunity Fund Institutional Class	LOGOX	NAS CM	Open End	Moderate Alloc (Balanced)	B-	C	B		Y	5,000,000
Scharf Multi-Asset Opportunity Fund Retail Class	LOGBX	NAS CM	Open End	Moderate Alloc (Balanced)	C+	C	B	Down	Y	10,000
Schneider Small Cap Value Fund	SCMVX	NAS CM	Open End	US Equity Small Cap (Small Company)	D	D	D	Down	Y	5,000
Schroder Emerging Markets Small Cap Fund Investor Shares	SMLNX	NAS CM	Open End	Global Emerg Mkts (Div Emerging Mkts)	C	C	C+		Y	250,000
Schroder Emerging Markets Small Cap Fund R6 Shares	SMLRX	NAS CM	Open End	Global Emerg Mkts (Div Emerging Mkts)	C	C	C+		Y	5,000,000
Schroder North American Equity Fund Class Investor	SNAEX	NAS CM	Open End	US Equity Large Cap Blend (Growth)	B-	C	B		Y	250,000
Schwab ® U.S. Large-Cap Growth Index Fund	SWLGX	NAS CM	Open End	US Equity Large Cap Growth (Growth)	D+	C-	B-	Up	Y	0
Schwab ® U.S. Large-Cap Value Index Fund	SWLVX	NAS CM	Open End	US Equity Large Cap Value (Growth & Income)	D+	D+	C+	Up	Y	0
Schwab ® U.S. Mid-Cap Index Fund	SWMCX	NAS CM	Open End	US Equity Mid Cap (Growth & Income)	D+	D+	C+	Up	Y	0
Schwab 1000 Index® Fund	SNXFX	NAS CM	Open End	US Equity Large Cap Blend (Growth & Income)	B-	C	B		Y	0
Schwab Balanced Fund™	SWOBX	NAS CM	Open End	Moderate Alloc (Balanced)	B-	C	B+		Y	0
Schwab Core Equity Fund™	SWANX	NAS CM	Open End	US Equity Large Cap Blend (Growth)	C+	C	B		Y	0
Schwab Dividend Equity Fund™	SWDSX	NAS CM	Open End	US Equity Large Cap Value (Equity-Income)	C+	C	B	Up	Y	0
Schwab Fundamental Emerging Mkts Large Company Index Fund	SFENX	NAS CM	Open End	Global Emerg Mkts (Div Emerging Mkts)	C+	C	B	Up	Y	0
Schwab Fundamental Global Real Estate Index Fund	SFREX	NAS CM	Open End	Real Estate Sector Equity (Real Estate)	B-	C+	B	Down	Y	0
Schwab Fundamental International Large Company Index Fund	SFNNX	NAS CM	Open End	Global Equity Large Cap (Foreign Stock)	C	C	B-		Y	0
Schwab Fundamental International Small Company Index Fund	SFILX	NAS CM	Open End	Global Equity Mid/Small Cap (Foreign Stock)	C	C-	C		Y	0
Schwab Fundamental US Large Company Index Fund	SFLNX	NAS CM	Open End	US Equity Large Cap Value (Growth & Income)	B-	C	B	Up	Y	0
Schwab Fundamental US Small Company Index Fund	SFSNX	NAS CM	Open End	US Equity Small Cap (Small Company)	C	C-	C+		Y	0
Schwab Global Real Estate Fund™	SWASX	NAS CM	Open End	Real Estate Sector Equity (Real Estate)	B-	C	B		Y	0
Schwab Health Care Fund™	SWHFX	NAS CM	Open End	Healthcare Sector Equity (Health)	C+	C	B	Down	Y	0
Schwab Hedged Equity Fund™	SWHEX	NAS CM	Open End	Long/Short Equity (Growth)	C	C-	C		Y	0
Schwab International Index Fund®	SWISX	NAS CM	Open End	Global Equity Large Cap (Foreign Stock)	C	C	B		Y	0
Schwab Large-Cap Growth Fund™	SWLSX	NAS CM	Open End	US Equity Large Cap Growth (Growth)	C+	C	B-		Y	0
Schwab MarketTrack All Equity Portfolio™	SWEGX	NAS CM	Open End	Aggressive Alloc (Growth)	C+	C	B	Up	Y	0
Schwab MarketTrack Balanced Portfolio™	SWBGX	NAS CM	Open End	Moderate Alloc (Asset Alloc)	B-	C	A-	Up	Y	0
Schwab MarketTrack Conservative Portfolio™	SWCGX	NAS CM	Open End	Cautious Alloc (Asset Alloc)	B	C	A-	Up	Y	0
Schwab MarketTrack Growth Portfolio™	SWHGX	NAS CM	Open End	Aggressive Alloc (Asset Alloc)	B-	C	B+	Up	Y	0
Schwab Small Cap Index Fund®	SWSSX	NAS CM	Open End	US Equity Small Cap (Small Company)	C	C	C+		Y	0
Schwab Small-Cap Equity Fund™	SWSCX	NAS CM	Open End	US Equity Small Cap (Small Company)	C	C-	C+		Y	0
Schwab Target 2010 Fund	SWBRX	NAS CM	Open End	Target Date (Asset Alloc)	B	C+	A-	Up	Y	0
Schwab Target 2010 Index Fund	SWYAX	NAS CM	Open End	Target Date (Asset Alloc)	C+	C	B		Y	0
Schwab Target 2015 Fund	SWGRX	NAS CM	Open End	Target Date (Asset Alloc)	B	C+	A-	Up	Y	0
Schwab Target 2015 Index Fund	SWYBX	NAS CM	Open End	Target Date (Asset Alloc)	C+	C	B		Y	0
Schwab Target 2020 Fund	SWCRX	NAS CM	Open End	Target Date (Asset Alloc)	B	C	A-	Up	Y	0
Schwab Target 2020 Index Fund	SWYLX	NAS CM	Open End	Target Date (Asset Alloc)	C+	C	B		Y	0
Schwab Target 2025 Fund	SWHRX	NAS CM	Open End	Target Date (Asset Alloc)	B-	C	A-	Up	Y	0
Schwab Target 2025 Index Fund	SWYDX	NAS CM	Open End	Target Date (Asset Alloc)	C+	C	B+		Y	0
Schwab Target 2030 Fund	SWDRX	NAS CM	Open End	Target Date (Asset Alloc)	B-	C	B+	Up	Y	0
Schwab Target 2030 Index Fund	SWYEX	NAS CM	Open End	Target Date (Asset Alloc)	C+	C	B		Y	0
Schwab Target 2035 Fund	SWIRX	NAS CM	Open End	Target Date (Asset Alloc)	B-	C	B+	Up	Y	0
Schwab Target 2035 Index Fund	SWYFX	NAS CM	Open End	Target Date (Asset Alloc)	C+	C	B	Up	Y	0
Schwab Target 2040 Fund	SWERX	NAS CM	Open End	Target Date (Asset Alloc)	B-	C	B	Up	Y	0
Schwab Target 2040 Index Fund	SWYGX	NAS CM	Open End	Target Date (Asset Alloc)	C+	C	B	Up	Y	0
Schwab Target 2045 Fund	SWMRX	NAS CM	Open End	Target Date (Asset Alloc)	B-	C	B	Up	Y	0
Schwab Target 2045 Index Fund	SWYHX	NAS CM	Open End	Target Date (Asset Alloc)	C+	C	B	Up	Y	0
Schwab Target 2050 Fund	SWNRX	NAS CM	Open End	Target Date (Asset Alloc)	C+	C	B	Up	Y	0
Schwab Target 2050 Index Fund	SWYMX	NAS CM	Open End	Target Date (Asset Alloc)	C+	C	B	Up	Y	0
Schwab Target 2055 Fund	SWORX	NAS CM	Open End	Target Date (Asset Alloc)	C+	C	B	Up	Y	0
Schwab Target 2055 Index Fund	SWYJX	NAS CM	Open End	Target Date (Asset Alloc)	C+	C	B	Up	Y	0
Schwab Target 2060 Fund	SWPRX	NAS CM	Open End	Target Date (Asset Alloc)	C+	C	B	Up	Y	0
Schwab Target 2060 Index Fund	SWYNX	NAS CM	Open End	Target Date (Asset Alloc)	C+	C	B	Up	Y	0

★ Expanded analysis of this fund is included in Section II.

	TOTAL RETURNS					PERFORMANCE				ASSETS		ASSET ALLOCATION & TURNOVER					BULL & BEAR		FEES		
Min Additional Investment	3-Month Total Return	6-Month Total Return	1-Year Total Return	3-Year Total Return	5-Year Total Return	Dividend Yield (TTM)	Expense Ratio	3-Yr Std Deviation	3-Year Beta	NAV	Total Assets (MIL)	%Cash	%Stocks	%Bonds	%Other	Turnover Ratio	Last Bull Market Total Return	Last Bear Market Total Return	Front End Fee (%)	Back End Fee (%)	Inception Date
	3.50	12.59	11.01	23.49	28.98	1.42	0.99	8.25	0.63	32.81	53.3	7	65	23	1	36					Dec-12
500	3.44	12.46	10.75	22.55	27.31	1.04	1.24	8.23	0.63	32.75	53.3	7	65	23	1	36					Jan-16
500	-9.29	7.69	-32.32	25.85	-10.17	0	1.16	28.76	1.5	8.68	30.1	0	100	0	0	84	40.62	-37.25			Sep-98
1,000	2.50	15.90	1.85	27.28		1.99	1.5	11.59	0.85	10.64	2.2	2	98	0	0	38					Aug-15
	2.50	15.90	1.85	27.24		1.99	1.35	11.54	0.84	10.64	2.2	2	98	0	0	38					Aug-15
1,000	3.76	17.44	8.90	47.13	58.52	1.83	0.33	12.23	1	16.83	1,002	6	94	0	0	46	24.21	-16.47			Sep-03
	4.65	22.63	11.51			0.85	0.04			47.03	147.4	0	100	0	0						Dec-17
	3.84	17.09	8.30			1.47	0.04			41.91	186.1	0	100	0	0						Dec-17
	4.10	22.41	7.69			0.96	0.04			43.63	317.0	1	99	0	0						Dec-17
	4.29	19.89	9.91	50.33	62.93	1.86	0.05	12.32	1	66.3	9,246	0	100	0	0	4	25.29	-17.17			Apr-91
	3.55	14.42	6.27	32.16	39.26	2.25	0.5	8.04	0.64	15.71	505.6	5	59	36	0	6	16.38	-10.26			Nov-96
	3.86	19.39	6.18	46.15	52.73	1.14	0.73	12.6	1.03	21.24	2,202	1	99	0	0	101	25.2	-19.06			Jul-96
	3.04	17.13	4.11	31.73	31.40	1.49	0.88	12.68	1.04	14.88	877.1	0	100	0	0	79	22.96	-15.07			Sep-03
	4.28	12.53	7.84	46.80	15.34	2.59	0.39	13.72	1.01	9.25	669.7	0	100	0	0	19	16.32	-27.15			Jan-08
	-0.71	15.03	5.58	25.68		3.54	0.39	11.84	1.01	11.61	199.3	1	99	0	0	16					Oct-14
	2.08	11.66	-1.66	30.40	6.89	3.15	0.25	11.4	0.99	8.81	1,383	0	100	0	0	13	10.42	-26.25			Apr-07
	1.23	11.01	-7.49	25.24	19.85	2.38	0.39	11.86	1	12.3	795.6	-1	101	0	0	26	10.39	-19.44			Jan-08
	3.54	17.24	7.08	39.34	49.38	2.32	0.25	12.65	1	16.93	5,093	0	100	0	0	10	23.3	-18.45			Apr-07
	1.65	16.30	-3.93	36.30	36.92	1.53	0.25	16.09	1	13.55	1,732	0	100	0	0	30	27.98	-25.46			Apr-07
	0.08	17.85	8.85	21.79	36.78	3.55	1.05	11.61	1.02	7.91	307.9	1	98	0	0	90	23.71	-21.34			May-07
	-0.28	8.42	8.89	32.06	51.15	0.88	0.8	13.03	1	24.58	802.8	0	100	0	0	45	18	-9.61			Jul-00
	-1.16	4.21	-3.46	18.45	23.24	0.5	1.67	8.4	0.6	15.33	227.6	43	57	0	0	180	14.71	-13.99			Sep-02
	3.73	14.61	1.40	31.37	11.87	2.77	0.06	11.1	0.99	20	5,167	0	100	0	0	5	14.07	-23.87			May-97
	3.54	20.00	5.43	52.35	63.79	0.38	0.99	13.65	1.01	17.52	182.6	0	100	0	0	88	28.44	-18.82			Oct-05
	3.14	16.50	3.01	40.00	38.18	1.88	0.52	12.1	0.97	18.71	685.2	1	99	0	0	5	21.8	-20.5			May-98
	3.03	12.26	5.13	25.95	29.32	2.03	0.5	7.32	0.58	18.31	540.9	6	59	35	0	8	14.09	-10.89			Nov-95
	2.94	10.03	5.78	18.64	23.18	2.18	0.49	4.96	0.38	16.09	255.4	7	39	54	0	9	9.94	-5.95			Nov-95
	3.04	14.43	4.25	33.46	34.94	1.92	0.51	9.8	0.79	22.99	814.3	6	79	15	0	7	18.18	-15.74			Nov-95
	2.12	17.94	-3.23	44.36	41.41	1.28	0.04	17.11	1	28.79	4,181	0	100	0	0	17	27.24	-23.72			May-97
	1.01	15.80	-5.94	38.61	33.72	0.05	1.09	17.97	1.03	16.93	607.9	1	99	0	0	111	29.07	-24.33			Jul-03
	2.95	9.95	5.87	18.91	23.47	2.48	0.33	4.68		13.26	52.5	8	35	56	0	16	10.84	-6.67			Jul-05
	3.03	9.90	6.88			1.79	0.08			11.21	26.8	8	35	56	0	30			0.00		Aug-16
	3.05	10.38	5.79	19.72	24.01	2.48	0.35	4.95		11.8	82.6	8	38	54	0	14	13.38	-9.47			Mar-08
	2.93	10.08	6.70			1.55	0.08			11.24	46.6	8	38	54	0	29					Aug-16
	3.06	11.08	5.47	23.61	26.81	2.39	0.41	5.76		14.13	557.1	7	43	51	0	18	15.69	-11.76			Jul-05
	3.04	10.87	6.74			2.03	0.08			11.52	142.4	8	43	50	0	13					Aug-16
	3.22	12.74	5.10	27.67	30.17	2.32	0.5	7.27		14.42	564.4	5	56	39	0	13	17.68	-13.59			Mar-08
	3.22	12.55	6.93			1.98	0.08			11.83	174.8	5	57	38	0	13					Aug-16
	3.20	13.93	4.57	30.52	32.46	2.29	0.57	8.41		15.45	995.3	3	66	31	0	14	19.14	-15.25			Jul-05
	3.34	13.79	6.94			1.97	0.08			12.04	238.0	4	66	29	0	8					Aug-16
	3.20	14.78	4.07	32.92	34.09	2.28	0.62	9.32		15.14	477.0	2	74	24	0	14	20.39	-16.49			Mar-08
	3.38	14.63	6.83			1.84	0.08			12.22	144.1	3	75	22	0	6					Aug-16
	3.23	15.62	3.60	35.01	35.65	2.27	0.67	10.16		16.28	1,020	2	81	17	0	17	21.4	-17.45			Jul-05
	3.43	15.40	6.61			1.92	0.08			12.36	169.1	2	81	16	0	2					Aug-16
	3.18	16.12	3.33	36.24	36.41	2.21	0.71	10.78		13.61	157.4	2	86	12	0	12					Jan-13
	3.48	16.10	6.51			1.93	0.08			12.47	102.6	2	87	11	0	7					Aug-16
	3.22	16.49	3.08	37.04	37.10	2.19	0.73	11.08		13.77	155.4	2	89	9	0	10					Jan-13
	3.47	16.37	6.41			1.86	0.08			12.51	104.9	1	90	9	0	0					Aug-16
	3.19	16.70	2.94	37.88	37.55	2.19	0.74	11.36		13.9	88.4	2	92	6	0	10					Jan-13
	3.45	16.62	6.32			1.87	0.08			12.56	60.4	1	93	6	0	6					Aug-16
	3.28	17.04	2.95			2.17	0.75			11.95	14.7	2	94	4	0	22					Aug-16
	3.45	16.80	6.39			1.85	0.08			12.58	71.3	1	95	4	0	2					Aug-16

	MARKET			FUND TYPE, CATEGORY & OBJECTIVE	RATINGS				MINIMUMS	
Fund Name	Ticker Symbol	Traded On	Fund Type	Category and (Prospectus Objective)	Overall Rating	Reward Rating	Risk Rating	Recent Up/ Downgrade	Open to New Investors	Min Initial Investment
Schwab Total Stock Market Index Fund®	SWTSX	NAS CM	Open End	US Equity Large Cap Blend (Growth & Income)	B-	C	B		Y	0
Schwab® International Core Equity Fund	SICNX	NAS CM	Open End	Global Equity Large Cap (Foreign Stock)	C	C-	C+		Y	0
Schwab® Monthly Income Fund - Enhanced Payout	SWKRX	NAS CM	Open End	Cautious Alloc (Asset Alloc)	B-	C	B+		Y	0
Schwab® Monthly Income Fund - Maximum Payout	SWLRX	NAS CM	Open End	Cautious Alloc (Asset Alloc)	B-	C	B	Up	Y	0
Schwab® Monthly Income Fund - Moderate Payout	SWJRX	NAS CM	Open End	Cautious Alloc (Asset Alloc)	B-	C	B+	Up	Y	0
Schwab® S&P 500 Index Fund	SWPPX	NAS CM	Open End	US Equity Large Cap Blend (Growth & Income)	B-	C	B		Y	0
Schwartz Value Focused Fund	RCMFX	NAS CM	Open End	US Equity Mid Cap (Growth)	C	C	B-		Y	2,500
Seafarer Overseas Growth & Income Institutional Cls	SIGIX	NAS CM	Open End	Global Emerg Mkts (Growth & Income)	C	C-	C+		Y	25,000
Seafarer Overseas Growth and Income Fund Investor Class	SFGIX	NAS CM	Open End	Global Emerg Mkts (Growth & Income)	C	D+	C+		Y	2,500
Seafarer Overseas Value Fund Institutional Class	SIVLX	NAS CM	Open End	Global Emerg Mkts (Foreign Stock)	C	D+	B		Y	25,000
Seafarer Overseas Value Fund Investor Class	SFVLX	NAS CM	Open End	Global Emerg Mkts (Foreign Stock)	C	D+	B	Up	Y	2,500
Second Nature Thematic Growth Fund Class A	CEGSX	NAS CM	Open End	US Equity Large Cap Blend (Growth)	U	U	U		Y	1,000
Second Nature Thematic Growth Fund Class I	CEGYX	NAS CM	Open End	US Equity Large Cap Blend (Growth)	U	U	U		Y	10,000
Sector Rotation Fund	NAVFX	NAS CM	Open End	Moderate Alloc (Growth)	C+	C	B	Up	Y	2,500
Securian AM Dynamic Managed Volatility Institutional Cls	VVMIX	NAS CM	Open End	Global Macro (Growth & Income)	B	C+	A-		Y	100,000
Securian AM Managed Volatility Equity Institutional Cls	VMEIX	NAS CM	Open End	Long/Short Equity (Growth & Income)	B-	C	A-	Up	Y	100,000
Securian AM Real Asset Income Institutional Cls Shares	VSDIX	NAS CM	Open End	Aggressive Alloc (Equity-Income)	C+	C	B-		Y	100,000
Segall Bryant & Hamill All Cap Fund	SBHAX	NAS CM	Open End	US Equity Large Cap Growth (Growth)	B-	C	B		Y	2,500
Segall Bryant & Hamill Emerging Markets Fund Class A	SBHEX	NAS CM	Open End	Global Emerg Mkts (Div Emerging Mkts)	C	C	C+		Y	2,500
Segall Bryant & Hamill Emerging Markets Fund Class I	SBEMX	NAS CM	Open End	Global Emerg Mkts (Div Emerging Mkts)	C	C	C+		Y	250,000
Segall Bryant & Hamill Fundament Int'l Small Cap Inst Cls	WIIFX	NAS CM	Open End	Global Equity Mid/Small Cap (Growth)	C	C	C	Up	Y	250,000
Segall Bryant & Hamill Fundament Int'l Small Cap Retail Cl	WTIFX	NAS CM	Open End	Global Equity Mid/Small Cap (Growth)	C	C	C	Up		2,500
Segall Bryant & Hamill Global Large Cap Institutional Cls	WIMVX	NAS CM	Open End	Global Equity Large Cap (Growth & Income)	B-	C+	B+	Up	Y	250,000
Segall Bryant & Hamill Global Large Cap Fund Retail Class	WTMVX	NAS CM	Open End	Global Equity Large Cap (Growth & Income)	B-	C+	B+	Up	Y	2,500
Segall Bryant & Hamill International Small Cap Cls A	SBHSX	NAS CM	Open End	Global Equity Mid/Small Cap (Small Company)	D+	D	D+		Y	2,500
Segall Bryant & Hamill International Small Cap Cls I	SBSIX	NAS CM	Open End	Global Equity Mid/Small Cap (Small Company)	D+	D	D+	Down	Y	250,000
Segall Bryant & Hamill Micro Cap Fund Retail Class	WTMIX	NAS CM	Open End	US Equity Small Cap (Growth)	C-	C-	C	Down	Y	2,500
Segall Bryant & Hamill Mid Cap Value Dividend Inst Cls	WIMCX	NAS CM	Open End	US Equity Mid Cap (Growth)	C+	C	B	Up	Y	250,000
Segall Bryant & Hamill Mid Cap Value Dividend Retail Cls	WTMCX	NAS CM	Open End	US Equity Mid Cap (Growth)	C+	C	B	Up	Y	2,500
Segall Bryant & Hamill Small Cap Growth Institutional Cls	WISGX	NAS CM	Open End	US Equity Small Cap (Small Company)	C+	C+	B	Down	Y	250,000
Segall Bryant & Hamill Small Cap Growth Fund Retail Class	WTSGX	NAS CM	Open End	US Equity Small Cap (Small Company)	C+	C+	B	Down	Y	2,500
Segall Bryant & Hamill Small Cap Value Dividend Inst Cls	WISVX	NAS CM	Open End	US Equity Small Cap (Small Company)	C-	D+	C	Down		250,000
Segall Bryant & Hamill Small Cap Value Dividend Retail Cls	WTSVX	NAS CM	Open End	US Equity Small Cap (Small Company)	C-	D+	C	Down		2,500
Segall Bryant & Hamill Small Cap Value Fund	SBHVX	NAS CM	Open End	US Equity Small Cap (Small Company)	C+	C	B	Down	Y	2,500
Segall Bryant & Hamill Smid Cap Value Dividend Inst Cls	WISDX	NAS CM	Open End	US Equity Mid Cap (Equity-Income)	C	C	C	Up	Y	250,000
Segall Bryant & Hamill Smid Cap Value Dividend Retail Cls	WTSDX	NAS CM	Open End	US Equity Mid Cap (Equity-Income)	C	C-	C	Up	Y	2,500
Segall Bryant & Hamill Workplace Equality Inst Cls	WEQIX	NAS CM	Open End	US Equity Large Cap Value (Growth)	B	C+	B+	Up	Y	250,000
Segall Bryant & Hamill Workplace Equality Retail Cls	WEQRX	NAS CM	Open End	US Equity Large Cap Value (Growth)	B	C+	B+	Up	Y	2,500
SEI Asset Allocation Trust Aggressive Strategy Cls D	SASDX	NAS CM	Open End	Moderate Alloc (Growth)	C+	C	B+	Up	Y	150,000
SEI Asset Allocation Trust Aggressive Strategy Cls F	SSGAX	NAS CM	Open End	Moderate Alloc (Growth)	B-	C	B+	Up	Y	100,000
SEI Asset Allocation Trust Aggressive Strategy Cls I	SEAIX	NAS CM	Open End	Moderate Alloc (Growth)	B-	C	B+	Up	Y	100,000
SEI Asset Alloc Trust Conservative Strategy Alloc Cls F	SMGAX	NAS CM	Open End	Moderate Alloc (Growth & Income)	B	C+	A-		Y	100,000
SEI Asset Allocation Trust Conservative Strategy Cls D	SSTDX	NAS CM	Open End	Cautious Alloc (Growth)	B-	C	B+	Up	Y	150,000
SEI Asset Allocation Trust Conservative Strategy Cls F	SVSAX	NAS CM	Open End	Cautious Alloc (Growth)	B-	C	A-		Y	100,000
SEI Asset Allocation Trust Conservative Strategy Cls I	SICIX	NAS CM	Open End	Cautious Alloc (Growth)	B-	C	B+		Y	100,000
SEI Asset Alloc Trust Core Mkt Strategy Alloc Cls F	SKTAX	NAS CM	Open End	Aggressive Alloc (Growth & Income)	C+	C	B	Up	Y	100,000
SEI Asset Allocation Trust Core Market Strategy Cls F	SOKAX	NAS CM	Open End	Cautious Alloc (Growth)	B-	C	A-	Up	Y	100,000
SEI Asset Allocation Trust Core Market Strategy Cls I	SCMSX	NAS CM	Open End	Cautious Alloc (Growth)	B	C	A-	Up	Y	100,000
SEI Asset Alloc Trust Defensive Strategy Alloc Cls F	STDAX	NAS CM	Open End	Moderate Alloc (Growth & Income)	B	C+	A-		Y	100,000
SEI Asset Alloc Trust Mkt Growth Strategy Alloc Cls F	SGOAX	NAS CM	Open End	Aggressive Alloc (Growth & Income)	C+	C	B	Up	Y	100,000
SEI Asset Allocation Trust Market Growth Strategy Cls D	SMKDX	NAS CM	Open End	Cautious Alloc (Growth)	B-	C	A-	Up	Y	150,000
SEI Asset Allocation Trust Market Growth Strategy Cls F	SRWAX	NAS CM	Open End	Cautious Alloc (Growth)	B-	C	A-	Up	Y	100,000

★ Expanded analysis of this fund is included in Section II.

Min Additional Investment	3-Month Total Return	6-Month Total Return	1-Year Total Return	3-Year Total Return	5-Year Total Return	Dividend Yield (TTM)	Expense Ratio	3-Yr Std Deviation	3-Year Beta	NAV	Total Assets (MIL)	%Cash	%Stocks	%Bonds	%Other	Turnover Ratio	Last Bull Market Total Return	Last Bear Market Total Return	Front End Fee (%)	Back End Fee (%)	Inception Date
	TOTAL RETURNS					PERFORMANCE				ASSETS		ASSET ALLOCATION & TURNOVER					BULL & BEAR		FEES		
	4.08	19.74	8.86	50.01	61.84	1.72	0.03	12.54	1	51.73	9,794	0	100	0	0	4	25.64	-17.46			Jun-99
	2.04	13.89	-3.64	23.66	9.31	2.53	0.86	11.75	1.04	10	1,060	0	100	0	0	98	15.65	-21.3			May-08
	2.99	9.56	6.11	14.18	18.81	2.43	0.35	4.13	0.28	11.42	80.7	4	32	64	0	9	7.06	-1.83			Mar-08
	2.92	7.86	6.62	10.24	16.09	2.55	0.21	2.97	0.14	10.2	45.5	4	17	78	0	11	3.96	0.61			Mar-08
	2.94	11.35	5.39	17.79	21.33	2.31	0.5	5.68	0.43	11.02	43.2	4	47	49	0	20	10.35	-5.89			Mar-08
	4.29	19.53	10.37	50.67	65.66	1.85	0.02	12.18	1	45.4	38,408	0	100	0	0	2	24.95	-16.17			May-97
	0.79	14.06	-1.90	31.35	6.36	0	1.26	13.05	0.97	26.76	21.7	7	93	0	0	34	17.75	-11.23			Dec-83
100	1.51	13.47	3.57	16.01	16.71	1.48	0.87	13.43	0.9	11.47	1,484	4	95	1	0	23					Feb-12
100	1.41	13.40	3.48	15.67	15.98	1.47	0.97	13.44	0.9	11.42	1,484	4	95	1	0	23					Feb-12
100	5.24	18.06	4.46	29.76		2.53	1.05	10.36	0.61	11.83	28.1	0	94	5	0	3					May-16
100	5.25	18.08	4.40	29.40		2.47	1.15	10.34	0.61	11.82	28.1	0	94	5	0	3					May-16
100	5.05	15.57					1.77			10.39	0.13	0	100	0	0				5.75		Aug-18
100	5.04	15.64					1.52			10.42	0.13	0	100	0	0						Aug-18
100	3.73	15.10	3.24	38.86	43.11	2.8	2.24	12.76	1.02	12.77	25.5	6	89	6	0	220	14.77	-14.76			Dec-09
1,000	4.06	13.84	10.98	37.50		1.33	0.61	8.13	0.64	12.73	58.9	30	31	39	0	7					Sep-15
1,000	3.33	11.12	7.85	23.92		1.54	0.73	8.14	0.6	12.32	39.7	5	89	5	0	12					Sep-15
1,000	1.15	15.82	8.41	12.03	23.93	2.8	0.77	10.29	1.36	11.32	81.9	1	77	12	0	56					Sep-12
500	6.32	22.10	11.47	42.04	51.97	0	0.98	12.57	0.97	15.8	104.3	3	97	0	0	37					Jul-13
500	1.80	13.40	-0.74	36.71	8.71	2.17	1.48	13.86	0.98	8.46	34.5	0	100	0	0	99	23.99		5.75		Jun-14
1,000	1.79	13.50	-0.50	37.75	9.57	2.47	1.23	13.86	0.98	8.49	34.5	0	100	0	0	99	24.16		0.80		Jun-11
	9.64	33.40	1.17	40.17	18.90	0.55	1.1	15.27	1.13	17.85	34.3	4	96	0	0	57	23.24	-19.2			Apr-16
25	9.61	33.33	1.06	39.49	18.24	0.41	1.25	15.27	1.13	16.76	34.3	4	96	0	0	57	23.24	-19.2			Dec-99
	4.42	15.76	10.84	30.86	35.12	2.34	0.74	10.13	0.74	10.65	48.4	2	98	0	0	59	22.75	-13.11			Sep-07
25	4.34	15.62	10.65	30.21	33.94	1.99	0.89	10.12	0.75	10.76	48.4	2	98	0	0	59	22.69	-13.1			Jun-88
500	-2.03	6.75	-13.78	13.68	5.34	2.29	1.28	13.1	1.03	11.06	282.0	0	99	0	1	111	15.99		5.75		Jun-14
1,000	-1.94	6.94	-13.47	14.63	6.59	2.59	1.03	13.07	1.03	11.08	282.0	0	99	0	1	111	16.16		0.50		May-11
25	-0.29	10.96	-11.34	28.80	23.54	0.43	1.05	17.08	0.94	10.32	3.5	0	100	0	0	87	28.18	-24.2			Jun-08
	4.19	17.86	1.37	23.13	37.38	1.14	0.84	13.35	0.98	25.34	77.9	4	96	0	0	125	19.64	-17.84			Apr-16
25	4.10	17.77	1.19	22.38	36.43	1.08	0.99	13.34	0.98	24.85	77.9	4	96	0	0	125	19.64	-17.84			Oct-98
	4.17	24.34	8.96	82.29	71.46	0	0.99	17.23	0.96	12.72	79.3	3	97	0	0	83					Dec-13
25	4.18	24.22	8.65	81.22	68.87	0	1.14	17.3	0.96	12.46	79.3	3	97	0	0	83					Dec-13
	1.77	13.77	-7.41	19.95	19.45	1.39	0.99	17.14	0.97	9.17	103.3	3	97	0	0	83	23.87	-20			Sep-07
25	1.79	13.62	-7.58	19.30	18.40	1.72	1.14	17.17	0.98	9.09	103.3	3	97	0	0	83	23.86	-20.06			Dec-04
500	1.77	17.00	5.32	46.78	44.71	0.59	0.99	13.71	0.76	12.59	143.3	9	91	0	-1	59					Jul-13
	3.46	18.36	-0.38			1.19	0.9			9.86	0.88	4	96	0	0	112					Dec-16
25	3.44	18.27	-0.60			0.99	1.05			9.9	0.88	4	96	0	0	112					Dec-16
	5.70	20.77	18.95	44.67	52.68	2.67	0.74	11.84	0.9	6.58	17.4	3	97	0	0	43	25.51	-15.8			Sep-07
25	5.65	20.87	18.78	43.69	51.01	3.11	0.89	11.8	0.9	6.41	17.4	3	97	0	0	43	25.43	-15.91			Jun-88
1,000	3.28	14.42	3.26	26.47	22.29	1.71	2.15	9.1	0.7	15.07	198.1	8	65	29	-2	12	21.16	-17.79			Mar-11
1,000	3.48	14.84	4.01	29.33	27.00	2.3	1.4	9.08	0.7	15.25	198.1	8	65	29	-2	12	21.74	-17.52			Nov-03
1,000	3.37	14.62	3.72	28.29	25.28	2.12	1.65	9.11	0.7	14.83	198.1	8	65	29	-2	12	21.55	-17.52			Nov-03
1,000	2.86	14.28	9.28	26.26	41.75	3.49	1.32	7.57	0.55	13.48	39.9	3	66	31	0	15	18.67	-10.15			Nov-03
1,000	2.22	6.42	4.71	8.76	10.79	1.27	1.88	2.71	0.33	10.86	78.6	18	23	59	0	13	4.96	-2.43			Mar-11
1,000	2.33	6.74	5.49	11.24	15.10	2	1.13	2.66	0.34	10.87	78.6	18	23	59	0	13	5.49	-1.94			Nov-03
1,000	2.32	6.75	5.23	10.47	13.76	1.72	1.38	2.73	0.33	11.07	78.6	18	23	59	0	13	5.33	-2.07			Nov-03
1,000	3.25	15.66	3.37	37.74	33.95	1.35	1.33	11.11	0.9	19.19	27.9	5	86	11	-3	17	22.42	-18.66			Nov-03
1,000	3.36	11.81	5.58	19.70	20.37	2.46	1.32	5.86	0.52	11.87	94.8	7	37	56	0	14	14.05	-8.99			Nov-03
1,000	3.46	12.07	5.93	19.79	22.04	2.19	1.57	5.91	0.54	13.03	94.8	7	37	56	0	14	13.83	-9.08			Nov-03
1,000	2.88	13.83	9.01	26.19	39.84	3.97	1.31	7.14	0.52	14.54	10.3	4	59	37	0	44	17.95	-9.7			Nov-03
1,000	3.24	15.66	3.38	37.72	33.98	1.35	1.33	11.11	0.89	24.15	135.2	5	86	11	-3	9	22.56	-18.54			Nov-03
1,000	3.13	12.47	4.12	20.45	17.62	1.65	2.12	7.12	0.54	13.29	226.8	7	48	45	0	12	17.37	-13.96			Mar-11
1,000	3.33	12.82	4.89	23.13	22.11	2.38	1.37	7.17	0.54	13.36	226.8	7	48	45	0	12	17.92	-13.58			Nov-03

Fund Name	MARKET Ticker Symbol	Traded On	FUND TYPE, CATEGORY & OBJECTIVE Fund Type	Category and (Prospectus Objective)	RATINGS Overall Rating	Reward Rating	Risk Rating	Recent Up/ Downgrade	Open to New Investors	MINIMUMS Min Initial Investment
SEI Asset Allocation Trust Market Growth Strategy Cls I	SMGSX	NAS CM	Open End	Cautious Alloc (Growth)	B-	C	A-	Up	Y	100,000
SEI Asset Alloc Trust Moderate Strategy Alloc Cls F	SXMAX	NAS CM	Open End	Aggressive Alloc (Growth & Income)	B	C+	A-		Y	100,000
SEI Asset Allocation Trust Moderate Strategy Fund Class D	SMSDX	NAS CM	Open End	Cautious Alloc (Growth)	B-	C	B+		Y	150,000
SEI Asset Allocation Trust Moderate Strategy Fund Class F	SMOAX	NAS CM	Open End	Cautious Alloc (Growth)	B	C+	A-	Up	Y	100,000
SEI Asset Allocation Trust Moderate Strategy Fund Class I	SMSIX	NAS CM	Open End	Cautious Alloc (Growth)	B-	C	B+		Y	100,000
SEI Asset Alloc Trust Tax-Managed Aggress Strat Cls F	SISAX	NAS CM	Open End	Aggressive Alloc (Growth)	B-	C	B	Up	Y	100,000
SEI Catholic Values Trust Catholic Values Equity Cls F	CAVAX	NAS CM	Open End	US Equity Large Cap Blend (Growth)	C+	C	B	Up	Y	500
SEI Catholic Values Trust Catholic Values Equity Cls Y	CAVYX	NAS CM	Open End	US Equity Large Cap Blend (Growth)	C+	C	B	Up	Y	500
SEI Inst Intl Trust Emerging Mkts Equity Cls F	SIEMX	NAS CM	Open End	Global Emerg Mkts (Div Emerging Mkts)	C	C	C+		Y	100,000
SEI Inst Intl Trust Emerging Mkts Equity Cls Y	SEQFX	NAS CM	Open End	Global Emerg Mkts (Div Emerging Mkts)	C	C	C+		Y	100,000
SEI Inst Intl Trust Intl Equity Cls F	SEITX	NAS CM	Open End	Global Equity Large Cap (Foreign Stock)	C	C	B-		Y	100,000
SEI Inst Intl Trust Intl Equity Cls I	SEEIX	NAS CM	Open End	Global Equity Large Cap (Foreign Stock)	C	C	B-		Y	100,000
SEI Inst Intl Trust Intl Equity Cls Y	SEFCX	NAS CM	Open End	Global Equity Large Cap (Foreign Stock)	C	C	B-		Y	100,000
SEI Inst Investments Trust Dynamic Asset Allocation Cls A	SDLAX	NAS CM	Open End	US Equity Large Cap Blend (Asset Alloc)	B-	C	B	Up	Y	100,000
SEI Inst Investments Trust Emerging Mkts Equity Cls A	SMQFX	NAS CM	Open End	Global Emerg Mkts (Div Emerging Mkts)	C	C	C+		Y	100,000
SEI Inst Investments Trust Extended Mkt Index Cls A	SMXAX	NAS CM	Open End	US Equity Mid Cap (Growth)	C+	C	B-		Y	100,000
SEI Inst Investments Trust Global Managed Volatility Cls A	SGMAX	NAS CM	Open End	Global Equity Large Cap (World Stock)	B-	C	A-	Down	Y	100,000
SEI Inst Inv Trust Large Cap Disciplined Eq Cls A	SCPAX	NAS CM	Open End	US Equity Large Cap Blend (Growth)	C+	C	B		Y	100,000
SEI Institutional Investments Trust Large Cap Fund Class A	SLCAX	NAS CM	Open End	US Equity Large Cap Blend (Growth & Income)	B-	C	B		Y	100,000
SEI Institutional Investments Trust Large Cap Index Cls A	LCIAX	NAS CM	Open End	US Equity Large Cap Blend (Growth)	B-	C	B		Y	100,000
SEI Inst Investments Trust Multi-Asset Real Return Cls A	SEIAX	NAS CM	Open End	Cautious Alloc (Growth & Income)	C	C	C		Y	100,000
SEI Institutional Investments Trust S&P 500 Index Cls A	SPINX	NAS CM	Open End	US Equity Large Cap Blend (Growth)	B-	C	B		Y	100,000
SEI Inst Inv Trust Screened World Eq Ex-US Cls A	SSEAX	NAS CM	Open End	Global Equity Large Cap (Growth)	C	C	B		Y	100,000
SEI Institutional Investments Trust Small Cap Fund Class A	SLPAX	NAS CM	Open End	US Equity Small Cap (Small Company)	C	C	C+		Y	100,000
SEI Institutional Investments Trust Small Cap II Cls A	SECAX	NAS CM	Open End	US Equity Small Cap (Small Company)	C	C	C+	Down	Y	100,000
SEI Inst Investments Trust Small/Mid Cap Equity Cls A	SSMAX	NAS CM	Open End	US Equity Small Cap (Growth)	C	C	B-		Y	100,000
SEI Inst Inv Trust U.S. Eq Factor Alloc Cls A	SEHAX	NAS CM	Open End	US Equity Large Cap Blend (Growth & Income)	D	D+	C+	Up	Y	100,000
SEI Inst Investments Trust U.S. Managed Volatility Cls A	SVYAX	NAS CM	Open End	US Equity Large Cap Value (Growth)	B	C+	A-		Y	100,000
SEI Inst Investments Trust World Equity Ex-US Cls A	WEUSX	NAS CM	Open End	Global Equity Large Cap (Growth)	C	C	B-		Y	100,000
SEI Inst Managed Trust Dynamic Asset Allocation Cls F	SDYAX	NAS CM	Open End	US Equity Large Cap Blend (Asset Alloc)	B-	C	B	Up	Y	100,000
SEI Inst Managed Trust Dynamic Asset Allocation Cls Y	SDYYX	NAS CM	Open End	US Equity Large Cap Blend (Asset Alloc)	B-	C	B	Up	Y	100,000
SEI Inst Managed Trust Global Managed Volatility Cls F	SVTAX	NAS CM	Open End	Global Equity Large Cap (Growth)	B-	C	B+		Y	100,000
SEI Inst Managed Trust Global Managed Volatility Cls I	SGMIX	NAS CM	Open End	Global Equity Large Cap (Growth)	B-	C	B+		Y	100,000
SEI Inst Managed Trust Global Managed Volatility Cls Y	SGLYX	NAS CM	Open End	Global Equity Large Cap (Growth)	B-	C	B+		Y	100,000
SEI Institutional Managed Trust Large Cap Fund Class F	SLGAX	NAS CM	Open End	US Equity Large Cap Blend (Growth & Income)	B-	C	B	Up	Y	100,000
SEI Institutional Managed Trust Large Cap Fund Class Y	SLYCX	NAS CM	Open End	US Equity Large Cap Blend (Growth & Income)	B-	C	B	Up	Y	100,000
SEI Institutional Managed Trust Large Cap Growth Cls F	SELCX	NAS CM	Open End	US Equity Large Cap Growth (Growth & Income)	B-	C+	B	Down	Y	100,000
SEI Institutional Managed Trust Large Cap Growth Cls I	SPGIX	NAS CM	Open End	US Equity Large Cap Growth (Growth & Income)	B-	C+	B	Down	Y	100,000
SEI Institutional Managed Trust Large Cap Growth Cls Y	SLRYX	NAS CM	Open End	US Equity Large Cap Growth (Growth & Income)	B-	C+	B	Down	Y	100,000
SEI Institutional Managed Trust Large Cap Index Cls F	SLGFX	NAS CM	Open End	US Equity Large Cap Blend (Growth)	D	C-	B-		Y	100,000
SEI Institutional Managed Trust Large Cap Value Cls F	TRMVX	NAS CM	Open End	US Equity Large Cap Value (Growth & Income)	B-	C	B	Up	Y	100,000
SEI Institutional Managed Trust Large Cap Value Cls I	SEUIX	NAS CM	Open End	US Equity Large Cap Value (Growth & Income)	B-	C	B	Up	Y	100,000
SEI Institutional Managed Trust Large Cap Value Cls Y	SVAYX	NAS CM	Open End	US Equity Large Cap Value (Growth & Income)	B-	C	B	Up	Y	100,000
SEI Inst Managed Trust Long/Short Alternative Cls F	SNAAX	NAS CM	Open End	Multialternative (Growth)	C	C-	B		Y	100,000
SEI Inst Managed Trust Long/Short Alternative Cls Y	SLSFX	NAS CM	Open End	Multialternative (Growth)	C	C	B		Y	100,000
SEI Institutional Managed Trust Mid-Cap Fund Class Y	SFDYX	NAS CM	Open End	US Equity Mid Cap (Growth)	C+	C	B-	Up	Y	100,000
SEI Institutional Managed Trust Mid-Cap Portfolio Cls F	SEMCX	NAS CM	Open End	US Equity Mid Cap (Growth)	C+	C	B-	Up	Y	100,000
SEI Institutional Managed Trust Mid-Cap Portfolio Cls I	SIPIX	NAS CM	Open End	US Equity Mid Cap (Growth)	C+	C	B-	Up	Y	100,000
SEI Inst Managed Trust Multi-Asset Accumulation Cls F	SAAAX	NAS CM	Open End	Moderate Alloc (Growth & Income)	B	C+	A-	Up	Y	100,000
SEI Inst Managed Trust Multi-Asset Accumulation Cls Y	SMOYX	NAS CM	Open End	Moderate Alloc (Growth & Income)	B	C+	A-	Up	Y	100,000
SEI Inst Managed Trust Multi-Asset Capital Stability Cls F	SCLAX	NAS CM	Open End	Cautious Alloc (Growth & Income)	B-	C	B+	Up	Y	100,000
SEI Inst Managed Trust Multi-Asset Capital Stability Cls Y	SMLYX	NAS CM	Open End	Cautious Alloc (Growth & Income)	B-	C	B+	Up	Y	100,000

★ Expanded analysis of this fund is included in Section II.

Min Additional Investment	TOTAL RETURNS 3-Month Total Return	6-Month Total Return	1-Year Total Return	3-Year Total Return	5-Year Total Return	PERFORMANCE Dividend Yield (TTM)	Expense Ratio	3-Yr Std Deviation	3-Year Beta	ASSETS NAV	Total Assets (MIL)	ASSET ALLOCATION & TURNOVER %Cash	%Stocks	%Bonds	%Other	Turnover Ratio	BULL & BEAR Last Bull Market Total Return	Last Bear Market Total Return	FEES Front End Fee (%)	Back End Fee (%)	Inception Date
1,000	3.31	12.77	4.70	22.28	20.62	2.17	1.62	7.18	0.54	13.16	226.8	7	48	45	0	12	17.72	-13.63			Nov-03
1,000	3.11	15.02	8.11	31.70	42.33	2.63	1.31	8.69	0.69	20.51	84.5	3	80	17	0	15	19.04	-12.44			Nov-03
1,000	2.97	9.47	6.09	13.56	17.25	1.46	2	4.36	0.47	12.48	173.9	10	34	55	0	12	8.28	-4.15			Mar-11
1,000	3.16	9.94	6.96	16.21	21.83	2.18	1.25	4.35	0.47	12.52	173.9	10	34	55	0	12	8.81	-3.78			Nov-03
1,000	3.17	9.76	6.66	15.42	20.33	1.87	1.5	4.39	0.47	12.87	173.9	10	34	55	0	12	8.63	-3.94			Nov-03
1,000	3.21	15.66	3.39	37.70	33.95	1.34	1.33	11.07	0.89	21.52	79.4	5	87	11	-3	8	22.59	-18.85			Nov-03
100	3.57	19.10	4.51	46.97		1.15	1.24	13.05	1.02	12.47	277.0	5	95	0	0	49					Apr-15
100	3.58	19.27	4.61	47.38		1.3	0.99	13.02	1.02	12.44	277.0	5	95	0	0	49					May-15
1,000	0.17	11.04	-1.99	31.25	7.62	0.57	1.69	13.9	0.99	11.56	1,767	7	96	0	-3	70	16.66	-28.57			Jan-95
1,000	0.25	11.15	-1.76	32.26	8.88	0.94	1.44	13.91	0.99	11.56	1,767	7	96	0	-3	70	16.66	-28.57			Dec-14
1,000	3.14	14.10	-2.59	25.17	11.13	1.41	1.09	11.47	1.02	10.84	4,141	6	97	0	-3	40	12.8	-24.29			Dec-89
1,000	3.03	13.97	-2.87	24.12	9.68	1.08	1.34	11.42	1.02	10.85	4,141	6	97	0	-3	40	12.55	-24.32			Jan-02
1,000	3.14	14.24	-2.43	26.03	12.28	1.82	0.84	11.45	1.02	10.83	4,141	6	97	0	-3	40	12.8	-24.29			Dec-14
1,000	3.70	18.06	7.78	44.37	69.96	0.6	0.07	11.83	0.96	20.98	2,285	2	93	0	5	12	14.07	-9.21			Jul-10
1,000	2.03	12.41	-1.00	26.32		1.86	0.64	12.39	0.97	9.51	1,064	7	92	1	0	97					Oct-14
1,000	3.16	20.68	2.53	48.31	47.59	1.44	0.06	15.19	1	15.52	1,002	10	98	0	-8	64					Feb-13
1,000	2.71	13.08	7.87	31.21		3.49	0.24	8.44	0.72	12.1	2,606					37					Feb-16
1,000	3.09	17.18	6.60	41.08	55.41	1.6	0.19	12.32	1.01	10.98	2,137	6	97	0	-3	134	26.04	-17.29			Aug-03
1,000	3.26	17.74	7.84	45.45	50.63	1.59	0.2	12.19	0.98	15.71	1,137	8	95	0	-3	68	26.8	-17.64			Jun-96
1,000	4.21	19.85	9.94	50.54	64.15	2	0.03	12.32	1	186.11	1,743	4	98	0	-2	16	25.45	-17.03			Apr-02
1,000	0.38	4.10	0.93	-0.86	-7.07	3.49	0.72	3.45	1.02	7.86	923.8	-33	0	105	27	22	3.48				Jul-11
1,000	4.32	19.53	10.40	50.70	65.96	2.12	0.05	12.19	1	15.82	4,131	3	98	0	-1	25					Dec-13
1,000	3.89	16.24	1.35	42.17	25.35	1.93	0.36	11.79	1.02	10.95	104.4	3	96	0	0	56	15.7	-24.86			Jun-08
1,000	3.40	18.10	-2.29	33.95	31.44	0.9	0.43	16.07	0.93	14.57	284.6	12	97	0	-8	115	29.25	-26.09			Jun-96
1,000	2.70	19.41	-1.76	39.39	37.64	0.63	0.43	16.46	0.95	10.63	371.1	18	97	0	-14	127					Apr-12
1,000	3.83	19.27	-0.10	37.34	36.18	0.76	0.42	15.28	0.98	11.03	1,263	16	96	0	-12	107	28.44	-24.22			Dec-03
1,000	3.89	18.77	8.72			1.52	0.05			10.9	803.3	1	99	0	0						Apr-18
1,000	3.01	15.21	11.53	36.65	60.54	2.31	0.23	9.32	0.7	13.71	1,237	2	98	0	0	58	18.02	-9.7			Dec-08
1,000	3.14	15.94	0.06	34.17	14.38	2.14	0.32	11.79	1.02	12.8	8,797	10	93	0	-3	75	16.57	-24.18			Mar-05
1,000	3.46	17.56	6.95	41.46		1.75	1.19	11.82	0.96	13.12	804.6	3	93	0	4						Jul-15
1,000	3.54	17.63	7.24	42.40		2	0.5	11.78	0.96	13.14	804.6	3	93	0	4						Jul-15
1,000	3.78	14.12	7.63	25.77	49.39	2.43	1.24	8.49	0.7	11.23	1,317	2	98	0	0		9.73	-4.04			Jul-06
1,000	3.87	14.01	7.39	24.93	47.61	2.22	1.49	8.55	0.71	10.98	1,317	2	98	0	0		9.47	-4.19			Jun-07
1,000	3.97	14.31	7.92	26.81	51.19	2.67	0.86	8.54	0.7	11.26	1,317	2	98	0	0		9.73	-4.05			Dec-14
1,000	3.35	17.72	6.37	47.71	49.59	1.07	0.94	12.84	1.03	13.85	2,358	3	99	0	-1		26.3	-17.99			Sep-09
1,000	3.41	17.87	6.64	48.80	51.28	1.3	0.64	12.84	1.03	13.86	2,358	3	99	0	-1		26.3	-17.99			Dec-14
1,000	4.40	22.35	10.41	61.32	69.70	0.25	0.98	13.42	0.98	36.03	1,515	2	98	0	-1		28.32	-16.58			Dec-94
1,000	4.34	22.21	10.18	60.28	67.79	0.07	1.23	13.42	0.98	35.09	1,515	2	98	0	-1		28.15	-16.67			Aug-01
1,000	4.46	22.48	10.67	62.52	71.25	0.47	0.64	13.45	0.99	36.07	1,515	2	98	0	-1		28.32	-16.58			Oct-15
1,000	4.18	19.78	9.78			1.66	0.64			10.44	387.1	2	98	0	0						Jan-18
1,000	1.83	13.81	3.24	38.40	33.18	1.85	0.93	12.91	1.06	23.19	1,362	2	98	0	0		25.47	-19.82			Apr-87
1,000	1.76	13.73	3.04	37.52	31.73	1.63	1.18	12.92	1.06	23.21	1,362	2	98	0	0		25.3	-19.88			Aug-01
1,000	1.89	13.99	3.55	39.51	34.41	2.09	0.64	12.93	1.06	23.2	1,362	2	98	0	0		25.47	-19.82			Oct-15
1,000	1.89	5.78	-0.40	16.64		0.79	1.44	5.59	0.82	9.69	31.9	82	14	4	0						Dec-14
1,000	1.98	5.86	-0.13	17.40		0.95	0.9	5.56	0.81	9.74	31.9	82	14	4	0						Apr-15
1,000	1.91	18.35	1.99	39.97	47.53	0.96	0.73	14.38	1.06	25.18	108.8	4	96	0	0		29.09	-23.76			Oct-15
1,000	1.84	18.18	1.77	38.91	46.17	0.73	0.99	14.39	1.06	25.16	108.8	4	96	0	0		29.09	-23.76			Feb-93
1,000	1.79	18.04	1.52	37.95	44.56	0.54	1.24	14.38	1.06	25.12	108.8	4	96	0	0		28.95	-23.85			Oct-07
1,000	5.27	16.38	8.87	19.59	22.36	2.6	1.29	7.45	0.51	10.37	2,886	18	21	61	0						Apr-12
1,000	5.34	16.51	9.21	20.43	23.69	2.82	1.04	7.46	0.51	10.44	2,886	18	21	61	0						Dec-14
1,000	1.97	4.86	3.85	7.86	9.42	0.51	0.98	1.96	0.71	10.34	732.4	52	14	34	0						Apr-12
1,000	2.06	4.96	3.95	8.17	9.95	0.61	0.73	1.92	0.74	10.36	732.4	52	14	34	0						Dec-14

	MARKET			FUND TYPE, CATEGORY & OBJECTIVE	RATINGS				MINIMUMS	
Fund Name	Ticker Symbol	Traded On	Fund Type	Category and (Prospectus Objective)	Overall Rating	Reward Rating	Risk Rating	Recent Up/ Downgrade	Open to New Investors	Min Initial Investment
SEI Institutional Managed Trust Multi-Asset Income Cls F	SIOAX	NAS CM	Open End	Moderate Alloc (Income)	B-	C+	B	Down	Y	100,000
SEI Institutional Managed Trust Multi-Asset Income Cls Y	SLIYX	NAS CM	Open End	Moderate Alloc (Income)	B-	C+	B	Down	Y	100,000
SEI Inst Managed Trust Multi-Asset Inflation Managed Cls F	SIFAX	NAS CM	Open End	Cautious Alloc (Income)	C-	C-	C		Y	100,000
SEI Inst Managed Trust Multi-Asset Inflation Managed Cls Y	SLFYX	NAS CM	Open End	Cautious Alloc (Income)	C-	C-	C		Y	100,000
SEI Inst Managed Trust Multi-Strategy Alternative Cls F	SMSAX	NAS CM	Open End	Multialternative (Balanced)	C	C-	B-		Y	100,000
SEI Inst Managed Trust Multi-Strategy Alternative Cls Y	SMUYX	NAS CM	Open End	Multialternative (Balanced)	C	C-	B-		Y	100,000
SEI Institutional Managed Trust Real Estate Fund Class F	SETAX	NAS CM	Open End	Real Estate Sector Equity (Real Estate)	C+	C	B-	Down	Y	100,000
SEI Institutional Managed Trust Real Estate Fund Class I	SEIRX	NAS CM	Open End	Real Estate Sector Equity (Real Estate)	C+	C	B-	Down	Y	100,000
SEI Institutional Managed Trust Real Estate Fund Class Y	SREYX	NAS CM	Open End	Real Estate Sector Equity (Real Estate)	C+	C	B-	Down	Y	100,000
SEI Institutional Managed Trust S&P 500 Index Fund Class F	SSPIX	NAS CM	Open End	US Equity Large Cap Blend (Growth)	B-	C	B		Y	100,000
SEI Institutional Managed Trust S&P 500 Index Fund Class I	SPIIX	NAS CM	Open End	US Equity Large Cap Blend (Growth)	B-	C	B		Y	100,000
SEI Institutional Managed Trust Small Cap Fund Class F	SLLAX	NAS CM	Open End	US Equity Small Cap (Small Company)	C	C	C+		Y	100,000
SEI Institutional Managed Trust Small Cap Fund Class Y	SMYFX	NAS CM	Open End	US Equity Small Cap (Small Company)	C	C	C+		Y	100,000
SEI Institutional Managed Trust Small Cap Growth Cls F	SSCGX	NAS CM	Open End	US Equity Small Cap (Small Company)	C	C	C+	Down	Y	100,000
SEI Institutional Managed Trust Small Cap Growth Cls I	SPWIX	NAS CM	Open End	US Equity Small Cap (Small Company)	C	C	C+	Down	Y	100,000
SEI Institutional Managed Trust Small Cap Growth Cls Y	SMAYX	NAS CM	Open End	US Equity Small Cap (Small Company)	C	C	C+	Down	Y	100,000
SEI Institutional Managed Trust Small Cap Value Cls F	SESVX	NAS CM	Open End	US Equity Small Cap (Small Company)	C	C-	C		Y	100,000
SEI Institutional Managed Trust Small Cap Value Cls I	SMVIX	NAS CM	Open End	US Equity Small Cap (Small Company)	C	C-	C		Y	100,000
SEI Institutional Managed Trust Small Cap Value Cls Y	SPVYX	NAS CM	Open End	US Equity Small Cap (Small Company)	C	C-	C		Y	100,000
SEI Inst Managed Trust Tax Managed Large Cap Cls Y	STLYX	NAS CM	Open End	US Equity Large Cap Blend (Growth)	B-	C	B	Up	Y	100,000
SEI Inst Managed Trust Tax-Managed Intl Managed Vol Cls F	SMINX	NAS CM	Open End	Global Equity Large Cap (Foreign Stock)	C	D+	C+	Up	Y	100,000
SEI Inst Managed Trust Tax-Managed Intl Managed Vol Cls Y	SIMYX	NAS CM	Open End	Global Equity Large Cap (Foreign Stock)	C	D+	B-	Up	Y	100,000
SEI Inst Managed Trust Tax-Managed Large Cap Cls F	TMLCX	NAS CM	Open End	US Equity Large Cap Blend (Growth)	B-	C	B	Up	Y	100,000
SEI Inst Managed Trust Tax-Managed Managed Vol Cls Y	STVYX	NAS CM	Open End	US Equity Large Cap Value (Asset Alloc)	B	C+	B+		Y	100,000
SEI Inst Managed Trust Tax-Managed Small/Mid Cap Cls F	STMSX	NAS CM	Open End	US Equity Small Cap (Growth & Income)	C	C	C		Y	100,000
SEI Inst Managed Trust Tax-Managed Small/Mid Cap Cls Y	STMPX	NAS CM	Open End	US Equity Small Cap (Growth & Income)	C	C	C+		Y	100,000
SEI Inst Managed Trust Tax-Managed Volatility Cls F	TMMAX	NAS CM	Open End	US Equity Large Cap Value (Asset Alloc)	B	C+	B+		Y	100,000
SEI Inst Managed Trust U.S. Managed Volatility Cls F	SVOAX	NAS CM	Open End	US Equity Large Cap Value (Growth)	B	C+	A-		Y	100,000
SEI Inst Managed Trust U.S. Managed Volatility Cls I	SEVIX	NAS CM	Open End	US Equity Large Cap Value (Growth)	B	C+	A-		Y	100,000
SEI Inst Managed Trust U.S. Managed Volatility Cls Y	SUSYX	NAS CM	Open End	US Equity Large Cap Value (Growth)	B	C+	A-		Y	100,000
SEI World Select Equity Fund Class A	SWSAX	NAS CM	Open End	Global Equity Large Cap (World Stock)	D+	D	C		Y	100,000
Selected American Shares Fund Class D	SLADX	NAS CM	Open End	US Equity Large Cap Blend (Growth & Income)	C	C	C+		Y	10,000
Selected American Shares Fund Class S	SLASX	NAS CM	Open End	US Equity Large Cap Blend (Growth & Income)	C	C	C+		Y	1,000
Selected International Fund Class D	SLSDX	NAS CM	Open End	Global Equity Large Cap (Foreign Stock)	C	C-	C		Y	10,000
Selected International Fund Class S	SLSSX	NAS CM	Open End	Global Equity Large Cap (Foreign Stock)	C	C-	C		Y	1,000
Selective Opportunity Fund Foundation Class	SLCTX	NAS CM	Open End	US Equity Large Cap Blend (Growth & Income)	C	C-	B		Y	10,000
Selective Opportunity Fund Service Class	SLCSX	NAS CM	Open End	US Equity Large Cap Blend (Growth & Income)	C	C-	B-		Y	10,000
Sequoia Fund	SEQUX	NAS CM	Open End	US Equity Large Cap Growth (Growth)	B	B-	B	Up		5,000
Seven Canyons Strategic Income Fund Investor Class	WASIX	NAS CM	Open End	US Equity Mid Cap (Income)	B-	C	B+	Up	Y	2,000
Seven Canyons World Innovators Fund Institutional Class	WIGTX	NAS CM	Open End	Global Equity Mid/Small Cap (World Stock)	C+	C	B	Up	Y	100,000
Seven Canyons World Innovators Fund Investor Class	WAGTX	NAS CM	Open End	Global Equity Mid/Small Cap (World Stock)	C+	C	B	Up	Y	2,000
Sextant Core Fund	SCORX	NAS CM	Open End	Moderate Alloc (Growth)	B-	C	A-		Y	1,000
Sextant Global High Income Fund	SGHIX	NAS CM	Open End	Cautious Alloc (Income)	B-	C	B+	Down	Y	1,000
Sextant Growth Fund	SSGFX	NAS CM	Open End	US Equity Large Cap Growth (Growth)	B-	C+	B	Down	Y	1,000
Sextant Growth Fund	SGZFX	NAS CM	Open End	US Equity Large Cap Growth (Growth)	B-	C+	B	Down	Y	1,000
Sextant International Fund	SSIFX	NAS CM	Open End	Global Equity Large Cap (Foreign Stock)	B	B	B+	Up	Y	1,000
Sextant International Fund Z Shares	SIFZX	NAS CM	Open End	Global Equity Large Cap (Foreign Stock)	B	B	B+	Up	Y	1,000
SGA International Equity Fund Institutional Shares	SGLCX	NAS CM	Open End	Global Equity Large Cap (Growth & Income)	C	D+	C+	Up	Y	1,000,000
SGA International Equity Fund Investor Shares	SGNLX	NAS CM	Open End	Global Equity Large Cap (Growth & Income)	C	D+	C+	Up	Y	10,000
SGI Global Equity Fund Class I	SGLIX	NAS CM	Open End	Global Equity Large Cap (Growth)	B	B-	B+	Up	Y	1,000,000
SGI U.S. Large Cap Equity Fund Class A	LVOLX	NAS CM	Open End	US Equity Large Cap Blend (Growth)	B-	C+	B	Down	Y	2,500
SGI U.S. Large Cap Equity Fund Class C	SGICX	NAS CM	Open End	US Equity Large Cap Blend (Growth)	B-	C+	B		Y	2,500

★ Expanded analysis of this fund is included in Section II.

Min Additional Investment	TOTAL RETURNS: 3-Month Total Return	6-Month Total Return	1-Year Total Return	3-Year Total Return	5-Year Total Return	PERFORMANCE: Dividend Yield (TTM)	Expense Ratio	3-Yr Std Deviation	3-Year Beta	ASSETS: NAV	Total Assets (MIL)	ASSET ALLOCATION & TURNOVER: %Cash	%Stocks	%Bonds	%Other	Turnover Ratio	BULL & BEAR: Last Bull Market Total Return	Last Bear Market Total Return	FEES: Front End Fee (%)	Back End Fee (%)	Inception Date
1,000	3.29	10.38	9.03	21.23	28.46	3.52	1.21	3.61	0.31	11.05	968.1	5	11	82	0						Apr-12
1,000	3.32	10.43	9.13	21.59	29.01	3.6	0.96	3.61	0.32	11.05	968.1	5	11	82	0						Dec-14
1,000	0.36	3.74	0.21	-2.95	-9.65	1.83	1.76	3.46	1.02	8.31	867.1	-9	13	76	20	32					Apr-12
1,000	0.36	3.87	0.47	-2.29	-8.72	2.09	1.5	3.54	1.04	8.31	867.1	-9	13	76	20	32					Dec-14
1,000	1.16	3.58	0.18	8.33	4.33	1.65	2.9	3.32	6.83	9.53	482.1	60	17	22	1		2.17	-5.15			Mar-10
1,000	1.27	3.81	0.45	9.06	5.40	1.91	1.65	3.33	7.02	9.53	482.1	60	17	22	1		2.17	-5.15			Apr-15
1,000	1.92	18.32	9.95	13.34	43.48	1.18	1.24	12.78	0.98	16.01	131.7	2	98	0	0		29.77	-16.4			Nov-03
1,000	1.87	18.19	9.66	12.57	41.90	1	1.49	12.77	0.98	15.99	131.7	2	98	0	0		29.68	-16.49			Oct-07
1,000	1.98	18.48	10.22	14.16	45.06	1.39	0.89	12.82	0.98	16.01	131.7	2	98	0	0		29.77	-16.4			Dec-14
1,000	4.26	19.46	10.20	49.42	63.35	1.89	0.29	12.19	1	68.18	845.3	1	99	0	0		24.89	-16.44			Feb-96
1,000	4.14	19.22	9.75	48.04	61.14	1.51	0.8	12.19	1	68.56	845.3	1	99	0	0		24.73	-16.5			Jun-02
1,000	3.26	19.19	-3.91	30.14	23.19	0.01	1.24	16.73	0.97	11.43	626.6	7	98	0	-4		29.05	-26.67			Sep-09
1,000	3.29	19.29	-3.67	31.06	24.56	0.06	0.89	16.72	0.97	11.54	626.6	7	98	0	-4		29.05	-26.67			Dec-14
1,000	1.03	16.57	-2.26	46.39	42.73	0	1.24	16.23	0.92	33.33	341.4	9	97	0	-7		31.12	-26.87			Apr-92
1,000	0.92	16.42	-2.54	45.26	40.91	0	1.49	16.24	0.92	31.69	341.4	9	97	0	-7		31.04	-27.03			Aug-01
1,000	1.08	16.74	-2.03	47.46	44.04	0	0.86	16.24	0.92	33.68	341.4	9	97	0	-7		31.12	-26.87			Oct-15
1,000	1.42	15.31	-6.90	21.86	16.27	0.92	1.24	17.28	0.98	21.08	323.9	7	96	0	-3		28.26	-24.56			Dec-94
1,000	1.38	15.23	-7.09	21.11	15.02	0.71	1.49	17.29	0.98	20.87	323.9	7	96	0	-3		28.16	-24.65			Feb-02
1,000	1.44	15.44	-6.70	22.78	17.34	1.17	0.89	17.27	0.98	21.09	323.9	7	96	0	-3		28.26	-24.56			Oct-15
1,000	3.40	17.50	6.75	47.87	49.06	1.24	0.64	12.44	1	27.23	3,990	2	99	0	-1		26.84	-18.01			Dec-14
1,000	1.30	9.61	-1.08			2.49	1.4			10.83	375.1	6	94	0	0						Oct-16
1,000	1.49	9.81	-0.70			2.75	0.86			10.85	375.1	6	94	0	0						Oct-16
1,000	3.34	17.38	6.48	46.79	47.44	1	0.9	12.42	1	27.22	3,990	2	99	0	-1		26.84	-18.01			Mar-98
1,000	4.12	15.99	12.29	35.35	59.03	1.69	0.75	9.03	0.67	17.22	1,075	2	98	0	0		16.47	-9.42			Apr-15
1,000	3.43	16.76	-3.66	33.76	29.88	0.28	1.23	15.06	0.97	21.35	889.3	14	97	0	-11		27.46	-23.58			Oct-00
1,000	3.48	16.93	-3.44	34.66	31.20	0.5	0.89	15.08	0.97	21.38	889.3	14	97	0	-11		27.46	-23.58			Dec-14
1,000	3.99	15.77	12.01	34.26	57.37	1.46	1.23	9.01	0.67	17.21	1,075	2	98	0	0		16.47	-9.42			Dec-07
1,000	3.48	15.74	11.54	33.58	54.71	1.52	0.9	9.34	0.7	17.4	1,822	2	98	0	0		17.94	-10.1			Oct-04
1,000	3.35	15.60	11.25	32.58	52.75	1.29	1.15	9.36	0.7	17.39	1,822	2	98	0	0		17.74	-10.24			Jun-07
1,000	3.54	15.96	11.82	34.65	56.44	1.75	0.65	9.34	0.7	17.41	1,822	2	98	0	0		17.94	-10.1			Dec-14
1,000	1.93	14.10	-0.82			2.91	0.3			10.03	760.9					68					Jun-17
25	3.63	18.30	-0.58	41.72	46.67	0.89	0.65	15	1.17	34.04	1,834	1	96	0	3	24	22.9	-19.64			May-04
25	3.56	18.10	-0.89	40.40	44.30	0.59	0.97	15.01	1.17	33.99	1,834	1	96	0	3	24	22.66	-19.76			Feb-33
25	0.81	18.11	-7.18	32.55	18.47	0.51	0.89	15.79	1.25	12.39	65.1	1	99	0	0	31	19.79	-32.59			May-04
25	0.73	17.91	-7.47	31.08	16.09	0.11	1.15	15.73	1.25	12.31	65.1	1	99	0	0	31	19.29	-32.71			Jan-39
	-3.41	14.78	3.74			0	1.31			11.88	92.1	20	80	0	0	82					Jan-17
	-3.49	14.67	3.57			0	1.38			11.88	92.1	20	80	0	0	82					Mar-18
	5.50	21.86	9.96	52.76	29.73	0	1	11.92	0.9	154.84	3,933	5	95	0	0	27	25.23	-11.48			Jul-70
100	2.83	13.20	3.27	26.99	17.59	3.44	1.43	10.76	0.88	12.14	34.5	8	87	5	0	72	22.9	-14.78			Feb-06
5,000	2.02	13.07	2.09	48.42	41.39	0	1.55	11.74	0.88	16.7	128.5	25	75	0	0	159	22.84	-13.21			Feb-16
100	2.48	13.64	1.98	45.18	41.06	0	1.75	11.76	0.88	16.49	128.5	25	75	0	0	159	22.84	-13.21			Dec-00
25	3.94	13.32	9.77	24.84	22.65	1.26	0.88	7.62	0.99	13.69	14.9	4	59	37	0	30	11.88	-9.78			Mar-07
25	2.40	10.17	8.60	36.04	23.28	3.41	0.75	7.16	0.52	11.48	9.9	23	37	38	0	10					Mar-12
25	5.90	23.62	14.76	59.10	56.01	0.13	0.92	13.39	1.06	30.66	42.0	1	99	0	0	17	22.65	-16.86			Apr-87
25	5.96	23.84	15.13	59.77	56.66	0.46	0.7	13.4	1.06	30.54	42.0	1	99	0	0	17	22.65	-16.86			Jun-17
25	6.29	21.99	17.87	53.86	34.16	0.81	1.05	10.64	0.83	18.08	98.5	23	77	0	0	2	10.31	-15.6			Sep-95
25	6.34	22.11	18.13	54.67	34.86	1.01	0.84	10.65	0.83	18.11	98.5	23	77	0	0	2	10.31	-15.6			Jun-17
	1.61	12.53	-2.63			1.52	0.95			10.68	6.1	1	99	0	0	45					Sep-16
	1.62	12.32	-2.90			1.2	1.2			10.66	6.1	1	99	0	0	45					Sep-16
	5.42	18.62	14.33	40.89	44.48	1.26	0.84	11.03	0.81	32.48	21.8	3	97	0	0	247	27.97	-14.29			Apr-09
	3.97	19.02	10.79	39.10	67.43	0.3	1.23	11.27	0.88	17.77	487.5	1	99	0	0	31			5.25		Nov-15
	3.77	18.64	10.02	36.13	60.49	0	1.98	11.24	0.88	17.31	487.5	1	99	0	0	31					Dec-15

	MARKET			FUND TYPE, CATEGORY & OBJECTIVE	RATINGS				MINIMUMS	
Fund Name	Ticker Symbol	Traded On	Fund Type	Category and (Prospectus Objective)	Overall Rating	Reward Rating	Risk Rating	Recent Up/ Downgrade	Open to New Investors	Min Initial Investment
SGI U.S. Large Cap Equity Fund Class I	SILVX	NAS CM	Open End	US Equity Large Cap Blend (Growth)	B-	C+	B	Down	Y	1,000,000
SGI U.S. Small Cap Equity Fund Class A	LVSMX	NAS CM	Open End	US Equity Small Cap (Small Company)	C	C	C+	Up	Y	1,000
SGI U.S. Small Cap Equity Fund Class C	SMLVX	NAS CM	Open End	US Equity Small Cap (Small Company)	C	C-	C+	Up	Y	2,500
SGI U.S. Small Cap Equity Fund Class I	SCLVX	NAS CM	Open End	US Equity Small Cap (Small Company)	C	C	C+	Up	Y	1,000,000
SharesPost 100 Fund	PRIVX	NAS CM	Closed End	Equity Miscellaneous (Equity-Income)	B-	C+	B		Y	2,500
SharesPost 100 Fund Class L Shares	PRLVX	NAS CM	Closed End	Equity Miscellaneous (Equity-Income)	D	D+	C+		Y	2,500
SharesPost 100 Fund I	PIIVX	NAS CM	Closed End	Equity Miscellaneous (Equity-Income)	D+	D+	B	Up	Y	1,000,000
Shelton BDC Income Fund Institutional Class	LOAIX	NAS CM	Open End	Financials Sector Equity (Income)	B-	C+	B		Y	500,000
Shelton BDC Income Fund Investor Class	LOANX	NAS CM	Open End	Financials Sector Equity (Income)	B-	C+	B		Y	1,000
Shelton Capital Management Core Value Fund Class K	EQTKX	NAS CM	Open End	US Equity Large Cap Value (Equity-Income)	B-	C	B	Up	Y	1,000
Shelton Capital Management Core Value Fund Direct Shares	EQTIX	NAS CM	Open End	US Equity Large Cap Value (Equity-Income)	B-	C	B	Up	Y	1,000
Shelton Capital Management Nasdaq-100 Index Fund Class K	NDXKX	NAS CM	Open End	US Equity Large Cap Growth (Growth)	B-	C+	B	Down	Y	1,000
Shelton Capital Management Nasdaq-100 Index Direct Shares	NASDX	NAS CM	Open End	US Equity Large Cap Growth (Growth)	B-	C+	B	Down	Y	1,000
Shelton Capital Management S&P 500 Index Fund Class K	SPXKX	NAS CM	Open End	US Equity Large Cap Blend (Growth & Income)	B-	C	B		Y	1,000
Shelton Capital Management S&P 500 Index Direct Shares	SPFIX	NAS CM	Open End	US Equity Large Cap Blend (Growth & Income)	B-	C	B		Y	1,000
Shelton Capital Management S&P Midcap Index Fund Class K	MIDKX	NAS CM	Open End	US Equity Mid Cap (Growth)	C+	C	B-	Up	Y	1,000
Shelton Capital Management S&P Midcap Index Direct Shares	SPMIX	NAS CM	Open End	US Equity Mid Cap (Growth)	C+	C	B-	Up	Y	1,000
Shelton Capital Management S&P Smallcap Index Fund Class K	SMLKX	NAS CM	Open End	US Equity Small Cap (Small Company)	C	C-	C		Y	1,000
Shelton Capital Mgmt S&P Smallcap Index Direct Shares	SMCIX	NAS CM	Open End	US Equity Small Cap (Small Company)	C	C-	C+		Y	1,000
Shelton Green Alpha Fund	NEXTX	NAS CM	Open End	US Equity Mid Cap (Growth)	C+	C	B-	Up	Y	1,000
Shelton International Select Equity Institutional Cls	SISEX	NAS CM	Open End	Global Equity Large Cap (Foreign Stock)	C	C	B-		Y	500,000
Shelton International Select Equity Fund Investor Class	SISLX	NAS CM	Open End	Global Equity Large Cap (Foreign Stock)	C	C	B-		Y	1,000
Shelton Real Estate Income Fund Institutional Class	RENIX	NAS CM	Open End	Real Estate Sector Equity (Real Estate)	C+	C	C+	Down	Y	500,000
Shelton Real Estate Income Fund Investor Class	RENTX	NAS CM	Open End	Real Estate Sector Equity (Real Estate)	C	C	C+	Down	Y	1,000
Shelton Tactical Credit Institutional	DEBIX	NAS CM	Open End	Long/Short Credit (Growth & Income)	B-	C+	B+	Up	Y	1,000,000
Shelton Tactical Credit Investor	DEBTX	NAS CM	Open End	Long/Short Credit (Growth & Income)	B-	C+	B	Up	Y	2,500
Sierra Total Return Fund Class T	SRNTX	NAS CM	Closed End	Cautious Alloc (Growth & Income)	C	D+	A-	Up	Y	2,500
Silk Invest New Horizons Frontier Fund Institutional Class	FSNHX	NAS CM	Open End	Global Emerg Mkts (Growth)	D	D	D+			100,000
SilverPepper Commodity Strategies Global Macro Advisor Cls	SPCAX	NAS CM	Open End	Commodities Broad Basket (Growth & Income)	D+	D	C-	Down	Y	5,000
SilverPepper Commodity Strategies Global Macro Inst Cls	SPCIX	NAS CM	Open End	Commodities Broad Basket (Growth & Income)	D+	D	C-	Down	Y	5,000
SilverPepper Merger Arbitrage Fund Advisor Class	SPABX	NAS CM	Open End	Market Neutral (Growth & Income)	C	C	B		Y	5,000
SilverPepper Merger Arbitrage Fund Institutional Class	SPAIX	NAS CM	Open End	Market Neutral (Growth & Income)	C+	C	B		Y	5,000
SIM Global Core Managed Volatility Fund Class Z Shares	SIMVX	NAS CM	Open End	Global Equity Large Cap (Growth)	U	U	U		Y	500
SIM U.S. Core Managed Volatility Fund Class Z Shares	SIMUX	NAS CM	Open End	US Equity Large Cap Blend (Growth)	U	U	U		Y	500
Sims Total Return Fund	SIMFX	NAS CM	Open End	US Equity Large Cap Value (Growth & Income)	C	C-	C	Down		500
Sirios Long/Short Fund Institutional Class	SLHIX	NAS CM	Open End	Long/Short Equity (Growth)	D	D+	B		Y	100,000
Sirius S&P Strategic Large-Cap Allocation Fund	SSPLX	NAS CM	Open End	Long/Short Equity (Growth & Income)	C	C-	C	Up	Y	2,500
Sit Balanced Fund	SIBAX	NAS CM	Open End	Moderate Alloc (Balanced)	B	C	A-	Up	Y	5,000
Sit Developing Markets Growth Fund	SDMGX	NAS CM	Open End	Global Emerg Mkts (Div Emerging Mkts)	C	C	C+		Y	5,000
Sit Dividend Growth Fund Class I	SDVGX	NAS CM	Open End	US Equity Large Cap Blend (Equity-Income)	B-	C	B	Up	Y	100,000
Sit Dividend Growth Fund Class S	SDVSX	NAS CM	Open End	US Equity Large Cap Blend (Equity-Income)	B-	C	B	Up	Y	5,000
Sit ESG Growth Fund Class I	IESGX	NAS CM	Open End	US Equity Large Cap Blend (Growth)	C+	C	B		Y	100,000
Sit ESG Growth Fund Class S	SESGX	NAS CM	Open End	US Equity Large Cap Blend (Growth)	C+	C	B		Y	5,000
Sit Global Dividend Growth Fund Class I	GDGIX	NAS CM	Open End	US Equity Large Cap Blend (Equity-Income)	B-	C	B	Up	Y	100,000
Sit Global Dividend Growth Fund Class S	GDGSX	NAS CM	Open End	US Equity Large Cap Blend (Equity-Income)	B-	C	B	Up	Y	5,000
Sit International Growth Fund	SNGRX	NAS CM	Open End	Global Equity Large Cap (Foreign Stock)	C	C-	B-		Y	5,000
Sit Large Cap Growth Fund	SNIGX	NAS CM	Open End	US Equity Large Cap Growth (Growth)	B-	C+	B	Down	Y	5,000
Sit Mid Cap Growth Fund	NBNGX	NAS CM	Open End	US Equity Mid Cap (Growth)	C+	C	B		Y	5,000
Sit Small Cap Dividend Growth Fund Class I	SSCDX	NAS CM	Open End	US Equity Small Cap (Small Company)	C	C	B-		Y	100,000
Sit Small Cap Dividend Growth Fund Class S	SDFSX	NAS CM	Open End	US Equity Small Cap (Small Company)	C	C	B-		Y	5,000
Sit Small Cap Growth Fund	SSMGX	NAS CM	Open End	US Equity Mid Cap (Small Company)	C+	C	C+	Up	Y	5,000
SkyBridge Dividend Value Fund Class A	SKYAX	NAS CM	Open End	US Equity Large Cap Value (Equity-Income)	C-	C-	C	Down	Y	1,000

★ Expanded analysis of this fund is included in Section II.

	TOTAL RETURNS					PERFORMANCE				ASSETS		ASSET ALLOCATION & TURNOVER					BULL & BEAR		FEES		
Min Additional Investment	3-Month Total Return	6-Month Total Return	1-Year Total Return	3-Year Total Return	5-Year Total Return	Dividend Yield (TTM)	Expense Ratio	3-Yr Std Deviation	3-Year Beta	NAV	Total Assets (MIL)	%Cash	%Stocks	%Bonds	%Other	Turnover Ratio	Last Bull Market Total Return	Last Bear Market Total Return	Front End Fee (%)	Back End Fee (%)	Inception Date
	4.05	19.16	11.09	40.14	69.46	0.62	0.98	11.26	0.88	17.72	487.5	1	99	0	0	31					Feb-12
	1.92	13.31	-4.06	30.38		0.28	1.69	14.57	0.81	11.66	38.8	3	97	0	0	95			5.25		Mar-16
	1.77	12.93	-4.73	27.49		0.01	2.44	14.62	0.81	11.44	38.8	3	97	0	0	95					Mar-16
	2.00	13.49	-3.73	31.29		0.36	1.44	14.62	0.81	11.69	38.8	3	97	0	0	95					Mar-16
	-1.47	3.34	1.62	15.66	29.47	0	2.5	5.92		29.39	--	35	38	0	11	2			5.75		Mar-14
	-1.51	3.17	1.34			0	2.75			29.29	--	35	38	0	11	2			4.25		May-18
	-1.40	3.47	1.86			0	2.25			29.5	--	35	38	0	11	2					Nov-17
2,500	1.99	13.62	7.78	27.46	20.08	6.94	10.27	12.52	0.83	8.71	6.9	1	84	0	9	30					May-14
1,000	2.01	13.69	7.71	26.71	20.34	8.66	10.52	12.46	0.83	8.65	6.9	1	84	0	9	30			4.50		May-14
100	3.39	16.13	5.19	26.77	33.60	2.49	1.28	10.84	0.85	19.95	154.6	4	96	0	0	35	21.71	-16.83			Oct-03
100	3.53	16.40	5.72	28.75	36.99	2.87	0.78	10.86	0.85	20.25	154.6	4	96	0	0	35	22.14	-16.66			Sep-96
100	3.63	21.78	9.36	72.39	97.65	0.22	1	14.84	0.98	18.23	637.6	0	100	0	0	2	27.96	-10.97			Oct-03
100	3.69	22.01	9.88	74.94	102.58	0.61	0.51	14.84	0.98	18.76	637.6	0	100	0	0	2	28.5	-10.82			Jan-00
100	4.10	18.98	9.50	47.55	60.24	1.1	1	12.24	1	56.14	193.0	0	100	0	0	3	24.41	-16.28			Oct-03
100	4.24	19.29	10.07	49.79	64.31	1.56	0.5	12.22	1	56.17	193.0	0	100	0	0	3	24.72	-16.08			Apr-92
100	2.75	18.41	0.40	36.30	42.31	0.52	1.16	15.17	1	24.22	114.2	1	99	0	0	12	26.99	-22.53			Oct-03
100	2.89	18.70	0.92	38.37	45.91	0.87	0.66	15.17	1	24.6	114.2	1	99	0	0	12	27.34	-22.37			Apr-92
100	1.68	13.58	-6.13	36.68	44.22	0.26	1.31	17.56	0.98	20.75	69.9	1	99	0	0	18	29.62	-21.81			Oct-03
100	1.78	13.82	-5.69	38.70	47.85	0.66	0.8	17.55	0.98	21.31	69.9	1	99	0	0	18	29.94	-21.67			Oct-96
100	8.18	32.23	14.77	42.04	23.25	0.08	1.3	18.12	1.38	18.63	53.4	1	99	0	0	13					Mar-13
2,500	3.55	16.84	0.31	35.07	-11.74	0.21	1.17			21.29	58.6	11	89	0	0	65	21.76	-28.97			Dec-08
1,000	3.51	16.72	0.10	35.99	-11.57	0.15	1.38			21.21	58.6	11	89	0	0	65	21.54	-29.03	5.75		Jul-09
2,500	2.36	18.04	12.07	14.41	36.69	2.88	1.16	10	0.71	9.04	5.8	1	98	0	0	38					Jun-13
1,000	2.34	17.82	11.74	13.55	35.30	3.01	1.41	9.96	0.71	9.25	5.8	1	98	0	0	38			4.50		Jun-13
100	1.53	4.04	3.13	9.79	14.97	3.69	4.97	3.72	0.22	10.67	98.1	9	0	84	4	63					Dec-13
100	1.58	4.02	2.89	9.08	13.58	3.52	5.22	3.65	0.2	10.67	98.1	9	0	84	4	63					Dec-13
1,000	2.03	4.82	6.18			5.22	3.86			25.25	--								2.00		Jun-17
1,000	-4.59	0.48	-14.83	-4.03		2.58	1.74	10.38	0.7	8.3	37.1	3	97	0	0	39					May-16
100	-1.71	2.56	-3.06	-4.81	-16.07	5.47	2.03	6.76	0.66	8.01	121.1	75	16	0	9	1,040					Oct-13
100	-1.82	2.54	-3.03	-4.82	-15.68	5.34	1.99	6.77	0.66	8.05	121.1	75	16	0	9	1,040					Oct-13
100	-0.45	1.94	1.38	5.34	17.92	0	2.93	1.78	0.04	10.99	63.0	17	48	0	35	385					Oct-13
100	-0.35	2.10	1.72	6.15	19.33	0	2.68	1.76	0.04	11.15	63.0	17	48	0	35	385					Oct-13
500	2.69	14.52					2.55			11.83	4.6	15	85	0	0						Dec-18
500	2.99	15.54					2.4			12.04	3.1	15	85	0	0						Dec-18
500	-11.59	-5.23	-4.13	3.89	-7.20	0	3.41	10.21	0.33		7.0	23	77	0	0	63	16.28	-13.41			Sep-86
	4.83	14.07	8.55			0.12	2.1			10.62	26.8	16	84	0	0						May-18
100	1.21	7.00	-2.27	1.88		0	2.21	8.45	0.53	9.16	20.0	12	87	1	0	469					Oct-14
100	3.52	13.42	7.97	34.22	44.75	1.21	1.03	8.01	0.18	25.06	34.5	5	60	35	0	50	16.15	-9.35			Dec-93
100	0.18	12.80	-4.43	39.32	8.40	0.47	1.43	14.22	0.96	16.21	10.0	5	95	0	0	30	16.64	-24.42			Jul-94
100	3.42	16.83	8.37	39.80	52.72	2.31	0.7	11.6	0.94	14.45	254.0	1	99	0	0	68	23.2	-15.98			Dec-03
100	3.31	16.68	8.11	38.73	50.79	2.08	0.95	11.56	0.94	14.37	254.0	1	99	0	0	68	23.04	-16			Mar-06
100	5.09	16.79	8.30	33.21		1.22	1			13.21	6.3	6	94	0	0	15					Jul-16
100	5.02	16.66	8.01	32.21		1.1	1.25			13.16	6.3	6	94	0	0	15					Jul-16
100	4.81	17.08	9.18	31.92	30.82	1.7	1	11.52	0.98	16.34	34.1	4	96	0	0	20	21.04	-19.2			Sep-08
100	4.82	16.94	8.98	30.94	29.25	1.46	1.25	11.58	0.98	16.33	34.1	4	96	0	0	20	20.86	-19.26			Sep-08
100	5.67	20.12	3.55	23.34	10.25	1.05	1.51	12.86	1.06	17.13	23.5	2	98	0	0	16	19.32	-24.38			Nov-91
100	4.16	20.37	10.54	58.04	71.66	0.33	1	13.01	0.96	42.53	116.6	3	97	0	0	15	25.21	-15.52			Sep-82
100	5.72	25.68	11.75	46.92	43.37	0	1.25	14.53	0.99	18.84	169.2	6	94	0	0	29	32.46	-22.79			Sep-82
100	4.73	19.53	-0.54	26.58		1.24	1	15.48	0.86	11.89	16.5	5	96	0	0	30					Mar-15
100	4.67	19.36	-0.79	25.54		0.99	1.25	15.44	0.86	11.88	16.5	5	96	0	0	30					Mar-15
100	5.96	25.98	6.44	44.90	32.70	0	1.5	16.19	0.89	55.46	99.6	7	93	0	0	29	30.28	-22			Jul-94
50	-1.86	4.17	-8.70	11.89	24.32	3.09	1.25	14.29	0.94	7.87	68.9	2	98	0	0	43			5.75		Jun-14

	MARKET			FUND TYPE, CATEGORY & OBJECTIVE	RATINGS				MINIMUMS	
Fund Name	Ticker Symbol	Traded On	Fund Type	Category and (Prospectus Objective)	Overall Rating	Reward Rating	Risk Rating	Recent Up/ Downgrade	Open to New Investors	Min Initial Investment
SkyBridge Dividend Value Fund Class C	SKYCX	NAS CM	Open End	US Equity Large Cap Value (Equity-Income)	C-	D+	C	Down	Y	1,000
SkyBridge Dividend Value Fund Class I	SKYIX	NAS CM	Open End	US Equity Large Cap Value (Equity-Income)	C-	C-	C	Down	Y	50,000
Small Cap Value Fund	SCAPX	NAS CM	Open End	US Equity Small Cap (Small Company)	D+	D+	D	Down	Y	100,000
Small/Mid Cap Growth Fund Institutional Class	TRSMX	NAS CM	Open End	US Equity Mid Cap (Growth)	C+	C	B-	Down	Y	100,000
Smead Value Fund Class A	SVFAX	NAS CM	Open End	US Equity Large Cap Value (Growth)	B-	C	B		Y	3,000
Smead Value Fund Class I1	SVFFX	NAS CM	Open End	US Equity Large Cap Value (Growth)	B-	C	B		Y	1,000,000
Smead Value Fund Class R1	SVFDX	NAS CM	Open End	US Equity Large Cap Value (Growth)	B-	C	B		Y	25,000
Smead Value Fund Class R2	SVFKX	NAS CM	Open End	US Equity Large Cap Value (Growth)	B-	C	B+	Down	Y	25,000
Smead Value Fund Class Y	SVFYX	NAS CM	Open End	US Equity Large Cap Value (Growth)	B-	C	B+		Y	10,000,000
Smead Value Fund Investor Class	SMVLX	NAS CM	Open End	US Equity Large Cap Value (Growth)	B-	C	B		Y	3,000
SMI 50/40/10 Fund	SMILX	NAS CM	Open End	Aggressive Alloc (Growth & Income)	C	C	C	Up	Y	500
SMI Dynamic Allocation Fund	SMIDX	NAS CM	Open End	Moderate Alloc (Growth & Income)	C	C-	C+	Up	Y	500
Smith Group Large Cap Core Growth Fund Institutional Class	BSLGX	NAS CM	Open End	US Equity Large Cap Blend (Growth)	C	C	B-	Down	Y	25,000
Smith Group Large Cap Core Growth Fund Investor Class	BSLNX	NAS CM	Open End	US Equity Large Cap Blend (Growth)	C	C	B-	Down	Y	2,500
Snow Capital Long/Short Opportunity Fund Class A	SNOAX	NAS CM	Open End	Long/Short Equity (Growth)	C	C	B		Y	2,500
Snow Capital Long/Short Opportunity Fund Class C	SNOCX	NAS CM	Open End	Long/Short Equity (Growth)	C	C	B-		Y	2,500
Snow Capital Long/Short Opportunity Cls Institutional	SNOIX	NAS CM	Open End	Long/Short Equity (Growth)	C+	C	B	Up	Y	2,500
Snow Capital Small Cap Value Fund Class A	SNWAX	NAS CM	Open End	US Equity Small Cap (Small Company)	C-	D+	C	Down	Y	2,500
Snow Capital Small Cap Value Fund Class C	SNWCX	NAS CM	Open End	US Equity Small Cap (Small Company)	C-	D+	C-	Down	Y	2,500
Snow Capital Small Cap Value Fund Institutional Class	SNWIX	NAS CM	Open End	US Equity Small Cap (Small Company)	C-	D+	C	Down	Y	2,500
Sound Mind Investing Fund	SMIFX	NAS CM	Open End	Aggressive Alloc (Asset Alloc)	C	C	C+		Y	500
Sound Shore Fund Institutional Class	SSHVX	NAS CM	Open End	US Equity Large Cap Value (Growth)	C+	C	B	Up	Y	1,000,000
Sound Shore Fund Investor Class	SSHFX	NAS CM	Open End	US Equity Large Cap Value (Growth)	C+	C	B	Up	Y	10,000
Soundwatch Hedged Equity Fund Institutional Class	BHHEX	NAS CM	Open End	Long/Short Equity (Growth)	C	C	B		Y	2,500,000
Source Capital Inc	SOR	NYSE	Closed End	Moderate Alloc (Growth & Income)	C	C	C-		Y	
Sparrow Growth Fund Class A	SGFFX	NAS CM	Open End	US Equity Mid Cap (Growth)	C+	C+	C	Down	Y	1,000
Sparrow Growth Fund Class C	SGFCX	NAS CM	Open End	US Equity Mid Cap (Growth)	C+	C+	C	Down	Y	1,000
Sparrow Growth Fund No-Load Class	SGNFX	NAS CM	Open End	US Equity Mid Cap (Growth)	C+	C+	C	Down	Y	2,500
Special Opportunities Fund	SPE	NYSE	Closed End	Moderate Alloc (Municipal Bond - Natl)	C	C	C-	Up	Y	
Spectrum Advisors Preferred Fund Investor Class	SAPEX	NAS CM	Open End	Global Macro (Growth)	C+	C	B	Up	Y	1,000
Spirit of America Energy Fund Class A	SOAEX	NAS CM	Open End	Energy Sector Equity ()	D+	D+	C-	Down	Y	500
Spirit of America Energy Fund Class C	SACEX	NAS CM	Open End	Energy Sector Equity ()	D+	D	D+	Down	Y	500
Spirit of America Income & Opportunity Fund Class A	SOAOX	NAS CM	Open End	Cautious Alloc (Growth & Income)	B-	C+	B		Y	500
Spirit of America Income & Opportunity Fund Class C	SACOX	NAS CM	Open End	Cautious Alloc (Growth & Income)	B-	C+	B	Up	Y	500
Spirit of America Large Cap Value Fund A	SOAVX	NAS CM	Open End	US Equity Large Cap Blend (Growth & Income)	C+	C	B		Y	500
Spirit of America Large Cap Value Fund Class C	SACVX	NAS CM	Open End	US Equity Large Cap Blend (Growth & Income)	C+	C	B		Y	500
Spirit of America Real Estate Income & Growth Fund Class A	SOAAX	NAS CM	Open End	Real Estate Sector Equity (Real Estate)	C+	C	B-		Y	500
Spirit of America Real Estate Income & Growth Fund Class C	SACRX	NAS CM	Open End	Real Estate Sector Equity (Real Estate)	C+	C	B-		Y	500
Sprott Focus Trust Inc.	FUND	NAS CM	Closed End	US Equity Mid Cap (World Stock)	C-	D+	C-	Down	Y	
Spyglass Growth Fund Institutional Shares	SPYGX	NAS CM	Open End	US Equity Mid Cap (Growth)	D+	C-	B-	Up	Y	100,000
SSgA Dynamic Small Cap Fund Class A	SSSDX	NAS CM	Open End	US Equity Small Cap (Small Company)	C	C-	C		Y	2,000
SSgA Dynamic Small Cap Fund Class I	SSSJX	NAS CM	Open End	US Equity Small Cap (Small Company)	C	C-	C		Y	1,000,000
SSgA Dynamic Small Cap Fund Class K	SSSKX	NAS CM	Open End	US Equity Small Cap (Small Company)	C	C-	C		Y	10,000,000
SSgA Dynamic Small Cap Fund N Class	SVSCX	NAS CM	Open End	US Equity Small Cap (Small Company)	C	C-	C			1,000
SSgA International Stock Selection Fund Class A	SSILX	NAS CM	Open End	Global Equity Large Cap (Foreign Stock)	C	D+	C+		Y	2,000
SSgA International Stock Selection Fund Class I	SSIPX	NAS CM	Open End	Global Equity Large Cap (Foreign Stock)	C	C-	B-		Y	1,000,000
SSgA International Stock Selection Fund Class K	SSIQX	NAS CM	Open End	Global Equity Large Cap (Foreign Stock)	C	C-	B-		Y	10,000,000
SSgA International Stock Selection Fund N Class	SSAIX	NAS CM	Open End	Global Equity Large Cap (Foreign Stock)	C	C-	B-			1,000
SSgA S&P 500 Index Fund N Class	SVSPX	NAS CM	Open End	US Equity Large Cap Blend (Growth)	B-	C	B		Y	10,000
STAAR Adaptive Discovery Fund	SITSX	NAS CM	Open End	US Equity Small Cap (Small Company)	C	C	C+		Y	1,000
STAAR Dynamic Capital Fund	SITLX	NAS CM	Open End	US Equity Large Cap Growth (Growth)	C+	C	B	Up	Y	1,000
STAAR International Fund	SITIX	NAS CM	Open End	Global Equity Large Cap (Foreign Stock)	C-	D+	C		Y	1,000

★ Expanded analysis of this fund is included in Section II.

Min Additional Investment	TOTAL RETURNS 3-Month Total Return	6-Month Total Return	1-Year Total Return	3-Year Total Return	5-Year Total Return	PERFORMANCE Dividend Yield (TTM)	Expense Ratio	3-Yr Std Deviation	3-Year Beta	ASSETS NAV	Total Assets (MIL)	ASSET ALLOCATION & TURNOVER %Cash	%Stocks	%Bonds	%Other	Turnover Ratio	BULL & BEAR Last Bull Market Total Return	Last Bear Market Total Return	FEES Front End Fee (%)	Back End Fee (%)	Inception Date
50	-2.10	3.80	-9.40	9.28	19.18	2.57	2	14.35	0.95	7.76	68.9	2	98	0	0	43				1.00	Oct-14
0	-1.91	4.31	-8.44	12.61	25.28	3.27	1	14.28	0.95	7.86	68.9	2	98	0	0	43					Apr-14
100	-17.46	-11.61	-31.72	20.75	-15.49	2.17	0.95	24.77		34.4	19.3	4	96	0	0	63	26.04	-21.96			Dec-05
100	8.72	23.86	6.97	42.88		0	1.01	14.47	0.82	13.96	7.6	3	97	0	0	30					Dec-14
100	6.87	16.61	12.02	50.32	56.28	0	1.19	12.67	0.93	47.58	1,198	2	98	0	0	11	29.88	-15.39	5.75		Jan-14
100	6.93	16.75	12.28	51.29	58.28	0.02	0.98	12.66	0.93	47.94	1,198	2	98	0	0	11	30.13	-15.31			Dec-09
100	6.77	16.41	11.65	48.89	54.04	0	1.5	12.66	0.93	46.95	1,198	2	98	0	0	11	29.69	-15.47			Nov-14
100	6.81	16.50	15.80	53.94	59.63	0	1.44	13.09	0.94	48.77	1,198	2	98	0	0	11	29.69	-15.47			Nov-14
100	6.97	16.87	12.44	51.98	59.22	0.16	0.84	12.66	0.93	48	1,198	2	98	0	0	11	29.88	-15.39			Nov-14
100	6.87	16.60	12.04	50.07	56.17	0	1.26	12.66	0.93	47.9	1,198	2	98	0	0	11	29.88	-15.39			Jan-08
50	1.76	8.36	-3.26	18.99		0.69	1.57	9.68	0.69	9.23	61.3	0	77	18	5	155					Apr-15
50	2.99	6.53	1.09	6.82	8.11	1.44	1.32	7.16	0.4	11.71	118.7	0	65	34	0	61					Feb-13
100	-1.10	14.24	0.48	42.97	52.46	0.54	0.79	14.29	1.13	8.98	34.5	1	99	0	0	42	27.07	-19.11			Jun-07
100	-1.21	14.12	0.24	41.88	50.85	0.35	1.04	14.29	1.13	8.97	34.5	1	99	0	0	42	26.88	-19.2			Feb-14
	1.22	11.78	-0.04	34.18	0.88	1.59	1.48	11.4	0.81	26.37	144.0	40	60	0	0	38	25.14	-26.88	5.25		Apr-06
	1.02	11.32	-0.81	31.18	-2.81	0.61	2.23	11.41	0.82	24.58	144.0	40	60	0	0	38	24.65	-27.03		1.00	Apr-06
	1.29	11.91	0.23	35.20	2.21	1.85	1.23	11.44	0.82	26.67	144.0	40	60	0	0	38	25.25	-26.8			Apr-06
	-0.26	16.89	-12.10	20.14	-4.50	0	1.52	21.86	1.22	30.65	29.7	1	99	0	0	52	33.83	-28.42	5.25		Nov-10
	-0.45	16.46	-12.75	17.46	-7.98	0	2.27	21.89	1.22	28.58	29.7	1	99	0	0	52	33.29	-28.67		1.00	Nov-10
	-0.19	17.05	-11.88	21.07	-3.26	0	1.27	21.88	1.22	31.37	29.7	1	99	0	0	52	34.04	-28.36			Nov-10
50	2.80	13.39	-4.25	31.45	26.95	0.39	2.04	12.44	0.92	9.52	154.8	5	94	0	1	164	18.04	-21.26			Dec-05
	4.52	17.76	4.21	35.64	33.92	1.06	0.75	13.48	1.08	43.27	1,737	4	96	0	0	56	26.27	-22.68			Dec-13
	4.47	17.68	4.05	35.03	32.84	0.97	0.9	13.49	1.08	43.06	1,737	4	96	0	0	56	26.27	-22.68			May-85
	2.25	10.07	2.60			0.99	0.7			17.7	95.4	10	90	0	0	8					Nov-16
	3.34	14.10	5.68	30.27	34.52	7.44	0	9.49		42.37	364.8	5	63	32	1	59	32.5	-26.52			Oct-68
50	3.80	32.58	10.41	82.19	75.61	0	2.21	21.53	1.4	27.26	23.5	0	100	0	0	43	29.55	-15.96	5.75		Oct-98
50	3.69	32.27	9.92	79.51	71.39	0	2.61	21.54	1.4	25.53	23.5	0	100	0	0	43	29.24	-16.13			Jan-12
100	3.93	32.81	10.73	83.49	77.75	0	1.94	21.55	1.4	26.39	23.5	0	100	0	0	43	29.89	-15.86			Nov-00
	1.44	13.33	1.47	23.79	25.56	1.62	0	8.87	0.64	15.5	131.8	18	92	19	10	66	14.02	-9.4			Jun-93
500	5.44	18.63	5.66	39.75		0.63	2.4	11.2	0.84	23.83	12.8	3	44	22	31	269					Jun-15
50	-4.02	14.20	-4.43	0.07		18.32	1.38	15.54	0.9	9.21	460.6	1	99	0	0	19			5.75		Jul-14
50	-4.27	13.75	-5.25	-2.05		18.98	2.13	15.56	0.9	8.89	460.6	1	99	0	0	19				1.00	Mar-16
50	2.98	10.22	6.76	13.03	16.97	5.07	1.27	4.96	1.23	9.7	23.4	2	30	57	0	4			4.75		Jul-13
50	2.68	9.62	5.99	11.18	12.22	4.32	2.02	4.98	1.24	9.68	23.4	2	30	57	0	4				1.00	Mar-16
50	4.51	18.62	8.33	39.46	43.13	3.67	1.52	12.23	1	21.08	100.4	0	98	0	0	13	25.17	-17.32	5.25		Aug-02
50	4.30	18.17	7.55	36.50	38.16	2.94	2.22	12.22	1	21.07	100.4	0	98	0	0	13	24.66	-17.57		1.00	Mar-16
50	2.61	19.76	10.55	16.85	34.74	3.54	1.54	12.8	0.95	11.54	89.1	0	97	0	0	4	29.14	-20.36	5.25		Jan-98
50	2.30	19.34	9.75	14.27	29.85	3.43	2.24	12.79	0.95	11.35	89.1	0	97	0	0	4	28.61	-20.6		1.00	Mar-16
	0.39	15.72	-6.18	21.83	4.99	2.26		14.56	0.76	7.54	196.2	2	97	0	2	31	16.21	-25.91			Mar-88
	-0.45	27.07	19.59			0	1			13.19	155.0	1	99	0	0						Dec-17
	0.33	12.04	-6.52	29.51	31.57	1.03	1.3	16.64	0.96	47.53	21.8	1	99	0	0	110	32.33	-23.3	5.25		Jul-14
	0.41	12.25	-6.20	30.66	33.38	1.36	1.05	16.64	0.96	47.83	21.8	1	99	0	0	110	32.33	-23.3			Jul-14
	0.41	12.25	-6.19	30.85	34.06	1.35	0.85	16.65	0.96	47.92	21.8	1	99	0	0	110	32.33	-23.3			Jul-14
100	0.35	12.11	-6.43	29.88	32.45	1.04	1.1	16.64	0.96	47.85	21.8	1	99	0	0	110	32.33	-23.3			Jul-92
	1.09	12.34	-1.93	20.21	3.73	5.1	1.2	11.03	0.97	10.19	225.1	2	98	0	0	72	12.24	-26.03	5.25		Jul-14
	1.08	12.52	-1.60	21.56	5.47	5.61	0.95	10.95	0.96	10.24	225.1	2	98	0	0	72	12.24	-26.03			Jul-14
	1.08	12.52	-1.56	21.79	5.96	5.66	0.75	10.94	0.96	10.24	225.1	2	98	0	0	72	12.24	-26.03			Jul-14
100	1.08	12.39	-1.78	20.85	4.75	5.36	1	10.96	0.96	10.25	225.1	2	98	0	0	72	12.24	-26.03			Mar-95
100	4.25	19.47	10.25	50.11	64.96	1.76	0.16	12.2	1	37.1	1,564	2	98	0	0	2	25.37	-16.41			Dec-92
50	2.54	15.00	-3.87	28.37	18.01	0	3.87	15.17	0.88	12.08	2.8	12	88	0	0	12	21.21	-23.24			Apr-96
50	3.19	16.89	4.52	27.94	27.49	0.01	3.72	11.32	0.9	13.87	2.9	18	81	0	0	16	19.2	-17.94			Apr-96
50	1.74	10.90	-4.69	15.07	-8.57	0	4.28	11.08	0.97	9.89	1.5	9	91	0	0	0	12.83	-23.97			Apr-96

Fund Name	Ticker Symbol	Traded On	Fund Type	Category and (Prospectus Objective)	Overall Rating	Reward Rating	Risk Rating	Recent Up/ Downgrade	Open to New Investors	Min Initial Investment
	MARKET		FUND TYPE, CATEGORY & OBJECTIVE		RATINGS				MINIMUMS	
STAAR Inv Trust - STAAR Disciplined Strategies Cls A	DSFAX	NAS CM	Open End	Aggressive Alloc (Multi-Asset Global)	C-	C-	C		Y	1,000
STAAR Inv Trust - STAAR Disciplined Strategies Cls C	DSFCX	NAS CM	Open End	Aggressive Alloc (Multi-Asset Global)	D+	D+	C		Y	1,000
STAAR Inv Trust - STAAR Disciplined Strategies Inst Cls	DSFNX	NAS CM	Open End	Aggressive Alloc (Multi-Asset Global)	C-	C-	C		Y	1,000,000
STAAR Inv Trust - STAAR Disciplined Strategies Inv Cls	SITAX	NAS CM	Open End	Aggressive Alloc (Multi-Asset Global)	C	C-	B-	Up	Y	1,000
Stadion Alternative Income Fund Class A	TACFX	NAS CM	Open End	Long/Short Equity (Growth & Income)	D	D	C-	Down	Y	1,000
Stadion Alternative Income Fund Class C	TACCX	NAS CM	Open End	Long/Short Equity (Growth & Income)	D	D	C-	Down	Y	1,000
Stadion Alternative Income Fund Class I	TACSX	NAS CM	Open End	Long/Short Equity (Growth & Income)	D	D	C-	Down	Y	0
Stadion Tactical Defensive Fund Class A	ETFRX	NAS CM	Open End	Moderate Alloc (Growth)	B-	C	A-	Up	Y	1,000
Stadion Tactical Defensive Fund Class C	ETFZX	NAS CM	Open End	Moderate Alloc (Growth)	B-	C	A-	Up	Y	1,000
Stadion Tactical Defensive Fund Class I	ETFWX	NAS CM	Open End	Moderate Alloc (Growth)	B	C	A-	Up	Y	0
Stadion Tactical Growth Fund Class A Shares	ETFAX	NAS CM	Open End	Moderate Alloc (Growth)	C+	C	B	Up	Y	1,000
Stadion Tactical Growth Fund Class C Shares	ETFCX	NAS CM	Open End	Moderate Alloc (Growth)	C+	C	B-	Up	Y	1,000
Stadion Tactical Growth Fund Class I Shares	ETFOX	NAS CM	Open End	Moderate Alloc (Growth)	C+	C	B		Y	0
Stadion Trilogy Alternative Return Fund Class A Shares	STTGX	NAS CM	Open End	Multialternative (Growth & Income)	D+	D	C		Y	1,000
Stadion Trilogy Alternative Return Fund Class C Shares	STTCX	NAS CM	Open End	Multialternative (Growth & Income)	D+	D	C-		Y	1,000
Stadion Trilogy Alternative Return Fund Class I Shares	STTIX	NAS CM	Open End	Multialternative (Growth & Income)	D+	D	C		Y	0
State Farm Balanced Fund	STFBX	NAS CM	Open End	Moderate Alloc (Balanced)	B	C+	B+		Y	250
State Farm Growth Fund	STFGX	NAS CM	Open End	US Equity Large Cap Blend (Growth)	B-	C+	B+		Y	250
State Street Asia Pacific Value Spotlight Fund Class K	SIDKX	NAS CM	Open End	Asia Equity (Growth)	C	C-	C+		Y	10,000,000
State Street Defensive Emerging Markets Equity Cls A	SSELX	NAS CM	Open End	Global Emerg Mkts (Div Emerging Mkts)	C	C	B-		Y	2,000
State Street Defensive Emerging Markets Equity Cls I	SSEOX	NAS CM	Open End	Global Emerg Mkts (Div Emerging Mkts)	C	C	B-		Y	1,000,000
State Street Defensive Emerging Markets Equity Cls K	SSEQX	NAS CM	Open End	Global Emerg Mkts (Div Emerging Mkts)	C	C	B-		Y	10,000,000
State Street Defensive Emerging Markets Equity Cls N	SSEMX	NAS CM	Open End	Global Emerg Mkts (Div Emerging Mkts)	C	C	B-			1,000
State Street Disciplined Global Equity Fund Class I	SSGMX	NAS CM	Open End	Global Equity Large Cap (Growth & Income)	B-	C	B+	Up	Y	1,000,000
State Street Disciplined Global Equity Portfolio			Open End	Global Equity Large Cap (Growth)	B-	C	B+	Up	Y	0
State Street Disciplined U.S. Equity Fund Class I	SSJIX	NAS CM	Open End	US Equity Large Cap Value (Growth)	B-	C	A		Y	1,000,000
State Street Emerging Markets Equity Index Fund Class K	SSKEX	NAS CM	Open End	Global Emerg Mkts (Div Emerging Mkts)	C	C	C+		Y	10,000,000
State Street Equity 500 Index Fund Administrative Shares	STFAX	NAS CM	Open End	US Equity Large Cap Blend (Growth & Income)	B-	C	B		Y	25,000,000
State Street Equity 500 Index Fund Class A	SSSVX	NAS CM	Open End	US Equity Large Cap Blend (Growth & Income)	B-	C	B		Y	2,000
State Street Equity 500 Index Fund Class I	SSSWX	NAS CM	Open End	US Equity Large Cap Blend (Growth & Income)	B-	C	B		Y	1,000,000
State Street Equity 500 Index Fund Class K	SSSYX	NAS CM	Open End	US Equity Large Cap Blend (Growth & Income)	B-	C	B		Y	10,000,000
State Street Equity 500 Index Fund Class R Shares	SSFRX	NAS CM	Open End	US Equity Large Cap Blend (Growth & Income)	B-	C	B		Y	25,000,000
State Street Equity 500 Index Fund Service Shares	STBIX	NAS CM	Open End	US Equity Large Cap Blend (Growth & Income)	B-	C	B		Y	25,000,000
State Street Equity 500 Index II Portfolio	SSEYX	NAS CM	Open End	US Equity Large Cap Blend (Growth & Income)	B-	C	B		Y	0
State Street European Value Spotlight Fund Class K	SIBKX	NAS CM	Open End	Europe Equity Large Cap (Growth)	D	D	D+	Down	Y	10,000,000
State Street Global Equity ex-U.S. Index Fund Class A	SSGHX	NAS CM	Open End	Global Equity Large Cap (Growth & Income)	C	C	B		Y	2,000
State Street Global Equity ex-U.S. Index Fund Class I	SSGJX	NAS CM	Open End	Global Equity Large Cap (Growth & Income)	C	C	B		Y	1,000,000
State Street Global Equity ex-U.S. Index Fund Class K	SSGLX	NAS CM	Open End	Global Equity Large Cap (Growth & Income)	C	C	B		Y	10,000,000
State Street Global Equity ex-U.S. Index Portfolio	SSGVX	NAS CM	Open End	Global Equity Large Cap (Growth & Income)	C	C	B		Y	0
State Street Hedged Intl Developed Equity Index Cls K	SSHQX	NAS CM	Open End	Global Equity Large Cap (Foreign Stock)	B-	C	B	Up	Y	10,000,000
State Street Inst Intl Equity Investment Cls	SIEIX	NAS CM	Open End	Global Equity Large Cap (Foreign Stock)	C	C	B-		Y	0
State Street Inst Intl Equity Service Cls	SIESX	NAS CM	Open End	Global Equity Large Cap (Foreign Stock)	C	C	B-		Y	5,000,000
State Street Inst Premier Growth Equity Investment Cls	SSPGX	NAS CM	Open End	US Equity Large Cap Growth (Growth)	B-	C	B	Down	Y	5,000,000
State Street Inst Premier Growth Equity Service Cls	SSPSX	NAS CM	Open End	US Equity Large Cap Growth (Growth)	B-	C	B	Down	Y	5,000,000
State Street Institutional Small-Cap Equity Investment Cls	SIVIX	NAS CM	Open End	US Equity Small Cap (Small Company)	C+	C	B-		Y	0
State Street Institutional Small-Cap Equity Service Cls	SSQSX	NAS CM	Open End	US Equity Small Cap (Small Company)	C+	C	C+		Y	5,000,000
State Street Institutional U.S. Equity Investment Cls	SUSIX	NAS CM	Open End	US Equity Large Cap Blend (Growth)	B-	C	B	Down	Y	5,000,000
State Street Institutional U.S. Equity Fund Service Class	SUSSX	NAS CM	Open End	US Equity Large Cap Blend (Growth)	B-	C	B	Down	Y	5,000,000
State Street International Value Spotlight Fund Class K	SIVSX	NAS CM	Open End	Global Equity Large Cap (Growth)	D+	D	C	Down	Y	10,000,000
State Street Small/Mid Cap Equity Index Fund Class A	SSMJX	NAS CM	Open End	US Equity Small Cap (Growth & Income)	C+	C	B-		Y	2,000
State Street Small/Mid Cap Equity Index Fund Class I	SSMLX	NAS CM	Open End	US Equity Small Cap (Growth & Income)	C+	C	B-		Y	1,000,000
State Street Small/Mid Cap Equity Index Fund Class K	SSMKX	NAS CM	Open End	US Equity Small Cap (Growth & Income)	C+	C	B-		Y	10,000,000

★ Expanded analysis of this fund is included in Section II.

Min Additional Investment	TOTAL RETURNS 3-Month Total Return	6-Month Total Return	1-Year Total Return	3-Year Total Return	5-Year Total Return	PERFORMANCE Dividend Yield (TTM)	Expense Ratio	3-Yr Std Deviation	3-Year Beta	ASSETS NAV	Total Assets (MIL)	ASSET ALLOCATION & TURNOVER %Cash	%Stocks	%Bonds	%Other	Turnover Ratio	BULL & BEAR Last Bull Market Total Return	Last Bear Market Total Return	FEES Front End Fee (%)	Back End Fee (%)	Inception Date
50	1.74	6.74	-5.01	10.77	-1.52		2.78	8.45	0.67	5.85	14.1	22	42	33	2	153	15.12	-20.51	4.75		Mar-19
50	1.55	6.35	-5.70	8.33	-5.12		3.53	8.43	0.66	5.84	14.1	22	42	33	2	153	14.62	-20.76		1.00	Mar-19
	1.73	6.99	-4.87	9.93	-0.23		2.53	8.42	0.66	5.85	14.1	22	42	33	2	153	15.28	-20.44			Mar-19
50	4.52	9.91	-2.26	12.93	2.49	0	2.54	8.33	0.61	6.01	14.1	22	42	33	2	153	15.28	-20.43			Apr-96
250	-2.77	-3.34	-4.97	-8.10	1.04	2.42	1.4	4.91	-0.25	8.79	6.1	5	95	0	0	7			5.75		Dec-12
250	-2.86	-3.73	-5.65	-10.07	-2.63	1.76	2.15	4.85	-0.24	8.7	6.1	5	95	0	0	7				1.00	Aug-15
	-2.65	-3.15	-4.65	-7.40	2.41	2.68	1.15	4.87	-0.25	8.77	6.1	5	95	0	0	7					Feb-13
250	1.77	8.21	5.68	33.24	23.63	0.4	2	9.1	1.11	13.98	100.3	15	50	34	0	335	6.68	-12.21	5.75		Sep-06
250	1.62	7.78	4.91	30.17	18.93	0.37	2.74	9.07	1.11	12.93	100.3	15	50	34	0	335	6.29	-12.53		1.00	Oct-09
	1.82	8.29	5.89	34.07	24.94	0.4	1.77	9.08	1.11	14.26	100.3	15	50	34	0	335	6.85	-12.18			May-10
250	0.77	8.74	0.39	28.32	28.61	0.27	1.77	9.76	0.97	12.07	546.0	18	67	12	3	82	20.22	-15.62	5.75		Apr-13
250	0.57	8.27	-0.41	25.37	23.93	0.22	2.52	9.78	0.98	11.56	546.0	18	67	12	3	82	19.7	-15.88		1.00	Apr-13
	0.86	8.83	0.65	29.32	30.32	0.28	1.52	9.78	0.98	12.23	546.0	18	67	12	3	82	20.4	-15.53			Apr-04
250	0.02	0.97	-1.96	2.03	4.94	1.58	1.71	4.46	0.71	10.53	64.4	3	50	46	0	55			5.75		Apr-12
250	-0.13	0.63	-2.64	-0.28	1.04	1.14	2.46	4.44	0.72	10.3	64.4	3	50	46	0	55				1.00	Apr-12
	0.04	1.05	-1.73	2.74	6.18	1.81	1.46	4.44	0.7	10.56	64.4	3	50	46	0	55					Apr-12
50	5.93	15.22	12.53	27.74	38.15	3.74	0.13	7.06	0.54	71.38	2,037	2	67	31	0	5	11.71	-9.09			Mar-68
50	4.57	17.07	12.69	37.54	49.22	2.47	0.12	10.85	0.85	83.44	5,231	1	99	0	0	0	19.37	-17.29			Mar-68
	2.42	-3.55	-0.09			1.88	0.75				2.3	7	93	0	0	37					Sep-16
	-0.16	5.99	2.90	22.13	-4.78	4.44	1.45	10.1	0.68	6.19	56.9	3	97	0	0	51	18.62	-27.77	5.25		Jul-14
	-0.16	5.77	2.83	22.60	-3.91	4.67	1.2	10.06	0.67	6.23	56.9	3	97	0	0	51	18.62	-27.77			Jul-14
	-0.15	5.91	3.12	23.01	-3.23	4.66	1	10.09	0.67	6.27	56.9	3	97	0	0	51	18.62	-27.77			Jul-14
100	-0.15	5.93	2.96	22.27	-4.27	4.37	1.25	10.08	0.67	6.25	56.9	3	97	0	0	51	18.62	-27.77			Mar-94
	2.37	13.25	7.52	31.01		3.96	0.95	9.01	0.74	12.05	2.3	1	99	0	0	64					Feb-16
	2.61	12.01	8.38	33.83		6.07	0	8.94	0.73	11	5.0	1	99	0	0	47					Feb-16
	-1.90	3.79	5.71			1.64	0.85				4.0	1	99	0	0	50					Feb-16
	0.60	10.82	1.05	35.81		2.06	0.17	13.88	1	13.21	688.4	5	95	0	0	7					Dec-15
	4.21	19.41	10.12	49.87	64.19	1.64	0.17	12.19	1	23.25	1,077	2	98	0	0	8	25.07	-16.4			Apr-01
	4.16	19.36	10.04	48.92	62.26	1.53	0.47	12.16	1	23.24	1,077	2	98	0	0	8	25	-16.44	5.25		Sep-14
	4.20	19.45	10.30	49.99	64.22	1.74	0.22	12.17	1	23.27	1,077	2	98	0	0	8	25.07	-16.4			Sep-14
	4.20	19.51	10.28	50.51	65.33	1.76	0.02	12.19	1	23.27	1,077	2	98	0	0	8	25.07	-16.4			Sep-14
	4.08	19.11	9.65	47.85	60.53	1.26	0.62	12.19	1	23.18	1,077	2	98	0	0	8	24.7	-16.6			Jun-05
	4.17	19.33	9.98	49.40	63.36	1.55	0.27	12.17	1	23.21	1,077	2	98	0	0	8	24.99	-16.5			Mar-03
	4.26	19.53	10.33	50.61		1.8	0.02	12.19	1	13.95	2,020	3	97	0	0	8					Aug-14
	-9.95	-14.75	-15.89			1.81	0.75				0.98	1	99	0	0	70					Sep-16
	3.00	13.87	1.13	30.61		2.25	0.52	11.36	0.99	9.6	326.3	3	97	0	0	4			5.25		Sep-14
	2.89	13.86	1.26	31.44		2.37	0.27	11.37	0.99	9.61	326.3	3	97	0	0	4					Sep-14
	3.10	14.09	1.44	32.04		2.61	0.07	11.38	0.99	9.63	326.3	3	97	0	0	4					Sep-14
	3.21	14.23	1.59	32.36		2.64	0.06	11.36	0.99	10.27	1,359	4	96	0	0	4					Sep-14
	3.47	15.37	4.68	40.19		4.87	0.2	9.56	0.98	10.13	3,456	45	55	0	0	14					May-15
	5.84	19.20	3.41	29.34	12.21	2.38	0.55	11.9	1.04	13.41	87.3	1	99	0	0	24	16.31	-25.76			Nov-97
	5.77	19.05	3.18	28.47	10.88	1.94	0.8	11.88	1.04	13.37	87.3	1	99	0	0	24	16.1	-25.86			Jan-01
	6.06	22.71	12.45	64.00	79.63	0.65	0.38	13.66	1.05	15.56	209.5	4	96	0	0	21	28.91	-16.75			Oct-99
	6.08	22.63	12.25	62.82	77.44	0.39	0.63	13.64	1.05	15.33	209.5	4	96	0	0	21	28.7	-16.78			Jan-01
	3.23	19.22	-1.19	43.65	43.58	0.21	0.88	16.43	0.95	17.24	1,315	5	95	0	0	38	28.78	-21.71			Aug-98
	3.17	19.07	-1.42	42.64	41.81	0.08	1.13	16.45	0.95	17.23	1,315	5	95	0	0	38	28.55	-21.73			Sep-05
	5.60	20.68	12.24	53.60	59.04	1.33	0.37	12.28	1	12.25	418.4	2	98	0	0	48	26.16	-18.65			Nov-97
	5.48	20.54	11.98	52.44	56.96	1.01	0.62	12.22	0.99	13.26	418.4	2	98	0	0	48	25.87	-18.66			Jan-01
	0.45	9.31	-7.95			2.07	0.75			8.8	1.8	2	98	0	0	63					Jul-16
	3.05	20.42	2.15	46.58		1.2	0.5	15.16	1	12.5	94.0	2	98	0	0	22			5.25		Oct-15
	3.13	20.61	2.38	47.68		1.39	0.25	15.14	1	12.52	94.0	2	98	0	0	22					Oct-15
	3.21	20.59	2.50	47.85		1.42	0.05	15.17	1	12.53	94.0	2	98	0	0	22					Aug-15

	MARKET			FUND TYPE, CATEGORY & OBJECTIVE	RATINGS				MINIMUMS	
Fund Name	Ticker Symbol	Traded On	Fund Type	Category and (Prospectus Objective)	Overall Rating	Reward Rating	Risk Rating	Recent Up/ Downgrade	Open to New Investors	Min Initial Investment
State Street Small/Mid Cap Equity Index Portfolio	SSMHX	NAS CM	Open End	US Equity Small Cap (Growth & Income)	C+	C	B-		Y	0
State Street Target Retirement 2015 Fund Class I	SSBFX	NAS CM	Open End	Target Date (Asset Alloc)	B	C+	A-		Y	1,000,000
State Street Target Retirement 2015 Fund Class K	SSBHX	NAS CM	Open End	Target Date (Asset Alloc)	B	C+	A		Y	10,000,000
State Street Target Retirement 2020 Fund Class I	SSBNX	NAS CM	Open End	Target Date (Asset Alloc)	B	C+	A		Y	1,000,000
State Street Target Retirement 2020 Fund Class K	SSBOX	NAS CM	Open End	Target Date (Asset Alloc)	B	C+	A		Y	10,000,000
State Street Target Retirement 2025 Fund Class I	SSBRX	NAS CM	Open End	Target Date (Asset Alloc)	B	C+	A-	Up	Y	1,000,000
State Street Target Retirement 2025 Fund Class K	SSBSX	NAS CM	Open End	Target Date (Asset Alloc)	B	C+	A-	Up	Y	10,000,000
State Street Target Retirement 2030 Fund Class I	SSBWX	NAS CM	Open End	Target Date (Asset Alloc)	B-	C	B+		Y	1,000,000
State Street Target Retirement 2030 Fund Class K	SSBYX	NAS CM	Open End	Target Date (Asset Alloc)	B-	C	B+	Up	Y	10,000,000
State Street Target Retirement 2035 Fund Class I	SSCJX	NAS CM	Open End	Target Date (Asset Alloc)	B-	C	B+	Up	Y	1,000,000
State Street Target Retirement 2035 Fund Class K	SSCKX	NAS CM	Open End	Target Date (Asset Alloc)	B-	C	B+	Up	Y	10,000,000
State Street Target Retirement 2040 Fund Class I	SSCNX	NAS CM	Open End	Target Date (Asset Alloc)	B-	C	B+	Up	Y	1,000,000
State Street Target Retirement 2040 Fund Class K	SSCQX	NAS CM	Open End	Target Date (Asset Alloc)	B-	C	B+	Up	Y	10,000,000
State Street Target Retirement 2045 Fund Class I	SSDDX	NAS CM	Open End	Target Date (Asset Alloc)	B-	C	B	Up	Y	1,000,000
State Street Target Retirement 2045 Fund Class K	SSDEX	NAS CM	Open End	Target Date (Asset Alloc)	B-	C	B	Up	Y	10,000,000
State Street Target Retirement 2050 Fund Class I	SSDJX	NAS CM	Open End	Target Date (Asset Alloc)	B-	C	B	Up	Y	1,000,000
State Street Target Retirement 2050 Fund Class K	SSDLX	NAS CM	Open End	Target Date (Asset Alloc)	B-	C	B	Up	Y	10,000,000
State Street Target Retirement 2055 Fund Class I	SSDOX	NAS CM	Open End	Target Date (Asset Alloc)	B-	C	B	Up	Y	1,000,000
State Street Target Retirement 2055 Fund Class K	SSDQX	NAS CM	Open End	Target Date (Asset Alloc)	B-	C	B	Up	Y	10,000,000
State Street Target Retirement 2060 Fund Class I	SSDWX	NAS CM	Open End	Target Date (Asset Alloc)	B-	C	B	Up	Y	1,000,000
State Street Target Retirement 2060 Fund Class K	SSDYX	NAS CM	Open End	Target Date (Asset Alloc)	B-	C	B	Up	Y	10,000,000
State Street Target Retirement Fund Class I	SSFNX	NAS CM	Open End	Target Date (Asset Alloc)	B	C+	A-		Y	1,000,000
State Street Target Retirement Fund Class K	SSFOX	NAS CM	Open End	Target Date (Asset Alloc)	B	C+	A-		Y	10,000,000
State Street U.S. Value Spotlight Fund Class K	SIEKX	NAS CM	Open End	US Equity Large Cap Value (Growth)	C	C-	C		Y	10,000,000
Steben Managed Futures Strategy Fund Class A	SKLAX	NAS CM	Open End	Alternative Miscellaneous (Income)	C-	D+	C	Up	Y	2,500
Steben Managed Futures Strategy Fund Class C	SKLCX	NAS CM	Open End	Alternative Miscellaneous (Income)	D+	D	C	Up	Y	2,500
Steben Managed Futures Strategy Fund Class I	SKLIX	NAS CM	Open End	Alternative Miscellaneous (Income)	C-	C-	C	Up	Y	1,000,000
Steben Managed Futures Strategy Fund Class N	SKLNX	NAS CM	Open End	Alternative Miscellaneous (Income)	C-	D+	C	Up	Y	2,500
Sterling Capital Behavioral International Equity Cls A	SBIAX	NAS CM	Open End	Global Equity Large Cap (Foreign Stock)	C	C-	C		Y	1,000
Sterling Capital Behavioral International Equity Cls C	SBIDX	NAS CM	Open End	Global Equity Large Cap (Foreign Stock)	C-	C-	C		Y	1,000
Sterling Capital Behavioral International Equity Cls R6	STRCX	NAS CM	Open End	Global Equity Large Cap (Foreign Stock)	C	C-	C		Y	0
Sterling Capital Behavioral Intl Equity Inst Shares	SBIIX	NAS CM	Open End	Global Equity Large Cap (Foreign Stock)	C	C-	C		Y	1,000,000
Sterling Capital Behavioral Large Cap Value Equity Fund A	BBTGX	NAS CM	Open End	US Equity Large Cap Value (Growth & Income)	C	C	C+		Y	1,000
Sterling Capital Behavioral Large Cap Value Equity Fund C	BCVCX	NAS CM	Open End	US Equity Large Cap Value (Growth & Income)	C	C	C+		Y	1,000
Sterling Capital Behavioral Large Cap Value Equity Cls R6	STRAX	NAS CM	Open End	US Equity Large Cap Value (Growth & Income)	C	C	C+		Y	0
Sterling Capital Behavioral Large Cap Value Equity Inst	BBISX	NAS CM	Open End	US Equity Large Cap Value (Growth & Income)	C	C	C+		Y	1,000,000
Sterling Capital Behavioral Small Cap Value Equity Cls A	SPSAX	NAS CM	Open End	US Equity Small Cap (Small Company)	C-	C-	C	Down	Y	1,000
Sterling Capital Behavioral Small Cap Value Equity Cls C	SPSDX	NAS CM	Open End	US Equity Small Cap (Small Company)	C-	D+	C		Y	1,000
Sterling Capital Behavioral Small Cap Value Equity Cls R	SPSRX	NAS CM	Open End	US Equity Small Cap (Small Company)	C-	C-	C	Down	Y	1,000
Sterling Capital Behavioral Small Cap Value Equity Cls R6	STRBX	NAS CM	Open End	US Equity Small Cap (Small Company)	C-	C-	C	Down	Y	0
Sterling Capital Behavioral Small Cap Value Eq Inst Shares	SPSCX	NAS CM	Open End	US Equity Small Cap (Small Company)	C-	C-	C	Down	Y	1,000,000
Sterling Capital Diversified Income Fund Class A	BCGAX	NAS CM	Open End	Cautious Alloc (Asset Alloc)	C+	C	B		Y	1,000
Sterling Capital Diversified Income Fund Class C	BCCCX	NAS CM	Open End	Cautious Alloc (Asset Alloc)	C+	C	B	Up	Y	1,000
Sterling Capital Diversified Income Institutional Shares	BMGTX	NAS CM	Open End	Cautious Alloc (Asset Alloc)	C+	C	B		Y	1,000,000
Sterling Capital Equity Income Fund Class A	BAEIX	NAS CM	Open End	US Equity Large Cap Value (Equity-Income)	B-	C+	B+	Down	Y	1,000
Sterling Capital Equity Income Fund Class C	BCEGX	NAS CM	Open End	US Equity Large Cap Value (Equity-Income)	B-	C	B+	Down	Y	1,000
Sterling Capital Equity Income Fund Class R	BAERX	NAS CM	Open End	US Equity Large Cap Value (Equity-Income)	B-	C+	B+	Down	Y	1,000
Sterling Capital Equity Income Fund Class R6	STREX	NAS CM	Open End	US Equity Large Cap Value (Equity-Income)	B	C+	B+		Y	0
Sterling Capital Equity Income Fund Institutional Shares	BEGIX	NAS CM	Open End	US Equity Large Cap Value (Equity-Income)	B	C+	B+		Y	1,000,000
Sterling Capital Mid Value Fund Class A	OVEAX	NAS CM	Open End	US Equity Mid Cap (Growth)	C	C	C+		Y	1,000
Sterling Capital Mid Value Fund Class C	OVECX	NAS CM	Open End	US Equity Mid Cap (Growth)	C	C-	C+		Y	1,000
Sterling Capital Mid Value Fund Class R	OVERX	NAS CM	Open End	US Equity Mid Cap (Growth)	C	C	C+		Y	1,000

★ Expanded analysis of this fund is included in Section II.

	TOTAL RETURNS					PERFORMANCE				ASSETS		ASSET ALLOCATION & TURNOVER					BULL & BEAR		FEES		
Min Additional Investment	3-Month Total Return	6-Month Total Return	1-Year Total Return	3-Year Total Return	5-Year Total Return	Dividend Yield (TTM)	Expense Ratio	3-Yr Std Deviation	3-Year Beta	NAV	Total Assets (MIL)	%Cash	%Stocks	%Bonds	%Other	Turnover Ratio	Last Bull Market Total Return	Last Bear Market Total Return	Front End Fee (%)	Back End Fee (%)	Inception Date
	3.18	20.64	2.47	48.01		1.45	0.03	15.17	1	12.33	355.0	2	98	0	0	22					Aug-15
	2.71	10.01	6.62	20.58		2.53	0.29	4.75	0.36	10.98	278.9	2	37	61	0	29					Sep-14
	2.80	10.01	6.65	20.65		2.56	0.09	4.72	0.35	10.98	278.9	2	37	61	0	29					Sep-14
	3.05	12.01	7.00	25.50		2.44	0.29	6.11	0.47	11.47	976.0	2	49	49	0	22					Sep-14
	3.14	12.00	7.11	25.68		2.45	0.09	6.15	0.47	11.48	976.0	2	49	49	0	22					Sep-14
	3.46	13.93	7.26	30.53		2.36	0.29	7.53	0.58	11.94	1,228	2	61	37	0	15					Sep-14
	3.55	13.90	7.26	30.66		2.37	0.09	7.48	0.58	11.96	1,228	2	61	37	0	15					Sep-14
	3.74	14.98	7.20	33.16		2.2	0.29	8.38	0.66	12.2	1,199	2	70	28	0	12					Sep-14
	3.73	14.95	7.28	33.33		2.21	0.09	8.34	0.65	12.22	1,199	2	70	28	0	12					Sep-14
	3.75	15.64	6.91	35.39		2.07	0.29	9.06	0.71	12.42	997.0	2	77	21	0	13					Sep-14
	3.75	15.70	6.99	35.59		2.07	0.09	9.06	0.71	12.45	997.0	2	77	21	0	13					Sep-14
	3.82	16.32	6.68	37.32		2.03	0.29	9.67	0.76	12.47	814.6	2	82	15	0	11					Sep-14
	3.82	16.30	6.70	37.37		2.05	0.09	9.7	0.77	12.48	814.6	2	82	15	0	11					Sep-14
	3.81	16.91	6.38	38.83		2.01	0.29	10.25	0.81	12.51	616.2	2	87	11	0	11					Sep-14
	3.81	16.91	6.40	38.91		2.02	0.09	10.26	0.81	12.51	616.2	2	87	11	0	11					Sep-14
	3.83	16.91	6.27	38.69		2.03	0.29	10.34	0.82	12.44	414.4	2	88	9	0	11					Sep-14
	3.75	16.91	6.29	38.73		2.04	0.09	10.4	0.82	12.44	414.4	2	88	9	0	11					Sep-14
	3.75	16.93	6.26	39.09		1.99	0.29	10.33	0.82	12.43	202.3	2	88	9	0	16					Sep-14
	3.76	16.96	6.27	38.98		1.99	0.09	10.32	0.82	12.41	202.3	2	88	9	0	16					Sep-14
	3.81	17.02	6.43	38.73		1.93	0.29	10.31	0.82	11.96	46.3	2	88	9	0	38					Sep-14
	3.90	17.02	6.43	38.80		1.93	0.09	10.34	0.82	11.96	46.3	2	88	9	0	38					Sep-14
	2.71	9.60	6.64	18.13		2.58	0.29	4.34	0.43	10.95	229.2	2	35	63	0	53					Sep-14
	2.72	9.62	6.66	17.96		2.58	0.09	4.35	0.44	10.93	229.2	2	35	63	0	53					Sep-14
	-2.64	-2.80	-1.52			1.09	0.65				1.1	9	91	0	0	50					Sep-16
100	2.87	2.14	2.69	-2.04	7.98	0	2.24	8.95	42.32	8.9745	68.2	22	0	65	13	19			5.75		Apr-14
100	2.68	1.76	1.92	-4.26	3.96	0	2.99	8.93	42.43	8.6084	68.2	22	0	65	13	19				1.00	Apr-14
25,000	2.93	2.27	2.94	-1.34	9.28	0	1.99	8.92	42.48	9.0911	68.2	22	0	65	13	19					Apr-14
100	2.87	2.14	2.69	-2.08	7.96	0	2.24	8.89	41.83	8.9715	68.2	22	0	65	13	19					Apr-14
0	1.03	9.79	-6.28	25.19		2.82	0.9	11.87	1.03	9.75	76.9	2	98	0	0	97			5.75		Nov-14
0	0.83	9.39	-6.97	22.40		2.22	1.65	11.87	1.03	9.66	76.9	2	98	0	0	97				1.00	Nov-14
	1.03	9.92	-6.05	25.94		3.12	0.6	11.85	1.03	9.75	76.9	2	98	0	0	97					Feb-18
0	1.03	9.92	-6.09	26.00		3.08	0.65	11.87	1.03	9.75	76.9	2	98	0	0	97					Nov-14
0	1.88	11.61	0.15	30.33	33.72	1.81	0.88	12.5	1	19.11	277.5	1	99	0	0	128	24.14	-19.93	5.75		Oct-92
0	1.70	11.20	-0.56	27.49	28.82	1.12	1.63	12.51	1	18.51	277.5	1	99	0	0	128	23.66	-20.21		1.00	Feb-01
	1.95	11.81	0.51	31.48	35.48	2.08	0.58	12.49	1	19.24	277.5	1	99	0	0	128	24.37	-19.87			Feb-18
0	1.93	11.79	0.41	31.33	35.32	2.03	0.63	12.49	1	19.23	277.5	1	99	0	0	128	24.37	-19.87			Oct-92
0	0.34	13.49	-9.16	26.77	22.77	0.95	1.05	17.31	0.99	14.72	209.1	1	99	0	0	128	23.73	-25.63	5.75		Feb-10
0	0.14	13.01	-9.84	23.85	18.15	0.29	1.8	17.28	0.99	14.07	209.1	1	99	0	0	128	23.18	-25.86		1.00	Feb-10
0	0.27	13.27	-9.43	25.81	21.00	0.82	1.3	17.3	0.99	14.59	209.1	1	99	0	0	128	24.01	-25.53			Feb-10
	0.40	13.59	-8.92	27.84	24.35	1.23	0.74	17.32	0.99	14.87	209.1	1	99	0	0	128	23.96	-25.53			Feb-18
0	0.40	13.60	-8.92	27.72	24.23	1.19	0.8	17.29	0.99	14.86	209.1	1	99	0	0	128	23.96	-25.53			Jan-97
0	1.50	7.47	3.29	10.88	15.90	4.76	1.44	4.81		10.36	17.1	7	36	54	0	48	10.21	-8.59	5.75		Jan-98
0	1.22	6.96	2.43	8.34	11.58	4.04	2.19	4.82		10.26	17.1	7	36	54	0	48	9.77	-8.89		1.00	Feb-01
0	1.54	7.53	3.50	11.59	17.32	4.95	1.19	4.79		10.49	17.1	7	36	54	0	48	10.35	-8.5			Oct-97
0	4.11	15.79	13.26	51.53	51.48	1.71	1.02	12.32	0.96	20.81	1,774	2	98	0	0	19	19.39	-10.26	5.75		Jun-04
0	3.96	15.34	12.47	48.21	45.90	1.01	1.77	12.3	0.96	20.6	1,774	2	98	0	0	19	18.89	-10.54		1.00	Jun-04
0	4.08	15.60	12.98	50.44	49.58	1.49	1.27	12.3	0.96	20.64	1,774	2	98	0	0	19	19.27	-10.3			Feb-10
	4.25	15.98	13.68	52.96	53.61	2.02	0.66	12.28	0.96	20.88	1,774	2	98	0	0	19	19.65	-10.19			Feb-18
0	4.22	15.92	13.61	52.75	53.40	1.93	0.77	12.32	0.96	20.88	1,774	2	98	0	0	19	19.65	-10.19			Jun-04
0	4.15	20.00	-3.22	29.51	28.16	0	1.18	17	1.25	16.8	451.2	2	98	0	0	35	26.25	-23.71	5.75		Aug-96
0	3.99	19.60	-3.91	26.67	23.45	0	1.93	17.03	1.25	14.58	451.2	2	98	0	0	35	25.77	-23.97		1.00	Jul-01
0	4.12	19.89	-3.39	28.66	26.52	0	1.43	17.03	1.25	16.15	451.2	2	98	0	0	35	26.05	-23.75			Feb-10

	MARKET			FUND TYPE, CATEGORY & OBJECTIVE	RATINGS				MINIMUMS	
Fund Name	Ticker Symbol	Traded On	Fund Type	Category and (Prospectus Objective)	Overall Rating	Reward Rating	Risk Rating	Recent Up/ Downgrade	Open to New Investors	Min Initial Investment
Sterling Capital Mid Value Fund Class R6	STRMX	NAS CM	Open End	US Equity Mid Cap (Growth)	C	C	C+		Y	0
Sterling Capital Mid Value Fund Institutional Shares	OVEIX	NAS CM	Open End	US Equity Mid Cap (Growth)	C	C	C+		Y	1,000,000
Sterling Capital SMID Opportunities Fund A Shares	SMDPX	NAS CM	Open End	US Equity Mid Cap (Growth)	C	C	B-	Down	Y	1,000
Sterling Capital SMID Opportunities Fund C Shares	SMDQX	NAS CM	Open End	US Equity Mid Cap (Growth)	C	C	C+	Down	Y	1,000
Sterling Capital SMID Opportunities Institutional Shares	SMDOX	NAS CM	Open End	US Equity Mid Cap (Growth)	C	C	B-	Down	Y	1,000,000
Sterling Capital Special Opportunities Fund Class A	BOPAX	NAS CM	Open End	US Equity Large Cap Growth (Growth)	B-	C	B		Y	1,000
Sterling Capital Special Opportunities Fund Class C	BOPCX	NAS CM	Open End	US Equity Large Cap Growth (Growth)	B-	C	B		Y	1,000
Sterling Capital Special Opportunities Fund Class R	BOPRX	NAS CM	Open End	US Equity Large Cap Growth (Growth)	B-	C	B		Y	1,000
Sterling Capital Special Opportunities Fund Class R6	STRSX	NAS CM	Open End	US Equity Large Cap Growth (Growth)	B-	C	B		Y	0
Sterling Capital Special Opp Inst Shares	BOPIX	NAS CM	Open End	US Equity Large Cap Growth (Growth)	B-	C	B		Y	1,000,000
Sterling Capital Strategic Allocation Balanced Cls A	BAMGX	NAS CM	Open End	Moderate Alloc (Balanced)	B-	C	A-	Up	Y	1,000
Sterling Capital Strategic Allocation Balanced Cls C	BCMCX	NAS CM	Open End	Moderate Alloc (Balanced)	B-	C	B+	Up	Y	1,000
Sterling Capital Strategic Allocation Balanced Inst Shares	BCGTX	NAS CM	Open End	Moderate Alloc (Balanced)	B-	C	A-	Up	Y	1,000,000
Sterling Capital Strategic Allocation Growth Fund Class A	BCMAX	NAS CM	Open End	Aggressive Alloc (Asset Alloc)	B-	C	B+	Up	Y	1,000
Sterling Capital Strategic Allocation Growth Fund Class C	BCGCX	NAS CM	Open End	Aggressive Alloc (Asset Alloc)	B-	C	B+	Up	Y	1,000
Sterling Capital Strategic Allocation Growth Inst Shares	BCMTX	NAS CM	Open End	Aggressive Alloc (Asset Alloc)	B-	C	B+	Up	Y	1,000,000
Sterling Capital Stratton Mid Cap Value Fund A Shares	STRLX	NAS CM	Open End	US Equity Mid Cap (Growth)	C+	C	B-	Up	Y	1,000
Sterling Capital Stratton Mid Cap Value Fund C Shares	STRNX	NAS CM	Open End	US Equity Mid Cap (Growth)	C	C	B-		Y	1,000
Sterling Capital Stratton Mid Cap Value Inst Shares	STRGX	NAS CM	Open End	US Equity Mid Cap (Growth)	C+	C	B-	Up	Y	1,000,000
Sterling Capital Stratton Real Estate Fund A Shares	STMMX	NAS CM	Open End	Real Estate Sector Equity (Real Estate)	C+	C+	B	Down	Y	1,000
Sterling Capital Stratton Real Estate Fund C Shares	STMOX	NAS CM	Open End	Real Estate Sector Equity (Real Estate)	C+	C	B-	Down	Y	1,000
Sterling Capital Stratton Real Estate Institutional Shares	STMDX	NAS CM	Open End	Real Estate Sector Equity (Real Estate)	B-	C+	B		Y	1,000,000
Sterling Capital Stratton Small Cap Value Fund A Shares	STSNX	NAS CM	Open End	US Equity Small Cap (Small Company)	C	C	C+		Y	1,000
Sterling Capital Stratton Small Cap Value Fund C Shares	STSOX	NAS CM	Open End	US Equity Small Cap (Small Company)	C	C	C+		Y	1,000
Sterling Capital Stratton Small Cap Value Inst Shares	STSCX	NAS CM	Open End	US Equity Small Cap (Small Company)	C	C	C+		Y	1,000,000
Stock Dividend Fund	SDIVX	NAS CM	Open End	US Equity Large Cap Value (Equity-Income)	C	C	B-	Down	Y	100,000
Stone Harbor 500 Plus Fund Institutional Class	SHERX	NAS CM	Open End	US Equity Large Cap Blend (Growth & Income)	C	C	B		Y	1,000,000
Stone Ridge Elements U.S. Portfolio	ELUSX	NAS CM	Open End	US Equity Large Cap Blend (Growth)	U	U	U		Y	0
Stone Ridge Elements U.S. Small Cap Portfolio	ELSMX	NAS CM	Open End	US Equity Small Cap (Small Company)	U	U	U		Y	0
Stralem Equity Fund	STEFX	NAS CM	Open End	US Equity Large Cap Blend (Growth)	B-	C	B+		Y	25,000
Strategic Advisers Fidelity Emerging Markets Fund	FGOMX	NAS CM	Open End	Global Emerg Mkts (Div Emerging Mkts)	U	U	U		Y	0
Strategic Advisers® Core Fund	FCSAX	NAS CM	Open End	US Equity Large Cap Blend (Growth)	B-	C	B		Y	0
Strategic Advisers® Emerging Markets Fund	FSAMX	NAS CM	Open End	Global Emerg Mkts (Div Emerging Mkts)	C	C	C+		Y	0
Strategic Advisers® Fidelity U.S. Total Stock Fund	FCTDX	NAS CM	Open End	US Equity Large Cap Blend (Growth)	D	D+	C+		Y	0
Strategic Advisers® Fidelity® International Fund	FUSIX	NAS CM	Open End	Global Equity Large Cap (Foreign Stock)	C	C	B		Y	0
Strategic Advisers® Growth Fund	FSGFX	NAS CM	Open End	US Equity Large Cap Growth (Growth)	C+	C	B		Y	0
Strategic Advisers® International Fund	FILFX	NAS CM	Open End	Global Equity Large Cap (Foreign Stock)	C	C	B		Y	0
Strategic Advisers® Small-Mid Cap Fund	FSCFX	NAS CM	Open End	US Equity Small Cap (Growth)	C+	C	C+	Up	Y	0
Strategic Advisers® Value Fund	FVSAX	NAS CM	Open End	US Equity Large Cap Value (Growth)	B-	C	B	Up	Y	0
Stringer Growth Fund Class A Shares	SRGAX	NAS CM	Open End	Aggressive Alloc (Growth)	C+	C	B	Up	Y	5,000
Stringer Growth Fund Class C Shares	SRGCX	NAS CM	Open End	Aggressive Alloc (Growth)	C+	C	B	Up	Y	5,000
Stringer Growth Fund Institutional Class Shares	SRGIX	NAS CM	Open End	Aggressive Alloc (Growth)	C+	C	B	Up	Y	1,000,000
Superfund Managed Futures Strategy Fund Class A	SUPRX	NAS CM	Open End	Alternative Miscellaneous (Growth & Income)	C+	C+	C+	Up	Y	2,500
Superfund Managed Futures Strategy Fund Class I	SUPIX	NAS CM	Open End	Alternative Miscellaneous (Growth & Income)	C+	C+	C+	Up	Y	100,000
Swan Defined Risk Emerging Markets Fund Class A	SDFAX	NAS CM	Open End	Long/Short Equity (Growth & Income)	C	C-	C+		Y	2,500
Swan Defined Risk Emerging Markets Fund Class C	SDFCX	NAS CM	Open End	Long/Short Equity (Growth & Income)	C	C-	C		Y	2,500
Swan Defined Risk Emerging Markets Fund Class I	SDFIX	NAS CM	Open End	Long/Short Equity (Growth & Income)	C	C-	C+		Y	100,000
Swan Defined Risk Emerging Markets Fund Class Y Shares	SDFYX	NAS CM	Open End	Long/Short Equity (Growth & Income)	C	C-	C+		Y	25,000,000
Swan Defined Risk Foreign Developed Fund Class A	SDJAX	NAS CM	Open End	Long/Short Equity (Foreign Stock)	C	C-	C+	Up	Y	2,500
Swan Defined Risk Foreign Developed Fund Class C	SDJCX	NAS CM	Open End	Long/Short Equity (Foreign Stock)	C-	D+	C		Y	2,500
Swan Defined Risk Foreign Developed Fund Class I	SDJIX	NAS CM	Open End	Long/Short Equity (Foreign Stock)	C	C-	C+	Up	Y	100,000
Swan Defined Risk Foreign Developed Fund Class Y Shares	SDJYX	NAS CM	Open End	Long/Short Equity (Foreign Stock)	C	C-	C+	Up	Y	25,000,000

★ Expanded analysis of this fund is included in Section II.

	TOTAL RETURNS					PERFORMANCE				ASSETS		ASSET ALLOCATION & TURNOVER					BULL & BEAR		FEES		
Min Additional Investment	3-Month Total Return	6-Month Total Return	1-Year Total Return	3-Year Total Return	5-Year Total Return	Dividend Yield (TTM)	Expense Ratio	3-Yr Std Deviation	3-Year Beta	NAV	Total Assets (MIL)	%Cash	%Stocks	%Bonds	%Other	Turnover Ratio	Last Bull Market Total Return	Last Bear Market Total Return	Front End Fee (%)	Back End Fee (%)	Inception Date
	4.25	20.25	-2.82	30.77	29.97	0.14	0.82	17.03	1.25	17.16	451.2	2	98	0	0	35	26.52	-23.66			Feb-18
0	4.25	20.18	-2.90	30.59	29.80	0.07	0.93	17.02	1.25	17.15	451.2	2	98	0	0	35	26.52	-23.66			Aug-96
0	8.52	26.36	12.56			0	1.05			12.99	9.4	2	98	0	0	46			5.75		Sep-16
0	8.39	25.91	11.71			0	1.8			12.78	9.4	2	98	0	0	46				1.00	Sep-16
0	8.56	26.45	12.79			0	0.8			13.05	9.4	2	98	0	0	46					Sep-16
0	2.60	18.52	8.26	41.10	54.42	0	1.11	13.13	1.01	24.44	1,067	0	100	0	0	23	21.66	-18.05	5.75		Jun-03
0	2.41	18.07	7.45	37.95	48.74	0	1.86	13.1	1.01	19.92	1,067	0	100	0	0	23	21.17	-18.31		1.00	Jun-03
0	2.53	18.38	8.00	39.99	52.53	0	1.36	13.11	1.01	24.66	1,067	0	100	0	0	23	21.51	-18.12			Feb-10
	2.69	18.72	8.62	42.29	56.58	0.06	0.77	13.15	1.01	25.87	1,067	0	100	0	0	23	21.81	-17.93			Feb-18
0	2.66	18.68	8.56	42.16	56.44	0.02	0.86	13.13	1.01	25.85	1,067	0	100	0	0	23	21.81	-17.93			Jun-03
0	2.68	10.72	3.99	23.78	22.88	2.12	1.13	7.08		12.05	26.7	2	60	38	0	14	14.06	-15.09	5.75		Jan-98
0	2.46	10.31	3.17	20.98	18.34	1.4	1.88	7.05		11.81	26.7	2	60	38	0	14	13.49	-15.33		1.00	Feb-01
0	2.63	10.84	4.22	24.70	24.43	2.35	0.88	7.05		12.14	26.7	2	60	38	0	14	14.11	-14.9			Oct-97
0	2.39	11.72	3.26	28.05	24.61	1.91	1.23	8.65		12.08	21.6	3	74	22	0	18	16.71	-18.65	5.75		Jan-98
0	2.22	11.28	2.57	25.16	19.97	1.29	1.98	8.62		11.62	21.6	3	74	22	0	18	16.24	-18.94		1.00	Feb-01
0	2.54	11.89	3.51	29.01	26.19	2.16	0.98	8.63		12.11	21.6	3	74	22	0	18	16.96	-18.61			Oct-97
0	3.13	17.64	0.76	35.58	32.22	0.22	1.21	13.48	1	62.26	60.9	4	96	0	0	14	24.05	-25.54	5.75		Nov-15
0	2.92	17.24	0.05	32.61	27.43	0	1.96	13.47	1	60.86	60.9	4	96	0	0	14	23.51	-25.77		1.00	Nov-15
0	3.18	17.77	1.01	36.59	33.87	0.43	0.96	13.49	1	62.48	60.9	4	96	0	0	14	24.23	-25.46			Sep-72
0	1.04	17.31	11.01	16.86	48.72	1.94	1.07	12.63	0.99	39.4	99.1	2	98	0	0	8	28.33	-16.68	5.75		Nov-15
0	0.86	16.86	10.16	14.26	43.32	1.28	1.82	12.62	0.99	39.19	99.1	2	98	0	0	8	27.77	-16.94		1.00	Nov-15
0	1.12	17.46	11.28	17.72	50.61	2.15	0.82	12.62	0.99	39.48	99.1	2	98	0	0	8	28.52	-16.59			May-80
0	2.79	15.59	-2.01	34.26	27.51	0.18	1.27	16.5	0.92	77.66	998.2	4	96	0	0	16	22.99	-21.27	5.75		Nov-15
0	2.58	15.17	-2.75	31.28	22.84	0	2.02	16.49	0.92	75.68	998.2	4	96	0	0	16	22.46	-21.52		1.00	Nov-15
0	2.84	15.74	-1.76	35.26	29.06	0.36	1.02	16.5	0.92	77.99	998.2	4	96	0	0	16	23.17	-21.19			Apr-93
100	-0.64	7.35	-1.83	45.71	29.41	2.45	0.85	13.37	0.94	27.72	28.3	2	97	0	0	29	22.4	-13.54			Dec-04
250,000	4.43	19.27	10.03			2.46	0.63			10.83	2.8	10	-3	94	0	60					Jan-17
	2.50						0.45				614.4										Mar-17
	1.30						0.65				422.8										Mar-17
100	2.15	16.98	10.84	33.23	44.34	1.04	0.97	11.67	0.92	8.54	90.9	4	96	0	0	32	20.23	-11.35			Jan-00
	1.78	13.55					0.67			11.39	2,149	8	88	0	4						Oct-18
	4.11	19.52	8.85	51.09	59.42	1.49	0.39	12.46	1.02	18.49	25,971	2	99	-1	0	98	25.06	-18.78			Dec-09
	1.59	13.03	1.24	34.94	11.41	1.53	0.75	14.03	1	10.53	4,994	9	86	0	5	57	17.83	-24.81			Sep-10
	3.60	18.82	6.12			0.97	0.35			10.35	24,325	2	98	0	0	126					Mar-18
	4.68	16.46	1.84	29.67	18.31	1.38	0.74	11.07	0.98	10.13	7,393	8	92	0	0	9	15.86	-24.58			Mar-07
	3.80	21.45	8.00	59.76	73.24	0.62	0.34	13.65	1.02	18.57	9,998	1	99	0	0	38	26	-17.56			Jun-10
	3.24	14.56	-0.36	29.34	14.34	1.81	0.63	11.21	1	10.32	16,029	4	96	0	0	39	15.67	-22.74			Mar-06
	3.40	20.84	0.49	43.91	39.84	0.65	0.46	15.74	1.01	13.97	8,012	2	98	0	0	82	27.42	-24.07			Jun-05
	3.02	15.54	5.04	40.05	44.73	2.02	0.28	13.06	1.07	19.4	9,966	1	99	0	0	23	24.54	-18.6			Dec-08
250	2.80	14.07	2.93	25.86	24.14	0.69	1.56	10.03	0.87	11.75	30.8	8	86	5	0	68			5.50		Mar-13
250	2.55	13.78	2.29	23.18	19.66	0	2.31	10.01	0.87	11.64	30.8	8	86	5	0	68			1.00	1.00	Mar-13
5,000	2.79	14.17	3.13	26.71	25.60	1.08	1.31	10.01	0.87	11.76	30.8	8	86	5	0	68					Mar-13
500	7.34	18.05	14.30	25.26	16.01	0	0	15.25	62.68	9.35	11.0	88	0	0	12	0			5.75		Dec-13
1,000	7.28	18.16	14.44	25.98	17.35	0	0	15.26	63.04	9.43	11.0	88	0	0	12	0			5.75		Dec-13
500	-0.90	2.92	-1.71	13.47		0.27	2.28	8.45	0.57	9.86	46.1	2	98	0	0	7			5.50		Dec-14
500	-1.13	2.56	-2.43	10.85		0	3.03	8.54	0.58	9.6	46.1	2	98	0	0	7				1.00	Dec-14
500	-0.90	3.01	-1.47	14.16		0.59	2.03	8.53	0.58	9.91	46.1	2	98	0	0	7					Dec-14
500	-0.79	3.32	-1.33	13.92			1.64	8.47	0.57	9.94	46.1	2	98	0	0	7					Dec-18
500	1.38	6.22	-0.91	9.82		0.77	2.16	6.78	0.58	10.24	41.6	3	97	0	0	4			5.50		Dec-15
500	1.20	5.85	-1.68	7.35		0.15	2.91	6.75	0.57	10.12	41.6	3	97	0	0	4				1.00	Dec-15
500	1.48	6.32	-0.70	10.65		1.14	1.91	6.81	0.58	10.25	41.6	3	97	0	0	4					Dec-15
500	1.58	6.53	-0.51	10.86			1.53	6.8	0.58	10.27	41.6	3	97	0	0	4					Dec-18

	MARKET			FUND TYPE, CATEGORY & OBJECTIVE	RATINGS					MINIMUMS
Fund Name	Ticker Symbol	Traded On	Fund Type	Category and (Prospectus Objective)	Overall Rating	Reward Rating	Risk Rating	Recent Up/ Downgrade	Open to New Investors	Min Initial Investment
Swan Defined Risk Fund Class A Shares	SDRAX	NAS CM	Open End	Long/Short Equity (Growth)	C	C	B-		Y	2,500
Swan Defined Risk Fund Class C Shares	SDRCX	NAS CM	Open End	Long/Short Equity (Growth)	C	C	C+		Y	2,500
Swan Defined Risk Fund Class I Shares	SDRIX	NAS CM	Open End	Long/Short Equity (Growth)	C+	C	B	Up	Y	100,000
Swan Defined Risk Fund Class Y Shares	SDRYX	NAS CM	Open End	Long/Short Equity (Growth)	C+	C	B	Up	Y	25,000,000
Swan Defined Risk Growth Fund Class A Shares	SDAAX	NAS CM	Open End	Alternative Miscellaneous (Growth)	U	U	U		Y	2,500
Swan Defined Risk Growth Fund Class C Shares	SDACX	NAS CM	Open End	Alternative Miscellaneous (Growth)	U	U	U		Y	2,500
Swan Defined Risk Growth Fund Class I Shares	SDAIX	NAS CM	Open End	Alternative Miscellaneous (Growth)	U	U	U		Y	100,000
Swan Defined Risk Growth Fund Class Y Shares	SDAYX	NAS CM	Open End	Alternative Miscellaneous (Growth)	U	U	U		Y	25,000,000
Swan Defined Risk U.S. Small Cap Fund Class A	SDCAX	NAS CM	Open End	Long/Short Equity (Small Company)	C	C-	C+		Y	2,500
Swan Defined Risk U.S. Small Cap Fund Class C	SDCCX	NAS CM	Open End	Long/Short Equity (Small Company)	C	C-	C+		Y	2,500
Swan Defined Risk U.S. Small Cap Fund Class I	SDCIX	NAS CM	Open End	Long/Short Equity (Small Company)	C	C-	B-		Y	100,000
Swan Defined Risk U.S. Small Cap Fund Class Y Shares	SDCYX	NAS CM	Open End	Long/Short Equity (Small Company)	C	C-	B-		Y	25,000,000
Swiss Helvetia Fund Inc	SWZ	NYSE	Closed End	Equity Miscellaneous (Europe Stock)	C	C	C-	Up	Y	
Symmetry Panoramic Alternatives Fund Class I Shares	SPATX	NAS CM	Open End	Multialternative (Growth & Income)	U	U	U		Y	1,000
Symmetry Panoramic Global Equity Fund Class I Shares	SPGEX	NAS CM	Open End	Global Equity Large Cap (Growth)	U	U	U		Y	1,000
Symmetry Panoramic International Equity Cls I Shares	SPILX	NAS CM	Open End	Global Equity Large Cap (Growth)	U	U	U		Y	1,000
Symmetry Panoramic Tax-Managed Global Equity Cls I Shares	SPGTX	NAS CM	Open End	Global Equity Large Cap (Growth)	U	U	U		Y	1,000
Symmetry Panoramic US Equity Fund Class I Shares	SPUSX	NAS CM	Open End	US Equity Large Cap Blend (Growth)	U	U	U		Y	1,000
Symons Value Institutional Fund Class II	SVTIX	NAS CM	Open End	US Equity Large Cap Value (Growth)	C+	C	B-	Up	Y	5,000
T. Rowe Price Africa & Middle East Fund	TRAMX	NAS CM	Open End	Equity Miscellaneous (Foreign Stock)	C	C	B		Y	2,500
T. Rowe Price Africa & Middle East Fund I Class	PRAMX	NAS CM	Open End	Equity Miscellaneous (Foreign Stock)	C	C	B		Y	1,000,000
T. Rowe Price Asia Opportunities Fund	TRAOX	NAS CM	Open End	Asia ex-Japan Equity (Pacific Stock)	C	C	B-		Y	2,500
T. Rowe Price Asia Opportunities Fund Advisor Class	PAAOX	NAS CM	Open End	Asia ex-Japan Equity (Pacific Stock)	C	C	B-		Y	2,500
T. Rowe Price Asia Opportunities Fund I Class	TRASX	NAS CM	Open End	Asia ex-Japan Equity (Pacific Stock)	C	C	B-		Y	1,000,000
T. Rowe Price Balanced Fund	RPBAX	NAS CM	Open End	Moderate Alloc (Balanced)	B	C	A-	Up	Y	2,500
T. Rowe Price Balanced I Class	RBAIX	NAS CM	Open End	Moderate Alloc (Balanced)	B	C	A-	Up	Y	1,000,000
T. Rowe Price Blue Chip Growth Fund	TRBCX	NAS CM	Open End	US Equity Large Cap Growth (Growth)	B-	C+	B	Down	Y	2,500
T. Rowe Price Blue Chip Growth Fund Advisor Class	PABGX	NAS CM	Open End	US Equity Large Cap Growth (Growth)	B-	C+	B	Down	Y	2,500
T. Rowe Price Blue Chip Growth Fund Class R	RRBGX	NAS CM	Open End	US Equity Large Cap Growth (Growth)	B-	C+	B	Down	Y	2,500
T. Rowe Price Blue Chip Growth Fund I Class	TBCIX	NAS CM	Open End	US Equity Large Cap Growth (Growth)	B-	C+	B	Down	Y	1,000,000
T. Rowe Price Capital Appreciation Fund	PRWCX	NAS CM	Open End	Moderate Alloc (Growth)	B	B-	A	Down		2,500
T. Rowe Price Capital Appreciation Fund Advisor Class	PACLX	NAS CM	Open End	Moderate Alloc (Growth)	B	B-	A	Down		2,500
T. Rowe Price Capital Appreciation Fund I Class	TRAIX	NAS CM	Open End	Moderate Alloc (Growth)	B	B-	A	Down	Y	1,000,000
T. Rowe Price Capital Opportunity Fund	PRCOX	NAS CM	Open End	US Equity Large Cap Blend (Growth)	B-	C+	B	Down	Y	2,500
T. Rowe Price Capital Opportunity Fund Advisor Class	PACOX	NAS CM	Open End	US Equity Large Cap Blend (Growth)	B-	C+	B		Y	2,500
T. Rowe Price Capital Opportunity Fund Class R	RRCOX	NAS CM	Open End	US Equity Large Cap Blend (Growth)	B-	C	B		Y	2,500
T. Rowe Price Capital Opportunity Fund I Class	PCCOX	NAS CM	Open End	US Equity Large Cap Blend (Growth)	B-	C+	B	Down	Y	1,000,000
T. Rowe Price Communications & Technology Fund I Class	TTMIX	NAS CM	Open End	Communications Sector Equity (Comm)	B	B-	B	Up	Y	1,000,000
T. Rowe Price Communications & Technology Investor Cls	PRMTX	NAS CM	Open End	Communications Sector Equity (Comm)	B	B-	B	Up	Y	2,500
T. Rowe Price Diversified Mid Cap Growth Fund	PRDMX	NAS CM	Open End	US Equity Mid Cap (Growth)	B	B-	B		Y	2,500
T. Rowe Price Diversified Mid Cap Growth Fund I Class	RPTTX	NAS CM	Open End	US Equity Mid Cap (Growth)	B	B-	B		Y	1,000,000
T. Rowe Price Dividend Growth Fund	PRDGX	NAS CM	Open End	US Equity Large Cap Blend (Equity-Income)	B	B-	A-		Y	2,500
T. Rowe Price Dividend Growth Fund Advisor Class	TADGX	NAS CM	Open End	US Equity Large Cap Blend (Equity-Income)	B	B-	A-		Y	2,500
T. Rowe Price Dividend Growth Fund I Class	PDGIX	NAS CM	Open End	US Equity Large Cap Blend (Equity-Income)	B	B-	A-		Y	1,000,000
T. Rowe Price Emerging Europe Fund	TREMX	NAS CM	Open End	Equity Miscellaneous (Foreign Stock)	C+	C	B-	Up	Y	2,500
T. Rowe Price Emerging Europe Fund I Class	TTEEX	NAS CM	Open End	Equity Miscellaneous (Foreign Stock)	C+	C	B-	Up	Y	1,000,000
T. Rowe Price Emerging Markets Discovery Stock Fund	PRIJX	NAS CM	Open End	Global Emerg Mkts (Div Emerging Mkts)	C+	C	B	Up	Y	2,500
T. Rowe Price Emerging Markets Discovery Stock Advisor Cls	PAIJX	NAS CM	Open End	Global Emerg Mkts (Div Emerging Mkts)	C+	C	B	Up	Y	2,500
T. Rowe Price Emerging Markets Discovery Stock I Cls	REVIX	NAS CM	Open End	Global Emerg Mkts (Div Emerging Mkts)	C+	C	B	Up	Y	1,000,000
T. Rowe Price Emerging Markets Stock Fund	PRMSX	NAS CM	Open End	Global Emerg Mkts (Div Emerging Mkts)	C	C	C+		Y	2,500
T. Rowe Price Emerging Markets Stock Fund I Class	PRZIX	NAS CM	Open End	Global Emerg Mkts (Div Emerging Mkts)	C	C	C+		Y	1,000,000
T. Rowe Price Equity Income Fund	PRFDX	NAS CM	Open End	US Equity Large Cap Value (Equity-Income)	B-	C	B	Up	Y	2,500

★ Expanded analysis of this fund is included in Section II.

	TOTAL RETURNS					PERFORMANCE				ASSETS		ASSET ALLOCATION & TURNOVER					BULL & BEAR		FEES		
Min Additional Investment	3-Month Total Return	6-Month Total Return	1-Year Total Return	3-Year Total Return	5-Year Total Return	Dividend Yield (TTM)	Expense Ratio	3-Yr Std Deviation	3-Year Beta	NAV	Total Assets (MIL)	%Cash	%Stocks	%Bonds	%Other	Turnover Ratio	Last Bull Market Total Return	Last Bear Market Total Return	Front End Fee (%)	Back End Fee (%)	Inception Date
500	2.23	9.30	1.66	13.10	12.91	0.65	1.52	7.62	0.58	12.8	2,068	1	99	0	0	9			5.50		Jul-12
500	2.10	9.01	0.96	10.57	8.86	0	2.27	7.66	0.59	12.58	2,068	1	99	0	0	9				1.00	Oct-12
500	2.30	9.53	1.96	13.94	14.39	0.91	1.27	7.67	0.59	12.86	2,068	1	99	0	0	9					Jul-12
500	2.38	9.62	2.04	14.03	14.48		1.14	7.65	0.59	12.87	2,068	1	99	0	0	9					Dec-18
500	2.62	13.50					1.73			11.38	3.8	13	87	0	0				5.50		Dec-18
500	2.52	13.80					2.48			11.38	3.8	13	87	0	0						Dec-18
500	2.62	13.50					1.48			11.38	3.8	13	87	0	0						Dec-18
500	2.61	14.00					1.1			11.4	3.8	13	87	0	0						Dec-18
500	0.42	10.06	-3.79	17.33		0	1.99	10.72	0.62	11.92	41.7	1	99	0	0	1			5.50		Dec-15
500	0.17	9.62	-4.51	14.71		0	2.74	10.72	0.62	11.62	41.7	1	99	0	0	1				1.00	Dec-15
500	0.41	10.18	-3.53	18.31		0	1.74	10.74	0.62	12.01	41.7	1	99	0	0	1					Dec-15
500	0.50	10.27	-3.45	18.41			1.36	10.74	0.62	12.02	41.7	1	99	0	0	1					Dec-18
	6.30	16.31	9.16	27.52	14.18	52.97	1.06	11.81	0.93	9.27	123.0	0	89	0	11	21	10.79	-20.92			Aug-87
100	0.10	2.07					2.04			9.8	0.86	-83	37	109	22						Nov-18
100	2.78	15.44					0.76			10.7	534.9	3	97	0	0						Nov-18
100	1.70	11.41					0.95			10.71	284.3	4	96	0	0						Nov-18
100	2.55	16.67					0.79			10.82	23.8	2	97	0	1						Nov-18
100	3.49	18.28					0.67			10.67	526.1	3	97	0	0						Nov-18
250	3.11	13.81	4.78	11.51	21.56	1.92	0.98	10.22	0.67	8.96	26.4	10	90	0	0	76	13.04	-7.34			Dec-06
100	4.06	11.01	3.09	32.27	5.70	1.8	1.36	12.1		9.47	131.0	1	99	0	0	52	18.48	-17.11			Sep-07
	4.06	11.15	3.33	32.70	6.05	2.01	1.13	12.06		9.47	131.0	1	99	0	0	52	18.48	-17.11			Mar-17
100	-1.27	13.02	1.44	47.18	50.25	0.61	1.13	14.29	0.94	14.75	129.7	4	94	0	2	79					May-14
100	-1.34	12.83	1.30	46.32	48.94	0.54	1.25	14.35	0.94	14.68	129.7	4	94	0	2	79					May-14
	-1.20	13.19	1.76	47.81	50.90	0.95	0.84	14.3	0.94	14.76	129.7	4	94	0	2	79					Mar-17
100	3.35	13.79	6.66	33.27	36.40	2.06	0.58	7.71	1.12	23.93	4,405	1	65	33	0	68	17	-11.83			Dec-39
	3.35	13.89	6.79	33.83	37.10	2.18	0.46	7.7	1.11	23.93	4,405	1	65	33	0	68	17	-11.83			Dec-15
100	4.04	21.92	10.33	81.45	100.36	0	0.7	14.3	1.07	116.06	63,955	0	100	0	0	27	31.15	-14.81			Jun-93
100	3.97	21.75	10.03	79.97	97.68	0	0.97	14.3	1.07	114	63,955	0	100	0	0	27	30.97	-14.89			Mar-00
100	3.90	21.60	9.75	78.59	95.13	0	1.23	14.29	1.07	109.41	63,955	0	100	0	0	27	30.8	-15.02			Sep-02
	4.07	21.99	10.47	82.15	101.28	0.05	0.57	14.3	1.07	116.24	63,955	0	100	0	0	27	31.15	-14.81			Dec-15
100	4.91	18.17	15.20	41.40	63.23	2.06	0.71	7.56	0.59	31.15	35,084	8	60	27	0	65	19.66	-12.48			Jun-86
100	4.83	18.01	14.86	40.14	60.83	1.78	1	7.54	0.58	30.79	35,084	8	60	27	0	65	19.45	-12.56			Dec-04
	4.91	18.24	15.31	41.81	63.81	2.15	0.59	7.54	0.58	31.18	35,084	8	60	27	0	65	19.66	-12.48			Dec-15
100	4.33	20.44	10.21	53.43	68.26	0.99	0.5	12.35	1.01	28.16	784.8	1	100	0	0	34	25.56	-16.51			Nov-94
100	4.27	20.26	9.89	52.15	65.91	0.69	0.82	12.35	1.01	28.07	784.8	1	100	0	0	34	25.33	-16.7			Dec-04
100	4.17	20.03	9.51	50.73	63.44	0.52	1.12	12.36	1.01	27.92	784.8	1	100	0	0	34	25.09	-16.73			Dec-04
	4.37	20.53	10.38	54.01	68.90	1.13	0.38	12.34	1.01	28.18	784.8	1	100	0	0	34	25.56	-16.51			Nov-16
	5.22	25.86	12.80	73.54	99.88	0.25	0.66	14.78	1	117.37	6,154	2	98	0	0	7	24.55	-16.87			Mar-16
100	5.19	25.78	12.67	72.94	99.15	0.15	0.78	14.77	1	117.21	6,154	2	98	0	0	7	24.55	-16.87			Oct-93
100	7.10	29.24	17.19	65.74	81.21	0.25	0.83	13.75	0.95	34.69	1,347	0	100	0	0	20	28.51	-22.88			Dec-03
	7.12	29.31	17.33	66.27	81.79	0.36	0.69	13.74	0.95	34.72	1,347	0	100	0	0	20	28.51	-22.88			May-17
100	6.10	20.92	16.72	50.05	72.23	1.55	0.64	10.32	0.82	49.39	11,498	5	95	0	0	17	23.59	-15.25			Dec-92
100	6.02	20.76	16.42	48.83	69.93	1.3	0.91	10.32	0.82	49.34	11,498	5	95	0	0	17	23.4	-15.37			Dec-05
	6.12	21.00	16.88	50.64	72.95	1.65	0.51	10.31	0.82	49.38	11,498	5	95	0	0	17	23.59	-15.25			Dec-15
100	9.50	20.73	10.18	40.48	-8.90	2.7	1.42	14.64	0.87	15.55	160.2	0	100	0	0	42	18.76	-34.24			Aug-00
	9.57	20.88	10.58	41.55	-8.20	3.02	1.09	14.64	0.87	15.57	160.2	0	100	0	0	42	18.76	-34.24			Mar-17
100	2.62	14.35	8.73	50.98		1.46	1.29	13.38	0.93	13.7	136.5	4	94	0	0	70					Sep-15
100	2.55	14.04	8.32	49.68		1.1	1.65	13.4	0.94	13.64	136.5	4	94	0	0	70					Sep-15
	2.61	14.42	8.89	51.64		1.6	1.09	13.36	0.93	13.72	136.5	4	94	0	0	70					Mar-17
100	1.75	16.19	3.33	42.60	30.25	0.53	1.22	14.94	1.04	43.4	12,675	4	96	0	0	18	17.68	-26.02			Mar-95
	1.75	16.26	3.59	43.44	31.15	0.67	1.07	14.94	1.04	43.46	12,675	4	96	0	0	18	17.68	-26.02			Aug-15
100	4.28	16.64	5.50	38.49	37.56	2.26	0.64	12.26	1	31.25	20,244	3	95	0	0	16	23.56	-18.08			Oct-85

	MARKET			FUND TYPE, CATEGORY & OBJECTIVE	RATINGS				MINIMUMS	
Fund Name	Ticker Symbol	Traded On	Fund Type	Category and (Prospectus Objective)	Overall Rating	Reward Rating	Risk Rating	Recent Up/ Downgrade	Open to New Investors	Min Initial Investment
T. Rowe Price Equity Income Fund Advisor Class	PAFDX	NAS CM	Open End	US Equity Large Cap Value (Equity-Income)	B-	C	B	Up	Y	0
T. Rowe Price Equity Income Fund Class R	RRFDX	NAS CM	Open End	US Equity Large Cap Value (Equity-Income)	B-	C	B	Up	Y	0
T. Rowe Price Equity Income Fund I Class	REIPX	NAS CM	Open End	US Equity Large Cap Value (Equity-Income)	B-	C	B	Up	Y	1,000,000
T. Rowe Price Equity Index 500 Fund	PREIX	NAS CM	Open End	US Equity Large Cap Blend (Growth & Income)	B-	C	B		Y	2,500
T. Rowe Price Equity Index 500 Fund I Class	PRUIX	NAS CM	Open End	US Equity Large Cap Blend (Growth & Income)	B-	C	B		Y	1,000,000
T. Rowe Price European Stock Fund	PRESX	NAS CM	Open End	Europe Equity Large Cap (Europe Stock)	C	C	B-		Y	2,500
T. Rowe Price European Stock Fund I Class	TEUIX	NAS CM	Open End	Europe Equity Large Cap (Europe Stock)	C	C	B-		Y	1,000,000
T. Rowe Price Extended Equity Market Index Fund	PEXMX	NAS CM	Open End	US Equity Mid Cap (Growth)	C+	C	B-		Y	2,500
T. Rowe Price Financial Services Fund	PRISX	NAS CM	Open End	Financials Sector Equity (Financial)	C+	C	B	Up	Y	2,500
T. Rowe Price Financial Services Fund I Class	TFIFX	NAS CM	Open End	Financials Sector Equity (Financial)	C+	C	B	Up	Y	1,000,000
T. Rowe Price Global Allocation Fund	RPGAX	NAS CM	Open End	Moderate Alloc (Growth & Income)	B-	C	A-	Up	Y	2,500
T. Rowe Price Global Allocation Fund Advisor Class	PAFGX	NAS CM	Open End	Moderate Alloc (Growth & Income)	B-	C	A-	Up	Y	2,500
T. Rowe Price Global Allocation Fund I Class	TGAFX	NAS CM	Open End	Moderate Alloc (Growth & Income)	B-	C	A-	Up	Y	1,000,000
T. Rowe Price Global Consumer Fund	PGLOX	NAS CM	Open End	Consumer Goods Sec Equity (Growth)	C+	C	B	Up	Y	2,500
T. Rowe Price Global Growth Stock Fund	RPGEX	NAS CM	Open End	Global Equity Large Cap (Growth)	C+	C	B		Y	2,500
T. Rowe Price Global Growth Stock Fund Advisor Class	PAGLX	NAS CM	Open End	Global Equity Large Cap (Growth)	C+	C	B		Y	2,500
T. Rowe Price Global Growth Stock Fund I Class	RGGIX	NAS CM	Open End	Global Equity Large Cap (Growth)	C+	C	B	Down	Y	1,000,000
T. Rowe Price Global Industrials Fund	RPGIX	NAS CM	Open End	Industrials Sector Equity (Growth)	C+	C	B	Up	Y	2,500
T. Rowe Price Global Industrials Fund I Class	TRGAX	NAS CM	Open End	Industrials Sector Equity (Growth)	C+	C	B	Up	Y	1,000,000
T. Rowe Price Global Real Estate Fund	TRGRX	NAS CM	Open End	Real Estate Sector Equity (Real Estate)	B-	C	B	Up	Y	2,500
T. Rowe Price Global Real Estate Fund Advisor Class	PAGEX	NAS CM	Open End	Real Estate Sector Equity (Real Estate)	B-	C	B	Up	Y	2,500
T. Rowe Price Global Real Estate Fund I Class	TIRGX	NAS CM	Open End	Real Estate Sector Equity (Real Estate)	B-	C	B+	Up	Y	1,000,000
T. Rowe Price Global Stock Fund	PRGSX	NAS CM	Open End	Global Equity Large Cap (World Stock)	B-	C	B		Y	2,500
T. Rowe Price Global Stock Fund Advisor Class	PAGSX	NAS CM	Open End	Global Equity Large Cap (World Stock)	B-	C	B		Y	2,500
T. Rowe Price Global Stock Fund I Class	TRGLX	NAS CM	Open End	Global Equity Large Cap (World Stock)	B-	C	B		Y	1,000,000
T. Rowe Price Global Technology Fund	PRGTX	NAS CM	Open End	Technology Sector Equity (Technology)	C+	C+	C+		Y	2,500
T. Rowe Price Global Technology Fund I Class	PGTIX	NAS CM	Open End	Technology Sector Equity (Technology)	C+	C+	C+		Y	1,000,000
T. Rowe Price Growth and Income Fund	PRGIX	NAS CM	Open End	US Equity Large Cap Blend (Growth & Income)	B	C+	B+		Y	2,500
T. Rowe Price Growth and Income Fund I Class	TGTIX	NAS CM	Open End	US Equity Large Cap Blend (Growth & Income)	B	C+	B+		Y	1,000,000
T. Rowe Price Growth Stock Fund	PRGFX	NAS CM	Open End	US Equity Large Cap Growth (Growth)	B-	C	B	Down	Y	2,500
T. Rowe Price Growth Stock Fund Advisor Class	TRSAX	NAS CM	Open End	US Equity Large Cap Growth (Growth)	B-	C	B	Down	Y	2,500
T. Rowe Price Growth Stock Fund I Class	PRUFX	NAS CM	Open End	US Equity Large Cap Growth (Growth)	B-	C+	B	Down	Y	1,000,000
T. Rowe Price Growth Stock Fund R Class	RRGSX	NAS CM	Open End	US Equity Large Cap Growth (Growth)	B-	C	B	Down	Y	2,500
T. Rowe Price Health Sciences Fund	PRHSX	NAS CM	Open End	Healthcare Sector Equity (Health)	C+	C	B	Down		2,500
T. Rowe Price Health Sciences Fund I Class	THISX	NAS CM	Open End	Healthcare Sector Equity (Health)	C+	C	B	Down	Y	1,000,000
T. Rowe Price Institutional Africa & Middle East Fund	TRIAX	NAS CM	Open End	Equity Miscellaneous (Foreign Stock)	C	C	B		Y	1,000,000
T. Rowe Price Institutional Emerging Markets Equity Fund	IEMFX	NAS CM	Open End	Global Emerg Mkts (Div Emerging Mkts)	C	C	C+			1,000,000
T. Rowe Price Institutional Frontier Markets Equity Fund	PRFFX	NAS CM	Open End	Global Emerg Mkts (Growth)	C	C-	C+	Up	Y	1,000,000
T. Rowe Price Inst Global Focused Growth Equity Fund	TRGSX	NAS CM	Open End	Global Equity Large Cap (World Stock)	B-	C	B	Down	Y	1,000,000
T. Rowe Price Institutional Global Growth Equity Fund	RPIGX	NAS CM	Open End	Global Equity Large Cap (Growth)	C+	C	B		Y	1,000,000
T. Rowe Price Institutional Global Value Equity Fund	PRIGX	NAS CM	Open End	Global Equity Large Cap (World Stock)	C+	C	B	Up	Y	1,000,000
T. Rowe Price Institutional International Core Equity Fund	TRCEX	NAS CM	Open End	Global Equity Large Cap (World Stock)	C	C	C+		Y	1,000,000
T. Rowe Price Inst Intl Disciplined Equity Fund	RPICX	NAS CM	Open End	Global Equity Large Cap (Foreign Stock)	C+	C	B	Up	Y	1,000,000
T. Rowe Price Inst Intl Growth Equity Fund	PRFEX	NAS CM	Open End	Global Equity Large Cap (Foreign Stock)	C	C	B		Y	1,000,000
T. Rowe Price Institutional Large Cap Core Growth Fund	TPLGX	NAS CM	Open End	US Equity Large Cap Growth (Growth)	B-	C+	B	Down	Y	1,000,000
T. Rowe Price Institutional Large Cap Growth Fund	TRLGX	NAS CM	Open End	US Equity Large Cap Growth (Growth)	B-	C+	B	Down	Y	1,000,000
T. Rowe Price Institutional Large Cap Value Fund	TILCX	NAS CM	Open End	US Equity Large Cap Value (Growth)	B-	C	B	Up	Y	1,000,000
T. Rowe Price Institutional Mid-Cap Equity Growth Fund	PMEGX	NAS CM	Open End	US Equity Mid Cap (Growth)	B-	C+	B	Down		1,000,000
T. Rowe Price Institutional Small-Cap Stock Fund	TRSSX	NAS CM	Open End	US Equity Small Cap (Small Company)	B-	C+	B	Down		1,000,000
T. Rowe Price Institutional U.S. Structured Research Fund	TRISX	NAS CM	Open End	US Equity Large Cap Blend (Growth)	B-	C+	B	Down	Y	1,000,000
T. Rowe Price International Disciplined Equity Advisor Cls	PRNCX	NAS CM	Open End	Global Equity Large Cap (Foreign Stock)	C+	C	B	Up	Y	2,500
T. Rowe Price International Disciplined Equity I Cls	RICIX	NAS CM	Open End	Global Equity Large Cap (Foreign Stock)	C+	C	B	Up	Y	1,000,000

★ Expanded analysis of this fund is included in Section II.

	TOTAL RETURNS					PERFORMANCE				ASSETS		ASSET ALLOCATION & TURNOVER					BULL & BEAR		FEES		
Min Additional Investment	3-Month Total Return	6-Month Total Return	1-Year Total Return	3-Year Total Return	5-Year Total Return	Dividend Yield (TTM)	Expense Ratio	3-Yr Std Deviation	3-Year Beta	NAV	Total Assets (MIL)	%Cash	%Stocks	%Bonds	%Other	Turnover Ratio	Last Bull Market Total Return	Last Bear Market Total Return	Front End Fee (%)	Back End Fee (%)	Inception Date
	4.26	16.53	5.22	37.32	35.65	1.97	0.94	12.28	1	31.19	20,244	3	95	0	0	16	23.35	-18.18			Mar-00
	4.13	16.29	4.89	36.13	33.78	1.67	1.22	12.27	1	31.12	20,244	3	95	0	0	16	23.19	-18.29			Sep-02
	4.35	16.71	5.63	38.91	38.07	2.32	0.54	12.27	1	31.27	20,244	3	95	0	0	16	23.56	-18.08			Dec-15
100	4.25	19.45	10.20	49.94	64.36	1.85	0.19	12.2	1	78.34	29,526	1	99	0	0	7	24.92	-16.37			Mar-90
	4.29	19.52	10.36	50.60	65.27	1.99	0.06	12.19	1	78.35	29,526	1	99	0	0	7	24.92	-16.37			Aug-15
100	5.87	18.54	4.31	27.83	6.75	2.27	0.97	12.74	1	20.71	985.4	3	97	0	0	32	21.42	-27.29			Feb-90
	5.93	18.68	4.44	28.24	7.08	2.46	0.84	12.78	1	20.71	985.4	3	97	0	0	32	21.42	-27.29			Mar-17
100	2.95	20.28	1.58	46.26	44.98	1.04	0.35	15.44	1.01	28.58	911.0	3	97	0	0	21	28.84	-23.93			Jan-98
100	6.40	17.85	2.47	61.01	57.17	1.39	0.87	14.07	1.02	26.4	763.8	9	91	0	0	34	32.83	-27.62			Sep-96
	6.44	17.95	2.65	61.68	57.82	1.57	0.72	14.06	1.02	26.41	763.8	9	91	0	0	34	32.83	-27.62			Nov-16
100	3.34	13.25	5.01	28.99	29.37	1.76	0.94	7.35	1.02	12.99	699.8	3	52	32	12	48					May-13
100	3.27	13.03	4.68	28.04	28.18	1.54	1.25	7.36	1.02	12.92	699.8	3	52	32	12	48					May-13
	3.33	13.31	5.08	29.69	30.20	1.83	0.84	7.38	1.02	13.02	699.8	3	52	32	12	48					Mar-16
100	3.21	19.01	6.81	30.38		1.08	1.05	12.23	0.99	12.83	19.5	3	97	0	0	91					Jun-16
100	3.17	22.28	7.87	57.57	58.94	0	0.92	12.98	1.08	28.31	457.8	0	100	0	0	120	23.39	-22.44			Oct-08
100	3.14	22.15	7.71	57.00	58.12	0	1.1	12.98	1.08	28.17	457.8	0	100	0	0	120	23.27	-22.48			Oct-08
	3.24	22.40	8.14	58.43	59.80	0.21	0.69	12.97	1.08	28.35	457.8	0	100	0	0	120	23.39	-22.44			Mar-17
100	5.67	22.31	9.43	43.13	39.04	0.22	1.05	14.25	1.01	12.66	23.5	1	99	0	0	72					Oct-13
	5.75	22.51	9.73	44.07	39.95	0.51	0.74	14.28	1.02	12.68	23.5	1	99	0	0	72					May-17
100	0.35	15.08	6.41	10.69	22.00	2.35	0.97	11.14	0.98	20.28	136.7	2	96	0	2	16	24.54	-17.87			Oct-08
100	0.25	14.97	6.18	10.16	21.18	2.13	1.15	11.12	0.98	20.13	136.7	2	96	0	2	16	24.51	-17.9			Oct-08
	0.35	15.20	6.62	11.36	22.74	2.54	0.74	11.17	0.98	20.28	136.7	2	96	0	2	16	24.54	-17.87			Nov-16
100	2.90	22.26	7.43	67.92	76.48	0.16	0.82	14.05	1.14	41.74	1,848	1	98	0	1	104	21.89	-22.7			Dec-95
100	2.83	22.09	7.11	66.45	74.04	0	1.09	14.04	1.14	41.34	1,848	1	98	0	1	104	21.7	-22.82			Apr-06
	2.93	22.34	7.57	68.43	77.03	0.27	0.68	14.05	1.14	41.78	1,848	1	98	0	1	104	21.89	-22.7			Mar-17
100	3.04	25.59	5.67	81.48	129.67	0	0.91	19.75	1.12	15.21	4,922	4	96	0	0	289	29.67	-20.38			Sep-00
	3.11	25.68	5.84	82.13	130.50	0.16	0.77	19.74	1.12	15.22	4,922	4	96	0	0	289	29.67	-20.38			Nov-16
100	5.35	19.53	12.57	46.01	66.08	1.2	0.65	11.01	0.87	28.68	1,982	4	96	0	0	73	23.7	-16.61			Dec-82
	5.34	19.57	12.64	46.31	66.42	1.29	0.56	11.01	0.87	28.68	1,982	4	96	0	0	73	23.7	-16.61			Nov-16
100	3.79	21.42	8.30	72.77	89.60	0.15	0.66	13.87	1.04	68.7	55,454	2	98	0	0	42	31.05	-16.52			Apr-50
100	3.71	21.27	8.02	71.46	87.22	0	0.92	13.86	1.04	66.97	55,454	2	98	0	0	42	30.83	-16.58			Dec-01
	3.83	21.51	8.45	73.56	90.72	0.28	0.52	13.87	1.04	68.79	55,454	2	98	0	0	42	31.05	-16.52			Aug-15
100	3.66	21.11	7.73	70.17	84.85	0	1.18	13.88	1.04	64.53	55,454	2	98	0	0	42	30.64	-16.69			Sep-02
100	1.73	19.35	10.39	49.89	83.42	0	0.77	17.01	1.15	78.74	13,215	0	100	0	0	43	31.05	-14.4			Dec-95
	1.76	19.43	10.52	50.41	84.12	0	0.66	17.01	1.15	78.78	13,215	0	100	0	0	43	31.05	-14.4			Mar-16
	3.50	10.12	2.40	32.05	6.80	2.65	1.18	12.04		6.2	104.8	1	99	0	0	50	18.68	-16.95			Apr-08
	1.72	16.26	3.51	43.22	31.13	0.76	1.1	14.9	1.04	39.53	1,817	4	96	0	0	14	18.17	-25.99			Oct-02
	4.17	10.99	-0.57	23.87		1.58	1.39	10.93	0.91	9.49	46.8	1	98	0	1	56					Sep-14
	2.91	22.32	7.58	68.55	77.27	0.3	0.75	13.93	1.13	12	58.3	2	97	0	2	112	21.68	-22.42			Jun-06
	2.97	21.91	7.60	58.24	60.43	0.33	0.73	12.99	1.09	28.76	203.0	0	100	0	0	76	23.87	-22.52			Oct-08
	3.34	14.96	2.65	30.33	26.58	1.8	0.75	11.06	0.96	12.06	10.5	4	96	0	0	100					Jul-12
	2.17	12.61	-3.19	30.30	11.65	7.44	0.75	12.15	1.07	12.23	31.1	0	100	0	0	32	17.05	-23.43			Oct-10
	2.44	12.13	3.64	25.70	15.29	3.4	0.75	10.37	0.89	10.9	273.0	10	87	0	2	147	16.84	-18.69			Jul-10
	3.50	17.43	2.82	34.58	23.38	1.52	0.75	12.34	1.04	23.03	59.5	3	97	0	1	39	19.27	-23.72			Sep-89
	4.07	22.01	10.54	81.91	101.46	0.13	0.56	14.26	1.07	45.51	4,004	0	100	0	0	27	31	-14.79			Sep-03
	3.00	19.19	9.96	87.94	102.29	0.22	0.56	13.73	0.98	42.17	19,125	3	97	0	0	33	29.76	-16.72			Oct-01
	4.32	16.96	6.22	37.57	44.54	2.09	0.57	12.09	0.99	22.89	3,438	2	97	0	0	28	23.79	-20.44			Mar-00
	7.26	26.93	16.65	64.64	89.34	0.2	0.61	13.45	0.91	60.56	7,975	2	98	0	0	36	25.84	-20.61			Jul-96
	5.82	25.73	10.93	61.87	65.59	0.18	0.66	14.77	0.85	25.26	5,261	2	98	0	0	39	32.48	-24.06			Mar-00
	4.39	20.57	10.52	54.21	69.41	1.26	0.38	12.38	1.01	13.07	800.3	1	99	0	0	47	25.66	-16.39			Oct-07
100	2.42	12.05	3.34	24.04		1.74	1	10.41	0.89	10.13	110.1	10	87	0	2	153					Aug-14
	2.52	12.16	3.68	25.02		2.12	0.69	10.38	0.89	10.14	110.1	10	87	0	2	153					Mar-17

	MARKET			FUND TYPE, CATEGORY & OBJECTIVE	RATINGS				MINIMUMS	
Fund Name	Ticker Symbol	Traded On	Fund Type	Category and (Prospectus Objective)	Overall Rating	Reward Rating	Risk Rating	Recent Up/ Downgrade	Open to New Investors	Min Initial Investment
T. Rowe Price Intl Disciplined Equity Inv Cls	PRCNX	NAS CM	Open End	Global Equity Large Cap (Foreign Stock)	C+	C	B	Up	Y	2,500
T. Rowe Price International Discovery Fund	PRIDX	NAS CM	Open End	Global Equity Mid/Small Cap (Foreign Stock)	C	C	C+		Y	2,500
T. Rowe Price International Discovery Fund I Class	TIDDX	NAS CM	Open End	Global Equity Mid/Small Cap (Foreign Stock)	C	C	C+		Y	1,000,000
T. Rowe Price International Equity Index Fund	PIEQX	NAS CM	Open End	Global Equity Large Cap (Growth)	C	C	B		Y	2,500
T. Rowe Price International Stock Fund	PRITX	NAS CM	Open End	Global Equity Large Cap (Foreign Stock)	C	C	B		Y	2,500
T. Rowe Price International Stock Fund Advisor Class	PAITX	NAS CM	Open End	Global Equity Large Cap (Foreign Stock)	C	C	B-		Y	2,500
T. Rowe Price International Stock Fund Class R	RRITX	NAS CM	Open End	Global Equity Large Cap (Foreign Stock)	C	C	B-		Y	2,500
T. Rowe Price International Stock Fund I Class	PRIUX	NAS CM	Open End	Global Equity Large Cap (Foreign Stock)	C	C	B		Y	1,000,000
T. Rowe Price International Value Equity Fund	TRIGX	NAS CM	Open End	Global Equity Large Cap (Foreign Stock)	C-	D+	C		Y	2,500
T. Rowe Price International Value Equity Advisor Cls	PAIGX	NAS CM	Open End	Global Equity Large Cap (Foreign Stock)	C-	D+	C		Y	2,500
T. Rowe Price International Value Equity Fund Class I	TRTIX	NAS CM	Open End	Global Equity Large Cap (Foreign Stock)	C-	D+	C		Y	1,000,000
T. Rowe Price International Value Equity Fund Class R	RRIGX	NAS CM	Open End	Global Equity Large Cap (Foreign Stock)	C-	D+	C		Y	2,500
T. Rowe Price Japan Fund	PRJPX	NAS CM	Open End	Japan Equity (Pacific Stock)	C	C	C+		Y	2,500
T. Rowe Price Japan Fund I Class	RJAIX	NAS CM	Open End	Japan Equity (Pacific Stock)	C	C	C+		Y	1,000,000
T. Rowe Price Latin America Fund	PRLAX	NAS CM	Open End	Latin America Equity (Foreign Stock)	C	C	C+		Y	2,500
T. Rowe Price Latin America Fund I Class	RLAIX	NAS CM	Open End	Latin America Equity (Foreign Stock)	C	C	C+		Y	1,000,000
T. Rowe Price Mid-Cap Growth Fund	RPMGX	NAS CM	Open End	US Equity Mid Cap (Growth)	B-	C+	B	Down		2,500
T. Rowe Price Mid-Cap Growth Fund Advisor Class	PAMCX	NAS CM	Open End	US Equity Mid Cap (Growth)	B-	C+	B	Down		2,500
T. Rowe Price Mid-Cap Growth Fund I Class	RPTIX	NAS CM	Open End	US Equity Mid Cap (Growth)	B-	C+	B	Down	Y	1,000,000
T. Rowe Price Mid-Cap Growth Fund R Class	RRMGX	NAS CM	Open End	US Equity Mid Cap (Growth)	B-	C+	B	Down		2,500
T. Rowe Price Mid-Cap Value Fund	TRMCX	NAS CM	Open End	US Equity Mid Cap (Growth)	C	C	B-			2,500
T. Rowe Price Mid-Cap Value Fund Advisor Class	TAMVX	NAS CM	Open End	US Equity Mid Cap (Growth)	C	C	B-			2,500
T. Rowe Price Mid-Cap Value Fund I Class	TRMIX	NAS CM	Open End	US Equity Mid Cap (Growth)	C	C	B-		Y	1,000,000
T. Rowe Price Mid-Cap Value Fund R Class	RRMVX	NAS CM	Open End	US Equity Mid Cap (Growth)	C	C	C+			2,500
T. Rowe Price Multi-Strategy Total Return Fund I Class	TMSSX	NAS CM	Open End	Moderate Alloc (Growth & Income)	D	D+	C+		Y	1,000,000
T. Rowe Price Multi-Strategy Total Return Investor Cls	TMSRX	NAS CM	Open End	Moderate Alloc (Growth & Income)	D	D+	C+		Y	2,500
T. Rowe Price New America Growth Fund	PRWAX	NAS CM	Open End	US Equity Large Cap Growth (Growth)	B-	C+	B	Down	Y	2,500
T. Rowe Price New America Growth Fund Advisor Class	PAWAX	NAS CM	Open End	US Equity Large Cap Growth (Growth)	B-	C+	B	Down	Y	0
T. Rowe Price New America Growth Fund I Class	PNAIX	NAS CM	Open End	US Equity Large Cap Growth (Growth)	B-	C+	B	Down	Y	1,000,000
T. Rowe Price New Asia Fund	PRASX	NAS CM	Open End	Asia ex-Japan Equity (Pacific Stock)	C	C	C+		Y	2,500
T. Rowe Price New Asia Fund I Class	PNSIX	NAS CM	Open End	Asia ex-Japan Equity (Pacific Stock)	C	C	C+		Y	1,000,000
T. Rowe Price New Era Fund	PRNEX	NAS CM	Open End	Natl Resources Sec Equity (Natl Res)	C	C-	C		Y	2,500
T. Rowe Price New Era Fund I Class	TRNEX	NAS CM	Open End	Natl Resources Sec Equity (Natl Res)	C	C-	C		Y	1,000,000
T. Rowe Price New Horizons Fund	PRNHX	NAS CM	Open End	US Equity Mid Cap (Aggr Growth)	B	B	B			2,500
T. Rowe Price New Horizons Fund I Class	PRJIX	NAS CM	Open End	US Equity Mid Cap (Aggr Growth)	B	B	B		Y	1,000,000
T. Rowe Price Overseas Stock Fund	TROSX	NAS CM	Open End	Global Equity Large Cap (Growth)	C	C	B-		Y	2,500
T. Rowe Price Overseas Stock Fund Advisor Class	PAEIX	NAS CM	Open End	Global Equity Large Cap (Growth)	C	C	C+		Y	2,500
T. Rowe Price Overseas Stock Fund I Class	TROIX	NAS CM	Open End	Global Equity Large Cap (Growth)	C	C	B-		Y	1,000,000
T. Rowe Price Personal Strategy Balanced Fund	TRPBX	NAS CM	Open End	Moderate Alloc (Balanced)	B	C	A-	Up	Y	2,500
T. Rowe Price Personal Strategy Balanced Fund I Class	TPPAX	NAS CM	Open End	Moderate Alloc (Balanced)	B	C	A-	Up	Y	1,000,000
T. Rowe Price Personal Strategy Growth Fund	TRSGX	NAS CM	Open End	Aggressive Alloc (Asset Alloc)	B-	C	B+	Up	Y	2,500
T. Rowe Price Personal Strategy Growth Fund I Class	TGIPX	NAS CM	Open End	Aggressive Alloc (Asset Alloc)	B-	C	B+	Up	Y	1,000,000
T. Rowe Price Personal Strategy Income Fund	PRSIX	NAS CM	Open End	Cautious Alloc (Asset Alloc)	B	C+	A	Up	Y	2,500
T. Rowe Price Personal Strategy Income Fund I Class	PPIPX	NAS CM	Open End	Cautious Alloc (Asset Alloc)	B	C+	A	Up	Y	1,000,000
T. Rowe Price QM Global Equity Fund	TQGEX	NAS CM	Open End	Global Equity Large Cap (Growth)	C+	C	B	Up	Y	2,500
T. Rowe Price QM Global Equity Fund Advisor Class	TQGAX	NAS CM	Open End	Global Equity Large Cap (Growth)	C+	C	B	Up	Y	2,500
T. Rowe Price QM Global Equity Fund I Class	TQGIX	NAS CM	Open End	Global Equity Large Cap (Growth)	C+	C	B	Up	Y	1,000,000
T. Rowe Price QM U.S. Small & Mid-Cap Core Equity Fund	TQSMX	NAS CM	Open End	US Equity Mid Cap (Growth)	C+	C	B-	Up	Y	2,500
T. Rowe Price QM U.S. Small & Mid-Cap Core Equity Adv Cls	TQSAX	NAS CM	Open End	US Equity Mid Cap (Growth)	C+	C	B-	Up	Y	2,500
T. Rowe Price QM U.S. Small & Mid-Cap Core Equity I Cls	TQSIX	NAS CM	Open End	US Equity Mid Cap (Growth)	C+	C	B-	Up	Y	1,000,000
T. Rowe Price QM U.S. Small-Cap Growth Equity Fund	PRDSX	NAS CM	Open End	US Equity Small Cap (Small Company)	C+	C	B-	Down	Y	2,500
T. Rowe Price QM U.S. Small-Cap Growth Equity Advisor Cls	TQAAX	NAS CM	Open End	US Equity Small Cap (Small Company)	C+	C	B-		Y	2,500

★ Expanded analysis of this fund is included in Section II.

TOTAL RETURNS						PERFORMANCE				ASSETS		ASSET ALLOCATION & TURNOVER					BULL & BEAR		FEES		
Min Additional Investment	3-Month Total Return	6-Month Total Return	1-Year Total Return	3-Year Total Return	5-Year Total Return	Dividend Yield (TTM)	Expense Ratio	3-Yr Std Deviation	3-Year Beta	NAV	Total Assets (MIL)	%Cash	%Stocks	%Bonds	%Other	Turnover Ratio	Last Bull Market Total Return	Last Bear Market Total Return	Front End Fee (%)	Back End Fee (%)	Inception Date
100	2.51	12.22	3.60	24.58		1.44	0.9	10.37	0.89	10.19	110.1	10	87	0	2	153					Aug-14
100	2.87	16.20	-6.72	38.37	38.84	0.48	1.2	12.34	1	63.95	7,857	4	94	0	2	32	20.32	-21.75			Dec-88
	2.90	16.29	-6.57	38.93	39.48	0.63	1.07	12.34	1	64.02	7,857	4	94	0	2	32	20.32	-21.75			Dec-15
100	3.18	13.60	0.03	29.51	11.12	2.65	0.46	11.29	0.99	13.61	580.8	0	100	0	0	11	14.19	-24.21			Nov-00
100	3.31	17.16	2.60	34.10	22.78	1.37	0.81	12.34	1.04	17.47	14,957	3	97	0	1	37	19.24	-23.53			May-80
100	3.23	17.08	2.37	33.04	21.62	1.03	1.07	12.32	1.04	17.54	14,957	3	97	0	1	37	19.14	-23.61			Mar-00
100	3.15	16.86	2.01	31.81	19.33	0.83	1.39	12.34	1.04	17.32	14,957	3	97	0	1	37	18.97	-23.7			Sep-02
	3.31	17.24	2.79	34.74	23.60	1.53	0.66	12.33	1.04	17.47	14,957	3	97	0	1	37	19.24	-23.53			Aug-15
100	2.05	11.22	-4.26	15.02	-4.17	2.24	0.81	11.77	1.04	13.38	10,427	2	98	0	0	58	15.56	-24.46			Dec-98
100	1.94	11.07	-4.52	14.09	-5.32	1.69	1.07	11.76	1.04	13.64	10,427	2	98	0	0	58	15.43	-24.59			Sep-02
	2.06	11.34	-4.10	15.54	-3.52	2.47	0.66	11.75	1.04	13.35	10,427	2	98	0	0	58	15.56	-24.46			Aug-15
100	1.89	10.90	-4.81	13.10	-6.73	1.56	1.39	11.78	1.04	13.42	10,427	2	98	0	0	58	15.18	-24.66			Sep-02
100	1.53	12.73	-4.51	35.35	52.39	0.68	0.95	13.25	1.12	13.9	747.3	2	98	0	0	34	6.94	-6.84			Dec-91
	1.53	12.81	-4.36	35.62	52.70	0.81	0.85	13.31	1.13	13.91	747.3	2	98	0	0	34	6.94	-6.84			Mar-17
100	6.54	16.45	25.71	40.16	7.43	1.24	1.29	20.44	0.94	25.55	603.6	5	93	0	0	26	13.11	-29.34			Dec-93
	6.63	16.59	25.98	40.77	7.90	1.44	1.09	20.43	0.94	25.57	603.6	5	93	0	0	26	13.11	-29.34			Mar-17
100	6.92	25.70	15.93	61.36	83.75	0.12	0.75	12.92	0.88	94.91	33,863	6	94	0	0	25	25.27	-20.15			Jun-92
100	6.85	25.57	15.64	60.12	81.40	0	1.02	12.93	0.88	91.78	33,863	6	94	0	0	25	25.11	-20.24			Mar-00
	6.96	25.76	16.06	61.98	84.63	0.23	0.62	12.92	0.88	94.94	33,863	6	94	0	0	25	25.27	-20.15			Aug-15
100	6.79	25.38	15.31	58.84	79.06	0	1.28	12.91	0.88	88.77	33,863	6	94	0	0	25	24.92	-20.33			Sep-02
100	1.22	12.68	-2.91	27.38	35.84	1	0.78	12.46	0.92	27.37	12,865	8	92	0	0	34	20.73	-19.44			Jun-96
100	1.15	12.51	-3.15	26.37	34.12	0.64	1.05	12.47	0.92	27.25	12,865	8	92	0	0	34	20.56	-19.5			Sep-02
	1.25	12.72	-2.80	27.89	36.49	1.13	0.65	12.45	0.92	27.37	12,865	8	92	0	0	34	20.73	-19.44			Aug-15
100	1.05	12.34	-3.43	25.41	32.42	0.41	1.3	12.46	0.92	26.75	12,865	8	92	0	0	34	20.4	-19.62			Sep-02
	1.35	4.87	1.35			1.83	1.12			9.69	61.9	26	4	66	0	82					Feb-18
100	1.35	4.87	1.35			1.83	1.17			9.69	61.9	26	4	66	0	82					Feb-18
100	5.34	23.16	11.90	77.09	95.65	0.17	0.79	13.66	0.99	53.01	5,248	4	95	0	1	78	21.8	-16.67			Sep-85
	5.29	22.99	11.61	75.68	93.05	0	1.06	13.65	0.99	51.72	5,248	4	95	0	1	78	21.63	-16.74			Dec-05
	5.38	23.23	12.05	77.82	96.56	0.29	0.66	13.66	0.99	53.03	5,248	4	95	0	1	78	21.8	-16.67			Dec-15
100	-0.39	14.80	0.19	38.19	29.52	1.24	0.93	14.63	0.97	17.68	2,779	2	97	0	1	50	20.01	-19.4			Sep-90
	-0.33	14.86	0.31	38.63	30.02	1.34	0.82	14.6	0.97	17.7	2,779	2	97	0	1	50	20.01	-19.4			Dec-15
100	0.88	14.42	-6.15	13.89	-13.80	1.49	0.69	14.43		34.19	3,523	1	98	0	0	52	17.09	-30.95			Jan-69
	0.91	14.52	-6.00	14.36	-13.38	1.64	0.56	14.44		34.21	3,523	1	98	0	0	52	17.09	-30.95			Dec-15
100	8.02	31.98	18.01	93.51	107.76	0	0.77	14.31	0.77	62.88	27,636	2	98	0	0	39	31.94	-18.11			Jun-60
	8.06	32.05	18.15	94.26	108.79	0	0.65	14.3	0.77	62.99	27,636	2	98	0	0	39	31.94	-18.11			Aug-15
100	1.95	12.52	-3.02	29.28	11.70	2	0.81	11.85	1.05	10.42	17,207	4	96	0	0	14	16.86	-23.21			Dec-06
100	1.97	12.30	-3.25	28.18	10.30	1.83	1.1	11.89	1.05	10.31	17,207	4	96	0	0	14	16.69	-23.29			Aug-15
	2.05	12.54	-2.92	29.83	12.43	2.09	0.66	11.86	1.05	10.41	17,207	4	96	0	0	14	16.86	-23.21			Aug-15
100	3.39	13.44	6.67	32.90	35.71	1.83	0.73	7.18	1.04	23.67	2,433	2	58	33	6	60	18.19	-13.12			Jul-94
	3.43	13.49	6.80	33.41	36.23	1.91	0.62	7.2	1.04	23.68	2,433	2	58	33	6	60	18.19	-13.12			Mar-16
100	3.55	15.98	6.40	41.07	42.25	1.33	0.79	9.38	1.02	34.39	2,481	1	78	16	5	56	22.31	-16.94			Jul-94
	3.60	16.06	6.55	41.64	42.87	1.39	0.66	9.38	1.02	34.46	2,481	1	78	16	5	56	22.31	-16.94			Mar-16
100	3.02	10.66	6.52	24.60	28.03	2.28	0.62	5.1	1.04	19.63	2,243	8	39	47	6	63	13.89	-9.48			Jul-94
	3.08	10.66	6.58	24.93	28.38	2.38	0.52	5.08	1.04	19.62	2,243	8	39	47	6	63	13.89	-9.48			Mar-16
100	4.08	18.81	7.26	40.13		1.51	0.72	11.18	0.98	13.26	19.7	0	99	0	0	18					Apr-16
100	4.08	18.63	6.90	38.74		1.21	1.04	11.15	0.98	13.24	19.7	0	99	0	0	18					Apr-16
	4.16	18.94	7.37	40.63		1.66	0.59	11.17	0.98	13.25	19.7	0	99	0	0	18					Apr-16
100	4.65	21.82	4.01	43.95		0.39	0.86	14.17	0.91	15.07	93.1	1	99	0	0	25					Feb-16
100	4.58	21.68	3.78	42.74		0.13	1.14	14.17	0.91	15.04	93.1	1	99	0	0	25					Feb-16
	4.71	21.98	4.23	44.67		0.52	0.69	14.18	0.91	15.09	93.1	1	99	0	0	25					Feb-16
100	5.33	24.97	6.84	56.59	66.40	0	0.8	15.45	0.89	38.48	7,978	0	100	0	0	18	30.19	-23.8			Jun-97
100	5.24	24.80	6.51	55.23	64.14	0	1.07	15.44	0.89	38.34	7,978	0	100	0	0	18	30	-23.88			Jul-16

	MARKET			FUND TYPE, CATEGORY & OBJECTIVE	RATINGS					MINIMUMS
Fund Name	Ticker Symbol	Traded On	Fund Type	Category and (Prospectus Objective)	Overall Rating	Reward Rating	Risk Rating	Recent Up/ Downgrade	Open to New Investors	Min Initial Investment
T. Rowe Price QM U.S. Small-Cap Growth Equity Fund I Class	TQAIX	NAS CM	Open End	US Equity Small Cap (Small Company)	C+	C	B-	Down	Y	1,000,000
T. Rowe Price QM U.S. Value Equity Fund	TQMVX	NAS CM	Open End	US Equity Large Cap Value (Growth)	C+	C	B	Up	Y	2,500
T. Rowe Price QM U.S. Value Equity Fund Advisor Class	TQVAX	NAS CM	Open End	US Equity Large Cap Value (Growth)	C+	C	B	Up	Y	2,500
T. Rowe Price QM U.S. Value Equity Fund I Class	TQVIX	NAS CM	Open End	US Equity Large Cap Value (Growth)	C+	C	B	Up	Y	1,000,000
T. Rowe Price Real Assets Fund	PRAFX	NAS CM	Open End	Aggressive Alloc (Real Estate)	C+	C	B		Y	2,500
T. Rowe Price Real Assets Fund I Class	PRIKX	NAS CM	Open End	Aggressive Alloc (Real Estate)	C+	C	B		Y	1,000,000
T. Rowe Price Real Estate Fund	TRREX	NAS CM	Open End	Real Estate Sector Equity (Real Estate)	C+	C	B-	Down	Y	2,500
T. Rowe Price Real Estate Fund Advisor Class	PAREX	NAS CM	Open End	Real Estate Sector Equity (Real Estate)	C+	C	B-	Down	Y	2,500
T. Rowe Price Real Estate Fund I Class	TIRRX	NAS CM	Open End	Real Estate Sector Equity (Real Estate)	C+	C	B-	Down	Y	1,000,000
T. Rowe Price Retirement 2005 Fund	TRRFX	NAS CM	Open End	Target Date (Asset Alloc)	B	C+	A	Up	Y	2,500
T. Rowe Price Retirement 2005 Fund Advisor Class	PARGX	NAS CM	Open End	Target Date (Asset Alloc)	B	C+	A-	Up	Y	0
T. Rowe Price Retirement 2005 Fund Class R	RRTLX	NAS CM	Open End	Target Date (Asset Alloc)	B	C+	A-	Up	Y	0
T. Rowe Price Retirement 2010 Fund	TRRAX	NAS CM	Open End	Target Date (Asset Alloc)	B	C+	A	Up	Y	2,500
T. Rowe Price Retirement 2010 Fund Advisor Class	PARAX	NAS CM	Open End	Target Date (Asset Alloc)	B	C+	A	Up	Y	0
T. Rowe Price Retirement 2010 Fund Class R	RRTAX	NAS CM	Open End	Target Date (Asset Alloc)	B	C+	A-	Up	Y	0
T. Rowe Price Retirement 2015 Fund	TRRGX	NAS CM	Open End	Target Date (Asset Alloc)	B	C+	A	Up	Y	2,500
T. Rowe Price Retirement 2015 Fund Advisor Class	PARHX	NAS CM	Open End	Target Date (Asset Alloc)	B	C+	A	Up	Y	0
T. Rowe Price Retirement 2015 Fund Class R	RRTMX	NAS CM	Open End	Target Date (Asset Alloc)	B	C	A	Up	Y	0
T. Rowe Price Retirement 2020 Fund	TRRBX	NAS CM	Open End	Target Date (Asset Alloc)	B	C	A-	Up	Y	2,500
T. Rowe Price Retirement 2020 Fund Advisor Class	PARBX	NAS CM	Open End	Target Date (Asset Alloc)	B	C	A-	Up	Y	0
T. Rowe Price Retirement 2020 Fund Class R	RRTBX	NAS CM	Open End	Target Date (Asset Alloc)	B	C	A-	Up	Y	0
T. Rowe Price Retirement 2025 Fund	TRRHX	NAS CM	Open End	Target Date (Asset Alloc)	B-	C	A-	Up	Y	2,500
T. Rowe Price Retirement 2025 Fund Advisor Class	PARJX	NAS CM	Open End	Target Date (Asset Alloc)	B-	C	A-	Up	Y	0
T. Rowe Price Retirement 2025 Fund Class R	RRTNX	NAS CM	Open End	Target Date (Asset Alloc)	B-	C	A-	Up	Y	0
T. Rowe Price Retirement 2030 Fund	TRRCX	NAS CM	Open End	Target Date (Asset Alloc)	B-	C	B+	Up	Y	2,500
T. Rowe Price Retirement 2030 Fund Advisor Class	PARCX	NAS CM	Open End	Target Date (Asset Alloc)	B-	C	B+	Up	Y	0
T. Rowe Price Retirement 2030 Fund Class R	RRTCX	NAS CM	Open End	Target Date (Asset Alloc)	B-	C	B+	Up	Y	0
T. Rowe Price Retirement 2035 Fund	TRRJX	NAS CM	Open End	Target Date (Asset Alloc)	B-	C	B+	Up	Y	2,500
T. Rowe Price Retirement 2035 Fund Advisor Class	PARKX	NAS CM	Open End	Target Date (Asset Alloc)	B-	C	B+	Up	Y	0
T. Rowe Price Retirement 2035 Fund Class R	RRTPX	NAS CM	Open End	Target Date (Asset Alloc)	B-	C	B+	Up	Y	0
T. Rowe Price Retirement 2040 Fund	TRRDX	NAS CM	Open End	Target Date (Asset Alloc)	B-	C	B+	Up	Y	2,500
T. Rowe Price Retirement 2040 Fund Advisor Class	PARDX	NAS CM	Open End	Target Date (Asset Alloc)	B-	C	B+	Up	Y	0
T. Rowe Price Retirement 2040 Fund Class R	RRTDX	NAS CM	Open End	Target Date (Asset Alloc)	B-	C	B+	Up	Y	0
T. Rowe Price Retirement 2045 Fund	TRRKX	NAS CM	Open End	Target Date (Asset Alloc)	B-	C	B+	Up	Y	2,500
T. Rowe Price Retirement 2045 Fund Advisor Class	PARLX	NAS CM	Open End	Target Date (Asset Alloc)	B-	C	B+	Up	Y	0
T. Rowe Price Retirement 2045 Fund Class R	RRTRX	NAS CM	Open End	Target Date (Asset Alloc)	B-	C	B	Up	Y	0
T. Rowe Price Retirement 2050 Fund	TRRMX	NAS CM	Open End	Target Date (Asset Alloc)	B-	C	B+	Up	Y	2,500
T. Rowe Price Retirement 2050 Fund Advisor Class	PARFX	NAS CM	Open End	Target Date (Asset Alloc)	B-	C	B+	Up	Y	0
T. Rowe Price Retirement 2050 Fund Class R	RRTFX	NAS CM	Open End	Target Date (Asset Alloc)	B-	C	B	Up	Y	0
T. Rowe Price Retirement 2055 Fund	TRRNX	NAS CM	Open End	Target Date (Asset Alloc)	B-	C	B+	Up	Y	2,500
T. Rowe Price Retirement 2055 Fund Advisor Class	PAROX	NAS CM	Open End	Target Date (Asset Alloc)	B-	C	B	Up	Y	0
T. Rowe Price Retirement 2055 Fund Class R	RRTVX	NAS CM	Open End	Target Date (Asset Alloc)	B-	C	B	Up	Y	0
T. Rowe Price Retirement 2060 Fund	TRRLX	NAS CM	Open End	Target Date (Asset Alloc)	B-	C	B+	Up	Y	2,500
T. Rowe Price Retirement 2060 Fund Advisor Class	TRRYX	NAS CM	Open End	Target Date (Asset Alloc)	B-	C	B+	Up	Y	0
T. Rowe Price Retirement 2060 Fund R Class	TRRZX	NAS CM	Open End	Target Date (Asset Alloc)	B-	C	B	Up	Y	0
T. Rowe Price Retirement Balanced Fund	TRRIX	NAS CM	Open End	Cautious Alloc (Asset Alloc)	B	C+	A	Up	Y	2,500
T. Rowe Price Retirement Balanced Fund Advisor Class	PARIX	NAS CM	Open End	Cautious Alloc (Asset Alloc)	B	C+	A-	Up	Y	0
T. Rowe Price Retirement Balanced Fund Class R	RRTIX	NAS CM	Open End	Cautious Alloc (Asset Alloc)	B	C	A-	Up	Y	0
T. Rowe Price Retirement Balanced I Fund I Class	TRPTX	NAS CM	Open End	Cautious Alloc (Asset Alloc)	B	C+	A	Up	Y	1,000,000
T. Rowe Price Retirement I 2005 Fund I Class	TRPFX	NAS CM	Open End	Target Date (Asset Alloc)	B	C+	A	Up	Y	1,000,000
T. Rowe Price Retirement I 2010 Fund I Class	TRPAX	NAS CM	Open End	Target Date (Asset Alloc)	B	C+	A	Up	Y	1,000,000
T. Rowe Price Retirement I 2015 Fund I Class	TRFGX	NAS CM	Open End	Target Date (Asset Alloc)	B	C+	A	Up	Y	1,000,000

★ Expanded analysis of this fund is included in Section II.

	TOTAL RETURNS					PERFORMANCE				ASSETS		ASSET ALLOCATION & TURNOVER					BULL & BEAR		FEES		
Min Additional Investment	3-Month Total Return	6-Month Total Return	1-Year Total Return	3-Year Total Return	5-Year Total Return	Dividend Yield (TTM)	Expense Ratio	3-Yr Std Deviation	3-Year Beta	NAV	Total Assets (MIL)	%Cash	%Stocks	%Bonds	%Other	Turnover Ratio	Last Bull Market Total Return	Last Bear Market Total Return	Front End Fee (%)	Back End Fee (%)	Inception Date
	5.38	25.06	6.98	57.23	67.21	0	0.66	15.46	0.89	38.57	7,978	0	100	0	0	18	30.19	-23.8			Mar-16
100	2.59	14.68	2.64	34.23		2.01	0.71	13.86	1.13	13.04	20.2	2	98	0	0	29					Feb-16
100	2.44	14.42	2.32	33.14		1.72	0.99	13.79	1.12	13.01	20.2	2	98	0	0	29					Feb-16
	2.59	14.77	2.81	34.94		2.16	0.54	13.86	1.13	13.05	20.2	2	98	0	0	29					Feb-16
100	1.14	14.95	1.45	15.41	3.35	2.25	0.81	11.39	0.82	11.53	3,117	3	96	0	0	54	17.15	-25.21			Jul-10
	1.23	14.96	1.55	15.95	3.83	2.43	0.66	11.39	0.82	11.52	3,117	3	96	0	0	54	17.15	-25.21			Aug-15
100	-0.02	16.54	5.87	8.48	35.53	2.58	0.78	12.93	0.98	28.4	3,916	1	99	0	0	4	32.33	-16.36			Oct-97
100	-0.05	16.43	5.63	7.64	33.91	2.31	1.03	12.94	0.98	28.8	3,916	1	99	0	0	4	32.2	-16.46			Dec-04
	0.04	16.70	6.09	9.02	36.30	2.75	0.61	12.93	0.98	28.42	3,916	1	99	0	0	4	32.33	-16.36			Dec-15
100	3.11	10.24	6.61	20.60	24.14	2.2	0.54	4.67	1.15	13.56	1,348	4	36	60	0	35	13	-9.33			Feb-04
	2.97	10.02	6.31	19.68	22.55	1.92	0.79	4.65	1.14	13.5	1,348	4	36	60	0	35	12.84	-9.44			May-07
	3.03	9.95	6.09	18.86	21.14	1.63	1.04	4.65	1.14	13.59	1,348	4	36	60	0	35	12.63	-9.51			May-07
100	3.22	10.94	6.71	22.55	26.10	2.11	0.54	5.18	1.11	17.94	4,043	3	41	55	0	31	14.72	-11.09			Sep-02
	3.12	10.73	6.43	21.65	24.56	1.86	0.79	5.16	1.1	17.84	4,043	3	41	55	0	31	14.57	-11.15			Oct-03
	3.08	10.68	6.16	20.70	22.96	1.6	1.04	5.2	1.11	17.72	4,043	3	41	55	0	31	14.43	-11.27			Oct-03
100	3.28	11.81	6.59	25.69	28.98	2.06	0.57	5.9	1.09	14.48	6,435	3	48	49	0	33	16.77	-12.97			Feb-04
	3.21	11.68	6.38	24.76	27.50	1.81	0.82	5.9	1.09	14.43	6,435	3	48	49	0	33	16.64	-13.09			May-07
	3.10	11.56	6.11	23.80	25.82	1.5	1.07	5.9	1.09	14.28	6,435	3	48	49	0	33	16.46	-13.17			May-07
100	3.38	13.11	6.65	29.75	32.68	1.92	0.61	6.98	1.15	21.99	18,453	3	57	40	0	30	18.62	-14.71			Sep-02
	3.36	12.94	6.39	28.79	31.01	1.68	0.86	6.98	1.15	21.81	18,453	3	57	40	0	30	18.38	-14.74			Oct-03
	3.30	12.80	6.08	27.82	29.41	1.39	1.11	6.97	1.15	21.59	18,453	3	57	40	0	30	18.31	-14.85			Oct-03
100	3.48	14.20	6.55	33.12	35.63	1.74	0.64	7.86	1.11	17.53	17,282	3	65	32	0	30	20.04	-16.08			Feb-04
	3.44	14.07	6.33	32.13	34.03	1.53	0.89	7.85	1.11	17.42	17,282	3	65	32	0	30	19.93	-16.22			May-07
	3.36	13.88	6.00	31.06	32.27	1.27	1.14	7.84	1.11	17.22	17,282	3	65	32	0	30	19.76	-16.31			May-07
100	3.60	15.23	6.47	36.35	38.41	1.62	0.67	8.71	1.06	25.56	21,904	2	73	24	0	28	21.5	-17.37			Sep-02
	3.51	15.09	6.16	35.25	36.65	1.38	0.92	8.72	1.06	25.31	21,904	2	73	24	0	28	21.39	-17.53			Oct-03
	3.46	14.94	5.93	34.24	34.97	1.13	1.17	8.7	1.06	25.08	21,904	2	73	24	0	28	21.24	-17.63			Oct-03
100	3.64	16.08	6.27	38.74	40.30	1.46	0.7	9.39	1.02	18.76	13,494	2	79	18	0	25	22.42	-18.29			Feb-04
	3.55	15.91	6.04	37.73	38.52	1.22	0.95	9.44	1.02	18.65	13,494	2	79	18	0	25	22.2	-18.41			May-07
	3.54	15.77	5.74	36.64	36.83	0.97	1.2	9.42	1.02	18.42	13,494	2	79	18	0	25	22.17	-18.54			May-07
100	3.68	16.73	6.20	40.85	41.84	1.37	0.72	9.99	1.01	26.72	15,448	2	85	13	0	23	22.82	-18.65			Sep-02
	3.64	16.61	5.91	39.77	40.05	1.1	0.97	9.96	1.01	26.46	15,448	2	85	13	0	23	22.7	-18.73			Oct-03
	3.55	16.40	5.63	38.75	38.32	0.86	1.22	9.96	1.01	26.25	15,448	2	85	13	0	23	22.53	-18.82			Oct-03
100	3.64	17.10	6.05	41.49	42.43	1.29	0.72	10.32	1.01	18.21	8,839	2	88	9	0	27	22.77	-18.49			May-05
	3.61	16.94	5.83	40.39	40.62	1.04	0.97	10.28	1.01	18.08	8,839	2	88	9	0	27	22.55	-18.56			May-07
	3.53	16.80	5.57	39.35	38.94	0.79	1.22	10.29	1.01	17.86	8,839	2	88	9	0	27	22.4	-18.68			May-07
100	3.71	17.16	6.11	41.53	42.41	1.23	0.72	10.3	0.98	15.36	7,437	2	88	10	0	30	22.77	-18.52			Dec-06
	3.68	16.99	5.86	40.48	40.72	0.99	0.97	10.3	0.98	15.21	7,437	2	88	10	0	30	22.53	-18.61			Dec-06
	3.57	16.83	5.52	39.41	38.91	0.75	1.22	10.29	0.98	15.06	7,437	2	88	10	0	30	22.28	-18.62			Dec-06
100	3.66	17.16	6.08	41.34	42.34	1.16	0.72	10.32	0.98	15.56	3,834	2	88	10	0	36	22.72	-18.45			Dec-06
	3.62	16.96	5.82	40.39	40.62	0.98	0.97	10.33	0.98	15.44	3,834	2	88	10	0	36	22.56	-18.59			May-07
	3.51	16.84	5.48	39.31	38.80	0.74	1.22	10.3	0.98	15.33	3,834	2	88	10	0	36	22.48	-18.63			May-07
100	3.70	17.14	6.06	41.42	42.32	1.1	0.72	10.3	0.97	12.3	750.9	2	88	10	0	35					Jun-14
	3.64	17.03	5.81	40.35	40.67	0.95	0.97	10.29	0.96	12.23	750.9	2	88	10	0	35					Jun-14
	3.57	16.90	5.54	39.29	38.90	0.71	1.22	10.32	0.97	12.17	750.9	2	88	10	0	35					Jun-14
100	3.00	10.35	6.19	20.56	23.16	1.81	0.52	4.86	1.19	15.17	2,153	4	39	56	0	25	11.7	-8.39			Sep-02
	2.93	10.21	5.97	19.78	21.67	1.61	0.77	4.91	1.2	15.18	2,153	4	39	56	0	25	11.46	-8.48			Oct-03
	2.87	10.08	5.67	18.85	20.12	1.34	1.02	4.87	1.19	15.17	2,153	4	39	56	0	25	11.39	-8.58			Oct-03
	3.13	10.39	6.40	20.99		1.95	0.38	4.84	1.19	11.49	342.1	4	39	56	0	46					Sep-15
	3.15	10.31	6.85	21.04		1.93	0.4	4.67	1.14	11.76	255.2	4	36	60	0	55					Sep-15
	3.17	10.89	6.83	23.01		1.88	0.39	5.15	1.1	12.01	691.4	4	41	55	0	50					Sep-15
	3.38	11.91	6.77	26.17		1.93	0.43	5.91	1.09	12.21	1,341	3	48	49	0	50					Sep-15

	MARKET			FUND TYPE, CATEGORY & OBJECTIVE	RATINGS				MINIMUMS	
Fund Name	Ticker Symbol	Traded On	Fund Type	Category and (Prospectus Objective)	Overall Rating	Reward Rating	Risk Rating	Recent Up/ Downgrade	Open to New Investors	Min Initial Investment
T. Rowe Price Retirement I 2020 Fund I Class	TRBRX	NAS CM	Open End	Target Date (Asset Alloc)	B	C+	A-	Up	Y	1,000,000
T. Rowe Price Retirement I 2025 Fund I Class	TRPHX	NAS CM	Open End	Target Date (Asset Alloc)	B-	C	A-	Up	Y	1,000,000
T. Rowe Price Retirement I 2030 Fund I Class	TRPCX	NAS CM	Open End	Target Date (Asset Alloc)	B-	C	B+	Up	Y	1,000,000
T. Rowe Price Retirement I 2035 Fund I Class	TRPJX	NAS CM	Open End	Target Date (Asset Alloc)	B-	C	B+	Up	Y	1,000,000
T. Rowe Price Retirement I 2040 Fund I Class	TRPDX	NAS CM	Open End	Target Date (Asset Alloc)	B-	C	B+	Up	Y	1,000,000
T. Rowe Price Retirement I 2045 Fund I Class	TRPKX	NAS CM	Open End	Target Date (Asset Alloc)	B-	C	B+	Up	Y	1,000,000
T. Rowe Price Retirement I 2050 Fund I Class	TRPMX	NAS CM	Open End	Target Date (Asset Alloc)	B-	C	B+	Up	Y	1,000,000
T. Rowe Price Retirement I 2055 Fund I Class	TRPNX	NAS CM	Open End	Target Date (Asset Alloc)	B-	C	B+	Up	Y	1,000,000
T. Rowe Price Retirement I 2060 Fund I Class	TRPLX	NAS CM	Open End	Target Date (Asset Alloc)	B-	C	B+	Up	Y	1,000,000
T. Rowe Price Retirement Income 2020 Fund	TRLAX	NAS CM	Open End	Target Date (Asset Alloc)	C	D+	B	Up	Y	25,000
T. Rowe Price Science and Technology Fund	PRSCX	NAS CM	Open End	Technology Sector Equity (Technology)	C+	C+	B-		Y	2,500
T. Rowe Price Science and Technology Fund Advisor Class	PASTX	NAS CM	Open End	Technology Sector Equity (Technology)	C+	C+	B-		Y	2,500
T. Rowe Price Science and Technology Fund I Class	TSNIX	NAS CM	Open End	Technology Sector Equity (Technology)	C+	C+	B-		Y	1,000,000
T. Rowe Price Small-Cap Stock Fund	OTCFX	NAS CM	Open End	US Equity Small Cap (Small Company)	B-	C+	B	Down		2,500
T. Rowe Price Small-Cap Stock Fund Advisor Class	PASSX	NAS CM	Open End	US Equity Small Cap (Small Company)	B-	C+	B	Down		2,500
T. Rowe Price Small-Cap Stock Fund I Class	OTIIX	NAS CM	Open End	US Equity Small Cap (Small Company)	B-	C+	B	Down	Y	1,000,000
T. Rowe Price Small-Cap Value Fund	PRSVX	NAS CM	Open End	US Equity Small Cap (Small Company)	C+	C	B-	Up	Y	2,500
T. Rowe Price Small-Cap Value Fund Advisor Class	PASVX	NAS CM	Open End	US Equity Small Cap (Small Company)	C+	C	B-	Up	Y	2,500
T. Rowe Price Small-Cap Value Fund I Class	PRVIX	NAS CM	Open End	US Equity Small Cap (Small Company)	C+	C	B-	Up	Y	1,000,000
T. Rowe Price Spectrum Growth Fund	PRSGX	NAS CM	Open End	US Equity Large Cap Growth (Growth)	B-	C	B	Up	Y	2,500
T. Rowe Price Spectrum International Fund	PSILX	NAS CM	Open End	Global Equity Large Cap (Growth)	C	C	B-		Y	2,500
T. Rowe Price Target 2005 Fund	TRARX	NAS CM	Open End	Target Date (Asset Alloc)	B	C+	A-	Up	Y	2,500
T. Rowe Price Target 2005 Fund Advisor Class	PANRX	NAS CM	Open End	Target Date (Asset Alloc)	B	C+	A-	Up	Y	0
T. Rowe Price Target 2005 Fund I Class	TFRRX	NAS CM	Open End	Target Date (Asset Alloc)	B	C+	A	Up	Y	1,000,000
T. Rowe Price Target 2010 Fund	TRROX	NAS CM	Open End	Target Date (Asset Alloc)	B	C+	A	Up	Y	2,500
T. Rowe Price Target 2010 Fund Advisor Class	PAERX	NAS CM	Open End	Target Date (Asset Alloc)	B	C+	A-	Up	Y	0
T. Rowe Price Target 2010 Fund I Class	TORFX	NAS CM	Open End	Target Date (Asset Alloc)	B	C+	A	Up	Y	1,000,000
T. Rowe Price Target 2015 Fund	TRRTX	NAS CM	Open End	Target Date (Asset Alloc)	B	C+	A	Up	Y	2,500
T. Rowe Price Target 2015 Fund Advisor Class	PAHRX	NAS CM	Open End	Target Date (Asset Alloc)	B	C+	A-	Up	Y	0
T. Rowe Price Target 2015 Fund I Class	TTRTX	NAS CM	Open End	Target Date (Asset Alloc)	B	C+	A	Up	Y	1,000,000
T. Rowe Price Target 2020 Fund	TRRUX	NAS CM	Open End	Target Date (Asset Alloc)	B	C+	A	Up	Y	2,500
T. Rowe Price Target 2020 Fund Advisor Class	PAIRX	NAS CM	Open End	Target Date (Asset Alloc)	B	C+	A	Up	Y	0
T. Rowe Price Target 2020 Fund I Class	TTURX	NAS CM	Open End	Target Date (Asset Alloc)	B	C+	A	Up	Y	1,000,000
T. Rowe Price Target 2025 Fund	TRRVX	NAS CM	Open End	Target Date (Asset Alloc)	B	C	A	Up	Y	2,500
T. Rowe Price Target 2025 Fund Advisor Class	PAJRX	NAS CM	Open End	Target Date (Asset Alloc)	B	C	A	Up	Y	0
T. Rowe Price Target 2025 Fund I Class	TRVVX	NAS CM	Open End	Target Date (Asset Alloc)	B	C+	A	Up	Y	1,000,000
T. Rowe Price Target 2030 Fund	TRRWX	NAS CM	Open End	Target Date (Asset Alloc)	B	C	A-	Up	Y	2,500
T. Rowe Price Target 2030 Fund Advisor Class	PAKRX	NAS CM	Open End	Target Date (Asset Alloc)	B	C	A-	Up	Y	0
T. Rowe Price Target 2030 Fund I Class	TWRRX	NAS CM	Open End	Target Date (Asset Alloc)	B	C	A-	Up	Y	1,000,000
T. Rowe Price Target 2035 Fund	RPGRX	NAS CM	Open End	Target Date (Asset Alloc)	B-	C	A-	Up	Y	2,500
T. Rowe Price Target 2035 Fund Advisor Class	PATVX	NAS CM	Open End	Target Date (Asset Alloc)	B-	C	A-	Up	Y	0
T. Rowe Price Target 2035 Fund I Class	TPGPX	NAS CM	Open End	Target Date (Asset Alloc)	B-	C	A-	Up	Y	1,000,000
T. Rowe Price Target 2040 Fund	TRHRX	NAS CM	Open End	Target Date (Asset Alloc)	B-	C	B+	Up	Y	2,500
T. Rowe Price Target 2040 Fund Advisor Class	PAHHX	NAS CM	Open End	Target Date (Asset Alloc)	B-	C	B+	Up	Y	0
T. Rowe Price Target 2040 Fund I Class	TRXRX	NAS CM	Open End	Target Date (Asset Alloc)	B-	C	B+	Up	Y	1,000,000
T. Rowe Price Target 2045 Fund	RPTFX	NAS CM	Open End	Target Date (Asset Alloc)	B-	C	B+	Up	Y	2,500
T. Rowe Price Target 2045 Fund Advisor Class	PAFFX	NAS CM	Open End	Target Date (Asset Alloc)	B-	C	B+	Up	Y	0
T. Rowe Price Target 2045 Fund I Class	TRFWX	NAS CM	Open End	Target Date (Asset Alloc)	B-	C	B+	Up	Y	1,000,000
T. Rowe Price Target 2050 Fund	TRFOX	NAS CM	Open End	Target Date (Asset Alloc)	B-	C	B+	Up	Y	2,500
T. Rowe Price Target 2050 Fund Advisor Class	PAOFX	NAS CM	Open End	Target Date (Asset Alloc)	B-	C	B+	Up	Y	0
T. Rowe Price Target 2050 Fund I Class	TOORX	NAS CM	Open End	Target Date (Asset Alloc)	B-	C	B+	Up	Y	1,000,000
T. Rowe Price Target 2055 Fund	TRFFX	NAS CM	Open End	Target Date (Asset Alloc)	B-	C	B+	Up	Y	2,500

★ Expanded analysis of this fund is included in Section II.

	TOTAL RETURNS					PERFORMANCE				ASSETS		ASSET ALLOCATION & TURNOVER					BULL & BEAR		FEES		
Min Additional Investment	3-Month Total Return	6-Month Total Return	1-Year Total Return	3-Year Total Return	5-Year Total Return	Dividend Yield (TTM)	Expense Ratio	3-Yr Std Deviation	3-Year Beta	NAV	Total Assets (MIL)	%Cash	%Stocks	%Bonds	%Other	Turnover Ratio	Last Bull Market Total Return	Last Bear Market Total Return	Front End Fee (%)	Back End Fee (%)	Inception Date
	3.42	13.20	6.73	30.21		1.78	0.47	6.91	1.14	12.69	4,743	3	57	40	0	39					Sep-15
	3.58	14.31	6.74	33.56		1.65	0.5	7.84	1.11	13.02	4,995	2	66	32	0	36					Sep-15
	3.59	15.31	6.56	36.71		1.55	0.53	8.68	1.06	13.25	6,369	2	73	24	0	34					Sep-15
	3.69	16.19	6.41	39.21		1.48	0.56	9.41	1.02	13.49	4,238	2	80	18	0	30					Sep-15
	3.72	16.79	6.29	41.33		1.35	0.58	9.97	1.01	13.63	4,999	2	85	13	0	27					Sep-15
	3.69	17.13	6.18	41.94		1.31	0.59	10.32	1.01	13.74	3,051	2	88	10	0	25					Sep-15
	3.70	17.26	6.21	41.97		1.35	0.59	10.31	0.98	13.72	2,999	2	88	10	0	24					Sep-15
	3.76	17.26	6.21	42.01		1.27	0.59	10.31	0.98	13.79	1,350	2	88	10	0	24					Sep-15
	3.78	17.26	6.27	41.97		1.25	0.59	10.32	0.97	13.72	346.3	2	88	10	0	27					Sep-15
100	3.34	13.03	6.46			4.32	0.71			9.98	41.1	3	57	40	0	38					May-17
100	2.51	26.22	5.16	77.95	108.60	0	0.79	17.16	1.2	39.52	5,994	11	89	0	0	109	20.99	-19			Sep-87
100	2.45	26.05	4.90	76.59	106.10	0	1.06	17.16	1.2	38.85	5,994	11	89	0	0	109	20.84	-19.05			Mar-00
	2.54	26.30	5.30	78.71	109.48	0	0.66	17.18	1.2	39.52	5,994	11	89	0	0	109	20.99	-19			Mar-16
100	5.66	25.53	10.63	60.66	63.35	0	0.89	14.73	0.84	51.28	10,220	3	97	0	0	34	32.01	-23.84			Jun-56
100	5.60	25.35	10.34	59.37	61.17	0	1.16	14.72	0.84	50.72	10,220	3	97	0	0	34	31.84	-23.93			Mar-00
	5.70	25.60	10.77	61.33	64.19	0	0.75	14.73	0.84	51.31	10,220	3	97	0	0	34	32.01	-23.84			Aug-15
100	4.51	18.70	0.01	44.80	42.62	0.34	0.85	15.62	0.9	46.97	9,888	2	98	0	0	19	28.42	-21.85			Jun-88
100	4.44	18.54	-0.05	43.70	40.69	0	1.1	15.63	0.9	46.79	9,888	2	98	0	0	19	28.23	-21.92			Mar-00
	4.53	18.75	0.11	45.30	43.30	0.45	0.73	15.62	0.9	46.98	9,888	2	98	0	0	19	28.42	-21.85			Aug-15
100	3.79	18.42	5.10	46.58	46.53	1.06	0.77	11.74	0.9	23.52	3,696	2	98	0	0	11	24.65	-19.4			Jun-90
100	2.77	14.98	0.14	29.04	14.73	1.65	0.9	11.92	1.02	13.35	1,524	1	99	0	0	15	18.13	-23.53			Dec-96
100	3.10	10.01	6.65	19.35	22.86	1.94	0.54	4.44	1.09	11.64	37.6	4	34	62	0	44					Aug-13
	3.00	9.79	6.34	18.48	21.39	1.51	0.79	4.38	1.07	11.66	37.6	4	34	62	0	44					Aug-13
	3.09	10.00	6.74	19.67	23.19	2.02	0.4	4.42	1.08	11.65	37.6	4	34	62	0	44					Feb-16
100	3.10	10.12	6.64	19.98	23.47	2.01	0.52	4.56	0.97	11.64	67.6	4	35	60	0	49					Aug-13
	3.09	10.11	6.42	19.14	21.93	1.5	0.79	4.55	0.97	11.65	67.6	4	35	60	0	49					Aug-13
	3.18	10.31	6.82	20.49	23.88	2.09	0.39	4.61	0.98	11.66	67.6	4	35	60	0	49					Feb-16
100	3.21	10.60	6.69	21.59	24.74	1.93	0.53	4.84	0.89	11.89	197.4	4	38	58	0	40					Aug-13
	3.13	10.42	6.27	20.53	22.98	1.56	0.81	4.8	0.88	11.86	197.4	4	38	58	0	40					Aug-13
	3.21	10.51	6.65	21.76	24.92	1.97	0.42	4.79	0.88	11.88	197.4	4	38	58	0	40					Feb-16
100	3.21	11.32	6.44	24.31	27.04	1.67	0.59	5.49	0.9	12.19	322.8	3	44	52	0	37					Aug-13
	3.14	11.17	6.17	23.24	25.27	1.36	0.84	5.54	0.91	12.14	322.8	3	44	52	0	37					Aug-13
	3.21	11.31	6.52	24.61	27.47	1.75	0.45	5.56	0.91	12.2	322.8	3	44	52	0	37					Feb-16
100	3.30	12.21	6.37	27.13	29.73	1.48	0.61	6.28	0.88	12.49	350.7	3	52	45	0	31					Aug-13
	3.23	12.15	6.09	26.22	28.00	1.17	0.86	6.28	0.88	12.46	350.7	3	52	45	0	31					Aug-13
	3.30	12.32	6.42	27.61	30.22	1.59	0.47	6.3	0.89	12.49	350.7	3	52	45	0	31					Feb-16
100	3.39	13.29	6.40	30.40	32.85	1.51	0.65	7.16	0.87	12.78	349.2	3	59	38	0	34					Aug-13
	3.32	13.14	6.14	29.43	31.27	1.21	0.9	7.12	0.86	12.74	349.2	3	59	38	0	34					Aug-13
	3.39	13.39	6.50	30.83	33.40	1.66	0.51	7.11	0.86	12.78	349.2	3	59	38	0	34					Feb-16
100	3.50	14.34	6.44	33.30	35.68	1.41	0.68	7.94	0.86	12.99	233.4	3	66	31	0	30					Aug-13
	3.43	14.08	6.09	32.27	33.91	1.12	0.93	7.91	0.85	12.96	233.4	3	66	31	0	30					Aug-13
	3.58	14.42	6.61	33.93	36.32	1.56	0.54	7.89	0.85	13.01	233.4	3	66	31	0	30					Feb-16
100	3.59	15.23	6.36	35.83	37.86	1.39	0.7	8.6	0.87	13.24	202.5	2	72	25	0	31					Aug-13
	3.53	15.09	6.20	34.87	36.17	1.17	0.95	8.67	0.88	13.19	202.5	2	72	25	0	31					Aug-13
	3.59	15.31	6.54	36.37	38.41	1.53	0.56	8.63	0.87	13.25	202.5	2	72	25	0	31					Feb-16
100	3.67	15.82	6.35	37.86	39.47	1.29	0.71	9.14	0.89	13.54	164.1	2	78	20	0	25					Aug-13
	3.52	15.69	6.03	36.78	37.65	1.08	0.96	9.15	0.89	13.49	164.1	2	78	20	0	25					Aug-13
	3.74	15.99	6.53	38.38	40.12	1.43	0.57	9.18	0.9	13.56	164.1	2	78	20	0	25					Feb-16
100	3.71	16.41	6.23	39.59	40.77	1.23	0.72	9.7	0.92	13.69	120.1	2	82	15	0	27					Aug-13
	3.57	16.29	5.94	38.47	39.03	0.99	0.97	9.66	0.92	13.63	120.1	2	82	15	0	27					Aug-13
	3.70	16.49	6.36	40.07	41.26	1.34	0.58	9.69	0.92	13.7	120.1	2	82	15	0	27					Feb-16
100	3.65	16.83	6.06	40.76	41.76	1.17	0.72	10.04	0.95	13.6	72.8	2	86	12	0	32					Aug-13

	MARKET		FUND TYPE, CATEGORY & OBJECTIVE		RATINGS				MINIMUMS	
Fund Name	Ticker Symbol	Traded On	Fund Type	Category and (Prospectus Objective)	Overall Rating	Reward Rating	Risk Rating	Recent Up/ Downgrade	Open to New Investors	Min Initial Investment
T. Rowe Price Target 2055 Fund Advisor Class	PAFTX	NAS CM	Open End	Target Date (Asset Alloc)	B-	C	B+	Up	Y	0
T. Rowe Price Target 2055 Fund I Class	TRPPX	NAS CM	Open End	Target Date (Asset Alloc)	B-	C	B+	Up	Y	1,000,000
T. Rowe Price Target 2060 Fund	TRTFX	NAS CM	Open End	Target Date (Asset Alloc)	B-	C	B+	Up	Y	2,500
T. Rowe Price Target 2060 Fund Advisor Class	TRTGX	NAS CM	Open End	Target Date (Asset Alloc)	B-	C	B+	Up	Y	0
T. Rowe Price Target 2060 Fund I Class	TTOIX	NAS CM	Open End	Target Date (Asset Alloc)	B-	C	B+	Up	Y	1,000,000
T. Rowe Price Tax-Efficient Equity Fund	PREFX	NAS CM	Open End	US Equity Large Cap Growth (Growth)	B-	B-	B	Down	Y	2,500
T. Rowe Price Tax-Efficient Equity Fund I Class	TEEFX	NAS CM	Open End	US Equity Large Cap Growth (Growth)	B-	B-	B	Down	Y	1,000,000
T. Rowe Price Total Equity Market Index Fund	POMIX	NAS CM	Open End	US Equity Large Cap Blend (Growth)	B-	C	B		Y	2,500
T. Rowe Price U.S. Large-Cap Core Fund	TRULX	NAS CM	Open End	US Equity Large Cap Blend (Growth)	B	C+	B+		Y	2,500
T. Rowe Price U.S. Large-Cap Core Fund Advisor Class	PAULX	NAS CM	Open End	US Equity Large Cap Blend (Growth)	B	C+	B+		Y	2,500
T. Rowe Price U.S. Large-Cap Core Fund I Class	RCLIX	NAS CM	Open End	US Equity Large Cap Blend (Growth)	B	C+	B+		Y	1,000,000
T. Rowe Price Value Fund	TRVLX	NAS CM	Open End	US Equity Large Cap Value (Growth)	B-	C	B	Up	Y	2,500
T. Rowe Price Value Fund Advisor Class	PAVLX	NAS CM	Open End	US Equity Large Cap Value (Growth)	B-	C	B	Up	Y	2,500
T. Rowe Price Value Fund I Class	TRPIX	NAS CM	Open End	US Equity Large Cap Value (Growth)	B-	C	B	Up	Y	1,000,000
Taiwan Fund Inc	TWN	NYSE	Closed End	Greater China Equity (Pacific Stock)	D+	C-	D+	Down	Y	
Tanaka Growth Fund	TGFRX	NAS CM	Open End	US Equity Mid Cap (Growth)	D+	D	C-	Down	Y	2,000
Target 2015 Allocation Fund Class B			Open End	Target Date (Asset Alloc)	B	C	A-	Up	Y	0
Target 2015 Allocation Portfolio Class K			Open End	Target Date (Asset Alloc)	B	C	A-	Up	Y	0
Target 2025 Allocation Fund Class B			Open End	Target Date (Asset Alloc)	B-	C	B+	Up	Y	0
Target 2025 Allocation Portfolio Class K			Open End	Target Date (Asset Alloc)	B-	C	B+	Up	Y	0
Target 2035 Allocation Fund Class B			Open End	Target Date (Asset Alloc)	B-	C	B+	Up	Y	0
Target 2035 Allocation Portfolio Class K			Open End	Target Date (Asset Alloc)	B-	C	B+	Up	Y	0
Target 2045 Allocation Fund Class B			Open End	Target Date (Asset Alloc)	B-	C	B	Up	Y	0
Target 2045 Allocation Portfolio Class K			Open End	Target Date (Asset Alloc)	B-	C	B	Up	Y	0
Target 2055 Allocation Portfolio Class B			Open End	Target Date (Asset Alloc)	C+	C	B	Up	Y	0
Target 2055 Allocation Portfolio Class K			Open End	Target Date (Asset Alloc)	C+	C	B	Up	Y	0
Tarkio Fund	TARKX	NAS CM	Open End	US Equity Mid Cap (Growth)	C	C-	C		Y	2,500
Taylor Frigon Core Growth Fund	TFCGX	NAS CM	Open End	US Equity Large Cap Growth (Growth)	C+	C	B-	Up	Y	5,000
TCM Small Cap Growth Fund	TCMSX	NAS CM	Open End	US Equity Small Cap (Small Company)	C+	C	C+	Down	Y	2,500
TCW Artificial Intelligence Equity Fund Class I	TGFTX	NAS CM	Open End	Technology Sector Equity (Growth)	C-	D+	C+	Up	Y	2,000
TCW Artificial Intelligence Equity Fund Class N	TGJNX	NAS CM	Open End	Technology Sector Equity (Growth)	C-	D+	C+	Up	Y	2,000
TCW Conservative Allocation Fund Class Institutional	TGPCX	NAS CM	Open End	Cautious Alloc (Income)	B	C	A-	Up	Y	2,000
TCW Conservative Allocation Fund Class N	TGPNX	NAS CM	Open End	Cautious Alloc (Income)	B-	C	A-		Y	2,000
TCW Developing Markets Equity Fund Class I	TGDMX	NAS CM	Open End	Global Emerg Mkts (Growth)	C-	C-	C		Y	2,000
TCW Developing Markets Equity Fund Class N	TGDPX	NAS CM	Open End	Global Emerg Mkts (Growth)	C-	C-	C		Y	2,000
TCW Emerging Markets Multi-Asset Opportunities I Share Cls	TGMAX	NAS CM	Open End	Global Emerg Mkts (Div Emerging Mkts)	C	C	B		Y	2,000
TCW Emerging Markets Multi-Asset Opportunities N Share Cls	TGMEX	NAS CM	Open End	Global Emerg Mkts (Div Emerging Mkts)	C	C	B		Y	2,000
TCW Enhanced Commodity Strategy Fund Class I	TGGWX	NAS CM	Open End	Commodities Broad Basket (Growth)	C-	D+	C	Up	Y	2,000
TCW Enhanced Commodity Strategy Fund Class N	TGABX	NAS CM	Open End	Commodities Broad Basket (Growth)	C-	D+	C	Up	Y	2,000
TCW Global Real Estate Fund Class I	TGREX	NAS CM	Open End	Real Estate Sector Equity (Real Estate)	C+	C	B-		Y	2,000
TCW Global Real Estate Fund Class N	TGRYX	NAS CM	Open End	Real Estate Sector Equity (Real Estate)	C+	C	B-		Y	2,000
TCW International Small Cap Fund Class I	TGICX	NAS CM	Open End	Global Equity Mid/Small Cap (Small Company)	C-	C-	C-		Y	2,000
TCW International Small Cap Fund Class N	TGNIX	NAS CM	Open End	Global Equity Mid/Small Cap (Small Company)	C-	C-	C-		Y	2,000
TCW New America Premier Equities Fund Class I	TGUSX	NAS CM	Open End	US Equity Large Cap Blend (Growth)	B+	B+	B	Up	Y	2,000
TCW New America Premier Equities Fund Class N	TGUNX	NAS CM	Open End	US Equity Large Cap Blend (Growth)	B+	B+	B	Up	Y	2,000
TCW Relative Value Dividend Appreciation Fund Class I	TGDFX	NAS CM	Open End	US Equity Large Cap Value (Equity-Income)	C	C	B-		Y	2,000
TCW Relative Value Dividend Appreciation Fund Class N	TGIGX	NAS CM	Open End	US Equity Large Cap Value (Equity-Income)	C	C	B-		Y	2,000
TCW Relative Value Large Cap Fund Class Institutional	TGDIX	NAS CM	Open End	US Equity Large Cap Value (Growth)	C	C	C+		Y	2,000
TCW Relative Value Large Cap Fund Class N	TGDVX	NAS CM	Open End	US Equity Large Cap Value (Growth)	C	C	C+		Y	2,000
TCW Relative Value Mid Cap Fund Class I	TGVOX	NAS CM	Open End	US Equity Mid Cap (Growth)	C	C	C		Y	2,000
TCW Relative Value Mid Cap Fund Class N	TGVNX	NAS CM	Open End	US Equity Mid Cap (Growth)	C	C	C		Y	2,000
TCW Select Equities Fund Class I	TGCEX	NAS CM	Open End	US Equity Large Cap Growth (Growth)	B-	B-	B	Down	Y	2,000

★ Expanded analysis of this fund is included in Section II.

	TOTAL RETURNS					PERFORMANCE				ASSETS		ASSET ALLOCATION & TURNOVER					BULL & BEAR		FEES		
Min Additional Investment	3-Month Total Return	6-Month Total Return	1-Year Total Return	3-Year Total Return	5-Year Total Return	Dividend Yield (TTM)	Expense Ratio	3-Yr Std Deviation	3-Year Beta	NAV	Total Assets (MIL)	%Cash	%Stocks	%Bonds	%Other	Turnover Ratio	Last Bull Market Total Return	Last Bear Market Total Return	Front End Fee (%)	Back End Fee (%)	Inception Date
	3.67	16.70	5.85	39.75	40.01	0.92	0.97	10.07	0.95	13.55	72.8	2	86	12	0	32					Aug-13
	3.73	16.92	6.27	41.37	42.38	1.27	0.58	10.04	0.95	13.61	72.8	2	86	12	0	32					Feb-16
100	3.70	17.16	6.03	41.03	41.98	1.15	0.73	10.32	0.97	11.74	23.6	2	88	10	0	29					Jun-14
	3.61	17.03	5.87	40.04	40.40	0.94	0.98	10.29	0.96	11.75	23.6	2	88	10	0	29					Jun-14
	3.79	17.23	6.27	41.69	42.64	1.27	0.59	10.32	0.97	11.77	23.6	2	88	10	0	29					Feb-16
100	6.23	26.79	14.56	70.55	88.16	0.14	0.77	13.56	0.98	35.63	510.0	0	100	0	0	12	26.78	-17.65			Dec-00
	6.23	26.79	14.63	70.72	88.35	0.19	0.69	13.53	0.98	35.63	510.0	0	100	0	0	12	26.78	-17.65			Jul-17
100	4.14	19.78	8.82	49.42	60.99	1.48	0.3	12.56	1	32.88	1,942	3	97	0	0	7	25.56	-17.93			Jan-98
100	5.31	19.45	12.40	45.40	68.92	1.01	0.75	11.01	0.87	25.36	571.8	3	97	0	0	77	24.35	-17.74			Jun-09
100	5.27	19.34	12.12	44.27	66.96	0.71	1.02	11.03	0.87	25.35	571.8	3	97	0	0	77	24.38	-17.77			Jun-09
	5.35	19.58	12.58	46.04	69.67	1.16	0.59	11.02	0.87	25.4	571.8	3	97	0	0	77	24.35	-17.74			Nov-16
100	4.65	18.74	8.94	40.07	43.67	1.39	0.78	11.17	0.9	35.98	24,947	1	98	0	0	146	24.92	-20.63			Sep-94
100	4.61	18.63	8.70	39.10	42.03	1.12	1.02	11.16	0.9	35.39	24,947	1	98	0	0	146	24.77	-20.7			Mar-00
	4.71	18.85	9.10	40.71	44.55	1.54	0.63	11.18	0.9	36	24,947	1	98	0	0	146	24.92	-20.64			Aug-15
	-2.60	9.87	-8.10	26.51	12.57	0	0	15.01	0.95	19.44	157.7	0	97	0	3	112	2.74	-19.59			Dec-86
500	2.65	15.05	-8.30	-0.46	-6.66	0	2.29	18.48		19.33	10.2	1	100	0	0	19	25.02	-24.85			Dec-98
	2.68	9.87	5.16	22.04	19.81	1.69	1.1	5.62	1.04	8.82	47.9	2	44	53	0	20	12.06	-12.43			Aug-06
	2.80	10.13	5.47	22.99	21.37	1.94	0.85	5.65	1.05	8.82	47.9	2	44	53	0	20	12.19	-12.43			Dec-11
	2.97	12.38	4.97	30.02	27.02	1.59	1.1	8.05	1.14	11.48	164.7	1	66	33	0	17	15.22	-15.58			Aug-06
	3.06	12.59	5.25	30.98	28.74	1.83	0.85	8.05	1.15	11.49	164.7	1	66	33	0	17	15.36	-15.58			Dec-11
	3.32	14.03	5.03	34.68	30.96	1.45	1.1	9.46	1.04	12.16	147.1	1	79	20	0	12	17.41	-17.66			Aug-06
	3.32	14.13	5.23	35.56	32.51	1.69	0.85	9.46	1.04	12.17	147.1	1	79	20	0	12	17.54	-17.66			Dec-11
	3.38	15.05	4.84	38.40	33.56	1.42	1.1	10.46	1.04	12.3	115.4	1	89	11	0	8	19.28	-19.65			Aug-06
	3.46	15.25	5.14	39.44	35.27	1.67	0.85	10.46	1.04	12.3	115.4	1	89	11	0	8	19.43	-19.65			Dec-11
	3.63	16.53	4.88	42.78		1.4	1.1	11.7	1.12	11.76	30.8	1	99	0	0	4					Apr-15
	3.62	16.63	5.07	43.81		1.64	0.85	11.68	1.12	11.78	30.8	1	99	0	0	4					Apr-15
100	0.49	28.34	1.59	55.04	59.14	0.53	1	22.88	1.71	20.42	110.6	0	100	0	0	28	25.69				Jun-11
100	7.20	31.85	14.51			0	1.45			15.48	16.6	3	97	0	0	27					Dec-16
500	6.32	28.02	6.91	74.13	73.94	0	0.94	16.98	0.94	35.13	442.4	2	98	0	0	126	32.17	-28.14			Oct-04
250	4.25	23.59	5.11			0	0.9			12.73	2.9	3	97	0	0	74					Aug-17
250	4.17	23.49	5.03			0	1			12.72	2.9	3	97	0	0	74					Aug-17
250	3.37	11.47	6.71	17.85	24.60	1.68	0.98	5.02		11.93	30.0	10	36	54	0	20	10.72	-8.15			Nov-06
250	3.37	11.26	6.41	16.48	21.72	1.36	1.37	5.02		11.94	30.0	10	36	54	0	20	10.66	-8.15			Nov-06
250	-1.10	8.23	-11.41	22.13		0.41	1.25	14	0.94	9.86	5.5	10	90	0	0	163					Jun-15
250	-1.20	8.24	-11.42	22.01		0.41	1.25	14.04	0.94	9.85	5.5	10	90	0	0	163					Jun-15
250	0.72	10.02	-1.33	24.21	12.92	1.37	1	10.4		11.08	109.6	5	52	43	0	161					Jun-13
250	0.63	9.87	-1.51	24.08	12.84	1.38	1.2	10.38		11.02	109.6	5	52	43	0	161					Jun-13
250	-0.20	6.01	-5.65	-3.35	-35.36	2.49	0.7	8.64	1	4.86	1.2	6	0	84	10	76	3.66	-20.7			Mar-11
250	-0.40	5.80	-5.84	-3.55	-35.47	2.49	0.75	8.71	1.01	4.85	1.2	6	0	84	10	76	3.66	-20.78			Mar-11
250	3.18	18.86	8.62	12.59		2.38	1	10.41	0.85	10.38	6.2	7	93	0	0	122					Nov-14
250	3.24	18.78	8.45	12.38		2.24	1.15	10.43	0.85	10.38	6.2	7	93	0	0	122					Nov-14
250	1.26	10.20	-14.37	22.26	1.14	0.37	1	14.46	1.14	9.61	9.9	7	93	0	0	213	17.77	-29.8			Feb-11
250	1.15	10.08	-14.52	22.11	1.06	0.37	1.2	14.43	1.13	9.61	9.9	7	93	0	0	213	17.72	-29.87			Feb-11
250	9.01	33.33	23.12	102.99		0.04	0.8	12.91	0.92	20.08	97.5	8	91	0	0	50					Jan-16
250	8.96	33.20	22.99	102.79		0.04	1	12.92	0.92	20.06	97.5	8	91	0	0	50					Jan-16
250	5.38	20.07	3.83	29.82	31.43	1.99	0.73	13.89	1.11	17.89	338.3	1	99	0	0	18	29.37	-21.39			Oct-04
250	5.36	20.04	3.60	29.06	29.87	1.81	0.95	13.86	1.11	18.22	338.3	1	99	0	0	18	29.22	-21.52			Sep-86
250	4.10	19.94	1.28	31.97	29.69	1.5	0.72	15.48	1.24	18.76	196.2	0	100	0	0	20	29.05	-23.45			Dec-03
250	4.00	19.79	1.06	31.04	28.12	1.29	0.95	15.46	1.24	18.7	196.2	0	100	0	0	20	28.84	-23.57			Dec-97
250	2.81	19.75	-8.43	38.61	19.70	0.65	0.9	18.9	1.38	21.22	82.2	1	99	0	0	23	33.08	-25.98			Oct-97
250	2.79	19.74	-8.52	38.05	18.70	0.5	1	18.91	1.38	20.62	82.2	1	99	0	0	23	32.92	-26.14			Oct-00
250	6.07	27.39	15.28	70.77	86.84	0	0.77	14.45	1.02	27.58	945.5	2	98	0	0	15	23.84	-12.32			Feb-93

	MARKET		FUND TYPE, CATEGORY & OBJECTIVE		RATINGS				MINIMUMS	
Fund Name	Ticker Symbol	Traded On	Fund Type	Category and (Prospectus Objective)	Overall Rating	Reward Rating	Risk Rating	Recent Up/ Downgrade	Open to New Investors	Min Initial Investment
TCW Select Equities Fund Class N	TGCNX	NAS CM	Open End	US Equity Large Cap Growth (Growth)	B-	B-	B-	Down	Y	2,000
Teberg Fund	TEBRX	NAS CM	Open End	Moderate Alloc (Growth & Income)	B-	C	B	Up	Y	2,000
Tekla Healthcare Investors	HQH	NYSE	Closed End	Healthcare Sector Equity (Health)	C	C	C		Y	
Tekla Healthcare Opportunities Fund	THQ	NYSE	Closed End	Healthcare Sector Equity (Health)	C	C	C+	Down	Y	
Tekla Life Sciences Investors	HQL	NYSE	Closed End	Healthcare Sector Equity (Health)	C	C	C-		Y	
Tekla World Healthcare Fund	THW	NYSE	Closed End	Healthcare Sector Equity (Growth & Income)	C	C	C+		Y	
Templeton China World Fund Class A	TCWAX	NAS CM	Open End	Greater China Equity (Growth)	C	C-	B-		Y	1,000
Templeton China World Fund Class Advisor	TACWX	NAS CM	Open End	Greater China Equity (Growth)	C	C-	B-		Y	100,000
Templeton China World Fund Class C	TCWCX	NAS CM	Open End	Greater China Equity (Growth)	C	C-	B-		Y	1,000
Templeton China World Fund Class R6	FCWRX	NAS CM	Open End	Greater China Equity (Growth)	C	C-	B-		Y	1,000,000
Templeton Developing Markets Trust Class A	TEDMX	NAS CM	Open End	Global Emerg Mkts (Growth)	C	C	B-		Y	1,000
Templeton Developing Markets Trust Class Advisor	TDADX	NAS CM	Open End	Global Emerg Mkts (Growth)	C	C	B-		Y	100,000
Templeton Developing Markets Trust Class C	TDMTX	NAS CM	Open End	Global Emerg Mkts (Growth)	C	C	C+		Y	1,000
Templeton Developing Markets Trust Class R6	FDEVX	NAS CM	Open End	Global Emerg Mkts (Growth)	C	C	B-		Y	1,000,000
Templeton Developing Markets Trust Class Retirement	TDMRX	NAS CM	Open End	Global Emerg Mkts (Growth)	C	C	C+		Y	1,000
Templeton Dragon Fund Inc	TDF	NYSE	Closed End	Greater China Equity (Pacific Stock)	C-	C-	C-	Down	Y	
Templeton Emerging Markets Balanced Fund Advisor Class	TZEMX	NAS CM	Open End	Global Emerg Mkts (Growth & Income)	C	C	B		Y	100,000
Templeton Emerging Markets Balanced Fund Class A	TAEMX	NAS CM	Open End	Global Emerg Mkts (Growth & Income)	C	C	B		Y	1,000
Templeton Emerging Markets Balanced Fund Class C			Open End	Global Emerg Mkts (Growth & Income)	C	C	B-		Y	1,000
Templeton Emerging Markets Balanced Fund Class R			Open End	Global Emerg Mkts (Growth & Income)	C	C	B		Y	1,000
Templeton Emerging Markets Balanced Fund Class R6	FEBQX	NAS CM	Open End	Global Emerg Mkts (Growth & Income)	C	C	B		Y	1,000,000
Templeton Emerging Markets Fund Inc.	EMF	NYSE	Closed End	Global Emerg Mkts (World Stock)	C	C	C-		Y	
Templeton Emerging Markets Small Cap Fund Class A	TEMMX	NAS CM	Open End	Global Emerg Mkts (Growth)	C	C-	C+		Y	1,000
Templeton Emerging Markets Small Cap Fund Class Advisor	TEMZX	NAS CM	Open End	Global Emerg Mkts (Growth)	C	C-	C+		Y	100,000
Templeton Emerging Markets Small Cap Fund Class C	TCEMX	NAS CM	Open End	Global Emerg Mkts (Growth)	C	C-	C+		Y	1,000
Templeton Emerging Markets Small Cap Fund Class R6	FTEQX	NAS CM	Open End	Global Emerg Mkts (Growth)	C	C-	C+		Y	0
Templeton Emerging Markets Small Cap Fund Class Retirement	FTESX	NAS CM	Open End	Global Emerg Mkts (Growth)	C	C-	C+		Y	1,000
Templeton Foreign Fund Class A	TEMFX	NAS CM	Open End	Global Equity Large Cap (Foreign Stock)	C-	D+	C	Down	Y	1,000
Templeton Foreign Fund Class Advisor	TFFAX	NAS CM	Open End	Global Equity Large Cap (Foreign Stock)	C-	D+	C	Down	Y	100,000
Templeton Foreign Fund Class C	TEFTX	NAS CM	Open End	Global Equity Large Cap (Foreign Stock)	C-	D	C	Down	Y	1,000
Templeton Foreign Fund Class R	TEFRX	NAS CM	Open End	Global Equity Large Cap (Foreign Stock)	C-	D+	C	Down	Y	1,000
Templeton Foreign Fund Class R6	FTFGX	NAS CM	Open End	Global Equity Large Cap (Foreign Stock)	C-	D+	C+	Down	Y	1,000,000
Templeton Frontier Markets Fund Class A	TFMAX	NAS CM	Open End	Global Emerg Mkts (Growth)	C-	D+	C			1,000
Templeton Frontier Markets Fund Class Adv	FFRZX	NAS CM	Open End	Global Emerg Mkts (Growth)	C-	D+	C			100,000
Templeton Frontier Markets Fund Class C	FFRMX	NAS CM	Open End	Global Emerg Mkts (Growth)	D+	D+	C			1,000
Templeton Frontier Markets Fund Class R			Open End	Global Emerg Mkts (Growth)	C-	D+	C	Up		1,000
Templeton Frontier Markets Fund Class R6	FFMRX	NAS CM	Open End	Global Emerg Mkts (Growth)	C-	D+	C			0
Templeton Global Balanced Fund Class A	TAGBX	NAS CM	Open End	Moderate Alloc (Balanced)	C	D+	C+		Y	1,000
Templeton Global Balanced Fund Class A1	TINCX	NAS CM	Open End	Moderate Alloc (Balanced)	C	D+	C+			1,000
Templeton Global Balanced Fund Class Advisor	TZINX	NAS CM	Open End	Moderate Alloc (Balanced)	C	C-	C+		Y	100,000
Templeton Global Balanced Fund Class C	FCGBX	NAS CM	Open End	Moderate Alloc (Balanced)	C-	D+	C	Down	Y	1,000
Templeton Global Balanced Fund Class C1	TCINX	NAS CM	Open End	Moderate Alloc (Balanced)	C-	D+	C	Down		1,000
Templeton Global Balanced Fund Class R6	FGGBX	NAS CM	Open End	Moderate Alloc (Balanced)	C	C-	C+		Y	1,000,000
Templeton Global Balanced Fund Class Retirement			Open End	Moderate Alloc (Balanced)	C-	D+	C+	Down	Y	1,000
Templeton Global Smaller Companies Fund Class A	TEMGX	NAS CM	Open End	Global Equity Mid/Small Cap (World Stock)	C	C-	B-		Y	1,000
Templeton Global Smaller Companies Fund Class Advisor	TGSAX	NAS CM	Open End	Global Equity Mid/Small Cap (World Stock)	C	C-	B-		Y	100,000
Templeton Global Smaller Companies Fund Class C	TESGX	NAS CM	Open End	Global Equity Mid/Small Cap (World Stock)	C	C-	B-		Y	1,000
Templeton Global Smaller Companies Fund Class R6	FBOGX	NAS CM	Open End	Global Equity Mid/Small Cap (World Stock)	C	C-	B-		Y	1,000,000
Templeton Growth Fund, Inc. Class A	TEPLX	NAS CM	Open End	Global Equity Large Cap (World Stock)	C-	D+	C	Down	Y	1,000
Templeton Growth Fund, Inc. Class Advisor	TGADX	NAS CM	Open End	Global Equity Large Cap (World Stock)	C-	C-	C	Down	Y	100,000
Templeton Growth Fund, Inc. Class C	FTGQX	NAS CM	Open End	Global Equity Large Cap (World Stock)	C-	D+	C	Down	Y	1,000
Templeton Growth Fund, Inc. Class R6	FTGFX	NAS CM	Open End	Global Equity Large Cap (World Stock)	C-	C-	C	Down	Y	1,000,000

★ Expanded analysis of this fund is included in Section II.

Min Additional Investment	3-Month Total Return	6-Month Total Return	1-Year Total Return	3-Year Total Return	5-Year Total Return	Dividend Yield (TTM)	Expense Ratio	3-Yr Std Deviation	3-Year Beta	NAV	Total Assets (MIL)	%Cash	%Stocks	%Bonds	%Other	Turnover Ratio	Last Bull Market Total Return	Last Bear Market Total Return	Front End Fee (%)	Back End Fee (%)	Inception Date
	TOTAL RETURNS					PERFORMANCE				ASSETS		ASSET ALLOCATION & TURNOVER					BULL & BEAR		FEES		
250	6.00	27.20	15.03	69.60	84.61	0	1	14.45	1.02	24.55	945.5	2	98	0	0	15	23.65	-12.45			Feb-99
100	2.95	15.36	5.40	29.56	24.17	0.68	2.07	11.07	0.87	11.86	28.2	2	78	18	0	2	10.55	-6.45			Apr-02
	0.43	14.48	2.77	20.39	21.42	0	0	18.53	0.82	22.31	953.6	5	91	0	1	46	31.92	-12.09			Apr-87
	1.29	11.23	10.16	32.63		0.32	1.44	15.9	0.66	19.47	807.3	5	102	17	-25	40					Jul-14
	0.34	16.35	0.73	33.43	33.02	0	1.66	20.06	0.89	18.35	421.4	7	88	0	2	37	38.67	-12.53			May-92
	2.05	12.96	8.51	18.95		0.42	1.86	14.68		13.89	418.9	6	104	17	-28	55					Jun-15
	-3.09	10.59	-2.57	43.58	23.41	1.42	1.85	14.93	0.88	18.79	237.5	3	97	0	0	12	20.64	-23.09	5.50		Sep-93
	-3.06	10.68	-2.35	44.69	25.00	1.59	1.6	14.95	0.88	18.96	237.5	3	97	0	0	12	20.82	-22.97			Aug-03
	-3.25	10.12	-3.27	40.44	18.91	0.04	2.6	14.93	0.88	18.71	237.5	3	97	0	0	12	20.16	-23.32		1.00	Sep-93
	-3.02	10.77	-2.18	45.52	26.32	1.71	1.43	14.93	0.88	18.91	237.5	3	97	0	0	12	20.64	-23.09			May-13
	0.97	14.56	3.52	44.66	15.66	1.19	1.39	14.38	1.01	20.69	1,297	2	98	0	0	10	17.42	-24.75	5.50		Oct-91
	1.03	14.70	3.74	45.73	17.19	1.45	1.14	14.38	1.01	20.59	1,297	2	98	0	0	10	17.64	-24.68			Jan-97
	0.80	14.16	2.80	41.54	11.50	0	2.14	14.39	1.01	20.15	1,297	2	98	0	0	10	16.92	-24.99		1.00	May-95
	1.13	14.78	3.90	46.57	18.22	1.58	1.01	14.38	1.01	20.57	1,297	2	98	0	0	10	17.42	-24.75			May-13
	0.94	14.41	3.25	43.58	14.29	0.97	1.64	14.37	1.01	20.32	1,297	2	98	0	0	10	17.31	-24.84			Jan-02
	-3.55	14.75	-3.54	40.23	34.64	3.08		16.2	0.96	21.7	738.7	1	98	0	1	14	20.6	-18.7			Sep-94
	2.74	10.17	4.02	32.40	13.28	4.85	1.24	10.46		9.98	34.0	7	57	36	0	22					Oct-11
	2.57	10.04	3.65	31.42	11.86	4.63	1.49	10.44		9.97	34.0	7	57	36	0	22			5.50		Oct-11
	2.36	9.67	2.93	28.44	7.61	3.97	2.24	10.42		9.88	34.0	7	57	36	0	22				1.00	Oct-11
	2.53	9.92	3.42	30.54	10.47	4.44	1.74	10.4		9.98	34.0	7	57	36	0	22					Oct-11
	2.67	10.24	4.02	32.52	13.39	4.94	1.11	10.36		9.97	34.0	7	57	36	0	22					Aug-17
	1.55	14.92	5.51	50.71	14.79	1.16		14.25	1	16.94	287.8	1	98	0	0	12	15.33	-26.83			Feb-87
	-1.45	9.33	-1.73	22.88	12.68	0	1.85	11.47	0.84	13.58	868.7	4	96	0	0	12	14.85	-28.92	5.50		Oct-06
	-1.43	9.38	-1.53	23.79	14.10	0.1	1.6	11.45	0.84	13.76	868.7	4	96	0	0	12	14.94	-28.79			Oct-06
	-1.61	8.92	-2.42	20.14	8.59	0	2.6	11.45	0.84	12.81	868.7	4	96	0	0	12	14.26	-29.07		1.00	Oct-06
	-1.36	9.56	-1.31	24.22	14.50	0.31	1.49	11.44	0.83	13.75	868.7	4	96	0	0	12	14.94	-28.79			Aug-17
	-1.54	9.20	-1.97	21.95	11.39	0	2.1	11.46	0.84	13.41	868.7	4	96	0	0	12	14.6	-28.92			Oct-06
	-0.41	7.06	-5.90	19.72	-5.39	2.49	1.1	11.89	0.99	7.12	4,937	3	97	0	0	23	11.11	-25.03	5.50		Oct-82
	-0.42	7.18	-5.72	20.56	-4.17	2.79	0.85	11.88	0.98	7.01	4,937	3	97	0	0	23	11.21	-24.9			Jan-97
	-0.70	6.65	-6.69	17.11	-8.86	0.3	1.85	11.8	0.98	7.05	4,937	3	97	0	0	23	10.52	-25.22		1.00	May-95
	-0.57	6.90	-6.14	18.79	-6.51	2.29	1.35	11.95	0.99	6.97	4,937	3	97	0	0	23	10.83	-25.03			Jan-02
	-0.42	7.19	-5.66	21.16	-3.23	2.99	0.69	11.88	0.99	7	4,937	3	97	0	0	23	11.11	-25.03			May-13
	1.96	9.27	-3.13	10.24	-29.27	0	2.01	12.84	0.78	11.43	60.9	3	97	0	0	49	15.77	-19.55	5.50		Oct-08
	1.94	9.41	-2.84	11.07	-28.42	0.18	1.76	12.79	0.78	11.51	60.9	3	97	0	0	49	15.94	-19.46			Oct-08
	1.74	8.82	-3.81	7.94	-31.79	0	2.76	12.85	0.78	11.1	60.9	3	97	0	0	49	15.33	-19.81		1.00	Oct-08
	1.89	9.06	-3.33	9.49	-30.09	0	2.26	12.86	0.78	11.31	60.9	3	97	0	0	49	15.6	-19.61			Oct-08
	2.04	9.43	-2.77	11.65	-27.70	0.48	1.54	12.85	0.78	11.48	60.9	3	97	0	0	49	15.94	-19.46			May-13
	-0.08	5.52	-2.49	17.77	3.84	4.34	1.19	9.19	0.74	2.84	1,212	9	69	22	0	46	15.66	-17.46	5.50		Sep-11
	0.26	5.50	-2.15	17.73	4.17	4.33	1.19	9.18	0.73	2.85	1,212	9	69	22	0	46	16.09	-17.54	3.75		Jul-05
	-0.02	5.24	-2.24	18.17	5.16	4.59	0.94	9.24	0.73	2.85	1,212	9	69	22	0	46	16.17	-17.37			Jul-05
	0.06	5.14	-2.94	15.28	0.39	3.55	1.94	9.37	0.75	2.83	1,212	9	69	22	0	46	15.73	-17.7		1.00	Jul-11
	0.15	5.26	-2.63	16.68	2.02	3.82	1.59	9.31	0.74	2.85	1,212	9	69	22	0	46	15.85	-17.44		1.00	Jul-05
	0.35	5.68	-2.13	19.05	5.78	4.69	0.85	9.11	0.73	2.85	1,212	9	69	22	0	46	16.17	-17.38			May-13
	-0.15	5.36	-2.74	16.78	2.82	4.06	1.44	9.13	0.73	2.85	1,212	9	69	22	0	46	15.88	-17.32			Jul-05
	0.66	15.75	-3.75	31.07	14.11	0.71	1.33	12.91	0.96	9.11	1,185	5	95	0	0	33	18.8	-27.3	5.50		Jun-81
	0.77	15.94	-3.51	32.17	15.64	0.98	1.08	12.86	0.96	9.16	1,185	5	95	0	0	33	18.83	-27.23			Jan-97
	0.58	15.30	-4.42	28.15	10.03	0	2.08	12.9	0.96	8.59	1,185	5	95	0	0	33	18.11	-27.54		1.00	May-95
	0.88	16.11	-3.26	32.89	16.69	1.11	0.96	12.91	0.96	9.15	1,185	5	95	0	0	33	18.8	-27.3			May-13
	-0.49	8.09	-5.81	23.34	2.97	1.82	1.03	12.78	1.07	22.31	11,011	2	98	0	0	29	17.73	-22.83	5.50		Nov-54
	-0.44	8.28	-5.56	24.28	4.26	2.09	0.78	12.79	1.07	22.35	11,011	2	98	0	0	29	17.9	-22.77			Jan-97
	-0.72	7.71	-6.51	20.60	-0.80		1.78	12.76	1.07	21.91	11,011	2	98	0	0	29	17.21	-23.07		1.00	Oct-18
	-0.40	8.35	-5.47	24.61	4.77	2.15	0.72	12.78	1.07	22.31	11,011	2	98	0	0	29	17.72	-22.83			May-13

	MARKET			FUND TYPE, CATEGORY & OBJECTIVE	RATINGS					MINIMUMS
Fund Name	Ticker Symbol	Traded On	Fund Type	Category and (Prospectus Objective)	Overall Rating	Reward Rating	Risk Rating	Recent Up/ Downgrade	Open to New Investors	Min Initial Investment
Templeton Growth Fund, Inc. Class Retirement	TEGRX	NAS CM	Open End	Global Equity Large Cap (World Stock)	C-	D+	C	Down	Y	1,000
Templeton Inst Foreign Smaller Companies Series Adv	TFSCX	NAS CM	Open End	Global Equity Mid/Small Cap (Foreign Stock)	C	C	C+			1,000,000
Templeton Inst Intl Equity Series Primary Shares	TFEQX	NAS CM	Open End	Global Equity Large Cap (Foreign Stock)	C-	C-	C	Down	Y	1,000,000
Templeton Inst Intl Equity Series Service Shares	TFESX	NAS CM	Open End	Global Equity Large Cap (Foreign Stock)	C-	D+	C	Down	Y	1,000,000
Templeton Institutional Global Equity Fund Class Advisor	TGESX	NAS CM	Open End	Global Equity Large Cap (Growth)	C	C-	C+		Y	1,000,000
Templeton World Fund Class A	TEMWX	NAS CM	Open End	Global Equity Large Cap (World Stock)	C	C-	C+		Y	1,000
Templeton World Fund Class Advisor	TWDAX	NAS CM	Open End	Global Equity Large Cap (World Stock)	C	C-	C+		Y	100,000
Templeton World Fund Class C	TEWTX	NAS CM	Open End	Global Equity Large Cap (World Stock)	C	C-	C+		Y	1,000
Templeton World Fund Class R6	FTWRX	NAS CM	Open End	Global Equity Large Cap (World Stock)	C	C-	C+		Y	1,000,000
TETON Convertible Securities Fund Class A	WEIAX	NAS CM	Open End	Convertibles (Growth & Income)	B	C+	B+		Y	1,000
TETON Convertible Securities Fund Class AAA	WESRX	NAS CM	Open End	Convertibles (Growth & Income)	B	C+	B+		Y	1,000
TETON Convertible Securities Fund Class C	WEICX	NAS CM	Open End	Convertibles (Growth & Income)	B-	C+	B+		Y	1,000
TETON Convertible Securities Fund Institutional Class	WESIX	NAS CM	Open End	Convertibles (Growth & Income)	B-	C+	B	Down	Y	100,000
TETON Westwood Balanced Fund Class A	WEBCX	NAS CM	Open End	Moderate Alloc (Balanced)	B	C	A-	Up	Y	1,000
TETON Westwood Balanced Fund Class AAA	WEBAX	NAS CM	Open End	Moderate Alloc (Balanced)	B	C+	A-	Up	Y	1,000
TETON Westwood Balanced Fund Class C	WBCCX	NAS CM	Open End	Moderate Alloc (Balanced)	B-	C	A-		Y	1,000
TETON Westwood Balanced Fund Class Institutional	WBBIX	NAS CM	Open End	Moderate Alloc (Balanced)	B	C+	A-	Up	Y	500,000
TETON Westwood Equity Fund Class A	WEECX	NAS CM	Open End	US Equity Large Cap Blend (Growth)	B-	C	B		Y	1,000
TETON Westwood Equity Fund Class AAA	WESWX	NAS CM	Open End	US Equity Large Cap Blend (Growth)	B-	C	B		Y	1,000
TETON Westwood Equity Fund Class C	WEQCX	NAS CM	Open End	US Equity Large Cap Blend (Growth)	B-	C	B	Up	Y	1,000
TETON Westwood Equity Fund Institutional Class	WEEIX	NAS CM	Open End	US Equity Large Cap Blend (Growth)	B-	C	B+		Y	500,000
TETON Westwood Mighty Mites Class Institutional	WEIMX	NAS CM	Open End	US Equity Small Cap (Small Company)	C	C-	C		Y	500,000
TETON Westwood Mighty Mites Fund Class A	WMMAX	NAS CM	Open End	US Equity Small Cap (Small Company)	C	C-	C		Y	1,000
TETON Westwood Mighty Mites Fund Class AAA	WEMMX	NAS CM	Open End	US Equity Small Cap (Small Company)	C	C-	C		Y	1,000
TETON Westwood Mighty Mites Fund Class C	WMMCX	NAS CM	Open End	US Equity Small Cap (Small Company)	C	C-	C		Y	1,000
TETON Westwood SmallCap Equity Fund Class A	WWSAX	NAS CM	Open End	US Equity Small Cap (Small Company)	C	C-	C+		Y	1,000
TETON Westwood SmallCap Equity Fund Class AAA	WESCX	NAS CM	Open End	US Equity Small Cap (Small Company)	C	C-	C+		Y	1,000
TETON Westwood SmallCap Equity Fund Class C	WWSCX	NAS CM	Open End	US Equity Small Cap (Small Company)	C	C-	C+		Y	1,000
TETON Westwood SmallCap Equity Fund Class Institutional	WWSIX	NAS CM	Open End	US Equity Small Cap (Small Company)	C	C-	B-		Y	500,000
THB Asset Management MicroCap Institutional Cls Shares	THBIX	NAS CM	Open End	US Equity Small Cap (Small Company)	C	C-	C		Y	100,000
THB Asset Management MicroCap Fund Investor Class Shares	THBVX	NAS CM	Open End	US Equity Small Cap (Small Company)	C	C-	C		Y	100
The Arbitrage Event-Driven Fund Class A	AGEAX	NAS CM	Open End	Market Neutral (Growth)	C	C	B-		Y	2,000
The Arbitrage Event-Driven Fund Class C	AEFCX	NAS CM	Open End	Market Neutral (Growth)	C	C	B-		Y	2,000
The Arbitrage Event-Driven Fund Class I	AEDNX	NAS CM	Open End	Market Neutral (Growth)	C+	C	B+	Down	Y	100,000
The Arbitrage Event-Driven Fund ClassR	AEDFX	NAS CM	Open End	Market Neutral (Growth)	C+	C	B		Y	2,000
The Arbitrage Fund Class A	ARGAX	NAS CM	Open End	Market Neutral (Growth)	C+	C	B		Y	2,000
The Arbitrage Fund Class C	ARBCX	NAS CM	Open End	Market Neutral (Growth)	C	C	B-		Y	2,000
The Arbitrage Fund Class Institutional	ARBNX	NAS CM	Open End	Market Neutral (Growth)	B-	C	B+		Y	100,000
The Arbitrage Fund Class R	ARBFX	NAS CM	Open End	Market Neutral (Growth)	C+	C	B	Down	Y	2,000
The BeeHive Fund	BEEHX	NAS CM	Open End	US Equity Large Cap Growth (Growth)	C+	C	B	Down	Y	2,500
The Central and Eastern Europe Fund, Inc.	CEE	NYSE	Closed End	Equity Miscellaneous (Europe Stock)	C	B-	D+	Up	Y	
The Cook & Bynum Fund	COBYX	NAS CM	Open End	US Equity Large Cap Blend (World Stock)	C	D+	C+	Up	Y	5,000
The Covered Bridge Fund Class A	TCBAX	NAS CM	Open End	Long/Short Equity (Growth & Income)	B-	C	A-		Y	2,500
The Covered Bridge Fund Class I	TCBIX	NAS CM	Open End	Long/Short Equity (Growth & Income)	B-	C	A-		Y	1,000,000
The Cushing® Energy Income Fund Common	SRF	NYSE	Closed End	Energy Sector Equity (Income)	D	D	D+	Down	Y	
The Cushing® Renaissance Fund Common	SZC	NYSE	Closed End	Energy Sector Equity (Growth & Income)	C-	C-	C-	Down	Y	
The Disciplined Growth Investors Fund	DGIFX	NAS CM	Open End	Aggressive Alloc (Balanced)	B-	C	B+	Down	Y	10,000
The European Equity Fund Inc	EEA	NYSE	Closed End	Europe Equity Large Cap (Europe Stock)	C-	C-	D+		Y	
The Gabelli Global Rising Income and Dividend Fund AAA	GAGCX	NAS CM	Open End	Moderate Alloc (Growth & Income)	C	C-	C+		Y	1,000
The Gabelli Global Small & Mid Cap Value Trust	GGZ	NYSE	Closed End	Global Equity Mid/Small Cap (World Stock)	C-	C-	C-		Y	
The Gabelli Multimedia Trust Inc.	GGT	NYSE	Closed End	US Equity Large Cap Growth (Comm)	C	C	C-		Y	
The Gold Bullion Strategy Fund Advisor Class	QGLCX	NAS CM	Open End	Commodities Specified (Precious Metals)	C-	D	C		Y	1,000

★ Expanded analysis of this fund is included in Section II.

	TOTAL RETURNS					PERFORMANCE				ASSETS		ASSET ALLOCATION & TURNOVER					BULL & BEAR		FEES		
Min Additional Investment	3-Month Total Return	6-Month Total Return	1-Year Total Return	3-Year Total Return	5-Year Total Return	Dividend Yield (TTM)	Expense Ratio	3-Yr Std Deviation	3-Year Beta	NAV	Total Assets (MIL)	%Cash	%Stocks	%Bonds	%Other	Turnover Ratio	Last Bull Market Total Return	Last Bear Market Total Return	Front End Fee (%)	Back End Fee (%)	Inception Date
	-0.54	7.96	-6.02	22.44	1.70	1.52	1.28	12.76	1.07	22.09	11,011	2	98	0	0	29	17.56	-22.9			Jan-02
	1.58	15.50	-4.74	31.31	16.60	0.91	1.01	13.09	1.06	20.56	769.8	5	95	0	0	34	18.37	-19.78			Oct-02
	-0.35	6.75	-6.26	21.69	-1.24	2.2	0.81	11.87	1	15.8	2,410	3	97	0	0	26	13.57	-24.51			Oct-90
	-0.43	6.64	-6.44	21.04	-2.02	1.87	0.96	11.86	1	15.89	2,410	3	97	0	0	26	13.4	-24.5			Sep-06
	0.24	9.70	-4.60	28.03	6.81	1.67	0.85	12.51	1.06	8.25	216.6	4	96	0	0	34	19.17	-18.99			Mar-08
	-0.37	8.96	-3.75	27.84	5.90	4.4	1.05	12.17	1.08	13.37	3,420	1	99	0	0	28	18.04	-20.39	5.50		Jan-78
	-0.37	8.99	-3.58	28.73	7.15	4.7	0.8	12.17	1.08	13.33	3,420	1	99	0	0	28	18.31	-20.32			May-06
	-0.54	8.52	-4.54	24.98	1.91	1.92	1.8	12.17	1.08	12.86	3,420	1	99	0	0	28	17.55	-20.65		1.00	May-95
	-0.29	9.09	-3.51	29.10	7.61	4.75	0.74	12.18	1.08	13.32	3,420	1	99	0	0	28	18.04	-20.39			May-13
	4.28	16.14	7.32	42.56	31.39	1.16	1.4	8.55	0.96	14.21	43.4	5	7	0	0	35	15.63	-12.61	4.00		May-01
	4.41	16.32	7.60	43.65	33.00	1.43	1.15	8.5	0.95	13.75	43.4	5	7	0	0	35	15.71	-12.57			Sep-97
	4.14	15.88	6.78	40.41	28.10	0.71	1.9	8.49	0.95	15.17	43.4	5	7	0	0	35	15.2	-12.81		1.00	Nov-01
	4.38	16.40	7.84	44.75	34.76	1.65	0.9	8.5	0.95	13.79	43.4	5	7	0	0	35	15.99	-12.46			Jan-08
	4.01	12.01	7.54	26.10	32.93	0.81	1.59	7.38	-0.1	11.47	58.0	3	65	32	0	27	15.39	-12.1	4.00		Apr-93
	4.00	12.12	7.77	26.96	34.53	1.04	1.34	7.4	-0.1	11.39	58.0	3	65	32	0	27	15.5	-11.96			Oct-91
	3.82	11.72	6.96	24.10	29.62	0.26	2.09	7.41	-0.11	11.68	58.0	3	65	32	0	27	15.07	-12.31		1.00	Sep-01
	4.08	12.29	8.06	27.87	36.30	1.28	1.09	7.39	-0.11	11.37	58.0	3	65	32	0	27	15.76	-11.92			Jan-08
	4.73	16.47	8.28	38.21	47.36	0.35	1.85	11.48	0.9	12.16	55.4	1	99	0	0	33	24.69	-20.36	4.00		Jan-94
	4.72	16.66	8.51	39.28	49.10	0.63	1.6	11.47	0.9	12.18	55.4	1	99	0	0	33	24.9	-20.3			Jan-87
	4.61	16.18	7.74	36.16	43.67	0	2.35	11.46	0.9	11.34	55.4	1	99	0	0	33	24.2	-20.5		1.00	Feb-01
	4.83	16.84	8.85	40.29	51.01	0.88	1.35	11.51	0.9	12.14	55.4	1	99	0	0	33	24.95	-20.18			Jan-08
	1.25	11.69	-5.77	31.20	28.49	0	1.15	14.25	0.78	26.55	1,062	6	89	5	0	9	19.8	-19.15			Jan-08
	1.10	11.38	-6.26	29.26	25.27	0	1.65	14.26	0.78	24.76	1,062	6	89	5	0	9	19.48	-19.32	4.00		Nov-01
	1.17	11.56	-5.98	30.25	26.93	0	1.4	14.26	0.78	25.85	1,062	6	89	5	0	9	19.7	-19.24			May-98
	0.98	11.11	-6.69	27.34	22.24	0	2.15	14.25	0.78	21.5	1,062	6	89	5	0	9	19.17	-19.49		1.00	Aug-01
	2.48	18.46	-4.00	48.03	40.84	0	1.5	17.62	1	17.32	43.3	7	93	0	0	32	26.4	-28.89	4.00		Nov-01
	2.57	18.64	-3.75	49.19	42.65	0	1.25	17.59	1	18.33	43.3	7	93	0	0	32	26.53	-28.8			Apr-97
	2.38	18.23	-4.49	45.90	37.44	0	2	17.62	1	14.59	43.3	7	93	0	0	32	26.02	-29.02		1.00	Nov-01
	2.68	18.78	-3.53	50.33	44.51	0.11	1	17.62	1	19.1	43.3	7	93	0	0	32	26.85	-28.79			Jan-08
2,500	1.19	9.55	-8.26	50.10	33.83	0	1.25	16.68	0.91	16.05	81.1	1	99	0	0	35					Mar-12
	1.10	9.30	-8.63	48.20	30.77	0	1.75	16.7	0.91	15.5	81.1	1	99	0	0	35					Mar-12
	0.31	2.26	1.02	7.66	-2.91	1.53	2.2	2.75	-0.37	9.47	133.9	31	45	21	0	421	8.57	-4.38	3.25		May-13
	0.10	1.97	0.36	5.22	-6.45	0.58	2.95	2.74	0.1	9.29	133.9	31	45	21	0	421	8.1	-4.68	3.25	1.00	Jun-12
	0.31	2.35	1.34	8.42	-1.68	1.74	1.95	2.79	0.03	9.55	133.9	31	45	21	0	421	8.73	-4.28	3.25		Oct-10
	0.42	2.37	1.16	7.67	-2.82	1.46	2.2	2.81	-0.61	9.48	133.9	31	45	21	0	421	8.53	-4.19	3.25		Oct-10
	0.31	1.33	3.44	7.62	10.79	0.53	1.94	1.87	-2.83	12.89	1,736	46	51	2	0	362	1.67	1.64	2.50		May-13
	0.24	0.98	2.77	5.26	6.80	0	2.69	1.87	-4.21	12.33	1,736	46	51	2	0	362	1.22	1.32		1.00	Jun-12
	0.45	1.44	3.73	8.44	12.23	0.73	1.69	1.87	-3.57	13.31	1,736	46	51	2	0	362	1.87	1.69			Oct-03
	0.38	1.33	3.47	7.68	10.85	0.48	1.94	1.91	-3.23	12.92	1,736	46	51	2	0	362	1.67	1.64			Sep-00
500	8.15	27.54	16.40	40.50	32.25	0.78	0.99	13.94	1.08	16.58	128.1	6	94	0	0	10	20.8	-21.6			Sep-08
	12.40	22.33	20.63	60.99	10.31	3.23		14.19	0.88	31.17	213.3	7	92	0	-1	119	17.34	-34.89			Mar-90
1,000	0.43	8.99	-1.74	5.97	11.17	0.19	1.49	10.14	0.64	13.93	121.2	15	85	0	0	5	11.7	-2.47			Jul-09
1,000	2.54	11.80	5.34	27.64	27.57	1.51	1.73	10.03	0.76	9.38	85.0	2	98	0	0	186			5.25		Oct-13
1,000	2.62	11.87	5.53	28.50	29.07	1.76	1.48	9.96	0.76	9.34	85.0	2	98	0	0	186					Oct-13
	-5.30	17.51	-19.93	-6.61	-86.57	0	1.75	22.81		8.51	21.1	4	83	13	0	40					Feb-12
	-0.62	16.84	-4.05	31.71	-14.39	2.48		15.68		17.19	134.2	10	67	23	0	74					Sep-12
	0.17	16.05	6.09	42.33	51.80	0.76	0.78	11.59	0.87	20.66	235.6	1	71	28	0	18	24.51				Aug-11
	3.98	16.58	-1.09	24.43	9.30	0.73		12.45	0.83	10.19	80.6	3	97	0	0	58	14.7	-33.34			Jul-86
	2.80	10.58	-1.92	18.81	19.61	0.79	1.67	10.67	1.52	25.28	51.2	1	99	0	0	20	2.99	-11.1			Feb-94
	-0.65	11.93	-4.24	21.47	23.79	1.04	1.65	12.72		13.6	131.9	6	89	5	0	80					Jun-14
	3.33	19.26	-1.48	33.17	24.87	11.29	1.7	16.24	1.31	7.97	196.2	2	98	0	0	21	20.89	-26.76			Nov-94
250	8.91	9.73	10.79	-1.45	-5.90	0.95	2.08	11.01	0	23.27	76.1	24	7	69	0	167					Apr-16

	MARKET			FUND TYPE, CATEGORY & OBJECTIVE	RATINGS				MINIMUMS	
Fund Name	Ticker Symbol	Traded On	Fund Type	Category and (Prospectus Objective)	Overall Rating	Reward Rating	Risk Rating	Recent Up/ Downgrade	Open to New Investors	Min Initial Investment
The Gold Bullion Strategy Fund Investor Class	QGLDX	NAS CM	Open End	Commodities Specified (Precious Metals)	C-	D	C+	Down	Y	1,000
The Gold Bullion Strategy Portfolio			Open End	Commodities Specified (Precious Metals)	C-	D	C+	Down	Y	0
The Hartford Balanced Income Fund Class A	HBLAX	NAS CM	Open End	Cautious Alloc (Balanced)	B	C+	B+		Y	2,000
The Hartford Balanced Income Fund Class C	HBLCX	NAS CM	Open End	Cautious Alloc (Balanced)	B-	C+	B		Y	2,000
The Hartford Balanced Income Fund Class F	HBLFX	NAS CM	Open End	Cautious Alloc (Balanced)	B	C+	B+		Y	1,000,000
The Hartford Balanced Income Fund Class I	HBLIX	NAS CM	Open End	Cautious Alloc (Balanced)	B	C+	B+		Y	2,000
The Hartford Balanced Income Fund Class R3	HBLRX	NAS CM	Open End	Cautious Alloc (Balanced)	B	C+	B+		Y	0
The Hartford Balanced Income Fund Class R4	HBLSX	NAS CM	Open End	Cautious Alloc (Balanced)	B	C+	B+		Y	0
The Hartford Balanced Income Fund Class R5	HBLTX	NAS CM	Open End	Cautious Alloc (Balanced)	B	C+	B+		Y	0
The Hartford Balanced Income Fund Class R6	HBLVX	NAS CM	Open End	Cautious Alloc (Balanced)	B	B-	B+		Y	0
The Hartford Balanced Income Fund Class Y	HBLYX	NAS CM	Open End	Cautious Alloc (Balanced)	B	C+	B+		Y	250,000
The Hartford Capital Appreciation Fund Class A	ITHAX	NAS CM	Open End	US Equity Large Cap Blend (Growth)	B-	C+	B		Y	2,000
The Hartford Capital Appreciation Fund Class C	HCACX	NAS CM	Open End	US Equity Large Cap Blend (Growth)	B-	C+	B		Y	2,000
The Hartford Capital Appreciation Fund Class F	HCAFX	NAS CM	Open End	US Equity Large Cap Blend (Growth)	B-	C+	B		Y	1,000,000
The Hartford Capital Appreciation Fund Class I	ITHIX	NAS CM	Open End	US Equity Large Cap Blend (Growth)	B-	C+	B		Y	2,000
The Hartford Capital Appreciation Fund Class R3	ITHRX	NAS CM	Open End	US Equity Large Cap Blend (Growth)	B-	C+	B		Y	0
The Hartford Capital Appreciation Fund Class R4	ITHSX	NAS CM	Open End	US Equity Large Cap Blend (Growth)	B-	C+	B		Y	0
The Hartford Capital Appreciation Fund Class R5	ITHTX	NAS CM	Open End	US Equity Large Cap Blend (Growth)	B-	C+	B		Y	0
The Hartford Capital Appreciation Fund Class R6	ITHVX	NAS CM	Open End	US Equity Large Cap Blend (Growth)	B-	C+	B		Y	0
The Hartford Capital Appreciation Fund Class Y	HCAYX	NAS CM	Open End	US Equity Large Cap Blend (Growth)	B-	C+	B		Y	250,000
The Hartford Dividend and Growth Fund Class A	IHGIX	NAS CM	Open End	US Equity Large Cap Value (Equity-Income)	B-	C	B+		Y	2,000
The Hartford Dividend and Growth Fund Class C	HDGCX	NAS CM	Open End	US Equity Large Cap Value (Equity-Income)	B-	C	B		Y	2,000
The Hartford Dividend and Growth Fund Class F	HDGFX	NAS CM	Open End	US Equity Large Cap Value (Equity-Income)	B-	C	B+		Y	1,000,000
The Hartford Dividend and Growth Fund Class I	HDGIX	NAS CM	Open End	US Equity Large Cap Value (Equity-Income)	B-	C	B+		Y	2,000
The Hartford Dividend and Growth Fund Class R3	HDGRX	NAS CM	Open End	US Equity Large Cap Value (Equity-Income)	B-	C	B		Y	0
The Hartford Dividend and Growth Fund Class R4	HDGSX	NAS CM	Open End	US Equity Large Cap Value (Equity-Income)	B-	C	B+		Y	0
The Hartford Dividend and Growth Fund Class R5	HDGTX	NAS CM	Open End	US Equity Large Cap Value (Equity-Income)	B-	C	B+		Y	0
The Hartford Dividend and Growth Fund Class R6	HDGVX	NAS CM	Open End	US Equity Large Cap Value (Equity-Income)	B-	C	B+		Y	0
The Hartford Dividend and Growth Fund Class Y	HDGYX	NAS CM	Open End	US Equity Large Cap Value (Equity-Income)	B-	C	B+		Y	250,000
The Hartford Equity Income Fund Class A	HQIAX	NAS CM	Open End	US Equity Large Cap Value (Equity-Income)	B-	C+	B+		Y	2,000
The Hartford Equity Income Fund Class C	HQICX	NAS CM	Open End	US Equity Large Cap Value (Equity-Income)	B-	C	B		Y	2,000
The Hartford Equity Income Fund Class F	HQIFX	NAS CM	Open End	US Equity Large Cap Value (Equity-Income)	B-	C+	B+		Y	1,000,000
The Hartford Equity Income Fund Class I	HQIIX	NAS CM	Open End	US Equity Large Cap Value (Equity-Income)	B-	C+	B+		Y	2,000
The Hartford Equity Income Fund Class R3	HQIRX	NAS CM	Open End	US Equity Large Cap Value (Equity-Income)	B-	C	B		Y	0
The Hartford Equity Income Fund Class R4	HQISX	NAS CM	Open End	US Equity Large Cap Value (Equity-Income)	B-	C	B+		Y	0
The Hartford Equity Income Fund Class R5	HQITX	NAS CM	Open End	US Equity Large Cap Value (Equity-Income)	B-	C+	B+		Y	0
The Hartford Equity Income Fund Class R6	HQIVX	NAS CM	Open End	US Equity Large Cap Value (Equity-Income)	B-	C+	B+		Y	0
The Hartford Equity Income Fund Class Y	HQIYX	NAS CM	Open End	US Equity Large Cap Value (Equity-Income)	B-	C+	B+		Y	250,000
The Hartford Global All-Asset Fund Class A	HLAAX	NAS CM	Open End	Moderate Alloc (Asset Alloc)	C+	C	B+	Up	Y	5,000
The Hartford Global All-Asset Fund Class Y	HLAYX	NAS CM	Open End	Moderate Alloc (Asset Alloc)	C+	C	B+	Up	Y	250,000
The Hartford Global Real Asset Fund Class C	HRLCX	NAS CM	Open End	Moderate Alloc (Asset Alloc)	C	C-	C+		Y	5,000
The Hartford Growth Opportunities Fund Class A	HGOAX	NAS CM	Open End	US Equity Large Cap Growth (Growth)	B-	B-	B-	Down	Y	2,000
The Hartford Growth Opportunities Fund Class C	HGOCX	NAS CM	Open End	US Equity Large Cap Growth (Growth)	B-	B-	B-		Y	2,000
The Hartford Growth Opportunities Fund Class F	HGOFX	NAS CM	Open End	US Equity Large Cap Growth (Growth)	B-	B-	B-	Down	Y	1,000,000
The Hartford Growth Opportunities Fund Class I	HGOIX	NAS CM	Open End	US Equity Large Cap Growth (Growth)	B-	B-	B-	Down	Y	2,000
The Hartford Growth Opportunities Fund Class R3	HGORX	NAS CM	Open End	US Equity Large Cap Growth (Growth)	B-	B-	B-	Down	Y	0
The Hartford Growth Opportunities Fund Class R4	HGOSX	NAS CM	Open End	US Equity Large Cap Growth (Growth)	B-	B-	B-	Down	Y	0
The Hartford Growth Opportunities Fund Class R5	HGOTX	NAS CM	Open End	US Equity Large Cap Growth (Growth)	B-	B-	B-	Down	Y	0
The Hartford Growth Opportunities Fund Class R6	HGOVX	NAS CM	Open End	US Equity Large Cap Growth (Growth)	B-	B-	B-	Down	Y	0
The Hartford Growth Opportunities Fund Class Y	HGOYX	NAS CM	Open End	US Equity Large Cap Growth (Growth)	B-	B-	B-	Down	Y	250,000
The Hartford Healthcare Fund Class A	HGHAX	NAS CM	Open End	Healthcare Sector Equity (Health)	C+	C	B-		Y	2,000
The Hartford Healthcare Fund Class C	HGHCX	NAS CM	Open End	Healthcare Sector Equity (Health)	C+	C	B-		Y	2,000

★ Expanded analysis of this fund is included in Section II.

Min Additional Investment	TOTAL RETURNS: 3-Month Total Return	6-Month Total Return	1-Year Total Return	3-Year Total Return	5-Year Total Return	PERFORMANCE: Dividend Yield (TTM)	Expense Ratio	3-Yr Std Deviation	3-Year Beta	ASSETS: NAV	Total Assets (MIL)	ASSET ALLOCATION & TURNOVER: %Cash	%Stocks	%Bonds	%Other	Turnover Ratio	BULL & BEAR: Last Bull Market Total Return	Last Bear Market Total Return	FEES: Front End Fee (%)	Back End Fee (%)	Inception Date
1,000	9.07	10.05	11.47	0.34	-2.75	1.4	1.48	11.02	0	23.45	76.1	24	7	69	0	167					Jul-13
	9.41	10.78	11.86	0.55	-2.40	10.43	1.69	11.13	0.01	22.19	10.7	15	5	80	0	253					Nov-13
50	4.04	13.03	10.34	23.88	33.22	2.58	0.9	5.85		14.41	12,315	4	41	54	0	48	14.09	-5.43	5.50		Jul-06
50	3.84	12.57	9.50	21.10	28.34	1.91	1.65	5.85		14.19	12,315	4	41	54	0	48	13.7	-5.79		1.00	Jul-06
	4.12	13.20	10.77	25.09	35.53	2.89	0.57	5.89		14.42	12,315	4	41	54	0	48	14.61	-5.26			Feb-17
50	4.11	13.16	10.61	24.78	34.89	2.82	0.65	5.89		14.41	12,315	4	41	54	0	48	14.33	-5.42			Feb-10
	4.03	12.88	9.98	22.65	31.16	2.24	1.28	5.88		14.47	12,315	4	41	54	0	48	13.99	-5.59			May-10
	4.02	12.94	10.31	23.73	33.16	2.52	0.98	5.89		14.47	12,315	4	41	54	0	48	14.15	-5.45			May-10
	4.07	13.15	10.59	24.68	34.83	2.77	0.68	5.88		14.49	12,315	4	41	54	0	48	14.26	-5.31			May-10
	4.15	13.22	10.73	25.07	35.49	2.86	0.58	5.85		14.57	12,315	4	41	54	0	48	14.61	-5.26			Nov-14
	4.06	13.18	10.67	24.93	35.36	2.81	0.67	5.84		14.57	12,315	4	41	54	0	48	14.61	-5.26			Jul-06
50	5.91	23.55	10.99	52.12	52.58	0.26	1.07	12.38	0.96	36.87	7,165	3	95	0	2	108	23.42	-25.61	5.50		Jul-96
50	5.72	23.11	10.12	48.71	47.08	0	1.82	12.39	0.96	26.95	7,165	3	95	0	2	108	22.91	-25.82	2.50	1.00	Jul-98
	6.00	23.78	11.39	53.79	55.48	0.54	0.71	12.39	0.96	37.06	7,165	3	95	0	2	108	23.76	-25.46			Feb-17
50	6.00	23.73	11.30	53.39	54.84	0.46	0.79	12.39	0.96	37.07	7,165	3	95	0	2	108	23.68	-25.55			Aug-06
	5.82	23.36	10.61	50.60	50.14	0	1.43	12.39	0.96	41.24	7,165	3	95	0	2	108	23.26	-25.7			Dec-06
	5.91	23.57	10.94	51.99	52.45	0.11	1.11	12.37	0.96	42.78	7,165	3	95	0	2	108	23.45	-25.6			Dec-06
	5.99	23.72	11.26	53.37	54.72	0.37	0.81	12.39	0.96	43.7	7,165	3	95	0	2	108	23.71	-25.5			Dec-06
	6.02	23.81	11.39	53.80	55.44	0.46	0.71	12.4	0.96	43.99	7,165	3	95	0	2	108	23.76	-25.46			Nov-14
	6.00	23.78	11.36	53.72	55.41	0.45	0.75	12.38	0.96	43.97	7,165	3	95	0	2	108	23.76	-25.46			Jul-96
50	3.48	16.04	9.54	43.20	50.06	1.42	1	11.44	0.91	24.77	8,710	3	97	0	0	31	22.11	-17.37	5.50		Jul-96
50	3.29	15.56	8.66	39.93	44.53	0.7	1.76	11.44	0.91	23.85	8,710	3	97	0	0	31	21.57	-17.59	2.50	1.00	Jul-98
	3.59	16.25	9.94	44.78	52.87	1.75	0.64	11.45	0.91	24.62	8,710	3	97	0	0	31	22.41	-17.22			Feb-17
50	3.53	16.14	9.84	44.27	51.82	1.67	0.73	11.45	0.91	24.63	8,710	3	97	0	0	31	22.3	-17.29			Aug-06
	3.37	15.82	9.12	41.65	47.49	1.06	1.35	11.43	0.91	25.14	8,710	3	97	0	0	31	21.9	-17.47			Dec-06
	3.46	16.02	9.52	42.98	49.80	1.33	1.05	11.44	0.91	25.33	8,710	3	97	0	0	31	22.11	-17.34			Dec-06
	3.54	16.13	9.82	44.27	52.06	1.61	0.74	11.44	0.91	25.43	8,710	3	97	0	0	31	22.37	-17.27			Dec-06
	3.60	16.22	9.96	44.75	52.73	1.7	0.65	11.46	0.91	25.44	8,710	3	97	0	0	31	22.41	-17.22			Nov-14
	3.54	16.20	9.87	44.60	52.68	1.65	0.69	11.45	0.91	25.44	8,710	3	97	0	0	31	22.41	-17.22			Jul-96
50	3.98	16.73	9.77	36.44	46.05	1.74	1	11.02	0.89	19.43	4,020	1	99	0	0	22	24.53	-14.05	5.50		Aug-03
50	3.74	16.32	8.95	33.35	40.69	1.03	1.75	11.02	0.89	19.33	4,020	1	99	0	0	22	23.99	-14.31	2.50	1.00	Aug-03
	4.09	16.98	10.15	37.85	48.64	2.07	0.66	11.02	0.89	19.31	4,020	1	99	0	0	22	24.87	-13.93			Feb-17
50	4.01	16.90	10.02	37.35	47.78	1.96	0.75	11	0.89	19.31	4,020	1	99	0	0	22	24.71	-13.96			Aug-06
	3.88	16.57	9.34	34.90	43.44	1.4	1.37	10.99	0.89	19.46	4,020	1	99	0	0	22	24.34	-14.19			Dec-06
	3.94	16.71	9.71	36.22	45.69	1.67	1.06	11.02	0.89	19.49	4,020	1	99	0	0	22	24.46	-14.01			Dec-06
	4.05	16.91	10.05	37.47	47.88	1.94	0.76	11.05	0.89	19.59	4,020	1	99	0	0	22	24.77	-13.98			Dec-06
	4.07	17.00	10.15	37.88	48.67	2.03	0.66	11.02	0.89	19.64	4,020	1	99	0	0	22	24.87	-13.93			Nov-14
	4.06	16.96	10.08	37.72	48.49	1.98	0.71	11.03	0.89	19.64	4,020	1	99	0	0	22	24.87	-13.93			Aug-03
50	3.37	11.88	2.15	23.84	19.09	9.17	1.24	7.05		9.79	156.8	14	49	36	0	62	11.51	-15.63	5.50		May-10
	3.46	12.07	2.47	25.12	21.17	9.51	0.8	7.1		9.84	156.8	14	49	36	0	62	11.72	-15.51			May-10
50	0.79	9.59	-3.74	12.55	-15.11	1.02	2.02	9.28		8.91	296.5	8	65	13	15	111	7.54	-20.47		1.00	May-10
50	5.73	29.43	11.52	69.46	94.38	0	1.11	15.93	1.11	41.29	5,201	7	88	0	2	122	26.92	-23.05	5.50		Feb-02
50	5.54	28.95	10.69	65.69	87.26	0	1.85	15.93	1.11	21.51	5,201	7	88	0	2	122	26.39	-23.25	2.50	1.00	Feb-02
	5.84	29.67	11.95	71.37	97.95	0	0.74	15.95	1.11	44	5,201	7	88	0	2	122	27.27	-22.88			Feb-17
50	5.81	29.60	11.83	70.75	96.68	0	0.83	15.94	1.11	43.87	5,201	7	88	0	2	122	27.06	-22.93			Aug-06
	5.65	29.22	11.16	67.79	91.16	0	1.46	15.94	1.11	41.3	5,201	7	88	0	2	122	26.71	-23.13			Dec-06
	5.71	29.39	11.47	69.28	94.07	0	1.15	15.94	1.11	44.24	5,201	7	88	0	2	122	26.94	-23			Dec-06
	5.80	29.57	11.80	70.80	96.95	0	0.85	15.94	1.11	46.83	5,201	7	88	0	2	122	27.14	-22.9			Dec-06
	5.83	29.65	11.94	71.33	97.85	0	0.74	15.94	1.11	47.7	5,201	7	88	0	2	122	27.27	-22.88			Nov-14
	5.83	29.66	11.89	71.24	97.81	0	0.79	15.94	1.11	47.69	5,201	7	88	0	2	122	27.27	-22.88			Feb-02
50	1.42	17.44	6.53	34.25	58.83	0	1.28	16.08	1.09	34.81	1,315	2	98	0	0	27	22.44	-12.92	5.50		May-00
50	1.24	17.00	5.75	31.31	53.04	0	2.03	16.03	1.08	27.66	1,315	2	98	0	0	27	21.98	-13.19	2.50	1.00	May-00

	MARKET		FUND TYPE, CATEGORY & OBJECTIVE		RATINGS				MINIMUMS	
Fund Name	Ticker Symbol	Traded On	Fund Type	Category and (Prospectus Objective)	Overall Rating	Reward Rating	Risk Rating	Recent Up/ Downgrade	Open to New Investors	Min Initial Investment
The Hartford Healthcare Fund Class F	HGHFX	NAS CM	Open End	Healthcare Sector Equity (Health)	C+	C	B		Y	1,000,000
The Hartford Healthcare Fund Class I	HGHIX	NAS CM	Open End	Healthcare Sector Equity (Health)	C+	C	B		Y	2,000
The Hartford Healthcare Fund Class R3	HGHRX	NAS CM	Open End	Healthcare Sector Equity (Health)	C+	C	B-		Y	0
The Hartford Healthcare Fund Class R4	HGHSX	NAS CM	Open End	Healthcare Sector Equity (Health)	C+	C	B-		Y	0
The Hartford Healthcare Fund Class R5	HGHTX	NAS CM	Open End	Healthcare Sector Equity (Health)	C+	C	B		Y	0
The Hartford Healthcare Fund Class R6	HGHVX	NAS CM	Open End	Healthcare Sector Equity (Health)	C+	C	B		Y	0
The Hartford Healthcare Fund Class Y	HGHYX	NAS CM	Open End	Healthcare Sector Equity (Health)	C+	C	B		Y	250,000
The Hartford International Opportunities Fund Class A	IHOAX	NAS CM	Open End	Global Equity Large Cap (Foreign Stock)	C	C	C+		Y	2,000
The Hartford International Opportunities Fund Class C	HIOCX	NAS CM	Open End	Global Equity Large Cap (Foreign Stock)	C	C-	C+	Up	Y	2,000
The Hartford International Opportunities Fund Class F	IHOFX	NAS CM	Open End	Global Equity Large Cap (Foreign Stock)	C	C	C+		Y	1,000,000
The Hartford International Opportunities Fund Class I	IHOIX	NAS CM	Open End	Global Equity Large Cap (Foreign Stock)	C	C	C+		Y	2,000
The Hartford International Opportunities Fund Class R3	IHORX	NAS CM	Open End	Global Equity Large Cap (Foreign Stock)	C	C-	C+	Up	Y	0
The Hartford International Opportunities Fund Class R4	IHOSX	NAS CM	Open End	Global Equity Large Cap (Foreign Stock)	C	C	C+		Y	0
The Hartford International Opportunities Fund Class R5	IHOTX	NAS CM	Open End	Global Equity Large Cap (Foreign Stock)	C	C	C+		Y	0
The Hartford International Opportunities Fund Class R6	IHOVX	NAS CM	Open End	Global Equity Large Cap (Foreign Stock)	C	C	C+		Y	0
The Hartford International Opportunities Fund Class Y	HAOYX	NAS CM	Open End	Global Equity Large Cap (Foreign Stock)	C	C	C+		Y	250,000
The Hartford International Value Fund Class Y	HILYX	NAS CM	Open End	Global Equity Large Cap (Foreign Stock)	C	C-	C			250,000
The Hartford MidCap Fund Class A	HFMCX	NAS CM	Open End	US Equity Mid Cap (Growth)	C+	C	B-		Y	2,000
The Hartford MidCap Fund Class C	HMDCX	NAS CM	Open End	US Equity Mid Cap (Growth)	C+	C	B-		Y	2,000
The Hartford MidCap Fund Class F	HMDFX	NAS CM	Open End	US Equity Mid Cap (Growth)	C+	C	B-	Down	Y	1,000,000
The Hartford MidCap Fund Class I	HFMIX	NAS CM	Open End	US Equity Mid Cap (Growth)	C+	C	B-	Down	Y	2,000
The Hartford MidCap Fund Class R3	HFMRX	NAS CM	Open End	US Equity Mid Cap (Growth)	C+	C	B-		Y	0
The Hartford MidCap Fund Class R4	HFMSX	NAS CM	Open End	US Equity Mid Cap (Growth)	C+	C	B-		Y	0
The Hartford MidCap Fund Class R5	HFMTX	NAS CM	Open End	US Equity Mid Cap (Growth)	C+	C	B-	Down	Y	0
The Hartford MidCap Fund Class R6	HFMVX	NAS CM	Open End	US Equity Mid Cap (Growth)	C+	C	B-	Down	Y	0
The Hartford MidCap Fund Class Y	HMDYX	NAS CM	Open End	US Equity Mid Cap (Growth)	C+	C	B-	Down	Y	250,000
The Hartford Small Company Fund Class A	IHSAX	NAS CM	Open End	US Equity Small Cap (Small Company)	C+	C+	C+	Down	Y	2,000
The Hartford Small Company Fund Class C	HSMCX	NAS CM	Open End	US Equity Small Cap (Small Company)	C+	C	C+	Down	Y	2,000
The Hartford Small Company Fund Class F	IHSFX	NAS CM	Open End	US Equity Small Cap (Small Company)	C+	C+	C+	Down	Y	1,000,000
The Hartford Small Company Fund Class I	IHSIX	NAS CM	Open End	US Equity Small Cap (Small Company)	C+	C+	C+	Down	Y	2,000
The Hartford Small Company Fund Class R3	IHSRX	NAS CM	Open End	US Equity Small Cap (Small Company)	C+	C	C+	Down	Y	0
The Hartford Small Company Fund Class R4	IHSSX	NAS CM	Open End	US Equity Small Cap (Small Company)	C+	C+	C+	Down	Y	0
The Hartford Small Company Fund Class R5	IHSUX	NAS CM	Open End	US Equity Small Cap (Small Company)	C+	C+	C+	Down	Y	0
The Hartford Small Company Fund Class R6	IHSVX	NAS CM	Open End	US Equity Small Cap (Small Company)	C+	C+	C+	Down	Y	0
The Hartford Small Company Fund Class Y	HSCYX	NAS CM	Open End	US Equity Small Cap (Small Company)	C+	C+	C+	Down	Y	250,000
The India Fund Inc	IFN	NYSE	Closed End	India Equity (Pacific Stock)	C	C	C+	Up	Y	
The Investment House Growth Fund	TIHGX	NAS CM	Open End	US Equity Large Cap Growth (Growth)	C+	C	B-	Down	Y	1,000
The Merger Fund® Institutional Class	MERIX	NAS CM	Open End	Market Neutral (Growth)	B	C	A-		Y	1,000,000
The Merger Fund® Investor Class	MERFX	NAS CM	Open End	Market Neutral (Growth)	B	C	A+		Y	2,000
The MP 63 Fund	DRIPX	NAS CM	Open End	US Equity Large Cap Blend (Growth)	B-	C+	B+	Down	Y	0
The Texas Fund Class I	BIGTX	NAS CM	Open End	US Equity Mid Cap (Growth)	C	C-	C		Y	50,000
The Tocqueville Gold Fund Institutional Class	TGLIX	NAS CM	Open End	Precious Metals Sector Equity (Precious Metals)	D	D	D+		Y	1,000,000
The Tocqueville Phoenix Fund	TOPHX	NAS CM	Open End	US Equity Mid Cap (Growth)	C	D+	C+		Y	1,000
The Water Island Long/Short Fund Class A	ATQAX	NAS CM	Open End	Long/Short Equity (Growth)	C+	C	B+		Y	2,000
The Water Island Long/Short Fund Class C	ATQCX	NAS CM	Open End	Long/Short Equity (Growth)	C+	C	B+		Y	2,000
The Water Island Long/Short Fund Class I	ATQIX	NAS CM	Open End	Long/Short Equity (Growth)	C+	C	B+		Y	100,000
The Water Island Long/Short Fund Class R	ATQFX	NAS CM	Open End	Long/Short Equity (Growth)	C+	C	B+		Y	2,000
Theta Income Fund Institutional Class	LQTIX	NAS CM	Open End	Long/Short Equity (Income)	C	C	C+		Y	1,000
Third Avenue Real Estate Value Fund Institutional Class	TAREX	NAS CM	Open End	Real Estate Sector Equity (Real Estate)	C	D+	B-		Y	100,000
Third Avenue Real Estate Value Fund Investor Class	TVRVX	NAS CM	Open End	Real Estate Sector Equity (Real Estate)	C	D+	B-		Y	2,500
Third Avenue Real Estate Value Fund Z Class	TARZX	NAS CM	Open End	Real Estate Sector Equity (Real Estate)	C	D+	B-		Y	1,000,000
Third Avenue Small Cap Value Fund Institutional Class	TASCX	NAS CM	Open End	US Equity Small Cap (Small Company)	C	C-	C+		Y	100,000

★ Expanded analysis of this fund is included in Section II.

	TOTAL RETURNS					PERFORMANCE				ASSETS		ASSET ALLOCATION & TURNOVER					BULL & BEAR		FEES		
Min Additional Investment	3-Month Total Return	6-Month Total Return	1-Year Total Return	3-Year Total Return	5-Year Total Return	Dividend Yield (TTM)	Expense Ratio	3-Yr Std Deviation	3-Year Beta	NAV	Total Assets (MIL)	%Cash	%Stocks	%Bonds	%Other	Turnover Ratio	Last Bull Market Total Return	Last Bear Market Total Return	Front End Fee (%)	Back End Fee (%)	Inception Date
	1.51	17.65	6.90	35.77	61.90	0	0.9	16.04	1.08	36.86	1,315	2	98	0	0	27	22.78	-12.72			Feb-17
50	1.49	17.58	6.80	35.32	60.99	0	1	16.07	1.09	36.77	1,315	2	98	0	0	27	22.74	-12.81			Aug-06
	1.33	17.25	6.17	32.94	56.31	0	1.61	16.04	1.08	35.75	1,315	2	98	0	0	27	22.37	-13.01			Dec-06
	1.39	17.43	6.46	34.16	58.69	0	1.3	16.04	1.09	37.79	1,315	2	98	0	0	27	22.56	-12.89			Dec-06
	1.48	17.61	6.80	35.35	61.03	0	1.02	16.05	1.09	39.73	1,315	2	98	0	0	27	22.82	-12.81			Dec-06
	1.51	17.66	6.89	35.74	61.86		0.9	16.04	1.08	40.28	1,315	2	98	0	0	27	22.78	-12.72			Feb-19
	1.51	17.64	6.87	35.71	61.83	0	0.96	16.04	1.08	40.27	1,315	2	98	0	0	27	22.78	-12.72			May-00
50	3.91	18.90	-0.43	25.75	12.86	1.12	1.11	12.99	1.11	15.66	3,641	2	98	0	0	76	18.13	-23.19	5.50		Jul-96
50	3.72	18.52	-1.17	23.02	8.72	0.24	1.87	12.95	1.1	13.63	3,641	2	98	0	0	76	17.67	-23.47		1.00	Jul-98
	4.07	19.21	0.02	27.43	15.41	1.57	0.71	12.98	1.11	15.57	3,641	2	98	0	0	76	18.51	-23.04			Feb-17
50	4.01	19.14	-0.11	26.86	14.68	1.45	0.8	12.99	1.11	15.56	3,641	2	98	0	0	76	18.33	-23.07			May-08
	3.84	18.80	-0.72	24.67	11.37	0.8	1.42	12.97	1.1	15.92	3,641	2	98	0	0	76	18.02	-23.22			Dec-06
	3.97	19.00	-0.36	25.86	13.08	1.07	1.12	12.97	1.1	16.22	3,641	2	98	0	0	76	18.21	-23.15			Dec-06
	4.06	19.14	-0.09	27.05	14.79	1.4	0.81	13.01	1.11	16.37	3,641	2	98	0	0	76	18.45	-23.05			Dec-06
	4.04	19.18	-0.03	27.41	15.32	1.48	0.71	12.96	1.1	16.46	3,641	2	98	0	0	76	18.51	-23.04			Nov-14
	4.04	19.10	-0.08	27.22	15.23	1.44	0.76	13	1.11	16.46	3,641	2	98	0	0	76	18.51	-23.04			Jul-96
	1.60	9.28	-5.44	32.35	14.42	2.63	0.9	12.68	1.08	14.59	2,473	5	95	0	0	22	14.54	-22.48			May-10
50	4.75	27.35	8.20	58.73	63.08	0	1.11	14.93	0.95	30.63	13,927	0	100	0	0	37	29.28	-25.59	5.50		Dec-97
50	4.56	26.91	7.37	55.19	57.12	0	1.86	14.91	0.95	21.08	13,927	0	100	0	0	37	28.78	-25.83	2.50	1.00	Jul-98
	4.88	27.61	8.60	60.52	66.19	0	0.75	14.93	0.95	31.79	13,927	0	100	0	0	37	29.71	-25.48			Feb-17
50	4.82	27.55	8.51	59.93	65.12	0	0.82	14.92	0.95	31.71	13,927	0	100	0	0	37	29.49	-25.56			Feb-09
	4.69	27.17	7.81	57.08	60.41	0	1.47	14.93	0.95	34.35	13,927	0	100	0	0	37	29.15	-25.72			May-09
	4.75	27.34	8.14	58.51	62.86	0	1.16	14.89	0.95	35.91	13,927	0	100	0	0	37	29.31	-25.6			May-09
	4.86	27.53	8.47	60.05	65.39	0	0.85	14.92	0.95	37.1	13,927	0	100	0	0	37	29.6	-25.53			May-09
	4.86	27.56	8.58	60.46	66.19	0	0.75	14.92	0.95	37.53	13,927	0	100	0	0	37	29.71	-25.48			Nov-14
	4.86	27.56	8.53	60.37	66.04	0	0.79	14.91	0.95	37.49	13,927	0	100	0	0	37	29.71	-25.48			Dec-97
50	4.73	29.77	9.44	68.99	46.62	0	1.35	18.15	1.01	20.79	624.3	6	93	0	0	104	26.36	-24.9	5.50		Jul-96
50	4.52	29.22	8.61	65.17	41.34	0	2.13	18.17	1.01	13.62	624.3	6	93	0	0	104	25.85	-25.12	2.50	1.00	Jul-98
	4.81	29.99	9.87	71.13	50.07	0	0.91	18.14	1.01	22.19	624.3	6	93	0	0	104	26.74	-24.71			Feb-17
50	4.79	29.94	9.72	70.19	48.49	0	1.08	18.16	1.01	22.09	624.3	6	93	0	0	104	26.52	-24.79			Aug-06
	4.63	29.56	9.19	67.96	45.16	0	1.56	18.18	1.01	22.79	624.3	6	93	0	0	104	26.24	-24.94			Dec-06
	4.72	29.80	9.52	69.48	47.41	0	1.26	18.16	1.01	24.39	624.3	6	93	0	0	104	26.43	-24.83			Dec-06
	4.81	30.00	9.86	71.00	49.67	0	0.96	18.18	1.01	25.91	624.3	6	93	0	0	104	26.69	-24.74			Dec-06
	4.82	30.04	9.93	70.17	50.15	0	0.91	18.19	1.01	26.49	624.3	6	93	0	0	104	26.74	-24.71			Nov-14
	4.79	30.00	9.89	71.16	50.10	0	0.96	18.15	1.01	26.47	624.3	6	93	0	0	104	26.74	-24.71			Jul-96
	2.75	4.92	1.99	26.77	44.62	2.88	1.33	16.19	0.95	23.7	637.6	1	99	0	0	13	-5.14	-20.8			Feb-94
100	4.28	23.29	7.54	69.29	78.44	0	1.43	15	1.14	38.21	122.8	1	99	0	0	5	33.64	-15.66			Dec-01
500	0.42	2.82	4.61	16.07	14.96	1.35	1.71	2.62	-1.32	16.72	3,039	60	30	8	2	155	4.35	-4.06			Aug-13
	0.35	2.68	4.28	15.05	13.18	1.07	2.01	2.63	-0.97	16.82	3,039	60	30	8	2	155	4.35	-4.06			Jan-89
	3.88	18.62	13.25	40.41	54.48	1.74	0.75	11.77	0.93	22.48	71.3	1	99	0	0	6	24.1	-16.92			Mar-99
	-2.12	8.87	-9.78	25.71	-2.91	0.28	1.62	15.08	1	10.15	10.5	15	85	0	0	44					Sep-13
	11.50	19.23	6.06	-14.31	-17.84		1.18	22.93	0.08	36.32	982.2	3	83	0	14	9	-7.82	-17.44			Apr-19
100	2.34	14.59	-5.58	21.22	-5.84	0.03	1.26	17.84	0.97	20.1	189.9	10	90	0	0	40	35.75	-27.43			Nov-93
	0.10	5.40	-0.46	9.52		0	2.42	4.37	1.11	9.94	2.2					520			3.25		Dec-14
	0.10	5.40	-0.46	9.52		0	3.17	4.37	1.11	9.94	2.2					520				1.00	Dec-14
	0.10	5.40	-0.46	9.52		0	2.17	4.37	1.11	9.94	2.2					520					Dec-14
	0.10	5.40	-0.46	9.52		0	2.42	4.37	1.11	9.94	2.2					520					Dec-14
100	0.87	4.17	1.80	7.86	9.95	1.51	1.25	3.36		51.01	378.7	7	0	93	1	8					Mar-14
1,000	-2.85	13.17	-6.60	16.56	14.88	1.55	1.12	13.33	0.97	27.92	1,168	4	96	0	0	27	27.72	-22.46			Sep-98
1,000	-2.93	13.02	-6.84	15.67	13.42	1.2	1.4	13.32	0.97	27.76	1,168	4	96	0	0	27	27.52	-22.53			Dec-09
1,000	-2.85	13.22	-6.52	16.66	14.98	1.69	1.03	13.31	0.97	27.91	1,168	4	96	0	0	27	27.72	-22.46			Mar-18
1,000	2.55	14.33	-4.88	30.59	27.53	0	1.15	15.53	0.86	18.43	208.1	2	98	0	0	44	18.41	-19.64			Apr-97

Fund Name	Ticker Symbol	Traded On	Fund Type	Category and (Prospectus Objective)	Overall Rating	Reward Rating	Risk Rating	Recent Up/ Downgrade	Open to New Investors	Min Initial Investment
	MARKET		FUND TYPE, CATEGORY & OBJECTIVE		RATINGS				MINIMUMS	
Third Avenue Small Cap Value Fund Z Class	TASZX	NAS CM	Open End	US Equity Small Cap (Small Company)	C	C-	C+		Y	1,000,000
Third Avenue Small-Cap Value Fund Investor Class	TVSVX	NAS CM	Open End	US Equity Small Cap (Small Company)	C	C-	C+		Y	2,500
Third Avenue Value Fund Institutional Class	TAVFX	NAS CM	Open End	Global Equity Large Cap (Growth)	D+	D	C-	Down	Y	100,000
Third Avenue Value Fund Investor Class	TVFVX	NAS CM	Open End	Global Equity Large Cap (Growth)	D+	D	C-	Down	Y	2,500
Third Avenue Value Fund Z Class	TAVZX	NAS CM	Open End	Global Equity Large Cap (Growth)	D+	D	C-	Down	Y	1,000,000
Thomas White American Opportunities Fund Investor Class	TWAOX	NAS CM	Open End	US Equity Mid Cap (Growth)	C+	C	B		Y	2,500
Thomas White Emerging Markets Fund Class I	TWIIX	NAS CM	Open End	Global Emerg Mkts (Div Emerging Mkts)	C	C	C+		Y	1,000,000
Thomas White Emerging Markets Fund Investor Class	TWEMX	NAS CM	Open End	Global Emerg Mkts (Div Emerging Mkts)	C	C	C+		Y	2,500
Thomas White International Fund Class I	TWWIX	NAS CM	Open End	Global Equity Large Cap (Foreign Stock)	C	C	C+		Y	1,000,000
Thomas White International Fund Investor Class	TWWDX	NAS CM	Open End	Global Equity Large Cap (Foreign Stock)	C	C-	C+		Y	2,500
Thompson LargeCap Fund	THPGX	NAS CM	Open End	US Equity Large Cap Blend (Growth)	C+	C	B-	Up	Y	250
Thompson MidCap Fund	THPMX	NAS CM	Open End	US Equity Mid Cap (Growth)	C	C-	C+		Y	250
Thornburg Better World International Fund Class A	TBWAX	NAS CM	Open End	Global Equity Large Cap (Growth)	C	C	B		Y	5,000
Thornburg Better World International Fund Class C	TBWCX	NAS CM	Open End	Global Equity Large Cap (Growth)	C	C	B		Y	5,000
Thornburg Better World International Fund Class I	TBWIX	NAS CM	Open End	Global Equity Large Cap (Growth)	C	C	B		Y	2,500,000
Thornburg Core Growth Fund Class A	THCGX	NAS CM	Open End	US Equity Large Cap Growth (Growth)	C+	C	B-	Down	Y	5,000
Thornburg Core Growth Fund Class C	TCGCX	NAS CM	Open End	US Equity Large Cap Growth (Growth)	C+	C	B-	Down	Y	5,000
Thornburg Core Growth Fund Class I	THIGX	NAS CM	Open End	US Equity Large Cap Growth (Growth)	C+	C	B-	Down	Y	2,500,000
Thornburg Core Growth Fund Class R3	THCRX	NAS CM	Open End	US Equity Large Cap Growth (Growth)	C+	C	B-	Down	Y	0
Thornburg Core Growth Fund Class R4	TCGRX	NAS CM	Open End	US Equity Large Cap Growth (Growth)	C+	C	B-	Down	Y	0
Thornburg Core Growth Fund Class R5	THGRX	NAS CM	Open End	US Equity Large Cap Growth (Growth)	C+	C	B-	Down	Y	0
Thornburg Developing World Fund Class A	THDAX	NAS CM	Open End	Global Emerg Mkts (Growth)	C	C	C+		Y	5,000
Thornburg Developing World Fund Class C	THDCX	NAS CM	Open End	Global Emerg Mkts (Growth)	C	C	C+		Y	5,000
Thornburg Developing World Fund Class I	THDIX	NAS CM	Open End	Global Emerg Mkts (Growth)	C	C	C+		Y	2,500,000
Thornburg Developing World Fund Class R5	THDRX	NAS CM	Open End	Global Emerg Mkts (Growth)	C	C	C+		Y	0
Thornburg Developing World Fund Class R6	TDWRX	NAS CM	Open End	Global Emerg Mkts (Growth)	C	C	C+		Y	0
Thornburg Global Opportunities Fund Class A	THOAX	NAS CM	Open End	Global Equity Large Cap (Growth)	C-	D+	C+	Down	Y	5,000
Thornburg Global Opportunities Fund Class C	THOCX	NAS CM	Open End	Global Equity Large Cap (Growth)	C-	D+	C+		Y	5,000
Thornburg Global Opportunities Fund Class I	THOIX	NAS CM	Open End	Global Equity Large Cap (Growth)	C	D+	C+		Y	2,500,000
Thornburg Global Opportunities Fund Class R3	THORX	NAS CM	Open End	Global Equity Large Cap (Growth)	C-	D+	C+	Down	Y	0
Thornburg Global Opportunities Fund Class R4	THOVX	NAS CM	Open End	Global Equity Large Cap (Growth)	C-	D+	C+	Down	Y	0
Thornburg Global Opportunities Fund Class R5	THOFX	NAS CM	Open End	Global Equity Large Cap (Growth)	C-	D+	C+	Down	Y	0
Thornburg Global Opportunities Fund Class R6	THOGX	NAS CM	Open End	Global Equity Large Cap (Growth)	C	D+	C+		Y	0
Thornburg International Growth Fund Class A	TIGAX	NAS CM	Open End	Global Equity Large Cap (Growth)	C	C	C+		Y	5,000
Thornburg International Growth Fund Class C	TIGCX	NAS CM	Open End	Global Equity Large Cap (Growth)	C	C	C+		Y	5,000
Thornburg International Growth Fund Class I	TINGX	NAS CM	Open End	Global Equity Large Cap (Growth)	C	C	C+		Y	2,500,000
Thornburg International Growth Fund Class R3	TIGVX	NAS CM	Open End	Global Equity Large Cap (Growth)	C	C	C+		Y	0
Thornburg International Growth Fund Class R4	TINVX	NAS CM	Open End	Global Equity Large Cap (Growth)	C	C	C+		Y	0
Thornburg International Growth Fund Class R5	TINFX	NAS CM	Open End	Global Equity Large Cap (Growth)	C	C	C+		Y	0
Thornburg International Growth Fund Class R6	THGIX	NAS CM	Open End	Global Equity Large Cap (Growth)	C	C	C+		Y	0
Thornburg International Value Fund Class A	TGVAX	NAS CM	Open End	Global Equity Large Cap (Multi-Asset Global)	C	C	C+		Y	5,000
Thornburg International Value Fund Class C	THGCX	NAS CM	Open End	Global Equity Large Cap (Multi-Asset Global)	C	C-	C+	Up	Y	5,000
Thornburg International Value Fund Class I	TGVIX	NAS CM	Open End	Global Equity Large Cap (Multi-Asset Global)	C	C	C+		Y	2,500,000
Thornburg International Value Fund Class R3	TGVRX	NAS CM	Open End	Global Equity Large Cap (Multi-Asset Global)	C	C	C+		Y	0
Thornburg International Value Fund Class R4	THVRX	NAS CM	Open End	Global Equity Large Cap (Multi-Asset Global)	C	C	C+		Y	0
Thornburg International Value Fund Class R5	TIVRX	NAS CM	Open End	Global Equity Large Cap (Multi-Asset Global)	C	C	C+		Y	0
Thornburg International Value Fund Class R6	TGIRX	NAS CM	Open End	Global Equity Large Cap (Multi-Asset Global)	C	C	C+		Y	0
Thornburg Investment Income Builder Fund Class A	TIBAX	NAS CM	Open End	Flexible Alloc (Equity-Income)	B-	C	A-		Y	5,000
Thornburg Investment Income Builder Fund Class C	TIBCX	NAS CM	Open End	Flexible Alloc (Equity-Income)	B-	C	A-	Up	Y	5,000
Thornburg Investment Income Builder Fund Class I	TIBIX	NAS CM	Open End	Flexible Alloc (Equity-Income)	B	C	A-	Up	Y	2,500,000
Thornburg Investment Income Builder Fund Class R3	TIBRX	NAS CM	Open End	Flexible Alloc (Equity-Income)	B-	C	A-		Y	0
Thornburg Investment Income Builder Fund Class R4	TIBGX	NAS CM	Open End	Flexible Alloc (Equity-Income)	B-	C	A-		Y	0

★ Expanded analysis of this fund is included in Section II.

	TOTAL RETURNS					PERFORMANCE				ASSETS		ASSET ALLOCATION & TURNOVER					BULL & BEAR		FEES		
Min Additional Investment	3-Month Total Return	6-Month Total Return	1-Year Total Return	3-Year Total Return	5-Year Total Return	Dividend Yield (TTM)	Expense Ratio	3-Yr Std Deviation	3-Year Beta	NAV	Total Assets (MIL)	%Cash	%Stocks	%Bonds	%Other	Turnover Ratio	Last Bull Market Total Return	Last Bear Market Total Return	Front End Fee (%)	Back End Fee (%)	Inception Date
1,000	2.55	14.38	-4.82	30.72	27.66	0	1.05	15.51	0.86	18.45	208.1	2	98	0	0	44	18.41	-19.64			Mar-18
1,000	2.49	14.20	-5.19	29.56	25.91	0	1.4	15.47	0.86	18.09	208.1	2	98	0	0	44	18.3	-19.71			Dec-09
1,000	-2.04	10.82	-11.90	13.58	0.73	0.43	1.15	15.43	1.23	41.68	742.5	10	91	0	0	72	17.95	-26.9			Nov-90
1,000	-2.11	10.69	-12.11	12.75	-0.52	0.09	1.4	15.42	1.23	41.71	742.5	10	91	0	0	72	17.8	-26.98			Dec-09
1,000	-2.02	10.87	-11.80	13.74	0.87	0.55	1.05	15.42	1.23	41.69	742.5	10	91	0	0	72	17.95	-26.9			Mar-18
100	3.47	21.20	7.83	32.19	40.36	0.26	1.34	13.25	0.96	17.55	45.5	0	100	0	0	21	25.52	-19.66			Mar-99
100	1.25	14.05	1.57	25.15	2.04	1.04	1.1	14.73	1.03	11.28	39.4	2	98	0	0	34	20.8	-27.1			Aug-12
100	1.18	14.00	1.40	24.20	0.81	1.04	1.35	14.79	1.03	11.15	39.4	2	98	0	0	34	20.8	-27.1			Jun-10
100	3.24	14.88	-0.39	23.32	2.47	1.72	0.99	12.99	1.12	15.28	126.2	0	100	0	0	38	18.48	-23.85			Aug-12
100	3.16	14.77	-0.65	22.42	1.25	1.71	1.24	12.98	1.12	15.3	126.2	0	100	0	0	38	18.48	-23.85			Jun-94
50	3.46	20.20	5.72	44.65	42.25	0.75	1.03	15.76	1.23	69.78	123.5	0	100	0	0	29	27.58	-21.59			Feb-92
50	2.72	22.43	-5.28	30.09	23.27	0.23	1.15	18.32	1.32	11.68	43.0	0	100	0	0	30	27.23	-23.04			Mar-08
100	4.09	14.95	-0.33	29.42		1.06	1.83	12.09	0.97	13.22	70.2	6	94	0	0				4.50		Sep-15
100	3.88	14.51	-0.94	27.30		0.27	2.38	12.06	0.97	13.1	70.2	6	94	0	0					1.00	Sep-15
100	4.32	15.35	0.39	32.55		1.58	1.09	12.12	0.98	13.52	70.2	6	94	0	0						Sep-15
100	2.99	22.37	4.87	57.47	51.94	0	1.34	14.45	0.99	40.25	641.3	7	93	0	0		37.95	-20.98	4.50		Dec-00
100	2.78	21.85	3.91	53.67	46.04	0	2.14	14.43	0.99	34.73	641.3	7	93	0	0		37.23	-21.21		1.00	Dec-00
100	3.07	22.59	5.23	59.24	54.90	0	0.99	14.43	0.99	43.25	641.3	7	93	0	0		38.32	-20.77			Nov-03
	2.96	22.29	4.69	56.81	51.00	0	1.5	14.46	0.99	39.94	641.3	7	93	0	0		37.95	-20.98			Jul-03
	2.98	22.33	4.80	57.32	51.82	0	1.4	14.44	0.99	40.37	641.3	7	93	0	0		37.99	-20.93			Feb-07
	3.07	22.58	5.23	59.21	54.92	0	0.99	14.46	0.99	43.21	641.3	7	93	0	0		38.38	-20.84			Oct-05
100	3.82	19.61	8.97	35.07	9.76	0.72	1.48	13.95	0.96	21.16	868.2	4	96	0	0		25.19	-25.32	4.50		Dec-09
100	3.66	19.16	8.13	31.93	5.67	0	2.25	13.96	0.96	20.08	868.2	4	96	0	0		24.73	-25.57		1.00	Dec-09
100	3.99	19.87	9.46	36.70	12.10	1.1	1.09	13.95	0.96	21.59	868.2	4	96	0	0		25.75	-25.19			Dec-09
	3.96	19.88	9.48	36.66	12.14	1.09	1.09	13.96	0.96	21.52	868.2	4	96	0	0		25.75	-25.19			Feb-13
	3.94	19.86	9.51	36.98	12.61	1.19	0.99	13.95	0.96	21.6	868.2	4	96	0	0		25.75	-25.19			Feb-13
100	0.65	13.94	-5.84	23.19	18.73	1.99	1.28	14.16	1.14	27.79	1,376	3	97	0	0		18.44	-23.6	4.50		Jul-06
100	0.44	13.49	-6.58	20.39	14.30	0.93	2.03	14.16	1.14	26.82	1,376	3	97	0	0		17.85	-23.78		1.00	Jul-06
100	0.72	14.12	-5.56	24.41	20.78	2.34	0.97	14.17	1.14	27.88	1,376	3	97	0	0		18.8	-23.43			Jul-06
	0.58	13.81	-6.01	22.54	17.72	1.66	1.5	14.17	1.14	27.52	1,376	3	97	0	0		18.41	-23.58			Feb-08
	0.62	13.89	-5.94	22.92	18.27	1.78	1.4	14.19	1.14	27.55	1,376	3	97	0	0		18.55	-23.54			Feb-08
	0.72	14.15	-5.51	24.44	20.78	2.35	0.99	14.17	1.14	27.91	1,376	3	97	0	0		18.79	-23.41			Feb-08
	0.75	14.21	-5.41	24.69	21.06	2.51	0.85	14.17	1.14	27.97	1,376	3	97	0	0		18.8	-23.43			Apr-17
100	1.47	17.34	-6.82	36.59	20.65	0.1	1.32	14.36	1.08	21.99	1,520	7	93	0	0		14.59	-12.44	4.50		Feb-07
100	1.29	16.90	-7.51	33.51	16.14	0	2.08	14.36	1.08	20.4	1,520	7	93	0	0		13.98	-12.67		1.00	Feb-07
100	1.56	17.59	-6.47	38.17	23.04	0.44	0.99	14.37	1.08	22.66	1,520	7	93	0	0		14.82	-12.18			Feb-07
	1.44	17.24	-6.96	36.03	19.94	0	1.5	14.37	1.08	21.76	1,520	7	93	0	0		14.49	-12.4			Feb-08
	1.48	17.32	-6.85	36.42	20.56	0	1.4	14.39	1.08	21.87	1,520	7	93	0	0		14.63	-12.31			Feb-08
	1.56	17.53	-6.50	38.09	23.03	0.43	0.99	14.37	1.08	22.72	1,520	7	93	0	0		14.86	-12.16			Feb-08
	1.60	17.60	-6.40	38.48	23.64	0.54	0.89	14.36	1.08	22.78	1,520	7	93	0	0		14.82	-12.18			Feb-13
100	4.34	21.32	3.62	27.16	20.66	1.2	1.27	13.55	1.16	23.27	3,517	9	91	0	0		15.19	-24.25	4.50		May-98
100	4.07	20.78	2.73	24.22	16.15	0	2.02	13.52	1.16	20.69	3,517	9	91	0	0		14.66	-24.49		1.00	May-98
100	4.42	21.52	3.92	28.49	22.80	1.46	0.91	13.54	1.16	24.05	3,517	9	91	0	0		15.44	-24.14			Mar-01
	4.30	21.26	3.44	26.56	19.63	0.96	1.45	13.54	1.16	23.27	3,517	9	91	0	0		15.04	-24.3			Jul-03
	4.33	21.32	3.61	27.26	20.79	1.19	1.25	13.54	1.16	23.1	3,517	9	91	0	0		15.2	-24.24			Feb-07
	4.38	21.48	3.90	28.26	22.46	1.41	0.99	13.55	1.16	24.03	3,517	9	91	0	0		15.36	-24.17			Feb-05
	4.44	21.62	4.11	29.05	23.77	1.64	0.83	13.53	1.16	23.96	3,517	9	91	0	0		15.19	-24.25			May-12
100	2.52	10.24	6.44	27.80	21.15	4.23	1.33	8.5		21.58	14,496	4	87	8	1		11.07	-12.08	4.50		Dec-02
100	2.29	9.87	5.63	24.99	16.81	3.52	2.08	8.49		21.55	14,496	4	87	8	1		10.59	-12.35		1.00	Dec-02
100	2.52	10.37	6.69	28.85	22.98	4.47	1.04	8.52		21.73	14,496	4	87	8	1		11.29	-12			Nov-03
	2.39	10.06	6.07	26.56	19.22	3.88	1.68	8.52		21.57	14,496	4	87	8	1		10.9	-12.24			Feb-05
	2.46	10.11	6.15	26.84	19.73	4.29	1.58	8.52		21.6	14,496	4	87	8	1		11.01	-12.22			Feb-08

Fund Name	MARKET Ticker Symbol	Traded On	FUND TYPE, CATEGORY & OBJECTIVE Fund Type	Category and (Prospectus Objective)	RATINGS Overall Rating	Reward Rating	Risk Rating	Recent Up/ Downgrade	MINIMUMS Open to New Investors	Min Initial Investment
Thornburg Investment Income Builder Fund Class R5	TIBMX	NAS CM	Open End	Flexible Alloc (Equity-Income)	B	C	A-	Up	Y	0
Thornburg Investment Income Builder Fund Class R6	TIBOX	NAS CM	Open End	Flexible Alloc (Equity-Income)	B	C	A-	Up	Y	0
Thornburg Long/Short Equity Fund Class I	THLSX	NAS CM	Open End	Long/Short Equity (Growth)	C	C-	B		Y	2,500,000
Thornburg Summit Fund Class I	TSUMX	NAS CM	Open End	Moderate Alloc (Growth & Income)	U	U	U		Y	2,500,000
Thornburg Value Fund Class A	TVAFX	NAS CM	Open End	US Equity Large Cap Blend (Growth)	C+	C	B		Y	5,000
Thornburg Value Fund Class C	TVCFX	NAS CM	Open End	US Equity Large Cap Blend (Growth)	C+	C	B		Y	5,000
Thornburg Value Fund Class I	TVIFX	NAS CM	Open End	US Equity Large Cap Blend (Growth)	C+	C	B		Y	2,500,000
Thornburg Value Fund Class R3	TVRFX	NAS CM	Open End	US Equity Large Cap Blend (Growth)	C+	C	B		Y	0
Thornburg Value Fund Class R4	TVIRX	NAS CM	Open End	US Equity Large Cap Blend (Growth)	C+	C	B		Y	0
Thornburg Value Fund Class R5	TVRRX	NAS CM	Open End	US Equity Large Cap Blend (Growth)	C+	C	B		Y	0
Thrivent Aggressive Allocation Fund Class A	TAAAX	NAS CM	Open End	Aggressive Alloc (Asset Alloc)	B-	C	B	Up	Y	2,000
Thrivent Aggressive Allocation Fund Class S	TAAIX	NAS CM	Open End	Aggressive Alloc (Asset Alloc)	B-	C	B	Up	Y	2,000
Thrivent Aggressive Allocation Portfolio			Open End	Aggressive Alloc (Asset Alloc)	U	U	U		Y	0
Thrivent Balanced Income Plus Fund Class A	AABFX	NAS CM	Open End	Moderate Alloc (Balanced)	B-	C	A-	Up	Y	2,000
Thrivent Balanced Income Plus Fund Class S	IBBFX	NAS CM	Open End	Moderate Alloc (Balanced)	B-	C	A-	Up	Y	2,000
Thrivent Balanced Income Plus Portfolio			Open End	Moderate Alloc (Balanced)	U	U	U		Y	0
Thrivent Diversified Income Plus Fund Class A	AAHYX	NAS CM	Open End	Cautious Alloc (Growth & Income)	B	C+	A-	Up	Y	2,000
Thrivent Diversified Income Plus Fund Class S	THYFX	NAS CM	Open End	Cautious Alloc (Growth & Income)	B	C+	A	Up	Y	2,000
Thrivent Diversified Income Plus Portfolio			Open End	Cautious Alloc (Income)	U	U	U		Y	0
Thrivent Global Stock Fund Class A	AALGX	NAS CM	Open End	Global Equity Large Cap (Growth)	C+	C	B	Up	Y	2,000
Thrivent Global Stock Fund Class S	IILGX	NAS CM	Open End	Global Equity Large Cap (Growth)	C+	C	B	Up	Y	2,000
Thrivent Growth and Income Plus Portfolio			Open End	Aggressive Alloc (Growth & Income)	U	U	U		Y	0
Thrivent International Allocation Fund Class A	TWAAX	NAS CM	Open End	Global Equity Large Cap (Multi-Asset Global)	C	C-	B-		Y	2,000
Thrivent International Allocation Fund Class S	TWAIX	NAS CM	Open End	Global Equity Large Cap (Multi-Asset Global)	C	C	B-		Y	2,000
Thrivent Large Cap Growth Fund Class A	AAAGX	NAS CM	Open End	US Equity Large Cap Growth (Growth)	C+	C	B	Down	Y	2,000
Thrivent Large Cap Growth Fund Class S	THLCX	NAS CM	Open End	US Equity Large Cap Growth (Growth)	C+	C	B	Down	Y	2,000
Thrivent Large Cap Growth Portfolio			Open End	US Equity Large Cap Growth (Growth)	U	U	U		Y	0
Thrivent Large Cap Index Portfolio			Open End	US Equity Large Cap Blend (Growth & Income)	U	U	U		Y	0
Thrivent Large Cap Stock Portfolio			Open End	Global Equity (Growth)	U	U	U		Y	0
Thrivent Large Cap Value Fund Class A	AAUTX	NAS CM	Open End	US Equity Large Cap Value (Growth)	C+	C	B		Y	2,000
Thrivent Large Cap Value Fund Class S	TLVIX	NAS CM	Open End	US Equity Large Cap Value (Growth)	C+	C	B		Y	2,000
Thrivent Large Cap Value Portfolio			Open End	US Equity Large Cap Value (Growth)	U	U	U		Y	0
Thrivent Low Volatility Equity Fund Class S	TLVOX	NAS CM	Open End	Global Equity Large Cap (World Stock)	C	C	B		Y	2,000
Thrivent Mid Cap Index Portfolio			Open End	US Equity Mid Cap (Growth)	U	U	U		Y	0
Thrivent Mid Cap Stock Fund Class A	AASCX	NAS CM	Open End	US Equity Mid Cap (Growth)	C+	C	B	Up	Y	2,000
Thrivent Mid Cap Stock Fund Class S	TMSIX	NAS CM	Open End	US Equity Mid Cap (Growth)	C+	C	B	Up	Y	2,000
Thrivent Mid Cap Stock Portfolio			Open End	US Equity Mid Cap (Growth)	U	U	U		Y	0
Thrivent Moderate Allocation Fund Class A	THMAX	NAS CM	Open End	Moderate Alloc (Asset Alloc)	B-	C	B+	Up	Y	2,000
Thrivent Moderate Allocation Fund Class S	TMAIX	NAS CM	Open End	Moderate Alloc (Asset Alloc)	B-	C	B+	Up	Y	2,000
Thrivent Moderate Allocation Portfolio			Open End	Moderate Alloc (Growth)	U	U	U		Y	0
Thrivent Moderately Aggressive Allocation Fund Class A	TMAAX	NAS CM	Open End	Aggressive Alloc (Asset Alloc)	B-	C	B+	Up	Y	2,000
Thrivent Moderately Aggressive Allocation Fund Class S	TMAFX	NAS CM	Open End	Aggressive Alloc (Asset Alloc)	B-	C	B+	Up	Y	2,000
Thrivent Moderately Aggressive Allocation Portfolio			Open End	Aggressive Alloc (Growth)	U	U	U		Y	0
Thrivent Moderately Conservative Allocation Fund Class A	TCAAX	NAS CM	Open End	Cautious Alloc (Asset Alloc)	B	C+	A-	Up	Y	2,000
Thrivent Moderately Conservative Allocation Fund Class S	TCAIX	NAS CM	Open End	Cautious Alloc (Asset Alloc)	B	C+	A-		Y	2,000
Thrivent Moderately Conservative Allocation Portfolio			Open End	Cautious Alloc (Growth)	U	U	U		Y	0
Thrivent Partner All Cap Portfolio			Open End	US Equity Large Cap Growth (Growth)	U	U	U		Y	0
Thrivent Partner Emerging Markets Equity Cls A Shares	TPEAX	NAS CM	Open End	Global Emerg Mkts (Div Emerging Mkts)	C	C	C+		Y	2,000
Thrivent Partner Emerging Markets Equity Fund Class S	TPEIX	NAS CM	Open End	Global Emerg Mkts (Div Emerging Mkts)	C	C	C+		Y	2,000
Thrivent Partner Emerging Markets Equity Portfolio			Open End	Emerging Markets Equity (Div Emerging Mkts)	U	U	U		Y	0
Thrivent Partner Growth Stock Portfolio			Open End	US Equity Large Cap Growth (Growth & Income)	U	U	U		Y	0
Thrivent Partner Healthcare Portfolio			Open End	Healthcare Sector Equity (Health)	U	U	U		Y	0

★ Expanded analysis of this fund is included in Section II.

	TOTAL RETURNS					PERFORMANCE				ASSETS		ASSET ALLOCATION & TURNOVER					BULL & BEAR		FEES		
Min Additional Investment	3-Month Total Return	6-Month Total Return	1-Year Total Return	3-Year Total Return	5-Year Total Return	Dividend Yield (TTM)	Expense Ratio	3-Yr Std Deviation	3-Year Beta	NAV	Total Assets (MIL)	%Cash	%Stocks	%Bonds	%Other	Turnover Ratio	Last Bull Market Total Return	Last Bear Market Total Return	Front End Fee (%)	Back End Fee (%)	Inception Date
	2.55	10.32	6.56	28.44	22.22	4.7	1.17	8.49		21.72	14,496	4	87	8	1		11.15	-12.04			Feb-07
	2.55	10.44	6.77	28.51	21.82	4.54	0.98	8.53		21.66	14,496	4	87	8	1		11.07	-12.08			Apr-17
100	-2.00	6.31	-1.52	18.46	25.42	0	2.82			10.77	208.9	67	32	0	0		15.8	-4.19			Dec-16
100	2.66						1.12			10.41	35.0	16	40	40	3						Mar-19
100	1.50	16.31	2.08	40.21	47.37	0.41	1.33	13.39	1.07	70.21	885.7	3	97	0	0		17.68	-25.1	4.50		Oct-95
100	1.28	15.81	1.14	36.85	41.69	0	2.11	13.38	1.07	63.85	885.7	3	97	0	0		17.18	-25.34		1.00	Oct-95
100	1.58	16.52	2.43	41.76	50.18	0.69	0.99	13.39	1.07	72.33	885.7	3	97	0	0		17.97	-25			Nov-98
	1.49	16.30	2.06	40.21	47.48	0.31	1.35	13.39	1.07	69.85	885.7	3	97	0	0		17.66	-25.14			Jul-03
	1.52	16.36	2.16	40.64	48.23	0.4	1.25	13.39	1.07	70.62	885.7	3	97	0	0		17.7	-25.08			Feb-07
	1.57	16.52	2.42	41.73	50.18	0.69	0.99	13.39	1.07	72.22	885.7	3	97	0	0		17.89	-25.02			Feb-05
50	3.28	17.07	5.68	44.38	43.15	0.73	1.23	11.28	0.91	15.42	1,377	24	89	7	-21	52	20.5	-19.91	4.50		Jun-05
50	3.31	17.21	5.91	45.67	45.47	0.95	0.93	11.28	0.91	15.58	1,377	24	89	7	-21	52	20.79	-19.8			Jun-05
	2.27	4.85	15.44	32.64	74.62	0.65	0.76	10.22	0.96		1,365	6	85	4	5	63	20.69	-19.72			Apr-05
50	2.71	11.43	4.07	22.05	25.21	2.62	1.09	6.63	0.58	12.6	385.8	12	49	42	-6	149	18.02	-15.43	4.50		Dec-97
50	2.70	11.51	4.30	23.16	27.26	2.9	0.76	6.62	0.57	12.56	385.8	12	49	42	-6	149	18.32	-15.24			Dec-97
	1.69	2.28	7.64	17.89	42.28	2.23	0.68	5.96	0.55		407.1	3	49	39	7	151	17.04	-9.51			Jun-95
50	2.48	9.38	4.79	19.48	21.47	3.2	1.05	4.52	0.39	7.29	1,004	15	26	70	-16	143	13.54	-9.03	4.50		Jan-97
50	2.57	9.48	4.96	20.50	23.08	3.48	0.78	4.54	0.39	7.22	1,004	15	26	70	-16	143	13.69	-8.93			Dec-97
	1.37	1.71	5.59	15.71	31.28	2.97	0.54	4.12	0.37		693.2	0	30	59	5	146	14	-8.95			Mar-98
50	2.89	15.55	2.57	38.01	34.18	1.08	1.01	11.59	1.01	25.92	1,807	12	98	0	-10	52	24.78	-20.82	4.50		Jul-87
50	3.02	15.78	2.91	39.51	36.79	1.39	0.65	11.6	1.01	26.19	1,807	12	98	0	-10	52	25.11	-20.66			Dec-97
	2.09	2.94	9.49	19.62	40.81	1.83	0.93	7.72	0.71		98.9	4	69	22	4	131	20.64	-19.39			Apr-08
50	2.44	13.55	-0.64	22.65	8.28	1.7	1.2	10.84	0.94	10.05	871.9	18	97	0	-16	75	14.44	-20.41	4.50		Feb-08
50	2.63	13.85	-0.15	24.19	10.55	2.12	0.79	10.8	0.94	10.11	871.9	18	97	0	-16	75	14.7	-20.35			Feb-08
50	3.51	21.25	9.36	64.73	73.49	0	1.15	14.3	1.12	11.18	1,116	2	98	0	0	62	27.18	-20.07	4.50		Oct-99
50	3.56	21.57	9.69	66.67	76.66	0	0.82	14.31	1.12	12.51	1,116	2	98	0	0	62	27.53	-19.96			Oct-99
	6.22	15.32	28.03	51.78	126.80	0.32	0.44	13.1	1.11		1,300	1	99	0	0	59	28.18	-19.88			Jan-87
	2.47	3.93	15.51	38.49	89.78	1.2	0.25	10.28	1		980.8	0	100	0	0	3	24.78	-16.4			Jun-95
	1.85	3.80	13.51	28.80	70.16	1.15	0.66	11.08	1.03		1,118	1	98	0	0	59	24.76	-20.37			Mar-01
50	3.91	15.21	4.55	40.61	41.54	1.14	0.91	13.69	1.03	22.03	1,117	4	96	0	0	18	25.11	-21.59	4.50		Oct-99
50	3.98	15.40	4.90	42.16	44.37	1.49	0.53	13.69	1.03	22.18	1,117	4	96	0	0	18	25.47	-21.4			Oct-99
	1.65	1.02	14.06	30.62	69.52	1.27	0.64	12.76	1.18		1,571	1	99	0	0	18	25.43	-21.52			Nov-01
50	3.70	15.39	11.98			1.1	1.2			11.77	14.6	6	98	0	-4	58					Feb-17
	4.35	5.73	16.87	35.23	87.08	0.8	0.27	11.3	1		419.6	0	100	0	0	18	27.56	-22.67			Mar-01
50	1.78	17.10	2.25	51.84	61.15	0.15	1.06	14.09	0.9	23.41	2,234	8	92	0	0	34	25.34	-25.91	4.50		Jun-93
50	1.82	17.27	2.49	53.21	63.90	0.37	0.72	14.09	0.9	26.75	2,234	8	92	0	0	34	25.75	-25.75			Dec-97
	3.67	5.10	18.09	55.58	119.56	0.32	0.67	12.21	1.02		1,766	8	92	0	0	30	25.55	-25.72			Mar-01
50	3.24	12.82	6.57	27.39	29.42	1.71	1.06	6.92	0.55	13.93	2,525	19	54	47	-20	133	14.4	-13.16	4.50		Jun-05
50	3.29	12.98	6.89	28.40	31.36	1.94	0.79	6.92	0.55	13.97	2,525	19	54	47	-20	133	14.68	-12.97			Jun-05
	1.30	1.63	7.86	20.32	45.49	1.54	0.64	6.42	0.6		10,118	7	50	40	3	155	14.37	-12.67			Apr-05
50	3.37	15.23	6.29	35.87	36.05	1.24	1.12	9.1	0.73	14.99	2,981	19	70	26	-15	86	17.99	-17.07	4.50		Jun-05
50	3.41	15.38	6.58	36.82	38.00	1.45	0.87	9.12	0.73	15.12	2,981	19	70	26	-15	86	18.23	-16.97			Jun-05
	1.64	2.76	11.12	26.06	59.04	1.12	0.71	8.52	0.8		6,229	7	68	21	4	104	17.96	-16.79			Apr-05
50	3.11	10.81	6.88	19.75	23.20	2.09	1.03	4.96	0.38	12.53	932.0	18	34	66	-19	175	10.64	-9.23	4.50		Jun-05
50	3.16	10.89	7.13	20.64	24.95	2.33	0.76	4.91	0.38	12.56	932.0	18	34	66	-19	175	10.8	-8.97			Jun-05
	0.85	0.39	4.51	14.59	32.16	1.75	0.6	4.36	0.39		5,091	7	31	59	3	207	10.32	-8.67			Apr-05
	2.01	3.31	12.79	25.65	81.90	0.45	0.81	10.61	0.98		110.3	1	99	0	0	51	25.62	-20.62			Nov-01
50	3.78	15.40	10.05	24.28	-2.17	0.36	1.65	13.83	0.95	9.59	14.8	2	98	0	0	26			4.50		Aug-12
50	3.81	15.53	10.38	25.40	-0.56	0.56	1.32	13.78	0.95	9.52	14.8	2	98	0	0	26					Aug-12
	-11.13	-7.65	-0.87	9.42	14.69	0.67	1.2	15.08	0.9		95.7	3	97	0	0	15	21.11	-18.39			Apr-08
	4.92	12.56	25.24	55.16	134.72	0.07	0.79	12.98	1.09		213.5	1	98	0	1	52	30.83	-16.67			Nov-01
	5.75	8.74	7.58	0.32	67.07	0.24	0.88	15.67	1.1		196.3	4	96	0	0	212	19.4	-17.07			Apr-08

Fund Name	MARKET Ticker Symbol	Traded On	FUND TYPE, CATEGORY & OBJECTIVE Fund Type	Category and (Prospectus Objective)	RATINGS Overall Rating	Reward Rating	Risk Rating	Recent Up/ Downgrade	Open to New Investors	MINIMUMS Min Initial Investment
Thrivent Partner Worldwide Allocation Portfolio			Open End	Alloc (Asset Alloc)	U	U	U		Y	0
Thrivent Real Estate Securities Portfolio			Open End	Real Estate Sector Equity (Real Estate)	U	U	U		Y	0
Thrivent Small Cap Growth Fund Class S	TSCGX	NAS CM	Open End	US Equity Small Cap (Small Company)	D	D+	C+		Y	2,000
Thrivent Small Cap Index Portfolio	US88589M1053		Open End	US Equity Small Cap (Small Company)	U	U	U		Y	0
Thrivent Small Cap Stock Fund Class A	AASMX	NAS CM	Open End	US Equity Small Cap (Small Company)	C+	C	B-		Y	2,000
Thrivent Small Cap Stock Fund Class S	TSCSX	NAS CM	Open End	US Equity Small Cap (Small Company)	C+	C	B-		Y	2,000
Thrivent Small Cap Stock Portfolio			Open End	US Equity Small Cap (Small Company)	U	U	U		Y	0
TIAA-CREF Emerging Markets Equity Fund Advisor Class	TEMHX	NAS CM	Open End	Global Emerg Mkts (Div Emerging Mkts)	C	C-	C		Y	0
TIAA-CREF Emerging Markets Equity Fund Class W	TEMVX	NAS CM	Open End	Global Emerg Mkts (Div Emerging Mkts)	C	C-	C		Y	0
TIAA-CREF Emerging Markets Equity Fund Institutional Class	TEMLX	NAS CM	Open End	Global Emerg Mkts (Div Emerging Mkts)	C	C-	C		Y	2,000,000
TIAA-CREF Emerging Markets Equity Fund Premier Class	TEMPX	NAS CM	Open End	Global Emerg Mkts (Div Emerging Mkts)	C	C-	C		Y	0
TIAA-CREF Emerging Markets Equity Fund Retail Class	TEMRX	NAS CM	Open End	Global Emerg Mkts (Div Emerging Mkts)	C	C-	C		Y	2,500
TIAA-CREF Emerging Markets Equity Fund Retirement Class	TEMSX	NAS CM	Open End	Global Emerg Mkts (Div Emerging Mkts)	C	C-	C		Y	0
TIAA-CREF Emerging Markets Equity Index Fund Advisor Class	TEQHX	NAS CM	Open End	Global Emerg Mkts (Div Emerging Mkts)	C	C	C+		Y	0
TIAA-CREF Emerging Markets Equity Index Fund Class W	TENWX	NAS CM	Open End	Global Emerg Mkts (Div Emerging Mkts)	C	C	C+		Y	0
TIAA-CREF Emerging Markets Equity Index Institutional Cls	TEQLX	NAS CM	Open End	Global Emerg Mkts (Div Emerging Mkts)	C	C	C+		Y	10,000,000
TIAA-CREF Emerging Markets Equity Index Fund Premier Class	TEQPX	NAS CM	Open End	Global Emerg Mkts (Div Emerging Mkts)	C	C	C+		Y	0
TIAA-CREF Emerging Markets Equity Index Fund Retail Class	TEQKX	NAS CM	Open End	Global Emerg Mkts (Div Emerging Mkts)	C	C	C+		Y	2,500
TIAA-CREF Emerging Markets Equity Index Retirement Cls	TEQSX	NAS CM	Open End	Global Emerg Mkts (Div Emerging Mkts)	C	C	C+		Y	0
TIAA-CREF Equity Index Fund Advisor Class	TEIHX	NAS CM	Open End	US Equity Large Cap Blend (Growth)	B-	C	B		Y	0
TIAA-CREF Equity Index Fund Class W	TEQWX	NAS CM	Open End	US Equity Large Cap Blend (Growth)	B-	C	B		Y	0
TIAA-CREF Equity Index Fund Institutional Class	TIEIX	NAS CM	Open End	US Equity Large Cap Blend (Growth)	B-	C	B		Y	10,000,000
TIAA-CREF Equity Index Fund Premier Class	TCEPX	NAS CM	Open End	US Equity Large Cap Blend (Growth)	B-	C	B		Y	0
TIAA-CREF Equity Index Fund Retail Class	TINRX	NAS CM	Open End	US Equity Large Cap Blend (Growth)	B-	C	B		Y	2,500
TIAA-CREF Equity Index Fund Retirement Class	TIQRX	NAS CM	Open End	US Equity Large Cap Blend (Growth)	B-	C	B		Y	0
TIAA-CREF Growth & Income Fund Advisor Class	TGIHX	NAS CM	Open End	US Equity Large Cap Growth (Growth & Income)	C+	C	B		Y	0
TIAA-CREF Growth & Income Fund Class W	TGIWX	NAS CM	Open End	US Equity Large Cap Growth (Growth & Income)	C+	C	B		Y	0
TIAA-CREF Growth & Income Fund Institutional Class	TIGRX	NAS CM	Open End	US Equity Large Cap Growth (Growth & Income)	C+	C	B		Y	2,000,000
TIAA-CREF Growth & Income Fund Premier Class	TRPGX	NAS CM	Open End	US Equity Large Cap Growth (Growth & Income)	C+	C	B		Y	0
TIAA-CREF Growth & Income Fund Retail Class	TIIRX	NAS CM	Open End	US Equity Large Cap Growth (Growth & Income)	C+	C	B-		Y	2,500
TIAA-CREF Growth & Income Fund Retirement Class	TRGIX	NAS CM	Open End	US Equity Large Cap Growth (Growth & Income)	C+	C	B-		Y	0
TIAA-CREF International Equity Fund Advisor Class	TIEHX	NAS CM	Open End	Global Equity Large Cap (Foreign Stock)	C-	D+	C		Y	0
TIAA-CREF International Equity Fund Class W	TIEWX	NAS CM	Open End	Global Equity Large Cap (Foreign Stock)	C-	D+	C		Y	0
TIAA-CREF International Equity Fund Institutional Class	TIIEX	NAS CM	Open End	Global Equity Large Cap (Foreign Stock)	C-	D+	C		Y	2,000,000
TIAA-CREF International Equity Fund Premier Class	TREPX	NAS CM	Open End	Global Equity Large Cap (Foreign Stock)	C-	D+	C		Y	0
TIAA-CREF International Equity Fund Retail Class	TIERX	NAS CM	Open End	Global Equity Large Cap (Foreign Stock)	C-	D+	C		Y	2,500
TIAA-CREF International Equity Fund Retirement Class	TRERX	NAS CM	Open End	Global Equity Large Cap (Foreign Stock)	C-	D+	C		Y	0
TIAA-CREF International Equity Index Fund Advisor Class	TCIHX	NAS CM	Open End	Global Equity Large Cap (Foreign Stock)	C	C	B		Y	0
TIAA-CREF International Equity Index Fund Class W	TCIWX	NAS CM	Open End	Global Equity Large Cap (Foreign Stock)	C	C	B		Y	0
TIAA-CREF International Equity Index Institutional Cls	TCIEX	NAS CM	Open End	Global Equity Large Cap (Foreign Stock)	C	C	B		Y	10,000,000
TIAA-CREF International Equity Index Fund Premier Class	TRIPX	NAS CM	Open End	Global Equity Large Cap (Foreign Stock)	C	C	B		Y	0
TIAA-CREF International Equity Index Fund Retirement Class	TRIEX	NAS CM	Open End	Global Equity Large Cap (Foreign Stock)	C	C	B		Y	0
TIAA-CREF International Opportunities Fund Advisor Class	TIOHX	NAS CM	Open End	Global Equity Large Cap (Foreign Stock)	C	C	C+		Y	0
TIAA-CREF International Opportunities Fund Class W	TIOVX	NAS CM	Open End	Global Equity Large Cap (Foreign Stock)	C	C	C+		Y	0
TIAA-CREF International Opportunities Institutional Cls	TIOIX	NAS CM	Open End	Global Equity Large Cap (Foreign Stock)	C	C	C+		Y	2,000,000
TIAA-CREF International Opportunities Fund Premier Class	TIOPX	NAS CM	Open End	Global Equity Large Cap (Foreign Stock)	C	C	C+		Y	0
TIAA-CREF International Opportunities Fund Retail Class	TIOSX	NAS CM	Open End	Global Equity Large Cap (Foreign Stock)	C	C	C+		Y	2,500
TIAA-CREF International Opportunities Retirement Cls	TIOTX	NAS CM	Open End	Global Equity Large Cap (Foreign Stock)	C	C	C+		Y	0
TIAA-CREF Large Cap Growth Fund Advisor Class	TILHX	NAS CM	Open End	US Equity Large Cap Growth (Growth)	B-	C+	B	Down	Y	0
TIAA-CREF Large Cap Growth Fund Class W	TILWX	NAS CM	Open End	US Equity Large Cap Growth (Growth)	B-	C+	B	Down	Y	0
TIAA-CREF Large Cap Value Fund Advisor Class	TRLHX	NAS CM	Open End	US Equity Large Cap Value (Growth & Income)	C	C	B-		Y	0
TIAA-CREF Large Cap Value Fund Class W	TRLWX	NAS CM	Open End	US Equity Large Cap Value (Growth & Income)	C	C	B-		Y	0

★ Expanded analysis of this fund is included in Section II.

Min Additional Investment	TOTAL RETURNS 3-Month Total Return	6-Month Total Return	1-Year Total Return	3-Year Total Return	5-Year Total Return	PERFORMANCE Dividend Yield (TTM)	Expense Ratio	3-Yr Std Deviation	3-Year Beta	ASSETS NAV	Total Assets (MIL)	ASSET ALLOCATION & TURNOVER %Cash	%Stocks	%Bonds	%Other	Turnover Ratio	BULL & BEAR Last Bull Market Total Return	Last Bear Market Total Return	FEES Front End Fee (%)	Back End Fee (%)	Inception Date
	-3.48	-2.36	5.71	15.51	36.36	2.01	0.88	10.38	0.83		1,975	2	89	9	1	88	14.73	-20.52			Apr-08
	7.85	0.85	1.60	17.79	51.99	1.64	0.85	13.21			172.2	0	99	0	0	15	31.59	-16.3			Apr-03
50	3.46	25.30	4.43			0	1.25			11.34	7.1	5	98	0	-2	32					Feb-18
	9.44	12.30	26.36	47.98	104.36	0.73	0.27	13.75	1		548.1	0	100	0	0	16	29.23	-22.12			Jun-95
50	2.77	20.51	2.00	58.18	60.45	0	1.17	16.58	0.9	19.62	710.1	3	97	0	0	63	26.53	-27.62	4.50		Jul-96
50	2.81	20.73	2.26	59.71	63.51	0	0.81	16.57	0.9	24.46	710.1	3	97	0	0	63	26.97	-27.41			Dec-97
	5.33	7.27	21.64	46.33	101.53	0.3	0.73	12.99	0.89		606.3	2	98	0	0	44	26.54	-27.23			Mar-01
	-0.79	13.84	1.32	39.85	10.80	0.47	1	15.93	1.09	11.18	1,599	7	93	0	0	127	17.87	-27.28			Dec-15
	-0.61	14.35	2.02	40.78	11.66		0	15.93	1.09	11.23	1,599	7	93	0	0	127	17.87	-27.28			Sep-18
1,000	-0.79	13.84	1.33	39.82	10.91	0.47	0.91	15.89	1.09	11.18	1,599	7	93	0	0	127	17.87	-27.28			Aug-10
	-0.79	13.83	1.22	39.33	10.07	0.31	1.06	15.96	1.1	11.19	1,599	7	93	0	0	127	17.73	-27.3			Aug-10
100	-0.88	13.74	1.05	38.33	8.85	0	1.27	15.96	1.1	11.17	1,599	7	93	0	0	127	17.46	-27.35			Aug-10
	-0.80	13.78	1.22	38.96	9.68	0.3	1.16	15.92	1.09	11.14	1,599	7	93	0	0	127	17.57	-27.39			Aug-10
	0.45	10.90	1.23	36.06	12.85	1.95	0.34	14.07	1.01	11.09	2,477	0	100	0	0	27	18.63	-27.25			Dec-15
	0.54	11.12	1.46	36.69	13.37		0	14.03	1.01	11.09	2,477	0	100	0	0	27	18.63	-27.25			Sep-18
1,000	0.54	11.02	1.31	36.49	13.21	2.19	0.2	14.03	1.01	11.08	2,477	0	100	0	0	27	18.63	-27.25			Aug-10
	0.45	10.94	1.20	35.86	12.34	2.01	0.35	14.08	1.01	11.05	2,477	0	100	0	0	27	18.59	-27.33			Aug-10
100	0.45	10.94	1.05	34.97	11.19	1.79	0.57	14.06	1.01	11.05	2,477	0	100	0	0	27	18.37	-27.38			Aug-10
	0.45	10.85	1.10	35.42	11.76	1.92	0.45	14.11	1.01	11.03	2,477	0	100	0	0	27	18.58	-27.36			Aug-10
	4.00	19.62	8.78	49.79	61.90	1.63	0.19	12.51	1	21.58	21,187	0	100	0	0	5	25.73	-17.79			Dec-15
	4.09	19.73	9.00	50.21	62.46		0	12.52	1	21.6	21,187	0	100	0	0	5	25.73	-17.79			Sep-18
1,000	4.04	19.67	8.93	50.12	62.37	1.72	0.05	12.52	1	21.59	21,187	0	100	0	0	5	25.73	-17.79			Jul-99
	4.05	19.60	8.79	49.51	61.14	1.54	0.2	12.54	1	21.54	21,187	0	100	0	0	5	25.51	-17.73			Sep-09
100	4.02	19.52	8.65	48.87	60.09	1.42	0.33	12.53	1	21.98	21,187	0	100	0	0	5	25.34	-17.79			Mar-06
	4.03	19.53	8.66	49.07	60.38	1.45	0.3	12.53	1	21.91	21,187	0	100	0	0	5	25.53	-17.86			Mar-06
	4.67	21.19	6.77	50.03	61.74	1.05	0.49	13.03	1.05	14.49	6,704	0	100	0	0	59	26.19	-16.09			Dec-15
	4.79	21.50	7.19	50.91	62.67		0	13.01	1.05	14.48	6,704	0	100	0	0	59	26.2	-16.09			Sep-18
1,000	4.61	21.26	6.87	50.45	62.18	1.13	0.4	13.04	1.06	14.48	6,704	0	100	0	0	59	26.19	-16.09			Jul-99
	4.57	21.04	6.61	49.70	60.87	0.98	0.55	12.97	1.05	14.49	6,704	0	100	0	0	59	26.09	-16.24			Sep-09
100	4.57	20.99	6.54	48.99	59.76	0.57	0.69	13.02	1.05	19.8	6,704	0	100	0	0	59	25.93	-16.19			Mar-06
	4.53	21.04	6.54	49.17	60.07	0.87	0.65	12.98	1.05	14.75	6,704	0	100	0	0	59	26	-16.24			Oct-02
	3.01	13.58	-9.27	20.16	2.18	0	0.61	14.8	1.28	10.95	4,857	5	95	0	0	73	18.75	-31.19			Dec-15
	3.17	13.89	-8.79	20.97	2.98		0	14.73	1.27	10.74	4,857	5	95	0	0	73	18.75	-31.19			Sep-18
1,000	2.98	13.57	-9.17	20.47	2.55	2.14	0.48	14.77	1.28	10.71	4,857	5	95	0	0	73	18.75	-31.19			Jul-99
	2.98	13.48	-9.30	19.91	1.81	1.96	0.63	14.75	1.27	10.69	4,857	5	95	0	0	73	18.61	-31.25			Sep-09
100	3.02	13.31	-9.49	19.45	1.02	2.89	0.8	14.69	1.27	6.81	4,857	5	95	0	0	73	18.53	-31.24			Mar-06
	2.96	13.45	-9.38	19.59	1.28	1.76	0.73	14.74	1.27	11.13	4,857	5	95	0	0	73	18.44	-31.19			Oct-02
	3.65	14.48	1.32	31.19	12.25	2.88	0.2	11.05	0.99	19.29	12,069	2	98	0	0	4	13.47	-23.25			Dec-15
	3.65	14.59	1.47	31.55	12.70		0	11.06	0.99	19.31	12,069	2	98	0	0	4	13.47	-23.25			Sep-18
1,000	3.64	14.59	1.46	31.53	12.68	3	0.06	11.05	0.99	19.31	12,069	2	98	0	0	4	13.47	-23.25			Oct-02
	3.60	14.50	1.27	30.94	11.80	2.83	0.21	11.04	0.99	19.26	12,069	2	98	0	0	4	13.44	-23.28			Sep-09
	3.62	14.43	1.19	30.54	11.24	2.67	0.31	11.06	0.99	19.74	12,069	2	98	0	0	4	13.34	-23.3			Oct-02
	5.08	22.27	-0.39	43.63	26.36	1.08	0.71	13.99	1.14	13.23	1,759	6	94	0	0	21					Dec-15
	5.23	22.64	0.00	43.82	26.53		0	13.94	1.14	13.27	1,759	6	94	0	0	21					Sep-18
1,000	4.99	22.27	-0.38	43.64	26.72	1.15	0.62	13.92	1.14	13.23	1,759	6	94	0	0	21					Apr-13
	4.99	22.11	-0.54	43.04	25.84	1.01	0.78	13.94	1.14	13.25	1,759	6	94	0	0	21					Apr-13
100	5.00	22.06	-0.73	41.96	24.26	0.72	1.02	13.98	1.14	13.22	1,759	6	94	0	0	21					Apr-13
	5.02	22.14	-0.58	42.63	25.25	0.99	0.87	13.95	1.14	13.18	1,759	6	94	0	0	21					Apr-13
	3.06	22.29	9.16	69.54	90.14	0.46	0.52	13.87	1.01	21.17	5,691	1	99	0	0	90	26.63	-15.36			Dec-15
	3.10	22.51	9.50	70.35	91.05		0	13.86	1.01	21.22	5,691	1	99	0	0	90	26.63	-15.36			Sep-18
	4.47	18.06	1.61	29.78	30.97	1.76	0.49	13.3	1.08	17.06	6,034	1	99	0	0	53	26.97	-22.95			Dec-15
	4.58	18.33	1.93	29.54	30.65		0	13.32	1.08	17.1	6,034	1	99	0	0	53	26.97	-22.95			Sep-18

	MARKET			FUND TYPE, CATEGORY & OBJECTIVE	RATINGS				MINIMUMS	
Fund Name	Ticker Symbol	Traded On	Fund Type	Category and (Prospectus Objective)	Overall Rating	Reward Rating	Risk Rating	Recent Up/ Downgrade	Open to New Investors	Min Initial Investment
TIAA-CREF Large-Cap Growth Fund Institutional Class	TILGX	NAS CM	Open End	US Equity Large Cap Growth (Growth)	B-	C+	B	Down	Y	2,000,000
TIAA-CREF Large-Cap Growth Fund Premier Class	TILPX	NAS CM	Open End	US Equity Large Cap Growth (Growth)	C+	C+	B	Down	Y	0
TIAA-CREF Large-Cap Growth Fund Retail Class	TIRTX	NAS CM	Open End	US Equity Large Cap Growth (Growth)	B-	C+	B	Down	Y	2,500
TIAA-CREF Large-Cap Growth Fund Retirement Class	TILRX	NAS CM	Open End	US Equity Large Cap Growth (Growth)	C+	C+	B	Down	Y	0
TIAA-CREF Large-Cap Growth Index Fund Advisor Class	TRIHX	NAS CM	Open End	US Equity Large Cap Growth (Growth)	B-	C+	B	Down	Y	0
TIAA-CREF Large-Cap Growth Index Fund Institutional Class	TILIX	NAS CM	Open End	US Equity Large Cap Growth (Growth)	B-	C+	B	Down	Y	10,000,000
TIAA-CREF Large-Cap Growth Index Fund Retirement Class	TRIRX	NAS CM	Open End	US Equity Large Cap Growth (Growth)	B-	C+	B	Down	Y	0
TIAA-CREF Large-Cap Value Fund Institutional Class	TRLIX	NAS CM	Open End	US Equity Large Cap Value (Growth & Income)	C	C	B-		Y	2,000,000
TIAA-CREF Large-Cap Value Fund Premier Class	TRCPX	NAS CM	Open End	US Equity Large Cap Value (Growth & Income)	C	C	B-		Y	0
TIAA-CREF Large-Cap Value Fund Retail Class	TCLCX	NAS CM	Open End	US Equity Large Cap Value (Growth & Income)	C	C	B-		Y	2,500
TIAA-CREF Large-Cap Value Fund Retirement Class	TRLCX	NAS CM	Open End	US Equity Large Cap Value (Growth & Income)	C	C	B-		Y	0
TIAA-CREF Large-Cap Value Index Fund Advisor Class	THCVX	NAS CM	Open End	US Equity Large Cap Value (Growth & Income)	B-	C	B	Up	Y	0
TIAA-CREF Large-Cap Value Index Fund Institutional Class	TILVX	NAS CM	Open End	US Equity Large Cap Value (Growth & Income)	B-	C	B	Up	Y	10,000,000
TIAA-CREF Large-Cap Value Index Fund Retirement Class	TRCVX	NAS CM	Open End	US Equity Large Cap Value (Growth & Income)	B-	C	B	Up	Y	0
TIAA-CREF Lifecycle 2010 Fund Advisor Class	TCLHX	NAS CM	Open End	Target Date (Asset Alloc)	B	C+	A	Up	Y	0
TIAA-CREF Lifecycle 2010 Fund Institutional Class	TCTIX	NAS CM	Open End	Target Date (Asset Alloc)	B	C+	A	Up	Y	2,000,000
TIAA-CREF Lifecycle 2010 Fund Premier Class	TCTPX	NAS CM	Open End	Target Date (Asset Alloc)	B	C+	A	Up	Y	0
TIAA-CREF Lifecycle 2010 Fund Retirement Class	TCLEX	NAS CM	Open End	Target Date (Asset Alloc)	B	C+	A-	Up	Y	0
TIAA-CREF Lifecycle 2015 Fund Advisor Class	TCNHX	NAS CM	Open End	Target Date (Asset Alloc)	B	C	A	Up	Y	0
TIAA-CREF Lifecycle 2015 Fund Institutional Class	TCNIX	NAS CM	Open End	Target Date (Asset Alloc)	B	C	A	Up	Y	2,000,000
TIAA-CREF Lifecycle 2015 Fund Premier Class	TCFPX	NAS CM	Open End	Target Date (Asset Alloc)	B	C	A	Up	Y	0
TIAA-CREF Lifecycle 2015 Fund Retirement Class	TCLIX	NAS CM	Open End	Target Date (Asset Alloc)	B	C	A-	Up	Y	0
TIAA-CREF Lifecycle 2020 Fund Advisor Class	TCWHX	NAS CM	Open End	Target Date (Asset Alloc)	B	C	A-	Up	Y	0
TIAA-CREF Lifecycle 2020 Fund Institutional Class	TCWIX	NAS CM	Open End	Target Date (Asset Alloc)	B	C	A-	Up	Y	2,000,000
TIAA-CREF Lifecycle 2020 Fund Premier Class	TCWPX	NAS CM	Open End	Target Date (Asset Alloc)	B	C	A-	Up	Y	0
TIAA-CREF Lifecycle 2020 Fund Retirement Class	TCLTX	NAS CM	Open End	Target Date (Asset Alloc)	B	C	A-	Up	Y	0
TIAA-CREF Lifecycle 2025 Fund Advisor Class	TCQHX	NAS CM	Open End	Target Date (Asset Alloc)	B-	C	A-	Up	Y	0
TIAA-CREF Lifecycle 2025 Fund Institutional Class	TCYIX	NAS CM	Open End	Target Date (Asset Alloc)	B-	C	A-	Up	Y	2,000,000
TIAA-CREF Lifecycle 2025 Fund Premier Class	TCQPX	NAS CM	Open End	Target Date (Asset Alloc)	B-	C	A-	Up	Y	0
TIAA-CREF Lifecycle 2025 Fund Retirement Class	TCLFX	NAS CM	Open End	Target Date (Asset Alloc)	B-	C	A-	Up	Y	0
TIAA-CREF Lifecycle 2030 Fund Advisor Class	TCHHX	NAS CM	Open End	Target Date (Asset Alloc)	B-	C	B+	Up	Y	0
TIAA-CREF Lifecycle 2030 Fund Institutional Class	TCRIX	NAS CM	Open End	Target Date (Asset Alloc)	B-	C	B+	Up	Y	2,000,000
TIAA-CREF Lifecycle 2030 Fund Premier Class	TCHPX	NAS CM	Open End	Target Date (Asset Alloc)	B-	C	B+	Up	Y	0
TIAA-CREF Lifecycle 2030 Fund Retirement Class	TCLNX	NAS CM	Open End	Target Date (Asset Alloc)	B-	C	B+	Up	Y	0
TIAA-CREF Lifecycle 2035 Fund Advisor Class	TCYHX	NAS CM	Open End	Target Date (Asset Alloc)	B-	C	B	Up	Y	0
TIAA-CREF Lifecycle 2035 Fund Institutional Class	TCIIX	NAS CM	Open End	Target Date (Asset Alloc)	B-	C	B	Up	Y	2,000,000
TIAA-CREF Lifecycle 2035 Fund Premier Class	TCYPX	NAS CM	Open End	Target Date (Asset Alloc)	B-	C	B	Up	Y	0
TIAA-CREF Lifecycle 2035 Fund Retirement Class	TCLRX	NAS CM	Open End	Target Date (Asset Alloc)	B-	C	B	Up	Y	0
TIAA-CREF Lifecycle 2040 Fund Advisor Class	TCZHX	NAS CM	Open End	Target Date (Asset Alloc)	B-	C	B	Up	Y	0
TIAA-CREF Lifecycle 2040 Fund Institutional Class	TCOIX	NAS CM	Open End	Target Date (Asset Alloc)	B-	C	B	Up	Y	2,000,000
TIAA-CREF Lifecycle 2040 Fund Premier Class	TCZPX	NAS CM	Open End	Target Date (Asset Alloc)	B-	C	B	Up	Y	0
TIAA-CREF Lifecycle 2040 Fund Retirement Class	TCLOX	NAS CM	Open End	Target Date (Asset Alloc)	B-	C	B	Up	Y	0
TIAA-CREF Lifecycle 2045 Fund Advisor Class	TTFHX	NAS CM	Open End	Target Date (Asset Alloc)	C+	C	B	Up	Y	0
TIAA-CREF Lifecycle 2045 Fund Institutional Class	TTFIX	NAS CM	Open End	Target Date (Asset Alloc)	C+	C	B	Up	Y	2,000,000
TIAA-CREF Lifecycle 2045 Fund Premier Class	TTFPX	NAS CM	Open End	Target Date (Asset Alloc)	C+	C	B	Up	Y	0
TIAA-CREF Lifecycle 2045 Fund Retirement Class	TTFRX	NAS CM	Open End	Target Date (Asset Alloc)	C+	C	B	Up	Y	0
TIAA-CREF Lifecycle 2050 Fund Advisor Class	TFTHX	NAS CM	Open End	Target Date (Asset Alloc)	C+	C	B	Up	Y	0
TIAA-CREF Lifecycle 2050 Fund Institutional Class	TFTIX	NAS CM	Open End	Target Date (Asset Alloc)	C+	C	B	Up	Y	2,000,000
TIAA-CREF Lifecycle 2050 Fund Premier Class	TCLPX	NAS CM	Open End	Target Date (Asset Alloc)	C+	C	B	Up	Y	0
TIAA-CREF Lifecycle 2050 Fund Retirement Class	TLFRX	NAS CM	Open End	Target Date (Asset Alloc)	C+	C	B	Up	Y	0
TIAA-CREF Lifecycle 2055 Fund Advisor Class	TTRHX	NAS CM	Open End	Target Date (Asset Alloc)	C+	C	B	Up	Y	0
TIAA-CREF Lifecycle 2055 Fund Institutional Class	TTRIX	NAS CM	Open End	Target Date (Asset Alloc)	C+	C	B	Up	Y	2,000,000

★ Expanded analysis of this fund is included in Section II.

Min Additional Investment	3-Month Total Return	6-Month Total Return	1-Year Total Return	3-Year Total Return	5-Year Total Return	Dividend Yield (TTM)	Expense Ratio	3-Yr Std Deviation	3-Year Beta	NAV	Total Assets (MIL)	%Cash	%Stocks	%Bonds	%Other	Turnover Ratio	Last Bull Market Total Return	Last Bear Market Total Return	Front End Fee (%)	Back End Fee (%)	Inception Date
	TOTAL RETURNS					PERFORMANCE				ASSETS		ASSET ALLOCATION & TURNOVER					BULL & BEAR		FEES		
1,000	3.01	22.28	9.16	69.83	90.47	0.51	0.41	13.86	1.01	21.18	5,691	1	99	0	0	90	26.63	-15.36			Mar-06
	2.96	22.17	9.01	69.03	89.09	0.31	0.57	13.89	1.02	21.16	5,691	1	99	0	0	90	26.5	-15.46			Sep-09
100	2.92	22.09	8.86	68.18	87.45	0.22	0.72	13.86	1.01	21.11	5,691	1	99	0	0	90	26.29	-15.46			Mar-06
	2.98	22.18	8.94	68.43	87.99	0.3	0.67	13.86	1.01	21.04	5,691	1	99	0	0	90	26.48	-15.49			Mar-06
	4.57	22.50	11.36	65.64	86.35	1.06	0.19	13.38	1	33.15	7,194	0	100	0	0	28	26.54	-15.26			Dec-15
1,000	4.60	22.60	11.51	66.15	87.02	1.16	0.05	13.39	1	33.19	7,194	0	100	0	0	28	26.54	-15.26			Oct-02
	4.56	22.46	11.22	64.95	84.63	0.91	0.3	13.4	1	33.42	7,194	0	100	0	0	28	26.43	-15.43			Oct-02
1,000	4.53	18.13	1.67	29.86	31.66	1.82	0.4	13.31	1.08	17.07	6,034	1	99	0	0	53	27.13	-22.87			Oct-02
	4.41	17.94	1.52	29.28	30.67	1.64	0.55	13.3	1.08	17.02	6,034	1	99	0	0	53	26.99	-22.9			Sep-09
100	4.42	17.89	1.37	28.69	29.63	1.67	0.71	13.32	1.08	16.27	6,034	1	99	0	0	53	26.91	-22.95			Oct-02
	4.42	17.97	1.45	28.93	30.05	1.53	0.65	13.33	1.08	17	6,034	1	99	0	0	53	26.97	-22.95			Oct-02
	3.79	17.06	8.29	35.22	42.52	2.34	0.19	12.08	1	19.96	6,476	0	100	0	0	27	24.25	-18.73			Dec-15
1,000	3.84	17.09	8.43	35.67	42.99	2.41	0.06	12.08	1	20	6,476	0	100	0	0	27	24.25	-18.73			Oct-02
	3.72	16.90	8.14	34.58	41.13	2.12	0.3	12.09	1	20.33	6,476	0	100	0	0	27	24.12	-18.8			Oct-02
	3.04	10.67	5.81	23.64	27.18	2.89	0.45	5.2	1.11	11.51	1,197	3	35	56	5	21	13.55	-9.17			Dec-15
1,000	3.04	10.57	5.74	23.60	27.62	2.91	0.37	5.18	1.11	11.5	1,197	3	35	56	5	21	13.72	-9.09			Jan-07
	2.96	10.50	5.58	23.09	26.72	2.76	0.52	5.25	1.12	11.47	1,197	3	35	56	5	21	13.62	-9.1			Sep-09
	3.01	10.52	5.55	22.73	26.12	2.21	0.62	5.2	1.11	13.65	1,197	3	35	56	5	21	13.55	-9.17			Oct-04
	3.05	11.26	5.64	25.36	28.69	2.95	0.46	5.77	1.07	9.78	1,836	3	40	52	5	19	15.04	-11.06			Dec-15
1,000	3.16	11.37	5.76	25.56	29.40	2.95	0.38	5.8	1.07	9.79	1,836	3	40	52	5	19	15.25	-10.9			Jan-07
	3.06	11.18	5.60	24.97	28.41	2.81	0.53	5.74	1.06	9.74	1,836	3	40	52	5	19	15.19	-11.02			Sep-09
	3.03	11.18	5.44	24.60	27.76	2.13	0.63	5.8	1.07	12.23	1,836	3	40	52	5	19	15.04	-11.06			Oct-04
	3.16	12.09	5.44	28.05	30.85	2.83	0.47	6.5	1.08	10.1	3,815	3	46	46	5	17	16.81	-12.98			Dec-15
1,000	3.06	12.09	5.51	28.15	31.49	2.89	0.39	6.49	1.07	10.1	3,815	3	46	46	5	17	16.95	-12.9			Jan-07
	3.07	12.01	5.34	27.52	30.47	2.74	0.54	6.48	1.07	10.07	3,815	3	46	46	5	17	16.86	-13.02			Sep-09
	3.03	11.95	5.23	27.17	29.86	2.03	0.64	6.5	1.08	12.92	3,815	3	46	46	5	17	16.81	-12.98			Oct-04
	3.20	13.17	5.10	30.89	33.16	2.75	0.49	7.53	1.07	10.31	4,611	3	54	38	5	16	18.49	-14.94			Dec-15
1,000	3.30	13.28	5.25	31.17	33.86	2.78	0.41	7.48	1.06	10.32	4,611	3	54	38	5	16	18.62	-14.9			Jan-07
	3.11	13.12	4.99	30.47	32.76	2.65	0.56	7.47	1.06	10.26	4,611	3	54	38	5	16	18.69	-15.03			Sep-09
	3.16	13.03	4.95	30.17	32.19	1.93	0.66	7.52	1.06	13.35	4,611	3	54	38	5	16	18.49	-14.94			Oct-04
	3.29	14.36	4.82	33.94	35.40	2.66	0.5	8.55	1.05	10.35	4,590	3	63	29	5	12	20.17	-16.79			Dec-15
1,000	3.29	14.36	4.89	34.08	36.08	2.72	0.42	8.54	1.05	10.35	4,590	3	63	29	5	12	20.39	-16.75			Jan-07
	3.20	14.20	4.72	33.39	34.98	2.58	0.57	8.53	1.05	10.29	4,590	3	63	29	5	12	20.19	-16.78			Sep-09
	3.16	14.20	4.63	33.02	34.34	1.83	0.67	8.54	1.05	13.67	4,590	3	63	29	5	12	20.17	-16.79			Oct-04
	3.35	15.40	4.52	36.91	37.30	2.61	0.51	9.55	1.04	10.49	4,640	2	72	21	5	13	21.72	-18.57			Dec-15
1,000	3.34	15.38	4.56	36.97	37.98	2.64	0.43	9.55	1.04	10.5	4,640	2	72	21	5	13	21.94	-18.49			Jan-07
	3.25	15.32	4.39	36.37	36.97	2.49	0.58	9.55	1.04	10.46	4,640	2	72	21	5	13	21.86	-18.62			Sep-09
	3.28	15.30	4.27	35.96	36.26	1.73	0.68	9.55	1.04	14.16	4,640	2	72	21	5	13	21.72	-18.57			Oct-04
	3.35	16.44	3.97	39.61	39.11	2.54	0.52	10.64	1.09	10.48	5,523	2	81	12	5	14	22.24	-18.97			Dec-15
1,000	3.35	16.31	4.00	39.70	39.66	2.57	0.44	10.56	1.08	10.48	5,523	2	81	12	5	14	22.35	-18.83			Jan-07
	3.36	16.36	3.92	39.20	38.74	2.42	0.59	10.66	1.09	10.45	5,523	2	81	12	5	14	22.27	-18.96			Sep-09
	3.27	16.26	3.81	38.70	38.04	1.63	0.69	10.61	1.08	14.51	5,523	2	81	12	5	14	22.24	-18.97			Oct-04
	3.35	17.16	3.65	40.82	40.71	2.32	0.53	11.32	1.12	12.63	3,155	2	88	5	5	11	22.42	-18.94			Dec-15
1,000	3.27	17.06	3.58	40.75	40.64	2.32	0.45	11.29	1.11	12.62	3,155	2	88	5	5	11	22.42	-18.94			Nov-07
	3.28	17.05	3.51	40.11	39.62	2.19	0.6	11.33	1.12	12.56	3,155	2	88	5	5	11	22.2	-18.87			Sep-09
	3.21	16.89	3.32	39.71	38.89	2.1	0.7	11.32	1.12	12.52	3,155	2	88	5	5	11	22.24	-18.93			Nov-07
	3.33	17.28	3.51	41.14	41.06	2.3	0.53	11.44	1.1	12.69	2,130	2	90	4	5	10	22.33	-18.82			Dec-15
1,000	3.33	17.28	3.60	41.18	41.10	2.31	0.45	11.48	1.1	12.69	2,130	2	90	4	5	10	22.33	-18.82			Nov-07
	3.27	17.16	3.36	40.55	39.97	2.17	0.6	11.43	1.1	12.63	2,130	2	90	4	5	10	22.25	-18.84			Sep-09
	3.28	17.11	3.34	40.16	39.39	2.08	0.7	11.43	1.1	12.59	2,130	2	90	4	5	10	22.17	-18.9			Nov-07
	3.35	17.35	3.49	41.56	41.51	2.27	0.53	11.57	1.1	14.47	751.3	2	91	3	5	9	22.58	-18.89			Dec-15
1,000	3.35	17.45	3.50	41.61	41.56	2.27	0.45	11.58	1.1	14.47	751.3	2	91	3	5	9	22.58	-18.9			Apr-11

Fund Name	Ticker Symbol	Traded On	Fund Type	Category and (Prospectus Objective)	Overall Rating	Reward Rating	Risk Rating	Recent Up/ Downgrade	Open to New Investors	Min Initial Investment
	MARKET		FUND TYPE, CATEGORY & OBJECTIVE		RATINGS				MINIMUMS	
TIAA-CREF Lifecycle 2055 Fund Premier Class	TTRPX	NAS CM	Open End	Target Date (Asset Alloc)	C+	C	B	Up	Y	0
TIAA-CREF Lifecycle 2055 Fund Retirement Class	TTRLX	NAS CM	Open End	Target Date (Asset Alloc)	C+	C	B	Up	Y	0
TIAA-CREF Lifecycle 2060 Fund Advisor Class	TLXHX	NAS CM	Open End	Target Date (Asset Alloc)	C+	C	B	Up	Y	0
TIAA-CREF Lifecycle 2060 Fund Institutional Class	TLXNX	NAS CM	Open End	Target Date (Asset Alloc)	C+	C	B	Up	Y	2,000,000
TIAA-CREF Lifecycle 2060 Fund Premier Class	TLXPX	NAS CM	Open End	Target Date (Asset Alloc)	C+	C	B	Up	Y	0
TIAA-CREF Lifecycle 2060 Fund Retirement Class	TLXRX	NAS CM	Open End	Target Date (Asset Alloc)	C+	C	B	Up	Y	0
TIAA-CREF Lifecycle Index 2010 Fund Advisor Class	TLTHX	NAS CM	Open End	Target Date (Asset Alloc)	B	C+	A		Y	0
TIAA-CREF Lifecycle Index 2010 Fund Institutional Class	TLTIX	NAS CM	Open End	Target Date (Asset Alloc)	B	C+	A		Y	10,000,000
TIAA-CREF Lifecycle Index 2010 Fund Premier Class	TLTPX	NAS CM	Open End	Target Date (Asset Alloc)	B	C+	A	Up	Y	0
TIAA-CREF Lifecycle Index 2010 Fund Retirement Class	TLTRX	NAS CM	Open End	Target Date (Asset Alloc)	B	C+	A-	Up	Y	0
TIAA-CREF Lifecycle Index 2015 Fund Advisor Class	TLFAX	NAS CM	Open End	Target Date (Asset Alloc)	B	C+	A	Up	Y	0
TIAA-CREF Lifecycle Index 2015 Fund Institutional Class	TLFIX	NAS CM	Open End	Target Date (Asset Alloc)	B	C+	A	Up	Y	10,000,000
TIAA-CREF Lifecycle Index 2015 Fund Premier Class	TLFPX	NAS CM	Open End	Target Date (Asset Alloc)	B	C+	A	Up	Y	0
TIAA-CREF Lifecycle Index 2015 Fund Retirement Class	TLGRX	NAS CM	Open End	Target Date (Asset Alloc)	B	C+	A	Up	Y	0
TIAA-CREF Lifecycle Index 2020 Fund Advisor Class	TLWHX	NAS CM	Open End	Target Date (Asset Alloc)	B	C+	A	Up	Y	0
TIAA-CREF Lifecycle Index 2020 Fund Institutional Class	TLWIX	NAS CM	Open End	Target Date (Asset Alloc)	B	C+	A	Up	Y	10,000,000
TIAA-CREF Lifecycle Index 2020 Fund Premier Class	TLWPX	NAS CM	Open End	Target Date (Asset Alloc)	B	C+	A	Up	Y	0
TIAA-CREF Lifecycle Index 2020 Fund Retirement Class	TLWRX	NAS CM	Open End	Target Date (Asset Alloc)	B	C+	A	Up	Y	0
TIAA-CREF Lifecycle Index 2025 Fund Advisor Class	TLQHX	NAS CM	Open End	Target Date (Asset Alloc)	B	C	A-	Up	Y	0
TIAA-CREF Lifecycle Index 2025 Fund Institutional Class	TLQIX	NAS CM	Open End	Target Date (Asset Alloc)	B	C+	A-	Up	Y	10,000,000
TIAA-CREF Lifecycle Index 2025 Fund Premier Class	TLVPX	NAS CM	Open End	Target Date (Asset Alloc)	B	C	A-	Up	Y	0
TIAA-CREF Lifecycle Index 2025 Fund Retirement Class	TLQRX	NAS CM	Open End	Target Date (Asset Alloc)	B	C	A-	Up	Y	0
TIAA-CREF Lifecycle Index 2030 Fund Advisor Class	TLHHX	NAS CM	Open End	Target Date (Asset Alloc)	B	C	A-	Up	Y	0
TIAA-CREF Lifecycle Index 2030 Fund Institutional Class	TLHIX	NAS CM	Open End	Target Date (Asset Alloc)	B	C	A-	Up	Y	10,000,000
TIAA-CREF Lifecycle Index 2030 Fund Premier Class	TLHPX	NAS CM	Open End	Target Date (Asset Alloc)	B-	C	A-		Y	0
TIAA-CREF Lifecycle Index 2030 Fund Retirement Class	TLHRX	NAS CM	Open End	Target Date (Asset Alloc)	B-	C	A-		Y	0
TIAA-CREF Lifecycle Index 2035 Fund Advisor Class	TLYHX	NAS CM	Open End	Target Date (Asset Alloc)	B-	C	B+	Up	Y	0
TIAA-CREF Lifecycle Index 2035 Fund Institutional Class	TLYIX	NAS CM	Open End	Target Date (Asset Alloc)	B-	C	B+	Up	Y	10,000,000
TIAA-CREF Lifecycle Index 2035 Fund Premier Class	TLYPX	NAS CM	Open End	Target Date (Asset Alloc)	B-	C	B+	Up	Y	0
TIAA-CREF Lifecycle Index 2035 Fund Retirement Class	TLYRX	NAS CM	Open End	Target Date (Asset Alloc)	B-	C	B+	Up	Y	0
TIAA-CREF Lifecycle Index 2040 Fund Advisor Class	TLZHX	NAS CM	Open End	Target Date (Asset Alloc)	B-	C	B+	Up	Y	0
TIAA-CREF Lifecycle Index 2040 Fund Institutional Class	TLZIX	NAS CM	Open End	Target Date (Asset Alloc)	B-	C	B+	Up	Y	10,000,000
TIAA-CREF Lifecycle Index 2040 Fund Premier Class	TLPRX	NAS CM	Open End	Target Date (Asset Alloc)	B-	C	B+	Up	Y	0
TIAA-CREF Lifecycle Index 2040 Fund Retirement Class	TLZRX	NAS CM	Open End	Target Date (Asset Alloc)	B-	C	B+	Up	Y	0
TIAA-CREF Lifecycle Index 2045 Fund Advisor Class	TLMHX	NAS CM	Open End	Target Date (Asset Alloc)	B-	C	B	Up	Y	0
TIAA-CREF Lifecycle Index 2045 Fund Institutional Class	TLXIX	NAS CM	Open End	Target Date (Asset Alloc)	B-	C	B	Up	Y	10,000,000
TIAA-CREF Lifecycle Index 2045 Fund Premier Class	TLMPX	NAS CM	Open End	Target Date (Asset Alloc)	B-	C	B	Up	Y	0
TIAA-CREF Lifecycle Index 2045 Fund Retirement Class	TLMRX	NAS CM	Open End	Target Date (Asset Alloc)	B-	C	B	Up	Y	0
TIAA-CREF Lifecycle Index 2050 Fund Advisor Class	TLLHX	NAS CM	Open End	Target Date (Asset Alloc)	B-	C	B	Up	Y	0
TIAA-CREF Lifecycle Index 2050 Fund Institutional Class	TLLIX	NAS CM	Open End	Target Date (Asset Alloc)	B-	C	B	Up	Y	10,000,000
TIAA-CREF Lifecycle Index 2050 Fund Premier Class	TLLPX	NAS CM	Open End	Target Date (Asset Alloc)	B-	C	B	Up	Y	0
TIAA-CREF Lifecycle Index 2050 Fund Retirement Class	TLLRX	NAS CM	Open End	Target Date (Asset Alloc)	B-	C	B	Up	Y	0
TIAA-CREF Lifecycle Index 2055 Fund Advisor Class	TTIHX	NAS CM	Open End	Target Date (Asset Alloc)	B-	C	B	Up	Y	0
TIAA-CREF Lifecycle Index 2055 Fund Institutional Class	TTIIX	NAS CM	Open End	Target Date (Asset Alloc)	B-	C	B	Up	Y	10,000,000
TIAA-CREF Lifecycle Index 2055 Fund Premier Class	TTIPX	NAS CM	Open End	Target Date (Asset Alloc)	B-	C	B	Up	Y	0
TIAA-CREF Lifecycle Index 2055 Fund Retirement Class	TTIRX	NAS CM	Open End	Target Date (Asset Alloc)	B-	C	B	Up	Y	0
TIAA-CREF Lifecycle Index 2060 Fund Advisor Class	TVIHX	NAS CM	Open End	Target Date (Asset Alloc)	B-	C	B	Up	Y	0
TIAA-CREF Lifecycle Index 2060 Fund Institutional Class	TVIIX	NAS CM	Open End	Target Date (Asset Alloc)	B-	C	B	Up	Y	10,000,000
TIAA-CREF Lifecycle Index 2060 Fund Premier Class	TVIPX	NAS CM	Open End	Target Date (Asset Alloc)	B-	C	B	Up	Y	0
TIAA-CREF Lifecycle Index 2060 Fund Retirement Class	TVITX	NAS CM	Open End	Target Date (Asset Alloc)	B-	C	B	Up	Y	0
TIAA-CREF Lifecycle Index Retirement Income Advisor Cls	TLIHX	NAS CM	Open End	Target Date (Asset Alloc)	B	C+	A		Y	0
TIAA-CREF Lifecycle Index Retmnt Income Inst Cls	TRILX	NAS CM	Open End	Target Date (Asset Alloc)	B	C+	A		Y	10,000,000

★ Expanded analysis of this fund is included in Section II.

	TOTAL RETURNS					PERFORMANCE				ASSETS		ASSET ALLOCATION & TURNOVER					BULL & BEAR		FEES		
Min Additional Investment	3-Month Total Return	6-Month Total Return	1-Year Total Return	3-Year Total Return	5-Year Total Return	Dividend Yield (TTM)	Expense Ratio	3-Yr Std Deviation	3-Year Beta	NAV	Total Assets (MIL)	%Cash	%Stocks	%Bonds	%Other	Turnover Ratio	Last Bull Market Total Return	Last Bear Market Total Return	Front End Fee (%)	Back End Fee (%)	Inception Date
	3.29	17.34	3.35	41.02	40.51	2.14	0.6	11.6	1.11	14.41	751.3	2	91	3	5	9	22.47	-18.9			Apr-11
	3.29	17.24	3.24	40.62	39.77	2.05	0.7	11.57	1.1	14.41	751.3	2	91	3	5	9	22.54	-19			Apr-11
	3.31	17.47	3.32	41.67		2.21	0.53	11.75	1.11	11.83	138.7	3	91	1	5	37					Dec-15
1,000	3.40	17.57	3.43	41.90		2.23	0.45	11.77	1.11	11.84	138.7	3	91	1	5	37					Sep-14
	3.23	17.39	3.21	41.22		2.12	0.6	11.71	1.1	11.81	138.7	3	91	1	5	37					Sep-14
	3.32	17.41	3.19	40.76		2.02	0.7	11.69	1.1	11.8	138.7	3	91	1	5	37					Sep-14
	3.17	10.54	7.01	21.92	26.95	2.2	0.18	5.02	1.08	15.62	458.2	3	40	59	-2	16	12.36	-7.55			Dec-15
1,000	3.17	10.62	7.06	22.01	27.14	2.24	0.1	5.06	1.08	15.62	458.2	3	40	59	-2	16	12.36	-7.55			Sep-09
	3.11	10.43	6.84	21.41	26.06	2.1	0.25	5.04	1.08	15.56	458.2	3	40	59	-2	16	12.28	-7.65			Sep-09
	3.06	10.41	6.77	21.09	25.49	2.01	0.35	5.02	1.08	15.48	458.2	3	40	59	-2	16	12.23	-7.66			Sep-09
	3.22	11.23	7.11	23.94	28.99	2.2	0.18	5.56	1.03	16.34	921.7	3	45	54	-2	11	13.79	-9.37			Dec-15
1,000	3.22	11.23	7.13	24.02	28.98	2.22	0.1	5.56	1.03	16.33	921.7	3	45	54	-2	11	13.79	-9.37			Sep-09
	3.17	11.14	6.93	23.44	28.02	2.09	0.25	5.58	1.04	16.26	921.7	3	45	54	-2	11	13.61	-9.31			Sep-09
	3.18	11.10	6.91	23.16	27.47	2	0.35	5.55	1.03	16.21	921.7	3	45	54	-2	11	13.62	-9.4			Sep-09
	3.34	12.03	7.16	26.53	31.11	2.13	0.18	6.25	1.04	17.31	2,329	3	50	49	-2	8	15.35	-11.23			Dec-15
1,000	3.34	12.03	7.21	26.75	31.35	2.18	0.1	6.22	1.03	17.32	2,329	3	50	49	-2	8	15.35	-11.22			Sep-09
	3.29	11.95	7.01	26.13	30.35	2.04	0.25	6.24	1.04	17.23	2,329	3	50	49	-2	8	15.28	-11.33			Sep-09
	3.24	11.85	6.92	25.80	29.72	1.95	0.35	6.22	1.03	17.17	2,329	3	50	49	-2	8	15.06	-11.25			Sep-09
	3.39	13.00	7.14	29.70	33.83	2.08	0.18	7.13	1.01	18.25	3,034	3	58	41	-2	7	16.89	-13.11			Dec-15
1,000	3.45	13.05	7.21	29.92	34.14	2.14	0.1	7.13	1.01	18.27	3,034	3	58	41	-2	7	16.89	-13.11			Sep-09
	3.41	12.98	7.08	29.29	33.14	2.01	0.25	7.13	1.01	18.19	3,034	3	58	41	-2	7	16.81	-13.13			Sep-09
	3.36	12.90	7.00	28.93	32.45	1.92	0.35	7.12	1.01	18.11	3,034	3	58	41	-2	7	16.75	-13.22			Sep-09
	3.50	14.00	7.16	32.84	36.55	2.08	0.18	8.04	0.99	19.21	3,218	2	66	33	-2	5	18.49	-14.98			Dec-15
1,000	3.49	14.05	7.26	33.18	36.89	2.12	0.1	8.03	0.99	19.23	3,218	2	66	33	-2	5	18.49	-14.98			Sep-09
	3.45	13.99	7.13	32.56	35.90	1.98	0.25	8.05	0.99	19.14	3,218	2	66	33	-2	5	18.43	-15.01			Sep-09
	3.42	13.86	6.99	32.07	35.11	1.9	0.35	8.04	0.99	19.05	3,218	2	66	33	-2	5	18.33	-15.03			Sep-09
	3.55	14.97	7.10	36.26	39.12	2.07	0.18	8.95	0.98	20.12	2,924	2	74	25	-1	5	20.16	-16.77			Dec-15
1,000	3.54	15.02	7.19	36.39	39.34	2.1	0.1	8.95	0.98	20.14	2,924	2	74	25	-1	5	20.16	-16.77			Sep-09
	3.56	14.97	7.01	35.81	38.37	1.97	0.25	8.95	0.98	20.04	2,924	2	74	25	-1	5	20.1	-16.81			Sep-09
	3.52	14.91	6.93	35.40	37.65	1.88	0.35	8.95	0.98	19.95	2,924	2	74	25	-1	5	20.01	-16.82			Sep-09
	3.59	15.96	6.98	39.38	41.56	2.02	0.18	9.88	1.01	20.77	3,096	2	82	17	-1	3	20.73	-17.19			Dec-15
1,000	3.63	16.01	7.05	39.66	41.84	2.08	0.1	9.85	1.01	20.79	3,096	2	82	17	-1	3	20.73	-17.19			Sep-09
	3.60	15.91	6.92	39.01	40.70	1.95	0.25	9.87	1.01	20.68	3,096	2	82	17	-1	3	20.67	-17.23			Sep-09
	3.56	15.86	6.78	38.58	40.05	1.86	0.35	9.87	1.01	20.6	3,096	2	82	17	-1	3	20.58	-17.31			Sep-09
	3.62	16.64	6.85	40.69	42.79	2.01	0.18	10.54	1.04	20.88	2,060	1	89	10	-1	3	20.6	-17.09			Dec-15
1,000	3.67	16.69	6.92	41.03	43.14	2.08	0.1	10.52	1.04	20.9	2,060	1	89	10	-1	3	20.6	-17.09			Sep-09
	3.58	16.59	6.73	40.35	41.98	1.95	0.25	10.52	1.04	20.8	2,060	1	89	10	-1	3	20.64	-17.26			Sep-09
	3.60	16.54	6.65	39.94	41.34	1.86	0.35	10.5	1.04	20.71	2,060	1	89	10	-1	3	20.54	-17.21			Sep-09
	3.60	16.76	6.79	41.19	43.39	2.04	0.18	10.66	1.03	20.96	1,571	1	90	9	0	3	20.72	-17.17			Dec-15
1,000	3.65	16.81	6.88	41.50	43.71	2.07	0.1	10.65	1.03	20.98	1,571	1	90	9	0	3	20.72	-17.17			Sep-09
	3.62	16.77	6.75	40.92	42.65	1.95	0.25	10.65	1.03	20.88	1,571	1	90	9	0	3	20.67	-17.21			Sep-09
	3.58	16.67	6.62	40.47	41.90	1.86	0.35	10.68	1.03	20.78	1,571	1	90	9	0	3	20.56	-17.29			Sep-09
	3.58	16.85	6.72	41.80	43.95	2.03	0.18	10.79	1.03	16.78	660.4	1	92	7	0	5	20.72	-17.2			Dec-15
1,000	3.63	16.99	6.88	42.06	44.21	2.06	0.1	10.83	1.04	16.8	660.4	1	92	7	0	5	20.72	-17.2			Apr-11
	3.58	16.80	6.69	41.37	43.13	1.94	0.25	10.79	1.03	16.75	660.4	1	92	7	0	5	20.73	-17.3			Apr-11
	3.59	16.77	6.59	40.91	42.35	1.85	0.35	10.77	1.03	16.71	660.4	1	92	7	0	5	20.65	-17.3			Apr-11
	3.60	17.02	6.82	42.40		2.01	0.18	10.9	1.03	12.92	166.9	1	93	6	0	32					Dec-15
1,000	3.69	17.13	6.86	42.50		2.05	0.1	10.97	1.04	12.92	166.9	1	93	6	0	32					Sep-14
	3.61	16.95	6.64	41.86		1.93	0.25	10.93	1.04	12.9	166.9	1	93	6	0	32					Sep-14
	3.53	16.89	6.58	41.35		1.87	0.35	10.93	1.04	12.87	166.9	1	93	6	0	32					Sep-14
	3.11	10.35	6.99	20.90	26.03	2.32	0.18	4.83	1.19	14.72	383.8	3	39	60	-2	26	10.66	-5.3			Dec-15
1,000	3.12	10.38	7.02	20.98	26.16	2.35	0.1	4.81	1.18	14.72	383.8	3	39	60	-2	26	10.66	-5.3			Sep-09

	MARKET			FUND TYPE, CATEGORY & OBJECTIVE	RATINGS				MINIMUMS	
Fund Name	Ticker Symbol	Traded On	Fund Type	Category and (Prospectus Objective)	Overall Rating	Reward Rating	Risk Rating	Recent Up/ Downgrade	Open to New Investors	Min Initial Investment
TIAA-CREF Lifecycle Index Retirement Income Premier Cls	TLIPX	NAS CM	Open End	Target Date (Asset Alloc)	B	C+	A		Y	0
TIAA-CREF Lifecycle Index Retirement Income Retirement Cls	TRCIX	NAS CM	Open End	Target Date (Asset Alloc)	B	C+	A-	Up	Y	0
TIAA-CREF Lifecycle Retirement Income Fund Advisor Class	TLRHX	NAS CM	Open End	Target Date (Asset Alloc)	B	C+	A	Up	Y	0
TIAA-CREF Lifecycle Retirement Income Institutional Cls	TLRIX	NAS CM	Open End	Target Date (Asset Alloc)	B	C+	A	Up	Y	2,000,000
TIAA-CREF Lifecycle Retirement Income Fund Premier Class	TPILX	NAS CM	Open End	Target Date (Asset Alloc)	B	C+	A-	Up	Y	0
TIAA-CREF Lifecycle Retirement Income Fund Retail Class	TLRRX	NAS CM	Open End	Target Date (Asset Alloc)	B	C+	A-	Up	Y	2,500
TIAA-CREF Lifecycle Retirement Income Retirement Cls	TLIRX	NAS CM	Open End	Target Date (Asset Alloc)	B	C+	A-	Up	Y	0
TIAA-CREF Lifestyle Aggressive Growth Fund Advisor Class	TSAHX	NAS CM	Open End	Aggressive Alloc (Asset Alloc)	C+	C	B	Up	Y	0
TIAA-CREF Lifestyle Aggressive Growth Institutional Cls	TSAIX	NAS CM	Open End	Aggressive Alloc (Asset Alloc)	C+	C	B	Up	Y	2,000,000
TIAA-CREF Lifestyle Aggressive Growth Fund Premier Class	TSAPX	NAS CM	Open End	Aggressive Alloc (Asset Alloc)	C+	C	B	Up	Y	0
TIAA-CREF Lifestyle Aggressive Growth Fund Retail Class	TSALX	NAS CM	Open End	Aggressive Alloc (Asset Alloc)	C+	C	B	Up	Y	2,500
TIAA-CREF Lifestyle Aggressive Growth Retirement Cls	TSARX	NAS CM	Open End	Aggressive Alloc (Asset Alloc)	C+	C	B	Up	Y	0
TIAA-CREF Lifestyle Conservative Fund Advisor Class	TLSHX	NAS CM	Open End	Cautious Alloc (Asset Alloc)	B	C	A-	Up	Y	0
TIAA-CREF Lifestyle Conservative Fund Institutional Class	TCSIX	NAS CM	Open End	Cautious Alloc (Asset Alloc)	B	C	A-	Up	Y	2,000,000
TIAA-CREF Lifestyle Conservative Fund Premier Class	TLSPX	NAS CM	Open End	Cautious Alloc (Asset Alloc)	B	C	A-	Up	Y	0
TIAA-CREF Lifestyle Conservative Fund Retail Class	TSCLX	NAS CM	Open End	Cautious Alloc (Asset Alloc)	B	C	A-	Up	Y	2,500
TIAA-CREF Lifestyle Conservative Fund Retirement Class	TSCTX	NAS CM	Open End	Cautious Alloc (Asset Alloc)	B	C	A-	Up	Y	0
TIAA-CREF Lifestyle Growth Fund Advisor Class	TSGHX	NAS CM	Open End	Aggressive Alloc (Asset Alloc)	B-	C	B	Up	Y	0
TIAA-CREF Lifestyle Growth Fund Institutional Class	TSGGX	NAS CM	Open End	Aggressive Alloc (Asset Alloc)	B-	C	B	Up	Y	2,000,000
TIAA-CREF Lifestyle Growth Fund Premier Class	TSGPX	NAS CM	Open End	Aggressive Alloc (Asset Alloc)	B-	C	B	Up	Y	0
TIAA-CREF Lifestyle Growth Fund Retail Class	TSGLX	NAS CM	Open End	Aggressive Alloc (Asset Alloc)	B-	C	B	Up	Y	2,500
TIAA-CREF Lifestyle Growth Fund Retirement Class	TSGRX	NAS CM	Open End	Aggressive Alloc (Asset Alloc)	B-	C	B	Up	Y	0
TIAA-CREF Lifestyle Income Fund Advisor Class	TSIHX	NAS CM	Open End	Cautious Alloc (Asset Alloc)	B	C	A-	Up	Y	0
TIAA-CREF Lifestyle Income Fund Institutional Class	TSITX	NAS CM	Open End	Cautious Alloc (Asset Alloc)	B	C	A-	Up	Y	2,000,000
TIAA-CREF Lifestyle Income Fund Premier Class	TSIPX	NAS CM	Open End	Cautious Alloc (Asset Alloc)	B	C	A-	Up	Y	0
TIAA-CREF Lifestyle Income Fund Retail Class	TSILX	NAS CM	Open End	Cautious Alloc (Asset Alloc)	B-	C	A-		Y	2,500
TIAA-CREF Lifestyle Income Fund Retirement Class	TLSRX	NAS CM	Open End	Cautious Alloc (Asset Alloc)	B	C	A-	Up	Y	0
TIAA-CREF Lifestyle Moderate Fund Advisor Class	TSMHX	NAS CM	Open End	Moderate Alloc (Asset Alloc)	B-	C	B+	Up	Y	0
TIAA-CREF Lifestyle Moderate Fund Institutional Class	TSIMX	NAS CM	Open End	Moderate Alloc (Asset Alloc)	B-	C	B+	Up	Y	2,000,000
TIAA-CREF Lifestyle Moderate Fund Premier Class	TSMPX	NAS CM	Open End	Moderate Alloc (Asset Alloc)	B-	C	B+	Up	Y	0
TIAA-CREF Lifestyle Moderate Fund Retail Class	TSMLX	NAS CM	Open End	Moderate Alloc (Asset Alloc)	B-	C	B+	Up	Y	2,500
TIAA-CREF Lifestyle Moderate Fund Retirement Class	TSMTX	NAS CM	Open End	Moderate Alloc (Asset Alloc)	B-	C	B+	Up	Y	0
TIAA-CREF Managed Allocation Fund Institutional Class	TIMIX	NAS CM	Open End	Moderate Alloc (Growth)	B-	C	B+	Up	Y	2,000,000
TIAA-CREF Managed Allocation Fund Retail Class	TIMRX	NAS CM	Open End	Moderate Alloc (Growth)	B-	C	B+	Up	Y	2,500
TIAA-CREF Managed Allocation Fund Retirement Class	TITRX	NAS CM	Open End	Moderate Alloc (Growth)	B-	C	B+	Up	Y	0
TIAA-CREF Mid-Cap Growth Fund Advisor Class	TCMHX	NAS CM	Open End	US Equity Mid Cap (Growth)	C+	C+	B-	Down	Y	0
TIAA-CREF Mid-Cap Growth Fund Institutional Class	TRPWX	NAS CM	Open End	US Equity Mid Cap (Growth)	C+	C+	B-	Down	Y	2,000,000
TIAA-CREF Mid-Cap Growth Fund Premier Class	TRGPX	NAS CM	Open End	US Equity Mid Cap (Growth)	C+	C+	B-	Down	Y	0
TIAA-CREF Mid-Cap Growth Fund Retail Class	TCMGX	NAS CM	Open End	US Equity Mid Cap (Growth)	C+	C+	B-		Y	2,500
TIAA-CREF Mid-Cap Growth Fund Retirement Class	TRGMX	NAS CM	Open End	US Equity Mid Cap (Growth)	C+	C+	B-		Y	0
TIAA-CREF Mid-Cap Value Fund Advisor Class	TRVHX	NAS CM	Open End	US Equity Mid Cap (Growth & Income)	C	C	B-		Y	0
TIAA-CREF Mid-Cap Value Fund Institutional Class	TIMVX	NAS CM	Open End	US Equity Mid Cap (Growth & Income)	C	C	B-		Y	2,000,000
TIAA-CREF Mid-Cap Value Fund Premier Class	TRVPX	NAS CM	Open End	US Equity Mid Cap (Growth & Income)	C	C	B-		Y	0
TIAA-CREF Mid-Cap Value Fund Retail Class	TCMVX	NAS CM	Open End	US Equity Mid Cap (Growth & Income)	C	C	B-		Y	2,500
TIAA-CREF Mid-Cap Value Fund Retirement Class	TRVRX	NAS CM	Open End	US Equity Mid Cap (Growth & Income)	C	C	B-		Y	0
TIAA-CREF Quant International Equity Fund Advisor Class	TEIEX	NAS CM	Open End	Global Equity Large Cap (Foreign Stock)	C	C	B-		Y	0
TIAA-CREF Quant International Equity Fund Class W	TEIWX	NAS CM	Open End	Global Equity Large Cap (Foreign Stock)	C	C	B-		Y	0
TIAA-CREF Quant International Equity Institutional Cls	TFIIX	NAS CM	Open End	Global Equity Large Cap (Foreign Stock)	C	C	B-		Y	2,000,000
TIAA-CREF Quant International Small-Cap Equity Advisor Cls	TAISX	NAS CM	Open End	Global Equity Mid/Small Cap (Small Company)	D+	D	C-		Y	0
TIAA-CREF Quant International Small-Cap Equity Cls W	TAIWX	NAS CM	Open End	Global Equity Mid/Small Cap (Small Company)	D+	D	C-		Y	0
TIAA-CREF Quant Intl Small-Cap Equity Inst Cls	TIISX	NAS CM	Open End	Global Equity Mid/Small Cap (Small Company)	D+	D	C-		Y	2,000,000
TIAA-CREF Quant International Small-Cap Equity Premier Cls	TPISX	NAS CM	Open End	Global Equity Mid/Small Cap (Small Company)	D+	D	C-		Y	0

★ Expanded analysis of this fund is included in Section II.

	TOTAL RETURNS					PERFORMANCE				ASSETS		ASSET ALLOCATION & TURNOVER					BULL & BEAR		FEES		
Min Additional Investment	3-Month Total Return	6-Month Total Return	1-Year Total Return	3-Year Total Return	5-Year Total Return	Dividend Yield (TTM)	Expense Ratio	3-Yr Std Deviation	3-Year Beta	NAV	Total Assets (MIL)	%Cash	%Stocks	%Bonds	%Other	Turnover Ratio	Last Bull Market Total Return	Last Bear Market Total Return	Front End Fee (%)	Back End Fee (%)	Inception Date
	3.08	10.31	6.87	20.37	25.16	2.21	0.25	4.84	1.19	14.71	383.8	3	39	60	-2	26	10.49	-5.29			Sep-09
	3.06	10.26	6.77	20.12	24.54	2.12	0.35	4.84	1.19	14.7	383.8	3	39	60	-2	26	10.53	-5.33			Sep-09
	2.96	10.41	5.79	22.36	26.49	2.67	0.45	4.99	1.22	11.59	541.1	3	34	58	5	18	11.85	-6.9			Dec-15
1,000	3.08	10.43	5.85	22.47	26.66	2.72	0.37	5	1.22	11.59	541.1	3	34	58	5	18	11.85	-6.9			Nov-07
	2.95	10.25	5.60	21.94	25.62	2.57	0.52	4.98	1.22	11.58	541.1	3	34	58	5	18	11.77	-6.96			Sep-09
100	2.93	10.21	5.50	21.49	25.02	2.48	0.62	5.02	1.23	11.57	541.1	3	34	58	5	18	11.68	-6.88			Nov-07
	2.93	10.22	5.50	21.51	25.04	2.48	0.62	5.02	1.23	11.56	541.1	3	34	58	5	18	11.73	-6.94			Nov-07
	3.33	18.62	2.74	42.79	41.60	2.14	0.63	12.5	1.14	16.43	125.4	2	98	0	0	38					Dec-15
1,000	3.39	18.54	2.73	42.92	41.72	2.18	0.55	12.51	1.14	16.43	125.4	2	98	0	0	38					Dec-11
	3.32	18.48	2.61	42.37	40.76	2.03	0.7	12.54	1.15	16.47	125.4	2	98	0	0	38					Dec-11
100	3.28	18.39	2.39	41.57	39.45	1.89	0.85	12.56	1.15	16.35	125.4	2	98	0	0	38					Dec-11
	3.28	18.36	2.45	41.89	39.92	1.94	0.8	12.49	1.14	16.37	125.4	2	98	0	0	38					Dec-11
	2.87	10.70	5.20	21.83	25.87	2.52	0.54	5.41	1.12	12.61	240.4	4	38	57	0	13					Dec-15
1,000	2.90	10.75	5.28	21.98	26.06	2.59	0.46	5.39	1.11	12.61	240.4	4	38	57	0	13					Dec-11
	2.86	10.66	5.12	21.43	25.10	2.44	0.61	5.4	1.11	12.62	240.4	4	38	57	0	13					Dec-11
100	2.84	10.53	5.01	20.94	24.31	2.34	0.73	5.37	1.1	12.59	240.4	4	38	57	0	13					Dec-11
	2.84	10.63	5.03	21.10	24.44	2.36	0.71	5.4	1.11	12.6	240.4	4	38	57	0	13					Dec-11
	3.34	16.22	3.81	35.89	37.00	2.22	0.59	10.2	1.11	15.47	170.6	3	78	19	0	18					Dec-15
1,000	3.33	16.30	3.87	36.17	37.38	2.27	0.52	10.22	1.12	15.48	170.6	3	78	19	0	18					Dec-11
	3.33	16.21	3.69	35.57	36.26	2.17	0.67	10.2	1.11	15.48	170.6	3	78	19	0	18					Dec-11
100	3.28	16.13	3.56	34.94	35.32	2	0.8	10.17	1.11	15.4	170.6	3	78	19	0	18					Dec-11
	3.28	16.11	3.60	35.06	35.57	2.03	0.77	10.19	1.11	15.42	170.6	3	78	19	0	18					Dec-11
	2.51	7.61	5.46	14.61	19.29	2.65	0.5	3.08	0.96	11.18	73.1	5	19	75	0	19					Dec-15
1,000	2.53	7.64	5.49	14.67	19.28	2.67	0.42	3.06	0.95	11.18	73.1	5	19	75	0	19					Dec-11
	2.48	7.55	5.24	14.15	18.31	2.53	0.57	3.1	0.97	11.19	73.1	5	19	75	0	19					Dec-11
100	2.45	7.49	5.11	13.64	17.56	2.4	0.69	3.05	0.96	11.17	73.1	5	19	75	0	19					Dec-11
	2.46	7.51	5.23	13.84	17.71	2.43	0.67	3.07	0.96	11.17	73.1	5	19	75	0	19					Dec-11
	3.30	13.85	4.96	29.27	32.51	2.46	0.57	7.84	1.14	14.12	366.8	4	58	38	0	10					Dec-15
1,000	3.32	13.88	5.03	29.49	32.79	2.53	0.49	7.86	1.14	14.12	366.8	4	58	38	0	10					Dec-11
	3.28	13.86	4.79	28.90	31.92	2.38	0.64	7.78	1.13	14.15	366.8	4	58	38	0	10					Dec-11
100	3.26	13.76	4.68	28.41	31.08	2.27	0.76	7.83	1.13	14.1	366.8	4	58	38	0	10					Dec-11
	3.19	13.77	4.70	28.48	31.11	2.29	0.74	7.84	1.14	14.1	366.8	4	58	38	0	10					Dec-11
1,000	3.28	13.82	5.18	29.77	33.59	2.69	0.39	7.81	1.13	12.68	867.7	3	58	38	0	12	16.67	-12.09			Mar-06
100	3.21	13.63	4.98	28.81	31.92	2.44	0.64	7.74	1.12	12.72	867.7	3	58	38	0	12	16.47	-12.16			Mar-06
	3.22	13.69	5.00	28.85	31.98	2.45	0.64	7.78	1.13	12.67	867.7	3	58	38	0	12	16.41	-12.12			Mar-06
	5.62	30.39	12.22	55.91	57.59	0.29	0.56	15.18	1.04	22.91	1,510	1	99	0	0	70	29.96	-24.1			Dec-15
1,000	5.62	30.39	12.22	56.02	57.78	0.33	0.47	15.18	1.04	22.91	1,510	1	99	0	0	70	29.96	-24.1			Oct-02
	5.61	30.28	12.13	55.35	56.65	0.18	0.62	15.18	1.04	22.76	1,510	1	99	0	0	70	29.87	-24.15			Sep-09
100	5.57	30.23	11.96	54.63	55.43	0.04	0.77	15.2	1.04	22.14	1,510	1	99	0	0	70	29.62	-24.17			Oct-02
	5.57	30.19	11.97	54.82	55.85	0.09	0.72	15.22	1.04	22.16	1,510	1	99	0	0	70	29.8	-24.2			Oct-02
	3.15	19.36	0.69	26.45	29.17	1.68	0.51	14.15	1.06	20.28	3,155	1	99	0	0	25	25.96	-21.16			Dec-15
1,000	3.15	19.41	0.82	26.74	29.52	1.76	0.42	14.11	1.06	20.3	3,155	1	99	0	0	25	25.96	-21.16			Oct-02
	3.10	19.32	0.66	26.15	28.55	1.58	0.57	14.12	1.06	20.25	3,155	1	99	0	0	25	25.83	-21.2			Sep-09
100	3.08	19.26	0.51	25.63	27.62	1.51	0.72	14.13	1.06	19.69	3,155	1	99	0	0	25	25.72	-21.2			Oct-02
	3.12	19.28	0.54	25.80	27.91	1.48	0.67	14.13	1.06	20.16	3,155	1	99	0	0	25	25.74	-21.22			Oct-02
	2.68	14.15	-0.80	27.17	8.63	3.09	0.49	11.78	1.05	7.26	1,858	1	99	0	0	106	14.14	-23.44			Dec-15
	2.82	14.46	-0.36	27.88	9.40		0	11.74	1.04	7.28	1,858	1	99	0	0	106	14.14	-23.44			Sep-18
1,000	2.54	14.15	-0.74	27.39	8.98	3.14	0.4	11.72	1.04	7.26	1,858	1	99	0	0	106	14.14	-23.44			Nov-07
	0.90	11.66	-8.43			2.83	0.8			10.05	948.7	1	98	0	0	89					Dec-16
	1.20	12.11	-7.93				0			10.09	948.7	1	98	0	0	89					Sep-18
1,000	0.90	11.66	-8.45			2.81	0.71			10.05	948.7	1	98	0	0	89					Dec-16
	0.89	11.62	-8.56			1.68	0.87			10.18	948.7	1	98	0	0	89					Dec-16

	MARKET			FUND TYPE, CATEGORY & OBJECTIVE	RATINGS				MINIMUMS	
Fund Name	Ticker Symbol	Traded On	Fund Type	Category and (Prospectus Objective)	Overall Rating	Reward Rating	Risk Rating	Recent Up/ Downgrade	Open to New Investors	Min Initial Investment
TIAA-CREF Quant International Small-Cap Equity Retail Cls	TLISX	NAS CM	Open End	Global Equity Mid/Small Cap (Small Company)	D+	D	C-		Y	2,500
TIAA-CREF Quant Intl Small-Cap Equity Retmnt Cls	TTISX	NAS CM	Open End	Global Equity Mid/Small Cap (Small Company)	D+	D	C-		Y	0
TIAA-CREF Quant Large-Cap Growth Fund Advisor Class	TECGX	NAS CM	Open End	US Equity Large Cap Growth (Growth & Income)	C+	C	B	Down	Y	0
TIAA-CREF Quant Large-Cap Growth Fund Class W	TECWX	NAS CM	Open End	US Equity Large Cap Growth (Growth & Income)	C+	C	B	Down	Y	0
TIAA-CREF Quant Large-Cap Growth Fund Institutional Class	TLIIX	NAS CM	Open End	US Equity Large Cap Growth (Growth & Income)	C+	C	B	Down	Y	2,000,000
TIAA-CREF Quant Large-Cap Value Fund Advisor Class	TELCX	NAS CM	Open End	US Equity Large Cap Value (Growth & Income)	C+	C	B	Up	Y	0
TIAA-CREF Quant Large-Cap Value Fund Class W	TELWX	NAS CM	Open End	US Equity Large Cap Value (Growth & Income)	B-	C	B	Up	Y	0
TIAA-CREF Quant Large-Cap Value Fund Institutional Class	TEVIX	NAS CM	Open End	US Equity Large Cap Value (Growth & Income)	B-	C	B	Up	Y	2,000,000
TIAA-CREF Quant Small/Mid-Cap Equity Fund Advisor Class	TSMNX	NAS CM	Open End	US Equity Small Cap (Growth)	C+	C	B-	Up	Y	0
TIAA-CREF Quant Small/Mid-Cap Equity Fund Class W	TSMUX	NAS CM	Open End	US Equity Small Cap (Growth)	C+	C	B-	Up	Y	0
TIAA-CREF Quant Small/Mid-Cap Equity Institutional Cls	TSMWX	NAS CM	Open End	US Equity Small Cap (Growth)	C+	C	B-	Up	Y	2,000,000
TIAA-CREF Quant Small/Mid-Cap Equity Fund Premier Class	TSMMX	NAS CM	Open End	US Equity Small Cap (Growth)	C+	C	B-	Up	Y	0
TIAA-CREF Quant Small/Mid-Cap Equity Fund Retail Class	TSMEX	NAS CM	Open End	US Equity Small Cap (Growth)	C+	C	B-	Up	Y	2,500
TIAA-CREF Quant Small/Mid-Cap Equity Fund Retirement Class	TSMOX	NAS CM	Open End	US Equity Small Cap (Growth)	C+	C	B-	Up	Y	0
TIAA-CREF Quant Small-Cap Equity Fund Advisor Class	TSCHX	NAS CM	Open End	US Equity Small Cap (Small Company)	C	C	C+		Y	0
TIAA-CREF Quant Small-Cap Equity Fund Class W	TSCWX	NAS CM	Open End	US Equity Small Cap (Small Company)	C	C	C+		Y	0
TIAA-CREF Quant Small-Cap Equity Fund Institutional Class	TISEX	NAS CM	Open End	US Equity Small Cap (Small Company)	C	C	C+		Y	2,000,000
TIAA-CREF Quant Small-Cap Equity Fund Premier Class	TSRPX	NAS CM	Open End	US Equity Small Cap (Small Company)	C	C	C+		Y	0
TIAA-CREF Quant Small-Cap Equity Fund Retail Class	TCSEX	NAS CM	Open End	US Equity Small Cap (Small Company)	C	C	C+		Y	2,500
TIAA-CREF Quant Small-Cap Equity Fund Retirement Class	TRSEX	NAS CM	Open End	US Equity Small Cap (Small Company)	C	C	C+		Y	0
TIAA-CREF Real Estate Securities Fund Advisor Class	TIRHX	NAS CM	Open End	Real Estate Sector Equity (Real Estate)	B	B-	B	Up	Y	0
TIAA-CREF Real Estate Securities Fund Institutional Class	TIREX	NAS CM	Open End	Real Estate Sector Equity (Real Estate)	B	B-	B	Up	Y	2,000,000
TIAA-CREF Real Estate Securities Fund Premier Class	TRRPX	NAS CM	Open End	Real Estate Sector Equity (Real Estate)	B-	B-	B		Y	0
TIAA-CREF Real Estate Securities Fund Retail Class	TCREX	NAS CM	Open End	Real Estate Sector Equity (Real Estate)	B-	C+	B		Y	2,500
TIAA-CREF Real Estate Securities Fund Retirement Class	TRRSX	NAS CM	Open End	Real Estate Sector Equity (Real Estate)	B-	B-	B		Y	0
TIAA-CREF S&P 500 Index Fund Advisor Class	TISAX	NAS CM	Open End	US Equity Large Cap Blend (Growth)	B-	C	B		Y	0
TIAA-CREF S&P 500 Index Fund Institutional Class	TISPX	NAS CM	Open End	US Equity Large Cap Blend (Growth)	B-	C	B		Y	10,000,000
TIAA-CREF S&P 500 Index Fund Retirement Class	TRSPX	NAS CM	Open End	US Equity Large Cap Blend (Growth)	B-	C	B		Y	0
TIAA-CREF Small-Cap Blend Index Fund Advisor Class	TRHBX	NAS CM	Open End	US Equity Small Cap (Growth)	C	C	C+		Y	0
TIAA-CREF Small-Cap Blend Index Fund Institutional Class	TISBX	NAS CM	Open End	US Equity Small Cap (Growth)	C	C	C+		Y	10,000,000
TIAA-CREF Small-Cap Blend Index Fund Retirement Class	TRBIX	NAS CM	Open End	US Equity Small Cap (Growth)	C	C	C+		Y	0
TIAA-CREF Social Choice Equity Fund Advisor Class	TICHX	NAS CM	Open End	US Equity Large Cap Blend (Growth)	B-	C	B		Y	0
TIAA-CREF Social Choice Equity Fund Institutional Class	TISCX	NAS CM	Open End	US Equity Large Cap Blend (Growth)	B-	C	B		Y	2,000,000
TIAA-CREF Social Choice Equity Fund Premier Class	TRPSX	NAS CM	Open End	US Equity Large Cap Blend (Growth)	B-	C	B		Y	0
TIAA-CREF Social Choice Equity Fund Retail Class	TICRX	NAS CM	Open End	US Equity Large Cap Blend (Growth)	B-	C	B		Y	2,500
TIAA-CREF Social Choice Equity Fund Retirement Class	TRSCX	NAS CM	Open End	US Equity Large Cap Blend (Growth)	B-	C	B		Y	0
TIAA-CREF Social Choice International Equity Advisor Cls	TSOHX	NAS CM	Open End	Global Equity Large Cap (Foreign Stock)	C	C	B		Y	0
TIAA-CREF Social Choice Intl Equity Inst Cls	TSONX	NAS CM	Open End	Global Equity Large Cap (Foreign Stock)	C	C	B		Y	2,000,000
TIAA-CREF Social Choice International Equity Premier Cls	TSOPX	NAS CM	Open End	Global Equity Large Cap (Foreign Stock)	C	C	B		Y	0
TIAA-CREF Social Choice International Equity Retail Cls	TSORX	NAS CM	Open End	Global Equity Large Cap (Foreign Stock)	C	C	B		Y	2,500
TIAA-CREF Social Choice Intl Equity Retmnt Cls	TSOEX	NAS CM	Open End	Global Equity Large Cap (Foreign Stock)	C	C	B		Y	0
TIAA-CREF Social Choice Low Carbon Equity Advisor Cls	TCCHX	NAS CM	Open End	US Equity Large Cap Blend (Growth)	B-	C	B		Y	0
TIAA-CREF Social Choice Low Carbon Equity Inst Cls	TNWCX	NAS CM	Open End	US Equity Large Cap Blend (Growth)	B-	C	B		Y	2,000,000
TIAA-CREF Social Choice Low Carbon Equity Premier Cls	TPWCX	NAS CM	Open End	US Equity Large Cap Blend (Growth)	B-	C	B		Y	0
TIAA-CREF Social Choice Low Carbon Equity Retail Cls	TLWCX	NAS CM	Open End	US Equity Large Cap Blend (Growth)	B-	C	B		Y	2,500
TIAA-CREF Social Choice Low Carbon Equity Retirement Cls	TEWCX	NAS CM	Open End	US Equity Large Cap Blend (Growth)	B-	C	B		Y	0
Timothy Aggressive Growth Fund Class A	TAAGX	NAS CM	Open End	US Equity Mid Cap (Aggr Growth)	C	C	C+		Y	1,000
Timothy Aggressive Growth Fund Class C	TCAGX	NAS CM	Open End	US Equity Mid Cap (Aggr Growth)	C	C	C+		Y	1,000
Timothy Plan Aggressive Growth Fund Class I	TIAGX	NAS CM	Open End	US Equity Mid Cap (Aggr Growth)	C	C	C+		Y	100,000
Timothy Plan Conservative Growth Fund Class A	TCGAX	NAS CM	Open End	Cautious Alloc (Growth)	C+	C-	B	Up	Y	1,000
Timothy Plan Conservative Growth Fund Class C	TCVCX	NAS CM	Open End	Cautious Alloc (Growth)	C	C-	B-		Y	1,000
Timothy Plan Defensive Strategies Fund Class A	TPDAX	NAS CM	Open End	Moderate Alloc (Growth)	C	C	B-		Y	1,000

★ Expanded analysis of this fund is included in Section II.

	TOTAL RETURNS					PERFORMANCE				ASSETS		ASSET ALLOCATION & TURNOVER					BULL & BEAR		FEES		
Min Additional Investment	3-Month Total Return	6-Month Total Return	1-Year Total Return	3-Year Total Return	5-Year Total Return	Dividend Yield (TTM)	Expense Ratio	3-Yr Std Deviation	3-Year Beta	NAV	Total Assets (MIL)	%Cash	%Stocks	%Bonds	%Other	Turnover Ratio	Last Bull Market Total Return	Last Bear Market Total Return	Front End Fee (%)	Back End Fee (%)	Inception Date
100	0.90	11.51	-8.76			2.06	1.14			10.07	948.7	1	98	0	0	89					Dec-16
	0.90	11.54	-8.55			2.47	0.97			10.05	948.7	1	98	0	0	89					Dec-16
	4.00	20.57	8.23	62.05	82.38	0.93	0.43	13.42	1	14.3	2,839	0	100	0	0	84	27.66	-15.01			Dec-15
	4.07	20.87	8.59	62.43	82.98		0	13.48	1	14.3	2,839	0	100	0	0	84	27.66	-15.01			Sep-18
1,000	4.00	20.60	8.34	62.06	82.57	1.08	0.32	13.48	1	14.28	2,839	0	100	0	0	84	27.66	-15.01			Nov-07
	2.75	14.80	5.30	30.21	34.74	2.22	0.41	12.53	1.03	10.08	2,655	0	100	0	0	84	24.87	-18.77			Dec-15
	2.84	15.11	5.52	30.96	35.66		0	12.5	1.03	10.13	2,655	0	100	0	0	84	24.87	-18.77			Sep-18
1,000	2.74	14.88	5.22	30.59	35.27	2.25	0.32	12.5	1.03	10.11	2,655	0	100	0	0	84	24.87	-18.77			Nov-07
	3.84	22.47	4.44			0.65	0.59			12.15	695.9	0	100	0	0	64					Aug-16
	4.01	22.92	4.88				0			12.17	695.9	0	100	0	0	64					Sep-18
1,000	3.84	22.50	4.46			0.73	0.5			12.14	695.9	0	100	0	0	64					Aug-16
	3.76	22.42	4.29			0.59	0.66			12.12	695.9	0	100	0	0	64					Aug-16
100	3.78	22.26	4.10			0.43	0.88			12.08	695.9	0	100	0	0	64					Aug-16
	3.77	22.34	4.23			0.54	0.76			12.1	695.9	0	100	0	0	64					Aug-16
	2.64	19.49	-0.47	47.97	47.99	0.63	0.48	16.91	0.98	16.67	3,164	0	100	0	0	87	28.53	-25.74			Dec-15
	2.76	19.78	-0.15	48.60	48.63		0	16.91	0.98	16.71	3,164	0	100	0	0	87	28.53	-25.74			Sep-18
1,000	2.64	19.56	-0.44	48.16	48.19	0.7	0.41	16.92	0.98	16.68	3,164	0	100	0	0	87	28.53	-25.74			Oct-02
	2.60	19.46	-0.58	47.51	47.04	0.54	0.56	16.94	0.98	16.57	3,164	0	100	0	0	87	28.43	-25.79			Sep-09
100	2.56	19.43	-0.69	46.84	45.97	0.44	0.71	16.9	0.98	15.98	3,164	0	100	0	0	87	28.15	-25.81			Oct-02
	2.59	19.48	-0.66	47.12	46.39	0.44	0.66	16.93	0.98	16.19	3,164	0	100	0	0	87	28.3	-25.83			Oct-02
	2.88	21.13	13.88	25.53	56.95	1.86	0.65	12.28	0.96	17.32	2,461	2	98	0	0	34	32.49	-17.14			Dec-15
1,000	2.91	21.21	14.02	25.94	57.58	1.97	0.51	12.24	0.96	17.31	2,461	2	98	0	0	34	32.49	-17.14			Oct-02
	2.87	21.10	13.84	25.35	56.37	1.83	0.66	12.27	0.96	17.32	2,461	2	98	0	0	34	32.37	-17.28			Sep-09
100	2.86	20.99	13.67	24.72	55.22	1.72	0.81	12.29	0.96	17.17	2,461	2	98	0	0	34	32.09	-17.24			Oct-02
	2.84	21.07	13.73	24.99	55.63	1.66	0.76	12.26	0.96	18.05	2,461	2	98	0	0	34	32.28	-17.25			Oct-02
	4.25	19.43	10.22	50.19	65.21	1.68	0.2	12.19	1	32.57	5,201	0	100	0	0	8	25.03	-16.26			Dec-15
1,000	4.28	19.49	10.34	50.58	65.78	1.79	0.05	12.19	1	32.61	5,201	0	100	0	0	8	25.03	-16.26			Oct-02
	4.21	19.38	10.09	49.49	63.74	1.56	0.3	12.16	1	32.39	5,201	0	100	0	0	8	24.77	-16.33			Oct-02
	2.05	17.85	-3.36	44.32	42.02	1.16	0.21	17.08	1	20.4	3,027	0	100	0	0	20	27.94	-25.08			Dec-15
1,000	2.10	17.89	-3.22	44.71	42.50	1.28	0.06	17.07	1	20.42	3,027	0	100	0	0	20	27.94	-25.08			Oct-02
	2.04	17.74	-3.47	43.65	40.74	1.04	0.31	17.1	1	20.5	3,027	0	100	0	0	20	27.79	-25.16			Oct-02
	3.76	19.32	8.93	49.38	55.44	1.44	0.22	12.36	0.98	19.57	4,522	1	99	0	0	29	23.79	-17.52			Dec-15
1,000	3.76	19.31	8.97	49.37	55.53	1.48	0.17	12.36	0.98	19.58	4,522	1	99	0	0	29	23.79	-17.52			Jul-99
	3.72	19.26	8.74	48.67	54.26	1.35	0.33	12.34	0.98	19.5	4,522	1	99	0	0	29	23.68	-17.57			Sep-09
100	3.69	19.19	8.63	48.09	53.39	1.37	0.45	12.32	0.98	17.39	4,522	1	99	0	0	29	23.54	-17.55			Mar-06
	3.70	19.24	8.66	48.26	53.55	1.22	0.42	12.35	0.98	19.89	4,522	1	99	0	0	29	23.61	-17.67			Oct-02
	4.25	14.80	1.93	30.71		2.15	0.49	11.28	1.01	10.78	183.3	3	97	0	0	16					Dec-15
1,000	4.35	14.80	1.98	30.87		2.2	0.4	11.31	1.01	10.78	183.3	3	97	0	0	16					Aug-15
	4.25	14.78	1.78	30.29		1.85	0.55	11.24	1	10.79	183.3	3	97	0	0	16					Aug-15
100	4.16	14.60	1.58	29.52		1.85	0.74	11.3	1.01	10.75	183.3	3	97	0	0	16					Aug-15
	4.26	14.72	1.71	29.84		1.96	0.65	11.23	1	10.75	183.3	3	97	0	0	16					Aug-15
	4.06	19.38	8.91	48.24		1.29	0.41	12.39	0.98	13.3	207.5	2	98	0	0	45					Dec-15
1,000	4.06	19.38	9.01	48.52		1.37	0.32	12.36	0.98	13.3	207.5	2	98	0	0	45					Aug-15
	4.05	19.33	8.84	48.04		1.24	0.47	12.38	0.98	13.33	207.5	2	98	0	0	45					Aug-15
100	4.00	19.13	8.61	47.01		1.1	0.64	12.36	0.98	13.26	207.5	2	98	0	0	45					Aug-15
	4.08	19.24	8.77	47.52		1.16	0.57	12.34	0.98	13.26	207.5	2	98	0	0	45					Aug-15
	4.18	21.99	1.45	36.21	22.02	0	1.74	14.7	0.98	8.21	26.2	8	92	0	0	85	31.59	-22.09	5.50		Oct-00
	4.08	21.65	0.89	33.16	17.63	0	2.49	14.74	0.98	6.63	26.2	8	92	0	0	85	31.1	-22.44		1.00	Feb-04
25,000	4.23	22.22	1.78	37.26	23.50	0	1.49	14.72	0.98	8.36	26.2	8	92	0	0	85	31.59	-22.09			Aug-13
	2.81	10.86	2.27	10.49	7.18	0	2.45	6.53	0.88	10.61	46.9	10	47	41	3	7	12.64	-10.75	5.50		Oct-00
	2.68	10.51	1.56	8.17	3.27	0	3.2	6.51	0.88	9.56	46.9	10	47	41	3	7	12.13	-11.01		1.00	Feb-04
	2.38	9.97	2.76	4.86	0.94	0.92	1.42	6.5	1.01	11.58	41.0	3	45	31	21	51	12.68	-7.08	5.50		Nov-09

	MARKET		FUND TYPE, CATEGORY & OBJECTIVE		RATINGS				MINIMUMS	
Fund Name	Ticker Symbol	Traded On	Fund Type	Category and (Prospectus Objective)	Overall Rating	Reward Rating	Risk Rating	Recent Up/ Downgrade	Open to New Investors	Min Initial Investment
Timothy Plan Defensive Strategies Fund Class C	TPDCX	NAS CM	Open End	Moderate Alloc (Growth)	C	C	C+		Y	1,000
Timothy Plan Defensive Strategies Fund Class I	TPDIX	NAS CM	Open End	Moderate Alloc (Growth)	C	C	B-		Y	100,000
Timothy Plan Emerging Markets Class A	TPEMX	NAS CM	Open End	Global Emerg Mkts (Div Emerging Mkts)	C	C	B-		Y	1,000
Timothy Plan Emerging Markets Class C	TPECX	NAS CM	Open End	Global Emerg Mkts (Div Emerging Mkts)	C	C-	C+		Y	1,000
Timothy Plan Emerging Markets Fund Class I	TIEMX	NAS CM	Open End	Global Emerg Mkts (Div Emerging Mkts)	C	C	B-		Y	100,000
Timothy Plan Growth & Income Fund Class A	TGIAX	NAS CM	Open End	Moderate Alloc (Growth & Income)	C-	D+	C	Up	Y	1,000
Timothy Plan Growth & Income Fund Class C	TGCIX	NAS CM	Open End	Moderate Alloc (Growth & Income)	D+	D+	C		Y	1,000
Timothy Plan Growth & Income Fund Class I	TIGIX	NAS CM	Open End	Moderate Alloc (Growth & Income)	C-	D+	C	Up	Y	100,000
Timothy Plan International Fund Class A	TPIAX	NAS CM	Open End	Global Equity Large Cap (Foreign Stock)	C	C-	C+	Up	Y	1,000
Timothy Plan International Fund Class C	TPICX	NAS CM	Open End	Global Equity Large Cap (Foreign Stock)	C	C-	C+	Up	Y	1,000
Timothy Plan International Fund Class I	TPIIX	NAS CM	Open End	Global Equity Large Cap (Foreign Stock)	C	C-	C+		Y	100,000
Timothy Plan Israel Common Values Fund Class A	TPAIX	NAS CM	Open End	Equity Miscellaneous (Growth)	B	B	B		Y	1,000
Timothy Plan Israel Common Values Fund Class C	TPCIX	NAS CM	Open End	Equity Miscellaneous (Growth)	B	B	B		Y	1,000
Timothy Plan Israel Common Values Fund Class I	TICIX	NAS CM	Open End	Equity Miscellaneous (Growth)	B	B	B		Y	100,000
Timothy Plan Large/Mid Cap Growth Fund Class A	TLGAX	NAS CM	Open End	US Equity Large Cap Growth (Growth)	C+	C	B-	Up	Y	1,000
Timothy Plan Large/Mid Cap Growth Fund Class C	TLGCX	NAS CM	Open End	US Equity Large Cap Growth (Growth)	C+	C	B-	Up	Y	1,000
Timothy Plan Large/Mid Cap Growth Fund Class I	TPLIX	NAS CM	Open End	US Equity Large Cap Growth (Growth)	C+	C	B-	Up	Y	100,000
Timothy Plan Large/Mid Cap Value Fund Class A	TLVAX	NAS CM	Open End	US Equity Mid Cap (Growth)	C+	C	B		Y	1,000
Timothy Plan Large/Mid Cap Value Fund Class C	TLVCX	NAS CM	Open End	US Equity Mid Cap (Growth)	C+	C	B		Y	1,000
Timothy Plan Large/Mid Cap Value Fund Class I	TMVIX	NAS CM	Open End	US Equity Mid Cap (Growth)	C+	C	B		Y	100,000
Timothy Plan Smal Cap Value Fund Class C	TSVCX	NAS CM	Open End	US Equity Small Cap (Small Company)	C	C	C+		Y	1,000
Timothy Plan Small Cap Value Fund Class A	TPLNX	NAS CM	Open End	US Equity Small Cap (Small Company)	C	C	C+		Y	1,000
Timothy Plan Small Cap Value Fund Class I	TPVIX	NAS CM	Open End	US Equity Small Cap (Small Company)	C	C	C+		Y	100,000
Timothy Plan Strategic Growth Fund Class A	TSGAX	NAS CM	Open End	Moderate Alloc (Growth)	C	C-	B		Y	1,000
Timothy Plan Strategic Growth Fund Class C	TSGCX	NAS CM	Open End	Moderate Alloc (Growth)	C	C-	B		Y	1,000
TOBAM Emerging Markets Fund Class I	TBMIX	NAS CM	Open End	Global Emerg Mkts (Div Emerging Mkts)	C-	D+	C	Up	Y	500,000
Tocqueville Fund	TOCQX	NAS CM	Open End	US Equity Large Cap Blend (Growth)	B-	C	B		Y	1,000
Tocqueville Gold Fund	TGLDX	NAS CM	Open End	Precious Metals Sector Equity (Precious Metals)	D	D	D+	Down	Y	1,000
Tocqueville Opportunity Fund	TOPPX	NAS CM	Open End	US Equity Mid Cap (Growth)	C	C+	C	Down	Y	1,000
Tocqueville Select Fund	TSELX	NAS CM	Open End	US Equity Small Cap (Growth & Income)	C-	D+	C+	Down	Y	1,000
Toews Tactical Defensive Alpha Fund	TTDAX	NAS CM	Open End	Long/Short Equity (Growth)	B-	C	B+	Up	Y	10,000
Toews Tactical Growth Allocation Fund	THGWX	NAS CM	Open End	Moderate Alloc (Growth)	C+	C	B	Up	Y	10,000
Toews Tactical Monument Fund	THLGX	NAS CM	Open End	Long/Short Equity (Growth)	B-	B-	B		Y	10,000
Toews Tactical Oceana Fund	THIDX	NAS CM	Open End	Long/Short Equity (Growth)	C	C-	B-		Y	10,000
Toews Tactical Opportunity Fund	THSMX	NAS CM	Open End	Long/Short Equity (Growth)	C	C	B-		Y	10,000
TOPS® Aggressive Growth ETF Portfolio Class 1			Open End	Aggressive Alloc (Aggr Growth)	C+	C	B	Up	Y	0
TOPS® Aggressive Growth ETF Portfolio Class 2			Open End	Aggressive Alloc (Aggr Growth)	C+	C	B	Up	Y	0
TOPS® Aggressive Growth ETF Portfolio Investor Class			Open End	Aggressive Alloc (Aggr Growth)	C+	C	B	Up	Y	0
TOPS® Aggressive Growth ETF Portfolio Service Class Shares			Open End	Aggressive Alloc (Aggr Growth)	C+	C	B		Y	0
TOPS® Balanced ETF Portfolio Class 1			Open End	Moderate Alloc (Balanced)	B-	C	A-	Up	Y	0
TOPS® Balanced ETF Portfolio Class 2			Open End	Moderate Alloc (Balanced)	B-	C	A-	Up	Y	0
TOPS® Balanced ETF Portfolio Investor Class			Open End	Moderate Alloc (Balanced)	B-	C	A-	Up	Y	0
TOPS® Balanced ETF Portfolio Service Class Shares			Open End	Moderate Alloc (Balanced)	B-	C	A-		Y	0
TOPS® Conservative ETF Portfolio Class 1			Open End	Cautious Alloc (Growth & Income)	B-	C	A-		Y	0
TOPS® Conservative ETF Portfolio Class 2			Open End	Cautious Alloc (Growth & Income)	B-	C	A-		Y	0
TOPS® Conservative ETF Portfolio Investor Class			Open End	Cautious Alloc (Growth & Income)	B-	C	A-		Y	0
TOPS® Conservative ETF Portfolio Service Class Shares			Open End	Cautious Alloc (Growth & Income)	B-	C	A-		Y	0
TOPS® Growth ETF Portfolio Class 1			Open End	Aggressive Alloc (Growth)	B-	C	B	Up	Y	0
TOPS® Growth ETF Portfolio Class 2			Open End	Aggressive Alloc (Growth)	B-	C	B	Up	Y	0
TOPS® Growth ETF Portfolio Investor Class			Open End	Aggressive Alloc (Growth)	B-	C	B	Up	Y	0
TOPS® Growth ETF Portfolio Service Class Shares			Open End	Aggressive Alloc (Growth)	B-	C	B		Y	0
TOPS® Managed Risk Balanced ETF Portfolio Class 1			Open End	Cautious Alloc (Balanced)	B-	C	B+	Up		0

★Expanded analysis of this fund is included in Section II.

	TOTAL RETURNS					PERFORMANCE				ASSETS		ASSET ALLOCATION & TURNOVER					BULL & BEAR		FEES		
Min Additional Investment	3-Month Total Return	6-Month Total Return	1-Year Total Return	3-Year Total Return	5-Year Total Return	Dividend Yield (TTM)	Expense Ratio	3-Yr Std Deviation	3-Year Beta	NAV	Total Assets (MIL)	%Cash	%Stocks	%Bonds	%Other	Turnover Ratio	Last Bull Market Total Return	Last Bear Market Total Return	Front End Fee (%)	Back End Fee (%)	Inception Date
	2.22	9.62	1.99	2.46	-2.88	0.16	2.17	6.45	1	11.05	41.0	3	45	31	21	51	12.09	-7.35		1.00	Nov-09
25,000	2.48	10.19	3.01	5.61	2.17	1.22	1.17	6.5	1.01	11.57	41.0	3	45	31	21	51	12.68	-7.08			Aug-13
	5.25	13.98	5.42	26.62	-9.95	0.74	2.62	13.02	0.8	9.21	23.5	11	87	0	2	12			5.50		Dec-12
	5.03	13.54	4.66	23.80	-13.27	0	3.37	13.05	0.81	8.97	23.5	11	87	0	2	12				1.00	Dec-12
25,000	5.22	14.04	5.59	27.64	-8.80	1	2.37	12.96	0.8	9.26	23.5	11	87	0	2	12					Aug-13
	2.39	8.04	-2.26	3.23	-2.30	0.28	1.71	7.61	0.72	10.4	30.3	37	26	37	0	56			5.50		Oct-13
	2.03	7.51	-3.10	0.90	-5.89	0	2.46	7.57	0.72	10.01	30.3	37	26	37	0	56				1.00	Oct-13
25,000	2.34	8.12	-2.05	3.95	-1.08	0.47	1.46	7.6	0.72	10.47	30.3	37	26	37	0	56					Oct-13
	3.23	15.17	-3.68	19.27	2.86	1.06	1.71	12.55	1.07	9.26	96.7	4	96	0	0	19	16.04	-27.17	5.50		May-07
	2.97	14.81	-4.39	16.74	-0.97	0.16	2.46	12.53	1.07	8.99	96.7	4	96	0	0	19	15.52	-27.38		1.00	May-07
25,000	3.34	15.42	-3.35	20.36	4.16	1.35	1.45	12.54	1.07	9.28	96.7	4	96	0	0	19	16.04	-27.17			Aug-13
	6.61	20.77	17.81	52.60	34.98	0	1.85	11.39		16.92	72.0	9	91	0	0	9			5.50		Oct-11
	6.39	20.28	16.87	49.18	29.98	0	2.6	11.35		16.13	72.0	9	91	0	0	9				1.00	Oct-11
25,000	6.63	20.86	18.08	53.63	36.68	0	1.7	11.36		17.03	72.0	9	91	0	0	9					Aug-13
	3.57	20.22	3.97	31.76	35.25	0	1.53	13.79	0.98	8.68	88.8	4	96	0	0	57	28.17	-20.07	5.50		Oct-00
	3.41	19.79	3.31	28.71	30.34	0	2.28	13.76	0.97	6.96	88.8	4	96	0	0	57	27.54	-20.19		1.00	Feb-04
25,000	3.63	20.27	4.25	32.72	37.05	0	1.28	13.76	0.97	8.84	88.8	4	96	0	0	57	28.17	-20.07			Aug-13
	4.89	19.23	6.46	33.99	38.12	0.28	1.46	12.29	0.97	18.66	216.3	4	96	0	0	24	22.59	-18.8	5.50		Jul-99
	4.70	18.75	5.65	31.04	33.02	0	2.21	12.32	0.97	14.69	216.3	4	96	0	0	24	22.05	-19.06		1.00	Feb-04
25,000	4.95	19.31	6.72	34.98	39.89	0.54	1.21	12.28	0.96	18.84	216.3	4	96	0	0	24	22.59	-18.8			Aug-13
	5.92	22.53	-2.81	38.31	33.62	0	2.25	17.09	0.97	11.8	149.9	3	97	0	0	58	32.51	-24.83		1.00	Feb-04
	6.20	23.07	-2.04	41.43	38.69	0	1.5	17.08	0.97	17.28	149.9	3	97	0	0	58	33.17	-24.65	5.50		Mar-94
25,000	6.29	23.29	-1.76	42.52	40.48	0	1.25	17.07	0.97	17.57	149.9	3	97	0	0	58	33.17	-24.65			Aug-13
	3.21	13.42	1.19	13.43	6.31	0	2.62	8.87	0.9	9.63	36.3	8	67	22	3	8	18.82	-19.3	5.50		Oct-00
	3.12	13.02	0.39	10.85	2.38	0	3.37	8.91	0.9	8.59	36.3	8	67	22	3	8	18.55	-20.38		1.00	Feb-04
100	0.00	7.86	-5.33			1.07	1.1			10.7	104.1	1	99	0	0	33					Apr-17
100	4.56	18.64	10.66	43.18	43.87	0.86	1.25	12.07	0.96	36.66	280.5	0	100	0	0	19	21.17	-18.2			Jan-87
100	11.42	19.15	5.99	-14.37	-17.90	0	1.43	22.91	0.08	36.27	982.2	3	83	0	14	9	-7.82	-17.44			Jun-98
100	9.31	39.72	12.48	82.94	78.68	0	1.27	20.92	1.13	29.58	100.1	0	100	0	0	151	30.48	-21.27			Aug-94
100	-0.17	14.42	-6.38	16.36	-4.08	0	1.26	18.58	1.12	11.58	38.0	4	96	0	0	27	27.28	-27.47			Sep-08
100	5.66	17.76	8.61	31.32		0.37	1.28	9.89	0.75	11.93	118.9	11	0	89	0	933					Jan-16
100	3.26	10.35	6.54	17.43	3.41	1.09	1.38	6.27	0.36	10.76	18.4	18	0	81	0	749	0.08	-12.82			Aug-10
100	4.08	14.09	15.38	31.70	14.37	0.23	1.29	8.65	0.5	11.98	30.6	20	0	79	0	752	7.1	-13.79			Jun-10
100	3.63	10.94	1.83	16.51	0.06	0.95	1.29	7.62	0.52	9.12	31.5	19	0	80	0	761	-16.42	-11.31			Jun-10
100	3.18	10.32	5.70	11.31	-9.54	0.21	1.29	8.71	0.33	10.04	42.3	20	0	80	0	756	7.13	-19.08			Jun-10
	2.69	16.08	3.40	38.38	37.32	1.05	0.32	11.76	0.94	14.87	19.4	3	97	0	0	39	21.82	-22.13			Apr-11
	2.65	15.93	3.13	37.32	35.52	0.92	0.57	11.74	0.94	14.7	19.4	3	97	0	0	39	21.57	-22.13			Apr-11
	2.40	15.06	2.38	35.72	30.74	0.86	0.82	11.6	0.92	15.83	19.4	3	97	0	0	39	21.39	-22.21			Jul-15
	2.52	15.22	2.92	38.97	34.69		0.62	11.74	0.94	14.7	19.4	3	97	0	0	39	21.57	-22.13			Apr-19
	2.49	10.79	5.05	20.74	21.90	1.27	0.35	6.26	0.48	12.73	22.0	4	49	46	0	45	14.09	-10.7			Apr-11
	2.42	10.64	4.73	19.81	20.04	1.17	0.6	6.28	0.48	12.27	22.0	4	49	46	0	45	13.98	-10.7			Apr-11
	2.27	10.14	4.35	19.39	17.86	1.1	0.85	6.2	0.48	13.08	22.0	4	49	46	0	45	13.81	-10.79			Jul-15
	2.34	10.27	4.64	20.63	19.65		0.65	6.28	0.48	12.27	22.0	4	49	46	0	45	13.98	-10.7			Apr-19
	2.35	8.17	5.21	15.51	15.97	1.42	0.37	3.89	0.29	12.17	12.3	5	30	65	0	47	10.44	-5.85			Apr-11
	2.28	8.05	4.96	14.57	14.49	1.25	0.62	3.91	0.3	12.08	12.3	5	30	65	0	47	10.34	-5.95			Apr-11
	1.88	7.52	4.72	14.57	13.41	1.21	0.87	3.87	0.29	12.47	12.3	5	30	65	0	47	10.18	-6.05			Jul-15
	2.11	7.78	4.88	15.02	14.21		0.67	3.91	0.3	12.08	12.3	5	30	65	0	47	10.34	-5.95			Apr-19
	2.77	14.82	3.96	33.77	31.31	1.29	0.34	10.28	0.81	15.18	31.2	3	84	13	0	43	20.22	-13.04			Apr-11
	2.68	14.70	3.73	32.80	29.75	1.17	0.59	10.28	0.81	14.9	31.2	3	84	13	0	43	20.11	-13.53			Apr-11
	2.47	13.84	3.23	31.63	25.73	1.08	0.84	10.05	0.79	16.21	31.2	3	84	13	0	43	19.93	-13.62			Jul-15
	2.49	14.01	3.51	34.25	28.96		0.64	10.28	0.81	14.9	31.2	3	84	13	0	43	20.11	-13.53			Apr-19
	2.54	9.55	4.26	18.22	15.16	1.93	0.53	5.93	0.45	11.69	519.3	14	45	42	0	48	7.76				Jun-11

	MARKET		FUND TYPE, CATEGORY & OBJECTIVE		RATINGS				MINIMUMS	
Fund Name	Ticker Symbol	Traded On	Fund Type	Category and (Prospectus Objective)	Overall Rating	Reward Rating	Risk Rating	Recent Up/ Downgrade	Open to New Investors	Min Initial Investment
TOPS® Managed Risk Balanced ETF Portfolio Class 2			Open End	Cautious Alloc (Balanced)	B-	C	B+	Up	Y	0
TOPS® Managed Risk Balanced ETF Portfolio Class 3			Open End	Cautious Alloc (Balanced)	B-	C	B+	Up	Y	0
TOPS® Managed Risk Balanced ETF Portfolio Class 4			Open End	Cautious Alloc (Balanced)	B-	C	B+	Up	Y	0
TOPS® Managed Risk Balanced ETF Portfolio Investor Class			Open End	Cautious Alloc (Balanced)	B-	C	B+	Up	Y	0
TOPS® Managed Risk Flex ETF Portfolio			Open End	Cautious Alloc (Growth & Income)	B-	C	B+	Up	Y	0
TOPS® Managed Risk Growth ETF Portfolio Class 1			Open End	Aggressive Alloc (Growth)	B-	C	B+	Up		0
TOPS® Managed Risk Growth ETF Portfolio Class 2			Open End	Aggressive Alloc (Growth)	B-	C	B+	Up	Y	0
TOPS® Managed Risk Growth ETF Portfolio Class 3 Shares			Open End	Aggressive Alloc (Growth)	B-	C	B+	Up	Y	0
TOPS® Managed Risk Growth ETF Portfolio Class 4 Shares			Open End	Aggressive Alloc (Growth)	C+	C	B+	Up	Y	0
TOPS® Managed Risk Growth ETF Portfolio Investor Class			Open End	Aggressive Alloc (Growth)	B-	C	B+	Up	Y	0
TOPS® Managed Risk Moderate Growth ETF Portfolio Class 1			Open End	Moderate Alloc (Growth)	B-	C	B+	Up		0
TOPS® Managed Risk Moderate Growth ETF Portfolio Class 2			Open End	Moderate Alloc (Growth)	B-	C	B+	Up	Y	0
TOPS® Managed Risk Moderate Growth ETF Port Cls 3 Shares			Open End	Moderate Alloc (Growth)	B-	C	B+	Up	Y	0
TOPS® Managed Risk Moderate Growth ETF Port Cls 4 Shares			Open End	Moderate Alloc (Growth)	B-	C	B+	Up	Y	0
TOPS® Managed Risk Moderate Growth ETF Portfolio Inv Cls			Open End	Moderate Alloc (Growth)	B-	C	B+	Up	Y	0
TOPS® Moderate Growth ETF Portfolio Class 1			Open End	Moderate Alloc (Growth)	B-	C	A-	Up	Y	0
TOPS® Moderate Growth ETF Portfolio Class 2			Open End	Moderate Alloc (Growth)	B-	C	A-	Up	Y	0
TOPS® Moderate Growth ETF Portfolio Investor Class			Open End	Moderate Alloc (Growth)	B-	C	A-	Up	Y	0
TOPS® Moderate Growth ETF Portfolio Service Class Shares			Open End	Moderate Alloc (Growth)	B-	C	A-		Y	0
Toreador Core Fund Institutional Class	TORZX	NAS CM	Open End	US Equity Large Cap Value (Growth)	C+	C	B	Up	Y	10,000
Toreador Core Fund Investor Class	TORLX	NAS CM	Open End	US Equity Large Cap Value (Growth)	C+	C	B	Up	Y	1,000
Toreador Explorer Fund Institutional Shares	TMRZX	NAS CM	Open End	US Equity Small Cap (Growth)	C	C-	C		Y	10,000
Toreador Explorer Fund Investor Shares	TMRLX	NAS CM	Open End	US Equity Small Cap (Growth)	C-	C-	C	Down	Y	1,000
Toreador International Fund Class Institutional	TMRIX	NAS CM	Open End	Global Equity Large Cap (Growth)	C-	D+	C		Y	100,000
Toreador International Fund Investor Class	TMRFX	NAS CM	Open End	Global Equity Large Cap (Growth)	C-	D+	C		Y	2,500
Toreador Select Fund Institutional Class Shares	TOSZX	NAS CM	Open End	US Equity Large Cap Blend (Growth)	C	C	B		Y	10,000
Toreador Select Fund Investor Class Shares	TOSLX	NAS CM	Open End	US Equity Large Cap Blend (Growth)	C	C	B		Y	1,000
Torray Fund	TORYX	NAS CM	Open End	US Equity Large Cap Value (Growth)	B-	C	B	Up	Y	2,000
TorrayResolute Small/Mid Cap Growth Fund Investor Class	TRSDX	NAS CM	Open End	US Equity Mid Cap (Growth)	C+	C	B-	Down	Y	1,000
Tortoise Energy Independence Fund, Inc	NDP	NYSE	Closed End	Energy Sector Equity (Growth & Income)	D	D-	D		Y	
Tortoise Energy Infrastructure Corporation	TYG	NYSE	Closed End	Energy Sector Equity (Natl Res)	C-	C-	C	Down	Y	
Tortoise Essential Assets Income Term	TEAF	NYSE	Closed End	Equity Miscellaneous (Income)	U	U	U		Y	
Tortoise Midstream Energy Fund	NTG	NYSE	Closed End	Energy Sector Equity (Natl Res)	C-	D+	C-	Down	Y	
Tortoise MLP & Pipeline Fund A Class	TORTX	NAS CM	Open End	Energy Sector Equity ()	C	C	C+	Down	Y	2,500
Tortoise MLP & Pipeline Fund C Class Shares	TORCX	NAS CM	Open End	Energy Sector Equity ()	C	C	C+	Down	Y	2,500
Tortoise MLP & Pipeline Fund lInstitutional Class	TORIX	NAS CM	Open End	Energy Sector Equity ()	C	C	C+	Down	Y	1,000,000
Tortoise Pipeline & Energy Fund	TTP	NYSE	Closed End	Energy Sector Equity (Natl Res)	D+	D+	D+	Down	Y	
Tortoise Power and Energy Infrastructure Fund	TPZ	NYSE	Closed End	Energy Sector Equity (Natl Res)	C-	C-	C-	Down	Y	
Tortoise Select Opportunity Fund A Class	TOPTX	NAS CM	Open End	Energy Sector Equity (Growth & Income)	D	D	D	Down	Y	2,500
Tortoise Select Opportunity Fund C Class	TOPCX	NAS CM	Open End	Energy Sector Equity (Growth & Income)	D	D	D	Down	Y	2,500
Tortoise Select Opportunity Fund Institutional Class	TOPIX	NAS CM	Open End	Energy Sector Equity (Growth & Income)	D	D	D	Down	Y	1,000,000
Touchstone Anti-Benchmark® International Core Equity Cls Y	TYBAX	NAS CM	Open End	Global Equity Large Cap (Growth)	U	U	U		Y	2,500
Touchstone Anti-Benchmark® Intl Core Equity Inst Cls	TIABX	NAS CM	Open End	Global Equity Large Cap (Growth)	U	U	U		Y	500,000
Touchstone Anti-Benchmark® US Core Equity Fund Class Y	TABYX	NAS CM	Open End	US Equity Large Cap Blend (Growth)	U	U	U		Y	2,500
Touchstone Anti-Benchmark® US Core Equity Inst Cls	TABOX	NAS CM	Open End	US Equity Large Cap Blend (Growth)	U	U	U		Y	500,000
Touchstone Balanced Fund Class A	SEBLX	NAS CM	Open End	Moderate Alloc (Balanced)	B	C+	A-		Y	2,500
Touchstone Balanced Fund Class Y	SIBLX	NAS CM	Open End	Moderate Alloc (Balanced)	B	C+	A-		Y	2,500
Touchstone Credit Opportunities II Fund Class A	TMARX	NAS CM	Open End	Market Neutral (Growth)	C	C	B-		Y	2,500
Touchstone Credit Opportunities II Fund Class Y	TMAYX	NAS CM	Open End	Market Neutral (Growth)	C	C	B-		Y	2,500
Touchstone Credit Opportunities II Fund Institutional	TARBX	NAS CM	Open End	Market Neutral (Growth)	C	C	B-		Y	500,000
Touchstone Dynamic Diversified Income Fund A	TBAAX	NAS CM	Open End	Cautious Alloc (Income)	B-	C	B+		Y	2,500
Touchstone Dynamic Diversified Income Fund Y	TBAYX	NAS CM	Open End	Cautious Alloc (Income)	B-	C	A-		Y	2,500

★ Expanded analysis of this fund is included in Section II.

	TOTAL RETURNS					PERFORMANCE				ASSETS		ASSET ALLOCATION & TURNOVER					BULL & BEAR		FEES		
Min Additional Investment	3-Month Total Return	6-Month Total Return	1-Year Total Return	3-Year Total Return	5-Year Total Return	Dividend Yield (TTM)	Expense Ratio	3-Yr Std Deviation	3-Year Beta	NAV	Total Assets (MIL)	%Cash	%Stocks	%Bonds	%Other	Turnover Ratio	Last Bull Market Total Return	Last Bear Market Total Return	Front End Fee (%)	Back End Fee (%)	Inception Date
	2.47	9.42	3.98	17.25	13.68	1.66	0.78	5.97	0.46	11.61	519.3	14	45	42	0	48	7.55				Jun-11
	2.29	8.91	3.70	17.10	12.71	1.59	0.88	5.92	0.45	11.65	519.3	14	45	42	0	48	7.49				May-12
	2.33	8.89	3.51	16.33	11.42	1.3	1.13	5.92	0.45	11.43	519.3	14	45	42	0	48	7.33				May-12
	2.24	8.45	3.55	16.54	11.90	1.57	1.03	5.62	0.43	12.36	519.3	14	45	42	0	48	7.4				Jul-15
	2.43	9.36	3.59	17.50	11.68	1.15	0.98	6.22	0.48	11.8	144.3	13	49	37	0	44					Aug-13
	2.77	10.95	3.25	25.49	12.16	1.79	0.53	8.79	0.67	11.85	854.7	13	76	11	0	50	7.7	-8.62			Apr-11
	2.70	10.72	2.97	24.46	10.67	1.53	0.78	8.83	0.67	11.77	854.7	13	76	11	0	50	7.59	-8.62			Apr-11
	2.55	10.11	2.70	24.16	9.52	1.46	0.88	8.87	0.68	11.71	854.7	13	76	11	0	50	7.48	-8.75			May-12
	2.44	9.95	2.44	23.22	8.19	0.83	1.13	8.82	0.67	11.77	854.7	13	76	11	0	50	7.32	-8.85			May-12
	2.41	9.63	2.64	23.61	9.05	1.46	1.03	8.43	0.64	12.35	854.7	13	76	11	0	50	7.38	-8.81			Jul-15
	2.62	10.46	3.67	22.98	15.16	1.88	0.53	7.46	0.58	12.14	868.6	13	58	29	0	38	8.15				Jun-11
	2.54	10.32	3.38	21.97	13.68	1.62	0.78	7.46	0.58	12.07	868.6	13	58	29	0	38	8.03				Jun-11
	2.39	9.71	3.05	21.77	12.58	1.56	0.88	7.47	0.58	12.03	868.6	13	58	29	0	38	7.93				May-12
	2.31	9.66	2.82	20.94	11.25	1.27	1.13	7.42	0.57	11.96	868.6	13	58	29	0	38	7.77				May-12
	2.23	9.20	2.99	21.09	11.82	1.53	1.03	7.01	0.54	12.86	868.6	13	58	29	0	38	7.83				Jul-15
	2.62	12.72	4.64	27.26	26.89	1.34	0.34	8.08	0.64	12.49	33.4	4	64	32	0	33	16.08	-15.04			Apr-11
	2.55	12.53	4.39	26.35	25.14	1.24	0.59	8.12	0.64	12.03	33.4	4	64	32	0	33	15.96	-15.04			Apr-11
	2.24	11.85	4.46	25.53	21.77	1.13	0.84	7.78	0.61	13.27	33.4	4	64	32	0	33	15.79	-15.13			Jul-15
	2.48	12.06	4.30	27.45	24.62		0.64	8.13	0.64	12.04	33.4	4	64	32	0	33	15.96	-15.05			Apr-19
100	3.97	17.45	2.86	55.41	52.01	0.49	0.95	13.65	1.04	14.13	81.7	1	99	0	0	75	21.73	-19.02			Sep-09
100	3.91	17.33	2.66	54.32	50.14	0.39	1.2	13.66	1.04	14.08	81.7	1	99	0	0	75	21.58	-19.12			Jun-06
100	1.13	13.87	-6.22	39.63		0.18	0.83	17.73	1.01	10.67	20.8	8	92	0	0	83					Jun-15
100	0.95	13.53	-6.56	38.31		0	1.08	17.69	1.01	10.57	20.8	8	92	0	0	83					Jun-15
10,000	0.34	12.03	-6.17	17.38	-2.55	2.53	0.84	11.26	0.99	17.6	17.1	0	97	0	3	66	6.25	-31.72			Dec-12
100	0.30	11.92	-6.42	16.41	-3.81	2.61	1.09	11.28	0.99	16.42	17.1	0	97	0	3	66	6.25	-31.72			Dec-12
100	4.07	20.24	8.44			0.46	0.75			12.77	83.9	1	99	0	0	212					Feb-17
100	4.08	20.09	8.32			0.49	1			12.73	83.9	1	99	0	0	212					Feb-17
500	4.33	15.79	6.40	26.24	35.48	1.43	1.08	11.47	0.89	49.58	411.7	12	88	0	0	4	17.75	-12.28			Dec-90
100	8.65	23.74	6.72	41.93		0	1.26	14.47	0.82	13.81	7.6	3	97	0	0	30					Dec-14
	-16.89	-2.02	-38.89	-39.43	-63.66	7.14		26.67	1.14	6.13	90.5	5	93	0	0	144					Jul-12
	-1.96	19.35	0.52	3.78	-31.55	2.81	2.13	22.07	1.14	23.35	1,252	-13	148	-31	-12	18	19.7	-10.72			Feb-04
	-2.55						2.01			19.31	260.5										Mar-19
	-2.32	20.01	-0.02	-0.19	-27.80	2.94	3.66	20.89		14.37	908.3	-15	149	-34	-7	14	14.26	-10.72			Jul-10
100	-0.45	22.37	0.97	13.12	-17.25	3.73	1.18	16.79	0.9	12.96	4,147	0	100	0	0	14	26.23		5.75		May-11
100	-0.60	21.95	0.23	10.83	-20.12	2.95	1.93	16.75	0.9	12.88	4,147	0	100	0	0	14	25.72			1.00	Sep-12
100	-0.42	22.51	1.24	14.08	-16.07	3.95	0.96	16.81	0.9	13.06	4,147	0	100	0	0	14	26.45				May-11
	-4.51	22.45	-6.77	-4.00	-40.30	0	2.57	22.72		16.15	161.8	0	96	0	0	14					Oct-11
	-1.26	13.66	4.10	9.96	-6.14	4.37	1.51	11.93		20.3	141.1	0	58	64	-34	31	14.66	-6.4			Jul-09
100	-1.22	13.46	-16.85	-8.05	-34.52	0	1.35	20.8	1.16	8.09	25.0	1	99	0	0	100			5.75		Sep-13
100	-1.39	13.06	-17.39	-10.15	-36.85	0	2.1	20.79	1.16	7.79	25.0	1	99	0	0	100				1.00	Sep-13
100	-1.09	13.66	-16.58	-7.31	-33.59	0	1.1	20.83	1.16	8.15	25.0	1	99	0	0	100					Sep-13
50	0.00	6.77					0.69			10.08	36.5	26	74	0	0						Nov-18
50	0.00	6.77					0.59			10.08	36.5	26	74	0	0						Nov-18
50	3.86	16.03					0.54			10.49	26.4	1	99	0	0						Nov-18
50	3.86	16.04					0.44			10.49	26.4	1	99	0	0						Nov-18
50	4.27	14.68	10.12	34.76	41.39	1.46	1.02	7.7	0.63	22.18	338.5	2	67	31	0		18.14	-11.36	5.00		Nov-38
50	4.31	14.80	10.32	35.59	42.83	1.66	0.82	7.69	0.62	22.01	338.5	2	67	31	0		18.16	-11.32			Aug-07
50	1.44	5.94	2.06	4.53	10.14	1.56	1.14	3.25	18.4	9.8	57.0	5	88	3	0	254			5.00		Sep-13
50	1.43	5.98	2.29	5.47	11.78	2.07	0.89	3.29	18.99	9.91	57.0	5	88	3	0	254					Sep-13
50	1.52	6.17	2.48	5.86	12.44	2.15	0.79	3.26	19.6	9.97	57.0	5	88	3	0	254					Sep-13
50	2.50	10.05	5.62	16.42	18.93	4.15	1.22	5.34	0.34	13.03	75.0	5	28	57	7	20	14.22	-11.21	5.00		Sep-04
50	2.47	10.06	5.78	17.25	20.38	4.38	0.97	5.3	0.34	13.05	75.0	5	28	57	7	20	14.34	-11.07			Dec-05

	MARKET			FUND TYPE, CATEGORY & OBJECTIVE	RATINGS				MINIMUMS	
Fund Name	Ticker Symbol	Traded On	Fund Type	Category and (Prospectus Objective)	Overall Rating	Reward Rating	Risk Rating	Recent Up/ Downgrade	Open to New Investors	Min Initial Investment
Touchstone Dynamic Equity Fund Class A	TDEAX	NAS CM	Open End	Long/Short Equity (Growth)	C	C-	C	Up	Y	2,500
Touchstone Dynamic Equity Fund Class Y	TDEYX	NAS CM	Open End	Long/Short Equity (Growth)	C	C-	C	Up	Y	2,500
Touchstone Dynamic Equity Fund Institutional Class	TDELX	NAS CM	Open End	Long/Short Equity (Growth)	C	C-	C	Up	Y	500,000
Touchstone Dynamic Global Allocation Fund A	TSMAX	NAS CM	Open End	Moderate Alloc (Growth)	B-	C	B+	Up	Y	2,500
Touchstone Dynamic Global Allocation Fund Y	TSMYX	NAS CM	Open End	Moderate Alloc (Growth)	B-	C	B+	Up	Y	2,500
Touchstone Focused Fund Class A	TFOAX	NAS CM	Open End	US Equity Large Cap Blend (Growth)	C+	C	B		Y	2,500
Touchstone Focused Fund Class Y	TFFYX	NAS CM	Open End	US Equity Large Cap Blend (Growth)	C+	C	B		Y	2,500
Touchstone Focused Fund Institutional	TFFIX	NAS CM	Open End	US Equity Large Cap Blend (Growth)	C+	C	B		Y	500,000
Touchstone Growth Opportunities Fund Class A	TGVFX	NAS CM	Open End	US Equity Large Cap Growth (Growth)	C+	C+	B	Down	Y	2,500
Touchstone Growth Opportunities Fund Class Y	TGVYX	NAS CM	Open End	US Equity Large Cap Growth (Growth)	B-	C+	B	Down	Y	2,500
Touchstone Growth Opportunities Fund Institutional Class	TGVVX	NAS CM	Open End	US Equity Large Cap Growth (Growth)	B-	C+	B	Down	Y	500,000
Touchstone International Equity Fund Class A	SWRLX	NAS CM	Open End	Global Equity Large Cap (Foreign Stock)	C	C-	B-		Y	2,500
Touchstone International Equity Fund Class Y	SIIEX	NAS CM	Open End	Global Equity Large Cap (Foreign Stock)	C	C-	B-		Y	2,500
Touchstone International Equity Fund Institutional USD	TOIIX	NAS CM	Open End	Global Equity Large Cap (Foreign Stock)	C	C-	B-		Y	500,000
Touchstone International Growth Opportunities Fund Class A	TGGAX	NAS CM	Open End	Global Equity Large Cap (Growth)	C	C	C		Y	2,500
Touchstone International Growth Opportunities Fund Class Y	TYGGX	NAS CM	Open End	Global Equity Large Cap (Growth)	C	C	C		Y	2,500
Touchstone Intl Growth Opp Inst Cls	DSMGX	NAS CM	Open End	Global Equity Large Cap (Growth)	C	C	C		Y	500,000
Touchstone International Small Cap Fund Class A	TNSAX	NAS CM	Open End	Global Equity Mid/Small Cap (Small Company)	C-	C-	C	Up	Y	2,500
Touchstone International Small Cap Fund Class Y	TNSYX	NAS CM	Open End	Global Equity Mid/Small Cap (Small Company)	C-	C-	C	Up	Y	2,500
Touchstone International Small Cap Fund Institutional	TNSIX	NAS CM	Open End	Global Equity Mid/Small Cap (Small Company)	C-	C-	C	Up	Y	500,000
Touchstone Large Cap Focused Fund Class A	SENCX	NAS CM	Open End	US Equity Large Cap Blend (Growth & Income)	B-	C	B+	Down	Y	2,500
Touchstone Large Cap Focused Fund Class Y	SICWX	NAS CM	Open End	US Equity Large Cap Blend (Growth & Income)	B-	C+	B+	Down	Y	2,500
Touchstone Large Cap Focused Fund Institutional Class	SCRLX	NAS CM	Open End	US Equity Large Cap Blend (Growth & Income)	B-	C+	B+	Down	Y	500,000
Touchstone Large Cap Fund Class A	TACLX	NAS CM	Open End	US Equity Large Cap Blend (Growth)	B-	C	B		Y	2,500
Touchstone Large Cap Fund Class Y	TLCYX	NAS CM	Open End	US Equity Large Cap Blend (Growth)	B-	C	B		Y	2,500
Touchstone Large Cap Fund Institutional Class	TLCIX	NAS CM	Open End	US Equity Large Cap Blend (Growth)	B-	C	B		Y	500,000
Touchstone Large Company Growth Fund Class A	TSAGX	NAS CM	Open End	US Equity Large Cap Growth (Growth)	C+	C	B	Down	Y	2,500
Touchstone Large Company Growth Fund Class Institutional	DSMLX	NAS CM	Open End	US Equity Large Cap Growth (Growth)	B-	C+	B	Down	Y	500,000
Touchstone Large Company Growth Fund Class Y	TLGYX	NAS CM	Open End	US Equity Large Cap Growth (Growth)	B-	C+	B	Down	Y	2,500
Touchstone Mid Cap Fund Class A	TMAPX	NAS CM	Open End	US Equity Mid Cap (Growth)	B-	B-	B		Y	2,500
Touchstone Mid Cap Fund Class Y	TMCPX	NAS CM	Open End	US Equity Mid Cap (Growth)	B	B-	B	Up	Y	2,500
Touchstone Mid Cap Fund Class Z	TMCTX	NAS CM	Open End	US Equity Mid Cap (Growth)	B	B-	B	Up	Y	2,500
Touchstone Mid Cap Fund Institutional	TMPIX	NAS CM	Open End	US Equity Mid Cap (Growth)	B	B-	B	Up	Y	500,000
Touchstone Mid Cap Growth Fund Class A	TEGAX	NAS CM	Open End	US Equity Mid Cap (Growth)	B-	B-	B	Down	Y	2,500
Touchstone Mid Cap Growth Fund Class Y	TEGYX	NAS CM	Open End	US Equity Mid Cap (Growth)	B-	B-	B	Down	Y	2,500
Touchstone Mid Cap Growth Fund Institutional Class	TEGIX	NAS CM	Open End	US Equity Mid Cap (Growth)	B-	B-	B	Down	Y	500,000
Touchstone Mid Cap Value Class A	TCVAX	NAS CM	Open End	US Equity Mid Cap (Growth)	C	C	B-		Y	2,500
Touchstone Mid Cap Value Fund Class Y	TCVYX	NAS CM	Open End	US Equity Mid Cap (Growth)	C	C	B-		Y	2,500
Touchstone Mid Cap Value Institutional Class	TCVIX	NAS CM	Open End	US Equity Mid Cap (Growth)	C+	C	B-	Up	Y	500,000
Touchstone Premium Yield Equity Fund Class A	TPYAX	NAS CM	Open End	US Equity Large Cap Value (Growth & Income)	C+	C	B		Y	2,500
Touchstone Premium Yield Equity Fund Class Y	TPYYX	NAS CM	Open End	US Equity Large Cap Value (Growth & Income)	C+	C	B		Y	2,500
Touchstone Sands Capital Emerging Markets Growth Cls A	TSMGX	NAS CM	Open End	Global Emerg Mkts (Growth)	C	C	C		Y	2,500
Touchstone Sands Capital Emerging Markets Growth Cls Y	TSEMX	NAS CM	Open End	Global Emerg Mkts (Growth)	C	C	C		Y	2,500
Touchstone Sands Capital Emerging Mkts Growth Inst Cls	TSEGX	NAS CM	Open End	Global Emerg Mkts (Growth)	C	C	C		Y	500,000
Touchstone Sands Capital Institutional Growth Fund	CISGX	NAS CM	Open End	US Equity Large Cap Growth (Growth)	C+	C+	B-	Down		500,000
Touchstone Sands Capital Select Growth Fund Class A	TSNAX	NAS CM	Open End	US Equity Large Cap Growth (Growth)	C+	C+	B-	Down		2,500
Touchstone Sands Capital Select Growth Fund Class Y	CFSIX	NAS CM	Open End	US Equity Large Cap Growth (Growth)	C+	C+	B-	Down		2,500
Touchstone Sands Capital Select Growth Fund Class Z	PTSGX	NAS CM	Open End	US Equity Large Cap Growth (Growth)	C+	C+	B-	Down		2,500
Touchstone Small Cap Class A	TSFAX	NAS CM	Open End	US Equity Small Cap (Small Company)	C+	C	B-			2,500
Touchstone Small Cap Class Y	TSFYX	NAS CM	Open End	US Equity Small Cap (Small Company)	C+	C	B-			2,500
Touchstone Small Cap Institutional Class	TSFIX	NAS CM	Open End	US Equity Small Cap (Small Company)	C+	C	B-			500,000
Touchstone Small Cap Value Fund Class A	TVOAX	NAS CM	Open End	US Equity Small Cap (Small Company)	C	C-	C		Y	2,500

★ Expanded analysis of this fund is included in Section II.

Min Additional Investment	TOTAL RETURNS: 3-Month Total Return	6-Month Total Return	1-Year Total Return	3-Year Total Return	5-Year Total Return	PERFORMANCE: Dividend Yield (TTM)	Expense Ratio	3-Yr Std Deviation	3-Year Beta	ASSETS: NAV	Total Assets (MIL)	ASSET ALLOCATION & TURNOVER: %Cash	%Stocks	%Bonds	%Other	Turnover Ratio	BULL & BEAR: Last Bull Market Total Return	Last Bear Market Total Return	FEES: Front End Fee (%)	Back End Fee (%)	Inception Date
50	2.29	9.33	-2.80	8.44	16.56	0	2.3	7.88	0.59	15.57	44.1	9	91	0	0	267	17.13	-9.85	5.00		Mar-05
50	2.34	9.45	-2.54	9.45	18.51	0.96	1.95	7.88	0.59	15.74	44.1	9	91	0	0	267	17.3	-9.73			Jun-78
50	2.39	9.48	-2.50	9.48	18.49	0.92	1.96	7.87	0.59	15.81	44.1	9	91	0	0	267	17.31	-9.72			Dec-05
50	2.66	12.14	2.89	21.10	16.42	2.11	1.21	7.54	0.65	11.78	87.4	4	59	37	0	40	18.04	-15.31	5.00		Sep-04
50	2.78	12.35	3.11	22.00	17.89	2.31	0.96	7.54	0.65	11.9	87.4	4	59	37	0	40	18.3	-15.25			Dec-05
50	2.15	15.93	4.30	31.38	40.48	0.03	1.2	13.23	1.04	43.59	971.2	0	100	0	0	12	26.39	-18.51	5.00		Sep-03
50	2.22	16.09	4.59	32.53	42.48	0.58	0.91	13.22	1.04	44.07	971.2	0	100	0	0	12	26.65	-18.48			Feb-99
50	2.24	16.13	4.68	32.82	43.13	0.65	0.83	13.23	1.04	44.26	971.2	0	100	0	0	12	26.71	-18.43			Dec-06
50	5.19	25.76	11.41	63.04	58.92	0	1.24	13.83	1	34.41	132.3	1	99	0	0	94	26.53	-23.09	5.00		Sep-95
50	5.29	25.91	11.72	64.28	60.94	0	0.99	13.83	1	35.57	132.3	1	99	0	0	94	26.68	-23.02			Feb-09
50	5.28	25.97	11.82	64.78	61.68	0.07	0.89	13.83	1	36.03	132.3	1	99	0	0	94	26.78	-22.98			Feb-09
50	1.75	12.34	-0.78	21.22	14.48	1.49	1.31	12.27	1.01	15.65	155.4	9	91	0	0		15.61	-24.11	5.00		Mar-93
50	1.84	12.53	-0.47	22.33	16.51	1.74	1	12.24	1.01	15.44	155.4	9	91	0	0		15.99	-24.01			Aug-07
50	1.91	12.63	-0.38	21.98	15.20	1.86	0.9	12.23	1.01	15.42	155.4	9	91	0	0		15.61	-24.11			Oct-17
50	3.55	23.92	-1.78	47.62	51.43	0	1.24	16.69	1.3	21.29	34.7	0	100	0	0	109			5.00		Aug-16
50	3.63	24.07	-1.52	48.47	53.07	0.09	0.99	16.68	1.3	21.39	34.7	0	100	0	0	109					Aug-16
50	3.57	24.11	-1.45	49.04	53.66	0.18	0.89	16.68	1.3	21.46	34.7	0	100	0	0	109					Mar-12
50	4.42	17.22	-7.42	14.99	11.87	1.14	1.56	13.54	1.06	15.11	201.5	1	99	0	0	94	18.86	-21.29	5.00		Jul-03
50	4.46	17.40	-7.16	15.82	13.29	1.41	1.31	13.53	1.06	15.45	201.5	1	99	0	0	94	18.91	-21.23			Dec-96
50	4.50	17.46	-7.10	16.21	13.96	1.46	1.19	13.56	1.06	15.54	201.5	1	99	0	0	94	19.18	-21.13			Dec-06
50	3.95	18.43	10.51	53.35	65.50	0.56	1.03	11.72	0.96	43.37	1,732	2	98	0	0		24.14	-16.97	5.00		Jan-34
50	4.04	18.59	10.80	54.52	67.73	0.78	0.75	11.72	0.96	43.24	1,732	2	98	0	0		24.35	-16.83			May-07
50	4.06	18.62	10.87	54.91	68.09	0.84	0.68	11.71	0.96	43.31	1,732	2	98	0	0		24.14	-16.97			Dec-14
50	1.95	14.52	7.04	38.57		0.59	1.03	12.1	0.94	14.11	284.3	2	98	0	0	10			5.00		Jul-14
50	2.02	14.68	7.31	39.62		0.88	0.78	12.09	0.94	14.14	284.3	2	98	0	0	10					Jul-14
50	2.01	14.74	7.42	40.10		0.99	0.68	12.12	0.94	14.16	284.3	2	98	0	0	10					Jul-14
50	4.47	24.34	10.38	67.95	82.04	0	1.23	14.66	1.03	42.5	225.7	0	100	0	0	44	29.9	-16.3	5.00		Aug-16
50	4.55	24.52	10.73	69.67	84.83	0	0.88	14.67	1.03	42.95	225.7	0	100	0	0	44	30.09	-16.22			Aug-09
50	4.54	24.47	10.66	69.19	84.31	0	0.98	14.66	1.03	42.82	225.7	0	100	0	0	44	30.08	-16.22			Aug-16
50	5.83	23.18	12.35	55.23	61.82	0.06	1.21	12.68	0.89	36.61	1,350	2	98	0	0	46	22.29	-19.01	5.00		May-07
50	5.89	23.31	12.62	56.40	63.83	0.11	0.96	12.7	0.89	37.02	1,350	2	98	0	0	46	22.48	-18.9			Jan-03
50	5.84	23.19	12.34	55.26	61.77	0.06	1.21	12.69	0.89	36.38	1,350	2	98	0	0	46	22.21	-19			Apr-06
50	5.94	23.38	12.71	56.73	64.43	0.13	0.89	12.69	0.89	37.09	1,350	2	98	0	0	46	22.56	-18.9			Jan-12
50	5.57	29.08	13.73	64.53	71.42	0	1.3	13.99	0.94	30.89	1,212	3	97	0	0	71	24.65	-25.99	5.00		Oct-94
50	5.63	29.24	14.01	65.81	73.66	0	1.03	13.99	0.94	32.22	1,212	3	97	0	0	71	24.81	-25.85			Feb-09
50	5.65	29.24	14.05	66.01	74.25	0	1	13.99	0.94	32.53	1,212	3	97	0	0	71	24.92	-25.88			Apr-11
50	2.54	18.32	-0.14	22.61	33.34	0.49	1.23	14.18	1.06	17.59	741.3	0	100	0	0	31	25.37	-23.27	5.00		Sep-09
50	2.60	18.45	0.06	23.51	34.92	0.73	0.98	14.2	1.06	17.67	741.3	0	100	0	0	31	25.54	-23.23			Sep-09
50	2.68	18.56	0.19	24.00	35.93	0.85	0.85	14.2	1.06	17.77	741.3	0	100	0	0	31	25.74	-23.17			Sep-09
50	2.24	12.84	2.36	22.12	19.33	2.14	1.2	12.38	0.96	8.49	53.8	1	99	0	0	68	20.46	-9.27	5.00		Dec-07
50	2.32	12.89	2.52	22.98	20.77	2.39	0.95	12.36	0.95	8.46	53.8	1	99	0	0	68	20.51	-9.18			Aug-08
50	-0.07	16.38	-0.51	37.05	21.97		1.61	15.5	0.97	13.14	1,048	4	96	0	0	31			5.00		Nov-18
50	-0.07	16.37	-0.37	37.69	22.89	0	1.35	15.45	0.96	13.15	1,048	4	96	0	0	31					May-14
50	0.00	16.49	-0.30	38.03	23.45	0	1.26	15.5	0.97	13.21	1,048	4	96	0	0	31					May-14
50	4.24	27.99	11.33	86.43	78.17	0	0.8	17.64	1.18	24.05	1,947	4	96	0	0	22	35.22	-11.8			Jan-05
50	4.12	27.71	10.47	83.23	73.92	0	1.43	17.68	1.18	13.87	1,839	4	96	0	0	21	34.71	-11.99	5.00		Nov-10
50	4.25	27.91	10.75	84.58	76.10	0	1.17	17.66	1.18	14.94	1,839	4	96	0	0	21	34.72	-11.8			Aug-04
50	4.12	27.66	10.45	83.25	73.95	0	1.42	17.7	1.18	13.89	1,839	4	96	0	0	21	34.61	-11.99			Aug-00
50	3.31	19.94	0.89	19.09	13.34	0	1.26	16.35	0.89	12.15	79.2	3	97	0	0	29	34.24	-17.88	5.00		Sep-09
50	3.42	20.17	1.24	20.12	14.88	0	1.01	16.37	0.89	12.39	79.2	3	97	0	0	29	34.46	-17.8			Sep-09
50	3.43	20.25	1.32	20.40	15.34	0	0.93	16.3	0.89	12.35	79.2	3	97	0	0	29	34.54	-17.7			Sep-09
50	2.04	15.23	-5.99	23.87	12.66	0.13	1.46	16.7	0.95	23.98	97.1	3	97	0	0	49	30.36	-22.65	5.00		Mar-02

Fund Name	MARKET Ticker Symbol	Traded On	FUND TYPE, CATEGORY & OBJECTIVE Fund Type	Category and (Prospectus Objective)	RATINGS Overall Rating	Reward Rating	Risk Rating	Recent Up/ Downgrade	MINIMUMS Open to New Investors	Min Initial Investment
Touchstone Small Cap Value Fund Class Y	TVOYX	NAS CM	Open End	US Equity Small Cap (Small Company)	C	C-	C		Y	2,500
Touchstone Small Cap Value Fund Institutional Class	TVOIX	NAS CM	Open End	US Equity Small Cap (Small Company)	C	C-	C		Y	500,000
Touchstone Small Company Fund Class A	SAGWX	NAS CM	Open End	US Equity Small Cap (Small Company)	C	C	B-	Down	Y	2,500
Touchstone Small Company Fund Class R6	SSRRX	NAS CM	Open End	US Equity Small Cap (Small Company)	C	C	B-	Down	Y	50,000
Touchstone Small Company Fund Class Y	SIGWX	NAS CM	Open End	US Equity Small Cap (Small Company)	C	C	B-	Down	Y	2,500
Touchstone Small Company Fund Institutional USD	TICSX	NAS CM	Open End	US Equity Small Cap (Small Company)	C	C	B-	Down	Y	500,000
Touchstone Sustainability and Impact Equity Fund Class A	TEQAX	NAS CM	Open End	Global Equity Large Cap (Growth)	C+	C	B	Up	Y	2,500
Touchstone Sustainability and Impact Equity Fund Class Y	TIQIX	NAS CM	Open End	Global Equity Large Cap (Growth)	C+	C	B	Up	Y	2,500
Touchstone Sustainability & Impact Equity Inst Cls	TROCX	NAS CM	Open End	Global Equity Large Cap (Growth)	C+	C	B	Up	Y	500,000
Touchstone Value Fund Class A	TVLAX	NAS CM	Open End	US Equity Large Cap Value (Growth)	B-	C	B		Y	2,500
Touchstone Value Fund Class Y	TVLYX	NAS CM	Open End	US Equity Large Cap Value (Growth)	B-	C	B		Y	2,500
Touchstone Value Fund Institutional	TVLIX	NAS CM	Open End	US Equity Large Cap Value (Growth)	B-	C	B		Y	500,000
Towle Deep Value Fund	TDVFX	NAS CM	Open End	US Equity Small Cap (Growth)	D	D	D	Down	Y	5,000
Transamerica Asset Allocation Conservative Portfolio Cls A	ICLAX	NAS CM	Open End	Cautious Alloc (Asset Alloc)	B-	C	A-	Up	Y	1,000
Transamerica Asset Allocation Conservative Portfolio Cls C	ICLLX	NAS CM	Open End	Cautious Alloc (Asset Alloc)	B-	C	B+	Up	Y	1,000
Transamerica Asset Allocation Conservative Portfolio Cls I	TACIX	NAS CM	Open End	Cautious Alloc (Asset Alloc)	B-	C	A-	Up	Y	1,000,000
Transamerica Asset Allocation Conservative Portfolio Cls R	ICVRX	NAS CM	Open End	Cautious Alloc (Asset Alloc)	B-	C	B+	Up	Y	0
Transamerica Asset Allocation Growth Portfolio Class A	IAAAX	NAS CM	Open End	Aggressive Alloc (Asset Alloc)	C+	C	B	Up	Y	1,000
Transamerica Asset Allocation Growth Portfolio Class C	IAALX	NAS CM	Open End	Aggressive Alloc (Asset Alloc)	C	C	B		Y	1,000
Transamerica Asset Allocation Growth Portfolio Class I	TAGIX	NAS CM	Open End	Aggressive Alloc (Asset Alloc)	C+	C	B	Up	Y	1,000,000
Transamerica Asset Allocation Growth Portfolio Class R	IGWRX	NAS CM	Open End	Aggressive Alloc (Asset Alloc)	C+	C	B	Up	Y	0
Transamerica Asset Allocation Intermediate Horizon R	TAARX	NAS CM	Open End	Moderate Alloc (Asset Alloc)	B-	C	B	Up	Y	0
Transamerica Asset Allocation Intermediate Horizon R4	TAAFX	NAS CM	Open End	Moderate Alloc (Asset Alloc)	B-	C	A-		Y	0
Transamerica Asset Allocation Long Horizon R	TALRX	NAS CM	Open End	Aggressive Alloc (Asset Alloc)	C+	C	B	Up	Y	0
Transamerica Asset Allocation Long Horizon R4	TALFX	NAS CM	Open End	Aggressive Alloc (Asset Alloc)	C+	C	B	Up	Y	0
Transamerica Asset Alloc Moderate Growth Port Cls A	IMLAX	NAS CM	Open End	Moderate Alloc (Asset Alloc)	B-	C	B+	Up	Y	1,000
Transamerica Asset Alloc Moderate Growth Port Cls C	IMLLX	NAS CM	Open End	Moderate Alloc (Asset Alloc)	C+	C	B+	Up	Y	1,000
Transamerica Asset Alloc Moderate Growth Port Cls I	TMGIX	NAS CM	Open End	Moderate Alloc (Asset Alloc)	B-	C	B+	Up	Y	1,000,000
Transamerica Asset Alloc Moderate Growth Port Cls R	IMGRX	NAS CM	Open End	Moderate Alloc (Asset Alloc)	B-	C	B+	Up	Y	0
Transamerica Asset Allocation Moderate Portfolio Class A	IMOAX	NAS CM	Open End	Cautious Alloc (Asset Alloc)	B-	C	B+	Up	Y	1,000
Transamerica Asset Allocation Moderate Portfolio Class C	IMOLX	NAS CM	Open End	Cautious Alloc (Asset Alloc)	B-	C	B+	Up	Y	1,000
Transamerica Asset Allocation Moderate Portfolio Class I	TMMIX	NAS CM	Open End	Cautious Alloc (Asset Alloc)	B-	C	A-	Up	Y	1,000,000
Transamerica Asset Allocation Moderate Portfolio Class R	IMDRX	NAS CM	Open End	Cautious Alloc (Asset Alloc)	B-	C	B+	Up	Y	0
Transamerica Balanced II I3	TBLTX	NAS CM	Open End	Moderate Alloc (Balanced)	B	C+	A-		Y	0
Transamerica Balanced II R	TBLRX	NAS CM	Open End	Moderate Alloc (Balanced)	B	C+	A-		Y	0
Transamerica Capital Growth Fund Class A	IALAX	NAS CM	Open End	US Equity Large Cap Growth (Growth)	C+	C+	B-		Y	1,000
Transamerica Capital Growth Fund Class C	ILLLX	NAS CM	Open End	US Equity Large Cap Growth (Growth)	C+	C+	B-		Y	1,000
Transamerica Capital Growth Fund Class I	TFOIX	NAS CM	Open End	US Equity Large Cap Growth (Growth)	B-	C+	B-	Up	Y	1,000,000
Transamerica Capital Growth Fund Class I2			Open End	US Equity Large Cap Growth (Growth)	B-	C+	B-	Up	Y	0
Transamerica ClearTrack® 2015 R1	TCFTX	NAS CM	Open End	Target Date (Asset Alloc)	B-	C	B+	Up	Y	0
Transamerica ClearTrack® 2015 R3	TCTGX	NAS CM	Open End	Target Date (Asset Alloc)	B-	C	B+	Up	Y	0
Transamerica ClearTrack® 2015 R6	TDKTX	NAS CM	Open End	Target Date (Asset Alloc)	B-	C	A-	Up	Y	0
Transamerica ClearTrack® 2020 R1	TCHTX	NAS CM	Open End	Target Date (Asset Alloc)	B-	C	B+	Up	Y	0
Transamerica ClearTrack® 2020 R3	TCTJX	NAS CM	Open End	Target Date (Asset Alloc)	B-	C	A-	Up	Y	0
Transamerica ClearTrack® 2020 R6	TCSUX	NAS CM	Open End	Target Date (Asset Alloc)	B-	C	A-	Up	Y	0
Transamerica ClearTrack® 2025 R1	TDITX	NAS CM	Open End	Target Date (Asset Alloc)	B-	C	A-	Up	Y	0
Transamerica ClearTrack® 2025 R3	TCTKX	NAS CM	Open End	Target Date (Asset Alloc)	B-	C	A-	Up	Y	0
Transamerica ClearTrack® 2025 R6	TDOTX	NAS CM	Open End	Target Date (Asset Alloc)	B	C	A-	Up	Y	0
Transamerica ClearTrack® 2030 R1	TDFTX	NAS CM	Open End	Target Date (Asset Alloc)	B-	C	B+	Up	Y	0
Transamerica ClearTrack® 2030 R3	TCTLX	NAS CM	Open End	Target Date (Asset Alloc)	B-	C	A-	Up	Y	0
Transamerica ClearTrack® 2030 R6	TDHTX	NAS CM	Open End	Target Date (Asset Alloc)	B-	C	A-	Up	Y	0
Transamerica ClearTrack® 2035 R1	TCETX	NAS CM	Open End	Target Date (Asset Alloc)	B-	C	B+	Up	Y	0

★ Expanded analysis of this fund is included in Section II.

	TOTAL RETURNS					PERFORMANCE				ASSETS		ASSET ALLOCATION & TURNOVER					BULL & BEAR		FEES		
Min Additional Investment	3-Month Total Return	6-Month Total Return	1-Year Total Return	3-Year Total Return	5-Year Total Return	Dividend Yield (TTM)	Expense Ratio	3-Yr Std Deviation	3-Year Beta	NAV	Total Assets (MIL)	%Cash	%Stocks	%Bonds	%Other	Turnover Ratio	Last Bull Market Total Return	Last Bear Market Total Return	Front End Fee (%)	Back End Fee (%)	Inception Date
50	2.10	15.38	-5.73	24.82	14.11	0.37	1.21	16.71	0.95	24.02	97.1	3	97	0	0	49	30.61	-22.41			Mar-11
50	2.10	15.43	-5.62	25.31	14.87	0.49	1.06	16.69	0.95	23.99	97.1	3	97	0	0	49	30.76	-22.55			Mar-11
50	0.41	15.82	-0.73	44.14	47.99	0	1.19	16.02	0.91	4.83	1,096	4	96	0	0		23.66	-20.31	5.00		Mar-93
50	0.40	15.92	-0.58	45.82	50.87	0.11	0.74	15.91	0.9	4.95	1,096	4	96	0	0		23.66	-20.31			Dec-14
50	0.37	15.86	-0.78	45.09	50.06	0.05	0.9	16	0.91	5.33	1,096	4	96	0	0		23.91	-20.08			May-07
50	0.37	15.90	-0.91	44.38	48.23	0.08	0.8	15.95	0.91	5.32	1,096	4	96	0	0		23.65	-20.31			Oct-17
50	4.46	14.19	3.74	39.23	41.28	0.76	1.17	13.01	1.11	20.83	737.8	1	99	0	0	40	22.05	-10.77	5.00		Dec-97
50	4.54	14.34	4.01	40.28	43.09	0.99	0.9	12.99	1.11	21.6	737.8	1	99	0	0	40	22.19	-10.66			Nov-04
50	4.54	14.33	4.02	40.48	42.98	0.99	0.89	13	1.11	21.62	737.8	1	99	0	0	40	22.05	-10.77			May-15
50	4.27	15.72	8.53	37.54	41.10	1.5	1.08	12.29	0.99	9.41	337.8	4	96	0	0	24	24.73	-16.53	5.00		Jul-03
50	4.44	15.81	8.81	38.52	42.99	1.76	0.83	12.36	0.99	9.45	337.8	4	96	0	0	24	25.01	-16.52			Sep-98
50	4.37	15.93	8.96	39.17	43.93	1.87	0.68	12.33	0.99	9.42	337.8	4	96	0	0	24	24.89	-16.35			Dec-06
500	-2.89	10.12	-21.54	16.94	9.42	0	1.2	28.47	1.56	12.73	98.0	3	96	0	0	41					Oct-11
50	2.55	8.76	4.53	16.66	20.17	1.71	1.21	4.42	0.46	10.61	797.1	4	29	64	1	20	9.92	-8.33	5.50		Mar-02
50	2.37	8.28	3.71	14.04	15.82	0.84	1.97	4.4	0.46	10.53	797.1	4	29	64	1	20	9.53	-8.49		1.00	Nov-02
	2.61	8.86	4.73	17.45	21.56	1.9	1	4.37	0.46	10.64	797.1	4	29	64	1	20	10.15	-8.14			Nov-09
	2.42	8.55	4.04	15.31	17.93	1.28	1.57	4.35	0.46	10.73	797.1	4	29	64	1	20	9.81	-8.45			Jun-06
50	2.14	14.73	0.88	30.79	33.53	0.99	1.44	11.22	0.86	12.85	1,196	5	92	0	1	32	21.27	-20.07	5.50		Mar-02
50	1.96	14.31	0.08	27.83	28.65	0	2.19	11.21	0.86	12.46	1,196	5	92	0	1	32	20.83	-20.29		1.00	Nov-02
	2.22	14.95	1.15	31.78	35.34	1.2	1.19	11.25	0.86	12.84	1,196	5	92	0	1	32	21.5	-19.9			Nov-09
	2.08	14.67	0.58	29.69	31.60	0.55	1.72	11.28	0.86	12.74	1,196	5	92	0	1	32	21.15	-20.15			Jun-06
	2.90	11.87	4.82	23.46	23.95	2.28	1.15	6.65	0.53	10.38	360.1	5	50	45	0	27	13.84	-10.53			May-17
	2.96	12.01	5.09	24.36	25.48	2.53	0.9	6.69	0.53	10.38	360.1	5	50	45	0	27	14.01	-10.44			Sep-00
	3.26	16.56	3.07	35.68	32.55	2	1.26	11.41	0.92	10.26	210.7	2	89	9	0	30	21.83	-19.09			May-17
	3.33	16.70	3.34	36.71	34.23	2.24	1.01	11.39	0.91	10.26	210.7	2	89	9	0	30	22.01	-19.01			Sep-00
50	2.32	12.19	2.51	24.93	27.74	1.56	1.33	8.25	0.62	11.87	2,061	4	64	29	1	32	16.82	-16.28	5.50		Mar-02
50	2.13	11.78	1.70	22.09	23.02	0.01	2.08	8.22	0.62	11.95	2,061	4	64	29	1	32	16.36	-16.5		1.00	Nov-02
	2.33	12.32	2.74	25.78	29.23	1.76	1.09	8.25	0.62	11.86	2,061	4	64	29	1	32	17.1	-16.2			Nov-09
	2.24	12.03	2.20	23.91	25.94	1.17	1.6	8.18	0.62	11.82	2,061	4	64	29	1	32	16.78	-16.43			Jun-06
50	2.45	10.16	3.59	20.05	23.16	1.87	1.26	5.97	0.44	11.27	1,457	4	44	50	1	25	13.34	-11.77	5.50		Mar-02
50	2.26	9.80	2.79	17.30	18.68	0.49	2.01	5.97	0.44	11.31	1,457	4	44	50	1	25	12.93	-12.06		1.00	Nov-02
	2.54	10.28	3.83	20.89	24.67	2.06	1.04	6.01	0.44	11.26	1,457	4	44	50	1	25	13.47	-11.61			Nov-09
	2.46	10.10	3.37	19.14	21.69	1.59	1.51	5.98	0.44	11.22	1,457	4	44	50	1	25	13.22	-11.83			Jun-06
	3.85	14.02	8.99	30.78	39.55	1.86	0.59	7.6	0.61	10.69	120.7	6	55	38	0	60	16.42	-9.27			Sep-17
	3.62	13.74	8.54	29.60	38.28	1.38	1.09	7.62	0.62	10.69	120.7	6	55	38	0	60	16.42	-9.27			Jul-94
50	7.32	28.59	14.36	98.99	117.29	0	1.19	16.46	1.06	30.31	2,036	6	94	0	0	40	20.94	-16.25	5.50		Mar-99
50	7.11	28.05	13.51	94.57	109.41	0	1.93	16.44	1.06	23.78	2,036	6	94	0	0	40	20.55	-16.53		1.00	Nov-02
	7.39	28.73	14.66	100.63	120.36	0	0.94	16.46	1.06	31.94	2,036	6	94	0	0	40	21.35	-16.08			Nov-09
	7.89	28.02	14.47	104.00	120.26	0	0.83	16.45	1.06	15.12	2,036	6	94	0	0	40	21.49	-16.25			Sep-11
	3.06	10.84	5.28	18.05		1.59	1.2	5.83	1.59	10.43	40.2	2	44	54	0	23					Mar-15
	3.16	11.06	5.78	19.44			0.95	5.81	1.59	10.43	40.2	2	44	54	0	23					Mar-19
	3.24	11.21	6.06	20.36		2.28	0.55	5.82	1.6	10.51	40.2	2	44	54	0	23					Mar-15
	3.17	11.09	4.88	19.33		1.48	1.2	6.3	1.43	10.41	57.4	2	49	49	0	25					Mar-15
	3.27	11.31	5.40	20.74			0.95	6.27	1.42	10.41	57.4	2	49	49	0	25					Mar-19
	3.24	11.35	5.57	21.54		2.17	0.55	6.26	1.42	10.49	57.4	2	49	49	0	25					Mar-15
	3.03	12.43	5.66	21.91		1.43	1.2	6.87	1.32	10.85	75.4	3	55	43	0	25					Mar-15
	3.13	12.63	6.08	23.28			0.95	6.86	1.31	10.84	75.4	3	55	43	0	25					Mar-19
	3.20	12.78	6.34	24.22		2.11	0.55	6.86	1.32	10.94	75.4	3	55	43	0	25					Mar-15
	3.16	13.16	5.63	24.16		1.39	1.2	7.58	1.15	11.09	57.6	3	62	35	0	26					Mar-15
	3.26	13.46	6.14	25.65			0.95	7.57	1.15	11.08	57.6	3	62	35	0	26					Mar-19
	3.32	13.60	6.40	26.60		2.06	0.55	7.6	1.15	11.19	57.6	3	62	35	0	26					Mar-15
	3.12	13.90	5.32	27.22		1.43	1.2	8.55	1.06	11.22	60.1	3	71	26	0	24					Mar-15

	MARKET			FUND TYPE, CATEGORY & OBJECTIVE	RATINGS				MINIMUMS	
Fund Name	Ticker Symbol	Traded On	Fund Type	Category and (Prospectus Objective)	Overall Rating	Reward Rating	Risk Rating	Recent Up/ Downgrade	Open to New Investors	Min Initial Investment
Transamerica ClearTrack® 2035 R3	TCTMX	NAS CM	Open End	Target Date (Asset Alloc)	B-	C	B+	Up	Y	0
Transamerica ClearTrack® 2035 R6	TCHDX	NAS CM	Open End	Target Date (Asset Alloc)	B-	C	B+	Up	Y	0
Transamerica ClearTrack® 2040 R1	TCRTX	NAS CM	Open End	Target Date (Asset Alloc)	B-	C	B+	Up	Y	0
Transamerica ClearTrack® 2040 R3	TCTQX	NAS CM	Open End	Target Date (Asset Alloc)	B-	C	B+	Up	Y	0
Transamerica ClearTrack® 2040 R6	TCKTX	NAS CM	Open End	Target Date (Asset Alloc)	B-	C	B+	Up	Y	0
Transamerica ClearTrack® 2045 R1	TCPTX	NAS CM	Open End	Target Date (Asset Alloc)	B-	C	B	Up	Y	0
Transamerica ClearTrack® 2045 R3	TCTTX	NAS CM	Open End	Target Date (Asset Alloc)	B-	C	B	Up	Y	0
Transamerica ClearTrack® 2045 R6	TCOTX	NAS CM	Open End	Target Date (Asset Alloc)	B-	C	B	Up	Y	0
Transamerica ClearTrack® 2050 R1	TRNTX	NAS CM	Open End	Target Date (Asset Alloc)	B-	C	B	Up	Y	0
Transamerica ClearTrack® 2050 R3	TCTUX	NAS CM	Open End	Target Date (Asset Alloc)	B-	C	B	Up	Y	0
Transamerica ClearTrack® 2050 R6	TCMTX	NAS CM	Open End	Target Date (Asset Alloc)	B-	C	B	Up	Y	0
Transamerica ClearTrack® 2055 R1	TCTOX	NAS CM	Open End	Target Date (Asset Alloc)	C	D+	B	Up	Y	0
Transamerica ClearTrack® 2055 R3	TCTVX	NAS CM	Open End	Target Date (Asset Alloc)	C-	D+	B	Up	Y	0
Transamerica ClearTrack® 2055 R6	TCTSX	NAS CM	Open End	Target Date (Asset Alloc)	C	D+	B	Up	Y	0
Transamerica ClearTrack® 2060 R1	TCSOX	NAS CM	Open End	Target Date (Asset Alloc)	C	D+	B	Up	Y	0
Transamerica ClearTrack® 2060 R3	TCTYX	NAS CM	Open End	Target Date (Asset Alloc)	C-	D+	B	Up	Y	0
Transamerica ClearTrack® 2060 R6	TCSSX	NAS CM	Open End	Target Date (Asset Alloc)	C	D+	B	Up	Y	0
Transamerica ClearTrack® Retirement Income R1	TCITX	NAS CM	Open End	Target Date (Asset Alloc)	B-	C	B		Y	0
Transamerica ClearTrack® Retirement Income R3	TCTZX	NAS CM	Open End	Target Date (Asset Alloc)	B-	C	B+		Y	0
Transamerica ClearTrack® Retirement Income R6	TCJTX	NAS CM	Open End	Target Date (Asset Alloc)	B-	C+	B+		Y	0
Transamerica Concentrated Growth Fund Class A	TORAX	NAS CM	Open End	US Equity Large Cap Growth (Growth)	B-	C+	B	Down	Y	1,000
Transamerica Concentrated Growth Fund Class C	TCCGX	NAS CM	Open End	US Equity Large Cap Growth (Growth)	B-	C	B	Down	Y	1,000
Transamerica Concentrated Growth Fund Class I	TOREX	NAS CM	Open End	US Equity Large Cap Growth (Growth)	B-	C+	B	Down	Y	1,000,000
Transamerica Concentrated Growth Fund Class I2			Open End	US Equity Large Cap Growth (Growth)	B-	C+	B	Down	Y	0
Transamerica Dividend Focused Class A	TDFAX	NAS CM	Open End	US Equity Large Cap Value (Growth & Income)	C+	C	B	Up	Y	1,000
Transamerica Dividend Focused Class C	TDFCX	NAS CM	Open End	US Equity Large Cap Value (Growth & Income)	C	C	B-		Y	1,000
Transamerica Dividend Focused Class I	TDFIX	NAS CM	Open End	US Equity Large Cap Value (Growth & Income)	C+	C	B	Up	Y	1,000,000
Transamerica Dividend Focused Class I2	TRDIX	NAS CM	Open End	US Equity Large Cap Value (Growth & Income)	C+	C	B	Up	Y	0
Transamerica Dividend Focused Class R6	TADFX	NAS CM	Open End	US Equity Large Cap Value (Growth & Income)	C+	C	B	Up	Y	0
Transamerica Dynamic Allocation Fund Class A	ATTRX	NAS CM	Open End	Moderate Alloc (Growth & Income)	B-	C	B	Up	Y	1,000
Transamerica Dynamic Allocation Fund Class C	CTTRX	NAS CM	Open End	Moderate Alloc (Growth & Income)	C+	C	B	Up	Y	1,000
Transamerica Dynamic Allocation Fund Class I	ITTOX	NAS CM	Open End	Moderate Alloc (Growth & Income)	B-	C	B	Up	Y	1,000,000
Transamerica Dynamic Income Fund Class A	IGTAX	NAS CM	Open End	Cautious Alloc (Income)	C+	C	B	Down	Y	1,000
Transamerica Dynamic Income Fund Class C	IGTCX	NAS CM	Open End	Cautious Alloc (Income)	C	C	B-		Y	1,000
Transamerica Dynamic Income Fund Class I	IGTIX	NAS CM	Open End	Cautious Alloc (Income)	C+	C	B	Down	Y	1,000,000
Transamerica Emerging Markets Equity Fund Class A	AEMTX	NAS CM	Open End	Global Emerg Mkts (Div Emerging Mkts)	C	C	C		Y	1,000
Transamerica Emerging Markets Equity Fund Class C	CEMTX	NAS CM	Open End	Global Emerg Mkts (Div Emerging Mkts)	C	C-	C	Up	Y	1,000
Transamerica Emerging Markets Equity Fund Class I	IEMTX	NAS CM	Open End	Global Emerg Mkts (Div Emerging Mkts)	C	C	C		Y	1,000,000
Transamerica Emerging Markets Equity Fund Class I2			Open End	Global Emerg Mkts (Div Emerging Mkts)	C	C	C		Y	0
Transamerica Event Driven Fund Class I	TENIX	NAS CM	Open End	Multialternative (Growth)	B-	C	B+	Up	Y	1,000,000
Transamerica Event Driven Fund Class I2			Open End	Multialternative (Growth)	B-	C	B+	Up	Y	0
Transamerica Global Equity Class A	IMNAX	NAS CM	Open End	Global Equity Large Cap (Growth)	C+	C	B	Up	Y	1,000
Transamerica Global Equity Class C	IMNCX	NAS CM	Open End	Global Equity Large Cap (Growth)	C+	C	B	Up	Y	1,000
Transamerica Global Equity Class I	TMUIX	NAS CM	Open End	Global Equity Large Cap (Growth)	C+	C	B	Up	Y	1,000,000
Transamerica Global Equity Class R6	TAGEX	NAS CM	Open End	Global Equity Large Cap (Growth)	C+	C	B	Up	Y	0
Transamerica Global Multifactor Macro Class I2			Open End	Global Macro (Growth & Income)	C	C	C+		Y	0
Transamerica Global Real Estate Securities Fund Class I2	TRSIX	NAS CM	Open End	Real Estate Sector Equity (Real Estate)	C+	C	B		Y	0
Transamerica Growth Fund Class I2	TJNIX	NAS CM	Open End	US Equity Large Cap Growth (Growth)	C+	C+	B	Down	Y	0
Transamerica Growth Fund Class R6	TAGOX	NAS CM	Open End	US Equity Large Cap Growth (Growth)	C+	C+	B	Down	Y	0
Transamerica International Equity A	TRWAX	NAS CM	Open End	Global Equity Large Cap (Foreign Stock)	C	C-	C	Up	Y	1,000
Transamerica International Equity C	TRWCX	NAS CM	Open End	Global Equity Large Cap (Foreign Stock)	C-	D+	C		Y	1,000
Transamerica International Equity I	TSWIX	NAS CM	Open End	Global Equity Large Cap (Foreign Stock)	C	C-	C		Y	1,000,000

★ Expanded analysis of this fund is included in Section II.

	TOTAL RETURNS					PERFORMANCE				ASSETS		ASSET ALLOCATION & TURNOVER					BULL & BEAR		FEES		
Min Additional Investment	3-Month Total Return	6-Month Total Return	1-Year Total Return	3-Year Total Return	5-Year Total Return	Dividend Yield (TTM)	Expense Ratio	3-Yr Std Deviation	3-Year Beta	NAV	Total Assets (MIL)	%Cash	%Stocks	%Bonds	%Other	Turnover Ratio	Last Bull Market Total Return	Last Bear Market Total Return	Front End Fee (%)	Back End Fee (%)	Inception Date
	3.31	14.30	5.85	28.83			0.95	8.52	1.05	11.21	60.1	3	71	26	0	24					Mar-19
	3.28	14.34	6.02	29.67		2.1	0.55	8.54	1.06	11.32	60.1	3	71	26	0	24					Mar-15
	3.26	14.83	5.21	30.70		1.35	1.2	9.36	1	11.38	52.7	2	77	20	0	20					Mar-15
	3.27	14.96	5.56	32.23			0.95	9.36	1	11.35	52.7	2	77	20	0	20					Mar-19
	3.31	15.08	5.80	33.20		2.02	0.55	9.35	1	11.52	52.7	2	77	20	0	20					Mar-15
	3.37	16.05	5.11	33.23		1.3	1.2	10.44	1.01	11.64	35.3	2	88	10	0	15					Mar-15
	3.38	16.21	5.45	34.76			0.95	10.42	1.01	11.61	35.3	2	88	10	0	15					Mar-19
	3.43	16.35	5.70	35.75		1.95	0.55	10.38	1	11.74	35.3	2	88	10	0	15					Mar-15
	3.33	16.15	4.81	33.47		1.32	1.2	10.66	0.98	11.79	27.5	2	91	6	0	13					Mar-15
	3.33	16.32	5.16	34.95			0.95	10.66	0.98	11.76	27.5	2	91	6	0	13					Mar-19
	3.47	16.55	5.50	36.07		1.98	0.55	10.65	0.98	11.9	27.5	2	91	6	0	13					Mar-15
	3.30	16.50	4.80			1.26	1.2			10.94	0.61	2	91	7	0	35					Jul-17
	3.41	16.66	5.19				0.95			10.91	0.61	2	91	7	0	35					Mar-19
	3.39	16.72	5.37			1.88	0.55			10.96	0.61	2	91	7	0	35					Jul-17
	3.21	16.40	4.74			1.27	1.2			10.93	0.59	2	91	7	0	35					Jul-17
	3.31	16.55	5.12				0.95			10.91	0.59	2	91	7	0	35					Mar-19
	3.39	16.71	5.40			1.9	0.55			10.96	0.59	2	91	7	0	35					Jul-17
	2.90	9.83	6.45	14.25		1.65	1.2	4.47		10.27	67.1	3	30	67	0	24					Mar-15
	3.00	10.05	6.86	15.52			0.95	4.51		10.28	67.1	3	30	67	0	24					Mar-19
	3.08	10.21	7.14	16.41		2.34	0.55	4.51		10.36	67.1	3	30	67	0	24					Mar-15
50	2.98	20.82	11.87	49.48	55.28	0	1.2	11.8	0.84	17.58	176.6	2	98	0	0	23	25.81	-12.85	5.50		Mar-14
50	2.80	20.41	11.14	46.54	50.00	0	1.86	11.82	0.84	16.87	176.6	2	98	0	0	23	25.27	-13.13		1.00	Mar-14
	3.06	20.96	12.27	50.96	57.43	0	0.87	11.8	0.84	17.48	176.6	2	98	0	0	23	26	-12.76			Dec-10
	3.10	20.27	12.40	53.08	57.28	0.09	0.77	11.83	0.84	17.74	176.6	2	98	0	0	23	26	-12.76			Mar-14
50	1.52	13.55	2.10	27.89	33.17	2.05	1.03	12.64	1.03	9.21	531.3	1	99	0	0	22			5.50		Jan-13
50	1.31	13.10	1.25	24.72	27.79	1.18	1.86	12.65	1.03	9.17	531.3	1	99	0	0	22				1.00	Jan-13
	1.67	13.79	2.30	28.58	34.43	2.21	0.85	12.61	1.02	9.21	531.3	1	99	0	0	22					Jan-13
	1.70	13.85	2.41	28.97	35.01	2.31	0.75	12.67	1.03	9.21	531.3	1	99	0	0	22					Jan-13
	1.70	13.85	2.41	28.98	35.02	2.31	0.75	12.57	1.02	9.21	531.3	1	99	0	0	22					May-15
50	2.78	9.13	2.01	21.70	18.74	1.01	1.27	7.22	0.56	12.18	15.7	2	68	30	0	25			5.50		Oct-12
50	2.55	8.74	1.26	19.06	14.43	0.08	2.02	7.24	0.56	12.06	15.7	2	68	30	0	25				1.00	Oct-12
	2.87	9.26	2.30	22.70	20.27	1.19	1.02	7.25	0.56	12.15	15.7	2	68	30	0	25					Oct-12
50	2.20	9.12	5.74	9.14	12.11	4.74	1.27	5.19	0.92	9.16	185.6	1	30	69	0	23			4.75		Oct-11
50	2.02	8.76	5.08	6.65	8.00	4.04	2.02	5.21	0.92	9.12	185.6	1	30	69	0	23				1.00	Oct-11
	2.27	9.26	6.01	9.93	13.45	4.98	1.02	5.19	0.92	9.16	185.6	1	30	69	0	23					Oct-11
50	0.30	9.15	-5.23	27.51	0.72	0.29	1.53	14.47	1.02	9.9	851.3	1	99	0	0	75			5.50		Apr-12
50	0.10	8.77	-5.77	25.17	-2.39	0	2.23	14.45	1.02	9.79	851.3	1	99	0	0	75				1.00	Apr-12
	0.50	9.46	-4.71	29.27	2.87	0.93	1.2	14.47	1.02	9.95	851.3	1	99	0	0	75					Apr-12
	0.40	9.35	-4.67	29.42	3.30	1.07	1.1	14.42	1.02	9.94	851.3	1	99	0	0	75					Apr-12
	2.41	7.94	1.11	13.99		0.04	1.49	4.6	18.83	10.6	104.8	10	3	12	-4	514					Nov-16
	2.45	7.95	1.13	13.97		0.04	1.6	4.64	19.05	10.45	104.8	10	3	12	-4	514					Mar-15
50	3.75	14.72	3.47	38.67	28.84	0.02	1.35	12.91	1.11	14.1	109.7	2	98	0	0	36	16.05	-24.31	5.50		Mar-06
50	3.62	14.33	2.77	35.66	24.09	0	2.1	12.92	1.11	13.72	109.7	2	98	0	0	36	15.54	-24.46		1.00	Mar-06
	3.82	14.87	3.76	39.82	30.59	0.21	1.1	12.88	1.11	14.13	109.7	2	98	0	0	36	16.25	-24.15			Nov-09
	3.82	14.87	3.77	40.03	30.60	0.29	1.02	12.92	1.11	14.13	109.7	2	98	0	0	36	16.05	-24.31			May-15
	1.09	2.32	2.20	6.24		0	1.61	5.24	-1.98	9.25	78.5	65	6	10	20						Mar-15
	1.04	16.93	6.92	9.80	17.08	2.79	1.58	11.26	1.02	14.39	21.6	1	99	0	0	150	22.37	-18.92			Nov-05
	2.88	21.99	7.78	73.60	89.17	0	0.9	14.92	1.08	8.21	195.9	1	99	0	0	42	26.55	-13.8			Nov-05
	2.88	22.17	7.78	73.61	89.19	0	0.9	14.9	1.08	8.21	195.9	1	99	0	0	42	26.55	-13.8			May-15
50	2.28	10.82	-4.71	21.33	4.41	1.58	1.23	11.93	1.06	16.99	4,884	1	99	0	0	21	17.07	-22.2	5.50		Mar-11
50	2.07	10.42	-5.43	18.66	0.83	0.73	1.94	11.93	1.06	16.73	4,884	1	99	0	0	21	16.58	-22.35		1.00	Mar-11
	2.38	11.03	-4.39	22.53	6.32	1.96	0.89	11.94	1.06	17.2	4,884	1	99	0	0	21	17.32	-22.06			Dec-92

	MARKET			FUND TYPE, CATEGORY & OBJECTIVE	RATINGS				MINIMUMS	
Fund Name	Ticker Symbol	Traded On	Fund Type	Category and (Prospectus Objective)	Overall Rating	Reward Rating	Risk Rating	Recent Up/ Downgrade	Open to New Investors	Min Initial Investment
Transamerica International Equity I2	TRWIX	NAS CM	Open End	Global Equity Large Cap (Foreign Stock)	C	C-	C		Y	0
Transamerica International Equity I3	TRWTX	NAS CM	Open End	Global Equity Large Cap (Foreign Stock)	C	C-	C		Y	0
Transamerica International Equity Index VP Initial	I9CL1	NAS CM	Open End	Global Equity Large Cap (Growth)	U	U	U		Y	0
Transamerica International Equity R	TRWRX	NAS CM	Open End	Global Equity Large Cap (Foreign Stock)	C	C-	C	Up	Y	0
Transamerica International Equity R4	TRWFX	NAS CM	Open End	Global Equity Large Cap (Foreign Stock)	C	C-	C		Y	0
Transamerica International Equity R6	TAINX	NAS CM	Open End	Global Equity Large Cap (Foreign Stock)	C	C-	C		Y	0
Transamerica International Growth Class A	TGRHX	NAS CM	Open End	Global Equity Large Cap (Foreign Stock)	C	C	B-		Y	1,000
Transamerica International Growth Class I	TGRGX	NAS CM	Open End	Global Equity Large Cap (Foreign Stock)	C	C	B-		Y	1,000,000
Transamerica International Growth Class I2			Open End	Global Equity Large Cap (Foreign Stock)	C	C	B-		Y	0
Transamerica International Growth Class R6	TGRFX	NAS CM	Open End	Global Equity Large Cap (Foreign Stock)	C	C	B-		Y	0
Transamerica International Small Cap Value Class I	TISVX	NAS CM	Open End	Global Equity Mid/Small Cap (Small Company)	C	C-	C			1,000,000
Transamerica International Small Cap Value Class I2			Open End	Global Equity Mid/Small Cap (Small Company)	C	C-	C			0
Transamerica International Stock Class A	TIHAX	NAS CM	Open End	Global Equity Large Cap (Foreign Stock)	U	U	U		Y	1,000
Transamerica International Stock Class I	TIHBX	NAS CM	Open End	Global Equity Large Cap (Foreign Stock)	U	U	U		Y	1,000,000
Transamerica International Stock Class I2	TIHIX	NAS CM	Open End	Global Equity Large Cap (Foreign Stock)	U	U	U		Y	0
Transamerica International Stock Class R6	TIHJX	NAS CM	Open End	Global Equity Large Cap (Foreign Stock)	U	U	U		Y	0
Transamerica International Value Class I2	TIHCX	NAS CM	Open End	Global Equity Large Cap (Growth & Income)	U	U	U		Y	0
Transamerica Large Cap Value Fund Class A	TWQAX	NAS CM	Open End	US Equity Large Cap Value (Growth)	C	C	B	Down	Y	1,000
Transamerica Large Cap Value Fund Class C	TWQCX	NAS CM	Open End	US Equity Large Cap Value (Growth)	C	C	B	Down	Y	1,000
Transamerica Large Cap Value Fund Class I	TWQIX	NAS CM	Open End	US Equity Large Cap Value (Growth)	C	C	B	Down	Y	1,000,000
Transamerica Large Cap Value Fund Class I2	TWQZX	NAS CM	Open End	US Equity Large Cap Value (Growth)	C	C	B	Down	Y	0
Transamerica Large Cap Value Fund Class R6	TALCX	NAS CM	Open End	US Equity Large Cap Value (Growth)	C	C	B	Down	Y	0
Transamerica Large Core Fund Class I3	TLATX	NAS CM	Open End	US Equity Large Cap Blend (Growth & Income)	B-	C	B		Y	0
Transamerica Large Core Fund Class R	TLARX	NAS CM	Open End	US Equity Large Cap Blend (Growth & Income)	B-	C	B	Up	Y	0
Transamerica Large Core Fund Class R4	TLAFX	NAS CM	Open End	US Equity Large Cap Blend (Growth & Income)	B-	C	B	Up	Y	0
Transamerica Large Growth Fund Class I3	TGWTX	NAS CM	Open End	US Equity Large Cap Growth (Growth)	C+	C+	B	Down	Y	0
Transamerica Large Growth Fund Class R	TGWRX	NAS CM	Open End	US Equity Large Cap Growth (Growth)	C+	C+	B	Down	Y	0
Transamerica Large Growth Fund Class R4	TGWFX	NAS CM	Open End	US Equity Large Cap Growth (Growth)	C+	C+	B	Down	Y	0
Transamerica Large Value Opportunities Fund Class I3	TLOTX	NAS CM	Open End	US Equity Large Cap Value (Growth)	B-	C	B	Up	Y	0
Transamerica Large Value Opportunities Fund Class R	TLORX	NAS CM	Open End	US Equity Large Cap Value (Growth)	B-	C	B	Up	Y	0
Transamerica Large Value Opportunities Fund Class R4	TLOFX	NAS CM	Open End	US Equity Large Cap Value (Growth)	B-	C	B	Up	Y	0
Transamerica Long/Short Strategy Fund Class I2			Open End	Long/Short Equity (Growth)	B	C	A-	Up	Y	0
Transamerica Managed Futures Strategy Fund Class I2			Open End	Alternative Miscellaneous (Growth & Income)	D	D	D+		Y	0
Transamerica Mid Cap Growth A	MCGAX	NAS CM	Open End	US Equity Mid Cap (Growth)	C	C	C+	Down	Y	1,000
Transamerica Mid Cap Growth C	MGTCX	NAS CM	Open End	US Equity Mid Cap (Growth)	C	C	C+	Down	Y	1,000
Transamerica Mid Cap Growth I	IMCGX	NAS CM	Open End	US Equity Mid Cap (Growth)	C	C	C+	Down	Y	1,000,000
Transamerica Mid Cap Growth I2			Open End	US Equity Mid Cap (Growth)	C	C	C+	Down	Y	0
Transamerica Mid Cap Growth I3	TMITX	NAS CM	Open End	US Equity Mid Cap (Growth)	C	C	C+	Down	Y	0
Transamerica Mid Cap Growth R	TMIRX	NAS CM	Open End	US Equity Mid Cap (Growth)	C	C	C+	Down	Y	0
Transamerica Mid Cap Value Fund Class I2			Open End	US Equity Mid Cap (Growth)	C+	C	B	Up		0
Transamerica Mid Cap Value Opportunities A	MCVAX	NAS CM	Open End	US Equity Mid Cap (Growth)	B-	C	B	Up	Y	1,000
Transamerica Mid Cap Value Opportunities C	MCVCX	NAS CM	Open End	US Equity Mid Cap (Growth)	B-	C	B	Up	Y	1,000
Transamerica Mid Cap Value Opportunities I	MVTIX	NAS CM	Open End	US Equity Mid Cap (Growth)	B-	C	B		Y	1,000,000
Transamerica Mid Cap Value Opportunities I2			Open End	US Equity Mid Cap (Growth)	B-	C	B		Y	0
Transamerica Mid Cap Value Opportunities I3	TOTTX	NAS CM	Open End	US Equity Mid Cap (Growth)	B-	C	B		Y	0
Transamerica Mid Cap Value Opportunities R	TOTRX	NAS CM	Open End	US Equity Mid Cap (Growth)	B-	C	B	Up	Y	0
Transamerica Mid Cap Value Opportunities R4	TOTFX	NAS CM	Open End	US Equity Mid Cap (Growth)	B-	C	B	Up	Y	0
Transamerica Mid Cap Value Opportunities R6	MVTRX	NAS CM	Open End	US Equity Mid Cap (Growth)	B-	C	B		Y	0
Transamerica MLP & Energy Income Class A	TMLAX	NAS CM	Open End	Energy Sector Equity (Growth & Income)	C	C	C		Y	1,000
Transamerica MLP & Energy Income Class C	TMCLX	NAS CM	Open End	Energy Sector Equity (Growth & Income)	C-	C-	C	Down	Y	1,000
Transamerica MLP & Energy Income Class I	TMLPX	NAS CM	Open End	Energy Sector Equity (Growth & Income)	C	C	C		Y	1,000,000
Transamerica MLP & Energy Income Class I2			Open End	Energy Sector Equity (Growth & Income)	C	C	C		Y	0

★ Expanded analysis of this fund is included in Section II.

	TOTAL RETURNS					PERFORMANCE				ASSETS		ASSET ALLOCATION & TURNOVER					BULL & BEAR		FEES		
Min Additional Investment	3-Month Total Return	6-Month Total Return	1-Year Total Return	3-Year Total Return	5-Year Total Return	Dividend Yield (TTM)	Expense Ratio	3-Yr Std Deviation	3-Year Beta	NAV	Total Assets (MIL)	%Cash	%Stocks	%Bonds	%Other	Turnover Ratio	Last Bull Market Total Return	Last Bear Market Total Return	Front End Fee (%)	Back End Fee (%)	Inception Date
	2.37	11.09	-4.27	22.93	6.86	2.06	0.79	11.93	1.06	17.22	4,884	1	99	0	0	21	17.39	-22.06			Mar-11
	2.42	11.15	-4.25	22.79	6.19	2.05	0.79	11.9	1.05	17.34	4,884	1	99	0	0	21	17.32	-22.06			Dec-92
	1.27	4.82					0.18				10.5	3	95	0	2						Jan-18
	2.23	10.85	-4.74	20.97	3.58	1.48	1.28	11.92	1.05	17.36	4,884	1	99	0	0	21	16.98	-22.22			Mar-17
	2.30	10.94	-4.51	21.81	4.82	1.76	1.04	11.93	1.06	17.33	4,884	1	99	0	0	21	17.15	-22.14			Mar-17
	2.41	11.11	-4.28	22.92	6.41	2.04	0.79	11.96	1.06	17.39	4,884	1	99	0	0	21	17.32	-22.06			May-15
50	3.45	16.34	0.03	27.60	11.34	1.33	1.2	11.89	1.05	7.19	1,110	2	98	0	0		18.78	-23.49	5.50		Mar-18
	3.29	16.31	0.21	28.40	12.60	1.39	1.05	11.87	1.05	7.2	1,110	2	98	0	0		18.95	-23.41			Mar-18
	4.06	16.23	1.31	30.53	12.64	1.85	0.83	11.83	1.04	7.18	1,110	2	98	0	0		18.95	-23.41			Jun-08
	3.44	16.47	0.53	28.81	12.96	1.55	0.83	11.81	1.04	7.21	1,110	2	98	0	0		18.95	-23.41			Mar-18
	2.31	10.46	-7.65	27.29	15.38	1.74	1.12	11.59	0.91	11.93	522.9	13	87	0	0	20					Jan-13
	2.39	10.54	-7.52	27.65	15.88	1.86	1.02	11.57	0.91	11.95	522.9	13	87	0	0	20					Jan-13
50	2.26	12.85					1.28			9.48	1.9	2	98	0	0				5.50		Sep-18
	2.37	12.96					1.03			9.5	1.9	2	98	0	0						Sep-18
	2.37	12.96					1.03			9.5	1.9	2	98	0	0						Sep-18
	2.37	12.96					1.03			9.5	1.9	2	98	0	0						Sep-18
	1.70	11.73					1			9.52	9.6	1	99	0	0	3					Aug-18
50	0.26	14.71	0.85	31.87	46.73	1.34	1.08	14.4	1.14	11.15	2,079	2	98	0	0	139	22.86	-19.17	5.50		Nov-10
50	0.06	14.26	0.08	28.98	41.39	0.63	1.8	14.43	1.14	11.08	2,079	2	98	0	0	139	22.36	-19.38		1.00	Nov-10
	0.24	14.77	1.04	32.83	48.64	1.6	0.8	14.46	1.15	11.22	2,079	2	98	0	0	139	22.99	-19			Nov-10
	0.27	14.84	1.15	33.24	49.41	1.7	0.69	14.42	1.14	11.21	2,079	2	98	0	0	139	23.16	-18.99			Nov-10
	0.27	14.84	1.15	33.24	49.42	1.7	0.69	14.39	1.14	11.21	2,079	2	98	0	0	139	23.16	-18.99			May-15
	3.13	17.03	7.46	49.66	52.74	1.35	0.56	12.27	0.99	9.71	262.9	0	100	0	0	130	25.89	-16.17			Mar-17
	2.90	16.61	6.91	47.67	49.96	0.89	1.05	12.3	0.99	9.71	262.9	0	100	0	0	130	25.7	-16.26			Mar-17
	2.94	16.72	7.14	48.69	51.76	1.08	0.84	12.26	0.99	9.71	262.9	0	100	0	0	130	25.89	-16.18			Sep-00
	4.29	23.96	10.69	70.12	89.27	0.08	0.7	14.5	1.07	12.9	826.9	1	99	0	0	34	27.2	-16.9			Mar-17
	4.13	23.60	10.18	67.91	85.87	0	1.19	14.47	1.06	12.83	826.9	1	99	0	0	34	27.02	-16.98			Mar-17
	4.20	23.72	10.41	69.19	88.23	0	0.9	14.49	1.07	12.88	826.9	1	99	0	0	34	27.2	-16.9			Sep-00
	1.76	14.25	5.07	38.70	34.22	1.94	0.49	12.45	1.05	9.15	563.6	0	100	0	0	137	25.64	-18.18			May-17
	1.63	14.09	4.60	36.93	31.85	1.45	0.98	12.5	1.05	9.16	563.6	0	100	0	0	137	25.46	-18.27			May-17
	1.81	14.23	4.92	38.07	33.61	1.7	0.74	12.52	1.06	9.16	563.6	0	100	0	0	137	25.64	-18.18			Sep-00
	3.10	7.86	5.86	24.22	18.45	0	4.06	5.34	17.33	6.31	10.3	70	30	0	0	728	5.82	-7.47			Jan-07
	1.79	2.50	-1.07	-17.82	-1.51	0	1.46	7.85		7.36	138.3	70	0	2	28		-4.08	-5.4			Sep-10
50	8.46	30.21	3.80	43.59	41.26	0.06	1.24	15.62	1	9.87	75.8	1	99	0	0	61	23.11	-22.5	5.50		Oct-13
50	8.36	29.76	3.06	40.50	36.01	0	2.01	15.64	1.01	9.33	75.8	1	99	0	0	61	22.58	-22.74		1.00	Oct-13
	8.59	30.45	4.01	44.63	43.05	0.26	0.95	15.69	1.01	9.98	75.8	1	99	0	0	61	23.11	-22.5			Oct-13
	8.60	29.47	3.29	46.78	42.49	0	0.82	15.68	1.01	10.04	75.8	1	99	0	0	61	23.11	-22.5			Oct-13
	8.54	30.42	3.83	44.70	42.34	0.35	0.83	15.66	1.01	10.03	75.8	1	99	0	0	61	23.11	-22.49			Oct-13
	8.46	30.24	3.59	43.99	41.99	0	1.34	15.68	1.01	9.99	75.8	1	99	0	0	61	22.93	-22.58			Mar-17
	3.22	19.40	4.60	30.10	41.68	1.44	0.91	12.9	0.97	12.8	142.9	1	99	0	0	19	27.74	-17.55			Nov-05
50	2.78	17.69	6.09	28.31	44.83	0.9	1.2	12.28	0.89	11.44	1,708	7	93	0	0	85			5.50		Apr-14
50	2.81	17.42	5.43	25.60	39.79	0.18	1.88	12.26	0.89	11.32	1,708	7	93	0	0	85				1.00	Apr-14
	3.03	18.13	6.46	29.43	46.95	1.14	0.85	12.28	0.89	11.53	1,708	7	93	0	0	85					Apr-14
	3.12	18.11	6.60	29.89	47.57	1.26	0.75	12.24	0.89	11.54	1,708	7	93	0	0	85					Apr-14
	3.11	18.14	6.49	29.55	45.86	1.26	0.75	12.29	0.89	11.59	1,708	7	93	0	0	85					Apr-14
	3.02	17.90	6.04	27.70	42.35	0.69	1.25	12.27	0.89	11.59	1,708	7	93	0	0	85					Mar-17
	3.02	18.02	6.32	28.73	44.21	1.05	0.9	12.27	0.89	11.59	1,708	7	93	0	0	85					Mar-17
	3.10	18.08	6.47	29.70	46.02	1.26	0.75	12.29	0.89	11.62	1,708	7	93	0	0	85					Jul-16
50	-0.79	20.08	0.94	11.18	-27.91	3.75	1.6	15.76	0.89	7.02	285.2	1	98	1	0	33			5.50		Apr-13
50	-0.99	19.70	0.29	8.74	-30.60	3.19	2.35	15.8	0.89	7	285.2	1	98	1	0	33				1.00	Apr-13
	-0.72	20.26	1.28	12.19	-26.86	3.99	1.3	15.77	0.89	7.02	285.2	1	98	1	0	33					Apr-13
	-0.69	20.32	1.39	12.53	-26.48	4.06	1.2	15.75	0.89	7.02	285.2	1	98	1	0	33					Apr-13

	MARKET			FUND TYPE, CATEGORY & OBJECTIVE	RATINGS				MINIMUMS	
Fund Name	Ticker Symbol	Traded On	Fund Type	Category and (Prospectus Objective)	Overall Rating	Reward Rating	Risk Rating	Recent Up/ Downgrade	Open to New Investors	Min Initial Investment
Transamerica Multi-Asset Income Fund Class A	TASHX	NAS CM	Open End	Cautious Alloc (Income)	B	C+	A	Up	Y	1,000
Transamerica Multi-Asset Income Fund Class C	TCSHX	NAS CM	Open End	Cautious Alloc (Income)	B	C	A-	Up	Y	1,000
Transamerica Multi-Asset Income Fund Class I	TSHIX	NAS CM	Open End	Cautious Alloc (Income)	B	C+	A	Up	Y	1,000,000
Transamerica Multi-Asset Income Fund Class I2			Open End	Cautious Alloc (Income)	B	C+	A	Up	Y	0
Transamerica Multi-Cap Growth Class A	ITSAX	NAS CM	Open End	US Equity Large Cap Growth (Growth)	C+	C	B-	Down	Y	1,000
Transamerica Multi-Cap Growth Class C	ITSLX	NAS CM	Open End	US Equity Large Cap Growth (Growth)	C+	C	B-	Down	Y	1,000
Transamerica Multi-Cap Growth Class I	TGPIX	NAS CM	Open End	US Equity Large Cap Growth (Growth)	C+	C	B	Down	Y	1,000,000
Transamerica Multi-Cap Growth Class I2			Open End	US Equity Large Cap Growth (Growth)	C+	C	B	Down	Y	0
Transamerica Multi-Managed Balanced Fund Class A	IBALX	NAS CM	Open End	Moderate Alloc (Balanced)	B	C+	A-		Y	1,000
Transamerica Multi-Managed Balanced Fund Class C	IBLLX	NAS CM	Open End	Moderate Alloc (Balanced)	B-	C	A-		Y	1,000
Transamerica Multi-Managed Balanced Fund Class I	TBLIX	NAS CM	Open End	Moderate Alloc (Balanced)	B	C+	A-		Y	1,000,000
Transamerica Multi-Managed Balanced Fund Class R6	TAMMX	NAS CM	Open End	Moderate Alloc (Balanced)	B	C+	A-		Y	0
Transamerica Multi-Mgr Alternative Strat Port Cls A	IMUAX	NAS CM	Open End	Multialternative (Growth)	C+	C	B	Up	Y	1,000
Transamerica Multi-Mgr Alternative Strat Port Cls C	IMUCX	NAS CM	Open End	Multialternative (Growth)	C	C-	B-		Y	1,000
Transamerica Multi-Mgr Alternative Strat Port Cls I	TASIX	NAS CM	Open End	Multialternative (Growth)	C+	C	B	Up	Y	1,000,000
Transamerica Multi-Mgr Alternative Strat Port Cls R6	TAMAX	NAS CM	Open End	Multialternative (Growth)	C+	C	B	Up	Y	0
Transamerica Small Cap Core Fund Class A	SCCAX	NAS CM	Open End	US Equity Small Cap (Small Company)	C-	D+	C-	Down	Y	1,000
Transamerica Small Cap Core Fund Class C	SCCCX	NAS CM	Open End	US Equity Small Cap (Small Company)	D+	D+	C-	Down	Y	1,000
Transamerica Small Cap Core Fund Class I	ISMTX	NAS CM	Open End	US Equity Small Cap (Small Company)	C-	D+	C-	Down	Y	1,000,000
Transamerica Small Cap Core Fund Class I2			Open End	US Equity Small Cap (Small Company)	C-	D+	C-	Down	Y	0
Transamerica Small Cap Core Fund Class I3	TCCTX	NAS CM	Open End	US Equity Small Cap (Small Company)	C-	D+	C-	Down	Y	0
Transamerica Small Cap Core Fund Class R	TCCRX	NAS CM	Open End	US Equity Small Cap (Small Company)	C-	D+	C-	Down	Y	0
Transamerica Small Cap Core Fund Class R4	TCCFX	NAS CM	Open End	US Equity Small Cap (Small Company)	C-	D+	C-	Down	Y	0
Transamerica Small Cap Growth A	ASGTX	NAS CM	Open End	US Equity Small Cap (Small Company)	C+	C	C+		Y	1,000
Transamerica Small Cap Growth C	CSGTX	NAS CM	Open End	US Equity Small Cap (Small Company)	C+	C	C+		Y	1,000
Transamerica Small Cap Growth I	ISCGX	NAS CM	Open End	US Equity Small Cap (Small Company)	C+	C	C+		Y	1,000,000
Transamerica Small Cap Growth I2			Open End	US Equity Small Cap (Small Company)	C+	C	C+		Y	0
Transamerica Small Cap Growth I3	TSPTX	NAS CM	Open End	US Equity Small Cap (Small Company)	C+	C	C+		Y	0
Transamerica Small Cap Growth R	TSPRX	NAS CM	Open End	US Equity Small Cap (Small Company)	C+	C	C+		Y	0
Transamerica Small Cap Growth R4	TSPFX	NAS CM	Open End	US Equity Small Cap (Small Company)	C+	C	C+		Y	0
Transamerica Small Cap Growth R6	RTSGX	NAS CM	Open End	US Equity Small Cap (Small Company)	C+	C	C+		Y	0
Transamerica Small Cap Value A	TSLAX	NAS CM	Open End	US Equity Small Cap (Small Company)	C-	D+	C	Down	Y	1,000
Transamerica Small Cap Value C	TSLCX	NAS CM	Open End	US Equity Small Cap (Small Company)	D+	D+	C	Down	Y	1,000
Transamerica Small Cap Value I	TSLIX	NAS CM	Open End	US Equity Small Cap (Small Company)	C-	D+	C	Down	Y	1,000,000
Transamerica Small Cap Value I2			Open End	US Equity Small Cap (Small Company)	C-	D+	C	Down	Y	0
Transamerica Small Cap Value I3	TSLTX	NAS CM	Open End	US Equity Small Cap (Small Company)	C-	D+	C	Down	Y	0
Transamerica Small Cap Value R	TRSLX	NAS CM	Open End	US Equity Small Cap (Small Company)	C-	D+	C		Y	0
Transamerica Small Cap Value R6	TSLRX	NAS CM	Open End	US Equity Small Cap (Small Company)	C-	D+	C	Down	Y	0
Transamerica Small/Mid Cap Value Fund Class A	IIVAX	NAS CM	Open End	US Equity Mid Cap (Growth & Income)	C+	C	B	Up	Y	1,000
Transamerica Small/Mid Cap Value Fund Class C	IIVLX	NAS CM	Open End	US Equity Mid Cap (Growth & Income)	C+	C	B	Up	Y	1,000
Transamerica Small/Mid Cap Value Fund Class I	TSVIX	NAS CM	Open End	US Equity Mid Cap (Growth & Income)	C+	C	B	Up	Y	1,000,000
Transamerica Small/Mid Cap Value Fund Class I2	TSMVX	NAS CM	Open End	US Equity Mid Cap (Growth & Income)	C+	C	B	Up	Y	0
Transamerica Small/Mid Cap Value Fund Class R6	TASMX	NAS CM	Open End	US Equity Mid Cap (Growth & Income)	C+	C	B	Up	Y	0
Transamerica Stock Index R	TSTRX	NAS CM	Open End	US Equity Large Cap Blend (Growth & Income)	B-	C	B		Y	0
Transamerica Stock Index R4	TSTFX	NAS CM	Open End	US Equity Large Cap Blend (Growth & Income)	B-	C	B		Y	0
Transamerica U.S. Equity Index VP Initial	I9CJ1	NAS CM	Open End	US Equity Large Cap Blend (Growth)	U	U	U		Y	0
Transamerica US Growth Class A	TADAX	NAS CM	Open End	US Equity Large Cap Growth (Growth)	B-	C+	B	Down	Y	1,000
Transamerica US Growth Class C	TADCX	NAS CM	Open End	US Equity Large Cap Growth (Growth)	B-	C+	B	Down	Y	1,000
Transamerica US Growth Class I	TDEIX	NAS CM	Open End	US Equity Large Cap Growth (Growth)	B-	C+	B	Down	Y	1,000,000
Transamerica US Growth Class I2			Open End	US Equity Large Cap Growth (Growth)	B-	C+	B	Down	Y	0
Transamerica US Growth Class T	TWMTX	NAS CM	Open End	US Equity Large Cap Growth (Growth)	B-	C+	B	Down	Y	1,000
Trend Aggregation Dividend & Income Institutional Shares	TRDVX	NAS CM	Open End	US Equity Large Cap Blend (Equity-Income)	D	D+	C		Y	1,000

★ Expanded analysis of this fund is included in Section II.

Min Additional Investment	TOTAL RETURNS: 3-Month Total Return	6-Month Total Return	1-Year Total Return	3-Year Total Return	5-Year Total Return	PERFORMANCE: Dividend Yield (TTM)	Expense Ratio	3-Yr Std Deviation	3-Year Beta	ASSETS: NAV	Total Assets (MIL)	ASSET ALLOCATION & TURNOVER: %Cash	%Stocks	%Bonds	%Other	Turnover Ratio	BULL & BEAR: Last Bull Market Total Return	Last Bear Market Total Return	FEES: Front End Fee (%)	Back End Fee (%)	Inception Date
50	2.75	11.16	6.65	28.33	31.41	3.24	1.08	6.72	0.54	11.15	187.1	4	44	44	0	38			5.50		Mar-14
50	2.57	10.81	5.82	25.49	26.60	2.56	1.8	6.69	0.54	11.11	187.1	4	44	44	0	38				1.00	Mar-14
	2.75	11.33	6.85	29.26	33.03	3.51	0.72	6.69	0.54	11.15	187.1	4	44	44	0	38					Mar-14
	2.76	11.30	7.01	27.59	26.50	3.72	0.78	6.72	0.54	10.67	187.1	4	44	44	0	38					Mar-14
50	3.95	19.67	7.91	40.12	14.03	0	1.25	13.26	0.94	7.36	262.6	1	99	0	0	32	17.39	-22.22	5.50		Mar-00
50	3.59	19.13	7.06	36.85	9.67	0	2	13.3	0.94	5.48	262.6	1	99	0	0	32	17.1	-22.41		1.00	Nov-02
	3.89	19.85	8.29	41.49	15.98	0.05	0.92	13.39	0.95	8.27	262.6	1	99	0	0	32	17.9	-21.91			Nov-09
	3.86	18.80	7.49	43.21	15.88	0.23	0.77	13.31	0.94	8.42	262.6	1	99	0	0	32	17.98	-21.95			Nov-05
50	3.60	13.67	8.53	29.78	38.23	1.27	1.03	7.62	0.62	27.89	988.5	7	56	37	0	48	16.03	-9.13	5.50		Dec-94
50	3.44	13.21	7.71	26.85	33.23	0.55	1.79	7.63	0.62	27.37	988.5	7	56	37	0	48	15.61	-9.31		1.00	Nov-02
	3.68	13.80	8.76	30.63	39.90	1.46	0.82	7.63	0.62	28.03	988.5	7	56	37	0	48	16.33	-8.93			Nov-09
	3.70	13.86	8.87	31.05	40.17	1.57	0.71	7.65	0.62	28.03	988.5	7	56	37	0	48	16.03	-9.13			May-15
50	1.86	6.39	2.39	7.26	3.15	1.56	2.17	3.9	0.84	9.81	94.1	30	16	36	6	11	5.68	-8.3	5.50		Dec-06
50	1.66	6.06	1.63	4.87	-0.61	0.36	2.9	3.83	0.83	9.79	94.1	30	16	36	6	11	5.27	-8.55		1.00	Dec-06
	1.87	6.53	2.72	8.28	4.85	1.87	1.82	3.88	0.83	9.78	94.1	30	16	36	6	11	5.96	-8.11			Nov-09
	1.95	6.55	2.73	8.57	4.86	1.98	1.72	3.88	0.83	9.91	94.1	30	16	36	6	11	5.68	-8.3			May-15
50	-3.67	8.37	-12.11	17.38	8.90	0.61	1.3	18.29	1.04	9.71	185.6	3	97	0	0	86	24.37	-22.92	5.50		Oct-13
50	-3.72	8.01	-12.63	14.82	4.85	0	2.05	18.32	1.04	9.57	185.6	3	97	0	0	86	23.83	-23.16		1.00	Oct-13
	-3.56	8.45	-11.88	18.15	10.17	0.88	1.02	18.37	1.05	9.75	185.6	3	97	0	0	86	24.37	-22.92			Oct-13
	-4.84	6.88	-13.33	19.23	8.98	0.97	0.92	18.33	1.04	9.77	185.6	3	97	0	0	86	24.37	-22.92			Oct-13
	-3.51	8.58	-11.87	18.79	9.33	0.97	0.92	18.3	1.04	9.87	185.6	3	97	0	0	86	24.37	-22.92			Mar-17
	-3.71	8.23	-12.25	17.18	7.31	0.38	1.42	18.32	1.04	9.86	185.6	3	97	0	0	86	24.19	-23			Mar-17
	-3.51	8.57	-12.05	18.21	8.79	0.62	1.1	18.33	1.04	9.88	185.6	3	97	0	0	86	24.37	-22.92			Sep-00
50	7.51	24.32	3.92	50.60	65.37	0	1.4	16.43	0.91	6.44	143.2	4	96	0	0	55			5.50		Aug-12
50	7.28	23.97	3.15	47.19	59.39	0	2.15	16.41	0.91	5.74	143.2	4	96	0	0	55				1.00	Aug-12
	7.53	24.48	4.22	51.55	67.49	0	1.11	16.48	0.91	6.71	143.2	4	96	0	0	55					Aug-12
	7.55	24.63	4.45	52.13	68.62	0	1	16.47	0.91	6.83	143.2	4	96	0	0	55					Aug-12
	7.55	24.63	4.16	49.04	63.66	0	1	16.57	0.92	6.83	143.2	4	96	0	0	55					Aug-12
	7.49	24.35	3.90	46.78	59.57	0	1.5	16.5	0.91	6.74	143.2	4	96	0	0	55					Mar-17
	7.42	24.76	4.19	48.22	61.94	0	1.15	16.46	0.91	6.8	143.2	4	96	0	0	55					Mar-17
	7.55	24.63	4.31	52.16	67.09	0	1.01	16.53	0.92	6.83	143.2	4	96	0	0	55					Jul-16
50	1.46	14.30	-8.27	19.99	2.72	0.54	1.3	18.72	1.05	9.67	261.0	1	99	0	0	84	28.06	-21.39	5.50		Apr-12
50	1.16	13.85	-8.97	17.40	-1.01	0	2.01	18.67	1.05	9.53	261.0	1	99	0	0	84	27.51	-21.64		1.00	Apr-12
	1.45	14.43	-7.93	21.08	4.19	0.81	1.02	18.7	1.05	9.75	261.0	1	99	0	0	84	28.25	-21.31			Apr-12
	0.10	12.79	-9.41	21.74	2.99	0.81	0.91	18.73	1.05	9.76	261.0	1	99	0	0	84	28.25	-21.31			Apr-12
	1.45	14.40	-8.14	21.11	18.87	0.81	0.92	18.69	1.05	9.77	261.0	1	99	0	0	84	28.25	-21.31			Jan-03
	1.45	14.26	-8.39	19.43	16.06	0.21	1.41	18.76	1.05	9.77	261.0	1	99	0	0	84	27.87	-21.48			Apr-17
	1.44	14.46	-7.97	21.23	18.99	0.81	0.9	18.7	1.05	9.81	261.0	1	99	0	0	84	28.25	-21.31			Jul-16
50	3.05	17.15	0.77	41.30	37.90	0.5	1.29	14.29	0.93	24.93	832.2	4	96	0	0	61	29.22	-25.84	5.50		Apr-01
50	2.85	16.65	0.05	38.43	33.26	0	1.96	14.3	0.93	21.22	832.2	4	96	0	0	61	28.68	-26.01		1.00	Nov-02
	3.14	17.31	1.14	42.78	40.35	0.81	0.94	14.3	0.93	25.88	832.2	4	96	0	0	61	29.53	-25.72			Nov-09
	3.18	17.38	1.22	43.17	41.03	0.91	0.84	14.31	0.93	25.93	832.2	4	96	0	0	61	29.52	-25.65			Nov-05
	3.20	17.39	1.22	43.21	40.49	0.91	0.84	14.31	0.93	26.05	832.2	4	96	0	0	61	29.22	-25.84			May-15
	4.12	19.19	9.65	48.16	61.55	1.41	0.61	12.15	1	12.04	518.3	1	99	0	0	12	24.72	-16.43			Apr-17
	4.21	19.38	9.97	49.48	63.81	1.77	0.3	12.16	1	12.04	518.3	1	99	0	0	12	24.9	-16.34			Sep-00
	3.55	9.12					0.14				25.8	6	94	0	0						Jan-18
50	5.39	25.00	12.50	63.39	84.54	0	1.16	14.2	1.05	21.3	1,126	0	100	0	0	27	27.2	-20.04	5.50		Nov-09
50	5.12	24.43	11.52	59.40	77.26	0	1.96	14.24	1.05	19.71	1,126	0	100	0	0	27	26.67	-20.28		1.00	Nov-09
	5.46	25.15	12.81	64.83	87.45	0	0.87	14.21	1.05	21.79	1,126	0	100	0	0	27	27.62	-20			Nov-09
	5.81	24.69	12.83	67.42	87.73	0	0.75	14.19	1.05	21.76	1,126	0	100	0	0	27	27.74	-19.86			Nov-09
50	5.45	25.23	12.85	65.06	87.90	0	0.81	14.2	1.05	61.84	1,126	0	100	0	0	27	27.72	-19.86	8.50		Feb-12
500	3.13	7.04	2.45			0.33	1.62			9.87	83.3	18	65	17	0						May-18

	MARKET		FUND TYPE, CATEGORY & OBJECTIVE		RATINGS				MINIMUMS	
Fund Name	Ticker Symbol	Traded On	Fund Type	Category and (Prospectus Objective)	Overall Rating	Reward Rating	Risk Rating	Recent Up/ Downgrade	Open to New Investors	Min Initial Investment
Trend Aggregation Growth Fund Institutional Shares	TRAGX	NAS CM	Open End	US Equity Large Cap Growth (Growth)	D	D+	C		Y	1,000
Tributary Balanced Fund Class Institutional Plus	FOBPX	NAS CM	Open End	Moderate Alloc (Balanced)	B	C+	A-		Y	5,000,000
Tributary Balanced Fund Institutional Class	FOBAX	NAS CM	Open End	Moderate Alloc (Balanced)	B	C+	A-		Y	1,000
Tributary Growth Opportunities Cls Institutional Plus	FOGPX	NAS CM	Open End	US Equity Mid Cap (Growth)	C+	C+	B	Down	Y	5,000,000
Tributary Growth Opportunities Fund Institutional Class	FOGRX	NAS CM	Open End	US Equity Mid Cap (Growth)	C+	C+	B	Down	Y	1,000
Tributary Small Company Fund Institutional Class	FOSCX	NAS CM	Open End	US Equity Small Cap (Small Company)	C	C-	C+		Y	1,000
Tributary Small Company Fund Institutional Plus Class	FOSBX	NAS CM	Open End	US Equity Small Cap (Small Company)	C	C-	B-		Y	5,000,000
Tri-Continental Corporation	TY	NYSE	Closed End	Aggressive Alloc (Growth & Income)	C	C	C-		Y	
Trillium P21 Global Equity Fund Class Institutional	PORIX	NAS CM	Open End	Global Equity Large Cap (World Stock)	B-	C	B	Up	Y	100,000
Trillium P21 Global Equity Fund Class R	PORTX	NAS CM	Open End	Global Equity Large Cap (World Stock)	B-	C	B	Up	Y	5,000
Trillium Small/Mid Cap Fund Institutional Class	TSMDX	NAS CM	Open End	US Equity Mid Cap (Growth)	C	C	B-		Y	100,000
TS&W Equity Portfolio Institutional Class Shares	TSWEX	NAS CM	Open End	US Equity Large Cap Value (Growth & Income)	B-	C	B+		Y	2,500
Tweedy, Browne Global Value Fund	TBGVX	NAS CM	Open End	Global Equity Large Cap (Foreign Stock)	B-	C	A-	Up	Y	2,500
Tweedy, Browne Global Value Fund II - Currency Unhedged	TBCUX	NAS CM	Open End	Global Equity Large Cap (Foreign Stock)	C+	C	B+	Up		2,500
Tweedy, Browne Value Fund	TWEBX	NAS CM	Open End	Global Equity Large Cap (Growth)	B-	C	A-	Up	Y	2,500
Tweedy, Browne Worldwide High Dividend Yield Value Fund	TBHDX	NAS CM	Open End	Global Equity Large Cap (Growth)	B	C	A-	Up	Y	2,500
Two Oaks Diversified Growth & Income Class A Shares	TWOAX	NAS CM	Open End	Aggressive Alloc (Growth & Income)	C+	C	B		Y	2,500
U.S. Global Investors All American Equity Fund	GBTFX	NAS CM	Open End	US Equity Large Cap Blend (Growth)	C+	C	B	Down	Y	5,000
U.S. Global Investors China Region Fund Investor Class	USCOX	NAS CM	Open End	Greater China Equity (Pacific Stock)	C-	C-	C-		Y	5,000
U.S. Global Investors Emerging Europe Fund	EUROX	NAS CM	Open End	Equity Miscellaneous (Europe Stock)	C	C	C+		Y	5,000
U.S. Global Investors Global Resources Fund	PSPFX	NAS CM	Open End	Natl Resources Sec Equity (Natl Res)	D	D	D		Y	5,000
U.S. Global Investors Gold and Precious Metals Fund	USERX	NAS CM	Open End	Precious Metals Sector Equity (Precious Metals)	D	D	D+	Down	Y	5,000
U.S. Global Investors Holmes Macro Trends Fund	MEGAX	NAS CM	Open End	US Equity Mid Cap (Growth)	C+	C-	B		Y	5,000
U.S. Global Investors World Precious Minerals Fund	UNWPX	NAS CM	Open End	Precious Metals Sector Equity (Precious Metals)	D-	D-	D-	Down	Y	5,000
UBS Dynamic Alpha Fund Class A	BNAAX	NAS CM	Open End	Global Macro (Asset Alloc)	C	D+	C+	Up	Y	1,000
UBS Dynamic Alpha Fund Class P	BNAYX	NAS CM	Open End	Global Macro (Asset Alloc)	C	D+	B-	Up	Y	5,000,000
UBS Emerging Markets Equity Opportunity Fund Class P	UEMPX	NAS CM	Open End	Global Emerg Mkts (Growth)	D	D+	C		Y	5,000,000
UBS Emerging Markets Equity Opportunity Fund Class P2	EMPTX	NAS CM	Open End	Global Emerg Mkts (Growth)	D	D+	C		Y	25,000,000
UBS Engage For Impact Fund Class P	UEIPX	NAS CM	Open End	Global Equity Large Cap (Growth & Income)	U	U	U		Y	5,000,000
UBS Global Allocation Fund Class A	BNGLX	NAS CM	Open End	Moderate Alloc (Asset Alloc)	B-	C	B+	Up	Y	1,000
UBS Global Allocation Fund Class P	BPGLX	NAS CM	Open End	Moderate Alloc (Asset Alloc)	B-	C	A-	Up	Y	5,000,000
UBS International Sustainable Equity Fund Class A	BNIEX	NAS CM	Open End	Global Equity Large Cap (Foreign Stock)	C	C	B-		Y	1,000
UBS International Sustainable Equity Fund Class P	BNUEX	NAS CM	Open End	Global Equity Large Cap (Foreign Stock)	C	C	B-		Y	5,000,000
UBS U.S. Allocation Fund Class A	PWTAX	NAS CM	Open End	Moderate Alloc (Asset Alloc)	B-	C	B	Up	Y	1,000
UBS U.S. Allocation Fund Class P	PWTYX	NAS CM	Open End	Moderate Alloc (Asset Alloc)	B-	C	B+	Up	Y	5,000,000
UBS U.S. Small Cap Growth Fund Class A	BNSCX	NAS CM	Open End	US Equity Small Cap (Small Company)	C+	C	C+		Y	1,000
UBS U.S. Small Cap Growth Fund Class P	BISCX	NAS CM	Open End	US Equity Small Cap (Small Company)	C+	C	C+		Y	5,000,000
UBS U.S. Sustainable Equity Fund Class A	BNEQX	NAS CM	Open End	US Equity Large Cap Blend (Growth & Income)	C+	C	B	Down	Y	1,000
UBS U.S. Sustainable Equity Fund Class P	BPEQX	NAS CM	Open End	US Equity Large Cap Blend (Growth & Income)	C+	C	B	Down	Y	5,000,000
Undiscovered Managers Behavioral Value Fund Class A	UBVAX	NAS CM	Open End	US Equity Small Cap (Growth)	C	C-	C+			1,000
Undiscovered Managers Behavioral Value Fund Class C	UBVCX	NAS CM	Open End	US Equity Small Cap (Growth)	C	C-	C			1,000
Undiscovered Managers Behavioral Value Fund Class I	UBVSX	NAS CM	Open End	US Equity Small Cap (Growth)	C	C-	C+		Y	1,000,000
Undiscovered Managers Behavioral Value Fund Class L	UBVLX	NAS CM	Open End	US Equity Small Cap (Growth)	C	C-	C+		Y	3,000,000
Undiscovered Managers Behavioral Value Fund Class R2	UBVRX	NAS CM	Open End	US Equity Small Cap (Growth)	C	C-	C+		Y	0
Undiscovered Managers Behavioral Value Fund Class R3	UBVTX	NAS CM	Open End	US Equity Small Cap (Growth)	C	C-	C+		Y	0
Undiscovered Managers Behavioral Value Fund Class R4	UBVUX	NAS CM	Open End	US Equity Small Cap (Growth)	C	C-	C+		Y	0
Undiscovered Managers Behavioral Value Fund Class R5	UBVVX	NAS CM	Open End	US Equity Small Cap (Growth)	C	C-	C+		Y	0
Undiscovered Managers Behavioral Value Fund Class R6	UBVFX	NAS CM	Open End	US Equity Small Cap (Growth)	C	C-	C+		Y	15,000,000
Union Street Partners Value Fund Advisor Class	USPFX	NAS CM	Open End	US Equity Large Cap Value (Growth)	C	C	C+	Down	Y	2,500
Union Street Partners Value Fund C Class	USPCX	NAS CM	Open End	US Equity Large Cap Value (Growth)	C	C	C+	Down	Y	2,500
Union Street Partners Value Fund Class A Shares	USPVX	NAS CM	Open End	US Equity Large Cap Value (Growth)	C	C	C+	Down	Y	2,500
Upright Assets Allocation Plus Fund	UPAAX	NAS CM	Open End	Cautious Alloc (Multi-Asset Global)	D	D	D-		Y	2,000

★ Expanded analysis of this fund is included in Section II.

Min Additional Investment	TOTAL RETURNS 3-Month Total Return	6-Month Total Return	1-Year Total Return	3-Year Total Return	5-Year Total Return	PERFORMANCE Dividend Yield (TTM)	Expense Ratio	3-Yr Std Deviation	3-Year Beta	ASSETS NAV	Total Assets (MIL)	ASSET ALLOCATION & TURNOVER %Cash	%Stocks	%Bonds	%Other	Turnover Ratio	BULL & BEAR Last Bull Market Total Return	Last Bear Market Total Return	FEES Front End Fee (%)	Back End Fee (%)	Inception Date
500	3.24	10.55	1.30			0.33	1.8			9.85	93.1	-3	98	4	0						May-18
50	3.45	13.37	8.37	29.82	34.08	1.12	0.85	7.73		17.21	72.7	4	62	34	0		17.03	-9.92			Oct-11
50	3.41	13.30	8.16	29.06	32.82	0.89	1.04	7.72		17.38	72.7	4	62	34	0		17.01	-9.92			Aug-96
50	3.17	23.77	11.80	53.38	55.22	0	0.94	14.4	0.98	17.23	144.7	2	98	0	0		29.94	-24.36			Oct-11
50	3.12	23.69	11.61	52.52	53.67	0	1.13	14.4	0.98	16.81	144.7	2	98	0	0		29.78	-24.36			Apr-98
50	1.35	15.02	-2.60	33.70	40.63	0	1.22	16.91	0.97	27.64	826.3	5	95	0	0		26.46	-21.38			Jun-96
50	1.38	15.14	-2.43	34.53	42.08	0.09	0.99	16.9	0.97	27.83	826.3	5	95	0	0		26.67	-21.31			Dec-10
	2.71	16.05	6.98	45.75	52.31	3.22	0.56	10.59	0.86	30.03	1,617	0	71	16	-3	63	25.71	-14.7			Jan-29
1,000	4.74	18.48	8.80	46.61	45.69	0.8	1.02	10.99	0.95	44.61	559.3	4	96	0	0	12	14.05	-19.46			Mar-07
100	4.67	18.32	8.51	45.47	43.77	0.54	1.29	10.99	0.95	44.81	559.3	4	96	0	0	12	13.82	-19.52			Sep-99
1,000	3.95	19.41	0.32	40.31		0.12	0.98	16.01	0.98	12.36	19.9	0	100	0	0	19					Aug-15
100	3.69	13.47	8.55	38.04	38.87	1.38	1.7	11.51	0.88	12.27	34.5	8	92	0	0	60	22.18	-20.88			Jul-92
200	3.71	12.63	4.43	28.54	22.16	1.34	1.36	8.82	0.84	27.91	8,252	5	91	4	0	6	14.63	-14.18			Jun-93
200	4.10	11.96	2.77	27.64	9.70	1.23	1.37	10.39	0.89	15.72	511.2	14	86	0	0	2	12.62	-14			Oct-09
200	2.03	12.15	5.59	30.88	22.60	1.02	1.37	9.25	0.81	20.02	453.2	8	92	0	0	9	17.1	-15.19			Dec-93
200	5.11	13.81	7.08	37.11	18.09	2.35	1.37	9.78	0.78	8.82	155.8	8	92	0	0	6	12.4	-11.79			Sep-07
1,000	2.71	15.03	2.29	22.53	28.20	1.12	1.72	10.53	0.76	13.2	27.9	5	79	17	0	15	16.12	-10.52	5.75		Apr-02
100	2.97	10.96	2.18	10.08	4.66	0.59	1.86	10.93	0.83	24.59	14.0	0	97	3	0	244	26.04	-18.31			Mar-81
100	-0.90	17.02	-16.02	28.82	12.60	0.87	2.66	18.38	0.98	8.73	15.3	1	99	0	0	109	8.78	-29			Feb-94
100	9.66	18.57	5.61	35.16	-11.59	0	2.43	14.26	0.59	7.15	33.8	2	99	0	0	81	15.06	-32.67			Mar-97
100	2.88	6.92	-15.89	2.61	-49.07	4.43	1.57	14.17	0.77	4.63	60.8	4	86	8	3	119	15.48	-31.76			Aug-83
100	11.26	21.76	6.62	-8.91	9.75	1.48	1.78	26.12	0.17	8	102.3	4	92	3	1	74	-12.37	-18.04			Jul-74
100	-0.52	10.91	1.33	39.38	22.48	0	1.77	13.72	0.92	16.97	36.2	0	96	3	1	245	23.57	-21.9			Oct-94
100	5.90	8.71	-10.35	-41.24	-32.91	16.42	1.54	25.85	0.38	2.87	72.2	3	95	1	2	55	-9.38	-28.46			Nov-85
100	1.11	4.77	0.59	4.35	-4.83	0.87	1.37	4.03	-0.2	6.36	49.5	49	22	28	0	31	5.43	-2.09	5.50		Jan-05
0	1.39	4.99	0.82	5.33	-3.52	1.08	1.12	3.96	-0.2	6.52	49.5	49	22	28	0	31	5.5	-2.05			Jan-05
	0.65	14.85	-0.78				1.16			9.28	222.9	3	97	0	0	0					Jan-19
	0.86	15.22	-0.46			0.52	0.41			9.31	222.9	3	97	0	0	0					May-18
100	1.59	17.22					0.85			10.82	15.9	2	98	0	0						Oct-18
100	2.69	12.24	3.97	25.23	21.20	0	1.29	7.81	0.67	12.56	268.0	29	59	12	0	54	12.36	-15.98	5.50		Jun-97
0	2.79	12.40	4.21	26.14	22.76	0	1.04	7.8	0.67	12.87	268.0	29	59	12	0	54	12.56	-15.86			Aug-92
100	3.73	14.79	-0.13	32.69	20.46	0.58	1.26	12.32	1.07	10.01	156.4	3	97	0	0	43	19.69	-27.94	5.50		Jun-97
0	3.82	14.87	0.09	33.62	21.85	0.78	1.01	12.35	1.07	10.04	156.4	3	97	0	0	43	19.81	-27.81			Aug-93
100	3.43	16.67	5.71	30.67	36.77	1	1.02	9.62	0.77	46.68	236.9	22	58	20	0	132	18.79	-12.16	5.50		May-93
0	3.49	16.81	5.99	31.71	38.62	1.17	0.76	9.6	0.77	47.65	236.9	22	58	20	0	132	18.99	-12.08			May-93
100	6.56	29.80	5.95	67.88	58.59	0	1.25	19.59	1.09	19.47	122.5	4	96	0	0	67	32.05	-21.63	5.50		Dec-98
0	6.64	29.95	6.23	69.15	60.69	0	1	19.6	1.09	21.82	122.5	4	96	0	0	67	32.3	-21.52			Sep-97
100	5.13	24.28	6.94	48.19	52.43	0.88	0.95	15.48	1.2	36.44	30.4	0	100	0	0	166	24.86	-19.44	5.50		Jun-97
0	5.17	24.44	7.20	49.25	54.28	1.09	0.7	15.46	1.19	36.6	30.4	0	100	0	0	166	25	-19.29			Feb-94
50	2.08	16.88	-5.16	30.10	37.83	0.82	1.37	17.81	0.98	60.63	5,377	6	94	0	0		43.24	-27.32	5.25		Jun-04
50	1.95	16.58	-5.62	28.16	34.41	0.38	1.87	17.81	0.98	56.73	5,377	6	94	0	0		42.84	-27.49		1.00	Jun-04
	2.14	17.01	-4.92	31.07	39.55	1.07	1.12	17.81	0.98	62.04	5,377	6	94	0	0		43.43	-27.3			Apr-13
	2.16	17.09	-4.79	31.67	40.59	1.22	0.97	17.81	0.98	62.25	5,377	6	94	0	0		43.43	-27.3			Dec-98
	2.00	16.73	-5.39	29.12	36.11	0.69	1.62	17.82	0.98	59.98	5,377	6	94	0	0		43.01	-27.45			Apr-13
	2.07	16.86	-5.16	30.21	38.35	1.13	1.37	17.81	0.98	60.14	5,377	6	94	0	0		43.22	-27.38			Feb-17
	2.12	17.01	-4.92	31.20	40.09	1.13	1.12	17.82	0.98	61.89	5,377	6	94	0	0		43.43	-27.3			Feb-17
	2.16	17.11	-4.78	31.67	40.60	1.27	0.97	17.8	0.98	62.2	5,377	6	94	0	0		43.43	-27.3			Feb-17
	2.19	17.15	-4.69	32.06	41.28	1.32	0.87	17.83	0.98	62.36	5,377	6	94	0	0		43.43	-27.3			Apr-13
50	1.31	15.46	-1.19	35.74	32.33	0.82	1.35	15.69	1.2	17.77	30.3	7	92	0	0	26	21.44	-18.35			Apr-16
50	1.00	14.87	-2.19	31.70	26.25	0	2.35	15.69	1.2	17.14	30.3	7	92	0	0	26	20.94	-18.64		1.00	Apr-11
50	1.20	15.26	-1.48	34.75	31.08	1.1	1.6	15.68	1.2	17.67	30.3	7	92	0	0	26	21.43	-18.35	5.75		Dec-10
100	-0.96	-0.41	-14.47			0	1.75			7.21	0.80	44	53	0	4	53					Oct-17

	MARKET			FUND TYPE, CATEGORY & OBJECTIVE	RATINGS					MINIMUMS
Fund Name	Ticker Symbol	Traded On	Fund Type	Category and (Prospectus Objective)	Overall Rating	Reward Rating	Risk Rating	Recent Up/ Downgrade	Open to New Investors	Min Initial Investment
Upright Growth & Income Fund	UPDDX	NAS CM	Open End	US Equity Large Cap Value (Growth & Income)	D	D	D-		Y	2,000
Upright Growth Fund	UPUPX	NAS CM	Open End	Technology Sector Equity (Growth)	D-	D-	D	Down	Y	2,000
USA Mutuals Navigator Fund Institutional Class	UNAVX	NAS CM	Open End	Long/Short Equity (Growth)	C-	C-	C+	Up	Y	2,000
USA Mutuals Vice Fund Class A Shares	VICAX	NAS CM	Open End	US Equity Large Cap Blend (Growth)	C	C	C+		Y	2,000
USA Mutuals Vice Fund Class C Shares	VICCX	NAS CM	Open End	US Equity Large Cap Blend (Growth)	C	C-	C+		Y	2,000
USA Mutuals Vice Fund Institutional Class	VICVX	NAS CM	Open End	US Equity Large Cap Blend (Growth)	C	C	C+		Y	2,000
USA Mutuals Vice Fund Investor Class Shares	VICEX	NAS CM	Open End	US Equity Large Cap Blend (Growth)	C	C	C+		Y	2,000
USAA Aggressive Growth Fund	USAUX	NAS CM	Open End	US Equity Large Cap Growth (Aggr Growth)	B-	C	B	Down	Y	3,000
USAA Aggressive Growth Fund Institutional Shares	UIAGX	NAS CM	Open End	US Equity Large Cap Growth (Aggr Growth)	B-	C	B	Down	Y	1,000,000
USAA Capital Growth Fund	USCGX	NAS CM	Open End	Global Equity Large Cap (Growth)	C+	C	B	Up	Y	3,000
USAA Capital Growth Fund Institutional Shares	UICGX	NAS CM	Open End	Global Equity Large Cap (Growth)	C+	C	B	Up	Y	1,000,000
USAA Cornerstone Aggressive Fund	UCAGX	NAS CM	Open End	Aggressive Alloc (Growth)	B-	C	B+	Up	Y	500
USAA Cornerstone Conservative Fund	USCCX	NAS CM	Open End	Cautious Alloc (Asset Alloc)	B-	C+	B+		Y	500
USAA Cornerstone Equity Fund	UCEQX	NAS CM	Open End	Global Equity Large Cap (Growth)	C+	C	B	Up	Y	500
USAA Cornerstone Moderate Fund	USBSX	NAS CM	Open End	Moderate Alloc (Balanced)	B-	C	B+	Up	Y	500
USAA Cornerstone Moderately Aggressive Fund	USCRX	NAS CM	Open End	Moderate Alloc (Multi-Asset Global)	B-	C	B+	Up	Y	500
USAA Cornerstone Moderately Conservative Fund	UCMCX	NAS CM	Open End	Cautious Alloc (Balanced)	B-	C	B+	Up	Y	500
USAA Emerging Markets Fund	USEMX	NAS CM	Open End	Global Emerg Mkts (Div Emerging Mkts)	C	C	C+		Y	3,000
USAA Emerging Markets Fund Adviser Shares	UAEMX	NAS CM	Open End	Global Emerg Mkts (Div Emerging Mkts)	C	C	C+		Y	3,000
USAA Emerging Markets Fund Institutional Shares	UIEMX	NAS CM	Open End	Global Emerg Mkts (Div Emerging Mkts)	C	C	C+		Y	1,000,000
USAA Extended Market Index Fund	USMIX	NAS CM	Open End	US Equity Mid Cap (Growth)	C+	C	B-		Y	3,000
USAA Global Equity Income Fund Fund Shares	UGEIX	NAS CM	Open End	Global Equity Large Cap (Equity-Income)	B-	C	B+	Up	Y	3,000
USAA Global Equity Income Fund Institutional Shares	UIGEX	NAS CM	Open End	Global Equity Large Cap (Equity-Income)	B-	C	B+	Up	Y	1,000,000
USAA Global Managed Volatility Fund Fund Shares	UGMVX	NAS CM	Open End	Global Equity Large Cap (Equity-Income)	B-	C	B+	Up	Y	3,000
USAA Global Managed Volatility Fund Institutional Shares	UGOFX	NAS CM	Open End	Global Equity Large Cap (Equity-Income)	B-	C	B+	Up	Y	1,000,000
USAA Growth & Income Fund	USGRX	NAS CM	Open End	US Equity Large Cap Blend (Growth & Income)	C+	C	B		Y	3,000
USAA Growth & Income Fund Adviser Shares	USGIX	NAS CM	Open End	US Equity Large Cap Blend (Growth & Income)	C+	C	B	Up	Y	3,000
USAA Growth & Income Fund Institutional Shares	UIGIX	NAS CM	Open End	US Equity Large Cap Blend (Growth & Income)	C+	C	B		Y	1,000,000
USAA Growth and Tax Strategy Fund	USBLX	NAS CM	Open End	Cautious Alloc (Asset Alloc)	B	C+	A-		Y	3,000
USAA Growth Fund	USAAX	NAS CM	Open End	US Equity Large Cap Growth (Growth)	B-	C+	B	Down	Y	3,000
USAA Growth Fund Institutional Shares	UIGRX	NAS CM	Open End	US Equity Large Cap Growth (Growth)	B-	C+	B	Down	Y	1,000,000
USAA Income Stock Fund	USISX	NAS CM	Open End	US Equity Large Cap Value (Equity-Income)	B-	C	B+	Down	Y	3,000
USAA Income Stock Fund Institutional Shares	UIISX	NAS CM	Open End	US Equity Large Cap Value (Equity-Income)	B-	C	B+	Down	Y	1,000,000
USAA Income Stock Fund R6 Shares	URISX	NAS CM	Open End	US Equity Large Cap Value (Equity-Income)	B-	C	B+	Down	Y	0
USAA International Fund	USIFX	NAS CM	Open End	Global Equity Large Cap (Foreign Stock)	C	C	B		Y	3,000
USAA International Fund Adviser Shares	UAIFX	NAS CM	Open End	Global Equity Large Cap (Foreign Stock)	C	C	B		Y	3,000
USAA International Fund Institutional Shares	UIIFX	NAS CM	Open End	Global Equity Large Cap (Foreign Stock)	C	C	B		Y	1,000,000
USAA International Fund R6 Shares	URITX	NAS CM	Open End	Global Equity Large Cap (Foreign Stock)	C	C	B		Y	0
USAA Managed Allocation Fund	UMAFX	NAS CM	Open End	Moderate Alloc (Asset Alloc)	C	C-	C+	Up	Y	0
USAA Nasdaq 100 Index Fund R6 Shares	URNQX	NAS CM	Open End	US Equity Large Cap Growth (Growth)	B-	C+	B		Y	0
USAA NASDAQ-100 Index Fund	USNQX	NAS CM	Open End	US Equity Large Cap Growth (Growth)	B-	C+	B		Y	3,000
USAA Precious Metals and Minerals Fund	USAGX	NAS CM	Open End	Precious Metals Sector Equity (Precious Metals)	D+	D	C-	Down	Y	3,000
USAA Precious Metals and Minerals Fund Adviser Shares	UPMMX	NAS CM	Open End	Precious Metals Sector Equity (Precious Metals)	D+	D	C-	Down	Y	3,000
USAA Precious Metals & Minerals Institutional Shares	UIPMX	NAS CM	Open End	Precious Metals Sector Equity (Precious Metals)	D+	D	C	Down	Y	1,000,000
USAA S&P 500 Index Fund Member Shares	USSPX	NAS CM	Open End	US Equity Large Cap Blend (Growth & Income)	B-	C	B		Y	3,000
USAA S&P 500 Index Fund Reward Shares	USPRX	NAS CM	Open End	US Equity Large Cap Blend (Growth & Income)	B-	C	B		Y	100,000
USAA Science & Technology Fund	USSCX	NAS CM	Open End	Technology Sector Equity (Technology)	B-	C+	B-		Y	3,000
USAA Science & Technology Fund Adviser Shares	USTCX	NAS CM	Open End	Technology Sector Equity (Technology)	C+	C+	B-	Down	Y	3,000
USAA Small Cap Stock Fund	USCAX	NAS CM	Open End	US Equity Small Cap (Small Company)	C	C	C+	Down	Y	3,000
USAA Small Cap Stock Fund Institutional Shares	UISCX	NAS CM	Open End	US Equity Small Cap (Small Company)	C	C	C+	Down	Y	1,000,000
USAA Target Managed Allocation Fund	UTMAX	NAS CM	Open End	Moderate Alloc (Asset Alloc)	B-	C	B	Up	Y	0
USAA Target Retirement 2020 Fund	URTNX	NAS CM	Open End	Target Date (Asset Alloc)	B	C	A-	Up	Y	500

★ Expanded analysis of this fund is included in Section II.

	TOTAL RETURNS					PERFORMANCE				ASSETS		ASSET ALLOCATION & TURNOVER					BULL & BEAR		FEES		
Min Additional Investment	3-Month Total Return	6-Month Total Return	1-Year Total Return	3-Year Total Return	5-Year Total Return	Dividend Yield (TTM)	Expense Ratio	3-Yr Std Deviation	3-Year Beta	NAV	Total Assets (MIL)	%Cash	%Stocks	%Bonds	%Other	Turnover Ratio	Last Bull Market Total Return	Last Bear Market Total Return	Front End Fee (%)	Back End Fee (%)	Inception Date
100	-0.39	0.39	-14.04			0	1.95			7.53	0.82	39	62	0	-1	31					Oct-17
100	-2.47	0.69	-36.04	-56.79	-53.33	0	2.4	36.39	1.2	4.33	10.3	3	98	0	0	129	34.71	-20.89			Jan-99
100	3.18	16.38	8.80			0.09	2			22.72	90.4	36	46	18	0	0					Oct-17
100	2.89	20.36	-1.41	21.86	27.78	0.34	1.49	14.52	1.01	29.75	157.4	0	100	0	0	15	30.04	-13.93	5.75		Dec-11
100	2.68	19.90	-2.19	19.38	23.27	0.11	2.24	14.48	1	29.14	157.4	0	100	0	0	15	29.56	-14.2		1.00	Dec-11
100	2.93	20.47	-1.19	23.18	29.73	0.46	1.24	14.5	1.01	30.33	157.4	0	100	0	0	15	30.04	-13.93			Apr-14
100	2.87	20.31	-1.43	22.03	27.93	0.33	1.49	14.5	1.01	29.92	157.4	0	100	0	0	15	30.04	-13.93			Aug-02
50	4.75	21.07	9.14	61.42	76.99	0.15	0.75	14.34	1.05	44.3	1,659	2	98	0	0	57	26.56	-18.73			Oct-81
	4.73	21.07	9.15	61.47	77.74	0.24	0.7	14.35	1.05	44.93	1,659	2	98	0	0	57	26.82	-18.55			Aug-08
50	0.89	13.54	0.45	37.86	42.29	1.38	1.15	12.48	1.07	11.32	939.0	0	100	0	0	22	19.28	-22.05			Oct-00
	0.97	13.61	0.50	38.06	42.90	1.42	1.1	12.54	1.07	11.35	939.0	0	100	0	0	22	19.28	-22.05			Aug-15
50	2.57	12.59	2.72	25.89	19.24	1.38	1.21	9.03	0.79	12.34	369.0	3	73	23	0	65					Jun-12
50	3.12	8.74	6.88	15.45	18.89	2.91	0.69	3.46	0.82	10.91	199.6	3	20	76	0	5					Jun-12
50	2.99	15.55	2.90	34.75	29.72	1.63	0.85	11.42	1	14.78	214.7	2	96	1	0	38					Jun-12
50	2.53	9.93	4.01	19.44	16.02	2.09	1.08	5.96	0.5	14.5	1,199	5	43	51	0	51	12.47	-13.37			Sep-95
50	2.50	10.65	3.41	20.95	16.07	1.09	1.07	6.95	0.6	24.93	2,877	4	54	41	0	56	10.64	-13.98			Aug-84
50	2.50	8.87	4.47	15.97	14.83	2.15	0.97	4.97	0.91	11.19	232.4	5	38	55	0	45					Jun-12
50	1.78	14.68	2.11	27.37	3.01	1.12	1.46	13.91	0.97	18.2	801.7	9	91	0	0	59	14.97	-28.85			Nov-94
	1.68	14.52	1.87	26.49	1.89	0.86	1.75	13.91	0.97	18.13	801.7	9	91	0	0	59	14.71	-28.97			Aug-10
	1.85	14.80	2.33	28.10	4.19	1.36	1.28	13.92	0.97	18.15	801.7	9	91	0	0	59	15.14	-28.77			Aug-08
50	2.94	20.38	1.64	45.49	43.14	0.83	0.43	15.22	1	19.25	765.2	0	100	0	0	12	28.3	-23.55			Oct-00
50	3.62	14.32	7.03	26.97		2.33	1	9.65	0.98	10.8	83.3	2	98	0	0	15					Aug-15
	3.68	14.41	7.16	27.11		2.45	0.9	9.67	0.98	10.81	83.3	2	98	0	0	15					Aug-15
50	2.98	14.45	5.02	33.47	23.32	1.36	1.07	9.8	0.86	10.69	1,059	2	98	0	0	35	11.32	-12.57			Jul-13
	3.04	14.49	5.26	34.33	24.80	1.52	0.87	9.85	0.86	10.82	1,059	2	98	0	0	35	11.32	-12.57			Jul-08
50	3.76	16.98	4.68	47.06	49.10	0.9	0.88	13.32	1.04	23.83	1,871	3	97	0	0	23	24.4	-19.56			Jun-93
	3.71	16.84	4.37	45.81	46.99	0.65	1.15	13.32	1.04	23.75	1,871	3	97	0	0	23	24.14	-19.69			Aug-10
	3.74	16.98	4.69	47.22	49.36	0.94	0.84	13.32	1.04	23.8	1,871	3	97	0	0	23	24.4	-19.56			Aug-15
50	3.44	11.84	8.18	25.20	38.69	2.3	0.62	6.04	0.46	20.77	543.4	1	46	53	0	10	14.66	-4.01			Jan-89
50	5.42	22.99	14.42	60.44	82.65	0.27	0.94	13.58	0.99	31.5	2,860	1	99	0	0	19	24.34	-17.28			Apr-71
	5.43	23.01	14.47	60.77	83.26	0.28	0.89	13.59	0.99	31.43	2,860	1	99	0	0	19	24.32	-17.21			Aug-08
50	3.36	15.64	9.73	35.16	44.93	2.09	0.76	10.44	0.84	19.68	2,891	1	99	0	0	23	22.9	-16.68			May-87
	3.32	15.55	9.72	35.19	45.14	2.12	0.72	10.44	0.84	19.65	2,891	1	99	0	0	23	22.9	-16.52			Aug-08
	3.34	15.65	9.79	35.50	45.30	2.18	0.65	10.42	0.84	19.66	2,891	1	99	0	0	23	22.9	-16.68			Dec-16
50	5.02	16.28	2.14	36.95	20.85	1.37	1.08	11.18	1	30.49	3,895	1	99	0	0	36	18.96	-23.19			Jul-88
	4.94	16.14	1.87	35.87	19.26	1.08	1.35	11.18	1	30.36	3,895	1	99	0	0	36	18.71	-23.28			Aug-10
	5.04	16.34	2.22	37.33	21.48	1.43	1	11.17	1	30.4	3,895	1	99	0	0	36	19.07	-23.08			Aug-08
	5.10	16.48	2.35	37.23	21.09		0.85	11.17	1	30.46	3,895	1	99	0	0	36	18.96	-23.19			Aug-18
	1.94	11.17	0.06	9.44	6.85	0.97	0.91	9.88	0.67	11.54	751.3	0	48	52	0	97	9.1	-1.59			Feb-10
	4.16	22.49	9.73	79.50	106.40	0.63	0.4	15.14	1	21.51	2,154	3	97	0	0	5	27.52	-10.94			Mar-17
50	4.16	22.49	9.66	79.12	105.96	0.54	0.48	15.12	1	21.51	2,154	3	97	0	0	5	27.52	-10.94			Oct-00
50	12.14	24.65	11.53	-10.13	-8.79	0	1.23	25.34	0.03	14.31	586.0	1	99	0	0	13	-15.77	-12.02			Aug-84
	12.11	24.64	11.40	-10.32	-9.08	0	1.3	25.34	0.03	14.16	586.0	1	99	0	0	13	-15.95	-12.13			Aug-10
	12.23	24.80	12.05	-8.96	-7.17	0	1	25.32	0.03	14.59	586.0	1	99	0	0	13	-15.68	-11.93			Aug-08
50	4.24	19.43	10.13	49.78	64.22	1.63	0.25	12.2		41.35	7,716	2	97	0	0	4	24.94	-16.36			May-96
50	4.27	19.48	10.26	50.22	65.02	1.72	0.15	12.19		41.37	7,716	2	97	0	0	4	25.01	-16.31			May-02
50	5.54	28.77	12.17	76.67	105.03	0	1.04	16.39	1.18	27.79	1,459	1	99	0	0	56	24.72	-16.27			Aug-97
	5.47	28.57	11.87	75.27	102.50	0	1.31	16.4	1.18	26.95	1,459	1	99	0	0	56	24.55	-16.38			Aug-10
50	4.26	19.66	-1.04	41.33	35.00	0.2	1.06	17.17	1	16.61	1,601	4	96	0	0	68	27.55	-24.05			Aug-99
	4.28	19.68	-0.90	41.79	35.97	0.25	0.95	17.21	1	16.78	1,601	4	96	0	0	68	27.79	-23.91			Aug-08
	3.11	13.88	2.92	22.62		1.28	0.86	8.98	0.76	10.58	525.8	1	65	33	0	195					Aug-15
50	2.90	10.14	5.49	22.77	22.21	2.32	0.69	5.54	0.92	12.38	585.9	2	44	54	0	34	11.14	-9.19			Jul-08

	MARKET			FUND TYPE, CATEGORY & OBJECTIVE	RATINGS				MINIMUMS	
Fund Name	Ticker Symbol	Traded On	Fund Type	Category and (Prospectus Objective)	Overall Rating	Reward Rating	Risk Rating	Recent Up/ Downgrade	Open to New Investors	Min Initial Investment
USAA Target Retirement 2030 Fund	URTRX	NAS CM	Open End	Target Date (Asset Alloc)	B-	C	A-	Up	Y	500
USAA Target Retirement 2040 Fund	URFRX	NAS CM	Open End	Target Date (Asset Alloc)	B-	C	B+	Up	Y	500
USAA Target Retirement 2050 Fund	URFFX	NAS CM	Open End	Target Date (Asset Alloc)	B-	C	B+	Up	Y	500
USAA Target Retirement 2060 Fund	URSIX	NAS CM	Open End	Target Date (Asset Alloc)	B-	C	B+	Up	Y	500
USAA Target Retirement Income Fund	URINX	NAS CM	Open End	Target Date (Asset Alloc)	B	C+	A-	Up	Y	500
USAA Value Fund	UVALX	NAS CM	Open End	US Equity Large Cap Value (Growth)	C+	C	B	Up	Y	3,000
USAA Value Fund Adviser Shares	UAVAX	NAS CM	Open End	US Equity Large Cap Value (Growth)	C+	C	B-	Up	Y	3,000
USAA Value Fund Institutional Shares	UIVAX	NAS CM	Open End	US Equity Large Cap Value (Growth)	C+	C	B	Up	Y	1,000,000
USAA World Growth Fund	USAWX	NAS CM	Open End	Global Equity Large Cap (World Stock)	B-	C+	B	Up	Y	3,000
USAA World Growth Fund Adviser Shares	USWGX	NAS CM	Open End	Global Equity Large Cap (World Stock)	B-	C+	B	Up	Y	3,000
USAA World Growth Fund Institutional Shares	UIWGX	NAS CM	Open End	Global Equity Large Cap (World Stock)	B-	C+	B	Up	Y	1,000,000
USCA Premium Buy-Write Fund Institutional Class Shares	SHLDX	NAS CM	Open End	Long/Short Equity (Growth & Income)	C	C	B-		Y	10,000
USQ Core Real Estate Fund Class I Shares	USQIX	NAS CM	Closed End	Real Estate Sector Equity (Real Estate)	C-	D+	A-	Up	Y	25,000
USQ Core Real Estate Fund Class IS Shares	USQSX	NAS CM	Closed End	Real Estate Sector Equity (Real Estate)	C-	D+	A-	Up	Y	2,500
VALIC Company I Asset Allocation Fund	VCAAX	NAS CM	Open End	Moderate Alloc (Asset Alloc)	C+	C	B	Up	Y	0
VALIC Company I Blue Chip Growth Fund	VCBCX	NAS CM	Open End	US Equity Large Cap Growth (Growth)	B-	C+	B	Down	Y	0
VALIC Company I Broad Cap Value Income Fund	VBCVX	NAS CM	Open End	US Equity Large Cap Value (Growth)	C+	C	B	Up	Y	0
VALIC Company I Core Equity Fund	VCCEX	NAS CM	Open End	US Equity Large Cap Blend (Growth)	C+	C	B	Down	Y	0
VALIC Company I Dividend Value Fund	VCIGX	NAS CM	Open End	US Equity Large Cap Value (Growth)	B-	C	B	Up	Y	0
VALIC Company I Dynamic Allocation Fund	VDAFX	NAS CM	Open End	Moderate Alloc (Asset Alloc)	B-	C	B+	Up	Y	0
VALIC Company I Emerging Economies Fund	VCGEX	NAS CM	Open End	Global Emerg Mkts (Div Emerging Mkts)	C	C	C+		Y	0
VALIC Company I Global Real Estate Fund	VGREX	NAS CM	Open End	Real Estate Sector Equity (Real Estate)	B-	C+	B+		Y	0
VALIC Company I Global Strategy Fund	VGLSX	NAS CM	Open End	Moderate Alloc (World Stock)	C	C-	B		Y	0
VALIC Company I Growth & Income Fund	VCGAX	NAS CM	Open End	US Equity Large Cap Blend (Growth)	B-	C	B		Y	0
VALIC Company I Growth Fund	VCULX	NAS CM	Open End	US Equity Large Cap Growth (Aggr Growth)	B-	C+	B		Y	0
VALIC Company I Health Sciences Fund	VCHSX	NAS CM	Open End	Healthcare Sector Equity (Health)	C+	C	B	Down	Y	0
VALIC Company I International Equities Index Fund	VCIEX	NAS CM	Open End	Global Equity Large Cap (Foreign Stock)	C	C	B		Y	0
VALIC Company I International Growth Fund	VCINX	NAS CM	Open End	Global Equity Large Cap (Foreign Stock)	C+	C	B	Up	Y	0
VALIC Company I International Socially Responsible Fund	VCSOX	NAS CM	Open End	Global Equity Large Cap (World Stock)	B-	C	B	Up	Y	0
VALIC Company I International Value	VCFVX	NAS CM	Open End	Global Equity Large Cap (Foreign Stock)	C-	D+	C		Y	0
VALIC Company I Large Cap Core Fund	VLCCX	NAS CM	Open End	US Equity Large Cap Blend (Growth)	C+	C	B		Y	0
VALIC Company I Large Capital Growth Fund	VLCGX	NAS CM	Open End	US Equity Large Cap Growth (Growth)	B	B	B+		Y	0
VALIC Company I Mid Cap Index Fund	VMIDX	NAS CM	Open End	US Equity Mid Cap (Growth)	C+	C	B-	Up	Y	0
VALIC Company I Mid Cap Strategic Growth Fund	VMSGX	NAS CM	Open End	US Equity Mid Cap (Growth)	B-	B-	B	Down	Y	0
VALIC Company I Nasdaq-100 Index Fund	VCNIX	NAS CM	Open End	US Equity Large Cap Growth (Growth)	B-	C+	B		Y	0
VALIC Company I Science & Technology Fund	VCSTX	NAS CM	Open End	Technology Sector Equity (Technology)	B-	C+	B-	Down	Y	0
VALIC Company I Small Cap Aggressive Growth Fund	VSAGX	NAS CM	Open End	US Equity Small Cap (Small Company)	C+	C+	C+		Y	0
VALIC Company I Small Cap Fund	VCSMX	NAS CM	Open End	US Equity Small Cap (Small Company)	C+	C	B-		Y	0
VALIC Company I Small Cap Index Fund	VCSLX	NAS CM	Open End	US Equity Small Cap (Small Company)	C	C	C+		Y	0
VALIC Company I Small Cap Special Values Fund	VSSVX	NAS CM	Open End	US Equity Small Cap (Small Company)	C	C	C+		Y	0
VALIC Company I Small-Mid Growth Fund	VSSGX	NAS CM	Open End	US Equity Mid Cap (Small Company)	C+	C+	B-	Down	Y	0
VALIC Company I Stock Index Fund	VSTIX	NAS CM	Open End	US Equity Large Cap Blend (Growth)	B-	C	B		Y	0
VALIC Company I Value Fund	VAVAX	NAS CM	Open End	US Equity Large Cap Value (Growth)	C+	C	B	Up	Y	0
VALIC Company II Aggressive Growth Lifestyle Fund	VAGLX	NAS CM	Open End	Aggressive Alloc (Aggr Growth)	B-	C	B	Up	Y	0
VALIC Company II Capital Appreciation Fund	VCCAX	NAS CM	Open End	US Equity Large Cap Growth (Growth)	C+	C	B	Down	Y	0
VALIC Company II Conservative Growth Lifestyle Fund	VCGLX	NAS CM	Open End	Cautious Alloc (Growth)	B-	C	A-	Up	Y	0
VALIC Company II International Opportunities Fund	VISEX	NAS CM	Open End	Global Equity Mid/Small Cap (Foreign Stock)	C	C	C+		Y	0
VALIC Company II Large Cap Value Fund	VACVX	NAS CM	Open End	US Equity Large Cap Value (Growth)	C+	C	B	Up	Y	0
VALIC Company II Mid Cap Growth Fund	VAMGX	NAS CM	Open End	US Equity Mid Cap (Growth)	C+	C	B-	Down	Y	0
VALIC Company II Mid Cap Value Fund	VMCVX	NAS CM	Open End	US Equity Mid Cap (Growth)	C	C	B-		Y	0
VALIC Company II Moderate Growth Lifestyle Fund	VMGLX	NAS CM	Open End	Moderate Alloc (Growth)	B-	C	B+	Up	Y	0
VALIC Company II Small Cap Growth Fund	VASMX	NAS CM	Open End	US Equity Small Cap (Small Company)	C+	C+	C+	Down	Y	0

★ Expanded analysis of this fund is included in Section II.

	TOTAL RETURNS					PERFORMANCE				ASSETS		ASSET ALLOCATION & TURNOVER					BULL & BEAR		FEES		
Min Additional Investment	3-Month Total Return	6-Month Total Return	1-Year Total Return	3-Year Total Return	5-Year Total Return	Dividend Yield (TTM)	Expense Ratio	3-Yr Std Deviation	3-Year Beta	NAV	Total Assets (MIL)	%Cash	%Stocks	%Bonds	%Other	Turnover Ratio	Last Bull Market Total Return	Last Bear Market Total Return	Front End Fee (%)	Back End Fee (%)	Inception Date
50	3.03	12.01	4.88	27.74	25.43	2.11	0.75	7.5	0.92	13.24	1,319	2	62	35	0	36	14.8	-13.31			Jul-08
50	3.15	13.45	4.51	31.24	27.58	1.92	0.79	9.04	0.92	13.41	1,480	2	76	22	0	35	17.79	-17.41			Jul-08
50	3.12	13.87	4.23	32.42	28.48	1.81	0.83	9.47	0.91	13.54	850.3	2	81	17	0	36	19.59	-19.48			Jul-08
50	3.13	13.83	4.13	31.81	28.16	1.8	0.88	9.47	0.89	12.51	108.5	2	81	17	0	36					Jul-13
50	2.69	8.34	5.87	16.69	17.82	2.55	0.65	3.83	0.94	11.44	336.3	3	28	69	0	29	8.18	-5.72			Jul-08
50	3.37	17.10	3.70	33.25	32.30	1.11	0.96	14.18	1.13	19.31	1,271	0	100	0	0	29	25.94	-20.91			Aug-01
	3.32	16.96	3.38	32.05	30.47	0.76	1.27	14.16	1.12	19.24	1,271	0	100	0	0	29	25.6	-21.1			Aug-10
	3.42	17.16	3.80	33.58	33.02	1.1	0.88	14.17	1.12	19.32	1,271	0	100	0	0	29	26.04	-20.85			Aug-08
50	5.44	21.79	11.32	43.12	41.62	0.8	1.1	11.64	1	32.92	1,389	0	100	0	0	10	22.88	-19.73			Oct-92
	5.40	21.65	11.04	42.02	39.84	0.55	1.35	11.62	1	32.98	1,389	0	100	0	0	10	22.68	-19.86			Aug-10
	5.47	21.81	11.38	43.28	41.88	0.58	1	11.62	1	32.95	1,389	0	100	0	0	10	22.88	-19.73			Aug-15
1,000	1.00	7.74	4.56			4.52	1.18			10.11	24.8	7	86	5	2	74					Nov-16
100	1.60	2.51	5.45			4.02	0.96			25.74	--	10	0	0	90						Sep-17
100	1.60	2.51	5.45			4.02	1.21			25.74	--	10	0	0	90						Sep-17
	1.78	10.09	1.62	20.77	20.89	1.49	0.78	8.26		10.29	152.4	17	63	20	0	84	17.25	-11.01			Sep-83
	3.97	21.78	10.26	80.71	99.04	0	0.83	14.29	1.07	20.38	828.5	1	100	0	0	24	30.72	-14.72			Nov-00
	3.34	16.34	3.97	39.58	39.93	1.32	0.85	13.57	1.1	14.84	53.7	0	100	0	0	24	23.79	-18.7			Dec-05
	2.11	15.59	5.23	47.34	50.57	1.14	0.75	12.83	1.02	21.26	239.0	0	100	0	0	50	26.14	-20.5			Apr-94
	2.30	13.64	5.40	34.74	47.62	1.88	0.81	12.1	0.98	11.55	991.7	5	95	0	0	54	21.58	-11.77			Dec-00
	3.42	13.76	6.67	31.85	27.39	1.21	0.91	9.3		12.08	212.2	3	71	26	0	15					Dec-12
	1.35	11.49	-0.18	36.08	10.07	1.71	0.93	14.72	1.03	8.24	879.0	1	99	0	0	53	23.04	-23.59			Dec-05
	0.99	16.51	8.71	20.95	29.82	3.58	0.86	10.81	0.95	8.14	473.6	2	96	0	2	50	24.38	-20.95			Mar-08
	0.46	7.00	-0.33	21.33	7.63	2.26	0.65	8.63		10.71	336.0	18	58	24	0	30	14.03	-15.21			Dec-05
	4.01	18.69	9.16	47.72	59.01	0.87	0.85	12.53	1.02	21.78	125.8	1	99	0	0	43	25.43	-19.73			Apr-94
	4.29	21.90	8.74	63.37	72.52	0.39	0.74	13.47	1	17.47	1,157	1	99	0	0	58	27.53	-17.31			Dec-05
	1.69	19.27	10.21	48.90	81.39	0	1.06	17	1.15	21.01	802.2	1	98	0	0	44	31.23	-14.69			Nov-00
	3.48	14.29	0.72	29.36	10.42	3.37	0.43	10.96	0.98	7.13	1,148	3	97	0	0	17	13.49	-23.64			Oct-89
	4.30	22.81	6.54	46.96	29.79	0.62	0.88	11.84	0.9	11.88	485.5	6	94	0	0	130	18.39	-23.08			Dec-00
	3.56	17.89	6.20	40.26	40.29	1.74	0.62	11.1	0.97	27.34	381.9	1	99	0	0	5	19.07	-19.87			Oct-89
	1.89	11.73	-5.25	20.82	-5.09	2.89	0.72	12.8	1.06	9.68	738.2	2	98	0	0	30	10.58	-24.66			Dec-05
	4.53	19.97	9.48	42.15	57.34	0.88	0.84	12.62	1.01	11.76	177.2	2	98	0	0	59	25.46	-19.99			Dec-05
	5.67	25.25	18.59	66.05	81.71	0.54	0.75	12.28	0.89	16.76	508.4	1	99	0	0	21	24.24	-18.87			Dec-04
	2.96	19.03	1.01	37.80	45.59	1.34	0.35	15.16	1	25.31	3,112	1	99	0	0	15	27.72	-22.66			Oct-91
	7.71	30.07	15.44	66.45	68.20	0.01	0.82	14.33	0.98	16.61	323.2	2	96	0	0	40	20.85	-21.72			Dec-04
	4.04	22.37	9.46	78.76	105.73	0.39	0.53	15.13	1	15.16	535.7	6	94	0	0	3	27.52	-10.87			Oct-00
	4.41	28.47	11.03	94.59	118.59	0	0.97	17.08	1.03	27.91	1,488	5	94	0	0	84	22.34	-19.41			Apr-94
	7.14	33.32	7.24	92.25	89.55	0	0.99	17.38	0.96	15.14	172.3	3	97	0	0	74	27.94	-25.72			Dec-05
	4.75	21.55	3.30	46.39	43.84	0.43	0.93	15.22	0.88	11.02	301.9	3	96	0	0	25	30.5	-24.89			Dec-00
	1.98	17.81	-3.52	43.31	40.06	1.09	0.4	17.13	1	20.08	1,081	3	97	0	0	17	27.61	-25.15			May-92
	3.48	18.48	-2.04	37.55	42.03	1.28	0.87	16.18	0.91	11.87	232.4	5	95	0	0	37	28.85	-24.04			Dec-05
	7.12	30.02	13.32	59.41	62.77	0	0.95	15.04	0.88	13.83	124.7	3	97	0	0	62	26.35	-23.2			Dec-05
	4.21	19.38	10.06	49.41	63.52	1.5	0.34	12.19	1	42	4,941	0	100	0	0	3	24.84	-16.35			Apr-87
	3.60	16.98	5.74	33.38	38.88	1.32	0.85	12.51	1.02	18.68	122.9	2	98	0	0	19	27.4	-20.63			Dec-01
	2.93	15.30	3.87	30.94	30.66	1.94	0.87	10.04		10.21	592.8	3	79	18	0	49	19.17	-13.97			Sep-98
	2.31	17.88	8.86	50.74	64.49	0.23	0.85	13.57	1	14.78	103.9	1	99	0	0	124	28.01	-19.41			Sep-98
	2.83	11.30	5.13	18.49	19.36	2.88	0.89	6		11.81	328.8	4	41	54	0	44	12.89	-7.54			Sep-98
	2.55	16.10	-5.59	33.19	31.97	0.96	1	13.4	1.05	19.02	602.6	2	98	0	0	46	14.72	-24.2			Sep-98
	4.38	16.63	4.29	38.15	42.24	1.22	0.81	13.34	1.09	20.43	279.6	1	99	0	0	90	24.41	-22.39			Sep-98
	4.74	27.57	8.48	59.74	61.32	0	0.85	14.88	0.92	10.57	246.3	0	100	0	0	35	24.82	-23.55			Sep-98
	4.39	19.36	1.09	30.83	29.07	0.53	1.05	14.66	1.09	17.4	765.0	2	98	0	0	44	31.5	-25.59			Sep-98
	3.09	13.84	4.79	26.65	27.82	2.11	0.87	8.31		13.91	952.4	3	62	35	0	47	16.62	-11.43			Sep-98
	2.71	28.39	5.39	94.56	88.94	0	1.16	18.56	1.04	17.36	199.1	2	98	0	0	63	30.69	-28.15			Sep-98

	MARKET			FUND TYPE, CATEGORY & OBJECTIVE	RATINGS				MINIMUMS	
Fund Name	Ticker Symbol	Traded On	Fund Type	Category and (Prospectus Objective)	Overall Rating	Reward Rating	Risk Rating	Recent Up/ Downgrade	Open to New Investors	Min Initial Investment
VALIC Company II Small Cap Value Fund	VCSVX	NAS CM	Open End	US Equity Small Cap (Growth)	C-	C-	C	Down	Y	0
VALIC Company II U.S. Socially Responsible Fund	VCSRX	NAS CM	Open End	US Equity Large Cap Blend (Growth)	B-	C+	B		Y	0
Value Line Asset Allocation Fund Institutional Class	VLAIX	NAS CM	Open End	Moderate Alloc (Asset Alloc)	B+	B	A-	Up	Y	100,000
Value Line Asset Allocation Fund Investor Class	VLAAX	NAS CM	Open End	Moderate Alloc (Asset Alloc)	B+	B	A-	Up	Y	1,000
Value Line Capital Appreciation Fund, Inc. Inst Cls	VLIIX	NAS CM	Open End	Aggressive Alloc (Growth & Income)	B-	C	B		Y	100,000
Value Line Capital Appreciation Fund, Inc. Investor Class	VALIX	NAS CM	Open End	Aggressive Alloc (Growth & Income)	B-	C	B		Y	1,000
Value Line Larger Companies Focused Institutional Cls	VLLIX	NAS CM	Open End	US Equity Large Cap Growth (Growth)	C+	C+	B	Down	Y	100,000
Value Line Larger Companies Focused Fund Investor Class	VALLX	NAS CM	Open End	US Equity Large Cap Growth (Growth)	C+	C+	B	Down	Y	1,000
Value Line Mid Cap Focused Fund	VLIFX	NAS CM	Open End	US Equity Mid Cap (Growth)	B+	B	B+	Up	Y	1,000
Value Line Mid Cap Focused Fund Institutional Class	VLMIX	NAS CM	Open End	US Equity Mid Cap (Growth)	B+	B	B+	Up	Y	100,000
Value Line Premier Growth Fund	VALSX	NAS CM	Open End	US Equity Mid Cap (Growth)	B	B	B		Y	1,000
Value Line Small Cap Opportunities Institutional Cls	VLEIX	NAS CM	Open End	US Equity Small Cap (Small Company)	C+	C	B	Down	Y	100,000
Value Line Small Cap Opportunities Fund Investor Class	VLEOX	NAS CM	Open End	US Equity Small Cap (Small Company)	C+	C	B	Down	Y	1,000
VanEck CM Commodity Index Fund Class A	CMCAX	NAS CM	Open End	Commodities Broad Basket (Growth & Income)	C-	D+	C	Down	Y	1,000
VanEck CM Commodity Index Fund Class I	COMIX	NAS CM	Open End	Commodities Broad Basket (Growth & Income)	C-	D+	C	Down	Y	1,000,000
VanEck CM Commodity Index Fund Class Y	CMCYX	NAS CM	Open End	Commodities Broad Basket (Growth & Income)	C-	D+	C	Down	Y	1,000
VanEck Emerging Markets Fund Class A	GBFAX	NAS CM	Open End	Global Emerg Mkts (Div Emerging Mkts)	C	C	C		Y	1,000
VanEck Emerging Markets Fund Class C	EMRCX	NAS CM	Open End	Global Emerg Mkts (Div Emerging Mkts)	C	C	C		Y	1,000
VanEck Emerging Markets Fund Class I	EMRIX	NAS CM	Open End	Global Emerg Mkts (Div Emerging Mkts)	C	C	C		Y	1,000,000
VanEck Emerging Markets Fund Class Y	EMRYX	NAS CM	Open End	Global Emerg Mkts (Div Emerging Mkts)	C	C	C		Y	1,000
VanEck Global Hard Assets Fund Class A	GHAAX	NAS CM	Open End	Natl Resources Sec Equity (Natl Res)	D	D	D	Down	Y	1,000
VanEck Global Hard Assets Fund Class C	GHACX	NAS CM	Open End	Natl Resources Sec Equity (Natl Res)	D	D	D	Down	Y	1,000
VanEck Global Hard Assets Fund Class I	GHAIX	NAS CM	Open End	Natl Resources Sec Equity (Natl Res)	D	D	D	Down	Y	1,000,000
VanEck Global Hard Assets Fund Class Y	GHAYX	NAS CM	Open End	Natl Resources Sec Equity (Natl Res)	D	D	D	Down	Y	1,000
VanEck International Investors Gold Fund Class A	INIVX	NAS CM	Open End	Precious Metals Sector Equity (Precious Metals)	D+	D	C-	Down	Y	1,000
VanEck International Investors Gold Fund Class C	IIGCX	NAS CM	Open End	Precious Metals Sector Equity (Precious Metals)	D	D	C-	Down	Y	1,000
VanEck International Investors Gold Fund Class I	INIIX	NAS CM	Open End	Precious Metals Sector Equity (Precious Metals)	D+	D	C-	Down	Y	1,000,000
VanEck International Investors Gold Fund Class Y	INIYX	NAS CM	Open End	Precious Metals Sector Equity (Precious Metals)	D+	D	C-	Down	Y	1,000
VanEck Morningstar Wide Moat Fund Class I	MWMIX	NAS CM	Open End	US Equity Large Cap Blend (Growth)	D+	C-	B-	Up	Y	1,000,000
VanEck Morningstar Wide Moat Fund Class Z	MWMZX	NAS CM	Open End	US Equity Large Cap Blend (Growth)	D+	C-	B-	Up	Y	0
VanEck NDR Managed Allocation Fund Class A	NDRMX	NAS CM	Open End	Moderate Alloc (Asset Alloc)	C	D+	B-	Up	Y	1,000
VanEck NDR Managed Allocation Fund Class I	NDRUX	NAS CM	Open End	Moderate Alloc (Asset Alloc)	C	D+	B-		Y	1,000,000
VanEck NDR Managed Allocation Fund Class Y	NDRYX	NAS CM	Open End	Moderate Alloc (Asset Alloc)	C	D+	B-		Y	1,000
★ Vanguard 500 Index Fund Admiral Shares	VFIAX	NAS CM	Open End	US Equity Large Cap Blend (Growth)	B-	C	B		Y	3,000
★ Vanguard 500 Index Fund Investor Shares	VFINX	NAS CM	Open End	US Equity Large Cap Blend (Growth)	B-	C	B		Y	3,000
Vanguard Alternative Strategies Fund Investor Shares	VASFX	NAS CM	Open End	Multialternative (Growth & Income)	B-	C	B	Up	Y	250,000
Vanguard Balanced Index Fund Admiral Shares	VBIAX	NAS CM	Open End	Moderate Alloc (Balanced)	B	C+	A-		Y	10,000
Vanguard Balanced Index Fund Institutional Shares	VBAIX	NAS CM	Open End	Moderate Alloc (Balanced)	B	C+	A-		Y	5,000,000
Vanguard Balanced Index Fund Investor Shares	VBINX	NAS CM	Open End	Moderate Alloc (Balanced)	B	C+	A-		Y	3,000
Vanguard Capital Opportunity Fund Admiral Shares	VHCAX	NAS CM	Open End	US Equity Large Cap Growth (Growth)	C+	C	B	Down		50,000
Vanguard Capital Opportunity Fund Investor Shares	VHCOX	NAS CM	Open End	US Equity Large Cap Growth (Growth)	C+	C	B	Down		3,000
Vanguard Capital Value Fund Investor Shares	VCVLX	NAS CM	Open End	US Equity Mid Cap (Growth)	C+	C	B	Up	Y	3,000
Vanguard Communication Services Index Fund Admiral Class	VTCAX	NAS CM	Open End	Communications Sector Equity (Comm)	C-	C-	C	Down	Y	100,000
Vanguard Consumer Discretionary Index Fund Admiral Shares	VCDAX	NAS CM	Open End	Consumer Goods Sec Equity ()	C+	C	B	Down	Y	100,000
Vanguard Consumer Staples Index Fund Class Admiral Shares	VCSAX	NAS CM	Open End	Consumer Goods Sec Equity ()	C	C	C+	Down	Y	100,000
★ Vanguard Developed Markets Index Fund Admiral Shares	VTMGX	NAS CM	Open End	Global Equity Large Cap (Foreign Stock)	C	C	B		Y	3,000
Vanguard Developed Markets Index Institutional Plus Shares	VDIPX	NAS CM	Open End	Global Equity Large Cap (Foreign Stock)	C	C	B		Y	100,000,000
Vanguard Developed Markets Index Fund Institutional Shares	VTMNX	NAS CM	Open End	Global Equity Large Cap (Foreign Stock)	C	C	B		Y	5,000,000
★ Vanguard Developed Markets Index Fund Investor Shares	VDVIX	NAS CM	Open End	Global Equity Large Cap (Foreign Stock)	C	C	B		Y	3,000
Vanguard Diversified Equity Fund Investor Shares	VDEQX	NAS CM	Open End	US Equity Large Cap Growth (Growth & Income)	C+	C	B	Down	Y	3,000
Vanguard Dividend Appreciation Index Fund Admiral Shares	VDADX	NAS CM	Open End	US Equity Large Cap Blend (Equity-Income)	B	C+	B+		Y	3,000
Vanguard Dividend Appreciation Index Fund Investor Shares	VDAIX	NAS CM	Open End	US Equity Large Cap Blend (Equity-Income)	B	C+	B+		Y	3,000

★ Expanded analysis of this fund is included in Section II.

Min Additional Investment	TOTAL RETURNS 3-Month Total Return	6-Month Total Return	1-Year Total Return	3-Year Total Return	5-Year Total Return	PERFORMANCE Dividend Yield (TTM)	Expense Ratio	3-Yr Std Deviation	3-Year Beta	ASSETS NAV	Total Assets (MIL)	ASSET ALLOCATION & TURNOVER %Cash	%Stocks	%Bonds	%Other	Turnover Ratio	BULL & BEAR Last Bull Market Total Return	Last Bear Market Total Return	FEES Front End Fee (%)	Back End Fee (%)	Inception Date
	0.22	12.45	-9.71	24.78	21.88	1.58	0.95	17.86	1.03	11.35	340.8	2	98	0	0	46	27.34	-28.13			Sep-98
	4.49	20.27	10.85	48.72	63.24	1.43	0.56	12.21	1	21.96	730.4	4	96	0	0	5	24.76	-16.44			Sep-98
100	6.22	20.36	17.65	43.72	56.11	0.56	0.87	8.06	0.6	37.35	743.6	8	63	28	0	19	20.19	-10.9			Oct-15
100	6.15	20.17	17.35	42.65	54.71	0.32	1.12	8.08	0.6	37.23	743.6	8	63	28	0	19	20.19	-10.9			Aug-93
100	3.45	22.22	8.76	54.57	55.73	0	0.87	13.73		10.78	503.7	4	85	11	0	86	13.68	-12.81			Oct-15
100	3.44	22.12	8.51	53.33	55.64	0	1.12	13.74		10.82	503.7	4	85	11	0	86	13.68	-12.81			Sep-52
100	2.78	24.58	9.10	76.86	96.56	0	0.9	17.05	1.17	31.32	311.1	1	99	0	0	36	24.04	-18.36			Oct-15
100	2.69	24.40	8.84	75.86	95.82	0	1.15	17.03	1.17	31.2	311.1	1	99	0	0	36	24.04	-18.36			Mar-72
100	8.63	29.08	26.38	68.39	89.95	0	1.18	11.72	0.87	24.41	329.8	8	92	0	0	10	22.18	-13.59			Mar-50
100	8.73	29.30	26.67	69.20	90.85	0	0.93	11.75	0.87	24.53	329.8	8	92	0	0	10	22.18	-13.59			Aug-17
100	8.15	29.56	23.10	65.21	74.95	0	1.2	12.08	0.92	39.13	450.9	5	95	0	0	8	26.62	-16.14			May-56
100	6.08	21.96	10.64	52.81	65.39	0	0.96	14.07	0.78	51.8	464.6	6	94	0	0	20	27.45	-16.57			Oct-15
100	6.02	21.83	10.36	51.64	63.83	0	1.21	14.08	0.79	51.22	464.6	6	94	0	0	20	27.45	-16.57			Jun-93
100	-2.14	6.27	-6.78	1.98	-34.54	0.53	0.95	9.72	1	4.57	528.8	75	0	7	18	0	5.51	-17.64	5.75		Dec-10
	-2.30	6.37	-6.58	2.70	-33.67	0.77	0.65	9.74	1	4.67	528.8	75	0	7	18	0	5.75	-17.52	0.00		Dec-10
100	-2.10	6.39	-6.66	2.62	-33.68	0.71	0.7	9.79	1	4.66	528.8	75	0	7	18	0	5.62	-17.52	0.00		Dec-10
100	5.52	22.27	1.44	39.92	15.07	0.02	1.5	16.03	1.1	17.18	2,103	3	91	0	0	39	21.4	-29.65	5.75		Dec-93
100	5.31	21.80	0.65	36.72	10.51	0	2.27	16.02	1.1	15.25	2,103	3	91	0	0	39	21.05	-29.92		1.00	Oct-03
	5.70	22.63	2.00	42.11	17.96	0.57	1	16.06	1.1	18.15	2,103	3	91	0	0	39	21.81	-29.48			Dec-07
100	5.62	22.45	1.89	41.65	17.36	0.49	1.1	16.05	1.1	17.45	2,103	3	91	0	0	39	21.72	-29.67			Apr-10
100	-0.72	13.88	-19.62	-11.70	-46.57	0	1.38	20.5	1	28.88	1,110	5	95	0	0	16	14.32	-29.5	5.75		Nov-94
100	-0.92	13.38	-20.27	-13.79	-48.67	0	2.2	20.48	1	24.57	1,110	5	95	0	0	16	13.84	-29.74		1.00	Nov-94
	-0.62	14.08	-19.27	-10.58	-45.49	0.31	0.95	20.52	1	30.38	1,110	5	95	0	0	16	14.61	-29.4			May-06
100	-0.63	13.98	-19.41	-11.03	-45.90	0.07	1.13	20.51	1	29.51	1,110	5	95	0	0	16	14.5	-29.45			Apr-10
100	15.47	24.39	8.59	-10.29	-5.87	2.35	1.45	26.33	1.01	9.33	666.0	0	100	0	0	35	-15.18	-16.5	5.75		Feb-56
100	15.12	23.77	7.73	-12.37	-9.40	2.72	2.2	26.31	1.01	8.07	666.0	0	100	0	0	35	-15.59	-16.77		1.00	Oct-03
	15.52	24.53	9.05	-9.19	-3.84	1.81	1	26.3	1.01	12.13	666.0	0	100	0	0	35	-15	-16.42			Oct-06
100	15.47	24.51	8.98	-9.46	-4.40	2.3	1.1	26.31	1.01	9.55	666.0	0	100	0	0	35	-15.1	-16.44			Apr-10
	3.09	17.48	12.36			1.61	0.59			27.95	7.0	1	99	0	0	76					Nov-17
	3.13	17.51	12.48			1.65	0.49			27.98	7.0	1	99	0	0	76					Nov-17
100	0.60	6.35	-0.97	16.83		0.81	1.36	7.33		28.1	40.3	2	69	29	0	202			5.75		May-16
	0.67	6.52	-0.65	17.89		1.1	1.06	7.34		28.24	40.3	2	69	29	0	202					May-16
100	0.67	6.49	-0.71	17.70		1.01	1.11	7.32		28.22	40.3	2	69	29	0	202					May-16
1	4.29	19.55	10.38	50.75	66.01	1.97	0.04	12.19	1	271.39	483,171	1	99	0	0	4	25.08	-16.27			Nov-00
1	4.27	19.49	10.26	50.30	65.15	1.87	0.14	12.19	1	271.41	483,171	1	99	0	0	4	24.99	-16.31			Aug-76
1	0.65	5.44	7.26	5.60		1.21	0.66	3.6		21.48	316.3	22	63	1	14	131					Aug-15
1	3.73	14.35	8.90	31.94	43.05	2.21	0.07	7.52		37.07	41,955	1	59	40	0	44	16.1	-8.96			Nov-00
1	3.73	14.35	8.94	32.01	43.15	2.22	0.06	7.5		37.08	41,955	1	59	40	0	44	16.1	-8.96			Dec-00
1	3.70	14.28	8.78	31.48	42.15	2.1	0.18	7.51		37.08	41,955	1	59	40	0	44	15.97	-9.03			Nov-92
1	0.97	14.85	4.90	65.83	74.25	0.75	0.36	15.7	1.03	150.06	16,867	3	97	0	0	10	20.61	-21.72			Nov-01
1	0.96	14.80	4.83	65.46	73.64	0.66	0.43	15.69	1.03	64.97	16,867	3	97	0	0	10	20.56	-21.75			Aug-95
1	2.99	17.53	0.87	30.32	8.80	2.31	0.29	14.66	1.16	13.07	795.9	3	97	0	0	47	28.41	-29.64			Dec-01
1	3.93	17.88	3.10	-2.77	15.46	0.94	0.1	13.65	0.95	44.13	2,102	1	99	0	0	84	10.49	-13.47			Mar-05
1	4.38	20.99	7.04	54.31	76.78	1.11	0.1	14.98	1.02	92.88	3,412	1	99	0	0	28	32.24	-15.14			Jul-05
1	3.22	15.33	13.72	16.52	46.76	2.45	0.1	11.46	1	73.39	5,685	0	100	0	0	8	16.23	-4.25			Jan-04
1	3.26	14.33	-0.01	30.61	13.45	2.78	0.07	11.36	1	13.4	114,759	4	96	0	0	3	13.27	-23.3			Aug-99
1	3.28	14.36	0.04	30.74	13.65	2.8	0.04	11.35	1	20.98	114,759	4	96	0	0	3	13.27	-23.3			Apr-14
1	3.26	14.32	0.00	30.72	13.51	2.8	0.05	11.35	1	13.42	114,759	4	96	0	0	3	13.31	-23.28			Jan-01
1	3.27	14.25	-0.01	30.31	12.89	2.69	0.16	11.34	1	10.38	114,759	4	96	0	0	3	13.21	-23.33			Dec-13
1	4.35	20.76	8.06	52.20	58.53	0.99	0.36	13.18	1.04	37.1	1,801	3	96	0	0	8	27.14	-19.21			Jun-05
1	5.54	19.97	15.60	49.52	64.21	1.76	0.08	11.64	1	31.28	44,334	0	100	0	0	16	21.09	-14.22			Dec-13
1	5.52	19.93	15.56	49.24	63.59	1.71	0.14	11.63	1	46.12	44,334	0	100	0	0	16	21.03	-14.25			Apr-06

	MARKET			FUND TYPE, CATEGORY & OBJECTIVE	RATINGS				MINIMUMS	
Fund Name	Ticker Symbol	Traded On	Fund Type	Category and (Prospectus Objective)	Overall Rating	Reward Rating	Risk Rating	Recent Up/ Downgrade	Open to New Investors	Min Initial Investment
Vanguard Dividend Growth Fund Investor Shares	VDIGX	NAS CM	Open End	US Equity Large Cap Blend (Equity-Income)	B	B	A-		Y	0
Vanguard Emerging Markets Select Stock Investor Shares	VMMSX	NAS CM	Open End	Global Emerg Mkts (Div Emerging Mkts)	C	C	B-		Y	3,000
Vanguard Emerging Markets Stock Index Fund Admiral Shares	VEMAX	NAS CM	Open End	Global Emerg Mkts (Div Emerging Mkts)	C	C	C+		Y	3,000
Vanguard Emerging Mkts Stock Index Inst Plus Shares	VEMRX	NAS CM	Open End	Global Emerg Mkts (Div Emerging Mkts)	C	C	C+		Y	100,000,000
Vanguard Emerging Markets Stock Index Institutional Shares	VEMIX	NAS CM	Open End	Global Emerg Mkts (Div Emerging Mkts)	C	C	C+		Y	5,000,000
Vanguard Emerging Markets Stock Index Fund Investor Shares	VEIEX	NAS CM	Open End	Global Emerg Mkts (Div Emerging Mkts)	C	C	C+		Y	3,000
Vanguard Energy Fund Admiral Shares	VGELX	NAS CM	Open End	Energy Sector Equity (Natl Res)	C-	D+	C-		Y	50,000
Vanguard Energy Fund Investor Shares	VGENX	NAS CM	Open End	Energy Sector Equity (Natl Res)	C-	D+	C-		Y	3,000
Vanguard Energy Index Fund Admiral Shares	VENAX	NAS CM	Open End	Energy Sector Equity (Natl Res)	D+	D	D+	Down	Y	100,000
Vanguard Equity-Income Fund Admiral Shares	VEIRX	NAS CM	Open End	US Equity Large Cap Value (Equity-Income)	B-	C	B+	Down	Y	50,000
Vanguard Equity-Income Fund Investor Shares	VEIPX	NAS CM	Open End	US Equity Large Cap Value (Equity-Income)	B-	C	B+	Down	Y	3,000
Vanguard European Stock Index Fund Admiral Shares	VEUSX	NAS CM	Open End	Europe Equity Large Cap (Europe Stock)	C	C	B-		Y	3,000
Vanguard European Stock Index Institutional Plus Shares	VEUPX	NAS CM	Open End	Europe Equity Large Cap (Europe Stock)	C	C	B-		Y	100,000,000
Vanguard European Stock Index Fund Institutional Shares	VESIX	NAS CM	Open End	Europe Equity Large Cap (Europe Stock)	C	C	B-		Y	5,000,000
Vanguard European Stock Index Fund Investor Shares	VEURX	NAS CM	Open End	Europe Equity Large Cap (Europe Stock)	C	C	B-		Y	3,000
Vanguard Explorer Fund Admiral Shares	VEXRX	NAS CM	Open End	US Equity Small Cap (Growth)	C+	C	B-	Down	Y	50,000
Vanguard Explorer Fund Investor Class	VEXPX	NAS CM	Open End	US Equity Small Cap (Growth)	C+	C	B-	Down	Y	3,000
Vanguard Explorer Value Fund Investor Shares	VEVFX	NAS CM	Open End	US Equity Small Cap (Growth)	C	C	C+		Y	3,000
Vanguard Extended Market Index Fund Admiral Shares	VEXAX	NAS CM	Open End	US Equity Mid Cap (Growth)	C+	C	B-		Y	3,000
Vanguard Extended Market Index Institutional Plus Shares	VEMPX	NAS CM	Open End	US Equity Mid Cap (Growth)	C+	C	B-		Y	100,000,000
Vanguard Extended Market Index Fund Institutional Shares	VIEIX	NAS CM	Open End	US Equity Mid Cap (Growth)	C+	C	B-		Y	5,000,000
Vanguard Extended Market Index Fund Investor Shares	VEXMX	NAS CM	Open End	US Equity Mid Cap (Growth)	C+	C	B-		Y	3,000
Vanguard Financials Index Fund Admiral Shares	VFAIX	NAS CM	Open End	Financials Sector Equity (Financial)	C+	C	B-	Up	Y	100,000
Vanguard FTSE All-World ex-US Index Fund Admiral Shares	VFWAX	NAS CM	Open End	Global Equity Large Cap (Foreign Stock)	C	C	B		Y	3,000
Vanguard FTSE All-World ex-US Index Inst Plus Shares	VFWPX	NAS CM	Open End	Global Equity Large Cap (Foreign Stock)	C	C	B		Y	100,000,000
Vanguard FTSE All-World ex-US Index Institutional Shares	VFWSX	NAS CM	Open End	Global Equity Large Cap (Foreign Stock)	C	C	B		Y	5,000,000
Vanguard FTSE All-World ex-US Index Fund Investor Shares	VFWIX	NAS CM	Open End	Global Equity Large Cap (Foreign Stock)	C	C	B		Y	3,000
Vanguard FTSE All-World ex-US Small Capital Ind Admiral Sh	VFSAX	NAS CM	Open End	Global Equity Mid/Small Cap (Foreign Stock)	C	C-	C		Y	3,000
Vanguard FTSE All-World ex-US Small Capital Ind Inv Shares	VFSVX	NAS CM	Open End	Global Equity Mid/Small Cap (Foreign Stock)	C	C-	C		Y	3,000
Vanguard FTSE All-World ex-US Small-Cap Index Inst Shares	VFSNX	NAS CM	Open End	Global Equity Mid/Small Cap (Foreign Stock)	C	C-	C		Y	5,000,000
Vanguard FTSE Social Index Fund Admiral	VFTAX	NAS CM	Open End	US Equity Large Cap Blend (Growth)	B-	C+	B	Down	Y	3,000
Vanguard FTSE Social Index Fund Institutional Shares	VFTNX	NAS CM	Open End	US Equity Large Cap Blend (Growth)	B-	C+	B	Down	Y	5,000,000
Vanguard FTSE Social Index Fund Investor Shares	VFTSX	NAS CM	Open End	US Equity Large Cap Blend (Growth)	B-	C+	B	Down	Y	3,000
Vanguard Global Capital Cycles Fund Investor Shares	VGPMX	NAS CM	Open End	Precious Metals Sector Equity (Precious Metals)	D	D	D		Y	3,000
Vanguard Global Equity Fund Investor Shares	VHGEX	NAS CM	Open End	Global Equity Large Cap (World Stock)	B-	C	B	Up	Y	3,000
Vanguard Global ex-U.S. Real Estate Index Admiral Shares	VGRLX	NAS CM	Open End	Real Estate Sector Equity (Real Estate)	C+	C	B		Y	3,000
Vanguard Global ex-U.S. Real Estate Index Inst Shares	VGRNX	NAS CM	Open End	Real Estate Sector Equity (Real Estate)	C+	C	B		Y	5,000,000
Vanguard Global ex-U.S. Real Estate Index Investor Shares	VGXRX	NAS CM	Open End	Real Estate Sector Equity (Real Estate)	C+	C	B	Up	Y	3,000
Vanguard Global Minimum Volatility Fund Admiral Shares	VMNVX	NAS CM	Open End	Global Equity Mid/Small Cap (World Stock)	B	B-	A-		Y	50,000
Vanguard Global Minimum Volatility Fund Investor Shares	VMVFX	NAS CM	Open End	Global Equity Mid/Small Cap (World Stock)	B	B-	A-		Y	3,000
Vanguard Global Wellesley Income Fund Admiral Shares	VGYAX	NAS CM	Open End	Moderate Alloc (Income)	D+	D+	B-	Up	Y	50,000
Vanguard Global Wellesley Income Fund Investor Shares	VGWIX	NAS CM	Open End	Moderate Alloc (Income)	D+	D+	B-	Up	Y	3,000
Vanguard Global Wellington Fund Admiral Shares	VGWAX	NAS CM	Open End	Moderate Alloc (Growth)	D+	D+	B-	Up	Y	50,000
Vanguard Global Wellington Fund Investor Shares	VGWLX	NAS CM	Open End	Moderate Alloc (Growth)	D+	D+	B-	Up	Y	3,000
Vanguard Growth and Income Fund Admiral Shares	VGIAX	NAS CM	Open End	US Equity Large Cap Blend (Growth & Income)	B-	C	B		Y	50,000
Vanguard Growth and Income Fund Investor Shares	VQNPX	NAS CM	Open End	US Equity Large Cap Blend (Growth & Income)	B-	C	B		Y	3,000
Vanguard Growth Index Fund Admiral Shares	VIGAX	NAS CM	Open End	US Equity Large Cap Growth (Growth)	B-	C+	B		Y	3,000
Vanguard Growth Index Fund Institutional Shares	VIGIX	NAS CM	Open End	US Equity Large Cap Growth (Growth)	B-	C+	B		Y	5,000,000
Vanguard Growth Index Fund Investor Shares	VIGRX	NAS CM	Open End	US Equity Large Cap Growth (Growth)	B-	C+	B		Y	3,000
Vanguard Health Care Fund Admiral Shares	VGHAX	NAS CM	Open End	Healthcare Sector Equity (Health)	C	C-	B-	Down	Y	50,000
Vanguard Health Care Fund Investor Shares	VGHCX	NAS CM	Open End	Healthcare Sector Equity (Health)	C	C-	B-	Down	Y	0
Vanguard Health Care Index Fund Admiral Shares	VHCIX	NAS CM	Open End	Healthcare Sector Equity (Health)	B-	C	B		Y	100,000

★Expanded analysis of this fund is included in Section II.

Min Additional Investment	TOTAL RETURNS 3-Month Total Return	6-Month Total Return	1-Year Total Return	3-Year Total Return	5-Year Total Return	PERFORMANCE Dividend Yield (TTM)	Expense Ratio	3-Yr Std Deviation	3-Year Beta	ASSETS NAV	Total Assets (MIL)	ASSET ALLOCATION & TURNOVER %Cash	%Stocks	%Bonds	%Other	Turnover Ratio	BULL & BEAR Last Bull Market Total Return	Last Bear Market Total Return	FEES Front End Fee (%)	Back End Fee (%)	Inception Date
	6.32	22.14	19.04	49.45	70.52	1.73	0.22	10.6	0.8	29.36	36,582	2	98	0	0	23	20.46	-10.03			May-92
1	1.05	13.48	6.16	41.68	13.13	2.24	0.94	13.91	1.02	21.96	710.8	6	93	0	0	76	20.13				Jun-11
1	0.70	12.57	3.21	32.07	12.07	2.54	0.14	13.3	1.01	35.38	87,848	2	97	0	0	11	18.73	-27.19			Jun-06
1	0.71	12.61	3.29	32.30	12.37	2.62	0.08	13.29	1.01	89.49	87,848	2	97	0	0	11	18.81	-27.16			Dec-10
1	0.68	12.59	3.26	32.19	12.24	2.58	0.1	13.29	1.01	26.9	87,848	2	97	0	0	11	18.79	-27.16			Jun-00
1	0.67	12.51	3.08	31.46	11.13	2.42	0.29	13.29	1.01	26.95	87,848	2	97	0	0	11	18.65	-27.23			May-94
1	-1.56	13.84	-11.61	7.47	-23.60	2.53	0.29	17.47	1.08	92.02	7,612	5	95	0	0	31	19.32	-27.57			Nov-01
1	-1.58	13.81	-11.68	7.21	-23.88	2.46	0.37	17.47	1.08	49.04	7,612	5	95	0	0	31	19.28	-27.59			May-84
1	-4.06	12.57	-16.52	-1.89	-31.25	3.17	0.1	21.13	1	42.5	4,033	1	99	0	0	5	22.63	-26.89			Oct-04
1	3.43	15.80	9.72	39.19	53.85	2.73	0.18	10.85	0.96	75.33	35,525	4	96	0	0	37	23.56	-12.06			Aug-01
1	3.41	15.75	9.63	38.80	53.14	2.65	0.27	10.84	0.96	35.94	35,525	4	96	0	0	37	23.5	-12.12			Mar-88
1	4.31	16.13	1.18	32.67	7.96	3.25	0.1	12.36	0.98	68.72	19,546	3	97	0	0	6	15.27	-27.18			Aug-01
1	4.33	16.15	1.21	32.86	8.07	3.28	0.07	12.36	0.98	130.94	19,546	3	97	0	0	6	15.16	-27.21			Dec-14
1	4.33	16.14	1.20	32.72	8.07	3.27	0.08	12.36	0.98	29.3	19,546	3	97	0	0	6	15.33	-27.17			May-00
1	4.30	16.06	1.07	32.12	7.19	3.13	0.23	12.35	0.98	29.52	19,546	3	97	0	0	6	15.16	-27.21			Jun-90
1	4.20	23.76	7.08	65.67	61.66	0.38	0.34	16.15	0.97	95.26	16,510	5	95	0	0	50	28.24	-23.24			Nov-01
1	4.18	23.69	6.97	65.10	60.64	0.26	0.46	16.15	0.97	102.36	16,510	5	95	0	0	50	28.12	-23.29			Dec-67
1	4.23	18.42	-2.44	36.21	34.18	1	0.56	15.83	1.03	34.45	688.2	8	92	0	0	31	27.77	-22.89			Mar-10
1	3.03	20.60	2.03	47.18	46.20	1.32	0.07	15.23	1	89.98	69,501	3	97	0	0	10	28.84	-23.87			Nov-00
1	3.04	20.63	2.06	47.28	46.43	1.34	0.05	15.23	1	222.06	69,501	3	97	0	0	10	28.89	-23.87			Jan-11
1	3.03	20.63	2.05	47.24	46.33	1.33	0.06	15.23	1	89.98	69,501	3	97	0	0	10	28.86	-23.87			Jul-97
1	3.00	20.54	1.92	46.63	45.28	1.2	0.19	15.23	1	90.04	69,501	3	97	0	0	10	28.75	-23.91			Dec-87
1	7.60	18.69	4.74	57.02	64.45	2.16	0.1	16.91	1	34.61	7,989	0	100	0	0	3	31.67	-26.3			Feb-04
1	2.85	13.85	1.32	31.77	12.83	2.87	0.11	11.43	1	31.69	38,749	0	97	0	3	6	14.74	-24.47			Sep-11
1	2.88	13.88	1.39	31.94	13.08	2.92	0.06	11.44	1	106.4	38,749	0	97	0	3	6	14.79	-24.45			Dec-10
1	2.87	13.87	1.38	31.86	12.94	2.91	0.08	11.44	1	100.48	38,749	0	97	0	3	6	14.76	-24.46			Apr-07
1	2.82	13.80	1.25	31.34	12.18	2.79	0.2	11.45	1.01	20.12	38,749	0	97	0	3	6	14.58	-24.5			Mar-07
1	1.52	12.97	-6.30	24.09	9.61		0.16	12.12	1	25.93	6,647	7	92	0	1	15	14.02	-25.77			Feb-19
1	1.51	12.92	-6.37	23.73	8.96	2.58	0.22	12.11	1	40.06	6,647	7	92	0	1	15	13.89	-25.86			Apr-09
1	1.54	13.00	-6.27	24.18	9.74	2.68	0.11	12.11	1	200.68	6,647	7	92	0	1	15	14.04	-25.77			Apr-09
1	4.54	20.04	11.28	57.90	72.16		0.14	12.21	1	27.25	5,942	0	100	0	0	8	23.1	-15.74			Feb-19
1	4.58	20.05	11.32	58.19	72.72	1.6	0.12	12.23	1	19.62	5,942	0	100	0	0	8	23.22	-15.62			Jan-03
1	4.56	20.03	11.27	57.89	72.15	1.55	0.18	12.22	1	19.61	5,942	0	100	0	0	8	23.1	-15.74			May-00
1	3.21	14.38	-16.14	-24.32	-26.27	1.21	0.33	21.7	0.98	8.03	1,359	7	92	0	0	110	-1	-25.25			May-84
1	4.45	18.71	6.40	47.54	42.82	1.27	0.48	11.66	1.01	30.95	6,524	5	94	0	1	40	20.05	-22.16			Aug-95
1	-0.08	13.86	5.47	25.89	24.85	3.44	0.12	11.52	1.01	35.72	6,762	4	95	0	1	7	19.43	-21.55			Feb-11
1	-0.07	13.86	5.47	25.97	24.95	3.44	0.11	11.52	1.01	119	6,762	4	95	0	1	7	19.47	-21.55			Apr-11
1	-0.10	13.78	5.29	25.23	23.71	3.31	0.31	11.5	1.01	23.57	6,762	4	95	0	1	7	19.36	-21.65			Nov-10
1	4.13	15.30	9.73	35.60	60.81	2.1	0.15	7.59	0.65	28.47	3,803	3	97	0	0	24					Dec-13
1	4.02	15.23	9.64	35.25	60.10	2.03	0.23	7.57	0.65	14.22	3,803	3	97	0	0	24					Dec-13
1	3.07	9.52	6.30			2.44	0.33			24.95	461.5	3	37	60	0	39					Oct-17
1	3.04	9.48	6.21			2.34	0.43			19.96	461.5	3	37	60	0	39					Oct-17
1	3.81	13.32	8.85			2.12	0.36			26.38	996.0	2	65	32	1						Oct-17
1	3.75	13.27	8.69			2.02	0.46			21.1	996.0	2	65	32	1						Oct-17
1	3.69	18.52	8.93	48.24	64.92	1.58	0.23	12.36	1.01	79.53	11,292	3	97	0	0	83	26.15	-16.43			May-01
1	3.67	18.46	8.83	47.79	64.05	1.49	0.33	12.36	1.01	48.73	11,292	3	97	0	0	83	26.1	-16.5			Dec-86
1	4.74	23.51	10.44	59.99	76.29	1.11	0.05	13.4	1	84.14	90,346	0	100	0	0	11	27.48	-15.16			Nov-00
1	4.74	23.53	10.46	60.05	76.39	1.12	0.04	13.41	1	84.15	90,346	0	100	0	0	11	27.49	-15.15			May-98
1	4.70	23.42	10.30	59.42	75.16	0.99	0.17	13.4	1	84.16	90,346	0	100	0	0	11	27.39	-15.2			Nov-92
1	-0.96	8.12	7.35	23.45	49.21	1.12	0.28	14.39	1.11	82.15	44,748	3	96	0	1	16	14.6	-7.49			Nov-01
	-0.97	8.10	7.30	23.26	48.84	1.06	0.34	14.39	1.11	194.79	44,748	3	96	0	1	16	14.57	-7.5			May-84
1	1.47	11.35	11.45	41.15	67.87	2	0.1	14.15	1	86.99	10,619	0	100	0	0	6	20.86	-11.28			Feb-04

	MARKET			FUND TYPE, CATEGORY & OBJECTIVE	RATINGS				MINIMUMS	
Fund Name	Ticker Symbol	Traded On	Fund Type	Category and (Prospectus Objective)	Overall Rating	Reward Rating	Risk Rating	Recent Up/ Downgrade	Open to New Investors	Min Initial Investment
Vanguard High Dividend Yield Index Fund Admiral	VHYAX	NAS CM	Open End	US Equity Large Cap Value (Equity-Income)	B-	C	B+		Y	3,000
Vanguard High Dividend Yield Index Fund Investor Shares	VHDYX	NAS CM	Open End	US Equity Large Cap Value (Equity-Income)	B-	C	B+		Y	3,000
Vanguard Industrials Index Fund Admiral Shares	VINAX	NAS CM	Open End	Industrials Sector Equity ()	C+	C	B-		Y	100,000
Vanguard Information Technology Index Fund Admiral Shares	VITAX	NAS CM	Open End	Technology Sector Equity ()	B	B-	B		Y	100,000
Vanguard Institutional Index Institutional Plus Shares	VIIIX	NAS CM	Open End	US Equity Large Cap Blend (Growth & Income)	B-	C	B		Y	100,000,000
Vanguard Institutional Index Fund Institutional Shares	VINIX	NAS CM	Open End	US Equity Large Cap Blend (Growth & Income)	B-	C	B		Y	5,000,000
Vanguard Inst Target Retmnt 2015 Inst Shares	VITVX	NAS CM	Open End	Target Date (Asset Alloc)	B	C+	A	Up	Y	100,000,000
Vanguard Inst Target Retmnt 2020 Inst Shares	VITWX	NAS CM	Open End	Target Date (Asset Alloc)	B	C+	A	Up	Y	100,000,000
Vanguard Inst Target Retmnt 2025 Inst Shares	VRIVX	NAS CM	Open End	Target Date (Asset Alloc)	B	C	A-	Up	Y	100,000,000
Vanguard Inst Target Retmnt 2030 Inst Shares	VTTWX	NAS CM	Open End	Target Date (Asset Alloc)	B-	C	A-	Up	Y	100,000,000
Vanguard Inst Target Retmnt 2035 Inst Shares	VITFX	NAS CM	Open End	Target Date (Asset Alloc)	B-	C	B+	Up	Y	100,000,000
Vanguard Inst Target Retmnt 2040 Inst Shares	VIRSX	NAS CM	Open End	Target Date (Asset Alloc)	B-	C	B+	Up	Y	100,000,000
Vanguard Inst Target Retmnt 2045 Inst Shares	VITLX	NAS CM	Open End	Target Date (Asset Alloc)	B-	C	B	Up	Y	100,000,000
Vanguard Inst Target Retmnt 2050 Inst Shares	VTRLX	NAS CM	Open End	Target Date (Asset Alloc)	B-	C	B	Up	Y	100,000,000
Vanguard Inst Target Retmnt 2055 Inst Shares	VIVLX	NAS CM	Open End	Target Date (Asset Alloc)	B-	C	B	Up	Y	100,000,000
Vanguard Inst Target Retmnt 2060 Inst Shares	VILVX	NAS CM	Open End	Target Date (Asset Alloc)	B-	C	B	Up	Y	100,000,000
Vanguard Inst Target Retmnt 2065 Inst Shares	VSXFX	NAS CM	Open End	Target Date (Asset Alloc)	C	D+	B	Up	Y	100,000,000
Vanguard Inst Target Retmnt Income Inst Shares	VITRX	NAS CM	Open End	Target Date (Asset Alloc)	B	C+	A-		Y	100,000,000
Vanguard Inst Total Stock Mkt Index Inst Plus Shares	VITPX	NAS CM	Open End	US Equity Large Cap Blend (Growth)	B-	C	B		Y	100,000,000
Vanguard Inst Total Stock Mkt Index Inst Shares	VITNX	NAS CM	Open End	US Equity Large Cap Blend (Growth)	B-	C	B		Y	5,000,000
Vanguard Instl 500 Index Trust	VFFSX	NAS CM	Open End	US Equity Large Cap Blend (Growth)	B-	C	B		Y	5 Billion
Vanguard Instl Extended Market Index Trust	VSEMX	NAS CM	Open End	US Equity Mid Cap (Growth)	C+	C	B-		Y	3 Billion
Vanguard Instl Total International Index Trust	VTISX	NAS CM	Open End	Global Equity Large Cap (Foreign Stock)	C	C	B		Y	3 Billion
Vanguard Intl Dividend Appreciation Index Admiral Shares	VIAAX	NAS CM	Open End	Global Equity Large Cap (Foreign Stock)	C+	C	B	Up	Y	3,000
Vanguard Intl Dividend Appreciation Index Inv Shares	VIAIX	NAS CM	Open End	Global Equity Large Cap (Foreign Stock)	C+	C	B	Up	Y	3,000
Vanguard International Explorer Fund Investor Shares	VINEX	NAS CM	Open End	Global Equity Mid/Small Cap (Foreign Stock)	C	C-	C	Up	Y	3,000
Vanguard International Growth Fund Admiral Shares	VWILX	NAS CM	Open End	Global Equity Large Cap (Foreign Stock)	C	C	C+		Y	50,000
Vanguard International Growth Fund Investor Shares	VWIGX	NAS CM	Open End	Global Equity Large Cap (Foreign Stock)	C	C	C+		Y	3,000
Vanguard Intl High Dividend Yield Index Admiral Shares	VIHAX	NAS CM	Open End	Global Equity Large Cap (Foreign Stock)	C+	C	B	Up	Y	3,000
Vanguard Intl High Dividend Yield Index Inv Shares	VIHIX	NAS CM	Open End	Global Equity Large Cap (Foreign Stock)	C+	C	B	Up	Y	3,000
Vanguard International Value Fund Investor Shares	VTRIX	NAS CM	Open End	Global Equity Large Cap (Foreign Stock)	C	C	B		Y	3,000
Vanguard Large Cap Index Fund Admiral Shares	VLCAX	NAS CM	Open End	US Equity Large Cap Blend (Growth)	B-	C	B		Y	3,000
Vanguard Large Cap Index Fund Institutional Shares	VLISX	NAS CM	Open End	US Equity Large Cap Blend (Growth)	B-	C	B		Y	5,000,000
Vanguard Large Cap Index Fund Investor Shares	VLACX	NAS CM	Open End	US Equity Large Cap Blend (Growth)	B-	C	B		Y	3,000
Vanguard LifeStrategy Conservative Growth Investor Shares	VSCGX	NAS CM	Open End	Cautious Alloc (Asset Alloc)	B	C+	A-		Y	3,000
Vanguard LifeStrategy Growth Fund Investor Shares	VASGX	NAS CM	Open End	Aggressive Alloc (Asset Alloc)	B-	C	B+	Up	Y	3,000
Vanguard LifeStrategy Income Fund Investor Shares	VASIX	NAS CM	Open End	Cautious Alloc (Asset Alloc)	B	C+	A-		Y	3,000
Vanguard LifeStrategy Moderate Growth Fund Investor Shares	VSMGX	NAS CM	Open End	Moderate Alloc (Asset Alloc)	B	C	A-	Up	Y	3,000
Vanguard Managed Payout Fund Investor Shares	VPGDX	NAS CM	Open End	Moderate Alloc (Growth & Income)	B-	C	A-	Up	Y	25,000
Vanguard Market Neutral Fund Institutional Shares	VMNIX	NAS CM	Open End	Market Neutral (Growth & Income)	D	D	D	Down	Y	5,000,000
Vanguard Market Neutral Fund Investor Shares	VMNFX	NAS CM	Open End	Market Neutral (Growth & Income)	D	D	D	Down	Y	250,000
Vanguard Materials Index Fund Admiral Shares	VMIAX	NAS CM	Open End	Natl Resources Sec Equity ()	C	C	C+		Y	100,000
Vanguard Mega Cap Growth Index Fund Institutional Shares	VMGAX	NAS CM	Open End	US Equity Large Cap Growth (Growth)	B-	C+	B		Y	5,000,000
Vanguard Mega Cap Index Fund Institutional Shares	VMCTX	NAS CM	Open End	US Equity Large Cap Blend (Growth)	B-	C	B		Y	5,000,000
Vanguard Mega Cap Value Index Fund Institutional Shares	VMVLX	NAS CM	Open End	US Equity Large Cap Value (Growth & Income)	B-	C	B+	Down	Y	5,000,000
Vanguard Mid-Cap Growth Fund Investor Shares	VMGRX	NAS CM	Open End	US Equity Mid Cap (Growth)	B-	C+	B-		Y	3,000
Vanguard Mid-Cap Growth Index Fund Admiral Shares	VMGMX	NAS CM	Open End	US Equity Mid Cap (Growth)	B-	C+	B		Y	3,000
Vanguard Mid-Cap Growth Index Fund Investor Shares	VMGIX	NAS CM	Open End	US Equity Mid Cap (Growth)	B-	C+	B		Y	3,000
★ Vanguard Mid-Cap Index Fund Admiral Shares	VIMAX	NAS CM	Open End	US Equity Mid Cap (Growth)	C+	C	B		Y	3,000
Vanguard Mid-Cap Index Fund Institutional Plus Shares	VMCPX	NAS CM	Open End	US Equity Mid Cap (Growth)	C+	C	B		Y	100,000,000
Vanguard Mid-Cap Index Fund Institutional Shares	VMCIX	NAS CM	Open End	US Equity Mid Cap (Growth)	C+	C	B		Y	5,000,000
★ Vanguard Mid-Cap Index Fund Investor Shares	VIMSX	NAS CM	Open End	US Equity Mid Cap (Growth)	C+	C	B		Y	3,000

★ Expanded analysis of this fund is included in Section II.

	TOTAL RETURNS					PERFORMANCE				ASSETS		ASSET ALLOCATION & TURNOVER					BULL & BEAR		FEES		
Min Additional Investment	3-Month Total Return	6-Month Total Return	1-Year Total Return	3-Year Total Return	5-Year Total Return	Dividend Yield (TTM)	Expense Ratio	3-Yr Std Deviation	3-Year Beta	NAV	Total Assets (MIL)	%Cash	%Stocks	%Bonds	%Other	Turnover Ratio	Last Bull Market Total Return	Last Bear Market Total Return	Front End Fee (%)	Back End Fee (%)	Inception Date
1	2.74	14.67	8.73	36.30	53.73		0.08	11.23	1	26.34	33,225	0	100	0	0	13	21.91	-11.18			Feb-19
1	2.72	14.60	8.58	35.99	53.19	2.99	0.14	11.22	1	34.61	33,225	0	100	0	0	13	21.84	-11.22			Nov-06
1	4.59	23.37	9.27	47.55	53.91	1.67	0.1	16.78	1	74.92	3,800	1	99	0	0	4	30.04	-25.06			May-06
1	5.44	28.43	17.80	106.59	133.78	1.2	0.1	16.08	1	108.02	22,786	0	100	0	0	7	29.16	-14.12			Mar-04
1	4.30	19.56	10.40	50.85	66.21	1.98	0.02	12.19	1	266.32	228,885	1	99	0	0	6	25.1	-16.26			Jul-97
1	4.29	19.55	10.39	50.77	66.06	1.96	0.04	12.19	1	266.31	228,885	1	99	0	0	6	25.08	-16.26			Jul-90
1	3.04	10.16	6.54	22.26		2.35	0.09	4.82	0.43	22.65	8,725	2	37	61	0	15					Jun-15
1	3.21	11.84	6.58	26.51		2.27	0.09	6.22	0.47	23.41	23,929	2	50	48	0	8					Jun-15
1	3.38	13.05	6.68	29.73		2.21	0.09	7.22	0.55	23.81	32,422	2	59	39	0	9					Jun-15
1	3.39	13.86	6.45	32.42		2.2	0.09	8.07	0.62	24.06	30,368	2	66	31	0	7					Jun-15
1	3.44	14.73	6.27	35.13		2.17	0.09	8.93	0.69	24.3	27,817	2	74	24	0	8					Jun-15
1	3.45	15.53	6.03	37.75		2.11	0.09	9.79	0.76	24.54	24,336	2	81	16	0	7					Jun-15
1	3.47	16.17	5.88	38.78		2.07	0.09	10.35	0.8	24.71	20,743	2	87	10	0	6					Jun-15
1	3.47	16.15	5.86	38.68		2.03	0.09	10.36	0.8	24.75	15,332	2	87	10	0	5					Jun-15
1	3.50	16.19	5.95	38.79		1.96	0.09	10.33	0.8	24.82	7,409	2	87	10	0	5					Jun-15
1	3.50	16.14	5.94	38.74		1.92	0.09	10.38	0.8	24.82	2,279	2	87	10	0	5					Jun-15
1	3.55	16.22	5.92			1.56	0.09			22.71	203.5	2	88	10	0	28					Jul-17
1	2.90	9.01	6.56	17.19		2.55	0.09	3.8	0.5	22.07	6,193	2	28	69	0	13					Jun-15
1	4.09	19.77	9.02	50.45	62.77	1.92	0.02	12.54	1	63.46	39,445	1	99	0	0	7	25.85	-17.66			May-01
1	4.09	19.76	9.03	50.37	62.65	1.92	0.03	12.54	1	63.46	39,445	1	99	0	0	7	25.84	-17.67			Aug-01
1	4.30	19.56	10.41	50.89	65.80	2	0.01	12.19	1	143.81	483,171	1	99	0	0	4	24.99	-16.31			Jun-16
1	3.05	20.65	2.09	47.41	46.06	1.37	0.02	15.23	1	144.59	69,501	3	97	0	0	10	28.75	-23.91			Jun-16
1	2.76	13.81	0.64	31.25	12.37	2.92	0.05	11.45	1	119.4	381,622	4	96	0	0	3	14.58	-24.35			Jun-16
1	5.83	19.33	6.21	29.93		1.37	0.25	11.46	1	32.98	1,378	1	99	0	0	36					Mar-16
1	5.79	19.23	6.09	29.54		1.26	0.35	11.47	1	27.15	1,378	1	99	0	0	36					Mar-16
1	1.68	13.11	-11.71	25.52	16.71	1.61	0.39	14.37	1.12	16.91	3,312	7	93	0	0	40	15.1	-25.66			Nov-96
1	3.22	19.11	-0.39	55.70	38.87	1.46	0.32	15.53	1.27	93.98	37,113	5	95	0	0	16	19.77	-25.55			Aug-01
1	3.17	19.02	-0.53	55.06	37.95	1.32	0.45	15.51	1.27	29.53	37,113	5	95	0	0	16	19.73	-25.6			Sep-81
1	2.58	11.85	2.61	30.68		4.15	0.32	10.94	1.01	29.73	1,328	3	97	0	0	10					Mar-16
1	2.50	11.73	2.44	30.24		4.01	0.42	10.93	1	24.56	1,328	3	97	0	0	10					Feb-16
1	2.41	12.57	-0.39	30.32	6.71	2.55	0.38	11.12	0.96	35.98	10,204	5	95	0	0	28	15.06	-24.2			May-83
1	4.28	19.63	10.30	51.20	65.13	1.96	0.05	12.22	1	68.05	22,808	1	99	0	0	4	25.36	-16.74			Feb-04
1	4.28	19.64	10.32	51.24	65.22	1.97	0.04	12.21	1	280.08	22,808	1	99	0	0	4	25.39	-16.75			Jun-05
1	4.25	19.56	10.18	50.67	64.14	1.84	0.17	12.21	1	54.44	22,808	1	99	0	0	4	25.26	-16.81			Jan-04
1	3.20	10.58	7.07	20.97	27.82	2.58	0.12	4.84	0.51	20.35	10,103	2	38	60	0	11	10.32	-7.41			Sep-94
1	3.44	15.04	6.14	34.91	37.41	2.31	0.14	9.21	0.71	34.02	15,573	2	77	20	0	10	18.14	-16.17			Sep-94
1	3.06	8.36	7.44	14.30	22.56	2.72	0.11	3.14	0.71	15.9	4,449	2	19	79	0	9	6.3	-2.5			Sep-94
1	3.34	12.80	6.66	27.85	32.79	2.45	0.13	6.97	0.32	27.55	16,723	2	58	40	0	12	14.1	-11.41			Sep-94
1	1.88	9.94	4.15	21.70	25.01	13.95	0.32	6.32	0.56	16.85	1,803	9	63	20	8	17	14.98	-12.59			May-08
1	-5.66	-10.38	-10.57	-9.82	-5.89	1.15	1.74	5.4	-38.53	10.33	1,027	103	-3	0	0	110	-0.09	2.59			Oct-98
1	-5.63	-10.35	-10.57	-9.91	-6.24	1.08	1.8	5.38	-37.79	10.38	1,027	103	-3	0	0	110	-0.19	2.58			Nov-98
1	4.77	17.87	-0.52	34.73	27.99	1.94	0.1	15.63	1	65.34	2,485	0	100	0	0	5	29.14	-28.04			Feb-04
1	4.47	22.61	9.73	62.46	80.08	0.79	0.06	13.46	1	257.19	4,447	0	100	0	0	9	27.58	-13.66			Apr-08
1	4.26	18.98	10.85	52.71	67.84	1.98	0.06	12.08	1	199.76	2,060	0	100	0	0	4	25.18	-15.74			Feb-08
1	4.02	15.55	11.43	44.01	57.38	2.72	0.06	11.85	1	159.74	2,619	0	100	0	0	8	22.7	-17.81			Mar-08
1	5.73	29.17	13.30	59.32	61.55	0.31	0.36	14.31	0.98	28.56	4,765	5	95	0	0	75	28.63	-18.47			Dec-97
1	4.81	26.54	12.04	52.04	62.31	0.7	0.07	13.63	1	64.29	14,046	1	99	0	0	25	26.99	-21.74			Sep-11
1	4.78	26.48	11.91	51.49	61.34	0.58	0.19	13.63	1	58.74	14,046	1	99	0	0	25	26.87	-21.78			Aug-06
1	4.36	22.96	7.83	43.90	52.92	1.52	0.05	13.29	1	207.01	105,461	1	99	0	0	16	26.38	-21.36			Nov-01
1	4.36	22.98	7.85	43.98	53.10	1.54	0.03	13.3	1	225.53	105,461	1	99	0	0	16	26.41	-21.34			Dec-10
1	4.36	22.98	7.85	43.93	53.00	1.53	0.04	13.3	1	45.73	105,461	1	99	0	0	16	26.43	-21.37			May-98
1	4.33	22.89	7.69	43.38	52.02	1.4	0.17	13.28	1	45.64	105,461	1	99	0	0	16	26.27	-21.4			May-98

	MARKET			FUND TYPE, CATEGORY & OBJECTIVE	RATINGS				MINIMUMS	
Fund Name	Ticker Symbol	Traded On	Fund Type	Category and (Prospectus Objective)	Overall Rating	Reward Rating	Risk Rating	Recent Up/ Downgrade	Open to New Investors	Min Initial Investment
Vanguard Mid-Cap Value Index Fund Admiral Shares	VMVAX	NAS CM	Open End	US Equity Mid Cap (Growth)	C+	C	B	Up	Y	3,000
Vanguard Mid-Cap Value Index Fund Investor Shares	VMVIX	NAS CM	Open End	US Equity Mid Cap (Growth)	C+	C	B	Up	Y	3,000
Vanguard Pacific Stock Index Fund Admiral Shares	VPADX	NAS CM	Open End	Asia Equity (Pacific Stock)	C	C	C+		Y	3,000
Vanguard Pacific Stock Index Fund Institutional Shares	VPKIX	NAS CM	Open End	Asia Equity (Pacific Stock)	C	C	C+		Y	5,000,000
Vanguard Pacific Stock Index Fund Investor Shares	VPACX	NAS CM	Open End	Asia Equity (Pacific Stock)	C	C	C+		Y	3,000
Vanguard PRIMECAP Core Fund Investor Shares	VPCCX	NAS CM	Open End	US Equity Large Cap Blend (Growth)	B-	C	B			3,000
Vanguard PRIMECAP Fund Admiral Shares	VPMAX	NAS CM	Open End	US Equity Large Cap Growth (Growth)	B-	C	B			50,000
Vanguard PRIMECAP Fund Investor Shares	VPMCX	NAS CM	Open End	US Equity Large Cap Growth (Growth)	B-	C	B			3,000
Vanguard Real Estate II Index Fund	VRTPX	NAS CM	Open End	Real Estate Sector Equity (Real Estate)	C-	C	C+	Up	Y	100,000,000
Vanguard Real Estate Index Fund Admiral Shares	VGSLX	NAS CM	Open End	Real Estate Sector Equity (Real Estate)	C	C	C+	Down	Y	3,000
Vanguard Real Estate Index Fund Institutional Shares	VGSNX	NAS CM	Open End	Real Estate Sector Equity (Real Estate)	C	C	C+	Down	Y	5,000,000
Vanguard Real Estate Index Fund Investor Shares	VGSIX	NAS CM	Open End	Real Estate Sector Equity (Real Estate)	C	C	C+	Down	Y	3,000
Vanguard Russell 1000 Growth Index Institutional Shares	VRGWX	NAS CM	Open End	US Equity Large Cap Growth (Growth)	B-	C+	B	Down	Y	5,000,000
Vanguard Russell 1000 Index Fund Institutional Shares	VRNIX	NAS CM	Open End	US Equity Large Cap Blend (Growth)	B-	C	B		Y	5,000,000
Vanguard Russell 1000 Value Index Institutional Shares	VRVIX	NAS CM	Open End	US Equity Large Cap Value (Growth & Income)	B-	C	B	Up	Y	5,000,000
Vanguard Russell 2000 Growth Index Institutional Shares	VRTGX	NAS CM	Open End	US Equity Small Cap (Small Company)	C	C	C+	Down	Y	5,000,000
Vanguard Russell 2000 Index Fund Institutional Shares	VRTIX	NAS CM	Open End	US Equity Small Cap (Small Company)	C	C	C+		Y	5,000,000
Vanguard Russell 2000 Value Index Institutional Shares	VRTVX	NAS CM	Open End	US Equity Small Cap (Small Company)	C	C-	C		Y	5,000,000
Vanguard Russell 3000 Index Fund Institutional Shares	VRTTX	NAS CM	Open End	US Equity Large Cap Blend (Growth)	B-	C	B		Y	5,000,000
Vanguard S&P 500 Value Index Fund Institutional Shares	VSPVX	NAS CM	Open End	US Equity Large Cap Value (Growth & Income)	B-	C	B	Up	Y	5,000,000
Vanguard S&P Mid-Cap 400 Growth Index Institutional Shares	VMFGX	NAS CM	Open End	US Equity Mid Cap (Growth & Income)	C+	C	B-	Up	Y	5,000,000
Vanguard S&P Mid-Cap 400 Index Fund Institutional Shares	VSPMX	NAS CM	Open End	US Equity Mid Cap (Growth & Income)	C+	C	B-	Up	Y	5,000,000
Vanguard S&P Mid-Cap 400 Value Index Institutional Shares	VMFVX	NAS CM	Open End	US Equity Mid Cap (Growth & Income)	C+	C	B		Y	5,000,000
Vanguard S&P Small-Cap 600 Index Fund Institutional Shares	VSMSX	NAS CM	Open End	US Equity Small Cap (Growth & Income)	C	C-	C+	Down	Y	5,000,000
Vanguard S&P Small-Cap 600 Value Index Inst Shares	VSMVX	NAS CM	Open End	US Equity Small Cap (Growth & Income)	C	C-	C		Y	5,000,000
Vanguard Selected Value Fund Investor Shares	VASVX	NAS CM	Open End	US Equity Mid Cap (Growth & Income)	C	C	B-		Y	3,000
Vanguard Small Cap Value Index Fund Admiral Shares	VSIAX	NAS CM	Open End	US Equity Small Cap (Small Company)	C	C	B-		Y	3,000
Vanguard Small Capitalization Growth Index Investor Shares	VISGX	NAS CM	Open End	US Equity Small Cap (Small Company)	C+	C	B-	Down	Y	3,000
Vanguard Small Capitalization Index Fund Investor Shares	NAESX	NAS CM	Open End	US Equity Small Cap (Small Company)	C+	C	B-		Y	3,000
Vanguard Small Capitalization Value Index Investor Shares	VISVX	NAS CM	Open End	US Equity Small Cap (Small Company)	C	C	B-		Y	3,000
Vanguard Small-Cap Growth Index Fund Admiral Shares	VSGAX	NAS CM	Open End	US Equity Small Cap (Small Company)	C+	C	B-	Down	Y	3,000
Vanguard Small-Cap Growth Index Fund Institutional Shares	VSGIX	NAS CM	Open End	US Equity Small Cap (Small Company)	C+	C	B-	Down	Y	5,000,000
Vanguard Small-Cap Index Fund Admiral Shares	VSMAX	NAS CM	Open End	US Equity Small Cap (Small Company)	C+	C	B-		Y	3,000
Vanguard Small-Cap Index Fund Institutional Plus Shares	VSCPX	NAS CM	Open End	US Equity Small Cap (Small Company)	C+	C	B-		Y	100,000,000
Vanguard Small-Cap Index Fund Institutional Shares	VSCIX	NAS CM	Open End	US Equity Small Cap (Small Company)	C+	C	B-		Y	5,000,000
Vanguard Small-Cap Value Index Fund Institutional Shares	VSIIX	NAS CM	Open End	US Equity Small Cap (Small Company)	C	C	B-		Y	5,000,000
Vanguard Star Fund Investor Shares	VGSTX	NAS CM	Open End	Moderate Alloc (Balanced)	B-	C	B+	Up	Y	1,000
Vanguard Strategic Equity Fund Investor Shares	VSEQX	NAS CM	Open End	US Equity Mid Cap (Aggr Growth)	C	C	C+		Y	3,000
Vanguard Strategic Small-Cap Equity Fund Investor Shares	VSTCX	NAS CM	Open End	US Equity Small Cap (Small Company)	C	C-	C		Y	3,000
Vanguard Target Retirement 2015 Fund Investor Shares	VTXVX	NAS CM	Open End	Target Date (Growth & Income)	B	C+	A	Up	Y	1,000
Vanguard Target Retirement 2020 Fund Investor Shares	VTWNX	NAS CM	Open End	Target Date (Growth & Income)	B	C+	A	Up	Y	1,000
Vanguard Target Retirement 2025 Fund Investor Shares	VTTVX	NAS CM	Open End	Target Date (Growth & Income)	B	C	A-	Up	Y	1,000
Vanguard Target Retirement 2030 Fund Investor Shares	VTHRX	NAS CM	Open End	Target Date (Growth & Income)	B-	C	A-	Up	Y	1,000
Vanguard Target Retirement 2035 Fund Investor Shares	VTTHX	NAS CM	Open End	Target Date (Growth & Income)	B-	C	B+	Up	Y	1,000
Vanguard Target Retirement 2040 Fund Investor Shares	VFORX	NAS CM	Open End	Target Date (Growth & Income)	B-	C	B+	Up	Y	1,000
Vanguard Target Retirement 2045 Fund Investor Shares	VTIVX	NAS CM	Open End	Target Date (Growth & Income)	B-	C	B	Up	Y	1,000
Vanguard Target Retirement 2050 Fund Investor Shares	VFIFX	NAS CM	Open End	Target Date (Growth & Income)	B-	C	B	Up	Y	1,000
Vanguard Target Retirement 2055 Fund Investor Shares	VFFVX	NAS CM	Open End	Target Date (Growth & Income)	B-	C	B	Up	Y	1,000
Vanguard Target Retirement 2060 Fund Investor Shares	VTTSX	NAS CM	Open End	Target Date (Growth & Income)	B-	C	B	Up	Y	1,000
Vanguard Target Retirement 2065 Fund Investor Shares	VLXVX	NAS CM	Open End	Target Date (Growth & Income)	C	D+	B	Up	Y	1,000
Vanguard Target Retirement Income Fund Investor Shares	VTINX	NAS CM	Open End	Target Date (Growth & Income)	B	C+	A-		Y	1,000
Vanguard Tax-Managed Balanced Fund Admiral Shares	VTMFX	NAS CM	Open End	Cautious Alloc (Balanced)	B	C+	A		Y	10,000

★ Expanded analysis of this fund is included in Section II.

	TOTAL RETURNS					PERFORMANCE				ASSETS		ASSET ALLOCATION & TURNOVER					BULL & BEAR		FEES		
Min Additional Investment	3-Month Total Return	6-Month Total Return	1-Year Total Return	3-Year Total Return	5-Year Total Return	Dividend Yield (TTM)	Expense Ratio	3-Yr Std Deviation	3-Year Beta	NAV	Total Assets (MIL)	%Cash	%Stocks	%Bonds	%Other	Turnover Ratio	Last Bull Market Total Return	Last Bear Market Total Return	Front End Fee (%)	Back End Fee (%)	Inception Date
1	3.86	19.19	3.52	36.04	43.62	2.43	0.07	13.52	1	57.71	19,070	0	100	0	0	17	25.77	-20.99			Sep-11
1	3.83	19.14	3.42	35.57	42.75	2.3	0.19	13.52	1	43.87	19,070	0	100	0	0	17	25.66	-21			Aug-06
1	1.38	10.23	-2.59	29.44	21.74	2.79	0.1	11.43	1.01	81.97	6,749	2	98	0	0	4	10.23	-15.25			Aug-01
1	1.37	10.23	-2.57	29.44	21.83	2.81	0.08	11.44	1.01	12.54	6,749	2	98	0	0	4	10.34	-15.24			May-00
1	1.41	10.17	-2.66	28.95	20.92	2.68	0.23	11.43	1.01	12.64	6,749	2	98	0	0	4	10.18	-15.32			Jun-90
1	2.89	14.99	6.99	56.21	68.16	1.13	0.46	14.24	1.12	26.69	10,783	3	97	0	0	9	18.7	-17.64			Dec-04
1	2.18	14.23	6.18	64.11	76.57	1.13	0.31	14.31	1.13	136.92	64,289	4	96	0	0	8	20.42	-18.36			Nov-01
1	2.17	14.19	6.11	63.77	75.96	1.05	0.38	14.31	1.13	132.09	64,289	4	96	0	0	8	20.34	-18.38			Nov-84
1	1.73	19.59	12.22			3.83	0.08			21.16	7,175	0	100	0	0	24					Sep-17
1	1.73	19.56	12.21	13.70	44.59	4.04	0.12	13.17		124.05	64,152	1	99	0	0	24	31.27	-16.26			Nov-01
1	1.76	19.56	12.25	13.76	44.73	4.06	0.1	13.18		19.2	64,152	1	99	0	0	24	31.24	-16.24			Dec-03
1	1.68	19.46	12.04	13.19	43.57	3.89	0.26	13.18		29.08	64,152	1	99	0	0	24	31.21	-16.32			May-96
1	4.62	22.62	11.49	66.15	86.89	1.03	0.08	13.4	1	311.83	5,828	0	100	0	0	15	26.6	-15.4			Dec-10
1	4.23	19.85	9.97	50.45	63.65	1.77	0.08	12.31	1	261.08	3,540	0	100	0	0	9	25.48	-17.08			Oct-10
1	3.83	17.13	8.44	35.66	42.72	2.34	0.08	12.1	1	217.9	3,851	0	100	0	0	16	24.35	-18.82			Dec-10
1	2.79	21.76	-0.33	53.93	52.88	0.73	0.08	17.45	1	279.14	801.8	3	97	0	0	35	28.12	-25.44			May-11
1	2.11	17.95	-3.22	44.58	41.76	1.28	0.08	17.1	1	239.51	2,435	3	97	0	0	19	27.77	-25.08			Dec-10
1	1.38	14.05	-6.20	35.12	30.44	1.86	0.08	17.31	1	207.5	401.7	2	98	0	0	30	27.35	-24.77			Jul-12
1	4.08	19.71	8.93	50.05	61.94	1.76	0.08	12.52	1	259.41	1,349	0	100	0	0	14	25.64	-17.76			Nov-10
1	3.99	17.56	8.59	37.24	45.80	2.4	0.08	12.97	1	246.58	1,095	0	100	0	0	20	25.79	-19.65			Mar-15
1	3.53	20.39	1.86	41.40	53.69	0.99	0.08	14.51	1	279.62	967.7	1	99	0	0	43	25.63	-20.97			Mar-11
1	3.02	19.13	1.29	38.78	47.30	1.45	0.08	15.13	1	261.62	2,258	1	99	0	0	12	27.88	-22.61			Mar-11
1	2.48	17.84	0.75	35.19	39.38	1.72	0.08	16.18	1	246.27	921.3	1	99	0	0	36	30.21	-24.19			Nov-10
1	1.84	14.28	-4.93	43.33	50.19	1.22	0.08	17.88	1	287.48	2,310	2	98	0	0	13	29.45	-22.07			Apr-11
1	1.24	14.35	-7.20	36.82	40.17	1.77	0.08	18.6	1	268.53	423.6	1	99	0	0	34	31.25	-22.71			Nov-14
1	4.60	19.19	-0.67	32.16	25.70	1.76	0.36	15.24	1.12	26.57	8,089	6	94	0	0	31	23.1	-19.11			Feb-96
1	2.00	16.43	-1.56	34.41	38.12	2.24	0.07	15.76	1	56.08	30,407	1	99	0	0	18	28.1	-23.97			Sep-11
1	3.80	25.54	6.65	56.08	53.44	0.52	0.19	16.06	1	52.42	24,806	2	98	0	0	22	29.39	-25.13			May-98
1	2.84	20.58	2.14	43.81	44.67	1.36	0.17	15.66	1	75.08	92,923	2	98	0	0	15	28.67	-24.56			Oct-60
1	1.98	16.37	-1.66	33.92	37.26	2.12	0.19	15.76	1	31.3	30,407	1	99	0	0	18	27.94	-23.97			May-98
1	3.82	25.61	6.78	56.65	54.39	0.64	0.07	16.06	1	65.52	24,806	2	98	0	0	22	29.48	-25.13			Sep-11
1	3.81	25.63	6.77	56.67	54.46	0.65	0.06	16.06	1	52.47	24,806	2	98	0	0	22	29.55	-25.08			May-00
1	2.86	20.65	2.26	44.31	45.53	1.48	0.05	15.66	1	75.09	92,923	2	98	0	0	15	28.76	-24.5			Nov-00
1	2.87	20.66	2.28	44.40	45.71	1.5	0.03	15.66	1	216.74	92,923	2	98	0	0	15	28.79	-24.5			Dec-10
1	2.86	20.66	2.27	44.35	45.61	1.49	0.04	15.67	1	75.09	92,923	2	98	0	0	15	28.75	-24.5			Jul-97
1	2.01	16.47	-1.54	34.46	38.19	2.25	0.06	15.76	1	31.35	30,407	1	99	0	0	18	28.1	-23.96			Dec-99
1	3.61	14.14	6.57	33.54	37.26	2.2	0.31	8.16		26.75	21,973	4	60	36	0	11	15.79	-11.43			Mar-85
1	1.78	19.00	-0.32	40.39	43.18	1.15	0.17	15.97	1.08	32	7,280	2	98	0	0	82	29.14	-22.23			Aug-95
1	-0.50	13.40	-8.06	32.05	31.61	1.09	0.29	17.76	1.07	31.64	1,540	2	98	0	0	88	27.99	-24.06			Apr-06
1	2.98	10.06	6.40	22.09	26.98	2.35	0.13	4.82	0.44	15.21	15,775	2	37	61	0	7	13.57	-9.63			Oct-03
1	3.20	11.78	6.49	26.29	31.06	2.29	0.13	6.22	0.47	31.87	32,912	2	50	48	0	10	15.15	-11.62			Jun-06
1	3.34	12.99	6.61	29.52	33.61	2.26	0.13	7.23	0.55	19.13	43,560	2	59	39	0	8	16.65	-13.45			Oct-03
1	3.40	13.86	6.41	32.25	35.37	2.19	0.14	8.06	0.62	34.91	38,403	2	66	31	0	9	18.22	-15.23			Jun-06
1	3.42	14.64	6.21	34.91	37.01	2.16	0.14	8.91	0.68	21.46	36,493	2	74	24	0	8	19.76	-16.99			Oct-03
1	3.45	15.50	6.00	37.65	38.58	2.1	0.14	9.76	0.75	37.09	28,470	2	81	16	0	8	20.19	-17.37			Jun-06
1	3.50	16.13	5.89	38.61	39.46	2.07	0.15	10.34	0.8	23.32	26,144	2	87	10	0	7	20.17	-17.34			Oct-03
1	3.47	16.12	5.85	38.52	39.41	2.1	0.15	10.35	0.8	37.52	18,853	2	87	10	0	7	20.15	-17.4			Jun-06
1	3.48	16.13	5.87	38.56	39.20	2.04	0.15	10.33	0.8	40.73	9,695	2	87	10	0	5	20.27	-17.27			Aug-10
1	3.48	16.14	5.85	38.50	39.17	1.99	0.15	10.34	0.8	35.97	4,079	2	87	10	0	3					Jan-12
1	3.52	16.17	5.84			1.6	0.15			22.63	365.2	2	88	10	0	1					Jul-17
1	2.96	8.97	6.54	17.10	22.80	2.52	0.12	3.78	0.51	13.72	16,765	2	28	69	0	6	8.71	-3			Oct-03
1	3.06	11.76	8.26	26.86	39.02	2.15	0.09	5.94	0.46	32.64	5,208	1	47	52	0	11	14.31	-6.48			Sep-94

	MARKET		FUND TYPE, CATEGORY & OBJECTIVE		RATINGS				MINIMUMS	
Fund Name	Ticker Symbol	Traded On	Fund Type	Category and (Prospectus Objective)	Overall Rating	Reward Rating	Risk Rating	Recent Up/ Downgrade	Open to New Investors	Min Initial Investment
Vanguard Tax-Managed Capital Appreciation Admiral Shares	VTCLX	NAS CM	Open End	US Equity Large Cap Blend (Growth)	B-	C	B		Y	10,000
Vanguard Tax-Managed Capital Appreciation Inst Shares	VTCIX	NAS CM	Open End	US Equity Large Cap Blend (Growth)	B-	C	B		Y	5,000,000
Vanguard Tax-Managed Small Cap Fund Admiral Shares	VTMSX	NAS CM	Open End	US Equity Small Cap (Small Company)	C	C-	C+	Down	Y	10,000
Vanguard Tax-Managed Small-Cap Fund Institutional Shares	VTSIX	NAS CM	Open End	US Equity Small Cap (Small Company)	C	C-	C+	Down	Y	5,000,000
★ Vanguard Total International Stock Index Admiral Shares	VTIAX	NAS CM	Open End	Global Equity Large Cap (Foreign Stock)	C	C	B		Y	3,000
Vanguard Total Intl Stock Index Inst Plus Shares	VTPSX	NAS CM	Open End	Global Equity Large Cap (Foreign Stock)	C	C	B		Y	100,000,000
Vanguard Total Intl Stock Index Inst Shares	VTSNX	NAS CM	Open End	Global Equity Large Cap (Foreign Stock)	C	C	B		Y	5,000,000
★ Vanguard Total International Stock Index Investor Shares	VGTSX	NAS CM	Open End	Global Equity Large Cap (Foreign Stock)	C	C	B		Y	0
★ Vanguard Total Stock Market Index Fund Admiral Shares	VTSAX	NAS CM	Open End	US Equity Large Cap Blend (Growth)	B-	C	B		Y	3,000
Vanguard Total Stock Mkt Index Inst Plus Shares	VSMPX	NAS CM	Open End	US Equity Large Cap Blend (Growth)	B-	C	B		Y	100,000,000
Vanguard Total Stock Mkt Index Inst Select Shares	VSTSX	NAS CM	Open End	US Equity Large Cap Blend (Growth)	B-	C	B		Y	5 Billion
Vanguard Total Stock Market Index Institutional Shares	VITSX	NAS CM	Open End	US Equity Large Cap Blend (Growth)	B-	C	B		Y	5,000,000
★ Vanguard Total Stock Market Index Fund Investor Shares	VTSMX	NAS CM	Open End	US Equity Large Cap Blend (Growth)	B-	C	B		Y	3,000
Vanguard Total World Stock Index Fund Admiral	VTWAX	NAS CM	Open End	Global Equity Large Cap (World Stock)	B-	C	B	Up	Y	3,000
Vanguard Total World Stock Index Fund Institutional Shares	VTWIX	NAS CM	Open End	Global Equity Large Cap (World Stock)	B-	C	B	Up	Y	5,000,000
Vanguard Total World Stock Index Investor Shares	VTWSX	NAS CM	Open End	Global Equity Large Cap (World Stock)	B-	C	B	Up	Y	3,000
Vanguard U.S. Multifactor Fund Admiral™ Shares	VFMFX	NAS CM	Open End	US Equity Mid Cap (Growth)	D	D	C-		Y	50,000
Vanguard U.S. Value Fund Investor Shares	VUVLX	NAS CM	Open End	US Equity Large Cap Value (Growth & Income)	C+	C	B-	Up	Y	3,000
Vanguard Utilities Index Fund Admiral Shares	VUIAX	NAS CM	Open End	Utilities Sector Equity (Utility)	B	B	B		Y	100,000
Vanguard Value Index Fund Admiral Shares	VVIAX	NAS CM	Open End	US Equity Large Cap Value (Growth)	B-	C	B+		Y	3,000
Vanguard Value Index Fund Institutional Shares	VIVIX	NAS CM	Open End	US Equity Large Cap Value (Growth)	B-	C	B+		Y	5,000,000
Vanguard Value Index Fund Investor Shares	VIVAX	NAS CM	Open End	US Equity Large Cap Value (Growth)	B-	C	B+		Y	3,000
Vanguard Wellesley® Income Fund Admiral™ Shares	VWIAX	NAS CM	Open End	Cautious Alloc (Income)	B	B-	B+		Y	50,000
Vanguard Wellesley® Income Fund Investor Shares	VWINX	NAS CM	Open End	Cautious Alloc (Income)	B	B-	B+		Y	3,000
★ Vanguard Wellington™ Fund Admiral™ Shares	VWENX	NAS CM	Open End	Moderate Alloc (Growth & Income)	B	C+	A			50,000
★ Vanguard Wellington™ Fund Investor Shares	VWELX	NAS CM	Open End	Moderate Alloc (Growth & Income)	B	C+	A-			3,000
Vanguard Windsor™ Fund Admiral™ Shares	VWNEX	NAS CM	Open End	US Equity Large Cap Value (Growth & Income)	C+	C	B	Up	Y	50,000
Vanguard Windsor™ Fund Investor Share	VWNDX	NAS CM	Open End	US Equity Large Cap Value (Growth & Income)	C+	C	B	Up	Y	3,000
Vanguard Windsor™ II Fund Admiral™ Shares	VWNAX	NAS CM	Open End	US Equity Large Cap Value (Growth & Income)	C+	C	B		Y	50,000
Vanguard Windsor™ II Fund Investor Share	VWNFX	NAS CM	Open End	US Equity Large Cap Value (Growth & Income)	C+	C	B		Y	3,000
Variant Alternative Income Fund Institutional Class	NICHX	NAS CM	Closed End	Multialternative (Income)	U	U	U		Y	1,000,000
Variant Alternative Income Fund Investor Class	UNIQX	NAS CM	Closed End	Multialternative (Income)	U	U	U		Y	25,000
Vericimetry U.S. Small Cap Value Fund	VYSVX	NAS CM	Open End	US Equity Small Cap (Small Company)	C-	C-	C	Down	Y	0
Verplanck Balanced Fund			Open End	Moderate Alloc (Growth & Income)	U	U	U		Y	0
Versus Capital Multi-Manager Real Estate Income LLC Cls I	VCMIX	NAS CM	Closed End	Real Estate Sector Equity (Real Estate)	B	C+	A-		Y	10,000,000
Versus Capital Real Assets Fund	VCRRX	NAS CM	Closed End	Alloc Miscellaneous (Growth & Income)	C-	D+	B	Up	Y	10,000,000
Vert Global Sustainable Real Estate Institutional Cls	VGSRX	NAS CM	Open End	Real Estate Sector Equity (Real Estate)	D+	C-	C+	Up	Y	10,000
Victory Diversified Stock Fund Class A	SRVEX	NAS CM	Open End	US Equity Large Cap Blend (Growth)	C+	C	B-	Up	Y	2,500
Victory Diversified Stock Fund Class C	VDSCX	NAS CM	Open End	US Equity Large Cap Blend (Growth)	C+	C	B-	Up	Y	2,500
Victory Diversified Stock Fund Class I	VDSIX	NAS CM	Open End	US Equity Large Cap Blend (Growth)	C+	C	B-	Up	Y	2,000,000
Victory Diversified Stock Fund Class R	GRINX	NAS CM	Open End	US Equity Large Cap Blend (Growth)	C+	C	B-	Up	Y	0
Victory Diversified Stock Fund Class R6	VDSRX	NAS CM	Open End	US Equity Large Cap Blend (Growth)	C+	C	B-	Up	Y	0
Victory Diversified Stock Fund Class Y	VDSYX	NAS CM	Open End	US Equity Large Cap Blend (Growth)	C+	C	B-	Up	Y	1,000,000
Victory Global Natural Resources Fund Class A	RSNRX	NAS CM	Open End	Natl Resources Sec Equity (Natl Res)	D-	D-	D	Down	Y	2,500
Victory Global Natural Resources Fund Class C	RGNCX	NAS CM	Open End	Natl Resources Sec Equity (Natl Res)	D-	D-	D	Down	Y	2,500
Victory Global Natural Resources Fund Class R	RSNKX	NAS CM	Open End	Natl Resources Sec Equity (Natl Res)	D-	D-	D	Down	Y	0
Victory Global Natural Resources Fund Class Y	RSNYX	NAS CM	Open End	Natl Resources Sec Equity (Natl Res)	D-	D-	D	Down	Y	1,000,000
Victory INCORE Investment Grade Convertible Fund Class A	SBFCX	NAS CM	Open End	Convertibles (Convertible Bond)	B	C	A		Y	2,500
Victory INCORE Investment Grade Convertible Fund Class I	VICIX	NAS CM	Open End	Convertibles (Convertible Bond)	B	C	A		Y	2,000,000
Victory Integrity Discovery Fund Class A	MMEAX	NAS CM	Open End	US Equity Small Cap (Small Company)	C-	C-	C	Down	Y	2,500
Victory Integrity Discovery Fund Class C	MMECX	NAS CM	Open End	US Equity Small Cap (Small Company)	C-	C-	C	Down	Y	2,500
Victory Integrity Discovery Fund Class R	MMERX	NAS CM	Open End	US Equity Small Cap (Small Company)	C-	C-	C	Down	Y	0

★ Expanded analysis of this fund is included in Section II.

Min Additional Investment	TOTAL RETURNS: 3-Month Total Return	6-Month Total Return	1-Year Total Return	3-Year Total Return	5-Year Total Return	PERFORMANCE: Dividend Yield (TTM)	Expense Ratio	3-Yr Std Deviation	3-Year Beta	ASSETS: NAV	Total Assets (MIL)	ASSET ALLOCATION & TURNOVER: %Cash	%Stocks	%Bonds	%Other	Turnover Ratio	BULL & BEAR: Last Bull Market Total Return	Last Bear Market Total Return	FEES: Front End Fee (%)	Back End Fee (%)	Inception Date
1	4.41	20.11	10.11	52.09	65.46	1.62	0.09	12.31	1	151.51	10,675	0	100	0	0	6	25.84	-17.39			Nov-01
1	4.42	20.14	10.15	52.23	65.74	1.65	0.06	12.31	1	75.29	10,675	0	100	0	0	6	25.88	-17.38			Feb-99
1	1.91	14.64	-4.69	42.76	49.92	1.19	0.09	17.76	0.99	63.16	6,618	1	99	0	0	29	29.56	-21.87			Mar-99
1	1.91	14.66	-4.66	42.89	50.19	1.22	0.06	17.76	0.99	63.31	6,618	1	99	0	0	29	29.64	-21.89			Apr-99
1	2.74	13.76	0.56	31.00	12.35	2.9	0.11	11.46	1	28.34	381,622	4	96	0	0	3	14.52	-24.32			Nov-10
1	2.74	13.79	0.62	31.16	12.59	2.93	0.07	11.45	1	113.35	381,622	4	96	0	0	3	14.61	-24.32			Nov-10
1	2.74	13.79	0.61	31.10	12.48	2.93	0.08	11.45	1	113.33	381,622	4	96	0	0	3	14.59	-24.32			Nov-10
	2.71	13.73	0.49	30.72	11.94	2.84	0.17	11.45	1	16.94	381,622	4	96	0	0	3	14.58	-24.35			Apr-96
1	4.08	19.74	8.99	50.32	62.39	1.82	0.04	12.53	1	73.04	814,086	1	99	0	0	3	25.82	-17.71			Nov-00
1	4.09	19.73	9.00	50.40	62.38	1.84	0.02	12.53	1	136.99	814,086	1	99	0	0	3	25.72	-17.74			Apr-15
1	4.09	19.74	9.01	50.46	62.18	1.85	0.01	12.53	1	143.74	814,086	1	99	0	0	3	25.72	-17.74			Jun-16
1	4.09	19.73	9.00	50.35	62.44	1.83	0.03	12.53	1	73.05	814,086	1	99	0	0	3	25.82	-17.68			Jul-97
1	4.05	19.66	8.87	49.86	61.54	1.73	0.14	12.52	1	73.01	814,086	1	99	0	0	3	25.72	-17.74			Apr-92
1	3.49	17.11	5.20	41.02	36.20		0.1	11.45	1	26.66	17,539	1	99	0	0	9	19.31	-21.12			Feb-19
1	3.49	17.09	5.17	41.01	36.22	2.24	0.08	11.46	1	153.69	17,539	1	99	0	0	9	19.31	-21.1			Oct-08
1	3.49	17.05	5.10	40.66	35.56	2.16	0.17	11.45	1	30.67	17,539	1	99	0	0	9	19.18	-21.14			Jun-08
1	1.30	13.57	-3.11			1.7	0.18			24.4	33.4	0	100	0	0	58					Feb-18
1	2.39	13.80	1.56	31.90	37.11	2.07	0.22	13.3	1.06	17.97	1,495	1	99	0	0	75	25.88	-18.36			Jun-00
1	3.32	14.80	18.24	30.52	63.21	2.92	0.1	10.58	1	66.7	4,967	0	100	0	0	4	8.77	1.41			Apr-04
1	3.77	15.91	9.87	43.37	55.54	2.58	0.05	12.02	1	43.3	80,262	0	100	0	0	8	23.26	-18.39			Nov-00
1	3.77	15.91	9.91	43.41	55.66	2.59	0.04	12.02	1	43.3	80,262	0	100	0	0	8	23.28	-18.38			Jul-98
1	3.76	15.85	9.78	42.86	54.60	2.45	0.17	12.02	1	43.32	80,262	0	100	0	0	8	23.17	-18.46			Nov-92
1	3.62	11.06	10.21	20.42	33.08	2.99	0.16	4.57	0.72	64.53	55,740	5	37	58	0	36	11.06	-1.88			May-01
1	3.58	11.03	10.10	20.14	32.58	2.93	0.23	4.57	0.72	26.64	55,740	5	37	58	0	36	11.01	-1.9			Jul-70
1	3.91	13.56	10.37	33.92	43.83	2.61	0.17	7.32	0.58	71.41	105,381	2	66	32	0	34	16.35	-10.37			May-01
1	3.89	13.51	10.28	33.60	43.27	2.53	0.25	7.32	0.58	41.35	105,381	2	66	32	0	34	16.28	-10.37			Jul-29
1	3.56	16.68	1.82	38.88	35.61	1.96	0.21	13.68	1.1	70.28	18,870	4	96	0	0	33	26.57	-21.09			Nov-01
1	3.49	16.58	1.70	38.43	34.90	1.87	0.31	13.68	1.1	20.84	18,870	4	96	0	0	33	26.51	-21.14			Oct-58
1	3.87	17.12	7.16	38.63	41.10	2.26	0.25	12.65	1.03	63.48	46,296	4	96	0	0	29	25.42	-17.14			May-01
1	3.84	17.05	7.07	38.31	40.54	2.19	0.33	12.65	1.03	35.78	46,296	4	96	0	0	29	25.37	-17.18			Jun-85
	2.97	6.14					2.83			25.84	--	16	24	2	58						Sep-18
	2.79	5.91					3.08			25.85	--	16	24	2	58						Oct-18
	1.11	12.74	-10.49	25.77	18.13	0.84	0.61	17.95	1.02	16.85	201.1	3	97	0	0	46					Dec-11
	3.69	12.44					0			104.24	881.0	3	50	47	0						Aug-18
	1.35	4.07	5.84	17.74	38.32	4.38	1.25	1.37		28.33	--	3	14	3	79	13					Jul-12
	1.56	5.07	3.56			3.38	1.46			25.42	--										Sep-17
	0.58	16.16	6.63			3.13	0.5			10.45	24.1	0	100	0	0						Oct-17
50	4.48	17.86	4.40	35.05	35.56	0.46	1.05	13.29	1.05	16.89	307.4	1	99	0	0	112	26.59	-22.59	5.75		Oct-89
50	4.22	17.31	3.48	31.67	29.95	0	1.89	13.25	1.04	15.79	307.4	1	99	0	0	112	26	-22.9		1.00	Feb-02
	4.49	17.97	4.67	36.13	37.29	0.69	0.79	13.3	1.05	16.85	307.4	1	99	0	0	112	26.89	-22.53			Aug-07
	4.43	17.73	4.14	33.97	33.67	0.22	1.34	13.32	1.05	16.55	307.4	1	99	0	0	112	26.38	-22.67			Mar-99
	4.57	18.08	4.71	36.32	37.62	0.72	0.78	13.29	1.05	16.86	307.4	1	99	0	0	112	26.59	-22.59			Mar-14
	4.48	18.01	4.62	35.84	36.93	0.66	0.86	13.28	1.05	16.88	307.4	1	99	0	0	112	26.59	-22.59			Jan-13
50	-22.45	-12.37	-52.77	-48.65	-68.70	0	1.48	24.49	1.3	11.05	335.3	5	95	0	0	26	18.82	-25.21	5.75		Nov-95
50	-22.62	-12.71	-53.17	-49.89	-69.93	0	2.28	24.47	1.29	9.95	335.3	5	95	0	0	26	18.35	-25.44		1.00	May-07
	-22.55	-12.56	-52.99	-49.22	-69.27	0	1.86	24.48	1.29	10.44	335.3	5	95	0	0	26	18.55	-25.34			Dec-06
100	-22.38	-12.27	-52.63	-48.17	-68.20	0	1.15	24.49	1.3	11.51	335.3	5	95	0	0	26	19.08	-25.1			May-07
50	2.93	10.66	7.63	36.64	41.13	2.09	1.27	6.78		16.71	213.9	4	11	0	0	41	9.86	-12.18	2.00		Apr-88
	3.07	10.95	8.11	38.33	44.14	2.57	0.94	6.79		16.69	213.9	4	11	0	0	41	10.22	-12.07			Aug-07
250	0.68	12.23	-12.01	35.21	37.75	0	1.54	18.52	1.03	32.29	132.4	3	97	0	0	45	36.13	-24.84	5.75		Dec-96
250	0.49	11.74	-12.74	32.05	32.39	0	2.32	18.5	1.03	22.36	132.4	3	97	0	0	45	35.55	-25.1		1.00	Mar-97
	0.52	11.90	-12.49	33.08	34.43	0	2.08	18.5	1.03	30.36	132.4	3	97	0	0	45	35.9	-24.92			Jul-04

	MARKET		FUND TYPE, CATEGORY & OBJECTIVE		RATINGS				MINIMUMS	
Fund Name	Ticker Symbol	Traded On	Fund Type	Category and (Prospectus Objective)	Overall Rating	Reward Rating	Risk Rating	Recent Up/ Downgrade	Open to New Investors	Min Initial Investment
Victory Integrity Discovery Fund Class Y	MMEYX	NAS CM	Open End	US Equity Small Cap (Small Company)	C-	C-	C	Down	Y	1,000,000
Victory Integrity Mid-Cap Value Fund Class A	MAIMX	NAS CM	Open End	US Equity Mid Cap (Growth)	C	C	B-		Y	2,500
Victory Integrity Mid-Cap Value Fund Class R6	MRIMX	NAS CM	Open End	US Equity Mid Cap (Growth)	C+	C	B-	Up	Y	0
Victory Integrity Mid-Cap Value Fund Class Y	MYIMX	NAS CM	Open End	US Equity Mid Cap (Growth)	C	C	B-		Y	1,000,000
Victory Integrity Small/Mid-Cap Value Fund Class A	MAISX	NAS CM	Open End	US Equity Mid Cap (Growth)	C	C	B-		Y	2,500
Victory Integrity Small/Mid-Cap Value Fund Class R6	MIRSX	NAS CM	Open End	US Equity Mid Cap (Growth)	C	C	B-		Y	0
Victory Integrity Small/Mid-Cap Value Fund Class Y	MYISX	NAS CM	Open End	US Equity Mid Cap (Growth)	C	C	B-		Y	1,000,000
Victory Integrity Small-Cap Value Fund Class A	VSCVX	NAS CM	Open End	US Equity Small Cap (Small Company)	C	C-	C		Y	2,500
Victory Integrity Small-Cap Value Fund Class C	MCVSX	NAS CM	Open End	US Equity Small Cap (Small Company)	C	C-	C		Y	2,500
Victory Integrity Small-Cap Value Fund Class R	MRVSX	NAS CM	Open End	US Equity Small Cap (Small Company)	C	C-	C		Y	0
Victory Integrity Small-Cap Value Fund Class R6	MVSSX	NAS CM	Open End	US Equity Small Cap (Small Company)	C	C-	C		Y	0
Victory Integrity Small-Cap Value Fund Class Y	VSVIX	NAS CM	Open End	US Equity Small Cap (Small Company)	C	C-	C		Y	1,000,000
Victory Market Neutral Income Fund Class A	CBHAX	NAS CM	Open End	Market Neutral (Income)	C+	C	B	Down	Y	2,500
Victory Market Neutral Income Fund Class C	CBHCX	NAS CM	Open End	Market Neutral (Income)	C	C	B	Down	Y	2,500
Victory Market Neutral Income Fund Class I	CBHIX	NAS CM	Open End	Market Neutral (Income)	B-	C	B+		Y	2,000,000
Victory Munder Mid-Cap Core Growth Fund Class A	MGOAX	NAS CM	Open End	US Equity Mid Cap (Growth)	C+	C	B-	Up	Y	2,500
Victory Munder Mid-Cap Core Growth Fund Class C	MGOTX	NAS CM	Open End	US Equity Mid Cap (Growth)	C+	C	B-	Up	Y	2,500
Victory Munder Mid-Cap Core Growth Fund Class R	MMSRX	NAS CM	Open End	US Equity Mid Cap (Growth)	C+	C	B-	Up	Y	0
Victory Munder Mid-Cap Core Growth Fund Class R6	MGOSX	NAS CM	Open End	US Equity Mid Cap (Growth)	C+	C	B-	Up	Y	0
Victory Munder Mid-Cap Core Growth Fund Class Y	MGOYX	NAS CM	Open End	US Equity Mid Cap (Growth)	C+	C	B-	Up	Y	1,000,000
Victory Munder Multi-Cap Fund Class A	MNNAX	NAS CM	Open End	US Equity Large Cap Growth (Growth)	C+	C	B-	Up	Y	2,500
Victory Munder Multi-Cap Fund Class C	MNNCX	NAS CM	Open End	US Equity Large Cap Growth (Growth)	C	C	B-		Y	2,500
Victory Munder Multi-Cap Fund Class Y	MNNYX	NAS CM	Open End	US Equity Large Cap Growth (Growth)	C+	C	B-	Up	Y	1,000,000
Victory Munder Small Cap Growth Fund Class A	MASCX	NAS CM	Open End	US Equity Small Cap (Growth)	B-	C+	B-		Y	2,500
Victory Munder Small Cap Growth Fund Class I	MIGSX	NAS CM	Open End	US Equity Small Cap (Growth)	B-	C+	B-		Y	2,000,000
Victory Munder Small Cap Growth Fund Class Y	MYSGX	NAS CM	Open End	US Equity Small Cap (Growth)	B-	C+	B-		Y	1,000,000
Victory NewBridge Large Cap Growth Fund Class A	VFGAX	NAS CM	Open End	US Equity Large Cap Growth (Growth)	C+	C	B-	Down	Y	2,500
Victory NewBridge Large Cap Growth Fund Class C	VFGCX	NAS CM	Open End	US Equity Large Cap Growth (Growth)	C+	C	B-	Down	Y	2,500
Victory NewBridge Large Cap Growth Fund Class I	VFGIX	NAS CM	Open End	US Equity Large Cap Growth (Growth)	C+	C	B-	Down	Y	2,000,000
Victory NewBridge Large Cap Growth Fund Class Y	VFGYX	NAS CM	Open End	US Equity Large Cap Growth (Growth)	C+	C	B-	Down	Y	1,000,000
Victory RS Global Fund Class A	RSGGX	NAS CM	Open End	Global Equity Large Cap (Growth)	B-	C+	B		Y	2,500
Victory RS Global Fund Class C	RGGCX	NAS CM	Open End	Global Equity Large Cap (Growth)	B-	C	B		Y	2,500
Victory RS Global Fund Class R	RGGKX	NAS CM	Open End	Global Equity Large Cap (Growth)	B-	C+	B		Y	0
Victory RS Global Fund Class R6	RGGRX	NAS CM	Open End	Global Equity Large Cap (Growth)	B-	C+	B		Y	0
Victory RS Global Fund Class Y	RGGYX	NAS CM	Open End	Global Equity Large Cap (Growth)	B-	C+	B		Y	1,000,000
Victory RS Growth Fund Class A	RSGRX	NAS CM	Open End	US Equity Large Cap Growth (Growth)	C+	C	B-	Down	Y	2,500
Victory RS Growth Fund Class C	RGWCX	NAS CM	Open End	US Equity Large Cap Growth (Growth)	C+	C	C+	Down	Y	2,500
Victory RS Growth Fund Class R	RSGKX	NAS CM	Open End	US Equity Large Cap Growth (Growth)	C+	C	C+	Down	Y	0
Victory RS Growth Fund Class Y	RGRYX	NAS CM	Open End	US Equity Large Cap Growth (Growth)	C+	C	B-	Down	Y	1,000,000
Victory RS International Fund Class A	GUBGX	NAS CM	Open End	Global Equity Large Cap (Foreign Stock)	B-	C	B	Up	Y	2,500
Victory RS International Fund Class C	RIGCX	NAS CM	Open End	Global Equity Large Cap (Foreign Stock)	C+	C	B	Up	Y	2,500
Victory RS International Fund Class R	RIGKX	NAS CM	Open End	Global Equity Large Cap (Foreign Stock)	B-	C	B	Up	Y	0
Victory RS International Fund Class R6	RSIRX	NAS CM	Open End	Global Equity Large Cap (Foreign Stock)	B-	C	B		Y	0
Victory RS International Fund Class Y	RSIGX	NAS CM	Open End	Global Equity Large Cap (Foreign Stock)	B-	C	B	Up	Y	1,000,000
Victory RS Investors Fund Class A	RSINX	NAS CM	Open End	US Equity Mid Cap (Growth)	B-	C+	B	Up	Y	2,500
Victory RS Investors Fund Class C	RIVCX	NAS CM	Open End	US Equity Mid Cap (Growth)	C+	C	B	Up	Y	2,500
Victory RS Investors Fund Class R	RSIKX	NAS CM	Open End	US Equity Mid Cap (Growth)	C+	C	B	Up	Y	0
Victory RS Investors Fund Class Y	RSIYX	NAS CM	Open End	US Equity Mid Cap (Growth)	B-	C+	B	Up	Y	1,000,000
Victory RS Large Cap Alpha Fund Class A	GPAFX	NAS CM	Open End	US Equity Large Cap Blend (Growth)	C+	C	B		Y	2,500
Victory RS Large Cap Alpha Fund Class C	RCOCX	NAS CM	Open End	US Equity Large Cap Blend (Growth)	C+	C	B	Up	Y	2,500
Victory RS Large Cap Alpha Fund Class R	RCEKX	NAS CM	Open End	US Equity Large Cap Blend (Growth)	C+	C	B	Up	Y	0
Victory RS Large Cap Alpha Fund Class Y	RCEYX	NAS CM	Open End	US Equity Large Cap Blend (Growth)	C+	C	B		Y	1,000,000

★ Expanded analysis of this fund is included in Section II.

	TOTAL RETURNS					PERFORMANCE				ASSETS		ASSET ALLOCATION & TURNOVER					BULL & BEAR		FEES		
Min Additional Investment	3-Month Total Return	6-Month Total Return	1-Year Total Return	3-Year Total Return	5-Year Total Return	Dividend Yield (TTM)	Expense Ratio	3-Yr Std Deviation	3-Year Beta	NAV	Total Assets (MIL)	%Cash	%Stocks	%Bonds	%Other	Turnover Ratio	Last Bull Market Total Return	Last Bear Market Total Return	Front End Fee (%)	Back End Fee (%)	Inception Date
	0.73	12.35	-11.81	36.15	39.43	0	1.28	18.52	1.03	35.65	132.4	3	97	0	0	45	36.33	-24.78			Dec-96
250	3.59	18.90	0.36	31.99	31.80	1.03	1	14.67	1.1	17.86	85.4	2	98	0	0	73	29.63		5.75		Jul-11
	3.68	19.10	0.72	33.28	33.79	1.23	0.6	14.68	1.1	18.02	85.4	2	98	0	0	73	29.93				Dec-15
	3.68	19.10	0.57	32.97	33.64	1.24	0.75	14.63	1.1	18.02	85.4	2	98	0	0	73	29.92				Jul-11
250	3.79	18.35	-1.66	35.98	24.84	0.71	1.13	16.48	1.07	16.7	134.9	3	97	0	0	77	30.85		5.75		Jul-11
	3.80	18.50	-1.38	37.23	26.71	0.92	0.83	16.47	1.07	16.91	134.9	3	97	0	0	77	31.15				Mar-15
	3.81	18.48	-1.45	37.00	26.40	0.92	0.88	16.47	1.07	16.86	134.9	3	97	0	0	77	31.15				Jul-11
50	2.85	16.34	-7.16	30.61	22.65	0	1.5	18.52	1.06	32.38	2,327	2	98	0	0	70	27.41	-25.04	5.75		Mar-04
50	2.72	15.99	-7.78	28.08	18.52	0	2.13	18.53	1.06	27.85	2,327	2	98	0	0	70	26.82	-25.26		1.00	May-11
	2.82	16.20	-7.39	29.62	21.11	0	1.75	18.53	1.06	31.33	2,327	2	98	0	0	70	27.21	-25.11			May-11
	2.99	16.64	-6.67	32.73	25.83	0.49	0.95	18.54	1.06	33.7	2,327	2	98	0	0	70	27.41	-25.04			Jun-12
	2.95	16.56	-6.83	32.03	24.78	0.3	1.12	18.54	1.06	33.49	2,327	2	98	0	0	70	27.56	-24.97			Jul-05
50	1.15	0.58	1.99	13.21	13.81	2.83	0.75	3.54	-17.14	9.51	87.9	14	86	0	0	69			5.75		Nov-12
50	0.96	0.23	1.18	10.63	9.59	2.14	1.5	3.52	-16.5	9.43	87.9	14	86	0	0	69				1.00	Nov-12
	1.20	0.69	2.25	14.00	15.36	3.08	0.4	3.52	-16.34	9.55	87.9	14	86	0	0	69					Nov-12
50	4.91	22.67	4.18	38.90	39.22	0	1.28	13.6	0.99	22.96	1,465	0	100	0	0	50	27.54	-18.99	5.75		Jul-00
50	4.76	22.24	3.50	36.14	34.55	0	1.96	13.58	0.98	15.96	1,465	0	100	0	0	50	26.98	-19.27		1.00	Jul-00
	4.78	22.41	3.85	37.72	37.36	0	1.57	13.59	0.99	21.16	1,465	0	100	0	0	50	27.38	-19.09			Jul-04
	4.94	22.83	4.56	40.65	42.24	0	0.84	13.59	0.99	26	1,465	0	100	0	0	50	27.73	-18.92			Jun-12
	4.98	22.82	4.46	40.02	41.06	0	1.01	13.59	0.99	25.37	1,465	0	100	0	0	50	27.73	-18.92			Jun-98
250	4.08	17.17	2.86	39.01	47.23	0	1.36	13.6	0.93	38.75	387.4	0	100	0	0	123	26.51	-20.71	5.75		Aug-96
250	4.07	16.97	2.21	35.93	41.63	0	2.16	13.6	0.93	30.11	387.4	0	100	0	0	123	25.92	-20.92		1.00	Nov-98
	4.17	17.37	3.20	40.50	49.98	0	1	13.61	0.93	42.42	387.4	0	100	0	0	123	26.66	-20.61			Jun-98
50	8.15	28.87	10.06	80.35		0	1.4	16.52	0.9	13.39	9.3	1	99	0	0	62			5.75		May-15
	8.21	29.02	10.44	81.76		0	1.15	16.53	0.91	13.56	9.3	1	99	0	0	62					May-15
	8.21	28.73	9.84	80.47		0	1.25	16.53	0.91	13.44	9.3	1	99	0	0	62					May-15
50	2.29	20.12	3.67	47.77	58.06	0	1.36	15.17	1.08	5.79	18.2	3	97	0	0	41	25.94	-18.2	5.75		Dec-03
50	1.99	19.71	2.87	44.30	51.82	0	2.1	15.02	1.08	2.55	18.2	3	97	0	0	41	25.29	-18.48		1.00	Dec-03
	2.23	20.26	4.02	49.52	60.99	0	0.95	15.06	1.08	6.41	18.2	3	97	0	0	41	26.15	-18.14			Mar-11
	2.33	20.43	3.96	49.29	60.44	0	1.02	15.1	1.08	6.13	18.2	3	97	0	0	41	25.94	-18.2			Jan-13
50	5.02	18.68	9.46	48.23	52.63	1.14	0.85	10.69	0.93	13.59	55.8	1	99	0	0	58	21.27		5.75		May-11
50	4.70	18.30	8.59	44.85	46.79	0.58	1.6	10.71	0.93	13.12	55.8	1	99	0	0	58	20.61			1.00	May-11
	4.89	18.57	9.18	80.41	84.41	0.75	1.1	14.03	0.91	16.92	55.8	1	99	0	0	58	20.95				May-11
	5.09	19.00	9.79	49.48	54.88		0.55	10.72	0.93	10.15	55.8	1	99	0	0	58	21.51				May-19
	4.98	18.88	9.68	49.33	54.72	1.38	0.6	10.71	0.93	13.47	55.8	1	99	0	0	58	21.51				May-11
50	4.36	25.33	7.29	58.93	70.51	0	1.1	14.36	1.04	20.33	260.5	3	97	0	0	87	25.55	-15.95	5.75		May-92
50	4.11	24.77	6.35	55.05	63.55	0	1.93	14.33	1.04	16.97	260.5	3	97	0	0	87	24.37	-16.34		1.00	Jun-07
	4.21	24.93	6.62	56.07	65.35	0	1.71	14.35	1.04	18.54	260.5	3	97	0	0	87	25.25	-16.14			Nov-06
	4.44	25.44	7.56	60.21	72.78	0	0.83	14.36	1.04	21.15	260.5	3	97	0	0	87	25.75	-15.86			May-07
50	3.46	15.76	4.60	37.83	22.53	1.62	1.13	10.31	0.91	12.26	50.5	7	93	0	0	52	18.6	-25.14	5.75		Feb-93
50	3.24	15.26	3.77	34.61	17.65	1.46	1.88	10.27	0.91	8.91	50.5	7	93	0	0	52	18.12	-25.37		1.00	Aug-00
	3.42	15.64	4.33	36.64	20.38	1.46	1.38	10.31	0.91	11.46	50.5	7	93	0	0	52	18.23	-25.26			May-01
	3.44	15.75	4.59	37.81	22.52		0.83	10.31	0.91	10.14	50.5	7	93	0	0	52	18.6	-25.14			May-19
	3.51	15.81	4.80	38.80	23.97	1.82	0.88	10.32	0.92	12.08	50.5	7	93	0	0	52	18.86	-25.05			Mar-09
50	4.83	22.83	9.46	39.96	31.00	0	1.33	12.69	0.95	13.02	42.1	3	97	0	0	56	31.07	-23.97	5.75		Nov-05
50	4.70	22.28	8.66	36.93	26.29	0	2.07	12.72	0.95	11.58	42.1	3	97	0	0	56	30.44	-24.17		1.00	Jul-07
	4.63	22.41	8.72	37.39	27.24	0	1.95	12.7	0.95	11.74	42.1	3	97	0	0	56	30.6	-23.99			Jan-07
	4.87	22.92	9.73	41.08	32.82	0	1.05	12.67	0.95	13.35	42.1	3	97	0	0	56	31.19	-23.86			May-07
50	4.61	19.48	6.64	41.51	43.19	0.64	0.89	12.44	0.98	50.1	544.6	3	97	0	0	59	25.1	-24.79	5.75		Jun-72
50	4.41	19.01	5.79	38.16	37.56	0	1.69	12.44	0.98	42.31	544.6	3	97	0	0	59	24.5	-25.02		1.00	Aug-00
	4.51	19.23	6.25	39.97	40.57	0.26	1.26	12.43	0.98	49.77	544.6	3	97	0	0	59	24.77	-24.91			May-01
	4.67	19.59	6.86	42.40	44.70	0.81	0.68	12.43	0.98	49.92	544.6	3	97	0	0	59	25.28	-24.68			May-07

	MARKET		FUND TYPE, CATEGORY & OBJECTIVE		RATINGS				MINIMUMS	
Fund Name	Ticker Symbol	Traded On	Fund Type	Category and (Prospectus Objective)	Overall Rating	Reward Rating	Risk Rating	Recent Up/ Downgrade	Open to New Investors	Min Initial Investment
Victory RS Mid Cap Growth Fund Class A	RSMOX	NAS CM	Open End	US Equity Mid Cap (Growth)	C+	C+	B-		Y	2,500
Victory RS Mid Cap Growth Fund Class C	RMOCX	NAS CM	Open End	US Equity Mid Cap (Growth)	C+	C	B-		Y	2,500
Victory RS Mid Cap Growth Fund Class R	RSMKX	NAS CM	Open End	US Equity Mid Cap (Growth)	C+	C+	B-		Y	0
Victory RS Mid Cap Growth Fund Class R6	RMORX	NAS CM	Open End	US Equity Mid Cap (Growth)	C+	C+	B-		Y	0
Victory RS Mid Cap Growth Fund Class Y	RMOYX	NAS CM	Open End	US Equity Mid Cap (Growth)	C+	C+	B-		Y	1,000,000
Victory RS Partners Fund Class A	RSPFX	NAS CM	Open End	US Equity Small Cap (Small Company)	C+	C	B	Up		2,500
Victory RS Partners Fund Class R	RSPKX	NAS CM	Open End	US Equity Small Cap (Small Company)	C+	C	B	Up		0
Victory RS Partners Fund Class Y	RSPYX	NAS CM	Open End	US Equity Small Cap (Small Company)	C+	C	B	Up		1,000,000
Victory RS Science and Technology Fund Class A	RSIFX	NAS CM	Open End	Technology Sector Equity (Technology)	C+	C+	C+	Down	Y	2,500
Victory RS Science and Technology Fund Class C	RINCX	NAS CM	Open End	Technology Sector Equity (Technology)	C+	C+	C+	Down	Y	2,500
Victory RS Science and Technology Fund Class R	RIFKX	NAS CM	Open End	Technology Sector Equity (Technology)	C+	C+	C+	Down	Y	0
Victory RS Science and Technology Fund Class Y	RIFYX	NAS CM	Open End	Technology Sector Equity (Technology)	C+	C+	C+	Down	Y	1,000,000
Victory RS Select Growth Fund Class A	RSDGX	NAS CM	Open End	US Equity Mid Cap (Growth)	C+	C	C+		Y	2,500
Victory RS Select Growth Fund Class C	RSGFX	NAS CM	Open End	US Equity Mid Cap (Growth)	C+	C	C+	Up	Y	2,500
Victory RS Select Growth Fund Class R	RSDKX	NAS CM	Open End	US Equity Mid Cap (Growth)	C+	C	C+	Up	Y	0
Victory RS Select Growth Fund Class R6	RSSRX	NAS CM	Open End	US Equity Mid Cap (Growth)	C+	C	C+		Y	0
Victory RS Select Growth Fund Class Y	RSSYX	NAS CM	Open End	US Equity Mid Cap (Growth)	C+	C	C+		Y	1,000,000
Victory RS Small Cap Equity Fund Class A	GPSCX	NAS CM	Open End	US Equity Small Cap (Small Company)	C+	C+	C+			2,500
Victory RS Small Cap Equity Fund Class C	RSCCX	NAS CM	Open End	US Equity Small Cap (Small Company)	C+	C+	C+			2,500
Victory RS Small Cap Equity Fund Class R	RSCKX	NAS CM	Open End	US Equity Small Cap (Small Company)	C+	C+	C+			0
Victory RS Small Cap Equity Fund Class Y	RSCYX	NAS CM	Open End	US Equity Small Cap (Small Company)	C+	C+	C+			1,000,000
Victory RS Small Cap Growth Fund Class A	RSEGX	NAS CM	Open End	US Equity Small Cap (Small Company)	C+	C+	C+			2,500
Victory RS Small Cap Growth Fund Class C	REGWX	NAS CM	Open End	US Equity Small Cap (Small Company)	C+	C+	C+	Up		2,500
Victory RS Small Cap Growth Fund Class R	RSEKX	NAS CM	Open End	US Equity Small Cap (Small Company)	C+	C+	C+	Up		0
Victory RS Small Cap Growth Fund Class R6	RSEJX	NAS CM	Open End	US Equity Small Cap (Small Company)	C+	C+	C+		Y	0
Victory RS Small Cap Growth Fund Class Y	RSYEX	NAS CM	Open End	US Equity Small Cap (Small Company)	C+	C+	C+			1,000,000
Victory RS Value Fund Class A	RSVAX	NAS CM	Open End	US Equity Mid Cap (Growth)	B-	C+	B	Up	Y	2,500
Victory RS Value Fund Class C	RVACX	NAS CM	Open End	US Equity Mid Cap (Growth)	C+	C	B	Up	Y	2,500
Victory RS Value Fund Class R	RSVKX	NAS CM	Open End	US Equity Mid Cap (Growth)	B-	C	B	Up	Y	0
Victory RS Value Fund Class Y	RSVYX	NAS CM	Open End	US Equity Mid Cap (Growth)	B-	C+	B	Up	Y	1,000,000
Victory S&P 500 Index Fund Class A	MUXAX	NAS CM	Open End	US Equity Large Cap Blend (Growth)	B-	C	B		Y	2,500
Victory S&P 500 Index Fund Class R	MUXRX	NAS CM	Open End	US Equity Large Cap Blend (Growth)	B-	C	B		Y	0
Victory S&P 500 Index Fund Class Y	MUXYX	NAS CM	Open End	US Equity Large Cap Blend (Growth)	B-	C	B		Y	1,000,000
Victory Sophus Emerging Markets Fund Class A	GBEMX	NAS CM	Open End	Global Emerg Mkts (Div Emerging Mkts)	C	C	C		Y	2,500
Victory Sophus Emerging Markets Fund Class C	REMGX	NAS CM	Open End	Global Emerg Mkts (Div Emerging Mkts)	C	C	C		Y	2,500
Victory Sophus Emerging Markets Fund Class R	REMKX	NAS CM	Open End	Global Emerg Mkts (Div Emerging Mkts)	C	C	C		Y	0
Victory Sophus Emerging Markets Fund Class R6	RSERX	NAS CM	Open End	Global Emerg Mkts (Div Emerging Mkts)	C	C	C		Y	0
Victory Sophus Emerging Markets Fund Class Y	RSENX	NAS CM	Open End	Global Emerg Mkts (Div Emerging Mkts)	C	C	C		Y	1,000,000
Victory Sophus Emerging Markets Small Cap Fund Class A	RSMSX	NAS CM	Open End	Global Emerg Mkts (Div Emerging Mkts)	C	C	C	Up	Y	2,500
Victory Sophus Emerging Markets Small Cap Fund Class C	RSMGX	NAS CM	Open End	Global Emerg Mkts (Div Emerging Mkts)	C	C-	C	Up	Y	2,500
Victory Sophus Emerging Markets Small Cap Fund Class Y	RSMYX	NAS CM	Open End	Global Emerg Mkts (Div Emerging Mkts)	C	C	C	Up	Y	1,000,000
Victory Special Value Fund Class A	SSVSX	NAS CM	Open End	US Equity Large Cap Blend (Growth & Income)	C+	C	B-	Up	Y	2,500
Victory Special Value Fund Class C	VSVCX	NAS CM	Open End	US Equity Large Cap Blend (Growth & Income)	C	C	B-		Y	2,500
Victory Special Value Fund Class I	VSPIX	NAS CM	Open End	US Equity Large Cap Blend (Growth & Income)	C+	C	B-	Up	Y	2,000,000
Victory Special Value Fund Class R	VSVGX	NAS CM	Open End	US Equity Large Cap Blend (Growth & Income)	C+	C	B-	Up	Y	0
Victory Special Value Fund Class Y	VSVYX	NAS CM	Open End	US Equity Large Cap Blend (Growth & Income)	C+	C	B-	Up	Y	1,000,000
Victory Strategic Allocation Fund Class A	SBALX	NAS CM	Open End	Multialternative (Balanced)	B-	C	A-	Up	Y	2,500
Victory Strategic Allocation Fund Class C	VBFCX	NAS CM	Open End	Multialternative (Balanced)	B-	C	B+	Up	Y	2,500
Victory Strategic Allocation Fund Class I	VBFIX	NAS CM	Open End	Multialternative (Balanced)	B-	C	A-	Up	Y	2,000,000
Victory Strategic Allocation Fund Class R	VBFGX	NAS CM	Open End	Multialternative (Balanced)	B-	C	B+	Up	Y	0
Victory Sycamore Established Value Fund Class A	VETAX	NAS CM	Open End	US Equity Mid Cap (Growth)	C+	C	B	Up	Y	2,500
Victory Sycamore Established Value Fund Class C	VEVCX	NAS CM	Open End	US Equity Mid Cap (Growth)	C+	C	B	Up	Y	2,500

★ Expanded analysis of this fund is included in Section II.

	TOTAL RETURNS					PERFORMANCE				ASSETS		ASSET ALLOCATION & TURNOVER					BULL & BEAR		FEES		
Min Additional Investment	3-Month Total Return	6-Month Total Return	1-Year Total Return	3-Year Total Return	5-Year Total Return	Dividend Yield (TTM)	Expense Ratio	3-Yr Std Deviation	3-Year Beta	NAV	Total Assets (MIL)	%Cash	%Stocks	%Bonds	%Other	Turnover Ratio	Last Bull Market Total Return	Last Bear Market Total Return	Front End Fee (%)	Back End Fee (%)	Inception Date
50	7.39	31.86	13.81	52.21	62.90	0	1.2	15.1	1.02	25.99	531.5	3	97	0	0	126	30.29	-18.96	5.75		Jul-95
50	7.17	31.23	12.77	48.14	55.83	0	2.11	15.08	1.02	22.56	531.5	3	97	0	0	126	29.69	-19.34		1.00	May-07
	7.21	31.45	13.12	49.60	58.47	0	1.8	15.09	1.02	23.78	531.5	3	97	0	0	126	29.89	-19.14			Dec-06
	7.46	32.08	14.13	53.27	64.04	0	0.94	15.09	1.02	27.05	531.5	3	97	0	0	126	30.29	-18.96			Nov-16
	7.47	32.04	14.10	53.36	64.94	0	0.95	15.09	1.02	27.03	531.5	3	97	0	0	126	30.45	-18.88			May-07
50	6.08	23.76	7.59	45.79	26.95	0.26	1.45	13.38	0.72	24.58	432.1	6	93	0	0	62	24.61	-24.41	5.75		Jul-95
	6.00	23.47	7.20	44.24	24.62	0	1.81	13.39	0.72	22.25	432.1	6	93	0	0	62	24.26	-24.61			Oct-06
	6.16	23.88	7.92	47.21	28.97	0.52	1.12	13.4	0.72	26.19	432.1	6	93	0	0	62	24.84	-24.35			May-07
50	3.26	32.09	8.99	120.11	145.64	0	1.47	19.34	1.01	23.75	276.6	4	96	0	0	83	24.1	-26.76	5.75		Nov-95
50	2.99	31.51	8.04	114.88	135.97	0	2.28	19.33	1.01	18.57	276.6	4	96	0	0	83	23.52	-26.98		1.00	May-07
	3.09	31.75	8.48	117.34	140.22	0	1.93	19.33	1.01	20.29	276.6	4	96	0	0	83	23.68	-26.96			Jan-07
	3.31	32.16	9.20	121.65	148.68	0	1.24	19.33	1.01	25.56	276.6	4	96	0	0	83	24.27	-26.64			May-07
50	8.05	27.73	7.98	48.48	50.99	0	1.4	15.14	0.88	36.48	256.9	1	99	0	0	79	28.7	-19.38	5.75		Aug-96
50	7.82	27.19	7.14	45.01	45.17	0	2.18	15.13	0.88	29.89	256.9	1	99	0	0	79	28.2	-19.88		1.00	Nov-07
	7.92	27.40	7.44	46.32	47.32	0	1.91	15.14	0.88	30.36	256.9	1	99	0	0	79	28.3	-19.68			Feb-07
	8.15	27.92	8.34	49.78	52.31	0	1.06	15.13	0.88	38.48	256.9	1	99	0	0	79	28.7	-19.38			Nov-16
	8.11	27.90	8.26	49.64	52.96	0	1.14	15.14	0.88	38.36	256.9	1	99	0	0	79	28.95	-19.3			May-09
50	7.08	33.41	7.00	92.05	86.41	0	1.22	17.51	0.97	17.09	71.6	1	99	0	0	77	28.64	-25.68	5.75		May-97
50	7.03	32.87	6.19	87.24	78.87	0	2.1	17.51	0.97	5.78	71.6	1	99	0	0	77	27.87	-25.96		1.00	Aug-00
	6.93	33.16	6.45	89.29	82.31	0	1.75	17.51	0.97	13.57	71.6	1	99	0	0	77	28.33	-25.77			May-01
	7.15	33.53	7.18	92.93	87.38	0	1.1	17.46	0.96	17.52	71.6	1	99	0	0	77	28.78	-25.56			May-07
50	6.99	32.96	6.22	88.22	81.55	0	1.4	17.51	0.97	80.26	2,206	2	98	0	0	86	27.99	-25.07	5.75		Nov-87
50	6.78	32.45	5.41	83.98	74.76	0	2.16	17.5	0.97	68.28	2,206	2	98	0	0	86	26.41	-25.47		1.00	Sep-07
	6.87	32.67	5.71	85.84	77.90	0	1.86	17.51	0.97	73.21	2,206	2	98	0	0	86	27.56	-25.28			Jan-07
	7.09	33.20	6.58	89.46	82.74	0	1.06	17.51	0.97	83.97	2,206	2	98	0	0	86	27.99	-25.07			Jul-17
	7.06	33.14	6.49	89.71	84.02	0	1.13	17.51	0.97	83.83	2,206	2	98	0	0	86	28.23	-24.98			May-07
50	4.43	22.98	9.41	40.04	38.84	0.51	1.3	12.87	0.94	24.72	391.4	5	95	0	0	65	24.37	-26.03	5.75		Jun-93
50	4.22	22.55	8.56	36.86	33.57	0	2.07	12.85	0.94	21.95	391.4	5	95	0	0	65	23.81	-26.25		1.00	May-07
	4.32	22.74	8.95	38.41	36.08	0.21	1.69	12.86	0.94	23.42	391.4	5	95	0	0	65	24.03	-26.13			Dec-06
	4.49	23.12	9.59	40.99	40.38	0.73	1.06	12.88	0.94	25.34	391.4	5	95	0	0	65	24.52	-25.94			May-07
250	4.13	19.18	9.79	48.46	61.62	1.46	0.55	12.18	1	21.07	234.6	1	99	0	0	2	24.6	-16.52	2.50		Dec-92
	4.03	18.93	9.31	46.48	58.24	1.08	0.97	12.2	1	21.01	234.6	1	99	0	0	2	24.33	-16.64			Jul-04
	4.10	19.26	9.92	49.15	63.00	1.57	0.39	12.19	1	21.22	234.6	1	99	0	0	2	24.68	-16.46			Nov-91
50	1.04	11.69	-5.68	36.14	14.81	0.67	1.34	15.26	1.07	19.39	375.8	0	100	0	0	118	24.88	-27.86	5.75		May-97
50	0.83	11.23	-6.43	32.91	10.33	0.01	2.14	15.28	1.08	14.46	375.8	0	100	0	0	118	24.26	-28.11		1.00	Aug-00
	1.00	11.54	-5.87	35.14	13.38	0.47	1.58	15.26	1.07	18.17	375.8	0	100	0	0	118	24.58	-28			May-01
	1.13	11.87	-5.24	37.74	16.17	1.04	0.89	15.26	1.07	19.69	375.8	0	100	0	0	118	24.88	-27.86			Nov-16
	1.13	11.86	-5.33	37.53	16.77	1.01	0.99	15.25	1.07	19.52	375.8	0	100	0	0	118	24.92	-27.81			Mar-09
50	1.61	14.42	-5.26	32.05	13.50	0	1.79	13.83	1.03	6.9	5.4	0	100	0	0	200			5.75		Jan-14
50	1.45	14.02	-5.91	26.49	7.16	0	2.54	13.87	1.02	6.26	5.4	0	100	0	0	200				1.00	Jan-14
	1.77	14.64	-5.02	33.13	15.22	0	1.54	13.8	1.03	6.89	5.4	0	100	0	0	200					Jan-14
50	4.04	16.91	3.67	32.66	29.14	0.11	1.27	13.23	1.04	24.68	58.0	0	100	0	0	113	26.68	-26.94	5.75		Dec-93
50	3.83	16.39	2.76	29.09	23.44	0	2.2	13.22	1.04	21.65	58.0	0	100	0	0	113	26.03	-27.21		1.00	Feb-03
	4.12	16.98	3.86	33.07	30.09	0.17	1.15	13.22	1.04	25	58.0	0	100	0	0	113	27	-26.86			Aug-07
	4.02	16.77	3.40	31.57	27.36	0	1.56	13.23	1.04	23.53	58.0	0	100	0	0	113	26.49	-27.04			Dec-99
	4.10	16.99	3.90	33.52	30.72	0.18	1.1	13.22	1.04	24.85	58.0	0	100	0	0	113	26.68	-26.94			Jan-13
50	2.77	11.32	3.90	22.49	25.90	2.47	1.2	6.91	0.59	16.21	26.1	4	84	12	0	40	16.98	-14.01	5.75		Dec-93
50	2.64	10.99	3.18	19.78	21.47	1.89	1.95	6.88	0.59	15.94	26.1	4	84	12	0	40	16.45	-14.25		1.00	Feb-03
	2.82	11.47	4.13	23.41	27.38	2.69	0.95	6.84	0.59	16.29	26.1	4	84	12	0	40	17.18	-13.87			Aug-07
	2.72	11.14	3.60	21.51	24.08	2.25	1.45	6.89	0.59	16.17	26.1	4	84	12	0	40	16.8	-14.13			Dec-99
50	4.63	20.00	5.44	38.71	56.09	0.94	0.89	13	0.97	39.1	11,223	2	98	0	0	36	26.28	-20.78	5.75		May-00
50	4.43	19.56	4.65	35.52	50.42	0.27	1.68	13	0.97	38.23	11,223	2	98	0	0	36	25.79	-21		1.00	Mar-16

	MARKET			FUND TYPE, CATEGORY & OBJECTIVE	RATINGS				MINIMUMS	
Fund Name	Ticker Symbol	Traded On	Fund Type	Category and (Prospectus Objective)	Overall Rating	Reward Rating	Risk Rating	Recent Up/ Downgrade	Open to New Investors	Min Initial Investment
Victory Sycamore Established Value Fund Class I	VEVIX	NAS CM	Open End	US Equity Mid Cap (Growth)	C+	C	B		Y	2,000,000
Victory Sycamore Established Value Fund Class R	GETGX	NAS CM	Open End	US Equity Mid Cap (Growth)	C+	C	B	Up	Y	0
Victory Sycamore Established Value Fund Class R6	VEVRX	NAS CM	Open End	US Equity Mid Cap (Growth)	C+	C	B		Y	0
Victory Sycamore Established Value Fund Class Y	VEVYX	NAS CM	Open End	US Equity Mid Cap (Growth)	C+	C	B	Up	Y	1,000,000
Victory Sycamore Small Company Opportunity Fund Class A	SSGSX	NAS CM	Open End	US Equity Small Cap (Small Company)	C+	C	B		Y	2,500
Victory Sycamore Small Company Opportunity Fund Class I	VSOIX	NAS CM	Open End	US Equity Small Cap (Small Company)	C+	C	B		Y	2,000,000
Victory Sycamore Small Company Opportunity Fund Class R	GOGFX	NAS CM	Open End	US Equity Small Cap (Small Company)	C+	C	B		Y	0
Victory Sycamore Small Company Opportunity Fund Class Y	VSOYX	NAS CM	Open End	US Equity Small Cap (Small Company)	C+	C	B		Y	1,000,000
Victory Sycamore Small Company Opportunity Fund R6	VSORX	NAS CM	Open End	US Equity Small Cap (Small Company)	C+	C	B		Y	0
Victory Trivalent Emerging Markets Small-Cap Fund Class A	MAEMX	NAS CM	Open End	Global Emerg Mkts (Div Emerging Mkts)	C	C-	C		Y	2,500
Victory Trivalent Emerging Markets Small-Cap Fund Class Y	MYEMX	NAS CM	Open End	Global Emerg Mkts (Div Emerging Mkts)	C	C-	C		Y	1,000,000
Victory Trivalent International Fund-Core Equity Class A	MAICX	NAS CM	Open End	Global Equity Large Cap (Growth)	C	C	B-		Y	2,500
Victory Trivalent International Fund-Core Equity Class C	MICCX	NAS CM	Open End	Global Equity Large Cap (Growth)	C	C	B-		Y	2,500
Victory Trivalent International Fund-Core Equity Class I	MICIX	NAS CM	Open End	Global Equity Large Cap (Growth)	C	C	B-		Y	2,000,000
Victory Trivalent International Fund-Core Equity Class R6	MAIRX	NAS CM	Open End	Global Equity Large Cap (Growth)	C	C	B-		Y	0
Victory Trivalent International Fund-Core Equity Class Y	MICYX	NAS CM	Open End	Global Equity Large Cap (Growth)	C	C	B-		Y	1,000,000
Victory Trivalent International Small-Cap Fund Class A	MISAX	NAS CM	Open End	Global Equity Mid/Small Cap (Small Company)	C	C	C+		Y	2,500
Victory Trivalent International Small-Cap Fund Class C	MCISX	NAS CM	Open End	Global Equity Mid/Small Cap (Small Company)	C	C	C		Y	2,500
Victory Trivalent International Small-Cap Fund Class I	MISIX	NAS CM	Open End	Global Equity Mid/Small Cap (Small Company)	C	C	C+		Y	2,000,000
Victory Trivalent International Small-Cap Fund Class R6	MSSIX	NAS CM	Open End	Global Equity Mid/Small Cap (Small Company)	C	C	C+		Y	0
Victory Trivalent International Small-Cap Fund Class Y	MYSIX	NAS CM	Open End	Global Equity Mid/Small Cap (Small Company)	C	C	C+		Y	1,000,000
Victory US 500 Enhanced Volatility Wtd Index Fund Class A	CUHAX	NAS CM	Open End	US Equity Large Cap Blend (Growth & Income)	C	C	C+	Up	Y	2,500
Victory US 500 Enhanced Volatility Wtd Index Fund Class C	CUHCX	NAS CM	Open End	US Equity Large Cap Blend (Growth & Income)	C	C	C+	Up	Y	2,500
Victory US 500 Enhanced Volatility Wtd Index Fund Class I	CUHIX	NAS CM	Open End	US Equity Large Cap Blend (Growth & Income)	C	C	B-	Up	Y	2,000,000
Villere Balanced Fund Investor Class	VILLX	NAS CM	Open End	Moderate Alloc (Balanced)	C+	C	B-		Y	2,000
Villere Equity Fund	VLEQX	NAS CM	Open End	US Equity Mid Cap (Growth)	C	C	C+	Down	Y	2,000
Virtus Aviva Multi-Strategy Target Return Fund Class A	VMSAX	NAS CM	Open End	Global Macro (Growth & Income)	C	D+	C+	Up	Y	2,500
Virtus Aviva Multi-Strategy Target Return Fund Class C	VCMSX	NAS CM	Open End	Global Macro (Growth & Income)	C-	D	C	Up	Y	2,500
Virtus Aviva Multi-Strategy Target Return Fund Class I	VMSIX	NAS CM	Open End	Global Macro (Growth & Income)	C	D+	B-	Up	Y	100,000
Virtus Aviva Multi-Strategy Target Return Fund Class R6	VMSRX	NAS CM	Open End	Global Macro (Growth & Income)	C	D+	B-	Up	Y	0
Virtus Ceredex Large-Cap Value Equity Fund Class A	SVIIX	NAS CM	Open End	US Equity Large Cap Value (Growth)	C+	C	B		Y	2,500
Virtus Ceredex Large-Cap Value Equity Fund Class C	SVIFX	NAS CM	Open End	US Equity Large Cap Value (Growth)	C+	C	B		Y	2,500
Virtus Ceredex Large-Cap Value Equity Fund Class I	STVTX	NAS CM	Open End	US Equity Large Cap Value (Growth)	C+	C	B		Y	100,000
Virtus Ceredex Large-Cap Value Equity Fund Class R6	STVZX	NAS CM	Open End	US Equity Large Cap Value (Growth)	C+	C	B		Y	2,500,000
Virtus Ceredex Mid-Cap Value Equity Fund Class A	SAMVX	NAS CM	Open End	US Equity Mid Cap (Growth)	B-	C	B		Y	2,500
Virtus Ceredex Mid-Cap Value Equity Fund Class C	SMVFX	NAS CM	Open End	US Equity Mid Cap (Growth)	B-	C	B		Y	2,500
Virtus Ceredex Mid-Cap Value Equity Fund Class I	SMVTX	NAS CM	Open End	US Equity Mid Cap (Growth)	B-	C	B		Y	100,000
Virtus Ceredex Mid-Cap Value Equity Fund Class R6	SMVZX	NAS CM	Open End	US Equity Mid Cap (Growth)	B-	C	B		Y	2,500,000
Virtus Ceredex Small-Cap Value Equity Fund Class A	SASVX	NAS CM	Open End	US Equity Small Cap (Small Company)	C	C-	C+			2,500
Virtus Ceredex Small-Cap Value Equity Fund Class C	STCEX	NAS CM	Open End	US Equity Small Cap (Small Company)	C	C-	C+			2,500
Virtus Ceredex Small-Cap Value Equity Fund Class I	SCETX	NAS CM	Open End	US Equity Small Cap (Small Company)	C	C-	C+			100,000
Virtus Ceredex Small-Cap Value Equity Fund Class R6	VVERX	NAS CM	Open End	US Equity Small Cap (Small Company)	C	C-	C+		Y	2,500,000
Virtus Duff & Phelps Global Infrastructure Fund Class A	PGUAX	NAS CM	Open End	Infrastructure Sector Equity (Growth & Income)	B	B	B		Y	2,500
Virtus Duff & Phelps Global Infrastructure Fund Class C	PGUCX	NAS CM	Open End	Infrastructure Sector Equity (Growth & Income)	B-	B-	B	Down	Y	2,500
Virtus Duff & Phelps Global Infrastructure Fund Class I	PGIUX	NAS CM	Open End	Infrastructure Sector Equity (Growth & Income)	B	B	B		Y	100,000
Virtus Duff & Phelps Global Infrastructure Fund Class R6	VGIRX	NAS CM	Open End	Infrastructure Sector Equity (Growth & Income)	B	B	B		Y	0
Virtus Duff & Phelps Global Real Estate Securities Cls A	VGSAX	NAS CM	Open End	Real Estate Sector Equity (Real Estate)	B-	C+	B		Y	2,500
Virtus Duff & Phelps Global Real Estate Securities Cls C	VGSCX	NAS CM	Open End	Real Estate Sector Equity (Real Estate)	B-	C	B		Y	2,500
Virtus Duff & Phelps Global Real Estate Securities Cls I	VGISX	NAS CM	Open End	Real Estate Sector Equity (Real Estate)	B-	C+	B		Y	100,000
Virtus Duff & Phelps Global Real Estate Securities Cls R6	VRGEX	NAS CM	Open End	Real Estate Sector Equity (Real Estate)	B	C+	B	Up	Y	0
Virtus Duff & Phelps Intl Real Estate Securities Cls A	PXRAX	NAS CM	Open End	Real Estate Sector Equity (Real Estate)	B	B-	B	Up	Y	2,500
Virtus Duff & Phelps Intl Real Estate Securities Cls C	PXRCX	NAS CM	Open End	Real Estate Sector Equity (Real Estate)	B-	C+	B	Up	Y	2,500

★ Expanded analysis of this fund is included in Section II.

	TOTAL RETURNS					PERFORMANCE				ASSETS		ASSET ALLOCATION & TURNOVER					BULL & BEAR		FEES		
Min Additional Investment	3-Month Total Return	6-Month Total Return	1-Year Total Return	3-Year Total Return	5-Year Total Return	Dividend Yield (TTM)	Expense Ratio	3-Yr Std Deviation	3-Year Beta	NAV	Total Assets (MIL)	%Cash	%Stocks	%Bonds	%Other	Turnover Ratio	Last Bull Market Total Return	Last Bear Market Total Return	Front End Fee (%)	Back End Fee (%)	Inception Date
	4.72	20.20	5.79	39.96	58.60	1.22	0.59	13	0.97	39.12	11,223	2	98	0	0	36	26.56	-20.66			Mar-10
	4.56	19.88	5.22	37.91	54.62	0.77	1.1	13	0.97	38.57	11,223	2	98	0	0	36	26.16	-20.84			Aug-83
	4.72	20.21	5.79	40.18	58.95	1.24	0.57	13	0.97	39.13	11,223	2	98	0	0	36	26.16	-20.84			Mar-14
	4.71	20.20	5.77	39.92	58.04	1.2	0.62	13.02	0.97	39.12	11,223	2	98	0	0	36	26.16	-20.84			Jan-13
50	5.17	17.49	2.98	49.39	55.62	0.21	1.22	15.8	0.89	43.72	5,444	3	97	0	0	43	26.83	-20.81	5.75		Mar-99
	5.26	17.67	3.34	50.88	58.20	0.53	0.88	15.81	0.89	44.2	5,444	3	97	0	0	43	27.08	-20.69			Aug-07
	5.10	17.34	2.75	48.39	53.87	0.07	1.44	15.8	0.89	40.73	5,444	3	97	0	0	43	26.63	-20.87			Aug-83
	5.22	17.59	3.19	49.95	56.64	0.39	1.06	15.8	0.89	43.91	5,444	3	97	0	0	43	26.63	-20.87			Jan-13
	5.29	17.73	3.36	50.94	56.83	0.55	0.87	15.81	0.89	44.15	5,444	3	97	0	0	43	26.63	-20.87			Dec-15
250	-1.09	10.20	-5.96	28.43	18.25	1.25	1.75	13.41	1.01	11.77	8.9	1	99	0	0	93			5.75		Jul-13
	-1.09	10.29	-5.76	29.33	19.61	1.37	1.5	13.37	1.01	11.78	8.9	1	99	0	0	93					Jul-13
50	2.07	14.09	-1.54	28.67	11.37	1.82	0.97	11.98	1.04	6.88	22.1	0	100	0	0	51	17.1	-27.05	5.75		Aug-07
50	1.93	13.62	-2.18	25.73	7.33	1.02	1.72	11.97	1.03	6.84	22.1	0	100	0	0	51	16.52	-27.43		1.00	Aug-07
	2.21	14.40	-1.04	30.09	13.81	2.01	0.62	11.97	1.03	6.91	22.1	0	100	0	0	51	17.3	-27.01			Aug-07
	2.21	14.19	-1.11	30.17	13.95	2.06	0.57	11.94	1.03	6.92	22.1	0	100	0	0	51	17.3	-27.01			Mar-15
	2.23	14.11	-1.33	29.63	12.79	2.01	0.72	11.96	1.03	6.87	22.1	0	100	0	0	51	17.21	-27.05			Aug-07
250	2.92	16.56	-7.12	30.59	23.90	0.69	1.39	13.71	1.09	13.02	1,805	1	99	0	0	62	19.63	-23.11	5.75		Aug-07
250	2.82	16.16	-7.77	27.66	19.37	0	2.14	13.73	1.09	12.72	1,805	1	99	0	0	62	19.11	-23.34		1.00	Aug-07
	3.14	16.81	-6.69	32.17	26.44	1.08	0.99	13.79	1.09	13.13	1,805	1	99	0	0	62	20.14	-23			Aug-07
	3.04	16.72	-6.85	31.61	25.55	0.96	1.12	13.76	1.09	13.19	1,805	1	99	0	0	62	20.14	-23			Jun-12
	3.07	16.69	-6.87	31.54	25.48	0.94	1.14	13.75	1.09	13.07	1,805	1	99	0	0	62	19.91	-23.08			Aug-07
50	4.76	12.71	-0.01	36.35	45.27	0.76	0.99	12.06	1	14.26	95.6	1	99	0	0	45			5.75		Nov-12
50	4.53	12.32	-0.73	33.18	39.74	0.24	1.74	12.03	1	13.9	95.6	1	99	0	0	45				1.00	Nov-12
	4.83	12.85	0.23	37.31	47.01	0.99	0.74	12.04	1	14.26	95.6	1	99	0	0	45					Nov-12
500	4.73	18.81	1.65	30.39	13.70	0.98	0.97	11.93	0.81	22.99	241.3	8	72	20	0	23	22.09	-12.82			Sep-99
500	5.66	21.52	0.50	31.54	7.86	0	1.23	14.37	0.95	12.31	42.3	17	83	0	0	24					May-13
100	1.59	7.06	0.63	2.25		1.32	1.74	5.52	9.97	9.55	38.3	62	20	18	0	113			5.75		Jul-15
100	1.40	6.69	-0.03	0.09		0.41	2.49	5.45	9.88	9.41	38.3	62	20	18	0	113				1.00	Jul-15
	1.59	7.15	0.85	3.03		1.62	1.49	5.53	10.26	9.58	38.3	62	20	18	0	113					Jul-15
	1.69	7.15	1.00	3.21		1.66	1.43	5.49	10.03	9.59	38.3	62	20	18	0	113					Nov-16
100	3.83	16.92	6.48	33.55	36.12	1.46	1.24	12.91	1.05	12.99	1,277	1	99	0	0		24.72	-19.48	5.75		Feb-93
100	3.71	16.62	5.95	31.67	33.01	0.88	1.72	12.93	1.05	12.56	1,277	1	99	0	0		24.15	-19.65		1.00	Jun-95
	3.94	17.18	6.76	34.74	38.02	1.71	0.97	12.92	1.05	13.16	1,277	1	99	0	0		24.85	-19.34			Feb-93
	4.00	17.27	7.00	35.70	39.75	1.92	0.72	12.96	1.06	13.24	1,277	1	99	0	0		24.85	-19.34			Aug-14
100	4.33	20.27	6.53	41.73	38.28	0.7	1.38	13.49	1.01	12.04	3,123	4	96	0	0		29.68	-27.84	5.75		Oct-03
100	4.18	19.99	6.10	39.91	35.52	0.09	1.79	13.56	1.01	11.7	3,123	4	96	0	0		29.28	-28.05		1.00	Nov-01
	4.35	20.49	6.89	43.17	40.48	0.99	1.01	13.53	1.01	12.23	3,123	4	96	0	0		30.01	-27.77			Nov-01
	4.42	20.55	7.07	44.11	42.37	1.14	0.79	13.48	1	12.26	3,123	4	96	0	0		30.01	-27.77			Aug-14
100	1.92	13.93	-4.90	24.76	29.54	1.34	1.46	16.71	0.91	9.54	588.4	0	100	0	0		23.01	-20.87	5.75		Oct-03
100	1.82	13.71	-5.33	23.31	27.06	0.86	1.9	16.71	0.91	8.35	588.4	0	100	0	0		22.57	-21.14		1.00	Jun-97
	1.93	14.12	-4.66	25.92	31.55	1.63	1.18	16.7	0.91	9.99	588.4	0	100	0	0		23.25	-20.78			Jan-97
	2.03	14.24	-4.56	26.04	31.68		0.88	16.71	0.91	10	588.4	0	100	0	0		23.25	-20.78			Feb-19
100	4.99	22.52	16.24	30.81	30.90	1.64	1.25	9.91	1	15.99	103.6	1	99	0	0	36	16.3	-9.58	5.75		Dec-04
100	4.82	22.10	15.35	27.89	26.10	0.97	2	9.91	1	15.93	103.6	1	99	0	0	36	15.91	-9.95		1.00	Dec-04
	5.06	22.66	16.49	31.78	32.54	1.85	1.01	9.92	1	16	103.6	1	99	0	0	36	16.45	-9.54			Jun-08
	5.08	22.62	16.54	31.38	31.47	1.94	0.93	9.91	1	15.99	103.6	1	99	0	0	36	16.3	-9.58			Jan-18
100	2.37	18.47	10.39	20.33	40.46	1.33	1.4	11.1	0.98	32.77	217.8	3	96	0	2	41	25.75	-18.06	5.75		Mar-09
100	2.17	18.01	9.55	17.62	35.25	1.93	2.15	11.08	0.98	31.51	217.8	3	96	0	2	41	25.22	-18.28		1.00	Mar-09
	2.44	18.62	10.67	21.21	42.22	2.89	1.15	11.1	0.98	32.29	217.8	3	96	0	2	41	25.93	-17.93			Mar-09
	2.50	18.75	10.87	21.69	42.79	2.97	0.95	11.08	0.98	32.35	217.8	3	96	0	2	41	25.93	-17.93			Nov-16
100	1.83	16.66	8.40	25.11	29.74	3.45	1.5	11.3	0.97	7.77	45.7	4	92	0	4	38	18.47	-20.99	5.75		Oct-07
100	1.57	16.21	7.59	22.17	24.94	2.89	2.25	11.32	0.97	7.74	45.7	4	92	0	4	38	17.96	-21.33		1.00	Oct-07

	MARKET		FUND TYPE, CATEGORY & OBJECTIVE		RATINGS				MINIMUMS	
Fund Name	Ticker Symbol	Traded On	Fund Type	Category and (Prospectus Objective)	Overall Rating	Reward Rating	Risk Rating	Recent Up/ Downgrade	Open to New Investors	Min Initial Investment
Virtus Duff & Phelps Intl Real Estate Securities Cls I	PXRIX	NAS CM	Open End	Real Estate Sector Equity (Real Estate)	B	B-	B	Up	Y	100,000
Virtus Duff & Phelps Real Estate Securities Fund Class A	PHRAX	NAS CM	Open End	Real Estate Sector Equity (Real Estate)	C+	C	B-	Down	Y	2,500
Virtus Duff & Phelps Real Estate Securities Fund Class C	PHRCX	NAS CM	Open End	Real Estate Sector Equity (Real Estate)	C+	C	B-	Down	Y	2,500
Virtus Duff & Phelps Real Estate Securities Fund Class I	PHRIX	NAS CM	Open End	Real Estate Sector Equity (Real Estate)	C+	C	B-	Down	Y	100,000
Virtus Duff & Phelps Real Estate Securities Fund Class R6	VRREX	NAS CM	Open End	Real Estate Sector Equity (Real Estate)	C+	C	B-	Down	Y	0
Virtus Duff & Phelps Select MLP and Energy Fund Class A	VLPAX	NAS CM	Open End	Energy Sector Equity (Growth & Income)	D+	D+	C	Down	Y	2,500
Virtus Duff & Phelps Select MLP and Energy Fund Class C	VLPCX	NAS CM	Open End	Energy Sector Equity (Growth & Income)	D+	D	C-	Down	Y	2,500
Virtus Duff & Phelps Select MLP and Energy Fund Class I	VLPIX	NAS CM	Open End	Energy Sector Equity (Growth & Income)	C-	D+	C	Down	Y	100,000
Virtus Global Dividend & Income Fund Inc.	ZTR	NYSE	Closed End	Aggressive Alloc (Growth)	C	C	C-	Up	Y	
Virtus Herzfeld Fund Class A	VHFAX	NAS CM	Open End	Moderate Alloc (Growth & Income)	C+	C	B	Up	Y	2,500
Virtus Herzfeld Fund Class C	VHFCX	NAS CM	Open End	Moderate Alloc (Growth & Income)	B-	C	B	Up	Y	2,500
Virtus Herzfeld Fund Class I	VHFIX	NAS CM	Open End	Moderate Alloc (Growth & Income)	B-	C	B	Up	Y	100,000
Virtus Horizon Wealth Masters Fund Class A	VWMAX	NAS CM	Open End	US Equity Mid Cap (Growth)	C	C-	C+		Y	2,500
Virtus Horizon Wealth Masters Fund Class C	VWMCX	NAS CM	Open End	US Equity Mid Cap (Growth)	C	C-	C+		Y	2,500
Virtus Horizon Wealth Masters Fund Class I	VWMIX	NAS CM	Open End	US Equity Mid Cap (Growth)	C	C	B-		Y	100,000
Virtus KAR Capital Growth Fund Class A	PSTAX	NAS CM	Open End	US Equity Large Cap Growth (Growth)	C+	C	C+	Down	Y	2,500
Virtus KAR Capital Growth Fund Class C	SSTFX	NAS CM	Open End	US Equity Large Cap Growth (Growth)	C+	C	C+		Y	2,500
Virtus KAR Capital Growth Fund Class I	PLXGX	NAS CM	Open End	US Equity Large Cap Growth (Growth)	C+	C	B-	Down	Y	100,000
Virtus KAR Capital Growth Fund Class R6	VCGRX	NAS CM	Open End	US Equity Large Cap Growth (Growth)	C+	C	C+	Down	Y	0
Virtus KAR Emerging Markets Small-Cap Fund Class A	VAESX	NAS CM	Open End	Global Emerg Mkts (Small Company)	B-	C	B	Up	Y	2,500
Virtus KAR Emerging Markets Small-Cap Fund Class C	VCESX	NAS CM	Open End	Global Emerg Mkts (Small Company)	C+	C	B	Up	Y	2,500
Virtus KAR Emerging Markets Small-Cap Fund Class I	VIESX	NAS CM	Open End	Global Emerg Mkts (Small Company)	B-	C	B	Up	Y	100,000
Virtus KAR Global Quality Dividend Fund Class A	PPTAX	NAS CM	Open End	Global Equity Large Cap (Growth)	B	C+	B+		Y	2,500
Virtus KAR Global Quality Dividend Fund Class C	PPTCX	NAS CM	Open End	Global Equity Large Cap (Growth)	B-	C	B+	Down	Y	2,500
Virtus KAR Global Quality Dividend Fund Class I	PIPTX	NAS CM	Open End	Global Equity Large Cap (Growth)	B	C+	A-		Y	100,000
Virtus KAR International Small-Cap Fund Class A	VISAX	NAS CM	Open End	Global Equity Mid/Small Cap (Growth)	C+	C	B	Up	Y	2,500
Virtus KAR International Small-Cap Fund Class C	VCISX	NAS CM	Open End	Global Equity Mid/Small Cap (Growth)	C+	C	B	Up	Y	2,500
Virtus KAR International Small-Cap Fund Class I	VIISX	NAS CM	Open End	Global Equity Mid/Small Cap (Growth)	C+	C	B	Up	Y	100,000
Virtus KAR International Small-Cap Fund Class R6	VRISX	NAS CM	Open End	Global Equity Mid/Small Cap (Growth)	C+	C	B	Up	Y	0
Virtus KAR Long/Short Equity Fund Class A	VLSAX	NAS CM	Open End	Long/Short Equity (Growth)	U	U	U		Y	2,500
Virtus KAR Long/Short Equity Fund Class C	VLSCX	NAS CM	Open End	Long/Short Equity (Growth)	U	U	U		Y	2,500
Virtus KAR Long/Short Equity Fund Class I	VLSIX	NAS CM	Open End	Long/Short Equity (Growth)	U	U	U		Y	100,000
Virtus KAR Long/Short Equity Fund Class R6	VLSRX	NAS CM	Open End	Long/Short Equity (Growth)	U	U	U		Y	2,500,000
Virtus KAR Mid-Cap Core Fund Class A	VMACX	NAS CM	Open End	US Equity Mid Cap (Growth)	B-	C+	B	Down	Y	2,500
Virtus KAR Mid-Cap Core Fund Class C	VMCCX	NAS CM	Open End	US Equity Mid Cap (Growth)	B-	C	B	Down	Y	2,500
Virtus KAR Mid-Cap Core Fund Class I	VIMCX	NAS CM	Open End	US Equity Mid Cap (Growth)	B-	C+	B	Down	Y	100,000
Virtus KAR Mid-Cap Core Fund Class R6	VRMCX	NAS CM	Open End	US Equity Mid Cap (Growth)	B-	C+	B	Down	Y	0
Virtus KAR Mid-Cap Growth Fund Class A	PHSKX	NAS CM	Open End	US Equity Mid Cap (Growth)	B	B+	B		Y	2,500
Virtus KAR Mid-Cap Growth Fund Class C	PSKCX	NAS CM	Open End	US Equity Mid Cap (Growth)	B	B	B-		Y	2,500
Virtus KAR Mid-Cap Growth Fund Class I	PICMX	NAS CM	Open End	US Equity Mid Cap (Growth)	B	B+	B		Y	100,000
Virtus KAR Mid-Cap Growth Fund Class R6	VRMGX	NAS CM	Open End	US Equity Mid Cap (Growth)	B	B+	B		Y	0
Virtus KAR Small-Cap Core Fund Class A	PKSAX	NAS CM	Open End	US Equity Mid Cap (Small Company)	B	B+	B		Y	2,500
Virtus KAR Small-Cap Core Fund Class C	PKSCX	NAS CM	Open End	US Equity Mid Cap (Small Company)	B	B	B	Up	Y	2,500
Virtus KAR Small-Cap Core Fund Class I	PKSFX	NAS CM	Open End	US Equity Mid Cap (Small Company)	B	B+	B		Y	100,000
Virtus KAR Small-Cap Core Fund Class R6	VSCRX	NAS CM	Open End	US Equity Mid Cap (Small Company)	B	B+	B		Y	0
Virtus KAR Small-Cap Growth Fund Class A	PSGAX	NAS CM	Open End	US Equity Small Cap (Small Company)	B+	B+	B	Up	Y	2,500
Virtus KAR Small-Cap Growth Fund Class C	PSGCX	NAS CM	Open End	US Equity Small Cap (Small Company)	B+	B+	B	Up	Y	2,500
Virtus KAR Small-Cap Growth Fund Class I	PXSGX	NAS CM	Open End	US Equity Small Cap (Small Company)	B+	B+	B	Up	Y	100,000
Virtus KAR Small-Cap Growth Fund Class R6	VRSGX	NAS CM	Open End	US Equity Small Cap (Small Company)	B+	B+	B	Up	Y	0
Virtus KAR Small-Cap Value Fund Class A	PQSAX	NAS CM	Open End	US Equity Small Cap (Small Company)	C	C	C+	Down	Y	2,500
Virtus KAR Small-Cap Value Fund Class C	PQSCX	NAS CM	Open End	US Equity Small Cap (Small Company)	C	C	C+	Down	Y	2,500
Virtus KAR Small-Cap Value Fund Class I	PXQSX	NAS CM	Open End	US Equity Small Cap (Small Company)	C	C	C+	Down	Y	100,000

★ Expanded analysis of this fund is included in Section II.

	TOTAL RETURNS					PERFORMANCE				ASSETS		ASSET ALLOCATION & TURNOVER					BULL & BEAR		FEES		
Min Additional Investment	3-Month Total Return	6-Month Total Return	1-Year Total Return	3-Year Total Return	5-Year Total Return	Dividend Yield (TTM)	Expense Ratio	3-Yr Std Deviation	3-Year Beta	NAV	Total Assets (MIL)	%Cash	%Stocks	%Bonds	%Other	Turnover Ratio	Last Bull Market Total Return	Last Bear Market Total Return	Front End Fee (%)	Back End Fee (%)	Inception Date
	1.86	16.74	8.72	25.98	31.43	3.84	1.25	11.3	0.97	7.74	45.7	4	92	0	4	38	18.79	-20.99			Oct-07
100	1.94	18.27	8.78	11.47	40.47	1.78	1.38	12.58	0.94	24.32	582.4	1	99	0	0	12	32.69	-16.45	5.75		Mar-95
100	1.80	17.84	8.05	9.10	35.45	1.08	2.07	12.58	0.94	24.26	582.4	1	99	0	0	12	32.13	-16.69		1.00	Jul-03
	2.06	18.47	9.12	12.42	42.38	2.05	1.08	12.58	0.94	24.27	582.4	1	99	0	0	12	32.91	-16.34			Dec-06
	2.09	18.59	9.32	12.99	43.41	2.18	0.9	12.6	0.94	24.29	582.4	1	99	0	0	12	32.69	-16.45			Nov-14
100	-1.34	18.28	-6.40	6.07		3.65	1.43	17.37	0.96	9.06	9.1	8	90	0	3	29			5.75		Sep-15
100	-1.53	17.75	-7.21	3.45		2.97	2.18	17.35	0.96	9.02	9.1	8	90	0	3	29				1.00	Sep-15
	-1.33	18.34	-6.23	6.71		3.95	1.18	17.37	0.96	9.03	9.1	8	90	0	3	29					Sep-15
	4.92	16.67	8.79	16.91	13.56	4.37	1.15	10.77		10.51	258.2	1	61	37	0	43	12.2	-8.19			Sep-88
100	1.59	14.16	2.75	29.84	30.47	4.31	3.26	9.74	0.8	11.15	53.5	4	65	24	-3	69			5.75		Sep-12
100	1.32	13.71	1.97	26.89	25.67	3.6	4.01	9.78	0.81	11.09	53.5	4	65	24	-3	69				1.00	Sep-12
	1.57	14.31	2.96	30.67	32.09	4.59	3.01	9.79	0.81	11.15	53.5	4	65	24	-3	69					Sep-12
100	1.42	17.10	-4.51	35.90	25.07	0	1.25	15.58	1.15	16.36	52.7	0	100	0	0	27			5.75		Sep-12
100	1.22	16.62	-5.23	32.98	20.50	0	2	15.58	1.15	15.71	52.7	0	100	0	0	27				1.00	Sep-12
	1.47	17.19	-4.26	37.01	26.67	0	1	15.6	1.15	16.49	52.7	0	100	0	0	27					Sep-12
100	5.61	31.20	10.08	66.66	89.09	0	1.22	16.2	1.15	17.49	530.2	1	99	0	0		30.45	-23.26	5.75		Oct-95
100	5.37	30.74	9.21	62.83	81.98	0	2	16.18	1.15	13.14	530.2	1	99	0	0		29.95	-23.58		1.00	Nov-97
	5.62	31.38	10.30	67.77	91.38	0	0.99	16.22	1.15	18.21	530.2	1	99	0	0		30.83	-23.26			Sep-06
	5.69	31.50	10.19	67.07	89.55	0	0.78	16.18	1.15	18.2	530.2	1	99	0	0		30.45	-23.27			Jan-18
100	0.32	13.08	2.21	49.68	27.10	0.28	1.89	10.76	0.71	12.36	100.8	8	89	0	3	24			5.75		Dec-13
100	0.16	12.71	1.48	46.38	22.53	0	2.64	10.78	0.71	12.32	100.8	8	89	0	3	24				1.00	Dec-13
	0.48	13.21	2.52	50.72	28.70	0.33	1.64	10.75	0.71	12.42	100.8	8	89	0	3	24					Dec-13
100	3.88	14.50	10.59	28.97	35.60	0.42	1.35	9.17	0.84	14.45	38.2	3	97	0	0		23.75	-16.97	5.75		Jul-05
100	3.72	14.07	9.77	26.03	30.59	0	2.1	9.13	0.84	13.94	38.2	3	97	0	0		23.21	-17.25		1.00	Jul-05
	3.95	14.67	10.94	29.97	37.40	0.76	1.1	9.12	0.84	14.46	38.2	3	97	0	0		23.9	-16.86			Jun-08
100	2.29	14.74	-1.37	55.80	45.34	0.37	1.58	10.4	0.79	17.35	1,458	8	88	0	4	21			5.75		Sep-12
100	2.09	14.34	-2.04	52.40	40.12	0	2.29	10.38	0.79	17.06	1,458	8	88	0	4	21				1.00	Sep-12
	2.29	14.83	-1.13	56.93	47.19	0.62	1.31	10.39	0.79	17.42	1,458	8	88	0	4	21					Sep-12
	2.40	14.96	-1.02	57.48	47.95	0.67	1.22	10.4	0.79	17.44	1,458	8	88	0	4	21					Nov-14
100	7.08	27.50					2.29			12.24	10.2	29	71	0	0				5.75		Dec-18
100	6.92	26.97					3.04			12.19	10.2	29	71	0	0						Dec-18
	7.16	27.70					2.04			12.26	10.2	29	71	0	0						Dec-18
	7.16	27.70					1.97			12.26	10.2	29	71	0	0						Dec-18
100	6.11	21.66	9.72	55.30	83.05	0	1.2	12.64	0.9	34.71	396.5	5	95	0	0		24.22	-16.33	5.75		Jun-09
100	5.89	21.23	8.92	51.84	76.31	0	1.95	12.63	0.9	32.32	396.5	5	95	0	0		23.63	-16.6		1.00	Jun-09
	6.15	21.77	9.98	56.43	85.27	0	0.95	12.63	0.9	35.34	396.5	5	95	0	0		24.42	-16.25			Jun-09
	6.18	21.86	10.10	56.70	85.58	0	0.87	12.64	0.9	35.39	396.5	5	95	0	0		24.42	-16.25			Jan-18
100	9.48	36.50	19.48	99.81	115.01	0	1.41	15.45	0.98	39.49	427.4	6	94	0	0		31.22	-26.82	5.75		Dec-75
100	9.27	36.00	18.62	95.41	107.21	0	2.16	15.44	0.98	31.09	427.4	6	94	0	0		30.64	-27.07		1.00	Jan-01
	9.54	36.67	19.79	101.37	117.76	0	1.16	15.45	0.98	40.84	427.4	6	94	0	0		31.41	-26.73			Sep-07
	9.60	36.84	20.06	101.20	116.50	0	0.91	15.45	0.98	40.97	427.4	6	94	0	0		31.22	-26.82			Jan-18
100	5.13	28.66	12.56	87.73	110.13	0	1.31	15.64	0.8	36.85	1,508	2	98	0	0		22.39	-14.04	5.75		Aug-02
100	4.95	28.19	11.77	83.62	102.46	0	2.04	15.64	0.8	30.74	1,508	2	98	0	0		21.88	-14.28		1.00	Aug-02
	5.19	28.82	12.88	89.22	112.80	0.11	1.03	15.65	0.8	38.88	1,508	2	98	0	0		22.49	-13.87			Oct-96
	5.23	28.89	12.97	89.69	113.78	0.16	0.96	15.64	0.8	39.03	1,508	2	98	0	0		22.49	-13.87			Nov-14
100	8.04	32.61	19.06	127.25	167.25	0	1.41	13.84	0.66	38.26	5,214	2	98	0	0		21.34	-8.26	5.75		Jun-06
100	7.87	32.12	18.21	122.19	157.56	0	2.14	13.84	0.66	34.26	5,214	2	98	0	0		20.69	-8.57		1.00	Jun-06
	8.10	32.77	19.37	129.01	170.62	0	1.14	13.84	0.66	39.09	5,214	2	98	0	0		21.43	-8.17			Jun-06
	8.14	32.84	19.52	129.36	171.03	0	1.04	13.82	0.66	39.15	5,214	2	98	0	0		21.44	-8.17			Jan-18
100	3.13	15.22	-2.96	30.43	46.29	0.73	1.27	15.74	0.85	17.78	576.1	3	97	0	0		20.84	-16.19	5.75		Jun-06
100	2.84	14.72	-3.72	27.50	40.95	0	1.97	15.72	0.85	17.37	576.1	3	97	0	0		20.34	-16.45		1.00	Jun-06
	3.13	15.31	-2.77	31.39	48.20	1.15	0.99	15.74	0.85	17.77	576.1	3	97	0	0		21.18	-16.15			Jun-06

	MARKET		FUND TYPE, CATEGORY & OBJECTIVE		RATINGS				MINIMUMS	
Fund Name	Ticker Symbol	Traded On	Fund Type	Category and (Prospectus Objective)	Overall Rating	Reward Rating	Risk Rating	Recent Up/ Downgrade	Open to New Investors	Min Initial Investment
Virtus KAR Small-Cap Value Fund Class R6	VQSRX	NAS CM	Open End	US Equity Small Cap (Small Company)	C	C	C+	Down	Y	0
Virtus KAR Small-Mid Cap Core Fund Class A	VKSAX	NAS CM	Open End	US Equity Mid Cap (Growth)	D	C-	C+		Y	2,500
Virtus KAR Small-Mid Cap Core Fund Class C	VKSCX	NAS CM	Open End	US Equity Mid Cap (Growth)	D	C-	C+		Y	2,500
Virtus KAR Small-Mid Cap Core Fund Class I	VKSIX	NAS CM	Open End	US Equity Mid Cap (Growth)	D	C-	C+		Y	100,000
Virtus KAR Small-Mid Cap Core Fund Class R6	VKSRX	NAS CM	Open End	US Equity Mid Cap (Growth)	D	C-	C+		Y	0
Virtus Rampart Alternatives Diversifier Fund Class A	PDPAX	NAS CM	Open End	Multialternative (Growth)	B-	C	B+	Up	Y	2,500
Virtus Rampart Alternatives Diversifier Fund Class C	PDPCX	NAS CM	Open End	Multialternative (Growth)	C+	C	B	Up	Y	2,500
Virtus Rampart Alternatives Diversifier Fund Class I	VADIX	NAS CM	Open End	Multialternative (Growth)	B-	C	B+	Up	Y	100,000
Virtus Rampart Enhanced Core Equity Fund Class A	PDIAX	NAS CM	Open End	US Equity Large Cap Blend (Growth & Income)	C+	C	B-		Y	2,500
Virtus Rampart Enhanced Core Equity Fund Class C	PGICX	NAS CM	Open End	US Equity Large Cap Blend (Growth & Income)	C+	C	B-	Up	Y	2,500
Virtus Rampart Enhanced Core Equity Fund Class I	PXIIX	NAS CM	Open End	US Equity Large Cap Blend (Growth & Income)	C+	C	B-		Y	100,000
Virtus Rampart Enhanced Core Equity Fund Class R6	VECRX	NAS CM	Open End	US Equity Large Cap Blend (Growth & Income)	C+	C	B-		Y	0
Virtus Rampart Equity Trend Fund Class A	VAPAX	NAS CM	Open End	US Equity Large Cap Blend (Growth)	C	C	B-		Y	2,500
Virtus Rampart Equity Trend Fund Class C	VAPCX	NAS CM	Open End	US Equity Large Cap Blend (Growth)	C	C	C+		Y	2,500
Virtus Rampart Equity Trend Fund Class I	VAPIX	NAS CM	Open End	US Equity Large Cap Blend (Growth)	C	C	B-		Y	100,000
Virtus Rampart Equity Trend Fund Class R6	VRPAX	NAS CM	Open End	US Equity Large Cap Blend (Growth)	C	C	B-		Y	0
Virtus Rampart Multi-Asset Trend Fund Class A	VAAAX	NAS CM	Open End	Moderate Alloc (Growth)	C+	C	B+	Up	Y	2,500
Virtus Rampart Multi-Asset Trend Fund Class C	VAACX	NAS CM	Open End	Moderate Alloc (Growth)	C	C-	B		Y	2,500
Virtus Rampart Multi-Asset Trend Fund Class I	VAISX	NAS CM	Open End	Moderate Alloc (Growth)	C+	C	B+	Up	Y	100,000
Virtus Rampart Sector Trend Fund Class A	PWBAX	NAS CM	Open End	US Equity Large Cap Blend (Growth)	C+	C	B	Up	Y	2,500
Virtus Rampart Sector Trend Fund Class C	PWBCX	NAS CM	Open End	US Equity Large Cap Blend (Growth)	C+	C	B	Up	Y	2,500
Virtus Rampart Sector Trend Fund Class I	VARIX	NAS CM	Open End	US Equity Large Cap Blend (Growth)	C+	C	B	Up	Y	100,000
Virtus SGA Global Growth A Class	SGAAX	NAS CM	Open End	Global Equity Large Cap (World Stock)	B	B-	B		Y	2,500
Virtus SGA Global Growth C Class	SGACX	NAS CM	Open End	Global Equity Large Cap (World Stock)	B	B-	B		Y	1,000
Virtus SGA Global Growth I Class	SGAPX	NAS CM	Open End	Global Equity Large Cap (World Stock)	B	B-	B		Y	2,500
Virtus SGA Global Growth R6 Class	SGARX	NAS CM	Open End	Global Equity Large Cap (World Stock)	B	B	B		Y	250,000
Virtus SGA International Growth Fund Class A	SCIIX	NAS CM	Open End	Global Equity Large Cap (Foreign Stock)	B-	C+	B	Up	Y	2,500
Virtus SGA International Growth Fund Class I	STITX	NAS CM	Open End	Global Equity Large Cap (Foreign Stock)	B-	C+	B	Up	Y	100,000
Virtus SGA International Growth Fund Class R6	SCIZX	NAS CM	Open End	Global Equity Large Cap (Foreign Stock)	B-	C+	B	Up	Y	2,500,000
Virtus Silvant Large-Cap Growth Stock Fund Class A	STCIX	NAS CM	Open End	US Equity Large Cap Growth (Growth)	C+	C+	B	Down	Y	2,500
Virtus Silvant Large-Cap Growth Stock Fund Class C	STCFX	NAS CM	Open End	US Equity Large Cap Growth (Growth)	C+	C	B-	Down	Y	2,500
Virtus Silvant Large-Cap Growth Stock Fund Class I	STCAX	NAS CM	Open End	US Equity Large Cap Growth (Growth)	C+	C+	B	Down	Y	100,000
Virtus Silvant Large-Cap Growth Stock Fund Class R6	STCZX	NAS CM	Open End	US Equity Large Cap Growth (Growth)	C+	C+	B	Down	Y	2,500,000
Virtus Silvant Small-Cap Growth Stock Fund Class A	SCGIX	NAS CM	Open End	US Equity Small Cap (Small Company)	C+	C	C+	Down	Y	2,500
Virtus Silvant Small-Cap Growth Stock Fund Class C	SSCFX	NAS CM	Open End	US Equity Small Cap (Small Company)	C+	C	C+		Y	2,500
Virtus Silvant Small-Cap Growth Stock Fund Class I	SSCTX	NAS CM	Open End	US Equity Small Cap (Small Company)	C+	C	C+	Down	Y	100,000
Virtus Tactical Allocation Fund Class A	NAINX	NAS CM	Open End	Moderate Alloc (Asset Alloc)	B-	C	B	Up	Y	2,500
Virtus Tactical Allocation Fund Class C	POICX	NAS CM	Open End	Moderate Alloc (Asset Alloc)	B-	C	B	Up	Y	2,500
Virtus Tactical Allocation Fund Class I	VTAIX	NAS CM	Open End	Moderate Alloc (Asset Alloc)	B-	C	B	Up	Y	100,000
Virtus Vontobel Emerging Markets Opportunities Cls A	HEMZX	NAS CM	Open End	Global Emerg Mkts (Div Emerging Mkts)	C	C	C+		Y	2,500
Virtus Vontobel Emerging Markets Opportunities Cls C	PICEX	NAS CM	Open End	Global Emerg Mkts (Div Emerging Mkts)	C	C	C+		Y	2,500
Virtus Vontobel Emerging Markets Opportunities Cls I	HIEMX	NAS CM	Open End	Global Emerg Mkts (Div Emerging Mkts)	C	C	C+		Y	100,000
Virtus Vontobel Emerging Markets Opportunities Cls R6	VREMX	NAS CM	Open End	Global Emerg Mkts (Div Emerging Mkts)	C	C	C+		Y	0
Virtus Vontobel Foreign Opportunities Fund Class A	JVIAX	NAS CM	Open End	Global Equity Large Cap (Foreign Stock)	C+	C	B-	Up	Y	2,500
Virtus Vontobel Foreign Opportunities Fund Class C	JVICX	NAS CM	Open End	Global Equity Large Cap (Foreign Stock)	C+	C	B-	Up	Y	2,500
Virtus Vontobel Foreign Opportunities Fund Class I	JVXIX	NAS CM	Open End	Global Equity Large Cap (Foreign Stock)	C+	C	B-	Up	Y	100,000
Virtus Vontobel Foreign Opportunities Fund Class R6	VFOPX	NAS CM	Open End	Global Equity Large Cap (Foreign Stock)	C+	C	B-	Up	Y	0
Virtus Vontobel Global Opportunities Fund Class A	NWWOX	NAS CM	Open End	Global Equity Large Cap (World Stock)	B	C+	B	Up	Y	2,500
Virtus Vontobel Global Opportunities Fund Class C	WWOCX	NAS CM	Open End	Global Equity Large Cap (World Stock)	B-	C+	B	Up	Y	2,500
Virtus Vontobel Global Opportunities Fund Class I	WWOIX	NAS CM	Open End	Global Equity Large Cap (World Stock)	B	B-	B+	Up	Y	100,000
Virtus Vontobel Global Opportunities Fund Class R6	VRGOX	NAS CM	Open End	Global Equity Large Cap (World Stock)	B	B-	B+	Up	Y	0
Virtus Vontobel Greater European Opportunities Cls A	VGEAX	NAS CM	Open End	Europe Equity Large Cap (Europe Stock)	C	C-	C+	Up	Y	2,500

★ Expanded analysis of this fund is included in Section II.

Min Additional Investment	TOTAL RETURNS 3-Month Total Return	6-Month Total Return	1-Year Total Return	3-Year Total Return	5-Year Total Return	PERFORMANCE Dividend Yield (TTM)	Expense Ratio	3-Yr Std Deviation	3-Year Beta	ASSETS NAV	Total Assets (MIL)	ASSET ALLOCATION & TURNOVER %Cash	%Stocks	%Bonds	%Other	Turnover Ratio	BULL & BEAR Last Bull Market Total Return	Last Bear Market Total Return	FEES Front End Fee (%)	Back End Fee (%)	Inception Date
	3.13	15.30	-2.72	31.64	48.47	1.23	0.9	15.73	0.85	17.78	576.1	3	97	0	0		21.18	-16.15			Nov-16
100	9.19	27.09	13.40			0	1.3			11.4	11.9	4	96	0	0				5.75		Mar-18
100	9.08	26.56	12.64			0	2.05			11.29	11.9	4	96	0	0					1.00	Mar-18
	9.37	27.28	13.82			0.09	1.05			11.43	11.9	4	96	0	0						Mar-18
	9.36	27.25	13.81			0.09	0.97			11.44	11.9	4	96	0	0						Mar-18
100	0.97	13.31	0.27	12.46	3.58	2.12	1.5	8.72	0.58	11.4	40.4	18	63	11	7	17	12.87	-14.86	5.75		Nov-05
100	0.70	12.79	-0.55	9.92	-0.24	0.83	2.25	8.71	0.58	11.37	40.4	18	63	11	7	17	12.35	-15.03		1.00	Nov-05
	1.06	13.47	0.53	13.40	4.92	2.51	1.24	8.72	0.58	11.37	40.4	18	63	11	7	17	13.02	-14.76			Oct-09
100	2.12	16.66	5.49	36.66	49.36	1.04	1.2	13.6	1.06	20.23	136.9	1	99	0	0		26.86	-20.05	5.75		Sep-97
100	1.97	16.15	4.68	33.62	43.87	0.19	1.95	13.59	1.06	18.05	136.9	1	99	0	0		26.28	-20.34		1.00	Sep-97
	2.17	16.77	5.73	37.70	51.29	1.28	0.95	13.62	1.06	20.19	136.9	1	99	0	0		27.13	-20.02			Nov-07
	2.23	16.80	5.81	37.19	49.95	1.47	0.91	13.6	1.06	20.16	136.9	1	99	0	0		26.86	-20.05			Jan-18
100	4.84	10.67	1.47	27.87	7.21	0	1.56	11.34	0.84	15.14	334.8	1	99	0	0	57	11.8	-11.57	5.75		Jul-10
100	4.57	10.16	0.69	25.08	3.38	0	2.29	11.34	0.84	14.41	334.8	1	99	0	0	57	11.26	-11.8		1.00	Jul-10
	4.85	10.76	1.72	28.71	8.46	0	1.3	11.34	0.84	15.33	334.8	1	99	0	0	57	11.91	-11.48			Jul-10
	4.89	10.84	1.84	29.23	9.16	0	1.2	11.33	0.84	15.43	334.8	1	99	0	0	57	11.91	-11.48			Nov-14
100	3.13	8.21	3.32	15.06	2.35	0.32	1.84	6.29	0.79	11.4	53.4	3	64	31	1	117	6.77	-8.58	5.75		Mar-11
100	3.00	7.85	2.61	12.50	-1.32	0	2.57	6.28	0.79	10.98	53.4	3	64	31	1	117	6.27	-8.78		1.00	Mar-11
	3.20	8.36	3.58	15.84	3.57	0.75	1.6	6.31	0.8	11.46	53.4	3	64	31	1	117	6.84	-8.39			Mar-11
100	3.93	11.37	2.27	22.77	16.73	0.93	0.98	10.83	0.83	13.22	212.9	1	99	0	0	324	12.84	-11.09	5.75		Aug-03
100	3.66	10.92	1.48	19.97	12.37	0.08	1.74	10.81	0.83	13	212.9	1	99	0	0	324	12.34	-11.29		1.00	Aug-03
	3.94	11.49	2.47	23.59	18.18	1.18	0.74	10.84	0.83	13.19	212.9	1	99	0	0	324	12.89	-10.9			Oct-09
50	5.99	25.04	14.04	60.91	81.25	0	1.39	12.86	1.04	21.22	60.4	8	92	0	0	54	25.45	-14.29	5.75		Oct-13
50	5.80	24.56	13.18	57.34	74.58	0	2.14	12.84	1.04	20.23	60.4	8	92	0	0	54	24.9	-14.56		1.00	Oct-13
50	5.98	25.07	14.08	60.92	81.36	0	1.14	12.84	1.04	21.25	60.4	8	92	0	0	54	25.63	-14.2			Oct-13
50	6.03	25.25	14.46	62.76	84.80	0	0.99	12.86	1.04	21.77	60.4	8	92	0	0	54	25.63	-14.2			Dec-10
100	9.21	24.29	11.09	46.95	37.25	0	1.42	11.62	0.87	10.09	58.4	3	97	0	0		16.34	-25.57	5.75		Jan-96
	9.31	24.46	11.35	47.89	38.82	0.29	1.2	11.6	0.87	10.29	58.4	3	97	0	0		16.58	-25.52			Jan-95
	9.32	24.44	11.44	48.20	39.26	0.34	1.1	11.58	0.87	10.31	58.4	3	97	0	0		16.58	-25.52			Sep-15
100	5.39	24.42	11.70	60.12	66.77	0	1.23	14.64	1.08	5.38	109.6	1	99	0	0		29.58	-16.87	5.75		Jun-92
100	5.60	23.66	10.88	57.00	61.30	0	1.9	14.52	1.07	1.61	109.6	1	99	0	0		29.08	-17.12		1.00	Jun-95
	5.40	24.37	11.94	61.41	68.65	0	0.97	14.76	1.09	7.89	109.6	1	99	0	0		29.79	-16.73			Jul-92
	5.49	24.45	12.13	62.18	69.94	0	0.9	14.69	1.08	7.97	109.6	1	99	0	0		29.58	-16.87			Aug-14
100	6.74	32.85	12.53	55.35	49.24	0	1.28	17.13	0.95	7.38	31.0	4	96	0	0		29.13	-25.63	5.75		Dec-99
100	6.58	32.05	11.62	52.15	44.05	0	1.94	17.06	0.94	2.04	31.0	4	96	0	0		28.58	-25.85		1.00	Oct-98
	6.80	32.92	12.59	55.89	49.98	0	1.16	17.12	0.95	9.67	31.0	4	96	0	0		29.3	-25.51			Oct-98
100	4.44	19.83	6.82	35.44	26.37	1.37	1.1	10.24	0.41	9.69	602.1	1	61	37	0		18.02	-12.03	5.75		Sep-40
100	4.15	19.37	5.84	32.31	21.57	0.54	1.86	10.22	0.41	9.97	602.1	1	61	37	0		17.5	-12.38		1.00	Aug-99
	4.41	19.86	6.86	35.48	26.41		0.85	10.24	0.41	9.68	602.1	1	61	37	0		18.02	-12.03			Jan-19
100	3.08	14.80	5.27	23.36	16.31	0.55	1.58	13.45	0.89	11.01	6,960	3	97	0	0	38	19.92	-12.73	5.75		Aug-99
100	3.00	14.40	4.55	20.81	12.18	0	2.25	13.44	0.89	10.64	6,960	3	97	0	0	38	19.28	-13.02		1.00	Jun-06
	3.16	14.91	5.65	24.58	18.04	0.92	1.23	13.45	0.89	11.4	6,960	3	97	0	0	38	20.07	-12.66			Oct-97
	3.35	15.13	5.85	25.16	18.74	1	0.98	13.5	0.9	11.41	6,960	3	97	0	0	38	20.07	-12.66			Nov-14
100	6.26	19.34	5.49	31.02	28.56	0.34	1.39	11.57	0.92	30.17	1,088	4	96	0	0	39	19.61	-14.03	5.75		Jul-90
100	6.07	18.94	4.76	28.28	24.01	0	2.05	11.55	0.92	29.32	1,088	4	96	0	0	39	19.13	-14.32		1.00	Oct-03
	6.31	19.51	5.79	32.13	30.33	0.8	1.07	11.58	0.92	30.13	1,088	4	96	0	0	39	19.8	-13.92			May-06
	6.35	19.61	5.89	32.54	30.80	0.93	0.95	11.56	0.92	30.13	1,088	4	96	0	0	39	19.61	-14.03			Nov-14
100	6.30	18.00	9.71	45.76	58.30	0.02	1.36	10.73	0.86	16.19	306.5	3	97	0	0	38	21.61	-9.08	5.75		May-60
100	6.15	17.65	8.94	42.67	52.60	0	2.11	10.7	0.85	13.46	306.5	3	97	0	0	38	21.22	-9.41		1.00	Dec-98
	6.43	18.32	10.15	47.08	60.47	0.2	1.09	10.72	0.86	16.21	306.5	3	97	0	0	38	21.61	-9.08			Aug-12
	6.43	18.30	10.23	46.70	59.32	0.26	0.9	10.7	0.85	16.22	306.5	3	97	0	0	38	21.61	-9.08			Jan-18
100	6.38	18.07	1.88	17.64	13.57	0.92	1.45	11.73	0.87	11.5	4.9	4	96	0	0	22	20.4	-15.41	5.75		Apr-09

	MARKET			FUND TYPE, CATEGORY & OBJECTIVE	RATINGS				MINIMUMS	
Fund Name	Ticker Symbol	Traded On	Fund Type	Category and (Prospectus Objective)	Overall Rating	Reward Rating	Risk Rating	Recent Up/ Downgrade	Open to New Investors	Min Initial Investment
Virtus Vontobel Greater European Opportunities Cls C	VGECX	NAS CM	Open End	Europe Equity Large Cap (Europe Stock)	C	D+	C+	Up	Y	2,500
Virtus Vontobel Greater European Opportunities Cls I	VGEIX	NAS CM	Open End	Europe Equity Large Cap (Europe Stock)	C	C-	B-	Up	Y	100,000
Virtus Zevenbergen Innovative Growth Stock Fund Class A	SAGAX	NAS CM	Open End	US Equity Large Cap Growth (Aggr Growth)	B-	C+	B-	Up	Y	2,500
Virtus Zevenbergen Innovative Growth Stock Fund Class I	SCATX	NAS CM	Open End	US Equity Large Cap Growth (Aggr Growth)	B-	C+	B-	Up	Y	100,000
Vivaldi Merger Arbitrage Fund Class A	VARAX	NAS CM	Open End	Market Neutral (Growth)	C	C	B-	Down	Y	1,000
Vivaldi Merger Arbitrage Fund Class I	VARBX	NAS CM	Open End	Market Neutral (Growth)	C+	C	B-	Down	Y	500,000
Vivaldi Multi-Strategy Fund Class A	OMOAX	NAS CM	Open End	Multialternative (Growth)	B-	C	B	Up	Y	5,000
Vivaldi Multi-Strategy Fund Class I	OMOIX	NAS CM	Open End	Multialternative (Growth)	B-	C	B+		Y	100,000
Vivaldi Opportunities Fund	VAM	NYSE	Closed End	(Growth & Income)	D	D+	D+		Y	
Volumetric Fund	VOLMX	NAS CM	Open End	US Equity Large Cap Blend (Growth)	C+	C	B	Up	Y	500
Vontobel U.S. Equity Institutional Fund Class I	VTUIX	NAS CM	Open End	US Equity Large Cap Growth (Growth)	D	C-	B-		Y	1,000,000
Voya Asia Pacific High Dividend Equity Income Fund	IAE	NYSE	Closed End	Asia ex-Japan Equity (Pacific Stock)	C-	C-	C-		Y	
Voya Australia Index Portfolio Class I	IAIIX	NAS CM	Open End	Equity Miscellaneous (Pacific Stock)	C+	C	B	Up	Y	0
Voya Balanced Income Portfolio Class A	IIFAX	NAS CM	Open End	Moderate Alloc (Income)	B	B-	A		Y	0
Voya Balanced Income Portfolio Class I	IIFIX	NAS CM	Open End	Moderate Alloc (Income)	B	B-	A		Y	0
Voya Balanced Income Portfolio Class S	IIFSX	NAS CM	Open End	Moderate Alloc (Income)	B	B-	A		Y	0
Voya Balanced Income Portfolio Class S2	IIFTX	NAS CM	Open End	Moderate Alloc (Income)	B	B-	A		Y	0
Voya Balanced Portfolio Class I	IBPIX	NAS CM	Open End	Moderate Alloc (Balanced)	B-	C	A-	Up	Y	0
Voya Balanced Portfolio Class S	IBPSX	NAS CM	Open End	Moderate Alloc (Balanced)	B-	C	A-	Up	Y	0
Voya CBRE Global Infrastructure Fund Class A	VCRAX	NAS CM	Open End	Infrastructure Sector Equity (Growth & Income)	B	B	B		Y	1,000
Voya CBRE Global Infrastructure Fund Class C	VCRCX	NAS CM	Open End	Infrastructure Sector Equity (Growth & Income)	B-	B-	B	Down	Y	1,000
Voya CBRE Global Infrastructure Fund Class I	VCRIX	NAS CM	Open End	Infrastructure Sector Equity (Growth & Income)	B	B	B		Y	250,000
Voya CBRE Global Infrastructure Fund Class W	VCGWX	NAS CM	Open End	Infrastructure Sector Equity (Growth & Income)	B	B	B		Y	1,000
Voya Corporate Leaders 100 Fund Class A	IACLX	NAS CM	Open End	US Equity Large Cap Blend (Growth)	B-	C	B		Y	1,000
Voya Corporate Leaders 100 Fund Class C	ICCLX	NAS CM	Open End	US Equity Large Cap Blend (Growth)	B-	C	B		Y	1,000
Voya Corporate Leaders 100 Fund Class I	IICLX	NAS CM	Open End	US Equity Large Cap Blend (Growth)	B-	C	B		Y	250,000
Voya Corporate Leaders 100 Fund Class O	IOCLX	NAS CM	Open End	US Equity Large Cap Blend (Growth)	B-	C	B		Y	1,000
Voya Corporate Leaders 100 Fund Class P3	VCLPX	NAS CM	Open End	US Equity Large Cap Blend (Growth)	B-	C	B		Y	0
Voya Corporate Leaders 100 Fund Class R	IRCLX	NAS CM	Open End	US Equity Large Cap Blend (Growth)	B-	C	B		Y	0
Voya Corporate Leaders 100 Fund Class R6	VCLRX	NAS CM	Open End	US Equity Large Cap Blend (Growth)	B-	C	B		Y	1,000,000
Voya Corporate Leaders 100 Fund Class W	IWCLX	NAS CM	Open End	US Equity Large Cap Blend (Growth)	B-	C	B		Y	1,000
Voya Corporate Leaders Trust Fund Series B	LEXCX	NAS CM	Open End	US Equity Large Cap Value (Growth & Income)	B-	C	B	Down	Y	1,000
Voya Emerging Markets High Dividend Equity Fund	IHD	NYSE	Closed End	Global Emerg Mkts (Equity-Income)	C-	C-	C-	Down	Y	
Voya Emerging Markets Index Portfolio Class I	IEPIX	NAS CM	Open End	Global Emerg Mkts (Div Emerging Mkts)	C	C	C+		Y	0
Voya Emerging Markets Index Portfolio Class P2	VPEPX	NAS CM	Open End	Global Emerg Mkts (Div Emerging Mkts)	C	C	C+		Y	0
Voya Emerging Markets Index Portfolio Class S	IEPSX	NAS CM	Open End	Global Emerg Mkts (Div Emerging Mkts)	C	C	C+		Y	0
Voya Euro STOXX 50® Index Portfolio Class A	IDJAX	NAS CM	Open End	Europe Equity Large Cap (Europe Stock)	C	C	C+		Y	0
Voya Euro STOXX 50® Index Portfolio Class I	IDJIX	NAS CM	Open End	Europe Equity Large Cap (Europe Stock)	C	C	B-		Y	0
Voya FTSE 100 Index® Portfolio Class A	IAFPX	NAS CM	Open End	Equity Miscellaneous (Europe Stock)	C	C-	B-		Y	0
Voya FTSE 100 Index® Portfolio Class I	IIFPX	NAS CM	Open End	Equity Miscellaneous (Europe Stock)	C	C	B-		Y	0
Voya Global Advantage and Premium Opportunity Fund	IGA	NYSE	Closed End	Global Equity Large Cap (World Stock)	C	C	C-		Y	
Voya Global Corporate Leaders® 100 Fund Class A	VGDAX	NAS CM	Open End	Global Equity Large Cap (Growth)	C+	C	B	Up	Y	1,000
Voya Global Corporate Leaders® 100 Fund Class I	VGDIX	NAS CM	Open End	Global Equity Large Cap (Growth)	C+	C	B	Up	Y	250,000
Voya Global Diversified Payment Fund Class A	IGPAX	NAS CM	Open End	Moderate Alloc (Growth & Income)	B-	C	B+	Up	Y	1,000
Voya Global Diversified Payment Fund Class C	IGPCX	NAS CM	Open End	Moderate Alloc (Growth & Income)	B-	C	B+	Up	Y	1,000
Voya Global Diversified Payment Fund Class I	IGPIX	NAS CM	Open End	Moderate Alloc (Growth & Income)	B-	C	B+	Up	Y	250,000
Voya Global Diversified Payment Fund Class R	IGPRX	NAS CM	Open End	Moderate Alloc (Growth & Income)	B-	C	B+	Up	Y	0
Voya Global Diversified Payment Fund Class R6	VTPRX	NAS CM	Open End	Moderate Alloc (Growth & Income)	B-	C	B+	Up	Y	1,000,000
Voya Global Diversified Payment Fund Class W	IGPWX	NAS CM	Open End	Moderate Alloc (Growth & Income)	B-	C	B+	Up	Y	1,000
Voya Global Equity Dividend and Premium Opportunity Fund	IGD	NYSE	Closed End	Global Equity Large Cap (World Stock)	C	C	C+		Y	
Voya Global Equity Dividend Fund Class A	IAGEX	NAS CM	Open End	Global Equity Large Cap (Equity-Income)	C+	C	B	Up	Y	1,000
Voya Global Equity Dividend Fund Class C	ICGEX	NAS CM	Open End	Global Equity Large Cap (Equity-Income)	C+	C	B	Up	Y	1,000

★Expanded analysis of this fund is included in Section II.

	TOTAL RETURNS					PERFORMANCE				ASSETS		ASSET ALLOCATION & TURNOVER					BULL & BEAR		FEES		
Min Additional Investment	3-Month Total Return	6-Month Total Return	1-Year Total Return	3-Year Total Return	5-Year Total Return	Dividend Yield (TTM)	Expense Ratio	3-Yr Std Deviation	3-Year Beta	NAV	Total Assets (MIL)	%Cash	%Stocks	%Bonds	%Other	Turnover Ratio	Last Bull Market Total Return	Last Bear Market Total Return	Front End Fee (%)	Back End Fee (%)	Inception Date
100	6.26	17.66	1.15	15.06	9.49	0	2.2	11.74	0.87	11.19	4.9	4	96	0	0	22	19.93	-15.7		1.00	Apr-09
	6.48	18.31	2.17	18.51	15.10	1.24	1.2	11.78	0.87	11.5	4.9	4	96	0	0	22	20.56	-15.3			Apr-09
100	9.08	38.24	21.78	122.49	105.50	0	1.26	20.56	1.35	28.45	222.4	1	99	0	0		23.82	-26.21	5.75		Feb-04
	9.15	38.39	22.03	123.85	107.55	0	1.01	20.55	1.35	30.28	222.4	1	99	0	0		24.14	-26.11			Feb-04
50	0.46	1.51	5.01	5.85	21.34	0.93	2.5	3.22	0.09	10.7	640.0	63	32	0	5	670	1.79	0.69	5.75		Oct-15
0	0.55	1.59	5.27	6.82	23.11	1.21	2.21	3.27	0.08	10.8	640.0	63	32	0	5	670	1.94	0.79			Oct-15
	1.44	8.13	6.41	6.44	14.79	1.21	3.17	3.88	10.49	26.72	45.4	21	25	36	15	275			5.00		Apr-12
	1.53	8.28	6.77	7.45	16.60	1.82	2.87	3.88	10.48	27.18	45.4	21	25	36	15	275					Apr-12
	1.75	7.90	4.46			8.47	4.26			14.23	80.1	-6	21	57	25	282					May-18
200	3.94	15.30	2.89	30.14	30.31	0	1.9	10.84	0.86	21.09	34.5	7	93	0	0	71	13.88	-16.65			Jan-79
	7.45	20.54	15.48			0.61	0.66			11.97	14.9	4	96	0	0	21					Mar-18
	-2.68	5.00	0.48	26.73	7.29	4.45	1.3	11.38		10.04	119.5	2	98	0	0	38	22.26	-24.97			Mar-07
	6.57	19.22	5.35	34.99	9.35	4.42	0.5	11.49	0.96	8.73	100.8	0	100	0	0	13	22	-26.47			Mar-11
	3.81	14.28	7.79	29.08	22.30	4.92	1.2	6.69		11.44	396.1	1	48	48	0	45	12.43	-11.2			Dec-06
	4.07	14.61	8.43	31.43	25.83	5.25	0.6	6.74		12	396.1	1	48	48	0	45	12.92	-10.98			Apr-06
	4.01	14.50	8.16	30.43	24.50	5	0.85	6.72		11.92	396.1	1	48	48	0	45	12.77	-11.07			Apr-06
	3.93	14.43	8.02	29.88	23.54	4.79	1	6.74		11.89	396.1	1	48	48	0	45	12.69	-11.18			May-06
	2.92	12.53	5.26	26.65	27.62	2.39	0.76	7.78	1.09	14.77	372.4	-3	44	59	0	184	15.37	-12.96			Apr-89
	2.85	12.36	4.98	25.73	26.07	2.13	1.01	7.78	1.09	14.7	372.4	-3	44	59	0	184	15.17	-13.03			May-03
	4.54	20.90	14.68	31.42	37.79	1.76	1.35	10.27	1.1	11.62	188.0	2	98	0	0	61			5.75		Oct-13
	4.37	20.53	13.79	28.71	33.02		2.1	10.23	1.09	11.6	188.0	2	98	0	0	61				1.00	Feb-19
	4.62	21.15	14.94	32.62	39.81	1.97	1.1	10.24	1.09	11.63	188.0	2	98	0	0	61					Jun-13
	4.53	21.04	14.84	32.50	39.69		1.1	10.22	1.09	11.62	188.0	2	98	0	0	61					Feb-19
	3.45	17.31	8.73	41.48	49.36	1.62	0.81	12.43	1.01	21.55	824.8	0	100	0	0	14	25.09	-16.52	5.75		Jun-08
	3.33	16.94	8.17	39.17	45.34	1.05	1.4	12.41	1.01	21.4	824.8	0	100	0	0	14	24.68	-16.82		1.00	Jun-08
	3.50	17.41	9.04	42.82	51.79	1.88	0.49	12.43	1.01	21.57	824.8	0	100	0	0	14	25.04	-16.41			Jun-08
	3.44	17.26	8.74	41.36	49.08	0	0.9	12.42	1.01	21.94	824.8	0	100	0	0	14	24.89	-16.5			Mar-12
	3.70	17.74	9.70	43.68	52.70	1.38	0	12.42	1.01	21.83	824.8	0	100	0	0	14	25.04	-16.41			Jun-18
	3.38	17.12	8.45	40.22	47.19	1.28	1.15	12.42	1.01	21.41	824.8	0	100	0	0	14	24.73	-16.59			Mar-12
	3.55	17.47	9.11	42.85	51.91	1.89	0.48	12.44	1.01	21.58	824.8	0	100	0	0	14	25.04	-16.41			Oct-14
	3.49	17.39	8.98	42.53	51.26	1.79	0.56	12.44	1.01	21.6	824.8	0	100	0	0	14	25.21	-16.4			Jun-08
50	2.28	16.73	10.32	40.62	41.55	1.84	0.59	13.17	0.96	40.19	815.8	0	100	0	0	0	24.85	-16.36			Nov-35
	-2.37	4.94	4.08	29.93	-1.73	2.83	1.45	11.33	0.78	8.5	161.8	3	97	0	0	53	15.03	-22.49			Apr-11
	0.54	10.66	0.88	34.11	10.05	2.42	0.54	14.12	1.01	11.47	678.5	0	100	0	0	12					Dec-11
	0.71	10.86	1.31	35.23	10.97	2.4	0.15	14.1	1.01	11.58	678.5	0	100	0	0	12					May-17
	0.52	10.59	0.69	33.88	9.36	2.15	0.79	14.16	1.02	11.55	678.5	0	100	0	0	12					Dec-11
	6.99	18.04	2.20	34.06	-0.25	1.86	0.94	14.44	0.99	10.51	373.2	0	99	0	0	11	7.41	-33.53			Aug-09
	7.00	18.30	2.66	35.95	2.29	2.47	0.44	14.46	0.99	10.57	373.2	0	99	0	0	11	7.71	-33.43			Aug-09
	0.52	12.67	-2.78	22.08	-4.79	3.78	0.93	11.51	0.97	8.24	227.0	-1	101	0	0	9	19.48	-20.94			Aug-09
	0.63	12.92	-2.32	23.96	-2.46	4.33	0.43	11.52	0.97	8.3	227.0	-1	101	0	0	9	19.81	-20.79			Aug-09
	1.52	12.18	4.62	35.25	33.50	4.56	0	8.74		11.53	211.1	4	96	0	0	70	17.32	-13.78			Oct-05
	3.77	15.88	6.89			2.26	0.92			11.82	4.2	0	99	0	0	22			5.75		Dec-16
	3.85	16.06	7.30			2.53	0.57			11.85	4.2	0	99	0	0	22					Dec-16
	2.95	10.54	3.86	18.41	17.91	3.37	1.24	6.33	1.24	7.75	443.9	2	58	37	2	80	13.76	-13.97	5.75		Jul-08
	2.70	10.06	3.11	15.69	13.58	2.69	1.99	6.24	1.22	8.02	443.9	2	58	37	2	80	13.31	-14.22		1.00	Aug-08
	2.91	10.50	4.06	19.41	19.60	3.69	0.95	6.26	1.22	7.71	443.9	2	58	37	2	80	14.1	-13.89			Jul-08
	3.00	10.48	3.80	17.79	16.78	3.07	1.49	6.24	1.22	7.76	443.9	2	58	37	2	80	13.61	-14.06			Aug-11
	2.91	10.49	4.06	19.41	19.60	3.69	0.99	6.25	1.22	7.71	443.9	2	58	37	2	80	14.1	-13.89			Feb-18
	2.92	10.52	4.07	19.31	19.46	3.7	0.99	6.25	1.22	7.69	443.9	2	58	37	2	80	13.98	-13.91			Jul-08
	2.66	10.48	2.65	23.60	13.03	4.2	1	8.79	0.72	6.99	678.6	4	96	0	0	39	8.99	-12.81			Mar-05
	3.80	14.53	4.34	29.84	15.39	2.23	0.86	10.67	0.91	13.85	60.8	4	95	0	0	33	15.53	-16.92	5.75		Sep-03
	3.55	14.04	3.58	26.85	11.14	1.39	1.61	10.64	0.9	13.76	60.8	4	95	0	0	33	14.99	-17.09		1.00	Oct-03

Fund Name	MARKET Ticker Symbol	Traded On	FUND TYPE, CATEGORY & OBJECTIVE Fund Type	Category and (Prospectus Objective)	RATINGS Overall Rating	Reward Rating	Risk Rating	Recent Up/ Downgrade	Open to New Investors	MINIMUMS Min Initial Investment
Voya Global Equity Dividend Fund Class I	IGEIX	NAS CM	Open End	Global Equity Large Cap (Equity-Income)	C+	C	B	Up	Y	250,000
Voya Global Equity Dividend Fund Class O	IDGEX	NAS CM	Open End	Global Equity Large Cap (Equity-Income)	C+	C	B	Up	Y	1,000
Voya Global Equity Dividend Fund Class W	IGEWX	NAS CM	Open End	Global Equity Large Cap (Equity-Income)	B-	C	B	Up	Y	1,000
Voya Global Equity Fund Class A	NAWGX	NAS CM	Open End	Global Equity Large Cap (World Stock)	B-	C	B	Up	Y	1,000
Voya Global Equity Fund Class C	NAWCX	NAS CM	Open End	Global Equity Large Cap (World Stock)	B-	C	B	Up	Y	1,000
Voya Global Equity Fund Class I	NAWIX	NAS CM	Open End	Global Equity Large Cap (World Stock)	B-	C	B+	Up	Y	250,000
Voya Global Equity Fund Class W	IGVWX	NAS CM	Open End	Global Equity Large Cap (World Stock)	B-	C	B+	Up	Y	1,000
Voya Global Equity Portfolio Class A	IGHAX	NAS CM	Open End	Global Equity Large Cap (Equity-Income)	B-	C	B	Up	Y	0
Voya Global Equity Portfolio Class I	IIGZX	NAS CM	Open End	Global Equity Large Cap (Equity-Income)	B-	C	B+	Up	Y	0
Voya Global Equity Portfolio Class S	IGHSX	NAS CM	Open End	Global Equity Large Cap (Equity-Income)	B-	C	B	Up	Y	0
Voya Global Equity Portfolio Class S2	IWTTX	NAS CM	Open End	Global Equity Large Cap (Equity-Income)	B-	C	B	Up	Y	0
Voya Global Equity Portfolio Class T	VGVTX	NAS CM	Open End	Global Equity Large Cap (Equity-Income)	B-	C	B	Up	Y	0
Voya Global Multi-Asset Fund Class A	ATLAX	NAS CM	Open End	Moderate Alloc (Asset Alloc)	B-	C	B+	Up	Y	1,000
Voya Global Multi-Asset Fund Class C	ACLGX	NAS CM	Open End	Moderate Alloc (Asset Alloc)	C+	C	B+	Up	Y	1,000
Voya Global Multi-Asset Fund Class I	ALEGX	NAS CM	Open End	Moderate Alloc (Asset Alloc)	B-	C	B+	Up	Y	250,000
Voya Global Multi-Asset Fund Class O	IDSIX	NAS CM	Open End	Moderate Alloc (Asset Alloc)	B-	C	B+	Up	Y	1,000
Voya Global Multi-Asset Fund Class W	IAFWX	NAS CM	Open End	Moderate Alloc (Asset Alloc)	B-	C	B+	Up	Y	1,000
Voya Global Multi-Asset Fund R6	VGMRX	NAS CM	Open End	Moderate Alloc (Asset Alloc)	C+	C	B+	Up	Y	1,000,000
Voya Global Perspectives Fund Class A	IAPVX	NAS CM	Open End	Cautious Alloc (Growth & Income)	B-	C	A-	Up	Y	1,000
Voya Global Perspectives Fund Class C	ICPVX	NAS CM	Open End	Cautious Alloc (Growth & Income)	B-	C	B+	Up	Y	1,000
Voya Global Perspectives Fund Class I	IIPVX	NAS CM	Open End	Cautious Alloc (Growth & Income)	B-	C	A-	Up	Y	250,000
Voya Global Perspectives Fund Class R	IRPVX	NAS CM	Open End	Cautious Alloc (Growth & Income)	B-	C	A-	Up	Y	0
Voya Global Perspectives Fund Class W	IWPVX	NAS CM	Open End	Cautious Alloc (Growth & Income)	B-	C	A-	Up	Y	1,000
Voya Global Perspectives Portfolio Class A	IPARX	NAS CM	Open End	Cautious Alloc (Growth & Income)	B-	C	A-	Up	Y	0
Voya Global Perspectives Portfolio Class I	IPIRX	NAS CM	Open End	Cautious Alloc (Growth & Income)	B-	C	A-	Up	Y	0
Voya Global Perspectives Portfolio Class S	IPSRX	NAS CM	Open End	Cautious Alloc (Growth & Income)	B-	C	A-	Up	Y	0
Voya Global Real Estate Fund Class A	IGLAX	NAS CM	Open End	Real Estate Sector Equity (Real Estate)	C+	C	B		Y	1,000
Voya Global Real Estate Fund Class C	IGCAX	NAS CM	Open End	Real Estate Sector Equity (Real Estate)	C+	C	B-		Y	1,000
Voya Global Real Estate Fund Class I	IGLIX	NAS CM	Open End	Real Estate Sector Equity (Real Estate)	C+	C	B		Y	250,000
Voya Global Real Estate Fund Class O	IDGTX	NAS CM	Open End	Real Estate Sector Equity (Real Estate)	C+	C	B		Y	1,000
Voya Global Real Estate Fund Class P3	VGRPX	NAS CM	Open End	Real Estate Sector Equity (Real Estate)	C-	C-	C	Down	Y	0
Voya Global Real Estate Fund Class R	IGARX	NAS CM	Open End	Real Estate Sector Equity (Real Estate)	C+	C	B		Y	0
Voya Global Real Estate Fund Class R6	VGRQX	NAS CM	Open End	Real Estate Sector Equity (Real Estate)	C+	C	B		Y	1,000,000
Voya Global Real Estate Fund Class W	IRGWX	NAS CM	Open End	Real Estate Sector Equity (Real Estate)	C+	C	B		Y	1,000
Voya Growth and Income Portfolio Class A	IAVGX	NAS CM	Open End	US Equity Large Cap Blend (Growth & Income)	B-	C+	B		Y	0
Voya Growth and Income Portfolio Class I	IIVGX	NAS CM	Open End	US Equity Large Cap Blend (Growth & Income)	B-	C+	B	Down	Y	0
Voya Growth and Income Portfolio Class S	ISVGX	NAS CM	Open End	US Equity Large Cap Blend (Growth & Income)	B-	C+	B		Y	0
Voya Growth and Income Portfolio Class S2	IGISX	NAS CM	Open End	US Equity Large Cap Blend (Growth & Income)	B-	C+	B		Y	0
Voya Hang Seng Index Portfolio Class A	IHSPX	NAS CM	Open End	Greater China Equity (Pacific Stock)	C	C	B-		Y	0
Voya Hang Seng Index Portfolio Class I	IHPIX	NAS CM	Open End	Greater China Equity (Pacific Stock)	C	C	B-		Y	0
Voya Hang Seng Index Portfolio Class S	IHPSX	NAS CM	Open End	Greater China Equity (Pacific Stock)	C	C	B-		Y	0
Voya Index Plus LargeCap Portfolio Class ADV	VIPAX	NAS CM	Open End	US Equity Large Cap Blend (Growth)	B-	C	B		Y	0
Voya Index Plus LargeCap Portfolio Class I	IPLIX	NAS CM	Open End	US Equity Large Cap Blend (Growth)	B-	C	B		Y	0
Voya Index Plus LargeCap Portfolio Class S	IPLSX	NAS CM	Open End	US Equity Large Cap Blend (Growth)	B-	C	B		Y	0
Voya Index Plus MidCap Portfolio Class I	IPMIX	NAS CM	Open End	US Equity Mid Cap (Growth)	C	C	B-		Y	0
Voya Index Plus MidCap Portfolio Class S	IPMSX	NAS CM	Open End	US Equity Mid Cap (Growth)	C	C	B-		Y	0
Voya Index Plus SmallCap Portfolio Class I	IPSIX	NAS CM	Open End	US Equity Small Cap (Small Company)	C-	C-	C	Down	Y	0
Voya Index Plus SmallCap Portfolio Class S	IPSSX	NAS CM	Open End	US Equity Small Cap (Small Company)	C-	C-	C	Down	Y	0
Voya Index Solution 2020 Portfolio Class ADV	IDXAX	NAS CM	Open End	Target Date (Asset Alloc)	B	C	A-	Up	Y	0
Voya Index Solution 2020 Portfolio Class I	IDXBX	NAS CM	Open End	Target Date (Asset Alloc)	B	C+	A	Up	Y	0
Voya Index Solution 2020 Portfolio Class S	IDXCX	NAS CM	Open End	Target Date (Asset Alloc)	B	C+	A-	Up	Y	0
Voya Index Solution 2020 Portfolio Class S2	IDXDX	NAS CM	Open End	Target Date (Asset Alloc)	B	C	A-	Up	Y	0

★ Expanded analysis of this fund is included in Section II.

Min Additional Investment	TOTAL RETURNS: 3-Month Total Return	6-Month Total Return	1-Year Total Return	3-Year Total Return	5-Year Total Return	PERFORMANCE: Dividend Yield (TTM)	Expense Ratio	3-Yr Std Deviation	3-Year Beta	ASSETS: NAV	Total Assets (MIL)	ASSET ALLOCATION & TURNOVER: %Cash	%Stocks	%Bonds	%Other	Turnover Ratio	BULL & BEAR: Last Bull Market Total Return	Last Bear Market Total Return	FEES: Front End Fee (%)	Back End Fee (%)	Inception Date
	3.83	14.59	4.62	30.77	16.79	2.49	0.61	10.67	0.9	13.87	60.8	4	95	0	0	33	15.52	-16.65			Aug-07
	3.80	14.56	4.25	29.69	15.30	1.91	0.86	10.67	0.91	13.86	60.8	4	95	0	0	33	15.43	-16.86			Nov-06
	3.88	14.64	4.66	30.83	16.89	2.23	0.61	10.67	0.9	15.54	60.8	4	95	0	0	33	15.41	-16.71			Feb-08
	2.85	14.87	5.54	37.46	21.38	3.11	0.85	10.52	0.91	36.15	245.5	0	100	0	0	140	-1.89	-15.06	5.75		Apr-93
	2.64	14.44	4.74	34.37	16.90	2.26	1.6	10.51	0.91	33.63	245.5	0	100	0	0	140	-2.31	-15.32		1.00	Apr-93
	2.90	15.02	5.78	38.45	22.88	3.43	0.6	10.52	0.91	36.48	245.5	0	100	0	0	140	-1.72	-14.93			Sep-06
	2.93	15.02	5.81	38.51	22.94	3.43	0.6	10.51	0.91	36.46	245.5	0	100	0	0	140	-1.76	-14.93			Jun-09
	2.84	14.78	5.34	36.41	28.23	2.75	1.11	10.47	0.9	10.37	590.7	0	100	0	0	147	11.89	-19.88			Jan-08
	2.97	15.04	5.76	38.43	31.14	3.84	0.61	10.45	0.9	10.37	590.7	0	100	0	0	147	12.09	-19.75			Mar-15
	2.89	14.91	5.53	37.39	29.75	3.28	0.86	10.43	0.9	10.41	590.7	0	100	0	0	147	12.09	-19.75			Jan-08
	2.79	14.72	5.37	36.71	28.70	2.94	1.01	10.46	0.9	10.27	590.7	0	100	0	0	147	11.99	-19.8			Mar-15
	2.73	14.59	5.14	35.81	27.26	2.57	1.21	10.43	0.9	10.32	590.7	0	100	0	0	147	11.76	-19.92			Mar-15
	3.18	12.39	3.19	25.40	21.61	2.14	1.15	8.28	1.17	11.66	141.4	2	66	31	1	78	14.4	-13.12	5.75		Jan-97
	3.06	11.93	2.44	22.63	17.12	1.19	1.9	8.25	1.17	11.76	141.4	2	66	31	1	78	13.93	-13.39		1.00	Jun-98
	3.22	12.50	3.43	26.30	23.10	2.21	0.9	8.29	1.17	11.86	141.4	2	66	31	1	78	14.66	-13.05			Jan-95
	3.02	12.25	2.90	25.01	21.25	1.97	1.15	8.23	1.16	11.57	141.4	2	66	31	1	78	14.5	-13.18			Nov-06
	3.31	12.53	3.53	26.40	23.18	2.23	0.9	8.21	1.16	11.85	141.4	2	66	31	1	78	14.64	-13.05			Aug-11
	4.01	12.96	3.22	25.27	22.09	1.03	0.9	8.25	1.16	11.91	141.4	2	66	31	1	78	14.66	-13.05			Sep-17
	2.75	12.60	4.48	21.07	20.60	2.78	1.23	7.5	1.05	11.19	58.3	4	59	37	0	23			5.75		Mar-13
	2.50	12.15	3.66	18.43	16.19	2.07	1.98	7.46	1.04	11.04	58.3	4	59	37	0	23				1.00	Mar-13
	2.74	12.70	4.70	21.95	22.06	3.05	0.98	7.47	1.04	11.21	58.3	4	59	37	0	23					Mar-13
	2.67	12.47	4.14	20.20	19.06	2.57	1.48	7.43	1.04	11.14	58.3	4	59	37	0	23					Mar-13
	2.74	12.68	4.68	21.96	22.11	3.04	0.98	7.42	1.04	11.23	58.3	4	59	37	0	23					Mar-13
	2.87	12.79	4.92	21.18	20.87	2.49	1.09	7.36	1.03	11.46	107.5	5	59	37	0	16					May-13
	2.93	12.98	5.24	22.47	22.77	2.81	0.83	7.41	1.04	11.57	107.5	5	59	37	0	16					May-13
	2.86	12.88	5.03	21.39	21.14	2.61	1.08	7.42	1.04	11.48	107.5	5	59	37	0	16					May-13
	0.86	16.51	7.97	10.49	16.20	2.29	1.26	11.18	0.99	15.72	502.1	0	99	0	1	107	22.07	-18.48	5.75		Nov-01
	0.67	16.12	7.16	8.06	11.95	2.16	2.01	11.15	0.99	12.51	502.1	0	99	0	1	107	21.6	-18.76		1.00	Jan-02
	0.98	16.75	8.30	11.46	17.90	2.5	1.01	11.17	0.99	15.71	502.1	0	99	0	1	107	22.3	-18.4			Jun-05
	0.86	16.60	7.90	10.45	16.16	1.82	1.26	11.18	0.99	15.78	502.1	0	99	0	1	107	22.07	-18.48			Nov-06
	-4.98	-4.17	-2.55	0.43	10.64		0	10.76	1.01		1,196	1	99	0	0	83	22.07	-18.48			Jun-18
	0.81	16.39	7.68	9.66	14.77	2.08	1.51	11.18	0.99	15.63	502.1	0	99	0	1	107	21.91	-18.6			Aug-11
	0.93	16.73	8.30	11.82	18.52	2.6	0.92	11.19	0.99	15.7	502.1	0	99	0	1	107	22.07	-18.48			Jul-14
	0.91	16.71	8.24	11.36	17.70	2.51	1.01	11.16	0.99	15.75	502.1	0	99	0	1	107	22.26	-18.44			Feb-08
	5.21	18.40	10.62	43.61	48.19	1.32	1.03	10.42	0.84	27.65	3,134	2	98	0	0	84	26.8	-18.17			Dec-06
	5.35	18.69	11.10	45.59	51.55	1.75	0.58	10.43	0.85	28.17	3,134	2	98	0	0	84	27.07	-17.98			Dec-79
	5.28	18.56	10.83	44.48	49.68	1.52	0.83	10.42	0.84	27.7	3,134	2	98	0	0	84	26.95	-18.09			Jun-03
	5.24	18.46	10.67	43.87	48.56	1.43	0.98	10.4	0.84	27.31	3,134	2	98	0	0	84	26.94	-18.18			Feb-09
	0.05	13.72	2.13	47.29	36.73	3.16	1.05	15.36	0.98	11.47	44.9	0	100	0	0	6	21.9	-26.23			May-09
	0.20	14.04	2.62	49.44	40.14	3.76	0.55	15.39	0.99	11.5	44.9	0	100	0	0	6	22.32	-26.11			May-09
	0.02	13.87	2.30	48.27	38.35	3.47	0.8	15.37	0.99	11.49	44.9	0	100	0	0	6	22.1	-26.17			May-09
	4.48	19.35	9.16	48.10	58.47		0.99	12.42	1.01	25.92	890.2	-1	101	0	0	72	23.94	-17.72			Aug-18
	4.60	19.64	9.71	50.34	62.48	1.53	0.49	12.42	1.01	26.22	890.2	-1	101	0	0	72	24.3	-17.55			Sep-96
	4.56	19.51	9.47	49.24	60.50	1.34	0.74	12.42	1.01	26	890.2	-1	101	0	0	72	24.15	-17.64			Jul-01
	2.48	19.12	-0.17	30.78	37.47	1.32	0.55	15.66	1.03	18.11	534.7	0	100	0	0	68	28.3	-22.34			Dec-97
	2.39	18.99	-0.41	29.79	35.74	1.05	0.8	15.68	1.03	17.8	534.7	0	100	0	0	68	28.07	-22.43			Jul-01
	1.35	13.53	-7.61	31.96	38.13	1.01	0.55	18.3	1.02	19.37	249.5	-1	101	0	0	67	27.02	-22.97			Dec-97
	1.29	13.35	-7.81	30.92	36.40	0.73	0.8	18.33	1.02	19.12	249.5	-1	101	0	0	67	26.87	-23.03			Jul-01
	2.99	10.26	5.84	21.24	24.81	1.09	0.89	5.47	0.91	13.43	366.8	-4	46	58	0	44					Oct-11
	3.13	10.55	6.44	23.21	27.59	1.39	0.39	5.45	0.9	13.82	366.8	-4	46	58	0	44					Oct-11
	3.07	10.44	6.16	22.29	26.21	1.19	0.64	5.45	0.9	13.75	366.8	-4	46	58	0	44					Oct-11
	3.09	10.42	6.04	21.71	25.27	0.98	0.79	5.44	0.9	13.67	366.8	-4	46	58	0	44					Oct-11

	MARKET		FUND TYPE, CATEGORY & OBJECTIVE		RATINGS					MINIMUMS
Fund Name	Ticker Symbol	Traded On	Fund Type	Category and (Prospectus Objective)	Overall Rating	Reward Rating	Risk Rating	Recent Up/ Downgrade	Open to New Investors	Min Initial Investment
Voya Index Solution 2020 Portfolio Class Z	VSZAX	NAS CM	Open End	Target Date (Asset Alloc)	B	C+	A	Up	Y	0
Voya Index Solution 2025 Portfolio Class ADV	ISDAX	NAS CM	Open End	Target Date (Asset Alloc)	B	C	A-	Up	Y	0
Voya Index Solution 2025 Portfolio Class I	ISDIX	NAS CM	Open End	Target Date (Asset Alloc)	B	C	A-	Up	Y	0
Voya Index Solution 2025 Portfolio Class S	ISDSX	NAS CM	Open End	Target Date (Asset Alloc)	B	C	A-	Up	Y	0
Voya Index Solution 2025 Portfolio Class S2	IXXVX	NAS CM	Open End	Target Date (Asset Alloc)	B	C	A-	Up	Y	0
Voya Index Solution 2025 Portfolio Class Z	VSZBX	NAS CM	Open End	Target Date (Asset Alloc)	B	C	A-	Up	Y	0
Voya Index Solution 2030 Portfolio Class ADV	IDXFX	NAS CM	Open End	Target Date (Asset Alloc)	B-	C	B+	Up	Y	0
Voya Index Solution 2030 Portfolio Class I	IDXGX	NAS CM	Open End	Target Date (Asset Alloc)	B-	C	A-	Up	Y	0
Voya Index Solution 2030 Portfolio Class S	IDXHX	NAS CM	Open End	Target Date (Asset Alloc)	B-	C	B+	Up	Y	0
Voya Index Solution 2030 Portfolio Class S2	IDXIX	NAS CM	Open End	Target Date (Asset Alloc)	B-	C	B+	Up	Y	0
Voya Index Solution 2030 Portfolio Class Z	VSZCX	NAS CM	Open End	Target Date (Asset Alloc)	B-	C	A-	Up	Y	0
Voya Index Solution 2035 Portfolio Class ADV	ISEAX	NAS CM	Open End	Target Date (Asset Alloc)	B-	C	B+	Up	Y	0
Voya Index Solution 2035 Portfolio Class I	ISEIX	NAS CM	Open End	Target Date (Asset Alloc)	B-	C	B+	Up	Y	0
Voya Index Solution 2035 Portfolio Class S	ISESX	NAS CM	Open End	Target Date (Asset Alloc)	B-	C	B+	Up	Y	0
Voya Index Solution 2035 Portfolio Class S2	IXISX	NAS CM	Open End	Target Date (Asset Alloc)	B-	C	B+	Up	Y	0
Voya Index Solution 2035 Portfolio Class Z	VSZDX	NAS CM	Open End	Target Date (Asset Alloc)	B-	C	B+	Up	Y	0
Voya Index Solution 2040 Portfolio Class ADV	IDXKX	NAS CM	Open End	Target Date (Asset Alloc)	B-	C	B+	Up	Y	0
Voya Index Solution 2040 Portfolio Class I	IDXLX	NAS CM	Open End	Target Date (Asset Alloc)	B-	C	B+	Up	Y	0
Voya Index Solution 2040 Portfolio Class S	IDXMX	NAS CM	Open End	Target Date (Asset Alloc)	B-	C	B+	Up	Y	0
Voya Index Solution 2040 Portfolio Class S2	IDXNX	NAS CM	Open End	Target Date (Asset Alloc)	B-	C	B+	Up	Y	0
Voya Index Solution 2040 Portfolio Class Z	VSZEX	NAS CM	Open End	Target Date (Asset Alloc)	B-	C	B+	Up	Y	0
Voya Index Solution 2045 Portfolio Class ADV	ISJAX	NAS CM	Open End	Target Date (Asset Alloc)	B-	C	B	Up	Y	0
Voya Index Solution 2045 Portfolio Class I	ISJIX	NAS CM	Open End	Target Date (Asset Alloc)	B-	C	B	Up	Y	0
Voya Index Solution 2045 Portfolio Class S	ISJSX	NAS CM	Open End	Target Date (Asset Alloc)	B-	C	B	Up	Y	0
Voya Index Solution 2045 Portfolio Class S2	ISVLX	NAS CM	Open End	Target Date (Asset Alloc)	B-	C	B	Up	Y	0
Voya Index Solution 2045 Portfolio Class Z	VSZFX	NAS CM	Open End	Target Date (Asset Alloc)	B-	C	B	Up	Y	0
Voya Index Solution 2050 Portfolio Class ADV	IDXPX	NAS CM	Open End	Target Date (Asset Alloc)	B-	C	B	Up	Y	0
Voya Index Solution 2050 Portfolio Class I	IDXQX	NAS CM	Open End	Target Date (Asset Alloc)	B-	C	B	Up	Y	0
Voya Index Solution 2050 Portfolio Class S	IDXRX	NAS CM	Open End	Target Date (Asset Alloc)	B-	C	B	Up	Y	0
Voya Index Solution 2050 Portfolio Class S2	IDXSX	NAS CM	Open End	Target Date (Asset Alloc)	B-	C	B	Up	Y	0
Voya Index Solution 2050 Portfolio Class Z	VSZGX	NAS CM	Open End	Target Date (Asset Alloc)	B-	C	B	Up	Y	0
Voya Index Solution 2055 Portfolio Class ADV	IISAX	NAS CM	Open End	Target Date (Asset Alloc)	B-	C	B	Up	Y	0
Voya Index Solution 2055 Portfolio Class I	IISNX	NAS CM	Open End	Target Date (Asset Alloc)	B-	C	B	Up	Y	0
Voya Index Solution 2055 Portfolio Class S	IISSX	NAS CM	Open End	Target Date (Asset Alloc)	B-	C	B	Up	Y	0
Voya Index Solution 2055 Portfolio Class S2	IISTX	NAS CM	Open End	Target Date (Asset Alloc)	B-	C	B	Up	Y	0
Voya Index Solution 2055 Portfolio Class Z	VSZHX	NAS CM	Open End	Target Date (Asset Alloc)	B-	C	B	Up	Y	0
Voya Index Solution 2060 Portfolio Class ADV	VPSAX	NAS CM	Open End	Target Date (Asset Alloc)	B-	C	B	Up	Y	0
Voya Index Solution 2060 Portfolio Class I	VISPX	NAS CM	Open End	Target Date (Asset Alloc)	B-	C	B	Up	Y	0
Voya Index Solution 2060 Portfolio Class S	VPISX	NAS CM	Open End	Target Date (Asset Alloc)	B-	C	B	Up	Y	0
Voya Index Solution 2060 Portfolio Class S2	VPSSX	NAS CM	Open End	Target Date (Asset Alloc)	B-	C	B	Up	Y	0
Voya Index Solution 2060 Portfolio Class Z	VSZIX	NAS CM	Open End	Target Date (Asset Alloc)	B-	C	B	Up	Y	0
Voya Index Solution Income Portfolio Class ADV	ISKAX	NAS CM	Open End	Target Date (Asset Alloc)	B-	C	B+		Y	0
Voya Index Solution Income Portfolio Class I	ISKIX	NAS CM	Open End	Target Date (Asset Alloc)	B	C+	A-	Up	Y	0
Voya Index Solution Income Portfolio Class S	ISKSX	NAS CM	Open End	Target Date (Asset Alloc)	B-	C	A-		Y	0
Voya Index Solution Income Portfolio Class S2	IIIPX	NAS CM	Open End	Target Date (Asset Alloc)	B-	C	B+		Y	0
Voya Index Solution Income Portfolio Class Z	VSZJX	NAS CM	Open End	Target Date (Asset Alloc)	B	C+	A-	Up	Y	0
Voya Infrastructure Industrials and Materials Fund	IDE	NYSE	Closed End	Industrials Sector Equity (Growth)	C-	C	C-	Down	Y	
Voya International High Dividend Equity Income Fund	IID	NYSE	Closed End	Global Equity Large Cap (Foreign Stock)	C-	C	C-		Y	
Voya International High Dividend Low Volatility Cls A	VGLAX	NAS CM	Open End	Global Equity Large Cap (Growth & Income)	C-	D+	C		Y	1,000
Voya International High Dividend Low Volatility Cls I	VGLIX	NAS CM	Open End	Global Equity Large Cap (Growth & Income)	C-	D+	C		Y	250,000
Voya International High Dividend Low Volatility Cls P3	VHDZX	NAS CM	Open End	Global Equity Large Cap (Growth & Income)	C-	D+	C		Y	0
Voya Intl High Dividend Low Volatility Portfolio Cls A	IFTAX	NAS CM	Open End	Global Equity Large Cap (Foreign Stock)	C	C-	C+		Y	0

★ Expanded analysis of this fund is included in Section II.

	TOTAL RETURNS					PERFORMANCE				ASSETS		ASSET ALLOCATION & TURNOVER					BULL & BEAR		FEES		
Min Additional Investment	3-Month Total Return	6-Month Total Return	1-Year Total Return	3-Year Total Return	5-Year Total Return	Dividend Yield (TTM)	Expense Ratio	3-Yr Std Deviation	3-Year Beta	NAV	Total Assets (MIL)	%Cash	%Stocks	%Bonds	%Other	Turnover Ratio	Last Bull Market Total Return	Last Bear Market Total Return	Front End Fee (%)	Back End Fee (%)	Inception Date
	3.26	10.73	6.63	23.85	28.57	1.38	0.19	5.47	0.91	13.93	366.8	-4	46	58	0	44					May-15
	3.05	11.75	5.81	25.78	26.26	1.2	0.89	6.92	0.98	11.12	1,005	3	53	43	0	35	15.28	-14.02			Mar-08
	3.25	12.05	6.38	27.60	29.48	1.65	0.39	6.87	0.98	11.43	1,005	3	53	43	0	35	15.65	-13.86			Mar-08
	3.19	11.99	6.16	26.71	27.97	1.4	0.64	6.9	0.98	11.3	1,005	3	53	43	0	35	15.53	-13.95			Mar-08
	3.06	11.79	5.93	26.14	26.85	1.21	0.79	6.87	0.98	11.09	1,005	3	53	43	0	35	15.34	-14			May-09
	3.31	12.26	6.72	28.41	30.53	1.63	0.19	6.94	0.99	11.53	1,005	3	53	43	0	35	15.65	-13.86			May-15
	3.24	13.31	5.85	29.32	30.29	0.93	0.89	8.18	1	15.57	523.4	3	66	31	0	33					Oct-11
	3.35	13.59	6.40	31.22	33.39	1.18	0.39	8.23	1.01	16.04	523.4	3	66	31	0	33					Oct-11
	3.31	13.48	6.10	30.33	31.82	0.99	0.64	8.2	1.01	15.91	523.4	3	66	31	0	33					Oct-11
	3.35	13.41	6.02	29.79	30.62	0.75	0.79	8.22	1.01	15.73	523.4	3	66	31	0	33					Oct-11
	3.39	13.67	6.57	31.94	34.12	1.18	0.19	8.19	1.01	16.13	523.4	3	66	31	0	33					May-15
	3.22	14.28	5.64	32.23	31.19	1.06	0.89	9.18	1	11.52	948.2	3	74	23	0	33	18.72	-17.4			Mar-08
	3.48	14.67	6.28	34.33	34.69	1.51	0.39	9.23	1.01	11.88	948.2	3	74	23	0	33	19.05	-17.22			Mar-08
	3.35	14.45	5.97	33.30	32.93	1.26	0.64	9.24	1.01	11.72	948.2	3	74	23	0	33	18.95	-17.4			Mar-08
	3.31	14.39	5.78	32.74	32.02	1.1	0.79	9.18	1	11.52	948.2	3	74	23	0	33	18.85	-17.37			May-09
	3.54	14.73	6.50	35.08	35.81	1.49	0.19	9.22	1.01	11.99	948.2	3	74	23	0	33	19.05	-17.22			May-15
	3.35	15.07	5.53	33.66	32.62	0.77	0.89	9.82	1	16.34	383.9	2	80	17	0	30					Oct-11
	3.45	15.31	6.04	35.59	35.73	0.99	0.39	9.79	1	16.79	383.9	2	80	17	0	30					Oct-11
	3.39	15.13	5.78	34.61	34.18	0.8	0.64	9.83	1.01	16.74	383.9	2	80	17	0	30					Oct-11
	3.38	15.06	5.58	34.08	33.11	0.74	0.79	9.81	1	16.5	383.9	2	80	17	0	30					Oct-11
	3.54	15.41	6.32	36.40	36.66	0.98	0.18	9.85	1.01	16.92	383.9	2	80	17	0	30					May-15
	3.37	15.69	5.37	34.62	32.86	0.91	0.89	10.38	1.03	11.94	653.7	2	86	11	0	31	19.99	-19.25			Mar-08
	3.51	16.02	5.86	36.73	36.21	1.34	0.39	10.4	1.03	12.38	653.7	2	86	11	0	31	20.25	-19.04			Mar-08
	3.48	15.88	5.58	35.64	34.51	1.1	0.64	10.4	1.03	12.18	653.7	2	86	11	0	31	20.18	-19.22			Mar-08
	3.36	15.76	5.46	34.99	33.51	0.92	0.79	10.37	1.02	11.97	653.7	2	86	11	0	31	20.11	-19.26			May-09
	3.56	16.18	6.16	37.47	37.21	1.33	0.17	10.43	1.03	12.49	653.7	2	86	11	0	31	20.25	-19.04			May-15
	3.43	15.94	5.39	34.89	33.30	0.66	0.89	10.57	1.02	16.58	258.0	2	88	9	0	28					Oct-11
	3.60	16.23	5.90	36.91	36.83	0.87	0.39	10.54	1.02	16.97	258.0	2	88	9	0	28					Oct-11
	3.49	16.07	5.66	35.93	35.28	0.69	0.64	10.58	1.02	16.9	258.0	2	88	9	0	28					Oct-11
	3.54	16.01	5.53	35.28	34.08	0.63	0.79	10.57	1.02	16.66	258.0	2	88	9	0	28					Oct-11
	3.64	16.34	6.18	37.70	37.82	0.86	0.17	10.55	1.02	17.08	258.0	2	88	9	0	28					May-15
	3.41	15.90	5.32	35.06	33.19	0.76	0.89	10.6	1.01	15.45	289.5	2	88	9	0	29	19.93	-19.21			Mar-10
	3.52	16.16	5.83	37.15	36.65	1.15	0.39	10.61	1.02	15.88	289.5	2	88	9	0	29	20.3	-19.09			Mar-10
	3.43	15.98	5.59	36.03	34.87	0.94	0.64	10.64	1.02	15.67	289.5	2	88	9	0	29	20.06	-19.17			Mar-10
	3.46	15.96	5.43	35.57	33.93	0.76	0.79	10.6	1.01	15.54	289.5	2	88	9	0	29	19.91	-19.2			Mar-10
	3.62	16.33	6.12	37.97	37.68	1.14	0.17	10.61	1.02	16.02	289.5	2	88	9	0	29	20.3	-19.09			May-15
	3.33	15.88	5.34	35.35		0.53	0.89	10.65	1.01	12.69	77.7	2	88	10	0	40					Feb-15
	3.52	16.27	5.93	37.38		0.76	0.39	10.64	1.01	12.93	77.7	2	88	10	0	40					Feb-15
	3.47	16.04	5.66	36.33		0.62	0.64	10.63	1.01	12.8	77.7	2	88	10	0	40					Feb-15
	3.40	15.90	5.43	35.60		0.39	0.79	10.6	1	12.75	77.7	2	88	10	0	40					Feb-15
	3.57	16.35	6.07	38.22		0.75	0.17	10.65	1.01	13.02	77.7	2	88	10	0	40					May-15
	2.84	8.72	5.71	15.05	18.55	1.62	0.89	4.16	1.02	10.47	469.7	-7	32	75	0	38	8.65	-4.56			Mar-08
	2.86	8.89	6.16	16.72	21.51	2.13	0.39	4.16	1.02	10.77	469.7	-7	32	75	0	38	9.13	-4.5			Mar-08
	2.79	8.78	5.93	15.90	20.01	1.89	0.64	4.14	1.01	10.65	469.7	-7	32	75	0	38	8.89	-4.52			Mar-08
	2.76	8.66	5.77	15.40	19.14	1.75	0.79	4.16	1.02	10.41	469.7	-7	32	75	0	38	8.79	-4.6			May-09
	2.93	9.03	6.42	17.41	22.48	2.12	0.18	4.15	1.02	10.86	469.7	-7	32	75	0	38	9.13	-4.5			May-15
	0.35	11.04	0.99	29.27	11.81	3.55		10.86		13.57	261.6	0	100	0	0	78	25.53	-27.88			Jan-10
	0.59	9.82	0.37	23.12	0.27	5.31	1.15	10.08	0.74	6.03	50.8	2	97	0	1	83	18.4	-23.54			Sep-07
	1.36	9.69	-0.30			3.12	0.9			9.69	9.4	1	99	0	0	129			5.75		Dec-16
	1.47	9.86	0.00			3.4	0.65			9.7	9.4	1	99	0	0	129					Dec-16
	1.62	10.03	0.14				0			9.72	9.4	1	99	0	0	129					Feb-19
	2.83	10.51	-3.05	23.40	-1.00	1.72	1.2	11.05	0.95	11.98	486.4	2	96	0	0	16	13.43	-25.08			Dec-06

	MARKET			FUND TYPE, CATEGORY & OBJECTIVE	RATINGS				MINIMUMS	
Fund Name	Ticker Symbol	Traded On	Fund Type	Category and (Prospectus Objective)	Overall Rating	Reward Rating	Risk Rating	Recent Up/ Downgrade	Open to New Investors	Min Initial Investment
Voya Intl High Dividend Low Volatility Portfolio Cls I	IFTIX	NAS CM	Open End	Global Equity Large Cap (Foreign Stock)	C	C-	C+		Y	0
Voya Intl High Dividend Low Volatility Portfolio Cls S	IFTSX	NAS CM	Open End	Global Equity Large Cap (Foreign Stock)	C	C-	C+		Y	0
Voya Intl High Dividend Low Volatility Portfolio Cls S2	ITFEX	NAS CM	Open End	Global Equity Large Cap (Foreign Stock)	C	C-	C+		Y	0
Voya International Index Portfolio Class A	IIIAX	NAS CM	Open End	Global Equity Large Cap (Foreign Stock)	C	C	B		Y	0
Voya International Index Portfolio Class I	IIIIX	NAS CM	Open End	Global Equity Large Cap (Foreign Stock)	C	C	B		Y	0
Voya International Index Portfolio Class P2	VIPPX	NAS CM	Open End	Global Equity Large Cap (Foreign Stock)	C	C	B		Y	0
Voya International Index Portfolio Class S	INTIX	NAS CM	Open End	Global Equity Large Cap (Foreign Stock)	C	C	B		Y	0
Voya International Index Portfolio Class S2	ISIIX	NAS CM	Open End	Global Equity Large Cap (Foreign Stock)	C	C	B		Y	0
Voya International Real Estate Fund Class A	IIRAX	NAS CM	Open End	Real Estate Sector Equity (Real Estate)	B-	C	B	Up	Y	1,000
Voya International Real Estate Fund Class C	IIRCX	NAS CM	Open End	Real Estate Sector Equity (Real Estate)	C+	C	B	Up	Y	1,000
Voya International Real Estate Fund Class I	IIRIX	NAS CM	Open End	Real Estate Sector Equity (Real Estate)	B-	C	B	Up	Y	250,000
Voya International Real Estate Fund Class W	IIRWX	NAS CM	Open End	Real Estate Sector Equity (Real Estate)	B-	C	B	Up	Y	1,000
Voya Japan TOPIX Index® Portfolio Class A	IJIAX	NAS CM	Open End	Japan Equity (Pacific Stock)	C	C-	C		Y	0
Voya Japan TOPIX Index® Portfolio Class I	IJIIX	NAS CM	Open End	Japan Equity (Pacific Stock)	C	C	C		Y	0
Voya Large Cap Growth Portfolio Class A	IEOPX	NAS CM	Open End	US Equity Large Cap Growth (Growth)	B-	C+	B	Down	Y	0
Voya Large Cap Growth Portfolio Class I	IEOHX	NAS CM	Open End	US Equity Large Cap Growth (Growth)	B-	C+	B	Down	Y	0
Voya Large Cap Growth Portfolio Class R6	VRLCX	NAS CM	Open End	US Equity Large Cap Growth (Growth)	B-	C+	B	Down	Y	0
Voya Large Cap Growth Portfolio Class S	IEOSX	NAS CM	Open End	US Equity Large Cap Growth (Growth)	B-	C+	B	Down	Y	0
Voya Large Cap Growth Portfolio Class S2	IEOTX	NAS CM	Open End	US Equity Large Cap Growth (Growth)	B-	C+	B	Down	Y	0
Voya Large Cap Value Fund Class A	IEDAX	NAS CM	Open End	US Equity Large Cap Value (Equity-Income)	B-	C	B	Up	Y	1,000
Voya Large Cap Value Fund Class C	IEDCX	NAS CM	Open End	US Equity Large Cap Value (Equity-Income)	B-	C	B	Up	Y	1,000
Voya Large Cap Value Fund Class I	IEDIX	NAS CM	Open End	US Equity Large Cap Value (Equity-Income)	B-	C	B	Up	Y	250,000
Voya Large Cap Value Fund Class O	ILVOX	NAS CM	Open End	US Equity Large Cap Value (Equity-Income)	B-	C	B	Up	Y	1,000
Voya Large Cap Value Fund Class R	IEDRX	NAS CM	Open End	US Equity Large Cap Value (Equity-Income)	B-	C	B	Up	Y	0
Voya Large Cap Value Fund Class R6	IEDZX	NAS CM	Open End	US Equity Large Cap Value (Equity-Income)	B-	C	B	Up	Y	1,000,000
Voya Large Cap Value Fund Class W	IWEDX	NAS CM	Open End	US Equity Large Cap Value (Equity-Income)	B-	C	B	Up	Y	1,000
Voya Large Cap Value Fund ClassP3	VLVPX	NAS CM	Open End	US Equity Large Cap Value (Equity-Income)	B-	C	B	Up	Y	0
Voya Large Cap Value Portfolio Class A	IPEAX	NAS CM	Open End	US Equity Large Cap Value (Equity-Income)	B-	C	B	Up	Y	0
Voya Large Cap Value Portfolio Class I	IPEIX	NAS CM	Open End	US Equity Large Cap Value (Equity-Income)	B-	C	B	Up	Y	0
Voya Large Cap Value Portfolio Class S	IPESX	NAS CM	Open End	US Equity Large Cap Value (Equity-Income)	B-	C	B	Up	Y	0
Voya Large Cap Value Portfolio Class S2	IPETX	NAS CM	Open End	US Equity Large Cap Value (Equity-Income)	B-	C	B	Up	Y	0
Voya Large Cap Value Portfolio R6	VLCRX	NAS CM	Open End	US Equity Large Cap Value (Equity-Income)	B-	C	B	Up	Y	0
Voya Large-Cap Growth Fund Class A	NLCAX	NAS CM	Open End	US Equity Large Cap Growth (Growth)	B-	C+	B	Down	Y	1,000
Voya Large-Cap Growth Fund Class C	NLCCX	NAS CM	Open End	US Equity Large Cap Growth (Growth)	B-	C+	B	Down	Y	1,000
Voya Large-Cap Growth Fund Class I	PLCIX	NAS CM	Open End	US Equity Large Cap Growth (Growth)	B-	C+	B	Down	Y	250,000
Voya Large-Cap Growth Fund Class P3	VPLCX	NAS CM	Open End	US Equity Large Cap Growth (Growth)	B-	C+	B	Down	Y	0
Voya Large-Cap Growth Fund Class R	VGORX	NAS CM	Open End	US Equity Large Cap Growth (Growth)	B-	C+	B	Down	Y	0
Voya Large-Cap Growth Fund Class R6	VGOSX	NAS CM	Open End	US Equity Large Cap Growth (Growth)	B-	C+	B	Down	Y	1,000,000
Voya Large-Cap Growth Fund Class W	IGOWX	NAS CM	Open End	US Equity Large Cap Growth (Growth)	B-	C+	B	Down	Y	1,000
Voya Mid Cap Research Enhanced Index Fund Class A	AIMAX	NAS CM	Open End	US Equity Mid Cap (Growth & Income)	C	C	B-		Y	1,000
Voya Mid Cap Research Enhanced Index Fund Class C	APMCX	NAS CM	Open End	US Equity Mid Cap (Growth & Income)	C	C	B-		Y	1,000
Voya Mid Cap Research Enhanced Index Fund Class I	AIMIX	NAS CM	Open End	US Equity Mid Cap (Growth & Income)	C	C	B-		Y	250,000
Voya Mid Cap Research Enhanced Index Fund Class O	IDMOX	NAS CM	Open End	US Equity Mid Cap (Growth & Income)	C	C	B-		Y	1,000
Voya Mid Cap Research Enhanced Index Fund Class P3	VMRPX	NAS CM	Open End	US Equity Mid Cap (Growth & Income)	C	C	B-		Y	0
Voya Mid Cap Research Enhanced Index Fund Class R	AIMRX	NAS CM	Open End	US Equity Mid Cap (Growth & Income)	C	C	B-		Y	0
Voya Mid Cap Research Enhanced Index Fund Class W	AIMWX	NAS CM	Open End	US Equity Mid Cap (Growth & Income)	C	C	B-		Y	1,000
Voya MidCap Opportunities Fund Class A	NMCAX	NAS CM	Open End	US Equity Mid Cap (Growth)	C+	C	B		Y	1,000
Voya MidCap Opportunities Fund Class C	NMCCX	NAS CM	Open End	US Equity Mid Cap (Growth)	C+	C	B-		Y	1,000
Voya MidCap Opportunities Fund Class I	NMCIX	NAS CM	Open End	US Equity Mid Cap (Growth)	C+	C	B		Y	250,000
Voya MidCap Opportunities Fund Class O	NMCOX	NAS CM	Open End	US Equity Mid Cap (Growth)	C+	C	B		Y	1,000
Voya MidCap Opportunities Fund Class P3	VPMOX	NAS CM	Open End	US Equity Mid Cap (Growth)	C+	C	B	Down	Y	0
Voya MidCap Opportunities Fund Class R	IMORX	NAS CM	Open End	US Equity Mid Cap (Growth)	C+	C	B		Y	0

★ Expanded analysis of this fund is included in Section II.

	TOTAL RETURNS					PERFORMANCE				ASSETS		ASSET ALLOCATION & TURNOVER					BULL & BEAR		FEES		
Min Additional Investment	3-Month Total Return	6-Month Total Return	1-Year Total Return	3-Year Total Return	5-Year Total Return	Dividend Yield (TTM)	Expense Ratio	3-Yr Std Deviation	3-Year Beta	NAV	Total Assets (MIL)	%Cash	%Stocks	%Bonds	%Other	Turnover Ratio	Last Bull Market Total Return	Last Bear Market Total Return	Front End Fee (%)	Back End Fee (%)	Inception Date
	2.96	10.76	-2.59	25.23	1.45	2.22	0.7	11.06	0.95	12.14	486.4	2	96	0	0	16	13.79	-24.91			Jan-06
	2.90	10.65	-2.82	24.24	0.25	1.93	0.95	11.05	0.95	12.05	486.4	2	96	0	0	16	13.63	-25.02			Jan-06
	2.97	10.59	-2.90	23.79	-0.47	0.65	1.1	11.05	0.95	12.11	486.4	2	96	0	0	16	13.43	-24.99			Feb-09
	3.56	14.28	0.65	28.18	7.85	2.58	0.94	11.1	0.99	9.78	1,611	-1	101	0	0	3	13.03	-23.39			Mar-08
	3.66	14.38	1.01	30.04	10.48	3.09	0.45	11.18	1	9.96	1,611	-1	101	0	0	3	13.35	-23.28			Mar-08
	3.63	14.54	1.30	30.79	11.11	3.07	0.15	11.08	0.99	10.02	1,611	-1	101	0	0	3	13.35	-23.28			May-17
	3.62	14.30	0.85	29.12	9.07	2.85	0.7	11.1	0.99	9.9	1,611	-1	101	0	0	3	13.28	-23.38			Mar-08
	3.49	14.19	0.62	28.50	8.21	2.73	0.85	11.09	0.99	9.88	1,611	-1	101	0	0	3	12.94	-23.3			Feb-09
	1.25	15.12	6.33	21.37	15.34	3.82	1.27	11.55	1.03	8.65	75.6	1	98	0	1	118	15.5	-20.66	5.75		Feb-06
	1.17	14.90	5.60	18.71	11.10	2.92	2.02	11.5	1.03	8.61	75.6	1	98	0	1	118	15.01	-20.89		1.00	Feb-06
	1.34	15.33	6.51	22.34	16.89	4.32	1.02	11.55	1.03	8.64	75.6	1	98	0	1	118	15.67	-20.57			Feb-06
	1.34	15.39	6.51	22.37	16.79	4.33	1.02	11.5	1.03	8.68	75.6	1	98	0	1	118	15.68	-20.62			Feb-08
	-0.17	7.13	-6.63	21.40	22.30	1.75	0.94	11.26	1.01	9.34	234.5	-1	101	0	0	5	3.19	-7			Aug-09
	-0.05	7.37	-6.18	23.24	25.44	2.41	0.44	11.23	1.01	9.42	234.5	-1	101	0	0	5	3.57	-6.86			Aug-09
	3.62	20.12	10.32	58.79	75.53	0.05	1.27	12.54	0.93	19.46	5,704	2	98	0	0	85	26.65	-14.51			Dec-06
	3.81	20.51	11.01	61.72	80.98	0.58	0.67	12.54	0.93	21.21	5,704	2	98	0	0	85	27.15	-14.35			May-05
	3.81	20.49	11.06	61.77	80.41	0.58	0.67	12.57	0.93	21.22	5,704	2	98	0	0	85	26.91	-14.37			Nov-15
	3.72	20.36	10.78	60.47	78.76	0.35	0.92	12.58	0.93	20.63	5,704	2	98	0	0	85	26.91	-14.37			May-04
	3.70	20.22	10.57	59.75	77.36	0.19	1.07	12.52	0.92	20.45	5,704	2	98	0	0	85	26.81	-14.48			May-04
	4.26	16.51	7.67	34.06	33.96	1.32	1.1	11.01	0.9	11.73	775.8	3	97	0	0	85	22.91	-15.74	5.75		Dec-07
	3.99	16.11	6.85	30.97	28.95	0.53	1.85	10.98	0.89	11.7	775.8	3	97	0	0	85	22.4	-15.97		1.00	Feb-08
	4.32	16.80	8.06	35.46	36.25	1.65	0.76	10.96	0.89	12.78	775.8	3	97	0	0	85	23.07	-15.56			Mar-10
	4.15	16.53	7.48	33.86	33.80	0.79	1.1	10.95	0.89	11.77	775.8	3	97	0	0	85	22.91	-15.74			Jan-13
	4.18	16.48	7.40	33.11	32.44	0.93	1.35	10.95	0.89	11.74	775.8	3	97	0	0	85	22.79	-15.81			Aug-11
	4.34	16.75	8.01	35.49	36.35	1.68	0.74	11	0.89	12.76	775.8	3	97	0	0	85	22.91	-15.74			May-13
	4.29	16.65	8.03	35.16	35.66	1.48	0.85	10.95	0.89	12.76	775.8	3	97	0	0	85	23.06	-15.6			Jun-09
	4.47	17.11	8.81	35.48	35.38	1.67	0	10.97	0.89	12.87	775.8	3	97	0	0	85	22.91	-15.74			Jun-18
	4.22	16.45	7.48	33.00	32.49	1.28	1.24	10.99	0.89	12.1	1,091	2	98	0	0	97	23.14	-15.8			May-07
	4.38	16.90	8.14	35.50	36.64	1.8	0.64	10.99	0.89	12.38	1,091	2	98	0	0	97	23.66	-15.62			May-07
	4.27	16.74	7.86	34.49	34.92	1.59	0.89	10.95	0.89	12.2	1,091	2	98	0	0	97	23.44	-15.72			May-07
	4.26	16.73	7.79	34.05	34.08	1.48	1.04	10.96	0.89	12.21	1,091	2	98	0	0	97	23.37	-15.76			Sep-13
	4.38	16.91	8.24	35.79	36.58	1.8	0.64	10.93	0.89	12.37	1,091	2	98	0	0	97	23.66	-15.62			Nov-15
	3.73	20.33	10.85	59.98	77.25	0.02	1.04	12.57	0.93	40.54	1,080	3	97	0	0	90	28.76	-14.56	5.75		Jul-97
	3.53	19.87	9.98	56.37	70.95	0	1.79	12.56	0.93	33.71	1,080	3	97	0	0	90	28.3	-14.82		1.00	Jul-97
	3.83	20.51	11.25	61.71	80.44	0.35	0.66	12.57	0.93	45.17	1,080	3	97	0	0	90	29.02	-14.44			Jan-02
	4.00	20.86	11.93	62.38	80.94	0.4	0	12.56	0.93	45.47	1,080	3	97	0	0	90	29.03	-14.45			Jun-18
	3.68	20.18	10.59	58.82	75.24	0	1.29	12.57	0.93	44.48	1,080	3	97	0	0	90	28.66	-14.62			May-14
	3.86	20.54	11.30	61.96	80.52	0.41	0.57	12.57	0.93	45.18	1,080	3	97	0	0	90	29.03	-14.45			Jun-15
	3.79	20.48	11.12	61.22	79.64	0.16	0.79	12.57	0.93	43.99	1,080	3	97	0	0	90	29.03	-14.45			Jul-97
	2.40	18.92	-0.43	29.28	27.10	0.85	0.95	15.64	1.03	15.33	131.1	0	100	0	0	83	27.67	-22.56	5.75		Feb-98
	2.24	18.60	-0.91	27.37	24.01	0.27	1.45	15.62	1.03	14.09	131.1	0	100	0	0	83	27.29	-22.69		1.00	Jun-98
	2.39	18.99	-0.20	30.18	28.71	0.87	0.7	15.64	1.03	15.85	131.1	0	100	0	0	83	27.84	-22.47			Feb-98
	2.36	18.86	-0.40	29.30	27.14	0	0.95	15.6	1.02	15.56	131.1	0	100	0	0	83	27.7	-22.57			Aug-01
	2.61	19.49	0.64	31.28	29.79	0.53	0	15.56	1.02	16.06	131.1	0	100	0	0	83	27.84	-22.47			Jun-18
	2.30	18.75	-0.74	28.32	25.56	0.51	1.2	15.65	1.03	15.07	131.1	0	100	0	0	83	27.49	-22.62			Oct-03
	2.47	19.04	-0.18	29.83	28.29	0.94	0.7	15.64	1.03	15.75	131.1	0	100	0	0	83	27.92	-22.47			Aug-11
	5.24	22.32	7.97	45.49	57.43	0	1.26	13.8	0.94	20.27	1,225	1	99	0	0	102	27.61	-19.96	5.75		Aug-98
	5.06	21.94	7.06	42.22	51.58	0	2.01	13.81	0.94	13.89	1,225	1	99	0	0	102	27.1	-20.24		1.00	Aug-98
	5.35	22.55	8.30	46.83	59.96	0	0.98	13.78	0.94	24.02	1,225	1	99	0	0	102	27.99	-19.82			Aug-98
	5.27	22.31	7.96	45.52	57.44	0	1.26	13.81	0.94	20.17	1,225	1	99	0	0	102	27.64	-19.96			Jun-08
	5.60	23.13	9.39	48.31	61.57	0	0	13.78	0.94	24.48	1,225	1	99	0	0	102	27.99	-19.82			Jun-18
	5.20	22.16	7.69	44.45	55.48	0	1.51	13.8	0.94	19.62	1,225	1	99	0	0	102	27.45	-19.99			Aug-11

Fund Name	MARKET Ticker Symbol	Traded On	FUND TYPE, CATEGORY & OBJECTIVE Fund Type	Category and (Prospectus Objective)	RATINGS Overall Rating	Reward Rating	Risk Rating	Recent Up/ Downgrade	MINIMUMS Open to New Investors	Min Initial Investment
Voya MidCap Opportunities Fund Class R6	IMOZX	NAS CM	Open End	US Equity Mid Cap (Growth)	C+	C	B		Y	1,000,000
Voya MidCap Opportunities Fund Class W	IMOWX	NAS CM	Open End	US Equity Mid Cap (Growth)	C+	C	B		Y	1,000
Voya MidCap Opportunities Portfolio Class A	IAMOX	NAS CM	Open End	US Equity Mid Cap (Growth)	C+	C	B		Y	0
Voya MidCap Opportunities Portfolio Class I	IIMOX	NAS CM	Open End	US Equity Mid Cap (Growth)	C+	C	B		Y	0
Voya MidCap Opportunities Portfolio Class S	ISMOX	NAS CM	Open End	US Equity Mid Cap (Growth)	C+	C	B		Y	0
Voya MidCap Opportunities Portfolio Class S2	IMOPX	NAS CM	Open End	US Equity Mid Cap (Growth)	C+	C	B		Y	0
Voya MidCap Opportunities Portfolio R6	VMCRX	NAS CM	Open End	US Equity Mid Cap (Growth)	C+	C	B		Y	0
Voya Multi-Manager Emerging Markets Equity Fund Class A	IEMHX	NAS CM	Open End	Global Emerg Mkts (Div Emerging Mkts)	C	C	C		Y	1,000
Voya Multi-Manager Emerging Markets Equity Fund Class C	IEMJX	NAS CM	Open End	Global Emerg Mkts (Div Emerging Mkts)	C	C	C		Y	1,000
Voya Multi-Manager Emerging Markets Equity Fund Class I	IEMGX	NAS CM	Open End	Global Emerg Mkts (Div Emerging Mkts)	C	C	C		Y	250,000
Voya Multi-Manager Emerging Markets Equity Fund Class P	VMEPX	NAS CM	Open End	Global Emerg Mkts (Div Emerging Mkts)	C	C	C		Y	0
Voya Multi-Manager Emerging Markets Equity Fund Class P3	VPMEX	NAS CM	Open End	Global Emerg Mkts (Div Emerging Mkts)	C	C	C+		Y	0
Voya Multi-Manager Emerging Markets Equity Fund Class R	IEMKX	NAS CM	Open End	Global Emerg Mkts (Div Emerging Mkts)	C	C	C		Y	0
Voya Multi-Manager Emerging Markets Equity Fund Class W	IEMLX	NAS CM	Open End	Global Emerg Mkts (Div Emerging Mkts)	C	C	C		Y	1,000
Voya Multi-Manager International Equity Fund Class I	IIGIX	NAS CM	Open End	Global Equity Large Cap (Foreign Stock)	C	C	B-		Y	250,000
Voya Multi-Manager International Equity Fund Class P	VIEPX	NAS CM	Open End	Global Equity Large Cap (Foreign Stock)	C	C	B-		Y	0
Voya Multi-Manager International Equity Fund Class P3	VMIPX	NAS CM	Open End	Global Equity Large Cap (Foreign Stock)	C	C	B-		Y	0
Voya Multi-Manager International Factors Fund Class I	IICFX	NAS CM	Open End	Global Equity Large Cap (Foreign Stock)	C	C	B-		Y	250,000
Voya Multi-Manager International Factors Fund Class P	VIFPX	NAS CM	Open End	Global Equity Large Cap (Foreign Stock)	C	C	B-		Y	0
Voya Multi-Manager International Factors Fund Class P3	VPMFX	NAS CM	Open End	Global Equity Large Cap (Foreign Stock)	C	C	B		Y	0
Voya Multi-Manager International Factors Fund Class W	IICWX	NAS CM	Open End	Global Equity Large Cap (Foreign Stock)	C	C	B-		Y	1,000
Voya Multi-Manager International Small Cap Fund Class A	NTKLX	NAS CM	Open End	Global Equity Mid/Small Cap (Small Company)	C	C-	C	Up	Y	1,000
Voya Multi-Manager International Small Cap Fund Class C	NARCX	NAS CM	Open End	Global Equity Mid/Small Cap (Small Company)	C	C-	C	Up	Y	1,000
Voya Multi-Manager International Small Cap Fund Class I	NAPIX	NAS CM	Open End	Global Equity Mid/Small Cap (Small Company)	C	C-	C	Up	Y	250,000
Voya Multi-Manager International Small Cap Fund Class O	NAPOX	NAS CM	Open End	Global Equity Mid/Small Cap (Small Company)	C	C-	C	Up	Y	1,000
Voya Multi-Manager International Small Cap Fund Class P3	VSCZX	NAS CM	Open End	Global Equity Mid/Small Cap (Small Company)	C	C-	C	Up	Y	0
Voya Multi-Manager International Small Cap Fund Class W	ISCWX	NAS CM	Open End	Global Equity Mid/Small Cap (Small Company)	C	C-	C	Up	Y	1,000
Voya Multi-Manager Mid Cap Value Fund Class I	IMCVX	NAS CM	Open End	US Equity Mid Cap (Growth)	C	C	B-		Y	250,000
Voya Multi-Manager Mid Cap Value Fund Class P	VMMCX	NAS CM	Open End	US Equity Mid Cap (Growth)	C	C	B-		Y	0
Voya Multi-Manager Mid Cap Value Fund P3	VMMPX	NAS CM	Open End	US Equity Mid Cap (Growth)	C	C	B-		Y	0
Voya Natural Resources Equity Income Fund	IRR	NYSE	Closed End	Energy Sector Equity (Natl Res)	D	D	D	Down	Y	
Voya Real Estate Fund Class A	CLARX	NAS CM	Open End	Real Estate Sector Equity (Real Estate)	C	C	C+	Down	Y	1,000
Voya Real Estate Fund Class C	CRCRX	NAS CM	Open End	Real Estate Sector Equity (Real Estate)	C	C	C+	Down	Y	1,000
Voya Real Estate Fund Class I	CRARX	NAS CM	Open End	Real Estate Sector Equity (Real Estate)	C	C	C+	Down	Y	250,000
Voya Real Estate Fund Class O	IDROX	NAS CM	Open End	Real Estate Sector Equity (Real Estate)	C	C	C+	Down	Y	1,000
Voya Real Estate Fund Class P3	VREPX	NAS CM	Open End	Real Estate Sector Equity (Real Estate)	C	C	C+	Down	Y	0
Voya Real Estate Fund Class R	CRWRX	NAS CM	Open End	Real Estate Sector Equity (Real Estate)	C	C	C+	Down	Y	0
Voya Real Estate Fund Class R6	VREQX	NAS CM	Open End	Real Estate Sector Equity (Real Estate)	C	C	C+	Down	Y	1,000,000
Voya Real Estate Fund Class W	IREWX	NAS CM	Open End	Real Estate Sector Equity (Real Estate)	C	C	C+	Down	Y	1,000
Voya Retirement Conservative Portfolio Class A	IRCAX	NAS CM	Open End	Cautious Alloc (Asset Alloc)	B-	C	B+		Y	0
Voya Retirement Conservative Portfolio Class I	IRCPX	NAS CM	Open End	Cautious Alloc (Asset Alloc)	B	C+	B+	Up	Y	0
Voya Retirement Growth Portfolio Class A	IRGPX	NAS CM	Open End	Aggressive Alloc (Asset Alloc)	B-	C	B+	Up	Y	0
Voya Retirement Growth Portfolio Class I	IIRGX	NAS CM	Open End	Aggressive Alloc (Asset Alloc)	B-	C	B+	Up	Y	0
Voya Retirement Moderate Growth Portfolio Class A	IRMGX	NAS CM	Open End	Moderate Alloc (Asset Alloc)	B-	C	A-	Up	Y	0
Voya Retirement Moderate Growth Portfolio Class I	IRGMX	NAS CM	Open End	Moderate Alloc (Asset Alloc)	B-	C	A-	Up	Y	0
Voya Retirement Moderate Portfolio Class A	IRMPX	NAS CM	Open End	Cautious Alloc (Asset Alloc)	B	C	A-	Up	Y	0
Voya Retirement Moderate Portfolio Class I	IRMIX	NAS CM	Open End	Cautious Alloc (Asset Alloc)	B	C	A-	Up	Y	0
Voya Russell Large Cap Growth Index Portfolio Class A	IRLAX	NAS CM	Open End	US Equity Large Cap Growth (Growth)	B-	C+	B		Y	0
Voya Russell Large Cap Growth Index Portfolio Class I	IRLNX	NAS CM	Open End	US Equity Large Cap Growth (Growth)	B-	C+	B		Y	0
Voya Russell Large Cap Growth Index Portfolio Class S	IRLSX	NAS CM	Open End	US Equity Large Cap Growth (Growth)	B-	C+	B		Y	0
Voya Russell Large Cap Index Portfolio Class A	IRLIX	NAS CM	Open End	US Equity Large Cap Blend (Growth & Income)	B-	C	B		Y	0
Voya Russell Large Cap Index Portfolio Class I	IIRLX	NAS CM	Open End	US Equity Large Cap Blend (Growth & Income)	B-	C	B		Y	0

★ Expanded analysis of this fund is included in Section II.

	TOTAL RETURNS					PERFORMANCE				ASSETS		ASSET ALLOCATION & TURNOVER					BULL & BEAR		FEES		
Min Additional Investment	3-Month Total Return	6-Month Total Return	1-Year Total Return	3-Year Total Return	5-Year Total Return	Dividend Yield (TTM)	Expense Ratio	3-Yr Std Deviation	3-Year Beta	NAV	Total Assets (MIL)	%Cash	%Stocks	%Bonds	%Other	Turnover Ratio	Last Bull Market Total Return	Last Bear Market Total Return	Front End Fee (%)	Back End Fee (%)	Inception Date
	5.34	22.55	8.44	47.29	60.80	0	0.87	13.8	0.94	24.23	1,225	1	99	0	0	102	27.99	-19.82			May-13
	5.31	22.48	8.26	46.67	59.48	0	1.01	13.79	0.94	23.59	1,225	1	99	0	0	102	27.78	-19.86			Jun-09
	5.26	22.39	8.00	45.55	57.48	0	1.16	13.77	0.94	13.39	1,972	3	97	0	0	102	27.63	-20.07			Dec-06
	5.45	22.63	8.50	47.74	61.51	0.08	0.66	13.8	0.94	14.74	1,972	3	97	0	0	102	27.99	-19.87			May-00
	5.41	22.51	8.25	46.63	59.54	0	0.91	13.8	0.94	13.82	1,972	3	97	0	0	102	27.77	-19.96			May-01
	5.24	22.42	8.02	45.84	58.26	0	1.06	13.79	0.94	13.65	1,972	3	97	0	0	102	27.7	-20.07			Feb-09
	5.45	22.63	8.50	47.74	61.39	0.08	0.66	13.81	0.94	14.74	1,972	3	97	0	0	102	27.99	-19.87			Nov-15
	2.10	14.94	0.57	38.40	7.52	0.51	1.58	15.28	1.08	12.15	411.2	1	99	0	0	53			5.75		Oct-11
	1.94	14.50	-0.16	35.46	3.58	0	2.33	15.3	1.08	12.08	411.2	1	99	0	0	53				1.00	Oct-11
	2.26	15.23	0.91	39.95	9.45	0.88	1.23	15.28	1.08	12.18	411.2	1	99	0	0	53					Oct-11
	2.51	15.61	1.24	40.41	9.81		0.15	15.28	1.08	12.22	411.2	1	99	0	0	53					Feb-19
	2.49	15.88	2.07	41.55	10.70	0.87	0	15.25	1.07	12.33	411.2	1	99	0	0	53					Jun-18
	2.09	14.81	0.33	37.42	6.12	0.37	1.83	15.29	1.08	12.17	411.2	1	99	0	0	53					Oct-11
	2.18	15.15	0.81	39.63	8.89	0.79	1.33	15.23	1.07	12.16	411.2	1	99	0	0	53					Oct-11
	3.64	16.15	-0.50	26.48	10.24	1.28	0.97	12.12	1.06	11.36	606.1	2	98	0	0	45	18.13	-22.86			Jan-11
	3.82	16.46	-0.23	26.81	10.53		0.15	12.11	1.06	11.39	606.1	2	98	0	0	45	18.13	-22.86			Feb-19
	3.89	16.66	0.51	27.77	11.36	1.26	0	12.07	1.06	11.48	606.1	2	98	0	0	45	18.13	-22.86			Jun-18
	1.49	11.52	-1.47	26.98	14.02	2.6	0.75	10.84	0.95	9.48	469.4	0	100	0	0	55	17.39	-24.26			Feb-11
	1.60	11.76	-1.26	27.25	14.26		0.15	10.89	0.95	9.5	469.4	0	100	0	0	55	17.39	-24.26			Feb-19
	1.70	11.94	-0.67	28.01	14.95	2.58	0	10.84	0.95	9.56	469.4	0	100	0	0	55	17.39	-24.26			Jun-18
	1.49	11.52	-1.47	26.99	14.01	2.6	0.75	10.85	0.95	9.48	469.4	0	100	0	0	55	17.39	-24.26			Aug-12
	2.01	14.20	-9.70	24.52	13.39	1.23	1.54	13.57	1.07	50.73	165.4	1	99	0	0	46	16.92	-24.72	5.75		Aug-94
	1.82	13.79	-10.37	21.94	9.63	0.45	2.29	13.57	1.07	46.78	165.4	1	99	0	0	46	16.5	-24.95		1.00	Aug-94
	2.10	14.42	-9.40	25.97	15.79	1.64	1.21	13.57	1.07	50.52	165.4	1	99	0	0	46	17.2	-24.6			Dec-05
	2.08	14.37	-9.53	24.97	14.03	0	1.54	13.57	1.07	50.85	165.4	1	99	0	0	46	16.99	-24.68			Jun-08
	2.42	14.80	-9.22	25.18	13.99		0	13.58	1.07	50.72	165.4	1	99	0	0	46	16.92	-24.72			Feb-19
	2.08	14.36	-9.45	25.70	15.29	1.23	1.29	13.57	1.07	62.27	165.4	1	99	0	0	46	17.15	-24.62			Feb-08
	2.67	18.66	-0.59	31.26	29.70	1.1	0.84	15.19	1.13	9.98	124.5	2	98	0	0	26					Oct-11
	2.88	18.90	-0.39	31.52	29.96		0.15	15.22	1.14	10	124.5	2	98	0	0	26					Feb-19
	2.85	19.28	0.31	32.46	30.88	1.09	0	15.24	1.14	10.08	124.5	2	98	0	0	26					Jun-18
	-3.07	9.82	-17.77	-7.07	-35.65	7.64	1.25	16.96	1.06	4.71	106.7	1	99	0	0	50	3.24	-12.61			Oct-06
	1.16	18.81	9.19	7.70	34.11	2.49	1.2	12.75	0.95	12.43	367.3	0	100	0	0	102	31.86	-15.95	5.75		Dec-02
	1.02	18.38	8.45	5.37	28.65	1.63	1.95	12.7	0.95	13.58	367.3	0	100	0	0	102	31.28	-16.17		1.00	Jan-03
	1.29	18.95	9.59	8.89	35.80	2.49	0.85	12.73	0.95	14.21	367.3	0	100	0	0	102	32.02	-15.78			Dec-96
	1.15	18.74	9.28	7.76	34.20	1.94	1.2	12.7	0.95	12.5	367.3	0	100	0	0	102	31.83	-15.92			Sep-04
	1.49	19.49	10.60	9.89	37.05	1.84	0	12.75	0.95	14.5	367.3	0	100	0	0	102	32.02	-15.78			Jun-18
	1.18	18.69	8.96	6.96	32.52	2.29	1.45	12.77	0.96	12.34	367.3	0	100	0	0	102	31.59	-15.97			Aug-11
	1.31	19.10	9.75	9.11	36.20	2.57	0.76	12.76	0.95	14.22	367.3	0	100	0	0	102	32.02	-15.78			Jul-14
	1.26	18.94	9.51	8.53	33.71	2	0.95	12.7	0.95	17.43	367.3	0	100	0	0	102	32.06	-15.85			Dec-07
	3.09	9.36	6.80	14.99	19.88	1.82	0.9	4	0.95	9.34	423.2	4	30	66	0	33	8.24	-2.83			Oct-07
	3.03	9.45	6.99	15.64	20.92	2.05	0.65	3.97	0.94	9.49	423.2	4	30	66	0	33	8.45	-2.61			Oct-07
	3.25	14.22	5.28	29.45	28.94	1.59	1.06	8.77	0.96	13.33	2,642	2	74	24	0	20	16.05	-14.6			Apr-06
	3.30	14.48	5.77	31.06	31.73	2.04	0.64	8.79	0.96	13.44	2,642	2	74	24	0	20	16.28	-14.42			Apr-06
	3.17	13.09	5.81	26.29	27.75	1.66	1.02	7.64	1.08	12.35	1,818	3	64	33	0	22	14.22	-12.02			Apr-06
	3.19	13.28	6.17	27.69	30.25	2.1	0.64	7.62	1.08	12.28	1,818	3	64	33	0	22	14.37	-11.87			Apr-06
	3.09	11.36	5.94	21.09	22.98	1.75	0.99	6	1.18	11.66	1,033	3	49	47	0	27	11.44	-8.23			Apr-06
	3.22	11.60	6.37	22.44	25.19	2.09	0.65	6.01	1.18	11.83	1,033	3	49	47	0	27	11.73	-8.18			Apr-06
	4.23	20.75	9.88	63.98	86.23	0.52	0.93	13.3	1	37.64	757.2	0	100	0	0	9	25.6	-13.17			Jul-15
	4.32	20.98	10.37	66.25	90.56	0.95	0.43	13.32	1	37.91	757.2	0	100	0	0	9	25.96	-12.99			May-09
	4.22	20.81	10.07	65.04	88.21	0.72	0.68	13.3	1	37.71	757.2	0	100	0	0	9	25.91	-13.11			May-09
	4.06	18.45	9.99	49.96	63.13	1.3	0.86	12.1	1	21.91	959.4	0	100	0	0	5	24.48	-15.74			Mar-08
	4.20	18.75	10.53	52.27	67.26	1.66	0.36	12.09	1	22.34	959.4	0	100	0	0	5	24.99	-15.46			Mar-08

	MARKET			FUND TYPE, CATEGORY & OBJECTIVE	RATINGS				MINIMUMS	
Fund Name	Ticker Symbol	Traded On	Fund Type	Category and (Prospectus Objective)	Overall Rating	Reward Rating	Risk Rating	Recent Up/ Downgrade	Open to New Investors	Min Initial Investment
Voya Russell Large Cap Index Portfolio Class S	IRLCX	NAS CM	Open End	US Equity Large Cap Blend (Growth & Income)	B-	C	B		Y	0
Voya Russell Large Cap Index Portfolio Class S2	IRLUX	NAS CM	Open End	US Equity Large Cap Blend (Growth & Income)	B-	C	B		Y	0
Voya Russell Large Cap Value Index Portfolio Class A	IRVAX	NAS CM	Open End	US Equity Large Cap Value (Growth & Income)	B-	C	B+	Up	Y	0
Voya Russell Large Cap Value Index Portfolio Class I	IRVIX	NAS CM	Open End	US Equity Large Cap Value (Growth & Income)	B-	C	B+		Y	0
Voya Russell Large Cap Value Index Portfolio Class S	IRVSX	NAS CM	Open End	US Equity Large Cap Value (Growth & Income)	B-	C	B+		Y	0
Voya Russell Mid Cap Growth Index Portfolio Class I	IRGJX	NAS CM	Open End	US Equity Mid Cap (Growth)	B-	C+	B	Down	Y	0
Voya Russell Mid Cap Growth Index Portfolio Class S	IRGUX	NAS CM	Open End	US Equity Mid Cap (Growth)	B-	C+	B		Y	0
Voya Russell Mid Cap Growth Index Portfolio Class S2	IRGVX	NAS CM	Open End	US Equity Mid Cap (Growth)	B-	C+	B		Y	0
Voya Russell Mid Cap Index Portfolio Class A	IRMAX	NAS CM	Open End	US Equity Mid Cap (Growth & Income)	C+	C	B		Y	0
Voya Russell Mid Cap Index Portfolio Class I	IIRMX	NAS CM	Open End	US Equity Mid Cap (Growth & Income)	C+	C	B		Y	0
Voya Russell Mid Cap Index Portfolio Class P2	VRMPX	NAS CM	Open End	US Equity Mid Cap (Growth & Income)	C+	C	B	Down	Y	0
Voya Russell Mid Cap Index Portfolio Class S	IRMCX	NAS CM	Open End	US Equity Mid Cap (Growth & Income)	C+	C	B		Y	0
Voya Russell Mid Cap Index Portfolio Class S2	IRMTX	NAS CM	Open End	US Equity Mid Cap (Growth & Income)	C+	C	B		Y	0
Voya Russell Small Cap Index Portfolio Class A	IRSIX	NAS CM	Open End	US Equity Small Cap (Small Company)	C	C	C+		Y	0
Voya Russell Small Cap Index Portfolio Class I	IIRSX	NAS CM	Open End	US Equity Small Cap (Small Company)	C	C	C+		Y	0
Voya Russell Small Cap Index Portfolio Class P2	VRSPX	NAS CM	Open End	US Equity Small Cap (Small Company)	C	C	C+		Y	0
Voya Russell Small Cap Index Portfolio Class S	IRSSX	NAS CM	Open End	US Equity Small Cap (Small Company)	C	C	C+		Y	0
Voya Russell Small Cap Index Portfolio Class S2	IRCIX	NAS CM	Open End	US Equity Small Cap (Small Company)	C	C	C+		Y	0
Voya Russia Fund Class A	LETRX	NAS CM	Open End	Equity Miscellaneous (Europe Stock)	B	B	B	Up	Y	1,000
Voya Russia Fund Class I	IIRFX	NAS CM	Open End	Equity Miscellaneous (Europe Stock)	B	B	B	Up	Y	250,000
Voya Russia Fund Class W	IWRFX	NAS CM	Open End	Equity Miscellaneous (Europe Stock)	B	B	B	Up	Y	1,000
Voya Small Company Fund Class A	AESAX	NAS CM	Open End	US Equity Small Cap (Small Company)	C	C	C+		Y	1,000
Voya Small Company Fund Class C	ASCCX	NAS CM	Open End	US Equity Small Cap (Small Company)	C	C-	C+		Y	1,000
Voya Small Company Fund Class I	AESGX	NAS CM	Open End	US Equity Small Cap (Small Company)	C	C	C+		Y	250,000
Voya Small Company Fund Class O	ISCOX	NAS CM	Open End	US Equity Small Cap (Small Company)	C	C	C+		Y	1,000
Voya Small Company Fund Class P3	VPSCX	NAS CM	Open End	US Equity Small Cap (Small Company)	C	C	C+		Y	0
Voya Small Company Fund Class R	VSMRX	NAS CM	Open End	US Equity Small Cap (Small Company)	C	C	C+		Y	0
Voya Small Company Fund Class R6	ISMZX	NAS CM	Open End	US Equity Small Cap (Small Company)	C	C	C+		Y	1,000,000
Voya Small Company Fund Class W	ISMWX	NAS CM	Open End	US Equity Small Cap (Small Company)	C	C	C+		Y	1,000
Voya Small Company Portfolio Class A	IASCX	NAS CM	Open End	US Equity Small Cap (Small Company)	C	C	C+		Y	0
Voya Small Company Portfolio Class I	IVCSX	NAS CM	Open End	US Equity Small Cap (Small Company)	C	C	C+		Y	0
Voya Small Company Portfolio Class S	IVPSX	NAS CM	Open End	US Equity Small Cap (Small Company)	C	C	C+		Y	0
Voya Small Company Portfolio R6	VSPRX	NAS CM	Open End	US Equity Small Cap (Small Company)	C	C	C+		Y	0
Voya SmallCap Opportunities Fund Class A	NSPAX	NAS CM	Open End	US Equity Small Cap (Small Company)	C	C	C+		Y	1,000
Voya SmallCap Opportunities Fund Class C	NSPCX	NAS CM	Open End	US Equity Small Cap (Small Company)	C	C	C		Y	1,000
Voya SmallCap Opportunities Fund Class I	NSPIX	NAS CM	Open End	US Equity Small Cap (Small Company)	C	C	C+		Y	250,000
Voya SmallCap Opportunities Fund Class P3	VSOPX	NAS CM	Open End	US Equity Small Cap (Small Company)	C	C	C+		Y	0
Voya SmallCap Opportunities Fund Class R	ISORX	NAS CM	Open End	US Equity Small Cap (Small Company)	C	C	C+		Y	0
Voya SmallCap Opportunities Fund Class R6	ISOZX	NAS CM	Open End	US Equity Small Cap (Small Company)	C	C	C+		Y	1,000,000
Voya SmallCap Opportunities Fund Class W	ISOWX	NAS CM	Open End	US Equity Small Cap (Small Company)	C	C	C+		Y	1,000
Voya SmallCap Opportunities Portfolio Class A	ISOPX	NAS CM	Open End	US Equity Small Cap (Small Company)	C	C	C+		Y	0
Voya SmallCap Opportunities Portfolio Class I	IVSOX	NAS CM	Open End	US Equity Small Cap (Small Company)	C	C	C+		Y	0
Voya SmallCap Opportunities Portfolio Class S	IVPOX	NAS CM	Open End	US Equity Small Cap (Small Company)	C	C	C+		Y	0
Voya SmallCap Opportunities Portfolio Class S2	ISCTX	NAS CM	Open End	US Equity Small Cap (Small Company)	C	C	C+		Y	0
Voya SmallCap Opportunities Portfolio R6	VRSCX	NAS CM	Open End	US Equity Small Cap (Small Company)	C	C	C+		Y	0
Voya SMID Cap Growth Fund Class A	VGROX	NAS CM	Open End	US Equity Mid Cap (Growth)	C	C	C+		Y	1,000
Voya SMID Cap Growth Fund Class I	VSMDX	NAS CM	Open End	US Equity Mid Cap (Growth)	C	C	C+		Y	250,000
Voya SMID Cap Growth Fund Class P3	VPSGX	NAS CM	Open End	US Equity Mid Cap (Growth)	C	C	C+		Y	0
Voya SMID Cap Growth Fund Class R6	VSGRX	NAS CM	Open End	US Equity Mid Cap (Growth)	C	C	C+		Y	1,000,000
Voya Solution 2020 Portfolio Class ADV	ISNAX	NAS CM	Open End	Target Date (Asset Alloc)	B	C+	A-	Up	Y	0
Voya Solution 2020 Portfolio Class I	ISNBX	NAS CM	Open End	Target Date (Asset Alloc)	B	C+	A	Up	Y	0
Voya Solution 2020 Portfolio Class S	ISNCX	NAS CM	Open End	Target Date (Asset Alloc)	B	C+	A	Up	Y	0

★ Expanded analysis of this fund is included in Section II.

Min Additional Investment	TOTAL RETURNS 3-Month Total Return	6-Month Total Return	1-Year Total Return	3-Year Total Return	5-Year Total Return	PERFORMANCE Dividend Yield (TTM)	Expense Ratio	3-Yr Std Deviation	3-Year Beta	ASSETS NAV	Total Assets (MIL)	ASSET ALLOCATION & TURNOVER %Cash	%Stocks	%Bonds	%Other	Turnover Ratio	BULL & BEAR Last Bull Market Total Return	Last Bear Market Total Return	FEES Front End Fee (%)	Back End Fee (%)	Inception Date
	4.14	18.57	10.26	51.11	65.13	1.42	0.61	12.1	1	22.2	959.4	0	100	0	0	5	24.65	-15.63			Mar-08
	4.09	18.48	10.08	50.44	63.91	1.19	0.76	12.07	1	22.88	959.4	0	100	0	0	5	24.6	-15.65			Feb-09
	3.91	15.81	9.82	34.61	39.66	1.95	0.93	11.86	1	22	382.7	0	100	0	0	14	23.39	-18.16			Jul-15
	4.04	16.12	10.44	36.63	43.16	2.47	0.43	11.88	1	22.2	382.7	0	100	0	0	14	23.75	-17.99			May-09
	3.97	15.98	10.16	35.56	41.36	2.22	0.68	11.87	1	22.06	382.7	0	100	0	0	14	23.55	-18.07			May-09
	5.30	27.19	13.45	58.59	66.49	0.79	0.4	14.4	1	33.56	302.5	0	100	0	0	31	27.43	-21.03			May-09
	5.23	27.03	13.16	57.40	64.39	0.53	0.65	14.39	1	33.5	302.5	0	100	0	0	31	27.3	-21.14			May-09
	5.19	26.92	13.01	56.72	63.20	0.41	0.8	14.39	1	33.44	302.5	0	100	0	0	31	27.2	-21.19			May-09
	3.84	21.86	6.85	39.52	44.98	1.06	0.91	13.38	1	12.21	1,469	0	100	0	0	11	25.91	-21.27			Mar-08
	4.05	22.20	7.47	41.69	48.78	1.51	0.41	13.42	1	12.72	1,469	0	100	0	0	11	26.18	-21.06			Mar-08
	4.02	22.34	7.64	42.45	49.59	1.5	0.16	13.42	1	12.8	1,469	0	100	0	0	11	26.18	-21.06			May-17
	3.95	22.08	7.19	40.59	46.86	1.26	0.66	13.44	1	12.54	1,469	0	100	0	0	11	26.03	-21.11			Mar-08
	3.91	21.97	7.05	39.98	45.84	1.12	0.81	13.4	1	12.33	1,469	0	100	0	0	11	25.94	-21.18			Feb-09
	1.78	17.43	-4.15	40.74	36.07	0.63	0.96	17.14	1	12.86	831.6	0	100	0	0	17	27.16	-25.11			Mar-08
	1.98	17.74	-3.64	42.89	39.55	1.11	0.46	17.17	1	13.35	831.6	0	100	0	0	17	27.47	-24.95			Mar-08
	2.03	17.86	-3.38	43.78	40.42	1.1	0.16	17.16	1	13.46	831.6	0	100	0	0	17	27.47	-24.95			May-17
	1.90	17.55	-3.84	41.93	37.78	0.82	0.71	17.13	1	13.23	831.6	0	100	0	0	17	27.34	-25.03			Mar-08
	1.89	17.51	-4.02	41.21	36.80	0.73	0.86	17.15	1	12.96	831.6	0	100	0	0	17	27.23	-25.04			Feb-09
	15.96	32.43	23.81	74.62	29.36	2.1	2	16.95	0.94	36.18	86.2	0	100	0	0	34	17.28	-34.93	5.75		Jul-96
	16.04	32.56	24.10	75.60	30.64	2.26	1.75	16.94	0.94	36.31	86.2	0	100	0	0	34	17.56	-34.73			Sep-09
	16.02	32.54	24.03	76.13	30.99	2.3	1.75	16.97	0.94	36.21	86.2	0	100	0	0	34	17.44	-34.9			Aug-11
	2.45	18.21	-4.92	29.68	34.98	0	1.36	16.95	0.98	11.29	518.7	3	97	0	0	79	30.07	-23.99	5.75		Apr-94
	2.23	17.85	-5.65	26.77	30.07	0	2.11	16.96	0.98	8.25	518.7	3	97	0	0	79	29.38	-24.17		1.00	Jun-98
	2.55	18.38	-4.50	31.01	37.20	0.14	1.05	16.94	0.98	14.04	518.7	3	97	0	0	79	30.28	-23.82			Jan-94
	2.45	18.13	-4.86	29.72	35.03	0	1.36	17.11	0.98	11.27	518.7	3	97	0	0	79	29.98	-23.94			Jun-08
	2.82	18.99	-3.50	32.39	38.65	0.25	0.01	16.92	0.98	14.22	518.7	3	97	0	0	79	30.28	-23.82			Jun-18
	2.63	18.69	-4.09	30.20	35.00	0.02	1.61	16.9	0.97	11.3	518.7	3	97	0	0	79	29.91	-23.98			Oct-16
	2.47	18.36	-4.50	31.23	37.68	0.25	0.96	16.94	0.98	14.05	518.7	3	97	0	0	79	30.28	-23.82			May-13
	2.48	18.34	-4.63	30.69	36.72	0	1.11	16.93	0.98	14	518.7	3	97	0	0	79	30.17	-23.87			Jun-09
	2.36	18.14	-4.70	29.97	36.21	0	1.4	16.85	0.97	14.83	531.9	4	96	0	0	96	30.08	-23.83			Dec-08
	2.48	18.45	-4.25	31.95	39.67	0.4	0.9	16.84	0.97	15.84	531.9	4	96	0	0	96	30.52	-23.68			Dec-96
	2.48	18.30	-4.44	30.98	37.99	0.13	1.15	16.86	0.97	15.35	531.9	4	96	0	0	96	30.35	-23.79			Nov-01
	2.54	18.43	-4.25	32.43	39.74	0.4	0.9	16.85	0.97	15.85	531.9	4	96	0	0	96	30.52	-23.68			Nov-15
	2.37	21.59	-5.21	35.02	35.08	0	1.36	18	1.02	48.65	721.2	2	98	0	0	88	30.94	-22.51	5.75		Jun-95
	2.19	21.10	-6.01	31.95	29.98	0	2.11	18	1.02	34.49	721.2	2	98	0	0	88	30.4	-22.73		1.00	Jun-95
	2.46	21.77	-4.88	36.26	37.12	0	1.07	17.99	1.02	54.35	721.2	2	98	0	0	88	31.26	-22.36			Apr-99
	2.74	22.44	-3.89	36.89	36.96	0	0.01	17.97	1.02	55.48	721.2	2	98	0	0	88	30.94	-22.51			Jun-18
	2.31	21.41	-5.46	34.00	33.40	0	1.61	17.99	1.02	47.22	721.2	2	98	0	0	88	30.72	-22.6			Aug-11
	2.48	21.85	-4.79	36.80	38.02	0	0.93	18	1.02	54.87	721.2	2	98	0	0	88	30.94	-22.51			May-13
	2.43	21.71	-4.96	36.06	36.80	0	1.11	17.99	1.02	53.41	721.2	2	98	0	0	88	31.15	-22.41			Dec-07
	2.43	21.55	-5.00	35.54	36.23	0	1.38	17.96	1.02	21.88	354.2	2	98	0	0	108	30.95	-22.39			Nov-08
	2.56	21.88	-4.50	37.61	39.74	0	0.88	17.96	1.02	24.78	354.2	2	98	0	0	108	31.3	-22.22			May-94
	2.50	21.78	-4.72	36.63	38.02	0	1.13	17.94	1.02	22.92	354.2	2	98	0	0	108	31.14	-22.28			May-01
	2.43	21.62	-4.88	36.01	36.97	0	1.28	17.92	1.02	22.27	354.2	2	98	0	0	108	31.03	-22.34			Feb-09
	2.56	21.88	-4.46	37.68	39.75	0	0.88	17.96	1.02	24.78	354.2	2	98	0	0	108	31.3	-22.22			Nov-15
	3.37	24.79	1.92			0	1.22			10.72	3.9	3	97	0	0	103			5.75		Dec-16
	3.44	24.85	2.18			0	0.97			10.8	3.9	3	97	0	0	103					Dec-16
	3.70	25.51	3.18			0	0.02			10.92	3.9	3	97	0	0	103					Jun-18
	3.44	24.85	2.18			0	0.95			10.8	3.9	3	97	0	0	103					Dec-16
	3.15	10.75	5.96	22.79	26.64	1.49	1.22	5.54	0.92	13.08	32.6	2	42	55	0	83					Oct-11
	3.23	11.00	6.58	24.55	29.79	1.84	0.72	5.55	0.92	13.42	32.6	2	42	55	0	83					Oct-11
	3.17	10.80	6.27	23.64	28.15	1.69	0.97	5.5	0.91	13.33	32.6	2	42	55	0	83					Oct-11

	MARKET		FUND TYPE, CATEGORY & OBJECTIVE		RATINGS				MINIMUMS	
Fund Name	Ticker Symbol	Traded On	Fund Type	Category and (Prospectus Objective)	Overall Rating	Reward Rating	Risk Rating	Recent Up/ Downgrade	Open to New Investors	Min Initial Investment
Voya Solution 2020 Portfolio Class S2	ISNDX	NAS CM	Open End	Target Date (Asset Alloc)	B	C+	A	Up	Y	0
Voya Solution 2020 Portfolio Class T	ISNEX	NAS CM	Open End	Target Date (Asset Alloc)	B	C	A-	Up	Y	0
Voya Solution 2025 Portfolio Class ADV	ISZAX	NAS CM	Open End	Target Date (Asset Alloc)	B-	C	A-	Up	Y	0
Voya Solution 2025 Portfolio Class I	ISZIX	NAS CM	Open End	Target Date (Asset Alloc)	B	C	A-	Up	Y	0
Voya Solution 2025 Portfolio Class S	ISZSX	NAS CM	Open End	Target Date (Asset Alloc)	B	C	A-	Up	Y	0
Voya Solution 2025 Portfolio Class S2	ISPBX	NAS CM	Open End	Target Date (Asset Alloc)	B-	C	A-	Up	Y	0
Voya Solution 2025 Portfolio Class T	ISZTX	NAS CM	Open End	Target Date (Asset Alloc)	B-	C	A-	Up	Y	0
Voya Solution 2030 Portfolio Class ADV	ISNFX	NAS CM	Open End	Target Date (Asset Alloc)	B-	C	B+	Up	Y	0
Voya Solution 2030 Portfolio Class I	ISNGX	NAS CM	Open End	Target Date (Asset Alloc)	B-	C	B+	Up	Y	0
Voya Solution 2030 Portfolio Class S	ISNHX	NAS CM	Open End	Target Date (Asset Alloc)	B-	C	B+	Up	Y	0
Voya Solution 2030 Portfolio Class S2	ISNIX	NAS CM	Open End	Target Date (Asset Alloc)	B-	C	B+	Up	Y	0
Voya Solution 2030 Portfolio Class T	ISNJX	NAS CM	Open End	Target Date (Asset Alloc)	B-	C	B+	Up	Y	0
Voya Solution 2035 Portfolio Class ADV	ISQAX	NAS CM	Open End	Target Date (Asset Alloc)	B-	C	B+	Up	Y	0
Voya Solution 2035 Portfolio Class I	ISQIX	NAS CM	Open End	Target Date (Asset Alloc)	B-	C	B+	Up	Y	0
Voya Solution 2035 Portfolio Class S	ISQSX	NAS CM	Open End	Target Date (Asset Alloc)	B-	C	B+	Up	Y	0
Voya Solution 2035 Portfolio Class S2	ISPCX	NAS CM	Open End	Target Date (Asset Alloc)	B-	C	B+	Up	Y	0
Voya Solution 2035 Portfolio Class T	ISQTX	NAS CM	Open End	Target Date (Asset Alloc)	B-	C	B+	Up	Y	0
Voya Solution 2040 Portfolio Class ADV	ISNKX	NAS CM	Open End	Target Date (Asset Alloc)	B-	C	B	Up	Y	0
Voya Solution 2040 Portfolio Class I	ISNLX	NAS CM	Open End	Target Date (Asset Alloc)	B-	C	B	Up	Y	0
Voya Solution 2040 Portfolio Class S	ISNMX	NAS CM	Open End	Target Date (Asset Alloc)	B-	C	B	Up	Y	0
Voya Solution 2040 Portfolio Class S2	ISNNX	NAS CM	Open End	Target Date (Asset Alloc)	B-	C	B	Up	Y	0
Voya Solution 2040 Portfolio Class T	ISNOX	NAS CM	Open End	Target Date (Asset Alloc)	B-	C	B	Up	Y	0
Voya Solution 2045 Portfolio Class ADV	ISRAX	NAS CM	Open End	Target Date (Asset Alloc)	B-	C	B	Up	Y	0
Voya Solution 2045 Portfolio Class I	ISRIX	NAS CM	Open End	Target Date (Asset Alloc)	B-	C	B	Up	Y	0
Voya Solution 2045 Portfolio Class S	ISRSX	NAS CM	Open End	Target Date (Asset Alloc)	B-	C	B	Up	Y	0
Voya Solution 2045 Portfolio Class S2	ISPDX	NAS CM	Open End	Target Date (Asset Alloc)	B-	C	B	Up	Y	0
Voya Solution 2045 Portfolio Class T	ISRTX	NAS CM	Open End	Target Date (Asset Alloc)	B-	C	B	Up	Y	0
Voya Solution 2050 Portfolio Class ADV	ISNPX	NAS CM	Open End	Target Date (Asset Alloc)	C+	C	B	Up	Y	0
Voya Solution 2050 Portfolio Class I	ISNQX	NAS CM	Open End	Target Date (Asset Alloc)	B-	C	B	Up	Y	0
Voya Solution 2050 Portfolio Class S	ISNRX	NAS CM	Open End	Target Date (Asset Alloc)	B-	C	B	Up	Y	0
Voya Solution 2050 Portfolio Class S2	ISNSX	NAS CM	Open End	Target Date (Asset Alloc)	B-	C	B	Up	Y	0
Voya Solution 2050 Portfolio Class T	ISNTX	NAS CM	Open End	Target Date (Asset Alloc)	C+	C	B	Up	Y	0
Voya Solution 2055 Portfolio Class ADV	IASPX	NAS CM	Open End	Target Date (Asset Alloc)	B-	C	B	Up	Y	0
Voya Solution 2055 Portfolio Class I	IISPX	NAS CM	Open End	Target Date (Asset Alloc)	B-	C	B	Up	Y	0
Voya Solution 2055 Portfolio Class S	ISSPX	NAS CM	Open End	Target Date (Asset Alloc)	B-	C	B	Up	Y	0
Voya Solution 2055 Portfolio Class S2	ITSPX	NAS CM	Open End	Target Date (Asset Alloc)	B-	C	B	Up	Y	0
Voya Solution 2055 Portfolio Class T	ISTPX	NAS CM	Open End	Target Date (Asset Alloc)	C+	C	B	Up	Y	0
Voya Solution 2060 Portfolio Class ADV	VSPAX	NAS CM	Open End	Target Date (Growth & Income)	C+	C	B	Up	Y	0
Voya Solution 2060 Portfolio Class I	VSIPX	NAS CM	Open End	Target Date (Growth & Income)	B-	C	B	Up	Y	0
Voya Solution 2060 Portfolio Class S	VSPSX	NAS CM	Open End	Target Date (Growth & Income)	B-	C	B	Up	Y	0
Voya Solution 2060 Portfolio Class S2	VSSPX	NAS CM	Open End	Target Date (Growth & Income)	B-	C	B	Up	Y	0
Voya Solution 2060 Portfolio Class T	VSPTX	NAS CM	Open End	Target Date (Growth & Income)	C+	C	B	Up	Y	0
Voya Solution Aggressive Portfolio Class A	IAVAX	NAS CM	Open End	Aggressive Alloc (Aggr Growth)	C+	C	B	Up	Y	0
Voya Solution Aggressive Portfolio Class I	IAVIX	NAS CM	Open End	Aggressive Alloc (Aggr Growth)	C+	C	B	Up	Y	0
Voya Solution Aggressive Portfolio Class R6	VYRMX	NAS CM	Open End	Aggressive Alloc (Aggr Growth)	C+	C	B	Up	Y	0
Voya Solution Aggressive Portfolio Class S	IAVSX	NAS CM	Open End	Aggressive Alloc (Aggr Growth)	C+	C	B	Up	Y	0
Voya Solution Aggressive Portfolio Class S2	IAVTX	NAS CM	Open End	Aggressive Alloc (Aggr Growth)	C+	C	B	Up	Y	0
Voya Solution Balanced Portfolio Class A	ISGAX	NAS CM	Open End	Moderate Alloc (Asset Alloc)	B-	C	A-	Up	Y	0
Voya Solution Balanced Portfolio Class I	ISGJX	NAS CM	Open End	Moderate Alloc (Asset Alloc)	B-	C	A-	Up	Y	0
Voya Solution Balanced Portfolio Class R6	VYRLX	NAS CM	Open End	Moderate Alloc (Asset Alloc)	B-	C	A-	Up	Y	0
Voya Solution Balanced Portfolio Class S	ISGKX	NAS CM	Open End	Moderate Alloc (Asset Alloc)	B-	C	A-	Up	Y	0
Voya Solution Balanced Portfolio Class S2	ISGTX	NAS CM	Open End	Moderate Alloc (Asset Alloc)	B-	C	A-	Up	Y	0

★ Expanded analysis of this fund is included in Section II.

	TOTAL RETURNS					PERFORMANCE				ASSETS		ASSET ALLOCATION & TURNOVER					BULL & BEAR		FEES		
Min Additional Investment	3-Month Total Return	6-Month Total Return	1-Year Total Return	3-Year Total Return	5-Year Total Return	Dividend Yield (TTM)	Expense Ratio	3-Yr Std Deviation	3-Year Beta	NAV	Total Assets (MIL)	%Cash	%Stocks	%Bonds	%Other	Turnover Ratio	Last Bull Market Total Return	Last Bear Market Total Return	Front End Fee (%)	Back End Fee (%)	Inception Date
	3.21	10.85	6.12	23.13	27.24	1.65	1.12	5.52	0.91	13.17	32.6	2	42	55	0	83					Oct-11
	3.07	10.66	5.82	22.05	25.39	1.36	1.42	5.56	0.92	13.07	32.6	2	42	55	0	83					Oct-11
	3.08	12.17	5.51	26.29	27.70	1.73	1.28	7.02	1	11.7	812.1	3	58	39	0	47	17.66	-16.08			Apr-05
	3.25	12.39	6.09	28.19	30.98	2.19	0.78	7	0.99	12.06	812.1	3	58	39	0	47	18.03	-15.91			Apr-05
	3.20	12.26	5.78	27.24	29.28	1.94	1.03	7	0.99	11.9	812.1	3	58	39	0	47	17.87	-15.95			Apr-05
	3.21	12.22	5.76	26.77	28.38	1.66	1.18	7.04	1	11.57	812.1	3	58	39	0	47	17.68	-15.96			May-09
	3.12	12.00	5.33	25.54	26.39	1.48	1.48	7.02	1	12.22	812.1	3	58	39	0	47	17.6	-16.13			Aug-05
	3.17	13.62	5.26	29.58	31.36	1.39	1.29	8.4	1.03	15.59	37.8	2	69	28	0	87					Oct-11
	3.27	13.90	5.80	31.42	34.73	1.73	0.79	8.37	1.03	16.06	37.8	2	69	28	0	87					Oct-11
	3.23	13.77	5.53	30.53	33.06	1.59	1.04	8.38	1.03	15.94	37.8	2	69	28	0	87					Oct-11
	3.21	13.66	5.37	29.92	31.96	1.46	1.19	8.37	1.03	15.72	37.8	2	69	28	0	87					Oct-11
	3.10	13.45	5.01	28.79	29.88	1.35	1.49	8.38	1.03	15.6	37.8	2	69	28	0	87					Oct-11
	3.16	14.42	4.74	31.84	31.03	1.49	1.33	9.35	1.02	12.06	832.1	2	78	19	0	50	20.95	-18.9			Apr-05
	3.32	14.77	5.24	33.85	34.39	1.95	0.83	9.45	1.03	12.43	832.1	2	78	19	0	50	21.28	-18.75			Apr-05
	3.28	14.67	5.02	32.84	32.71	1.71	1.08	9.45	1.03	12.27	832.1	2	78	19	0	50	21.12	-18.8			Apr-05
	3.23	14.56	4.92	32.36	31.79	1.59	1.23	9.34	1.02	11.8	832.1	2	78	19	0	50	20.98	-18.85			May-09
	3.19	14.44	4.58	31.13	29.88	1.24	1.53	9.39	1.03	12.6	832.1	2	78	19	0	50	20.73	-18.86			Aug-05
	3.28	15.23	4.47	33.37	33.11	1.24	1.33	10.12	1.04	16.34	31.3	2	84	13	0	81					Oct-11
	3.37	15.51	5.00	35.33	36.67	1.56	0.83	10.08	1.03	16.83	31.3	2	84	13	0	81					Oct-11
	3.28	15.36	4.72	34.37	34.80	1.4	1.08	10.08	1.03	16.67	31.3	2	84	13	0	81					Oct-11
	3.27	15.24	4.55	33.74	33.77	1.43	1.23	10.11	1.03	16.4	31.3	2	84	13	0	81					Oct-11
	3.17	15.06	4.26	32.58	31.81	1.16	1.53	10.09	1.03	16.27	31.3	2	84	13	0	81					Oct-11
	3.27	15.74	3.87	33.24	31.37	1.19	1.36	10.66	1.05	11.98	624.4	2	89	8	0	53	21.9	-19.77			Apr-05
	3.42	16.04	4.40	35.16	34.75	1.67	0.86	10.69	1.06	12.37	624.4	2	89	8	0	53	22.1	-19.6			Apr-05
	3.39	15.88	4.17	34.27	33.04	1.43	1.11	10.68	1.05	12.18	624.4	2	89	8	0	53	21.98	-19.67			Apr-05
	3.31	15.72	3.89	33.51	31.97	1.19	1.26	10.63	1.05	11.85	624.4	2	89	8	0	53	21.82	-19.72			May-09
	3.17	15.55	3.55	32.31	29.95	1.05	1.56	10.68	1.05	12.33	624.4	2	89	8	0	53	21.61	-19.78			Aug-05
	3.38	16.01	3.89	33.60	32.88	0.93	1.36	10.93	1.05	16.81	25.5	2	92	6	0	86					Oct-11
	3.51	16.33	4.39	35.55	36.50	1.18	0.86	10.94	1.05	17.38	25.5	2	92	6	0	86					Oct-11
	3.43	16.17	4.09	34.55	34.42	1.05	1.11	10.93	1.05	17.17	25.5	2	92	6	0	86					Oct-11
	3.42	16.04	3.95	33.90	33.55	0.99	1.26	10.91	1.05	16.92	25.5	2	92	6	0	86					Oct-11
	3.37	15.88	3.68	32.69	31.49	0.74	1.56	10.93	1.05	16.85	25.5	2	92	6	0	86					Oct-11
	3.34	15.98	3.86	33.73	31.98	0.99	1.36	10.93	1.04	14.22	205.3	2	92	5	0	62	21.77	-19.76			Mar-10
	3.48	16.29	4.36	35.75	35.36	1.44	0.86	10.91	1.04	14.56	205.3	2	92	5	0	62	22.15	-19.59			Mar-10
	3.38	16.07	4.08	34.75	33.62	1.21	1.11	10.91	1.04	14.37	205.3	2	92	5	0	62	21.91	-19.67			Mar-10
	3.40	16.00	3.94	34.08	32.63	1.07	1.26	10.93	1.04	14.28	205.3	2	92	5	0	62	21.85	-19.73			Mar-10
	3.35	15.93	3.67	32.91	30.85	0.65	1.56	10.93	1.04	14.48	205.3	2	92	5	0	62	21.69	-19.81			Mar-10
	3.26	15.89	3.73	33.73		0.85	1.37	10.93	1.03	12.03	14.1	2	93	5	0	84					Feb-15
	3.46	16.23	4.35	35.91		1.05	0.87	10.98	1.04	12.24	14.1	2	93	5	0	84					Feb-15
	3.33	16.05	3.98	34.73		0.92	1.12	10.97	1.04	12.07	14.1	2	93	5	0	84					Feb-15
	3.34	15.97	3.87	34.19		0.9	1.27	10.97	1.04	12.05	14.1	2	93	5	0	84					Feb-15
	3.27	15.76	3.51	32.90		0.47	1.57	10.97	1.04	11.97	14.1	2	93	5	0	84					Feb-15
	3.34	16.68	3.44	34.94	32.65	0.81	1.39	11.58	1.25	13.29	20.4	2	94	4	0	79					May-13
	3.49	16.89	3.94	36.94	35.87	1.2	0.89	11.56	1.25	13.63	20.4	2	94	4	0	79					May-13
	3.49	16.89	3.94	36.95	35.76	1.2	0.89	11.57	1.25	13.63	20.4	2	94	4	0	79					May-16
	3.38	16.75	3.67	35.98	34.21	0.98	1.14	11.52	1.25	13.45	20.4	2	94	4	0	79					May-13
	3.35	16.73	3.54	35.37	33.17	0.97	1.29	11.57	1.25	13.25	20.4	2	94	4	0	79					May-13
	2.99	12.76	5.15	25.58	27.06	1.54	1.3	7.74	1.09	9.98	56.6	2	64	33	0	60	17.86	-15.22			Jul-07
	3.17	13.16	5.67	27.71	30.38	2.04	0.8	7.76	1.09	10.4	56.6	2	64	33	0	60	18.28	-14.98			Jul-07
	3.17	13.16	5.67	27.58	30.38	2.04	0.8	7.75	1.09	10.4	56.6	2	64	33	0	60	18.28	-14.99			May-16
	3.05	12.93	5.41	26.65	28.80	1.82	1.05	7.71	1.08	10.13	56.6	2	64	33	0	60	18.07	-15.21			Jul-07
	3.05	12.83	5.21	26.02	27.67	1.34	1.2	7.74	1.08	10.11	56.6	2	64	33	0	60	17.89	-15.28			Apr-10

Fund Name	Ticker Symbol	Traded On	Fund Type	Category and (Prospectus Objective)	Overall Rating	Reward Rating	Risk Rating	Recent Up/ Downgrade	Open to New Investors	Min Initial Investment
	MARKET		FUND TYPE, CATEGORY & OBJECTIVE		RATINGS				MINIMUMS	
Voya Solution Conservative Portfolio Class A	ICGAX	NAS CM	Open End	Cautious Alloc (Asset Alloc)	B	C	A-	Up	Y	0
Voya Solution Conservative Portfolio Class I	ICGIX	NAS CM	Open End	Cautious Alloc (Asset Alloc)	B	C	A-	Up	Y	0
Voya Solution Conservative Portfolio Class R6	VYRPX	NAS CM	Open End	Cautious Alloc (Asset Alloc)	B	C	A-	Up	Y	0
Voya Solution Conservative Portfolio Class S	ICGSX	NAS CM	Open End	Cautious Alloc (Asset Alloc)	B	C	A-	Up	Y	0
Voya Solution Conservative Portfolio Class S2	ICGTX	NAS CM	Open End	Cautious Alloc (Asset Alloc)	B	C	A-	Up	Y	0
Voya Solution Income Portfolio Class ADV	ISWAX	NAS CM	Open End	Target Date (Asset Alloc)	B	C	A-	Up	Y	0
Voya Solution Income Portfolio Class I	ISWIX	NAS CM	Open End	Target Date (Asset Alloc)	B	C+	A-	Up	Y	0
Voya Solution Income Portfolio Class S	ISWSX	NAS CM	Open End	Target Date (Asset Alloc)	B	C+	A-	Up	Y	0
Voya Solution Income Portfolio Class S2	IJKBX	NAS CM	Open End	Target Date (Asset Alloc)	B	C+	A-	Up	Y	0
Voya Solution Income Portfolio Class T	ISWTX	NAS CM	Open End	Target Date (Asset Alloc)	B-	C	A-		Y	0
Voya Solution Moderately Aggressive Portfolio Class A	IAGAX	NAS CM	Open End	Aggressive Alloc (Asset Alloc)	B-	C	B	Up	Y	0
Voya Solution Moderately Aggressive Portfolio Class I	IAGIX	NAS CM	Open End	Aggressive Alloc (Asset Alloc)	B-	C	B+	Up	Y	0
Voya Solution Moderately Aggressive Portfolio Class R6	VYROX	NAS CM	Open End	Aggressive Alloc (Asset Alloc)	B-	C	B+	Up	Y	0
Voya Solution Moderately Aggressive Portfolio Class S	IAGSX	NAS CM	Open End	Aggressive Alloc (Asset Alloc)	B-	C	B+	Up	Y	0
Voya Solution Moderately Aggressive Portfolio Class S2	IAGTX	NAS CM	Open End	Aggressive Alloc (Asset Alloc)	B-	C	B	Up	Y	0
Voya Solution Moderately Conservative Portfolio Class A	ISPGX	NAS CM	Open End	Cautious Alloc (Asset Alloc)	B	C	A-	Up	Y	0
Voya Solution Moderately Conservative Portfolio Class I	ISPRX	NAS CM	Open End	Cautious Alloc (Asset Alloc)	B	C	A-	Up	Y	0
Voya Solution Moderately Conservative Portfolio Class R6	VYRNX	NAS CM	Open End	Cautious Alloc (Asset Alloc)	B	C	A-	Up	Y	0
Voya Solution Moderately Conservative Portfolio Class S	ISPSX	NAS CM	Open End	Cautious Alloc (Asset Alloc)	B	C	A-	Up	Y	0
Voya Solution Moderately Conservative Portfolio Class S2	ISPTX	NAS CM	Open End	Cautious Alloc (Asset Alloc)	B	C	A-	Up	Y	0
Voya Strategic Allocation Conservative Portfolio Class I	ISAIX	NAS CM	Open End	Cautious Alloc (Asset Alloc)	B	C	A-	Up	Y	0
Voya Strategic Allocation Conservative Portfolio Class S	ISCVX	NAS CM	Open End	Cautious Alloc (Asset Alloc)	B	C	A-	Up	Y	0
Voya Strategic Allocation Growth Portfolio Class I	ISAGX	NAS CM	Open End	Aggressive Alloc (Asset Alloc)	B-	C	B+	Up	Y	0
Voya Strategic Allocation Growth Portfolio Class S	ISGRX	NAS CM	Open End	Aggressive Alloc (Asset Alloc)	B-	C	B+	Up	Y	0
Voya Strategic Allocation Moderate Portfolio Class I	IIMDX	NAS CM	Open End	Moderate Alloc (Asset Alloc)	B-	C	A-	Up	Y	0
Voya Strategic Allocation Moderate Portfolio Class S	ISMDX	NAS CM	Open End	Moderate Alloc (Asset Alloc)	B-	C	A-	Up	Y	0
Voya Target In-Retirement Fund Class A	VTRVX	NAS CM	Open End	Target Date (Asset Alloc)	B	C	A-	Up	Y	1,000
Voya Target In-Retirement Fund Class I	ISOLX	NAS CM	Open End	Target Date (Asset Alloc)	B	C+	A-	Up	Y	250,000
Voya Target In-Retirement Fund Class R	VRRPX	NAS CM	Open End	Target Date (Asset Alloc)	B-	C	A-		Y	0
Voya Target In-Retirement Fund Class R6	VTRWX	NAS CM	Open End	Target Date (Asset Alloc)	B	C+	A-	Up	Y	1,000,000
Voya Target Retirement 2020 Fund Class A	VFTRX	NAS CM	Open End	Target Date (Asset Alloc)	B	C+	A-	Up	Y	1,000
Voya Target Retirement 2020 Fund Class I	IRSJX	NAS CM	Open End	Target Date (Asset Alloc)	B	C+	A	Up	Y	250,000
Voya Target Retirement 2020 Fund Class R	VRRGX	NAS CM	Open End	Target Date (Asset Alloc)	B	C	A-	Up	Y	0
Voya Target Retirement 2020 Fund Class R6	VTRBX	NAS CM	Open End	Target Date (Asset Alloc)	B	C+	A	Up	Y	1,000,000
Voya Target Retirement 2025 Fund Class A	VTRCX	NAS CM	Open End	Target Date (Asset Alloc)	B	C	A-	Up	Y	1,000
Voya Target Retirement 2025 Fund Class I	IRSLX	NAS CM	Open End	Target Date (Asset Alloc)	B	C	A-	Up	Y	250,000
Voya Target Retirement 2025 Fund Class R	VRRHX	NAS CM	Open End	Target Date (Asset Alloc)	B-	C	A-	Up	Y	0
Voya Target Retirement 2025 Fund Class R6	VTRDX	NAS CM	Open End	Target Date (Asset Alloc)	B	C	A-	Up	Y	1,000,000
Voya Target Retirement 2030 Fund Class A	VTREX	NAS CM	Open End	Target Date (Asset Alloc)	B-	C	B+	Up	Y	1,000
Voya Target Retirement 2030 Fund Class I	IRSMX	NAS CM	Open End	Target Date (Asset Alloc)	B-	C	B+	Up	Y	250,000
Voya Target Retirement 2030 Fund Class R6	VTRFX	NAS CM	Open End	Target Date (Asset Alloc)	B-	C	B+	Up	Y	1,000,000
Voya Target Retirement 2030 Fund ClassR	VRRIX	NAS CM	Open End	Target Date (Asset Alloc)	B-	C	B+	Up	Y	0
Voya Target Retirement 2035 Fund Class A	VTRGX	NAS CM	Open End	Target Date (Asset Alloc)	B-	C	B+	Up	Y	1,000
Voya Target Retirement 2035 Fund Class I	IRSNX	NAS CM	Open End	Target Date (Asset Alloc)	B-	C	B+	Up	Y	250,000
Voya Target Retirement 2035 Fund Class R	VRRJX	NAS CM	Open End	Target Date (Asset Alloc)	B-	C	B+	Up	Y	0
Voya Target Retirement 2035 Fund Class R6	VTRHX	NAS CM	Open End	Target Date (Asset Alloc)	B-	C	B+	Up	Y	1,000,000
Voya Target Retirement 2040 Fund Class A	VTRJX	NAS CM	Open End	Target Date (Asset Alloc)	B-	C	B+	Up	Y	1,000
Voya Target Retirement 2040 Fund Class I	IRSOX	NAS CM	Open End	Target Date (Asset Alloc)	B-	C	B+	Up	Y	250,000
Voya Target Retirement 2040 Fund Class R	VRRKX	NAS CM	Open End	Target Date (Asset Alloc)	B-	C	B+	Up	Y	0
Voya Target Retirement 2040 Fund Class R6	VTRKX	NAS CM	Open End	Target Date (Asset Alloc)	B-	C	B+	Up	Y	1,000,000
Voya Target Retirement 2045 Fund Class A	VTRMX	NAS CM	Open End	Target Date (Asset Alloc)	B-	C	B	Up	Y	1,000
Voya Target Retirement 2045 Fund Class I	IRSPX	NAS CM	Open End	Target Date (Asset Alloc)	B-	C	B	Up	Y	250,000

★ Expanded analysis of this fund is included in Section II.

	TOTAL RETURNS					PERFORMANCE				ASSETS		ASSET ALLOCATION & TURNOVER					BULL & BEAR		FEES		
Min Additional Investment	3-Month Total Return	6-Month Total Return	1-Year Total Return	3-Year Total Return	5-Year Total Return	Dividend Yield (TTM)	Expense Ratio	3-Yr Std Deviation	3-Year Beta	NAV	Total Assets (MIL)	%Cash	%Stocks	%Bonds	%Other	Turnover Ratio	Last Bull Market Total Return	Last Bear Market Total Return	Front End Fee (%)	Back End Fee (%)	Inception Date
	2.66	7.81	5.59	14.32	17.80	1.89	1.16	3.36	0.8	11.18	19.5	1	24	74	0	67	10.88	-8.23			Apr-10
	2.80	7.98	6.16	16.00	20.70	2.36	0.66	3.36	0.8	11.36	19.5	1	24	74	0	67	11.19	-7.97			Apr-10
	2.80	8.08	6.16	16.00	20.70	2.36	0.66	3.35	0.79	11.36	19.5	1	24	74	0	67	11.19	-7.97			May-16
	2.73	7.94	5.89	15.25	19.23	2.02	0.91	3.36	0.8	11.28	19.5	1	24	74	0	67	11.04	-8.11			Apr-10
	2.75	7.91	5.75	14.79	18.39	1.86	1.06	3.32	0.79	11.18	19.5	1	24	74	0	67	10.96	-8.13			Apr-10
	2.85	9.09	6.12	16.54	20.33	2.1	1.18	4.16	1.01	11.88	345.1	2	30	68	0	38	10.73	-8.23			Apr-05
	2.95	9.41	6.67	18.34	23.33	2.59	0.68	4.16	1.01	12.2	345.1	2	30	68	0	38	11.02	-8.05			Apr-05
	2.89	9.22	6.39	17.40	21.89	2.31	0.93	4.18	1.02	12.08	345.1	2	30	68	0	38	10.8	-8.11			Apr-05
	2.88	9.17	6.28	16.99	20.96	2.04	1.08	4.22	1.03	11.78	345.1	2	30	68	0	38	10.71	-8.19			May-09
	2.84	9.04	5.93	15.93	19.28	1.84	1.38	4.16	1.01	12.66	345.1	2	30	68	0	38	10.62	-8.24			Aug-05
	3.25	15.01	4.14	29.81	28.46	1.49	1.38	9.91	1.08	13.02	607.2	2	81	16	0	46	20.97	-19.15			Apr-10
	3.33	15.33	4.61	31.74	31.72	1.97	0.88	9.94	1.08	13.31	607.2	2	81	16	0	46	21.34	-18.99			Apr-10
	3.34	15.35	4.61	31.66	31.63	1.97	0.88	9.91	1.08	13.3	607.2	2	81	16	0	46	21.34	-18.99			May-16
	3.29	15.14	4.37	30.88	30.03	1.72	1.13	9.93	1.08	13.15	607.2	2	81	16	0	46	21.09	-19.06			Apr-10
	3.21	15.04	4.24	30.29	29.17	1.31	1.28	9.89	1.07	13.15	607.2	2	81	16	0	46	20.99	-19.17			Apr-10
	2.98	10.10	5.52	19.10	21.78	1.9	1.24	5.28	1.03	10.02	39.2	3	42	54	0	59	14.15	-11.39			Jul-07
	3.04	10.42	6.02	21.05	24.85	2.3	0.74	5.23	1.02	10.49	39.2	3	42	54	0	59	14.5	-11.16			Jul-07
	3.04	10.43	6.02	20.89	24.68	2.31	0.74	5.26	1.03	10.48	39.2	3	42	54	0	59	14.49	-11.16			May-16
	2.91	10.22	5.71	19.99	23.25	2.05	0.99	5.23	1.02	10.24	39.2	3	42	54	0	59	14.28	-11.3			Jul-07
	2.95	10.13	5.60	19.48	22.33	2.01	1.14	5.23	1.02	10.11	39.2	3	42	54	0	59	14.22	-11.38			Apr-10
	2.85	9.79	5.75	20.01	23.91	2.76	0.71	5.13	0.31	12.41	60.2	3	42	55	0	60	11.58	-7.91			Jul-95
	2.76	9.59	5.44	18.96	22.33	2.52	0.96	5.09	0.3	12.3	60.2	3	42	55	0	60	11.35	-7.94			Aug-05
	3.21	14.75	4.99	31.28	31.34	2.67	0.77	9.67	0.75	14.51	127.4	2	81	17	0	45	18.55	-16.67			Jul-95
	3.09	14.65	4.75	30.25	29.65	2.42	1.02	9.66	0.75	14.38	127.4	2	81	17	0	45	18.36	-16.74			Aug-05
	3.04	12.41	5.62	26.43	29.01	2.78	0.75	7.52	0.58	13.71	124.3	2	64	34	0	48	14.85	-12.39			Jul-95
	2.96	12.31	5.40	25.48	27.44	2.5	1	7.46	0.58	13.64	124.3	2	64	34	0	48	14.6	-12.42			Jun-05
	2.86	8.84	5.93	16.67	20.98	1.73	0.71	4.13	1.01	11.14	10.8	3	28	68	0	70			5.75		Dec-15
	2.94	8.98	6.28	17.57	22.48	1.97	0.45	4.1	1	11.18	10.8	3	28	68	0	70					Dec-12
	2.68	8.42	5.62	16.12	19.20	1.71	0.96	4.1	1	11.11	10.8	3	28	68	0	70					Jun-18
	2.85	8.91	6.21	17.57	22.59	1.99	0.45	4.09	1	11.17	10.8	3	28	68	0	70					Dec-15
	3.06	10.39	6.00	22.30	25.13	1.88	0.7	5.43	0.9	11.75	13.3	3	42	55	0	80			5.75		Dec-15
	3.14	10.55	6.37	23.27	26.94	2.13	0.43	5.39	0.89	11.81	13.3	3	42	55	0	80					Dec-12
	2.98	10.28	5.80	21.39	23.77	1.86	0.95	5.38	0.89	11.72	13.3	3	42	55	0	80					Jun-18
	3.14	10.56	6.37	23.41	26.85	2.13	0.43	5.42	0.9	11.81	13.3	3	42	55	0	80					Dec-15
	3.11	11.85	5.70	26.18	27.77	1.55	0.68	6.88	0.98	12.24	24.5	3	53	44	0	80			5.75		Dec-15
	3.10	11.94	5.98	27.12	29.32	1.74	0.43	6.91	0.98	12.29	24.5	3	53	44	0	80					Dec-12
	3.04	11.73	5.58	25.38	26.28	1.67	0.93	6.9	0.98	12.2	24.5	3	53	44	0	80					Jun-18
	3.27	12.09	6.12	27.43	29.64	1.78	0.43	6.91	0.98	12.29	24.5	3	53	44	0	80					Dec-15
	3.19	13.28	5.68	29.34	30.74	1.65	0.69	8.18	1	12.26	21.9	2	66	32	0	80			5.75		Dec-15
	3.26	13.47	5.98	30.39	32.55	1.84	0.43	8.22	1.01	12.32	21.9	2	66	32	0	80					Dec-12
	3.27	13.51	6.01	30.60	32.64	1.86	0.43	8.21	1.01	12.31	21.9	2	66	32	0	80					Dec-15
	3.11	13.12	5.43	28.43	29.26	1.66	0.94	8.2	1.01	12.23	21.9	2	66	32	0	80					Jun-18
	3.28	14.35	5.51	32.44	31.79	1.64	0.69	9.2	1.01	12.27	22.4	1	75	23	0	99			5.75		Dec-15
	3.26	14.39	5.78	33.52	33.63	1.88	0.44	9.18	1	12.32	22.4	1	75	23	0	99					Dec-12
	3.20	14.21	5.30	31.60	30.39	1.6	0.94	9.16	1	12.25	22.4	1	75	23	0	99					Jun-18
	3.35	14.54	5.90	33.54	33.64	1.9	0.44	9.2	1.01	12.31	22.4	1	75	23	0	99					Dec-15
	3.29	15.06	5.26	33.97	33.43	1.58	0.72	9.87	1.01	12.52	16.5	1	81	18	0	104			5.75		Dec-15
	3.28	15.19	5.50	34.99	35.08	1.8	0.46	9.85	1.01	12.57	16.5	1	81	18	0	104					Dec-12
	3.22	14.92	5.03	33.05	31.82	1.53	0.97	9.89	1.01	12.5	16.5	1	81	18	0	104					Jun-18
	3.37	15.25	5.55	35.20	35.29	1.83	0.46	9.86	1.01	12.56	16.5	1	81	18	0	104					Dec-15
	3.24	15.73	5.02	34.34	33.81	1.39	0.72	10.47	1.03	12.72	19.5	1	87	12	0	82			5.75		Dec-15
	3.31	15.88	5.37	35.51	35.74	1.63	0.45	10.46	1.03	12.77	19.5	1	87	12	0	82					Dec-12

	MARKET		FUND TYPE, CATEGORY & OBJECTIVE		RATINGS				MINIMUMS	
Fund Name	Ticker Symbol	Traded On	Fund Type	Category and (Prospectus Objective)	Overall Rating	Reward Rating	Risk Rating	Recent Up/ Downgrade	Open to New Investors	Min Initial Investment
Voya Target Retirement 2045 Fund Class R	VRRLX	NAS CM	Open End	Target Date (Asset Alloc)	B-	C	B	Up	Y	0
Voya Target Retirement 2045 Fund Class R6	VTRNX	NAS CM	Open End	Target Date (Asset Alloc)	B-	C	B	Up	Y	1,000,000
Voya Target Retirement 2050 Fund Class A	VTROX	NAS CM	Open End	Target Date (Asset Alloc)	B-	C	B	Up	Y	1,000
Voya Target Retirement 2050 Fund Class I	IRSQX	NAS CM	Open End	Target Date (Asset Alloc)	B-	C	B	Up	Y	250,000
Voya Target Retirement 2050 Fund Class R	VRRMX	NAS CM	Open End	Target Date (Asset Alloc)	B-	C	B	Up	Y	0
Voya Target Retirement 2050 Fund Class R6	VTRPX	NAS CM	Open End	Target Date (Asset Alloc)	B-	C	B	Up	Y	1,000,000
Voya Target Retirement 2055 Fund Class A	VTRQX	NAS CM	Open End	Target Date (Asset Alloc)	B-	C	B	Up	Y	1,000
Voya Target Retirement 2055 Fund Class I	IRSVX	NAS CM	Open End	Target Date (Asset Alloc)	B-	C	B	Up	Y	250,000
Voya Target Retirement 2055 Fund Class R	VRRNX	NAS CM	Open End	Target Date (Asset Alloc)	B-	C	B	Up	Y	0
Voya Target Retirement 2055 Fund Class R6	VTRRX	NAS CM	Open End	Target Date (Asset Alloc)	B-	C	B	Up	Y	1,000,000
Voya Target Retirement 2060 Fund Class A	VTRSX	NAS CM	Open End	Target Date (Asset Alloc)	B-	C	B	Up	Y	1,000
Voya Target Retirement 2060 Fund Class I	VRSAX	NAS CM	Open End	Target Date (Asset Alloc)	B-	C	B	Up	Y	250,000
Voya Target Retirement 2060 Fund Class R	VRROX	NAS CM	Open End	Target Date (Asset Alloc)	B-	C	B	Up	Y	0
Voya Target Retirement 2060 Fund Class R6	VTRUX	NAS CM	Open End	Target Date (Asset Alloc)	B-	C	B	Up	Y	1,000,000
Voya U.S. High Dividend Low Volatility Fund Class A	VHDAX	NAS CM	Open End	US Equity Large Cap Value (Equity-Income)	B-	C	B	Up	Y	1,000
Voya U.S. High Dividend Low Volatility Fund Class I	VHDIX	NAS CM	Open End	US Equity Large Cap Value (Equity-Income)	B-	C	B	Up	Y	250,000
Voya U.S. High Dividend Low Volatility Fund P3	VHDPX	NAS CM	Open End	US Equity Large Cap Value (Equity-Income)	B-	C	B	Up	Y	0
Voya U.S. Stock Index Portfolio Class A	ISIVX	NAS CM	Open End	US Equity Large Cap Blend (Growth)	B-	C	B		Y	0
Voya U.S. Stock Index Portfolio Class I	INGIX	NAS CM	Open End	US Equity Large Cap Blend (Growth)	B-	C	B		Y	0
Voya U.S. Stock Index Portfolio Class S	ISJBX	NAS CM	Open End	US Equity Large Cap Blend (Growth)	B-	C	B		Y	0
Voya U.S. Stock Index Portfolio Class S2	ISIPX	NAS CM	Open End	US Equity Large Cap Blend (Growth)	B-	C	B		Y	0
Voya U.S. Stock Index Portfolio P2	VPSPX	NAS CM	Open End	US Equity Large Cap Blend (Growth)	B-	C	B		Y	0
Vulcan Value Partners Fund	VVPLX	NAS CM	Open End	US Equity Large Cap Blend (Growth)	C+	C	B			5,000
Vulcan Value Partners Fund Institutional Class Shares			Open End	US Equity Large Cap Blend (Growth)	C+	C	B		Y	1,000,000
Vulcan Value Partners Small Cap Fund	VVPSX	NAS CM	Open End	US Equity Small Cap (Small Company)	C+	C	B	Up		5,000
Vulcan Value Partners Small Cap Institutional Cls Shares			Open End	US Equity Small Cap (Small Company)	C	C	B		Y	1,000,000
VY® American Century Small-Mid Cap Value Portfolio Class A	IASAX	NAS CM	Open End	US Equity Mid Cap (Growth)	C	C	B-		Y	0
VY® American Century Small-Mid Cap Value Portfolio Class I	IACIX	NAS CM	Open End	US Equity Mid Cap (Growth)	C+	C	B-	Up	Y	0
VY® American Century Small-Mid Cap Value Portfolio Class S	IASSX	NAS CM	Open End	US Equity Mid Cap (Growth)	C+	C	B-	Up	Y	0
VY® American Century Small-Mid Cap Value Portfolio Cls S2	ISMSX	NAS CM	Open End	US Equity Mid Cap (Growth)	C+	C	B-	Up	Y	0
VY® Baron Growth Portfolio Class A	IBSAX	NAS CM	Open End	US Equity Mid Cap (Small Company)	B-	B	B-		Y	0
VY® Baron Growth Portfolio Class I	IBGIX	NAS CM	Open End	US Equity Mid Cap (Small Company)	B	B	B-	Up	Y	0
VY® Baron Growth Portfolio Class R6	VYRBX	NAS CM	Open End	US Equity Mid Cap (Small Company)	B	B	B-	Up	Y	0
VY® Baron Growth Portfolio Class S	IBSSX	NAS CM	Open End	US Equity Mid Cap (Small Company)	B	B	B-	Up	Y	0
VY® Baron Growth Portfolio Class S2	IBCGX	NAS CM	Open End	US Equity Mid Cap (Small Company)	B-	B	B-		Y	0
VY® Clarion Global Real Estate Portfolio Class A	ICRNX	NAS CM	Open End	Real Estate Sector Equity (Real Estate)	C+	C	B		Y	0
VY® Clarion Global Real Estate Portfolio Class I	IRGIX	NAS CM	Open End	Real Estate Sector Equity (Real Estate)	C+	C	B		Y	0
VY® Clarion Global Real Estate Portfolio Class S	IRGTX	NAS CM	Open End	Real Estate Sector Equity (Real Estate)	C+	C	B		Y	0
VY® Clarion Global Real Estate Portfolio Class S2	IRGSX	NAS CM	Open End	Real Estate Sector Equity (Real Estate)	C+	C	B		Y	0
VY® Clarion Real Estate Portfolio Class A	ICRPX	NAS CM	Open End	Real Estate Sector Equity (Real Estate)	C	C	C+	Down	Y	0
VY® Clarion Real Estate Portfolio Class I	IVRIX	NAS CM	Open End	Real Estate Sector Equity (Real Estate)	C	C	C+	Down	Y	0
VY® Clarion Real Estate Portfolio Class S	IVRSX	NAS CM	Open End	Real Estate Sector Equity (Real Estate)	C	C	C+	Down	Y	0
VY® Clarion Real Estate Portfolio Class S2	IVRTX	NAS CM	Open End	Real Estate Sector Equity (Real Estate)	C	C	C+	Down	Y	0
VY® Columbia Contrarian Core Portfolio Class A	ISBAX	NAS CM	Open End	US Equity Large Cap Blend (Growth)	C+	C	B		Y	0
VY® Columbia Contrarian Core Portfolio Class I	ISFIX	NAS CM	Open End	US Equity Large Cap Blend (Growth)	C+	C	B		Y	0
VY® Columbia Contrarian Core Portfolio Class S	ISCSX	NAS CM	Open End	US Equity Large Cap Blend (Growth)	C+	C	B		Y	0
VY® Columbia Small Cap Value II Portfolio Class A	ICSAX	NAS CM	Open End	US Equity Small Cap (Small Company)	C	C-	C		Y	0
VY® Columbia Small Cap Value II Portfolio Class I	ICISX	NAS CM	Open End	US Equity Small Cap (Small Company)	C	C-	C		Y	0
VY® Columbia Small Cap Value II Portfolio Class R6	VYRDX	NAS CM	Open End	US Equity Small Cap (Small Company)	C	C-	C		Y	0
VY® Columbia Small Cap Value II Portfolio Class S	ICSSX	NAS CM	Open End	US Equity Small Cap (Small Company)	C	C-	C		Y	0
VY® Columbia Small Cap Value II Portfolio Class S2	ICVPX	NAS CM	Open End	US Equity Small Cap (Small Company)	C	C-	C		Y	0
VY® Invesco Comstock Portfolio Class A	IVKAX	NAS CM	Open End	US Equity Large Cap Value (Growth & Income)	C+	C	B-	Up	Y	0

★ Expanded analysis of this fund is included in Section II.

	TOTAL RETURNS					PERFORMANCE				ASSETS		ASSET ALLOCATION & TURNOVER					BULL & BEAR		FEES		
Min Additional Investment	3-Month Total Return	6-Month Total Return	1-Year Total Return	3-Year Total Return	5-Year Total Return	Dividend Yield (TTM)	Expense Ratio	3-Yr Std Deviation	3-Year Beta	NAV	Total Assets (MIL)	%Cash	%Stocks	%Bonds	%Other	Turnover Ratio	Last Bull Market Total Return	Last Bear Market Total Return	Front End Fee (%)	Back End Fee (%)	Inception Date
	3.17	15.61	4.81	33.45	32.34	1.35	0.97	10.44	1.03	12.69	19.5	1	87	12	0	82					Jun-18
	3.40	15.94	5.42	35.72	35.95	1.66	0.45	10.49	1.04	12.77	19.5	1	87	12	0	82					Dec-15
	3.31	16.03	5.05	34.57	33.94	1.56	0.72	10.67	1.03	12.45	12.5	1	88	10	0	86			5.75		Dec-15
	3.39	16.16	5.30	35.62	35.75	1.77	0.46	10.66	1.03	12.49	12.5	1	88	10	0	86					Dec-12
	3.23	15.85	4.72	33.53	32.32	1.49	0.97	10.69	1.03	12.43	12.5	1	88	10	0	86					Jun-18
	3.39	16.21	5.34	35.78	35.91	1.81	0.46	10.65	1.02	12.49	12.5	1	88	10	0	86					Dec-15
	3.28	15.99	5.02	34.86	34.37	1.48	0.72	10.68	1.02	12.58	12.2	1	89	10	0	71			5.75		Dec-15
	3.44	16.18	5.40	36.07	36.21	1.73	0.45	10.72	1.02	12.63	12.2	1	89	10	0	71					Dec-12
	3.20	15.74	4.62	33.71	32.52	1.42	0.97	10.71	1.02	12.55	12.2	1	89	10	0	71					Jun-18
	3.35	16.23	5.35	36.12	36.39	1.76	0.45	10.71	1.02	12.62	12.2	1	89	10	0	71					Dec-15
	3.21	15.93	4.97	34.68		1.53	0.71	10.68	1.01	11.56	5.4	1	88	10	0	69			5.75		Dec-15
	3.30	16.13	5.27	35.74		1.78	0.45	10.67	1.01	11.58	5.4	1	88	10	0	69					Dec-15
	3.30	15.90	4.76	33.94		1.5	0.96	10.73	1.02	11.55	5.4	1	88	10	0	69					Jun-18
	3.39	16.15	5.29	35.98		1.79	0.45	10.73	1.02	11.59	5.4	1	88	10	0	69					Dec-15
	4.50	17.57	10.19			1.63	0.8			12.03	325.7	0	100	0	0	33			5.75		Dec-16
	4.55	17.73	10.50			1.92	0.55			12.08	325.7	0	100	0	0	33					Dec-16
	4.70	17.98	10.94				0			12.13	325.7	0	100	0	0	33					Sep-18
	4.06	19.06	9.53	47.26	59.69	1.1	0.8	12.15	1	15.86	5,890	0	100	0	0	12	24.52	-16.55			May-09
	4.24	19.37	10.06	49.70	63.98	1.57	0.27	12.21	1	16.45	5,890	0	100	0	0	12	24.9	-16.36			May-04
	4.15	19.22	9.79	48.57	62.08	1.31	0.51	12.17	1	16.31	5,890	0	100	0	0	12	24.76	-16.45			Apr-07
	4.14	19.18	9.70	47.94	60.84	1.21	0.67	12.18	1	16.09	5,890	0	100	0	0	12	24.6	-16.45			Aug-07
	4.29	19.47	10.25	50.04	64.34	1.56	0.15	12.21	1	16.5	5,890	0	100	0	0	12	24.9	-16.36			May-17
500	4.68	21.15	5.65	45.41	42.73	0.39	1.09	14.45	1.11	21.02	1,300	3	97	0	0	50	30.52	-13.63			Dec-09
5,000	4.73	21.21	5.70	45.48	42.80		0.86	14.46	1.11	21.03	1,300	3	97	0	0	50	30.52	-13.63			May-19
500	4.93	22.01	4.60	37.82	32.63	0.62	1.27	16.71	0.84	17.24	504.3	2	98	0	0	68	29.7	-21.28			Dec-09
5,000	4.02	20.51	3.47	38.42	31.01		1.04	16.72	0.84	17.26	504.3	2	98	0	0	68	29.7	-21.28			May-19
	4.18	19.54	0.91	31.29	42.18	0.79	1.36	14.69	0.95	11.44	364.8	2	98	0	0	76	23.11	-19.89			May-02
	4.42	19.82	1.51	33.31	45.86	1.2	0.86	14.78	0.95	12.27	364.8	2	98	0	0	76	23.53	-19.72			May-02
	4.23	19.64	1.19	32.30	44.00	0.97	1.11	14.76	0.95	12.06	364.8	2	98	0	0	76	23.27	-19.71			May-02
	4.19	19.56	1.04	31.76	42.95	0.83	1.26	14.75	0.95	11.43	364.8	2	98	0	0	76	23.23	-19.83			Feb-09
	6.54	28.93	12.18	65.42	65.79	0	1.49	15.67	0.81	31.59	816.9	0	100	0	0	4	24.02	-19.48			May-02
	6.69	29.22	12.73	67.90	69.99	0	0.99	15.66	0.81	35.24	816.9	0	100	0	0	4	24.35	-19.32			May-02
	6.68	29.25	12.72	67.92	70.06	0	0.99	15.65	0.81	35.26	816.9	0	100	0	0	4	24.35	-19.32			May-16
	6.61	29.08	12.48	66.65	67.89	0	1.24	15.65	0.81	33.51	816.9	0	100	0	0	4	24.24	-19.39			May-02
	6.57	28.98	12.32	65.89	66.62	0	1.39	15.66	0.81	31.91	816.9	0	100	0	0	4	24.07	-19.44			Feb-09
	0.82	16.49	7.88	10.45	16.15	4.72	1.49	11.16	0.99	12.22	233.5	0	99	0	0	107	21.8	-18.52			Apr-06
	0.96	16.80	8.45	12.47	19.69	5.28	0.89	11.18	0.99	12.58	233.5	0	99	0	0	107	22.18	-18.28			Jan-06
	0.88	16.69	8.27	11.67	18.16	5.03	1.14	11.13	0.99	12.51	233.5	0	99	0	0	107	22.04	-18.4			Jan-06
	0.80	16.57	8.02	11.08	17.23	4.83	1.29	11.09	0.98	12.59	233.5	0	99	0	0	107	21.94	-18.45			May-06
	1.20	18.76	9.46	8.19	33.74	2.18	1.31	12.68	0.95	34.49	332.6	1	99	0	0	103	31.71	-16.19			Apr-06
	1.39	19.15	10.13	10.17	37.83	2.74	0.71	12.69	0.95	36.45	332.6	1	99	0	0	103	32.16	-15.95			May-03
	1.30	18.98	9.86	9.34	36.11	2.44	0.96	12.69	0.95	36.35	332.6	1	99	0	0	103	31.98	-16.06			Jan-89
	1.26	18.87	9.69	8.85	35.10	2.29	1.11	12.68	0.95	36.08	332.6	1	99	0	0	103	31.89	-16.12			Sep-02
	4.53	20.04	9.29	41.04	54.51	0.62	1.23	12.69	1.02	22.58	279.1	3	97	0	0	64	22.26	-20.1			Dec-01
	4.68	20.33	9.82	43.17	58.41	1.06	0.73	12.68	1.02	23.91	279.1	3	97	0	0	64	22.67	-19.98			Dec-01
	4.61	20.17	9.54	42.10	56.42	0.82	0.98	12.68	1.02	23.35	279.1	3	97	0	0	64	22.45	-20.01			Dec-01
	1.77	16.13	-7.00	28.21	24.55	0.02	1.37	17.69	1.01	16.63	168.7	3	97	0	0	41	30.11	-27.17			Dec-06
	1.94	16.44	-6.50	30.17	27.77	0.55	0.87	17.72	1.01	17.28	168.7	3	97	0	0	41	30.4	-26.95			Apr-06
	1.94	16.50	-6.50	30.23	27.76	0.55	0.87	17.72	1.01	17.29	168.7	3	97	0	0	41	30.4	-26.95			May-16
	1.89	16.32	-6.73	29.17	26.16	0.26	1.12	17.73	1.01	17.17	168.7	3	97	0	0	41	30.31	-27.02			May-06
	1.83	16.22	-6.91	28.61	25.22	0	1.27	17.69	1.01	16.62	168.7	3	97	0	0	41	30.19	-27.15			Feb-09
	2.72	15.70	0.55	40.57	32.90	1.09	1.24	14.65	1.17	19.97	457.1	5	95	0	0	29	24.82	-20.39			May-02

	MARKET		FUND TYPE, CATEGORY & OBJECTIVE		RATINGS				MINIMUMS	
Fund Name	Ticker Symbol	Traded On	Fund Type	Category and (Prospectus Objective)	Overall Rating	Reward Rating	Risk Rating	Recent Up/ Downgrade	Open to New Investors	Min Initial Investment
VY® Invesco Comstock Portfolio Class I	IVKIX	NAS CM	Open End	US Equity Large Cap Value (Growth & Income)	C+	C	B	Up	Y	0
VY® Invesco Comstock Portfolio Class S	IVKSX	NAS CM	Open End	US Equity Large Cap Value (Growth & Income)	C+	C	B-	Up	Y	0
VY® Invesco Equity and Income Portfolio Class A	IUAAX	NAS CM	Open End	Moderate Alloc (Equity-Income)	B-	C	B+	Up	Y	0
VY® Invesco Equity and Income Portfolio Class I	IUAIX	NAS CM	Open End	Moderate Alloc (Equity-Income)	B-	C	B+	Up	Y	0
VY® Invesco Equity and Income Portfolio Class S	IUASX	NAS CM	Open End	Moderate Alloc (Equity-Income)	B-	C	B+	Up	Y	0
VY® Invesco Equity and Income Portfolio Class S2	IVIPX	NAS CM	Open End	Moderate Alloc (Equity-Income)	B-	C	B+	Up	Y	0
VY® Invesco Growth and Income Portfolio Class A	IVGAX	NAS CM	Open End	US Equity Large Cap Value (Growth & Income)	C+	C	B	Up	Y	0
VY® Invesco Growth and Income Portfolio Class I	IVGIX	NAS CM	Open End	US Equity Large Cap Value (Growth & Income)	C+	C	B	Up	Y	0
VY® Invesco Growth and Income Portfolio Class S	IVGSX	NAS CM	Open End	US Equity Large Cap Value (Growth & Income)	C+	C	B	Up	Y	0
VY® Invesco Growth and Income Portfolio Class S2	IVITX	NAS CM	Open End	US Equity Large Cap Value (Growth & Income)	C+	C	B	Up	Y	0
VY® Invesco Oppenheimer Global Portfolio Class A	IGMAX	NAS CM	Open End	Global Equity Large Cap (World Stock)	C+	C	B-	Up	Y	0
VY® Invesco Oppenheimer Global Portfolio Class I	IGMIX	NAS CM	Open End	Global Equity Large Cap (World Stock)	C+	C	B-	Up	Y	0
VY® Invesco Oppenheimer Global Portfolio Class S	IGMSX	NAS CM	Open End	Global Equity Large Cap (World Stock)	C+	C	B-	Up	Y	0
VY® Invesco Oppenheimer Global Portfolio Class S2	IOGPX	NAS CM	Open End	Global Equity Large Cap (World Stock)	C+	C	B-	Up	Y	0
VY® JPMorgan Emerging Markets Equity Portfolio Class A	IJEAX	NAS CM	Open End	Global Emerg Mkts (Div Emerging Mkts)	C	C	C+		Y	0
VY® JPMorgan Emerging Markets Equity Portfolio Class I	IJEMX	NAS CM	Open End	Global Emerg Mkts (Div Emerging Mkts)	C	C	C+		Y	0
VY® JPMorgan Emerging Markets Equity Portfolio Class S	IJPIX	NAS CM	Open End	Global Emerg Mkts (Div Emerging Mkts)	C	C	C+		Y	0
VY® JPMorgan Emerging Markets Equity Portfolio Class S2	IJPTX	NAS CM	Open End	Global Emerg Mkts (Div Emerging Mkts)	C	C	C+		Y	0
VY® JPMorgan Mid Cap Value Portfolio Class A	IJMAX	NAS CM	Open End	US Equity Mid Cap (Growth)	C+	C	B	Up		0
VY® JPMorgan Mid Cap Value Portfolio Class I	IJMIX	NAS CM	Open End	US Equity Mid Cap (Growth)	C+	C	B	Up		0
VY® JPMorgan Mid Cap Value Portfolio Class S	IJMSX	NAS CM	Open End	US Equity Mid Cap (Growth)	C+	C	B	Up		0
VY® JPMorgan Mid Cap Value Portfolio Class S2	IJPMX	NAS CM	Open End	US Equity Mid Cap (Growth)	C+	C	B	Up		0
VY® JPMorgan Small Cap Core Equity Portfolio Class A	IJSAX	NAS CM	Open End	US Equity Small Cap (Small Company)	C	C	B-		Y	0
VY® JPMorgan Small Cap Core Equity Portfolio Class I	IJSIX	NAS CM	Open End	US Equity Small Cap (Small Company)	C	C	B-		Y	0
VY® JPMorgan Small Cap Core Equity Portfolio Class R6	VPRSX	NAS CM	Open End	US Equity Small Cap (Small Company)	C	C	B-		Y	0
VY® JPMorgan Small Cap Core Equity Portfolio Class S	IJSSX	NAS CM	Open End	US Equity Small Cap (Small Company)	C	C	B-		Y	0
VY® JPMorgan Small Cap Core Equity Portfolio Class S2	IJSTX	NAS CM	Open End	US Equity Small Cap (Small Company)	C	C	B-		Y	0
VY® Morgan Stanley Global Franchise Portfolio Class A	IGFAX	NAS CM	Open End	Global Equity Large Cap (World Stock)	B	B	B+		Y	0
VY® Morgan Stanley Global Franchise Portfolio Class R6	VPRDX	NAS CM	Open End	Global Equity Large Cap (World Stock)	B	B	B+		Y	0
VY® Morgan Stanley Global Franchise Portfolio Class S	IVGTX	NAS CM	Open End	Global Equity Large Cap (World Stock)	B	B	B+		Y	0
VY® Morgan Stanley Global Franchise Portfolio Class S2	IGFSX	NAS CM	Open End	Global Equity Large Cap (World Stock)	B	B	B+		Y	0
VY® T. Rowe Price Capital Appreciation Portfolio Class A	ITRAX	NAS CM	Open End	Moderate Alloc (Growth & Income)	B	B-	A	Down	Y	0
VY® T. Rowe Price Capital Appreciation Portfolio Class I	ITRIX	NAS CM	Open End	Moderate Alloc (Growth & Income)	B	B-	A	Down	Y	0
VY® T. Rowe Price Capital Appreciation Portfolio Class R6	VPRAX	NAS CM	Open End	Moderate Alloc (Growth & Income)	B	B-	A	Down	Y	0
VY® T. Rowe Price Capital Appreciation Portfolio Class S	ITCSX	NAS CM	Open End	Moderate Alloc (Growth & Income)	B	B-	A	Down	Y	0
VY® T. Rowe Price Capital Appreciation Portfolio Class S2	ITCTX	NAS CM	Open End	Moderate Alloc (Growth & Income)	B	B-	A	Down	Y	0
VY® T. Rowe Price Diversified Mid Cap Growth Port Cls A	IAXAX	NAS CM	Open End	US Equity Mid Cap (Aggr Growth)	B-	B-	B	Down	Y	0
VY® T. Rowe Price Diversified Mid Cap Growth Port Cls I	IAXIX	NAS CM	Open End	US Equity Mid Cap (Aggr Growth)	B-	B-	B	Down	Y	0
VY® T. Rowe Price Diversified Mid Cap Growth Port Cls R6	VYRIX	NAS CM	Open End	US Equity Mid Cap (Aggr Growth)	B	B-	B		Y	0
VY® T. Rowe Price Diversified Mid Cap Growth Port Cls S	IAXSX	NAS CM	Open End	US Equity Mid Cap (Aggr Growth)	B-	B-	B	Down	Y	0
VY® T. Rowe Price Diversified Mid Cap Growth Port Cls S2	IAXTX	NAS CM	Open End	US Equity Mid Cap (Aggr Growth)	B-	B-	B	Down	Y	0
VY® T. Rowe Price Equity Income Portfolio Class A	ITEAX	NAS CM	Open End	US Equity Large Cap Value (Equity-Income)	B-	C	B	Up	Y	0
VY® T. Rowe Price Equity Income Portfolio Class I	ITEIX	NAS CM	Open End	US Equity Large Cap Value (Equity-Income)	B-	C	B	Up	Y	0
VY® T. Rowe Price Equity Income Portfolio Class S	IRPSX	NAS CM	Open End	US Equity Large Cap Value (Equity-Income)	B-	C	B	Up	Y	0
VY® T. Rowe Price Equity Income Portfolio Class S2	ITETX	NAS CM	Open End	US Equity Large Cap Value (Equity-Income)	B-	C	B	Up	Y	0
VY® T. Rowe Price Growth Equity Portfolio Class A	IGEAX	NAS CM	Open End	US Equity Large Cap Growth (Growth)	B-	C	B	Down	Y	0
VY® T. Rowe Price Growth Equity Portfolio Class I	ITGIX	NAS CM	Open End	US Equity Large Cap Growth (Growth)	B-	C	B	Down	Y	0
VY® T. Rowe Price Growth Equity Portfolio Class S	ITGSX	NAS CM	Open End	US Equity Large Cap Growth (Growth)	B-	C	B	Down	Y	0
VY® T. Rowe Price Growth Equity Portfolio Class S2	ITRGX	NAS CM	Open End	US Equity Large Cap Growth (Growth)	B-	C	B	Down	Y	0
VY® T. Rowe Price International Stock Portfolio Class A	IMIOX	NAS CM	Open End	Global Equity Large Cap (Foreign Stock)	C	C	B-		Y	0
VY® T. Rowe Price International Stock Portfolio Class I	IMASX	NAS CM	Open End	Global Equity Large Cap (Foreign Stock)	C	C	B		Y	0
VY® T. Rowe Price International Stock Portfolio Class S	IMISX	NAS CM	Open End	Global Equity Large Cap (Foreign Stock)	C	C	B		Y	0

★ Expanded analysis of this fund is included in Section II.

	TOTAL RETURNS					PERFORMANCE				ASSETS		ASSET ALLOCATION & TURNOVER					BULL & BEAR		FEES		
Min Additional Investment	3-Month Total Return	6-Month Total Return	1-Year Total Return	3-Year Total Return	5-Year Total Return	Dividend Yield (TTM)	Expense Ratio	3-Yr Std Deviation	3-Year Beta	NAV	Total Assets (MIL)	%Cash	%Stocks	%Bonds	%Other	Turnover Ratio	Last Bull Market Total Return	Last Bear Market Total Return	Front End Fee (%)	Back End Fee (%)	Inception Date
	2.85	15.91	1.03	42.69	36.26	1.62	0.74	14.64	1.17	20.17	457.1	5	95	0	0	29	25.08	-20.16			May-02
	2.80	15.81	0.76	41.63	34.52	1.35	0.99	14.66	1.17	20.14	457.1	5	95	0	0	29	25.05	-20.28			May-02
	3.09	13.28	2.91	27.34	28.43	1.42	1.14	9.98	0.81	43.91	1,356	5	61	25	0	161	17.08	-15.4			Dec-01
	3.21	13.57	3.44	29.26	31.68	1.9	0.64	9.99	0.81	44.69	1,356	5	61	25	0	161	17.38	-15.19			Dec-01
	3.16	13.45	3.17	28.32	30.07	1.66	0.89	9.98	0.81	44.36	1,356	5	61	25	0	161	17.25	-15.32			Dec-01
	3.11	13.35	3.04	27.81	29.20	1.53	1.02	9.98	0.81	43.71	1,356	5	61	25	0	161	17.15	-15.36			Feb-09
	3.15	16.65	1.35	35.86	34.79	1.09	1.24	14.45	1.16	24.51	452.7	5	95	0	0	31	23.54	-20.18			Feb-04
	3.28	16.98	1.92	38.28	38.86	1.66	0.64	14.41	1.16	24.87	452.7	5	95	0	0	31	24.03	-20			Apr-06
	3.21	16.83	1.71	37.27	37.16	1.37	0.89	14.42	1.16	25.05	452.7	5	95	0	0	31	23.81	-20.07			Oct-93
	3.16	16.76	1.53	36.62	36.12	1.21	1.04	14.41	1.16	24.8	452.7	5	95	0	0	31	23.67	-20.1			Sep-02
	3.86	22.07	3.07	56.46	43.22	1.13	1.25	14.21	1.22	20.68	1,514	2	98	0	0	17	17.76	-22.99			May-02
	3.97	22.39	3.56	58.85	46.79	1.48	0.75	14.22	1.22	21.7	1,514	2	98	0	0	17	18.09	-22.93			May-02
	3.94	22.22	3.35	57.66	45.01	1.3	1	14.21	1.22	20.84	1,514	2	98	0	0	17	17.9	-22.96			May-02
	3.85	22.10	3.12	56.92	43.86	1.23	1.15	14.22	1.22	20.22	1,514	2	98	0	0	17	17.9	-23.06			Feb-09
	4.57	21.90	9.42	49.49	25.95	0.32	1.86	15.13	1.04	20.59	500.6	1	99	0	0	21	19.64	-25.64			Mar-06
	4.73	22.27	10.03	52.14	29.78	0.79	1.26	15.15	1.04	21.68	500.6	1	99	0	0	21	20.04	-25.46			Dec-05
	4.61	22.12	9.75	50.98	28.11	0.54	1.51	15.13	1.04	21.53	500.6	1	99	0	0	21	19.85	-25.53			Feb-98
	4.61	22.00	9.60	50.35	27.17	0.37	1.66	15.1	1.03	21.29	500.6	1	99	0	0	21	19.7	-25.55			Sep-02
	2.93	18.89	3.80	28.17	37.98	0.81	1.38	12.97	0.97	18.56	446.9	2	98	0	0	12	27.15	-17.89			May-02
	3.07	19.18	4.34	30.15	41.46	1.25	0.88	12.99	0.97	19.13	446.9	2	98	0	0	12	27.48	-17.71			May-02
	2.99	19.08	4.07	29.19	39.72	1.01	1.13	12.98	0.97	18.91	446.9	2	98	0	0	12	27.36	-17.81			May-02
	3.00	18.94	3.93	28.60	38.71	0.87	1.28	12.98	0.97	18.52	446.9	2	98	0	0	12	27.24	-17.81			Feb-09
	3.33	18.92	-1.56	43.85	45.27	0.09	1.45	16.57	0.96	18.6	781.5	1	99	0	0	43	29.96	-24.13			Aug-04
	3.52	19.36	-0.94	46.51	49.75	0.6	0.85	16.58	0.96	19.97	781.5	1	99	0	0	43	30.5	-24.01			May-04
	3.47	19.24	-0.99	46.38	48.94	0.6	0.85	16.6	0.96	19.95	781.5	1	99	0	0	43	30.27	-24.08			May-16
	3.47	19.22	-1.19	45.36	47.89	0.35	1.1	16.61	0.96	19.66	781.5	1	99	0	0	43	30.26	-24.08			May-02
	3.40	19.07	-1.34	44.71	46.73	0.18	1.25	16.57	0.96	19.41	781.5	1	99	0	0	43	30.12	-24.12			Sep-02
	4.96	21.30	14.81	48.91	63.44	0.73	1.54	10.42	0.75	16.91	413.4	4	96	0	0	27	17.72	-6.85			Dec-06
	5.16	21.67	15.47	51.66	67.65	1.16	0.94	10.39	0.75	18.13	413.4	4	96	0	0	27	18.03	-6.75			May-16
	5.04	21.51	15.17	50.38	66.23	0.92	1.19	10.39	0.75	18.13	413.4	4	96	0	0	27	18.03	-6.75			May-02
	5.03	21.44	15.03	49.77	65.02	0.76	1.34	10.37	0.75	17.95	413.4	4	96	0	0	27	17.99	-6.82			Sep-02
	4.75	17.87	14.58	39.09	58.97	1.65	1.24	7.58	0.59	28.22	7,145	7	61	27	1	75	19.2	-12.92			Dec-03
	4.92	18.23	15.26	41.61	63.81	2.04	0.64	7.58	0.59	29.63	7,145	7	61	27	1	75	19.65	-12.72			May-03
	4.91	18.22	15.29	41.69	63.11	2.04	0.64	7.58	0.59	29.65	7,145	7	61	27	1	75	19.45	-12.8			May-16
	4.85	18.06	14.99	40.60	61.80	1.82	0.89	7.56	0.58	29.61	7,145	7	61	27	1	75	19.45	-12.8			Jan-89
	4.81	17.99	14.94	39.97	60.60	1.71	1.04	7.57	0.59	29.37	7,145	7	61	27	1	75	19.35	-12.86			Sep-02
	7.03	28.69	16.20	62.75	76.38	0	1.27	13.65	0.86	11.57	1,109	0	99	0	0	19	27.7	-22.86			Dec-01
	7.11	29.11	16.81	65.21	80.95	0.15	0.77	13.7	0.86	12.95	1,109	0	99	0	0	19	27.99	-22.71			Dec-01
	7.11	28.98	16.70	65.19	81.10	0.15	0.77	13.68	0.86	12.95	1,109	0	99	0	0	19	27.99	-22.71			May-16
	7.06	28.97	16.53	63.92	78.71	0	1.02	13.67	0.86	12.42	1,109	0	99	0	0	19	27.8	-22.8			Dec-01
	6.98	28.76	16.32	63.16	77.31	0	1.17	13.75	0.86	11.64	1,109	0	99	0	0	19	27.74	-22.83			Feb-09
	4.19	16.41	4.93	36.96	34.15	1.56	1.21	12.3	1	12.41	817.9	2	96	1	0	16	23.42	-18.44			Jan-04
	4.35	16.71	5.54	39.42	38.31	2.04	0.61	12.32	1	12.71	817.9	2	96	1	0	16	23.83	-18.2			May-03
	4.17	16.48	5.21	38.37	36.44	1.81	0.86	12.3	1	12.72	817.9	2	96	1	0	16	23.59	-18.27			Jan-89
	4.24	16.48	5.13	37.79	35.57	1.71	1.01	12.32	1	12.51	817.9	2	96	1	0	16	23.52	-18.32			Sep-02
	3.66	21.15	7.77	70.14	84.88	0	1.21	13.86	1.04	85.16	1,929	1	97	0	0	47	30.54	-16.68			Dec-01
	3.79	21.45	8.32	72.71	89.56	0.21	0.71	13.87	1.04	93.9	1,929	1	97	0	0	47	30.96	-16.51			Nov-97
	3.71	21.30	8.03	71.40	87.20	0.04	0.96	13.86	1.04	89.57	1,929	1	97	0	0	47	30.75	-16.58			Dec-01
	3.67	21.21	7.88	70.65	85.81	0	1.11	13.86	1.04	86.57	1,929	1	97	0	0	47	30.65	-16.65			Feb-09
	3.18	16.78	2.05	32.06	19.17	1.4	1.36	12.37	1.04	15.86	212.5	2	97	0	0	35	19.48	-24.06			Jan-06
	3.29	17.15	2.70	34.40	22.78	1.91	0.76	12.4	1.05	15.98	212.5	2	97	0	0	35	19.89	-23.81			Apr-05
	3.31	17.08	2.45	33.48	21.26	1.66	1.01	12.37	1.04	15.9	212.5	2	97	0	0	35	19.63	-23.88			May-05

	MARKET		FUND TYPE, CATEGORY & OBJECTIVE		RATINGS				MINIMUMS	
Fund Name	Ticker Symbol	Traded On	Fund Type	Category and (Prospectus Objective)	Overall Rating	Reward Rating	Risk Rating	Recent Up/ Downgrade	Open to New Investors	Min Initial Investment
VY® Templeton Global Growth Portfolio Class A	IGGAX	NAS CM	Open End	Global Equity Large Cap (World Stock)	C-	D+	C	Down	Y	0
VY® Templeton Global Growth Portfolio Class I	IIGGX	NAS CM	Open End	Global Equity Large Cap (World Stock)	C	C-	C		Y	0
VY® Templeton Global Growth Portfolio Class S	ISGGX	NAS CM	Open End	Global Equity Large Cap (World Stock)	C-	C-	C	Down	Y	0
VY® Templeton Global Growth Portfolio Class S2	ICGGX	NAS CM	Open End	Global Equity Large Cap (World Stock)	C-	C-	C	Down	Y	0
Walden Asset Management Fund	WSBFX	NAS CM	Open End	Aggressive Alloc (Balanced)	B	C+	A-		Y	100,000
Walden Equity Fund	WSEFX	NAS CM	Open End	US Equity Large Cap Blend (Growth)	B-	C+	B+	Down	Y	100,000
Walden International Equity Fund	WIEFX	NAS CM	Open End	Global Equity Large Cap (Growth)	C+	C	B	Up	Y	1,000,000
Walden Midcap Fund	WAMFX	NAS CM	Open End	US Equity Mid Cap (Growth)	B-	C+	B	Down	Y	100,000
Walden Small Cap Fund	WASOX	NAS CM	Open End	US Equity Small Cap (Small Company)	C+	C	B	Down		100,000
Walden SMID Cap Fund	WASMX	NAS CM	Open End	US Equity Small Cap (Growth)	B-	C	B		Y	100,000
Walthausen Select Value Fund Class Retail	WSVRX	NAS CM	Open End	US Equity Small Cap (Growth)	C	C	C+		Y	2,500
Walthausen Select Value Fund Institutional Class	WSVIX	NAS CM	Open End	US Equity Small Cap (Growth)	C	C	C+		Y	100,000
Walthausen Select Value Fund R6 Class	WRSIX	NAS CM	Open End	US Equity Small Cap (Growth)	C	C	C+		Y	0
Walthausen Small Cap Value Fund	WSCVX	NAS CM	Open End	US Equity Small Cap (Small Company)	C-	C-	C	Down		2,500
Walthausen Small Cap Value Fund Institutional	WFICX	NAS CM	Open End	US Equity Small Cap (Small Company)	C-	C-	C	Down	Y	100,000
Wanger International	WSCAX	NAS CM	Open End	Global Equity Mid/Small Cap (Foreign Stock)	U	U	U		Y	0
Wanger International Select	WAFFX	NAS CM	Open End	Global Equity Large Cap (Foreign Stock)	U	U	U		Y	0
Wanger Select	WATWX	NAS CM	Open End	US Equity Mid Cap (Growth)	U	U	U		Y	0
Wanger USA	WUSAX	NAS CM	Open End	US Equity Small Cap (Aggr Growth)	U	U	U		Y	0
Wasatch Core Growth Fund	WGROX	NAS CM	Open End	US Equity Small Cap (Growth)	C+	C	B-	Down	Y	2,000
Wasatch Core Growth Fund Institutional Class Shares	WIGRX	NAS CM	Open End	US Equity Small Cap (Growth)	C+	C	B-	Down	Y	100,000
Wasatch Emerging India Fund® Institutional Class	WIINX	NAS CM	Open End	India Equity (Foreign Stock)	C+	C+	B-	Up	Y	100,000
Wasatch Emerging India Fund® Investor Class	WAINX	NAS CM	Open End	India Equity (Foreign Stock)	C+	C+	B-	Up	Y	2,000
Wasatch Emerging Markets Select Institutional Cls Shares	WIESX	NAS CM	Open End	Global Emerg Mkts (Div Emerging Mkts)	C	C	C+		Y	100,000
Wasatch Emerging Markets Select Fund Investor Class Shares	WAESX	NAS CM	Open End	Global Emerg Mkts (Div Emerging Mkts)	C	C	C+		Y	2,000
Wasatch Emerging Markets Small Cap Fund® Institutional Cls	WIEMX	NAS CM	Open End	Global Emerg Mkts (Div Emerging Mkts)	C	C	C		Y	100,000
Wasatch Emerging Markets Small Cap Fund® Investor Class	WAEMX	NAS CM	Open End	Global Emerg Mkts (Div Emerging Mkts)	C	C	C			2,000
Wasatch Frontier Emerging Small Countries Inv Cls Shares	WAFMX	NAS CM	Open End	Global Emerg Mkts (Growth)	C	C-	C+	Up		2,000
Wasatch Frontier Emerging Small Countries Fund® Inst Cls	WIFMX	NAS CM	Open End	Global Emerg Mkts (Growth)	C	C-	C+	Up	Y	100,000
Wasatch Global Opportunities Fund® Institutional Class	WIGOX	NAS CM	Open End	Global Equity Mid/Small Cap (World Stock)	C+	C	B-		Y	100,000
Wasatch Global Opportunities Fund® Investor Class	WAGOX	NAS CM	Open End	Global Equity Mid/Small Cap (World Stock)	C+	C	B-	Up	Y	2,000
Wasatch Global Value Fund™ Institutional Class Shares	WILCX	NAS CM	Open End	Global Equity Large Cap (Growth)	B-	C	B+		Y	100,000
Wasatch Global Value Fund™ Investor Class Shares	FMIEX	NAS CM	Open End	Global Equity Large Cap (Growth)	B-	C	B+		Y	2,000
Wasatch International Growth Fund® Institutional Class	WIIGX	NAS CM	Open End	Global Equity Mid/Small Cap (Foreign Stock)	C	C	C			100,000
Wasatch International Growth Fund® Investor Class	WAIGX	NAS CM	Open End	Global Equity Mid/Small Cap (Foreign Stock)	C	C	C			2,000
Wasatch Intl Opp Fund® Inst Cls	WIIOX	NAS CM	Open End	Global Equity Mid/Small Cap (Foreign Stock)	C+	C	B-	Up		100,000
Wasatch International Opportunities Fund® Investor Class	WAIOX	NAS CM	Open End	Global Equity Mid/Small Cap (Foreign Stock)	C	C	B-		Y	2,000
Wasatch Micro Cap Fund	WMICX	NAS CM	Open End	US Equity Small Cap (Growth & Income)	B-	B-	C+		Y	2,000
Wasatch Micro Cap Value Fund	WAMVX	NAS CM	Open End	US Equity Small Cap (Growth & Income)	C+	C+	B-		Y	2,000
Wasatch Small Cap Growth Fund® Institutional Class	WIAEX	NAS CM	Open End	US Equity Small Cap (Small Company)	B-	B-	B-	Down		100,000
Wasatch Small Cap Growth Fund® Investor Class	WAAEX	NAS CM	Open End	US Equity Small Cap (Small Company)	B-	B-	B-	Down		2,000
Wasatch Small Cap Value Fund	WMCVX	NAS CM	Open End	US Equity Small Cap (Small Company)	C+	C	B		Y	2,000
Wasatch Small Cap Value Fund Institutional Class Shares	WICVX	NAS CM	Open End	US Equity Small Cap (Small Company)	C+	C	B		Y	100,000
Wasatch Ultra Growth Fund	WAMCX	NAS CM	Open End	US Equity Small Cap (Growth)	B-	C+	B-	Down	Y	2,000
Water Island Credit Opportunities Fund Class A	AGCAX	NAS CM	Open End	Long/Short Credit (Growth & Income)	B-	C	A-		Y	2,000
Water Island Credit Opportunities Fund Class C	ARCCX	NAS CM	Open End	Long/Short Credit (Growth & Income)	C+	C	B		Y	2,000
Water Island Credit Opportunities Fund Class I	ACFIX	NAS CM	Open End	Long/Short Credit (Growth & Income)	B-	C	B+		Y	100,000
Water Island Credit Opportunities Fund Class R	ARCFX	NAS CM	Open End	Long/Short Credit (Growth & Income)	B-	C	B		Y	2,000
Waycross Long/Short Equity Fund	WAYEX	NAS CM	Open End	Long/Short Equity (Growth)	C+	C	B	Down	Y	5,000
WCM Alternatives: Credit Event Fund Institutional Class	WCFIX	NAS CM	Open End	Long/Short Credit (Growth & Income)	D+	D+	B	Up	Y	1,000,000
WCM Alternatives: Credit Event Fund Investor Class	WCFRX	NAS CM	Open End	Long/Short Credit (Growth & Income)	D+	D+	B	Up	Y	2,000
WCM Alternatives: Event-Driven Fund Institutional Class	WCEIX	NAS CM	Open End	Multialternative (Growth)	B	C+	A-		Y	1,000,000

★Expanded analysis of this fund is included in Section II.

Min Additional Investment	TOTAL RETURNS: 3-Month Total Return	6-Month Total Return	1-Year Total Return	3-Year Total Return	5-Year Total Return	PERFORMANCE: Dividend Yield (TTM)	Expense Ratio	3-Yr Std Deviation	3-Year Beta	ASSETS: NAV	Total Assets (MIL)	ASSET ALLOCATION & TURNOVER: %Cash	%Stocks	%Bonds	%Other	Turnover Ratio	BULL & BEAR: Last Bull Market Total Return	Last Bear Market Total Return	FEES: Front End Fee (%)	Back End Fee (%)	Inception Date
	-0.44	8.14	-5.57	24.52	1.83	2.61	1.43	13.14	1.1	8.9	133.5	1	97	0	0	27	18.06	-22.55			Dec-06
	-0.21	8.52	-4.95	26.80	5.01	3.11	0.83	13.24	1.1	9.29	133.5	1	97	0	0	27	18.58	-22.29			Apr-06
	-0.31	8.32	-5.22	25.86	3.71	2.77	1.08	13.15	1.1	9.37	133.5	1	97	0	0	27	18.4	-22.35			Oct-92
	-0.32	8.30	-5.37	25.25	2.90	2.59	1.23	13.21	1.1	9.26	133.5	1	97	0	0	27	18.31	-22.44			Sep-02
1,000	3.68	14.52	10.74	34.62	44.91	0.95	1	8.48	0.68	19.4	145.0	0	71	28	0	8	17.84	-11.54			Jun-99
1,000	4.57	19.76	13.65	51.45	62.67	0.75	1	11.9	0.96	24.48	229.5	1	99	0	0	7	24.65	-16.43			Jun-99
1,000	3.65	13.45	1.94	24.97		1.5	1.15	9.54	0.84	11.05	51.1	1	99	0	0	3					Jun-15
1,000	4.89	20.80	12.87	47.73	63.95	0.48	1	12.55	0.9	18.64	54.7	1	99	0	0	19	25.91				Aug-11
1,000	4.44	21.27	7.59	46.28	49.81	0.44	1	15.13	0.86	20.69	103.8	1	99	0	0	22	25.36	-21.59			Oct-08
1,000	4.23	20.05	7.87	51.36	55.99	0.47	1	13.83	0.86	17.96	56.5	2	98	0	0	19					Jun-12
100	5.87	18.95	-1.54	33.78	18.50	0	1.35	17.07	1.1	11.36	11.5	2	98	0	0	39	27.59	-22.86			Dec-10
1,000	5.91	19.01	-1.34	34.77	19.94	0	1.1	17.07	1.1	11.64	11.5	2	98	0	0	39	27.76	-22.74			Dec-10
	5.95	19.18	-1.18	35.16	20.29	0	0.98	17.11	1.1	11.74	11.5	2	98	0	0	39	27.76	-22.74			Nov-16
100	1.06	14.06	-8.74	29.51	14.49	0	1.21	19.41	1.09	18.98	391.1	2	98	0	0	46	28.93	-24.9			Feb-08
1,000	0.05	12.80	-9.79	30.31	13.22		0.98	19.41	1.09	18.99	391.1	2	98	0	0	46	28.93	-24.9			Dec-18
	-7.89	-10.32	-9.12	4.60	12.26	1.52	1.05	10.96	0.85		547.7	0	99	0	1	28	17.26	-21.76			May-95
	-7.95	-8.39	-9.41	-2.12	6.66	1.59	1.43	11.11	0.75		16.7	0	99	0	0	61	15.18	-18.72			Feb-99
	-14.34	-13.87	-10.39	16.28	19.28	0.01	0.73	11.91	0.94		122.7	0	100	0	0	18	26.66	-27.78			Feb-99
	-18.56	-19.32	-16.87	10.19	32.49	0	0.96	14.3	0.94		621.5	0	100	0	0	14	28.11	-24.29			May-95
100	7.60	25.25	7.79	68.86	80.74	0	1.18	15.69	0.85	74.14	2,352	1	99	0	0	27	22.67	-14.49			Dec-86
5,000	7.64	25.35	7.94	69.58	81.81	0	1.06	15.68	0.85	74.81	2,352	1	99	0	0	27	22.7	-14.49			Jan-12
5,000	1.43	7.86	5.88	57.54	94.14	0	1.51	16.91	0.86	4.25	281.7	1	99	0	0	48	0.94	-8.5			Feb-16
100	1.44	7.92	5.68	57.06	92.90	0	1.7	16.89	0.86	4.22	281.7	1	99	0	0	48	0.93	-8.5			Apr-11
5,000	3.02	17.18	2.74	30.51	13.06	0	1.21	15.21	0.88	11.59	46.1	2	98	0	0	44					Dec-12
100	2.98	17.06	2.51	29.43	11.61	0	1.51	15.14	0.88	11.39	46.1	2	98	0	0	44					Dec-12
5,000	2.33	14.35	-1.33	22.21	9.75	0	1.81	14.36	0.99	2.63	377.5	0	100	0	0	40	22.68	-17.86			Feb-16
100	2.74	14.41	-1.33	21.80	9.38	0	1.95	14.44	1	2.62	377.5	0	100	0	0	40	22.68	-17.87			Oct-07
100	8.42	19.91	10.54	8.42	-11.82	0	2.17	12.79	1.03	2.83	64.5	4	94	0	1	42					Jan-12
5,000	8.36	19.74	10.46	9.19	-11.54	0	1.98	12.82	1.02	2.85	64.5	4	94	0	1	42					Feb-16
5,000	7.76	27.11	8.85	62.25	59.64	0	1.36	15.01	1	3.61	126.6	2	98	0	0	40	20.88	-22.03			Feb-16
100	7.78	27.20	8.61	61.45	58.85	0	1.55	15.06	1.01	3.6	126.6	2	98	0	0	40	20.88	-22.03			Nov-08
5,000	1.43	11.90	5.74	31.28	31.74	2.21	0.95	10.32	0.82	7.77	163.0	2	98	0	0	72	20.82	-21.06			Jan-12
100	1.38	11.79	5.57	30.60	30.76	2.07	1.11	10.19	0.81	7.78	163.0	2	98	0	0	72	20.8	-21.06			Sep-96
5,000	4.53	19.88	-5.22	24.69	30.58	0.01	1.35	14.91	1.12	29.3	1,285	3	97	0	0	44	23.12	-21.37			Feb-16
100	4.54	19.86	-5.29	24.38	30.16	0	1.45	14.92	1.12	29.21	1,285	3	97	0	0	44	23.12	-21.37			Jun-02
5,000	8.43	23.70	3.29	35.96	49.48	0	1.95	13.6	0.95	3.6	494.7	5	95	0	0	36	17.76	-19.99			Feb-16
100	8.23	23.69	2.76	34.67	48.11	0	2.09	13.62	0.94	3.55	494.7	5	95	0	0	36	17.76	-19.99			Jan-05
100	7.16	28.88	9.57	93.38	90.49	0	1.65	16.86	0.82	7.63	471.5	1	98	0	1	54	28.63	-24.26			Jun-95
100	8.62	24.99	6.13	64.21	70.22	0.48	1.74	13.91	0.73	3.4	267.1	4	96	0	0	69	22.76	-22.22			Jul-03
5,000	8.83	32.50	17.75	81.93	78.59	0	1.05	16.56	0.87	42.48	1,805	0	98	0	1	36	26.45	-17.83			Feb-16
100	8.81	32.43	17.60	80.98	77.52	0	1.2	16.54	0.86	42.1	1,805	0	98	0	1	36	26.45	-17.83			Dec-86
100	5.15	17.78	1.72	52.86	48.36	0	1.2	15.44	0.86	7.75	771.2	2	98	0	0	46	23.39	-21.8			Dec-97
5,000	5.12	17.82	1.83	53.43	49.03	0	1.06	15.45	0.85	7.8	771.2	2	98	0	0	46	23.06	-21.8			Jan-12
100	5.12	26.18	13.00	103.06	101.73	0	1.25	17.54	0.93	26.26	623.4	10	89	0	1	44	19.86	-19.62			Aug-92
	1.07	3.54	2.95	8.96	8.59	3.31	1.7	1.65	8.31	9.67	58.0	24	-3	68	0	314			3.25		May-13
	0.88	3.04	2.18	6.62	4.76	2.57	2.45	1.67	7.72	9.68	58.0	24	-3	68	0	314			3.25	1.00	Oct-12
	1.14	3.67	3.20	9.81	9.98	3.56	1.45	1.62	8.17	9.67	58.0	24	-3	68	0	314			3.25		Oct-12
	0.97	3.42	2.84	8.85	8.56	3.32	1.7	1.62	7.17	9.71	58.0	24	-3	68	0	314			3.25		Oct-12
	2.96	16.95	3.99	25.44		0	2.9	10.68	0.82	11.45	45.5	50	50	0	0	43					Apr-15
500	3.77	9.64	6.21			1.5	1.78			10.46	4.0	9	33	33	21	192					Dec-17
	3.67	9.54	5.89			1.31	2.03			10.44	4.0	9	33	33	21	192					Dec-17
500	1.50	6.53	6.16	20.31	16.31	3.96	2.31	3.71	7.04	10.76	194.5	35	31	15	16	230					Jan-14

	MARKET			FUND TYPE, CATEGORY & OBJECTIVE	RATINGS				MINIMUMS	
Fund Name	Ticker Symbol	Traded On	Fund Type	Category and (Prospectus Objective)	Overall Rating	Reward Rating	Risk Rating	Recent Up/ Downgrade	Open to New Investors	Min Initial Investment
WCM Alternatives: Event-Driven Fund Investor Class	WCERX	NAS CM	Open End	Multialternative (Growth)	B	C+	A+		Y	2,000
WCM Focused Emerging Markets Fund Institutional Class	WCMEX	NAS CM	Open End	Global Emerg Mkts (Div Emerging Mkts)	C	C	C+		Y	100,000
WCM Focused Emerging Markets Fund Investor Class	WFEMX	NAS CM	Open End	Global Emerg Mkts (Div Emerging Mkts)	C	C	C+		Y	1,000
WCM Focused Global Growth Fund Institutional Class	WCMGX	NAS CM	Open End	Global Equity Large Cap (Growth)	B	B	B		Y	100,000
WCM Focused Global Growth Fund Investor Class	WFGGX	NAS CM	Open End	Global Equity Large Cap (Growth)	B	B	B		Y	1,000
WCM Focused International Growth Fund Institutional Class	WCMIX	NAS CM	Open End	Global Equity Large Cap (Foreign Stock)	B-	C+	B	Up	Y	100,000
WCM Focused International Growth Fund Investor Class	WCMRX	NAS CM	Open End	Global Equity Large Cap (Foreign Stock)	B-	C+	B	Up	Y	1,000
WCM International Small Cap Growth Institutional Cls	WCMSX	NAS CM	Open End	Global Equity Mid/Small Cap (Small Company)	C	C	C+		Y	100,000
Wealthfront Risk Parity Fund Class W	WFRPX	NAS CM	Open End	Cautious Alloc (Growth & Income)	D	D+	C+		Y	5,000,000
Weiss Alternative Balanced Risk Fund Class K	WEIKX	NAS CM	Open End	Multialternative (Balanced)	B	C+	A		Y	100,000
Weiss Alternative Balanced Risk Fund Investor Class	WEIZX	NAS CM	Open End	Multialternative (Balanced)	B	C+	A		Y	5,000
Weitz Balanced Fund - Investor Class	WBALX	NAS CM	Open End	Cautious Alloc (Balanced)	B	C+	A		Y	2,500
Weitz Balanced Fund Institutional Class	WBAIX	NAS CM	Open End	Cautious Alloc (Balanced)	B	C+	A		Y	1,000,000
Weitz Funds Hickory Fund	WEHIX	NAS CM	Open End	US Equity Mid Cap (Growth)	C+	C	B	Up	Y	2,500
Weitz Partners III Opportunity Fund Institutional Class	WPOPX	NAS CM	Open End	Long/Short Equity (Growth)	B-	C	B	Up	Y	1,000,000
Weitz Partners III Opportunity Fund Investor Class	WPOIX	NAS CM	Open End	Long/Short Equity (Growth)	B-	C	B	Up	Y	2,500
Weitz Partners Value Fund Institutional Class	WPVIX	NAS CM	Open End	US Equity Large Cap Blend (Growth)	C+	C	B		Y	1,000,000
Weitz Partners Value Fund Investor Class	WPVLX	NAS CM	Open End	US Equity Large Cap Blend (Growth)	C+	C	B		Y	2,500
Weitz Value Fund Institutional Class	WVAIX	NAS CM	Open End	US Equity Large Cap Growth (Growth)	B-	C	B		Y	1,000,000
Weitz Value Fund Investor Class	WVALX	NAS CM	Open End	US Equity Large Cap Growth (Growth)	B-	C	B		Y	2,500
Wellington Shields All-Cap Fund Institutional Shares	WSACX	NAS CM	Open End	US Equity Mid Cap (Growth)	C	C	B-		Y	5,000
Wellington Shields Small-Cap Fund Institutional Shares	WSSSX	NAS CM	Open End	US Equity Small Cap (Small Company)	C-	D+	C	Down	Y	5,000
Wells Fargo Absolute Return Fund - Class A	WARAX	NAS CM	Open End	Cautious Alloc (Growth & Income)	C+	C	B+	Up	Y	1,000
Wells Fargo Absolute Return Fund - Class Admin	WARDX	NAS CM	Open End	Cautious Alloc (Growth & Income)	C+	C	B+	Up	Y	1,000,000
Wells Fargo Absolute Return Fund - Class C	WARCX	NAS CM	Open End	Cautious Alloc (Growth & Income)	C	C-	B		Y	1,000
Wells Fargo Absolute Return Fund - Class Inst	WABIX	NAS CM	Open End	Cautious Alloc (Growth & Income)	C+	C	B+	Up	Y	1,000,000
Wells Fargo Absolute Return Fund - Class R	WARHX	NAS CM	Open End	Cautious Alloc (Growth & Income)	C+	C	B+	Up	Y	0
Wells Fargo Absolute Return Fund - Class R6	WARRX	NAS CM	Open End	Cautious Alloc (Growth & Income)	C+	C	B+	Up	Y	0
Wells Fargo Alternative Risk Premia Fund Class R6	WRPRX	NAS CM	Open End	Multialternative (Growth)	U	U	U			0
Wells Fargo Alternative Risk Premia Institutional Cls	WRPIX	NAS CM	Open End	Multialternative (Growth)	U	U	U			1,000,000
Wells Fargo Asia Pacific Fund - Class A	WFAAX	NAS CM	Open End	Asia Equity (Pacific Stock)	C	C-	C		Y	1,000
Wells Fargo Asia Pacific Fund - Class Admin	WFADX	NAS CM	Open End	Asia Equity (Pacific Stock)	C	C-	C		Y	1,000,000
Wells Fargo Asia Pacific Fund - Class C	WFCAX	NAS CM	Open End	Asia Equity (Pacific Stock)	C	C-	C	Up	Y	1,000
Wells Fargo Asia Pacific Fund - Class Inst	WFPIX	NAS CM	Open End	Asia Equity (Pacific Stock)	C	C-	C		Y	1,000,000
Wells Fargo Asset Allocation Fund - Class A	EAAFX	NAS CM	Open End	Moderate Alloc (Multi-Asset Global)	B-	C	B+	Up	Y	1,000
Wells Fargo Asset Allocation Fund - Class Admin	EAIFX	NAS CM	Open End	Moderate Alloc (Multi-Asset Global)	B-	C	B+	Up	Y	1,000,000
Wells Fargo Asset Allocation Fund - Class C	EACFX	NAS CM	Open End	Moderate Alloc (Multi-Asset Global)	B-	C	B+	Up	Y	1,000
Wells Fargo Asset Allocation Fund - Class Inst	EAAIX	NAS CM	Open End	Moderate Alloc (Multi-Asset Global)	B-	C	B+	Up	Y	1,000,000
Wells Fargo Asset Allocation Fund - Class R	EAXFX	NAS CM	Open End	Moderate Alloc (Multi-Asset Global)	B-	C	B+	Up	Y	0
Wells Fargo C&B Large Cap Value Fund - Class A	CBEAX	NAS CM	Open End	US Equity Large Cap Value (Growth)	C+	C	B	Up	Y	1,000
Wells Fargo C&B Large Cap Value Fund - Class Admin	CBLLX	NAS CM	Open End	US Equity Large Cap Value (Growth)	C+	C	B	Up	Y	1,000,000
Wells Fargo C&B Large Cap Value Fund - Class C	CBECX	NAS CM	Open End	US Equity Large Cap Value (Growth)	C+	C	B	Up	Y	1,000
Wells Fargo C&B Large Cap Value Fund - Class Inst	CBLSX	NAS CM	Open End	US Equity Large Cap Value (Growth)	C+	C	B		Y	1,000,000
Wells Fargo C&B Large Cap Value Fund Class R6	CBEJX	NAS CM	Open End	US Equity Large Cap Value (Growth)	C+	C	B		Y	0
Wells Fargo C&B Mid Cap Value Fund - Class A	CBMAX	NAS CM	Open End	US Equity Mid Cap (Growth)	C+	C	B	Up	Y	1,000
Wells Fargo C&B Mid Cap Value Fund - Class Admin	CBMIX	NAS CM	Open End	US Equity Mid Cap (Growth)	C+	C	B	Up	Y	1,000,000
Wells Fargo C&B Mid Cap Value Fund - Class C	CBMCX	NAS CM	Open End	US Equity Mid Cap (Growth)	C+	C	B	Up	Y	1,000
Wells Fargo C&B Mid Cap Value Fund - Class Inst	CBMSX	NAS CM	Open End	US Equity Mid Cap (Growth)	C+	C	B	Up	Y	1,000,000
Wells Fargo C&B Mid Cap Value Fund - Class R6	CBMYX	NAS CM	Open End	US Equity Mid Cap (Growth)	C+	C	B	Up	Y	0
Wells Fargo Capital Growth Fund - Class A	WFCGX	NAS CM	Open End	US Equity Large Cap Growth (Growth)	B	B	B		Y	1,000
Wells Fargo Capital Growth Fund - Class Admin	WFCDX	NAS CM	Open End	US Equity Large Cap Growth (Growth)	B	B	B		Y	1,000,000
Wells Fargo Capital Growth Fund - Class C	WFCCX	NAS CM	Open End	US Equity Large Cap Growth (Growth)	B	B-	B		Y	1,000

★ Expanded analysis of this fund is included in Section II.

	TOTAL RETURNS					PERFORMANCE				ASSETS		ASSET ALLOCATION & TURNOVER					BULL & BEAR		FEES		
Min Additional Investment	3-Month Total Return	6-Month Total Return	1-Year Total Return	3-Year Total Return	5-Year Total Return	Dividend Yield (TTM)	Expense Ratio	3-Yr Std Deviation	3-Year Beta	NAV	Total Assets (MIL)	%Cash	%Stocks	%Bonds	%Other	Turnover Ratio	Last Bull Market Total Return	Last Bear Market Total Return	Front End Fee (%)	Back End Fee (%)	Inception Date
	1.41	6.34	5.86	19.40	14.86	3.77	2.56	3.72	6.74	10.72	194.5	35	31	15	16	230					Mar-17
5,000	5.03	23.26	7.44	40.89	26.98	0.61	1.26	14.94	0.92	13.14	64.7	5	97	0	-1	47					Jun-13
100	4.97	23.25	7.47	40.96	26.70	0.62	1.51	14.9	0.92	13.09	64.7	5	97	0	-1	47					Jun-13
5,000	7.86	28.07	17.85	58.89	81.14	0	1.06	12.71	1.03	17.7	111.6	4	96	0	0	38					Jun-13
100	7.82	27.92	17.39	57.82	79.19	0	1.31	12.71	1.03	17.5	111.6	4	96	0	0	38					Jun-13
5,000	9.92	25.10	11.99	49.34	54.70	0.29	1.06	11.73	0.88	17.39	8,740	4	96	0	0	26	17.61				May-11
100	9.89	24.96	11.74	48.25	52.83	0.07	1.31	11.73	0.88	17.32	8,740	4	96	0	0	26	17.49				Aug-11
5,000	7.03	27.29	1.93	61.47		0	1.26	16.24	1.15	15.67	15.6	4	96	0	0	58					Nov-15
	5.63	20.52	12.10			1.6	0.25			10.03	926.1	394	0	0	-294						Jan-18
1,000	3.98	10.36	8.80	17.61		1.88	3.39	4.13	0.81	10.97	91.4	42	11	44	2	700					Dec-15
1,000	4.00	10.21	8.48	16.62		1.84	3.74	4.13	0.8	10.9	91.4	42	11	44	2	700				1.00	Feb-17
25	4.38	13.45	9.35	24.87	28.11	0.92	0.85	5.88	1.13	14.32	129.8	9	46	45	0	33	15.96	-10.19			Oct-03
25	4.38	13.45	9.35	24.87	28.11		0.7	5.88	1.13	14.32	129.8	9	46	45	0	33	15.96	-10.19			Mar-19
25	7.58	26.57	8.20	25.56	21.45	0	1.24	13.75	0.93	50.26	228.3	3	97	0	0	28	23.99	-18.31			Apr-93
25	3.72	24.52	14.33	31.50	23.21	0	1.63	12.68	0.86	15.58	658.2	18	82	0	0	38	20.5	-14.35			Dec-05
25	3.59	24.26	13.68	29.40	20.33	0	2.14	12.71	0.87	15	658.2	18	82	0	0	38	20.22	-14.35			Aug-11
25	6.13	23.34	8.62	29.35	21.74	0	0.99	14.03	1.08	30.34	594.9	4	96	0	0	38	22.48	-16.13			Jul-14
25	6.07	23.13	8.30	28.34	20.34	0	1.25	14.04	1.08	29.93	594.9	4	96	0	0	38	22.48	-16.13			Jun-83
25	7.61	25.01	14.64	43.18	40.68	0	0.99	12.24	0.94	44.81	819.2	4	96	0	0	32	22.24	-12.09			Jul-14
25	7.54	24.83	14.34	42.16	39.16	0	1.22	12.23	0.94	44.23	819.2	4	96	0	0	32	22.24	-12.09			May-86
500	3.62	16.31	-1.07	25.45	36.16	0	1.51	13.2	1	22.03	29.7	0	86	14	0	75	21.85	-21.51			Jan-95
500	0.86	11.46	-5.09	11.50	-3.64	0	1.51	16.25	0.84	18.66	13.9	0	84	16	0	57	18.08	-17.58			Jan-99
100	1.36	7.00	2.39	15.67	6.00	2.5	1.48	5.85	0.47	11.15	3,631	8	53	31	6	5	8.53	-4.02	5.75		Mar-12
	1.45	7.18	2.54	16.08	6.63	2.54	1.44	5.85	0.46	11.19	3,631	8	53	31	6	5	8.53	-4.02			Mar-12
100	1.29	6.72	1.68	13.21	2.14	1.67	2.23	5.89	0.47	10.95	3,631	8	53	31	6	5	8.02	-4.31		1.00	Mar-12
	1.54	7.20	2.74	16.99	7.92	2.9	1.13	5.84	0.46	11.16	3,631	8	53	31	6	5	8.49	-4.01			Nov-12
	1.36	6.92	2.28	14.92	5.63	2.31	1.73	5.83	0.46	11.12	3,631	8	53	31	6	5	8.33	-4.11			Oct-15
	1.54	7.20	2.84	17.30	8.44	2.99	1.12	5.84	0.46	11.16	3,631	8	53	31	6	5	8.49	-4.01			Oct-14
	-0.91						0.62			9.74	39.0										Jan-19
	-0.81						0.72			9.74	39.0										Jan-19
100	-0.97	8.69	-7.59	21.92	19.91	0.67	1.6	12.7	1.04	12.13	122.1	4	96	0	0	50	17.2	-19.4	5.75		Jul-07
	-0.99	8.64	-7.51	22.19	20.56	0.73	1.5	12.66	1.04	11.94	122.1	4	96	0	0	50	17.31	-19.36			Jul-10
100	-1.21	8.26	-8.27	19.24	15.49	0	2.35	12.69	1.04	11.4	122.1	4	96	0	0	50	16.69	-19.63		1.00	Jul-07
	-0.92	8.91	-7.20	23.28	22.02	1.07	1.25	12.73	1.05	11.85	122.1	4	96	0	0	50	17.44	-19.26			Jul-10
100	3.56	13.73	5.60	21.22	11.52	0.42	1.13	8.11		13.66	2,005	6	58	34	1	189	9.17	-8.23	5.75		Jul-96
	3.59	13.90	5.79	21.86	12.53	0.56	0.95	8.13		13.84	2,005	6	58	34	1	189	9.27	-8.11			Oct-02
100	3.38	13.37	4.79	18.53	7.43	0	1.88	8.12		13.14	2,005	6	58	34	1	189	8.67	-8.5		1.00	Oct-02
	3.63	13.89	5.96	22.52	13.66	0.78	0.8	8.18		13.69	2,005	6	58	34	1	189	9.17	-8.23			Nov-12
	3.44	13.60	5.32	20.29	10.13	0.16	1.38	8.13		13.53	2,005	6	58	34	1	189	8.91	-8.3			Oct-03
100	5.30	22.41	8.96	42.34	49.64	0.77	1.08	14.4	1.16	14.09	293.4	3	97	0	0	42	21.08	-15.57	5.75		Jul-04
	5.22	22.28	8.98	42.71	50.53	0.8	1	14.38	1.16	14.1	293.4	3	97	0	0	42	21.36	-15.47			Jul-04
100	5.05	21.89	8.11	39.12	44.03	0.05	1.83	14.39	1.16	13.92	293.4	3	97	0	0	42	20.63	-15.75		1.00	Jul-04
	5.29	22.54	9.26	43.76	52.30	1.08	0.75	14.39	1.16	14.13	293.4	3	97	0	0	42	21.31	-15.3			Jul-04
	5.28	22.53	9.36	44.12	52.69	1.16	0.65	14.41	1.16	14.14	293.4	3	97	0	0	42	21.31	-15.3			Nov-16
100	5.70	24.12	6.38	42.83	47.00	0.15	1.26	16.26	1.2	38.54	364.1	5	95	0	0	39	28.05	-19.79	5.75		Jul-04
	5.74	24.21	6.51	43.27	47.67	0.29	1.16	16.25	1.2	38.99	364.1	5	95	0	0	39	28.1	-19.75			Jul-04
100	5.51	23.67	5.60	39.65	41.58	0	2.01	16.25	1.2	35.99	364.1	5	95	0	0	39	27.52	-20.05		1.00	Jul-04
	5.79	24.35	6.76	44.32	49.48	0.52	0.91	16.25	1.2	38.86	364.1	5	95	0	0	39	28.24	-19.69			Jul-04
	5.82	24.42	6.84	44.42	49.59		0.81	16.26	1.2	38.87	364.1	5	95	0	0	39	28.24	-19.69			Aug-18
100	7.79	28.03	15.16	78.41	86.07	0	1.12	13.76	0.98	9.27	104.8	3	97	0	0	40	29.61	-21.14	5.75		Jul-07
	7.81	28.09	15.26	79.11	87.43	0	0.95	13.76	0.98	11.17	104.8	3	97	0	0	40	29.75	-21.06			Jun-03
100	7.56	27.49	14.28	74.52	79.29	0	1.87	13.71	0.98	6.26	104.8	3	97	0	0	40	29.03	-21.39		1.00	Jul-07

	MARKET			FUND TYPE, CATEGORY & OBJECTIVE	RATINGS				MINIMUMS	
Fund Name	Ticker Symbol	Traded On	Fund Type	Category and (Prospectus Objective)	Overall Rating	Reward Rating	Risk Rating	Recent Up/ Downgrade	Open to New Investors	Min Initial Investment
Wells Fargo Capital Growth Fund - Class Inst	WWCIX	NAS CM	Open End	US Equity Large Cap Growth (Growth)	B	B	B		Y	1,000,000
Wells Fargo Capital Growth Fund - Class R6	WFCRX	NAS CM	Open End	US Equity Large Cap Growth (Growth)	B	B	B		Y	0
Wells Fargo Classic Value Fund - Class A	EIVAX	NAS CM	Open End	US Equity Large Cap Blend (Growth)	B-	C+	B		Y	1,000
Wells Fargo Classic Value Fund - Class Admin	EIVDX	NAS CM	Open End	US Equity Large Cap Blend (Growth)	B-	C+	B		Y	1,000,000
Wells Fargo Classic Value Fund - Class Inst	EIVIX	NAS CM	Open End	US Equity Large Cap Blend (Growth)	B-	C+	B		Y	1,000,000
Wells Fargo Classic Value Fund - Class R	EIVTX	NAS CM	Open End	US Equity Large Cap Blend (Growth)	B-	C	B		Y	0
Wells Fargo Classic Value Fund - Class R6	EIVFX	NAS CM	Open End	US Equity Large Cap Blend (Growth)	B-	C+	B+		Y	0
Wells Fargo Classic Value Fund- Class C	EIVCX	NAS CM	Open End	US Equity Large Cap Blend (Growth)	B-	C	B		Y	1,000
Wells Fargo Common Stock Fund - Class A	SCSAX	NAS CM	Open End	US Equity Mid Cap (Growth)	C+	C	B		Y	1,000
Wells Fargo Common Stock Fund - Class Admin	SCSDX	NAS CM	Open End	US Equity Mid Cap (Growth)	C+	C	B		Y	1,000,000
Wells Fargo Common Stock Fund - Class C	STSAX	NAS CM	Open End	US Equity Mid Cap (Growth)	C+	C	B	Up	Y	1,000
Wells Fargo Common Stock Fund - Class Inst	SCNSX	NAS CM	Open End	US Equity Mid Cap (Growth)	C+	C	B		Y	1,000,000
Wells Fargo Common Stock Fund - Class R6	SCSRX	NAS CM	Open End	US Equity Mid Cap (Growth)	C+	C	B		Y	0
Wells Fargo Disciplined Small Cap Fund Administrator Class	NVSOX	NAS CM	Open End	US Equity Small Cap (Small Company)	C	C-	C		Y	1,000,000
Wells Fargo Disciplined Small Cap Fund Class A	WDSAX	NAS CM	Open End	US Equity Small Cap (Small Company)	C	C-	C		Y	1,000
Wells Fargo Disciplined Small Cap Fund Class R6	WSCJX	NAS CM	Open End	US Equity Small Cap (Small Company)	C	C-	C		Y	0
Wells Fargo Disciplined Small Cap Fund Institutional Class	WSCOX	NAS CM	Open End	US Equity Small Cap (Small Company)	C	C-	C		Y	1,000,000
Wells Fargo Disciplined U.S. Core Fund - Class A	EVSAX	NAS CM	Open End	US Equity Large Cap Blend (Growth)	C+	C	B		Y	1,000
Wells Fargo Disciplined U.S. Core Fund - Class Admin	EVSYX	NAS CM	Open End	US Equity Large Cap Blend (Growth)	C+	C	B		Y	1,000,000
Wells Fargo Disciplined U.S. Core Fund - Class C	EVSTX	NAS CM	Open End	US Equity Large Cap Blend (Growth)	C+	C	B	Up	Y	1,000
Wells Fargo Disciplined U.S. Core Fund - Class Inst	EVSIX	NAS CM	Open End	US Equity Large Cap Blend (Growth)	C+	C	B		Y	1,000,000
Wells Fargo Disciplined U.S. Core Fund - Class R	EVSHX	NAS CM	Open End	US Equity Large Cap Blend (Growth)	C+	C	B	Up	Y	0
Wells Fargo Disciplined U.S. Core Fund - Class R6	EVSRX	NAS CM	Open End	US Equity Large Cap Blend (Growth)	C+	C	B		Y	0
Wells Fargo Discovery Fund - Class A	WFDAX	NAS CM	Open End	US Equity Mid Cap (Growth)	B-	B	C+		Y	1,000
Wells Fargo Discovery Fund - Class Admin	WFDDX	NAS CM	Open End	US Equity Mid Cap (Growth)	B-	B	C+		Y	1,000,000
Wells Fargo Discovery Fund - Class C	WDSCX	NAS CM	Open End	US Equity Mid Cap (Growth)	B-	B-	C+		Y	1,000
Wells Fargo Discovery Fund - Class Inst	WFDSX	NAS CM	Open End	US Equity Mid Cap (Growth)	B-	B	C+		Y	1,000,000
Wells Fargo Discovery Fund - Class R6	WFDRX	NAS CM	Open End	US Equity Mid Cap (Growth)	B-	B	C+		Y	0
Wells Fargo Diversified Capital Builder Fund - Class A	EKBAX	NAS CM	Open End	Aggressive Alloc (Growth)	B-	C	B		Y	1,000
Wells Fargo Diversified Capital Builder Fund - Class Admin	EKBDX	NAS CM	Open End	Aggressive Alloc (Growth)	B-	C	B	Up	Y	1,000,000
Wells Fargo Diversified Capital Builder Fund - Class C	EKBCX	NAS CM	Open End	Aggressive Alloc (Growth)	B-	C	B	Up	Y	1,000
Wells Fargo Diversified Capital Builder Fund - Class Inst	EKBYX	NAS CM	Open End	Aggressive Alloc (Growth)	B-	C	B		Y	1,000,000
Wells Fargo Diversified Equity Fund - Class A	NVDAX	NAS CM	Open End	US Equity Large Cap Growth (Growth)	C+	C	B	Up	Y	1,000
Wells Fargo Diversified Equity Fund - Class Admin	NVDEX	NAS CM	Open End	US Equity Large Cap Growth (Growth)	C+	C	B		Y	1,000,000
Wells Fargo Diversified Equity Fund - Class C	WFDEX	NAS CM	Open End	US Equity Large Cap Growth (Growth)	C+	C	B	Up	Y	1,000
Wells Fargo Diversified Income Builder Fund - Class A	EKSAX	NAS CM	Open End	Cautious Alloc (Growth & Income)	B-	C+	B		Y	1,000
Wells Fargo Diversified Income Builder Fund - Class Admin	EKSDX	NAS CM	Open End	Cautious Alloc (Growth & Income)	B-	C+	B		Y	1,000,000
Wells Fargo Diversified Income Builder Fund - Class C	EKSCX	NAS CM	Open End	Cautious Alloc (Growth & Income)	B-	C+	B	Up	Y	1,000
Wells Fargo Diversified Income Builder Fund - Class Inst	EKSYX	NAS CM	Open End	Cautious Alloc (Growth & Income)	B-	C+	B		Y	1,000,000
Wells Fargo Diversified Income Builder Fund - Class R6	EKSRX	NAS CM	Open End	Cautious Alloc (Growth & Income)	B-	C+	B		Y	0
Wells Fargo Diversified International Fund - Class A	SILAX	NAS CM	Open End	Global Equity Large Cap (Foreign Stock)	C	C	B		Y	1,000
Wells Fargo Diversified International Fund - Class Admin	WFIEX	NAS CM	Open End	Global Equity Large Cap (Foreign Stock)	C	C	B		Y	1,000,000
Wells Fargo Diversified International Fund - Class C	WFECX	NAS CM	Open End	Global Equity Large Cap (Foreign Stock)	C	C	B-		Y	1,000
Wells Fargo Diversified International Fund - Class Inst	WFISX	NAS CM	Open End	Global Equity Large Cap (Foreign Stock)	C	C	B		Y	1,000,000
Wells Fargo Diversified International Fund - Class R6	WDIRX	NAS CM	Open End	Global Equity Large Cap (Foreign Stock)	C	C	B		Y	0
Wells Fargo Dynamic Target 2015 Fund Class A	WDTAX	NAS CM	Open End	Target Date (Asset Alloc)	B	C+	A		Y	1,000
Wells Fargo Dynamic Target 2015 Fund Class C	WDTCX	NAS CM	Open End	Target Date (Asset Alloc)	B	C+	A-	Up	Y	1,000
Wells Fargo Dynamic Target 2015 Fund Class R4	WDTYX	NAS CM	Open End	Target Date (Asset Alloc)	B	C+	A		Y	0
Wells Fargo Dynamic Target 2015 Fund Class R6	WDTZX	NAS CM	Open End	Target Date (Asset Alloc)	B	C+	A		Y	0
Wells Fargo Dynamic Target 2020 Fund Class A	WDTDX	NAS CM	Open End	Target Date (Asset Alloc)	B	C+	A		Y	1,000
Wells Fargo Dynamic Target 2020 Fund Class C	WDTEX	NAS CM	Open End	Target Date (Asset Alloc)	B	C+	A	Up	Y	1,000
Wells Fargo Dynamic Target 2020 Fund Class R4	WDTGX	NAS CM	Open End	Target Date (Asset Alloc)	B	C+	A		Y	0

★ Expanded analysis of this fund is included in Section II.

Min Additional Investment	3-Month Total Return	6-Month Total Return	1-Year Total Return	3-Year Total Return	5-Year Total Return	Dividend Yield (TTM)	Expense Ratio	3-Yr Std Deviation	3-Year Beta	NAV	Total Assets (MIL)	%Cash	%Stocks	%Bonds	%Other	Turnover Ratio	Last Bull Market Total Return	Last Bear Market Total Return	Front End Fee (%)	Back End Fee (%)	Inception Date
	TOTAL RETURNS					PERFORMANCE				ASSETS		ASSET ALLOCATION & TURNOVER					BULL & BEAR		FEES		
	7.87	28.16	15.51	80.38	89.68	0	0.71	13.76	0.98	12.06	104.8	3	97	0	0	40	29.88	-20.95			Apr-05
	7.80	28.27	15.62	80.54	90.07	0	0.61	13.75	0.98	12.16	104.8	3	97	0	0	40	29.75	-21.06			Nov-12
100	5.57	20.73	11.30	41.92	44.51	0.87	1.11	12.37	1	12.87	863.1	1	99	0	0	21	23.6	-19.49	5.75		Aug-06
	5.62	20.80	11.39	42.54	45.63	1.01	0.95	12.35	0.99	13.53	863.1	1	99	0	0	21	23.67	-19.41			Jul-10
	5.62	20.91	11.71	43.62	47.47	1.24	0.7	12.34	0.99	12.95	863.1	1	99	0	0	21	23.75	-19.33			Aug-06
	5.53	20.55	10.94	40.85	42.68	0.72	1.36	12.34	0.99	12.96	863.1	1	99	0	0	21	23.57	-19.41			Mar-13
	5.67	20.91	12.60	44.93	48.27	2.33	0.65	12.36	0.99	12.66	863.1	1	99	0	0	21	23.75	-19.33			Nov-12
100	5.39	20.28	10.47	38.71	39.07	0.14	1.86	12.36	1	12.51	863.1	1	99	0	0	21	22.86	-19.7		1.00	Aug-06
100	5.57	22.03	6.33	46.37	41.36	0	1.26	14	0.88	21.21	1,109	1	98	0	1	33	27.41	-22.39	5.75		Nov-00
	5.64	22.11	6.53	47.07	42.46	0	1.11	14.03	0.89	21.7	1,109	1	98	0	1	33	27.54	-22.33			Jul-10
100	5.39	21.62	5.58	43.20	36.22	0	2.01	14.01	0.89	14.85	1,109	1	98	0	1	33	26.88	-22.63		1.00	Nov-00
	5.69	22.27	6.79	48.21	44.30	0	0.86	14.03	0.89	22.45	1,109	1	98	0	1	33	27.64	-22.24			Jul-10
	5.72	22.32	6.82	48.26	44.48	0	0.83	14.04	0.89	22.52	1,109	1	98	0	1	33	27.41	-22.39			Jun-13
	2.26	15.61	-8.48	24.90	31.29	0.15	0.91	16.14	0.93	8.59	67.4	2	96	0	2	176	23.81	-22.83			Aug-93
100	2.86	16.46	-7.90	25.70	32.13		0.99	15.97	0.92	8.63	67.4	2	96	0	2	176	23.81	-22.83	5.75		Jul-18
	2.35	15.69	-8.20	26.00	32.45	0.39	0.56	16.07	0.92	8.7	67.4	2	96	0	2	176	23.8	-22.83			Nov-16
	2.35	15.73	-8.24	25.90	32.91	0.3	0.66	16.11	0.92	8.68	67.4	2	96	0	2	176	23.81	-22.83			Oct-14
100	3.15	17.05	6.22	41.10	56.47	1.05	0.83	12.42	1.02	17.02	1,179	0	100	0	0	73	25.84	-16.77	5.75		Feb-90
	3.18	17.11	6.29	41.47	57.46	1.03	0.74	12.4	1.01	17.52	1,179	0	100	0	0	73	26.01	-16.78			Feb-95
100	2.96	16.66	5.39	37.92	50.79	0.33	1.58	12.41	1.02	15.61	1,179	0	100	0	0	73	25.29	-17.08		1.00	Jun-99
	3.28	17.30	6.58	42.62	59.46	1.41	0.48	12.39	1.01	17.29	1,179	0	100	0	0	73	26.13	-16.63			Jul-10
	3.12	16.96	5.95	40.06	54.60	1.03	1.08	12.41	1.02	17.17	1,179	0	100	0	0	73	25.66	-16.86			Sep-15
	3.30	17.39	6.70	42.99	59.09	1.5	0.4	12.43	1.02	17.48	1,179	0	100	0	0	73	25.84	-16.77			Sep-15
100	10.74	38.02	17.44	76.95	76.21	0	1.21	15.96	0.93	34.74	2,582	2	93	0	5	67	33.96	-22.85	5.75		Jul-07
	10.73	38.04	17.51	77.35	76.97	0	1.13	15.96	0.93	36.1	2,582	2	93	0	5	67	34	-22.77			Apr-05
100	10.53	37.48	16.53	73.02	69.66	0	1.96	15.94	0.92	29.6	2,582	2	93	0	5	67	33.38	-23.09		1.00	Jul-07
	10.81	38.23	17.81	78.72	79.23	0	0.88	15.97	0.93	38.11	2,582	2	93	0	5	67	34.25	-22.69			Aug-06
	10.86	38.27	17.91	79.22	80.03	0	0.78	15.96	0.93	38.37	2,582	2	93	0	5	67	34	-22.77			Jun-13
100	4.48	19.41	10.53	41.94	57.86	1.08	1.12	11.95		10.57	1,087	1	79	18	2	31	21.35	-23.2	5.75		Jan-98
	4.50	19.43	10.61	42.38	59.01	1.15	1.04	11.95		10.58	1,087	1	79	18	2	31	21.45	-23.09			Jul-10
100	4.31	18.90	9.71	38.88	52.20	0.38	1.87	11.93		10.55	1,087	1	79	18	2	31	20.71	-23.43		1.00	Jan-98
	4.59	19.60	10.97	43.53	60.81	1.39	0.78	12.02		10.5	1,087	1	79	18	2	31	21.7	-23.1			Jan-98
100	4.25	18.75	6.12	44.38	43.80	0.46	1.25	12.38		22.79	159.1	2	97	0	1	70	24.74	-19.56	5.75		May-96
	4.27	18.88	6.37	45.48	45.56	0.67	1	12.39		22.91	159.1	2	97	0	1	70	24.89	-19.49			Nov-94
100	4.01	18.28	5.31	41.18	38.48	0	2	12.36		19.67	159.1	2	97	0	1	70	24.18	-19.81		1.00	Oct-98
100	2.39	12.09	6.89	24.21	30.42	3.53	0.85	6.18		6.09	708.3	-1	28	66	0	50	14	-10.82	5.75		Apr-87
	2.46	12.24	6.95	24.67	31.31	3.67	0.77	6.27		5.95	708.3	-1	28	66	0	50	14.13	-10.8			Jul-10
100	2.36	11.86	6.07	21.64	25.81	2.8	1.6	6.25		6.11	708.3	-1	28	66	0	50	13.49	-11.23		1.00	Feb-93
	2.53	12.58	7.24	25.74	32.96	3.93	0.52	6.22		5.95	708.3	-1	28	66	0	50	14.06	-10.74			Jan-97
	2.55	12.43	7.37	24.77	31.00		0.42	6.23		5.94	708.3	-1	28	66	0	50	14	-10.82			Aug-18
100	3.69	13.17	1.32	28.74	9.62	2	1.36	11.64	1.03	12.63	100.8	-1	98	1	2	39	17.76	-24.3	5.75		Sep-97
	3.79	13.29	1.42	29.13	10.20	2.07	1.26	11.63	1.03	12.87	100.8	-1	98	1	2	39	17.88	-24.17			Nov-99
100	3.56	12.80	0.56	25.89	5.62	1.03	2.11	11.67	1.03	11.63	100.8	-1	98	1	2	39	17.24	-24.53		1.00	Apr-98
	3.81	13.35	1.62	30.18	11.73	2.6	1	11.6	1.02	11.97	100.8	-1	98	1	2	39	18.18	-24.17			Aug-06
	3.77	13.42	1.74	30.38	11.49	2.48	0.9	11.64	1.03	12.93	100.8	-1	98	1	2	39	17.76	-24.3			Sep-15
100	2.96	11.69	7.42	26.45		1.1	0.68	6.05	1.11	10.41	5.6	7	43	50	0	45			5.75		Nov-15
100	2.67	11.17	6.57	23.54		0.4	1.43	6.01	1.1	10.35	5.6	7	43	50	0	45				1.00	Nov-15
	2.96	11.69	7.74	27.50		1.37	0.37	6.01	1.1	10.41	5.6	7	43	50	0	45					Nov-15
	2.96	11.80	7.92	28.11		1.51	0.22	6.06	1.11	10.42	5.6	7	43	50	0	45					Nov-15
100	2.98	12.36	7.58	29.98		0.99	0.68	6.77	1.11	10.36	5.9	9	51	40	0	42			5.75		Nov-15
100	2.68	11.91	6.73	26.98		0.24	1.43	6.72	1.1	10.33	5.9	9	51	40	0	42				1.00	Nov-15
	2.96	12.43	7.83	30.92		1.21	0.37	6.74	1.11	10.4	5.9	9	51	40	0	42					Nov-15

Fund Name	Ticker Symbol	Traded On	Fund Type	Category and (Prospectus Objective)	Overall Rating	Reward Rating	Risk Rating	Recent Up/ Downgrade	Open to New Investors	Min Initial Investment
	MARKET			FUND TYPE, CATEGORY & OBJECTIVE	RATINGS				MINIMUMS	
Wells Fargo Dynamic Target 2020 Fund Class R6	WDTHX	NAS CM	Open End	Target Date (Asset Alloc)	B	C+	A		Y	0
Wells Fargo Dynamic Target 2025 Fund Class A	WDTIX	NAS CM	Open End	Target Date (Asset Alloc)	B	C	A-	Up	Y	1,000
Wells Fargo Dynamic Target 2025 Fund Class C	WDTJX	NAS CM	Open End	Target Date (Asset Alloc)	B-	C	A-	Up	Y	1,000
Wells Fargo Dynamic Target 2025 Fund Class R4	WDTLX	NAS CM	Open End	Target Date (Asset Alloc)	B	C+	A-	Up	Y	0
Wells Fargo Dynamic Target 2025 Fund Class R6	WDTMX	NAS CM	Open End	Target Date (Asset Alloc)	B	C+	A-	Up	Y	0
Wells Fargo Dynamic Target 2030 Fund Class A	WDTNX	NAS CM	Open End	Target Date (Asset Alloc)	B-	C	A-		Y	1,000
Wells Fargo Dynamic Target 2030 Fund Class C	WDTOX	NAS CM	Open End	Target Date (Asset Alloc)	B-	C	B+	Up	Y	1,000
Wells Fargo Dynamic Target 2030 Fund Class R4	WDTQX	NAS CM	Open End	Target Date (Asset Alloc)	B-	C	A-		Y	0
Wells Fargo Dynamic Target 2030 Fund Class R6	WDTSX	NAS CM	Open End	Target Date (Asset Alloc)	B-	C	A-		Y	0
Wells Fargo Dynamic Target 2035 Fund Class A	WDTTX	NAS CM	Open End	Target Date (Asset Alloc)	B-	C	B+		Y	1,000
Wells Fargo Dynamic Target 2035 Fund Class C	WDCTX	NAS CM	Open End	Target Date (Asset Alloc)	B-	C	B+	Up	Y	1,000
Wells Fargo Dynamic Target 2035 Fund Class R4	WDTVX	NAS CM	Open End	Target Date (Asset Alloc)	B-	C	B+		Y	0
Wells Fargo Dynamic Target 2035 Fund Class R6	WDTWX	NAS CM	Open End	Target Date (Asset Alloc)	B-	C	B+		Y	0
Wells Fargo Dynamic Target 2040 Fund Class A	WTDAX	NAS CM	Open End	Target Date (Asset Alloc)	B-	C	B+		Y	1,000
Wells Fargo Dynamic Target 2040 Fund Class C	WTDCX	NAS CM	Open End	Target Date (Asset Alloc)	B-	C	B+	Up	Y	1,000
Wells Fargo Dynamic Target 2040 Fund Class R4	WTDEX	NAS CM	Open End	Target Date (Asset Alloc)	B-	C	B+		Y	0
Wells Fargo Dynamic Target 2040 Fund Class R6	WTDFX	NAS CM	Open End	Target Date (Asset Alloc)	B-	C	B+		Y	0
Wells Fargo Dynamic Target 2045 Fund Class A	WTDGX	NAS CM	Open End	Target Date (Asset Alloc)	B-	C	B+	Up	Y	1,000
Wells Fargo Dynamic Target 2045 Fund Class C	WTDHX	NAS CM	Open End	Target Date (Asset Alloc)	B-	C	B+	Up	Y	1,000
Wells Fargo Dynamic Target 2045 Fund Class R4	WTDJX	NAS CM	Open End	Target Date (Asset Alloc)	B-	C	B+		Y	0
Wells Fargo Dynamic Target 2045 Fund Class R6	WTDKX	NAS CM	Open End	Target Date (Asset Alloc)	B-	C	B+		Y	0
Wells Fargo Dynamic Target 2050 Fund Class A	WTDLX	NAS CM	Open End	Target Date (Asset Alloc)	B-	C	B+	Up	Y	1,000
Wells Fargo Dynamic Target 2050 Fund Class C	WTDMX	NAS CM	Open End	Target Date (Asset Alloc)	B-	C	B+	Up	Y	1,000
Wells Fargo Dynamic Target 2050 Fund Class R4	WTDOX	NAS CM	Open End	Target Date (Asset Alloc)	B-	C	B+	Up	Y	0
Wells Fargo Dynamic Target 2050 Fund Class R6	WTDPX	NAS CM	Open End	Target Date (Asset Alloc)	B-	C	B+		Y	0
Wells Fargo Dynamic Target 2055 Fund Class A	WTDQX	NAS CM	Open End	Target Date (Asset Alloc)	B-	C	B+	Up	Y	1,000
Wells Fargo Dynamic Target 2055 Fund Class C	WTDRX	NAS CM	Open End	Target Date (Asset Alloc)	B-	C	B+	Up	Y	1,000
Wells Fargo Dynamic Target 2055 Fund Class R4	WTDTX	NAS CM	Open End	Target Date (Asset Alloc)	B-	C	B+	Up	Y	0
Wells Fargo Dynamic Target 2055 Fund Class R6	WTDUX	NAS CM	Open End	Target Date (Asset Alloc)	B-	C	B+		Y	0
Wells Fargo Dynamic Target 2060 Fund Class A	WTDVX	NAS CM	Open End	Target Date (Asset Alloc)	B-	C	B+	Up	Y	1,000
Wells Fargo Dynamic Target 2060 Fund Class C	WTDWX	NAS CM	Open End	Target Date (Asset Alloc)	B-	C	B+	Up	Y	1,000
Wells Fargo Dynamic Target 2060 Fund Class R4	WTDZX	NAS CM	Open End	Target Date (Asset Alloc)	B-	C	B+	Up	Y	0
Wells Fargo Dynamic Target 2060 Fund Class R6	WTSZX	NAS CM	Open End	Target Date (Asset Alloc)	B-	C	B+		Y	0
Wells Fargo Dynamic Target Today Fund Class A	WDYAX	NAS CM	Open End	Target Date (Asset Alloc)	B	C+	A		Y	1,000
Wells Fargo Dynamic Target Today Fund Class C	WDYCX	NAS CM	Open End	Target Date (Asset Alloc)	B	C+	A-	Up	Y	1,000
Wells Fargo Dynamic Target Today Fund Class R4	WDYYX	NAS CM	Open End	Target Date (Asset Alloc)	B	C+	A		Y	0
Wells Fargo Dynamic Target Today Fund Class R6	WDYZX	NAS CM	Open End	Target Date (Asset Alloc)	B	C+	A		Y	0
Wells Fargo Emerging Growth Fund - Class A	WEMAX	NAS CM	Open End	US Equity Small Cap (Growth)	C+	C+	C+			1,000
Wells Fargo Emerging Growth Fund - Class Admin	WFGDX	NAS CM	Open End	US Equity Small Cap (Growth)	C+	C+	C+			1,000,000
Wells Fargo Emerging Growth Fund - Class C	WEMCX	NAS CM	Open End	US Equity Small Cap (Growth)	C+	C	C+			1,000
Wells Fargo Emerging Growth Fund - Class Inst	WEMIX	NAS CM	Open End	US Equity Small Cap (Growth)	C+	C+	C+			1,000,000
Wells Fargo Emerging Growth Fund - Class R6	WEGRX	NAS CM	Open End	US Equity Small Cap (Growth)	C+	C+	C+		Y	0
Wells Fargo Emerging Markets Equity Fund - Class A	EMGAX	NAS CM	Open End	Global Emerg Mkts (Div Emerging Mkts)	C	C	C+			1,000
Wells Fargo Emerging Markets Equity Fund - Class Admin	EMGYX	NAS CM	Open End	Global Emerg Mkts (Div Emerging Mkts)	C	C	C+			1,000,000
Wells Fargo Emerging Markets Equity Fund - Class C	EMGCX	NAS CM	Open End	Global Emerg Mkts (Div Emerging Mkts)	C	C	C+			1,000
Wells Fargo Emerging Markets Equity Fund - Class Inst	EMGNX	NAS CM	Open End	Global Emerg Mkts (Div Emerging Mkts)	C	C	C+			1,000,000
Wells Fargo Emerging Markets Equity Fund - Class R6	EMGDX	NAS CM	Open End	Global Emerg Mkts (Div Emerging Mkts)	C	C	C+			0
Wells Fargo Emerging Markets Equity Income Fund - Class A	EQIAX	NAS CM	Open End	Global Emerg Mkts (Div Emerging Mkts)	C	C	B-		Y	1,000
Wells Fargo Emerging Markets Equity Income - Cls Admin	EQIDX	NAS CM	Open End	Global Emerg Mkts (Div Emerging Mkts)	C	C	B-		Y	1,000,000
Wells Fargo Emerging Markets Equity Income Fund - Class C	EQICX	NAS CM	Open End	Global Emerg Mkts (Div Emerging Mkts)	C	C-	B-		Y	1,000
Wells Fargo Emerging Markets Equity Income - Cls Inst	EQIIX	NAS CM	Open End	Global Emerg Mkts (Div Emerging Mkts)	C	C	B		Y	1,000,000
Wells Fargo Emerging Markets Equity Income Fund - Class R	EQIHX	NAS CM	Open End	Global Emerg Mkts (Div Emerging Mkts)	C	C	B-		Y	0

★ Expanded analysis of this fund is included in Section II.

	TOTAL RETURNS					PERFORMANCE				ASSETS		ASSET ALLOCATION & TURNOVER					BULL & BEAR		FEES		
Min Additional Investment	3-Month Total Return	6-Month Total Return	1-Year Total Return	3-Year Total Return	5-Year Total Return	Dividend Yield (TTM)	Expense Ratio	3-Yr Std Deviation	3-Year Beta	NAV	Total Assets (MIL)	%Cash	%Stocks	%Bonds	%Other	Turnover Ratio	Last Bull Market Total Return	Last Bear Market Total Return	Front End Fee (%)	Back End Fee (%)	Inception Date
	3.06	12.54	8.00	31.61		1.35	0.22	6.77	1.11	10.41	5.9	9	51	40	0	42					Nov-15
100	3.04	13.02	7.02	32.70		0.87	0.68	7.79	1.1	10.5	7.6	7	62	31	0	41			5.75		Nov-15
100	2.84	12.58	6.19	29.56		0.13	1.43	7.8	1.1	10.47	7.6	7	62	31	0	41				1.00	Nov-15
	3.12	13.18	7.31	33.76		1.05	0.37	7.76	1.1	10.56	7.6	7	62	31	0	41					Nov-15
	3.12	13.29	7.49	34.47		1.19	0.22	7.78	1.1	10.57	7.6	7	62	31	0	41					Nov-15
100	3.09	13.65	7.11	36.18		0.72	0.68	8.52	1.04	10.32	6.4	9	68	23	0	37			5.75		Nov-15
100	2.91	13.27	6.32	33.13		0.48	1.43	8.52	1.04	10.24	6.4	9	68	23	0	37				1.00	Nov-15
	3.17	13.92	7.41	37.43		0.9	0.37	8.56	1.04	10.39	6.4	9	68	23	0	37					Nov-15
	3.27	14.03	7.59	38.02		1.04	0.22	8.55	1.04	10.4	6.4	9	68	23	0	37					Nov-15
100	3.13	14.20	7.18	38.96		0.63	0.68	9.15	0.99	10.21	5.7	7	74	18	0	34			5.75		Nov-15
100	2.83	13.75	6.36	35.78		0	1.43	9.13	0.99	10.17	5.7	7	74	18	0	34				1.00	Nov-15
	3.11	14.36	7.49	40.17		0.8	0.37	9.1	0.99	10.27	5.7	7	74	18	0	34					Nov-15
	3.21	14.47	7.67	40.77		0.94	0.22	9.05	0.98	10.28	5.7	7	74	18	0	34					Nov-15
100	2.95	14.22	6.75	39.85		0.49	0.68	9.54	0.97	10.12	5.9	7	80	13	0	32			5.75		Nov-15
100	2.85	13.88	6.02	36.94		0	1.43	9.56	0.97	10.09	5.9	7	80	13	0	32				1.00	Nov-15
	3.13	14.47	7.20	41.33		0.72	0.37	9.55	0.97	10.2	5.9	7	80	13	0	32					Nov-15
	3.13	14.59	7.30	41.93		0.86	0.22	9.58	0.97	10.21	5.9	7	80	13	0	32					Nov-15
100	2.96	14.56	6.48	40.20		0.6	0.68	9.95	0.98	10.07	5.4	8	84	8	0	31			5.75		Nov-15
100	2.87	14.10	5.68	37.13		0	1.43	9.94	0.98	10.03	5.4	8	84	8	0	31				1.00	Nov-15
	3.04	14.70	6.77	41.51		0.7	0.37	9.92	0.97	10.14	5.4	8	84	8	0	31					Nov-15
	3.04	14.81	6.93	42.08		0.82	0.22	9.88	0.97	10.15	5.4	8	84	8	0	31					Nov-15
100	3.07	14.56	6.21	39.97		0.42	0.68	10.14	0.97	10.07	5.3	8	87	5	0	31			5.75		Nov-15
100	2.88	14.15	5.49	36.97		0	1.43	10.12	0.97	10	5.3	8	87	5	0	31				1.00	Nov-15
	3.05	14.75	6.53	41.29		0.68	0.37	10.06	0.96	10.11	5.3	8	87	5	0	31					Nov-15
	3.16	14.86	6.71	41.89		0.82	0.22	10.09	0.97	10.12	5.3	8	87	5	0	31					Nov-15
100	3.07	14.56	6.22	39.96		0.43	0.68	10.12	0.96	10.07	5.2	8	87	5	0	31			5.75		Nov-15
100	2.88	14.17	5.50	36.79		0	1.43	10.12	0.96	9.99	5.2	8	87	5	0	31				1.00	Nov-15
	3.06	14.77	6.53	41.09		0.67	0.37	10.09	0.96	10.1	5.2	8	87	5	0	31					Nov-15
	3.16	14.88	6.76	41.90		0.85	0.22	10.1	0.96	10.11	5.2	8	87	5	0	31					Nov-15
100	2.96	14.54	6.24	40.01		0.5	0.68	10.1	0.96	10.08	5.4	8	87	5	0	31			5.75		Nov-15
100	2.76	14.23	5.40	36.81		0	1.43	10.08	0.96	10.03	5.4	8	87	5	0	31				1.00	Nov-15
	3.15	14.81	6.64	41.26		0.67	0.37	10.11	0.96	10.15	5.4	8	87	5	0	31					Nov-15
	3.14	14.93	6.73	42.02		0.81	0.22	10.1	0.96	10.16	5.4	8	87	5	0	31					Nov-15
100	2.82	10.48	7.55	21.56		1.32	0.68	4.86	1.18	10.54	5.7	7	33	60	0	48			5.75		Nov-15
100	2.64	10.08	6.77	18.86		0.57	1.43	4.9	1.19	10.48	5.7	7	33	60	0	48				1.00	Nov-15
	2.93	10.71	7.92	22.68		1.54	0.37	4.88	1.18	10.54	5.7	7	33	60	0	48					Nov-15
	3.02	10.81	8.10	23.26		1.68	0.22	4.87	1.18	10.55	5.7	7	33	60	0	48					Nov-15
100	6.35	25.30	5.13	73.86	69.66	0	1.28	18.08	0.99	14.56	790.6	1	94	0	5	47	32.13	-23.48	5.75		Mar-08
	6.40	25.29	5.16	74.56	70.76	0	1.2	18.07	0.99	15.11	790.6	1	94	0	5	47	32.24	-23.38			Jan-07
100	6.12	24.70	4.29	69.94	63.34	0	2.03	18.04	0.99	12.47	790.6	1	94	0	5	47	31.47	-23.65		1.00	Mar-08
	6.46	25.43	5.51	76.18	73.34	0	0.9	18.07	0.99	15.98	790.6	1	94	0	5	47	32.41	-23.26			Mar-08
	6.44	25.74	5.66	75.39	71.57		0.85	18.09	0.99	16.02	790.6	1	94	0	5	47	32.24	-23.38			Aug-18
100	1.25	14.65	1.70	32.28	13.98	0.32	1.59	14.19	0.99	24.25	3,908	4	92	0	4	11	11.66	-20.4	5.75		Sep-94
	1.27	14.72	1.79	32.63	14.60	0.45	1.47	14.21	0.99	25.4	3,908	4	92	0	4	11	11.84	-20.36			Sep-94
100	1.09	14.25	0.94	29.33	9.79	0	2.34	14.21	0.99	20.28	3,908	4	92	0	4	11	11.21	-20.65		1.00	Sep-94
	1.36	14.86	2.07	33.78	16.20	0.75	1.2	14.21	0.99	25.27	3,908	4	92	0	4	11	11.94	-20.24			Jul-10
	1.36	14.91	2.12	33.98	16.53	0.79	1.16	14.21	0.99	25.27	3,908	4	92	0	4	11	11.84	-20.36			Jun-13
100	0.88	9.60	4.58	22.70	8.18	2.1	1.62	12.92	0.89	11.21	615.9	2	98	0	0	69			5.75		May-12
	0.90	9.69	4.77	23.49	9.39	2.2	1.45	12.93	0.89	11.31	615.9	2	98	0	0	69					May-12
100	0.70	9.18	3.72	19.91	4.15	1.37	2.37	12.86	0.89	11.15	615.9	2	98	0	0	69				1.00	May-12
	0.97	9.76	4.93	24.11	10.40	2.43	1.22	12.89	0.89	11.24	615.9	2	98	0	0	69					May-12
	0.83	9.47	4.33	21.77	7.38	1.87	1.87	12.88	0.89	11.23	615.9	2	98	0	0	69					Sep-15

Fund Name	MARKET Ticker Symbol	Traded On	FUND TYPE, CATEGORY & OBJECTIVE Fund Type	Category and (Prospectus Objective)	RATINGS Overall Rating	Reward Rating	Risk Rating	Recent Up/ Downgrade	Open to New Investors	MINIMUMS Min Initial Investment
Wells Fargo Emerging Markets Equity Income Fund - Class R6	EQIRX	NAS CM	Open End	Global Emerg Mkts (Div Emerging Mkts)	C	C	B		Y	0
Wells Fargo Endeavor Select Fund - Class A	STAEX	NAS CM	Open End	US Equity Large Cap Growth (Growth)	B	B	B		Y	1,000
Wells Fargo Endeavor Select Fund - Class Admin	WECDX	NAS CM	Open End	US Equity Large Cap Growth (Growth)	B	B	B		Y	1,000,000
Wells Fargo Endeavor Select Fund - Class C	WECCX	NAS CM	Open End	US Equity Large Cap Growth (Growth)	B	B-	B		Y	1,000
Wells Fargo Endeavor Select Fund - Class Inst	WFCIX	NAS CM	Open End	US Equity Large Cap Growth (Growth)	B	B	B		Y	1,000,000
Wells Fargo Enterprise Fund - Class A	SENAX	NAS CM	Open End	US Equity Mid Cap (Growth)	B	B	B-		Y	1,000
Wells Fargo Enterprise Fund - Class Admin	SEPKX	NAS CM	Open End	US Equity Mid Cap (Growth)	B	B	B-		Y	1,000,000
Wells Fargo Enterprise Fund - Class C	WENCX	NAS CM	Open End	US Equity Mid Cap (Growth)	B	B	B-	Up	Y	1,000
Wells Fargo Enterprise Fund - Class Inst	WFEIX	NAS CM	Open End	US Equity Mid Cap (Growth)	B	B	B-		Y	1,000,000
Wells Fargo Enterprise Fund - Class R6	WENRX	NAS CM	Open End	US Equity Mid Cap (Growth)	B	B	B-		Y	0
Wells Fargo Factor Enhanced Emerging Markets Fund	WEEMX	NAS CM	Open End	Global Emerg Mkts (Div Emerging Mkts)	D	D	C-	Down	Y	0
Wells Fargo Factor Enhanced International Fund	WINTX	NAS CM	Open End	Global Equity Large Cap (Foreign Stock)	C-	D	B-	Up	Y	0
Wells Fargo Factor Enhanced International Fund	WLECX	NAS CM	Open End	US Equity Large Cap Blend (Growth)	C-	C-	B	Up	Y	0
Wells Fargo Factor Enhanced Small Cap Fund	WFESX	NAS CM	Open End	US Equity Small Cap (Small Company)	D+	D	C		Y	0
Wells Fargo Global Dividend Opportunity Fund	EOD	NYSE	Closed End	Alloc Miscellaneous (World Stock)	C	C	C+		Y	
Wells Fargo Global Small Cap Fund Class A	EKGAX	NAS CM	Open End	Global Equity Mid/Small Cap (World Stock)	C+	C	B	Up	Y	1,000
Wells Fargo Global Small Cap Fund Class Admin	EKGYX	NAS CM	Open End	Global Equity Mid/Small Cap (World Stock)	C+	C	B	Up	Y	1,000,000
Wells Fargo Global Small Cap Fund Class C	EKGCX	NAS CM	Open End	Global Equity Mid/Small Cap (World Stock)	C+	C	B	Up	Y	1,000
Wells Fargo Global Small Cap Fund Class Inst	EKGIX	NAS CM	Open End	Global Equity Mid/Small Cap (World Stock)	C+	C	B	Up	Y	1,000,000
Wells Fargo Growth Balanced Fund - Class A	WFGBX	NAS CM	Open End	Moderate Alloc (Balanced)	B-	C	B+	Up	Y	1,000
Wells Fargo Growth Balanced Fund - Class Admin	NVGBX	NAS CM	Open End	Moderate Alloc (Balanced)	B-	C	B+	Up	Y	1,000,000
Wells Fargo Growth Balanced Fund - Class C	WFGWX	NAS CM	Open End	Moderate Alloc (Balanced)	B-	C	B+	Up	Y	1,000
Wells Fargo Growth Fund - Class A	SGRAX	NAS CM	Open End	US Equity Large Cap Growth (Growth)	B-	B-	B-	Down		1,000
Wells Fargo Growth Fund - Class Admin	SGRKX	NAS CM	Open End	US Equity Large Cap Growth (Growth)	B-	B-	B-	Down		1,000,000
Wells Fargo Growth Fund - Class C	WGFCX	NAS CM	Open End	US Equity Large Cap Growth (Growth)	B-	B-	B-	Down		1,000
Wells Fargo Growth Fund - Class Inst	SGRNX	NAS CM	Open End	US Equity Large Cap Growth (Growth)	B-	B-	B-	Down		1,000,000
Wells Fargo Growth Fund - Class R6	SGRHX	NAS CM	Open End	US Equity Large Cap Growth (Growth)	B-	B-	B-	Down	Y	0
Wells Fargo Index Asset Allocation Fund - Class A	SFAAX	NAS CM	Open End	Moderate Alloc (Asset Alloc)	B	C+	A-		Y	1,000
Wells Fargo Index Asset Allocation Fund - Class Admin	WFAIX	NAS CM	Open End	Moderate Alloc (Asset Alloc)	B	C+	A-		Y	1,000,000
Wells Fargo Index Asset Allocation Fund - Class C	WFALX	NAS CM	Open End	Moderate Alloc (Asset Alloc)	B-	C	A-		Y	1,000
Wells Fargo Index Asset Allocation Institutional Cls	WFATX	NAS CM	Open End	Moderate Alloc (Asset Alloc)	B	C+	A-		Y	1,000,000
Wells Fargo Index Fund - Class A	WFILX	NAS CM	Open End	US Equity Large Cap Blend (Growth)	B-	C	B		Y	1,000
Wells Fargo Index Fund - Class Admin	WFIOX	NAS CM	Open End	US Equity Large Cap Blend (Growth)	B-	C	B		Y	1,000,000
Wells Fargo Index Fund - Class C	WFINX	NAS CM	Open End	US Equity Large Cap Blend (Growth)	B-	C	B		Y	1,000
Wells Fargo International Equity Fund - Class A	WFEAX	NAS CM	Open End	Global Equity Large Cap (Foreign Stock)	C	C-	C		Y	1,000
Wells Fargo International Equity Fund - Class Admin	WFEDX	NAS CM	Open End	Global Equity Large Cap (Foreign Stock)	C	C-	C		Y	1,000,000
Wells Fargo International Equity Fund - Class C	WFEFX	NAS CM	Open End	Global Equity Large Cap (Foreign Stock)	C	C-	C		Y	1,000
Wells Fargo International Equity Fund - Class Inst	WFENX	NAS CM	Open End	Global Equity Large Cap (Foreign Stock)	C	C-	C		Y	1,000,000
Wells Fargo International Equity Fund - Class R	WFERX	NAS CM	Open End	Global Equity Large Cap (Foreign Stock)	C	C-	C		Y	0
Wells Fargo International Equity Fund - Class R6	WFEHX	NAS CM	Open End	Global Equity Large Cap (Foreign Stock)	C	C-	C		Y	0
Wells Fargo International Value Fund - Class A	WFFAX	NAS CM	Open End	Global Equity Large Cap (Foreign Stock)	C	C-	C		Y	1,000
Wells Fargo International Value Fund - Class Admin	WFVDX	NAS CM	Open End	Global Equity Large Cap (Foreign Stock)	C	C-	C		Y	1,000,000
Wells Fargo International Value Fund - Class C	WFVCX	NAS CM	Open End	Global Equity Large Cap (Foreign Stock)	C-	C-	C	Down	Y	1,000
Wells Fargo International Value Fund - Class Inst	WFVIX	NAS CM	Open End	Global Equity Large Cap (Foreign Stock)	C	C-	C		Y	1,000,000
Wells Fargo International Value Fund - Class R6	WFRVX	NAS CM	Open End	Global Equity Large Cap (Foreign Stock)	C	C-	C+		Y	0
Wells Fargo Intrinsic Small Cap Value Fund - Class A	WFSMX	NAS CM	Open End	US Equity Small Cap (Small Company)	C	C	C+		Y	1,000
Wells Fargo Intrinsic Small Cap Value Fund - Class Admin	WFSDX	NAS CM	Open End	US Equity Small Cap (Small Company)	C	C	C+		Y	1,000,000
Wells Fargo Intrinsic Small Cap Value Fund - Class C	WSCDX	NAS CM	Open End	US Equity Small Cap (Small Company)	C	C	C+		Y	1,000
Wells Fargo Intrinsic Small Cap Value Fund - Class Inst	WFSSX	NAS CM	Open End	US Equity Small Cap (Small Company)	C	C	C+		Y	1,000,000
Wells Fargo Intrinsic World Equity Fund - Class A	EWEAX	NAS CM	Open End	Global Equity Large Cap (World Stock)	B-	C	B	Up	Y	1,000
Wells Fargo Intrinsic World Equity Fund - Class Admin	EWEIX	NAS CM	Open End	Global Equity Large Cap (World Stock)	B-	C	B	Up	Y	1,000,000
Wells Fargo Intrinsic World Equity Fund - Class C	EWECX	NAS CM	Open End	Global Equity Large Cap (World Stock)	B-	C	B	Up	Y	1,000

★ Expanded analysis of this fund is included in Section II.

	TOTAL RETURNS					PERFORMANCE				ASSETS		ASSET ALLOCATION & TURNOVER					BULL & BEAR		FEES		
Min Additional Investment	3-Month Total Return	6-Month Total Return	1-Year Total Return	3-Year Total Return	5-Year Total Return	Dividend Yield (TTM)	Expense Ratio	3-Yr Std Deviation	3-Year Beta	NAV	Total Assets (MIL)	%Cash	%Stocks	%Bonds	%Other	Turnover Ratio	Last Bull Market Total Return	Last Bear Market Total Return	Front End Fee (%)	Back End Fee (%)	Inception Date
	0.99	9.79	5.02	24.44	10.63	2.51	1.17	12.91	0.89	11.23	615.9	2	98	0	0	69					Sep-15
100	7.84	27.71	15.25	80.86	87.39	0	1.21	13.72	0.97	8.11	128.1	1	99	0	0	36	29.22	-19.92	5.75		Dec-00
	7.74	27.87	15.43	82.00	89.48	0	1.01	13.74	0.97	8.9	128.1	1	99	0	0	36	29.48	-19.83			Apr-05
100	7.49	27.15	14.27	76.88	80.47	0	1.96	13.77	0.98	4.73	128.1	1	99	0	0	36	28.71	-20.16		1.00	Dec-00
	7.90	27.98	15.71	83.09	91.28	0	0.81	13.72	0.97	9.42	128.1	1	99	0	0	36	29.51	-19.74			Apr-05
100	9.33	35.60	18.39	68.45	68.54	0	1.18	14.69	1	50.84	782.5	1	93	0	6	62	32.55	-24.89	5.75		Feb-00
	9.35	35.66	18.51	68.86	69.47	0	1.1	14.69	1	54.01	782.5	1	93	0	6	62	32.57	-24.83			Aug-02
100	9.12	35.11	17.51	64.67	62.32	0	1.93	14.69	0.99	43.75	782.5	1	93	0	6	62	31.95	-25.1		1.00	Mar-08
	9.40	35.84	18.77	70.12	71.33	0	0.85	14.69	1	56.88	782.5	1	93	0	6	62	32.78	-24.76			Jun-03
	9.43	35.88	18.84	70.36	71.60	0	0.8	14.7	1	57.06	782.5	1	93	0	6	62	32.55	-24.89			Oct-14
	1.15	6.85	1.00			0.51	0			9.66	1.0	6	94	0	0	81					Aug-17
	3.14	13.88	1.18			0.71	0			10.5	1.00	4	96	0	0	47					Aug-17
	3.84	18.32	12.43			0.79	0			12.14	1.00	2	98	0	0	23					Aug-17
	1.54	15.21	-4.31			0.77	0			11.21	0.91	3	96	0	0	37					Aug-17
	3.19	14.44	10.35	16.15	5.08	10.32		9.77		5.9	266.5	4	66	19	0	45	9.68	-17.34			Mar-07
100	2.20	15.78	0.30	44.31	41.59	0.07	1.55	12.07	0.87	39.39	292.3	5	94	0	1	51	22.03	-29.06	5.75		Mar-88
	2.22	15.88	0.43	44.91	42.60	0.23	1.41	12.06	0.87	41.43	292.3	5	94	0	1	51	22.13	-29			Jan-97
100	2.01	15.36	-0.46	41.06	36.35	0	2.3	12.07	0.87	26.36	292.3	5	94	0	1	51	21.49	-29.27		1.00	Feb-93
	2.28	16.02	0.67	46.00	44.41	0.48	1.16	12.08	0.87	41.26	292.3	5	94	0	1	51	22.33	-28.92			Jul-10
100	3.55	13.66	5.47	27.82	32.36	2.62	1.13	8.06		47.16	226.4	6	48	34	11	114	20.33	-16.42	5.75		Oct-98
	3.57	13.74	5.66	28.70	33.91	3.35	0.95	8.07		41.71	226.4	6	48	34	11	114	20.51	-16.32			Nov-94
100	3.35	13.22	4.71	25.02	27.50	2.14	1.88	8.06		40.66	226.4	6	48	34	11	114	19.82	-16.7		1.00	Oct-98
100	7.24	29.71	13.85	77.03	83.15	0	1.16	15.29	1.08	34.92	4,621	0	96	0	4	37	31.01	-16.26	5.75		Feb-00
	7.30	29.83	14.09	78.06	84.98	0	0.96	15.29	1.08	40.82	4,621	0	96	0	4	37	31.17	-16.16			Aug-02
100	7.07	29.23	13.03	73.02	76.35	0	1.91	15.31	1.09	25.42	4,621	0	96	0	4	37	30.44	-16.5		1.00	Dec-02
	7.37	29.99	14.34	79.18	86.96	0	0.75	15.31	1.09	44.86	4,621	0	96	0	4	37	31.34	-16.11			Feb-00
	7.37	30.02	14.39	79.47	87.34	0	0.7	15.29	1.08	45	4,621	0	96	0	4	37	31.34	-16.11			Sep-15
100	3.44	13.82	8.70	29.25	44.74	0.89	1.08	7.4		34.66	1,325	2	55	43	0	9	18.56	-8.89	5.75		Nov-86
	3.48	13.91	8.89	29.93	46.19	1.06	0.9	7.41		34.67	1,325	2	55	43	0	9	18.69	-8.75			Nov-99
100	3.21	13.37	7.88	26.33	39.37	0.23	1.83	7.4		21.07	1,325	2	55	43	0	9	18.03	-9.19		1.00	Apr-98
	3.50	14.01	9.06	30.36	45.98	1.2	0.75	7.42		34.62	1,325	2	55	43	0	9	18.56	-8.89			Oct-16
100	4.17	19.28	9.92	48.87	62.42	1.34	0.45	12.19	1	52.94	1,196	2	98	0	0	3	24.64	-16.4	5.75		Nov-98
	4.24	19.43	10.14	49.78	64.29	1.42	0.25	12.2	1	53.77	1,196	2	98	0	0	3	24.85	-16.28			Feb-85
100	4.00	18.86	9.10	45.57	56.45	0.44	1.2	12.2	1	53.5	1,196	2	98	0	0	3	24.1	-16.67		1.00	Apr-99
100	1.52	10.66	-2.61	26.43	14.27	4.26	1.15	13.32	1.13	11.67	320.8	-17	110	0	7	62	14.53	-26	5.75		Jan-98
	1.55	10.73	-2.61	26.49	14.36	4.03	1.15	13.31	1.13	11.5	320.8	-17	110	0	7	62	14.43	-25.97			Jul-10
100	1.41	10.35	-3.32	23.69	10.19	2.24	1.9	13.28	1.13	11.58	320.8	-17	110	0	7	62	13.98	-26.26		1.00	Mar-98
	1.63	10.84	-2.37	27.35	15.73	5.05	0.85	13.32	1.13	11.58	320.8	-17	110	0	7	62	14.78	-25.94			Mar-98
	1.45	10.59	-2.86	25.48	12.95	3.41	1.4	13.28	1.13	11.9	320.8	-17	110	0	7	62	14.41	-26.13			Oct-03
	1.58	10.86	-2.32	27.49	15.50	5.24	0.8	13.32	1.13	11.6	320.8	-17	110	0	7	62	14.53	-26			Sep-15
100	0.70	8.75	-3.25	26.43	0.92	2.28	1.35	11.56	0.98	14.28	901.1	2	92	0	6	15	10.83	-22.95	5.75		Oct-03
	0.69	8.76	-3.21	26.71	1.25	2.1	1.25	11.57	0.99	14.39	901.1	2	92	0	6	15	11	-22.88			Apr-05
100	0.50	8.34	-3.97	23.53	-2.88	1.35	2.1	11.56	0.98	13.9	901.1	2	92	0	6	15	10.36	-23.2		1.00	Apr-05
	0.78	8.95	-2.89	27.77	2.77	2.49	1	11.56	0.98	14.12	901.1	2	92	0	6	15	11.08	-22.84			Aug-06
	0.78	8.95	-2.81	27.00	1.38		0.9	11.57	0.98	14.11	901.1	2	92	0	6	15	10.83	-22.95			Jul-18
100	3.00	19.60	-3.94	32.33	28.63	0	1.36	17.57	0.98	31.18	66.6	3	97	0	0	34	31.17	-28	5.75		Mar-08
	3.04	19.70	-3.80	32.90	29.64	0	1.21	17.56	0.98	31.83	66.6	3	97	0	0	34	31.35	-27.93			Apr-05
100	2.82	19.17	-4.67	29.41	23.90	0	2.11	17.53	0.98	28.77	66.6	3	97	0	0	34	30.47	-28.21		1.00	Mar-08
	3.09	19.80	-3.61	33.70	30.94	0	1.01	17.56	0.98	32.3	66.6	3	97	0	0	34	31.42	-27.85			Apr-05
100	5.09	17.46	6.80	46.53	37.20	0.75	1.35	11.8	1	21.05	149.7	0	94	0	6	20	26.67	-17.25	5.75		Apr-96
	5.11	17.49	6.94	46.91	38.28	0.76	1.25	11.78	1	20.95	149.7	0	94	0	6	20	26.87	-17.19			May-07
100	4.90	17.05	6.04	43.27	32.18	0	2.1	11.8	1	20.11	149.7	0	94	0	6	20	26.18	-17.52		1.00	May-07

	MARKET			FUND TYPE, CATEGORY & OBJECTIVE	RATINGS				MINIMUMS	
Fund Name	Ticker Symbol	Traded On	Fund Type	Category and (Prospectus Objective)	Overall Rating	Reward Rating	Risk Rating	Recent Up/ Downgrade	Open to New Investors	Min Initial Investment
Wells Fargo Intrinsic World Equity Fund - Class Inst	EWENX	NAS CM	Open End	Global Equity Large Cap (World Stock)	B-	C	B	Up	Y	1,000,000
Wells Fargo Large Cap Core Fund - Class A	EGOAX	NAS CM	Open End	US Equity Large Cap Blend (Growth)	C+	C	B		Y	1,000
Wells Fargo Large Cap Core Fund - Class Admin	WFLLX	NAS CM	Open End	US Equity Large Cap Blend (Growth)	C+	C	B		Y	1,000,000
Wells Fargo Large Cap Core Fund - Class C	EGOCX	NAS CM	Open End	US Equity Large Cap Blend (Growth)	C+	C	B-		Y	1,000
Wells Fargo Large Cap Core Fund - Class Inst	EGOIX	NAS CM	Open End	US Equity Large Cap Blend (Growth)	C+	C	B		Y	1,000,000
Wells Fargo Large Cap Core Fund - Class R	EGOHX	NAS CM	Open End	US Equity Large Cap Blend (Growth)	C+	C	B		Y	0
Wells Fargo Large Cap Core Fund - Class R6	EGORX	NAS CM	Open End	US Equity Large Cap Blend (Growth)	C+	C	B		Y	0
Wells Fargo Large Cap Growth Fund - Class A	STAFX	NAS CM	Open End	US Equity Large Cap Growth (Growth)	B-	B-	B	Down	Y	1,000
Wells Fargo Large Cap Growth Fund - Class Admin	STDFX	NAS CM	Open End	US Equity Large Cap Growth (Growth)	B-	B-	B	Down	Y	1,000,000
Wells Fargo Large Cap Growth Fund - Class C	STOFX	NAS CM	Open End	US Equity Large Cap Growth (Growth)	B-	C+	B	Down	Y	1,000
Wells Fargo Large Cap Growth Fund - Class Inst	STNFX	NAS CM	Open End	US Equity Large Cap Growth (Growth)	B-	B-	B	Down	Y	1,000,000
Wells Fargo Large Cap Growth Fund - Class R	STMFX	NAS CM	Open End	US Equity Large Cap Growth (Growth)	B-	C+	B	Down	Y	0
Wells Fargo Large Cap Growth Fund - Class R4	SLGRX	NAS CM	Open End	US Equity Large Cap Growth (Growth)	B-	B-	B	Down	Y	0
Wells Fargo Large Cap Growth Fund - Class R6	STFFX	NAS CM	Open End	US Equity Large Cap Growth (Growth)	B-	B-	B	Down	Y	0
Wells Fargo Large Company Value Fund - Class A	WLCAX	NAS CM	Open End	US Equity Large Cap Value (Growth)	C+	C	B	Up	Y	1,000
Wells Fargo Large Company Value Fund - Class Admin	WWIDX	NAS CM	Open End	US Equity Large Cap Value (Growth)	C+	C	B	Up	Y	1,000,000
Wells Fargo Large Company Value Fund - Class C	WFLVX	NAS CM	Open End	US Equity Large Cap Value (Growth)	C+	C	B	Up	Y	1,000
Wells Fargo Large Company Value Fund - Class Inst	WLCIX	NAS CM	Open End	US Equity Large Cap Value (Growth)	B-	C	B	Up	Y	1,000,000
Wells Fargo Large Company Value Fund Class R6	WTLVX	NAS CM	Open End	US Equity Large Cap Value (Growth)	B-	C	B	Up	Y	0
Wells Fargo Low Volatility U.S. Equity Administrator Cls	WLVDX	NAS CM	Open End	US Equity Large Cap Blend (Growth)	B-	C	B	Up	Y	1,000,000
Wells Fargo Low Volatility U.S. Equity Fund Class A	WLVLX	NAS CM	Open End	US Equity Large Cap Blend (Growth)	B-	C	B	Up	Y	1,000
Wells Fargo Low Volatility U.S. Equity Fund Class C	WLVKX	NAS CM	Open End	US Equity Large Cap Blend (Growth)	C+	C	B	Up	Y	1,000
Wells Fargo Low Volatility U.S. Equity Fund Class R6	WLVJX	NAS CM	Open End	US Equity Large Cap Blend (Growth)	B-	C	B+	Up	Y	0
Wells Fargo Low Volatility U.S. Equity Institutional Cls	WLVOX	NAS CM	Open End	US Equity Large Cap Blend (Growth)	B-	C	B+	Up	Y	1,000,000
Wells Fargo Moderate Balanced Fund - Class A	WFMAX	NAS CM	Open End	Cautious Alloc (Balanced)	B	C	A-	Up	Y	1,000
Wells Fargo Moderate Balanced Fund - Class Admin	NVMBX	NAS CM	Open End	Cautious Alloc (Balanced)	B	C+	A-	Up	Y	1,000,000
Wells Fargo Moderate Balanced Fund - Class C	WFBCX	NAS CM	Open End	Cautious Alloc (Balanced)	B-	C	A-	Up	Y	1,000
Wells Fargo Moderate Balanced Fund - Class Institutional	WFMYX	NAS CM	Open End	Cautious Alloc (Balanced)	B	C+	A-	Up	Y	0
Wells Fargo Omega Growth Fund - Class A	EKOAX	NAS CM	Open End	US Equity Large Cap Growth (Growth)	B-	B-	B	Down	Y	1,000
Wells Fargo Omega Growth Fund - Class Admin	EOMYX	NAS CM	Open End	US Equity Large Cap Growth (Growth)	B	B-	B		Y	1,000,000
Wells Fargo Omega Growth Fund - Class C	EKOCX	NAS CM	Open End	US Equity Large Cap Growth (Growth)	B-	B-	B	Down	Y	1,000
Wells Fargo Omega Growth Fund - Class Inst	EKONX	NAS CM	Open End	US Equity Large Cap Growth (Growth)	B	B-	B		Y	1,000,000
Wells Fargo Omega Growth Fund - Class R	EKORX	NAS CM	Open End	US Equity Large Cap Growth (Growth)	B-	B-	B	Down	Y	0
Wells Fargo Opportunity Fund - Class A	SOPVX	NAS CM	Open End	US Equity Large Cap Growth (Growth)	B-	C	B		Y	1,000
Wells Fargo Opportunity Fund - Class Admin	WOFDX	NAS CM	Open End	US Equity Large Cap Growth (Growth)	B-	C	B		Y	1,000,000
Wells Fargo Opportunity Fund - Class C	WFOPX	NAS CM	Open End	US Equity Large Cap Growth (Growth)	C+	C	B		Y	1,000
Wells Fargo Opportunity Fund - Class Inst	WOFNX	NAS CM	Open End	US Equity Large Cap Growth (Growth)	B-	C	B		Y	1,000,000
Wells Fargo Precious Metals Fund - Class A	EKWAX	NAS CM	Open End	Precious Metals Sector Equity (Precious Metals)	D+	D+	C-	Down	Y	1,000
Wells Fargo Precious Metals Fund - Class Admin	EKWDX	NAS CM	Open End	Precious Metals Sector Equity (Precious Metals)	D+	D+	C-	Down	Y	1,000,000
Wells Fargo Precious Metals Fund - Class C	EKWCX	NAS CM	Open End	Precious Metals Sector Equity (Precious Metals)	D+	D	C-	Down	Y	1,000
Wells Fargo Precious Metals Fund - Class Inst	EKWYX	NAS CM	Open End	Precious Metals Sector Equity (Precious Metals)	D+	D+	C-	Down	Y	1,000,000
Wells Fargo Premier Large Company Growth Fund - Class A	EKJAX	NAS CM	Open End	US Equity Large Cap Growth (Growth)	B-	B-	B	Down	Y	1,000
Wells Fargo Premier Large Company Growth - Cls Admin	WFPDX	NAS CM	Open End	US Equity Large Cap Growth (Growth)	B-	B-	B	Down	Y	1,000,000
Wells Fargo Premier Large Company Growth Fund - Class C	EKJCX	NAS CM	Open End	US Equity Large Cap Growth (Growth)	B-	B-	B-	Down	Y	1,000
Wells Fargo Premier Large Company Growth Fund - Class Inst	EKJYX	NAS CM	Open End	US Equity Large Cap Growth (Growth)	B-	B-	B	Down	Y	1,000,000
Wells Fargo Premier Large Company Growth Fund - Class R4	EKJRX	NAS CM	Open End	US Equity Large Cap Growth (Growth)	B-	B-	B	Down	Y	0
Wells Fargo Premier Large Company Growth Fund - Class R6	EKJFX	NAS CM	Open End	US Equity Large Cap Growth (Growth)	B-	B-	B	Down	Y	0
Wells Fargo Small Cap Value Fund - Class A	SMVAX	NAS CM	Open End	US Equity Small Cap (Small Company)	C	C-	C		Y	1,000
Wells Fargo Small Cap Value Fund - Class Admin	SMVDX	NAS CM	Open End	US Equity Small Cap (Small Company)	C	C-	C		Y	1,000,000
Wells Fargo Small Cap Value Fund - Class C	SMVCX	NAS CM	Open End	US Equity Small Cap (Small Company)	C-	C-	C	Down	Y	1,000
Wells Fargo Small Cap Value Fund - Class Inst	WFSVX	NAS CM	Open End	US Equity Small Cap (Small Company)	C	C-	C		Y	1,000,000
Wells Fargo Small Cap Value Fund - Class R6	SMVRX	NAS CM	Open End	US Equity Small Cap (Small Company)	C	C-	C		Y	0

★ Expanded analysis of this fund is included in Section II.

Min Additional Investment	TOTAL RETURNS 3-Month Total Return	6-Month Total Return	1-Year Total Return	3-Year Total Return	5-Year Total Return	PERFORMANCE Dividend Yield (TTM)	Expense Ratio	3-Yr Std Deviation	3-Year Beta	ASSETS NAV	Total Assets (MIL)	ASSET ALLOCATION & TURNOVER %Cash	%Stocks	%Bonds	%Other	Turnover Ratio	BULL & BEAR Last Bull Market Total Return	Last Bear Market Total Return	FEES Front End Fee (%)	Back End Fee (%)	Inception Date
	5.21	17.71	7.24	48.26	40.08	1.12	0.95	11.78	1	21	149.7	0	94	0	6	20	27.02	-17.12			Jul-10
100	2.84	17.32	3.51	49.95	51.34	0.77	1.08	14.11	1.13	18.42	1,029	1	99	0	0	33	30.38	-19.74	5.75		Dec-07
	2.86	17.43	3.64	50.44	52.48	0.81	0.97	14.13	1.13	18.66	1,029	1	99	0	0	33	30.42	-19.5			Jul-10
100	2.61	16.87	2.74	46.60	45.70	0	1.83	14.09	1.13	18.08	1,029	1	99	0	0	33	29.83	-19.91		1.00	Dec-07
	2.94	17.63	3.96	51.86	54.73	1.15	0.67	14.13	1.13	18.54	1,029	1	99	0	0	33	30.74	-19.5			Dec-07
	2.73	17.17	3.23	48.84	50.34	0.54	1.33	14.1	1.13	18.42	1,029	1	99	0	0	33	30.55	-19.59			Sep-15
	2.89	17.59	3.95	56.45	59.35	1.13	0.65	14.13	1.12	18.51	1,029	1	99	0	0	33	30.74	-19.5			Sep-15
100	5.44	25.07	12.22	70.48	78.06	0	1.07	14.3	1.04	43.6	1,016	0	96	0	3	34	28.5	-14.14	5.75		Jul-10
	5.46	25.12	12.35	71.09	79.14	0	0.95	14.31	1.04	44.23	1,016	0	96	0	3	34	28.63	-14.06			Jul-10
100	5.22	24.58	11.37	66.65	71.46	0	1.82	14.3	1.04	38.87	1,016	0	96	0	3	34	27.99	-14.44		1.00	Jul-10
	5.51	25.26	12.57	72.07	81.16	0	0.75	14.31	1.04	45.17	1,016	0	96	0	3	34	28.82	-14.01			Jul-10
	5.36	24.88	11.93	69.12	75.79	0	1.32	14.31	1.04	42.26	1,016	0	96	0	3	34	28.63	-14.1			Jun-12
	5.50	25.20	12.52	71.87	80.65	0	0.8	14.3	1.04	45.06	1,016	0	96	0	3	34	28.82	-14.01			Nov-12
	5.53	25.31	12.68	72.63	81.99	0.03	0.65	14.32	1.05	45.39	1,016	0	96	0	3	34	28.82	-14.01			Nov-12
100	3.57	14.96	4.53	33.14	29.32	1.77	0.84	12.19	1	12.89	216.7	2	98	0	0	258	23.84	-19.18	5.75		Mar-08
	3.55	14.93	4.59	33.50	30.17	1.85	0.76	12.14	0.99	13.02	216.7	2	98	0	0	258	24.09	-19.12			Dec-01
100	3.34	14.46	3.68	30.14	24.54	0.66	1.59	12.16	0.99	13.31	216.7	2	98	0	0	258	23.39	-19.49		1.00	Mar-08
	3.63	15.09	4.93	34.55	31.76	2.15	0.51	12.14	0.99	13	216.7	2	98	0	0	258	24.14	-18.98			Mar-08
	3.65	15.14	4.98	34.53	31.18	2.27	0.41	12.17	0.99	13	216.7	2	98	0	0	258	24.09	-19.13			Apr-17
	5.53	19.27	12.61			1.54	0.66			11.82	38.8	2	98	0	0	75					Oct-16
100	5.53	19.25	12.48			1.45	0.74			11.83	38.8	2	98	0	0	75			5.75		Oct-16
100	5.37	18.90	11.76			0.91	1.49			11.76	38.8	2	98	0	0	75				1.00	Oct-16
	5.70	19.57	13.10			1.85	0.31			11.85	38.8	2	98	0	0	75					Oct-16
	5.61	19.35	12.90			1.78	0.41			11.84	38.8	2	98	0	0	75					Oct-16
100	2.94	10.72	5.85	20.15	25.71	1.77	1.15	5.41		20.96	129.2	9	34	55	1	113	13.3	-9.72	5.75		Jan-04
	3.01	10.88	6.15	21.11	27.25	2.02	0.9	5.4		21.19	129.2	9	34	55	1	113	13.51	-9.61			Nov-94
100	2.72	10.33	5.08	17.51	21.07	1.18	1.9	5.41		20.39	129.2	9	34	55	1	113	12.87	-10.02		1.00	Jan-04
	3.00	10.91	6.25	21.22	27.37		0.8	5.42		21.23	129.2	9	34	55	1	113	13.51	-9.61			Aug-18
100	7.48	28.98	15.14	78.15	77.00	0	1.28	14.27	1.02	54.15	836.3	3	97	0	0	48	32.36	-22.96	5.75		Apr-68
	7.52	29.11	15.36	79.13	78.79	0	1.1	14.27	1.02	59.43	836.3	3	97	0	0	48	32.53	-22.86			Jan-97
100	7.28	28.53	14.30	74.20	70.47	0	2.03	14.27	1.02	35.18	836.3	3	97	0	0	48	31.77	-23.2		1.00	Aug-93
	7.61	29.28	15.66	80.52	81.04	0	0.85	14.29	1.02	61.49	836.3	3	97	0	0	48	32.7	-22.79			Jul-10
	7.41	28.83	14.86	76.85	74.78	0	1.53	14.27	1.02	50.85	836.3	3	97	0	0	48	32.15	-23.04			Oct-03
100	4.12	20.84	7.95	47.58	47.66	0	1.18	12.49	0.97	42.37	1,721	2	98	0	0	30	23.75	-22.99	5.75		Feb-00
	4.16	20.96	8.16	48.49	49.20	0.02	1	12.5	0.98	46.73	1,721	2	98	0	0	30	23.92	-22.91			Aug-02
100	3.89	20.37	7.13	44.27	42.20	0	1.93	12.49	0.97	39.17	1,721	2	98	0	0	30	23.22	-23.23		1.00	Mar-08
	4.21	21.09	8.42	49.58	51.06	0.24	0.75	12.5	0.97	47.71	1,721	2	98	0	0	30	24.1	-22.87			Jul-10
100	14.02	25.28	15.24	-10.52	-4.49	0	1.09	25.5	0.93	38.7	308.2	1	99	0	0	19	-13.28	-11.64	5.75		Jan-98
	14.02	25.36	15.40	-10.15	-3.83	0	0.95	25.5	0.93	39.1	308.2	1	99	0	0	19	-13.22	-11.57			Jul-10
100	13.78	24.81	14.40	-12.51	-8.00	0	1.84	25.47	0.93	34	308.2	1	99	0	0	19	-13.66	-11.9		1.00	Jan-98
	14.08	25.48	15.59	-9.69	-3.09	0	0.79	25.51	0.93	39.44	308.2	1	99	0	0	19	-13.11	-11.49			Feb-00
100	6.70	27.71	14.03	74.06	77.96	0	1.11	14.41	1.04	14.01	2,423	0	96	0	4	45	30.37	-14.97	5.75		Jan-98
	6.71	27.79	14.06	74.61	79.11	0	1	14.46	1.05	14.3	2,423	0	96	0	4	45	30.45	-14.96			Jul-10
100	6.50	27.09	13.08	70.02	71.24	0	1.86	14.42	1.04	10.32	2,423	0	96	0	4	45	29.8	-15.27		1.00	Jan-98
	6.82	27.96	14.48	76.29	81.76	0	0.7	14.45	1.05	14.87	2,423	0	96	0	4	45	30.61	-14.84			Jun-99
	6.82	27.91	14.39	75.68	80.79	0	0.8	14.45	1.05	14.71	2,423	0	96	0	4	45	30.37	-14.97			Nov-12
	6.87	28.04	14.57	76.53	82.25	0	0.65	14.41	1.04	14.93	2,423	0	96	0	4	45	30.37	-14.97			Nov-12
100	2.45	16.29	-10.18	27.76	17.84	0	1.29	17.08	0.94	12.92	423.0	2	98	0	0	37	20.62	-22.31	5.75		Nov-00
	2.53	16.36	-9.98	28.53	19.02	0	1.09	17.08	0.94	14.15	423.0	2	98	0	0	37	20.79	-22.25			Jul-10
100	2.29	15.92	-10.79	24.93	13.50	0	2.04	17.07	0.94	7.57	423.0	2	98	0	0	37	20.12	-22.57		1.00	Nov-00
	2.50	16.40	-9.82	29.21	20.17	0	0.89	17.1	0.94	14.33	423.0	2	98	0	0	37	20.88	-22.18			Jul-07
	2.56	16.53	-9.74	29.47	20.51	0	0.84	17.12	0.94	14.38	423.0	2	98	0	0	37	20.62	-22.31			Jun-13

Fund Name	MARKET Ticker Symbol	Traded On	FUND TYPE, CATEGORY & OBJECTIVE Fund Type	Category and (Prospectus Objective)	RATINGS Overall Rating	Reward Rating	Risk Rating	Recent Up/ Downgrade	MINIMUMS Open to New Investors	Min Initial Investment
Wells Fargo Small Company Growth Fund - Class A	WFSAX	NAS CM	Open End	US Equity Small Cap (Small Company)	C+	C	C+	Down	Y	1,000
Wells Fargo Small Company Growth Fund - Class Admin	NVSCX	NAS CM	Open End	US Equity Small Cap (Small Company)	C+	C	C+	Down	Y	1,000,000
Wells Fargo Small Company Growth Fund - Class C	WSMCX	NAS CM	Open End	US Equity Small Cap (Small Company)	C+	C	C+		Y	1,000
Wells Fargo Small Company Growth Fund - Class Inst	WSCGX	NAS CM	Open End	US Equity Small Cap (Small Company)	C+	C	C+	Down	Y	1,000,000
Wells Fargo Small Company Growth Fund - Class R6	WSCRX	NAS CM	Open End	US Equity Small Cap (Small Company)	C+	C	C+	Down	Y	0
Wells Fargo Small Company Value Fund - Class A	SCVAX	NAS CM	Open End	US Equity Small Cap (Small Company)	C-	C-	C	Down	Y	1,000
Wells Fargo Small Company Value Fund - Class Admin	SCVIX	NAS CM	Open End	US Equity Small Cap (Small Company)	C-	C-	C	Down	Y	1,000,000
Wells Fargo Small Company Value Fund - Class C	SCVFX	NAS CM	Open End	US Equity Small Cap (Small Company)	C-	C-	C	Down	Y	1,000
Wells Fargo Small Company Value Fund - Class Inst	SCVNX	NAS CM	Open End	US Equity Small Cap (Small Company)	C-	C-	C	Down	Y	1,000,000
Wells Fargo Small Company Value Fund Class R6	SCVJX	NAS CM	Open End	US Equity Small Cap (Small Company)	C-	C-	C	Down	Y	0
Wells Fargo Special Mid Cap Value Fund - Class A	WFPAX	NAS CM	Open End	US Equity Mid Cap (Growth)	C+	C	B		Y	1,000
Wells Fargo Special Mid Cap Value Fund - Class Admin	WFMDX	NAS CM	Open End	US Equity Mid Cap (Growth)	C+	C	B		Y	1,000,000
Wells Fargo Special Mid Cap Value Fund - Class C	WFPCX	NAS CM	Open End	US Equity Mid Cap (Growth)	C+	C	B		Y	1,000
Wells Fargo Special Mid Cap Value Fund - Class Inst	WFMIX	NAS CM	Open End	US Equity Mid Cap (Growth)	C+	C	B		Y	1,000,000
Wells Fargo Special Mid Cap Value Fund - Class R	WFHHX	NAS CM	Open End	US Equity Mid Cap (Growth)	C+	C	B		Y	0
Wells Fargo Special Mid Cap Value Fund - Class R6	WFPRX	NAS CM	Open End	US Equity Mid Cap (Growth)	C+	C	B		Y	0
Wells Fargo Special Small Cap Value Fund - Class A	ESPAX	NAS CM	Open End	US Equity Small Cap (Small Company)	C	C	C+		Y	1,000
Wells Fargo Special Small Cap Value Fund - Class Admin	ESPIX	NAS CM	Open End	US Equity Small Cap (Small Company)	C	C	C+		Y	1,000,000
Wells Fargo Special Small Cap Value Fund - Class C	ESPCX	NAS CM	Open End	US Equity Small Cap (Small Company)	C	C	C+		Y	1,000
Wells Fargo Special Small Cap Value Fund - Class Inst	ESPNX	NAS CM	Open End	US Equity Small Cap (Small Company)	C	C	B-		Y	1,000,000
Wells Fargo Special Small Cap Value Fund - Class R	ESPHX	NAS CM	Open End	US Equity Small Cap (Small Company)	C	C	C+		Y	0
Wells Fargo Special Small Cap Value Fund - Class R6	ESPRX	NAS CM	Open End	US Equity Small Cap (Small Company)	C	C	B-		Y	0
Wells Fargo Specialized Technology Fund - Class A	WFSTX	NAS CM	Open End	Technology Sector Equity (Technology)	C+	C+	B-	Down	Y	1,000
Wells Fargo Specialized Technology Fund - Class Admin	WFTDX	NAS CM	Open End	Technology Sector Equity (Technology)	C+	C+	B-	Down	Y	1,000,000
Wells Fargo Specialized Technology Fund - Class C	WFTCX	NAS CM	Open End	Technology Sector Equity (Technology)	C+	C+	B-	Down	Y	1,000
Wells Fargo Specialized Technology Institutional Cls	WFTIX	NAS CM	Open End	Technology Sector Equity (Technology)	C+	C+	B-	Down	Y	1,000,000
Wells Fargo Target 2010 Fund - Class A	STNRX	NAS CM	Open End	Target Date (Asset Alloc)	B-	C	B	Up	Y	1,000
Wells Fargo Target 2010 Fund - Class Admin	WFLGX	NAS CM	Open End	Target Date (Asset Alloc)	B-	C	B+	Up	Y	1,000,000
Wells Fargo Target 2010 Fund - Class C	WFOCX	NAS CM	Open End	Target Date (Asset Alloc)	C+	C	B		Y	1,000
Wells Fargo Target 2010 Fund - Class R	WFARX	NAS CM	Open End	Target Date (Asset Alloc)	C+	C	B		Y	0
Wells Fargo Target 2010 Fund - Class R4	WFORX	NAS CM	Open End	Target Date (Asset Alloc)	B-	C	B+		Y	0
Wells Fargo Target 2010 Fund - Class R6	WFOAX	NAS CM	Open End	Target Date (Asset Alloc)	B-	C	B+		Y	0
Wells Fargo Target 2015 Fund - Class A	WFACX	NAS CM	Open End	Target Date (Asset Alloc)	B-	C	B+		Y	1,000
Wells Fargo Target 2015 Fund - Class Admin	WFFFX	NAS CM	Open End	Target Date (Asset Alloc)	B-	C	B+		Y	1,000,000
Wells Fargo Target 2015 Fund - Class R	WFBRX	NAS CM	Open End	Target Date (Asset Alloc)	C+	C	B		Y	0
Wells Fargo Target 2015 Fund - Class R4	WFSRX	NAS CM	Open End	Target Date (Asset Alloc)	B-	C	B+		Y	0
Wells Fargo Target 2015 Fund - Class R6	WFSCX	NAS CM	Open End	Target Date (Asset Alloc)	B-	C	B+		Y	0
Wells Fargo Target 2020 Fund - Class A	STTRX	NAS CM	Open End	Target Date (Asset Alloc)	B-	C	B+		Y	1,000
Wells Fargo Target 2020 Fund - Class Admin	WFLPX	NAS CM	Open End	Target Date (Asset Alloc)	B-	C	B+		Y	1,000,000
Wells Fargo Target 2020 Fund - Class C	WFLAX	NAS CM	Open End	Target Date (Asset Alloc)	C+	C	B+		Y	1,000
Wells Fargo Target 2020 Fund - Class R	WFURX	NAS CM	Open End	Target Date (Asset Alloc)	B-	C	B+		Y	0
Wells Fargo Target 2020 Fund - Class R4	WFLRX	NAS CM	Open End	Target Date (Asset Alloc)	B-	C+	B+		Y	0
Wells Fargo Target 2020 Fund - Class R6	WFOBX	NAS CM	Open End	Target Date (Asset Alloc)	B	C+	A-		Y	0
Wells Fargo Target 2025 Fund - Class A	WFAYX	NAS CM	Open End	Target Date (Asset Alloc)	B-	C	A-		Y	1,000
Wells Fargo Target 2025 Fund - Class Admin	WFTRX	NAS CM	Open End	Target Date (Asset Alloc)	B-	C	A-		Y	1,000,000
Wells Fargo Target 2025 Fund - Class R	WFHRX	NAS CM	Open End	Target Date (Asset Alloc)	B-	C	B+		Y	0
Wells Fargo Target 2025 Fund - Class R4	WFGRX	NAS CM	Open End	Target Date (Asset Alloc)	B	C+	A-	Up	Y	0
Wells Fargo Target 2025 Fund - Class R6	WFTYX	NAS CM	Open End	Target Date (Asset Alloc)	B	C+	A-	Up	Y	0
Wells Fargo Target 2030 Fund - Class A	STHRX	NAS CM	Open End	Target Date (Asset Alloc)	B	C	A-	Up	Y	1,000
Wells Fargo Target 2030 Fund - Class Admin	WFLIX	NAS CM	Open End	Target Date (Asset Alloc)	B	C	A-	Up	Y	1,000,000
Wells Fargo Target 2030 Fund - Class C	WFDMX	NAS CM	Open End	Target Date (Asset Alloc)	B-	C	B+	Up	Y	1,000
Wells Fargo Target 2030 Fund - Class R	WFJRX	NAS CM	Open End	Target Date (Asset Alloc)	B-	C	A-	Up	Y	0

★ Expanded analysis of this fund is included in Section II.

	TOTAL RETURNS					PERFORMANCE				ASSETS		ASSET ALLOCATION & TURNOVER					BULL & BEAR		FEES		
Min Additional Investment	3-Month Total Return	6-Month Total Return	1-Year Total Return	3-Year Total Return	5-Year Total Return	Dividend Yield (TTM)	Expense Ratio	3-Yr Std Deviation	3-Year Beta	NAV	Total Assets (MIL)	%Cash	%Stocks	%Bonds	%Other	Turnover Ratio	Last Bull Market Total Return	Last Bear Market Total Return	Front End Fee (%)	Back End Fee (%)	Inception Date
100	3.17	20.32	0.48	54.30	43.57	0	1.33	17.73	1	52.69	1,888	4	90	0	6	37	30.26	-26.79	5.75		Jan-04
	3.21	20.38	0.60	54.85	44.61	0	1.2	17.73	1	54.97	1,888	4	90	0	6	37	30.48	-26.73			Nov-94
100	2.98	19.84	-0.26	50.83	38.27	0	2.08	17.71	1	45.95	1,888	4	90	0	6	37	29.7	-27.02		1.00	Jan-04
	3.27	20.54	0.86	56.01	46.38	0	0.95	17.73	1	56.5	1,888	4	90	0	6	37	30.64	-26.64			Mar-08
	3.28	20.55	0.91	56.28	46.59	0	0.9	17.74	1	56.65	1,888	4	90	0	6	37	30.48	-26.73			Oct-14
100	1.29	12.37	-9.88	34.52	25.83	0.64	1.15	16.91	0.96	25.88	62.9	0	98	0	2	144	33.54	-26.17	5.75		Jan-02
	1.30	12.38	-9.81	34.97	26.79	0.55	1.05	16.92	0.96	26.49	62.9	0	98	0	2	144	33.84	-26.15			Jan-02
100	1.10	11.90	-10.56	31.47	21.19	0	1.9	16.89	0.96	22.93	62.9	0	98	0	2	144	33.03	-26.41		1.00	Aug-02
	1.33	12.49	-9.62	35.84	28.04	1.05	0.85	16.91	0.96	26.56	62.9	0	98	0	2	144	33.88	-26.05			Jul-10
	1.37	12.55	-9.54	36.06	27.82	1.05	0.75	16.9	0.96	26.62	62.9	0	98	0	2	144	33.84	-26.15			Oct-16
100	5.28	23.16	8.30	33.68	41.94	0.44	1.16	12.69	0.94	38.66	8,542	4	96	0	0	37	26.09	-22.26	5.75		Jul-07
	5.32	23.19	8.40	34.00	42.60	0.43	1.08	12.68	0.94	39.36	8,542	4	96	0	0	37	26.18	-22.2			Apr-05
100	5.11	22.71	7.51	30.68	36.73	0	1.91	12.68	0.94	37	8,542	4	96	0	0	37	25.51	-22.46		1.00	Jul-07
	5.36	23.35	8.66	34.99	44.39	0.75	0.83	12.69	0.94	39.67	8,542	4	96	0	0	37	26.37	-22.11			Apr-05
	5.21	23.00	8.03	32.68	40.85	0.35	1.41	12.68	0.94	39.14	8,542	4	96	0	0	37	26.19	-22.19			Sep-15
	5.41	23.43	8.77	35.41	45.05	0.85	0.73	12.7	0.94	39.72	8,542	4	96	0	0	37	26.37	-22.11			Jun-13
100	3.56	18.10	-1.93	36.29	41.06	0.42	1.31	15.94	0.9	32.87	3,240	12	86	0	2	32	29.92	-22.37	5.75		May-93
	3.59	18.19	-1.85	36.71	42.09	0.46	1.2	15.96	0.9	33.72	3,240	12	86	0	2	32	30.09	-22.28			Jul-96
100	3.33	17.65	-2.67	33.26	35.87	0	2.06	15.94	0.9	29.45	3,240	12	86	0	2	32	29.34	-22.61		1.00	Dec-00
	3.62	18.33	-1.60	37.80	43.77	0.78	0.94	15.95	0.9	33.75	3,240	12	86	0	2	32	30.2	-22.22			Jul-10
	3.47	17.98	-2.17	35.39	39.45	0.35	1.56	15.96	0.9	33.33	3,240	12	86	0	2	32	29.73	-22.45			Sep-15
	3.65	18.38	-1.52	38.05	43.92	0.85	0.88	15.96	0.9	33.74	3,240	12	86	0	2	32	29.92	-22.37			Oct-14
100	3.75	26.18	13.89	109.67	123.45	0	1.39	17.79	1.07	13.83	494.4	7	89	0	4	107	20.66	-21.45	5.75		Sep-00
	3.73	26.20	14.07	110.39	124.71	0	1.29	17.86	1.07	14.16	494.4	7	89	0	4	107	20.75	-21.31			Jul-10
100	3.46	25.63	13.07	104.83	115.02	0	2.14	17.8	1.07	10.44	494.4	7	89	0	4	107	20.03	-21.62		1.00	Sep-00
	3.85	26.41	14.37	111.67	125.58	0	1.04	17.82	1.07	14.26	494.4	7	89	0	4	107	20.66	-21.45			Nov-16
100	2.93	9.35	6.94	10.60	12.69	2.25	0.65	4.13	0.82	10.47	66.4	2	31	67	0	45	5.83	-2.49	5.75		Mar-94
	2.91	9.37	7.03	10.95	13.36	2.3	0.54	4.1	0.82	10.62	66.4	2	31	67	0	45	5.9	-2.43			Nov-99
100	2.68	8.91	6.11	8.15	8.53	1.48	1.4	4.13	0.82	10.6	66.4	2	31	67	0	45	5.36	-2.81		1.00	Dec-98
	2.78	9.18	6.61	9.82	11.26	2.01	0.9	4.13	0.82	10.38	66.4	2	31	67	0	45	5.68	-2.59			Jun-13
	2.97	9.49	7.29	11.69	14.51	2.52	0.34	4.09	0.82	10.61	66.4	2	31	67	0	45	5.83	-2.49			Nov-12
	3.02	9.59	7.38	12.22	15.33	2.68	0.19	4.1	0.82	10.59	66.4	2	31	67	0	45	6.18	-2.34			Jun-04
100	2.66	9.43	6.61	11.95	14.66	2.15	0.65	4.69	0.81	7.27	77.6	2	36	62	0	44	7.86	-4.53	5.75		Nov-12
	2.88	9.81	6.97	12.43	15.90	2.19	0.54	4.67	0.8	7.48	77.6	2	36	62	0	44	7.69	-4.74			Jun-07
	2.80	9.68	6.60	11.13	13.62	1.84	0.9	4.66	0.8	7.43	77.6	2	36	62	0	44	7.7	-4.63			Jun-13
	2.99	10.12	7.36	13.01	16.95	2.45	0.34	4.69	0.8	7.34	77.6	2	36	62	0	44	7.86	-4.53			Nov-12
	2.90	10.04	7.35	13.45	17.68	2.56	0.19	4.65	0.8	7.33	77.6	2	36	62	0	44	7.85	-4.53			Jun-07
100	2.88	10.57	6.78	15.35	18.06	3.27	0.65	5.34	0.84	12.13	407.1	2	42	55	0	43	9.78	-7.48	5.75		Mar-94
	2.90	10.60	6.85	15.65	18.66	3.25	0.54	5.33	0.84	12.41	407.1	2	42	55	0	43	9.94	-7.47			Nov-99
100	2.77	10.21	5.96	12.77	13.70	2.45	1.4	5.35	0.84	11.87	407.1	2	42	55	0	43	9.38	-7.82		1.00	Dec-98
	2.82	10.38	6.51	14.54	16.69	3.17	0.9	5.29	0.83	12.01	407.1	2	42	55	0	43	9.63	-7.58			Jun-13
	3.04	10.70	7.10	16.42	19.96	3.48	0.34	5.3	0.84	12.51	407.1	2	42	55	0	43	9.78	-7.48			Nov-12
	3.04	10.80	7.32	16.97	20.89	3.74	0.19	5.31	0.84	12.51	407.1	2	42	55	0	43	10.18	-7.34			Jun-04
100	2.83	11.32	6.52	19.34	21.38	2.17	0.65	6.11	0.84	5.8	298.8	2	52	45	0	43	12.8	-10.42	5.75		Nov-12
	2.96	11.53	6.81	19.97	22.25	2.04	0.54	6.2	0.86	5.9	298.8	2	52	45	0	43	12.69	-10.64			Jun-07
	2.87	11.28	6.27	17.52	18.89	2.08	0.9	6.19	0.85	5.72	298.8	2	52	45	0	43	12.63	-10.51			Jun-13
	2.99	11.64	6.79	20.40	23.15	2.43	0.34	6.09	0.84	5.85	298.8	2	52	45	0	43	12.8	-10.42			Nov-12
	3.17	11.85	7.16	21.07	24.31	2.58	0.19	6.29	0.87	5.85	298.8	2	52	45	0	43	12.8	-10.42			Jun-07
100	2.96	12.29	6.25	24.01	25.03	2.34	0.65	7.19	0.87	12.51	571.0	3	62	35	0	43	15.11	-13.77	5.75		Mar-94
	2.97	12.35	6.39	24.47	25.83	2.32	0.54	7.2	0.87	12.82	571.0	3	62	35	0	43	15.22	-13.7			Mar-94
100	2.75	11.91	5.46	21.21	20.41	1.77	1.4	7.17	0.87	11.93	571.0	3	62	35	0	43	14.59	-13.99		1.00	Dec-98
	2.96	12.18	6.05	22.88	23.30	2.18	0.9	7.2	0.87	12.52	571.0	3	62	35	0	43	15.05	-13.79			Jun-13

	MARKET		FUND TYPE, CATEGORY & OBJECTIVE		RATINGS				MINIMUMS	
Fund Name	Ticker Symbol	Traded On	Fund Type	Category and (Prospectus Objective)	Overall Rating	Reward Rating	Risk Rating	Recent Up/ Downgrade	Open to New Investors	Min Initial Investment
Wells Fargo Target 2030 Fund - Class R4	WTHRX	NAS CM	Open End	Target Date (Asset Alloc)	B	C	A-	Up	Y	0
Wells Fargo Target 2030 Fund - Class R6	WFOOX	NAS CM	Open End	Target Date (Asset Alloc)	B	C	A-	Up	Y	0
Wells Fargo Target 2035 Fund - Class A	WFQBX	NAS CM	Open End	Target Date (Asset Alloc)	B-	C	A-	Up	Y	1,000
Wells Fargo Target 2035 Fund - Class Admin	WFQWX	NAS CM	Open End	Target Date (Asset Alloc)	B-	C	A-	Up	Y	1,000,000
Wells Fargo Target 2035 Fund - Class R	WFKRX	NAS CM	Open End	Target Date (Asset Alloc)	B-	C	B+	Up	Y	0
Wells Fargo Target 2035 Fund - Class R4	WTTRX	NAS CM	Open End	Target Date (Asset Alloc)	B-	C	A-		Y	0
Wells Fargo Target 2035 Fund - Class R6	WFQRX	NAS CM	Open End	Target Date (Asset Alloc)	B-	C	A-		Y	0
Wells Fargo Target 2040 Fund - Class A	STFRX	NAS CM	Open End	Target Date (Asset Alloc)	B-	C	B+	Up	Y	1,000
Wells Fargo Target 2040 Fund - Class Admin	WFLWX	NAS CM	Open End	Target Date (Asset Alloc)	B-	C	B+	Up	Y	1,000,000
Wells Fargo Target 2040 Fund - Class C	WFOFX	NAS CM	Open End	Target Date (Asset Alloc)	B-	C	B+	Up	Y	1,000
Wells Fargo Target 2040 Fund - Class R	WFMRX	NAS CM	Open End	Target Date (Asset Alloc)	B-	C	B+	Up	Y	0
Wells Fargo Target 2040 Fund - Class R4	WTFRX	NAS CM	Open End	Target Date (Asset Alloc)	B-	C	B+	Up	Y	0
Wells Fargo Target 2040 Fund - Class R6	WFOSX	NAS CM	Open End	Target Date (Asset Alloc)	B-	C	B+	Up	Y	0
Wells Fargo Target 2045 Fund - Class A	WFQVX	NAS CM	Open End	Target Date (Asset Alloc)	B-	C	B+	Up	Y	1,000
Wells Fargo Target 2045 Fund - Class Admin	WFQYX	NAS CM	Open End	Target Date (Asset Alloc)	B-	C	B+	Up	Y	1,000,000
Wells Fargo Target 2045 Fund - Class R	WFNRX	NAS CM	Open End	Target Date (Asset Alloc)	B-	C	B+	Up	Y	0
Wells Fargo Target 2045 Fund - Class R4	WFFRX	NAS CM	Open End	Target Date (Asset Alloc)	B-	C	B+	Up	Y	0
Wells Fargo Target 2045 Fund - Class R6	WFQPX	NAS CM	Open End	Target Date (Asset Alloc)	B-	C	B+	Up	Y	0
Wells Fargo Target 2050 Fund - Class A	WFQAX	NAS CM	Open End	Target Date (Asset Alloc)	B-	C	B+	Up	Y	1,000
Wells Fargo Target 2050 Fund - Class Admin	WFQDX	NAS CM	Open End	Target Date (Asset Alloc)	B-	C	B+	Up	Y	1,000,000
Wells Fargo Target 2050 Fund - Class C	WFQCX	NAS CM	Open End	Target Date (Asset Alloc)	B-	C	B+	Up	Y	1,000
Wells Fargo Target 2050 Fund - Class R	WFWRX	NAS CM	Open End	Target Date (Asset Alloc)	B-	C	B+	Up	Y	0
Wells Fargo Target 2050 Fund - Class R4	WQFRX	NAS CM	Open End	Target Date (Asset Alloc)	B-	C	B+	Up	Y	0
Wells Fargo Target 2050 Fund - Class R6	WFQFX	NAS CM	Open End	Target Date (Asset Alloc)	B-	C	B+	Up	Y	0
Wells Fargo Target 2055 Fund - Class A	WFQZX	NAS CM	Open End	Target Date (Asset Alloc)	B-	C	B+	Up	Y	1,000
Wells Fargo Target 2055 Fund - Class Admin	WFLHX	NAS CM	Open End	Target Date (Asset Alloc)	B-	C	B+	Up	Y	1,000,000
Wells Fargo Target 2055 Fund - Class R	WFYRX	NAS CM	Open End	Target Date (Asset Alloc)	B-	C	B+	Up	Y	0
Wells Fargo Target 2055 Fund - Class R4	WFVRX	NAS CM	Open End	Target Date (Asset Alloc)	B-	C	B+	Up	Y	0
Wells Fargo Target 2055 Fund - Class R6	WFQUX	NAS CM	Open End	Target Date (Asset Alloc)	B-	C	B+	Up	Y	0
Wells Fargo Target 2060 Fund - Class A	WFAFX	NAS CM	Open End	Target Date (Asset Alloc)	B-	C	B+	Up	Y	1,000
Wells Fargo Target 2060 Fund - Class Admin	WFDFX	NAS CM	Open End	Target Date (Asset Alloc)	B-	C	B+	Up	Y	1,000,000
Wells Fargo Target 2060 Fund - Class C	WFCFX	NAS CM	Open End	Target Date (Asset Alloc)	B-	C	B+	Up	Y	1,000
Wells Fargo Target 2060 Fund - Class R	WFRFX	NAS CM	Open End	Target Date (Asset Alloc)	B-	C	B+	Up	Y	0
Wells Fargo Target 2060 Fund - Class R4	WFSFX	NAS CM	Open End	Target Date (Asset Alloc)	B-	C	B+	Up	Y	0
Wells Fargo Target 2060 Fund - Class R6	WFUFX	NAS CM	Open End	Target Date (Asset Alloc)	B-	C	B+	Up	Y	0
Wells Fargo Target Today Fund - Class A	STWRX	NAS CM	Open End	Target Date (Asset Alloc)	B-	C	B	Up	Y	1,000
Wells Fargo Target Today Fund - Class Admin	WFLOX	NAS CM	Open End	Target Date (Asset Alloc)	B-	C	B	Up	Y	1,000,000
Wells Fargo Target Today Fund - Class C	WFODX	NAS CM	Open End	Target Date (Asset Alloc)	C+	C	B	Up	Y	1,000
Wells Fargo Target Today Fund - Class R	WFRRX	NAS CM	Open End	Target Date (Asset Alloc)	C+	C	B		Y	0
Wells Fargo Target Today Fund - Class R4	WOTRX	NAS CM	Open End	Target Date (Asset Alloc)	B-	C	B		Y	0
Wells Fargo Target Today Fund - Class R6	WOTDX	NAS CM	Open End	Target Date (Asset Alloc)	B-	C	B+		Y	0
Wells Fargo Traditional Small Cap Growth Fund - Class A	EGWAX	NAS CM	Open End	US Equity Small Cap (Growth)	B-	B-	C+	Down	Y	1,000
Wells Fargo Traditional Small Cap Growth - Cls Admin	EGWDX	NAS CM	Open End	US Equity Small Cap (Growth)	B-	B-	C+	Down	Y	1,000,000
Wells Fargo Traditional Small Cap Growth Fund - Class C	EGWCX	NAS CM	Open End	US Equity Small Cap (Growth)	B-	B-	C+	Down	Y	1,000
Wells Fargo Traditional Small Cap Growth Fund - Class Inst	EGRYX	NAS CM	Open End	US Equity Small Cap (Growth)	B-	B-	C+	Down	Y	1,000,000
Wells Fargo Utilities and High Income Fund	ERH	AMEX	Closed End	Moderate Alloc (Balanced)	C	B-	C-	Down	Y	
Wells Fargo Utility and Telecommunications Fund - Class A	EVUAX	NAS CM	Open End	Utilities Sector Equity (Utility)	B	B	B		Y	1,000
Wells Fargo Utility & Telecommunications - Cls Admin	EVUDX	NAS CM	Open End	Utilities Sector Equity (Utility)	B	B	B		Y	1,000,000
Wells Fargo Utility and Telecommunications Fund - Class C	EVUCX	NAS CM	Open End	Utilities Sector Equity (Utility)	B	B	B		Y	1,000
Wells Fargo Utility & Telecommunications - Cls Inst	EVUYX	NAS CM	Open End	Utilities Sector Equity (Utility)	B	B	B		Y	1,000,000
Wells Fargo WealthBuilder Conservative Allocation Cls A	WCAFX	NAS CM	Open End	Cautious Alloc (Income)	B-	C	B		Y	1,000
Wells Fargo WealthBuilder Conservative Allocation Inst Cls	WCYFX	NAS CM	Open End	Cautious Alloc (Income)	B-	C	B	Up	Y	1,000,000

★ Expanded analysis of this fund is included in Section II.

Min Additional Investment	TOTAL RETURNS 3-Month Total Return	6-Month Total Return	1-Year Total Return	3-Year Total Return	5-Year Total Return	PERFORMANCE Dividend Yield (TTM)	Expense Ratio	3-Yr Std Deviation	3-Year Beta	ASSETS NAV	Total Assets (MIL)	ASSET ALLOCATION & TURNOVER %Cash	%Stocks	%Bonds	%Other	Turnover Ratio	BULL & BEAR Last Bull Market Total Return	Last Bear Market Total Return	FEES Front End Fee (%)	Back End Fee (%)	Inception Date
	3.05	12.54	6.60	25.22	27.06	2.56	0.34	7.17	0.87	12.83	571.0	3	62	35	0	43	15.22	-13.7			Nov-12
	3.13	12.66	6.81	25.73	28.05	2.74	0.19	7.2	0.87	12.81	571.0	3	62	35	0	43	15.5	-13.55			Jun-04
100	2.95	13.14	5.98	28.20	27.82	2.1	0.65	8.14	0.88	7.66	263.1	3	72	25	0	41	17.59	-15.96	5.75		Nov-12
	3.05	13.28	6.12	28.67	28.64	1.91	0.54	8.19	0.89	7.76	263.1	3	72	25	0	41	17.47	-16.16			Jun-07
	2.93	13.03	5.75	27.26	26.22	1.93	0.9	8.13	0.88	7.72	263.1	3	72	25	0	41	17.42	-16.05			Jun-13
	3.08	13.25	6.32	29.44	29.94	2.37	0.34	8.26	0.9	7.69	263.1	3	72	25	0	41	17.59	-15.96			Nov-12
	3.08	13.42	6.52	30.07	30.98	2.52	0.19	8.17	0.89	7.69	263.1	3	72	25	0	41	17.59	-15.96			Jun-07
100	2.95	13.78	5.76	31.50	30.06	2.21	0.65	8.93	0.91	14.61	505.8	3	79	18	0	40	18.75	-17.81	5.75		Mar-94
	2.99	13.86	5.88	31.95	30.80	2.17	0.54	8.9	0.9	15.11	505.8	3	79	18	0	40	18.86	-17.82			Nov-99
100	2.74	13.32	4.93	28.59	25.26	1.68	1.4	8.94	0.91	13.1	505.8	3	79	18	0	40	18.24	-18.08		1.00	Jul-98
	2.89	13.62	5.47	30.58	28.47	2.03	0.9	8.92	0.91	14.59	505.8	3	79	18	0	40	18.58	-17.9			Jun-13
	3.06	13.90	6.03	32.78	32.09	2.41	0.34	8.93	0.91	15.15	505.8	3	79	18	0	40	18.75	-17.81			Nov-12
	3.06	14.00	6.17	33.30	33.08	2.58	0.19	8.89	0.9	15.14	505.8	3	79	18	0	40	19.1	-17.64			Jun-04
100	3.05	14.22	5.63	33.93	31.61	2.05	0.65	9.49	0.93	8.43	151.5	3	84	13	0	39	19.68	-18.3	5.75		Nov-12
	3.00	14.24	5.69	34.28	32.32	1.84	0.54	9.42	0.92	8.58	151.5	3	84	13	0	39	19.53	-18.47			Jun-07
	2.87	14.09	5.37	32.84	29.93	1.78	0.9	9.43	0.92	8.58	151.5	3	84	13	0	39	19.51	-18.39			Jun-13
	3.03	14.26	5.94	35.09	33.65	2.32	0.34	9.46	0.93	8.49	151.5	3	84	13	0	39	19.68	-18.3			Nov-12
	3.04	14.47	6.04	35.67	34.64	2.49	0.19	9.46	0.93	8.46	151.5	3	84	13	0	39	19.68	-18.3			Jun-07
100	3.06	14.39	5.58	34.68	32.13	2.27	0.65	9.63	0.92	7.39	230.7	3	87	10	0	39	19.75	-18.33	5.75		Nov-12
	3.05	14.50	5.59	35.24	32.95	2.3	0.54	9.66	0.92	7.42	230.7	3	87	10	0	39	19.58	-18.42			Jun-07
100	2.80	14.01	4.69	31.79	27.31	1.66	1.4	9.7	0.93	7.32	230.7	3	87	10	0	39	19.23	-18.59		1.00	Nov-12
	2.92	14.19	5.24	33.72	30.44	2.13	0.9	9.67	0.92	7.4	230.7	3	87	10	0	39	19.58	-18.42			Jun-13
	3.04	14.61	5.91	36.01	34.24	2.55	0.34	9.72	0.93	7.45	230.7	3	87	10	0	39	19.75	-18.33			Nov-12
	3.04	14.63	5.98	36.49	35.25	2.7	0.19	9.72	0.93	7.44	230.7	3	87	10	0	39	19.75	-18.33			Jun-07
100	3.01	14.43	5.59	34.67	32.14	2.31	0.65	9.63	0.92	11.97	38.7	3	87	10	0	39	19.48		5.75		Nov-12
	3.00	14.42	5.66	35.05	32.77	2.38	0.54	9.7	0.92	11.98	38.7	3	87	10	0	39	19.26				Jul-11
	2.87	14.24	5.28	33.64	30.46	2.1	0.9	9.65	0.92	11.79	38.7	3	87	10	0	39	19.3				Jun-13
	3.08	14.57	5.95	35.92	34.23	2.55	0.34	9.69	0.92	12.03	38.7	3	87	10	0	39	19.48				Nov-12
	3.17	14.70	6.11	36.58	35.28	2.67	0.19	9.7	0.92	12.01	38.7	3	87	10	0	39	19.48				Jul-11
100	2.95	14.49	5.56	34.53		2.07	0.65	9.76	0.93	11.85	20.1	3	87	10	0	39			5.75		Jun-15
	3.03	14.53	5.70	35.13		2.35	0.54	9.72	0.92	11.9	20.1	3	87	10	0	39					Jun-15
100	2.87	14.10	4.88	31.71		1.72	1.4	9.74	0.93	11.81	20.1	3	87	10	0	39				1.00	Jun-15
	2.92	14.37	5.36	33.56		2.16	0.9	9.73	0.92	11.62	20.1	3	87	10	0	39					Jun-15
	3.06	14.70	5.90	35.93		2.48	0.34	9.71	0.92	12.09	20.1	3	87	10	0	39					Jun-15
	3.08	14.77	6.04	36.33		2.74	0.19	9.72	0.92	12.04	20.1	3	87	10	0	39					Jun-15
100	2.96	9.05	7.09	10.18	12.07	2.25	0.65	3.88	0.9	8.95	69.7	2	29	69	0	45	4.47	-0.65	5.75		Mar-94
	2.91	9.22	7.11	10.49	12.66	2.28	0.54	3.87	0.9	9.2	69.7	2	29	69	0	45	4.62	-0.6			Nov-99
100	2.68	8.71	6.34	7.81	7.95	1.39	1.4	3.89	0.9	9.21	69.7	2	29	69	0	45	4.03	-1		1.00	Dec-98
	2.90	8.95	6.82	9.37	10.69	1.99	0.9	3.9	0.91	8.92	69.7	2	29	69	0	45	4.32	-0.75			Jun-13
	2.96	9.21	7.36	10.75	13.39	2.5	0.34	3.85	0.89	9.19	69.7	2	29	69	0	45	4.47	-0.65			Nov-12
	3.00	9.31	7.43	11.57	14.65	2.65	0.19	3.86	0.9	9.17	69.7	2	29	69	0	45	4.72	-0.46			Jun-04
100	9.86	35.97	17.04	82.31	71.40	0	1.25	16.95	0.92	14.59	102.0	3	89	0	8	155	30.55	-27.64	5.75		Jun-95
	9.84	36.00	17.07	83.30	72.70	0	1.17	17	0.93	16.96	102.0	3	89	0	8	155	30.7	-27.57			Jul-10
100	9.60	35.50	16.14	78.37	65.13	0	2	16.96	0.92	12.67	102.0	3	89	0	8	155	29.97	-27.85		1.00	Jul-10
	9.97	36.20	17.41	84.29	74.38	0	0.92	16.98	0.92	17.53	102.0	3	89	0	8	155	30.83	-27.52			Nov-97
	3.44	13.78	11.77	22.04	29.73	6.93		8.75	0.66	12.99	120.2	10	56	30	0	109	11.62	-11.75			Apr-04
100	5.44	19.28	22.80	33.04	47.59	1.29	1.14	10.7	0.92	25.26	425.3	2	96	0	0	10	15.24	-5.23	5.75		Jan-94
	5.52	19.41	23.06	33.85	49.06	1.46	0.95	10.74	0.92	25.29	425.3	2	96	0	0	10	15.34	-5.13			Jul-10
100	5.28	18.81	21.91	30.10	42.14	0.48	1.89	10.71	0.92	25.31	425.3	2	96	0	0	10	14.72	-5.53		1.00	Sep-94
	5.53	19.48	23.25	34.51	50.32	1.61	0.78	10.73	0.92	25.25	425.3	2	96	0	0	10	15.43	-5.11			Feb-94
100	2.63	8.96	6.07	12.91	13.37	1.95	1.16	3.8		10.02	256.0	4	15	77	3	192	8.02	-5.74	5.75		Feb-17
	2.73	8.91	6.03	11.80	12.25		0.83	3.76		9.99	256.0	4	15	77	3	192	8.02	-5.74			Jul-18

	MARKET		FUND TYPE, CATEGORY & OBJECTIVE		RATINGS				MINIMUMS	
Fund Name	Ticker Symbol	Traded On	Fund Type	Category and (Prospectus Objective)	Overall Rating	Reward Rating	Risk Rating	Recent Up/ Downgrade	Open to New Investors	Min Initial Investment
Wells Fargo WealthBuilder Equity Fund Class A	WEAFX	NAS CM	Open End	Aggressive Alloc (Growth)	C+	C	B	Up	Y	1,000
Wells Fargo WealthBuilder Equity Fund Institutional Class	WEAYX	NAS CM	Open End	Aggressive Alloc (Growth)	C+	C	B	Up	Y	1,000,000
Wells Fargo WealthBuilder Growth Allocation Fund Class A	WGAFX	NAS CM	Open End	Aggressive Alloc (Growth)	B-	C	B+	Up	Y	1,000
Wells Fargo WealthBuilder Growth Allocation Inst Cls	WGAYX	NAS CM	Open End	Aggressive Alloc (Growth)	B-	C	B	Up	Y	1,000,000
Wells Fargo WealthBuilder Growth Balanced Fund Class A	WGBAX	NAS CM	Open End	Moderate Alloc (Balanced)	B-	C	A-	Up	Y	1,000
Wells Fargo WealthBuilder Growth Balanced Inst Cls	WGBIX	NAS CM	Open End	Moderate Alloc (Balanced)	B-	C	A-	Up	Y	1,000,000
Wells Fargo WealthBuilder Moderate Balanced Fund Class A	WMBGX	NAS CM	Open End	Cautious Alloc (Balanced)	B	C	A-	Up	Y	1,000
Wells Fargo WealthBuilder Moderate Balanced Inst Cls	WMBZX	NAS CM	Open End	Cautious Alloc (Balanced)	B-	C	A-	Up	Y	1,000,000
WesMark Balanced Fund	WMBLX	NAS CM	Open End	Moderate Alloc (Balanced)	B-	C	A-	Up	Y	1,000
WesMark Growth Fund	WMKGX	NAS CM	Open End	US Equity Large Cap Growth (Growth)	C+	C	B		Y	1,000
WesMark Small Company Growth Fund	WMKSX	NAS CM	Open End	US Equity Small Cap (Small Company)	C	C-	C+		Y	1,000
WesMark Tactical Opportunity Fund	WMKTX	NAS CM	Open End	Moderate Alloc (Growth)	C	C	B	Up	Y	1,000
West Loop Realty Fund Class A Shares	REIAX	NAS CM	Open End	Real Estate Sector Equity (Real Estate)	C+	C	B-	Down	Y	2,500
West Loop Realty Fund Class C Shares	REICX	NAS CM	Open End	Real Estate Sector Equity (Real Estate)	C+	C	B-	Down	Y	2,500
West Loop Realty Fund Institutional Class Shares	REIIX	NAS CM	Open End	Real Estate Sector Equity (Real Estate)	C+	C	B-	Down	Y	1,000,000
Westfield Capital Dividend Growth Fund Institutional Class	WDIVX	NAS CM	Open End	US Equity Large Cap Blend (Equity-Income)	B-	C	B		Y	50,000
Westfield Capital Dividend Growth Fund Investor Class	WCDGX	NAS CM	Open End	US Equity Large Cap Blend (Equity-Income)	B-	C	B		Y	2,500
Westfield Capital Large Cap Growth Inst Cls Shares	WCLGX	NAS CM	Open End	US Equity Large Cap Growth (Growth)	C+	C	B	Down	Y	50,000
Westfield Capital Large Cap Growth Investor Cls Shares	WCLCX	NAS CM	Open End	US Equity Large Cap Growth (Growth)	C+	C	B	Down	Y	2,500
Westwood Emerging Markets Fund A Class Shares	WWEAX	NAS CM	Open End	Global Emerg Mkts (Div Emerging Mkts)	C	C	C+		Y	5,000
Westwood Emerging Markets Fund Institutional Shares	WWEMX	NAS CM	Open End	Global Emerg Mkts (Div Emerging Mkts)	C	C	B-		Y	100,000
Westwood Flexible Income Fund Institutional Shares	WFLEX	NAS CM	Open End	Cautious Alloc (Growth & Income)	U	U	U		Y	5,000
Westwood Income Opportunity Fund A Class	WWIAX	NAS CM	Open End	Moderate Alloc (Income)	B-	C	B+		Y	5,000
Westwood Income Opportunity Fund Institutional Class	WHGIX	NAS CM	Open End	Moderate Alloc (Income)	B-	C+	B+		Y	100,000
Westwood LargeCap Value Fund A Class	WWLAX	NAS CM	Open End	US Equity Large Cap Blend (Growth)	B-	C	B+		Y	5,000
Westwood LargeCap Value Fund Institutional Class	WHGLX	NAS CM	Open End	US Equity Large Cap Blend (Growth)	B-	C	B+		Y	100,000
Westwood Low Volatility Equity Fund Institutional Class	WLVIX	NAS CM	Open End	US Equity Large Cap Blend (Growth & Income)	B-	C	B+		Y	5,000
Westwood Market Neutral Income Fund Institutional Shares	WMNIX	NAS CM	Open End	Market Neutral (Convertible Bond)	C+	C	B		Y	5,000
Westwood Market Neutral Income Fund Ultra Shares	WMNUX	NAS CM	Open End	Market Neutral (Convertible Bond)	C+	C	B		Y	250,000
Westwood MLP & Strategic Energy Institutional Shares	WMLPX	NAS CM	Open End	Energy Sector Equity (Growth & Income)	D+	D	C-	Down	Y	5,000
Westwood SmallCap Fund Institutional Class	WHGSX	NAS CM	Open End	US Equity Small Cap (Growth)	C	C	C+		Y	5,000
Westwood SMidCap Fund Institutional Class	WHGMX	NAS CM	Open End	US Equity Mid Cap (Growth)	C+	C	B-	Up	Y	5,000
Westwood SMidCap Plus Fund Institutional Class	WHGPX	NAS CM	Open End	US Equity Mid Cap (Growth)	C+	C	B-	Up	Y	5,000
Westwood Strategic Convertibles Fund Institutional Shares	WSCIX	NAS CM	Open End	Convertibles (Convertible Bond)	B-	C	A-		Y	5,000
Westwood Worldwide Income Opportunity Institutional Shares	WWIOX	NAS CM	Open End	Moderate Alloc (Equity-Income)	B-	C	B+	Up	Y	5,000
White Oak Select Growth Fund	WOGSX	NAS CM	Open End	US Equity Large Cap Growth (Growth)	C+	C	B	Down	Y	2,000
Wildermuth Endowment Fund Class A	WESFX	NAS CM	Closed End	Moderate Alloc (Growth & Income)	B-	C+	B+		Y	2,500
Wildermuth Endowment Fund Class C	WEFCX	NAS CM	Closed End	Moderate Alloc (Growth & Income)	B	C	A+	Up	Y	2,500
Wildermuth Endowment Fund Class I	WEIFX	NAS CM	Closed End	Moderate Alloc (Growth & Income)	B	C+	A-	Up	Y	1,000,000
William Blair Emerging Markets Fund Class N	WBENX	NAS CM	Open End	Global Emerg Mkts (Div Emerging Mkts)	C	C	C	Up		2,500
William Blair Emerging Markets Growth Fund Class I	WBEIX	NAS CM	Open End	Global Emerg Mkts (Div Emerging Mkts)	C	C	C	Up		500,000
William Blair Emerging Markets Growth Fund Class R6	BIEMX	NAS CM	Open End	Global Emerg Mkts (Div Emerging Mkts)	C	C	C			5,000,000
William Blair Emerging Markets Leaders Fund Class I	WBELX	NAS CM	Open End	Global Emerg Mkts (Div Emerging Mkts)	C	C	C+		Y	500,000
William Blair Emerging Markets Leaders Fund Class N	WELNX	NAS CM	Open End	Global Emerg Mkts (Div Emerging Mkts)	C	C	C+		Y	2,500
William Blair Emerging Markets Leaders Fund R6 Class	WELIX	NAS CM	Open End	Global Emerg Mkts (Div Emerging Mkts)	C	C	C+		Y	5,000,000
William Blair Emerging Markets Small Cap Growth Cls I	BESIX	NAS CM	Open End	Global Emerg Mkts (Div Emerging Mkts)	C-	D+	C			500,000
William Blair Emerging Markets Small Cap Growth Cls N	WESNX	NAS CM	Open End	Global Emerg Mkts (Div Emerging Mkts)	C-	D+	C			2,500
William Blair Emerging Markets Small Cap Growth R6 Cls	WESJX	NAS CM	Open End	Global Emerg Mkts (Div Emerging Mkts)	C-	D+	C			5,000,000
William Blair Global Leaders Fund Class I	WGFIX	NAS CM	Open End	Global Equity Large Cap (World Stock)	C+	C	B-	Up	Y	500,000
William Blair Global Leaders Fund Class N	WGGNX	NAS CM	Open End	Global Equity Large Cap (World Stock)	C+	C	B-	Up	Y	2,500
William Blair Global Leaders Fund R6 Class	BGGIX	NAS CM	Open End	Global Equity Large Cap (World Stock)	C+	C	B-	Up	Y	5,000,000
William Blair Growth Fund Class I	BGFIX	NAS CM	Open End	US Equity Large Cap Growth (Growth)	B	B-	B		Y	500,000

★ Expanded analysis of this fund is included in Section II.

	TOTAL RETURNS					PERFORMANCE				ASSETS		ASSET ALLOCATION & TURNOVER					BULL & BEAR		FEES		
Min Additional Investment	3-Month Total Return	6-Month Total Return	1-Year Total Return	3-Year Total Return	5-Year Total Return	Dividend Yield (TTM)	Expense Ratio	3-Yr Std Deviation	3-Year Beta	NAV	Total Assets (MIL)	%Cash	%Stocks	%Bonds	%Other	Turnover Ratio	Last Bull Market Total Return	Last Bear Market Total Return	Front End Fee (%)	Back End Fee (%)	Inception Date
100	3.24	15.80	3.69	41.09	35.20	1.26	1.25	11.43		17.51	419.4	7	92	0	0	63	25.33	-20.15	5.75		Feb-17
	3.29	15.85	3.85	39.88	34.05		0.92	11.4		17.54	419.4	7	92	0	0	63	25.33	-20.15			Jul-18
100	2.97	14.43	4.51	34.61	30.51	1.6	1.26	9.67		12.13	295.6	3	66	20	9	93	24.11	-20.94	5.75		Feb-17
	3.05	14.52	4.74	33.55	29.49		0.93	9.7		12.14	295.6	3	66	20	9	93	24.11	-20.94			Jul-18
100	2.89	12.45	5.09	27.38	25.42	1.73	1.23	7.64		12.1	599.9	4	50	40	6	129	20.84	-18.21	5.75		Feb-17
	2.97	12.65	5.23	26.35	24.42		0.89	7.67		12.11	599.9	4	50	40	6	129	20.84	-18.21			Jul-18
100	2.71	10.65	5.48	20.15	19.74	1.64	1.22	5.6		10.61	434.6	4	34	59	3	161	13.76	-11.65	5.75		Feb-17
	2.80	10.79	5.82	19.35	18.95		0.88	5.59		10.63	434.6	4	34	59	3	161	13.76	-11.65			Jul-18
100	3.49	11.26	6.82	23.07	28.15	1.7	1.24	7.35	0.58	12.91	109.5	3	62	35	0	35	16.31	-7.8			Apr-98
100	3.18	18.95	6.26	45.94	40.26	0.19	1.14	12.74	1.02	19.75	328.9	6	94	0	0	37	25.31	-22.71			Apr-97
100	-0.73	15.60	-4.01	31.25	20.23	0	1.26	17.03	0.96	12.15	92.4	5	95	0	0	88	23.6	-24.05			Dec-93
100	2.62	10.24	3.10			0.54	1.74			10.95	39.0	4	57	34	5	145					Mar-17
100	2.41	19.96	11.30	13.78	46.42	1.13	1.35	12.77	0.94	14.5	59.4	3	97	0	0	22			5.75		Dec-13
100	2.15	19.42	10.37	11.26	40.92	0.4	2.1	12.73	0.94	14.44	59.4	3	97	0	0	22				1.00	Dec-13
100,000	2.40	20.00	11.50	14.62	48.14	1.37	1.1	12.75	0.94	14.51	59.4	3	97	0	0	22					Dec-13
	5.49	19.63	10.17	48.90	54.16	1.12	0.95	11.35	0.9	11.7	125.9	2	98	0	0	69	20.25	-14.14			Jul-13
	5.39	19.44	9.87	47.81	52.73	0.92	1.2	11.33	0.9	11.73	125.9	2	98	0	0	69	20.25	-14.14			Jul-13
	4.89	23.60	10.45	65.92	73.25	0.11	0.85	14.1	1.04	6.86	33.3	2	98	0	0	60	24.59				Jul-11
	4.78	23.41	10.08	64.50	70.88	0	1.1	14.15	1.04	7.01	33.3	2	98	0	0	60	24.58				Jul-11
	2.33	12.47	5.94	23.83	5.03	1.38	1.48	13.22	0.89	9.65	267.6	2	98	0	0	23			5.00		Dec-12
	2.44	12.60	6.17	24.85	6.37	1.67	1.23	13.28	0.89	9.65	267.6	2	98	0	0	23					Dec-12
	3.09	7.77					1.29			10.57	3.7	16	12	34	0						Dec-18
	2.97	11.49	6.95	18.91	22.31	1.98	1.1	6.38	-0.15	15.45	1,342	16	44	31	0	42	12.93	-6.64	5.00		Dec-07
	3.04	11.71	7.22	19.82	23.88	2.22	0.85	6.38	-0.16	15.46	1,342	16	44	31	0	42	13.04	-6.52			Dec-05
	4.81	16.52	8.45	40.45	50.74	1.25	0.9	11.42	0.92	12.62	234.6	5	95	0	0	49	24.72	-19.96	5.00		Dec-07
	4.83	16.71	8.73	41.40	52.52	1.38	0.65	11.38	0.92	12.57	234.6	5	95	0	0	49	24.79	-19.85			Jun-06
	4.84	17.16	9.81	32.46	38.96	3.45	0.75	10.02	0.79	6.28	4.7	1	72	0	0	26	21.02	-14.13			Aug-01
	1.60	4.72	5.75	8.79		2.04	1.27	1.99	27.9	10.13	34.3	6	-29	0	-22	88					May-15
	1.61	4.75	5.81	9.02		2.1	1.12	2	28.44	10.13	34.3	6	-29	0	-22	88					May-15
	-2.96	15.39	-8.56	-1.34		5.01	1.01	15.72	0.87	6.32	15.8	2	98	0	0	44					Dec-14
	5.80	22.15	-1.77	46.51	46.17	0.66	0.99	17.41	0.98	16.76	398.3	2	98	0	0	50	33.68	-23.74			Apr-07
	3.84	18.98	1.01	30.58	23.12	0.7	0.88	13.74	0.86	13.79	189.6	1	99	0	0	58	26.27	-24.21			Dec-05
	5.65	22.33	4.42	28.40	25.60	1.53	0.81	13.23	0.82	13.64	18.0	0	100	0	0	51	23.66	-22.44			Mar-11
	3.07	13.23	5.85	26.45		0.47	0.86	7.77	0.84	11.12	37.7	0	0	0	0	175					May-15
	2.47	9.45	5.20	16.60		1.89	0.98	6.11	0.5	10.48	1.7	32	38	22	0	33					May-15
25	-0.04	14.30	6.84	56.31	71.98	0.56	0.93	14.59	1.13	95.4	363.0	2	98	0	0	14	21.3	-16.2			Aug-92
	4.05	5.78	5.79	31.74		2.68	3.27	4.42	0.27	13.57	--	8	55	13	20	55			5.75		Dec-14
100	3.84	5.36	4.96	28.76		2.76	4.02	4.41	0.26	13.21	--	8	55	13	20	55				1.00	Mar-16
	4.09	5.89	6.06	32.86		2.66	3.02			13.69	--	8	55	13	20	55					Apr-17
1,000	3.61	16.00	-2.03	32.79	12.58	0.79	1.52	14.76	1.02	12.9	815.6	2	97	0	0	113	21.11	-22.94			Jun-05
	3.65	16.11	-1.76	33.72	13.90	1.17	1.27	14.75	1.02	13.04	815.6	2	97	0	0	113	21.26	-22.86			Jun-05
	3.70	16.25	-1.69	34.11	14.53	1.26	1.19	14.75	1.02	13.16	815.6	2	97	0	0	113	21.44	-22.79			Jun-05
	2.87	17.07	3.52	36.10	15.79	1.12	1.15	14.35	0.99	9.67	223.7	3	97	0	0	52	20.12	-23.03			Mar-08
1,000	2.77	16.84	3.19	34.99	14.03	0.68	1.4	14.4	0.99	9.64	223.7	3	97	0	0	52	19.96	-23.15			May-10
	2.87	17.09	3.52	36.25	16.15	1.21	1.1	14.42	0.99	9.66	223.7	3	97	0	0	52	20.2	-23.01			Mar-08
	1.25	9.44	-7.80	12.20	8.99	0.14	1.3	12.97	0.94	15.3	281.9	1	98	0	1	187					Oct-11
1,000	1.13	9.35	-8.05	11.19	7.32	0	1.55	13	0.94	15.2	281.9	1	98	0	1	187					Oct-11
	1.25	9.49	-7.75	12.42	9.40	0.24	1.25	12.99	0.94	15.33	281.9	1	98	0	1	187					Dec-12
	4.67	21.66	4.43	50.62	49.99	0.36	0.9	13.77	1.16	13.87	209.3	2	98	0	0	49	27.07	-18.8			Oct-07
1,000	4.53	21.50	4.14	49.18	47.80	0	1.15	13.74	1.16	13.84	209.3	2	98	0	0	49	26.97	-18.93			Oct-07
	4.60	21.66	4.44	50.76	50.35	0.42	0.85	13.76	1.16	13.87	209.3	2	98	0	0	49	27.07	-18.8			Dec-12
	4.99	23.93	14.42	64.60	74.67	0	0.91	12.6	0.89	11.34	259.9	1	99	0	0	46	25.68	-17.02			Oct-99

	MARKET			FUND TYPE, CATEGORY & OBJECTIVE	RATINGS				MINIMUMS	
Fund Name	Ticker Symbol	Traded On	Fund Type	Category and (Prospectus Objective)	Overall Rating	Reward Rating	Risk Rating	Recent Up/ Downgrade	Open to New Investors	Min Initial Investment
William Blair Growth Fund Class N	WBGSX	NAS CM	Open End	US Equity Large Cap Growth (Growth)	B	B-	B		Y	2,500
William Blair Growth Fund Class R6	BGFRX	NAS CM	Open End	US Equity Large Cap Growth (Growth)	B	B-	B		Y	1,000,000
William Blair Inst Intl Developed Plus Cls Inst	WIIEX	NAS CM	Open End	Global Equity Large Cap (Foreign Stock)	C	C	B-		Y	5,000,000
William Blair Institutional International Growth Fund	WBIIX	NAS CM	Open End	Global Equity Large Cap (Foreign Stock)	C	C	C+			5,000,000
William Blair Intl Developed Plus Cls Inst	WIEIX	NAS CM	Open End	Global Equity Large Cap (Foreign Stock)	C	C	B-		Y	500,000
William Blair International Developed Plus Fund Class N	WIENX	NAS CM	Open End	Global Equity Large Cap (Foreign Stock)	C	C	C+		Y	2,500
William Blair International Growth Fund Class I	BIGIX	NAS CM	Open End	Global Equity Large Cap (Foreign Stock)	C	C	C+			500,000
William Blair International Growth Fund Class N	WBIGX	NAS CM	Open End	Global Equity Large Cap (Foreign Stock)	C	C	C+			2,500
William Blair International Growth Fund Class R6	WBIRX	NAS CM	Open End	Global Equity Large Cap (Foreign Stock)	C	C	C+		Y	1,000,000
William Blair International Leaders Fund Class I Shares	WILIX	NAS CM	Open End	Global Equity Large Cap (Growth)	C+	C	B-	Up	Y	500,000
William Blair International Leaders Fund Class N Shares	WILNX	NAS CM	Open End	Global Equity Large Cap (Growth)	C+	C	B-	Up	Y	2,500
William Blair International Leaders Fund R6 Class Shares	WILJX	NAS CM	Open End	Global Equity Large Cap (Growth)	C+	C	B-	Up	Y	5,000,000
William Blair International Small Cap Growth Fund Class I	WISIX	NAS CM	Open End	Global Equity Mid/Small Cap (Foreign Stock)	C	C-	C	Up		500,000
William Blair International Small Cap Growth Fund Class N	WISNX	NAS CM	Open End	Global Equity Mid/Small Cap (Foreign Stock)	C	C-	C	Up		2,500
William Blair International Small Cap Growth Fund Class R6	WIISX	NAS CM	Open End	Global Equity Mid/Small Cap (Foreign Stock)	C	C-	C	Up		5,000,000
William Blair Large Cap Growth Fund Class I	LCGFX	NAS CM	Open End	US Equity Large Cap Growth (Growth)	B	B-	B		Y	500,000
William Blair Large Cap Growth Fund Class N	LCGNX	NAS CM	Open End	US Equity Large Cap Growth (Growth)	B	B-	B		Y	2,500
William Blair Large Cap Growth Fund Class R6	LCGJX	NAS CM	Open End	US Equity Large Cap Growth (Growth)	B	B-	B		Y	1,000,000
William Blair Macro Allocation Fund Class I	WMCIX	NAS CM	Open End	Multialternative (Asset Alloc)	C+	C	B+		Y	500,000
William Blair Macro Allocation Fund Class N	WMCNX	NAS CM	Open End	Multialternative (Asset Alloc)	C+	C	B		Y	2,500
William Blair Macro Allocation Fund R6 Class	WMCJX	NAS CM	Open End	Multialternative (Asset Alloc)	C+	C	B+		Y	5,000,000
William Blair Mid Cap Growth Fund Class I	WCGIX	NAS CM	Open End	US Equity Mid Cap (Growth)	B	B	B	Up	Y	500,000
William Blair Mid Cap Growth Fund Class N	WCGNX	NAS CM	Open End	US Equity Mid Cap (Growth)	B	B	B	Up	Y	2,500
William Blair Mid Cap Growth Fund Class R6	WCGJX	NAS CM	Open End	US Equity Mid Cap (Growth)	B	B	B		Y	1,000,000
William Blair Small Cap Growth Fund Class I	WBSIX	NAS CM	Open End	US Equity Small Cap (Small Company)	C+	C	B-		Y	500,000
William Blair Small Cap Growth Fund Class N	WBSNX	NAS CM	Open End	US Equity Small Cap (Small Company)	C+	C	B-		Y	2,500
William Blair Small Cap Growth Fund Class R6	WBSRX	NAS CM	Open End	US Equity Small Cap (Small Company)	C+	C	B-		Y	1,000,000
William Blair Small Cap Value Fund Class I	BVDIX	NAS CM	Open End	US Equity Small Cap (Small Company)	C	C-	C+		Y	500,000
William Blair Small Cap Value Fund Class N	WBVDX	NAS CM	Open End	US Equity Small Cap (Small Company)	C	C-	C+		Y	2,500
William Blair Small Cap Value Fund Class R6	BVDRX	NAS CM	Open End	US Equity Small Cap (Small Company)	C	C-	C+		Y	1,000,000
William Blair Small-Mid Cap Growth Fund Class I	WSMDX	NAS CM	Open End	US Equity Mid Cap (Small Company)	B-	C+	B-		Y	500,000
William Blair Small-Mid Cap Growth Fund Class N	WSMNX	NAS CM	Open End	US Equity Mid Cap (Small Company)	B-	C+	B-		Y	2,500
William Blair Small-Mid Cap Growth Fund Class R6	WSMRX	NAS CM	Open End	US Equity Mid Cap (Small Company)	B-	C+	B-		Y	1,000,000
William Blair Small-Mid Cap Value Fund Class I	WSMIX	NAS CM	Open End	US Equity Small Cap (Growth)	C	C	B-		Y	500,000
William Blair Small-Mid Cap Value Fund Class N	BSMNX	NAS CM	Open End	US Equity Small Cap (Growth)	C	C	C+		Y	2,500
William Blair Small-Mid Cap Value Fund Class R6	BSMRX	NAS CM	Open End	US Equity Small Cap (Growth)	C	C	B-		Y	1,000,000
Williston Basin/Mid-North America Stock Fund Class A	ICPAX	NAS CM	Open End	Energy Sector Equity (Growth)	D	D	D	Down	Y	1,000
Williston Basin/Mid-North America Stock Fund Class C	ICPUX	NAS CM	Open End	Energy Sector Equity (Growth)	D	D	D	Down	Y	1,000
Williston Basin/Mid-North America Stock Fund Class I	ICWIX	NAS CM	Open End	Energy Sector Equity (Growth)	D	D	D	Down	Y	1,000
Wilmington Diversified Income Fund Class A	WDIAX	NAS CM	Open End	Moderate Alloc (Balanced)	B	C	A-	Up	Y	1,000
Wilmington Diversified Income Fund Class I	WDIIX	NAS CM	Open End	Moderate Alloc (Balanced)	B	C	A-	Up	Y	100,000
Wilmington Global Alpha Equities Fund Class A	WRAAX	NAS CM	Open End	Long/Short Equity (Growth)	B-	C+	B		Y	1,000
Wilmington Global Alpha Equities Fund Class I	WRAIX	NAS CM	Open End	Long/Short Equity (Growth)	B	C+	A	Up	Y	100,000
Wilmington International Fund Class A	WINAX	NAS CM	Open End	Global Equity Large Cap (Foreign Stock)	C	C	B-		Y	1,000
Wilmington International Fund Class Institutional	WINIX	NAS CM	Open End	Global Equity Large Cap (Foreign Stock)	C	C	B-		Y	100,000
Wilmington Large-Cap Strategy Fund Class Institutional	WMLIX	NAS CM	Open End	US Equity Large Cap Blend (Growth)	B-	C	B		Y	100,000
Wilmington Real Asset Fund Class A	WMMRX	NAS CM	Open End	Moderate Alloc (Growth & Income)	B-	C	B+	Up	Y	1,000
Wilmington Real Asset Fund Class Institutional	WMRIX	NAS CM	Open End	Moderate Alloc (Growth & Income)	B-	C	B+		Y	100,000
Wilshire 5000 Index Portfolio Class Institutional	WINDX	NAS CM	Open End	US Equity Large Cap Blend (Growth)	B-	C	B		Y	250,000
Wilshire 5000 Index Portfolio Investment Class Shares	WFIVX	NAS CM	Open End	US Equity Large Cap Blend (Growth)	B-	C	B		Y	1,000
Wilshire International Equity Institutional Cls Shares	WLTTX	NAS CM	Open End	Global Equity Large Cap (Foreign Stock)	C	C	B		Y	250,000
Wilshire International Equity Fund Investment Class Shares	WLCTX	NAS CM	Open End	Global Equity Large Cap (Foreign Stock)	C	C	B		Y	2,500

★ Expanded analysis of this fund is included in Section II.

	TOTAL RETURNS					PERFORMANCE				ASSETS		ASSET ALLOCATION & TURNOVER					BULL & BEAR		FEES		
Min Additional Investment	3-Month Total Return	6-Month Total Return	1-Year Total Return	3-Year Total Return	5-Year Total Return	Dividend Yield (TTM)	Expense Ratio	3-Yr Std Deviation	3-Year Beta	NAV	Total Assets (MIL)	%Cash	%Stocks	%Bonds	%Other	Turnover Ratio	Last Bull Market Total Return	Last Bear Market Total Return	Front End Fee (%)	Back End Fee (%)	Inception Date
1,000	4.87	23.78	14.07	63.18	72.06	0	1.2	12.63	0.89	9.68	259.9	1	99	0	0	46	25.54	-17.2			Mar-46
	4.86	23.77	14.06	63.17	72.05		0.83	12.63	0.89	11.34	259.9	1	99	0	0	46	25.54	-17.2			May-19
	5.25	21.29	3.43	31.29	20.68	2.94	0.9	12.32	1.05	14.41	20.5	8	92	0	0	68	17.57	-23			Dec-04
	5.05	20.21	0.10	31.14	17.94	0.98	0.97	12.59	1.05	16	1,797	2	98	0	0	82	20.71	-21.77			Jul-02
	5.68	21.78	3.73	29.34	18.76	1.45	1	12.27	1.04	16.55	24.4	2	98	0	0	65	17.07	-23.31			May-04
1,000	5.59	21.55	3.50	28.38	17.28	1.04	1.25	12.25	1.04	16.41	24.4	2	98	0	0	65	16.84	-23.37			May-04
	5.11	20.20	-0.09	30.72	17.15	0.93	1.13	12.65	1.05	28.14	2,170	2	98	0	0	78	20.45	-22.14			Oct-99
1,000	5.00	19.99	-0.42	29.55	15.38	0.41	1.45	12.64	1.05	27.48	2,170	2	98	0	0	78	20.3	-22.3			Oct-92
	5.04	20.04	-0.39	29.60	15.42		1.05	12.65	1.05	28.14	2,170	2	98	0	0	78	20.3	-22.3			May-19
	6.03	21.36	4.44	42.99	40.66	0.74	0.9	12.76	1.06	16.7	545.1	3	97	0	0	33					Aug-12
1,000	5.98	21.28	4.18	41.74	39.08	0.35	1.15	12.79	1.06	16.64	545.1	3	97	0	0	33					Aug-12
	6.09	21.45	4.53	43.34	41.45	0.81	0.85	12.81	1.06	16.7	545.1	3	97	0	0	33					Nov-12
	5.42	19.63	-6.10	20.96	14.69	1	1.18	13.94	1.14	12.43	308.5	3	97	0	0	88	16.34	-20.9			Nov-05
1,000	5.39	19.41	-6.34	19.89	12.97	0.57	1.48	13.95	1.14	12.3	308.5	3	97	0	0	88	16.15	-21.05			Nov-05
	5.40	19.63	-6.06	21.22	15.18	1.21	1.08	13.98	1.14	12.49	308.5	3	97	0	0	88	16.5	-20.8			Nov-05
	7.29	25.53	16.32	77.29	101.32	0.09	0.65	12.2	0.87	15.73	230.6	1	99	0	0	47	31.15	-17.63			Dec-99
1,000	7.20	25.35	16.01	75.93	98.80	0	0.9	12.21	0.87	14.88	230.6	1	99	0	0	47	31.08	-17.78			Dec-99
	7.37	25.62	16.40	77.41	101.46		0.6	12.21	0.87	15.73	230.6	1	99	0	0	47	31.15	-17.63			May-19
	1.65	2.72	3.08	9.42	3.46	3.16	1.13	4.93	-10.7	11.68	892.1	36	28	54	-18	36					Nov-11
1,000	1.56	2.63	2.77	8.47	2.00	2.35	1.41	4.92	-11.23	11.69	892.1	36	28	54	-18	36					Nov-11
	1.65	2.72	3.14	9.68	3.93	3.38	1.05	4.96	-11.25	11.68	892.1	36	28	54	-18	36					Oct-13
	5.73	29.05	13.04	56.61	62.69	0	0.95	13.2	0.88	12.17	68.7	1	99	0	0	58	24.68	-17.72			Feb-06
1,000	5.60	28.84	12.75	55.53	60.69	0	1.2	13.22	0.89	11.3	68.7	1	99	0	0	58	24.47	-17.78			Feb-06
	5.73	29.05	13.04	56.61	62.69		0.9	13.2	0.88	12.17	68.7	1	99	0	0	58	24.68	-17.72			May-19
	2.75	20.32	1.14	73.37	72.64	0	1.25	16.16	0.9	30.96	707.1	3	97	0	0	74	28.8	-25.75			Dec-99
1,000	2.67	20.17	0.88	72.08	70.44	0	1.5	16.17	0.9	27.64	707.1	3	97	0	0	74	28.62	-25.84			Dec-99
	2.75	20.32	1.14	73.37	72.64		1.15	16.16	0.9	30.96	707.1	3	97	0	0	74	28.8	-25.75			May-19
	2.85	17.21	-3.09	27.84	28.77	0.23	1.25	17.05	0.97	18.04	452.6	3	97	0	0	56	25.59	-24.22			Oct-99
1,000	2.76	17.00	-3.35	26.92	27.19	0	1.5	17.04	0.97	17.48	452.6	3	97	0	0	56	25.37	-24.29			Dec-96
	2.79	17.03	-3.31	26.96	27.23		1.16	17.05	0.97	18.05	452.6	3	97	0	0	56	25.37	-24.29			May-19
	6.29	25.88	9.90	68.20	87.17	0	1.1	14.82	0.87	27.53	2,840	2	98	0	0	46	23.99	-20.8			Dec-03
1,000	6.23	25.71	9.65	66.90	84.83	0	1.35	14.77	0.87	26.06	2,840	2	98	0	0	46	23.97	-20.91			Dec-03
	6.29	25.87	9.90	68.20	87.17		1.04	14.82	0.87	27.54	2,840	2	98	0	0	46	23.98	-20.8			May-19
	2.47	17.81	-1.73	26.53	29.95	0.6	1	15.38	1.01	10.78	1.7	1	99	0	0	104					Dec-11
1,000	2.45	17.67	-2.03	25.56	28.21	0.21	1.25	15.39	1.01	10.85	1.7	1	99	0	0	104					Dec-11
	2.56	17.92	-1.64	26.65	30.07		0.95	15.4	1.01	10.79	1.7	1	99	0	0	104					May-19
50	-3.52	17.42	-19.14	-9.81	-41.89	0.52	1.49	23.66	1.34	4.38	207.4	0	100	0	0		30.02	-32.64	5.00		Apr-99
50	-3.56	17.02	-19.51	-11.08	-43.36	0	1.99	23.59	1.34	4.33	207.4	0	100	0	0		29.64	-32.78		1.00	May-14
50	-3.31	17.79	-18.66	-8.48	-41.03	1.22	0.99	23.54	1.34	4.37	207.4	0	100	0	0		30.02	-32.64			Aug-16
25	2.86	10.77	5.82	23.68	23.01	3.55	0.75	6.71	0.5	10.55	39.5	3	60	37	0	85	14.16	-15.14	5.50		Feb-99
25	2.83	10.79	5.97	24.45	24.44	3.8	0.5	6.76	0.5	10.55	39.5	3	60	37	0	85	14.35	-15.05			Jun-10
25	3.05	9.02	6.58	19.88	14.47	1.1	1.5	4.15	0.59	11.48	177.0	14	86	0	0	58			5.50		Jan-12
25	3.01	9.12	6.77	20.73	15.93	1.15	1.25	4.16	0.6	11.6	177.0	14	86	0	0	58					Jan-12
25	2.33	14.00	-1.13	30.31	12.40	1.62	1	12.05	1.03	8.37	572.2	7	93	0	0	75	12.56	-25.11	5.50		Dec-05
25	2.35	14.10	-0.87	31.01	13.23	1.74	0.87	12.09	1.04	8.44	572.2	7	93	0	0	75	12.62	-24.94			Jun-98
25	4.16	19.73	9.61	51.41	64.60	1.57	0.25	12.47	1.01	23.28	517.3	0	100	0	0	15	25.78	-17.05			Jul-03
25	0.58	11.54	3.77	11.89	7.74	2.94	1.09	8.06	0.7	14.49	313.8	4	67	26	4	438	10.95	-10.44	5.50		Dec-05
25	0.64	11.73	3.99	12.73	9.07	3.09	0.84	8.05	0.7	14.65	313.8	4	67	26	4	438	11.17	-10.38			Jul-03
100,000	3.88	19.05	8.72	48.58	60.30	1.55	0.33	12.31	0.98	21.93	191.9	2	98	0	0	1	24.97	-17.6			Feb-99
100	3.79	18.82	8.35	47.24	58.12	1.3	0.6	12.33	0.98	21.9	191.9	2	98	0	0	1	24.82	-17.69			Feb-99
100,000	4.17	14.77	2.22	29.97	16.06	0.63	1.25	11.66	1	10.49	383.0	3	97	0	0	96	24.61	-19.45			Nov-07
100	4.11	14.67	1.89	29.00	14.59	0.37	1.51	11.65	1	10.63	383.0	3	97	0	0	96	24.41	-19.56			Nov-07

Fund Name	MARKET Ticker Symbol	Traded On	FUND TYPE, CATEGORY & OBJECTIVE Fund Type	Category and (Prospectus Objective)	RATINGS Overall Rating	Reward Rating	Risk Rating	Recent Up/ Downgrade	MINIMUMS Open to New Investors	Min Initial Investment
Wilshire Large Company Growth Portfolio Cls Institutional	WLCGX	NAS CM	Open End	US Equity Large Cap Growth (Growth)	C+	C	B	Down	Y	250,000
Wilshire Large Company Growth Port Inv Cls Shares	DTLGX	NAS CM	Open End	US Equity Large Cap Growth (Growth)	C+	C	B	Down	Y	2,500
Wilshire Large Company Value Portfolio Cls Institutional	WLCVX	NAS CM	Open End	US Equity Large Cap Value (Growth)	C+	C	B	Up	Y	250,000
Wilshire Large Company Value Port Inv Cls Shares	DTLVX	NAS CM	Open End	US Equity Large Cap Value (Growth)	C+	C	B	Up	Y	2,500
Wilshire Small Company Growth Portfolio Cls Institutional	WSMGX	NAS CM	Open End	US Equity Small Cap (Small Company)	C+	C	C+		Y	250,000
Wilshire Small Company Growth Port Inv Cls Shares	DTSGX	NAS CM	Open End	US Equity Small Cap (Small Company)	C+	C	C+		Y	2,500
Wilshire Small Company Value Fund Class Institutional	WSMVX	NAS CM	Open End	US Equity Small Cap (Small Company)	C	C-	C		Y	250,000
Wilshire Small Company Value Port Inv Cls Shares	DTSVX	NAS CM	Open End	US Equity Small Cap (Small Company)	C	C-	C		Y	2,500
Wireless Fund	WIREX	NAS CM	Open End	Technology Sector Equity (Comm)	B-	C+	B	Down	Y	5,000
WOA All Asset I Class I Shares	WOAIX	NAS CM	Open End	Moderate Alloc (Growth & Income)	B	C	A-	Up	Y	1,000,000
WP International Companies Income Plus Institutional Cls	WPITX	NAS CM	Open End	Global Equity Large Cap (Equity-Income)	C	C	C		Y	2,000
WP Large Cap Income Plus Fund Institutional Class	WPLCX	NAS CM	Open End	US Equity Large Cap Value (Growth)	C+	C	C+	Down	Y	2,000
WP Smaller Companies Income Plus Fund Institutional Class	WPSMX	NAS CM	Open End	US Equity Small Cap (Small Company)	C	C	C		Y	2,000
WPG Partners Small/Micro Cap Value Fund	WPGTX	NAS CM	Open End	US Equity Small Cap (Small Company)	D+	D+	C-	Down	Y	100,000
WSTCM Sector Select Risk - Managed Institutional Shares	WSTIX	NAS CM	Open End	Flexible Alloc (Growth & Income)	C	C-	C	Up	Y	100,000
WSTCM Sector Select Risk - Managed Fund Investor Shares	WSTEX	NAS CM	Open End	Flexible Alloc (Growth & Income)	C-	C-	C		Y	1,000
WV Concentrated Equities Fund Class A Shares	WVCAX	NAS CM	Open End	US Equity Mid Cap (Growth)	C-	C-	C		Y	1,000
WV Concentrated Equities Fund Class I Shares	WVCIX	NAS CM	Open End	US Equity Mid Cap (Growth)	C-	C-	C		Y	500,000
YCG Enhanced Fund	YCGEX	NAS CM	Open End	US Equity Large Cap Blend (Growth)	B	B	B		Y	2,500
Yorktown Capital Income Fund Class A	APIGX	NAS CM	Open End	Aggressive Alloc (Growth & Income)	B	C	A	Up		1,000
Yorktown Capital Income Fund Class Institutional	AFAAX	NAS CM	Open End	Aggressive Alloc (Growth & Income)	B	C	A	Up	Y	1,000,000
Yorktown Capital Income Fund Class L	AFDDX	NAS CM	Open End	Aggressive Alloc (Growth & Income)	B-	C	A-	Up	Y	1,000
Yorktown Growth Fund Class A	AFGGX	NAS CM	Open End	Global Equity Large Cap (Growth)	C+	C	B-	Up	Y	1,000
Yorktown Growth Fund Class Institutional	APGRX	NAS CM	Open End	Global Equity Large Cap (Growth)	C+	C	B-	Up	Y	1,000,000
Yorktown Growth Fund Class L	APITX	NAS CM	Open End	Global Equity Large Cap (Growth)	C+	C	B-	Up	Y	1,000
Yorktown Master Allocation Fund Class A	APIFX	NAS CM	Open End	US Equity Mid Cap (Asset Alloc)	C	C-	B-		Y	1,000
Yorktown Master Allocation Fund Class Institutional	APMAX	NAS CM	Open End	US Equity Mid Cap (Asset Alloc)	C	C	B-		Y	1,000,000
Yorktown Master Allocation Fund Class L	APILX	NAS CM	Open End	US Equity Mid Cap (Asset Alloc)	C	C-	B-		Y	1,000
Yorktown Mid-Cap Fund Class A	YWBAX	NAS CM	Open End	US Equity Mid Cap (Growth)	D	D	D	Down	Y	1,000
Yorktown Mid-Cap Fund Class L	YWBLX	NAS CM	Open End	US Equity Mid Cap (Growth)	D	D	D	Down	Y	1,000
Yorktown Mid-Cap Fund Institutional Class	YWBIX	NAS CM	Open End	US Equity Mid Cap (Growth)	D	D	D	Down	Y	1,000,000
Yorktown Multi-Asset Income Fund Class A	APIUX	NAS CM	Open End	Cautious Alloc (Income)	B-	C	B+	Up	Y	1,000
Yorktown Multi-Asset Income Fund Class C	AFFCX	NAS CM	Open End	Cautious Alloc (Income)	B-	C	B+	Up	Y	1,000
Yorktown Multi-Asset Income Fund Class Institutional	APIIX	NAS CM	Open End	Cautious Alloc (Income)	B-	C	B	Up	Y	1,000,000
Yorktown Multi-Asset Income Fund Class L	AFFIX	NAS CM	Open End	Cautious Alloc (Income)	C+	C	B	Up	Y	1,000
Yorktown Small-Cap Fund Class A	YOVAX	NAS CM	Open End	US Equity Small Cap (Small Company)	C	C-	C+		Y	1,000
Yorktown Small-Cap Fund Class L	YOVLX	NAS CM	Open End	US Equity Small Cap (Small Company)	C	C-	C+		Y	1,000
Yorktown Small-Cap Fund Institutional Class	YOVIX	NAS CM	Open End	US Equity Small Cap (Small Company)	C	C	C+		Y	1,000,000
Zacks All-Cap Core Fund Institutional Class	CZOVX	NAS CM	Open End	US Equity Large Cap Blend (Growth & Income)	B-	C	B		Y	5,000
Zacks Dividend Fund Institutional Class Shares	ZDIIX	NAS CM	Open End	US Equity Large Cap Value (Equity-Income)	B-	C	B+	Down	Y	5,000
Zacks Dividend Fund Investor Class	ZDIVX	NAS CM	Open End	US Equity Large Cap Value (Equity-Income)	B-	C	B+		Y	2,500
Zacks Market Neutral Fund Institutional Class	ZMNIX	NAS CM	Open End	Market Neutral (Growth & Income)	D	D	C-	Down	Y	5,000
Zacks Market Neutral Fund Investor Class	ZMNVX	NAS CM	Open End	Market Neutral (Growth & Income)	D	D	C-		Y	2,500
Zacks Small-Cap Core Fund Institutional Class	ZSCIX	NAS CM	Open End	US Equity Small Cap (Small Company)	C	C	C		Y	5,000
Zacks Small-Cap Core Fund Investor Class	ZSCCX	NAS CM	Open End	US Equity Small Cap (Small Company)	C	C	C		Y	2,500
Zevenbergen Genea Fund Institutional Class	ZVGIX	NAS CM	Open End	US Equity Large Cap Growth (Technology)	C+	B-	C+	Up	Y	50,000
Zevenbergen Genea Fund Investor Class	ZVGNX	NAS CM	Open End	US Equity Large Cap Growth (Technology)	C+	B-	C+	Up	Y	2,500
Zevenbergen Growth Fund Institutional Class	ZVNIX	NAS CM	Open End	US Equity Large Cap Growth (Growth)	C+	C+	C+		Y	50,000
Zevenbergen Growth Fund Investor Class	ZVNBX	NAS CM	Open End	US Equity Large Cap Growth (Growth)	C+	C+	C+		Y	2,500

★ Expanded analysis of this fund is included in Section II.

Min Additional Investment	TOTAL RETURNS 3-Month Total Return	6-Month Total Return	1-Year Total Return	3-Year Total Return	5-Year Total Return	PERFORMANCE Dividend Yield (TTM)	Expense Ratio	3-Yr Std Deviation	3-Year Beta	ASSETS NAV	Total Assets (MIL)	ASSET ALLOCATION & TURNOVER %Cash	%Stocks	%Bonds	%Other	Turnover Ratio	BULL & BEAR Last Bull Market Total Return	Last Bear Market Total Return	FEES Front End Fee (%)	Back End Fee (%)	Inception Date
100,000	3.97	21.67	10.17	56.20	76.40	0	0.98	14.02	1.03	43.95	213.5	2	98	0	0	69	27.7	-17.85			Jul-96
100	3.90	21.46	9.83	54.77	73.64	0	1.31	14.03	1.03	40.17	213.5	2	98	0	0	69	27.4	-17.93			Sep-92
100,000	3.29	15.16	3.14	34.76	32.38	1.69	0.97	13.02	1.06	19.44	190.8	1	99	0	0	65	26.04	-21.48			Jul-96
100	3.20	14.97	2.83	33.89	30.84	1.41	1.24	13	1.06	19.65	190.8	1	99	0	0	65	25.85	-21.65			Sep-92
100,000	5.33	21.90	2.40	49.44	62.32	0	1.1	16.46	0.93	28.61	62.9	3	97	0	0	92	25.97	-25.09			Jul-96
100	5.26	21.72	2.12	48.29	60.15	0	1.35	16.46	0.93	26.17	62.9	3	97	0	0	92	25.72	-25.21			Oct-92
100,000	2.36	15.02	-8.68	29.21	29.82	0.46	1.1	17.27	0.98	21.2	58.7	4	96	0	0	74	26.77	-25.15			Jul-96
100	2.32	14.91	-8.87	28.32	28.10	0.21	1.35	17.27	0.98	20.72	58.7	4	96	0	0	74	26.43	-25.42			Sep-92
100	2.46	23.28	13.69	61.60	78.71	0	1.96	14.63	0.92	12.07	5.5	2	98	0	0	79	14.85	-20.86			Apr-00
25,000	2.56	10.93	5.80	25.46	17.61	0.99	1.43	6.14		12.38	262.0	1	31	68	0	139					Mar-12
100	3.65	32.24	0.57	24.60		0	3.81	17.34	1.18	12.18	10.2	3	97	0	0	0					Dec-15
100	7.48	40.70	13.94	68.13	54.86	0.08	2.84	18.53	1.32	15.66	39.8	3	97	0	0						Oct-13
100	7.22	45.68	4.47	41.61		0	3.98	24.3	1.68	14.7	9.8	5	95	0	0	0					Jan-16
5,000	0.43	15.79	-10.06	10.92	-8.83	0.32	1.1	18.81	1.06	14	24.4	5	95	0	0	80	31.34	-28.94			Mar-72
1,000	-0.90	1.96	-4.88	8.37	8.54	0	1.62	8.63	0.55	9.85	14.4	7	68	19	6	268					Dec-13
250	-0.91	1.88	-5.10	7.61	7.20	0	1.87	9.05	0.59	9.75	14.4	7	68	19	6	268					Dec-13
50	-1.68	10.71	-3.25			0	1.62			18.08	90.0	5	92	0	0	184			5.75		Apr-17
	-1.57	10.93	-2.96			0	1.37			18.16	90.0	5	92	0	0	184					Apr-17
100	7.65	27.44	16.60	58.09	73.02	0.31	1.19	11.12	0.85	19.27	251.4	0	97	3	0	21					Dec-12
100	1.95	6.53	5.26	28.69	21.26	1.17	1.56	7.05	0.5	30.46	24.4	1	76	9	0	126	18.29	-15.81	5.75		Apr-88
100,000	2.04	6.67	5.52	29.91	23.61	1.33	1.31	7.07	0.5	31.53	24.4	1	76	9	0	126	18.63	-15.64			Jun-04
100	1.79	6.16	4.49	26.08	17.59	0.63	2.31	7.05	0.5	28.91	24.4	1	76	9	0	126	17.94	-16			Jun-04
100	6.11	22.13	5.02	42.31	38.31	0	1.45	12.48	1.05	15.45	57.9	1	99	0	0	61	26.23	-21.52	5.75		Jul-04
100,000	6.07	22.08	4.98	42.32	38.33	0	1.45	12.49	1.05	16.42	57.9	1	99	0	0	61	25.55	-21.9			May-13
100	5.87	21.48	3.95	38.06	31.50	0	2.45	12.47	1.05	12.44	57.9	1	99	0	0	61	25.55	-21.9			Jun-85
100	1.52	12.77	-1.54	23.20	13.29	0.02	2.54	11.4	0.96	23.93	18.7	5	91	2	0	24	20.91	-20.64	5.75		Mar-09
100,000	1.61	12.93	-1.26	24.32	15.51	0.29	2.29	11.42	0.96	25.84	18.7	5	91	2	0	24	20.91	-20.64			May-13
100	1.33	12.42	-2.28	20.63	9.85	0	3.29	11.44	0.96	21.98	18.7	5	91	2	0	24	20.52	-20.82			Mar-09
100	-4.83	8.03	-19.41	-11.67		0	1.38	17.8	1.21	8.07	15.5	7	93	0	0	54			5.75		May-16
100	-5.05	7.49	-19.99	-13.54		0	2.13	17.77	1.21	7.89	15.5	7	93	0	0	54					May-16
100,000	-4.80	8.12	-19.22	-10.98		0.19	1.13	17.79	1.21	8.12	15.5	7	93	0	0	54					May-16
100	1.12	10.10	2.62	22.08	13.07	4.92	1.13	6.58	1.71	10.1	657.9	4	26	62	0	48	13.1	-12.74	5.75		Jul-97
100	1.09	9.99	2.17	20.39	10.35	4.89	1.63	6.6	1.7	9.34	657.9	4	26	62	0	48	12.77	-12.92		1.00	May-16
100,000	1.28	10.51	3.18	24.02	16.00	5.16	0.63	6.58	1.71	10.61	657.9	4	26	62	0	48	13.52	-12.4			Apr-10
100	1.07	9.90	2.21	20.37	10.34	4.76	1.63	6.56	1.71	9.52	657.9	4	26	62	0	48	12.79	-12.72			Jul-04
100	5.00	19.12	0.79	40.22		0.12	1.48	16.5	0.89	11.96	31.5	6	94	0	0	42			5.75		May-16
100	4.74	18.68	-0.02	36.90		0	2.23	16.46	0.89	11.69	31.5	6	94	0	0	42					May-16
100,000	5.06	19.32	1.03	41.22		0.19	1.23	16.5	0.89	12.04	31.5	6	94	0	0	42					May-16
1,000	4.26	18.93	9.37	44.87	54.42	0.38	1	11.56	0.91	25.19	42.0	3	97	0	0	29	22.27	-17.06	5.75		Dec-05
1,000	4.59	16.39	11.57	39.04	47.77	1.93	1.05	10.95	0.89	20.72	71.5	2	97	0	0	25					Jan-17
100	4.58	16.25	11.32	38.29	46.97	1.71	1.3	10.93	0.89	20.73	71.5	2	97	0	0	25					Jan-14
1,000	-0.39	-0.15	-1.94	-5.33	5.70	0	2.94	4.29	-9.29	12.61	9.6	21	1	0	78	152	3.18	2.7		1.00	Jul-08
100	-0.52	-0.29	-2.20	-5.87	6.73	0	3.19	4.25	-7.6	13.31	9.6	21	1	0	78	152	3.63	3.04	5.75		Jul-08
1,000	2.99	15.31	-5.41	42.06	44.29	0	1.14	16.84	0.94	25.82	117.2	0	99	0	1	129	28.69				Feb-14
100	2.91	15.20	-5.63	40.97	42.32	0	1.39	16.83	0.94	25.38	117.2	0	99	0	1	129	28.69				Jun-11
500	4.33	34.54	11.87	150.69		0	1.1	23.74	1.49	23.33	44.8	1	99	0	0	22					Aug-15
100	4.24	34.36	11.67	148.87		0	1.4	23.71	1.49	23.11	44.8	1	99	0	0	22					Aug-15
500	8.78	38.95	16.65	113.45		0	1	20.73	1.37	19.19	20.1	1	99	0	0	31					Aug-15
100	8.75	38.75	16.41	111.92		0	1.3	20.71	1.37	19.01	20.1	1	99	0	0	31					Aug-15

Section II:
Analysis of 100 Largest Stock Mutual Funds

Detailed analysis of the 100 Largest Open End and Closed End Stock Mutual Funds. Funds are listed by their asset size.

Section II: Contents

This section contains an expanded analysis of the 100 Largest Stock Mutual Funds, with current and historical Weiss Investment Ratings, key rating factors, summary financial data and performance charts. Funds are listed by their asset size.

TOP ROW

Fund Name
Describes the fund's assets, regions of investments and investment strategies. Many funds have similar names, so you want to make sure the fund you look up is really the one you are interested in evaluating.

Overall Rating
The Weiss rating measured on a scale from A to E based on each fund's risk and performance. See the preceding section, "What Our Ratings Mean," for an explanation of each letter grade rating.

BUY-HOLD-SELL Indicator
Funds that are rated in the A or B range are, in our opinion, a potential BUY. Funds in the C range will indicate a HOLD status. Funds in the D or E range will indicate a SELL status.

Ticker Symbol
An arrangement of characters (usually letters) representing a particular security listed on an exchange or otherwise traded publicly. When a company issues securities to the public marketplace, it selects an available ticker symbol for its securities which investors use to place trade orders. Every listed security has a unique ticker symbol, facilitating the vast array of trade orders that flow through the financial markets every day. If a ticker symbol is not assigned to a particular fund, the International Securities Identification Number (ISIN) is displayed.

Traded On (Exchange)
The stock exchange on which the fund is listed. The core function of a stock exchange is to ensure fair and orderly trading, as well as efficient dissemination of price information. Exchanges such as: NYSE (New York Stock Exchange), AMEX (American Stock Exchange), NNM (NASDAQ National Market), and NASQ (NASDAQ Small Cap) give companies, governments and other groups a platform to sell securities to the investing public. NASDAQ CM is abbreviated as NAS in this section.

NAV (Net Asset Value)
A fund's price per share. The value is calculated by dividing the total value of all the securities in the portfolio, less any liabilities, by the number of fund shares outstanding.

Total Assets ($)
The total of all assets listed on the institution's balance sheet. This figure primarily consists of loans, investments, and fixed assets. Total Assets are displayed in dollars.

Dividend Yield (TTM)
Trailing twelve months dividends paid out relative to the share price. Expressed as a percentage and measures how much cash flow an investor is getting for each invested dollar. **Trailing Twelve Months (TTM)** is a representation of a fund's financial performance over the most recent 12 months. TTM uses the latest available financial data from a company's interim, quarterly or annual reports.

Turnover Ratio
The percentage of a mutual fund or other investment vehicle's holdings that have been replaced with other holdings in a given year. Generally, low turnover ratio is favorable, because high turnover equates to higher brokerage transaction fees, which reduce fund returns.

Expense Ratio
A measure of what it costs an investment company to operate a mutual fund. An expense ratio is determined through an annual calculation, where a fund's operating expenses are divided by the average dollar value of its assets under management. Operating expenses may include money spent on administration and management of the fund, advertising, etc. An expense ratio of 1 percent per annum means that each year 1 percent of the fund's total assets will be used to cover expenses.

LEFT COLUMN

Ratings

Reward Rating
This is based on the total return over a period of up to five years, including net asset value and price growth. The total return figure is stated net of the expenses and fees charged by the fund. Based on proprietary modeling the individual components of the risk and reward ratings are calculated and weighted and the final rating is generated.

Risk Rating
This is includes the risk ratings of component stocks where applicable and also includes the financial stability of the fund, turnover where applicable, together with the level of volatility as measured by the fund's daily returns over a period of up to five years. Funds with greater stability are considered less risky and receive a higher risk rating. Funds with greater volatility are considered riskier, and will receive a lower risk rating. In addition to considering the fund's volatility, the risk rating also considers an assessment of the valuation and quality of a fund's holdings.

Recent Upgrade/Downgrade
An "Up" or "Down" indicates that the Weiss Mutual Fund rating has changed since the publication of the last print edition. If a fund has had a rating change since March 31, 2019, the change is identified with an "Up" or "Down."

Fund Information

Fund Type
Describes the fund's assets, regions of investments and investment strategies.

Open End Fund
A type of mutual fund that does not have restrictions on the amount of shares the fund will issue. If demand is high enough, the fund will continue to issue shares no matter how many investors there are. Open-end funds also buy back shares when investors wish to sell.

Closed End Fund
They are launched through an Initial Public Offering in order to raise money and then trade in the open market just like a stock or an ETF. They only issue a set amount of shares and, although their value is also based on the Net Asset Value, the actual price of the fund is affected by supply and demand, allowing it to trade at prices above or below its real value.

Category
Identifies funds according to their actual investment styles as measured by their portfolio holdings. This categorization allows investors to spread their money around in a mix of funds with a variety of risk and return characteristics.

Sub-Category
A subdivision of funds, usually with common characteristics as the category.

Prospectus Objective
Gives a general idea of a fund's overall investment approach and goals.

Inception Date
The date on which the fund began its operations. The commencement date indicates when a fund began investing in the market. Many investors prefer funds with longer operating histories. Funds with longer histories have longer track records and can thereby provide investors with a more long-standing picture of their performance.

Open to New Investments
Indicates whether the fund accepts investments from those who are not existing investors. A "Y" in this column identifies that the fund accepts new investors. No data in this column indicates that the fund is closed to new investors. The fund may be closed to new investors because the fund's asset base is getting too large to effectively execute its investing style. Although, the fund may be closed, in most cases, existing investors are able to add to their holdings.

Minimum Initial Investment
The smallest investment amount a fund will accept to establish a new account. This amount could be $0 or any other number set by the fund.

Minimum Subsequent Investment
The smallest additional investment amount a fund will accept in an existing account.

Front End Fee
A commission or sales charge applied at the time of the initial purchase of an investment. The fee percentage is generally based on the amount of the investment. Larger investments, both initial and cumulative, generally receive percentage discounts based on the dollar value invested. Fees are displayed as a percent.

Back End Fee
A fee that investors pay when withdrawing money from an investment within a specified number of years, usually five to 10 years. The back-end load is designed to discourage withdrawals and typically declines for each year that a shareholder remains in a fund. The fee is a percentage of the value of the share being sold. Fees are displayed as a percent.

Total Returns (%)

3-Month Total Return
The rate of return on an investment over three months that includes interest, capital gains, dividends and distributions realized.

6-Month Total Return
The rate of return on an investment over six months that includes interest, capital gains, dividends and distributions realized.

1-Year Total Return
The rate of return on an investment over one year that includes interest, capital gains, dividends and distributions realized.

3-Year Total Return
The rate of return on an investment over three years that includes interest, capital gains, dividends and distributions realized.

5-Year Total Return
The rate of return on an investment over five years that includes interest, capital gains, dividends and distributions realized.

Last Bull Market Total Return
The fund's total return (the rate of return on an investment over a period of time that includes interest, capital gains, dividends and distributions realized) during the last market upswing. A **Bull Market** is a financial market condition in which prices are rising or are expected to rise. Bull markets are characterized by optimism, investor confidence and expectations that strong results will continue.

Last Bear Market Total Return
The fund's total return (the rate of return on an investment over a period of time that includes interest, capital gains, dividends and distributions realized) during the last market downturn. A **Bear Market** is a financial market condition in which the prices of securities are falling, investors anticipate losses, and selling of securities increases.

3-Year Standard Deviation

A statistical measurement of dispersion about an average, which depicts how widely the returns varied over the past three years. Investors use the standard deviation of historical performance to try to predict the range of returns that are most likely for a given fund. When a fund has a high standard deviation, the predicted range of performance is wide, implying greater volatility. Standard deviation is most appropriate for measuring risk if it is for a fund that is an investor's only holding. The figure cannot be combined for more than one fund because the standard deviation for a portfolio of multiple funds is a function of not only the individual standard deviations, but also of the degree of correlation among the funds' returns. If a fund's returns follow a normal distribution, then approximately 68 percent of the time they will fall within one standard deviation of the mean return for the fund, and 95 percent of the time within two standard deviations.

3-Year Beta

A three year measure of volatility, or systematic risk, of a security in comparison to the market as a whole. A beta of less than 1 means that the security will be less volatile than the market, a beta larger than 1 means more volatility. Beta value cannot be calculated if less than 24 months of pricing is available.

Company Information

Provider

The legal company that issues the fund.

Manager/Tenure (Years)

The name of the manager and the number of years spent managing the fund.

Website

The company's web address.

Address

The company’s street address.

Phone Number

The company's phone number.

RIGHT COLUMN

Performance Chart
A graphical representation of the fund's total returns over the past year.

Ratings History

Indicates the fund's Overall, Risk and Reward Ratings for the previous five years. Ratings are listed as of June 30, 2019 (Q2-19), December 31, 2018 (Q4-18), December 31, 2017 (Q4-17), December 31, 2016 (Q4-16), and December 31, 2015 (Q4-15).

Overall Rating
The Weiss rating measured on a scale from A to E based on each fund's risk and performance. See the preceding section, "What Our Ratings Mean," for an explanation of each letter grade rating.

Risk Rating
This is includes the risk ratings of component stocks where applicable and also includes the financial stability of the fund, turnover where applicable, together with the level of volatility as measured by the fund's daily returns over a period of up to five years. Funds with greater stability are considered less risky and receive a higher risk rating. Funds with greater volatility are considered riskier, and will receive a lower risk rating. In addition to considering the fund's volatility, the risk rating also considers an assessment of the valuation and quality of a fund's holdings.

Reward Rating
This is based on the total return over a period of up to five years, including net asset value and price growth. The total return figure is stated net of the expenses and fees charged by the fund. Based on proprietary modeling the individual components of the risk and reward ratings are calculated and weighted and the final rating is generated.

Asset & Performance History

Indicates the fund's NAV (Net Asset Value) and 1-Year Total Return for the previous 6 years.

NAV (Net Asset Value)
A fund's price per share. The value is calculated by dividing the total value of all the securities in the portfolio, less any liabilities, by the number of fund shares outstanding.

1-Year Total Return
The rate of return on an investment over one year that includes interest, capital gains, dividends and distributions realized.

Total Assets ($)
The total of all assets listed on the institution's balance sheet. This figure primarily consists of loans, investments, and fixed assets. Total Assets are displayed in dollars.

Asset Allocation

Indicates the percentage of assets in each category. Used as an investment strategy that attempts to balance risk versus reward by adjusting the percentage of each asset in an investment portfolio according to the investor's risk tolerance, goals and investment time frame. Allocation percentages may not add up to 100%. Negative values reflect short positions.

%Cash

The percentage of the fund's assets invested in short-term obligations, usually less than 90 days, that provide a return in the form of interest payments. This type of investment generally offers a low return compared to other investments but has a low risk level.

%Stocks

The percentage of the fund's assets invested in stock.

%US Stocks

The percentage of the fund's assets invested in US stock.

%Bonds

The percentage of the fund's assets invested in bonds. A bond is an unsecured debt security issued by companies, municipalities, states and sovereign governments to raise funds. When a company issues a bond it borrows money from the bondholder to boost the business, in exchange the bondholder receives the principal amount back plus the interest on the determined maturity date.

%US Bonds

The percentage of the fund's assets invested in US bonds.

%Other

The percentage of the fund's assets invested in other financial instruments.

Services Offered

Services offered by the fund provider. Such services can include:

Systematic Withdrawal Plan

A plan offered by mutual funds that pays specific amounts to shareholders at predetermined intervals.

Institutional Only

This indicates if the fund is offered to institutional clients only (pension funds, mutual funds, money managers, insurance companies, investment banks, commercial trusts, endowment funds, hedge funds, and some hedge fund investors).

Phone Exchange

This indicates that investors can move money between different funds within the same fund family over the phone.

Wire Redemption

This indicates whether or not investors can redeem electronically.

Qualified Investment

Under a qualified plan, an investor may invest in the variable annuity with pretax dollars through an employee pension plan, such as a 401(k) or 403(b). Money builds up on a tax-deferred basis, and when the qualified investor makes a withdrawal or annuitizes, all contributions received are taxable income.

Investment Strategy

A set of rules, behaviors or procedures, designed to guide an investor's selection of an investment portfolio. Individuals have different profit objectives, and their individual skills make different tactics and strategies appropriate.

Top Holdings

The highest amount of publicly traded assets held by a fund. These publicly traded assets may include company stock, mutual funds or other investment vehicles.

Vanguard Total Stock Market Index Fund Investor Shares B- BUY

Ticker	Traded On	NAV	Total Assets ($)	Dividend Yield (TTM)	Turnover Ratio	Expense Ratio
VTSMX	NAS CM	73.01	$814,086,000,000	1.73	3	0.14

Ratings

Reward	C
Risk	B
Recent Upgrade/Downgrade	

Fund Information

Fund Type	Open End
Category	US Equity Large Cap Blend
Sub-Category	Large Blend
Prospectus Objective	Growth
Inception Date	Apr-92
Open to New Investments	Y
Minimum Initial Investment	3,000
Minimum Subsequent Investment	1
Front End Fee	
Back End Fee	

Total Returns (%)

3-Month	6-Month	1-Year	3-Year	5-Year
4.05	19.66	8.87	49.86	61.54

Last Bull Market	25.72
Last Bear Market	-17.74
3-Year Standard Deviation	12.52
3-Year Beta	1

Company Information

Provider	Vanguard
Manager/Tenure	Gerard C. O'Reilly (24), Walter Nejman (3)
Website	http://www.vanguard.com
Address	Vanguard 100 Vanguard Boulevard Malvern PA 19355 United States
Phone Number	877-662-7447

Ratings History

Date	Overall Rating	Risk Rating	Reward Rating
Q2-19	B-	B	C
Q4-18	C	B	C
Q4-17	B	B	B
Q4-16	B	B	B
Q4-15	C+	B-	C

Asset & Performance History

Date	NAV	1-Year Total Return
2018	62.08	-5.25
2017	66.7	21.05
2016	56.06	12.53
2015	50.78	0.29
2014	51.58	12.42
2013	46.67	33.34

Total Assets: $814,086,000,000

Asset Allocation

Asset	%
Cash	1%
Stocks	99%
US Stocks	98%
Bonds	0%
US Bonds	0%
Other	0%

Services Offered: Systematic Withdrawal Plan, Automatic Investment Plan, Phone Exchange, Wire Redemption

Investment Strategy: The investment seeks to track the performance of a benchmark index that measures the investment return of the overall stock market. The fund employs an indexing investment approach designed to track the performance of the CRSP US Total Market Index, which represents approximately 100% of the investable U.S. stock market and includes large-, mid-, small-, and micro-cap stocks regularly traded on the New York Stock Exchange and Nasdaq. It invests by sampling the index, meaning that it holds a broadly diversified collection of securities that, in the aggregate, approximates the full index in terms of key characteristics. **Top Holdings:** Microsoft Corp Apple Inc Amazon.com Inc Facebook Inc A Berkshire Hathaway Inc B

Vanguard Total Stock Market Index Fund Admiral Shares B- BUY

Ticker	Traded On	NAV	Total Assets ($)	Dividend Yield (TTM)	Turnover Ratio	Expense Ratio
VTSAX	NAS CM	73.04	$814,086,000,000	1.82	3	0.04

Ratings

Reward	C
Risk	B
Recent Upgrade/Downgrade	

Fund Information

Fund Type	Open End
Category	US Equity Large Cap Blend
Sub-Category	Large Blend
Prospectus Objective	Growth
Inception Date	Nov-00
Open to New Investments	Y
Minimum Initial Investment	3,000
Minimum Subsequent Investment	1
Front End Fee	
Back End Fee	

Total Returns (%)

3-Month	6-Month	1-Year	3-Year	5-Year
4.08	19.74	8.99	50.32	62.39

Last Bull Market	25.82
Last Bear Market	-17.71
3-Year Standard Deviation	12.53
3-Year Beta	1

Company Information

Provider	Vanguard
Manager/Tenure	Gerard C. O'Reilly (24), Walter Nejman (3)
Website	http://www.vanguard.com
Address	Vanguard 100 Vanguard Boulevard Malvern PA 19355 United States
Phone Number	877-662-7447

Ratings History

Date	Overall Rating	Risk Rating	Reward Rating
Q2-19	B-	B	C+
Q4-18	C+	B	C
Q4-17	B	B	B
Q4-16	B	B	B
Q4-15	C+	B-	C

Asset & Performance History

Date	NAV	1-Year Total Return
2018	62.09	-5.17
2017	66.72	21.16
2016	56.08	12.66
2015	50.79	0.38
2014	51.6	12.55
2013	46.69	33.52

Total Assets: $814,086,000,000

Asset Allocation

Asset	%
Cash	1%
Stocks	99%
US Stocks	98%
Bonds	0%
US Bonds	0%
Other	0%

Services Offered: Systematic Withdrawal Plan, Automatic Investment Plan, Phone Exchange, Wire Redemption

Investment Strategy: The investment seeks to track the performance of a benchmark index that measures the investment return of the overall stock market. The fund employs an indexing investment approach designed to track the performance of the CRSP US Total Market Index, which represents approximately 100% of the investable U.S. stock market and includes large-, mid-, small-, and micro-cap stocks regularly traded on the New York Stock Exchange and Nasdaq. It invests by sampling the index, meaning that it holds a broadly diversified collection of securities that, in the aggregate, approximates the full index in terms of key characteristics. **Top Holdings:** Microsoft Corp Apple Inc Amazon.com Inc Facebook Inc A Berkshire Hathaway Inc B

Vanguard 500 Index Fund Admiral Shares B- BUY

Ticker	Traded On	NAV	Total Assets ($)	Dividend Yield (TTM)	Turnover Ratio	Expense Ratio
VFIAX	NAS CM	271.39	$483,171,000,000	1.97	4	0.04

Ratings

Reward	C
Risk	B
Recent Upgrade/Downgrade	

Fund Information

Fund Type	Open End
Category	US Equity Large Cap Blend
Sub-Category	Large Blend
Prospectus Objective	Growth
Inception Date	Nov-00
Open to New Investments	Y
Minimum Initial Investment	3,000
Minimum Subsequent Investment	1
Front End Fee	
Back End Fee	

Total Returns (%)

3-Month	6-Month	1-Year	3-Year	5-Year
4.29	19.55	10.38	50.75	66.01

Last Bull Market	25.08
Last Bear Market	-16.27
3-Year Standard Deviation	12.19
3-Year Beta	1

Company Information

Provider	Vanguard
Manager/Tenure	Donald M. Butler (3), Michelle Louie (1)
Website	http://www.vanguard.com
Address	Vanguard 100 Vanguard Boulevard Malvern PA 19355 United States
Phone Number	877-662-7447

Ratings History

Date	Overall Rating	Risk Rating	Reward Rating
Q2-19	B-	B	C+
Q4-18	C+	B	C
Q4-17	B	B	B
Q4-16	B	B	B
Q4-15	C+	C+	C

Asset & Performance History

Date	NAV	1-Year Total Return
2018	231.44	-4.42
2017	246.82	21.78
2016	206.57	11.92
2015	188.48	1.36
2014	189.89	13.64
2013	170.36	32.33

Total Assets: $483,171,000,000

Asset Allocation

Asset	%
Cash	1%
Stocks	99%
US Stocks	99%
Bonds	0%
US Bonds	0%
Other	0%

Services Offered: Systematic Withdrawal Plan, Automatic Investment Plan, Phone Exchange, Wire Redemption

Investment Strategy: The investment seeks to track the performance of a benchmark index that measures the investment return of large-capitalization stocks. The fund employs an indexing investment approach designed to track the performance of the Standard & Poor's 500 Index, a widely recognized benchmark of U.S. stock market performance that is dominated by the stocks of large U.S. companies. The advisor attempts to replicate the target index by investing all, or substantially all, of its assets in the stocks that make up the index, holding each stock in approximately the same proportion as its weighting in the index. **Top Holdings:** Microsoft Corp Apple Inc Amazon.com Inc Facebook Inc A Berkshire Hathaway Inc B

Vanguard 500 Index Fund Investor Shares B- BUY

Ticker	Traded On	NAV	Total Assets ($)	Dividend Yield (TTM)	Turnover Ratio	Expense Ratio
VFINX	NAS CM	271.41	$483,171,000,000	1.87	4	0.14

Ratings

Reward	C
Risk	B
Recent Upgrade/Downgrade	

Fund Information

Fund Type	Open End
Category	US Equity Large Cap Blend
Sub-Category	Large Blend
Prospectus Objective	Growth
Inception Date	Aug-76
Open to New Investments	Y
Minimum Initial Investment	3,000
Minimum Subsequent Investment	1
Front End Fee	
Back End Fee	

Total Returns (%)

3-Month	6-Month	1-Year	3-Year	5-Year
4.27	19.49	10.26	50.30	65.15

Last Bull Market	24.99
Last Bear Market	-16.31
3-Year Standard Deviation	12.19
3-Year Beta	1

Company Information

Provider	Vanguard
Manager/Tenure	Donald M. Butler (3), Michelle Louie (1)
Website	http://www.vanguard.com
Address	Vanguard 100 Vanguard Boulevard Malvern PA 19355 United States
Phone Number	877-662-7447

Ratings History

Date	Overall Rating	Risk Rating	Reward Rating
Q2-19	B-	B	C+
Q4-18	C+	B	C
Q4-17	B	B	B
Q4-16	B	B	B
Q4-15	C+	C+	C

Asset & Performance History

Date	NAV	1-Year Total Return
2018	231.44	-4.52
2017	246.82	21.66
2016	206.57	11.81
2015	188.48	1.24
2014	189.89	13.5
2013	170.36	32.17

Total Assets: $483,171,000,000

Asset Allocation

Asset	%
Cash	1%
Stocks	99%
US Stocks	99%
Bonds	0%
US Bonds	0%
Other	0%

Services Offered: Systematic Withdrawal Plan, Automatic Investment Plan, Phone Exchange, Wire Redemption

Investment Strategy: The investment seeks to track the performance of a benchmark index that measures the investment return of large-capitalization stocks. The fund employs an indexing investment approach designed to track the performance of the Standard & Poor's 500 Index, a widely recognized benchmark of U.S. stock market performance that is dominated by the stocks of large U.S. companies. The advisor attempts to replicate the target index by investing all, or substantially all, of its assets in the stocks that make up the index, holding each stock in approximately the same proportion as its weighting in the index. **Top Holdings:** Microsoft Corp Apple Inc Amazon.com Inc Facebook Inc A Berkshire Hathaway Inc B

Vanguard Total International Stock Index Fund Admiral Shares — C HOLD

Ticker	Traded On	NAV	Total Assets ($)	Dividend Yield (TTM)	Turnover Ratio	Expense Ratio
VTIAX	NAS CM	28.34	$381,622,000,000	2.9	3	0.11

Ratings

Reward	C
Risk	B
Recent Upgrade/Downgrade	

Fund Information

Fund Type	Open End
Category	Global Equity Large Cap
Sub-Category	Foreign Large Blend
Prospectus Objective	Foreign Stock
Inception Date	Nov-10
Open to New Investments	Y
Minimum Initial Investment	3,000
Minimum Subsequent Investment	1
Front End Fee	
Back End Fee	

Total Returns (%)

3-Month	6-Month	1-Year	3-Year	5-Year
2.74	13.76	0.56	31.00	12.35

Last Bull Market	14.52
Last Bear Market	-24.32
3-Year Standard Deviation	11.46
3-Year Beta	1

Company Information

Provider	Vanguard
Manager/Tenure	Michael Perre (10), Christine D. Franquin (1)
Website	http://www.vanguard.com
Address	Vanguard 100 Vanguard Boulevard Malvern PA 19355 United States
Phone Number	877-662-7447

Ratings History

Date	Overall Rating	Risk Rating	Reward Rating
Q2-19	C	B-	C-
Q4-18	C-	C	D+
Q4-17	B-	B-	B-
Q4-16	C-	C	D+
Q4-15	C	B	C-

Asset & Performance History

Date	NAV	1-Year Total Return
2018	25.37	-14.43
2017	30.52	27.55
2016	24.63	4.67
2015	24.24	-4.25
2014	26	-4.17
2013	28.01	15.14

Total Assets: $381,622,000,000

Asset Allocation

Asset	%
Cash	4%
Stocks	96%
US Stocks	1%
Bonds	0%
US Bonds	0%
Other	0%

Services Offered: Systematic Withdrawal Plan, Automatic Investment Plan, Phone Exchange, Wire Redemption

Investment Strategy: The investment seeks to track the performance of a benchmark index that measures the investment return of stocks issued by companies located in developed and emerging markets, excluding the United States. The fund employs an indexing investment approach designed to track the performance of the FTSE Global All Cap ex US Index, a float-adjusted market-capitalization-weighted index designed to measure equity market performance of companies located in developed and emerging markets, excluding the United States. It invests all, or substantially all, of its assets in the common stocks included in its target index. **Top Holdings:** Nestle SA Tencent Holdings Ltd Alibaba Group Holding Ltd ADR Taiwan Semiconductor Manufacturing Co Ltd Samsung Electronics Co Ltd

Vanguard Total International Stock Index Fund Investor Shares — C HOLD

Ticker	Traded On	NAV	Total Assets ($)	Dividend Yield (TTM)	Turnover Ratio	Expense Ratio
VGTSX	NAS CM	16.94	$381,622,000,000	2.84	3	0.17

Ratings

Reward	C
Risk	B
Recent Upgrade/Downgrade	

Fund Information

Fund Type	Open End
Category	Global Equity Large Cap
Sub-Category	Foreign Large Blend
Prospectus Objective	Foreign Stock
Inception Date	Apr-96
Open to New Investments	Y
Minimum Initial Investment	0
Minimum Subsequent Investment	
Front End Fee	
Back End Fee	

Total Returns (%)

3-Month	6-Month	1-Year	3-Year	5-Year
2.71	13.73	0.49	30.72	11.94

Last Bull Market	14.58
Last Bear Market	-24.35
3-Year Standard Deviation	11.45
3-Year Beta	1

Company Information

Provider	Vanguard
Manager/Tenure	Michael Perre (10), Christine D. Franquin (1)
Website	http://www.vanguard.com
Address	Vanguard 100 Vanguard Boulevard Malvern PA 19355 United States
Phone Number	877-662-7447

Ratings History

Date	Overall Rating	Risk Rating	Reward Rating
Q2-19	C	B-	C-
Q4-18	C-	C	D+
Q4-17	B-	B-	B-
Q4-16	C-	C	D+
Q4-15	C	B	C-

Asset & Performance History

Date	NAV	1-Year Total Return
2018	15.17	-14.44
2017	18.24	27.39
2016	14.73	4.65
2015	14.49	-4.37
2014	15.55	-4.23
2013	16.75	15.04

Total Assets: $381,622,000,000

Asset Allocation

Asset	%
Cash	4%
Stocks	96%
US Stocks	1%
Bonds	0%
US Bonds	0%
Other	0%

Services Offered: Systematic Withdrawal Plan, Automatic Investment Plan, Phone Exchange, Wire Redemption

Investment Strategy: The investment seeks to track the performance of a benchmark index that measures the investment return of stocks issued by companies located in developed and emerging markets, excluding the United States. The fund employs an indexing investment approach designed to track the performance of the FTSE Global All Cap ex US Index, a float-adjusted market-capitalization-weighted index designed to measure equity market performance of companies located in developed and emerging markets, excluding the United States. It invests all, or substantially all, of its assets in the common stocks included in its target index. **Top Holdings:** Nestle SA Tencent Holdings Ltd Alibaba Group Holding Ltd ADR Taiwan Semiconductor Manufacturing Co Ltd Samsung Electronics Co Ltd

American Funds The Growth Fund of America® Class 529-F B- BUY

Ticker	Traded On	NAV	Total Assets ($)	Dividend Yield (TTM)	Turnover Ratio	Expense Ratio
CGFFX	NAS CM	49.62	$193,270,000,000	0.74	28	0.47

Ratings

Reward	C
Risk	B
Recent Upgrade/Downgrade	

Fund Information

Fund Type	Open End
Category	US Equity Large Cap Growth
Sub-Category	Large Growth
Prospectus Objective	Growth
Inception Date	Sep-02
Open to New Investments	Y
Minimum Initial Investment	250
Minimum Subsequent Investment	50
Front End Fee	
Back End Fee	

Total Returns (%)

3-Month	6-Month	1-Year	3-Year	5-Year
3.50	18.67	5.02	58.08	71.36

Last Bull Market	24.26
Last Bear Market	-18.95
3-Year Standard Deviation	12.97
3-Year Beta	1.01

Company Information

Provider	American Funds
Manager/Tenure	Donald D. O'Neal (25), Michael T. Kerr (20), J. Blair Frank (17), 10 others
Website	http://www.americanfunds.com
Address	American Funds 333 South Hope Street Los Angeles CA 90071-1406 United States
Phone Number	800-421-4225

Ratings History

Date	Overall Rating	Risk Rating	Reward Rating
Q2-19	C+	B	C
Q4-18	C	B-	C
Q4-17	B	B	B
Q4-16	B	B	B
Q4-15	C+	C+	C+

Asset & Performance History

Date	NAV	1-Year Total Return
2018	42.12	-2.73
2017	48.91	26.3
2016	41.55	8.61
2015	40.84	5.48
2014	42.26	9.45
2013	42.62	33.99

Total Assets: $193,270,000,000

Asset Allocation

Asset	%
Cash	6%
Stocks	93%
US Stocks	82%
Bonds	0%
US Bonds	0%
Other	0%

Services Offered: Systematic Withdrawal Plan, Automatic Investment Plan, Qualified Investment, Phone Exchange, Retirement Investment

Investment Strategy: The investment seeks growth of capital. The fund invests primarily in common stocks and seeks to invest in companies that appear to offer superior opportunities for growth of capital. It may invest up to 25% of its assets in securities of issuers domiciled outside the United States. The investment adviser uses a system of multiple portfolio managers in managing the fund's assets. Under this approach, the portfolio of the fund is divided into segments managed by individual managers who decide how their respective segments will be invested. **Top Holdings:** Facebook Inc A Microsoft Corp Amazon.com Inc Netflix Inc Alphabet Inc Class C

American Funds The Growth Fund of America® Class F-2 B- BUY

Ticker	Traded On	NAV	Total Assets ($)	Dividend Yield (TTM)	Turnover Ratio	Expense Ratio
GFFFX	NAS CM	50.23	$193,270,000,000	0.76	28	0.42

Ratings

Reward	C
Risk	B
Recent Upgrade/Downgrade	

Fund Information

Fund Type	Open End
Category	US Equity Large Cap Growth
Sub-Category	Large Growth
Prospectus Objective	Growth
Inception Date	Aug-08
Open to New Investments	Y
Minimum Initial Investment	250
Minimum Subsequent Investment	50
Front End Fee	
Back End Fee	

Total Returns (%)

3-Month	6-Month	1-Year	3-Year	5-Year
3.52	18.71	5.09	58.38	72.02

Last Bull Market	24.36
Last Bear Market	-18.91
3-Year Standard Deviation	12.97
3-Year Beta	1.01

Company Information

Provider	American Funds
Manager/Tenure	Donald D. O'Neal (25), Michael T. Kerr (20), J. Blair Frank (17), 10 others
Website	http://www.americanfunds.com
Address	American Funds 333 South Hope Street Los Angeles CA 90071-1406 United States
Phone Number	800-421-4225

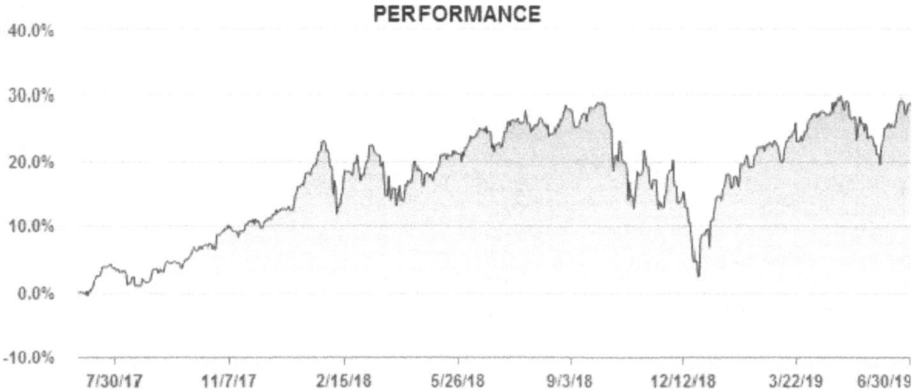

Ratings History

Date	Overall Rating	Risk Rating	Reward Rating
Q2-19	C+	B	C
Q4-18	C	B-	C
Q4-17	B	B	B
Q4-16	B	B	B
Q4-15	C+	C+	C+

Asset & Performance History

Date	NAV	1-Year Total Return
2018	42.62	-2.68
2017	49.42	26.38
2016	41.95	8.69
2015	41.21	5.6
2014	42.6	9.53
2013	42.95	34.15

Total Assets: $193,270,000,000

Asset Allocation

Asset	%
Cash	6%
Stocks	93%
US Stocks	82%
Bonds	0%
US Bonds	0%
Other	0%

Services Offered: Systematic Withdrawal Plan, Automatic Investment Plan, Qualified Investment, Phone Exchange, Retirement Investment

Investment Strategy: The investment seeks growth of capital. The fund invests primarily in common stocks and seeks to invest in companies that appear to offer superior opportunities for growth of capital. It may invest up to 25% of its assets in securities of issuers domiciled outside the United States. The investment adviser uses a system of multiple portfolio managers in managing the fund's assets. Under this approach, the portfolio of the fund is divided into segments managed by individual managers who decide how their respective segments will be invested. **Top Holdings:** Facebook Inc A Microsoft Corp Amazon.com Inc Netflix Inc Alphabet Inc Class C

American Funds The Growth Fund of America® Class R-6 — B- BUY

Ticker	Traded On	NAV	Total Assets ($)	Dividend Yield (TTM)	Turnover Ratio	Expense Ratio
RGAGX	NAS CM	50.4	$193,270,000,000	0.84	28	0.33

Ratings

Reward	C
Risk	B
Recent Upgrade/Downgrade	

Fund Information

Fund Type	Open End
Category	US Equity Large Cap Growth
Sub-Category	Large Growth
Prospectus Objective	Growth
Inception Date	May-09
Open to New Investments	Y
Minimum Initial Investment	250
Minimum Subsequent Investment	50
Front End Fee	
Back End Fee	

Total Returns (%)

3-Month	6-Month	1-Year	3-Year	5-Year
3.53	18.75	5.18	58.82	72.86

Last Bull Market	24.41
Last Bear Market	-18.89
3-Year Standard Deviation	12.96
3-Year Beta	1.01

Company Information

Provider	American Funds
Manager/Tenure	Donald D. O'Neal (25), Michael T. Kerr (20), J. Blair Frank (17), 10 others
Website	http://www.americanfunds.com
Address	American Funds 333 South Hope Street Los Angeles CA 90071-1406 United States
Phone Number	800-421-4225

Ratings History

Date	Overall Rating	Risk Rating	Reward Rating
Q2-19	C+	B	C
Q4-18	C	B-	C
Q4-17	B	B	B
Q4-16	B	B	B
Q4-15	B-	B+	C+

Asset & Performance History

Date	NAV	1-Year Total Return
2018	42.75	-2.6
2017	49.56	26.52
2016	42.05	8.81
2015	41.29	5.69
2014	42.68	9.63
2013	43.01	34.29

Total Assets: $193,270,000,000

Asset Allocation

Asset	%
Cash	6%
Stocks	93%
US Stocks	82%
Bonds	0%
US Bonds	0%
Other	0%

Services Offered: Automatic Investment Plan, Qualified Investment, Phone Exchange

Investment Strategy: The investment seeks growth of capital. The fund invests primarily in common stocks and seeks to invest in companies that appear to offer superior opportunities for growth of capital. It may invest up to 25% of its assets in securities of issuers domiciled outside the United States. The investment adviser uses a system of multiple portfolio managers in managing the fund's assets. Under this approach, the portfolio of the fund is divided into segments managed by individual managers who decide how their respective segments will be invested. **Top Holdings:** Facebook Inc A Microsoft Corp Amazon.com Inc Netflix Inc Alphabet Inc Class C

American Funds The Growth Fund of America® Class F-1 — C+ HOLD

Ticker	Traded On	NAV	Total Assets ($)	Dividend Yield (TTM)	Turnover Ratio	Expense Ratio
GFAFX	NAS CM	49.97	$193,270,000,000	0.47	28	0.69

Ratings

Reward	C
Risk	B
Recent Upgrade/Downgrade	Down

Fund Information

Fund Type	Open End
Category	US Equity Large Cap Growth
Sub-Category	Large Growth
Prospectus Objective	Growth
Inception Date	Mar-01
Open to New Investments	Y
Minimum Initial Investment	250
Minimum Subsequent Investment	50
Front End Fee	
Back End Fee	

Total Returns (%)

3-Month	6-Month	1-Year	3-Year	5-Year
3.43	18.52	4.80	57.06	69.68

Last Bull Market	24.17
Last Bear Market	-18.97
3-Year Standard Deviation	12.97
3-Year Beta	1.01

Company Information

Provider	American Funds
Manager/Tenure	Donald D. O'Neal (25), Michael T. Kerr (20), J. Blair Frank (17), 10 others
Website	http://www.americanfunds.com
Address	American Funds 333 South Hope Street Los Angeles CA 90071-1406 United States
Phone Number	800-421-4225

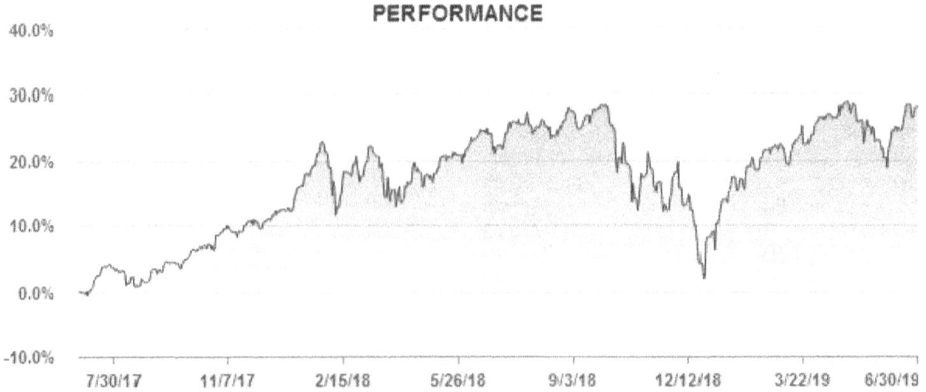

Ratings History

Date	Overall Rating	Risk Rating	Reward Rating
Q2-19	C+	B	C
Q4-18	C	B-	C
Q4-17	B	B	B
Q4-16	B	B	B
Q4-15	B-	B+	C+

Asset & Performance History

Date	NAV	1-Year Total Return
2018	42.46	-2.96
2017	49.22	26.07
2016	41.77	8.37
2015	41.05	5.33
2014	42.44	9.23
2013	42.74	33.79

Total Assets: $193,270,000,000

Asset Allocation

Asset	%
Cash	6%
Stocks	93%
US Stocks	82%
Bonds	0%
US Bonds	0%
Other	0%

Services Offered: Systematic Withdrawal Plan, Automatic Investment Plan, Qualified Investment, Phone Exchange, Retirement Investment

Investment Strategy: The investment seeks growth of capital. The fund invests primarily in common stocks and seeks to invest in companies that appear to offer superior opportunities for growth of capital. It may invest up to 25% of its assets in securities of issuers domiciled outside the United States. The investment adviser uses a system of multiple portfolio managers in managing the fund's assets. Under this approach, the portfolio of the fund is divided into segments managed by individual managers who decide how their respective segments will be invested. **Top Holdings:** Facebook Inc A Microsoft Corp Amazon.com Inc Netflix Inc Alphabet Inc Class C

American Funds The Growth Fund of America® Class R-1 C+ HOLD

Ticker	Traded On	NAV	Total Assets ($)	Dividend Yield (TTM)	Turnover Ratio	Expense Ratio
RGAAX	NAS CM	46.8	$193,270,000,000	0	28	1.43

Ratings

Reward	C
Risk	B
Recent Upgrade/Downgrade	

Fund Information

Fund Type	Open End
Category	US Equity Large Cap Growth
Sub-Category	Large Growth
Prospectus Objective	Growth
Inception Date	Jun-02
Open to New Investments	Y
Minimum Initial Investment	250
Minimum Subsequent Investment	50
Front End Fee	
Back End Fee	

Total Returns (%)

3-Month	6-Month	1-Year	3-Year	5-Year
3.26	18.12	4.04	53.66	63.64

Last Bull Market	23.63
Last Bear Market	-19.26
3-Year Standard Deviation	12.97
3-Year Beta	1.01

Company Information

Provider	American Funds
Manager/Tenure	Donald D. O'Neal (25), Michael T. Kerr (20), J. Blair Frank (17), 10 others
Website	http://www.americanfunds.com
Address	American Funds 333 South Hope Street Los Angeles CA 90071-1406 United States
Phone Number	800-421-4225

PERFORMANCE

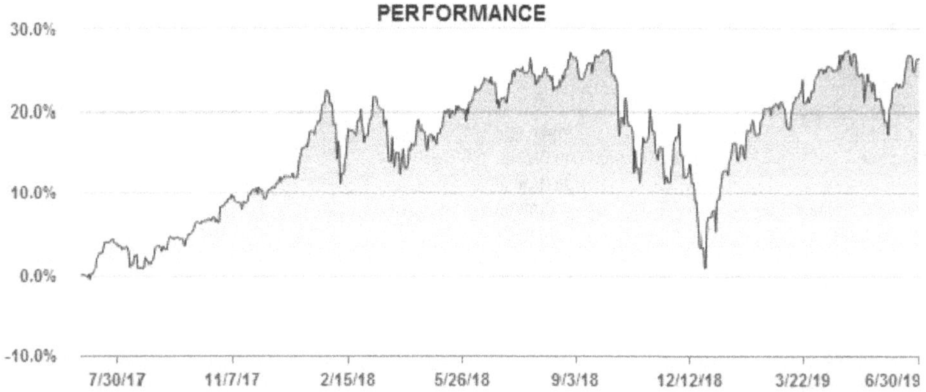

Ratings History

Date	Overall Rating	Risk Rating	Reward Rating
Q2-19	C+	B	C
Q4-18	C	C+	C
Q4-17	B	B	B
Q4-16	B	B	B
Q4-15	C+	C+	C+

Asset & Performance History

Date	NAV	1-Year Total Return
2018	39.91	-3.66
2017	46.65	25.15
2016	39.86	7.6
2015	39.36	4.55
2014	40.9	8.44
2013	41.54	32.8

Total Assets: $193,270,000,000

Asset Allocation

Asset	%
Cash	6%
Stocks	93%
US Stocks	82%
Bonds	0%
US Bonds	0%
Other	0%

Services Offered: Automatic Investment Plan, Qualified Investment, Phone Exchange

Investment Strategy: The investment seeks growth of capital. The fund invests primarily in common stocks and seeks to invest in companies that appear to offer superior opportunities for growth of capital. It may invest up to 25% of its assets in securities of issuers domiciled outside the United States. The investment adviser uses a system of multiple portfolio managers in managing the fund's assets. Under this approach, the portfolio of the fund is divided into segments managed by individual managers who decide how their respective segments will be invested. **Top Holdings:** Facebook Inc A Microsoft Corp Amazon.com Inc Netflix Inc Alphabet Inc Class C

American Funds The Growth Fund of America® Class A B- BUY

Ticker	Traded On	NAV	Total Assets ($)	Dividend Yield (TTM)	Turnover Ratio	Expense Ratio
AGTHX	NAS CM	50.34	$193,270,000,000	0.55	28	0.62

Ratings

Reward	C
Risk	B
Recent Upgrade/Downgrade	

Fund Information

Fund Type	Open End
Category	US Equity Large Cap Growth
Sub-Category	Large Growth
Prospectus Objective	Growth
Inception Date	Nov-73
Open to New Investments	Y
Minimum Initial Investment	250
Minimum Subsequent Investment	50
Front End Fee	5.75
Back End Fee	

Total Returns (%)

3-Month	6-Month	1-Year	3-Year	5-Year
3.47	18.58	4.86	57.40	70.19

Last Bull Market	24.15
Last Bear Market	-19.01
3-Year Standard Deviation	12.97
3-Year Beta	1.01

Company Information

Provider	American Funds
Manager/Tenure	Donald D. O'Neal (25), Michael T. Kerr (20), J. Blair Frank (17), 10 others
Website	http://www.americanfunds.com
Address	American Funds 333 South Hope Street Los Angeles CA 90071-1406 United States
Phone Number	800-421-4225

PERFORMANCE

Ratings History

Date	Overall Rating	Risk Rating	Reward Rating
Q2-19	C+	B	C
Q4-18	C	B-	C
Q4-17	B	B	B
Q4-16	B	B	B
Q4-15	C+	C+	C+

Asset & Performance History

Date	NAV	1-Year Total Return
2018	42.76	-2.88
2017	49.54	26.13
2016	42.04	8.45
2015	41.29	5.36
2014	42.68	9.3
2013	43	33.79

Total Assets: $193,270,000,000

Asset Allocation

Asset	%
Cash	6%
Stocks	93%
US Stocks	82%
Bonds	0%
US Bonds	0%
Other	0%

Services Offered: Systematic Withdrawal Plan, Automatic Investment Plan, Phone Exchange, Retirement Investment

Investment Strategy: The investment seeks growth of capital. The fund invests primarily in common stocks and seeks to invest in companies that appear to offer superior opportunities for growth of capital. It may invest up to 25% of its assets in securities of issuers domiciled outside the United States. The investment adviser uses a system of multiple portfolio managers in managing the fund's assets. Under this approach, the portfolio of the fund is divided into segments managed by individual managers who decide how their respective segments will be invested. **Top Holdings:** Facebook Inc A Microsoft Corp Amazon.com Inc Netflix Inc Alphabet Inc Class C

American Funds The Growth Fund of America® Class R-5 B- BUY

Ticker	Traded On	NAV	Total Assets ($)	Dividend Yield (TTM)	Turnover Ratio	Expense Ratio
RGAFX	NAS CM	50.33	$193,270,000,000	0.78	28	0.38

Ratings

Reward	C
Risk	B
Recent Upgrade/Downgrade	

Fund Information

Fund Type	Open End
Category	US Equity Large Cap Growth
Sub-Category	Large Growth
Prospectus Objective	Growth
Inception Date	May-02
Open to New Investments	Y
Minimum Initial Investment	250
Minimum Subsequent Investment	50
Front End Fee	
Back End Fee	

Total Returns (%)

3-Month	6-Month	1-Year	3-Year	5-Year
3.53	18.73	5.13	58.57	72.42

Last Bull Market	24.39
Last Bear Market	-18.89
3-Year Standard Deviation	12.98
3-Year Beta	1.01

Company Information

Provider	American Funds
Manager/Tenure	Donald D. O'Neal (25), Michael T. Kerr (20), J. Blair Frank (17), 10 others
Website	http://www.americanfunds.com
Address	American Funds 333 South Hope Street Los Angeles CA 90071-1406 United States
Phone Number	800-421-4225

PERFORMANCE

Ratings History

Date	Overall Rating	Risk Rating	Reward Rating
Q2-19	C+	B	C
Q4-18	C	B-	C
Q4-17	B	B	B
Q4-16	B	B	B
Q4-15	C+	C+	C+

Asset & Performance History

Date	NAV	1-Year Total Return
2018	42.69	-2.66
2017	49.49	26.43
2016	42	8.75
2015	41.24	5.65
2014	42.63	9.6
2013	42.95	34.2

Total Assets: $193,270,000,000

Asset Allocation

Asset	%
Cash	6%
Stocks	93%
US Stocks	82%
Bonds	0%
US Bonds	0%
Other	0%

Services Offered: Automatic Investment Plan, Qualified Investment, Phone Exchange

Investment Strategy: The investment seeks growth of capital. The fund invests primarily in common stocks and seeks to invest in companies that appear to offer superior opportunities for growth of capital. It may invest up to 25% of its assets in securities of issuers domiciled outside the United States. The investment adviser uses a system of multiple portfolio managers in managing the fund's assets. Under this approach, the portfolio of the fund is divided into segments managed by individual managers who decide how their respective segments will be invested. **Top Holdings:** Facebook Inc A Microsoft Corp Amazon.com Inc Netflix Inc Alphabet Inc Class C

American Funds The Growth Fund of America® Class 529-C C+ HOLD

Ticker	Traded On	NAV	Total Assets ($)	Dividend Yield (TTM)	Turnover Ratio	Expense Ratio
CGFCX	NAS CM	46.16	$193,270,000,000	0	28	1.47

Ratings

Reward	C
Risk	B
Recent Upgrade/Downgrade	

Fund Information

Fund Type	Open End
Category	US Equity Large Cap Growth
Sub-Category	Large Growth
Prospectus Objective	Growth
Inception Date	Feb-02
Open to New Investments	Y
Minimum Initial Investment	250
Minimum Subsequent Investment	50
Front End Fee	
Back End Fee	1.00

Total Returns (%)

3-Month	6-Month	1-Year	3-Year	5-Year
3.24	18.08	4.01	53.50	63.15

Last Bull Market	23.54
Last Bear Market	-19.3
3-Year Standard Deviation	12.95
3-Year Beta	1.01

Company Information

Provider	American Funds
Manager/Tenure	Donald D. O'Neal (25), Michael T. Kerr (20), J. Blair Frank (17), 10 others
Website	http://www.americanfunds.com
Address	American Funds 333 South Hope Street Los Angeles CA 90071-1406 United States
Phone Number	800-421-4225

PERFORMANCE

Ratings History

Date	Overall Rating	Risk Rating	Reward Rating
Q2-19	C+	B	C
Q4-18	C	C+	C
Q4-17	B	B	B
Q4-16	B	B	B
Q4-15	C+	C+	C+

Asset & Performance History

Date	NAV	1-Year Total Return
2018	39.37	-3.68
2017	46.1	25.06
2016	39.45	7.54
2015	39	4.47
2014	40.59	8.34
2013	41.29	32.68

Total Assets: $193,270,000,000

Asset Allocation

Asset	%
Cash	6%
Stocks	93%
US Stocks	82%
Bonds	0%
US Bonds	0%
Other	0%

Services Offered: Systematic Withdrawal Plan, Automatic Investment Plan, Qualified Investment, Phone Exchange, Retirement Investment

Investment Strategy: The investment seeks growth of capital. The fund invests primarily in common stocks and seeks to invest in companies that appear to offer superior opportunities for growth of capital. It may invest up to 25% of its assets in securities of issuers domiciled outside the United States. The investment adviser uses a system of multiple portfolio managers in managing the fund's assets. Under this approach, the portfolio of the fund is divided into segments managed by individual managers who decide how their respective segments will be invested. **Top Holdings:** Facebook Inc A Microsoft Corp Amazon.com Inc Netflix Inc Alphabet Inc Class C

American Funds The Growth Fund of America® Class R-2 C+ HOLD

Ticker	Traded On	NAV	Total Assets ($)	Dividend Yield (TTM)	Turnover Ratio	Expense Ratio
RGABX	NAS CM	47.34	$193,270,000,000	0	28	1.42

Ratings

Reward	C
Risk	B
Recent Upgrade/Downgrade	

Fund Information

Fund Type	Open End
Category	US Equity Large Cap Growth
Sub-Category	Large Growth
Prospectus Objective	Growth
Inception Date	May-02
Open to New Investments	Y
Minimum Initial Investment	250
Minimum Subsequent Investment	50
Front End Fee	
Back End Fee	

Total Returns (%)

3-Month	6-Month	1-Year	3-Year	5-Year
3.27	18.11	4.04	53.71	63.85

Last Bull Market	23.64
Last Bear Market	-19.22
3-Year Standard Deviation	12.96
3-Year Beta	1.01

Company Information

Provider	American Funds
Manager/Tenure	Donald D. O'Neal (25), Michael T. Kerr (20), J. Blair Frank (17), 10 others
Website	http://www.americanfunds.com
Address	American Funds 333 South Hope Street Los Angeles CA 90071-1406 United States
Phone Number	800-421-4225

PERFORMANCE

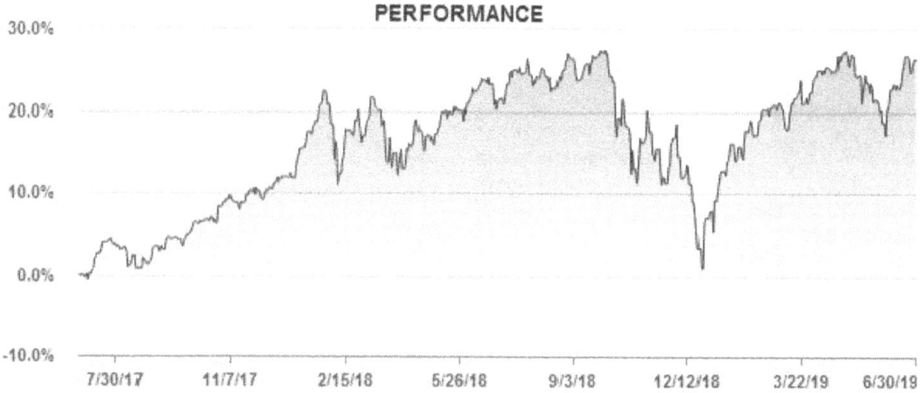

Ratings History

Date	Overall Rating	Risk Rating	Reward Rating
Q2-19	C+	B	C
Q4-18	C	C+	C
Q4-17	B	B	B
Q4-16	B	B	B
Q4-15	C+	C+	C+

Asset & Performance History

Date	NAV	1-Year Total Return
2018	40.37	-3.66
2017	47.13	25.16
2016	40.24	7.64
2015	39.7	4.62
2014	41.2	8.48
2013	41.8	32.9

Total Assets: $193,270,000,000

Asset Allocation

Asset	%
Cash	6%
Stocks	93%
US Stocks	82%
Bonds	0%
US Bonds	0%
Other	0%

Services Offered: Automatic Investment Plan, Qualified Investment, Phone Exchange

Investment Strategy: The investment seeks growth of capital. The fund invests primarily in common stocks and seeks to invest in companies that appear to offer superior opportunities for growth of capital. It may invest up to 25% of its assets in securities of issuers domiciled outside the United States. The investment adviser uses a system of multiple portfolio managers in managing the fund's assets. Under this approach, the portfolio of the fund is divided into segments managed by individual managers who decide how their respective segments will be invested. **Top Holdings:** Facebook Inc A Microsoft Corp Amazon.com Inc Netflix Inc Alphabet Inc Class C

American Funds The Growth Fund of America® Class C C+ HOLD

Ticker	Traded On	NAV	Total Assets ($)	Dividend Yield (TTM)	Turnover Ratio	Expense Ratio
GFACX	NAS CM	46.02	$193,270,000,000	0	28	1.42

Ratings

Reward	C
Risk	B
Recent Upgrade/Downgrade	

Fund Information

Fund Type	Open End
Category	US Equity Large Cap Growth
Sub-Category	Large Growth
Prospectus Objective	Growth
Inception Date	Mar-01
Open to New Investments	Y
Minimum Initial Investment	250
Minimum Subsequent Investment	50
Front End Fee	
Back End Fee	1.00

Total Returns (%)

3-Month	6-Month	1-Year	3-Year	5-Year
3.25	18.12	4.04	53.67	63.57

Last Bull Market	23.6
Last Bear Market	-19.27
3-Year Standard Deviation	12.97
3-Year Beta	1.01

Company Information

Provider	American Funds
Manager/Tenure	Donald D. O'Neal (25), Michael T. Kerr (20), J. Blair Frank (17), 10 others
Website	http://www.americanfunds.com
Address	American Funds 333 South Hope Street Los Angeles CA 90071-1406 United States
Phone Number	800-421-4225

PERFORMANCE

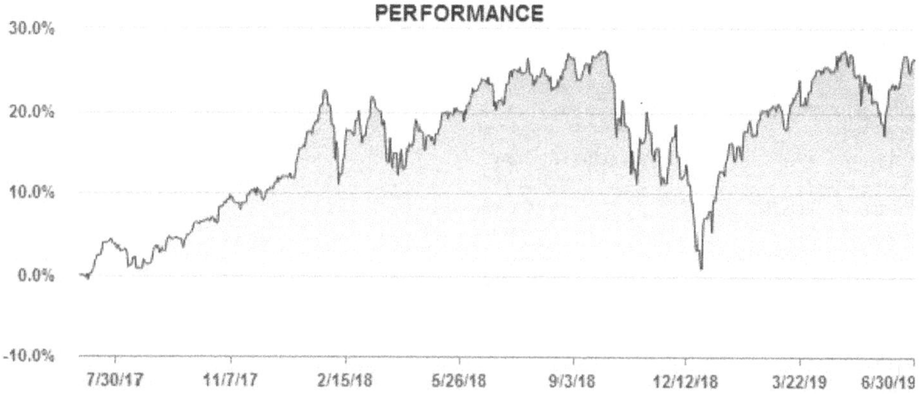

Ratings History

Date	Overall Rating	Risk Rating	Reward Rating
Q2-19	C+	B	C
Q4-18	C	C+	C
Q4-17	B	B	B
Q4-16	B	B	B
Q4-15	C+	C+	C+

Asset & Performance History

Date	NAV	1-Year Total Return
2018	39.24	-3.65
2017	45.95	25.12
2016	39.31	7.6
2015	38.85	4.51
2014	40.43	8.43
2013	41.11	32.74

Total Assets: $193,270,000,000

Asset Allocation

Asset	%
Cash	6%
Stocks	93%
US Stocks	82%
Bonds	0%
US Bonds	0%
Other	0%

Services Offered: Systematic Withdrawal Plan, Automatic Investment Plan, Phone Exchange, Retirement Investment

Investment Strategy: The investment seeks growth of capital. The fund invests primarily in common stocks and seeks to invest in companies that appear to offer superior opportunities for growth of capital. It may invest up to 25% of its assets in securities of issuers domiciled outside the United States. The investment adviser uses a system of multiple portfolio managers in managing the fund's assets. Under this approach, the portfolio of the fund is divided into segments managed by individual managers who decide how their respective segments will be invested. **Top Holdings:** Facebook Inc A Microsoft Corp Amazon.com Inc Netflix Inc Alphabet Inc Class C

American Funds The Growth Fund of America® Class R-5E B- BUY

Ticker	Traded On	NAV	Total Assets ($)	Dividend Yield (TTM)	Turnover Ratio	Expense Ratio
RGAHX	NAS CM	49.9	$193,270,000,000	0.79	28	0.45

Ratings

Reward	C
Risk	B
Recent Upgrade/Downgrade	

Fund Information

Fund Type	Open End
Category	US Equity Large Cap Growth
Sub-Category	Large Growth
Prospectus Objective	Growth
Inception Date	Nov-15
Open to New Investments	Y
Minimum Initial Investment	250
Minimum Subsequent Investment	50
Front End Fee	
Back End Fee	

Total Returns (%)

3-Month	6-Month	1-Year	3-Year	5-Year
3.50	18.69	5.03	58.14	71.09

Last Bull Market	24.15
Last Bear Market	-19
3-Year Standard Deviation	12.98
3-Year Beta	1.01

Company Information

Provider	American Funds
Manager/Tenure	Donald D. O'Neal (25), Michael T. Kerr (20), J. Blair Frank (17), 10 others
Website	http://www.americanfunds.com
Address	American Funds 333 South Hope Street Los Angeles CA 90071-1406 United States
Phone Number	800-421-4225

PERFORMANCE

Ratings History

Date	Overall Rating	Risk Rating	Reward Rating
Q2-19	C+	B	C
Q4-18	C	B-	C
Q4-17	B	B	B
Q4-16	B	B	B
Q4-15			

Asset & Performance History

Date	NAV	1-Year Total Return
2018	42.35	-2.73
2017	49.18	26.35
2016	41.77	8.56
2015	41.14	5.37
2014		9.3
2013		33.79

Total Assets: $193,270,000,000

Asset Allocation

Asset	%
Cash	6%
Stocks	93%
US Stocks	82%
Bonds	0%
US Bonds	0%
Other	0%

Services Offered: Automatic Investment Plan, Qualified Investment, Phone Exchange

Investment Strategy: The investment seeks growth of capital. The fund invests primarily in common stocks and seeks to invest in companies that appear to offer superior opportunities for growth of capital. It may invest up to 25% of its assets in securities of issuers domiciled outside the United States. The investment adviser uses a system of multiple portfolio managers in managing the fund's assets. Under this approach, the portfolio of the fund is divided into segments managed by individual managers who decide how their respective segments will be invested. **Top Holdings:** Facebook Inc A Microsoft Corp Amazon.com Inc Netflix Inc Alphabet Inc Class C

American Funds The Growth Fund of America® Class 529-E C+ HOLD

Ticker	Traded On	NAV	Total Assets ($)	Dividend Yield (TTM)	Turnover Ratio	Expense Ratio
CGFEX	NAS CM	49.17	$193,270,000,000	0.25	28	0.93

Ratings

Reward	C
Risk	B
Recent Upgrade/Downgrade	

Fund Information

Fund Type	Open End
Category	US Equity Large Cap Growth
Sub-Category	Large Growth
Prospectus Objective	Growth
Inception Date	Mar-02
Open to New Investments	Y
Minimum Initial Investment	250
Minimum Subsequent Investment	50
Front End Fee	
Back End Fee	

Total Returns (%)

3-Month	6-Month	1-Year	3-Year	5-Year
3.38	18.39	4.54	55.94	67.50

Last Bull Market	23.94
Last Bear Market	-19.13
3-Year Standard Deviation	12.97
3-Year Beta	1.01

Company Information

Provider	American Funds
Manager/Tenure	Donald D. O'Neal (25), Michael T. Kerr (20), J. Blair Frank (17), 10 others
Website	http://www.americanfunds.com
Address	American Funds 333 South Hope Street Los Angeles CA 90071-1406 United States
Phone Number	800-421-4225

PERFORMANCE

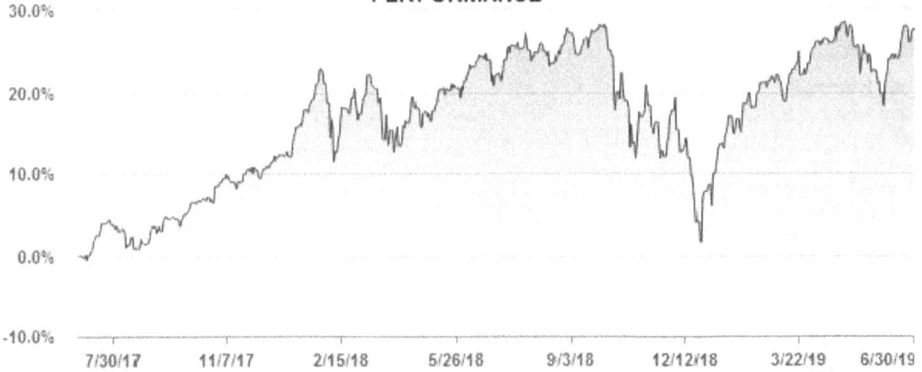

Ratings History

Date	Overall Rating	Risk Rating	Reward Rating
Q2-19	C+	B	C
Q4-18	C	C+	C
Q4-17	B	B	B
Q4-16	B	B	B
Q4-15	C+	C+	C+

Asset & Performance History

Date	NAV	1-Year Total Return
2018	41.83	-3.18
2017	48.55	25.73
2016	41.27	8.11
2015	40.59	5.03
2014	42.01	8.91
2013	42.4	33.38

Total Assets: $193,270,000,000

Asset Allocation

Asset	%
Cash	6%
Stocks	93%
US Stocks	82%
Bonds	0%
US Bonds	0%
Other	0%

Services Offered: Systematic Withdrawal Plan, Automatic Investment Plan, Qualified Investment, Phone Exchange, Retirement Investment

Investment Strategy: The investment seeks growth of capital. The fund invests primarily in common stocks and seeks to invest in companies that appear to offer superior opportunities for growth of capital. It may invest up to 25% of its assets in securities of issuers domiciled outside the United States. The investment adviser uses a system of multiple portfolio managers in managing the fund's assets. Under this approach, the portfolio of the fund is divided into segments managed by individual managers who decide how their respective segments will be invested. **Top Holdings:** Facebook Inc A Microsoft Corp Amazon.com Inc Netflix Inc Alphabet Inc Class C

American Funds The Growth Fund of America® Class 529-A C+ HOLD

Ticker	Traded On	NAV	Total Assets ($)	Dividend Yield (TTM)	Turnover Ratio	Expense Ratio
CGFAX	NAS CM	49.74	$193,270,000,000	0.49	28	0.69

Ratings

Reward	C
Risk	B
Recent Upgrade/Downgrade	

Fund Information

Fund Type	Open End
Category	US Equity Large Cap Growth
Sub-Category	Large Growth
Prospectus Objective	Growth
Inception Date	Feb-02
Open to New Investments	Y
Minimum Initial Investment	250
Minimum Subsequent Investment	50
Front End Fee	5.75
Back End Fee	

Total Returns (%)

3-Month	6-Month	1-Year	3-Year	5-Year
3.45	18.54	4.78	57.05	69.52

Last Bull Market	24.13
Last Bear Market	-19.02
3-Year Standard Deviation	12.98
3-Year Beta	1.01

Company Information

Provider	American Funds
Manager/Tenure	Donald D. O'Neal (25), Michael T. Kerr (20), J. Blair Frank (17), 10 others
Website	http://www.americanfunds.com
Address	American Funds 333 South Hope Street Los Angeles CA 90071-1406 United States
Phone Number	800-421-4225

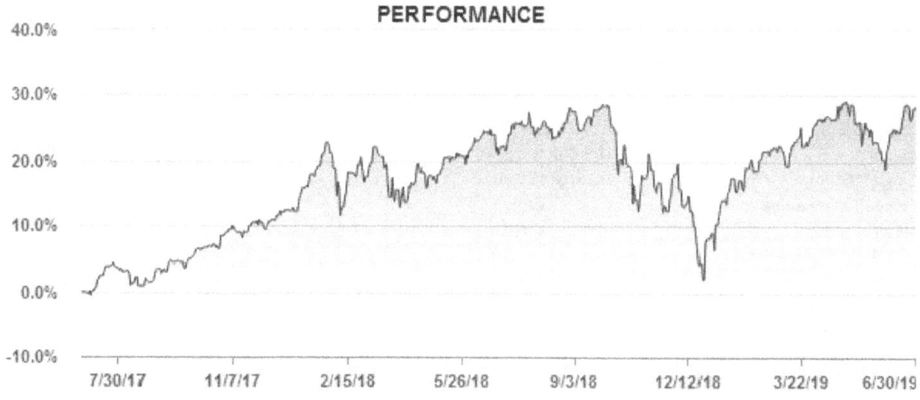

Ratings History

Date	Overall Rating	Risk Rating	Reward Rating
Q2-19	C+	B	C
Q4-18	C	B-	C
Q4-17	B	B	B
Q4-16	B	B	B
Q4-15	C+	C+	C+

Asset & Performance History

Date	NAV	1-Year Total Return
2018	42.26	-2.98
2017	49.03	26.05
2016	41.65	8.35
2015	40.94	5.29
2014	42.34	9.19
2013	42.7	33.69

Total Assets: $193,270,000,000

Asset Allocation

Asset	%
Cash	6%
Stocks	93%
US Stocks	82%
Bonds	0%
US Bonds	0%
Other	0%

Services Offered: Systematic Withdrawal Plan, Automatic Investment Plan, Qualified Investment, Phone Exchange, Retirement Investment

Investment Strategy: The investment seeks growth of capital. The fund invests primarily in common stocks and seeks to invest in companies that appear to offer superior opportunities for growth of capital. It may invest up to 25% of its assets in securities of issuers domiciled outside the United States. The investment adviser uses a system of multiple portfolio managers in managing the fund's assets. Under this approach, the portfolio of the fund is divided into segments managed by individual managers who decide how their respective segments will be invested. **Top Holdings:** Facebook Inc A Microsoft Corp Amazon.com Inc Netflix Inc Alphabet Inc Class C

American Funds The Growth Fund of America® Class R-4 C+ HOLD

Ticker	Traded On	NAV	Total Assets ($)	Dividend Yield (TTM)	Turnover Ratio	Expense Ratio
RGAEX	NAS CM	49.84	$193,270,000,000	0.49	28	0.68

Ratings

Reward	C
Risk	B
Recent Upgrade/Downgrade	Down

Fund Information

Fund Type	Open End
Category	US Equity Large Cap Growth
Sub-Category	Large Growth
Prospectus Objective	Growth
Inception Date	May-02
Open to New Investments	Y
Minimum Initial Investment	250
Minimum Subsequent Investment	50
Front End Fee	
Back End Fee	

Total Returns (%)

3-Month	6-Month	1-Year	3-Year	5-Year
3.46	18.55	4.82	57.18	69.89

Last Bull Market	24.14
Last Bear Market	-19
3-Year Standard Deviation	12.97
3-Year Beta	1.01

Company Information

Provider	American Funds
Manager/Tenure	Donald D. O'Neal (25), Michael T. Kerr (20), J. Blair Frank (17), 10 others
Website	http://www.americanfunds.com
Address	American Funds 333 South Hope Street Los Angeles CA 90071-1406 United States
Phone Number	800-421-4225

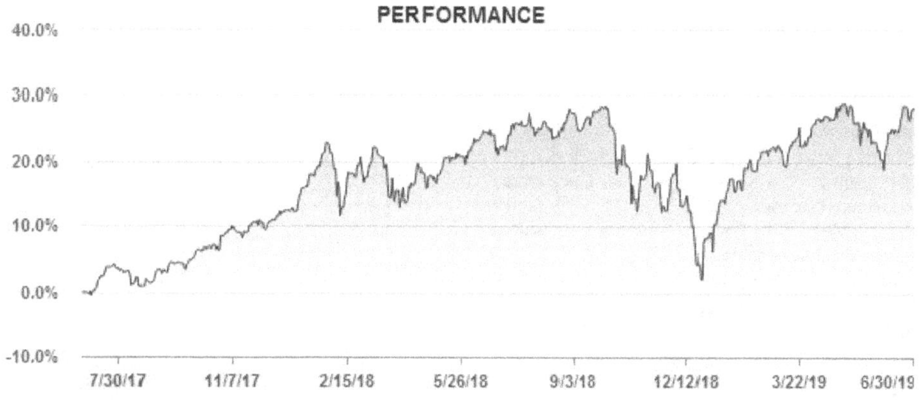

Ratings History

Date	Overall Rating	Risk Rating	Reward Rating
Q2-19	C+	B	C
Q4-18	C	B-	C
Q4-17	B	B	B
Q4-16	B	B	B
Q4-15	C+	C+	C+

Asset & Performance History

Date	NAV	1-Year Total Return
2018	42.34	-2.95
2017	49.1	26.08
2016	41.69	8.43
2015	40.97	5.33
2014	42.37	9.25
2013	42.72	33.82

Total Assets: $193,270,000,000

Asset Allocation

Asset	%
Cash	6%
Stocks	93%
US Stocks	82%
Bonds	0%
US Bonds	0%
Other	0%

Services Offered: Automatic Investment Plan, Qualified Investment, Phone Exchange

Investment Strategy: The investment seeks growth of capital. The fund invests primarily in common stocks and seeks to invest in companies that appear to offer superior opportunities for growth of capital. It may invest up to 25% of its assets in securities of issuers domiciled outside the United States. The investment adviser uses a system of multiple portfolio managers in managing the fund's assets. Under this approach, the portfolio of the fund is divided into segments managed by individual managers who decide how their respective segments will be invested. **Top Holdings:** Facebook Inc A Microsoft Corp Amazon.com Inc Netflix Inc Alphabet Inc Class C

American Funds The Growth Fund of America® Class R-3 C+ HOLD

Ticker	Traded On	NAV	Total Assets ($)	Dividend Yield (TTM)	Turnover Ratio	Expense Ratio
RGACX	NAS CM	49.27	$193,270,000,000	0.18	28	0.98

Ratings

Reward	C
Risk	B
Recent Upgrade/Downgrade	

Fund Information

Fund Type	Open End
Category	US Equity Large Cap Growth
Sub-Category	Large Growth
Prospectus Objective	Growth
Inception Date	May-02
Open to New Investments	Y
Minimum Initial Investment	250
Minimum Subsequent Investment	50
Front End Fee	
Back End Fee	

Total Returns (%)

3-Month	6-Month	1-Year	3-Year	5-Year
3.37	18.38	4.49	55.74	67.36

Last Bull Market	23.96
Last Bear Market	-19.09
3-Year Standard Deviation	12.97
3-Year Beta	1.01

Company Information

Provider	American Funds
Manager/Tenure	Donald D. O'Neal (25), Michael T. Kerr (20), J. Blair Frank (17), 10 others
Website	http://www.americanfunds.com
Address	American Funds 333 South Hope Street Los Angeles CA 90071-1406 United States
Phone Number	800-421-4225

Ratings History

Date	Overall Rating	Risk Rating	Reward Rating
Q2-19	C+	B	C
Q4-18	C	C+	C
Q4-17	B	B	B
Q4-16	B	B	B
Q4-15	C+	C+	C+

Asset & Performance History

Date	NAV	1-Year Total Return
2018	41.92	-3.24
2017	48.63	25.7
2016	41.32	8.11
2015	40.62	5.03
2014	42.02	8.94
2013	42.39	33.42

Total Assets: $193,270,000,000

Asset Allocation

Asset	%
Cash	6%
Stocks	93%
US Stocks	82%
Bonds	0%
US Bonds	0%
Other	0%

Services Offered: Automatic Investment Plan, Qualified Investment, Phone Exchange

Investment Strategy: The investment seeks growth of capital. The fund invests primarily in common stocks and seeks to invest in companies that appear to offer superior opportunities for growth of capital. It may invest up to 25% of its assets in securities of issuers domiciled outside the United States. The investment adviser uses a system of multiple portfolio managers in managing the fund's assets. Under this approach, the portfolio of the fund is divided into segments managed by individual managers who decide how their respective segments will be invested. **Top Holdings:** Facebook Inc A Microsoft Corp Amazon.com Inc Netflix Inc Alphabet Inc Class C

American Funds The Growth Fund of America® Class R-2E C+ HOLD

Ticker	Traded On	NAV	Total Assets ($)	Dividend Yield (TTM)	Turnover Ratio	Expense Ratio
RGEBX	NAS CM	49.27	$193,270,000,000	0.18	28	1.12

Ratings

Reward	C
Risk	B
Recent Upgrade/Downgrade	

Fund Information

Fund Type	Open End
Category	US Equity Large Cap Growth
Sub-Category	Large Growth
Prospectus Objective	Growth
Inception Date	Aug-14
Open to New Investments	Y
Minimum Initial Investment	250
Minimum Subsequent Investment	50
Front End Fee	
Back End Fee	

Total Returns (%)

3-Month	6-Month	1-Year	3-Year	5-Year
3.33	18.29	4.35	55.11	66.75

Last Bull Market	23.89
Last Bear Market	-19.13
3-Year Standard Deviation	12.97
3-Year Beta	1.01

Company Information

Provider	American Funds
Manager/Tenure	Donald D. O'Neal (25), Michael T. Kerr (20), J. Blair Frank (17), 10 others
Website	http://www.americanfunds.com
Address	American Funds 333 South Hope Street Los Angeles CA 90071-1406 United States
Phone Number	800-421-4225

Ratings History

Date	Overall Rating	Risk Rating	Reward Rating
Q2-19	C+	B	C
Q4-18	C	C+	C
Q4-17	B	B	B
Q4-16	B	B	B
Q4-15	C+	C+	C+

Asset & Performance History

Date	NAV	1-Year Total Return
2018	41.95	-3.37
2017	48.73	25.52
2016	41.48	7.98
2015	40.88	4.97
2014	42.57	9.09
2013		33.31

Total Assets: $193,270,000,000

Asset Allocation

Asset	%
Cash	6%
Stocks	93%
US Stocks	82%
Bonds	0%
US Bonds	0%
Other	0%

Services Offered: Automatic Investment Plan, Qualified Investment, Phone Exchange

Investment Strategy: The investment seeks growth of capital. The fund invests primarily in common stocks and seeks to invest in companies that appear to offer superior opportunities for growth of capital. It may invest up to 25% of its assets in securities of issuers domiciled outside the United States. The investment adviser uses a system of multiple portfolio managers in managing the fund's assets. Under this approach, the portfolio of the fund is divided into segments managed by individual managers who decide how their respective segments will be invested. **Top Holdings:** Facebook Inc A Microsoft Corp Amazon.com Inc Netflix Inc Alphabet Inc Class C

American Funds EuroPacific Growth Fund® Class R-5 — C HOLD

Ticker	Traded On	NAV	Total Assets ($)	Dividend Yield (TTM)	Turnover Ratio	Expense Ratio
RERFX	NAS CM	52.77	$161,594,000,000	1.5	35	0.53

Ratings

Reward	C
Risk	B-
Recent Upgrade/Downgrade	

Fund Information

Fund Type	Open End
Category	Global Equity Large Cap
Sub-Category	Foreign Large Growth
Prospectus Objective	Foreign Stock
Inception Date	May-02
Open to New Investments	Y
Minimum Initial Investment	250
Minimum Subsequent Investment	50
Front End Fee	
Back End Fee	

Total Returns (%)

3-Month	6-Month	1-Year	3-Year	5-Year
3.86	18.11	1.85	37.42	24.19

Last Bull Market	17.05
Last Bear Market	-23.93
3-Year Standard Deviation	12.38
3-Year Beta	1.06

Company Information

Provider	American Funds
Manager/Tenure	Mark E. Denning (27), Carl M. Kawaja (18), Nicholas J. Grace (17), 6 others
Website	http://www.americanfunds.com
Address	American Funds 333 South Hope Street Los Angeles CA 90071-1406 United States
Phone Number	800-421-4225

Ratings History

Date	Overall Rating	Risk Rating	Reward Rating
Q2-19	C	B-	C-
Q4-18	D+	C-	D+
Q4-17	B	B	B
Q4-16	C	C+	C-
Q4-15	C	C	C

Asset & Performance History

Date	NAV	1-Year Total Return
2018	44.95	-14.95
2017	56.09	31.08
2016	45.01	1
2015	45.27	-0.53
2014	47.04	-2.35
2013	48.98	20.53

Total Assets: $161,594,000,000

Asset Allocation

Asset	%
Cash	6%
Stocks	94%
US Stocks	1%
Bonds	0%
US Bonds	0%
Other	0%

Services Offered: Automatic Investment Plan, Qualified Investment, Phone Exchange

Investment Strategy: The investment seeks long-term growth of capital. The fund invests primarily in common stocks of issuers in Europe and the Pacific Basin that the investment adviser believes have the potential for growth. Growth stocks are stocks that the investment adviser believes have the potential for above-average capital appreciation. It normally will invest at least 80% of its net assets in securities of issuers in Europe and the Pacific Basin. The fund may invest a portion of its assets in common stocks and other securities of companies in emerging markets. **Top Holdings:** AIA Group Ltd Airbus SE Alibaba Group Holding Ltd ADR Reliance Industries Ltd HDFC Bank Ltd

American Funds EuroPacific Growth Fund® Class R-1 — C HOLD

Ticker	Traded On	NAV	Total Assets ($)	Dividend Yield (TTM)	Turnover Ratio	Expense Ratio
RERAX	NAS CM	50.62	$161,594,000,000	0.59	35	1.6

Ratings

Reward	C
Risk	C+
Recent Upgrade/Downgrade	

Fund Information

Fund Type	Open End
Category	Global Equity Large Cap
Sub-Category	Foreign Large Growth
Prospectus Objective	Foreign Stock
Inception Date	Jun-02
Open to New Investments	Y
Minimum Initial Investment	250
Minimum Subsequent Investment	50
Front End Fee	
Back End Fee	

Total Returns (%)

3-Month	6-Month	1-Year	3-Year	5-Year
3.60	17.50	0.79	33.13	17.77

Last Bull Market	16.33
Last Bear Market	-24.28
3-Year Standard Deviation	12.36
3-Year Beta	1.06

Company Information

Provider	American Funds
Manager/Tenure	Mark E. Denning (27), Carl M. Kawaja (18), Nicholas J. Grace (17), 6 others
Website	http://www.americanfunds.com
Address	American Funds 333 South Hope Street Los Angeles CA 90071-1406 United States
Phone Number	800-421-4225

Ratings History

Date	Overall Rating	Risk Rating	Reward Rating
Q2-19	C	C+	C-
Q4-18	C-	C-	C-
Q4-17	B-	B	B-
Q4-16	C-	C	D+
Q4-15	C	C	C

Asset & Performance History

Date	NAV	1-Year Total Return
2018	43.28	-15.84
2017	54.14	29.7
2016	43.54	-0.08
2015	43.82	-1.57
2014	45.55	-3.37
2013	47.43	19.25

Total Assets: $161,594,000,000

Asset Allocation

Asset	%
Cash	6%
Stocks	94%
US Stocks	1%
Bonds	0%
US Bonds	0%
Other	0%

Services Offered: Automatic Investment Plan, Qualified Investment, Phone Exchange

Investment Strategy: The investment seeks long-term growth of capital. The fund invests primarily in common stocks of issuers in Europe and the Pacific Basin that the investment adviser believes have the potential for growth. Growth stocks are stocks that the investment adviser believes have the potential for above-average capital appreciation. It normally will invest at least 80% of its net assets in securities of issuers in Europe and the Pacific Basin. The fund may invest a portion of its assets in common stocks and other securities of companies in emerging markets. **Top Holdings:** AIA Group Ltd Airbus SE Alibaba Group Holding Ltd ADR Reliance Industries Ltd HDFC Bank Ltd

American Funds EuroPacific Growth Fund® Class 529-F-1 C HOLD

Ticker	Traded On	NAV	Total Assets ($)	Dividend Yield (TTM)	Turnover Ratio	Expense Ratio
CEUFX	NAS CM	52.19	$161,594,000,000	1.42	35	0.65

Ratings

Reward	C
Risk	B-
Recent Upgrade/Downgrade	

Fund Information

Fund Type	Open End
Category	Global Equity Large Cap
Sub-Category	Foreign Large Growth
Prospectus Objective	Foreign Stock
Inception Date	Sep-02
Open to New Investments	Y
Minimum Initial Investment	250
Minimum Subsequent Investment	50
Front End Fee	
Back End Fee	

Total Returns (%)

3-Month	6-Month	1-Year	3-Year	5-Year
3.83	18.05	1.74	36.92	23.37

Last Bull Market	16.95
Last Bear Market	-23.96
3-Year Standard Deviation	12.37
3-Year Beta	1.06

Company Information

Provider	American Funds
Manager/Tenure	Mark E. Denning (27), Carl M. Kawaja (18), Nicholas J. Grace (17), 6 others
Website	http://www.americanfunds.com
Address	American Funds 333 South Hope Street Los Angeles CA 90071-1406 United States
Phone Number	800-421-4225

Ratings History

Date	Overall Rating	Risk Rating	Reward Rating
Q2-19	C	C+	C-
Q4-18	D+	C-	D+
Q4-17	B	B	B
Q4-16	C	C+	C-
Q4-15	C	C	C

Asset & Performance History

Date	NAV	1-Year Total Return
2018	44.47	-15.04
2017	55.53	30.92
2016	44.59	0.82
2015	44.87	-0.65
2014	46.63	-2.49
2013	48.57	20.36

Total Assets: $161,594,000,000

Asset Allocation

Asset	%
Cash	6%
Stocks	94%
US Stocks	1%
Bonds	0%
US Bonds	0%
Other	0%

Services Offered: Systematic Withdrawal Plan, Automatic Investment Plan, Phone Exchange

Investment Strategy: The investment seeks long-term growth of capital. The fund invests primarily in common stocks of issuers in Europe and the Pacific Basin that the investment adviser believes have the potential for growth. Growth stocks are stocks that the investment adviser believes have the potential for above-average capital appreciation. It normally will invest at least 80% of its net assets in securities of issuers in Europe and the Pacific Basin. The fund may invest a portion of its assets in common stocks and other securities of companies in emerging markets. **Top Holdings:** AIA Group Ltd Airbus SE Alibaba Group Holding Ltd ADR Reliance Industries Ltd HDFC Bank Ltd

American Funds EuroPacific Growth Fund® Class R-5E C HOLD

Ticker	Traded On	NAV	Total Assets ($)	Dividend Yield (TTM)	Turnover Ratio	Expense Ratio
RERHX	NAS CM	52.46	$161,594,000,000	1.47	35	0.62

Ratings

Reward	C
Risk	B-
Recent Upgrade/Downgrade	

Fund Information

Fund Type	Open End
Category	Global Equity Large Cap
Sub-Category	Foreign Large Growth
Prospectus Objective	Foreign Stock
Inception Date	Nov-15
Open to New Investments	Y
Minimum Initial Investment	250
Minimum Subsequent Investment	50
Front End Fee	
Back End Fee	

Total Returns (%)

3-Month	6-Month	1-Year	3-Year	5-Year
3.84	18.05	1.76	37.06	23.20

Last Bull Market	16.84
Last Bear Market	-24.03
3-Year Standard Deviation	12.37
3-Year Beta	1.06

Company Information

Provider	American Funds
Manager/Tenure	Mark E. Denning (27), Carl M. Kawaja (18), Nicholas J. Grace (17), 6 others
Website	http://www.americanfunds.com
Address	American Funds 333 South Hope Street Los Angeles CA 90071-1406 United States
Phone Number	800-421-4225

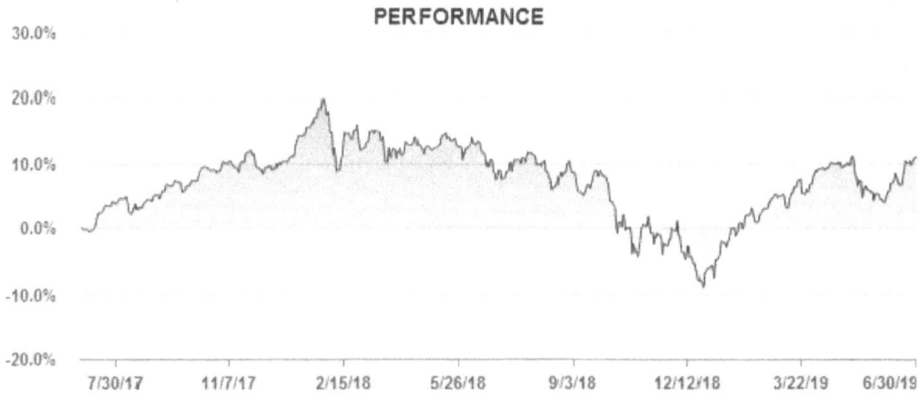

Ratings History

Date	Overall Rating	Risk Rating	Reward Rating
Q2-19	C	C+	C-
Q4-18	D+	C-	D+
Q4-17	B	B	B
Q4-16	C	C+	C-
Q4-15			

Asset & Performance History

Date	NAV	1-Year Total Return
2018	44.7	-15
2017	55.82	30.98
2016	44.84	0.81
2015	45.21	-0.79
2014		-2.64
2013		20.15

Total Assets: $161,594,000,000

Asset Allocation

Asset	%
Cash	6%
Stocks	94%
US Stocks	1%
Bonds	0%
US Bonds	0%
Other	0%

Services Offered: Automatic Investment Plan, Qualified Investment, Phone Exchange

Investment Strategy: The investment seeks long-term growth of capital. The fund invests primarily in common stocks of issuers in Europe and the Pacific Basin that the investment adviser believes have the potential for growth. Growth stocks are stocks that the investment adviser believes have the potential for above-average capital appreciation. It normally will invest at least 80% of its net assets in securities of issuers in Europe and the Pacific Basin. The fund may invest a portion of its assets in common stocks and other securities of companies in emerging markets. **Top Holdings:** AIA Group Ltd Airbus SE Alibaba Group Holding Ltd ADR Reliance Industries Ltd HDFC Bank Ltd

American Funds EuroPacific Growth Fund® Class R-2E — C HOLD

Ticker	Traded On	NAV	Total Assets ($)	Dividend Yield (TTM)	Turnover Ratio	Expense Ratio
REEBX	NAS CM	52.28	$161,594,000,000	0.25	35	1.3

Ratings

Reward	C
Risk	B-
Recent Upgrade/Downgrade	

Fund Information

Fund Type	Open End
Category	Global Equity Large Cap
Sub-Category	Foreign Large Growth
Prospectus Objective	Foreign Stock
Inception Date	Aug-14
Open to New Investments	Y
Minimum Initial Investment	250
Minimum Subsequent Investment	50
Front End Fee	
Back End Fee	

Total Returns (%)

3-Month	6-Month	1-Year	3-Year	5-Year
3.68	17.69	1.07	34.34	19.86

Last Bull Market	16.59
Last Bear Market	-24.14
3-Year Standard Deviation	12.38
3-Year Beta	1.06

Company Information

Provider	American Funds
Manager/Tenure	Mark E. Denning (27), Carl M. Kawaja (18), Nicholas J. Grace (17), 6 others
Website	http://www.americanfunds.com
Address	American Funds 333 South Hope Street Los Angeles CA 90071-1406 United States
Phone Number	800-421-4225

Ratings History

Date	Overall Rating	Risk Rating	Reward Rating
Q2-19	C	C+	C-
Q4-18	C-	C-	C-
Q4-17	B	B	B-
Q4-16	C	C+	C-
Q4-15	C	C	C

Asset & Performance History

Date	NAV	1-Year Total Return
2018	44.63	-15.61
2017	55.39	30.13
2016	44.51	0.28
2015	44.9	-1.19
2014	46.96	-2.94
2013		19.72

Total Assets: $161,594,000,000

Asset Allocation

Asset	%
Cash	6%
Stocks	94%
US Stocks	1%
Bonds	0%
US Bonds	0%
Other	0%

Services Offered: Automatic Investment Plan, Qualified Investment, Phone Exchange

Investment Strategy: The investment seeks long-term growth of capital. The fund invests primarily in common stocks of issuers in Europe and the Pacific Basin that the investment adviser believes have the potential for growth. Growth stocks are stocks that the investment adviser believes have the potential for above-average capital appreciation. It normally will invest at least 80% of its net assets in securities of issuers in Europe and the Pacific Basin. The fund may invest a portion of its assets in common stocks and other securities of companies in emerging markets. **Top Holdings:** AIA Group Ltd Airbus SE Alibaba Group Holding Ltd ADR Reliance Industries Ltd HDFC Bank Ltd

American Funds EuroPacific Growth Fund® Class F-1 — C HOLD

Ticker	Traded On	NAV	Total Assets ($)	Dividend Yield (TTM)	Turnover Ratio	Expense Ratio
AEGFX	NAS CM	52.64	$161,594,000,000	1.15	35	0.87

Ratings

Reward	C
Risk	B-
Recent Upgrade/Downgrade	

Fund Information

Fund Type	Open End
Category	Global Equity Large Cap
Sub-Category	Foreign Large Growth
Prospectus Objective	Foreign Stock
Inception Date	Mar-01
Open to New Investments	Y
Minimum Initial Investment	250
Minimum Subsequent Investment	50
Front End Fee	
Back End Fee	

Total Returns (%)

3-Month	6-Month	1-Year	3-Year	5-Year
3.79	17.91	1.54	36.09	22.19

Last Bull Market	16.84
Last Bear Market	-24.04
3-Year Standard Deviation	12.38
3-Year Beta	1.06

Company Information

Provider	American Funds
Manager/Tenure	Mark E. Denning (27), Carl M. Kawaja (18), Nicholas J. Grace (17), 6 others
Website	http://www.americanfunds.com
Address	American Funds 333 South Hope Street Los Angeles CA 90071-1406 United States
Phone Number	800-421-4225

Ratings History

Date	Overall Rating	Risk Rating	Reward Rating
Q2-19	C	C+	C-
Q4-18	C-	C-	C-
Q4-17	B	B	B
Q4-16	C	C+	C-
Q4-15	C	C	C

Asset & Performance History

Date	NAV	1-Year Total Return
2018	44.87	-15.23
2017	55.96	30.68
2016	44.91	0.65
2015	45.16	-0.85
2014	46.91	-2.66
2013	48.8	20.13

Total Assets: $161,594,000,000

Asset Allocation

Asset	%
Cash	6%
Stocks	94%
US Stocks	1%
Bonds	0%
US Bonds	0%
Other	0%

Services Offered: Systematic Withdrawal Plan, Automatic Investment Plan, Qualified Investment, Phone Exchange

Investment Strategy: The investment seeks long-term growth of capital. The fund invests primarily in common stocks of issuers in Europe and the Pacific Basin that the investment adviser believes have the potential for growth. Growth stocks are stocks that the investment adviser believes have the potential for above-average capital appreciation. It normally will invest at least 80% of its net assets in securities of issuers in Europe and the Pacific Basin. The fund may invest a portion of its assets in common stocks and other securities of companies in emerging markets. **Top Holdings:** AIA Group Ltd Airbus SE Alibaba Group Holding Ltd ADR Reliance Industries Ltd HDFC Bank Ltd

American Funds EuroPacific Growth Fund® Class R-6 — C HOLD

Ticker	Traded On	NAV	Total Assets ($)	Dividend Yield (TTM)	Turnover Ratio	Expense Ratio
RERGX	NAS CM	52.82	$161,594,000,000	1.55	35	0.49

Ratings

Reward	C
Risk	B-
Recent Upgrade/Downgrade	

Fund Information

Fund Type	Open End
Category	Global Equity Large Cap
Sub-Category	Foreign Large Growth
Prospectus Objective	Foreign Stock
Inception Date	May-09
Open to New Investments	Y
Minimum Initial Investment	250
Minimum Subsequent Investment	50
Front End Fee	
Back End Fee	

Total Returns (%)

3-Month	6-Month	1-Year	3-Year	5-Year
3.87	18.13	1.91	37.62	24.47

Last Bull Market	17.06
Last Bear Market	-23.91
3-Year Standard Deviation	12.37
3-Year Beta	1.06

Company Information

Provider	American Funds
Manager/Tenure	Mark E. Denning (27), Carl M. Kawaja (18), Nicholas J. Grace (17), 6 others
Website	http://www.americanfunds.com
Address	American Funds 333 South Hope Street Los Angeles CA 90071-1406 United States
Phone Number	800-421-4225

PERFORMANCE

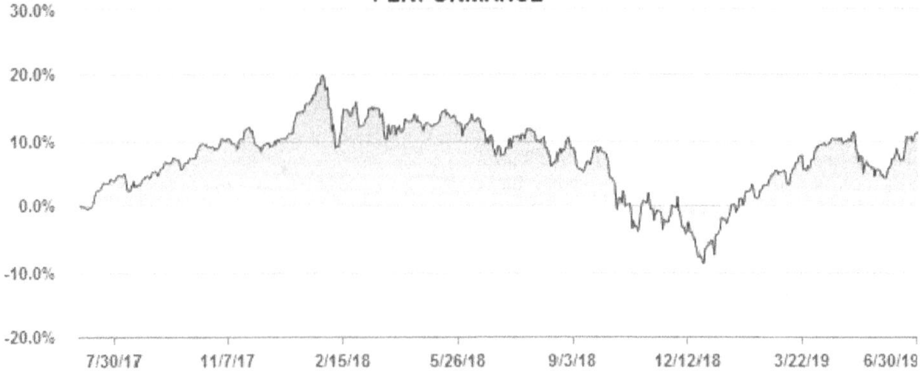

Ratings History

Date	Overall Rating	Risk Rating	Reward Rating
Q2-19	C	B-	C-
Q4-18	D+	C-	D+
Q4-17	B	B	B
Q4-16	C	C+	C-
Q4-15	C	C	C

Asset & Performance History

Date	NAV	1-Year Total Return
2018	44.99	-14.9
2017	56.14	31.17
2016	45.04	1.01
2015	45.32	-0.48
2014	47.09	-2.29
2013	49.03	20.57

Total Assets: $161,594,000,000

Asset Allocation

Asset	%
Cash	6%
Stocks	94%
US Stocks	1%
Bonds	0%
US Bonds	0%
Other	0%

Services Offered: Automatic Investment Plan, Qualified Investment, Phone Exchange

Investment Strategy: The investment seeks long-term growth of capital. The fund invests primarily in common stocks of issuers in Europe and the Pacific Basin that the investment adviser believes have the potential for growth. Growth stocks are stocks that the investment adviser believes have the potential for above-average capital appreciation. It normally will invest at least 80% of its net assets in securities of issuers in Europe and the Pacific Basin. The fund may invest a portion of its assets in common stocks and other securities of companies in emerging markets. **Top Holdings:** AIA Group Ltd Airbus SE Alibaba Group Holding Ltd ADR Reliance Industries Ltd HDFC Bank Ltd

American Funds EuroPacific Growth Fund® Class A — C HOLD

Ticker	Traded On	NAV	Total Assets ($)	Dividend Yield (TTM)	Turnover Ratio	Expense Ratio
AEPGX	NAS CM	52.89	$161,594,000,000	1.21	35	0.83

Ratings

Reward	C
Risk	B-
Recent Upgrade/Downgrade	

Fund Information

Fund Type	Open End
Category	Global Equity Large Cap
Sub-Category	Foreign Large Growth
Prospectus Objective	Foreign Stock
Inception Date	Apr-84
Open to New Investments	Y
Minimum Initial Investment	250
Minimum Subsequent Investment	50
Front End Fee	5.75
Back End Fee	

Total Returns (%)

3-Month	6-Month	1-Year	3-Year	5-Year
3.79	17.95	1.56	36.25	22.37

Last Bull Market	16.84
Last Bear Market	-24.03
3-Year Standard Deviation	12.38
3-Year Beta	1.06

Company Information

Provider	American Funds
Manager/Tenure	Mark E. Denning (27), Carl M. Kawaja (18), Nicholas J. Grace (17), 6 others
Website	http://www.americanfunds.com
Address	American Funds 333 South Hope Street Los Angeles CA 90071-1406 United States
Phone Number	800-421-4225

PERFORMANCE

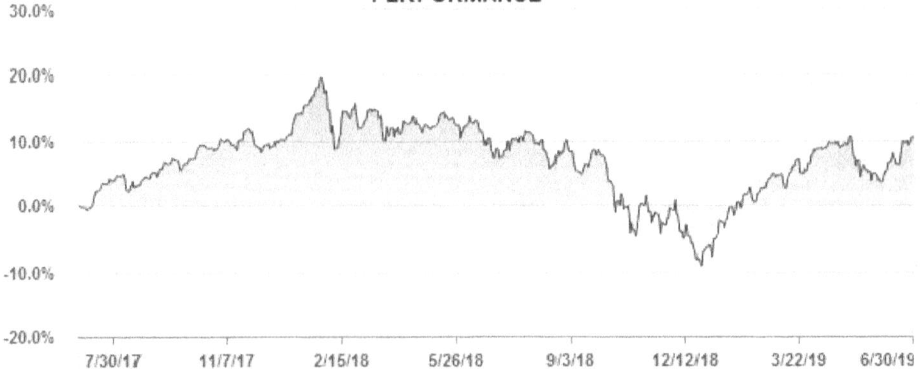

Ratings History

Date	Overall Rating	Risk Rating	Reward Rating
Q2-19	C	C+	C-
Q4-18	D+	C-	D+
Q4-17	B	B	B
Q4-16	C	C+	C-
Q4-15	C	C	C

Asset & Performance History

Date	NAV	1-Year Total Return
2018	45.08	-15.19
2017	56.22	30.72
2016	45.11	0.66
2015	45.37	-0.82
2014	47.13	-2.64
2013	49.07	20.15

Total Assets: $161,594,000,000

Asset Allocation

Asset	%
Cash	6%
Stocks	94%
US Stocks	1%
Bonds	0%
US Bonds	0%
Other	0%

Services Offered: Systematic Withdrawal Plan, Automatic Investment Plan, Phone Exchange

Investment Strategy: The investment seeks long-term growth of capital. The fund invests primarily in common stocks of issuers in Europe and the Pacific Basin that the investment adviser believes have the potential for growth. Growth stocks are stocks that the investment adviser believes have the potential for above-average capital appreciation. It normally will invest at least 80% of its net assets in securities of issuers in Europe and the Pacific Basin. The fund may invest a portion of its assets in common stocks and other securities of companies in emerging markets. **Top Holdings:** AIA Group Ltd Airbus SE Alibaba Group Holding Ltd ADR Reliance Industries Ltd HDFC Bank Ltd

American Funds EuroPacific Growth Fund® Class R-2 C HOLD

Ticker	Traded On	NAV	Total Assets ($)	Dividend Yield (TTM)	Turnover Ratio	Expense Ratio
RERBX	NAS CM	51.08	$161,594,000,000	0.6	35	1.59

Ratings

Reward C
Risk C+
Recent Upgrade/Downgrade

Fund Information

Fund Type	Open End
Category	Global Equity Large Cap
Sub-Category	Foreign Large Growth
Prospectus Objective	Foreign Stock
Inception Date	May-02
Open to New Investments	Y
Minimum Initial Investment	250
Minimum Subsequent Investment	50
Front End Fee	
Back End Fee	

Total Returns (%)

3-Month	6-Month	1-Year	3-Year	5-Year
3.61	17.50	0.79	33.18	17.87

Last Bull Market	16.33
Last Bear Market	-24.29
3-Year Standard Deviation	12.36
3-Year Beta	1.05

Company Information

Provider: American Funds
Manager/Tenure: Mark E. Denning (27), Carl M. Kawaja (18), Nicholas J. Grace (17), 6 others
Website: http://www.americanfunds.com
Address: American Funds 333 South Hope Street Los Angeles CA 90071-1406 United States
Phone Number: 800-421-4225

PERFORMANCE

Ratings History

Date	Overall Rating	Risk Rating	Reward Rating
Q2-19	C	C+	C-
Q4-18	C-	C-	C-
Q4-17	B	B	B-
Q4-16	C-	C	D+
Q4-15	C	C	C

Asset & Performance History

Date	NAV	1-Year Total Return
2018	43.67	-15.85
2017	54.61	29.72
2016	43.9	-0.06
2015	44.15	-1.52
2014	45.87	-3.37
2013	47.75	19.26

Total Assets: $161,594,000,000

Asset Allocation

Asset	%
Cash	6%
Stocks	94%
US Stocks	1%
Bonds	0%
US Bonds	0%
Other	0%

Services Offered: Automatic Investment Plan, Qualified Investment, Phone Exchange

Investment Strategy: The investment seeks long-term growth of capital. The fund invests primarily in common stocks of issuers in Europe and the Pacific Basin that the investment adviser believes have the potential for growth. Growth stocks are stocks that the investment adviser believes have the potential for above-average capital appreciation. It normally will invest at least 80% of its net assets in securities of issuers in Europe and the Pacific Basin. The fund may invest a portion of its assets in common stocks and other securities of companies in emerging markets. **Top Holdings:** AIA Group Ltd Airbus SE Alibaba Group Holding Ltd ADR Reliance Industries Ltd HDFC Bank Ltd

American Funds EuroPacific Growth Fund® Class R-4 C HOLD

Ticker	Traded On	NAV	Total Assets ($)	Dividend Yield (TTM)	Turnover Ratio	Expense Ratio
REREX	NAS CM	51.76	$161,594,000,000	1.22	35	0.84

Ratings

Reward C
Risk B-
Recent Upgrade/Downgrade

Fund Information

Fund Type	Open End
Category	Global Equity Large Cap
Sub-Category	Foreign Large Growth
Prospectus Objective	Foreign Stock
Inception Date	Jun-02
Open to New Investments	Y
Minimum Initial Investment	250
Minimum Subsequent Investment	50
Front End Fee	
Back End Fee	

Total Returns (%)

3-Month	6-Month	1-Year	3-Year	5-Year
3.77	17.93	1.56	36.19	22.34

Last Bull Market	16.84
Last Bear Market	-24.05
3-Year Standard Deviation	12.38
3-Year Beta	1.06

Company Information

Provider: American Funds
Manager/Tenure: Mark E. Denning (27), Carl M. Kawaja (18), Nicholas J. Grace (17), 6 others
Website: http://www.americanfunds.com
Address: American Funds 333 South Hope Street Los Angeles CA 90071-1406 United States
Phone Number: 800-421-4225

PERFORMANCE

Ratings History

Date	Overall Rating	Risk Rating	Reward Rating
Q2-19	C	C+	C-
Q4-18	C-	C-	C-
Q4-17	B	B	B
Q4-16	C	C+	C-
Q4-15	C	C	C

Asset & Performance History

Date	NAV	1-Year Total Return
2018	44.12	-15.21
2017	55.09	30.7
2016	44.25	0.68
2015	44.51	-0.82
2014	46.26	-2.65
2013	48.18	20.16

Total Assets: $161,594,000,000

Asset Allocation

Asset	%
Cash	6%
Stocks	94%
US Stocks	1%
Bonds	0%
US Bonds	0%
Other	0%

Services Offered: Automatic Investment Plan, Qualified Investment, Phone Exchange

Investment Strategy: The investment seeks long-term growth of capital. The fund invests primarily in common stocks of issuers in Europe and the Pacific Basin that the investment adviser believes have the potential for growth. Growth stocks are stocks that the investment adviser believes have the potential for above-average capital appreciation. It normally will invest at least 80% of its net assets in securities of issuers in Europe and the Pacific Basin. The fund may invest a portion of its assets in common stocks and other securities of companies in emerging markets. **Top Holdings:** AIA Group Ltd Airbus SE Alibaba Group Holding Ltd ADR Reliance Industries Ltd HDFC Bank Ltd

American Funds EuroPacific Growth Fund® Class C — C HOLD

Ticker	Traded On	NAV	Total Assets ($)	Dividend Yield (TTM)	Turnover Ratio	Expense Ratio
AEPCX	NAS CM	51.48	$161,594,000,000	0.54	35	1.61

Ratings

Reward	C
Risk	C+
Recent Upgrade/Downgrade	

Fund Information

Fund Type	Open End
Category	Global Equity Large Cap
Sub-Category	Foreign Large Growth
Prospectus Objective	Foreign Stock
Inception Date	Mar-01
Open to New Investments	Y
Minimum Initial Investment	250
Minimum Subsequent Investment	50
Front End Fee	
Back End Fee	1.00

Total Returns (%)

3-Month	6-Month	1-Year	3-Year	5-Year
3.58	17.48	0.79	33.09	17.68

Last Bull Market	16.33
Last Bear Market	-24.28
3-Year Standard Deviation	12.37
3-Year Beta	1.06

Company Information

Provider: American Funds
Manager/Tenure: Mark E. Denning (27), Carl M. Kawaja (18), Nicholas J. Grace (17), 6 others
Website: http://www.americanfunds.com
Address: American Funds 333 South Hope Street Los Angeles CA 90071-1406 United States
Phone Number: 800-421-4225

PERFORMANCE

Ratings History

Date	Overall Rating	Risk Rating	Reward Rating
Q2-19	C	C+	C-
Q4-18	C-	C-	C-
Q4-17	B-	B	B-
Q4-16	C-	C	D+
Q4-15	C	C	C

Asset & Performance History

Date	NAV	1-Year Total Return
2018	44.02	-15.85
2017	55	29.7
2016	44.19	-0.11
2015	44.4	-1.59
2014	46.13	-3.39
2013	48.01	19.22

Total Assets: $161,594,000,000

Asset Allocation

Asset	%
Cash	6%
Stocks	94%
US Stocks	1%
Bonds	0%
US Bonds	0%
Other	0%

Services Offered: Systematic Withdrawal Plan, Automatic Investment Plan, Phone Exchange

Investment Strategy: The investment seeks long-term growth of capital. The fund invests primarily in common stocks of issuers in Europe and the Pacific Basin that the investment adviser believes have the potential for growth. Growth stocks are stocks that the investment adviser believes have the potential for above-average capital appreciation. It normally will invest at least 80% of its net assets in securities of issuers in Europe and the Pacific Basin. The fund may invest a portion of its assets in common stocks and other securities of companies in emerging markets. **Top Holdings:** AIA Group Ltd Airbus SE Alibaba Group Holding Ltd ADR Reliance Industries Ltd HDFC Bank Ltd

American Funds EuroPacific Growth Fund® Class F-2 — C HOLD

Ticker	Traded On	NAV	Total Assets ($)	Dividend Yield (TTM)	Turnover Ratio	Expense Ratio
AEPFX	NAS CM	52.72	$161,594,000,000	1.46	35	0.58

Ratings

Reward	C
Risk	B-
Recent Upgrade/Downgrade	

Fund Information

Fund Type	Open End
Category	Global Equity Large Cap
Sub-Category	Foreign Large Growth
Prospectus Objective	Foreign Stock
Inception Date	Aug-08
Open to New Investments	Y
Minimum Initial Investment	250
Minimum Subsequent Investment	50
Front End Fee	
Back End Fee	

Total Returns (%)

3-Month	6-Month	1-Year	3-Year	5-Year
3.85	18.09	1.82	37.22	23.85

Last Bull Market	17.03
Last Bear Market	-23.96
3-Year Standard Deviation	12.39
3-Year Beta	1.06

Company Information

Provider: American Funds
Manager/Tenure: Mark E. Denning (27), Carl M. Kawaja (18), Nicholas J. Grace (17), 6 others
Website: http://www.americanfunds.com
Address: American Funds 333 South Hope Street Los Angeles CA 90071-1406 United States
Phone Number: 800-421-4225

PERFORMANCE

Ratings History

Date	Overall Rating	Risk Rating	Reward Rating
Q2-19	C	C+	C-
Q4-18	D+	C-	D+
Q4-17	B	B	B
Q4-16	C	C+	C-
Q4-15	C	C	C

Asset & Performance History

Date	NAV	1-Year Total Return
2018	44.91	-14.98
2017	56.04	31.02
2016	44.97	0.91
2015	45.25	-0.57
2014	47.02	-2.4
2013	48.98	20.44

Total Assets: $161,594,000,000

Asset Allocation

Asset	%
Cash	6%
Stocks	94%
US Stocks	1%
Bonds	0%
US Bonds	0%
Other	0%

Services Offered: Systematic Withdrawal Plan, Automatic Investment Plan, Qualified Investment, Phone Exchange

Investment Strategy: The investment seeks long-term growth of capital. The fund invests primarily in common stocks of issuers in Europe and the Pacific Basin that the investment adviser believes have the potential for growth. Growth stocks are stocks that the investment adviser believes have the potential for above-average capital appreciation. It normally will invest at least 80% of its net assets in securities of issuers in Europe and the Pacific Basin. The fund may invest a portion of its assets in common stocks and other securities of companies in emerging markets. **Top Holdings:** AIA Group Ltd Airbus SE Alibaba Group Holding Ltd ADR Reliance Industries Ltd HDFC Bank Ltd

American Funds EuroPacific Growth Fund® Class 529-A — C HOLD

Ticker	Traded On	NAV	Total Assets ($)	Dividend Yield (TTM)	Turnover Ratio	Expense Ratio
CEUAX	NAS CM	52.22	$161,594,000,000	1.18	35	0.89

Ratings

Reward	C
Risk	B-
Recent Upgrade/Downgrade	

Fund Information

Fund Type	Open End
Category	Global Equity Large Cap
Sub-Category	Foreign Large Growth
Prospectus Objective	Foreign Stock
Inception Date	Feb-02
Open to New Investments	Y
Minimum Initial Investment	250
Minimum Subsequent Investment	50
Front End Fee	5.75
Back End Fee	

Total Returns (%)

3-Month	6-Month	1-Year	3-Year	5-Year
3.77	17.89	1.49	36.00	22.03

Last Bull Market	16.82
Last Bear Market	-24.05
3-Year Standard Deviation	12.38
3-Year Beta	1.06

Company Information

Provider	American Funds
Manager/Tenure	Mark E. Denning (27), Carl M. Kawaja (18), Nicholas J. Grace (17), 6 others
Website	http://www.americanfunds.com
Address	American Funds 333 South Hope Street Los Angeles CA 90071-1406 United States
Phone Number	800-421-4225

PERFORMANCE

Ratings History

Date	Overall Rating	Risk Rating	Reward Rating
Q2-19	C	C+	C-
Q4-18	C-	C-	C-
Q4-17	B	B	B
Q4-16	C	C+	C-
Q4-15	C	C	C

Asset & Performance History

Date	NAV	1-Year Total Return
2018	44.52	-15.25
2017	55.57	30.65
2016	44.63	0.62
2015	44.9	-0.9
2014	46.67	-2.66
2013	48.59	20.08

Total Assets: $161,594,000,000

Asset Allocation

Asset	%
Cash	6%
Stocks	94%
US Stocks	1%
Bonds	0%
US Bonds	0%
Other	0%

Services Offered: Systematic Withdrawal Plan, Automatic Investment Plan, Phone Exchange

Investment Strategy: The investment seeks long-term growth of capital. The fund invests primarily in common stocks of issuers in Europe and the Pacific Basin that the investment adviser believes have the potential for growth. Growth stocks are stocks that the investment adviser believes have the potential for above-average capital appreciation. It normally will invest at least 80% of its net assets in securities of issuers in Europe and the Pacific Basin. The fund may invest a portion of its assets in common stocks and other securities of companies in emerging markets. **Top Holdings:** AIA Group Ltd Airbus SE Alibaba Group Holding Ltd ADR Reliance Industries Ltd HDFC Bank Ltd

American Funds EuroPacific Growth Fund® Class R-3 — C HOLD

Ticker	Traded On	NAV	Total Assets ($)	Dividend Yield (TTM)	Turnover Ratio	Expense Ratio
RERCX	NAS CM	51.71	$161,594,000,000	0.91	35	1.14

Ratings

Reward	C
Risk	B-
Recent Upgrade/Downgrade	

Fund Information

Fund Type	Open End
Category	Global Equity Large Cap
Sub-Category	Foreign Large Growth
Prospectus Objective	Foreign Stock
Inception Date	May-02
Open to New Investments	Y
Minimum Initial Investment	250
Minimum Subsequent Investment	50
Front End Fee	
Back End Fee	

Total Returns (%)

3-Month	6-Month	1-Year	3-Year	5-Year
3.71	17.76	1.24	34.97	20.53

Last Bull Market	16.64
Last Bear Market	-24.13
3-Year Standard Deviation	12.37
3-Year Beta	1.06

Company Information

Provider	American Funds
Manager/Tenure	Mark E. Denning (27), Carl M. Kawaja (18), Nicholas J. Grace (17), 6 others
Website	http://www.americanfunds.com
Address	American Funds 333 South Hope Street Los Angeles CA 90071-1406 United States
Phone Number	800-421-4225

PERFORMANCE

Ratings History

Date	Overall Rating	Risk Rating	Reward Rating
Q2-19	C	C+	C-
Q4-18	C-	C-	C-
Q4-17	B	B	B
Q4-16	C	C+	C-
Q4-15	C	C	C

Asset & Performance History

Date	NAV	1-Year Total Return
2018	44.11	-15.47
2017	55.09	30.31
2016	44.25	0.38
2015	44.5	-1.12
2014	46.24	-2.91
2013	48.13	19.78

Total Assets: $161,594,000,000

Asset Allocation

Asset	%
Cash	6%
Stocks	94%
US Stocks	1%
Bonds	0%
US Bonds	0%
Other	0%

Services Offered: Automatic Investment Plan, Qualified Investment, Phone Exchange

Investment Strategy: The investment seeks long-term growth of capital. The fund invests primarily in common stocks of issuers in Europe and the Pacific Basin that the investment adviser believes have the potential for growth. Growth stocks are stocks that the investment adviser believes have the potential for above-average capital appreciation. It normally will invest at least 80% of its net assets in securities of issuers in Europe and the Pacific Basin. The fund may invest a portion of its assets in common stocks and other securities of companies in emerging markets. **Top Holdings:** AIA Group Ltd Airbus SE Alibaba Group Holding Ltd ADR Reliance Industries Ltd HDFC Bank Ltd

American Funds EuroPacific Growth Fund® Class 529-E C HOLD

Ticker	Traded On	NAV	Total Assets ($)	Dividend Yield (TTM)	Turnover Ratio	Expense Ratio
CEUEX	NAS CM	51.72	$161,594,000,000	0.96	35	1.12

Ratings

Reward	C
Risk	B-
Recent Upgrade/Downgrade	

Fund Information

Fund Type	Open End
Category	Global Equity Large Cap
Sub-Category	Foreign Large Growth
Prospectus Objective	Foreign Stock
Inception Date	Mar-02
Open to New Investments	Y
Minimum Initial Investment	250
Minimum Subsequent Investment	50
Front End Fee	
Back End Fee	

Total Returns (%)

3-Month	6-Month	1-Year	3-Year	5-Year
3.71	17.76	1.29	35.07	20.59

Last Bull Market	16.64
Last Bear Market	-24.14
3-Year Standard Deviation	12.38
3-Year Beta	1.06

Company Information

Provider	American Funds
Manager/Tenure	Mark E. Denning (27), Carl M. Kawaja (18), Nicholas J. Grace (17), 6 others
Website	http://www.americanfunds.com
Address	American Funds 333 South Hope Street Los Angeles CA 90071-1406 United States
Phone Number	800-421-4225

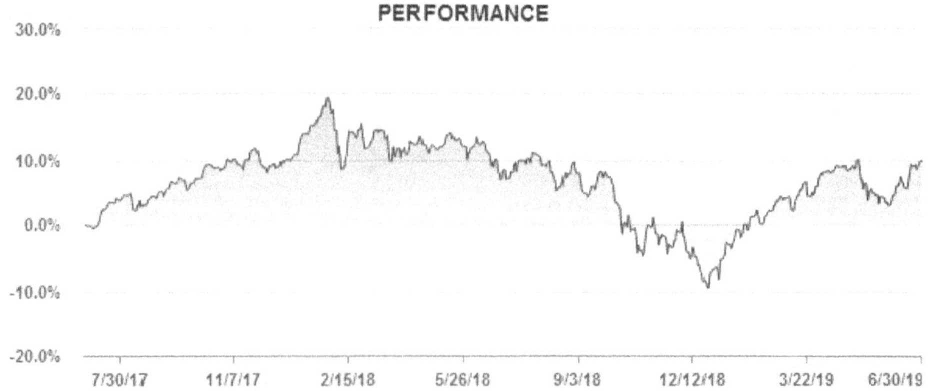

Ratings History

Date	Overall Rating	Risk Rating	Reward Rating
Q2-19	C	C+	C-
Q4-18	C-	C-	C-
Q4-17	B	B	B
Q4-16	C	C+	C-
Q4-15	C	C	C

Asset & Performance History

Date	NAV	1-Year Total Return
2018	44.12	-15.43
2017	55.11	30.33
2016	44.28	0.38
2015	44.55	-1.13
2014	46.31	-2.92
2013	48.22	19.78

Total Assets: $161,594,000,000

Asset Allocation

Asset	%
Cash	6%
Stocks	94%
US Stocks	1%
Bonds	0%
US Bonds	0%
Other	0%

Services Offered: Systematic Withdrawal Plan, Automatic Investment Plan, Phone Exchange

Investment Strategy: The investment seeks long-term growth of capital. The fund invests primarily in common stocks of issuers in Europe and the Pacific Basin that the investment adviser believes have the potential for growth. Growth stocks are stocks that the investment adviser believes have the potential for above-average capital appreciation. It normally will invest at least 80% of its net assets in securities of issuers in Europe and the Pacific Basin. The fund may invest a portion of its assets in common stocks and other securities of companies in emerging markets. **Top Holdings:** AIA Group Ltd Airbus SE Alibaba Group Holding Ltd ADR Reliance Industries Ltd HDFC Bank Ltd

American Funds EuroPacific Growth Fund® Class 529-C C HOLD

Ticker	Traded On	NAV	Total Assets ($)	Dividend Yield (TTM)	Turnover Ratio	Expense Ratio
CEUCX	NAS CM	50.94	$161,594,000,000	0.55	35	1.66

Ratings

Reward	C
Risk	C+
Recent Upgrade/Downgrade	

Fund Information

Fund Type	Open End
Category	Global Equity Large Cap
Sub-Category	Foreign Large Growth
Prospectus Objective	Foreign Stock
Inception Date	Feb-02
Open to New Investments	Y
Minimum Initial Investment	250
Minimum Subsequent Investment	50
Front End Fee	
Back End Fee	1.00

Total Returns (%)

3-Month	6-Month	1-Year	3-Year	5-Year
3.57	17.48	0.75	32.92	17.40

Last Bull Market	16.27
Last Bear Market	-24.31
3-Year Standard Deviation	12.37
3-Year Beta	1.06

Company Information

Provider	American Funds
Manager/Tenure	Mark E. Denning (27), Carl M. Kawaja (18), Nicholas J. Grace (17), 6 others
Website	http://www.americanfunds.com
Address	American Funds 333 South Hope Street Los Angeles CA 90071-1406 United States
Phone Number	800-421-4225

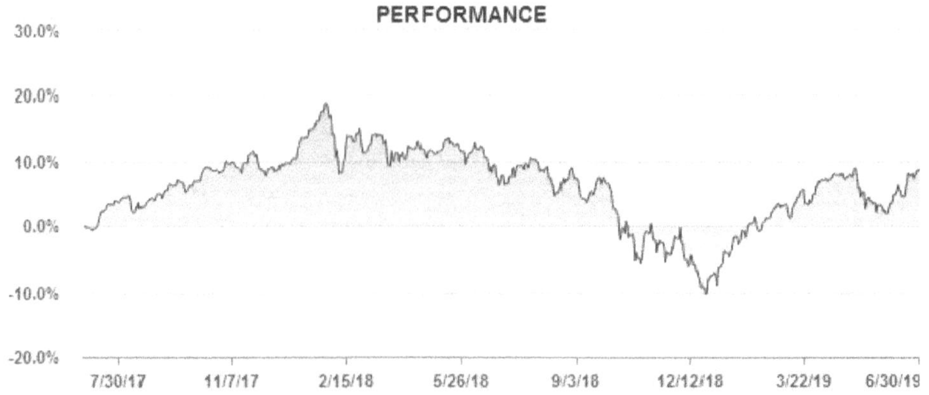

Ratings History

Date	Overall Rating	Risk Rating	Reward Rating
Q2-19	C	C+	C-
Q4-18	C-	C-	C-
Q4-17	B-	B	B-
Q4-16	C-	C	D+
Q4-15	C	C	C

Asset & Performance History

Date	NAV	1-Year Total Return
2018	43.56	-15.88
2017	54.47	29.64
2016	43.77	-0.17
2015	44.04	-1.65
2014	45.78	-3.46
2013	47.68	19.14

Total Assets: $161,594,000,000

Asset Allocation

Asset	%
Cash	6%
Stocks	94%
US Stocks	1%
Bonds	0%
US Bonds	0%
Other	0%

Services Offered: Systematic Withdrawal Plan, Automatic Investment Plan, Phone Exchange

Investment Strategy: The investment seeks long-term growth of capital. The fund invests primarily in common stocks of issuers in Europe and the Pacific Basin that the investment adviser believes have the potential for growth. Growth stocks are stocks that the investment adviser believes have the potential for above-average capital appreciation. It normally will invest at least 80% of its net assets in securities of issuers in Europe and the Pacific Basin. The fund may invest a portion of its assets in common stocks and other securities of companies in emerging markets. **Top Holdings:** AIA Group Ltd Airbus SE Alibaba Group Holding Ltd ADR Reliance Industries Ltd HDFC Bank Ltd

American Funds American Balanced Fund® Class R-1 — B BUY

Ticker	Traded On	NAV	Total Assets ($)	Dividend Yield (TTM)	Turnover Ratio	Expense Ratio
RLBAX	NAS CM	27.13	$146,710,000,000	1.09	72	1.37

Ratings

Reward	C
Risk	A
Recent Upgrade/Downgrade	Up

Fund Information

Fund Type	Open End
Category	Moderate Alloc
Sub-Category	Alloc--50% to 70% Equity
Prospectus Objective	Balanced
Inception Date	May-02
Open to New Investments	Y
Minimum Initial Investment	250
Minimum Subsequent Investment	50
Front End Fee	
Back End Fee	

Total Returns (%)

3-Month	6-Month	1-Year	3-Year	5-Year
2.61	11.04	6.11	27.01	37.25

Last Bull Market	16.93
Last Bear Market	-10.27
3-Year Standard Deviation	6.98
3-Year Beta	0.56

Company Information

Provider	American Funds
Manager/Tenure	Hilda L. Applbaum (20), Gregory D. Johnson (16), Alan N. Berro (13), 7 others
Website	http://www.americanfunds.com
Address	American Funds 333 South Hope Street Los Angeles CA 90071-1406 United States
Phone Number	800-421-4225

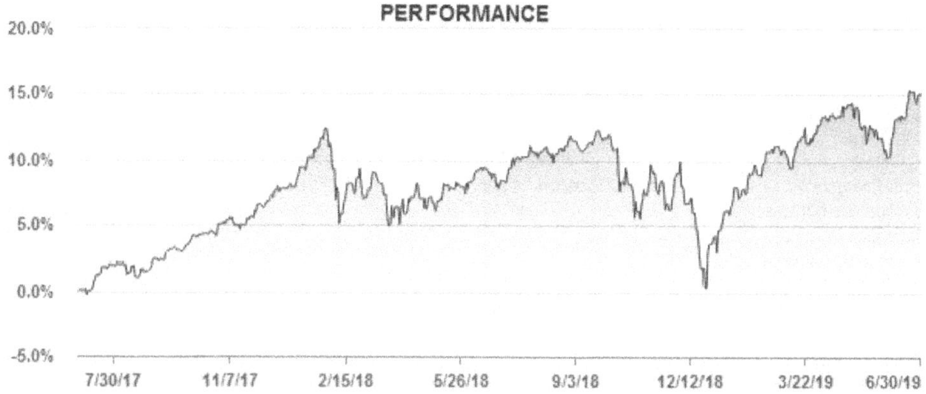

Ratings History

Date	Overall Rating	Risk Rating	Reward Rating
Q2-19	B	A-	C
Q4-18	C	B-	C
Q4-17	B	B+	C+
Q4-16	B	B+	B-
Q4-15	C+	B-	C

Asset & Performance History

Date	NAV	1-Year Total Return
2018	24.72	-3.48
2017	26.96	14.55
2016	24.64	7.74
2015	23.68	0.88
2014	24.61	8.05
2013	24.28	20.76

Total Assets: $146,710,000,000

Asset Allocation

Asset	%
Cash	6%
Stocks	62%
US Stocks	54%
Bonds	32%
US Bonds	29%
Other	0%

Services Offered: Automatic Investment Plan, Qualified Investment, Phone Exchange

Investment Strategy: The investment seeks conservation of capital, current income and long-term growth of capital and income. The fund uses a balanced approach to invest in a broad range of securities, including common stocks and investment-grade bonds. It also invests in securities issued and guaranteed by the U.S. government and by federal agencies and instrumentalities. In addition, the fund may invest a portion of its assets in common stocks, most of which have a history of paying dividends, bonds and other securities of issuers domiciled outside the United States. **Top Holdings:** Microsoft Corp UnitedHealth Group Inc The Home Depot Inc Berkshire Hathaway Inc A Philip Morris International Inc

American Funds American Balanced Fund® Class 529-C — B BUY

Ticker	Traded On	NAV	Total Assets ($)	Dividend Yield (TTM)	Turnover Ratio	Expense Ratio
CLBCX	NAS CM	27.29	$146,710,000,000	1.05	72	1.41

Ratings

Reward	C
Risk	A
Recent Upgrade/Downgrade	Up

Fund Information

Fund Type	Open End
Category	Moderate Alloc
Sub-Category	Alloc--50% to 70% Equity
Prospectus Objective	Balanced
Inception Date	Feb-02
Open to New Investments	Y
Minimum Initial Investment	250
Minimum Subsequent Investment	50
Front End Fee	
Back End Fee	1.00

Total Returns (%)

3-Month	6-Month	1-Year	3-Year	5-Year
2.62	11.03	6.12	26.92	36.89

Last Bull Market	16.81
Last Bear Market	-10.27
3-Year Standard Deviation	7
3-Year Beta	0.56

Company Information

Provider	American Funds
Manager/Tenure	Hilda L. Applbaum (20), Gregory D. Johnson (16), Alan N. Berro (13), 7 others
Website	http://www.americanfunds.com
Address	American Funds 333 South Hope Street Los Angeles CA 90071-1406 United States
Phone Number	800-421-4225

Ratings History

Date	Overall Rating	Risk Rating	Reward Rating
Q2-19	B-	A-	C
Q4-18	C	B-	C
Q4-17	B	B	C+
Q4-16	B	B+	B-
Q4-15	C+	B-	C

Asset & Performance History

Date	NAV	1-Year Total Return
2018	24.86	-3.53
2017	27.11	14.54
2016	24.75	7.63
2015	23.79	0.88
2014	24.7	7.89
2013	24.38	20.67

Total Assets: $146,710,000,000

Asset Allocation

Asset	%
Cash	6%
Stocks	62%
US Stocks	54%
Bonds	32%
US Bonds	29%
Other	0%

Services Offered: Systematic Withdrawal Plan, Automatic Investment Plan, Qualified Investment, Phone Exchange, Retirement Investment

Investment Strategy: The investment seeks conservation of capital, current income and long-term growth of capital and income. The fund uses a balanced approach to invest in a broad range of securities, including common stocks and investment-grade bonds. It also invests in securities issued and guaranteed by the U.S. government and by federal agencies and instrumentalities. In addition, the fund may invest a portion of its assets in common stocks, most of which have a history of paying dividends, bonds and other securities of issuers domiciled outside the United States. **Top Holdings:** Microsoft Corp UnitedHealth Group Inc The Home Depot Inc Berkshire Hathaway Inc A Philip Morris International Inc

American Funds American Balanced Fund® Class R-6 B BUY

Ticker	Traded On	NAV	Total Assets ($)	Dividend Yield (TTM)	Turnover Ratio	Expense Ratio
RLBGX	NAS CM	27.34	$146,710,000,000	2.11	72	0.28

Ratings

Reward	C
Risk	A
Recent Upgrade/Downgrade	

Fund Information

Fund Type	Open End
Category	Moderate Alloc
Sub-Category	Alloc--50% to 70% Equity
Prospectus Objective	Balanced
Inception Date	May-09
Open to New Investments	Y
Minimum Initial Investment	250
Minimum Subsequent Investment	50
Front End Fee	
Back End Fee	

Total Returns (%)

3-Month	6-Month	1-Year	3-Year	5-Year
2.90	11.67	7.31	31.26	44.98

Last Bull Market	17.71
Last Bear Market	-9.86
3-Year Standard Deviation	7.01
3-Year Beta	0.56

Company Information

Provider	American Funds
Manager/Tenure	Hilda L. Applbaum (20), Gregory D. Johnson (16), Alan N. Berro (13), 7 others
Website	http://www.americanfunds.com
Address	American Funds 333 South Hope Street Los Angeles CA 90071-1406 United States
Phone Number	800-421-4225

PERFORMANCE

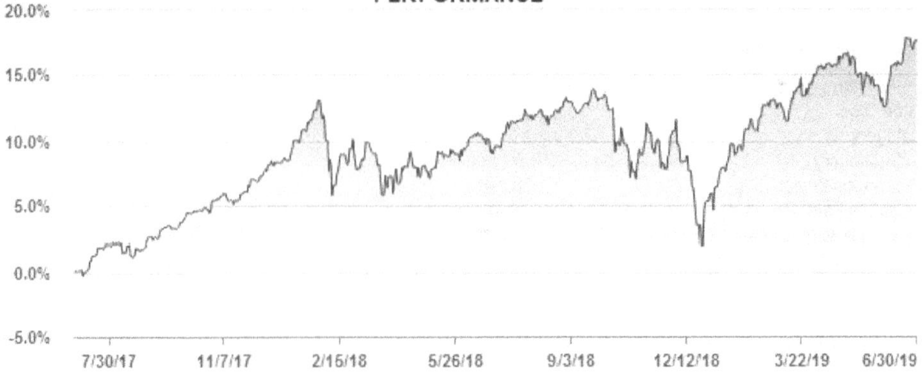

Ratings History

Date	Overall Rating	Risk Rating	Reward Rating
Q2-19	B	A	C
Q4-18	C	B	C
Q4-17	B	A-	B-
Q4-16	B	B+	B-
Q4-15	C+	B-	C

Asset & Performance History

Date	NAV	1-Year Total Return
2018	24.91	-2.42
2017	27.16	15.84
2016	24.81	8.89
2015	23.84	2.02
2014	24.76	9.21
2013	24.42	22.11

Total Assets: $146,710,000,000

Asset Allocation

Asset	%
Cash	6%
Stocks	62%
US Stocks	54%
Bonds	32%
US Bonds	29%
Other	0%

Services Offered: Automatic Investment Plan, Qualified Investment, Phone Exchange

Investment Strategy: The investment seeks conservation of capital, current income and long-term growth of capital and income. The fund uses a balanced approach to invest in a broad range of securities, including common stocks and investment-grade bonds. It also invests in securities issued and guaranteed by the U.S. government and by federal agencies and instrumentalities. In addition, the fund may invest a portion of its assets in common stocks, most of which have a history of paying dividends, bonds and other securities of issuers domiciled outside the United States. **Top Holdings:** Microsoft Corp UnitedHealth Group Inc The Home Depot Inc Berkshire Hathaway Inc A Philip Morris International Inc

American Funds American Balanced Fund® Class 529-F B BUY

Ticker	Traded On	NAV	Total Assets ($)	Dividend Yield (TTM)	Turnover Ratio	Expense Ratio
CLBFX	NAS CM	27.26	$146,710,000,000	2	72	0.41

Ratings

Reward	C
Risk	A
Recent Upgrade/Downgrade	

Fund Information

Fund Type	Open End
Category	Moderate Alloc
Sub-Category	Alloc--50% to 70% Equity
Prospectus Objective	Balanced
Inception Date	Sep-02
Open to New Investments	Y
Minimum Initial Investment	250
Minimum Subsequent Investment	50
Front End Fee	
Back End Fee	

Total Returns (%)

3-Month	6-Month	1-Year	3-Year	5-Year
2.84	11.59	7.15	30.73	43.89

Last Bull Market	17.57
Last Bear Market	-9.91
3-Year Standard Deviation	7
3-Year Beta	0.56

Company Information

Provider	American Funds
Manager/Tenure	Hilda L. Applbaum (20), Gregory D. Johnson (16), Alan N. Berro (13), 7 others
Website	http://www.americanfunds.com
Address	American Funds 333 South Hope Street Los Angeles CA 90071-1406 United States
Phone Number	800-421-4225

PERFORMANCE

Ratings History

Date	Overall Rating	Risk Rating	Reward Rating
Q2-19	B	A	C
Q4-18	C	B	C
Q4-17	B	A-	B-
Q4-16	B	B+	B-
Q4-15	C+	B-	C

Asset & Performance History

Date	NAV	1-Year Total Return
2018	24.84	-2.55
2017	27.09	15.68
2016	24.75	8.74
2015	23.78	1.81
2014	24.71	9.05
2013	24.37	21.88

Total Assets: $146,710,000,000

Asset Allocation

Asset	%
Cash	6%
Stocks	62%
US Stocks	54%
Bonds	32%
US Bonds	29%
Other	0%

Services Offered: Systematic Withdrawal Plan, Automatic Investment Plan, Qualified Investment, Phone Exchange, Retirement Investment

Investment Strategy: The investment seeks conservation of capital, current income and long-term growth of capital and income. The fund uses a balanced approach to invest in a broad range of securities, including common stocks and investment-grade bonds. It also invests in securities issued and guaranteed by the U.S. government and by federal agencies and instrumentalities. In addition, the fund may invest a portion of its assets in common stocks, most of which have a history of paying dividends, bonds and other securities of issuers domiciled outside the United States. **Top Holdings:** Microsoft Corp UnitedHealth Group Inc The Home Depot Inc Berkshire Hathaway Inc A Philip Morris International Inc

American Funds American Balanced Fund® Class R-2E — B BUY

Ticker	Traded On	NAV	Total Assets ($)	Dividend Yield (TTM)	Turnover Ratio	Expense Ratio
RAMHX	NAS CM	27.22	$146,710,000,000	1.38	72	1.08

Ratings

Reward	C
Risk	A
Recent Upgrade/Downgrade	

Fund Information

Fund Type	Open End
Category	Moderate Alloc
Sub-Category	Alloc--50% to 70% Equity
Prospectus Objective	Balanced
Inception Date	Aug-14
Open to New Investments	Y
Minimum Initial Investment	250
Minimum Subsequent Investment	50
Front End Fee	
Back End Fee	

Total Returns (%)

3-Month	6-Month	1-Year	3-Year	5-Year
2.68	11.21	6.46	28.17	40.26

Last Bull Market	17.22
Last Bear Market	-10.09
3-Year Standard Deviation	7.01
3-Year Beta	0.56

Company Information

Provider	American Funds
Manager/Tenure	Hilda L. Applbaum (20), Gregory D. Johnson (16), Alan N. Berro (13), 7 others
Website	http://www.americanfunds.com
Address	American Funds 333 South Hope Street Los Angeles CA 90071-1406 United States
Phone Number	800-421-4225

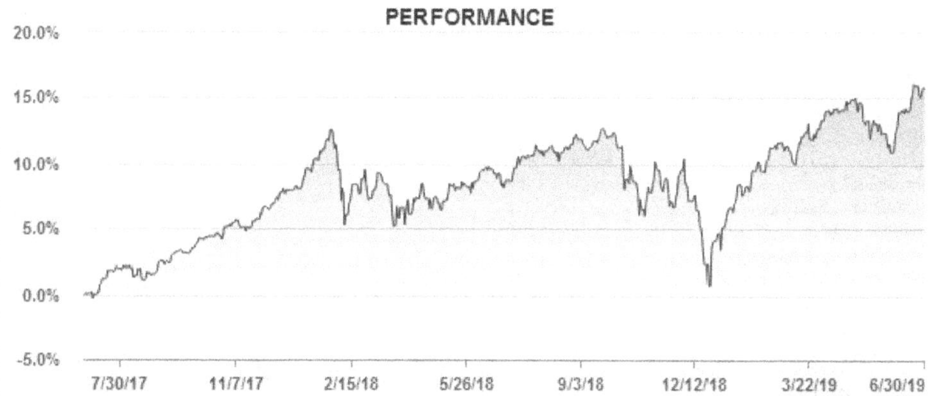

Ratings History

Date	Overall Rating	Risk Rating	Reward Rating
Q2-19	B	A-	C
Q4-18	C	B	C
Q4-17	B	A-	C+
Q4-16	B	B+	B-
Q4-15	C+	B-	C

Asset & Performance History

Date	NAV	1-Year Total Return
2018	24.8	-3.19
2017	27.05	14.88
2016	24.74	8.1
2015	23.77	1.6
2014	24.75	8.67
2013		21.29

Total Assets: $146,710,000,000

Asset Allocation

Asset	%
Cash	6%
Stocks	62%
US Stocks	54%
Bonds	32%
US Bonds	29%
Other	0%

Services Offered: Automatic Investment Plan, Qualified Investment, Phone Exchange

Investment Strategy: The investment seeks conservation of capital, current income and long-term growth of capital and income. The fund uses a balanced approach to invest in a broad range of securities, including common stocks and investment-grade bonds. It also invests in securities issued and guaranteed by the U.S. government and by federal agencies and instrumentalities. In addition, the fund may invest a portion of its assets in common stocks, most of which have a history of paying dividends, bonds and other securities of issuers domiciled outside the United States. **Top Holdings:** Microsoft Corp UnitedHealth Group Inc The Home Depot Inc Berkshire Hathaway Inc A Philip Morris International Inc

American Funds American Balanced Fund® Class R-3 — B BUY

Ticker	Traded On	NAV	Total Assets ($)	Dividend Yield (TTM)	Turnover Ratio	Expense Ratio
RLBCX	NAS CM	27.18	$146,710,000,000	1.5	72	0.93

Ratings

Reward	C
Risk	A
Recent Upgrade/Downgrade	

Fund Information

Fund Type	Open End
Category	Moderate Alloc
Sub-Category	Alloc--50% to 70% Equity
Prospectus Objective	Balanced
Inception Date	Jun-02
Open to New Investments	Y
Minimum Initial Investment	250
Minimum Subsequent Investment	50
Front End Fee	
Back End Fee	

Total Returns (%)

3-Month	6-Month	1-Year	3-Year	5-Year
2.72	11.25	6.61	28.72	40.31

Last Bull Market	17.22
Last Bear Market	-10.05
3-Year Standard Deviation	7
3-Year Beta	0.56

Company Information

Provider	American Funds
Manager/Tenure	Hilda L. Applbaum (20), Gregory D. Johnson (16), Alan N. Berro (13), 7 others
Website	http://www.americanfunds.com
Address	American Funds 333 South Hope Street Los Angeles CA 90071-1406 United States
Phone Number	800-421-4225

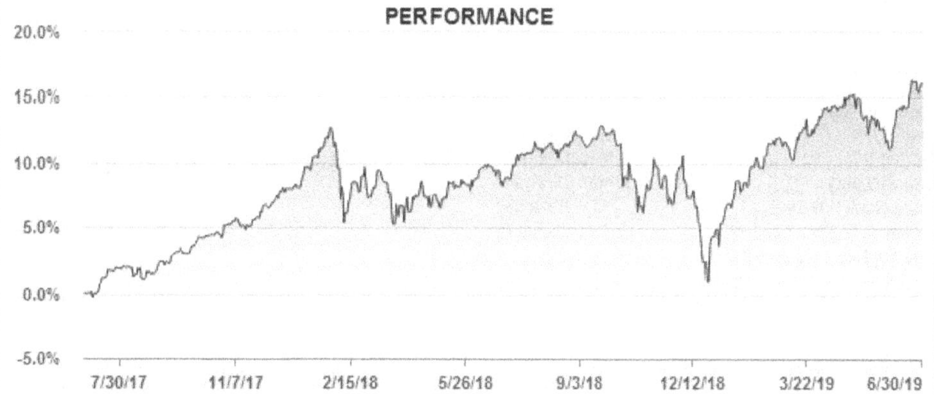

Ratings History

Date	Overall Rating	Risk Rating	Reward Rating
Q2-19	B	A-	C
Q4-18	C	B	C
Q4-17	B	A-	C+
Q4-16	B	B+	B-
Q4-15	C+	B-	C

Asset & Performance History

Date	NAV	1-Year Total Return
2018	24.77	-3.03
2017	27.01	15.05
2016	24.69	8.24
2015	23.72	1.33
2014	24.65	8.51
2013	24.32	21.32

Total Assets: $146,710,000,000

Asset Allocation

Asset	%
Cash	6%
Stocks	62%
US Stocks	54%
Bonds	32%
US Bonds	29%
Other	0%

Services Offered: Automatic Investment Plan, Qualified Investment, Phone Exchange

Investment Strategy: The investment seeks conservation of capital, current income and long-term growth of capital and income. The fund uses a balanced approach to invest in a broad range of securities, including common stocks and investment-grade bonds. It also invests in securities issued and guaranteed by the U.S. government and by federal agencies and instrumentalities. In addition, the fund may invest a portion of its assets in common stocks, most of which have a history of paying dividends, bonds and other securities of issuers domiciled outside the United States. **Top Holdings:** Microsoft Corp UnitedHealth Group Inc The Home Depot Inc Berkshire Hathaway Inc A Philip Morris International Inc

American Funds American Balanced Fund® Class F-1 — B BUY

Ticker	Traded On	NAV	Total Assets ($)	Dividend Yield (TTM)	Turnover Ratio	Expense Ratio
BALFX	NAS CM	27.31	$146,710,000,000	1.77	72	0.64

Ratings

Reward	C
Risk	A
Recent Upgrade/Downgrade	

Fund Information

Fund Type	Open End
Category	Moderate Alloc
Sub-Category	Alloc--50% to 70% Equity
Prospectus Objective	Balanced
Inception Date	Mar-01
Open to New Investments	Y
Minimum Initial Investment	250
Minimum Subsequent Investment	50
Front End Fee	
Back End Fee	

Total Returns (%)

3-Month	6-Month	1-Year	3-Year	5-Year
2.82	11.44	6.93	29.88	42.33

Last Bull Market	17.4
Last Bear Market	-9.96
3-Year Standard Deviation	7
3-Year Beta	0.56

Company Information

Provider	American Funds
Manager/Tenure	Hilda L. Applbaum (20), Gregory D. Johnson (16), Alan N. Berro (13), 7 others
Website	http://www.americanfunds.com
Address	American Funds 333 South Hope Street Los Angeles CA 90071-1406 United States
Phone Number	800-421-4225

Ratings History

Date	Overall Rating	Risk Rating	Reward Rating
Q2-19	B	A	C
Q4-18	C	B	C
Q4-17	B	A-	B-
Q4-16	B	B+	B-
Q4-15	C+	B-	C

Asset & Performance History

Date	NAV	1-Year Total Return
2018	24.88	-2.77
2017	27.13	15.39
2016	24.79	8.5
2015	23.82	1.66
2014	24.74	8.79
2013	24.41	21.7

Total Assets: $146,710,000,000

Asset Allocation

Asset	%
Cash	6%
Stocks	62%
US Stocks	54%
Bonds	32%
US Bonds	29%
Other	0%

Services Offered: Systematic Withdrawal Plan, Automatic Investment Plan, Qualified Investment, Phone Exchange, Retirement Investment

Investment Strategy: The investment seeks conservation of capital, current income and long-term growth of capital and income. The fund uses a balanced approach to invest in a broad range of securities, including common stocks and investment-grade bonds. It also invests in securities issued and guaranteed by the U.S. government and by federal agencies and instrumentalities. In addition, the fund may invest a portion of its assets in common stocks, most of which have a history of paying dividends, bonds and other securities of issuers domiciled outside the United States. **Top Holdings:** Microsoft Corp UnitedHealth Group Inc The Home Depot Inc Berkshire Hathaway Inc A Philip Morris International Inc

American Funds American Balanced Fund® Class A — B BUY

Ticker	Traded On	NAV	Total Assets ($)	Dividend Yield (TTM)	Turnover Ratio	Expense Ratio
ABALX	NAS CM	27.33	$146,710,000,000	1.84	72	0.57

Ratings

Reward	C
Risk	A
Recent Upgrade/Downgrade	

Fund Information

Fund Type	Open End
Category	Moderate Alloc
Sub-Category	Alloc--50% to 70% Equity
Prospectus Objective	Balanced
Inception Date	Jul-75
Open to New Investments	Y
Minimum Initial Investment	250
Minimum Subsequent Investment	50
Front End Fee	5.75
Back End Fee	

Total Returns (%)

3-Month	6-Month	1-Year	3-Year	5-Year
2.79	11.47	7.00	30.14	42.84

Last Bull Market	17.46
Last Bear Market	-9.96
3-Year Standard Deviation	7.01
3-Year Beta	0.56

Company Information

Provider	American Funds
Manager/Tenure	Hilda L. Applbaum (20), Gregory D. Johnson (16), Alan N. Berro (13), 7 others
Website	http://www.americanfunds.com
Address	American Funds 333 South Hope Street Los Angeles CA 90071-1406 United States
Phone Number	800-421-4225

Ratings History

Date	Overall Rating	Risk Rating	Reward Rating
Q2-19	B	A	C
Q4-18	C	B	C
Q4-17	B	A-	B-
Q4-16	B	B+	B-
Q4-15	C+	B-	C

Asset & Performance History

Date	NAV	1-Year Total Return
2018	24.9	-2.7
2017	27.15	15.47
2016	24.81	8.61
2015	23.83	1.72
2014	24.75	8.84
2013	24.42	21.73

Total Assets: $146,710,000,000

Asset Allocation

Asset	%
Cash	6%
Stocks	62%
US Stocks	54%
Bonds	32%
US Bonds	29%
Other	0%

Services Offered: Systematic Withdrawal Plan, Automatic Investment Plan, Phone Exchange, Retirement Investment

Investment Strategy: The investment seeks conservation of capital, current income and long-term growth of capital and income. The fund uses a balanced approach to invest in a broad range of securities, including common stocks and investment-grade bonds. It also invests in securities issued and guaranteed by the U.S. government and by federal agencies and instrumentalities. In addition, the fund may invest a portion of its assets in common stocks, most of which have a history of paying dividends, bonds and other securities of issuers domiciled outside the United States. **Top Holdings:** Microsoft Corp UnitedHealth Group Inc The Home Depot Inc Berkshire Hathaway Inc A Philip Morris International Inc

American Funds American Balanced Fund® Class R-5 — B BUY

Ticker	Traded On	NAV	Total Assets ($)	Dividend Yield (TTM)	Turnover Ratio	Expense Ratio
RLBFX	NAS CM	27.36	$146,710,000,000	2.06	72	0.33

Ratings

Reward	C
Risk	A
Recent Upgrade/Downgrade	

Fund Information

Fund Type	Open End
Category	Moderate Alloc
Sub-Category	Alloc--50% to 70% Equity
Prospectus Objective	Balanced
Inception Date	May-02
Open to New Investments	Y
Minimum Initial Investment	250
Minimum Subsequent Investment	50
Front End Fee	
Back End Fee	

Total Returns (%)

3-Month	6-Month	1-Year	3-Year	5-Year
2.89	11.63	7.25	31.09	44.59

Last Bull Market	17.67
Last Bear Market	-9.88
3-Year Standard Deviation	7
3-Year Beta	0.56

Company Information

Provider	American Funds
Manager/Tenure	Hilda L. Applbaum (20), Gregory D. Johnson (16), Alan N. Berro (13), 7 others
Website	http://www.americanfunds.com
Address	American Funds 333 South Hope Street Los Angeles CA 90071-1406 United States
Phone Number	800-421-4225

Ratings History

Date	Overall Rating	Risk Rating	Reward Rating
Q2-19	B	A	C
Q4-18	C	B	C
Q4-17	B	A-	B-
Q4-16	B	B+	B-
Q4-15	C+	B-	C

Asset & Performance History

Date	NAV	1-Year Total Return
2018	24.93	-2.46
2017	27.18	15.77
2016	24.83	8.87
2015	23.85	1.97
2014	24.77	9.15
2013	24.43	22.04

Total Assets: $146,710,000,000

Asset Allocation

Asset	%
Cash	6%
Stocks	62%
US Stocks	54%
Bonds	32%
US Bonds	29%
Other	0%

Services Offered: Automatic Investment Plan, Qualified Investment, Phone Exchange

Investment Strategy: The investment seeks conservation of capital, current income and long-term growth of capital and income. The fund uses a balanced approach to invest in a broad range of securities, including common stocks and investment-grade bonds. It also invests in securities issued and guaranteed by the U.S. government and by federal agencies and instrumentalities. In addition, the fund may invest a portion of its assets in common stocks, most of which have a history of paying dividends, bonds and other securities of issuers domiciled outside the United States. **Top Holdings:** Microsoft Corp UnitedHealth Group Inc The Home Depot Inc Berkshire Hathaway Inc A Philip Morris International Inc

American Funds American Balanced Fund® Class F-2 — B BUY

Ticker	Traded On	NAV	Total Assets ($)	Dividend Yield (TTM)	Turnover Ratio	Expense Ratio
AMBFX	NAS CM	27.31	$146,710,000,000	2.02	72	0.38

Ratings

Reward	C
Risk	A
Recent Upgrade/Downgrade	

Fund Information

Fund Type	Open End
Category	Moderate Alloc
Sub-Category	Alloc--50% to 70% Equity
Prospectus Objective	Balanced
Inception Date	Aug-08
Open to New Investments	Y
Minimum Initial Investment	250
Minimum Subsequent Investment	50
Front End Fee	
Back End Fee	

Total Returns (%)

3-Month	6-Month	1-Year	3-Year	5-Year
2.84	11.58	7.17	30.85	44.21

Last Bull Market	17.66
Last Bear Market	-9.91
3-Year Standard Deviation	7.01
3-Year Beta	0.56

Company Information

Provider	American Funds
Manager/Tenure	Hilda L. Applbaum (20), Gregory D. Johnson (16), Alan N. Berro (13), 7 others
Website	http://www.americanfunds.com
Address	American Funds 333 South Hope Street Los Angeles CA 90071-1406 United States
Phone Number	800-421-4225

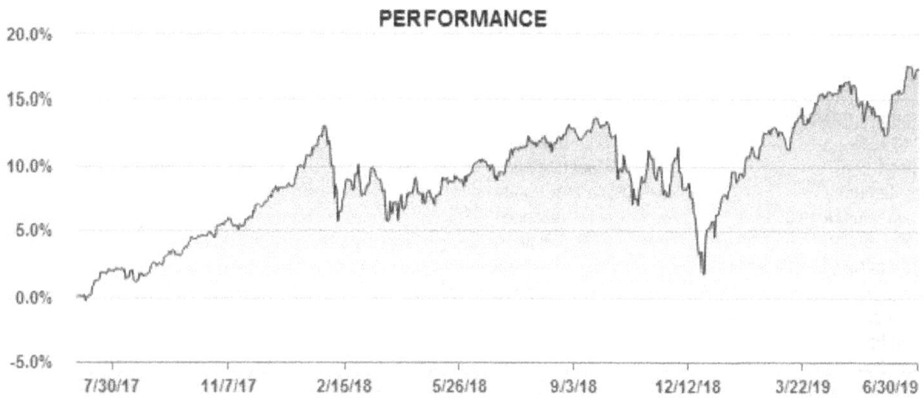

Ratings History

Date	Overall Rating	Risk Rating	Reward Rating
Q2-19	B	A	C
Q4-18	C	B	C
Q4-17	B	A-	B-
Q4-16	B	B+	B-
Q4-15	C+	B-	C

Asset & Performance History

Date	NAV	1-Year Total Return
2018	24.88	-2.51
2017	27.13	15.69
2016	24.79	8.8
2015	23.82	1.92
2014	24.74	9.07
2013	24.41	21.98

Total Assets: $146,710,000,000

Asset Allocation

Asset	%
Cash	6%
Stocks	62%
US Stocks	54%
Bonds	32%
US Bonds	29%
Other	0%

Services Offered: Systematic Withdrawal Plan, Automatic Investment Plan, Qualified Investment, Phone Exchange, Retirement Investment

Investment Strategy: The investment seeks conservation of capital, current income and long-term growth of capital and income. The fund uses a balanced approach to invest in a broad range of securities, including common stocks and investment-grade bonds. It also invests in securities issued and guaranteed by the U.S. government and by federal agencies and instrumentalities. In addition, the fund may invest a portion of its assets in common stocks, most of which have a history of paying dividends, bonds and other securities of issuers domiciled outside the United States. **Top Holdings:** Microsoft Corp UnitedHealth Group Inc The Home Depot Inc Berkshire Hathaway Inc A Philip Morris International Inc

American Funds American Balanced Fund® Class C — B BUY

Ticker	Traded On	NAV	Total Assets ($)	Dividend Yield (TTM)	Turnover Ratio	Expense Ratio
BALCX	NAS CM	27.15	$146,710,000,000	1.11	72	1.36

Ratings

Reward	C
Risk	A
Recent Upgrade/Downgrade	Up

Fund Information

Fund Type	Open End
Category	Moderate Alloc
Sub-Category	Alloc--50% to 70% Equity
Prospectus Objective	Balanced
Inception Date	Mar-01
Open to New Investments	Y
Minimum Initial Investment	250
Minimum Subsequent Investment	50
Front End Fee	
Back End Fee	1.00

Total Returns (%)

3-Month	6-Month	1-Year	3-Year	5-Year
2.62	11.04	6.18	27.08	37.32

Last Bull Market	16.89
Last Bear Market	-10.23
3-Year Standard Deviation	7
3-Year Beta	0.56

Company Information

Provider	American Funds
Manager/Tenure	Hilda L. Applbaum (20), Gregory D. Johnson (16), Alan N. Berro (13), 7 others
Website	http://www.americanfunds.com
Address	American Funds 333 South Hope Street Los Angeles CA 90071-1406 United States
Phone Number	800-421-4225

Ratings History

Date	Overall Rating	Risk Rating	Reward Rating
Q2-19	B	A-	C
Q4-18	C	B-	C
Q4-17	B	B+	C+
Q4-16	B	B+	B-
Q4-15	C+	B-	C

Asset & Performance History

Date	NAV	1-Year Total Return
2018	24.74	-3.44
2017	26.98	14.58
2016	24.66	7.69
2015	23.71	0.93
2014	24.63	8.03
2013	24.3	20.72

Total Assets: $146,710,000,000

Asset Allocation

Asset	%
Cash	6%
Stocks	62%
US Stocks	54%
Bonds	32%
US Bonds	29%
Other	0%

Services Offered: Systematic Withdrawal Plan, Automatic Investment Plan, Phone Exchange, Retirement Investment

Investment Strategy: The investment seeks conservation of capital, current income and long-term growth of capital and income. The fund uses a balanced approach to invest in a broad range of securities, including common stocks and investment-grade bonds. It also invests in securities issued and guaranteed by the U.S. government and by federal agencies and instrumentalities. In addition, the fund may invest a portion of its assets in common stocks, most of which have a history of paying dividends, bonds and other securities of issuers domiciled outside the United States. **Top Holdings:** Microsoft Corp UnitedHealth Group Inc The Home Depot Inc Berkshire Hathaway Inc A Philip Morris International Inc

American Funds American Balanced Fund® Class R-5E — B BUY

Ticker	Traded On	NAV	Total Assets ($)	Dividend Yield (TTM)	Turnover Ratio	Expense Ratio
RLEFX	NAS CM	27.31	$146,710,000,000	1.89	72	0.41

Ratings

Reward	C
Risk	A
Recent Upgrade/Downgrade	

Fund Information

Fund Type	Open End
Category	Moderate Alloc
Sub-Category	Alloc--50% to 70% Equity
Prospectus Objective	Balanced
Inception Date	Nov-15
Open to New Investments	Y
Minimum Initial Investment	250
Minimum Subsequent Investment	50
Front End Fee	
Back End Fee	

Total Returns (%)

3-Month	6-Month	1-Year	3-Year	5-Year
2.88	11.55	7.14	30.72	43.57

Last Bull Market	17.46
Last Bear Market	-9.96
3-Year Standard Deviation	7
3-Year Beta	0.56

Company Information

Provider	American Funds
Manager/Tenure	Hilda L. Applbaum (20), Gregory D. Johnson (16), Alan N. Berro (13), 7 others
Website	http://www.americanfunds.com
Address	American Funds 333 South Hope Street Los Angeles CA 90071-1406 United States
Phone Number	800-421-4225

Ratings History

Date	Overall Rating	Risk Rating	Reward Rating
Q2-19	B	A	C
Q4-18	C	B	C
Q4-17	B	A-	B-
Q4-16	B	B+	B-
Q4-15			

Asset & Performance History

Date	NAV	1-Year Total Return
2018	24.88	-2.57
2017	27.12	15.7
2016	24.78	8.65
2015	23.82	1.79
2014		8.84
2013		21.73

Total Assets: $146,710,000,000

Asset Allocation

Asset	%
Cash	6%
Stocks	62%
US Stocks	54%
Bonds	32%
US Bonds	29%
Other	0%

Services Offered: Automatic Investment Plan, Qualified Investment, Phone Exchange

Investment Strategy: The investment seeks conservation of capital, current income and long-term growth of capital and income. The fund uses a balanced approach to invest in a broad range of securities, including common stocks and investment-grade bonds. It also invests in securities issued and guaranteed by the U.S. government and by federal agencies and instrumentalities. In addition, the fund may invest a portion of its assets in common stocks, most of which have a history of paying dividends, bonds and other securities of issuers domiciled outside the United States. **Top Holdings:** Microsoft Corp UnitedHealth Group Inc The Home Depot Inc Berkshire Hathaway Inc A Philip Morris International Inc

American Funds American Balanced Fund® Class R-2 B BUY

Ticker	Traded On	NAV	Total Assets ($)	Dividend Yield (TTM)	Turnover Ratio	Expense Ratio
RLBBX	NAS CM	27.15	$146,710,000,000	1.09	72	1.37

Ratings

Reward	C
Risk	A
Recent Upgrade/Downgrade	Up

Fund Information

Fund Type	Open End
Category	Moderate Alloc
Sub-Category	Alloc--50% to 70% Equity
Prospectus Objective	Balanced
Inception Date	May-02
Open to New Investments	Y
Minimum Initial Investment	250
Minimum Subsequent Investment	50
Front End Fee	
Back End Fee	

Total Returns (%)

3-Month	6-Month	1-Year	3-Year	5-Year
2.65	11.08	6.15	27.09	37.43

Last Bull Market	16.93
Last Bear Market	-10.26
3-Year Standard Deviation	7
3-Year Beta	0.56

Company Information

Provider	American Funds
Manager/Tenure	Hilda L. Applbaum (20), Gregory D. Johnson (16), Alan N. Berro (13), 7 others
Website	http://www.americanfunds.com
Address	American Funds 333 South Hope Street Los Angeles CA 90071-1406 United States
Phone Number	800-421-4225

Ratings History

Date	Overall Rating	Risk Rating	Reward Rating
Q2-19	B-	A-	C
Q4-18	C	B-	C
Q4-17	B	B+	C+
Q4-16	B	B+	B-
Q4-15	C+	B-	C

Asset & Performance History

Date	NAV	1-Year Total Return
2018	24.74	-3.46
2017	26.98	14.57
2016	24.66	7.74
2015	23.7	0.97
2014	24.62	8.03
2013	24.3	20.86

Total Assets: $146,710,000,000

Asset Allocation

Asset	%
Cash	6%
Stocks	62%
US Stocks	54%
Bonds	32%
US Bonds	29%
Other	0%

Services Offered: Automatic Investment Plan, Qualified Investment, Phone Exchange

Investment Strategy: The investment seeks conservation of capital, current income and long-term growth of capital and income. The fund uses a balanced approach to invest in a broad range of securities, including common stocks and investment-grade bonds. It also invests in securities issued and guaranteed by the U.S. government and by federal agencies and instrumentalities. In addition, the fund may invest a portion of its assets in common stocks, most of which have a history of paying dividends, bonds and other securities of issuers domiciled outside the United States. **Top Holdings:** Microsoft Corp UnitedHealth Group Inc The Home Depot Inc Berkshire Hathaway Inc A Philip Morris International Inc

American Funds American Balanced Fund® Class 529-E B BUY

Ticker	Traded On	NAV	Total Assets ($)	Dividend Yield (TTM)	Turnover Ratio	Expense Ratio
CLBEX	NAS CM	27.27	$146,710,000,000	1.55	72	0.89

Ratings

Reward	C
Risk	A
Recent Upgrade/Downgrade	

Fund Information

Fund Type	Open End
Category	Moderate Alloc
Sub-Category	Alloc--50% to 70% Equity
Prospectus Objective	Balanced
Inception Date	Mar-02
Open to New Investments	Y
Minimum Initial Investment	250
Minimum Subsequent Investment	50
Front End Fee	
Back End Fee	

Total Returns (%)

3-Month	6-Month	1-Year	3-Year	5-Year
2.76	11.33	6.68	28.95	40.56

Last Bull Market	17.24
Last Bear Market	-10.14
3-Year Standard Deviation	7.01
3-Year Beta	0.56

Company Information

Provider	American Funds
Manager/Tenure	Hilda L. Applbaum (20), Gregory D. Johnson (16), Alan N. Berro (13), 7 others
Website	http://www.americanfunds.com
Address	American Funds 333 South Hope Street Los Angeles CA 90071-1406 United States
Phone Number	800-421-4225

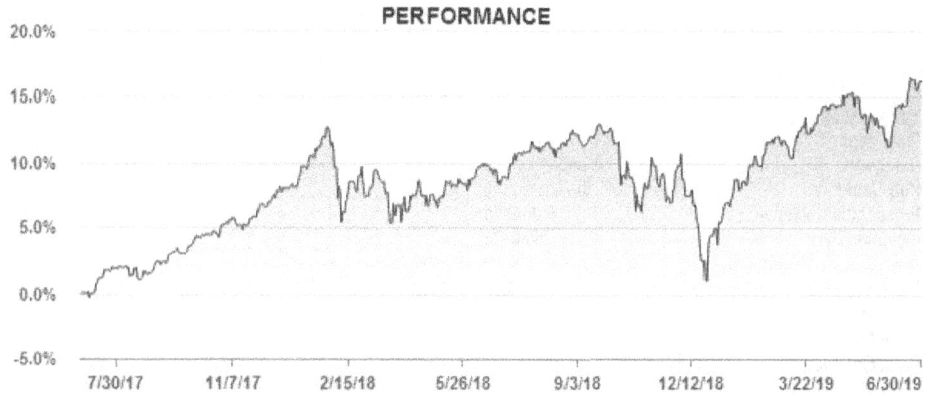

Ratings History

Date	Overall Rating	Risk Rating	Reward Rating
Q2-19	B	A-	C
Q4-18	C	B	C
Q4-17	B	A-	C+
Q4-16	B	B+	B-
Q4-15	C+	B-	C

Asset & Performance History

Date	NAV	1-Year Total Return
2018	24.84	-3.01
2017	27.09	15.1
2016	24.76	8.24
2015	23.79	1.38
2014	24.71	8.49
2013	24.38	21.3

Total Assets: $146,710,000,000

Asset Allocation

Asset	%
Cash	6%
Stocks	62%
US Stocks	54%
Bonds	32%
US Bonds	29%
Other	0%

Services Offered: Systematic Withdrawal Plan, Automatic Investment Plan, Qualified Investment, Phone Exchange, Retirement Investment

Investment Strategy: The investment seeks conservation of capital, current income and long-term growth of capital and income. The fund uses a balanced approach to invest in a broad range of securities, including common stocks and investment-grade bonds. It also invests in securities issued and guaranteed by the U.S. government and by federal agencies and instrumentalities. In addition, the fund may invest a portion of its assets in common stocks, most of which have a history of paying dividends, bonds and other securities of issuers domiciled outside the United States. **Top Holdings:** Microsoft Corp UnitedHealth Group Inc The Home Depot Inc Berkshire Hathaway Inc A Philip Morris International Inc

American Funds American Balanced Fund® Class R-4 B BUY

Ticker	Traded On	NAV	Total Assets ($)	Dividend Yield (TTM)	Turnover Ratio	Expense Ratio
RLBEX	NAS CM	27.28	$146,710,000,000	1.78	72	0.63

Ratings

Reward	C
Risk	A
Recent Upgrade/Downgrade	

Fund Information

Fund Type	Open End
Category	Moderate Alloc
Sub-Category	Alloc--50% to 70% Equity
Prospectus Objective	Balanced
Inception Date	Jun-02
Open to New Investments	Y
Minimum Initial Investment	250
Minimum Subsequent Investment	50
Front End Fee	
Back End Fee	

Total Returns (%)

3-Month	6-Month	1-Year	3-Year	5-Year
2.82	11.46	6.95	29.88	42.49

Last Bull Market	17.41
Last Bear Market	-9.98
3-Year Standard Deviation	6.99
3-Year Beta	0.56

Company Information

Provider	American Funds
Manager/Tenure	Hilda L. Applbaum (20), Gregory D. Johnson (16), Alan N. Berro (13), 7 others
Website	http://www.americanfunds.com
Address	American Funds 333 South Hope Street Los Angeles CA 90071-1406 United States
Phone Number	800-421-4225

Ratings History

Date	Overall Rating	Risk Rating	Reward Rating
Q2-19	B	A	C
Q4-18	C	B	C
Q4-17	B	A-	B-
Q4-16	B	B+	B-
Q4-15	C+	B-	C

Asset & Performance History

Date	NAV	1-Year Total Return
2018	24.85	-2.77
2017	27.1	15.43
2016	24.76	8.49
2015	23.8	1.67
2014	24.72	8.85
2013	24.38	21.68

Total Assets: $146,710,000,000

Asset Allocation

Asset	%
Cash	6%
Stocks	62%
US Stocks	54%
Bonds	32%
US Bonds	29%
Other	0%

Services Offered: Automatic Investment Plan, Qualified Investment, Phone Exchange

Investment Strategy: The investment seeks conservation of capital, current income and long-term growth of capital and income. The fund uses a balanced approach to invest in a broad range of securities, including common stocks and investment-grade bonds. It also invests in securities issued and guaranteed by the U.S. government and by federal agencies and instrumentalities. In addition, the fund may invest a portion of its assets in common stocks, most of which have a history of paying dividends, bonds and other securities of issuers domiciled outside the United States. **Top Holdings:** Microsoft Corp UnitedHealth Group Inc The Home Depot Inc Berkshire Hathaway Inc A Philip Morris International Inc

American Funds American Balanced Fund® Class 529-A B BUY

Ticker	Traded On	NAV	Total Assets ($)	Dividend Yield (TTM)	Turnover Ratio	Expense Ratio
CLBAX	NAS CM	27.28	$146,710,000,000	1.76	72	0.65

Ratings

Reward	C
Risk	A
Recent Upgrade/Downgrade	

Fund Information

Fund Type	Open End
Category	Moderate Alloc
Sub-Category	Alloc--50% to 70% Equity
Prospectus Objective	Balanced
Inception Date	Feb-02
Open to New Investments	Y
Minimum Initial Investment	250
Minimum Subsequent Investment	50
Front End Fee	5.75
Back End Fee	

Total Returns (%)

3-Month	6-Month	1-Year	3-Year	5-Year
2.78	11.45	6.88	29.80	42.22

Last Bull Market	17.38
Last Bear Market	-10.01
3-Year Standard Deviation	7.01
3-Year Beta	0.56

Company Information

Provider	American Funds
Manager/Tenure	Hilda L. Applbaum (20), Gregory D. Johnson (16), Alan N. Berro (13), 7 others
Website	http://www.americanfunds.com
Address	American Funds 333 South Hope Street Los Angeles CA 90071-1406 United States
Phone Number	800-421-4225

Ratings History

Date	Overall Rating	Risk Rating	Reward Rating
Q2-19	B	A	C
Q4-18	C	B	C
Q4-17	B	A-	B-
Q4-16	B	B+	B-
Q4-15	C+	B-	C

Asset & Performance History

Date	NAV	1-Year Total Return
2018	24.86	-2.78
2017	27.11	15.42
2016	24.77	8.49
2015	23.8	1.62
2014	24.72	8.76
2013	24.39	21.59

Total Assets: $146,710,000,000

Asset Allocation

Asset	%
Cash	6%
Stocks	62%
US Stocks	54%
Bonds	32%
US Bonds	29%
Other	0%

Services Offered: Systematic Withdrawal Plan, Automatic Investment Plan, Qualified Investment, Phone Exchange, Retirement Investment

Investment Strategy: The investment seeks conservation of capital, current income and long-term growth of capital and income. The fund uses a balanced approach to invest in a broad range of securities, including common stocks and investment-grade bonds. It also invests in securities issued and guaranteed by the U.S. government and by federal agencies and instrumentalities. In addition, the fund may invest a portion of its assets in common stocks, most of which have a history of paying dividends, bonds and other securities of issuers domiciled outside the United States. **Top Holdings:** Microsoft Corp UnitedHealth Group Inc The Home Depot Inc Berkshire Hathaway Inc A Philip Morris International Inc

Fidelity® Contrafund® Fund C+ HOLD

Ticker	Traded On	NAV	Total Assets ($)	Dividend Yield (TTM)	Turnover Ratio	Expense Ratio
FCNTX	NAS CM	13.18	$121,774,000,000	0	32	0.82

Ratings

Reward	C
Risk	B
Recent Upgrade/Downgrade	Down

Fund Information

Fund Type	Open End
Category	US Equity Large Cap Growth
Sub-Category	Large Growth
Prospectus Objective	Growth
Inception Date	May-67
Open to New Investments	Y
Minimum Initial Investment	0
Minimum Subsequent Investment	
Front End Fee	
Back End Fee	

Total Returns (%)

3-Month	6-Month	1-Year	3-Year	5-Year
5.43	21.87	7.91	64.96	80.53

Last Bull Market	24.33
Last Bear Market	-14.42
3-Year Standard Deviation	13.74
3-Year Beta	1.04

Company Information

Provider	Fidelity Investments
Manager/Tenure	William Danoff (28)
Website	http://www.institutional.fidelity.com
Address	Fidelity Investments 82 Devonshire Street Boston MA 2109 United States
Phone Number	617-563-7000

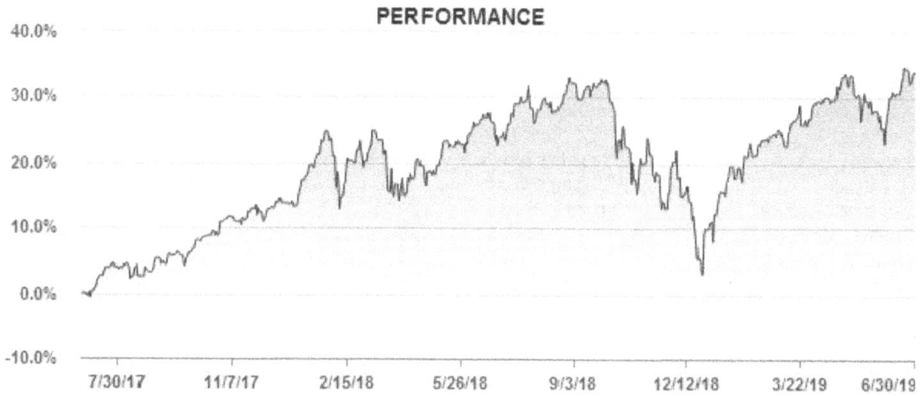

Ratings History

Date	Overall Rating	Risk Rating	Reward Rating
Q2-19	C+	B	C
Q4-18	C+	B	C
Q4-17	A-	A-	A-
Q4-16	B	B	B-
Q4-15	B	A	C+

Asset & Performance History

Date	NAV	1-Year Total Return
2018	11.01	-2.12
2017	12.24	32.26
2016	9.85	3.37
2015	9.89	6.46
2014	9.8	9.55
2013	9.61	34.14

Total Assets: $121,774,000,000

Asset Allocation

Asset	%
Cash	2%
Stocks	97%
US Stocks	91%
Bonds	0%
US Bonds	0%
Other	0%

Services Offered: Phone Exchange, Wire Redemption, Retirement Investment

Investment Strategy: The investment seeks capital appreciation. The fund normally invests primarily in common stocks. It invests in securities of companies whose value the advisor believes is not fully recognized by the public. The fund invests in domestic and foreign issuers. It invests in either "growth" stocks or "value" stocks or both. The fund uses fundamental analysis of factors such as each issuer's financial condition and industry position, as well as market and economic conditions to select investments. **Top Holdings:** Amazon.com Inc Facebook Inc A Berkshire Hathaway Inc A Microsoft Corp Salesforce.com Inc

Fidelity® Contrafund® Fund Class K C+ HOLD

Ticker	Traded On	NAV	Total Assets ($)	Dividend Yield (TTM)	Turnover Ratio	Expense Ratio
FCNKX	NAS CM	13.19	$121,774,000,000	0	32	0.73

Ratings

Reward	C
Risk	B
Recent Upgrade/Downgrade	Down

Fund Information

Fund Type	Open End
Category	US Equity Large Cap Growth
Sub-Category	Large Growth
Prospectus Objective	Growth
Inception Date	May-08
Open to New Investments	Y
Minimum Initial Investment	0
Minimum Subsequent Investment	
Front End Fee	
Back End Fee	

Total Returns (%)

3-Month	6-Month	1-Year	3-Year	5-Year
5.51	21.97	8.01	65.44	81.41

Last Bull Market	24.41
Last Bear Market	-14.38
3-Year Standard Deviation	13.75
3-Year Beta	1.04

Company Information

Provider	Fidelity Investments
Manager/Tenure	William Danoff (28)
Website	http://www.institutional.fidelity.com
Address	Fidelity Investments 82 Devonshire Street Boston MA 2109 United States
Phone Number	617-563-7000

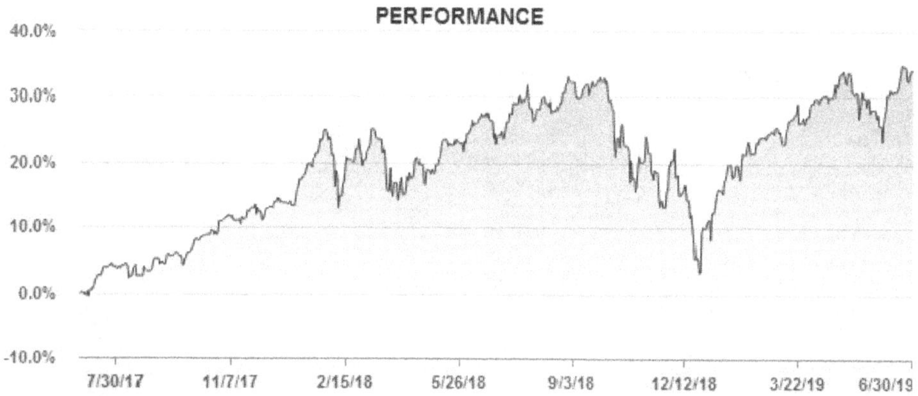

Ratings History

Date	Overall Rating	Risk Rating	Reward Rating
Q2-19	C+	B	C
Q4-18	C+	B	C
Q4-17	A-	A-	A-
Q4-16	B	B	B-
Q4-15	B	A	C+

Asset & Performance History

Date	NAV	1-Year Total Return
2018	11.01	-2.06
2017	12.24	32.38
2016	9.84	3.47
2015	9.88	6.55
2014	9.79	9.67
2013	9.61	34.29

Total Assets: $121,774,000,000

Asset Allocation

Asset	%
Cash	2%
Stocks	97%
US Stocks	91%
Bonds	0%
US Bonds	0%
Other	0%

Services Offered: Qualified Investment, Phone Exchange

Investment Strategy: The investment seeks capital appreciation. The fund normally invests primarily in common stocks. It invests in securities of companies whose value the advisor believes is not fully recognized by the public. The fund invests in domestic and foreign issuers. It invests in either "growth" stocks or "value" stocks or both. The fund uses fundamental analysis of factors such as each issuer's financial condition and industry position, as well as market and economic conditions to select investments. **Top Holdings:** Amazon.com Inc Facebook Inc A Berkshire Hathaway Inc A Microsoft Corp Salesforce.com Inc

American Funds Washington Mutual Investors Fund Class R-5E — B- BUY

Ticker	Traded On	NAV	Total Assets ($)	Dividend Yield (TTM)	Turnover Ratio	Expense Ratio
RWMHX	NAS CM	45.77	$118,091,000,000	1.98	25	0.41

Ratings

Reward	C
Risk	B+
Recent Upgrade/Downgrade	Down

Fund Information

Fund Type	Open End
Category	US Equity Large Cap Blend
Sub-Category	Large Blend
Prospectus Objective	Growth & Income
Inception Date	Nov-15
Open to New Investments	Y
Minimum Initial Investment	250
Minimum Subsequent Investment	50
Front End Fee	
Back End Fee	

Total Returns (%)

3-Month	6-Month	1-Year	3-Year	5-Year
4.09	15.73	10.32	46.74	58.86

Last Bull Market	20.97
Last Bear Market	-12.51
3-Year Standard Deviation	10.51
3-Year Beta	0.84

Company Information

Provider	American Funds
Manager/Tenure	Alan N. Berro (22), Jeffrey T. Lager (15), Alan J. Wilson (6), 4 others
Website	http://www.americanfunds.com
Address	American Funds 333 South Hope Street Los Angeles CA 90071-1406 United States
Phone Number	800-421-4225

Ratings History

Date	Overall Rating	Risk Rating	Reward Rating
Q2-19	B-	B+	C
Q4-18	C+	B	C
Q4-17	B	B	B
Q4-16	B	B	B
Q4-15			

Asset & Performance History

Date	NAV	1-Year Total Return
2018	41.02	-2.78
2017	45.61	20.32
2016	40.92	13.5
2015	38.43	-0.14
2014		11.22
2013		31.9

Total Assets: $118,091,000,000

Asset Allocation

Asset	%
Cash	4%
Stocks	96%
US Stocks	87%
Bonds	0%
US Bonds	0%
Other	0%

Services Offered: Systematic Withdrawal Plan, Automatic Investment Plan, Qualified Investment, Phone Exchange

Investment Strategy: The investment seeks to produce income and to provide an opportunity for growth of principal consistent with sound common stock investing. The fund invests primarily in common stocks of established companies that are listed on, or meet the financial listing requirements of, the New York Stock Exchange and have a strong record of earnings and dividends. Its advisor strives to maintain a fully invested, diversified portfolio, consisting primarily of high-quality common stocks. **Top Holdings:** Microsoft Corp Intel Corp Broadcom Inc Boeing Co Merck & Co Inc

American Funds Washington Mutual Investors Fund Class 529-C — B- BUY

Ticker	Traded On	NAV	Total Assets ($)	Dividend Yield (TTM)	Turnover Ratio	Expense Ratio
CWMCX	NAS CM	45.44	$118,091,000,000	1.04	25	1.4

Ratings

Reward	C
Risk	B+
Recent Upgrade/Downgrade	Down

Fund Information

Fund Type	Open End
Category	US Equity Large Cap Blend
Sub-Category	Large Blend
Prospectus Objective	Growth & Income
Inception Date	Feb-02
Open to New Investments	Y
Minimum Initial Investment	250
Minimum Subsequent Investment	50
Front End Fee	
Back End Fee	1.00

Total Returns (%)

3-Month	6-Month	1-Year	3-Year	5-Year
3.85	15.16	9.26	42.51	51.60

Last Bull Market	20.35
Last Bear Market	-12.85
3-Year Standard Deviation	10.51
3-Year Beta	0.84

Company Information

Provider	American Funds
Manager/Tenure	Alan N. Berro (22), Jeffrey T. Lager (15), Alan J. Wilson (6), 4 others
Website	http://www.americanfunds.com
Address	American Funds 333 South Hope Street Los Angeles CA 90071-1406 United States
Phone Number	800-421-4225

Ratings History

Date	Overall Rating	Risk Rating	Reward Rating
Q2-19	B-	B+	C
Q4-18	C+	B	C
Q4-17	B-	B	B-
Q4-16	B	B	B-
Q4-15	B	A-	C+

Asset & Performance History

Date	NAV	1-Year Total Return
2018	40.73	-3.72
2017	45.28	19.19
2016	40.59	12.43
2015	38.13	-1.01
2014	40.63	10.25
2013	39.15	30.77

Total Assets: $118,091,000,000

Asset Allocation

Asset	%
Cash	4%
Stocks	96%
US Stocks	87%
Bonds	0%
US Bonds	0%
Other	0%

Services Offered: Systematic Withdrawal Plan, Automatic Investment Plan, Qualified Investment, Phone Exchange, Retirement Investment

Investment Strategy: The investment seeks to produce income and to provide an opportunity for growth of principal consistent with sound common stock investing. The fund invests primarily in common stocks of established companies that are listed on, or meet the financial listing requirements of, the New York Stock Exchange and have a strong record of earnings and dividends. Its advisor strives to maintain a fully invested, diversified portfolio, consisting primarily of high-quality common stocks. **Top Holdings:** Microsoft Corp Intel Corp Broadcom Inc Boeing Co Merck & Co Inc

American Funds Washington Mutual Investors Fund Class R-3 — B- BUY

Ticker	Traded On	NAV	Total Assets ($)	Dividend Yield (TTM)	Turnover Ratio	Expense Ratio
RWMCX	NAS CM	45.42	$118,091,000,000	1.47	25	0.92

Ratings

Reward	C
Risk	B+
Recent Upgrade/Downgrade	Down

Fund Information

Fund Type	Open End
Category	US Equity Large Cap Blend
Sub-Category	Large Blend
Prospectus Objective	Growth & Income
Inception Date	Jun-02
Open to New Investments	Y
Minimum Initial Investment	250
Minimum Subsequent Investment	50
Front End Fee	
Back End Fee	

Total Returns (%)

3-Month	6-Month	1-Year	3-Year	5-Year
3.97	15.43	9.74	44.51	55.32

Last Bull Market	20.78
Last Bear Market	-12.67
3-Year Standard Deviation	10.51
3-Year Beta	0.84

Company Information

Provider	American Funds
Manager/Tenure	Alan N. Berro (22), Jeffrey T. Lager (15), Alan J. Wilson (6), 4 others
Website	http://www.americanfunds.com
Address	American Funds 333 South Hope Street Los Angeles CA 90071-1406 United States
Phone Number	800-421-4225

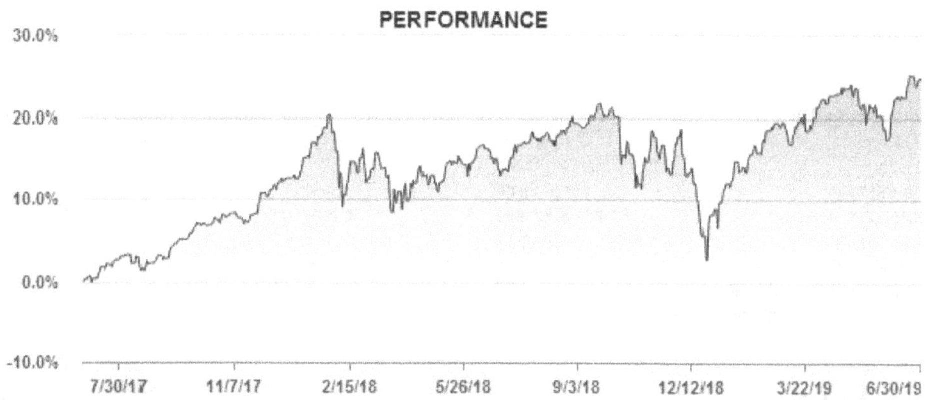

Ratings History

Date	Overall Rating	Risk Rating	Reward Rating
Q2-19	B-	B+	C
Q4-18	C+	B	C
Q4-17	B-	B	B-
Q4-16	B	B	B
Q4-15	B	A-	C+

Asset & Performance History

Date	NAV	1-Year Total Return
2018	40.71	-3.29
2017	45.27	19.73
2016	40.64	12.99
2015	38.17	-0.5
2014	40.67	10.82
2013	39.18	31.46

Total Assets: $118,091,000,000

Asset Allocation

Asset	%
Cash	4%
Stocks	96%
US Stocks	87%
Bonds	0%
US Bonds	0%
Other	0%

Services Offered: Systematic Withdrawal Plan, Automatic Investment Plan, Qualified Investment, Phone Exchange

Investment Strategy: The investment seeks to produce income and to provide an opportunity for growth of principal consistent with sound common stock investing. The fund invests primarily in common stocks of established companies that are listed on, or meet the financial listing requirements of, the New York Stock Exchange and have a strong record of earnings and dividends. Its advisor strives to maintain a fully invested, diversified portfolio, consisting primarily of high-quality common stocks. **Top Holdings:** Microsoft Corp Intel Corp Broadcom Inc Boeing Co Merck & Co Inc

American Funds Washington Mutual Investors Fund Class R-5 — B- BUY

Ticker	Traded On	NAV	Total Assets ($)	Dividend Yield (TTM)	Turnover Ratio	Expense Ratio
RWMFX	NAS CM	45.81	$118,091,000,000	2.03	25	0.32

Ratings

Reward	C
Risk	B+
Recent Upgrade/Downgrade	Down

Fund Information

Fund Type	Open End
Category	US Equity Large Cap Blend
Sub-Category	Large Blend
Prospectus Objective	Growth & Income
Inception Date	May-02
Open to New Investments	Y
Minimum Initial Investment	250
Minimum Subsequent Investment	50
Front End Fee	
Back End Fee	

Total Returns (%)

3-Month	6-Month	1-Year	3-Year	5-Year
4.11	15.78	10.39	47.14	60.00

Last Bull Market	21.19
Last Bear Market	-12.46
3-Year Standard Deviation	10.51
3-Year Beta	0.84

Company Information

Provider	American Funds
Manager/Tenure	Alan N. Berro (22), Jeffrey T. Lager (15), Alan J. Wilson (6), 4 others
Website	http://www.americanfunds.com
Address	American Funds 333 South Hope Street Los Angeles CA 90071-1406 United States
Phone Number	800-421-4225

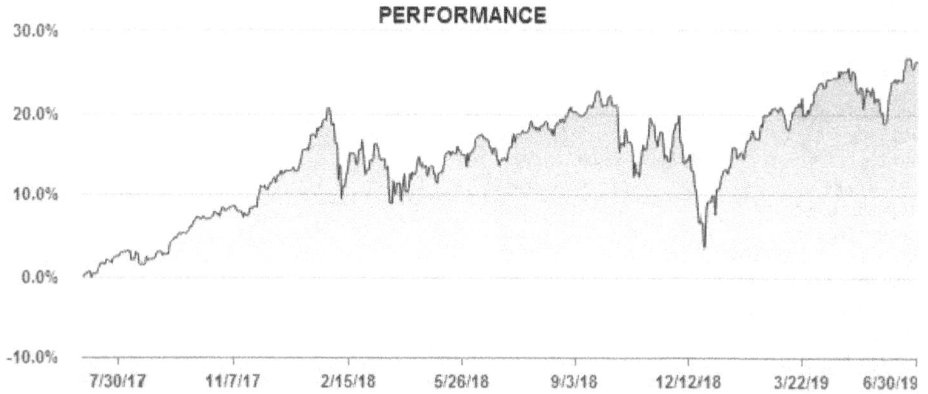

Ratings History

Date	Overall Rating	Risk Rating	Reward Rating
Q2-19	B-	B+	C
Q4-18	C+	B	C
Q4-17	B	B	B
Q4-16	B	B	B
Q4-15	B	A	C+

Asset & Performance History

Date	NAV	1-Year Total Return
2018	41.05	-2.72
2017	45.63	20.46
2016	40.93	13.68
2015	38.42	0.07
2014	40.93	11.48
2013	39.41	32.26

Total Assets: $118,091,000,000

Asset Allocation

Asset	%
Cash	4%
Stocks	96%
US Stocks	87%
Bonds	0%
US Bonds	0%
Other	0%

Services Offered: Systematic Withdrawal Plan, Automatic Investment Plan, Qualified Investment, Phone Exchange

Investment Strategy: The investment seeks to produce income and to provide an opportunity for growth of principal consistent with sound common stock investing. The fund invests primarily in common stocks of established companies that are listed on, or meet the financial listing requirements of, the New York Stock Exchange and have a strong record of earnings and dividends. Its advisor strives to maintain a fully invested, diversified portfolio, consisting primarily of high-quality common stocks. **Top Holdings:** Microsoft Corp Intel Corp Broadcom Inc Boeing Co Merck & Co Inc

American Funds Washington Mutual Investors Fund Class R-2E B- BUY

Ticker	Traded On	NAV	Total Assets ($)	Dividend Yield (TTM)	Turnover Ratio	Expense Ratio
RWEBX	NAS CM	45.61	$118,091,000,000	1.35	25	1.07

Ratings

Reward	C
Risk	B+
Recent Upgrade/Downgrade	Down

Fund Information

Fund Type	Open End
Category	US Equity Large Cap Blend
Sub-Category	Large Blend
Prospectus Objective	Growth & Income
Inception Date	Aug-14
Open to New Investments	Y
Minimum Initial Investment	250
Minimum Subsequent Investment	50
Front End Fee	
Back End Fee	

Total Returns (%)

3-Month	6-Month	1-Year	3-Year	5-Year
3.92	15.33	9.58	43.88	54.98

Last Bull Market	20.71
Last Bear Market	-12.64
3-Year Standard Deviation	10.52
3-Year Beta	0.84

Company Information

Provider	American Funds
Manager/Tenure	Alan N. Berro (22), Jeffrey T. Lager (15), Alan J. Wilson (6), 4 others
Website	http://www.americanfunds.com
Address	American Funds 333 South Hope Street Los Angeles CA 90071-1406 United States
Phone Number	800-421-4225

PERFORMANCE

Ratings History

Date	Overall Rating	Risk Rating	Reward Rating
Q2-19	B-	B+	C
Q4-18	C+	B	C
Q4-17	B-	B	B-
Q4-16	B	B	B
Q4-15	B	A-	C+

Asset & Performance History

Date	NAV	1-Year Total Return
2018	40.88	-3.43
2017	45.46	19.57
2016	40.81	12.86
2015	38.34	-0.37
2014	40.92	10.96
2013		31.42

Total Assets: $118,091,000,000

Asset Allocation

Asset	%
Cash	4%
Stocks	96%
US Stocks	87%
Bonds	0%
US Bonds	0%
Other	0%

Services Offered: Systematic Withdrawal Plan, Automatic Investment Plan, Qualified Investment, Phone Exchange

Investment Strategy: The investment seeks to produce income and to provide an opportunity for growth of principal consistent with sound common stock investing. The fund invests primarily in common stocks of established companies that are listed on, or meet the financial listing requirements of, the New York Stock Exchange and have a strong record of earnings and dividends. Its advisor strives to maintain a fully invested, diversified portfolio, consisting primarily of high-quality common stocks. **Top Holdings:** Microsoft Corp Intel Corp Broadcom Inc Boeing Co Merck & Co Inc

American Funds Washington Mutual Investors Fund Class 529-F-1 B- BUY

Ticker	Traded On	NAV	Total Assets ($)	Dividend Yield (TTM)	Turnover Ratio	Expense Ratio
CWMFX	NAS CM	45.6	$118,091,000,000	1.97	25	0.4

Ratings

Reward	C
Risk	B+
Recent Upgrade/Downgrade	Down

Fund Information

Fund Type	Open End
Category	US Equity Large Cap Blend
Sub-Category	Large Blend
Prospectus Objective	Growth & Income
Inception Date	Sep-02
Open to New Investments	Y
Minimum Initial Investment	250
Minimum Subsequent Investment	50
Front End Fee	
Back End Fee	

Total Returns (%)

3-Month	6-Month	1-Year	3-Year	5-Year
4.09	15.73	10.31	46.79	59.28

Last Bull Market	21.04
Last Bear Market	-12.48
3-Year Standard Deviation	10.51
3-Year Beta	0.84

Company Information

Provider	American Funds
Manager/Tenure	Alan N. Berro (22), Jeffrey T. Lager (15), Alan J. Wilson (6), 4 others
Website	http://www.americanfunds.com
Address	American Funds 333 South Hope Street Los Angeles CA 90071-1406 United States
Phone Number	800-421-4225

PERFORMANCE

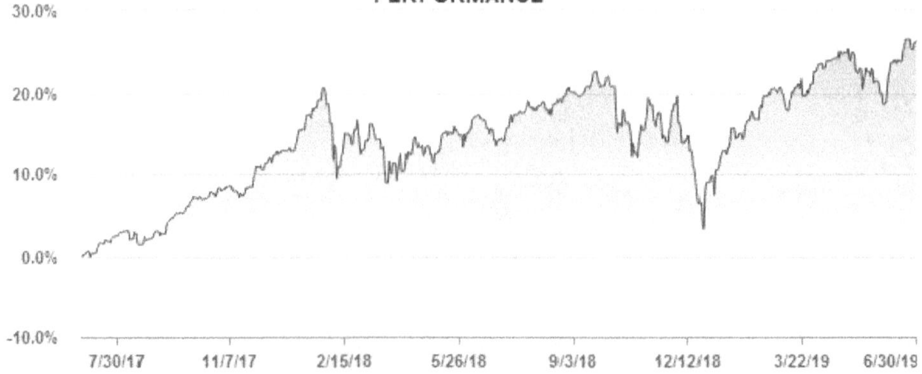

Ratings History

Date	Overall Rating	Risk Rating	Reward Rating
Q2-19	B-	B+	C
Q4-18	C+	B	C
Q4-17	B	B	B
Q4-16	B	B	B
Q4-15	B	A	C+

Asset & Performance History

Date	NAV	1-Year Total Return
2018	40.87	-2.77
2017	45.44	20.34
2016	40.78	13.56
2015	38.29	-0.03
2014	40.8	11.35
2013	39.3	32.08

Total Assets: $118,091,000,000

Asset Allocation

Asset	%
Cash	4%
Stocks	96%
US Stocks	87%
Bonds	0%
US Bonds	0%
Other	0%

Services Offered: Systematic Withdrawal Plan, Automatic Investment Plan, Qualified Investment, Phone Exchange, Retirement Investment

Investment Strategy: The investment seeks to produce income and to provide an opportunity for growth of principal consistent with sound common stock investing. The fund invests primarily in common stocks of established companies that are listed on, or meet the financial listing requirements of, the New York Stock Exchange and have a strong record of earnings and dividends. Its advisor strives to maintain a fully invested, diversified portfolio, consisting primarily of high-quality common stocks. **Top Holdings:** Microsoft Corp Intel Corp Broadcom Inc Boeing Co Merck & Co Inc

American Funds Washington Mutual Investors Fund Class 529-A B- BUY

Ticker	Traded On	NAV	Total Assets ($)	Dividend Yield (TTM)	Turnover Ratio	Expense Ratio
CWMAX	NAS CM	45.72	$118,091,000,000	1.74	25	0.63

Ratings

Reward	C
Risk	B+
Recent Upgrade/Downgrade	Down

Fund Information

Fund Type	Open End
Category	US Equity Large Cap Blend
Sub-Category	Large Blend
Prospectus Objective	Growth & Income
Inception Date	Feb-02
Open to New Investments	Y
Minimum Initial Investment	250
Minimum Subsequent Investment	50
Front End Fee	5.75
Back End Fee	

Total Returns (%)

3-Month	6-Month	1-Year	3-Year	5-Year
4.02	15.58	10.04	45.76	57.47

Last Bull Market	20.91
Last Bear Market	-12.56
3-Year Standard Deviation	10.5
3-Year Beta	0.84

Company Information

Provider	American Funds
Manager/Tenure	Alan N. Berro (22), Jeffrey T. Lager (15), Alan J. Wilson (6), 4 others
Website	http://www.americanfunds.com
Address	American Funds 333 South Hope Street Los Angeles CA 90071-1406 United States
Phone Number	800-421-4225

Ratings History

Date	Overall Rating	Risk Rating	Reward Rating
Q2-19	B-	B+	C
Q4-18	C+	B	C
Q4-17	B	B	B-
Q4-16	B	B	B
Q4-15	B	A-	C+

Asset & Performance History

Date	NAV	1-Year Total Return
2018	40.98	-3
2017	45.55	20.09
2016	40.87	13.31
2015	38.37	-0.24
2014	40.87	11.08
2013	39.37	31.8

Total Assets: $118,091,000,000

Asset Allocation

Asset	%
Cash	4%
Stocks	96%
US Stocks	87%
Bonds	0%
US Bonds	0%
Other	0%

Services Offered: Systematic Withdrawal Plan, Automatic Investment Plan, Qualified Investment, Phone Exchange, Retirement Investment

Investment Strategy: The investment seeks to produce income and to provide an opportunity for growth of principal consistent with sound common stock investing. The fund invests primarily in common stocks of established companies that are listed on, or meet the financial listing requirements of, the New York Stock Exchange and have a strong record of earnings and dividends. Its advisor strives to maintain a fully invested, diversified portfolio, consisting primarily of high-quality common stocks. **Top Holdings:** Microsoft Corp Intel Corp Broadcom Inc Boeing Co Merck & Co Inc

American Funds Washington Mutual Investors Fund Class R-1 B- BUY

Ticker	Traded On	NAV	Total Assets ($)	Dividend Yield (TTM)	Turnover Ratio	Expense Ratio
RWMAX	NAS CM	45.32	$118,091,000,000	1.05	25	1.37

Ratings

Reward	C
Risk	B+
Recent Upgrade/Downgrade	Down

Fund Information

Fund Type	Open End
Category	US Equity Large Cap Blend
Sub-Category	Large Blend
Prospectus Objective	Growth & Income
Inception Date	May-02
Open to New Investments	Y
Minimum Initial Investment	250
Minimum Subsequent Investment	50
Front End Fee	
Back End Fee	

Total Returns (%)

3-Month	6-Month	1-Year	3-Year	5-Year
3.84	15.19	9.27	42.59	51.89

Last Bull Market	20.43
Last Bear Market	-12.83
3-Year Standard Deviation	10.51
3-Year Beta	0.84

Company Information

Provider	American Funds
Manager/Tenure	Alan N. Berro (22), Jeffrey T. Lager (15), Alan J. Wilson (6), 4 others
Website	http://www.americanfunds.com
Address	American Funds 333 South Hope Street Los Angeles CA 90071-1406 United States
Phone Number	800-421-4225

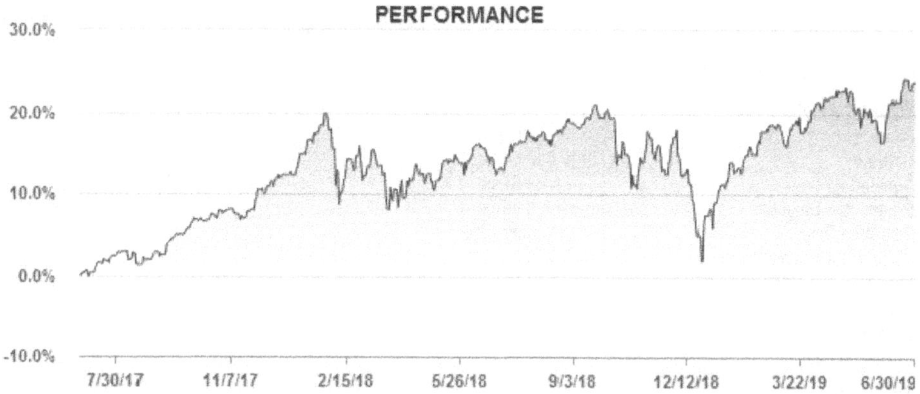

Ratings History

Date	Overall Rating	Risk Rating	Reward Rating
Q2-19	B-	B+	C
Q4-18	C+	B	C
Q4-17	B-	B	B-
Q4-16	B	B	B-
Q4-15	B	A-	C+

Asset & Performance History

Date	NAV	1-Year Total Return
2018	40.63	-3.7
2017	45.17	19.19
2016	40.56	12.5
2015	38.1	-0.95
2014	40.6	10.31
2013	39.13	30.89

Total Assets: $118,091,000,000

Asset Allocation

Asset	%
Cash	4%
Stocks	96%
US Stocks	87%
Bonds	0%
US Bonds	0%
Other	0%

Services Offered: Systematic Withdrawal Plan, Automatic Investment Plan, Qualified Investment, Phone Exchange

Investment Strategy: The investment seeks to produce income and to provide an opportunity for growth of principal consistent with sound common stock investing. The fund invests primarily in common stocks of established companies that are listed on, or meet the financial listing requirements of, the New York Stock Exchange and have a strong record of earnings and dividends. Its advisor strives to maintain a fully invested, diversified portfolio, consisting primarily of high-quality common stocks. **Top Holdings:** Microsoft Corp Intel Corp Broadcom Inc Boeing Co Merck & Co Inc

American Funds Washington Mutual Investors Fund Class R-6 B- BUY

Ticker	Traded On	NAV	Total Assets ($)	Dividend Yield (TTM)	Turnover Ratio	Expense Ratio
RWMGX	NAS CM	45.86	$118,091,000,000	2.07	25	0.27

Ratings

Reward	C
Risk	B+
Recent Upgrade/Downgrade	Down

Fund Information

Fund Type	Open End
Category	US Equity Large Cap Blend
Sub-Category	Large Blend
Prospectus Objective	Growth & Income
Inception Date	May-09
Open to New Investments	Y
Minimum Initial Investment	250
Minimum Subsequent Investment	50
Front End Fee	
Back End Fee	

Total Returns (%)

3-Month	6-Month	1-Year	3-Year	5-Year
4.14	15.82	10.47	47.40	60.43

Last Bull Market	21.2
Last Bear Market	-12.43
3-Year Standard Deviation	10.52
3-Year Beta	0.84

Company Information

Provider	American Funds
Manager/Tenure	Alan N. Berro (22), Jeffrey T. Lager (15), Alan J. Wilson (6), 4 others
Website	http://www.americanfunds.com
Address	American Funds 333 South Hope Street Los Angeles CA 90071-1406 United States
Phone Number	800-421-4225

Ratings History

Date	Overall Rating	Risk Rating	Reward Rating
Q2-19	B-	B+	C
Q4-18	C+	B	C
Q4-17	B	B	B
Q4-16	B	B	B
Q4-15	B	A	C+

Asset & Performance History

Date	NAV	1-Year Total Return
2018	41.09	-2.66
2017	45.67	20.53
2016	40.96	13.73
2015	38.45	0.12
2014	40.96	11.53
2013	39.44	32.33

Total Assets: $118,091,000,000

Asset Allocation

Asset	%
Cash	4%
Stocks	96%
US Stocks	87%
Bonds	0%
US Bonds	0%
Other	0%

Services Offered: Systematic Withdrawal Plan, Automatic Investment Plan, Qualified Investment, Phone Exchange

Investment Strategy: The investment seeks to produce income and to provide an opportunity for growth of principal consistent with sound common stock investing. The fund invests primarily in common stocks of established companies that are listed on, or meet the financial listing requirements of, the New York Stock Exchange and have a strong record of earnings and dividends. Its advisor strives to maintain a fully invested, diversified portfolio, consisting primarily of high-quality common stocks. **Top Holdings:** Microsoft Corp Intel Corp Broadcom Inc Boeing Co Merck & Co Inc

American Funds Washington Mutual Investors Fund Class R-2 B- BUY

Ticker	Traded On	NAV	Total Assets ($)	Dividend Yield (TTM)	Turnover Ratio	Expense Ratio
RWMBX	NAS CM	45.13	$118,091,000,000	1.07	25	1.37

Ratings

Reward	C
Risk	B+
Recent Upgrade/Downgrade	Down

Fund Information

Fund Type	Open End
Category	US Equity Large Cap Blend
Sub-Category	Large Blend
Prospectus Objective	Growth & Income
Inception Date	May-02
Open to New Investments	Y
Minimum Initial Investment	250
Minimum Subsequent Investment	50
Front End Fee	
Back End Fee	

Total Returns (%)

3-Month	6-Month	1-Year	3-Year	5-Year
3.84	15.18	9.24	42.58	51.99

Last Bull Market	20.48
Last Bear Market	-12.82
3-Year Standard Deviation	10.49
3-Year Beta	0.84

Company Information

Provider	American Funds
Manager/Tenure	Alan N. Berro (22), Jeffrey T. Lager (15), Alan J. Wilson (6), 4 others
Website	http://www.americanfunds.com
Address	American Funds 333 South Hope Street Los Angeles CA 90071-1406 United States
Phone Number	800-421-4225

Ratings History

Date	Overall Rating	Risk Rating	Reward Rating
Q2-19	B-	B+	C
Q4-18	C+	B	C
Q4-17	B-	B	B-
Q4-16	B	B	B-
Q4-15	B	A-	C+

Asset & Performance History

Date	NAV	1-Year Total Return
2018	40.47	-3.72
2017	45.02	19.21
2016	40.43	12.53
2015	37.98	-0.91
2014	40.48	10.34
2013	39.02	30.94

Total Assets: $118,091,000,000

Asset Allocation

Asset	%
Cash	4%
Stocks	96%
US Stocks	87%
Bonds	0%
US Bonds	0%
Other	0%

Services Offered: Systematic Withdrawal Plan, Automatic Investment Plan, Qualified Investment, Phone Exchange

Investment Strategy: The investment seeks to produce income and to provide an opportunity for growth of principal consistent with sound common stock investing. The fund invests primarily in common stocks of established companies that are listed on, or meet the financial listing requirements of, the New York Stock Exchange and have a strong record of earnings and dividends. Its advisor strives to maintain a fully invested, diversified portfolio, consisting primarily of high-quality common stocks. **Top Holdings:** Microsoft Corp Intel Corp Broadcom Inc Boeing Co Merck & Co Inc

American Funds Washington Mutual Investors Fund Class C B- BUY

Ticker	Traded On	NAV	Total Assets ($)	Dividend Yield (TTM)	Turnover Ratio	Expense Ratio
WSHCX	NAS CM	45.2	$118,091,000,000	1.1	25	1.34

Ratings

Reward	C
Risk	B+
Recent Upgrade/Downgrade	Down

Fund Information

Fund Type	Open End
Category	US Equity Large Cap Blend
Sub-Category	Large Blend
Prospectus Objective	Growth & Income
Inception Date	Mar-01
Open to New Investments	Y
Minimum Initial Investment	250
Minimum Subsequent Investment	50
Front End Fee	
Back End Fee	1.00

Total Returns (%)

3-Month	6-Month	1-Year	3-Year	5-Year
3.86	15.19	9.29	42.69	52.03

Last Bull Market	20.4
Last Bear Market	-12.8
3-Year Standard Deviation	10.51
3-Year Beta	0.84

Company Information

Provider	American Funds
Manager/Tenure	Alan N. Berro (22), Jeffrey T. Lager (15), Alan J. Wilson (6), 4 others
Website	http://www.americanfunds.com
Address	American Funds 333 South Hope Street Los Angeles CA 90071-1406 United States
Phone Number	800-421-4225

Ratings History

Date	Overall Rating	Risk Rating	Reward Rating
Q2-19	B-	B+	C
Q4-18	C+	B	C
Q4-17	B-	B	B-
Q4-16	B	B	B-
Q4-15	B	A-	C+

Asset & Performance History

Date	NAV	1-Year Total Return
2018	40.52	-3.7
2017	45.08	19.25
2016	40.47	12.48
2015	38.03	-0.92
2014	40.52	10.32
2013	39.05	30.86

Total Assets: $118,091,000,000

Asset Allocation

Asset	%
Cash	4%
Stocks	96%
US Stocks	87%
Bonds	0%
US Bonds	0%
Other	0%

Services Offered: Systematic Withdrawal Plan, Automatic Investment Plan, Phone Exchange, Retirement Investment

Investment Strategy: The investment seeks to produce income and to provide an opportunity for growth of principal consistent with sound common stock investing. The fund invests primarily in common stocks of established companies that are listed on, or meet the financial listing requirements of, the New York Stock Exchange and have a strong record of earnings and dividends. Its advisor strives to maintain a fully invested, diversified portfolio, consisting primarily of high-quality common stocks. **Top Holdings:** Microsoft Corp Intel Corp Broadcom Inc Boeing Co Merck & Co Inc

American Funds Washington Mutual Investors Fund Class F-2 B- BUY

Ticker	Traded On	NAV	Total Assets ($)	Dividend Yield (TTM)	Turnover Ratio	Expense Ratio
WMFFX	NAS CM	45.79	$118,091,000,000	1.99	25	0.36

Ratings

Reward	C
Risk	B+
Recent Upgrade/Downgrade	Down

Fund Information

Fund Type	Open End
Category	US Equity Large Cap Blend
Sub-Category	Large Blend
Prospectus Objective	Growth & Income
Inception Date	Aug-08
Open to New Investments	Y
Minimum Initial Investment	250
Minimum Subsequent Investment	50
Front End Fee	
Back End Fee	

Total Returns (%)

3-Month	6-Month	1-Year	3-Year	5-Year
4.10	15.73	10.35	46.94	59.58

Last Bull Market	21.12
Last Bear Market	-12.44
3-Year Standard Deviation	10.51
3-Year Beta	0.84

Company Information

Provider	American Funds
Manager/Tenure	Alan N. Berro (22), Jeffrey T. Lager (15), Alan J. Wilson (6), 4 others
Website	http://www.americanfunds.com
Address	American Funds 333 South Hope Street Los Angeles CA 90071-1406 United States
Phone Number	800-421-4225

Ratings History

Date	Overall Rating	Risk Rating	Reward Rating
Q2-19	B-	B+	C
Q4-18	C+	B	C
Q4-17	B	B	B
Q4-16	B	B	B
Q4-15	B	A	C+

Asset & Performance History

Date	NAV	1-Year Total Return
2018	41.04	-2.72
2017	45.61	20.38
2016	40.92	13.62
2015	38.41	0.01
2014	40.92	11.41
2013	39.41	32.18

Total Assets: $118,091,000,000

Asset Allocation

Asset	%
Cash	4%
Stocks	96%
US Stocks	87%
Bonds	0%
US Bonds	0%
Other	0%

Services Offered: Systematic Withdrawal Plan, Automatic Investment Plan, Qualified Investment, Phone Exchange, Retirement Investment

Investment Strategy: The investment seeks to produce income and to provide an opportunity for growth of principal consistent with sound common stock investing. The fund invests primarily in common stocks of established companies that are listed on, or meet the financial listing requirements of, the New York Stock Exchange and have a strong record of earnings and dividends. Its advisor strives to maintain a fully invested, diversified portfolio, consisting primarily of high-quality common stocks. **Top Holdings:** Microsoft Corp Intel Corp Broadcom Inc Boeing Co Merck & Co Inc

American Funds Washington Mutual Investors Fund Class A — B- BUY

Ticker	Traded On	NAV	Total Assets ($)	Dividend Yield (TTM)	Turnover Ratio	Expense Ratio
AWSHX	NAS CM	45.84	$118,091,000,000	1.81	25	0.59

Ratings

Reward	C
Risk	B+
Recent Upgrade/Downgrade	Down

Fund Information

Fund Type	Open End
Category	US Equity Large Cap Blend
Sub-Category	Large Blend
Prospectus Objective	Growth & Income
Inception Date	Jul-52
Open to New Investments	Y
Minimum Initial Investment	250
Minimum Subsequent Investment	50
Front End Fee	5.75
Back End Fee	

Total Returns (%)

3-Month	6-Month	1-Year	3-Year	5-Year
4.05	15.64	10.16	46.15	58.16

Last Bull Market	20.97
Last Bear Market	-12.51
3-Year Standard Deviation	10.51
3-Year Beta	0.84

Company Information

Provider	American Funds
Manager/Tenure	Alan N. Berro (22), Jeffrey T. Lager (15), Alan J. Wilson (6), 4 others
Website	http://www.americanfunds.com
Address	American Funds 333 South Hope Street Los Angeles CA 90071-1406 United States
Phone Number	800-421-4225

Ratings History

Date	Overall Rating	Risk Rating	Reward Rating
Q2-19	B-	B+	C
Q4-18	C+	B	C
Q4-17	B	B	B-
Q4-16	B	B	B
Q4-15	B	A-	C+

Asset & Performance History

Date	NAV	1-Year Total Return
2018	41.08	-2.91
2017	45.65	20.19
2016	40.95	13.4
2015	38.44	-0.16
2014	40.95	11.22
2013	39.43	31.9

Total Assets: $118,091,000,000

Asset Allocation

Asset	%
Cash	4%
Stocks	96%
US Stocks	87%
Bonds	0%
US Bonds	0%
Other	0%

Services Offered: Systematic Withdrawal Plan, Automatic Investment Plan, Phone Exchange, Retirement Investment

Investment Strategy: The investment seeks to produce income and to provide an opportunity for growth of principal consistent with sound common stock investing. The fund invests primarily in common stocks of established companies that are listed on, or meet the financial listing requirements of, the New York Stock Exchange and have a strong record of earnings and dividends. Its advisor strives to maintain a fully invested, diversified portfolio, consisting primarily of high-quality common stocks. **Top Holdings:** Microsoft Corp Intel Corp Broadcom Inc Boeing Co Merck & Co Inc

American Funds Washington Mutual Investors Fund Class 529-E — B- BUY

Ticker	Traded On	NAV	Total Assets ($)	Dividend Yield (TTM)	Turnover Ratio	Expense Ratio
CWMEX	NAS CM	45.44	$118,091,000,000	1.52	25	0.87

Ratings

Reward	C
Risk	B+
Recent Upgrade/Downgrade	Down

Fund Information

Fund Type	Open End
Category	US Equity Large Cap Blend
Sub-Category	Large Blend
Prospectus Objective	Growth & Income
Inception Date	Mar-02
Open to New Investments	Y
Minimum Initial Investment	250
Minimum Subsequent Investment	50
Front End Fee	
Back End Fee	

Total Returns (%)

3-Month	6-Month	1-Year	3-Year	5-Year
3.96	15.45	9.80	44.74	55.59

Last Bull Market	20.76
Last Bear Market	-12.67
3-Year Standard Deviation	10.51
3-Year Beta	0.84

Company Information

Provider	American Funds
Manager/Tenure	Alan N. Berro (22), Jeffrey T. Lager (15), Alan J. Wilson (6), 4 others
Website	http://www.americanfunds.com
Address	American Funds 333 South Hope Street Los Angeles CA 90071-1406 United States
Phone Number	800-421-4225

Ratings History

Date	Overall Rating	Risk Rating	Reward Rating
Q2-19	B-	B+	C
Q4-18	C+	B	C
Q4-17	B	B	B-
Q4-16	B	B	B
Q4-15	B	A-	C+

Asset & Performance History

Date	NAV	1-Year Total Return
2018	40.73	-3.25
2017	45.3	19.8
2016	40.66	13.02
2015	38.19	-0.48
2014	40.69	10.83
2013	39.2	31.44

Total Assets: $118,091,000,000

Asset Allocation

Asset	%
Cash	4%
Stocks	96%
US Stocks	87%
Bonds	0%
US Bonds	0%
Other	0%

Services Offered: Systematic Withdrawal Plan, Automatic Investment Plan, Qualified Investment, Phone Exchange, Retirement Investment

Investment Strategy: The investment seeks to produce income and to provide an opportunity for growth of principal consistent with sound common stock investing. The fund invests primarily in common stocks of established companies that are listed on, or meet the financial listing requirements of, the New York Stock Exchange and have a strong record of earnings and dividends. Its advisor strives to maintain a fully invested, diversified portfolio, consisting primarily of high-quality common stocks. **Top Holdings:** Microsoft Corp Intel Corp Broadcom Inc Boeing Co Merck & Co Inc

American Funds Washington Mutual Investors Fund Class F-1 B- BUY

Ticker	Traded On	NAV	Total Assets ($)	Dividend Yield (TTM)	Turnover Ratio	Expense Ratio
WSHFX	NAS CM	45.65	$118,091,000,000	1.74	25	0.64

Ratings

Reward	C
Risk	B+
Recent Upgrade/Downgrade	Down

Fund Information

Fund Type	Open End
Category	US Equity Large Cap Blend
Sub-Category	Large Blend
Prospectus Objective	Growth & Income
Inception Date	Mar-01
Open to New Investments	Y
Minimum Initial Investment	250
Minimum Subsequent Investment	50
Front End Fee	
Back End Fee	

Total Returns (%)

3-Month	6-Month	1-Year	3-Year	5-Year
4.02	15.58	10.06	45.75	57.48

Last Bull Market	20.97
Last Bear Market	-12.56
3-Year Standard Deviation	10.52
3-Year Beta	0.84

Company Information

Provider	American Funds
Manager/Tenure	Alan N. Berro (22), Jeffrey T. Lager (15), Alan J. Wilson (6), 4 others
Website	http://www.americanfunds.com
Address	American Funds 333 South Hope Street Los Angeles CA 90071-1406 United States
Phone Number	800-421-4225

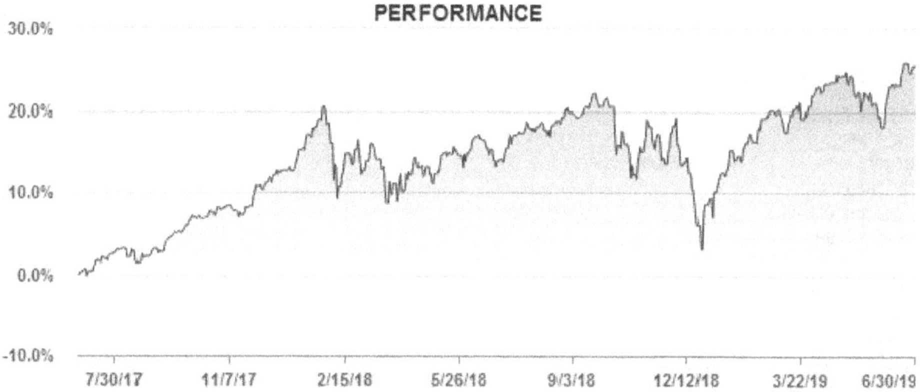

Ratings History

Date	Overall Rating	Risk Rating	Reward Rating
Q2-19	B-	B+	C
Q4-18	C+	B	C
Q4-17	B	B	B-
Q4-16	B	B	B
Q4-15	B	A-	C+

Asset & Performance History

Date	NAV	1-Year Total Return
2018	40.91	-3.01
2017	45.48	20.06
2016	40.81	13.3
2015	38.32	-0.22
2014	40.82	11.12
2013	39.31	31.81

Total Assets: $118,091,000,000

Asset Allocation

Asset	%
Cash	4%
Stocks	96%
US Stocks	87%
Bonds	0%
US Bonds	0%
Other	0%

Services Offered: Systematic Withdrawal Plan, Automatic Investment Plan, Qualified Investment, Phone Exchange, Retirement Investment

Investment Strategy: The investment seeks to produce income and to provide an opportunity for growth of principal consistent with sound common stock investing. The fund invests primarily in common stocks of established companies that are listed on, or meet the financial listing requirements of, the New York Stock Exchange and have a strong record of earnings and dividends. Its advisor strives to maintain a fully invested, diversified portfolio, consisting primarily of high-quality common stocks. **Top Holdings:** Microsoft Corp Intel Corp Broadcom Inc Boeing Co Merck & Co Inc

American Funds Washington Mutual Investors Fund Class R-4 B- BUY

Ticker	Traded On	NAV	Total Assets ($)	Dividend Yield (TTM)	Turnover Ratio	Expense Ratio
RWMEX	NAS CM	45.57	$118,091,000,000	1.75	25	0.62

Ratings

Reward	C
Risk	B+
Recent Upgrade/Downgrade	Down

Fund Information

Fund Type	Open End
Category	US Equity Large Cap Blend
Sub-Category	Large Blend
Prospectus Objective	Growth & Income
Inception Date	May-02
Open to New Investments	Y
Minimum Initial Investment	250
Minimum Subsequent Investment	50
Front End Fee	
Back End Fee	

Total Returns (%)

3-Month	6-Month	1-Year	3-Year	5-Year
4.03	15.59	10.07	45.82	57.64

Last Bull Market	20.95
Last Bear Market	-12.54
3-Year Standard Deviation	10.5
3-Year Beta	0.84

Company Information

Provider	American Funds
Manager/Tenure	Alan N. Berro (22), Jeffrey T. Lager (15), Alan J. Wilson (6), 4 others
Website	http://www.americanfunds.com
Address	American Funds 333 South Hope Street Los Angeles CA 90071-1406 United States
Phone Number	800-421-4225

Ratings History

Date	Overall Rating	Risk Rating	Reward Rating
Q2-19	B-	B+	C
Q4-18	C+	B	C
Q4-17	B	B	B-
Q4-16	B	B	B
Q4-15	B	A-	C+

Asset & Performance History

Date	NAV	1-Year Total Return
2018	40.85	-2.99
2017	45.42	20.11
2016	40.76	13.35
2015	38.27	-0.22
2014	40.78	11.15
2013	39.28	31.84

Total Assets: $118,091,000,000

Asset Allocation

Asset	%
Cash	4%
Stocks	96%
US Stocks	87%
Bonds	0%
US Bonds	0%
Other	0%

Services Offered: Systematic Withdrawal Plan, Automatic Investment Plan, Qualified Investment, Phone Exchange

Investment Strategy: The investment seeks to produce income and to provide an opportunity for growth of principal consistent with sound common stock investing. The fund invests primarily in common stocks of established companies that are listed on, or meet the financial listing requirements of, the New York Stock Exchange and have a strong record of earnings and dividends. Its advisor strives to maintain a fully invested, diversified portfolio, consisting primarily of high-quality common stocks. **Top Holdings:** Microsoft Corp Intel Corp Broadcom Inc Boeing Co Merck & Co Inc

Vanguard Developed Markets Index Fund Investor Shares — C HOLD

Ticker	Traded On	NAV	Total Assets ($)	Dividend Yield (TTM)	Turnover Ratio	Expense Ratio
VDVIX	NAS CM	10.38	$114,759,000,000	2.69	3	0.16

Ratings

Reward	C
Risk	B
Recent Upgrade/Downgrade	

Fund Information

Fund Type	Open End
Category	Global Equity Large Cap
Sub-Category	Foreign Large Blend
Prospectus Objective	Foreign Stock
Inception Date	Dec-13
Open to New Investments	Y
Minimum Initial Investment	3,000
Minimum Subsequent Investment	1
Front End Fee	
Back End Fee	

Total Returns (%)

3-Month	6-Month	1-Year	3-Year	5-Year
3.27	14.25	-0.01	30.31	12.89

Last Bull Market	13.21
Last Bear Market	-23.33
3-Year Standard Deviation	11.34
3-Year Beta	1

Company Information

Provider	Vanguard
Manager/Tenure	Christine D. Franquin (6), Michael Perre (1)
Website	http://www.vanguard.com
Address	Vanguard 100 Vanguard Boulevard Malvern PA 19355 United States
Phone Number	877-662-7447

Ratings History

Date	Overall Rating	Risk Rating	Reward Rating
Q2-19	C	B-	C-
Q4-18	C-	C	D+
Q4-17	B-	B	B-
Q4-16	C-	C	D+
Q4-15	C-	C	C-

Asset & Performance History

Date	NAV	1-Year Total Return
2018	9.26	-14.56
2017	11.16	26.3
2016	9.09	2.35
2015	9.15	-0.28
2014	9.42	-5.82
2013	10.34	21.96

Total Assets: $114,759,000,000

Asset Allocation

Asset	%
Cash	4%
Stocks	96%
US Stocks	1%
Bonds	0%
US Bonds	0%
Other	0%

Services Offered: Systematic Withdrawal Plan, Automatic Investment Plan, Phone Exchange, Wire Redemption

Investment Strategy: The investment seeks to track the performance of the FTSE Developed All Cap ex US Index. The fund employs an indexing investment approach designed to track the performance of the FTSE Developed All Cap ex US Index, a market-capitalization-weighted index that is made up of approximately 3,885 common stocks of large-, mid-, and small-cap companies located in Canada and the major markets of Europe and the Pacific region. The adviser attempts to replicate the target index by investing all, or substantially all, of its assets in the stocks that make up the index, holding each stock in approximately the same proportion as its weighting in the index. **Top Holdings:** Nestle SA Roche Holding AG Dividend Right Cert. Novartis AG HSBC Holdings PLC Samsung Electronics Co Ltd

Vanguard Developed Markets Index Fund Admiral Shares — C HOLD

Ticker	Traded On	NAV	Total Assets ($)	Dividend Yield (TTM)	Turnover Ratio	Expense Ratio
VTMGX	NAS CM	13.4	$114,759,000,000	2.78	3	0.07

Ratings

Reward	C
Risk	B
Recent Upgrade/Downgrade	

Fund Information

Fund Type	Open End
Category	Global Equity Large Cap
Sub-Category	Foreign Large Blend
Prospectus Objective	Foreign Stock
Inception Date	Aug-99
Open to New Investments	Y
Minimum Initial Investment	3,000
Minimum Subsequent Investment	1
Front End Fee	
Back End Fee	

Total Returns (%)

3-Month	6-Month	1-Year	3-Year	5-Year
3.26	14.33	-0.01	30.61	13.45

Last Bull Market	13.27
Last Bear Market	-23.3
3-Year Standard Deviation	11.36
3-Year Beta	1

Company Information

Provider	Vanguard
Manager/Tenure	Christine D. Franquin (6), Michael Perre (1)
Website	http://www.vanguard.com
Address	Vanguard 100 Vanguard Boulevard Malvern PA 19355 United States
Phone Number	877-662-7447

Ratings History

Date	Overall Rating	Risk Rating	Reward Rating
Q2-19	C	B-	C-
Q4-18	C-	C	D+
Q4-17	B	B	B-
Q4-16	C-	C	D+
Q4-15	C-	C	C-

Asset & Performance History

Date	NAV	1-Year Total Return
2018	11.96	-14.45
2017	14.41	26.39
2016	11.74	2.45
2015	11.82	-0.18
2014	12.17	-5.66
2013	13.35	22.06

Total Assets: $114,759,000,000

Asset Allocation

Asset	%
Cash	4%
Stocks	96%
US Stocks	1%
Bonds	0%
US Bonds	0%
Other	0%

Services Offered: Systematic Withdrawal Plan, Automatic Investment Plan, Phone Exchange, Wire Redemption

Investment Strategy: The investment seeks to track the performance of the FTSE Developed All Cap ex US Index. The fund employs an indexing investment approach designed to track the performance of the FTSE Developed All Cap ex US Index, a market-capitalization-weighted index that is made up of approximately 3,885 common stocks of large-, mid-, and small-cap companies located in Canada and the major markets of Europe and the Pacific region. The adviser attempts to replicate the target index by investing all, or substantially all, of its assets in the stocks that make up the index, holding each stock in approximately the same proportion as its weighting in the index. **Top Holdings:** Nestle SA Roche Holding AG Dividend Right Cert. Novartis AG HSBC Holdings PLC Samsung Electronics Co Ltd

American Funds The Income Fund of America® Class F-1 B BUY

Ticker	Traded On	NAV	Total Assets ($)	Dividend Yield (TTM)	Turnover Ratio	Expense Ratio
IFAFX	NAS CM	22.43	$109,899,000,000	2.88	70	0.64

Ratings

Reward	C
Risk	A-
Recent Upgrade/Downgrade	Up

Fund Information

Fund Type	Open End
Category	Aggressive Alloc
Sub-Category	Alloc--70% to 85% Equity
Prospectus Objective	Income
Inception Date	Mar-01
Open to New Investments	Y
Minimum Initial Investment	250
Minimum Subsequent Investment	50
Front End Fee	
Back End Fee	

Total Returns (%)

3-Month	6-Month	1-Year	3-Year	5-Year
2.59	11.11	6.43	24.63	30.89

Last Bull Market	14.52
Last Bear Market	-10.11
3-Year Standard Deviation	7.12
3-Year Beta	0.56

Company Information

Provider	American Funds
Manager/Tenure	Dina N. Perry (27), Hilda L. Applbaum (21), Andrew B. Suzman (19), 6 others
Website	http://www.americanfunds.com
Address	American Funds 333 South Hope Street Los Angeles CA 90071-1406 United States
Phone Number	800-421-4225

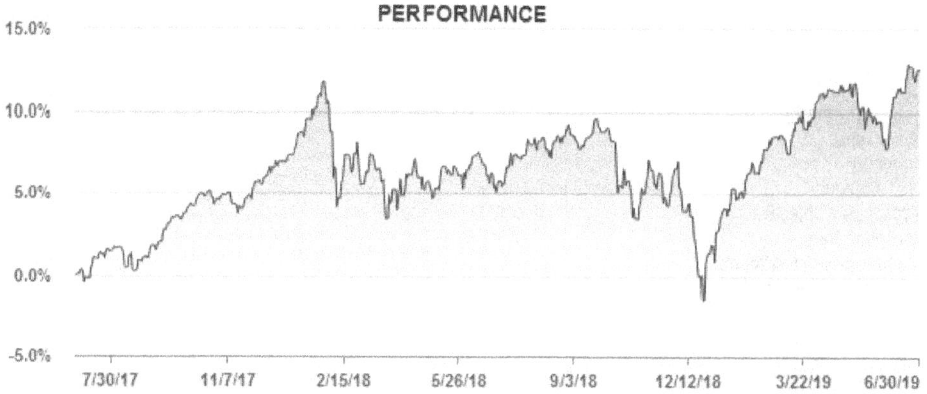

Ratings History

Date	Overall Rating	Risk Rating	Reward Rating
Q2-19	B	A-	C
Q4-18	C	B-	C
Q4-17	B-	B	C+
Q4-16	B-	B	B-
Q4-15	B-	B+	C

Asset & Performance History

Date	NAV	1-Year Total Return
2018	20.58	-5.16
2017	23.31	13.24
2016	21.62	10.5
2015	20.18	-1.55
2014	21.53	8.31
2013	20.6	18.09

Total Assets: $109,899,000,000

Asset Allocation

Asset	%
Cash	7%
Stocks	66%
US Stocks	48%
Bonds	27%
US Bonds	24%
Other	0%

Services Offered: Systematic Withdrawal Plan, Automatic Investment Plan, Qualified Investment, Phone Exchange, Retirement Investment

Investment Strategy: The investment seeks to provide investors with current income while secondarily striving for capital growth. Normally the fund invests primarily in income-producing securities. These include equity securities, such as dividend-paying common stocks, and debt securities, such as interest-paying bonds. Generally at least 60% of the fund's assets will be invested in common stocks and other equity-type securities. The fund may also invest up to 30% of its assets in equity securities of issuers domiciled outside the United States, including issuers in developing countries. **Top Holdings:** Merck & Co Inc Microsoft Corp United States Treasury Notes 2.62% United States Treasury Bills 0.39% Verizon Communications Inc

American Funds The Income Fund of America® Class A B BUY

Ticker	Traded On	NAV	Total Assets ($)	Dividend Yield (TTM)	Turnover Ratio	Expense Ratio
AMECX	NAS CM	22.5	$109,899,000,000	2.96	70	0.55

Ratings

Reward	C
Risk	A-
Recent Upgrade/Downgrade	Up

Fund Information

Fund Type	Open End
Category	Aggressive Alloc
Sub-Category	Alloc--70% to 85% Equity
Prospectus Objective	Income
Inception Date	Nov-73
Open to New Investments	Y
Minimum Initial Investment	250
Minimum Subsequent Investment	50
Front End Fee	5.75
Back End Fee	

Total Returns (%)

3-Month	6-Month	1-Year	3-Year	5-Year
2.65	11.23	6.55	25.02	31.51

Last Bull Market	14.52
Last Bear Market	-10.07
3-Year Standard Deviation	7.16
3-Year Beta	0.56

Company Information

Provider	American Funds
Manager/Tenure	Dina N. Perry (27), Hilda L. Applbaum (21), Andrew B. Suzman (19), 6 others
Website	http://www.americanfunds.com
Address	American Funds 333 South Hope Street Los Angeles CA 90071-1406 United States
Phone Number	800-421-4225

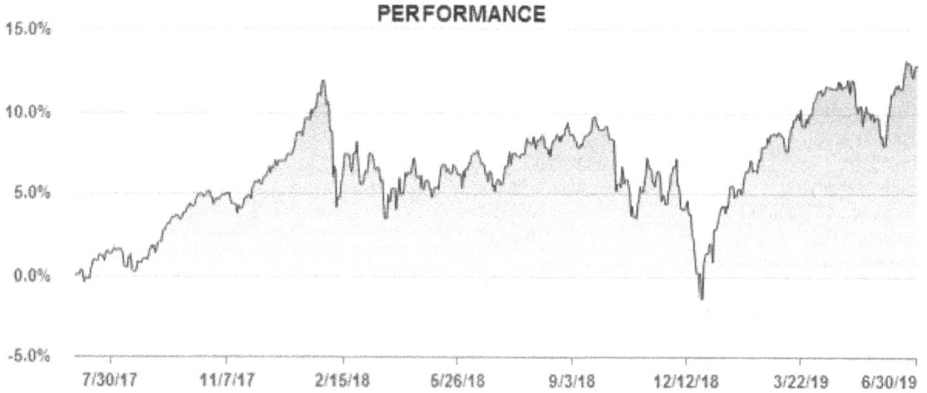

Ratings History

Date	Overall Rating	Risk Rating	Reward Rating
Q2-19	B	A-	C
Q4-18	C	B-	C
Q4-17	B-	B	C+
Q4-16	B-	B	B-
Q4-15	B-	B+	C

Asset & Performance History

Date	NAV	1-Year Total Return
2018	20.63	-5.11
2017	23.37	13.37
2016	21.67	10.57
2015	20.23	-1.47
2014	21.58	8.39
2013	20.65	18.25

Total Assets: $109,899,000,000

Asset Allocation

Asset	%
Cash	7%
Stocks	66%
US Stocks	48%
Bonds	27%
US Bonds	24%
Other	0%

Services Offered: Systematic Withdrawal Plan, Automatic Investment Plan, Phone Exchange, Retirement Investment

Investment Strategy: The investment seeks to provide investors with current income while secondarily striving for capital growth. Normally the fund invests primarily in income-producing securities. These include equity securities, such as dividend-paying common stocks, and debt securities, such as interest-paying bonds. Generally at least 60% of the fund's assets will be invested in common stocks and other equity-type securities. The fund may also invest up to 30% of its assets in equity securities of issuers domiciled outside the United States, including issuers in developing countries. **Top Holdings:** Merck & Co Inc Microsoft Corp United States Treasury Notes 2.62% United States Treasury Bills 0.39% Verizon Communications Inc

American Funds The Income Fund of America® Class R-5 B BUY

Ticker	Traded On	NAV	Total Assets ($)	Dividend Yield (TTM)	Turnover Ratio	Expense Ratio
RIDFX	NAS CM	22.49	$109,899,000,000	3.18	70	0.33

Ratings

Reward	C
Risk	A-
Recent Upgrade/Downgrade	Up

Fund Information

Fund Type	Open End
Category	Aggressive Alloc
Sub-Category	Alloc--70% to 85% Equity
Prospectus Objective	Income
Inception Date	May-02
Open to New Investments	Y
Minimum Initial Investment	250
Minimum Subsequent Investment	50
Front End Fee	
Back End Fee	

Total Returns (%)

3-Month	6-Month	1-Year	3-Year	5-Year
2.67	11.31	6.75	25.87	33.00

Last Bull Market	14.72
Last Bear Market	-9.97
3-Year Standard Deviation	7.13
3-Year Beta	0.56

Company Information

Provider	American Funds
Manager/Tenure	Dina N. Perry (27), Hilda L. Applbaum (21), Andrew B. Suzman (19), 6 others
Website	http://www.americanfunds.com
Address	American Funds 333 South Hope Street Los Angeles CA 90071-1406 United States
Phone Number	800-421-4225

Ratings History

Date	Overall Rating	Risk Rating	Reward Rating
Q2-19	B	A-	C+
Q4-18	C	B-	C
Q4-17	B-	B	C+
Q4-16	B-	B	B-
Q4-15	C+	C+	C

Asset & Performance History

Date	NAV	1-Year Total Return
2018	20.63	-4.85
2017	23.36	13.56
2016	21.67	10.88
2015	20.22	-1.29
2014	21.58	8.68
2013	20.64	18.47

Total Assets: $109,899,000,000

Asset Allocation

Asset	%
Cash	7%
Stocks	66%
US Stocks	48%
Bonds	27%
US Bonds	24%
Other	0%

Services Offered: Automatic Investment Plan, Qualified Investment, Phone Exchange

Investment Strategy: The investment seeks to provide investors with current income while secondarily striving for capital growth. Normally the fund invests primarily in income-producing securities. These include equity securities, such as dividend-paying common stocks, and debt securities, such as interest-paying bonds. Generally at least 60% of the fund's assets will be invested in common stocks and other equity-type securities. The fund may also invest up to 30% of its assets in equity securities of issuers domiciled outside the United States, including issuers in developing countries. **Top Holdings:** Merck & Co Inc Microsoft Corp United States Treasury Notes 2.62% United States Treasury Bills 0.39% Verizon Communications Inc

American Funds The Income Fund of America® Class R-5E B BUY

Ticker	Traded On	NAV	Total Assets ($)	Dividend Yield (TTM)	Turnover Ratio	Expense Ratio
RIDHX	NAS CM	22.47	$109,899,000,000	3.1	70	0.42

Ratings

Reward	C
Risk	A-
Recent Upgrade/Downgrade	Up

Fund Information

Fund Type	Open End
Category	Aggressive Alloc
Sub-Category	Alloc--70% to 85% Equity
Prospectus Objective	Income
Inception Date	Nov-15
Open to New Investments	Y
Minimum Initial Investment	250
Minimum Subsequent Investment	50
Front End Fee	
Back End Fee	

Total Returns (%)

3-Month	6-Month	1-Year	3-Year	5-Year
2.69	11.33	6.66	25.42	31.99

Last Bull Market	14.52
Last Bear Market	-10.07
3-Year Standard Deviation	7.14
3-Year Beta	0.56

Company Information

Provider	American Funds
Manager/Tenure	Dina N. Perry (27), Hilda L. Applbaum (21), Andrew B. Suzman (19), 6 others
Website	http://www.americanfunds.com
Address	American Funds 333 South Hope Street Los Angeles CA 90071-1406 United States
Phone Number	800-421-4225

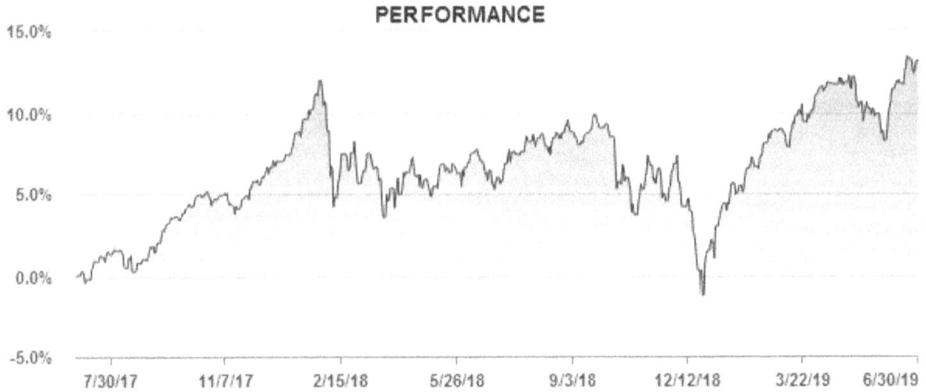

Ratings History

Date	Overall Rating	Risk Rating	Reward Rating
Q2-19	B	A-	C
Q4-18	C	B-	C
Q4-17	B-	B	C+
Q4-16	B-	B	B-
Q4-15			

Asset & Performance History

Date	NAV	1-Year Total Return
2018	20.61	-4.94
2017	23.34	13.46
2016	21.66	10.64
2015	20.22	-1.46
2014		8.39
2013		18.25

Total Assets: $109,899,000,000

Asset Allocation

Asset	%
Cash	7%
Stocks	66%
US Stocks	48%
Bonds	27%
US Bonds	24%
Other	0%

Services Offered: Automatic Investment Plan, Qualified Investment, Phone Exchange

Investment Strategy: The investment seeks to provide investors with current income while secondarily striving for capital growth. Normally the fund invests primarily in income-producing securities. These include equity securities, such as dividend-paying common stocks, and debt securities, such as interest-paying bonds. Generally at least 60% of the fund's assets will be invested in common stocks and other equity-type securities. The fund may also invest up to 30% of its assets in equity securities of issuers domiciled outside the United States, including issuers in developing countries. **Top Holdings:** Merck & Co Inc Microsoft Corp United States Treasury Notes 2.62% United States Treasury Bills 0.39% Verizon Communications Inc

American Funds The Income Fund of America® Class R-2E B- BUY

Ticker	Traded On	NAV	Total Assets ($)	Dividend Yield (TTM)	Turnover Ratio	Expense Ratio
RIEBX	NAS CM	22.44	$109,899,000,000	2.48	70	1.08

Ratings

Reward	C
Risk	A-
Recent Upgrade/Downgrade	Up

Fund Information

Fund Type	Open End
Category	Aggressive Alloc
Sub-Category	Alloc--70% to 85% Equity
Prospectus Objective	Income
Inception Date	Aug-14
Open to New Investments	Y
Minimum Initial Investment	250
Minimum Subsequent Investment	50
Front End Fee	
Back End Fee	

Total Returns (%)

3-Month	6-Month	1-Year	3-Year	5-Year
2.53	10.94	5.98	23.06	28.56

Last Bull Market	14.28
Last Bear Market	-10.2
3-Year Standard Deviation	7.14
3-Year Beta	0.56

Company Information

Provider	American Funds
Manager/Tenure	Dina N. Perry (27), Hilda L. Applbaum (21), Andrew B. Suzman (19), 6 others
Website	http://www.americanfunds.com
Address	American Funds 333 South Hope Street Los Angeles CA 90071-1406 United States
Phone Number	800-421-4225

Ratings History

Date	Overall Rating	Risk Rating	Reward Rating
Q2-19	B-	A-	C
Q4-18	C	B-	C-
Q4-17	B-	B	C+
Q4-16	B-	B	C+
Q4-15	B-	B+	C

Asset & Performance History

Date	NAV	1-Year Total Return
2018	20.58	-5.58
2017	23.31	12.75
2016	21.63	10.06
2015	20.2	-1.92
2014	21.57	8.15
2013		17.83

Total Assets: $109,899,000,000

Asset Allocation

Asset	%
Cash	7%
Stocks	66%
US Stocks	48%
Bonds	27%
US Bonds	24%
Other	0%

Services Offered: Automatic Investment Plan, Qualified Investment, Phone Exchange

Investment Strategy: The investment seeks to provide investors with current income while secondarily striving for capital growth. Normally the fund invests primarily in income-producing securities. These include equity securities, such as dividend-paying common stocks, and debt securities, such as interest-paying bonds. Generally at least 60% of the fund's assets will be invested in common stocks and other equity-type securities. The fund may also invest up to 30% of its assets in equity securities of issuers domiciled outside the United States, including issuers in developing countries. **Top Holdings:** Merck & Co Inc Microsoft Corp United States Treasury Notes 2.62% United States Treasury Bills 0.39% Verizon Communications Inc

American Funds The Income Fund of America® Class F-2 B BUY

Ticker	Traded On	NAV	Total Assets ($)	Dividend Yield (TTM)	Turnover Ratio	Expense Ratio
AMEFX	NAS CM	22.47	$109,899,000,000	3.13	70	0.38

Ratings

Reward	C
Risk	A-
Recent Upgrade/Downgrade	Up

Fund Information

Fund Type	Open End
Category	Aggressive Alloc
Sub-Category	Alloc--70% to 85% Equity
Prospectus Objective	Income
Inception Date	Aug-08
Open to New Investments	Y
Minimum Initial Investment	250
Minimum Subsequent Investment	50
Front End Fee	
Back End Fee	

Total Returns (%)

3-Month	6-Month	1-Year	3-Year	5-Year
2.65	11.29	6.70	25.63	32.61

Last Bull Market	14.63
Last Bear Market	-10
3-Year Standard Deviation	7.14
3-Year Beta	0.56

Company Information

Provider	American Funds
Manager/Tenure	Dina N. Perry (27), Hilda L. Applbaum (21), Andrew B. Suzman (19), 6 others
Website	http://www.americanfunds.com
Address	American Funds 333 South Hope Street Los Angeles CA 90071-1406 United States
Phone Number	800-421-4225

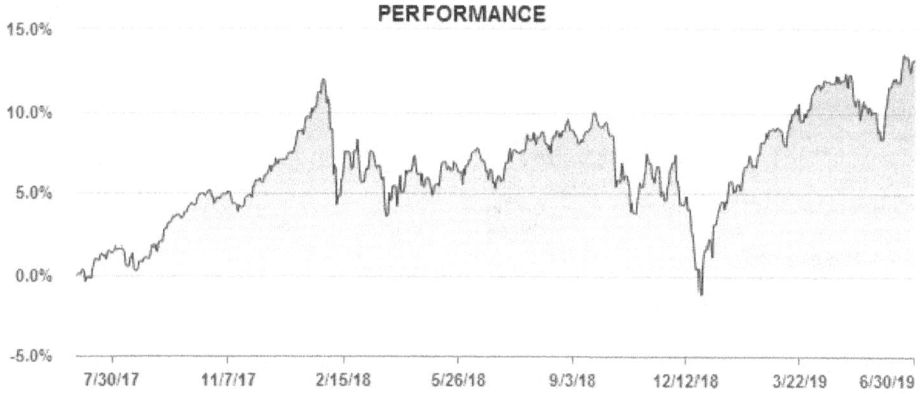

Ratings History

Date	Overall Rating	Risk Rating	Reward Rating
Q2-19	B	A-	C+
Q4-18	C	B-	C
Q4-17	B-	B	C+
Q4-16	B-	B	B-
Q4-15	C	C	C

Asset & Performance History

Date	NAV	1-Year Total Return
2018	20.61	-4.95
2017	23.35	13.57
2016	21.65	10.78
2015	20.21	-1.35
2014	21.57	8.64
2013	20.63	18.4

Total Assets: $109,899,000,000

Asset Allocation

Asset	%
Cash	7%
Stocks	66%
US Stocks	48%
Bonds	27%
US Bonds	24%
Other	0%

Services Offered: Systematic Withdrawal Plan, Automatic Investment Plan, Qualified Investment, Phone Exchange, Retirement Investment

Investment Strategy: The investment seeks to provide investors with current income while secondarily striving for capital growth. Normally the fund invests primarily in income-producing securities. These include equity securities, such as dividend-paying common stocks, and debt securities, such as interest-paying bonds. Generally at least 60% of the fund's assets will be invested in common stocks and other equity-type securities. The fund may also invest up to 30% of its assets in equity securities of issuers domiciled outside the United States, including issuers in developing countries. **Top Holdings:** Merck & Co Inc Microsoft Corp United States Treasury Notes 2.62% United States Treasury Bills 0.39% Verizon Communications Inc

American Funds The Income Fund of America® Class R-6 B BUY

Ticker	Traded On	NAV	Total Assets ($)	Dividend Yield (TTM)	Turnover Ratio	Expense Ratio
RIDGX	NAS CM	22.5	$109,899,000,000	3.22	70	0.28

Ratings

Reward	C
Risk	A
Recent Upgrade/Downgrade	Up

Fund Information

Fund Type	Open End
Category	Aggressive Alloc
Sub-Category	Alloc--70% to 85% Equity
Prospectus Objective	Income
Inception Date	May-09
Open to New Investments	Y
Minimum Initial Investment	250
Minimum Subsequent Investment	50
Front End Fee	
Back End Fee	

Total Returns (%)

3-Month	6-Month	1-Year	3-Year	5-Year
2.68	11.33	6.80	26.05	33.32

Last Bull Market	14.74
Last Bear Market	-9.94
3-Year Standard Deviation	7.14
3-Year Beta	0.56

Company Information

Provider	American Funds
Manager/Tenure	Dina N. Perry (27), Hilda L. Applbaum (21), Andrew B. Suzman (19), 6 others
Website	http://www.americanfunds.com
Address	American Funds 333 South Hope Street Los Angeles CA 90071-1406 United States
Phone Number	800-421-4225

PERFORMANCE

Ratings History

Date	Overall Rating	Risk Rating	Reward Rating
Q2-19	B	A-	C+
Q4-18	C	B-	C
Q4-17	B-	B	C+
Q4-16	B-	B	B-
Q4-15	C+	C+	C

Asset & Performance History

Date	NAV	1-Year Total Return
2018	20.64	-4.8
2017	23.37	13.67
2016	21.67	10.88
2015	20.23	-1.24
2014	21.59	8.73
2013	20.65	18.52

Total Assets: $109,899,000,000

Asset Allocation

Asset	%
Cash	7%
Stocks	66%
US Stocks	48%
Bonds	27%
US Bonds	24%
Other	0%

Services Offered: Automatic Investment Plan, Qualified Investment, Phone Exchange

Investment Strategy: The investment seeks to provide investors with current income while secondarily striving for capital growth. Normally the fund invests primarily in income-producing securities. These include equity securities, such as dividend-paying common stocks, and debt securities, such as interest-paying bonds. Generally at least 60% of the fund's assets will be invested in common stocks and other equity-type securities. The fund may also invest up to 30% of its assets in equity securities of issuers domiciled outside the United States, including issuers in developing countries. **Top Holdings:** Merck & Co Inc Microsoft Corp United States Treasury Notes 2.62% United States Treasury Bills 0.39% Verizon Communications Inc

American Funds The Income Fund of America® Class 529-C B- BUY

Ticker	Traded On	NAV	Total Assets ($)	Dividend Yield (TTM)	Turnover Ratio	Expense Ratio
CIMCX	NAS CM	22.38	$109,899,000,000	2.17	70	1.4

Ratings

Reward	C
Risk	A-
Recent Upgrade/Downgrade	Up

Fund Information

Fund Type	Open End
Category	Aggressive Alloc
Sub-Category	Alloc--70% to 85% Equity
Prospectus Objective	Income
Inception Date	Feb-02
Open to New Investments	Y
Minimum Initial Investment	250
Minimum Subsequent Investment	50
Front End Fee	
Back End Fee	1.00

Total Returns (%)

3-Month	6-Month	1-Year	3-Year	5-Year
2.41	10.74	5.64	21.86	26.00

Last Bull Market	13.96
Last Bear Market	-10.41
3-Year Standard Deviation	7.14
3-Year Beta	0.56

Company Information

Provider	American Funds
Manager/Tenure	Dina N. Perry (27), Hilda L. Applbaum (21), Andrew B. Suzman (19), 6 others
Website	http://www.americanfunds.com
Address	American Funds 333 South Hope Street Los Angeles CA 90071-1406 United States
Phone Number	800-421-4225

PERFORMANCE

Ratings History

Date	Overall Rating	Risk Rating	Reward Rating
Q2-19	B-	B+	C
Q4-18	C	B-	C-
Q4-17	B-	B	C+
Q4-16	B-	B	C+
Q4-15	B-	B+	C

Asset & Performance History

Date	NAV	1-Year Total Return
2018	20.53	-5.87
2017	23.25	12.4
2016	21.55	9.64
2015	20.12	-2.35
2014	21.47	7.45
2013	20.55	17.2

Total Assets: $109,899,000,000

Asset Allocation

Asset	%
Cash	7%
Stocks	66%
US Stocks	48%
Bonds	27%
US Bonds	24%
Other	0%

Services Offered: Systematic Withdrawal Plan, Automatic Investment Plan, Qualified Investment, Phone Exchange, Retirement Investment

Investment Strategy: The investment seeks to provide investors with current income while secondarily striving for capital growth. Normally the fund invests primarily in income-producing securities. These include equity securities, such as dividend-paying common stocks, and debt securities, such as interest-paying bonds. Generally at least 60% of the fund's assets will be invested in common stocks and other equity-type securities. The fund may also invest up to 30% of its assets in equity securities of issuers domiciled outside the United States, including issuers in developing countries. **Top Holdings:** Merck & Co Inc Microsoft Corp United States Treasury Notes 2.62% United States Treasury Bills 0.39% Verizon Communications Inc

American Funds The Income Fund of America® Class 529-E B BUY

Ticker	Traded On	NAV	Total Assets ($)	Dividend Yield (TTM)	Turnover Ratio	Expense Ratio
CIMEX	NAS CM	22.37	$109,899,000,000	2.67	70	0.87

Ratings

Reward	C
Risk	A-
Recent Upgrade/Downgrade	Up

Fund Information

Fund Type	Open End
Category	Aggressive Alloc
Sub-Category	Alloc--70% to 85% Equity
Prospectus Objective	Income
Inception Date	Feb-02
Open to New Investments	Y
Minimum Initial Investment	250
Minimum Subsequent Investment	50
Front End Fee	
Back End Fee	

Total Returns (%)

3-Month	6-Month	1-Year	3-Year	5-Year
2.54	11.03	6.16	23.81	29.38

Last Bull Market	14.32
Last Bear Market	-10.21
3-Year Standard Deviation	7.17
3-Year Beta	0.56

Company Information

Provider	American Funds
Manager/Tenure	Dina N. Perry (27), Hilda L. Applbaum (21), Andrew B. Suzman (19), 6 others
Website	http://www.americanfunds.com
Address	American Funds 333 South Hope Street Los Angeles CA 90071-1406 United States
Phone Number	800-421-4225

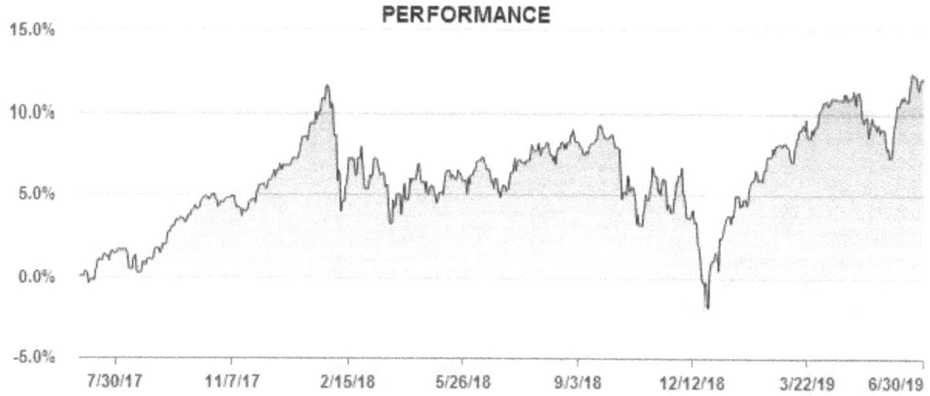

Ratings History

Date	Overall Rating	Risk Rating	Reward Rating
Q2-19	B-	A-	C
Q4-18	C	B-	C-
Q4-17	B-	B	C+
Q4-16	B-	B	C+
Q4-15	B-	B+	C

Asset & Performance History

Date	NAV	1-Year Total Return
2018	20.52	-5.4
2017	23.25	12.98
2016	21.57	10.27
2015	20.13	-1.82
2014	21.48	8.01
2013	20.56	17.81

Total Assets: $109,899,000,000

Asset Allocation

Asset	%
Cash	7%
Stocks	66%
US Stocks	48%
Bonds	27%
US Bonds	24%
Other	0%

Services Offered: Systematic Withdrawal Plan, Automatic Investment Plan, Qualified Investment, Phone Exchange, Retirement Investment

Investment Strategy: The investment seeks to provide investors with current income while secondarily striving for capital growth. Normally the fund invests primarily in income-producing securities. These include equity securities, such as dividend-paying common stocks, and debt securities, such as interest-paying bonds. Generally at least 60% of the fund's assets will be invested in common stocks and other equity-type securities. The fund may also invest up to 30% of its assets in equity securities of issuers domiciled outside the United States, including issuers in developing countries. **Top Holdings:** Merck & Co Inc Microsoft Corp United States Treasury Notes 2.62% United States Treasury Bills 0.39% Verizon Communications Inc

American Funds The Income Fund of America® Class R-4 B BUY

Ticker	Traded On	NAV	Total Assets ($)	Dividend Yield (TTM)	Turnover Ratio	Expense Ratio
RIDEX	NAS CM	22.45	$109,899,000,000	2.89	70	0.63

Ratings

Reward	C
Risk	A-
Recent Upgrade/Downgrade	Up

Fund Information

Fund Type	Open End
Category	Aggressive Alloc
Sub-Category	Alloc--70% to 85% Equity
Prospectus Objective	Income
Inception Date	Jun-02
Open to New Investments	Y
Minimum Initial Investment	250
Minimum Subsequent Investment	50
Front End Fee	
Back End Fee	

Total Returns (%)

3-Month	6-Month	1-Year	3-Year	5-Year
2.59	11.17	6.43	24.73	31.02

Last Bull Market	14.43
Last Bear Market	-10.06
3-Year Standard Deviation	7.14
3-Year Beta	0.56

Company Information

Provider	American Funds
Manager/Tenure	Dina N. Perry (27), Hilda L. Applbaum (21), Andrew B. Suzman (19), 6 others
Website	http://www.americanfunds.com
Address	American Funds 333 South Hope Street Los Angeles CA 90071-1406 United States
Phone Number	800-421-4225

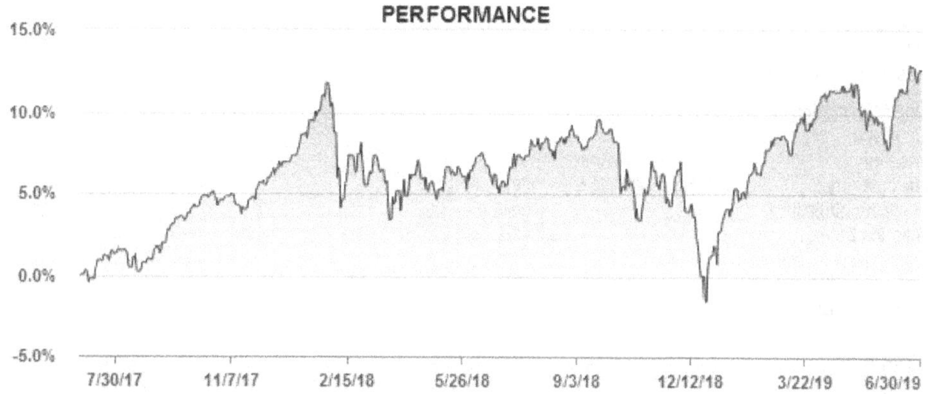

Ratings History

Date	Overall Rating	Risk Rating	Reward Rating
Q2-19	B	A-	C
Q4-18	C	B-	C
Q4-17	B-	B	C+
Q4-16	B-	B	B-
Q4-15	B-	B+	C

Asset & Performance History

Date	NAV	1-Year Total Return
2018	20.59	-5.2
2017	23.33	13.31
2016	21.63	10.52
2015	20.19	-1.6
2014	21.55	8.32
2013	20.62	18.14

Total Assets: $109,899,000,000

Asset Allocation

Asset	%
Cash	7%
Stocks	66%
US Stocks	48%
Bonds	27%
US Bonds	24%
Other	0%

Services Offered: Automatic Investment Plan, Qualified Investment, Phone Exchange

Investment Strategy: The investment seeks to provide investors with current income while secondarily striving for capital growth. Normally the fund invests primarily in income-producing securities. These include equity securities, such as dividend-paying common stocks, and debt securities, such as interest-paying bonds. Generally at least 60% of the fund's assets will be invested in common stocks and other equity-type securities. The fund may also invest up to 30% of its assets in equity securities of issuers domiciled outside the United States, including issuers in developing countries. **Top Holdings:** Merck & Co Inc Microsoft Corp United States Treasury Notes 2.62% United States Treasury Bills 0.39% Verizon Communications Inc

American Funds The Income Fund of America® Class 529-F-1 B BUY

Ticker	Traded On	NAV	Total Assets ($)	Dividend Yield (TTM)	Turnover Ratio	Expense Ratio
CIMFX	NAS CM	22.43	$109,899,000,000	3.12	70	0.4

Ratings

Reward	C
Risk	A-
Recent Upgrade/Downgrade	Up

Fund Information

Fund Type	Open End
Category	Aggressive Alloc
Sub-Category	Alloc--70% to 85% Equity
Prospectus Objective	Income
Inception Date	Sep-02
Open to New Investments	Y
Minimum Initial Investment	250
Minimum Subsequent Investment	50
Front End Fee	
Back End Fee	

Total Returns (%)

3-Month	6-Month	1-Year	3-Year	5-Year
2.65	11.25	6.64	25.55	32.35

Last Bull Market	14.61
Last Bear Market	-10.03
3-Year Standard Deviation	7.14
3-Year Beta	0.56

Company Information

Provider	American Funds
Manager/Tenure	Dina N. Perry (27), Hilda L. Applbaum (21), Andrew B. Suzman (19), 6 others
Website	http://www.americanfunds.com
Address	American Funds 333 South Hope Street Los Angeles CA 90071-1406 United States
Phone Number	800-421-4225

Ratings History

Date	Overall Rating	Risk Rating	Reward Rating
Q2-19	B	A-	C
Q4-18	C	B-	C
Q4-17	B-	B	C+
Q4-16	B-	B	B-
Q4-15	C	C	C

Asset & Performance History

Date	NAV	1-Year Total Return
2018	20.58	-4.93
2017	23.31	13.52
2016	21.62	10.76
2015	20.18	-1.4
2014	21.54	8.54
2013	20.61	18.37

Total Assets: $109,899,000,000

Asset Allocation

Asset	%
Cash	7%
Stocks	66%
US Stocks	48%
Bonds	27%
US Bonds	24%
Other	0%

Services Offered: Systematic Withdrawal Plan, Automatic Investment Plan, Qualified Investment, Phone Exchange, Retirement Investment

Investment Strategy: The investment seeks to provide investors with current income while secondarily striving for capital growth. Normally the fund invests primarily in income-producing securities. These include equity securities, such as dividend-paying common stocks, and debt securities, such as interest-paying bonds. Generally at least 60% of the fund's assets will be invested in common stocks and other equity-type securities. The fund may also invest up to 30% of its assets in equity securities of issuers domiciled outside the United States, including issuers in developing countries. **Top Holdings:** Merck & Co Inc Microsoft Corp United States Treasury Notes 2.62% United States Treasury Bills 0.39% Verizon Communications Inc

American Funds The Income Fund of America® Class C B- BUY

Ticker	Traded On	NAV	Total Assets ($)	Dividend Yield (TTM)	Turnover Ratio	Expense Ratio
IFACX	NAS CM	22.2	$109,899,000,000	2.24	70	1.34

Ratings

Reward	C
Risk	A-
Recent Upgrade/Downgrade	Up

Fund Information

Fund Type	Open End
Category	Aggressive Alloc
Sub-Category	Alloc--70% to 85% Equity
Prospectus Objective	Income
Inception Date	Mar-01
Open to New Investments	Y
Minimum Initial Investment	250
Minimum Subsequent Investment	50
Front End Fee	
Back End Fee	1.00

Total Returns (%)

3-Month	6-Month	1-Year	3-Year	5-Year
2.44	10.80	5.70	22.11	26.42

Last Bull Market	13.95
Last Bear Market	-10.32
3-Year Standard Deviation	7.14
3-Year Beta	0.56

Company Information

Provider	American Funds
Manager/Tenure	Dina N. Perry (27), Hilda L. Applbaum (21), Andrew B. Suzman (19), 6 others
Website	http://www.americanfunds.com
Address	American Funds 333 South Hope Street Los Angeles CA 90071-1406 United States
Phone Number	800-421-4225

Ratings History

Date	Overall Rating	Risk Rating	Reward Rating
Q2-19	B-	B+	C
Q4-18	C	B-	C-
Q4-17	B-	B	C+
Q4-16	B-	B	C+
Q4-15	B-	B+	C

Asset & Performance History

Date	NAV	1-Year Total Return
2018	20.36	-5.85
2017	23.08	12.48
2016	21.41	9.67
2015	20	-2.24
2014	21.34	7.52
2013	20.43	17.27

Total Assets: $109,899,000,000

Asset Allocation

Asset	%
Cash	7%
Stocks	66%
US Stocks	48%
Bonds	27%
US Bonds	24%
Other	0%

Services Offered: Systematic Withdrawal Plan, Automatic Investment Plan, Phone Exchange, Retirement Investment

Investment Strategy: The investment seeks to provide investors with current income while secondarily striving for capital growth. Normally the fund invests primarily in income-producing securities. These include equity securities, such as dividend-paying common stocks, and debt securities, such as interest-paying bonds. Generally at least 60% of the fund's assets will be invested in common stocks and other equity-type securities. The fund may also invest up to 30% of its assets in equity securities of issuers domiciled outside the United States, including issuers in developing countries. **Top Holdings:** Merck & Co Inc Microsoft Corp United States Treasury Notes 2.62% United States Treasury Bills 0.39% Verizon Communications Inc

American Funds The Income Fund of America® Class R-3 B BUY

Ticker	Traded On	NAV	Total Assets ($)	Dividend Yield (TTM)	Turnover Ratio	Expense Ratio
RIDCX	NAS CM	22.4	$109,899,000,000	2.61	70	0.93

Ratings

Reward	C
Risk	A-
Recent Upgrade/Downgrade	Up

Fund Information

Fund Type	Open End
Category	Aggressive Alloc
Sub-Category	Alloc--70% to 85% Equity
Prospectus Objective	Income
Inception Date	Jun-02
Open to New Investments	Y
Minimum Initial Investment	250
Minimum Subsequent Investment	50
Front End Fee	
Back End Fee	

Total Returns (%)

3-Month	6-Month	1-Year	3-Year	5-Year
2.53	10.98	6.13	23.55	29.07

Last Bull Market	14.29
Last Bear Market	-10.22
3-Year Standard Deviation	7.17
3-Year Beta	0.56

Company Information

Provider	American Funds
Manager/Tenure	Dina N. Perry (27), Hilda L. Applbaum (21), Andrew B. Suzman (19), 6 others
Website	http://www.americanfunds.com
Address	American Funds 333 South Hope Street Los Angeles CA 90071-1406 United States
Phone Number	800-421-4225

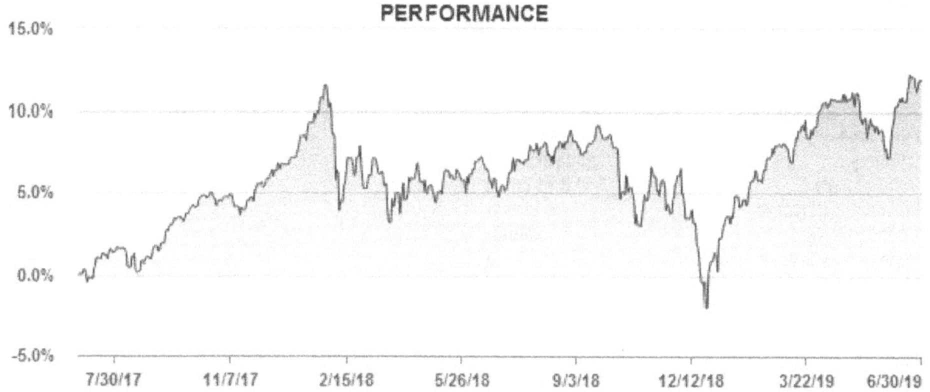

Ratings History

Date	Overall Rating	Risk Rating	Reward Rating
Q2-19	B-	A-	C
Q4-18	C	B-	C-
Q4-17	B-	B	C+
Q4-16	B-	B	C+
Q4-15	B-	B+	C

Asset & Performance History

Date	NAV	1-Year Total Return
2018	20.55	-5.46
2017	23.28	12.94
2016	21.59	10.16
2015	20.16	-1.85
2014	21.51	8.01
2013	20.58	17.76

Total Assets: $109,899,000,000

Asset Allocation

Asset	%
Cash	7%
Stocks	66%
US Stocks	48%
Bonds	27%
US Bonds	24%
Other	0%

Services Offered: Automatic Investment Plan, Qualified Investment, Phone Exchange

Investment Strategy: The investment seeks to provide investors with current income while secondarily striving for capital growth. Normally the fund invests primarily in income-producing securities. These include equity securities, such as dividend-paying common stocks, and debt securities, such as interest-paying bonds. Generally at least 60% of the fund's assets will be invested in common stocks and other equity-type securities. The fund may also invest up to 30% of its assets in equity securities of issuers domiciled outside the United States, including issuers in developing countries. **Top Holdings:** Merck & Co Inc Microsoft Corp United States Treasury Notes 2.62% United States Treasury Bills 0.39% Verizon Communications Inc

American Funds The Income Fund of America® Class 529-A B BUY

Ticker	Traded On	NAV	Total Assets ($)	Dividend Yield (TTM)	Turnover Ratio	Expense Ratio
CIMAX	NAS CM	22.44	$109,899,000,000	2.88	70	0.63

Ratings

Reward	C
Risk	A-
Recent Upgrade/Downgrade	Up

Fund Information

Fund Type	Open End
Category	Aggressive Alloc
Sub-Category	Alloc--70% to 85% Equity
Prospectus Objective	Income
Inception Date	Feb-02
Open to New Investments	Y
Minimum Initial Investment	250
Minimum Subsequent Investment	50
Front End Fee	5.75
Back End Fee	

Total Returns (%)

3-Month	6-Month	1-Year	3-Year	5-Year
2.59	11.17	6.43	24.66	30.89

Last Bull Market	14.49
Last Bear Market	-10.13
3-Year Standard Deviation	7.13
3-Year Beta	0.56

Company Information

Provider	American Funds
Manager/Tenure	Dina N. Perry (27), Hilda L. Applbaum (21), Andrew B. Suzman (19), 6 others
Website	http://www.americanfunds.com
Address	American Funds 333 South Hope Street Los Angeles CA 90071-1406 United States
Phone Number	800-421-4225

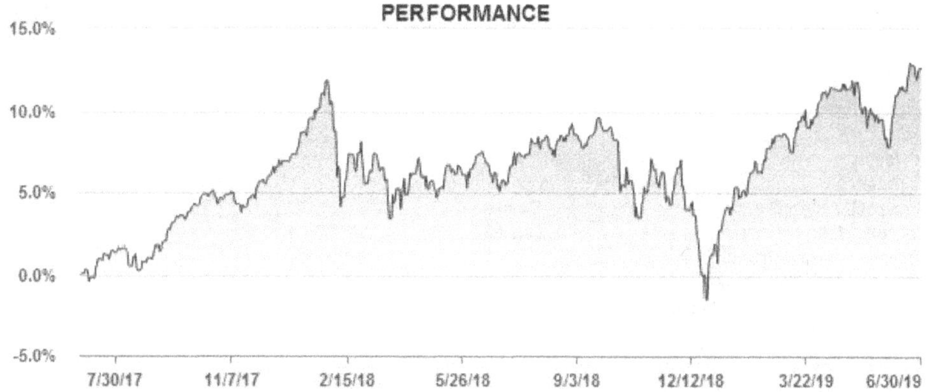

Ratings History

Date	Overall Rating	Risk Rating	Reward Rating
Q2-19	B	A-	C
Q4-18	C	B-	C
Q4-17	B-	B	C+
Q4-16	B-	B	B-
Q4-15	B-	B+	C

Asset & Performance History

Date	NAV	1-Year Total Return
2018	20.59	-5.16
2017	23.32	13.27
2016	21.63	10.5
2015	20.19	-1.57
2014	21.54	8.3
2013	20.61	18.11

Total Assets: $109,899,000,000

Asset Allocation

Asset	%
Cash	7%
Stocks	66%
US Stocks	48%
Bonds	27%
US Bonds	24%
Other	0%

Services Offered: Systematic Withdrawal Plan, Automatic Investment Plan, Qualified Investment, Phone Exchange, Retirement Investment

Investment Strategy: The investment seeks to provide investors with current income while secondarily striving for capital growth. Normally the fund invests primarily in income-producing securities. These include equity securities, such as dividend-paying common stocks, and debt securities, such as interest-paying bonds. Generally at least 60% of the fund's assets will be invested in common stocks and other equity-type securities. The fund may also invest up to 30% of its assets in equity securities of issuers domiciled outside the United States, including issuers in developing countries. **Top Holdings:** Merck & Co Inc Microsoft Corp United States Treasury Notes 2.62% United States Treasury Bills 0.39% Verizon Communications Inc

American Funds The Income Fund of America® Class R-1 B- BUY

Ticker	Traded On	NAV	Total Assets ($)	Dividend Yield (TTM)	Turnover Ratio	Expense Ratio
RIDAX	NAS CM	22.36	$109,899,000,000	2.18	70	1.38

Ratings

Reward	C
Risk	A-
Recent Upgrade/Downgrade	Up

Fund Information

Fund Type	Open End
Category	Aggressive Alloc
Sub-Category	Alloc--70% to 85% Equity
Prospectus Objective	Income
Inception Date	Jun-02
Open to New Investments	Y
Minimum Initial Investment	250
Minimum Subsequent Investment	50
Front End Fee	
Back End Fee	

Total Returns (%)

3-Month	6-Month	1-Year	3-Year	5-Year
2.46	10.75	5.66	21.99	26.22

Last Bull Market	14
Last Bear Market	-10.38
3-Year Standard Deviation	7.14
3-Year Beta	0.56

Company Information

Provider	American Funds
Manager/Tenure	Dina N. Perry (27), Hilda L. Applbaum (21), Andrew B. Suzman (19), 6 others
Website	http://www.americanfunds.com
Address	American Funds 333 South Hope Street Los Angeles CA 90071-1406 United States
Phone Number	800-421-4225

PERFORMANCE

Ratings History

Date	Overall Rating	Risk Rating	Reward Rating
Q2-19	B-	B+	C
Q4-18	C	B-	C-
Q4-17	B-	B	C+
Q4-16	B-	B	C+
Q4-15	B-	B+	C

Asset & Performance History

Date	NAV	1-Year Total Return
2018	20.5	-5.9
2017	23.23	12.42
2016	21.55	9.68
2015	20.12	-2.29
2014	21.47	7.56
2013	20.54	17.21

Total Assets: $109,899,000,000

Asset Allocation

Asset	%
Cash	7%
Stocks	66%
US Stocks	48%
Bonds	27%
US Bonds	24%
Other	0%

Services Offered: Automatic Investment Plan, Qualified Investment, Phone Exchange

Investment Strategy: The investment seeks to provide investors with current income while secondarily striving for capital growth. Normally the fund invests primarily in income-producing securities. These include equity securities, such as dividend-paying common stocks, and debt securities, such as interest-paying bonds. Generally at least 60% of the fund's assets will be invested in common stocks and other equity-type securities. The fund may also invest up to 30% of its assets in equity securities of issuers domiciled outside the United States, including issuers in developing countries. **Top Holdings:** Merck & Co Inc Microsoft Corp United States Treasury Notes 2.62% United States Treasury Bills 0.39% Verizon Communications Inc

American Funds The Income Fund of America® Class R-2 B- BUY

Ticker	Traded On	NAV	Total Assets ($)	Dividend Yield (TTM)	Turnover Ratio	Expense Ratio
RIDBX	NAS CM	22.23	$109,899,000,000	2.2	70	1.37

Ratings

Reward	C
Risk	A-
Recent Upgrade/Downgrade	Up

Fund Information

Fund Type	Open End
Category	Aggressive Alloc
Sub-Category	Alloc--70% to 85% Equity
Prospectus Objective	Income
Inception Date	May-02
Open to New Investments	Y
Minimum Initial Investment	250
Minimum Subsequent Investment	50
Front End Fee	
Back End Fee	

Total Returns (%)

3-Month	6-Month	1-Year	3-Year	5-Year
2.44	10.78	5.66	21.94	26.30

Last Bull Market	13.99
Last Bear Market	-10.37
3-Year Standard Deviation	7.13
3-Year Beta	0.56

Company Information

Provider	American Funds
Manager/Tenure	Dina N. Perry (27), Hilda L. Applbaum (21), Andrew B. Suzman (19), 6 others
Website	http://www.americanfunds.com
Address	American Funds 333 South Hope Street Los Angeles CA 90071-1406 United States
Phone Number	800-421-4225

PERFORMANCE

Ratings History

Date	Overall Rating	Risk Rating	Reward Rating
Q2-19	B-	B+	C
Q4-18	C	B-	C-
Q4-17	B-	B	C+
Q4-16	B-	B	C+
Q4-15	B-	B+	C

Asset & Performance History

Date	NAV	1-Year Total Return
2018	20.39	-5.87
2017	23.11	12.45
2016	21.44	9.69
2015	20.02	-2.27
2014	21.37	7.51
2013	20.46	17.33

Total Assets: $109,899,000,000

Asset Allocation

Asset	%
Cash	7%
Stocks	66%
US Stocks	48%
Bonds	27%
US Bonds	24%
Other	0%

Services Offered: Automatic Investment Plan, Qualified Investment, Phone Exchange

Investment Strategy: The investment seeks to provide investors with current income while secondarily striving for capital growth. Normally the fund invests primarily in income-producing securities. These include equity securities, such as dividend-paying common stocks, and debt securities, such as interest-paying bonds. Generally at least 60% of the fund's assets will be invested in common stocks and other equity-type securities. The fund may also invest up to 30% of its assets in equity securities of issuers domiciled outside the United States, including issuers in developing countries. **Top Holdings:** Merck & Co Inc Microsoft Corp United States Treasury Notes 2.62% United States Treasury Bills 0.39% Verizon Communications Inc

Vanguard Mid-Cap Index Fund Investor Shares C+ HOLD

Ticker	Traded On	NAV	Total Assets ($)	Dividend Yield (TTM)	Turnover Ratio	Expense Ratio
VIMSX	NAS CM	45.64	$105,461,000,000	1.4	16	0.17

Ratings

Reward	C
Risk	B
Recent Upgrade/Downgrade	

Fund Information

Fund Type	Open End
Category	US Equity Mid Cap
Sub-Category	Mid-Cap Blend
Prospectus Objective	Growth
Inception Date	May-98
Open to New Investments	Y
Minimum Initial Investment	3,000
Minimum Subsequent Investment	1
Front End Fee	
Back End Fee	

Total Returns (%)

3-Month	6-Month	1-Year	3-Year	5-Year
4.33	22.89	7.69	43.38	52.02

Last Bull Market	26.27
Last Bear Market	-21.4
3-Year Standard Deviation	13.28
3-Year Beta	1

Company Information

Provider	Vanguard
Manager/Tenure	Donald M. Butler (21), Michael A. Johnson (3)
Website	http://www.vanguard.com
Address	Vanguard 100 Vanguard Boulevard Malvern PA 19355 United States
Phone Number	877-662-7447

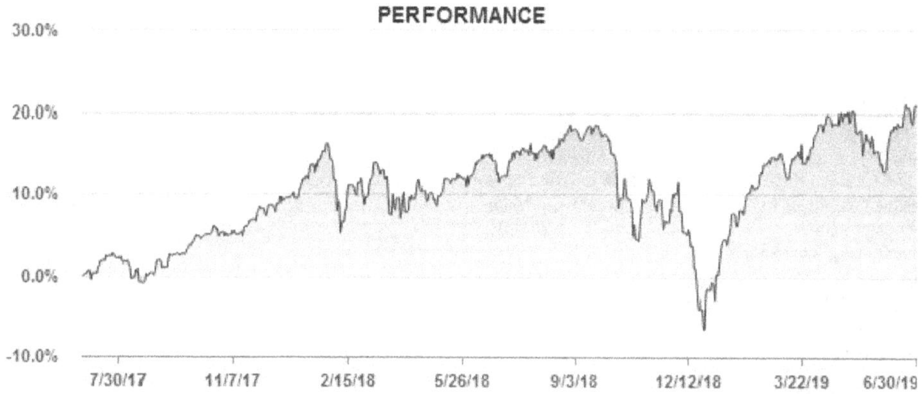

Ratings History

Date	Overall Rating	Risk Rating	Reward Rating
Q2-19	C+	B	C
Q4-18	C	C+	C-
Q4-17	B-	B-	B-
Q4-16	B	B	B
Q4-15	C+	B-	C

Asset & Performance History

Date	NAV	1-Year Total Return
2018	37.71	-9.33
2017	42.23	19.11
2016	35.92	11.07
2015	32.79	-1.45
2014	33.72	13.6
2013	30.02	34.99

Total Assets: $105,461,000,000

Asset Allocation

Asset	%
Cash	1%
Stocks	99%
US Stocks	97%
Bonds	0%
US Bonds	0%
Other	0%

Services Offered: Systematic Withdrawal Plan, Automatic Investment Plan, Phone Exchange, Wire Redemption

Investment Strategy: The investment seeks to track the performance of a benchmark index that measures the investment return of mid-capitalization stocks. The fund employs an indexing investment approach designed to track the performance of the CRSP US Mid Cap Index, a broadly diversified index of stocks of mid-size U.S. companies. The advisor attempts to replicate the target index by investing all, or substantially all, of its assets in the stocks that make up the index, holding each stock in approximately the same proportion as its weighting in the index. **Top Holdings:** Roper Technologies Inc Worldpay Inc Class A Fiserv Inc Moody's Corporation Red Hat Inc

Vanguard Mid-Cap Index Fund Admiral Shares C+ HOLD

Ticker	Traded On	NAV	Total Assets ($)	Dividend Yield (TTM)	Turnover Ratio	Expense Ratio
VIMAX	NAS CM	207.01	$105,461,000,000	1.52	16	0.05

Ratings

Reward	C
Risk	B
Recent Upgrade/Downgrade	

Fund Information

Fund Type	Open End
Category	US Equity Mid Cap
Sub-Category	Mid-Cap Blend
Prospectus Objective	Growth
Inception Date	Nov-01
Open to New Investments	Y
Minimum Initial Investment	3,000
Minimum Subsequent Investment	1
Front End Fee	
Back End Fee	

Total Returns (%)

3-Month	6-Month	1-Year	3-Year	5-Year
4.36	22.96	7.83	43.90	52.92

Last Bull Market	26.38
Last Bear Market	-21.36
3-Year Standard Deviation	13.29
3-Year Beta	1

Company Information

Provider	Vanguard
Manager/Tenure	Donald M. Butler (21), Michael A. Johnson (3)
Website	http://www.vanguard.com
Address	Vanguard 100 Vanguard Boulevard Malvern PA 19355 United States
Phone Number	877-662-7447

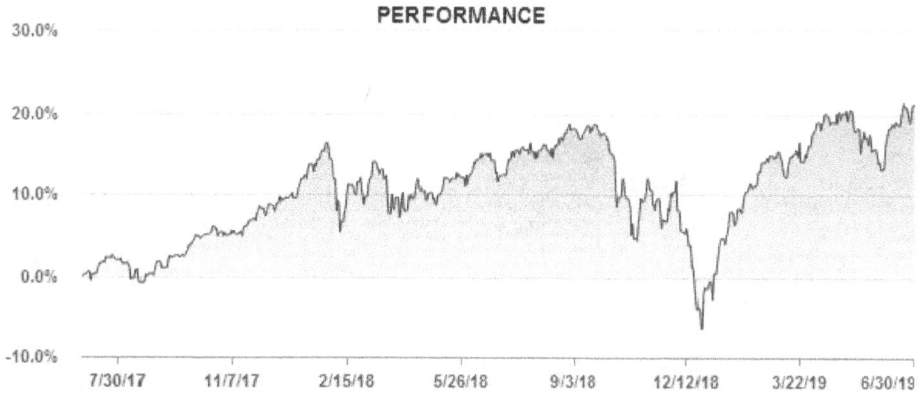

Ratings History

Date	Overall Rating	Risk Rating	Reward Rating
Q2-19	C+	B	C
Q4-18	C	C+	C-
Q4-17	B-	B-	B-
Q4-16	B	B	B
Q4-15	C+	B-	C

Asset & Performance History

Date	NAV	1-Year Total Return
2018	171.04	-9.23
2017	191.55	19.25
2016	162.94	11.22
2015	148.72	-1.33
2014	152.97	13.76
2013	136.19	35.15

Total Assets: $105,461,000,000

Asset Allocation

Asset	%
Cash	1%
Stocks	99%
US Stocks	97%
Bonds	0%
US Bonds	0%
Other	0%

Services Offered: Systematic Withdrawal Plan, Automatic Investment Plan, Phone Exchange, Wire Redemption

Investment Strategy: The investment seeks to track the performance of a benchmark index that measures the investment return of mid-capitalization stocks. The fund employs an indexing investment approach designed to track the performance of the CRSP US Mid Cap Index, a broadly diversified index of stocks of mid-size U.S. companies. The advisor attempts to replicate the target index by investing all, or substantially all, of its assets in the stocks that make up the index, holding each stock in approximately the same proportion as its weighting in the index. **Top Holdings:** Roper Technologies Inc Worldpay Inc Class A Fiserv Inc Moody's Corporation Red Hat Inc

Vanguard Wellington™ Fund Admiral™ Shares — B BUY

Ticker	Traded On	NAV	Total Assets ($)	Dividend Yield (TTM)	Turnover Ratio	Expense Ratio
VWENX	NAS CM	71.41	$105,381,000,000	2.61	34	0.17

Ratings

Reward	C+
Risk	A
Recent Upgrade/Downgrade	

Fund Information

Fund Type	Open End
Category	Moderate Alloc
Sub-Category	Alloc--50% to 70% Equity
Prospectus Objective	Growth & Income
Inception Date	May-01
Open to New Investments	
Minimum Initial Investment	50,000
Minimum Subsequent Investment	1
Front End Fee	
Back End Fee	

Total Returns (%)

3-Month	6-Month	1-Year	3-Year	5-Year
3.91	13.56	10.37	33.92	43.83

Last Bull Market	16.35
Last Bear Market	-10.37
3-Year Standard Deviation	7.32
3-Year Beta	0.58

Company Information

Provider	Vanguard
Manager/Tenure	Edward P. Bousa (16), Loren L. Moran (2), Michael E. Stack (2), 1 other
Website	http://www.vanguard.com
Address	Vanguard 100 Vanguard Boulevard Malvern PA 19355 United States
Phone Number	877-662-7447

PERFORMANCE

Ratings History

Date	Overall Rating	Risk Rating	Reward Rating
Q2-19	B	A-	C+
Q4-18	C	B	C
Q4-17	B-	B	B-
Q4-16	B	B+	B-
Q4-15	C+	B-	C

Asset & Performance History

Date	NAV	1-Year Total Return
2018	64.1	-3.34
2017	72.58	14.81
2016	67.45	11.09
2015	63.54	0.14
2014	67.61	9.89
2013	65.53	19.75

Total Assets: $105,381,000,000

Asset Allocation

Asset	%
Cash	2%
Stocks	66%
US Stocks	54%
Bonds	32%
US Bonds	26%
Other	0%

Services Offered: Systematic Withdrawal Plan, Automatic Investment Plan, Phone Exchange, Wire Redemption

Investment Strategy: The investment seeks to provide long-term capital appreciation and moderate current income. The fund invests 60% to 70% of its assets in dividend-paying and, to a lesser extent, non-dividend-paying common stocks of established large companies. The remaining 30% to 40% of the fund's assets are invested mainly in fixed income securities that the advisor believes will generate a moderate level of current income. These securities include investment-grade corporate bonds, with some exposure to U.S. Treasury and government agency bonds, and mortgage-backed securities. **Top Holdings:** Microsoft Corp Verizon Communications Inc JPMorgan Chase & Co Bank of America Corporation Alphabet Inc A

Vanguard Wellington™ Fund Investor Shares — B BUY

Ticker	Traded On	NAV	Total Assets ($)	Dividend Yield (TTM)	Turnover Ratio	Expense Ratio
VWELX	NAS CM	41.35	$105,381,000,000	2.53	34	0.25

Ratings

Reward	C+
Risk	A-
Recent Upgrade/Downgrade	

Fund Information

Fund Type	Open End
Category	Moderate Alloc
Sub-Category	Alloc--50% to 70% Equity
Prospectus Objective	Growth & Income
Inception Date	Jul-29
Open to New Investments	
Minimum Initial Investment	3,000
Minimum Subsequent Investment	1
Front End Fee	
Back End Fee	

Total Returns (%)

3-Month	6-Month	1-Year	3-Year	5-Year
3.89	13.51	10.28	33.60	43.27

Last Bull Market	16.28
Last Bear Market	-10.37
3-Year Standard Deviation	7.32
3-Year Beta	0.58

Company Information

Provider	Vanguard
Manager/Tenure	Edward P. Bousa (16), Loren L. Moran (2), Michael E. Stack (2), 1 other
Website	http://www.vanguard.com
Address	Vanguard 100 Vanguard Boulevard Malvern PA 19355 United States
Phone Number	877-662-7447

PERFORMANCE

Ratings History

Date	Overall Rating	Risk Rating	Reward Rating
Q2-19	B	A-	C+
Q4-18	C	B	C
Q4-17	B-	B	B-
Q4-16	B	B+	B-
Q4-15	C+	B-	C

Asset & Performance History

Date	NAV	1-Year Total Return
2018	37.12	-3.42
2017	42.03	14.72
2016	39.06	11.01
2015	36.79	0.05
2014	39.15	9.82
2013	37.94	19.66

Total Assets: $105,381,000,000

Asset Allocation

Asset	%
Cash	2%
Stocks	66%
US Stocks	54%
Bonds	32%
US Bonds	26%
Other	0%

Services Offered: Systematic Withdrawal Plan, Automatic Investment Plan, Phone Exchange, Wire Redemption

Investment Strategy: The investment seeks to provide long-term capital appreciation and moderate current income. The fund invests 60% to 70% of its assets in dividend-paying and, to a lesser extent, non-dividend-paying common stocks of established large companies. The remaining 30% to 40% of the fund's assets are invested mainly in fixed income securities that the advisor believes will generate a moderate level of current income. These securities include investment-grade corporate bonds, with some exposure to U.S. Treasury and government agency bonds, and mortgage-backed securities. **Top Holdings:** Microsoft Corp Verizon Communications Inc JPMorgan Chase & Co Bank of America Corporation Alphabet Inc A

American Funds Capital Income Builder® Class 529-E C+ HOLD

Ticker	Traded On	NAV	Total Assets ($)	Dividend Yield (TTM)	Turnover Ratio	Expense Ratio
CIREX	NAS CM	61.1	$104,371,000,000	3.21	73	0.89

Ratings

Reward	C
Risk	B
Recent Upgrade/Downgrade	

Fund Information

Fund Type	Open End
Category	Flexible Alloc
Sub-Category	World Alloc
Prospectus Objective	Equity-Income
Inception Date	Mar-02
Open to New Investments	Y
Minimum Initial Investment	250
Minimum Subsequent Investment	50
Front End Fee	
Back End Fee	

Total Returns (%)

3-Month	6-Month	1-Year	3-Year	5-Year
1.85	10.66	5.41	17.49	19.29

Last Bull Market	12.54
Last Bear Market	-10.09
3-Year Standard Deviation	7.07
3-Year Beta	0.58

Company Information

Provider	American Funds
Manager/Tenure	James B. Lovelace (27), Joyce E. Gordon (19), David A. Hoag (15), 8 others
Website	http://www.americanfunds.com
Address	American Funds 333 South Hope Street Los Angeles CA 90071-1406 United States
Phone Number	800-421-4225

PERFORMANCE

Ratings History

Date	Overall Rating	Risk Rating	Reward Rating
Q2-19	B-	B+	C
Q4-18	C	C	D+
Q4-17	B-	B	C+
Q4-16	C+	B	C
Q4-15	B-	B+	C

Asset & Performance History

Date	NAV	1-Year Total Return
2018	56.33	-7.3
2017	62.81	13.88
2016	57.64	6.59
2015	55.84	-3.25
2014	59.57	6.26
2013	58.54	14.5

Total Assets: $104,371,000,000

Asset Allocation

Asset	%
Cash	4%
Stocks	71%
US Stocks	37%
Bonds	25%
US Bonds	23%
Other	0%

Services Offered: Systematic Withdrawal Plan, Automatic Investment Plan, Qualified Investment, Phone Exchange, Retirement Investment

Investment Strategy: The investment seeks (1) to provide a level of current income that exceeds the average yield on U.S. stocks generally and (2) to provide a growing stream of income over the years. The fund normally will invest at least 90% of its assets in income-producing securities (with at least 50% of its assets in common stocks and other equity securities). It invests primarily in a broad range of income-producing securities, including common stocks and bonds. In seeking to provide the investors with a level of current income that exceeds the average yield on U.S. stocks, the fund generally looks to the average yield on stocks of companies listed on the S&P 500 Index.

Top Holdings: AbbVie Inc Novartis AG Broadcom Inc Verizon Communications Inc Coca-Cola Co

American Funds Capital Income Builder® Class R-3 C+ HOLD

Ticker	Traded On	NAV	Total Assets ($)	Dividend Yield (TTM)	Turnover Ratio	Expense Ratio
RIRCX	NAS CM	61.11	$104,371,000,000	3.15	73	0.95

Ratings

Reward	C
Risk	B
Recent Upgrade/Downgrade	

Fund Information

Fund Type	Open End
Category	Flexible Alloc
Sub-Category	World Alloc
Prospectus Objective	Equity-Income
Inception Date	Jun-02
Open to New Investments	Y
Minimum Initial Investment	250
Minimum Subsequent Investment	50
Front End Fee	
Back End Fee	

Total Returns (%)

3-Month	6-Month	1-Year	3-Year	5-Year
1.83	10.63	5.34	17.30	19.04

Last Bull Market	12.55
Last Bear Market	-10.1
3-Year Standard Deviation	7.07
3-Year Beta	0.58

Company Information

Provider	American Funds
Manager/Tenure	James B. Lovelace (27), Joyce E. Gordon (19), David A. Hoag (15), 8 others
Website	http://www.americanfunds.com
Address	American Funds 333 South Hope Street Los Angeles CA 90071-1406 United States
Phone Number	800-421-4225

PERFORMANCE

Ratings History

Date	Overall Rating	Risk Rating	Reward Rating
Q2-19	B-	B+	C
Q4-18	C	C	D+
Q4-17	B-	B	C+
Q4-16	C+	B	C
Q4-15	B-	B+	C

Asset & Performance History

Date	NAV	1-Year Total Return
2018	56.34	-7.36
2017	62.82	13.82
2016	57.65	6.54
2015	55.85	-3.28
2014	59.58	6.22
2013	58.55	14.5

Total Assets: $104,371,000,000

Asset Allocation

Asset	%
Cash	4%
Stocks	71%
US Stocks	37%
Bonds	25%
US Bonds	23%
Other	0%

Services Offered: Automatic Investment Plan, Qualified Investment, Phone Exchange

Investment Strategy: The investment seeks (1) to provide a level of current income that exceeds the average yield on U.S. stocks generally and (2) to provide a growing stream of income over the years. The fund normally will invest at least 90% of its assets in income-producing securities (with at least 50% of its assets in common stocks and other equity securities). It invests primarily in a broad range of income-producing securities, including common stocks and bonds. In seeking to provide the investors with a level of current income that exceeds the average yield on U.S. stocks, the fund generally looks to the average yield on stocks of companies listed on the S&P 500 Index.

Top Holdings: AbbVie Inc Novartis AG Broadcom Inc Verizon Communications Inc Coca-Cola Co

American Funds Capital Income Builder® Class A

C+ HOLD

Ticker	Traded On	NAV	Total Assets ($)	Dividend Yield (TTM)	Turnover Ratio	Expense Ratio
CAIBX	NAS CM	61.1	$104,371,000,000	3.5	73	0.58

Ratings

Reward	C
Risk	B
Recent Upgrade/Downgrade	

Fund Information

Fund Type	Open End
Category	Flexible Alloc
Sub-Category	World Alloc
Prospectus Objective	Equity-Income
Inception Date	Jul-87
Open to New Investments	Y
Minimum Initial Investment	250
Minimum Subsequent Investment	50
Front End Fee	5.75
Back End Fee	

Total Returns (%)

3-Month	6-Month	1-Year	3-Year	5-Year
1.92	10.83	5.71	18.54	21.19

Last Bull Market	12.77
Last Bear Market	-9.97
3-Year Standard Deviation	7.08
3-Year Beta	0.58

Company Information

Provider	American Funds
Manager/Tenure	James B. Lovelace (27), Joyce E. Gordon (19), David A. Hoag (15), 8 others
Website	http://www.americanfunds.com
Address	American Funds 333 South Hope Street Los Angeles CA 90071-1406 United States
Phone Number	800-421-4225

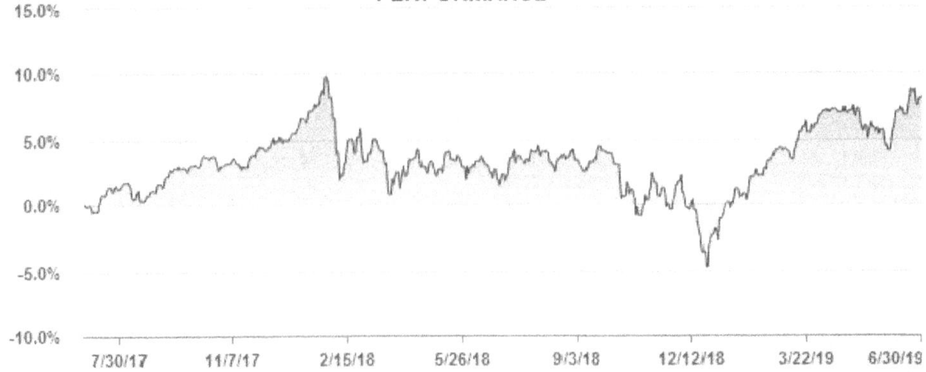

Ratings History

Date	Overall Rating	Risk Rating	Reward Rating
Q2-19	B-	B+	C
Q4-18	C	C+	D+
Q4-17	B-	B	C+
Q4-16	C+	B	C
Q4-15	C+	B-	C

Asset & Performance History

Date	NAV	1-Year Total Return
2018	56.33	-7.03
2017	62.82	14.24
2016	57.64	6.9
2015	55.85	-2.92
2014	59.58	6.61
2013	58.55	14.9

Total Assets: $104,371,000,000

Asset Allocation

Asset	%
Cash	4%
Stocks	71%
US Stocks	37%
Bonds	25%
US Bonds	23%
Other	0%

Services Offered: Systematic Withdrawal Plan, Automatic Investment Plan, Phone Exchange, Retirement Investment

Investment Strategy: The investment seeks (1) to provide a level of current income that exceeds the average yield on U.S. stocks generally and (2) to provide a growing stream of income over the years. The fund normally will invest at least 90% of its assets in income-producing securities (with at least 50% of its assets in common stocks and other equity securities). It invests primarily in a broad range of income-producing securities, including common stocks and bonds. In seeking to provide the investors with a level of current income that exceeds the average yield on U.S. stocks, the fund generally looks to the average yield on stocks of companies listed on the S&P 500 Index.

Top Holdings: AbbVie Inc Novartis AG Broadcom Inc Verizon Communications Inc Coca-Cola Co

American Funds Capital Income Builder® Class C

C+ HOLD

Ticker	Traded On	NAV	Total Assets ($)	Dividend Yield (TTM)	Turnover Ratio	Expense Ratio
CIBCX	NAS CM	61.22	$104,371,000,000	2.71	73	1.37

Ratings

Reward	C
Risk	B
Recent Upgrade/Downgrade	Up

Fund Information

Fund Type	Open End
Category	Flexible Alloc
Sub-Category	World Alloc
Prospectus Objective	Equity-Income
Inception Date	Mar-01
Open to New Investments	Y
Minimum Initial Investment	250
Minimum Subsequent Investment	50
Front End Fee	
Back End Fee	1.00

Total Returns (%)

3-Month	6-Month	1-Year	3-Year	5-Year
1.73	10.39	4.90	15.78	16.47

Last Bull Market	12.25
Last Bear Market	-10.26
3-Year Standard Deviation	7.07
3-Year Beta	0.58

Company Information

Provider	American Funds
Manager/Tenure	James B. Lovelace (27), Joyce E. Gordon (19), David A. Hoag (15), 8 others
Website	http://www.americanfunds.com
Address	American Funds 333 South Hope Street Los Angeles CA 90071-1406 United States
Phone Number	800-421-4225

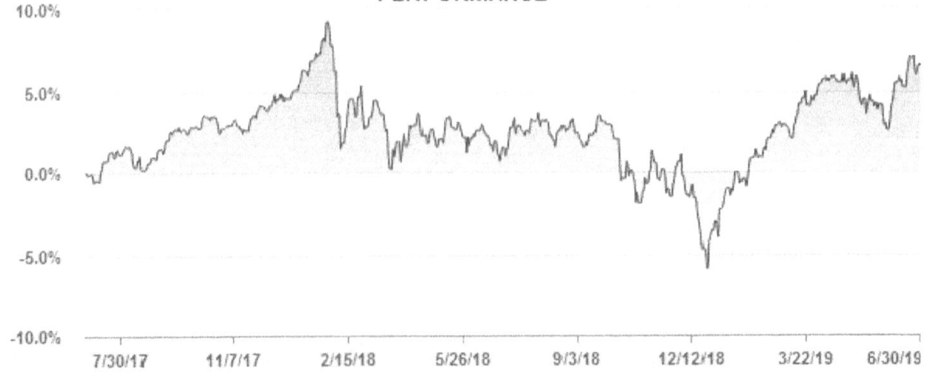

Ratings History

Date	Overall Rating	Risk Rating	Reward Rating
Q2-19	C+	B	C
Q4-18	C-	C	D+
Q4-17	B-	B	C+
Q4-16	C+	B	C
Q4-15	B-	B+	C

Asset & Performance History

Date	NAV	1-Year Total Return
2018	56.43	-7.75
2017	62.9	13.32
2016	57.71	6.07
2015	55.9	-3.71
2014	59.63	5.77
2013	58.59	13.99

Total Assets: $104,371,000,000

Asset Allocation

Asset	%
Cash	4%
Stocks	71%
US Stocks	37%
Bonds	25%
US Bonds	23%
Other	0%

Services Offered: Systematic Withdrawal Plan, Automatic Investment Plan, Phone Exchange, Retirement Investment

Investment Strategy: The investment seeks (1) to provide a level of current income that exceeds the average yield on U.S. stocks generally and (2) to provide a growing stream of income over the years. The fund normally will invest at least 90% of its assets in income-producing securities (with at least 50% of its assets in common stocks and other equity securities). It invests primarily in a broad range of income-producing securities, including common stocks and bonds. In seeking to provide the investors with a level of current income that exceeds the average yield on U.S. stocks, the fund generally looks to the average yield on stocks of companies listed on the S&P 500 Index.

Top Holdings: AbbVie Inc Novartis AG Broadcom Inc Verizon Communications Inc Coca-Cola Co

American Funds Capital Income Builder® Class R-5E — C+ HOLD

Ticker	Traded On	NAV	Total Assets ($)	Dividend Yield (TTM)	Turnover Ratio	Expense Ratio
RIRHX	NAS CM	61.02	$104,371,000,000	3.66	73	0.44

Ratings

Reward	C
Risk	B
Recent Upgrade/Downgrade	

Fund Information

Fund Type	Open End
Category	Flexible Alloc
Sub-Category	World Alloc
Prospectus Objective	Equity-Income
Inception Date	Nov-15
Open to New Investments	Y
Minimum Initial Investment	250
Minimum Subsequent Investment	50
Front End Fee	
Back End Fee	

Total Returns (%)

3-Month	6-Month	1-Year	3-Year	5-Year
1.97	10.93	5.88	19.05	21.77

Last Bull Market	12.77
Last Bear Market	-9.97
3-Year Standard Deviation	7.09
3-Year Beta	0.58

Company Information

Provider	American Funds
Manager/Tenure	James B. Lovelace (27), Joyce E. Gordon (19), David A. Hoag (15), 8 others
Website	http://www.americanfunds.com
Address	American Funds 333 South Hope Street Los Angeles CA 90071-1406 United States
Phone Number	800-421-4225

PERFORMANCE

Ratings History

Date	Overall Rating	Risk Rating	Reward Rating
Q2-19	B-	B+	C
Q4-18	C	C+	D+
Q4-17	B-	B	C+
Q4-16	C+	B	C
Q4-15			

Asset & Performance History

Date	NAV	1-Year Total Return
2018	56.25	-6.89
2017	62.74	14.4
2016	57.58	6.99
2015	55.82	-2.91
2014		6.61
2013		14.9

Total Assets: $104,371,000,000

Asset Allocation

Asset	%
Cash	4%
Stocks	71%
US Stocks	37%
Bonds	25%
US Bonds	23%
Other	0%

Services Offered: Automatic Investment Plan, Qualified Investment, Phone Exchange

Investment Strategy: The investment seeks (1) to provide a level of current income that exceeds the average yield on U.S. stocks generally and (2) to provide a growing stream of income over the years. The fund normally will invest at least 90% of its assets in income-producing securities (with at least 50% of its assets in common stocks and other equity securities). It invests primarily in a broad range of income-producing securities, including common stocks and bonds. In seeking to provide the investors with a level of current income that exceeds the average yield on U.S. stocks, the fund generally looks to the average yield on stocks of companies listed on the S&P 500 Index.

Top Holdings: AbbVie Inc Novartis AG Broadcom Inc Verizon Communications Inc Coca-Cola Co

American Funds Capital Income Builder® Class F-1 — C+ HOLD

Ticker	Traded On	NAV	Total Assets ($)	Dividend Yield (TTM)	Turnover Ratio	Expense Ratio
CIBFX	NAS CM	61.1	$104,371,000,000	3.43	73	0.66

Ratings

Reward	C
Risk	B
Recent Upgrade/Downgrade	

Fund Information

Fund Type	Open End
Category	Flexible Alloc
Sub-Category	World Alloc
Prospectus Objective	Equity-Income
Inception Date	Mar-01
Open to New Investments	Y
Minimum Initial Investment	250
Minimum Subsequent Investment	50
Front End Fee	
Back End Fee	

Total Returns (%)

3-Month	6-Month	1-Year	3-Year	5-Year
1.90	10.78	5.65	18.28	20.73

Last Bull Market	12.75
Last Bear Market	-9.97
3-Year Standard Deviation	7.08
3-Year Beta	0.58

Company Information

Provider	American Funds
Manager/Tenure	James B. Lovelace (27), Joyce E. Gordon (19), David A. Hoag (15), 8 others
Website	http://www.americanfunds.com
Address	American Funds 333 South Hope Street Los Angeles CA 90071-1406 United States
Phone Number	800-421-4225

PERFORMANCE

Ratings History

Date	Overall Rating	Risk Rating	Reward Rating
Q2-19	B-	B+	C
Q4-18	C	C+	D+
Q4-17	B-	B	C+
Q4-16	C+	B	C
Q4-15	C+	B-	C

Asset & Performance History

Date	NAV	1-Year Total Return
2018	56.33	-7.08
2017	62.81	14.13
2016	57.64	6.83
2015	55.85	-2.99
2014	59.59	6.55
2013	58.55	14.82

Total Assets: $104,371,000,000

Asset Allocation

Asset	%
Cash	4%
Stocks	71%
US Stocks	37%
Bonds	25%
US Bonds	23%
Other	0%

Services Offered: Systematic Withdrawal Plan, Automatic Investment Plan, Qualified Investment, Phone Exchange, Retirement Investment

Investment Strategy: The investment seeks (1) to provide a level of current income that exceeds the average yield on U.S. stocks generally and (2) to provide a growing stream of income over the years. The fund normally will invest at least 90% of its assets in income-producing securities (with at least 50% of its assets in common stocks and other equity securities). It invests primarily in a broad range of income-producing securities, including common stocks and bonds. In seeking to provide the investors with a level of current income that exceeds the average yield on U.S. stocks, the fund generally looks to the average yield on stocks of companies listed on the S&P 500 Index.

Top Holdings: AbbVie Inc Novartis AG Broadcom Inc Verizon Communications Inc Coca-Cola Co

Section III:
Best All-Around Stock Mutual Funds

Investment Ratings and analysis of the Best All-Around Stock Mutual Funds. Funds are listed in order by their one-year returns and overall rating.

Section III: Contents

This section contains Weiss Investment Ratings, key rating factors, and summary financial data for our selections for "Best All-Around Stock Mutual Funds." We have selected funds with better returns, lower expense and with a maximum initial investment of $5,000 or less required. Funds are listed in order by their one-year returns and overall rating.

Fund Name

Describes the fund's assets, regions of investments and investment strategies. Many funds have similar names, so you want to make sure the fund you look up is really the one you are interested in evaluating.

Ticker Symbol

An arrangement of characters (usually letters) representing a particular security listed on an exchange or otherwise traded publicly. When a company issues securities to the public marketplace, it selects an available ticker symbol for its securities which investors use to place trade orders. Every listed security has a unique ticker symbol, facilitating the vast array of trade orders that flow through the financial markets every day. If a ticker symbol is not assigned to a particular fund, the International Securities Identification Number (ISIN) is displayed.

RATINGS

Overall Rating

The Weiss rating measured on a scale from A to E based on each fund's risk and performance. See the preceding section, "What Our Ratings Mean," for an explanation of each letter grade rating.

Reward Rating

This is based on the total return over a period of up to five years, including net asset value and price growth. The total return figure is stated net of the expenses and fees charged by the fund. Based on proprietary modeling the individual components of the risk and reward ratings are calculated and weighted and the final rating is generated.

Risk Rating

This is includes the risk ratings of component stocks where applicable and also includes the financial stability of the fund, turnover where applicable, together with the level of volatility as measured by the fund's daily returns over a period of up to five years. Funds with greater stability are considered less risky and receive a higher risk rating. Funds with greater volatility are considered riskier, and will receive a lower risk rating. In addition to considering the fund's volatility, the risk rating also considers an assessment of the valuation and quality of a fund's holdings.

Recent Upgrade/Downgrade

An "Up" or "Down" indicates that the Weiss Mutual Fund rating has changed since the publication of the last print edition. If a fund has had a rating change since March 31, 2019, the change is identified with an "Up" or "Down."

TOTAL RETURNS & PERFORMANCE

3-Month Total Return
The rate of return on an investment over three months that includes interest, capital gains, dividends and distributions realized.

6-Month Total Return
The rate of return on an investment over six months that includes interest, capital gains, dividends and distributions realized.

1-Year Total Return
The rate of return on an investment over one year that includes interest, capital gains, dividends and distributions realized.

3-Year Total Return
The rate of return on an investment over three years that includes interest, capital gains, dividends and distributions realized.

5-Year Total Return
The rate of return on an investment over five years that includes interest, capital gains, dividends and distributions realized.

ASSETS

NAV (Net Asset Value)
A fund's price per share. The value is calculated by dividing the total value of all the securities in the portfolio, less any liabilities, by the number of fund shares outstanding.

Total Assets (MIL)
The total of all assets listed on the institution's balance sheet. This figure primarily consists of loans, investments, and fixed assets. Total Assets are displayed in millions.

NEW INVESTORS

Telephone
The company's phone number.

Open to New Investors
Indicates whether the fund accepts investments from those who are not existing investors. A "Y" in this column identifies that the fund accepts new investors. No data in this column indicates that the fund is closed to new investors. The fund may be closed to new investors because the fund's asset base is getting too large to effectively execute its investing style. Although, the fund may be closed, in most cases, existing investors are able to add to their holdings.

		RATINGS				TOTAL RETURNS & PERFORMANCE					ASSETS		NEW INVESTORS	
Fund Name	Ticker Symbol	Overall Rating	Reward Rating	Risk Rating	Recent Up/ Downgrade	3-Month Total Return	6-Month Total Return	1-Year Total Return	3-Year Total Return	5-Year Total Return	NAV	Total Assets (MIL)	Telephone	Open to New Investors
Eaton Vance-Atlanta Capital Focused Growth Fund Class A	EAALX	B+	B+	A-	Up	6.83	27.40	26.22	83.15	93.59	11.25	71.7		Y
Calvert Equity Fund Class A	CSIEX	B+	B	A-	Up	7.11	26.50	24.67	71.16	89.28	52.22	2,937	301-951-4881	Y
Eaton Vance Atlanta Capital Select Equity Fund Class A	ESEAX	B	B	B+		8.31	27.13	22.60	55.09	78.59	24.74	489.2		Y
DF Dent Premier Growth Fund Investor Shares	DFDPX	B	B+	B		9.83	32.94	21.13	84.80	94.20	35.75	209.4		Y
Davenport Equity Opportunities Fund	DEOPX	B-	B-	B	Up	8.82	30.23	19.01	50.70	53.57	20	448.6		Y
MFS Massachusetts Investors Growth Stock Fund Class R6	MIGNX	B	B	B+		5.43	25.06	18.70	67.40	84.61	32.38	7,515	877-960-6077	Y
MFS Massachusetts Investors Growth Stock Fund Class I	MGTIX	B	B	B+		5.40	25.04	18.63	66.91	83.68	32.35	7,515	877-960-6077	Y
MFS Massachusetts Investors Growth Stock Fund Class R4	MIGKX	B	B	B+		5.40	25.02	18.60	66.86	83.64	31.62	7,515	877-960-6077	Y
MFS Massachusetts Investors Growth Stock Fund Class A	MIGFX	B	B	B+		5.33	24.88	18.34	65.68	81.49	31.37	7,515	877-960-6077	Y
MFS Massachusetts Investors Growth Stock Fund Class 529A	EISTX	B	B	B+		5.32	24.84	18.29	65.49	81.16	30.85	7,515	877-960-6077	Y
MFS Massachusetts Investors Growth Stock Fund Class R3	MIGHX	B	B	B+		5.29	24.84	18.28	65.62	81.32	31	7,515	877-960-6077	Y
MFS Massachusetts Investors Growth Stock Fund Class R2	MIRGX	B	B	B+		5.25	24.70	18.01	64.40	79.11	30.44	7,515	877-960-6077	Y
Value Line Asset Allocation Fund Investor Class	VLAAX	B+	B	A-	Up	6.15	20.17	17.35	42.65	54.71	37.23	743.6	800-243-2729	Y
Fidelity® Select Insurance Portfolio	FSPCX	B-	B-	B	Up	10.81	24.37	17.32	47.89	64.32	63.1	260.3	617-563-7000	Y
Janus Henderson VIT Enterprise Portfolio Institutional Cls	JAAGX	B	B-	B		7.31	27.98	17.30	73.71	101.11	79.89	1,393	877-335-2687	Y
Franklin DynaTech Fund Class A	FKDNX	B-	B-	B-	Down	6.64	31.22	17.13	97.19	115.57	85.11	7,895	650-312-2000	Y
Janus Henderson VIT Enterprise Portfolio Service Class		B	B-	B		7.25	27.83	17.02	72.44	98.64	74.78	1,384	877-335-2687	Y
Franklin DynaTech Fund Class R	FDNRX	B-	B-	B-	Down	6.57	31.05	16.84	95.73	112.91	82.5	7,895	650-312-2000	Y
VY® T. Rowe Price Diversified Mid Cap Growth Port Cls I	IAXIX	B-	B-	B	Down	7.11	29.11	16.81	65.21	80.95	12.95	1,109	800-366-0066	Y
T. Rowe Price Dividend Growth Fund	PRDGX	B	B-	A-		6.10	20.92	16.72	50.05	72.23	49.39	11,498	410-345-2000	Y
VY® T. Rowe Price Diversified Mid Cap Growth Port Cls R6	VYRIX	B	B-	B		7.11	28.98	16.70	65.19	81.10	12.95	1,109	800-366-0066	Y
Janus Henderson Enterprise Fund Class T	JAENX	B	B-	B		7.15	27.65	16.62	69.98	94.98	137.46	19,965	877-335-2687	Y
VY® T. Rowe Price Diversified Mid Cap Growth Port Cls S	IAXSX	B-	B-	B	Down	7.06	28.97	16.53	63.92	78.71	12.42	1,109	800-366-0066	Y
T. Rowe Price Dividend Growth Fund Advisor Class	TADGX	B	B-	A-		6.02	20.76	16.42	48.83	69.93	49.34	11,498	410-345-2000	Y
Janus Henderson Enterprise Fund Class A	JDMAX	B	B-	B		7.09	27.52	16.37	68.88	92.86	134.72	19,965	877-335-2687	Y
Janus Henderson Enterprise Fund Class S	JGRTX	B	B-	B		7.08	27.50	16.33	68.70	92.54	134.02	19,965	877-335-2687	Y
Bridgeway Blue Chip Index Fund	BRLIX	B	C+	B+		5.19	19.34	16.25	50.56	67.67	14.99	505.2	800-661-3550	Y
Ivy Science and Technology Fund Class I	ISTIX	B-	B	B-		9.36	35.04	15.97	93.25	66.48	79.3	7,179		Y
Vanguard Dividend Appreciation Index Fund Admiral Shares	VDADX	B	C+	B+		5.54	19.97	15.60	49.52	64.21	31.28	44,334	877-662-7447	Y
Vanguard Dividend Appreciation Index Fund Investor Shares	VDAIX	B	C+	B+		5.52	19.93	15.56	49.24	63.59	46.12	44,334	877-662-7447	Y
ClearBridge Dividend Strategy Fund Class 1	LCBOX	B	B-	B+		5.56	20.53	15.48	46.02	58.51	24.54	6,398	877-721-1926	Y
TCW Select Equities Fund Class I	TGCEX	B-	B-	B	Down	6.07	27.39	15.28	70.77	86.84	27.58	945.5	213-244-0000	Y
ClearBridge Dividend Strategy Fund Class FI	LBRIX	B	B-	B+		5.55	20.37	15.25	44.76	56.25	24.48	6,398	877-721-1926	Y
ClearBridge Dividend Strategy Fund Class A	SOPAX	B	B-	B+		5.50	20.38	15.18	44.80	56.34	24.53	6,398	877-721-1926	Y
Loomis Sayles Growth Fund Class A	LGRRX	B-	C+	B	Down	5.10	22.68	15.13	63.47	93.66	16.28	8,854	800-862-4863	Y
Sextant Growth Fund	SGZFX	B-	C+	B	Down	5.96	23.84	15.13	59.77	56.66	30.54	42.0		Y
TCW Select Equities Fund Class N	TGCNX	B-	B-	B-	Down	6.00	27.20	15.03	69.60	84.61	24.55	945.5	213-244-0000	Y
MFS Growth Fund Class R6	MFEKX	B	B-	B		6.57	26.71	14.94	74.17	97.15	117.89	22,365	877-960-6077	Y
City National Rochdale U.S. Core Equity Cls Servicing	CNRVX	B	B-	B+		7.22	23.30	14.88	59.75	70.21	18.58	314.9		Y
MFS Growth Fund Class I	MFEIX	B	B-	B		6.56	26.65	14.84	73.69	96.22	117.53	22,365	877-960-6077	Y
MFS Growth Fund Class R4	MFEJX	B	B-	B		6.55	26.66	14.84	73.67	96.19	114.23	22,365	877-960-6077	Y
Baron Global Advantage Fund Retail Shares	BGAFX	B	B	C+	Up	6.77	35.40	14.79	102.43	87.56	26.62	215.8	800-992-2766	Y
Sextant Growth Fund	SSGFX	B-	C+	B	Down	5.90	23.62	14.76	59.10	56.01	30.66	42.0		Y
AAM/Bahl & Gaynor Income Growth Fund Class A	AFNAX	B	B-	B+		5.06	17.85	14.75	42.51	55.84	18.68	1,173	800-617-0004	Y
City National Rochdale U.S. Core Equity Fund Class N	CNRWX	B	B-	B+		7.17	23.20	14.63	58.60	68.05	18.55	314.9		Y
ClearBridge Appreciation Fund Class A	SHAPX	B	C+	B+		5.90	19.13	14.59	46.52	61.29	25.65	6,450	877-721-1926	Y
MFS Growth Fund Class A	MFEGX	B	B-	B		6.48	26.49	14.56	72.41	93.83	110.16	22,365	877-960-6077	Y
T. Rowe Price Tax-Efficient Equity Fund	PREFX	B-	B-	B	Down	6.23	26.79	14.56	70.55	88.16	35.63	510.0	410-345-2000	Y
MFS Growth Fund Class R3	MFEHX	B	B-	B		6.48	26.49	14.55	72.38	93.75	109.59	22,365	877-960-6077	Y
ClearBridge Appreciation Fund Class FI	LMPIX	B	C+	B+		5.87	19.06	14.49	46.31	61.01	25.79	6,450	877-721-1926	Y
Jensen Quality Growth Fund Class J	JENSX	B	C+	B+		2.49	18.35	14.47	55.43	83.41	50.69	7,522	800-992-4144	Y
USAA Growth Fund	USAAX	B-	C+	B	Down	5.42	22.99	14.42	60.44	82.65	31.5	2,860	800-235-8396	Y

		RATINGS				TOTAL RETURNS & PERFORMANCE					ASSETS		NEW INVESTORS	
Fund Name	Ticker Symbol	Overall Rating	Reward Rating	Risk Rating	Recent Up/ Downgrade	3-Month Total Return	6-Month Total Return	1-Year Total Return	3-Year Total Return	5-Year Total Return	NAV	Total Assets (MIL)	Telephone	Open to New Investors
GuideStone Funds Growth Equity Fund Investor Class	GGEZX	B-	C+	B	Down	5.19	25.02	14.00	71.28	83.05	26.09	1,613	214-720-1171	Y
American Beacon The London Company Income Equity A Cls	ABCAX	B-	C	B+		2.43	17.08	13.96	34.44	50.09	18.19	1,114	800-658-5811	Y
American Beacon The London Company Income Equity Inv Cls	ABCVX	B-	C	B+		2.41	17.03	13.92	34.51	50.31	18.3	1,114	800-658-5811	Y
MFAM Global Opportunities Fund Investor Shares	FOOLX	B-	B-	B	Up	6.93	26.97	13.82	64.62	60.33	25.28	469.5		Y
Franklin Rising Dividends Fund Class A	FRDPX	B-	C+	B	Down	4.99	21.83	13.69	46.50	58.92	66.62	19,187	650-312-2000	Y
Sterling Capital Equity Income Fund Class R6	STREX	B	C+	B+		4.25	15.98	13.68	52.96	53.61	20.88	1,774	800-228-1872	Y
Mairs & Power Growth Fund Investor Class	MPGFX	B-	C	B	Down	2.73	17.46	13.68	36.89	50.24	122.92	4,404	800-304-7404	Y
Congress Large Cap Growth Fund Retail Class	CAMLX	B	B-	B		5.02	23.35	13.59	60.28	69.96	31.37	326.0	888-688-1299	Y
Franklin Rising Dividends Fund Class R	FRDRX	B-	C+	B	Down	4.92	21.68	13.40	45.41	56.95	66.37	19,187	650-312-2000	Y
Carillon Eagle Growth & Income Fund Class R6	HIGUX	B	C+	A-		3.73	15.46	13.37	44.23	50.80	21.2	812.9	800-421-4184	Y
MFS Massachusetts Investors Trust Class R6	MITJX	B	C+	B		5.45	22.14	13.32	54.41	65.72	31.02	5,716	877-960-6077	Y
Sterling Capital Equity Income Fund Class A	BAEIX	B-	C+	B+	Down	4.11	15.79	13.26	51.53	51.48	20.81	1,774	800-228-1872	Y
The MP 63 Fund	DRIPX	B-	C+	B+	Down	3.88	18.62	13.25	40.41	54.48	22.48	71.3		Y
MFS Massachusetts Investors Trust Class R4	MITDX	B	C+	B		5.41	22.05	13.24	53.97	64.95	32.32	5,716	877-960-6077	Y
MFS Massachusetts Investors Trust Class I	MITIX	B	C+	B		5.40	22.07	13.23	54.04	65.02	31.02	5,716	877-960-6077	Y
Columbia Dividend Income Fund Institutional 2 Class	CDDRX	B	C+	B+		4.11	17.57	13.05	44.96	63.72	23.07	14,746	800-345-6611	Y
MFS Massachusetts Investors Trust Class A	MITTX	B	C+	B		5.34	21.93	12.98	52.95	63.09	32	5,716	877-960-6077	Y
Columbia Dividend Income Fund Advisor Class	CVIRX	B	C+	B+		4.09	17.51	12.95	44.58	62.82	23.09	14,746	800-345-6611	Y
MFS Massachusetts Investors Trust Class R3	MITHX	B-	C+	B	Down	5.36	21.91	12.94	52.89	62.96	31.68	5,716	877-960-6077	Y
Columbia Dividend Income Fund Institutional Class	GSFTX	B	C+	B+		4.11	17.50	12.92	44.59	62.84	22.7	14,746	800-345-6611	Y
MFS Massachusetts Investors Trust Class 529A	EAMTX	B-	C+	B	Down	5.32	21.88	12.88	52.65	62.64	31.1	5,716	877-960-6077	Y
Red Oak Technology Select Fund	ROGSX	B-	C+	B	Down	1.69	21.87	12.86	92.44	118.24	28.75	629.2	888-462-5386	Y
VY® Baron Growth Portfolio Class I	IBGIX	B	B	B-	Up	6.69	29.22	12.73	67.90	69.99	35.24	816.9	800-366-0066	Y
VY® Baron Growth Portfolio Class R6	VYRBX	B	B	B-	Up	6.68	29.25	12.72	67.92	70.06	35.26	816.9	800-366-0066	Y
T. Rowe Price Communications & Technology Investor Cls	PRMTX	B	B-	B	Up	5.19	25.78	12.67	72.94	99.15	117.21	6,154	410-345-2000	Y
Columbia Dividend Income Fund Class A	LBSAX	B-	C+	B+	Down	4.05	17.38	12.65	43.49	60.81	22.68	14,746	800-345-6611	Y
Queens Road Value Fund	QRVLX	B-	C	B+	Down	4.00	17.55	12.65	44.31	54.00	24.17	41.7	888-353-0261	Y
MFS Massachusetts Investors Trust Class R2	MIRTX	B-	C+	B	Down	5.25	21.76	12.63	51.72	60.91	30.32	5,716	877-960-6077	Y
Franklin Growth Series Class A	FKGRX	B-	C+	B	Down	5.73	23.07	12.58	61.92	76.87	109.61	15,253	650-312-2000	Y
Buffalo Large Cap Fund	BUFEX	B-	C+	B	Down	4.77	21.68	12.46	60.62	86.03	32.49	72.5	800-492-8332	Y
Nationwide Ziegler NYSE Arca Tech 100 Index Fund Class A	NWJCX	B-	C+	B	Down	3.67	22.76	12.37	80.68	88.50	90.81	678.0	800-848-0920	Y
Franklin Growth Series Class R	FGSRX	B-	C+	B	Down	5.67	22.92	12.31	60.71	74.65	109.13	15,253	650-312-2000	Y
DFA U.S. Large Cap Growth Portfolio Institutional Class	DUSLX	B-	C+	B	Down	4.19	20.61	12.25	57.22	74.07	21.27	2,140	512-306-7400	Y
Buffalo Growth Fund	BUFGX	B-	B-	B	Down	6.85	24.39	12.19	59.08	70.03	26.82	177.2	800-492-8332	Y
BNY Mellon Appreciation Fund, Inc. - Class I	DGIGX	B	B-	B	Up	5.85	21.52	12.17	50.77	52.20	32.03	1,640		Y
BNY Mellon Appreciation Fund, Inc. - Investor Shares	DGAGX	B	B-	B	Up	5.79	21.41	11.89	49.80	51.22	32.23	1,640		Y
Elfun Trusts	ELFNX	B-	C+	B	Down	6.35	21.29	11.70	57.70	71.17	60.38	2,789	617-664-7338	Y
Janus Henderson Growth And Income Fund Class T	JAGIX	B-	C	B+	Down	3.87	15.98	11.47	54.85	67.26	56.98	5,718	877-335-2687	Y
Conestoga SMid Cap Fund Investors Class	CCSMX	B-	B	C+		8.64	27.90	11.40	86.33	82.18	16.96	113.5	800-320-7790	Y
Principal Equity Income Fund Institutional Class	PEIIX	B-	C+	B+	Down	5.44	18.00	11.39	46.53	54.92	32.11	7,444	800-787-1621	Y
Janus Henderson Growth And Income Fund Class A	JDNAX	B-	C	B+	Down	3.85	15.94	11.39	54.48	66.61	56.94	5,718	877-335-2687	Y
Sarofim Equity Fund	SRFMX	B-	B-	B		5.51	21.73	11.37	49.64	50.11	12.43	94.3		Y
Frost Growth Equity Fund Investor Class Shares	FACEX	B-	C+	B	Down	4.44	21.92	11.30	71.75	83.30	13.4	327.2		Y
Vanguard FTSE Social Index Fund Admiral	VFTAX	B-	C+	B	Down	4.54	20.04	11.28	57.90	72.16	27.25	5,942	877-662-7447	Y
Vanguard FTSE Social Index Fund Investor Shares	VFTSX	B-	C+	B	Down	4.56	20.03	11.27	57.89	72.15	19.61	5,942	877-662-7447	Y
Janus Henderson Growth And Income Fund Class S	JADGX	B-	C	B+	Down	3.80	15.86	11.19	53.67	65.12	56.93	5,718	877-335-2687	Y
Homestead Funds Value Fund	HOVLX	B-	C	B	Down	3.71	17.24	11.19	45.42	54.39	53.31	938.5		Y
Baron Fifth Avenue Growth Fund Retail Class	BFTHX	B-	C+	B-	Down	6.54	27.39	11.16	86.63	95.26	32.55	310.0	800-992-2766	Y
Principal Equity Income Fund R-5 Class	PEIQX	B-	C	B+		5.38	17.89	11.13	45.49	53.04	32.08	7,444	800-787-1621	Y
Nationwide Geneva Mid Cap Growth Fund Class A	NWHVX	B-	C+	B-		6.31	24.69	11.07	49.22	65.31	21.71	606.5	800-848-0920	Y
Principal Equity Income Fund Class J	PEIJX	B-	C	B+		5.34	17.84	10.99	44.99	52.04	32.11	7,444	800-787-1621	Y
Principal Equity Income Fund R-4 Class	PEIPX	B-	C	B+		5.32	17.80	10.97	44.91	52.08	32.03	7,444	800-787-1621	Y

		RATINGS				TOTAL RETURNS & PERFORMANCE					ASSETS		NEW INVESTORS	
Fund Name	Ticker Symbol	Overall Rating	Reward Rating	Risk Rating	Recent Up/ Downgrade	3-Month Total Return	6-Month Total Return	1-Year Total Return	3-Year Total Return	5-Year Total Return	NAV	Total Assets (MIL)	Telephone	Open to New Investors
Principal Equity Income Fund Class A	PQIAX	B-	C	B+		5.35	17.81	10.96	44.94	51.99	32.07	7,444	800-787-1621	Y
MFS Value Fund Class R6	MEIKX	B-	C	B	Up	5.10	19.52	10.92	37.22	51.40	41.33	48,073	877-960-6077	Y
MainStay Epoch U.S. Equity Yield Fund Class R6	EPLDX	B-	C+	B+	Down	3.10	15.41	10.85	31.43	50.84	16.63	1,056	800-624-6782	Y
VALIC Company II U.S. Socially Responsible Fund	VCSRX	B-	C+	B		4.49	20.27	10.85	48.72	63.24	21.96	730.4		Y
MFS Value Fund Class R4	MEIJX	B-	C	B	Up	5.07	19.46	10.83	36.84	50.65	41.34	48,073	877-960-6077	Y
MFS Value Fund Class I	MEIIX	B-	C	B	Up	5.07	19.47	10.82	36.82	50.65	41.58	48,073	877-960-6077	Y
Principal Equity Income Fund R-3 Class	PEIOX	B-	C	B+		5.28	17.68	10.77	44.13	50.61	31.97	7,444	800-787-1621	Y
Harbor Strategic Growth Fund Investor Class	HISWX	B-	C+	B	Down	5.96	22.33	10.73	47.18	62.78	21.31	105.1	800-422-1050	Y
DWS Equity 500 Index Fund - Class R6	BTIRX	B-	C	B	Down	4.24	19.45	10.60	50.33	64.77	197.44	624.3		Y
MainStay Epoch U.S. Equity Yield Fund Class R1	EPLRX	B-	C	B+	Down	3.05	15.23	10.57	30.79	50.12	16.62	1,056	800-624-6782	Y
DWS S&P 500 Index Fund - Class R6	SXPRX	B-	C	B		4.22	19.41	10.57	50.18	64.61	31.56	1,006		Y
DWS Equity 500 Index Fund - Class S	BTIEX	B-	C	B		4.23	19.41	10.54	50.11	64.37	194.23	624.3		Y
Sit Large Cap Growth Fund	SNIGX	B-	C+	B	Down	4.16	20.37	10.54	58.04	71.66	42.53	116.6	800-332-5580	Y
Voya Russell Large Cap Index Portfolio Class I	IIRLX	B-	C	B		4.20	18.75	10.53	52.27	67.26	22.34	959.4	800-366-0066	Y
DWS S&P 500 Index Fund - Class S	SCPIX	B-	C	B		4.23	19.41	10.51	49.99	64.08	31.56	1,006		Y
AXA/Mutual Large Cap Eq Managed Vol Port Cls K		B-	C	B+	Down	6.47	10.14	10.49	43.14	62.33		615.7	877-222-2144	Y
Vanguard Growth Index Fund Admiral Shares	VIGAX	B-	C+	B		4.74	23.51	10.44	59.99	76.29	84.14	90,346	877-662-7447	Y
Fidelity® 500 Index Fund	FXAIX	B-	C	B		4.29	19.55	10.40	50.84	66.20	102.66	198,287	617-563-7000	Y
Vanguard 500 Index Fund Admiral Shares	VFIAX	B-	C	B		4.29	19.55	10.38	50.75	66.01	271.39	483,171	877-662-7447	Y
Schwab® S&P 500 Index Fund	SWPPX	B-	C	B		4.29	19.53	10.37	50.67	65.66	45.4	38,408	877-824-5615	Y
Voya Russell Large Cap Growth Index Portfolio Class I	IRLNX	B-	C+	B		4.32	20.98	10.37	66.25	90.56	37.91	757.2	800-366-0066	Y
DFA U.S. Large Company Portfolio	DFUSX	B-	C	B		4.29	19.50	10.33	50.70	65.78	22.68	9,457	512-306-7400	Y
Northern Stock Index Fund	NOSIX	B-	C	B		4.29	19.53	10.32	50.46	65.47	33.99	8,781	800-595-9111	Y
Vanguard Large Cap Index Fund Admiral Shares	VLCAX	B-	C	B		4.28	19.63	10.30	51.20	65.13	68.05	22,808	877-662-7447	Y
Vanguard Growth Index Fund Investor Shares	VIGRX	B-	C+	B		4.70	23.42	10.30	59.42	75.16	84.16	90,346	877-662-7447	Y
MM S&P 500® Index Fund Class I	MMIZX	B-	C	B		4.26	19.53	10.28	50.37	65.25	17.62	3,372		Y
PGIM QMA Stock Index Fund- Class R6	PQSIX	B-	C	B		4.28	19.47	10.27	50.03	64.68	47.92	923.4	800-225-1852	Y
Voya Russell Large Cap Index Portfolio Class S	IRLCX	B-	C	B		4.14	18.57	10.26	51.11	65.13	22.2	959.4	800-366-0066	Y
Vanguard 500 Index Fund Investor Shares	VFINX	B-	C	B		4.27	19.49	10.26	50.30	65.15	271.41	483,171	877-662-7447	Y
PGIM QMA Stock Index Fund- Class I	PDSIX	B-	C	B		4.26	19.48	10.25	50.15	64.96	47.9	923.4	800-225-1852	Y
Voya U.S. Stock Index Portfolio P2	VPSPX	B-	C	B		4.29	19.47	10.25	50.04	64.34	16.5	5,890	800-366-0066	Y
JNL/Mellon S&P 500 Index Fund Class I		B-	C	B		4.27	19.47	10.25	49.74	63.60	23.68	8,414		Y
DWS S&P 500 Index Fund - Class A	SXPAX	B-	C	B		4.14	19.26	10.25	48.82	61.88	31.49	1,006		Y
Principal LargeCap S&P 500 Index Fund Institutional Class	PLFIX	B-	C	B		4.24	19.46	10.24	50.15	64.91	18.41	5,904	800-787-1621	Y
TIAA-CREF S&P 500 Index Fund Advisor Class	TISAX	B-	C	B		4.25	19.43	10.22	50.19	65.21	32.57	5,201	877-518-9161	Y
BNY Mellon Institutional S&P 500 Stock Index Fund Class I	DSPIX	B-	C	B		4.26	19.48	10.22	50.07	64.70	56.62	2,625		Y
T. Rowe Price Equity Index 500 Fund	PREIX	B-	C	B		4.25	19.45	10.20	49.94	64.36	78.34	29,526	410-345-2000	Y
iShares S&P 500 Index Fund Service Shares	BSPSX	B-	C	B		4.24	19.40	10.20	49.93	64.46	349.04	19,490	800-441-7762	Y
PGIM QMA Stock Index Fund- Class Z	PSIFX	B-	C	B		4.26	19.44	10.20	49.88	64.51	47.91	923.4	800-225-1852	Y
Columbia Large Cap Index Fund Institutional 2 Class	CLXRX	B-	C	B		4.25	19.44	10.19	49.98	64.66	49.69	3,370	800-345-6611	Y
Vanguard Large Cap Index Fund Investor Shares	VLACX	B-	C	B		4.25	19.56	10.18	50.67	64.14	54.44	22,808	877-662-7447	Y
Columbia Large Cap Index Fund Institutional Class	NINDX	B-	C	B		4.25	19.43	10.17	49.98	64.65	48.91	3,370	800-345-6611	Y
MM S&P 500® Index Fund Class R5	MIEZX	B-	C	B		4.24	19.45	10.14	49.91	64.44	17.68	3,372		Y
USAA S&P 500 Index Fund Member Shares	USSPX	B-	C	B		4.24	19.43	10.13	49.78	64.22	41.35	7,716	800-235-8396	Y
GuideStone Funds Equity Index Fund Investor Class	GEQZX	B-	C	B		4.35	19.42	10.12	50.56	64.01	32.38	1,905	214-720-1171	Y
TIAA-CREF S&P 500 Index Fund Retirement Class	TRSPX	B-	C	B		4.21	19.38	10.09	49.49	63.74	32.39	5,201	877-518-9161	Y
Voya Russell Large Cap Index Portfolio Class S2	IRLUX	B-	C	B		4.09	18.48	10.08	50.44	63.91	22.88	959.4	800-366-0066	Y
iShares S&P 500 Index Fund Investor P Shares	BSPPX	B-	C	B		4.21	19.33	10.07	49.58	63.88	348.69	19,490	800-441-7762	Y
Shelton Capital Management S&P 500 Index Direct Shares	SPFIX	B-	C	B		4.24	19.29	10.07	49.79	64.31	56.17	193.0	800-955-9988	Y
Voya Russell Large Cap Growth Index Portfolio Class S	IRLSX	B-	C+	B		4.22	20.81	10.07	65.04	88.21	37.71	757.2	800-366-0066	Y
Voya U.S. Stock Index Portfolio Class I	INGIX	B-	C	B		4.24	19.37	10.06	49.70	63.98	16.45	5,890	800-366-0066	Y
VALIC Company I Stock Index Fund	VSTIX	B-	C	B		4.21	19.38	10.06	49.41	63.52	42	4,941		Y

Fund Name	Ticker Symbol	RATINGS: Overall Rating	Reward Rating	Risk Rating	Recent Up/ Downgrade	TOTAL RETURNS & PERFORMANCE: 3-Month Total Return	6-Month Total Return	1-Year Total Return	3-Year Total Return	5-Year Total Return	ASSETS: NAV	Total Assets (MIL)	NEW INVESTORS: Telephone	Open to New Investors
iShares S&P 500 Index Fund Investor A Shares	**BSPAX**	**B-**	C	B		4.20	19.32	10.05	49.34	63.38	348.95	19,490	800-441-7762	Y
Invesco S&P 500 Index Fund Class Y	**SPIDX**	**B-**	C	B		4.22	19.34	10.05	49.43	63.60	32.08	1,394	800-659-1005	Y
State Street Equity 500 Index Fund Class A	**SSSVX**	**B-**	C	B		4.16	19.36	10.04	48.92	62.26	23.24	1,077	617-664-7338	Y
Principal LargeCap S&P 500 Index Fund Class J	**PSPJX**	**B-**	C	B		4.23	19.39	10.04	49.24	62.96	18.22	5,904	800-787-1621	Y
American Century Ultra® Fund Y Class	**AULYX**	**B-**	C+	B	Down	3.35	22.17	10.02	72.89	89.29	50.79	12,123	800-444-4015	Y
American Century Ultra® Fund R6 Class	**AULDX**	**B-**	C+	B	Down	3.34	22.15	10.01	73.40	91.19	50.73	12,123	800-444-4015	Y

Section IV: Consistent Return BUY Stock Mutual Funds

Investment Ratings and analysis of the Consistent Return BUY Stock Mutual Funds. Funds are listed in order by their five-year returns and overall rating.

Section IV: Contents

This section contains Weiss Investment Ratings, key rating factors, and summary financial data for our selections for "Consistent Return BUY Stock Mutual Funds." If your priority is to achieve a consistent return over at least a five-year period, including the last three months then check out this listing. We have selected the highest rated funds with excellent five-year returns with a size of invested assets to give them a substantial base. At the same time, we have looked for the smallest initial investment we could find. Funds are listed in order by their five-year returns and overall rating.

Fund Name

Describes the fund's assets, regions of investments and investment strategies. Many funds have similar names, so you want to make sure the fund you look up is really the one you are interested in evaluating.

Ticker Symbol

An arrangement of characters (usually letters) representing a particular security listed on an exchange or otherwise traded publicly. When a company issues securities to the public marketplace, it selects an available ticker symbol for its securities which investors use to place trade orders. Every listed security has a unique ticker symbol, facilitating the vast array of trade orders that flow through the financial markets every day. If a ticker symbol is not assigned to a particular fund, the International Securities Identification Number (ISIN) is displayed.

RATINGS

Overall Rating

The Weiss rating measured on a scale from A to E based on each fund's risk and performance. See the preceding section, "What Our Ratings Mean," for an explanation of each letter grade rating.

Reward Rating

This is based on the total return over a period of up to five years, including net asset value and price growth. The total return figure is stated net of the expenses and fees charged by the fund. Based on proprietary modeling the individual components of the risk and reward ratings are calculated and weighted and the final rating is generated.

Risk Rating

This is includes the risk ratings of component stocks where applicable and also includes the financial stability of the fund, turnover where applicable, together with the level of volatility as measured by the fund's daily returns over a period of up to five years. Funds with greater stability are considered less risky and receive a higher risk rating. Funds with greater volatility are considered riskier, and will receive a lower risk rating. In addition to considering the fund's volatility, the risk rating also considers an assessment of the valuation and quality of a fund's holdings.

Recent Upgrade/Downgrade
An "Up" or "Down" indicates that the Weiss Mutual Fund rating has changed since the publication of the last print edition. If a fund has had a rating change since March 31, 2019, the change is identified with an "Up" or "Down."

TOTAL RETURNS & PERFORMANCE

3-Month Total Return
The rate of return on an investment over three months that includes interest, capital gains, dividends and distributions realized.

6-Month Total Return
The rate of return on an investment over six months that includes interest, capital gains, dividends and distributions realized.

1-Year Total Return
The rate of return on an investment over one year that includes interest, capital gains, dividends and distributions realized.

3-Year Total Return
The rate of return on an investment over three years that includes interest, capital gains, dividends and distributions realized.

5-Year Total Return
The rate of return on an investment over five years that includes interest, capital gains, dividends and distributions realized.

ASSETS

NAV (Net Asset Value)
A fund's price per share. The value is calculated by dividing the total value of all the securities in the portfolio, less any liabilities, by the number of fund shares outstanding.

Total Assets (MIL)
The total of all assets listed on the institution's balance sheet. This figure primarily consists of loans, investments, and fixed assets. Total Assets are displayed in millions.

NEW INVESTORS

Telephone
The company's phone number.

Open to New Investors
Indicates whether the fund accepts investments from those who are not existing investors. A "Y" in this column identifies that the fund accepts new investors. No data in this column indicates that the fund is closed to new investors. The fund may be closed to new investors because the fund's asset base is getting too large to effectively execute its investing style. Although, the fund may be closed, in most cases, existing investors are able to add to their holdings.

		RATINGS				TOTAL RETURNS & PERFORMANCE					ASSETS		NEW INVESTORS	
Fund Name	Ticker Symbol	Overall Rating	Reward Rating	Risk Rating	Recent Up/ Downgrade	3-Month Total Return	6-Month Total Return	1-Year Total Return	3-Year Total Return	5-Year Total Return	NAV	Total Assets (MIL)	Telephone	Open to New Investors
Virtus KAR Small-Cap Growth Fund Class R6	VRSGX	B+	B+	B	Up	8.14	32.84	19.52	129.36	171.03	39.15	5,214	800-243-1574	Y
BlackRock Technology Opportunities Fund Investor A Shares	BGSAX	B-	B	B-	Down	5.78	30.72	13.31	123.22	149.42	31.01	1,831	800-441-7762	Y
BlackRock Technology Opportunities Fund Class R Shares	BGSRX	B-	B-	B-	Down	5.69	30.52	13.01	121.49	146.03	31.3	1,831	800-441-7762	Y
Morgan Stanley Insight Fund Class A	CPOAX	B-	B-	B	Up	9.05	38.27	25.76	130.63	143.84	44.87	2,027	855-332-5306	Y
Columbia Global Technology Growth Institutional 2 Cls	CTHRX	B-	C+	B-	Down	5.17	26.95	11.08	105.39	143.42	37.63	1,512	800-345-6611	Y
BlackRock Technology Opportunities Fund Investor C Shares	BGSCX	B-	B-	B-	Down	5.59	30.24	12.48	118.31	139.77	26.15	1,831	800-441-7762	Y
Fidelity® Select IT Services Portfolio	FBSOX	B	B+	B		5.68	33.93	20.91	99.10	139.65	71.43	3,670	617-563-7000	Y
Morgan Stanley Insight Fund Class C	MSCMX	B-	B-	B	Up	8.85	37.81	24.88	125.49	134.85	31.53	2,027	855-332-5306	Y
Fidelity® Select Software & IT Services Portfolio	FSCSX	B	B-	B		6.23	27.05	15.44	101.09	134.79	18.52	7,272	617-563-7000	Y
MFS Technology Fund Class R6	MTCLX	B-	B-	B-	Down	6.15	27.50	10.38	94.73	131.72	48.45	1,278	877-960-6077	Y
MFS Technology Fund Class I	MTCIX	B-	B-	B-	Down	6.13	27.41	10.27	94.14	130.59	48.1	1,278	877-960-6077	Y
MFS Technology Fund Class R4	MTCJX	B-	B-	B-	Down	6.14	27.45	10.27	94.14	130.56	46.8	1,278	877-960-6077	Y
Fidelity® Select Medical Technology and Devices Portfolio	FSMEX	B-	C+	B	Down	5.07	21.14	17.75	72.31	129.16	56.48	6,711	617-563-7000	Y
MFS Technology Fund Class A	MTCAX	B-	B-	B-	Down	6.05	27.25	9.99	92.65	127.79	44.82	1,278	877-960-6077	Y
MFS Technology Fund Class R3	MTCHX	B-	B-	B-	Down	6.06	27.27	9.99	92.65	127.70	44.8	1,278	877-960-6077	Y
JNL/Mellon Capital Information Technology Sector Cls I		B-	B-	B-	Down	5.37	28.35	14.09	99.60	126.02	19.42	3,007		Y
MFS Technology Fund Class R2	MTERX	B-	C+	B-	Down	6.00	27.12	9.73	91.25	124.93	42.56	1,278	877-960-6077	Y
JNL/Mellon Capital Information Technology Sector Cls A		B-	B-	B-	Down	5.26	28.07	13.66	97.86	123.09	18.98	3,007		Y
Morgan Stanley Inst Fund, Inc. Growth Portfolio Cls A	MSEGX	B-	C+	B-		7.16	29.41	15.15	102.15	122.83	50.69	7,525	855-332-5306	Y
Fidelity Advisor® Growth Opportunities Fund Class Z	FZAHX	B	C+	B	Down	3.92	26.75	22.29	108.07	120.89	90.29	6,286	617-563-7000	Y
Transamerica Capital Growth Fund Class I2		B-	C+	B-	Up	7.89	28.02	14.47	104.00	120.26	15.12	2,036	888-233-4339	Y
Federated Kaufmann Small Cap Fund Class R6 Shares	FKALX	B	B	B		5.41	31.06	19.03	115.24	120.16	42.28	3,149	800-341-7400	Y
Fidelity Advisor® Growth Opportunities Fund I Class	FAGCX	B	C+	B	Down	3.88	26.68	22.14	107.31	119.51	89.53	6,286	617-563-7000	Y
Federated Kaufmann Small Cap Fund Class R Shares	FKKSX	B	B	B		5.29	30.76	18.50	113.80	118.85	42.12	3,149	800-341-7400	Y
VALIC Company I Science & Technology Fund	VCSTX	B-	C+	B-	Down	4.41	28.47	11.03	94.59	118.59	27.91	1,488		Y
Fidelity Advisor® Growth Opportunities Fund Class A	FAGAX	B	C+	B	Down	3.80	26.49	21.80	105.57	116.44	82.68	6,286	617-563-7000	Y
Franklin DynaTech Fund Class A	FKDNX	B-	B-	B-	Down	6.64	31.22	17.13	97.19	115.57	85.11	7,895	650-312-2000	Y
Fidelity Advisor® Growth Opportunities Fund Class M	FAGOX	B	C+	B	Down	3.76	26.36	21.53	104.17	113.99	81.87	6,286	617-563-7000	Y
Virtus KAR Small-Cap Core Fund Class R6	VSCRX	B	B+	B		5.23	28.89	12.97	89.69	113.78	39.03	1,508	800-243-1574	Y
Franklin DynaTech Fund Class R	FDNRX	B-	B-	B-	Down	6.57	31.05	16.84	95.73	112.91	82.5	7,895	650-312-2000	Y
Brown Advisory Sustainable Growth Fund Investor Shares	BIAWX	B	B	B		6.27	26.73	18.68	75.43	111.21	26.07	1,373	800-540-6807	Y
Brown Advisory Sustainable Growth Fund Advisor Shares	BAWAX	B	B-	B		6.22	26.55	18.38	74.12	108.67	25.59	1,373	800-540-6807	Y
Fidelity Advisor® Growth Opportunities Fund Class C	FACGX	B-	C+	B	Down	3.61	26.02	20.88	100.98	108.48	70.5	6,286	617-563-7000	Y
Franklin DynaTech Fund Class C	FDYNX	B-	B-	B-	Down	6.45	30.73	16.24	92.83	107.65	70.61	7,895	650-312-2000	Y
USAA Nasdaq 100 Index Fund R6 Shares	URNQX	B-	C+	B		4.16	22.49	9.73	79.50	106.40	21.51	2,154	800-235-8396	Y
AB Growth Fund Advisor Class	AGRYX	B-	C+	B	Down	4.27	23.25	14.64	77.62	105.54	88.88	1,145	212-969-1000	Y
JPMorgan Large Cap Growth Fund Class R5	JLGRX	B-	B-	B-	Down	7.57	29.86	14.14	89.55	104.83	43.44	15,920	800-480-4111	Y
BlackRock Mid-Cap Growth Equity Portfolio Inv A Shares	BMGAX	B	B+	B		9.22	33.22	18.59	91.17	103.59	25.66	4,326	800-441-7762	Y
JPMorgan Large Cap Growth Fund Class R4	JLGQX	B-	B-	B-	Down	7.52	29.73	13.95	88.52	102.93	42.45	15,920	800-480-4111	Y
AB Growth Fund Class K	AGFKX	B-	C+	B	Down	4.18	23.04	14.27	76.04	102.76	82.81	1,145	212-969-1000	Y
AB Large Cap Growth Fund Advisor Class	APGYX	B-	C+	B	Down	4.22	21.96	13.76	71.69	102.37	58.97	9,074	212-969-1000	Y
Janus Henderson VIT Enterprise Portfolio Institutional Cls	JAAGX	B	B-	B		7.31	27.98	17.30	73.71	101.11	79.89	1,393	877-335-2687	Y
BlackRock Mid-Cap Growth Equity Portfolio Class R	BMRRX	B	B+	B		9.20	33.11	18.38	89.75	101.08	25.23	4,326	800-441-7762	Y
JPMorgan Large Cap Growth Fund Class A	OLGAX	B-	B-	B-	Down	7.46	29.58	13.66	87.39	101.02	41.87	15,920	800-480-4111	Y
Hartford Growth Opportunities HLS Fund Class IA	HAGOX	B-	B-	B-	Down	6.08	30.13	12.61	72.05	100.93	43.44	1,655	888-843-7824	Y
Principal Blue Chip Fund Class R-6	PGBHX	B	B	B		7.10	27.01	18.72	79.67	100.75	25.48	4,088	800-787-1621	Y
Principal Blue Chip Fund Institutional Class	PBCKX	B	B	B		7.11	26.99	18.63	79.54	100.61	25.45	4,088	800-787-1621	Y
JPMorgan Large Cap Growth Fund Class R3	JLGPX	B-	B-	B-	Down	7.45	29.57	13.67	87.16	100.46	42.1	15,920	800-480-4111	Y
AB Growth Fund Class R	AGFRX	B-	C+	B	Down	4.11	22.87	13.92	74.44	99.59	77.89	1,145	212-969-1000	Y
Fidelity® Series Blue Chip Growth Fund	FSBDX	B-	C+	B	Down	3.32	21.24	10.66	85.40	99.55	15.24	6,162	617-563-7000	Y
Principal Blue Chip Fund Class R-5	PGBGX	B	B	B		7.06	26.91	18.42	78.47	99.29	25.32	4,088	800-787-1621	Y
John Hancock Funds II Blue Chip Growth Fund Class NAV	JHBCX	B-	C+	B	Down	4.02	21.83	10.17	80.76	99.28	41.35	4,014	800-225-5913	Y

		RATINGS				TOTAL RETURNS & PERFORMANCE					ASSETS		NEW INVESTORS	
Fund Name	Ticker Symbol	Overall Rating	Reward Rating	Risk Rating	Recent Up/ Downgrade	3-Month Total Return	6-Month Total Return	1-Year Total Return	3-Year Total Return	5-Year Total Return	NAV	Total Assets (MIL)	Telephone	Open to New Investors
AB Large Cap Growth Fund Class K	ALCKX	B-	C+	B	Down	4.11	21.74	13.39	69.97	99.13	54.64	9,074	212-969-1000	Y
Principal Blue Chip Fund Class J	PBCJX	B	B	B		7.01	26.84	18.35	78.46	98.81	25.33	4,088	800-787-1621	Y
John Hancock Funds II Blue Chip Growth Fund Class 1	JIBCX	B-	C+	B	Down	4.00	21.81	10.11	80.48	98.79	41.27	4,014	800-225-5913	Y
Janus Henderson VIT Enterprise Portfolio Service Class		B	B-	B		7.25	27.83	17.02	72.44	98.64	74.78	1,384	877-335-2687	Y
MassMutual Select Blue Chip Growth Fund Class I	MBCZX	B-	C+	B	Down	4.52	22.31	12.59	75.90	98.49	23.08	3,215		Y
JPMorgan Large Cap Growth Fund Class R2	JLGZX	B-	B-	B-	Down	7.40	29.39	13.38	85.89	98.46	40.32	15,920	800-480-4111	Y
Hartford Growth Opportunities HLS Fund Class IB	HBGOX	B-	B-	B-	Down	6.02	30.00	12.33	70.73	98.40	41.33	1,655	888-843-7824	Y
Principal Blue Chip Fund Class R-4	PGBFX	B	B	B		7.04	26.84	18.28	77.93	98.21	25.23	4,088	800-787-1621	Y
The Hartford Growth Opportunities Fund Class R6	HGOVX	B-	B-	B-	Down	5.83	29.65	11.94	71.33	97.85	47.7	5,201	888-843-7824	Y
MassMutual Select Blue Chip Growth Fund Class R5	MBCSX	B-	C+	B	Down	4.48	22.28	12.53	75.39	97.48	23.05	3,215		Y
MFS Growth Fund Class R6	MFEKX	B	B-	B		6.57	26.71	14.94	74.17	97.15	117.89	22,365	877-960-6077	Y
The Hartford Growth Opportunities Fund Class R5	HGOTX	B-	B-	B-	Down	5.80	29.57	11.80	70.80	96.95	46.83	5,201	888-843-7824	Y
JNL/BlackRock Large Cap Select Growth Fund Class I		B-	C+	B	Down	5.92	25.14	10.61	79.35	96.82	44	3,738		Y
MassMutual Select Blue Chip Growth Fund Service Class	MBCYX	B-	C+	B	Down	4.48	22.20	12.41	74.96	96.56	22.84	3,215		Y
Principal Blue Chip Fund Class R-3	PGBEX	B	B	B		6.99	26.68	18.08	76.86	96.38	25.07	4,088	800-787-1621	Y
BlackRock Mid-Cap Growth Equity Portfolio Inv C Shares	BMGCX	B	B+	B		9.02	32.77	17.70	87.04	96.31	19.94	4,326	800-441-7762	Y
MFS Growth Fund Class I	MFEIX	B	B-	B		6.56	26.65	14.84	73.69	96.22	117.53	22,365	877-960-6077	Y
AB Large Cap Growth Fund Class R	ABPRX	B-	C+	B	Down	4.03	21.55	13.05	68.46	96.20	51.09	9,074	212-969-1000	Y
MFS Growth Fund Class R4	MFEJX	B	B-	B		6.55	26.66	14.84	73.67	96.19	114.23	22,365	877-960-6077	Y
JPMorgan Large Cap Growth Fund Class C	OLGCX	B-	B-	B-	Down	7.33	29.26	13.11	84.58	96.07	32.33	15,920	800-480-4111	Y
Hartford Growth Opportunities HLS Fund Class IC	HCGOX	B-	B-	B-	Down	5.95	29.81	12.06	69.49	95.99	42.19	1,655	888-843-7824	Y
Principal Blue Chip Fund Class A	PBLAX	B	B	B		7.01	26.79	18.23	77.45	95.92	25.03	4,088	800-787-1621	Y
John Hancock Funds II Blue Chip Growth Fund Class A	JBGAX	B-	C+	B	Down	3.91	21.60	9.76	78.70	95.86	40.64	4,014	800-225-5913	Y
MassMutual Select Blue Chip Growth Administrative Cls	MBCLX	B-	C+	B	Down	4.41	22.09	12.24	74.32	95.45	22.49	3,215		Y
Laudus U.S. Large Cap Growth Fund	LGILX	B-	C+	B	Down	5.91	25.04	10.48	78.92	95.11	22.57	2,384	888-832-4386	Y
Principal LargeCap Growth Fund I Class R-6	PLCGX	B-	C+	B	Down	4.37	23.45	13.23	78.74	95.05	15.74	9,006	800-787-1621	Y
JNL/Mellon Capital Nasdaq® 100 Index Fund Class I		B-	C+	B	Down	4.16	22.54	9.86	79.65	95.03	17.99	2,980		Y
Principal LargeCap Growth Fund I Institutional Class	PLGIX	B-	C+	B	Down	4.30	23.43	13.12	78.46	94.84	15.75	9,006	800-787-1621	Y
JNL/BlackRock Large Cap Select Growth Fund Class A		B-	C+	B	Down	5.83	24.97	10.25	77.97	94.54	42.09	3,738		Y
MassMutual Select Blue Chip Growth Fund Class R4	MBGFX	B-	C+	B	Down	4.38	22.02	12.09	73.58	94.16	21.44	3,215		Y
MFS Mid Cap Growth Fund Class R6	OTCKX	B	B	B		9.23	31.10	17.68	73.62	94.15	21.41	5,405	877-960-6077	Y
The Hartford Growth Opportunities Fund Class R4	HGOSX	B-	B-	B-	Down	5.71	29.39	11.47	69.28	94.07	44.24	5,201	888-843-7824	Y
MFS Growth Fund Class A	MFEGX	B	B-	B		6.48	26.49	14.56	72.41	93.83	110.16	22,365	877-960-6077	Y
MFS Growth Fund Class R3	MFEHX	B	B-	B		6.48	26.49	14.55	72.38	93.75	109.59	22,365	877-960-6077	Y
Putnam Growth Opportunities Fund Class R6	PGOEX	B	B-	B		6.52	25.76	16.24	82.59	93.24	39	5,747	617-292-1000	Y
MFS Mid Cap Growth Fund Class R4	OTCJX	B	B	B		9.20	31.06	17.54	73.03	93.13	20.76	5,405	877-960-6077	Y
MFS Mid Cap Growth Fund Class I	OTCIX	B	B	B		9.19	31.07	17.57	73.14	93.11	21.26	5,405	877-960-6077	Y
MassMutual Select Blue Chip Growth Fund Class A	MBCGX	B-	C+	B	Down	4.37	21.96	12.00	73.01	93.06	21.49	3,215		Y
ClearBridge Large Cap Growth Fund Class O	LCMMX	B-	C+	B	Down	5.21	22.88	13.68	64.55	93.05	52.83	14,233	877-721-1926	Y
T. Rowe Price New America Growth Fund Advisor Class	PAWAX	B-	C+	B	Down	5.29	22.99	11.61	75.68	93.05	51.72	5,248	410-345-2000	Y
Principal LargeCap Growth Fund I R-5 Class	PPUPX	B-	C+	B	Down	4.28	23.28	12.93	77.43	92.84	15.09	9,006	800-787-1621	Y
Principal LargeCap Growth Fund I Class J	PLGJX	B-	C+	B	Down	4.28	23.39	12.99	77.74	92.62	12.66	9,006	800-787-1621	Y
JNL/Mellon Capital Nasdaq® 100 Index Fund Class A		B-	C+	B		4.07	22.37	9.47	78.24	92.59	27.35	2,980		Y
Putnam Growth Opportunities Fund Class R5	PGODX	B	B-	B		6.50	25.71	16.12	82.01	92.29	39.11	5,747	617-292-1000	Y
Putnam Growth Opportunities Fund Class Y	PGOYX	B	B-	B		6.50	25.70	16.10	81.78	91.88	38.78	5,747	617-292-1000	Y
Principal LargeCap Growth Fund I R-4 Class	PPUSX	B-	C+	B	Down	4.25	23.18	12.80	76.88	91.67	14.45	9,006	800-787-1621	Y
MassMutual Select Blue Chip Growth Fund Class R3	MBCNX	B-	C+	B	Down	4.33	21.82	11.83	72.29	91.64	19.98	3,215		Y
MFS Growth Fund Class R2	MEGRX	B	B-	B		6.43	26.34	14.27	71.10	91.36	103.7	22,365	877-960-6077	Y
Federated Kaufmann Fund Class R Shares	KAUFX	B-	C+	B	Down	5.46	27.65	14.37	77.40	91.17	6.37	6,797	800-341-7400	Y
The Hartford Growth Opportunities Fund Class R3	HGORX	B-	B-	B-	Down	5.65	29.22	11.16	67.79	91.16	41.3	5,201	888-843-7824	Y
TIAA-CREF Large Cap Growth Fund Class W	TILWX	B-	C+	B	Down	3.10	22.51	9.50	70.35	91.05	21.22	5,691	877-518-9161	Y
JNL/T. Rowe Price Established Growth Fund Class I		B-	C+	B	Down	3.80	21.77	8.50	73.55	90.86	47.42	9,825		Y

		RATINGS				TOTAL RETURNS & PERFORMANCE					ASSETS		NEW INVESTORS	
Fund Name	Ticker Symbol	Overall Rating	Reward Rating	Risk Rating	Recent Up/ Downgrade	3-Month Total Return	6-Month Total Return	1-Year Total Return	3-Year Total Return	5-Year Total Return	NAV	Total Assets (MIL)	Telephone	Open to New Investors
MFS Mid Cap Growth Fund Class A	OTCAX	B	B	B		9.11	30.82	17.23	71.73	90.74	19.99	5,405	877-960-6077	Y
Ivy Large Cap Growth Fund Class I	IYGIX	B	B-	B		6.93	25.17	14.97	74.73	90.71	25.76	4,284		Y
MFS Mid Cap Growth Fund Class R3	OTCHX	B	B	B		9.12	30.82	17.23	71.66	90.62	19.86	5,405	877-960-6077	Y
MFS Mid Cap Growth Fund Class 529A	EAMCX	B	B	B		9.06	30.87	17.24	71.58	90.50	19.37	5,405	877-960-6077	Y
TIAA-CREF Large Cap Growth Fund Advisor Class	TILHX	B-	C+	B	Down	3.06	22.29	9.16	69.54	90.14	21.17	5,691	877-518-9161	Y
Principal LargeCap Growth Fund I Class A	PLGAX	B-	C+	B	Down	4.25	23.17	12.76	76.12	90.10	15.2	9,006	800-787-1621	Y
BlackRock Capital Appreciation Fund Investor A Shares	MDFGX	B-	C+	B	Down	5.04	23.93	9.31	74.23	90.07	28.73	3,270	800-441-7762	Y
ClearBridge Large Cap Growth Fund Class A	SBLGX	B-	C+	B	Down	5.09	22.65	13.28	62.86	90.06	47.42	14,233	877-721-1926	Y
Principal LargeCap Growth Fund I R-3 Class	PPUMX	B-	C+	B	Down	4.20	23.10	12.61	75.84	89.87	14.12	9,006	800-787-1621	Y
VY® T. Rowe Price Growth Equity Portfolio Class I	ITGIX	B-	C	B	Down	3.79	21.45	8.32	72.71	89.56	93.9	1,929	800-366-0066	Y
Putnam Growth Opportunities Fund Class A	POGAX	B	B-	B		6.43	25.50	15.78	80.39	89.48	37.05	5,747	617-292-1000	Y
Calvert Equity Fund Class A	CSIEX	B+	B	A-	Up	7.11	26.50	24.67	71.16	89.28	52.22	2,937	301-951-4881	Y
MainStay Large Cap Growth Fund Class R6	MLRSX	B-	C+	B	Down	4.60	24.43	11.98	74.53	89.14	10.44	11,931	800-624-6782	Y
John Hancock Funds II Blue Chip Growth Fund Class C	JBGCX	B-	C+	B	Down	3.71	21.15	8.94	74.78	88.75	39.06	4,014	800-225-5913	Y
Ivy Large Cap Growth Fund Class Y	WLGYX	B	B-	B		6.84	24.91	14.58	73.61	88.74	24.97	4,284		Y
JNL/T. Rowe Price Established Growth Fund Class A		B-	C	B	Down	3.71	21.57	8.16	72.20	88.63	45.76	9,825		Y
Principal Blue Chip Fund Class C	PBLCX	B	B	B		6.83	26.36	17.40	73.48	88.60	23.92	4,088	800-787-1621	Y
MFS Mid Cap Growth Fund Class R2	MCPRX	B	B	B		9.00	30.71	16.94	70.44	88.29	18.77	5,405	877-960-6077	Y
Principal LargeCap Growth Fund I R-2 Class	PPUNX	B-	C+	B	Down	4.22	23.01	12.38	74.98	88.22	12.83	9,006	800-787-1621	Y
Ivy Large Cap Growth Fund Class A	WLGAX	B	B-	B		6.86	24.94	14.62	73.36	88.13	24.29	4,284		Y
Transamerica US Growth Class T	TWMTX	B-	C+	B	Down	5.45	25.23	12.85	65.06	87.90	61.84	1,126	888-233-4339	Y
Ivy Large Cap Growth Fund Class E	ILCEX	B	B-	B		6.83	24.90	14.50	73.01	87.78	24.22	4,284		Y
Transamerica US Growth Class I2		B-	C+	B	Down	5.81	24.69	12.83	67.42	87.73	21.76	1,126	888-233-4339	Y
BlackRock Capital Appreciation Fund R Shares	MRFGX	B-	C+	B	Down	4.99	23.78	9.03	72.82	87.57	23.27	3,270	800-441-7762	Y
Brown Advisory Growth Equity Fund Investor Shares	BIAGX	B	B-	B		5.51	27.53	16.49	71.81	87.55	24.5	2,359	800-540-6807	Y
Wells Fargo Growth Fund - Class R6	SGRHX	B-	B-	B-	Down	7.37	30.02	14.39	79.47	87.34	45	4,621	800-222-8222	Y
ClearBridge Large Cap Growth Fund Class R	LMPLX	B-	C+	B	Down	5.02	22.48	12.93	61.46	87.30	45.32	14,233	877-721-1926	Y
VY® T. Rowe Price Growth Equity Portfolio Class S	ITGSX	B-	C	B	Down	3.71	21.30	8.03	71.40	87.20	89.57	1,929	800-366-0066	Y
Putnam Growth Opportunities Fund Class R	PGORX	B	B-	B		6.36	25.39	15.52	79.10	87.10	35.6	5,747	617-292-1000	Y
DWS Capital Growth Fund - Class R6	SDGZX	B-	B-	B	Down	5.86	25.93	13.61	67.27	87.02	81.44	1,562		Y
Principal LargeCap Growth Fund I R-1 Class	PCRSX	B-	C+	B	Down	4.11	22.85	12.22	74.10	86.84	13.17	9,006	800-787-1621	Y
MFS Growth Fund Class B	MEGBX	B-	B-	B	Down	6.29	26.02	13.70	68.57	86.66	87.63	22,365	877-960-6077	Y
John Hancock U.S. Global Leaders Growth Fund Class A	USGLX	B	B-	B+		5.10	23.95	18.72	62.31	86.65	51.02	1,524	800-225-5913	Y
MFS Growth Fund Class R1	MFELX	B-	B-	B	Down	6.29	26.02	13.70	68.56	86.65	87.25	22,365	877-960-6077	Y
MFS Growth Fund Class C	MFECX	B-	B-	B	Down	6.29	26.03	13.70	68.57	86.62	86.92	22,365	877-960-6077	Y
TIAA-CREF Large-Cap Growth Index Fund Advisor Class	TRIHX	B-	C+	B	Down	4.57	22.50	11.36	65.64	86.35	33.15	7,194	877-518-9161	Y
VY® T. Rowe Price Growth Equity Portfolio Class S2	ITRGX	B-	C	B	Down	3.67	21.21	7.88	70.65	85.81	86.57	1,929	800-366-0066	Y
American Century Select Fund R6 Class	ASDEX	B-	C+	B	Down	4.75	22.47	9.56	64.09	85.50	76.52	3,154	800-444-4015	Y
John Hancock U.S. Global Leaders Growth Fund Class R2	USLYX	B	B-	B+		5.06	23.88	18.57	61.61	85.32	53.95	1,524	800-225-5913	Y
Brown Advisory Growth Equity Fund Advisor Shares	BAGAX	B-	B-	B	Down	5.43	27.35	16.21	70.51	85.27	23.09	2,359	800-540-6807	Y
Ivy Large Cap Growth Fund Class R	WLGRX	B-	B-	B	Down	6.72	24.71	14.18	71.58	84.99	23.16	4,284		Y
VY® T. Rowe Price Growth Equity Portfolio Class A	IGEAX	B-	C	B	Down	3.66	21.15	7.77	70.14	84.88	85.16	1,929	800-366-0066	Y
Putnam Growth Opportunities Fund Class M	PGOMX	B	B-	B		6.27	25.22	15.20	77.70	84.78	33.01	5,747	617-292-1000	Y
Amana Mutual Funds Trust Growth Fund Investor	AMAGX	B	B-	B+		3.42	22.78	20.01	68.32	84.68	42.03	2,119	888-732-6262	Y
Optimum Large Cap Growth Fund Institutional Class	OILGX	B-	C	B	Down	4.41	22.12	10.67	69.73	84.68	18.93	1,728		Y
DWS Capital Growth Fund - Class A	SDGAX	B-	B-	B	Down	5.78	25.74	13.27	65.71	84.63	80.84	1,562		Y
TIAA-CREF Large-Cap Growth Index Fund Retirement Class	TRIRX	B-	C+	B	Down	4.56	22.46	11.22	64.95	84.63	33.42	7,194	877-518-9161	Y
MFS Massachusetts Investors Growth Stock Fund Class R6	MIGNX	B	B	B+		5.43	25.06	18.70	67.40	84.61	32.38	7,515	877-960-6077	Y
Transamerica US Growth Class A	TADAX	B-	C+	B	Down	5.39	25.00	12.50	63.39	84.54	21.3	1,126	888-233-4339	Y
MFS Mid Cap Growth Fund Class C	OTCCX	B	B	B		8.95	30.42	16.42	68.00	83.76	15.82	5,405	877-960-6077	Y
MFS Mid Cap Growth Fund Class B	OTCBX	B	B	B		8.93	30.43	16.40	67.91	83.72	16.33	5,405	877-960-6077	Y
JNL/T. Rowe Price Mid-Cap Growth Fund Class I		B-	C+	B	Down	6.91	25.82	15.90	61.17	83.70	55.69	6,233		Y

		RATINGS				TOTAL RETURNS & PERFORMANCE					ASSETS		NEW INVESTORS	
Fund Name	Ticker Symbol	Overall Rating	Reward Rating	Risk Rating	Recent Up/ Downgrade	3-Month Total Return	6-Month Total Return	1-Year Total Return	3-Year Total Return	5-Year Total Return	NAV	Total Assets (MIL)	Telephone	Open to New Investors
American Century Select Fund Y Class	ASLWX	B-	C+	B	Down	4.74	22.47	9.56	63.61	83.69	76.61	3,154	800-444-4015	Y
MFS Massachusetts Investors Growth Stock Fund Class I	MGTIX	B	B	B+		5.40	25.04	18.63	66.91	83.68	32.35	7,515	877-960-6077	Y
MFS Mid Cap Growth Fund Class R1	OTCGX	B	B	B		8.91	30.41	16.41	67.94	83.68	16.25	5,405	877-960-6077	Y
MFS Massachusetts Investors Growth Stock Fund Class R4	MIGKX	B	B	B+		5.40	25.02	18.60	66.86	83.64	31.62	7,515	877-960-6077	Y
Putnam Sustainable Leaders Fund Class Y	PNOYX	B	B-	B		6.60	26.23	15.76	75.78	83.59	100.65	4,727	617-292-1000	Y
MFS Mid Cap Growth Fund Class 529C	ECGRX	B	B	B		8.91	30.31	16.34	67.74	83.33	15.39	5,405	877-960-6077	Y
MFS Mid Cap Growth Fund Class 529B	EBCGX	B	B	B		8.90	30.32	16.32	67.65	83.29	15.9	5,405	877-960-6077	Y
ClearBridge Large Cap Growth Fund Class C	SLCCX	B-	C+	B	Down	4.92	22.21	12.48	59.42	83.29	37.52	14,233	877-721-1926	Y
American Century NT Growth Fund G Class	ACLTX	B-	C+	B	Down	5.59	23.94	12.79	70.19	83.27	17.55	1,103	800-444-4015	Y
GuideStone Funds Growth Equity Fund Investor Class	GGEZX	B-	C+	B	Down	5.19	25.02	14.00	71.28	83.05	26.09	1,613	214-720-1171	Y
American Century Select Fund R5 Class	ASLGX	B-	C+	B	Down	4.69	22.36	9.35	62.99	82.99	76.55	3,154	800-444-4015	Y
Great-West T. Rowe Price Mid Cap Growth Institutional Cls	MXYKX	B-	C+	B	Down	6.70	24.51	15.14	63.01	82.72	8.5	1,864		Y
BlackRock Capital Appreciation Fund Investor C Shares	MCFGX	B-	C+	B	Down	4.81	23.42	8.43	70.13	82.55	20.37	3,270	800-441-7762	Y
Putnam Growth Opportunities Fund Class B	POGBX	B	B-	B		6.23	25.07	14.94	76.41	82.52	30.83	5,747	617-292-1000	Y
Putnam Growth Opportunities Fund Class C	POGCX	B	B-	B		6.25	25.06	14.95	76.41	82.51	31.43	5,747	617-292-1000	Y
Optimum Large Cap Growth Fund Class A	OALGX	B-	C	B	Down	4.31	21.90	10.32	68.40	82.31	17.42	1,728		Y
Calvert Equity Fund Class C	CSECX	B+	B	A-	Up	6.90	26.00	23.74	67.30	82.25	28.78	2,937	301-951-4881	Y
Wells Fargo Premier Large Company Growth Fund - Class R6	EKJFX	B-	B-	B	Down	6.87	28.04	14.57	76.53	82.25	14.93	2,423	800-222-8222	Y
Fidelity Advisor® Equity Growth Fund Class Z	FZAFX	B-	C+	B	Down	4.33	22.82	10.59	72.90	82.05	13.72	3,243	617-563-7000	Y
Putnam Sustainable Leaders Fund Class R6 Shares	PSLGX	B	B-	B		6.63	26.30	15.89	75.18	82.04	100.88	4,727	617-292-1000	Y
Wells Fargo Large Cap Growth Fund - Class R6	STFFX	B-	B-	B	Down	5.53	25.31	12.68	72.63	81.99	45.39	1,016	800-222-8222	Y
American Century Growth Fund R6 Class	AGRDX	B-	C+	B	Down	5.51	23.54	11.59	67.24	81.67	35.42	7,952	800-444-4015	Y
JNL/T. Rowe Price Mid-Cap Growth Fund Class A		B-	C+	B	Down	6.83	25.65	15.59	59.93	81.60	52.99	6,233		Y
Fidelity® Growth Discovery Fund Class K	FGDKX	B-	C+	B	Down	4.48	22.62	10.46	71.98	81.59	37.78	2,073	617-563-7000	Y
MFS Massachusetts Investors Growth Stock Fund Class A	MIGFX	B	B	B+		5.33	24.88	18.34	65.68	81.49	31.37	7,515	877-960-6077	Y
Ivy Large Cap Growth Fund Class C	WLGCX	B-	B-	B	Down	6.66	24.48	13.69	69.52	81.33	19.52	4,284		Y
MFS Massachusetts Investors Growth Stock Fund Class R3	MIGHX	B	B	B+		5.29	24.84	18.28	65.62	81.32	31	7,515	877-960-6077	Y
Putnam Sustainable Leaders Fund Class A	PNOPX	B	B-	B		6.52	26.07	15.45	74.46	81.30	92.99	4,727	617-292-1000	Y
MFS Massachusetts Investors Growth Stock Fund Class 529A	EISTX	B	B	B+		5.32	24.84	18.29	65.49	81.16	30.85	7,515	877-960-6077	Y
VY® T. Rowe Price Diversified Mid Cap Growth Port Cls R6	VYRIX	B	B-	B		7.11	28.98	16.70	65.19	81.10	12.95	1,109	800-366-0066	Y
Voya Large Cap Growth Portfolio Class I	IEOHX	B-	C+	B	Down	3.81	20.51	11.01	61.72	80.98	21.21	5,704	800-366-0066	Y
DWS Capital Growth Fund - Class R	SDGRX	B-	B-	B	Down	5.76	25.61	12.88	63.73	80.96	79.1	1,562		Y
VY® T. Rowe Price Diversified Mid Cap Growth Port Cls I	IAXIX	B-	B-	B	Down	7.11	29.11	16.81	65.21	80.95	12.95	1,109	800-366-0066	Y
Voya Large-Cap Growth Fund Class P3	VPLCX	B-	C+	B	Down	4.00	20.86	11.93	62.38	80.94	45.47	1,080	800-366-0066	Y
Fidelity Advisor® Equity Growth Fund I Class	EQPGX	B-	C+	B	Down	4.29	22.72	10.42	72.20	80.85	13.61	3,243	617-563-7000	Y
Wells Fargo Premier Large Company Growth Fund - Class R4	EKJRX	B-	B-	B	Down	6.82	27.91	14.39	75.68	80.79	14.71	2,423	800-222-8222	Y
PRINCIPAL MIDCAP FUND Class R-6	PMAQX	B	B	B		9.25	31.62	18.20	63.73	80.76	29.51	16,562	800-787-1621	Y
Federated Kaufmann Large Cap Fund Class R6	KLCSX	B	B-	B		7.28	28.31	17.97	66.62	80.76	27.69	3,453	800-341-7400	Y
Wells Fargo Large Cap Growth Fund - Class R4	SLGRX	B-	B-	B	Down	5.50	25.20	12.52	71.87	80.65	45.06	1,016	800-222-8222	Y
Fidelity® Growth Discovery Fund	FDSVX	B-	C+	B	Down	4.42	22.57	10.33	71.41	80.51	37.74	2,073	617-563-7000	Y
Eventide Gilead Class N	ETGLX	B	B	B		3.13	33.80	16.43	91.18	80.47	41.76	2,652		Y
Voya Large Cap Growth Portfolio Class R6	VRLCX	B-	C+	B	Down	3.81	20.49	11.06	61.77	80.41	21.22	5,704	800-366-0066	Y
Alger Spectra Fund Class I	ASPIX	B-	C+	B	Down	5.88	23.30	9.82	66.26	80.37	22.49	6,218	800-992-3863	Y
Alger Spectra Fund Class A	SPECX	B-	C+	B	Down	5.85	23.22	9.78	66.08	80.19	22.23	6,218	800-992-3863	Y
Glenmede Quantitative U.S. Large Cap Growth Eq Port	GTLLX	B-	C+	B	Down	5.59	22.43	11.32	59.18	80.09	31.88	3,492	800-442-8299	Y
Eventide Gilead Class A	ETAGX	B	B	B		3.10	33.75	16.35	90.85	80.06	41.57	2,652		Y
Wells Fargo Discovery Fund - Class R6	WFDRX	B-	B	C+		10.86	38.27	17.91	79.22	80.03	38.37	2,582	800-222-8222	Y
Great-West T. Rowe Price Mid Cap Growth Investor Cls	MXMGX	B-	C+	B	Down	6.54	24.23	14.65	61.27	79.96	29.78	1,864		Y
Brown Advisory Small-Cap Growth Fund Investor Shares	BIASX	B-	B-	B-	Down	7.79	32.59	14.40	59.02	79.90	22.13	1,347	800-540-6807	Y
American Century Growth Fund Y Class	AGYWX	B-	C+	B	Down	5.50	23.54	11.58	66.73	79.84	35.47	7,952	800-444-4015	Y
Alger Capital Appreciation Institutional Fund Class I	ALARX	B-	C+	B	Down	5.31	22.84	9.90	65.70	79.84	34.85	3,523	800-992-3863	Y
John Hancock U.S. Global Leaders Growth Fund Class C	USLCX	B	B-	B+		4.91	23.47	17.86	58.67	79.74	41.81	1,524	800-225-5913	Y

		RATINGS				TOTAL RETURNS & PERFORMANCE					ASSETS		NEW INVESTORS	
Fund Name	Ticker Symbol	Overall Rating	Reward Rating	Risk Rating	Recent Up/ Downgrade	3-Month Total Return	6-Month Total Return	1-Year Total Return	3-Year Total Return	5-Year Total Return	NAV	Total Assets (MIL)	Telephone	Open to New Investors
Voya Large-Cap Growth Fund Class W	IGOWX	B-	C+	B	Down	3.79	20.48	11.12	61.22	79.64	43.99	1,080	800-366-0066	Y
Alger Capital Appreciation Fund Class A	ACAAX	B-	C+	B	Down	5.25	22.76	9.73	65.61	79.42	26.64	2,866	800-992-3863	Y
American Century Growth Fund R5 Class	AGWUX	B-	C+	B	Down	5.47	23.45	11.44	66.19	79.25	35.47	7,952	800-444-4015	Y
Invesco Oppenheimer Discovery Mid Cap Growth Fund Y	OEGYX	B-	B-	C+		9.00	31.41	14.91	59.30	79.23	24.93	1,557	800-659-1005	Y
MFS Massachusetts Investors Growth Stock Fund Class R2	MIRGX	B	B	B+		5.25	24.70	18.01	64.40	79.11	30.44	7,515	877-960-6077	Y
MassMutual Select Mid Cap Growth Fund Class I	MEFZX	B-	C+	B	Down	6.00	25.81	15.13	59.42	79.11	23.49	8,748		Y
Putnam Sustainable Leaders Fund Class R	PNORX	B	B-	B		6.47	25.90	15.17	73.15	79.05	89.28	4,727	617-292-1000	Y
JNL/Mellon Capital Consumer Discretionary Sector Cls I		B-	C+	B		4.51	21.19	8.05	55.86	78.84	24.53	1,299		Y
Voya Large Cap Growth Portfolio Class S	IEOSX	B-	C+	B	Down	3.72	20.36	10.78	60.47	78.76	20.63	5,704	800-366-0066	Y
VY® T. Rowe Price Diversified Mid Cap Growth Port Cls S	IAXSX	B-	B-	B	Down	7.06	28.97	16.53	63.92	78.71	12.42	1,109	800-366-0066	Y
Fidelity Advisor® Equity Growth Fund Class A	EPGAX	B-	C+	B	Down	4.31	22.58	10.15	70.90	78.46	12.32	3,243	617-563-7000	Y
MassMutual Select Mid Cap Growth Fund Class R5	MGRFX	B-	C+	B	Down	5.97	25.68	14.98	58.92	78.19	23.24	8,748		Y
Wells Fargo Large Cap Growth Fund - Class A	STAFX	B-	B-	B	Down	5.44	25.07	12.22	70.48	78.06	43.6	1,016	800-222-8222	Y
Wells Fargo Premier Large Company Growth Fund - Class A	EKJAX	B-	B-	B	Down	6.70	27.71	14.03	74.06	77.96	14.01	2,423	800-222-8222	Y
Brown Advisory Small-Cap Growth Fund Advisor Shares	BASAX	B-	B-	B-	Down	7.74	32.43	14.07	57.79	77.74	21.15	1,347	800-540-6807	Y
Great-West T. Rowe Price Mid Cap Growth Fund Class L	MXTMX	B-	C+	B	Down	6.48	24.19	14.48	60.05	77.60	6.55	1,864		Y
Voya Large Cap Growth Portfolio Class S2	IEOTX	B-	C+	B	Down	3.70	20.22	10.57	59.75	77.36	20.45	5,704	800-366-0066	Y
VY® T. Rowe Price Diversified Mid Cap Growth Port Cls S2	IAXTX	B-	B-	B	Down	6.98	28.76	16.32	63.16	77.31	11.64	1,109	800-366-0066	Y
MassMutual Select Mid Cap Growth Fund Service Class	MEFYX	B-	C+	B	Down	5.89	25.66	14.87	58.41	77.28	22.62	8,748		Y
Transamerica US Growth Class C	TADCX	B-	C+	B	Down	5.12	24.43	11.52	59.40	77.26	19.71	1,126	888-233-4339	Y
Voya Large-Cap Growth Fund Class A	NLCAX	B-	C+	B	Down	3.73	20.33	10.85	59.98	77.25	40.54	1,080	800-366-0066	Y
DWS Capital Growth Fund - Class C	SDGCX	B-	C+	B	Down	5.57	25.22	12.35	61.60	77.18	67.21	1,562		Y
Invesco Oppenheimer Discovery Mid Cap Growth Fund A	OEGAX	B-	B-	C+	Up	8.96	31.26	14.69	58.20	77.12	22	1,557	800-659-1005	Y
John Hancock Funds II Mid Cap Stock Fund Class NAV	JHMSX	B-	B-	B-	Down	5.25	32.19	15.05	73.82	76.95	22.83	1,643	800-225-5913	Y
Franklin Growth Series Class A	FKGRX	B-	C+	B	Down	5.73	23.07	12.58	61.92	76.87	109.61	15,253	650-312-2000	Y
Putnam Sustainable Leaders Fund Class M	PNOMX	B	B-	B		6.39	25.75	14.88	71.86	76.81	78.02	4,727	617-292-1000	Y
Hartford Core Equity Fund Class R6	HAITX	B-	C+	B	Down	5.44	20.95	13.49	51.03	76.80	32.56	4,986	888-843-7824	Y
JNL/Mellon Capital Consumer Discretionary Sector Cls A		B-	C+	B		4.43	20.95	7.72	54.52	76.63	24.01	1,299		Y
John Hancock Funds II Mid Cap Stock Fund Class 1	JIMSX	B-	B-	B-	Down	5.27	32.18	14.97	73.59	76.54	22.55	1,643	800-225-5913	Y
MassMutual Select Mid Cap Growth Fund Administrative Class	MMELX	B-	C+	B	Down	5.89	25.59	14.76	57.98	76.47	21.54	8,748		Y
VY® T. Rowe Price Diversified Mid Cap Growth Port Cls A	IAXAX	B-	B-	B	Down	7.03	28.69	16.20	62.75	76.38	11.57	1,109	800-366-0066	Y
Fidelity Advisor® Equity Growth Fund Class M	FAEGX	B-	C+	B	Down	4.14	22.45	9.91	69.67	76.37	12.05	3,243	617-563-7000	Y
Wells Fargo Discovery Fund - Class A	WFDAX	B-	B	C+		10.74	38.02	17.44	76.95	76.21	34.74	2,582	800-222-8222	Y
Hartford Core Equity Fund Class R5	HGITX	B-	C+	B	Down	5.36	20.88	13.37	50.55	76.12	32.41	4,986	888-843-7824	Y
Wells Fargo Large Cap Growth Fund - Class R	STMFX	B-	C+	B	Down	5.36	24.88	11.93	69.12	75.79	42.26	1,016	800-222-8222	Y
Optimum Large Cap Growth Fund Class C	OCLGX	B-	C	B	Down	4.16	21.48	9.58	64.73	75.65	14.25	1,728		Y
Alger Capital Appreciation Institutional Fund Class R	ACARX	B-	C+	B	Down	5.19	22.55	9.40	63.40	75.62	30.59	3,523	800-992-3863	Y
Voya Large Cap Growth Portfolio Class A	IEOPX	B-	C+	B	Down	3.62	20.12	10.32	58.79	75.53	19.46	5,704	800-366-0066	Y
MassMutual Select Mid Cap Growth Fund Class R4	MEFFX	B-	C+	B	Down	5.85	25.48	14.59	57.29	75.26	19.89	8,748		Y
Voya Large-Cap Growth Fund Class R	VGORX	B-	C+	B	Down	3.68	20.18	10.59	58.82	75.24	44.48	1,080	800-366-0066	Y
MFS Massachusetts Investors Growth Stock Fund Class B	MIGBX	B	B-	B		5.09	24.35	17.39	61.94	74.75	26.81	7,515	877-960-6077	Y
MFS Massachusetts Investors Growth Stock Fund Class 529B	EMIVX	B	B-	B		5.06	24.25	17.36	62.06	74.67	25.92	7,515	877-960-6077	Y
MFS Massachusetts Investors Growth Stock Fund Class C	MIGDX	B	B-	B		5.09	24.33	17.36	61.91	74.65	26.62	7,515	877-960-6077	Y
Franklin Growth Series Class R	FGSRX	B-	C+	B	Down	5.67	22.92	12.31	60.71	74.65	109.13	15,253	650-312-2000	Y
MFS Massachusetts Investors Growth Stock Fund Class R1	MIGMX	B	B-	B		5.09	24.32	17.37	61.85	74.64	26.22	7,515	877-960-6077	Y
Putnam Sustainable Leaders Fund Class B	PNOBX	B	B-	B		6.33	25.58	14.59	70.57	74.63	68.68	4,727	617-292-1000	Y
Putnam Sustainable Leaders Fund Class C	PNOCX	B	B-	B		6.34	25.59	14.61	70.59	74.62	76.06	4,727	617-292-1000	Y
Federated Kaufmann Large Cap Fund Class R Shares	KLCKX	B	B-	B		7.08	27.89	17.13	63.18	74.47	25.4	3,453	800-341-7400	Y
MassMutual Select Mid Cap Growth Fund Class A	MEFAX	B-	C+	B	Down	5.84	25.41	14.45	56.80	74.24	19.74	8,748		Y
MFS Massachusetts Investors Growth Stock Fund Class 529C	EMICX	B	B-	B		5.03	24.26	17.26	61.56	74.13	25.66	7,515	877-960-6077	Y
DFA U.S. Large Cap Growth Portfolio Institutional Class	DUSLX	B-	C+	B	Down	4.19	20.61	12.25	57.22	74.07	21.27	2,140	512-306-7400	Y
Pioneer Fundamental Growth Fund Class A	PIGFX	B	C+	B		4.58	20.74	14.39	53.58	73.73	25.32	6,012	617-742-7825	Y

		RATINGS				TOTAL RETURNS & PERFORMANCE					ASSETS		NEW INVESTORS	
Fund Name	Ticker Symbol	Overall Rating	Reward Rating	Risk Rating	Recent Up/ Downgrade	3-Month Total Return	6-Month Total Return	1-Year Total Return	3-Year Total Return	5-Year Total Return	NAV	Total Assets (MIL)	Telephone	Open to New Investors
Hartford Core Equity Fund Class R4	HGISX	B-	C+	B	Down	5.34	20.75	13.10	49.31	73.67	33.11	4,986	888-843-7824	Y
Fidelity® Focused Stock Fund	FTQGX	B-	C+	B	Down	4.39	21.74	14.00	70.45	73.49	25.19	2,876	617-563-7000	Y
MassMutual Select Mid Cap Growth Fund Class R3	MEFNX	B-	C+	B	Down	5.79	25.38	14.31	56.11	73.01	18.08	8,748		Y
VALIC Company I Growth Fund	VCULX	B-	C+	B		4.29	21.90	8.74	63.37	72.52	17.47	1,157		Y
Franklin Growth Opportunities Fund Class A	FGRAX	B-	C+	B-		6.00	27.53	11.12	66.79	72.05	40.07	3,802	650-312-2000	Y
Fidelity Advisor® Equity Growth Fund Class C	EPGCX	B-	C+	B	Down	4.04	22.03	9.32	66.94	71.70	10.3	3,243	617-563-7000	Y
JNL/JPMorgan MidCap Growth Fund Class I		B-	B-	B-	Down	6.69	31.21	16.40	68.42	71.67	39.51	2,373		Y
Wells Fargo Large Cap Growth Fund - Class C	STOFX	B-	C+	B	Down	5.22	24.58	11.37	66.65	71.46	38.87	1,016	800-222-8222	Y
Wells Fargo Premier Large Company Growth Fund - Class C	EKJCX	B-	B-	B-	Down	6.50	27.09	13.08	70.02	71.24	10.32	2,423	800-222-8222	Y
Elfun Trusts	ELFNX	B-	C+	B	Down	6.35	21.29	11.70	57.70	71.17	60.38	2,789	617-664-7338	Y
Pioneer Fundamental Growth Fund Class R	PFGRX	B	C+	B		4.53	20.61	14.10	52.22	71.13	24.87	6,012	617-742-7825	Y
PACE Large Co Growth Equity Investments Class A	PLAAX	B-	C+	B		6.99	23.87	11.68	58.74	70.98	23.87	1,217	212-882-5586	Y
Voya Large-Cap Growth Fund Class C	NLCCX	B-	C+	B	Down	3.53	19.87	9.98	56.37	70.95	33.71	1,080	800-366-0066	Y
Hartford Core Equity Fund Class R3	HGIRX	B-	C+	B	Down	5.23	20.52	12.70	47.88	70.92	32.59	4,986	888-843-7824	Y
Hartford Stock HLS Fund Class IA	HSTAX	B	B	B+		5.95	21.69	18.43	49.25	70.73	94.42	1,496	888-843-7824	Y
MFS Core Equity Fund Class R6	MRGKX	B-	C+	B	Down	5.53	21.95	11.76	58.56	70.67	34.5	2,665	877-960-6077	Y
Vanguard Dividend Growth Fund Investor Shares	VDIGX	B	B	A-		6.32	22.14	19.04	49.45	70.52	29.36	36,582	877-662-7447	Y
Franklin Growth Series Class C	FRGSX	B-	C+	B		5.54	22.62	11.75	58.31	70.33	100.01	15,253	650-312-2000	Y
Franklin Growth Opportunities Fund Class R	FKARX	B-	C+	B-		5.93	27.40	10.88	65.60	70.06	38.03	3,802	650-312-2000	Y
MFS Core Equity Fund Class I	MRGRX	B-	C+	B	Down	5.51	21.91	11.66	58.22	69.97	34.43	2,665	877-960-6077	Y
MFS Core Equity Fund Class R4	MRGJX	B-	C+	B	Down	5.51	21.90	11.66	58.18	69.93	32.72	2,665	877-960-6077	Y
JNL/JPMorgan MidCap Growth Fund Class A		B-	B-	B-	Down	6.62	31.06	16.06	67.13	69.67	38.31	2,373		Y
Wells Fargo Discovery Fund - Class C	WDSCX	B-	B-	C+		10.53	37.48	16.53	73.02	69.66	29.6	2,582	800-222-8222	Y
Ivy Mid Cap Growth Fund Class I	IYMIX	B-	C+	B	Down	4.90	28.59	14.41	71.09	69.60	28.87	4,525		Y
JPMorgan Mid Cap Growth Fund Class R5	JMGFX	B-	B-	B-	Down	6.57	30.88	15.88	67.16	69.10	38.9	4,565	800-480-4111	Y
Hartford Stock HLS Fund Class IB	HIBSX	B	B	B+		5.89	21.54	18.14	48.14	68.61	94.31	1,496	888-843-7824	Y
Pioneer Fundamental Growth Fund Class C	FUNCX	B	C+	B		4.46	20.38	13.72	50.56	68.07	22.91	6,012	617-742-7825	Y
MFS Core Equity Fund Class A	MRGAX	B-	C+	B	Down	5.46	21.78	11.39	57.04	67.85	32.42	2,665	877-960-6077	Y
MFS Core Equity Fund Class R3	MRGHX	B-	C+	B	Down	5.44	21.77	11.38	56.98	67.81	32.33	2,665	877-960-6077	Y
JPMorgan Mid Cap Growth Fund Class R4	JMGQX	B-	B-	B-	Down	6.53	30.76	15.65	66.17	67.63	38.3	4,565	800-480-4111	Y
Pioneer Disciplined Growth Fund Class A	PINDX	B-	C+	B	Down	4.72	23.47	11.23	54.25	67.53	16.83	1,318	617-742-7825	Y
Ivy Mid Cap Growth Fund Class Y	WMGYX	B-	C+	B	Down	4.78	28.34	13.98	69.63	67.36	27.8	4,525		Y
MFS Research Fund Class R6	MFRKX	B-	C+	B	Down	5.97	22.60	12.33	53.18	67.13	43.6	5,837	877-960-6077	Y
Ivy Mid Cap Growth Fund Class A	WMGAX	B-	C+	B	Down	4.78	28.32	13.98	69.48	67.00	26.5	4,525		Y
JNL Multi-Manager Small Cap Growth Fund Class I		B-	B-	C+	Down	7.18	31.32	10.99	84.60	66.98	32.24	2,375		Y
Ivy Science and Technology Fund Class I	ISTIX	B-	B	B-		9.36	35.04	15.97	93.25	66.48	79.3	7,179		Y
MFS Research Fund Class R4	MFRJX	B-	C+	B	Down	5.96	22.58	12.24	52.81	66.42	43.69	5,837	877-960-6077	Y
MFS Research Fund Class I	MRFIX	B-	C+	B	Down	5.97	22.58	12.24	52.78	66.42	44.88	5,837	877-960-6077	Y
Ivy Mid Cap Growth Fund Class E	IMCEX	B-	C+	B	Down	4.79	28.27	13.88	69.36	66.35	25.77	4,525		Y
MFS New Discovery Fund Class R6	MNDKX	B-	C+	B-	Down	9.05	32.85	13.42	80.16	66.34	32.27	1,451	877-960-6077	Y
Fidelity® 500 Index Fund	FXAIX	B-	C	B		4.29	19.55	10.40	50.84	66.20	102.66	198,287	617-563-7000	Y
KP Large Cap Equity Fund Institutional Shares	KPLCX	B-	C	B		3.74	18.94	8.59	52.78	66.05	13.31	2,927		Y
MFS Core Equity Fund Class R2	MRERX	B-	C+	B	Down	5.40	21.63	11.12	55.89	65.81	31.6	2,665	877-960-6077	Y
DFA U.S. Large Company Portfolio	DFUSX	B-	C	B		4.29	19.50	10.33	50.70	65.78	22.68	9,457	512-306-7400	Y
MFS Massachusetts Investors Trust Class R6	MITJX	B	C+	B		5.45	22.14	13.32	54.41	65.72	31.02	5,716	877-960-6077	Y
Schwab® S&P 500 Index Fund	SWPPX	B-	C	B		4.29	19.53	10.37	50.67	65.66	45.4	38,408	877-824-5615	Y
JPMorgan Mid Cap Growth Fund Class R3	JMGPX	B-	B-	B-		6.47	30.61	15.38	64.97	65.59	38.01	4,565	800-480-4111	Y
MFS New Discovery Fund Class R4	MNDJX	B-	C+	B-	Down	9.00	32.75	13.29	79.72	65.48	30.03	1,451	877-960-6077	Y
JPMorgan Mid Cap Growth Fund Class A	OSGIX	B-	B-	B-		6.46	30.61	15.37	64.93	65.35	32.94	4,565	800-480-4111	Y
MFS New Discovery Fund Class I	MNDIX	B-	C+	B-	Down	9.01	32.73	13.29	79.59	65.32	31.91	1,451	877-960-6077	Y
MM S&P 500® Index Fund Class I	MMIZX	B-	C	B		4.26	19.53	10.28	50.37	65.25	17.62	3,372		Y
TIAA-CREF S&P 500 Index Fund Advisor Class	TISAX	B-	C	B		4.25	19.43	10.22	50.19	65.21	32.57	5,201	877-518-9161	Y

Fund Name	Ticker Symbol	RATINGS: Overall Rating	Reward Rating	Risk Rating	Recent Up/ Downgrade	TOTAL RETURNS & PERFORMANCE: 3-Month Total Return	6-Month Total Return	1-Year Total Return	3-Year Total Return	5-Year Total Return	ASSETS: NAV	Total Assets (MIL)	NEW INVESTORS: Telephone	Open to New Investors
JNL Multi-Manager Small Cap Growth Fund Class A		B-	B-	C+	Down	7.10	31.17	10.69	83.30	65.04	30.59	2,375		Y
MFS Massachusetts Investors Trust Class I	MITIX	B	C+	B		5.40	22.07	13.23	54.04	65.02	31.02	5,716	877-960-6077	Y
MFS Massachusetts Investors Trust Class R4	MITDX	B	C+	B		5.41	22.05	13.24	53.97	64.95	32.32	5,716	877-960-6077	Y
Columbia Mid Cap Growth Fund Institutional 2 Class	CMGVX	B-	B-	B		6.46	27.22	11.62	55.32	64.92	26.36	1,744	800-345-6611	Y
Principal LargeCap S&P 500 Index Fund Institutional Class	PLFIX	B-	C	B		4.24	19.46	10.24	50.15	64.91	18.41	5,904	800-787-1621	Y
American Century Heritage Fund R6 Class	ATHDX	B-	B-	B		7.07	29.64	16.57	55.39	64.86	23.92	4,738	800-444-4015	Y
Principal Capital Appreciation Fund Institutional Class	PWCIX	B-	C+	B	Down	5.34	20.51	12.50	51.24	64.77	49.63	1,758	800-787-1621	Y
BNY Mellon Institutional S&P 500 Stock Index Fund Class I	DSPIX	B-	C	B		4.26	19.48	10.22	50.07	64.70	56.62	2,625		Y
Columbia Large Cap Index Fund Institutional 2 Class	CLXRX	B-	C	B		4.25	19.44	10.19	49.98	64.66	49.69	3,370	800-345-6611	Y
DWS S&P 500 Index Fund - Class R6	SXPRX	B-	C	B		4.22	19.41	10.57	50.18	64.61	31.56	1,006		Y
Ivy Science And Technology Fund Class Y	WSTYX	B-	B	C+		9.31	34.92	15.73	91.93	64.54	75.45	7,179		Y
MM S&P 500® Index Fund Class R5	MIEZX	B-	C	B		4.24	19.45	10.14	49.91	64.44	17.68	3,372		Y
MFS Research Fund Class A	MFRFX	B-	C+	B	Down	5.91	22.44	12.01	51.70	64.41	43.69	5,837	877-960-6077	Y
MFS Research Fund Class R3	MFRHX	B-	C+	B	Down	5.91	22.44	11.99	51.68	64.36	43.32	5,837	877-960-6077	Y
Voya U.S. Stock Index Portfolio P2	VPSPX	B-	C	B		4.29	19.47	10.25	50.04	64.34	16.5	5,890	800-366-0066	Y
Ivy Science And Technology Fund Class A	WSTAX	B-	B	C+		9.30	34.89	15.71	91.86	64.27	71.05	7,179		Y
GuideStone Funds Equity Index Fund Investor Class	GEQZX	B-	C	B		4.35	19.42	10.12	50.56	64.01	32.38	1,905	214-720-1171	Y
Voya U.S. Stock Index Portfolio Class I	INGIX	B-	C	B		4.24	19.37	10.06	49.70	63.98	16.45	5,890	800-366-0066	Y
iShares S&P 500 Index Fund Investor P Shares	BSPPX	B-	C	B		4.21	19.33	10.07	49.58	63.88	348.69	19,490	800-441-7762	Y
VY® T. Rowe Price Capital Appreciation Portfolio Class I	ITRIX	B	B-	A	Down	4.92	18.23	15.26	41.61	63.81	29.63	7,145	800-366-0066	Y
TIAA-CREF S&P 500 Index Fund Retirement Class	TRSPX	B-	C	B		4.21	19.38	10.09	49.49	63.74	32.39	5,201	877-518-9161	Y
Columbia Dividend Income Fund Institutional 2 Class	CDDRX	B	C+	B+		4.11	17.57	13.05	44.96	63.72	23.07	14,746	800-345-6611	Y
JPMorgan Mid Cap Growth Fund Class R2	JMGZX	B-	C+	B-		6.39	30.43	15.09	63.83	63.72	35.91	4,565	800-480-4111	Y
JNL/Mellon S&P 500 Index Fund Class I		B-	C	B		4.27	19.47	10.25	49.74	63.60	23.68	8,414		Y
Invesco S&P 500 Index Fund Class Y	SPIDX	B-	C	B		4.22	19.34	10.05	49.43	63.60	32.08	1,394	800-659-1005	Y
VALIC Company I Stock Index Fund	VSTIX	B-	C	B		4.21	19.38	10.06	49.41	63.52	42	4,941		Y
Ivy Science and Technology Fund Class E	ISTEX	B-	B	C+		9.27	34.82	15.55	91.34	63.41	70.35	7,179		Y
iShares S&P 500 Index Fund Investor A Shares	BSPAX	B-	C	B		4.20	19.32	10.05	49.34	63.38	348.95	19,490	800-441-7762	Y
MFS New Discovery Fund Class A	MNDAX	B-	C+	B-	Down	8.94	32.57	13.02	78.26	63.30	28.12	1,451	877-960-6077	Y
MM S&P 500® Index Fund Class Service Class	MMIEX	B-	C	B		4.23	19.40	9.98	49.21	63.27	17.72	3,372		Y
American Century Heritage Fund Y Class	ATHYX	B-	B-	B		7.02	29.64	16.57	54.94	63.26	23.92	4,738	800-444-4015	Y
MFS New Discovery Fund Class R3	MNDHX	B-	C+	B-	Down	8.92	32.59	12.99	78.17	63.21	28.07	1,451	877-960-6077	Y
VY® T. Rowe Price Capital Appreciation Portfolio Class R6	VPRAX	B	B-	A	Down	4.91	18.22	15.29	41.69	63.11	29.65	7,145	800-366-0066	Y
MFS Massachusetts Investors Trust Class A	MITTX	B	C+	B		5.34	21.93	12.98	52.95	63.09	32	5,716	877-960-6077	Y
Great-West S&P 500® Index Fund Institutional Class	MXKWX	B-	C	B		4.34	18.88	9.67	51.81	63.08	9.9	2,973		Y
MFS Massachusetts Investors Trust Class R3	MITHX	B-	C+	B	Down	5.36	21.91	12.94	52.89	62.96	31.68	5,716	877-960-6077	Y
Principal LargeCap S&P 500 Index Fund Class J	PSPJX	B-	C	B		4.23	19.39	10.04	49.24	62.96	18.22	5,904	800-787-1621	Y
Schwab 1000 Index® Fund	SNXFX	B-	C	B		4.29	19.89	9.91	50.33	62.93	66.3	9,246	877-824-5615	Y
Principal LargeCap S&P 500 Index Fund R-5 Class	PLFPX	B-	C	B		4.18	19.29	9.95	49.01	62.90	18.67	5,904	800-787-1621	Y
American Century Heritage Fund R5 Class	ATHGX	B-	C+	B		7.02	29.58	16.38	54.43	62.73	23.61	4,738	800-444-4015	Y
Principal Capital Appreciation Fund R-5 Class	PCAQX	B-	C+	B	Down	5.27	20.35	12.20	50.08	62.69	49.13	1,758	800-787-1621	Y
MFS Massachusetts Investors Trust Class 529A	EAMTX	B-	C+	B	Down	5.32	21.88	12.88	52.65	62.64	31.1	5,716	877-960-6077	Y
JPMorgan Tax Aware Equity Fund Class A	JPEAX	B-	C	B		4.37	19.09	8.90	52.98	62.63	35.81	1,278	800-480-4111	Y
PIMCO StocksPLUS® Absolute Return Fund Class A	PTOAX	B-	C	B		4.47	20.52	9.19	54.56	62.59	10.41	2,030	866-746-2602	Y
JPMorgan Equity Index Fund Class A	OGEAX	B-	C	B		4.17	19.27	9.87	48.81	62.52	44.9	4,510	800-480-4111	Y
TIAA-CREF Equity Index Fund Class W	TEQWX	B-	C	B		4.09	19.73	9.00	50.21	62.46	21.6	21,187	877-518-9161	Y
Wells Fargo Index Fund - Class A	WFILX	B-	C	B		4.17	19.28	9.92	48.87	62.42	52.94	1,196	800-222-8222	Y
Principal LargeCap S&P 500 Index Fund Class A	PLSAX	B-	C	B		4.18	19.31	9.90	48.86	62.38	18.41	5,904	800-787-1621	Y
John Hancock Funds II Capital Appreciation Value Cls NAV	JCAVX	B	B-	A		4.92	18.14	15.04	41.07	62.35	11.72	1,654	800-225-5913	Y
MFS Research Fund Class R2	MSRRX	B-	C+	B	Down	5.85	22.27	11.71	50.54	62.33	42.1	5,837	877-960-6077	Y
MM S&P 500® Index Fund Class Administrative Class	MIEYX	B-	C	B		4.14	19.24	9.85	48.71	62.33	17.35	3,372		Y
Fidelity® Total Market Index Fund	FSKAX	B-	C	B		4.08	19.74	8.88	50.30	62.30	83.41	48,079	617-563-7000	Y

		RATINGS				TOTAL RETURNS & PERFORMANCE					ASSETS		NEW INVESTORS	
Fund Name	Ticker Symbol	Overall Rating	Reward Rating	Risk Rating	Recent Up/ Downgrade	3-Month Total Return	6-Month Total Return	1-Year Total Return	3-Year Total Return	5-Year Total Return	NAV	Total Assets (MIL)	Telephone	Open to New Investors
Voya U.S. Stock Index Portfolio Class S	ISJBX	B-	C	B		4.15	19.22	9.79	48.57	62.08	16.31	5,890	800-366-0066	Y
DFA Tax Managed U.S. Equity Portfolio	DTMEX	B-	C	B		4.21	19.58	8.80	50.68	62.06	31.7	3,900	512-306-7400	Y
JNL/Mellon S&P 500 Index Fund Class A		B-	C	B		4.15	19.24	9.84	48.61	61.93	23.05	8,414		Y
JNL/American Funds Growth-Income Fund Class I		B-	C	B+		3.22	16.81	6.94	51.93	61.92	25.57	7,247		Y
TIAA-CREF Equity Index Fund Advisor Class	TEIHX	B-	C	B		4.00	19.62	8.78	49.79	61.90	21.58	21,187	877-518-9161	Y
DWS S&P 500 Index Fund - Class A	SXPAX	B-	C	B		4.14	19.26	10.25	48.82	61.88	31.49	1,006		Y
Schwab Total Stock Market Index Fund®	SWTSX	B-	C	B		4.08	19.74	8.86	50.01	61.84	51.73	9,794	877-824-5615	Y
VY® T. Rowe Price Capital Appreciation Portfolio Class S	ITCSX	B	B-	A	Down	4.85	18.06	14.99	40.60	61.80	29.61	7,145	800-366-0066	Y
Principal LargeCap S&P 500 Index Fund R-4 Class	PLFSX	B-	C	B		4.11	19.21	9.83	48.44	61.80	18.49	5,904	800-787-1621	Y
Principal Capital Appreciation Fund Class A	CMNWX	B-	C+	B	Down	5.23	20.29	12.06	49.59	61.78	48.24	1,758	800-787-1621	Y
Principal Capital Appreciation Fund R-4 Class	PCAPX	B-	C+	B	Down	5.23	20.30	12.06	49.55	61.72	48.88	1,758	800-787-1621	Y
Ivy Science and Technology Fund Class R	WSTRX	B-	B-	C+		9.20	34.65	15.31	89.89	61.66	68.69	7,179		Y
MFS Core Equity Fund Class C	MRGCX	B-	C+	B	Down	5.24	21.33	10.54	53.45	61.64	27.87	2,665	877-960-6077	Y
MFS Core Equity Fund Class B	MRGBX	B-	C+	B	Down	5.25	21.30	10.56	53.54	61.64	28.24	2,665	877-960-6077	Y
MFS Core Equity Fund Class R1	MRGGX	B-	C+	B	Down	5.25	21.29	10.55	53.50	61.63	27.85	2,665	877-960-6077	Y
Invesco S&P 500 Index Fund Class A	SPIAX	B-	C	B		4.17	19.23	9.84	48.40	61.61	31.68	1,394	800-659-1005	Y
Principal MidCap Growth Fund III Institutional Class	PPIMX	B-	C+	B-		7.32	28.14	13.30	57.57	61.60	12.02	1,126	800-787-1621	Y
ClearBridge Appreciation Fund Class A	SHAPX	B	C+	B+		5.90	19.13	14.59	46.52	61.29	25.65	6,450	877-721-1926	Y
MFS New Discovery Fund Class R2	MNDRX	B-	C+	B-	Down	8.85	32.39	12.72	76.87	61.23	25.95	1,451	877-960-6077	Y
JPMorgan Mid Cap Growth Fund Class C	OMGCX	B-	C+	B-		6.33	30.28	14.78	62.43	61.20	25.34	4,565	800-480-4111	Y
MM S&P 500® Index Fund Class R4	MIEAX	B-	C	B		4.19	19.20	9.76	48.19	61.19	17.13	3,372		Y
TIAA-CREF Equity Index Fund Premier Class	TCEPX	B-	C	B		4.05	19.60	8.79	49.51	61.14	21.54	21,187	877-518-9161	Y
Pioneer Fund Class A	PIODX	B	B-	B+		6.68	19.88	14.76	53.47	61.06	29.33	5,068	617-742-7825	Y
ClearBridge Appreciation Fund Class FI	LMPIX	B	C+	B+		5.87	19.06	14.49	46.31	61.01	25.79	6,450	877-721-1926	Y
MFS Massachusetts Investors Trust Class R2	MIRTX	B-	C+	B	Down	5.25	21.76	12.63	51.72	60.91	30.32	5,716	877-960-6077	Y
Voya U.S. Stock Index Portfolio Class S2	ISIPX	B-	C	B		4.14	19.18	9.70	47.94	60.84	16.09	5,890	800-366-0066	Y
Pioneer Disciplined Growth Fund Class C	INDCX	B-	C+	B		4.51	22.94	10.32	50.50	60.79	14.36	1,318	617-742-7825	Y
MainStay MacKay S&P 500 Index Fund Investor Class	MYSPX	B-	C	B		4.12	19.14	9.71	47.88	60.76	47.74	1,023	800-624-6782	Y
Great-West S&P 500® Index Fund Investor Class	MXVIX	B-	C	B		4.31	18.63	9.31	50.21	60.71	22.77	2,973		Y
VY® T. Rowe Price Capital Appreciation Portfolio Class S2	ITCTX	B	B-	A	Down	4.81	17.99	14.94	39.97	60.60	29.37	7,145	800-366-0066	Y
FAM Value Fund Investor Class	FAMVX	B-	C+	B		7.48	21.77	12.43	47.11	60.52	79.8	1,337		Y
American Funds Washington Mutual Investors Fund Class R-6	RWMGX	B-	C	B+	Down	4.14	15.82	10.47	47.40	60.43	45.86	118,091	800-421-4225	Y
MM S&P 500® Index Fund Class A	MMFFX	B-	C	B		4.10	19.13	9.58	47.62	60.42	17	3,372		Y
TIAA-CREF Equity Index Fund Retirement Class	TIQRX	B-	C	B		4.03	19.53	8.66	49.07	60.38	21.91	21,187	877-518-9161	Y
Principal LargeCap S&P 500 Index Fund R-3 Class	PLFMX	B-	C	B		4.12	19.19	9.67	47.66	60.37	18.44	5,904	800-787-1621	Y
JNL/T. Rowe Price Capital Appreciation Fund Class I		B	B-	A	Down	4.88	18.08	15.22	40.55	60.22	16.32	4,959		Y
Principal Capital Appreciation Fund R-3 Class	PCAOX	B-	C+	B	Down	5.20	20.19	11.84	48.68	60.19	48.33	1,758	800-787-1621	Y
JNL/American Funds Growth-Income Fund Class A		B-	C	B		3.19	16.67	6.64	50.83	60.06	25.19	7,247		Y
Columbia Mid Cap Growth Fund Class R	CMGRX	B-	C+	B-		6.30	26.86	10.99	52.58	60.02	22.76	1,744	800-345-6611	Y
American Funds Washington Mutual Investors Fund Class R-5	RWMFX	B-	C	B+	Down	4.11	15.78	10.39	47.14	60.00	45.81	118,091	800-421-4225	Y
Morgan Stanley Inst Fund, Inc. Global Franchise Port Cls C	MSGFX	B	B	B+		4.87	21.07	14.19	46.47	59.92	26.66	1,742	855-332-5306	Y
Voya U.S. Stock Index Portfolio Class A	ISIVX	B-	C	B		4.06	19.06	9.53	47.26	59.69	15.86	5,890	800-366-0066	Y
Delaware U.S. Growth Fund Class R6	DUZRX	B-	C	B		7.81	21.69	10.91	54.79	59.66	24.57	2,446		Y
American Funds Washington Mutual Investors Fund Class F-2	WMFFX	B-	C	B+	Down	4.10	15.73	10.35	46.94	59.58	45.79	118,091	800-421-4225	Y
Principal MidCap Growth Fund III R-5 Class	PPQPX	B-	C+	B-		7.19	27.99	13.02	56.35	59.54	12.07	1,126	800-787-1621	Y
Delaware U.S. Growth Fund Institutional Class	DEUIX	B-	C	B		7.75	21.57	10.65	53.95	59.53	24.46	2,446		Y
Nationwide S&P 500 Index Fund Class R	GRMRX	B-	C	B		4.10	19.11	9.57	47.30	59.52	15.21	1,069	800-848-0920	Y
JNL/T. Rowe Price Capital Appreciation Fund		B	B-	A		4.76	17.91	14.88	39.86	59.43	16.26	4,959		Y
Strategic Advisers® Core Fund	FCSAX	B-	C	B		4.11	19.52	8.85	51.09	59.42	18.49	25,971	617-563-7000	Y
American Funds Washington Mutual Investors Cls 529-F-1	CWMFX	B-	C	B+	Down	4.09	15.73	10.31	46.79	59.28	45.6	118,091	800-421-4225	Y
MM S&P 500® Index Fund Class R3	MMINX	B-	C	B		4.07	19.05	9.40	46.97	59.21	16.62	3,372		Y
DFA U.S. Large Cap Equity Portfolio Institutional Class	DUSQX	B-	C	B		4.28	19.96	8.90	50.74	59.10	18.09	1,626	512-306-7400	Y

		RATINGS				TOTAL RETURNS & PERFORMANCE					ASSETS		NEW INVESTORS	
Fund Name	Ticker Symbol	Overall Rating	Reward Rating	Risk Rating	Recent Up/ Downgrade	3-Month Total Return	6-Month Total Return	1-Year Total Return	3-Year Total Return	5-Year Total Return	NAV	Total Assets (MIL)	Telephone	Open to New Investors
Invesco Oppenheimer Main Street Fund Class R6	OMSIX	B-	C+	B		5.90	22.57	12.16	42.79	59.09	47.51	9,574	800-659-1005	Y
VY® T. Rowe Price Capital Appreciation Portfolio Class A	ITRAX	B	B-	A	Down	4.75	17.87	14.58	39.09	58.97	28.22	7,145	800-366-0066	Y
American Century Equity Income Fund R6 Class	AEUDX	B	C+	A-		4.61	16.66	12.53	36.26	58.94	9.04	11,975	800-444-4015	Y
Franklin Rising Dividends Fund Class A	FRDPX	B-	C+	B	Down	4.99	21.83	13.69	46.50	58.92	66.62	19,187	650-312-2000	Y
Principal LargeCap S&P 500 Index Fund R-2 Class	PLFNX	B-	C	B		4.04	19.03	9.45	46.86	58.88	18.51	5,904	800-787-1621	Y
American Funds Washington Mutual Investors Fund Class R-5E	RWMHX	B-	C	B+	Down	4.09	15.73	10.32	46.74	58.86	45.77	118,091	800-421-4225	Y
Columbia Dividend Income Fund Class R	CDIRX	B-	C+	B+	Down	3.98	17.22	12.42	42.46	58.85	22.7	14,746	800-345-6611	Y
Principal Capital Appreciation Fund R-2 Class	PCANX	B-	C+	B	Down	5.15	20.08	11.64	47.90	58.77	48.37	1,758	800-787-1621	Y
GE RSP U.S. Equity Fund	GESSX	B-	C	B	Down	5.50	20.33	12.05	53.63	58.75	54.98	5,348	617-664-7338	Y
ClearBridge Appreciation Fund Class R	LMPPX	B	C+	B+		5.83	18.92	14.27	45.11	58.73	25.58	6,450	877-721-1926	Y
Great-West S&P 500® Index Fund Class L	MXVJX	B-	C	B		4.26	18.45	9.04	49.06	58.70	17.42	2,973		Y
Principal MidCap Growth Fund III Class J	PPQJX	B-	C+	B-		7.12	27.80	12.88	55.66	58.56	9.47	1,126	800-787-1621	Y
ClearBridge Dividend Strategy Fund Class 1	LCBOX	B	B-	B+		5.56	20.53	15.48	46.02	58.51	24.54	6,398	877-721-1926	Y
Ivy Science And Technology Fund Class C	WSTCX	B-	B-	C+		9.10	34.41	14.87	87.68	58.50	59.21	7,179		Y
Principal MidCap Growth Fund III R-4 Class	PPQSX	B-	C+	B-		7.19	27.87	12.90	55.57	58.42	11.47	1,126	800-787-1621	Y
MFS Research Fund Class C	MFRCX	B-	C+	B		5.70	21.98	11.14	48.27	58.33	38.89	5,837	877-960-6077	Y
Lord Abbett Calibrated Dividend Growth Fund Class R6	LAMHX	B-	C+	B+	Down	4.10	17.62	12.99	40.30	58.32	15.71	2,400	201-827-2000	Y
MFS Research Fund Class B	MFRBX	B-	C+	B		5.71	21.97	11.14	48.30	58.31	39.19	5,837	877-960-6077	Y
MFS Research Fund Class R1	MFRLX	B-	C+	B		5.71	21.96	11.13	48.25	58.28	38.09	5,837	877-960-6077	Y
American Funds Washington Mutual Investors Fund Class A	AWSHX	B-	C	B+	Down	4.05	15.64	10.16	46.15	58.16	45.84	118,091	800-421-4225	Y
Lord Abbett Calibrated Dividend Growth Fund Class F3	LRMAX	B-	C+	B+	Down	4.10	17.62	12.91	40.19	58.07	15.71	2,400	201-827-2000	Y
MFS Massachusetts Investors Trust Class 529B	EBMTX	B-	C+	B	Down	5.04	21.31	12.49	50.18	58.02	29.08	5,716	877-960-6077	Y
Ivy Accumulative Fund Class I	IATIX	B-	C	B		5.65	25.44	14.07	47.78	57.97	10.65	1,338		Y
Pioneer Fund Class R	PIORX	B	B-	B+		6.61	19.65	14.31	51.53	57.91	29.48	5,068	617-742-7825	Y
Principal LargeCap S&P 500 Index Fund R-1 Class	PLPIX	B-	C	B		4.02	19.00	9.33	46.25	57.89	18.35	5,904	800-787-1621	Y
Wells Fargo Diversified Capital Builder Fund - Class A	EKBAX	B-	C	B		4.48	19.41	10.53	41.94	57.86	10.57	1,087	800-222-8222	Y
Principal Capital Appreciation Fund R-1 Class	PCAMX	B-	C+	B		5.10	19.97	11.49	47.30	57.70	48.18	1,758	800-787-1621	Y
Invesco Oppenheimer Main Street Fund Class Y	MIGYX	B-	C+	B		5.87	22.47	11.98	42.03	57.68	47.58	9,574	800-659-1005	Y
Lord Abbett Calibrated Dividend Growth Fund Class R5	LAMTX	B-	C+	B+	Down	4.04	17.52	12.87	39.91	57.64	15.64	2,400	201-827-2000	Y
American Funds Washington Mutual Investors Fund Class R-4	RWMEX	B-	C	B+	Down	4.03	15.59	10.07	45.82	57.64	45.57	118,091	800-421-4225	Y
iShares S&P 500 Index Fund Investor C1 Shares	BSPZX	B-	C	B		4.02	18.90	9.23	46.11	57.56	350.28	19,490	800-441-7762	Y
American Funds Washington Mutual Investors Fund Class F-1	WSHFX	B-	C	B+	Down	4.02	15.58	10.06	45.75	57.48	45.65	118,091	800-421-4225	Y
American Funds Washington Mutual Investors Cls 529-A	CWMAX	B-	C	B+	Down	4.02	15.58	10.04	45.76	57.47	45.72	118,091	800-421-4225	Y
American Century Equity Income Fund Y Class	AEIYX	B	C+	A-		4.61	16.66	12.53	36.06	57.46	9.04	11,975	800-444-4015	Y
Lord Abbett Calibrated Dividend Growth Fund Class F	LAMFX	B-	C+	B+	Down	4.05	17.55	12.88	39.79	57.26	15.51	2,400	201-827-2000	Y
JPMorgan Equity Index Fund Class C	OEICX	B-	C	B		4.04	18.93	9.23	46.09	57.16	44.45	4,510	800-480-4111	Y
Ivy Accumulative Fund Class N	IATNX	B-	C	B		5.79	25.62	14.30	47.57	57.02	10.59	1,338		Y
Franklin Rising Dividends Fund Class R	FRDRX	B-	C+	B	Down	4.92	21.68	13.40	45.41	56.95	66.37	19,187	650-312-2000	Y
MFS Massachusetts Investors Trust Class C	MITCX	B-	C+	B		5.14	21.47	12.12	49.46	56.93	30.26	5,716	877-960-6077	Y
American Funds New Perspective Fund® Class R-6	RNPGX	B-	C	B	Up	4.35	19.85	7.37	52.50	56.91	44.8	89,711	800-421-4225	Y
MFS Massachusetts Investors Trust Class R1	MITGX	B-	C+	B		5.14	21.45	12.06	49.46	56.90	30.06	5,716	877-960-6077	Y
MFS Massachusetts Investors Trust Class B	MITBX	B-	C+	B		5.11	21.46	12.09	49.45	56.90	30.93	5,716	877-960-6077	Y
Principal MidCap Growth Fund III R-3 Class	PPQMX	B-	C+	B-		7.06	27.71	12.64	54.75	56.88	11.06	1,126	800-787-1621	Y
American Century Equity Income Fund R5 Class	AEIUX	B	C+	A-		4.46	16.47	12.26	35.50	56.82	9.02	11,975	800-444-4015	Y
Morgan Stanley Pathway Funds Large Cap Equity Fund	TLGUX	B-	C	B		3.54	18.87	8.80	45.90	56.72	19.27	1,584	855-332-5306	Y
MFS Massachusetts Investors Trust Class 529C	ECITX	B-	C+	B		5.11	21.40	12.03	49.21	56.56	28.66	5,716	877-960-6077	Y
Franklin Convertible Securities Fund Class A	FISCX	B	C+	A-		5.54	20.81	14.81	54.39	56.55	22.73	3,864	650-312-2000	Y
American Funds New Perspective Fund® Class R-5	RNPFX	B-	C	B	Up	4.36	19.82	7.31	52.26	56.53	44.73	89,711	800-421-4225	Y
Neuberger Berman Multi-Cap Opportunities Fund Class A	NMUAX	B-	C	B	Down	3.45	17.24	8.92	56.69	56.50	18.56	1,208	212-476-9000	Y
Goldman Sachs Growth Opportunities Fund Class P	GGQPX	B-	B-	B		7.01	27.83	15.60	53.85	56.49	22.87	1,315	800-526-7384	Y
PIMCO StocksPLUS® Absolute Return Fund Class C	PSOCX	B-	C	B	Up	4.18	20.06	8.36	51.02	56.49	9.35	2,030	866-746-2602	Y
Wells Fargo Index Fund - Class C	WFINX	B-	C	B		4.00	18.86	9.10	45.57	56.45	53.5	1,196	800-222-8222	Y

		RATINGS				TOTAL RETURNS & PERFORMANCE					ASSETS		NEW INVESTORS	
Fund Name	Ticker Symbol	Overall Rating	Reward Rating	Risk Rating	Recent Up/ Downgrade	3-Month Total Return	6-Month Total Return	1-Year Total Return	3-Year Total Return	5-Year Total Return	NAV	Total Assets (MIL)	Telephone	Open to New Investors
ClearBridge Dividend Strategy Fund Class A	SOPAX	B	B-	B+		5.50	20.38	15.18	44.80	56.34	24.53	6,398	877-721-1926	Y
JPMorgan Equity Income Fund Class R5	OIERX	B-	C	B+	Down	4.28	16.79	11.66	43.67	56.29	18.16	23,652	800-480-4111	Y
DWS S&P 500 Index Fund - Class C	SXPCX	B-	C	B		3.97	18.80	9.44	45.62	56.29	31.42	1,006		Y
Ivy Accumulative Fund Class Y	IATYX	B-	C	B		5.59	25.23	13.87	46.87	56.28	10.57	1,338		Y
ClearBridge Dividend Strategy Fund Class FI	LBRIX	B	B-	B+		5.55	20.37	15.25	44.76	56.25	24.48	6,398	877-721-1926	Y
American Funds New Perspective Fund® Class F-2	ANWFX	B-	C	B	Up	4.32	19.79	7.26	52.02	56.12	44.61	89,711	800-421-4225	Y
Principal LargeCap S&P 500 Index Fund Class C	PLICX	B-	C	B		3.99	18.79	9.01	45.15	55.84	17.95	5,904	800-787-1621	Y
Invesco Oppenheimer Main Street Fund Class A	MSIGX	B-	C	B		5.81	22.33	11.72	41.07	55.83	48.04	9,574	800-659-1005	Y
Lord Abbett Calibrated Dividend Growth Fund Class R4	LAMSX	B-	C+	B+	Down	4.02	17.42	12.60	38.86	55.77	15.48	2,400	201-827-2000	Y
Lord Abbett Calibrated Dividend Growth Fund Class A	LAMAX	B-	C+	B+	Down	3.95	17.40	12.58	38.82	55.75	15.49	2,400	201-827-2000	Y
Invesco S&P 500 Index Fund Class C	SPICX	B-	C	B		3.95	18.78	8.98	45.08	55.71	30.48	1,394	800-659-1005	Y
ClearBridge Appreciation Fund Class C	SAPCX	B-	C+	B+	Down	5.70	18.69	13.80	43.44	55.70	24.63	6,450	877-721-1926	Y
American Funds New Perspective Fund® Class 529-F	CNPFX	B-	C	B	Up	4.33	19.75	7.21	51.81	55.66	44.07	89,711	800-421-4225	Y
Goldman Sachs Growth Opportunities Fund Investor Class	GGOTX	B-	B-	B		7.00	27.81	15.49	53.45	55.62	19.39	1,315	800-526-7384	Y
The Hartford Capital Appreciation Fund Class R6	ITHVX	B-	C+	B		6.02	23.81	11.39	53.80	55.44	43.99	7,165	888-843-7824	Y
TIAA-CREF Social Choice Equity Fund Advisor Class	TICHX	B-	C	B		3.76	19.32	8.93	49.38	55.44	19.57	4,522	877-518-9161	Y
American Funds New Perspective Fund® Class R-5E	RNPHX	B-	C	B	Up	4.34	19.81	7.26	51.78	55.28	44.44	89,711	800-421-4225	Y
Principal Capital Appreciation Fund Class C	CMNCX	B-	C+	B		5.00	19.77	11.14	45.93	55.23	32.28	1,758	800-787-1621	Y
PGIM Jennison Mid-Cap Growth Fund- Class R4	PEGGX	B-	C+	B		6.98	29.34	14.08	50.94	55.14	32.79	3,442	800-225-1852	Y
Mercer Global Low Volatility Equity Fund Class Y-3	MGLVX	B	C+	B+		50.24	68.02	58.18	68.19	55.04	13.74	1,019		Y
Principal Equity Income Fund Institutional Class	PEIIX	B-	C+	B+	Down	5.44	18.00	11.39	46.53	54.92	32.11	7,444	800-787-1621	Y
Pioneer Fund Class C	PCODX	B	C+	B+		6.48	19.38	13.86	49.81	54.81	25.1	5,068	617-742-7825	Y
The Hartford Capital Appreciation Fund Class R5	ITHTX	B-	C+	B		5.99	23.72	11.26	53.37	54.72	43.7	7,165	888-843-7824	Y
JPMorgan Equity Income Fund Class R4	OIEQX	B-	C	B+	Down	4.19	16.66	11.45	42.91	54.72	18.13	23,652	800-480-4111	Y
American Funds New Perspective Fund® Class A	ANWPX	B-	C	B	Up	4.28	19.65	7.05	51.13	54.55	44.75	89,711	800-421-4225	Y
Franklin Small-Mid Cap Growth Fund Class A	FRSGX	B-	C+	B		5.42	28.37	14.38	56.09	54.36	37.51	3,324	650-312-2000	Y
TIAA-CREF Social Choice Equity Fund Premier Class	TRPSX	B-	C	B		3.72	19.26	8.74	48.67	54.26	19.5	4,522	877-518-9161	Y
Russell Investments Tax-Managed U.S. Large Cap Cls M	RTMTX	B-	C	B	Up	4.46	18.96	8.68	45.15	54.24	44.48	3,396	800-426-7969	Y
ClearBridge Dividend Strategy Fund Class R	LMMRX	B	B-	B+		5.41	20.12	14.77	43.53	54.17	24.36	6,398	877-721-1926	Y
Ivy Accumulative Fund Class R	IATLX	B-	C	B		5.60	25.14	13.51	45.52	54.07	10.55	1,338		Y
Lord Abbett Calibrated Dividend Growth Fund Class R3	LAMRX	B-	C+	B+	Down	3.97	17.26	12.36	37.93	54.00	15.42	2,400	201-827-2000	Y
Russell Investments Tax-Managed U.S. Large Cap Cls S	RETSX	B-	C	B	Up	4.43	18.89	8.56	44.85	53.92	44.49	3,396	800-426-7969	Y
Invesco Oppenheimer Main Street Fund Class R	OMGNX	B-	C	B		5.73	22.17	11.41	39.95	53.83	46.99	9,574	800-659-1005	Y
JNL/WCM Focused International Equity Fund Class I		B-	C+	B	Up	10.06	25.52	12.23	49.54	53.72	16.08	1,456		Y
Goldman Sachs Growth Opportunities Fund Class A	GGOAX	B-	C+	B		6.92	27.61	15.15	52.21	53.64	18.07	1,315	800-526-7384	Y
Sterling Capital Equity Income Fund Class R6	STREX	B	C+	B+		4.25	15.98	13.68	52.96	53.61	20.88	1,774	800-228-1872	Y
TIAA-CREF Social Choice Equity Fund Retirement Class	TRSCX	B-	C	B		3.70	19.24	8.66	48.26	53.55	19.89	4,522	877-518-9161	Y
Nuveen Santa Barbara Dividend Growth Fund Class R3	NBDRX	B-	C+	B		5.64	18.96	12.22	42.53	53.36	43.72	3,357	312-917-8146	Y
Hartford Dividend and Growth HLS Fund Class IA	HIADX	B-	C	B+		3.60	16.44	10.06	45.10	53.36	23.01	3,214	888-843-7824	Y
PGIM Jennison Mid-Cap Growth Fund- Class R2	PEGEX	B-	C+	B		6.87	29.17	13.75	49.78	53.18	32.63	3,442	800-225-1852	Y
Franklin Rising Dividends Fund Class C	FRDTX	B-	C+	B	Down	4.80	21.37	12.84	43.24	53.05	65.27	19,187	650-312-2000	Y
Principal Equity Income Fund R-5 Class	PEIQX	B-	C	B+		5.38	17.89	11.13	45.49	53.04	32.08	7,444	800-787-1621	Y
Lord Abbett Calibrated Dividend Growth Fund Class R2	LAMQX	B-	C+	B+	Down	3.86	17.22	12.17	37.32	52.99	15.66	2,400	201-827-2000	Y
JNL/WCM Focused International Equity Fund		B-	C+	B	Up	9.98	25.33	11.95	48.77	52.93	16.08	1,456		Y
JPMorgan Equity Income Fund Class R3	OIEPX	B-	C	B+	Down	4.15	16.49	11.19	41.94	52.90	17.81	23,652	800-480-4111	Y
JPMorgan U.S. Research Enhanced Equity Fund Class A	JDEAX	B-	C	B		4.13	19.00	9.39	48.30	52.85	27.38	5,820	800-480-4111	Y
JPMorgan Equity Income Fund Class A	OIEIX	B-	C	B+	Down	4.20	16.53	11.17	41.87	52.83	17.83	23,652	800-480-4111	Y
WCM Focused International Growth Fund Investor Class	WCMRX	B-	C+	B	Up	9.89	24.96	11.74	48.25	52.83	17.32	8,740	949-380-0200	Y
The Hartford Dividend and Growth Fund Class R6	HDGVX	B-	C	B+		3.60	16.22	9.96	44.75	52.73	25.44	8,710	888-843-7824	Y
Invesco Equally-Weighted S&P 500 Fund Class Y	VADDX	B-	C	B		3.65	20.02	7.90	43.00	52.70	62.1	7,665	800-659-1005	Y
Goldman Sachs Growth Opportunities Fund Service Class	GGOSX	B-	C+	B		6.85	27.50	14.96	51.53	52.60	16.83	1,315	800-526-7384	Y
Franklin Small-Mid Cap Growth Fund Class R	FSMRX	B-	C+	B		5.33	28.21	14.12	54.95	52.46	33.95	3,324	650-312-2000	Y

		RATINGS				TOTAL RETURNS & PERFORMANCE					ASSETS		NEW INVESTORS	
Fund Name	Ticker Symbol	Overall Rating	Reward Rating	Risk Rating	Recent Up/ Downgrade	3-Month Total Return	6-Month Total Return	1-Year Total Return	3-Year Total Return	5-Year Total Return	NAV	Total Assets (MIL)	Telephone	Open to New Investors
The Hartford Capital Appreciation Fund Class R4	ITHSX	B-	C+	B		5.91	23.57	10.94	51.99	52.45	42.78	7,165	888-843-7824	Y
BNY Mellon Appreciation Fund, Inc. - Class I	DGIGX	B	B-	B	Up	5.85	21.52	12.17	50.77	52.20	32.03	1,640		Y
Wells Fargo Diversified Capital Builder Fund - Class C	EKBCX	B-	C	B	Up	4.31	18.90	9.71	38.88	52.20	10.55	1,087	800-222-8222	Y
Principal Equity Income Fund R-4 Class	PEIPX	B-	C	B+		5.32	17.80	10.97	44.91	52.08	32.03	7,444	800-787-1621	Y
The Hartford Dividend and Growth Fund Class R5	HDGTX	B-	C	B+		3.54	16.13	9.82	44.27	52.06	25.43	8,710	888-843-7824	Y
Principal Equity Income Fund Class J	PEIJX	B-	C	B+		5.34	17.84	10.99	44.99	52.04	32.11	7,444	800-787-1621	Y
Russell Investments Tax-Managed U.S. Large Cap Cls E	RTLEX	B-	C	B	Up	4.36	18.73	8.28	43.75	52.04	44.48	3,396	800-426-7969	Y
Russell Investments Tax-Managed U.S. Large Cap Cls A	RTLAX	B-	C	B	Up	4.36	18.71	8.27	43.76	52.02	44.02	3,396	800-426-7969	Y
Principal Equity Income Fund Class A	PQIAX	B-	C	B+		5.35	17.81	10.96	44.94	51.99	32.07	7,444	800-787-1621	Y
Fidelity® Export and Multinational Fund Class K	FEXKX	B-	C	B		3.53	16.06	8.69	39.30	51.89	20.81	1,680	617-563-7000	Y
Goldman Sachs Growth Opportunities Fund Class R	GGORX	B-	C+	B		6.90	27.51	14.89	51.18	51.79	16.87	1,315	800-526-7384	Y
Voya Growth and Income Portfolio Class I	IIVGX	B-	C+	B	Down	5.35	18.69	11.10	45.59	51.55	28.17	3,134	800-366-0066	Y
Sterling Capital Equity Income Fund Class A	BAEIX	B-	C+	B+	Down	4.11	15.79	13.26	51.53	51.48	20.81	1,774	800-228-1872	Y
Hartford Dividend and Growth HLS Fund Class IB	HDGBX	B-	C	B		3.48	16.32	9.79	44.00	51.43	22.87	3,214	888-843-7824	Y
MFS Value Fund Class R6	MEIKX	B-	C	B	Up	5.10	19.52	10.92	37.22	51.40	41.33	48,073	877-960-6077	Y
ClearBridge Dividend Strategy Fund Class C	SBPLX	B	B-	B+		5.32	19.89	14.36	41.79	51.01	24.16	6,398	877-721-1926	Y
Fidelity® Export and Multinational Fund	FEXPX	B-	C	B		3.52	16.01	8.59	38.82	50.99	20.86	1,680	617-563-7000	Y
JPMorgan Equity Income Fund Class R2	OIEFX	B-	C	B+	Down	4.10	16.34	10.89	40.76	50.95	17.74	23,652	800-480-4111	Y
Franklin Convertible Securities Fund Class C	FROTX	B	C+	A-		5.34	20.38	13.93	50.96	50.83	22.37	3,864	650-312-2000	Y
Goldman Sachs U.S. Equity Dividend & Premium Cls P	GSFPX	B-	C	B		3.07	16.03	6.54	34.55	50.83	13.01	2,934	800-526-7384	Y
Invesco Equally-Weighted S&P 500 Fund Class A	VADAX	B-	C	B		3.59	19.87	7.63	41.95	50.82	61.46	7,665	800-659-1005	Y
Neuberger Berman Large Cap Value Fund Class R6	NRLCX	B	C+	A-		4.33	15.66	14.80	54.02	50.65	31.07	1,707	212-476-9000	Y
MFS Value Fund Class R4	MEIJX	B-	C	B	Up	5.07	19.46	10.83	36.84	50.65	41.34	48,073	877-960-6077	Y
MFS Value Fund Class I	MEIIX	B-	C	B	Up	5.07	19.47	10.82	36.82	50.65	41.58	48,073	877-960-6077	Y
Principal Equity Income Fund R-3 Class	PEIOX	B-	C	B+		5.28	17.68	10.77	44.13	50.61	31.97	7,444	800-787-1621	Y
The Hartford Capital Appreciation Fund Class R3	ITHRX	B-	C+	B		5.82	23.36	10.61	50.60	50.14	41.24	7,165	888-843-7824	Y
Lord Abbett Calibrated Dividend Growth Fund Class C	LAMCX	B-	C+	B		3.81	16.97	11.77	35.76	50.12	15.29	2,400	201-827-2000	Y
Nicholas Fund	NICSX	B-	C	B		5.33	22.64	16.19	43.00	49.94	66.58	2,826	800-544-6547	Y
Hartford Capital Appreciation HLS Fund Class IA	HIACX	B-	C+	B		4.77	22.43	9.46	49.51	49.94	48.46	4,447	888-843-7824	Y
Goldman Sachs U.S. Equity Dividend & Premium Investor Cls	GVIRX	B-	C	B		3.04	15.94	6.38	34.12	49.91	13.02	2,934	800-526-7384	Y
The Hartford Dividend and Growth Fund Class R4	HDGSX	B-	C	B+		3.46	16.02	9.52	42.98	49.80	25.33	8,710	888-843-7824	Y
Voya Growth and Income Portfolio Class S	ISVGX	B-	C+	B		5.28	18.56	10.83	44.48	49.68	27.7	3,134	800-366-0066	Y
Sterling Capital Equity Income Fund Class R	BAERX	B-	C+	B+	Down	4.08	15.60	12.98	50.44	49.58	20.64	1,774	800-228-1872	Y
BlackRock Equity Dividend Fund Investor A Shares	MDDVX	B-	C	B	Up	4.67	16.34	7.30	39.75	49.58	21.39	19,552	800-441-7762	Y
Principal Equity Income Fund R-2 Class	PEINX	B-	C	B+		5.25	17.61	10.58	43.38	49.30	32.08	7,444	800-787-1621	Y
State Farm Growth Fund	STFGX	B-	C+	B+		4.57	17.07	12.69	37.54	49.22	83.44	5,231		Y
JPMorgan Equity Income Fund Class C	OINCX	B-	C	B+		4.06	16.29	10.66	39.76	49.06	17.47	23,652	800-480-4111	Y
Franklin Small-Mid Cap Growth Fund Class C	FRSIX	B-	C+	B		5.22	27.88	13.65	52.73	48.78	25.18	3,324	650-312-2000	Y
MFS Value Fund Class A	MEIAX	B-	C	B	Up	5.01	19.32	10.55	35.77	48.77	41.35	48,073	877-960-6077	Y
MFS Value Fund Class R3	MEIHX	B-	C	B	Up	5.01	19.31	10.54	35.79	48.76	41.18	48,073	877-960-6077	Y
MFS Value Fund Class 529A	EAVLX	B-	C	B	Up	5.00	19.30	10.52	35.73	48.70	41	48,073	877-960-6077	Y
The Hartford Equity Income Fund Class R6	HQIVX	B-	C+	B+		4.07	17.00	10.15	37.88	48.67	19.64	4,020	888-843-7824	Y
Voya Growth and Income Portfolio Class S2	IGISX	B-	C+	B		5.24	18.46	10.67	43.87	48.56	27.31	3,134	800-366-0066	Y
Principal Equity Income Fund R-1 Class	PIEMX	B-	C	B+		5.22	17.51	10.44	42.76	48.26	31.93	7,444	800-787-1621	Y
Voya Growth and Income Portfolio Class A	IAVGX	B-	C+	B		5.21	18.40	10.62	43.61	48.19	27.65	3,134	800-366-0066	Y
Hartford Capital Appreciation HLS Fund Class IB	HIBCX	B-	C+	B	Up	4.70	22.26	9.19	48.40	48.07	47.66	4,447	888-843-7824	Y
Goldman Sachs Growth Opportunities Fund Class C	GGOCX	B-	C+	B		6.74	27.10	14.29	48.86	47.98	10.13	1,315	800-526-7384	Y
The Hartford Equity Income Fund Class R5	HQITX	B-	C+	B+		4.05	16.91	10.05	37.47	47.88	19.59	4,020	888-843-7824	Y
Lord Abbett Affiliated Fund Class R6	LAFVX	B-	C	B+		3.85	15.82	8.62	40.25	47.86	15.06	6,252	201-827-2000	Y
Principal LargeCap Value Fund III Institutional Class	PLVIX	B-	C	B		4.47	16.37	8.92	40.09	47.84	16.56	2,138	800-787-1621	Y
BNY Mellon Income Stock Fund Class I	BMIIX	B-	C	B	Up	5.16	17.13	6.47	38.05	47.72	8.81	1,011	800-645-6561	Y
Wells Fargo Opportunity Fund - Class A	SOPVX	B-	C	B		4.12	20.84	7.95	47.58	47.66	42.37	1,721	800-222-8222	Y

		RATINGS				TOTAL RETURNS & PERFORMANCE					ASSETS		NEW INVESTORS	
Fund Name	Ticker Symbol	Overall Rating	Reward Rating	Risk Rating	Recent Up/ Downgrade	3-Month Total Return	6-Month Total Return	1-Year Total Return	3-Year Total Return	5-Year Total Return	NAV	Total Assets (MIL)	Telephone	Open to New Investors
The Hartford Dividend and Growth Fund Class R3	HDGRX	B-	C	B		3.37	15.82	9.12	41.65	47.49	25.14	8,710	888-843-7824	Y
Lord Abbett Affiliated Fund Class R5	LAFTX	B-	C	B+	Up	3.85	15.84	8.54	39.99	47.47	15.03	6,252	201-827-2000	Y
MFS Aggressive Growth Allocation Fund Class I	MIAGX	B-	C+	B		5.01	20.69	8.65	44.30	47.29	24.73	1,882	877-960-6077	Y
MFS Aggressive Growth Allocation Fund Class R4	MAALX	B-	C+	B		5.03	20.68	8.63	44.26	47.28	24.39	1,882	877-960-6077	Y
Lord Abbett Affiliated Fund Class F	LAAFX	B-	C	B+	Up	3.84	15.78	8.53	39.57	47.14	14.96	6,252	201-827-2000	Y
Lord Abbett Affiliated Fund Class F3	LTFOX	B-	C	B+		3.85	15.80	8.68	39.95	47.05	15.07	6,252	201-827-2000	Y
MFS Value Fund Class R2	MVRRX	B-	C	B	Up	4.92	19.15	10.27	34.78	46.93	40.92	48,073	877-960-6077	Y
American Funds 2050 Target Date Retirement Fund® Class R-6	RFITX	B-	C	B+	Up	3.29	15.90	6.09	41.89	46.81	15.67	9,824	800-421-4225	Y
Fidelity® Mid-Cap Stock Fund Class K	FKMCX	B-	C	B		4.85	18.50	6.34	44.86	46.69	35.25	7,698	617-563-7000	Y
American Funds 2055 Target Date Retirement Fund® Class R-6	RFKTX	B-	C	B+	Up	3.26	15.87	5.99	41.72	46.62	19.63	5,208	800-421-4225	Y
Multi-Manager Value Strategies Fund Institutional Class	CZMVX	B-	C	B	Up	4.67	18.14	8.85	42.33	46.55	13.69	3,055	800-345-6611	Y
Principal Equity Income Fund Class C	PEUCX	B-	C	B+		5.16	17.38	10.19	41.75	46.48	31.21	7,444	800-787-1621	Y
JNL/S&P Managed Aggressive Growth Fund Class I		B-	C	B	Up	4.44	19.42	7.78	47.25	46.44	24.65	2,272		Y
Fidelity® Dividend Growth Fund Class K	FDGKX	B-	C	B		3.75	16.68	9.15	40.47	46.33	29.3	6,902	617-563-7000	Y
American Funds 2050 Target Date Retirement Fund® Class R-5	REITX	B-	C	B+	Up	3.21	15.85	5.94	41.55	46.32	15.71	9,824	800-421-4225	Y
American Funds 2055 Target Date Retirement Fund® Class R-5	REKTX	B-	C	B+	Up	3.26	15.83	5.99	41.58	46.28	19.61	5,208	800-421-4225	Y
Hartford Capital Appreciation HLS Fund Class IC	HCPCX	B-	C	B	Up	4.65	22.12	8.92	47.27	46.26	47.92	4,447	888-843-7824	Y
American Funds 2045 Target Date Retirement Fund® Class R-6	RFHTX	B-	C	B+	Up	3.29	15.71	6.08	41.39	46.24	15.98	11,753	800-421-4225	Y
American Funds 2050 Target Date Retirement Fund® Class F-2	FBITX	B-	C	B+	Up	3.24	15.76	5.90	41.37	46.01	15.57	9,824	800-421-4225	Y
Lord Abbett Affiliated Fund Class R4	LAFSX	B-	C	B	Up	3.81	15.72	8.24	38.93	45.98	14.93	6,252	201-827-2000	Y
American Funds 2055 Target Date Retirement Fund® Class F-2	FBJTX	B-	C	B+	Up	3.23	15.83	5.92	41.36	45.94	19.46	5,208	800-421-4225	Y
American Funds 2055 Target Date Retirement Fund® Cls R-5E	RHJTX	B-	C	B+	Up	3.30	15.82	5.88	41.25	45.93	19.4	5,208	800-421-4225	Y
American Funds 2050 Target Date Retirement Fund® Cls R-5E	RHITX	B-	C	B+	Up	3.25	15.79	5.88	41.24	45.93	15.54	9,824	800-421-4225	Y
Lord Abbett Affiliated Fund Class A	LAFFX	B-	C	B	Up	3.81	15.70	8.24	38.89	45.93	14.95	6,252	201-827-2000	Y
American Funds 2045 Target Date Retirement Fund® Class R-5	REHTX	B-	C	B+	Up	3.28	15.72	5.99	41.10	45.92	16.04	11,753	800-421-4225	Y
Principal LargeCap Value Fund III R-5 Class	PPSRX	B-	C	B		4.38	16.23	8.65	39.02	45.87	16.68	2,138	800-787-1621	Y
Multi-Manager Value Strategies Fund Class A	CDEIX	B-	C	B	Up	4.64	17.98	8.65	41.66	45.86	13.84	3,055	800-345-6611	Y
Fidelity® Mid-Cap Stock Fund	FMCSX	B-	C	B	Up	4.81	18.39	6.22	44.31	45.83	35.23	7,698	617-563-7000	Y
The Hartford Equity Income Fund Class R4	HQISX	B-	C	B+		3.94	16.71	9.71	36.22	45.69	19.49	4,020	888-843-7824	Y
JNL/S&P Managed Aggressive Growth Fund Class A		B-	C	B	Up	4.38	19.26	7.44	46.47	45.66	24.52	2,272		Y
American Funds 2045 Target Date Retirement Fund® Class F-2	FBHTX	B-	C	B+	Up	3.24	15.72	5.99	40.98	45.49	15.9	11,753	800-421-4225	Y
Fidelity® Dividend Growth Fund	FDGFX	B-	C	B		3.67	16.62	9.03	40.01	45.47	29.32	6,902	617-563-7000	Y
Principal LargeCap Value Fund III Class J	PLVJX	B-	C	B		4.41	16.25	8.62	38.82	45.45	16.31	2,138	800-787-1621	Y
MFS Aggressive Growth Allocation Fund Class A	MAAGX	B-	C+	B	Up	4.92	20.47	8.31	43.19	45.40	24.3	1,882	877-960-6077	Y
MFS Value Fund Class 529B	EBVLX	B-	C	B	Up	4.81	18.99	10.28	34.31	45.40	40.55	48,073	877-960-6077	Y
MFS Aggressive Growth Allocation Fund Class R3	MAAHX	B-	C+	B	Up	4.91	20.50	8.32	43.16	45.38	24.1	1,882	877-960-6077	Y
American Funds 2045 Target Date Retirement Fund® Cls R-5E	RHHTX	B-	C	B+	Up	3.19	15.63	5.87	40.70	45.34	15.83	11,753	800-421-4225	Y
USAA Income Stock Fund R6 Shares	URISX	B-	C	B+	Down	3.34	15.65	9.79	35.50	45.30	19.66	2,891	800-235-8396	Y
MFS Aggressive Growth Allocation Fund Class 529A	EAGTX	B-	C+	B	Up	4.95	20.52	8.33	43.05	45.17	24.13	1,882	877-960-6077	Y
Principal LargeCap Value Fund III R-4 Class	PPSSX	B-	C	B	Up	4.41	16.22	8.56	38.59	45.10	16.55	2,138	800-787-1621	Y
George Putnam Balanced Fund Class R6	PGEJX	B	C+	A-		4.80	15.98	10.51	36.76	45.05	20.46	1,292	617-292-1000	Y
Franklin Equity Income Fund Class A	FISEX	B-	C	B+	Down	3.83	15.69	9.84	37.96	44.70	25.47	2,260	650-312-2000	Y
George Putnam Balanced Fund Class R5	PGELX	B	C+	A-		4.80	15.96	10.46	36.54	44.54	20.56	1,292	617-292-1000	Y
Columbia Large Cap Value Fund Institutional 2 Class	RSEDX	B-	C	B	Up	4.48	19.07	8.61	38.36	44.54	13.58	1,984	800-345-6611	Y
JNL/T. Rowe Price Value Fund Class I		B-	C	B	Up	4.75	18.83	9.16	40.53	44.40	16.97	4,398		Y
American Funds 2055 Target Date Retirement Fund® Class A	AAMTX	B-	C	B+	Up	3.18	15.63	5.62	40.39	44.34	19.45	5,208	800-421-4225	Y
Lord Abbett Affiliated Fund Class R3	LAFRX	B-	C	B	Up	3.74	15.55	8.10	38.01	44.33	14.95	6,252	201-827-2000	Y
American Funds 2050 Target Date Retirement Fund® Class A	AALTX	B-	C	B+	Up	3.17	15.66	5.68	40.43	44.32	15.58	9,824	800-421-4225	Y
George Putnam Balanced Fund Class Y	PGEYX	B	C+	A-		4.72	15.86	10.39	36.29	44.24	20.45	1,292	617-292-1000	Y
Old Westbury All Cap Core Fund	OWACX	B-	B-	B		5.95	22.33	11.46	52.26	44.22	18.51	1,989	212-708-9100	Y
American Funds 2050 Target Date Retirement Fund® Class R-4	RDITX	B-	C	B+	Up	3.18	15.71	5.67	40.30	44.21	15.54	9,824	800-421-4225	Y
American Funds 2055 Target Date Retirement Fund® Class F-1	FAJTX	B-	C	B+	Up	3.20	15.67	5.64	40.31	44.20	19.34	5,208	800-421-4225	Y

		RATINGS				TOTAL RETURNS & PERFORMANCE					ASSETS		NEW INVESTORS	
Fund Name	Ticker Symbol	Overall Rating	Reward Rating	Risk Rating	Recent Up/ Downgrade	3-Month Total Return	6-Month Total Return	1-Year Total Return	3-Year Total Return	5-Year Total Return	NAV	Total Assets (MIL)	Telephone	Open to New Investors
American Funds 2055 Target Date Retirement Fund® Class R-4	RDJTX	B-	C	B+	Up	3.18	15.67	5.63	40.29	44.13	19.41	5,208	800-421-4225	Y
American Funds 2050 Target Date Retirement Fund® Class F-1	FAITX	B-	C	B+	Up	3.19	15.69	5.61	40.34	44.09	15.48	9,824	800-421-4225	Y
American Funds 2045 Target Date Retirement Fund® Class A	AAHTX	B-	C	B+	Up	3.18	15.56	5.67	39.94	43.92	15.89	11,753	800-421-4225	Y
Principal LargeCap Value Fund III R-3 Class	PPSFX	B-	C	B	Up	4.38	16.10	8.35	37.81	43.71	17.37	2,138	800-787-1621	Y
MFS Aggressive Growth Allocation Fund Class R2	MAWAX	B-	C	B	Up	4.89	20.35	8.08	42.14	43.59	23.77	1,882	877-960-6077	Y
MFS Global Equity Fund Class R6	MWEMX	B-	C+	B	Up	5.54	21.94	11.71	44.15	43.58	46.23	3,024	877-960-6077	Y
The Hartford Equity Income Fund Class R3	HQIRX	B-	C	B		3.88	16.57	9.34	34.90	43.44	19.46	4,020	888-843-7824	Y
TIAA-CREF Lifecycle Index 2050 Fund Advisor Class	TLLHX	B-	C	B	Up	3.60	16.76	6.79	41.19	43.39	20.96	1,571	877-518-9161	Y
JPMorgan Value Advantage Fund Class R5	JVARX	B-	C	B	Up	3.84	17.90	7.40	39.43	43.27	35.62	10,840	800-480-4111	Y
Fidelity® Series Large Cap Value Index Fund	FIOOX	B-	C	B		3.86	17.18	8.60	36.03	43.22	12.89	4,259	617-563-7000	Y
Columbia Convertible Securities Fund Institutional 2 Class	COCRX	B	C+	A-	Down	5.32	18.54	11.32	49.63	43.20	21.87	1,276	800-345-6611	Y
Franklin Equity Income Fund Class R	FREIX	B-	C	B+	Down	3.77	15.58	9.58	37.02	42.96	25.47	2,260	650-312-2000	Y
MFS Global Equity Fund Class R4	MWELX	B-	C+	B	Up	5.51	21.88	11.60	43.78	42.89	45.12	3,024	877-960-6077	Y
MFS Global Equity Fund Class I	MWEIX	B-	C+	B	Up	5.52	21.89	11.60	43.77	42.89	46.21	3,024	877-960-6077	Y
TIAA-CREF Lifecycle Index 2045 Fund Advisor Class	TLMHX	B-	C	B	Up	3.62	16.64	6.85	40.69	42.79	20.88	2,060	877-518-9161	Y
JPMorgan Value Advantage Fund Class R4	JVAQX	B-	C	B	Up	3.82	17.81	7.27	38.88	42.70	35.52	10,840	800-480-4111	Y
JNL/T. Rowe Price Value Fund Class A		B-	C	B	Up	4.65	18.70	8.83	39.54	42.69	16.18	4,398		Y
TIAA-CREF Lifecycle Index 2050 Fund Premier Class	TLLPX	B-	C	B	Up	3.62	16.77	6.75	40.92	42.65	20.88	1,571	877-518-9161	Y
TIAA-CREF Large-Cap Value Index Fund Advisor Class	THCVX	B-	C	B	Up	3.79	17.06	8.29	35.22	42.52	19.96	6,476	877-518-9161	Y
George Putnam Balanced Fund Class A	PGEOX	B	C+	A-		4.67	15.73	10.10	35.29	42.42	20.37	1,292	617-292-1000	Y
Principal LargeCap Value Fund III R-2 Class	PPSNX	B-	C	B	Up	4.28	15.96	8.13	36.96	42.35	16.56	2,138	800-787-1621	Y
JNL/S&P Managed Growth Fund Class I		B-	C	B+	Up	4.15	17.81	7.53	42.96	42.13	20.83	5,416		Y
TIAA-CREF Lifecycle Index 2045 Fund Premier Class	TLMPX	B-	C	B	Up	3.58	16.59	6.73	40.35	41.98	20.8	2,060	877-518-9161	Y
TIAA-CREF Lifecycle Index 2050 Fund Retirement Class	TLLRX	B-	C	B	Up	3.58	16.67	6.62	40.47	41.90	20.78	1,571	877-518-9161	Y
Eaton Vance Large-Cap Value Fund Class A	EHSTX	B-	C+	B		5.78	20.20	10.88	39.75	41.88	19.54	1,726		Y
TIAA-CREF Lifecycle Index 2040 Fund Advisor Class	TLZHX	B-	C	B+	Up	3.59	15.96	6.98	39.38	41.56	20.77	3,096	877-518-9161	Y
ClearBridge Large Cap Value Fund Class 1	LCLIX	B-	C	B		5.36	19.40	9.90	37.47	41.51	33.04	1,676	877-721-1926	Y
Principal LargeCap Value Fund III R-1 Class	PESAX	B-	C	B	Up	4.30	15.88	8.07	36.56	41.50	16.49	2,138	800-787-1621	Y
JNL/S&P Managed Growth Fund Class A		B-	C	B+	Up	4.06	17.59	7.19	42.21	41.38	20.72	5,416		Y
TIAA-CREF Lifecycle Index 2045 Fund Retirement Class	TLMRX	B-	C	B	Up	3.60	16.54	6.65	39.94	41.34	20.71	2,060	877-518-9161	Y
TIAA-CREF Large-Cap Value Index Fund Retirement Class	TRCVX	B-	C	B	Up	3.72	16.90	8.14	34.58	41.13	20.33	6,476	877-518-9161	Y
MFS Global Equity Fund Class R3	MWEHX	B-	C+	B	Up	5.45	21.72	11.32	42.69	41.12	44.65	3,024	877-960-6077	Y
MFS Global Equity Fund Class A	MWEFX	B-	C+	B	Up	5.44	21.71	11.30	42.67	41.11	44.96	3,024	877-960-6077	Y
MFS Growth Allocation Fund Class I	MGWIX	B	C+	B+	Up	4.86	18.48	8.85	37.98	40.98	21.54	5,102	877-960-6077	Y
JPMorgan Value Advantage Fund Class R3	JVAPX	B-	C	B	Up	3.78	17.67	7.00	37.87	40.96	35.08	10,840	800-480-4111	Y
MFS Growth Allocation Fund Class R4	MAGJX	B	C+	B+	Up	4.86	18.51	8.89	37.99	40.93	21.32	5,102	877-960-6077	Y
Fidelity® Four-in-One Index Fund	FFNOX	B-	C	B+	Up	3.86	16.39	6.87	38.37	40.91	46.42	6,296	617-563-7000	Y
Fidelity Advisor Freedom® 2045 Fund Class Z6	FCGLX	B-	C	B	Up	3.93	17.44	6.06	41.07	40.77	11.25	1,452	617-563-7000	Y
Fidelity Advisor Freedom® 2050 Fund Class Z6	FVGLX	B-	C	B	Up	3.91	17.33	6.03	40.94	40.73	11.23	1,178	617-563-7000	Y
T. Rowe Price Retirement 2050 Fund Advisor Class	PARFX	B-	C	B+	Up	3.68	16.99	5.86	40.48	40.72	15.21	7,437	410-345-2000	Y
Fidelity Advisor Freedom® 2040 Fund Class Z6	FKGLX	B-	C	B	Up	3.87	17.37	5.99	41.14	40.72	14.4	2,233	617-563-7000	Y
TIAA-CREF Lifecycle Index 2040 Fund Premier Class	TLPRX	B-	C	B+	Up	3.60	15.91	6.92	39.01	40.70	20.68	3,096	877-518-9161	Y
George Putnam Balanced Fund Class R	PGPRX	B	C+	A-		4.63	15.60	9.82	34.27	40.68	20.3	1,292	617-292-1000	Y
T. Rowe Price Retirement 2045 Fund Advisor Class	PARLX	B-	C	B+	Up	3.61	16.94	5.83	40.39	40.62	18.08	8,839	410-345-2000	Y
T. Rowe Price Retirement 2055 Fund Advisor Class	PAROX	B-	C	B	Up	3.62	16.96	5.82	40.39	40.62	15.44	3,834	410-345-2000	Y
Fidelity Freedom® Index 2050 Fund Investor Class	FIPFX	B-	C	B	Up	3.80	16.94	6.87	39.82	40.60	20.11	2,652	617-563-7000	Y
Fidelity Advisor Freedom® 2035 Fund Class Z6	FHGLX	B-	C	B	Up	3.91	16.82	6.11	40.86	40.59	13.52	2,474	617-563-7000	Y
Fidelity Freedom® Index 2055 Fund Investor Class	FDEWX	B-	C	B	Up	3.80	16.92	6.92	39.88	40.58	15.88	1,167	617-563-7000	Y
Hartford Checks and Balances Fund Class R5	HCKTX	B	C+	A-		4.17	15.55	9.75	35.04	40.56	9.42	1,555	888-843-7824	Y
Fidelity Freedom® Index 2045 Fund Investor Class	FIOFX	B-	C	B	Up	3.78	16.97	6.89	39.90	40.56	20.02	2,954	617-563-7000	Y
Fidelity Freedom® Index 2040 Fund Investor Class	FBIFX	B-	C	B	Up	3.80	16.97	6.88	39.84	40.53	19.88	4,515	617-563-7000	Y
Fidelity Freedom® Index 2035 Fund Investor Class	FIHFX	B-	C	B+	Up	3.79	16.43	7.06	39.67	40.43	19.74	4,405	617-563-7000	Y

		RATINGS				TOTAL RETURNS & PERFORMANCE					ASSETS		NEW INVESTORS	
Fund Name	Ticker Symbol	Overall Rating	Reward Rating	Risk Rating	Recent Up/ Downgrade	3-Month Total Return	6-Month Total Return	1-Year Total Return	3-Year Total Return	5-Year Total Return	NAV	Total Assets (MIL)	Telephone	Open to New Investors
Columbia Large Cap Value Fund Class R	RDEIX	B-	C	B	Up	4.36	18.79	8.04	36.09	40.41	13.49	1,984	800-345-6611	Y
JPMorgan Value Advantage Fund Class A	JVAAX	B-	C	B	Up	3.77	17.68	6.99	37.76	40.13	35.46	10,840	800-480-4111	Y
ClearBridge Large Cap Value Fund Class A	SINAX	B-	C	B	Up	5.31	19.28	9.66	36.62	40.09	33.06	1,676	877-721-1926	Y
MFS Aggressive Growth Allocation Fund Class B	MBAGX	B-	C	B	Up	4.77	20.07	7.57	40.03	40.09	23.93	1,882	877-960-6077	Y
Fidelity Advisor Freedom® 2050 Fund Class Z	FIJRX	B-	C	B	Up	3.87	17.32	5.73	40.30	40.08	11.19	1,178	617-563-7000	Y
MFS Aggressive Growth Allocation Fund Class C	MCAGX	B-	C	B	Up	4.77	20.08	7.55	40.07	40.07	23.68	1,882	877-960-6077	Y
TIAA-CREF Lifecycle Index 2040 Fund Retirement Class	TLZRX	B-	C	B+	Up	3.56	15.86	6.78	38.58	40.05	20.6	3,096	877-518-9161	Y
T. Rowe Price Retirement 2040 Fund Advisor Class	PARDX	B-	C	B+	Up	3.64	16.61	5.91	39.77	40.05	26.46	15,448	410-345-2000	Y
Fidelity Advisor Freedom® 2040 Fund Class Z	FIJPX	B-	C	B	Up	3.81	17.26	5.79	40.46	40.04	14.34	2,233	617-563-7000	Y
Fidelity Advisor Freedom® 2050 Fund Class I	FFFPX	B-	C	B	Up	3.83	17.21	5.70	40.25	40.04	11.25	1,178	617-563-7000	Y
MFS Aggressive Growth Allocation Fund Class R1	MAAFX	B-	C	B	Up	4.76	20.04	7.54	40.05	40.03	23.3	1,882	877-960-6077	Y
Eaton Vance Large-Cap Value Fund Class R	ERSTX	B-	C	B		5.67	20.04	10.63	38.66	40.02	19.48	1,726		Y
Fidelity Advisor Freedom® 2045 Fund Class Z	FIJQX	B-	C	B	Up	3.84	17.27	5.80	40.31	40.02	11.19	1,452	617-563-7000	Y
Fidelity Advisor Freedom® 2035 Fund Class Z	FIJOX	B-	C	B	Up	3.79	16.72	5.88	40.27	40.00	13.45	2,474	617-563-7000	Y
Fidelity Advisor Freedom® 2035 Fund Class I	FITHX	B-	C	B	Up	3.83	16.71	5.84	40.21	39.94	13.54	2,474	617-563-7000	Y
Fidelity Advisor Freedom® 2040 Fund Class I	FIFFX	B-	C	B	Up	3.84	17.24	5.70	40.34	39.92	14.43	2,233	617-563-7000	Y
Fidelity Advisor Freedom® 2045 Fund Class I	FFFIX	B-	C	B	Up	3.76	17.22	5.72	40.21	39.91	11.26	1,452	617-563-7000	Y
MFS Aggressive Growth Allocation Fund Class 529C	ECAAX	B-	C	B	Up	4.76	20.04	7.49	39.88	39.76	23.3	1,882	877-960-6077	Y
MFS Aggressive Growth Allocation Fund Class 529B	EBAAX	B-	C	B	Up	4.74	20.02	7.47	39.82	39.69	23.62	1,882	877-960-6077	Y
Vanguard Target Retirement 2045 Fund Investor Shares	VTIVX	B-	C	B	Up	3.50	16.13	5.89	38.61	39.46	23.32	26,144	877-662-7447	Y
JPMorgan Value Advantage Fund Class R2	JGAQX	B-	C	B	Up	3.70	17.50	6.75	37.06	39.43	35.24	10,840	800-480-4111	Y
Vanguard Target Retirement 2050 Fund Investor Shares	VFIFX	B-	C	B	Up	3.47	16.12	5.85	38.52	39.41	37.52	18,853	877-662-7447	Y
MFS Global Equity Fund Class R2	MEQRX	B-	C+	B	Up	5.38	21.57	11.05	41.64	39.35	43.62	3,024	877-960-6077	Y
BlackRock LifePath® Index 2055 Fund Investor P Shares	LIVPX	B-	C	B	Up	3.09	16.85	6.41	37.26	39.34	15.77	1,157	800-441-7762	Y
American Century NT Large Company Value Fund G Class	ACLLX	B-	C	B		4.33	17.78	9.56	36.25	39.33	11.14	1,603	800-444-4015	Y
MFS Growth Allocation Fund Class R3	MAGEX	B	C+	B+	Up	4.80	18.36	8.58	36.93	39.23	21.14	5,102	877-960-6077	Y
Vanguard Target Retirement 2055 Fund Investor Shares	VFFVX	B-	C	B	Up	3.48	16.13	5.87	38.56	39.20	40.73	9,695	877-662-7447	Y
BlackRock LifePath® Index 2050 Fund Investor P Shares	LIPPX	B-	C	B	Up	3.07	16.88	6.39	37.21	39.20	15.46	2,524	800-441-7762	Y
MFS Growth Allocation Fund Class A	MAGWX	B	C+	B+	Up	4.76	18.30	8.58	36.88	39.19	21.33	5,102	877-960-6077	Y
Vanguard Target Retirement 2060 Fund Investor Shares	VTTSX	B-	C	B	Up	3.48	16.14	5.85	38.50	39.17	35.97	4,079	877-662-7447	Y
Columbia Convertible Securities Fund Class R	CVBRX	B	C+	A-		5.17	18.24	10.70	47.09	39.08	21.66	1,276	800-345-6611	Y
BlackRock LifePath® Index 2055 Fund Investor A Shares	LIVAX	B-	C	B	Up	3.09	16.87	6.36	37.11	39.01	15.78	1,157	800-441-7762	Y
Principal Strategic Asset Mgmt Strategic Growth Inst Cls	PSWIX	B-	C	B	Up	4.20	17.65	6.50	38.10	39.00	17.61	1,875	800-787-1621	Y
ClearBridge Large Cap Value Fund Class A2	LIVVX	B-	C	B	Up	5.27	19.17	9.51	36.02	38.98	33.03	1,676	877-721-1926	Y
MFS Growth Allocation Fund Class 529A	EAGWX	B	C+	B+	Up	4.75	18.28	8.56	36.74	38.94	21.15	5,102	877-960-6077	Y
T. Rowe Price Retirement 2045 Fund Class R	RRTRX	B-	C	B	Up	3.53	16.80	5.57	39.35	38.94	17.86	8,839	410-345-2000	Y
BlackRock LifePath® Index 2050 Fund Investor A Shares	LIPAX	B-	C	B	Up	3.14	16.89	6.42	37.15	38.93	15.48	2,524	800-441-7762	Y
T. Rowe Price Retirement 2050 Fund Class R	RRTFX	B-	C	B	Up	3.57	16.83	5.52	39.41	38.91	15.06	7,437	410-345-2000	Y
American Century Inv One Choice 2050 Port R6 Cls	ARFEX	B-	C	B	Up	3.66	16.27	5.70	35.63	38.88	12.43	1,121	800-444-4015	Y
BlackRock LifePath® Index 2045 Fund Investor P Shares	LIHPX	B-	C	B	Up	3.17	16.58	6.50	36.76	38.83	15.21	2,339	800-441-7762	Y
T. Rowe Price Retirement 2055 Fund Class R	RRTVX	B-	C	B	Up	3.51	16.84	5.48	39.31	38.80	15.33	3,834	410-345-2000	Y
Fidelity® Equity-Income Fund Class K	FEIKX	B-	C	B		3.75	17.27	9.37	37.25	38.69	58.33	6,371	617-563-7000	Y
T. Rowe Price Retirement 2035 Fund Advisor Class	PARKX	B-	C	B+	Up	3.55	15.91	6.04	37.73	38.52	18.65	13,494	410-345-2000	Y
BlackRock LifePath® Index 2045 Fund Investor A Shares	LIHAX	B-	C	B	Up	3.10	16.51	6.45	36.60	38.47	15.22	2,339	800-441-7762	Y
Fidelity Advisor Freedom® 2050 Fund Class A	FFFLX	B-	C	B	Up	3.81	17.06	5.53	39.27	38.33	11.17	1,178	617-563-7000	Y
T. Rowe Price Retirement 2040 Fund Class R	RRTDX	B-	C	B+	Up	3.55	16.40	5.63	38.75	38.32	26.25	15,448	410-345-2000	Y
Fidelity Advisor Freedom® 2045 Fund Class A	FFFZX	B-	C	B	Up	3.72	17.05	5.45	39.18	38.26	11.18	1,452	617-563-7000	Y
Fidelity Advisor Freedom® 2040 Fund Class A	FAFFX	B-	C	B	Up	3.81	17.12	5.52	39.27	38.24	14.33	2,233	617-563-7000	Y
MainStay MacKay Convertible Fund Investor Class	MCINX	B-	C	B+	Down	3.38	16.54	7.43	37.31	38.15	17.79	1,433	800-624-6782	Y
Fidelity Advisor Freedom® 2035 Fund Class A	FATHX	B-	C	B	Up	3.80	16.59	5.58	39.15	38.14	13.43	2,474	617-563-7000	Y
Principal LifeTime 2050 Fund Institutional Class	PPLIX	B-	C	B	Up	3.97	17.96	5.90	38.76	37.97	15.43	2,274	800-787-1621	Y
Fidelity® Equity-Income Fund	FEQIX	B-	C	B		3.72	17.20	9.26	36.82	37.93	58.36	6,371	617-563-7000	Y

		RATINGS				TOTAL RETURNS & PERFORMANCE					ASSETS		NEW INVESTORS	
Fund Name	Ticker Symbol	Overall Rating	Reward Rating	Risk Rating	Recent Up/ Downgrade	3-Month Total Return	6-Month Total Return	1-Year Total Return	3-Year Total Return	5-Year Total Return	NAV	Total Assets (MIL.)	Telephone	Open to New Investors
Principal Strategic Asset Mgmt Strategic Growth Cls J	PSWJX	B-	C	B	Up	4.13	17.54	6.35	37.42	37.61	17.38	1,875	800-787-1621	Y
Principal Strat Asset Mgmt Cons Growth Inst Cls	PCWIX	B-	C	B+	Up	3.87	15.55	6.82	35.73	37.57	16.63	3,032	800-787-1621	Y
MFS Growth Allocation Fund Class R2	MGALX	B-	C+	B+		4.72	18.21	8.34	35.93	37.50	20.83	5,102	877-960-6077	Y
KP Retirement Path 2045 Fund Institutional Shares	KPRGX	B-	C	B+	Up	3.59	15.57	5.48	39.42	37.25	11.8	1,071		Y
Principal Strategic Asset Mgmt Strategic Growth R-5 Cls	PSGFX	B-	C	B	Up	4.12	17.46	6.24	37.08	37.24	17.42	1,875	800-787-1621	Y
PIMCO StocksPLUS® International (U.S. Dollar-Hedged) Cls A	PIPAX	B-	C	B	Up	3.91	16.76	4.10	46.04	37.19	7.49	3,084	866-746-2602	Y
BlackRock LifePath® Index 2040 Fund Investor P Shares	LIKPX	B-	C	B+	Up	3.13	15.73	6.47	34.91	37.09	14.84	5,278	800-441-7762	Y
BlackRock LifePath® Index 2040 Fund Investor A Shares	LIKAX	B-	C	B+	Up	3.21	15.84	6.49	34.80	36.87	14.86	5,278	800-441-7762	Y
John Hancock Funds II Equity Income Fund Class NAV		B-	C	B	Up	4.31	16.63	5.16	38.17	36.85	18.6	1,796	800-225-5913	Y
T. Rowe Price Retirement 2035 Fund Class R	RRTPX	B-	C	B+	Up	3.54	15.77	5.74	36.64	36.83	18.42	13,494	410-345-2000	Y
ClearBridge Large Cap Value Fund Class R	LCBVX	B-	C	B	Up	5.19	18.97	9.03	34.96	36.78	33.1	1,676	877-721-1926	Y
Voya Large Cap Value Portfolio Class I	IPEIX	B-	C	B	Up	4.38	16.90	8.14	35.50	36.64	12.38	1,091	800-366-0066	Y
JPMorgan SmartRetirement® 2045 Fund Class R5	JSAIX	B-	C	B	Up	3.52	16.26	5.44	35.69	36.60	21.2	4,379	800-480-4111	Y
JPMorgan SmartRetirement® 2050 Fund Class R5	JTSIX	B-	C	B	Up	3.51	16.20	5.44	35.63	36.59	21.25	3,936	800-480-4111	Y
Voya Large Cap Value Portfolio R6	VLCRX	B-	C	B	Up	4.38	16.91	8.24	35.79	36.58	12.37	1,091	800-366-0066	Y
Principal Strategic Asset Mgmt Strategic Growth Cls A	SACAX	B-	C	B	Up	4.08	17.38	6.12	36.72	36.55	18.1	1,875	800-787-1621	Y
JPMorgan SmartRetirement® 2055 Fund Class R5	JFFIX	B-	C	B	Up	3.50	16.18	5.45	35.56	36.54	23.86	1,800	800-480-4111	Y
Fidelity Advisor Freedom® 2050 Fund Class M	FFFQX	B-	C	B	Up	3.66	16.86	5.20	38.11	36.53	11.09	1,178	617-563-7000	Y
Fidelity Advisor Freedom® 2040 Fund Class M	FTFFX	B-	C	B	Up	3.72	16.92	5.26	38.27	36.52	14.24	2,233	617-563-7000	Y
Principal Strategic Asset Mgmt Strategic Growth R-4 Cls	PSGLX	B-	C	B	Up	4.10	17.41	6.16	36.64	36.50	17.48	1,875	800-787-1621	Y
Fidelity Advisor Freedom® 2045 Fund Class M	FFFTX	B-	C	B	Up	3.71	16.94	5.17	38.22	36.47	11.07	1,452	617-563-7000	Y
John Hancock Funds II Equity Income Fund Class 1	JIEMX	B-	C	B	Up	4.24	16.58	5.05	37.91	36.43	18.62	1,796	800-225-5913	Y
Fidelity Advisor Freedom® 2035 Fund Class M	FTTHX	B-	C	B	Up	3.72	16.36	5.32	38.07	36.40	13.28	2,474	617-563-7000	Y
JPMorgan SmartRetirement® 2040 Fund Class R5	SMTIX	B-	C	B	Up	3.56	15.90	5.47	35.42	36.26	22.16	6,144	800-480-4111	Y
Principal LifeTime 2040 Fund Institutional Class	PTDIX	B-	C	B	Up	3.85	16.87	6.04	36.28	36.14	15.36	3,821	800-787-1621	Y
Principal LifeTime 2050 Fund R-5 Class	PTEFX	B-	C	B	Up	3.92	17.72	5.56	37.59	36.13	15.36	2,274	800-787-1621	Y
JPMorgan SmartRetirement® 2045 Fund Class R4	JSAQX	B-	C	B	Up	3.50	16.14	5.27	35.12	36.03	21.13	4,379	800-480-4111	Y
JPMorgan SmartRetirement® 2050 Fund Class R4	JTSQX	B-	C	B	Up	3.49	16.14	5.26	35.04	35.99	21.18	3,936	800-480-4111	Y
JPMorgan SmartRetirement® 2055 Fund Class R4	JFFQX	B-	C	B	Up	3.48	16.11	5.32	34.99	35.97	23.81	1,800	800-480-4111	Y
MFS Global Equity Fund Class B	MWEBX	B-	C	B	Up	5.25	21.26	10.48	39.53	35.93	41.28	3,024	877-960-6077	Y
MFS Global Equity Fund Class C	MWECX	B-	C	B	Up	5.23	21.28	10.50	39.51	35.93	39.38	3,024	877-960-6077	Y
MFS Global Equity Fund Class R1	MWEGX	B-	C	B	Up	5.24	21.28	10.49	39.50	35.92	40.34	3,024	877-960-6077	Y
Principal LifeTime 2050 Fund Class J	PFLJX	B-	C	B	Up	3.95	17.84	5.60	37.72	35.83	14.97	2,274	800-787-1621	Y
John Hancock Funds II Multimanager 2035 Lifetime Cls 1	JLHOX	B-	C	B+	Up	3.23	15.76	4.90	36.91	35.71	11.16	1,042	800-225-5913	Y
John Hancock Funds II Multimanager 2035 Lifetime Cls R5	JLHHX	B-	C	B+	Up	3.23	15.76	4.88	36.88	35.68	11.16	1,042	800-225-5913	Y
JPMorgan SmartRetirement® 2040 Fund Class R4	SMTQX	B-	C	B	Up	3.54	15.80	5.35	34.83	35.67	22.06	6,144	800-480-4111	Y
T. Rowe Price Equity Income Fund Advisor Class	PAFDX	B-	C	B	Up	4.26	16.53	5.22	37.32	35.65	31.19	20,244	410-345-2000	Y
Principal LifeTime 2050 Fund Class A	PPEAX	B-	C	B	Up	3.88	17.71	5.50	37.16	35.43	15.5	2,274	800-787-1621	Y
Principal LifeTime 2050 Fund R-4 Class	PTESX	B-	C	B	Up	3.86	17.65	5.46	37.13	35.29	15.32	2,274	800-787-1621	Y
Principal Strategic Asset Mgmt Strategic Growth R-3 Cls	PSGPX	B-	C	B	Up	4.02	17.30	5.93	35.84	35.20	17.33	1,875	800-787-1621	Y
JNL Aggressive Growth Allocation Fund Class I		B-	C	B	Up	4.27	17.84	5.80	37.24	34.94	13.67	1,491		Y
Voya Large Cap Value Portfolio Class S	IPESX	B-	C	B	Up	4.27	16.74	7.86	34.49	34.92	12.2	1,091	800-366-0066	Y
JPMorgan SmartRetirement® 2050 Fund Class A	JTSAX	B-	C	B	Up	3.46	16.11	5.17	34.59	34.92	21.14	3,936	800-480-4111	Y
JPMorgan SmartRetirement® 2045 Fund Class A	JSAAX	B-	C	B	Up	3.46	16.09	5.16	34.61	34.89	21.1	4,379	800-480-4111	Y
JPMorgan SmartRetirement® 2055 Fund Class A	JFFAX	B-	C	B	Up	3.44	16.04	5.17	34.51	34.83	23.8	1,800	800-480-4111	Y
Principal LifeTime 2035 Fund Institutional Class	LTIUX	B-	C	B+	Up	3.83	16.06	6.17	34.49	34.75	12.18	1,256	800-787-1621	Y
Principal LifeTime 2040 Fund Class J	PTDJX	B-	C	B	Up	3.81	16.72	5.88	35.59	34.62	15.22	3,821	800-787-1621	Y
JPMorgan SmartRetirement® 2040 Fund Class A	SMTAX	B-	C	B	Up	3.46	15.69	5.15	34.32	34.53	22.03	6,144	800-480-4111	Y
Principal LifeTime 2040 Fund R-5 Class	PTDPX	B-	C	B	Up	3.80	16.71	5.77	35.28	34.36	15.28	3,821	800-787-1621	Y
JPMorgan SmartRetirement® 2045 Fund Class R3	JSAPX	B-	C	B	Up	3.45	16.02	5.05	34.12	34.35	21.03	4,379	800-480-4111	Y
JPMorgan SmartRetirement® 2050 Fund Class R3	JTSPX	B-	C	B	Up	3.46	15.98	5.06	34.03	34.31	21.07	3,936	800-480-4111	Y
JPMorgan SmartRetirement® 2055 Fund Class R3	JFFPX	B-	C	B	Up	3.43	15.97	5.06	33.95	34.26	23.73	1,800	800-480-4111	Y

Fund Name	Ticker Symbol	Overall Rating	Reward Rating	Risk Rating	Recent Up/ Downgrade	3-Month Total Return	6-Month Total Return	1-Year Total Return	3-Year Total Return	5-Year Total Return	NAV	Total Assets (MIL)	Telephone	Open to New Investors
		RATINGS				TOTAL RETURNS & PERFORMANCE					ASSETS		NEW INVESTORS	
JNL Aggressive Growth Allocation Fund Class A		B-	C	B	Up	4.21	17.64	5.42	36.54	34.24	13.6	1,491		Y
John Hancock Funds II Multimanager 2035 Lifetime Cls R4	JLHGX	B-	C	B+	Up	3.14	15.68	4.65	36.09	34.23	11.14	1,042	800-225-5913	Y
Principal LifeTime 2050 Fund R-3 Class	PTERX	B-	C	B	Up	3.88	17.64	5.30	36.40	34.14	15.23	2,274	800-787-1621	Y
MFS Growth Allocation Fund Class B	MBGWX	B-	C+	B+	Up	4.60	17.91	7.80	33.89	34.11	21.13	5,102	877-960-6077	Y
Voya Large Cap Value Portfolio Class S2	IPETX	B-	C	B	Up	4.26	16.73	7.79	34.05	34.08	12.21	1,091	800-366-0066	Y
MFS Growth Allocation Fund Class R1	MAGMX	B-	C+	B+	Up	4.60	17.88	7.77	33.92	34.05	20.43	5,102	877-960-6077	Y
Optimum Large Cap Value Fund Institutional Class	OILVX	B-	C	B	Up	4.53	17.99	9.27	35.98	33.99	16.59	1,637		Y
Principal Strategic Asset Mgmt Strategic Growth R-2 Cls	PSGVX	B-	C	B	Up	4.01	17.24	5.74	35.16	33.97	17.34	1,875	800-787-1621	Y
T. Rowe Price Equity Income Fund Class R	RRFDX	B-	C	B	Up	4.13	16.29	4.89	36.13	33.78	31.12	20,244	410-345-2000	Y
Principal LifeTime 2040 Fund Class A	PTDAX	B-	C	B	Up	3.79	16.67	5.73	34.90	33.70	15.06	3,821	800-787-1621	Y
Principal LifeTime 2040 Fund R-4 Class	PTDSX	B-	C	B	Up	3.83	16.65	5.71	34.85	33.64	15.18	3,821	800-787-1621	Y

Section V:
High Performance Stock Mutual Funds

Investment Ratings and analysis of High Performance Stock Mutual Funds. Funds are listed in order by their five-year returns and overall rating.

Section V: Contents

This section contains Weiss Investment Ratings, key rating factors, and summary financial data for our selections for "High Performance Stock Mutual Funds." If your priority is to achieve the highest return, balanced with the amount of risk we have chosen the top mutual funds with the best financial performance. Not just "Buy" rated these funds have hit our demanding criteria of being in the top 25% of total returns for funds over a number of time-periods. Keep in mind that past performance alone is not always a guide to future performance. Funds are listed in order by their five-year returns and overall rating.

Fund Name

Describes the fund's assets, regions of investments and investment strategies. Many funds have similar names, so you want to make sure the fund you look up is really the one you are interested in evaluating.

Ticker Symbol

An arrangement of characters (usually letters) representing a particular security listed on an exchange or otherwise traded publicly. When a company issues securities to the public marketplace, it selects an available ticker symbol for its securities which investors use to place trade orders. Every listed security has a unique ticker symbol, facilitating the vast array of trade orders that flow through the financial markets every day. If a ticker symbol is not assigned to a particular fund, the International Securities Identification Number (ISIN) is displayed.

RATINGS

Overall Rating

The Weiss rating measured on a scale from A to E based on each fund's risk and performance. See the preceding section, "What Our Ratings Mean," for an explanation of each letter grade rating.

Reward Rating

This is based on the total return over a period of up to five years, including net asset value and price growth. The total return figure is stated net of the expenses and fees charged by the fund. Based on proprietary modeling the individual components of the risk and reward ratings are calculated and weighted and the final rating is generated.

Risk Rating

This is includes the risk ratings of component stocks where applicable and also includes the financial stability of the fund, turnover where applicable, together with the level of volatility as measured by the fund's daily returns over a period of up to five years. Funds with greater stability are considered less risky and receive a higher risk rating. Funds with greater volatility are considered riskier, and will receive a lower risk rating. In addition to considering the fund's volatility, the risk rating also considers an assessment of the valuation and quality of a fund's holdings.

Recent Upgrade/Downgrade
An "Up" or "Down" indicates that the Weiss Mutual Fund rating has changed since the publication of the last print edition. If a fund has had a rating change since March 31, 2019, the change is identified with an "Up" or "Down."

TOTAL RETURNS & PERFORMANCE

3-Month Total Return
The rate of return on an investment over three months that includes interest, capital gains, dividends and distributions realized.

6-Month Total Return
The rate of return on an investment over six months that includes interest, capital gains, dividends and distributions realized.

1-Year Total Return
The rate of return on an investment over one year that includes interest, capital gains, dividends and distributions realized.

3-Year Total Return
The rate of return on an investment over three years that includes interest, capital gains, dividends and distributions realized.

5-Year Total Return
The rate of return on an investment over five years that includes interest, capital gains, dividends and distributions realized.

ASSETS

NAV (Net Asset Value)
A fund's price per share. The value is calculated by dividing the total value of all the securities in the portfolio, less any liabilities, by the number of fund shares outstanding.

Total Assets (MIL)
The total of all assets listed on the institution's balance sheet. This figure primarily consists of loans, investments, and fixed assets. Total Assets are displayed in millions.

NEW INVESTORS

Telephone
The company's phone number.

Open to New Investors
Indicates whether the fund accepts investments from those who are not existing investors. A "Y" in this column identifies that the fund accepts new investors. No data in this column indicates that the fund is closed to new investors. The fund may be closed to new investors because the fund's asset base is getting too large to effectively execute its investing style. Although, the fund may be closed, in most cases, existing investors are able to add to their holdings.

		RATINGS				TOTAL RETURNS & PERFORMANCE					ASSETS		NEW INVESTORS	
Fund Name	Ticker Symbol	Overall Rating	Reward Rating	Risk Rating	Recent Up/ Downgrade	3-Month Total Return	6-Month Total Return	1-Year Total Return	3-Year Total Return	5-Year Total Return	NAV	Total Assets (MIL)	Telephone	Open to New Investors
BlackRock Technology Opportunities Fund Investor A Shares	BGSAX	B-	B	B-	Down	5.78	30.72	13.31	123.22	149.42	31.01	1,831	800-441-7762	Y
BlackRock Technology Opportunities Fund Class R Shares	BGSRX	B-	B-	B-	Down	5.69	30.52	13.01	121.49	146.03	31.3	1,831	800-441-7762	Y
Morgan Stanley Insight Fund Class A	CPOAX	B-	B-	B	Up	9.05	38.27	25.76	130.63	143.84	44.87	2,027	855-332-5306	Y
Columbia Global Technology Growth Institutional 2 Cls	CTHRX	B-	C+	B-	Down	5.17	26.95	11.08	105.39	143.42	37.63	1,512	800-345-6611	Y
BlackRock Technology Opportunities Fund Investor C Shares	BGSCX	B-	B-	B-	Down	5.59	30.24	12.48	118.31	139.77	26.15	1,831	800-441-7762	Y
Fidelity® Select IT Services Portfolio	FBSOX	B	B+	B		5.68	33.93	20.91	99.10	139.65	71.43	3,670	617-563-7000	Y
Morgan Stanley Insight Fund Class C	MSCMX	B-	B-	B	Up	8.85	37.81	24.88	125.49	134.85	31.53	2,027	855-332-5306	Y
Fidelity® Select Software & IT Services Portfolio	FSCSX	B	B-	B		6.23	27.05	15.44	101.09	134.79	18.52	7,272	617-563-7000	Y
JNL/Mellon Capital Information Technology Sector Cls I		B-	B-	B-	Down	5.37	28.35	14.09	99.60	126.02	19.42	3,007		Y
JNL/Mellon Capital Information Technology Sector Cls A		B-	B-	B-	Down	5.26	28.07	13.66	97.86	123.09	18.98	3,007		Y
Morgan Stanley Inst Fund, Inc. Growth Portfolio Cls A	MSEGX	B-	C+	B-		7.16	29.41	15.15	102.15	122.83	50.69	7,525	855-332-5306	Y
Fidelity Advisor® Growth Opportunities Fund Class Z	FZAHX	B	C+	B	Down	3.92	26.75	22.29	108.07	120.89	90.29	6,286	617-563-7000	Y
Transamerica Capital Growth Fund Class I2		B-	C+	B-	Up	7.89	28.02	14.47	104.00	120.26	15.12	2,036	888-233-4339	Y
Fidelity Advisor® Growth Opportunities Fund I Class	FAGCX	B	C+	B	Down	3.88	26.68	22.14	107.31	119.51	89.53	6,286	617-563-7000	Y
Federated Kaufmann Small Cap Fund Class R Shares	FKKSX	B	B	B		5.29	30.76	18.50	113.80	118.85	42.12	3,149	800-341-7400	Y
VALIC Company I Science & Technology Fund	VCSTX	B-	C+	B-	Down	4.41	28.47	11.03	94.59	118.59	27.91	1,488		Y
Fidelity Advisor® Growth Opportunities Fund Class A	FAGAX	B	C+	B	Down	3.80	26.49	21.80	105.57	116.44	82.68	6,286	617-563-7000	Y
Franklin DynaTech Fund Class A	FKDNX	B-	B-	B-	Down	6.64	31.22	17.13	97.19	115.57	85.11	7,895	650-312-2000	Y
Fidelity Advisor® Growth Opportunities Fund Class M	FAGOX	B	C+	B	Down	3.76	26.36	21.53	104.17	113.99	81.87	6,286	617-563-7000	Y
Virtus KAR Small-Cap Core Fund Class R6	VSCRX	B	B+	B		5.23	28.89	12.97	89.69	113.78	39.03	1,508	800-243-1574	Y
Franklin DynaTech Fund Class R	FDNRX	B-	B-	B-	Down	6.57	31.05	16.84	95.73	112.91	82.5	7,895	650-312-2000	Y
Fidelity Advisor® Growth Opportunities Fund Class C	FACGX	B-	C+	B	Down	3.61	26.02	20.88	100.98	108.48	70.5	6,286	617-563-7000	Y
Franklin DynaTech Fund Class C	FDYNX	B-	B-	B-	Down	6.45	30.73	16.24	92.83	107.65	70.61	7,895	650-312-2000	Y
BlackRock Mid-Cap Growth Equity Portfolio Inv A Shares	BMGAX	B	B+	B		9.22	33.22	18.59	91.17	103.59	25.66	4,326	800-441-7762	Y
BlackRock Mid-Cap Growth Equity Portfolio Class R	BMRRX	B	B+	B		9.20	33.11	18.38	89.75	101.08	25.23	4,326	800-441-7762	Y
BlackRock Mid-Cap Growth Equity Portfolio Inv C Shares	BMGCX	B	B+	B		9.02	32.77	17.70	87.04	96.31	19.94	4,326	800-441-7762	Y
Wells Fargo Growth Fund - Class R6	SGRHX	B-	B-	B-	Down	7.37	30.02	14.39	79.47	87.34	45	4,621	800-222-8222	Y
VY® T. Rowe Price Diversified Mid Cap Growth Port Cls R6	VYRIX	B	B-	B		7.11	28.98	16.70	65.19	81.10	12.95	1,109	800-366-0066	Y
VY® T. Rowe Price Diversified Mid Cap Growth Port Cls I	IAXIX	B-	B-	B	Down	7.11	29.11	16.81	65.21	80.95	12.95	1,109	800-366-0066	Y
Federated Kaufmann Large Cap Fund Class R6	KLCSX	B	B-	B		7.28	28.31	17.97	66.62	80.76	27.69	3,453	800-341-7400	Y
Eventide Gilead Class N	ETGLX	B	B	B		3.13	33.80	16.43	91.18	80.47	41.76	2,652		Y
Glenmede Quantitative U.S. Large Cap Growth Eq Port	GTLLX	B-	C+	B	Down	5.59	22.43	11.32	59.18	80.09	31.88	3,492	800-442-8299	Y
Eventide Gilead Class A	ETAGX	B	B	B		3.10	33.75	16.35	90.85	80.06	41.57	2,652		Y
Wells Fargo Discovery Fund - Class R6	WFDRX	B-	B	C+		10.86	38.27	17.91	79.22	80.03	38.37	2,582	800-222-8222	Y
Brown Advisory Small-Cap Growth Fund Investor Shares	BIASX	B-	B-	B-	Down	7.79	32.59	14.40	59.02	79.90	22.13	1,347	800-540-6807	Y
Invesco Oppenheimer Discovery Mid Cap Growth Fund Y	OEGYX	B-	B-	C+		9.00	31.41	14.91	59.30	79.23	24.93	1,557	800-659-1005	Y
VY® T. Rowe Price Diversified Mid Cap Growth Port Cls S	IAXSX	B-	B-	B	Down	7.06	28.97	16.53	63.92	78.71	12.42	1,109	800-366-0066	Y
Brown Advisory Small-Cap Growth Fund Advisor Shares	BASAX	B-	B-	B-	Down	7.74	32.43	14.07	57.79	77.74	21.15	1,347	800-540-6807	Y
VY® T. Rowe Price Diversified Mid Cap Growth Port Cls S2	IAXTX	B-	B-	B	Down	6.98	28.76	16.32	63.16	77.31	11.64	1,109	800-366-0066	Y
Invesco Oppenheimer Discovery Mid Cap Growth Fund A	OEGAX	B-	B-	C+	Up	8.96	31.26	14.69	58.20	77.12	22	1,557	800-659-1005	Y
John Hancock Funds II Mid Cap Stock Fund Class NAV	JHMSX	B-	B-	B-	Down	5.25	32.19	15.05	73.82	76.95	22.83	1,643	800-225-5913	Y
John Hancock Funds II Mid Cap Stock Fund Class 1	JIMSX	B-	B-	B-	Down	5.27	32.18	14.97	73.59	76.54	22.55	1,643	800-225-5913	Y
VY® T. Rowe Price Diversified Mid Cap Growth Port Cls A	IAXAX	B-	B-	B	Down	7.03	28.69	16.20	62.75	76.38	11.57	1,109	800-366-0066	Y
Wells Fargo Discovery Fund - Class A	WFDAX	B-	B	C+		10.74	38.02	17.44	76.95	76.21	34.74	2,582	800-222-8222	Y
Federated Kaufmann Large Cap Fund Class R Shares	KLCKX	B	B-	B		7.08	27.89	17.13	63.18	74.47	25.4	3,453	800-341-7400	Y
Eventide Gilead Class C	ETCGX	B	B	B-		2.89	33.27	15.50	86.63	73.38	38.37	2,652		Y
JNL/JPMorgan MidCap Growth Fund Class I		B-	B-	B-	Down	6.69	31.21	16.40	68.42	71.67	39.51	2,373		Y
JNL/JPMorgan MidCap Growth Fund Class A		B-	B-	B-	Down	6.62	31.06	16.06	67.13	69.67	38.31	2,373		Y
Wells Fargo Discovery Fund - Class C	WDSCX	B-	B-	C+		10.53	37.48	16.53	73.02	69.66	29.6	2,582	800-222-8222	Y
Ivy Mid Cap Growth Fund Class I	IYMIX	B-	C+	B	Down	4.90	28.59	14.41	71.09	69.60	28.87	4,525		Y
JPMorgan Mid Cap Growth Fund Class R5	JMGFX	B-	B-	B-	Down	6.57	30.88	15.88	67.16	69.10	38.9	4,565	800-480-4111	Y
JPMorgan Mid Cap Growth Fund Class R4	JMGQX	B-	B-	B-	Down	6.53	30.76	15.65	66.17	67.63	38.3	4,565	800-480-4111	Y

		RATINGS				TOTAL RETURNS & PERFORMANCE					ASSETS		NEW INVESTORS	
Fund Name	Ticker Symbol	Overall Rating	Reward Rating	Risk Rating	Recent Up/ Downgrade	3-Month Total Return	6-Month Total Return	1-Year Total Return	3-Year Total Return	5-Year Total Return	NAV	Total Assets (MIL)	Telephone	Open to New Investors
Ivy Mid Cap Growth Fund Class Y	WMGYX	B-	C+	B	Down	4.78	28.34	13.98	69.63	67.36	27.8	4,525		Y
Ivy Mid Cap Growth Fund Class A	WMGAX	B-	C+	B	Down	4.78	28.32	13.98	69.48	67.00	26.5	4,525		Y
JNL Multi-Manager Small Cap Growth Fund Class I		B-	B-	C+	Down	7.18	31.32	10.99	84.60	66.98	32.24	2,375		Y
Ivy Science and Technology Fund Class I	ISTIX	B-	B	B-		9.36	35.04	15.97	93.25	66.48	79.3	7,179		Y
Ivy Mid Cap Growth Fund Class E	IMCEX	B-	C+	B	Down	4.79	28.27	13.88	69.36	66.35	25.77	4,525		Y
MFS New Discovery Fund Class R6	MNDKX	B-	C+	B-	Down	9.05	32.85	13.42	80.16	66.34	32.27	1,451	877-960-6077	Y
JPMorgan Mid Cap Growth Fund Class R3	JMGPX	B-	B-	B-		6.47	30.61	15.38	64.97	65.59	38.01	4,565	800-480-4111	Y
MFS New Discovery Fund Class R4	MNDJX	B-	C+	B-	Down	9.00	32.75	13.29	79.72	65.48	30.03	1,451	877-960-6077	Y
JPMorgan Mid Cap Growth Fund Class A	OSGIX	B-	B-	B-		6.46	30.61	15.37	64.93	65.35	32.94	4,565	800-480-4111	Y
MFS New Discovery Fund Class I	MNDIX	B-	C+	B-	Down	9.01	32.73	13.29	79.59	65.32	31.91	1,451	877-960-6077	Y
JNL Multi-Manager Small Cap Growth Fund Class A		B-	B-	C+	Down	7.10	31.17	10.69	83.30	65.04	30.59	2,375		Y
Columbia Mid Cap Growth Fund Institutional 2 Class	CMGVX	B-	B-	B		6.46	27.22	11.62	55.32	64.92	26.36	1,744	800-345-6611	Y
American Century Heritage Fund R6 Class	ATHDX	B-	B-	B		7.07	29.64	16.57	55.39	64.86	23.92	4,738	800-444-4015	Y
Ivy Science And Technology Fund Class Y	WSTYX	B-	B	C+		9.31	34.92	15.73	91.93	64.54	75.45	7,179		Y
Ivy Science And Technology Fund Class A	WSTAX	B-	B	C+		9.30	34.89	15.71	91.86	64.27	71.05	7,179		Y
JPMorgan Mid Cap Growth Fund Class R2	JMGZX	B-	C+	B-		6.39	30.43	15.09	63.83	63.72	35.91	4,565	800-480-4111	Y
Ivy Science and Technology Fund Class E	ISTEX	B-	B	C+		9.27	34.82	15.55	91.34	63.41	70.35	7,179		Y
MFS New Discovery Fund Class A	MNDAX	B-	C+	B-	Down	8.94	32.57	13.02	78.26	63.30	28.12	1,451	877-960-6077	Y
American Century Heritage Fund Y Class	ATHYX	B-	B-	B		7.02	29.64	16.57	54.94	63.26	23.92	4,738	800-444-4015	Y
MFS New Discovery Fund Class R3	MNDHX	B-	C+	B-	Down	8.92	32.59	12.99	78.17	63.21	28.07	1,451	877-960-6077	Y
American Century Heritage Fund R5 Class	ATHGX	B-	C+	B		7.02	29.58	16.38	54.43	62.73	23.61	4,738	800-444-4015	Y
PIMCO StocksPLUS® Absolute Return Fund Class A	PTOAX	B-	C	B		4.47	20.52	9.19	54.56	62.59	10.41	2,030	866-746-2602	Y
Cohen & Steers Real Estate Securities Fund, Inc. Class Z	CSZIX	B-	C+	B-		2.89	20.40	13.73	21.82	62.33	16.62	5,566	212-832-3232	Y
Ivy Science and Technology Fund Class R	WSTRX	B-	B-	C+		9.20	34.65	15.31	89.89	61.66	68.69	7,179		Y
Principal MidCap Growth Fund III Institutional Class	PPIMX	B-	C+	B-		7.32	28.14	13.30	57.57	61.60	12.02	1,126	800-787-1621	Y
MFS New Discovery Fund Class R2	MNDRX	B-	C+	B-	Down	8.85	32.39	12.72	76.87	61.23	25.95	1,451	877-960-6077	Y
JPMorgan Mid Cap Growth Fund Class C	OMGCX	B-	C+	B-		6.33	30.28	14.78	62.43	61.20	25.34	4,565	800-480-4111	Y
Columbia Mid Cap Growth Fund Class R	CMGRX	B-	C+	B-		6.30	26.86	10.99	52.58	60.02	22.76	1,744	800-345-6611	Y
Principal MidCap Growth Fund III R-5 Class	PPQPX	B-	C+	B-		7.19	27.99	13.02	56.35	59.54	12.07	1,126	800-787-1621	Y
Principal MidCap Growth Fund III Class J	PPQJX	B-	C+	B-		7.12	27.80	12.88	55.66	58.56	9.47	1,126	800-787-1621	Y
Principal MidCap Growth Fund III R-4 Class	PPQSX	B-	C+	B-		7.19	27.87	12.90	55.57	58.42	11.47	1,126	800-787-1621	Y
TIAA-CREF Real Estate Securities Fund Advisor Class	TIRHX	B	B-	B	Up	2.88	21.13	13.88	25.53	56.95	17.32	2,461	877-518-9161	Y
Principal MidCap Growth Fund III R-3 Class	PPQMX	B-	C+	B-		7.06	27.71	12.64	54.75	56.88	11.06	1,126	800-787-1621	Y
Principal Real Estate Securities Fund Institutional Class	PIREX	B-	C+	B		3.11	21.57	14.51	21.46	56.66	26.2	4,636	800-787-1621	Y
PIMCO StocksPLUS® Absolute Return Fund Class C	PSOCX	B-	C	B	Up	4.18	20.06	8.36	51.02	56.49	9.35	2,030	866-746-2602	Y
TIAA-CREF Real Estate Securities Fund Premier Class	TRRPX	B-	B-	B		2.87	21.10	13.84	25.35	56.37	17.32	2,461	877-518-9161	Y
TIAA-CREF Real Estate Securities Fund Retirement Class	TRRSX	B-	B-	B		2.84	21.07	13.73	24.99	55.63	18.05	2,461	877-518-9161	Y
Principal Real Estate Securities Fund R-5 Class	PREPX	B-	C+	B		3.10	21.51	14.38	20.84	55.24	25.27	4,636	800-787-1621	Y
Principal Real Estate Securities Fund Class J	PREJX	B-	C+	B		3.07	21.46	14.27	20.64	54.67	25.39	4,636	800-787-1621	Y
Franklin Small-Mid Cap Growth Fund Class A	FRSGX	B-	C+	B		5.42	28.37	14.38	56.09	54.36	37.51	3,324	650-312-2000	Y
Principal Real Estate Securities Fund R-4 Class	PRETX	B-	C+	B		3.04	21.38	14.17	20.36	54.22	25.21	4,636	800-787-1621	Y
Principal Real Estate Securities Fund Class A	PRRAX	B-	C+	B		3.02	21.34	14.15	20.17	53.70	26.18	4,636	800-787-1621	Y
Principal Real Estate Securities Fund R-3 Class	PRERX	B-	C+	B		3.00	21.27	13.98	19.71	52.83	25.51	4,636	800-787-1621	Y
Franklin Small-Mid Cap Growth Fund Class R	FSMRX	B-	C+	B		5.33	28.21	14.12	54.95	52.46	33.95	3,324	650-312-2000	Y
Principal Real Estate Securities Fund R-2 Class	PRENX	B-	C+	B		2.94	21.19	13.80	19.05	51.46	24.86	4,636	800-787-1621	Y
Hartford Capital Appreciation HLS Fund Class IA	HIACX	B-	C+	B		4.77	22.43	9.46	49.51	49.94	48.46	4,447	888-843-7824	Y
EQ/Janus Enterprise Portfolio Class K		B-	C	B	Down	3.27	14.41	9.60	63.10	49.15		1,035	877-222-2144	Y
Neuberger Berman Large Cap Value Fund Class A	NPNAX	B	C+	A-		4.18	15.40	14.40	52.86	48.86	31.09	1,707	212-476-9000	Y
Franklin Small-Mid Cap Growth Fund Class C	FRSIX	B-	C+	B		5.22	27.88	13.65	52.73	48.78	25.18	3,324	650-312-2000	Y
Hartford Capital Appreciation HLS Fund Class IB	HIBCX	B-	C+	B	Up	4.70	22.26	9.19	48.40	48.07	47.66	4,447	888-843-7824	Y
EQ/Janus Enterprise Portfolio Class IA		B-	C	B	Down	3.18	14.22	9.34	61.85	47.27		1,035	877-222-2144	Y
EQ/Janus Enterprise Portfolio Class IB		B-	C	B	Down	3.17	14.20	9.31	61.90	47.24		1,035	877-222-2144	Y

Fund Name	Ticker Symbol	RATINGS: Overall Rating	Reward Rating	Risk Rating	Recent Up/ Downgrade	TOTAL RETURNS & PERFORMANCE: 3-Month Total Return	6-Month Total Return	1-Year Total Return	3-Year Total Return	5-Year Total Return	ASSETS: NAV	Total Assets (MIL)	NEW INVESTORS: Telephone	Open to New Investors
Neuberger Berman Large Cap Value Fund Class R3	NPNRX	B	C+	A-		4.14	15.25	14.12	51.56	46.82	31.13	1,707	212-476-9000	Y
Fidelity® Mid-Cap Stock Fund Class K	FKMCX	B-	C	B		4.85	18.50	6.34	44.86	46.69	35.25	7,698	617-563-7000	Y
Hartford Capital Appreciation HLS Fund Class IC	HCPCX	B-	C	B	Up	4.65	22.12	8.92	47.27	46.26	47.92	4,447	888-843-7824	Y
Fidelity® Mid-Cap Stock Fund	FMCSX	B-	C	B	Up	4.81	18.39	6.22	44.31	45.83	35.23	7,698	617-563-7000	Y
MFS Global Real Estate Fund Class R4	MGLMX	B	B-	B+		2.80	17.90	11.28	23.93	42.51	17.25	2,002	877-960-6077	Y
Federated MDT Large Cap Value Fund Class R6	FSTLX	B-	C	B		2.61	15.73	6.72	39.16	38.90	27.2	1,161	800-341-7400	Y
Franklin Mutual Shares Fund Class A	TESIX	B-	C	B	Up	3.21	14.33	4.22	25.73	23.29	27.27	12,661	650-312-2000	Y

Section VI: Low Volatility Stock Mutual Funds

Investment Ratings and analysis of Low Volatility Stock Mutual Funds. Funds are listed in order by their beta (lowest to highest) and overall rating.

Section VI: Contents

This section contains Weiss Investment Ratings, key rating factors, and summary financial data for our selections for "Low Volatility Stock Mutual Funds". If ultimate safety is your top priority, the top recommended mutual funds with the lowest volatility may be your best bet. These funds may have lower performance ratings than some other funds, but can provide a safe place for your savings. Funds are listed in order by their beta (lowest to highest) and overall rating.

Fund Name

Describes the fund's assets, regions of investments and investment strategies. Many funds have similar names, so you want to make sure the fund you look up is really the one you are interested in evaluating.

Ticker Symbol

An arrangement of characters (usually letters) representing a particular security listed on an exchange or otherwise traded publicly. When a company issues securities to the public marketplace, it selects an available ticker symbol for its securities which investors use to place trade orders. Every listed security has a unique ticker symbol, facilitating the vast array of trade orders that flow through the financial markets every day. If a ticker symbol is not assigned to a particular fund, the International Securities Identification Number (ISIN) is displayed.

RATINGS

Overall Rating

The Weiss rating measured on a scale from A to E based on each fund's risk and performance. See the preceding section, "What Our Ratings Mean," for an explanation of each letter grade rating.

Reward Rating

This is based on the total return over a period of up to five years, including net asset value and price growth. The total return figure is stated net of the expenses and fees charged by the fund. Based on proprietary modeling the individual components of the risk and reward ratings are calculated and weighted and the final rating is generated.

Risk Rating

This is includes the risk ratings of component stocks where applicable and also includes the financial stability of the fund, turnover where applicable, together with the level of volatility as measured by the fund's daily returns over a period of up to five years. Funds with greater stability are considered less risky and receive a higher risk rating. Funds with greater volatility are considered riskier, and will receive a lower risk rating. In addition to considering the fund's volatility, the risk rating also considers an assessment of the valuation and quality of a fund's holdings.

Recent Upgrade/Downgrade

An "Up" or "Down" indicates that the Weiss Mutual Fund rating has changed since the publication of the last print edition. If a fund has had a rating change since March 31, 2019, the change is identified with an "Up" or "Down."

TOTAL RETURNS & PERFORMANCE

3-Month Total Return
The rate of return on an investment over three months that includes interest, capital gains, dividends and distributions realized.

6-Month Total Return
The rate of return on an investment over six months that includes interest, capital gains, dividends and distributions realized.

1-Year Total Return
The rate of return on an investment over one year that includes interest, capital gains, dividends and distributions realized.

3-Year Total Return
The rate of return on an investment over three years that includes interest, capital gains, dividends and distributions realized.

5-Year Total Return
The rate of return on an investment over five years that includes interest, capital gains, dividends and distributions realized.

3-Year Beta
A three year measure of volatility, or systematic risk, of a security in comparison to the market as a whole. A beta of less than 1 means that the security will be less volatile than the market, a beta larger than 1 means more volatility. Beta value cannot be calculated if less than 24 months of pricing is available.

ASSETS

NAV (Net Asset Value)
A fund's price per share. The value is calculated by dividing the total value of all the securities in the portfolio, less any liabilities, by the number of fund shares outstanding.

Total Assets (MIL)
The total of all assets listed on the institution's balance sheet. This figure primarily consists of loans, investments, and fixed assets. Total Assets are displayed in millions.

NEW INVESTORS

Telephone
The company's phone number.

Open to New Investors
Indicates whether the fund accepts investments from those who are not existing investors. A "Y" in this column identifies that the fund accepts new investors. No data in this column indicates that the fund is closed to new investors. The fund may be closed to new investors because the fund's asset base is getting too large to effectively execute its investing style. Although, the fund may be closed, in most cases, existing investors are able to add to their holdings.

		RATINGS				TOTAL RETURNS & PERFORMANCE						ASSETS		NEW INVESTORS	
Fund Name	Ticker Symbol	Overall Rating	Reward Rating	Risk Rating	Recent Up/ Downgrade	3-Month Total Return	6-Month Total Return	1-Year Total Return	3-Year Total Return	5-Year Total Return	3-Year Beta	NAV	Total Assets (MIL)	Telephone	Open to New Investors
Franklin Managed Income Fund Class R	FBFQX	B	C+	A		2.85	11.67	8.52	24.85	26.91	0.04	12.58	3,561	650-312-2000	Y
Franklin Managed Income Fund Class A	FBLAX	B	C+	A		2.92	11.74	8.72	25.78	28.41	0.05	12.54	3,561	650-312-2000	Y
Franklin Managed Income Fund Class C	FBMCX	B	C+	A-		2.68	11.37	7.93	22.96	23.85	0.06	12.42	3,561	650-312-2000	Y
Berwyn Income Fund	BERIX	B-	C	A-		2.20	6.25	3.49	14.20	13.91	0.07	13.15	1,146	610-296-1400	Y
American Funds College 2021 Fund Class 529F1	CTOFX	B-	C	B+		2.15	5.07	6.11	9.19	14.54	0.07	11.39	1,949	800-421-4225	Y
American Funds College 2021 Fund Class 529-A	CTOAX	B-	C	B	Up	1.97	4.99	5.77	8.40	13.28	0.07	11.35	1,949	800-421-4225	Y
American Funds College 2021 Fund Class 529-E	CTOEX	B-	C	B	Up	1.98	4.92	5.58	7.69	11.97	0.07	11.3	1,949	800-421-4225	Y
Russell Investments LifePoints Balanced Strategy Cls A	RBLAX	B-	C	A-	Up	1.97	9.36	2.96	19.46	19.19	0.15	10.86	1,516	800-426-7969	Y
Russell Investments LifePoints Balanced Strategy Cls R4	RBLUX	B-	C	A-	Up	2.05	9.43	2.92	19.32	19.04	0.15	10.9	1,516	800-426-7969	Y
Russell Investments LifePoints Balanced Strategy Cls E	RBLEX	B-	C	B+	Up	1.96	9.30	2.86	19.12	18.63	0.15	10.92	1,516	800-426-7969	Y
Russell Investments LifePoints Balanced Strategy Cls R1	RBLRX	B-	C	A-	Up	2.03	9.42	3.18	20.14	20.52	0.16	11.03	1,516	800-426-7969	Y
Russell Investments LifePoints Balanced Strategy Cls S	RBLSX	B-	C	A-	Up	2.03	9.43	3.13	20.01	20.09	0.16	11.02	1,516	800-426-7969	Y
Russell Investments LifePoints Balanced Strategy Cls R5	RBLVX	B-	C	B+	Up	1.96	9.32	2.71	18.45	17.64	0.16	10.9	1,516	800-426-7969	Y
American Funds College 2024 Fund Class 529F1	CTFFX	B	C+	A-		2.51	7.19	7.06	16.88	21.67	0.21	12.22	1,942	800-421-4225	Y
American Funds College 2024 Fund Class 529-A	CFTAX	B	C+	A-		2.44	6.94	6.72	16.09	20.23	0.21	12.17	1,942	800-421-4225	Y
American Funds College 2024 Fund Class 529-E	CTFEX	B	C+	B+		2.45	6.87	6.54	15.25	18.80	0.21	12.12	1,942	800-421-4225	Y
American Funds College 2024 Fund Class 529-C	CTFCX	B-	C	B+		2.29	6.66	6.05	13.48	15.77	0.21	12.01	1,942	800-421-4225	Y
Fidelity Advisor® Real Estate Income Fund Class I	FRIRX	B	B-	B		2.95	11.65	9.92	21.92	37.50	0.24	12.3	6,194	617-563-7000	Y
Fidelity Advisor® Real Estate Income Fund Class Z	FIKMX	B	B-	B		2.98	11.70	10.03	21.95	37.44	0.25	12.3	6,194	617-563-7000	Y
Fidelity® Real Estate Income Fund	FRIFX	B	B-	B		2.94	11.69	9.96	21.88	37.35	0.25	12.35	6,194	617-563-7000	Y
Fidelity Advisor® Real Estate Income Fund Class M	FRIQX	B	B-	B		2.88	11.53	9.61	20.86	35.51	0.25	12.29	6,194	617-563-7000	Y
Fidelity Advisor® Real Estate Income Fund Class A	FRINX	B	B-	B		2.89	11.46	9.64	20.95	35.70	0.25	12.28	6,194	617-563-7000	Y
Fidelity Advisor® Real Estate Income Fund Class C	FRIOX	B	B-	B		2.72	11.15	8.82	18.28	30.75	0.25	12.15	6,194	617-563-7000	Y
MFS Diversified Income Fund Class R6	DIFHX	B	C+	B		2.91	11.60	9.20	19.71	28.57	0.31	12.76	3,710	877-960-6077	Y
MFS Diversified Income Fund Class I	DIFIX	B	C+	B		2.81	11.47	9.01	19.28	27.75	0.31	12.75	3,710	877-960-6077	Y
BlackRock Multi-Asset Income Portfolio Investor C Shares	BCICX	B	C+	B+	Up	2.50	9.77	6.17	16.68	15.02	0.31	10.83	16,425	800-441-7762	Y
MFS Diversified Income Fund Class R4	DIFGX	B	C+	B		2.89	11.55	9.10	19.38	27.85	0.31	12.76	3,710	877-960-6077	Y
MFS Diversified Income Fund Class R3	DIFFX	B-	C+	B	Down	2.83	11.42	8.83	18.49	26.27	0.31	12.76	3,710	877-960-6077	Y
MFS Diversified Income Fund Class A	DIFAX	B-	C+	B	Down	2.83	11.42	8.83	18.49	26.27	0.31	12.76	3,710	877-960-6077	Y
MFS Diversified Income Fund Class R2	DIFEX	B-	C+	B	Down	2.77	11.20	8.57	17.62	24.72	0.31	12.75	3,710	877-960-6077	Y
MFS Diversified Income Fund Class C	DIFCX	B-	C+	B	Down	2.65	10.93	8.04	15.88	21.65	0.31	12.75	3,710	877-960-6077	Y
MFS Diversified Income Fund Class R1	DIFDX	B-	C+	B	Down	2.65	10.94	7.95	15.89	21.66	0.31	12.74	3,710	877-960-6077	Y
BlackRock Multi-Asset Income Portfolio Investor A Shares	BAICX	B	C+	A-		2.60	10.05	6.95	19.19	19.30	0.32	10.84	16,425	800-441-7762	Y
JPMorgan Investor Conservative Growth Fund Class C	OCGCX	B-	C	A-		2.56	8.57	5.23	16.02	17.51	0.32	12.52	3,419	800-480-4111	Y
Fidelity Freedom® Index 2015 Fund Investor Class	FLIFX	B	C+	A	Up	3.21	11.09	7.00	25.11	28.19	0.33	15.5	1,404	617-563-7000	Y
JPMorgan Investor Conservative Growth Fund Class A	OICAX	B	C+	A-	Up	2.69	8.78	5.80	18.03	20.74	0.33	12.58	3,419	800-480-4111	Y
American Funds College 2027 Fund Class 529F1	CTSFX	B	C+	A		2.87	9.25	7.16	22.61	26.31	0.34	12.87	1,582	800-421-4225	Y
American Funds College 2027 Fund Class 529-A	CSTAX	B	C+	A		2.80	9.11	6.83	21.83	25.01	0.34	12.81	1,582	800-421-4225	Y
American Funds College 2027 Fund Class 529-E	CTSEX	B	C+	A-		2.66	8.91	6.58	20.90	23.36	0.34	12.71	1,582	800-421-4225	Y
Principal Strategic Asset Mgmt Conservative Balanced Cls J	PCBJX	B	C+	A-	Up	3.01	10.46	6.08	21.25	24.31	0.34	11.77	1,676	800-787-1621	Y
American Funds College 2027 Fund Class 529-C	CTSCX	B	C+	A-	Up	2.60	8.69	6.02	19.04	20.20	0.34	12.63	1,582	800-421-4225	Y
Invesco Oppenheimer Capital Income Fund Class C	OPECX	B-	C	B+	Up	1.86	8.10	4.28	11.97	13.91	0.34	9.89	2,283	800-659-1005	Y
Principal Strat Asset Mgmt Cons Balanced Inst Cls	PCCIX	B	C+	A-	Up	3.04	10.55	6.31	21.79	25.49	0.35	11.81	1,676	800-787-1621	Y
Principal Strat Asset Mgmt Cons Balanced R-5 Cls	PCBFX	B	C+	A-	Up	2.98	10.35	5.96	20.83	23.96	0.35	11.8	1,676	800-787-1621	Y
Principal Strat Asset Mgmt Cons Balanced R-4 Cls	PCBLX	B	C+	A-	Up	2.90	10.31	5.79	20.42	23.15	0.35	11.8	1,676	800-787-1621	Y
Principal Strat Asset Mgmt Cons Balanced R-3 Cls	PCBPX	B	C+	A-	Up	2.90	10.22	5.65	19.74	22.09	0.35	11.79	1,676	800-787-1621	Y
Principal Strat Asset Mgmt Cons Balanced R-2 Cls	PCNSX	B	C+	A-	Up	2.84	10.09	5.49	19.10	20.97	0.35	11.87	1,676	800-787-1621	Y
Principal Strategic Asset Mgmt Conservative Balanced Cls C	SCIPX	B-	C	A-	Up	2.75	9.90	5.12	17.87	18.91	0.35	11.81	1,676	800-787-1621	Y
Invesco Balanced-Risk Allocation Fund Class Y	ABRYX	B-	C	A-	Up	2.16	10.74	3.56	15.62	19.42	0.35	11.34	3,369	800-659-1005	Y
Invesco Oppenheimer Capital Income Fund Class A	OPPEX	B-	C	B+	Up	2.19	8.63	5.22	14.63	18.43	0.35	10.24	2,283	800-659-1005	Y
Invesco Balanced-Risk Allocation Fund Class A	ABRZX	B-	C	A-	Up	2.10	10.62	3.33	14.79	17.98	0.35	11.14	3,369	800-659-1005	Y
Invesco Oppenheimer Capital Income Fund Class R	OCINX	B-	C	B+	Up	2.16	8.52	4.92	13.81	16.95	0.35	10.09	2,283	800-659-1005	Y

		RATINGS				TOTAL RETURNS & PERFORMANCE					ASSETS		NEW INVESTORS		
Fund Name	Ticker Symbol	Overall Rating	Reward Rating	Risk Rating	Recent Up/ Downgrade	3-Month Total Return	6-Month Total Return	1-Year Total Return	3-Year Total Return	5-Year Total Return	3-Year Beta	NAV	Total Assets (MIL)	Telephone	Open to New Investors
Invesco Balanced-Risk Allocation Fund Class R	ABRRX	B-	C	B+	Up	2.05	10.52	3.11	13.88	16.49	0.35	10.92	3,369	800-659-1005	Y
Invesco Balanced-Risk Allocation Fund Class C	ABRCX	B-	C	B+	Up	1.93	10.14	2.53	12.23	13.57	0.35	10.53	3,369	800-659-1005	Y
Invesco Oppenheimer Capital Income Fund Class Y	OCIYX	B-	C	B	Up	2.25	8.75	5.46	15.46	19.76	0.35	10.23	2,283	800-659-1005	Y
Principal Strategic Asset Mgmt Conservative Balanced Cls A	SAIPX	B	C+	A-	Up	3.01	10.35	5.88	20.58	23.54	0.36	11.94	1,676	800-787-1621	Y
Fidelity Freedom® 2015 Fund	FFVFX	B	C	A	Up	2.87	10.54	5.20	25.97	29.16	0.36	12.73	8,745	617-563-7000	Y
Principal Strat Asset Mgmt Cons Balanced R-1 Cls	PCSSX	B	C+	A-	Up	2.83	10.09	5.33	18.69	20.17	0.36	11.77	1,676	800-787-1621	Y
Fidelity Freedom® 2015 Fund Class K6	FPTKX	B	C	A	Up	2.93	10.63	5.31	26.35	29.55	0.37	12.69	8,745	617-563-7000	Y
American Funds Tax-Advantaged Growth & Inc Port Cls A	TAIAX	B	C+	A		2.87	10.14	6.85	24.68	34.09	0.38	13.8	2,661	800-421-4225	Y
American Funds Tax-Advantaged Growth & Inc Port Cls C	TAICX	B	C+	A	Up	2.64	9.71	6.10	22.03	29.39	0.38	13.71	2,661	800-421-4225	Y
John Hancock Funds II Multimgr Lifest Mod Cls 5	JHLMX	B	C+	A-	Up	3.00	11.03	6.15	21.28	22.53	0.38	13.4	3,179	800-225-5913	Y
John Hancock Funds II Multimgr Lifest Mod Cls A	JALMX	B	C	A-	Up	2.89	10.75	5.69	19.77	20.00	0.38	13.46	3,179	800-225-5913	Y
John Hancock Funds II Multimgr Lifest Mod Cls R3	JRLMX	B	C	A-	Up	2.84	10.74	5.54	18.96	18.51	0.38	13.44	3,179	800-225-5913	Y
John Hancock Funds II Multimgr Lifest Mod Cls C	JCLMX	B-	C	B+	Up	2.71	10.46	4.96	17.32	15.89	0.38	13.47	3,179	800-225-5913	Y
American Funds Tax-Advantaged Growth & Inc Port Cls F-1	TAIFX	B	C+	A		2.86	10.13	6.89	24.69	34.17	0.39	13.8	2,661	800-421-4225	Y
American Funds Tax-Advantaged Growth & Inc Port Cls F-2	TXIFX	B	C+	A		2.92	10.24	7.08	25.65	35.87	0.39	13.82	2,661	800-421-4225	Y
John Hancock Funds II Multimgr Lifest Mod Cls 1	JILMX	B	C+	A-	Up	2.99	11.07	6.09	21.06	22.27	0.39	13.42	3,179	800-225-5913	Y
John Hancock Funds II Multimgr Lifest Mod Cls R5	JTLMX	B	C+	A-	Up	2.99	10.98	6.08	21.00	22.02	0.39	13.42	3,179	800-225-5913	Y
John Hancock Funds II Multimgr Lifest Mod Cls R1	JPLMX	B-	C	A-	Up	2.81	10.60	5.36	18.61	17.85	0.39	13.44	3,179	800-225-5913	Y
John Hancock Funds II Multimgr Lifest Mod Cls R4	JSLMX	B	C	A-	Up	2.86	10.89	5.80	20.26	20.77	0.4	13.4	3,179	800-225-5913	Y
John Hancock Funds II Multimgr Lifest Mod Cls R2	JQLMX	B	C	A-	Up	2.87	10.74	5.61	19.37	19.38	0.4	13.41	3,179	800-225-5913	Y
BlackRock LifePath® Index 2020 Fund Investor P Shares	LIQPX	B	C+	A-	Up	3.15	11.07	6.42	21.84	25.92	0.41	13	4,737	800-441-7762	Y
BlackRock LifePath® Index 2020 Fund Investor A Shares	LIQAX	B	C+	A-	Up	3.15	11.01	6.38	21.72	25.71	0.41	13.01	4,737	800-441-7762	Y
Fidelity Advisor Asset Manager® 40% Fund I Class	FFNIX	B	C	A-	Up	2.76	10.16	4.88	21.10	24.71	0.41	11.75	1,776	617-563-7000	Y
Fidelity Advisor Asset Manager® 40% Fund Class A	FFNAX	B-	C	A-	Up	2.70	9.99	4.58	20.08	23.03	0.41	11.75	1,776	617-563-7000	Y
JPMorgan Income Builder Fund Class A Shares	JNBAX	B	C+	A	Up	3.07	10.49	7.02	22.92	22.37	0.42	10.63	13,005	800-480-4111	Y
Fidelity Freedom® 2010 Fund Class K6	FOTKX	B	C+	A	Up	2.81	9.46	5.38	23.22	26.52	0.42	15.42	5,806	617-563-7000	Y
JPMorgan Income Builder Fund Class C Shares	JNBCX	B	C+	A-	Up	2.95	10.13	6.50	21.12	19.33	0.42	10.6	13,005	800-480-4111	Y
Fidelity Freedom® 2010 Fund	FFFCX	B	C+	A	Up	2.75	9.38	5.27	22.90	26.20	0.42	15.47	5,806	617-563-7000	Y
Fidelity Asset Manager® 40% Fund	FFANX	B	C	A-	Up	2.77	10.17	4.92	21.22	24.92	0.42	11.75	1,776	617-563-7000	Y
Fidelity Advisor Asset Manager® 40% Fund Class Z	FIKYX	B	C	A-	Up	2.69	10.08	4.84	21.13	24.83	0.42	11.75	1,776	617-563-7000	Y
Fidelity Advisor Asset Manager® 40% Fund Class M	FFNTX	B-	C	A-	Up	2.64	9.83	4.37	19.13	21.37	0.42	11.73	1,776	617-563-7000	Y
Fidelity Advisor Asset Manager® 40% Fund Class C	FFNCX	B-	C	B+	Up	2.51	9.62	3.88	17.37	18.44	0.43	11.69	1,776	617-563-7000	Y
Principal Strategic Asset Mgmt Flexible Income Inst Cls	PIFIX	B	C+	A-		2.85	8.94	6.67	17.59	21.69	0.44	12.17	2,643	800-787-1621	Y
Vanguard Target Retirement 2015 Fund Investor Shares	VTXVX	B	C+	A	Up	2.98	10.06	6.40	22.09	26.98	0.44	15.21	15,775	877-662-7447	Y
American Funds Conservative Growth & Inc Port Cls R-6	RINGX	B	C+	A		2.47	10.42	7.28	23.32	29.45	0.44	12.65	5,248	800-421-4225	Y
American Funds Conservative Growth & Inc Port Cls R-5	RINFX	B	C+	A-		2.54	10.39	7.22	23.24	29.13	0.44	12.66	5,248	800-421-4225	Y
American Funds Conservative Growth & Inc Port Cls R-5E	RGOFX	B	C+	A-		2.45	10.28	7.15	22.82	28.72	0.44	12.62	5,248	800-421-4225	Y
Goldman Sachs Income Builder Fund Investor Class	GKIRX	B	C+	B+		3.96	14.10	9.58	24.03	21.68	0.44	23.7	1,587	800-526-7384	Y
American Funds Conservative Growth & Inc Port Cls F-2	INPEX	B	C+	A-		2.45	10.28	7.09	22.97	28.74	0.44	12.64	5,248	800-421-4225	Y
Principal Strategic Asset Mgmt Flexible Income R-4 Cls	PFILX	B	C+	A-		2.77	8.74	6.23	16.33	19.49	0.44	12.15	2,643	800-787-1621	Y
American Funds Conservative Growth & Inc Port Cls 529-F-1	CIPFX	B	C+	A-		2.45	10.29	7.10	22.77	28.35	0.44	12.63	5,248	800-421-4225	Y
Goldman Sachs Income Builder Fund Class P	GGKPX	B	C+	B+		3.66	13.83	9.42	23.30	20.33	0.44	23.77	1,587	800-526-7384	Y
American Funds Conservative Growth & Inc Port Cls A	INPAX	B	C+	A-		2.40	10.19	6.97	22.19	27.37	0.44	12.63	5,248	800-421-4225	Y
American Funds Conservative Growth & Inc Port Cls F-1	INPFX	B	C+	A-		2.39	10.16	6.91	22.01	27.19	0.44	12.64	5,248	800-421-4225	Y
American Funds Conservative Growth & Inc Port Cls 529-A	CIPAX	B	C+	A-		2.40	10.18	6.84	21.92	26.85	0.44	12.62	5,248	800-421-4225	Y
Goldman Sachs Income Builder Fund Class A	GSBFX	B	C+	B+		3.88	13.99	9.35	23.14	20.17	0.44	23.25	1,587	800-526-7384	Y
Principal Strategic Asset Mgmt Flexible Income R-3 Cls	PFIPX	B	C+	A-	Up	2.72	8.63	6.03	15.65	18.36	0.44	12.14	2,643	800-787-1621	Y
American Funds Conservative Growth & Inc Port Cls 529-E	CIPEX	B	C+	A-	Up	2.33	10.06	6.67	21.17	25.52	0.44	12.62	5,248	800-421-4225	Y
American Funds Conservative Growth & Inc Port Cls R-3	RNCCX	B	C+	A-	Up	2.33	10.05	6.62	21.01	25.35	0.44	12.61	5,248	800-421-4225	Y
Principal Strategic Asset Mgmt Flexible Income R-2 Cls	PFIVX	B	C+	B+	Up	2.68	8.51	5.93	15.01	17.37	0.44	12.15	2,643	800-787-1621	Y
American Funds Conservative Growth & Inc Port Cls R-2	RINBX	B-	C	B+		2.24	9.81	6.13	19.47	22.58	0.44	12.57	5,248	800-421-4225	Y
American Funds Conservative Growth & Inc Port Cls C	INPCX	B-	C	B+		2.23	9.88	6.22	19.51	22.69	0.44	12.57	5,248	800-421-4225	Y

		RATINGS				TOTAL RETURNS & PERFORMANCE						ASSETS		NEW INVESTORS	
Fund Name	Ticker Symbol	Overall Rating	Reward Rating	Risk Rating	Recent Up/ Downgrade	3-Month Total Return	6-Month Total Return	1-Year Total Return	3-Year Total Return	5-Year Total Return	3-Year Beta	NAV	Total Assets (MIL)	Telephone	Open to New Investors
American Funds Conservative Growth & Inc Port Cls 529-C	CIPCX	B-	C	B+		2.22	9.76	6.17	19.27	22.26	0.44	12.58	5,248	800-421-4225	Y
American Funds Conservative Growth & Inc Port Cls R-1	RNCAX	B-	C	B+		2.20	9.74	6.02	19.32	22.48	0.44	12.58	5,248	800-421-4225	Y
Goldman Sachs Income Builder Fund Class C	GSBCX	B-	C+	B+		3.67	13.53	8.52	20.35	15.75	0.44	22.84	1,587	800-526-7384	Y
Transamerica Asset Allocation Moderate Portfolio Class A	IMOAX	B-	C	B+	Up	2.45	10.16	3.59	20.05	23.16	0.44	11.27	1,457	888-233-4339	Y
Transamerica Asset Allocation Moderate Portfolio Class R	IMDRX	B-	C	B+	Up	2.46	10.10	3.37	19.14	21.69	0.44	11.22	1,457	888-233-4339	Y
Transamerica Asset Allocation Moderate Portfolio Class C	IMOLX	B-	C	B+	Up	2.26	9.80	2.79	17.30	18.68	0.44	11.31	1,457	888-233-4339	Y
Principal Strategic Asset Management Flexible Income Cls J	PFIJX	B	C+	A-		2.84	8.83	6.50	17.09	20.61	0.45	12.1	2,643	800-787-1621	Y
Principal Strategic Asset Mgmt Flexible Income R-5 Cls	PFIFX	B	C+	A-		2.80	8.72	6.35	16.66	20.25	0.45	12.14	2,643	800-787-1621	Y
American Funds Conservative Growth & Inc Port Cls R-4	RINEX	B	C+	A-		2.39	10.17	6.91	22.09	27.24	0.45	12.63	5,248	800-421-4225	Y
American Funds Conservative Growth & Inc Port Cls ABLE-A	CIPGX	B	C	A-		2.39	10.11	6.95	22.19	27.27	0.45	12.61	5,248	800-421-4225	Y
Putnam Dynamic Asset Allocation Conservative Fund Class R6	PCCEX	B	C+	A-	Up	2.72	9.48	5.41	17.82	24.76	0.45	10.76	1,088	617-292-1000	Y
Franklin Conservative Allocation Fund Class R	FTCRX	B	C	A-	Up	2.20	9.53	5.19	19.86	17.35	0.45	14.37	1,196	650-312-2000	Y
American Funds Conservative Growth & Inc Port Cls R-2E	RNBEX	B	C	A-	Up	2.30	9.97	6.42	20.57	25.87	0.45	12.63	5,248	800-421-4225	Y
Principal Strategic Asset Mgmt Flexible Income R-1 Cls	PFIGX	B-	C+	B+		2.59	8.40	5.67	14.47	16.55	0.45	12.1	2,643	800-787-1621	Y
Franklin Conservative Allocation Fund Class C	FTCCX	B-	C	A-	Up	2.03	9.28	4.65	18.04	14.44	0.45	14.13	1,196	650-312-2000	Y
Putnam Dynamic Asset Allocation Conservative Fund Class R	PACRX	B-	C	B+	Up	2.59	9.12	4.75	15.64	20.94	0.45	11.03	1,088	617-292-1000	Y
Principal Strategic Asset Management Flexible Income Cls A	SAUPX	B	C+	A-		2.77	8.73	6.33	16.45	19.86	0.46	12.21	2,643	800-787-1621	Y
Franklin Conservative Allocation Fund Class A	FTCIX	B	C	A-	Up	2.26	9.70	5.46	20.72	18.80	0.46	14.43	1,196	650-312-2000	Y
Fidelity Advisor Asset Manager® 30% Fund Class Z	FIKWX	B	C	A-	Up	2.55	8.57	5.07	17.56	21.73	0.46	11.15	1,679	617-563-7000	Y
Fidelity Asset Manager® 30% Fund	FTANX	B	C	A-	Up	2.53	8.65	5.04	17.53	21.70	0.46	11.15	1,679	617-563-7000	Y
Putnam Dynamic Asset Allocation Conservative Fund Class R5	PACDX	B	C	A-	Up	2.71	9.45	5.26	17.60	24.28	0.46	10.75	1,088	617-292-1000	Y
Putnam Dynamic Asset Allocation Conservative Fund Class Y	PACYX	B-	C	A-		2.69	9.32	5.20	17.32	23.93	0.46	10.75	1,088	617-292-1000	Y
Principal Strategic Asset Management Flexible Income Cls C	SCUPX	B-	C	B+		2.60	8.33	5.49	13.90	15.40	0.46	12.08	2,643	800-787-1621	Y
Putnam Dynamic Asset Allocation Conservative Fund Class A	PACAX	B-	C	B+		2.64	9.23	4.98	16.57	22.43	0.46	10.71	1,088	617-292-1000	Y
Putnam Dynamic Asset Allocation Conservative Fund Class M	PACMX	B-	C	B+	Up	2.55	8.98	4.52	14.81	19.50	0.46	10.58	1,088	617-292-1000	Y
Putnam Dynamic Asset Allocation Conservative Fund Class B	PACBX	B-	C	B+	Up	2.47	8.92	4.23	14.02	18.02	0.46	10.62	1,088	617-292-1000	Y
Fidelity Advisor Asset Manager® 30% Fund I Class	FTINX	B	C	A-	Up	2.52	8.62	4.97	17.25	21.28	0.47	11.15	1,679	617-563-7000	Y
Fidelity Advisor Asset Manager® 30% Fund Class A	FTAAX	B-	C	A-		2.45	8.50	4.79	16.47	19.86	0.47	11.16	1,679	617-563-7000	Y
Fidelity Advisor Asset Manager® 30% Fund Class M	FTTNX	B-	C	A-		2.40	8.32	4.44	15.53	18.31	0.47	11.14	1,679	617-563-7000	Y
Fidelity Advisor Asset Manager® 20% Fund Class A	FTAWX	B-	C	B+		2.06	6.74	4.58	12.58	15.88	0.47	13.4	5,044	617-563-7000	Y
Putnam Dynamic Asset Allocation Conservative Fund Class C	PACCX	B-	C	B+	Up	2.39	8.86	4.17	13.90	17.98	0.47	10.56	1,088	617-292-1000	Y
Principal Global Diversified Income Fund Class R-6	PGBLX	B	C+	A-	Up	2.77	9.71	6.00	18.18	19.64	0.48	13.59	7,703	800-787-1621	Y
Principal Global Diversified Income Fund Class A	PGBAX	B	C+	B+	Up	2.59	9.47	5.60	17.05	17.75	0.48	13.66	7,703	800-787-1621	Y
Fidelity Advisor Asset Manager® 20% Fund Class Z	FIKVX	B-	C	A-		2.14	6.88	4.86	13.67	17.70	0.48	13.42	5,044	617-563-7000	Y
Fidelity Asset Manager® 20% Fund	FASIX	B-	C	A-		2.21	6.94	4.91	13.73	17.76	0.48	13.43	5,044	617-563-7000	Y
Fidelity Advisor Asset Manager® 20% Fund I Class	FTIWX	B-	C	A-		2.20	6.92	4.86	13.58	17.52	0.48	13.42	5,044	617-563-7000	Y
Fidelity Advisor Asset Manager® 20% Fund Class M	FTDWX	B-	C	B+		2.01	6.58	4.32	11.74	14.42	0.48	13.37	5,044	617-563-7000	Y
Fidelity Advisor Asset Manager® 30% Fund Class C	FCANX	B-	C	B+	Up	2.27	8.03	3.93	13.84	15.34	0.48	11.08	1,679	617-563-7000	Y
Principal Global Diversified Income Fund Class C	PGDCX	B-	C	B+	Up	2.41	9.04	4.84	14.38	13.42	0.48	13.57	7,703	800-787-1621	Y
Principal Global Diversified Income Institutional Cls	PGDIX	B	C+	A-	Up	2.77	9.70	5.98	18.21	19.66	0.49	13.6	7,703	800-787-1621	Y
Fidelity Advisor Asset Manager® 20% Fund Class C	FTCWX	B-	C	B+	Up	1.87	6.36	3.78	10.02	11.55	0.49	13.32	5,044	617-563-7000	Y
USAA Cornerstone Moderate Fund	USBSX	B-	C	B+	Up	2.53	9.93	4.01	19.44	16.02	0.5	14.5	1,199	800-235-8396	Y
Vanguard Target Retirement Income Fund Investor Shares	VTINX	B	C+	A-		2.96	8.97	6.54	17.10	22.80	0.51	13.72	16,765	877-662-7447	Y
Fidelity Freedom® Income Fund	FFFAX	B	C+	A-	Up	2.45	7.16	5.33	15.72	19.51	0.51	11.59	3,400	617-563-7000	Y
EQ/Franklin Balanced Managed Volatility Portfolio Class K		B-	C	A-		1.58	4.77	3.57	22.88	25.35	0.51		1,145	877-222-2144	Y
EQ/Franklin Balanced Managed Volatility Portfolio Class IB		B-	C	A-		1.58	4.68	3.39	22.07	23.88	0.51		1,145	877-222-2144	Y
EQ/Franklin Balanced Managed Volatility Portfolio Class IA		B-	C	A-		1.49	4.59	3.30	21.96	23.77	0.51		1,145	877-222-2144	Y
MFS Conservative Allocation Fund Class I	MACIX	B	C+	A		3.94	12.36	8.18	22.46	26.94	0.52	16.05	2,934	877-960-6077	Y
MFS Conservative Allocation Fund Class R4	MACJX	B	C+	A		3.90	12.41	8.18	22.43	26.94	0.52	15.91	2,934	877-960-6077	Y
MFS Conservative Allocation Fund Class R3	MACNX	B	C+	A		3.81	12.25	7.85	21.47	25.35	0.52	15.76	2,934	877-960-6077	Y
MFS Conservative Allocation Fund Class A	MACFX	B	C+	A		3.85	12.21	7.85	21.52	25.38	0.52	15.9	2,934	877-960-6077	Y
MFS Conservative Allocation Fund Class R2	MCARX	B	C+	A	Up	3.84	12.16	7.69	20.65	23.86	0.52	15.44	2,934	877-960-6077	Y

Fund Name	Ticker Symbol	RATINGS: Overall Rating	Reward Rating	Risk Rating	Recent Up/ Downgrade	TOTAL RETURNS & PERFORMANCE: 3-Month Total Return	6-Month Total Return	1-Year Total Return	3-Year Total Return	5-Year Total Return	3-Year Beta	ASSETS: NAV	Total Assets (Mil)	NEW INVESTORS: Telephone	Open to New Investors
Fidelity Freedom® Income Fund Class K6	FYTKX	B	C+	A-	Up	2.49	7.14	5.40	15.90	19.70	0.52	11.57	3,400	617-563-7000	Y
MFS Conservative Allocation Fund Class R1	MACKX	B	C+	A-	Up	3.68	11.84	7.06	18.87	20.82	0.52	15.34	2,934	877-960-6077	Y
MFS Conservative Allocation Fund Class 529B	EBCAX	B	C+	A-	Up	3.67	11.77	7.03	18.65	20.49	0.52	15.56	2,934	877-960-6077	Y
MFS Conservative Allocation Fund Class 529C	ECACX	B	C+	A-	Up	3.69	11.84	7.09	18.71	20.47	0.52	15.5	2,934	877-960-6077	Y
John Hancock Funds II Multimgr Lifest Cons Cls R2	JQLCX	B-	C	B+		2.69	8.41	5.80	12.95	14.04	0.52	12.97	2,376	800-225-5913	Y
MFS Conservative Allocation Fund Class 529A	ECLAX	B	C+	A		3.79	12.19	7.86	21.38	25.14	0.53	15.81	2,934	877-960-6077	Y
MFS Conservative Allocation Fund Class C	MACVX	B	C+	A-	Up	3.66	11.79	7.11	18.81	20.74	0.53	15.66	2,934	877-960-6077	Y
MFS Conservative Allocation Fund Class B	MACBX	B	C+	A-	Up	3.68	11.79	7.06	18.86	20.80	0.53	15.82	2,934	877-960-6077	Y
John Hancock Funds II Multimgr Lifest Cons Cls R5	JTLRX	B-	C+	B+		2.80	8.64	6.28	14.43	16.47	0.53	12.96	2,376	800-225-5913	Y
John Hancock Funds II Multimgr Lifest Cons Cls 1	JILCX	B-	C+	B+		2.80	8.65	6.37	14.48	16.74	0.53	12.96	2,376	800-225-5913	Y
John Hancock Funds II Multimgr Lifest Cons Cls R4	JSLCX	B-	C	B+		2.75	8.54	6.14	13.77	15.32	0.53	12.96	2,376	800-225-5913	Y
John Hancock Funds II Multimgr Lifest Cons Cls A	JALRX	B-	C	B+		2.70	8.53	5.97	13.30	14.68	0.53	12.99	2,376	800-225-5913	Y
John Hancock Funds II Multimgr Lifest Cons Cls R3	JRLCX	B-	C	B+	Up	2.67	8.37	5.72	12.62	13.39	0.53	12.95	2,376	800-225-5913	Y
John Hancock Funds II Multimgr Lifest Cons Cls R1	JPLCX	B-	C	B	Up	2.62	8.27	5.54	12.05	12.53	0.53	12.97	2,376	800-225-5913	Y
John Hancock Funds II Multimgr Lifest Cons Cls C	JCLCX	B-	C	B	Up	2.53	8.07	5.24	10.90	10.67	0.53	12.99	2,376	800-225-5913	Y
BlackRock LifePath® Index Retirement Investor P Shares	LIRPX	B	C+	A-	Up	3.14	10.65	6.60	19.51	24.05	0.55	12.57	2,499	800-441-7762	Y
BlackRock LifePath® Index Retirement Investor A Shares	LIRAX	B	C+	A-	Up	3.14	10.60	6.55	19.27	23.72	0.55	12.58	2,499	800-441-7762	Y
Cohen & Steers Preferred Sec & Income Fund, Inc. Cls R	CPRRX	B	B-	B	Up	3.75	10.96	7.87	17.63	29.92	0.76	13.78	7,347	212-832-3232	Y
Cohen & Steers Preferred Sec & Income Fund, Inc. Cls F	CPXFX	B	B-	B	Up	3.87	11.22	8.40	19.39	33.14	0.77	13.79	7,347	212-832-3232	Y
Cohen & Steers Preferred Sec & Income Fund, Inc. Cls Z	CPXZX	B	B-	B	Up	3.95	11.30	8.48	19.50	33.27	0.77	13.8	7,347	212-832-3232	Y
Cohen & Steers Preferred Sec & Income Fund, Inc. Cls A	CPXAX	B	B-	B	Up	3.87	11.05	8.11	18.26	30.95	0.77	13.77	7,347	212-832-3232	Y
Cohen & Steers Preferred Sec & Income Fund, Inc. Cls C	CPXCX	B-	C+	B	Up	3.72	10.76	7.38	15.94	26.77	0.77	13.69	7,347	212-832-3232	Y
American Funds 2020 Target Date Retirement Fund® Class R-6	RRCTX	B	C+	A		2.79	10.27	6.51	24.38	30.73	0.78	12.88	15,535	800-421-4225	Y
American Funds 2020 Target Date Retirement Fund® Class R-5	RECTX	B	C+	A	Up	2.78	10.23	6.51	24.22	30.43	0.78	12.92	15,535	800-421-4225	Y
American Funds 2020 Target Date Retirement Fund® Cls R-5E	RHCTX	B	C+	A	Up	2.81	10.26	6.42	23.87	30.03	0.78	12.78	15,535	800-421-4225	Y
American Funds 2020 Target Date Retirement Fund® Class F-2	FBCTX	B	C+	A	Up	2.80	10.24	6.47	24.07	30.09	0.78	12.81	15,535	800-421-4225	Y
American Funds 2020 Target Date Retirement Fund® Class F-1	FAOTX	B	C+	A	Up	2.65	10.01	6.11	23.04	28.34	0.78	12.74	15,535	800-421-4225	Y
American Funds 2020 Target Date Retirement Fund® Class A	AACTX	B	C+	A	Up	2.72	10.04	6.16	23.14	28.49	0.78	12.82	15,535	800-421-4225	Y
American Funds 2020 Target Date Retirement Fund® Class R-3	RCCTX	B	C	A	Up	2.66	9.94	5.84	22.02	26.49	0.78	12.71	15,535	800-421-4225	Y
American Funds 2020 Target Date Retirement Fund® Cls R-2E	RBEHX	B	C	A-	Up	2.60	9.84	5.67	21.39	26.16	0.78	12.61	15,535	800-421-4225	Y
American Funds 2020 Target Date Retirement Fund® Class R-2	RBCTX	B	C	A-	Up	2.52	9.66	5.39	20.38	23.89	0.78	12.59	15,535	800-421-4225	Y
American Funds 2020 Target Date Retirement Fund® Class C	CCCTX	B	C	A-	Up	2.52	9.75	5.38	20.42	23.75	0.78	12.6	15,535	800-421-4225	Y
American Funds 2020 Target Date Retirement Fund® Class R-1	RACTX	B	C	A-	Up	2.51	9.72	5.34	20.24	23.58	0.78	12.64	15,535	800-421-4225	Y
American Funds 2020 Target Date Retirement Fund® Class R-4	RDCTX	B	C+	A	Up	2.72	10.06	6.21	23.09	28.51	0.79	12.8	15,535	800-421-4225	Y
Principal Preferred Securities Fund R-4 Class	PQARX	B	B-	B	Up	3.49	10.36	6.89	16.71	27.03	0.79	10	5,513	800-787-1621	Y
Principal Preferred Securities Fund R-3 Class	PNARX	B	C+	B	Up	3.43	10.23	6.67	16.11	25.88	0.79	10.02	5,513	800-787-1621	Y
Principal Preferred Securities Fund R-1 Class	PUSAX	B-	C+	B	Up	3.34	10.04	6.33	14.97	23.97	0.79	10.04	5,513	800-787-1621	Y
Principal Global Investors Funds Preferred Securities R-6	PPREX	B	B-	B+	Up	3.55	10.45	7.22	17.93	29.22	0.8	10.09	5,513	800-787-1621	Y
Principal Preferred Securities Fund Institutional Class	PPSIX	B	B-	B+	Up	3.52	10.40	7.10	17.72	29.00	0.8	10.09	5,513	800-787-1621	Y
Principal Preferred Securities Fund R-5 Class	PPARX	B	B-	B+	Up	3.50	10.36	6.97	17.18	27.92	0.8	10.05	5,513	800-787-1621	Y
Principal Preferred Securities Fund Class J	PPSJX	B	B-	B+	Up	3.43	10.26	6.87	16.90	27.27	0.8	9.88	5,513	800-787-1621	Y
Principal Preferred Securities Fund Class A	PPSAX	B	B-	B+	Up	3.43	10.30	6.89	16.84	27.31	0.8	10.17	5,513	800-787-1621	Y
Principal Preferred Securities Fund R-2 Class	PPRSX	B	C+	B	Up	3.40	10.06	6.50	15.45	24.78	0.8	9.98	5,513	800-787-1621	Y
Principal Preferred Securities Fund Class C	PRFCX	B-	C+	B	Up	3.34	9.89	6.09	14.30	22.59	0.8	10.16	5,513	800-787-1621	Y
Franklin K2 Alternative Strategies Fund Class A	FAAAX	B-	C	A-	Up	1.95	6.68	2.87	13.09	13.53	0.81	11.49	1,238	650-312-2000	Y
Franklin K2 Alternative Strategies Fund Class R	FSKKX	B-	C	B+	Up	1.86	6.48	2.51	12.28	11.73	0.81	11.49	1,238	650-312-2000	Y
American Funds 2015 Target Date Retirement Fund® Cls R-5E	RHBTX	B	C+	A		2.62	9.64	6.45	20.99	27.14	0.84	11.71	5,129	800-421-4225	Y
American Funds 2015 Target Date Retirement Fund® Class A	AABTX	B	C+	A-	Up	2.61	9.49	6.28	20.27	25.70	0.84	11.76	5,129	800-421-4225	Y
American Funds 2015 Target Date Retirement Fund® Class R-3	RCJTX	B	C	A-	Up	2.54	9.47	5.95	19.17	23.80	0.84	11.67	5,129	800-421-4225	Y
American Funds 2015 Target Date Retirement Fund® Class R-1	RAJTX	B-	C	A-	Up	2.39	9.15	5.39	17.48	20.84	0.84	11.56	5,129	800-421-4225	Y
American Funds 2015 Target Date Retirement Fund® Class R-5	REJTX	B	C+	A		2.68	9.73	6.57	21.29	27.60	0.85	11.84	5,129	800-421-4225	Y
American Funds 2015 Target Date Retirement Fund® Class R-6	RFJTX	B	C+	A		2.69	9.76	6.65	21.57	27.93	0.85	11.8	5,129	800-421-4225	Y

		RATINGS				TOTAL RETURNS & PERFORMANCE						ASSETS		NEW INVESTORS	
Fund Name	Ticker Symbol	Overall Rating	Reward Rating	Risk Rating	Recent Up/ Downgrade	3-Month Total Return	6-Month Total Return	1-Year Total Return	3-Year Total Return	5-Year Total Return	3-Year Beta	NAV	Total Assets (MIL)	Telephone	Open to New Investors
American Funds 2015 Target Date Retirement Fund® Class F-2	FBBTX	B	C+	A		2.62	9.71	6.52	21.16	27.27	0.85	11.75	5,129	800-421-4225	Y
American Funds 2015 Target Date Retirement Fund® Class F-1	FAKTX	B	C+	A-	Up	2.63	9.55	6.20	20.18	25.61	0.85	11.69	5,129	800-421-4225	Y
American Funds 2015 Target Date Retirement Fund® Class R-4	RDBTX	B	C+	A-	Up	2.61	9.60	6.34	20.28	25.79	0.85	11.75	5,129	800-421-4225	Y
American Funds 2015 Target Date Retirement Fund® Cls R-2E	RBEJX	B	C	A-	Up	2.57	9.35	5.81	18.72	23.62	0.85	11.57	5,129	800-421-4225	Y
American Funds 2015 Target Date Retirement Fund® Class C	CCBTX	B-	C	A-		2.38	9.14	5.54	17.63	21.09	0.85	11.58	5,129	800-421-4225	Y
American Funds 2015 Target Date Retirement Fund® Class R-2	RBJTX	B-	C	A-		2.48	9.15	5.46	17.54	21.28	0.85	11.57	5,129	800-421-4225	Y
JNL Institutional Alt 50 Fund Class I		B-	C	A-	Up	2.83	10.57	4.64	18.13	13.79	0.85	17.78	2,302		Y
JNL Institutional Alt 50 Fund Class A		B-	C	A-	Up	2.73	10.43	4.30	17.47	13.15	0.85	17.68	2,302		Y
KP Retirement Path 2020 Fund Institutional Shares	KPRBX	B	C+	A		3.01	10.75	6.42	23.12	26.68	0.86	10.92	1,053		Y
Nuveen Preferred Securities & Income Fund Class R3	NPSTX	B	C+	B	Up	3.46	10.38	6.94	17.70	25.82	0.87	17.06	3,523	312-917-8146	Y
American Funds 2010 Target Date Retirement Fund® Class R-2	RBATX	B-	C	A-		2.34	8.54	5.32	16.07	19.57	0.87	10.93	3,349	800-421-4225	Y
American Funds 2010 Target Date Retirement Fund® Class R-6	RFTTX	B	C+	A		2.67	9.22	6.57	20.07	26.17	0.88	11.13	3,349	800-421-4225	Y
American Funds 2010 Target Date Retirement Fund® Class F-2	FBATX	B	C+	A		2.50	9.06	6.33	19.59	25.41	0.88	11.07	3,349	800-421-4225	Y
American Funds 2010 Target Date Retirement Fund® Cls R-5E	RHATX	B	C+	A-		2.59	9.08	6.37	19.44	25.48	0.88	11.05	3,349	800-421-4225	Y
American Funds 2010 Target Date Retirement Fund® Class R-4	RDATX	B	C+	A-	Up	2.49	8.95	6.07	18.68	23.96	0.88	11.07	3,349	800-421-4225	Y
American Funds 2010 Target Date Retirement Fund® Class F-1	FAATX	B	C+	A-	Up	2.41	8.88	6.11	18.59	23.77	0.88	11.03	3,349	800-421-4225	Y
American Funds 2010 Target Date Retirement Fund® Class R-3	RCATX	B	C+	A-	Up	2.41	8.79	5.80	17.62	22.02	0.88	11.01	3,349	800-421-4225	Y
American Funds 2010 Target Date Retirement Fund® Cls R-2E	RBEAX	B	C	A-	Up	2.43	8.76	5.72	17.17	21.92	0.88	10.92	3,349	800-421-4225	Y
American Funds 2010 Target Date Retirement Fund® Class C	CCATX	B-	C	A-		2.34	8.64	5.41	16.10	19.44	0.88	10.93	3,349	800-421-4225	Y
American Funds 2010 Target Date Retirement Fund® Class R-5	REATX	B	C+	A-		2.57	9.19	6.49	19.82	25.90	0.89	11.16	3,349	800-421-4225	Y
American Funds 2010 Target Date Retirement Fund® Class A	AAATX	B	C+	A-	Up	2.49	8.93	6.19	18.77	24.07	0.89	11.09	3,349	800-421-4225	Y
American Funds 2010 Target Date Retirement Fund® Class R-1	RAATX	B-	C	A-		2.31	8.53	5.30	15.98	19.17	0.89	11.06	3,349	800-421-4225	Y
JPMorgan SmartRetirement® 2020 Fund Class R4	JTTQX	B	C	A-	Up	3.13	11.11	5.86	23.17	27.16	0.94	19.28	5,793	800-480-4111	Y
JPMorgan SmartRetirement® 2020 Fund Class A	JTTAX	B	C	A-	Up	3.11	11.02	5.73	22.86	26.21	0.94	19.25	5,793	800-480-4111	Y
JPMorgan SmartRetirement® 2020 Fund Class R3	JTTPX	B	C	A-	Up	3.08	10.95	5.51	22.19	25.52	0.94	19.17	5,793	800-480-4111	Y
JPMorgan SmartRetirement® 2020 Fund Class R2	JTTZX	B-	C	A-	Up	3.01	10.84	5.27	21.50	24.17	0.94	19.19	5,793	800-480-4111	Y
JPMorgan SmartRetirement® 2020 Fund Class C	JTTCX	B-	C	A-	Up	2.97	10.71	5.08	20.53	22.22	0.94	19.16	5,793	800-480-4111	Y
JPMorgan SmartRetirement® 2020 Fund Class R5	JTTIX	B	C	A-	Up	3.16	11.18	5.98	23.69	27.70	0.95	19.34	5,793	800-480-4111	Y
JNL/S&P Managed Conservative Fund Class A		B	C	A-	Up	2.68	8.33	5.90	15.39	15.99	0.97	14.17	1,272		Y
JNL/S&P Managed Conservative Fund Class I		B	C+	A-		2.74	8.47	6.28	15.71	16.32	0.97	14.21	1,272		Y

Section VII:
BUY Rated Stock Mutual Funds by Category

Investment Ratings and analysis for BUY Rated Stock Mutual Funds by Category. Within Category, funds are listed in alphabetical order.

Section VII: Contents

This section contains Weiss Investment Ratings, key rating factors, and summary financial data for BUY Rated Stock Mutual Funds by Category. Within category, funds are listed in alphabetical order.

Fund Name
Describes the fund's assets, regions of investments and investment strategies. Many funds have similar names, so you want to make sure the fund you look up is really the one you are interested in evaluating.

Ticker Symbol
An arrangement of characters (usually letters) representing a particular security listed on an exchange or otherwise traded publicly. When a company issues securities to the public marketplace, it selects an available ticker symbol for its securities which investors use to place trade orders. Every listed security has a unique ticker symbol, facilitating the vast array of trade orders that flow through the financial markets every day. If a ticker symbol is not assigned to a particular fund, the International Securities Identification Number (ISIN) is displayed.

RATINGS

Overall Rating
The Weiss rating measured on a scale from A to E based on each fund's risk and performance. See the preceding section, "What Our Ratings Mean," for an explanation of each letter grade rating.

Reward Rating
This is based on the total return over a period of up to five years, including net asset value and price growth. The total return figure is stated net of the expenses and fees charged by the fund. Based on proprietary modeling the individual components of the risk and reward ratings are calculated and weighted and the final rating is generated.

Risk Rating
This is includes the risk ratings of component stocks where applicable and also includes the financial stability of the fund, turnover where applicable, together with the level of volatility as measured by the fund's daily returns over a period of up to five years. Funds with greater stability are considered less risky and receive a higher risk rating. Funds with greater volatility are considered riskier, and will receive a lower risk rating. In addition to considering the fund's volatility, the risk rating also considers an assessment of the valuation and quality of a fund's holdings.

Recent Upgrade/Downgrade
An "Up" or "Down" indicates that the Weiss Mutual Fund rating has changed since the publication of the last print edition. If a fund has had a rating change since March 31, 2019, the change is identified with an "Up" or "Down."

TOTAL RETURNS & PERFORMANCE

3-Month Total Return
The rate of return on an investment over three months that includes interest, capital gains, dividends and distributions realized.

6-Month Total Return
The rate of return on an investment over six months that includes interest, capital gains, dividends and distributions realized.

1-Year Total Return
The rate of return on an investment over one year that includes interest, capital gains, dividends and distributions realized.

3-Year Total Return
The rate of return on an investment over three years that includes interest, capital gains, dividends and distributions realized.

5-Year Total Return
The rate of return on an investment over five years that includes interest, capital gains, dividends and distributions realized.

ASSETS

NAV (Net Asset Value)
A fund's price per share. The value is calculated by dividing the total value of all the securities in the portfolio, less any liabilities, by the number of fund shares outstanding.

Total Assets (MIL)
The total of all assets listed on the institution's balance sheet. This figure primarily consists of loans, investments, and fixed assets. Total Assets are displayed in millions.

NEW INVESTORS

Telephone
The company's phone number.

Open to New Investors
Indicates whether the fund accepts investments from those who are not existing investors. A "Y" in this column identifies that the fund accepts new investors. No data in this column indicates that the fund is closed to new investors. The fund may be closed to new investors because the fund's asset base is getting too large to effectively execute its investing style. Although, the fund may be closed, in most cases, existing investors are able to add to their holdings.

Category: Aggressive Allocation

Fund Name	Ticker Symbol	RATINGS: Overall Rating	Reward Rating	Risk Rating	Recent Up/ Downgrade	TOTAL RETURNS & PERFORMANCE: 3-Month Total Return	6-Month Total Return	1-Year Total Return	3-Year Total Return	5-Year Total Return	ASSETS: NAV	Total Assets (MIL)	NEW INVESTORS: Telephone	Open to New Investors
1789 Growth and Income Fund Class Class C	PSECX	B-	C	B+		5.74	16.09	7.95	18.91	19.65	13.17	24.7	617-399-0900	Y
1789 Growth and Income Fund Class P	PSEPX	B-	C	B+		5.94	16.63	9.02	22.50	25.88	13.25	24.7	617-399-0900	Y
American Century Inv One Choice Port®: Aggressive Inv Cls	AOGIX	B-	C	B	Up	3.53	15.98	4.83	33.79	35.63	16.69	1,332	800-444-4015	Y
American Century Inv One Choice Port®: Aggressive R Cls	AORYX	B-	C	B	Up	3.41	15.76	4.36	31.80	32.33	16.67	1,332	800-444-4015	Y
American Century Strategic Allocation: Aggressive A Cls	ACVAX	B-	C	B	Up	3.66	16.29	5.20	33.29	34.03	7.92	782.1	800-444-4015	Y
American Century Strategic Allocation: Aggressive C Cls	ASTAX	B-	C	B	Up	3.48	15.76	4.36	30.40	29.07	7.71	782.1	800-444-4015	Y
American Century Strategic Allocation: Aggressive I Cls	AAAIX	B-	C	B	Up	3.72	16.41	5.65	35.00	36.90	7.8	782.1	800-444-4015	Y
American Century Strategic Allocation: Aggressive Inv Cls	TWSAX	B-	C	B	Up	3.69	16.29	5.38	34.08	35.57	7.85	782.1	800-444-4015	Y
American Century Strategic Allocation: Aggressive R Cls	AAARX	B-	C	B	Up	3.53	16.00	4.80	32.16	32.13	7.9	782.1	800-444-4015	Y
American Century Strategic Allocation: Aggressive R5 Cls	ASAUX	B-	C	B+	Up	3.85	16.56	5.64	34.69	36.19	7.81	782.1	800-444-4015	Y
American Century Strategic Allocation: Aggressive R6 Cls	AAAUX	B-	C	B+	Up	3.73	16.46	5.70	35.53	37.90	7.78	782.1	800-444-4015	Y
American Funds College 2030 Fund Class 529-A	CTHAX	B	C	A	Up	2.95	11.02	5.95	27.26	28.95	13.6	1,785	800-421-4225	Y
American Funds College 2030 Fund Class 529-C	CTYCX	B	C	A	Up	2.76	10.66	5.11	24.36	23.90	13.39	1,785	800-421-4225	Y
American Funds College 2030 Fund Class 529-E	CTHEX	B	C	A	Up	2.97	11.00	5.75	26.41	27.31	13.52	1,785	800-421-4225	Y
American Funds College 2030 Fund Class 529F1	CTHFX	B	C+	A	Up	3.01	11.23	6.20	28.16	30.28	13.66	1,785	800-421-4225	Y
American Funds College 2033 Fund Class 529-A	CTLAX	B-	C	A-	Up	2.95	12.77	4.85	32.65		11.83	1,073	800-421-4225	Y
American Funds College 2033 Fund Class 529-C	CTLCX	B-	C	B+	Up	2.80	12.37	4.09	29.51		11.71	1,073	800-421-4225	Y
American Funds College 2033 Fund Class 529-E	CTLEX	▪ B-	C	A-	Up	2.88	12.61	4.57	31.57		11.78	1,073	800-421-4225	Y
American Funds College 2033 Fund Class 529-F-1	CTLFX	B-	C	A-	Up	3.03	12.92	5.10	33.51		11.88	1,073	800-421-4225	Y
American Funds Growth and Income Portfolio Class 529-A	CGNAX	B-	C	B+	Up	2.65	13.64	4.92	31.85	35.58	15.05	9,679	800-421-4225	Y
American Funds Growth and Income Portfolio Class 529-C	CGNCX	B-	C	B+	Up	2.47	13.24	4.08	28.91	30.37	14.98	9,679	800-421-4225	Y
American Funds Growth and Income Portfolio Class 529-E	CGNEX	B-	C	B+	Up	2.60	13.56	4.70	31.01	33.97	15.02	9,679	800-421-4225	Y
American Funds Growth and Income Portfolio Class 529-F-1	CGNFX	B-	C	B+	Up	2.71	13.75	5.10	32.82	37.02	15.06	9,679	800-421-4225	Y
American Funds Growth and Income Portfolio Class A	GAIOX	B-	C	B+	Up	2.66	13.73	4.95	32.11	36.08	15.06	9,679	800-421-4225	Y
American Funds Growth and Income Portfolio Class ABLE-A	CGNGX	B-	C	B+	Up	2.67	13.68	4.96	32.05	35.86	15.04	9,679	800-421-4225	Y
American Funds Growth and Income Portfolio Class C	GAITX	B-	C	B+	Up	2.42	13.20	4.14	29.13	30.88	14.96	9,679	800-421-4225	Y
American Funds Growth and Income Portfolio Class F-1	GAIFX	B-	C	B+	Up	2.65	13.72	4.92	31.96	35.78	15.06	9,679	800-421-4225	Y
American Funds Growth and Income Portfolio Class F-2	GAIEX	B-	C	B+	Up	2.71	13.82	5.19	32.95	37.57	15.08	9,679	800-421-4225	Y
American Funds Growth and Income Portfolio Class F-3	GAIHX	B-	C	B+	Up	2.74	13.90	5.31	33.34	38.02	15.06	9,679	800-421-4225	Y
American Funds Growth and Income Portfolio Class R-1	RGNAX	B-	C	B+	Up	2.43	13.21	4.15	29.04	30.82	14.99	9,679	800-421-4225	Y
American Funds Growth and Income Portfolio Class R-2	RGNBX	B-	C	B+	Up	2.50	13.32	4.17	29.15	30.86	14.95	9,679	800-421-4225	Y
American Funds Growth and Income Portfolio Class R-2E	RBEGX	B-	C	B+	Up	2.56	13.48	4.45	30.23	33.83	15.02	9,679	800-421-4225	Y
American Funds Growth and Income Portfolio Class R-3	RAICX	B-	C	B+	Up	2.59	13.55	4.65	30.84	33.80	15.01	9,679	800-421-4225	Y
American Funds Growth and Income Portfolio Class R-4	RGNEX	B-	C	B+	Up	2.66	13.65	4.95	31.96	35.86	15.05	9,679	800-421-4225	Y
American Funds Growth and Income Portfolio Class R-5	RGNFX	B-	C	B+	Up	2.72	13.91	5.23	33.18	37.85	15.11	9,679	800-421-4225	Y
American Funds Growth and Income Portfolio Class R-5E	RGQFX	B-	C	B+	Up	2.71	13.77	5.10	32.86	37.31	15.04	9,679	800-421-4225	Y
American Funds Growth and Income Portfolio Class R-6	RGNGX	B-	C	B+	Up	2.74	13.88	5.23	33.34	38.23	15.08	9,679	800-421-4225	Y
American Funds The Income Fund of America® Class 529-A	CIMAX	B	C	A-	Up	2.59	11.17	6.43	24.66	30.89	22.44	109,899	800-421-4225	Y
American Funds The Income Fund of America® Class 529-C	CIMCX	B-	C	A-	Up	2.41	10.74	5.64	21.86	26.00	22.38	109,899	800-421-4225	Y
American Funds The Income Fund of America® Class 529-E	CIMEX	B	C	A-	Up	2.54	11.03	6.16	23.81	29.38	22.37	109,899	800-421-4225	Y
American Funds The Income Fund of America® Class 529-F-1	CIMFX	B	C	A-	Up	2.65	11.25	6.64	25.55	32.35	22.43	109,899	800-421-4225	Y
American Funds The Income Fund of America® Class A	AMECX	B	C	A-	Up	2.65	11.23	6.55	25.02	31.51	22.5	109,899	800-421-4225	Y
American Funds The Income Fund of America® Class C	IFACX	B-	C	A-	Up	2.44	10.80	5.70	22.11	26.42	22.2	109,899	800-421-4225	Y
American Funds The Income Fund of America® Class F-1	IFAFX	B	C	A-	Up	2.59	11.11	6.43	24.63	30.89	22.43	109,899	800-421-4225	Y
American Funds The Income Fund of America® Class F-2	AMEFX	B	C	A-	Up	2.65	11.29	6.70	25.63	32.61	22.47	109,899	800-421-4225	Y
American Funds The Income Fund of America® Class F-3	FIFAX	B	C	A	Up	2.68	11.34	6.80	25.78	32.31	22.48	109,899	800-421-4225	Y
American Funds The Income Fund of America® Class R-1	RIDAX	B-	C	A-	Up	2.46	10.75	5.66	21.99	26.22	22.36	109,899	800-421-4225	Y
American Funds The Income Fund of America® Class R-2	RIDBX	B-	C	A-	Up	2.44	10.78	5.66	21.94	26.30	22.23	109,899	800-421-4225	Y
American Funds The Income Fund of America® Class R-2E	RIEBX	B-	C	A-	Up	2.53	10.94	5.98	23.06	28.56	22.44	109,899	800-421-4225	Y
American Funds The Income Fund of America® Class R-3	RIDCX	B	C	A-	Up	2.53	10.98	6.13	23.55	29.07	22.4	109,899	800-421-4225	Y
American Funds The Income Fund of America® Class R-4	RIDEX	B	C	A-	Up	2.59	11.17	6.43	24.73	31.02	22.45	109,899	800-421-4225	Y
American Funds The Income Fund of America® Class R-5	RIDFX	B	C	A-	Up	2.67	11.31	6.75	25.87	33.00	22.49	109,899	800-421-4225	Y

Category: Aggressive Allocation (con't)

Fund Name	Ticker Symbol	RATINGS: Overall Rating	Reward Rating	Risk Rating	Recent Up/ Downgrade	TOTAL RETURNS & PERFORMANCE: 3-Month Total Return	6-Month Total Return	1-Year Total Return	3-Year Total Return	5-Year Total Return	ASSETS: NAV	Total Assets (MIL)	NEW INVESTORS: Telephone	Open to New Investors
American Funds The Income Fund of America® Class R-5E	RIDHX	B	C	A-	Up	2.69	11.33	6.66	25.42	31.99	22.47	109,899	800-421-4225	Y
American Funds The Income Fund of America® Class R-6	RIDGX	B	C	A	Up	2.68	11.33	6.80	26.05	33.32	22.5	109,899	800-421-4225	Y
Archer Balanced Fund	ARCHX	B-	C	B+	Up	4.18	13.99	7.82	25.27	34.86	13.35	36.7		Y
BlackRock 80/20 Target Allocation Fund Class A	BAAPX	B-	C	B	Up	3.41	15.65	5.38	31.82	32.61	12.49	370.0	800-441-7762	Y
BlackRock 80/20 Target Allocation Fund Class C	BCAPX	B-	C	B	Up	3.26	15.20	4.62	28.91	27.81	12.07	370.0	800-441-7762	Y
BlackRock 80/20 Target Allocation Fund Class Institutional	BIAPX	B-	C	B	Up	3.50	15.84	5.67	33.12	34.98	12.74	370.0	800-441-7762	Y
BlackRock 80/20 Target Allocation Fund Class K	BKAPX	B-	C	B	Up	3.51	15.87	5.69	33.18	35.05	12.74	370.0	800-441-7762	Y
BlackRock 80/20 Target Allocation Fund Class R	BRAPX	B-	C	B	Up	3.34	15.48	5.15	31.04	31.52	12.4	370.0	800-441-7762	Y
BMO Aggressive Allocation Fund Class I	BDSHX	B-	C	B	Up	2.83	16.62	4.77	40.14	38.26	8.7	171.7	800-236-3863	Y
BMO Aggressive Allocation Fund Class R6	BDSQX	B-	C	B	Up	2.71	16.62	4.77	40.54	39.15	8.7	171.7	800-236-3863	Y
BMO Growth Allocation Fund Class I	BABHX	B-	C	B+	Up	2.60	14.40	4.55	33.72	32.31	9.45	117.6	800-236-3863	Y
BMO Growth Allocation Fund Class R3	BABRX	B-	C	B	Up	2.48	14.23	4.02	31.84	29.12	9.47	117.6	800-236-3863	Y
BMO Growth Allocation Fund Class R6	BABQX	B-	C	B+	Up	2.71	14.64	4.76	34.42	33.35	9.47	117.6	800-236-3863	Y
BMO Growth Allocation Fund Class Y	BABYX	B-	C	B+	Up	2.60	14.38	4.32	32.75	30.77	9.46	117.6	800-236-3863	Y
Boston Trust Asset Management Fund	BTBFX	B	C+	A-		3.85	15.85	12.52	37.69	51.66	50.92	527.2	617-814-1215	Y
Buffalo Flexible Income Fund	BUFBX	B-	C	B		0.37	12.91	3.79	26.19	25.13	15.24	600.4	800-492-8332	Y
Calamos Growth & Income Fund Class A	CVTRX	B-	C	B+		4.00	16.66	8.30	38.96	44.34	32.72	2,018	800-582-6959	Y
Calamos Growth & Income Fund Class C	CVTCX	B-	C	B+	Up	3.80	16.24	7.51	35.93	38.96	32.98	2,018	800-582-6959	Y
Calamos Growth & Income Fund Institutional Class	CGIIX	B-	C	B+		4.08	16.81	8.56	40.05	46.12	31.35	2,018	800-582-6959	Y
Calamos® Growth & Income Portfolio		B-	C	B+		3.93	16.56	7.92	36.61	40.11	16.03	26.7	800-582-6959	Y
Calvert Aggressive Allocation Fund Class A	CAAAX	B-	C	B	Up	4.04	17.50	7.44	40.39	40.87	20.34	163.8	301-951-4881	Y
Calvert Aggressive Allocation Fund Class C	CAACX	B-	C	B	Up	3.85	17.09	6.68	37.33	34.90	17.26	163.8	301-951-4881	Y
Charter Aggressive Growth Portfolio Class B		B-	C	B	Up	2.39	14.16	2.72	30.68	19.40	11.19	8.0	877-222-2144	Y
Columbia Capital Allocation Aggressive Portfolio Adv Cls	CPDAX	B-	C	B	Up	3.28	16.07	4.54	36.77	40.03	12.05	719.8	800-345-6611	Y
Columbia Capital Allocation Aggressive Portfolio Class A	AXBAX	B-	C	B	Up	3.19	15.98	4.30	35.75	38.27	12.31	719.8	800-345-6611	Y
Columbia Capital Allocation Aggressive Portfolio Class R	CPARX	B-	C	B	Up	3.11	15.81	3.95	34.74	36.49	12.19	719.8	800-345-6611	Y
Columbia Capital Alloc Aggressive Port Inst 2 Cls	CPANX	B-	C	B	Up	3.28	16.08	4.56	36.96	40.37	12.04	719.8	800-345-6611	Y
Columbia Capital Alloc Aggressive Port Inst 3 Cls	CPDIX	B-	C	B	Up	3.20	16.10	4.54	37.08	40.63	12.03	719.8	800-345-6611	Y
Columbia Capital Allocation Aggressive Portfolio Inst Cls	CPAZX	B-	C	B	Up	3.22	16.08	4.55	36.82	39.95	12.26	719.8	800-345-6611	Y
Davis Appreciation & Income Fund Class A	RPFCX	B-	C	B	Up	2.03	11.56	0.82	28.10	14.34	40.05	189.7	800-279-0279	Y
Davis Appreciation & Income Fund Class Y	DCSYX	B-	C	B	Up	2.08	11.75	1.13	29.31	15.87	40.22	189.7	800-279-0279	Y
Eaton Vance Tax-Managed Equity Asset Allocation Cls A	EAEAX	B-	C	B		3.75	18.34	7.12	42.00	44.87	21.8	515.6		Y
Eaton Vance Tax-Managed Equity Asset Allocation Cls B	EBEAX	B-	C	B	Up	3.58	17.91	6.31	38.82	39.49	20.54	515.6		
Eaton Vance Tax-Managed Equity Asset Allocation Cls C	ECEAX	B-	C	B	Up	3.58	17.90	6.28	38.83	39.53	20.22	515.6		Y
Eaton Vance Tax-Managed Equity Asset Allocation Cls I	EIEAX	B-	C	B		3.86	18.50	7.38	43.08	46.20	21.77	515.6		Y
EQ/Aggressive Strategy Growth Portfolio Class IB		B-	C	B	Up	3.10	14.09	4.04	33.81	33.94	15.38	4,054	877-222-2144	Y
EQ/Franklin Templeton Alloc Managed Vol Port Cls IA		B-	C	B+	Up	2.85	13.45	3.94	30.51	24.87	9.06	1,100	877-222-2144	Y
EQ/Franklin Templeton Alloc Managed Vol Port Cls IB		B-	C	B	Up	2.85	13.45	3.94	30.64	24.87	9.06	1,100	877-222-2144	Y
EQ/Growth Strategy Fund Class IA		B-	C	B+	Up	2.92	12.84	4.26	29.57	30.33	18.72	5,349	877-222-2144	Y
EQ/Growth Strategy Fund Class IB		B-	C	B+	Up	2.86	12.76	4.20	29.55	30.22	18.74	5,349	877-222-2144	Y
EQ/Moderate-Plus Allocation Portfolio Class K		B-	C	B+	Up	3.02	13.17	4.11	30.93	29.30	11.31	8,764	877-222-2144	Y
EQ/Premier VIP Moderate-Plus Allocation Fund Class A		B-	C	B+	Up	2.93	13.07	3.91	29.96	27.70	11.29	8,764	877-222-2144	Y
EQ/Premier VIP Moderate-Plus Allocation Fund Class B		B-	C	B+	Up	2.93	13.07	3.91	29.95	27.69	11.3	8,764	877-222-2144	Y
Fallen Angels Income Fund	FAINX	B	C+	A-		5.76	15.98	13.13	35.23	34.65	13.11	9.0		Y
Fidelity Advisor® Strategic Dividend & Income® Cls A	FASDX	B	C+	A-		2.44	14.70	8.61	27.28	39.17	15.18	4,835	617-563-7000	Y
Fidelity Advisor® Strategic Dividend & Income® Cls C	FCSDX	B-	C	B+	Down	2.31	14.29	7.84	24.43	34.05	15.1	4,835	617-563-7000	Y
Fidelity Advisor® Strategic Dividend & Income® Cls M	FTSDX	B	C+	B+		2.45	14.55	8.34	26.35	37.44	15.17	4,835	617-563-7000	Y
Fidelity Advisor® Strategic Dividend & Income® Cls Z	FIQWX	B	C+	A-		2.59	14.89	9.01	28.38	41.15	15.25	4,835	617-563-7000	Y
Fidelity Advisor® Strategic Dividend & Income® I Cls	FSIDX	B	C+	A-		2.56	14.86	8.93	28.29	41.05	15.25	4,835	617-563-7000	Y
Fidelity® Four-in-One Index Fund	FFNOX	B-	C	B+	Up	3.86	16.39	6.87	38.37	40.91	46.42	6,296	617-563-7000	Y
Fidelity® Strategic Dividend & Income® Fund	FSDIX	B	C+	A-		2.55	14.90	8.93	28.35	41.13	15.29	4,835	617-563-7000	Y
Franklin Corefolio Allocation Fund Advisor Class	FCAZX	B-	C	B	Up	3.73	18.31	5.69	44.52	41.43	19.31	763.2	650-312-2000	Y

Category: Aggressive Allocation (con't)

Fund Name	Ticker Symbol	RATINGS: Overall Rating	Reward Rating	Risk Rating	Recent Up/ Downgrade	TOTAL RETURNS & PERFORMANCE: 3-Month Total Return	6-Month Total Return	1-Year Total Return	3-Year Total Return	5-Year Total Return	ASSETS: NAV	Total Assets (MIL)	NEW INVESTORS: Telephone	Open to New Investors
Franklin Corefolio Allocation Fund Class R6	FTLQX	B-	C	B	Up	3.78	18.38	5.78	44.82	41.73	19.31	763.2	650-312-2000	Y
Franklin Growth Allocation Fund Advisor Class	FGTZX	B-	C	B+	Up	3.10	15.36	6.58	35.76	34.85	18.92	1,221	650-312-2000	Y
Franklin Growth Allocation Fund Class A	FGTIX	B-	C	B+	Up	3.06	15.24	6.33	34.71	33.23	18.82	1,221	650-312-2000	Y
Franklin Growth Allocation Fund Class C	FTGTX	B-	C	B+	Up	2.81	14.77	5.48	31.68	28.29	18.26	1,221	650-312-2000	Y
Franklin Growth Allocation Fund Class R	FGTRX	B-	C	B+	Up	2.99	15.06	6.05	33.70	31.56	18.56	1,221	650-312-2000	Y
Franklin Growth Allocation Fund Class R6		B-	C	B+	Up	3.10	15.37	6.66	36.21	35.77	18.91	1,221	650-312-2000	Y
Franklin Mutual Shares Fund Class A	TESIX	B-	C	B	Up	3.21	14.33	4.22	25.73	23.29	27.27	12,661	650-312-2000	Y
Franklin Mutual Shares Fund Class Z	MUTHX	B-	C	B	Up	3.29	14.48	4.50	26.68	24.92	27.59	12,661	650-312-2000	Y
Franklin NextStep Growth Fund Advisor Class	FNGVX	B-	C	B+	Up	3.32	14.29	5.97	27.67		12.54	7.2	650-312-2000	Y
Franklin NextStep Growth Fund Class A	FNGBX	B-	C	B+	Up	3.23	14.02	5.63	26.61		12.5	7.2	650-312-2000	Y
Franklin NextStep Growth Fund Class C	FNGCX	B-	C	B+	Up	3.04	13.55	4.81	23.83		12.36	7.2	650-312-2000	Y
Great-West Moderately Aggressive Profile Fund Class L	MXFPX	B-	C	B+	Up	2.62	12.98	3.58	29.08	30.27	9.3	679.5		Y
Great-West Moderately Aggressive Profile Institutional Cls	MXHRX	B-	C	B+	Up	2.83	13.31	4.31	31.50	33.89	9.88	679.5		Y
Great-West Moderately Aggressive Profile Investor Cls	MXBPX	B-	C	B+	Up	2.75	13.18	3.95	30.05	32.04	7.8	679.5		Y
GuideStone Funds Growth Allocation Institutional Cls	GGRYX	B-	C	B+	Up	3.68	15.60	5.87	34.29	27.91	12.67	1,207	214-720-1171	Y
GuideStone Funds Growth Allocation Fund Investor Class	GCOZX	B-	C	B+	Up	3.60	15.41	5.66	33.35	26.76	12.65	1,207	214-720-1171	Y
Hartford Growth Allocation Fund Class A	HRAAX	B-	C	B+	Up	3.35	15.53	5.21	33.63	24.04	12.64	619.3	888-843-7824	Y
Hartford Growth Allocation Fund Class C	HRACX	B-	C	B	Up	3.12	15.03	4.33	30.63	19.46	12.55	619.3	888-843-7824	Y
Hartford Growth Allocation Fund Class F	HRAFX	B-	C	B+	Up	3.37	15.74	5.57	34.81	25.13	12.57	619.3	888-843-7824	Y
Hartford Growth Allocation Fund Class I	HRAIX	B-	C	B+	Up	3.45	15.74	5.55	34.86	26.08	12.57	619.3	888-843-7824	Y
Hartford Growth Allocation Fund Class R3	HRARX	B-	C	B+	Up	3.26	15.34	4.84	32.32	22.06	12.33	619.3	888-843-7824	Y
Hartford Growth Allocation Fund Class R4	HRASX	B-	C	B+	Up	3.36	15.51	5.17	33.60	23.91	12.58	619.3	888-843-7824	Y
Hartford Growth Allocation Fund Class R5	HRATX	B-	C	B+	Up	3.34	15.63	5.49	34.74	25.81	12.65	619.3	888-843-7824	Y
Hennessy Total Return Fund Investor Class	HDOGX	B	C	A		1.12	9.87	10.34	27.25	40.68	13.97	76.4	800-966-4354	Y
ICON Equity Income Fund Class A	IEQAX	B-	C	B	Up	4.46	18.23	5.76	33.26	41.03	18.13	83.2	303-790-1600	Y
ICON Equity Income Fund Class C	IOECX	B-	C	B	Up	4.27	17.84	5.02	30.35	35.81	18.35	83.2	303-790-1600	Y
ICON Equity Income Fund Class S	IOEZX	B-	C	B	Up	4.57	18.39	6.08	34.38	42.85	18.18	83.2	303-790-1600	Y
Invesco Growth Allocation Fund Class A	AADAX	B-	C	B+	Up	3.21	14.47	4.69	28.90	23.62	16.37	988.8	800-659-1005	Y
Invesco Growth Allocation Fund Class C	AADCX	B-	C	B+	Up	2.99	14.02	3.82	26.08	19.09	16.18	988.8	800-659-1005	Y
Invesco Growth Allocation Fund Class R	AADRX	B-	C	B+	Up	3.16	14.36	4.40	27.97	22.12	16.32	988.8	800-659-1005	Y
Invesco Growth Allocation Fund Class R6	AAESX	B-	C	B+	Up	3.32	14.70	5.05	30.32	25.88	16.46	988.8	800-659-1005	Y
Invesco Growth Allocation Fund Class S	AADSX	B-	C	B+	Up	3.28	14.56	4.75	29.33	24.29	16.36	988.8	800-659-1005	Y
Invesco Growth Allocation Fund Class Y	AADYX	B-	C	B+	Up	3.28	14.65	4.93	29.96	25.20	16.35	988.8	800-659-1005	Y
Invesco Growth Allocation Fund R5 Class	AADIX	B-	C	B+	Up	3.32	14.62	4.99	30.32	25.88	16.46	988.8	800-659-1005	Y
Invesco Oppenheimer Port Series: Active Alloc Cls A	OAAAX	B-	C	B	Up	3.25	15.77	4.02	30.66	27.94	14.9	2,355	800-659-1005	Y
Invesco Oppenheimer Port Series: Active Alloc Cls C	OAACX	B-	C	B	Up	3.04	15.30	3.21	27.64	23.17	14.54	2,355	800-659-1005	Y
Invesco Oppenheimer Port Series: Active Alloc Cls R	OAANX	B-	C	B	Up	3.20	15.62	3.70	29.61	26.28	14.8	2,355	800-659-1005	Y
Invesco Oppenheimer Port Series: Active Alloc Cls R5	PAAJX	B-	C	B		3.35	15.95	4.34	31.68	29.54	14.91	2,355	800-659-1005	Y
Invesco Oppenheimer Port Series: Active Alloc Cls R6	PAAQX	B-	C	B		3.35	15.95	4.34	31.68	29.54	14.91	2,355	800-659-1005	Y
Invesco Oppenheimer Port Series: Active Alloc Cls Y	OAAYX	B-	C	B	Up	3.34	15.95	4.34	31.67	29.54	15.12	2,355	800-659-1005	Y
InvestEd Growth Portfolio	WAGRX	B-	C	B+	Up	3.30	14.00	6.05	36.73	37.44	11.56	117.4	888-923-3355	Y
JNL Aggressive Growth Allocation Fund Class A		B-	C	B	Up	4.21	17.64	5.42	36.54	34.24	13.6	1,491		Y
JNL Aggressive Growth Allocation Fund Class I		B-	C	B	Up	4.27	17.84	5.80	37.24	34.94	13.67	1,491		Y
JNL Growth Allocation Fund Class A		B-	C	B+	Up	4.00	16.39	6.01	32.74	32.08	14.27	2,369		Y
JNL Growth Allocation Fund Class I		B-	C	B+	Up	4.06	16.58	6.30	33.29	32.63	14.34	2,369		Y
JNL iShares Tactical Growth A		B-	C	B	Up	2.77	13.98	2.86	31.62	34.68	14.43	239.9		Y
JNL iShares Tactical Growth I		B-	C	B	Up	2.76	14.10	3.15	32.35	35.42	14.48	239.9		Y
JNL/American Funds Growth Allocation Fund Class A		B-	C	B+	Up	3.38	15.22	6.11	38.79	39.58	17.71	2,631		Y
JNL/American Funds Growth Allocation Fund Class I		B-	C	B+	Up	3.42	15.42	6.45	39.57	40.37	17.81	2,631		Y
JNL/Mellon Index 5 Fund Class A		B-	C	B	Up	3.02	14.33	2.75	31.98	33.63	15.31	1,371		Y
JNL/Mellon Index 5 Fund Class I		B-	C	B	Up	3.21	14.57	3.14	32.84	34.50	15.41	1,371		Y
JNL/S&P Managed Aggressive Growth Fund Class A		B-	C	B	Up	4.38	19.26	7.44	46.47	45.66	24.52	2,272		Y

Category: Aggressive Allocation (con't)

Fund Name	Ticker Symbol	RATINGS Overall Rating	Reward Rating	Risk Rating	Recent Up/ Downgrade	TOTAL RETURNS & PERFORMANCE 3-Month Total Return	6-Month Total Return	1-Year Total Return	3-Year Total Return	5-Year Total Return	ASSETS NAV	Total Assets (MIL)	NEW INVESTORS Telephone	Open to New Investors
JNL/S&P Managed Aggressive Growth Fund Class I		B-	C	B	Up	4.44	19.42	7.78	47.25	46.44	24.65	2,272		Y
JNL/S&P Managed Growth Fund Class A		B-	C	B+	Up	4.06	17.59	7.19	42.21	41.38	20.72	5,416		Y
JNL/S&P Managed Growth Fund Class I		B-	C	B+	Up	4.15	17.81	7.53	42.96	42.13	20.83	5,416		Y
John Hancock Funds II Multimgr Lifest Growth Cls 1	JILGX	B-	C	B+	Up	3.07	15.29	4.48	34.02	32.11	15.08	11,094	800-225-5913	Y
John Hancock Funds II Multimgr Lifest Growth Cls 5	JHLGX	B-	C	B+	Up	3.08	15.31	4.55	34.27	32.49	15.06	11,094	800-225-5913	Y
John Hancock Funds II Multimgr Lifest Growth Cls A	JALGX	B-	C	B+	Up	3.06	15.12	4.15	32.64	29.79	15.15	11,094	800-225-5913	Y
John Hancock Funds II Multimgr Lifest Growth Cls B	JBLGX	B-	C	B	Up	2.78	14.68	3.37	29.83	25.24	15.15	11,094	800-225-5913	
John Hancock Funds II Multimgr Lifest Growth Cls C	JCLGX	B-	C	B	Up	2.78	14.70	3.38	29.87	25.21	15.13	11,094	800-225-5913	Y
John Hancock Funds II Multimgr Lifest Growth Cls I	JTGIX	B-	C	B+	Up	3.07	15.30	4.48	33.80	31.88	15.07	11,094	800-225-5913	Y
John Hancock Funds II Multimgr Lifest Growth Cls R1	JPLGX	B-	C	B+	Up	2.91	14.89	3.80	31.22	27.55	15.2	11,094	800-225-5913	Y
John Hancock Funds II Multimgr Lifest Growth Cls R2	JQLGX	B-	C	B+	Up	2.94	15.00	4.02	32.17	29.07	15.02	11,094	800-225-5913	Y
John Hancock Funds II Multimgr Lifest Growth Cls R3	JRLGX	B-	C	B+	Up	2.93	14.91	3.91	31.69	28.18	15.1	11,094	800-225-5913	Y
John Hancock Funds II Multimgr Lifest Growth Cls R4	JSLGX	B-	C	B+	Up	3.06	15.23	4.27	33.20	30.72	15.13	11,094	800-225-5913	Y
John Hancock Funds II Multimgr Lifest Growth Cls R5	JTLGX	B-	C	B+	Up	3.05	15.27	4.50	34.03	32.01	15.17	11,094	800-225-5913	Y
John Hancock Funds II Multimgr Lifest Growth Cls R6	JULGX	B-	C	B+	Up	3.07	15.29	4.52	34.18	32.40	15.08	11,094	800-225-5913	Y
John Hancock Funds II Strategic Equity Allocation Fund NAV		B-	C	B	Up	3.44	16.76	4.73	40.54	39.95	11.42	7,560	800-225-5913	Y
John Hancock Funds Multi-Ind Lifestyle Aggress Port Cls 1	JIIOX	B-	C	B	Up	3.41	17.27	5.39	39.79	40.70	11.81	348.1	800-225-5913	Y
John Hancock Funds Multi-Ind Lifestyle Aggress Port Cls R6	JIIRX	B-	C	B	Up	3.50	17.26	5.44	40.05	40.96	11.82	348.1	800-225-5913	Y
John Hancock Funds Multi-Index Lifestyle Growth Port Cls 1	JLGOX	B-	C	B+	Up	3.36	15.18	6.04	32.92	35.49	11.68	837.8	800-225-5913	Y
John Hancock Funds Multi-Ind Lifestyle Growth Port Cls R6	JLGSX	B-	C	B+	Up	3.35	15.17	6.06	33.01	35.50	11.69	837.8	800-225-5913	Y
JPMorgan Investor Growth & Income Fund Class A	ONGIX	B-	C	B+	Up	3.28	13.92	5.44	32.80	33.83	16.94	2,900	800-480-4111	Y
JPMorgan Investor Growth & Income Fund Class C	ONECX	B-	C	B+	Up	3.11	13.54	4.77	30.52	30.14	16.41	2,900	800-480-4111	Y
JPMorgan Investor Growth & Income Fund Class I	ONGFX	B-	C	B+	Up	3.27	14.03	5.62	33.76	35.54	16.64	2,900	800-480-4111	Y
JPMorgan Investor Growth & Income Fund Class R6	JFBUX	B-	C	B+	Up	3.32	14.10	5.85	34.15	35.93	16.64	2,900	800-480-4111	Y
JPMorgan Investor Growth Fund Class A	ONGAX	B-	C	B	Up	3.51	16.66	4.94	40.44	41.39	20.16	2,783	800-480-4111	Y
JPMorgan Investor Growth Fund Class C	OGGCX	B-	C	B	Up	3.37	16.28	4.30	38.05	37.50	18.67	2,783	800-480-4111	Y
JPMorgan Investor Growth Fund Class I	ONIFX	B-	C	B	Up	3.60	16.77	5.18	41.53	43.23	20.62	2,783	800-480-4111	Y
JPMorgan Investor Growth Fund Class R6	JFTUX	B-	C	B	Up	3.59	16.86	5.35	41.87	43.57	20.61	2,783	800-480-4111	Y
Ladenburg Growth Fund Class A	LGWAX	B-	C	B	Up	3.05	15.44	4.71	30.30		12.48	59.5	877-803-6583	Y
Ladenburg Growth Fund Class C	LGWCX	B-	C	B	Up	2.92	15.01	3.91	27.35		12.33	59.5	877-803-6583	Y
Ladenburg Growth Fund Class I	LGWIX	B-	C	B	Up	3.14	15.66	4.99	30.85		12.48	59.5	877-803-6583	Y
Madison Aggressive Allocation Fund Class A	MAGSX	B-	C	B+	Up	2.88	13.63	5.97	31.71	34.99	11.75	64.1	800-767-0300	Y
Madison Aggressive Allocation Fund Class B	MAGBX	B-	C	B+	Up	2.70	13.22	5.22	28.85	30.08	11.39	64.1	800-767-0300	Y
Madison Aggressive Allocation Fund Class C	MAACX	B-	C	B+	Up	2.70	13.20	5.22	28.82	30.05	11.4	64.1	800-767-0300	Y
Manning & Napier Pro-Blend Maximum Term Series Class I	MNHIX	B-	C	B	Up	4.23	18.78	6.94	40.32	34.31	9.21	399.2	585-325-6880	Y
Manning & Napier Pro-Blend Maximum Term Series Class L	MNHCX	B-	C	B	Up	3.97	18.13	5.90	36.16	27.78	9.86	399.2	585-325-6880	Y
Manning & Napier Pro-Blend Maximum Term Series Class R	MNHRX	B-	C	B	Up	4.11	18.47	6.47	38.30	31.06	12.33	399.2	585-325-6880	Y
Manning & Napier Pro-Blend Maximum Term Series Class S	EXHAX	B-	C	B	Up	4.21	18.61	6.68	39.30	32.69	20.81	399.2	585-325-6880	Y
Manning & Napier Pro-Blend Maximum Term Series Class W	MNHWX	B-	C	B		4.41	18.84	6.89	39.56	32.94	20.81	399.2	585-325-6880	Y
MassMutual RetireSMART Growth Fund Administrative Class	MRGLX	B-	C	B	Up	3.92	17.68	5.75	39.45	32.27	10.58	119.0		Y
MassMutual RetireSMART Growth Fund Class A	MRRAX	B-	C	B	Up	3.92	17.55	5.55	38.35	30.67	10.58	119.0		Y
MassMutual RetireSMART Growth Fund Class I	MRGUX	B-	C	B	Up	4.03	17.83	6.15	40.73	34.35	10.57	119.0		Y
MassMutual RetireSMART Growth Fund Class R3	MRGVX	B-	C	B	Up	3.88	17.43	5.42	37.78	29.77	10.44	119.0		Y
MassMutual RetireSMART Growth Fund Class R4	MRGZX	B-	C	B	Up	3.87	17.66	5.65	38.82	31.29	10.46	119.0		Y
MassMutual RetireSMART Growth Fund Class R5	MRRSX	B-	C	B	Up	3.92	17.81	5.99	40.20	33.70	10.58	119.0		Y
MassMutual RetireSMART Growth Fund Service Class	MRGYX	B-	C	B	Up	4.02	17.77	5.97	39.84	33.05	10.6	119.0		Y
MassMutual RetireSMART Moderate Growth Administrative Cls	MRSLX	B-	C	B+	Up	3.78	15.96	5.86	35.45	29.86	9.88	239.7		Y
MassMutual RetireSMART Moderate Growth Fund Class A	MOGAX	B-	C	B+	Up	3.65	15.88	5.64	34.36	28.16	9.92	239.7		Y
MassMutual RetireSMART Moderate Growth Fund Class I	MROUX	B-	C	B+	Up	3.79	16.15	6.25	36.46	31.68	9.85	239.7		Y
MassMutual RetireSMART Moderate Growth Fund Class R3	MROTX	B-	C	B+	Up	3.60	15.75	5.46	33.77	27.29	9.77	239.7		Y
MassMutual RetireSMART Moderate Growth Fund Class R4	MROZX	B-	C	B+	Up	3.70	15.97	5.75	34.77	28.83	9.8	239.7		Y
MassMutual RetireSMART Moderate Growth Fund Class R5	MRSSX	B-	C	B+	Up	3.78	16.13	6.10	36.30	31.17	9.86	239.7		Y

Category: Aggressive Allocation (con't)

		RATINGS				TOTAL RETURNS & PERFORMANCE					ASSETS		NEW INVESTORS	
Fund Name	Ticker Symbol	Overall Rating	Reward Rating	Risk Rating	Recent Up/ Downgrade	3-Month Total Return	6-Month Total Return	1-Year Total Return	3-Year Total Return	5-Year Total Return	NAV	Total Assets (MIL)	Telephone	Open to New Investors
MassMutual RetireSMART Moderate Growth Fund Service Class	MROYX	B-	C	B+	Up	3.77	16.07	5.97	35.77	30.41	9.89	239.7		Y
MFS Aggressive Growth Allocation Fund Class 529A	EAGTX	B-	C+	B	Up	4.95	20.52	8.33	43.05	45.17	24.13	1,882	877-960-6077	Y
MFS Aggressive Growth Allocation Fund Class 529B	EBAAX	B-	C	B	Up	4.74	20.02	7.47	39.82	39.69	23.62	1,882	877-960-6077	Y
MFS Aggressive Growth Allocation Fund Class 529C	ECAAX	B-	C	B	Up	4.76	20.04	7.49	39.88	39.76	23.3	1,882	877-960-6077	Y
MFS Aggressive Growth Allocation Fund Class A	MAAGX	B-	C+	B	Up	4.92	20.47	8.31	43.19	45.40	24.3	1,882	877-960-6077	Y
MFS Aggressive Growth Allocation Fund Class B	MBAGX	B-	C	B	Up	4.77	20.07	7.57	40.03	40.09	23.93	1,882	877-960-6077	Y
MFS Aggressive Growth Allocation Fund Class C	MCAGX	B-	C	B	Up	4.77	20.08	7.55	40.07	40.07	23.68	1,882	877-960-6077	Y
MFS Aggressive Growth Allocation Fund Class I	MIAGX	B-	C+	B		5.01	20.69	8.65	44.30	47.29	24.73	1,882	877-960-6077	Y
MFS Aggressive Growth Allocation Fund Class R1	MAAFX	B-	C	B	Up	4.76	20.04	7.54	40.05	40.03	23.3	1,882	877-960-6077	Y
MFS Aggressive Growth Allocation Fund Class R2	MAWAX	B-	C	B	Up	4.89	20.35	8.08	42.14	43.59	23.77	1,882	877-960-6077	Y
MFS Aggressive Growth Allocation Fund Class R3	MAAHX	B-	C+	B	Up	4.91	20.50	8.32	43.16	45.38	24.1	1,882	877-960-6077	Y
MFS Aggressive Growth Allocation Fund Class R4	MAALX	B-	C+	B		5.03	20.68	8.63	44.26	47.28	24.39	1,882	877-960-6077	Y
MFS Growth Allocation Fund Class 529A	EAGWX	B	C+	B+	Up	4.75	18.28	8.56	36.74	38.94	21.15	5,102	877-960-6077	Y
MFS Growth Allocation Fund Class 529B	EBGWX	B-	C+	B+	Up	4.60	17.87	7.78	33.70	33.83	20.9	5,102	877-960-6077	Y
MFS Growth Allocation Fund Class 529C	ECGWX	B-	C+	B+	Up	4.57	17.85	7.77	33.69	33.78	20.59	5,102	877-960-6077	Y
MFS Growth Allocation Fund Class A	MAGWX	B	C+	B+	Up	4.76	18.30	8.58	36.88	39.19	21.33	5,102	877-960-6077	Y
MFS Growth Allocation Fund Class B	MBGWX	B-	C+	B+	Up	4.60	17.91	7.80	33.89	34.11	21.13	5,102	877-960-6077	Y
MFS Growth Allocation Fund Class C	MCGWX	B-	C+	B+	Up	4.55	17.89	7.75	33.85	34.11	20.88	5,102	877-960-6077	Y
MFS Growth Allocation Fund Class I	MGWIX	B	C+	B+	Up	4.86	18.48	8.85	37.98	40.98	21.54	5,102	877-960-6077	Y
MFS Growth Allocation Fund Class R1	MAGMX	B-	C+	B+	Up	4.60	17.88	7.77	33.92	34.05	20.43	5,102	877-960-6077	Y
MFS Growth Allocation Fund Class R2	MGALX	B-	C+	B+		4.72	18.21	8.34	35.93	37.50	20.83	5,102	877-960-6077	Y
MFS Growth Allocation Fund Class R3	MAGEX	B	C+	B+	Up	4.80	18.36	8.58	36.93	39.23	21.14	5,102	877-960-6077	Y
MFS Growth Allocation Fund Class R4	MAGJX	B	C+	B+	Up	4.86	18.51	8.89	37.99	40.93	21.32	5,102	877-960-6077	Y
Morningstar Aggressive Growth ETF Asset Alloc Port Cls I		B-	C	B	Up	2.71	14.27	3.94	34.25	33.07	12.09	103.5	866-759-5679	Y
Morningstar Growth ETF Asset Allocation Portfolio Class I		B-	C	B+	Up	2.68	12.90	4.56	29.62	29.98	11.11	218.5	866-759-5679	Y
Nationwide Investor Destinations Aggressive Fund Class R6	GAIDX	B-	C	B	Up	3.58	17.31	4.59	38.09	35.72	9.43	998.2	800-848-0920	Y
Nationwide Inv Destinations Moderately Aggressive Cls A	NDMAX	B-	C	B	Up	3.45	15.72	4.90	33.13	31.15	9.6	1,563	800-848-0920	Y
Nationwide Inv Destinations Moderately Aggressive Cls C	NDMCX	B-	C	B	Up	3.29	15.35	4.18	30.27	26.50	9.26	1,563	800-848-0920	Y
Nationwide Inv Destinations Moderately Aggressive Cls R	GMARX	B-	C	B	Up	3.38	15.57	4.62	31.93	29.29	9.29	1,563	800-848-0920	Y
Nationwide Inv Destinations Moderately Aggressive Cls R6	GMIAX	B-	C	B+	Up	3.55	15.81	5.28	34.44	33.45	9.58	1,563	800-848-0920	Y
Nationwide Inv Destinations Mod Aggress Inst Serv Cls	NWWIX	B-	C	B+	Up	3.53	15.79	5.19	34.16	32.87	9.56	1,563	800-848-0920	Y
Nationwide Inv Destinations Moderately Aggressive Serv Cls	NDMSX	B-	C	B	Up	3.45	15.60	4.86	32.88	30.81	9.57	1,563	800-848-0920	Y
Pacific Funds Port Optimization Aggressive-Growth Adv Cls	POEDX	B-	C	B	Up	4.12	18.66	6.11	39.99	37.34	14.88	316.0	800-722-2333	Y
Pacific Funds Port Optimization Aggressive-Growth Cls A	POEAX	B-	C	B	Up	4.07	18.54	5.91	39.05	35.66	14.83	316.0	800-722-2333	Y
Pacific Funds Portfolio Optimization Growth Advisor Cls	PMADX	B-	C	B+	Up	3.90	16.73	5.98	33.50	33.36	13.32	872.6	800-722-2333	Y
Pacific Funds Portfolio Optimization Growth Fund Class A	PODAX	B-	C	B	Up	3.83	16.62	5.77	32.47	31.69	13.26	872.6	800-722-2333	Y
Pacific Funds Portfolio Optimization Growth Fund Class B	PODBX	B-	C	B	Up	3.59	16.12	4.92	29.54	26.85	12.96	872.6	800-722-2333	Y
Pacific Funds Portfolio Optimization Growth Fund Class C	PODCX	B-	C	B	Up	3.69	16.20	4.99	29.61	26.90	12.91	872.6	800-722-2333	Y
PIMCO StocksPLUS® Long Duration Fund Institutional Class	PSLDX	B	B	B-	Up	10.05	33.65	22.35	63.68	107.98	7.29	430.9	866-746-2602	Y
Praxis Genesis Growth Portfolio Class A	MGAFX	B-	C	B+	Up	3.21	14.11	4.81	31.63	30.94	15.09	69.2		Y
Principal Strategic Asset Mgmt Conservative Growth Cls A	SAGPX	B-	C	B+	Up	3.77	15.37	6.46	34.38	35.26	17.05	3,032	800-787-1621	Y
Principal Strategic Asset Mgmt Conservative Growth Cls C	SCGPX	B-	C	B+	Up	3.57	14.87	5.59	31.30	30.20	15.66	3,032	800-787-1621	Y
Principal Strategic Asset Mgmt Conservative Growth Cls J	PCGJX	B-	C	B+	Up	3.80	15.46	6.62	35.05	36.17	16.37	3,032	800-787-1621	Y
Principal Strat Asset Mgmt Cons Growth Inst Cls	PCWIX	B-	C	B+	Up	3.87	15.55	6.82	35.73	37.57	16.63	3,032	800-787-1621	Y
Principal Strategic Asset Mgmt Conservative Growth R-1 Cls	PCGGX	B-	C	B+	Up	3.59	15.03	5.88	32.26	31.67	16.43	3,032	800-787-1621	Y
Principal Strategic Asset Mgmt Conservative Growth R-2 Cls	PCGVX	B-	C	B+	Up	3.65	15.13	6.00	32.74	32.55	16.44	3,032	800-787-1621	Y
Principal Strategic Asset Mgmt Conservative Growth R-3 Cls	PCGPX	B-	C	B+	Up	3.74	15.23	6.20	33.45	33.77	16.35	3,032	800-787-1621	Y
Principal Strategic Asset Mgmt Conservative Growth R-4 Cls	PCWSX	B-	C	B+	Up	3.75	15.40	6.44	34.26	35.03	16.56	3,032	800-787-1621	Y
Principal Strategic Asset Mgmt Conservative Growth R-5 Cls	PCWPX	B-	C	B+	Up	3.76	15.44	6.53	34.70	35.82	16.52	3,032	800-787-1621	Y
Principal Strategic Asset Mgmt Strategic Growth Cls A	SACAX	B-	C	B	Up	4.08	17.38	6.12	36.72	36.55	18.1	1,875	800-787-1621	Y
Principal Strategic Asset Mgmt Strategic Growth Cls C	SWHCX	B-	C	B	Up	3.92	16.95	5.36	33.65	31.53	16.14	1,875	800-787-1621	Y
Principal Strategic Asset Mgmt Strategic Growth Cls J	PSWJX	B-	C	B	Up	4.13	17.54	6.35	37.42	37.61	17.38	1,875	800-787-1621	Y

Category: Aggressive Allocation (con't)

Fund Name	Ticker Symbol	RATINGS: Overall Rating	Reward Rating	Risk Rating	Recent Up/ Downgrade	TOTAL RETURNS & PERFORMANCE: 3-Month Total Return	6-Month Total Return	1-Year Total Return	3-Year Total Return	5-Year Total Return	ASSETS: NAV	Total Assets (MIL)	NEW INVESTORS: Telephone	Open to New Investors
Principal Strategic Asset Mgmt Strategic Growth Inst Cls	PSWIX	B-	C	B	Up	4.20	17.65	6.50	38.10	39.00	17.61	1,875	800-787-1621	Y
Principal Strategic Asset Mgmt Strategic Growth R-1 Cls	PSGGX	B-	C	B	Up	3.92	17.08	5.57	34.54	33.07	17.47	1,875	800-787-1621	Y
Principal Strategic Asset Mgmt Strategic Growth R-2 Cls	PSGVX	B-	C	B	Up	4.01	17.24	5.74	35.16	33.97	17.34	1,875	800-787-1621	Y
Principal Strategic Asset Mgmt Strategic Growth R-3 Cls	PSGPX	B-	C	B	Up	4.02	17.30	5.93	35.84	35.20	17.33	1,875	800-787-1621	Y
Principal Strategic Asset Mgmt Strategic Growth R-4 Cls	PSGLX	B-	C	B	Up	4.10	17.41	6.16	36.64	36.50	17.48	1,875	800-787-1621	Y
Principal Strategic Asset Mgmt Strategic Growth R-5 Cls	PSGFX	B-	C	B	Up	4.12	17.46	6.24	37.08	37.24	17.42	1,875	800-787-1621	Y
Prospector Capital Appreciation Fund	PCAFX	B	C+	B+		4.79	17.26	11.06	37.27	36.83	19.02	28.5	877-734-7862	Y
Putnam Dynamic Asset Allocation Growth Fund Class A	PAEAX	B-	C	B	Up	2.57	14.86	3.04	34.08	36.32	15.92	2,872	617-292-1000	Y
Putnam Dynamic Asset Allocation Growth Fund Class P		B-	C	B	Up	2.73	15.09	3.48	35.74	38.01	16.16	2,872	617-292-1000	
Putnam Dynamic Asset Allocation Growth Fund Class R	PASRX	B-	C	B	Up	2.51	14.71	2.81	33.03	34.65	15.51	2,872	617-292-1000	Y
Putnam Dynamic Asset Allocation Growth Fund Class R5	PADEX	B-	C	B	Up	2.67	14.98	3.32	35.21	38.13	16.11	2,872	617-292-1000	Y
Putnam Dynamic Asset Allocation Growth Fund Class R6	PAEEX	B-	C	B	Up	2.73	15.09	3.50	35.65	38.90	16.16	2,872	617-292-1000	Y
Putnam Dynamic Asset Allocation Growth Fund Class Y	PAGYX	B-	C	B	Up	2.67	14.97	3.31	35.12	38.05	16.12	2,872	617-292-1000	Y
QS Growth Fund Class A	SCHAX	B-	C	B	Up	2.13	13.55	3.13	30.26	24.57	15.33	730.9	877-721-1926	Y
QS Growth Fund Class C	SCHCX	B-	C	B	Up	1.95	13.17	2.46	27.65	20.44	14.19	730.9	877-721-1926	Y
QS Growth Fund Class I	LANIX	B-	C	B	Up	2.20	13.69	3.41	31.34	26.38	15.27	730.9	877-721-1926	Y
QS Growth Fund Class R	LLLRX	B-	C	B	Up	2.01	13.33	2.76	28.97	22.85	15.22	730.9	877-721-1926	Y
QS Moderate Growth Fund Class A	SCGRX	B-	C	B+	Up	2.24	12.34	4.14	28.20	25.41	15.31	463.3	877-721-1926	Y
QS Moderate Growth Fund Class C	SCGCX	B-	C	B+	Up	2.07	12.00	3.44	25.46	21.16	15.61	463.3	877-721-1926	Y
QS Moderate Growth Fund Class I	LLAIX	B-	C	B+	Up	2.39	12.54	4.49	29.36	27.26	15.18	463.3	877-721-1926	Y
QS Moderate Growth Fund Class R	LLMRX	B-	C	B+	Up	2.20	12.19	3.84	26.89	23.42	15.11	463.3	877-721-1926	Y
Russell Inv LifePoints Eq Growth Strategy Cls S	RELSX	B-	C	B+	Up	2.28	12.77	1.89	29.77	24.03	12.98	512.3	800-426-7969	Y
Russell Investments LifePoints Growth Strategy Cls A	RALAX	B-	C	B+	Up	2.22	10.84	2.25	25.10	20.35	11.96	1,109	800-426-7969	Y
Russell Investments LifePoints Growth Strategy Cls E	RALEX	B-	C	B+	Up	2.12	10.78	2.24	25.07	20.39	12.02	1,109	800-426-7969	Y
Russell Investments LifePoints Growth Strategy Cls R1	RALRX	B-	C	A-	Up	2.27	10.94	2.55	26.23	22.21	12.16	1,109	800-426-7969	Y
Russell Investments LifePoints Growth Strategy Cls R4	RALUX	B-	C	B+	Up	2.12	10.79	2.28	25.21	20.66	12.01	1,109	800-426-7969	Y
Russell Investments LifePoints Growth Strategy Cls R5	RALVX	B-	C	B+	Up	2.04	10.61	1.99	24.27	19.12	11.98	1,109	800-426-7969	Y
Schwab MarketTrack Growth Portfolio™	SWHGX	B-	C	B+	Up	3.04	14.43	4.25	33.46	34.94	22.99	814.3	877-824-5615	Y
SEI Asset Alloc Trust Moderate Strategy Alloc Cls F	SXMAX	B	C+	A-		3.11	15.02	8.11	31.70	42.33	20.51	84.5	800-342-5734	Y
SEI Asset Alloc Trust Tax-Managed Aggress Strat Cls F	SISAX	B-	C	B	Up	3.21	15.66	3.39	37.70	33.95	21.52	79.4	800-342-5734	Y
Sterling Capital Strategic Allocation Growth Fund Class A	BCMAX	B-	C	B+	Up	2.39	11.72	3.26	28.05	24.61	12.08	21.6	800-228-1872	Y
Sterling Capital Strategic Allocation Growth Fund Class C	BCGCX	B-	C	B+	Up	2.22	11.28	2.57	25.16	19.97	11.62	21.6	800-228-1872	Y
Sterling Capital Strategic Allocation Growth Inst Shares	BCMTX	B-	C	B+	Up	2.54	11.89	3.51	29.01	26.19	12.11	21.6	800-228-1872	Y
T. Rowe Price Personal Strategy Growth Fund	TRSGX	B-	C	B+	Up	3.55	15.98	6.40	41.07	42.25	34.39	2,481	410-345-2000	Y
T. Rowe Price Personal Strategy Growth Fund I Class	TGIPX	B-	C	B+	Up	3.60	16.06	6.55	41.64	42.87	34.46	2,481	410-345-2000	Y
The Disciplined Growth Investors Fund	DGIFX	B-	C	B+	Down	0.17	16.05	6.09	42.33	51.80	20.66	235.6	855-344-3863	Y
Thrivent Aggressive Allocation Fund Class A	TAAAX	B-	C	B	Up	3.28	17.07	5.68	44.38	43.15	15.42	1,377		Y
Thrivent Aggressive Allocation Fund Class S	TAAIX	B-	C	B	Up	3.31	17.21	5.91	45.67	45.47	15.58	1,377		Y
Thrivent Moderately Aggressive Allocation Fund Class A	TMAAX	B-	C	B+	Up	3.37	15.23	6.29	35.87	36.05	14.99	2,981		Y
Thrivent Moderately Aggressive Allocation Fund Class S	TMAFX	B-	C	B+	Up	3.41	15.38	6.58	36.82	38.00	15.12	2,981		Y
TIAA-CREF Lifestyle Growth Fund Advisor Class	TSGHX	B-	C	B	Up	3.34	16.22	3.81	35.89	37.00	15.47	170.6	877-518-9161	Y
TIAA-CREF Lifestyle Growth Fund Institutional Class	TSGGX	B-	C	B	Up	3.33	16.30	3.87	36.17	37.38	15.48	170.6	877-518-9161	Y
TIAA-CREF Lifestyle Growth Fund Premier Class	TSGPX	B-	C	B	Up	3.33	16.21	3.69	35.57	36.26	15.48	170.6	877-518-9161	Y
TIAA-CREF Lifestyle Growth Fund Retail Class	TSGLX	B-	C	B	Up	3.28	16.13	3.56	34.94	35.32	15.4	170.6	877-518-9161	Y
TIAA-CREF Lifestyle Growth Fund Retirement Class	TSGRX	B-	C	B	Up	3.28	16.11	3.60	35.06	35.57	15.42	170.6	877-518-9161	Y
TOPS® Growth ETF Portfolio Class 1		B-	C	B	Up	2.77	14.82	3.96	33.77	31.31	15.18	31.2	855-572-5945	Y
TOPS® Growth ETF Portfolio Class 2		B-	C	B	Up	2.68	14.70	3.73	32.80	29.75	14.9	31.2	855-572-5945	Y
TOPS® Growth ETF Portfolio Investor Class		B-	C	B	Up	2.47	13.84	3.23	31.63	25.73	16.21	31.2	855-572-5945	Y
TOPS® Growth ETF Portfolio Service Class Shares		B-	C	B		2.49	14.01	3.51	34.25	28.96	14.9	31.2	855-572-5945	Y
TOPS® Managed Risk Growth ETF Portfolio Class 1		B-	C	B+	Up	2.77	10.95	3.25	25.49	12.16	11.85	854.7	855-572-5945	
TOPS® Managed Risk Growth ETF Portfolio Class 2		B-	C	B+	Up	2.70	10.72	2.97	24.46	10.67	11.77	854.7	855-572-5945	Y
TOPS® Managed Risk Growth ETF Portfolio Class 3 Shares		B-	C	B+	Up	2.55	10.11	2.70	24.16	9.52	11.71	854.7	855-572-5945	Y

Category: Aggressive Allocation (con't)

Fund Name	Ticker Symbol	Overall Rating	Reward Rating	Risk Rating	Recent Up/ Downgrade	3-Month Total Return	6-Month Total Return	1-Year Total Return	3-Year Total Return	5-Year Total Return	NAV	Total Assets (MIL)	Telephone	Open to New Investors
		RATINGS				TOTAL RETURNS & PERFORMANCE					ASSETS		NEW INVESTORS	
TOPS® Managed Risk Growth ETF Portfolio Investor Class		B-	C	B+	Up	2.41	9.63	2.64	23.61	9.05	12.35	854.7	855-572-5945	Y
USAA Cornerstone Aggressive Fund	UCAGX	B-	C	B+	Up	2.57	12.59	2.72	25.89	19.24	12.34	369.0	800-235-8396	Y
VALIC Company II Aggressive Growth Lifestyle Fund	VAGLX	B-	C	B	Up	2.93	15.30	3.87	30.94	30.66	10.21	592.8		Y
Value Line Capital Appreciation Fund, Inc. Inst Cls	VLIIX	B-	C	B		3.45	22.22	8.76	54.57	55.73	10.78	503.7	800-243-2729	Y
Value Line Capital Appreciation Fund, Inc. Investor Class	VALIX	B-	C	B		3.44	22.12	8.51	53.33	55.64	10.82	503.7	800-243-2729	Y
Vanguard LifeStrategy Growth Fund Investor Shares	VASGX	B-	C	B+	Up	3.44	15.04	6.14	34.91	37.41	34.02	15,573	877-662-7447	Y
Voya Retirement Growth Portfolio Class A	IRGPX	B-	C	B+	Up	3.25	14.22	5.28	29.45	28.94	13.33	2,642	800-366-0066	Y
Voya Retirement Growth Portfolio Class I	IIRGX	B-	C	B+	Up	3.30	14.48	5.77	31.06	31.73	13.44	2,642	800-366-0066	Y
Voya Solution Moderately Aggressive Portfolio Class A	IAGAX	B-	C	B	Up	3.25	15.01	4.14	29.81	28.46	13.02	607.2	800-366-0066	Y
Voya Solution Moderately Aggressive Portfolio Class I	IAGIX	B-	C	B+	Up	3.33	15.33	4.61	31.74	31.72	13.31	607.2	800-366-0066	Y
Voya Solution Moderately Aggressive Portfolio Class R6	VYROX	B-	C	B+	Up	3.34	15.35	4.61	31.66	31.63	13.3	607.2	800-366-0066	Y
Voya Solution Moderately Aggressive Portfolio Class S	IAGSX	B-	C	B+	Up	3.29	15.14	4.37	30.88	30.03	13.15	607.2	800-366-0066	Y
Voya Solution Moderately Aggressive Portfolio Class S2	IAGTX	B-	C	B	Up	3.21	15.04	4.24	30.29	29.17	13.15	607.2	800-366-0066	Y
Voya Strategic Allocation Growth Portfolio Class I	ISAGX	B-	C	B+	Up	3.21	14.75	4.99	31.28	31.34	14.51	127.4	800-366-0066	Y
Voya Strategic Allocation Growth Portfolio Class S	ISGRX	B-	C	B+	Up	3.09	14.65	4.75	30.25	29.65	14.38	127.4	800-366-0066	Y
Walden Asset Management Fund	WSBFX	B	C+	A-		3.68	14.52	10.74	34.62	44.91	19.4	145.0	617-814-1215	Y
Wells Fargo Diversified Capital Builder Fund - Class A	EKBAX	B-	C	B		4.48	19.41	10.53	41.94	57.86	10.57	1,087	800-222-8222	Y
Wells Fargo Diversified Capital Builder Fund - Class Admin	EKBDX	B-	C	B	Up	4.50	19.43	10.61	42.38	59.01	10.58	1,087	800-222-8222	Y
Wells Fargo Diversified Capital Builder Fund - Class C	EKBCX	B-	C	B	Up	4.31	18.90	9.71	38.88	52.20	10.55	1,087	800-222-8222	Y
Wells Fargo Diversified Capital Builder Fund - Class Inst	EKBYX	B-	C	B		4.59	19.60	10.97	43.53	60.81	10.5	1,087	800-222-8222	Y
Wells Fargo WealthBuilder Growth Allocation Fund Class A	WGAFX	B-	C	B+	Up	2.97	14.43	4.51	34.61	30.51	12.13	295.6	800-222-8222	Y
Wells Fargo WealthBuilder Growth Allocation Inst Cls	WGAYX	B-	C	B	Up	3.05	14.52	4.74	33.55	29.49	12.14	295.6	800-222-8222	Y
Yorktown Capital Income Fund Class A	APIGX	B	C	A	Up	1.95	6.53	5.26	28.69	21.26	30.46	24.4	800-544-6060	
Yorktown Capital Income Fund Class Institutional	AFAAX	B	C	A	Up	2.04	6.67	5.52	29.91	23.61	31.53	24.4	800-544-6060	Y
Yorktown Capital Income Fund Class L	AFDDX	B-	C	A-	Up	1.79	6.16	4.49	26.08	17.59	28.91	24.4	800-544-6060	Y

Category: Alternative Miscellaneous

Fund Name	Ticker Symbol	Overall Rating	Reward Rating	Risk Rating	Recent Up/ Downgrade	3-Month Total Return	6-Month Total Return	1-Year Total Return	3-Year Total Return	5-Year Total Return	NAV	Total Assets (MIL)	Telephone	Open to New Investors
		RATINGS				TOTAL RETURNS & PERFORMANCE					ASSETS		NEW INVESTORS	
Catalyst/Exceed Defined Risk Fund Class A	CLPAX	B	C	A-	Up	3.17	13.17	6.54	30.26	22.02	10.74	12.2	866-447-4228	Y
Catalyst/Exceed Defined Risk Fund Class C	CLPCX	B-	C	A-	Up	2.91	12.76	5.64	26.93	17.10	10.25	12.2	866-447-4228	Y
Catalyst/Exceed Defined Risk Fund Class I	CLPFX	B	C	A-	Up	3.14	13.19	6.72	30.82	23.19	10.81	12.2	866-447-4228	Y

Category: Cautious Allocation

Fund Name	Ticker Symbol	Overall Rating	Reward Rating	Risk Rating	Recent Up/ Downgrade	3-Month Total Return	6-Month Total Return	1-Year Total Return	3-Year Total Return	5-Year Total Return	NAV	Total Assets (MIL)	Telephone	Open to New Investors
		RATINGS				TOTAL RETURNS & PERFORMANCE					ASSETS		NEW INVESTORS	
1290 DoubleLine Dynamic Allocation Fund Class A	TNXAX	B	C	A-	Up	3.48	12.61	7.65	21.88		10.98	60.6	212-554-1234	Y
1290 DoubleLine Dynamic Allocation Fund Class I	TNVDX	B	C+	A-	Up	3.58	12.71	7.93	22.74		10.99	60.6	212-554-1234	Y
1290 DoubleLine Dynamic Allocation Fund Class R	TNYRX	B-	C	A-	Up	3.49	12.51	7.38	21.03		10.97	60.6	212-554-1234	Y
AB All Market Income Portfolio Advisor Class	MRKYX	B-	C	B	Up	3.34	12.35	4.84	18.46		9.79	95.8	212-969-1000	Y
AB All Market Income Portfolio Class A	MRKAX	B-	C	B	Up	3.28	12.35	4.69	17.56		9.78	95.8	212-969-1000	Y
AB Conservative Wealth Strategy Advisor Class	ABPYX	B-	C	A-	Up	3.03	10.56	4.66	15.41	16.87	12.56	180.8	212-969-1000	Y
AB Conservative Wealth Strategy Class A	ABPAX	B-	C	A-	Up	3.04	10.51	4.48	14.62	15.53	12.51	180.8	212-969-1000	Y
AB Conservative Wealth Strategy Class I	APWIX	B-	C	A-	Up	3.08	10.53	4.66	15.31	16.72	12.7	180.8	212-969-1000	Y
AB Conservative Wealth Strategy Class K	APWKX	B-	C	B+	Up	2.97	10.44	4.38	14.21	14.90	12.48	180.8	212-969-1000	Y
AB Conservative Wealth Strategy Class R	APPRX	B-	C	B+	Up	2.87	10.22	3.99	13.17	13.15	12.51	180.8	212-969-1000	Y
AB Tax-Managed All Market Income Portfolio Advisor Class	AGIYX	B-	C+	B		3.70	12.17	7.67	20.12	21.29	12.65	105.5	212-969-1000	Y
AB Tax-Managed All Market Income Portfolio Class A	AGIAX	B-	C+	B		3.64	11.95	7.41	19.27	19.73	12.63	105.5	212-969-1000	Y

Category: Cautious Allocation (con't)

Fund Name	Ticker Symbol	RATINGS: Overall Rating	RATINGS: Reward Rating	RATINGS: Risk Rating	RATINGS: Recent Up/ Downgrade	TOTAL RETURNS & PERFORMANCE: 3-Month Total Return	6-Month Total Return	1-Year Total Return	3-Year Total Return	5-Year Total Return	ASSETS: NAV	Total Assets (MIL)	NEW INVESTORS: Telephone	Open to New Investors
AB Tax-Managed All Market Income Portfolio Class B	AGIBX	B-	C	B	Up	3.51	11.66	6.61	16.63	15.34	12.96	105.5	212-969-1000	
AB Tax-Managed All Market Income Portfolio Class C	AGICX	B-	C	B	Up	3.45	11.67	6.69	16.68	15.41	12.87	105.5	212-969-1000	Y
AC Alternatives® Income Fund Y Class	ALYNX	B-	C	B		0.69	5.13	3.23	14.62		9.68	297.0	800-444-4015	Y
AdvisorOne CLS Growth and Income Fund Class N	CLERX	B-	C	B+	Up	2.13	10.08	3.26	18.50	17.54	11.02	416.6		Y
AIG Income Explorer Fund Class A	IEAAX	B-	C	A-	Up	3.44	14.69	4.71	25.37	20.82	15.31	46.3	800-858-8850	Y
AIG Income Explorer Fund Class C	IEACX	B-	C	B+	Up	3.35	14.41	4.11	23.02	16.97	15.29	46.3	800-858-8850	Y
AIG Income Explorer Fund Class W	IEAWX	B-	C	A-	Up	3.49	14.82	4.92	26.13	22.02	15.31	46.3	800-858-8850	Y
AllianzGI Income & Growth Fund Class A	AZNAX	B-	C	B+		2.48	13.63	5.35	32.43	31.11	11	4,520	800-498-5413	Y
AllianzGI Income & Growth Fund Class C	AZNCX	B-	C	B+	Up	2.33	13.27	4.60	29.56	26.26	10.07	4,520	800-498-5413	Y
AllianzGI Income & Growth Fund Class P	AIGPX	B-	C	B+		2.56	13.82	5.64	33.48	32.81	11.29	4,520	800-498-5413	Y
AllianzGI Income & Growth Fund Class R	AIGRX	B-	C	B+		2.42	13.50	5.09	31.46	29.37	11	4,520	800-498-5413	Y
AllianzGI Income & Growth Fund Institutional Class	AZNIX	B-	C	B+		2.56	13.84	5.69	33.76	33.41	11.4	4,520	800-498-5413	Y
American Century Inv One Choice Port®: Cons Inv Cls	AOCIX	B-	C	A-	Up	3.19	11.31	5.23	20.24	23.68	13.69	1,239	800-444-4015	Y
American Century Inv One Choice Port®: Conservative R Cls	AORSX	B-	C	A-	Up	3.06	11.04	4.78	18.45	20.62	13.69	1,239	800-444-4015	Y
American Century Inv One Choice Port®: Very Cons Inv Cls	AONIX	B-	C	A-		2.84	8.66	5.75	13.79	18.43	12.13	424.9	800-444-4015	Y
American Century Inv One Choice Port®: Very Cons R Cls	AORHX	B-	C	B+	Up	2.71	8.39	5.22	12.09	15.49	12.14	424.9	800-444-4015	Y
American Century Multi-Asset Income Fund A Class	AMJAX	B-	C	B+		1.93	10.48	4.16	15.91		9.83	64.3	800-444-4015	Y
American Century Multi-Asset Income Fund I Class	AMJIX	B-	C	B+		2.05	10.83	4.72	17.57		9.84	64.3	800-444-4015	Y
American Century Multi-Asset Income Fund Investor Class	AMJVX	B-	C	B+		2.00	10.61	4.41	16.77		9.83	64.3	800-444-4015	Y
American Century Multi-Asset Income Fund R Class	AMJWX	B-	C	B	Up	1.87	10.36	4.01	15.07		9.83	64.3	800-444-4015	Y
American Century Multi-Asset Income Fund R5 Class	AMJGX	B-	C	B+		2.04	10.81	4.72	17.56		9.85	64.3	800-444-4015	Y
American Century Multi-Asset Income Fund R6 Class	AMJRX	B-	C	B+		2.08	10.90	4.87	18.09		9.84	64.3	800-444-4015	Y
American Century Multi-Asset Income Fund Y Class	AMJYX	B-	C	B+		2.08	10.78	4.87	17.97		9.84	64.3	800-444-4015	Y
American Century Multi-Asset Real Return Fund A Class	ASIDX	B-	C	B+	Up	2.23	11.53	5.07	17.67	5.30	10.53	11.8	800-444-4015	Y
American Century Multi-Asset Real Return Fund C Class	ASIZX	B-	C	B+	Up	2.02	11.03	4.25	14.99	1.39	10.09	11.8	800-444-4015	Y
American Century Multi-Asset Real Return Fund I Class	ASINX	B-	C	A-		2.39	11.82	5.55	19.29	7.73	10.69	11.8	800-444-4015	Y
American Century Multi-Asset Real Return Investor Cls	ASIOX	B-	C	A-		2.30	11.66	5.32	18.62	6.68	10.63	11.8	800-444-4015	Y
American Century Multi-Asset Real Return Fund R Class	ASIUX	B-	C	B+	Up	2.16	11.32	4.73	16.78	4.03	10.39	11.8	800-444-4015	Y
American Century Multi-Asset Real Return Fund R5 Class	AMRUX	B-	C	A-		2.29	11.71	5.45	19.21	7.66	10.68	11.8	800-444-4015	Y
American Century Strategic Allocation: Conservative A Cls	ACCAX	B-	C	A-	Up	2.99	11.20	5.17	18.81	21.17	5.64	417.3	800-444-4015	Y
American Century Strategic Allocation: Conservative C Cls	AACCX	B-	C	B+	Up	2.84	10.83	4.32	16.16	16.79	5.55	417.3	800-444-4015	Y
American Century Strategic Allocation: Conservative I Cls	ACCIX	B	C	A-	Up	3.29	11.41	5.64	20.39	24.05	5.65	417.3	800-444-4015	Y
American Century Strategic Alloc: Conservative Inv Cls	TWSCX	B	C	A-	Up	3.23	11.31	5.44	19.91	22.85	5.65	417.3	800-444-4015	Y
American Century Strategic Allocation: Conservative R Cls	AACRX	B-	C	A-	Up	2.93	11.10	4.93	18.01	19.85	5.63	417.3	800-444-4015	Y
American Century Strategic Allocation: Conservative R5 Cls	AACGX	B	C	A-	Up	3.28	11.39	5.64	20.40	23.36	5.66	417.3	800-444-4015	Y
American Century Strategic Allocation: Conservative R6 Cls	AACDX	B	C	A-	Up	3.14	11.49	5.80	20.93	24.97	5.65	417.3	800-444-4015	Y
American Funds College 2021 Fund Class 529-A	CTOAX	B-	C	B	Up	1.97	4.99	5.77	8.40	13.28	11.35	1,949	800-421-4225	Y
American Funds College 2021 Fund Class 529-E	CTOEX	B-	C	B	Up	1.98	4.92	5.58	7.69	11.97	11.3	1,949	800-421-4225	Y
American Funds College 2021 Fund Class 529F1	CTOFX	B-	C	B+		2.15	5.07	6.11	9.19	14.54	11.39	1,949	800-421-4225	Y
American Funds College 2024 Fund Class 529-A	CFTAX	B	C+	A-		2.44	6.94	6.72	16.09	20.23	12.17	1,942	800-421-4225	Y
American Funds College 2024 Fund Class 529-C	CTFCX	B-	C	B+		2.29	6.66	6.05	13.48	15.77	12.01	1,942	800-421-4225	Y
American Funds College 2024 Fund Class 529-E	CTFEX	B	C+	B+		2.45	6.87	6.54	15.25	18.80	12.12	1,942	800-421-4225	Y
American Funds College 2024 Fund Class 529F1	CTFFX	B	C+	A-		2.51	7.19	7.06	16.88	21.67	12.22	1,942	800-421-4225	Y
American Funds College 2027 Fund Class 529-A	CSTAX	B	C+	A		2.80	9.11	6.83	21.83	25.01	12.81	1,582	800-421-4225	Y
American Funds College 2027 Fund Class 529-C	CTSCX	B	C+	A-	Up	2.60	8.69	6.02	19.04	20.20	12.63	1,582	800-421-4225	Y
American Funds College 2027 Fund Class 529-E	CTSEX	B	C+	A-		2.66	8.91	6.58	20.90	23.36	12.71	1,582	800-421-4225	Y
American Funds College 2027 Fund Class 529F1	CTSFX	B	C+	A		2.87	9.25	7.16	22.61	26.31	12.87	1,582	800-421-4225	Y
American Funds Retmnt Income Port - Conservative Cls A	NAARX	B-	C+	B+		2.50	8.60	6.55	15.63		11.12	706.9	800-421-4225	Y
American Funds Retmnt Income Port - Conservative Cls C	NGCRX	B-	C	B		2.34	8.31	5.85	13.31		11.08	706.9	800-421-4225	Y
American Funds Retmnt Income Port - Conservative Cls F-1	FAFWX	B-	C+	B+		2.59	8.69	6.64	15.62		11.13	706.9	800-421-4225	Y
American Funds Retmnt Income Port - Conservative Cls F-2	FDFWX	B	C+	B+		2.65	8.80	6.87	16.44		11.14	706.9	800-421-4225	Y
American Funds Retmnt Income Port - Conservative Cls F-3	FICWX	B	C+	B+		2.58	8.86	6.89	16.56		11.13	706.9	800-421-4225	Y

Category: Cautious Allocation (con't)

		RATINGS				TOTAL RETURNS & PERFORMANCE					ASSETS		NEW INVESTORS	
Fund Name	Ticker Symbol	Overall Rating	Reward Rating	Risk Rating	Recent Up/ Downgrade	3-Month Total Return	6-Month Total Return	1-Year Total Return	3-Year Total Return	5-Year Total Return	NAV	Total Assets (MIL)	Telephone	Open to New Investors
American Funds Retmnt Income Port - Conservative Cls R-1	RARPX	B-	C	B		2.41	8.34	5.86	13.10		11.12	706.9	800-421-4225	Y
American Funds Retmnt Income Port - Conservative Cls R-2	RDRPX	B-	C	B		2.47	8.36	6.02	13.91		11.12	706.9	800-421-4225	Y
American Funds Retmnt Income Port - Conservative Cls R-2E	RGRPX	B	C+	B+		2.64	8.76	6.72	16.27		11.15	706.9	800-421-4225	Y
American Funds Retmnt Income Port - Conservative Cls R-3	RJRPX	B-	C	B+		2.48	8.50	6.25	14.55		11.14	706.9	800-421-4225	Y
American Funds Retmnt Income Port - Conservative Cls R-4	RMRPX	B-	C+	B+		2.60	8.70	6.60	15.63		11.13	706.9	800-421-4225	Y
American Funds Retmnt Income Port - Conservative Cls R-5	RQRPX	B	C+	B+		2.67	8.81	6.89	16.44		11.15	706.9	800-421-4225	Y
American Funds Retmnt Income Port - Conservative Cls R-5E	RROPX	B	C+	B+		2.55	8.68	6.73	16.30		11.13	706.9	800-421-4225	Y
American Funds Retmnt Income Port - Conservative Cls R-6	RTRPX	B	C+	B+		2.58	8.84	6.88	16.74		11.14	706.9	800-421-4225	Y
American Funds Tax-Advantaged Growth & Inc Port Cls A	TAIAX	B	C+	A		2.87	10.14	6.85	24.68	34.09	13.8	2,661	800-421-4225	Y
American Funds Tax-Advantaged Growth & Inc Port Cls C	TAICX	B	C+	A	Up	2.64	9.71	6.10	22.03	29.39	13.71	2,661	800-421-4225	Y
American Funds Tax-Advantaged Growth & Inc Port Cls F-1	TAIFX	B	C+	A		2.86	10.13	6.89	24.69	34.17	13.8	2,661	800-421-4225	Y
American Funds Tax-Advantaged Growth & Inc Port Cls F-2	TXIFX	B	C+	A		2.92	10.24	7.08	25.65	35.87	13.82	2,661	800-421-4225	Y
American Funds Tax-Advantaged Growth & Inc Port Cls F-3	TYIFX	B	C+	A		2.95	10.30	7.19	25.98	36.22	13.81	2,661	800-421-4225	Y
Ave Maria Bond Fund	AVEFX	B	C	A-	Up	2.08	5.46	5.74	10.92	16.52	11.58	347.3	888-726-9331	Y
Berwyn Income Fund	BERIX	B-	C	A-		2.20	6.25	3.49	14.20	13.91	13.15	1,146	610-296-1400	Y
BlackRock 20/80 Target Allocation Fund Class K	BKCPX	B	C+	B+	Up	2.92	8.53	7.01	15.32	22.26	11.65	289.4	800-441-7762	Y
BlackRock 20/80 Target Allocation Institutional Shares	BICPX	B	C+	B+	Up	2.92	8.60	6.98	15.14	22.18	11.65	289.4	800-441-7762	Y
BlackRock 20/80 Target Allocation Fund Investor A Shares	BACPX	B-	C	B+		2.86	8.39	6.66	14.08	20.05	11.5	289.4	800-441-7762	Y
BlackRock 20/80 Target Allocation Fund Investor C Shares	BCCPX	B-	C	B	Up	2.71	7.97	5.94	11.48	15.65	11.37	289.4	800-441-7762	Y
BlackRock 20/80 Target Allocation Fund R Shares	BRCPX	B-	C	B+		2.69	8.16	6.32	12.96	18.29	11.44	289.4	800-441-7762	Y
BlackRock 40/60 Target Allocation Fund Class K	BKMPX	B	C+	A	Up	3.15	10.89	7.05	21.84	27.84	11.79	365.6	800-441-7762	Y
BlackRock 40/60 Target Allocation Fund Class R Shares	BRMPX	B	C	A-	Up	3.01	10.66	6.49	19.91	24.59	11.63	365.6	800-441-7762	Y
BlackRock 40/60 Target Allocation Fund Institutional	BIMPX	B	C+	A	Up	3.16	10.87	7.04	21.69	27.68	11.78	365.6	800-441-7762	Y
BlackRock 40/60 Target Allocation Fund Investor A Shares	BAMPX	B	C+	A-	Up	3.09	10.75	6.70	20.57	25.59	11.68	365.6	800-441-7762	Y
BlackRock 40/60 Target Allocation Fund Investor C Shares	BCMPX	B-	C	A-	Up	2.86	10.31	5.93	17.84	20.88	11.53	365.6	800-441-7762	Y
BlackRock Dynamic High Income Portfolio Class K	BDHKX	B	C+	A-	Up	3.72	14.80	7.46	30.80		9.66	985.9	800-441-7762	Y
BlackRock Dynamic High Income Portfolio Institutional	BDHIX	B	C+	A-	Up	3.60	14.65	7.41	30.48		9.65	985.9	800-441-7762	Y
BlackRock Dynamic High Income Portfolio Investor A	BDHAX	B	C+	A-	Up	3.55	14.47	7.14	29.50		9.65	985.9	800-441-7762	Y
BlackRock Dynamic High Income Portfolio Investor C	BDHCX	B-	C	A-	Up	3.36	14.07	6.36	26.66		9.64	985.9	800-441-7762	Y
BlackRock Managed Income Fund Class K Shares	BLDRX	B	C+	A		2.23	6.43	5.88	13.55	22.30	9.99	378.5	800-441-7762	Y
BlackRock Managed Income Fund Institutional Shares	BLDIX	B	C+	A-		2.12	6.31	5.84	13.26	21.83	9.96	378.5	800-441-7762	Y
BlackRock Managed Income Fund Investor A Shares	BLADX	B	C+	A-		2.16	6.28	5.67	12.51	20.11	9.97	378.5	800-441-7762	Y
BlackRock Managed Income Fund Investor C Shares	BMICX	B-	C	B+		1.87	5.76	4.77	10.04	16.18	9.97	378.5	800-441-7762	Y
BMO Conservative Allocation Fund Class I	BDVIX	B-	C	B+		2.70	8.58	5.80	14.79	17.27	7.97	39.0	800-236-3863	Y
BMO Conservative Allocation Fund Class R3	BDVRX	B-	C	B+	Up	2.62	8.32	5.27	13.02	14.36	7.81	39.0	800-236-3863	Y
BMO Conservative Allocation Fund Class R6	BDVSX	B-	C	B+		2.67	8.48	5.87	15.16	18.05	7.67	39.0	800-236-3863	Y
BMO Conservative Allocation Fund Class Y	BDVYX	B-	C	B+		2.55	8.36	5.50	13.80	15.75	7.64	39.0	800-236-3863	Y
BMO Moderate Allocation Fund Class I	BMBHX	B	C	A-	Up	2.69	10.66	5.52	21.05	22.54	9.13	71.9	800-236-3863	Y
BMO Moderate Allocation Fund Class R3	BMBQX	B-	C	A-	Up	2.58	10.27	5.04	19.21	19.42	9.12	71.9	800-236-3863	Y
BMO Moderate Allocation Fund Class R6	BMBTX	B	C	A-	Up	2.69	10.66	5.63	21.64	23.45	9.13	71.9	800-236-3863	Y
BMO Moderate Allocation Fund Class Y	BMBYX	B	C	A-	Up	2.59	10.42	5.25	20.15	20.93	9.11	71.9	800-236-3863	Y
Calvert Conservative Allocation Fund Class A	CCLAX	B	C+	A		3.27	10.90	7.41	21.45	26.13	17.41	206.1	301-951-4881	Y
Calvert Conservative Allocation Fund Class C	CALCX	B	C+	A-	Up	3.05	10.49	6.61	18.70	20.99	17.2	206.1	301-951-4881	Y
Calvert Conservative Allocation Fund Class I	CFAIX	B	C+	B+	Up	3.33	11.03	7.79	22.66	27.42	17.42	206.1	301-951-4881	Y
Charter Conservative Portfolio Class B		B	C	A-	Up	2.43	8.55	4.95	16.68	14.39	10.55	38.7	877-222-2144	Y
Charter Moderate Portfolio Class B		B-	C	A-	Up	2.57	10.34	4.51	21.41	17.34	10.81	35.7	877-222-2144	Y
Columbia Capital Allocation Conservative Portfolio Adv Cls	CPCYX	B-	C	B+		2.58	8.04	5.22	13.51	17.93	10.05	227.6	800-345-6611	Y
Columbia Capital Allocation Conservative Portfolio Class A	ABDAX	B-	C	B+	Up	2.60	7.96	5.02	12.80	16.60	10.13	227.6	800-345-6611	Y
Columbia Capital Allocation Conservative Portfolio Class R	CBVRX	B-	C	B+	Up	2.54	7.72	4.66	11.85	15.04	10.12	227.6	800-345-6611	Y
Columbia Capital Alloc Conservative Port Inst 2 Cls	CPAOX	B-	C	B+		2.59	8.05	5.24	13.63	18.21	10.05	227.6	800-345-6611	Y
Columbia Capital Alloc Conservative Port Inst 3 Cls	CPDHX	B-	C	B+		2.71	8.09	5.30	13.82	18.50	10.04	227.6	800-345-6611	Y
Columbia Capital Alloc Conservative Port Inst Cls	CBVZX	B-	C	B+		2.67	8.10	5.29	13.66	18.06	10.12	227.6	800-345-6611	Y

Category: Cautious Allocation (con't)

		RATINGS				TOTAL RETURNS & PERFORMANCE					ASSETS		NEW INVESTORS	
Fund Name	Ticker Symbol	Overall Rating	Reward Rating	Risk Rating	Recent Up/ Downgrade	3-Month Total Return	6-Month Total Return	1-Year Total Return	3-Year Total Return	5-Year Total Return	NAV	Total Assets (MIL)	Telephone	Open to New Investors
Columbia Capital Alloc Moderate Conservative Port Adv Cls	CHWRX	B	C+	A-	Up	2.88	10.17	5.44	19.35	23.84	10.64	529.9	800-345-6611	Y
Columbia Capital Alloc Moderate Conservative Port Cls A	NLGAX	B	C	A-	Up	2.79	9.94	5.12	18.39	22.19	10.74	529.9	800-345-6611	Y
Columbia Capital Alloc Moderate Conservative Port Cls C	NIICX	B-	C	B+	Up	2.64	9.57	4.40	15.89	17.73	10.59	529.9	800-345-6611	Y
Columbia Capital Alloc Moderate Conservative Port Cls R	CLIRX	B-	C	A-	Up	2.72	9.78	4.85	17.59	20.64	10.76	529.9	800-345-6611	Y
Columbia Capital Alloc Mod Cons Port Inst 2 Cls	CLRRX	B	C+	A-	Up	2.88	10.20	5.37	19.48	24.04	10.63	529.9	800-345-6611	Y
Columbia Capital Alloc Mod Cons Port Inst 3 Cls	CPDGX	B	C+	A-	Up	2.84	10.15	5.39	19.58	24.35	10.48	529.9	800-345-6611	Y
Columbia Capital Alloc Moderate Conservative Port Inst Cls	NIPAX	B	C+	A-	Up	2.89	10.12	5.37	19.34	23.73	10.58	529.9	800-345-6611	Y
Columbia Capital Allocation Moderate Portfolio Advisor Cls	CPCZX	B-	C	A-	Up	3.22	12.76	5.53	25.91	31.01	10.99	1,492	800-345-6611	Y
Columbia Capital Allocation Moderate Portfolio Class A	ABUAX	B-	C	A-	Up	3.12	12.45	5.19	24.96	29.33	11.13	1,492	800-345-6611	Y
Columbia Capital Allocation Moderate Portfolio Class C	AMTCX	B-	C	A-	Up	2.95	12.15	4.44	22.15	24.54	11.04	1,492	800-345-6611	Y
Columbia Capital Allocation Moderate Portfolio Class R	CBMRX	B-	C	A-	Up	3.06	12.35	4.94	23.99	27.68	11.1	1,492	800-345-6611	Y
Columbia Capital Allocation Moderate Portfolio Inst 2 Cls	CPAMX	B-	C	A-	Up	3.23	12.67	5.54	26.02	31.22	10.98	1,492	800-345-6611	Y
Columbia Capital Allocation Moderate Portfolio Inst 3 Cls	CPDMX	B-	C	A-	Up	3.24	12.69	5.49	26.20	31.63	10.98	1,492	800-345-6611	Y
Columbia Capital Allocation Moderate Portfolio Inst Cls	CBMZX	B-	C	A-	Up	3.28	12.71	5.47	25.94	31.00	11.12	1,492	800-345-6611	Y
Columbia Flexible Capital Income Fund Advisor Class	CFCRX	B-	C+	B	Up	3.03	14.86	5.68	35.07	31.71	13.09	930.6	800-345-6611	Y
Columbia Flexible Capital Income Fund Class A	CFIAX	B-	C	B	Up	2.99	14.75	5.38	34.15	30.13	12.99	930.6	800-345-6611	Y
Columbia Flexible Capital Income Fund Class C	CFIGX	B-	C	B	Up	2.82	14.22	4.62	31.15	25.30	12.92	930.6	800-345-6611	Y
Columbia Flexible Capital Income Fund Class R	CFIRX	B-	C	B	Up	2.93	14.52	5.12	33.18	28.44	12.98	930.6	800-345-6611	Y
Columbia Flexible Capital Income Institutional 2 Cls	CFXRX	B-	C+	B	Up	3.04	14.87	5.72	35.32	32.07	13.1	930.6	800-345-6611	Y
Columbia Flexible Capital Income Institutional 3 Cls	CFCYX	B-	C+	B	Up	3.01	14.81	5.76	35.42	32.03	12.93	930.6	800-345-6611	Y
Columbia Flexible Capital Income Fund Institutional Class	CFIZX	B-	C	B	Up	2.98	14.80	5.65	35.04	31.66	12.98	930.6	800-345-6611	Y
Columbia Income Builder Fund Advisor Class	CNMRX	B	C+	B+		2.75	10.12	7.51	21.19	24.52	12.09	1,315	800-345-6611	Y
Columbia Income Builder Fund Class A	RBBAX	B	C+	B+	Up	2.69	10.02	7.27	20.26	22.96	12.05	1,315	800-345-6611	Y
Columbia Income Builder Fund Class C	RBBCX	B-	C+	B		2.49	9.57	6.44	17.51	18.45	12.1	1,315	800-345-6611	Y
Columbia Income Builder Fund Class R	CBURX	B-	C+	B		2.61	9.82	6.96	19.34	21.40	12.12	1,315	800-345-6611	Y
Columbia Income Builder Fund Institutional 2 Class	CKKRX	B	C+	B+		2.75	10.13	7.43	21.16	24.62	12.09	1,315	800-345-6611	Y
Columbia Income Builder Fund Institutional 3 Class	CIBYX	B	C+	B+		2.77	10.17	7.50	21.18	23.90	12.08	1,315	800-345-6611	Y
Columbia Income Builder Fund Institutional Class	CBUZX	B	C+	B+		2.76	10.16	7.44	21.16	24.49	12.05	1,315	800-345-6611	Y
Columbia Thermostat Fund Advisor Class	CTORX	B	C+	A		3.42	10.00	9.18	17.31	23.57	14.93	683.7	800-345-6611	Y
Columbia Thermostat Fund Class A	CTFAX	B	C+	A-		3.32	9.83	8.82	16.44	21.99	15.05	683.7	800-345-6611	Y
Columbia Thermostat Fund Class C	CTFDX	B-	C	B+	Down	3.17	9.47	8.10	13.90	17.52	15.11	683.7	800-345-6611	Y
Columbia Thermostat Fund Institutional 2 Class	CQTRX	B	C+	A		3.42	10.06	9.21	17.45	23.67	14.95	683.7	800-345-6611	Y
Columbia Thermostat Fund Institutional 3 Class	CYYYX	B	C+	A		3.49	10.08	9.29	17.66	24.02	14.93	683.7	800-345-6611	Y
Columbia Thermostat Fund Institutional Class	COTZX	B	C+	A		3.37	9.98	9.08	17.25	23.47	14.84	683.7	800-345-6611	Y
DFA Global Allocation 25/75 Portfolio Class R2	DFGPX	B-	C	A-		1.94	6.62	4.01	13.12	14.43	13.55	888.2	512-306-7400	Y
DFA Global Allocation 25/75 Portfolio Institutional Class	DGTSX	B-	C	A-		1.92	6.73	4.26	13.88	16.20	13.59	888.2	512-306-7400	Y
DWS Multi-Asset Conservative Allocation Fund - Class A	SPDAX	B-	C	B+	Up	2.88	11.09	5.06	17.23	16.18	13.32	84.4		Y
DWS Multi-Asset Conservative Allocation Fund - Class C	SPDCX	B-	C	B+	Up	2.69	10.68	4.28	14.61	11.89	13.32	84.4		Y
DWS Multi-Asset Conservative Allocation Fund - Class S	SPBAX	B-	C	A-	Up	2.96	11.16	5.26	18.05	17.58	13.29	84.4		Y
EQ/Conservative Allocation Portfolio Class K		B-	C	B+		2.26	6.62	5.30	11.66	14.71	9.5	1,062	877-222-2144	Y
EQ/Conservative Growth Strategy Fund Class IB		B-	C	A-		2.38	8.88	4.69	17.51	19.63	14.64	1,530	877-222-2144	Y
EQ/Conservative Growth Strategy Fund Class IB		B-	C	B+	Up	2.07	6.23	4.80	9.85	12.52	12.3	1,530	877-222-2144	Y
EQ/Conservative-Plus Allocation Portfolio Class K		B	C	A-	Up	2.60	9.21	4.96	19.03	20.59	9.87	1,235	877-222-2144	Y
EQ/Invesco Moderate Allocation Portfolio Class IB		B-	C	B+	Up	1.44	4.18	1.10	13.75			282.1	877-222-2144	Y
EQ/Premier VIP Conservative Allocation Fund Class A		B-	C	B+	Up	2.15	6.38	5.02	10.68	13.25	9.51	1,062	877-222-2144	Y
EQ/Premier VIP Conservative Allocation Fund Class B		B-	C	B+	Up	2.26	6.50	5.01	10.79	13.25	9.51	1,062	877-222-2144	Y
EQ/Premier VIP Conservative-Plus Allocation Fund Class A		B-	C	A-		2.39	8.98	4.58	18.02	18.97	9.85	1,235	877-222-2144	Y
EQ/Premier VIP Conservative-Plus Allocation Fund Class B		B-	C	A-		2.50	8.97	4.68	18.01	19.08	9.86	1,235	877-222-2144	Y
E-Valuator Conservative (15%-30%) RMS Fund R4 Class	EVFCX	B-	C	A-	Up	3.05	10.10	4.88	16.68	20.30	10.46	56.0	888-507-2798	Y
E-Valuator Conservative (15%-30%) RMS Fund Service Class	EVCLX	B-	C	A-	Up	3.06	10.26	5.13	17.61	21.27	10.42	56.0	888-507-2798	Y
E-Valuator Very Conservative (0%-15%) RMS Fund R4 Class	EVVCX	B-	C	B	Up	2.68	7.05	4.22	10.71	12.68	10.32	14.3	888-507-2798	Y
E-Valuator Very Conservative (0%-15%) RMS Service Cls	EVVLX	B-	C	B+	Up	2.71	7.12	4.40	11.52	14.06	10.22	14.3	888-507-2798	Y

Category: Cautious Allocation (con't)

Fund Name	Ticker Symbol	RATINGS: Overall Rating	Reward Rating	Risk Rating	Recent Up/ Downgrade	TOTAL RETURNS & PERFORMANCE: 3-Month Total Return	6-Month Total Return	1-Year Total Return	3-Year Total Return	5-Year Total Return	ASSETS: NAV	Total Assets (MIL)	NEW INVESTORS: Telephone	Open to New Investors
Federated Capital Income Fund Class A Shares	CAPAX	B-	C	B+	Up	2.64	10.90	3.29	16.74	9.33	7.86	1,239	800-341-7400	Y
Federated Capital Income Fund Class F Shares	CAPFX	B-	C	B+	Up	2.51	10.91	3.29	16.72	9.28	7.85	1,239	800-341-7400	Y
Federated Capital Income Fund Class R	CAPRX	B-	C	B+	Up	2.59	10.77	3.23	16.14	8.21	7.87	1,239	800-341-7400	Y
Federated Capital Income Fund Institutional Class	CAPSX	B-	C	B+	Up	2.70	11.02	3.68	17.75	10.70	7.87	1,239	800-341-7400	Y
Federated Muni and Stock Advantage Fund Class A Shares	FMUAX	B-	C	B+	Up	4.00	10.66	4.81	17.83	20.86	12.86	1,565	800-341-7400	Y
Federated Muni and Stock Advantage Fund Class B Shares	FMNBX	B-	C	B+	Up	3.89	10.34	4.10	15.22	16.53	12.86	1,565	800-341-7400	
Federated Muni and Stock Advantage Fund Class C Shares	FMUCX	B-	C	B+	Up	3.89	10.26	4.11	15.23	16.45	12.85	1,565	800-341-7400	Y
Federated Muni and Stock Advantage Fund Class F Shares	FMUFX	B-	C	B+	Up	4.00	10.66	4.81	17.83	20.86	12.86	1,565	800-341-7400	Y
Federated Muni & Stock Advantage Institutional Shares	FMUIX	B-	C	A-	Up	4.15	10.89	5.16	18.72	22.47	12.86	1,565	800-341-7400	Y
Fidelity Advisor Asset Manager® 20% Fund Class A	FTAWX	B-	C	B+		2.06	6.74	4.58	12.58	15.88	13.4	5,044	617-563-7000	Y
Fidelity Advisor Asset Manager® 20% Fund Class C	FTCWX	B-	C	B+	Up	1.87	6.36	3.78	10.02	11.55	13.32	5,044	617-563-7000	Y
Fidelity Advisor Asset Manager® 20% Fund Class M	FTDWX	B-	C	B+		2.01	6.58	4.32	11.74	14.42	13.37	5,044	617-563-7000	Y
Fidelity Advisor Asset Manager® 20% Fund Class Z	FIKVX	B-	C	A-		2.14	6.88	4.86	13.67	17.70	13.42	5,044	617-563-7000	Y
Fidelity Advisor Asset Manager® 20% Fund I Class	FTIWX	B-	C	A-		2.20	6.92	4.86	13.58	17.52	13.42	5,044	617-563-7000	Y
Fidelity Advisor Asset Manager® 30% Fund Class A	FTAAX	B-	C	A-		2.45	8.50	4.79	16.47	19.86	11.16	1,679	617-563-7000	Y
Fidelity Advisor Asset Manager® 30% Fund Class C	FCANX	B-	C	B+	Up	2.27	8.03	3.93	13.84	15.34	11.08	1,679	617-563-7000	Y
Fidelity Advisor Asset Manager® 30% Fund Class M	FTTNX	B-	C	A-		2.40	8.32	4.44	15.53	18.31	11.14	1,679	617-563-7000	Y
Fidelity Advisor Asset Manager® 30% Fund Class Z	FIKWX	B	C	A-	Up	2.55	8.57	5.07	17.56	21.73	11.15	1,679	617-563-7000	Y
Fidelity Advisor Asset Manager® 30% Fund I Class	FTINX	B	C	A-	Up	2.52	8.62	4.97	17.25	21.28	11.15	1,679	617-563-7000	Y
Fidelity Advisor Asset Manager® 40% Fund Class A	FFNAX	B-	C	A-	Up	2.70	9.99	4.58	20.08	23.03	11.75	1,776	617-563-7000	Y
Fidelity Advisor Asset Manager® 40% Fund Class C	FFNCX	B-	C	B+	Up	2.51	9.62	3.88	17.37	18.44	11.69	1,776	617-563-7000	Y
Fidelity Advisor Asset Manager® 40% Fund Class M	FFNTX	B-	C	A-	Up	2.64	9.83	4.37	19.13	21.37	11.73	1,776	617-563-7000	Y
Fidelity Advisor Asset Manager® 40% Fund Class Z	FIKYX	B	C	A-	Up	2.69	10.08	4.84	21.13	24.83	11.75	1,776	617-563-7000	Y
Fidelity Advisor Asset Manager® 40% Fund I Class	FFNIX	B	C	A-	Up	2.76	10.16	4.88	21.10	24.71	11.75	1,776	617-563-7000	Y
Fidelity Advisor Asset Manager® 50% Fund Class A	FFAMX	B-	C	A-	Up	2.90	11.48	4.32	23.54	25.62	18.15	9,299	617-563-7000	Y
Fidelity Advisor Asset Manager® 50% Fund Class C	FFCMX	B-	C	B+	Up	2.68	10.98	3.51	20.66	20.85	17.98	9,299	617-563-7000	Y
Fidelity Advisor Asset Manager® 50% Fund Class M	FFTMX	B-	C	A-	Up	2.84	11.36	4.11	22.57	24.02	18.13	9,299	617-563-7000	Y
Fidelity Advisor Asset Manager® 50% Fund Class Z	FIKZX	B-	C	A-	Up	2.98	11.68	4.69	24.67	27.55	18.19	9,299	617-563-7000	Y
Fidelity Advisor Asset Manager® 50% Fund I Class	FFIMX	B-	C	A-	Up	2.96	11.59	4.59	24.50	27.27	18.19	9,299	617-563-7000	Y
Fidelity Advisor® Multi-Asset Income Fund Class A	FWATX	B-	C+	B+	Down	4.66	13.52	10.23	22.03		10.92	82.7	617-563-7000	Y
Fidelity Advisor® Multi-Asset Income Fund Class C	FWBTX	B-	C	B+	Down	4.47	13.12	9.49	19.33		10.91	82.7	617-563-7000	Y
Fidelity Advisor® Multi-Asset Income Fund Class I	FAYZX	B-	C+	B+	Down	4.72	13.55	10.50	22.96		10.92	82.7	617-563-7000	Y
Fidelity Advisor® Multi-Asset Income Fund Class M	FAZYX	B-	C+	B+	Down	4.66	13.52	10.23	22.04		10.92	82.7	617-563-7000	Y
Fidelity Advisor® Multi-Asset Income Fund Class Z	FIWBX	B-	C+	B+	Down	4.74	13.60	10.57	23.03		10.92	82.7	617-563-7000	Y
Fidelity Advisor® Strategic Real Return Fund Class A	FSRAX	B-	C	B+	Up	0.86	6.93	1.40	7.55	0.93	8.35	373.1	617-563-7000	Y
Fidelity Advisor® Strategic Real Return Fund Class M	FSRTX	B-	C	B+	Up	0.84	7.04	1.39	7.51	0.88	8.36	373.1	617-563-7000	Y
Fidelity Advisor® Strategic Real Return Fund Class Z	FIQDX	B-	C	B+		0.94	7.27	1.74	8.56	2.37	8.37	373.1	617-563-7000	Y
Fidelity Advisor® Strategic Real Return Fund I Class	FSIRX	B-	C	B+		0.92	7.12	1.69	8.50	2.31	8.37	373.1	617-563-7000	Y
Fidelity Asset Manager® 20% Fund	FASIX	B-	C	A-		2.21	6.94	4.91	13.73	17.76	13.43	5,044	617-563-7000	Y
Fidelity Asset Manager® 30% Fund	FTANX	B	C	A-	Up	2.53	8.65	5.04	17.53	21.70	11.15	1,679	617-563-7000	Y
Fidelity Asset Manager® 40% Fund	FFANX	B	C	A-	Up	2.77	10.17	4.92	21.22	24.92	11.75	1,776	617-563-7000	Y
Fidelity Asset Manager® 50% Fund	FASMX	B-	C	A-	Up	2.95	11.63	4.67	24.66	27.54	18.23	9,299	617-563-7000	Y
Fidelity® Multi-Asset Income Fund	FMSDX	B	C+	B+		4.81	13.65	10.59	23.05		10.93	82.7	617-563-7000	Y
Fidelity® Strategic Real Return Fund	FSRRX	B-	C	B+		0.90	7.07	1.66	8.41	2.26	8.39	373.1	617-563-7000	Y
Franklin Conservative Allocation Fund Advisor Class	FTCZX	B	C	A	Up	2.33	9.82	5.72	21.70	20.36	14.43	1,196	650-312-2000	Y
Franklin Conservative Allocation Fund Class A	FTCIX	B	C	A-	Up	2.26	9.70	5.46	20.72	18.80	14.43	1,196	650-312-2000	Y
Franklin Conservative Allocation Fund Class C	FTCCX	B-	C	A-	Up	2.03	9.28	4.65	18.04	14.44	14.13	1,196	650-312-2000	Y
Franklin Conservative Allocation Fund Class R	FTCRX	B	C	A-	Up	2.20	9.53	5.19	19.86	17.35	14.37	1,196	650-312-2000	Y
Franklin Conservative Allocation Fund Class R6		B	C	A	Up	2.35	9.88	5.82	21.93	20.89	14.41	1,196	650-312-2000	Y
Franklin Income Fund Advisor Class	FRIAX	B-	C	A-	Down	1.34	12.01	6.01	26.26	17.66	2.3	72,795	650-312-2000	Y
Franklin Income Fund Class A	FKIQX	B-	C+	B		1.72	11.79	5.75	25.19	16.17	2.32	72,795	650-312-2000	Y
Franklin Income Fund Class A1	FKINX	B	C	A-		1.31	11.84	5.85	25.57	16.75	2.32	72,795	650-312-2000	Y

Category: Cautious Allocation (con't)

Fund Name	Ticker Symbol	RATINGS: Overall Rating	Reward Rating	Risk Rating	Recent Up/ Downgrade	TOTAL RETURNS & PERFORMANCE: 3-Month Total Return	6-Month Total Return	1-Year Total Return	3-Year Total Return	5-Year Total Return	ASSETS: NAV	Total Assets (MIL)	NEW INVESTORS: Telephone	Open to New Investors
Franklin Income Fund Class C	FCISX	B-	C+	B		1.59	11.85	5.67	23.78	14.04	2.36	72,795	650-312-2000	Y
Franklin Income Fund Class R	FISRX	B-	C	B		1.24	11.86	6.03	24.12	14.98	2.28	72,795	650-312-2000	Y
Franklin Income Fund Class R6	FNCFX	B-	C+	B	Down	1.80	12.00	6.53	26.42	18.56	2.31	72,795	650-312-2000	Y
Franklin NextStep Conservative Fund Advisor Class	FNCVX	B-	C	B+	Up	2.70	8.37	6.58	14.09		10.96	3.7	650-312-2000	Y
Franklin NextStep Conservative Fund Class A	FNCAX	B-	C	B+	Up	2.56	8.17	6.36	13.24		10.96	3.7	650-312-2000	Y
GMO Benchmark-Free Allocation Fund Class III	GBMFX	B-	C	B+	Up	1.58	7.44	3.06	18.23	9.74	26.84	10,633	617-330-7500	Y
GMO Benchmark-Free Allocation Fund Class IV	GBMBX	B-	C	B+	Up	1.62	7.48	3.12	18.38	10.02	26.84	10,633	617-330-7500	Y
GMO Benchmark-Free Allocation Series Fund Class PS	GBFPX	B-	C	B+	Up	1.46	7.24	2.83	18.00	9.52	10.36	630.3	617-330-7500	Y
GMO Benchmark-Free Allocation Series Fund Class R6	GBMRX	B-	C	B+	Up	1.56	7.35	2.94	17.72	9.15	10.37	630.3	617-330-7500	Y
GMO Global Asset Allocation Fund Class III	GMWAX	B-	C	A-	Up	2.67	10.61	4.95	22.65	14.91	32.63	1,789	617-330-7500	Y
GMO Global Asset Allocation Series Fund Class PS	GLAPX	B-	C	A-	Up	2.57	10.39	4.75	22.50	14.76	9.56	191.8	617-330-7500	Y
GMO Global Asset Allocation Series Fund Class R6	GATRX	B-	C	A-	Up	2.68	10.50	4.85	22.16	14.20	9.57	191.8	617-330-7500	Y
Goldman Sachs Income Builder Fund Class A	GSBFX	B	C+	B+		3.88	13.99	9.35	23.14	20.17	23.25	1,587	800-526-7384	Y
Goldman Sachs Income Builder Fund Class C	GSBCX	B-	C+	B+		3.67	13.53	8.52	20.35	15.75	22.84	1,587	800-526-7384	Y
Goldman Sachs Income Builder Fund Class P	GGKPX	B	C+	B+		3.66	13.83	9.42	23.30	20.33	23.77	1,587	800-526-7384	Y
Goldman Sachs Income Builder Fund Class R6	GSBUX	B	C+	A-		3.99	14.19	9.76	24.62	22.05	23.77	1,587	800-526-7384	Y
Goldman Sachs Income Builder Fund Institutional Class	GSBIX	B	C+	A-		3.98	14.18	9.75	24.54	22.54	23.77	1,587	800-526-7384	Y
Goldman Sachs Income Builder Fund Investor Class	GKIRX	B	C+	B+		3.96	14.10	9.58	24.03	21.68	23.7	1,587	800-526-7384	Y
Great-West Conservative Profile Fund Class L	MXIPX	B-	C	A-		1.94	7.66	4.18	15.43	17.13	9.34	796.9		Y
Great-West Conservative Profile Fund Institutional Class	MXKVX	B	C	A-	Up	2.19	8.17	4.85	17.69	20.58	9.9	796.9		Y
Great-West Conservative Profile Fund Investor Class	MXCPX	B-	C	A-		2.03	7.90	4.45	16.34	18.60	7.99	796.9		Y
Great-West Moderately Conservative Profile Fund Class L	MXHPX	B-	C	A-	Up	2.08	9.40	3.83	20.00	21.65	9.58	458.6		Y
Great-West Moderately Conservative Profile Inst Cls	MXJUX	B	C	A-	Up	2.28	9.75	4.47	22.26	25.04	9.87	458.6		Y
Great-West Moderately Conservative Profile Investor Cls	MXDPX	B-	C	A-		2.22	9.64	4.18	20.98	23.27	8.56	458.6		Y
Guggenheim Diversified Income Fund Class A	GUDAX	B	C+	B+	Up	2.32	7.86	4.43	16.24		26.7	7.2	212-518-9290	Y
Guggenheim Diversified Income Fund Class C	GUDCX	B-	C	B+	Up	2.10	7.46	3.68	13.68		26.73	7.2	212-518-9290	Y
Guggenheim Diversified Income Fund Class P	GUDPX	B	C+	B+	Up	2.29	7.87	4.45	16.24		26.7	7.2	212-518-9290	Y
Guggenheim Diversified Income Fund Institutional	GUDIX	B	C+	B+	Up	2.35	7.98	4.69	17.09		26.71	7.2	212-518-9290	Y
GuidePath® Absolute Return Allocation Institutional Shares	GIARX	B-	C	B		2.00	5.99	5.78	15.16	19.86	10.611	324.6	800-664-5345	Y
GuidePath® Absolute Return Allocation Fund Service Shares	GPARX	B-	C	B+	Down	1.86	5.67	5.15	13.15	16.35	10.596	324.6	800-664-5345	Y
GuidePath® Conservative Allocation Institutional Shares	GITTX	B	C+	A-	Up	3.09	10.97	6.52	19.13	15.92	9.977	363.8	603-888-5500	Y
GuidePath® Conservative Allocation Fund Service Shares	GPTCX	B-	C	B+		2.94	10.65	5.88	17.00	12.43	9.9	363.8	603-888-5500	Y
GuidePath® Multi-Asset Income Allocation Service Shares	GPMIX	B-	C	B		2.47	11.55	6.15	17.36	16.17	10.857	136.5	800-664-5345	Y
GuideStone Funds Balanced Allocation Institutional Cls	GBAYX	B	C+	A	Up	3.51	12.34	6.74	24.37	22.27	12.38	1,576	214-720-1171	Y
GuideStone Funds Balanced Allocation Fund Investor Class	GGIZX	B	C	A	Up	3.43	12.15	6.45	23.34	21.13	12.36	1,576	214-720-1171	Y
GuideStone Funds Conservative Allocation Institutional Cls	GCAYX	B	C	A-	Up	2.27	7.65	5.13	15.62	15.02	11.67	514.6	214-720-1171	Y
GuideStone Funds Conservative Allocation Investor Cls	GFIZX	B	C	A-	Up	2.28	7.56	4.98	14.83	14.10	11.66	514.6	214-720-1171	Y
Hartford Conservative Allocation Fund Class A	HCVAX	B	C	A-	Up	2.98	10.21	6.00	19.27	12.05	10.68	133.8	888-843-7824	Y
Hartford Conservative Allocation Fund Class C	HCVCX	B-	C	A-	Up	2.71	9.63	5.10	16.46	7.80	10.58	133.8	888-843-7824	Y
Hartford Conservative Allocation Fund Class F	HCVFX	B	C+	A-	Up	2.98	10.30	6.34	20.18	12.90	10.7	133.8	888-843-7824	Y
Hartford Conservative Allocation Fund Class I	HCVIX	B	C+	A-	Up	2.98	10.20	6.21	20.07	13.41	10.69	133.8	888-843-7824	Y
Hartford Conservative Allocation Fund Class R3	HCVRX	B	C	A-	Up	2.88	9.97	5.61	18.25	10.47	10.69	133.8	888-843-7824	Y
Hartford Conservative Allocation Fund Class R4	HCVSX	B	C	A-	Up	2.88	10.09	5.94	19.36	12.13	10.69	133.8	888-843-7824	Y
Hartford Conservative Allocation Fund Class R5	HCVTX	B	C+	A	Up	2.97	10.28	6.29	20.42	13.77	10.72	133.8	888-843-7824	Y
Hartford Multi-Asset Income Fund Class A	HAFAX	B	C+	A	Up	2.75	10.48	5.59	22.43	16.47	9.18	85.6	888-843-7824	Y
Hartford Multi-Asset Income Fund Class C	HAICX	B	C+	A	Up	2.55	10.06	4.88	19.89	12.37	9.19	85.6	888-843-7824	Y
Hartford Multi-Asset Income Fund Class F	HAFDX	B	C+	B+	Up	2.84	10.67	5.88	23.26	17.95	9.11	85.6	888-843-7824	Y
Hartford Multi-Asset Income Fund Class I	HAFIX	B	C+	A	Up	2.79	10.45	5.74	22.87	17.49	9.17	85.6	888-843-7824	Y
Hartford Multi-Asset Income Fund Class R3	HAFRX	B	C+	A	Up	2.83	10.52	5.61	22.14	15.51	9.19	85.6	888-843-7824	Y
Hartford Multi-Asset Income Fund Class R4	HAFSX	B	C+	A	Up	2.80	10.42	5.66	22.44	16.45	9.18	85.6	888-843-7824	Y
Hartford Multi-Asset Income Fund Class R5	HAFTX	B	C+	A	Up	2.80	10.46	5.74	22.80	17.24	9.17	85.6	888-843-7824	Y
Hartford Multi-Asset Income Fund Class R6	HAFVX	B	C+	B+	Up	2.82	10.60	5.82	23.14	17.84	9.17	85.6	888-843-7824	Y

Category: Cautious Allocation (con't)

		RATINGS				TOTAL RETURNS & PERFORMANCE					ASSETS		NEW INVESTORS	
Fund Name	Ticker Symbol	Overall Rating	Reward Rating	Risk Rating	Recent Up/ Downgrade	3-Month Total Return	6-Month Total Return	1-Year Total Return	3-Year Total Return	5-Year Total Return	NAV	Total Assets (MIL)	Telephone	Open to New Investors
Hartford Multi-Asset Income Fund Class Y	HAFYX	B	C+	A	Up	2.81	10.63	5.85	23.19	17.88	9.17	85.6	888-843-7824	Y
Invesco Conservative Allocation Fund Class A	CAAMX	B-	C	A-		2.92	10.33	6.05	16.78	16.29	11.63	297.0	800-659-1005	Y
Invesco Conservative Allocation Fund Class C	CACMX	B-	C	B+	Up	2.76	9.91	5.19	14.15	12.00	11.51	297.0	800-659-1005	Y
Invesco Conservative Allocation Fund Class R	CMARX	B-	C	A-	Up	2.96	10.22	5.80	15.93	14.94	11.59	297.0	800-659-1005	Y
Invesco Conservative Allocation Fund Class R6	CNSSX	B	C+	A-	Up	3.08	10.56	6.36	17.88	18.14	11.68	297.0	800-659-1005	Y
Invesco Conservative Allocation Fund Class S	CMASX	B	C	A-	Up	3.04	10.37	6.15	17.11	16.97	11.65	297.0	800-659-1005	Y
Invesco Conservative Allocation Fund Class Y	CAAYX	B	C+	A-	Up	3.08	10.48	6.32	17.67	17.86	11.62	297.0	800-659-1005	Y
Invesco Conservative Allocation Fund R5 Class	CMAIX	B	C+	A-	Up	3.08	10.45	6.36	17.78	18.04	11.68	297.0	800-659-1005	Y
Invesco Income Allocation Fund Class A	ALAAX	B-	C+	B	Down	2.67	10.37	7.35	16.89	24.18	11.6	540.0	800-659-1005	Y
Invesco Income Allocation Fund Class C	CLIAX	B-	C+	B		2.47	10.05	6.64	14.38	19.60	11.62	540.0	800-659-1005	Y
Invesco Income Allocation Fund Class R	RLIAX	B-	C+	B	Down	2.60	10.33	7.17	16.01	22.63	11.61	540.0	800-659-1005	Y
Invesco Income Allocation Fund Class R6	IIASX	B-	C+	B+	Down	2.73	10.51	7.61	17.77	25.63	11.6	540.0	800-659-1005	Y
Invesco Income Allocation Fund Class Y	ALAYX	B	C+	B+		2.73	10.51	7.62	17.77	25.75	11.6	540.0	800-659-1005	Y
Invesco Income Allocation Fund R5 Class	ILAAX	B-	C+	B+	Down	2.73	10.51	7.61	17.77	25.63	11.6	540.0	800-659-1005	Y
Invesco Multi-Asset Income Fund Class A	PIAFX	B-	C+	B	Down	2.86	12.36	7.85	21.33	32.44	10.75	658.5	800-659-1005	Y
Invesco Multi-Asset Income Fund Class C	PICFX	B-	C+	B		2.67	11.95	7.05	18.63	27.56	10.74	658.5	800-659-1005	Y
Invesco Multi-Asset Income Fund Class R	PIRFX	B-	C+	B		2.70	12.11	7.48	20.31	30.67	10.74	658.5	800-659-1005	Y
Invesco Multi-Asset Income Fund Class R5	IPNFX	B-	B-	B	Down	2.92	12.38	8.02	22.11	33.98	10.75	658.5	800-659-1005	Y
Invesco Multi-Asset Income Fund Class R6	PIFFX	B-	B-	B	Down	2.92	12.50	8.12	22.24	33.98	10.75	658.5	800-659-1005	Y
Invesco Multi-Asset Income Fund Class Y	PIYFX	B-	C+	B	Down	2.92	12.50	8.12	22.12	33.98	10.75	658.5	800-659-1005	Y
Invesco Oppenheimer Capital Income Fund Class A	OPPEX	B-	C	B+	Up	2.19	8.63	5.22	14.63	18.43	10.24	2,283	800-659-1005	Y
Invesco Oppenheimer Capital Income Fund Class C	OPECX	B-	C	B+	Up	1.86	8.10	4.28	11.97	13.91	9.89	2,283	800-659-1005	Y
Invesco Oppenheimer Capital Income Fund Class R	OCINX	B-	C	B+	Up	2.16	8.52	4.92	13.81	16.95	10.09	2,283	800-659-1005	Y
Invesco Oppenheimer Capital Income Fund Class R5	CPIFX	B-	C	B+		2.19	8.63	5.22	14.64	18.43	10.23	2,283	800-659-1005	Y
Invesco Oppenheimer Capital Income Fund Class R6	OCIIX	B-	C	B	Up	2.27	8.82	5.62	16.17	20.94	10.23	2,283	800-659-1005	Y
Invesco Oppenheimer Capital Income Fund Class Y	OCIYX	B-	C	B	Up	2.25	8.75	5.46	15.46	19.76	10.23	2,283	800-659-1005	Y
Invesco Oppenheimer Port Series: Conservative Inv Cls A	OACIX	B-	C	A-		3.16	9.39	6.11	16.19	18.13	9.78	578.8	800-659-1005	Y
Invesco Oppenheimer Port Series: Conservative Inv Cls C	OCCIX	B-	C	B+	Up	2.99	9.04	5.34	13.57	13.84	9.64	578.8	800-659-1005	Y
Invesco Oppenheimer Port Series: Conservative Inv Cls R	ONCIX	B-	C	B+	Up	3.06	9.30	5.88	15.34	16.70	9.75	578.8	800-659-1005	Y
Invesco Oppenheimer Port Series: Conservative Inv Cls R5	PXCIX	B	C+	A-		3.26	9.60	6.40	17.05	19.65	9.79	578.8	800-659-1005	Y
Invesco Oppenheimer Port Series: Conservative Inv Cls R6	PXCCX	B	C+	A-		3.26	9.60	6.40	17.05	19.65	9.79	578.8	800-659-1005	Y
Invesco Oppenheimer Port Series: Conservative Inv Cls Y	OYCIX	B	C+	A-	Up	3.25	9.58	6.39	17.03	19.64	9.83	578.8	800-659-1005	Y
Janus Henderson Global Allocation - Conservative Cls A	JCAAX	B-	C	B+	Up	2.87	8.76	3.46	15.44	13.97	12.53	195.6	877-335-2687	Y
Janus Henderson Global Allocation - Conservative Cls D	JMSCX	B-	C	B+	Up	2.94	8.90	3.69	16.14	15.06	12.59	195.6	877-335-2687	
Janus Henderson Global Allocation - Conservative Cls I	JCAIX	B-	C	B+	Up	2.86	8.91	3.70	16.23	15.37	12.58	195.6	877-335-2687	Y
Janus Henderson Global Allocation - Conservative Cls S	JCASX	B-	C	B+	Up	2.80	8.63	3.32	14.87	13.08	12.45	195.6	877-335-2687	Y
Janus Henderson Global Allocation - Conservative Cls T	JSPCX	B-	C	B+	Up	2.86	8.83	3.50	15.77	14.64	12.56	195.6	877-335-2687	Y
Janus Henderson Value Plus Income Fund Class A	JPVAX	B	C+	A-	Up	3.87	12.49	7.46	26.33	29.63	11.49	59.2	877-335-2687	Y
Janus Henderson Value Plus Income Fund Class C	JPVCX	B	C+	A-	Up	2.08	10.39	5.06	21.60	22.99	11.41	59.2	877-335-2687	Y
Janus Henderson Value Plus Income Fund Class D	JPVDX	B	C+	A		3.74	12.38	7.51	26.59	30.24	11.52	59.2	877-335-2687	Y
Janus Henderson Value Plus Income Fund Class I	JPVIX	B	C+	A		3.74	12.39	7.56	26.81	30.64	11.53	59.2	877-335-2687	Y
Janus Henderson Value Plus Income Fund Class N	JPVNX	B	C+	A		3.86	12.45	7.65	27.08	30.92	11.53	59.2	877-335-2687	Y
Janus Henderson Value Plus Income Fund Class S	JPVSX	B	C+	A-	Up	3.86	12.57	7.44	25.94	29.24	11.53	59.2	877-335-2687	Y
Janus Henderson Value Plus Income Fund Class T	JPVTX	B	C+	A		3.81	12.42	7.40	26.32	29.86	11.53	59.2	877-335-2687	Y
JNL Conservative Allocation Fund Class A		B	C+	A-	Up	2.95	9.43	7.00	16.34	15.98	12.53	409.2		Y
JNL Conservative Allocation Fund Class I		B	C+	A-		3.02	9.47	7.24	16.89	16.53	12.59	409.2		Y
JNL Institutional Alt 50 Fund Class A		B-	C	A-	Up	2.73	10.43	4.30	17.47	13.15	17.68	2,302		Y
JNL Institutional Alt 50 Fund Class I		B-	C	A-	Up	2.83	10.57	4.64	18.13	13.79	17.78	2,302		Y
JNL iShares Tactical Moderate A		B-	C	B+	Up	2.39	9.53	3.64	18.41	22.78	12.41	146.1		Y
JNL iShares Tactical Moderate I		B-	C	A-	Up	2.46	9.67	4.01	19.13	23.52	12.47	146.1		Y
JNL Moderate Allocation Fund Class A		B	C+	A-	Up	3.19	11.39	6.60	20.38	19.38	13.88	560.8		Y
JNL Moderate Allocation Fund Class I		B	C+	A-	Up	3.25	11.51	6.89	20.98	19.98	13.95	560.8		Y

Category: Cautious Allocation (con't)

		RATINGS				TOTAL RETURNS & PERFORMANCE					ASSETS		NEW INVESTORS	
Fund Name	Ticker Symbol	Overall Rating	Reward Rating	Risk Rating	Recent Up/ Downgrade	3-Month Total Return	6-Month Total Return	1-Year Total Return	3-Year Total Return	5-Year Total Return	NAV	Total Assets (MIL)	Telephone	Open to New Investors
JNL/Franklin Templeton Income Fund Class A		B	C	A		1.58	11.27	5.83	26.74	17.60	12.14	1,869		Y
JNL/Franklin Templeton Income Fund Class I		B-	C+	B+	Down	1.66	11.51	6.14	27.80	19.01	11.62	1,869		Y
JNL/S&P Managed Conservative Fund Class A		B	C	A-	Up	2.68	8.33	5.90	15.39	15.99	14.17	1,272		Y
JNL/S&P Managed Conservative Fund Class I		B	C+	A-		2.74	8.47	6.28	15.71	16.32	14.21	1,272		Y
JNL/S&P Managed Moderate Fund Class A		B	C	A	Up	3.00	10.91	6.26	23.66	23.45	16.46	2,974		Y
JNL/S&P Managed Moderate Fund Class I		B	C+	A		3.11	11.07	6.56	24.34	24.13	16.55	2,974		Y
John Hancock Funds II Multimgr Lifest Cons Cls 1	JILCX	B-	C+	B+		2.80	8.65	6.37	14.48	16.74	12.96	2,376	800-225-5913	Y
John Hancock Funds II Multimgr Lifest Cons Cls A	JALRX	B-	C	B+		2.70	8.53	5.97	13.30	14.68	12.99	2,376	800-225-5913	Y
John Hancock Funds II Multimgr Lifest Cons Cls B	JBLCX	B-	C	B	Up	2.53	8.07	5.15	10.90	10.57	12.99	2,376	800-225-5913	
John Hancock Funds II Multimgr Lifest Cons Cls C	JCLCX	B-	C	B	Up	2.53	8.07	5.24	10.90	10.67	12.99	2,376	800-225-5913	Y
John Hancock Funds II Multimgr Lifest Cons Cls I	JTOIX	B-	C+	B+		2.79	8.62	6.22	14.25	16.43	12.96	2,376	800-225-5913	Y
John Hancock Funds II Multimgr Lifest Cons Cls R1	JPLCX	B-	C	B	Up	2.62	8.27	5.54	12.05	12.53	12.97	2,376	800-225-5913	Y
John Hancock Funds II Multimgr Lifest Cons Cls R2	JQLCX	B-	C	B+		2.69	8.41	5.80	12.95	14.04	12.97	2,376	800-225-5913	Y
John Hancock Funds II Multimgr Lifest Cons Cls R3	JRLCX	B-	C	B+	Up	2.67	8.37	5.72	12.62	13.39	12.95	2,376	800-225-5913	Y
John Hancock Funds II Multimgr Lifest Cons Cls R4	JSLCX	B-	C	B+		2.75	8.54	6.14	13.77	15.32	12.96	2,376	800-225-5913	Y
John Hancock Funds II Multimgr Lifest Cons Cls R5	JTLRX	B-	C+	B+		2.80	8.64	6.28	14.43	16.47	12.96	2,376	800-225-5913	Y
John Hancock Funds II Multimgr Lifest Cons Cls R6	JULCX	B-	C+	B+		2.81	8.68	6.32	14.64	16.93	12.95	2,376	800-225-5913	Y
John Hancock Funds II Multimgr Lifest Mod Cls 1	JILMX	B	C+	A-	Up	2.99	11.07	6.09	21.06	22.27	13.42	3,179	800-225-5913	Y
John Hancock Funds II Multimgr Lifest Mod Cls 5	JHLMX	B	C+	A-	Up	3.00	11.03	6.15	21.28	22.53	13.4	3,179	800-225-5913	Y
John Hancock Funds II Multimgr Lifest Mod Cls A	JALMX	B	C	A-	Up	2.89	10.75	5.69	19.77	20.00	13.46	3,179	800-225-5913	Y
John Hancock Funds II Multimgr Lifest Mod Cls B	JBLMX	B-	C	B+	Up	2.71	10.39	4.96	17.25	15.80	13.45	3,179	800-225-5913	
John Hancock Funds II Multimgr Lifest Mod Cls C	JCLMX	B-	C	B+	Up	2.71	10.46	4.96	17.32	15.89	13.47	3,179	800-225-5913	Y
John Hancock Funds II Multimgr Lifest Mod Cls I	JTMIX	B	C+	A-	Up	2.98	11.05	6.03	20.93	21.97	13.41	3,179	800-225-5913	Y
John Hancock Funds II Multimgr Lifest Mod Cls R1	JPLMX	B-	C	A-	Up	2.81	10.60	5.36	18.61	17.85	13.44	3,179	800-225-5913	Y
John Hancock Funds II Multimgr Lifest Mod Cls R2	JQLMX	B	C	A-	Up	2.87	10.74	5.61	19.37	19.38	13.41	3,179	800-225-5913	Y
John Hancock Funds II Multimgr Lifest Mod Cls R3	JRLMX	B	C	A-	Up	2.84	10.74	5.54	18.96	18.51	13.44	3,179	800-225-5913	Y
John Hancock Funds II Multimgr Lifest Mod Cls R4	JSLMX	B	C	A-	Up	2.86	10.89	5.80	20.26	20.77	13.4	3,179	800-225-5913	Y
John Hancock Funds II Multimgr Lifest Mod Cls R5	JTLMX	B	C+	A-	Up	2.99	10.98	6.08	21.00	22.02	13.42	3,179	800-225-5913	Y
John Hancock Funds II Multimgr Lifest Mod Cls R6	JULMX	B	C+	A-	Up	3.00	11.11	6.14	21.26	22.51	13.4	3,179	800-225-5913	Y
John Hancock Funds Income Allocation Fund Class A	JIAFX	B-	C	B		2.62	9.83	6.45	14.15		9.86	6.2	800-225-5913	Y
John Hancock Funds Income Allocation Fund Class I	JIAIX	B-	C+	B		2.70	10.10	6.87	15.19		9.87	6.2	800-225-5913	Y
John Hancock Funds Income Allocation Fund Class R6	JIASX	B-	C+	B		2.72	10.03	6.98	15.53		9.87	6.2	800-225-5913	Y
John Hancock Funds Multi-Ind Lifestyle Cons Port Cls 1	JLCGX	B-	C+	B+		2.91	9.10	7.29	13.58	18.96	10.69	175.3	800-225-5913	Y
John Hancock Funds Multi-Ind Lifestyle Cons Port Cls R6	JLCSX	B-	C+	B+		2.92	9.11	7.43	13.81	19.32	10.7	175.3	800-225-5913	Y
John Hancock Funds Multi-Ind Lifestyle Mod Port Cls 1	JLMOX	B	C+	A-	Up	3.12	11.25	7.38	20.10	24.56	11.01	258.7	800-225-5913	Y
John Hancock Funds Multi-Ind Lifestyle Mod Port Cls R6	JLMRX	B	C+	A-		3.13	11.28	7.42	20.12	24.71	11.01	258.7	800-225-5913	Y
JPMorgan Income Builder Fund Class A Shares	JNBAX	B	C+	A	Up	3.07	10.49	7.02	22.92	22.37	10.63	13,005	800-480-4111	Y
JPMorgan Income Builder Fund Class C Shares	JNBCX	B	C+	A-	Up	2.95	10.13	6.50	21.12	19.33	10.6	13,005	800-480-4111	Y
JPMorgan Income Builder Fund Class I Shares	JNBSX	B	C+	A	Up	3.00	10.45	7.17	23.43	23.25	10.64	13,005	800-480-4111	Y
JPMorgan Income Builder Fund Class R6	JNBZX	B	C+	A	Up	3.02	10.49	7.27	23.61	23.43	10.64	13,005	800-480-4111	Y
JPMorgan Insurance Trust Global Allocation Portfolio Cls 1		B-	C	A-	Up	3.05	11.01	5.08	27.69		16.7	88.0	800-480-4111	Y
JPMorgan Insurance Trust Global Allocation Portfolio Cls 2		B-	C	A-	Up	3.05	10.83	4.82	26.76		16.66	88.0	800-480-4111	Y
JPMorgan Insurance Trust Income Builder Portfolio Class 1		B	C+	A-	Up	2.91	10.16	6.77	21.20		10.7	80.6	800-480-4111	Y
JPMorgan Insurance Trust Income Builder Portfolio Class 2		B	C+	A-	Up	2.90	10.07	6.47	20.29		10.68	80.6	800-480-4111	Y
JPMorgan Investor Conservative Growth Fund Class A	OICAX	B	C+	A-	Up	2.69	8.78	5.80	18.03	20.74	12.58	3,419	800-480-4111	Y
JPMorgan Investor Conservative Growth Fund Class C	OCGCX	B-	C	A-		2.56	8.57	5.23	16.02	17.51	12.52	3,419	800-480-4111	Y
JPMorgan Investor Conservative Growth Fund Class I	ONCFX	B	C+	A-	Up	2.73	8.97	6.02	18.88	22.31	12.66	3,419	800-480-4111	Y
JPMorgan Investor Conservative Growth Fund Class R6	JFLJX	B	C+	A-	Up	2.77	9.08	6.18	19.12	22.56	12.65	3,419	800-480-4111	Y
Ladenburg Income & Growth Fund Class A	LNOAX	B-	C	A-	Up	2.72	10.53	5.20	18.32		11.32	35.4	877-803-6583	Y
Ladenburg Income & Growth Fund Class C	LNOCX	B-	C	B+	Up	2.44	10.07	4.29	14.42		11.23	35.4	877-803-6583	Y
Ladenburg Income & Growth Fund Class I	LNOIX	B-	C	A-	Up	2.77	10.69	5.41	18.86		11.38	35.4	877-803-6583	Y
Ladenburg Income Fund Class A	LNCAX	B-	C	B+	Up	2.55	8.39	5.31	12.31		10.9	10.5	877-803-6583	Y

Category: Cautious Allocation (con't)

Fund Name	Ticker Symbol	RATINGS: Overall Rating	Reward Rating	Risk Rating	Recent Up/ Downgrade	TOTAL RETURNS & PERFORMANCE: 3-Month Total Return	6-Month Total Return	1-Year Total Return	3-Year Total Return	5-Year Total Return	ASSETS: NAV	Total Assets (MIL)	NEW INVESTORS: Telephone	Open to New Investors
Ladenburg Income Fund Class I	LNCIX	B-	C	B+		2.61	8.54	5.58	6.68		10.88	10.5	877-803-6583	Y
Madison Conservative Allocation Fund Class A	MCNAX	B	C+	A-	Up	2.68	9.07	6.46	16.81	21.54	10.75	69.1	800-767-0300	Y
Madison Conservative Allocation Fund Class B	MCNBX	B-	C	B+	Up	2.55	8.64	5.67	14.20	17.12	10.9	69.1	800-767-0300	Y
Madison Conservative Allocation Fund Class C	MCOCX	B-	C	B+	Up	2.54	8.63	5.67	14.30	17.11	10.91	69.1	800-767-0300	Y
MainStay Conservative Allocation Fund Class A	MCKAX	B-	C	B+	Up	2.34	10.00	3.46	17.08	16.74	11.77	453.1	800-624-6782	Y
MainStay Conservative Allocation Fund Class I	MCKIX	B-	C	B+	Up	2.55	10.28	3.85	18.15	18.52	11.89	453.1	800-624-6782	Y
MainStay Conservative Allocation Fund Class R2	MCKKX	B-	C	B+							11.78	453.1	800-624-6782	
MainStay Conservative Allocation Fund Class R3	MCKRX	B-	C	B+	Up	2.35	9.93	3.12	15.94	15.09	11.75	453.1	800-624-6782	Y
MainStay Conservative Allocation Fund Investor Class	MCKNX	B-	C	B+	Up	2.34	9.99	3.33	16.61	15.99	11.78	453.1	800-624-6782	Y
Manning & Napier Pro-Blend Conservative Term Series Cls I	MNCIX	B	C+	B+		2.86	9.06	6.93	17.01	16.65	10.4	907.1	585-325-6880	Y
Manning & Napier Pro-Blend Conservative Term Series Cls L	MNCCX	B-	C	B		2.57	8.57	5.82	13.61	10.99	9.96	907.1	585-325-6880	Y
Manning & Napier Pro-Blend Conservative Term Series Cls R	MNCRX	B-	C+	B+		2.65	8.77	6.32	15.37	13.76	9.96	907.1	585-325-6880	Y
Manning & Napier Pro-Blend Conservative Term Series Cls S	EXDAX	B	C+	B+	Up	2.77	8.93	6.64	16.37	15.43	13.9	907.1	585-325-6880	Y
Manning & Napier Pro-Blend Conservative Term Series Cls W	MNCWX	B	C+	B+		2.90	9.07	6.77	16.51	15.57	13.91	907.1	585-325-6880	Y
Manning & Napier Pro-Blend Moderate Term Series Class I	MNMIX	B	C+	A-	Up	3.19	11.01	6.36	19.91	16.32	9.88	410.2	585-325-6880	Y
Manning & Napier Pro-Blend Moderate Term Series Class L	MNMCX	B-	C	B+	Up	2.93	10.48	5.40	16.42	10.68	10.05	410.2	585-325-6880	Y
Manning & Napier Pro-Blend Moderate Term Series Class R	MNMRX	B-	C	B+		3.04	10.73	5.90	18.18	13.47	10.51	410.2	585-325-6880	Y
Manning & Napier Pro-Blend Moderate Term Series Class S	EXBAX	B-	C+	B+		3.18	10.96	6.21	19.14	15.01	13.63	410.2	585-325-6880	Y
Manning & Napier Pro-Blend Moderate Term Series Class W	MNMWX	B	C+	B+		3.28	11.07	6.31	19.26	15.13	13.62	410.2	585-325-6880	Y
MassMutual RetireSMART Conservative Administrative Cls	MRCLX	B	C+	A-	Up	3.09	9.30	6.37	16.70	17.72	9.99	217.5		Y
MassMutual RetireSMART Conservative Fund Class A	MCTAX	B	C	A-	Up	3.07	9.23	6.14	15.96	16.31	10.05	217.5		Y
MassMutual RetireSMART Conservative Fund Class I	MRCUX	B	C+	A-	Up	3.30	9.52	6.75	17.83	19.59	10	217.5		Y
MassMutual RetireSMART Conservative Fund Class R3	MRCVX	B-	C	A-		3.02	9.06	5.84	15.35	15.29	9.87	217.5		Y
MassMutual RetireSMART Conservative Fund Class R4	MRCZX	B	C+	A-	Up	3.12	9.27	6.21	16.18	16.90	9.9	217.5		Y
MassMutual RetireSMART Conservative Fund Class R5	MRCSX	B	C+	A-	Up	3.20	9.53	6.63	17.50	18.94	9.99	217.5		Y
MassMutual RetireSMART Conservative Fund Service Class	MRCYX	B	C+	A-	Up	3.09	9.31	6.42	17.08	18.20	9.98	217.5		Y
Meeder Conservative Allocation Fund Adviser Class	IFAAX	B-	C	A-		2.56	6.78	4.93	17.30	8.61	22.65	141.5		Y
Meeder Conservative Allocation Fund Institutional Class	IFAIX	B-	C	A-		2.60	6.86	5.10	17.74	9.03	22.7	141.5		Y
Meeder Conservative Allocation Fund Retail Class	FLRUX	B-	C	B+	Up	2.50	6.72	4.80	16.60	7.97	22.38	141.5		Y
Meeder Moderate Allocation Fund Adviser Class	DVOAX	B-	C	B+	Up	2.45	6.47	3.56	33.11		11.45	179.3		Y
Meeder Moderate Allocation Fund Institutional Class	DVOIX	B-	C	A-	Up	2.49	6.55	3.74	33.63		11.47	179.3		Y
Meeder Moderate Allocation Fund Retail Class	FLDOX	B-	C	B+	Up	2.41	6.38	3.33	32.14		11.43	179.3		Y
MFS Conservative Allocation Fund Class 529A	ECLAX	B	C+	A		3.79	12.19	7.86	21.38	25.14	15.81	2,934	877-960-6077	Y
MFS Conservative Allocation Fund Class 529B	EBCAX	B	C+	A-	Up	3.67	11.77	7.03	18.65	20.49	15.56	2,934	877-960-6077	Y
MFS Conservative Allocation Fund Class 529C	ECACX	B	C+	A-	Up	3.69	11.84	7.09	18.71	20.47	15.5	2,934	877-960-6077	Y
MFS Conservative Allocation Fund Class A	MACFX	B	C+	A		3.85	12.21	7.85	21.52	25.38	15.9	2,934	877-960-6077	Y
MFS Conservative Allocation Fund Class B	MACBX	B	C+	A-	Up	3.68	11.79	7.06	18.86	20.80	15.82	2,934	877-960-6077	Y
MFS Conservative Allocation Fund Class C	MACVX	B	C+	A-	Up	3.66	11.79	7.11	18.81	20.74	15.66	2,934	877-960-6077	Y
MFS Conservative Allocation Fund Class I	MACIX	B	C+	A		3.94	12.36	8.18	22.46	26.94	16.05	2,934	877-960-6077	Y
MFS Conservative Allocation Fund Class R1	MACKX	B	C+	A-	Up	3.68	11.84	7.06	18.87	20.82	15.34	2,934	877-960-6077	Y
MFS Conservative Allocation Fund Class R2	MCARX	B	C+	A	Up	3.84	12.16	7.69	20.65	23.86	15.44	2,934	877-960-6077	Y
MFS Conservative Allocation Fund Class R3	MACNX	B	C+	A		3.81	12.25	7.85	21.47	25.35	15.76	2,934	877-960-6077	Y
MFS Conservative Allocation Fund Class R4	MACJX	B	C+	A		3.90	12.41	8.18	22.43	26.94	15.91	2,934	877-960-6077	Y
MFS Diversified Income Fund Class A	DIFAX	B-	C+	B	Down	2.83	11.42	8.83	18.49	26.27	12.76	3,710	877-960-6077	Y
MFS Diversified Income Fund Class C	DIFCX	B-	C+	B	Down	2.65	10.93	8.04	15.88	21.65	12.75	3,710	877-960-6077	Y
MFS Diversified Income Fund Class I	DIFIX	B	C+	B		2.81	11.47	9.01	19.28	27.75	12.75	3,710	877-960-6077	Y
MFS Diversified Income Fund Class R1	DIFDX	B-	C+	B	Down	2.65	10.94	7.95	15.89	21.66	12.74	3,710	877-960-6077	Y
MFS Diversified Income Fund Class R2	DIFEX	B-	C+	B	Down	2.77	11.20	8.57	17.62	24.72	12.75	3,710	877-960-6077	Y
MFS Diversified Income Fund Class R3	DIFFX	B-	C+	B	Down	2.83	11.42	8.83	18.49	26.27	12.76	3,710	877-960-6077	Y
MFS Diversified Income Fund Class R4	DIFGX	B	C+	B		2.89	11.55	9.10	19.38	27.85	12.76	3,710	877-960-6077	Y
MFS Diversified Income Fund Class R6	DIFHX	B	C+	B		2.91	11.60	9.20	19.71	28.57	12.76	3,710	877-960-6077	Y
Morgan Stanley Inst Global Multi-Asset Income Port Cls I	MSGMX	B-	C	B+	Up	2.82	9.45	5.11	13.24		10.33	15.6	855-332-5306	Y

Category: Cautious Allocation (con't)

Fund Name	Ticker Symbol	RATINGS: Overall Rating	Reward Rating	Risk Rating	Recent Up/ Downgrade	TOTAL RETURNS & PERFORMANCE: 3-Month Total Return	6-Month Total Return	1-Year Total Return	3-Year Total Return	5-Year Total Return	ASSETS: NAV	Total Assets (MIL)	NEW INVESTORS: Telephone	Open to New Investors
Morgan Stanley Inst Global Multi-Asset Income Port Cls IS	MSMUX	B-	C	B+	Up	2.83	9.45	5.15	13.51		10.34	15.6	855-332-5306	Y
Morningstar Conservative ETF Asset Alloc Port Cls I		B-	C	B+		2.56	6.87	5.86	11.80	15.07	11.19	34.8	866-759-5679	Y
Morningstar Income & Growth ETF Asset Alloc Port Cls I		B	C	A-	Up	2.57	8.84	5.49	17.64	19.86	9.97	75.0	866-759-5679	Y
Nationwide Investor Destinations Conservative Fund Class A	NDCAX	B-	C	A-		2.27	6.96	4.80	11.90	15.83	10.12	659.9	800-848-0920	Y
Nationwide Investor Destinations Conservative Fund Class C	NDCCX	B-	C	B+	Up	2.09	6.61	4.05	9.43	11.68	10.07	659.9	800-848-0920	Y
Nationwide Investor Destinations Conservative Fund Class R	GCFRX	B-	C	B+	Up	2.19	6.80	4.48	10.76	14.11	10.1	659.9	800-848-0920	Y
Nationwide Investor Destinations Conservative Cls R6	GIMCX	B-	C	A-		2.24	7.10	5.14	12.95	17.81	10.17	659.9	800-848-0920	Y
Nationwide Inv Destinations Conservative Inst Service Cls	NWWLX	B-	C	A-		2.33	7.19	5.17	12.71	17.38	10.15	659.9	800-848-0920	Y
Nationwide Investor Destinations Conservative Service Cls	NDCSX	B-	C	A-		2.24	7.01	4.82	11.64	15.50	10.16	659.9	800-848-0920	Y
Nationwide Inv Destinations Moderately Conservative Cls A	NADCX	B	C	A-	Up	2.71	10.06	4.99	18.66	21.35	9.83	445.7	800-848-0920	Y
Nationwide Inv Destinations Moderately Conservative Cls C	NCDCX	B-	C	A-	Up	2.54	9.72	4.26	16.19	17.00	9.78	445.7	800-848-0920	Y
Nationwide Inv Destinations Moderately Conservative Cls R	GMMRX	B-	C	A-	Up	2.62	9.97	4.75	17.63	19.55	9.86	445.7	800-848-0920	Y
Nationwide Inv Destinations Moderately Conservative Cls R6	GMIMX	B	C	A-	Up	2.76	10.22	5.29	19.86	23.44	9.95	445.7	800-848-0920	Y
Nationwide Inv Destinations Mod Cons Inst Serv Cls	NWWKX	B	C	A-	Up	2.74	10.20	5.30	19.62	22.96	9.91	445.7	800-848-0920	Y
Nationwide Inv Destinations Mod Cons Serv Cls	NSDCX	B-	C	A-	Up	2.56	9.93	4.88	18.42	20.96	9.9	445.7	800-848-0920	Y
Neuberger Berman Global Allocation Fund Class A	NGLAX	B-	C	B+	Up	3.26	12.79	3.13	24.49	17.02	11.37	16.9	212-476-9000	Y
Neuberger Berman Global Allocation Fund Class R6	NRGLX	B-	C	B+	Up	3.33	12.91	3.41	25.82	19.12	11.45	16.9	212-476-9000	Y
Neuberger Berman Global Allocation Institutional Cls	NGLIX	B-	C	B+	Up	3.33	12.91	3.41	25.82	19.12	11.45	16.9	212-476-9000	Y
Neuberger Berman Multi-Asset Income Fund Class A	NANAX	B-	C	B+	Up	2.13	10.53	3.94	16.24		9.95	22.2	212-476-9000	Y
Neuberger Berman Multi-Asset Income Fund Class R6	NRANX	B-	C	B+	Up	2.25	10.78	4.41	17.80		9.95	22.2	212-476-9000	Y
Neuberger Berman Multi-Asset Income Institutional Cls	NANIX	B-	C	B+	Up	2.22	10.73	4.32	17.53		9.95	22.2	212-476-9000	Y
New Covenant Balanced Income Fund	NCBIX	B	C+	A-		2.79	9.71	6.76	18.93	24.05	21.41	78.4		Y
Nuveen NWQ Flexible Income Fund Class A	NWQAX	B	B-	B+	Up	3.61	11.94	7.06	20.99	26.41	21.62	1,248	312-917-8146	Y
Nuveen NWQ Flexible Income Fund Class C	NWQCX	B	C+	B	Up	3.37	11.43	6.22	18.22	21.70	21.57	1,248	312-917-8146	Y
Nuveen NWQ Flexible Income Fund Class I	NWQIX	B	B-	A-	Up	3.67	12.03	7.33	21.87	27.97	21.64	1,248	312-917-8146	Y
Nuveen NWQ Flexible Income Fund Class R6	NQWFX	B	B-	A-	Up	3.62	11.99	7.29	22.14	28.25	21.75	1,248	312-917-8146	Y
Nuveen Real Asset Income Fund Class A	NRIAX	B	B-	B		3.21	14.77	9.14	20.34	29.49	23.93	1,943	312-917-8146	Y
Nuveen Real Asset Income Fund Class C	NRICX	B-	C+	B		2.98	14.29	8.33	17.68	24.75	23.94	1,943	312-917-8146	Y
Nuveen Real Asset Income Fund Class I	NRIIX	B	B-	B		3.27	14.87	9.42	21.25	31.13	23.93	1,943	312-917-8146	Y
Nuveen Real Asset Income Fund Class R6	NRIFX	B	B-	B		3.27	14.92	9.56	21.56	31.46	24.05	1,943	312-917-8146	Y
Old Westbury Strategic Opportunities Fund	OWSOX	B-	C	B+	Up	2.17	11.92	2.68	23.67	19.81	7.51	5,193	212-708-9100	Y
Pacific Funds Portfolio Optimization Conservative Adv Cls	PLCDX	B-	C	B+	Up	2.92	9.08	5.80	15.49	17.79	10.57	248.4	800-722-2333	Y
Pacific Funds Portfolio Optimization Conservative Cls A	POAAX	B-	C	B+	Up	2.93	9.00	5.61	14.66	16.38	10.53	248.4	800-722-2333	Y
Pacific Funds Portfolio Optimization Conservative Cls B	POABX	B-	C	B	Up	2.70	8.46	4.74	12.12	12.12	10.25	248.4	800-722-2333	Y
Pacific Funds Portfolio Optimization Conservative Cls C	POACX	B-	C	B	Up	2.70	8.58	4.81	12.20	12.09	10.24	248.4	800-722-2333	Y
Pacific Funds Port Optimization Mod-Cons Adv Cls	PMCDX	B	C	A-	Up	3.34	11.43	5.93	20.63	22.67	11.11	363.1	800-722-2333	Y
Pacific Funds Port Optimization Mod-Cons Cls A	POBAX	B	C	A-	Up	3.26	11.26	5.65	19.79	21.16	11.06	363.1	800-722-2333	Y
Pacific Funds Port Optimization Mod-Cons Cls B	POBBX	B-	C	B+	Up	3.06	10.80	4.84	17.07	16.69	10.77	363.1	800-722-2333	Y
Pacific Funds Port Optimization Mod-Cons Cls C	POBCX	B-	C	B+	Up	3.06	10.81	4.79	17.12	16.77	10.76	363.1	800-722-2333	Y
Permanent Portfolio Permanent Portfolio Class A	PRPDX	B-	C	B+	Up	2.50	10.85	4.10	13.54	11.08	39.63	1,946	800-531-5142	Y
Permanent Portfolio Permanent Portfolio Class I	PRPFX	B-	C	B+	Up	2.55	10.97	4.34	14.35	12.44	39.75	1,946	800-531-5142	Y
PIMCO Inflation Response Multi-Asset Fund Class A	PZRMX	B-	C	A-		1.14	6.40	2.48	10.65	4.35	7.96	1,068	866-746-2602	Y
PIMCO Inflation Response Multi-Asset Fund Class I-2	PPRMX	B-	C	A-		1.19	6.67	2.86	11.91	6.18	8.05	1,068	866-746-2602	Y
PIMCO Inflation Response Multi-Asset Fund Institutional	PIRMX	B-	C	B		1.21	6.69	2.92	12.24	6.68	8.05	1,068	866-746-2602	Y
Praxis Genesis Conservative Portfolio Class A	MCONX	B	C+	B+	Up	2.92	9.02	6.79	15.59	20.29	11.9	24.5		Y
Principal Global Diversified Income Fund Class A	PGBAX	B	C+	B+	Up	2.59	9.47	5.60	17.05	17.75	13.66	7,703	800-787-1621	Y
Principal Global Diversified Income Fund Class C	PGDCX	B-	C	B+	Up	2.41	9.04	4.84	14.38	13.42	13.57	7,703	800-787-1621	Y
Principal Global Diversified Income Fund Class R-6	PGBLX	B	C+	A-	Up	2.77	9.71	6.00	18.18	19.64	13.59	7,703	800-787-1621	Y
Principal Global Diversified Income Institutional Cls	PGDIX	B	C+	A-	Up	2.77	9.70	5.98	18.21	19.66	13.6	7,703	800-787-1621	Y
Principal Strategic Asset Mgmt Conservative Balanced Cls A	SAIPX	B	C+	A-	Up	3.01	10.35	5.88	20.58	23.54	11.94	1,676	800-787-1621	Y
Principal Strategic Asset Mgmt Conservative Balanced Cls C	SCIPX	B-	C	A-	Up	2.75	9.90	5.12	17.87	18.91	11.81	1,676	800-787-1621	Y
Principal Strategic Asset Mgmt Conservative Balanced Cls J	PCBJX	B	C+	A-	Up	3.01	10.46	6.08	21.25	24.31	11.77	1,676	800-787-1621	Y

Category: Cautious Allocation (con't)

Fund Name	Ticker Symbol	RATINGS: Overall Rating	Reward Rating	Risk Rating	Recent Up/ Downgrade	TOTAL RETURNS & PERFORMANCE: 3-Month Total Return	6-Month Total Return	1-Year Total Return	3-Year Total Return	5-Year Total Return	ASSETS: NAV	Total Assets (MIL)	NEW INVESTORS: Telephone	Open to New Investors
Principal Strat Asset Mgmt Cons Balanced Inst Cls	PCCIX	B	C+	A-	Up	3.04	10.55	6.31	21.79	25.49	11.81	1,676	800-787-1621	Y
Principal Strat Asset Mgmt Cons Balanced R-1 Cls	PCSSX	B	C+	A-	Up	2.83	10.09	5.33	18.69	20.17	11.77	1,676	800-787-1621	Y
Principal Strat Asset Mgmt Cons Balanced R-2 Cls	PCNSX	B	C+	A-	Up	2.84	10.09	5.49	19.10	20.97	11.87	1,676	800-787-1621	Y
Principal Strat Asset Mgmt Cons Balanced R-3 Cls	PCBPX	B	C+	A-	Up	2.90	10.22	5.65	19.74	22.09	11.79	1,676	800-787-1621	Y
Principal Strat Asset Mgmt Cons Balanced R-4 Cls	PCBLX	B	C+	A-	Up	2.90	10.31	5.79	20.42	23.15	11.8	1,676	800-787-1621	Y
Principal Strat Asset Mgmt Cons Balanced R-5 Cls	PCBFX	B	C+	A-	Up	2.98	10.35	5.96	20.83	23.96	11.8	1,676	800-787-1621	Y
Principal Strategic Asset Management Flexible Income Cls A	SAUPX	B	C+	A-		2.77	8.73	6.33	16.45	19.86	12.21	2,643	800-787-1621	Y
Principal Strategic Asset Management Flexible Income Cls C	SCUPX	B-	C	B+		2.60	8.33	5.49	13.90	15.40	12.08	2,643	800-787-1621	Y
Principal Strategic Asset Management Flexible Income Cls J	PFIJX	B	C+	A-		2.84	8.83	6.50	17.09	20.61	12.1	2,643	800-787-1621	Y
Principal Strategic Asset Mgmt Flexible Income Inst Cls	PIFIX	B	C+	A-		2.85	8.94	6.67	17.59	21.69	12.17	2,643	800-787-1621	Y
Principal Strategic Asset Mgmt Flexible Income R-1 Cls	PFIGX	B-	C+	B+		2.59	8.40	5.67	14.47	16.55	12.1	2,643	800-787-1621	Y
Principal Strategic Asset Mgmt Flexible Income R-2 Cls	PFIVX	B	C+	B+	Up	2.68	8.51	5.93	15.01	17.37	12.15	2,643	800-787-1621	Y
Principal Strategic Asset Mgmt Flexible Income R-3 Cls	PFIPX	B	C+	A-	Up	2.72	8.63	6.03	15.65	18.36	12.14	2,643	800-787-1621	Y
Principal Strategic Asset Mgmt Flexible Income R-4 Cls	PFILX	B	C+	A-		2.77	8.74	6.23	16.33	19.49	12.15	2,643	800-787-1621	Y
Principal Strategic Asset Mgmt Flexible Income R-5 Cls	PFIFX	B	C+	A-		2.80	8.72	6.35	16.66	20.25	12.14	2,643	800-787-1621	Y
Putnam Dynamic Asset Allocation Conservative Fund Class A	PACAX	B-	C	B+		2.64	9.23	4.98	16.57	22.43	10.71	1,088	617-292-1000	Y
Putnam Dynamic Asset Allocation Conservative Fund Class B	PACBX	B-	C	B+	Up	2.47	8.92	4.23	14.02	18.02	10.62	1,088	617-292-1000	Y
Putnam Dynamic Asset Allocation Conservative Fund Class C	PACCX	B-	C	B+	Up	2.39	8.86	4.17	13.90	17.98	10.56	1,088	617-292-1000	Y
Putnam Dynamic Asset Allocation Conservative Fund Class M	PACMX	B-	C	B+	Up	2.55	8.98	4.52	14.81	19.50	10.58	1,088	617-292-1000	Y
Putnam Dynamic Asset Allocation Conservative Fund Class P		B-	C	B+		2.74	9.51	5.48	17.30	23.20	10.75	1,088	617-292-1000	
Putnam Dynamic Asset Allocation Conservative Fund Class R	PACRX	B-	C	B+	Up	2.59	9.12	4.75	15.64	20.94	11.03	1,088	617-292-1000	Y
Putnam Dynamic Asset Allocation Conservative Fund Class R5	PACDX	B	C	A-	Up	2.71	9.45	5.26	17.60	24.28	10.75	1,088	617-292-1000	Y
Putnam Dynamic Asset Allocation Conservative Fund Class R6	PCCEX	B	C+	A-	Up	2.72	9.48	5.41	17.82	24.76	10.76	1,088	617-292-1000	Y
Putnam Dynamic Asset Allocation Conservative Fund Class Y	PACYX	B-	C	A-		2.69	9.32	5.20	17.32	23.93	10.75	1,088	617-292-1000	Y
QCI Balanced Fund Institutional Class	QCIBX	B	C	A		2.23	12.61	9.91	27.33	31.75	12.03	64.4	252-442-4226	Y
QS Defensive Growth Fund Class A	SBCPX	B	C+	A-	Up	2.78	9.52	6.43	18.27	20.59	13.05	121.9	877-721-1926	Y
QS Defensive Growth Fund Class C	LWLAX	B-	C	B+	Up	2.67	9.15	5.74	15.82	16.39	13	121.9	877-721-1926	Y
QS Defensive Growth Fund Class C1	SBCLX	B-	C	B+		2.68	9.20	5.92	16.56	17.64	13.39	121.9	877-721-1926	
QS Defensive Growth Fund Class I	LMGIX	B	C+	A-		2.87	9.71	6.77	19.34	22.25	13.02	121.9	877-721-1926	Y
QS Defensive Growth Fund Class R	LMLRX	B	C	A-	Up	2.73	9.32	6.17	17.36	18.98	13.04	121.9	877-721-1926	Y
RiverFront Asset Allocation Income & Growth Class A	RCCAX	B-	C	B+	Up	1.99	8.81	3.95	14.18	15.75	10.42	8.5	866-759-5679	Y
RiverFront Asset Allocation Income & Growth Class I	RCIBX	B-	C	B+	Up	1.95	8.91	4.19	15.01	17.18	10.25	8.5	866-759-5679	Y
RiverFront Asset Allocation Income & Growth Class Investor	RCABX	B-	C	B+	Up	1.96	8.83	3.97	14.17	15.81	10.44	8.5	866-759-5679	Y
Russell Investments LifePoints Conservative Strategy Cls A	RCLAX	B-	C	B+	Up	2.01	6.58	4.39	10.47	13.14	9.76	209.6	800-426-7969	Y
Russell Investments LifePoints Conservative Strategy Cls E	RCLEX	B-	C	B+	Up	1.99	6.53	4.33	10.48	13.13	9.81	209.6	800-426-7969	Y
Russell Inv LifePoints Conservative Strategy Cls R1	RCLRX	B-	C	A-		2.07	6.83	4.74	11.77	15.35	9.85	209.6	800-426-7969	Y
Russell Inv LifePoints Conservative Strategy Cls R4	RCLUX	B-	C	B+		2.03	6.70	4.50	10.83	13.96	9.78	209.6	800-426-7969	Y
Russell Inv LifePoints Conservative Strategy Cls R5	RCLVX	B-	C	B+	Up	1.85	6.47	4.18	10.04	12.45	9.86	209.6	800-426-7969	Y
Russell Investments LifePoints Conservative Strategy Cls S	RCLSX	B-	C	B+		2.04	6.79	4.69	11.35	14.70	9.86	209.6	800-426-7969	Y
Russell Investments LifePoints Moderate Strategy Cls A	RMLAX	B-	C	A-	Up	2.09	7.91	3.68	15.03	17.55	10.23	357.9	800-426-7969	Y
Russell Investments LifePoints Moderate Strategy Cls C	RMLCX	B-	C	B+	Up	1.93	7.50	3.01	12.53	13.18	10.03	357.9	800-426-7969	Y
Russell Investments LifePoints Moderate Strategy Cls E	RMLEX	B-	C	A-	Up	2.08	7.88	3.60	14.75	17.18	10.26	357.9	800-426-7969	Y
Russell Investments LifePoints Moderate Strategy Cls R1	RMLRX	B-	C	A-	Up	2.07	7.95	3.96	15.94	19.10	10.31	357.9	800-426-7969	Y
Russell Investments LifePoints Moderate Strategy Cls R4	RMLUX	B-	C	A-	Up	2.09	7.89	3.67	14.98	17.61	10.25	357.9	800-426-7969	Y
Russell Investments LifePoints Moderate Strategy Cls R5	RMLVX	B-	C	A-	Up	1.98	7.74	3.45	14.23	16.19	10.29	357.9	800-426-7969	Y
Russell Investments LifePoints Moderate Strategy Cls S	RMLSX	B-	C	A-	Up	2.18	7.96	3.90	15.63	18.65	10.3	357.9	800-426-7969	Y
Russell Investments Multi-Strategy Income Fund Class A	RMYAX	B-	C	A-	Up	1.81	6.99	3.46	17.17		10.03	1,201	800-426-7969	Y
Russell Investments Multi-Strategy Income Fund Class C	RMYCX	B-	C	B+	Up	1.65	6.62	2.71	14.50		9.98	1,201	800-426-7969	Y
Russell Investments Multi-Strategy Income Fund Class E	RMYEX	B-	C	A-	Up	1.85	7.08	3.58	17.23		10.16	1,201	800-426-7969	Y
Russell Investments Multi-Strategy Income Fund Class M	RGYTX	B-	C	A-	Up	1.90	7.08	3.77	18.46		10.04	1,201	800-426-7969	Y
Russell Investments Multi-Strategy Income Fund Class S	RMYSX	B-	C	A-	Up	1.97	7.15	3.83	18.05		10.05	1,201	800-426-7969	Y
Russell Investments Multi-Strategy Income Fund Class Y	RMYYX	B	C	A-	Up	1.91	7.19	3.93	18.82		10.06	1,201	800-426-7969	Y

Category: Cautious Allocation (con't)

Fund Name	Ticker Symbol	Overall Rating	Reward Rating	Risk Rating	Recent Up/ Downgrade	3-Month Total Return	6-Month Total Return	1-Year Total Return	3-Year Total Return	5-Year Total Return	NAV	Total Assets (MIL)	Telephone	Open to New Investors
		RATINGS				TOTAL RETURNS & PERFORMANCE					ASSETS		NEW INVESTORS	
Schwab MarketTrack Conservative Portfolio™	SWCGX	B	C	A-	Up	2.94	10.03	5.78	18.64	23.18	16.09	255.4	877-824-5615	Y
Schwab® Monthly Income Fund - Enhanced Payout	SWKRX	B-	C	B+		2.99	9.56	6.11	14.18	18.81	11.42	80.7	877-824-5615	Y
Schwab® Monthly Income Fund - Maximum Payout	SWLRX	B-	C	B	Up	2.92	7.86	6.62	10.24	16.09	10.2	45.5	877-824-5615	Y
Schwab® Monthly Income Fund - Moderate Payout	SWJRX	B-	C	B+	Up	2.94	11.35	5.39	17.79	21.33	11.02	43.2	877-824-5615	Y
SEI Asset Allocation Trust Conservative Strategy Cls D	SSTDX	B-	C	B+	Up	2.22	6.42	4.71	8.76	10.79	10.86	78.6	800-342-5734	Y
SEI Asset Allocation Trust Conservative Strategy Cls F	SVSAX	B-	C	A-		2.33	6.74	5.49	11.24	15.10	10.87	78.6	800-342-5734	Y
SEI Asset Allocation Trust Conservative Strategy Cls I	SICIX	B-	C	B+		2.32	6.75	5.23	10.47	13.76	11.07	78.6	800-342-5734	Y
SEI Asset Allocation Trust Core Market Strategy Cls F	SOKAX	B-	C	A-	Up	3.36	11.81	5.58	19.70	20.37	11.87	94.8	800-342-5734	Y
SEI Asset Allocation Trust Core Market Strategy Cls I	SCMSX	B	C	A-	Up	3.46	12.07	5.93	19.79	22.04	13.03	94.8	800-342-5734	Y
SEI Asset Allocation Trust Market Growth Strategy Cls D	SMKDX	B-	C	A-	Up	3.13	12.47	4.12	20.45	17.62	13.29	226.8	800-342-5734	Y
SEI Asset Allocation Trust Market Growth Strategy Cls F	SRWAX	B-	C	A-	Up	3.33	12.82	4.89	23.13	22.11	13.36	226.8	800-342-5734	Y
SEI Asset Allocation Trust Market Growth Strategy Cls I	SMGSX	B-	C	A-	Up	3.31	12.77	4.70	22.28	20.62	13.16	226.8	800-342-5734	Y
SEI Asset Allocation Trust Moderate Strategy Fund Class D	SMSDX	B-	C	B+		2.97	9.47	6.09	13.56	17.25	12.48	173.9	800-342-5734	Y
SEI Asset Allocation Trust Moderate Strategy Fund Class F	SMOAX	B	C+	A-	Up	3.16	9.94	6.96	16.21	21.83	12.52	173.9	800-342-5734	Y
SEI Asset Allocation Trust Moderate Strategy Fund Class I	SMSIX	B-	C	B+		3.17	9.76	6.66	15.42	20.33	12.87	173.9	800-342-5734	Y
SEI Inst Managed Trust Multi-Asset Capital Stability Cls F	SCLAX	B-	C	B+	Up	1.97	4.86	3.85	7.86	9.42	10.34	732.4	800-342-5734	Y
SEI Inst Managed Trust Multi-Asset Capital Stability Cls Y	SMLYX	B-	C	B+	Up	2.06	4.96	3.95	8.17	9.95	10.36	732.4	800-342-5734	Y
Sextant Global High Income Fund	SGHIX	B-	C	B+	Down	2.40	10.17	8.60	36.04	23.28	11.48	9.9		Y
Spirit of America Income & Opportunity Fund Class A	SOAOX	B-	C+	B		2.98	10.22	6.76	13.03	16.97	9.7	23.4		Y
Spirit of America Income & Opportunity Fund Class C	SACOX	B-	C+	B	Up	2.68	9.62	5.99	11.18	12.22	9.68	23.4		Y
T. Rowe Price Personal Strategy Income Fund	PRSIX	B	C+	A	Up	3.02	10.66	6.52	24.60	28.03	19.63	2,243	410-345-2000	Y
T. Rowe Price Personal Strategy Income Fund I Class	PPIPX	B	C+	A	Up	3.08	10.66	6.58	24.93	28.38	19.62	2,243	410-345-2000	Y
T. Rowe Price Retirement Balanced Fund	TRRIX	B	C+	A	Up	3.00	10.35	6.19	20.56	23.16	15.17	2,153	410-345-2000	Y
T. Rowe Price Retirement Balanced Fund Advisor Class	PARIX	B	C+	A-	Up	2.93	10.21	5.97	19.78	21.67	15.18	2,153	410-345-2000	Y
T. Rowe Price Retirement Balanced Fund Class R	RRTIX	B	C	A-	Up	2.87	10.08	5.67	18.85	20.12	15.17	2,153	410-345-2000	Y
T. Rowe Price Retirement Balanced I Fund I Class	TRPTX	B	C+	A	Up	3.13	10.39	6.40	20.99		11.49	342.1	410-345-2000	Y
TCW Conservative Allocation Fund Class Institutional	TGPCX	B	C	A-	Up	3.37	11.47	6.71	17.85	24.60	11.93	30.0	213-244-0000	Y
TCW Conservative Allocation Fund Class N	TGPNX	B-	C	A-		3.37	11.26	6.41	16.48	21.72	11.94	30.0	213-244-0000	Y
The Hartford Balanced Income Fund Class A	HBLAX	B	C+	B+		4.04	13.03	10.34	23.88	33.22	14.41	12,315	888-843-7824	Y
The Hartford Balanced Income Fund Class C	HBLCX	B-	C+	B		3.84	12.57	9.50	21.10	28.34	14.19	12,315	888-843-7824	Y
The Hartford Balanced Income Fund Class F	HBLFX	B	C+	B+		4.12	13.20	10.77	25.09	35.53	14.42	12,315	888-843-7824	Y
The Hartford Balanced Income Fund Class I	HBLIX	B	C+	B+		4.11	13.16	10.61	24.78	34.89	14.41	12,315	888-843-7824	Y
The Hartford Balanced Income Fund Class R3	HBLRX	B	C+	B+		4.03	12.88	9.98	22.65	31.16	14.47	12,315	888-843-7824	Y
The Hartford Balanced Income Fund Class R4	HBLSX	B	C+	B+		4.02	12.94	10.31	23.73	33.16	14.47	12,315	888-843-7824	Y
The Hartford Balanced Income Fund Class R5	HBLTX	B	C+	B+		4.07	13.15	10.59	24.68	34.83	14.49	12,315	888-843-7824	Y
The Hartford Balanced Income Fund Class R6	HBLVX	B	B-	B+		4.15	13.22	10.73	25.07	35.49	14.57	12,315	888-843-7824	Y
The Hartford Balanced Income Fund Class Y	HBLYX	B	C+	B+		4.06	13.18	10.67	24.93	35.36	14.57	12,315	888-843-7824	Y
Thrivent Diversified Income Plus Fund Class A	AAHYX	B	C+	A-	Up	2.48	9.38	4.79	19.48	21.47	7.29	1,004		Y
Thrivent Diversified Income Plus Fund Class S	THYFX	B	C+	A	Up	2.57	9.48	4.96	20.50	23.08	7.22	1,004		Y
Thrivent Moderately Conservative Allocation Fund Class A	TCAAX	B	C+	A-	Up	3.11	10.81	6.88	19.75	23.20	12.53	932.0		Y
Thrivent Moderately Conservative Allocation Fund Class S	TCAIX	B	C+	A-		3.16	10.89	7.13	20.64	24.95	12.56	932.0		Y
TIAA-CREF Lifestyle Conservative Fund Advisor Class	TLSHX	B	C	A-	Up	2.87	10.70	5.20	21.83	25.87	12.61	240.4	877-518-9161	Y
TIAA-CREF Lifestyle Conservative Fund Institutional Class	TCSIX	B	C	A-	Up	2.90	10.75	5.28	21.98	26.06	12.61	240.4	877-518-9161	Y
TIAA-CREF Lifestyle Conservative Fund Premier Class	TLSPX	B	C	A-	Up	2.86	10.66	5.12	21.43	25.10	12.62	240.4	877-518-9161	Y
TIAA-CREF Lifestyle Conservative Fund Retail Class	TSCLX	B	C	A-	Up	2.84	10.53	5.01	20.94	24.31	12.59	240.4	877-518-9161	Y
TIAA-CREF Lifestyle Conservative Fund Retirement Class	TSCTX	B	C	A-	Up	2.84	10.63	5.03	21.10	24.44	12.6	240.4	877-518-9161	Y
TIAA-CREF Lifestyle Income Fund Advisor Class	TSIHX	B	C	A-	Up	2.51	7.61	5.46	14.61	19.29	11.18	73.1	877-518-9161	Y
TIAA-CREF Lifestyle Income Fund Institutional Class	TSITX	B	C	A-	Up	2.53	7.64	5.49	14.67	19.28	11.18	73.1	877-518-9161	Y
TIAA-CREF Lifestyle Income Fund Premier Class	TSIPX	B	C	A-	Up	2.48	7.55	5.24	14.15	18.31	11.19	73.1	877-518-9161	Y
TIAA-CREF Lifestyle Income Fund Retail Class	TSILX	B-	C	A-		2.45	7.49	5.11	13.64	17.56	11.17	73.1	877-518-9161	Y
TIAA-CREF Lifestyle Income Fund Retirement Class	TLSRX	B	C	A-	Up	2.46	7.51	5.23	13.84	17.71	11.17	73.1	877-518-9161	Y
TOPS® Conservative ETF Portfolio Class 1		B-	C	A-		2.35	8.17	5.21	15.51	15.97	12.17	12.3	855-572-5945	Y

Category: Cautious Allocation (con't)

Fund Name	Ticker Symbol	RATINGS: Overall Rating	Reward Rating	Risk Rating	Recent Up/ Downgrade	TOTAL RETURNS & PERFORMANCE: 3-Month Total Return	6-Month Total Return	1-Year Total Return	3-Year Total Return	5-Year Total Return	ASSETS: NAV	Total Assets (MIL)	NEW INVESTORS: Telephone	Open to New Investors
TOPS® Conservative ETF Portfolio Class 2		B-	C	A-		2.28	8.05	4.96	14.57	14.49	12.08	12.3	855-572-5945	Y
TOPS® Conservative ETF Portfolio Investor Class		B-	C	A-		1.88	7.52	4.72	14.57	13.41	12.47	12.3	855-572-5945	Y
TOPS® Conservative ETF Portfolio Service Class Shares		B-	C	A-		2.11	7.78	4.88	15.02	14.21	12.08	12.3	855-572-5945	Y
TOPS® Managed Risk Balanced ETF Portfolio Class 1		B-	C	B+	Up	2.54	9.55	4.26	18.22	15.16	11.69	519.3	855-572-5945	
TOPS® Managed Risk Balanced ETF Portfolio Class 2		B-	C	B+	Up	2.47	9.42	3.98	17.25	13.68	11.61	519.3	855-572-5945	Y
TOPS® Managed Risk Balanced ETF Portfolio Class 3		B-	C	B+	Up	2.29	8.91	3.70	17.10	12.71	11.65	519.3	855-572-5945	Y
TOPS® Managed Risk Balanced ETF Portfolio Class 4		B-	C	B+	Up	2.33	8.89	3.51	16.33	11.42	11.43	519.3	855-572-5945	Y
TOPS® Managed Risk Balanced ETF Portfolio Investor Class		B-	C	B+	Up	2.24	8.45	3.55	16.54	11.90	12.36	519.3	855-572-5945	Y
TOPS® Managed Risk Flex ETF Portfolio		B-	C	B+	Up	2.43	9.36	3.59	17.50	11.68	11.8	144.3	855-572-5945	Y
Touchstone Dynamic Diversified Income Fund A	TBAAX	B-	C	B+		2.50	10.05	5.62	16.42	18.93	13.03	75.0	800-543-0407	Y
Touchstone Dynamic Diversified Income Fund Y	TBAYX	B-	C	A-		2.47	10.06	5.78	17.25	20.38	13.05	75.0	800-543-0407	Y
Transamerica Asset Allocation Conservative Portfolio Cls A	ICLAX	B-	C	A-	Up	2.55	8.76	4.53	16.66	20.17	10.61	797.1	888-233-4339	Y
Transamerica Asset Allocation Conservative Portfolio Cls C	ICLLX	B-	C	B+	Up	2.37	8.28	3.71	14.04	15.82	10.53	797.1	888-233-4339	Y
Transamerica Asset Allocation Conservative Portfolio Cls I	TACIX	B-	C	A-	Up	2.61	8.86	4.73	17.45	21.56	10.64	797.1	888-233-4339	Y
Transamerica Asset Allocation Conservative Portfolio Cls R	ICVRX	B-	C	B+	Up	2.42	8.55	4.04	15.31	17.93	10.73	797.1	888-233-4339	Y
Transamerica Asset Allocation Moderate Portfolio Class A	IMOAX	B-	C	B+	Up	2.45	10.16	3.59	20.05	23.16	11.27	1,457	888-233-4339	Y
Transamerica Asset Allocation Moderate Portfolio Class C	IMOLX	B-	C	B+	Up	2.26	9.80	2.79	17.30	18.68	11.31	1,457	888-233-4339	Y
Transamerica Asset Allocation Moderate Portfolio Class I	TMMIX	B-	C	A-	Up	2.54	10.28	3.83	20.89	24.67	11.26	1,457	888-233-4339	Y
Transamerica Asset Allocation Moderate Portfolio Class R	IMDRX	B-	C	B+	Up	2.46	10.10	3.37	19.14	21.69	11.22	1,457	888-233-4339	Y
Transamerica Multi-Asset Income Fund Class A	TASHX	B	C+	A	Up	2.75	11.16	6.65	28.33	31.41	11.15	187.1	888-233-4339	Y
Transamerica Multi-Asset Income Fund Class C	TCSHX	B	C	A-	Up	2.57	10.81	5.82	25.49	26.60	11.11	187.1	888-233-4339	Y
Transamerica Multi-Asset Income Fund Class I	TSHIX	B	C+	A	Up	2.75	11.33	6.85	29.26	33.03	11.15	187.1	888-233-4339	Y
Transamerica Multi-Asset Income Fund Class I2		B	C+	A	Up	2.76	11.30	7.01	27.59	26.50	10.67	187.1	888-233-4339	Y
USAA Cornerstone Conservative Fund	USCCX	B-	C+	B+		3.12	8.74	6.88	15.45	18.89	10.91	199.6	800-235-8396	Y
USAA Cornerstone Moderately Conservative Fund	UCMCX	B-	C	B+	Up	2.50	8.87	4.47	15.97	14.83	11.19	232.4	800-235-8396	Y
USAA Growth and Tax Strategy Fund	USBLX	B	C+	A-		3.44	11.84	8.18	25.20	38.69	20.77	543.4	800-235-8396	Y
VALIC Company II Conservative Growth Lifestyle Fund	VCGLX	B-	C	A-	Up	2.83	11.30	5.13	18.49	19.36	11.81	328.8		Y
Vanguard LifeStrategy Conservative Growth Investor Shares	VSCGX	B	C+	A-		3.20	10.58	7.07	20.97	27.82	20.35	10,103	877-662-7447	Y
Vanguard LifeStrategy Income Fund Investor Shares	VASIX	B	C+	A-		3.06	8.36	7.44	14.30	22.56	15.9	4,449	877-662-7447	Y
Vanguard Tax-Managed Balanced Fund Admiral Shares	VTMFX	B	C+	A		3.06	11.76	8.26	26.86	39.02	32.64	5,208	877-662-7447	Y
Vanguard Wellesley® Income Fund Admiral™ Shares	VWIAX	B	B-	B+		3.62	11.06	10.21	20.42	33.08	64.53	55,740	877-662-7447	Y
Vanguard Wellesley® Income Fund Investor Shares	VWINX	B	B-	B+		3.58	11.03	10.10	20.14	32.58	26.64	55,740	877-662-7447	Y
Voya Global Perspectives Fund Class A	IAPVX	B-	C	A-	Up	2.75	12.60	4.48	21.07	20.60	11.19	58.3	800-366-0066	Y
Voya Global Perspectives Fund Class C	ICPVX	B-	C	B+	Up	2.50	12.15	3.66	18.43	16.19	11.04	58.3	800-366-0066	Y
Voya Global Perspectives Fund Class I	IIPVX	B-	C	A-	Up	2.74	12.70	4.70	21.95	22.06	11.21	58.3	800-366-0066	Y
Voya Global Perspectives Fund Class R	IRPVX	B-	C	A-	Up	2.67	12.47	4.14	20.20	19.06	11.14	58.3	800-366-0066	Y
Voya Global Perspectives Fund Class W	IWPVX	B-	C	A-	Up	2.74	12.68	4.68	21.96	22.11	11.23	58.3	800-366-0066	Y
Voya Global Perspectives Portfolio Class A	IPARX	B-	C	A-	Up	2.87	12.79	4.92	21.18	20.87	11.46	107.5	800-366-0066	Y
Voya Global Perspectives Portfolio Class I	IPIRX	B-	C	A-	Up	2.93	12.98	5.24	22.47	22.77	11.57	107.5	800-366-0066	Y
Voya Global Perspectives Portfolio Class S	IPSRX	B-	C	A-	Up	2.86	12.88	5.03	21.39	21.14	11.48	107.5	800-366-0066	Y
Voya Retirement Conservative Portfolio Class A	IRCAX	B-	C	B+		3.09	9.36	6.80	14.99	19.88	9.34	423.2	800-366-0066	Y
Voya Retirement Conservative Portfolio Class I	IRCPX	B	C+	B+	Up	3.03	9.45	6.99	15.64	20.92	9.49	423.2	800-366-0066	Y
Voya Retirement Moderate Portfolio Class A	IRMPX	B	C	A-	Up	3.09	11.36	5.94	21.09	22.98	11.66	1,033	800-366-0066	Y
Voya Retirement Moderate Portfolio Class I	IRMIX	B	C	A-	Up	3.22	11.60	6.37	22.44	25.19	11.83	1,033	800-366-0066	Y
Voya Solution Conservative Portfolio Class A	ICGAX	B	C	A-	Up	2.66	7.81	5.59	14.32	17.80	11.18	19.5	800-366-0066	Y
Voya Solution Conservative Portfolio Class I	ICGIX	B	C	A-	Up	2.80	7.98	6.16	16.00	20.70	11.36	19.5	800-366-0066	Y
Voya Solution Conservative Portfolio Class R6	VYRPX	B	C	A-	Up	2.80	8.08	6.16	16.00	20.70	11.36	19.5	800-366-0066	Y
Voya Solution Conservative Portfolio Class S	ICGSX	B	C	A-	Up	2.73	7.94	5.89	15.25	19.23	11.28	19.5	800-366-0066	Y
Voya Solution Conservative Portfolio Class S2	ICGTX	B	C	A-	Up	2.75	7.91	5.75	14.79	18.39	11.18	19.5	800-366-0066	Y
Voya Solution Moderately Conservative Portfolio Class A	ISPGX	B	C	A-	Up	2.98	10.10	5.52	19.10	21.78	10.02	39.2	800-366-0066	Y
Voya Solution Moderately Conservative Portfolio Class I	ISPRX	B	C	A-	Up	3.04	10.42	6.02	21.05	24.85	10.49	39.2	800-366-0066	Y
Voya Solution Moderately Conservative Portfolio Class R6	VYRNX	B	C	A-	Up	3.04	10.43	6.02	20.89	24.68	10.48	39.2	800-366-0066	Y

Category: Cautious Allocation (con't)

Fund Name	Ticker Symbol	Overall Rating	Reward Rating	Risk Rating	Recent Up/ Downgrade	3-Month Total Return	6-Month Total Return	1-Year Total Return	3-Year Total Return	5-Year Total Return	NAV	Total Assets (MIL)	Telephone	Open to New Investors
		RATINGS				TOTAL RETURNS & PERFORMANCE					ASSETS		NEW INVESTORS	
Voya Solution Moderately Conservative Portfolio Class S	ISPSX	B	C	A-	Up	2.91	10.22	5.71	19.99	23.25	10.24	39.2	800-366-0066	Y
Voya Solution Moderately Conservative Portfolio Class S2	ISPTX	B	C	A-	Up	2.95	10.13	5.60	19.48	22.33	10.11	39.2	800-366-0066	Y
Voya Strategic Allocation Conservative Portfolio Class I	ISAIX	B	C	A-	Up	2.85	9.79	5.75	20.01	23.91	12.41	60.2	800-366-0066	Y
Voya Strategic Allocation Conservative Portfolio Class S	ISCVX	B	C	A-	Up	2.76	9.59	5.44	18.96	22.33	12.3	60.2	800-366-0066	Y
Weitz Balanced Fund - Investor Class	WBALX	B	C+	A		4.38	13.45	9.35	24.87	28.11	14.32	129.8	800-304-9745	Y
Weitz Balanced Fund Institutional Class	WBAIX	B	C+	A		4.38	13.45	9.35	24.87	28.11	14.32	129.8	800-304-9745	Y
Wells Fargo Diversified Income Builder Fund - Class A	EKSAX	B-	C+	B		2.39	12.09	6.89	24.21	30.42	6.09	708.3	800-222-8222	Y
Wells Fargo Diversified Income Builder Fund - Class Admin	EKSDX	B-	C+	B		2.46	12.24	6.95	24.67	31.31	5.95	708.3	800-222-8222	Y
Wells Fargo Diversified Income Builder Fund - Class C	EKSCX	B-	C+	B	Up	2.36	11.86	6.07	21.64	25.81	6.11	708.3	800-222-8222	Y
Wells Fargo Diversified Income Builder Fund - Class Inst	EKSYX	B-	C+	B		2.53	12.58	7.24	25.74	32.96	5.95	708.3	800-222-8222	Y
Wells Fargo Diversified Income Builder Fund - Class R6	EKSRX	B-	C+	B		2.55	12.43	7.37	24.77	31.00	5.94	708.3	800-222-8222	Y
Wells Fargo Moderate Balanced Fund - Class A	WFMAX	B	C	A-	Up	2.94	10.72	5.85	20.15	25.71	20.96	129.2	800-222-8222	Y
Wells Fargo Moderate Balanced Fund - Class Admin	NVMBX	B	C+	A-	Up	3.01	10.88	6.15	21.11	27.25	21.19	129.2	800-222-8222	Y
Wells Fargo Moderate Balanced Fund - Class C	WFBCX	B-	C	A-	Up	2.72	10.33	5.08	17.51	21.07	20.39	129.2	800-222-8222	Y
Wells Fargo Moderate Balanced Fund - Class Institutional	WFMYX	B	C+	A-	Up	3.00	10.91	6.25	21.22	27.37	21.23	129.2	800-222-8222	Y
Wells Fargo WealthBuilder Conservative Allocation Cls A	WCAFX	B-	C	B		2.63	8.96	6.07	12.91	13.37	10.02	256.0	800-222-8222	Y
Wells Fargo WealthBuilder Conservative Allocation Inst Cls	WCYFX	B-	C	B	Up	2.73	8.91	6.03	11.80	12.25	9.99	256.0	800-222-8222	Y
Wells Fargo WealthBuilder Moderate Balanced Fund Class A	WMBGX	B	C	A-	Up	2.71	10.65	5.48	20.15	19.74	10.61	434.6	800-222-8222	Y
Wells Fargo WealthBuilder Moderate Balanced Inst Cls	WMBZX	B-	C	A-	Up	2.80	10.79	5.82	19.35	18.95	10.63	434.6	800-222-8222	Y
Yorktown Multi-Asset Income Fund Class A	APIUX	B-	C	B+	Up	1.12	10.10	2.62	22.08	13.07	10.1	657.9	800-544-6060	Y
Yorktown Multi-Asset Income Fund Class C	AFFCX	B-	C	B+	Up	1.09	9.99	2.17	20.39	10.35	9.34	657.9	800-544-6060	Y
Yorktown Multi-Asset Income Fund Class Institutional	APIIX	B-	C	B	Up	1.28	10.51	3.18	24.02	16.00	10.61	657.9	800-544-6060	Y

Category: Communications Sector Equity

Fund Name	Ticker Symbol	Overall Rating	Reward Rating	Risk Rating	Recent Up/ Downgrade	3-Month Total Return	6-Month Total Return	1-Year Total Return	3-Year Total Return	5-Year Total Return	NAV	Total Assets (MIL)	Telephone	Open to New Investors
		RATINGS				TOTAL RETURNS & PERFORMANCE					ASSETS		NEW INVESTORS	
Fidelity® Select Wireless Portfolio	FWRLX	B	B-	B	Up	4.86	18.72	12.74	49.55	48.91	9.7	261.5	617-563-7000	Y
Rydex Telecommunications Fund Class A	RYTLX	B-	C	B+	Up	0.00	11.94	4.22	22.50	19.48	46.03	4.5	800-820-0888	Y
Rydex Telecommunications Fund Class H	RYMAX	B-	C	B+		-0.02	11.97	4.43	22.84	19.43	44.87	4.5	800-820-0888	Y
Rydex Telecommunications Fund Class Investor	RYMIX	B-	C	B+		0.05	12.07	4.46	23.45	21.15	50.2	4.5	800-820-0888	Y
T. Rowe Price Communications & Technology Fund I Class	TTMIX	B	B-	B	Up	5.22	25.86	12.80	73.54	99.88	117.37	6,154	410-345-2000	Y
T. Rowe Price Communications & Technology Investor Cls	PRMTX	B	B-	B	Up	5.19	25.78	12.67	72.94	99.15	117.21	6,154	410-345-2000	Y

Category: Consumer Goods Sector Equity

Fund Name	Ticker Symbol	Overall Rating	Reward Rating	Risk Rating	Recent Up/ Downgrade	3-Month Total Return	6-Month Total Return	1-Year Total Return	3-Year Total Return	5-Year Total Return	NAV	Total Assets (MIL)	Telephone	Open to New Investors
		RATINGS				TOTAL RETURNS & PERFORMANCE					ASSETS		NEW INVESTORS	
Fidelity Advisor® Communication Services Class A	FGDMX	B-	C+	B		4.50	20.81	13.67	45.77	46.96	61.83	628.4	617-563-7000	Y
Fidelity Advisor® Communication Services Class C	FGHMX	B-	C	B		4.27	20.32	12.77	42.49	41.53	61.54	628.4	617-563-7000	Y
Fidelity Advisor® Communication Services Class I	FGJMX	B-	C+	B		4.58	21.02	14.00	46.94	48.88	61.95	628.4	617-563-7000	Y
Fidelity Advisor® Communication Services Class M	FGEMX	B-	C+	B		4.42	20.64	13.36	44.66	45.12	61.73	628.4	617-563-7000	Y
Fidelity Advisor® Communication Services Class Z	FGKMX	B-	C+	B		4.61	21.07	14.06	47.01	48.95	61.98	628.4	617-563-7000	Y
Fidelity Advisor® Consumer Discretionary Fund Class A	FCNAX	B-	C+	B		4.29	21.34	7.81	51.34	68.83	29.62	422.9	617-563-7000	Y
Fidelity Advisor® Consumer Discretionary Fund Class C	FCECX	B-	C+	B		4.10	20.91	7.04	48.01	62.64	23.82	422.9	617-563-7000	Y
Fidelity Advisor® Consumer Discretionary Fund Class M	FACPX	B-	C+	B		4.23	21.16	7.54	50.15	66.45	27.59	422.9	617-563-7000	Y
Fidelity Advisor® Consumer Discretionary Fund Class Z	FIJZX	B-	C+	B		4.39	21.61	8.25	52.78	71.38	32.07	422.9	617-563-7000	Y
Fidelity Advisor® Consumer Discretionary Fund I Class	FCNIX	B-	C+	B		4.33	21.50	8.11	52.59	71.17	32.03	422.9	617-563-7000	Y
Fidelity® Select Communication Services Portfolio	FBMPX	B-	C+	B		4.58	20.97	13.97	46.89	48.83	61.93	628.4	617-563-7000	Y
Fidelity® Select Consumer Discretionary Portfolio	FSCPX	B-	C+	B		4.35	21.52	8.22	52.98	73.72	46.81	462.2	617-563-7000	Y

Category: Consumer Goods Sector Equity (con't)

Fund Name	Ticker Symbol	RATINGS: Overall Rating	Reward Rating	Risk Rating	Recent Up/ Downgrade	TOTAL RETURNS & PERFORMANCE: 3-Month Total Return	6-Month Total Return	1-Year Total Return	3-Year Total Return	5-Year Total Return	ASSETS: NAV	Total Assets (MIL)	NEW INVESTORS: Telephone	Open to New Investors
Fidelity® Select Leisure Portfolio	FDLSX	B	B-	B+		8.23	24.81	16.71	60.50	70.77	15.96	511.3	617-563-7000	Y
JNL/Mellon Capital Consumer Discretionary Sector Cls A		B-	C+	B		4.43	20.95	7.72	54.52	76.63	24.01	1,299		Y
JNL/Mellon Capital Consumer Discretionary Sector Cls I		B-	C+	B		4.51	21.19	8.05	55.86	78.84	24.53	1,299		Y

Category: Convertibles

Fund Name	Ticker Symbol	RATINGS: Overall Rating	Reward Rating	Risk Rating	Recent Up/ Downgrade	TOTAL RETURNS & PERFORMANCE: 3-Month Total Return	6-Month Total Return	1-Year Total Return	3-Year Total Return	5-Year Total Return	ASSETS: NAV	Total Assets (MIL)	NEW INVESTORS: Telephone	Open to New Investors
1290 Convertible Securities Fund Class A	TNFAX	B-	C	B+	Down	3.56	17.77	7.04	35.83		11.12	24.8	212-554-1234	Y
1290 Convertible Securities Fund Class I	TNFIX	B-	C	B+	Down	3.63	17.92	7.21	36.85		11.12	24.8	212-554-1234	Y
1290 Convertible Securities Fund Class R	TNFRX	B-	C	B+		3.61	17.66	6.79	34.99		11.12	24.8	212-554-1234	Y
AllianzGI Convertible Fund Administrative Class	ANNAX	B	C+	A-		5.30	18.04	11.57	49.07	42.56	29.08	561.1	800-498-5413	
AllianzGI Convertible Fund Class A	ANZAX	B	C+	A-		5.41	18.14	11.66	48.93	42.14	29.39	561.1	800-498-5413	
AllianzGI Convertible Fund Class C	ANZCX	B-	C	A-	Down	5.19	17.69	10.80	45.67	37.06	29.75	561.1	800-498-5413	
AllianzGI Convertible Fund Class P	ANCMX	B	C+	A-		5.44	18.28	11.89	50.03	43.98	28.58	561.1	800-498-5413	
AllianzGI Convertible Fund Class R	ANZRX	B	C	A-		5.31	18.02	11.52	47.74	39.93	30.56	561.1	800-498-5413	
AllianzGI Convertible Fund Institutional Class	ANNPX	B	C+	A-		5.43	18.28	11.92	50.24	44.32	28.89	561.1	800-498-5413	
Calamos Convertible Fund Class A	CCVIX	B	C	A-		3.32	12.60	6.18	37.27	29.50	17.33	712.6	800-582-6959	Y
Calamos Convertible Fund Class C	CCVCX	B-	C	A-	Down	3.06	12.17	5.33	34.17	24.63	17.14	712.6	800-582-6959	Y
Calamos Convertible Fund Institutional Class	CICVX	B	C	A-		3.37	12.66	6.40	38.29	31.06	15.27	712.6	800-582-6959	Y
Calamos Global Convertible Fund Class A	CAGCX	B-	C	A-	Up	2.43	9.15	3.17	25.94		10.92	136.8	800-582-6959	Y
Calamos Global Convertible Fund Class C	CCGCX	B-	C	A-	Up	2.18	8.77	2.36	23.14		10.78	136.8	800-582-6959	Y
Calamos Global Convertible Fund Class I	CXGCX	B	C	A	Up	2.50	9.28	3.45	26.82		10.92	136.8	800-582-6959	Y
Columbia Convertible Securities Fund Advisor Class	COVRX	B	C+	A-	Down	5.29	18.48	11.23	49.31	42.58	21.89	1,276	800-345-6611	Y
Columbia Convertible Securities Fund Class A	PACIX	B	C+	A-	Down	5.23	18.31	10.97	48.15	40.79	21.67	1,276	800-345-6611	Y
Columbia Convertible Securities Fund Class C	PHIKX	B	C	A-		5.05	17.87	10.12	44.88	35.60	21.61	1,276	800-345-6611	Y
Columbia Convertible Securities Fund Class R	CVBRX	B	C+	A-		5.17	18.24	10.70	47.09	39.08	21.66	1,276	800-345-6611	Y
Columbia Convertible Securities Fund Institutional 2 Class	COCRX	B	C+	A-	Down	5.32	18.54	11.32	49.63	43.20	21.87	1,276	800-345-6611	Y
Columbia Convertible Securities Fund Institutional 3 Class	CSFYX	B	C+	A-	Down	5.34	18.53	11.33	49.79	43.35	22.04	1,276	800-345-6611	Y
Columbia Convertible Securities Fund Institutional Class	NCIAX	B	C+	A-	Down	5.29	18.48	11.22	49.24	42.56	21.7	1,276	800-345-6611	Y
Fidelity Advisor® Convertible Securities Fund Class A	FACVX	B	C	A-		5.82	18.63	10.93	34.69	23.64	29.43	1,533	617-563-7000	Y
Fidelity Advisor® Convertible Securities Fund Class C	FCCVX	B	C	A-		5.61	18.16	10.13	31.71	19.07	29.22	1,533	617-563-7000	Y
Fidelity Advisor® Convertible Securities Fund Class M	FTCVX	B	C	A-		5.74	18.44	10.60	33.50	21.82	29.44	1,533	617-563-7000	Y
Fidelity Advisor® Convertible Securities Fund Class Z	FIQVX	B	C	A-		5.93	18.86	11.34	35.97	25.51	29.51	1,533	617-563-7000	Y
Fidelity Advisor® Convertible Securities Fund I Class	FICVX	B	C	A-		5.87	18.75	11.22	35.80	25.31	29.5	1,533	617-563-7000	Y
Fidelity® Convertible Securities Fund	FCVSX	B	C	A-		5.86	18.76	11.25	35.86	25.41	29.55	1,533	617-563-7000	Y
Franklin Convertible Securities Fund Advisor Class	FCSZX	B	C+	B		5.56	20.99	15.09	55.53	58.54	22.73	3,864	650-312-2000	Y
Franklin Convertible Securities Fund Class A	FISCX	B	C+	A-		5.54	20.81	14.81	54.39	56.55	22.73	3,864	650-312-2000	Y
Franklin Convertible Securities Fund Class C	FROTX	B	C+	A-		5.34	20.38	13.93	50.96	50.83	22.37	3,864	650-312-2000	Y
Franklin Convertible Securities Fund Class R6	FCSKX	B	C+	B		5.60	21.01	15.22	56.02	59.40	22.87	3,864	650-312-2000	Y
Harbor Convertible Securities Fund Administrative Class	HRCSX	B	C	A		3.22	13.26	6.43	26.53	22.64	10.75	135.0	800-422-1050	Y
Harbor Convertible Securities Fund Institutional Class	HACSX	B-	C	B+	Down	3.28	13.37	7.01	27.73	24.54	10.77	135.0	800-422-1050	Y
Harbor Convertible Securities Fund Investor Class	HICSX	B	C	A		3.20	13.21	6.63	26.39	22.22	10.75	135.0	800-422-1050	Y
Harbor Convertible Securities Fund Retirement Class	HNCVX	B	C	A		3.30	13.43	7.00	28.02	24.72	10.76	135.0	800-422-1050	Y
Invesco Convertible Securities Fund Class A	CNSAX	B-	C	B+	Down	4.68	16.65	8.42	33.88	26.16	24.69	1,156	800-659-1005	Y
Invesco Convertible Securities Fund Class C	CNSCX	B-	C	B+		4.47	16.21	7.60	30.94	21.72	24.56	1,156	800-659-1005	Y
Invesco Convertible Securities Fund Class R6	CNSFX	B-	C	B+	Down	4.77	16.84	8.80	35.31	28.39	24.7	1,156	800-659-1005	Y
Invesco Convertible Securities Fund Class Y	CNSDX	B-	C	B+	Down	4.73	16.82	8.68	34.89	27.69	24.72	1,156	800-659-1005	Y
Invesco Convertible Securities Fund R5 Shares	CNSIX	B-	C	B+	Down	4.75	16.80	8.71	34.98	27.93	24.7	1,156	800-659-1005	Y
Lord Abbett Convertible Fund Class A	LACFX	B-	C+	B+	Down	4.69	17.21	8.25	46.00	35.58	13.64	739.6	201-827-2000	Y
Lord Abbett Convertible Fund Class C	LACCX	B-	C	B+		4.47	16.86	7.54	43.20	31.29	13.56	739.6	201-827-2000	Y
Lord Abbett Convertible Fund Class F	LBFFX	B-	C+	B+	Down	4.72	17.26	8.35	46.45	36.27	13.64	739.6	201-827-2000	Y

Category: Convertibles (con't)

Fund Name	Ticker Symbol	RATINGS: Overall Rating	Reward Rating	Risk Rating	Recent Up/ Downgrade	TOTAL RETURNS & PERFORMANCE: 3-Month Total Return	6-Month Total Return	1-Year Total Return	3-Year Total Return	5-Year Total Return	ASSETS: NAV	Total Assets (MIL)	NEW INVESTORS: Telephone	Open to New Investors
Lord Abbett Convertible Fund Class F3	LOCFX	B-	C+	B+	Down	4.79	17.39	8.49	46.84	37.02	13.73	739.6	201-827-2000	Y
Lord Abbett Convertible Fund Class I	LCFYX	B-	C	B+	Down	4.71	17.30	8.49	46.84	37.03	13.72	739.6	201-827-2000	Y
Lord Abbett Convertible Fund Class P	LCFPX	B-	C	B+	Down	4.63	17.04	7.93	44.89	34.32	13.86	739.6	201-827-2000	
Lord Abbett Convertible Fund Class R2	LBCQX	B-	C	B+		4.58	17.04	7.84	44.30	32.96	13.86	739.6	201-827-2000	Y
Lord Abbett Convertible Fund Class R3	LCFRX	B-	C	B+	Down	4.56	17.03	7.91	44.65	33.65	13.58	739.6	201-827-2000	Y
Lord Abbett Convertible Fund Class R4	LCFSX	B-	C	B+	Down	4.68	17.18	8.21	45.82	35.30	13.64	739.6	201-827-2000	Y
Lord Abbett Convertible Fund Class R5	LCFTX	B-	C	B		4.72	17.32	8.42	46.73	36.94	13.71	739.6	201-827-2000	Y
Lord Abbett Convertible Fund Class R6	LCFVX	B-	C+	B+	Down	4.71	17.29	8.49	46.96	37.15	13.73	739.6	201-827-2000	Y
MainStay MacKay Convertible Fund Class A	MCOAX	B-	C	B+	Down	3.36	16.64	7.54	37.95	39.23	17.79	1,433	800-624-6782	Y
MainStay MacKay Convertible Fund Class B	MCSVX	B-	C	B+		3.14	16.10	6.61	34.27	33.03	17.69	1,433	800-624-6782	
MainStay MacKay Convertible Fund Class C	MCCVX	B-	C	B+		3.15	16.13	6.61	34.23	33.07	17.67	1,433	800-624-6782	Y
MainStay MacKay Convertible Fund Class I	MCNVX	B-	C	B+	Down	3.45	16.81	7.91	39.35	41.35	17.82	1,433	800-624-6782	Y
MainStay MacKay Convertible Fund Investor Class	MCINX	B-	C	B+	Down	3.38	16.54	7.43	37.31	38.15	17.79	1,433	800-624-6782	Y
Miller Convertible Bond Fund Class A	MCFAX	B-	C	B+	Up	4.32	10.14	2.85	17.52	17.75	12.62	803.0	877-441-4434	Y
Miller Convertible Bond Fund Class I	MCIFX	B-	C	B+	Up	4.45	10.50	3.46	19.33	20.82	12.61	803.0	877-441-4434	Y
Putnam Convertible Securities Fund Class A	PCONX	B	C+	B+		4.82	17.87	9.11	41.69	33.50	25.13	732.1	617-292-1000	Y
Putnam Convertible Securities Fund Class B	PCNBX	B-	C	B+	Down	4.59	17.42	8.26	38.50	28.59	24.56	732.1	617-292-1000	Y
Putnam Convertible Securities Fund Class C	PRCCX	B-	C	B+	Down	4.60	17.42	8.31	38.51	28.57	24.81	732.1	617-292-1000	Y
Putnam Convertible Securities Fund Class M	PCNMX	B-	C+	B+	Down	4.66	17.56	8.57	39.56	30.21	24.83	732.1	617-292-1000	Y
Putnam Convertible Securities Fund Class R	PCVRX	B-	C+	B+	Down	4.77	17.77	8.83	40.66	31.84	25.01	732.1	617-292-1000	Y
Putnam Convertible Securities Fund Class R6 Shares	PCNTX	B	C+	B+		4.90	18.07	9.47	42.23	34.00	25.12	732.1	617-292-1000	Y
Putnam Convertible Securities Fund Class Y	PCGYX	B	C+	B+		4.88	18.03	9.39	42.76	35.20	25.11	732.1	617-292-1000	Y
TETON Convertible Securities Fund Class A	WEIAX	B	C+	B+		4.28	16.14	7.32	42.56	31.39	14.21	43.4		Y
TETON Convertible Securities Fund Class AAA	WESRX	B	C+	B+		4.41	16.32	7.60	43.65	33.00	13.75	43.4		Y
TETON Convertible Securities Fund Class C	WEICX	B-	C+	B+		4.14	15.88	6.78	40.41	28.10	15.17	43.4		Y
TETON Convertible Securities Fund Institutional Class	WESIX	B-	C+	B	Down	4.38	16.40	7.84	44.75	34.76	13.79	43.4		Y
Victory INCORE Investment Grade Convertible Fund Class A	SBFCX	B	C	A		2.93	10.66	7.63	36.64	41.13	16.71	213.9	800-539-3863	Y
Victory INCORE Investment Grade Convertible Fund Class I	VICIX	B	C	A		3.07	10.95	8.11	38.33	44.14	16.69	213.9	800-539-3863	Y
Westwood Strategic Convertibles Fund Institutional Shares	WSCIX	B-	C	A-		3.07	13.23	5.85	26.45		11.12	37.7		Y

Category: Equity Miscellaneous

Fund Name	Ticker Symbol	RATINGS: Overall Rating	Reward Rating	Risk Rating	Recent Up/ Downgrade	TOTAL RETURNS & PERFORMANCE: 3-Month Total Return	6-Month Total Return	1-Year Total Return	3-Year Total Return	5-Year Total Return	ASSETS: NAV	Total Assets (MIL)	NEW INVESTORS: Telephone	Open to New Investors
AMG Pantheon Fund, LLC Advisory Class	XPEAX	B	C+	B+	Up	3.67	4.46	7.49	40.01			--	800-835-3879	Y
AMG Pantheon Fund, LLC Brokerage Class	XPEBX	B	C+	B+	Up	3.48	4.22	6.98	38.11			--	800-835-3879	Y
AMG Pantheon Fund, LLC Institutional Class	XPEIX	B	C+	B+	Up	3.72	4.64	7.74	41.24			--	800-835-3879	Y
AMG Pantheon Fund, LLC Institutional Plus Class	XPEPX	B	C+	B+	Up	3.77	4.70	8.01	42.15			--	800-835-3879	Y
SharesPost 100 Fund	PRIVX	B-	C+	B		-1.47	3.34	1.62	15.66	29.47	29.39	--		Y
Timothy Plan Israel Common Values Fund Class A	TPAIX	B	B	B		6.61	20.77	17.81	52.60	34.98	16.92	72.0	800-662-0201	Y
Timothy Plan Israel Common Values Fund Class C	TPCIX	B	B	B		6.39	20.28	16.87	49.18	29.98	16.13	72.0	800-662-0201	Y
Timothy Plan Israel Common Values Fund Class I	TICIX	B	B	B		6.63	20.86	18.08	53.63	36.68	17.03	72.0	800-662-0201	Y
Voya Russia Fund Class A	LETRX	B	B	B	Up	15.96	32.43	23.81	74.62	29.36	36.18	86.2	800-366-0066	Y
Voya Russia Fund Class I	IIRFX	B	B	B	Up	16.04	32.56	24.10	75.60	30.64	36.31	86.2	800-366-0066	Y
Voya Russia Fund Class W	IWRFX	B	B	B	Up	16.02	32.54	24.03	76.13	30.99	36.21	86.2	800-366-0066	Y

Category: Financials Sector Equity

Fund Name	Ticker Symbol	Overall Rating	Reward Rating	Risk Rating	Recent Up/ Downgrade	3-Month Total Return	6-Month Total Return	1-Year Total Return	3-Year Total Return	5-Year Total Return	NAV	Total Assets (MIL)	Telephone	Open to New Investors
		RATINGS				TOTAL RETURNS & PERFORMANCE					ASSETS		NEW INVESTORS	
Fidelity® Select Consumer Finance Portfolio	FSVLX	B	B-	B	Up	6.63	26.64	12.33	69.47	58.80	16.93	153.4	617-563-7000	Y
Fidelity® Select Insurance Portfolio	FSPCX	B-	B-	B	Up	10.81	24.37	17.32	47.89	64.32	63.1	260.3	617-563-7000	Y
Kinetics Market Opportunities Fund Advisor Class A	KMKAX	B-	B-	C+	Up	9.18	25.13	9.65	88.58	68.14	26.98	89.1	800-930-3828	Y
Kinetics Market Opportunities Fund Advisor Class C	KMKCX	B-	B-	C+	Up	9.04	24.81	9.09	85.78	63.97	25.8	89.1	800-930-3828	Y
Kinetics Market Opportunities Fund Class Institutional	KMKYX	B-	B-	C+	Up	9.29	25.41	10.11	91.27	72.03	27.88	89.1	800-930-3828	Y
Kinetics Market Opportunities Fund No Load Class	KMKNX	B-	B-	C+	Up	9.23	25.29	9.90	89.98	70.23	27.44	89.1	800-930-3828	Y
Shelton BDC Income Fund Institutional Class	LOAIX	B-	C+	B		1.99	13.62	7.78	27.46	20.08	8.71	6.9	800-955-9988	Y
Shelton BDC Income Fund Investor Class	LOANX	B-	C+	B		2.01	13.69	7.71	26.71	20.34	8.65	6.9	800-955-9988	Y

Category: Flexible Allocation

Fund Name	Ticker Symbol	Overall Rating	Reward Rating	Risk Rating	Recent Up/ Downgrade	3-Month Total Return	6-Month Total Return	1-Year Total Return	3-Year Total Return	5-Year Total Return	NAV	Total Assets (MIL)	Telephone	Open to New Investors
		RATINGS				TOTAL RETURNS & PERFORMANCE					ASSETS		NEW INVESTORS	
American Funds Capital Income Builder® Class F-3	CFIHX	B-	C	B	Up	1.99	10.99	6.03	19.37	22.03	61.08	104,371	800-421-4225	Y
American Funds Capital Income Builder® Class R-6	RIRGX	B-	C	B	Up	2.00	10.99	6.03	19.61	23.00	61.09	104,371	800-421-4225	Y
Cavalier Tactical Economic Fund A Class	CAVMX	B-	C	B+		2.38	9.87	5.70	33.47	27.79	8.57	16.4	800-773-3863	Y
Cavalier Tactical Economic Fund C Class	CMSYX	B-	C	B+	Up	2.26	9.51	4.98	30.71	23.28	11.74	16.4	800-773-3863	Y
Cavalier Tactical Economic Fund Institutional Class	CMSFX	B-	C	B+		2.37	10.02	6.00	34.52	29.44	12.51	16.4	800-773-3863	Y
Crow Point Global Tactical Allocation Inst Cls Shares	CGHIX	B-	C	B+		1.43	11.57	4.81	19.87	8.04	9.16	20.9		Y
Crow Point Global Tactical Allocation Investor Cls Shares	CGHAX	B-	C	B+		1.44	11.61	5.03	19.44	7.04	9.13	20.9		Y
Federated Global Allocation Fund Class A Shares	FSTBX	B-	C	B+	Up	2.69	12.61	3.72	24.11	18.49	19.39	355.7	800-341-7400	Y
Federated Global Allocation Fund Class R Shares	FSBKX	B-	C	B+	Up	2.60	12.41	3.30	22.57	16.04	19.26	355.7	800-341-7400	Y
Federated Global Allocation Fund Class R6	FSBLX	B-	C	B+	Up	2.77	12.77	4.07	25.22	19.55	19.39	355.7	800-341-7400	Y
Federated Global Allocation Fund Institutional Shares	SBFIX	B-	C	B+	Up	2.80	12.81	4.05	25.28	20.27	19.51	355.7	800-341-7400	Y
First Eagle Global Fund Class A	SGENX	B-	C	A-	Up	3.63	14.34	5.56	23.92	25.80	57.95	50,427	800-334-2143	Y
First Eagle Global Fund Class C	FESGX	B-	C	B+	Up	3.43	13.91	4.76	21.14	21.13	55.68	50,427	800-334-2143	Y
First Eagle Global Fund Class I	SGIIX	B-	C	A-	Up	3.70	14.50	5.82	24.88	27.48	58.26	50,427	800-334-2143	Y
First Eagle Global Fund Class R3	EARGX	B-	C	B+	Up	3.59	14.28	5.42	23.48	25.11	58.16	50,427	800-334-2143	Y
First Eagle Global Fund Class R4	EAGRX	B-	C	A-	Up	3.66	14.43	5.70	24.18	26.06	58.26	50,427	800-334-2143	Y
First Eagle Global Fund Class R6	FEGRX	B-	C	A-	Up	3.71	14.54	5.91	24.82	26.72	58.28	50,427	800-334-2143	Y
Invesco Balanced-Risk Allocation Fund Class A	ABRZX	B-	C	A-	Up	2.10	10.62	3.33	14.79	17.98	11.14	3,369	800-659-1005	Y
Invesco Balanced-Risk Allocation Fund Class C	ABRCX	B-	C	B+	Up	1.93	10.14	2.53	12.23	13.57	10.53	3,369	800-659-1005	Y
Invesco Balanced-Risk Allocation Fund Class R	ABRRX	B-	C	B+	Up	2.05	10.52	3.11	13.88	16.49	10.92	3,369	800-659-1005	Y
Invesco Balanced-Risk Allocation Fund Class R6	ALLFX	B-	C	A-	Up	2.24	10.80	3.73	16.07	20.26	11.38	3,369	800-659-1005	Y
Invesco Balanced-Risk Allocation Fund Class Y	ABRYX	B-	C	A-	Up	2.16	10.74	3.56	15.62	19.42	11.34	3,369	800-659-1005	Y
Invesco Balanced-Risk Allocation Fund R5 Class	ABRIX	B-	C	A-	Up	2.25	10.82	3.74	15.79	19.77	11.36	3,369	800-659-1005	Y
Janus Henderson Dividend & Income Builder Fund Class A	HDAVX	B-	C	B+	Up	2.28	11.37	3.14	22.54	19.32	13.09	168.7	877-335-2687	Y
Janus Henderson Dividend & Income Builder Fund Class D	HDDVX	B-	C	B+	Up	2.30	11.41	3.33	23.23	20.62	13.09	168.7	877-335-2687	Y
Janus Henderson Dividend & Income Builder Fund Class I	HDIVX	B-	C	B+	Up	2.39	11.51	3.40	23.42	20.80	13.11	168.7	877-335-2687	Y
Janus Henderson Dividend & Income Builder Fund Class N	HDRVX	B-	C	B+	Up	2.41	11.55	3.47	23.39	20.70	13.08	168.7	877-335-2687	Y
Janus Henderson Dividend & Income Builder Fund Class S	HDQVX	B-	C	B+	Up	2.46	11.57	3.27	22.55	19.36	13.06	168.7	877-335-2687	Y
Janus Henderson Dividend & Income Builder Fund Class T	HDTVX	B-	C	B+	Up	2.30	11.41	3.28	23.04	20.43	13.08	168.7	877-335-2687	Y
Janus Henderson Global Allocation Fund - Growth Class A	JGCAX	B-	C	B+	Up	3.23	13.85	3.56	28.12	22.65	14.05	243.1	877-335-2687	Y
Janus Henderson Global Allocation Fund - Growth Class D	JNSGX	B-	C	B+	Up	3.35	13.99	3.76	28.76	23.68	14.17	243.1	877-335-2687	
Janus Henderson Global Allocation Fund - Growth Class I	JGCIX	B-	C	B+	Up	3.35	14.00	3.80	29.02	24.06	14.16	243.1	877-335-2687	Y
Janus Henderson Global Allocation Fund - Growth Class S	JGCSX	B-	C	B+	Up	3.25	13.77	3.40	27.43	21.56	13.96	243.1	877-335-2687	Y
Janus Henderson Global Allocation Fund - Growth Class T	JSPGX	B-	C	B+	Up	3.28	13.92	3.68	28.54	23.30	14.15	243.1	877-335-2687	Y
Power Momentum Index VIT Fund Class 1 shares		B-	C	B	Up	2.94	5.13	3.97	32.86	31.01	27.63	77.2	877-779-7462	Y
Thornburg Investment Income Builder Fund Class A	TIBAX	B-	C	A-		2.52	10.24	6.44	27.80	21.15	21.58	14,496	800-847-0200	Y

Category: Flexible Allocation (con't)

		RATINGS				TOTAL RETURNS & PERFORMANCE					ASSETS		NEW INVESTORS	
Fund Name	Ticker Symbol	Overall Rating	Reward Rating	Risk Rating	Recent Up/ Downgrade	3-Month Total Return	6-Month Total Return	1-Year Total Return	3-Year Total Return	5-Year Total Return	NAV	Total Assets (MIL)	Telephone	Open to New Investors
Thornburg Investment Income Builder Fund Class C	TIBCX	B-	C	A-	Up	2.29	9.87	5.63	24.99	16.81	21.55	14,496	800-847-0200	Y
Thornburg Investment Income Builder Fund Class I	TIBIX	B	C	A-	Up	2.52	10.37	6.69	28.85	22.98	21.73	14,496	800-847-0200	Y
Thornburg Investment Income Builder Fund Class R3	TIBRX	B-	C	A-		2.39	10.06	6.07	26.56	19.22	21.57	14,496	800-847-0200	Y
Thornburg Investment Income Builder Fund Class R4	TIBGX	B-	C	A-		2.46	10.11	6.15	26.84	19.73	21.6	14,496	800-847-0200	Y
Thornburg Investment Income Builder Fund Class R5	TIBMX	B	C	A-	Up	2.55	10.32	6.56	28.44	22.22	21.72	14,496	800-847-0200	Y
Thornburg Investment Income Builder Fund Class R6	TIBOX	B	C	A-	Up	2.55	10.44	6.77	28.51	21.82	21.66	14,496	800-847-0200	Y

Category: Global Emerging Markets

		RATINGS				TOTAL RETURNS & PERFORMANCE					ASSETS		NEW INVESTORS	
Fund Name	Ticker Symbol	Overall Rating	Reward Rating	Risk Rating	Recent Up/ Downgrade	3-Month Total Return	6-Month Total Return	1-Year Total Return	3-Year Total Return	5-Year Total Return	NAV	Total Assets (MIL)	Telephone	Open to New Investors
American Beacon Acadian Emerging Mkts Managed Vol A Cls	ACDAX	B-	C	B+	Up	1.24	7.41	5.69	26.93	7.00	10.58	21.1	800-658-5811	Y
American Beacon Acadian Emerging Mkts Managed Vol Inst Cls	ACDIX	B-	C	B+	Up	1.32	7.74	6.12	28.47	9.18	10.71	21.1	800-658-5811	Y
American Beacon Acadian Emerging Mkts Managed Vol Inv Cls	ACDPX	B-	C	B+	Up	1.24	7.55	5.70	27.01	7.17	10.54	21.1	800-658-5811	Y
American Beacon Acadian Emerging Mkts Managed Vol Y Cls	ACDYX	B-	C	B+	Up	1.33	7.68	5.95	28.10	8.63	10.65	21.1	800-658-5811	Y
BlackRock Emerging Markets Equity Strategies Fund Class K	BEFKX	B	C+	B+	Up	5.40	22.08	21.43	70.13		11.5	25.1	800-441-7762	Y
BlackRock Emerging Markets Equity Strategies Institutional	BEFIX	B	C+	B+	Up	5.31	21.95	21.31	69.92		11.5	25.1	800-441-7762	Y
BlackRock Emerging Markets Equity Strategies Investor A	BEFAX	B-	C+	B+		5.24	21.85	20.99	68.44		11.43	25.1	800-441-7762	Y
BlackRock Emerging Markets Equity Strategies Investor C	BEFCX	B-	C+	B+		5.04	21.39	20.12	64.87		11.46	25.1	800-441-7762	Y
Virtus KAR Emerging Markets Small-Cap Fund Class A	VAESX	B-	C	B	Up	0.32	13.08	2.21	49.68	27.10	12.36	100.8	800-243-1574	Y
Virtus KAR Emerging Markets Small-Cap Fund Class I	VIESX	B-	C	B	Up	0.48	13.21	2.52	50.72	28.70	12.42	100.8	800-243-1574	Y

Category: Global Equity Large Cap

		RATINGS				TOTAL RETURNS & PERFORMANCE					ASSETS		NEW INVESTORS	
Fund Name	Ticker Symbol	Overall Rating	Reward Rating	Risk Rating	Recent Up/ Downgrade	3-Month Total Return	6-Month Total Return	1-Year Total Return	3-Year Total Return	5-Year Total Return	NAV	Total Assets (MIL)	Telephone	Open to New Investors
1290 SmartBeta Equity Fund Class A	TNBAX	B	C+	B+	Up	5.36	18.57	11.76	37.74		12.96	23.6	212-554-1234	Y
1290 SmartBeta Equity Fund Class I	TNBIX	B	C+	B+	Up	5.44	18.75	12.03	38.68		12.98	23.6	212-554-1234	Y
1290 SmartBeta Equity Fund Class R	TNBRX	B	C+	B+	Up	5.28	18.39	11.50	36.64		12.94	23.6	212-554-1234	Y
1290 SmartBeta Equity Fund Class T	TNBCX	B	C+	B+	Up	5.36	18.66	11.94	38.71		12.97	23.6	212-554-1234	Y
AB Global Core Equity Portfolio Advisor Class	GCEYX	B-	C	B+		4.46	18.35	10.21	51.40		13.35	797.1	212-969-1000	Y
AB Global Core Equity Portfolio Class A	GCEAX	B-	C	B+		4.47	18.31	9.95	50.31		13.31	797.1	212-969-1000	Y
AB Global Core Equity Portfolio Class C	GCECX	B-	C	B+		4.21	17.80	9.12	46.95		13.1	797.1	212-969-1000	Y
AB Wealth Appreciation Strategy Advisor Class	AWAYX	B-	C	B	Up	3.15	16.26	4.28	36.08	29.86	16.37	1,303	212-969-1000	Y
AB Wealth Appreciation Strategy Class I	AWAIX	B-	C	B	Up	3.08	16.17	4.16	35.77	29.49	16.38	1,303	212-969-1000	Y
American Century Global Growth Fund A Class	AGGRX	B-	C+	B	Up	6.95	26.36	11.16	53.37	47.67	12.46	567.1	800-444-4015	Y
American Century Global Growth Fund I Class	AGGIX	B-	C+	B	Up	7.08	26.56	11.69	55.50	50.87	13.15	567.1	800-444-4015	Y
American Century Global Growth Fund Investor Class	TWGGX	B-	C+	B	Up	7.06	26.52	11.45	54.47	49.39	12.88	567.1	800-444-4015	Y
American Century Global Growth Fund R Class	AGORX	B-	C+	B	Up	6.83	26.16	10.83	52.11	45.66	12.2	567.1	800-444-4015	Y
American Century Global Growth Fund R5 Class	AGFGX	B-	C+	B	Up	7.08	26.56	11.60	55.12	50.02	13.15	567.1	800-444-4015	Y
American Century Global Growth Fund R6 Class	AGGDX	B-	C+	B	Up	7.13	26.75	11.81	56.23	52.07	13.22	567.1	800-444-4015	Y
American Century Global Growth Fund Y Class	AGYGX	B-	C+	B	Up	7.12	26.60	11.80	55.64	50.52	13.23	567.1	800-444-4015	Y
American Funds New Perspective Fund® Class 529-F	CNPFX	B-	C	B	Up	4.33	19.75	7.21	51.81	55.66	44.07	89,711	800-421-4225	Y
American Funds New Perspective Fund® Class A	ANWPX	B-	C	B	Up	4.28	19.65	7.05	51.13	54.55	44.75	89,711	800-421-4225	Y
American Funds New Perspective Fund® Class F-2	ANWFX	B-	C	B	Up	4.32	19.79	7.26	52.02	56.12	44.61	89,711	800-421-4225	Y
American Funds New Perspective Fund® Class F-3	FNPFX	B-	C	B	Up	4.35	19.86	7.36	52.22	55.67	44.78	89,711	800-421-4225	Y
American Funds New Perspective Fund® Class R-5	RNPFX	B-	C	B	Up	4.36	19.82	7.31	52.26	56.53	44.73	89,711	800-421-4225	Y
American Funds New Perspective Fund® Class R-5E	RNPHX	B-	C	B	Up	4.34	19.81	7.26	51.78	55.28	44.44	89,711	800-421-4225	Y
American Funds New Perspective Fund® Class R-6	RNPGX	B-	C	B	Up	4.35	19.85	7.37	52.50	56.91	44.8	89,711	800-421-4225	Y
Aristotle/Saul Global Opportunities Fund Class I	ARSOX	B-	C	B	Up	6.00	19.00	6.22	29.16	22.81	12.71	70.0		Y

Category: Global Equity Large Cap (con't)

Fund Name	Ticker Symbol	RATINGS: Overall Rating	Reward Rating	Risk Rating	Recent Up/ Downgrade	TOTAL RETURNS & PERFORMANCE: 3-Month Total Return	6-Month Total Return	1-Year Total Return	3-Year Total Return	5-Year Total Return	ASSETS: NAV	Total Assets (MIL)	NEW INVESTORS: Telephone	Open to New Investors
Artisan Global Equity Fund Institutional Shares	APHHX	B-	B-	B	Up	8.67	23.80	12.54	57.00	56.71	20.8	242.4	800-344-1770	Y
Artisan Global Equity Fund Investor Class	ARTHX	B-	C+	B	Up	8.60	23.65	12.27	55.85	55.27	20.7	242.4	800-344-1770	Y
Aspiriant Risk-Managed Equity Allocation Advisor Shares	RMEAX	B-	C	A-		1.89	10.72	7.52	32.36	29.27	13.42	1,182	877-997-9971	Y
Ave Maria World Equity Fund	AVEWX	B-	C	B	Up	5.99	20.89	9.71	38.52	28.65	15.74	67.1	888-726-9331	Y
Baron Global Advantage Fund Institutional Shares	BGAIX	B	B	C+	Up	6.84	35.56	15.09	103.69	89.49	26.99	215.8	800-992-2766	Y
Baron Global Advantage Fund R6 Shares	BGLUX	B	B	C+	Up	6.84	35.59	15.13	103.84	89.63	27.01	215.8	800-992-2766	Y
Baron Global Advantage Fund Retail Shares	BGAFX	B	B	C+	Up	6.77	35.40	14.79	102.43	87.56	26.62	215.8	800-992-2766	Y
BBH Partner - International Equity Cls Institutional	BBHLX	B-	C	B	Up	5.83	23.69	9.70	36.36	25.34	16.13	1,716	800-575-1265	Y
BlackRock Long-Horizon Equity Fund Class R Shares	MREGX	B-	C+	B		3.72	20.79	12.61	40.65	30.46	13.94	263.1	800-441-7762	Y
BlackRock Long-Horizon Equity Fund Institutional Shares	MAEGX	B	C+	B	Up	3.81	21.11	13.28	43.48	34.95	13.88	263.1	800-441-7762	Y
BlackRock Long-Horizon Equity Fund Investor A Shares	MDEGX	B-	C+	B		3.81	21.02	13.05	42.31	33.19	13.87	263.1	800-441-7762	Y
BlackRock Long-Horizon Equity Fund Investor C Shares	MCEGX	B-	C	B		3.59	20.43	12.17	39.05	28.08	13.85	263.1	800-441-7762	Y
BMO Global Low Volatility Equity Fund Class A	BAEGX	B	C+	A-	Up	1.58	11.27	7.67	25.51	36.81	11.55	34.6	800-236-3863	Y
BMO Global Low Volatility Equity Fund Class I	BGLBX	B	C+	A-	Up	1.66	11.51	8.02	26.50	38.50	11.62	34.6	800-236-3863	Y
BNY Mellon Global Equity Income Fund - Class A	DEQAX	B	C+	B+	Up	6.25	18.51	11.55	31.94	41.35	13.76	446.0		Y
BNY Mellon Global Equity Income Fund - Class C	DEQCX	B-	C	B+	Up	6.07	18.12	10.79	29.13	36.28	14.24	446.0		Y
BNY Mellon Global Equity Income Fund - Class I	DQEIX	B	C+	B+	Up	6.33	18.72	11.86	33.07	43.27	13.08	446.0		Y
BNY Mellon Global Equity Income Fund - Class Y	DEQYX	B	C+	B+	Up	6.27	18.69	11.93	33.26	43.78	13.06	446.0		Y
BNY Mellon Global Stock Fund - Class A	DGLAX	B	C+	B+		3.77	20.14	13.10	48.20	52.01	22.02	1,369		
BNY Mellon Global Stock Fund - Class C	DGLCX	B-	C+	B+	Down	3.54	19.71	12.25	44.91	46.36	21.32	1,369		
BNY Mellon Global Stock Fund - Class I	DGLRX	B	C+	B+		3.80	20.23	13.39	49.44	54.15	22.35	1,369		
BNY Mellon Global Stock Fund - Class Y	DGLYX	B	C+	B+		3.81	20.34	13.49	49.71	54.47	22.32	1,369		
BNY Mellon International Stock Fund Class A	DISAX	B-	C	B	Up	4.80	17.64	7.92	39.24	31.71	19.86	4,296		
BNY Mellon International Stock Fund Class C	DISCX	B-	C	B	Up	4.59	17.19	7.11	36.19	26.81	19.56	4,296		
BNY Mellon International Stock Fund Class I	DISRX	B-	C	B	Up	4.88	17.82	8.27	40.60	33.85	19.96	4,296		
BNY Mellon International Stock Fund Class Y	DISYX	B-	C	B	Up	4.89	17.81	8.28	40.67	33.94	19.73	4,296		
BNY Mellon Worldwide Growth Fund Class A	PGROX	B-	B-	B		6.12	22.18	11.90	46.13	44.96	52.36	715.0		Y
BNY Mellon Worldwide Growth Fund Class C	PGRCX	B-	C+	B	Up	5.92	21.74	11.10	42.94	39.73	45.2	715.0		Y
BNY Mellon Worldwide Growth Fund Class I	DPWRX	B	B-	B	Up	6.18	22.34	12.17	47.26	46.88	52.7	715.0		Y
BNY Mellon Worldwide Growth Fund Class Y	DPRIX	B	B-	B	Up	6.21	22.38	12.27	47.62	47.47	52.64	715.0		Y
Brown Advisory Global Leaders Fund Institutional Shares	BAFLX	B	B-	B	Up	4.88	21.14	10.56	60.26		15.24	232.9	800-540-6807	Y
Brown Advisory Global Leaders Fund Investor Shares	BIALX	B-	B-	B		4.88	21.06	10.49	60.15		15.23	232.9	800-540-6807	Y
Capital Group Global Equity Fund	CGLOX	B-	C	B	Up	4.08	18.35	8.43	46.11	45.00	15.8	661.2	213-486-9200	Y
Catalyst/MAP Global Equity Fund Class A	CAXAX	B-	C	A-	Up	3.36	13.19	5.39	38.32	32.57	14.75	62.7	866-447-4228	Y
Catalyst/MAP Global Equity Fund Class C	CAXCX	B-	C	A-	Up	3.15	12.76	4.57	35.11	27.48	14.4	62.7	866-447-4228	Y
Catalyst/MAP Global Equity Fund Class I	CAXIX	B-	C	A-		3.43	13.36	5.70	39.39	34.33	14.76	62.7	866-447-4228	Y
Columbia Global Equity Value Fund Advisor Class	RSEVX	B-	C	B	Up	3.27	15.77	6.53	40.25	28.45	12.92	752.8	800-345-6611	Y
Columbia Global Equity Value Fund Class A	IEVAX	B-	C	B	Up	3.22	15.72	6.29	39.28	26.89	12.86	752.8	800-345-6611	Y
Columbia Global Equity Value Fund Class C	REVCX	B-	C	B	Up	3.07	15.34	5.55	36.20	22.21	12.68	752.8	800-345-6611	Y
Columbia Global Equity Value Fund Class R	REVRX	B-	C	B	Up	3.16	15.53	6.03	38.22	25.27	12.82	752.8	800-345-6611	Y
Columbia Global Equity Value Fund Institutional 2 Class	RSEYX	B-	C	B	Up	3.31	15.91	6.63	40.74	29.08	12.85	752.8	800-345-6611	Y
Columbia Global Equity Value Fund Institutional 3 Class	CEVYX	B-	C	B	Up	3.33	15.92	6.68	40.95	29.54	12.5	752.8	800-345-6611	Y
Columbia Global Equity Value Fund Institutional Class	CEVZX	B-	C	B	Up	3.28	15.83	6.55	40.27	28.46	12.88	752.8	800-345-6611	Y
Columbia Select Global Equity Fund Advisor Class	CSGVX	B	B-	B		7.38	23.94	14.80	56.46	58.29	14.39	473.6	800-345-6611	Y
Columbia Select Global Equity Fund Class A	IGLGX	B	B-	B		7.36	23.78	14.48	55.89	57.71	14	473.6	800-345-6611	Y
Columbia Select Global Equity Fund Class C	RGCEX	B-	B-	B	Down	7.13	23.34	13.65	52.33	52.00	12.31	473.6	800-345-6611	Y
Columbia Select Global Equity Fund Class R	CGERX	B	B-	B		7.30	23.64	14.20	54.75	55.86	13.96	473.6	800-345-6611	Y
Columbia Select Global Equity Fund Institutional 2 Class	RGERX	B	B-	B		7.46	24.00	14.87	57.47	60.80	14.26	473.6	800-345-6611	Y
Columbia Select Global Equity Fund Institutional 3 Class	CSEYX	B	B-	B		7.47	24.03	14.97	57.30	59.14	14.09	473.6	800-345-6611	Y
Columbia Select Global Equity Fund Institutional Class	CGEZX	B	B-	B		7.41	23.93	14.77	56.98	59.82	14.19	473.6	800-345-6611	Y
Crossmark Steward Global Equity Income Fund Class A	SGIDX	B-	C	B	Up	2.93	14.70	3.78	37.81	45.28	31.18	312.4	800-262-6631	Y
Crossmark Steward Global Equity Income Fund Class C	SGIFX	B-	C	B	Up	2.68	14.27	3.10	35.69	41.16	5.13	312.4	800-262-6631	Y

Category: Global Equity Large Cap (con't)

Fund Name	Ticker Symbol	RATINGS: Overall Rating	Reward Rating	Risk Rating	Recent Up/ Downgrade	TOTAL RETURNS & PERFORMANCE: 3-Month Total Return	6-Month Total Return	1-Year Total Return	3-Year Total Return	5-Year Total Return	ASSETS: NAV	Total Assets (MIL)	NEW INVESTORS: Telephone	Open to New Investors
Crossmark Steward Global Equity Income Cls Institutional	SGISX	B-	C	B	Up	3.00	14.90	4.05	39.11	47.63	31.26	312.4	800-262-6631	Y
Crossmark Steward Global Equity Income Fund Class R6	SGIGX	B-	C	B	Up	3.14	15.01	4.16	38.58	47.06	4.83	312.4	800-262-6631	Y
Eaton Vance Hexavest Global Equity Fund Class A	EHGAX	B-	C	B	Up	2.29	11.58	4.69	21.46	28.86	12.04	65.4		Y
Eaton Vance Hexavest Global Equity Fund Class I	EHGIX	B-	C	B+	Up	2.28	11.66	4.93	22.33	30.48	12.06	65.4		Y
Fidelity Advisor® Global Equity Income Fund Class A	FBLYX	B-	C	B	Up	3.50	17.03	5.51	30.54	31.51	14.73	18.0	617-563-7000	Y
Fidelity Advisor® Global Equity Income Fund Class Z	FIQQX	B-	C	B	Up	3.54	17.23	5.83	31.65	33.27	14.76	18.0	617-563-7000	Y
Fidelity Advisor® Global Equity Income Fund I Class	FBUSX	B-	C	B	Up	3.54	17.24	5.75	31.55	33.17	14.75	18.0	617-563-7000	Y
Fidelity® Global Equity Income Fund	FGILX	B-	C	B	Up	3.40	16.72	5.75	32.21	33.59	14.08	69.2	617-563-7000	Y
Fidelity® SAI International Low Volatility Index Fund	FSKLX	B-	C	A-	Up	3.20	11.03	6.29	22.99		11.27	2,010	617-563-7000	Y
FMI International Fund	FMIJX	B-	C	B+	Up	2.73	11.89	1.74	25.97	30.84	31.88	7,290	800-811-5311	Y
FMI International Fund Institutional Class	FMIYX	B-	C	B+	Up	2.76	11.96	1.87	26.42	31.30	31.91	7,290	800-811-5311	Y
FPA Paramount Fund	FPRAX	B-	C	B	Up	5.08	17.06	5.70	48.66	31.57	21.06	165.6	800-982-4372	Y
Franklin Mutual Beacon Fund Class C	TEMEX	B-	C	B+	Up	2.31	14.30	5.56	30.52	26.37	15.5	3,440	650-312-2000	Y
Franklin Mutual Beacon Fund Class R6	FMBRX	B-	C	B	Up	2.54	14.94	6.70	34.87	33.45	15.69	3,440	650-312-2000	Y
Franklin Mutual Beacon Fund Class Z	BEGRX	B-	C	B+	Up	2.54	14.86	6.62	34.55	32.95	15.69	3,440	650-312-2000	Y
GAMCO Global Growth Fund Class A	GGGAX	B-	C+	B		5.45	23.13	10.19	58.83	52.53	36.51	105.4	914-921-5135	Y
GAMCO Global Growth Fund Class AAA	GICPX	B-	C+	B		5.48	23.16	10.22	58.83	52.57	36.53	105.4	914-921-5135	Y
GAMCO Global Growth Fund Class Institutional	GGGIX	B-	C+	B		5.54	23.33	10.52	61.38	57.09	37.32	105.4	914-921-5135	Y
Goldman Sachs Enhanced Div Global Eq Port Cls A	GADGX	B-	C	B+	Up	2.23	13.45	2.84	28.45	24.51	11.7	621.7	800-526-7384	Y
Goldman Sachs Enhanced Div Global Eq Port Cls P	GAFPX	B-	C	B	Up	2.32	13.55	3.23	29.83	26.90	11.79	621.7	800-526-7384	Y
Goldman Sachs Enhanced Div Global Eq Port Cls R6 Shares	GRGDX	B-	C	B	Up	2.31	13.64	3.22	29.92	26.98	11.8	621.7	800-526-7384	Y
Goldman Sachs Enhanced Div Global Eq Port Inst Cls	GIDGX	B-	C	B	Up	2.31	13.61	3.21	29.88	26.95	11.82	621.7	800-526-7384	Y
Guggenheim World Equity Income Fund Class A	SEQAX	B-	C	B	Up	2.37	13.01	2.96	23.02	21.20	15.13	79.0	212-518-9290	Y
Guggenheim World Equity Income Fund Class P	SEQPX	B-	C	B	Up	2.55	12.65	2.75	24.73	21.78	15.25	79.0	212-518-9290	Y
Guggenheim World Equity Income Fund Institutional Class	SEWIX	B-	C	B	Up	2.61	12.73	2.95	25.17	22.32	15.05	79.0	212-518-9290	Y
Guinness Atkinson Dividend Builder Fund	GAINX	B	C+	B+	Up	2.76	15.74	10.47	38.65	34.07	19.2	11.4	800-915-6566	Y
Harbor Global Leaders Fund Administrative Class	HRGAX	B	B-	B		6.48	24.44	16.56	64.99	61.74	29.22	89.9	800-422-1050	Y
Harbor Global Leaders Fund Institutional Class	HGGAX	B	B-	B		6.54	24.60	16.88	66.26	63.80	29.78	89.9	800-422-1050	Y
Harbor Global Leaders Fund Investor Class	HGGIX	B	B-	B		6.42	24.32	16.40	64.40	60.75	28.83	89.9	800-422-1050	Y
Harbor Global Leaders Fund Retirement Class	HNGIX	B	B-	B		6.57	24.60	16.94	66.55	64.17	29.83	89.9	800-422-1050	Y
Harding Loevner Global Equity Research Portfolio Inst Cls	HLRGX	B-	C	B	Up	4.03	18.14	8.48			12.37	6.8	877-435-8105	Y
Ivy Global Equity Income Fund Class I	IBIIX	B-	C	B	Up	2.72	14.48	4.45	27.07	24.31	12.1	760.9		Y
Ivy Global Equity Income Fund Class N	IICNX	B-	C	B	Up	2.75	14.54	4.60	27.62	25.17	12.11	760.9		Y
Janus Henderson Global Income Managed Volatility Cls A	JGDAX	B-	C+	B	Down	2.81	12.05	11.22	22.05	32.05	14.1	276.3	877-335-2687	Y
Janus Henderson Global Income Managed Volatility Cls C	JGDCX	B-	C	B		2.57	11.59	10.33	19.43	27.19	13.99	276.3	877-335-2687	Y
Janus Henderson Global Income Managed Volatility Cls D	JGDDX	B-	C+	B	Down	2.87	12.13	11.46	22.83	33.29	14.06	276.3	877-335-2687	Y
Janus Henderson Global Income Managed Volatility Cls I	JGDIX	B-	C+	B	Down	2.86	12.17	11.52	22.99	33.89	14.14	276.3	877-335-2687	Y
Janus Henderson Global Income Managed Volatility Cls N	JGGNX	B-	C+	B	Down	2.89	12.23	11.63	23.20	34.11	14.14	276.3	877-335-2687	Y
Janus Henderson Global Income Managed Volatility Cls S	JGDSX	B-	C+	B	Down	2.95	12.25	11.34	22.07	32.01	14.08	276.3	877-335-2687	Y
Janus Henderson Global Income Managed Volatility Cls T	JDGTX	B-	C+	B	Down	2.84	12.14	11.34	22.43	32.65	14.08	276.3	877-335-2687	Y
Janus Henderson Global Research Fund Class N	JDWNX	B-	C	B	Up	4.54	19.21	7.45	47.80	41.80	80.97	2,680	877-335-2687	Y
Janus Henderson Global Value Fund Class A	JPPAX	B-	C	B+	Up	1.92	11.11	6.47	25.73	20.53	14.29	197.1	877-335-2687	Y
Janus Henderson Global Value Fund Class C	JPPCX	B-	C	B+	Up	1.82	10.79	5.74	22.99	16.24	13.96	197.1	877-335-2687	Y
Janus Henderson Global Value Fund Class D	JNGOX	B-	C	B+		2.05	11.27	6.73	26.43	21.58	14.41	197.1	877-335-2687	
Janus Henderson Global Value Fund Class I	JPPIX	B-	C	A-		2.02	11.25	6.72	26.60	22.01	14.14	197.1	877-335-2687	Y
Janus Henderson Global Value Fund Class N	JPPNX	B-	C	A-		2.03	11.24	6.72	26.90	22.50	14.05	197.1	877-335-2687	Y
Janus Henderson Global Value Fund Class S	JPPSX	B-	C	B	Up	1.36	9.78	3.94	21.28	15.93	14.14	197.1	877-335-2687	Y
Janus Henderson Global Value Fund Class T	JGVAX	B-	C	B+		1.98	11.12	6.62	26.16	21.23	14.38	197.1	877-335-2687	Y
JNL/Epoch Global Shareholder Yield Fund Class I		B-	C	A-		2.17	16.13	6.55	27.69	23.74		29.9		Y
JNL/Mellon Capital MSCI World Index Fund Class A		B-	C	B	Up	3.94	17.73	6.15	36.24	37.53	25.83	351.3		Y
JNL/Mellon Capital MSCI World Index Fund Class I		B-	C	B	Up	4.04	17.93	6.53	37.20	38.50	25.97	351.3		Y
JNL/WCM Focused International Equity Fund		B-	C+	B	Up	9.98	25.33	11.95	48.77	52.93	16.08	1,456		Y

Category: Global Equity Large Cap (con't)

Fund Name	Ticker Symbol	RATINGS: Overall Rating	Reward Rating	Risk Rating	Recent Up/ Downgrade	TOTAL RETURNS & PERFORMANCE: 3-Month Total Return	6-Month Total Return	1-Year Total Return	3-Year Total Return	5-Year Total Return	ASSETS: NAV	Total Assets (MIL)	NEW INVESTORS: Telephone	Open to New Investors
JNL/WCM Focused International Equity Fund Class I		B-	C+	B	Up	10.06	25.52	12.23	49.54	53.72	16.08	1,456		Y
John Hancock Funds Global Equity Fund Class I	JGEFX	B-	C	B	Up	4.37	20.51	11.68	35.37	30.94	11.69	733.6	800-225-5913	Y
John Hancock Funds Global Equity Fund Class NAV		B-	C	B	Up	4.37	20.64	11.91	35.84	31.90	11.69	733.6	800-225-5913	Y
John Hancock Funds Global Equity Fund Class R4	JGETX	B-	C	B	Up	4.28	20.51	11.70	35.14	30.72	11.69	733.6	800-225-5913	Y
John Hancock Funds Global Equity Fund Class R6	JGEMX	B-	C	B	Up	4.37	20.51	11.90	35.79	31.86	11.69	733.6	800-225-5913	Y
JPMorgan Global Research Enhanced Index Fund Class I	JEITX	B-	C	B	Up	4.10	18.03	6.63	41.67	37.93	21.79	4,473	800-480-4111	Y
JPMorgan Global Research Enhanced Index Fund Class R6	JEIYX	B-	C	B	Up	4.16	18.10	6.73	41.88	38.14	21.53	4,473	800-480-4111	Y
Lazard Global Equity Select Portfolio Institutional Shares	GESIX	B-	C	B	Up	4.74	19.50	8.89	46.42	46.57	13.91	71.6	800-823-6300	Y
Lazard Global Equity Select Portfolio Open Shares	GESOX	B-	C	B	Up	4.66	19.41	8.64	45.14	44.42	13.9	71.6	800-823-6300	Y
Lazard Managed Equity Volatility Portfolio Inst Shares	MEVIX	B-	C	B+		2.70	15.74	8.47	31.84		12.13	25.4	800-823-6300	Y
Lazard Managed Equity Volatility Portfolio Open Shares	MEVOX	B-	C	B+		2.71	15.66	8.15	30.59		12.11	25.4	800-823-6300	Y
Longleaf Partners International Fund	LLINX	B-	C	B+		0.75	13.96	5.40	48.74	13.91	17.3	1,317	800-445-9469	Y
Loomis Sayles Global Growth Fund Class A	LSAGX	B-	B-	B	Up	5.20	24.55	13.15	57.60		14.56	66.7	800-862-4863	Y
Loomis Sayles Global Growth Fund Class C	LSCGX	B-	B-	B	Up	4.98	24.11	12.24	53.85		14.31	66.7	800-862-4863	Y
Loomis Sayles Global Growth Fund Class Y	LSGGX	B-	B-	B	Up	5.33	24.76	13.40	58.83		14.61	66.7	800-862-4863	Y
LSV Global Managed Volatility Fund Institutional Class	LSVFX	B-	C	A-	Up	1.27	10.79	5.51	27.24	30.07	11.08	22.1		Y
LSV Global Managed Volatility Fund Investor Class	LVAFX	B-	C	A-	Up	1.18	10.65	5.23	26.25	28.49	11.11	22.1		Y
Martin Currie International Unconstrained Equity Cls I	LUEIX	B-	C+	B	Up	7.86	25.57	12.50	39.95		12.62	5.7	877-721-1926	Y
Martin Currie International Unconstrained Equity Cls IS	LUISX	B-	C+	B	Up	7.77	25.59	12.51	40.12		12.61	5.7	877-721-1926	Y
Mercer Global Low Volatility Equity Fund Class Y-3	MGLVX	B	C+	B+		50.24	68.02	58.18	68.19	55.04	13.74	1,019		Y
MFAM Global Opportunities Fund Institutional Shares	FOIIX	B-	B-	B	Up	6.99	27.09	13.96	65.22	61.46	25.38	469.5		Y
MFAM Global Opportunities Fund Investor Shares	FOOLX	B-	B-	B	Up	6.93	26.97	13.82	64.62	60.33	25.28	469.5		Y
MFS Global Equity Fund Class A	MWEFX	B-	C+	B	Up	5.44	21.71	11.30	42.67	41.11	44.96	3,024	877-960-6077	Y
MFS Global Equity Fund Class B	MWEBX	B-	C	B	Up	5.25	21.26	10.48	39.53	35.93	41.28	3,024	877-960-6077	Y
MFS Global Equity Fund Class C	MWECX	B-	C	B	Up	5.23	21.28	10.50	39.51	35.93	39.38	3,024	877-960-6077	Y
MFS Global Equity Fund Class I	MWEIX	B-	C+	B	Up	5.52	21.89	11.60	43.77	42.89	46.21	3,024	877-960-6077	Y
MFS Global Equity Fund Class R1	MWEGX	B-	C	B	Up	5.24	21.28	10.49	39.50	35.92	40.34	3,024	877-960-6077	Y
MFS Global Equity Fund Class R2	MEQRX	B-	C+	B	Up	5.38	21.57	11.05	41.64	39.35	43.62	3,024	877-960-6077	Y
MFS Global Equity Fund Class R3	MWEHX	B-	C+	B	Up	5.45	21.72	11.32	42.69	41.12	44.65	3,024	877-960-6077	Y
MFS Global Equity Fund Class R4	MWELX	B-	C+	B	Up	5.51	21.88	11.60	43.78	42.89	45.12	3,024	877-960-6077	Y
MFS Global Equity Fund Class R6	MWEMX	B-	C+	B	Up	5.54	21.94	11.71	44.15	43.58	46.23	3,024	877-960-6077	Y
MFS Global Growth Fund Class A	MWOFX	B	B-	B	Up	5.58	22.17	11.96	54.13	55.12	44.8	468.4	877-960-6077	Y
MFS Global Growth Fund Class B	MWOBX	B-	C+	B		5.41	21.72	11.13	50.64	49.37	38.55	468.4	877-960-6077	Y
MFS Global Growth Fund Class C	MWOCX	B-	C+	B		5.40	21.71	11.13	50.67	49.38	38.06	468.4	877-960-6077	Y
MFS Global Growth Fund Class I	MWOIX	B	B-	B	Up	5.65	22.29	12.25	55.23	56.98	45.96	468.4	877-960-6077	Y
MFS Global Growth Fund Class R1	MWOGX	B-	C+	B		5.41	21.69	11.13	50.67	49.33	37.97	468.4	877-960-6077	Y
MFS Global Growth Fund Class R2	MGWRX	B-	B-	B		5.53	22.03	11.69	52.94	53.13	43.26	468.4	877-960-6077	Y
MFS Global Growth Fund Class R3	MWOHX	B	B-	B	Up	5.59	22.14	11.95	54.06	55.04	44.57	468.4	877-960-6077	Y
MFS Global Growth Fund Class R4	MWOJX	B	B-	B	Up	5.64	22.31	12.24	55.22	56.97	44.89	468.4	877-960-6077	Y
MFS Global Growth Fund Class R6	MWOKX	B	B-	B		5.68	22.33	12.31	55.58	57.58	45.95	468.4	877-960-6077	Y
MFS International Intrinsic Value Fund Class A	MGIAX	B-	C	B	Up	4.27	17.24	6.58	35.17	43.65	43.93	28,593	877-960-6077	
MFS International Intrinsic Value Fund Class I	MINIX	B-	C	B	Up	4.31	17.38	6.83	36.17	45.45	46.18	28,593	877-960-6077	
MFS International Intrinsic Value Fund Class R3	MINGX	B-	C	B	Up	4.25	17.23	6.55	35.14	43.62	43.6	28,593	877-960-6077	
MFS International Intrinsic Value Fund Class R4	MINHX	B-	C	B	Up	4.33	17.40	6.85	36.19	45.43	44.05	28,593	877-960-6077	
MFS International Intrinsic Value Fund Class R6	MINJX	B-	C	B	Up	4.35	17.44	6.95	36.59	46.18	44.1	28,593	877-960-6077	
MFS Low Volatility Global Equity Fund Class A	MVGAX	B	C+	A-		3.03	12.87	10.10	28.40	42.23	13.81	242.4	877-960-6077	Y
MFS Low Volatility Global Equity Fund Class B	MVGBX	B	C+	A-		2.87	12.47	9.32	25.52	36.73	13.73	242.4	877-960-6077	Y
MFS Low Volatility Global Equity Fund Class C	MVGCX	B	C+	A-		2.82	12.41	9.29	25.45	36.73	13.71	242.4	877-960-6077	Y
MFS Low Volatility Global Equity Fund Class I	MVGIX	B	C+	A-		3.16	12.98	10.43	29.35	43.82	13.81	242.4	877-960-6077	Y
MFS Low Volatility Global Equity Fund Class R1	MVGJX	B	C+	A-		2.88	12.53	9.31	25.46	36.80	13.79	242.4	877-960-6077	Y
MFS Low Volatility Global Equity Fund Class R2	MVGKX	B	C+	A-		3.04	12.72	9.88	27.38	40.24	13.82	242.4	877-960-6077	Y
MFS Low Volatility Global Equity Fund Class R3	MVGLX	B	C+	A-		3.10	12.93	10.14	28.31	42.08	13.83	242.4	877-960-6077	Y

Category: Global Equity Large Cap (con't)

Fund Name	Ticker Symbol	RATINGS: Overall Rating	Reward Rating	Risk Rating	Recent Up/ Downgrade	TOTAL RETURNS & PERFORMANCE: 3-Month Total Return	6-Month Total Return	1-Year Total Return	3-Year Total Return	5-Year Total Return	ASSETS: NAV	Total Assets (MIL)	NEW INVESTORS: Telephone	Open to New Investors
MFS Low Volatility Global Equity Fund Class R4	MVGMX	B	C+	A-		3.08	12.98	10.34	29.34	43.65	13.81	242.4	877-960-6077	Y
MFS Low Volatility Global Equity Fund Class R6	MVGNX	B	C+	A-		3.10	13.03	10.43	29.47	43.86	13.79	242.4	877-960-6077	Y
Mirova Global Sustainable Equity Fund Class A	ESGMX	B-	C+	B	Up	5.60	22.32	11.43	49.81		13.79	108.9	800-862-4863	Y
Mirova Global Sustainable Equity Fund Class C	ESGCX	B-	C	B	Up	5.41	21.84	10.60	46.47		13.48	108.9	800-862-4863	Y
Mirova Global Sustainable Equity Fund Class Y	ESGYX	B-	C+	B	Up	5.65	22.51	11.71	50.99		13.86	108.9	800-862-4863	Y
Morgan Stanley Inst Fund, Inc. Global Advantage Port Cls A	MIGPX	B-	C+	B-	Up	6.48	29.35	11.13	76.62	74.88	17.58	136.8	855-332-5306	Y
Morgan Stanley Inst Fund, Inc. Global Advantage Port Cls I	MIGIX	B-	C+	B-	Up	6.53	29.55	11.51	78.36	77.85	17.93	136.8	855-332-5306	Y
Morgan Stanley Inst Fund, Inc. Global Franchise Port Cls A	MSFBX	B	B	B+		5.05	21.45	15.01	49.79	65.88	27.23	1,742	855-332-5306	
Morgan Stanley Inst Fund, Inc. Global Franchise Port Cls C	MSGFX	B	B	B+		4.87	21.07	14.19	46.47	59.92	26.66	1,742	855-332-5306	Y
Morgan Stanley Inst Fund, Inc. Global Franchise Port Cls I	MSFAX	B+	B	B+	Up	5.16	21.68	15.36	51.00	68.20	27.89	1,742	855-332-5306	
Morgan Stanley Inst Fund, Inc. Global Franch Port Cls IS	MGISX	B+	B	B+	Up	5.16	21.68	15.42	51.28	68.59	27.89	1,742	855-332-5306	Y
Morgan Stanley Inst Fund, Inc. Global Franchise Port Cls L	MSFLX	B	B	B+		4.94	21.15	14.40	47.58	61.98	27.15	1,742	855-332-5306	
Morgan Stanley Inst Fund, Inc. Global Sustain Port Cls A	MGQAX	B	B-	B+		6.15	19.91	13.57	47.78	55.00	13.79	23.4	855-332-5306	Y
Morgan Stanley Inst Fund, Inc. Global Sustain Port Cls C	MSGQX	B	B-	B+		5.99	19.57	12.82	44.55	49.32	13.44	23.4	855-332-5306	Y
Morgan Stanley Inst Fund, Inc. Global Sustain Port Cls I	MGQIX	B	B-	B+		6.29	20.22	14.09	49.44	57.77	13.85	23.4	855-332-5306	Y
Morgan Stanley Inst Fund, Inc. Global Sustain Port Cls IS	MGQSX	B	B-	B+		6.37	20.22	14.16	49.57	57.95	13.85	23.4	855-332-5306	Y
Morgan Stanley Inst Fund, Inc. Global Sustain Port Cls L	MGQLX	B	B-	B+		6.05	19.61	13.04	45.50	51.10	13.66	23.4	855-332-5306	
Northern Global Sustainability Index Fund	NSRIX	B-	C	B	Up	4.08	17.54	7.65	39.75	36.95	14.54	742.4	800-595-9111	Y
Pax Ellevate Global Women's Leadership Individual Inv Cls	PXWEX	B-	C	B	Up	4.91	19.25	8.59	43.25	42.87	25.71	356.4	800-767-1729	Y
Pax Ellevate Global Women's Leadership Institutional Cls	PXWIX	B-	C+	B	Up	5.00	19.37	8.86	44.39	44.65	25.84	356.4	800-767-1729	Y
PIMCO StocksPLUS® International (U.S. Dollar-Hedged) Cls A	PIPAX	B-	C	B	Up	3.91	16.76	4.10	46.04	37.19	7.49	3,084	866-746-2602	Y
PIMCO StocksPLUS® International (U.S. Dollar-Hedged) Cls C	PIPCX	B-	C	B	Up	3.72	16.30	3.35	42.91	32.03	6.82	3,084	866-746-2602	Y
PIMCO StocksPLUS® Intl (U.S. Dollar-Hedged) Cls I-2	PIUHX	B-	C	B	Up	3.93	16.84	4.35	47.38	39.20	7.84	3,084	866-746-2602	Y
PIMCO StocksPLUS® International (U.S. Dollar-Hedged) I-3	PISNX	B-	C	B	Up	3.92	16.91	4.34	47.09	38.58	7.83	3,084	866-746-2602	Y
PIMCO StocksPLUS® Intl (U.S. Dollar-Hedged) Inst Cls	PISIX	B-	C	B	Up	3.90	16.87	4.51	47.81	39.82	7.92	3,084	866-746-2602	Y
Polen Global Growth Fund Institutional Class	PGIIX	B	B-	B		5.72	23.10	13.96	69.83		17.53	87.2	561-241-2425	Y
Polen Global Growth Fund Investor Class	PGIRX	B	B-	B		5.66	22.89	13.69	68.50		17.34	87.2	561-241-2425	Y
Principal Global Opportunities Fund Class A	PGLAX	B-	C	B	Up	1.65	13.19	3.84	28.45	22.76	3.69	17.5	800-787-1621	Y
Principal Global Opportunities Fund Institutional Class	PGOIX	B-	C	B	Up	1.83	13.45	4.79	31.31	27.22	3.88	17.5	800-787-1621	Y
QS Global Dividend Fund Class A	LGDAX	B-	C	B+		0.48	9.86	4.27	19.63	36.84	12.71	340.3	877-721-1926	Y
QS Global Dividend Fund Class A2	LMQSX	B-	C	B+		0.43	9.75	4.09	19.08	36.14	12.71	340.3	877-721-1926	Y
QS Global Dividend Fund Class C	LGDCX	B-	C	B	Up	0.26	9.36	3.54	17.12	31.90	12.74	340.3	877-721-1926	Y
QS Global Dividend Fund Class FI	LDIGX	B-	C	B+		0.54	9.81	4.24	19.34	36.18	12.71	340.3	877-721-1926	Y
QS Global Dividend Fund Class I	LTTMX	B-	C	B+		0.54	9.96	4.49	20.35	38.38	12.63	340.3	877-721-1926	Y
QS Global Dividend Fund Class IS	LDIFX	B-	C	B+		0.56	9.98	4.66	20.97	39.14	12.66	340.3	877-721-1926	Y
Ranger Quest For Income & Growth Institutional Cls	RFIDX	B-	C	B+	Up	5.69	17.37	8.18	28.92	18.35	12.82	14.4		Y
Ranger Quest for Income and Growth Investor	RFTDX	B-	C	B+	Up	5.59	17.21	8.00	27.80	16.65	12.65	14.4		Y
RBC Global Opportunities Fund Class I	RGOIX	B-	C+	B	Up	4.84	22.36	8.48	56.93		14.72	28.3	800-422-2766	Y
RBC Global Opportunities Fund Class R6	RGORX	B-	C+	B	Up	4.82	22.38	8.53	57.20		14.76	28.3	800-422-2766	Y
Russell Investments Global Equity Fund Class C	RGECX	B-	C	B	Up	2.91	14.97	3.15	37.51	32.24	9.52	1,574	800-426-7969	Y
Russell Investments Global Equity Fund Class E	RGEEX	B-	C	B	Up	3.17	15.40	3.84	40.49	37.21	9.74	1,574	800-426-7969	Y
Russell Investments Global Equity Fund Class M	RGDTX	B-	C	B	Up	3.29	15.59	4.28	42.06	39.44	9.71	1,574	800-426-7969	Y
Russell Investments Global Equity Fund Class S	RGESX	B-	C	B	Up	3.18	15.43	4.12	41.59	38.99	9.72	1,574	800-426-7969	Y
Russell Investments Global Equity Fund Class Y	RLGYX	B-	C	B	Up	3.18	15.57	4.31	42.34	40.32	9.72	1,574	800-426-7969	Y
Saturna Sustainable Equity Fund	SEEFX	B-	C+	B	Up	6.16	20.87	10.76	45.07		12.91	6.3		Y
Scharf Global Opportunity Fund Retail Class	WRLDX	B-	C	B+	Up	4.30	14.96	13.80	38.34		29.58	19.4	831-429-6513	Y
Segall Bryant & Hamill Global Large Cap Institutional Cls	WIMVX	B-	C+	B+	Up	4.42	15.76	10.84	30.86	35.12	10.65	48.4	312-474-1222	Y
Segall Bryant & Hamill Global Large Cap Fund Retail Class	WTMVX	B-	C+	B+	Up	4.34	15.62	10.65	30.21	33.94	10.76	48.4	312-474-1222	Y
SEI Inst Investments Trust Global Managed Volatility Cls A	SGMAX	B-	C	A-	Down	2.71	13.08	7.87	31.21		12.1	2,606	800-342-5734	Y
SEI Inst Managed Trust Global Managed Volatility Cls F	SVTAX	B-	C	B+		3.78	14.12	7.63	25.77	49.39	11.23	1,317	800-342-5734	Y
SEI Inst Managed Trust Global Managed Volatility Cls I	SGMIX	B-	C	B+		3.87	14.01	7.39	24.93	47.61	10.98	1,317	800-342-5734	Y
SEI Inst Managed Trust Global Managed Volatility Cls Y	SGLYX	B-	C	B+		3.97	14.31	7.92	26.81	51.19	11.26	1,317	800-342-5734	Y

Category: Global Equity Large Cap (con't)

Fund Name	Ticker Symbol	RATINGS: Overall Rating	Reward Rating	Risk Rating	Recent Up/ Downgrade	TOTAL RETURNS & PERFORMANCE: 3-Month Total Return	6-Month Total Return	1-Year Total Return	3-Year Total Return	5-Year Total Return	ASSETS: NAV	Total Assets (MIL)	NEW INVESTORS: Telephone	Open to New Investors
Sextant International Fund	SSIFX	B	B	B+	Up	6.29	21.99	17.87	53.86	34.16	18.08	98.5		Y
Sextant International Fund Z Shares	SIFZX	B	B	B+	Up	6.34	22.11	18.13	54.67	34.86	18.11	98.5		Y
SGI Global Equity Fund Class I	SGLIX	B	B-	B+	Up	5.42	18.62	14.33	40.89	44.48	32.48	21.8	888-251-4847	Y
State Street Disciplined Global Equity Fund Class I	SSGMX	B-	C	B+	Up	2.37	13.25	7.52	31.01		12.05	2.3	617-664-7338	Y
State Street Disciplined Global Equity Portfolio		B-	C	B+	Up	2.61	12.01	8.38	33.83		11	5.0	617-786-3000	Y
State Street Hedged Intl Developed Equity Index Cls K	SSHQX	B-	C	B	Up	3.47	15.37	4.68	40.19		10.13	3,456	617-664-7338	Y
T. Rowe Price Global Stock Fund	PRGSX	B-	C	B		2.90	22.26	7.43	67.92	76.48	41.74	1,848	410-345-2000	Y
T. Rowe Price Global Stock Fund Advisor Class	PAGSX	B-	C	B		2.83	22.09	7.11	66.45	74.04	41.34	1,848	410-345-2000	Y
T. Rowe Price Global Stock Fund I Class	TRGLX	B-	C	B		2.93	22.34	7.57	68.43	77.03	41.78	1,848	410-345-2000	Y
T. Rowe Price Inst Global Focused Growth Equity Fund	TRGSX	B-	C	B	Down	2.91	22.32	7.58	68.55	77.27	12	58.3	410-345-2000	Y
Trillium P21 Global Equity Fund Class Institutional	PORIX	B-	C	B	Up	4.74	18.48	8.80	46.61	45.69	44.61	559.3	866-209-1962	Y
Trillium P21 Global Equity Fund Class R	PORTX	B-	C	B	Up	4.67	18.32	8.51	45.47	43.77	44.81	559.3	866-209-1962	Y
Tweedy, Browne Global Value Fund	TBGVX	B-	C	A-	Up	3.71	12.63	4.43	28.54	22.16	27.91	8,252	800-432-4789	Y
Tweedy, Browne Value Fund	TWEBX	B-	C	A-	Up	2.03	12.15	5.59	30.88	22.60	20.02	453.2	800-432-4789	Y
Tweedy, Browne Worldwide High Dividend Yield Value Fund	TBHDX	B	C	A-	Up	5.11	13.81	7.08	37.11	18.09	8.82	155.8	800-432-4789	Y
USAA Global Equity Income Fund Fund Shares	UGEIX	B-	C	B+	Up	3.62	14.32	7.03	26.97		10.8	83.3	800-235-8396	Y
USAA Global Equity Income Fund Institutional Shares	UIGEX	B-	C	B+	Up	3.68	14.41	7.16	27.11		10.81	83.3	800-235-8396	Y
USAA Global Managed Volatility Fund Fund Shares	UGMVX	B-	C	B+	Up	2.98	14.45	5.02	33.47	23.32	10.69	1,059	800-235-8396	Y
USAA Global Managed Volatility Fund Institutional Shares	UGOFX	B-	C	B+	Up	3.04	14.49	5.26	34.33	24.80	10.82	1,059	800-235-8396	Y
USAA World Growth Fund	USAWX	B-	C+	B	Up	5.44	21.79	11.32	43.12	41.62	32.92	1,389	800-235-8396	Y
USAA World Growth Fund Adviser Shares	USWGX	B-	C+	B	Up	5.40	21.65	11.04	42.02	39.84	32.98	1,389	800-235-8396	Y
USAA World Growth Fund Institutional Shares	UIWGX	B-	C+	B	Up	5.47	21.81	11.38	43.28	41.88	32.95	1,389	800-235-8396	Y
VALIC Company I International Socially Responsible Fund	VCSOX	B-	C	B	Up	3.56	17.89	6.20	40.26	40.29	27.34	381.9		Y
Vanguard Global Equity Fund Investor Shares	VHGEX	B-	C	B	Up	4.45	18.71	6.40	47.54	42.82	30.95	6,524	877-662-7447	Y
Vanguard Total World Stock Index Fund Admiral	VTWAX	B-	C	B	Up	3.49	17.11	5.20	41.02	36.20	26.66	17,539	877-662-7447	Y
Vanguard Total World Stock Index Fund Institutional Shares	VTWIX	B-	C	B	Up	3.49	17.09	5.17	41.01	36.22	153.69	17,539	877-662-7447	Y
Vanguard Total World Stock Index Investor Shares	VTWSX	B-	C	B	Up	3.49	17.05	5.10	40.66	35.56	30.67	17,539	877-662-7447	Y
Victory RS Global Fund Class A	RSGGX	B-	C+	B		5.02	18.68	9.46	48.23	52.63	13.59	55.8	800-539-3863	Y
Victory RS Global Fund Class C	RGGCX	B-	C	B		4.70	18.30	8.59	44.85	46.79	13.12	55.8	800-539-3863	Y
Victory RS Global Fund Class R	RGGKX	B-	C+	B		4.89	18.57	9.18	80.41	84.41	16.92	55.8	800-539-3863	Y
Victory RS Global Fund Class R6	RGGRX	B-	C+	B		5.09	19.00	9.79	49.48	54.88	10.15	55.8	800-539-3863	Y
Victory RS Global Fund Class Y	RGGYX	B-	C+	B		4.98	18.88	9.68	49.33	54.72	13.47	55.8	800-539-3863	Y
Victory RS International Fund Class A	GUBGX	B-	C	B	Up	3.46	15.76	4.60	37.83	22.53	12.26	50.5	800-539-3863	Y
Victory RS International Fund Class R	RIGKX	B-	C	B	Up	3.42	15.64	4.33	36.64	20.38	11.46	50.5	800-539-3863	Y
Victory RS International Fund Class R6	RSIRX	B-	C	B		3.44	15.75	4.59	37.81	22.52	10.14	50.5	800-539-3863	Y
Victory RS International Fund Class Y	RSIGX	B-	C	B	Up	3.51	15.81	4.80	38.80	23.97	12.08	50.5	800-539-3863	Y
Virtus KAR Global Quality Dividend Fund Class A	PPTAX	B	C+	B+		3.88	14.50	10.59	28.97	35.60	14.45	38.2	800-243-1574	Y
Virtus KAR Global Quality Dividend Fund Class C	PPTCX	B-	C	B+	Down	3.72	14.07	9.77	26.03	30.59	13.94	38.2	800-243-1574	Y
Virtus KAR Global Quality Dividend Fund Class I	PIPTX	B	C+	A-		3.95	14.67	10.94	29.97	37.40	14.46	38.2	800-243-1574	Y
Virtus SGA Global Growth A Class	SGAAX	B	B-	B		5.99	25.04	14.04	60.91	81.25	21.22	60.4	800-243-1574	Y
Virtus SGA Global Growth C Class	SGACX	B	B-	B		5.80	24.56	13.18	57.34	74.58	20.23	60.4	800-243-1574	Y
Virtus SGA Global Growth I Class	SGAPX	B	B-	B		5.98	25.07	14.08	60.92	81.36	21.25	60.4	800-243-1574	Y
Virtus SGA Global Growth R6 Class	SGARX	B	B	B		6.03	25.25	14.46	62.76	84.80	21.77	60.4	800-243-1574	Y
Virtus SGA International Growth Fund Class A	SCIIX	B-	C+	B	Up	9.21	24.29	11.09	46.95	37.25	10.09	58.4	800-243-1574	Y
Virtus SGA International Growth Fund Class I	STITX	B-	C+	B	Up	9.31	24.46	11.35	47.89	38.82	10.29	58.4	800-243-1574	Y
Virtus SGA International Growth Fund Class R6	SCIZX	B-	C+	B	Up	9.32	24.44	11.44	48.20	39.26	10.31	58.4	800-243-1574	Y
Virtus Vontobel Global Opportunities Fund Class A	NWWOX	B	C+	B	Up	6.30	18.00	9.71	45.76	58.30	16.19	306.5	800-243-1574	Y
Virtus Vontobel Global Opportunities Fund Class C	WWOCX	B-	C+	B	Up	6.15	17.65	8.94	42.67	52.60	13.46	306.5	800-243-1574	Y
Virtus Vontobel Global Opportunities Fund Class I	WWOIX	B	B-	B+	Up	6.43	18.32	10.15	47.08	60.47	16.21	306.5	800-243-1574	Y
Virtus Vontobel Global Opportunities Fund Class R6	VRGOX	B	B-	B+	Up	6.43	18.30	10.23	46.70	59.32	16.22	306.5	800-243-1574	Y
Voya Global Equity Dividend Fund Class W	IGEWX	B-	C	B	Up	3.88	14.64	4.66	30.83	16.89	15.54	60.8	800-366-0066	Y
Voya Global Equity Fund Class A	NAWGX	B-	C	B	Up	2.85	14.87	5.54	37.46	21.38	36.15	245.5	800-366-0066	Y

Category: Global Equity Large Cap (con't)

Fund Name	Ticker Symbol	RATINGS: Overall Rating	Reward Rating	Risk Rating	Recent Up/ Downgrade	TOTAL RETURNS & PERFORMANCE: 3-Month Total Return	6-Month Total Return	1-Year Total Return	3-Year Total Return	5-Year Total Return	ASSETS: NAV	Total Assets (MIL)	NEW INVESTORS: Telephone	Open to New Investors
Voya Global Equity Fund Class C	NAWCX	B-	C	B	Up	2.64	14.44	4.74	34.37	16.90	33.63	245.5	800-366-0066	Y
Voya Global Equity Fund Class I	NAWIX	B-	C	B+	Up	2.90	15.02	5.78	38.45	22.88	36.48	245.5	800-366-0066	Y
Voya Global Equity Fund Class W	IGVWX	B-	C	B+	Up	2.93	15.02	5.81	38.51	22.94	36.46	245.5	800-366-0066	Y
Voya Global Equity Portfolio Class A	IGHAX	B-	C	B	Up	2.84	14.78	5.34	36.41	28.23	10.37	590.7	800-366-0066	Y
Voya Global Equity Portfolio Class I	IIGZX	B-	C	B+	Up	2.97	15.04	5.76	38.43	31.14	10.37	590.7	800-366-0066	Y
Voya Global Equity Portfolio Class S	IGHSX	B-	C	B	Up	2.89	14.91	5.53	37.39	29.75	10.41	590.7	800-366-0066	Y
Voya Global Equity Portfolio Class S2	IWTTX	B-	C	B	Up	2.79	14.72	5.37	36.71	28.70	10.27	590.7	800-366-0066	Y
Voya Global Equity Portfolio Class T	VGVTX	B-	C	B	Up	2.73	14.59	5.14	35.81	27.26	10.32	590.7	800-366-0066	Y
VY® Morgan Stanley Global Franchise Portfolio Class A	IGFAX	B	B	B+		4.96	21.30	14.81	48.91	63.44	16.91	413.4	800-366-0066	Y
VY® Morgan Stanley Global Franchise Portfolio Class R6	VPRDX	B	B	B+		5.16	21.67	15.47	51.66	67.65	18.13	413.4	800-366-0066	Y
VY® Morgan Stanley Global Franchise Portfolio Class S	IVGTX	B	B	B+		5.04	21.51	15.17	50.38	66.23	18.13	413.4	800-366-0066	Y
VY® Morgan Stanley Global Franchise Portfolio Class S2	IGFSX	B	B	B+		5.03	21.44	15.03	49.77	65.02	17.95	413.4	800-366-0066	Y
Wasatch Global Value Fund™ Institutional Class Shares	WILCX	B-	C	B+		1.43	11.90	5.74	31.28	31.74	7.77	163.0	800-551-1700	Y
Wasatch Global Value Fund™ Investor Class Shares	FMIEX	B-	C	B+		1.38	11.79	5.57	30.60	30.76	7.78	163.0	800-551-1700	Y
WCM Focused Global Growth Fund Institutional Class	WCMGX	B	B	B		7.86	28.07	17.85	58.89	81.14	17.7	111.6	949-380-0200	Y
WCM Focused Global Growth Fund Investor Class	WFGGX	B	B	B		7.82	27.92	17.39	57.82	79.19	17.5	111.6	949-380-0200	Y
WCM Focused International Growth Fund Institutional Class	WCMIX	B-	C+	B	Up	9.92	25.10	11.99	49.34	54.70	17.39	8,740	949-380-0200	Y
WCM Focused International Growth Fund Investor Class	WCMRX	B-	C+	B	Up	9.89	24.96	11.74	48.25	52.83	17.32	8,740	949-380-0200	Y
Wells Fargo Intrinsic World Equity Fund - Class A	EWEAX	B-	C	B	Up	5.09	17.46	6.80	46.53	37.20	21.05	149.7	800-222-8222	Y
Wells Fargo Intrinsic World Equity Fund - Class Admin	EWEIX	B-	C	B	Up	5.11	17.49	6.94	46.91	38.28	20.95	149.7	800-222-8222	Y
Wells Fargo Intrinsic World Equity Fund - Class C	EWECX	B-	C	B	Up	4.90	17.05	6.04	43.27	32.18	20.11	149.7	800-222-8222	Y
Wells Fargo Intrinsic World Equity Fund - Class Inst	EWENX	B-	C	B	Up	5.21	17.71	7.24	48.26	40.08	21	149.7	800-222-8222	Y

Category: Global Equity Mid/Small Cap

Fund Name	Ticker Symbol	RATINGS: Overall Rating	Reward Rating	Risk Rating	Recent Up/ Downgrade	TOTAL RETURNS & PERFORMANCE: 3-Month Total Return	6-Month Total Return	1-Year Total Return	3-Year Total Return	5-Year Total Return	ASSETS: NAV	Total Assets (MIL)	NEW INVESTORS: Telephone	Open to New Investors
Aberdeen International Small Cap Fund Class A	WVCCX	B-	C	B	Up	4.97	17.11	7.36	40.15	35.55	28.05	101.0	866-667-9231	Y
Aberdeen International Small Cap Fund Class C	CPVCX	B-	C	B	Up	4.82	16.75	6.66	37.33	31.03	25.43	101.0	866-667-9231	Y
Aberdeen International Small Cap Fund Class R	WPVAX	B-	C	B	Up	4.88	16.90	7.00	38.73	33.30	26.42	101.0	866-667-9231	Y
Aberdeen International Small Cap Fund Institutional Class	ABNIX	B-	C	B	Up	5.07	17.34	7.74	41.59	37.77	28.15	101.0	866-667-9231	Y
Aberdeen International Small Cap Institutional Service Cls	AGISX	B-	C	B	Up	5.02	17.22	7.55	40.87	36.39	28.24	101.0	866-667-9231	Y
New Alternatives Fund Class A	NALFX	B	B	B		6.42	21.91	15.19	35.83	27.09	58.6	208.9	800-423-8383	Y
New Alternatives Fund Investor Shares	NAEFX	B	B	B		6.35	21.78	14.93	34.83	25.55	58.39	208.9	800-423-8383	Y
Vanguard Global Minimum Volatility Fund Admiral Shares	VMNVX	B	B-	A-		4.13	15.30	9.73	35.60	60.81	28.47	3,803	877-662-7447	Y
Vanguard Global Minimum Volatility Fund Investor Shares	VMVFX	B	B-	A-		4.02	15.23	9.64	35.25	60.10	14.22	3,803	877-662-7447	Y

Category: Global Macro

Fund Name	Ticker Symbol	RATINGS: Overall Rating	Reward Rating	Risk Rating	Recent Up/ Downgrade	TOTAL RETURNS & PERFORMANCE: 3-Month Total Return	6-Month Total Return	1-Year Total Return	3-Year Total Return	5-Year Total Return	ASSETS: NAV	Total Assets (MIL)	NEW INVESTORS: Telephone	Open to New Investors
All Terrain Opportunity Fund Class Institutional	TERIX	B	C+	A-	Up	1.98	5.24	4.85	16.91		25.57	30.4		Y
Astor Macro Alternative Fund Class I	GBLMX	B-	C	B+		4.22	15.53	10.13	22.24		11.6	6.6	877-738-0333	Y
BNY Mellon Global Real Return Fund - Class A	DRRAX	B-	C	B	Up	4.03	8.94	9.19	8.79	16.43	15.22	2,614		Y
BNY Mellon Global Real Return Fund - Class I	DRRIX	B-	C	B+	Up	4.09	9.07	9.51	9.66	17.99	15.26	2,614		Y
BNY Mellon Global Real Return Fund - Class Y	DRRYX	B-	C	B+	Up	4.15	9.14	9.59	9.92	18.39	15.28	2,614		Y
DWS Global Macro Fund - Class A	DBISX	B-	C	A-	Down	1.96	6.59	6.00	25.36	20.89	9.86	32.4		Y
DWS Global Macro Fund - Class C	DBICX	B-	C	B+		1.76	6.21	5.17	22.58	16.45	9.23	32.4		Y
DWS Global Macro Fund - Class Inst	MGINX	B-	C	A-	Down	2.11	6.85	6.32	26.34	22.45	9.67	32.4		Y

Category: Global Macro (con't)

Fund Name	Ticker Symbol	RATINGS: Overall Rating	Reward Rating	Risk Rating	Recent Up/ Downgrade	TOTAL RETURNS & PERFORMANCE: 3-Month Total Return	6-Month Total Return	1-Year Total Return	3-Year Total Return	5-Year Total Return	ASSETS: NAV	Total Assets (MIL)	NEW INVESTORS: Telephone	Open to New Investors
DWS Global Macro Fund - Class R	DBITX	B-	C	B+		1.93	6.50	5.68	24.45	19.30	9.49	32.4		Y
DWS Global Macro Fund - Class S	DBIVX	B-	C	A-	Down	2.01	6.75	6.27	26.19	22.15	9.64	32.4		Y
MFS Global Alternative Strategy Fund Class A	DVRAX	B-	C	B		2.59	9.08	7.64	13.15	10.12	10.69	181.2	877-960-6077	Y
MFS Global Alternative Strategy Fund Class I	DVRIX	B-	C	B		2.67	9.12	7.93	13.89	11.46	10.76	181.2	877-960-6077	Y
MFS Global Alternative Strategy Fund Class R2	DVRHX	B-	C	B	Up	2.52	8.86	7.25	12.16	8.69	10.56	181.2	877-960-6077	Y
MFS Global Alternative Strategy Fund Class R3	DVRJX	B-	C	B		2.68	9.07	7.62	13.07	10.04	10.7	181.2	877-960-6077	Y
MFS Global Alternative Strategy Fund Class R4	DVRKX	B-	C	B		2.66	9.21	7.91	14.02	10.93	10.79	181.2	877-960-6077	Y
MFS Global Alternative Strategy Fund Class R6	DVRLX	B-	C+	B		2.75	9.19	7.96	14.25	11.95	10.81	181.2	877-960-6077	Y
PGIM QMA Global Tactical Allocation Fund- Class A	PTALX	B-	C	A-	Up	2.48	10.75	2.38	23.07		9.89	39.6	800-225-1852	Y
PGIM QMA Global Tactical Allocation Fund- Class C	PTCLX	B-	C	B+	Up	2.33	10.30	1.58	20.32		9.63	39.6	800-225-1852	Y
PGIM QMA Global Tactical Allocation Fund- Class R6	PTQLX	B-	C	A-	Up	2.57	10.80	2.57	23.87		9.95	39.6	800-225-1852	Y
PGIM QMA Global Tactical Allocation Fund- Class Z	PTZLX	B-	C	A-	Up	2.57	10.91	2.68	24.12		9.96	39.6	800-225-1852	Y
Securian AM Dynamic Managed Volatility Institutional Cls	VVMIX	B	C+	A-		4.06	13.84	10.98	37.50		12.73	58.9	800-665-6005	Y

Category: Health Care Sector Equity

Fund Name	Ticker Symbol	RATINGS: Overall Rating	Reward Rating	Risk Rating	Recent Up/ Downgrade	TOTAL RETURNS & PERFORMANCE: 3-Month Total Return	6-Month Total Return	1-Year Total Return	3-Year Total Return	5-Year Total Return	ASSETS: NAV	Total Assets (MIL)	NEW INVESTORS: Telephone	Open to New Investors
AllianzGI Health Sciences Fund Class A	RAGHX	B-	C	B		3.19	15.04	13.13	36.77	57.90	32.27	155.4	800-498-5413	Y
AllianzGI Health Sciences Fund Class C	RCGHX	B-	C	B		3.04	14.66	12.33	33.74	52.12	24.71	155.4	800-498-5413	Y
AllianzGI Health Sciences Fund Institutional Class	HLHIX	B-	C	B		3.31	15.27	13.54	38.19	60.41	32.76	155.4	800-498-5413	Y
BlackRock Health Sciences Opportunities Portfolio Class K	SHSKX	B-	C	B+	Down	1.22	11.74	11.94	46.89	81.52	62.6	7,136	800-441-7762	Y
BlackRock Health Sciences Opportunities Portfolio Class R	BHSRX	B-	C	B+	Down	1.03	11.34	11.17	43.81	76.64	58.05	7,136	800-441-7762	Y
BlackRock Health Sciences Opp Portfolio Inst Shares	SHSSX	B-	C	B+	Down	1.19	11.67	11.83	46.41	81.98	62.54	7,136	800-441-7762	Y
BlackRock Health Sciences Opp Portfolio Inv A Shares	SHSAX	B-	C	B+	Down	1.13	11.51	11.52	45.20	79.45	59.42	7,136	800-441-7762	Y
BlackRock Health Sciences Opp Portfolio Inv C Shares	SHSCX	B-	C	B+	Down	0.94	11.11	10.72	42.07	73.07	51.69	7,136	800-441-7762	Y
BlackRock Health Sciences Opp Portfolio Service Shares	SHISX	B-	C	B+	Down	1.12	11.50	11.50	45.16	79.40	59.65	7,136	800-441-7762	Y
DWS Health and Wellness Fund - Class A	SUHAX	B-	C	B		1.77	12.55	10.01	32.36	48.72	36.14	289.4		Y
DWS Health and Wellness Fund - Class Inst	SUHIX	B-	C	B		1.84	12.67	10.28	33.43	50.62	40.81	289.4		Y
DWS Health and Wellness Fund - Class S	SCHLX	B-	C	B		1.85	12.70	10.29	33.42	50.63	39.04	289.4		Y
Eaton Vance Worldwide Health Sciences Fund Class A	ETHSX	B-	C	B		1.90	14.73	15.90	29.97	45.49	11.76	1,026		Y
Eaton Vance Worldwide Health Sciences Fund Class B	EMHSX	B-	C	B		1.69	14.24	15.04	27.03	40.17	12.03	1,026		
Eaton Vance Worldwide Health Sciences Fund Class C	ECHSX	B-	C	B		1.71	14.25	15.01	27.00	40.23	11.86	1,026		Y
Eaton Vance Worldwide Health Sciences Fund Class I	EIHSX	B-	C	B		1.94	14.82	16.16	30.91	47.31	12.08	1,026		Y
Eaton Vance Worldwide Health Sciences Fund Class R	ERHSX	B-	C	B		1.86	14.58	15.61	28.97	43.73	12.57	1,026		Y
Fidelity® Select Medical Technology and Devices Portfolio	FSMEX	B-	C+	B	Down	5.07	21.14	17.75	72.31	129.16	56.48	6,711	617-563-7000	Y
Invesco Health Care Fund Class R6	GGHSX	B-	C	B		3.18	17.04	12.53	32.91	34.04	38.93	1,381	800-659-1005	Y
Invesco Health Care Fund Class Y	GGHYX	B-	C	B		3.18	17.00	12.46	33.02	34.84	38.87	1,381	800-659-1005	Y
Janus Henderson Global Life Sciences Fund Class D	JNGLX	B-	C	B		2.19	17.98	11.20	43.83	67.89	58.71	3,679	877-335-2687	
Janus Henderson Global Life Sciences Fund Class I	JFNIX	B-	C	B		2.20	18.01	11.30	44.13	68.30	58.82	3,679	877-335-2687	Y
Janus Henderson Global Life Sciences Fund Class N	JFNNX	B-	C	B		2.23	18.05	11.36	44.11	68.21	58.64	3,679	877-335-2687	Y
Janus Henderson Global Life Sciences Fund Class T	JAGLX	B-	C	B		2.18	17.94	11.12	43.46	67.14	58.44	3,679	877-335-2687	Y
JNL/Mellon Capital Healthcare Sector Fund Class A		B-	C	B		1.37	11.13	10.88	38.94	63.22	28.74	3,224		Y
JNL/Mellon Capital Healthcare Sector Fund Class I		B-	C	B		1.43	11.30	11.23	40.08	65.16	28.94	3,224		Y
Putnam Global Health Care Fund Class A	PHSTX	B-	C	B		1.36	13.33	7.50	24.04	38.12	51.24	1,287	617-292-1000	Y
Putnam Global Health Care Fund Class Y	PHSYX	B-	C	B		1.43	13.49	7.77	25.00	39.88	55.25	1,287	617-292-1000	Y
Vanguard Health Care Index Fund Admiral Shares	VHCIX	B-	C	B		1.47	11.35	11.45	41.15	67.87	86.99	10,619	877-662-7447	Y

Category: Infrastructure Sector Equity

Fund Name	Ticker Symbol	RATINGS Overall Rating	Reward Rating	Risk Rating	Recent Up/ Downgrade	TOTAL RETURNS & PERFORMANCE 3-Month Total Return	6-Month Total Return	1-Year Total Return	3-Year Total Return	5-Year Total Return	ASSETS NAV	Total Assets (MIL)	NEW INVESTORS Telephone	Open to New Investors
Aberdeen Global Infrastructure Fund Class A	AIAFX	B-	B-	B	Down	4.74	20.37	15.52	37.49	25.84	21.4	99.8	866-667-9231	Y
Aberdeen Global Infrastructure Fund Institutional Class	AIFRX	B-	B-	B	Down	4.80	20.56	15.79	38.47	27.42	21.43	99.8	866-667-9231	Y
Cohen & Steers Global Infrastructure Fund, Inc. Class A	CSUAX	B	B-	B		3.87	17.51	14.30	28.66	28.67	20.51	307.8	212-832-3232	Y
Cohen & Steers Global Infrastructure Fund, Inc. Class C	CSUCX	B-	C+	B	Down	3.70	17.11	13.53	26.14	24.51	20.47	307.8	212-832-3232	Y
Cohen & Steers Global Infrastructure Fund, Inc. Class I	CSUIX	B	B-	B		3.92	17.70	14.70	29.99	30.67	20.57	307.8	212-832-3232	Y
Cohen & Steers Global Infrastructure Fund, Inc. Class R	CSURX	B	B-	B		3.81	17.34	14.06	28.02	27.57	20.63	307.8	212-832-3232	Y
Cohen & Steers Global Infrastructure Fund, Inc. Class Z	CSUZX	B	B-	B		3.97	17.76	14.76	30.06	30.96	20.58	307.8	212-832-3232	Y
Cohen & Steers Infrastructure Fund	UTF	B	B	C+		5.18	25.62	20.12	41.37	40.22	26.56	2,266	212-832-3232	Y
Franklin Global Listed Infrastructure Fund Advisor Class	FLGZX	B	B	B	Up	7.10	22.25	12.89	33.86	32.45	14.88	63.2	650-312-2000	Y
Franklin Global Listed Infrastructure Fund Class A	FLGIX	B	B	B	Up	7.02	22.09	12.56	32.95	30.55	14.85	63.2	650-312-2000	Y
Franklin Global Listed Infrastructure Fund Class C	FLGDX	B-	B-	B		6.89	21.67	11.72	30.05	25.94	14.77	63.2	650-312-2000	Y
Franklin Global Listed Infrastructure Fund Class R	FLGRX	B	B	B	Up	7.00	21.99	12.30	32.06	29.18	14.84	63.2	650-312-2000	Y
Franklin Global Listed Infrastructure Fund Class R6	FILGX	B	B	B	Up	7.17	22.41	13.09	34.72	33.38	14.89	63.2	650-312-2000	Y
Frontier MFG Core Infrastructure Fund Institutional Class	FMGIX	B-	B-	B		5.39	18.50	14.65	25.68	42.60	17.16	510.9		Y
Frontier MFG Core Infrastructure Fund Service Class	FCIVX	B-	B-	B		5.42	18.56	14.59	25.65	42.57	17.2	510.9		Y
Invesco Global Infrastructure Fund Class A	GIZAX	B-	B-	B	Down	4.78	21.59	11.18	28.73	21.23	11.52	20.2	800-659-1005	Y
Invesco Global Infrastructure Fund Class C	GIZCX	B-	C+	B		4.60	21.07	10.39	25.81	16.68	11.5	20.2	800-659-1005	Y
Invesco Global Infrastructure Fund Class R	GIZRX	B-	B-	B	Down	4.81	21.44	10.91	27.78	19.72	11.52	20.2	800-659-1005	Y
Invesco Global Infrastructure Fund Class R5	GIZFX	B-	B-	B	Down	4.93	21.84	11.55	29.67	22.86	11.53	20.2	800-659-1005	Y
Invesco Global Infrastructure Fund Class R6	GIZSX	B-	B-	B	Down	4.93	21.84	11.55	29.80	22.86	11.53	20.2	800-659-1005	Y
Invesco Global Infrastructure Fund Class Y	GIZYX	B-	B-	B	Down	4.93	21.84	11.55	29.80	22.86	11.53	20.2	800-659-1005	Y
JHancock Infrastructure Fund Class A	JEEBX	B	C+	A-		3.70	15.03	12.96	25.82	29.46	12.91	306.4	800-225-5913	Y
JHancock Infrastructure Fund Class C	JEEFX	B-	C+	B+	Down	3.56	14.75	12.27	23.31	24.83	12.79	306.4	800-225-5913	Y
JHancock Infrastructure Fund Class I	JEEIX	B	C+	A-		3.77	15.29	13.30	26.99	31.29	12.92	306.4	800-225-5913	Y
JHancock Infrastructure Fund Class NAV	JEEDX	B	C+	A-		3.87	15.40	13.45	27.46	32.20	12.95	306.4	800-225-5913	Y
JHancock Infrastructure Fund Class R6		B	C+	A-		3.79	15.31	13.36	27.38	32.19	12.94	306.4	800-225-5913	Y
JNL/First State Global Infrastructure A		B-	C+	B	Down	4.43	19.33	13.48	20.21	4.92	15.06	1,028		Y
JNL/First State Global Infrastructure I		B-	C+	B	Down	4.48	19.47	13.80	21.02	6.10	15.15	1,028		Y
Lazard Global Listed Infrastructure Portfolio Inst Shares	GLIFX	B	B-	B	Up	4.47	14.20	9.67	43.12	64.96	15.27	6,725	800-823-6300	Y
Lazard Global Listed Infrastructure Portfolio Open Shares	GLFOX	B-	B-	B		4.48	14.13	9.39	42.08	62.95	15.29	6,725	800-823-6300	Y
Morgan Stanley Inst Fund, Inc. Global Infrastr Port Cls A	MTIPX	B-	C+	B		4.89	19.77	12.28	22.83	23.28	14.78	356.0	855-332-5306	Y
Morgan Stanley Inst Fund, Inc. Global Infrastr Port Cls I	MTIIX	B-	C+	B		4.95	19.88	12.55	23.71	24.90	14.83	356.0	855-332-5306	Y
Morgan Stanley Inst Fund, Inc. Global Infrastr Port Cls IR	MRGOX	B-	C+	B		5.02	19.98	12.60	23.76	24.95	14.83	356.0	855-332-5306	Y
Morgan Stanley Inst Fund, Inc. Global Infrastr Port Cls IS	MSGPX	B-	C+	B		5.02	19.98	12.59	23.81	24.94	14.83	356.0	855-332-5306	Y
Northern Multi-Manager Global Listed Infrastructure Fund	NMFIX	B-	C+	B-		4.81	16.90	7.81	29.11	20.45	12.54	1,027	800-595-9111	Y
Nuveen Global Infrastructure Fund Class A	FGIAX	B-	C+	B	Down	6.16	22.11	14.86	28.96	33.11	11.54	533.0	312-917-8146	Y
Nuveen Global Infrastructure Fund Class C	FGNCX	B-	C+	B		5.94	21.64	13.98	26.14	28.17	11.41	533.0	312-917-8146	Y
Nuveen Global Infrastructure Fund Class I	FGIYX	B-	B-	B	Down	6.18	22.31	15.10	29.93	34.77	11.51	533.0	312-917-8146	Y
Nuveen Global Infrastructure Fund Class R3	FGNRX	B-	C+	B	Down	6.06	21.95	14.56	27.98	31.40	11.72	533.0	312-917-8146	Y
Nuveen Global Infrastructure Fund Class R6	FGIWX	B-	B-	B	Down	6.35	22.48	15.28	30.49	35.35	11.55	533.0	312-917-8146	Y
PGIM Jennison Global Infrastructure Fund- Class A	PGJAX	B-	C+	B		4.88	20.63	11.52	26.40	18.04	14.33	49.0	800-225-1852	Y
PGIM Jennison Global Infrastructure Fund- Class C	PGJCX	B-	C	B		4.68	20.12	10.72	23.56	13.71	14.2	49.0	800-225-1852	Y
PGIM Jennison Global Infrastructure Fund- Class R6	PGJQX	B-	C+	B	Down	4.95	20.81	11.92	27.44	19.54	14.34	49.0	800-225-1852	Y
PGIM Jennison Global Infrastructure Fund- Class Z	PGJZX	B-	C+	B+	Down	5.03	20.80	11.91	27.50	19.59	14.35	49.0	800-225-1852	Y
RARE Global Infrastructure Value Fund Class IS	RGSVX	B-	C+	B-	Up	3.13	17.57	10.46	26.11		11.68	24.8	877-721-1926	Y
Reaves Utilities & Energy Infrastructure Cls Institutional	RSRFX	B-	C+	B		5.43	22.88	14.02	26.53	38.70	10.45	40.0		Y
Russell Investments Global Infrastructure Fund Class M	RGFTX	B-	C+	B-		5.42	20.94	12.05	26.76	27.61	11.38	469.3	800-426-7969	Y
Russell Investments Global Infrastructure Fund Class S	RGISX	B-	C+	B-		5.38	20.75	11.91	26.20	26.70	11.39	469.3	800-426-7969	Y
Russell Investments Global Infrastructure Fund Class Y	RGIYX	B-	C+	B-		5.52	20.91	12.13	27.02	27.88	11.4	469.3	800-426-7969	Y
Virtus Duff & Phelps Global Infrastructure Fund Class A	PGUAX	B	B	B		4.99	22.52	16.24	30.81	30.90	15.99	103.6	800-243-1574	Y
Virtus Duff & Phelps Global Infrastructure Fund Class C	PGUCX	B-	B-	B	Down	4.82	22.10	15.35	27.89	26.10	15.93	103.6	800-243-1574	Y
Virtus Duff & Phelps Global Infrastructure Fund Class I	PGIUX	B	B	B		5.06	22.66	16.49	31.78	32.54	16	103.6	800-243-1574	Y
Virtus Duff & Phelps Global Infrastructure Fund Class R6	VGIRX	B	B	B		5.08	22.62	16.54	31.38	31.47	15.99	103.6	800-243-1574	Y

Category: Infrastructure Sector Equity (con't)

Fund Name	Ticker Symbol	Overall Rating	Reward Rating	Risk Rating	Recent Up/Downgrade	3-Month Total Return	6-Month Total Return	1-Year Total Return	3-Year Total Return	5-Year Total Return	NAV	Total Assets (MIL)	Telephone	Open to New Investors
		RATINGS				TOTAL RETURNS & PERFORMANCE					ASSETS		NEW INVESTORS	
Voya CBRE Global Infrastructure Fund Class A	VCRAX	B	B	B		4.54	20.90	14.68	31.42	37.79	11.62	188.0	800-366-0066	Y
Voya CBRE Global Infrastructure Fund Class C	VCRCX	B-	B-	B	Down	4.37	20.53	13.79	28.71	33.02	11.6	188.0	800-366-0066	Y
Voya CBRE Global Infrastructure Fund Class I	VCRIX	B	B	B		4.62	21.15	14.94	32.62	39.81	11.63	188.0	800-366-0066	Y
Voya CBRE Global Infrastructure Fund Class W	VCGWX	B	B	B		4.53	21.04	14.84	32.50	39.69	11.62	188.0	800-366-0066	Y

Category: Long/Short Credit

Fund Name	Ticker Symbol	Overall Rating	Reward Rating	Risk Rating	Recent Up/Downgrade	3-Month Total Return	6-Month Total Return	1-Year Total Return	3-Year Total Return	5-Year Total Return	NAV	Total Assets (MIL)	Telephone	Open to New Investors
		RATINGS				TOTAL RETURNS & PERFORMANCE					ASSETS		NEW INVESTORS	
BrandywineGLOBAL - Alternative Credit Fund Class A	LMAPX	B	C+	A	Up	2.10	4.06	3.25	19.60	12.68	10.41	676.3	877-721-1926	Y
BrandywineGLOBAL - Alternative Credit Fund Class C	LMAQX	B	C	A-	Up	2.01	3.67	2.48	17.10	8.77	10.35	676.3	877-721-1926	Y
BrandywineGLOBAL - Alternative Credit Fund Class FI	LMAOX	B	C+	A	Up	2.10	3.96	3.15	19.54	12.46	10.38	676.3	877-721-1926	Y
BrandywineGLOBAL - Alternative Credit Fund Class I	LMANX	B	C+	A	Up	2.28	4.21	3.58	20.71	14.44	10.42	676.3	877-721-1926	Y
BrandywineGLOBAL - Alternative Credit Fund Class IS	LMAMX	B-	C+	B+	Up	2.29	4.25	3.67	21.05	14.90	10.44	676.3	877-721-1926	Y
Dunham Long/Short Credit Fund Class A	DAAIX	B	C+	A		1.19	4.05	4.00	28.97	17.10	9.23	71.6	800-442-4358	Y
Dunham Long/Short Credit Fund Class C	DCAIX	B	C+	A		0.69	3.45	2.95	25.91	12.40	8.98	71.6	800-442-4358	Y
Dunham Long/Short Credit Fund Class N	DNAIX	B	C+	A		1.01	3.95	4.00	29.75	18.31	9.25	71.6	800-442-4358	Y
Franklin K2 Long Short Credit Fund Advisor Class	FKLZX	B	C+	A-		1.44	3.84	3.89	15.51		10.52	117.9	650-312-2000	Y
Franklin K2 Long Short Credit Fund Class A	FKLSX	B	C+	A-		1.35	3.75	3.71	15.05		10.51	117.9	650-312-2000	Y
Franklin K2 Long Short Credit Fund Class C	FKLCX	B-	C	B+		1.17	3.30	2.71	11.84		10.31	117.9	650-312-2000	Y
Franklin K2 Long Short Credit Fund Class R	FKLRX	B-	C	B+		1.36	3.58	3.31	14.03		10.41	117.9	650-312-2000	Y
Franklin K2 Long Short Credit Fund Class R6	FKLQX	B	C+	A-		1.44	3.85	3.82	15.45		10.51	117.9	650-312-2000	Y
James Alpha Hedged High Income Portfolio Class A	INCAX	B-	C	B	Up	1.02	3.54	1.75	16.47	12.04	9.07	56.6	800-807-3863	Y
James Alpha Hedged High Income Portfolio Class I	INCIX	B-	C	B	Up	1.08	3.88	2.33	18.10	14.42	9.11	56.6	800-807-3863	Y
James Alpha Hedged High Income Portfolio Class S Shares	INCSX	B-	C+	B+		1.18	4.07	2.75	19.35	15.64	9.21	56.6	800-807-3863	Y
PIMCO Credit Opportunities Bond Fund Class A	PZCRX	B-	C+	B+		2.20	5.97	5.18	17.69	15.04	10.06	424.8	866-746-2602	Y
PIMCO Credit Opportunities Bond Fund Class C	PCCRX	B-	C+	B	Up	1.90	5.55	4.29	14.99	10.74	9.91	424.8	866-746-2602	Y
PIMCO Credit Opportunities Bond Fund Class I-2	PPCRX	B	C+	B+	Up	2.18	6.05	5.34	18.65	16.67	10	424.8	866-746-2602	Y
PIMCO Credit Opportunities Bond Fund Institutional Class	PCARX	B	C+	B+	Up	2.19	6.18	5.52	19.05	17.33	10.04	424.8	866-746-2602	Y
Shelton Tactical Credit Institutional	DEBIX	B-	C+	B+	Up	1.53	4.04	3.13	9.79	14.97	10.67	98.1	800-955-9988	Y
Shelton Tactical Credit Investor	DEBTX	B-	C+	B	Up	1.58	4.02	2.89	9.08	13.58	10.67	98.1	800-955-9988	Y
Water Island Credit Opportunities Fund Class A	AGCAX	B-	C	A-		1.07	3.54	2.95	8.96	8.59	9.67	58.0	800-285-4485	Y
Water Island Credit Opportunities Fund Class I	ACFIX	B-	C	B+		1.14	3.67	3.20	9.81	9.98	9.67	58.0	800-285-4485	Y
Water Island Credit Opportunities Fund Class R	ARCFX	B-	C	B		0.97	3.42	2.84	8.85	8.56	9.71	58.0	800-285-4485	Y

Category: Long/Short Equity

Fund Name	Ticker Symbol	Overall Rating	Reward Rating	Risk Rating	Recent Up/Downgrade	3-Month Total Return	6-Month Total Return	1-Year Total Return	3-Year Total Return	5-Year Total Return	NAV	Total Assets (MIL)	Telephone	Open to New Investors
		RATINGS				TOTAL RETURNS & PERFORMANCE					ASSETS		NEW INVESTORS	
361 Domestic Long/Short Equity Fund Class I	ADMZX	B-	C	B+	Up	1.82	11.77	1.82	18.70		10.63	47.4	866-361-1720	Y
361 Domestic Long/Short Equity Fund Class Y	ADMWX	B-	C	B+	Up	1.81	11.74	1.90	19.02		10.66	47.4	866-361-1720	Y
AB Select US Long/Short Portfolio Advisor Class	ASYLX	B	C	A-	Up	3.56	10.74	6.23	27.87	28.86	12.78	1,097	212-969-1000	Y
AB Select US Long/Short Portfolio Class A	ASLAX	B	C	A-	Up	3.46	10.59	5.93	26.86	27.19	12.53	1,097	212-969-1000	Y
AB Select US Long/Short Portfolio Class C	ASCLX	B-	C	A-	Up	3.31	10.23	5.10	24.02	22.53	11.85	1,097	212-969-1000	Y
AB Select US Long/Short Portfolio Class I	ASILX	B	C	A-	Up	3.55	10.81	6.22	28.02	29.23	12.81	1,097	212-969-1000	Y
AB Select US Long/Short Portfolio Class K	ASLKX	B	C	A-	Up	3.46	10.59	5.93	26.74	27.29	12.53	1,097	212-969-1000	Y
AB Select US Long/Short Portfolio Class R	ASRLX	B-	C	A-		3.44	10.51	5.69	25.78	25.69	12.3	1,097	212-969-1000	Y

Category: Long/Short Equity (con't)

		RATINGS				TOTAL RETURNS & PERFORMANCE					ASSETS		NEW INVESTORS	
Fund Name	Ticker Symbol	Overall Rating	Reward Rating	Risk Rating	Recent Up/ Downgrade	3-Month Total Return	6-Month Total Return	1-Year Total Return	3-Year Total Return	5-Year Total Return	NAV	Total Assets (MIL.)	Telephone	Open to New Investors
Absolute Capital Opportunities Fund Institutional Shares	CAPOX	B	C	A	Up	2.78	4.41	3.17	23.31		11.82	56.7	888-992-2765	Y
Alger Dynamic Opportunities Fund Class A	SPEDX	B-	C+	B		1.23	17.60	6.41	38.37	37.25	14.7	116.5	800-992-3863	Y
Alger Dynamic Opportunities Fund Class C	ADOCX	B-	C+	B	Up	1.11	17.18	5.62	35.30	32.10	13.64	116.5	800-992-3863	Y
Alger Dynamic Opportunities Fund Class Z	ADOZX	B-	C+	B		1.34	17.78	6.68	39.70	39.26	15.1	116.5	800-992-3863	Y
AllianzGI U.S. Equity-Hedged Fund Class A	AZUAX	B-	C	B+	Up	2.99	10.64	4.74	23.64	21.47	17.56	2.2	800-498-5413	Y
AllianzGI U.S. Equity-Hedged Fund Class C	AZUCX	B-	C	B	Up	2.87	10.23	4.01	20.89	17.08	16.8	2.2	800-498-5413	Y
AllianzGI U.S. Equity-Hedged Fund Class P	AZUPX	B-	C	B+	Up	3.06	10.71	4.95	24.20	22.34	17.15	2.2	800-498-5413	Y
AllianzGI U.S. Equity-Hedged Fund Institutional Class	AZUIX	B-	C	B+	Up	3.11	10.78	5.04	24.53	23.03	17.88	2.2	800-498-5413	Y
AMG FQ Long-Short Equity Fund Class I	MEQFX	B	C	A-	Up	3.24	7.36	6.54	46.79	50.46	15.79	85.5	800-835-3879	Y
AMG FQ Long-Short Equity Fund Class N	FQUAX	B-	C	A-		3.10	7.17	6.21	45.30	48.19	15.75	85.5	800-835-3879	Y
AMG River Road Long-Short Fund Class I	ALSIX	B-	C+	B+		4.03	13.46	11.74	26.97	23.20	12.89	22.5	800-835-3879	Y
AMG River Road Long-Short Fund Class N	ARLSX	B-	C+	B+		4.02	13.32	11.58	26.09	21.66	12.67	22.5	800-835-3879	Y
AMG River Road Long-Short Fund Class Z	ARLZX	B-	C+	B+		4.02	13.44	11.82	26.81	22.36	12.91	22.5	800-835-3879	Y
Anchor Tactical Equity Strategies Fund Institutional Class	ATESX	B-	C	B+	Up	6.41	11.90	12.50			11.94	128.2		Y
Balter L/S Small Cap Equity Fund Institutional Class	BEQIX	B-	C	A-		0.66	10.80	1.40	33.00	31.83		101.7		Y
Balter L/S Small Cap Equity Fund Investor Class	BEQRX	B-	C	B		1.13	11.15	1.53	32.47	30.64		101.7		Y
Bridgeway Managed Volatility Fund	BRBPX	B-	C	B+	Up	1.89	9.05	1.74	14.78	16.20	15.05	30.7	800-661-3550	Y
Calamos Hedged Equity Fund Class A	CAHEX	B-	C	B+	Up	1.99	8.62	4.62	23.33		11.65	203.4	800-582-6959	Y
Calamos Hedged Equity Fund Class C	CCHEX	B-	C	B	Up	1.76	8.18	3.82	20.71		11.5	203.4	800-582-6959	Y
Calamos Hedged Equity Fund Class I	CIHEX	B-	C	B+		2.03	8.74	4.89	24.38		11.63	203.4	800-582-6959	Y
Catalyst/Exceed Defined Shield Fund Class A	SHIEX	B-	C	B+	Up	3.65	13.48	5.75	29.12		9.87	31.2	866-447-4228	Y
Catalyst/Exceed Defined Shield Fund Class C	SHINX	B-	C	B+	Up	2.85	12.47	4.33	25.56		9.74	31.2	866-447-4228	Y
Catalyst/Exceed Defined Shield Fund Class I	SHIIX	B-	C	B+	Up	2.49	12.28	4.73	28.60		9.93	31.2	866-447-4228	Y
Diamond Hill Long Short Fund Class A	DIAMX	B-	C	B	Up	6.81	16.75	9.75	28.27	25.48	26.48	3,377	888-226-5595	
Diamond Hill Long Short Fund Class I	DHLSX	B-	C	B	Up	6.88	16.92	10.06	29.42	27.35	27.15	3,377	888-226-5595	
Diamond Hill Long-Short Fund Class Y	DIAYX	B-	C	B	Up	6.89	16.98	10.15	29.84	28.03	27.27	3,377	888-226-5595	
Fintrust Income and Opportunity Fund Class A	HROAX	B-	C	B+	Up	1.93	9.45	2.50	18.91		10.53	10.2	877-244-6235	Y
Fintrust Income and Opportunity Fund Institutional Class	HIOIX	B-	C	B+	Up	1.91	9.59	2.67	19.71		10.62	10.2	877-244-6235	Y
First Invs Hedged U.S. Equity Opp Adv Cls	FHEKX	B-	C	B	Up	5.10	16.38	9.68	26.56		12.36	315.8	800-423-4026	Y
First Invs Hedged U.S. Equity Opp Inst Cls	FHELX	B-	C	B	Up	5.08	16.43	9.85	26.97		12.4	315.8	800-423-4026	Y
FundX Tactical Upgrader Fund	TACTX	B-	C	A-	Down	0.39	0.22	1.87	25.46	29.79	25.17	49.9	866-455-3863	Y
Gotham Absolute Return Fund Institutional Class Shares	GARIX	B-	C	B	Up	0.88	7.08	2.84	20.58	12.64	14.82	925.7	877-974-6852	Y
Gotham Defensive Long 500 Fund Institutional Class	GDLFX	B-	C	B		1.11	8.67	7.92			12.65	12.7	877-974-6852	Y
Gotham Total Return Fund Institutional Class	GTRFX	B-	C	B+		0.54	6.34	4.59	38.11		12.9	33.2	877-974-6852	Y
Gotham Total Return Fund Investor Class	GTRNX	B-	C	B		0.54	6.27	4.40	37.13		12.88	33.2	877-974-6852	Y
James Alpha Managed Risk Domestic Equity Portfolio Class A	JDAEX	B	C	A	Up	1.28	8.47	5.99	18.63		10.24	31.8	800-807-3863	Y
James Alpha Managed Risk Domestic Equity Portfolio Class C	JDCEX	B-	C	A-		1.10	8.12	5.24	15.89		10.11	31.8	800-807-3863	Y
James Alpha Managed Risk Domestic Equity Portfolio Class I	JDIEX	B	C	A		1.37	8.62	6.51	20.02		10.33	31.8	800-807-3863	Y
James Alpha Managed Risk Domestic Eq Port Cls S Shares	JDSEX	B	C+	A		1.55	8.97	7.17	21.57		10.44	31.8	800-807-3863	Y
John Hancock Seaport Long/Short Fund Class A	JSFBX	B-	C	A-	Up	2.19	10.14	3.48	21.62	24.29	11.18	742.6	800-225-5913	Y
John Hancock Seaport Long/Short Fund Class C	JSFTX	B-	C	B+	Up	2.08	9.76	2.73	19.11	20.07	10.79	742.6	800-225-5913	Y
John Hancock Seaport Long/Short Fund Class I	JSFDX	B-	C	A-	Up	2.33	10.35	3.69	22.74	26.26	11.4	742.6	800-225-5913	Y
John Hancock Seaport Long/Short Fund Class NAV		B-	C	A-	Up	2.31	10.36	3.84	23.13	27.15	11.5	742.6	800-225-5913	Y
John Hancock Seaport Long/Short Fund Class R6	JSFRX	B-	C	A-	Up	2.31	10.36	3.93	23.13	27.15	11.5	742.6	800-225-5913	Y
JPMorgan Hedged Equity Fund Class A	JHQAX	B-	C	A-	Down	3.38	7.42	5.28	29.91	34.59	20.24	5,022	800-480-4111	Y
JPMorgan Hedged Equity Fund Class C	JHQCX	B-	C	B	Down	3.29	7.18	4.76	28.00	31.29	20.12	5,022	800-480-4111	Y
JPMorgan Hedged Equity Fund Class I	JHEQX	B-	C	A-	Down	3.44	7.54	5.49	30.91	36.30	20.29	5,022	800-480-4111	Y
JPMorgan Hedged Equity Fund Class R5	JHQPX	B-	C	B+		3.47	7.60	5.73	31.63	37.58	20.33	5,022	800-480-4111	Y
JPMorgan Hedged Equity Fund Class R6	JHQRX	B-	C	B+		3.49	7.70	5.79	31.83	37.95	20.33	5,022	800-480-4111	Y
LS Opportunity Fund - Institutional Class	LSOFX	B	C+	A-	Up	4.74	13.13	8.27	29.09	27.26	14.56	71.9		Y
MAI Managed Volatility Fund Institutional Class	MAIPX	B-	C	A-		2.60	11.49	6.12	21.52	24.06	11.79	140.6	866-624-9584	Y
MAI Managed Volatility Fund Investor Class	DIVPX	B-	C	A-		2.51	11.34	5.81	20.51	22.49	12.13	140.6	866-624-9584	Y

Category: Long/Short Equity (con't)

Fund Name	Ticker Symbol	RATINGS: Overall Rating	Reward Rating	Risk Rating	Recent Up/ Downgrade	TOTAL RETURNS & PERFORMANCE: 3-Month Total Return	6-Month Total Return	1-Year Total Return	3-Year Total Return	5-Year Total Return	ASSETS: NAV	Total Assets (MIL)	NEW INVESTORS: Telephone	Open to New Investors
MFS Managed Wealth Fund Class A	MNWAX	B	C+	B+	Up	2.79	7.39	6.33	15.22	16.65	11.04	41.4	877-960-6077	Y
MFS Managed Wealth Fund Class B	MNWBX	B-	C	B	Up	2.56	6.83	5.37	12.26	11.52	10.78	41.4	877-960-6077	Y
MFS Managed Wealth Fund Class C	MNWCX	B	C	A-	Up	2.58	6.87	5.40	12.21	11.54	10.73	41.4	877-960-6077	Y
MFS Managed Wealth Fund Class I	MNWIX	B	C+	B+	Up	2.88	7.47	6.48	15.64	17.30	11.07	41.4	877-960-6077	Y
MFS Managed Wealth Fund Class R1	MNWRX	B	C	A-	Up	2.56	6.83	5.37	12.26	11.52	10.78	41.4	877-960-6077	Y
MFS Managed Wealth Fund Class R2	MNWSX	B-	C+	B	Up	2.80	7.21	5.97	14.03	14.49	10.99	41.4	877-960-6077	Y
MFS Managed Wealth Fund Class R3	MNWTX	B-	C+	B+		2.79	7.28	6.23	14.90	15.91	11.05	41.4	877-960-6077	Y
MFS Managed Wealth Fund Class R4	MNWUX	B	C+	B+	Up	2.88	7.47	6.48	15.79	17.34	11.07	41.4	877-960-6077	Y
MFS Managed Wealth Fund Class R6	MNWZX	B	C+	A	Up	2.88	7.47	6.50	15.64	17.30	11.07	41.4	877-960-6077	Y
Nationwide Long/Short Equity Fund Class R6	NWLFX	B-	C	B	Up	1.44	11.46	1.00	17.77	27.24	14	22.5	800-848-0920	Y
Neuberger Berman Long Short Fund Class A	NLSAX	B-	C	B+	Up	3.91	11.86	3.32	18.93	16.12	14.33	2,606	212-476-9000	Y
Neuberger Berman Long Short Fund Institutional Class	NLSIX	B-	C	B+	Up	4.05	12.09	3.72	20.26	18.24	14.37	2,606	212-476-9000	Y
PIMCO RAE Worldwide Long/Short PLUS Institutional Cls	PWLIX	B	C	A-		0.68	6.35	6.00	23.35		10.12	1,629	866-746-2602	Y
RiverPark Long/Short Opportunity Fund Institutional Class	RLSIX	B-	C	B		5.79	17.24	6.86	48.46	34.75	12.78	88.1	888-564-4517	Y
RiverPark Long/Short Opportunity Fund Retail Class	RLSFX	B-	C	B		5.76	17.22	6.66	47.57	33.35	12.66	88.1	888-564-4517	Y
Salient Tactical Growth Fund Institutional Class	FTGWX	B-	C	B	Up	1.70	5.74	1.48	19.17	15.46	26.88	296.4	866-667-9228	Y
Salient Tactical Plus Fund Class A	SBTAX	B-	C	A-		2.09	3.62	6.18	28.25	24.39	11.71	55.6	866-667-9228	Y
Salient Tactical Plus Fund Class C	SBTCX	B-	C	A-	Up	1.80	3.20	5.41	25.28	19.60	11.26	55.6	866-667-9228	Y
Salient Tactical Plus Fund Class F	BTPIX	B	C	A-	Up	2.12	3.89	6.72	30.30	27.47	12.01	55.6	866-667-9228	Y
Salient Tactical Plus Fund Class I	SBTIX	B-	C	A-		2.07	3.68	6.43	29.13	25.63	11.82	55.6	866-667-9228	Y
Securian AM Managed Volatility Equity Institutional Cls	VMEIX	B-	C	A-	Up	3.33	11.12	7.85	23.92		12.32	39.7	800-665-6005	Y
The Covered Bridge Fund Class A	TCBAX	B-	C	A-		2.54	11.80	5.34	27.64	27.57	9.38	85.0		Y
The Covered Bridge Fund Class I	TCBIX	B-	C	A-		2.62	11.87	5.53	28.50	29.07	9.34	85.0		Y
Toews Tactical Defensive Alpha Fund	TTDAX	B-	C	B+	Up	5.66	17.76	8.61	31.32		11.93	118.9		Y
Toews Tactical Monument Fund	THLGX	B-	B-	B		4.08	14.09	15.38	31.70	14.37	11.98	30.6		Y
Transamerica Long/Short Strategy Fund Class I2		B	C	A-	Up	3.10	7.86	5.86	24.22	18.45	6.31	10.3	888-233-4339	Y
Weitz Partners III Opportunity Fund Institutional Class	WPOPX	B-	C	B	Up	3.72	24.52	14.33	31.50	23.21	15.58	658.2	800-304-9745	Y
Weitz Partners III Opportunity Fund Investor Class	WPOIX	B-	C	B	Up	3.59	24.26	13.68	29.40	20.33	15	658.2	800-304-9745	Y
Wilmington Global Alpha Equities Fund Class A	WRAAX	B-	C+	B		3.05	9.02	6.58	19.88	14.47	11.48	177.0	800-836-2211	Y
Wilmington Global Alpha Equities Fund Class I	WRAIX	B	C+	A	Up	3.01	9.12	6.77	20.73	15.93	11.6	177.0	800-836-2211	Y

Category: Market Neutral

Fund Name	Ticker Symbol	RATINGS: Overall Rating	Reward Rating	Risk Rating	Recent Up/ Downgrade	TOTAL RETURNS & PERFORMANCE: 3-Month Total Return	6-Month Total Return	1-Year Total Return	3-Year Total Return	5-Year Total Return	ASSETS: NAV	Total Assets (MIL)	NEW INVESTORS: Telephone	Open to New Investors
American Beacon SSI Alternative Income Institutional Cls	SSIJX	B-	C	B+							10.27	229.1	800-658-5811	Y
American Beacon SSI Alternative Income Fund --Y Class	PSCIX	B-	C	B+		1.48	4.26	3.76	12.20	9.90	10.27	229.1	800-658-5811	Y
American Beacon SSI Alternative Income Fund--Investor Cls	PSCAX	B-	C	B+		1.38	4.15	3.54	11.32	8.44	10.27	229.1	800-658-5811	Y
AQR Diversified Arbitrage Fund Class I	ADAIX	B	C+	A-	Up	2.21	5.72	4.25	23.01	9.57	9.24	486.8	203-742-3600	
AQR Diversified Arbitrage Fund Class N	ADANX	B	C+	A-	Up	2.21	5.59	3.95	22.13	8.36	9.24	486.8	203-742-3600	
AQR Diversified Arbitrage Fund Class R6	QDARX	B	C+	A-	Up	2.21	5.73	4.25	23.29	10.02	9.22	486.8	203-742-3600	Y
BlackRock Event Driven Equity Fund Institutional Shares	BILPX	B-	C+	B	Down	1.98	4.61	7.27	20.67	30.52	9.73	2,617	800-441-7762	Y
BlackRock Event Driven Equity Fund Investor A Shares	BALPX	B-	C+	B	Down	1.96	4.58	7.00	19.70	28.92	9.35	2,617	800-441-7762	Y
BlackRock Event Driven Equity Fund Investor C Shares	BCLPX	B-	C+	B		1.81	4.20	6.23	17.16	24.33	8.42	2,617	800-441-7762	Y
BlackRock Global Long/Short Equity Fund Class K	BGCKX	B	C	A		2.75	3.25	4.67	22.49	13.70	12.69	609.0	800-441-7762	Y
BlackRock Global Long/Short Equity Institutional Shares	BDMIX	B	C	A		2.67	3.17	4.58	22.29	13.41	12.66	609.0	800-441-7762	Y
BlackRock Global Long/Short Equity Fund Investor A Shares	BDMAX	B	C	A		2.62	3.05	4.27	21.33	11.84	12.5	609.0	800-441-7762	Y
BlackRock Global Long/Short Equity Fund Investor C Shares	BDMCX	B	C	A-	Up	2.47	2.74	3.56	18.64	7.86	12	609.0	800-441-7762	Y
Calamos Market Neutral Income Fund Class A	CVSIX	B-	C	B+		1.39	4.34	3.67	14.20	17.49	13.32	7,940	800-582-6959	Y
Calamos Market Neutral Income Fund Class C	CVSCX	B-	C	B	Up	1.18	3.91	2.87	11.62	13.15	13.55	7,940	800-582-6959	Y
Calamos Market Neutral Income Fund Institutional Class	CMNIX	B-	C	B+		1.47	4.50	3.89	15.07	18.95	13.15	7,940	800-582-6959	Y

Category: Market Neutral (con't)

		RATINGS				TOTAL RETURNS & PERFORMANCE					ASSETS		NEW INVESTORS	
Fund Name	Ticker Symbol	Overall Rating	Reward Rating	Risk Rating	Recent Up/ Downgrade	3-Month Total Return	6-Month Total Return	1-Year Total Return	3-Year Total Return	5-Year Total Return	NAV	Total Assets (MIL)	Telephone	Open to New Investors
Gabelli Enterprise Mergers and Acquisitions Fund Class A	EMAAX	B-	C	B+		1.27	6.24	2.76	15.11	16.87	14.3	145.2	914-921-5135	Y
Gabelli Enterprise Mergers and Acquisitions Fund Class AAA	EAAAX	B-	C	B+		1.32	6.35	2.99	15.83	18.21	14.55	145.2	914-921-5135	Y
Gabelli Enterprise Mergers and Acquisitions Fund Class Y	EMAYX	B-	C	A-		1.38	6.52	3.27	16.75	19.64	15.35	145.2	914-921-5135	Y
Guggenheim Market Neutral Real Estate Fund Class A	GUMAX	B	C+	A-	Up	3.97	6.47	7.68	17.42		26.97	8.6	212-518-9290	Y
Guggenheim Market Neutral Real Estate Fund Class C	GUMCX	B-	C	B+	Up	3.77	6.04	6.70	14.68		26.14	8.6	212-518-9290	Y
Guggenheim Market Neutral Real Estate Fund Class P	GUMPX	B	C+	A-	Up	3.98	6.48	7.36	16.98		26.12	8.6	212-518-9290	Y
Guggenheim Market Neutral Real Estate Fund Institutional	GUMNX	B	C+	A-	Up	4.04	6.61	7.80	18.07		26.75	8.6	212-518-9290	Y
Highland Merger Arbitrage Fund Class A	HMEAX	B-	C+	B		1.14	2.66	5.77	18.81		18.5	29.3	877-665-1287	Y
Highland Merger Arbitrage Fund Class C	HMECX	B-	C	B	Down	0.98	2.33	5.05	16.51		18.37	29.3	877-665-1287	Y
Highland Merger Arbitrage Fund Class Z	HMEZX	B-	C+	B		1.19	2.81	6.06	20.00		18.65	29.3	877-665-1287	Y
JNL/Nicholas Convertible Arbitrage Fund Class A		B	C	A		1.83	5.83	4.82	13.42	8.10	10.52	152.0		Y
JNL/Nicholas Convertible Arbitrage Fund Class I		B-	C+	B+		1.94	5.95	5.08	14.04	8.69	10.5	152.0		Y
JPMorgan Research Market Neutral Fund Class I	JMNSX	B-	C	B+	Up	1.46	1.66	3.82	11.58	4.52	13.9	68.3	800-480-4111	Y
JPMorgan Research Market Neutral Fund Class L	JPMNX	B-	C	B+	Up	1.50	1.69	3.95	12.02	5.39	14.23	68.3	800-480-4111	Y
Kellner Merger Fund Institutional Class	GAKIX	B-	C	B+	Up	0.45	2.60	1.97	8.84	11.90	11.03	164.0	212-350-0200	Y
The Arbitrage Fund Class Institutional	ARBNX	B-	C	B+		0.45	1.44	3.73	8.44	12.23	13.31	1,736	800-285-4485	Y
The Merger Fund® Institutional Class	MERIX	B	C	A-		0.42	2.82	4.61	16.07	14.96	16.72	3,039		Y
The Merger Fund® Investor Class	MERFX	B	C	A+		0.35	2.68	4.28	15.05	13.18	16.82	3,039		Y
Victory Market Neutral Income Fund Class I	CBHIX	B-	C	B+		1.20	0.69	2.25	14.00	15.36	9.55	87.9	800-539-3863	Y

Category: Moderate Allocation

		RATINGS				TOTAL RETURNS & PERFORMANCE					ASSETS		NEW INVESTORS	
Fund Name	Ticker Symbol	Overall Rating	Reward Rating	Risk Rating	Recent Up/ Downgrade	3-Month Total Return	6-Month Total Return	1-Year Total Return	3-Year Total Return	5-Year Total Return	NAV	Total Assets (MIL)	Telephone	Open to New Investors
1919 Socially Responsive Balanced Fund Class A	SSIAX	B	C+	B+		4.61	16.73	11.01	39.11	42.17	19.17	173.5		Y
1919 Socially Responsive Balanced Fund Class B	SESIX	B	C+	B+		4.49	16.31	10.22	35.30	36.22	18.59	173.5		
1919 Socially Responsive Balanced Fund Class C	SESLX	B	C+	B+		4.43	16.31	10.19	36.09	37.05	19.31	173.5		Y
1919 Socially Responsive Balanced Fund Class I	LMRNX	B	C+	B+		4.73	16.89	11.36	40.29	44.08	19.15	173.5		Y
AB All Market Total Return Portfolio Advisor Class	ABWYX	B-	C	A-	Up	4.04	14.35	6.22	22.64	21.34	15.69	729.1	212-969-1000	Y
AB All Market Total Return Portfolio Class A	ABWAX	B-	C	A-	Up	3.94	14.18	6.00	21.72	19.82	15.54	729.1	212-969-1000	Y
AB All Market Total Return Portfolio Class B	ABWBX	B-	C	B+	Up	3.75	13.75	5.23	18.99	15.36	15.47	729.1	212-969-1000	
AB All Market Total Return Portfolio Class C	ABWCX	B-	C	B+	Up	3.79	13.75	5.22	18.99	15.40	15.3	729.1	212-969-1000	Y
AB All Market Total Return Portfolio Class I	ABWIX	B-	C	A-	Up	4.07	14.27	6.23	22.53	21.17	15.85	729.1	212-969-1000	Y
AB All Market Total Return Portfolio Class K	ABWKX	B-	C	A-	Up	3.96	14.08	5.88	21.30	19.19	15.47	729.1	212-969-1000	Y
AB All Market Total Return Portfolio Class R	ABWRX	B-	C	B+	Up	3.91	14.00	5.55	20.26	17.35	15.39	729.1	212-969-1000	Y
AB Global Risk Allocation Fund Class A	CABNX	B-	C	B+	Up	2.76	12.89	3.30	19.46	16.20	16.72	229.5	212-969-1000	Y
AB Global Risk Allocation Fund Class Adv	CBSYX	B-	C	A-	Up	2.80	13.00	3.49	20.31	17.64	16.86	229.5	212-969-1000	Y
AB Global Risk Allocation Fund Class I	CABIX	B-	C	A-	Up	2.86	13.08	3.61	20.70	18.35	16.85	229.5	212-969-1000	Y
AB Global Risk Allocation Fund Class K	CBSKX	B-	C	B+	Up	2.77	12.93	3.23	19.34	16.02	16.68	229.5	212-969-1000	Y
AB Global Risk Allocation Fund Class R	CBSRX	B-	C	B+	Up	2.66	12.71	2.90	18.18	14.20	16.58	229.5	212-969-1000	Y
Aberdeen Diversified Income Fund Class A	GMAAX	B-	C	B+	Up	2.50	10.45	4.97	16.76	15.68	12.26	13.6	866-667-9231	Y
Aberdeen Diversified Income Fund Class I	GMAIX	B-	C	B+	Up	2.57	10.66	5.30	17.96	17.45	12.27	13.6	866-667-9231	Y
Aberdeen Diversified Income Cls Institutional Service	GAMSX	B-	C	B+	Up	2.59	10.64	5.21	17.65	17.17	12.21	13.6	866-667-9231	Y
Aberdeen Diversified Income Fund Class R	GMRRX	B-	C	B+	Up	2.36	10.21	4.60	15.94	13.77	12.15	13.6	866-667-9231	Y
Aberdeen Dynamic Allocation Fund Class A	GMMAX	B-	C	B+	Up	2.87	13.09	3.52	17.54	15.61	13.67	11.7	866-667-9231	Y
Aberdeen Dynamic Allocation Fund Class C	GMMCX	B-	C	B+	Up	2.73	12.76	2.83	15.17	11.71	13.38	11.7	866-667-9231	Y
Aberdeen Dynamic Allocation Cls Institutional Service	GAASX	B-	C	B+	Up	2.97	13.32	3.87	18.73	17.40	13.6	11.7	866-667-9231	Y
Aberdeen Dynamic Allocation Fund Class R	GAGRX	B-	C	B+	Up	2.80	12.94	3.14	16.37	13.53	13.59	11.7	866-667-9231	Y
Aberdeen Dynamic Allocation Fund Institutional Class	GMMIX	B-	C	B+	Up	2.95	13.24	3.82	18.70	17.48	13.65	11.7	866-667-9231	Y
Aberdeen Income Builder Fund Class A	AAADX	B	C+	B+	Up	3.01	13.04	7.96	37.54	37.61	16.42	90.5	866-667-9231	Y
Aberdeen Income Builder Fund Institutional Class	AADDX	B	C+	B+	Up	3.02	13.12	8.19	38.50	39.20	16.41	90.5	866-667-9231	Y
AIG Active Allocation Fund Class A	FBAAX	B-	C	B+	Up	2.03	10.97	1.96	23.66	24.61	16.68	130.0	800-858-8850	Y

Category: Moderate Allocation (con't)

Fund Name	Ticker Symbol	RATINGS: Overall Rating	Reward Rating	Risk Rating	Recent Up/ Downgrade	TOTAL RETURNS & PERFORMANCE: 3-Month Total Return	6-Month Total Return	1-Year Total Return	3-Year Total Return	5-Year Total Return	ASSETS: NAV	Total Assets (MIL)	NEW INVESTORS: Telephone	Open to New Investors
AIG Active Allocation Fund Class B	FBABX	B-	C	B	Up	1.88	10.56	1.32	21.20	20.48	16.52	130.0	800-858-8850	Y
AIG Active Allocation Fund Class C	FBACX	B-	C	B	Up	1.94	10.59	1.32	21.32	20.67	16.58	130.0	800-858-8850	Y
Alger Balanced Portfolio Class I-2	ABLOX	B	C	A-	Up	2.78	11.10	7.61	30.41	41.20	15.11	44.6	800-992-3863	Y
All Asset Growth – Alt 20 Portfolio Class IA		B-	C	B+	Up	2.76	12.97	3.69	29.01	23.47	20.91	333.6	877-222-2144	Y
All Asset Growth – Alt 20 Portfolio Class IB		B-	C	B+	Up	2.75	12.99	3.73	29.06	23.48	20.97	333.6	877-222-2144	Y
All Asset Growth – Alt 20 Portfolio Class K		B-	C	B+	Up	2.81	13.11	3.99	30.04	25.01	20.89	333.6	877-222-2144	Y
AllianzGI Global Allocation Fund Administrative Class	AGAMX	B-	C	B+	Up	3.38	12.20	5.27	21.52	17.32	11.34	324.5	800-498-5413	Y
AllianzGI Global Allocation Fund Class A	PALAX	B-	C	B+	Up	3.28	12.13	5.12	21.21	16.92	11.01	324.5	800-498-5413	Y
AllianzGI Global Allocation Fund Class C	PALCX	B-	C	B	Up	3.09	11.76	4.25	18.53	12.65	11.33	324.5	800-498-5413	Y
AllianzGI Global Allocation Fund Class P	AGAPX	B-	C	B+	Up	3.38	12.29	5.36	22.23	18.60	10.9	324.5	800-498-5413	Y
AllianzGI Global Allocation Fund Class R	AGARX	B-	C	B+	Up	3.26	12.01	4.98	20.54	15.99	10.9	324.5	800-498-5413	Y
AllianzGI Global Allocation Fund Class R6	AGASX	B-	C	B+	Up	3.44	12.40	5.55	22.45	18.45	10.75	324.5	800-498-5413	Y
AllianzGI Global Allocation Fund Institutional Class	PALLX	B-	C	B+	Up	3.36	12.32	5.44	21.98	18.30	10.98	324.5	800-498-5413	Y
AllianzGI Global Dynamic Allocation Administrative Cls	AGFAX	B-	C	B+	Up	3.68	11.73	3.88	20.07	11.99	19.42	182.3	800-498-5413	Y
AllianzGI Global Dynamic Allocation Fund Class A	ASGAX	B-	C	B+	Up	3.67	11.70	3.87	20.02	11.94	19.47	182.3	800-498-5413	Y
AllianzGI Global Dynamic Allocation Fund Class P	AGSPX	B-	C	B+	Up	3.69	11.85	4.05	20.64	12.91	19.34	182.3	800-498-5413	Y
AllianzGI Global Dynamic Allocation Fund Class R6	ADYFX	B-	C	B+	Up	3.73	11.85	4.13	21.09	13.58	19.43	182.3	800-498-5413	Y
AllianzGI Global Dynamic Allocation Institutional Cls	AGAIX	B-	C	B+	Up	3.72	11.83	4.08	20.97	13.40	19.75	182.3	800-498-5413	Y
ALPS/Stadion Core ETF Portfolio Class I		B-	C	A-	Up	2.82	11.90	5.36	32.50	24.02	12.03	17.4	866-759-5679	Y
ALPS/Stadion Core ETF Portfolio Class III	ALSTX	B-	C	A-	Up	2.76	11.66	5.06	31.04	22.16	12.25	17.4	866-759-5679	Y
American Beacon Balanced Fund Advisor Class	ABLSX	B-	C	B+	Up	3.78	14.81	5.17	29.31	27.66	15.05	273.6	800-658-5811	Y
American Beacon Balanced Fund C Class	ABCCX	B-	C	B+	Up	3.63	14.44	4.53	27.11	23.85	14.21	273.6	800-658-5811	Y
American Beacon Balanced Fund Class A	ABFAX	B-	C	B+	Up	3.87	14.91	5.34	29.99	28.57	14.08	273.6	800-658-5811	Y
American Beacon Balanced Fund Class Y	ACBYX	B-	C	B	Up	3.93	15.04	5.63	31.23	30.59	16.17	273.6	800-658-5811	Y
American Beacon Balanced Fund Institutional Class	AADBX	B-	C	B+	Up	3.91	15.02	5.54	31.07	30.69	16.05	273.6	800-658-5811	Y
American Beacon Balanced Fund Investor Class	AABPX	B-	C	B+	Up	3.86	14.87	5.41	30.01	28.76	14.11	273.6	800-658-5811	Y
American Century Balanced Fund I Class	ABINX	B	C	A-	Up	3.36	13.79	7.47	30.62	35.34	18.86	900.6	800-444-4015	Y
American Century Balanced Fund Investor Class	TWBIX	B-	C	A-		3.32	13.69	7.26	29.86	34.02	18.85	900.6	800-444-4015	Y
American Century Balanced Fund R5 Class	ABGNX	B	C	A-	Up	3.36	13.86	7.47	30.49	34.67	18.86	900.6	800-444-4015	Y
American Century Inv One Choice Port®: Moderate Inv Cls	AOMIX	B-	C	B+	Up	3.28	13.72	5.04	27.59	29.79	15.57	1,888	800-444-4015	Y
American Century Inv One Choice Port®: Moderate R Cls	AORMX	B-	C	B+	Up	3.15	13.45	4.51	25.69	26.66	15.57	1,888	800-444-4015	Y
American Century Strategic Allocation: Moderate A Cls	ACOAX	B-	C	B+	Up	3.46	13.93	5.28	27.02	28.03	6.51	909.9	800-444-4015	Y
American Century Strategic Allocation: Moderate C Cls	ASTCX	B-	C	B+	Up	3.21	13.62	4.63	24.17	23.48	6.42	909.9	800-444-4015	Y
American Century Strategic Allocation: Moderate I Cls	ASAMX	B-	C	B+	Up	3.50	14.12	5.72	28.61	30.95	6.53	909.9	800-444-4015	Y
American Century Strategic Allocation: Moderate Inv Cls	TWSMX	B-	C	B+	Up	3.40	14.21	5.52	27.88	29.68	6.53	909.9	800-444-4015	Y
American Century Strategic Allocation: Moderate R Cls	ASMRX	B-	C	B+	Up	3.36	13.89	5.05	25.92	26.43	6.47	909.9	800-444-4015	Y
American Century Strategic Allocation: Moderate R5 Cls	ASMUX	B-	C	B+	Up	3.65	14.29	5.88	28.42	30.22	6.54	909.9	800-444-4015	Y
American Century Strategic Allocation: Moderate R6 Cls	ASMDX	B-	C	B+	Up	3.57	14.22	5.88	29.24	31.80	6.52	909.9	800-444-4015	Y
American Funds American Balanced Fund® Class 529-A	CLBAX	B	C	A		2.78	11.45	6.88	29.80	42.22	27.28	146,710	800-421-4225	Y
American Funds American Balanced Fund® Class 529-C	CLBCX	B	C	A	Up	2.62	11.03	6.12	26.92	36.89	27.29	146,710	800-421-4225	Y
American Funds American Balanced Fund® Class 529-E	CLBEX	B	C	A		2.76	11.33	6.68	28.95	40.56	27.27	146,710	800-421-4225	Y
American Funds American Balanced Fund® Class 529-F	CLBFX	B	C	A		2.84	11.59	7.15	30.73	43.89	27.26	146,710	800-421-4225	Y
American Funds American Balanced Fund® Class A	ABALX	B	C	A		2.79	11.47	7.00	30.14	42.84	27.33	146,710	800-421-4225	Y
American Funds American Balanced Fund® Class C	BALCX	B	C	A	Up	2.62	11.04	6.18	27.08	37.32	27.15	146,710	800-421-4225	Y
American Funds American Balanced Fund® Class F-1	BALFX	B	C	A		2.82	11.44	6.93	29.88	42.33	27.31	146,710	800-421-4225	Y
American Funds American Balanced Fund® Class F-2	AMBFX	B	C	A		2.84	11.58	7.17	30.85	44.21	27.31	146,710	800-421-4225	Y
American Funds American Balanced Fund® Class F-3	AFMBX	B	C	A		2.90	11.63	7.31	31.09	43.88	27.32	146,710	800-421-4225	Y
American Funds American Balanced Fund® Class R-1	RLBAX	B	C	A	Up	2.61	11.04	6.11	27.01	37.25	27.13	146,710	800-421-4225	Y
American Funds American Balanced Fund® Class R-2	RLBBX	B	C	A	Up	2.65	11.08	6.15	27.09	37.43	27.15	146,710	800-421-4225	Y
American Funds American Balanced Fund® Class R-2E	RAMHX	B	C	A		2.68	11.21	6.46	28.17	40.26	27.22	146,710	800-421-4225	Y
American Funds American Balanced Fund® Class R-3	RLBCX	B	C	A		2.72	11.25	6.61	28.72	40.31	27.18	146,710	800-421-4225	Y
American Funds American Balanced Fund® Class R-4	RLBEX	B	C	A		2.82	11.46	6.95	29.88	42.49	27.28	146,710	800-421-4225	Y

Category: Moderate Allocation (con't)

Fund Name	Ticker Symbol	Overall Rating	Reward Rating	Risk Rating	Recent Up/ Downgrade	3-Month Total Return	6-Month Total Return	1-Year Total Return	3-Year Total Return	5-Year Total Return	NAV	Total Assets (MIL)	Telephone	Open to New Investors
		RATINGS				TOTAL RETURNS & PERFORMANCE					ASSETS		NEW INVESTORS	
American Funds American Balanced Fund® Class R-5	RLBFX	B	C	A		2.89	11.63	7.25	31.09	44.59	27.36	146,710	800-421-4225	Y
American Funds American Balanced Fund® Class R-5E	RLEFX	B	C	A		2.88	11.55	7.14	30.72	43.57	27.31	146,710	800-421-4225	Y
American Funds American Balanced Fund® Class R-6	RLBGX	B	C	A		2.90	11.67	7.31	31.26	44.98	27.34	146,710	800-421-4225	Y
American Funds Conservative Growth & Inc Port Cls 529-A	CIPAX	B	C+	A-		2.40	10.18	6.84	21.92	26.85	12.62	5,248	800-421-4225	Y
American Funds Conservative Growth & Inc Port Cls 529-C	CIPCX	B-	C	B+		2.22	9.76	6.17	19.27	22.26	12.58	5,248	800-421-4225	Y
American Funds Conservative Growth & Inc Port Cls 529-E	CIPEX	B	C+	A-	Up	2.33	10.06	6.67	21.17	25.52	12.62	5,248	800-421-4225	Y
American Funds Conservative Growth & Inc Port Cls 529-F-1	CIPFX	B	C+	A-		2.45	10.29	7.10	22.77	28.35	12.63	5,248	800-421-4225	Y
American Funds Conservative Growth & Inc Port Cls A	INPAX	B	C+	A-		2.40	10.19	6.97	22.19	27.37	12.63	5,248	800-421-4225	Y
American Funds Conservative Growth & Inc Port Cls ABLE-A	CIPGX	B	C	A-		2.39	10.11	6.95	22.19	27.27	12.61	5,248	800-421-4225	Y
American Funds Conservative Growth & Inc Port Cls C	INPCX	B-	C	B+		2.23	9.88	6.22	19.51	22.69	12.57	5,248	800-421-4225	Y
American Funds Conservative Growth & Inc Port Cls F-1	INPFX	B	C+	A-		2.39	10.16	6.91	22.01	27.19	12.64	5,248	800-421-4225	Y
American Funds Conservative Growth & Inc Port Cls F-2	INPEX	B	C+	A-		2.45	10.28	7.09	22.97	28.74	12.64	5,248	800-421-4225	Y
American Funds Conservative Growth & Inc Port Cls F-3	INPDX	B	C+	A		2.48	10.44	7.29	23.43	29.34	12.63	5,248	800-421-4225	Y
American Funds Conservative Growth & Inc Port Cls R-1	RNCAX	B-	C	B+		2.20	9.74	6.02	19.32	22.48	12.58	5,248	800-421-4225	Y
American Funds Conservative Growth & Inc Port Cls R-2	RINBX	B-	C	B+		2.24	9.81	6.13	19.47	22.58	12.57	5,248	800-421-4225	Y
American Funds Conservative Growth & Inc Port Cls R-2E	RNBEX	B	C	A-	Up	2.30	9.97	6.42	20.57	25.87	12.63	5,248	800-421-4225	Y
American Funds Conservative Growth & Inc Port Cls R-3	RNCCX	B	C+	A-	Up	2.33	10.05	6.62	21.01	25.35	12.61	5,248	800-421-4225	Y
American Funds Conservative Growth & Inc Port Cls R-4	RINEX	B	C+	A-		2.39	10.17	6.91	22.09	27.24	12.63	5,248	800-421-4225	Y
American Funds Conservative Growth & Inc Port Cls R-5	RINFX	B	C+	A-		2.54	10.39	7.22	23.24	29.13	12.66	5,248	800-421-4225	Y
American Funds Conservative Growth & Inc Port Cls R-5E	RGOFX	B	C+	A-		2.45	10.28	7.15	22.82	28.72	12.62	5,248	800-421-4225	Y
American Funds Conservative Growth & Inc Port Cls R-6	RINGX	B	C+	A		2.47	10.42	7.28	23.32	29.45	12.65	5,248	800-421-4225	Y
American Funds Global Balanced Fund Class 529-A	CBFAX	B-	C	A-	Up	2.21	11.47	4.53	19.79	18.85	32.76	19,381	800-421-4225	Y
American Funds Global Balanced Fund Class 529-C	CBFCX	B-	C	B+	Up	1.99	11.02	3.76	17.04	14.30	32.66	19,381	800-421-4225	Y
American Funds Global Balanced Fund Class 529-E	CBFEX	B-	C	A-	Up	2.12	11.33	4.31	18.97	17.49	32.73	19,381	800-421-4225	Y
American Funds Global Balanced Fund Class 529-F-1	CBFFX	B-	C	A-	Up	2.26	11.59	4.81	20.60	20.15	32.77	19,381	800-421-4225	Y
American Funds Global Balanced Fund Class A	GBLAX	B-	C	A-	Up	2.23	11.50	4.60	19.97	19.24	32.78	19,381	800-421-4225	Y
American Funds Global Balanced Fund Class C	GBLCX	B-	C	B+	Up	2.00	11.06	3.79	17.21	14.63	32.71	19,381	800-421-4225	Y
American Funds Global Balanced Fund Class F-1	GBLEX	B-	C	A-	Up	2.18	11.42	4.53	19.79	18.92	32.79	19,381	800-421-4225	Y
American Funds Global Balanced Fund Class F-2	GBLFX	B-	C	A-	Up	2.27	11.60	4.82	20.76	20.52	32.79	19,381	800-421-4225	Y
American Funds Global Balanced Fund Class F-3	GFBLX	B-	C	A-	Up	2.30	11.67	4.93	21.14	21.12	32.77	19,381	800-421-4225	Y
American Funds Global Balanced Fund Class R-1	RGBLX	B-	C	B+	Up	2.02	11.04	3.78	17.22	14.91	32.74	19,381	800-421-4225	Y
American Funds Global Balanced Fund Class R-2	RGBBX	B-	C	B+	Up	2.01	11.06	3.81	17.25	14.74	32.67	19,381	800-421-4225	Y
American Funds Global Balanced Fund Class R-2E	RGGHX	B-	C	B+	Up	2.09	11.21	4.12	18.29	17.24	32.71	19,381	800-421-4225	Y
American Funds Global Balanced Fund Class R-3	RGBCX	B-	C	A-	Up	2.15	11.30	4.27	18.83	17.33	32.73	19,381	800-421-4225	Y
American Funds Global Balanced Fund Class R-4	RGBEX	B-	C	A-	Up	2.19	11.45	4.57	19.87	19.07	32.77	19,381	800-421-4225	Y
American Funds Global Balanced Fund Class R-5	RGBFX	B-	C	A-	Up	2.28	11.62	4.90	20.96	20.85	32.82	19,381	800-421-4225	Y
American Funds Global Balanced Fund Class R-5E	RGBHX	B-	C	A-	Up	2.23	11.57	4.76	20.72	20.53	32.75	19,381	800-421-4225	Y
American Funds Global Balanced Fund Class R-6	RGBGX	B-	C	A-	Up	2.30	11.66	4.96	21.16	21.14	32.8	19,381	800-421-4225	Y
American Funds Moderate Growth & Inc Port Cls 529-A	CBAAX	B	C	A-	Up	3.02	12.52	6.27	28.33	34.52	15.01	8,894	800-421-4225	Y
American Funds Moderate Growth & Inc Port Cls 529-C	CBPCX	B-	C	A-	Up	2.77	12.11	5.43	25.46	29.46	14.95	8,894	800-421-4225	Y
American Funds Moderate Growth & Inc Port Cls 529-E	CBAEX	B	C	A-	Up	2.90	12.43	5.98	27.49	32.94	14.98	8,894	800-421-4225	Y
American Funds Moderate Growth & Inc Port Cls 529-F-1	CBAFX	B	C	A-	Up	3.08	12.70	6.53	29.28	36.09	15.03	8,894	800-421-4225	Y
American Funds Moderate Growth & Income Portfolio Cls A	BLPAX	B	C	A-	Up	2.96	12.53	6.23	28.52	34.94	15.01	8,894	800-421-4225	Y
American Funds Moderate Growth & Inc Port Cls ABLE-A	CBAGX	B	C	A-	Up	3.03	12.55	6.32	28.61	34.89	15.01	8,894	800-421-4225	Y
American Funds Moderate Growth & Income Portfolio Cls C	BLPCX	B-	C	A-	Up	2.79	12.08	5.50	25.71	29.93	14.92	8,894	800-421-4225	Y
American Funds Moderate Growth & Income Portfolio Cls F-1	BLPFX	B	C	A-	Up	2.95	12.51	6.20	28.36	34.66	15.01	8,894	800-421-4225	Y
American Funds Moderate Growth & Income Portfolio Cls F-2	BLPEX	B	C	A-	Up	3.01	12.62	6.47	29.44	36.47	15.03	8,894	800-421-4225	Y
American Funds Moderate Growth & Income Portfolio Cls F-3	BLPDX	B	C	A-	Up	3.04	12.70	6.59	29.73	36.88	15.01	8,894	800-421-4225	Y
American Funds Moderate Growth & Income Portfolio Cls R-1	RBAAX	B-	C	A-	Up	2.78	12.12	5.47	25.57	29.77	14.95	8,894	800-421-4225	Y
American Funds Moderate Growth & Income Portfolio Cls R-2	RBABX	B-	C	A-	Up	2.79	12.17	5.50	25.74	29.88	14.93	8,894	800-421-4225	Y
American Funds Moderate Growth & Income Portfolio Cls R-2E	RBBEX	B-	C	A-	Up	2.92	12.32	5.81	26.72	32.87	15.01	8,894	800-421-4225	Y
American Funds Moderate Growth & Income Portfolio Cls R-3	RBACX	B	C	A-	Up	2.96	12.41	6.00	27.33	32.77	14.98	8,894	800-421-4225	Y

Category: Moderate Allocation (con't)

Fund Name	Ticker Symbol	RATINGS: Overall Rating	Reward Rating	Risk Rating	Recent Up/ Downgrade	TOTAL RETURNS & PERFORMANCE: 3-Month Total Return	6-Month Total Return	1-Year Total Return	3-Year Total Return	5-Year Total Return	ASSETS: NAV	Total Assets (MIL)	NEW INVESTORS: Telephone	Open to New Investors
American Funds Moderate Growth & Income Portfolio Cls R-4	RBAEX	B	C	A-	Up	2.96	12.53	6.21	28.48	34.84	15.01	8,894	800-421-4225	Y
American Funds Moderate Growth & Income Portfolio Cls R-5	RBAFX	B	C	A-	Up	3.02	12.64	6.51	29.61	36.76	15.04	8,894	800-421-4225	Y
American Funds Moderate Growth & Income Portfolio Cls R-5E	RGPFX	B	C	A-	Up	3.00	12.61	6.43	29.21	36.23	15.02	8,894	800-421-4225	Y
American Funds Moderate Growth & Income Portfolio Cls R-6	RBAGX	B	C	A-	Up	3.03	12.75	6.64	29.80	37.10	15.04	8,894	800-421-4225	Y
American Funds Retmnt Income Portfolio - Enhanced Cls A	NDARX	B	C	A-	Up	2.42	10.95	6.16	22.90		11.68	980.0	800-421-4225	Y
American Funds Retmnt Income Portfolio - Enhanced Cls C	NDCRX	B-	C	B+	Up	2.26	10.64	5.45	20.42		11.65	980.0	800-421-4225	Y
American Funds Retmnt Income Portfolio - Enhanced Cls F-1	FCFWX	B	C	A-	Up	2.41	11.02	6.22	22.85		11.69	980.0	800-421-4225	Y
American Funds Retmnt Income Portfolio - Enhanced Cls F-2	FGFWX	B	C	A-	Up	2.47	11.13	6.46	23.73		11.7	980.0	800-421-4225	Y
American Funds Retmnt Income Portfolio - Enhanced Cls F-3	FIEWX	B	C	A-	Up	2.50	11.19	6.58	23.70		11.69	980.0	800-421-4225	Y
American Funds Retmnt Income Portfolio - Enhanced Cls R-1	RCRPX	B-	C	A-	Up	2.22	10.53	5.48	21.04		11.66	980.0	800-421-4225	Y
American Funds Retmnt Income Portfolio - Enhanced Cls R-2	RFRPX	B-	C	A-	Up	2.25	10.69	5.67	21.11		11.64	980.0	800-421-4225	Y
American Funds Retmnt Income Portfolio - Enhanced Cls R-2E	RIRPX	B	C	A-	Up	2.31	10.76	6.07	23.28		11.7	980.0	800-421-4225	Y
American Funds Retmnt Income Portfolio - Enhanced Cls R-3	RLRPX	B-	C	A-	Up	2.38	10.87	5.92	21.84		11.67	980.0	800-421-4225	Y
American Funds Retmnt Income Portfolio - Enhanced Cls R-4	RPRPX	B	C	A-	Up	2.44	10.97	6.24	23.13		11.69	980.0	800-421-4225	Y
American Funds Retmnt Income Portfolio - Enhanced Cls R-5	RXRPX	B	C	A-	Up	2.50	11.15	6.50	23.74		11.71	980.0	800-421-4225	Y
American Funds Retmnt Income Portfolio - Enhanced Cls R-5E	RRQPX	B	C	A-	Up	2.55	11.10	6.40	23.76		11.7	980.0	800-421-4225	Y
American Funds Retmnt Income Portfolio - Enhanced Cls R-6	RVRPX	B	C	A-	Up	2.50	11.08	6.48	24.07		11.7	980.0	800-421-4225	Y
American Funds Retmnt Income Portfolio - Moderate Cls A	NBARX	B	C+	A-	Up	2.50	9.76	6.45	19.31		11.38	912.1	800-421-4225	Y
American Funds Retmnt Income Portfolio - Moderate Cls C	NBCRX	B-	C	B+	Up	2.23	9.35	5.64	16.80		11.33	912.1	800-421-4225	Y
American Funds Retmnt Income Portfolio - Moderate Cls F-1	FBFWX	B	C	A-	Up	2.47	9.73	6.40	19.17		11.38	912.1	800-421-4225	Y
American Funds Retmnt Income Portfolio - Moderate Cls F-2	FHFWX	B	C+	A-	Up	2.45	9.84	6.57	20.03		11.39	912.1	800-421-4225	Y
American Funds Retmnt Income Portfolio - Moderate Cls F-3	FIMWX	B	C+	A-		2.56	9.90	6.77	20.28		11.38	912.1	800-421-4225	Y
American Funds Retmnt Income Portfolio - Moderate Cls R-1	RBRPX	B-	C	B+	Up	2.26	9.27	5.67	16.89		11.37	912.1	800-421-4225	Y
American Funds Retmnt Income Portfolio - Moderate Cls R-2	RERPX	B-	C	B+		2.35	9.50	5.89	17.61		11.36	912.1	800-421-4225	Y
American Funds Retmnt Income Portfolio - Moderate Cls R-2E	RHRPX	B	C+	A-	Up	2.51	9.79	6.55	19.91		11.4	912.1	800-421-4225	Y
American Funds Retmnt Income Portfolio - Moderate Cls R-3	RKRPX	B-	C	A-		2.43	9.53	6.11	18.70		11.37	912.1	800-421-4225	Y
American Funds Retmnt Income Portfolio - Moderate Cls R-4	RNRPX	B	C	A-	Up	2.47	9.73	6.43	19.55		11.39	912.1	800-421-4225	Y
American Funds Retmnt Income Portfolio - Moderate Cls R-5	RRRPX	B	C+	A-	Up	2.54	9.80	6.64	19.95		11.4	912.1	800-421-4225	Y
American Funds Retmnt Income Portfolio - Moderate Cls R-5E	RRPPX	B	C+	A-	Up	2.52	9.80	6.57	20.03		11.39	912.1	800-421-4225	Y
American Funds Retmnt Income Portfolio - Moderate Cls R-6	RURPX	B	C+	A-		2.55	9.87	6.76	20.44		11.4	912.1	800-421-4225	Y
AMG Chicago Equity Partners Balanced Fund Class I	MBESX	B-	C	B+	Up	3.44	11.71	4.78	29.36	38.54	17.17	265.6	800-835-3879	Y
AMG Chicago Equity Partners Balanced Fund Class N	MBEAX	B-	C	B+	Up	3.38	11.62	4.60	28.65	37.29	16.99	265.6	800-835-3879	Y
AMG Chicago Equity Partners Balanced Fund Class Z	MBEYX	B-	C	B+	Up	3.46	11.77	4.87	29.65	39.03	17.16	265.6	800-835-3879	Y
AMG FQ Global Risk-Balanced Fund Class I	MMASX	B-	C	B+	Up	4.75	16.10	6.23	23.40	24.09	16.29	54.2	800-835-3879	Y
AMG FQ Global Risk-Balanced Fund Class N	MMAVX	B-	C	B	Up	4.71	16.02	6.01	22.23	21.93	16.22	54.2	800-835-3879	Y
AMG FQ Global Risk-Balanced Fund Class Z	MMAFX	B-	C	B+	Up	4.76	16.20	6.41	23.81	24.71	16.28	54.2	800-835-3879	Y
AQR Multi-Asset Fund Class I	AQRIX	B-	C	A-		3.96	14.38	7.92	22.87	20.23	9.7	181.9	203-742-3600	
AQR Multi-Asset Fund Class N	AQRNX	B-	C	A-		3.98	14.31	7.63	21.81	18.64	9.66	181.9	203-742-3600	
AQR Multi-Asset Fund Class R6	AQRRX	B-	C	A-		4.07	14.52	8.05	23.08	20.53	9.7	181.9	203-742-3600	Y
AQR Risk Parity II HV Fund Class I	QRHIX	B-	C+	B	Up	7.66	23.65	10.25	27.80	21.29	8.99	29.8	203-742-3600	Y
AQR Risk Parity II HV Fund Class N	QRHNX	B-	C+	B	Up	7.66	23.48	10.02	26.66	19.47	8.99	29.8	203-742-3600	Y
AQR Risk Parity II HV Fund Class R6	QRHRX	B-	B-	B	Up	7.79	23.65	10.34	28.13	21.60	8.99	29.8	203-742-3600	Y
AQR Risk Parity II MV Fund Class I	QRMIX	B	C+	A-	Up	5.18	15.54	7.60	19.52	17.18	9.74	109.6	203-742-3600	Y
AQR Risk Parity II MV Fund Class N	QRMNX	B	C+	A-	Up	5.22	15.39	7.34	18.69	15.71	9.67	109.6	203-742-3600	Y
AQR Risk Parity II MV Fund Class R6	QRMRX	B	C+	A-	Up	5.29	15.65	7.83	20.02	17.74	9.75	109.6	203-742-3600	Y
Astor Dynamic Allocation Fund Class A	ASTLX	B-	C	B	Up	2.30	14.42	2.72	26.06	29.05	13.41	223.9	877-738-0333	Y
Astor Dynamic Allocation Fund Class I	ASTIX	B-	C	B	Up	2.35	14.64	2.95	26.98	30.65	13.45	223.9	877-738-0333	Y
BlackRock 60/40 Target Allocation Fund Class K	BKGPX	B-	C	A-	Up	3.45	13.55	6.31	27.30	30.37	13.23	850.9	800-441-7762	Y
BlackRock 60/40 Target Allocation Fund Class R Shares	BRGPX	B-	C	B+	Up	3.27	13.21	5.71	25.25	27.95	12.96	850.9	800-441-7762	Y
BlackRock 60/40 Target Allocation Institutional Shares	BIGPX	B-	C	A-	Up	3.45	13.55	6.29	27.24	31.41	13.23	850.9	800-441-7762	Y
BlackRock 60/40 Target Allocation Fund Investor A Shares	BAGPX	B-	C	B+	Up	3.35	13.35	5.96	25.98	29.10	13	850.9	800-441-7762	Y
BlackRock 60/40 Target Allocation Fund Investor C Shares	BCGPX	B-	C	B+	Up	3.09	12.93	5.13	23.10	24.46	12.7	850.9	800-441-7762	Y

Category: Moderate Allocation (con't)

		RATINGS				TOTAL RETURNS & PERFORMANCE					ASSETS		NEW INVESTORS	
Fund Name	Ticker Symbol	Overall Rating	Reward Rating	Risk Rating	Recent Up/ Downgrade	3-Month Total Return	6-Month Total Return	1-Year Total Return	3-Year Total Return	5-Year Total Return	NAV	Total Assets (MIL)	Telephone	Open to New Investors
BlackRock Balanced Capital Fund Class K	MKCPX	B	C+	A-		3.56	14.99	8.71	37.24	45.85	23.32	1,207	800-441-7762	Y
BlackRock Balanced Capital Fund Class R	MRBPX	B	C+	A-	Up	3.36	14.61	7.96	34.46	41.08	21.25	1,207	800-441-7762	Y
BlackRock Balanced Capital Fund Institutional Shares	MACPX	B	C+	A-		3.56	14.99	8.68	37.08	45.68	23.31	1,207	800-441-7762	Y
BlackRock Balanced Capital Fund Investor A Shares	MDCPX	B	C+	A-	Up	3.44	14.79	8.30	35.83	43.53	23.2	1,207	800-441-7762	Y
BlackRock Balanced Capital Fund Investor C Shares	MCCPX	B	C+	A-	Up	3.26	14.35	7.52	32.78	38.19	19.98	1,207	800-441-7762	Y
BlackRock Global Allocation Fund, Inc. Class K	MKLOX	B-	C	B+	Up	2.88	11.14	4.13	21.91	18.75	19.24	26,928	800-441-7762	Y
BlackRock Global Allocation Fund, Inc. Class R	MRLOX	B-	C	B+	Up	2.66	10.75	3.36	19.42	14.87	18.12	26,928	800-441-7762	Y
BlackRock Global Allocation Fund, Inc. Inst Shares	MALOX	B-	C	B+	Up	2.88	11.08	4.05	21.59	18.44	19.24	26,928	800-441-7762	Y
BlackRock Global Allocation Fund, Inc. Investor A Shares	MDLOX	B-	C	B+	Up	2.79	10.91	3.72	20.64	16.81	19.1	26,928	800-441-7762	Y
BlackRock Multi-Asset Income Portfolio Class K	BKMIX	B	C+	A-		2.77	10.32	7.27	20.33	21.05	10.85	16,425	800-441-7762	Y
BlackRock Multi-Asset Income Portfolio Inst Shares	BIICX	B	C+	A-		2.66	10.19	7.22	20.08	20.80	10.85	16,425	800-441-7762	Y
BlackRock Multi-Asset Income Portfolio Investor A Shares	BAICX	B	C+	A-		2.60	10.05	6.95	19.19	19.30	10.84	16,425	800-441-7762	Y
BlackRock Multi-Asset Income Portfolio Investor C Shares	BCICX	B	C+	B+	Up	2.50	9.77	6.17	16.68	15.02	10.83	16,425	800-441-7762	Y
BMO Balanced Allocation Fund Class I	BGRHX	B-	C	A-	Up	2.76	12.49	4.94	27.28	27.35	8.55	301.9	800-236-3863	Y
BMO Balanced Allocation Fund Class R3	BGRRX	B-	C	B+	Up	2.51	12.20	4.45	25.33	24.07	8.55	301.9	800-236-3863	Y
BMO Balanced Allocation Fund Class R6	BGRQX	B-	C	A-	Up	2.76	12.63	5.19	27.78	28.29	8.56	301.9	800-236-3863	Y
BMO Balanced Allocation Fund Class Y	BGRYX	B-	C	A-	Up	2.52	12.36	4.64	26.13	25.64	8.54	301.9	800-236-3863	Y
BNY Mellon Asset Allocation Fund Class M	MPBLX	B-	C	B+	Up	3.01	13.54	3.80	29.76	29.98	12.33	465.1	800-645-6561	Y
BNY Mellon Asset Allocation Fund Investor Class	MIBLX	B-	C	B+	Up	3.02	13.46	3.60	28.79	28.48	12.43	465.1	800-645-6561	Y
BNY Mellon Balanced Opportunity Fund - Class A	DBOAX	B-	C	B+		3.47	12.99	6.23	29.84	35.28	22.33	315.4		Y
BNY Mellon Balanced Opportunity Fund - Class C	DBOCX	B-	C	B+	Up	3.33	12.56	5.44	26.96	30.30	22.32	315.4		Y
BNY Mellon Balanced Opportunity Fund - Class J	THPBX	B-	C	A-		3.56	13.11	6.46	30.81	37.00	22.39	315.4		
BNY Mellon Balanced Opportunity Fund - Class Y	DBOYX	B-	C	A-		3.51	13.06	6.47	30.85	37.03	22.37	315.4		Y
BNY Mellon Balanced Opportunity Fund - Class Z	DBOZX	B-	C	A-		3.53	13.07	6.38	30.50	36.50	22.24	315.4		
BNY Mellon Balanced Opportunity Fund- Class I	DBORX	B-	C	A-		3.57	13.13	6.52	30.84	37.04	22.28	315.4		Y
Bruce Fund	BRUFX	B-	C	B		3.00	13.12	8.81	17.96	27.46	555	521.1		Y
Calvert Balanced Fund Class A	CSIFX	B	C+	A-		4.77	16.30	10.96	31.45	36.17	33.63	785.2	301-951-4881	Y
Calvert Balanced Fund Class C	CSGCX	B	C+	A-		4.57	15.88	10.12	28.43	30.97	32.52	785.2	301-951-4881	Y
Calvert Balanced Fund Class I	CBAIX	B	B-	A-		4.82	16.45	11.26	32.76	38.72	34.31	785.2	301-951-4881	Y
Calvert Balanced Fund Class R6	CBARX	B	C+	A-		4.85	16.42	11.07	31.59	36.31	34.32	785.2	301-951-4881	Y
Calvert Moderate Allocation Fund Class A	CMAAX	B	C+	A-	Up	3.45	14.17	7.50	31.76	34.10	19.39	325.1	301-951-4881	Y
Calvert Moderate Allocation Fund Class C	CMACX	B-	C	A-	Up	3.27	13.72	6.71	28.81	29.15	18.42	325.1	301-951-4881	Y
Catalyst/MAP Global Balanced Fund Class A	TRXAX	B	C	A	Up	1.91	8.25	4.28	19.39	18.61	11.65	23.4	866-447-4228	Y
Catalyst/MAP Global Balanced Fund Class C	TRXCX	B-	C	A-	Up	1.67	7.81	3.44	16.71	14.22	11.52	23.4	866-447-4228	Y
Catalyst/MAP Global Balanced Fund Class I	TRXIX	B	C	A	Up	1.97	8.46	4.54	20.38	20.39	11.67	23.4	866-447-4228	Y
Cavanal Hill Active Core Fund Class A	AABAX	B	C	A-	Up	2.92	12.05	6.08	23.14	29.24	13.36	47.4		Y
Cavanal Hill Active Core Fund Class C	AACBX	B-	C	A-	Up	2.83	11.76	5.42	20.63	24.81	13.36	47.4		Y
Cavanal Hill Active Core Fund Institutional Class	AIBLX	B	C	A-	Up	3.06	12.33	6.48	24.36	31.22	13.44	47.4		Y
Cavanal Hill Active Core Fund Investor Class	APBAX	B	C	A-	Up	2.93	12.14	6.22	23.40	29.83	13.4	47.4		Y
Charter Growth Portfolio Class B		B-	C	B+	Up	2.54	12.86	3.38	27.51	19.05	10.94	18.2	877-222-2144	Y
Charter Moderate Growth Portfolio Class B		B-	C	A-	Up	2.53	11.55	3.96	24.38	18.88	10.96	33.7	877-222-2144	Y
CIBC Atlas Income Opportunities Fund Institutional Class	AWIIX	B	C+	A-		4.11	15.07	10.77	35.22	39.40	12.06	404.1	312-368-7700	Y
Cohen & Steers REIT & Preferred Income Fund	RNP	B-	B	C+	Up	4.13	20.85	14.47	24.44	57.33	23.25	1,106	212-832-3232	Y
Columbia Adaptive Risk Allocation Fund Advisor Class	CARRX	B	C	A		3.00	12.50	7.05	23.74	25.77	10.98	2,996	800-345-6611	Y
Columbia Adaptive Risk Allocation Fund Class A	CRAAX	B	C	A		2.93	12.30	6.73	22.70	24.06	10.86	2,996	800-345-6611	Y
Columbia Adaptive Risk Allocation Fund Class C	CRACX	B	C	A-	Up	2.75	11.88	5.90	20.06	19.55	10.45	2,996	800-345-6611	Y
Columbia Adaptive Risk Allocation Fund Class R	CRKRX	B	C	A-	Up	2.97	12.22	6.52	21.95	22.64	10.74	2,996	800-345-6611	Y
Columbia Adaptive Risk Allocation Institutional 2 Cls	CRDRX	B	C	A		2.99	12.37	6.92	23.62	25.91	10.99	2,996	800-345-6611	Y
Columbia Adaptive Risk Allocation Institutional 3 Cls	CARYX	B	C	A		2.98	12.44	7.03	24.00	26.17	11.02	2,996	800-345-6611	Y
Columbia Adaptive Risk Allocation Fund Institutional Class	CRAZX	B	C	A		3.00	12.39	6.95	23.63	25.66	10.97	2,996	800-345-6611	Y
Columbia Balanced Fund Advisor Class	CBDRX	B-	C	A-		4.02	14.68	8.79	27.91	39.41	42.18	6,831	800-345-6611	Y
Columbia Balanced Fund Class A	CBLAX	B-	C	B+	Up	3.91	14.51	8.51	26.93	37.66	41.85	6,831	800-345-6611	Y

Category: Moderate Allocation (con't)

Fund Name	Ticker Symbol	RATINGS: Overall Rating	Reward Rating	Risk Rating	Recent Up/ Downgrade	TOTAL RETURNS & PERFORMANCE: 3-Month Total Return	6-Month Total Return	1-Year Total Return	3-Year Total Return	5-Year Total Return	ASSETS: NAV	Total Assets (MIL)	NEW INVESTORS: Telephone	Open to New Investors
Columbia Balanced Fund Class C	CBLCX	B-	C	B+	Up	3.73	14.07	7.70	24.10	32.60	41.75	6,831	800-345-6611	Y
Columbia Balanced Fund Class R	CBLRX	B-	C	B+	Up	3.84	14.37	8.24	25.99	35.96	41.86	6,831	800-345-6611	Y
Columbia Balanced Fund Institutional 2 Class	CLREX	B-	C	A-		3.99	14.68	8.83	28.09	39.91	41.79	6,831	800-345-6611	Y
Columbia Balanced Fund Institutional 3 Class	CBDYX	B-	C	A-		4.02	14.70	8.87	28.28	40.23	42.18	6,831	800-345-6611	Y
Columbia Balanced Fund Institutional Class	CBALX	B-	C	A-		4.01	14.65	8.80	27.91	39.40	41.77	6,831	800-345-6611	Y
Columbia Capital Alloc Moderate Aggressive Port Adv Cls	CGBRX	B-	C	B+	Up	3.25	14.55	5.14	31.57	36.04	12.19	2,027	800-345-6611	Y
Columbia Capital Alloc Moderate Aggressive Port Cls A	NBIAX	B-	C	B+	Up	3.22	14.35	4.84	30.55	34.45	12.08	2,027	800-345-6611	Y
Columbia Capital Alloc Moderate Aggressive Port Cls C	NBICX	B-	C	B+	Up	3.02	13.89	4.03	27.71	29.37	12.11	2,027	800-345-6611	Y
Columbia Capital Alloc Moderate Aggressive Port Cls R	CLBRX	B-	C	B+	Up	3.16	14.22	4.57	29.71	32.81	12.07	2,027	800-345-6611	Y
Columbia Capital Alloc Moderate Aggressive Port Cls V	CGGTX	B-	C	B+	Up	3.22	14.35	4.84	30.55	34.43	12.08	2,027	800-345-6611	
Columbia Capital Alloc Moderate Aggressive Port Inst 2 Cls	CLHRX	B-	C	B+	Up	3.35	14.59	5.20	31.84	36.61	12.18	2,027	800-345-6611	Y
Columbia Capital Alloc Moderate Aggressive Port Inst 3 Cls	CPHNX	B-	C	B+	Up	3.36	14.60	5.30	32.07	36.96	11.88	2,027	800-345-6611	Y
Columbia Capital Alloc Moderate Aggressive Port Inst Cls	NBGPX	B-	C	B+	Up	3.29	14.52	5.11	31.61	36.12	12.05	2,027	800-345-6611	Y
Columbia Global Opportunities Fund Advisor Class	CSDRX	B-	C	A-	Up	3.04	11.45	3.30	24.62	24.20	14.2	559.2	800-345-6611	Y
Columbia Global Opportunities Fund Class A	IMRFX	B-	C	A-	Up	2.92	11.22	2.98	23.61	22.67	14.07	559.2	800-345-6611	Y
Columbia Global Opportunities Fund Class R	CSARX	B-	C	B+	Up	2.88	11.18	2.81	22.74	21.08	13.92	559.2	800-345-6611	Y
Columbia Global Opportunities Fund Institutional 2 Class	CLNRX	B-	C	A-	Up	2.96	11.42	3.26	24.79	24.68	14.24	559.2	800-345-6611	Y
Columbia Global Opportunities Fund Institutional 3 Class	CGOYX	B-	C	A-	Up	2.97	11.39	3.31	24.48	23.54	14.18	559.2	800-345-6611	Y
Columbia Global Opportunities Fund Institutional Class	CSAZX	B-	C	A-	Up	2.98	11.40	3.24	24.59	24.28	14.16	559.2	800-345-6611	Y
Columbia Multi-Asset Income Fund Advisor Class	CLNFX	B-	C	B+	Up	3.06	12.37	5.61	17.31		9.44	151.8	800-345-6611	Y
Columbia Multi-Asset Income Fund Class A	CLNAX	B-	C	B+	Up	3.00	12.23	5.34	16.54		9.44	151.8	800-345-6611	Y
Columbia Multi-Asset Income Fund Institutional 2 Class	CLNVX	B-	C	B+	Up	3.07	12.27	5.65	17.45		9.44	151.8	800-345-6611	Y
Columbia Multi-Asset Income Fund Institutional 3 Class	CMUYX	B-	C	B+	Up	3.10	12.33	5.73	17.62		9.42	151.8	800-345-6611	Y
Columbia Multi-Asset Income Fund Institutional Class	CLNZX	B-	C	B+	Up	3.06	12.24	5.60	17.28		9.44	151.8	800-345-6611	Y
CornerCap Balanced Fund	CBLFX	B-	C	B+	Up	1.96	11.70	3.68	25.06	23.31	14.03	34.1	888-813-8637	Y
Davenport Balanced Income Fund	DBALX	B-	C	B+	Up	2.57	11.27	5.75	18.44		11.56	148.8		Y
Delaware Strategic Allocation Class A	DFBAX	B-	C	B+	Up	1.72	9.94	2.98	21.00	20.17	10.63	266.4		Y
Delaware Strategic Allocation Class C	DFBCX	B-	C	B+	Up	1.53	9.41	2.21	18.24	15.55	10.63	266.4		Y
Delaware Strategic Allocation Class R	DFBRX	B-	C	B+	Up	1.67	9.73	2.80	20.05	18.49	10.58	266.4		Y
Delaware Strategic Allocation Institutional Class	DFFIX	B-	C	B+	Up	1.78	10.06	3.32	21.85	21.58	10.64	266.4		Y
Delaware Wealth Builder Fund Class A	DDIAX	B-	C	B	Up	2.00	10.83	4.45	16.13	20.03	13.59	530.2		Y
Delaware Wealth Builder Fund Institutional Class	DDIIX	B-	C	B+	Up	2.07	10.98	4.72	17.01	21.56	13.59	530.2		Y
DFA Global Allocation 60/40 Portfolio Class R2	DFPRX	B-	C	A-	Up	2.69	11.75	3.95	25.48	24.28	18.33	4,253	512-306-7400	Y
DFA Global Allocation 60/40 Portfolio Institutional Class	DGSIX	B-	C	A-	Up	2.71	11.91	4.14	26.30	25.75	18.2	4,253	512-306-7400	Y
Dodge & Cox Balanced Fund	DODBX	B-	C	A-		2.68	11.25	5.57	36.68	37.98	99.55	14,775	415-981-1710	Y
DWS Global Income Builder Fund - Class A	KTRAX	B-	C	A-	Up	3.15	13.94	6.61	28.82	20.93	9.37	747.7		Y
DWS Global Income Builder Fund - Class C	KTRCX	B-	C	B+	Up	3.07	13.51	5.80	25.80	16.24	9.37	747.7		Y
DWS Global Income Builder Fund - Class Inst	KTRIX	B	C+	A-	Up	3.22	13.97	6.87	29.61	22.29	9.35	747.7		Y
DWS Global Income Builder Fund - Class R6	KTRZX	B	C+	A-	Up	3.24	14.02	6.98	30.09	22.42	9.35	747.7		Y
DWS Global Income Builder Fund - Class S	KTRSX	B	C+	A-	Up	3.32	14.06	6.84	29.63	22.19	9.37	747.7		Y
DWS Multi-Asset Moderate Allocation Fund - Class A	PLUSX	B-	C	B+	Up	2.87	12.85	4.16	24.50	19.94	9.66	27.8		Y
DWS Multi-Asset Moderate Allocation Fund - Class C	PLSCX	B-	C	B+	Up	2.66	12.48	3.37	21.69	15.48	9.64	27.8		Y
DWS Multi-Asset Moderate Allocation Fund - Class S	PPLSX	B-	C	B+	Up	2.87	12.99	4.44	25.35	21.42	9.65	27.8		Y
DWS RREEF Real Assets Fund - Class A	AAAAX	B	C+	A-		2.22	15.69	7.48	20.00	14.13	10.14	541.6		Y
DWS RREEF Real Assets Fund - Class C	AAAPX	B-	C	B+		2.04	15.22	6.60	17.27	9.81	10.06	541.6		Y
DWS RREEF Real Assets Fund - Class Inst	AAAZX	B	C+	A-		2.30	15.90	7.82	20.90	15.86	10.06	541.6		Y
DWS RREEF Real Assets Fund - Class R	AAAQX	B-	C	A-	Down	2.16	15.53	7.17	18.99	12.77	10.2	541.6		Y
DWS RREEF Real Assets Fund - Class R6	AAAVX	B	C+	A-		2.30	15.77	7.71	20.89	15.85	10.06	541.6		Y
DWS RREEF Real Assets Fund - Class S	AAASX	B	C+	A-		2.27	15.87	7.69	20.56	14.96	10.06	541.6		Y
DWS RREEF Real Assets Fund - Class T	AAAWX	B	C+	A-		2.22	15.69	7.59	20.14	14.64	10.14	541.6		Y
Eaton Vance Balanced Fund Class A	EVIFX	B	C+	A-		4.87	16.25	10.55	29.56	39.22	9.5	885.8		Y
Eaton Vance Balanced Fund Class B	EMIFX	B	C	A-	Up	4.56	15.75	9.60	26.60	33.96	9.54	885.8		

Category: Moderate Allocation (con't)

Fund Name	Ticker Symbol	RATINGS: Overall Rating	Reward Rating	Risk Rating	Recent Up/ Downgrade	TOTAL RETURNS & PERFORMANCE: 3-Month Total Return	6-Month Total Return	1-Year Total Return	3-Year Total Return	5-Year Total Return	ASSETS: NAV	Total Assets (MIL)	NEW INVESTORS: Telephone	Open to New Investors
Eaton Vance Balanced Fund Class C	ECIFX	B	C	A-	Up	4.65	15.88	9.67	26.54	34.15	9.54	885.8		Y
Eaton Vance Balanced Fund Class I	EIIFX	B	C+	A-		4.82	16.40	10.71	30.37	40.92	9.5	885.8		Y
Eaton Vance Balanced Fund Class R	ERIFX	B	C+	A-	Up	4.72	16.05	10.24	28.56	37.63	9.47	885.8		Y
Eaton Vance Balanced Fund Class R6	ESIFX	B	C+	A-		4.83	16.41	10.75	30.60	40.43	9.5	885.8		Y
Eaton Vance Global Income Builder Fund Class A	EDIAX	B-	C	B+	Up	3.64	14.86	5.84	26.67	26.76	9.09	302.5		Y
Eaton Vance Global Income Builder Fund Class C	EDICX	B-	C	B+	Up	3.37	14.48	4.99	23.88	22.15	8.99	302.5		Y
Eaton Vance Global Income Builder Fund Class I	EDIIX	B-	C	B+	Up	3.71	15.04	6.14	27.74	28.60	9.08	302.5		Y
Eaton Vance Global Income Builder Fund Class R	EDIRX	B-	C	B+	Up	3.59	14.78	5.47	25.62	25.14	9.06	302.5		Y
Elfun Diversified Fund	ELDFX	B	C	A-	Up	3.40	12.92	6.94	28.10	28.78	19.13	194.8	617-664-7338	Y
EQ/AB Dynamic Growth Portfolio Class IB		B-	C	B+	Up	1.47	4.92	-0.40	21.51			694.6	877-222-2144	Y
EQ/AB Dynamic Moderate Growth Portfolio Class IB		B-	C	B+	Up	1.33	4.69	0.21	19.29	21.63		2,674	877-222-2144	Y
EQ/Balanced Strategy Fund Class IA		B-	C	A-	Up	2.60	10.23	4.59	21.42	23.15	15.78	3,544	877-222-2144	Y
EQ/Balanced Strategy Fund Class IB		B-	C	A-	Up	2.60	10.21	4.59	21.47	23.12	15.8	3,544	877-222-2144	Y
EQ/Franklin Balanced Managed Volatility Portfolio Class IA		B-	C	A-		1.49	4.59	3.30	21.96	23.77		1,145	877-222-2144	Y
EQ/Franklin Balanced Managed Volatility Portfolio Class IB		B-	C	A-		1.58	4.68	3.39	22.07	23.88		1,145	877-222-2144	Y
EQ/Franklin Balanced Managed Volatility Portfolio Class K		B-	C	A-		1.58	4.77	3.57	22.88	25.35		1,145	877-222-2144	Y
EQ/Goldman Sachs Moderate Growth Alloc Port Cls IB		B-	C	B+	Up	1.90	5.37	2.29	18.64			582.5	877-222-2144	Y
EQ/Moderate Allocation Portfolio Class K		B-	C	A-	Up	2.73	10.45	4.67	22.86	23.01	14.31	7,296	877-222-2144	Y
EQ/Moderate Growth Strategy Fund Class IB		B-	C	A-	Up	2.72	11.50	4.41	25.46	26.73	17.43	7,250	877-222-2144	Y
EQ/Premier VIP Moderate Allocation Fund Class A		B-	C	A-	Up	2.66	10.30	4.39	21.86	21.40	14.29	7,296	877-222-2144	Y
EQ/Premier VIP Moderate Allocation Fund Class B		B-	C	A-	Up	2.61	10.31	4.35	21.86	21.37	14.17	7,296	877-222-2144	Y
E-Valuator Moderate (50%-70%) RMS Fund R4 Class Shares	EVFMX	B-	C	B	Up	3.28	14.46	3.99	26.81	29.86	10.68	173.9	888-507-2798	Y
E-Valuator Moderate (50%-70%) RMS Service Cls Shares	EVMLX	B-	C	B	Up	3.39	14.62	4.22	27.99	31.07	10.66	173.9	888-507-2798	Y
Eventide Multi-Asset Income Fund Class I	ETIMX	B-	C+	B	Up	3.57	13.34	6.81	19.70		10.9	111.5		Y
Federated MDT Balanced Fund Class A Shares	QABGX	B-	C	B+		3.09	14.27	7.07	33.48	33.60	18.65	160.1	800-341-7400	Y
Federated MDT Balanced Fund Class C Shares	QCBGX	B-	C	B+	Up	2.90	13.88	6.24	30.48	28.62	18.45	160.1	800-341-7400	Y
Federated MDT Balanced Fund Class R6 Shares	QKBGX	B-	C	B+		3.20	14.46	7.30	34.34	33.81	18.67	160.1	800-341-7400	Y
Federated MDT Balanced Fund Institutional Shares	QIBGX	B-	C	B+		3.14	14.43	7.34	34.48	35.18	18.71	160.1	800-341-7400	Y
Fidelity Advisor Asset Manager® 60% Fund Class A	FSAAX	B-	C	B+	Up	3.02	12.91	4.08	26.91	28.15	12.59	3,051	617-563-7000	Y
Fidelity Advisor Asset Manager® 60% Fund Class C	FSCNX	B-	C	B+	Up	2.91	12.56	3.34	24.25	23.48	12.36	3,051	617-563-7000	Y
Fidelity Advisor Asset Manager® 60% Fund Class M	FSATX	B-	C	B+	Up	3.04	12.79	3.78	26.10	26.57	12.52	3,051	617-563-7000	Y
Fidelity Advisor Asset Manager® 60% Fund Class Z	FIQAX	B-	C	B+	Up	3.26	13.23	4.46	28.30	30.38	12.66	3,051	617-563-7000	Y
Fidelity Advisor Asset Manager® 60% Fund I Class	FSNIX	B-	C	B+	Up	3.09	13.13	4.32	28.02	29.99	12.66	3,051	617-563-7000	Y
Fidelity Advisor Asset Manager® 70% Fund Class A	FAASX	B-	C	B+	Up	3.17	14.21	3.59	30.63	30.70	22.1	5,301	617-563-7000	Y
Fidelity Advisor Asset Manager® 70% Fund Class C	FCASX	B-	C	B	Up	3.00	13.83	2.86	27.72	25.83	21.97	5,301	617-563-7000	Y
Fidelity Advisor Asset Manager® 70% Fund Class M	FTASX	B-	C	B+	Up	3.12	14.09	3.34	29.67	29.05	22.1	5,301	617-563-7000	Y
Fidelity Advisor Asset Manager® 70% Fund Class Z	FIQBX	B-	C	B+	Up	3.26	14.48	3.99	32.01	32.80	22.13	5,301	617-563-7000	Y
Fidelity Advisor Asset Manager® 70% Fund I Class	FAAIX	B-	C	B+	Up	3.26	14.41	3.89	31.73	32.48	22.15	5,301	617-563-7000	Y
Fidelity Advisor® Balanced Fund Class A	FABLX	B-	C	B+		3.60	15.03	6.17	33.87	40.98	21.19	3,732	617-563-7000	Y
Fidelity Advisor® Balanced Fund Class C	FABCX	B-	C	B+	Up	3.37	14.64	5.37	30.89	35.81	21.01	3,732	617-563-7000	Y
Fidelity Advisor® Balanced Fund Class M	FAIGX	B-	C	B+	Up	3.49	14.88	5.87	32.91	39.27	21.44	3,732	617-563-7000	Y
Fidelity Advisor® Balanced Fund Class Z	FZAAX	B-	C	B+		3.70	15.31	6.57	35.44	43.86	21.65	3,732	617-563-7000	Y
Fidelity Advisor® Balanced Fund I Class	FAIOX	B-	C	B+		3.62	15.22	6.45	34.95	42.85	21.64	3,732	617-563-7000	Y
Fidelity Asset Manager® 60% Fund	FSANX	B-	C	B+	Up	3.18	13.14	4.37	28.19	30.26	12.65	3,051	617-563-7000	Y
Fidelity Asset Manager® 70% Fund	FASGX	B-	C	B+	Up	3.31	14.47	3.95	31.95	32.74	22.15	5,301	617-563-7000	Y
Fidelity® Balanced Fund	FBALX	B-	C	B+		3.69	15.41	6.61	35.28	43.39	23.6	33,544	617-563-7000	Y
Fidelity® Balanced Fund Class K	FBAKX	B-	C+	B+		3.66	15.43	6.71	35.64	44.04	23.6	33,544	617-563-7000	Y
Fidelity® Puritan® Fund	FPURX	B-	C	B+	Up	3.34	14.06	5.24	34.96	43.30	22.12	27,345	617-563-7000	Y
Fidelity® Puritan® Fund Class K	FPUKX	B-	C	B+	Up	3.36	14.15	5.34	35.35	44.02	22.11	27,345	617-563-7000	Y
First Eagle Global Income Builder Fund Class A	FEBAX	B-	C	A-	Up	2.40	10.28	3.91	21.69	16.43	12.04	1,501	800-334-2143	Y
First Eagle Global Income Builder Fund Class C	FEBCX	B-	C	B+	Up	2.13	9.81	3.06	18.94	12.05	12	1,501	800-334-2143	Y
First Eagle Global Income Builder Fund Class I	FEBIX	B-	C	A-	Up	2.47	10.45	4.10	22.68	17.92	12.01	1,501	800-334-2143	Y

Category: Moderate Allocation (con't)

		RATINGS				TOTAL RETURNS & PERFORMANCE					ASSETS		NEW INVESTORS	
Fund Name	Ticker Symbol	Overall Rating	Reward Rating	Risk Rating	Recent Up/ Downgrade	3-Month Total Return	6-Month Total Return	1-Year Total Return	3-Year Total Return	5-Year Total Return	NAV	Total Assets (MIL)	Telephone	Open to New Investors
First Eagle Global Income Builder Fund Class R3	FBRRX	B-	C	A-	Up	2.27	10.15	3.63	21.25	15.73	12.01	1,501	800-334-2143	Y
First Eagle Global Income Builder Fund Class R6	FEBRX	B-	C	A-	Up	2.47	10.37	4.13	22.78	18.02	12	1,501	800-334-2143	Y
First Investors Total Return Fund Advisor Class	FITUX	B-	C	B+	Up	4.51	13.64	6.96	23.17	25.01	18.9	881.0	800-423-4026	Y
First Investors Total Return Fund Institutional Class	FITVX	B-	C	B+	Up	4.47	13.74	7.13	23.49	25.39	18.94	881.0	800-423-4026	Y
First Investors Total Return Series Class A	FITRX	B-	C	B+	Up	4.37	13.49	6.69	21.98	22.86	18.8	881.0	800-423-4026	Y
First Investors Total Return Series Class B	FBTRX	B-	C	B	Up	2.69	9.67	2.45	16.91	16.97		850.2	800-423-4026	Y
FPA Crescent Fund	FPACX	B-	C	B+	Up	3.33	14.80	6.69	30.24	28.22	33.19	14,445	800-982-4372	Y
Franklin Managed Income Fund Advisor Class	FBFZX	B	C+	A		2.97	11.84	8.96	26.74	30.11	12.57	3,561	650-312-2000	Y
Franklin Managed Income Fund Class A	FBLAX	B	C+	A		2.92	11.74	8.72	25.78	28.41	12.54	3,561	650-312-2000	Y
Franklin Managed Income Fund Class C	FBMCX	B	C+	A-		2.68	11.37	7.93	22.96	23.85	12.42	3,561	650-312-2000	Y
Franklin Managed Income Fund Class R	FBFQX	B	C+	A		2.85	11.67	8.52	24.85	26.91	12.58	3,561	650-312-2000	Y
Franklin Managed Income Fund Class R6	FBFRX	B	C+	A		2.99	11.88	9.14	27.20	30.94	12.58	3,561	650-312-2000	Y
Franklin Moderate Allocation Fund Advisor Class	FMTZX	B	C	A-	Up	2.70	12.57	6.25	28.75	27.81	15.6	1,895	650-312-2000	Y
Franklin Moderate Allocation Fund Class A	FMTIX	B	C	A-	Up	2.63	12.45	6.05	27.82	26.18	15.59	1,895	650-312-2000	Y
Franklin Moderate Allocation Fund Class C	FTMTX	B-	C	A-	Up	2.45	12.00	5.19	24.95	21.55	15.12	1,895	650-312-2000	Y
Franklin Moderate Allocation Fund Class R	FTMRX	B-	C	A-	Up	2.57	12.27	5.76	26.79	24.62	15.56	1,895	650-312-2000	Y
Franklin Moderate Allocation Fund Class R6		B	C	A-	Up	2.66	12.56	6.32	29.07	28.38	15.58	1,895	650-312-2000	Y
Franklin NextStep Moderate Fund Advisor Class	FNMZX	B-	C	A-	Up	3.02	12.31	5.88	23.56		11.97	12.5	650-312-2000	Y
Franklin NextStep Moderate Fund Class A	FNMDX	B-	C	A-	Up	2.97	12.13	5.55	22.52		11.94	12.5	650-312-2000	Y
Franklin NextStep Moderate Fund Class C	FNMFX	B-	C	B+	Up	2.74	11.67	4.78	19.83		11.85	12.5	650-312-2000	Y
FundX Conservative Upgrader Fund	RELAX	B-	C	B+	Up	2.94	13.08	5.31	27.81	30.98	39.54	54.4	866-455-3863	Y
George Putnam Balanced Fund Class A	PGEOX	B	C+	A-		4.67	15.73	10.10	35.29	42.42	20.37	1,292	617-292-1000	Y
George Putnam Balanced Fund Class B	PGEBX	B	C+	A-		4.53	15.30	9.31	32.30	37.19	20.14	1,292	617-292-1000	Y
George Putnam Balanced Fund Class C	PGPCX	B	C+	A-		4.49	15.30	9.25	32.27	37.21	20.21	1,292	617-292-1000	Y
George Putnam Balanced Fund Class M	PGEMX	B	C+	A-		4.57	15.46	9.59	33.30	38.95	20.07	1,292	617-292-1000	Y
George Putnam Balanced Fund Class R	PGPRX	B	C+	A-		4.63	15.60	9.82	34.27	40.68	20.3	1,292	617-292-1000	Y
George Putnam Balanced Fund Class R5	PGELX	B	C+	A-		4.80	15.96	10.46	36.54	44.54	20.56	1,292	617-292-1000	Y
George Putnam Balanced Fund Class R6	PGEJX	B	C+	A-		4.80	15.98	10.51	36.76	45.05	20.46	1,292	617-292-1000	Y
George Putnam Balanced Fund Class Y	PGEYX	B	C+	A-		4.72	15.86	10.39	36.29	44.24	20.45	1,292	617-292-1000	Y
GMO Implementation Fund	GIMFX	B-	C	B+	Up	1.88	8.00	3.88	20.37	10.59	13.5	8,451	617-330-7500	Y
GMO Strategic Opportunities Allocation Fund Class III	GBATX	B-	C	B+	Up	2.54	11.70	4.21	25.74	16.37	20.13	913.5	617-330-7500	Y
Goldman Sachs Balanced Strategy Portfolio Class A	GIPAX	B-	C	B+	Up	2.95	10.54	4.99	17.69	16.59	11.31	517.7	800-526-7384	Y
Goldman Sachs Balanced Strategy Portfolio Class P	GAOPX	B-	C	A-	Up	3.05	10.75	5.40	18.91	18.74	11.31	517.7	800-526-7384	Y
Goldman Sachs Balanced Strategy Portfolio Class R	GIPRX	B-	C	B+	Up	2.90	10.45	4.75	16.74	15.32	11.27	517.7	800-526-7384	Y
Goldman Sachs Balanced Strategy Portfolio Class R6	GIPUX	B-	C	A-	Up	3.05	10.75	5.41	19.03	18.87	11.31	517.7	800-526-7384	Y
Goldman Sachs Balanced Strategy Portfolio Inst Cls	GIPIX	B-	C	A-	Up	3.05	10.74	5.40	18.99	18.83	11.31	517.7	800-526-7384	Y
Goldman Sachs Balanced Strategy Portfolio Investor Class	GIPTX	B-	C	A-	Up	3.03	10.61	5.27	18.55	18.03	11.26	517.7	800-526-7384	Y
Goldman Sachs Balanced Strategy Portfolio Service Class	GIPSX	B-	C	B+	Up	2.89	10.46	4.90	17.19	16.74	11.44	517.7	800-526-7384	Y
Goldman Sachs Growth and Income Strategy Portfolio Class A	GOIAX	B-	C	B+	Up	2.88	12.20	3.63	24.18	21.30	13.65	898.0	800-526-7384	Y
Goldman Sachs Growth and Income Strategy Portfolio Class P	GGSPX	B-	C	B+	Up	3.05	12.46	4.11	25.60	23.68	13.69	898.0	800-526-7384	Y
Goldman Sachs Growth and Income Strategy Portfolio Class R	GPIRX	B-	C	B+	Up	2.92	12.08	3.40	23.22	19.73	13.55	898.0	800-526-7384	Y
Goldman Sachs Growth & Income Strategy Portfolio Cls R6	GOIUX	B-	C	B+	Up	3.05	12.46	4.03	25.62	23.70	13.69	898.0	800-526-7384	Y
Goldman Sachs Growth & Income Strategy Portfolio Inst Cls	GOIIX	B-	C	B+	Up	3.12	12.54	4.09	25.66	23.73	13.7	898.0	800-526-7384	Y
Goldman Sachs Growth & Income Strategy Portfolio Inv Cls	GPITX	B-	C	B+	Up	3.03	12.39	3.90	25.16	22.87	13.59	898.0	800-526-7384	Y
Goldman Sachs Growth & Inc Strategy Port Serv Cls	GOISX	B-	C	B+	Up	2.93	12.17	3.51	23.73	20.63	13.62	898.0	800-526-7384	Y
Goldman Sachs Satellite Strategies Portfolio Class P	GMFPX	B-	C	B	Up	2.64	13.37	5.55	18.71	12.90	8.22	364.7	800-526-7384	Y
Goldman Sachs Satellite Strategies Portfolio Class R6	GXSUX	B-	C	B	Up	2.64	13.53	5.55	18.74	13.09	8.22	364.7	800-526-7384	Y
Goldman Sachs Satellite Strategies Portfolio Inst Cls	GXSIX	B-	C	B	Up	2.64	13.38	5.54	18.69	12.88	8.21	364.7	800-526-7384	Y
Goldman Sachs Satellite Strategies Portfolio Investor Cls	GXSTX	B-	C	B	Up	2.72	13.44	5.51	18.30	12.16	8.22	364.7	800-526-7384	Y
Goldman Sachs Tactical Tilt Overlay Fund Class P	GSLPX	B-	C	B+		0.40	5.82	3.20	8.65		9.81	3,298	312-362-3000	Y
Goldman Sachs Tactical Tilt Overlay Institutional Shares	TTIFX	B-	C	B+		0.49	5.98	3.27	8.73		10.1	3,298	800-526-7384	Y
Great-West Moderate Profile Fund Class L	MXGPX	B-	C	A-	Up	2.36	11.29	3.73	24.81	26.31	10.48	1,632		Y

Category: Moderate Allocation (con't)

Fund Name	Ticker Symbol	RATINGS: Overall Rating	Reward Rating	Risk Rating	Recent Up/ Downgrade	TOTAL RETURNS & PERFORMANCE: 3-Month Total Return	6-Month Total Return	1-Year Total Return	3-Year Total Return	5-Year Total Return	ASSETS: NAV	Total Assets (MIL)	NEW INVESTORS: Telephone	Open to New Investors
Great-West Moderate Profile Fund Institutional Class	MXITX	B-	C	A-	Up	2.47	11.65	4.37	27.07	29.75	9.95	1,632		Y
Great-West Moderate Profile Fund Investor Class	MXMPX	B-	C	A-	Up	2.37	11.48	3.97	25.73	27.89	6.86	1,632		Y
Great-West SecureFoundation® Balanced ETF Fund Class A	SFBPX	B-	C	A-	Up	2.89	12.29	4.93	27.41	30.68	13.58	34.2		Y
Great-West SecureFoundation® Balanced Fund Class L	MXLDX	B-	C	A-	Up	2.67	11.42	4.16	25.45	28.26	11.87	934.0		Y
Great-West SecureFoundation® Balanced Institutional Cls	MXCJX	B-	C	A-		2.77	11.71	4.79	27.79	31.84	9.69	934.0		Y
Great-West SecureFoundation® Balanced Fund Investor Class	MXSBX	B-	C	A-	Up	2.65	11.50	4.39	26.34	29.79	13.55	934.0		Y
Great-West SecureFoundation® Balanced Fund Service Class	MXSHX	B-	C	A-	Up	2.66	11.47	4.31	26.01	29.20	13.74	934.0		Y
Green Century Balanced Fund	GCBLX	B	C+	A		4.24	15.17	11.42	33.86	36.22	28.73	272.0	800-221-5519	Y
GuidePath® Tactical Allocation Fund Institutional Shares	GITUX	B-	C	B	Up	1.41	11.02	3.65	32.05	21.77	11.117	357.9	603-888-5500	Y
GuideStone Funds Defensive Mkt Strategies Inst Cls	GDMYX	B	C+	A		3.63	13.60	9.15	32.17	48.31	13.07	1,161	214-720-1171	Y
GuideStone Funds Defensive Market Strategies Investor Cls	GDMZX	B	C+	A		3.59	13.45	8.94	31.14	46.45	13.08	1,161	214-720-1171	Y
Hartford Balanced HLS Fund Class IA	HADAX	B-	C	B+	Up	3.72	13.88	7.28	28.31	36.93	31.17	2,064	888-843-7824	Y
Hartford Balanced HLS Fund Class IB	HAIBX	B-	C	B+	Up	3.70	13.77	7.03	27.37	35.24	31.64	2,064	888-843-7824	Y
Hartford Checks and Balances Fund Class A	HCKAX	B	C+	A-		4.01	15.26	9.54	34.08	38.79	9.4	1,555	888-843-7824	Y
Hartford Checks and Balances Fund Class C	HCKCX	B	C+	A-	Up	3.94	14.91	8.71	31.06	33.71	9.34	1,555	888-843-7824	Y
Hartford Checks and Balances Fund Class F	HCKFX	B	C+	A-		4.20	15.55	9.89	35.22	39.97	9.42	1,555	888-843-7824	Y
Hartford Checks and Balances Fund Class I	HCKIX	B	C+	A-		4.18	15.50	9.79	35.08	40.52	9.42	1,555	888-843-7824	Y
Hartford Checks and Balances Fund Class R3	HCKRX	B	C+	A-		3.93	15.13	9.19	32.64	36.25	9.36	1,555	888-843-7824	Y
Hartford Checks and Balances Fund Class R4	HCKSX	B	C+	A-		4.01	15.29	9.50	33.78	38.43	9.37	1,555	888-843-7824	Y
Hartford Checks and Balances Fund Class R5	HCKTX	B	C+	A-		4.17	15.55	9.75	35.04	40.56	9.42	1,555	888-843-7824	Y
Hartford Moderate Allocation Fund Class A	HBAAX	B-	C	A-	Up	3.16	13.01	5.38	26.92	18.80	11.72	415.4	888-843-7824	Y
Hartford Moderate Allocation Fund Class C	HBACX	B-	C	A-	Up	2.93	12.52	4.58	23.99	14.38	11.59	415.4	888-843-7824	Y
Hartford Moderate Allocation Fund Class F	HBADX	B-	C	A-	Up	3.24	13.18	5.74	27.86	19.69	11.76	415.4	888-843-7824	Y
Hartford Moderate Allocation Fund Class I	HBAIX	B-	C	A-	Up	3.24	13.18	5.65	27.93	20.56	11.76	415.4	888-843-7824	Y
Hartford Moderate Allocation Fund Class R3	HBARX	B-	C	A-	Up	3.03	12.81	4.99	25.52	16.73	11.53	415.4	888-843-7824	Y
Hartford Moderate Allocation Fund Class R4	HBASX	B-	C	A-	Up	3.17	13.03	5.40	26.65	18.52	11.71	415.4	888-843-7824	Y
Hartford Moderate Allocation Fund Class R5	HBATX	B-	C	A-	Up	3.24	13.17	5.68	27.76	20.35	11.77	415.4	888-843-7824	Y
Hartford Multi-Asset Income and Growth Fund Class A	ITTAX	B-	C	B+	Up	2.27	11.58	5.28	25.34	32.04	23.13	982.4	888-843-7824	Y
Hartford Multi-Asset Income and Growth Fund Class C	HAFCX	B-	C	B+	Up	2.14	11.22	4.57	22.68	27.50	23.15	982.4	888-843-7824	Y
Hartford Multi-Asset Income and Growth Fund Class F	ITTFX	B-	C	A-	Up	2.37	11.80	5.73	26.79	34.69	23.11	982.4	888-843-7824	Y
Hartford Multi-Asset Income and Growth Fund Class I	ITTIX	B-	C	A-	Up	2.35	11.76	5.66	26.44	34.16	23.12	982.4	888-843-7824	Y
Hartford Multi-Asset Income and Growth Fund Class R3	ITTRX	B-	C	B+	Up	2.22	11.46	4.98	24.28	30.27	23.39	982.4	888-843-7824	Y
Hartford Multi-Asset Income and Growth Fund Class R4	ITTSX	B-	C	B+	Up	2.28	11.60	5.31	25.31	32.20	23.46	982.4	888-843-7824	Y
Hartford Multi-Asset Income and Growth Fund Class R5	ITTTX	B-	C	B+	Up	2.36	11.71	5.57	26.43	34.13	23.47	982.4	888-843-7824	Y
Hartford Multi-Asset Income and Growth Fund Class R6	ITTVX	B-	C	A-	Up	2.38	11.80	5.69	26.72	34.62	23.48	982.4	888-843-7824	Y
Hartford Multi-Asset Income and Growth Fund Class Y	IHAYX	B-	C	A-	Up	2.36	11.78	5.63	26.64	34.54	23.48	982.4	888-843-7824	Y
Hennessy Balanced Fund Investor Class	HBFBX	B	C	A		0.94	7.32	7.34	20.88	27.08	12.4	12.4	800-966-4354	Y
Hennessy Equity and Income Fund Institutional Class	HEIIX	B	C	A-	Up	2.02	10.77	6.92	25.46	31.25	14.46	183.1	800-966-4354	Y
Hennessy Equity and Income Fund Investor Class	HEIFX	B-	C	A-		2.01	10.57	6.53	24.04	28.83	15.36	183.1	800-966-4354	Y
Hilton Tactical Income Fund Institutional Class	HCYIX	B	B-	A		3.60	11.30	7.43	22.73	26.99	17.1	132.6	646-572-3390	Y
Hilton Tactical Income Fund Investor Class	HCYAX	B	C+	A		3.48	11.12	7.14	21.80	25.33	17.07	132.6	646-572-3390	Y
Holland Balanced Fund	HOLBX	B-	C	B+		3.88	11.55	8.57	21.89	28.22	21.12	31.2		Y
Hundredfold Select Alternative Fund Investor Class	HFSAX	B-	C	B+		2.32	8.26	5.83	23.19	27.43	23.21	57.7	855-582-8006	Y
Hundredfold Select Alternative Fund Service Class	SFHYX	B	C	A	Up	2.13	7.80	4.90	19.93	21.83	22.08	57.7	855-582-8006	Y
Invesco Equity and Income Fund Class A	ACEIX	B-	C	B+	Up	3.30	13.75	3.47	29.18	30.89	10.25	13,588	800-659-1005	Y
Invesco Equity and Income Fund Class C	ACERX	B-	C	B	Up	3.07	13.38	2.65	26.34	26.02	10.05	13,588	800-659-1005	Y
Invesco Equity and Income Fund Class R	ACESX	B-	C	B+	Up	3.22	13.65	3.20	28.20	29.26	10.31	13,588	800-659-1005	Y
Invesco Equity and Income Fund Class R6	IEIFX	B-	C	B+	Up	3.40	13.99	3.89	30.78	33.49	10.24	13,588	800-659-1005	Y
Invesco Equity and Income Fund Class Y	ACETX	B-	C	B+	Up	3.36	13.89	3.73	30.17	32.54	10.25	13,588	800-659-1005	Y
Invesco Equity and Income Fund R5 Class	ACEKX	B-	C	B+	Up	3.38	13.93	3.80	30.40	32.87	10.25	13,588	800-659-1005	Y
Invesco Moderate Allocation Fund Class A	AMKAX	B-	C	A-	Up	3.02	12.53	5.25	23.98	20.70	13.33	712.0	800-659-1005	Y
Invesco Moderate Allocation Fund Class C	AMKCX	B-	C	B+	Up	2.84	12.11	4.48	21.24	16.30	13.23	712.0	800-659-1005	Y

Category: Moderate Allocation (con't)

Fund Name	Ticker Symbol	Overall Rating	Reward Rating	Risk Rating	Recent Up/ Downgrade	3-Month Total Return	6-Month Total Return	1-Year Total Return	3-Year Total Return	5-Year Total Return	NAV	Total Assets (MIL)	Telephone	Open to New Investors
		RATINGS				TOTAL RETURNS & PERFORMANCE					ASSETS		NEW INVESTORS	
Invesco Moderate Allocation Fund Class R	AMKRX	B-	C	A-	Up	2.96	12.32	4.99	22.99	19.21	13.3	712.0	800-659-1005	Y
Invesco Moderate Allocation Fund Class R6	AMLSX	B-	C	A-	Up	3.09	12.74	5.56	25.24	22.30	13.39	712.0	800-659-1005	Y
Invesco Moderate Allocation Fund Class S	AMKSX	B-	C	A-	Up	3.12	12.59	5.36	24.36	21.31	13.33	712.0	800-659-1005	Y
Invesco Moderate Allocation Fund Class Y	ABKYX	B-	C	A-	Up	3.08	12.65	5.51	24.90	22.22	13.35	712.0	800-659-1005	Y
Invesco Moderate Allocation Fund R5 Class	AMLIX	B-	C	A-	Up	3.08	12.64	5.56	25.14	22.21	13.39	712.0	800-659-1005	Y
Invesco Oppenheimer Portfolio Series: Moderate Inv Cls A	OAMIX	B-	C	B+	Up	3.39	13.53	5.33	25.79	25.72	12.5	1,571	800-659-1005	Y
Invesco Oppenheimer Portfolio Series: Moderate Inv Cls C	OCMIX	B-	C	B+	Up	3.20	13.14	4.55	22.94	21.05	12.22	1,571	800-659-1005	Y
Invesco Oppenheimer Portfolio Series: Moderate Inv Cls R	ONMIX	B-	C	B+	Up	3.33	13.43	5.10	24.74	24.07	12.41	1,571	800-659-1005	Y
Invesco Oppenheimer Portfolio Series: Moderate Inv Cls R5	PXMQX	B-	C	B+		3.48	13.77	5.59	26.72	27.24	12.51	1,571	800-659-1005	Y
Invesco Oppenheimer Portfolio Series: Moderate Inv Cls R6	PXMMX	B-	C	B+		3.48	13.77	5.59	26.72	27.24	12.51	1,571	800-659-1005	Y
Invesco Oppenheimer Portfolio Series: Moderate Inv Cls Y	OYMIX	B-	C	B+	Up	3.45	13.74	5.56	26.69	27.20	12.58	1,571	800-659-1005	Y
InvestEd Balanced Portfolio	WBLAX	B	C	A-	Up	3.05	12.21	6.33	29.48	29.24	10.47	80.0	888-923-3355	Y
InvestEd Conservative Portfolio	WICAX	B	C	A-	Up	2.77	9.54	6.46	19.03	18.09	11.13	76.2	888-923-3355	Y
Ivy Apollo Multi-Asset Income Fund Class A	IMAAX	B	C	A-	Up	1.91	10.30	4.81	20.12		10.59	459.8		Y
Ivy Apollo Multi-Asset Income Fund Class C	IMACX	B-	C	A-	Up	1.72	9.91	4.14	17.36		10.59	459.8		Y
Ivy Apollo Multi-Asset Income Fund Class I	IMAIX	B	C	A-	Up	2.02	10.53	5.33	21.31		10.59	459.8		Y
Ivy Apollo Multi-Asset Income Fund Class N	IMURX	B	C+	A	Up	2.12	10.52	5.37	21.85		10.6	459.8		Y
Ivy Apollo Multi-Asset Income Fund Class Y	IMAYX	B	C	A-	Up	1.91	10.31	4.83	20.28		10.59	459.8		Y
Ivy Asset Strategy Fund Class A	WASAX	B-	C	B+	Up	5.19	15.59	7.25	28.26	6.51	21.65	2,947		Y
Ivy Asset Strategy Fund Class B	WASBX	B-	C	B+	Up	4.97	15.10	6.39	25.37	2.54	20.09	2,947		
Ivy Asset Strategy Fund Class C	WASCX	B-	C	B+	Up	4.99	15.17	6.53	25.59	2.77	20.28	2,947		Y
Ivy Asset Strategy Fund Class E	IASEX	B-	C	B+	Up	5.26	15.71	7.36	28.79	6.88	21.74	2,947		Y
Ivy Asset Strategy Fund Class I	IVAEX	B-	C	B+	Up	5.28	15.78	7.53	29.33	7.95	21.97	2,947		Y
Ivy Asset Strategy Fund Class N	IASTX	B-	C	B+	Up	5.30	15.81	7.65	29.90	8.55	22.03	2,947		Y
Ivy Asset Strategy Fund Class R	IASRX	B-	C	B+	Up	5.13	15.42	6.89	27.06	4.76	21.36	2,947		Y
Ivy Asset Strategy Fund Class Y	WASYX	B-	C	B+	Up	5.23	15.62	7.31	28.44	6.66	21.72	2,947		Y
Ivy Balanced Fund Class A	IBNAX	B-	C	A-		3.01	13.33	7.12	24.83	25.41	24.21	2,490		Y
Ivy Balanced Fund Class B	IBNBX	B-	C	B+		2.85	12.94	6.35	22.14	20.90	23.93	2,490		
Ivy Balanced Fund Class C	IBNCX	B-	C	B+		2.87	12.91	6.39	22.24	21.11	24.02	2,490		Y
Ivy Balanced Fund Class I	IYBIX	B-	C	A-		3.12	13.47	7.43	25.77	27.02	24.21	2,490		Y
Ivy Balanced Fund Class N	IBARX	B-	C	A-		3.15	13.58	7.58	26.41	27.96	24.26	2,490		Y
Ivy Balanced Fund Class R	IYBFX	B-	C	B+		2.93	13.12	6.77	23.58	23.31	24.17	2,490		Y
Ivy Balanced Fund Class Y	IBNYX	B-	C	A-		3.05	13.33	7.17	24.92	25.51	24.22	2,490		Y
Ivy Wilshire Global Allocation Fund Class A	IWGAX	B-	C	B+	Up	2.52	11.55	3.52	19.77	1.54	8.11	1,227		
Ivy Wilshire Global Allocation Fund Class I	IWGIX	B-	C	B+	Up	2.62	11.83	3.98	20.95	3.21	8.22	1,227		Y
Ivy Wilshire Global Allocation Fund Class N	IWGNX	B-	C	B+	Up	2.65	11.84	3.95	20.41	2.08	8.12	1,227		Y
Ivy Wilshire Global Allocation Fund Class R	IWGRX	B-	C	B+	Up	2.40	11.41	3.36	19.08	0.46	8.1	1,227		Y
Ivy Wilshire Global Allocation Fund Class Y	IWGYX	B-	C	B+	Up	2.52	11.70	3.62	20.03	1.76	8.11	1,227		Y
Janus Henderson Adaptive Global Allocation Fund Class A	JAGAX	B-	C	A-	Up	2.28	9.78	4.22	25.28		10.32	75.1	877-335-2687	Y
Janus Henderson Adaptive Global Allocation Fund Class C	JAVCX	B-	C	A-	Up	2.58	10.04	3.95	23.10		10.3	75.1	877-335-2687	Y
Janus Henderson Adaptive Global Allocation Fund Class D	JAGDX	B-	C	A-	Up	2.27	9.89	4.30	25.63		10.33	75.1	877-335-2687	Y
Janus Henderson Adaptive Global Allocation Fund Class I	JVGIX	B-	C	A-	Up	2.27	9.87	4.32	26.05		10.35	75.1	877-335-2687	Y
Janus Henderson Adaptive Global Allocation Fund Class N	JAGNX	B-	C	A-	Up	2.37	9.97	4.46	26.27		10.36	75.1	877-335-2687	Y
Janus Henderson Adaptive Global Allocation Fund Class S	JAGSX	B-	C	A-	Up	2.47	10.10	4.32	25.14		10.35	75.1	877-335-2687	Y
Janus Henderson Adaptive Global Allocation Fund Class T	JVGTX	B-	C	A-	Up	2.37	10.00	4.32	25.70		10.34	75.1	877-335-2687	Y
Janus Henderson Balanced Fund Class A	JDBAX	B	C+	A		3.85	13.35	9.79	41.39	44.62	34.54	15,961	877-335-2687	Y
Janus Henderson Balanced Fund Class C	JABCX	B	C+	A		3.68	13.00	9.05	38.57	39.73	34.21	15,961	877-335-2687	Y
Janus Henderson Balanced Fund Class D	JANBX	B	C+	A		3.89	13.49	10.05	42.34	46.17	34.63	15,961	877-335-2687	
Janus Henderson Balanced Fund Class I	JBALX	B	C+	A		3.94	13.56	10.15	42.69	46.74	34.65	15,961	877-335-2687	Y
Janus Henderson Balanced Fund Class N	JABNX	B	C+	A		3.89	13.54	10.17	42.95	47.22	34.6	15,961	877-335-2687	Y
Janus Henderson Balanced Fund Class R	JDBRX	B	C+	A		3.74	13.16	9.40	39.80	41.86	34.34	15,961	877-335-2687	Y
Janus Henderson Balanced Fund Class S	JABRX	B	C+	A		3.84	13.30	9.69	40.87	43.67	34.54	15,961	877-335-2687	Y

Category: Moderate Allocation (con't)

Fund Name	Ticker Symbol	Overall Rating	Reward Rating	Risk Rating	Recent Up/ Downgrade	3-Month Total Return	6-Month Total Return	1-Year Total Return	3-Year Total Return	5-Year Total Return	NAV	Total Assets (MIL)	Telephone	Open to New Investors
		RATINGS				TOTAL RETURNS & PERFORMANCE					ASSETS		NEW INVESTORS	
Janus Henderson Balanced Fund Class T	JABAX	B	C+	A		3.90	13.46	9.95	41.96	45.49	34.59	15,961	877-335-2687	Y
Janus Henderson Global Allocation Fund - Moderate Class A	JMOAX	B-	C	B+	Up	3.03	10.91	3.32	21.48	17.95	12.9	230.4	877-335-2687	Y
Janus Henderson Global Allocation Fund - Moderate Class D	JNSMX	B-	C	A-	Up	3.09	11.03	3.44	22.22	18.99	12.98	230.4	877-335-2687	
Janus Henderson Global Allocation Fund - Moderate Class I	JMOIX	B-	C	A-	Up	3.09	11.04	3.53	22.38	19.30	12.97	230.4	877-335-2687	Y
Janus Henderson Global Allocation Fund - Moderate Class S	JMOSX	B-	C	B+	Up	2.97	10.83	3.14	20.94	16.99	12.79	230.4	877-335-2687	Y
Janus Henderson Global Allocation Fund - Moderate Class T	JSPMX	B-	C	A-	Up	3.02	10.97	3.37	21.91	18.62	12.94	230.4	877-335-2687	Y
Janus Henderson VIT Balanced Portfolio Institutional Class	JABLX	B	C+	A		3.95	13.49	10.17	42.44	46.44	36.67	4,318	877-335-2687	Y
Janus Henderson VIT Balanced Portfolio Service Class		B	C+	A		3.89	13.34	9.92	41.36	44.62	38.73	4,318	877-335-2687	Y
JNL Institutional Alt 25 Fund Class A		B-	C	A-	Up	3.12	12.71	5.13	25.05	21.04	17.82	2,729		Y
JNL Institutional Alt 25 Fund Class I		B-	C	A-	Up	3.22	12.91	5.47	25.75	21.72	17.92	2,729		Y
JNL iShares Tactical Moderate Growth A		B-	C	B+	Up	2.57	11.78	3.45	25.40	29.28	13.56	282.7		Y
JNL iShares Tactical Moderate Growth I		B-	C	B+	Up	2.63	11.92	3.76	26.14	30.05	13.61	282.7		Y
JNL Moderate Growth Allocation Fund Class A		B-	C	A-	Up	3.64	13.81	6.61	27.41	28.55	14.5	2,342		Y
JNL Moderate Growth Allocation Fund Class I		B	C	A-	Up	3.69	13.99	6.89	28.11	29.26	14.58	2,342		Y
JNL/American Funds Balanced Fund Class A		B-	C	B+	Up	2.22	12.29	5.37	27.82	25.64	11.51	1,325		Y
JNL/American Funds Balanced Fund Class I		B-	C	A-		2.22	12.42	5.73	28.94	27.07	11.94	1,325		Y
JNL/American Funds Moderate Growth Allocation Class A		B	C	A-	Up	2.78	12.29	5.44	29.08	31.47	15.89	2,346		Y
JNL/American Funds Moderate Growth Allocation Class I		B	C	A-	Up	2.83	12.53	5.75	29.81	32.22	15.98	2,346		Y
JNL/BlackRock Global Allocation Fund Class A		B-	C	B+	Up	2.86	11.15	3.87	21.43	17.66	12.55	3,603		Y
JNL/BlackRock Global Allocation Fund Class I		B-	C	B+	Up	3.00	11.32	4.25	22.39	19.08	12.68	3,603		Y
JNL/FPA + DoubleLine Flexible Allocation Fund Class I		B-	C	B+	Up	3.67	15.14	6.38	26.33	7.01	12.7	1,694		Y
JNL/JPMorgan Global Allocation Fund Class A		B-	C	B+	Up	2.98	11.82	3.35	22.21	19.54	11.73	53.4		Y
JNL/JPMorgan Global Allocation Fund Class I		B-	C	B+	Up	3.06	11.88	3.68	22.92	20.23	11.77	53.4		Y
JNL/S&P Managed Moderate Growth Fund Class A		B-	C	A-		3.33	13.86	6.24	31.91	30.85	18.89	5,832		Y
JNL/S&P Managed Moderate Growth Fund Class I		B	C	A-	Up	3.48	14.04	6.62	32.68	31.61	19	5,832		Y
JNL/T. Rowe Price Capital Appreciation Fund		B	B-	A		4.76	17.91	14.88	39.86	59.43	16.26	4,959		Y
JNL/T. Rowe Price Capital Appreciation Fund Class I		B	B-	A	Down	4.88	18.08	15.22	40.55	60.22	16.32	4,959		Y
JNL/T. Rowe Price Managed Volatility Balanced A		B-	C	B+	Up	3.43	15.00	6.30	27.00	21.75	12.65	518.0		Y
JNL/T. Rowe Price Managed Volatility Balanced I		B-	C	B+	Up	3.58	15.32	6.62	27.71	22.42	12.72	518.0		Y
JNL/WMC Balanced Fund Class A		B	C+	A-		3.24	12.93	9.20	30.41	38.52	24.53	8,240		Y
JNL/WMC Balanced Fund Class I		B	C+	A-		3.29	13.10	9.56	31.48	40.15	25.38	8,240		Y
John Hancock Balanced Fund Class A	SVBAX	B	C+	B+	Up	3.13	14.73	8.92	30.19	33.51	20.42	1,977	800-225-5913	Y
John Hancock Balanced Fund Class B	SVBBX	B-	C	B+		2.91	14.31	8.13	27.42	28.91	20.38	1,977	800-225-5913	
John Hancock Balanced Fund Class C	SVBCX	B-	C	B+		2.96	14.29	8.18	27.46	28.88	20.4	1,977	800-225-5913	Y
John Hancock Balanced Fund Class I	SVBIX	B	C+	B+		3.16	14.85	9.21	31.29	35.50	20.39	1,977	800-225-5913	Y
John Hancock Balanced Fund Class R1	JBAOX	B-	C	B+		2.98	14.46	8.50	28.76	31.21	20.51	1,977	800-225-5913	Y
John Hancock Balanced Fund Class R2	JBATX	B-	C+	B+		3.11	14.69	8.83	29.79	32.88	20.39	1,977	800-225-5913	Y
John Hancock Balanced Fund Class R3	JBAHX	B-	C	B+		3.06	14.61	8.66	29.31	31.98	20.47	1,977	800-225-5913	Y
John Hancock Balanced Fund Class R4	JBAFX	B	C+	B+	Up	3.16	14.80	9.04	30.76	34.53	20.51	1,977	800-225-5913	Y
John Hancock Balanced Fund Class R5	JBAVX	B	C+	B+		3.16	14.88	9.22	31.46	35.86	20.47	1,977	800-225-5913	Y
John Hancock Balanced Fund Class R6	JBAWX	B	C+	B+		3.23	14.95	9.30	31.69	36.30	20.42	1,977	800-225-5913	Y
John Hancock Funds II Capital Appreciation Value Cls NAV	JCAVX	B	B-	A		4.92	18.14	15.04	41.07	62.35	11.72	1,654	800-225-5913	Y
John Hancock Funds II Multimgr Lifest Bal Cls 1	JILBX	B-	C	A-	Up	3.08	13.28	5.38	28.10	27.65	14.53	10,927	800-225-5913	Y
John Hancock Funds II Multimgr Lifest Bal Cls 5	JHLAX	B-	C	A-	Up	3.09	13.30	5.44	28.29	27.98	14.54	10,927	800-225-5913	Y
John Hancock Funds II Multimgr Lifest Bal Cls A	JALBX	B-	C	A-	Up	2.97	12.98	4.97	26.69	25.33	14.63	10,927	800-225-5913	Y
John Hancock Funds II Multimgr Lifest Bal Cls B	JBLBX	B-	C	A-	Up	2.74	12.55	4.18	24.00	20.91	14.62	10,927	800-225-5913	
John Hancock Funds II Multimgr Lifest Bal Cls C	JCLBX	B-	C	A-	Up	2.66	12.54	4.18	23.98	20.86	14.63	10,927	800-225-5913	Y
John Hancock Funds II Multimgr Lifest Bal Cls I	JTBIX	B-	C	A-	Up	3.06	13.24	5.31	27.83	27.38	14.54	10,927	800-225-5913	Y
John Hancock Funds II Multimgr Lifest Bal Cls R1	JPLBX	B-	C	A-	Up	2.89	12.86	4.63	25.39	23.15	14.56	10,927	800-225-5913	Y
John Hancock Funds II Multimgr Lifest Bal Cls R2	JQLBX	B-	C	A-	Up	2.96	12.93	4.89	26.27	24.68	14.54	10,927	800-225-5913	Y
John Hancock Funds II Multimgr Lifest Bal Cls R3	JRLBX	B-	C	A-	Up	2.92	12.90	4.74	25.77	23.80	14.59	10,927	800-225-5913	Y
John Hancock Funds II Multimgr Lifest Bal Cls R4	JSLBX	B-	C	A-	Up	3.01	13.09	5.13	27.26	26.30	14.6	10,927	800-225-5913	Y

Category: Moderate Allocation (con't)

		RATINGS				TOTAL RETURNS & PERFORMANCE					ASSETS		NEW INVESTORS	
Fund Name	Ticker Symbol	Overall Rating	Reward Rating	Risk Rating	Recent Up/ Downgrade	3-Month Total Return	6-Month Total Return	1-Year Total Return	3-Year Total Return	5-Year Total Return	NAV	Total Assets (MIL)	Telephone	Open to New Investors
John Hancock Funds II Multimgr Lifest Bal Cls R5	JTSBX	B-	C	A-	Up	2.98	13.18	5.33	28.03	27.47	14.62	10,927	800-225-5913	Y
John Hancock Funds II Multimgr Lifest Bal Cls R6	JULBX	B-	C	A-	Up	3.02	13.21	5.42	28.18	27.87	14.53	10,927	800-225-5913	Y
John Hancock Funds Multi-Ind Lifestyle Balanced Port Cls 1	JIBOX	B	C	A-	Up	3.22	13.19	6.66	26.56	30.04	11.29	899.6	800-225-5913	Y
John Hancock Funds Multi-Ind Lifest Bal Cls R6	JIBRX	B	C	A-	Up	3.32	13.32	6.79	26.83	30.44	11.3	899.6	800-225-5913	Y
JPMorgan Diversified Fund Class A	JDVAX	B-	C	B+	Up	3.79	14.45	6.14	28.58	29.65	16.54	1,101	800-480-4111	Y
JPMorgan Diversified Fund Class C	JDVCX	B-	C	B+	Up	3.63	14.13	5.59	26.68	26.41	16.41	1,101	800-480-4111	Y
JPMorgan Diversified Fund Class I	JDVSX	B-	C	B+	Up	3.83	14.57	6.37	29.50	31.29	16.64	1,101	800-480-4111	Y
JPMorgan Diversified Fund Class L	JPDVX	B-	C	B+	Up	3.88	14.67	6.56	30.33	32.72	16.61	1,101	800-480-4111	Y
JPMorgan Diversified Fund Class R6	JDVZX	B-	C	B+	Up	3.90	14.73	6.64	30.52	32.91	16.61	1,101	800-480-4111	Y
JPMorgan Global Allocation Fund Class A	GAOAX	B-	C	A-	Up	2.92	10.30	4.49	26.18	25.97	18.63	3,623	800-480-4111	Y
JPMorgan Global Allocation Fund Class C	GAOCX	B-	C	A-	Up	2.83	10.09	4.02	24.29	22.88	18.37	3,623	800-480-4111	Y
JPMorgan Global Allocation Fund Class I	GAOSX	B-	C	A-	Up	2.96	10.51	4.78	27.15	27.58	18.72	3,623		Y
JPMorgan Global Allocation Fund Class R2	GAONX	B-	C	A-	Up	2.85	10.14	4.14	25.09	24.27	18.55	3,623	800-480-4111	Y
JPMorgan Global Allocation Fund Class R3	GAOTX	B-	C	A-	Up	2.89	10.31	4.44	26.11	25.91	18.72	3,623	800-480-4111	Y
JPMorgan Global Allocation Fund Class R4	GAOFX	B-	C	A-	Up	2.95	10.39	4.65	26.99	27.42	18.62	3,623	800-480-4111	Y
JPMorgan Global Allocation Fund Class R5	GAORX	B-	C	A-	Up	2.97	10.47	4.74	27.11	27.54	18.72	3,623	800-480-4111	Y
JPMorgan Global Allocation Fund Class R6	GAOZX	B-	C	A-	Up	3.00	10.56	4.91	27.47	27.90	18.71	3,623	800-480-4111	Y
JPMorgan Investor Balanced Fund Class A	OGIAX	B	C	A-	Up	3.02	11.53	5.52	25.59	27.72	15	4,768	800-480-4111	Y
JPMorgan Investor Balanced Fund Class C	OGBCX	B-	C	A-	Up	2.79	11.12	4.89	23.38	24.24	14.74	4,768	800-480-4111	Y
JPMorgan Investor Balanced Fund Class I	OIBFX	B	C	A-	Up	3.01	11.56	5.70	26.48	29.29	15.02	4,768	800-480-4111	Y
JPMorgan Investor Balanced Fund Class R6	JFQUX	B-	C	B+	Up	3.13	11.72	5.96	26.89	29.71	15.02	4,768	800-480-4111	Y
Ladenburg Growth & Income Fund Class A	LOWAX	B-	C	B+	Up	2.96	13.41	4.76	24.42		11.85	114.6	877-803-6583	Y
Ladenburg Growth & Income Fund Class C	LOWCX	B-	C	B+	Up	2.73	12.96	3.93	21.68		11.67	114.6	877-803-6583	Y
Ladenburg Growth & Income Fund Class I	LOWIX	B-	C	B+	Up	3.01	13.50	5.03	25.00		11.87	114.6	877-803-6583	Y
LK Balanced Fund Institutional Class Shares	LKBLX	B-	C+	B+	Down	5.57	15.45	9.06	34.24	26.73	50.19	29.6		Y
LKCM Balanced Fund	LKBAX	B	C+	A-		4.43	15.67	10.56	35.16	42.36	24.08	100.7	800-688-5526	Y
Loomis Sayles Global Allocation Fund Class A	LGMAX	B	C+	B+	Up	5.77	18.79	8.71	41.67	42.42	23.64	2,939	800-862-4863	Y
Loomis Sayles Global Allocation Fund Class C	LGMCX	B-	C	B+	Up	5.56	18.34	7.90	38.54	37.13	23.35	2,939	800-862-4863	Y
Loomis Sayles Global Allocation Fund Class N	LGMNX	B	C+	B+	Up	5.87	19.01	9.10	42.92	44.36	23.78	2,939	800-862-4863	Y
Loomis Sayles Global Allocation Fund Class Y	LSWWX	B	C+	B+	Up	5.82	19.00	9.00	42.78	44.22	23.79	2,939	800-862-4863	Y
Lord Abbett Multi-Asset Balanced Opportunity Fund Class C	BFLAX	B-	C	B+	Up	2.79	14.54	4.27	22.95	16.46	11.32	2,637	201-827-2000	Y
Lord Abbett Multi-Asset Balanced Opportunity Fund Class F	BLAFX	B-	C	B+	Up	2.98	15.03	5.14	26.34	21.81	11.39	2,637	201-827-2000	Y
Lord Abbett Multi-Asset Balanced Opportunity Fund Class F3	LOBFX	B-	C	B	Up	3.00	15.18	5.35	26.56	21.70	11.41	2,637	201-827-2000	Y
Lord Abbett Multi-Asset Balanced Opportunity Fund Class R2	BLAQX	B-	C	B+	Up	2.80	14.71	4.62	24.33	18.78	11.65	2,637	201-827-2000	Y
Lord Abbett Multi-Asset Balanced Opportunity Fund Class R5	BLATX	B-	C	B	Up	3.00	15.17	5.33	26.74	22.13	11.41	2,637	201-827-2000	Y
Lord Abbett Multi-Asset Balanced Opportunity Fund Class R6	BLAVX	B-	C	B	Up	3.01	15.08	5.26	26.90	22.20	11.4	2,637	201-827-2000	Y
Madison Diversified Income Fund Class A	MBLAX	B	C+	A		3.87	13.32	13.15	29.89	39.18	16.06	175.4	800-767-0300	Y
Madison Diversified Income Fund Class B	MBLNX	B	C+	A		3.65	12.87	12.30	26.98	34.10	16.17	175.4	800-767-0300	Y
Madison Diversified Income Fund Class C	MBLCX	B	C+	A		3.65	12.80	12.30	27.00	34.03	16.16	175.4	800-767-0300	Y
Madison Moderate Allocation Fund Class A	MMDAX	B	C+	A	Up	2.77	11.54	6.40	25.24	29.30	11.5	137.4	800-767-0300	Y
Madison Moderate Allocation Fund Class B	MMDRX	B	C	A-	Up	2.52	11.03	5.58	22.34	24.46	11.37	137.4	800-767-0300	Y
Madison Moderate Allocation Fund Class C	MMDCX	B	C	A-	Up	2.52	11.02	5.58	22.43	24.54	11.38	137.4	800-767-0300	Y
MainStay Balanced Fund Class A	MBNAX	B-	C	B+	Up	2.50	12.30	3.67	19.62	24.40	30.63	615.7	800-624-6782	Y
MainStay Balanced Fund Class I	MBAIX	B-	C	B+	Up	2.53	12.40	3.92	20.50	25.94	30.7	615.7	800-624-6782	Y
MainStay Balanced Fund Class R1	MBNRX	B-	C	B+	Up	2.50	12.37	3.82	20.12	25.32	30.66	615.7	800-624-6782	Y
MainStay Balanced Fund Class R2	MBCRX	B-	C	B+	Up	2.44	12.19	3.56	19.41	23.92	30.67	615.7	800-624-6782	Y
MainStay Balanced Fund Class R3	MBDRX	B-	C	B	Up	2.42	12.08	3.33	18.34	22.19	30.61	615.7	800-624-6782	Y
MainStay Balanced Fund Class R6	MBERX	B-	C	B+	Up	2.55	12.46	4.02	20.68	26.13	30.7	615.7	800-624-6782	Y
MainStay Balanced Fund Investor Class	MBINX	B-	C	B+	Up	2.41	12.16	3.45	18.97	23.36	30.66	615.7	800-624-6782	Y
MainStay Income Builder Fund Class A	MTRAX	B-	C+	B		2.78	11.70	8.26	21.83	23.65	19.4	1,506	800-624-6782	Y
MainStay Income Builder Fund Class B	MKTRX	B-	C	B		2.59	11.18	7.30	18.62	18.25	19.54	1,506	800-624-6782	
MainStay Income Builder Fund Class C	MCTRX	B-	C	B		2.54	11.21	7.32	18.60	18.22	19.5	1,506	800-624-6782	Y

Category: Moderate Allocation (con't)

Fund Name	Ticker Symbol	RATINGS: Overall Rating	Reward Rating	Risk Rating	Recent Up/ Downgrade	TOTAL RETURNS & PERFORMANCE: 3-Month Total Return	6-Month Total Return	1-Year Total Return	3-Year Total Return	5-Year Total Return	ASSETS: NAV	Total Assets (MIL)	NEW INVESTORS: Telephone	Open to New Investors
MainStay Income Builder Fund Class I	MTOIX	B-	C+	B	Down	2.87	11.84	8.56	22.72	25.27	19.59	1,506	800-624-6782	Y
MainStay Income Builder Fund Class R2	MTXRX	B-	C+	B		2.81	11.65	8.21	21.47	22.43	19.39	1,506	800-624-6782	Y
MainStay Income Builder Fund Class R3	MTXVX	B-	C+	B		2.69	11.46	7.89	20.55	20.36	19.4	1,506	800-624-6782	Y
MainStay Income Builder Fund Class R6	MTODX	B-	C+	B		2.90	11.89	8.67	20.57	20.19	19.59	1,506	800-624-6782	Y
MainStay Income Builder Fund Investor Class	MTINX	B-	C+	B		2.80	11.61	8.16	21.35	22.80	19.42	1,506	800-624-6782	Y
MainStay Moderate Allocation Class R3	MMRHX	B-	C	B+	Up	2.52	12.14	2.79	22.25	19.93	12.99	751.9	800-624-6782	Y
MainStay Moderate Allocation Fund Class A	MMRAX	B-	C	B+	Up	2.60	12.30	3.13	23.52	21.83	13.01	751.9	800-624-6782	Y
MainStay Moderate Allocation Fund Class I	MMRIX	B-	C	B+	Up	2.66	12.35	3.32	24.31	23.23	13.09	751.9	800-624-6782	Y
MainStay Moderate Allocation Fund Class R2	MMRKX	B-	C	B+							13.01	751.9	800-624-6782	
MainStay Moderate Allocation Fund Investor Class	MMRDX	B-	C	B+	Up	2.52	12.14	2.91	22.80	20.72	13.02	751.9	800-624-6782	Y
Mairs & Power Balanced Fund Investor Class	MAPOX	B	C+	B+		3.19	13.17	12.17	27.06	35.34	96.43	888.4	800-304-7404	Y
Manning & Napier Income Series Class I	MSMAX	B	C+	A		2.71	10.88	8.98	24.46	29.94	11.05	51.7	585-325-6880	Y
Manning & Napier Income Series Class S	MSMSX	B	C+	A		2.64	10.75	8.72	23.55	28.37	11.05	51.7	585-325-6880	Y
Manning & Napier Pro-Blend Extended Term Series Class I	MNBIX	B	C+	A-	Up	3.51	13.03	6.60	25.27	20.68	8.9	534.3	585-325-6880	Y
Manning & Napier Pro-Blend Extended Term Series Class L	MNECX	B-	C	A-	Up	3.20	12.44	5.47	21.51	14.77	9.76	534.3	585-325-6880	Y
Manning & Napier Pro-Blend Extended Term Series Class R	MNBRX	B	C+	A-	Up	3.33	12.75	5.99	23.36	17.72	10.59	534.3	585-325-6880	Y
Manning & Napier Pro-Blend Extended Term Series Class S	MNBAX	B	C+	A-	Up	3.38	12.86	6.29	24.33	19.16	17.54	534.3	585-325-6880	Y
Manning & Napier Pro-Blend Extended Term Series Class W	MNBWX	B	C+	A-		3.50	12.99	6.41	24.47	19.29	17.54	534.3	585-325-6880	Y
MassMutual Premier Balanced Fund Administrative Class	MMBLX	B-	C	B+	Up	2.92	11.97	5.43	30.23	33.73	11.97	124.4		Y
MassMutual Premier Balanced Fund Class A	MMBDX	B-	C	B+	Up	2.83	11.84	5.18	29.23	32.10	11.61	124.4		Y
MassMutual Premier Balanced Fund Class I	MBBIX	B-	C	B+	Up	2.93	12.13	5.73	31.46	35.89	11.92	124.4		Y
MassMutual Premier Balanced Fund Class R3	MMBRX	B-	C	B+	Up	2.78	11.71	4.97	28.64	31.11	11.44	124.4		Y
MassMutual Premier Balanced Fund Class R4	MBBRX	B-	C	B+	Up	2.85	11.96	5.21	29.71	32.73	11.51	124.4		Y
MassMutual Premier Balanced Fund Class R5	MBLDX	B-	C	B+	Up	2.93	12.13	5.63	31.05	35.00	11.92	124.4		Y
MassMutual Premier Balanced Fund Service Class	MBAYX	B-	C	B+	Up	2.94	12.02	5.53	30.65	34.32	12.58	124.4		Y
MassMutual RetireSMART Moderate Fund Administrative Class	MRMLX	B-	C	A-	Up	3.56	13.69	6.26	26.25	24.29	9.88	261.4		Y
MassMutual RetireSMART Moderate Fund Class A	MRMAX	B-	C	A-	Up	3.54	13.63	6.10	25.42	22.77	9.92	261.4		Y
MassMutual RetireSMART Moderate Fund Class I	MRMUX	B-	C	A-	Up	3.68	13.87	6.66	27.46	26.16	9.85	261.4		Y
MassMutual RetireSMART Moderate Fund Class R3	MRMTX	B-	C	A-	Up	3.48	13.42	5.94	24.91	21.98	9.8	261.4		Y
MassMutual RetireSMART Moderate Fund Class R4	MRMZX	B-	C	A-	Up	3.48	13.54	6.06	25.69	23.31	9.81	261.4		Y
MassMutual RetireSMART Moderate Fund Class R5	MROSX	B-	C	A-	Up	3.68	13.74	6.53	27.07	25.56	9.85	261.4		Y
MassMutual RetireSMART Moderate Fund Service Class	MRMYX	B-	C	A-	Up	3.66	13.66	6.39	26.75	24.87	9.9	261.4		Y
MassMutual Select BlackRock Global Allocation Admin Cls	MGSLX	B-	C	B+	Up	2.82	10.91	3.69	20.69	16.79	11.28	574.6		Y
MassMutual Select BlackRock Global Allocation Fund Class A	MGJAX	B-	C	B+	Up	2.73	10.77	3.44	19.81	15.34	10.9	574.6		Y
MassMutual Select BlackRock Global Allocation Fund Class I	MGJIX	B-	C	B+	Up	2.82	11.07	4.01	21.82	18.56	10.93	574.6		Y
MassMutual Select BlackRock Global Allocation Cls R3	MGJRX	B-	C	B+	Up	2.77	10.72	3.34	19.37	14.52	10.74	574.6		Y
MassMutual Select BlackRock Global Allocation Cls R4	MGJFX	B-	C	B+	Up	2.76	10.90	3.60	20.13	15.92	10.78	574.6		Y
MassMutual Select BlackRock Global Allocation Cls R5	MGSSX	B-	C	B+	Up	2.87	11.11	3.98	21.52	17.93	11.1	574.6		Y
MassMutual Select BlackRock Global Allocation Service Cls	MGSYX	B-	C	B+	Up	2.82	10.97	3.75	21.14	17.39	10.92	574.6		Y
Matisse Discounted Closed-End Strategy Inst Cls Shares	MDCEX	B	C+	A-	Up	0.37	16.94	8.36	36.45	34.59	10	45.3	252-442-4226	Y
Meeder Balanced Fund Institutional Class	BLNIX	B-	C	B	Up	2.25	6.29	2.98	24.39	22.20	11.76	399.7		Y
MFS Global Total Return Fund Class A	MFWTX	B-	C	B	Up	3.69	12.05	6.76	18.92	21.74	18.08	1,859	877-960-6077	Y
MFS Global Total Return Fund Class I	MFWIX	B-	C	B+	Up	3.79	12.18	7.04	19.83	23.25	17.89	1,859	877-960-6077	Y
MFS Global Total Return Fund Class R2	MGBRX	B-	C	B	Up	3.61	11.92	6.49	18.00	20.16	17.89	1,859	877-960-6077	Y
MFS Global Total Return Fund Class R3	MFWHX	B-	C	B	Up	3.70	12.09	6.79	19.00	21.82	18.03	1,859	877-960-6077	Y
MFS Global Total Return Fund Class R4	MFWJX	B-	C	B+	Up	3.80	12.23	7.08	19.85	23.29	18.11	1,859	877-960-6077	Y
MFS Global Total Return Fund Class R6	MFWLX	B-	C	B+	Up	3.76	12.24	7.09	20.17	23.84	17.89	1,859	877-960-6077	Y
MFS Moderate Allocation Fund Class 529A	EAMDX	B	C+	A-	Up	4.43	15.41	8.39	28.85	32.09	18.18	5,626	877-960-6077	Y
MFS Moderate Allocation Fund Class 529B	EBMDX	B	C+	A-	Up	4.26	15.01	7.65	26.03	27.21	17.87	5,626	877-960-6077	Y
MFS Moderate Allocation Fund Class 529C	ECMAX	B	C+	A-	Up	4.25	15.02	7.61	25.99	27.22	17.73	5,626	877-960-6077	Y
MFS Moderate Allocation Fund Class A	MAMAX	B	C+	A-	Up	4.42	15.48	8.44	29.05	32.38	18.28	5,626	877-960-6077	Y
MFS Moderate Allocation Fund Class B	MMABX	B	C+	A-	Up	4.28	15.05	7.65	26.21	27.53	18.07	5,626	877-960-6077	Y

Category: Moderate Allocation (con't)

Fund Name	Ticker Symbol	RATINGS: Overall Rating	Reward Rating	Risk Rating	Recent Up/ Downgrade	TOTAL RETURNS & PERFORMANCE: 3-Month Total Return	6-Month Total Return	1-Year Total Return	3-Year Total Return	5-Year Total Return	ASSETS: NAV	Total Assets (MIL)	NEW INVESTORS: Telephone	Open to New Investors
MFS Moderate Allocation Fund Class C	MMACX	B	C+	A-	Up	4.20	14.99	7.62	26.17	27.45	17.93	5,626	877-960-6077	Y
MFS Moderate Allocation Fund Class I	MMAIX	B	C+	A-		4.47	15.57	8.71	30.02	34.00	18.54	5,626	877-960-6077	Y
MFS Moderate Allocation Fund Class R1	MAMFX	B	C+	A-	Up	4.25	15.02	7.64	26.11	27.43	17.53	5,626	877-960-6077	Y
MFS Moderate Allocation Fund Class R2	MARRX	B	C+	A-	Up	4.40	15.31	8.18	28.09	30.71	17.87	5,626	877-960-6077	Y
MFS Moderate Allocation Fund Class R3	MAMHX	B	C+	A-	Up	4.45	15.48	8.45	28.99	32.35	18.13	5,626	877-960-6077	Y
MFS Moderate Allocation Fund Class R4	MAMJX	B	C+	A-		4.54	15.63	8.72	29.98	34.01	18.26	5,626	877-960-6077	Y
MFS Total Return Fund Class 529A	EATRX	B-	C	A-		3.72	13.36	8.57	24.01	32.59	19.13	7,506	877-960-6077	Y
MFS Total Return Fund Class 529B	EBTRX	B-	C	B+	Up	3.61	13.04	7.86	21.36	27.74	19.22	7,506	877-960-6077	Y
MFS Total Return Fund Class 529C	ECTRX	B-	C	B+	Up	3.48	12.92	7.76	21.20	27.65	19.3	7,506	877-960-6077	Y
MFS Total Return Fund Class A	MSFRX	B-	C	A-		3.72	13.40	8.64	24.22	32.90	19.19	7,506	877-960-6077	Y
MFS Total Return Fund Class B	MTRBX	B-	C	B+	Up	3.52	12.95	7.80	21.40	27.98	19.22	7,506	877-960-6077	Y
MFS Total Return Fund Class C	MTRCX	B-	C	B+	Up	3.49	13.00	7.81	21.39	27.97	19.32	7,506	877-960-6077	Y
MFS Total Return Fund Class I	MTRIX	B	C+	A-	Up	3.78	13.57	8.91	25.10	34.50	19.18	7,506	877-960-6077	Y
MFS Total Return Fund Class R1	MSFFX	B-	C	B+	Up	3.52	13.00	7.83	21.37	27.92	19.16	7,506	877-960-6077	Y
MFS Total Return Fund Class R2	MTRRX	B-	C	B+	Up	3.64	13.25	8.33	23.22	31.21	19.25	7,506	877-960-6077	Y
MFS Total Return Fund Class R3	MSFHX	B-	C	A-		3.71	13.39	8.63	24.17	32.83	19.2	7,506	877-960-6077	Y
MFS Total Return Fund Class R4	MSFJX	B	C+	A-	Up	3.78	13.55	8.90	25.12	34.59	19.21	7,506	877-960-6077	Y
MFS Total Return Fund Class R6	MSFKX	B	C+	A-	Up	3.80	13.62	9.00	25.41	35.12	19.19	7,506	877-960-6077	Y
Morgan Stanley Inst Trust Global Strategist Port Cls A	MBAAX	B-	C	A-	Up	3.35	12.16	5.74	25.59	17.31	15.4	398.8	855-332-5306	Y
Morgan Stanley Inst Trust Global Strategist Port Cls C	MSSOX	B-	C	A-	Up	3.19	11.79	4.95	22.66	12.99	15.16	398.8	855-332-5306	Y
Morgan Stanley Inst Trust Global Strategist Port Cls Inst	MPBAX	B-	C	A-	Up	3.46	12.36	6.08	26.74	19.21	15.54	398.8	855-332-5306	Y
Morgan Stanley Inst Trust Global Strategist Port Cls IS	MGPOX	B-	C	A-	Up	3.52	12.42	6.18	26.93	19.47	15.56	398.8	855-332-5306	Y
Morgan Stanley Inst Trust Global Strategist Port Cls L	MSDLX	B-	C	A-	Up	3.24	11.86	5.19	23.72	14.36	15.27	398.8	855-332-5306	
Morningstar Balanced ETF Asset Allocation Portfolio Cls I		B-	C	A-	Up	2.66	10.87	5.07	23.42	25.29	10.4	173.9	866-759-5679	Y
Nationwide Investor Destinations Moderate Fund Class A	NADMX	B-	C	A-	Up	3.08	13.05	5.17	26.09	26.11	9.47	1,274	800-848-0920	Y
Nationwide Investor Destinations Moderate Fund Class C	NCDMX	B-	C	B+	Up	2.85	12.59	4.41	23.40	21.64	9.25	1,274	800-848-0920	Y
Nationwide Investor Destinations Moderate Fund Class R	GMDRX	B-	C	A-	Up	2.99	12.81	4.90	24.99	24.31	9.17	1,274	800-848-0920	Y
Nationwide Investor Destinations Moderate Fund Class R6	GMDIX	B-	C	A-	Up	3.19	13.20	5.57	27.44	28.45	9.41	1,274	800-848-0920	Y
Nationwide Investor Destinations Moderate Cls Service	NSDMX	B-	C	A-	Up	2.97	12.98	5.04	25.92	25.86	9.41	1,274	800-848-0920	Y
Nationwide Inv Destinations Moderate Inst Service Cls	NWWJX	B-	C	A-	Up	3.16	13.16	5.47	27.14	27.89	9.4	1,274	800-848-0920	Y
New Covenant Balanced Growth Fund	NCBGX	B	C	A-	Up	3.10	13.07	7.10	29.30	33.69	103.44	293.8		Y
Northern Global Tactical Asset Allocation Fund	BBALX	B-	C	A-	Up	2.09	11.64	4.61	23.08	21.71	12.9	90.8	800-595-9111	Y
Oakmark Equity and Income Fund Class Advisor	OAYBX	B-	C	B+	Up	3.45	13.07	4.74	32.25	27.89	30.26	12,521	641-219-558	Y
Oakmark Equity and Income Fund Class Institutional	OANBX	B-	C	B+	Up	3.48	13.11	4.83	32.37	28.02	30.27	12,521	641-219-558	Y
Oakmark Equity And Income Fund Investor Class	OAKBX	B-	C	B+	Up	3.45	12.99	4.62	31.72	27.39	30.25	12,521	641-219-558	Y
Oakmark Equity And Income Fund Service Class	OARBX	B-	C	B+	Up	3.36	12.83	4.30	30.66	25.52	30.07	12,521	641-219-558	Y
Osterweis Strategic Investment Investment	OSTVX	B-	C+	B+		3.28	15.75	6.79	29.10	22.09	14.77	134.1	866-236-0050	Y
Pacific Funds Portfolio Optimization Moderate Advisor Cls	POMDX	B-	C	B+	Up	3.73	14.46	6.06	27.58	28.44	12.5	1,129	800-722-2333	Y
Pacific Funds Portfolio Optimization Moderate Fund Class A	POCAX	B-	C	B+	Up	3.66	14.32	5.80	26.64	26.86	12.45	1,129	800-722-2333	Y
Pacific Funds Portfolio Optimization Moderate Fund Class B	POMBX	B-	C	B+	Up	3.38	13.91	4.97	23.77	22.17	12.2	1,129	800-722-2333	Y
Pacific Funds Portfolio Optimization Moderate Fund Class C	POMCX	B-	C	B+	Up	3.39	13.84	4.93	23.85	22.09	12.17	1,129	800-722-2333	Y
Pax Balanced Fund Class Institutional	PAXIX	B	C+	A-	Up	3.78	13.16	7.60	27.81	33.93	23.84	1,810	800-767-1729	Y
Pax Balanced Fund Individual Investor Class	PAXWX	B	C	A-	Up	3.72	13.00	7.35	26.75	32.22	23.46	1,810	800-767-1729	Y
PGIM Balanced Fund- Class A	PIBAX	B-	C	B+	Up	2.84	12.40	5.23	27.04	34.74	15.51	924.4	800-225-1852	Y
PGIM Balanced Fund- Class B	PBFBX	B-	C	B+	Up	2.50	11.76	4.09	23.72	29.39	15.61	924.4	800-225-1852	
PGIM Balanced Fund- Class C	PABCX	B-	C	B+	Up	2.62	11.95	4.41	24.35	30.06	15.61	924.4	800-225-1852	Y
PGIM Balanced Fund- Class R	PALRX	B-	C	B+	Up	2.67	12.09	4.56	25.50	32.63	15.52	924.4	800-225-1852	Y
PGIM Balanced Fund- Class R6	PIBQX	B-	C	A-	Up	2.98	12.62	5.64	28.38	37.00	15.64	924.4	800-225-1852	Y
PGIM Balanced Fund- Class Z	PABFX	B-	C	B+	Up	2.87	12.55	5.52	28.15	36.76	15.63	924.4	800-225-1852	Y
PGIM Income Builder Fund-Class A	PCGAX	B-	C	B		2.49	14.36	7.33	17.89	19.48	9.67	406.2	800-225-1852	Y
PGIM Income Builder Fund-Class R	PCLRX	B-	C	B		2.53	14.21	7.08	17.14	18.10	9.66	406.2	800-225-1852	Y
PGIM Income Builder Fund-Class R6	PCGQX	B-	C	B+		2.64	14.53	7.55	18.83	21.04	9.74	406.2	800-225-1852	Y

Category: Moderate Allocation (con't)

Fund Name	Ticker Symbol	RATINGS: Overall Rating	Reward Rating	Risk Rating	Recent Up/ Downgrade	TOTAL RETURNS & PERFORMANCE: 3-Month Total Return	6-Month Total Return	1-Year Total Return	3-Year Total Return	5-Year Total Return	ASSETS: NAV	Total Assets (MIL)	NEW INVESTORS: Telephone	Open to New Investors
PGIM Income Builder Fund-Class Z	PDCZX	B-	C	B+		2.64	14.53	7.54	18.78	20.99	9.74	406.2	800-225-1852	Y
PIMCO All Asset Fund Administrative Class	PAALX	B-	C	A-	Up	2.62	8.38	4.67	21.28	12.90	11.74	18,004	866-746-2602	Y
PIMCO All Asset Fund Class A	PASAX	B-	C	A-	Up	2.59	8.30	4.56	20.61	11.69	11.73	18,004	866-746-2602	Y
PIMCO All Asset Fund Class C	PASCX	B-	C	B+	Up	2.37	7.91	3.70	17.86	7.50	11.67	18,004	866-746-2602	Y
PIMCO All Asset Fund Class I-2	PALPX	B-	C	A-	Up	2.65	8.44	4.82	21.82	13.74	11.75	18,004	866-746-2602	Y
PIMCO All Asset Fund Class R	PATRX	B-	C	B+	Up	2.47	8.15	4.25	19.68	10.28	11.65	18,004	866-746-2602	Y
PIMCO All Asset Fund I-3	PAANX	B-	C	A-	Up	2.61	8.48	4.76	21.56	13.27	11.75	18,004	866-746-2602	Y
PIMCO All Asset Fund Institutional Class	PAAIX	B-	C	A-	Up	2.68	8.60	5.03	22.22	14.33	11.72	18,004	866-746-2602	Y
PIMCO Global Multi-Asset Fund Class A	PGMAX	B-	C	A-	Up	1.12	9.77	3.98	24.20	22.14	12.65	397.2	866-746-2602	Y
PIMCO Global Multi-Asset Fund Class C	PGMCX	B-	C	A-	Up	0.90	9.31	3.21	21.36	17.63	12.28	397.2	866-746-2602	Y
PIMCO Global Multi-Asset Fund Class I-2	PGAPX	B	C	A-	Up	1.19	9.95	4.33	25.57	24.69	12.75	397.2	866-746-2602	Y
PIMCO Global Multi-Asset Fund Institutional Class	PGAIX	B	C	A-	Up	1.27	10.05	4.48	25.96	25.35	12.78	397.2	866-746-2602	Y
Pioneer Classic Balanced Fund Class A	AOBLX	B	C+	A-	Up	4.19	14.92	8.95	31.43	35.13	9.4	295.5	617-742-7825	Y
Pioneer Classic Balanced Fund Class C	PCBCX	B	C	A-	Up	3.99	14.53	8.12	28.60	30.12	9.34	295.5	617-742-7825	Y
Pioneer Classic Balanced Fund Class K	PCBKX	B	C+	A-	Up	4.19	14.94	9.16	32.45	36.78	9.39	295.5	617-742-7825	Y
Pioneer Classic Balanced Fund Class R	CBPRX	B	C+	A-	Up	4.07	14.64	8.68	30.58	33.70	9.42	295.5	617-742-7825	Y
Pioneer Classic Balanced Fund Class Y	AYBLX	B	C+	A-	Up	4.27	15.06	9.32	32.39	36.70	9.47	295.5	617-742-7825	Y
Plumb Balanced Fund	PLBBX	B-	C+	B	Down	4.22	18.75	8.16	50.40	54.63	32.29	110.2		Y
PNC Balanced Allocation Fund Class A	PBAAX	B-	C	A-	Up	3.54	12.78	5.90	24.64	26.73	12.26	17.9	800-622-3863	Y
PNC Balanced Allocation Fund Class C	PBCCX	B-	C	B+	Up	3.36	12.37	5.13	21.86	22.32	11.99	17.9	800-622-3863	Y
PNC Balanced Allocation Fund Class I	PBLIX	B-	C	A-	Up	3.56	12.85	6.16	25.45	28.33	12.2	17.9	800-622-3863	Y
Praxis Genesis Balanced Portfolio Class A	MBAPX	B	C	A-	Up	3.13	12.09	5.79	25.37	27.17	13.79	78.1		Y
Preserver Alternative Opportunities Institutional Shares	PAOIX	B-	C	B+	Up	3.20	14.41	4.18	22.56		11.59	21.1		Y
Principal Strategic Asset Mgmt Balanced Portfolio Cls A	SABPX	B	C	A-	Up	3.39	12.86	6.26	27.15	29.39	15.38	4,529	800-787-1621	Y
Principal Strategic Asset Mgmt Balanced Portfolio Cls C	SCBPX	B-	C	A-	Up	3.24	12.43	5.48	24.29	24.67	15.13	4,529	800-787-1621	Y
Principal Strategic Asset Mgmt Balanced Portfolio Cls J	PSAJX	B	C+	A-	Up	3.42	12.97	6.47	27.79	30.34	14.82	4,529	800-787-1621	Y
Principal Strategic Asset Mgmt Balanced Portfolio Inst Cls	PSBIX	B	C+	A-	Up	3.46	13.07	6.58	28.41	31.59	15.11	4,529	800-787-1621	Y
Principal Strategic Asset Mgmt Balanced Portfolio R-1 Cls	PSBGX	B-	C	A-	Up	3.29	12.67	5.75	25.16	26.02	15.09	4,529	800-787-1621	Y
Principal Strategic Asset Mgmt Balanced Portfolio R-2 Cls	PSBVX	B	C	A-	Up	3.36	12.67	5.95	25.67	26.87	15.04	4,529	800-787-1621	Y
Principal Strategic Asset Mgmt Balanced Portfolio R-3 Cls	PBAPX	B	C	A-	Up	3.33	12.79	6.07	26.25	27.93	15.07	4,529	800-787-1621	Y
Principal Strategic Asset Mgmt Balanced Portfolio R-4 Cls	PSBLX	B	C	A-	Up	3.44	12.92	6.25	26.97	29.19	15.1	4,529	800-787-1621	Y
Principal Strategic Asset Mgmt Balanced Portfolio R-5 Cls	PSBFX	B	C	A-	Up	3.40	12.96	6.33	27.43	29.91	15.09	4,529	800-787-1621	Y
Putnam Dynamic Asset Allocation Balanced Fund Class A	PABAX	B-	C	B+	Up	2.73	12.89	4.34	27.59	32.57	14.54	2,787	617-292-1000	Y
Putnam Dynamic Asset Allocation Balanced Fund Class B	PABBX	B-	C	B+	Up	2.54	12.43	3.53	24.81	27.75	14.48	2,787	617-292-1000	Y
Putnam Dynamic Asset Allocation Balanced Fund Class C	AABCX	B-	C	B+	Up	2.55	12.39	3.54	24.75	27.67	14.1	2,787	617-292-1000	Y
Putnam Dynamic Asset Allocation Balanced Fund Class M	PABMX	B-	C	B+	Up	2.61	12.55	3.81	25.74	29.34	14.51	2,787	617-292-1000	Y
Putnam Dynamic Asset Allocation Balanced Fund Class P		B-	C	B+	Up	2.83	13.07	4.74	28.50	33.51	14.58	2,787	617-292-1000	
Putnam Dynamic Asset Allocation Balanced Fund Class R	PAARX	B-	C	B+	Up	2.62	12.63	4.05	26.61	30.87	14.4	2,787	617-292-1000	Y
Putnam Dynamic Asset Allocation Balanced Fund Class R5	PAADX	B-	C	B+	Up	2.79	13.00	4.59	28.58	34.30	14.57	2,787	617-292-1000	Y
Putnam Dynamic Asset Allocation Balanced Fund Class R6	PAAEX	B-	C	B+	Up	2.82	13.06	4.70	28.89	34.98	14.57	2,787	617-292-1000	Y
Putnam Dynamic Asset Allocation Balanced Fund Class Y	PABYX	B-	C	B+	Up	2.80	13.00	4.59	28.58	34.26	14.57	2,787	617-292-1000	Y
QS Conservative Growth Fund Class A	SBBAX	B-	C	A-	Up	2.52	10.99	5.46	23.97	24.10	13.85	281.4	877-721-1926	Y
QS Conservative Growth Fund Class C	SCBCX	B-	C	A-	Up	2.30	10.56	4.72	21.32	19.65	14.51	281.4	877-721-1926	Y
QS Conservative Growth Fund Class I	LMEIX	B-	C	A-		2.59	11.10	5.76	24.97	25.66	13.84	281.4	877-721-1926	Y
QS Conservative Growth Fund Class R	LLARX	B-	C	A-	Up	2.50	10.79	5.17	22.90	22.24	13.89	281.4	877-721-1926	Y
QS Strategic Real Return Fund Class I	LRRIX	B-	C	B+	Up	1.69	11.30	0.77	12.59	-7.35	11.42	100.1	877-721-1926	Y
QS Strategic Real Return Fund Class IS	LRRSX	B-	C	B+	Up	1.71	11.47	0.96	12.96	-6.91	11.27	100.1	877-721-1926	Y
Rational Strategic Allocation Fund Class A	HBAFX	B-	C	A-	Up	1.16	7.92	3.76	21.73	22.45	9.72	9.8	800-253-0412	Y
Rational Strategic Allocation Fund Class C	RHSCX	B-	C	B+	Up	0.98	7.45	2.98	18.92	17.98	9.68	9.8	800-253-0412	Y
Rational Strategic Allocation Fund Class Institutional	RHSIX	B-	C	A-		1.23	8.00	3.95	22.53	23.34	9.68	9.8	800-253-0412	Y
RiverFront Asset Allocation Moderate Class A	RMOAX	B-	C	B+	Up	1.75	10.78	2.11	19.32	20.60	10.26	60.3	866-759-5679	Y
RiverFront Asset Allocation Moderate Class I	RMIIX	B-	C	B+	Up	1.79	10.83	2.30	20.14	22.03	10.27	60.3	866-759-5679	Y

Category: Moderate Allocation (con't)

Fund Name	Ticker Symbol	RATINGS: Overall Rating	Reward Rating	Risk Rating	Recent Up/ Downgrade	TOTAL RETURNS & PERFORMANCE: 3-Month Total Return	6-Month Total Return	1-Year Total Return	3-Year Total Return	5-Year Total Return	ASSETS: NAV	Total Assets (MIL)	NEW INVESTORS: Telephone	Open to New Investors
RiverFront Asset Allocation Moderate Class Investor	RMIAX	B-	C	B+	Up	1.73	10.80	2.13	19.33	20.61	10.27	60.3	866-759-5679	Y
RiverNorth Core Opportunity Fund Class I	RNCIX	B-	C	B+	Up	2.86	14.25	5.63	33.38	29.92	8.12	131.4	312-832-1440	Y
RiverNorth Core Opportunity Fund Class R	RNCOX	B-	C	B+	Up	3.17	14.65	5.55	31.27	29.04	8.13	131.4	312-832-1440	Y
Russell Investments LifePoints Balanced Strategy Cls A	RBLAX	B-	C	A-	Up	1.97	9.36	2.96	19.46	19.19	10.86	1,516	800-426-7969	Y
Russell Investments LifePoints Balanced Strategy Cls E	RBLEX	B-	C	B+	Up	1.96	9.30	2.86	19.12	18.63	10.92	1,516	800-426-7969	Y
Russell Investments LifePoints Balanced Strategy Cls R1	RBLRX	B-	C	A-	Up	2.03	9.42	3.18	20.14	20.52	11.03	1,516	800-426-7969	Y
Russell Investments LifePoints Balanced Strategy Cls R4	RBLUX	B-	C	A-	Up	2.05	9.43	2.92	19.32	19.04	10.9	1,516	800-426-7969	Y
Russell Investments LifePoints Balanced Strategy Cls R5	RBLVX	B-	C	B+	Up	1.96	9.32	2.71	18.45	17.64	10.9	1,516	800-426-7969	Y
Russell Investments LifePoints Balanced Strategy Cls S	RBLSX	B-	C	A-	Up	2.03	9.43	3.13	20.01	20.09	11.02	1,516	800-426-7969	Y
Scharf Multi-Asset Opportunity Fund Institutional Class	LOGOX	B-	C	B		3.50	12.59	11.01	23.49	28.98	32.81	53.3	831-429-6513	Y
Schwab Balanced Fund™	SWOBX	B-	C	B+		3.55	14.42	6.27	32.16	39.26	15.71	505.6	877-824-5615	Y
Schwab MarketTrack Balanced Portfolio™	SWBGX	B-	C	A-	Up	3.03	12.26	5.13	25.95	29.32	18.31	540.9	877-824-5615	Y
SEI Asset Allocation Trust Aggressive Strategy Cls F	SSGAX	B-	C	B+	Up	3.48	14.84	4.01	29.33	27.00	15.25	198.1	800-342-5734	Y
SEI Asset Allocation Trust Aggressive Strategy Cls I	SEAIX	B-	C	B+	Up	3.37	14.62	3.72	28.29	25.28	14.83	198.1	800-342-5734	Y
SEI Asset Alloc Trust Conservative Strategy Alloc Cls F	SMGAX	B	C+	A-		2.86	14.28	9.28	26.26	41.75	13.48	39.9	800-342-5734	Y
SEI Asset Alloc Trust Defensive Strategy Alloc Cls F	STDAX	B	C+	A-		2.88	13.83	9.01	26.19	39.84	14.54	10.3	800-342-5734	Y
SEI Inst Managed Trust Multi-Asset Accumulation Cls F	SAAAX	B	C+	A-	Up	5.27	16.38	8.87	19.59	22.36	10.37	2,886	800-342-5734	Y
SEI Inst Managed Trust Multi-Asset Accumulation Cls Y	SMOYX	B	C+	A-	Up	5.34	16.51	9.21	20.43	23.69	10.44	2,886	800-342-5734	Y
SEI Institutional Managed Trust Multi-Asset Income Cls F	SIOAX	B-	C+	B	Down	3.29	10.38	9.03	21.23	28.46	11.05	968.1	800-342-5734	Y
SEI Institutional Managed Trust Multi-Asset Income Cls Y	SLIYX	B-	C+	B	Down	3.32	10.43	9.13	21.59	29.01	11.05	968.1	800-342-5734	Y
Sextant Core Fund	SCORX	B-	C	A-		3.94	13.32	9.77	24.84	22.65	13.69	14.9		Y
Sit Balanced Fund	SIBAX	B	C	A-	Up	3.52	13.42	7.97	34.22	44.75	25.06	34.5	800-332-5580	Y
Stadion Tactical Defensive Fund Class A	ETFRX	B-	C	A-	Up	1.77	8.21	5.68	33.24	23.63	13.98	100.3	706-353-8737	Y
Stadion Tactical Defensive Fund Class C	ETFZX	B-	C	A-	Up	1.62	7.78	4.91	30.17	18.93	12.93	100.3	706-353-8737	Y
Stadion Tactical Defensive Fund Class I	ETFWX	B	C	A-	Up	1.82	8.29	5.89	34.07	24.94	14.26	100.3	706-353-8737	Y
State Farm Balanced Fund	STFBX	B	C+	B+		5.93	15.22	12.53	27.74	38.15	71.38	2,037		Y
Sterling Capital Strategic Allocation Balanced Cls A	BAMGX	B-	C	A-	Up	2.68	10.72	3.99	23.78	22.88	12.05	26.7	800-228-1872	Y
Sterling Capital Strategic Allocation Balanced Cls C	BCMCX	B-	C	B+	Up	2.46	10.31	3.17	20.98	18.34	11.81	26.7	800-228-1872	Y
Sterling Capital Strategic Allocation Balanced Inst Shares	BCGTX	B-	C	A-	Up	2.63	10.84	4.22	24.70	24.43	12.14	26.7	800-228-1872	Y
T. Rowe Price Balanced Fund	RPBAX	B	C	A-	Up	3.35	13.79	6.66	33.27	36.40	23.93	4,405	410-345-2000	Y
T. Rowe Price Balanced I Class	RBAIX	B	C	A-	Up	3.35	13.89	6.79	33.83	37.10	23.93	4,405	410-345-2000	Y
T. Rowe Price Capital Appreciation Fund	PRWCX	B	B-	A	Down	4.91	18.17	15.20	41.40	63.23	31.15	35,084	410-345-2000	
T. Rowe Price Capital Appreciation Fund Advisor Class	PACLX	B	B-	A	Down	4.83	18.01	14.86	40.14	60.83	30.79	35,084	410-345-2000	
T. Rowe Price Capital Appreciation Fund I Class	TRAIX	B	B-	A	Down	4.91	18.24	15.31	41.81	63.81	31.18	35,084	410-345-2000	Y
T. Rowe Price Global Allocation Fund	RPGAX	B-	C	A-	Up	3.34	13.25	5.01	28.99	29.37	12.99	699.8	410-345-2000	Y
T. Rowe Price Global Allocation Fund Advisor Class	PAFGX	B-	C	A-	Up	3.27	13.03	4.68	28.04	28.18	12.92	699.8	410-345-2000	Y
T. Rowe Price Global Allocation Fund I Class	TGAFX	B-	C	A-	Up	3.33	13.31	5.08	29.69	30.20	13.02	699.8	410-345-2000	Y
T. Rowe Price Personal Strategy Balanced Fund	TRPBX	B	C	A-	Up	3.39	13.44	6.67	32.90	35.71	23.67	2,433	410-345-2000	Y
T. Rowe Price Personal Strategy Balanced Fund I Class	TPPAX	B	C	A-	Up	3.43	13.49	6.80	33.41	36.23	23.68	2,433	410-345-2000	Y
Teberg Fund	TEBRX	B-	C	B	Up	2.95	15.36	5.40	29.56	24.17	11.86	28.2		Y
TETON Westwood Balanced Fund Class A	WEBCX	B	C	A-	Up	4.01	12.01	7.54	26.10	32.93	11.47	58.0		Y
TETON Westwood Balanced Fund Class AAA	WEBAX	B	C+	A-	Up	4.00	12.12	7.77	26.96	34.53	11.39	58.0		Y
TETON Westwood Balanced Fund Class C	WBCCX	B-	C	A-		3.82	11.72	6.96	24.10	29.62	11.68	58.0		Y
TETON Westwood Balanced Fund Class Institutional	WBBIX	B	C+	A-	Up	4.08	12.29	8.06	27.87	36.30	11.37	58.0		Y
Thrivent Balanced Income Plus Fund Class A	AABFX	B-	C	A-	Up	2.71	11.43	4.07	22.05	25.21	12.6	385.8		Y
Thrivent Balanced Income Plus Fund Class S	IBBFX	B-	C	A-	Up	2.70	11.51	4.30	23.16	27.26	12.56	385.8		Y
Thrivent Moderate Allocation Fund Class A	THMAX	B-	C	B+	Up	3.24	12.82	6.57	27.39	29.42	13.93	2,525		Y
Thrivent Moderate Allocation Fund Class S	TMAIX	B-	C	B+	Up	3.29	12.98	6.89	28.40	31.36	13.97	2,525		Y
TIAA-CREF Lifestyle Moderate Fund Advisor Class	TSMHX	B-	C	B+	Up	3.30	13.85	4.96	29.27	32.51	14.12	366.8	877-518-9161	Y
TIAA-CREF Lifestyle Moderate Fund Institutional Class	TSIMX	B-	C	B+	Up	3.32	13.88	5.03	29.49	32.79	14.12	366.8	877-518-9161	Y
TIAA-CREF Lifestyle Moderate Fund Premier Class	TSMPX	B-	C	B+	Up	3.28	13.86	4.79	28.90	31.92	14.15	366.8	877-518-9161	Y
TIAA-CREF Lifestyle Moderate Fund Retail Class	TSMLX	B-	C	B+	Up	3.26	13.76	4.68	28.41	31.08	14.1	366.8	877-518-9161	Y

Category: Moderate Allocation (con't)

Fund Name	Ticker Symbol	RATINGS: Overall Rating	Reward Rating	Risk Rating	Recent Up/ Downgrade	TOTAL RETURNS & PERFORMANCE: 3-Month Total Return	6-Month Total Return	1-Year Total Return	3-Year Total Return	5-Year Total Return	ASSETS: NAV	Total Assets (MIL)	NEW INVESTORS: Telephone	Open to New Investors
TIAA-CREF Lifestyle Moderate Fund Retirement Class	TSMTX	B-	C	B+	Up	3.19	13.77	4.70	28.48	31.11	14.1	366.8	877-518-9161	Y
TIAA-CREF Managed Allocation Fund Institutional Class	TIMIX	B-	C	B+	Up	3.28	13.82	5.18	29.77	33.59	12.68	867.7	877-518-9161	Y
TIAA-CREF Managed Allocation Fund Retail Class	TIMRX	B-	C	B+	Up	3.21	13.63	4.98	28.81	31.92	12.72	867.7	877-518-9161	Y
TIAA-CREF Managed Allocation Fund Retirement Class	TITRX	B-	C	B+	Up	3.22	13.69	5.00	28.85	31.98	12.67	867.7	877-518-9161	Y
TOPS® Balanced ETF Portfolio Class 1		B-	C	A-	Up	2.49	10.79	5.05	20.74	21.90	12.73	22.0	855-572-5945	Y
TOPS® Balanced ETF Portfolio Class 2		B-	C	A-	Up	2.42	10.64	4.73	19.81	20.04	12.27	22.0	855-572-5945	Y
TOPS® Balanced ETF Portfolio Investor Class		B-	C	A-	Up	2.27	10.14	4.35	19.39	17.86	13.08	22.0	855-572-5945	Y
TOPS® Balanced ETF Portfolio Service Class Shares		B-	C	A-		2.34	10.27	4.64	20.63	19.65	12.27	22.0	855-572-5945	Y
TOPS® Managed Risk Moderate Growth ETF Portfolio Class 1		B-	C	B+	Up	2.62	10.46	3.67	22.98	15.16	12.14	868.6	855-572-5945	
TOPS® Managed Risk Moderate Growth ETF Portfolio Class 2		B-	C	B+	Up	2.54	10.32	3.38	21.97	13.68	12.07	868.6	855-572-5945	Y
TOPS® Managed Risk Moderate Growth ETF Port Cls 3 Shares		B-	C	B+	Up	2.39	9.71	3.05	21.77	12.58	12.03	868.6	855-572-5945	Y
TOPS® Managed Risk Moderate Growth ETF Port Cls 4 Shares		B-	C	B+	Up	2.31	9.66	2.82	20.94	11.25	11.96	868.6	855-572-5945	Y
TOPS® Managed Risk Moderate Growth ETF Portfolio Inv Cls		B-	C	B+	Up	2.23	9.20	2.99	21.09	11.82	12.86	868.6	855-572-5945	Y
TOPS® Moderate Growth ETF Portfolio Class 1		B-	C	A-	Up	2.62	12.72	4.64	27.26	26.89	12.49	33.4	855-572-5945	Y
TOPS® Moderate Growth ETF Portfolio Class 2		B-	C	A-	Up	2.55	12.53	4.39	26.35	25.14	12.03	33.4	855-572-5945	Y
TOPS® Moderate Growth ETF Portfolio Investor Class		B-	C	A-	Up	2.24	11.85	4.46	25.53	21.77	13.27	33.4	855-572-5945	Y
TOPS® Moderate Growth ETF Portfolio Service Class Shares		B-	C	A-		2.48	12.06	4.30	27.45	24.62	12.04	33.4	855-572-5945	Y
Touchstone Balanced Fund Class A	SEBLX	B	C+	A-		4.27	14.68	10.12	34.76	41.39	22.18	338.5	800-543-0407	Y
Touchstone Balanced Fund Class Y	SIBLX	B	C+	A-		4.31	14.80	10.32	35.59	42.83	22.01	338.5	800-543-0407	Y
Touchstone Dynamic Global Allocation Fund A	TSMAX	B-	C	B+	Up	2.66	12.14	2.89	21.10	16.42	11.78	87.4	800-543-0407	Y
Touchstone Dynamic Global Allocation Fund Y	TSMYX	B-	C	B+	Up	2.78	12.35	3.11	22.00	17.89	11.9	87.4	800-543-0407	Y
Transamerica Asset Allocation Intermediate Horizon R	TAARX	B-	C	B	Up	2.90	11.87	4.82	23.46	23.95	10.38	360.1	888-233-4339	Y
Transamerica Asset Allocation Intermediate Horizon R4	TAAFX	B-	C	A-		2.96	12.01	5.09	24.36	25.48	10.38	360.1	888-233-4339	Y
Transamerica Asset Alloc Moderate Growth Port Cls A	IMLAX	B-	C	B+	Up	2.32	12.19	2.51	24.93	27.74	11.87	2,061	888-233-4339	Y
Transamerica Asset Alloc Moderate Growth Port Cls I	TMGIX	B-	C	B+	Up	2.33	12.32	2.74	25.78	29.23	11.86	2,061	888-233-4339	Y
Transamerica Asset Alloc Moderate Growth Port Cls R	IMGRX	B-	C	B+	Up	2.24	12.03	2.20	23.91	25.94	11.82	2,061	888-233-4339	Y
Transamerica Balanced II I3	TBLTX	B	C+	A-		3.85	14.02	8.99	30.78	39.55	10.69	120.7	888-233-4339	Y
Transamerica Balanced II R	TBLRX	B	C+	A-		3.62	13.74	8.54	29.60	38.28	10.69	120.7	888-233-4339	Y
Transamerica Dynamic Allocation Fund Class A	ATTRX	B-	C	B	Up	2.78	9.13	2.01	21.70	18.74	12.18	15.7	888-233-4339	Y
Transamerica Dynamic Allocation Fund Class I	ITTOX	B-	C	B	Up	2.87	9.26	2.30	22.70	20.27	12.15	15.7	888-233-4339	Y
Transamerica Multi-Managed Balanced Fund Class A	IBALX	B	C+	A-		3.60	13.67	8.53	29.78	38.23	27.89	988.5	888-233-4339	Y
Transamerica Multi-Managed Balanced Fund Class C	IBLLX	B-	C	A-		3.44	13.21	7.71	26.85	33.23	27.37	988.5	888-233-4339	Y
Transamerica Multi-Managed Balanced Fund Class I	TBLIX	B	C+	A-		3.68	13.80	8.76	30.63	39.90	28.03	988.5	888-233-4339	Y
Transamerica Multi-Managed Balanced Fund Class R6	TAMMX	B	C+	A-		3.70	13.86	8.87	31.05	40.17	28.03	988.5	888-233-4339	Y
Tributary Balanced Fund Class Institutional Plus	FOBPX	B	C+	A-		3.45	13.37	8.37	29.82	34.08	17.21	72.7		Y
Tributary Balanced Fund Institutional Class	FOBAX	B	C+	A-		3.41	13.30	8.16	29.06	32.82	17.38	72.7		Y
UBS Global Allocation Fund Class A	BNGLX	B-	C	B+	Up	2.69	12.24	3.97	25.23	21.20	12.56	268.0	212-882-5586	Y
UBS Global Allocation Fund Class P	BPGLX	B-	C	A-	Up	2.79	12.40	4.21	26.14	22.76	12.87	268.0	212-882-5586	Y
UBS U.S. Allocation Fund Class A	PWTAX	B-	C	B	Up	3.43	16.67	5.71	30.67	36.77	46.68	236.9	212-882-5586	Y
UBS U.S. Allocation Fund Class P	PWTYX	B-	C	B+	Up	3.49	16.81	5.99	31.71	38.62	47.65	236.9	212-882-5586	Y
USAA Cornerstone Moderate Fund	USBSX	B-	C	B+	Up	2.53	9.93	4.01	19.44	16.02	14.5	1,199	800-235-8396	Y
USAA Cornerstone Moderately Aggressive Fund	USCRX	B-	C	B+	Up	2.50	10.65	3.41	20.95	16.07	24.93	2,877	800-235-8396	Y
USAA Target Managed Allocation Fund	UTMAX	B-	C	B	Up	3.11	13.88	2.92	22.62		10.58	525.8	800-235-8396	Y
VALIC Company I Dynamic Allocation Fund	VDAFX	B-	C	B+	Up	3.42	13.76	6.67	31.85	27.39	12.08	212.2		Y
VALIC Company II Moderate Growth Lifestyle Fund	VMGLX	B-	C	B+	Up	3.09	13.84	4.79	26.65	27.82	13.91	952.4		Y
Value Line Asset Allocation Fund Institutional Class	VLAIX	B+	B	A-	Up	6.22	20.36	17.65	43.72	56.11	37.35	743.6	800-243-2729	Y
Value Line Asset Allocation Fund Investor Class	VLAAX	B+	B	A-	Up	6.15	20.17	17.35	42.65	54.71	37.23	743.6	800-243-2729	Y
Vanguard Balanced Index Fund Admiral Shares	VBIAX	B	C+	A-		3.73	14.35	8.90	31.94	43.05	37.07	41,955	877-662-7447	Y
Vanguard Balanced Index Fund Institutional Shares	VBAIX	B	C+	A-		3.73	14.35	8.94	32.01	43.15	37.08	41,955	877-662-7447	Y
Vanguard Balanced Index Fund Investor Shares	VBINX	B	C+	A-		3.70	14.28	8.78	31.48	42.15	37.08	41,955	877-662-7447	Y
Vanguard LifeStrategy Moderate Growth Fund Investor Shares	VSMGX	B	C	A-	Up	3.34	12.80	6.66	27.85	32.79	27.55	16,723	877-662-7447	Y
Vanguard Managed Payout Fund Investor Shares	VPGDX	B-	C	A-	Up	1.88	9.94	4.15	21.70	25.01	16.85	1,803	877-662-7447	Y

Category: Moderate Allocation (con't)

Fund Name	Ticker Symbol	Overall Rating	Reward Rating	Risk Rating	Recent Up/ Downgrade	3-Month Total Return	6-Month Total Return	1-Year Total Return	3-Year Total Return	5-Year Total Return	NAV	Total Assets (MIL)	Telephone	Open to New Investors
		RATINGS				TOTAL RETURNS & PERFORMANCE					ASSETS		NEW INVESTORS	
Vanguard Star Fund Investor Shares	VGSTX	B-	C	B+	Up	3.61	14.14	6.57	33.54	37.26	26.75	21,973	877-662-7447	Y
Vanguard Wellington™ Fund Admiral™ Shares	VWENX	B	C+	A		3.91	13.56	10.37	33.92	43.83	71.41	105,381	877-662-7447	
Vanguard Wellington™ Fund Investor Shares	VWELX	B	C+	A-		3.89	13.51	10.28	33.60	43.27	41.35	105,381	877-662-7447	
Virtus Herzfeld Fund Class C	VHFCX	B-	C	B	Up	1.32	13.71	1.97	26.89	25.67	11.09	53.5	800-243-1574	Y
Virtus Herzfeld Fund Class I	VHFIX	B-	C	B	Up	1.57	14.31	2.96	30.67	32.09	11.15	53.5	800-243-1574	Y
Virtus Tactical Allocation Fund Class A	NAINX	B-	C	B	Up	4.44	19.83	6.82	35.44	26.37	9.69	602.1	800-243-1574	Y
Virtus Tactical Allocation Fund Class C	POICX	B-	C	B	Up	4.15	19.37	5.84	32.31	21.57	9.97	602.1	800-243-1574	Y
Virtus Tactical Allocation Fund Class I	VTAIX	B-	C	B	Up	4.41	19.86	6.86	35.48	26.41	9.68	602.1	800-243-1574	Y
Voya Balanced Income Portfolio Class A	IIFAX	B	B-	A		3.81	14.28	7.79	29.08	22.30	11.44	396.1	800-366-0066	Y
Voya Balanced Income Portfolio Class I	IIFIX	B	B-	A		4.07	14.61	8.43	31.43	25.83	12	396.1	800-366-0066	Y
Voya Balanced Income Portfolio Class S	IIFSX	B	B-	A		4.01	14.50	8.16	30.43	24.50	11.92	396.1	800-366-0066	Y
Voya Balanced Income Portfolio Class S2	IIFTX	B	B-	A		3.93	14.43	8.02	29.88	23.54	11.89	396.1	800-366-0066	Y
Voya Balanced Portfolio Class I	IBPIX	B-	C	A-	Up	2.92	12.53	5.26	26.65	27.62	14.77	372.4	800-366-0066	Y
Voya Balanced Portfolio Class S	IBPSX	B-	C	A-	Up	2.85	12.36	4.98	25.73	26.07	14.7	372.4	800-366-0066	Y
Voya Global Diversified Payment Fund Class A	IGPAX	B-	C	B+	Up	2.95	10.54	3.86	18.41	17.91	7.75	443.9	800-366-0066	Y
Voya Global Diversified Payment Fund Class C	IGPCX	B-	C	B+	Up	2.70	10.06	3.11	15.69	13.58	8.02	443.9	800-366-0066	Y
Voya Global Diversified Payment Fund Class I	IGPIX	B-	C	B+	Up	2.91	10.50	4.06	19.41	19.60	7.71	443.9	800-366-0066	Y
Voya Global Diversified Payment Fund Class R	IGPRX	B-	C	B+	Up	3.00	10.48	3.80	17.79	16.78	7.76	443.9	800-366-0066	Y
Voya Global Diversified Payment Fund Class R6	VTPRX	B-	C	B+	Up	2.91	10.49	4.06	19.41	19.60	7.71	443.9	800-366-0066	Y
Voya Global Diversified Payment Fund Class W	IGPWX	B-	C	B+	Up	2.92	10.52	4.07	19.31	19.46	7.69	443.9	800-366-0066	Y
Voya Global Multi-Asset Fund Class A	ATLAX	B-	C	B+	Up	3.18	12.39	3.19	25.40	21.61	11.66	141.4	800-366-0066	Y
Voya Global Multi-Asset Fund Class I	ALEGX	B-	C	B+	Up	3.22	12.50	3.43	26.30	23.10	11.86	141.4	800-366-0066	Y
Voya Global Multi-Asset Fund Class O	IDSIX	B-	C	B+	Up	3.02	12.25	2.90	25.01	21.25	11.57	141.4	800-366-0066	Y
Voya Global Multi-Asset Fund Class W	IAFWX	B-	C	B+	Up	3.31	12.53	3.53	26.40	23.18	11.85	141.4	800-366-0066	Y
Voya Retirement Moderate Growth Portfolio Class A	IRMGX	B-	C	A-	Up	3.17	13.09	5.81	26.29	27.75	12.35	1,818	800-366-0066	Y
Voya Retirement Moderate Growth Portfolio Class I	IRGMX	B-	C	A-	Up	3.19	13.28	6.17	27.69	30.25	12.28	1,818	800-366-0066	Y
Voya Solution Balanced Portfolio Class A	ISGAX	B-	C	A-	Up	2.99	12.76	5.15	25.58	27.06	9.98	56.6	800-366-0066	Y
Voya Solution Balanced Portfolio Class I	ISGJX	B-	C	A-	Up	3.17	13.16	5.67	27.71	30.38	10.4	56.6	800-366-0066	Y
Voya Solution Balanced Portfolio Class R6	VYRLX	B-	C	A-	Up	3.17	13.16	5.67	27.58	30.38	10.4	56.6	800-366-0066	Y
Voya Solution Balanced Portfolio Class S	ISGKX	B-	C	A-	Up	3.05	12.93	5.41	26.65	28.80	10.13	56.6	800-366-0066	Y
Voya Solution Balanced Portfolio Class S2	ISGTX	B-	C	A-	Up	3.05	12.83	5.21	26.02	27.67	10.11	56.6	800-366-0066	Y
Voya Strategic Allocation Moderate Portfolio Class I	IIMDX	B-	C	A-	Up	3.04	12.41	5.62	26.43	29.01	13.71	124.3	800-366-0066	Y
Voya Strategic Allocation Moderate Portfolio Class S	ISMDX	B-	C	A-	Up	2.96	12.31	5.40	25.48	27.44	13.64	124.3	800-366-0066	Y
VY® Invesco Equity and Income Portfolio Class A	IUAAX	B-	C	B+	Up	3.09	13.28	2.91	27.34	28.43	43.91	1,356	800-366-0066	Y
VY® Invesco Equity and Income Portfolio Class I	IUAIX	B-	C	B+	Up	3.21	13.57	3.44	29.26	31.68	44.69	1,356	800-366-0066	Y
VY® Invesco Equity and Income Portfolio Class S	IUASX	B-	C	B+	Up	3.16	13.45	3.17	28.32	30.07	44.36	1,356	800-366-0066	Y
VY® Invesco Equity and Income Portfolio Class S2	IVIPX	B-	C	B+	Up	3.11	13.35	3.04	27.81	29.20	43.71	1,356	800-366-0066	Y
VY® T. Rowe Price Capital Appreciation Portfolio Class A	ITRAX	B	B-	A	Down	4.75	17.87	14.58	39.09	58.97	28.22	7,145	800-366-0066	Y
VY® T. Rowe Price Capital Appreciation Portfolio Class I	ITRIX	B	B-	A	Down	4.92	18.23	15.26	41.61	63.81	29.63	7,145	800-366-0066	Y
VY® T. Rowe Price Capital Appreciation Portfolio Class R6	VPRAX	B	B-	A	Down	4.91	18.22	15.29	41.69	63.11	29.65	7,145	800-366-0066	Y
VY® T. Rowe Price Capital Appreciation Portfolio Class S	ITCSX	B	B-	A	Down	4.85	18.06	14.99	40.60	61.80	29.61	7,145	800-366-0066	Y
VY® T. Rowe Price Capital Appreciation Portfolio Class S2	ITCTX	B	B-	A	Down	4.81	17.99	14.94	39.97	60.60	29.37	7,145	800-366-0066	Y
Wells Fargo Asset Allocation Fund - Class A	EAAFX	B-	C	B+	Up	3.56	13.73	5.60	21.22	11.52	13.66	2,005	800-222-8222	Y
Wells Fargo Asset Allocation Fund - Class Admin	EAIFX	B-	C	B+	Up	3.59	13.90	5.79	21.86	12.53	13.84	2,005	800-222-8222	Y
Wells Fargo Asset Allocation Fund - Class C	EACFX	B-	C	B+	Up	3.38	13.37	4.79	18.53	7.43	13.14	2,005	800-222-8222	Y
Wells Fargo Asset Allocation Fund - Class Inst	EAAIX	B-	C	B+	Up	3.63	13.89	5.96	22.52	13.66	13.69	2,005	800-222-8222	Y
Wells Fargo Asset Allocation Fund - Class R	EAXFX	B-	C	B+	Up	3.44	13.60	5.32	20.29	10.13	13.53	2,005	800-222-8222	Y
Wells Fargo Growth Balanced Fund - Class A	WFGBX	B-	C	B+	Up	3.55	13.66	5.47	27.82	32.36	47.16	226.4	800-222-8222	Y
Wells Fargo Growth Balanced Fund - Class Admin	NVGBX	B-	C	B+	Up	3.57	13.74	5.66	28.70	33.91	41.71	226.4	800-222-8222	Y
Wells Fargo Growth Balanced Fund - Class C	WFGWX	B-	C	B+	Up	3.35	13.22	4.71	25.02	27.50	40.66	226.4	800-222-8222	Y
Wells Fargo Index Asset Allocation Fund - Class A	SFAAX	B	C+	A-		3.44	13.82	8.70	29.25	44.74	34.66	1,325	800-222-8222	Y
Wells Fargo Index Asset Allocation Fund - Class Admin	WFAIX	B	C+	A-		3.48	13.91	8.89	29.93	46.19	34.67	1,325	800-222-8222	Y

Category: Moderate Allocation (con't)

Fund Name	Ticker Symbol	RATINGS: Overall Rating	Reward Rating	Risk Rating	Recent Up/ Downgrade	TOTAL RETURNS & PERFORMANCE: 3-Month Total Return	6-Month Total Return	1-Year Total Return	3-Year Total Return	5-Year Total Return	ASSETS: NAV	Total Assets (MIL)	NEW INVESTORS: Telephone	Open to New Investors
Wells Fargo Index Asset Allocation Fund - Class C	WFALX	B-	C	A-		3.21	13.37	7.88	26.33	39.37	21.07	1,325	800-222-8222	Y
Wells Fargo Index Asset Allocation Institutional Cls	WFATX	B	C+	A-		3.50	14.01	9.06	30.36	45.98	34.62	1,325	800-222-8222	Y
Wells Fargo WealthBuilder Growth Balanced Fund Class A	WGBAX	B-	C	A-	Up	2.89	12.45	5.09	27.38	25.42	12.1	599.9	800-222-8222	Y
Wells Fargo WealthBuilder Growth Balanced Inst Cls	WGBIX	B-	C	A-	Up	2.97	12.65	5.23	26.35	24.42	12.11	599.9	800-222-8222	Y
WesMark Balanced Fund	WMBLX	B-	C	A-	Up	3.49	11.26	6.82	23.07	28.15	12.91	109.5	800-861-1013	Y
Westwood Income Opportunity Fund A Class	WWIAX	B-	C	B+		2.97	11.49	6.95	18.91	22.31	15.45	1,342		Y
Westwood Income Opportunity Fund Institutional Class	WHGIX	B-	C+	B+		3.04	11.71	7.22	19.82	23.88	15.46	1,342		Y
Westwood Worldwide Income Opportunity Institutional Shares	WWIOX	B-	C	B+	Up	2.47	9.45	5.20	16.60		10.48	1.7		Y
Wildermuth Endowment Fund Class A	WESFX	B-	C+	B+		4.05	5.78	5.79	31.74		13.57	--	877-562-0856	Y
Wildermuth Endowment Fund Class C	WEFCX	B	C	A+	Up	3.84	5.36	4.96	28.76		13.21	--	877-562-0856	Y
Wildermuth Endowment Fund Class I	WEIFX	B	C+	A-	Up	4.09	5.89	6.06	32.86		13.69	--	877-562-0856	Y
Wilmington Diversified Income Fund Class A	WDIAX	B	C	A-	Up	2.86	10.77	5.82	23.68	23.01	10.55	39.5	800-836-2211	Y
Wilmington Diversified Income Fund Class I	WDIIX	B	C	A-	Up	2.83	10.79	5.97	24.45	24.44	10.55	39.5	800-836-2211	Y
Wilmington Real Asset Fund Class A	WMMRX	B-	C	B+	Up	0.58	11.54	3.77	11.89	7.74	14.49	313.8	800-836-2211	Y
Wilmington Real Asset Fund Class Institutional	WMRIX	B-	C	B+		0.64	11.73	3.99	12.73	9.07	14.65	313.8	800-836-2211	Y
WOA All Asset I Class I Shares	WOAIX	B	C	A-	Up	2.56	10.93	5.80	25.46	17.61	12.38	262.0	855-754-7935	Y

Category: Multialternative

Fund Name	Ticker Symbol	RATINGS: Overall Rating	Reward Rating	Risk Rating	Recent Up/ Downgrade	TOTAL RETURNS & PERFORMANCE: 3-Month Total Return	6-Month Total Return	1-Year Total Return	3-Year Total Return	5-Year Total Return	ASSETS: NAV	Total Assets (MIL)	NEW INVESTORS: Telephone	Open to New Investors
Aspiriant Defensive Allocation Fund	RMDFX	B-	C	B+	Up	2.13	7.46	3.23	14.36		10.51	1,323	877-997-9971	Y
BlackRock Systematic Multi-Strategy Institutional Shares	BIMBX	B	B-	A+		2.48	7.70	10.13	20.38		10.11	122.1	800-441-7762	Y
BlackRock Systematic Multi-Strategy Fund Investor A Shares	BAMBX	B	C+	A+		2.46	7.67	9.93	19.59		10.1	122.1	800-441-7762	Y
BlackRock Systematic Multi-Strategy Fund Investor C Shares	BMBCX	B	C+	A		2.29	7.28	9.01	16.89		10.09	122.1	800-441-7762	Y
BlackRock Total Factor Fund Class K	BSTKX	B	C+	A-	Up	0.59	5.48	3.80	16.71	18.79	10.2	218.3	800-441-7762	Y
BlackRock Total Factor Fund Institutional Shares	BSTIX	B	C+	A-	Up	0.59	5.58	3.77	16.65	18.73	10.2	218.3	800-441-7762	Y
BlackRock Total Factor Fund Investor A Shares	BSTAX	B	C+	A-	Up	0.49	5.39	3.48	15.72	17.13	10.16	218.3	800-441-7762	Y
BlackRock Total Factor Fund Investor C Shares	BSTCX	B-	C	B+	Up	0.39	4.98	2.73	13.16	12.95	10.11	218.3	800-441-7762	Y
Camelot Event Driven Fund Class A	EVDAX	B	C	A		2.08	11.46	4.86	29.46	24.68	14.19	30.1		Y
Camelot Event Driven Fund Institutional Class	EVDIX	B	C	A		2.21	11.70	5.24	30.51	26.34	14.32	30.1		Y
Catalyst/Millburn Hedge Strategy Fund Class A	MBXAX	B-	C	B+	Down	0.34	7.22	6.13	23.70	61.03	32.07	4,924	866-447-4228	Y
Catalyst/Millburn Hedge Strategy Fund Class I	MBXIX	B-	C	B+	Down	0.40	7.32	6.41	24.59	63.00	32.23	4,924	866-447-4228	Y
CCM Alternative Income Fund Institutional Shares	CCMNX	B-	C	B		0.76	4.65	3.21	13.00	8.89	9.28	55.5	877-272-1977	Y
Driehaus Event Driven Fund	DEVDX	B	B-	B	Up	4.45	18.26	9.64	26.36	12.59	11.72	68.0	877-779-0079	Y
Franklin K2 Alternative Strategies Fund Advisor Class	FABZX	B-	C	A-	Up	1.94	6.75	3.04	14.01	15.10	11.54	1,238	650-312-2000	Y
Franklin K2 Alternative Strategies Fund Class A	FAAAX	B-	C	A-	Up	1.95	6.68	2.87	13.09	13.53	11.49	1,238	650-312-2000	Y
Franklin K2 Alternative Strategies Fund Class R	FSKKX	B-	C	B+	Up	1.86	6.48	2.51	12.28	11.73	11.49	1,238	650-312-2000	Y
Franklin K2 Alternative Strategies Fund Class R6	FASRX	B-	C	A-	Up	1.94	6.83	3.13	14.31	15.58	11.56	1,238	650-312-2000	Y
Goldman Sachs Absolute Return Tracker Fund Class A	GARTX	B-	C	A-	Up	1.93	7.36	3.57	15.64	14.40	9.47	2,979	800-526-7384	Y
Goldman Sachs Absolute Return Tracker Fund Class C	GCRTX	B-	C	B+	Up	1.75	6.88	2.66	13.01	10.13	8.69	2,979	800-526-7384	Y
Goldman Sachs Absolute Return Tracker Fund Class P	GSGPX	B-	C	B	Up	1.98	7.48	3.86	17.05	16.73	9.76	2,979	800-526-7384	Y
Goldman Sachs Absolute Return Tracker Fund Class R	GRRTX	B-	C	B+	Up	1.87	7.21	3.28	14.84	12.96	9.21	2,979	800-526-7384	Y
Goldman Sachs Absolute Return Tracker Fund Class R6	GARUX	B-	C	A-	Up	2.09	7.60	3.96	16.98	16.69	9.76	2,979	800-526-7384	Y
Goldman Sachs Absolute Return Tracker Institutional Cls	GJRTX	B-	C	B	Up	2.08	7.59	3.94	17.03	16.70	9.77	2,979	800-526-7384	Y
Goldman Sachs Absolute Return Tracker Fund Investor Class	GSRTX	B-	C	A-	Up	2.00	7.44	3.78	16.56	15.87	9.67	2,979	800-526-7384	Y
Infinity Q Diversified Alpha Fund Institutional Class	IQDNX	B	C	A+		0.84	1.19	7.40	23.24		11.88	626.0		
Infinity Q Diversified Alpha Fund Investor Class	IQDAX	B	C	A+		0.76	1.02	7.18	22.33		11.77	626.0		
James Alpha Multi Strat Alternative Income Cls A Shares	JAAMX	B-	C	B+		0.26	12.20	2.91	14.91		9.13	14.0	800-807-3863	Y

Category: Multialternative (con't)

Fund Name	Ticker Symbol	RATINGS: Overall Rating	Reward Rating	Risk Rating	Recent Up/ Downgrade	TOTAL RETURNS & PERFORMANCE: 3-Month Total Return	6-Month Total Return	1-Year Total Return	3-Year Total Return	5-Year Total Return	ASSETS: NAV	Total Assets (MIL)	NEW INVESTORS: Telephone	Open to New Investors
James Alpha Multi Strat Alternative Income Cls C Shares	JACMX	B-	C	B	Up	0.18	11.88	2.16	12.31		8.97	14.0	800-807-3863	Y
James Alpha Multi Strat Alternative Income Cls I Shares	JAIMX	B-	C	B+		0.32	12.31	3.05	15.73		9.15	14.0	800-807-3863	Y
James Alpha Multi Strat Alternative Income Cls S Shares	JASMX	B-	C	B+		0.32	12.48	3.37	16.71		9.22	14.0	800-807-3863	Y
JNL Multi-Manager Alternative Fund Class A		B-	C	B+	Up	1.86	6.12	3.17	12.19		10.4	1,196		Y
JNL Multi-Manager Alternative Fund Class I		B-	C	A-	Up	1.95	6.31	3.45	12.83		10.44	1,196		Y
JNL/Westchester Capital Event Driven Fund Class A		B	C+	A+		1.43	6.76	5.47	21.30		10.58	310.7		Y
JNL/Westchester Capital Event Driven Fund Class I		B	C+	A+		1.44	6.91	5.70	21.90		10.52	310.7		Y
John Hancock Funds Alternative Asset Allocation Cls I	JAAIX	B-	C	B+	Up	1.67	6.35	3.32	10.71	7.65	14.55	575.7	800-225-5913	Y
John Hancock Funds Alternative Asset Allocation Cls R6	JAARX	B-	C	B+	Up	1.74	6.43	3.49	11.04	8.31	14.56	575.7	800-225-5913	Y
KCM Macro Trends Fund Class R-1	KCMTX	B-	C	B		1.97	9.88	4.11	40.17	32.20	11.34	94.4		Y
KCM Macro Trends Fund Institutional Class	KCMIX	B-	C	B+		1.97	9.95	4.35	40.90	32.90	11.38	94.4		Y
Litman Gregory Masters Alternative Strategies Inst Cls	MASFX	B-	C	B	Up	1.83	5.94	3.92	13.30	14.93	11.59	1,887	800-960-0188	Y
Natixis Funds Trust II ASG Global Alternatives Cls N	GAFNX	B-	C	B+	Up	2.01	6.92	1.44	18.67	6.31	11.11	1,125	800-862-4863	Y
Natixis Funds Trust II ASG Global Alternatives Cls Y	GAFYX	B-	C	B+	Up	2.02	6.82	1.38	18.55	6.19	11.11	1,125	800-862-4863	Y
Palmer Square Strategic Credit Fund Class A	PSQAX	B-	C	B	Down	0.41	1.82	1.90	14.75	2.49	8.56	7.2	866-933-9033	Y
Palmer Square Strategic Credit Fund Class I	PSQIX	B-	C	B+	Down	0.55	1.96	2.18	15.58	3.97	8.59	7.2	866-933-9033	Y
PIMCO Multi-Strategy Alternative Fund Class I-2	PXAPX	B-	C	B+	Up	0.43	3.60	3.22	10.69		10	136.1	866-746-2602	Y
PIMCO Multi-Strategy Alternative Fund Institutional Class	PXAIX	B-	C	B+		0.45	3.64	3.28	11.06		10.01	136.1	866-746-2602	Y
Transamerica Event Driven Fund Class I	TENIX	B-	C	B+	Up	2.41	7.94	1.11	13.99		10.6	104.8	888-233-4339	Y
Transamerica Event Driven Fund Class I2		B-	C	B+	Up	2.45	7.95	1.13	13.97		10.45	104.8	888-233-4339	Y
Vanguard Alternative Strategies Fund Investor Shares	VASFX	B-	C	B	Up	0.65	5.44	7.26	5.60		21.48	316.3	877-662-7447	Y
Victory Strategic Allocation Fund Class A	SBALX	B-	C	A-	Up	2.77	11.32	3.90	22.49	25.90	16.21	26.1	800-539-3863	Y
Victory Strategic Allocation Fund Class C	VBFCX	B-	C	B+	Up	2.64	10.99	3.18	19.78	21.47	15.94	26.1	800-539-3863	Y
Victory Strategic Allocation Fund Class I	VBFIX	B-	C	A-	Up	2.82	11.47	4.13	23.41	27.38	16.29	26.1	800-539-3863	Y
Victory Strategic Allocation Fund Class R	VBFGX	B-	C	B+	Up	2.72	11.14	3.60	21.51	24.08	16.17	26.1	800-539-3863	Y
Virtus Rampart Alternatives Diversifier Fund Class A	PDPAX	B-	C	B+	Up	0.97	13.31	0.27	12.46	3.58	11.4	40.4	800-243-1574	Y
Virtus Rampart Alternatives Diversifier Fund Class I	VADIX	B-	C	B+	Up	1.06	13.47	0.53	13.40	4.92	11.37	40.4	800-243-1574	Y
Vivaldi Multi-Strategy Fund Class A	OMOAX	B-	C	B	Up	1.44	8.13	6.41	6.44	14.79	26.72	45.4		Y
Vivaldi Multi-Strategy Fund Class I	OMOIX	B-	C	B+		1.53	8.28	6.77	7.45	16.60	27.18	45.4		Y
WCM Alternatives: Event-Driven Fund Institutional Class	WCEIX	B	C+	A-		1.50	6.53	6.16	20.31	16.31	10.76	194.5		Y
WCM Alternatives: Event-Driven Fund Investor Class	WCERX	B	C+	A+		1.41	6.34	5.86	19.40	14.86	10.72	194.5		Y
Weiss Alternative Balanced Risk Fund Class K	WEIKX	B	C+	A		3.98	10.36	8.80	17.61		10.97	91.4	212-415-4500	Y
Weiss Alternative Balanced Risk Fund Investor Class	WEIZX	B	C+	A		4.00	10.21	8.48	16.62		10.9	91.4	212-415-4500	Y

Category: Real Estate Sector Equity

Fund Name	Ticker Symbol	RATINGS: Overall Rating	Reward Rating	Risk Rating	Recent Up/ Downgrade	TOTAL RETURNS & PERFORMANCE: 3-Month Total Return	6-Month Total Return	1-Year Total Return	3-Year Total Return	5-Year Total Return	ASSETS: NAV	Total Assets (MIL)	NEW INVESTORS: Telephone	Open to New Investors
AB Global Real Estate Investment Fund Advisor Class	ARSYX	B-	C+	B+		0.05	15.40	8.07	20.45	32.04	15.07	143.3	212-969-1000	Y
AB Global Real Estate Investment Fund Class A	AREAX	B-	C	B+		0.04	15.33	7.87	19.59	30.46	15.24	143.3	212-969-1000	Y
AB Global Real Estate Investment Fund Class B	AREBX	B-	C	B		-0.17	14.77	6.94	16.72	25.31	15.04	143.3	212-969-1000	
AB Global Real Estate Investment Fund Class C	ARECX	B-	C	B		-0.13	14.85	7.05	16.87	25.68	15.09	143.3	212-969-1000	Y
AB Global Real Estate Investment Fund Class I	AEEIX	B-	C+	B+		0.12	15.48	8.22	20.81	32.70	15.18	143.3	212-969-1000	Y
AB Global Real Estate Investment Fund Class K	ARRKX	B-	C	B+		0.04	15.30	7.84	19.50	30.41	15.11	143.3	212-969-1000	Y
AB Global Real Estate Investment Fund Class R	ARRRX	B-	C	B+		-0.10	15.03	7.49	18.39	28.33	15.03	143.3	212-969-1000	Y
AB Global Real Estate Investment Fund II Class I	ARIIX	B	C+	B+		0.26	15.82	8.78	22.48	35.44	11.56	331.8	212-969-1000	Y
American Century Global Real Estate Fund A Class	ARYMX	B-	C	B	Up	2.59	18.96	11.23	18.73	29.64	12.67	64.9	800-444-4015	Y
American Century Global Real Estate Fund C Class	ARYTX	B-	C	B	Up	2.34	18.46	10.41	16.08	24.83	12.64	64.9	800-444-4015	Y
American Century Global Real Estate Fund I Class	ARYNX	B-	C	B		2.67	19.28	11.83	20.37	32.63	12.68	64.9	800-444-4015	Y
American Century Global Real Estate Fund Investor Class	ARYVX	B-	C	B		2.59	19.07	11.51	19.64	31.30	12.67	64.9	800-444-4015	Y

Category: Real Estate Sector Equity (con't)

Fund Name	Ticker Symbol	RATINGS: Overall Rating	Reward Rating	Risk Rating	Recent Up/ Downgrade	TOTAL RETURNS & PERFORMANCE: 3-Month Total Return	6-Month Total Return	1-Year Total Return	3-Year Total Return	5-Year Total Return	ASSETS: NAV	Total Assets (MIL)	NEW INVESTORS: Telephone	Open to New Investors
American Century Global Real Estate Fund R Class	ARYWX	B-	C	B	Up	2.50	18.74	10.95	17.82	27.99	12.67	64.9	800-444-4015	Y
American Century Global Real Estate Fund R5 Class	ARYGX	B-	C	B		2.67	19.17	11.73	20.30	32.56	12.68	64.9	800-444-4015	Y
American Century Global Real Estate Fund R6 Class	ARYDX	B-	C	B		2.75	19.28	12.00	20.92	33.65	12.68	64.9	800-444-4015	Y
American Century Global Real Estate Fund Y Class	ARYYX	B-	C	B		2.67	19.28	11.90	20.72	33.02	12.68	64.9	800-444-4015	Y
American Century NT Global Real Estate Fund G Class	ANRHX	B-	C+	B		2.91	19.66	12.74	22.38		10.59	363.9	800-444-4015	
American Century NT Global Real Estate Fund Investor Class	ANREX	B-	C	B		2.63	18.98	11.56	19.42		10.53	363.9	800-444-4015	
BlackRock Real Estate Securities Fund Institutional Shares	BIREX	B-	C+	B-		1.90	19.68	13.62	20.01	52.65	13.61	47.3	800-441-7762	Y
Bluerock Total Income+ Real Estate Fund Class A	TIPRX	B	C+	A		1.22	3.26	5.99	21.46	40.53	30.01	--		Y
Bluerock Total Income+ Real Estate Fund Class C	TIPPX	B	C+	A-		1.14	2.95	5.31	18.85	35.53	28.87	--		Y
Bluerock Total Income+ Real Estate Fund Class I	TIPWX	B	C+	A		1.25	3.34	6.22	22.30	42.47	30.47	--		Y
Bluerock Total Income+ Real Estate Fund Class L	TIPLX	B	C+	A-		1.17	3.13	5.72	20.88	39.86	29.85	--		Y
BNY Mellon Global Real Estate Securities - Class A	DRLAX	B-	C	B		0.73	15.57	8.59	16.57	30.47	9.58	694.3		Y
BNY Mellon Global Real Estate Securities Fund - Class C	DGBCX	B-	C	B	Up	0.42	15.10	7.83	13.85	25.65	9.38	694.3		Y
BNY Mellon Global Real Estate Securities Fund - Class I	DRLIX	B-	C	B		0.74	15.69	8.90	17.35	32.20	9.44	694.3		Y
BNY Mellon Global Real Estate Securities Fund - Class Y	DRLYX	B-	C	B		0.74	15.69	8.93	17.45	32.34	9.44	694.3		Y
Brookfield Global Listed Real Estate Fund Class A	BLRAX	B-	C	B	Up	-0.25	15.16	5.33	14.70	24.92	13.29	1,839	212-549-8400	Y
Brookfield Global Listed Real Estate Fund Class I	BLRIX	B-	C	B	Up	-0.12	15.27	5.59	15.59	26.49	13.3	1,839	212-549-8400	Y
Brookfield Global Listed Real Estate Fund Class Y	BLRYX	B-	C	B	Up	-0.12	15.34	5.58	15.66	26.56	13.32	1,839	212-549-8400	Y
Cohen & Steers Global Realty Shares, Inc. Class A	CSFAX	B	C+	B+		0.94	16.22	10.89	22.88	35.08	56.19	1,429	212-832-3232	Y
Cohen & Steers Global Realty Shares, Inc. Class C	CSFCX	B-	C+	B+		0.78	15.84	10.16	20.50	30.78	55.88	1,429	212-832-3232	Y
Cohen & Steers Global Realty Shares, Inc. Class I	CSSPX	B	C+	B+		1.03	16.41	11.26	24.15	37.45	56.47	1,429	212-832-3232	Y
Cohen & Steers Global Realty Shares, Inc. Class R	GRSRX	B	C+	B+		0.89	16.14	10.73	22.33	34.36	56.6	1,429	212-832-3232	Y
Cohen & Steers Global Realty Shares, Inc. Class Z	CSFZX	B	C+	B+		1.03	16.43	11.29	24.20	37.54	56.48	1,429	212-832-3232	Y
Cohen & Steers Institutional Realty Shares	CSRIX	B-	C+	B-		3.46	21.66	14.67	21.72	54.44	44.92	3,331	212-832-3232	Y
Cohen & Steers International Realty Fund Class A	IRFAX	B	C+	B+	Up	-0.78	12.90	7.79	29.50	25.66	12.37	631.9	212-832-3232	Y
Cohen & Steers International Realty Fund Class C	IRFCX	B	C+	B+	Up	-0.88	12.73	7.22	27.16	21.77	12.35	631.9	212-832-3232	Y
Cohen & Steers International Realty Fund Class I	IRFIX	B	B-	B+	Up	-0.69	13.19	8.20	30.91	27.89	12.45	631.9	212-832-3232	Y
Cohen & Steers International Realty Fund Class R	IRFRX	B	C+	B+	Up	-0.88	12.84	7.59	29.36	25.15	12.5	631.9	212-832-3232	Y
Cohen & Steers International Realty Fund Class Z	IRFZX	B	B-	B+	Up	-0.70	13.19	8.21	30.91	28.00	12.45	631.9	212-832-3232	Y
Cohen & Steers Real Estate Securities Fund, Inc. Class F	CREFX	B-	C+	B-		2.89	20.40	13.73	21.43	60.82	16.62	5,566	212-832-3232	Y
Cohen & Steers Real Estate Securities Fund, Inc. Cls Inst	CSDIX	B-	C+	B-		2.86	20.35	13.64	21.52	61.85	16.62	5,566	212-832-3232	Y
Cohen & Steers Real Estate Securities Fund, Inc. Class Z	CSZIX	B-	C+	B-		2.89	20.40	13.73	21.82	62.33	16.62	5,566	212-832-3232	Y
Davis Real Estate Fund Class A	RPFRX	B-	C+	B		1.64	18.95	10.57	19.57	51.04	42.12	261.5	800-279-0279	Y
Davis Real Estate Fund Class C	DRECX	B-	C	B		1.42	18.42	9.62	16.54	44.62	42.1	261.5	800-279-0279	Y
Davis Real Estate Fund Class Y	DREYX	B-	C+	B		1.72	19.08	10.81	20.42	52.73	42.73	261.5	800-279-0279	Y
DFA Global Real Estate Securities Portfolio	DFGEX	B-	C	B		1.82	17.53	11.91	17.45	39.04	11.73	8,527	512-306-7400	Y
DFA Intl Real Estate Securities Portfolio Inst Cls	DFITX	B-	C	B	Up	2.15	14.47	7.58	15.53	19.07	5.22	5,881	512-306-7400	Y
DWS RREEF Global Real Estate Securities Fund - Class A	RRGAX	B-	C	B+		0.63	15.74	9.75	17.57	31.39	9.49	750.9		Y
DWS RREEF Global Real Estate Securities Fund - Class C	RRGCX	B-	C	B+		0.53	15.37	9.03	14.95	26.59	9.47	750.9		Y
DWS RREEF Global Real Estate Securities Fund - Class Inst	RRGIX	B-	C+	B+		0.74	15.92	10.05	18.41	33.14	9.47	750.9		Y
DWS RREEF Global Real Estate Securities Fund - Class R6	RRGRX	B-	C+	B+		0.74	15.90	10.16	18.39	33.12	9.48	750.9		Y
DWS RREEF Global Real Estate Securities Fund - Class S	RRGTX	B-	C	B+		0.74	15.90	10.05	18.06	32.02	9.48	750.9		Y
DWS RREEF Global Real Estate Securities Fund - Class T	RRGUX	B-	C	B+		0.63	15.76	9.76	17.59	31.56	9.48	750.9		Y
Fidelity Advisor® Global Real Estate Fund Class I	FWRIX	B-	C	B	Up	1.60	16.32	9.40			10.76	6.4	617-563-7000	Y
Fidelity Advisor® Global Real Estate Fund Class Z	FIKKX	B-	C	B	Up	1.60	16.43	9.50			10.77	6.4	617-563-7000	Y
Fidelity Advisor® International Real Estate Fund Class A	FIRAX	B	C+	B+	Up	3.09	16.57	8.63	35.01	32.21	12.31	578.4	617-563-7000	Y
Fidelity Advisor® International Real Estate Fund Class C	FIRCX	B	C+	B+	Up	2.83	16.00	7.75	32.10	27.51	11.96	578.4	617-563-7000	Y
Fidelity Advisor® International Real Estate Fund Class I	FIRIX	B	B-	B+	Up	3.16	16.76	9.02	36.57	34.76	12.4	578.4	617-563-7000	Y
Fidelity Advisor® International Real Estate Fund Class M	FIRTX	B	C+	B+	Up	2.95	16.31	8.20	33.77	30.29	12.19	578.4	617-563-7000	Y
Fidelity Advisor® International Real Estate Fund Class Z	FIKLX	B	B-	B+	Up	3.15	16.74	8.98	36.27	34.00	12.41	578.4	617-563-7000	Y
Fidelity Advisor® Real Estate Income Fund Class A	FRINX	B	B-	B		2.89	11.46	9.64	20.95	35.70	12.28	6,194	617-563-7000	Y
Fidelity Advisor® Real Estate Income Fund Class C	FRIOX	B	B-	B		2.72	11.15	8.82	18.28	30.75	12.15	6,194	617-563-7000	Y

Category: Real Estate Sector Equity (con't)

Fund Name	Ticker Symbol	RATINGS: Overall Rating	Reward Rating	Risk Rating	Recent Up/ Downgrade	TOTAL RETURNS & PERFORMANCE: 3-Month Total Return	6-Month Total Return	1-Year Total Return	3-Year Total Return	5-Year Total Return	ASSETS: NAV	Total Assets (MIL)	NEW INVESTORS: Telephone	Open to New Investors
Fidelity Advisor® Real Estate Income Fund Class I	FRIRX	B	B-	B		2.95	11.65	9.92	21.92	37.50	12.3	6,194	617-563-7000	Y
Fidelity Advisor® Real Estate Income Fund Class M	FRIQX	B	B-	B		2.88	11.53	9.61	20.86	35.51	12.29	6,194	617-563-7000	Y
Fidelity Advisor® Real Estate Income Fund Class Z	FIKMX	B	B-	B		2.98	11.70	10.03	21.95	37.44	12.3	6,194	617-563-7000	Y
Fidelity® International Real Estate Fund	FIREX	B	B-	B+	Up	3.14	16.63	8.88	36.15	33.88	12.48	578.4	617-563-7000	Y
Fidelity® Real Estate Income Fund	FRIFX	B	B-	B		2.94	11.69	9.96	21.88	37.35	12.35	6,194	617-563-7000	Y
Fidelity® Series Real Estate Income Fund	FSREX	B	B-	A-		3.10	10.43	9.52	22.22	35.95	11.09	966.2	617-563-7000	
Gerstein Fisher Multi-Factor Global Real Estate Sec Fund	GFMRX	B-	C	B		0.39	15.86	8.90	17.05	36.67	11.73	144.5	800-846-6202	Y
Goldman Sachs Global Real Estate Securities Fund Class P	GGUPX	B-	C	B	Up	1.38	15.88	8.74	14.40		11.21	239.5	800-526-7384	Y
Goldman Sachs Global Real Estate Securities Fund Class R6	GARVX	B-	C	B	Up	1.47	15.98	8.73	14.49		11.22	239.5	800-526-7384	Y
Goldman Sachs Global Real Estate Securities Inst Cls	GARSX	B-	C	B	Up	1.47	15.94	8.71	14.47		11.24	239.5	800-526-7384	Y
Goldman Sachs Global Real Estate Securities Investor Cls	GARJX	B-	C	B	Up	1.43	15.90	8.57	13.96		11.22	239.5	800-526-7384	Y
Goldman Sachs International Real Estate Securities Cls A	GIRAX	B-	C	B	Up	-0.17	13.38	5.17	20.46	13.81	6.62	84.6	800-526-7384	Y
Goldman Sachs International Real Estate Securities Cls C	GIRCX	B-	C	B	Up	-0.34	13.12	4.31	17.81	9.77	6.68	84.6	800-526-7384	Y
Goldman Sachs International Real Estate Securities Cls P	GGEPX	B-	C	B	Up	0.01	13.75	5.49	22.03	16.09	6.39	84.6	800-526-7384	Y
Goldman Sachs International Real Estate Securities Cls R6	GIRUX	B-	C	B	Up	0.01	13.71	5.63	22.22	16.29	6.4	84.6	800-526-7384	Y
Goldman Sachs Intl Real Estate Securities Inst Cls	GIRIX	B-	C	B	Up	-0.14	13.71	5.46	21.96	16.02	6.4	84.6	800-526-7384	Y
Goldman Sachs Intl Real Estate Securities Inv Cls	GIRTX	B-	C	B	Up	-0.05	13.64	5.49	21.53	15.40	6.57	84.6	800-526-7384	Y
Griffin Institutional Access Real Estate Fund Class A	GIREX	B	C+	A-		1.47	5.09	6.77	19.85	41.37	27.24	--	310-469-6100	Y
Griffin Institutional Access Real Estate Fund Class C	GCREX	B	C+	A+		1.28	4.72	6.00	17.21	37.48	26.48	--	310-469-6100	Y
Griffin Institutional Access Real Estate Fund Class I	GRIFX	B	C+	A		1.50	5.22	7.03	20.76	42.72	27.51	--	310-469-6100	Y
Griffin Institutional Access Real Estate Fund Class L	GLREX	B	C+	A+		1.40	4.94	6.54	19.36	40.80	27.12	--	310-469-6100	Y
Griffin Institutional Access Real Estate Fund Class M	GMREX	B	C+	A-		1.36	4.84	6.31	18.35	39.61	26.9	--	310-469-6100	Y
Guggenheim Risk Managed Real Estate Fund Class A	GURAX	B	B	B		3.64	19.17	14.34	25.04	59.50	32.15	204.4	212-518-9290	Y
Guggenheim Risk Managed Real Estate Fund Class C	GURCX	B-	B-	B		3.44	18.75	13.50	22.24	53.59	31.94	204.4	212-518-9290	Y
Guggenheim Risk Managed Real Estate Fund Class P	GURPX	B	B-	B		3.67	19.21	14.35	24.97	59.53	32.35	204.4	212-518-9290	Y
Guggenheim Risk Managed Real Estate Fund Institutional	GURIX	B	B	B		3.73	19.37	14.63	26.11	61.83	32.53	204.4	212-518-9290	Y
GuideStone Funds Global Real Estate Securities Inst Cls	GREYX	B-	C	B+		0.76	16.09	9.41	18.58	32.78	10.13	242.1	214-720-1171	Y
GuideStone Funds Global Real Estate Securities Inv Cls	GREZX	B-	C	B+		0.63	15.89	9.06	17.52	31.35	10.16	242.1	214-720-1171	Y
Invesco Global Real Estate Fund Class A	AGREX	B-	C	B		0.46	15.75	8.42	17.52	24.64	13.07	798.6	800-659-1005	Y
Invesco Global Real Estate Fund Class C	CGREX	B-	C	B	Up	0.20	15.32	7.52	14.82	19.91	13.08	798.6	800-659-1005	Y
Invesco Global Real Estate Fund Class R	RGREX	B-	C	B		0.40	15.61	8.15	16.56	23.02	13.07	798.6	800-659-1005	Y
Invesco Global Real Estate Fund Class R6	FGREX	B-	C	B+		0.57	16.10	8.87	19.05	27.85	13.02	798.6	800-659-1005	Y
Invesco Global Real Estate Fund Class Y	ARGYX	B-	C	B+		0.44	15.91	8.61	18.33	26.10	13.06	798.6	800-659-1005	Y
Invesco Global Real Estate Fund R5 Class	IGREX	B-	C	B+		0.55	15.95	8.78	18.78	27.37	13.02	798.6	800-659-1005	Y
Invesco Global Real Estate Income Fund Class A	ASRAX	B-	C+	B+		1.22	13.19	7.47	15.49	24.12	9.37	743.0	800-659-1005	Y
Invesco Global Real Estate Income Fund Class C	ASRCX	B-	C	B		0.92	12.78	6.68	12.92	19.54	9.36	743.0	800-659-1005	Y
Invesco Global Real Estate Income Fund Class R5	ASRIX	B	C+	B+		1.30	13.41	7.88	16.69	26.22	9.36	743.0	800-659-1005	Y
Invesco Global Real Estate Income Fund Class R6	ASRFX	B	C+	B+		1.33	13.46	7.98	17.01	26.63	9.36	743.0	800-659-1005	Y
Invesco Global Real Estate Income Fund Class Y	ASRYX	B	C+	B+		1.28	13.37	7.75	16.38	25.71	9.34	743.0	800-659-1005	Y
iShares Developed Real Estate Index Fund Class K	BKRDX	B-	C	B+		0.05	15.13	8.54	16.55		10.89	2,013	800-441-7762	Y
iShares Developed Real Estate Index Institutional Shares	BIRDX	B-	C	B+		0.04	15.08	8.46	16.38		10.91	2,013	800-441-7762	Y
iShares Developed Real Estate Index Fund Investor A Shares	BARDX	B-	C	B+		-0.01	14.91	8.24	15.46		10.9	2,013	800-441-7762	Y
Ivy LaSalle Global Real Estate Fund Class A	IREAX	B-	C	B+	Up	-0.77	14.29	7.33	14.83	21.60	11	147.4		Y
Ivy LaSalle Global Real Estate Fund Class B	IREBX	B-	C	B	Up	-0.93	13.97	6.63	12.37	16.53	10.94	147.4		
Ivy LaSalle Global Real Estate Fund Class C	IRECX	B-	C	B	Up	-0.95	13.85	6.52	11.92	15.81	10.93	147.4		Y
Ivy LaSalle Global Real Estate Fund Class I	IRESX	B-	C	B+		-0.57	14.50	7.79	16.00	22.73	11.03	147.4		Y
Ivy LaSalle Global Real Estate Fund Class N	IRENX	B-	C	B+	Up	-0.63	14.51	7.80	15.81	22.63	11.04	147.4		Y
Ivy LaSalle Global Real Estate Fund Class R	IRERX	B-	C	B+	Up	-0.78	14.09	7.01	13.59	18.70	10.98	147.4		Y
Ivy LaSalle Global Real Estate Fund Class Y	IREYX	B-	C	B+	Up	-0.72	14.39	7.43	15.01	22.33	11.13	147.4		Y
James Alpha Global Real Estate Inv Port Cls A Shares	JAREX	B	B-	B		2.42	20.38	6.60	28.70	38.24	17.86	825.3	800-807-3863	Y
James Alpha Global Real Estate Inv Port Cls C Shares	JACRX	B-	C+	B	Down	2.25	19.95	5.84	25.93	33.43	18.03	825.3	800-807-3863	Y
James Alpha Global Real Estate Inv Port Cls I Shares	JARIX	B	B-	B		2.51	20.59	7.06	30.39	41.51	18.46	825.3	800-807-3863	Y

Category: Real Estate Sector Equity (con't)

Fund Name	Ticker Symbol	RATINGS: Overall Rating	Reward Rating	Risk Rating	Recent Up/ Downgrade	TOTAL RETURNS & PERFORMANCE: 3-Month Total Return	6-Month Total Return	1-Year Total Return	3-Year Total Return	5-Year Total Return	ASSETS: NAV	Total Assets (MIL)	NEW INVESTORS: Telephone	Open to New Investors
James Alpha Global Real Estate Inv Port Cls S Shares	JARSX	B	B-	B		2.60	20.81	7.38	30.44	40.11	18.58	825.3	800-807-3863	Y
Janus Henderson Global Real Estate Fund Class A	JERAX	B+	B	A-		3.08	19.98	11.94	35.09	38.79	12.48	358.4	877-335-2687	Y
Janus Henderson Global Real Estate Fund Class C	JERCX	B	B	A-		2.84	19.56	11.05	32.02	33.64	12.3	358.4	877-335-2687	Y
Janus Henderson Global Real Estate Fund Class D	JNGSX	B+	B	A-		3.11	20.04	12.06	35.69	39.81	12.56	358.4	877-335-2687	
Janus Henderson Global Real Estate Fund Class I	JERIX	B+	B	A-		3.13	20.10	12.28	36.20	40.56	12.55	358.4	877-335-2687	Y
Janus Henderson Global Real Estate Fund Class N	JERNX	B+	B	A-		3.15	20.15	12.35	36.35	40.71	12.55	358.4	877-335-2687	Y
Janus Henderson Global Real Estate Fund Class S	JERSX	B	B	A-		2.96	19.85	11.64	34.24	37.49	12.45	358.4	877-335-2687	Y
Janus Henderson Global Real Estate Fund Class T	JERTX	B+	B	A-		3.10	20.03	12.02	35.43	39.50	12.55	358.4	877-335-2687	Y
JNL/Invesco Global Real Estate Fund Class A		B-	C	B	Up	0.39	15.81	8.50	14.80	24.05	10.25	1,344		Y
JNL/Invesco Global Real Estate Fund Class I		B-	C	B+	Up	0.48	16.01	8.82	15.74	25.59	10.43	1,344		Y
MFS Global Real Estate Fund Class A	MGLAX	B	B-	B+		2.68	17.82	11.04	23.14	40.81	17.19	2,002	877-960-6077	Y
MFS Global Real Estate Fund Class B	MGLDX	B	C+	B+		2.54	17.35	10.26	20.49	35.63	17.31	2,002	877-960-6077	Y
MFS Global Real Estate Fund Class C	MGLCX	B	C+	B+		2.55	17.37	10.24	20.48	35.58	17.29	2,002	877-960-6077	Y
MFS Global Real Estate Fund Class I	MGLIX	B	B-	B+		2.80	17.98	11.40	24.09	42.47	17.25	2,002	877-960-6077	Y
MFS Global Real Estate Fund Class R1	MGLJX	B	C+	B+		2.50	17.34	10.20	20.40	35.63	17.18	2,002	877-960-6077	Y
MFS Global Real Estate Fund Class R2	MGLKX	B	B-	B+		2.67	17.64	10.77	22.21	39.10	17.27	2,002	877-960-6077	Y
MFS Global Real Estate Fund Class R3	MGLLX	B	B-	B+		2.73	17.80	11.11	23.18	40.92	17.27	2,002	877-960-6077	Y
MFS Global Real Estate Fund Class R4	MGLMX	B	B-	B+		2.80	17.90	11.28	23.93	42.51	17.25	2,002	877-960-6077	Y
MFS Global Real Estate Fund Class R6	MGLRX	B	B-	B+		2.79	17.93	11.43	24.37	42.98	17.29	2,002	877-960-6077	Y
Morgan Stanley Inst Fund, Inc. Global Real Est Cls IS	MGREX	B-	C	B	Up	-1.80	12.86	3.43	11.51	19.92	10.35	849.7	855-332-5306	Y
Morgan Stanley Inst Fund, Inc. Intl Real Estate Port Cls I	MSUAX	B-	C	B	Up	-1.34	12.60	3.16	21.05	12.27	19.12	20.6	855-332-5306	Y
Morgan Stanley Inst Fund, Inc. Intl Real Est Cls IS	MIREX	B-	C	B	Up	-1.29	12.61	3.20	21.16	12.40	19.11	20.6	855-332-5306	Y
Neuberger Berman Global Real Estate Fund Class A	NGRAX	B-	C+	B+	Down	1.34	17.08	11.21	21.94		11.48	4.0	212-476-9000	Y
Neuberger Berman Global Real Estate Fund Class C	NGRCX	B-	C	B		1.15	16.69	10.41	19.31		11.46	4.0	212-476-9000	Y
Neuberger Berman Global Real Estate Institutional Cls	NGRIX	B	C+	B+		1.42	17.35	11.66	23.40		11.49	4.0	212-476-9000	Y
Neuberger Berman Real Estate Fund Class A	NREAX	B-	C+	B	Down	3.41	21.67	15.07	21.27	47.93	14.01	476.9	212-476-9000	Y
Neuberger Berman Real Estate Fund Class R3	NRERX	B-	C+	B		3.27	21.47	14.73	20.34	46.04	13.98	476.9	212-476-9000	Y
Neuberger Berman Real Estate Fund Class R6	NRREX	B-	C+	B	Down	3.51	21.96	15.62	22.92	51.22	14.05	476.9	212-476-9000	Y
Neuberger Berman Real Estate Fund Institutional Class	NBRIX	B-	C+	B	Down	3.41	21.80	15.43	22.54	50.62	14.05	476.9	212-476-9000	Y
Neuberger Berman Real Estate Fund Trust Class	NBRFX	B-	C+	B	Down	3.44	21.76	15.26	21.91	49.25	14.01	476.9	212-476-9000	
Northern Global Real Estate Index Fund	NGREX	B-	C	B		0.27	15.29	7.71	18.97	29.29	10.98	2,123	800-595-9111	Y
Northern Multi-Manager Global Real Estate Fund	NMMGX	B-	C+	B+		1.68	16.59	9.29	19.18	27.90	11.23	102.1	800-595-9111	Y
PACE Global Real Estate Securities Investments Class A	PREAX	B-	C	B		-0.25	15.08	5.20	15.94	22.72	7.78	123.1	212-882-5586	Y
PACE Global Real Estate Securities Investments Class P	PREQX	B-	C	B		-0.13	15.23	5.48	16.95	24.13	7.49	123.1	212-882-5586	Y
PGIM Global Real Estate Fund- Class A	PURAX	B-	C	B+		0.83	17.43	10.88	17.99	25.82	25.62	1,922	800-225-1852	Y
PGIM Global Real Estate Fund- Class B	PURBX	B-	C	B	Up	0.61	16.94	9.96	15.41	21.35	25	1,922	800-225-1852	
PGIM Global Real Estate Fund- Class C	PURCX	B-	C	B	Up	0.72	17.16	10.38	16.04	22.02	25.02	1,922	800-225-1852	Y
PGIM Global Real Estate Fund- Class R	PURRX	B-	C	B	Up	0.81	17.37	10.78	17.43	24.73	25.54	1,922	800-225-1852	Y
PGIM Global Real Estate Fund- Class R2	PUREX	B-	C	B+		0.88	17.56	11.11	18.46	26.47	25.73	1,922	800-225-1852	Y
PGIM Global Real Estate Fund- Class R4	PURGX	B-	C	B+		0.98	17.73	11.41	19.39	28.11	25.75	1,922	800-225-1852	Y
PGIM Global Real Estate Fund- Class R6	PGRQX	B-	C+	B+		1.02	17.86	11.63	20.09	29.30	25.77	1,922	800-225-1852	Y
PGIM Global Real Estate Fund- Class Z	PURZX	B-	C	B+		1.02	17.81	11.56	19.62	28.35	25.78	1,922	800-225-1852	Y
PGIM Select Real Estate Fund- Class A	SREAX	B	B	B+		3.57	23.19	18.47	30.20		12.12	12.6	800-225-1852	Y
PGIM Select Real Estate Fund- Class C	SRECX	B	B-	B	Up	3.42	22.66	17.61	27.23		11.98	12.6	800-225-1852	Y
PGIM Select Real Estate Fund- Class R6	SREQX	B	B	B+		3.68	23.27	18.82	31.12		11.96	12.6	800-225-1852	Y
PGIM Select Real Estate Fund- Class Z	SREZX	B	B	B+		3.63	23.22	18.73	31.08		12.14	12.6	800-225-1852	Y
PGIM US Real Estate Fund- Class A	PJEAX	B-	C+	B-	Down	2.35	23.28	16.33	21.40	46.50	13.41	30.9	800-225-1852	Y
PGIM US Real Estate Fund- Class R6	PJEQX	B-	C+	B-	Down	2.41	23.42	16.59	22.40	48.49	13.43	30.9	800-225-1852	Y
PGIM US Real Estate Fund- Class Z	PJEZX	B-	C+	B-	Down	2.41	23.42	16.59	22.30	48.36	13.43	30.9	800-225-1852	Y
PREDEX Fund	PRDEX	B-	C	A-	Up	1.13	1.65	4.57	13.45		26.16	--		Y
Principal Global Real Estate Securities Fund Class A	POSAX	B	C+	B+	Up	1.33	16.91	10.44	22.73	35.48	9.53	3,881	800-787-1621	Y
Principal Global Real Estate Securities Fund Class C	POSCX	B-	C	B+		1.19	16.47	9.61	19.96	30.25	9.2	3,881	800-787-1621	Y

Category: Real Estate Sector Equity (con't)

Fund Name	Ticker Symbol	RATINGS: Overall Rating	Reward Rating	Risk Rating	Recent Up/ Downgrade	TOTAL RETURNS & PERFORMANCE: 3-Month Total Return	6-Month Total Return	1-Year Total Return	3-Year Total Return	5-Year Total Return	ASSETS: NAV	Total Assets (MIL)	NEW INVESTORS: Telephone	Open to New Investors
Principal Global Real Estate Securities Fund Class R-6	PGRSX	B	C+	B+	Up	1.45	17.08	10.88	24.12	38.23	10.25	3,881	800-787-1621	Y
Principal Global Real Estate Securities Institutional Cls	POSIX	B	C+	B+	Up	1.43	17.05	10.71	24.14	38.16	10.25	3,881	800-787-1621	Y
Principal Global Real Estate Securities Fund R-3	PGRKX	B-	C+	B+		1.30	16.77	10.28	22.30	35.37	10.24	3,881	800-787-1621	Y
Principal Global Real Estate Securities Fund R-4	PGRVX	B	C+	B+	Up	1.35	16.89	10.49	22.83	36.46	10.24	3,881	800-787-1621	Y
Principal Global Real Estate Securities Fund R-5	PGRUX	B	C+	B+	Up	1.41	17.10	10.65	23.54	37.49	10.26	3,881	800-787-1621	Y
Principal Real Estate Income Fund	PGZ	B-	B	C-		4.61	16.62	16.02	42.24	52.78	21.61	149.1	800-787-1621	Y
Principal Real Estate Securities Fund Class A	PRRAX	B-	C+	B		3.02	21.34	14.15	20.17	53.70	26.18	4,636	800-787-1621	Y
Principal Real Estate Securities Fund Class J	PREJX	B-	C+	B		3.07	21.46	14.27	20.64	54.67	25.39	4,636	800-787-1621	Y
Principal Real Estate Securities Fund Class R-6	PFRSX	B-	C+	B		3.14	21.63	14.63	21.51	56.09	26.19	4,636	800-787-1621	Y
Principal Real Estate Securities Fund Institutional Class	PIREX	B-	C+	B		3.11	21.57	14.51	21.46	56.66	26.2	4,636	800-787-1621	Y
Principal Real Estate Securities Fund R-2 Class	PRENX	B-	C+	B		2.94	21.19	13.80	19.05	51.46	24.86	4,636	800-787-1621	Y
Principal Real Estate Securities Fund R-3 Class	PRERX	B-	C+	B		3.00	21.27	13.98	19.71	52.83	25.51	4,636	800-787-1621	Y
Principal Real Estate Securities Fund R-4 Class	PRETX	B-	C+	B		3.04	21.38	14.17	20.36	54.22	25.21	4,636	800-787-1621	Y
Principal Real Estate Securities Fund R-5 Class	PREPX	B-	C+	B		3.10	21.51	14.38	20.84	55.24	25.27	4,636	800-787-1621	Y
REMS Intl Real Estate Value-Opp Founders Shares	REIFX	B-	C	B+		-1.53	11.31	2.63	37.79	30.91	10.92	77.1		Y
REMS International Real Estate Value-Opportunity Z Shares	REIZX	B-	C	B+		-1.51	11.29	2.58	37.73	30.84	11.04	77.1		Y
Resource Real Estate Diversified Income Fund Class A	RREDX	B	C+	A		1.92	8.17	7.93	26.77	40.04	10.47	--	855-747-9559	Y
Resource Real Estate Diversified Income Fund Class C	CRREX	B	C+	A		1.82	7.76	7.21	24.03	35.16	10.47	--	855-747-9559	Y
Resource Real Estate Diversified Income Fund Class D	DRREX	B	C+	A		1.78	7.81	7.35	24.85	36.99	10.63	--	855-747-9559	Y
Resource Real Estate Diversified Income Fund Class I	IRREX	B	C+	A		2.05	8.29	8.22	26.23	38.44	10.91	--	855-747-9559	Y
Resource Real Estate Diversified Income Fund Class L	LRREX	B	C+	A		1.95	8.03	7.76	26.24	39.46	10.48	--	855-747-9559	Y
Resource Real Estate Diversified Income Fund Class T	RRETX	B	C+	A		1.72	7.66	7.11	23.92	35.35	10.45	--	855-747-9559	Y
Resource Real Estate Diversified Income Fund Class U	URREX	B	C+	A		2.01	8.16	8.02	26.87	40.15	10.48	--	855-747-9559	Y
Resource Real Estate Diversified Income Cls W Shares	WRREX	B	C+	A		2.00	8.09	8.00	26.45	38.65	10.63	--	855-747-9559	Y
Russell Investments Global Real Estate Securities Cls A	RREAX	B-	C	B+		-0.54	14.50	7.09	15.98	24.85	33.76	879.3	800-426-7969	Y
Russell Investments Global Real Estate Securities Cls C	RRSCX	B-	C	B+	Up	-0.72	14.05	6.26	13.38	20.23	32.38	879.3	800-426-7969	Y
Russell Investments Global Real Estate Securities Cls E	RREEX	B-	C	B+		-0.53	14.49	7.09	15.95	24.85	33.86	879.3	800-426-7969	Y
Russell Investments Global Real Estate Securities Cls M	RETTX	B-	C	B+		-0.44	14.68	7.45	17.11	26.71	34.69	879.3	800-426-7969	Y
Russell Investments Global Real Estate Securities Cls R6	RRSRX	B-	C	B+		-0.43	14.70	7.53	17.46	27.11	34.73	879.3	800-426-7969	Y
Russell Investments Global Real Estate Securities Cls S	RRESX	B-	C	B+		-0.44	14.62	7.38	16.87	26.46	34.73	879.3	800-426-7969	Y
Russell Investments Global Real Estate Securities Cls Y	RREYX	B-	C	B+		-0.42	14.72	7.53	17.52	27.64	34.72	879.3	800-426-7969	Y
Salient Global Real Estate Fund Institutional Class	KIRYX	B-	C	B	Up	-0.79	14.78	2.24	25.58	20.17	13.94	41.5	866-667-9228	Y
Schwab Fundamental Global Real Estate Index Fund	SFREX	B-	C+	B	Down	-0.71	15.03	5.58	25.68		11.61	199.3	877-824-5615	Y
Schwab Global Real Estate Fund™	SWASX	B-	C	B		0.08	17.85	8.85	21.79	36.78	7.91	307.9	877-824-5615	Y
Sterling Capital Stratton Real Estate Institutional Shares	STMDX	B-	C+	B		1.12	17.46	11.28	17.72	50.61	39.48	99.1	800-228-1872	Y
T. Rowe Price Global Real Estate Fund	TRGRX	B-	C	B	Up	0.35	15.08	6.41	10.69	22.00	20.28	136.7	410-345-2000	Y
T. Rowe Price Global Real Estate Fund Advisor Class	PAGEX	B-	C	B	Up	0.25	14.97	6.18	10.16	21.18	20.13	136.7	410-345-2000	Y
T. Rowe Price Global Real Estate Fund I Class	TIRGX	B-	C	B+	Up	0.35	15.20	6.62	11.36	22.74	20.28	136.7	410-345-2000	Y
TIAA-CREF Real Estate Securities Fund Advisor Class	TIRHX	B	B-	B	Up	2.88	21.13	13.88	25.53	56.95	17.32	2,461	877-518-9161	Y
TIAA-CREF Real Estate Securities Fund Institutional Class	TIREX	B	B-	B	Up	2.91	21.21	14.02	25.94	57.58	17.31	2,461	877-518-9161	Y
TIAA-CREF Real Estate Securities Fund Premier Class	TRRPX	B-	B-	B		2.87	21.10	13.84	25.35	56.37	17.32	2,461	877-518-9161	Y
TIAA-CREF Real Estate Securities Fund Retail Class	TCREX	B-	C+	B		2.86	20.99	13.67	24.72	55.22	17.17	2,461	877-518-9161	Y
TIAA-CREF Real Estate Securities Fund Retirement Class	TRRSX	B-	B-	B		2.84	21.07	13.73	24.99	55.63	18.05	2,461	877-518-9161	Y
VALIC Company I Global Real Estate Fund	VGREX	B-	C+	B+		0.99	16.51	8.71	20.95	29.82	8.14	473.6		Y
Versus Capital Multi-Manager Real Estate Income LLC Cls I	VCMIX	B	C+	A-		1.35	4.07	5.84	17.74	38.32	28.33	--		Y
Virtus Duff & Phelps Global Real Estate Securities Cls A	VGSAX	B-	C+	B		2.37	18.47	10.39	20.33	40.46	32.77	217.8	800-243-1574	Y
Virtus Duff & Phelps Global Real Estate Securities Cls C	VGSCX	B-	C	B		2.17	18.01	9.55	17.62	35.25	31.51	217.8	800-243-1574	Y
Virtus Duff & Phelps Global Real Estate Securities Cls I	VGISX	B-	C+	B		2.44	18.62	10.67	21.21	42.22	32.29	217.8	800-243-1574	Y
Virtus Duff & Phelps Global Real Estate Securities Cls R6	VRGEX	B	C+	B	Up	2.50	18.75	10.87	21.69	42.79	32.35	217.8	800-243-1574	Y
Virtus Duff & Phelps Intl Real Estate Securities Cls A	PXRAX	B	B-	B	Up	1.83	16.66	8.40	25.11	29.74	7.77	45.7	800-243-1574	Y
Virtus Duff & Phelps Intl Real Estate Securities Cls C	PXRCX	B-	C+	B	Up	1.57	16.21	7.59	22.17	24.94	7.74	45.7	800-243-1574	Y
Virtus Duff & Phelps Intl Real Estate Securities Cls I	PXRIX	B	B-	B	Up	1.86	16.74	8.72	25.98	31.43	7.74	45.7	800-243-1574	Y

Category: Real Estate Sector Equity (con't)

Fund Name	Ticker Symbol	RATINGS: Overall Rating	Reward Rating	Risk Rating	Recent Up/ Downgrade	TOTAL RETURNS & PERFORMANCE: 3-Month Total Return	6-Month Total Return	1-Year Total Return	3-Year Total Return	5-Year Total Return	ASSETS: NAV	Total Assets (MIL)	NEW INVESTORS: Telephone	Open to New Investors
Voya International Real Estate Fund Class A	IIRAX	B-	C	B	Up	1.25	15.12	6.33	21.37	15.34	8.65	75.6	800-366-0066	Y
Voya International Real Estate Fund Class I	IIRIX	B-	C	B	Up	1.34	15.33	6.51	22.34	16.89	8.64	75.6	800-366-0066	Y
Voya International Real Estate Fund Class W	IIRWX	B-	C	B	Up	1.34	15.39	6.51	22.37	16.79	8.68	75.6	800-366-0066	Y

Category: Target Date

Fund Name	Ticker Symbol	RATINGS: Overall Rating	Reward Rating	Risk Rating	Recent Up/ Downgrade	TOTAL RETURNS & PERFORMANCE: 3-Month Total Return	6-Month Total Return	1-Year Total Return	3-Year Total Return	5-Year Total Return	ASSETS: NAV	Total Assets (MIL)	NEW INVESTORS: Telephone	Open to New Investors
AB Multi-Manager Select 2010 Fund Advisor Class	TDBYX	B	C	A-	Up	2.43	8.75	4.91	18.85		10.93	18.5	212-969-1000	Y
AB Multi-Manager Select 2010 Fund Class A	TDBAX	B	C	A-	Up	2.41	8.67	4.72	17.96		11.02	18.5	212-969-1000	Y
AB Multi-Manager Select 2010 Fund Class C	TDBCX	B-	C	B+	Up	2.23	8.26	3.93	15.35		11	18.5	212-969-1000	Y
AB Multi-Manager Select 2010 Fund Class I	TDIBX	B	C	A-	Up	2.48	8.85	5.00	18.87		10.33	18.5	212-969-1000	Y
AB Multi-Manager Select 2010 Fund Class K	TDBKX	B	C	A-	Up	2.47	8.71	4.78	18.00		10.35	18.5	212-969-1000	Y
AB Multi-Manager Select 2010 Fund Class R	TDBRX	B-	C	A-	Up	2.36	8.58	4.41	17.03		10.37	18.5	212-969-1000	Y
AB Multi-Manager Select 2010 Fund Class Z	TDBZX	B	C	A-	Up	2.47	8.84	4.98	18.84		10.34	18.5	212-969-1000	Y
AB Multi-Manager Select 2015 Fund Advisor Class	TDCYX	B	C	A-	Up	2.39	9.54	4.75	21.02		10.67	47.2	212-969-1000	Y
AB Multi-Manager Select 2015 Fund Class A	TDCAX	B-	C	A-	Up	2.32	9.44	4.41	20.04		10.54	47.2	212-969-1000	Y
AB Multi-Manager Select 2015 Fund Class C	TDCCX	B-	C	B+	Up	2.15	9.08	3.66	17.43		10.45	47.2	212-969-1000	Y
AB Multi-Manager Select 2015 Fund Class I	TDCIX	B	C	A-	Up	2.48	9.57	4.60	20.93		10.3	47.2	212-969-1000	Y
AB Multi-Manager Select 2015 Fund Class K	TDCKX	B-	C	A-	Up	2.38	9.45	4.40	20.08		10.3	47.2	212-969-1000	Y
AB Multi-Manager Select 2015 Fund Class R	TDCRX	B-	C	A-	Up	2.38	9.34	4.21	19.27		10.3	47.2	212-969-1000	Y
AB Multi-Manager Select 2015 Fund Class Z	TDCZX	B	C	A-	Up	2.39	9.49	4.64	20.90		10.26	47.2	212-969-1000	Y
AB Multi-Manager Select 2020 Fund Advisor Class	TDDYX	B-	C	A-	Up	2.49	10.34	4.69	23.39		10.67	101.9	212-969-1000	Y
AB Multi-Manager Select 2020 Fund Class A	TDDAX	B-	C	A-	Up	2.49	10.12	4.39	22.45		10.66	101.9	212-969-1000	Y
AB Multi-Manager Select 2020 Fund Class C	TDDCX	B-	C	A-	Up	2.33	9.79	3.62	19.77		10.54	101.9	212-969-1000	Y
AB Multi-Manager Select 2020 Fund Class I	TDDIX	B-	C	A-	Up	2.58	10.28	4.63	23.22		10.72	101.9	212-969-1000	Y
AB Multi-Manager Select 2020 Fund Class K	TDDKX	B-	C	A-	Up	2.45	10.12	4.31	22.48		10.44	101.9	212-969-1000	Y
AB Multi-Manager Select 2020 Fund Class R	TDDRX	B-	C	A-	Up	2.36	9.95	4.04	21.55		10.38	101.9	212-969-1000	Y
AB Multi-Manager Select 2020 Fund Class Z	TDDZX	B-	C	A-	Up	2.55	10.38	4.63	23.43		10.42	101.9	212-969-1000	Y
AB Multi-Manager Select 2025 Fund Advisor Class	TDGYX	B-	C	A-	Up	2.63	11.33	4.49	26.96		10.9	158.2	212-969-1000	Y
AB Multi-Manager Select 2025 Fund Class A	TDAGX	B-	C	A-	Up	2.54	11.23	4.29	25.99		10.89	158.2	212-969-1000	Y
AB Multi-Manager Select 2025 Fund Class C	TDCGX	B-	C	A-	Up	2.36	10.76	3.41	23.11		10.8	158.2	212-969-1000	Y
AB Multi-Manager Select 2025 Fund Class I	TDIGX	B-	C	A-	Up	2.59	11.26	4.42	26.79		10.67	158.2	212-969-1000	Y
AB Multi-Manager Select 2025 Fund Class K	TDGKX	B-	C	A-	Up	2.50	11.16	4.22	25.99		10.65	158.2	212-969-1000	Y
AB Multi-Manager Select 2025 Fund Class R	TDGRX	B-	C	A-	Up	2.52	11.05	3.96	25.05		10.55	158.2	212-969-1000	Y
AB Multi-Manager Select 2025 Fund Class Z	TDGZX	B-	C	A-	Up	2.60	11.30	4.53	26.95		10.63	158.2	212-969-1000	Y
AB Multi-Manager Select 2030 Fund Advisor Class	TDYHX	B-	C	A-	Up	2.66	12.17	4.40	30.09		11.15	136.1	212-969-1000	Y
AB Multi-Manager Select 2030 Fund Class A	TDHAX	B-	C	B+	Up	2.57	12.07	4.18	29.08		11.14	136.1	212-969-1000	Y
AB Multi-Manager Select 2030 Fund Class C	TDHCX	B-	C	B+	Up	2.42	11.68	3.47	26.37		10.99	136.1	212-969-1000	Y
AB Multi-Manager Select 2030 Fund Class I	TDIHX	B-	C	A-	Up	2.72	12.21	4.49	30.18		10.93	136.1	212-969-1000	Y
AB Multi-Manager Select 2030 Fund Class K	TDHKX	B-	C	B+	Up	2.63	12.13	4.24	29.18		10.9	136.1	212-969-1000	Y
AB Multi-Manager Select 2030 Fund Class R	TDHRX	B-	C	B+	Up	2.55	11.88	3.86	28.10		10.83	136.1	212-969-1000	Y
AB Multi-Manager Select 2030 Fund Class Z	TDHZX	B-	C	A-	Up	2.63	12.26	4.43	30.17		10.89	136.1	212-969-1000	Y
AB Multi-Manager Select 2035 Fund Advisor Class	TDMYX	B-	C	B+	Up	3.05	13.57	4.78	34.27		11.46	135.5	212-969-1000	Y
AB Multi-Manager Select 2035 Fund Class A	TDMAX	B-	C	B+	Up	2.97	13.40	4.50	33.22		11.42	135.5	212-969-1000	Y
AB Multi-Manager Select 2035 Fund Class C	TDMCX	B-	C	B+	Up	2.73	13.03	3.73	30.22		11.27	135.5	212-969-1000	Y
AB Multi-Manager Select 2035 Fund Class I	TDIMX	B-	C	B+	Up	3.01	13.58	4.74	34.20		11.29	135.5	212-969-1000	Y
AB Multi-Manager Select 2035 Fund Class K	TDMKX	B-	C	B+	Up	2.95	13.44	4.46	33.06		11.14	135.5	212-969-1000	Y
AB Multi-Manager Select 2035 Fund Class R	TDRMX	B-	C	B+	Up	2.88	13.31	4.26	32.19		11.06	135.5	212-969-1000	Y
AB Multi-Manager Select 2035 Fund Class Z	TDMZX	B-	C	B+	Up	2.96	13.57	4.66	34.07		11.13	135.5	212-969-1000	Y
AB Multi-Manager Select 2040 Fund Advisor Class	TDJYX	B-	C	B+	Up	3.27	14.66	4.87	36.44		11.34	86.5	212-969-1000	Y
AB Multi-Manager Select 2040 Fund Class A	TDJAX	B-	C	B+	Up	3.19	14.48	4.58	35.35		11.3	86.5	212-969-1000	Y

Category: Target Date (con't)

		RATINGS				TOTAL RETURNS & PERFORMANCE					ASSETS		NEW INVESTORS	
Fund Name	Ticker Symbol	Overall Rating	Reward Rating	Risk Rating	Recent Up/ Downgrade	3-Month Total Return	6-Month Total Return	1-Year Total Return	3-Year Total Return	5-Year Total Return	NAV	Total Assets (MIL)	Telephone	Open to New Investors
AB Multi-Manager Select 2040 Fund Class C	TDJCX	B-	C	B+	Up	3.05	14.13	3.83	32.44		11.14	86.5	212-969-1000	Y
AB Multi-Manager Select 2040 Fund Class I	TDJIX	B-	C	B+	Up	3.26	14.58	4.78	36.34		11.08	86.5	212-969-1000	Y
AB Multi-Manager Select 2040 Fund Class K	TDJKX	B-	C	B+	Up	3.18	14.43	4.54	35.35		11.02	86.5	212-969-1000	Y
AB Multi-Manager Select 2040 Fund Class R	TDJRX	B-	C	B+	Up	3.20	14.42	4.35	34.48		10.95	86.5	212-969-1000	Y
AB Multi-Manager Select 2040 Fund Class Z	TDJZX	B-	C	B+	Up	3.38	14.68	4.87	36.45		11.01	86.5	212-969-1000	Y
AB Multi-Manager Select 2045 Fund Advisor Class	TDNYX	B-	C	B+	Up	3.46	15.14	5.11	38.07		11.63	76.0	212-969-1000	Y
AB Multi-Manager Select 2045 Fund Class A	TDNAX	B-	C	B+	Up	3.40	15.03	4.75	36.83		11.55	76.0	212-969-1000	Y
AB Multi-Manager Select 2045 Fund Class C	TDNCX	B-	C	B	Up	3.13	14.54	3.97	33.82		11.5	76.0	212-969-1000	Y
AB Multi-Manager Select 2045 Fund Class I	TDNIX	B-	C	B+	Up	3.47	15.15	5.01	37.84		11.32	76.0	212-969-1000	Y
AB Multi-Manager Select 2045 Fund Class K	TDNKX	B-	C	B+	Up	3.41	14.95	4.72	36.94		11.22	76.0	212-969-1000	Y
AB Multi-Manager Select 2045 Fund Class R	TDNRX	B-	C	B	Up	3.32	14.90	4.51	35.86		11.18	76.0	212-969-1000	Y
AB Multi-Manager Select 2045 Fund Class Z	TDNZX	B-	C	B+	Up	3.51	15.22	5.05	37.89		11.2	76.0	212-969-1000	Y
AB Multi-Manager Select 2050 Fund Advisor Class	TDLYX	B-	C	B	Up	3.51	15.40	4.96	38.32		12.06	35.5	212-969-1000	Y
AB Multi-Manager Select 2050 Fund Class A	TDLAX	B-	C	B	Up	3.43	15.21	4.77	37.31		12.04	35.5	212-969-1000	Y
AB Multi-Manager Select 2050 Fund Class C	TDCLX	B-	C	B	Up	3.30	14.87	3.99	34.26		11.89	35.5	212-969-1000	Y
AB Multi-Manager Select 2050 Fund Class I	TDLIX	B-	C	B	Up	3.46	15.36	4.97	38.36		11.64	35.5	212-969-1000	Y
AB Multi-Manager Select 2050 Fund Class K	TDLKX	B-	C	B	Up	3.45	15.31	4.72	37.29		11.37	35.5	212-969-1000	Y
AB Multi-Manager Select 2050 Fund Class R	TDLRX	B-	C	B	Up	3.38	15.07	4.43	36.19		11.3	35.5	212-969-1000	Y
AB Multi-Manager Select 2050 Fund Class Z	TDLZX	B-	C	B	Up	3.55	15.43	5.02	38.40		11.37	35.5	212-969-1000	Y
AB Multi-Manager Select 2055 Fund Advisor Class	TDPYX	B-	C	B	Up	3.52	15.45	4.95	38.32		12.03	41.7	212-969-1000	Y
AB Multi-Manager Select 2055 Fund Class A	TDAPX	B-	C	B	Up	3.48	15.33	4.71	37.28		11.88	41.7	212-969-1000	Y
AB Multi-Manager Select 2055 Fund Class C	TDCPX	B-	C	B	Up	3.34	14.87	3.95	34.28		11.74	41.7	212-969-1000	Y
AB Multi-Manager Select 2055 Fund Class I	TDIPX	B-	C	B	Up	3.50	15.43	5.01	38.18		11.52	41.7	212-969-1000	Y
AB Multi-Manager Select 2055 Fund Class K	TDPKX	B-	C	B	Up	3.45	15.31	4.76	37.29		11.37	41.7	212-969-1000	Y
AB Multi-Manager Select 2055 Fund Class R	TDPRX	B-	C	B	Up	3.38	15.18	4.47	36.27		11.3	41.7	212-969-1000	Y
AB Multi-Manager Select 2055 Fund Class Z	TDPZX	B-	C	B	Up	3.55	15.43	4.96	38.35		11.37	41.7	212-969-1000	Y
AB Multi-Manager Select Retirement Allocation Advisor Cls	TDAYX	B-	C	A-		2.28	7.50	4.85	15.11		11.18	11.0	212-969-1000	Y
AB Multi-Manager Select Retirement Allocation Fund Class A	TDAAX	B-	C	A-		2.18	7.36	4.57	14.24		11.23	11.0	212-969-1000	Y
AB Multi-Manager Select Retirement Allocation Fund Class C	TDACX	B-	C	B+	Up	1.96	6.98	3.75	11.71		10.88	11.0	212-969-1000	Y
AB Multi-Manager Select Retirement Allocation Fund Class I	TDAIX	B-	C	A-		2.22	7.41	4.76	14.99		10.57	11.0	212-969-1000	Y
AB Multi-Manager Select Retirement Allocation Fund Class K	TDAKX	B-	C	A-		2.17	7.38	4.54	14.24		10.33	11.0	212-969-1000	Y
AB Multi-Manager Select Retirement Allocation Fund Class R	TDARX	B-	C	B+	Up	2.08	7.20	4.28	13.28		10.27	11.0	212-969-1000	Y
AB Multi-Manager Select Retirement Allocation Fund Class Z	TDAZX	B-	C	A-		2.27	7.49	4.91	15.17		10.33	11.0	212-969-1000	Y
AllianzGI Multi Asset Income Fund Administrative Class	ARAMX	B-	C	B		2.62	10.76	6.97	15.06	16.42	17.84	30.0	800-498-5413	Y
AllianzGI Multi Asset Income Fund Class A	AGRAX	B-	C+	B		3.45	11.65	7.73	17.01	18.29	17.54	30.0	800-498-5413	Y
AllianzGI Multi Asset Income Fund Class P	AGRPX	B-	C+	B		3.54	11.80	8.07	18.07	20.10	17.74	30.0	800-498-5413	Y
AllianzGI Multi Asset Income Fund Class R	ASRRX	B-	C+	B	Up	3.36	11.46	7.39	15.78	16.30	18.38	30.0	800-498-5413	Y
AllianzGI Multi Asset Income Fund Institutional Class	AVRNX	B-	C+	B		3.60	11.90	8.17	18.33	20.63	17.26	30.0	800-498-5413	Y
AllianzGI Multi Asset Income Fund R6 Class	AVRIX	B-	C+	B		3.62	11.92	8.20	18.45	20.75	17.27	30.0	800-498-5413	Y
AllianzGI Retirement 2020 Fund Administrative Class	AGLMX	B-	C	B+	Up	3.52	10.56	5.50	19.73	18.66	19.67	27.3	800-498-5413	Y
AllianzGI Retirement 2020 Fund Class A	AGLAX	B-	C	B+	Up	3.48	10.60	5.52	19.61	18.47	19.6	27.3	800-498-5413	Y
AllianzGI Retirement 2020 Fund Class P	AGLPX	B-	C	B+	Up	3.57	10.78	5.83	20.70	20.32	19.72	27.3	800-498-5413	Y
AllianzGI Retirement 2020 Fund R6 Class	AGNIX	B-	C	B+	Up	3.61	10.82	5.92	21.09	20.88	19.76	27.3	800-498-5413	Y
AllianzGI Retirement 2025 Fund Administrative Class	GVDAX	B-	C	B+	Up	3.41	11.55	4.96	23.37	22.03	17.57	37.9	800-498-5413	Y
AllianzGI Retirement 2025 Fund Class A	GVSAX	B-	C	B+	Up	3.42	11.59	4.89	23.20	21.77	17.51	37.9	800-498-5413	Y
AllianzGI Retirement 2025 Fund Class P	GVSPX	B-	C	A-	Up	3.43	11.69	5.19	24.37	23.64	17.48	37.9	800-498-5413	Y
AllianzGI Retirement 2025 Fund Class R	GVSRX	B-	C	B+	Up	3.32	11.33	4.51	21.90	19.63	17.38	37.9	800-498-5413	Y
AllianzGI Retirement 2025 Fund R6 Class	GVSIX	B-	C	A-	Up	3.48	11.79	5.27	24.69	24.27	17.53	37.9	800-498-5413	Y
AllianzGI Retirement 2030 Fund Administrative Class	ABAMX	B-	C	B+	Up	3.40	12.71	4.34	26.63	23.10	21.27	49.9	800-498-5413	Y
AllianzGI Retirement 2030 Fund Class A	ABLAX	B-	C	B+	Up	3.39	12.71	4.34	26.53	22.83	21.01	49.9	800-498-5413	Y
AllianzGI Retirement 2030 Fund Class C	ABLCX	B-	C	B+	Up	3.17	12.26	3.52	23.57	18.21	20.78	49.9	800-498-5413	Y
AllianzGI Retirement 2030 Fund Class P	ABLPX	B-	C	B+	Up	3.45	12.86	4.62	27.57	24.65	21.23	49.9	800-498-5413	Y

Category: Target Date (con't)

		RATINGS				TOTAL RETURNS & PERFORMANCE					ASSETS		NEW INVESTORS	
Fund Name	Ticker Symbol	Overall Rating	Reward Rating	Risk Rating	Recent Up/ Downgrade	3-Month Total Return	6-Month Total Return	1-Year Total Return	3-Year Total Return	5-Year Total Return	NAV	Total Assets (MIL)	Telephone	Open to New Investors
AllianzGI Retirement 2030 Fund Class R	ABLRX	B-	C	B+	Up	3.24	12.41	3.87	25.05	20.63	21.01	49.9	800-498-5413	Y
AllianzGI Retirement 2030 Fund R6 Class	ABLIX	B-	C	B+	Up	3.49	12.86	4.72	27.95	25.26	21.32	49.9	800-498-5413	Y
AllianzGI Retirement 2035 Fund Administrative Class	GVLAX	B-	C	B	Up	3.22	13.66	4.01	29.74	24.75	18.22	39.3	800-498-5413	Y
AllianzGI Retirement 2035 Fund Class A	GVRAX	B-	C	B	Up	3.13	13.56	3.97	29.49	24.43	18.08	39.3	800-498-5413	Y
AllianzGI Retirement 2035 Fund Class P	GVPAX	B-	C	B	Up	3.29	13.78	4.32	30.76	26.35	18.16	39.3	800-498-5413	Y
AllianzGI Retirement 2035 Fund Class R	GVRRX	B-	C	B	Up	3.09	13.43	3.63	28.17	22.26	17.99	39.3	800-498-5413	Y
AllianzGI Retirement 2035 Fund R6 Class	GVLIX	B-	C	B	Up	3.23	13.83	4.35	31.08	26.96	18.18	39.3	800-498-5413	Y
AllianzGI Retirement 2040 Fund Administrative Class	AVAMX	B-	C	B	Up	3.07	14.47	3.50	31.69	25.01	21.11	40.9	800-498-5413	Y
AllianzGI Retirement 2040 Fund Class P	AVSPX	B-	C	B	Up	3.15	14.68	3.82	32.70	26.72	21.24	40.9	800-498-5413	Y
AllianzGI Retirement 2040 Fund R6 Class	AVTIX	B-	C	B	Up	3.14	14.70	3.92	33.12	27.33	21.29	40.9	800-498-5413	Y
American Century Inv One Choice 2020 Port A Cls	ARBMX	B	C	A-	Up	2.92	10.98	5.30	20.71	22.94	12.33	1,695	800-444-4015	Y
American Century Inv One Choice 2020 Port C Cls	ARNCX	B-	C	A-	Up	2.75	10.59	4.49	18.06	18.41	12.32	1,695	800-444-4015	Y
American Century Inv One Choice 2020 Port I Cls	ARBSX	B	C	A-	Up	3.08	11.25	5.78	22.33	25.74	12.36	1,695	800-444-4015	Y
American Century Inv One Choice 2020 Port Inv Cls	ARBVX	B	C	A-	Up	3.00	11.16	5.57	21.60	24.49	12.35	1,695	800-444-4015	Y
American Century Inv One Choice 2020 Port R Cls	ARBRX	B-	C	A-	Up	2.92	10.89	5.04	19.81	21.41	12.32	1,695	800-444-4015	Y
American Century Inv One Choice 2020 Port R6 Cls	ARBDX	B	C+	A-	Up	3.10	11.35	5.95	22.70	26.50	11.28	1,695	800-444-4015	Y
American Century Inv One Choice 2025 Port A Cls	ARWAX	B-	C	A-	Up	3.08	11.88	5.38	22.59	24.85	14.69	2,660	800-444-4015	Y
American Century Inv One Choice 2025 Port C Cls	ARWCX	B-	C	A-	Up	2.94	11.48	4.64	19.90	20.24	14.66	2,660	800-444-4015	Y
American Century Inv One Choice 2025 Port I Cls	ARWFX	B	C	A-	Up	3.22	12.11	5.86	24.24	27.70	14.71	2,660	800-444-4015	Y
American Century Inv One Choice 2025 Port Inv Cls	ARWIX	B	C	A-	Up	3.15	11.95	5.64	23.51	26.43	14.7	2,660	800-444-4015	Y
American Century Inv One Choice 2025 Port R Cls	ARWRX	B-	C	A-	Up	3.02	11.65	5.11	21.61	23.22	14.66	2,660	800-444-4015	Y
American Century Inv One Choice 2025 Port R6 Cls	ARWDX	B	C	A-	Up	3.24	12.24	5.98	24.57	28.50	11.46	2,660	800-444-4015	Y
American Century Inv One Choice 2030 Port A Cls	ARCMX	B-	C	A-	Up	3.22	12.68	5.37	24.67	27.01	12.79	2,280	800-444-4015	Y
American Century Inv One Choice 2030 Port C Cls	ARWOX	B-	C	A-	Up	2.98	12.21	4.56	21.92	22.30	12.77	2,280	800-444-4015	Y
American Century Inv One Choice 2030 Port I Cls	ARCSX	B-	C	A-	Up	3.30	12.95	5.77	26.33	29.89	12.82	2,280	800-444-4015	Y
American Century Inv One Choice 2030 Port Inv Cls	ARCVX	B-	C	A-	Up	3.22	12.85	5.64	25.67	28.57	12.82	2,280	800-444-4015	Y
American Century Inv One Choice 2030 Port R Cls	ARCRX	B-	C	A-	Up	3.14	12.59	5.11	23.74	25.42	12.78	2,280	800-444-4015	Y
American Century Inv One Choice 2030 Port R6 Cls	ARCUX	B-	C	A-	Up	3.42	13.05	6.01	26.78	30.68	11.78	2,280	800-444-4015	Y
American Century Inv One Choice 2035 Port A Cls	ARYAX	B-	C	B+	Up	3.29	13.54	5.24	26.98	29.14	16.01	2,383	800-444-4015	Y
American Century Inv One Choice 2035 Port C Cls	ARLCX	B-	C	B+	Up	3.10	13.04	4.44	24.16	24.33	15.95	2,383	800-444-4015	Y
American Century Inv One Choice 2035 Port I Cls	ARLIX	B-	C	B+	Up	3.41	13.74	5.65	28.66	32.07	16.05	2,383	800-444-4015	Y
American Century Inv One Choice 2035 Port Inv Cls	ARYIX	B-	C	B+	Up	3.28	13.61	5.44	27.93	30.69	16.02	2,383	800-444-4015	Y
American Century Inv One Choice 2035 Port R Cls	ARYRX	B-	C	B+	Up	3.22	13.32	4.91	25.96	27.45	15.99	2,383	800-444-4015	Y
American Century Inv One Choice 2035 Port R6 Cls	ARLDX	B-	C	A-	Up	3.43	13.84	5.86	29.11	32.90	11.76	2,383	800-444-4015	Y
American Century Inv One Choice 2040 Port A Cls	ARDMX	B-	C	B+	Up	3.31	14.34	5.13	29.40	31.32	13.39	1,740	800-444-4015	Y
American Century Inv One Choice 2040 Port C Cls	ARNOX	B-	C	B+	Up	3.17	13.91	4.40	26.50	26.50	13.34	1,740	800-444-4015	Y
American Century Inv One Choice 2040 Port I Cls	ARDSX	B-	C	B+	Up	3.46	14.60	5.68	31.12	34.31	13.42	1,740	800-444-4015	Y
American Century Inv One Choice 2040 Port Inv Cls	ARDVX	B-	C	B+	Up	3.39	14.41	5.39	30.35	32.96	13.41	1,740	800-444-4015	Y
American Century Inv One Choice 2040 Port R Cls	ARDRX	B-	C	B+	Up	3.24	14.17	4.86	28.35	29.69	13.37	1,740	800-444-4015	Y
American Century Inv One Choice 2040 Port R6 Cls	ARDUX	B-	C	B+	Up	3.51	14.70	5.80	31.56	35.16	12.09	1,740	800-444-4015	Y
American Century Inv One Choice 2045 Port A Cls	AROAX	B-	C	B+	Up	3.45	15.15	5.14	31.71	33.62	16.79	1,690	800-444-4015	Y
American Century Inv One Choice 2045 Port C Cls	AROCX	B-	C	B+	Up	3.27	14.74	4.41	28.75	28.67	16.73	1,690	800-444-4015	Y
American Century Inv One Choice 2045 Port I Cls	AOOIX	B-	C	B+	Up	3.56	15.42	5.62	33.43	36.62	16.84	1,690	800-444-4015	Y
American Century Inv One Choice 2045 Port Inv Cls	AROIX	B-	C	B+	Up	3.50	15.29	5.41	32.59	35.21	16.81	1,690	800-444-4015	Y
American Century Inv One Choice 2045 Port R Cls	ARORX	B-	C	B+	Up	3.38	15.01	4.87	30.64	31.92	16.78	1,690	800-444-4015	Y
American Century Inv One Choice 2045 Port R6 Cls	ARDOX	B-	C	B+	Up	3.56	15.50	5.69	33.88	37.48	11.92	1,690	800-444-4015	Y
American Century Inv One Choice 2050 Port A Cls	ARFMX	B-	C	B	Up	3.53	15.93	5.11	33.31	34.96	13.75	1,121	800-444-4015	Y
American Century Inv One Choice 2050 Port C Cls	ARFDX	B-	C	B	Up	3.39	15.50	4.38	30.38	30.06	13.71	1,121	800-444-4015	Y
American Century Inv One Choice 2050 Port I Cls	ARFSX	B-	C	B	Up	3.68	16.25	5.66	35.14	38.08	13.8	1,121	800-444-4015	Y
American Century Inv One Choice 2050 Port Inv Cls	ARFVX	B-	C	B	Up	3.61	16.10	5.38	34.28	36.75	13.77	1,121	800-444-4015	Y
American Century Inv One Choice 2050 Port R Cls	ARFWX	B-	C	B	Up	3.46	15.75	4.84	32.31	33.25	13.74	1,121	800-444-4015	Y
American Century Inv One Choice 2050 Port R6 Cls	ARFEX	B-	C	B	Up	3.66	16.27	5.70	35.63	38.88	12.43	1,121	800-444-4015	Y

Category: Target Date (con't)

Fund Name	Ticker Symbol	RATINGS				TOTAL RETURNS & PERFORMANCE					ASSETS		NEW INVESTORS	
		Overall Rating	Reward Rating	Risk Rating	Recent Up/ Downgrade	3-Month Total Return	6-Month Total Return	1-Year Total Return	3-Year Total Return	5-Year Total Return	NAV	Total Assets (MIL)	Telephone	Open to New Investors
American Century Inv One Choice 2055 Port A Cls	AREMX	B-	C	B	Up	3.54	16.25	4.93	34.01	35.70	14.88	673.8	800-444-4015	Y
American Century Inv One Choice 2055 Port C Cls	AREFX	B-	C	B	Up	3.42	15.83	4.21	31.11	30.73	14.78	673.8	800-444-4015	Y
American Century Inv One Choice 2055 Port I Cls	ARENX	B-	C	B	Up	3.68	16.47	5.47	35.87	38.74	14.92	673.8	800-444-4015	Y
American Century Inv One Choice 2055 Port Inv Cls	AREVX	B-	C	B	Up	3.68	16.39	5.25	35.07	37.36	14.91	673.8	800-444-4015	Y
American Century Inv One Choice 2055 Port R Cls	AREOX	B-	C	B	Up	3.54	16.06	4.73	33.10	33.99	14.88	673.8	800-444-4015	Y
American Century Inv One Choice 2055 Port R6 Cls	AREUX	B-	C	B	Up	3.72	16.55	5.57	36.42	39.68	12.81	673.8	800-444-4015	Y
American Century Inv One Choice 2060 Port A Cls	ARGMX	B-	C	B	Up	3.60	16.47	4.90	34.45		12.94	138.2	800-444-4015	Y
American Century Inv One Choice 2060 Port C Cls	ARGHX	B-	C	B	Up	3.38	16.00	4.14	31.55		12.83	138.2	800-444-4015	Y
American Century Inv One Choice 2060 Port I Cls	ARGNX	B-	C	B	Up	3.75	16.72	5.45	36.29		12.98	138.2	800-444-4015	Y
American Century Inv One Choice 2060 Port Inv Cls	ARGVX	B-	C	B	Up	3.68	16.65	5.16	35.54		12.96	138.2	800-444-4015	Y
American Century Inv One Choice 2060 Port R Cls	ARGRX	B-	C	B	Up	3.52	16.29	4.64	33.44		12.92	138.2	800-444-4015	Y
American Century Inv One Choice 2060 Port R6 Cls	ARGDX	B-	C	B	Up	3.82	16.87	5.60	36.86		13.02	138.2	800-444-4015	Y
American Century Inv One Choice In Retmnt Port A Cls	ARTAX	B	C	A-	Up	2.93	10.88	5.37	19.67	21.83	13.17	1,520	800-444-4015	Y
American Century Inv One Choice In Retmnt Port C Cls	ATTCX	B-	C	A-	Up	2.75	10.53	4.59	17.14	17.39	13.13	1,520	800-444-4015	Y
American Century Inv One Choice In Retmnt Port I Cls	ATTIX	B	C	A-	Up	3.05	11.12	5.85	21.40	24.54	13.17	1,520	800-444-4015	Y
American Century Inv One Choice In Retmnt Port Inv Cls	ARTOX	B	C	A-	Up	2.92	10.93	5.64	20.59	23.29	13.16	1,520	800-444-4015	Y
American Century Inv One Choice In Retmnt Port R Cls	ARSRX	B-	C	A-	Up	2.87	10.75	5.11	18.90	20.33	13.16	1,520	800-444-4015	Y
American Century Inv One Choice In Retmnt Port R6 Cls	ARDTX	B	C+	A-	Up	3.08	11.24	6.02	21.68	25.26	10.85	1,520	800-444-4015	Y
American Funds 2010 Target Date Retirement Fund® Class A	AAATX	B	C+	A-	Up	2.49	8.93	6.19	18.77	24.07	11.09	3,349	800-421-4225	Y
American Funds 2010 Target Date Retirement Fund® Class C	CCATX	B-	C	A-		2.34	8.64	5.41	16.10	19.44	10.93	3,349	800-421-4225	Y
American Funds 2010 Target Date Retirement Fund® Class F-1	FAATX	B	C+	A-	Up	2.41	8.88	6.11	18.59	23.77	11.03	3,349	800-421-4225	Y
American Funds 2010 Target Date Retirement Fund® Class F-2	FBATX	B	C+	A		2.50	9.06	6.33	19.59	25.41	11.07	3,349	800-421-4225	Y
American Funds 2010 Target Date Retirement Fund® Class F-3	DJTFX	B	C+	A		2.58	9.14	6.48	19.93	26.02	11.1	3,349	800-421-4225	Y
American Funds 2010 Target Date Retirement Fund® Class R-1	RAATX	B-	C	A-		2.31	8.53	5.30	15.98	19.17	11.06	3,349	800-421-4225	Y
American Funds 2010 Target Date Retirement Fund® Class R-2	RBATX	B-	C	A-		2.34	8.54	5.32	16.07	19.57	10.93	3,349	800-421-4225	Y
American Funds 2010 Target Date Retirement Fund® Cls R-2E	RBEAX	B	C	A-	Up	2.43	8.76	5.72	17.17	21.92	10.92	3,349	800-421-4225	Y
American Funds 2010 Target Date Retirement Fund® Class R-3	RCATX	B	C+	A-	Up	2.41	8.79	5.80	17.62	22.02	11.01	3,349	800-421-4225	Y
American Funds 2010 Target Date Retirement Fund® Class R-4	RDATX	B	C+	A-	Up	2.49	8.95	6.07	18.68	23.96	11.07	3,349	800-421-4225	Y
American Funds 2010 Target Date Retirement Fund® Class R-5	REATX	B	C+	A-		2.57	9.19	6.49	19.82	25.90	11.16	3,349	800-421-4225	Y
American Funds 2010 Target Date Retirement Fund® Cls R-5E	RHATX	B	C+	A-		2.59	9.08	6.37	19.44	25.48	11.05	3,349	800-421-4225	Y
American Funds 2010 Target Date Retirement Fund® Class R-6	RFTTX	B	C+	A		2.67	9.22	6.57	20.07	26.17	11.13	3,349	800-421-4225	Y
American Funds 2015 Target Date Retirement Fund® Class A	AABTX	B	C+	A-	Up	2.61	9.49	6.28	20.27	25.70	11.76	5,129	800-421-4225	Y
American Funds 2015 Target Date Retirement Fund® Class C	CCBTX	B-	C	A-		2.38	9.14	5.54	17.63	21.09	11.58	5,129	800-421-4225	Y
American Funds 2015 Target Date Retirement Fund® Class F-1	FAKTX	B	C+	A-	Up	2.63	9.55	6.20	20.18	25.61	11.69	5,129	800-421-4225	Y
American Funds 2015 Target Date Retirement Fund® Class F-2	FBBTX	B	C+	A		2.62	9.71	6.52	21.16	27.27	11.75	5,129	800-421-4225	Y
American Funds 2015 Target Date Retirement Fund® Class F-3	FDBTX	B	C+	A		2.70	9.78	6.66	21.50	27.83	11.78	5,129	800-421-4225	Y
American Funds 2015 Target Date Retirement Fund® Class R-1	RAJTX	B-	C	A-	Up	2.39	9.15	5.39	17.48	20.84	11.56	5,129	800-421-4225	Y
American Funds 2015 Target Date Retirement Fund® Class R-2	RBJTX	B-	C	A-		2.48	9.15	5.46	17.54	21.28	11.57	5,129	800-421-4225	Y
American Funds 2015 Target Date Retirement Fund® Cls R-2E	RBEJX	B	C	A-	Up	2.57	9.35	5.81	18.72	23.62	11.57	5,129	800-421-4225	Y
American Funds 2015 Target Date Retirement Fund® Class R-3	RCJTX	B	C	A-	Up	2.54	9.47	5.95	19.17	23.80	11.67	5,129	800-421-4225	Y
American Funds 2015 Target Date Retirement Fund® Class R-4	RDBTX	B	C+	A-	Up	2.61	9.60	6.34	20.28	25.79	11.75	5,129	800-421-4225	Y
American Funds 2015 Target Date Retirement Fund® Class R-5	REJTX	B	C+	A		2.68	9.73	6.57	21.29	27.60	11.84	5,129	800-421-4225	Y
American Funds 2015 Target Date Retirement Fund® Cls R-5E	RHBTX	B	C+	A		2.62	9.64	6.45	20.99	27.14	11.71	5,129	800-421-4225	Y
American Funds 2015 Target Date Retirement Fund® Class R-6	RFJTX	B	C+	A		2.69	9.76	6.65	21.57	27.93	11.8	5,129	800-421-4225	Y
American Funds 2020 Target Date Retirement Fund® Class A	AACTX	B	C+	A	Up	2.72	10.04	6.16	23.14	28.49	12.82	15,535	800-421-4225	Y
American Funds 2020 Target Date Retirement Fund® Class C	CCCTX	B	C	A-	Up	2.52	9.75	5.38	20.42	23.75	12.6	15,535	800-421-4225	Y
American Funds 2020 Target Date Retirement Fund® Class F-1	FAOTX	B	C+	A	Up	2.65	10.01	6.11	23.04	28.34	12.74	15,535	800-421-4225	Y
American Funds 2020 Target Date Retirement Fund® Class F-2	FBCTX	B	C+	A	Up	2.80	10.24	6.47	24.07	30.09	12.81	15,535	800-421-4225	Y
American Funds 2020 Target Date Retirement Fund® Class F-3	FCCTX	B	C+	A	Up	2.80	10.21	6.53	24.38	30.60	12.84	15,535	800-421-4225	Y
American Funds 2020 Target Date Retirement Fund® Class R-1	RACTX	B	C	A-	Up	2.51	9.72	5.34	20.24	23.58	12.64	15,535	800-421-4225	Y
American Funds 2020 Target Date Retirement Fund® Class R-2	RBCTX	B	C	A-	Up	2.52	9.66	5.39	20.38	23.89	12.59	15,535	800-421-4225	Y
American Funds 2020 Target Date Retirement Fund® Cls R-2E	RBEHX	B	C	A-	Up	2.60	9.84	5.67	21.39	26.16	12.61	15,535	800-421-4225	Y

Category: Target Date (con't)

Fund Name	Ticker Symbol	RATINGS: Overall Rating	Reward Rating	Risk Rating	Recent Up/ Downgrade	TOTAL RETURNS & PERFORMANCE: 3-Month Total Return	6-Month Total Return	1-Year Total Return	3-Year Total Return	5-Year Total Return	ASSETS: NAV	Total Assets (MIL)	NEW INVESTORS: Telephone	Open to New Investors
American Funds 2020 Target Date Retirement Fund® Class R-3	RCCTX	B	C	A	Up	2.66	9.94	5.84	22.02	26.49	12.71	15,535	800-421-4225	Y
American Funds 2020 Target Date Retirement Fund® Class R-4	RDCTX	B	C+	A	Up	2.72	10.06	6.21	23.09	28.51	12.8	15,535	800-421-4225	Y
American Funds 2020 Target Date Retirement Fund® Class R-5	RECTX	B	C+	A	Up	2.78	10.23	6.51	24.22	30.43	12.92	15,535	800-421-4225	Y
American Funds 2020 Target Date Retirement Fund® Cls R-5E	RHCTX	B	C+	A	Up	2.81	10.26	6.42	23.87	30.03	12.78	15,535	800-421-4225	Y
American Funds 2020 Target Date Retirement Fund® Class R-6	RRCTX	B	C+	A		2.79	10.27	6.51	24.38	30.73	12.88	15,535	800-421-4225	Y
American Funds 2025 Target Date Retirement Fund® Class A	AADTX	B	C	A	Up	2.91	11.39	6.00	27.11	31.87	13.78	21,272	800-421-4225	Y
American Funds 2025 Target Date Retirement Fund® Class C	CCDTX	B	C	A-	Up	2.73	11.00	5.25	24.28	27.00	13.52	21,272	800-421-4225	Y
American Funds 2025 Target Date Retirement Fund® Class F-1	FAPTX	B	C	A	Up	2.93	11.39	6.03	27.09	31.83	13.69	21,272	800-421-4225	Y
American Funds 2025 Target Date Retirement Fund® Class F-2	FBDTX	B	C	A	Up	2.91	11.49	6.30	28.12	33.52	13.77	21,272	800-421-4225	Y
American Funds 2025 Target Date Retirement Fund® Class F-3	FDDTX	B	C	A	Up	2.98	11.56	6.36	28.33	33.93	13.8	21,272	800-421-4225	Y
American Funds 2025 Target Date Retirement Fund® Class R-1	RADTX	B	C	A-	Up	2.73	10.98	5.25	24.23	26.82	13.54	21,272	800-421-4225	Y
American Funds 2025 Target Date Retirement Fund® Class R-2	RBDTX	B	C	A-	Up	2.66	10.94	5.18	24.26	27.13	13.48	21,272	800-421-4225	Y
American Funds 2025 Target Date Retirement Fund® Cls R-2E	RBEDX	B	C	A	Up	2.80	11.15	5.51	25.41	29.50	13.55	21,272	800-421-4225	Y
American Funds 2025 Target Date Retirement Fund® Class R-3	RCDTX	B	C	A	Up	2.86	11.25	5.70	25.99	29.84	13.64	21,272	800-421-4225	Y
American Funds 2025 Target Date Retirement Fund® Class R-4	RDDTX	B	C	A	Up	2.91	11.42	6.06	27.10	31.89	13.75	21,272	800-421-4225	Y
American Funds 2025 Target Date Retirement Fund® Class R-5	REDTX	B	C	A	Up	2.96	11.56	6.34	28.23	33.82	13.89	21,272	800-421-4225	Y
American Funds 2025 Target Date Retirement Fund® Cls R-5E	RHDTX	B	C	A	Up	2.92	11.52	6.25	27.94	33.37	13.74	21,272	800-421-4225	Y
American Funds 2025 Target Date Retirement Fund® Class R-6	RFDTX	B	C+	A	Up	2.97	11.60	6.34	28.41	34.14	13.85	21,272	800-421-4225	Y
American Funds 2030 Target Date Retirement Fund® Class A	AAETX	B-	C	A-	Up	2.99	12.82	5.84	32.64	37.26	14.78	23,124	800-421-4225	Y
American Funds 2030 Target Date Retirement Fund® Class C	CCETX	B-	C	A-	Up	2.83	12.40	5.12	29.65	32.09	14.5	23,124	800-421-4225	Y
American Funds 2030 Target Date Retirement Fund® Class F-1	FAETX	B-	C	A-	Up	2.94	12.75	5.81	32.53	37.05	14.67	23,124	800-421-4225	Y
American Funds 2030 Target Date Retirement Fund® Class F-2	FBETX	B-	C	A-		3.13	12.99	6.15	33.68	38.94	14.78	23,124	800-421-4225	Y
American Funds 2030 Target Date Retirement Fund® Class F-3	FCETX	B	C	A-	Up	3.06	12.97	6.21	33.97	39.45	14.8	23,124	800-421-4225	Y
American Funds 2030 Target Date Retirement Fund® Class R-1	RAETX	B-	C	A-	Up	2.75	12.34	5.02	29.51	31.85	14.56	23,124	800-421-4225	Y
American Funds 2030 Target Date Retirement Fund® Class R-2	RBETX	B-	C	A-	Up	2.84	12.44	5.12	29.63	32.27	14.46	23,124	800-421-4225	Y
American Funds 2030 Target Date Retirement Fund® Cls R-2E	RBEEX	B-	C	A-	Up	2.89	12.52	5.43	30.84	34.60	14.55	23,124	800-421-4225	Y
American Funds 2030 Target Date Retirement Fund® Class R-3	RCETX	B-	C	A-	Up	2.88	12.63	5.56	31.33	35.01	14.62	23,124	800-421-4225	Y
American Funds 2030 Target Date Retirement Fund® Class R-4	RDETX	B-	C	A-	Up	3.00	12.85	5.91	32.62	37.17	14.75	23,124	800-421-4225	Y
American Funds 2030 Target Date Retirement Fund® Class R-5	REETX	B-	C	A-		3.04	12.96	6.18	33.72	39.19	14.9	23,124	800-421-4225	Y
American Funds 2030 Target Date Retirement Fund® Cls R-5E	RHETX	B-	C	A-	Up	3.07	12.94	6.11	33.41	38.71	14.74	23,124	800-421-4225	Y
American Funds 2030 Target Date Retirement Fund® Class R-6	RFETX	B	C	A-	Up	3.12	13.01	6.27	34.07	39.57	14.85	23,124	800-421-4225	Y
American Funds 2035 Target Date Retirement Fund® Class A	AAFTX	B-	C	B+	Up	3.11	14.66	5.72	37.38	41.48	15.25	18,453	800-421-4225	Y
American Funds 2035 Target Date Retirement Fund® Class C	CCFTX	B-	C	B+	Up	2.95	14.27	4.96	34.31	36.21	14.97	18,453	800-421-4225	Y
American Funds 2035 Target Date Retirement Fund® Class F-1	FAQTX	B-	C	B+	Up	3.12	14.66	5.75	37.27	41.35	15.17	18,453	800-421-4225	Y
American Funds 2035 Target Date Retirement Fund® Class F-2	FBFTX	B-	C	B+	Up	3.18	14.83	6.04	38.34	43.18	15.25	18,453	800-421-4225	Y
American Funds 2035 Target Date Retirement Fund® Class F-3	FDFTX	B-	C	B+	Up	3.17	14.89	6.09	38.72	43.70	15.27	18,453	800-421-4225	Y
American Funds 2035 Target Date Retirement Fund® Class R-1	RAFTX	B-	C	B+	Up	2.90	14.18	4.93	34.12	35.99	14.89	18,453	800-421-4225	Y
American Funds 2035 Target Date Retirement Fund® Class R-2	RBFTX	B-	C	B+	Up	2.89	14.25	4.99	34.19	36.30	14.91	18,453	800-421-4225	Y
American Funds 2035 Target Date Retirement Fund® Cls R-2E	RBEFX	B-	C	B+	Up	2.95	14.42	5.31	35.45	38.89	14.99	18,453	800-421-4225	Y
American Funds 2035 Target Date Retirement Fund® Class R-3	RCFTX	B-	C	B+	Up	3.00	14.50	5.43	36.01	39.25	15.08	18,453	800-421-4225	Y
American Funds 2035 Target Date Retirement Fund® Class R-4	RDFTX	B-	C	B+	Up	3.11	14.70	5.79	37.27	41.42	15.21	18,453	800-421-4225	Y
American Funds 2035 Target Date Retirement Fund® Class R-5	REFTX	B-	C	B+	Up	3.22	14.86	6.06	38.53	43.50	15.38	18,453	800-421-4225	Y
American Funds 2035 Target Date Retirement Fund® Cls R-5E	RHFTX	B-	C	B+	Up	3.11	14.79	5.99	38.17	43.07	15.21	18,453	800-421-4225	Y
American Funds 2035 Target Date Retirement Fund® Class R-6	RFFTX	B-	C	B+	Up	3.16	14.84	6.14	38.81	43.81	15.32	18,453	800-421-4225	Y
American Funds 2040 Target Date Retirement Fund® Class A	AAGTX	B-	C	B+	Up	3.10	15.27	5.71	39.03	42.93	15.62	16,065	800-421-4225	Y
American Funds 2040 Target Date Retirement Fund® Class C	CCGTX	B-	C	B+	Up	2.95	14.84	4.91	35.90	37.54	15.32	16,065	800-421-4225	Y
American Funds 2040 Target Date Retirement Fund® Class F-1	FAUTX	B-	C	B+	Up	3.18	15.29	5.70	38.96	42.78	15.53	16,065	800-421-4225	Y
American Funds 2040 Target Date Retirement Fund® Class F-2	FBGTX	B-	C	B+	Up	3.23	15.44	5.96	40.11	44.57	15.62	16,065	800-421-4225	Y
American Funds 2040 Target Date Retirement Fund® Class F-3	FCGTX	B-	C	B+	Up	3.23	15.49	6.08	40.36	45.03	15.65	16,065	800-421-4225	Y
American Funds 2040 Target Date Retirement Fund® Class R-1	RAKTX	B-	C	B+	Up	2.95	14.85	4.89	35.81	37.32	15.31	16,065	800-421-4225	Y
American Funds 2040 Target Date Retirement Fund® Class R-2	RBKTX	B-	C	B+	Up	2.96	14.90	4.91	35.91	37.71	15.26	16,065	800-421-4225	Y
American Funds 2040 Target Date Retirement Fund® Cls R-2E	RBEKX	B-	C	B+	Up	3.01	15.04	5.22	37.09	40.20	15.37	16,065	800-421-4225	Y

Category: Target Date (con't)

		RATINGS				TOTAL RETURNS & PERFORMANCE					ASSETS		NEW INVESTORS	
Fund Name	Ticker Symbol	Overall Rating	Reward Rating	Risk Rating	Recent Up/ Downgrade	3-Month Total Return	6-Month Total Return	1-Year Total Return	3-Year Total Return	5-Year Total Return	NAV	Total Assets (MIL)	Telephone	Open to New Investors
American Funds 2040 Target Date Retirement Fund® Class R-3	RCKTX	B-	C	B+	Up	3.06	15.11	5.41	37.73	40.66	15.46	16,065	800-421-4225	Y
American Funds 2040 Target Date Retirement Fund® Class R-4	RDGTX	B-	C	B+	Up	3.11	15.32	5.69	39.02	42.75	15.58	16,065	800-421-4225	Y
American Funds 2040 Target Date Retirement Fund® Class R-5	REGTX	B-	C	B+	Up	3.20	15.45	6.04	40.26	44.93	15.76	16,065	800-421-4225	Y
American Funds 2040 Target Date Retirement Fund® Cls R-5E	RHGTX	B-	C	B+	Up	3.24	15.49	5.91	39.84	44.44	15.58	16,065	800-421-4225	Y
American Funds 2040 Target Date Retirement Fund® Class R-6	RFGTX	B-	C	B+	Up	3.22	15.52	6.06	40.44	45.25	15.7	16,065	800-421-4225	Y
American Funds 2045 Target Date Retirement Fund® Class A	AAHTX	B-	C	B+	Up	3.18	15.56	5.67	39.94	43.92	15.89	11,753	800-421-4225	Y
American Funds 2045 Target Date Retirement Fund® Class C	CCHTX	B-	C	B+	Up	2.97	15.07	4.85	36.69	38.38	15.57	11,753	800-421-4225	Y
American Funds 2045 Target Date Retirement Fund® Class F-1	FATTX	B-	C	B+	Up	3.13	15.50	5.61	39.76	43.63	15.79	11,753	800-421-4225	Y
American Funds 2045 Target Date Retirement Fund® Class F-2	FBHTX	B-	C	B+	Up	3.24	15.72	5.99	40.98	45.49	15.9	11,753	800-421-4225	Y
American Funds 2045 Target Date Retirement Fund® Class F-3	FCHTX	B-	C	B+	Up	3.24	15.70	6.03	41.14	45.95	15.91	11,753	800-421-4225	Y
American Funds 2045 Target Date Retirement Fund® Class R-1	RAHTX	B-	C	B+	Up	2.98	15.01	4.82	36.58	38.23	15.55	11,753	800-421-4225	Y
American Funds 2045 Target Date Retirement Fund® Class R-2	RBHTX	B-	C	B+	Up	2.99	15.08	4.88	36.75	38.65	15.49	11,753	800-421-4225	Y
American Funds 2045 Target Date Retirement Fund® Cls R-2E	RBHHX	B-	C	B+	Up	3.09	15.26	5.16	37.97	41.24	15.63	11,753	800-421-4225	Y
American Funds 2045 Target Date Retirement Fund® Class R-3	RCHTX	B-	C	B+	Up	3.08	15.36	5.31	38.55	41.53	15.69	11,753	800-421-4225	Y
American Funds 2045 Target Date Retirement Fund® Class R-4	RDHTX	B-	C	B+	Up	3.18	15.52	5.66	39.81	43.68	15.85	11,753	800-421-4225	Y
American Funds 2045 Target Date Retirement Fund® Class R-5	REHTX	B-	C	B+	Up	3.28	15.72	5.99	41.10	45.92	16.04	11,753	800-421-4225	Y
American Funds 2045 Target Date Retirement Fund® Cls R-5E	RHHTX	B-	C	B+	Up	3.19	15.63	5.87	40.70	45.34	15.83	11,753	800-421-4225	Y
American Funds 2045 Target Date Retirement Fund® Class R-6	RFHTX	B-	C	B+	Up	3.29	15.71	6.08	41.39	46.24	15.98	11,753	800-421-4225	Y
American Funds 2050 Target Date Retirement Fund® Class A	AALTX	B-	C	B+	Up	3.17	15.66	5.68	40.43	44.32	15.58	9,824	800-421-4225	Y
American Funds 2050 Target Date Retirement Fund® Class C	CCITX	B-	C	B+	Up	2.97	15.18	4.82	37.14	38.84	15.25	9,824	800-421-4225	Y
American Funds 2050 Target Date Retirement Fund® Class F-1	FAITX	B-	C	B+	Up	3.19	15.69	5.61	40.34	44.09	15.48	9,824	800-421-4225	Y
American Funds 2050 Target Date Retirement Fund® Class F-2	FBITX	B-	C	B+	Up	3.24	15.76	5.90	41.37	46.01	15.57	9,824	800-421-4225	Y
American Funds 2050 Target Date Retirement Fund® Class F-3	DITFX	B-	C	B+	Up	3.30	15.88	6.04	41.73	46.50	15.61	9,824	800-421-4225	Y
American Funds 2050 Target Date Retirement Fund® Class R-1	RAITX	B-	C	B+	Up	2.97	15.20	4.80	37.08	38.68	15.23	9,824	800-421-4225	Y
American Funds 2050 Target Date Retirement Fund® Class R-2	RBITX	B-	C	B+	Up	3.04	15.28	4.88	37.17	39.08	15.24	9,824	800-421-4225	Y
American Funds 2050 Target Date Retirement Fund® Cls R-2E	RBHEX	B-	C	B+	Up	3.09	15.36	5.15	38.47	41.66	15.32	9,824	800-421-4225	Y
American Funds 2050 Target Date Retirement Fund® Class R-3	RCITX	B-	C	B+	Up	3.14	15.52	5.39	39.09	42.03	15.4	9,824	800-421-4225	Y
American Funds 2050 Target Date Retirement Fund® Class R-4	RDITX	B-	C	B+	Up	3.18	15.71	5.67	40.30	44.21	15.54	9,824	800-421-4225	Y
American Funds 2050 Target Date Retirement Fund® Class R-5	REITX	B-	C	B+	Up	3.21	15.85	5.94	41.55	46.32	15.71	9,824	800-421-4225	Y
American Funds 2050 Target Date Retirement Fund® Cls R-5E	RHITX	B-	C	B+	Up	3.25	15.79	5.88	41.24	45.93	15.54	9,824	800-421-4225	Y
American Funds 2050 Target Date Retirement Fund® Class R-6	RFITX	B-	C	B+	Up	3.29	15.90	6.09	41.89	46.81	15.67	9,824	800-421-4225	Y
American Funds 2055 Target Date Retirement Fund® Class A	AAMTX	B-	C	B+	Up	3.18	15.63	5.62	40.39	44.34	19.45	5,208	800-421-4225	Y
American Funds 2055 Target Date Retirement Fund® Class C	CCJTX	B-	C	B+	Up	3.02	15.26	4.89	37.19	38.84	19.1	5,208	800-421-4225	Y
American Funds 2055 Target Date Retirement Fund® Class F-1	FAJTX	B-	C	B+	Up	3.20	15.67	5.64	40.31	44.20	19.34	5,208	800-421-4225	Y
American Funds 2055 Target Date Retirement Fund® Class F-2	FBJTX	B-	C	B+	Up	3.23	15.83	5.92	41.36	45.94	19.46	5,208	800-421-4225	Y
American Funds 2055 Target Date Retirement Fund® Class F-3	FCJTX	B-	C	B+	Up	3.28	15.87	6.03	41.73	46.64	19.49	5,208	800-421-4225	Y
American Funds 2055 Target Date Retirement Fund® Class R-1	RAMTX	B-	C	B+	Up	3.03	15.26	4.86	37.14	38.66	19.03	5,208	800-421-4225	Y
American Funds 2055 Target Date Retirement Fund® Class R-2	RBMTX	B-	C	B+	Up	2.97	15.19	4.86	37.14	38.98	19.03	5,208	800-421-4225	Y
American Funds 2055 Target Date Retirement Fund® Cls R-2E	RBEMX	B-	C	B+	Up	3.12	15.42	5.22	38.50	41.78	19.16	5,208	800-421-4225	Y
American Funds 2055 Target Date Retirement Fund® Class R-3	RCMTX	B-	C	B+	Up	3.10	15.48	5.35	39.02	41.95	19.24	5,208	800-421-4225	Y
American Funds 2055 Target Date Retirement Fund® Class R-4	RDJTX	B-	C	B+	Up	3.18	15.67	5.63	40.29	44.13	19.41	5,208	800-421-4225	Y
American Funds 2055 Target Date Retirement Fund® Class R-5	REKTX	B-	C	B+	Up	3.26	15.83	5.99	41.58	46.28	19.61	5,208	800-421-4225	Y
American Funds 2055 Target Date Retirement Fund® Cls R-5E	RHJTX	B-	C	B+	Up	3.30	15.82	5.88	41.25	45.93	19.4	5,208	800-421-4225	Y
American Funds 2055 Target Date Retirement Fund® Class R-6	RFKTX	B-	C	B+	Up	3.26	15.87	5.99	41.72	46.62	19.63	5,208	800-421-4225	Y
American Funds 2060 Target Date Retirement Fund® Class A	AANTX	B-	C	B+	Up	3.19	15.57	5.64	40.27		12.91	1,670	800-421-4225	Y
American Funds 2060 Target Date Retirement Fund® Class C	CCKTX	B-	C	B+	Up	3.07	15.28	4.91	37.18		12.75	1,670	800-421-4225	Y
American Funds 2060 Target Date Retirement Fund® Class F-1	FAWTX	B-	C	B+	Up	3.19	15.66	5.60	40.15		12.92	1,670	800-421-4225	Y
American Funds 2060 Target Date Retirement Fund® Class F-2	FBKTX	B-	C	B+	Up	3.26	15.80	5.94	41.20		12.97	1,670	800-421-4225	Y
American Funds 2060 Target Date Retirement Fund® Class F-3	FCKTX	B-	C	B+	Up	3.27	15.84	5.94	41.70		12.94	1,670	800-421-4225	Y
American Funds 2060 Target Date Retirement Fund® Class R-1	RANTX	B-	C	B+	Up	3.05	15.31	4.95	37.27		12.8	1,670	800-421-4225	Y
American Funds 2060 Target Date Retirement Fund® Class R-2	RBNTX	B-	C	B+	Up	3.07	15.27	4.89	37.06		12.75	1,670	800-421-4225	Y
American Funds 2060 Target Date Retirement Fund® Cls R-2E	RBENX	B-	C	B+	Up	3.13	15.49	5.23	38.35		12.82	1,670	800-421-4225	Y

Category: Target Date (con't)

Fund Name	Ticker Symbol	RATINGS: Overall Rating	Reward Rating	Risk Rating	Recent Up/ Downgrade	TOTAL RETURNS & PERFORMANCE: 3-Month Total Return	6-Month Total Return	1-Year Total Return	3-Year Total Return	5-Year Total Return	ASSETS: NAV	Total Assets (MIL)	NEW INVESTORS: Telephone	Open to New Investors
American Funds 2060 Target Date Retirement Fund® Class R-3	RCNTX	B-	C	B+	Up	3.13	15.46	5.31	38.86		12.84	1,670	800-421-4225	Y
American Funds 2060 Target Date Retirement Fund® Class R-4	RDKTX	B-	C	B+	Up	3.19	15.68	5.63	40.14		12.91	1,670	800-421-4225	Y
American Funds 2060 Target Date Retirement Fund® Class R-5	REMTX	B-	C	B+	Up	3.25	15.87	5.95	41.53		12.99	1,670	800-421-4225	Y
American Funds 2060 Target Date Retirement Fund® Cls R-5E	RHKTX	B-	C	B+	Up	3.27	15.85	5.93	41.04		12.93	1,670	800-421-4225	Y
American Funds 2060 Target Date Retirement Fund® Class R-6	RFUTX	B-	C	B+	Up	3.33	15.86	6.00	41.66		13	1,670	800-421-4225	Y
BlackRock LifePath® Dynamic 2020 Fund Class K Shares	LPSCX	B	C+	A		3.32	12.68	7.29	26.30	28.94	15.48	296.3	800-441-7762	Y
BlackRock LifePath® Dynamic 2020 Fund Class R Shares	LPRMX	B	C+	A	Up	3.09	12.24	6.54	23.87	24.40	15.43	296.3	800-441-7762	Y
BlackRock LifePath® Dynamic 2020 Fund Institutional Shares	STLCX	B	C+	A	Up	3.25	12.52	7.02	25.62	27.33	15.55	296.3	800-441-7762	Y
BlackRock LifePath® Dynamic 2020 Fund Investor A Shares	LPRCX	B	C+	A	Up	3.14	12.35	6.71	24.64	25.78	14.19	296.3	800-441-7762	Y
BlackRock LifePath® Dynamic 2020 Fund Investor C Shares	LPCMX	B	C	A-	Up	2.97	11.94	5.90	21.71	20.95	15.31	296.3	800-441-7762	Y
BlackRock LifePath® Dynamic 2025 Fund Class K Shares	LPBKX	B	C+	A-	Up	3.28	13.91	7.39	30.24	32.01	13.12	58.5	800-441-7762	Y
BlackRock LifePath® Dynamic 2025 Fund Class R Shares	LPBRX	B	C	A-	Up	3.11	13.49	6.72	27.62	27.45	13.1	58.5	800-441-7762	Y
BlackRock LifePath® Dynamic 2025 Fund Institutional Shares	LPBIX	B	C+	A-	Up	3.20	13.75	7.10	29.31	30.30	13.25	58.5	800-441-7762	Y
BlackRock LifePath® Dynamic 2025 Fund Investor A Shares	LPBAX	B	C+	A-	Up	3.17	13.61	6.89	28.43	28.83	13.13	58.5	800-441-7762	Y
BlackRock LifePath® Dynamic 2025 Fund Investor C Shares	LPBCX	B-	C	A-	Up	2.91	13.12	6.04	25.37	23.83	13.05	58.5	800-441-7762	Y
BlackRock LifePath® Dynamic 2030 Fund Class K Shares	LPSDX	B	C+	A-	Up	3.30	15.23	7.32	34.14	35.25	13.48	338.3	800-441-7762	Y
BlackRock LifePath® Dynamic 2030 Fund Class R Shares	LPRNX	B-	C	A-		3.09	14.86	6.64	31.44	30.41	13.33	338.3	800-441-7762	Y
BlackRock LifePath® Dynamic 2030 Fund Institutional Shares	STLDX	B	C	A-	Up	3.17	15.11	7.07	33.23	33.48	13.5	338.3	800-441-7762	Y
BlackRock LifePath® Dynamic 2030 Fund Investor A Shares	LPRDX	B-	C	A-		3.17	14.98	6.82	32.23	31.84	12.91	338.3	800-441-7762	Y
BlackRock LifePath® Dynamic 2030 Fund Investor C Shares	LPCNX	B-	C	B+	Up	2.90	14.48	5.91	29.03	26.72	13.21	338.3	800-441-7762	Y
BlackRock LifePath® Dynamic 2035 Fund Class K Shares	LPJKX	B-	C	B+		3.22	16.17	6.98	36.80	37.10	14.14	54.4	800-441-7762	Y
BlackRock LifePath® Dynamic 2035 Fund Class R Shares	LPJRX	B-	C	B+	Up	3.06	15.76	6.28	34.15	32.41	13.88	54.4	800-441-7762	Y
BlackRock LifePath® Dynamic 2035 Fund Institutional Shares	LPJIX	B-	C	B+		3.14	16.00	6.79	36.04	35.56	13.96	54.4	800-441-7762	Y
BlackRock LifePath® Dynamic 2035 Fund Investor A Shares	LPJAX	B-	C	B+	Up	3.09	15.90	6.54	35.08	33.93	13.9	54.4	800-441-7762	Y
BlackRock LifePath® Dynamic 2035 Fund Investor C Shares	LPJCX	B-	C	B+	Up	2.93	15.51	5.72	31.88	28.75	13.75	54.4	800-441-7762	Y
BlackRock LifePath® Dynamic 2040 Fund Class K Shares	LPSFX	B-	C	B+	Up	3.21	17.31	6.77	39.63	39.17	16.97	275.9	800-441-7762	Y
BlackRock LifePath® Dynamic 2040 Fund Class R Shares	LPRKX	B-	C	B	Up	3.00	16.89	6.06	36.85	34.24	16.69	275.9	800-441-7762	Y
BlackRock LifePath® Dynamic 2040 Fund Institutional Shares	STLEX	B-	C	B+	Up	3.18	17.23	6.58	38.89	37.50	16.88	275.9	800-441-7762	Y
BlackRock LifePath® Dynamic 2040 Fund Investor A Shares	LPREX	B-	C	B+	Up	3.13	17.04	6.29	37.76	35.77	15.24	275.9	800-441-7762	Y
BlackRock LifePath® Dynamic 2040 Fund Investor C Shares	LPCKX	B-	C	B	Up	2.86	16.57	5.41	34.43	30.46	16.57	275.9	800-441-7762	Y
BlackRock LifePath® Dynamic 2045 Fund Class K Shares	LPHKX	B-	C	B	Up	3.14	17.74	6.48	40.60	39.50	14.93	36.7	800-441-7762	Y
BlackRock LifePath® Dynamic 2045 Fund Class R Shares	LPHRX	B-	C	B	Up	3.01	17.44	5.81	37.95	34.92	14.7	36.7	800-441-7762	Y
BlackRock LifePath® Dynamic 2045 Fund Institutional Shares	LPHIX	B-	C	B	Up	3.12	17.62	6.27	39.83	38.05	14.78	36.7	800-441-7762	Y
BlackRock LifePath® Dynamic 2045 Fund Investor A Shares	LPHAX	B-	C	B	Up	3.07	17.50	6.01	38.72	36.34	14.74	36.7	800-441-7762	Y
BlackRock LifePath® Dynamic 2045 Fund Investor C Shares	LPHCX	B-	C	B	Up	2.85	17.05	5.15	35.52	31.11	14.52	36.7	800-441-7762	Y
BlackRock LifePath® Dynamic 2050 Fund Class K Shares	LPSGX	B-	C	B	Up	3.21	17.52	6.21	40.90	39.83	19.88	105.5	800-441-7762	Y
BlackRock LifePath® Dynamic 2050 Fund Class R Shares	LPRPX	B-	C	B	Up	3.04	17.15	5.54	38.19	34.97	19.66	105.5	800-441-7762	Y
BlackRock LifePath® Dynamic 2050 Fund Institutional Shares	STLFX	B-	C	B	Up	3.17	17.44	5.99	40.15	38.14	19.82	105.5	800-441-7762	Y
BlackRock LifePath® Dynamic 2050 Fund Investor A Shares	LPRFX	B-	C	B	Up	3.12	17.25	5.72	39.06	36.40	19.74	105.5	800-441-7762	Y
BlackRock LifePath® Dynamic 2050 Porfolio Inv C Shares	LPCPX	B-	C	B	Up	2.91	16.79	4.92	35.77	31.20	19.48	105.5	800-441-7762	Y
BlackRock LifePath® Dynamic 2055 Fund Class K Shares	LPVKX	B-	C	B	Up	3.17	17.39	6.01	40.32	39.04	15.45	22.7	800-441-7762	Y
BlackRock LifePath® Dynamic 2055 Fund Class R Shares	LPVRX	B-	C	B	Up	3.05	17.07	5.35	37.65	34.11	15.14	22.7	800-441-7762	Y
BlackRock LifePath® Dynamic 2055 Fund Institutional Shares	LPVIX	B-	C	B	Up	3.17	17.33	5.82	39.57	37.45	15.26	22.7	800-441-7762	Y
BlackRock LifePath® Dynamic 2055 Fund Investor A Shares	LPVAX	B-	C	B	Up	3.12	17.17	5.58	38.51	35.69	15.18	22.7	800-441-7762	Y
BlackRock LifePath® Dynamic 2055 Fund Investor C Shares	LPVCX	B-	C	B	Up	2.90	16.67	4.72	35.27	30.43	14.96	22.7	800-441-7762	Y
BlackRock LifePath® Dynamic Retirement Fund Class K Shares	LPSAX	B	C+	A		3.30	12.20	7.29	23.27	26.84	10.68	116.3	800-441-7762	Y
BlackRock LifePath® Dynamic Retirement Fund Class R Shares	LPRRX	B	C+	A-	Up	3.21	11.91	6.70	20.98	22.42	10.62	116.3	800-441-7762	Y
BlackRock LifePath® Dynamic Retmnt Inst Shares	STLAX	B	C+	A		3.23	12.09	7.13	22.51	25.29	10.73	116.3	800-441-7762	Y
BlackRock LifePath® Dynamic Retirement Investor A Shares	LPRAX	B	C+	A	Up	3.22	11.91	6.85	21.70	23.79	9.34	116.3	800-441-7762	Y
BlackRock LifePath® Dynamic Retirement Investor C Shares	LPCRX	B	C+	A-	Up	2.93	11.51	5.99	18.67	19.01	10.58	116.3	800-441-7762	Y
BlackRock LifePath® Index 2020 Fund Class K Shares	LIMKX	B	C+	A-	Up	3.29	11.23	6.76	22.84	27.58	13.04	4,737	800-441-7762	Y
BlackRock LifePath® Index 2020 Fund Institutional Shares	LIQIX	B	C+	A-	Up	3.28	11.19	6.71	22.64	27.26	13.04	4,737	800-441-7762	Y

Category: Target Date (con't)

		RATINGS				TOTAL RETURNS & PERFORMANCE					ASSETS		NEW INVESTORS	
Fund Name	Ticker Symbol	Overall Rating	Reward Rating	Risk Rating	Recent Up/ Downgrade	3-Month Total Return	6-Month Total Return	1-Year Total Return	3-Year Total Return	5-Year Total Return	NAV	Total Assets (MIL)	Telephone	Open to New Investors
BlackRock LifePath® Index 2020 Fund Investor A Shares	LIQAX	B	C+	A-	Up	3.15	11.01	6.38	21.72	25.71	13.01	4,737	800-441-7762	Y
BlackRock LifePath® Index 2020 Fund Investor P Shares	LIQPX	B	C+	A-	Up	3.15	11.07	6.42	21.84	25.92	13	4,737	800-441-7762	Y
BlackRock LifePath® Index 2025 Fund Class K Shares	LIBKX	B	C+	A-	Up	3.21	12.62	6.83	26.58	30.95	13.67	3,720	800-441-7762	Y
BlackRock LifePath® Index 2025 Fund Institutional Shares	LIBIX	B	C+	A-	Up	3.28	12.67	6.78	26.38	30.72	13.67	3,720	800-441-7762	Y
BlackRock LifePath® Index 2025 Fund Investor A Shares	LILAX	B	C	A-	Up	3.15	12.48	6.52	25.42	29.01	13.65	3,720	800-441-7762	Y
BlackRock LifePath® Index 2025 Fund Investor P Shares	LILPX	B	C	A-	Up	3.17	12.44	6.56	25.64	29.32	13.63	3,720	800-441-7762	Y
BlackRock LifePath® Index 2030 Fund Class K Shares	LINKX	B-	C	A-		3.19	13.81	6.82	29.87	33.85	14.05	6,723	800-441-7762	Y
BlackRock LifePath® Index 2030 Fund Institutional Shares	LINIX	B-	C	A-		3.18	13.77	6.77	29.64	33.37	14.06	6,723	800-441-7762	Y
BlackRock LifePath® Index 2030 Fund Investor A Shares	LINAX	B-	C	A-		3.19	13.65	6.51	28.84	31.91	14.06	6,723	800-441-7762	Y
BlackRock LifePath® Index 2030 Fund Investor P Shares	LIDPX	B-	C	A-		3.19	13.70	6.56	28.90	32.18	14.05	6,723	800-441-7762	Y
BlackRock LifePath® Index 2035 Fund Class K Shares	LIJKX	B-	C	B+		3.24	14.92	6.84	33.08	36.56	14.52	3,312	800-441-7762	Y
BlackRock LifePath® Index 2035 Fund Institutional Shares	LIJIX	B-	C	B+		3.23	14.86	6.71	32.96	36.19	14.53	3,312	800-441-7762	Y
BlackRock LifePath® Index 2035 Fund Investor A Shares	LIJAX	B-	C	B+	Up	3.18	14.78	6.53	31.99	34.56	14.5	3,312	800-441-7762	Y
BlackRock LifePath® Index 2035 Fund Investor P Shares	LIJPX	B-	C	B+	Up	3.19	14.79	6.54	32.05	34.82	14.48	3,312	800-441-7762	Y
BlackRock LifePath® Index 2040 Fund Class K Shares	LIKKX	B-	C	B+	Up	3.20	15.97	6.79	36.00	38.89	14.88	5,278	800-441-7762	Y
BlackRock LifePath® Index 2040 Fund Institutional Shares	LIKIX	B-	C	B+	Up	3.19	15.94	6.75	35.80	38.54	14.88	5,278	800-441-7762	Y
BlackRock LifePath® Index 2040 Fund Investor A Shares	LIKAX	B-	C	B+	Up	3.21	15.84	6.49	34.80	36.87	14.86	5,278	800-441-7762	Y
BlackRock LifePath® Index 2040 Fund Investor P Shares	LIKPX	B-	C	B+	Up	3.13	15.73	6.47	34.91	37.09	14.84	5,278	800-441-7762	Y
BlackRock LifePath® Index 2045 Fund Class K Shares	LIHKX	B-	C	B	Up	3.23	16.69	6.81	37.85	40.64	15.27	2,339	800-441-7762	Y
BlackRock LifePath® Index 2045 Fund Institutional Shares	LIHIX	B-	C	B	Up	3.15	16.68	6.69	37.58	40.23	15.25	2,339	800-441-7762	Y
BlackRock LifePath® Index 2045 Fund Investor A Shares	LIHAX	B-	C	B	Up	3.10	16.51	6.45	36.60	38.47	15.22	2,339	800-441-7762	Y
BlackRock LifePath® Index 2045 Fund Investor P Shares	LIHPX	B-	C	B	Up	3.17	16.58	6.50	36.76	38.83	15.21	2,339	800-441-7762	Y
BlackRock LifePath® Index 2050 Fund Class K Shares	LIPKX	B-	C	B	Up	3.20	17.02	6.71	38.32	41.03	15.51	2,524	800-441-7762	Y
BlackRock LifePath® Index 2050 Fund Institutional Shares	LIPIX	B-	C	B	Up	3.19	16.97	6.66	38.11	40.67	15.51	2,524	800-441-7762	Y
BlackRock LifePath® Index 2050 Fund Investor A Shares	LIPAX	B-	C	B	Up	3.14	16.89	6.42	37.15	38.93	15.48	2,524	800-441-7762	Y
BlackRock LifePath® Index 2050 Fund Investor P Shares	LIPPX	B-	C	B	Up	3.07	16.88	6.39	37.21	39.20	15.46	2,524	800-441-7762	Y
BlackRock LifePath® Index 2055 Fund Class K Shares	LIVKX	B-	C	B	Up	3.21	17.07	6.72	38.35	41.16	15.82	1,157	800-441-7762	Y
BlackRock LifePath® Index 2055 Fund Institutional Shares	LIVIX	B-	C	B	Up	3.20	17.03	6.67	38.14	40.82	15.82	1,157	800-441-7762	Y
BlackRock LifePath® Index 2055 Fund Investor A Shares	LIVAX	B-	C	B	Up	3.09	16.87	6.36	37.11	39.01	15.78	1,157	800-441-7762	Y
BlackRock LifePath® Index 2055 Fund Investor P Shares	LIVPX	B-	C	B	Up	3.09	16.85	6.41	37.26	39.34	15.77	1,157	800-441-7762	Y
BlackRock LifePath® Index 2060 Fund Class K	LIZKX	B-	C	B	Up	3.19	17.05	6.75	38.65		14.02	260.8	800-441-7762	Y
BlackRock LifePath® Index 2060 Fund Institutional Shares	LIZIX	B-	C	B	Up	3.18	17.00	6.70	38.46		14.02	260.8	800-441-7762	Y
BlackRock LifePath® Index 2060 Fund Investor A Shares	LIZAX	B-	C	B	Up	3.13	16.85	6.41	37.41		13.99	260.8	800-441-7762	Y
BlackRock LifePath® Index 2060 Fund Investor P Shares	LIZPX	B-	C	B	Up	3.06	16.82	6.43	37.55		13.98	260.8	800-441-7762	Y
BlackRock LifePath® Index Retirement Fund Class K Shares	LIRKX	B	C+	A-	Up	3.21	10.74	6.77	20.31	25.50	12.58	2,499	800-441-7762	Y
BlackRock LifePath® Index Retirement Institutional Shares	LIRIX	B	C+	A-	Up	3.20	10.70	6.72	20.10	25.27	12.59	2,499	800-441-7762	Y
BlackRock LifePath® Index Retirement Investor A Shares	LIRAX	B	C+	A-	Up	3.14	10.60	6.55	19.27	23.72	12.58	2,499	800-441-7762	Y
BlackRock LifePath® Index Retirement Investor P Shares	LIRPX	B	C+	A-	Up	3.14	10.65	6.60	19.51	24.05	12.57	2,499	800-441-7762	Y
BlackRock LifePath® Smart Beta 2020 Fund Class K	BIPCX	B	C+	A	Up	2.89	11.59	6.79	25.80	27.12	10.71	19.1	800-441-7762	Y
BlackRock LifePath® Smart Beta 2020 Fund Class R Shares	BRPCX	B	C+	A-	Up	2.74	11.29	6.20	23.74	23.48	10.51	19.1	800-441-7762	Y
BlackRock LifePath® Smart Beta 2020 Institutional Shares	BLBIX	B	C+	A	Up	2.88	11.58	6.78	25.58	26.52	10.73	19.1	800-441-7762	Y
BlackRock LifePath® Smart Beta 2020 Fund Investor A Shares	BAPCX	B	C+	A	Up	2.71	11.43	6.49	24.58	24.98	10.64	19.1	800-441-7762	Y
BlackRock LifePath® Smart Beta 2025 Fund Class K	BIPDX	B	C	A-	Up	2.58	12.28	6.37	28.73	29.17	10.76	25.0	800-441-7762	Y
BlackRock LifePath® Smart Beta 2025 Fund Class R Shares	BRPDX	B	C	A-	Up	2.43	11.91	5.73	26.61	25.54	10.55	25.0	800-441-7762	Y
BlackRock LifePath® Smart Beta 2025 Institutional Shares	BLCIX	B	C	A-	Up	2.58	12.21	6.20	28.43	28.50	10.74	25.0	800-441-7762	Y
BlackRock LifePath® Smart Beta 2025 Fund Investor A Shares	BAPDX	B	C	A-	Up	2.60	12.06	6.03	27.63	27.10	10.67	25.0	800-441-7762	Y
BlackRock LifePath® Smart Beta 2030 Fund Class K	BIPEX	B-	C	A-	Up	2.49	12.84	5.69	30.88	30.23	10.33	25.0	800-441-7762	Y
BlackRock LifePath® Smart Beta 2030 Fund Class R Shares	BRPEX	B-	C	A-	Up	2.32	12.52	5.07	28.85	26.61	10.15	25.0	800-441-7762	Y
BlackRock LifePath® Smart Beta 2030 Institutional Shares	BLEIX	B-	C	A-	Up	2.39	12.66	5.62	30.70	29.69	10.31	25.0	800-441-7762	Y
BlackRock LifePath® Smart Beta 2030 Fund Investor A Shares	BAPEX	B-	C	A-	Up	2.41	12.58	5.38	29.72	28.08	10.23	25.0	800-441-7762	Y
BlackRock LifePath® Smart Beta 2035 Fund Class K	BIPGX	B-	C	B+	Up	2.23	13.24	5.01	32.99	30.47	11.01	18.6	800-441-7762	Y
BlackRock LifePath® Smart Beta 2035 Fund Class R Shares	BRPGX	B-	C	B+	Up	2.00	12.92	4.37	30.75	26.85	10.75	18.6	800-441-7762	Y

Category: Target Date (con't)

		RATINGS				TOTAL RETURNS & PERFORMANCE					ASSETS		NEW INVESTORS	
Fund Name	Ticker Symbol	Overall Rating	Reward Rating	Risk Rating	Recent Up/ Downgrade	3-Month Total Return	6-Month Total Return	1-Year Total Return	3-Year Total Return	5-Year Total Return	NAV	Total Assets (MIL)	Telephone	Open to New Investors
BlackRock LifePath® Smart Beta 2035 Institutional Shares	BLGIX	B-	C	B+	Up	2.14	13.16	4.85	32.63	30.03	11	18.6	800-441-7762	Y
BlackRock LifePath® Smart Beta 2035 Fund Investor A Shares	BAPGX	B-	C	B+	Up	2.16	13.01	4.63	31.69	28.34	10.91	18.6	800-441-7762	Y
BlackRock LifePath® Smart Beta 2040 Fund Class K	BIPHX	B-	C	B+	Up	1.88	13.50	4.03	33.09	30.68	10.89	16.8	800-441-7762	Y
BlackRock LifePath® Smart Beta 2040 Fund Class R Shares	BRPHX	B-	C	B+	Up	1.72	13.25	3.45	30.93	27.03	10.7	16.8	800-441-7762	Y
BlackRock LifePath® Smart Beta 2040 Institutional Shares	BLHIX	B-	C	B+	Up	1.88	13.51	3.93	32.67	30.00	10.88	16.8	800-441-7762	Y
BlackRock LifePath® Smart Beta 2040 Fund Investor A Shares	BAPHX	B-	C	B+	Up	1.80	13.39	3.73	31.85	28.61	10.78	16.8	800-441-7762	Y
BlackRock LifePath® Smart Beta 2045 Fund Class K	BIPJX	B-	C	B	Up	1.62	13.66	3.50	34.23	31.04	11.97	12.8	800-441-7762	Y
BlackRock LifePath® Smart Beta 2045 Fund Class R Shares	BRPJX	B-	C	B	Up	1.49	13.36	2.94	31.93	27.38	11.59	12.8	800-441-7762	Y
BlackRock LifePath® Smart Beta 2045 Institutional Shares	BLJIX	B-	C	B	Up	1.62	13.67	3.40	33.78	30.44	11.94	12.8	800-441-7762	Y
BlackRock LifePath® Smart Beta 2045 Fund Investor A Shares	BAPJX	B-	C	B	Up	1.65	13.53	3.20	32.81	28.87	11.75	12.8	800-441-7762	Y
BlackRock LifePath® Smart Beta 2050 Fund Class K	BIPKX	B-	C	B	Up	1.54	13.64	3.03	33.65	30.42	11.21	13.4	800-441-7762	Y
BlackRock LifePath® Smart Beta 2050 Fund Class R Shares	BRPKX	B-	C	B	Up	1.39	13.25	2.46	31.29	26.65	10.96	13.4	800-441-7762	Y
BlackRock LifePath® Smart Beta 2050 Institutional Shares	BLKIX	B-	C	B	Up	1.55	13.58	2.95	33.19	29.60	11.18	13.4	800-441-7762	Y
BlackRock LifePath® Smart Beta 2050 Fund Investor A Shares	BAPKX	B-	C	B	Up	1.48	13.43	2.69	32.18	28.02	11.04	13.4	800-441-7762	Y
BlackRock LifePath® Smart Beta 2055 Fund Class K Shares	BIPLX	B-	C	B	Up	1.45	13.62	2.91	33.22	30.81	11.91	8.6	800-441-7762	Y
BlackRock LifePath® Smart Beta 2055 Fund Class R Shares	BRPLX	B-	C	B	Up	1.30	13.29	2.28	30.88	27.03	11.69	8.6	800-441-7762	Y
BlackRock LifePath® Smart Beta 2055 Institutional Shares	BLLIX	B-	C	B	Up	1.37	13.55	2.83	32.75	30.18	11.89	8.6	800-441-7762	Y
BlackRock LifePath® Smart Beta 2055 Fund Investor A Shares	BAPLX	B-	C	B	Up	1.37	13.48	2.55	31.85	28.53	11.85	8.6	800-441-7762	Y
BlackRock LifePath® Smart Beta Retirement Fund Class K	BIPBX	B	C+	A-	Up	2.87	11.35	7.06	22.35	23.67	10.42	9.6	800-441-7762	Y
BlackRock LifePath® Smart Beta Retirement Cls R Shares	BRPBX	B	C+	A-	Up	2.69	11.16	6.52	20.41	20.29	10.32	9.6	800-441-7762	Y
BlackRock LifePath® Smart Beta Retmnt Inst Shares	BLAIX	B	C+	A-	Up	2.86	11.37	7.07	22.12	23.28	10.43	9.6	800-441-7762	Y
BlackRock LifePath® Smart Beta Retmnt Inv A Shares	BAPBX	B	C+	A-	Up	2.89	11.35	6.92	21.29	21.86	10.34	9.6	800-441-7762	Y
BMO In-Retirement Fund Class R3	BTRRX	B	C	A-	Up	2.78	10.40	5.09	17.91	17.76		8.1	800-236-3863	Y
BMO Target Retirement 2020 Fund Class R3	BTRFX	B-	C	A-	Up	3.08	13.98	4.77	26.41	24.40		49.0	800-236-3863	Y
BMO Target Retirement 2030 Fund Class R3	BTRKX	B-	C	B+	Up	3.46	17.51	4.38	32.70	28.69		65.6	800-236-3863	Y
BMO Target Retirement 2040 Fund Class R3	BTRPX	B-	C	B	Up	3.58	19.32	4.12	36.56	31.37		36.4	800-236-3863	Y
Dimensional 2005 Target Date Retmnt Income Inst Cls	DRIMX	B	C	A-	Up	2.61	7.64	4.91	13.61		10.81	6.7	512-306-7400	Y
Dimensional 2010 Target Date Retmnt Income Inst Cls	DRIBX	B	C+	A-	Up	3.23	9.39	5.64	14.97		11.03	19.8	512-306-7400	Y
Dimensional 2015 Target Date Retmnt Income Inst Cls	DRIQX	B	C+	B+	Up	3.41	9.96	5.53	15.25		11.13	50.8	512-306-7400	Y
Dimensional 2020 Target Date Retmnt Income Inst Cls	DRIRX	B	C+	A-	Up	3.55	10.83	5.41	18.12		11.37	114.8	512-306-7400	Y
Dimensional 2025 Target Date Retmnt Income Inst Cls	DRIUX	B	C+	A-	Up	3.66	12.55	5.26	23.03		11.76	156.7	512-306-7400	Y
Dimensional 2030 Target Date Retmnt Income Inst Cls	DRIWX	B-	C	B+	Up	3.55	13.54	5.06	27.66		12.01	155.9	512-306-7400	Y
Dimensional 2035 Target Date Retmnt Income Inst Cls	DRIGX	B-	C	B+	Up	3.34	13.98	5.10	32.22		12.14	124.1	512-306-7400	Y
Dimensional 2040 Target Date Retmnt Income Inst Cls	DRIHX	B-	C	B+	Up	3.03	14.25	4.68	36.30		12.41	102.9	512-306-7400	Y
Dimensional 2045 Target Date Retmnt Income Inst Cls	DRIIX	B-	C	B	Up	3.35	16.20	4.74	39.78		12.67	74.3	512-306-7400	Y
Dimensional 2050 Target Date Retmnt Income Inst Cls	DRIJX	B-	C	B	Up	3.37	16.37	4.84	39.98		12.63	61.1	512-306-7400	Y
Dimensional 2055 Target Date Retmnt Income Inst Cls	DRIKX	B-	C	B	Up	3.29	16.18	4.73	39.73		12.61	28.7	512-306-7400	Y
Dimensional 2060 Target Date Retmnt Income Inst Cls	DRILX	B-	C	B	Up	3.36	16.21	4.88	39.95		12.67	19.8	512-306-7400	Y
Dimensional Retirement Income Fund Institutional Class	TDIFX	B-	C	A-		2.29	7.04	4.66	12.44		10.75	17.8	512-306-7400	Y
Fidelity Advisor Freedom® 2005 Fund Class A	FFAVX	B	C+	A-	Up	2.77	8.50	5.65	19.10	21.68	11.49	171.1	617-563-7000	Y
Fidelity Advisor Freedom® 2005 Fund Class C	FCFVX	B	C	A-	Up	2.57	8.09	4.80	16.45	17.09	11.49	171.1	617-563-7000	Y
Fidelity Advisor Freedom® 2005 Fund Class I	FFIVX	B	C+	A		2.71	8.59	5.83	19.96	23.08	11.57	171.1	617-563-7000	Y
Fidelity Advisor Freedom® 2005 Fund Class M	FFTVX	B	C+	A-	Up	2.61	8.34	5.30	18.14	20.04	11.47	171.1	617-563-7000	Y
Fidelity Advisor Freedom® 2005 Fund Class Z	FIJHX	B	C+	A	Up	2.75	8.56	5.88	20.02	23.15	11.52	171.1	617-563-7000	Y
Fidelity Advisor Freedom® 2005 Fund Class Z6	FYGLX	B	C+	A		2.85	8.75	5.98	20.30	23.43	11.55	171.1	617-563-7000	Y
Fidelity Advisor Freedom® 2010 Fund Class A	FACFX	B	C+	A	Up	2.98	9.88	5.81	22.48	24.68	11.86	420.8	617-563-7000	Y
Fidelity Advisor Freedom® 2010 Fund Class C	FCFCX	B	C	A-	Up	2.77	9.43	4.94	19.66	19.96	11.74	420.8	617-563-7000	Y
Fidelity Advisor Freedom® 2010 Fund Class I	FCIFX	B	C+	A	Up	3.03	10.01	6.01	23.26	26.15	11.9	420.8	617-563-7000	Y
Fidelity Advisor Freedom® 2010 Fund Class M	FCFTX	B	C+	A-	Up	2.83	9.66	5.41	21.51	23.08	11.8	420.8	617-563-7000	Y
Fidelity Advisor Freedom® 2010 Fund Class Z	FIJJX	B	C+	A	Up	3.08	9.99	6.07	23.33	26.22	11.85	420.8	617-563-7000	Y
Fidelity Advisor Freedom® 2010 Fund Class Z6	FUGLX	B	C+	A	Up	2.99	10.07	6.07	23.59	26.49	11.88	420.8	617-563-7000	Y
Fidelity Advisor Freedom® 2015 Fund Class A	FFVAX	B	C+	A	Up	3.19	11.21	5.83	25.70	27.65	11.83	970.4	617-563-7000	Y

Category: Target Date (con't)

Fund Name	Ticker Symbol	Overall Rating	Reward Rating	Risk Rating	Recent Up/ Downgrade	3-Month Total Return	6-Month Total Return	1-Year Total Return	3-Year Total Return	5-Year Total Return	NAV	Total Assets (MIL)	Telephone	Open to New Investors
		RATINGS				TOTAL RETURNS & PERFORMANCE					ASSETS		NEW INVESTORS	
Fidelity Advisor Freedom® 2015 Fund Class C	FFVCX	B	C	A-	Up	2.88	10.74	5.03	22.83	22.85	11.71	970.4	617-563-7000	Y
Fidelity Advisor Freedom® 2015 Fund Class I	FFVIX	B	C+	A	Up	3.22	11.27	6.08	26.62	29.15	11.93	970.4	617-563-7000	Y
Fidelity Advisor Freedom® 2015 Fund Class M	FFVTX	B	C	A	Up	3.13	11.06	5.58	24.73	26.04	11.8	970.4	617-563-7000	Y
Fidelity Advisor Freedom® 2015 Fund Class Z	FIJKX	B	C+	A	Up	3.18	11.36	6.13	26.68	29.21	11.87	970.4	617-563-7000	Y
Fidelity Advisor Freedom® 2015 Fund Class Z6	FIGLX	B	C+	A	Up	3.19	11.35	6.24	27.01	29.55	11.9	970.4	617-563-7000	Y
Fidelity Advisor Freedom® 2020 Fund Class A	FDAFX	B	C	A-	Up	3.25	12.25	5.86	27.92	29.49	12.97	2,303	617-563-7000	Y
Fidelity Advisor Freedom® 2020 Fund Class C	FDCFX	B-	C	A-	Up	3.11	11.90	5.14	25.16	24.82	12.85	2,303	617-563-7000	Y
Fidelity Advisor Freedom® 2020 Fund Class I	FDIFX	B	C	A-	Up	3.36	12.39	6.20	28.94	31.19	13.08	2,303	617-563-7000	Y
Fidelity Advisor Freedom® 2020 Fund Class M	FDTFX	B	C	A-	Up	3.19	12.10	5.61	27.01	27.94	12.96	2,303	617-563-7000	Y
Fidelity Advisor Freedom® 2020 Fund Class Z	FIJLX	B	C+	A-	Up	3.37	12.44	6.25	28.99	31.24	13.01	2,303	617-563-7000	Y
Fidelity Advisor Freedom® 2020 Fund Class Z6	FOGLX	B	C+	A-	Up	3.35	12.50	6.33	29.37	31.63	13.04	2,303	617-563-7000	Y
Fidelity Advisor Freedom® 2025 Fund Class A	FATWX	B-	C	A-	Up	3.45	13.21	5.98	30.24	31.25	12.97	2,966	617-563-7000	Y
Fidelity Advisor Freedom® 2025 Fund Class C	FCTWX	B-	C	A-	Up	3.25	12.86	5.14	27.35	26.44	12.76	2,966	617-563-7000	Y
Fidelity Advisor Freedom® 2025 Fund Class I	FITWX	B	C	A-	Up	3.47	13.33	6.15	31.23	32.90	13.09	2,966	617-563-7000	Y
Fidelity Advisor Freedom® 2025 Fund Class M	FTTWX	B-	C	A-	Up	3.38	13.12	5.64	29.26	29.64	12.99	2,966	617-563-7000	Y
Fidelity Advisor Freedom® 2025 Fund Class Z	FIJMX	B	C	A-	Up	3.57	13.48	6.31	31.43	33.11	13.02	2,966	617-563-7000	Y
Fidelity Advisor Freedom® 2025 Fund Class Z6	FPGLX	B	C	A-	Up	3.55	13.54	6.43	31.84	33.53	13.06	2,966	617-563-7000	Y
Fidelity Advisor Freedom® 2030 Fund Class A	FAFEX	B-	C	B+	Up	3.62	14.85	5.93	35.49	35.32	13.92	3,066	617-563-7000	Y
Fidelity Advisor Freedom® 2030 Fund Class C	FCFEX	B-	C	B+	Up	3.49	14.48	5.18	32.51	30.32	13.64	3,066	617-563-7000	Y
Fidelity Advisor Freedom® 2030 Fund Class I	FEFIX	B-	C	B+	Up	3.73	15.08	6.21	36.47	37.02	14.01	3,066	617-563-7000	Y
Fidelity Advisor Freedom® 2030 Fund Class M	FTFEX	B-	C	B+	Up	3.59	14.71	5.65	34.44	33.68	13.84	3,066	617-563-7000	Y
Fidelity Advisor Freedom® 2030 Fund Class Z	FIJNX	B-	C	B+	Up	3.76	15.08	6.30	36.58	37.14	13.93	3,066	617-563-7000	Y
Fidelity Advisor Freedom® 2030 Fund Class Z6	FDGLX	B-	C	B+	Up	3.81	15.21	6.44	37.11	37.67	13.97	3,066	617-563-7000	Y
Fidelity Advisor Freedom® 2035 Fund Class A	FATHX	B-	C	B	Up	3.80	16.59	5.58	39.15	38.14	13.43	2,474	617-563-7000	Y
Fidelity Advisor Freedom® 2035 Fund Class C	FCTHX	B-	C	B	Up	3.55	16.04	4.78	36.06	33.06	13.01	2,474	617-563-7000	Y
Fidelity Advisor Freedom® 2035 Fund Class I	FITHX	B-	C	B	Up	3.83	16.71	5.84	40.21	39.94	13.54	2,474	617-563-7000	Y
Fidelity Advisor Freedom® 2035 Fund Class M	FTTHX	B-	C	B	Up	3.72	16.36	5.32	38.07	36.40	13.28	2,474	617-563-7000	Y
Fidelity Advisor Freedom® 2035 Fund Class Z	FIJOX	B-	C	B	Up	3.79	16.72	5.88	40.27	40.00	13.45	2,474	617-563-7000	Y
Fidelity Advisor Freedom® 2035 Fund Class Z6	FHGLX	B-	C	B	Up	3.91	16.82	6.11	40.86	40.59	13.52	2,474	617-563-7000	Y
Fidelity Advisor Freedom® 2040 Fund Class A	FAFFX	B-	C	B	Up	3.81	17.12	5.52	39.27	38.24	14.33	2,233	617-563-7000	Y
Fidelity Advisor Freedom® 2040 Fund Class C	FCFFX	B-	C	B	Up	3.51	16.62	4.63	36.11	33.06	13.9	2,233	617-563-7000	Y
Fidelity Advisor Freedom® 2040 Fund Class I	FIFFX	B-	C	B	Up	3.84	17.24	5.70	40.34	39.92	14.43	2,233	617-563-7000	Y
Fidelity Advisor Freedom® 2040 Fund Class M	FTFFX	B-	C	B	Up	3.72	16.92	5.26	38.27	36.52	14.24	2,233	617-563-7000	Y
Fidelity Advisor Freedom® 2040 Fund Class Z	FIJPX	B-	C	B	Up	3.81	17.26	5.79	40.46	40.04	14.34	2,233	617-563-7000	Y
Fidelity Advisor Freedom® 2040 Fund Class Z6	FKGLX	B-	C	B	Up	3.87	17.37	5.99	41.14	40.72	14.4	2,233	617-563-7000	Y
Fidelity Advisor Freedom® 2045 Fund Class A	FFFZX	B-	C	B	Up	3.72	17.05	5.45	39.18	38.26	11.18	1,452	617-563-7000	Y
Fidelity Advisor Freedom® 2045 Fund Class C	FFFJX	B-	C	B	Up	3.58	16.64	4.69	36.16	33.18	10.9	1,452	617-563-7000	Y
Fidelity Advisor Freedom® 2045 Fund Class I	FFFIX	B-	C	B	Up	3.76	17.22	5.72	40.21	39.91	11.26	1,452	617-563-7000	Y
Fidelity Advisor Freedom® 2045 Fund Class M	FFFTX	B-	C	B	Up	3.71	16.94	5.17	38.22	36.47	11.07	1,452	617-563-7000	Y
Fidelity Advisor Freedom® 2045 Fund Class Z	FIJQX	B-	C	B	Up	3.84	17.27	5.80	40.31	40.02	11.19	1,452	617-563-7000	Y
Fidelity Advisor Freedom® 2045 Fund Class Z6	FCGLX	B-	C	B	Up	3.93	17.44	6.06	41.07	40.77	11.25	1,452	617-563-7000	Y
Fidelity Advisor Freedom® 2050 Fund Class A	FFFLX	B-	C	B	Up	3.81	17.06	5.53	39.27	38.33	11.17	1,178	617-563-7000	Y
Fidelity Advisor Freedom® 2050 Fund Class C	FFFYX	B-	C	B	Up	3.52	16.65	4.71	36.12	33.18	10.93	1,178	617-563-7000	Y
Fidelity Advisor Freedom® 2050 Fund Class I	FFFPX	B-	C	B	Up	3.83	17.21	5.70	40.25	40.04	11.25	1,178	617-563-7000	Y
Fidelity Advisor Freedom® 2050 Fund Class M	FFFQX	B-	C	B	Up	3.66	16.86	5.20	38.11	36.53	11.09	1,178	617-563-7000	Y
Fidelity Advisor Freedom® 2050 Fund Class Z	FIJRX	B-	C	B	Up	3.87	17.32	5.73	40.30	40.08	11.19	1,178	617-563-7000	Y
Fidelity Advisor Freedom® 2050 Fund Class Z6	FVGLX	B-	C	B	Up	3.91	17.33	6.03	40.94	40.73	11.23	1,178	617-563-7000	Y
Fidelity Advisor Freedom® 2055 Fund Class A	FHFAX	B-	C	B	Up	3.83	17.15	5.47	39.28	38.35	12.45	672.2	617-563-7000	Y
Fidelity Advisor Freedom® 2055 Fund Class C	FHFCX	B-	C	B	Up	3.54	16.67	4.71	36.13	33.12	12.28	672.2	617-563-7000	Y
Fidelity Advisor Freedom® 2055 Fund Class I	FHFIX	B-	C	B	Up	3.79	17.24	5.70	40.27	40.00	12.5	672.2	617-563-7000	Y
Fidelity Advisor Freedom® 2055 Fund Class M	FHFTX	B-	C	B	Up	3.63	16.90	5.12	38.12	36.44	12.36	672.2	617-563-7000	Y
Fidelity Advisor Freedom® 2055 Fund Class Z	FIJSX	B-	C	B	Up	3.87	17.30	5.83	40.44	40.17	12.43	672.2	617-563-7000	Y

Category: Target Date (con't)

Fund Name	Ticker Symbol	Overall Rating	Reward Rating	Risk Rating	Recent Up/ Downgrade	3-Month Total Return	6-Month Total Return	1-Year Total Return	3-Year Total Return	5-Year Total Return	NAV	Total Assets (MIL)	Telephone	Open to New Investors
		RATINGS				TOTAL RETURNS & PERFORMANCE					ASSETS		NEW INVESTORS	
Fidelity Advisor Freedom® 2055 Fund Class Z6	FBGLX	B-	C	B	Up	3.87	17.35	5.95	40.96	40.69	12.48	672.2	617-563-7000	Y
Fidelity Advisor Freedom® 2060 Fund Class A	FDKPX	B-	C	B	Up	3.80	17.17	5.55	39.34		11.24	172.8	617-563-7000	Y
Fidelity Advisor Freedom® 2060 Fund Class C	FDKSX	B-	C	B	Up	3.62	16.63	4.67	36.11		11.21	172.8	617-563-7000	Y
Fidelity Advisor Freedom® 2060 Fund Class I	FDKQX	B-	C	B	Up	3.84	17.26	5.79	40.28		11.29	172.8	617-563-7000	Y
Fidelity Advisor Freedom® 2060 Fund Class M	FDKTX	B-	C	B	Up	3.74	16.89	5.21	38.18		11.22	172.8	617-563-7000	Y
Fidelity Advisor Freedom® 2060 Fund Class Z	FIJTX	B-	C	B	Up	3.81	17.28	5.84	40.34		11.24	172.8	617-563-7000	Y
Fidelity Advisor Freedom® 2060 Fund Class Z6	FNGLX	B-	C	B	Up	3.90	17.44	6.02	40.97		11.29	172.8	617-563-7000	Y
Fidelity Advisor Freedom® Income Fund Class A	FAFAX	B	C+	A-	Up	2.47	7.25	5.34	15.06	17.95	10.89	229.1	617-563-7000	Y
Fidelity Advisor Freedom® Income Fund Class C	FCAFX	B-	C	B+		2.33	6.89	4.68	12.57	13.70	10.87	229.1	617-563-7000	Y
Fidelity Advisor Freedom® Income Fund Class I	FIAFX	B	C+	A-	Up	2.62	7.44	5.69	15.98	19.47	10.93	229.1	617-563-7000	Y
Fidelity Advisor Freedom® Income Fund Class M	FTAFX	B	C	A-	Up	2.51	7.05	5.18	14.21	16.49	10.88	229.1	617-563-7000	Y
Fidelity Advisor Freedom® Income Fund Class Z	FIJUX	B	C+	A-	Up	2.56	7.37	5.70	16.00	19.49	10.92	229.1	617-563-7000	Y
Fidelity Advisor Freedom® Income Fund Class Z6	FEGLX	B	C+	A-		2.56	7.40	5.76	16.16	19.66	10.91	229.1	617-563-7000	Y
Fidelity Advisor Managed Retirement 2005 Fund Class A	FIOAX	B	C+	A-	Up	2.47	7.28	5.11	18.26	21.12	58.63	5.4	617-563-7000	Y
Fidelity Advisor Managed Retirement 2005 Fund Class C	FIOCX	B	C	A-	Up	2.29	6.87	4.34	15.64	16.68	58.34	5.4	617-563-7000	Y
Fidelity Advisor Managed Retirement 2005 Fund Class I	FIOIX	B	C+	A		2.55	7.41	5.38	19.17	22.64	58.62	5.4	617-563-7000	Y
Fidelity Advisor Managed Retirement 2005 Fund Class M	FIOTX	B	C+	A-	Up	2.43	7.15	4.87	17.40	19.62	58.66	5.4	617-563-7000	Y
Fidelity Advisor Managed Retirement 2010 Fund Class A	FRQAX	B	C+	A-	Up	2.63	8.38	5.10	21.17	23.79	56.35	9.3	617-563-7000	Y
Fidelity Advisor Managed Retirement 2010 Fund Class C	FRQCX	B	C	A-	Up	2.44	7.97	4.31	18.49	19.24	55.9	9.3	617-563-7000	Y
Fidelity Advisor Managed Retirement 2010 Fund Class I	FRQIX	B	C+	A	Up	2.70	8.52	5.36	22.08	25.36	56.37	9.3	617-563-7000	Y
Fidelity Advisor Managed Retirement 2010 Fund Class M	FRQTX	B	C+	A-	Up	2.57	8.25	4.85	20.27	22.26	56.48	9.3	617-563-7000	Y
Fidelity Advisor Managed Retirement 2015 Fund Class A	FARSX	B	C	A	Up	2.76	9.44	5.06	23.29	25.68	53.13	4.5	617-563-7000	Y
Fidelity Advisor Managed Retirement 2015 Fund Class C	FCRSX	B-	C	A-	Up	2.55	9.00	4.28	20.52	21.03	52.82	4.5	617-563-7000	Y
Fidelity Advisor Managed Retirement 2015 Fund Class I	FRASX	B	C+	A	Up	2.82	9.57	5.32	24.21	27.26	53.12	4.5	617-563-7000	Y
Fidelity Advisor Managed Retirement 2015 Fund Class M	FTRSX	B	C	A-	Up	2.69	9.30	4.80	22.36	24.11	53.22	4.5	617-563-7000	Y
Fidelity Advisor Managed Retirement Income Fund Class A	FRAMX	B	C	A-	Up	2.46	7.04	5.14	14.49	17.53	57.75	6.4	617-563-7000	Y
Fidelity Advisor Managed Retirement Income Fund Class C	FRCMX	B-	C	A-	Up	2.27	6.65	4.37	11.94	13.22	57.59	6.4	617-563-7000	Y
Fidelity Advisor Managed Retirement Income Fund Class I	FRIMX	B	C+	A-	Up	2.51	7.19	5.42	15.37	19.02	57.72	6.4	617-563-7000	Y
Fidelity Advisor Managed Retirement Income Fund Class M	FRTMX	B	C	A-	Up	2.39	6.92	4.89	13.65	16.08	57.83	6.4	617-563-7000	Y
Fidelity Advisor Simplicity RMD 2005 Fund Class A	FARPX	B	C+	A-	Up	2.43	7.22	5.05	19.34	22.05	58.24	17.9	617-563-7000	Y
Fidelity Advisor Simplicity RMD 2005 Fund Class C	FCRPX	B	C	A-	Up	2.22	6.81	4.25	16.66	17.53	57.92	17.9	617-563-7000	Y
Fidelity Advisor Simplicity RMD 2005 Fund Class I	FRAPX	B	C+	A		2.50	7.36	5.33	20.24	23.58	58.22	17.9	617-563-7000	Y
Fidelity Advisor Simplicity RMD 2005 Fund Class M	FTRPX	B	C+	A-	Up	2.36	7.08	4.79	18.42	20.52	58.19	17.9	617-563-7000	Y
Fidelity Advisor Simplicity RMD 2010 Fund Class A	FIARX	B	C+	A-	Up	2.58	8.40	5.02	21.83	24.36	53.51	10.6	617-563-7000	Y
Fidelity Advisor Simplicity RMD 2010 Fund Class C	FICRX	B	C	A-	Up	2.38	7.96	4.22	19.10	19.76	53.14	10.6	617-563-7000	Y
Fidelity Advisor Simplicity RMD 2010 Fund Class I	FIIRX	B	C+	A	Up	2.62	8.51	5.26	22.72	25.91	53.52	10.6	617-563-7000	Y
Fidelity Advisor Simplicity RMD 2010 Fund Class M	FTIRX	B	C+	A-	Up	2.51	8.24	4.75	20.91	22.81	53.54	10.6	617-563-7000	Y
Fidelity Advisor Simplicity RMD 2015 Fund Class A	FURAX	B	C	A	Up	2.68	9.52	4.94	23.89	26.15	59.42	20.9	617-563-7000	Y
Fidelity Advisor Simplicity RMD 2015 Fund Class C	FURCX	B-	C	A-	Up	2.49	8.60	3.66	20.56	20.95	58.47	20.9	617-563-7000	Y
Fidelity Advisor Simplicity RMD 2015 Fund Class I	FURIX	B	C+	A	Up	2.76	9.66	5.20	24.86	27.90	59.5	20.9	617-563-7000	Y
Fidelity Advisor Simplicity RMD 2015 Fund Class M	FURTX	B	C	A-	Up	2.64	9.40	4.68	22.95	24.58	59.38	20.9	617-563-7000	Y
Fidelity Advisor Simplicity RMD 2020 Fund Class A	FARWX	B	C	A-	Up	2.82	10.68	4.83	25.83	27.85	59.94	42.6	617-563-7000	Y
Fidelity Advisor Simplicity RMD 2020 Fund Class C	FCRWX	B-	C	A-	Up	2.62	10.26	4.06	23.00	23.14	59.04	42.6	617-563-7000	Y
Fidelity Advisor Simplicity RMD 2020 Fund Class I	FIIWX	B	C	A	Up	2.87	10.81	5.10	26.75	29.43	59.85	42.6	617-563-7000	Y
Fidelity Advisor Simplicity RMD 2020 Fund Class M	FTRWX	B-	C	A-	Up	2.75	10.54	4.58	24.86	26.25	59.98	42.6	617-563-7000	Y
Fidelity Advisor Simplicity RMD Income Fund Class A	FRNAX	B	C+	A-	Up	2.41	6.99	5.08	16.35	19.28	58.51	19.7	617-563-7000	Y
Fidelity Advisor Simplicity RMD Income Fund Class C	FRNCX	B-	C	A-	Up	2.22	6.31	4.05	13.48	14.61	58.09	19.7	617-563-7000	Y
Fidelity Advisor Simplicity RMD Income Fund Class I	FRNIX	B	C+	A-		2.48	7.13	5.35	17.24	20.81	58.54	19.7	617-563-7000	Y
Fidelity Advisor Simplicity RMD Income Fund Class M	FRNTX	B	C	A-	Up	2.34	6.86	4.83	15.48	17.81	58.5	19.7	617-563-7000	Y
Fidelity Advisor® Managed Retirement 2020 Fund Class A	FARVX	B	C	A-	Up	2.88	10.46	5.02	25.05	27.20	51.33	4.6	617-563-7000	Y
Fidelity Advisor® Managed Retirement 2020 Fund Class C	FCRVX	B-	C	A-	Up	2.70	10.04	4.24	22.25	22.52	50.67	4.6	617-563-7000	Y
Fidelity Advisor® Managed Retirement 2020 Fund Class I	FIIVX	B	C	A	Up	2.96	10.58	5.28	25.99	28.81	51.34	4.6	617-563-7000	Y

Category: Target Date (con't)

Fund Name	Ticker Symbol	Overall Rating	Reward Rating	Risk Rating	Recent Up/ Downgrade	3-Month Total Return	6-Month Total Return	1-Year Total Return	3-Year Total Return	5-Year Total Return	NAV	Total Assets (MIL)	Telephone	Open to New Investors
Fidelity Advisor® Managed Retirement 2020 Fund Class M	FTRVX	B	C	A-	Up	2.81	10.30	4.74	24.09	25.62	51.29	4.6	617-563-7000	Y
Fidelity Advisor® Managed Retirement 2025 Fund Class A	FARFX	B	C	A-	Up	2.95	11.19	4.98	26.37	28.28	52.87	20.7	617-563-7000	Y
Fidelity Advisor® Managed Retirement 2025 Fund Class C	FCRFX	B-	C	A-	Up	2.77	10.76	4.19	23.57	23.56	52.12	20.7	617-563-7000	Y
Fidelity Advisor® Managed Retirement 2025 Fund Class I	FIRFX	B	C	A	Up	3.03	11.32	5.24	27.35	29.91	52.98	20.7	617-563-7000	Y
Fidelity Advisor® Managed Retirement 2025 Fund Class M	FITTX	B-	C	A-	Up	2.89	11.06	4.71	25.44	26.69	52.86	20.7	617-563-7000	Y
Fidelity Freedom® 2005 Fund	FFFVX	B	C+	A-	Up	2.63	8.22	5.33	19.75	23.31	12.32	971.9	617-563-7000	Y
Fidelity Freedom® 2005 Fund Class K6	FITKX	B	C+	A	Up	2.60	8.29	5.44	19.86	23.43	12.28	971.9	617-563-7000	Y
Fidelity Freedom® 2010 Fund	FFFCX	B	C+	A	Up	2.75	9.38	5.27	22.90	26.20	15.47	5,806	617-563-7000	Y
Fidelity Freedom® 2010 Fund Class K6	FOTKX	B	C+	A	Up	2.81	9.46	5.38	23.22	26.52	15.42	5,806	617-563-7000	Y
Fidelity Freedom® 2015 Fund	FFVFX	B	C	A	Up	2.87	10.54	5.20	25.97	29.16	12.73	8,745	617-563-7000	Y
Fidelity Freedom® 2015 Fund Class K6	FPTKX	B	C	A	Up	2.93	10.63	5.31	26.35	29.55	12.69	8,745	617-563-7000	Y
Fidelity Freedom® 2020 Fund	FFFDX	B-	C	A-	Up	2.96	11.56	5.10	28.19	31.09	15.86	27,514	617-563-7000	Y
Fidelity Freedom® 2020 Fund Class K6	FATKX	B	C	A-	Up	3.09	11.65	5.29	28.63	31.54	15.82	27,514	617-563-7000	Y
Fidelity Freedom® 2025 Fund	FFTWX	B-	C	A-	Up	3.08	12.42	4.98	30.35	32.75	13.85	27,510	617-563-7000	Y
Fidelity Freedom® 2025 Fund Class K6	FDTKX	B-	C	A-	Up	3.16	12.53	5.26	30.87	33.28	13.82	27,510	617-563-7000	Y
Fidelity Freedom® 2030 Fund	FFFEX	B-	C	B+	Up	3.19	13.78	4.71	35.34	36.80	17.15	32,616	617-563-7000	Y
Fidelity Freedom® 2030 Fund Class K6	FGTKX	B-	C	B+	Up	3.21	13.89	4.90	35.98	37.44	17.11	32,616	617-563-7000	Y
Fidelity Freedom® 2035 Fund	FFTHX	B-	C	B	Up	3.28	15.18	4.08	38.82	39.40	14.32	22,552	617-563-7000	Y
Fidelity Freedom® 2035 Fund Class K6	FWTKX	B-	C	B	Up	3.29	15.31	4.35	39.50	40.08	14.28	22,552	617-563-7000	Y
Fidelity Freedom® 2040 Fund	FFFFX	B-	C	B	Up	3.13	15.62	3.92	38.76	39.30	9.98	22,805	617-563-7000	Y
Fidelity Freedom® 2040 Fund Class K6	FHTKX	B-	C	B	Up	3.21	15.75	4.09	39.43	39.97	9.95	22,805	617-563-7000	Y
Fidelity Freedom® 2045 Fund	FFFGX	B-	C	B	Up	3.23	15.67	3.92	38.88	39.39	11.33	14,123	617-563-7000	Y
Fidelity Freedom® 2045 Fund Class K6	FJTKX	B-	C	B	Up	3.23	15.81	4.16	39.63	40.15	11.29	14,123	617-563-7000	Y
Fidelity Freedom® 2050 Fund	FFFHX	B-	C	B	Up	3.19	15.64	3.91	38.85	39.36	11.41	12,207	617-563-7000	Y
Fidelity Freedom® 2050 Fund Class K6	FZTKX	B-	C	B	Up	3.27	15.77	4.14	39.60	40.11	11.38	12,207	617-563-7000	Y
Fidelity Freedom® 2055 Fund	FDEEX	B-	C	B	Up	3.13	15.57	3.84	38.70	39.26	12.99	5,480	617-563-7000	Y
Fidelity Freedom® 2055 Fund Class K6	FCTKX	B-	C	B	Up	3.22	15.79	4.17	39.44	40.01	12.97	5,480	617-563-7000	Y
Fidelity Freedom® 2060 Fund	FDKVX	B-	C	B	Up	3.10	15.58	3.83	38.60		11.71	1,450	617-563-7000	Y
Fidelity Freedom® 2060 Fund Class K6	FVTKX	B-	C	B	Up	3.17	15.79	4.09	39.32		11.7	1,450	617-563-7000	Y
Fidelity Freedom® Income Fund	FFFAX	B	C+	A-	Up	2.45	7.16	5.33	15.72	19.51	11.59	3,400	617-563-7000	Y
Fidelity Freedom® Income Fund Class K6	FYTKX	B	C+	A-	Up	2.49	7.14	5.40	15.90	19.70	11.57	3,400	617-563-7000	Y
Fidelity Freedom® Index 2005 Institutional Premium Cls	FFGFX	B	C+	A		2.90	8.52	6.67	18.49	21.96	13.82	141.1	617-563-7000	Y
Fidelity Freedom® Index 2005 Fund Investor Class	FJIFX	B	C+	A		2.88	8.51	6.60	18.32	21.70	13.82	141.1	617-563-7000	Y
Fidelity Freedom® Index 2010 Institutional Premium Cls	FFWTX	B	C+	A		3.08	9.83	6.91	21.91	25.29	14.53	605.6	617-563-7000	Y
Fidelity Freedom® Index 2010 Fund Investor Class	FKIFX	B	C+	A		3.08	9.82	6.86	21.72	25.00	14.53	605.6	617-563-7000	Y
Fidelity Freedom® Index 2015 Institutional Premium Cls	FIWFX	B	C+	A	Up	3.29	11.18	7.06	25.42	28.59	15.5	1,404	617-563-7000	Y
Fidelity Freedom® Index 2015 Fund Investor Class	FLIFX	B	C+	A	Up	3.21	11.09	7.00	25.11	28.19	15.5	1,404	617-563-7000	Y
Fidelity Freedom® Index 2020 Institutional Premium Cls	FIWTX	B	C+	A	Up	3.38	12.22	7.21	27.79	30.76	16.49	4,742	617-563-7000	Y
Fidelity Freedom® Index 2020 Fund Investor Class	FPIFX	B	C+	A	Up	3.43	12.27	7.15	27.57	30.53	16.5	4,742	617-563-7000	Y
Fidelity Freedom® Index 2025 Institutional Premium Cls	FFEDX	B	C+	A-	Up	3.54	13.23	7.30	30.14	32.87	17.59	5,167	617-563-7000	Y
Fidelity Freedom® Index 2025 Fund Investor Class	FQIFX	B	C+	A-	Up	3.52	13.22	7.24	29.94	32.58	17.59	5,167	617-563-7000	Y
Fidelity Freedom® Index 2030 Institutional Premium Cls	FFEGX	B-	C	B+		3.66	14.75	7.33	35.66	37.28	18.6	6,278	617-563-7000	Y
Fidelity Freedom® Index 2030 Fund Investor Class	FXIFX	B-	C	B+		3.71	14.74	7.34	35.46	36.98	18.6	6,278	617-563-7000	Y
Fidelity Freedom® Index 2035 Institutional Premium Cls	FFEZX	B-	C	B+	Up	3.76	16.38	7.06	39.89	40.73	19.74	4,405	617-563-7000	Y
Fidelity Freedom® Index 2035 Fund Investor Class	FIHFX	B-	C	B+	Up	3.79	16.43	7.06	39.67	40.43	19.74	4,405	617-563-7000	Y
Fidelity Freedom® Index 2040 Institutional Premium Cls	FFIZX	B-	C	B	Up	3.81	16.98	6.99	40.15	40.84	19.88	4,515	617-563-7000	Y
Fidelity Freedom® Index 2040 Fund Investor Class	FBIFX	B-	C	B	Up	3.80	16.97	6.88	39.84	40.53	19.88	4,515	617-563-7000	Y
Fidelity Freedom® Index 2045 Institutional Premium Cls	FFOLX	B-	C	B	Up	3.84	16.98	7.01	40.10	40.86	20.03	2,954	617-563-7000	Y
Fidelity Freedom® Index 2045 Fund Investor Class	FIOFX	B-	C	B	Up	3.78	16.97	6.89	39.90	40.56	20.02	2,954	617-563-7000	Y
Fidelity Freedom® Index 2050 Institutional Premium Cls	FFOPX	B-	C	B	Up	3.81	16.95	6.98	40.11	40.99	20.11	2,652	617-563-7000	Y
Fidelity Freedom® Index 2050 Fund Investor Class	FIPFX	B-	C	B	Up	3.80	16.94	6.87	39.82	40.60	20.11	2,652	617-563-7000	Y
Fidelity Freedom® Index 2055 Institutional Premium Cls	FFLDX	B-	C	B	Up	3.81	16.93	6.97	40.12	40.77	15.89	1,167	617-563-7000	Y

Category: Target Date (con't)

		RATINGS				TOTAL RETURNS & PERFORMANCE					ASSETS		NEW INVESTORS	
Fund Name	Ticker Symbol	Overall Rating	Reward Rating	Risk Rating	Recent Up/ Downgrade	3-Month Total Return	6-Month Total Return	1-Year Total Return	3-Year Total Return	5-Year Total Return	NAV	Total Assets (MIL)	Telephone	Open to New Investors
Fidelity Freedom® Index 2055 Fund Investor Class	FDEWX	B-	C	B	Up	3.80	16.92	6.92	39.88	40.58	15.88	1,167	617-563-7000	Y
Fidelity Freedom® Index 2060 Institutional Premium Cls	FFLEX	B-	C	B	Up	3.83	17.04	6.97	40.11		12.95	362.1	617-563-7000	Y
Fidelity Freedom® Index 2060 Fund Investor Class	FDKLX	B-	C	B	Up	3.83	16.93	6.93	39.86		12.94	362.1	617-563-7000	Y
Fidelity Freedom® Index Income Institutional Premium Cls	FFGZX	B	C+	A-		2.68	7.30	6.44	14.45	17.98	12.21	395.4	617-563-7000	Y
Fidelity Freedom® Index Income Fund Investor Class	FIKFX	B	C+	A-		2.66	7.35	6.44	14.32	17.78	12.23	395.4	617-563-7000	Y
Fidelity Managed Retirement 2005 Fund	FIROX	B	C+	A		2.54	7.40	5.37	19.17	22.64	58.65	5.4	617-563-7000	Y
Fidelity Managed Retirement 2010 Fund	FIRQX	B	C+	A	Up	2.69	8.52	5.36	22.08	25.35	56.38	9.3	617-563-7000	Y
Fidelity Managed Retirement 2015 Fund	FIRSX	B	C+	A	Up	2.80	9.55	5.31	24.19	27.24	53.11	4.5	617-563-7000	Y
Fidelity Managed Retirement 2020 Fund	FIRVX	B	C	A	Up	2.95	10.60	5.29	25.97	28.79	51.34	4.6	617-563-7000	Y
Fidelity Managed Retirement 2025 Fund	FIXRX	B	C	A	Up	3.04	11.34	5.24	27.33	29.92	52.91	20.7	617-563-7000	Y
Fidelity Managed Retirement Income Fund	FIRMX	B	C+	A-	Up	2.51	7.18	5.41	15.36	19.01	57.74	6.4	617-563-7000	Y
Fidelity Simplicity RMD 2005 Fund	FIRPX	B	C+	A		2.48	7.35	5.30	20.22	23.56	58.2	17.9	617-563-7000	Y
Fidelity Simplicity RMD 2010 Fund	FIRRX	B	C+	A	Up	2.63	8.52	5.28	22.72	25.91	53.51	10.6	617-563-7000	Y
Fidelity Simplicity RMD 2015 Fund	FIRUX	B	C+	A	Up	2.76	9.66	5.19	24.82	27.73	59.38	20.9	617-563-7000	Y
Fidelity Simplicity RMD 2020 Fund	FIRWX	B	C	A	Up	2.87	10.82	5.09	26.75	29.43	59.85	42.6	617-563-7000	Y
Fidelity Simplicity RMD Income Fund	FIRNX	B	C+	A-		2.47	7.12	5.36	17.23	20.79	58.51	19.7	617-563-7000	Y
Franklin LifeSmart™ 2020 Retirement Target Advisor Cls	FLROX	B	C	A-	Up	2.09	9.30	4.93	21.59	19.94	11.84	43.2	650-312-2000	Y
Franklin LifeSmart™ 2020 Retirement Target Fund Class A	FLRMX	B-	C	A-	Up	2.03	9.21	4.78	20.64	18.33	11.81	43.2	650-312-2000	Y
Franklin LifeSmart™ 2020 Retirement Target Fund Class C	FLRQX	B-	C	A-	Up	1.93	8.79	4.00	18.01	14.06	11.74	43.2	650-312-2000	Y
Franklin LifeSmart™ 2020 Retirement Target Fund Class R	FLRVX	B-	C	A-	Up	1.96	9.07	4.49	19.69	16.84	11.8	43.2	650-312-2000	Y
Franklin LifeSmart™ 2020 Retirement Target Fund Class R6	FRTSX	B	C	A-	Up	2.10	9.33	5.07	21.77	20.23	11.84	43.2	650-312-2000	Y
Franklin LifeSmart™ 2025 Retirement Target Advisor Cls	FLRFX	B-	C	A-	Up	2.58	11.91	5.42	26.66	24.25	12.66	122.8	650-312-2000	Y
Franklin LifeSmart™ 2025 Retirement Target Fund Class A	FTRTX	B-	C	A-	Up	2.52	11.72	5.17	25.64	22.61	12.63	122.8	650-312-2000	Y
Franklin LifeSmart™ 2025 Retirement Target Fund Class C	FTTCX	B-	C	A-	Up	2.36	11.36	4.37	22.86	18.21	12.42	122.8	650-312-2000	Y
Franklin LifeSmart™ 2025 Retirement Target Fund Class R	FRELX	B-	C	A-	Up	2.46	11.63	4.91	24.69	21.18	12.58	122.8	650-312-2000	Y
Franklin LifeSmart™ 2025 Retirement Target Fund Class R6	FTLMX	B-	C	A-	Up	2.59	11.93	5.47	26.85	24.54	12.67	122.8	650-312-2000	Y
Franklin LifeSmart™ 2030 Retirement Target Advisor Cls	FLRZX	B-	C	A-	Up	2.73	13.07	5.42	29.14	27.81	12.75	53.2	650-312-2000	Y
Franklin LifeSmart™ 2030 Retirement Target Fund Class A	FLRSX	B-	C	A-	Up	2.68	12.99	5.18	28.18	26.13	12.71	53.2	650-312-2000	Y
Franklin LifeSmart™ 2030 Retirement Target Fund Class C	FLRTX	B-	C	B+	Up	2.43	12.58	4.36	25.40	21.54	12.56	53.2	650-312-2000	Y
Franklin LifeSmart™ 2030 Retirement Target Fund Class R	FLRWX	B-	C	A-	Up	2.54	12.79	4.84	27.17	24.58	12.69	53.2	650-312-2000	Y
Franklin LifeSmart™ 2030 Retirement Target Fund Class R6	FLERX	B-	C	A-	Up	2.74	13.18	5.47	29.33	28.08	12.76	53.2	650-312-2000	Y
Franklin LifeSmart™ 2035 Retirement Target Advisor Cls	FLRHX	B-	C	B+	Up	2.83	13.97	5.45	31.13	28.36	13.52	116.5	650-312-2000	Y
Franklin LifeSmart™ 2035 Retirement Target Fund Class A	FRTAX	B-	C	B+	Up	2.74	13.79	5.20	30.03	26.70	13.4	116.5	650-312-2000	Y
Franklin LifeSmart™ 2035 Retirement Target Fund Class C	FTRCX	B-	C	B+	Up	2.54	13.39	4.41	27.19	22.12	13.08	116.5	650-312-2000	Y
Franklin LifeSmart™ 2035 Retirement Target Fund Class R	FLRGX	B-	C	B+	Up	2.71	13.69	4.91	29.15	25.23	13.38	116.5	650-312-2000	Y
Franklin LifeSmart™ 2035 Retirement Target Fund Class R6	FMTLX	B-	C	B+	Up	2.78	13.92	5.46	31.18	28.68	13.5	116.5	650-312-2000	Y
Franklin LifeSmart™ 2040 Retirement Target Advisor Cls	FLSHX	B-	C	B+	Up	2.83	14.21	5.41	31.89	30.30	13.04	44.4	650-312-2000	Y
Franklin LifeSmart™ 2040 Retirement Target Fund Class A	FLADX	B-	C	B+	Up	2.73	14.16	5.24	31.09	28.64	12.98	44.4	650-312-2000	Y
Franklin LifeSmart™ 2040 Retirement Target Fund Class C	FLOLX	B-	C	B+	Up	2.46	13.68	4.39	28.03	23.98	12.75	44.4	650-312-2000	Y
Franklin LifeSmart™ 2040 Retirement Target Fund Class R	FLSGX	B-	C	B+	Up	2.63	13.97	4.99	30.09	27.26	12.96	44.4	650-312-2000	Y
Franklin LifeSmart™ 2040 Retirement Target Fund Class R6	FLREX	B-	C	B+	Up	2.77	14.31	5.56	32.13	30.71	13.06	44.4	650-312-2000	Y
Franklin LifeSmart™ 2045 Retirement Target Advisor Cls	FLRLX	B-	C	B+	Up	2.89	14.64	5.41	32.24	29.29	13.6	82.2	650-312-2000	Y
Franklin LifeSmart™ 2045 Retirement Target Fund Class A	FTTAX	B-	C	B+	Up	2.80	14.46	5.15	31.26	27.60	13.49	82.2	650-312-2000	Y
Franklin LifeSmart™ 2045 Retirement Target Fund Class C	FLRIX	B-	C	B+	Up	2.61	14.02	4.37	28.37	23.03	13.13	82.2	650-312-2000	Y
Franklin LifeSmart™ 2045 Retirement Target Fund Class R	FLRJX	B-	C	B+	Up	2.70	14.22	4.86	30.14	26.01	13.42	82.2	650-312-2000	Y
Franklin LifeSmart™ 2045 Retirement Target Fund Class R6	FMLTX	B-	C	B+	Up	2.84	14.59	5.40	32.39	29.57	13.59	82.2	650-312-2000	Y
Franklin LifeSmart™ 2050 Retirement Target Advisor Cls	FLSOX	B-	C	B+	Up	2.82	14.68	5.48	32.47	31.41	13.26	40.5	650-312-2000	Y
Franklin LifeSmart™ 2050 Retirement Target Fund Class A	FLSJX	B-	C	B+	Up	2.81	14.56	5.24	31.50	29.75	13.18	40.5	650-312-2000	Y
Franklin LifeSmart™ 2050 Retirement Target Fund Class C	FLSKX	B-	C	B+	Up	2.57	14.01	4.40	28.47	24.99	13.08	40.5	650-312-2000	Y
Franklin LifeSmart™ 2050 Retirement Target Fund Class R	FLSNX	B-	C	B+	Up	2.62	14.35	4.87	30.47	28.07	13.17	40.5	650-312-2000	Y
Franklin LifeSmart™ 2050 Retirement Target Fund Class R6	FRLEX	B-	C	B+	Up	2.84	14.71	5.56	32.70	31.73	13.26	40.5	650-312-2000	Y
Franklin LifeSmart™ 2055 Retirement Target Advisor Cls	FLTKX	B-	C	B+	Up	2.78	14.52	5.32	32.77		11.11	15.0	650-312-2000	Y

Category: Target Date (con't)

Fund Name	Ticker Symbol	RATINGS: Overall Rating	Reward Rating	Risk Rating	Recent Up/ Downgrade	TOTAL RETURNS & PERFORMANCE: 3-Month Total Return	6-Month Total Return	1-Year Total Return	3-Year Total Return	5-Year Total Return	ASSETS: NAV	Total Assets (MIL)	NEW INVESTORS: Telephone	Open to New Investors
Franklin LifeSmart™ 2055 Retirement Target Fund Class A	FLTFX	B-	C	B+	Up	2.75	14.51	5.15	31.83		11.1	15.0	650-312-2000	Y
Franklin LifeSmart™ 2055 Retirement Target Fund Class C	FLTNX	B-	C	B+	Up	2.57	14.03	4.33	29.02		10.95	15.0	650-312-2000	Y
Franklin LifeSmart™ 2055 Retirement Target Fund Class R	FLSBX	B-	C	B+	Up	2.67	14.35	4.82	30.93		11.06	15.0	650-312-2000	Y
Franklin LifeSmart™ 2055 Retirement Target Fund Class R6	FLSZX	B-	C	B+	Up	2.88	14.63	5.47	33.09		11.12	15.0	650-312-2000	Y
Franklin LifeSmart™ Retirement Income Fund Advisor Class	FLRDX	B-	C	B		1.92	8.52	5.49	15.62	14.35	11.02	51.6	650-312-2000	Y
Franklin LifeSmart™ Retirement Income Fund Class A	FTRAX	B-	C	B		1.87	8.31	5.24	14.79	12.93	10.98	51.6	650-312-2000	Y
Franklin LifeSmart™ Retirement Income Fund Class R6	FLMTX	B-	C	B		1.93	8.54	5.54	15.79	14.64	11.03	51.6	650-312-2000	Y
Goldman Sachs Target Date 2020 Portfolio A Shares	GTAHX	B	C+	A-		3.54	11.69	7.99	17.59	24.51	9.36	7.2	800-526-7384	Y
Goldman Sachs Target Date 2020 Portfolio Inst Shares	GTIHX	B	C+	A-		3.63	12.02	8.48	19.08	26.71	9.41	7.2	800-526-7384	Y
Goldman Sachs Target Date 2020 Portfolio Investor Shares	GTMHX	B	C+	A-		3.64	11.91	8.34	18.59	26.19	9.39	7.2	800-526-7384	Y
Goldman Sachs Target Date 2020 Portfolio R Shares	GTRHX	B	C+	B+		3.53	11.68	7.83	16.95	23.21	9.37	7.2	800-526-7384	Y
Goldman Sachs Target Date 2020 Portfolio R6 Shares	GTZHX	B	C+	A-		3.63	11.89	8.48	19.09	26.72	9.41	7.2	800-526-7384	Y
Goldman Sachs Target Date 2020 Portfolio Service Shares	GTVHX	B	C+	A-		3.53	11.66	7.93	17.43	24.33	9.38	7.2	800-526-7384	Y
Goldman Sachs Target Date 2030 Portfolio A Shares	GTAJX	B	C	A-	Up	3.50	13.30	7.08	25.61	31.48	9.45	5.5	800-526-7384	Y
Goldman Sachs Target Date 2030 Portfolio Inst Shares	GTIJX	B	C	A-	Up	3.60	13.51	7.51	27.20	33.81	9.49	5.5	800-526-7384	Y
Goldman Sachs Target Date 2030 Portfolio Investor Shares	GTMJX	B	C	A-	Up	3.61	13.54	7.45	26.67	33.25	9.47	5.5	800-526-7384	Y
Goldman Sachs Target Date 2030 Portfolio R Shares	GTRJX	B	C	A-	Up	3.50	13.19	6.85	24.83	30.01	9.44	5.5	800-526-7384	Y
Goldman Sachs Target Date 2030 Portfolio R6 Shares	GTZJX	B	C+	A-	Up	3.60	13.51	7.51	27.23	33.84	9.49	5.5	800-526-7384	Y
Goldman Sachs Target Date 2030 Portfolio Service Shares	GTVJX	B	C	A-	Up	3.50	13.29	7.00	25.40	31.26	9.46	5.5	800-526-7384	Y
Goldman Sachs Target Date 2040 Portfolio A Shares	GTAMX	B-	C	B+		3.40	15.00	7.09	29.59	35.45	9.12	7.8	800-526-7384	Y
Goldman Sachs Target Date 2040 Portfolio Inst Shares	GTIMX	B-	C	B+		3.49	15.20	7.54	31.06	37.67	9.17	7.8	800-526-7384	Y
Goldman Sachs Target Date 2040 Portfolio Investor Shares	GTMMX	B-	C	B+		3.39	15.11	7.28	30.51	37.09	9.14	7.8	800-526-7384	Y
Goldman Sachs Target Date 2040 Portfolio R Shares	GTRMX	B-	C	B+		3.17	14.75	6.77	28.52	33.67	9.1	7.8	800-526-7384	Y
Goldman Sachs Target Date 2040 Portfolio R6 Shares	GTZMX	B-	C	A-		3.49	15.20	7.43	31.06	37.67	9.17	7.8	800-526-7384	Y
Goldman Sachs Target Date 2040 Portfolio Service Shares	GTVMX	B-	C	B+		3.28	14.84	6.88	29.16	35.01	9.13	7.8	800-526-7384	Y
Goldman Sachs Target Date 2050 Portfolio A Shares	GTASX	B-	C	B+	Up	3.22	15.70	6.18	32.24	39.82	10.24	7.2	800-526-7384	Y
Goldman Sachs Target Date 2050 Portfolio Inst Shares	GTIPX	B-	C	B+	Up	3.31	15.86	6.62	33.82	42.23	10.3	7.2	800-526-7384	Y
Goldman Sachs Target Date 2050 Portfolio Investor Shares	GTMAX	B-	C	B+	Up	3.31	15.89	6.47	33.30	41.68	10.28	7.2	800-526-7384	Y
Goldman Sachs Target Date 2050 Portfolio R Shares	GTRSX	B-	C	B+	Up	3.11	15.54	5.91	31.28	38.09	10.26	7.2	800-526-7384	Y
Goldman Sachs Target Date 2050 Portfolio R6 Shares	GTZSX	B-	C	B+	Up	3.31	15.86	6.63	33.86	42.27	10.3	7.2	800-526-7384	Y
Goldman Sachs Target Date 2050 Portfolio Service Shares	GTVSX	B-	C	B+	Up	3.21	15.65	6.07	31.91	39.47	10.27	7.2	800-526-7384	Y
Great-West Lifetime 2015 Fund Class L	MXABX	B	C	A-	Up	2.55	10.10	4.96	21.30	22.90	10.1	849.7		Y
Great-West Lifetime 2025 Fund Class L	MXANX	B-	C	A-	Up	2.93	11.99	5.04	26.81	27.29	9.86	1,710		Y
Great-West Lifetime 2035 Fund Class L	MXAZX	B-	C	B+	Up	3.10	14.46	4.62	33.69	32.11	9.85	1,556		Y
Great-West Lifetime 2045 Fund Class L	MXBHX	B-	C	B	Up	3.14	15.67	3.93	36.27	32.63	10.11	908.6		Y
Great-West Lifetime 2055 Fund Class L	MXBTX	B-	C	B	Up	3.20	15.67	3.78	36.35	31.84	9.86	389.0		Y
Great-West Lifetime Conservative 2015 Institutional Cls	MXMAX	B	C+	A-	Up	2.54	8.59	5.53	18.43	21.55	9.46	58.4		Y
Great-West Lifetime Conservative 2015 Fund Investor Class	MXLTX	B	C	A-	Up	2.44	8.31	5.16	17.22	19.80	12.2	58.4		Y
Great-West Lifetime Conservative 2015 Fund Service Class	MXLUX	B	C	A-	Up	2.46	8.30	5.00	16.92	19.19	12.29	58.4		Y
Great-West Lifetime Conservative 2025 Institutional Cls	MXOZX	B	C+	A	Up	2.77	9.95	5.74	22.58	25.10	8.7	142.8		Y
Great-West Lifetime Conservative 2025 Fund Investor Class	MXALX	B	C	A-	Up	2.71	9.83	5.48	21.38	23.31	12.9	142.8		Y
Great-West Lifetime Conservative 2025 Fund Service Class	MXBLX	B	C	A-	Up	2.64	9.73	5.34	20.93	22.69	12.95	142.8		Y
Great-West Lifetime Conservative 2035 Institutional Cls	MXRCX	B	C	A-	Up	3.03	12.07	5.67	29.14	30.25	7.7	138.2		Y
Great-West Lifetime Conservative 2035 Fund Investor Class	MXGLX	B-	C	A-	Up	2.89	11.95	5.36	27.86	28.39	13.83	138.2		Y
Great-West Lifetime Conservative 2035 Fund Service Class	MXHLX	B-	C	A-	Up	2.91	11.94	5.19	27.46	27.77	13.89	138.2		Y
Great-West Lifetime Conservative 2045 Institutional Cls	MXUCX	B-	C	B+	Up	3.23	14.50	5.11	35.13	34.23	7.18	88.2		Y
Great-West Lifetime Conservative 2045 Fund Investor Class	MXMLX	B-	C	B+	Up	3.16	14.35	4.80	33.75	32.28	14.56	88.2		Y
Great-West Lifetime Conservative 2045 Fund Service Class	MXNLX	B-	C	B+	Up	3.11	14.28	4.66	33.30	31.63	14.57	88.2		Y
Great-West Lifetime Conservative 2055 Institutional Cls	MXXFX	B-	C	B+	Up	3.25	15.04	4.65	36.33	33.92	7.81	44.2		Y
Great-West Lifetime Conservative 2055 Fund Investor Class	MXSLX	B-	C	B	Up	3.21	14.94	4.40	34.88	32.07	14.69	44.2		Y
Great-West Lifetime Conservative 2055 Fund Service Class	MXTLX	B-	C	B	Up	3.10	14.88	4.22	34.46	31.33	14.71	44.2		Y
Great-West SecureFoundation® Lifetime 2020 Fund Class L	MXLFX	B-	C	A-	Up	2.72	10.85	4.63	23.44	25.75	12.01	52.2		Y

Category: Target Date (con't)

Fund Name	Ticker Symbol	RATINGS: Overall Rating	Reward Rating	Risk Rating	Recent Up/ Downgrade	TOTAL RETURNS & PERFORMANCE: 3-Month Total Return	6-Month Total Return	1-Year Total Return	3-Year Total Return	5-Year Total Return	ASSETS: NAV	Total Assets (MIL)	NEW INVESTORS: Telephone	Open to New Investors
Great-West SecureFoundation® Lifetime 2020 Investor Cls	MXSMX	B-	C	A-	Up	2.76	11.07	4.86	24.42	27.30	11.9	52.2		Y
Great-West SecureFoundation® Lifetime 2020 Service Cls	MXSPX	B-	C	A-	Up	2.78	10.96	4.80	24.08	26.77	11.95	52.2		Y
Great-West SecureFoundation® Lifetime 2025 Fund Class L	MXLHX	B-	C	A-	Up	2.62	10.86	4.55	23.46	25.51	9.63	61.4		Y
Great-West SecureFoundation® Lifetime 2025 Investor Cls	MXSNX	B-	C	A-	Up	2.74	10.98	4.77	24.37	27.09	11.03	61.4		Y
Great-West SecureFoundation® Lifetime 2025 Service Cls	MXSOX	B-	C	A-	Up	2.71	10.93	4.69	23.92	26.44	11.2	61.4		Y
Great-West SecureFoundation® Lifetime 2030 Fund Class L	MXLIX	B-	C	A-	Up	2.76	11.41	4.65	27.08	27.62	12.68	78.9		Y
Great-West SecureFoundation® Lifetime 2030 Investor Cls	MXSQX	B-	C	A-	Up	2.73	11.51	4.86	27.99	29.03	12.48	78.9		Y
Great-West SecureFoundation® Lifetime 2030 Service Cls	MXASX	B-	C	A-	Up	2.74	11.38	4.72	27.67	28.46	12.55	78.9		Y
Great-West SecureFoundation® Lifetime 2035 Fund Class L	MXLJX	B-	C	B+	Up	2.93	12.70	4.29	31.89	30.94	10.17	53.4		Y
Great-West SecureFoundation® Lifetime 2035 Investor Cls	MXSRX	B-	C	B+	Up	2.88	12.69	4.35	32.24	31.55	11.8	53.4		Y
Great-West SecureFoundation® Lifetime 2035 Service Cls	MXSSX	B-	C	B+	Up	2.83	12.69	4.26	31.90	30.91	11.98	53.4		Y
Great-West SecureFoundation® Lifetime 2040 Fund Class L	MXLKX	B-	C	B+	Up	2.86	13.75	3.81	35.37	32.99	12.78	64.0		Y
Great-West SecureFoundation® Lifetime 2040 Investor Cls	MXDSX	B-	C	B+	Up	2.90	13.71	3.86	35.59	33.19	12.66	64.0		Y
Great-West SecureFoundation® Lifetime 2040 Service Cls	MXESX	B-	C	B+	Up	2.83	13.70	3.76	35.14	32.51	12.7	64.0		Y
Great-West SecureFoundation® Lifetime 2045 Fund Class L	MXLNX	B-	C	B	Up	2.95	14.40	3.51	36.61	33.14	10.16	26.9		Y
Great-West SecureFoundation® Lifetime 2045 Investor Cls	MXSTX	B-	C	B	Up	2.90	14.25	3.40	36.93	33.61	12.02	26.9		Y
Great-West SecureFoundation® Lifetime 2045 Service Cls	MXSWX	B-	C	B	Up	2.91	14.30	3.35	36.60	32.97	11.99	26.9		Y
Great-West SecureFoundation® Lifetime 2050 Fund Class L	MXLOX	B-	C	B	Up	2.93	14.41	3.16	36.75	32.85	12.82	21.1		Y
Great-West SecureFoundation® Lifetime 2050 Investor Cls	MXFSX	B-	C	B	Up	2.90	14.44	3.24	37.42	33.44	12.76	21.1		Y
Great-West SecureFoundation® Lifetime 2050 Service Cls	MXHSX	B-	C	B	Up	2.89	14.42	3.15	36.97	32.73	12.78	21.1		Y
Great-West SecureFoundation® Lifetime 2055 Fund Class L	MXLPX	B-	C	B	Up	2.93	14.43	3.07	37.21	32.64	10.44	10.5		Y
Great-West SecureFoundation® Lifetime 2055 Investor Cls	MXSYX	B-	C	B	Up	2.88	14.42	3.10	37.39	32.86	12.35	10.5		Y
Great-West SecureFoundation® Lifetime 2055 Service Cls	MXSZX	B-	C	B	Up	2.86	14.43	3.06	37.09	32.18	12.43	10.5		Y
GuideStone Funds MyDestination 2015 Fund Institutional	GMTYX	B	C+	A	Up	3.19	10.46	6.54	23.19	23.40	10.34	648.9	214-720-1171	Y
GuideStone Funds MyDestination 2015 Fund Investor Class	GMTZX	B	C+	A	Up	3.09	10.24	6.27	22.48	22.69	10.33	648.9	214-720-1171	Y
GuideStone Funds MyDestination 2025 Fund Institutional	GMWYX	B	C	A-	Up	3.43	12.29	6.61	28.60	26.73	10.23	1,301	214-720-1171	Y
GuideStone Funds MyDestination 2025 Fund Investor Class	GMWZX	B	C	A-	Up	3.33	12.17	6.34	27.97	26.11	10.23	1,301	214-720-1171	Y
GuideStone Funds MyDestination 2035 Fund Institutional	GMHYX	B-	C	B+	Up	3.67	14.76	6.18	35.17	28.03	9.87	815.6	214-720-1171	Y
GuideStone Funds MyDestination 2035 Fund Investor Class	GMHZX	B-	C	B+	Up	3.57	14.65	5.81	34.40	27.31	9.86	815.6	214-720-1171	Y
GuideStone Funds MyDestination 2045 Fund Institutional	GMYYX	B-	C	B	Up	3.72	15.93	5.70	39.17	30.02	9.46	615.3	214-720-1171	Y
GuideStone Funds MyDestination 2045 Fund Investor Class	GMFZX	B-	C	B	Up	3.73	15.80	5.44	38.37	29.28	9.45	615.3	214-720-1171	Y
GuideStone Funds MyDestination 2055 Fund Institutional	GMGYX	B-	C	B	Up	3.75	16.21	5.51	40.49	31.18	13.26	180.3	214-720-1171	Y
GuideStone Funds MyDestination 2055 Fund Investor Class	GMGZX	B-	C	B	Up	3.68	16.14	5.30	39.86	30.59	13.24	180.3	214-720-1171	Y
Harbor Target Retirement 2015 Fund Institutional Class	HARGX	B	C+	A-	Up	3.02	9.20	5.70	18.67	19.00	10.91	3.9	800-422-1050	Y
Harbor Target Retirement 2020 Fund Institutional Class	HARJX	B	C+	A	Up	3.30	11.11	5.58	22.41	22.05	9.7	25.8	800-422-1050	Y
Harbor Target Retirement 2025 Fund Institutional Class	HARMX	B	C	A-	Up	3.61	12.82	5.78	25.10	23.64	12.32	19.6	800-422-1050	Y
Harbor Target Retirement 2030 Fund Institutional Class	HARPX	B-	C	A-	Up	3.69	13.65	5.47	27.39	24.90	8.99	32.0	800-422-1050	Y
Harbor Target Retirement 2035 Fund Institutional Class	HARUX	B-	C	B+	Up	3.85	14.96	5.12	30.64	27.32	14.29	19.4	800-422-1050	Y
Harbor Target Retirement 2040 Fund Institutional Class	HARYX	B-	C	B+	Up	4.08	16.29	4.77	33.59	30.23	8.92	28.6	800-422-1050	Y
Harbor Target Retirement 2045 Fund Institutional Class	HACCX	B-	C	B	Up	4.14	16.97	4.43	36.54	32.32	15.09	14.9	800-422-1050	Y
Harbor Target Retirement Income Fund Institutional Class	HARAX	B	C+	A-	Up	2.96	9.03	5.78	16.98	18.77	9.08	13.5	800-422-1050	Y
Invesco Balanced-Risk Retirement 2020 Fund Class A	AFTAX	B-	C	A-	Up	1.55	7.15	2.88	11.62	14.24	9.13	46.3	800-659-1005	Y
Invesco Balanced-Risk Retirement 2020 Fund Class AX	VRCAX	B-	C	A-	Up	1.55	7.15	2.88	11.75	14.24	9.13	46.3	800-659-1005	
Invesco Balanced-Risk Retirement 2020 Fund Class R	ATFRX	B-	C	B+	Up	1.45	7.09	2.55	10.86	12.93	9.06	46.3	800-659-1005	Y
Invesco Balanced-Risk Retirement 2020 Fund Class R6	VRCFX	B-	C	A-		1.65	7.33	3.19	12.47	15.64	9.22	46.3	800-659-1005	Y
Invesco Balanced-Risk Retirement 2020 Fund Class RX	VRCRX	B-	C	B+	Up	1.45	6.96	2.55	10.86	12.93	9.06	46.3	800-659-1005	
Invesco Balanced-Risk Retirement 2020 Fund Class Y	AFTYX	B-	C	A-		1.66	7.38	3.10	12.43	15.73	9.16	46.3	800-659-1005	Y
Invesco Balanced-Risk Retirement 2020 Fund R5 Class	AFTSX	B-	C	A-		1.65	7.33	3.19	12.60	15.89	9.22	46.3	800-659-1005	Y
Invesco Balanced-Risk Retirement 2030 Fund Class A	TNAAX	B-	C	A-	Up	2.22	10.78	3.53	15.55	19.45	8.73	56.5	800-659-1005	Y
Invesco Balanced-Risk Retirement 2030 Fund Class AX	VREAX	B-	C	A-	Up	2.22	10.77	3.52	15.54	19.56	8.74	56.5	800-659-1005	
Invesco Balanced-Risk Retirement 2030 Fund Class C	TNACX	B-	C	B+	Up	1.90	10.33	2.62	13.17	15.21	8.54	56.5	800-659-1005	Y
Invesco Balanced-Risk Retirement 2030 Fund Class CX	VRECX	B-	C	B+	Up	2.02	10.46	2.74	13.31	15.35	8.55	56.5	800-659-1005	

Category: Target Date (con't)

Fund Name	Ticker Symbol	RATINGS				TOTAL RETURNS & PERFORMANCE					ASSETS		NEW INVESTORS	
		Overall Rating	Reward Rating	Risk Rating	Recent Up/ Downgrade	3-Month Total Return	6-Month Total Return	1-Year Total Return	3-Year Total Return	5-Year Total Return	NAV	Total Assets (MIL)	Telephone	Open to New Investors
Invesco Balanced-Risk Retirement 2030 Fund Class R	TNARX	B-	C	B+	Up	2.12	10.61	3.19	14.77	18.01	8.65	56.5	800-659-1005	Y
Invesco Balanced-Risk Retirement 2030 Fund Class R6	TNAFX	B-	C	A-	Up	2.32	10.95	3.74	16.44	20.91	8.81	56.5	800-659-1005	Y
Invesco Balanced-Risk Retirement 2030 Fund Class RX	VRERX	B-	C	B+	Up	2.12	10.61	3.20	14.92	18.16	8.65	56.5	800-659-1005	
Invesco Balanced-Risk Retirement 2030 Fund Class Y	TNAYX	B-	C	A-	Up	2.21	10.99	3.75	16.36	20.95	8.78	56.5	800-659-1005	Y
Invesco Balanced-Risk Retirement 2030 Fund R5 Class	TNAIX	B-	C	A-	Up	2.32	10.95	3.74	16.44	20.90	8.81	56.5	800-659-1005	Y
Invesco Balanced-Risk Retirement 2040 Fund Class A	TNDAX	B-	C	B+	Up	2.45	12.46	3.81	17.58	22.39	7.94	42.2	800-659-1005	Y
Invesco Balanced-Risk Retirement 2040 Fund Class AX	VRGAX	B-	C	B+	Up	2.45	12.48	3.82	17.61	22.41	7.93	42.2	800-659-1005	
Invesco Balanced-Risk Retirement 2040 Fund Class C	TNDCX	B-	C	B+	Up	2.23	12.13	3.09	15.34	18.25	7.76	42.2	800-659-1005	Y
Invesco Balanced-Risk Retirement 2040 Fund Class CX	VRGCX	B-	C	B+	Up	2.24	12.01	3.10	15.22	18.13	7.74	42.2	800-659-1005	
Invesco Balanced-Risk Retirement 2040 Fund Class R	TNDRX	B-	C	B+	Up	2.47	12.42	3.58	16.95	21.06	7.87	42.2	800-659-1005	Y
Invesco Balanced-Risk Retirement 2040 Fund Class R6	TNDFX	B-	C	B+	Up	2.43	12.51	4.05	18.36	23.87	8	42.2	800-659-1005	Y
Invesco Balanced-Risk Retirement 2040 Fund Class RX	VRGRX	B-	C	B+	Up	2.34	12.42	3.58	16.79	20.91	7.87	42.2	800-659-1005	
Invesco Balanced-Risk Retirement 2040 Fund Class Y	TNDYX	B-	C	B+	Up	2.56	12.69	4.06	18.55	23.92	7.99	42.2	800-659-1005	Y
Invesco Balanced-Risk Retirement 2040 Fund R5 Class	TNDIX	B-	C	B+	Up	2.56	12.67	4.05	18.37	23.87	8	42.2	800-659-1005	Y
Invesco Balanced-Risk Retirement 2050 Fund Class A	TNEAX	B-	C	B+	Up	2.63	14.05	4.20	19.65	25.15	7.79	31.5	800-659-1005	Y
Invesco Balanced-Risk Retirement 2050 Fund Class AX	VRIAX	B-	C	B+	Up	2.63	14.03	4.19	19.62	25.13	7.8	31.5	800-659-1005	
Invesco Balanced-Risk Retirement 2050 Fund Class C	TNECX	B-	C	B	Up	2.56	13.77	3.33	17.30	20.80	7.6	31.5	800-659-1005	Y
Invesco Balanced-Risk Retirement 2050 Fund Class CX	VRICX	B-	C	B	Up	2.56	13.77	3.46	17.31	20.96	7.6	31.5	800-659-1005	
Invesco Balanced-Risk Retirement 2050 Fund Class R	TNERX	B-	C	B+	Up	2.65	14.03	3.96	18.88	23.86	7.72	31.5	800-659-1005	Y
Invesco Balanced-Risk Retirement 2050 Fund Class R5	TNEIX	B-	C	B+	Up	2.74	14.26	4.30	20.39	26.75	7.85	31.5	800-659-1005	Y
Invesco Balanced-Risk Retirement 2050 Fund Class R6	TNEFX	B-	C	B+	Up	2.87	14.39	4.56	20.51	26.73	7.87	31.5	800-659-1005	Y
Invesco Balanced-Risk Retirement 2050 Fund Class RX	VRIRX	B-	C	B+	Up	2.65	14.01	3.96	18.87	23.85	7.73	31.5	800-659-1005	
Invesco Balanced-Risk Retirement 2050 Fund Class Y	TNEYX	B-	C	B+	Up	2.88	14.26	4.44	20.57	26.79	7.85	31.5	800-659-1005	Y
Invesco Balanced-Risk Retirement Now Fund Class A	IANAX	B-	C	A-	Up	1.56	6.82	2.99	10.48	12.44	8.45	18.9	800-659-1005	Y
Invesco Balanced-Risk Retirement Now Fund Class AX	VIRAX	B-	C	A-	Up	1.56	6.83	2.99	10.49	12.58	8.44	18.9	800-659-1005	
Invesco Balanced-Risk Retirement Now Fund Class CX	VIRCX	B-	C	B+	Up	1.38	6.46	2.28	8.18	8.65	8.07	18.9	800-659-1005	
Invesco Balanced-Risk Retirement Now Fund Class R	IANRX	B-	C	B+	Up	1.46	6.53	2.59	9.68	10.93	8.32	18.9	800-659-1005	Y
Invesco Balanced-Risk Retirement Now Fund Class R6	IANFX	B-	C	A-		1.53	6.85	3.14	11.16	13.84	8.57	18.9	800-659-1005	Y
Invesco Balanced-Risk Retirement Now Fund Class RX	VIRRX	B-	C	B+	Up	1.46	6.66	2.72	9.69	11.19	8.32	18.9	800-659-1005	
Invesco Balanced-Risk Retirement Now Fund Class Y	IANYX	B-	C	A-		1.53	6.84	3.14	11.28	13.84	8.58	18.9	800-659-1005	Y
Invesco Balanced-Risk Retirement Now Fund R5 Class	IANIX	B-	C	A-		1.53	6.85	3.14	11.16	13.72	8.57	18.9	800-659-1005	Y
John Hancock Funds II Multimanager 2010 Lifetime Cls 1	JLAOX	B	C+	A	Up	3.02	10.62	6.52	21.69	23.55	8.85	194.6	800-225-5913	Y
John Hancock Funds II Multimanager 2010 Lifetime Cls A	JLAAX	B	C+	A-	Up	2.90	10.48	6.21	20.46	21.37	8.85	194.6	800-225-5913	Y
John Hancock Funds II Multimanager 2010 Lifetime Cls I	JHRLX	B	C+	A	Up	3.02	10.76	6.58	21.61	23.24	8.85	194.6	800-225-5913	Y
John Hancock Funds II Multimanager 2010 Lifetime Cls R1	JLADX	B	C+	A-	Up	2.80	10.40	5.85	19.53	19.72	8.81	194.6	800-225-5913	Y
John Hancock Funds II Multimanager 2010 Lifetime Cls R2	JLAEX	B	C+	A-	Up	2.91	10.49	6.11	20.16	20.84	8.84	194.6	800-225-5913	Y
John Hancock Funds II Multimanager 2010 Lifetime Cls R3	JLAFX	B	C+	A-	Up	2.80	10.26	5.83	19.51	19.83	8.81	194.6	800-225-5913	Y
John Hancock Funds II Multimanager 2010 Lifetime Cls R4	JLAGX	B	C+	A-	Up	2.91	10.63	6.27	20.95	22.41	8.84	194.6	800-225-5913	Y
John Hancock Funds II Multimanager 2010 Lifetime Cls R5	JLAHX	B	C+	A	Up	3.02	10.76	6.52	21.71	23.68	8.85	194.6	800-225-5913	Y
John Hancock Funds II Multimanager 2010 Lifetime Cls R6	JLAIX	B	C+	A	Up	3.02	10.74	6.70	22.02	24.01	8.86	194.6	800-225-5913	Y
John Hancock Funds II Multimanager 2015 Lifetime Cls 1	JLBOX	B	C+	A	Up	3.05	11.35	6.35	23.96	25.39	9.12	306.0	800-225-5913	Y
John Hancock Funds II Multimanager 2015 Lifetime Cls A	JLBAX	B	C	A-	Up	3.04	11.20	5.92	22.67	23.13	9.13	306.0	800-225-5913	Y
John Hancock Funds II Multimanager 2015 Lifetime Cls I	JHREX	B	C+	A	Up	3.04	11.47	6.28	23.84	25.17	9.13	306.0	800-225-5913	Y
John Hancock Funds II Multimanager 2015 Lifetime Cls R1	JLBDX	B	C	A-	Up	2.82	10.98	5.53	21.34	21.09	9.09	306.0	800-225-5913	Y
John Hancock Funds II Multimanager 2015 Lifetime Cls R2	JLBKX	B	C	A-	Up	2.94	11.27	5.84	22.21	22.56	9.08	306.0	800-225-5913	Y
John Hancock Funds II Multimanager 2015 Lifetime Cls R3	JLBFX	B	C	A-	Up	2.82	10.98	5.65	21.72	21.71	9.09	306.0	800-225-5913	Y
John Hancock Funds II Multimanager 2015 Lifetime Cls R4	JLBGX	B	C+	A-	Up	3.05	11.38	6.13	23.27	24.18	9.1	306.0	800-225-5913	Y
John Hancock Funds II Multimanager 2015 Lifetime Cls R5	JLBHX	B	C+	A	Up	3.05	11.49	6.23	23.95	25.38	9.12	306.0	800-225-5913	Y
John Hancock Funds II Multimanager 2015 Lifetime Cls R6	JLBJX	B	C+	A	Up	3.16	11.47	6.41	24.15	25.82	9.13	306.0	800-225-5913	Y
John Hancock Funds II Multimanager 2020 Lifetime Cls 1	JLDOX	B	C	A	Up	3.11	12.45	6.12	27.36	28.29	9.93	845.5	800-225-5913	Y
John Hancock Funds II Multimanager 2020 Lifetime Cls A	JLDAX	B	C	A-	Up	3.11	12.31	5.68	26.03	25.99	9.94	845.5	800-225-5913	Y
John Hancock Funds II Multimanager 2020 Lifetime Cls I	JHRVX	B	C	A	Up	3.10	12.42	6.04	27.34	28.17	9.95	845.5	800-225-5913	Y

Category: Target Date (con't)

Fund Name	Ticker Symbol	RATINGS: Overall Rating	Reward Rating	Risk Rating	Recent Up/ Downgrade	TOTAL RETURNS & PERFORMANCE: 3-Month Total Return	6-Month Total Return	1-Year Total Return	3-Year Total Return	5-Year Total Return	ASSETS: NAV	Total Assets (MIL)	NEW INVESTORS: Telephone	Open to New Investors
John Hancock Funds II Multimanager 2020 Lifetime Cls R1	JLDDX	B-	C	A-	Up	2.91	12.00	5.32	24.72	23.83	9.89	845.5	800-225-5913	Y
John Hancock Funds II Multimanager 2020 Lifetime Cls R2	JLDEX	B	C	A-	Up	3.02	12.13	5.58	25.65	25.39	9.89	845.5	800-225-5913	Y
John Hancock Funds II Multimanager 2020 Lifetime Cls R3	JLDFX	B-	C	A-	Up	2.91	12.11	5.40	25.05	24.42	9.9	845.5	800-225-5913	Y
John Hancock Funds II Multimanager 2020 Lifetime Cls R4	JLDGX	B	C	A	Up	3.12	12.37	5.88	26.63	27.04	9.9	845.5	800-225-5913	Y
John Hancock Funds II Multimanager 2020 Lifetime Cls R5	JLDHX	B	C	A	Up	3.11	12.45	6.10	27.33	28.26	9.93	845.5	800-225-5913	Y
John Hancock Funds II Multimanager 2020 Lifetime Cls R6	JLDIX	B	C	A	Up	3.12	12.48	6.09	27.49	28.55	9.91	845.5	800-225-5913	Y
John Hancock Funds II Multimanager 2025 Lifetime Cls 1	JLEOX	B-	C	A-	Up	3.14	13.65	5.71	30.97	31.29	10.49	1,267	800-225-5913	Y
John Hancock Funds II Multimanager 2025 Lifetime Cls A	JLEAX	B-	C	A-	Up	3.13	13.45	5.34	29.72	28.94	10.54	1,267	800-225-5913	Y
John Hancock Funds II Multimanager 2025 Lifetime Cls I	JHRNX	B-	C	A-	Up	3.24	13.63	5.64	30.95	31.05	10.5	1,267	800-225-5913	Y
John Hancock Funds II Multimanager 2025 Lifetime Cls R1	JLEDX	B-	C	A-	Up	3.05	13.31	5.05	28.56	27.03	10.47	1,267	800-225-5913	Y
John Hancock Funds II Multimanager 2025 Lifetime Cls R2	JLEEX	B-	C	A-	Up	3.15	13.43	5.27	29.34	28.45	10.47	1,267	800-225-5913	Y
John Hancock Funds II Multimanager 2025 Lifetime Cls R3	JLEFX	B-	C	A-	Up	3.05	13.31	4.99	28.71	27.43	10.47	1,267	800-225-5913	Y
John Hancock Funds II Multimanager 2025 Lifetime Cls R4	JLEGX	B-	C	A-	Up	3.14	13.62	5.56	30.33	30.11	10.51	1,267	800-225-5913	Y
John Hancock Funds II Multimanager 2025 Lifetime Cls R5	JLEHX	B-	C	A-	Up	3.14	13.65	5.70	30.96	31.27	10.49	1,267	800-225-5913	Y
John Hancock Funds II Multimanager 2025 Lifetime Cls R6	JLEIX	B-	C	A-	Up	3.24	13.77	5.78	31.33	31.78	10.49	1,267	800-225-5913	Y
John Hancock Funds II Multimanager 2030 Lifetime Cls 1	JLFOX	B-	C	B+	Up	3.16	14.83	5.39	34.48	33.86	10.76	1,246	800-225-5913	Y
John Hancock Funds II Multimanager 2030 Lifetime Cls A	JLFAX	B-	C	B+	Up	3.05	14.66	5.02	32.99	31.40	10.79	1,246	800-225-5913	Y
John Hancock Funds II Multimanager 2030 Lifetime Cls I	JHRGX	B-	C	B+	Up	3.16	14.83	5.32	34.22	33.50	10.76	1,246	800-225-5913	Y
John Hancock Funds II Multimanager 2030 Lifetime Cls R1	JLFDX	B-	C	B+	Up	2.97	14.40	4.68	31.74	29.27	10.72	1,246	800-225-5913	Y
John Hancock Funds II Multimanager 2030 Lifetime Cls R2	JLFEX	B-	C	B+	Up	3.17	14.65	4.95	32.75	30.93	10.72	1,246	800-225-5913	Y
John Hancock Funds II Multimanager 2030 Lifetime Cls R3	JLFFX	B-	C	B+	Up	3.07	14.49	4.75	32.18	29.97	10.74	1,246	800-225-5913	Y
John Hancock Funds II Multimanager 2030 Lifetime Cls R4	JLFGX	B-	C	B+	Up	3.17	14.74	5.13	33.67	32.51	10.74	1,246	800-225-5913	Y
John Hancock Funds II Multimanager 2030 Lifetime Cls R5	JLFHX	B-	C	B+	Up	3.16	14.85	5.29	34.50	33.77	10.75	1,246	800-225-5913	Y
John Hancock Funds II Multimanager 2030 Lifetime Cls R6	JLFIX	B-	C	B+	Up	3.16	14.85	5.45	34.60	34.23	10.75	1,246	800-225-5913	Y
John Hancock Funds II Multimanager 2035 Lifetime Cls 1	JLHOX	B-	C	B+	Up	3.23	15.76	4.90	36.91	35.71	11.16	1,042	800-225-5913	Y
John Hancock Funds II Multimanager 2035 Lifetime Cls A	JLHAX	B-	C	B	Up	3.16	15.64	4.58	35.47	33.26	11.09	1,042	800-225-5913	Y
John Hancock Funds II Multimanager 2035 Lifetime Cls I	JHRMX	B-	C	B+	Up	3.14	15.66	4.74	36.53	35.24	11.15	1,042	800-225-5913	Y
John Hancock Funds II Multimanager 2035 Lifetime Cls R1	JLHDX	B-	C	B	Up	3.07	15.46	4.24	34.13	31.06	11.05	1,042	800-225-5913	Y
John Hancock Funds II Multimanager 2035 Lifetime Cls R2	JLHEX	B-	C	B	Up	3.14	15.55	4.44	35.19	32.78	11.14	1,042	800-225-5913	Y
John Hancock Funds II Multimanager 2035 Lifetime Cls R3	JLHFX	B-	C	B	Up	3.07	15.43	4.28	34.52	31.70	11.07	1,042	800-225-5913	Y
John Hancock Funds II Multimanager 2035 Lifetime Cls R4	JLHGX	B-	C	B+	Up	3.14	15.68	4.65	36.09	34.23	11.14	1,042	800-225-5913	Y
John Hancock Funds II Multimanager 2035 Lifetime Cls R5	JLHHX	B-	C	B+	Up	3.23	15.76	4.88	36.88	35.68	11.16	1,042	800-225-5913	Y
John Hancock Funds II Multimanager 2035 Lifetime Cls R6	JLHIX	B-	C	B+	Up	3.24	15.78	4.88	37.15	35.97	11.15	1,042	800-225-5913	Y
John Hancock Funds II Multimanager 2040 Lifetime Cls 1	JLIOX	B-	C	B	Up	3.22	16.52	4.70	38.67	37.24	11.21	843.9	800-225-5913	Y
John Hancock Funds II Multimanager 2040 Lifetime Cls A	JLIAX	B-	C	B	Up	3.14	16.28	4.31	37.11	34.66	11.14	843.9	800-225-5913	Y
John Hancock Funds II Multimanager 2040 Lifetime Cls I	JHRDX	B-	C	B	Up	3.12	16.40	4.53	38.38	36.84	11.21	843.9	800-225-5913	Y
John Hancock Funds II Multimanager 2040 Lifetime Cls R1	JLIDX	B-	C	B	Up	3.06	16.09	4.00	35.79	32.58	11.11	843.9	800-225-5913	Y
John Hancock Funds II Multimanager 2040 Lifetime Cls R2	JLIEX	B-	C	B	Up	3.13	16.21	4.22	36.80	34.15	11.18	843.9	800-225-5913	Y
John Hancock Funds II Multimanager 2040 Lifetime Cls R3	JLIFX	B-	C	B	Up	3.15	16.23	4.13	36.27	33.21	11.1	843.9	800-225-5913	Y
John Hancock Funds II Multimanager 2040 Lifetime Cls R4	JLIGX	B-	C	B	Up	3.14	16.38	4.46	37.72	35.74	11.15	843.9	800-225-5913	Y
John Hancock Funds II Multimanager 2040 Lifetime Cls R5	JLIHX	B-	C	B	Up	3.22	16.51	4.69	38.61	37.17	11.22	843.9	800-225-5913	Y
John Hancock Funds II Multimanager 2040 Lifetime Cls R6	JLIIX	B-	C	B	Up	3.22	16.54	4.77	38.92	37.51	11.2	843.9	800-225-5913	Y
John Hancock Funds II Multimanager 2045 Lifetime Cls 1	JLJOX	B-	C	B	Up	3.18	16.73	4.59	38.77	37.35	11.02	762.5	800-225-5913	Y
John Hancock Funds II Multimanager 2045 Lifetime Cls A	JLJAX	B-	C	B	Up	3.20	16.48	4.28	37.35	34.92	10.95	762.5	800-225-5913	Y
John Hancock Funds II Multimanager 2045 Lifetime Cls I	JHROX	B-	C	B	Up	3.18	16.63	4.51	38.52	37.00	11.01	762.5	800-225-5913	Y
John Hancock Funds II Multimanager 2045 Lifetime Cls R1	JLJDX	B-	C	B	Up	3.02	16.31	3.89	35.94	32.74	10.91	762.5	800-225-5913	Y
John Hancock Funds II Multimanager 2045 Lifetime Cls R2	JLJEX	B-	C	B	Up	3.09	16.41	4.19	37.04	34.28	10.99	762.5	800-225-5913	Y
John Hancock Funds II Multimanager 2045 Lifetime Cls R3	JLJFX	B-	C	B	Up	3.11	16.39	4.04	36.37	33.34	10.93	762.5	800-225-5913	Y
John Hancock Funds II Multimanager 2045 Lifetime Cls R4	JLJGX	B-	C	B	Up	3.10	16.57	4.34	37.89	35.93	10.97	762.5	800-225-5913	Y
John Hancock Funds II Multimanager 2045 Lifetime Cls R5	JLJHX	B-	C	B	Up	3.27	16.70	4.64	38.80	37.39	11.04	762.5	800-225-5913	Y
John Hancock Funds II Multimanager 2045 Lifetime Cls R6	JLJIX	B-	C	B	Up	3.18	16.75	4.65	39.02	37.62	11.01	762.5	800-225-5913	Y
John Hancock Funds Multi-Index 2010 Lifetime Port Cls 1	JRLDX	B	C+	A-		3.15	11.02	7.63	20.74	25.12	10.47	26.8	800-225-5913	Y

Category: Target Date (con't)

Fund Name	Ticker Symbol	RATINGS: Overall Rating	Reward Rating	Risk Rating	Recent Up/ Downgrade	TOTAL RETURNS & PERFORMANCE: 3-Month Total Return	6-Month Total Return	1-Year Total Return	3-Year Total Return	5-Year Total Return	ASSETS: NAV	Total Assets (MIL)	NEW INVESTORS: Telephone	Open to New Investors
John Hancock Funds Multi-Index 2010 Lifetime Port Cls R6	JRLHX	B	C+	A-		3.25	11.13	7.78	20.90	25.53	10.48	26.8	800-225-5913	Y
John Hancock Funds Multi-Index 2015 Lifetime Port Cls 1	JRLIX	B	C+	A		3.25	11.70	7.56	23.02	26.87	10.78	41.4	800-225-5913	Y
John Hancock Funds Multi-Index 2015 Lifetime Port Cls R6	JRLLX	B	C+	A		3.25	11.70	7.52	23.20	27.18	10.78	41.4	800-225-5913	Y
John Hancock Funds Multi-Index 2020 Lifetime Port Cls 1	JRLOX	B	C	A	Up	3.18	12.46	7.06	26.06	29.50	11.01	139.1	800-225-5913	Y
John Hancock Funds Multi-Index 2020 Lifetime Port Cls R6	JRTAX	B	C+	A	Up	3.28	12.56	7.11	26.35	29.93	11.02	139.1	800-225-5913	Y
John Hancock Funds Multi-Ind 2020 Preserv Port Cls 1	JRWOX	B-	C+	B+		2.85	7.75	7.23	14.19	18.76	11.53	646.6	800-225-5913	Y
John Hancock Funds Multi-Ind 2020 Preserv Port Cls R1	JRWQX	B-	C	B+		2.66	7.43	6.41	11.96	15.21	11.56	646.6	800-225-5913	Y
John Hancock Funds Multi-Ind 2020 Preserv Port Cls R2	JRWRX	B-	C+	B+		2.75	7.53	6.68	12.64	16.08	11.56	646.6	800-225-5913	Y
John Hancock Funds Multi-Ind 2020 Preserv Port Cls R4	JRWPX	B-	C+	B+		2.75	7.62	7.04	13.78	18.03	11.57	646.6	800-225-5913	Y
John Hancock Funds Multi-Ind 2020 Preserv Port Cls R6	JRWSX	B-	C+	B+	Down	2.85	7.85	7.28	14.35	19.04	11.54	646.6	800-225-5913	Y
John Hancock Funds Multi-Index 2025 Lifetime Port Cls 1	JRTBX	B-	C	A-	Up	3.22	13.59	6.69	29.85	32.74	11.2	220.4	800-225-5913	Y
John Hancock Funds Multi-Index 2025 Lifetime Port Cls R6	JRTFX	B-	C	A-		3.31	13.57	6.74	30.15	33.18	11.21	220.4	800-225-5913	Y
John Hancock Funds Multi-Ind 2025 Preserv Port Cls 1	JREOX	B	C+	A-	Up	3.04	10.09	6.92	21.17	24.70	12.54	1,272	800-225-5913	Y
John Hancock Funds Multi-Ind 2025 Preserv Port Cls R1	JREQX	B	C+	A-	Up	2.86	9.69	6.27	18.65	20.45	12.56	1,272	800-225-5913	Y
John Hancock Funds Multi-Ind 2025 Preserv Port Cls R2	JRERX	B	C+	A-	Up	2.95	9.79	6.47	19.77	22.52	12.56	1,272	800-225-5913	Y
John Hancock Funds Multi-Ind 2025 Preserv Port Cls R4	JREPX	B	C+	A-	Up	3.02	10.04	6.90	20.80	23.92	12.6	1,272	800-225-5913	Y
John Hancock Funds Multi-Ind 2025 Preserv Port Cls R6	JRESX	B	C+	A		3.04	10.09	6.98	21.34	24.91	12.54	1,272	800-225-5913	Y
John Hancock Funds Multi-Index 2030 Lifetime Port Cls 1	JRTGX	B-	C	B+	Up	3.34	14.75	6.42	33.49	35.53	11.43	245.2	800-225-5913	Y
John Hancock Funds Multi-Index 2030 Lifetime Port Cls R6	JRTJX	B-	C	B+	Up	3.34	14.75	6.48	33.70	35.94	11.43	245.2	800-225-5913	Y
John Hancock Funds Multi-Ind 2030 Preserv Port Cls 1	JRHOX	B	C	A-	Up	3.20	12.25	6.66	27.81	30.07	13.19	1,390	800-225-5913	Y
John Hancock Funds Multi-Ind 2030 Preserv Port Cls R1	JRHQX	B	C	A-	Up	3.03	11.93	6.04	25.47	25.95	13.22	1,390	800-225-5913	Y
John Hancock Funds Multi-Ind 2030 Preserv Port Cls R2	JRHRX	B	C	A-	Up	3.12	11.96	6.20	26.13	27.09	13.19	1,390	800-225-5913	Y
John Hancock Funds Multi-Ind 2030 Preserv Port Cls R4	JRHPX	B	C	A-	Up	3.11	12.08	6.47	27.37	29.30	13.26	1,390	800-225-5913	Y
John Hancock Funds Multi-Ind 2030 Preserv Port Cls R6	JRHSX	B	C	A-	Up	3.21	12.17	6.65	28.01	30.41	13.18	1,390	800-225-5913	Y
John Hancock Funds Multi-Index 2035 Lifetime Port Cls 1	JRTKX	B-	C	B+	Up	3.39	15.70	6.11	36.21	37.58	11.57	227.8	800-225-5913	Y
John Hancock Funds Multi-Index 2035 Lifetime Port Cls R6	JRTNX	B-	C	B+	Up	3.39	15.69	6.17	36.42	38.00	11.57	227.8	800-225-5913	Y
John Hancock Funds Multi-Ind 2035 Preserv Port Cls 1	JRYOX	B-	C	B+	Up	3.28	13.80	6.37	32.06	33.45	13.52	1,213	800-225-5913	Y
John Hancock Funds Multi-Ind 2035 Preserv Port Cls R1	JRYQX	B-	C	B+	Up	3.11	13.47	5.66	29.60	29.25	13.56	1,213	800-225-5913	Y
John Hancock Funds Multi-Ind 2035 Preserv Port Cls R2	JRYRX	B-	C	B+	Up	3.12	13.60	5.88	30.19	30.46	13.53	1,213	800-225-5913	Y
John Hancock Funds Multi-Ind 2035 Preserv Port Cls R4	JRYPX	B-	C	B+	Up	3.26	13.80	6.25	31.58	32.62	13.6	1,213	800-225-5913	Y
John Hancock Funds Multi-Ind 2035 Preserv Port Cls R6	JRYSX	B-	C	B+	Up	3.28	13.88	6.35	32.24	33.75	13.53	1,213	800-225-5913	Y
John Hancock Funds Multi-Index 2040 Lifetime Port Cls 1	JRTTX	B-	C	B	Up	3.44	16.40	5.89	38.05	39.45	11.71	194.6	800-225-5913	Y
John Hancock Funds Multi-Index 2040 Lifetime Port Cls R6	JRTWX	B-	C	B	Up	3.44	16.40	5.95	38.13	39.80	11.71	194.6	800-225-5913	Y
John Hancock Funds Multi-Ind 2040 Preserv Port Cls 1	JRROX	B-	C	B+	Up	3.38	14.79	6.23	34.71	35.55	13.73	961.1	800-225-5913	Y
John Hancock Funds Multi-Ind 2040 Preserv Port Cls R1	JRRQX	B-	C	B+	Up	3.15	14.40	5.41	32.02	31.36	13.74	961.1	800-225-5913	Y
John Hancock Funds Multi-Ind 2040 Preserv Port Cls R2	JRRRX	B-	C	B+	Up	3.23	14.59	5.72	33.13	32.86	13.74	961.1	800-225-5913	Y
John Hancock Funds Multi-Ind 2040 Preserv Port Cls R4	JRRPX	B-	C	B+	Up	3.29	14.71	6.03	34.11	34.61	13.8	961.1	800-225-5913	Y
John Hancock Funds Multi-Ind 2040 Preserv Port Cls R6	JRRSX	B-	C	B+	Up	3.39	14.82	6.29	34.85	35.83	13.71	961.1	800-225-5913	Y
John Hancock Funds Multi-Index 2045 Lifetime Port Cls 1	JRLQX	B-	C	B	Up	3.44	16.61	5.84	38.13	39.21	11.72	169.5	800-225-5913	Y
John Hancock Funds Multi-Index 2045 Lifetime Port Cls R6	JRLVX	B-	C	B	Up	3.43	16.71	5.98	38.32	39.67	11.73	169.5	800-225-5913	Y
John Hancock Funds Multi-Ind 2045 Preserv Port Cls 1	JRVOX	B-	C	B+	Up	3.35	15.28	6.10	35.72	36.49	13.88	779.6	800-225-5913	Y
John Hancock Funds Multi-Ind 2045 Preserv Port Cls R1	JRVQX	B-	C	B+	Up	3.19	14.88	5.37	32.86	31.80	13.89	779.6	800-225-5913	Y
John Hancock Funds Multi-Ind 2045 Preserv Port Cls R2	JRVRX	B-	C	B+	Up	3.26	14.97	5.67	33.96	33.58	13.9	779.6	800-225-5913	Y
John Hancock Funds Multi-Ind 2045 Preserv Port Cls R4	JRVPX	B-	C	B+	Up	3.33	15.19	6.00	35.25	35.58	13.95	779.6	800-225-5913	Y
John Hancock Funds Multi-Ind 2045 Preserv Port Cls R6	JRVSX	B-	C	B+	Up	3.42	15.36	6.24	36.02	36.83	13.89	779.6	800-225-5913	Y
John Hancock Funds Multi-Index 2050 Lifetime Port Cls 1	JRLWX	B-	C	B	Up	3.40	16.53	5.81	38.03	39.51	11.84	119.5	800-225-5913	Y
John Hancock Funds Multi-Index 2050 Lifetime Port Cls R6	JRLZX	B-	C	B	Up	3.49	16.65	5.96	38.26	39.96	11.84	119.5	800-225-5913	Y
John Hancock Funds Multi-Ind 2050 Preserv Port Cls 1	JRIOX	B-	C	B+	Up	3.35	15.34	6.12	35.90	36.67	12.33	617.8	800-225-5913	Y
John Hancock Funds Multi-Ind 2050 Preserv Port Cls R1	JRIQX	B-	C	B+	Up	3.17	14.99	5.40	33.19	32.33	12.35	617.8	800-225-5913	Y
John Hancock Funds Multi-Ind 2050 Preserv Port Cls R2	JRINX	B-	C	B+	Up	3.26	15.11	5.62	34.15	34.03	12.34	617.8	800-225-5913	Y
John Hancock Funds Multi-Ind 2050 Preserv Port Cls R4	JRIPX	B-	C	B+	Up	3.33	15.27	6.04	35.27	35.60	12.38	617.8	800-225-5913	Y
John Hancock Funds Multi-Ind 2050 Preserv Port Cls R6	JRISX	B-	C	B+	Up	3.43	15.44	6.19	36.12	36.92	12.33	617.8	800-225-5913	Y

Category: Target Date (con't)

		RATINGS				TOTAL RETURNS & PERFORMANCE					ASSETS		NEW INVESTORS	
Fund Name	Ticker Symbol	Overall Rating	Reward Rating	Risk Rating	Recent Up/ Downgrade	3-Month Total Return	6-Month Total Return	1-Year Total Return	3-Year Total Return	5-Year Total Return	NAV	Total Assets (MIL)	Telephone	Open to New Investors
John Hancock Funds Multi-Index 2055 Lifetime Port Cls 1	JLKZX	B-	C	B	Up	3.44	16.63	5.82	38.11	39.57	11.71	82.4	800-225-5913	Y
John Hancock Funds Multi-Index 2055 Lifetime Port Cls R6	JLKYX	B-	C	B	Up	3.35	16.53	5.89	38.23	39.88	11.7	82.4	800-225-5913	Y
John Hancock Funds Multi-Ind 2055 Preserv Port Cls 1	JRIYX	B-	C	B+	Up	3.37	15.36	6.08	35.80	36.80	11.04	270.3	800-225-5913	Y
John Hancock Funds Multi-Ind 2055 Preserv Port Cls R1	JRITX	B-	C	B+	Up	3.28	15.15	5.61	33.95	33.59	11.02	270.3	800-225-5913	Y
John Hancock Funds Multi-Ind 2055 Preserv Port Cls R2	JRIUX	B-	C	B+	Up	3.27	15.13	5.68	34.63	35.00	11.03	270.3	800-225-5913	Y
John Hancock Funds Multi-Ind 2055 Preserv Port Cls R4	JRIVX	B-	C	B+	Up	3.36	15.34	6.03	35.44	36.21	11.05	270.3	800-225-5913	Y
John Hancock Funds Multi-Ind 2055 Preserv Port Cls R6	JRIWX	B-	C	B+	Up	3.36	15.34	6.13	35.97	37.23	11.05	270.3	800-225-5913	Y
John Hancock Funds Multi-Index 2060 Lifetime Port Cls 1	JRODX	B-	C	B	Up	3.45	16.60	5.87	38.22		12.29	25.9	800-225-5913	Y
John Hancock Funds Multi-Index 2060 Lifetime Port Cls R6	JIEHX	B-	C	B	Up	3.45	16.60	5.93	38.41		12.29	25.9	800-225-5913	Y
John Hancock Funds Multi-Ind 2060 Preserv Port Cls 1	JCHOX	B-	C	B+	Up	3.37	15.36	6.11	35.76		11.94	89.4	800-225-5913	Y
John Hancock Funds Multi-Ind 2060 Preserv Port Cls R1	JKIMX	B-	C	B+	Up	3.29	15.05	5.64	33.92		11.92	89.4	800-225-5913	Y
John Hancock Funds Multi-Ind 2060 Preserv Port Cls R2	JSATX	B-	C	B+	Up	3.29	15.15	5.84	34.81		11.93	89.4	800-225-5913	Y
John Hancock Funds Multi-Ind 2060 Preserv Port Cls R4	JPORX	B-	C	B+	Up	3.37	15.25	5.97	35.31		11.94	89.4	800-225-5913	Y
John Hancock Funds Multi-Ind 2060 Preserv Port Cls R6	JTFOX	B-	C	B+	Up	3.37	15.34	6.16	35.92		11.95	89.4	800-225-5913	Y
John Hancock Funds Multi-Ind Income Preserv Port Cls 1	JRFOX	B-	C	B+		2.44	6.50	6.72	10.34	15.09	11.29	368.7	800-225-5913	Y
John Hancock Funds Multi-Ind Income Preserv Port Cls R1	JRFQX	B-	C	B+	Up	2.26	6.09	6.02	8.37	11.88	11.31	368.7	800-225-5913	Y
John Hancock Funds Multi-Ind Income Preserv Port Cls R2	JRFNX	B-	C	B+	Up	2.35	6.20	6.21	8.97	13.03	11.3	368.7	800-225-5913	Y
John Hancock Funds Multi-Ind Income Preserv Port Cls R4	JRFPX	B-	C	B+		2.44	6.40	6.58	9.92	14.37	11.3	368.7	800-225-5913	Y
John Hancock Funds Multi-Ind Income Preserv Port Cls R6	JRFSX	B-	C+	B+		2.45	6.41	6.78	10.41	15.28	11.28	368.7	800-225-5913	Y
John Hancock Funds Multimanager 2050 Lifetime Port Cls 1	JLKOX	B-	C	B	Up	3.20	16.73	4.69	38.80	37.33	11.93	413.0	800-225-5913	Y
John Hancock Funds Multimanager 2050 Lifetime Port Cls A	JLKAX	B-	C	B	Up	3.20	16.51	4.32	37.39	34.79	11.92	413.0	800-225-5913	Y
John Hancock Funds Multimanager 2050 Lifetime Port Cls I	JHRPX	B-	C	B	Up	3.20	16.61	4.53	38.51	36.94	11.93	413.0	800-225-5913	Y
John Hancock Funds Multimanager 2050 Lifetime Port Cls R1	JLKDX	B-	C	B	Up	3.03	16.34	3.96	36.02	32.64	11.89	413.0	800-225-5913	Y
John Hancock Funds Multimanager 2050 Lifetime Port Cls R2	JLKEX	B-	C	B	Up	3.11	16.52	4.21	37.03	34.34	11.92	413.0	800-225-5913	Y
John Hancock Funds Multimanager 2050 Lifetime Port Cls R3	JLKFX	B-	C	B	Up	3.03	16.34	4.03	36.41	33.47	11.89	413.0	800-225-5913	Y
John Hancock Funds Multimanager 2050 Lifetime Port Cls R4	JLKGX	B-	C	B	Up	3.20	16.63	4.44	38.00	36.05	11.92	413.0	800-225-5913	Y
John Hancock Funds Multimanager 2050 Lifetime Port Cls R5	JLKHX	B-	C	B	Up	3.19	16.71	4.60	38.80	37.33	11.94	413.0	800-225-5913	Y
John Hancock Funds Multimanager 2050 Lifetime Port Cls R6	JLKRX	B-	C	B	Up	3.28	16.81	4.75	39.09	37.76	11.95	413.0	800-225-5913	Y
John Hancock Funds Multimanager 2055 Lifetime Port Cls 1	JLKUX	B-	C	B	Up	3.25	16.71	4.66	38.78	37.29	11.1	207.8	800-225-5913	Y
John Hancock Funds Multimanager 2055 Lifetime Port Cls A	JLKLX	B-	C	B	Up	3.07	16.40	4.21	37.31	34.58	11.07	207.8	800-225-5913	Y
John Hancock Funds Multimanager 2055 Lifetime Port Cls I	JHRTX	B-	C	B	Up	3.25	16.71	4.68	38.54	37.01	11.1	207.8	800-225-5913	Y
John Hancock Funds Multimanager 2055 Lifetime Port Cls R1	JLKMX	B-	C	B	Up	3.16	16.40	4.24	36.97	34.02	11.07	207.8	800-225-5913	Y
John Hancock Funds Multimanager 2055 Lifetime Port Cls R2	JLKNX	B-	C	B	Up	3.07	16.40	4.17	37.35	35.00	11.07	207.8	800-225-5913	Y
John Hancock Funds Multimanager 2055 Lifetime Port Cls R3	JLKPX	B-	C	B	Up	3.07	16.31	4.03	36.50	33.54	11.05	207.8	800-225-5913	Y
John Hancock Funds Multimanager 2055 Lifetime Port Cls R4	JLKQX	B-	C	B	Up	3.25	16.73	4.57	38.38	36.41	11.09	207.8	800-225-5913	Y
John Hancock Funds Multimanager 2055 Lifetime Port Cls R5	JLKSX	B-	C	B	Up	3.25	16.71	4.64	38.82	37.33	11.1	207.8	800-225-5913	Y
John Hancock Funds Multimanager 2055 Lifetime Port Cls R6	JLKTX	B-	C	B	Up	3.25	16.71	4.72	38.99	37.62	11.1	207.8	800-225-5913	Y
John Hancock Funds Multimanager 2060 Lifetime Port Cls 1	JRETX	B-	C	B	Up	3.22	16.68	4.63	38.53		12.17	80.5	800-225-5913	Y
John Hancock Funds Multimanager 2060 Lifetime Port Cls A	JJERX	B-	C	B	Up	3.05	16.50	4.25	36.99		12.14	80.5	800-225-5913	Y
John Hancock Funds Multimanager 2060 Lifetime Port Cls I	JMENX	B-	C	B	Up	3.13	16.68	4.56	38.29		12.17	80.5	800-225-5913	Y
John Hancock Funds Multimanager 2060 Lifetime Port Cls R1	JTLOX	B-	C	B	Up	3.05	16.39	4.13	36.61		12.14	80.5	800-225-5913	Y
John Hancock Funds Multimanager 2060 Lifetime Port Cls R2	JVIMX	B-	C	B	Up	3.14	16.60	4.36	37.59		12.15	80.5	800-225-5913	Y
John Hancock Funds Multimanager 2060 Lifetime Port Cls R3	JGTHX	B-	C	B	Up	3.05	16.39	4.13	36.61		12.14	80.5	800-225-5913	Y
John Hancock Funds Multimanager 2060 Lifetime Port Cls R4	JROUX	B-	C	B	Up	3.22	16.69	4.55	38.07		12.16	80.5	800-225-5913	Y
John Hancock Funds Multimanager 2060 Lifetime Port Cls R5	JGHTX	B-	C	B	Up	3.13	16.69	4.59	38.55		12.16	80.5	800-225-5913	Y
John Hancock Funds Multimanager 2060 Lifetime Port Cls R6	JESRX	B-	C	B	Up	3.22	16.77	4.69	38.84		12.18	80.5	800-225-5913	Y
JPMorgan SmartRetirement® 2020 Fund Class A	JTTAX	B	C	A-	Up	3.11	11.02	5.73	22.86	26.21	19.25	5,793	800-480-4111	Y
JPMorgan SmartRetirement® 2020 Fund Class C	JTTCX	B-	C	A-	Up	2.97	10.71	5.08	20.53	22.22	19.16	5,793	800-480-4111	Y
JPMorgan SmartRetirement® 2020 Fund Class I	JTTSX	B	C	A-	Up	3.19	11.17	5.88	23.34	26.93	19.32	5,793	800-480-4111	Y
JPMorgan SmartRetirement® 2020 Fund Class R2	JTTZX	B-	C	A-	Up	3.01	10.84	5.27	21.50	24.17	19.19	5,793	800-480-4111	Y
JPMorgan SmartRetirement® 2020 Fund Class R3	JTTPX	B	C	A-	Up	3.08	10.95	5.51	22.19	25.52	19.17	5,793	800-480-4111	Y
JPMorgan SmartRetirement® 2020 Fund Class R4	JTTQX	B	C	A-	Up	3.13	11.11	5.86	23.17	27.16	19.28	5,793	800-480-4111	Y

Category: Target Date (con't)

Fund Name	Ticker Symbol	RATINGS Overall Rating	Reward Rating	Risk Rating	Recent Up/ Downgrade	TOTAL RETURNS & PERFORMANCE 3-Month Total Return	6-Month Total Return	1-Year Total Return	3-Year Total Return	5-Year Total Return	ASSETS NAV	Total Assets (MIL)	NEW INVESTORS Telephone	Open to New Investors
JPMorgan SmartRetirement® 2020 Fund Class R5	JTTIX	B	C	A-	Up	3.16	11.18	5.98	23.69	27.70	19.34	5,793	800-480-4111	Y
JPMorgan SmartRetirement® 2020 Fund Class R6	JTTYX	B	C	A-	Up	3.19	11.21	6.04	24.08	28.21	19.34	5,793	800-480-4111	Y
JPMorgan SmartRetirement® 2025 Fund Class A	JNSAX	B-	C	A-	Up	3.32	12.71	5.80	26.50	29.35	19.22	7,239	800-480-4111	Y
JPMorgan SmartRetirement® 2025 Fund Class C	JNSCX	B-	C	A-	Up	3.18	12.39	5.19	24.21	25.36	19.15	7,239	800-480-4111	Y
JPMorgan SmartRetirement® 2025 Fund Class I	JNSSX	B-	C	A-	Up	3.41	12.81	6.01	27.04	30.13	19.27	7,239		Y
JPMorgan SmartRetirement® 2025 Fund Class R2	JNSZX	B-	C	A-	Up	3.24	12.51	5.42	25.14	27.36	19.15	7,239	800-480-4111	Y
JPMorgan SmartRetirement® 2025 Fund Class R3	JNSPX	B-	C	A-	Up	3.31	12.67	5.71	26.04	28.82	19.16	7,239	800-480-4111	Y
JPMorgan SmartRetirement® 2025 Fund Class R4	JNSQX	B-	C	A-	Up	3.36	12.77	5.95	26.87	30.32	19.22	7,239	800-480-4111	Y
JPMorgan SmartRetirement® 2025 Fund Class R5	JNSIX	B-	C	A-	Up	3.38	12.90	6.13	27.51	30.97	19.29	7,239	800-480-4111	Y
JPMorgan SmartRetirement® 2025 Fund Class R6	JNSYX	B-	C	A-	Up	3.41	12.92	6.23	27.83	31.49	19.29	7,239	800-480-4111	Y
JPMorgan SmartRetirement® 2030 Fund Class A	JSMAX	B-	C	B+	Up	3.47	14.07	5.82	30.40	32.15	21	7,977	800-480-4111	Y
JPMorgan SmartRetirement® 2030 Fund Class C	JSMCX	B-	C	B+	Up	3.30	13.77	5.20	28.03	28.00	20.8	7,977	800-480-4111	Y
JPMorgan SmartRetirement® 2030 Fund Class I	JSMSX	B-	C	B+	Up	3.50	14.16	6.02	30.91	32.92	21.06	7,977		Y
JPMorgan SmartRetirement® 2030 Fund Class R2	JSMZX	B-	C	B+	Up	3.33	13.86	5.38	29.00	30.07	20.92	7,977	800-480-4111	Y
JPMorgan SmartRetirement® 2030 Fund Class R3	JSMNX	B-	C	B+	Up	3.44	14.07	5.72	29.95	31.58	20.94	7,977	800-480-4111	Y
JPMorgan SmartRetirement® 2030 Fund Class R4	JSMQX	B-	C	B+	Up	3.51	14.18	5.97	30.87	33.17	21.02	7,977	800-480-4111	Y
JPMorgan SmartRetirement® 2030 Fund Class R5	JSMIX	B-	C	B+	Up	3.52	14.23	6.08	31.42	33.73	21.11	7,977	800-480-4111	Y
JPMorgan SmartRetirement® 2030 Fund Class R6	JSMYX	B-	C	B+	Up	3.55	14.31	6.24	31.83	34.26	21.11	7,977	800-480-4111	Y
JPMorgan SmartRetirement® 2035 Fund Class A	SRJAX	B-	C	B+	Up	3.38	14.72	5.26	31.89	32.86	20.4	6,229	800-480-4111	Y
JPMorgan SmartRetirement® 2035 Fund Class C	SRJCX	B-	C	B+	Up	3.27	14.43	4.70	29.57	28.76	20.23	6,229	800-480-4111	Y
JPMorgan SmartRetirement® 2035 Fund Class I	SRJSX	B-	C	B+	Up	3.46	14.84	5.46	32.48	33.71	20.51	6,229	800-480-4111	Y
JPMorgan SmartRetirement® 2035 Fund Class R2	SRJZX	B-	C	B+	Up	3.35	14.58	4.89	30.56	30.84	20.34	6,229	800-480-4111	Y
JPMorgan SmartRetirement® 2035 Fund Class R3	SRJPX	B-	C	B+	Up	3.38	14.65	5.14	31.35	32.27	20.32	6,229	800-480-4111	Y
JPMorgan SmartRetirement® 2035 Fund Class R4	SRJQX	B-	C	B+	Up	3.46	14.80	5.41	32.39	33.99	20.47	6,229	800-480-4111	Y
JPMorgan SmartRetirement® 2035 Fund Class R5	SRJIX	B-	C	B+	Up	3.49	14.87	5.59	32.91	34.52	20.52	6,229	800-480-4111	Y
JPMorgan SmartRetirement® 2035 Fund Class R6	SRJYX	B-	C	B+	Up	3.56	15.02	5.69	33.40	35.04	20.53	6,229	800-480-4111	Y
JPMorgan SmartRetirement® 2040 Fund Class A	SMTAX	B-	C	B	Up	3.46	15.69	5.15	34.32	34.53	22.03	6,144	800-480-4111	Y
JPMorgan SmartRetirement® 2040 Fund Class C	SMTCX	B-	C	B	Up	3.28	15.35	4.54	31.88	30.38	21.72	6,144	800-480-4111	Y
JPMorgan SmartRetirement® 2040 Fund Class I	SMTSX	B-	C	B	Up	3.49	15.78	5.36	34.92	35.38	22.1	6,144	800-480-4111	Y
JPMorgan SmartRetirement® 2040 Fund Class R2	SMTZX	B-	C	B	Up	3.37	15.51	4.78	32.99	32.51	21.92	6,144	800-480-4111	Y
JPMorgan SmartRetirement® 2040 Fund Class R3	SMTPX	B-	C	B	Up	3.39	15.59	5.02	33.80	33.96	21.96	6,144	800-480-4111	Y
JPMorgan SmartRetirement® 2040 Fund Class R4	SMTQX	B-	C	B	Up	3.54	15.80	5.35	34.83	35.67	22.06	6,144	800-480-4111	Y
JPMorgan SmartRetirement® 2040 Fund Class R5	SMTIX	B-	C	B	Up	3.56	15.90	5.47	35.42	36.26	22.16	6,144	800-480-4111	Y
JPMorgan SmartRetirement® 2040 Fund Class R6	SMTYX	B-	C	B	Up	3.58	15.93	5.58	35.85	36.80	22.16	6,144	800-480-4111	Y
JPMorgan SmartRetirement® 2045 Fund Class A	JSAAX	B-	C	B	Up	3.46	16.09	5.16	34.61	34.89	21.1	4,379	800-480-4111	Y
JPMorgan SmartRetirement® 2045 Fund Class C	JSACX	B-	C	B	Up	3.31	15.75	4.57	32.18	30.69	20.91	4,379	800-480-4111	Y
JPMorgan SmartRetirement® 2045 Fund Class I	JSASX	B-	C	B	Up	3.54	16.17	5.32	35.19	35.73	21.18	4,379	800-480-4111	Y
JPMorgan SmartRetirement® 2045 Fund Class R2	JSAZX	B-	C	B	Up	3.38	15.84	4.75	33.23	32.80	21.02	4,379	800-480-4111	Y
JPMorgan SmartRetirement® 2045 Fund Class R3	JSAPX	B-	C	B	Up	3.45	16.02	5.05	34.12	34.35	21.03	4,379	800-480-4111	Y
JPMorgan SmartRetirement® 2045 Fund Class R4	JSAQX	B-	C	B	Up	3.50	16.14	5.27	35.12	36.03	21.13	4,379	800-480-4111	Y
JPMorgan SmartRetirement® 2045 Fund Class R5	JSAIX	B-	C	B	Up	3.52	16.26	5.44	35.69	36.60	21.2	4,379	800-480-4111	Y
JPMorgan SmartRetirement® 2045 Fund Class R6	JSAYX	B-	C	B	Up	3.60	16.35	5.60	36.12	37.14	21.2	4,379	800-480-4111	Y
JPMorgan SmartRetirement® 2050 Fund Class A	JTSAX	B-	C	B	Up	3.46	16.11	5.17	34.59	34.92	21.14	3,936	800-480-4111	Y
JPMorgan SmartRetirement® 2050 Fund Class C	JTSCX	B-	C	B	Up	3.31	15.73	4.53	32.13	30.67	20.92	3,936	800-480-4111	Y
JPMorgan SmartRetirement® 2050 Fund Class I	JTSSX	B-	C	B	Up	3.54	16.19	5.32	35.16	35.74	21.22	3,936	800-480-4111	Y
JPMorgan SmartRetirement® 2050 Fund Class R2	JTSZX	B-	C	B	Up	3.38	15.87	4.76	33.15	32.77	21.05	3,936	800-480-4111	Y
JPMorgan SmartRetirement® 2050 Fund Class R3	JTSPX	B-	C	B	Up	3.46	15.98	5.06	34.03	34.31	21.07	3,936	800-480-4111	Y
JPMorgan SmartRetirement® 2050 Fund Class R4	JTSQX	B-	C	B	Up	3.49	16.14	5.26	35.04	35.99	21.18	3,936	800-480-4111	Y
JPMorgan SmartRetirement® 2050 Fund Class R5	JTSIX	B-	C	B	Up	3.51	16.20	5.44	35.63	36.59	21.25	3,936	800-480-4111	Y
JPMorgan SmartRetirement® 2050 Fund Class R6	JTSYX	B-	C	B	Up	3.59	16.28	5.55	36.04	37.18	21.26	3,936	800-480-4111	Y
JPMorgan SmartRetirement® 2055 Fund Class A	JFFAX	B-	C	B	Up	3.44	16.04	5.17	34.51	34.83	23.8	1,800	800-480-4111	Y
JPMorgan SmartRetirement® 2055 Fund Class C	JFFCX	B-	C	B	Up	3.27	15.69	4.55	32.04	30.64	23.66	1,800	800-480-4111	Y

Category: Target Date (con't)

Fund Name	Ticker Symbol	Overall Rating	Reward Rating	Risk Rating	Recent Up/ Downgrade	3-Month Total Return	6-Month Total Return	1-Year Total Return	3-Year Total Return	5-Year Total Return	NAV	Total Assets (MIL)	Telephone	Open to New Investors
		RATINGS				TOTAL RETURNS & PERFORMANCE					ASSETS		NEW INVESTORS	
JPMorgan SmartRetirement® 2055 Fund Class I	JFFSX	B-	C	B	Up	3.48	16.09	5.33	35.00	35.63	23.84	1,800	800-480-4111	Y
JPMorgan SmartRetirement® 2055 Fund Class R2	JFFRX	B-	C	B	Up	3.35	15.81	4.80	33.08	32.75	23.75	1,800	800-480-4111	Y
JPMorgan SmartRetirement® 2055 Fund Class R3	JFFPX	B-	C	B	Up	3.43	15.97	5.06	33.95	34.26	23.73	1,800	800-480-4111	Y
JPMorgan SmartRetirement® 2055 Fund Class R4	JFFQX	B-	C	B	Up	3.48	16.11	5.32	34.99	35.97	23.81	1,800	800-480-4111	Y
JPMorgan SmartRetirement® 2055 Fund Class R5	JFFIX	B-	C	B	Up	3.50	16.18	5.45	35.56	36.54	23.86	1,800	800-480-4111	Y
JPMorgan SmartRetirement® 2055 Fund Class R6	JFFYX	B-	C	B	Up	3.53	16.26	5.60	35.95	37.05	23.87	1,800	800-480-4111	Y
JPMorgan SmartRetirement® Blend 2020 Fund Class I	JSSRX	B	C	A-	Up	2.89	10.38	5.66	22.36	26.13	19.53	842.3	800-480-4111	Y
JPMorgan SmartRetirement® Blend 2020 Fund Class R2	JIORX	B-	C	A-	Up	2.78	10.10	5.12	20.54	23.30	19.52	842.3	800-480-4111	Y
JPMorgan SmartRetirement® Blend 2020 Fund Class R3	JSTKX	B	C	A-	Up	2.83	10.26	5.42	21.69	25.47	19.51	842.3	800-480-4111	Y
JPMorgan SmartRetirement® Blend 2020 Fund Class R4	JSTLX	B	C	A-	Up	2.89	10.39	5.66	22.58	27.02	19.55	842.3	800-480-4111	Y
JPMorgan SmartRetirement® Blend 2020 Fund Class R5	JBSRX	B	C+	A-	Up	2.93	10.45	5.82	22.93	27.26	19.54	842.3	800-480-4111	Y
JPMorgan SmartRetirement® Blend 2020 Fund Class R6	JSYRX	B	C+	A-	Up	3.00	10.52	5.98	23.26	27.73	19.55	842.3	800-480-4111	Y
JPMorgan SmartRetirement® Blend 2025 Fund Class I	JBSSX	B	C	A-	Up	3.07	12.02	5.88	25.90	29.34	20.85	1,109	800-480-4111	Y
JPMorgan SmartRetirement® Blend 2025 Fund Class R2	JBRSX	B-	C	A-	Up	2.95	11.75	5.38	24.04	26.38	20.84	1,109	800-480-4111	Y
JPMorgan SmartRetirement® Blend 2025 Fund Class R3	JBTUX	B-	C	A-	Up	3.01	11.90	5.64	25.31	28.70	20.82	1,109	800-480-4111	Y
JPMorgan SmartRetirement® Blend 2025 Fund Class R4	JBTBX	B	C	A-	Up	3.06	12.03	5.89	26.26	30.33	20.87	1,109	800-480-4111	Y
JPMorgan SmartRetirement® Blend 2025 Fund Class R5	JBBSX	B	C	A-	Up	3.11	12.09	6.04	26.54	30.49	20.86	1,109	800-480-4111	Y
JPMorgan SmartRetirement® Blend 2025 Fund Class R6	JBYSX	B	C	A-	Up	3.13	12.17	6.14	26.89	30.98	20.86	1,109	800-480-4111	Y
JPMorgan SmartRetirement® Blend 2030 Fund Class I	JRBEX	B-	C	B+	Up	3.05	13.13	5.76	29.34	31.97	21.85	1,167	800-480-4111	Y
JPMorgan SmartRetirement® Blend 2030 Fund Class R2	JRBRX	B-	C	B+	Up	2.93	12.87	5.24	27.42	29.03	21.86	1,167	800-480-4111	Y
JPMorgan SmartRetirement® Blend 2030 Fund Class R3	JUTPX	B-	C	B+	Up	3.04	12.98	5.49	28.55	31.10	21.81	1,167	800-480-4111	Y
JPMorgan SmartRetirement® Blend 2030 Fund Class R4	JUTUX	B-	C	B+	Up	3.05	13.12	5.75	29.52	32.74	21.88	1,167	800-480-4111	Y
JPMorgan SmartRetirement® Blend 2030 Fund Class R5	JRBBX	B-	C	A-	Up	3.14	13.21	5.92	29.94	33.17	21.86	1,167	800-480-4111	Y
JPMorgan SmartRetirement® Blend 2030 Fund Class R6	JRBYX	B-	C	A-	Up	3.16	13.28	6.03	30.35	33.65	21.87	1,167	800-480-4111	Y
JPMorgan SmartRetirement® Blend 2035 Fund Class I	JPSRX	B-	C	B+	Up	3.13	14.15	5.72	31.76	33.96	22.8	954.0	800-480-4111	Y
JPMorgan SmartRetirement® Blend 2035 Fund Class R2	JPRRX	B-	C	B+	Up	3.01	13.92	5.20	29.81	30.95	22.78	954.0	800-480-4111	Y
JPMorgan SmartRetirement® Blend 2035 Fund Class R3	JPTLX	B-	C	B+	Up	3.07	14.05	5.47	31.03	33.25	22.77	954.0	800-480-4111	Y
JPMorgan SmartRetirement® Blend 2035 Fund Class R4	JPTKX	B-	C	B+	Up	3.13	14.21	5.73	32.06	34.97	22.83	954.0	800-480-4111	Y
JPMorgan SmartRetirement® Blend 2035 Fund Class R5	JPBRX	B-	C	B+	Up	3.16	14.27	5.89	32.42	35.14	22.82	954.0	800-480-4111	Y
JPMorgan SmartRetirement® Blend 2035 Fund Class R6	JPYRX	B-	C	B+	Up	3.19	14.30	5.99	32.72	35.65	22.82	954.0	800-480-4111	Y
JPMorgan SmartRetirement® Blend 2040 Fund Class I	JOBEX	B-	C	B+	Up	3.12	15.01	5.62	34.31	35.88	23.27	868.2	800-480-4111	Y
JPMorgan SmartRetirement® Blend 2040 Fund Class R2	JOBRX	B-	C	B+	Up	3.01	14.74	5.12	32.29	32.80	23.25	868.2	800-480-4111	Y
JPMorgan SmartRetirement® Blend 2040 Fund Class R3	JNTEX	B-	C	B+	Up	3.10	14.94	5.42	33.48	34.95	23.24	868.2	800-480-4111	Y
JPMorgan SmartRetirement® Blend 2040 Fund Class R4	JNTNX	B-	C	B+	Up	3.12	15.03	5.63	34.46	36.62	23.29	868.2	800-480-4111	Y
JPMorgan SmartRetirement® Blend 2040 Fund Class R5	JOBBX	B-	C	B+	Up	3.15	15.10	5.78	34.85	37.02	23.28	868.2	800-480-4111	Y
JPMorgan SmartRetirement® Blend 2040 Fund Class R6	JOBYX	B-	C	B+	Up	3.18	15.18	5.93	35.30	37.61	23.29	868.2	800-480-4111	Y
JPMorgan SmartRetirement® Blend 2045 Fund Class I	JMSSX	B-	C	B+	Up	3.14	15.43	5.58	34.35	36.04	23.43	689.7	800-480-4111	Y
JPMorgan SmartRetirement® Blend 2045 Fund Class R2	JNARX	B-	C	B	Up	3.03	15.12	5.07	32.38	32.95	23.41	689.7	800-480-4111	Y
JPMorgan SmartRetirement® Blend 2045 Fund Class R3	JNTOX	B-	C	B	Up	3.09	15.27	5.31	33.69	35.40	23.38	689.7	800-480-4111	Y
JPMorgan SmartRetirement® Blend 2045 Fund Class R4	JNTLX	B-	C	B+	Up	3.14	15.42	5.61	34.69	37.10	23.43	689.7	800-480-4111	Y
JPMorgan SmartRetirement® Blend 2045 Fund Class R5	JMBRX	B-	C	B+	Up	3.18	15.48	5.72	34.99	37.21	23.43	689.7	800-480-4111	Y
JPMorgan SmartRetirement® Blend 2045 Fund Class R6	JMYAX	B-	C	B+	Up	3.20	15.54	5.86	35.40	37.82	23.46	689.7	800-480-4111	Y
JPMorgan SmartRetirement® Blend 2050 Fund Class I	JNEAX	B-	C	B+	Up	3.10	15.39	5.59	34.46	36.10	23.37	508.1	800-480-4111	Y
JPMorgan SmartRetirement® Blend 2050 Fund Class R2	JNNRX	B-	C	B	Up	3.00	15.13	5.11	32.52	33.02	23.34	508.1	800-480-4111	Y
JPMorgan SmartRetirement® Blend 2050 Fund Class R3	JNTKX	B-	C	B+	Up	3.05	15.30	5.37	33.81	35.40	23.35	508.1	800-480-4111	Y
JPMorgan SmartRetirement® Blend 2050 Fund Class R4	JNTPX	B-	C	B+	Up	3.15	15.41	5.61	34.79	37.07	23.38	508.1	800-480-4111	Y
JPMorgan SmartRetirement® Blend 2050 Fund Class R5	JNABX	B-	C	B+	Up	3.15	15.51	5.79	35.12	37.28	23.37	508.1	800-480-4111	Y
JPMorgan SmartRetirement® Blend 2050 Fund Class R6	JNYAX	B-	C	B+	Up	3.17	15.53	5.85	35.49	37.78	23.38	508.1	800-480-4111	Y
JPMorgan SmartRetirement® Blend 2055 Fund Class I	JPTBX	B-	C	B+	Up	3.08	15.40	5.56	34.23	36.17	23.18	259.1	800-480-4111	Y
JPMorgan SmartRetirement® Blend 2055 Fund Class R2	JTRBX	B-	C	B	Up	3.02	15.17	5.10	32.24	33.10	23.16	259.1	800-480-4111	Y
JPMorgan SmartRetirement® Blend 2055 Fund Class R3	JTTUX	B-	C	B	Up	3.08	15.27	5.37	33.55	35.50	23.14	259.1	800-480-4111	Y
JPMorgan SmartRetirement® Blend 2055 Fund Class R4	JTTLX	B-	C	B+	Up	3.13	15.41	5.62	34.54	37.18	23.17	259.1	800-480-4111	Y

Category: Target Date (con't)

		RATINGS				TOTAL RETURNS & PERFORMANCE					ASSETS		NEW INVESTORS	
Fund Name	Ticker Symbol	Overall Rating	Reward Rating	Risk Rating	Recent Up/ Downgrade	3-Month Total Return	6-Month Total Return	1-Year Total Return	3-Year Total Return	5-Year Total Return	NAV	Total Assets (MIL)	Telephone	Open to New Investors
JPMorgan SmartRetirement® Blend 2055 Fund Class R5	JTBBX	B-	C	B+	Up	3.16	15.47	5.77	34.82	37.34	23.18	259.1	800-480-4111	Y
JPMorgan SmartRetirement® Blend 2055 Fund Class R6	JTYBX	B-	C	B+	Up	3.19	15.54	5.87	35.24	37.90	23.2	259.1	800-480-4111	Y
JPMorgan SmartRetirement® Blend Inc Fund Class R3	JITLX	B	C	A-	Up	2.70	9.20	5.37	17.42	20.34	17.52	421.2	800-480-4111	Y
JPMorgan SmartRetirement® Blend Inc Fund Class R4	JITKX	B	C+	A-	Up	2.83	9.43	5.66	18.36	21.91	17.52	421.2	800-480-4111	Y
JPMorgan SmartRetirement® Blend Income Fund Class I	JIJSX	B	C+	A-	Up	2.82	9.44	5.67	18.09	21.06	17.52	421.2	800-480-4111	Y
JPMorgan SmartRetirement® Blend Income Fund Class R2	JIRBX	B-	C	B+	Up	2.64	9.14	5.12	16.28	18.30	17.51	421.2	800-480-4111	Y
JPMorgan SmartRetirement® Blend Income Fund Class R5	JIBBX	B	C+	A-	Up	2.80	9.46	5.79	18.61	22.05	17.51	421.2	800-480-4111	Y
JPMorgan SmartRetirement® Blend Income Fund Class R6	JIYBX	B	C+	A-	Up	2.83	9.54	5.90	18.94	22.51	17.52	421.2	800-480-4111	Y
JPMorgan SmartRetirement® Income Fund Class A	JSRAX	B	C+	A-	Up	2.98	9.88	5.65	18.40	20.85	18.14	3,326	800-480-4111	Y
JPMorgan SmartRetirement® Income Fund Class C	JSRCX	B-	C	B+	Up	2.83	9.54	5.01	16.17	17.06	18.07	3,326	800-480-4111	Y
JPMorgan SmartRetirement® Income Fund Class I	JSRSX	B	C+	A-	Up	3.01	9.96	5.82	18.84	21.59	18.18	3,326	800-480-4111	Y
JPMorgan SmartRetirement® Income Fund Class R2	JSIZX	B-	C	A-	Up	2.93	9.72	5.24	17.06	18.91	18.11	3,326	800-480-4111	Y
JPMorgan SmartRetirement® Income Fund Class R3	JSIPX	B-	C	A-	Up	2.97	9.85	5.51	17.69	20.15	18.08	3,326	800-480-4111	Y
JPMorgan SmartRetirement® Income Fund Class R4	JSIQX	B	C+	A-	Up	3.00	9.94	5.78	18.58	21.66	18.15	3,326	800-480-4111	Y
JPMorgan SmartRetirement® Income Fund Class R5	JSIIX	B	C+	A-	Up	3.03	10.02	5.91	19.11	22.21	18.21	3,326	800-480-4111	Y
JPMorgan SmartRetirement® Income Fund Class R6	JSIYX	B	C+	A-	Up	3.05	10.10	6.02	19.48	22.67	18.21	3,326	800-480-4111	Y
KP Retirement Path 2015 Fund Institutional Shares	KPRAX	B	C+	A		3.03	9.91	6.66	19.58	24.06	10.53	469.8		Y
KP Retirement Path 2020 Fund Institutional Shares	KPRBX	B	C+	A		3.01	10.75	6.42	23.12	26.68	10.92	1,053		Y
KP Retirement Path 2025 Fund Institutional Shares	KPRCX	B	C	A	Up	3.21	12.17	6.36	27.81	29.74	11.24	1,353		Y
KP Retirement Path 2030 Fund Institutional Shares	KPRDX	B-	C	A-		3.34	13.49	6.12	32.45	32.58	11.44	1,344		Y
KP Retirement Path 2035 Fund Institutional Shares	KPREX	B-	C	B+	Up	3.38	14.49	5.82	35.84	34.89	11.61	1,504		Y
KP Retirement Path 2040 Fund Institutional Shares	KPRFX	B-	C	B+	Up	3.53	15.22	5.57	38.03	36.41	11.73	1,377		Y
KP Retirement Path 2045 Fund Institutional Shares	KPRGX	B-	C	B+	Up	3.59	15.57	5.48	39.42	37.25	11.8	1,071		Y
KP Retirement Path 2050 Fund Institutional Shares	KPRHX	B-	C	B+	Up	3.55	15.82	5.34	39.82	37.60	11.93	654.3		Y
KP Retirement Path 2055 Fund Institutional Shares	KPRIX	B-	C	B	Up	3.62	16.02	5.33	39.92	37.96	12.02	228.8		Y
KP Retirement Path 2060 Fund Institutional Shares	KPRJX	B-	C	B	Up	3.62	16.02	5.27	40.05	38.04	11.73	47.6		Y
Manning & Napier Target 2015 Series Class I	MTJIX	B	C+	B+	Up	2.81	9.57	6.05	18.03	14.36	11.62	1.3	585-325-6880	Y
Manning & Napier Target 2015 Series Class K	MTJKX	B-	C+	B+		2.71	9.38	5.81	17.15	12.90	11.59	1.3	585-325-6880	Y
Manning & Napier Target 2015 Series Class R	MTJRX	B-	C	B+		2.96	9.57	5.82	16.58	11.83	11.79	1.3	585-325-6880	Y
Manning & Napier Target 2020 Series Class I	MTNIX	B	C+	A-	Up	3.21	11.26	6.33	20.64	16.62	9.95	55.7	585-325-6880	Y
Manning & Napier Target 2020 Series Class K	MTNKX	B	C+	B+	Up	3.17	11.03	5.95	19.78	15.07	9.89	55.7	585-325-6880	Y
Manning & Napier Target 2020 Series Class R	MTNRX	B-	C	B+		3.13	10.98	5.76	18.94	13.73	9.75	55.7	585-325-6880	Y
Manning & Napier Target 2025 Series Class I	MTOAX	B	C+	A-	Up	3.32	11.93	6.35	22.90	18.08	12.59	66.3	585-325-6880	Y
Manning & Napier Target 2025 Series Class K	MTOKX	B	C+	A-	Up	3.17	11.75	5.96	21.89	16.49	12.6	66.3	585-325-6880	Y
Manning & Napier Target 2025 Series Class R	MTORX	B	C+	A-	Up	3.14	11.60	5.80	21.12	15.11	12.63	66.3	585-325-6880	Y
Manning & Napier Target 2030 Series Class I	MTPIX	B	C+	A-	Up	3.40	13.24	6.23	26.79	21.68	10.2	77.2	585-325-6880	Y
Manning & Napier Target 2030 Series Class K	MTPKX	B	C+	A-	Up	3.37	13.09	5.99	25.78	20.02	10.08	77.2	585-325-6880	Y
Manning & Napier Target 2030 Series Class R	MTPRX	B	C+	A-	Up	3.30	13.00	5.77	24.97	18.66	9.98	77.2	585-325-6880	Y
Manning & Napier Target 2035 Series Class I	MTQIX	B	C+	B+	Up	3.72	14.74	6.37	30.56	25.06	13.26	44.7	585-325-6880	Y
Manning & Napier Target 2035 Series Class K	MTQKX	B-	C+	B+	Up	3.61	14.58	6.05	29.45	23.45	13.18	44.7	585-325-6880	Y
Manning & Napier Target 2035 Series Class R	MTQRX	B-	C	B+	Up	3.58	14.52	5.83	28.53	21.97	13.22	44.7	585-325-6880	Y
Manning & Napier Target 2040 Series Class I	MTTIX	B-	C+	B+	Up	3.96	16.21	6.38	34.22	28.31	10.24	50.5	585-325-6880	Y
Manning & Napier Target 2040 Series Class K	MTTKX	B-	C	B+	Up	3.93	15.93	6.00	33.15	26.55	10.13	50.5	585-325-6880	Y
Manning & Napier Target 2040 Series Class R	MTTRX	B-	C	B+	Up	3.77	15.87	5.80	32.13	24.96	10.03	50.5	585-325-6880	Y
Manning & Napier Target 2045 Series Class I	MTUIX	B-	C	B	Up	4.13	17.67	6.36	37.74	31.68	13.37	24.9	585-325-6880	Y
Manning & Napier Target 2045 Series Class K	MTUKX	B-	C	B	Up	4.08	17.48	6.03	36.67	30.06	13.31	24.9	585-325-6880	Y
Manning & Napier Target 2045 Series Class R	MTURX	B-	C	B	Up	4.04	17.37	5.81	35.55	28.39	13.19	24.9	585-325-6880	Y
Manning & Napier Target 2050 Series Class I	MTYIX	B-	C	B	Up	4.31	18.81	6.48	39.48	33.39	10.58	29.4	585-325-6880	Y
Manning & Napier Target 2050 Series Class K	MTYKX	B-	C	B	Up	4.28	18.67	6.32	38.50	31.77	10.48	29.4	585-325-6880	Y
Manning & Napier Target 2050 Series Class R	MTYRX	B-	C	B	Up	4.16	18.40	5.98	37.31	30.01	10.31	29.4	585-325-6880	Y
Manning & Napier Target 2055 Series Class I	MTZIX	B-	C	B	Up	4.38	18.81	6.58	39.48	33.57	13.3	12.3	585-325-6880	Y
Manning & Napier Target 2055 Series Class K	MTZKX	B-	C	B	Up	4.27	18.66	6.26	38.37	31.86	13.15	12.3	585-325-6880	Y

Category: Target Date (con't)

Fund Name	Ticker Symbol	Overall Rating	Reward Rating	Risk Rating	Recent Up/ Downgrade	3-Month Total Return	6-Month Total Return	1-Year Total Return	3-Year Total Return	5-Year Total Return	NAV	Total Assets (MIL)	Telephone	Open to New Investors
		RATINGS				TOTAL RETURNS & PERFORMANCE					ASSETS		NEW INVESTORS	
Manning & Napier Target 2055 Series Class R	MTZRX	B-	C	B	Up	4.26	18.46	6.02	37.32	30.31	12.96	12.3	585-325-6880	Y
Manning & Napier Target 2060 Series Class I	MTKIX	B-	C	B	Up	4.36	18.78	6.49	39.48		11.93	11.6	585-325-6880	Y
Manning & Napier Target 2060 Series Class K	MTKKX	B-	C	B	Up	4.29	18.60	6.26	38.47		11.92	11.6	585-325-6880	Y
Manning & Napier Target 2060 Series Class R	MTKRX	B-	C	B	Up	4.22	18.36	5.88	37.38		11.86	11.6	585-325-6880	Y
Manning & Napier Target Income Series Class I	MTDIX	B	C+	B+	Up	2.77	9.16	6.54	16.43	15.98	10.33	77.6	585-325-6880	Y
Manning & Napier Target Income Series Class K	MTDKX	B-	C+	B+		2.74	9.04	6.31	15.65	14.63	10.28	77.6	585-325-6880	Y
Manning & Napier Target Income Series Class R	MTDRX	B-	C	B+		2.68	8.84	5.99	14.70	13.12	10.13	77.6	585-325-6880	Y
MassMutual RetireSMART by JPMorgan 2020 Administrative Cls	MRTYX	B	C+	A	Up	3.17	11.16	6.10	26.38	23.68	12.35	385.8		Y
MassMutual RetireSMART by JPMorgan 2020 Fund Class A	MRTAX	B	C+	A	Up	3.19	11.03	5.94	25.51	22.24	12.28	385.8		Y
MassMutual RetireSMART by JPMorgan 2020 Fund Class I	MRTDX	B	C+	A	Up	3.34	11.36	6.50	27.57	25.58	12.35	385.8		Y
MassMutual RetireSMART by JPMorgan 2020 Fund Class R3	MRTNX	B	C	A-	Up	3.11	11.00	5.76	24.93	21.24	11.9	385.8		Y
MassMutual RetireSMART by JPMorgan 2020 Fund Class R4	MRTHX	B	C+	A	Up	3.24	11.11	6.03	25.94	22.88	12.1	385.8		Y
MassMutual RetireSMART by JPMorgan 2020 Fund Class R5	MRTBX	B	C+	A	Up	3.26	11.38	6.35	27.20	25.06	12.33	385.8		Y
MassMutual RetireSMART by JPMorgan 2020 Fund Service Class	MRTSX	B	C+	A	Up	3.24	11.21	6.22	26.81	24.23	12.4	385.8		Y
MassMutual RetireSMART by JPMorgan 2025 Administrative Cls	MMIYX	B	C	A-	Up	3.52	12.92	6.58	31.46	27.37	12.32	279.2		Y
MassMutual RetireSMART by JPMorgan 2025 Fund Class A	MMSDX	B	C	A-	Up	3.38	12.75	6.26	30.44	25.69	12.2	279.2		Y
MassMutual RetireSMART by JPMorgan 2025 Fund Class I	MMNUX	B	C+	A-	Up	3.52	13.00	6.79	32.59	29.17	12.34	279.2		Y
MassMutual RetireSMART by JPMorgan 2025 Fund Class R3	MMNRX	B-	C	A-	Up	3.41	12.65	6.12	29.89	24.77	12.11	279.2		Y
MassMutual RetireSMART by JPMorgan 2025 Fund Class R4	MMNZX	B	C	A-	Up	3.49	12.81	6.41	30.90	26.45	12.15	279.2		Y
MassMutual RetireSMART by JPMorgan 2025 Fund Class R5	MMNTX	B	C+	A-	Up	3.57	13.06	6.76	32.40	28.75	12.46	279.2		Y
MassMutual RetireSMART by JPMorgan 2025 Fund Service Class	MMISX	B	C	A-	Up	3.51	12.97	6.64	31.84	28.02	12.36	279.2		Y
MassMutual RetireSMART by JPMorgan 2030 Administrative Cls	MRYYX	B-	C	B+	Up	3.60	14.12	6.52	34.43	29.17	12.36	510.0		Y
MassMutual RetireSMART by JPMorgan 2030 Fund Class A	MRYAX	B-	C	B+	Up	3.54	14.02	6.28	33.40	27.63	12.28	510.0		Y
MassMutual RetireSMART by JPMorgan 2030 Fund Class I	MRYUX	B-	C	A-	Up	3.68	14.31	6.82	35.73	31.27	12.38	510.0		Y
MassMutual RetireSMART by JPMorgan 2030 Fund Class R3	MRYNX	B-	C	B+	Up	3.54	13.86	6.12	32.85	26.60	11.99	510.0		Y
MassMutual RetireSMART by JPMorgan 2030 Fund Class R4	MRYZX	B-	C	B+	Up	3.57	14.04	6.40	33.87	28.23	12.18	510.0		Y
MassMutual RetireSMART by JPMorgan 2030 Fund Class R5	MRYTX	B-	C	A-	Up	3.70	14.27	6.70	35.19	30.51	12.33	510.0		Y
MassMutual RetireSMART by JPMorgan 2030 Fund Service Class	MRYSX	B-	C	B+	Up	3.67	14.18	6.62	34.79	29.81	12.4	510.0		Y
MassMutual RetireSMART by JPMorgan 2035 Administrative Cls	MMXYX	B-	C	B+	Up	3.67	14.81	5.98	35.62	29.97	12.71	219.1		Y
MassMutual RetireSMART by JPMorgan 2035 Fund Class A	MMXAX	B-	C	B+	Up	3.53	14.64	5.70	34.64	28.30	12.6	219.1		Y
MassMutual RetireSMART by JPMorgan 2035 Fund Class I	MMXUX	B-	C	B+	Up	3.69	14.93	6.32	36.92	31.90	12.62	219.1		Y
MassMutual RetireSMART by JPMorgan 2035 Fund Class R3	MMXNX	B-	C	B+	Up	3.56	14.57	5.57	33.97	27.40	12.5	219.1		Y
MassMutual RetireSMART by JPMorgan 2035 Fund Class R4	MMXZX	B-	C	B+	Up	3.55	14.63	5.78	34.90	28.94	12.53	219.1		Y
MassMutual RetireSMART by JPMorgan 2035 Fund Class R5	MMXTX	B-	C	B+	Up	3.69	14.90	6.23	36.38	31.24	12.64	219.1		Y
MassMutual RetireSMART by JPMorgan 2035 Fund Service Class	MMXSX	B-	C	B+	Up	3.65	14.85	6.07	35.96	30.56	12.76	219.1		Y
MassMutual RetireSMART by JPMorgan 2040 Administrative Cls	MRFYX	B-	C	B+	Up	3.68	15.58	5.77	36.00	30.34	12.09	331.9		Y
MassMutual RetireSMART by JPMorgan 2040 Fund Class A	MRFAX	B-	C	B+	Up	3.62	15.48	5.57	35.08	28.75	12.01	331.9		Y
MassMutual RetireSMART by JPMorgan 2040 Fund Class I	MRFUX	B-	C	B+	Up	3.77	15.77	6.15	37.30	32.21	12.11	331.9		Y
MassMutual RetireSMART by JPMorgan 2040 Fund Class R3	MFRNX	B-	C	B+	Up	3.63	15.49	5.43	34.56	27.80	11.7	331.9		Y
MassMutual RetireSMART by JPMorgan 2040 Fund Class R4	MRFZX	B-	C	B+	Up	3.65	15.64	5.67	35.53	29.43	11.9	331.9		Y
MassMutual RetireSMART by JPMorgan 2040 Fund Class R5	MRFTX	B-	C	B+	Up	3.68	15.78	5.99	36.98	31.67	12.1	331.9		Y
MassMutual RetireSMART by JPMorgan 2040 Fund Service Class	MFRSX	B-	C	B+	Up	3.66	15.71	5.86	36.42	30.99	12.15	331.9		Y
MassMutual RetireSMART by JPMorgan 2045 Administrative Cls	MMKYX	B-	C	B	Up	3.77	16.17	5.93	36.92	30.92	12.64	140.5		Y
MassMutual RetireSMART by JPMorgan 2045 Fund Class A	MMKAX	B-	C	B	Up	3.72	16.01	5.61	35.80	29.33	12.53	140.5		Y
MassMutual RetireSMART by JPMorgan 2045 Fund Class I	MMKUX	B-	C	B+	Up	3.84	16.31	6.28	38.22	32.97	12.69	140.5		Y
MassMutual RetireSMART by JPMorgan 2045 Fund Class R3	MMKNX	B-	C	B	Up	3.67	15.85	5.50	35.29	28.31	12.42	140.5		Y
MassMutual RetireSMART by JPMorgan 2045 Fund Class R4	MMKZX	B-	C	B	Up	3.74	16.12	5.78	36.25	29.98	12.46	140.5		Y
MassMutual RetireSMART by JPMorgan 2045 Fund Class R5	MMKTX	B-	C	B	Up	3.84	16.30	6.14	37.78	32.30	12.7	140.5		Y
MassMutual RetireSMART by JPMorgan 2045 Fund Service Class	MMKSX	B-	C	B+	Up	3.76	16.11	5.96	37.19	31.55	12.68	140.5		Y
MassMutual RetireSMART by JPMorgan 2050 Administrative Cls	MMRYX	B-	C	B	Up	3.79	16.20	6.01	39.13	32.46	8.75	196.0		Y
MassMutual RetireSMART by JPMorgan 2050 Fund Class A	MMARX	B-	C	B	Up	3.69	16.02	5.75	38.17	30.87	8.69	196.0		Y
MassMutual RetireSMART by JPMorgan 2050 Fund Class I	MMRUX	B-	C	B+	Up	3.79	16.20	6.27	40.40	34.35	8.75	196.0		Y

Category: Target Date (con't)

Fund Name	Ticker Symbol	RATINGS: Overall Rating	Reward Rating	Risk Rating	Recent Up/ Downgrade	TOTAL RETURNS & PERFORMANCE: 3-Month Total Return	6-Month Total Return	1-Year Total Return	3-Year Total Return	5-Year Total Return	ASSETS: NAV	Total Assets (MIL)	NEW INVESTORS: Telephone	Open to New Investors
MassMutual RetireSMART by JPMorgan 2050 Fund Class R3	MMRNX	B-	C	B	Up	3.62	15.96	5.69	37.52	29.95	8.57	196.0		Y
MassMutual RetireSMART by JPMorgan 2050 Fund Class R4	MMRZX	B-	C	B	Up	3.72	15.97	5.87	38.50	31.46	8.64	196.0		Y
MassMutual RetireSMART by JPMorgan 2050 Fund Class R5	MMRTX	B-	C	B	Up	3.80	16.22	6.22	39.95	33.94	8.74	196.0		Y
MassMutual RetireSMART by JPMorgan 2050 Fund Service Class	MMTSX	B-	C	B	Up	3.78	16.29	6.21	39.62	33.15	8.78	196.0		Y
MassMutual RetireSMART by JPMorgan 2055 Administrative Cls	MMWYX	B-	C	B	Up	3.70	16.15	6.11	39.43	32.78	10.64	59.9		Y
MassMutual RetireSMART by JPMorgan 2055 Fund Class A	MMWAX	B-	C	B	Up	3.70	15.92	5.87	38.41	31.16	10.63	59.9		Y
MassMutual RetireSMART by JPMorgan 2055 Fund Class I	MMWZX	B-	C	B+	Up	3.79	16.23	6.37	40.70	34.81	10.67	59.9		Y
MassMutual RetireSMART by JPMorgan 2055 Fund Class R3	MMWTX	B-	C	B	Up	3.63	15.82	5.69	37.71	30.12	10.54	59.9		Y
MassMutual RetireSMART by JPMorgan 2055 Fund Class R4	MMWEX	B-	C	B	Up	3.72	15.99	5.90	38.77	31.83	10.59	59.9		Y
MassMutual RetireSMART by JPMorgan 2055 Fund Class R5	MMWUX	B-	C	B	Up	3.78	16.21	6.33	40.25	34.02	10.68	59.9		Y
MassMutual RetireSMART by JPMorgan 2055 Fund Service Class	MMWSX	B-	C	B	Up	3.68	16.19	6.20	39.85	33.42	10.69	59.9		Y
MassMutual RetireSMART by JPMorgan 2060 Administrative Cls	MMWFX	B-	C	B	Up	3.78	16.14	6.07	39.19		10.43	15.2		Y
MassMutual RetireSMART by JPMorgan 2060 Fund Class A	MMWDX	B-	C	B	Up	3.68	16.03	5.85	38.15		10.42	15.2		Y
MassMutual RetireSMART by JPMorgan 2060 Fund Class I	MMWIX	B-	C	B	Up	3.76	16.33	6.40	40.33		10.47	15.2		Y
MassMutual RetireSMART by JPMorgan 2060 Fund Class R3	MMWBX	B-	C	B	Up	3.69	15.99	5.77	37.62		10.37	15.2		Y
MassMutual RetireSMART by JPMorgan 2060 Fund Class R4	MMWCX	B-	C	B	Up	3.78	16.14	5.96	38.51		10.43	15.2		Y
MassMutual RetireSMART by JPMorgan 2060 Fund Class R5	MMWHX	B-	C	B	Up	3.87	16.35	6.40	39.99		10.46	15.2		Y
MassMutual RetireSMART by JPMorgan 2060 Fund Service Class	MMWGX	B-	C	B	Up	3.77	16.12	6.13	39.48		10.44	15.2		Y
MassMutual RetireSMART by JPMorgan In Retmnt Admin Cls	MDRYX	B	C	A-	Up	3.09	10.22	5.61	17.25	17.22	11.64	200.1		Y
MassMutual RetireSMART by JPMorgan In Retirement Cls A	MRDAX	B-	C	A-	Up	3.04	10.02	5.29	16.34	15.67	11.52	200.1		Y
MassMutual RetireSMART by JPMorgan In Retirement Cls I	MDRVX	B	C+	A-	Up	3.11	10.37	5.90	18.25	18.89	11.6	200.1		Y
MassMutual RetireSMART by JPMorgan In Retirement Cls R3	MDRNX	B-	C	A-	Up	2.89	9.86	5.17	15.71	14.81	11.36	200.1		Y
MassMutual RetireSMART by JPMorgan In Retirement Cls R4	MDRZX	B-	C	A-	Up	3.05	10.08	5.37	16.65	16.31	11.46	200.1		Y
MassMutual RetireSMART by JPMorgan In Retirement Cls R5	MDRTX	B	C+	A-	Up	3.19	10.34	5.85	17.95	18.25	11.63	200.1		Y
MassMutual RetireSMART by JPMorgan In Retmnt Service Cls	MDRSX	B	C+	A-	Up	3.10	10.22	5.71	17.63	17.72	11.64	200.1		Y
MFS Lifetime 2020 Fund Class A	MFLAX	B	C+	A-		3.19	10.34	6.75	18.98	23.04	13.23	341.2	877-960-6077	Y
MFS Lifetime 2020 Fund Class B	MFLBX	B	C	A-	Up	3.05	10.04	6.02	16.39	18.61	13.15	341.2	877-960-6077	Y
MFS Lifetime 2020 Fund Class C	MFLCX	B	C	A-	Up	3.02	9.94	5.97	16.34	18.50	12.94	341.2	877-960-6077	Y
MFS Lifetime 2020 Fund Class I	MFLIX	B	C+	A		3.33	10.61	7.06	19.95	24.70	13.34	341.2	877-960-6077	Y
MFS Lifetime 2020 Fund Class R1	MFLEX	B	C	A-	Up	3.05	10.04	5.95	16.37	18.57	13.15	341.2	877-960-6077	Y
MFS Lifetime 2020 Fund Class R2	MFLGX	B	C+	A-	Up	3.22	10.33	6.49	18.15	21.61	13.13	341.2	877-960-6077	Y
MFS Lifetime 2020 Fund Class R3	MFLHX	B	C+	A-		3.27	10.42	6.78	19.03	23.15	13.24	341.2	877-960-6077	Y
MFS Lifetime 2020 Fund Class R4	MFLJX	B	C+	A		3.33	10.53	7.00	19.93	24.68	13.33	341.2	877-960-6077	Y
MFS Lifetime 2020 Fund Class R6	MFLKX	B	C+	A		3.33	10.63	7.14	20.35	25.11	13.32	341.2	877-960-6077	Y
MFS Lifetime 2025 Fund Class A	LTTAX	B	C+	A	Up	3.66	12.54	7.06	25.01	28.57	13.28	305.8	877-960-6077	Y
MFS Lifetime 2025 Fund Class B	LTTBX	B	C+	A-	Up	3.37	12.09	6.24	22.18	23.72	13.16	305.8	877-960-6077	Y
MFS Lifetime 2025 Fund Class C	LTTCX	B	C	A-	Up	3.39	12.07	6.22	22.08	23.76	13.09	305.8	877-960-6077	Y
MFS Lifetime 2025 Fund Class I	LTTIX	B	C+	A	Up	3.73	12.67	7.23	25.87	30.14	13.33	305.8	877-960-6077	Y
MFS Lifetime 2025 Fund Class R1	LTTRX	B	C	A-	Up	3.37	12.08	6.16	22.18	23.75	13.17	305.8	877-960-6077	Y
MFS Lifetime 2025 Fund Class R2	LTTSX	B	C+	A	Up	3.52	12.34	6.67	24.00	26.89	13.2	305.8	877-960-6077	Y
MFS Lifetime 2025 Fund Class R3	LTTTX	B	C+	A	Up	3.59	12.46	6.94	24.85	28.42	13.26	305.8	877-960-6077	Y
MFS Lifetime 2025 Fund Class R4	LTTUX	B	C+	A	Up	3.72	12.65	7.24	25.86	30.13	13.35	305.8	877-960-6077	Y
MFS Lifetime 2025 Fund Class R6	LTTKX	B	C+	A	Up	3.72	12.75	7.39	26.27	30.55	13.35	305.8	877-960-6077	Y
MFS Lifetime 2030 Fund Class A	MLTAX	B-	C	B+		3.93	15.29	6.97	32.17	34.81	15.83	591.8	877-960-6077	Y
MFS Lifetime 2030 Fund Class B	MLTBX	B-	C	B+	Up	3.72	14.80	6.18	29.25	29.89	15.59	591.8	877-960-6077	Y
MFS Lifetime 2030 Fund Class C	MLTCX	B-	C	B+	Up	3.74	14.90	6.20	29.29	29.92	15.5	591.8	877-960-6077	Y
MFS Lifetime 2030 Fund Class I	MLTIX	B	C+	A-	Up	3.98	15.37	7.23	32.85	36.22	15.91	591.8	877-960-6077	Y
MFS Lifetime 2030 Fund Class R1	MLTEX	B-	C	B+	Up	3.78	14.90	6.23	29.25	29.90	15.65	591.8	877-960-6077	Y
MFS Lifetime 2030 Fund Class R2	MLTGX	B-	C	B+	Up	3.91	15.22	6.74	31.29	33.23	15.67	591.8	877-960-6077	Y
MFS Lifetime 2030 Fund Class R3	MLTHX	B-	C	B+		3.95	15.33	7.02	32.22	34.84	15.79	591.8	877-960-6077	Y
MFS Lifetime 2030 Fund Class R4	MLTJX	B	C+	A-	Up	3.98	15.43	7.22	33.22	36.51	15.93	591.8	877-960-6077	Y
MFS Lifetime 2030 Fund Class R6	MLTKX	B	C+	A-	Up	3.98	15.51	7.37	33.70	37.09	15.93	591.8	877-960-6077	Y

Category: Target Date (con't)

Fund Name	Ticker Symbol	RATINGS: Overall Rating	Reward Rating	Risk Rating	Recent Up/ Downgrade	TOTAL RETURNS & PERFORMANCE: 3-Month Total Return	6-Month Total Return	1-Year Total Return	3-Year Total Return	5-Year Total Return	ASSETS: NAV	Total Assets (MIL)	NEW INVESTORS: Telephone	Open to New Investors
MFS Lifetime 2035 Fund Class A	LFEAX	B-	C	B+	Up	4.06	17.11	6.68	35.59	38.23	15.12	298.6	877-960-6077	Y
MFS Lifetime 2035 Fund Class B	LFEBX	B-	C	B+	Up	3.87	16.64	5.89	32.64	33.15	15	298.6	877-960-6077	Y
MFS Lifetime 2035 Fund Class C	LFECX	B-	C	B+	Up	3.89	16.71	5.95	32.60	33.17	14.94	298.6	877-960-6077	Y
MFS Lifetime 2035 Fund Class I	LFEDX	B-	C	B+	Up	4.12	17.26	6.94	36.23	39.57	15.15	298.6	877-960-6077	Y
MFS Lifetime 2035 Fund Class R1	LFERX	B-	C	B+	Up	3.88	16.65	5.90	32.57	33.18	14.99	298.6	877-960-6077	Y
MFS Lifetime 2035 Fund Class R2	LFESX	B-	C	B+	Up	4.00	16.92	6.41	34.55	36.52	15.06	298.6	877-960-6077	Y
MFS Lifetime 2035 Fund Class R3	LFETX	B-	C	B+	Up	4.05	17.09	6.71	35.64	38.16	15.14	298.6	877-960-6077	Y
MFS Lifetime 2035 Fund Class R4	LFEUX	B-	C	B+	Up	4.17	17.27	6.99	36.59	39.95	15.21	298.6	877-960-6077	Y
MFS Lifetime 2035 Fund Class R6	LFEKX	B-	C	B+	Up	4.10	17.27	7.08	37.11	40.47	15.21	298.6	877-960-6077	Y
MFS Lifetime 2040 Fund Class A	MLFAX	B-	C	B	Up	4.06	17.76	6.44	37.48	39.97	16.64	426.8	877-960-6077	Y
MFS Lifetime 2040 Fund Class B	MLFBX	B-	C	B	Up	3.84	17.28	5.58	34.40	34.71	16.49	426.8	877-960-6077	Y
MFS Lifetime 2040 Fund Class C	MLFCX	B-	C	B	Up	3.89	17.29	5.64	34.40	34.71	16.28	426.8	877-960-6077	Y
MFS Lifetime 2040 Fund Class I	MLFIX	B-	C	B	Up	4.10	17.87	6.68	38.17	41.33	16.75	426.8	877-960-6077	Y
MFS Lifetime 2040 Fund Class R1	MLFEX	B-	C	B	Up	3.85	17.28	5.63	34.37	34.77	16.42	426.8	877-960-6077	Y
MFS Lifetime 2040 Fund Class R2	MLFGX	B-	C	B	Up	3.96	17.60	6.09	36.39	38.11	16.5	426.8	877-960-6077	Y
MFS Lifetime 2040 Fund Class R3	MLFHX	B-	C	B	Up	4.00	17.69	6.37	37.42	39.82	16.63	426.8	877-960-6077	Y
MFS Lifetime 2040 Fund Class R4	MLFJX	B-	C	B	Up	4.09	17.90	6.66	38.50	41.66	16.79	426.8	877-960-6077	Y
MFS Lifetime 2040 Fund Class R6	MLFKX	B-	C	B	Up	4.15	17.90	6.75	39.01	42.18	16.79	426.8	877-960-6077	Y
MFS Lifetime 2045 Fund Class A	LTMAX	B-	C	B	Up	4.04	18.16	6.22	37.88	40.38	15.68	207.6	877-960-6077	Y
MFS Lifetime 2045 Fund Class B	LTMBX	B-	C	B	Up	3.80	17.62	5.41	34.83	35.15	15.55	207.6	877-960-6077	Y
MFS Lifetime 2045 Fund Class C	LTMDX	B-	C	B	Up	3.82	17.64	5.40	34.71	35.05	15.47	207.6	877-960-6077	Y
MFS Lifetime 2045 Fund Class I	LTMKX	B-	C	B	Up	4.09	18.24	6.44	39.10	42.26	15.75	207.6	877-960-6077	Y
MFS Lifetime 2045 Fund Class R1	LTMRX	B-	C	B	Up	3.81	17.65	5.40	34.77	35.13	15.53	207.6	877-960-6077	Y
MFS Lifetime 2045 Fund Class R2	LTMSX	B-	C	B	Up	4.01	17.96	5.91	36.84	38.55	15.56	207.6	877-960-6077	Y
MFS Lifetime 2045 Fund Class R3	LTMTX	B-	C	B	Up	4.05	18.09	6.18	37.90	40.24	15.66	207.6	877-960-6077	Y
MFS Lifetime 2045 Fund Class R4	LTMUX	B-	C	B	Up	4.10	18.27	6.43	38.84	41.99	15.73	207.6	877-960-6077	Y
MFS Lifetime 2045 Fund Class R6	LTMLX	B-	C	B	Up	4.10	18.27	6.60	39.36	42.52	15.73	207.6	877-960-6077	Y
MFS Lifetime 2050 Fund Class A	MFFSX	B-	C	B	Up	4.00	18.04	6.15	37.81	40.24	18.97	216.5	877-960-6077	Y
MFS Lifetime 2050 Fund Class B	MFFRX	B-	C	B	Up	3.83	17.62	5.35	34.71	35.06	18.69	216.5	877-960-6077	Y
MFS Lifetime 2050 Fund Class C	MFFDX	B-	C	B	Up	3.85	17.65	5.35	34.70	35.03	18.59	216.5	877-960-6077	Y
MFS Lifetime 2050 Fund Class I	MFFIX	B-	C	B	Up	4.11	18.20	6.43	38.95	42.11	18.96	216.5	877-960-6077	Y
MFS Lifetime 2050 Fund Class R1	MFFMX	B-	C	B	Up	3.85	17.64	5.39	34.76	35.04	18.6	216.5	877-960-6077	Y
MFS Lifetime 2050 Fund Class R2	MFFNX	B-	C	B	Up	4.05	18.03	5.97	36.91	38.58	18.72	216.5	877-960-6077	Y
MFS Lifetime 2050 Fund Class R3	MFFOX	B-	C	B	Up	4.03	18.11	6.22	37.89	40.24	18.84	216.5	877-960-6077	Y
MFS Lifetime 2050 Fund Class R4	MFFPX	B-	C	B	Up	4.12	18.21	6.45	38.91	42.07	18.95	216.5	877-960-6077	Y
MFS Lifetime 2050 Fund Class R6	MFFKX	B-	C	B	Up	4.17	18.36	6.62	39.42	42.58	18.95	216.5	877-960-6077	Y
MFS Lifetime 2055 Fund Class A	LFIAX	B-	C	B	Up	4.01	18.06	6.15	37.76	40.26	16.08	107.2	877-960-6077	Y
MFS Lifetime 2055 Fund Class B	LFIBX	B-	C	B	Up	3.83	17.66	5.34	34.64	35.02	15.99	107.2	877-960-6077	Y
MFS Lifetime 2055 Fund Class C	LFICX	B-	C	B	Up	3.79	17.64	5.33	34.60	34.98	15.87	107.2	877-960-6077	Y
MFS Lifetime 2055 Fund Class I	LFIIX	B-	C	B	Up	4.07	18.22	6.43	38.21	41.44	16.09	107.2	877-960-6077	Y
MFS Lifetime 2055 Fund Class R1	LFIRX	B-	C	B	Up	3.85	17.70	5.41	34.55	34.99	15.89	107.2	877-960-6077	Y
MFS Lifetime 2055 Fund Class R2	LFISX	B-	C	B	Up	3.96	17.93	5.88	36.64	38.43	15.98	107.2	877-960-6077	Y
MFS Lifetime 2055 Fund Class R3	LFITX	B-	C	B	Up	4.07	18.14	6.22	37.75	40.20	16.08	107.2	877-960-6077	Y
MFS Lifetime 2055 Fund Class R4	LFIUX	B-	C	B	Up	4.12	18.21	6.47	38.76	42.01	16.16	107.2	877-960-6077	Y
MFS Lifetime 2055 Fund Class R6	LFIKX	B-	C	B	Up	4.12	18.28	6.57	39.31	42.57	16.17	107.2	877-960-6077	Y
MFS Lifetime Income Fund Class 529A	MLLQX	B	C+	A-	Up	3.16	10.37	6.66	15.88	19.69	10.32	585.6	877-960-6077	Y
MFS Lifetime Income Fund Class 529B	MLLRX	B-	C	B+		2.97	9.95	5.87	13.30	15.29	10.32	585.6	877-960-6077	Y
MFS Lifetime Income Fund Class 529C	MLLSX	B-	C	B+		2.87	9.84	5.76	13.20	15.19	10.31	585.6	877-960-6077	Y
MFS Lifetime Income Fund Class A	MLLAX	B	C+	A-	Up	3.10	10.31	6.67	16.00	19.90	12.6	585.6	877-960-6077	Y
MFS Lifetime Income Fund Class B	MLLBX	B-	C	B+		2.91	9.89	5.87	13.42	15.49	12.6	585.6	877-960-6077	Y
MFS Lifetime Income Fund Class C	MLLCX	B-	C	B+		2.99	9.98	5.87	13.42	15.49	12.6	585.6	877-960-6077	Y
MFS Lifetime Income Fund Class I	MLLIX	B	C+	A-		3.16	10.45	6.93	16.87	21.40	12.6	585.6	877-960-6077	Y

Category: Target Date (con't)

Fund Name	Ticker Symbol	Overall Rating	Reward Rating	Risk Rating	Recent Up/ Downgrade	3-Month Total Return	6-Month Total Return	1-Year Total Return	3-Year Total Return	5-Year Total Return	NAV	Total Assets (MIL)	Telephone	Open to New Investors
		RATINGS				TOTAL RETURNS & PERFORMANCE					ASSETS		NEW INVESTORS	
MFS Lifetime Income Fund Class R1	MLLEX	B-	C	B+		2.99	10.06	5.95	13.50	15.57	12.62	585.6	877-960-6077	Y
MFS Lifetime Income Fund Class R2	MLLGX	B	C+	A-	Up	3.12	10.25	6.48	15.12	18.41	12.61	585.6	877-960-6077	Y
MFS Lifetime Income Fund Class R3	MLLHX	B	C+	A-	Up	3.10	10.31	6.67	15.99	19.90	12.6	585.6	877-960-6077	Y
MFS Lifetime Income Fund Class R4	MLLJX	B	C+	A-		3.16	10.44	6.93	16.87	21.40	12.6	585.6	877-960-6077	Y
MFS Lifetime Income Fund Class R6	MLLKX	B	C+	A-		3.26	10.56	7.09	17.53	22.10	12.64	585.6	877-960-6077	Y
Nationwide Destination 2010 Fund Class A	NWDAX	B-	C	A-	Up	2.65	9.75	4.82	17.54	19.26	8.14	17.3	800-848-0920	Y
Nationwide Destination 2010 Fund Class C	NWDCX	B-	C	B+	Up	2.50	9.49	4.22	15.33	15.37	8.08	17.3	800-848-0920	Y
Nationwide Destination 2010 Fund Class R	NWDBX	B-	C	A-	Up	2.47	9.51	4.57	16.57	17.59	8.11	17.3	800-848-0920	Y
Nationwide Destination 2010 Fund Class R6	NWDIX	B	C	A-	Up	2.77	10.02	5.35	19.29	22.09	8.15	17.3	800-848-0920	Y
Nationwide Destination 2010 Institutional Service Cls	NWDSX	B	C	A-	Up	2.65	9.88	5.35	19.14	21.65	8.14	17.3	800-848-0920	Y
Nationwide Destination 2015 Fund Class A	NWEAX	B-	C	A-	Up	2.64	10.31	4.60	20.21	21.06	8.3	67.0	800-848-0920	Y
Nationwide Destination 2015 Fund Class C	NWECX	B-	C	B+	Up	2.52	10.04	4.14	18.21	17.60	8.25	67.0	800-848-0920	Y
Nationwide Destination 2015 Fund Class R	NWEBX	B-	C	A-	Up	2.70	10.19	4.44	19.32	19.44	8.27	67.0	800-848-0920	Y
Nationwide Destination 2015 Fund Class R6	NWEIX	B	C	A-	Up	2.75	10.67	5.21	21.91	23.98	8.33	67.0	800-848-0920	Y
Nationwide Destination 2015 Institutional Service Cls	NWESX	B-	C	A-	Up	2.70	10.42	4.95	21.03	22.32	8.31	67.0	800-848-0920	Y
Nationwide Destination 2020 Fund Class A	NWAFX	B-	C	A-	Up	2.90	11.54	4.93	23.44	23.09	9.04	208.3	800-848-0920	Y
Nationwide Destination 2020 Fund Class C	NWFCX	B-	C	A-	Up	2.68	11.13	4.18	21.03	19.09	8.91	208.3	800-848-0920	Y
Nationwide Destination 2020 Fund Class R	NWFTX	B-	C	A-	Up	2.85	11.30	4.57	22.38	21.27	9.01	208.3	800-848-0920	Y
Nationwide Destination 2020 Fund Class R6	NWFIX	B	C	A-	Up	3.01	11.73	5.44	25.20	25.89	9.1	208.3	800-848-0920	Y
Nationwide Destination 2020 Institutional Service Cls	NWFSX	B-	C	A-	Up	2.96	11.65	5.20	24.24	24.31	9.06	208.3	800-848-0920	Y
Nationwide Destination 2025 Fund Class A	NWHAX	B-	C	A-	Up	2.92	12.44	4.72	26.36	24.89	9.34	298.2	800-848-0920	Y
Nationwide Destination 2025 Fund Class C	NWHCX	B-	C	B+	Up	2.68	12.00	4.02	24.10	21.05	9.23	298.2	800-848-0920	Y
Nationwide Destination 2025 Fund Class R	NWHBX	B-	C	A-	Up	2.87	12.34	4.46	25.32	23.10	9.31	298.2	800-848-0920	Y
Nationwide Destination 2025 Fund Class R6	NWHIX	B-	C	A-	Up	3.14	12.75	5.21	28.27	27.86	9.41	298.2	800-848-0920	Y
Nationwide Destination 2025 Institutional Service Cls	NWHSX	B-	C	A-	Up	2.98	12.56	4.98	27.23	26.17	9.35	298.2	800-848-0920	Y
Nationwide Destination 2030 Fund Class A	NWIAX	B-	C	B+	Up	3.14	13.72	4.90	29.24	27.11	8.94	314.9	800-848-0920	Y
Nationwide Destination 2030 Fund Class C	NWICX	B-	C	B+	Up	2.93	13.47	4.37	27.15	23.65	8.83	314.9	800-848-0920	Y
Nationwide Destination 2030 Fund Class R	NWBIX	B-	C	B+	Up	3.09	13.64	4.75	28.38	25.54	8.89	314.9	800-848-0920	Y
Nationwide Destination 2030 Fund Class R6	NWIIX	B-	C	B+	Up	3.24	14.00	5.48	31.14	30.32	9.01	314.9	800-848-0920	Y
Nationwide Destination 2030 Institutional Service Cls	NWISX	B-	C	B+	Up	3.20	13.83	5.14	30.09	28.63	8.95	314.9	800-848-0920	Y
Nationwide Destination 2035 Fund Class A	NWLAX	B-	C	B+	Up	3.14	14.72	4.83	31.25	28.66	9.64	265.4	800-848-0920	Y
Nationwide Destination 2035 Fund Class C	NWLCX	B-	C	B+	Up	2.97	14.42	4.29	28.86	24.74	9.43	265.4	800-848-0920	Y
Nationwide Destination 2035 Fund Class R	NWLBX	B-	C	B+	Up	3.21	14.68	4.69	30.21	27.02	9.58	265.4	800-848-0920	Y
Nationwide Destination 2035 Fund Class R6	NWLIX	B-	C	B+	Up	3.24	15.01	5.33	33.03	31.65	9.71	265.4	800-848-0920	Y
Nationwide Destination 2035 Institutional Service Cls	NWLSX	B-	C	B+	Up	3.20	14.85	5.10	32.13	30.09	9.65	265.4	800-848-0920	Y
Nationwide Destination 2040 Fund Class A	NWMAX	B-	C	B	Up	3.18	15.63	4.78	33.08	30.69	9.41	222.2	800-848-0920	Y
Nationwide Destination 2040 Fund Class C	NWMCX	B-	C	B	Up	3.19	15.38	4.33	31.15	27.20	9.35	222.2	800-848-0920	Y
Nationwide Destination 2040 Fund Class R	NWMDX	B-	C	B	Up	3.25	15.57	4.63	32.14	29.02	9.36	222.2	800-848-0920	Y
Nationwide Destination 2040 Fund Class R6	NWMHX	B-	C	B	Up	3.39	15.88	5.38	35.24	33.85	9.5	222.2	800-848-0920	Y
Nationwide Destination 2040 Institutional Service Cls	NWMSX	B-	C	B	Up	3.34	15.80	5.14	34.24	32.31	9.47	222.2	800-848-0920	Y
Nationwide Destination 2045 Fund Class A	NWNAX	B-	C	B	Up	3.27	16.06	4.85	35.20	32.31	9.84	174.6	800-848-0920	Y
Nationwide Destination 2045 Fund Class C	NWNCX	B-	C	B	Up	3.19	15.84	4.31	32.77	28.33	9.7	174.6	800-848-0920	Y
Nationwide Destination 2045 Fund Class R	NWNBX	B-	C	B	Up	3.24	15.96	4.53	34.13	30.53	9.75	174.6	800-848-0920	Y
Nationwide Destination 2045 Fund Class R6	NWNIX	B-	C	B	Up	3.48	16.49	5.45	37.28	35.55	9.91	174.6	800-848-0920	Y
Nationwide Destination 2045 Institutional Service Cls	NWNSX	B-	C	B	Up	3.34	16.25	5.13	36.17	33.79	9.82	174.6	800-848-0920	Y
Nationwide Destination 2050 Fund Class A	NWOAX	B-	C	B	Up	3.30	16.39	4.78	35.66	32.90	8.63	146.5	800-848-0920	Y
Nationwide Destination 2050 Fund Class C	NWOCX	B-	C	B	Up	3.24	15.97	4.16	33.54	29.13	8.44	146.5	800-848-0920	Y
Nationwide Destination 2050 Fund Class R	NWOBX	B-	C	B	Up	3.29	16.08	4.46	34.58	30.99	8.5	146.5	800-848-0920	Y
Nationwide Destination 2050 Fund Class R6	NWOIX	B-	C	B	Up	3.42	16.62	5.29	37.62	36.05	8.65	146.5	800-848-0920	Y
Nationwide Destination 2050 Institutional Service Cls	NWOSX	B-	C	B	Up	3.37	16.40	5.04	36.75	34.36	8.62	146.5	800-848-0920	Y
Nationwide Destination 2055 Fund Class A	NTDAX	B-	C	B	Up	3.30	16.47	4.59	36.16	33.22	13.24	81.9	800-848-0920	Y
Nationwide Destination 2055 Fund Class R	NTDTX	B-	C	B	Up	3.33	16.39	4.35	35.25	31.50	13.21	81.9	800-848-0920	Y

Category: Target Date (con't)

Fund Name	Ticker Symbol	RATINGS: Overall Rating	Reward Rating	Risk Rating	Recent Up/ Downgrade	TOTAL RETURNS & PERFORMANCE: 3-Month Total Return	6-Month Total Return	1-Year Total Return	3-Year Total Return	5-Year Total Return	ASSETS: NAV	Total Assets (MIL)	NEW INVESTORS: Telephone	Open to New Investors
Nationwide Destination 2055 Fund Class R6	NTDIX	B-	C	B	Up	3.49	16.84	5.17	38.30	36.53	13.32	81.9	800-848-0920	Y
Nationwide Destination 2055 Institutional Service Cls	NTDSX	B-	C	B	Up	3.43	16.61	4.91	37.23	34.82	13.31	81.9	800-848-0920	Y
Nationwide Destination 2060 Fund Class A	NWWRX	B-	C	B	Up	3.36	16.52	4.67	36.31		10.88	22.5	800-848-0920	Y
Nationwide Destination 2060 Fund Class R	NWWTX	B-	C	B	Up	3.21	16.31	4.36	35.29		10.86	22.5	800-848-0920	Y
Nationwide Destination 2060 Fund Class R6	NWWUX	B-	C	B	Up	3.48	16.76	5.08	38.21		10.9	22.5	800-848-0920	Y
Nationwide Destination 2060 Institutional Service Cls	NWWVX	B-	C	B	Up	3.41	16.75	4.93	37.25		10.9	22.5	800-848-0920	Y
PIMCO RealPath Blend 2020 Fund Administrative Class	PBZDX	B	C+	A	Up	3.10	10.94	6.24	23.40		11.13	48.6	866-746-2602	Y
PIMCO RealPath Blend 2020 Fund Class A	PBZAX	B	C+	A-	Up	3.14	10.92	5.99	22.66		11.13	48.6	866-746-2602	Y
PIMCO RealPath Blend 2020 Fund Institutional Class	PBZNX	B	C+	A	Up	3.16	11.06	6.49	24.32		11.14	48.6	866-746-2602	Y
PIMCO RealPath Blend 2025 Fund Administrative Class	PPZDX	B	C+	A	Up	3.14	12.19	6.19	25.70		11.31	58.4	866-746-2602	Y
PIMCO RealPath Blend 2025 Fund Class A	PPZAX	B	C	A-	Up	3.17	12.16	6.03	24.89		11.31	58.4	866-746-2602	Y
PIMCO RealPath Blend 2025 Fund Institutional Class	PPZRX	B	C+	A	Up	3.20	12.40	6.43	26.71		11.33	58.4	866-746-2602	Y
PIMCO RealPath Blend 2030 Fund Administrative Class	PBPRX	B	C	A-	Up	3.28	13.71	6.49	29.41		11.52	79.9	866-746-2602	Y
PIMCO RealPath Blend 2030 Fund Class A	PBPAX	B-	C	A-	Up	3.22	13.61	6.27	28.54		11.5	79.9	866-746-2602	Y
PIMCO RealPath Blend 2030 Fund Institutional Class	PBPNX	B	C	A-	Up	3.43	13.93	6.83	30.41		11.54	79.9	866-746-2602	Y
PIMCO RealPath Blend 2035 Fund Administrative Class	PDGDX	B-	C	B+	Up	3.38	14.48	6.42	31.57		11.57	65.7	866-746-2602	Y
PIMCO RealPath Blend 2035 Fund Class A	PDGAX	B-	C	B+	Up	3.30	14.28	6.15	30.55		11.61	65.7	866-746-2602	Y
PIMCO RealPath Blend 2035 Fund Institutional Class	PDGZX	B-	C	B+	Up	3.35	14.59	6.67	32.53		11.58	65.7	866-746-2602	Y
PIMCO RealPath Blend 2040 Fund Administrative Class	PVPRX	B-	C	B+	Up	3.31	15.07	6.20	32.60		11.69	84.8	866-746-2602	Y
PIMCO RealPath Blend 2040 Fund Class A	PVPAX	B-	C	B+	Up	3.27	14.87	5.98	31.57		11.67	84.8	866-746-2602	Y
PIMCO RealPath Blend 2040 Fund Institutional Class	PVPNX	B-	C	B+	Up	3.37	15.17	6.44	33.65		11.71	84.8	866-746-2602	Y
PIMCO RealPath Blend 2045 Fund Administrative Class	PVQDX	B-	C	B+	Up	3.28	15.55	6.21	33.59		11.65	84.7	866-746-2602	Y
PIMCO RealPath Blend 2045 Fund Class A	PVQAX	B-	C	B+	Up	3.22	15.44	5.87	32.49		11.64	84.7	866-746-2602	Y
PIMCO RealPath Blend 2045 Fund Institutional Class	PVQNX	B-	C	B+	Up	3.33	15.65	6.44	34.46		11.67	84.7	866-746-2602	Y
PIMCO RealPath Blend 2050 Fund Administrative Class	PPQDX	B-	C	B+	Up	3.27	15.99	6.21	34.08		11.71	105.8	866-746-2602	Y
PIMCO RealPath Blend 2050 Fund Class A	PPQAX	B-	C	B+	Up	3.22	15.81	5.99	33.14		11.67	105.8	866-746-2602	Y
PIMCO RealPath Blend 2050 Fund Institutional Class	PPQZX	B-	C	B+	Up	3.41	16.18	6.53	35.21		11.74	105.8	866-746-2602	Y
PIMCO RealPath Blend 2055 Fund Administrative Class	PRQDX	B-	C	B+	Up	3.18	15.74	6.01	33.68		11.78	35.4	866-746-2602	Y
PIMCO RealPath Blend 2055 Fund Class A	PRQAX	B-	C	B+	Up	3.21	15.68	5.86	32.65		11.73	35.4	866-746-2602	Y
PIMCO RealPath Blend 2055 Fund Institutional Class	PRQZX	B-	C	B+	Up	3.32	15.95	6.40	34.81		11.79	35.4	866-746-2602	Y
PIMCO RealPath Blend Income Fund Administrative Class	PBRDX	B	C+	A	Up	3.10	10.73	6.43	22.54		11.28	40.2	866-746-2602	Y
PIMCO RealPath Blend Income Fund Class A	PBRAX	B	C+	A-	Up	3.16	10.67	6.25	21.67		11.24	40.2	866-746-2602	Y
PIMCO RealPath Blend Income Fund Institutional Class	PBRNX	B	C+	A	Up	3.26	10.86	6.69	23.42		11.28	40.2	866-746-2602	Y
Principal LifeTime 2010 Fund Class A	PENAX	B	C+	A-	Up	3.03	9.97	5.65	19.09	20.39	13.23	764.1	800-787-1621	Y
Principal LifeTime 2010 Fund Class J	PTAJX	B	C+	A-	Up	3.07	10.07	5.88	19.73	21.40	13.08	764.1	800-787-1621	Y
Principal LifeTime 2010 Fund Institutional Class	PTTIX	B	C+	A-	Up	3.13	10.23	6.04	20.36	22.62	13.14	764.1	800-787-1621	Y
Principal LifeTime 2010 Fund R-1 Class	PVASX	B-	C	A-	Up	2.90	9.72	5.12	17.21	17.32	13.11	764.1	800-787-1621	Y
Principal LifeTime 2010 Fund R-2 Class	PTANX	B	C	A-	Up	2.90	9.77	5.26	17.73	18.19	13.11	764.1	800-787-1621	Y
Principal LifeTime 2010 Fund R-3 Class	PTAMX	B	C+	A-	Up	3.00	9.89	5.52	18.44	19.26	13.04	764.1	800-787-1621	Y
Principal LifeTime 2010 Fund R-4 Class	PTASX	B	C+	A-	Up	3.07	9.97	5.69	19.07	20.39	13.07	764.1	800-787-1621	Y
Principal LifeTime 2010 Fund R-5 Class	PTAPX	B	C+	A-	Up	3.07	10.05	5.77	19.44	21.01	13.08	764.1	800-787-1621	Y
Principal LifeTime 2015 Fund Institutional Class	LTINX	B	C+	A-	Up	3.39	11.42	6.13	23.63	25.24	10.05	416.8	800-787-1621	Y
Principal LifeTime 2015 Fund R-1 Class	LTSGX	B-	C	A-	Up	3.05	10.86	5.23	20.31	19.85	9.79	416.8	800-787-1621	Y
Principal LifeTime 2015 Fund R-2 Class	LTASX	B	C	A-	Up	3.13	11.02	5.42	20.95	20.69	9.87	416.8	800-787-1621	Y
Principal LifeTime 2015 Fund R-3 Class	LTAPX	B	C	A-	Up	3.15	11.06	5.56	21.45	21.82	9.81	416.8	800-787-1621	Y
Principal LifeTime 2015 Fund R-4 Class	LTSLX	B	C	A-	Up	3.23	11.17	5.81	22.23	22.97	9.9	416.8	800-787-1621	Y
Principal LifeTime 2015 Fund R-5 Class	LTPFX	B	C	A-	Up	3.33	11.27	5.92	22.72	23.68	9.91	416.8	800-787-1621	Y
Principal LifeTime 2020 Fund Class A	PTBAX	B-	C	A-	Up	3.44	12.71	5.73	25.07	25.72	14.13	4,126	800-787-1621	Y
Principal LifeTime 2020 Fund Class J	PLFJX	B-	C	A-	Up	3.56	12.81	5.99	25.84	26.85	13.96	4,126	800-787-1621	Y
Principal LifeTime 2020 Fund Institutional Class	PLWIX	B	C	A-	Up	3.61	12.92	6.14	26.50	28.11	14.04	4,126	800-787-1621	Y
Principal LifeTime 2020 Fund R-1 Class	PWASX	B-	C	A-	Up	3.33	12.41	5.20	23.21	22.61	13.95	4,126	800-787-1621	Y
Principal LifeTime 2020 Fund R-2 Class	PTBNX	B-	C	A-	Up	3.40	12.56	5.41	23.73	23.45	13.96	4,126	800-787-1621	Y

Category: Target Date (con't)

		RATINGS				TOTAL RETURNS & PERFORMANCE					ASSETS		NEW INVESTORS	
Fund Name	Ticker Symbol	Overall Rating	Reward Rating	Risk Rating	Recent Up/ Downgrade	3-Month Total Return	6-Month Total Return	1-Year Total Return	3-Year Total Return	5-Year Total Return	NAV	Total Assets (MIL)	Telephone	Open to New Investors
Principal LifeTime 2020 Fund R-3 Class	PTBMX	B-	C	A-	Up	3.42	12.63	5.54	24.34	24.57	13.9	4,126	800-787-1621	Y
Principal LifeTime 2020 Fund R-4 Class	PTBSX	B-	C	A-	Up	3.49	12.69	5.78	25.07	25.72	13.93	4,126	800-787-1621	Y
Principal LifeTime 2020 Fund R-5 Class	PTBPX	B-	C	A-	Up	3.48	12.77	5.87	25.40	26.43	13.96	4,126	800-787-1621	Y
Principal LifeTime 2025 Fund Institutional Class	LTSTX	B-	C	B+	Up	3.79	14.22	6.39	29.50	30.96	11.48	1,573	800-787-1621	Y
Principal LifeTime 2025 Fund R-1 Class	LTSNX	B-	C	B+	Up	3.50	13.75	5.45	26.22	25.32	11.21	1,573	800-787-1621	Y
Principal LifeTime 2025 Fund R-2 Class	LTADX	B-	C	B+	Up	3.59	13.83	5.66	26.73	26.26	11.25	1,573	800-787-1621	Y
Principal LifeTime 2025 Fund R-3 Class	LTVPX	B-	C	B+	Up	3.59	13.82	5.84	27.34	27.32	11.24	1,573	800-787-1621	Y
Principal LifeTime 2025 Fund R-4 Class	LTEEX	B-	C	B+	Up	3.64	14.00	5.99	28.08	28.55	11.36	1,573	800-787-1621	Y
Principal LifeTime 2025 Fund R-5 Class	LTPDX	B-	C	B+	Up	3.73	14.12	6.13	28.63	29.29	11.4	1,573	800-787-1621	Y
Principal LifeTime 2030 Fund Class A	PTCAX	B-	C	B+	Up	3.71	15.05	5.63	30.41	30.30	14.5	5,552	800-787-1621	Y
Principal LifeTime 2030 Fund Class J	PLTJX	B-	C	B+	Up	3.81	15.24	5.84	31.21	31.42	14.42	5,552	800-787-1621	Y
Principal LifeTime 2030 Fund Institutional Class	PMTIX	B-	C	B+	Up	3.80	15.32	6.01	31.79	32.74	14.46	5,552	800-787-1621	Y
Principal LifeTime 2030 Fund R-1 Class	PXASX	B-	C	B+	Up	3.60	14.86	5.11	28.44	27.04	14.36	5,552	800-787-1621	Y
Principal LifeTime 2030 Fund R-2 Class	PTCNX	B-	C	B+	Up	3.59	14.82	5.19	28.95	27.86	14.42	5,552	800-787-1621	Y
Principal LifeTime 2030 Fund R-3 Class	PTCMX	B-	C	B+	Up	3.74	15.04	5.47	29.67	29.11	14.4	5,552	800-787-1621	Y
Principal LifeTime 2030 Fund R-4 Class	PTCSX	B-	C	B+	Up	3.75	15.10	5.62	30.36	30.25	14.93	5,552	800-787-1621	Y
Principal LifeTime 2030 Fund R-5 Class	PTCPX	B-	C	B+	Up	3.73	15.11	5.72	30.76	31.01	14.44	5,552	800-787-1621	Y
Principal LifeTime 2035 Fund Institutional Class	LTIUX	B-	C	B+	Up	3.83	16.06	6.17	34.49	34.75	12.18	1,256	800-787-1621	Y
Principal LifeTime 2035 Fund R-1 Class	LTANX	B-	C	B+	Up	3.64	15.54	5.22	31.12	29.07	11.94	1,256	800-787-1621	Y
Principal LifeTime 2035 Fund R-2 Class	LTVIX	B-	C	B+	Up	3.64	15.65	5.40	31.71	29.91	11.93	1,256	800-787-1621	Y
Principal LifeTime 2035 Fund R-3 Class	LTAOX	B-	C	B+	Up	3.63	15.70	5.59	32.34	31.04	11.98	1,256	800-787-1621	Y
Principal LifeTime 2035 Fund R-4 Class	LTSEX	B-	C	B+	Up	3.78	15.91	5.76	33.10	32.37	12.08	1,256	800-787-1621	Y
Principal LifeTime 2035 Fund R-5 Class	LTPEX	B-	C	B+	Up	3.68	15.84	5.83	33.46	33.04	12.11	1,256	800-787-1621	Y
Principal LifeTime 2040 Fund Class A	PTDAX	B-	C	B	Up	3.79	16.67	5.73	34.90	33.70	15.06	3,821	800-787-1621	Y
Principal LifeTime 2040 Fund Class J	PTDJX	B-	C	B	Up	3.81	16.72	5.88	35.59	34.62	15.22	3,821	800-787-1621	Y
Principal LifeTime 2040 Fund Institutional Class	PTDIX	B-	C	B	Up	3.85	16.87	6.04	36.28	36.14	15.36	3,821	800-787-1621	Y
Principal LifeTime 2040 Fund R-1 Class	PYASX	B-	C	B	Up	3.68	16.39	5.18	32.81	30.26	15.2	3,821	800-787-1621	Y
Principal LifeTime 2040 Fund R-2 Class	PTDNX	B-	C	B	Up	3.74	16.47	5.33	33.29	31.13	15.24	3,821	800-787-1621	Y
Principal LifeTime 2040 Fund R-3 Class	PTDMX	B-	C	B	Up	3.76	16.50	5.48	34.04	32.31	15.15	3,821	800-787-1621	Y
Principal LifeTime 2040 Fund R-4 Class	PTDSX	B-	C	B	Up	3.83	16.65	5.71	34.85	33.64	15.18	3,821	800-787-1621	Y
Principal LifeTime 2040 Fund R-5 Class	PTDPX	B-	C	B	Up	3.80	16.71	5.77	35.28	34.36	15.28	3,821	800-787-1621	Y
Principal LifeTime 2045 Fund Institutional Class	LTRIX	B-	C	B	Up	3.90	17.39	5.93	37.53	37.05	12.78	910.1	800-787-1621	Y
Principal LifeTime 2045 Fund R-1 Class	LTRGX	B-	C	B	Up	3.68	16.85	4.99	33.95	31.12	12.38	910.1	800-787-1621	Y
Principal LifeTime 2045 Fund R-2 Class	LTRSX	B-	C	B	Up	3.68	17.03	5.15	34.47	32.06	12.38	910.1	800-787-1621	Y
Principal LifeTime 2045 Fund R-3 Class	LTRVX	B-	C	B	Up	3.83	17.15	5.42	35.27	33.28	12.46	910.1	800-787-1621	Y
Principal LifeTime 2045 Fund R-4 Class	LTRLX	B-	C	B	Up	3.79	17.18	5.55	36.01	34.47	12.57	910.1	800-787-1621	Y
Principal LifeTime 2045 Fund R-5 Class	LTRDX	B-	C	B	Up	3.87	17.35	5.73	36.57	35.30	12.6	910.1	800-787-1621	Y
Principal LifeTime 2050 Fund Class A	PPEAX	B-	C	B	Up	3.88	17.71	5.50	37.16	35.43	15.5	2,274	800-787-1621	Y
Principal LifeTime 2050 Fund Class J	PFLJX	B-	C	B	Up	3.95	17.84	5.60	37.72	35.83	14.97	2,274	800-787-1621	Y
Principal LifeTime 2050 Fund Institutional Class	PPLIX	B-	C	B	Up	3.97	17.96	5.90	38.76	37.97	15.43	2,274	800-787-1621	Y
Principal LifeTime 2050 Fund R-3 Class	PTERX	B-	C	B	Up	3.88	17.64	5.30	36.40	34.14	15.23	2,274	800-787-1621	Y
Principal LifeTime 2050 Fund R-4 Class	PTESX	B-	C	B	Up	3.86	17.65	5.46	37.13	35.29	15.32	2,274	800-787-1621	Y
Principal LifeTime 2050 Fund R-5 Class	PTEFX	B-	C	B	Up	3.92	17.72	5.56	37.59	36.13	15.36	2,274	800-787-1621	Y
Principal LifeTime 2055 Fund Institutional Class	LTFIX	B-	C	B	Up	3.96	18.27	5.74	39.34	38.49	13.64	458.4	800-787-1621	Y
Principal LifeTime Hybrid 2015 Fund Class J	PHJMX	B	C	A-	Up	2.85	10.36	5.14	20.45		11.17	101.1	800-787-1621	Y
Principal LifeTime Hybrid 2015 Fund Class R-3	PHTCX	B	C	A-	Up	2.85	10.29	5.06	20.17		11.17	101.1	800-787-1621	Y
Principal LifeTime Hybrid 2015 Fund Class R-5	PHTRX	B	C	A-	Up	2.94	10.46	5.35	21.11		11.18	101.1	800-787-1621	Y
Principal LifeTime Hybrid 2015 Fund Institutional Class	PHTMX	B	C	A-	Up	2.94	10.46	5.34	21.11		11.19	101.1	800-787-1621	Y
Principal LifeTime Hybrid 2015 Fund R-6	PLRRX	B	C	A-	Up	2.93	10.45	5.44	21.20		11.21	101.1	800-787-1621	Y
Principal LifeTime Hybrid 2020 Fund Class J	PHJTX	B-	C	A-	Up	3.00	11.52	5.09	23.26		11.3	315.9	800-787-1621	Y
Principal LifeTime Hybrid 2020 Fund Class R-3	PHWIX	B-	C	A-	Up	2.90	11.48	4.93	22.89		11.32	315.9	800-787-1621	Y
Principal LifeTime Hybrid 2020 Fund Class R-5	PHTIX	B-	C	A-	Up	3.00	11.65	5.22	23.85		11.33	315.9	800-787-1621	Y

Category: Target Date (con't)

		RATINGS				TOTAL RETURNS & PERFORMANCE					ASSETS		NEW INVESTORS	
Fund Name	Ticker Symbol	Overall Rating	Reward Rating	Risk Rating	Recent Up/ Downgrade	3-Month Total Return	6-Month Total Return	1-Year Total Return	3-Year Total Return	5-Year Total Return	NAV	Total Assets (MIL)	Telephone	Open to New Investors
Principal LifeTime Hybrid 2020 Fund Institutional Class	PHTTX	B-	C	A-	Up	3.09	11.75	5.31	23.96		11.34	315.9	800-787-1621	Y
Principal LifeTime Hybrid 2020 Fund R-6	PLTTX	B-	C	A-	Up	3.09	11.69	5.36	24.17		11.34	315.9	800-787-1621	Y
Principal LifeTime Hybrid 2025 Fund Class J	PHJQX	B-	C	B+	Up	3.20	12.76	4.80	25.84		11.58	220.4	800-787-1621	Y
Principal LifeTime Hybrid 2025 Fund Class R-3	PHTPX	B-	C	B+	Up	3.11	12.63	4.75	25.49		11.59	220.4	800-787-1621	Y
Principal LifeTime Hybrid 2025 Fund Class R-5	PHTOX	B-	C	B+	Up	3.20	12.80	5.04	26.46		11.6	220.4	800-787-1621	Y
Principal LifeTime Hybrid 2025 Fund Institutional Class	PHTQX	B-	C	B+	Up	3.29	12.90	5.13	26.57		11.61	220.4	800-787-1621	Y
Principal LifeTime Hybrid 2025 Fund R-6	PLFTX	B-	C	B+	Up	3.28	12.94	5.17	26.61		11.62	220.4	800-787-1621	Y
Principal LifeTime Hybrid 2030 Fund Class J	PHJNX	B-	C	B+	Up	3.35	13.85	4.71	28.54		11.72	266.4	800-787-1621	Y
Principal LifeTime Hybrid 2030 Fund Class R-3	PHTLX	B-	C	B+	Up	3.25	13.71	4.66	28.17		11.73	266.4	800-787-1621	Y
Principal LifeTime Hybrid 2030 Fund Class R-5	PHTKX	B-	C	B+	Up	3.34	13.88	4.94	29.16		11.75	266.4	800-787-1621	Y
Principal LifeTime Hybrid 2030 Fund Institutional Class	PHTNX	B-	C	B+	Up	3.42	13.98	5.03	29.27		11.76	266.4	800-787-1621	Y
Principal LifeTime Hybrid 2030 Fund R-6	PLZTX	B-	C	B+	Up	3.34	14.04	4.99	29.24		11.75	266.4	800-787-1621	Y
Principal LifeTime Hybrid 2035 Fund Class J	PHJJX	B-	C	B+	Up	3.36	14.91	4.67	30.94		11.97	160.9	800-787-1621	Y
Principal LifeTime Hybrid 2035 Fund Class R-3	PHTHX	B-	C	B+	Up	3.36	14.86	4.69	30.65		11.99	160.9	800-787-1621	Y
Principal LifeTime Hybrid 2035 Fund Class R-5	PHTGX	B-	C	B+	Up	3.35	14.93	4.88	31.55		12	160.9	800-787-1621	Y
Principal LifeTime Hybrid 2035 Fund Institutional Class	PHTJX	B-	C	B+	Up	3.44	15.02	4.97	31.66		12.01	160.9	800-787-1621	Y
Principal LifeTime Hybrid 2035 Fund R-6	PLRTX	B-	C	B+	Up	3.52	15.15	5.09	31.92		12.03	160.9	800-787-1621	Y
Principal LifeTime Hybrid 2040 Fund Class J	PHJEX	B-	C	B	Up	3.52	15.68	4.50	32.58		12.03	185.6	800-787-1621	Y
Principal LifeTime Hybrid 2040 Fund Class R-3	PLHBX	B-	C	B	Up	3.43	15.64	4.45	32.42		12.05	185.6	800-787-1621	Y
Principal LifeTime Hybrid 2040 Fund Class R-5	PHTZX	B-	C	B	Up	3.43	15.71	4.64	33.33		12.06	185.6	800-787-1621	Y
Principal LifeTime Hybrid 2040 Fund Institutional Class	PLTQX	B-	C	B	Up	3.51	15.81	4.73	33.43		12.07	185.6	800-787-1621	Y
Principal LifeTime Hybrid 2040 Fund R-6	PLMTX	B-	C	B	Up	3.51	15.82	4.85	33.56		12.09	185.6	800-787-1621	Y
Principal LifeTime Hybrid 2045 Fund Class J	PHJYX	B-	C	B	Up	3.49	16.18	4.33	33.92		12.14	99.3	800-787-1621	Y
Principal LifeTime Hybrid 2045 Fund Class R-3	PHTWX	B-	C	B	Up	3.40	16.06	4.21	33.55		12.16	99.3	800-787-1621	Y
Principal LifeTime Hybrid 2045 Fund Class R-5	PHTVX	B-	C	B	Up	3.48	16.22	4.49	34.58		12.17	99.3	800-787-1621	Y
Principal LifeTime Hybrid 2045 Fund Institutional Class	PHTYX	B-	C	B	Up	3.57	16.32	4.57	34.69		12.18	99.3	800-787-1621	Y
Principal LifeTime Hybrid 2045 Fund R-6	PLNTX	B-	C	B	Up	3.56	16.32	4.58	34.81		12.19	99.3	800-787-1621	Y
Principal LifeTime Hybrid Income Fund Class J	PHJFX	B-	C	B+		2.60	8.12	5.35	13.21		10.64	54.8	800-787-1621	Y
Principal LifeTime Hybrid Income Fund Class R-3	PHTEX	B-	C	B+		2.60	8.12	5.44	13.04		10.65	54.8	800-787-1621	Y
Principal LifeTime Hybrid Income Fund Class R-5	PHTDX	B-	C	A-		2.59	8.19	5.63	13.81		10.66	54.8	800-787-1621	Y
Principal LifeTime Hybrid Income Fund Institutional Class	PHTFX	B-	C	A-		2.69	8.29	5.73	13.92		10.67	54.8	800-787-1621	Y
Principal LifeTime Hybrid Income Fund R-6	PLTYX	B-	C	A-		2.69	8.28	5.73	13.90		10.68	54.8	800-787-1621	Y
Principal LifeTime Strategic Income Fund Class A	PALTX	B-	C	A-		2.95	8.96	5.80	14.91	16.99	12.2	426.8	800-787-1621	Y
Principal LifeTime Strategic Income Fund Class J	PLSJX	B	C+	A-	Up	2.99	8.98	5.97	15.44	17.71	12.03	426.8	800-787-1621	Y
Principal LifeTime Strategic Income Institutional Cls	PLSIX	B	C+	A-	Up	3.06	9.17	6.25	16.19	19.20	12.1	426.8	800-787-1621	Y
Principal LifeTime Strategic Income Fund R-1 Class	PLAIX	B-	C	B+	Up	2.88	8.66	5.32	13.17	14.08	12.12	426.8	800-787-1621	Y
Principal LifeTime Strategic Income Fund R-2 Class	PLSNX	B-	C	B+	Up	2.88	8.78	5.43	13.66	14.87	12.12	426.8	800-787-1621	Y
Principal LifeTime Strategic Income Fund R-3 Class	PLSMX	B-	C	B+	Up	3.00	8.86	5.66	14.28	15.92	11.99	426.8	800-787-1621	Y
Principal LifeTime Strategic Income Fund R-4 Class	PLSSX	B-	C	A-		2.91	8.95	5.84	14.80	16.93	12.01	426.8	800-787-1621	Y
Principal LifeTime Strategic Income Fund R-5 Class	PLSPX	B	C+	A-	Up	2.98	8.97	5.97	15.32	17.68	12.09	426.8	800-787-1621	Y
Putnam Retirement Income Fund Lifestyle 1 Class A	PRMAX	B-	C	B+	Up	2.18	7.19	3.03	11.84	13.06	17.51	114.2	617-292-1000	Y
Putnam Retirement Income Fund Lifestyle 1 Class M	PRMMX	B-	C	B+	Up	2.07	7.04	2.76	11.04	11.61	17.56	114.2	617-292-1000	Y
Putnam Retirement Income Fund Lifestyle 1 Class R	PRMKX	B-	C	B+	Up	2.12	7.06	2.76	11.01	11.58	17.5	114.2	617-292-1000	Y
Putnam Retirement Income Fund Lifestyle 1 Class Y	PRMYX	B-	C	A-	Up	2.24	7.36	3.33	12.76	14.50	17.58	114.2	617-292-1000	Y
Putnam RetirementReady 2020 Fund Class A	PRRMX	B-	C	B+	Up	2.24	7.78	3.25	14.60	16.64	19.1	208.5	617-292-1000	Y
Putnam RetirementReady 2020 Fund Class M		B-	C	B+	Up	2.11	7.49	2.73	12.86	13.73	18.82	208.5	617-292-1000	Y
Putnam RetirementReady 2020 Fund Class R		B-	C	B+	Up	2.16	7.58	2.94	13.77	15.16	18.37	208.5	617-292-1000	Y
Putnam RetirementReady 2020 Fund Class R6	PMRGX	B-	C	A-	Up	2.31	7.92	3.60	15.70	18.37	21.68	208.5	617-292-1000	Y
Putnam RetirementReady 2020 Fund Class Y	PRRNX	B-	C	A-	Up	2.26	7.84	3.47	15.43	18.08	21.64	208.5	617-292-1000	Y
Putnam RetirementReady 2025 Fund Class A	PRROX	B-	C	B+	Up	2.34	9.09	3.37	18.43	20.83	21.83	147.8	617-292-1000	Y
Putnam RetirementReady 2025 Fund Class B		B-	C	B+	Up	2.16	8.70	2.62	15.83	16.40	20.25	147.8	617-292-1000	Y
Putnam RetirementReady 2025 Fund Class C		B-	C	B+	Up	2.12	8.71	2.61	15.78	16.40	20.14	147.8	617-292-1000	Y

Category: Target Date (con't)

		RATINGS				TOTAL RETURNS & PERFORMANCE					ASSETS		NEW INVESTORS	
Fund Name	Ticker Symbol	Overall Rating	Reward Rating	Risk Rating	Recent Up/ Downgrade	3-Month Total Return	6-Month Total Return	1-Year Total Return	3-Year Total Return	5-Year Total Return	NAV	Total Assets (MIL)	Telephone	Open to New Investors
Putnam RetirementReady 2025 Fund Class M		B-	C	B+	Up	2.23	8.85	2.87	16.67	17.90	20.61	147.8	617-292-1000	Y
Putnam RetirementReady 2025 Fund Class R		B-	C	B+	Up	2.30	9.02	3.11	17.54	19.35	20.44	147.8	617-292-1000	Y
Putnam RetirementReady 2025 Fund Class R6	PRMFX	B-	C	A-	Up	2.41	9.27	3.73	19.65	22.70	22.02	147.8	617-292-1000	Y
Putnam RetirementReady 2025 Fund Class Y	PRRPX	B-	C	A-	Up	2.42	9.26	3.66	19.33	22.37	21.98	147.8	617-292-1000	Y
Putnam RetirementReady 2030 Fund Class A	PRRQX	B-	C	B+	Up	2.44	10.64	3.43	23.00	25.30	21.8	213.9	617-292-1000	Y
Putnam RetirementReady 2030 Fund Class B		B-	C	B+	Up	2.27	10.27	2.70	20.35	20.77	20.64	213.9	617-292-1000	Y
Putnam RetirementReady 2030 Fund Class C		B-	C	B+	Up	2.24	10.26	2.71	20.32	20.76	20.54	213.9	617-292-1000	Y
Putnam RetirementReady 2030 Fund Class M		B-	C	B+	Up	2.32	10.40	2.95	21.23	22.25	21.12	213.9	617-292-1000	Y
Putnam RetirementReady 2030 Fund Class R		B-	C	B+	Up	2.37	10.55	3.21	22.17	23.83	20.66	213.9	617-292-1000	Y
Putnam RetirementReady 2030 Fund Class R6	PREZX	B-	C	A-	Up	2.54	10.86	3.84	24.27	27.26	25.43	213.9	617-292-1000	Y
Putnam RetirementReady 2030 Fund Class Y	PRRTX	B-	C	A-	Up	2.50	10.80	3.73	23.94	26.92	25.39	213.9	617-292-1000	Y
Putnam RetirementReady 2035 Fund Class A	PRRWX	B-	C	B+	Up	2.46	12.08	3.21	27.06	29.07	22.04	137.8	617-292-1000	Y
Putnam RetirementReady 2035 Fund Class B		B-	C	B+	Up	2.29	11.64	2.43	24.25	24.28	20.06	137.8	617-292-1000	Y
Putnam RetirementReady 2035 Fund Class C		B-	C	B+	Up	2.25	11.64	2.43	24.22	24.25	19.91	137.8	617-292-1000	Y
Putnam RetirementReady 2035 Fund Class M		B-	C	B+	Up	2.37	11.78	2.68	25.18	25.87	21.16	137.8	617-292-1000	Y
Putnam RetirementReady 2035 Fund Class R		B-	C	B+	Up	2.41	11.91	2.94	26.12	27.45	21.18	137.8	617-292-1000	Y
Putnam RetirementReady 2035 Fund Class R6	PREGX	B-	C	B+	Up	2.60	12.27	3.59	28.43	31.08	26.36	137.8	617-292-1000	Y
Putnam RetirementReady 2035 Fund Class Y	PRRYX	B-	C	B+	Up	2.53	12.18	3.45	27.99	30.63	26.31	137.8	617-292-1000	Y
Putnam RetirementReady 2040 Fund Class A	PRRZX	B-	C	B+	Up	2.53	13.29	3.06	30.44	32.08	21.88	163.9	617-292-1000	Y
Putnam RetirementReady 2040 Fund Class B		B-	C	B+	Up	2.31	12.87	2.32	27.52	27.24	19.89	163.9	617-292-1000	Y
Putnam RetirementReady 2040 Fund Class C		B-	C	B+	Up	2.35	12.90	2.35	27.60	27.24	19.54	163.9	617-292-1000	Y
Putnam RetirementReady 2040 Fund Class M		B-	C	B+	Up	2.42	13.06	2.57	28.54	28.85	20.25	163.9	617-292-1000	Y
Putnam RetirementReady 2040 Fund Class R		B-	C	B+	Up	2.50	13.22	2.84	29.51	30.48	22.94	163.9	617-292-1000	Y
Putnam RetirementReady 2040 Fund Class R6	PREHX	B-	C	B+	Up	2.60	13.50	3.40	31.79	34.10	26.41	163.9	617-292-1000	Y
Putnam RetirementReady 2040 Fund Class Y	PRZZX	B-	C	B+	Up	2.60	13.46	3.34	31.48	33.78	26.39	163.9	617-292-1000	Y
Putnam RetirementReady 2045 Fund Class A	PRVLX	B-	C	B	Up	2.59	14.08	3.04	32.71	34.06	19.79	75.1	617-292-1000	Y
Putnam RetirementReady 2045 Fund Class B		B-	C	B	Up	2.43	13.68	2.31	29.85	29.16	17.67	75.1	617-292-1000	Y
Putnam RetirementReady 2045 Fund Class C		B-	C	B	Up	2.43	13.65	2.30	29.82	29.10	17.65	75.1	617-292-1000	Y
Putnam RetirementReady 2045 Fund Class M		B-	C	B	Up	2.46	13.76	2.52	30.72	30.76	19.16	75.1	617-292-1000	Y
Putnam RetirementReady 2045 Fund Class R		B-	C	B	Up	2.54	13.91	2.79	31.77	32.41	20.53	75.1	617-292-1000	Y
Putnam RetirementReady 2045 Fund Class R6	PREKX	B-	C	B	Up	2.29	13.80	2.99	33.62	35.64	24.58	75.1	617-292-1000	Y
Putnam RetirementReady 2045 Fund Class Y	PRVYX	B-	C	B	Up	2.67	14.20	3.29	33.72	35.74	24.53	75.1	617-292-1000	Y
Putnam RetirementReady 2050 Fund Class A	PRRJX	B-	C	B	Up	2.64	14.53	3.17	33.96	35.00	17.87	68.9	617-292-1000	Y
Putnam RetirementReady 2050 Fund Class M		B-	C	B	Up	2.49	14.23	2.65	31.98	31.65	18.04	68.9	617-292-1000	Y
Putnam RetirementReady 2050 Fund Class R	PRRKX	B-	C	B	Up	2.55	14.39	2.91	33.04	33.34	17.63	68.9	617-292-1000	Y
Putnam RetirementReady 2050 Fund Class R6	PREUX	B-	C	B	Up	2.27	14.24	3.07	34.78	36.52	18.03	68.9	617-292-1000	Y
Putnam RetirementReady 2050 Fund Class Y	PRRUX	B-	C	B	Up	2.67	14.65	3.41	34.94	36.68	18.04	68.9	617-292-1000	Y
Putnam RetirementReady 2055 Fund Class A	PRRFX	B-	C	B	Up	2.71	14.79	3.22	34.71	35.54	10.96	25.5	617-292-1000	Y
Putnam RetirementReady 2055 Fund Class R6	PREVX	B-	C	B	Up	2.31	14.51	3.19	35.73	37.27	11.09	25.5	617-292-1000	Y
Putnam RetirementReady 2055 Fund Class Y	PRTLX	B-	C	B	Up	2.69	14.86	3.39	35.74	37.28	11.06	25.5	617-292-1000	Y
Putnam RetirementReady 2060 Fund Class R6	PEFGX	B-	C	B	Up	2.23	14.51	2.99	35.72		11.03	2.2	617-292-1000	Y
Putnam RetirementReady 2060 Fund Class Y	PRTYX	B-	C	B	Up	2.80	15.05	3.46	36.12		11.01	2.2	617-292-1000	Y
Schwab Target 2010 Fund	SWBRX	B	C+	A-	Up	2.95	9.95	5.87	18.91	23.47	13.26	52.5	877-824-5615	Y
Schwab Target 2015 Fund	SWGRX	B	C+	A-	Up	3.05	10.38	5.79	19.72	24.01	11.8	82.6	877-824-5615	Y
Schwab Target 2020 Fund	SWCRX	B	C	A-	Up	3.06	11.08	5.47	23.61	26.81	14.13	557.1	877-824-5615	Y
Schwab Target 2025 Fund	SWHRX	B-	C	A-	Up	3.22	12.74	5.10	27.67	30.17	14.42	564.4	877-824-5615	Y
Schwab Target 2030 Fund	SWDRX	B-	C	B+	Up	3.20	13.93	4.57	30.52	32.46	15.45	995.3	877-824-5615	Y
Schwab Target 2035 Fund	SWIRX	B-	C	B+	Up	3.20	14.78	4.07	32.92	34.09	15.14	477.0	877-824-5615	Y
Schwab Target 2040 Fund	SWERX	B-	C	B	Up	3.23	15.62	3.60	35.01	35.65	16.28	1,020	877-824-5615	Y
Schwab Target 2045 Fund	SWMRX	B-	C	B	Up	3.18	16.12	3.33	36.24	36.41	13.61	157.4	877-824-5615	Y
State Street Target Retirement 2015 Fund Class I	SSBFX	B	C+	A-		2.71	10.01	6.62	20.58		10.98	278.9	617-664-7338	Y
State Street Target Retirement 2015 Fund Class K	SSBHX	B	C+	A		2.80	10.01	6.65	20.65		10.98	278.9	617-664-7338	Y

Category: Target Date (con't)

Fund Name	Ticker Symbol	RATINGS: Overall Rating	RATINGS: Reward Rating	RATINGS: Risk Rating	RATINGS: Recent Up/ Downgrade	TOTAL RETURNS & PERFORMANCE: 3-Month Total Return	6-Month Total Return	1-Year Total Return	3-Year Total Return	5-Year Total Return	ASSETS: NAV	Total Assets (MIL)	NEW INVESTORS: Telephone	Open to New Investors
State Street Target Retirement 2020 Fund Class I	SSBNX	B	C+	A		3.05	12.01	7.00	25.50		11.47	976.0	617-664-7338	Y
State Street Target Retirement 2020 Fund Class K	SSBOX	B	C+	A		3.14	12.00	7.11	25.68		11.48	976.0	617-664-7338	Y
State Street Target Retirement 2025 Fund Class I	SSBRX	B	C+	A-	Up	3.46	13.93	7.26	30.53		11.94	1,228	617-664-7338	Y
State Street Target Retirement 2025 Fund Class K	SSBSX	B	C+	A-	Up	3.55	13.90	7.26	30.66		11.96	1,228	617-664-7338	Y
State Street Target Retirement 2030 Fund Class I	SSBWX	B-	C	B+		3.74	14.98	7.20	33.16		12.2	1,199	617-664-7338	Y
State Street Target Retirement 2030 Fund Class K	SSBYX	B-	C	B+	Up	3.73	14.95	7.28	33.33		12.22	1,199	617-664-7338	Y
State Street Target Retirement 2035 Fund Class I	SSCJX	B-	C	B+	Up	3.75	15.64	6.91	35.39		12.42	997.0	617-664-7338	Y
State Street Target Retirement 2035 Fund Class K	SSCKX	B-	C	B+	Up	3.75	15.70	6.99	35.59		12.45	997.0	617-664-7338	Y
State Street Target Retirement 2040 Fund Class I	SSCNX	B-	C	B+	Up	3.82	16.32	6.68	37.32		12.47	814.6	617-664-7338	Y
State Street Target Retirement 2040 Fund Class K	SSCQX	B-	C	B+	Up	3.82	16.30	6.70	37.37		12.48	814.6	617-664-7338	Y
State Street Target Retirement 2045 Fund Class I	SSDDX	B-	C	B	Up	3.81	16.91	6.38	38.83		12.51	616.2	617-664-7338	Y
State Street Target Retirement 2045 Fund Class K	SSDEX	B-	C	B	Up	3.81	16.91	6.40	38.91		12.51	616.2	617-664-7338	Y
State Street Target Retirement 2050 Fund Class I	SSDJX	B-	C	B	Up	3.83	16.91	6.27	38.69		12.44	414.4	617-664-7338	Y
State Street Target Retirement 2050 Fund Class K	SSDLX	B-	C	B	Up	3.75	16.91	6.29	38.73		12.44	414.4	617-664-7338	Y
State Street Target Retirement 2055 Fund Class I	SSDOX	B-	C	B	Up	3.75	16.93	6.26	39.09		12.43	202.3	617-664-7338	Y
State Street Target Retirement 2055 Fund Class K	SSDQX	B-	C	B	Up	3.76	16.96	6.27	38.98		12.41	202.3	617-664-7338	Y
State Street Target Retirement 2060 Fund Class I	SSDWX	B-	C	B	Up	3.81	17.02	6.43	38.73		11.96	46.3	617-664-7338	Y
State Street Target Retirement 2060 Fund Class K	SSDYX	B-	C	B	Up	3.90	17.02	6.43	38.80		11.96	46.3	617-664-7338	Y
State Street Target Retirement Fund Class I	SSFNX	B	C+	A-		2.71	9.60	6.64	18.13		10.95	229.2	617-664-7338	Y
State Street Target Retirement Fund Class K	SSFOX	B	C+	A-		2.72	9.62	6.66	17.96		10.93	229.2	617-664-7338	Y
T. Rowe Price Retirement 2005 Fund	TRRFX	B	C+	A	Up	3.11	10.24	6.61	20.60	24.14	13.56	1,348	410-345-2000	Y
T. Rowe Price Retirement 2005 Fund Advisor Class	PARGX	B	C+	A-	Up	2.97	10.02	6.31	19.68	22.55	13.5	1,348	410-345-2000	Y
T. Rowe Price Retirement 2005 Fund Class R	RRTLX	B	C+	A-	Up	3.03	9.95	6.09	18.86	21.14	13.59	1,348	410-345-2000	Y
T. Rowe Price Retirement 2010 Fund	TRRAX	B	C+	A	Up	3.22	10.94	6.71	22.55	26.10	17.94	4,043	410-345-2000	Y
T. Rowe Price Retirement 2010 Fund Advisor Class	PARAX	B	C+	A	Up	3.12	10.73	6.43	21.65	24.56	17.84	4,043	410-345-2000	Y
T. Rowe Price Retirement 2010 Fund Class R	RRTAX	B	C+	A-	Up	3.08	10.68	6.16	20.70	22.96	17.72	4,043	410-345-2000	Y
T. Rowe Price Retirement 2015 Fund	TRRGX	B	C+	A	Up	3.28	11.81	6.59	25.69	28.98	14.48	6,435	410-345-2000	Y
T. Rowe Price Retirement 2015 Fund Advisor Class	PARHX	B	C+	A	Up	3.21	11.68	6.38	24.76	27.50	14.43	6,435	410-345-2000	Y
T. Rowe Price Retirement 2015 Fund Class R	RRTMX	B	C	A	Up	3.10	11.56	6.11	23.80	25.82	14.28	6,435	410-345-2000	Y
T. Rowe Price Retirement 2020 Fund	TRRBX	B	C	A-	Up	3.38	13.11	6.65	29.75	32.68	21.99	18,453	410-345-2000	Y
T. Rowe Price Retirement 2020 Fund Advisor Class	PARBX	B	C	A-	Up	3.36	12.94	6.39	28.79	31.01	21.81	18,453	410-345-2000	Y
T. Rowe Price Retirement 2020 Fund Class R	RRTBX	B	C	A-	Up	3.30	12.80	6.08	27.82	29.41	21.59	18,453	410-345-2000	Y
T. Rowe Price Retirement 2025 Fund	TRRHX	B-	C	A-	Up	3.48	14.20	6.55	33.12	35.63	17.53	17,282	410-345-2000	Y
T. Rowe Price Retirement 2025 Fund Advisor Class	PARJX	B-	C	A-	Up	3.44	14.07	6.33	32.13	34.03	17.42	17,282	410-345-2000	Y
T. Rowe Price Retirement 2025 Fund Class R	RRTNX	B-	C	A-	Up	3.36	13.88	6.00	31.06	32.27	17.22	17,282	410-345-2000	Y
T. Rowe Price Retirement 2030 Fund	TRRCX	B-	C	B+	Up	3.60	15.23	6.47	36.35	38.41	25.56	21,904	410-345-2000	Y
T. Rowe Price Retirement 2030 Fund Advisor Class	PARCX	B-	C	B+	Up	3.51	15.09	6.16	35.25	36.65	25.31	21,904	410-345-2000	Y
T. Rowe Price Retirement 2030 Fund Class R	RRTCX	B-	C	B+	Up	3.46	14.94	5.93	34.24	34.97	25.08	21,904	410-345-2000	Y
T. Rowe Price Retirement 2035 Fund	TRRJX	B-	C	B+	Up	3.64	16.08	6.27	38.74	40.30	18.76	13,494	410-345-2000	Y
T. Rowe Price Retirement 2035 Fund Advisor Class	PARKX	B-	C	B+	Up	3.55	15.91	6.04	37.73	38.52	18.65	13,494	410-345-2000	Y
T. Rowe Price Retirement 2035 Fund Class R	RRTPX	B-	C	B+	Up	3.54	15.77	5.74	36.64	36.83	18.42	13,494	410-345-2000	Y
T. Rowe Price Retirement 2040 Fund	TRRDX	B-	C	B+	Up	3.68	16.73	6.20	40.85	41.84	26.72	15,448	410-345-2000	Y
T. Rowe Price Retirement 2040 Fund Advisor Class	PARDX	B-	C	B+	Up	3.64	16.61	5.91	39.77	40.05	26.46	15,448	410-345-2000	Y
T. Rowe Price Retirement 2040 Fund Class R	RRTDX	B-	C	B+	Up	3.55	16.40	5.63	38.75	38.32	26.25	15,448	410-345-2000	Y
T. Rowe Price Retirement 2045 Fund	TRRKX	B-	C	B+	Up	3.64	17.10	6.05	41.49	42.43	18.21	8,839	410-345-2000	Y
T. Rowe Price Retirement 2045 Fund Advisor Class	PARLX	B-	C	B+	Up	3.61	16.94	5.83	40.39	40.62	18.08	8,839	410-345-2000	Y
T. Rowe Price Retirement 2045 Fund Class R	RRTRX	B-	C	B	Up	3.53	16.80	5.57	39.35	38.94	17.86	8,839	410-345-2000	Y
T. Rowe Price Retirement 2050 Fund	TRRMX	B-	C	B+	Up	3.71	17.16	6.11	41.53	42.41	15.36	7,437	410-345-2000	Y
T. Rowe Price Retirement 2050 Fund Advisor Class	PARFX	B-	C	B+	Up	3.68	16.99	5.86	40.48	40.72	15.21	7,437	410-345-2000	Y
T. Rowe Price Retirement 2050 Fund Class R	RRTFX	B-	C	B	Up	3.57	16.83	5.52	39.41	38.91	15.06	7,437	410-345-2000	Y
T. Rowe Price Retirement 2055 Fund	TRRNX	B-	C	B+	Up	3.66	17.16	6.08	41.34	42.34	15.56	3,834	410-345-2000	Y
T. Rowe Price Retirement 2055 Fund Advisor Class	PAROX	B-	C	B	Up	3.62	16.96	5.82	40.39	40.62	15.44	3,834	410-345-2000	Y

Category: Target Date (con't)

Fund Name	Ticker Symbol	RATINGS: Overall Rating	Reward Rating	Risk Rating	Recent Up/ Downgrade	TOTAL RETURNS & PERFORMANCE: 3-Month Total Return	6-Month Total Return	1-Year Total Return	3-Year Total Return	5-Year Total Return	ASSETS: NAV	Total Assets (MIL)	NEW INVESTORS: Telephone	Open to New Investors
T. Rowe Price Retirement 2055 Fund Class R	RRTVX	B-	C	B	Up	3.51	16.84	5.48	39.31	38.80	15.33	3,834	410-345-2000	Y
T. Rowe Price Retirement 2060 Fund	TRRLX	B-	C	B+	Up	3.70	17.14	6.06	41.42	42.32	12.3	750.9	410-345-2000	Y
T. Rowe Price Retirement 2060 Fund Advisor Class	TRRYX	B-	C	B+	Up	3.64	17.03	5.81	40.35	40.67	12.23	750.9	410-345-2000	Y
T. Rowe Price Retirement 2060 Fund R Class	TRRZX	B-	C	B	Up	3.57	16.90	5.54	39.29	38.90	12.17	750.9	410-345-2000	Y
T. Rowe Price Retirement I 2005 Fund I Class	TRPFX	B	C+	A	Up	3.15	10.31	6.85	21.04		11.76	255.2	410-345-2000	Y
T. Rowe Price Retirement I 2010 Fund I Class	TRPAX	B	C+	A	Up	3.17	10.89	6.83	23.01		12.01	691.4	410-345-2000	Y
T. Rowe Price Retirement I 2015 Fund I Class	TRFGX	B	C+	A	Up	3.38	11.91	6.77	26.17		12.21	1,341	410-345-2000	Y
T. Rowe Price Retirement I 2020 Fund I Class	TRBRX	B	C+	A-	Up	3.42	13.20	6.73	30.21		12.69	4,743	410-345-2000	Y
T. Rowe Price Retirement I 2025 Fund I Class	TRPHX	B-	C	A-	Up	3.58	14.31	6.74	33.56		13.02	4,995	410-345-2000	Y
T. Rowe Price Retirement I 2030 Fund I Class	TRPCX	B-	C	B+	Up	3.59	15.31	6.56	36.71		13.25	6,369	410-345-2000	Y
T. Rowe Price Retirement I 2035 Fund I Class	TRPJX	B-	C	B+	Up	3.69	16.19	6.41	39.21		13.49	4,238	410-345-2000	Y
T. Rowe Price Retirement I 2040 Fund I Class	TRPDX	B-	C	B+	Up	3.72	16.79	6.29	41.33		13.63	4,999	410-345-2000	Y
T. Rowe Price Retirement I 2045 Fund I Class	TRPKX	B-	C	B+	Up	3.69	17.13	6.18	41.94		13.74	3,051	410-345-2000	Y
T. Rowe Price Retirement I 2050 Fund I Class	TRPMX	B-	C	B+	Up	3.70	17.26	6.21	41.97		13.72	2,999	410-345-2000	Y
T. Rowe Price Retirement I 2055 Fund I Class	TRPNX	B-	C	B+	Up	3.76	17.26	6.21	42.01		13.79	1,350	410-345-2000	Y
T. Rowe Price Retirement I 2060 Fund I Class	TRPLX	B-	C	B+	Up	3.78	17.26	6.27	41.97		13.72	346.3	410-345-2000	Y
T. Rowe Price Target 2005 Fund	TRARX	B	C+	A-	Up	3.10	10.01	6.65	19.35	22.86	11.64	37.6	410-345-2000	Y
T. Rowe Price Target 2005 Fund Advisor Class	PANRX	B	C+	A-	Up	3.00	9.79	6.34	18.48	21.39	11.66	37.6	410-345-2000	Y
T. Rowe Price Target 2005 Fund I Class	TFRRX	B	C+	A	Up	3.09	10.00	6.74	19.67	23.19	11.65	37.6	410-345-2000	Y
T. Rowe Price Target 2010 Fund	TRROX	B	C+	A	Up	3.10	10.12	6.64	19.98	23.47	11.64	67.6	410-345-2000	Y
T. Rowe Price Target 2010 Fund Advisor Class	PAERX	B	C+	A-	Up	3.09	10.11	6.42	19.14	21.93	11.65	67.6	410-345-2000	Y
T. Rowe Price Target 2010 Fund I Class	TORFX	B	C+	A	Up	3.18	10.31	6.82	20.49	23.88	11.66	67.6	410-345-2000	Y
T. Rowe Price Target 2015 Fund	TRRTX	B	C+	A	Up	3.21	10.60	6.69	21.59	24.74	11.89	197.4	410-345-2000	Y
T. Rowe Price Target 2015 Fund Advisor Class	PAHRX	B	C+	A-	Up	3.13	10.42	6.27	20.53	22.98	11.86	197.4	410-345-2000	Y
T. Rowe Price Target 2015 Fund I Class	TTRTX	B	C+	A	Up	3.21	10.51	6.65	21.76	24.92	11.88	197.4	410-345-2000	Y
T. Rowe Price Target 2020 Fund	TRRUX	B	C+	A	Up	3.21	11.32	6.44	24.31	27.04	12.19	322.8	410-345-2000	Y
T. Rowe Price Target 2020 Fund Advisor Class	PAIRX	B	C+	A	Up	3.14	11.17	6.17	23.24	25.27	12.14	322.8	410-345-2000	Y
T. Rowe Price Target 2020 Fund I Class	TTURX	B	C+	A	Up	3.21	11.31	6.52	24.61	27.47	12.2	322.8	410-345-2000	Y
T. Rowe Price Target 2025 Fund	TRRVX	B	C	A	Up	3.30	12.21	6.37	27.13	29.73	12.49	350.7	410-345-2000	Y
T. Rowe Price Target 2025 Fund Advisor Class	PAJRX	B	C	A	Up	3.23	12.15	6.09	26.22	28.00	12.46	350.7	410-345-2000	Y
T. Rowe Price Target 2025 Fund I Class	TRVVX	B	C+	A	Up	3.30	12.32	6.42	27.61	30.22	12.49	350.7	410-345-2000	Y
T. Rowe Price Target 2030 Fund	TRRWX	B	C	A-	Up	3.39	13.29	6.40	30.40	32.85	12.78	349.2	410-345-2000	Y
T. Rowe Price Target 2030 Fund Advisor Class	PAKRX	B	C	A-	Up	3.32	13.14	6.14	29.43	31.27	12.74	349.2	410-345-2000	Y
T. Rowe Price Target 2030 Fund I Class	TWRRX	B	C	A-	Up	3.39	13.39	6.50	30.83	33.40	12.78	349.2	410-345-2000	Y
T. Rowe Price Target 2035 Fund	RPGRX	B-	C	A-	Up	3.50	14.34	6.44	33.30	35.68	12.99	233.4	410-345-2000	Y
T. Rowe Price Target 2035 Fund Advisor Class	PATVX	B-	C	A-	Up	3.43	14.08	6.09	32.27	33.91	12.96	233.4	410-345-2000	Y
T. Rowe Price Target 2035 Fund I Class	TPGPX	B-	C	A-	Up	3.58	14.42	6.61	33.93	36.32	13.01	233.4	410-345-2000	Y
T. Rowe Price Target 2040 Fund	TRHRX	B-	C	B+	Up	3.59	15.23	6.36	35.83	37.86	13.24	202.5	410-345-2000	Y
T. Rowe Price Target 2040 Fund Advisor Class	PAHHX	B-	C	B+	Up	3.53	15.09	6.20	34.87	36.17	13.19	202.5	410-345-2000	Y
T. Rowe Price Target 2040 Fund I Class	TRXRX	B-	C	B+	Up	3.59	15.31	6.54	36.37	38.41	13.25	202.5	410-345-2000	Y
T. Rowe Price Target 2045 Fund	RPTFX	B-	C	B+	Up	3.67	15.82	6.35	37.86	39.47	13.54	164.1	410-345-2000	Y
T. Rowe Price Target 2045 Fund Advisor Class	PAFFX	B-	C	B+	Up	3.52	15.69	6.03	36.78	37.65	13.49	164.1	410-345-2000	Y
T. Rowe Price Target 2045 Fund I Class	TRFWX	B-	C	B+	Up	3.74	15.99	6.53	38.38	40.12	13.56	164.1	410-345-2000	Y
T. Rowe Price Target 2050 Fund	TRFOX	B-	C	B+	Up	3.71	16.41	6.23	39.59	40.77	13.69	120.1	410-345-2000	Y
T. Rowe Price Target 2050 Fund Advisor Class	PAOFX	B-	C	B+	Up	3.57	16.29	5.94	38.47	39.03	13.63	120.1	410-345-2000	Y
T. Rowe Price Target 2050 Fund I Class	TOORX	B-	C	B+	Up	3.70	16.49	6.36	40.07	41.26	13.7	120.1	410-345-2000	Y
T. Rowe Price Target 2055 Fund	TRFFX	B-	C	B+	Up	3.65	16.83	6.06	40.76	41.76	13.6	72.8	410-345-2000	Y
T. Rowe Price Target 2055 Fund Advisor Class	PAFTX	B-	C	B+	Up	3.67	16.70	5.85	39.75	40.01	13.55	72.8	410-345-2000	Y
T. Rowe Price Target 2055 Fund I Class	TRPPX	B-	C	B+	Up	3.73	16.92	6.27	41.37	42.38	13.61	72.8	410-345-2000	Y
T. Rowe Price Target 2060 Fund	TRTFX	B-	C	B+	Up	3.70	17.16	6.03	41.03	41.98	11.74	23.6	410-345-2000	Y
T. Rowe Price Target 2060 Fund Advisor Class	TRTGX	B-	C	B+	Up	3.61	17.03	5.87	40.04	40.40	11.75	23.6	410-345-2000	Y
T. Rowe Price Target 2060 Fund I Class	TTOIX	B-	C	B+	Up	3.79	17.23	6.27	41.69	42.64	11.77	23.6	410-345-2000	Y

Category: Target Date (con't)

Fund Name	Ticker Symbol	RATINGS: Overall Rating	Reward Rating	Risk Rating	Recent Up/ Downgrade	TOTAL RETURNS & PERFORMANCE: 3-Month Total Return	6-Month Total Return	1-Year Total Return	3-Year Total Return	5-Year Total Return	ASSETS: NAV	Total Assets (MIL)	NEW INVESTORS: Telephone	Open to New Investors
Target 2015 Allocation Fund Class B		B	C	A-	Up	2.68	9.87	5.16	22.04	19.81	8.82	47.9	877-222-2144	Y
Target 2015 Allocation Portfolio Class K		B	C	A-	Up	2.80	10.13	5.47	22.99	21.37	8.82	47.9	877-222-2144	Y
Target 2025 Allocation Fund Class B		B-	C	B+	Up	2.97	12.38	4.97	30.02	27.02	11.48	164.7	877-222-2144	Y
Target 2025 Allocation Portfolio Class K		B-	C	B+	Up	3.06	12.59	5.25	30.98	28.74	11.49	164.7	877-222-2144	Y
Target 2035 Allocation Fund Class B		B-	C	B+	Up	3.32	14.03	5.03	34.68	30.96	12.16	147.1	877-222-2144	Y
Target 2035 Allocation Portfolio Class K		B-	C	B+	Up	3.32	14.13	5.23	35.56	32.51	12.17	147.1	877-222-2144	Y
Target 2045 Allocation Fund Class B		B-	C	B	Up	3.38	15.05	4.84	38.40	33.56	12.3	115.4	877-222-2144	Y
Target 2045 Allocation Portfolio Class K		B-	C	B	Up	3.46	15.25	5.14	39.44	35.27	12.3	115.4	877-222-2144	Y
TIAA-CREF Lifecycle 2010 Fund Advisor Class	TCLHX	B	C+	A	Up	3.04	10.67	5.81	23.64	27.18	11.51	1,197	877-518-9161	Y
TIAA-CREF Lifecycle 2010 Fund Institutional Class	TCTIX	B	C+	A	Up	3.04	10.57	5.74	23.60	27.62	11.5	1,197	877-518-9161	Y
TIAA-CREF Lifecycle 2010 Fund Premier Class	TCTPX	B	C+	A	Up	2.96	10.50	5.58	23.09	26.72	11.47	1,197	877-518-9161	Y
TIAA-CREF Lifecycle 2010 Fund Retirement Class	TCLEX	B	C+	A-	Up	3.01	10.52	5.55	22.73	26.12	13.65	1,197	877-518-9161	Y
TIAA-CREF Lifecycle 2015 Fund Advisor Class	TCNHX	B	C	A	Up	3.05	11.26	5.64	25.36	28.69	9.78	1,836	877-518-9161	Y
TIAA-CREF Lifecycle 2015 Fund Institutional Class	TCNIX	B	C	A	Up	3.16	11.37	5.76	25.56	29.40	9.79	1,836	877-518-9161	Y
TIAA-CREF Lifecycle 2015 Fund Premier Class	TCFPX	B	C	A	Up	3.06	11.18	5.60	24.97	28.41	9.74	1,836	877-518-9161	Y
TIAA-CREF Lifecycle 2015 Fund Retirement Class	TCLIX	B	C	A-	Up	3.03	11.18	5.44	24.60	27.76	12.23	1,836	877-518-9161	Y
TIAA-CREF Lifecycle 2020 Fund Advisor Class	TCWHX	B	C	A-	Up	3.16	12.09	5.44	28.05	30.85	10.1	3,815	877-518-9161	Y
TIAA-CREF Lifecycle 2020 Fund Institutional Class	TCWIX	B	C	A-	Up	3.06	12.09	5.51	28.15	31.49	10.1	3,815	877-518-9161	Y
TIAA-CREF Lifecycle 2020 Fund Premier Class	TCWPX	B	C	A-	Up	3.07	12.01	5.34	27.52	30.47	10.07	3,815	877-518-9161	Y
TIAA-CREF Lifecycle 2020 Fund Retirement Class	TCLTX	B	C	A-	Up	3.03	11.95	5.23	27.17	29.86	12.92	3,815	877-518-9161	Y
TIAA-CREF Lifecycle 2025 Fund Advisor Class	TCQHX	B-	C	A-	Up	3.20	13.17	5.10	30.89	33.16	10.31	4,611	877-518-9161	Y
TIAA-CREF Lifecycle 2025 Fund Institutional Class	TCYIX	B-	C	A-	Up	3.30	13.28	5.25	31.17	33.86	10.32	4,611	877-518-9161	Y
TIAA-CREF Lifecycle 2025 Fund Premier Class	TCQPX	B-	C	A-	Up	3.11	13.12	4.99	30.47	32.76	10.26	4,611	877-518-9161	Y
TIAA-CREF Lifecycle 2025 Fund Retirement Class	TCLFX	B-	C	A-	Up	3.16	13.03	4.95	30.17	32.19	13.35	4,611	877-518-9161	Y
TIAA-CREF Lifecycle 2030 Fund Advisor Class	TCHHX	B-	C	B+	Up	3.29	14.36	4.82	33.94	35.40	10.35	4,590	877-518-9161	Y
TIAA-CREF Lifecycle 2030 Fund Institutional Class	TCRIX	B-	C	B+	Up	3.29	14.36	4.89	34.08	36.08	10.35	4,590	877-518-9161	Y
TIAA-CREF Lifecycle 2030 Fund Premier Class	TCHPX	B-	C	B+	Up	3.20	14.20	4.72	33.39	34.98	10.29	4,590	877-518-9161	Y
TIAA-CREF Lifecycle 2030 Fund Retirement Class	TCLNX	B-	C	B+	Up	3.16	14.20	4.63	33.02	34.34	13.67	4,590	877-518-9161	Y
TIAA-CREF Lifecycle 2035 Fund Advisor Class	TCYHX	B-	C	B	Up	3.35	15.40	4.52	36.91	37.30	10.49	4,640	877-518-9161	Y
TIAA-CREF Lifecycle 2035 Fund Institutional Class	TCIIX	B-	C	B	Up	3.34	15.38	4.56	36.97	37.98	10.5	4,640	877-518-9161	Y
TIAA-CREF Lifecycle 2035 Fund Premier Class	TCYPX	B-	C	B	Up	3.25	15.32	4.39	36.37	36.97	10.46	4,640	877-518-9161	Y
TIAA-CREF Lifecycle 2035 Fund Retirement Class	TCLRX	B-	C	B	Up	3.28	15.30	4.27	35.96	36.26	14.16	4,640	877-518-9161	Y
TIAA-CREF Lifecycle 2040 Fund Advisor Class	TCZHX	B-	C	B	Up	3.35	16.44	3.97	39.61	39.11	10.48	5,523	877-518-9161	Y
TIAA-CREF Lifecycle 2040 Fund Institutional Class	TCOIX	B-	C	B	Up	3.35	16.31	4.00	39.70	39.66	10.48	5,523	877-518-9161	Y
TIAA-CREF Lifecycle 2040 Fund Premier Class	TCZPX	B-	C	B	Up	3.36	16.36	3.92	39.20	38.74	10.45	5,523	877-518-9161	Y
TIAA-CREF Lifecycle 2040 Fund Retirement Class	TCLOX	B-	C	B	Up	3.27	16.26	3.81	38.70	38.04	14.51	5,523	877-518-9161	Y
TIAA-CREF Lifecycle Index 2010 Fund Advisor Class	TLTHX	B	C+	A		3.17	10.54	7.01	21.92	26.95	15.62	458.2	877-518-9161	Y
TIAA-CREF Lifecycle Index 2010 Fund Institutional Class	TLTIX	B	C+	A		3.17	10.62	7.06	22.01	27.14	15.62	458.2	877-518-9161	Y
TIAA-CREF Lifecycle Index 2010 Fund Premier Class	TLTPX	B	C+	A	Up	3.11	10.43	6.84	21.41	26.06	15.56	458.2	877-518-9161	Y
TIAA-CREF Lifecycle Index 2010 Fund Retirement Class	TLTRX	B	C+	A-	Up	3.06	10.41	6.77	21.09	25.49	15.48	458.2	877-518-9161	Y
TIAA-CREF Lifecycle Index 2015 Fund Advisor Class	TLFAX	B	C+	A	Up	3.22	11.23	7.11	23.94	28.99	16.34	921.7	877-518-9161	Y
TIAA-CREF Lifecycle Index 2015 Fund Institutional Class	TLFIX	B	C+	A	Up	3.22	11.23	7.13	24.02	28.98	16.33	921.7	877-518-9161	Y
TIAA-CREF Lifecycle Index 2015 Fund Premier Class	TLFPX	B	C+	A	Up	3.17	11.14	6.93	23.44	28.02	16.26	921.7	877-518-9161	Y
TIAA-CREF Lifecycle Index 2015 Fund Retirement Class	TLGRX	B	C+	A	Up	3.18	11.10	6.91	23.16	27.47	16.21	921.7	877-518-9161	Y
TIAA-CREF Lifecycle Index 2020 Fund Advisor Class	TLWHX	B	C+	A	Up	3.34	12.03	7.16	26.53	31.11	17.31	2,329	877-518-9161	Y
TIAA-CREF Lifecycle Index 2020 Fund Institutional Class	TLWIX	B	C+	A	Up	3.34	12.03	7.21	26.75	31.35	17.32	2,329	877-518-9161	Y
TIAA-CREF Lifecycle Index 2020 Fund Premier Class	TLWPX	B	C+	A	Up	3.29	11.95	7.01	26.13	30.35	17.23	2,329	877-518-9161	Y
TIAA-CREF Lifecycle Index 2020 Fund Retirement Class	TLWRX	B	C+	A	Up	3.24	11.85	6.92	25.80	29.72	17.17	2,329	877-518-9161	Y
TIAA-CREF Lifecycle Index 2025 Fund Advisor Class	TLQHX	B	C	A-	Up	3.39	13.00	7.14	29.70	33.83	18.25	3,034	877-518-9161	Y
TIAA-CREF Lifecycle Index 2025 Fund Institutional Class	TLQIX	B	C+	A-	Up	3.45	13.05	7.21	29.92	34.14	18.27	3,034	877-518-9161	Y
TIAA-CREF Lifecycle Index 2025 Fund Premier Class	TLVPX	B	C	A-	Up	3.41	12.98	7.08	29.29	33.14	18.19	3,034	877-518-9161	Y
TIAA-CREF Lifecycle Index 2025 Fund Retirement Class	TLQRX	B	C	A-	Up	3.36	12.90	7.00	28.93	32.45	18.11	3,034	877-518-9161	Y

Category: Target Date (con't)

		RATINGS				TOTAL RETURNS & PERFORMANCE					ASSETS		NEW INVESTORS	
Fund Name	Ticker Symbol	Overall Rating	Reward Rating	Risk Rating	Recent Up/ Downgrade	3-Month Total Return	6-Month Total Return	1-Year Total Return	3-Year Total Return	5-Year Total Return	NAV	Total Assets (MIL)	Telephone	Open to New Investors
TIAA-CREF Lifecycle Index 2030 Fund Advisor Class	TLHHX	B	C	A-	Up	3.50	14.00	7.16	32.84	36.55	19.21	3,218	877-518-9161	Y
TIAA-CREF Lifecycle Index 2030 Fund Institutional Class	TLHIX	B	C	A-	Up	3.49	14.05	7.26	33.18	36.89	19.23	3,218	877-518-9161	Y
TIAA-CREF Lifecycle Index 2030 Fund Premier Class	TLHPX	B-	C	A-		3.45	13.99	7.13	32.56	35.90	19.14	3,218	877-518-9161	Y
TIAA-CREF Lifecycle Index 2030 Fund Retirement Class	TLHRX	B-	C	A-		3.42	13.86	6.99	32.07	35.11	19.05	3,218	877-518-9161	Y
TIAA-CREF Lifecycle Index 2035 Fund Advisor Class	TLYHX	B-	C	B+	Up	3.55	14.97	7.10	36.26	39.12	20.12	2,924	877-518-9161	Y
TIAA-CREF Lifecycle Index 2035 Fund Institutional Class	TLYIX	B-	C	B+	Up	3.54	15.02	7.19	36.39	39.34	20.14	2,924	877-518-9161	Y
TIAA-CREF Lifecycle Index 2035 Fund Premier Class	TLYPX	B-	C	B+	Up	3.56	14.97	7.01	35.81	38.37	20.04	2,924	877-518-9161	Y
TIAA-CREF Lifecycle Index 2035 Fund Retirement Class	TLYRX	B-	C	B+	Up	3.52	14.91	6.93	35.40	37.65	19.95	2,924	877-518-9161	Y
TIAA-CREF Lifecycle Index 2040 Fund Advisor Class	TLZHX	B-	C	B+	Up	3.59	15.96	6.98	39.38	41.56	20.77	3,096	877-518-9161	Y
TIAA-CREF Lifecycle Index 2040 Fund Institutional Class	TLZIX	B-	C	B+	Up	3.63	16.01	7.05	39.66	41.84	20.79	3,096	877-518-9161	Y
TIAA-CREF Lifecycle Index 2040 Fund Premier Class	TLPRX	B-	C	B+	Up	3.60	15.91	6.92	39.01	40.70	20.68	3,096	877-518-9161	Y
TIAA-CREF Lifecycle Index 2040 Fund Retirement Class	TLZRX	B-	C	B+	Up	3.56	15.86	6.78	38.58	40.05	20.6	3,096	877-518-9161	Y
TIAA-CREF Lifecycle Index 2045 Fund Advisor Class	TLMHX	B-	C	B	Up	3.62	16.64	6.85	40.69	42.79	20.88	2,060	877-518-9161	Y
TIAA-CREF Lifecycle Index 2045 Fund Institutional Class	TLXIX	B-	C	B	Up	3.67	16.69	6.92	41.03	43.14	20.9	2,060	877-518-9161	Y
TIAA-CREF Lifecycle Index 2045 Fund Premier Class	TLMPX	B-	C	B	Up	3.58	16.59	6.73	40.35	41.98	20.8	2,060	877-518-9161	Y
TIAA-CREF Lifecycle Index 2045 Fund Retirement Class	TLMRX	B-	C	B	Up	3.60	16.54	6.65	39.94	41.34	20.71	2,060	877-518-9161	Y
TIAA-CREF Lifecycle Index 2050 Fund Advisor Class	TLLHX	B-	C	B	Up	3.60	16.76	6.79	41.19	43.39	20.96	1,571	877-518-9161	Y
TIAA-CREF Lifecycle Index 2050 Fund Institutional Class	TLLIX	B-	C	B	Up	3.65	16.81	6.88	41.50	43.71	20.98	1,571	877-518-9161	Y
TIAA-CREF Lifecycle Index 2050 Fund Premier Class	TLLPX	B-	C	B	Up	3.62	16.77	6.75	40.92	42.65	20.88	1,571	877-518-9161	Y
TIAA-CREF Lifecycle Index 2050 Fund Retirement Class	TLLRX	B-	C	B	Up	3.58	16.67	6.62	40.47	41.90	20.78	1,571	877-518-9161	Y
TIAA-CREF Lifecycle Index 2055 Fund Advisor Class	TTIHX	B-	C	B	Up	3.58	16.85	6.72	41.80	43.95	16.78	660.4	877-518-9161	Y
TIAA-CREF Lifecycle Index 2055 Fund Institutional Class	TTIIX	B-	C	B	Up	3.63	16.99	6.88	42.06	44.21	16.8	660.4	877-518-9161	Y
TIAA-CREF Lifecycle Index 2055 Fund Premier Class	TTIPX	B-	C	B	Up	3.58	16.80	6.69	41.37	43.13	16.75	660.4	877-518-9161	Y
TIAA-CREF Lifecycle Index 2055 Fund Retirement Class	TTIRX	B-	C	B	Up	3.59	16.77	6.59	40.91	42.35	16.71	660.4	877-518-9161	Y
TIAA-CREF Lifecycle Index 2060 Fund Advisor Class	TVIHX	B-	C	B	Up	3.60	17.02	6.82	42.40		12.92	166.9	877-518-9161	Y
TIAA-CREF Lifecycle Index 2060 Fund Institutional Class	TVIIX	B-	C	B	Up	3.69	17.13	6.86	42.50		12.92	166.9	877-518-9161	Y
TIAA-CREF Lifecycle Index 2060 Fund Premier Class	TVIPX	B-	C	B	Up	3.61	16.95	6.64	41.86		12.9	166.9	877-518-9161	Y
TIAA-CREF Lifecycle Index 2060 Fund Retirement Class	TVITX	B-	C	B	Up	3.53	16.89	6.58	41.35		12.87	166.9	877-518-9161	Y
TIAA-CREF Lifecycle Index Retirement Income Advisor Cls	TLIHX	B	C+	A		3.11	10.35	6.99	20.90	26.03	14.72	383.8	877-518-9161	Y
TIAA-CREF Lifecycle Index Retmnt Income Inst Cls	TRILX	B	C+	A		3.12	10.38	7.02	20.98	26.16	14.72	383.8	877-518-9161	Y
TIAA-CREF Lifecycle Index Retirement Income Premier Cls	TLIPX	B	C+	A		3.08	10.31	6.87	20.37	25.16	14.71	383.8	877-518-9161	Y
TIAA-CREF Lifecycle Index Retirement Income Retirement Cls	TRCIX	B	C+	A-	Up	3.06	10.26	6.77	20.12	24.54	14.7	383.8	877-518-9161	Y
TIAA-CREF Lifecycle Retirement Income Fund Advisor Class	TLRHX	B	C+	A	Up	2.96	10.41	5.79	22.36	26.49	11.59	541.1	877-518-9161	Y
TIAA-CREF Lifecycle Retirement Income Institutional Cls	TLRIX	B	C+	A	Up	3.08	10.43	5.85	22.47	26.66	11.59	541.1	877-518-9161	Y
TIAA-CREF Lifecycle Retirement Income Fund Premier Class	TPILX	B	C+	A-	Up	2.95	10.25	5.60	21.94	25.62	11.58	541.1	877-518-9161	Y
TIAA-CREF Lifecycle Retirement Income Fund Retail Class	TLRRX	B	C+	A-	Up	2.93	10.21	5.50	21.49	25.02	11.57	541.1	877-518-9161	Y
TIAA-CREF Lifecycle Retirement Income Retirement Cls	TLIRX	B	C+	A-	Up	2.93	10.22	5.50	21.51	25.04	11.56	541.1	877-518-9161	Y
Transamerica ClearTrack® 2015 R1	TCFTX	B-	C	B+	Up	3.06	10.84	5.28	18.05		10.43	40.2	888-233-4339	Y
Transamerica ClearTrack® 2015 R3	TCTGX	B-	C	B+	Up	3.16	11.06	5.78	19.44		10.43	40.2	888-233-4339	Y
Transamerica ClearTrack® 2015 R6	TDKTX	B-	C	A-	Up	3.24	11.21	6.06	20.36		10.51	40.2	888-233-4339	Y
Transamerica ClearTrack® 2020 R1	TCHTX	B-	C	B+	Up	3.17	11.09	4.88	19.33		10.41	57.4	888-233-4339	Y
Transamerica ClearTrack® 2020 R3	TCTJX	B-	C	A-	Up	3.27	11.31	5.40	20.74		10.41	57.4	888-233-4339	Y
Transamerica ClearTrack® 2020 R6	TCSUX	B-	C	A-	Up	3.24	11.35	5.57	21.54		10.49	57.4	888-233-4339	Y
Transamerica ClearTrack® 2025 R1	TDITX	B-	C	A-	Up	3.03	12.43	5.66	21.91		10.85	75.4	888-233-4339	Y
Transamerica ClearTrack® 2025 R3	TCTKX	B-	C	A-	Up	3.13	12.63	6.08	23.28		10.84	75.4	888-233-4339	Y
Transamerica ClearTrack® 2025 R6	TDOTX	B	C	A-	Up	3.20	12.78	6.34	24.22		10.94	75.4	888-233-4339	Y
Transamerica ClearTrack® 2030 R1	TDFTX	B-	C	B+	Up	3.16	13.16	5.63	24.16		11.09	57.6	888-233-4339	Y
Transamerica ClearTrack® 2030 R3	TCTLX	B-	C	A-	Up	3.26	13.46	6.14	25.65		11.08	57.6	888-233-4339	Y
Transamerica ClearTrack® 2030 R6	TDHTX	B-	C	A-	Up	3.32	13.60	6.40	26.60		11.19	57.6	888-233-4339	Y
Transamerica ClearTrack® 2035 R1	TCETX	B-	C	B+	Up	3.12	13.90	5.32	27.22		11.22	60.1	888-233-4339	Y
Transamerica ClearTrack® 2035 R3	TCTMX	B-	C	B+	Up	3.31	14.30	5.85	28.83		11.21	60.1	888-233-4339	Y
Transamerica ClearTrack® 2035 R6	TCHDX	B-	C	B+	Up	3.28	14.34	6.02	29.67		11.32	60.1	888-233-4339	Y

Category: Target Date (con't)

Fund Name	Ticker Symbol	Overall Rating	Reward Rating	Risk Rating	Recent Up/ Downgrade	3-Month Total Return	6-Month Total Return	1-Year Total Return	3-Year Total Return	5-Year Total Return	NAV	Total Assets (MIL)	Telephone	Open to New Investors
		RATINGS				TOTAL RETURNS & PERFORMANCE					ASSETS		NEW INVESTORS	
Transamerica ClearTrack® 2040 R1	TCRTX	B-	C	B+	Up	3.26	14.83	5.21	30.70		11.38	52.7	888-233-4339	Y
Transamerica ClearTrack® 2040 R3	TCTQX	B-	C	B+	Up	3.27	14.96	5.56	32.23		11.35	52.7	888-233-4339	Y
Transamerica ClearTrack® 2040 R6	TCKTX	B-	C	B+	Up	3.31	15.08	5.80	33.20		11.52	52.7	888-233-4339	Y
Transamerica ClearTrack® 2045 R1	TCPTX	B-	C	B	Up	3.37	16.05	5.11	33.23		11.64	35.3	888-233-4339	Y
Transamerica ClearTrack® 2045 R3	TCTTX	B-	C	B	Up	3.38	16.21	5.45	34.76		11.61	35.3	888-233-4339	Y
Transamerica ClearTrack® 2045 R6	TCOTX	B-	C	B	Up	3.43	16.35	5.70	35.75		11.74	35.3	888-233-4339	Y
Transamerica ClearTrack® 2050 R1	TRNTX	B-	C	B	Up	3.33	16.15	4.81	33.47		11.79	27.5	888-233-4339	Y
Transamerica ClearTrack® 2050 R3	TCTUX	B-	C	B	Up	3.33	16.32	5.16	34.95		11.76	27.5	888-233-4339	Y
Transamerica ClearTrack® 2050 R6	TCMTX	B-	C	B	Up	3.47	16.55	5.50	36.07		11.9	27.5	888-233-4339	Y
Transamerica ClearTrack® Retirement Income R1	TCITX	B-	C	B		2.90	9.83	6.45	14.25		10.27	67.1	888-233-4339	Y
Transamerica ClearTrack® Retirement Income R3	TCTZX	B-	C	B+		3.00	10.05	6.86	15.52		10.28	67.1	888-233-4339	Y
Transamerica ClearTrack® Retirement Income R6	TCJTX	B-	C+	B+		3.08	10.21	7.14	16.41		10.36	67.1	888-233-4339	Y
USAA Target Retirement 2020 Fund	URTNX	B	C	A-	Up	2.90	10.14	5.49	22.77	22.21	12.38	585.9	800-235-8396	Y
USAA Target Retirement 2030 Fund	URTRX	B-	C	A-	Up	3.03	12.01	4.88	27.74	25.43	13.24	1,319	800-235-8396	Y
USAA Target Retirement 2040 Fund	URFRX	B-	C	B+	Up	3.15	13.45	4.51	31.24	27.58	13.41	1,480	800-235-8396	Y
USAA Target Retirement 2050 Fund	URFFX	B-	C	B+	Up	3.12	13.87	4.23	32.42	28.48	13.54	850.3	800-235-8396	Y
USAA Target Retirement 2060 Fund	URSIX	B-	C	B+	Up	3.13	13.83	4.13	31.81	28.16	12.51	108.5	800-235-8396	Y
USAA Target Retirement Income Fund	URINX	B	C+	A-	Up	2.69	8.34	5.87	16.69	17.82	11.44	336.3	800-235-8396	Y
Vanguard Inst Target Retmnt 2015 Inst Shares	VITVX	B	C+	A	Up	3.04	10.16	6.54	22.26		22.65	8,725	877-662-7447	Y
Vanguard Inst Target Retmnt 2020 Inst Shares	VITWX	B	C+	A	Up	3.21	11.84	6.58	26.51		23.41	23,929	877-662-7447	Y
Vanguard Inst Target Retmnt 2025 Inst Shares	VRIVX	B	C	A-	Up	3.38	13.05	6.68	29.73		23.81	32,422	877-662-7447	Y
Vanguard Inst Target Retmnt 2030 Inst Shares	VTTWX	B-	C	A-	Up	3.39	13.86	6.45	32.42		24.06	30,368	877-662-7447	Y
Vanguard Inst Target Retmnt 2035 Inst Shares	VITFX	B-	C	B+	Up	3.44	14.73	6.27	35.13		24.3	27,817	877-662-7447	Y
Vanguard Inst Target Retmnt 2040 Inst Shares	VIRSX	B-	C	B+	Up	3.45	15.53	6.03	37.75		24.54	24,336	877-662-7447	Y
Vanguard Inst Target Retmnt 2045 Inst Shares	VITLX	B-	C	B	Up	3.47	16.17	5.88	38.78		24.71	20,743	877-662-7447	Y
Vanguard Inst Target Retmnt 2050 Inst Shares	VTRLX	B-	C	B	Up	3.47	16.15	5.86	38.68		24.75	15,332	877-662-7447	Y
Vanguard Inst Target Retmnt 2055 Inst Shares	VIVLX	B-	C	B	Up	3.50	16.19	5.95	38.79		24.82	7,409	877-662-7447	Y
Vanguard Inst Target Retmnt 2060 Inst Shares	VILVX	B-	C	B	Up	3.50	16.14	5.94	38.74		24.82	2,279	877-662-7447	Y
Vanguard Inst Target Retmnt Income Inst Shares	VITRX	B	C+	A-		2.90	9.01	6.56	17.19		22.07	6,193	877-662-7447	Y
Vanguard Target Retirement 2015 Fund Investor Shares	VTXVX	B	C+	A	Up	2.98	10.06	6.40	22.09	26.98	15.21	15,775	877-662-7447	Y
Vanguard Target Retirement 2020 Fund Investor Shares	VTWNX	B	C+	A	Up	3.20	11.78	6.49	26.29	31.06	31.87	32,912	877-662-7447	Y
Vanguard Target Retirement 2025 Fund Investor Shares	VTTVX	B	C	A-	Up	3.34	12.99	6.61	29.52	33.61	19.13	43,560	877-662-7447	Y
Vanguard Target Retirement 2030 Fund Investor Shares	VTHRX	B-	C	A-	Up	3.40	13.86	6.41	32.25	35.37	34.91	38,403	877-662-7447	Y
Vanguard Target Retirement 2035 Fund Investor Shares	VTTHX	B-	C	B+	Up	3.42	14.64	6.21	34.91	37.01	21.46	36,493	877-662-7447	Y
Vanguard Target Retirement 2040 Fund Investor Shares	VFORX	B-	C	B+	Up	3.45	15.50	6.00	37.65	38.58	37.09	28,470	877-662-7447	Y
Vanguard Target Retirement 2045 Fund Investor Shares	VTIVX	B-	C	B	Up	3.50	16.13	5.89	38.61	39.46	23.32	26,144	877-662-7447	Y
Vanguard Target Retirement 2050 Fund Investor Shares	VFIFX	B-	C	B	Up	3.47	16.12	5.85	38.52	39.41	37.52	18,853	877-662-7447	Y
Vanguard Target Retirement 2055 Fund Investor Shares	VFFVX	B-	C	B	Up	3.48	16.13	5.87	38.56	39.20	40.73	9,695	877-662-7447	Y
Vanguard Target Retirement 2060 Fund Investor Shares	VTTSX	B-	C	B	Up	3.48	16.14	5.85	38.50	39.17	35.97	4,079	877-662-7447	Y
Vanguard Target Retirement Income Fund Investor Shares	VTINX	B	C+	A-		2.96	8.97	6.54	17.10	22.80	13.72	16,765	877-662-7447	Y
Voya Index Solution 2020 Portfolio Class ADV	IDXAX	B	C	A-	Up	2.99	10.26	5.84	21.24	24.81	13.43	366.8	800-366-0066	Y
Voya Index Solution 2020 Portfolio Class I	IDXBX	B	C+	A	Up	3.13	10.55	6.44	23.21	27.59	13.82	366.8	800-366-0066	Y
Voya Index Solution 2020 Portfolio Class S	IDXCX	B	C+	A-	Up	3.07	10.44	6.16	22.29	26.21	13.75	366.8	800-366-0066	Y
Voya Index Solution 2020 Portfolio Class S2	IDXDX	B	C	A-	Up	3.09	10.42	6.04	21.71	25.27	13.67	366.8	800-366-0066	Y
Voya Index Solution 2020 Portfolio Class Z	VSZAX	B	C+	A	Up	3.26	10.73	6.63	23.85	28.57	13.93	366.8	800-366-0066	Y
Voya Index Solution 2025 Portfolio Class ADV	ISDAX	B	C	A-	Up	3.05	11.75	5.81	25.78	26.26	11.12	1,005	800-366-0066	Y
Voya Index Solution 2025 Portfolio Class I	ISDIX	B	C	A-	Up	3.25	12.05	6.38	27.60	29.48	11.43	1,005	800-366-0066	Y
Voya Index Solution 2025 Portfolio Class S	ISDSX	B	C	A-	Up	3.19	11.99	6.16	26.71	27.97	11.3	1,005	800-366-0066	Y
Voya Index Solution 2025 Portfolio Class S2	IXXVX	B	C	A-	Up	3.06	11.79	5.93	26.14	26.85	11.09	1,005	800-366-0066	Y
Voya Index Solution 2025 Portfolio Class Z	VSZBX	B	C	A-	Up	3.31	12.26	6.72	28.41	30.53	11.53	1,005	800-366-0066	Y
Voya Index Solution 2030 Portfolio Class ADV	IDXFX	B-	C	B+	Up	3.24	13.31	5.85	29.32	30.29	15.57	523.4	800-366-0066	Y
Voya Index Solution 2030 Portfolio Class I	IDXGX	B-	C	A-	Up	3.35	13.59	6.40	31.22	33.39	16.04	523.4	800-366-0066	Y

Category: Target Date (con't)

Fund Name	Ticker Symbol	RATINGS: Overall Rating	Reward Rating	Risk Rating	Recent Up/ Downgrade	TOTAL RETURNS & PERFORMANCE: 3-Month Total Return	6-Month Total Return	1-Year Total Return	3-Year Total Return	5-Year Total Return	ASSETS: NAV	Total Assets (MIL)	NEW INVESTORS: Telephone	Open to New Investors
Voya Index Solution 2030 Portfolio Class S	IDXHX	B-	C	B+	Up	3.31	13.48	6.10	30.33	31.82	15.91	523.4	800-366-0066	Y
Voya Index Solution 2030 Portfolio Class S2	IDXIX	B-	C	B+	Up	3.35	13.41	6.02	29.79	30.62	15.73	523.4	800-366-0066	Y
Voya Index Solution 2030 Portfolio Class Z	VSZCX	B-	C	A-	Up	3.39	13.67	6.57	31.94	34.12	16.13	523.4	800-366-0066	Y
Voya Index Solution 2035 Portfolio Class ADV	ISEAX	B-	C	B+	Up	3.22	14.28	5.64	32.23	31.19	11.52	948.2	800-366-0066	Y
Voya Index Solution 2035 Portfolio Class I	ISEIX	B-	C	B+	Up	3.48	14.67	6.28	34.33	34.69	11.88	948.2	800-366-0066	Y
Voya Index Solution 2035 Portfolio Class S	ISESX	B-	C	B+	Up	3.35	14.45	5.97	33.30	32.93	11.72	948.2	800-366-0066	Y
Voya Index Solution 2035 Portfolio Class S2	IXISX	B-	C	B+	Up	3.31	14.39	5.78	32.74	32.02	11.52	948.2	800-366-0066	Y
Voya Index Solution 2035 Portfolio Class Z	VSZDX	B-	C	B+	Up	3.54	14.73	6.50	35.08	35.81	11.99	948.2	800-366-0066	Y
Voya Index Solution 2040 Portfolio Class ADV	IDXKX	B-	C	B+	Up	3.35	15.07	5.53	33.66	32.62	16.34	383.9	800-366-0066	Y
Voya Index Solution 2040 Portfolio Class I	IDXLX	B-	C	B+	Up	3.45	15.31	6.04	35.59	35.73	16.79	383.9	800-366-0066	Y
Voya Index Solution 2040 Portfolio Class S	IDXMX	B-	C	B+	Up	3.39	15.13	5.78	34.61	34.18	16.74	383.9	800-366-0066	Y
Voya Index Solution 2040 Portfolio Class S2	IDXNX	B-	C	B+	Up	3.38	15.06	5.58	34.08	33.11	16.5	383.9	800-366-0066	Y
Voya Index Solution 2040 Portfolio Class Z	VSZEX	B-	C	B+	Up	3.54	15.41	6.32	36.40	36.66	16.92	383.9	800-366-0066	Y
Voya Index Solution 2045 Portfolio Class ADV	ISJAX	B-	C	B	Up	3.37	15.69	5.37	34.62	32.86	11.94	653.7	800-366-0066	Y
Voya Index Solution 2045 Portfolio Class I	ISJIX	B-	C	B	Up	3.51	16.02	5.86	36.73	36.21	12.38	653.7	800-366-0066	Y
Voya Index Solution 2045 Portfolio Class S	ISJSX	B-	C	B	Up	3.48	15.88	5.58	35.64	34.51	12.18	653.7	800-366-0066	Y
Voya Index Solution 2045 Portfolio Class S2	ISVLX	B-	C	B	Up	3.36	15.76	5.46	34.99	33.51	11.97	653.7	800-366-0066	Y
Voya Index Solution 2045 Portfolio Class Z	VSZFX	B-	C	B	Up	3.56	16.18	6.16	37.47	37.21	12.49	653.7	800-366-0066	Y
Voya Index Solution 2050 Portfolio Class ADV	IDXPX	B-	C	B	Up	3.43	15.94	5.39	34.89	33.30	16.58	258.0	800-366-0066	Y
Voya Index Solution 2050 Portfolio Class I	IDXQX	B-	C	B	Up	3.60	16.23	5.90	36.91	36.83	16.97	258.0	800-366-0066	Y
Voya Index Solution 2050 Portfolio Class S	IDXRX	B-	C	B	Up	3.49	16.07	5.66	35.93	35.28	16.9	258.0	800-366-0066	Y
Voya Index Solution 2050 Portfolio Class S2	IDXSX	B-	C	B	Up	3.54	16.01	5.53	35.28	34.08	16.66	258.0	800-366-0066	Y
Voya Index Solution 2050 Portfolio Class Z	VSZGX	B-	C	B	Up	3.64	16.34	6.18	37.70	37.82	17.08	258.0	800-366-0066	Y
Voya Index Solution 2055 Portfolio Class ADV	IISAX	B-	C	B	Up	3.41	15.90	5.32	35.06	33.19	15.45	289.5	800-366-0066	Y
Voya Index Solution 2055 Portfolio Class I	IISNX	B-	C	B	Up	3.52	16.16	5.83	37.15	36.65	15.88	289.5	800-366-0066	Y
Voya Index Solution 2055 Portfolio Class S	IISSX	B-	C	B	Up	3.43	15.98	5.59	36.03	34.87	15.67	289.5	800-366-0066	Y
Voya Index Solution 2055 Portfolio Class S2	IISTX	B-	C	B	Up	3.46	15.96	5.43	35.57	33.93	15.54	289.5	800-366-0066	Y
Voya Index Solution 2055 Portfolio Class Z	VSZHX	B-	C	B	Up	3.62	16.33	6.12	37.97	37.68	16.02	289.5	800-366-0066	Y
Voya Index Solution 2060 Portfolio Class ADV	VPSAX	B-	C	B	Up	3.33	15.88	5.34	35.35		12.69	77.7	800-366-0066	Y
Voya Index Solution 2060 Portfolio Class I	VISPX	B-	C	B	Up	3.52	16.27	5.93	37.38		12.93	77.7	800-366-0066	Y
Voya Index Solution 2060 Portfolio Class S	VPISX	B-	C	B	Up	3.47	16.04	5.66	36.33		12.8	77.7	800-366-0066	Y
Voya Index Solution 2060 Portfolio Class S2	VPSSX	B-	C	B	Up	3.40	15.90	5.43	35.60		12.75	77.7	800-366-0066	Y
Voya Index Solution 2060 Portfolio Class Z	VSZIX	B-	C	B	Up	3.57	16.35	6.07	38.22		13.02	77.7	800-366-0066	Y
Voya Index Solution Income Portfolio Class ADV	ISKAX	B-	C	B+		2.84	8.72	5.71	15.05	18.55	10.47	469.7	800-366-0066	Y
Voya Index Solution Income Portfolio Class I	ISKIX	B	C+	A-	Up	2.86	8.89	6.16	16.72	21.51	10.77	469.7	800-366-0066	Y
Voya Index Solution Income Portfolio Class S	ISKSX	B-	C	A-		2.79	8.78	5.93	15.90	20.01	10.65	469.7	800-366-0066	Y
Voya Index Solution Income Portfolio Class S2	IIIPX	B-	C	B+		2.76	8.66	5.77	15.40	19.14	10.41	469.7	800-366-0066	Y
Voya Index Solution Income Portfolio Class Z	VSZJX	B	C+	A-	Up	2.93	9.03	6.42	17.41	22.48	10.86	469.7	800-366-0066	Y
Voya Solution 2020 Portfolio Class ADV	ISNAX	B	C+	A-	Up	3.15	10.75	5.96	22.79	26.64	13.08	32.6	800-366-0066	Y
Voya Solution 2020 Portfolio Class I	ISNBX	B	C+	A	Up	3.23	11.00	6.58	24.55	29.79	13.42	32.6	800-366-0066	Y
Voya Solution 2020 Portfolio Class S	ISNCX	B	C+	A	Up	3.17	10.80	6.27	23.64	28.15	13.33	32.6	800-366-0066	Y
Voya Solution 2020 Portfolio Class S2	ISNDX	B	C+	A	Up	3.21	10.85	6.12	23.13	27.24	13.17	32.6	800-366-0066	Y
Voya Solution 2020 Portfolio Class T	ISNEX	B	C	A-	Up	3.07	10.66	5.82	22.05	25.39	13.07	32.6	800-366-0066	Y
Voya Solution 2025 Portfolio Class ADV	ISZAX	B-	C	A-	Up	3.08	12.17	5.51	26.29	27.70	11.7	812.1	800-366-0066	Y
Voya Solution 2025 Portfolio Class I	ISZIX	B	C	A-	Up	3.25	12.39	6.09	28.19	30.98	12.06	812.1	800-366-0066	Y
Voya Solution 2025 Portfolio Class S	ISZSX	B	C	A-	Up	3.20	12.26	5.78	27.24	29.28	11.9	812.1	800-366-0066	Y
Voya Solution 2025 Portfolio Class S2	ISPBX	B-	C	A-	Up	3.21	12.22	5.76	26.77	28.38	11.57	812.1	800-366-0066	Y
Voya Solution 2025 Portfolio Class T	ISZTX	B-	C	A-	Up	3.12	12.00	5.33	25.54	26.39	12.22	812.1	800-366-0066	Y
Voya Solution 2030 Portfolio Class ADV	ISNFX	B-	C	B+	Up	3.17	13.62	5.26	29.58	31.36	15.59	37.8	800-366-0066	Y
Voya Solution 2030 Portfolio Class I	ISNGX	B-	C	B+	Up	3.27	13.90	5.80	31.42	34.73	16.06	37.8	800-366-0066	Y
Voya Solution 2030 Portfolio Class S	ISNHX	B-	C	B+	Up	3.23	13.77	5.53	30.53	33.06	15.94	37.8	800-366-0066	Y
Voya Solution 2030 Portfolio Class S2	ISNIX	B-	C	B+	Up	3.21	13.66	5.37	29.92	31.96	15.72	37.8	800-366-0066	Y

Category: Target Date (con't)

Fund Name	Ticker Symbol	Overall Rating	Reward Rating	Risk Rating	Recent Up/ Downgrade	3-Month Total Return	6-Month Total Return	1-Year Total Return	3-Year Total Return	5-Year Total Return	NAV	Total Assets (MIL)	Telephone	Open to New Investors
		RATINGS				TOTAL RETURNS & PERFORMANCE					ASSETS		NEW INVESTORS	
Voya Solution 2030 Portfolio Class T	ISNJX	B-	C	B+	Up	3.10	13.45	5.01	28.79	29.88	15.6	37.8	800-366-0066	Y
Voya Solution 2035 Portfolio Class ADV	ISQAX	B-	C	B+	Up	3.16	14.42	4.74	31.84	31.03	12.06	832.1	800-366-0066	Y
Voya Solution 2035 Portfolio Class I	ISQIX	B-	C	B+	Up	3.32	14.77	5.24	33.85	34.39	12.43	832.1	800-366-0066	Y
Voya Solution 2035 Portfolio Class S	ISQSX	B-	C	B+	Up	3.28	14.67	5.02	32.84	32.71	12.27	832.1	800-366-0066	Y
Voya Solution 2035 Portfolio Class S2	ISPCX	B-	C	B+	Up	3.23	14.56	4.92	32.36	31.79	11.8	832.1	800-366-0066	Y
Voya Solution 2035 Portfolio Class T	ISQTX	B-	C	B+	Up	3.19	14.44	4.58	31.13	29.88	12.6	832.1	800-366-0066	Y
Voya Solution 2040 Portfolio Class ADV	ISNKX	B-	C	B	Up	3.28	15.23	4.47	33.37	33.11	16.34	31.3	800-366-0066	Y
Voya Solution 2040 Portfolio Class I	ISNLX	B-	C	B	Up	3.37	15.51	5.00	35.33	36.67	16.83	31.3	800-366-0066	Y
Voya Solution 2040 Portfolio Class S	ISNMX	B-	C	B	Up	3.28	15.36	4.72	34.37	34.80	16.67	31.3	800-366-0066	Y
Voya Solution 2040 Portfolio Class S2	ISNNX	B-	C	B	Up	3.27	15.24	4.55	33.74	33.77	16.4	31.3	800-366-0066	Y
Voya Solution 2040 Portfolio Class T	ISNOX	B-	C	B	Up	3.17	15.06	4.26	32.58	31.81	16.27	31.3	800-366-0066	Y
Voya Solution 2045 Portfolio Class ADV	ISRAX	B-	C	B	Up	3.27	15.74	3.87	33.24	31.37	11.98	624.4	800-366-0066	Y
Voya Solution 2045 Portfolio Class I	ISRIX	B-	C	B	Up	3.42	16.04	4.40	35.16	34.75	12.37	624.4	800-366-0066	Y
Voya Solution 2045 Portfolio Class S	ISRSX	B-	C	B	Up	3.39	15.88	4.17	34.27	33.04	12.18	624.4	800-366-0066	Y
Voya Solution 2045 Portfolio Class S2	ISPDX	B-	C	B	Up	3.31	15.72	3.89	33.51	31.97	11.85	624.4	800-366-0066	Y
Voya Solution 2045 Portfolio Class T	ISRTX	B-	C	B	Up	3.17	15.55	3.55	32.31	29.95	12.33	624.4	800-366-0066	Y
Voya Solution 2050 Portfolio Class I	ISNQX	B-	C	B	Up	3.51	16.33	4.39	35.55	36.50	17.38	25.5	800-366-0066	Y
Voya Solution 2050 Portfolio Class S	ISNRX	B-	C	B	Up	3.43	16.17	4.09	34.55	34.42	17.17	25.5	800-366-0066	Y
Voya Solution 2050 Portfolio Class S2	ISNSX	B-	C	B	Up	3.42	16.04	3.95	33.90	33.55	16.92	25.5	800-366-0066	Y
Voya Solution 2055 Portfolio Class ADV	IASPX	B-	C	B	Up	3.34	15.98	3.86	33.73	31.98	14.22	205.3	800-366-0066	Y
Voya Solution 2055 Portfolio Class I	IISPX	B-	C	B	Up	3.48	16.29	4.36	35.75	35.36	14.56	205.3	800-366-0066	Y
Voya Solution 2055 Portfolio Class S	ISSPX	B-	C	B	Up	3.38	16.07	4.08	34.75	33.62	14.37	205.3	800-366-0066	Y
Voya Solution 2055 Portfolio Class S2	ITSPX	B-	C	B	Up	3.40	16.00	3.94	34.08	32.63	14.28	205.3	800-366-0066	Y
Voya Solution 2060 Portfolio Class I	VSIPX	B-	C	B	Up	3.46	16.23	4.35	35.91		12.24	14.1	800-366-0066	Y
Voya Solution 2060 Portfolio Class S	VSPSX	B-	C	B	Up	3.33	16.05	3.98	34.73		12.07	14.1	800-366-0066	Y
Voya Solution 2060 Portfolio Class S2	VSSPX	B-	C	B	Up	3.34	15.97	3.87	34.19		12.05	14.1	800-366-0066	Y
Voya Solution Income Portfolio Class ADV	ISWAX	B	C	A-	Up	2.85	9.09	6.12	16.54	20.33	11.88	345.1	800-366-0066	Y
Voya Solution Income Portfolio Class I	ISWIX	B	C+	A-	Up	2.95	9.41	6.67	18.34	23.33	12.2	345.1	800-366-0066	Y
Voya Solution Income Portfolio Class S	ISWSX	B	C+	A-	Up	2.89	9.22	6.39	17.40	21.89	12.08	345.1	800-366-0066	Y
Voya Solution Income Portfolio Class S2	IJKBX	B	C+	A-	Up	2.88	9.17	6.28	16.99	20.96	11.78	345.1	800-366-0066	Y
Voya Solution Income Portfolio Class T	ISWTX	B-	C	A-		2.84	9.04	5.93	15.93	19.28	12.66	345.1	800-366-0066	Y
Voya Target In-Retirement Fund Class A	VTRVX	B	C	A-	Up	2.86	8.84	5.93	16.67	20.98	11.14	10.8	800-366-0066	Y
Voya Target In-Retirement Fund Class I	ISOLX	B	C+	A-	Up	2.94	8.98	6.28	17.57	22.48	11.18	10.8	800-366-0066	Y
Voya Target In-Retirement Fund Class R	VRRPX	B-	C	A-		2.68	8.42	5.62	16.12	19.20	11.11	10.8	800-366-0066	Y
Voya Target In-Retirement Fund Class R6	VTRWX	B	C+	A-	Up	2.85	8.91	6.21	17.57	22.59	11.17	10.8	800-366-0066	Y
Voya Target Retirement 2020 Fund Class A	VFTRX	B	C+	A-	Up	3.06	10.39	6.00	22.30	25.13	11.75	13.3	800-366-0066	Y
Voya Target Retirement 2020 Fund Class I	IRSJX	B	C+	A	Up	3.14	10.55	6.37	23.27	26.94	11.81	13.3	800-366-0066	Y
Voya Target Retirement 2020 Fund Class R	VRRGX	B	C	A-	Up	2.98	10.28	5.80	21.39	23.77	11.72	13.3	800-366-0066	Y
Voya Target Retirement 2020 Fund Class R6	VTRBX	B	C+	A	Up	3.14	10.56	6.37	23.41	26.85	11.81	13.3	800-366-0066	Y
Voya Target Retirement 2025 Fund Class A	VTRCX	B	C	A-	Up	3.11	11.85	5.70	26.18	27.77	12.24	24.5	800-366-0066	Y
Voya Target Retirement 2025 Fund Class I	IRSLX	B	C	A-	Up	3.10	11.94	5.98	27.12	29.32	12.29	24.5	800-366-0066	Y
Voya Target Retirement 2025 Fund Class R	VRRHX	B-	C	A-	Up	3.04	11.73	5.58	25.38	26.28	12.2	24.5	800-366-0066	Y
Voya Target Retirement 2025 Fund Class R6	VTRDX	B	C	A-	Up	3.27	12.09	6.12	27.43	29.64	12.29	24.5	800-366-0066	Y
Voya Target Retirement 2030 Fund Class A	VTREX	B-	C	B+	Up	3.19	13.28	5.68	29.34	30.74	12.26	21.9	800-366-0066	Y
Voya Target Retirement 2030 Fund Class I	IRSMX	B-	C	B+	Up	3.26	13.47	5.98	30.39	32.55	12.32	21.9	800-366-0066	Y
Voya Target Retirement 2030 Fund Class R6	VTRFX	B-	C	B+	Up	3.27	13.51	6.01	30.60	32.64	12.31	21.9	800-366-0066	Y
Voya Target Retirement 2030 Fund ClassR	VRRIX	B-	C	B+	Up	3.11	13.12	5.43	28.43	29.26	12.23	21.9	800-366-0066	Y
Voya Target Retirement 2035 Fund Class A	VTRGX	B-	C	B+	Up	3.28	14.35	5.51	32.44	31.79	12.27	22.4	800-366-0066	Y
Voya Target Retirement 2035 Fund Class I	IRSNX	B-	C	B+	Up	3.26	14.39	5.78	33.52	33.63	12.32	22.4	800-366-0066	Y
Voya Target Retirement 2035 Fund Class R	VRRJX	B-	C	B+	Up	3.20	14.21	5.30	31.60	30.39	12.25	22.4	800-366-0066	Y
Voya Target Retirement 2035 Fund Class R6	VTRHX	B-	C	B+	Up	3.35	14.54	5.90	33.54	33.64	12.31	22.4	800-366-0066	Y
Voya Target Retirement 2040 Fund Class A	VTRJX	B-	C	B+	Up	3.29	15.06	5.26	33.97	33.43	12.52	16.5	800-366-0066	Y

Category: Target Date (con't)

Fund Name	Ticker Symbol	Overall Rating	Reward Rating	Risk Rating	Recent Up/ Downgrade	3-Month Total Return	6-Month Total Return	1-Year Total Return	3-Year Total Return	5-Year Total Return	NAV	Total Assets (MIL)	Telephone	Open to New Investors
Voya Target Retirement 2040 Fund Class I	IRSOX	B-	C	B+	Up	3.28	15.19	5.50	34.99	35.08	12.57	16.5	800-366-0066	Y
Voya Target Retirement 2040 Fund Class R	VRRKX	B-	C	B+	Up	3.22	14.92	5.03	33.05	31.82	12.5	16.5	800-366-0066	Y
Voya Target Retirement 2040 Fund Class R6	VTRKX	B-	C	B+	Up	3.37	15.25	5.55	35.20	35.29	12.56	16.5	800-366-0066	Y
Voya Target Retirement 2045 Fund Class A	VTRMX	B-	C	B	Up	3.24	15.73	5.02	34.34	33.81	12.72	19.5	800-366-0066	Y
Voya Target Retirement 2045 Fund Class I	IRSPX	B-	C	B	Up	3.31	15.88	5.37	35.51	35.74	12.77	19.5	800-366-0066	Y
Voya Target Retirement 2045 Fund Class R	VRRLX	B-	C	B	Up	3.17	15.61	4.81	33.45	32.34	12.69	19.5	800-366-0066	Y
Voya Target Retirement 2045 Fund Class R6	VTRNX	B-	C	B	Up	3.40	15.94	5.42	35.72	35.95	12.77	19.5	800-366-0066	Y
Voya Target Retirement 2050 Fund Class A	VTROX	B-	C	B	Up	3.31	16.03	5.05	34.57	33.94	12.45	12.5	800-366-0066	Y
Voya Target Retirement 2050 Fund Class I	IRSQX	B-	C	B	Up	3.39	16.16	5.30	35.62	35.75	12.49	12.5	800-366-0066	Y
Voya Target Retirement 2050 Fund Class R	VRRMX	B-	C	B	Up	3.23	15.85	4.72	33.53	32.32	12.43	12.5	800-366-0066	Y
Voya Target Retirement 2050 Fund Class R6	VTRPX	B-	C	B	Up	3.39	16.21	5.34	35.78	35.91	12.49	12.5	800-366-0066	Y
Voya Target Retirement 2055 Fund Class A	VTRQX	B-	C	B	Up	3.28	15.99	5.02	34.86	34.37	12.58	12.2	800-366-0066	Y
Voya Target Retirement 2055 Fund Class I	IRSVX	B-	C	B	Up	3.44	16.18	5.40	36.07	36.21	12.63	12.2	800-366-0066	Y
Voya Target Retirement 2055 Fund Class R	VRRNX	B-	C	B	Up	3.20	15.74	4.62	33.71	32.52	12.55	12.2	800-366-0066	Y
Voya Target Retirement 2055 Fund Class R6	VTRRX	B-	C	B	Up	3.35	16.23	5.35	36.12	36.39	12.62	12.2	800-366-0066	Y
Voya Target Retirement 2060 Fund Class A	VTRSX	B-	C	B	Up	3.21	15.93	4.97	34.68		11.56	5.4	800-366-0066	Y
Voya Target Retirement 2060 Fund Class I	VRSAX	B-	C	B	Up	3.30	16.13	5.27	35.74		11.58	5.4	800-366-0066	Y
Voya Target Retirement 2060 Fund Class R	VRROX	B-	C	B	Up	3.30	15.90	4.76	33.94		11.55	5.4	800-366-0066	Y
Voya Target Retirement 2060 Fund Class R6	VTRUX	B-	C	B	Up	3.39	16.15	5.29	35.98		11.59	5.4	800-366-0066	Y
Wells Fargo Dynamic Target 2015 Fund Class A	WDTAX	B	C+	A		2.96	11.69	7.42	26.45		10.41	5.6	800-222-8222	Y
Wells Fargo Dynamic Target 2015 Fund Class C	WDTCX	B	C+	A-	Up	2.67	11.17	6.57	23.54		10.35	5.6	800-222-8222	Y
Wells Fargo Dynamic Target 2015 Fund Class R4	WDTYX	B	C+	A		2.96	11.69	7.74	27.50		10.41	5.6	800-222-8222	Y
Wells Fargo Dynamic Target 2015 Fund Class R6	WDTZX	B	C+	A		2.96	11.80	7.92	28.11		10.42	5.6	800-222-8222	Y
Wells Fargo Dynamic Target 2020 Fund Class A	WDTDX	B	C+	A		2.98	12.36	7.58	29.98		10.36	5.9	800-222-8222	Y
Wells Fargo Dynamic Target 2020 Fund Class C	WDTEX	B	C+	A	Up	2.68	11.91	6.73	26.98		10.33	5.9	800-222-8222	Y
Wells Fargo Dynamic Target 2020 Fund Class R4	WDTGX	B	C+	A		2.96	12.43	7.83	30.92		10.4	5.9	800-222-8222	Y
Wells Fargo Dynamic Target 2020 Fund Class R6	WDTHX	B	C+	A		3.06	12.54	8.00	31.61		10.41	5.9	800-222-8222	Y
Wells Fargo Dynamic Target 2025 Fund Class A	WDTIX	B	C	A-	Up	3.04	13.02	7.02	32.70		10.5	7.6	800-222-8222	Y
Wells Fargo Dynamic Target 2025 Fund Class C	WDTJX	B-	C	A-	Up	2.84	12.58	6.19	29.56		10.47	7.6	800-222-8222	Y
Wells Fargo Dynamic Target 2025 Fund Class R4	WDTLX	B	C+	A-	Up	3.12	13.18	7.31	33.76		10.56	7.6	800-222-8222	Y
Wells Fargo Dynamic Target 2025 Fund Class R6	WDTMX	B	C+	A-	Up	3.12	13.29	7.49	34.47		10.57	7.6	800-222-8222	Y
Wells Fargo Dynamic Target 2030 Fund Class A	WDTNX	B-	C	A-		3.09	13.65	7.11	36.18		10.32	6.4	800-222-8222	Y
Wells Fargo Dynamic Target 2030 Fund Class C	WDTOX	B-	C	B+	Up	2.91	13.27	6.32	33.13		10.24	6.4	800-222-8222	Y
Wells Fargo Dynamic Target 2030 Fund Class R4	WDTQX	B-	C	A-		3.17	13.92	7.41	37.43		10.39	6.4	800-222-8222	Y
Wells Fargo Dynamic Target 2030 Fund Class R6	WDTSX	B-	C	A-		3.27	14.03	7.59	38.02		10.4	6.4	800-222-8222	Y
Wells Fargo Dynamic Target 2035 Fund Class A	WDTTX	B-	C	B+		3.13	14.20	7.18	38.96		10.21	5.7	800-222-8222	Y
Wells Fargo Dynamic Target 2035 Fund Class C	WDCTX	B-	C	B+	Up	2.83	13.75	6.36	35.78		10.17	5.7	800-222-8222	Y
Wells Fargo Dynamic Target 2035 Fund Class R4	WDTVX	B-	C	B+		3.11	14.36	7.49	40.17		10.27	5.7	800-222-8222	Y
Wells Fargo Dynamic Target 2035 Fund Class R6	WDTWX	B-	C	B+		3.21	14.47	7.67	40.77		10.28	5.7	800-222-8222	Y
Wells Fargo Dynamic Target 2040 Fund Class A	WTDAX	B-	C	B+		2.95	14.22	6.75	39.85		10.12	5.9	800-222-8222	Y
Wells Fargo Dynamic Target 2040 Fund Class C	WTDCX	B-	C	B+	Up	2.85	13.88	6.02	36.94		10.09	5.9	800-222-8222	Y
Wells Fargo Dynamic Target 2040 Fund Class R4	WTDEX	B-	C	B+		3.13	14.47	7.20	41.33		10.2	5.9	800-222-8222	Y
Wells Fargo Dynamic Target 2040 Fund Class R6	WTDFX	B-	C	B+		3.13	14.59	7.30	41.93		10.21	5.9	800-222-8222	Y
Wells Fargo Dynamic Target 2045 Fund Class A	WTDGX	B-	C	B+	Up	2.96	14.56	6.48	40.20		10.07	5.4	800-222-8222	Y
Wells Fargo Dynamic Target 2045 Fund Class C	WTDHX	B-	C	B+	Up	2.87	14.10	5.68	37.13		10.03	5.4	800-222-8222	Y
Wells Fargo Dynamic Target 2045 Fund Class R4	WTDJX	B-	C	B+		3.04	14.70	6.77	41.51		10.14	5.4	800-222-8222	Y
Wells Fargo Dynamic Target 2045 Fund Class R6	WTDKX	B-	C	B+		3.04	14.81	6.93	42.08		10.15	5.4	800-222-8222	Y
Wells Fargo Dynamic Target 2050 Fund Class A	WTDLX	B-	C	B+	Up	3.07	14.56	6.21	39.97		10.07	5.3	800-222-8222	Y
Wells Fargo Dynamic Target 2050 Fund Class C	WTDMX	B-	C	B+	Up	2.88	14.15	5.49	36.97		10	5.3	800-222-8222	Y
Wells Fargo Dynamic Target 2050 Fund Class R4	WTDOX	B-	C	B+	Up	3.05	14.75	6.53	41.29		10.11	5.3	800-222-8222	Y
Wells Fargo Dynamic Target 2050 Fund Class R6	WTDPX	B-	C	B+		3.16	14.86	6.71	41.89		10.12	5.3	800-222-8222	Y
Wells Fargo Dynamic Target 2055 Fund Class A	WTDQX	B-	C	B+	Up	3.07	14.56	6.22	39.96		10.07	5.2	800-222-8222	Y

Category: Target Date (con't)

Fund Name	Ticker Symbol	RATINGS: Overall Rating	Reward Rating	Risk Rating	Recent Up/ Downgrade	TOTAL RETURNS & PERFORMANCE: 3-Month Total Return	6-Month Total Return	1-Year Total Return	3-Year Total Return	5-Year Total Return	ASSETS: NAV	Total Assets (MIL)	NEW INVESTORS: Telephone	Open to New Investors
Wells Fargo Dynamic Target 2055 Fund Class C	WTDRX	B-	C	B+	Up	2.88	14.17	5.50	36.79		9.99	5.2	800-222-8222	Y
Wells Fargo Dynamic Target 2055 Fund Class R4	WTDTX	B-	C	B+	Up	3.06	14.77	6.53	41.09		10.1	5.2	800-222-8222	Y
Wells Fargo Dynamic Target 2055 Fund Class R6	WTDUX	B-	C	B+		3.16	14.88	6.76	41.90		10.11	5.2	800-222-8222	Y
Wells Fargo Dynamic Target 2060 Fund Class A	WTDVX	B-	C	B+	Up	2.96	14.54	6.24	40.01		10.08	5.4	800-222-8222	Y
Wells Fargo Dynamic Target 2060 Fund Class C	WTDWX	B-	C	B+	Up	2.76	14.23	5.40	36.81		10.03	5.4	800-222-8222	Y
Wells Fargo Dynamic Target 2060 Fund Class R4	WTDZX	B-	C	B+	Up	3.15	14.81	6.64	41.26		10.15	5.4	800-222-8222	Y
Wells Fargo Dynamic Target 2060 Fund Class R6	WTSZX	B-	C	B+		3.14	14.93	6.73	42.02		10.16	5.4	800-222-8222	Y
Wells Fargo Dynamic Target Today Fund Class A	WDYAX	B	C+	A		2.82	10.48	7.55	21.56		10.54	5.7	800-222-8222	Y
Wells Fargo Dynamic Target Today Fund Class C	WDYCX	B	C+	A-	Up	2.64	10.08	6.77	18.86		10.48	5.7	800-222-8222	Y
Wells Fargo Dynamic Target Today Fund Class R4	WDYYX	B	C+	A		2.93	10.71	7.92	22.68		10.54	5.7	800-222-8222	Y
Wells Fargo Dynamic Target Today Fund Class R6	WDYZX	B	C+	A		3.02	10.81	8.10	23.26		10.55	5.7	800-222-8222	Y
Wells Fargo Target 2010 Fund - Class A	STNRX	B-	C	B	Up	2.93	9.35	6.94	10.60	12.69	10.47	66.4	800-222-8222	Y
Wells Fargo Target 2010 Fund - Class Admin	WFLGX	B-	C	B+	Up	2.91	9.37	7.03	10.95	13.36	10.62	66.4	800-222-8222	Y
Wells Fargo Target 2010 Fund - Class R4	WFORX	B-	C	B+		2.97	9.49	7.29	11.69	14.51	10.61	66.4	800-222-8222	Y
Wells Fargo Target 2010 Fund - Class R6	WFOAX	B-	C	B+		3.02	9.59	7.38	12.22	15.33	10.59	66.4	800-222-8222	Y
Wells Fargo Target 2015 Fund - Class A	WFACX	B-	C	B+		2.66	9.43	6.61	11.95	14.66	7.27	77.6	800-222-8222	Y
Wells Fargo Target 2015 Fund - Class Admin	WFFFX	B-	C	B+		2.88	9.81	6.97	12.43	15.90	7.48	77.6	800-222-8222	Y
Wells Fargo Target 2015 Fund - Class R4	WFSRX	B-	C	B+		2.99	10.12	7.36	13.01	16.95	7.34	77.6	800-222-8222	Y
Wells Fargo Target 2015 Fund - Class R6	WFSCX	B-	C	B+		2.90	10.04	7.35	13.45	17.68	7.33	77.6	800-222-8222	Y
Wells Fargo Target 2020 Fund - Class A	STTRX	B-	C	B+		2.88	10.57	6.78	15.35	18.06	12.13	407.1	800-222-8222	Y
Wells Fargo Target 2020 Fund - Class Admin	WFLPX	B-	C	B+		2.90	10.60	6.85	15.65	18.66	12.41	407.1	800-222-8222	Y
Wells Fargo Target 2020 Fund - Class R	WFURX	B-	C	B+		2.82	10.38	6.51	14.54	16.69	12.01	407.1	800-222-8222	Y
Wells Fargo Target 2020 Fund - Class R4	WFLRX	B-	C+	B+		3.04	10.70	7.10	16.42	19.96	12.51	407.1	800-222-8222	Y
Wells Fargo Target 2020 Fund - Class R6	WFOBX	B	C+	A-		3.04	10.80	7.32	16.97	20.89	12.51	407.1	800-222-8222	Y
Wells Fargo Target 2025 Fund - Class A	WFAYX	B-	C	A-		2.83	11.32	6.52	19.34	21.38	5.8	298.8	800-222-8222	Y
Wells Fargo Target 2025 Fund - Class Admin	WFTRX	B-	C	A-		2.96	11.53	6.81	19.97	22.25	5.9	298.8	800-222-8222	Y
Wells Fargo Target 2025 Fund - Class R	WFHRX	B-	C	B+		2.87	11.28	6.27	17.52	18.89	5.72	298.8	800-222-8222	Y
Wells Fargo Target 2025 Fund - Class R4	WFGRX	B	C+	A-	Up	2.99	11.64	6.79	20.40	23.15	5.85	298.8	800-222-8222	Y
Wells Fargo Target 2025 Fund - Class R6	WFTYX	B	C+	A-	Up	3.17	11.85	7.16	21.07	24.31	5.85	298.8	800-222-8222	Y
Wells Fargo Target 2030 Fund - Class A	STHRX	B	C	A-	Up	2.96	12.29	6.25	24.01	25.03	12.51	571.0	800-222-8222	Y
Wells Fargo Target 2030 Fund - Class Admin	WFLIX	B	C	A-	Up	2.97	12.35	6.39	24.47	25.83	12.82	571.0	800-222-8222	Y
Wells Fargo Target 2030 Fund - Class C	WFDMX	B-	C	B+	Up	2.75	11.91	5.46	21.21	20.41	11.93	571.0	800-222-8222	Y
Wells Fargo Target 2030 Fund - Class R	WFJRX	B-	C	A-	Up	2.96	12.18	6.05	22.88	23.30	12.52	571.0	800-222-8222	Y
Wells Fargo Target 2030 Fund - Class R4	WTHRX	B	C	A-	Up	3.05	12.54	6.60	25.22	27.06	12.83	571.0	800-222-8222	Y
Wells Fargo Target 2030 Fund - Class R6	WFOOX	B	C	A-	Up	3.13	12.66	6.81	25.73	28.05	12.81	571.0	800-222-8222	Y
Wells Fargo Target 2035 Fund - Class A	WFQBX	B-	C	A-	Up	2.95	13.14	5.98	28.20	27.82	7.66	263.1	800-222-8222	Y
Wells Fargo Target 2035 Fund - Class Admin	WFQWX	B-	C	A-	Up	3.05	13.28	6.12	28.67	28.64	7.76	263.1	800-222-8222	Y
Wells Fargo Target 2035 Fund - Class R	WFKRX	B-	C	B+	Up	2.93	13.03	5.75	27.26	26.22	7.72	263.1	800-222-8222	Y
Wells Fargo Target 2035 Fund - Class R4	WTTRX	B-	C	A-		3.08	13.25	6.32	29.44	29.94	7.69	263.1	800-222-8222	Y
Wells Fargo Target 2035 Fund - Class R6	WFQRX	B-	C	A-		3.08	13.42	6.52	30.07	30.98	7.69	263.1	800-222-8222	Y
Wells Fargo Target 2040 Fund - Class A	STFRX	B-	C	B+	Up	2.95	13.78	5.76	31.50	30.06	14.61	505.8	800-222-8222	Y
Wells Fargo Target 2040 Fund - Class Admin	WFLWX	B-	C	B+	Up	2.99	13.86	5.88	31.95	30.80	15.11	505.8	800-222-8222	Y
Wells Fargo Target 2040 Fund - Class C	WFOFX	B-	C	B+	Up	2.74	13.32	4.93	28.59	25.26	13.1	505.8	800-222-8222	Y
Wells Fargo Target 2040 Fund - Class R	WFMRX	B-	C	B+	Up	2.89	13.62	5.47	30.58	28.47	14.59	505.8	800-222-8222	Y
Wells Fargo Target 2040 Fund - Class R4	WTFRX	B-	C	B+	Up	3.06	13.90	6.03	32.78	32.09	15.15	505.8	800-222-8222	Y
Wells Fargo Target 2040 Fund - Class R6	WFOSX	B-	C	B+	Up	3.06	14.00	6.17	33.30	33.08	15.14	505.8	800-222-8222	Y
Wells Fargo Target 2045 Fund - Class A	WFQVX	B-	C	B+	Up	3.05	14.22	5.63	33.93	31.61	8.43	151.5	800-222-8222	Y
Wells Fargo Target 2045 Fund - Class Admin	WFQYX	B-	C	B+	Up	3.00	14.24	5.69	34.28	32.32	8.58	151.5	800-222-8222	Y
Wells Fargo Target 2045 Fund - Class R	WFNRX	B-	C	B+	Up	2.87	14.09	5.37	32.84	29.93	8.58	151.5	800-222-8222	Y
Wells Fargo Target 2045 Fund - Class R4	WFFRX	B-	C	B+	Up	3.03	14.26	5.94	35.09	33.65	8.49	151.5	800-222-8222	Y
Wells Fargo Target 2045 Fund - Class R6	WFQPX	B-	C	B+	Up	3.04	14.47	6.04	35.67	34.64	8.46	151.5	800-222-8222	Y
Wells Fargo Target 2050 Fund - Class A	WFQAX	B-	C	B+	Up	3.06	14.39	5.58	34.68	32.13	7.39	230.7	800-222-8222	Y

Category: Target Date (con't)

Fund Name	Ticker Symbol	RATINGS Overall Rating	Reward Rating	Risk Rating	Recent Up/ Downgrade	TOTAL RETURNS & PERFORMANCE 3-Month Total Return	6-Month Total Return	1-Year Total Return	3-Year Total Return	5-Year Total Return	ASSETS NAV	Total Assets (MIL)	NEW INVESTORS Telephone	Open to New Investors
Wells Fargo Target 2050 Fund - Class Admin	WFQDX	B-	C	B+	Up	3.05	14.50	5.59	35.24	32.95	7.42	230.7	800-222-8222	Y
Wells Fargo Target 2050 Fund - Class C	WFQCX	B-	C	B+	Up	2.80	14.01	4.69	31.79	27.31	7.32	230.7	800-222-8222	Y
Wells Fargo Target 2050 Fund - Class R	WFWRX	B-	C	B+	Up	2.92	14.19	5.24	33.72	30.44	7.4	230.7	800-222-8222	Y
Wells Fargo Target 2050 Fund - Class R4	WQFRX	B-	C	B+	Up	3.04	14.61	5.91	36.01	34.24	7.45	230.7	800-222-8222	Y
Wells Fargo Target 2050 Fund - Class R6	WFQFX	B-	C	B+	Up	3.04	14.63	5.98	36.49	35.25	7.44	230.7	800-222-8222	Y
Wells Fargo Target 2055 Fund - Class A	WFQZX	B-	C	B+	Up	3.01	14.43	5.59	34.67	32.14	11.97	38.7	800-222-8222	Y
Wells Fargo Target 2055 Fund - Class Admin	WFLHX	B-	C	B+	Up	3.00	14.42	5.66	35.05	32.77	11.98	38.7	800-222-8222	Y
Wells Fargo Target 2055 Fund - Class R	WFYRX	B-	C	B+	Up	2.87	14.24	5.28	33.64	30.46	11.79	38.7	800-222-8222	Y
Wells Fargo Target 2055 Fund - Class R4	WFVRX	B-	C	B+	Up	3.08	14.57	5.95	35.92	34.23	12.03	38.7	800-222-8222	Y
Wells Fargo Target 2055 Fund - Class R6	WFQUX	B-	C	B+	Up	3.17	14.70	6.11	36.58	35.28	12.01	38.7	800-222-8222	Y
Wells Fargo Target 2060 Fund - Class A	WFAFX	B-	C	B+	Up	2.95	14.49	5.56	34.53		11.85	20.1	800-222-8222	Y
Wells Fargo Target 2060 Fund - Class Admin	WFDFX	B-	C	B+	Up	3.03	14.53	5.70	35.13		11.9	20.1	800-222-8222	Y
Wells Fargo Target 2060 Fund - Class C	WFCFX	B-	C	B+	Up	2.87	14.10	4.88	31.71		11.81	20.1	800-222-8222	Y
Wells Fargo Target 2060 Fund - Class R	WFRFX	B-	C	B+	Up	2.92	14.37	5.36	33.56		11.62	20.1	800-222-8222	Y
Wells Fargo Target 2060 Fund - Class R4	WFSFX	B-	C	B+	Up	3.06	14.70	5.90	35.93		12.09	20.1	800-222-8222	Y
Wells Fargo Target 2060 Fund - Class R6	WFUFX	B-	C	B+	Up	3.08	14.77	6.04	36.33		12.04	20.1	800-222-8222	Y
Wells Fargo Target Today Fund - Class A	STWRX	B-	C	B	Up	2.96	9.05	7.09	10.18	12.07	8.95	69.7	800-222-8222	Y
Wells Fargo Target Today Fund - Class Admin	WFLOX	B-	C	B	Up	2.91	9.22	7.11	10.49	12.66	9.2	69.7	800-222-8222	Y
Wells Fargo Target Today Fund - Class R4	WOTRX	B-	C	B		2.96	9.21	7.36	10.75	13.39	9.19	69.7	800-222-8222	Y
Wells Fargo Target Today Fund - Class R6	WOTDX	B-	C	B+		3.00	9.31	7.43	11.57	14.65	9.17	69.7	800-222-8222	Y

Category: Technology Sector Equity

Fund Name	Ticker Symbol	RATINGS Overall Rating	Reward Rating	Risk Rating	Recent Up/ Downgrade	TOTAL RETURNS & PERFORMANCE 3-Month Total Return	6-Month Total Return	1-Year Total Return	3-Year Total Return	5-Year Total Return	ASSETS NAV	Total Assets (MIL)	NEW INVESTORS Telephone	Open to New Investors
Berkshire Focus Fund	BFOCX	B-	B-	C+		1.69	33.66	18.64	133.77	126.36	29.42	293.1	877-526-0707	Y
BlackRock Technology Opportunities Fund Class R Shares	BGSRX	B-	B-	B-	Down	5.69	30.52	13.01	121.49	146.03	31.3	1,831	800-441-7762	Y
BlackRock Technology Opportunities Institutional Shares	BGSIX	B-	B	B-	Down	5.84	30.85	13.59	125.01	152.86	33.46	1,831	800-441-7762	Y
BlackRock Technology Opportunities Fund Investor A Shares	BGSAX	B-	B	B-	Down	5.78	30.72	13.31	123.22	149.42	31.01	1,831	800-441-7762	Y
BlackRock Technology Opportunities Fund Investor C Shares	BGSCX	B-	B-	B-	Down	5.59	30.24	12.48	118.31	139.77	26.15	1,831	800-441-7762	Y
BlackRock Technology Opportunities Fund Service Shares	BSTSX	B-	B	B-	Down	5.79	30.72	13.31	123.47	150.03	31.69	1,831	800-441-7762	Y
Columbia Global Technology Growth Fund Advisor Class	CTYRX	B-	C+	B-	Down	5.14	26.88	10.99	104.86	142.19	37.38	1,512	800-345-6611	Y
Columbia Global Technology Growth Fund Class A	CTCAX	B-	C+	B-	Down	5.10	26.72	10.73	103.45	139.20	35.42	1,512	800-345-6611	Y
Columbia Global Technology Growth Institutional 2 Cls	CTHRX	B-	C+	B-	Down	5.17	26.95	11.08	105.39	143.42	37.63	1,512	800-345-6611	Y
Columbia Global Technology Growth Institutional 3 Cls	CGTUX	B-	C+	B-	Down	5.18	26.95	11.14	105.67	143.28	37.73	1,512	800-345-6611	Y
Columbia Global Technology Growth Fund Institutional Class	CMTFX	B-	C+	B-	Down	5.13	26.87	10.98	104.89	142.21	36.87	1,512	800-345-6611	Y
Fidelity® Select IT Services Portfolio	FBSOX	B	B+	B		5.68	33.93	20.91	99.10	139.65	71.43	3,670	617-563-7000	Y
Fidelity® Select Software & IT Services Portfolio	FSCSX	B	B-	B		6.23	27.05	15.44	101.09	134.79	18.52	7,272	617-563-7000	Y
Goldman Sachs Technology Opportunities Fund Class A	GITAX	B-	B-	B	Down	5.93	26.51	13.34	91.13	115.08	23.19	484.2	800-526-7384	Y
Goldman Sachs Technology Opportunities Fund Class C	GITCX	B-	B-	B	Down	5.76	26.06	12.55	87.00	107.32	17.99	484.2	800-526-7384	Y
Goldman Sachs Technology Opportunities Fund Class P	GSJPX	B-	B-	B	Down	6.04	26.68	13.80	93.46	119.44	26.3	484.2	800-526-7384	Y
Goldman Sachs Technology Opportunities Cls R6 Shares	GTORX	B-	B-	B	Down	6.04	26.68	13.80	93.46	119.44	26.3	484.2	800-526-7384	Y
Goldman Sachs Technology Opportunities Institutional Cls	GITIX	B-	B-	B	Down	6.00	26.69	13.76	93.41	119.38	26.29	484.2	800-526-7384	Y
Goldman Sachs Technology Opportunities Fund Investor Class	GISTX	B-	B-	B	Down	6.04	26.65	13.67	92.58	117.84	25.8	484.2	800-526-7384	Y
Goldman Sachs Technology Opportunities Fund Service Class	GITSX	B-	B-	B	Down	5.86	26.35	13.19	90.48	113.96	22.58	484.2	800-526-7384	Y
Ivy Science And Technology Fund Class A	WSTAX	B-	B	C+		9.30	34.89	15.71	91.86	64.27	71.05	7,179		Y
Ivy Science And Technology Fund Class B	WSTBX	B-	B-	C+		9.06	34.33	14.75	87.28	57.97	56.54	7,179		
Ivy Science And Technology Fund Class C	WSTCX	B-	B-	C+		9.10	34.41	14.87	87.68	58.50	59.21	7,179		Y
Ivy Science and Technology Fund Class E	ISTEX	B-	B	C+		9.27	34.82	15.55	91.34	63.41	70.35	7,179		Y

Category: Technology Sector Equity (con't)

Fund Name	Ticker Symbol	Overall Rating	Reward Rating	Risk Rating	Recent Up/ Downgrade	3-Month Total Return	6-Month Total Return	1-Year Total Return	3-Year Total Return	5-Year Total Return	NAV	Total Assets (MIL)	Telephone	Open to New Investors
		RATINGS				TOTAL RETURNS & PERFORMANCE					ASSETS		NEW INVESTORS	
Ivy Science and Technology Fund Class I	ISTIX	B-	B	B-		9.36	35.04	15.97	93.25	66.48	79.3	7,179		Y
Ivy Science and Technology Fund Class N	ISTNX	B-	B	B-		9.40	35.16	16.17	94.16	67.59	79.91	7,179		Y
Ivy Science and Technology Fund Class R	WSTRX	B-	B-	C+		9.20	34.65	15.31	89.89	61.66	68.69	7,179		Y
Ivy Science And Technology Fund Class Y	WSTYX	B-	B	C+		9.31	34.92	15.73	91.93	64.54	75.45	7,179		Y
Janus Henderson Global Technology Fund Class A	JATAX	B-	B-	B	Down	5.02	28.26	12.79	109.79	129.29	36.35	3,008	877-335-2687	Y
Janus Henderson Global Technology Fund Class C	JAGCX	B-	B-	B-	Down	4.86	27.85	12.02	105.44	121.63	32.96	3,008	877-335-2687	Y
Janus Henderson Global Technology Fund Class D	JNGTX	B	B-	B		5.08	28.38	13.00	110.95	131.61	37.22	3,008	877-335-2687	
Janus Henderson Global Technology Fund Class I	JATIX	B	B-	B		5.09	28.43	13.08	111.49	132.52	37.53	3,008	877-335-2687	Y
Janus Henderson Global Technology Fund Class N	JATNX	B	B-	B		5.12	28.45	13.17	111.58	131.99	37.11	3,008	877-335-2687	Y
Janus Henderson Global Technology Fund Class S	JATSX	B-	B-	B	Down	4.99	28.15	12.57	108.79	127.82	35.73	3,008	877-335-2687	Y
Janus Henderson Global Technology Fund Class T	JAGTX	B-	B-	B	Down	5.08	28.34	12.93	110.46	130.76	36.99	3,008	877-335-2687	Y
Janus Henderson VIT Global Technology Portfolio Inst Cls	JGLTX	B	B-	B		5.17	28.42	13.18	112.48	134.93	13.08	452.4	877-335-2687	Y
Janus Henderson VIT Global Technology Port Serv Cls		B-	B-	B	Down	-2.57	18.99	4.75	95.56	115.12	13.22	452.4	877-335-2687	Y
JNL/Mellon Capital Information Technology Sector Cls A		B-	B-	B-	Down	5.26	28.07	13.66	97.86	123.09	18.98	3,007		Y
JNL/Mellon Capital Information Technology Sector Cls I		B-	B-	B-	Down	5.37	28.35	14.09	99.60	126.02	19.42	3,007		Y
MFS Technology Fund Class A	MTCAX	B-	B-	B-	Down	6.05	27.25	9.99	92.65	127.79	44.82	1,278	877-960-6077	Y
MFS Technology Fund Class I	MTCIX	B-	B-	B-	Down	6.13	27.41	10.27	94.14	130.59	48.1	1,278	877-960-6077	Y
MFS Technology Fund Class R2	MTERX	B-	C+	B-	Down	6.00	27.12	9.73	91.25	124.93	42.56	1,278	877-960-6077	Y
MFS Technology Fund Class R3	MTCHX	B-	B-	B-	Down	6.06	27.27	9.99	92.65	127.70	44.8	1,278	877-960-6077	Y
MFS Technology Fund Class R4	MTCJX	B-	B-	B-	Down	6.14	27.45	10.27	94.14	130.56	46.8	1,278	877-960-6077	Y
MFS Technology Fund Class R6	MTCLX	B-	B-	B-	Down	6.15	27.50	10.38	94.73	131.72	48.45	1,278	877-960-6077	Y
Nationwide Ziegler NYSE Arca Tech 100 Index Fund Class A	NWJCX	B-	C+	B	Down	3.67	22.76	12.37	80.68	88.50	90.81	678.0	800-848-0920	Y
Nationwide Ziegler NYSE Arca Tech 100 Index Fund Class C	NWJDX	B-	C+	B	Down	3.48	22.30	11.55	76.75	81.67	80.39	678.0	800-848-0920	Y
Nationwide Ziegler NYSE Arca Tech 100 Index Fund Class R6	NWJEX	B-	C+	B	Down	3.75	22.97	12.76	82.60	91.84	91.72	678.0	800-848-0920	Y
Nationwide Ziegler NYSE Arca Tech 100 Index Inst Serv Cls	NWJFX	B-	C+	B	Down	3.74	22.91	12.64	81.92	90.65	91.75	678.0	800-848-0920	Y
Red Oak Technology Select Fund	ROGSX	B-	C+	B	Down	1.69	21.87	12.86	92.44	118.24	28.75	629.2	888-462-5386	Y
Rydex Technology Fund Class A	RYTHX	B-	C+	B-	Down	3.89	26.77	12.33	87.76	94.14	98.19	76.2	800-820-0888	Y
Rydex Technology Fund Class H	RYTAX	B-	C+	B-	Down	3.90	26.77	12.34	87.79	93.58	96.01	76.2	800-820-0888	Y
Rydex Technology Fund Class Investor	RYTIX	B-	C+	B	Down	3.95	26.93	12.60	89.17	96.53	105.8	76.2	800-820-0888	Y
Saratoga Technology & Communications Portfolio Class A	STPAX	B-	C+	B	Down	1.84	22.27	11.69	79.25	102.46	22.12	56.2	800-807-3863	Y
Saratoga Technology & Communications Portfolio Class C	STPCX	B-	C+	B	Down	1.72	21.90	11.03	76.11	96.43	17.7	56.2	800-807-3863	Y
Saratoga Technology & Communications Portfolio Cls Inst	STPIX	B-	C+	B	Down	1.99	22.55	12.16	81.45	106.54	24.56	56.2	800-807-3863	Y
USAA Science & Technology Fund	USSCX	B-	C+	B-		5.54	28.77	12.17	76.67	105.03	27.79	1,459	800-235-8396	Y
VALIC Company I Science & Technology Fund	VCSTX	B-	C+	B-	Down	4.41	28.47	11.03	94.59	118.59	27.91	1,488		Y
Vanguard Information Technology Index Fund Admiral Shares	VITAX	B	B-	B		5.44	28.43	17.80	106.59	133.78	108.02	22,786	877-662-7447	Y
Wireless Fund	WIREX	B-	C+	B	Down	2.46	23.28	13.69	61.60	78.71	12.07	5.5	800-590-0898	Y

Category: Trading Tools

Fund Name	Ticker Symbol	Overall Rating	Reward Rating	Risk Rating	Recent Up/ Downgrade	3-Month Total Return	6-Month Total Return	1-Year Total Return	3-Year Total Return	5-Year Total Return	NAV	Total Assets (MIL)	Telephone	Open to New Investors
		RATINGS				TOTAL RETURNS & PERFORMANCE					ASSETS		NEW INVESTORS	
ProFunds Bull Fund Investor Class	BLPIX	B-	C	B	Up	3.81	18.45	8.40	42.61	51.39	134.28	75.4	614-470-8626	Y
ProFunds Consumer Services UltraSector Fund Investor Class	CYPIX	B-	B-	C+		9.74	33.59	16.61	81.41	120.38	138.32	48.0	614-470-8626	Y
ProFunds Consumer Services UltraSector Fund Service Class	CYPSX	B-	B-	C+	Up	9.47	32.92	15.46	76.07	109.64	118.93	48.0	614-470-8626	Y
ProFunds Utilities UltraSector Fund Investor Class	UTPIX	B	B	C+	Up	3.92	20.32	23.09	32.67	76.09	54.53	27.6	614-470-8626	Y
ProFunds Utilities UltraSector Fund Service Class	UTPSX	B	B	C+	Up	3.66	19.77	21.96	28.78	67.51	51.25	27.6	614-470-8626	Y

Category: US Equity Large Cap Blend

Fund Name	Ticker Symbol	RATINGS: Overall Rating	Reward Rating	Risk Rating	Recent Up/ Downgrade	TOTAL RETURNS & PERFORMANCE: 3-Month Total Return	6-Month Total Return	1-Year Total Return	3-Year Total Return	5-Year Total Return	ASSETS: NAV	Total Assets (MIL)	NEW INVESTORS: Telephone	Open to New Investors
AAM/Bahl & Gaynor Income Growth Fund Class A	AFNAX	B	B-	B+		5.06	17.85	14.75	42.51	55.84	18.68	1,173	800-617-0004	Y
AAM/Bahl & Gaynor Income Growth Fund Class C	AFYCX	B	C+	B+		4.86	17.39	13.86	39.30	49.96	18.5	1,173	800-617-0004	Y
AAM/Bahl & Gaynor Income Growth Fund Class I	AFNIX	B	B-	B+		5.15	17.99	15.07	43.62	58.02	18.73	1,173	800-617-0004	Y
Aberdeen U.S. Multi-Cap Equity Fund Class A	GXXAX	B-	C+	B		4.66	22.17	9.44	48.03	48.70	12.34	363.3	866-667-9231	Y
Aberdeen U.S. Multi-Cap Equity Fund Class C	GXXCX	B-	C+	B		4.49	21.79	8.61	44.91	43.40	10.45	363.3	866-667-9231	Y
Aberdeen U.S. Multi-Cap Equity Fund Class R	GGLRX	B-	C+	B		4.58	22.03	9.04	46.20	46.15	11.41	363.3	866-667-9231	Y
Aberdeen U.S. Multi-Cap Equity Fund Institutional Class	GGLIX	B-	C+	B		4.81	22.41	9.84	49.45	50.96	13.27	363.3	866-667-9231	Y
Aberdeen U.S. Multi-Cap Equity Institutional Service Cls	GXXIX	B-	C+	B		4.75	22.40	9.76	48.95	50.25	13.22	363.3	866-667-9231	Y
Advisory Research All Cap Value Fund	ADVGX	B-	C	B+	Down	7.19	19.47	14.26	56.06	52.37	11.47	9.8	312-565-1414	Y
Alger Growth & Income Fund Class A	ALBAX	B-	C	B		3.53	15.42	9.25	43.98	54.92	41.24	114.1	800-992-3863	Y
Alger Growth & Income Fund Class C	ALBCX	B-	C	B		3.32	15.00	8.42	40.74	49.19	40.67	114.1	800-992-3863	Y
Alger Growth & Income Fund Class Z	AGIZX	B-	C	B		3.63	15.63	9.66	45.39	57.28	41.27	114.1	800-992-3863	Y
Alger Growth & Income Portfolio I-2	AIGOX	B-	C	B		3.99	15.97	9.88	45.47	56.67	21.16	30.1	800-992-3863	Y
AllianzGI Best Styles U.S. Equity Fund Class A	AABUX	B-	C	B	Up	3.86	17.55	7.11	49.07		16.14	92.2	800-498-5413	Y
AllianzGI Best Styles U.S. Equity Fund Class P	ALBPX	B-	C	B		3.89	17.64	7.22	49.84		16	92.2	800-498-5413	Y
AllianzGI Best Styles U.S. Equity Fund Class R6	ALSEX	B-	C	B		3.92	17.69	7.35	50.34		16.16	92.2	800-498-5413	Y
AllianzGI Best Styles U.S. Equity Fund Institutional Class	ABTLX	B-	C	B		3.88	17.66	7.24	49.93		16.05	92.2	800-498-5413	Y
Amana Mutual Funds Trust Income Fund Institutional	AMINX	B-	C	B	Down	1.20	13.94	11.66	35.52	44.13	50.86	1,340	888-732-6262	Y
Amana Mutual Funds Trust Income Fund Investor	AMANX	B-	C	B	Down	1.11	13.78	11.36	34.54	42.35	51.06	1,340	888-732-6262	Y
American Century Sustainable Equity Fund A Class	AFDAX	B-	C	B		5.15	20.39	10.99	55.17	61.24	28.99	307.1	800-444-4015	Y
American Century Sustainable Equity Fund C Class	AFDCX	B-	C	B		4.92	19.92	10.11	51.66	55.29	28.35	307.1	800-444-4015	Y
American Century Sustainable Equity Fund G Class	AFEGX	B-	C	B		5.29	20.55	11.14	55.38	61.45	29.21	307.1	800-444-4015	Y
American Century Sustainable Equity Fund I Class	AFEIX	B-	C+	B		5.27	20.66	11.49	57.29	64.89	29.14	307.1	800-444-4015	Y
American Century Sustainable Equity Fund Investor Class	AFDIX	B-	C+	B		5.21	20.52	11.25	56.30	63.29	29.07	307.1	800-444-4015	Y
American Century Sustainable Equity Fund R Class	AFDRX	B-	C	B		5.06	20.21	10.68	53.93	59.25	28.84	307.1	800-444-4015	Y
American Century Sustainable Equity Fund R5 Class	AFDGX	B-	C+	B		5.27	20.64	11.48	56.65	62.77	29.16	307.1	800-444-4015	Y
American Century Sustainable Equity Fund R6 Class	AFEDX	B-	C	B		5.25	20.51	11.10	55.33	61.40	29.18	307.1	800-444-4015	Y
American Century Sustainable Equity Fund Y Class	AFYDX	B-	C+	B		5.30	20.72	11.65	57.16	63.30	29.18	307.1	800-444-4015	Y
American Funds Fundamental Investors® Class 529-A	CFNAX	B-	C	B	Up	2.78	15.79	5.32	45.18	58.89	59.17	100,949	800-421-4225	Y
American Funds Fundamental Investors® Class 529-C	CFNCX	B-	C	B	Up	2.59	15.36	4.53	41.90	52.87	59.16	100,949	800-421-4225	Y
American Funds Fundamental Investors® Class 529-E	CFNEX	B-	C	B	Up	2.73	15.68	5.08	44.18	57.04	59.12	100,949	800-421-4225	Y
American Funds Fundamental Investors® Class 529-F-1	CFNFX	B-	C	B	Up	2.86	15.96	5.58	46.16	60.67	59.12	100,949	800-421-4225	Y
American Funds Fundamental Investors® Class A	ANCFX	B-	C	B	Up	2.80	15.85	5.39	45.53	59.56	59.27	100,949	800-421-4225	Y
American Funds Fundamental Investors® Class C	AFICX	B-	C	B	Up	2.59	15.39	4.57	42.10	53.33	58.94	100,949	800-421-4225	Y
American Funds Fundamental Investors® Class F-1	AFIFX	B-	C	B	Up	2.78	15.80	5.32	45.19	58.99	59.23	100,949	800-421-4225	Y
American Funds Fundamental Investors® Class F-2	FINFX	B-	C	B	Up	2.85	15.96	5.60	46.34	61.11	59.25	100,949	800-421-4225	Y
American Funds Fundamental Investors® Class F-3	FUNFX	B-	C	B	Up	2.87	16.02	5.71	46.52	60.64	59.25	100,949	800-421-4225	Y
American Funds Fundamental Investors® Class R-1	RFNAX	B-	C	B	Up	2.60	15.38	4.54	42.02	53.26	58.94	100,949	800-421-4225	Y
American Funds Fundamental Investors® Class R-2	RFNBX	B-	C	B	Up	2.60	15.38	4.54	42.06	53.42	58.9	100,949	800-421-4225	Y
American Funds Fundamental Investors® Class R-2E	RFEBX	B-	C	B	Up	2.69	15.58	4.87	43.37	56.37	58.96	100,949	800-421-4225	Y
American Funds Fundamental Investors® Class R-3	RFNCX	B-	C	B	Up	2.72	15.66	5.04	43.97	56.81	59.11	100,949	800-421-4225	Y
American Funds Fundamental Investors® Class R-4	RFNEX	B-	C	B	Up	2.79	15.82	5.34	45.26	59.16	59.13	100,949	800-421-4225	Y
American Funds Fundamental Investors® Class R-5	RFNFX	B-	C	B	Up	2.88	16.00	5.67	46.61	61.58	59.32	100,949	800-421-4225	Y
American Funds Fundamental Investors® Class R-5E	RFNHX	B-	C	B	Up	2.84	15.96	5.58	46.18	60.35	59.16	100,949	800-421-4225	Y
American Funds Fundamental Investors® Class R-6	RFNGX	B-	C	B	Up	2.87	16.02	5.71	46.81	61.96	59.28	100,949	800-421-4225	Y
American Funds Investment Company of America® Class 529-A	CICAX	B-	C	B	Up	2.16	14.34	4.20	37.70	48.30	38.05	96,708	800-421-4225	Y
American Funds Investment Company of America® Class 529-C	CICCX	B-	C	B	Up	1.98	13.92	3.45	34.62	42.75	37.96	96,708	800-421-4225	Y
American Funds Investment Company of America® class 529-E	CICEX	B-	C	B	Up	2.11	14.23	3.97	36.74	46.54	37.92	96,708	800-421-4225	Y
American Funds Investment Company of America® class 529-F	CICFX	B-	C	B	Up	2.23	14.49	4.46	38.66	49.98	38	96,708	800-421-4225	Y
American Funds Investment Company of America® Class A	AIVSX	B-	C	B	Up	2.15	14.38	4.29	38.05	48.97	38.15	96,708	800-421-4225	Y
American Funds Investment Company of America® Class C	AICCX	B-	C	B	Up	1.98	13.95	3.47	34.82	43.15	37.72	96,708	800-421-4225	Y
American Funds Investment Company of America® Class F-1	AICFX	B-	C	B	Up	2.16	14.33	4.20	37.70	48.30	38.05	96,708	800-421-4225	Y

Category: US Equity Large Cap Blend (con't)

		RATINGS				TOTAL RETURNS & PERFORMANCE					ASSETS		NEW INVESTORS	
Fund Name	Ticker Symbol	Overall Rating	Reward Rating	Risk Rating	Recent Up/ Downgrade	3-Month Total Return	6-Month Total Return	1-Year Total Return	3-Year Total Return	5-Year Total Return	NAV	Total Assets (MIL)	Telephone	Open to New Investors
American Funds Investment Company of America® Class F-2	ICAFX	B-	C	B	Up	2.20	14.48	4.48	38.78	50.32	38.13	96,708	800-421-4225	Y
American Funds Investment Company of America® Class F-3	FFICX	B-	C	B	Up	2.25	14.57	4.58	38.98	49.97	38.14	96,708	800-421-4225	Y
American Funds Investment Company of America® Class R-1	RICAX	B-	C	B	Up	1.97	13.93	3.44	34.73	43.05	37.82	96,708	800-421-4225	Y
American Funds Investment Company of America® Class R-2	RICBX	B-	C	B	Up	1.97	13.91	3.43	34.71	43.11	37.87	96,708	800-421-4225	Y
American Funds Investment Company of America® Class R-2E	RIBEX	B-	C	B	Up	2.06	14.08	3.76	35.96	45.70	38.03	96,708	800-421-4225	Y
American Funds Investment Company of America® Class R-3	RICCX	B-	C	B	Up	2.10	14.17	3.91	36.55	46.25	38	96,708	800-421-4225	Y
American Funds Investment Company of America® Class R-4	RICEX	B-	C	B	Up	2.17	14.35	4.22	37.79	48.54	38.04	96,708	800-421-4225	Y
American Funds Investment Company of America® Class R-5	RICFX	B-	C	B	Up	2.24	14.54	4.56	39.03	50.75	38.15	96,708	800-421-4225	Y
American Funds Investment Company of America® Class R-5E	RICHX	B-	C	B	Up	2.19	14.48	4.44	38.63	49.66	38.12	96,708	800-421-4225	Y
American Funds Investment Company of America® Class R-6	RICGX	B-	C	B	Up	2.25	14.54	4.58	39.24	51.11	38.14	96,708	800-421-4225	Y
American Funds Washington Mutual Investors Cls 529-A	CWMAX	B-	C	B+	Down	4.02	15.58	10.04	45.76	57.47	45.72	118,091	800-421-4225	Y
American Funds Washington Mutual Investors Cls 529-C	CWMCX	B-	C	B+	Down	3.85	15.16	9.26	42.51	51.60	45.44	118,091	800-421-4225	Y
American Funds Washington Mutual Investors Cls 529-E	CWMEX	B-	C	B+	Down	3.96	15.45	9.80	44.74	55.59	45.44	118,091	800-421-4225	Y
American Funds Washington Mutual Investors Cls 529-F-1	CWMFX	B-	C	B+	Down	4.09	15.73	10.31	46.79	59.28	45.6	118,091	800-421-4225	Y
American Funds Washington Mutual Investors Fund Class A	AWSHX	B-	C	B+	Down	4.05	15.64	10.16	46.15	58.16	45.84	118,091	800-421-4225	Y
American Funds Washington Mutual Investors Fund Class C	WSHCX	B-	C	B+	Down	3.86	15.19	9.29	42.69	52.03	45.2	118,091	800-421-4225	Y
American Funds Washington Mutual Investors Fund Class F-1	WSHFX	B-	C	B+	Down	4.02	15.58	10.06	45.75	57.48	45.65	118,091	800-421-4225	Y
American Funds Washington Mutual Investors Fund Class F-2	WMFFX	B-	C	B+	Down	4.10	15.73	10.35	46.94	59.58	45.79	118,091	800-421-4225	Y
American Funds Washington Mutual Investors Fund Class F-3	FWMIX	B-	C	B+	Down	4.12	15.78	10.45	47.08	59.18	45.81	118,091	800-421-4225	Y
American Funds Washington Mutual Investors Fund Class R-1	RWMAX	B-	C	B+	Down	3.84	15.19	9.27	42.59	51.89	45.32	118,091	800-421-4225	Y
American Funds Washington Mutual Investors Fund Class R-2	RWMBX	B-	C	B+	Down	3.84	15.18	9.24	42.58	51.99	45.13	118,091	800-421-4225	Y
American Funds Washington Mutual Investors Fund Class R-2E	RWEBX	B-	C	B+	Down	3.92	15.33	9.58	43.88	54.98	45.61	118,091	800-421-4225	Y
American Funds Washington Mutual Investors Fund Class R-3	RWMCX	B-	C	B+	Down	3.97	15.43	9.74	44.51	55.32	45.42	118,091	800-421-4225	Y
American Funds Washington Mutual Investors Fund Class R-4	RWMEX	B-	C	B+	Down	4.03	15.59	10.07	45.82	57.64	45.57	118,091	800-421-4225	Y
American Funds Washington Mutual Investors Fund Class R-5	RWMFX	B-	C	B+	Down	4.11	15.78	10.39	47.14	60.00	45.81	118,091	800-421-4225	Y
American Funds Washington Mutual Investors Fund Class R-5E	RWMHX	B-	C	B+	Down	4.09	15.73	10.32	46.74	58.86	45.77	118,091	800-421-4225	Y
American Funds Washington Mutual Investors Fund Class R-6	RWMGX	B-	C	B+	Down	4.14	15.82	10.47	47.40	60.43	45.86	118,091	800-421-4225	Y
AMG Yacktman Fund Class I	YACKX	B	C+	A		2.82	11.33	10.59	42.11	49.97	21.11	8,349	800-835-3879	Y
AQR Large Cap Defensive Style Fund Class I	AUEIX	B	B-	B+		4.96	19.63	14.69	52.52	87.98	22.18	4,368	203-742-3600	Y
AQR Large Cap Defensive Style Fund Class N	AUENX	B	B-	B+		4.88	19.49	14.40	51.40	85.68	22.13	4,368	203-742-3600	Y
AQR Large Cap Defensive Style Fund Class R6	QUERX	B	B-	B+		4.97	19.66	14.79	52.96	88.77	22.15	4,368	203-742-3600	Y
Asset Management Fund Large Cap Equity Fund Class AMF	IICAX	B-	C	B	Down	1.54	15.68	7.67	43.38	49.05	7.96	41.3	800-247-9780	Y
Asset Management Fund Large Cap Equity Fund Class H	IICHX	B-	C	B	Down	1.60	15.88	7.93	44.25	50.30	7.93	41.3	800-247-9780	Y
ATM Large Cap Managed Volatility Portfolio Class K		B-	C	B	Up	2.73	6.70	4.11	41.71	58.26		3,360	877-222-2144	Y
Ave Maria Rising Dividend Fund	AVEDX	B-	C	B		3.70	18.64	10.00	42.10	45.38	18.5	892.5	888-726-9331	Y
AXA/Mutual Large Cap Eq Managed Vol Port Cls K		B-	C	B+	Down	6.47	10.14	10.49	43.14	62.33		615.7	877-222-2144	Y
BBH Core Select Fund Class N	BBTEX	B-	C	B	Down	7.04	20.03	13.51	40.84	43.23	15.34	767.5	800-575-1265	
BBH Core Select Retail Class Shares	BBTRX	B-	C	B		7.08	20.17	13.31	39.99	41.71	4.23	767.5	800-575-1265	
BlackRock Advantage Large Cap Core Fund Class K	MLRKX	B-	C	B		3.46	18.99	7.90	55.56	60.44	16.82	2,736	800-441-7762	Y
BlackRock Advantage Large Cap Core Fund Class R	MRLRX	B-	C	B		3.39	18.69	7.35	53.13	56.09	15	2,736	800-441-7762	Y
BlackRock Advantage Large Cap Core Institutional Shares	MALRX	B-	C	B		3.52	18.99	7.93	55.50	60.38	16.82	2,736	800-441-7762	Y
BlackRock Advantage Large Cap Core Fund Investor A Shares	MDLRX	B-	C	B		3.41	18.86	7.61	54.33	58.25	16.15	2,736	800-441-7762	Y
BlackRock Advantage Large Cap Core Fund Investor C Shares	MCLRX	B-	C	B	Up	3.25	18.40	6.82	50.73	52.07	13.71	2,736	800-441-7762	Y
BlackRock Advantage Large Cap Core Fund Service Shares	MSLRX	B-	C	B	Up	3.47	18.90	7.70	53.97	57.65	16.75	2,736	800-441-7762	Y
BlackRock Exchange Portfolio BlackRock Shares	STSEX	B-	C+	B+	Down	5.97	18.18	15.92	44.85	49.07	1178.35	178.4	800-441-7762	Y
BlackRock Impact U.S. Equity Fund Class K	BIRKX	B-	C	B		3.92	20.33	8.63	53.53		13.49	80.0	800-441-7762	Y
BlackRock Impact U.S. Equity Fund Institutional Shares	BIRIX	B-	C	B		3.93	20.24	8.50	53.29		13.48	80.0	800-441-7762	Y
BlackRock Impact U.S. Equity Fund Investor A Shares	BIRAX	B-	C	B		3.86	20.10	8.27	52.10		13.44	80.0	800-441-7762	Y
BNY Mellon Appreciation Fund, Inc. - Class I	DGIGX	B	B-	B	Up	5.85	21.52	12.17	50.77	52.20	32.03	1,640		Y
BNY Mellon Appreciation Fund, Inc. - Class Y	DGYGX	B	B-	B	Up	5.86	21.55	12.22	51.19	53.76	32.1	1,640		Y
BNY Mellon Appreciation Fund, Inc. - Investor Shares	DGAGX	B	B-	B	Up	5.79	21.41	11.89	49.80	51.22	32.23	1,640		Y
BNY Mellon Institutional S&P 500 Stock Index Fund Class I	DSPIX	B-	C	B		4.26	19.48	10.22	50.07	64.70	56.62	2,625		Y

Category: US Equity Large Cap Blend (con't)

Fund Name	Ticker Symbol	RATINGS: Overall Rating	Reward Rating	Risk Rating	Recent Up/ Downgrade	TOTAL RETURNS & PERFORMANCE: 3-Month Total Return	6-Month Total Return	1-Year Total Return	3-Year Total Return	5-Year Total Return	ASSETS: NAV	Total Assets (MIL)	NEW INVESTORS: Telephone	Open to New Investors
BNY Mellon S&P 500 Index Fund	PEOPX	B-	C	B		4.18	19.29	9.87	48.70	62.19	51.99	2,357		Y
BNY Mellon Sustainable U.S. Equity Fund Class A	DTCAX	B-	C+	B		5.38	20.93	14.25	45.42	45.36	12.13	322.8		Y
BNY Mellon Sustainable U.S. Equity Fund Class C	DTCCX	B-	C	B		5.25	20.37	13.42	42.14	39.95	10.22	322.8		Y
BNY Mellon Sustainable U.S. Equity Fund Class I	DRTCX	B-	C+	B		5.50	21.10	14.63	46.74	47.56	12.45	322.8		Y
BNY Mellon Sustainable U.S. Equity Fund Class Y	DTCYX	B-	C+	B		5.51	21.03	14.66	46.64	47.17	12.43	322.8		Y
BNY Mellon Sustainable U.S. Equity Fund Class Z	DRTHX	B-	C+	B		5.42	21.01	14.45	46.21	46.73	12.44	322.8		
BNY Mellon Tax Managed Growth Fund Class A	DTMGX	B-	C+	B	Down	5.36	20.91	11.31	46.49	45.81	29.26	106.7		Y
BNY Mellon Tax Managed Growth Fund Class C	DPTAX	B-	C+	B		5.17	20.46	10.50	43.20	40.43	27.33	106.7		Y
BNY Mellon Tax Managed Growth Fund Class I	DPTRX	B-	C+	B	Down	5.40	21.06	11.64	47.59	47.70	29.34	106.7		Y
BNY Mellon Tax-Sensitive Large Cap Multi-Strategy Cls Inv	MTSIX	B-	C	B		4.33	18.52	8.13	51.00	59.53	16.38	321.1	800-645-6561	Y
BNY Mellon Tax-Sensitive Large Cap Multi-Strategy Cls M	MTSMX	B-	C	B		4.38	18.67	8.38	52.06	61.58	15.95	321.1	800-645-6561	Y
Boston Trust Equity Fund	BTEFX	B	C+	B+		4.65	19.34	14.49	49.62	61.31	26.78	146.0	617-814-1215	Y
Boyar Value Fund	BOYAX	B-	C	B	Up	4.46	13.66	5.22	30.68	43.43	26.45	26.5		Y
Bretton Fund	BRTNX	B-	C+	B	Down	5.70	21.29	13.68	55.05	59.09	36.11	36.6		Y
Bridgeway Blue Chip Index Fund	BRLIX	B	C+	B+		5.19	19.34	16.25	50.56	67.67	14.99	505.2	800-661-3550	Y
Bright Rock Quality Large Cap Fund Institutional Class	BQLCX	B-	C	B		4.58	18.25	11.39	31.14	44.93	17.46	246.6	781-982-6593	Y
Bright Rock Quality Large Cap Fund Investor Class	BQLIX	B-	C	B		4.50	18.12	11.07	30.07	42.98	17.9	246.6	781-982-6593	Y
Brown Advisory Equity Income Fund Advisor Shares	BADAX	B-	C+	B	Down	4.76	20.19	12.67	40.86	43.13	14.14	89.7	800-540-6807	Y
Brown Advisory Equity Income Fund Inst Shares	BAFDX	B	C+	B+		4.86	20.41	13.11	42.47	45.95	14.15	89.7	800-540-6807	Y
Brown Advisory Equity Income Fund Investor Shares	BIADX	B	C+	B		4.82	20.32	13.03	41.90	45.02	14.15	89.7	800-540-6807	Y
Buffalo Dividend Focus Fund	BUFDX	B-	C	B		4.05	16.25	8.39	41.74	56.36	17.26	60.3	800-492-8332	Y
Calamos Opportunistic Value Fund Class A	CVAAX	B-	C	B	Up	3.30	15.75	6.77	38.73	33.09	13.74	44.7	800-582-6959	Y
Calamos Opportunistic Value Fund Class C	CVACX	B-	C	B	Up	3.09	15.30	6.04	35.69	28.20	11.98	44.7	800-582-6959	Y
Calamos Opportunistic Value Fund Institutional Class	CVAIX	B-	C	B	Up	3.36	15.83	7.05	39.69	34.71	14.12	44.7	800-582-6959	Y
Calvert US Large Cap Core Responsible Index Fund Class A	CSXAX	B-	C	B	Down	4.45	20.36	11.75	51.22	64.72	24.41	1,843	301-951-4881	Y
Calvert US Large Cap Core Responsible Index Fund Class C	CSXCX	B-	C	B		4.28	19.95	10.93	47.85	58.68	22.9	1,843	301-951-4881	Y
Calvert US Large Cap Core Responsible Index Fund Class I	CISIX	B-	C	B	Down	4.54	20.54	12.07	52.72	67.92	25.05	1,843	301-951-4881	Y
Calvert US Large Cap Core Responsible Index Fund Class R6	CSXRX	B-	C	B	Down	4.55	20.56	12.10	52.69	67.88	25.03	1,843	301-951-4881	Y
Central Securities Corporation	CET	B-	B	C-	Up	7.31	24.04	13.91	71.92	69.08	36.72	935.7		Y
Centre American Select Equity Fund Institutional Class	DHANX	B-	C	B	Up	0.27	12.44	2.07	37.87	45.06	10.84	114.5	855-298-4236	Y
Centre American Select Equity Fund Investor Class	DHAMX	B-	C	B	Up	0.09	12.22	1.50	36.52	43.35	10.74	114.5	855-298-4236	Y
CIBC Atlas Disciplined Equity Fund Institutional Class	AWEIX	B-	C+	B+	Down	5.28	19.94	14.17	56.12	73.61	21.11	1,146	312-368-7700	Y
Clarkston Fund Institutional Class	CILGX	B-	C	B+		4.90	20.28	11.99	32.29		12.19	52.2	844-680-6562	Y
ClearBridge Appreciation Fund Class A	SHAPX	B	C+	B+		5.90	19.13	14.59	46.52	61.29	25.65	6,450	877-721-1926	Y
ClearBridge Appreciation Fund Class C	SAPCX	B-	C+	B+	Down	5.70	18.69	13.80	43.44	55.70	24.63	6,450	877-721-1926	Y
ClearBridge Appreciation Fund Class FI	LMPIX	B	C+	B+		5.87	19.06	14.49	46.31	61.01	25.79	6,450	877-721-1926	Y
ClearBridge Appreciation Fund Class I	SAPYX	B	B-	B+		5.94	19.27	14.91	47.81	63.62	25.49	6,450	877-721-1926	Y
ClearBridge Appreciation Fund Class IS	LMESX	B	B-	B+		5.96	19.31	15.02	48.20	64.38	25.57	6,450	877-721-1926	Y
ClearBridge Appreciation Fund Class R	LMPPX	B	C+	B+		5.83	18.92	14.27	45.11	58.73	25.58	6,450	877-721-1926	Y
ClearBridge Dividend Strategy Fund Class 1	LCBOX	B	B-	B+		5.56	20.53	15.48	46.02	58.51	24.54	6,398	877-721-1926	Y
ClearBridge Dividend Strategy Fund Class A	SOPAX	B	B-	B+		5.50	20.38	15.18	44.80	56.34	24.53	6,398	877-721-1926	Y
ClearBridge Dividend Strategy Fund Class C	SBPLX	B	B-	B+		5.32	19.89	14.36	41.79	51.01	24.16	6,398	877-721-1926	Y
ClearBridge Dividend Strategy Fund Class FI	LBRIX	B	B-	B+		5.55	20.37	15.25	44.76	56.25	24.48	6,398	877-721-1926	Y
ClearBridge Dividend Strategy Fund Class I	SOPYX	B	B-	B+		5.59	20.52	15.52	46.15	58.72	25.22	6,398	877-721-1926	Y
ClearBridge Dividend Strategy Fund Class IS	LCBEX	B	B-	B+		5.60	20.58	15.61	46.46	59.35	25.25	6,398	877-721-1926	Y
ClearBridge Dividend Strategy Fund Class R	LMMRX	B	B-	B+		5.41	20.12	14.77	43.53	54.17	24.36	6,398	877-721-1926	Y
Coho Relative Value Equity Fund Advisor Class	COHOX	B-	C	B+		-0.42	9.95	4.19	28.76	45.08	14.03	573.3		Y
Coho Relative Value Equity Fund Institutional Class	COHIX	B-	C	B+		-0.42	10.00	4.36	29.32	45.98	14.07	573.3		Y
Columbia Contrarian Core Fund Institutional 3 Class	COFYX	B-	C	B	Up	4.68	20.45	9.74	43.08	58.89	26.15	9,914	800-345-6611	Y
Columbia Disciplined Core Fund Advisor Class	CLCQX	B-	C	B		1.99	16.05	7.14	49.55	63.08	12.29	4,509	800-345-6611	Y
Columbia Disciplined Core Fund Class A	AQEAX	B-	C	B		2.01	15.91	6.93	48.52	61.13	12.16	4,509	800-345-6611	Y
Columbia Disciplined Core Fund Class C	RDCEX	B-	C	B		1.79	15.45	6.11	45.10	55.19	11.88	4,509	800-345-6611	Y

Category: US Equity Large Cap Blend (con't)

Fund Name	Ticker Symbol	RATINGS: Overall Rating	Reward Rating	Risk Rating	Recent Up/ Downgrade	TOTAL RETURNS & PERFORMANCE: 3-Month Total Return	6-Month Total Return	1-Year Total Return	3-Year Total Return	5-Year Total Return	ASSETS: NAV	Total Assets (MIL)	NEW INVESTORS: Telephone	Open to New Investors
Columbia Disciplined Core Fund Class R	CLQRX	B-	C	B		1.84	15.72	6.56	47.39	58.95	12.14	4,509	800-345-6611	Y
Columbia Disciplined Core Fund Institutional 2 Class	RSIPX	B-	C	B		2.09	16.07	7.22	49.79	63.65	12.2	4,509	800-345-6611	Y
Columbia Disciplined Core Fund Institutional 3 Class	CCQYX	B-	C	B		1.99	16.11	7.25	50.03	63.33	12.25	4,509	800-345-6611	Y
Columbia Disciplined Core Fund Institutional Class	CCRZX	B-	C	B		2.08	16.12	7.17	49.67	63.09	12.24	4,509	800-345-6611	Y
Columbia Large Cap Enhanced Core Fund Advisor Class	CECFX	B-	C	B		1.95	15.89	6.65	48.87	61.02	23.51	552.5	800-345-6611	Y
Columbia Large Cap Enhanced Core Fund Class A	NMIAX	B-	C	B		1.88	15.73	6.38	47.81	58.97	23.79	552.5	800-345-6611	Y
Columbia Large Cap Enhanced Core Fund Class R	CCERX	B-	C	B		1.80	15.57	6.07	46.71	57.05	23.72	552.5	800-345-6611	Y
Columbia Large Cap Enhanced Core Institutional 2 Cls	CLNCX	B-	C	B		1.94	15.90	6.71	49.27	61.77	23.65	552.5	800-345-6611	Y
Columbia Large Cap Enhanced Core Institutional 3 Cls	CECYX	B-	C	B		1.97	15.98	6.77	49.45	62.07	23.76	552.5	800-345-6611	Y
Columbia Large Cap Enhanced Core Fund Institutional Class	NMIMX	B-	C	B		1.93	15.88	6.63	48.87	60.98	23.75	552.5	800-345-6611	Y
Columbia Large Cap Index Fund Class A	NEIAX	B-	C	B		4.18	19.28	9.91	48.85	62.61	48.6	3,370	800-345-6611	Y
Columbia Large Cap Index Fund Institutional 2 Class	CLXRX	B-	C	B		4.25	19.44	10.19	49.98	64.66	49.69	3,370	800-345-6611	Y
Columbia Large Cap Index Fund Institutional 3 Class	CLPYX	B-	C	B		4.24	19.43	10.18	49.99	64.66	48.11	3,370	800-345-6611	Y
Columbia Large Cap Index Fund Institutional Class	NINDX	B-	C	B		4.25	19.43	10.17	49.98	64.65	48.91	3,370	800-345-6611	Y
Columbia Select Large Cap Equity Fund Advisor Class	CLSRX	B-	C	B		4.47	19.32	9.75	52.06	68.09	14.13	726.8	800-345-6611	Y
Columbia Select Large Cap Equity Fund Class A	NSGAX	B-	C	B		4.38	19.21	9.51	51.03	66.01	14.3	726.8	800-345-6611	Y
Columbia Select Large Cap Equity Fund Class C	NSGCX	B-	C	B		4.21	18.83	8.69	47.67	60.02	13.01	726.8	800-345-6611	Y
Columbia Select Large Cap Equity Institutional 2 Cls	CLCRX	B-	C	B		4.47	19.41	9.86	52.39	68.78	14.64	726.8	800-345-6611	Y
Columbia Select Large Cap Equity Institutional 3 Cls	CLEYX	B-	C	B		4.54	19.49	9.92	52.62	68.71	13.98	726.8	800-345-6611	Y
Columbia Select Large Cap Equity Fund Institutional Class	NSEPX	B-	C	B		4.45	19.33	9.78	52.10	68.13	14.19	726.8	800-345-6611	Y
Concorde Wealth Management Fund	CONWX	B-	C	A-		2.66	12.54	5.55	24.44	19.86	15.79	26.0		Y
Cornerstone Strategic Value Fund	CLM	B	B	C+	Up	4.13	18.94	11.62	55.30	53.52	11.09	805.0	828-210-8184	Y
Cornerstone Total Return Fund Inc	CRF	B	B	C+	Up	3.85	19.02	11.12	54.11	65.59	10.73	411.6		Y
Crawford Dividend Growth Fund Class C	CDGCX	B-	C	B+	Down	5.28	19.18	12.51	36.67	34.65	11.48	49.4		Y
Crawford Dividend Growth Fund Class Institutional	CDGIX	B-	C+	B+	Down	5.51	19.70	13.67	40.89	41.51	11.57	49.4		Y
Davidson Multi-Cap Equity Fund Class A	DFMAX	B-	C	B		3.22	17.42	7.71	40.01	44.80	25.27	112.0		Y
Davidson Multi-Cap Equity Fund Class I	DFMIX	B-	C	B		3.31	17.53	7.96	41.06	46.62	25.27	112.0		Y
Dearborn Partners Rising Dividend Fund Class A Shares	DRDAX	B	C+	B+		4.97	19.90	18.32	37.67	53.57	16.66	257.3	888-983-3380	Y
Dearborn Partners Rising Dividend Fund Class C Shares	DRDCX	B	C+	B+		4.81	19.52	17.40	34.66	47.93	16.59	257.3	888-983-3380	Y
Dearborn Partners Rising Dividend Fund Class I Shares	DRDIX	B	B-	B+		5.10	20.01	18.59	38.75	55.53	16.68	257.3	888-983-3380	Y
DFA Enhanced U.S. Large Company Portfolio Inst Cls	DFELX	B-	C+	B		4.52	20.78	11.33	49.53	65.86	13.51	349.9	512-306-7400	Y
DFA Tax Managed U.S. Equity Portfolio	DTMEX	B-	C	B		4.21	19.58	8.80	50.68	62.06	31.7	3,900	512-306-7400	Y
DFA U.S. Large Cap Equity Portfolio Institutional Class	DUSQX	B-	C	B		4.28	19.96	8.90	50.74	59.10	18.09	1,626	512-306-7400	Y
DFA U.S. Large Company Portfolio	DFUSX	B-	C	B		4.29	19.50	10.33	50.70	65.78	22.68	9,457	512-306-7400	Y
DoubleLine Shiller Enhanced CAPE® Class I	DSEEX	B-	B-	B	Down	4.93	22.88	13.63	61.94	89.04	15.42	6,666	877-354-6311	Y
DoubleLine Shiller Enhanced CAPE® Class N	DSENX	B-	B-	B		4.80	22.74	13.29	60.69	86.55	15.4	6,666	877-354-6311	Y
DWS Core Equity Fund - Class Inst	SUWIX	B-	C	B		4.10	19.37	7.64	50.25	66.27	26.88	3,784		Y
DWS Core Equity Fund - Class R6	SUWZX	B-	C	B		4.08	19.37	7.66	50.49	66.35	26.85	3,784		Y
DWS Core Equity Fund - Class S	SCDGX	B-	C	B		4.10	19.35	7.58	50.12	65.98	26.82	3,784		Y
DWS Equity 500 Index Fund - Class Inst	BTIIX	B-	C	B	Down	4.24	19.44	10.60	50.33	64.78	197.47	624.3		Y
DWS Equity 500 Index Fund - Class R6	BTIRX	B-	C	B	Down	4.24	19.45	10.60	50.33	64.77	197.44	624.3		Y
DWS Equity 500 Index Fund - Class S	BTIEX	B-	C	B		4.23	19.41	10.54	50.11	64.37	194.23	624.3		Y
DWS S&P 500 Index Fund - Class A	SXPAX	B-	C	B		4.14	19.26	10.25	48.82	61.88	31.49	1,006		Y
DWS S&P 500 Index Fund - Class C	SXPCX	B-	C	B		3.97	18.80	9.44	45.62	56.29	31.42	1,006		Y
DWS S&P 500 Index Fund - Class R6	SXPRX	B-	C	B		4.22	19.41	10.57	50.18	64.61	31.56	1,006		Y
DWS S&P 500 Index Fund - Class S	SCPIX	B-	C	B		4.23	19.41	10.51	49.99	64.08	31.56	1,006		Y
Eaton Vance Dividend Builder Fund Class A	EVTMX	B-	C+	B		4.70	18.45	10.09	40.01	54.07	14.56	895.2		Y
Eaton Vance Dividend Builder Fund Class C	ECTMX	B-	C	B		4.47	17.94	9.24	36.88	48.31	14.65	895.2		Y
Eaton Vance Dividend Builder Fund Class I	EIUTX	B-	C+	B		4.77	18.61	10.37	41.11	55.96	14.55	895.2		Y
Eaton Vance Stock Fund Class A	EAERX	B-	C+	B		6.19	23.61	12.31	46.27	59.21	18.01	95.1		Y
Eaton Vance Stock Fund Class C	ECERX	B-	C	B		5.92	23.10	11.45	43.02	53.34	17.53	95.1		Y
Eaton Vance Stock Fund Institutional Class	EIERX	B-	C+	B		6.24	23.74	12.57	47.38	61.19	18.03	95.1		Y

Category: US Equity Large Cap Blend (con't)

Fund Name	Ticker Symbol	Overall Rating	Reward Rating	Risk Rating	Recent Up/ Downgrade	3-Month Total Return	6-Month Total Return	1-Year Total Return	3-Year Total Return	5-Year Total Return	NAV	Total Assets (MIL)	Telephone	Open to New Investors
		RATINGS				TOTAL RETURNS & PERFORMANCE					ASSETS		NEW INVESTORS	
Eaton Vance Tax-Managed Growth 1.0 Fund	CAPEX	B-	C	B		3.26	18.58	8.82	50.00	62.57	1256.92	967.7		
EQ/500 Managed Volatility Portfolio Class IB		B-	C	B	Up	2.67	6.93	4.21	41.45	57.40		9,448	877-222-2144	Y
EQ/500 Managed Volatility Portfolio Class K		B-	C	B	Up	2.73	7.10	4.49	42.52	59.37		9,448	877-222-2144	Y
EQ/Common Stock Index Portfolio Class IA		B-	C	B		2.18	7.78	4.38	43.49	58.44		5,878	877-222-2144	Y
EQ/Common Stock Index Portfolio Class IB		B-	C	B		2.17	7.76	4.38	43.51	58.42		5,878	877-222-2144	Y
EQ/Equity 500 Index Portfolio Class IA		B-	C	B		2.74	7.99	5.42	44.33	61.65		5,977	877-222-2144	Y
EQ/Equity 500 Index Portfolio Class IB		B-	C	B		2.73	7.99	5.43	44.30	61.64		5,977	877-222-2144	Y
EQ/Equity 500 Index Portfolio Class K		B-	C	B		2.79	8.10	5.67	45.40	63.55		5,977	877-222-2144	Y
EQ/Large Cap Core Managed Volatility Portfolio Class K		B-	C	B	Up	2.69	7.10	3.82	43.67	59.24		2,468	877-222-2144	Y
Federated Max-Cap Index Fund Class C Shares	MXCCX	B-	C	B		-0.04	14.18	4.84	39.77	49.92	9.59	321.0	800-341-7400	Y
Federated Max-Cap Index Fund Class R Shares	FMXKX	B-	C	B		0.14	14.39	5.25	41.17	52.43	9.79	321.0	800-341-7400	Y
Federated Max-Cap Index Fund Institutional Shares	FISPX	B-	C	B		0.31	14.80	6.06	44.30	58.15	9.97	321.0	800-341-7400	Y
Federated Max-Cap Index Fund Service Shares	FMXSX	B-	C	B		0.13	14.54	5.64	42.87	55.74	9.81	321.0	800-341-7400	Y
Fidelity Advisor® Dividend Growth Fund Class A	FADAX	B-	C	B		3.54	16.31	8.91	38.88	43.48	15.76	999.5	617-563-7000	Y
Fidelity Advisor® Dividend Growth Fund Class C	FDGCX	B-	C	B	Up	3.29	15.86	8.03	35.70	38.04	14.75	999.5	617-563-7000	Y
Fidelity Advisor® Dividend Growth Fund Class M	FDGTX	B-	C	B		3.43	16.17	8.57	37.77	41.70	15.66	999.5	617-563-7000	Y
Fidelity Advisor® Dividend Growth Fund Class Z	FZADX	B-	C	B+		3.58	16.51	9.31	40.49	46.30	17.07	999.5	617-563-7000	Y
Fidelity Advisor® Dividend Growth Fund I Class	FDGIX	B-	C	B+		3.64	16.52	9.19	39.93	45.23	16.78	999.5	617-563-7000	Y
Fidelity® 500 Index Fund	FXAIX	B-	C	B		4.29	19.55	10.40	50.84	66.20	102.66	198,287	617-563-7000	Y
Fidelity® Dividend Growth Fund	FDGFX	B-	C	B		3.67	16.62	9.03	40.01	45.47	29.32	6,902	617-563-7000	Y
Fidelity® Dividend Growth Fund Class K	FDGKX	B-	C	B		3.75	16.68	9.15	40.47	46.33	29.3	6,902	617-563-7000	Y
Fidelity® Export and Multinational Fund	FEXPX	B-	C	B		3.52	16.01	8.59	38.82	50.99	20.86	1,680	617-563-7000	Y
Fidelity® Export and Multinational Fund Class K	FEXKX	B-	C	B		3.53	16.06	8.69	39.30	51.89	20.81	1,680	617-563-7000	Y
Fidelity® Large Cap Core Enhanced Index Fund	FLCEX	B-	C	B		3.10	16.66	8.47	49.56	60.06	15.26	833.4	617-563-7000	Y
Fidelity® SAI U.S. Large Cap Index Fund	FLCPX	B-	C	B	Up	4.34	19.60	10.42	50.82		15.86	13,172	617-563-7000	Y
Fidelity® SAI U.S. Low Volatility Index Fund	FSUVX	B	B-	A-		5.05	18.40	17.01	42.66		14.54	3,432	617-563-7000	Y
Fidelity® Total Market Index Fund	FSKAX	B-	C	B		4.08	19.74	8.88	50.30	62.30	83.41	48,079	617-563-7000	Y
First Eagle U.S. Value Fund Class A	FEVAX	B-	C	A-		3.32	14.68	6.77	31.13	33.07	18.67	1,655	800-334-2143	Y
First Eagle U.S. Value Fund Class C	FEVCX	B-	C	A-		3.07	14.20	5.91	28.10	28.06	17.77	1,655	800-334-2143	Y
First Eagle U.S. Value Fund Class I	FEVIX	B-	C	A-		3.37	14.79	7.00	32.13	34.79	19.01	1,655	800-334-2143	Y
First Eagle U.S. Value Fund Class R3	EARVX	B-	C	A-		3.21	14.55	6.60	30.68	32.39	18.97	1,655	800-334-2143	Y
First Eagle U.S. Value Fund Class R6	FEVRX	B-	C	A-		3.42	14.85	7.09	32.22	34.80	19.02	1,655	800-334-2143	Y
FMI Large Cap Fund	FMIHX	B	C+	B+		5.34	17.55	9.72	46.56	53.86	20.09	5,115	800-811-5311	
FMI Large Cap Fund Institutional Class	FMIQX	B	C+	B+		5.40	17.64	9.89	47.03	54.35	20.07	5,115	800-811-5311	Y
Fort Pitt Capital Total Return Fund	FPCGX	B-	C	B+	Down	2.63	17.84	9.65	55.46	57.91	26.88	73.5		Y
Franklin Rising Dividends Fund Advisor Class	FRDAX	B-	C+	B	Down	5.06	21.98	13.98	47.62	60.94	66.59	19,187	650-312-2000	Y
Franklin Rising Dividends Fund Class A	FRDPX	B-	C+	B	Down	4.99	21.83	13.69	46.50	58.92	66.62	19,187	650-312-2000	Y
Franklin Rising Dividends Fund Class C	FRDTX	B-	C+	B	Down	4.80	21.37	12.84	43.24	53.05	65.27	19,187	650-312-2000	Y
Franklin Rising Dividends Fund Class R	FRDRX	B-	C+	B	Down	4.92	21.68	13.40	45.41	56.95	66.37	19,187	650-312-2000	Y
Franklin Rising Dividends Fund R6 Class	FRISX	B-	C+	B	Down	5.08	22.03	14.03	48.09	61.96	66.59	19,187	650-312-2000	Y
Frontier MFG Global Plus Fund Institutional Class	FMGPX	B	B-	A-		6.36	18.86	15.22	57.30		13.04	330.9		Y
Frontier MFG Global Plus Fund Service Class	FMPSX	B	B-	A-		6.36	18.77	15.08	56.94		13.03	330.9		Y
Gabelli Asset Fund Class A	GATAX	B-	C	B	Up	3.75	16.51	5.64	37.09	34.36	56.44	2,316	914-921-5135	Y
Gabelli Asset Fund Class AAA	GABAX	B-	C	B	Up	3.74	16.48	5.64	37.09	34.36	57.08	2,316	914-921-5135	Y
Gabelli Asset Fund Class C	GATCX	B-	C	B	Up	3.56	16.08	4.86	34.05	29.41	51.66	2,316	914-921-5135	Y
Gabelli Asset Fund Class I	GABIX	B-	C	B	Up	3.82	16.63	5.90	38.11	36.04	56.99	2,316	914-921-5135	Y
GE RSP U.S. Equity Fund	GESSX	B-	C	B	Down	5.50	20.33	12.05	53.63	58.75	54.98	5,348	617-664-7338	Y
Glenmede Quantitative U.S. Large Cap Core Equity Portfolio	GTLOX	B-	C	B	Up	2.34	14.12	3.65	43.51	56.58	26.6	2,596	800-442-8299	Y
Glenmede Quantitative U.S. Large Cap Core Eq Inst Shares	GTLIX	B-	C	B	Up	2.39	14.21	3.86	44.37	57.68	26.62	2,596	800-442-8299	Y
Glenmede Responsible ESG U.S. Equity Portfolio	RESGX	B-	C	B	Up	2.24	14.33	5.39	49.21		14.28	22.5	800-442-8299	Y
Glenmede Strategic Equity Portfolio	GTCEX	B-	C	B		3.35	19.25	8.56	50.65	67.32	26.16	255.7	800-442-8299	Y
Glenmede Women in Leadership U.S. Equity Portfolio	GWILX	B-	C	B	Up	3.29	15.64	5.89	44.72		13.61	20.1	800-442-8299	Y

Category: US Equity Large Cap Blend (con't)

Fund Name	Ticker Symbol	Overall Rating	Reward Rating	Risk Rating	Recent Up/ Downgrade	3-Month Total Return	6-Month Total Return	1-Year Total Return	3-Year Total Return	5-Year Total Return	NAV	Total Assets (MIL)	Telephone	Open to New Investors
		RATINGS				TOTAL RETURNS & PERFORMANCE					ASSETS		NEW INVESTORS	
GMO Quality Fund Class III	GQETX	B-	C+	B+	Down	3.64	18.19	14.09	58.54	79.85	23.91	6,700	617-330-7500	Y
GMO Quality Fund Class IV	GQEFX	B	C+	B+		3.63	18.21	14.13	58.70	80.27	23.95	6,700	617-330-7500	Y
GMO Quality Fund Class VI	GQLOX	B	C+	B+		3.68	18.24	14.19	59.00	80.75	23.92	6,700	617-330-7500	Y
GMO Quality Series Fund Class PS	GQPSX	B-	C+	B+	Down	3.54	17.70	13.72	57.48	78.89	11.1	78.6	617-330-7500	Y
GMO Quality Series Fund Class R6	GQURX	B-	C+	B+	Down	3.64	17.83	13.75	57.93	79.40	11.1	78.6	617-330-7500	Y
Goldman Sachs U.S. Equity Dividend & Premium Cls A	GSPAX	B-	C	B	Up	2.88	15.67	6.09	33.12	48.02	13.04	2,934	800-526-7384	Y
Goldman Sachs U.S. Equity Dividend & Premium Cls C	GSPQX	B-	C	B	Up	2.78	15.33	5.30	30.16	42.59	12.99	2,934	800-526-7384	Y
Goldman Sachs U.S. Equity Dividend & Premium Cls P	GSFPX	B-	C	B		3.07	16.03	6.54	34.55	50.83	13.01	2,934	800-526-7384	Y
Goldman Sachs U.S. Equity Dividend & Premium Cls R6	GIDWX	B-	C	B		3.00	15.94	6.46	34.55	50.83	13	2,934	800-526-7384	Y
Goldman Sachs U.S. Equity Dividend & Premium Inst Cls	GSPKX	B-	C	B		3.07	15.92	6.52	34.62	50.90	13.01	2,934	800-526-7384	Y
Goldman Sachs U.S. Equity Dividend & Premium Investor Cls	GVIRX	B-	C	B		3.04	15.94	6.38	34.12	49.91	13.02	2,934	800-526-7384	Y
Gotham Enhanced 500 Fund Institutional Class	GENFX	B-	C	B		0.00	9.23	4.47	50.54		11.71	27.7	877-974-6852	Y
Gotham Enhanced 500 Plus Fund Institutional Class	GEFPX	B-	C	B		1.85	13.80	7.87			11.54	2.9	877-974-6852	Y
Gotham Enhanced Index Plus Fund Institutional Class	GENDX	B-	C	B	Up	1.93	15.30	6.55			12.13	3.3	877-974-6852	Y
Gotham Index Plus Fund Institutional Class	GINDX	B-	C	B		1.85	9.21	5.26	54.60		14.82	746.7	877-974-6852	Y
Gotham Index Plus Fund Investor Class	GNNDX	B-	C	B		1.78	9.07	5.07	53.54		14.79	746.7	877-974-6852	Y
Great Lakes Disciplined Equity Fund Institutional Class	GLDNX	B-	C	B		4.20	20.54	10.27	44.78	58.59	15.57	43.7		Y
Great-West S&P 500® Index Fund Class L	MXVJX	B-	C	B		4.26	18.45	9.04	49.06	58.70	17.42	2,973		Y
Great-West S&P 500® Index Fund Institutional Class	MXKWX	B-	C	B		4.34	18.88	9.67	51.81	63.08	9.9	2,973		Y
Great-West S&P 500® Index Fund Investor Class	MXVIX	B-	C	B		4.31	18.63	9.31	50.21	60.71	22.77	2,973		Y
Guggenheim StylePlus - Large Core Fund Institutional	GILIX	B-	C	B	Up	3.67	18.46	7.95	48.09	63.84	20.02	202.8	212-518-9290	Y
GuideStone Funds Equity Index Fund Institutional Class	GEQYX	B-	C	B		4.40	19.57	10.43	51.78	65.98	32.36	1,905	214-720-1171	Y
GuideStone Funds Equity Index Fund Investor Class	GEQZX	B-	C	B		4.35	19.42	10.12	50.56	64.01	32.38	1,905	214-720-1171	Y
Harbor Large Cap Value Fund Administrative Class	HRLVX	B-	C	B	Up	6.07	19.89	7.54	48.23	60.04	15.67	1,146	800-422-1050	Y
Harbor Large Cap Value Fund Institutional Class	HAVLX	B-	C	B	Up	6.13	20.05	7.76	49.45	62.17	15.66	1,146	800-422-1050	Y
Harbor Large Cap Value Fund Retirement Class	HNLVX	B-	C	B	Up	6.17	20.10	7.91	49.75	62.70	15.66	1,146	800-422-1050	Y
Hartford Core Equity Fund Class A	HAIAX	B-	C+	B	Down	5.31	20.75	13.11	49.41	73.69	32.11	4,986	888-843-7824	Y
Hartford Core Equity Fund Class C	HGICX	B-	C+	B		5.14	20.32	12.25	46.12	67.43	29.25	4,986	888-843-7824	Y
Hartford Core Equity Fund Class F	HGIFX	B-	C+	B	Down	5.40	20.93	13.48	50.97	76.79	32.18	4,986	888-843-7824	Y
Hartford Core Equity Fund Class I	HGIIX	B-	C+	B	Down	5.40	20.89	13.39	50.51	76.17	32.17	4,986	888-843-7824	Y
Hartford Core Equity Fund Class R3	HGIRX	B-	C+	B	Down	5.23	20.52	12.70	47.88	70.92	32.59	4,986	888-843-7824	Y
Hartford Core Equity Fund Class R4	HGISX	B-	C+	B	Down	5.34	20.75	13.10	49.31	73.67	33.11	4,986	888-843-7824	Y
Hartford Core Equity Fund Class R5	HGITX	B-	C+	B	Down	5.36	20.88	13.37	50.55	76.12	32.41	4,986	888-843-7824	Y
Hartford Core Equity Fund Class R6	HAITX	B-	C+	B	Down	5.44	20.95	13.49	51.03	76.80	32.56	4,986	888-843-7824	Y
Hartford Core Equity Fund Class Y	HGIYX	B-	C+	B	Down	5.37	20.91	13.43	50.83	76.63	32.55	4,986	888-843-7824	Y
Hartford Disciplined Equity HLS Fund Class IA	HIAGX	B-	C+	B	Down	5.36	21.02	13.29	50.03	75.84	16.29	633.2	888-843-7824	Y
Hartford Disciplined Equity HLS Fund Class IB	HBGIX	B-	C+	B	Down	5.30	20.88	12.98	48.93	73.69	16.09	633.2	888-843-7824	Y
Hartford Stock HLS Fund Class IA	HSTAX	B	B	B+		5.95	21.69	18.43	49.25	70.73	94.42	1,496	888-843-7824	Y
Hartford Stock HLS Fund Class IB	HIBSX	B	B	B+		5.89	21.54	18.14	48.14	68.61	94.31	1,496	888-843-7824	Y
Homestead Stock Index Fund	HSTIX	B-	C	B		4.01	19.00	9.58	48.13	61.45	22.04	153.3		Y
Independent Franchise Partners US Equity Fund	IFPUX	B	C+	B+	Up	2.34	20.96	10.19	41.64	66.30	18.35	2,161		Y
Index Funds S&P 500® Equal Weight No Load Shares	INDEX	B-	C	B		3.62	20.00	7.97	43.46		32.33	43.0	844-464-6339	Y
Integrity Growth & Income Fund Class A	IGIAX	B	C+	B+		5.25	19.45	16.63	47.63	44.07	58.27	38.7	800-276-1262	Y
Integrity Growth & Income Fund Class C	IGIUX	B	C+	B+		5.13	19.18	16.13	45.01	39.71	57.71	38.7	800-276-1262	Y
Integrity Growth & Income Fund Class I	IGIVX	B	C+	B+		5.32	19.60	16.92	48.78	45.20	58.32	38.7	800-276-1262	Y
Invesco Equally-Weighted S&P 500 Fund Class A	VADAX	B-	C	B		3.59	19.87	7.63	41.95	50.82	61.46	7,665	800-659-1005	Y
Invesco Equally-Weighted S&P 500 Fund Class R6	VADFX	B-	C	B		3.68	20.10	8.03	43.53	53.67	62.2	7,665	800-659-1005	Y
Invesco Equally-Weighted S&P 500 Fund Class Y	VADDX	B-	C	B		3.65	20.02	7.90	43.00	52.70	62.1	7,665	800-659-1005	Y
Invesco Oppenheimer Main Street Fund Class A	MSIGX	B-	C	B		5.81	22.33	11.72	41.07	55.83	48.04	9,574	800-659-1005	Y
Invesco Oppenheimer Main Street Fund Class R	OMGNX	B-	C	B		5.73	22.17	11.41	39.95	53.83	46.99	9,574	800-659-1005	Y
Invesco Oppenheimer Main Street Fund Class R5	MSJFX	B-	C	B		5.81	22.33	11.72	41.06	55.83	48.05	9,574	800-659-1005	Y
Invesco Oppenheimer Main Street Fund Class R6	OMSIX	B-	C+	B		5.90	22.57	12.16	42.79	59.09	47.51	9,574	800-659-1005	Y

Category: US Equity Large Cap Blend (con't)

Fund Name	Ticker Symbol	RATINGS: Overall Rating	Reward Rating	Risk Rating	Recent Up/ Downgrade	TOTAL RETURNS & PERFORMANCE: 3-Month Total Return	6-Month Total Return	1-Year Total Return	3-Year Total Return	5-Year Total Return	ASSETS: NAV	Total Assets (MIL)	NEW INVESTORS: Telephone	Open to New Investors
Invesco Oppenheimer Main Street Fund Class Y	MIGYX	B-	C+	B		5.87	22.47	11.98	42.03	57.68	47.58	9,574	800-659-1005	Y
Invesco S&P 500 Index Fund Class A	SPIAX	B-	C	B		4.17	19.23	9.84	48.40	61.61	31.68	1,394	800-659-1005	Y
Invesco S&P 500 Index Fund Class C	SPICX	B-	C	B		3.95	18.78	8.98	45.08	55.71	30.48	1,394	800-659-1005	Y
Invesco S&P 500 Index Fund Class Y	SPIDX	B-	C	B		4.22	19.34	10.05	49.43	63.60	32.08	1,394	800-659-1005	Y
Invesco S&P 500 Index Fund ClassR6	SPISX	B-	C	B		4.22	19.38	10.12	49.57	63.76	32.09	1,394	800-659-1005	Y
iShares Edge MSCI Min Vol USA Index Fund Class K	BKMVX	B-	C	B+		5.48	19.93	18.50	39.87		12.98	22.3	800-441-7762	Y
iShares Edge MSCI Min Vol USA Index Institutional Shares	BIMVX	B-	C	B+		5.56	19.81	18.45	39.72		12.98	22.3	800-441-7762	Y
iShares Russell 1000 Large-Cap Index Fund Class K	BRGKX	B-	C	B		4.26	19.88	9.98	50.47	63.87	19.37	352.0	800-441-7762	Y
iShares Russell 1000 Large-Cap Index Institutional Shares	BRGNX	B-	C	B		4.17	19.76	9.89	50.23	63.43	19.44	352.0	800-441-7762	Y
iShares Russell 1000 Large-Cap Index Investor A Shares	BRGAX	B-	C	B		4.14	19.68	9.67	49.09	61.33	19.33	352.0	800-441-7762	Y
iShares S&P 500 Index Fund Class K	WFSPX	B-	C	B		4.29	19.52	10.41	50.78	66.02	349.13	19,490	800-441-7762	Y
iShares S&P 500 Index Fund Institutional Shares	BSPIX	B-	C	B		4.27	19.47	10.33	50.46	65.44	349.05	19,490	800-441-7762	Y
iShares S&P 500 Index Fund Investor A Shares	BSPAX	B-	C	B		4.20	19.32	10.05	49.34	63.38	348.95	19,490	800-441-7762	Y
iShares S&P 500 Index Fund Investor C1 Shares	BSPZX	B-	C	B		4.02	18.90	9.23	46.11	57.56	350.28	19,490	800-441-7762	Y
iShares S&P 500 Index Fund Investor P Shares	BSPPX	B-	C	B		4.21	19.33	10.07	49.58	63.88	348.69	19,490	800-441-7762	Y
iShares S&P 500 Index Fund Service Shares	BSPSX	B-	C	B		4.24	19.40	10.20	49.93	64.46	349.04	19,490	800-441-7762	Y
iShares Total U.S. Stock Market Index Fund Class K	BKTSX	B-	C	B		4.16	19.89	9.06	50.08		13.99	1,073	800-441-7762	Y
iShares Total U.S. Stock Market Index Institutional Shares	BITSX	B-	C	B		4.14	19.77	9.00	49.92		13.99	1,073	800-441-7762	Y
iShares Total U.S. Stock Market Index Investor A Shares	BASMX	B-	C	B		4.02	19.66	8.69	48.72		13.96	1,073	800-441-7762	Y
Jamestown Equity Fund	JAMEX	B-	C	B	Up	2.45	16.93	8.08	40.65	38.43	22.26	37.6	866-738-1126	Y
Janus Henderson Growth And Income Fund Class A	JDNAX	B-	C	B+	Down	3.85	15.94	11.39	54.48	66.61	56.94	5,718	877-335-2687	Y
Janus Henderson Growth And Income Fund Class C	JGICX	B-	C	B+	Down	3.66	15.51	10.55	51.11	60.56	56.17	5,718	877-335-2687	Y
Janus Henderson Growth And Income Fund Class D	JNGIX	B-	C	B+	Down	3.90	16.06	11.60	55.30	68.01	57.03	5,718	877-335-2687	
Janus Henderson Growth And Income Fund Class I	JGINX	B-	C	B+	Down	3.92	16.09	11.68	55.65	68.61	57.06	5,718	877-335-2687	Y
Janus Henderson Growth And Income Fund Class N	JDNNX	B-	C	B+	Down	3.94	16.12	11.71	55.65	68.38	56.97	5,718	877-335-2687	Y
Janus Henderson Growth And Income Fund Class R	JDNRX	B-	C	B+	Down	3.72	15.66	10.86	52.41	62.89	56.58	5,718	877-335-2687	Y
Janus Henderson Growth And Income Fund Class S	JADGX	B-	C	B+	Down	3.80	15.86	11.19	53.67	65.12	56.93	5,718	877-335-2687	Y
Janus Henderson Growth And Income Fund Class T	JAGIX	B-	C	B+	Down	3.87	15.98	11.47	54.85	67.26	56.98	5,718	877-335-2687	Y
Janus Henderson VIT U.S. Low Vol Port Serv Shares		B-	C+	B+	Down	5.02	18.61	15.01	29.18	60.53	17.99	1,048	877-335-2687	Y
JNL/American Funds Growth-Income Fund Class A		B-	C	B		3.19	16.67	6.64	50.83	60.06	25.19	7,247		Y
JNL/American Funds Growth-Income Fund Class I		B-	C	B+		3.22	16.81	6.94	51.93	61.92	25.57	7,247		Y
JNL/Mellon S&P 500 Index Fund Class A		B-	C	B		4.15	19.24	9.84	48.61	61.93	23.05	8,414		Y
JNL/Mellon S&P 500 Index Fund Class I		B-	C	B		4.27	19.47	10.25	49.74	63.60	23.68	8,414		Y
John Hancock ESG Large Cap Core Fund Class A	JHJAX	B-	C	B		4.63	19.86	13.89	51.69		14	61.0	800-225-5913	Y
John Hancock ESG Large Cap Core Fund Class C	JHJCX	B-	C	B		4.45	19.34	13.02	48.25		13.82	61.0	800-225-5913	Y
John Hancock ESG Large Cap Core Fund Class I	JHJIX	B-	C	B		4.70	19.93	14.17	52.86		14.02	61.0	800-225-5913	Y
John Hancock ESG Large Cap Core Fund Class R6	JHJRX	B-	C	B		4.77	20.01	14.28	53.40		14.03	61.0	800-225-5913	Y
Johnson Enhanced Return Fund	JENHX	B-	C+	B		4.92	21.54	11.87	49.10	66.52	16.93	157.4		Y
Johnson Equity Income Fund	JEQIX	B	B	B+		5.95	22.15	17.54	59.13	55.38	27.24	349.0		Y
JPMorgan Equity Index Fund Class A	OGEAX	B-	C	B		4.17	19.27	9.87	48.81	62.52	44.9	4,510	800-480-4111	Y
JPMorgan Equity Index Fund Class C	OEICX	B-	C	B		4.04	18.93	9.23	46.09	57.16	44.45	4,510	800-480-4111	Y
JPMorgan Equity Index Fund Class I	HLEIX	B-	C	B		4.26	19.44	10.16	49.94	64.59	44.97	4,510	800-480-4111	Y
JPMorgan Equity Index Fund Class R6	OGFAX	B-	C	B		4.27	19.53	10.32	50.61	65.34	44.98	4,510	800-480-4111	Y
JPMorgan Insurance Trust U.S. Equity Portfolio Class 1		B-	C	B		4.37	19.60	9.21	52.66	62.24	29.03	111.2	800-480-4111	Y
JPMorgan Insurance Trust U.S. Equity Portfolio Class 2		B-	C	B		4.20	18.64	8.25	53.04	59.17	28.67	111.2		Y
JPMorgan Intrepid Sustainable Equity Fund Class A Shares	JICAX	B-	C	B		4.02	18.42	9.90	49.07	56.69	41.85	30.7	800-480-4111	Y
JPMorgan Intrepid Sustainable Equity Fund Class C Shares	JICCX	B-	C	B		3.87	18.13	9.36	46.84	52.86	40.98	30.7	800-480-4111	Y
JPMorgan Intrepid Sustainable Equity Fund I Class	JIISX	B-	C	B		4.07	18.56	10.17	50.16	58.69	42.15	30.7	800-480-4111	Y
JPMorgan U.S. Equity Fund Class I	JUESX	B-	C	B		4.56	19.81	9.46	50.93	60.80	15.91	14,317	800-480-4111	Y
JPMorgan U.S. Equity Fund Class L	JMUEX	B-	C	B		4.52	19.79	9.59	51.56	61.85	15.93	14,317	800-480-4111	Y
JPMorgan U.S. Equity Fund Class R4	JUEQX	B-	C	B		4.57	19.77	9.43	50.91	61.16	15.89	14,317	800-480-4111	Y
JPMorgan U.S. Equity Fund Class R5	JUSRX	B-	C	B		4.59	19.87	9.59	51.66	62.13	15.94	14,317	800-480-4111	Y

Category: US Equity Large Cap Blend (con't)

Fund Name	Ticker Symbol	RATINGS: Overall Rating	Reward Rating	Risk Rating	Recent Up/ Downgrade	TOTAL RETURNS & PERFORMANCE: 3-Month Total Return	6-Month Total Return	1-Year Total Return	3-Year Total Return	5-Year Total Return	ASSETS: NAV	Total Assets (MIL)	NEW INVESTORS: Telephone	Open to New Investors
JPMorgan U.S. Equity Fund Class R6	JUEMX	B-	C	B		4.61	19.88	9.73	52.12	62.81	15.97	14,317		Y
JPMorgan U.S. Research Enhanced Equity Fund Class A	JDEAX	B-	C	B		4.13	19.00	9.39	48.30	52.85	27.38	5,820	800-480-4111	Y
JPMorgan U.S. Research Enhanced Equity Fund Class I	JDESX	B-	C	B		4.19	19.13	9.64	49.40	54.73	27.65	5,820	800-480-4111	Y
JPMorgan U.S. Research Enhanced Equity Fund Class L	JPIEX	B-	C	B		4.24	19.17	9.66	49.45	55.28	27.61	5,820	800-480-4111	Y
JPMorgan U.S. Research Enhanced Equity Fund Class R6	JDEUX	B-	C	B		4.22	19.22	9.78	49.97	56.08	27.62	5,820	800-480-4111	Y
KP Large Cap Equity Fund Institutional Shares	KPLCX	B-	C	B		3.74	18.94	8.59	52.78	66.05	13.31	2,927		Y
Lazard US Equity Concentrated Portfolio Inst Shares	LEVIX	B-	C	B	Down	5.16	22.69	11.35	40.17	65.52	15.68	1,292	800-823-6300	Y
Lazard US Equity Concentrated Portfolio Open Shares	LEVOX	B-	C	B	Down	5.05	22.51	11.02	39.02	63.04	15.78	1,292	800-823-6300	Y
Lazard US Equity Concentrated Portfolio R6 Shares	RLUEX	B-	C	B	Down	5.15	22.71	11.36	40.13	65.47	15.72	1,292	800-823-6300	Y
Lazard US Equity Select Portfolio Institutional Shares	LZUSX	B-	C+	B	Down	4.74	19.74	11.63	49.59	51.64	12.13	78.9	800-823-6300	Y
Lazard US Equity Select Portfolio Open Shares	LZUOX	B-	C+	B	Down	4.64	19.54	11.24	48.33	49.42	12.17	78.9	800-823-6300	Y
Lazard US Equity Select Portfolio R6 Shares	RLUSX	B-	C+	B	Down	4.74	19.72	11.62	49.70	52.03	12.14	78.9	800-823-6300	Y
Lord Abbett Calibrated Dividend Growth Fund Class A	LAMAX	B-	C+	B+	Down	3.95	17.40	12.58	38.82	55.75	15.49	2,400	201-827-2000	Y
Lord Abbett Calibrated Dividend Growth Fund Class C	LAMCX	B-	C+	B		3.81	16.97	11.77	35.76	50.12	15.29	2,400	201-827-2000	Y
Lord Abbett Calibrated Dividend Growth Fund Class F	LAMFX	B-	C+	B+	Down	4.05	17.55	12.88	39.79	57.26	15.51	2,400	201-827-2000	Y
Lord Abbett Calibrated Dividend Growth Fund Class F3	LRMAX	B-	C+	B+	Down	4.10	17.62	12.91	40.19	58.07	15.71	2,400	201-827-2000	Y
Lord Abbett Calibrated Dividend Growth Fund Class I	LAMYX	B-	C+	B+	Down	4.04	17.60	12.87	39.88	57.71	15.65	2,400	201-827-2000	Y
Lord Abbett Calibrated Dividend Growth Fund Class P	LAMPX	B-	C+	B+	Down	3.92	17.29	12.38	37.96	54.16	15.59	2,400	201-827-2000	
Lord Abbett Calibrated Dividend Growth Fund Class R2	LAMQX	B-	C+	B+	Down	3.86	17.22	12.17	37.32	52.99	15.66	2,400	201-827-2000	Y
Lord Abbett Calibrated Dividend Growth Fund Class R3	LAMRX	B-	C+	B+	Down	3.97	17.26	12.36	37.93	54.00	15.42	2,400	201-827-2000	Y
Lord Abbett Calibrated Dividend Growth Fund Class R4	LAMSX	B-	C+	B+	Down	4.02	17.42	12.60	38.86	55.77	15.48	2,400	201-827-2000	Y
Lord Abbett Calibrated Dividend Growth Fund Class R5	LAMTX	B-	C+	B+	Down	4.04	17.52	12.87	39.91	57.64	15.64	2,400	201-827-2000	Y
Lord Abbett Calibrated Dividend Growth Fund Class R6	LAMHX	B-	C+	B+	Down	4.10	17.62	12.99	40.30	58.32	15.71	2,400	201-827-2000	Y
MainStay MacKay S&P 500 Index Fund Class A	MSXAX	B-	C	B		4.18	19.25	9.91	48.52	61.77	47.82	1,023	800-624-6782	Y
MainStay MacKay S&P 500 Index Fund Class I	MSPIX	B-	C	B		4.23	19.41	10.17	49.62	63.80	48.53	1,023	800-624-6782	Y
MainStay MacKay S&P 500 Index Fund Investor Class	MYSPX	B-	C	B		4.12	19.14	9.71	47.88	60.76	47.74	1,023	800-624-6782	Y
Mairs & Power Growth Fund Investor Class	MPGFX	B-	C	B	Down	2.73	17.46	13.68	36.89	50.24	122.92	4,404	800-304-7404	Y
Marathon Value Portfolio	MVPFX	B-	C	B		3.62	19.51	10.70	40.62	48.76	29.15	61.8		Y
Marshfield Concentrated Opportunity Fund	MRFOX	B+	B+	A-	Up	6.29	26.58	24.74	87.24		17.38	71.5		Y
MassMutual Premier Main Street Fund Administrative Class	MMSLX	B-	C	B		5.79	22.32	11.50	40.56	54.71	10.96	126.1		Y
MassMutual Premier Main Street Fund Class I	MSZIX	B-	C+	B		5.88	22.43	11.89	41.75	56.88	10.97	126.1		Y
MassMutual Premier Main Street Fund Class R4	MSSRX	B-	C	B		5.73	22.17	11.31	39.91	53.47	10.69	126.1		Y
MassMutual Premier Main Street Fund Class R5	MMSSX	B-	C	B		5.88	22.43	11.76	41.44	56.23	10.97	126.1		Y
MassMutual Premier Main Street Fund Service Class	MMSYX	B-	C	B		5.84	22.31	11.63	40.91	55.34	11.4	126.1		Y
MassMutual Select Equity Opportunities Administrative Cls	MMFVX	B	B	B+		6.01	20.19	14.66	73.27	60.69	17.26	659.5		Y
MassMutual Select Equity Opportunities Fund Class A	MFVAX	B	B	B+		5.95	20.01	14.36	72.05	58.67	16.37	659.5		Y
MassMutual Select Equity Opportunities Fund Class I	MFVZX	B	B	B+		6.12	20.36	14.97	74.88	63.12	17.85	659.5		Y
MassMutual Select Equity Opportunities Fund Class R3	MFVNX	B	B	B+		5.98	20.01	14.25	71.26	57.52	15.05	659.5		Y
MassMutual Select Equity Opportunities Fund Class R4	MFVFX	B	B	B+		6.00	20.10	14.53	72.57	59.47	16.07	659.5		Y
MassMutual Select Equity Opportunities Fund Class R5	MFVSX	B	B	B+		6.09	20.33	14.90	74.38	62.30	17.93	659.5		Y
MassMutual Select Equity Opportunities Fund Service Class	MMFYX	B	B	B+		6.04	20.30	14.76	73.85	61.48	17.54	659.5		Y
Metropolitan West AlphaTrak 500 Fund	MWATX	B-	C+	B	Down	4.60	20.51	11.52	60.41	75.50	11.16	30.4	800-241-4671	Y
MFS Core Equity Fund Class A	MRGAX	B-	C+	B	Down	5.46	21.78	11.39	57.04	67.85	32.42	2,665	877-960-6077	Y
MFS Core Equity Fund Class B	MRGBX	B-	C+	B	Down	5.25	21.30	10.56	53.54	61.64	28.24	2,665	877-960-6077	Y
MFS Core Equity Fund Class C	MRGCX	B-	C+	B	Down	5.24	21.33	10.54	53.45	61.64	27.87	2,665	877-960-6077	Y
MFS Core Equity Fund Class I	MRGRX	B-	C+	B	Down	5.51	21.91	11.66	58.22	69.97	34.43	2,665	877-960-6077	Y
MFS Core Equity Fund Class R1	MRGGX	B-	C+	B	Down	5.25	21.29	10.55	53.50	61.63	27.85	2,665	877-960-6077	Y
MFS Core Equity Fund Class R2	MRERX	B-	C+	B	Down	5.40	21.63	11.12	55.89	65.81	31.6	2,665	877-960-6077	Y
MFS Core Equity Fund Class R3	MRGHX	B-	C+	B	Down	5.44	21.77	11.38	56.98	67.81	32.33	2,665	877-960-6077	Y
MFS Core Equity Fund Class R4	MRGJX	B-	C+	B	Down	5.51	21.90	11.66	58.18	69.93	32.72	2,665	877-960-6077	Y
MFS Core Equity Fund Class R6	MRGKX	B-	C+	B	Down	5.53	21.95	11.76	58.56	70.67	34.5	2,665	877-960-6077	Y
MFS Low Volatility Equity Fund Class A	MLVAX	B	B-	A-		5.79	19.64	16.70	41.48	66.27	15.9	258.2	877-960-6077	Y

Category: US Equity Large Cap Blend (con't)

Fund Name	Ticker Symbol	RATINGS				TOTAL RETURNS & PERFORMANCE					ASSETS		NEW INVESTORS	
		Overall Rating	Reward Rating	Risk Rating	Recent Up/ Downgrade	3-Month Total Return	6-Month Total Return	1-Year Total Return	3-Year Total Return	5-Year Total Return	NAV	Total Assets (MIL)	Telephone	Open to New Investors
MFS Low Volatility Equity Fund Class B	MLVBX	B	B-	A-		5.61	19.24	15.85	38.34	60.14	15.89	258.2	877-960-6077	Y
MFS Low Volatility Equity Fund Class C	MLVGX	B	B-	A-		5.63	19.24	15.85	38.38	60.15	15.84	258.2	877-960-6077	Y
MFS Low Volatility Equity Fund Class I	MLVHX	B	B-	A-		5.92	19.83	17.05	42.68	68.42	15.92	258.2	877-960-6077	Y
MFS Low Volatility Equity Fund Class R1	MLVMX	B	B-	A-		5.60	19.19	15.81	38.43	60.23	15.93	258.2	877-960-6077	Y
MFS Low Volatility Equity Fund Class R2	MLVOX	B	B-	A-		5.77	19.47	16.40	40.42	64.38	15.98	258.2	877-960-6077	Y
MFS Low Volatility Equity Fund Class R3	MLVPX	B	B-	A-		5.84	19.63	16.70	41.58	66.38	15.96	258.2	877-960-6077	Y
MFS Low Volatility Equity Fund Class R4	MLVRX	B	B-	A-		5.91	19.80	17.02	42.62	68.40	15.93	258.2	877-960-6077	Y
MFS Low Volatility Equity Fund Class R6	MLVTX	B	B-	A-		5.86	19.85	17.04	43.02	69.09	15.93	258.2	877-960-6077	Y
MFS Massachusetts Investors Trust Class 529A	EAMTX	B-	C+	B	Down	5.32	21.88	12.88	52.65	62.64	31.1	5,716	877-960-6077	Y
MFS Massachusetts Investors Trust Class 529B	EBMTX	B-	C+	B	Down	5.04	21.31	12.49	50.18	58.02	29.08	5,716	877-960-6077	Y
MFS Massachusetts Investors Trust Class 529C	ECITX	B-	C+	B		5.11	21.40	12.03	49.21	56.56	28.66	5,716	877-960-6077	Y
MFS Massachusetts Investors Trust Class A	MITTX	B	C+	B		5.34	21.93	12.98	52.95	63.09	32	5,716	877-960-6077	Y
MFS Massachusetts Investors Trust Class B	MITBX	B-	C+	B		5.11	21.46	12.09	49.45	56.90	30.93	5,716	877-960-6077	Y
MFS Massachusetts Investors Trust Class C	MITCX	B-	C+	B		5.14	21.47	12.12	49.46	56.93	30.26	5,716	877-960-6077	Y
MFS Massachusetts Investors Trust Class I	MITIX	B	C+	B		5.40	22.07	13.23	54.04	65.02	31.02	5,716	877-960-6077	Y
MFS Massachusetts Investors Trust Class R1	MITGX	B-	C+	B		5.14	21.45	12.06	49.46	56.90	30.06	5,716	877-960-6077	Y
MFS Massachusetts Investors Trust Class R2	MIRTX	B-	C+	B	Down	5.25	21.76	12.63	51.72	60.91	30.32	5,716	877-960-6077	Y
MFS Massachusetts Investors Trust Class R3	MITHX	B-	C+	B	Down	5.36	21.91	12.94	52.89	62.96	31.68	5,716	877-960-6077	Y
MFS Massachusetts Investors Trust Class R4	MITDX	B	C+	B		5.41	22.05	13.24	53.97	64.95	32.32	5,716	877-960-6077	Y
MFS Massachusetts Investors Trust Class R6	MITJX	B	C+	B		5.45	22.14	13.32	54.41	65.72	31.02	5,716	877-960-6077	Y
MFS Research Fund Class A	MFRFX	B-	C+	B	Down	5.91	22.44	12.01	51.70	64.41	43.69	5,837	877-960-6077	Y
MFS Research Fund Class B	MFRBX	B-	C+	B		5.71	21.97	11.14	48.30	58.31	39.19	5,837	877-960-6077	Y
MFS Research Fund Class C	MFRCX	B-	C+	B		5.70	21.98	11.14	48.27	58.33	38.89	5,837	877-960-6077	Y
MFS Research Fund Class I	MRFIX	B-	C+	B	Down	5.97	22.58	12.24	52.78	66.42	44.88	5,837	877-960-6077	Y
MFS Research Fund Class R1	MFRLX	B-	C+	B		5.71	21.96	11.13	48.25	58.28	38.09	5,837	877-960-6077	Y
MFS Research Fund Class R2	MSRRX	B-	C+	B	Down	5.85	22.27	11.71	50.54	62.33	42.1	5,837	877-960-6077	Y
MFS Research Fund Class R3	MFRHX	B-	C+	B	Down	5.91	22.44	11.99	51.68	64.36	43.32	5,837	877-960-6077	Y
MFS Research Fund Class R4	MFRJX	B-	C+	B	Down	5.96	22.58	12.24	52.81	66.42	43.69	5,837	877-960-6077	Y
MFS Research Fund Class R6	MFRKX	B-	C+	B	Down	5.97	22.60	12.33	53.18	67.13	43.6	5,837	877-960-6077	Y
MM S&P 500® Index Fund Class A	MMFFX	B-	C	B		4.10	19.13	9.58	47.62	60.42	17	3,372		Y
MM S&P 500® Index Fund Class Administrative Class	MIEYX	B-	C	B		4.14	19.24	9.85	48.71	62.33	17.35	3,372		Y
MM S&P 500® Index Fund Class I	MMIZX	B-	C	B		4.26	19.53	10.28	50.37	65.25	17.62	3,372		Y
MM S&P 500® Index Fund Class R3	MMINX	B-	C	B		4.07	19.05	9.40	46.97	59.21	16.62	3,372		Y
MM S&P 500® Index Fund Class R4	MIEAX	B-	C	B		4.19	19.20	9.76	48.19	61.19	17.13	3,372		Y
MM S&P 500® Index Fund Class R5	MIEZX	B-	C	B		4.24	19.45	10.14	49.91	64.44	17.68	3,372		Y
MM S&P 500® Index Fund Class Service Class	MMIEX	B-	C	B		4.23	19.40	9.98	49.21	63.27	17.72	3,372		Y
Morgan Stanley Pathway Funds Large Cap Equity Fund	TLGUX	B-	C	B		3.54	18.87	8.80	45.90	56.72	19.27	1,584	855-332-5306	Y
Mutual of America Inst Funds Inc Equity Index Fund	MAEQX	B-	C	B		4.32	19.59	10.35	50.33	65.39	12.2391	51.8		Y
Nationwide Diamond Hill Large Cap Concentrated Cls A	NWGHX	B-	C+	B		7.49	21.65	12.46	45.19	51.03	6.63	24.3	800-848-0920	Y
Nationwide Diamond Hill Large Cap Concentrated Cls R6	NWGJX	B-	C+	B		7.58	21.83	12.86	46.69	53.81	6.65	24.3	800-848-0920	Y
Nationwide Diamond Hill Large Cap Conc Inst Serv Cls	NWGKX	B-	C+	B		7.65	21.75	12.69	46.11	52.94	6.69	24.3	800-848-0920	Y
Nationwide Dynamic U.S. Growth Fund Class A	NMFAX	B-	C+	B		5.62	23.61	12.07	62.04	72.84	9.28	245.3	800-848-0920	Y
Nationwide Dynamic U.S. Growth Fund Class C	GCGRX	B-	C+	B		5.34	23.05	11.07	57.96	65.94	6	245.3	800-848-0920	Y
Nationwide Dynamic U.S. Growth Fund Class R	GGFRX	B-	C+	B		5.38	23.17	11.52	59.97	70.13	8.92	245.3	800-848-0920	Y
Nationwide Dynamic U.S. Growth Fund Class R6	MUIGX	B-	C+	B		5.70	23.73	12.37	63.43	75.50	10.03	245.3	800-848-0920	Y
Nationwide Dynamic U.S. Growth Fund Eagle Class	NWAEX	B-	C+	B		5.62	23.59	12.27	63.30	75.36	10.11	245.3	800-848-0920	Y
Nationwide Dynamic U.S. Growth Institutional Service Cls	NGISX	B-	C+	B		5.62	23.59	12.15	62.50	73.75	10.1	245.3	800-848-0920	Y
Nationwide S&P 500 Index Fund Class A	GRMAX	B-	C	B		4.11	19.19	9.75	48.26	61.36	15.27	1,069	800-848-0920	Y
Nationwide S&P 500 Index Fund Class C	GRMCX	B-	C	B		3.99	18.86	9.03	45.35	56.28	14.88	1,069	800-848-0920	Y
Nationwide S&P 500 Index Fund Class R	GRMRX	B-	C	B		4.10	19.11	9.57	47.30	59.52	15.21	1,069	800-848-0920	Y
Nationwide S&P 500 Index Fund Class R6	GRMIX	B-	C	B		4.26	19.50	10.21	50.14	64.85	15.42	1,069	800-848-0920	Y
Nationwide S&P 500 Index Fund Institutional Service Class	GRISX	B-	C	B		4.20	19.32	9.96	48.97	62.90	15.38	1,069	800-848-0920	Y

Category: US Equity Large Cap Blend (con't)

Fund Name	Ticker Symbol	Overall Rating	Reward Rating	Risk Rating	Recent Up/ Downgrade	3-Month Total Return	6-Month Total Return	1-Year Total Return	3-Year Total Return	5-Year Total Return	NAV	Total Assets (Mil.)	Telephone	Open to New Investors
		RATINGS				TOTAL RETURNS & PERFORMANCE					ASSETS		NEW INVESTORS	
Nationwide S&P 500 Index Fund Service Class	GRMSX	B-	C	B		4.19	19.27	9.78	48.40	61.72	15.29	1,069	800-848-0920	Y
Neuberger Berman Advisers Mgmt Trust Sustainable Eq Cls I		B-	C	B		1.81	14.49	3.01	39.89	46.53	25.83	575.1	212-476-9000	Y
Neuberger Berman Advisers Mgmt Trust Sustainable Eq Cls S		B-	C	B		1.72	14.34	2.78	38.93	44.98	25.91	575.1	212-476-9000	Y
Neuberger Berman Multi-Cap Opportunities Fund Class A	NMUAX	B-	C	B	Down	3.45	17.24	8.92	56.69	56.50	18.56	1,208	212-476-9000	Y
Neuberger Berman Multi-Cap Opportunities Fund Class C	NMUCX	B-	C	B		3.28	16.90	8.15	53.32	50.94	18.53	1,208	212-476-9000	Y
Neuberger Berman Multi-Cap Opportunities Institutional Cls	NMULX	B-	C	B	Down	3.57	17.49	9.37	58.40	59.46	18.54	1,208	212-476-9000	Y
Neuberger Berman Sustainable Equity Fund Class A	NRAAX	B-	C	B		1.74	14.41	2.76	39.45	45.60	37.22	1,912	212-476-9000	Y
Neuberger Berman Sustainable Equity Fund Class R6	NRSRX	B-	C	B		1.86	14.70	3.26	41.32	48.89	37.13	1,912	212-476-9000	Y
Neuberger Berman Sustainable Equity Institutional Cls	NBSLX	B-	C	B		1.83	14.62	3.17	41.02	48.36	37.14	1,912	212-476-9000	Y
Neuberger Berman Sustainable Equity Fund Investor Class	NBSRX	B-	C	B		1.80	14.52	2.98	40.23	46.99	37.21	1,912	212-476-9000	
Neuberger Berman Sustainable Equity Fund Trust Class	NBSTX	B-	C	B		1.74	14.40	2.80	39.53	45.74	37.24	1,912	212-476-9000	
New Covenant Growth Fund	NCGFX	B-	C	B		3.57	18.64	7.20	46.84	49.01	42.86	448.8		Y
North Square Oak Ridge Dividend Growth Fund Class A	ORDAX	B	C+	B+		6.46	18.40	13.66	53.83	62.70	17.1271	13.3		Y
North Square Oak Ridge Dividend Growth Fund Class I	ORDNX	B	C+	B+		6.48	18.49	13.85	54.98	64.64	17.2473	13.3		Y
Northern Stock Index Fund	NOSIX	B-	C	B		4.29	19.53	10.32	50.46	65.47	33.99	8,781	800-595-9111	Y
Nuveen Santa Barbara Dividend Growth Fund Class A	NSBAX	B	C+	B		5.70	19.11	12.52	43.63	55.28	43.38	3,357	312-917-8146	Y
Nuveen Santa Barbara Dividend Growth Fund Class C	NSBCX	B-	C+	B		5.50	18.69	11.68	40.44	49.55	43.36	3,357	312-917-8146	Y
Nuveen Santa Barbara Dividend Growth Fund Class I	NSBRX	B	B-	B		5.77	19.28	12.80	44.70	57.26	43.33	3,357	312-917-8146	Y
Nuveen Santa Barbara Dividend Growth Fund Class R3	NBDRX	B-	C+	B		5.64	18.96	12.22	42.53	53.36	43.72	3,357	312-917-8146	Y
Nuveen Santa Barbara Dividend Growth Fund Class R6	NSBFX	B	B-	B		5.78	19.30	12.87	45.03	57.79	43.77	3,357	312-917-8146	Y
Optimum Large Cap Value Fund Class A	OALVX	B-	C	B	Up	4.48	17.80	8.99	34.97	32.31	16.54	1,637		Y
Optimum Large Cap Value Fund Class C	OCLVX	B-	C	B	Up	4.28	17.41	8.21	31.96	27.45	16.32	1,637		Y
Optimum Large Cap Value Fund Institutional Class	OILVX	B-	C	B	Up	4.53	17.99	9.27	35.98	33.99	16.59	1,637		Y
Osterweis Fund	OSTFX	B-	C	B		3.50	20.05	9.59	32.73	22.22	16.82	128.5	866-236-0050	Y
Pacific Funds Large-Cap Advisor Class	PFCDX	B-	C	B	Up	3.97	17.43	7.49	45.58		13.07	21.4	800-722-2333	Y
Pacific Funds Large-Cap Class A	PFLAX	B-	C	B	Up	3.84	17.28	7.18	44.48		12.96	21.4	800-722-2333	Y
Pacific Funds Large-Cap S Class	PFKIX	B-	C	B		3.97	17.50	7.59	45.95		12.82	21.4	800-722-2333	Y
Parnassus Core Equity Fund - Institutional Shares	PRILX	B	B-	B+		6.12	21.30	17.43	52.37	63.97	46.76	17,021	999-350-5	Y
Parnassus Core Equity Fund - Investor Shares	PRBLX	B	B-	B+		6.07	21.20	17.21	51.44	62.31	46.7	17,021	999-350-5	Y
Parnassus Core Equity Fund - Investor Shares	TRFAX	B-	C	B		2.24	15.88	5.27	35.45	50.33	16.85	17,021		Y
Parnassus Core Equity Fund - Investor Shares	TRFTX	B-	C	B		2.31	16.08	5.52	36.56	52.37	17.25	17,021		Y
Payson Total Return Fund	PBFDX	B-	C	B	Down	3.43	18.61	10.33	55.13	51.14	20	112.9		Y
Pear Tree Quality Fund Institutional Shares	QGIAX	B-	C+	B	Down	3.41	18.37	14.04	54.26	75.00	20.87	140.5	800-326-2151	Y
Pear Tree Quality Fund Ordinary Shares	USBOX	B-	C+	B	Down	3.32	18.13	13.66	52.68	72.36	19.28	140.5	800-326-2151	Y
PGIM Jennison Equity Income Fund- Class A	SPQAX	B-	C	B	Up	2.64	14.86	7.12	25.76	26.87	14.28	1,381	800-225-1852	Y
PGIM Jennison Equity Income Fund- Class R6	PJIQX	B-	C	B	Up	2.73	15.13	7.48	27.08	29.12	14.29	1,381	800-225-1852	Y
PGIM Jennison Equity Income Fund- Class Z	JDEZX	B-	C	B	Up	2.72	15.02	7.42	26.69	28.44	14.26	1,381	800-225-1852	Y
PGIM Jennison Rising Dividend Fund- Class R6	PJDQX	B-	C	B	Up	6.05	21.30	11.29	38.96	50.24	13.39	15.9	800-225-1852	Y
PGIM Jennison Rising Dividend Fund- Class Z	PJDZX	B-	C	B	Up	6.04	21.29	11.37	39.06	50.34	13.4	15.9	800-225-1852	Y
PGIM QMA Stock Index Fund- Class A	PSIAX	B-	C	B		4.19	19.27	9.88	48.63	62.18	47.71	923.4	800-225-1852	Y
PGIM QMA Stock Index Fund- Class C	PSICX	B-	C	B		4.00	18.86	9.15	45.73	57.04	47.25	923.4	800-225-1852	Y
PGIM QMA Stock Index Fund- Class I	PDSIX	B-	C	B		4.26	19.48	10.25	50.15	64.96	47.9	923.4	800-225-1852	Y
PGIM QMA Stock Index Fund- Class R6	PQSIX	B-	C	B		4.28	19.47	10.27	50.03	64.68	47.92	923.4	800-225-1852	Y
PGIM QMA Stock Index Fund- Class Z	PSIFX	B-	C	B		4.26	19.44	10.20	49.88	64.51	47.91	923.4	800-225-1852	Y
PIMCO StocksPLUS® Absolute Return Fund Class A	PTOAX	B-	C	B		4.47	20.52	9.19	54.56	62.59	10.41	2,030	866-746-2602	Y
PIMCO StocksPLUS® Absolute Return Fund Class C	PSOCX	B-	C	B	Up	4.18	20.06	8.36	51.02	56.49	9.35	2,030	866-746-2602	Y
PIMCO StocksPLUS® Absolute Return Fund Class I-2	PTOPX	B-	C	B		4.51	20.67	9.46	55.99	65.01	10.47	2,030	866-746-2602	Y
PIMCO StocksPLUS® Absolute Return Fund I-3	PSPNX	B-	C	B		4.50	20.66	9.46	55.58	64.37	10.46	2,030	866-746-2602	Y
PIMCO StocksPLUS® Absolute Return Fund Institutional Class	PSPTX	B-	C+	B		4.56	20.76	9.63	56.42	65.93	10.62	2,030	866-746-2602	Y
PIMCO StocksPLUS® Fund Administrative Class	PPLAX	B-	C+	B		4.50	20.45	10.20	50.89	63.11	9.65	845.6	866-746-2602	Y
PIMCO StocksPLUS® Fund Class A	PSPAX	B-	C+	B		4.42	20.51	10.06	50.38	61.80	9.54	845.6	866-746-2602	Y
PIMCO StocksPLUS® Fund Class C	PSPCX	B-	C	B		4.28	20.04	9.41	47.95	57.71	8.93	845.6	866-746-2602	Y

Category: US Equity Large Cap Blend (con't)

		RATINGS				TOTAL RETURNS & PERFORMANCE					ASSETS		NEW INVESTORS	
Fund Name	Ticker Symbol	Overall Rating	Reward Rating	Risk Rating	Recent Up/ Downgrade	3-Month Total Return	6-Month Total Return	1-Year Total Return	3-Year Total Return	5-Year Total Return	NAV	Total Assets (MIL)	Telephone	Open to New Investors
PIMCO StocksPLUS® Fund Class I-2	PSKPX	B-	C+	B		4.50	20.63	10.38	51.63	64.24	10.42	845.6	866-746-2602	Y
PIMCO StocksPLUS® Fund Class R	PSPRX	B-	C+	B		4.33	20.32	9.82	49.11	59.79	9.87	845.6	866-746-2602	Y
PIMCO StocksPLUS® Fund I-3	PSTNX	B-	C+	B		4.45	20.62	10.33	51.13	63.36	10.41	845.6	866-746-2602	Y
PIMCO StocksPLUS® Fund Institutional Class	PSTKX	B-	C+	B		4.50	20.60	10.48	52.01	64.97	10.45	845.6	866-746-2602	Y
Pin Oak Equity Fund	POGSX	B-	C	B		2.58	16.93	3.85	53.70	58.54	69.73	247.2	888-462-5386	Y
Pioneer Fund Class A	PIODX	B	B-	B+		6.68	19.88	14.76	53.47	61.06	29.33	5,068	617-742-7825	Y
Pioneer Fund Class C	PCODX	B	C+	B+		6.48	19.38	13.86	49.81	54.81	25.1	5,068	617-742-7825	Y
Pioneer Fund Class R	PIORX	B	B-	B+		6.61	19.65	14.31	51.53	57.91	29.48	5,068	617-742-7825	Y
Pioneer Fund Class Y	PYODX	B	B-	B+		6.76	20.04	15.06	54.48	63.14	29.75	5,068	617-742-7825	Y
Port Street Quality Growth Fund Institutional Class	PSQGX	B	C	A		2.16	10.85	8.70	29.10	39.10	13.69	114.1		Y
PRIMECAP Odyssey Stock Fund	POSKX	B-	C	B	Up	3.28	15.70	6.40	54.14	64.64	33	10,114	800-729-2307	Y
Principal Capital Appreciation Fund Class A	CMNWX	B-	C+	B	Down	5.23	20.29	12.06	49.59	61.78	48.24	1,758	800-787-1621	Y
Principal Capital Appreciation Fund Class C	CMNCX	B-	C+	B		5.00	19.77	11.14	45.93	55.23	32.28	1,758	800-787-1621	Y
Principal Capital Appreciation Fund Institutional Class	PWCIX	B-	C+	B	Down	5.34	20.51	12.50	51.24	64.77	49.63	1,758	800-787-1621	Y
Principal Capital Appreciation Fund R-1 Class	PCAMX	B-	C+	B		5.10	19.97	11.49	47.30	57.70	48.18	1,758	800-787-1621	Y
Principal Capital Appreciation Fund R-2 Class	PCANX	B-	C+	B	Down	5.15	20.08	11.64	47.90	58.77	48.37	1,758	800-787-1621	Y
Principal Capital Appreciation Fund R-3 Class	PCAOX	B-	C+	B	Down	5.20	20.19	11.84	48.68	60.19	48.33	1,758	800-787-1621	Y
Principal Capital Appreciation Fund R-4 Class	PCAPX	B-	C+	B	Down	5.23	20.30	12.06	49.55	61.72	48.88	1,758	800-787-1621	Y
Principal Capital Appreciation Fund R-5 Class	PCAQX	B-	C+	B	Down	5.27	20.35	12.20	50.08	62.69	49.13	1,758	800-787-1621	Y
Principal LargeCap S&P 500 Index Fund Class A	PLSAX	B-	C	B		4.18	19.31	9.90	48.86	62.38	18.41	5,904	800-787-1621	Y
Principal LargeCap S&P 500 Index Fund Class C	PLICX	B-	C	B		3.99	18.79	9.01	45.15	55.84	17.95	5,904	800-787-1621	Y
Principal LargeCap S&P 500 Index Fund Class J	PSPJX	B-	C	B		4.23	19.39	10.04	49.24	62.96	18.22	5,904	800-787-1621	Y
Principal LargeCap S&P 500 Index Fund Institutional Class	PLFIX	B-	C	B		4.24	19.46	10.24	50.15	64.91	18.41	5,904	800-787-1621	Y
Principal LargeCap S&P 500 Index Fund R-1 Class	PLPIX	B-	C	B		4.02	19.00	9.33	46.25	57.89	18.35	5,904	800-787-1621	Y
Principal LargeCap S&P 500 Index Fund R-2 Class	PLFNX	B-	C	B		4.04	19.03	9.45	46.86	58.88	18.51	5,904	800-787-1621	Y
Principal LargeCap S&P 500 Index Fund R-3 Class	PLFMX	B-	C	B		4.12	19.19	9.67	47.66	60.37	18.44	5,904	800-787-1621	Y
Principal LargeCap S&P 500 Index Fund R-4 Class	PLFSX	B-	C	B		4.11	19.21	9.83	48.44	61.80	18.49	5,904	800-787-1621	Y
Principal LargeCap S&P 500 Index Fund R-5 Class	PLFPX	B-	C	B		4.18	19.29	9.95	49.01	62.90	18.67	5,904	800-787-1621	Y
Putnam Research Fund Class A	PNRAX	B-	C+	B		5.66	20.64	10.52	53.31	60.36	33.02	329.9	617-292-1000	Y
Putnam Research Fund Class B	PRFBX	B-	C+	B		5.44	20.22	9.66	49.88	54.43	30.2	329.9	617-292-1000	Y
Putnam Research Fund Class C	PRACX	B-	C+	B		5.45	20.19	9.67	49.87	54.46	30.18	329.9	617-292-1000	Y
Putnam Research Fund Class M	PRFMX	B-	C+	B		5.50	20.32	9.94	51.03	56.37	31.26	329.9	617-292-1000	Y
Putnam Research Fund Class R	PRSRX	B-	C+	B		5.57	20.50	10.23	52.18	58.37	32.56	329.9	617-292-1000	Y
Putnam Research Fund Class R6 Shares	PLJMX	B-	C+	B	Down	5.73	20.91	10.93	55.26	62.96	33.53	329.9	617-292-1000	Y
Putnam Research Fund Class Y	PURYX	B-	C+	B		5.70	20.78	10.75	54.42	62.36	33.36	329.9	617-292-1000	Y
QS S&P 500 Index Fund Class A	SBSPX	B-	C	B		4.15	19.21	9.76	48.27	61.57	26.8	272.2	877-721-1926	Y
QS S&P 500 Index Fund Class D	SBSDX	B-	C	B		4.20	19.34	9.99	49.23	63.17	27.02	272.2	877-721-1926	Y
Russell Investments Sustainable Equity Fund Class A	REQAX	B-	C	B+	Down	3.50	16.09	10.25	39.32	57.36	52.51	452.3	800-426-7969	Y
Russell Investments Sustainable Equity Fund Class C	REQCX	B-	C	B+	Down	3.33	15.65	9.39	36.20	51.55	51.8	452.3	800-426-7969	Y
Russell Investments Sustainable Equity Fund Class E	REQEX	B-	C	B+	Down	3.49	16.07	10.25	39.32	57.36	52.65	452.3	800-426-7969	Y
Russell Investments Sustainable Equity Fund Class S	REQTX	B-	C+	B+	Down	3.57	16.23	10.55	40.50	59.49	52.62	452.3	800-426-7969	Y
Russell Investments Sustainable Equity Fund Class Y	REUYX	B-	C+	B+	Down	3.61	16.33	10.72	41.19	60.91	52.53	452.3	800-426-7969	Y
Rydex S&P 500 Fund Class A	RYSOX	B-	C	B		3.84	18.50	8.49	43.41	52.74	53.53	163.5	800-820-0888	Y
Rydex S&P 500 Fund Class H	RYSPX	B-	C	B		3.86	18.50	8.51	43.42	52.74	53.53	163.5	800-820-0888	Y
SA U.S. Core Market Fund Investor Class	SAMKX	B-	C	B		4.11	19.46	9.29	51.33	60.68	24.8	755.5		Y
SA U.S. Core Market Fund Select Class	SAALX	B-	C	B		4.17	19.59	9.51	51.94	61.33	24.72	755.5		Y
Sarofim Equity Fund	SRFMX	B-	B-	B		5.51	21.73	11.37	49.64	50.11	12.43	94.3		Y
Schroder North American Equity Fund Class Investor	SNAEX	B-	C	B		3.76	17.44	8.90	47.13	58.52	16.83	1,002	800-464-3108	Y
Schwab 1000 Index® Fund	SNXFX	B-	C	B		4.29	19.89	9.91	50.33	62.93	66.3	9,246	877-824-5615	Y
Schwab Total Stock Market Index Fund®	SWTSX	B-	C	B		4.08	19.74	8.86	50.01	61.84	51.73	9,794	877-824-5615	Y
Schwab® S&P 500 Index Fund	SWPPX	B-	C	B		4.29	19.53	10.37	50.67	65.66	45.4	38,408	877-824-5615	Y
SEI Inst Investments Trust Dynamic Asset Allocation Cls A	SDLAX	B-	C	B	Up	3.70	18.06	7.78	44.37	69.96	20.98	2,285	800-342-5734	Y

Category: US Equity Large Cap Blend (con't)

Fund Name	Ticker Symbol	RATINGS: Overall Rating	Reward Rating	Risk Rating	Recent Up/ Downgrade	TOTAL RETURNS & PERFORMANCE: 3-Month Total Return	6-Month Total Return	1-Year Total Return	3-Year Total Return	5-Year Total Return	ASSETS: NAV	Total Assets (MIL)	NEW INVESTORS: Telephone	Open to New Investors
SEI Institutional Investments Trust Large Cap Fund Class A	SLCAX	B-	C	B		3.26	17.74	7.84	45.45	50.63	15.71	1,137	800-342-5734	Y
SEI Institutional Investments Trust Large Cap Index Cls A	LCIAX	B-	C	B		4.21	19.85	9.94	50.54	64.15	186.11	1,743	800-342-5734	Y
SEI Institutional Investments Trust S&P 500 Index Cls A	SPINX	B-	C	B		4.32	19.53	10.40	50.70	65.96	15.82	4,131	800-342-5734	Y
SEI Inst Managed Trust Dynamic Asset Allocation Cls F	SDYAX	B-	C	B	Up	3.46	17.56	6.95	41.46		13.12	804.6	800-342-5734	Y
SEI Inst Managed Trust Dynamic Asset Allocation Cls Y	SDYYX	B-	C	B	Up	3.54	17.63	7.24	42.40		13.14	804.6	800-342-5734	Y
SEI Institutional Managed Trust Large Cap Fund Class F	SLGAX	B-	C	B	Up	3.35	17.72	6.37	47.71	49.59	13.85	2,358	800-342-5734	Y
SEI Institutional Managed Trust Large Cap Fund Class Y	SLYCX	B-	C	B	Up	3.41	17.87	6.64	48.80	51.28	13.86	2,358	800-342-5734	Y
SEI Institutional Managed Trust S&P 500 Index Fund Class F	SSPIX	B-	C	B		4.26	19.46	10.20	49.42	63.35	68.18	845.3	800-342-5734	Y
SEI Institutional Managed Trust S&P 500 Index Fund Class I	SPIIX	B-	C	B		4.14	19.22	9.75	48.04	61.14	68.56	845.3	800-342-5734	Y
SEI Inst Managed Trust Tax Managed Large Cap Cls Y	STLYX	B-	C	B	Up	3.40	17.50	6.75	47.87	49.06	27.23	3,990	800-342-5734	Y
SEI Inst Managed Trust Tax-Managed Large Cap Cls F	TMLCX	B-	C	B	Up	3.34	17.38	6.48	46.79	47.44	27.22	3,990	800-342-5734	Y
SGI U.S. Large Cap Equity Fund Class A	LVOLX	B-	C+	B	Down	3.97	19.02	10.79	39.10	67.43	17.77	487.5	888-251-4847	Y
SGI U.S. Large Cap Equity Fund Class C	SGICX	B-	C+	B		3.77	18.64	10.02	36.13	60.49	17.31	487.5	888-251-4847	Y
SGI U.S. Large Cap Equity Fund Class I	SILVX	B-	C+	B	Down	4.05	19.16	11.09	40.14	69.46	17.72	487.5	888-251-4847	Y
Shelton Capital Management S&P 500 Index Fund Class K	SPXKX	B-	C	B		4.10	18.98	9.50	47.55	60.24	56.14	193.0	800-955-9988	Y
Shelton Capital Management S&P 500 Index Direct Shares	SPFIX	B-	C	B		4.24	19.29	10.07	49.79	64.31	56.17	193.0	800-955-9988	Y
Sit Dividend Growth Fund Class I	SDVGX	B-	C	B	Up	3.42	16.83	8.37	39.80	52.72	14.45	254.0	800-332-5580	Y
Sit Dividend Growth Fund Class S	SDVSX	B-	C	B	Up	3.31	16.68	8.11	38.73	50.79	14.37	254.0	800-332-5580	Y
Sit Global Dividend Growth Fund Class I	GDGIX	B-	C	B	Up	4.81	17.08	9.18	31.92	30.82	16.34	34.1	800-332-5580	Y
Sit Global Dividend Growth Fund Class S	GDGSX	B-	C	B	Up	4.82	16.94	8.98	30.94	29.25	16.33	34.1	800-332-5580	Y
SSgA S&P 500 Index Fund N Class	SVSPX	B-	C	B		4.25	19.47	10.25	50.11	64.96	37.1	1,564	617-664-7338	Y
State Farm Growth Fund	STFGX	B-	C+	B+		4.57	17.07	12.69	37.54	49.22	83.44	5,231		Y
State Street Equity 500 Index Fund Administrative Shares	STFAX	B-	C	B		4.21	19.41	10.12	49.87	64.19	23.25	1,077	617-664-7338	Y
State Street Equity 500 Index Fund Class A	SSSVX	B-	C	B		4.16	19.36	10.04	48.92	62.26	23.24	1,077	617-664-7338	Y
State Street Equity 500 Index Fund Class I	SSSWX	B-	C	B		4.20	19.45	10.30	49.99	64.22	23.27	1,077	617-664-7338	Y
State Street Equity 500 Index Fund Class K	SSSYX	B-	C	B		4.20	19.51	10.28	50.51	65.33	23.27	1,077	617-664-7338	Y
State Street Equity 500 Index Fund Class R Shares	SSFRX	B-	C	B		4.08	19.11	9.65	47.85	60.53	23.18	1,077	617-664-7338	Y
State Street Equity 500 Index Fund Service Shares	STBIX	B-	C	B		4.17	19.33	9.98	49.40	63.36	23.21	1,077	617-664-7338	Y
State Street Equity 500 Index II Portfolio	SSEYX	B-	C	B		4.26	19.53	10.33	50.61		13.95	2,020	617-664-7338	Y
State Street Institutional U.S. Equity Investment Cls	SUSIX	B-	C	B	Down	5.60	20.68	12.24	53.60	59.04	12.25	418.4	617-664-7338	Y
State Street Institutional U.S. Equity Fund Service Class	SUSSX	B-	C	B	Down	5.48	20.54	11.98	52.44	56.96	13.26	418.4	617-664-7338	Y
Stralem Equity Fund	STEFX	B-	C	B+		2.15	16.98	10.84	33.23	44.34	8.54	90.9		Y
Strategic Advisers® Core Fund	FCSAX	B-	C	B		4.11	19.52	8.85	51.09	59.42	18.49	25,971	617-563-7000	Y
T. Rowe Price Capital Opportunity Fund	PRCOX	B-	C+	B	Down	4.33	20.44	10.21	53.43	68.26	28.16	784.8	410-345-2000	Y
T. Rowe Price Capital Opportunity Fund Advisor Class	PACOX	B-	C+	B		4.27	20.26	9.89	52.15	65.91	28.07	784.8	410-345-2000	Y
T. Rowe Price Capital Opportunity Fund Class R	RRCOX	B-	C	B		4.17	20.03	9.51	50.73	63.44	27.92	784.8	410-345-2000	Y
T. Rowe Price Capital Opportunity Fund I Class	PCCOX	B-	C+	B	Down	4.37	20.53	10.38	54.01	68.90	28.18	784.8	410-345-2000	Y
T. Rowe Price Dividend Growth Fund	PRDGX	B	B-	A-		6.10	20.92	16.72	50.05	72.23	49.39	11,498	410-345-2000	Y
T. Rowe Price Dividend Growth Fund Advisor Class	TADGX	B	B-	A-		6.02	20.76	16.42	48.83	69.93	49.34	11,498	410-345-2000	Y
T. Rowe Price Dividend Growth Fund I Class	PDGIX	B	B-	A-		6.12	21.00	16.88	50.64	72.95	49.38	11,498	410-345-2000	Y
T. Rowe Price Equity Index 500 Fund	PREIX	B-	C	B		4.25	19.45	10.20	49.94	64.36	78.34	29,526	410-345-2000	Y
T. Rowe Price Equity Index 500 Fund I Class	PRUIX	B-	C	B		4.29	19.52	10.36	50.60	65.27	78.35	29,526	410-345-2000	Y
T. Rowe Price Growth and Income Fund	PRGIX	B	C+	B+		5.35	19.53	12.57	46.01	66.08	28.68	1,982	410-345-2000	Y
T. Rowe Price Growth and Income Fund I Class	TGTIX	B	C+	B+		5.34	19.57	12.64	46.31	66.42	28.68	1,982	410-345-2000	Y
T. Rowe Price Institutional U.S. Structured Research Fund	TRISX	B-	C+	B	Down	4.39	20.57	10.52	54.21	69.41	13.07	800.3	410-345-2000	Y
T. Rowe Price Total Equity Market Index Fund	POMIX	B-	C	B		4.14	19.78	8.82	49.42	60.99	32.88	1,942	410-345-2000	Y
T. Rowe Price U.S. Large-Cap Core Fund	TRULX	B	C+	B+		5.31	19.45	12.40	45.40	68.92	25.36	571.8	410-345-2000	Y
T. Rowe Price U.S. Large-Cap Core Fund Advisor Class	PAULX	B	C+	B+		5.27	19.34	12.12	44.27	66.96	25.35	571.8	410-345-2000	Y
T. Rowe Price U.S. Large-Cap Core Fund I Class	RCLIX	B	C+	B+		5.35	19.58	12.58	46.04	69.67	25.4	571.8	410-345-2000	Y
TCW New America Premier Equities Fund Class I	TGUSX	B+	B+	B	Up	9.01	33.33	23.12	102.99		20.08	97.5	213-244-0000	Y
TCW New America Premier Equities Fund Class N	TGUNX	B+	B+	B	Up	8.96	33.20	22.99	102.79		20.06	97.5	213-244-0000	Y
TETON Westwood Equity Fund Class A	WEECX	B-	C	B		4.73	16.47	8.28	38.21	47.36	12.16	55.4		Y

Category: US Equity Large Cap Blend (con't)

Fund Name	Ticker Symbol	RATINGS: Overall Rating	RATINGS: Reward Rating	RATINGS: Risk Rating	RATINGS: Recent Up/ Downgrade	TOTAL RETURNS & PERFORMANCE: 3-Month Total Return	6-Month Total Return	1-Year Total Return	3-Year Total Return	5-Year Total Return	ASSETS: NAV	Total Assets (MIL)	NEW INVESTORS: Telephone	Open to New Investors
TETON Westwood Equity Fund Class AAA	WESWX	B-	C	B		4.72	16.66	8.51	39.28	49.10	12.18	55.4		Y
TETON Westwood Equity Fund Class C	WEQCX	B-	C	B	Up	4.61	16.18	7.74	36.16	43.67	11.34	55.4		Y
TETON Westwood Equity Fund Institutional Class	WEEIX	B-	C	B+		4.83	16.84	8.85	40.29	51.01	12.14	55.4		Y
The Hartford Capital Appreciation Fund Class A	ITHAX	B-	C+	B		5.91	23.55	10.99	52.12	52.58	36.87	7,165	888-843-7824	Y
The Hartford Capital Appreciation Fund Class C	HCACX	B-	C+	B		5.72	23.11	10.12	48.71	47.08	26.95	7,165	888-843-7824	Y
The Hartford Capital Appreciation Fund Class F	HCAFX	B-	C+	B		6.00	23.78	11.39	53.79	55.48	37.06	7,165	888-843-7824	Y
The Hartford Capital Appreciation Fund Class I	ITHIX	B-	C+	B		6.00	23.73	11.30	53.39	54.84	37.07	7,165	888-843-7824	Y
The Hartford Capital Appreciation Fund Class R3	ITHRX	B-	C+	B		5.82	23.36	10.61	50.60	50.14	41.24	7,165	888-843-7824	Y
The Hartford Capital Appreciation Fund Class R4	ITHSX	B-	C+	B		5.91	23.57	10.94	51.99	52.45	42.78	7,165	888-843-7824	Y
The Hartford Capital Appreciation Fund Class R5	ITHTX	B-	C+	B		5.99	23.72	11.26	53.37	54.72	43.7	7,165	888-843-7824	Y
The Hartford Capital Appreciation Fund Class R6	ITHVX	B-	C+	B		6.02	23.81	11.39	53.80	55.44	43.99	7,165	888-843-7824	Y
The Hartford Capital Appreciation Fund Class Y	HCAYX	B-	C+	B		6.00	23.78	11.36	53.72	55.41	43.97	7,165	888-843-7824	Y
The MP 63 Fund	DRIPX	B-	C+	B+	Down	3.88	18.62	13.25	40.41	54.48	22.48	71.3		Y
TIAA-CREF Equity Index Fund Advisor Class	TEIHX	B-	C	B		4.00	19.62	8.78	49.79	61.90	21.58	21,187	877-518-9161	Y
TIAA-CREF Equity Index Fund Class W	TEQWX	B-	C	B		4.09	19.73	9.00	50.21	62.46	21.6	21,187	877-518-9161	Y
TIAA-CREF Equity Index Fund Institutional Class	TIEIX	B-	C	B		4.04	19.67	8.93	50.12	62.37	21.59	21,187	877-518-9161	Y
TIAA-CREF Equity Index Fund Premier Class	TCEPX	B-	C	B		4.05	19.60	8.79	49.51	61.14	21.54	21,187	877-518-9161	Y
TIAA-CREF Equity Index Fund Retail Class	TINRX	B-	C	B		4.02	19.52	8.65	48.87	60.09	21.98	21,187	877-518-9161	Y
TIAA-CREF Equity Index Fund Retirement Class	TIQRX	B-	C	B		4.03	19.53	8.66	49.07	60.38	21.91	21,187	877-518-9161	Y
TIAA-CREF S&P 500 Index Fund Advisor Class	TISAX	B-	C	B		4.25	19.43	10.22	50.19	65.21	32.57	5,201	877-518-9161	Y
TIAA-CREF S&P 500 Index Fund Institutional Class	TISPX	B-	C	B		4.28	19.49	10.34	50.58	65.78	32.61	5,201	877-518-9161	Y
TIAA-CREF S&P 500 Index Fund Retirement Class	TRSPX	B-	C	B		4.21	19.38	10.09	49.49	63.74	32.39	5,201	877-518-9161	Y
TIAA-CREF Social Choice Equity Fund Advisor Class	TICHX	B-	C	B		3.76	19.32	8.93	49.38	55.44	19.57	4,522	877-518-9161	Y
TIAA-CREF Social Choice Equity Fund Institutional Class	TISCX	B-	C	B		3.76	19.31	8.97	49.37	55.53	19.58	4,522	877-518-9161	Y
TIAA-CREF Social Choice Equity Fund Premier Class	TRPSX	B-	C	B		3.72	19.26	8.74	48.67	54.26	19.5	4,522	877-518-9161	Y
TIAA-CREF Social Choice Equity Fund Retail Class	TICRX	B-	C	B		3.69	19.19	8.63	48.09	53.39	17.39	4,522	877-518-9161	Y
TIAA-CREF Social Choice Equity Fund Retirement Class	TRSCX	B-	C	B		3.70	19.24	8.66	48.26	53.55	19.89	4,522	877-518-9161	Y
TIAA-CREF Social Choice Low Carbon Equity Advisor Cls	TCCHX	B-	C	B		4.06	19.38	8.91	48.24		13.3	207.5	877-518-9161	Y
TIAA-CREF Social Choice Low Carbon Equity Inst Cls	TNWCX	B-	C	B		4.06	19.38	9.01	48.52		13.3	207.5	877-518-9161	Y
TIAA-CREF Social Choice Low Carbon Equity Premier Cls	TPWCX	B-	C	B		4.05	19.33	8.84	48.04		13.33	207.5	877-518-9161	Y
TIAA-CREF Social Choice Low Carbon Equity Retail Cls	TLWCX	B-	C	B		4.00	19.13	8.61	47.01		13.26	207.5	877-518-9161	Y
TIAA-CREF Social Choice Low Carbon Equity Retirement Cls	TEWCX	B-	C	B		4.08	19.24	8.77	47.52		13.26	207.5	877-518-9161	Y
Tocqueville Fund	TOCQX	B-	C	B		4.56	18.64	10.66	43.18	43.87	36.66	280.5	212-698-0800	Y
Touchstone Large Cap Focused Fund Class A	SENCX	B-	C	B+	Down	3.95	18.43	10.51	53.35	65.50	43.37	1,732	800-543-0407	Y
Touchstone Large Cap Focused Fund Class Y	SICWX	B-	C+	B+	Down	4.04	18.59	10.80	54.52	67.73	43.24	1,732	800-543-0407	Y
Touchstone Large Cap Focused Fund Institutional Class	SCRLX	B-	C+	B+	Down	4.06	18.62	10.87	54.91	68.09	43.31	1,732	800-543-0407	Y
Touchstone Large Cap Fund Class A	TACLX	B-	C	B		1.95	14.52	7.04	38.57		14.11	284.3	800-543-0407	Y
Touchstone Large Cap Fund Class Y	TLCYX	B-	C	B		2.02	14.68	7.31	39.62		14.14	284.3	800-543-0407	Y
Touchstone Large Cap Fund Institutional Class	TLCIX	B-	C	B		2.01	14.74	7.42	40.10		14.16	284.3	800-543-0407	Y
Transamerica Large Core Fund Class I3	TLATX	B-	C	B		3.13	17.03	7.46	49.66	52.74	9.71	262.9	888-233-4339	Y
Transamerica Large Core Fund Class R	TLARX	B-	C	B	Up	2.90	16.61	6.91	47.67	49.96	9.71	262.9	888-233-4339	Y
Transamerica Large Core Fund Class R4	TLAFX	B-	C	B	Up	2.94	16.72	7.14	48.69	51.76	9.71	262.9	888-233-4339	Y
Transamerica Stock Index R	TSTRX	B-	C	B		4.12	19.19	9.65	48.16	61.55	12.04	518.3	888-233-4339	Y
Transamerica Stock Index R4	TSTFX	B-	C	B		4.21	19.38	9.97	49.48	63.81	12.04	518.3	888-233-4339	Y
USAA S&P 500 Index Fund Member Shares	USSPX	B-	C	B		4.24	19.43	10.13	49.78	64.22	41.35	7,716	800-235-8396	Y
USAA S&P 500 Index Fund Reward Shares	USPRX	B-	C	B		4.27	19.48	10.26	50.22	65.02	41.37	7,716	800-235-8396	Y
VALIC Company I Growth & Income Fund	VCGAX	B-	C	B		4.01	18.69	9.16	47.72	59.01	21.78	125.8		Y
VALIC Company I Stock Index Fund	VSTIX	B-	C	B		4.21	19.38	10.06	49.41	63.52	42	4,941		Y
VALIC Company II U.S. Socially Responsible Fund	VCSRX	B-	C+	B		4.49	20.27	10.85	48.72	63.24	21.96	730.4		Y
Vanguard 500 Index Fund Admiral Shares	VFIAX	B-	C	B		4.29	19.55	10.38	50.75	66.01	271.39	483,171	877-662-7447	Y
Vanguard 500 Index Fund Investor Shares	VFINX	B-	C	B		4.27	19.49	10.26	50.30	65.15	271.41	483,171	877-662-7447	Y
Vanguard Dividend Appreciation Index Fund Admiral Shares	VDADX	B	C+	B+		5.54	19.97	15.60	49.52	64.21	31.28	44,334	877-662-7447	Y

Category: US Equity Large Cap Blend (con't)

Fund Name	Ticker Symbol	RATINGS: Overall Rating	Reward Rating	Risk Rating	Recent Up/ Downgrade	TOTAL RETURNS & PERFORMANCE: 3-Month Total Return	6-Month Total Return	1-Year Total Return	3-Year Total Return	5-Year Total Return	ASSETS: NAV	Total Assets (MIL)	NEW INVESTORS: Telephone	Open to New Investors
Vanguard Dividend Appreciation Index Fund Investor Shares	VDAIX	B	C+	B+		5.52	19.93	15.56	49.24	63.59	46.12	44,334	877-662-7447	Y
Vanguard Dividend Growth Fund Investor Shares	VDIGX	B	B	A-		6.32	22.14	19.04	49.45	70.52	29.36	36,582	877-662-7447	Y
Vanguard FTSE Social Index Fund Admiral	VFTAX	B-	C+	B	Down	4.54	20.04	11.28	57.90	72.16	27.25	5,942	877-662-7447	Y
Vanguard FTSE Social Index Fund Institutional Shares	VFTNX	B-	C+	B	Down	4.58	20.05	11.32	58.19	72.72	19.62	5,942	877-662-7447	Y
Vanguard FTSE Social Index Fund Investor Shares	VFTSX	B-	C+	B	Down	4.56	20.03	11.27	57.89	72.15	19.61	5,942	877-662-7447	Y
Vanguard Growth and Income Fund Admiral Shares	VGIAX	B-	C	B		3.69	18.52	8.93	48.24	64.92	79.53	11,292	877-662-7447	Y
Vanguard Growth and Income Fund Investor Shares	VQNPX	B-	C	B		3.67	18.46	8.83	47.79	64.05	48.73	11,292	877-662-7447	Y
Vanguard Institutional Index Institutional Plus Shares	VIIIX	B-	C	B		4.30	19.56	10.40	50.85	66.21	266.32	228,885	877-662-7447	Y
Vanguard Institutional Index Fund Institutional Shares	VINIX	B-	C	B		4.29	19.55	10.39	50.77	66.06	266.31	228,885	877-662-7447	Y
Vanguard Inst Total Stock Mkt Index Inst Plus Shares	VITPX	B-	C	B		4.09	19.77	9.02	50.45	62.77	63.46	39,445	877-662-7447	Y
Vanguard Inst Total Stock Mkt Index Inst Shares	VITNX	B-	C	B		4.09	19.76	9.03	50.37	62.65	63.46	39,445	877-662-7447	Y
Vanguard Instl 500 Index Trust	VFFSX	B-	C	B		4.30	19.56	10.41	50.89	65.80	143.81	483,171	877-662-7447	Y
Vanguard Large Cap Index Fund Admiral Shares	VLCAX	B-	C	B		4.28	19.63	10.30	51.20	65.13	68.05	22,808	877-662-7447	Y
Vanguard Large Cap Index Fund Institutional Shares	VLISX	B-	C	B		4.28	19.64	10.32	51.24	65.22	280.08	22,808	877-662-7447	Y
Vanguard Large Cap Index Fund Investor Shares	VLACX	B-	C	B		4.25	19.56	10.18	50.67	64.14	54.44	22,808	877-662-7447	Y
Vanguard Mega Cap Index Fund Institutional Shares	VMCTX	B-	C	B		4.26	18.98	10.85	52.71	67.84	199.76	2,060	877-662-7447	Y
Vanguard PRIMECAP Core Fund Investor Shares	VPCCX	B-	C	B		2.89	14.99	6.99	56.21	68.16	26.69	10,783	877-662-7447	
Vanguard Russell 1000 Index Fund Institutional Shares	VRNIX	B-	C	B		4.23	19.85	9.97	50.45	63.65	261.08	3,540	877-662-7447	Y
Vanguard Russell 3000 Index Fund Institutional Shares	VRTTX	B-	C	B		4.08	19.71	8.93	50.05	61.94	259.41	1,349	877-662-7447	Y
Vanguard Tax-Managed Capital Appreciation Admiral Shares	VTCLX	B-	C	B		4.41	20.11	10.11	52.09	65.46	151.51	10,675	877-662-7447	Y
Vanguard Tax-Managed Capital Appreciation Inst Shares	VTCIX	B-	C	B		4.42	20.14	10.15	52.23	65.74	75.29	10,675	877-662-7447	Y
Vanguard Total Stock Market Index Fund Admiral Shares	VTSAX	B-	C	B		4.08	19.74	8.99	50.32	62.39	73.04	814,086	877-662-7447	Y
Vanguard Total Stock Mkt Index Inst Plus Shares	VSMPX	B-	C	B		4.09	19.73	9.00	50.40	62.38	136.99	814,086	877-662-7447	Y
Vanguard Total Stock Mkt Index Inst Select Shares	VSTSX	B-	C	B		4.09	19.74	9.01	50.46	62.18	143.74	814,086	877-662-7447	Y
Vanguard Total Stock Market Index Institutional Shares	VITSX	B-	C	B		4.09	19.73	9.00	50.35	62.44	73.05	814,086	877-662-7447	Y
Vanguard Total Stock Market Index Fund Investor Shares	VTSMX	B-	C	B		4.05	19.66	8.87	49.86	61.54	73.01	814,086	877-662-7447	Y
Victory S&P 500 Index Fund Class A	MUXAX	B-	C	B		4.13	19.18	9.79	48.46	61.62	21.07	234.6	800-539-3863	Y
Victory S&P 500 Index Fund Class R	MUXRX	B-	C	B		4.03	18.93	9.31	46.48	58.24	21.01	234.6	800-539-3863	Y
Victory S&P 500 Index Fund Class Y	MUXYX	B-	C	B		4.10	19.26	9.92	49.15	63.00	21.22	234.6	800-539-3863	Y
Voya Corporate Leaders 100 Fund Class A	IACLX	B-	C	B		3.45	17.31	8.73	41.48	49.36	21.55	824.8	800-366-0066	Y
Voya Corporate Leaders 100 Fund Class C	ICCLX	B-	C	B		3.33	16.94	8.17	39.17	45.34	21.4	824.8	800-366-0066	Y
Voya Corporate Leaders 100 Fund Class I	IICLX	B-	C	B		3.50	17.41	9.04	42.82	51.79	21.57	824.8	800-366-0066	Y
Voya Corporate Leaders 100 Fund Class O	IOCLX	B-	C	B		3.44	17.26	8.74	41.36	49.08	21.94	824.8	800-366-0066	Y
Voya Corporate Leaders 100 Fund Class P3	VCLPX	B-	C	B		3.70	17.74	9.70	43.68	52.70	21.83	824.8	800-366-0066	Y
Voya Corporate Leaders 100 Fund Class R	IRCLX	B-	C	B		3.38	17.12	8.45	40.22	47.19	21.41	824.8	800-366-0066	Y
Voya Corporate Leaders 100 Fund Class R6	VCLRX	B-	C	B		3.55	17.47	9.11	42.85	51.91	21.58	824.8	800-366-0066	Y
Voya Corporate Leaders 100 Fund Class W	IWCLX	B-	C	B		3.49	17.39	8.98	42.53	51.26	21.6	824.8	800-366-0066	Y
Voya Growth and Income Portfolio Class A	IAVGX	B-	C+	B		5.21	18.40	10.62	43.61	48.19	27.65	3,134	800-366-0066	Y
Voya Growth and Income Portfolio Class I	IIVGX	B-	C+	B	Down	5.35	18.69	11.10	45.59	51.55	28.17	3,134	800-366-0066	Y
Voya Growth and Income Portfolio Class S	ISVGX	B-	C+	B		5.28	18.56	10.83	44.48	49.68	27.7	3,134	800-366-0066	Y
Voya Growth and Income Portfolio Class S2	IGISX	B-	C+	B		5.24	18.46	10.67	43.87	48.56	27.31	3,134	800-366-0066	Y
Voya Index Plus LargeCap Portfolio Class ADV	VIPAX	B-	C	B		4.48	19.35	9.16	48.10	58.47	25.92	890.2	800-366-0066	Y
Voya Index Plus LargeCap Portfolio Class I	IPLIX	B-	C	B		4.60	19.64	9.71	50.34	62.48	26.22	890.2	800-366-0066	Y
Voya Index Plus LargeCap Portfolio Class S	IPLSX	B-	C	B		4.56	19.51	9.47	49.24	60.50	26	890.2	800-366-0066	Y
Voya Russell Large Cap Index Portfolio Class A	IRLIX	B-	C	B		4.06	18.45	9.99	49.96	63.13	21.91	959.4	800-366-0066	Y
Voya Russell Large Cap Index Portfolio Class I	IIRLX	B-	C	B		4.20	18.75	10.53	52.27	67.26	22.34	959.4	800-366-0066	Y
Voya Russell Large Cap Index Portfolio Class S	IRLCX	B-	C	B		4.14	18.57	10.26	51.11	65.13	22.2	959.4	800-366-0066	Y
Voya Russell Large Cap Index Portfolio Class S2	IRLUX	B-	C	B		4.09	18.48	10.08	50.44	63.91	22.88	959.4	800-366-0066	Y
Voya U.S. Stock Index Portfolio Class A	ISIVX	B-	C	B		4.06	19.06	9.53	47.26	59.69	15.86	5,890	800-366-0066	Y
Voya U.S. Stock Index Portfolio Class I	INGIX	B-	C	B		4.24	19.37	10.06	49.70	63.98	16.45	5,890	800-366-0066	Y
Voya U.S. Stock Index Portfolio Class S	ISJBX	B-	C	B		4.15	19.22	9.79	48.57	62.08	16.31	5,890	800-366-0066	Y
Voya U.S. Stock Index Portfolio Class S2	ISIPX	B-	C	B		4.14	19.18	9.70	47.94	60.84	16.09	5,890	800-366-0066	Y

Category: US Equity Large Cap Blend (con't)

Fund Name	Ticker Symbol	Overall Rating	Reward Rating	Risk Rating	Recent Up/ Downgrade	3-Month Total Return	6-Month Total Return	1-Year Total Return	3-Year Total Return	5-Year Total Return	NAV	Total Assets (MIL)	Telephone	Open to New Investors
		RATINGS				TOTAL RETURNS & PERFORMANCE					ASSETS		NEW INVESTORS	
Voya U.S. Stock Index Portfolio P2	VPSPX	B-	C	B		4.29	19.47	10.25	50.04	64.34	16.5	5,890	800-366-0066	Y
Walden Equity Fund	WSEFX	B-	C+	B+	Down	4.57	19.76	13.65	51.45	62.67	24.48	229.5	617-814-1215	Y
Wells Fargo Classic Value Fund - Class A	EIVAX	B-	C+	B		5.57	20.73	11.30	41.92	44.51	12.87	863.1	800-222-8222	Y
Wells Fargo Classic Value Fund - Class Admin	EIVDX	B-	C+	B		5.62	20.80	11.39	42.54	45.63	13.53	863.1	800-222-8222	Y
Wells Fargo Classic Value Fund - Class Inst	EIVIX	B-	C+	B		5.62	20.91	11.71	43.62	47.47	12.95	863.1	800-222-8222	Y
Wells Fargo Classic Value Fund - Class R	EIVTX	B-	C	B		5.53	20.55	10.94	40.85	42.68	12.96	863.1	800-222-8222	Y
Wells Fargo Classic Value Fund - Class R6	EIVFX	B-	C+	B+		5.67	20.91	12.60	44.93	48.27	12.66	863.1	800-222-8222	Y
Wells Fargo Classic Value Fund- Class C	EIVCX	B-	C	B		5.39	20.28	10.47	38.71	39.07	12.51	863.1	800-222-8222	Y
Wells Fargo Index Fund - Class A	WFILX	B-	C	B		4.17	19.28	9.92	48.87	62.42	52.94	1,196	800-222-8222	Y
Wells Fargo Index Fund - Class Admin	WFIOX	B-	C	B		4.24	19.43	10.14	49.78	64.29	53.77	1,196	800-222-8222	Y
Wells Fargo Index Fund - Class C	WFINX	B-	C	B		4.00	18.86	9.10	45.57	56.45	53.5	1,196	800-222-8222	Y
Wells Fargo Low Volatility U.S. Equity Administrator Cls	WLVDX	B-	C	B	Up	5.53	19.27	12.61			11.82	38.8	800-222-8222	Y
Wells Fargo Low Volatility U.S. Equity Fund Class A	WLVLX	B-	C	B	Up	5.53	19.25	12.48			11.83	38.8	800-222-8222	Y
Wells Fargo Low Volatility U.S. Equity Fund Class R6	WLVJX	B-	C	B+	Up	5.70	19.57	13.10			11.85	38.8	800-222-8222	Y
Wells Fargo Low Volatility U.S. Equity Institutional Cls	WLVOX	B-	C	B+	Up	5.61	19.35	12.90			11.84	38.8	800-222-8222	Y
Westfield Capital Dividend Growth Fund Institutional Class	WDIVX	B-	C	B		5.49	19.63	10.17	48.90	54.16	11.7	125.9		Y
Westfield Capital Dividend Growth Fund Investor Class	WCDGX	B-	C	B		5.39	19.44	9.87	47.81	52.73	11.73	125.9		Y
Westwood LargeCap Value Fund A Class	WWLAX	B-	C	B+		4.81	16.52	8.45	40.45	50.74	12.62	234.6		Y
Westwood LargeCap Value Fund Institutional Class	WHGLX	B-	C	B+		4.83	16.71	8.73	41.40	52.52	12.57	234.6		Y
Westwood Low Volatility Equity Fund Institutional Class	WLVIX	B-	C	B+		4.84	17.16	9.81	32.46	38.96	6.28	4.7		Y
Wilmington Large-Cap Strategy Fund Class Institutional	WMLIX	B-	C	B		4.16	19.73	9.61	51.41	64.60	23.28	517.3	800-836-2211	Y
Wilshire 5000 Index Portfolio Class Institutional	WINDX	B-	C	B		3.88	19.05	8.72	48.58	60.30	21.93	191.9	888-200-6796	Y
Wilshire 5000 Index Portfolio Investment Class Shares	WFIVX	B-	C	B		3.79	18.82	8.35	47.24	58.12	21.9	191.9	888-200-6796	Y
YCG Enhanced Fund	YCGEX	B	B	B		7.65	27.44	16.60	58.09	73.02	19.27	251.4		Y
Zacks All-Cap Core Fund Institutional Class	CZOVX	B-	C	B		4.26	18.93	9.37	44.87	54.42	25.19	42.0		Y

Category: US Equity Large Cap Growth

Fund Name	Ticker Symbol	Overall Rating	Reward Rating	Risk Rating	Recent Up/ Downgrade	3-Month Total Return	6-Month Total Return	1-Year Total Return	3-Year Total Return	5-Year Total Return	NAV	Total Assets (MIL)	Telephone	Open to New Investors
		RATINGS				TOTAL RETURNS & PERFORMANCE					ASSETS		NEW INVESTORS	
AB Concentrated Growth Fund Advisor Class	WPSGX	B	B	B+		7.31	28.87	22.96	77.67	84.73	40.93	587.5	212-969-1000	Y
AB Concentrated Growth Fund Class A	WPASX	B	B	B+		7.22	28.70	22.67	76.33	82.44	40.35	587.5	212-969-1000	Y
AB Concentrated Growth Fund Class C	WPCSX	B	B-	B+		7.04	28.27	21.74	72.44	75.85	38.61	587.5	212-969-1000	Y
AB Concentrated Growth Fund Class I	WPSIX	B	B	B+		7.32	28.93	22.99	77.74	84.94	41	587.5	212-969-1000	Y
AB Concentrated Growth Fund Class K	WPSKX	B	B	B+		7.25	28.74	22.66	76.37	82.55	40.36	587.5	212-969-1000	Y
AB Concentrated Growth Fund Class R	WPRSX	B	B	B+		7.19	28.58	22.37	75.02	80.26	39.76	587.5	212-969-1000	Y
AB Concentrated Growth Fund Class Z	WPSZX	B	B	B+		7.30	28.90	23.00	77.80	84.86	40.98	587.5	212-969-1000	Y
AB Core Opportunities Fund Advisor Class	ADGYX	B-	C	B+	Down	3.95	15.89	9.24	51.10	69.31	19.98	259.1	212-969-1000	Y
AB Core Opportunities Fund Class A	ADGAX	B-	C	B+	Down	3.92	15.76	9.00	50.00	67.04	19.31	259.1	212-969-1000	Y
AB Core Opportunities Fund Class B	ADGBX	B-	C	B+	Down	3.87	15.67	8.81	49.20	65.43	16.9	259.1	212-969-1000	
AB Core Opportunities Fund Class C	ADGCX	B-	C	B+	Down	3.72	15.38	8.21	46.67	61.08	15.6	259.1	212-969-1000	Y
AB Core Opportunities Fund Class I	ADGIX	B-	C	B+	Down	3.95	15.90	9.25	51.21	69.45	20.26	259.1	212-969-1000	Y
AB Core Opportunities Fund Class K	ADGKX	B-	C	B+	Down	3.88	15.78	8.94	49.87	67.04	19.51	259.1	212-969-1000	Y
AB Core Opportunities Fund Class R	ADGRX	B-	C	B+	Down	3.86	15.64	8.68	48.82	64.98	18.55	259.1	212-969-1000	Y
AB Core Opportunities Fund Class Z	ADGZX	B-	C	B+	Down	3.99	15.99	9.36	51.57	69.86	20.31	259.1	212-969-1000	Y
AB Growth Fund Advisor Class	AGRYX	B-	C+	B	Down	4.27	23.25	14.64	77.62	105.54	88.88	1,145	212-969-1000	Y
AB Growth Fund Class A	AGRFX	B-	C+	B	Down	4.21	23.10	14.37	76.30	102.97	80.56	1,145	212-969-1000	Y
AB Growth Fund Class B	AGBBX	B-	C+	B	Down	4.01	22.64	13.46	72.25	95.02	36.51	1,145	212-969-1000	
AB Growth Fund Class C	AGRCX	B-	C+	B	Down	4.02	22.65	13.53	72.38	95.42	37.25	1,145	212-969-1000	Y
AB Growth Fund Class I	AGFIX	B-	C+	B	Down	4.29	23.30	14.77	78.29	106.72	88.56	1,145	212-969-1000	Y

Category: US Equity Large Cap Growth (con't)

Fund Name	Ticker Symbol	RATINGS: Overall Rating	Reward Rating	Risk Rating	Recent Up/ Downgrade	TOTAL RETURNS & PERFORMANCE: 3-Month Total Return	6-Month Total Return	1-Year Total Return	3-Year Total Return	5-Year Total Return	ASSETS: NAV	Total Assets (MIL)	NEW INVESTORS: Telephone	Open to New Investors
AB Growth Fund Class K	AGFKX	B-	C+	B	Down	4.18	23.04	14.27	76.04	102.76	82.81	1,145	212-969-1000	Y
AB Growth Fund Class R	AGFRX	B-	C+	B	Down	4.11	22.87	13.92	74.44	99.59	77.89	1,145	212-969-1000	Y
AB Large Cap Growth Fund Advisor Class	APGYX	B-	C+	B	Down	4.22	21.96	13.76	71.69	102.37	58.97	9,074	212-969-1000	Y
AB Large Cap Growth Fund Class A	APGAX	B-	C+	B	Down	4.15	21.81	13.47	70.37	99.81	53.67	9,074	212-969-1000	Y
AB Large Cap Growth Fund Class B	APGBX	B-	C+	B	Down	3.93	21.31	12.57	66.52	91.95	38.3	9,074	212-969-1000	
AB Large Cap Growth Fund Class C	APGCX	B-	C+	B	Down	3.95	21.35	12.63	66.61	92.50	38.92	9,074	212-969-1000	Y
AB Large Cap Growth Fund Class I	ALLIX	B-	C+	B	Down	4.21	21.94	13.76	71.71	102.68	58.63	9,074	212-969-1000	Y
AB Large Cap Growth Fund Class K	ALCKX	B-	C+	B	Down	4.11	21.74	13.39	69.97	99.13	54.64	9,074	212-969-1000	Y
AB Large Cap Growth Fund Class R	ABPRX	B-	C+	B	Down	4.03	21.55	13.05	68.46	96.20	51.09	9,074	212-969-1000	Y
AB Large Cap Growth Fund Class Z	APGZX	B-	C+	B	Down	4.23	22.02	13.87	72.16	102.62	58.79	9,074	212-969-1000	Y
AB Select US Equity Portfolio Advisor Class	AUUYX	B-	C+	B		5.26	18.50	9.33	49.54	62.52	16.78	225.6	212-969-1000	Y
AB Select US Equity Portfolio Class A	AUUAX	B-	C	B		5.13	18.30	9.07	48.36	60.50	16.8	225.6	212-969-1000	Y
AB Select US Equity Portfolio Class C	AUUCX	B-	C	B	Up	4.98	17.84	8.26	45.15	54.65	15.78	225.6	212-969-1000	Y
AB Select US Equity Portfolio Class I	AUUIX	B-	C+	B		5.26	18.48	9.38	49.56	62.59	16.6	225.6	212-969-1000	Y
AB Select US Equity Portfolio Class K	AUUKX	B-	C	B		5.19	18.24	8.99	48.04	59.82	16.59	225.6	212-969-1000	Y
AB Select US Equity Portfolio Class R	AUURX	B-	C	B	Up	5.13	18.10	8.76	47.15	58.26	16.37	225.6	212-969-1000	Y
Aberdeen Focused U.S. Equity Fund Class A	MLSAX	B-	C	B	Down	4.19	20.60	11.57	33.18	33.52	7.2	20.0	866-667-9231	Y
Aberdeen Focused U.S. Equity Fund Class C	MLSCX	B-	C	B	Down	4.21	20.00	11.07	31.09	29.52	1.98	20.0	866-667-9231	Y
Aberdeen Focused U.S. Equity Fund Class R	GLSRX	B-	C	B	Down	3.90	20.15	11.10	31.76	31.04	6.38	20.0	866-667-9231	Y
Aberdeen Focused U.S. Equity Fund Institutional Class	GGUIX	B-	C	B	Down	4.16	20.68	11.91	34.50	35.73	7.76	20.0	866-667-9231	Y
Aberdeen Focused U.S. Equity Institutional Service Cls	AELSX	B-	C	B	Down	4.16	20.57	11.86	33.86	34.46	7.5	20.0	866-667-9231	Y
AC Alternatives® Disciplined Long Short Fund I Class	ACDKX	B-	C	B+		-0.57	5.65	1.71	24.93	34.11	17.37	51.1	800-444-4015	Y
AC Alternatives® Disciplined Long Short Investor Cls	ACDJX	B-	C	B+		-0.63	5.55	1.49	24.16	32.85	17.28	51.1	800-444-4015	Y
AIG Focused Alpha Large-Cap Fund Class A	SFLAX	B-	C+	B	Down	5.50	21.46	10.44	65.97	75.85	28.75	647.6	800-858-8850	Y
AIG Focused Alpha Large-Cap Fund Class C	SFLCX	B-	C+	B	Down	5.33	21.04	9.67	62.73	70.21	26.86	647.6	800-858-8850	Y
AIG Focused Alpha Large-Cap Fund Class W	SFLWX	B-	C+	B	Down	5.52	21.52	10.54	66.55	77.04	29.24	647.6	800-858-8850	Y
Akre Focus Fund Institutional Class	AKRIX	B+	B+	A-	Up	6.03	27.50	23.17	84.63	106.99	43.9	11,002	877-862-9556	Y
Akre Focus Fund Retail Class	AKREX	B+	B+	A-	Up	5.92	27.27	22.82	83.12	104.23	42.88	11,002	877-862-9556	Y
Akre Focus Fund Supra Institutional Class	AKRSX	B+	B+	A-	Up	6.04	27.53	23.28	85.18	107.69	44.05	11,002	877-862-9556	Y
Alger Capital Appreciation Fund Class A	ACAAX	B-	C+	B	Down	5.25	22.76	9.73	65.61	79.42	26.64	2,866	800-992-3863	Y
Alger Capital Appreciation Fund Class Z	ACAZX	B-	C+	B	Down	5.35	23.00	10.14	67.42	82.51	27.54	2,866	800-992-3863	Y
Alger Capital Appreciation Institutional Fund Class I	ALARX	B-	C+	B	Down	5.31	22.84	9.90	65.70	79.84	34.85	3,523	800-992-3863	Y
Alger Capital Appreciation Institutional Fund Class R	ACARX	B-	C+	B	Down	5.19	22.55	9.40	63.40	75.62	30.59	3,523	800-992-3863	Y
Alger Capital Appreciation Institutional Fund Class Y	ACAYX	B-	C+	B	Down	5.44	23.10	10.38	67.21	81.48	35.22	3,523	800-992-3863	Y
Alger Capital Appreciation Institutional Fund Class Z-2	ACIZX	B-	C+	B	Down	5.42	23.07	10.29	67.17	81.44	35.2	3,523	800-992-3863	Y
Alger Capital Appreciation Portfolio Class I-2	ALVOX	B-	C+	B	Down	5.54	23.04	10.83	67.23	82.35	82.97	494.3	800-992-3863	Y
Alger Capital Appreciation Portfolio Class S		B-	C+	B	Down	5.48	22.88	10.55	65.93	79.94	78.44	494.3	800-992-3863	Y
Alger Focus Equity Fund Class A	ALAFX	B-	C+	B	Down	5.21	22.86	9.50	74.84	92.98	36.54	524.3	800-992-3863	Y
Alger Focus Equity Fund Class C	ALCFX	B-	C+	B	Down	5.03	22.43	8.68	70.95	85.83	34.65	524.3	800-992-3863	Y
Alger Focus Equity Fund Class I	ALGRX	B-	C+	B	Down	5.23	22.94	9.57	74.97	93.58	36.76	524.3	800-992-3863	Y
Alger Focus Equity Fund Class Y	ALGYX	B-	C+	B	Down	5.31	23.11	9.92	76.38	95.14	37.44	524.3	800-992-3863	Y
Alger Focus Equity Fund Class Z	ALZFX	B-	C+	B	Down	5.29	23.09	9.87	76.50	96.30	37.36	524.3	800-992-3863	Y
Alger Responsible Investing Fund Class Z	ALGZX	B-	C+	B		4.79	21.85	9.81	61.83	64.20	11.15	61.3	800-992-3863	Y
Alger Spectra Fund Class A	SPECX	B-	C+	B	Down	5.85	23.22	9.78	66.08	80.19	22.23	6,218	800-992-3863	Y
Alger Spectra Fund Class I	ASPIX	B-	C+	B	Down	5.88	23.30	9.82	66.26	80.37	22.49	6,218	800-992-3863	Y
Alger Spectra Fund Class Y	ASPYX	B-	C+	B	Down	5.95	23.53	10.08	66.54	80.69	22.94	6,218	800-992-3863	Y
Alger Spectra Fund Class Z	ASPZX	B-	C+	B	Down	5.91	23.41	10.12	67.70	83.06	22.93	6,218	800-992-3863	Y
Amana Mutual Funds Trust Growth Fund Institutional	AMIGX	B	B-	B+		3.47	22.94	20.27	69.54	86.81	42.23	2,119	888-732-6262	Y
Amana Mutual Funds Trust Growth Fund Investor	AMAGX	B	B-	B+		3.42	22.78	20.01	68.32	84.68	42.03	2,119	888-732-6262	Y
American Century All Cap Growth Fund A Class	ACAQX	B-	C+	B		5.29	23.47	10.01	55.20	70.22	33.61	1,189	800-444-4015	Y
American Century All Cap Growth Fund I Class	ACAJX	B-	C+	B		5.43	23.75	10.54	57.34	74.12	35.32	1,189	800-444-4015	Y
American Century All Cap Growth Fund Investor Class	TWGTX	B-	C+	B		5.36	23.60	10.28	56.34	72.37	34.56	1,189	800-444-4015	Y

Category: US Equity Large Cap Growth (con't)

Fund Name	Ticker Symbol	RATINGS: Overall Rating	Reward Rating	Risk Rating	Recent Up/ Downgrade	TOTAL RETURNS & PERFORMANCE: 3-Month Total Return	6-Month Total Return	1-Year Total Return	3-Year Total Return	5-Year Total Return	ASSETS: NAV	Total Assets (MIL)	NEW INVESTORS: Telephone	Open to New Investors
American Century Growth Fund A Class	TCRAX	B-	C+	B	Down	5.34	23.19	10.92	64.25	76.26	33.51	7,952	800-444-4015	Y
American Century Growth Fund C Class	TWRCX	B-	C+	B	Down	5.14	22.71	10.08	60.56	69.74	31.5	7,952	800-444-4015	Y
American Century Growth Fund I Class	TWGIX	B-	C+	B	Down	5.47	23.48	11.41	66.48	80.32	35.44	7,952	800-444-4015	Y
American Century Growth Fund Investor Class	TWCGX	B-	C+	B	Down	5.40	23.33	11.19	65.46	78.47	34.73	7,952	800-444-4015	Y
American Century Growth Fund R Class	AGWRX	B-	C+	B	Down	5.27	23.01	10.62	62.97	74.05	32.55	7,952	800-444-4015	Y
American Century Growth Fund R5 Class	AGWUX	B-	C+	B	Down	5.47	23.45	11.44	66.19	79.25	35.47	7,952	800-444-4015	Y
American Century Growth Fund R6 Class	AGRDX	B-	C+	B	Down	5.51	23.54	11.59	67.24	81.67	35.42	7,952	800-444-4015	Y
American Century Growth Fund Y Class	AGYWX	B-	C+	B	Down	5.50	23.54	11.58	66.73	79.84	35.47	7,952	800-444-4015	Y
American Century Inv Focused Dynamic Growth Adv Cls	ACFDX	B-	C+	B		3.72	23.49	10.53	82.96	80.90	28.44	195.9	800-444-4015	Y
American Century Investments Focused Dynamic Growth G Cls	ACFGX	B-	C+	B		3.93	23.85	11.09	85.55	85.14	29.48	195.9	800-444-4015	Y
American Century Investments Focused Dynamic Growth I Cls	ACFSX	B-	C+	B		3.86	23.78	11.03	85.43	85.03	28.99	195.9	800-444-4015	Y
American Century Inv Focused Dynamic Growth Inv Cls	ACFOX	B-	C+	B		3.78	23.63	10.78	84.37	83.22	28.77	195.9	800-444-4015	Y
American Century Investments Focused Dynamic Growth R6 Cls	ACFNX	B-	C+	B		3.88	23.85	11.17	86.05	85.65	29.44	195.9	800-444-4015	Y
American Century NT Growth Fund G Class	ACLTX	B-	C+	B	Down	5.59	23.94	12.79	70.19	83.27	17.55	1,103	800-444-4015	Y
American Century Select Fund A Class	TWCAX	B-	C+	B	Down	4.59	22.11	8.90	61.16	80.03	73.33	3,154	800-444-4015	Y
American Century Select Fund I Class	TWSIX	B-	C+	B	Down	4.70	22.38	9.39	63.35	84.12	76.54	3,154	800-444-4015	Y
American Century Select Fund Investor Class	TWCIX	B-	C+	B	Down	4.64	22.26	9.17	62.37	82.29	75.18	3,154	800-444-4015	Y
American Century Select Fund R Class	ASERX	B-	C+	B	Down	4.52	21.95	8.62	59.95	77.78	72.55	3,154	800-444-4015	Y
American Century Select Fund R5 Class	ASLGX	B-	C+	B	Down	4.69	22.36	9.35	62.99	82.99	76.55	3,154	800-444-4015	Y
American Century Select Fund R6 Class	ASDEX	B-	C+	B	Down	4.75	22.47	9.56	64.09	85.50	76.52	3,154	800-444-4015	Y
American Century Select Fund Y Class	ASLWX	B-	C+	B	Down	4.74	22.47	9.56	63.61	83.69	76.61	3,154	800-444-4015	Y
American Century Ultra® Fund I Class	TWUIX	B-	C+	B	Down	3.30	22.07	9.87	72.63	89.76	50.65	12,123	800-444-4015	Y
American Century Ultra® Fund Investor Class	TWCUX	B-	C+	B	Down	3.26	21.96	9.63	71.59	87.86	48.76	12,123	800-444-4015	Y
American Century Ultra® Fund R5 Class	AULGX	B-	C+	B	Down	3.30	22.09	9.86	72.35	88.69	50.68	12,123	800-444-4015	Y
American Century Ultra® Fund R6 Class	AULDX	B-	C+	B	Down	3.34	22.15	10.01	73.40	91.19	50.73	12,123	800-444-4015	Y
American Century Ultra® Fund Y Class	AULYX	B-	C+	B	Down	3.35	22.17	10.02	72.89	89.29	50.79	12,123	800-444-4015	Y
American Funds AMCAP Fund® Class 529-A	CAFAX	B-	C	B	Up	3.06	17.16	5.07	49.58	56.99	31.84	67,763	800-421-4225	Y
American Funds AMCAP Fund® Class 529-C	CAFCX	B-	C	B	Up	2.87	16.70	4.29	46.18	51.05	28.12	67,763	800-421-4225	Y
American Funds AMCAP Fund® Class 529-E	CAFEX	B-	C	B	Up	2.98	17.01	4.83	48.52	55.15	30.91	67,763	800-421-4225	Y
American Funds AMCAP Fund® Class 529-F-1	CAFFX	B-	C	B		3.10	17.28	5.31	50.53	58.64	32.13	67,763	800-421-4225	Y
American Funds AMCAP Fund® Class A	AMCPX	B-	C	B		3.09	17.18	5.15	49.91	57.62	32.23	67,763	800-421-4225	Y
American Funds AMCAP Fund® Class C	AMPCX	B-	C	B	Up	2.85	16.72	4.32	46.32	51.41	27.96	67,763	800-421-4225	Y
American Funds AMCAP Fund® Class F-1	AMPFX	B-	C	B	Up	3.08	17.15	5.07	49.57	57.15	31.93	67,763	800-421-4225	Y
American Funds AMCAP Fund® Class F-2	AMCFX	B-	C	B		3.13	17.28	5.36	50.78	59.20	32.47	67,763	800-421-4225	Y
American Funds AMCAP Fund® Class F-3	FMACX	B-	C	B		3.18	17.39	5.48	51.04	58.80	32.3	67,763	800-421-4225	Y
American Funds AMCAP Fund® Class R-1	RAFAX	B-	C	B	Up	2.88	16.75	4.34	46.37	51.53	28.82	67,763	800-421-4225	Y
American Funds AMCAP Fund® Class R-2	RAFBX	B-	C	B	Up	2.88	16.71	4.33	46.38	51.60	28.81	67,763	800-421-4225	Y
American Funds AMCAP Fund® Class R-2E	RAEBX	B-	C	B	Up	2.93	16.90	4.63	47.73	54.48	31.78	67,763	800-421-4225	Y
American Funds AMCAP Fund® Class R-3	RAFCX	B-	C	B	Up	2.96	16.98	4.78	48.33	54.98	31.1	67,763	800-421-4225	Y
American Funds AMCAP Fund® Class R-4	RAFEX	B-	C	B	Up	3.08	17.16	5.11	49.68	57.32	31.92	67,763	800-421-4225	Y
American Funds AMCAP Fund® Class R-5	RAFFX	B-	C	B		3.14	17.33	5.42	51.05	59.73	32.73	67,763	800-421-4225	Y
American Funds AMCAP Fund® Class R-5E	RAEFX	B-	C	B		3.11	17.31	5.34	50.71	58.52	32.29	67,763	800-421-4225	Y
American Funds AMCAP Fund® Class R-6	RAFGX	B-	C	B		3.14	17.38	5.46	51.27	60.10	32.65	67,763	800-421-4225	Y
American Funds Growth Portfolio Class 529-A	CGPAX	B-	C	B	Up	3.18	17.25	4.30	46.17	48.35	18.48	8,323	800-421-4225	Y
American Funds Growth Portfolio Class 529-E	CGPEX	B-	C	B	Up	3.08	17.10	4.02	45.14	46.39	18.35	8,323	800-421-4225	Y
American Funds Growth Portfolio Class 529-F-1	CGPFX	B-	C	B	Up	3.22	17.39	4.54	47.20	49.91	18.56	8,323	800-421-4225	Y
American Funds Growth Portfolio Class A	GWPAX	B-	C	B	Up	3.17	17.30	4.33	46.43	48.79	18.51	8,323	800-421-4225	Y
American Funds Growth Portfolio Class ABLE-A	CGQGX	B-	C	B	Up	3.18	17.30	4.36	46.34	48.56	18.44	8,323	800-421-4225	Y
American Funds Growth Portfolio Class F-1	GWPFX	B-	C	B	Up	3.17	17.31	4.31	46.27	48.42	18.5	8,323	800-421-4225	Y
American Funds Growth Portfolio Class F-2	GWPEX	B-	C	B	Up	3.27	17.43	4.60	47.45	50.39	18.59	8,323	800-421-4225	Y
American Funds Growth Portfolio Class F-3	GWPDX	B-	C	B	Up	3.28	17.55	4.72	47.84	50.98	18.55	8,323	800-421-4225	Y
American Funds Growth Portfolio Class R-2E	RBGEX	B-	C	B	Up	3.04	17.04	3.88	44.36	46.04	18.27	8,323	800-421-4225	Y

Category: US Equity Large Cap Growth (con't)

Fund Name	Ticker Symbol	RATINGS: Overall Rating	Reward Rating	Risk Rating	Recent Up/ Downgrade	TOTAL RETURNS & PERFORMANCE: 3-Month Total Return	6-Month Total Return	1-Year Total Return	3-Year Total Return	5-Year Total Return	ASSETS: NAV	Total Assets (MIL)	NEW INVESTORS: Telephone	Open to New Investors
American Funds Growth Portfolio Class R-3	RGPCX	B-	C	B	Up	3.08	17.14	4.03	45.01	46.27	18.38	8,323	800-421-4225	Y
American Funds Growth Portfolio Class R-4	RGWEX	B-	C	B	Up	3.18	17.33	4.34	46.37	48.57	18.48	8,323	800-421-4225	Y
American Funds Growth Portfolio Class R-5	RGWFX	B-	C	B	Up	3.26	17.42	4.62	47.58	50.72	18.67	8,323	800-421-4225	Y
American Funds Growth Portfolio Class R-5E	RGSFX	B-	C	B	Up	3.24	17.40	4.58	47.32	50.25	18.48	8,323	800-421-4225	Y
American Funds Growth Portfolio Class R-6	RGWGX	B-	C	B	Up	3.27	17.46	4.70	47.82	51.11	18.63	8,323	800-421-4225	Y
American Funds The Growth Fund of America® Class 529-F	CGFFX	B-	C	B		3.50	18.67	5.02	58.08	71.36	49.62	193,270	800-421-4225	Y
American Funds The Growth Fund of America® Class A	AGTHX	B-	C	B		3.47	18.58	4.86	57.40	70.19	50.34	193,270	800-421-4225	Y
American Funds The Growth Fund of America® Class F-2	GFFFX	B-	C	B		3.52	18.71	5.09	58.38	72.02	50.23	193,270	800-421-4225	Y
American Funds The Growth Fund of America® Class F-3	GAFFX	B-	C	B		3.53	18.76	5.19	58.50	71.39	50.37	193,270	800-421-4225	Y
American Funds The Growth Fund of America® Class R-5	RGAFX	B-	C	B		3.53	18.73	5.13	58.57	72.42	50.33	193,270	800-421-4225	Y
American Funds The Growth Fund of America® Class R-5E	RGAHX	B-	C	B		3.50	18.69	5.03	58.14	71.09	49.9	193,270	800-421-4225	Y
American Funds The Growth Fund of America® Class R-6	RGAGX	B-	C	B		3.53	18.75	5.18	58.82	72.86	50.4	193,270	800-421-4225	Y
American Funds The New Economy Fund® Class 529-A	CNGAX	B-	C	B	Up	1.70	17.59	2.62	62.70	59.43	44.78	21,429	800-421-4225	Y
American Funds The New Economy Fund® Class 529-E	CNGEX	B-	C	B	Up	1.63	17.43	2.38	61.59	57.51	44.05	21,429	800-421-4225	Y
American Funds The New Economy Fund® Class 529-F	CNGFX	B-	C	B	Up	1.72	17.68	2.84	63.75	61.06	44.72	21,429	800-421-4225	Y
American Funds The New Economy Fund® Class A	ANEFX	B-	C	B	Up	1.70	17.60	2.69	63.02	59.97	45.29	21,429	800-421-4225	Y
American Funds The New Economy Fund® Class F-1	ANFFX	B-	C	B	Up	1.67	17.56	2.62	62.71	59.55	45.45	21,429	800-421-4225	Y
American Funds The New Economy Fund® Class F-2	NEFFX	B-	C	B	Up	1.75	17.75	2.92	64.07	61.76	45.23	21,429	800-421-4225	Y
American Funds The New Economy Fund® Class F-3	FNEFX	B-	C	B	Up	1.79	17.82	3.02	64.31	61.25	45.35	21,429	800-421-4225	Y
American Funds The New Economy Fund® Class R-3	RNGCX	B-	C	B	Up	1.61	17.42	2.34	61.40	57.38	44.15	21,429	800-421-4225	Y
American Funds The New Economy Fund® Class R-4	RNGEX	B-	C	B	Up	1.70	17.60	2.66	62.87	59.82	44.83	21,429	800-421-4225	Y
American Funds The New Economy Fund® Class R-5	RNGFX	B-	C	B	Up	1.78	17.77	2.99	64.37	62.25	45.58	21,429	800-421-4225	Y
American Funds The New Economy Fund® Class R-5E	RNGHX	B-	C	B	Up	1.73	17.71	2.87	63.92	61.01	45.05	21,429	800-421-4225	Y
American Funds The New Economy Fund® Class R-6	RNGGX	B-	C	B	Up	1.79	17.79	3.02	64.60	62.64	45.4	21,429	800-421-4225	Y
AMG Managers Brandywine Blue Fund Class I	BLUEX	B-	C+	B-		6.94	27.57	11.96	62.43	71.99	50.38	188.3	800-835-3879	Y
AMG Managers Montag & Caldwell Growth Fund Class I	MCGIX	B-	C+	B	Down	5.38	21.40	13.96	45.95	57.47	18.6	508.2	800-835-3879	Y
AMG Managers Montag & Caldwell Growth Fund Class N	MCGFX	B-	C+	B	Down	5.29	21.32	13.81	45.10	55.75	18.49	508.2	800-835-3879	Y
AMG Renaissance Large Cap Growth Fund Class I	MRLSX	B-	C	B		5.65	22.99	13.87	55.72	66.26	12.89	90.1	800-835-3879	Y
AMG Renaissance Large Cap Growth Fund Class N	MRLTX	B-	C	B		5.62	22.92	13.60	54.42	63.83	12.76	90.1	800-835-3879	Y
AMG Renaissance Large Cap Growth Fund Class Z	MRLIX	B-	C	B	Down	5.65	23.03	13.88	56.13	67.35	12.71	90.1	800-835-3879	Y
Ave Maria Growth Fund	AVEGX	B	B	B		6.31	26.03	15.49	65.88	83.25	35.19	746.1	888-726-9331	Y
Baron Fifth Avenue Growth Fund Class R6	BFTUX	B-	C+	B-	Down	6.60	27.59	11.42	88.06	97.00	33.25	310.0	800-992-2766	Y
Baron Fifth Avenue Growth Fund Institutional Class	BFTIX	B-	C+	B-	Down	6.60	27.60	11.43	88.00	97.76	33.24	310.0	800-992-2766	Y
Baron Fifth Avenue Growth Fund Retail Class	BFTHX	B-	C+	B-	Down	6.54	27.39	11.16	86.63	95.26	32.55	310.0	800-992-2766	Y
Baron Opportunity Fund Institutional Class	BIOIX	B-	B-	B	Down	6.05	29.90	15.98	98.80	89.63	23.46	473.5	800-992-2766	Y
Baron Opportunity Fund R6 Shares	BIOUX	B-	B-	B	Down	6.09	29.92	16.01	98.89	88.70	23.49	473.5	800-992-2766	Y
Baron Opportunity Fund Retail Class	BIOPX	B-	C+	B	Down	6.02	29.76	15.73	97.25	87.14	22.54	473.5	800-992-2766	Y
Barrett Growth Fund	BGRWX	B	B-	B	Up	6.17	22.95	13.69	55.85	69.60	22.34	28.1	877-363-6333	Y
BFS Equity Fund	BFSAX	B	B-	B	Up	6.31	24.31	15.49	54.29	59.14	16.67	39.0	860-527-8050	Y
BlackRock Advantage Large Cap Growth Fund Class K	BMCKX	B-	C+	B		4.25	21.93	9.26	65.14	55.12	16.47	815.9	800-441-7762	Y
BlackRock Advantage Large Cap Growth Institutional Shares	CMVIX	B-	C+	B		4.25	21.93	9.13	65.81	56.73	16.47	815.9	800-441-7762	Y
BlackRock Advantage Large Cap Growth Investor A Shares	BMCAX	B-	C+	B		4.19	21.71	8.86	64.41	54.43	15.7	815.9	800-441-7762	Y
BlackRock Advantage Large Cap Growth Fund Service Shares	CMVSX	B-	C+	B		4.20	21.76	8.89	64.45	54.42	16.17	815.9	800-441-7762	Y
BlackRock Capital Appreciation Fund Institutional Shares	MAFGX	B-	C+	B	Down	5.10	24.11	9.61	75.70	92.72	31.3	3,270	800-441-7762	Y
BlackRock Capital Appreciation Fund Investor A Shares	MDFGX	B-	C+	B	Down	5.04	23.93	9.31	74.23	90.07	28.73	3,270	800-441-7762	Y
BlackRock Capital Appreciation Fund Investor C Shares	MCFGX	B-	C+	B	Down	4.81	23.42	8.43	70.13	82.55	20.37	3,270	800-441-7762	Y
BlackRock Capital Appreciation Fund K Shares	BFGBX	B-	C+	B	Down	5.14	24.17	9.73	76.31	93.84	31.49	3,270	800-441-7762	Y
BlackRock Capital Appreciation Fund R Shares	MRFGX	B-	C+	B	Down	4.99	23.78	9.03	72.82	87.57	23.27	3,270	800-441-7762	Y
BlackRock Focus Growth Fund Institutional Shares	MAFOX	B-	C+	B	Down	5.47	24.31	10.74	76.41	104.02	5.04	218.6	800-441-7762	Y
BlackRock Focus Growth Fund Investor A Shares	MDFOX	B-	C+	B	Down	5.49	24.25	10.45	75.33	100.69	4.63	218.6	800-441-7762	Y
BlackRock Focus Growth Fund Investor C Shares	MCFOX	B-	C+	B	Down	5.08	23.58	9.32	70.99	93.30	3.75	218.6	800-441-7762	Y
BlackRock Large Cap Focus Growth Fund Class K	MLHKX	B-	B-	B	Down	5.69	24.65	10.56	82.87	98.13	13.63	975.6	800-441-7762	Y

Category: US Equity Large Cap Growth (con't)

Fund Name	Ticker Symbol	RATINGS: Overall Rating	Reward Rating	Risk Rating	Recent Up/ Downgrade	TOTAL RETURNS & PERFORMANCE: 3-Month Total Return	6-Month Total Return	1-Year Total Return	3-Year Total Return	5-Year Total Return	ASSETS: NAV	Total Assets (MIL)	NEW INVESTORS: Telephone	Open to New Investors
BlackRock Large Cap Focus Growth Fund Class R	MRLHX	B-	C+	B	Down	5.56	24.26	9.97	79.84	92.83	11.07	975.6	800-441-7762	Y
BlackRock Large Cap Focus Growth Fund Institutional Shares	MALHX	B-	B-	B	Down	5.69	24.65	10.55	82.84	98.10	13.63	975.6	800-441-7762	Y
BlackRock Large Cap Focus Growth Fund Investor A Shares	MDLHX	B-	C+	B	Down	5.61	24.47	10.16	81.17	95.16	12.48	975.6	800-441-7762	Y
BlackRock Large Cap Focus Growth Fund Investor C Shares	MCLHX	B-	C+	B	Down	5.44	23.97	9.30	76.87	87.46	9.15	975.6	800-441-7762	Y
BlackRock Large Cap Focus Growth Fund Service Shares	MSLHX	B-	C+	B	Down	5.58	24.46	10.21	81.26	95.23	13.51	975.6	800-441-7762	Y
BMO Large-Cap Growth Fund Class A	BALGX	B-	C	B	Down	2.35	17.85	8.60	60.99	83.43	17.82	495.8	800-236-3863	Y
BMO Large-Cap Growth Fund Class I	MLCIX	B-	C	B	Down	2.44	17.99	8.92	62.18	85.85	18.03	495.8	800-236-3863	Y
BMO Large-Cap Growth Fund Class R6	BLGRX	B-	C	B	Down	2.49	18.10	9.09	62.98	86.09	18.07	495.8	800-236-3863	Y
BMO Large-Cap Growth Fund Class Y	MASTX	B-	C	B	Down	2.35	17.89	8.62	61.02	83.46	17.85	495.8	800-236-3863	Y
BNY Mellon Large Cap Securities Inc	DREVX	B-	C	B	Down	4.13	18.71	12.38	48.65	59.36	12.06	1,274		Y
BNY Mellon Research Growth Fund, Inc. Class Y	DRYQX	B-	C+	B	Down	3.34	22.38	11.02	56.27	71.90	15.21	1,710		Y
BNY Mellon Research Growth Fund, Inc. Class Z	DREQX	B-	C+	B	Down	3.40	22.28	10.99	55.84	71.20	15.55	1,710		
BNY Mellon U.S. Equity Fund Class A	DPUAX	B-	C	B	Down	4.66	20.73	13.41	56.06	64.06	19.95	614.3		
BNY Mellon U.S. Equity Fund Class C	DPUCX	B-	C	B	Down	4.48	20.31	12.57	52.57	57.92	18.41	614.3		
BNY Mellon U.S. Equity Fund Class I	DPUIX	B-	C	B	Down	4.76	20.99	13.80	57.65	66.81	20.01	614.3		
BNY Mellon U.S. Equity Fund Class Y	DPUYX	B-	C	B	Down	4.76	20.97	13.84	57.72	66.96	20	614.3		
Bridge Builder Large Cap Growth Fund	BBGLX	B-	C+	B	Down	4.49	22.00	13.75	59.91		14.64	6,997		Y
Bridges Investment Fund	BRGIX	B-	C	B		4.68	20.02	8.70	54.64	54.46	68.16	180.3		Y
Brown Advisory Flexible Equity Fund Advisor Shares	BAFAX	B-	C+	B		4.66	20.46	8.51	58.79	62.00	22.9	483.5	800-540-6807	Y
Brown Advisory Flexible Equity Fund Institutional Shares	BAFFX	B-	C+	B		4.75	20.69	8.94	60.78	65.25	22.92	483.5	800-540-6807	Y
Brown Advisory Flexible Equity Fund Investor Shares	BIAFX	B-	C+	B		4.71	20.61	8.76	59.97	64.11	22.88	483.5	800-540-6807	Y
Brown Advisory Growth Equity Fund Advisor Shares	BAGAX	B-	B-	B	Down	5.43	27.35	16.21	70.51	85.27	23.09	2,359	800-540-6807	Y
Brown Advisory Growth Equity Fund Institutional Shares	BAFGX	B	B-	B		5.57	27.63	16.68	72.58	89.02	24.8	2,359	800-540-6807	Y
Brown Advisory Growth Equity Fund Investor Shares	BIAGX	B	B-	B		5.51	27.53	16.49	71.81	87.55	24.5	2,359	800-540-6807	Y
Brown Advisory Sustainable Growth Fund Advisor Shares	BAWAX	B	B-	B		6.22	26.55	18.38	74.12	108.67	25.59	1,373	800-540-6807	Y
Brown Advisory Sustainable Growth Institutional Shares	BAFWX	B	B	B		6.32	26.87	18.89	76.24	112.84	26.39	1,373	800-540-6807	Y
Brown Advisory Sustainable Growth Fund Investor Shares	BIAWX	B	B	B		6.27	26.73	18.68	75.43	111.21	26.07	1,373	800-540-6807	Y
Buffalo Growth Fund	BUFGX	B-	B-	B	Down	6.85	24.39	12.19	59.08	70.03	26.82	177.2	800-492-8332	Y
Buffalo Large Cap Fund	BUFEX	B-	C+	B	Down	4.77	21.68	12.46	60.62	86.03	32.49	72.5	800-492-8332	Y
Calvert Equity Fund Class A	CSIEX	B+	B	A-	Up	7.11	26.50	24.67	71.16	89.28	52.22	2,937	301-951-4881	Y
Calvert Equity Fund Class C	CSECX	B+	B	A-	Up	6.90	26.00	23.74	67.30	82.25	28.78	2,937	301-951-4881	Y
Calvert Equity Fund Class I	CEYIX	B+	B+	A-	Up	7.16	26.64	25.00	72.86	93.00	60.84	2,937	301-951-4881	Y
Calvert Equity Fund Class R6	CEYRX	B+	B	A-	Up	7.18	26.67	25.05	72.01	90.23	60.74	2,937	301-951-4881	Y
Calvert US Large Cap Growth Responsible Index Fund Class A	CGJAX	B-	C+	B	Down	4.20	22.06	13.73	62.50		29.26	88.6	301-951-4881	Y
Calvert US Large Cap Growth Responsible Index Fund Class I	CGJIX	B-	C+	B	Down	4.24	22.24	14.06	64.12		29.46	88.6	301-951-4881	Y
Capital Group U.S. Equity Fund	CUSEX	B	C+	B+		4.80	20.80	12.70	48.76	61.46	23.7	240.5	213-486-9200	Y
Christopher Weil & Company Core Investment Fund	CWCFX	B-	C	B		6.42	18.21	6.75	45.71	42.03	14.41	40.1		Y
CIBC Atlas All Cap Growth Fund Institutional Class	AWGIX	B-	B-	B-	Down	7.45	28.08	12.65	73.24	84.60	29.83	185.4	312-368-7700	Y
CIBC Atlas Equity Income Fund Institutional Class	AWYIX	B	C+	B+		5.78	19.41	14.87	48.80	44.55	40.33	127.5	312-368-7700	Y
City National Rochdale U.S. Core Equity Cls Institutional	CNRUX	B	B	B+		7.27	23.41	15.14	60.95	72.38	18.76	314.9		Y
City National Rochdale U.S. Core Equity Fund Class N	CNRWX	B	B-	B+		7.17	23.20	14.63	58.60	68.05	18.55	314.9		Y
City National Rochdale U.S. Core Equity Cls Servicing	CNRVX	B	B-	B+		7.22	23.30	14.88	59.75	70.21	18.58	314.9		Y
ClearBridge Large Cap Growth Fund Class A	SBLGX	B-	C+	B	Down	5.09	22.65	13.28	62.86	90.06	47.42	14,233	877-721-1926	Y
ClearBridge Large Cap Growth Fund Class C	SLCCX	B-	C+	B	Down	4.92	22.21	12.48	59.42	83.29	37.52	14,233	877-721-1926	Y
ClearBridge Large Cap Growth Fund Class I	SBLYX	B-	C+	B	Down	5.20	22.85	13.63	64.34	93.01	52.78	14,233	877-721-1926	Y
ClearBridge Large Cap Growth Fund Class IS	LSITX	B-	C+	B	Down	5.21	22.91	13.75	64.78	93.73	52.84	14,233	877-721-1926	Y
ClearBridge Large Cap Growth Fund Class O	LCMMX	B-	C+	B	Down	5.21	22.88	13.68	64.55	93.05	52.83	14,233	877-721-1926	Y
ClearBridge Large Cap Growth Fund Class R	LMPLX	B-	C+	B	Down	5.02	22.48	12.93	61.46	87.30	45.32	14,233	877-721-1926	Y
ClearBridge Sustainability Leaders Fund Class A	CLSUX	B-	C+	B	Down	6.56	22.16	14.78	56.00		14.44	10.4	877-721-1926	Y
ClearBridge Sustainability Leaders Fund Class FI	LCSTX	B-	C+	B	Down	6.54	22.09	14.75	56.29		14.48	10.4	877-721-1926	Y
ClearBridge Sustainability Leaders Fund Class I	LCISX	B-	C+	B	Down	6.66	22.45	15.23	57.90		14.56	10.4	877-721-1926	Y
ClearBridge Sustainability Leaders Fund Class IS	LCILX	B-	C+	B	Down	6.65	22.41	15.22	57.98		14.58	10.4	877-721-1926	Y

Category: US Equity Large Cap Growth (con't)

Fund Name	Ticker Symbol	RATINGS: Overall Rating	Reward Rating	Risk Rating	Recent Up/ Downgrade	TOTAL RETURNS & PERFORMANCE: 3-Month Total Return	6-Month Total Return	1-Year Total Return	3-Year Total Return	5-Year Total Return	ASSETS: NAV	Total Assets (MIL)	NEW INVESTORS: Telephone	Open to New Investors
Commerce Growth Fund	CFGRX	B	B-	B		6.75	23.95	16.09	62.19	92.36	36.02	156.6		Y
Congress Large Cap Growth Fund Institutional Class	CMLIX	B	B-	B		5.10	23.52	13.90	61.14	81.37	31.5	326.0	888-688-1299	Y
Congress Large Cap Growth Fund Retail Class	CAMLX	B	B-	B		5.02	23.35	13.59	60.28	69.96	31.37	326.0	888-688-1299	Y
Davenport Core Fund	DAVPX	B-	C+	B		6.05	22.23	11.79	48.50	56.55	25.04	548.4		Y
Delaware Select Growth Fund Class A	DVEAX	B-	C	B		6.11	24.57	11.35	57.16	49.79	34.52	312.8		
Delaware Select Growth Fund Class C	DVECX	B-	C	B		5.87	24.09	10.49	53.64	44.22	20.91	312.8		
Delaware Select Growth Fund Class R	DFSRX	B-	C	B		6.02	24.39	11.08	55.95	47.90	31.67	312.8		
Delaware Select Growth Fund Institutional Class	VAGGX	B-	C	B		6.17	24.68	11.62	58.33	51.66	38.69	312.8		
Delaware U.S. Growth Fund Class R6	DUZRX	B-	C	B		7.81	21.69	10.91	54.79	59.66	24.57	2,446		Y
Delaware U.S. Growth Fund Institutional Class	DEUIX	B-	C	B		7.75	21.57	10.65	53.95	59.53	24.46	2,446		Y
DF Dent Premier Growth Fund Investor Shares	DFDPX	B	B+	B		9.83	32.94	21.13	84.80	94.20	35.75	209.4		Y
DFA U.S. Large Cap Growth Portfolio Institutional Class	DUSLX	B-	C+	B	Down	4.19	20.61	12.25	57.22	74.07	21.27	2,140	512-306-7400	Y
Dunham Focused Large Cap Growth Fund Class A	DAFGX	B-	C+	B	Down	5.75	27.84	17.22	77.61	90.95	24.24	109.5	800-442-4358	Y
Dunham Focused Large Cap Growth Fund Class N	DNFGX	B-	C+	B	Down	5.81	28.03	17.51	79.00	93.52	24.75	109.5	800-442-4358	Y
DWS Capital Growth Fund - Class A	SDGAX	B-	B-	B	Down	5.78	25.74	13.27	65.71	84.63	80.84	1,562		Y
DWS Capital Growth Fund - Class C	SDGCX	B-	C+	B	Down	5.57	25.22	12.35	61.60	77.18	67.21	1,562		Y
DWS Capital Growth Fund - Class Institutional	SDGTX	B-	B-	B	Down	5.85	25.88	13.51	66.85	86.91	81.7	1,562		Y
DWS Capital Growth Fund - Class R	SDGRX	B-	B-	B	Down	5.76	25.61	12.88	63.73	80.96	79.1	1,562		Y
DWS Capital Growth Fund - Class R6	SDGZX	B-	B-	B	Down	5.86	25.93	13.61	67.27	87.02	81.44	1,562		Y
DWS Capital Growth Fund - Class S	SCGSX	B-	B-	B	Down	5.86	25.91	13.55	66.96	87.00	81.83	1,562		Y
DWS Large Cap Focus Growth Fund - Class A	SGGAX	B-	B-	B	Down	6.48	25.78	14.18	62.43	84.99	49.61	255.0		Y
DWS Large Cap Focus Growth Fund - Class C	SGGCX	B-	B-	B	Down	6.28	25.28	13.34	58.79	78.14	41.12	255.0		Y
DWS Large Cap Focus Growth Fund - Class Inst	SGGIX	B-	B-	B	Down	6.53	25.89	14.45	63.61	87.29	52.66	255.0		Y
DWS Large Cap Focus Growth Fund - Class S	SCQGX	B-	B-	B	Down	6.54	25.93	14.49	63.69	87.32	51.95	255.0		Y
Eaton Vance Atlanta Capital Focused Growth Fund Class C	EAGCX	B+	B+	A-	Up	6.70	26.83	25.19	79.16	86.40	10.35	71.7		Y
Eaton Vance Atlanta Capital Select Equity Fund Class A	ESEAX	B	B	B+		8.31	27.13	22.60	55.09	78.59	24.74	489.2		Y
Eaton Vance Atlanta Capital Select Equity Fund Class C	ESECX	B	B	B+		8.13	26.65	21.70	51.67	71.93	23.52	489.2		Y
Eaton Vance Atlanta Capital Select Equity Fund Class I	ESEIX	B	B	B+		8.39	27.30	22.97	56.26	80.87	25.18	489.2		Y
Eaton Vance Atlanta Capital Select Equity Fund Class R6	ESERX	B	B	B+		8.42	27.30	23.02	56.38	81.02	25.22	489.2		Y
Eaton Vance Focused Growth Opportunities Fund Class A	EAFGX	B-	C	B	Down	1.55	20.16	8.55	59.02	76.87	22.23	262.9		Y
Eaton Vance Focused Growth Opportunities Fund Class I	EIFGX	B-	C	B	Down	1.61	20.34	8.81	60.22	79.02	22.6	262.9		Y
Eaton Vance Tax-Managed Growth 1.1 Fund Class A	ETTGX	B-	C	B		3.17	18.41	8.49	48.62	60.06	56.52	1,653		
Eaton Vance Tax-Managed Growth 1.1 Fund Class I	EITMX	B-	C	B		3.24	18.57	8.77	49.75	62.07	52.79	1,653		
Eaton Vance Tax-Managed Growth 1.2 Fund Class A	EXTGX	B-	C	B		3.16	18.35	8.34	47.97	58.82	25.4	836.5		Y
Eaton Vance Tax-Managed Growth 1.2 Institutional Cls	EITGX	B-	C	B		3.24	18.51	8.62	49.12	60.89	25.48	836.5		Y
Eaton Vance-Atlanta Capital Focused Growth Fund Class A	EAALX	B+	B+	A-	Up	6.83	27.40	26.22	83.15	93.59	11.25	71.7		Y
Eaton Vance-Atlanta Capital Focused Growth Fund Class I	EILGX	B+	B+	A-	Up	6.90	27.58	26.52	84.57	96.01	9.76	71.7		Y
Edgewood Growth Fund Class Institutional	EGFIX	B-	B-	B	Down	5.34	23.56	9.80	84.10	105.95	35.29	15,209	800-791-4226	Y
Edgewood Growth Fund Retail Class	EGFFX	B-	C+	B	Down	5.20	23.26	9.34	81.96	101.95	33.75	15,209	800-791-4226	Y
Elfun Trusts	ELFNX	B-	C+	B	Down	6.35	21.29	11.70	57.70	71.17	60.38	2,789	617-664-7338	Y
Ensemble Fund	ENSBX	B-	C+	B	Down	6.61	26.26	11.71	67.44		14.18	30.2	800-785-8165	Y
EQ/Capital Guardian Research Portfolio Class IA		B-	C	B	Down	3.53	11.56	7.62	53.21	74.22		422.3	877-222-2144	Y
EQ/Capital Guardian Research Portfolio Class IB		B-	C	B	Down	3.48	11.54	7.61	53.13	74.19		422.3	877-222-2144	Y
EQ/Capital Guardian Research Portfolio Class K		B-	C	B	Down	3.57	11.72	7.89	54.33	76.41		422.3	877-222-2144	Y
EQ/ClearBridge Large Cap Growth Portfolio Class IA		B-	C	B	Down	5.40	13.81	9.57	55.46	63.95		381.2	877-222-2144	Y
EQ/ClearBridge Large Cap Growth Portfolio Class IB		B-	C	B	Down	5.42	13.85	9.47	55.45	63.85		381.2	877-222-2144	Y
EQ/ClearBridge Large Cap Growth Portfolio Class K		B-	C	B	Down	5.49	14.00	9.81	56.60	65.86		381.2	877-222-2144	Y
EQ/Large Cap Growth Managed Volatility Portfolio Class IA		B-	C	B		4.19	11.15	6.99	55.85	76.75		5,030	877-222-2144	Y
EQ/Large Cap Growth Managed Volatility Portfolio Class IB		B-	C	B		4.22	11.18	7.00	55.88	76.80		5,030	877-222-2144	Y
EQ/Large Cap Growth Managed Volatility Portfolio Class K		B-	C	B		4.25	11.30	7.27	57.05	79.00		5,030	877-222-2144	Y
EQ/Loomis Sayles Growth Portfolio Class IA		B-	C	B		5.13	12.98	9.05	63.54	97.80		674.6	877-222-2144	Y
EQ/Loomis Sayles Growth Portfolio Class IB		B-	C	B		5.10	12.92	8.88	63.39	97.45		674.6	877-222-2144	Y

Category: US Equity Large Cap Growth (con't)

Fund Name	Ticker Symbol	Overall Rating	Reward Rating	Risk Rating	Recent Up/ Downgrade	3-Month Total Return	6-Month Total Return	1-Year Total Return	3-Year Total Return	5-Year Total Return	NAV	Total Assets (MIL)	Telephone	Open to New Investors
		RATINGS				TOTAL RETURNS & PERFORMANCE					ASSETS		NEW INVESTORS	
EQ/Loomis Sayles Growth Portfolio Class K		B-	C	B		5.13	13.03	9.22	64.76	99.34		674.6	877-222-2144	Y
EQ/T. Rowe Price Growth Stock Portfolio Class IA		B-	C	B	Down	2.93	13.22	5.44	64.17	89.48		1,584	877-222-2144	Y
EQ/T. Rowe Price Growth Stock Portfolio Class IB		B-	C	B	Down	2.91	13.21	5.43	64.14	89.45		1,584	877-222-2144	Y
EQ/T. Rowe Price Growth Stock Portfolio Class K		B-	C	B	Down	2.97	13.36	5.69	65.37	91.82		1,584	877-222-2144	Y
FDP BlackRock Capital Appreciation Institutional Shares	MADDX	B-	C+	B	Down	5.86	24.98	10.32	63.67	65.74	16.06	69.4		Y
FDP BlackRock Capital Appreciation Fund Investor A Shares	MDDDX	B-	C+	B	Down	5.81	24.81	10.03	62.45	63.62	15.29	69.4		Y
Federated Kaufmann Large Cap Fund Class A	KLCAX	B	B-	B		7.19	28.09	17.59	65.05	77.98	26.81	3,453	800-341-7400	Y
Federated Kaufmann Large Cap Fund Class C	KLCCX	B	B-	B		6.95	27.57	16.66	61.22	71.11	24.29	3,453	800-341-7400	Y
Federated Kaufmann Large Cap Fund Class R Shares	KLCKX	B	B-	B		7.08	27.89	17.13	63.18	74.47	25.4	3,453	800-341-7400	Y
Federated Kaufmann Large Cap Fund Class R6	KLCSX	B	B-	B		7.28	28.31	17.97	66.62	80.76	27.69	3,453	800-341-7400	Y
Federated Kaufmann Large Cap Fund Institutional Shares	KLCIX	B	B-	B		7.27	28.26	17.85	66.34	80.17	27.59	3,453	800-341-7400	Y
Federated MDT Large Cap Growth Fund Class A Shares	QALGX	B-	C+	B	Down	5.00	24.35	13.00	73.70	67.99	20.58	128.8	800-341-7400	Y
Federated MDT Large Cap Growth Fund Class B Shares	QBLGX	B-	C+	B	Down	4.82	23.89	12.17	69.78	61.69	18.46	128.8	800-341-7400	Y
Federated MDT Large Cap Growth Fund Class C Shares	QCLGX	B-	C+	B	Down	4.79	23.85	12.11	69.72	61.79	17.91	128.8	800-341-7400	Y
Federated MDT Large Cap Growth Fund Institutional Shares	QILGX	B-	C+	B	Down	5.06	24.52	13.25	75.02	70.15	21.58	128.8	800-341-7400	Y
Fidelity Advisor® Equity Growth Fund Class A	EPGAX	B-	C+	B	Down	4.31	22.58	10.15	70.90	78.46	12.32	3,243	617-563-7000	Y
Fidelity Advisor® Equity Growth Fund Class C	EPGCX	B-	C+	B	Down	4.04	22.03	9.32	66.94	71.70	10.3	3,243	617-563-7000	Y
Fidelity Advisor® Equity Growth Fund Class M	FAEGX	B-	C+	B	Down	4.14	22.45	9.91	69.67	76.37	12.05	3,243	617-563-7000	Y
Fidelity Advisor® Equity Growth Fund Class Z	FZAFX	B-	C+	B	Down	4.33	22.82	10.59	72.90	82.05	13.72	3,243	617-563-7000	Y
Fidelity Advisor® Equity Growth Fund I Class	EQPGX	B-	C+	B	Down	4.29	22.72	10.42	72.20	80.85	13.61	3,243	617-563-7000	Y
Fidelity Advisor® Growth Opportunities Fund Class A	FAGAX	B	C+	B	Down	3.80	26.49	21.80	105.57	116.44	82.68	6,286	617-563-7000	Y
Fidelity Advisor® Growth Opportunities Fund Class C	FACGX	B-	C+	B	Down	3.61	26.02	20.88	100.98	108.48	70.5	6,286	617-563-7000	Y
Fidelity Advisor® Growth Opportunities Fund Class M	FAGOX	B	C+	B	Down	3.76	26.36	21.53	104.17	113.99	81.87	6,286	617-563-7000	Y
Fidelity Advisor® Growth Opportunities Fund Class Z	FZAHX	B	C+	B	Down	3.92	26.75	22.29	108.07	120.89	90.29	6,286	617-563-7000	Y
Fidelity Advisor® Growth Opportunities Fund I Class	FAGCX	B	C+	B	Down	3.88	26.68	22.14	107.31	119.51	89.53	6,286	617-563-7000	Y
Fidelity Advisor® Series Equity Growth Fund	FMFMX	B-	C+	B	Down	4.66	23.35	11.07	76.28	85.12	14.58	982.5	617-563-7000	Y
Fidelity Advisor® Series Growth Opportunities Fund	FAOFX	B	B-	B+	Down	3.87	27.39	24.09	113.52	126.10	15.02	650.7	617-563-7000	Y
Fidelity® Focused Stock Fund	FTQGX	B-	C+	B	Down	4.39	21.74	14.00	70.45	73.49	25.19	2,876	617-563-7000	Y
Fidelity® Growth Discovery Fund	FDSVX	B-	C+	B	Down	4.42	22.57	10.33	71.41	80.51	37.74	2,073	617-563-7000	Y
Fidelity® Growth Discovery Fund Class K	FGDKX	B-	C+	B	Down	4.48	22.62	10.46	71.98	81.59	37.78	2,073	617-563-7000	Y
Fidelity® SAI U.S. Quality Index Fund	FUQIX	B-	C+	B	Down	2.47	20.14	11.51	58.09		14.91	8,393	617-563-7000	Y
Fidelity® Series Blue Chip Growth Fund	FSBDX	B-	C+	B	Down	3.32	21.24	10.66	85.40	99.55	15.24	6,162	617-563-7000	Y
Franklin DynaTech Fund Advisor Class	FDYZX	B-	B	B-	Down	6.70	31.38	17.42	98.68	118.27	87.86	7,895	650-312-2000	Y
Franklin DynaTech Fund Class A	FKDNX	B-	B-	B-	Down	6.64	31.22	17.13	97.19	115.57	85.11	7,895	650-312-2000	Y
Franklin DynaTech Fund Class C	FDYNX	B-	B-	B-	Down	6.45	30.73	16.24	92.83	107.65	70.61	7,895	650-312-2000	Y
Franklin DynaTech Fund Class R	FDNRX	B-	B-	B-	Down	6.57	31.05	16.84	95.73	112.91	82.5	7,895	650-312-2000	Y
Franklin DynaTech Fund Class R6	FDTRX	B-	B	B-	Down	6.73	31.46	17.53	99.50	119.90	88.74	7,895	650-312-2000	Y
Franklin Growth Fund Advisor Class	FCGAX	B-	C+	B	Down	5.80	23.23	12.85	63.13	79.08	109.91	15,253	650-312-2000	Y
Franklin Growth Opportunities Fund Advisor Class	FRAAX	B-	C+	B-		6.08	27.72	11.39	68.03	74.30	43.44	3,802	650-312-2000	Y
Franklin Growth Opportunities Fund Class A	FGRAX	B-	C+	B-		6.00	27.53	11.12	66.79	72.05	40.07	3,802	650-312-2000	Y
Franklin Growth Opportunities Fund Class R	FKARX	B-	C+	B-		5.93	27.40	10.88	65.60	70.06	38.03	3,802	650-312-2000	Y
Franklin Growth Opportunities Fund Class R6	FOPPX	B-	B-	B-		6.10	27.75	11.48	68.82	75.74	44	3,802	650-312-2000	Y
Franklin Growth Series Class A	FKGRX	B-	C+	B	Down	5.73	23.07	12.58	61.92	76.87	109.61	15,253	650-312-2000	Y
Franklin Growth Series Class C	FRGSX	B-	C+	B		5.54	22.62	11.75	58.31	70.33	100.01	15,253	650-312-2000	Y
Franklin Growth Series Class R	FGSRX	B-	C+	B	Down	5.67	22.92	12.31	60.71	74.65	109.13	15,253	650-312-2000	Y
Franklin Growth Series Class R6	FIFRX	B-	C+	B	Down	5.82	23.29	12.96	63.76	80.41	109.83	15,253	650-312-2000	Y
Frontier MFG Global Equity Fund Institutional Class	FMGEX	B	B-	A-		6.30	18.86	15.06	57.84	64.21	19.72	1,125		
Frost Growth Equity Fund Class Institutional	FICEX	B-	C+	B	Down	4.45	21.97	11.51	73.08	85.52	13.6	327.2		Y
Frost Growth Equity Fund Investor Class Shares	FACEX	B-	C+	B	Down	4.44	21.92	11.30	71.75	83.30	13.4	327.2		Y
GAMCO Growth Fund Class A	GGCAX	B-	B-	B	Down	4.26	23.37	11.90	68.57	83.37	66.77	707.3	914-921-5135	Y
GAMCO Growth Fund Class AAA	GABGX	B-	B-	B	Down	4.26	23.35	11.91	68.56	83.37	66.75	707.3	914-921-5135	Y
GAMCO Growth Fund Class C	GGCCX	B-	C+	B	Down	4.07	22.93	11.07	64.85	76.65	57.73	707.3	914-921-5135	Y

Category: US Equity Large Cap Growth (con't)

Fund Name	Ticker Symbol	Overall Rating	Reward Rating	Risk Rating	Recent Up/ Downgrade	3-Month Total Return	6-Month Total Return	1-Year Total Return	3-Year Total Return	5-Year Total Return	NAV	Total Assets (MIL)	Telephone	Open to New Investors
GAMCO Growth Fund Class I	GGCIX	B-	B-	B	Down	4.33	23.52	12.18	69.83	85.70	68.42	707.3	914-921-5135	Y
Glenmede Quantitative U.S. Large Cap Growth Eq Port	GTLLX	B-	C+	B	Down	5.59	22.43	11.32	59.18	80.09	31.88	3,492	800-442-8299	Y
Glenmede Quantitative U.S. Large Cap Growth Eq Inst Shares	GTILX	B-	C+	B	Down	5.63	22.57	11.55	60.14	81.39	31.9	3,492	800-442-8299	Y
Goldman Sachs Blue Chip Fund Class A	GAGVX	B-	C+	B+	Down	4.20	19.14	12.45	49.01	49.82	13.38	11.3	800-526-7384	Y
Goldman Sachs Blue Chip Fund Class C	GCGVX	B-	C+	B	Down	4.00	18.65	11.64	45.63	44.26	12.72	11.3	800-526-7384	Y
Goldman Sachs Blue Chip Fund Class P	GALPX	B-	C+	B+	Down	4.32	19.25	12.86	50.47	52.57	13.5	11.3	800-526-7384	Y
Goldman Sachs Blue Chip Fund Class R	GRGVX	B-	C+	B+	Down	4.10	18.92	12.11	47.74	47.91	13.45	11.3	800-526-7384	Y
Goldman Sachs Blue Chip Fund Class R6	GDEUX	B-	C+	B+	Down	4.32	19.25	12.84	50.59	52.72	13.5	11.3	800-526-7384	Y
Goldman Sachs Blue Chip Fund Institutional Class	GINGX	B-	C+	B+	Down	4.32	19.25	12.91	50.54	52.64	13.5	11.3	800-526-7384	Y
Goldman Sachs Blue Chip Fund Investor Class	GIRGX	B-	C+	B+	Down	4.32	19.25	12.76	50.07	51.59	13.5	11.3	800-526-7384	Y
Goldman Sachs Capital Growth Fund Class A	GSCGX	B-	C+	B		4.90	21.51	9.83	60.90	73.55	22.87	904.0	800-526-7384	Y
Goldman Sachs Capital Growth Fund Class C	GSPCX	B-	C+	B		4.70	21.05	9.13	57.46	67.23	14.03	904.0	800-526-7384	Y
Goldman Sachs Capital Growth Fund Class P	GGGPX	B-	C+	B	Down	4.99	21.79	10.32	61.69	74.40	26.26	904.0	800-526-7384	Y
Goldman Sachs Capital Growth Fund Class R	GSPRX	B-	C+	B		4.80	21.37	9.61	59.72	71.37	21.58	904.0	800-526-7384	Y
Goldman Sachs Capital Growth Fund Class R6	GSPUX	B-	C+	B		4.95	21.74	10.27	62.83	76.34	26.26	904.0	800-526-7384	Y
Goldman Sachs Capital Growth Fund Institutional Class	GSPIX	B-	C+	B		4.98	21.75	10.29	62.84	77.05	26.3	904.0	800-526-7384	Y
Goldman Sachs Capital Growth Fund Investor Class	GSPTX	B-	C+	B		4.94	21.66	10.13	62.10	75.75	23.36	904.0	800-526-7384	Y
Goldman Sachs Capital Growth Fund Service Class	GSPSX	B-	C+	B		4.88	21.45	9.74	60.41	72.66	21.68	904.0	800-526-7384	Y
Goldman Sachs Concentrated Growth Fund Class A	GCGAX	B-	C+	B	Down	5.47	24.78	11.03	58.26	68.26	17.52	149.1	800-526-7384	Y
Goldman Sachs Concentrated Growth Fund Class P	GACPX	B-	C+	B	Down	5.54	25.03	11.46	59.96	71.52	18.83	149.1	800-526-7384	Y
Goldman Sachs Concentrated Growth Fund Class R6	GCGUX	B-	C+	B	Down	5.54	24.95	11.45	59.91	71.50	18.83	149.1	800-526-7384	Y
Goldman Sachs Concentrated Growth Fund Institutional Class	GCRIX	B-	C+	B	Down	5.59	25.03	11.44	59.91	71.47	18.88	149.1	800-526-7384	Y
Goldman Sachs Concentrated Growth Fund Investor Class	GGCTX	B-	C+	B	Down	5.55	24.89	11.29	59.41	70.36	17.86	149.1	800-526-7384	Y
Goldman Sachs Flexible Cap Fund Class A	GALLX	B-	C+	B		4.48	20.48	9.37	54.13	66.74	11.88	18.6	800-526-7384	Y
Goldman Sachs Flexible Cap Fund Class P	GGZPX	B-	C+	B		4.64	20.65	9.77	55.75	69.92	12.85	18.6	800-526-7384	Y
Goldman Sachs Flexible Cap Fund Class R	GRLLX	B-	C+	B		4.41	20.23	9.09	52.96	64.64	11.35	18.6	800-526-7384	Y
Goldman Sachs Flexible Cap Fund Class R6	GFCUX	B-	C+	B		4.56	20.56	9.75	55.72	69.87	12.84	18.6	800-526-7384	Y
Goldman Sachs Flexible Cap Fund Institutional Class	GILLX	B-	C+	B		4.63	20.61	9.77	55.75	69.91	12.87	18.6	800-526-7384	Y
Goldman Sachs Flexible Cap Fund Investor Class	GSLLX	B-	C+	B		4.57	20.49	9.64	55.11	68.71	12.58	18.6	800-526-7384	Y
Goldman Sachs Strategic Growth Fund Class A	GGRAX	B-	C+	B	Down	4.52	23.23	10.28	62.44	77.26	9.23	164.7	800-526-7384	Y
Goldman Sachs Strategic Growth Fund Class P	GSPPX	B-	C+	B	Down	4.66	23.44	10.68	64.29	80.66	10.32	164.7	800-526-7384	Y
Goldman Sachs Strategic Growth Fund Class R	GSTRX	B-	C+	B	Down	4.48	23.05	9.94	61.28	75.20	8.86	164.7	800-526-7384	Y
Goldman Sachs Strategic Growth Fund Class R6	GGRUX	B-	C+	B	Down	4.55	23.41	10.65	64.45	80.73	10.33	164.7	800-526-7384	Y
Goldman Sachs Strategic Growth Fund Institutional Class	GSTIX	B-	C+	B	Down	4.54	23.36	10.61	64.30	80.67	10.35	164.7	800-526-7384	Y
Goldman Sachs Strategic Growth Fund Investor Class	GSTTX	B-	C+	B	Down	4.56	23.32	10.48	63.59	79.40	10.31	164.7	800-526-7384	Y
Government Street Equity Fund	GVEQX	B-	C	B	Up	4.13	17.10	7.91	41.95	47.38	76.19	57.8		Y
Great-West Large Cap Growth Fund Institutional Class	MXGSX	B-	B-	B	Down	6.54	24.79	13.96	73.98	90.36	10.73	784.2		Y
Great-West Large Cap Growth Fund Investor Class	MXLGX	B-	B-	B	Down	6.56	24.62	13.64	72.25	86.87	10.17	784.2		Y
Green Century Equity Fund Individual Investor Class	GCEQX	B-	C	B	Down	4.18	19.32	10.66	49.98	62.45	45.23	295.0	800-221-5519	Y
Green Century Equity Fund Institutional Class	GCEUX	B-	C	B	Down	4.26	19.50	11.01	50.53	63.05	45.17	295.0	800-221-5519	Y
Guggenheim RBP® Large-Cap Defensive Fund Class A	TVDAX	B-	C+	B		6.33	21.74	11.29	44.48	52.15	10.75	15.4	212-518-9290	Y
Guggenheim RBP® Large-Cap Defensive Fund Class C	TVDCX	B-	C+	B		6.13	21.40	10.54	41.36	46.95	10.38	15.4	212-518-9290	Y
Guggenheim RBP® Large-Cap Defensive Fund Class I	TVIDX	B-	C+	B		6.36	21.89	11.56	45.60	54.47	11.19	15.4	212-518-9290	Y
Guggenheim RBP® Large-Cap Defensive Fund Class P	TVFDX	B-	C+	B		6.32	21.73	11.22	44.48	52.67	11.09	15.4	212-518-9290	Y
Guggenheim RBP® Large-Cap Market Fund Class A	TVMAX	B-	C	B		4.89	22.82	9.14	51.51	54.74	10.71	15.4	212-518-9290	Y
Guggenheim RBP® Large-Cap Market Fund Class I	TVIMX	B-	C	B		4.95	22.90	9.43	52.60	57.13	11.43	15.4	212-518-9290	Y
Guggenheim RBP® Large-Cap Market Fund Class P	TVFMX	B-	C	B		4.83	22.77	9.15	51.25	55.10	11.05	15.4	212-518-9290	Y
GuideStone Funds Growth Equity Fund Institutional Class	GGEYX	B-	C+	B	Down	5.26	25.19	14.29	72.64	85.44	26.25	1,613	214-720-1171	Y
GuideStone Funds Growth Equity Fund Investor Class	GGEZX	B-	C+	B	Down	5.19	25.02	14.00	71.28	83.05	26.09	1,613	214-720-1171	Y
Harbor Strategic Growth Fund Administrative Class	HSRGX	B	B-	B		5.97	22.31	12.34	49.44	65.28	21.65	105.1	800-422-1050	Y
Harbor Strategic Growth Fund Institutional Class	MVSGX	B	B-	B		6.01	22.48	12.61	50.59	67.39	21.68	105.1	800-422-1050	Y
Harbor Strategic Growth Fund Investor Class	HISWX	B-	C+	B	Down	5.96	22.33	10.73	47.18	62.78	21.31	105.1	800-422-1050	Y

Category: US Equity Large Cap Growth (con't)

Fund Name	Ticker Symbol	RATINGS: Overall Rating	Reward Rating	Risk Rating	Recent Up/ Downgrade	TOTAL RETURNS & PERFORMANCE: 3-Month Total Return	6-Month Total Return	1-Year Total Return	3-Year Total Return	5-Year Total Return	ASSETS: NAV	Total Assets (MIL)	NEW INVESTORS: Telephone	Open to New Investors
Harbor Strategic Growth Fund Retirement Class	HNGSX	B	B-	B		6.06	22.52	12.69	50.90	67.74	21.7	105.1	800-422-1050	Y
Hartford Capital Appreciation HLS Fund Class IA	HIACX	B-	C+	B		4.77	22.43	9.46	49.51	49.94	48.46	4,447	888-843-7824	Y
Hartford Capital Appreciation HLS Fund Class IB	HIBCX	B-	C+	B	Up	4.70	22.26	9.19	48.40	48.07	47.66	4,447	888-843-7824	Y
Hartford Capital Appreciation HLS Fund Class IC	HCPCX	B-	C	B	Up	4.65	22.12	8.92	47.27	46.26	47.92	4,447	888-843-7824	Y
Hartford Growth Opportunities HLS Fund Class IA	HAGOX	B-	B-	B-	Down	6.08	30.13	12.61	72.05	100.93	43.44	1,655	888-843-7824	Y
Hartford Growth Opportunities HLS Fund Class IB	HBGOX	B-	B-	B-	Down	6.02	30.00	12.33	70.73	98.40	41.33	1,655	888-843-7824	Y
Hartford Growth Opportunities HLS Fund Class IC	HCGOX	B-	B-	B-	Down	5.95	29.81	12.06	69.49	95.99	42.19	1,655	888-843-7824	Y
Homestead Growth Fund	HNASX	B-	C+	B	Down	3.01	19.23	9.63	86.92	99.08	11.34	228.0		Y
HVIA Equity Fund Institutional Class	HVEIX	B-	C	B		4.12	21.13	11.78			14.13	19.5		Y
Ivy Accumulative Fund Class A	IATAX	B-	C	B		5.59	25.38	13.86	46.85	56.26	10.57	1,338		
Ivy Accumulative Fund Class I	IATIX	B-	C	B		5.65	25.44	14.07	47.78	57.97	10.65	1,338		Y
Ivy Accumulative Fund Class N	IATNX	B-	C	B		5.79	25.62	14.30	47.57	57.02	10.59	1,338		Y
Ivy Accumulative Fund Class R	IATLX	B-	C	B		5.60	25.14	13.51	45.52	54.07	10.55	1,338		Y
Ivy Accumulative Fund Class Y	IATYX	B-	C	B		5.59	25.23	13.87	46.87	56.28	10.57	1,338		Y
Ivy Large Cap Growth Fund Class A	WLGAX	B	B-	B		6.86	24.94	14.62	73.36	88.13	24.29	4,284		Y
Ivy Large Cap Growth Fund Class B	WLGBX	B-	B-	B	Down	6.65	24.38	13.61	68.80	79.94	17.8	4,284		
Ivy Large Cap Growth Fund Class C	WLGCX	B-	B-	B	Down	6.66	24.48	13.69	69.52	81.33	19.52	4,284		Y
Ivy Large Cap Growth Fund Class E	ILCEX	B	B-	B		6.83	24.90	14.50	73.01	87.78	24.22	4,284		Y
Ivy Large Cap Growth Fund Class I	IYGIX	B	B-	B		6.93	25.17	14.97	74.73	90.71	25.76	4,284		Y
Ivy Large Cap Growth Fund Class N	ILGRX	B	B-	B		6.92	25.14	14.99	75.39	91.99	25.93	4,284		Y
Ivy Large Cap Growth Fund Class R	WLGRX	B-	B-	B	Down	6.72	24.71	14.18	71.58	84.99	23.16	4,284		Y
Ivy Large Cap Growth Fund Class Y	WLGYX	B	B-	B		6.84	24.91	14.58	73.61	88.74	24.97	4,284		Y
Jackson Square Large-Cap Growth Fund Institutional Class	JSPIX	B-	C	B		7.62	21.39	10.86	54.91	60.65	11.86	121.1		Y
Jackson Square Large-Cap Growth Fund Investor Class	JSPJX	B-	C	B		7.46	21.14	10.52	53.61	58.51	11.8	121.1		Y
Jackson Square Large-Cap Growth Fund IS Class	DPLGX	B-	C	B		7.63	21.43	10.89	54.94	60.68	11.84	121.1		Y
Jackson Square Select 20 Growth Fund IS Class	DPCEX	B-	C	B		7.56	22.98	12.59	49.24	50.91	6.26	5.6		Y
Janus Henderson Forty Fund Class A	JDCAX	B-	C+	B	Down	6.00	24.43	12.53	68.42	99.62	36.21	12,447	877-335-2687	Y
Janus Henderson Forty Fund Class C	JACCX	B-	C+	B	Down	5.82	24.11	11.81	65.31	93.90	29.44	12,447	877-335-2687	Y
Janus Henderson Forty Fund Class D	JFRDX	B-	C+	B	Down	6.05	24.60	12.83	69.31	100.52	35.05	12,447	877-335-2687	Y
Janus Henderson Forty Fund Class I	JCAPX	B-	C+	B	Down	6.08	24.64	12.90	70.03	102.91	37.68	12,447	877-335-2687	Y
Janus Henderson Forty Fund Class N	JFRNX	B-	C+	B	Down	6.08	24.68	12.98	70.38	103.65	37.83	12,447	877-335-2687	Y
Janus Henderson Forty Fund Class R	JDCRX	B-	C+	B	Down	5.89	24.21	12.15	66.59	96.17	32.16	12,447	877-335-2687	Y
Janus Henderson Forty Fund Class S	JARTX	B-	C+	B	Down	5.95	24.36	12.41	67.86	98.80	34.71	12,447	877-335-2687	Y
Janus Henderson Forty Fund Class T	JACTX	B-	C+	B	Down	6.03	24.56	12.73	69.19	101.30	35.5	12,447	877-335-2687	Y
Janus Henderson Research Fund Class A	JRAAX	B-	C+	B		5.22	24.17	12.74	56.43	72.15	49.57	13,727	877-335-2687	Y
Janus Henderson Research Fund Class C	JRACX	B-	C+	B		5.05	23.75	11.95	53.26	66.30	46.15	13,727	877-335-2687	Y
Janus Henderson Research Fund Class D	JNRFX	B-	C+	B	Down	5.26	24.27	12.97	57.37	73.89	49.96	13,727	877-335-2687	
Janus Henderson Research Fund Class I	JRAIX	B-	C+	B	Down	5.29	24.33	13.05	57.71	74.53	49.87	13,727	877-335-2687	Y
Janus Henderson Research Fund Class N	JRANX	B-	C+	B	Down	5.29	24.36	13.13	58.06	75.21	49.87	13,727	877-335-2687	Y
Janus Henderson Research Fund Class R	JRARX	B-	C+	B		5.07	23.92	12.27	54.58	69.12	49.52	13,727	877-335-2687	Y
Janus Henderson Research Fund Class S	JRASX	B-	C+	B		5.15	24.05	12.55	55.73	70.92	48.74	13,727	877-335-2687	Y
Janus Henderson Research Fund Class T	JAMRX	B-	C+	B	Down	5.24	24.23	12.85	56.95	73.18	49.98	13,727	877-335-2687	Y
Janus Henderson U.S. Growth Opportunities Fund Class A	HGRAX	B-	C+	B	Down	5.26	24.36	15.91	51.81		16.18	28.3	877-335-2687	Y
Janus Henderson U.S. Growth Opportunities Fund Class C	HGRCX	B-	C+	B	Down	5.10	23.91	15.17	48.69		15.65	28.3	877-335-2687	Y
Janus Henderson U.S. Growth Opportunities Fund Class D	HGRDX	B-	C+	B	Down	5.28	24.42	16.21	52.82		16.35	28.3	877-335-2687	Y
Janus Henderson U.S. Growth Opportunities Fund Class I	HGRIX	B-	C+	B	Down	5.34	24.48	16.35	53.01		16.37	28.3	877-335-2687	Y
Janus Henderson U.S. Growth Opportunities Fund Class N	HGRRX	B-	C+	B	Down	5.35	24.54	16.39	52.73		16.34	28.3	877-335-2687	Y
Janus Henderson U.S. Growth Opportunities Fund Class S	HGRSX	B-	C+	B	Down	5.36	24.54	16.03	51.89		16.29	28.3	877-335-2687	Y
Janus Henderson U.S. Growth Opportunities Fund Class T	HGRTX	B-	C+	B	Down	5.28	24.37	16.07	52.63		16.33	28.3	877-335-2687	Y
Janus Henderson VIT Forty Portfolio Institutional Class	JACAX	B-	C+	B	Down	5.84	24.88	13.14	71.81	105.03	39.99	806.9	877-335-2687	Y
Janus Henderson VIT Forty Portfolio Service Class		B-	C+	B	Down	5.77	24.71	12.83	70.53	102.44	37.44	806.9	877-335-2687	Y
Janus Henderson VIT Research Portfolio Institutional Class	JAGRX	B-	C+	B	Down	5.30	24.39	13.24	58.03	75.08	37.09	496.8	877-335-2687	Y

Category: US Equity Large Cap Growth (con't)

Fund Name	Ticker Symbol	RATINGS: Overall Rating	Reward Rating	Risk Rating	Recent Up/ Downgrade	TOTAL RETURNS & PERFORMANCE: 3-Month Total Return	6-Month Total Return	1-Year Total Return	3-Year Total Return	5-Year Total Return	ASSETS: NAV	Total Assets (MIL)	NEW INVESTORS: Telephone	Open to New Investors
Janus Henderson VIT Research Portfolio Service Class		B-	C+	B	Down	5.25	24.22	12.98	56.88	72.90	36.06	496.8	877-335-2687	Y
Jensen Quality Growth Fund Class I	JENIX	B	C+	B+		2.55	18.50	14.77	56.62	85.75	50.69	7,522	800-992-4144	Y
Jensen Quality Growth Fund Class J	JENSX	B	C+	B+		2.49	18.35	14.47	55.43	83.41	50.69	7,522	800-992-4144	Y
Jensen Quality Growth Fund Class Y	JENYX	B	C+	B+		2.57	18.54	14.85	56.80	85.03	50.68	7,522	800-992-4144	Y
Jensen Quality Growth FundClass R	JENRX	B	C+	B+		2.38	18.13	14.06	53.70	80.11	50.46	7,522	800-992-4144	Y
JNL/American Funds Growth Fund A		B-	C	B	Down	2.81	17.32	5.56	61.78	76.39	24.85	926.4		Y
JNL/American Funds Growth Fund Class I		B-	C	B		2.92	17.48	5.93	62.61	77.37	25	926.4		Y
JNL/BlackRock Large Cap Select Growth Fund Class A		B-	C+	B	Down	5.83	24.97	10.25	77.97	94.54	42.09	3,738		Y
JNL/BlackRock Large Cap Select Growth Fund Class I		B-	C+	B	Down	5.92	25.14	10.61	79.35	96.82	44	3,738		Y
JNL/Mellon Capital Nasdaq® 100 Index Fund Class A		B-	C+	B		4.07	22.37	9.47	78.24	92.59	27.35	2,980		Y
JNL/Mellon Capital Nasdaq® 100 Index Fund Class I		B-	C+	B	Down	4.16	22.54	9.86	79.65	95.03	17.99	2,980		Y
JNL/T. Rowe Price Established Growth Fund Class A		B-	C	B	Down	3.71	21.57	8.16	72.20	88.63	45.76	9,825		Y
JNL/T. Rowe Price Established Growth Fund Class I		B-	C+	B	Down	3.80	21.77	8.50	73.55	90.86	47.42	9,825		Y
JNL/Vanguard Capital Growth Fund Class A		B-	C	B	Up	1.88	12.92	5.41	59.29	68.72	11.88	348.6		Y
JNL/Vanguard Capital Growth Fund Class I		B-	C	B		1.87	12.94	5.75	60.83	71.37	11.95	348.6		Y
John Hancock ESG All Cap Core Fund Class I	JHKIX	B-	C	B		4.07	19.51	10.19	49.91		13.29	27.1	800-225-5913	Y
John Hancock ESG All Cap Core Fund Class R6	JHKRX	B-	C	B		4.07	19.51	10.33	50.37		13.29	27.1	800-225-5913	Y
John Hancock Funds II Blue Chip Growth Fund Class 1	JIBCX	B-	C+	B	Down	4.00	21.81	10.11	80.48	98.79	41.27	4,014	800-225-5913	Y
John Hancock Funds II Blue Chip Growth Fund Class A	JBGAX	B-	C+	B	Down	3.91	21.60	9.76	78.70	95.86	40.64	4,014	800-225-5913	Y
John Hancock Funds II Blue Chip Growth Fund Class C	JBGCX	B-	C+	B	Down	3.71	21.15	8.94	74.78	88.75	39.06	4,014	800-225-5913	Y
John Hancock Funds II Blue Chip Growth Fund Class NAV	JHBCX	B-	C+	B	Down	4.02	21.83	10.17	80.76	99.28	41.35	4,014	800-225-5913	Y
John Hancock U.S. Global Leaders Growth Fund Class A	USGLX	B	B-	B+		5.10	23.95	18.72	62.31	86.65	51.02	1,524	800-225-5913	Y
John Hancock U.S. Global Leaders Growth Fund Class B	USLBX	B	B-	B+		4.92	23.49	17.87	58.71	79.79	41.79	1,524	800-225-5913	
John Hancock U.S. Global Leaders Growth Fund Class C	USLCX	B	B-	B+		4.91	23.47	17.86	58.67	79.74	41.81	1,524	800-225-5913	Y
John Hancock U.S. Global Leaders Growth Fund Class I	USLIX	B	B-	B+		5.16	24.10	19.01	63.52	89.06	55.34	1,524	800-225-5913	Y
John Hancock U.S. Global Leaders Growth Fund Class R2	USLYX	B	B-	B+		5.06	23.88	18.57	61.61	85.32	53.95	1,524	800-225-5913	Y
John Hancock U.S. Global Leaders Growth Fund Class R6	UGLSX	B	B-	B+		5.19	24.17	19.15	64.02	90.05	55.73	1,524	800-225-5913	Y
John Hancock U.S. Quality Growth Fund Class A	JSGAX	B-	B-	B	Down	5.60	24.02	12.42	66.06	81.08	17.14	850.6	800-225-5913	Y
John Hancock U.S. Quality Growth Fund Class C	JSGCX	B-	C+	B	Down	5.41	23.54	11.61	62.36	74.56	16.74	850.6	800-225-5913	Y
John Hancock U.S. Quality Growth Fund Class I	JSGIX	B-	B-	B	Down	5.62	24.13	12.69	67.27	83.47	17.28	850.6	800-225-5913	Y
John Hancock U.S. Quality Growth Fund Class NAV		B-	B-	B	Down	5.67	24.26	12.84	67.86	84.85	17.31	850.6	800-225-5913	Y
John Hancock U.S. Quality Growth Fund Class R2	JSGRX	B-	B-	B	Down	5.54	23.90	12.32	65.46	80.64	17.31	850.6	800-225-5913	Y
John Hancock U.S. Quality Growth Fund Class R4	JHSGX	B-	B-	B	Down	5.61	23.99	12.56	66.73	82.45	17.31	850.6	800-225-5913	Y
John Hancock U.S. Quality Growth Fund Class R6	JSGTX	B-	B-	B	Down	5.67	24.24	12.83	67.89	84.88	17.32	850.6	800-225-5913	Y
JPMorgan Equity Focus Fund Class A	JPFAX	B-	C+	B		4.50	19.26	9.22	57.54	62.42	30.15	106.8	800-480-4111	Y
JPMorgan Equity Focus Fund Class C	JPFCX	B-	C	B		4.38	18.99	8.67	55.19	58.40	29.01	106.8	800-480-4111	Y
JPMorgan Equity Focus Fund Class I	JPFSX	B-	C+	B		4.57	19.43	9.50	58.76	64.50	30.6	106.8	800-480-4111	Y
JPMorgan Equity Focus Fund Class R6	JPFRX	B-	C+	B		4.63	19.57	9.68	59.02	64.77	30.48	106.8	800-480-4111	Y
JPMorgan Large Cap Growth Fund Class A	OLGAX	B-	B-	B-	Down	7.46	29.58	13.66	87.39	101.02	41.87	15,920	800-480-4111	Y
JPMorgan Large Cap Growth Fund Class C	OLGCX	B-	B-	B-	Down	7.33	29.26	13.11	84.58	96.07	32.33	15,920	800-480-4111	Y
JPMorgan Large Cap Growth Fund Class I	SEEGX	B-	B-	B-	Down	7.54	29.72	13.95	88.55	102.97	42.46	15,920	800-480-4111	Y
JPMorgan Large Cap Growth Fund Class R2	JLGZX	B-	B-	B-	Down	7.40	29.39	13.38	85.89	98.46	40.32	15,920	800-480-4111	Y
JPMorgan Large Cap Growth Fund Class R3	JLGPX	B-	B-	B-	Down	7.45	29.57	13.67	87.16	100.46	42.1	15,920	800-480-4111	Y
JPMorgan Large Cap Growth Fund Class R4	JLGQX	B-	B-	B-	Down	7.52	29.73	13.95	88.52	102.93	42.45	15,920	800-480-4111	Y
JPMorgan Large Cap Growth Fund Class R5	JLGRX	B-	B-	B-	Down	7.57	29.86	14.14	89.55	104.83	43.44	15,920	800-480-4111	Y
JPMorgan Large Cap Growth Fund Class R6	JLGMX	B-	B-	B-	Down	7.59	29.91	14.23	90.08	105.80	43.78	15,920	800-480-4111	Y
JPMorgan Tax Aware Equity Fund Class A	JPEAX	B-	C	B		4.37	19.09	8.90	52.98	62.63	35.81	1,278	800-480-4111	Y
JPMorgan Tax Aware Equity Fund Class R6	JPELX	B-	C+	B		4.50	19.41	9.40	55.07	66.26	36.02	1,278	800-480-4111	Y
Laudus U.S. Large Cap Growth Fund	LGILX	B-	C+	B	Down	5.91	25.04	10.48	78.92	95.11	22.57	2,384	888-832-4386	Y
LKCM Equity Fund Institutional Class	LKEQX	B-	C	B	Down	4.10	20.63	9.87	51.25	53.24	27.89	361.1	800-688-5526	Y
Logan Capital Large Cap Growth Fund Institutional Class	LGNGX	B-	B-	B-		5.13	29.99	10.06	72.81	82.15	25.57	35.8		Y
Logan Capital Large Cap Growth Fund Investor Class	LGNHX	B-	B-	B-		5.06	29.81	9.78	71.76	80.02	25.12	35.8		Y

Category: US Equity Large Cap Growth (con't)

Fund Name	Ticker Symbol	RATINGS: Overall Rating	Reward Rating	Risk Rating	Recent Up/ Downgrade	TOTAL RETURNS & PERFORMANCE: 3-Month Total Return	6-Month Total Return	1-Year Total Return	3-Year Total Return	5-Year Total Return	ASSETS: NAV	Total Assets (MIL)	NEW INVESTORS: Telephone	Open to New Investors
Loomis Sayles Growth Fund Class A	LGRRX	B-	C+	B	Down	5.10	22.68	15.13	63.47	93.66	16.28	8,854	800-862-4863	Y
Loomis Sayles Growth Fund Class C	LGRCX	B-	C+	B	Down	4.89	22.13	14.24	59.81	86.47	14.79	8,854	800-862-4863	Y
Loomis Sayles Growth Fund Class N	LGRNX	B-	C+	B	Down	5.19	22.83	15.48	65.16	96.80	17.43	8,854	800-862-4863	Y
Loomis Sayles Growth Fund Class Y	LSGRX	B-	C+	B	Down	5.18	22.81	15.43	64.71	95.99	17.44	8,854	800-862-4863	Y
Madison Investors Fund Class A	MNVAX	B	B-	A-		5.52	20.83	18.19	54.44	72.17	22.91	329.3	800-767-0300	Y
Madison Investors Fund Class R6	MNVRX	B	B-	A-		5.60	21.11	18.72	56.43	75.95	23.17	329.3	800-767-0300	Y
Madison Investors Fund Class Y	MINVX	B	B-	A-		5.56	20.96	18.51	55.52	74.28	22.96	329.3	800-767-0300	Y
MainStay Large Cap Growth Fund Class I	MLAIX	B-	C+	B	Down	4.64	24.36	11.86	73.98	88.20	10.36	11,931	800-624-6782	Y
MainStay Large Cap Growth Fund Class R6	MLRSX	B-	C+	B	Down	4.60	24.43	11.98	74.53	89.14	10.44	11,931	800-624-6782	Y
Manning & Napier Equity Series Class S	EXEYX	B-	C+	B	Down	4.13	21.38	9.04	55.27	51.38	13.34	65.6	585-325-6880	Y
Manning & Napier Equity Series Class W	MEYWX	B-	C+	B		4.36	21.65	9.28	55.61	51.72	13.38	65.6	585-325-6880	Y
MassMutual Select Blue Chip Growth Administrative Cls	MBCLX	B-	C+	B	Down	4.41	22.09	12.24	74.32	95.45	22.49	3,215		Y
MassMutual Select Blue Chip Growth Fund Class A	MBCGX	B-	C+	B	Down	4.37	21.96	12.00	73.01	93.06	21.49	3,215		Y
MassMutual Select Blue Chip Growth Fund Class I	MBCZX	B-	C+	B	Down	4.52	22.31	12.59	75.90	98.49	23.08	3,215		Y
MassMutual Select Blue Chip Growth Fund Class R3	MBCNX	B-	C+	B	Down	4.33	21.82	11.83	72.29	91.64	19.98	3,215		Y
MassMutual Select Blue Chip Growth Fund Class R4	MBGFX	B-	C+	B	Down	4.38	22.02	12.09	73.58	94.16	21.44	3,215		Y
MassMutual Select Blue Chip Growth Fund Class R5	MBCSX	B-	C+	B	Down	4.48	22.28	12.53	75.39	97.48	23.05	3,215		Y
MassMutual Select Blue Chip Growth Fund Service Class	MBCYX	B-	C+	B	Down	4.48	22.20	12.41	74.96	96.56	22.84	3,215		Y
MassMutual Select Fundamental Growth Administrative Cls	MOTLX	B-	C+	B	Down	3.59	21.59	11.51	61.49	80.22	7.49	140.2		Y
MassMutual Select Fundamental Growth Fund Class A	MOTAX	B-	C+	B	Down	3.66	21.47	11.33	60.35	78.29	7.07	140.2		Y
MassMutual Select Fundamental Growth Fund Class I	MOTZX	B-	C+	B	Down	3.66	21.84	11.84	62.92	82.99	7.92	140.2		Y
MassMutual Select Fundamental Growth Fund Class R3	MOTNX	B-	C+	B	Down	3.54	21.32	11.06	59.43	76.62	6.43	140.2		Y
MassMutual Select Fundamental Growth Fund Class R4	MFGFX	B-	C+	B	Down	3.56	21.42	11.34	60.94	78.96	6.97	140.2		Y
MassMutual Select Fundamental Growth Fund Class R5	MOTCX	B-	C+	B	Down	3.78	21.74	11.82	62.64	82.30	7.95	140.2		Y
MassMutual Select Fundamental Growth Fund Service Class	MOTYX	B-	C+	B	Down	3.75	21.69	11.71	62.16	81.43	7.74	140.2		Y
Meridian Enhanced Equity Fund® A Class	MRAEX	B-	B-	C		8.01	31.42	10.92	81.41	81.05	18.32	64.5	800-446-6662	Y
Meridian Enhanced Equity Fund® Class C	MRCEX	B-	B-	C		7.83	31.00	10.31	78.92	76.40	18.17	64.5	800-446-6662	Y
Meridian Enhanced Equity Fund® Investor Class	MRIEX	B-	B	C		8.10	31.61	11.27	82.46	82.92	18.4	64.5	800-446-6662	Y
Meridian Enhanced Equity Fund® Legacy Class	MEIFX	B-	B	C+		8.09	31.54	11.26	83.40	84.04	18.43	64.5	800-446-6662	
MFS Growth Fund Class A	MFEGX	B	B-	B		6.48	26.49	14.56	72.41	93.83	110.16	22,365	877-960-6077	Y
MFS Growth Fund Class B	MEGBX	B-	B-	B	Down	6.29	26.02	13.70	68.57	86.66	87.63	22,365	877-960-6077	Y
MFS Growth Fund Class C	MFECX	B-	B-	B	Down	6.29	26.03	13.70	68.57	86.62	86.92	22,365	877-960-6077	Y
MFS Growth Fund Class I	MFEIX	B	B-	B		6.56	26.65	14.84	73.69	96.22	117.53	22,365	877-960-6077	Y
MFS Growth Fund Class R1	MFELX	B-	B-	B	Down	6.29	26.02	13.70	68.56	86.65	87.25	22,365	877-960-6077	Y
MFS Growth Fund Class R2	MEGRX	B	B-	B		6.43	26.34	14.27	71.10	91.36	103.7	22,365	877-960-6077	Y
MFS Growth Fund Class R3	MFEHX	B	B-	B		6.48	26.49	14.55	72.38	93.75	109.59	22,365	877-960-6077	Y
MFS Growth Fund Class R4	MFEJX	B	B-	B		6.55	26.66	14.84	73.67	96.19	114.23	22,365	877-960-6077	Y
MFS Growth Fund Class R6	MFEKX	B	B-	B		6.57	26.71	14.94	74.17	97.15	117.89	22,365	877-960-6077	Y
MFS Massachusetts Investors Growth Stock Fund Class 529A	EISTX	B	B	B+		5.32	24.84	18.29	65.49	81.16	30.85	7,515	877-960-6077	Y
MFS Massachusetts Investors Growth Stock Fund Class 529B	EMIVX	B	B-	B		5.06	24.25	17.36	62.06	74.67	25.92	7,515	877-960-6077	Y
MFS Massachusetts Investors Growth Stock Fund Class 529C	EMICX	B	B-	B		5.03	24.26	17.26	61.56	74.13	25.66	7,515	877-960-6077	Y
MFS Massachusetts Investors Growth Stock Fund Class A	MIGFX	B	B	B+		5.33	24.88	18.34	65.68	81.49	31.37	7,515	877-960-6077	Y
MFS Massachusetts Investors Growth Stock Fund Class B	MIGBX	B	B-	B		5.09	24.35	17.39	61.94	74.75	26.81	7,515	877-960-6077	Y
MFS Massachusetts Investors Growth Stock Fund Class C	MIGDX	B	B-	B		5.09	24.33	17.36	61.91	74.65	26.62	7,515	877-960-6077	Y
MFS Massachusetts Investors Growth Stock Fund Class I	MGTIX	B	B	B+		5.40	25.04	18.63	66.91	83.68	32.35	7,515	877-960-6077	Y
MFS Massachusetts Investors Growth Stock Fund Class R1	MIGMX	B	B-	B		5.09	24.32	17.37	61.85	74.64	26.22	7,515	877-960-6077	Y
MFS Massachusetts Investors Growth Stock Fund Class R2	MIRGX	B	B	B+		5.25	24.70	18.01	64.40	79.11	30.44	7,515	877-960-6077	Y
MFS Massachusetts Investors Growth Stock Fund Class R3	MIGHX	B	B	B+		5.29	24.84	18.28	65.62	81.32	31	7,515	877-960-6077	Y
MFS Massachusetts Investors Growth Stock Fund Class R4	MIGKX	B	B	B+		5.40	25.02	18.60	66.86	83.64	31.62	7,515	877-960-6077	Y
MFS Massachusetts Investors Growth Stock Fund Class R6	MIGNX	B	B	B+		5.43	25.06	18.70	67.40	84.61	32.38	7,515	877-960-6077	Y
Monetta Core Growth Fund	MYIFX	B-	C	B		3.88	20.31	8.11	53.59	62.51	22.21	90.1	800-684-3416	Y
Monteagle Informed Investor Growth Fund Class I	MIIFX	B-	C	B+		2.73	9.06	4.10	30.60	41.31	10.5	10.6		Y

Category: US Equity Large Cap Growth (con't)

Fund Name	Ticker Symbol	Overall Rating	Reward Rating	Risk Rating	Recent Up/ Downgrade	3-Month Total Return	6-Month Total Return	1-Year Total Return	3-Year Total Return	5-Year Total Return	NAV	Total Assets (MIL)	Telephone	Open to New Investors
		RATINGS				TOTAL RETURNS & PERFORMANCE					ASSETS		NEW INVESTORS	
Morgan Stanley Insight Fund Class A	CPOAX	B-	B-	B	Up	9.05	38.27	25.76	130.63	143.84	44.87	2,027	855-332-5306	Y
Morgan Stanley Insight Fund Class C	MSCMX	B-	B-	B	Up	8.85	37.81	24.88	125.49	134.85	31.53	2,027	855-332-5306	Y
Morgan Stanley Insight Fund Class I	CPODX	B	B-	B	Up	9.11	38.51	26.12	132.71	147.74	49.96	2,027	855-332-5306	Y
Morgan Stanley Insight Fund Class IS	MCRTX	B	B-	B	Up	9.11	38.47	26.14	133.01	148.41	50.21	2,027	855-332-5306	Y
Morgan Stanley Insight Fund Class L	CPOCX	B-	B-	B	Up	8.93	37.98	25.22	127.18	137.75	32.01	2,027	855-332-5306	
Morgan Stanley Inst Fund, Inc. Advantage Portfolio Cls A	MAPPX	B	B	B		7.18	27.42	16.31	78.58	109.83	25.97	397.1	855-332-5306	Y
Morgan Stanley Inst Fund, Inc. Advantage Portfolio Cls C	MSPRX	B	B-	B		7.01	26.98	15.43	74.80	102.41	25.32	397.1	855-332-5306	Y
Morgan Stanley Inst Fund, Inc. Advantage Portfolio Cls I	MPAIX	B	B	B		7.26	27.63	16.65	80.39	113.42	26.56	397.1	855-332-5306	
Morgan Stanley Inst Fund, Inc. Advantage Portfolio Cls IS	MADSX	B	B	B		7.29	27.61	16.70	80.61	113.85	26.62	397.1	855-332-5306	Y
Morgan Stanley Inst Fund, Inc. Advantage Portfolio Cls L	MAPLX	B	B	B		7.25	27.56	16.51	79.76	112.32	26.47	397.1	855-332-5306	
Morgan Stanley Inst Fund, Inc. Growth Portfolio Cls A	MSEGX	B-	C+	B-		7.16	29.41	15.15	102.15	122.83	50.69	7,525	855-332-5306	Y
Morgan Stanley Inst Fund, Inc. Growth Portfolio Cls I	MSEQX	B-	C+	B-		7.23	29.57	15.45	103.81	125.88	53.49	7,525	855-332-5306	Y
Morgan Stanley Inst Fund, Inc. Growth Portfolio Cls IR	MGHRX	B-	C+	B-		7.26	29.61	15.54	103.98	126.06	53.88	7,525	855-332-5306	Y
Morgan Stanley Inst Fund, Inc. Growth Portfolio Cls IS	MGRPX	B-	C+	B-		7.26	29.61	15.54	104.29	126.91	53.88	7,525	855-332-5306	Y
Natixis Funds Trust I U.S. Equity Opportunities Cls A	NEFSX	B-	C	B		4.94	21.26	8.17	58.76	76.64	36.26	998.7	800-862-4863	Y
Natixis Funds Trust I U.S. Equity Opportunities Cls N	NESNX	B-	C	B		5.05	21.50	8.57	60.03	78.05	42.81	998.7	800-862-4863	Y
Natixis Funds Trust I U.S. Equity Opportunities Cls Y	NESYX	B-	C	B		5.01	21.41	8.46	59.97	78.89	42.74	998.7	800-862-4863	Y
Neuberger Berman Guardian Fund Class Institutional	NGDLX	B-	C+	B	Up	5.82	22.32	8.56	52.39	56.39	17.81	1,242	212-476-9000	Y
Nicholas Fund	NICSX	B-	C	B		5.33	22.64	16.19	43.00	49.94	66.58	2,826	800-544-6547	Y
NorthQuest Capital Fund	NQCFX	B-	C+	B	Down	2.35	22.22	12.10	48.78	58.42	18.26	4.6		Y
Nuveen Winslow Large-Cap Growth Fund Class R6	NWCFX	B-	C+	B	Down	4.63	24.20	11.76	74.92	90.83	41.51	725.9	312-917-8146	Y
Old Westbury All Cap Core Fund	OWACX	B-	B-	B		5.95	22.33	11.46	52.26	44.22	18.51	1,989	212-708-9100	Y
Optimum Large Cap Growth Fund Class A	OALGX	B-	C	B	Down	4.31	21.90	10.32	68.40	82.31	17.42	1,728		Y
Optimum Large Cap Growth Fund Class C	OCLGX	B-	C	B	Down	4.16	21.48	9.58	64.73	75.65	14.25	1,728		Y
Optimum Large Cap Growth Fund Institutional Class	OILGX	B-	C	B	Down	4.41	22.12	10.67	69.73	84.68	18.93	1,728		Y
PACE Large Co Growth Equity Investments Class A	PLAAX	B-	C+	B		6.99	23.87	11.68	58.74	70.98	23.87	1,217	212-882-5586	Y
PACE Large Co Growth Equity Investments Class P	PCLCX	B-	C+	B		7.08	24.00	11.99	59.96	73.13	24.95	1,217	212-882-5586	Y
PACE Large Co Growth Equity Investments Class Y	PLAYX	B-	C+	B		7.10	24.02	12.02	60.03	73.28	25.19	1,217	212-882-5586	Y
Parnassus Fund	PARNX	B-	C	B		4.26	21.15	11.08	47.26	52.30	48.68	951.8	999-350-5	Y
Parnassus Fund Institutional Shares	PFPRX	B-	C	B		4.28	21.24	11.27	47.94	53.25	48.69	951.8	999-350-5	Y
Pax ESG Beta Quality Fund Class A	PXGAX	B-	C	B+	Down	2.83	16.33	9.08	44.97	55.29	19.88	224.1	800-767-1729	Y
Pax ESG Beta Quality Fund Individual Investor Class	PXWGX	B-	C	B+	Down	2.82	16.28	9.05	44.95	55.25	19.93	224.1	800-767-1729	Y
Pax ESG Beta Quality Fund Institutional Class	PWGIX	B-	C	B+	Down	2.90	16.45	9.33	46.09	57.24	20.53	224.1	800-767-1729	Y
PF Growth Fund Class P		B	B-	B		6.69	27.24	15.02	75.02	97.88	29	185.9	800-722-2333	Y
PGIM Jennison Diversified Growth Fund-Class A	TBDAX	B-	C	B		3.74	20.81	7.30	60.61	66.55	13.29	243.8	800-225-1852	Y
PGIM Jennison Diversified Growth Fund-Class R6	TBDQX	B-	C	B		3.74	21.01	7.56	61.12	67.08	13.3	243.8	800-225-1852	Y
PGIM Jennison Diversified Growth Fund-Class Z	TBDZX	B-	C	B		3.74	21.01	7.56	61.12	67.08	13.3	243.8	800-225-1852	Y
Pioneer Disciplined Growth Fund Class A	PINDX	B-	C+	B	Down	4.72	23.47	11.23	54.25	67.53	16.83	1,318	617-742-7825	Y
Pioneer Disciplined Growth Fund Class C	INDCX	B-	C+	B		4.51	22.94	10.32	50.50	60.79	14.36	1,318	617-742-7825	Y
Pioneer Disciplined Growth Fund Class Y	INYDX	B-	C+	B	Down	4.78	23.57	11.38	55.22	69.55	17.3	1,318	617-742-7825	Y
Pioneer Fundamental Growth Fund Class A	PIGFX	B	C+	B		4.58	20.74	14.39	53.58	73.73	25.32	6,012	617-742-7825	Y
Pioneer Fundamental Growth Fund Class C	FUNCX	B	C+	B		4.46	20.38	13.72	50.56	68.07	22.91	6,012	617-742-7825	Y
Pioneer Fundamental Growth Fund Class K Shares	PFGKX	B	B-	B		4.70	21.00	14.92	55.60	77.59	25.35	6,012	617-742-7825	Y
Pioneer Fundamental Growth Fund Class R	PFGRX	B	C+	B		4.53	20.61	14.10	52.22	71.13	24.87	6,012	617-742-7825	Y
Pioneer Fundamental Growth Fund Class Y	FUNYX	B	B-	B		4.70	20.95	14.79	55.15	76.57	25.57	6,012	617-742-7825	Y
Polen Growth Fund Institutional Class	POLIX	B	B	B+		5.82	24.43	18.75	75.80	116.68	31.42	3,924	561-241-2425	Y
Polen Growth Fund Investor Class	POLRX	B	B	B		5.77	24.30	18.44	74.45	113.87	30.79	3,924	561-241-2425	Y
Praxis Growth Index Fund Class A	MGNDX	B-	C+	B	Down	4.66	21.15	12.28	61.68	80.67	26.48	301.1		Y
Praxis Growth Index Fund Class I	MMDEX	B-	B-	B	Down	4.74	21.37	12.66	63.61	84.25	26.71	301.1		Y
Principal Blue Chip Fund Class A	PBLAX	B	B	B		7.01	26.79	18.23	77.45	95.92	25.03	4,088	800-787-1621	Y
Principal Blue Chip Fund Class C	PBLCX	B	B	B		6.83	26.36	17.40	73.48	88.60	23.92	4,088	800-787-1621	Y
Principal Blue Chip Fund Class J	PBCJX	B	B	B		7.01	26.84	18.35	78.46	98.81	25.33	4,088	800-787-1621	Y

Category: US Equity Large Cap Growth (con't)

Fund Name	Ticker Symbol	RATINGS: Overall Rating	Reward Rating	Risk Rating	Recent Up/ Downgrade	TOTAL RETURNS & PERFORMANCE: 3-Month Total Return	6-Month Total Return	1-Year Total Return	3-Year Total Return	5-Year Total Return	ASSETS: NAV	Total Assets (MIL)	NEW INVESTORS: Telephone	Open to New Investors
Principal Blue Chip Fund Class R-3	PGBEX	B	B	B		6.99	26.68	18.08	76.86	96.38	25.07	4,088	800-787-1621	Y
Principal Blue Chip Fund Class R-4	PGBFX	B	B	B		7.04	26.84	18.28	77.93	98.21	25.23	4,088	800-787-1621	Y
Principal Blue Chip Fund Class R-5	PGBGX	B	B	B		7.06	26.91	18.42	78.47	99.29	25.32	4,088	800-787-1621	Y
Principal Blue Chip Fund Class R-6	PGBHX	B	B	B		7.10	27.01	18.72	79.67	100.75	25.48	4,088	800-787-1621	Y
Principal Blue Chip Fund Institutional Class	PBCKX	B	B	B		7.11	26.99	18.63	79.54	100.61	25.45	4,088	800-787-1621	Y
Principal LargeCap Growth Fund I Class A	PLGAX	B-	C+	B	Down	4.25	23.17	12.76	76.12	90.10	15.2	9,006	800-787-1621	Y
Principal LargeCap Growth Fund I Class J	PLGJX	B-	C+	B	Down	4.28	23.39	12.99	77.74	92.62	12.66	9,006	800-787-1621	Y
Principal LargeCap Growth Fund I Class R-6	PLCGX	B-	C+	B	Down	4.37	23.45	13.23	78.74	95.05	15.74	9,006	800-787-1621	Y
Principal LargeCap Growth Fund I Institutional Class	PLGIX	B-	C+	B	Down	4.30	23.43	13.12	78.46	94.84	15.75	9,006	800-787-1621	Y
Principal LargeCap Growth Fund I R-1 Class	PCRSX	B-	C+	B	Down	4.11	22.85	12.22	74.10	86.84	13.17	9,006	800-787-1621	Y
Principal LargeCap Growth Fund I R-2 Class	PPUNX	B-	C+	B	Down	4.22	23.01	12.38	74.98	88.22	12.83	9,006	800-787-1621	Y
Principal LargeCap Growth Fund I R-3 Class	PPUMX	B-	C+	B	Down	4.20	23.10	12.61	75.84	89.87	14.12	9,006	800-787-1621	Y
Principal LargeCap Growth Fund I R-4 Class	PPUSX	B-	C+	B	Down	4.25	23.18	12.80	76.88	91.67	14.45	9,006	800-787-1621	Y
Principal LargeCap Growth Fund I R-5 Class	PPUPX	B-	C+	B	Down	4.28	23.28	12.93	77.43	92.84	15.09	9,006	800-787-1621	Y
ProFunds Large Cap Growth Fund Investor Class	LGPIX	B-	C+	B		4.07	20.29	10.01	54.53	68.51	95.02	36.0	614-470-8626	Y
ProFunds Large Cap Growth Fund Service Class	LGPSX	B-	C+	B		3.81	19.70	8.93	49.97	60.35	79.77	36.0	614-470-8626	Y
Provident Trust Strategy Fund	PROVX	B-	C+	B	Down	2.55	14.46	6.27	57.58	71.53	15.67	179.4	855-739-9950	Y
Putnam Growth Opportunities Fund Class A	POGAX	B	B-	B		6.43	25.50	15.78	80.39	89.48	37.05	5,747	617-292-1000	Y
Putnam Growth Opportunities Fund Class B	POGBX	B	B-	B		6.23	25.07	14.94	76.41	82.52	30.83	5,747	617-292-1000	Y
Putnam Growth Opportunities Fund Class C	POGCX	B	B-	B		6.25	25.06	14.95	76.41	82.51	31.43	5,747	617-292-1000	Y
Putnam Growth Opportunities Fund Class M	PGOMX	B	B-	B		6.27	25.22	15.20	77.70	84.78	33.01	5,747	617-292-1000	Y
Putnam Growth Opportunities Fund Class R	PGORX	B	B-	B		6.36	25.39	15.52	79.10	87.10	35.6	5,747	617-292-1000	Y
Putnam Growth Opportunities Fund Class R5	PGODX	B	B-	B		6.50	25.71	16.12	82.01	92.29	39.11	5,747	617-292-1000	Y
Putnam Growth Opportunities Fund Class R6	PGOEX	B	B-	B		6.52	25.76	16.24	82.59	93.24	39	5,747	617-292-1000	Y
Putnam Growth Opportunities Fund Class Y	PGOYX	B	B-	B		6.50	25.70	16.10	81.78	91.88	38.78	5,747	617-292-1000	Y
Putnam Sustainable Leaders Fund Class A	PNOPX	B	B-	B		6.52	26.07	15.45	74.46	81.30	92.99	4,727	617-292-1000	Y
Putnam Sustainable Leaders Fund Class B	PNOBX	B	B-	B		6.33	25.58	14.59	70.57	74.63	68.68	4,727	617-292-1000	Y
Putnam Sustainable Leaders Fund Class C	PNOCX	B	B-	B		6.34	25.59	14.61	70.59	74.62	76.06	4,727	617-292-1000	Y
Putnam Sustainable Leaders Fund Class M	PNOMX	B	B-	B		6.39	25.75	14.88	71.86	76.81	78.02	4,727	617-292-1000	Y
Putnam Sustainable Leaders Fund Class R	PNORX	B	B-	B		6.47	25.90	15.17	73.15	79.05	89.28	4,727	617-292-1000	Y
Putnam Sustainable Leaders Fund Class R6 Shares	PSLGX	B	B-	B		6.63	26.30	15.89	75.18	82.04	100.88	4,727	617-292-1000	Y
Putnam Sustainable Leaders Fund Class Y	PNOYX	B	B-	B		6.60	26.23	15.76	75.78	83.59	100.65	4,727	617-292-1000	Y
Rational Dynamic Brands Fund Class A	HSUAX	B-	C	B		3.22	13.91	5.42	39.61	23.66	27.18	31.6	800-253-0412	Y
Rational Dynamic Brands Fund Class C	HSUCX	B-	C	B		2.98	13.28	4.70	37.05	20.17	24.48	31.6	800-253-0412	Y
Rational Dynamic Brands Fund Institutional Class	HSUTX	B-	C	B		3.24	14.06	5.69	40.65	25.24	38.77	31.6	800-253-0412	Y
RiverPark Large Growth Fund Class Institutional	RPXIX	B-	C+	B		7.38	25.15	9.87	70.12	61.47	22.84	53.9	888-564-4517	Y
RMB Dividend Growth Fund Class I	RMBDX	B	C+	B+		4.56	19.28	13.12	47.24	61.72	14.13	35.6		Y
RMB Fund Class A	RMBHX	B	B-	B		5.20	24.92	14.71	59.37	55.95	25.86	101.6		Y
RMB Fund Class C	RMBJX	B	B-	B		5.00	24.45	13.90	55.86	50.18	21.17	101.6		Y
RMB Fund Class I	RMBGX	B	B-	B		5.27	25.04	15.04	60.37	56.92	25.96	101.6		Y
Russell Investments Tax-Managed U.S. Large Cap Cls A	RTLAX	B-	C	B	Up	4.36	18.71	8.27	43.76	52.02	44.02	3,396	800-426-7969	Y
Russell Investments Tax-Managed U.S. Large Cap Cls E	RTLEX	B-	C	B	Up	4.36	18.73	8.28	43.75	52.04	44.48	3,396	800-426-7969	Y
Russell Investments Tax-Managed U.S. Large Cap Cls M	RTMTX	B-	C	B	Up	4.46	18.96	8.68	45.15	54.24	44.48	3,396	800-426-7969	Y
Russell Investments Tax-Managed U.S. Large Cap Cls S	RETSX	B-	C	B	Up	4.43	18.89	8.56	44.85	53.92	44.49	3,396	800-426-7969	Y
Segall Bryant & Hamill All Cap Fund	SBHAX	B-	C	B		6.32	22.10	11.47	42.04	51.97	15.8	104.3	312-474-1222	Y
SEI Institutional Managed Trust Large Cap Growth Cls F	SELCX	B-	C+	B	Down	4.40	22.35	10.41	61.32	69.70	36.03	1,515	800-342-5734	Y
SEI Institutional Managed Trust Large Cap Growth Cls I	SPGIX	B-	C+	B	Down	4.34	22.21	10.18	60.28	67.79	35.09	1,515	800-342-5734	Y
SEI Institutional Managed Trust Large Cap Growth Cls Y	SLRYX	B-	C+	B	Down	4.46	22.48	10.67	62.52	71.25	36.07	1,515	800-342-5734	Y
Sequoia Fund	SEQUX	B	B-	B	Up	5.50	21.86	9.96	52.76	29.73	154.84	3,933	800-686-6884	
Sextant Growth Fund	SGZFX	B-	C+	B	Down	5.96	23.84	15.13	59.77	56.66	30.54	42.0		Y
Sextant Growth Fund	SSGFX	B-	C+	B	Down	5.90	23.62	14.76	59.10	56.01	30.66	42.0		Y
Shelton Capital Management Nasdaq-100 Index Fund Class K	NDXKX	B-	C+	B	Down	3.63	21.78	9.36	72.39	97.65	18.23	637.6	800-955-9988	Y

Category: US Equity Large Cap Growth (con't)

Fund Name	Ticker Symbol	RATINGS Overall Rating	Reward Rating	Risk Rating	Recent Up/Downgrade	TOTAL RETURNS & PERFORMANCE 3-Month Total Return	6-Month Total Return	1-Year Total Return	3-Year Total Return	5-Year Total Return	ASSETS NAV	Total Assets (MIL)	NEW INVESTORS Telephone	Open to New Investors
Shelton Capital Management Nasdaq-100 Index Direct Shares	NASDX	B-	C+	B	Down	3.69	22.01	9.88	74.94	102.58	18.76	637.6	800-955-9988	Y
Sit Large Cap Growth Fund	SNIGX	B-	C+	B	Down	4.16	20.37	10.54	58.04	71.66	42.53	116.6	800-332-5580	Y
State Street Inst Premier Growth Equity Investment Cls	SSPGX	B-	C	B	Down	6.06	22.71	12.45	64.00	79.63	15.56	209.5	617-664-7338	Y
State Street Inst Premier Growth Equity Service Cls	SSPSX	B-	C	B	Down	6.08	22.63	12.25	62.82	77.44	15.33	209.5	617-664-7338	Y
Sterling Capital Special Opportunities Fund Class A	BOPAX	B-	C	B		2.60	18.52	8.26	41.10	54.42	24.44	1,067	800-228-1872	Y
Sterling Capital Special Opportunities Fund Class C	BOPCX	B-	C	B		2.41	18.07	7.45	37.95	48.74	19.92	1,067	800-228-1872	Y
Sterling Capital Special Opportunities Fund Class R	BOPRX	B-	C	B		2.53	18.38	8.00	39.99	52.53	24.66	1,067	800-228-1872	Y
Sterling Capital Special Opportunities Fund Class R6	STRSX	B-	C	B		2.69	18.72	8.62	42.29	56.58	25.87	1,067	800-228-1872	Y
Sterling Capital Special Opp Inst Shares	BOPIX	B-	C	B		2.66	18.68	8.56	42.16	56.44	25.85	1,067	800-228-1872	Y
T. Rowe Price Blue Chip Growth Fund	TRBCX	B-	C+	B	Down	4.04	21.92	10.33	81.45	100.36	116.06	63,955	410-345-2000	Y
T. Rowe Price Blue Chip Growth Fund Advisor Class	PABGX	B-	C+	B	Down	3.97	21.75	10.03	79.97	97.68	114	63,955	410-345-2000	Y
T. Rowe Price Blue Chip Growth Fund Class R	RRBGX	B-	C+	B	Down	3.90	21.60	9.75	78.59	95.13	109.41	63,955	410-345-2000	Y
T. Rowe Price Blue Chip Growth Fund I Class	TBCIX	B-	C+	B	Down	4.07	21.99	10.47	82.15	101.28	116.24	63,955	410-345-2000	Y
T. Rowe Price Growth Stock Fund	PRGFX	B-	C	B	Down	3.79	21.42	8.30	72.77	89.60	68.7	55,454	410-345-2000	Y
T. Rowe Price Growth Stock Fund Advisor Class	TRSAX	B-	C	B	Down	3.71	21.27	8.02	71.46	87.22	66.97	55,454	410-345-2000	Y
T. Rowe Price Growth Stock Fund I Class	PRUFX	B-	C+	B	Down	3.83	21.51	8.45	73.56	90.72	68.79	55,454	410-345-2000	Y
T. Rowe Price Growth Stock Fund R Class	RRGSX	B-	C	B	Down	3.66	21.11	7.73	70.17	84.85	64.53	55,454	410-345-2000	Y
T. Rowe Price Institutional Large Cap Core Growth Fund	TPLGX	B-	C+	B	Down	4.07	22.01	10.54	81.91	101.46	45.51	4,004	410-345-2000	Y
T. Rowe Price Institutional Large Cap Growth Fund	TRLGX	B-	C+	B	Down	3.00	19.19	9.96	87.94	102.29	42.17	19,125	410-345-2000	Y
T. Rowe Price New America Growth Fund	PRWAX	B-	C+	B	Down	5.34	23.16	11.90	77.09	95.65	53.01	5,248	410-345-2000	Y
T. Rowe Price New America Growth Fund Advisor Class	PAWAX	B-	C+	B	Down	5.29	22.99	11.61	75.68	93.05	51.72	5,248	410-345-2000	Y
T. Rowe Price New America Growth Fund I Class	PNAIX	B-	C+	B	Down	5.38	23.23	12.05	77.82	96.56	53.03	5,248	410-345-2000	Y
T. Rowe Price Spectrum Growth Fund	PRSGX	B-	C	B	Up	3.79	18.42	5.10	46.58	46.53	23.52	3,696	410-345-2000	Y
T. Rowe Price Tax-Efficient Equity Fund	PREFX	B-	B-	B	Down	6.23	26.79	14.56	70.55	88.16	35.63	510.0	410-345-2000	Y
T. Rowe Price Tax-Efficient Equity Fund I Class	TEEFX	B-	B-	B	Down	6.23	26.79	14.63	70.72	88.35	35.63	510.0	410-345-2000	Y
TCW Select Equities Fund Class I	TGCEX	B-	B-	B	Down	6.07	27.39	15.28	70.77	86.84	27.58	945.5	213-244-0000	Y
TCW Select Equities Fund Class N	TGCNX	B-	B-	B-	Down	6.00	27.20	15.03	69.60	84.61	24.55	945.5	213-244-0000	Y
The Hartford Growth Opportunities Fund Class A	HGOAX	B-	B-	B-	Down	5.73	29.43	11.52	69.46	94.38	41.29	5,201	888-843-7824	Y
The Hartford Growth Opportunities Fund Class C	HGOCX	B-	B-	B-		5.54	28.95	10.69	65.69	87.26	21.51	5,201	888-843-7824	Y
The Hartford Growth Opportunities Fund Class F	HGOFX	B-	B-	B-	Down	5.84	29.67	11.95	71.37	97.95	44	5,201	888-843-7824	Y
The Hartford Growth Opportunities Fund Class I	HGOIX	B-	B-	B-	Down	5.81	29.60	11.83	70.75	96.68	43.87	5,201	888-843-7824	Y
The Hartford Growth Opportunities Fund Class R3	HGORX	B-	B-	B-	Down	5.65	29.22	11.16	67.79	91.16	41.3	5,201	888-843-7824	Y
The Hartford Growth Opportunities Fund Class R4	HGOSX	B-	B-	B-	Down	5.71	29.39	11.47	69.28	94.07	44.24	5,201	888-843-7824	Y
The Hartford Growth Opportunities Fund Class R5	HGOTX	B-	B-	B-	Down	5.80	29.57	11.80	70.80	96.95	46.83	5,201	888-843-7824	Y
The Hartford Growth Opportunities Fund Class R6	HGOVX	B-	B-	B-	Down	5.83	29.65	11.94	71.33	97.85	47.7	5,201	888-843-7824	Y
The Hartford Growth Opportunities Fund Class Y	HGOYX	B-	B-	B-	Down	5.83	29.66	11.89	71.24	97.81	47.69	5,201	888-843-7824	Y
TIAA-CREF Large Cap Growth Fund Advisor Class	TILHX	B-	C+	B	Down	3.06	22.29	9.16	69.54	90.14	21.17	5,691	877-518-9161	Y
TIAA-CREF Large Cap Growth Fund Class W	TILWX	B-	C+	B	Down	3.10	22.51	9.50	70.35	91.05	21.22	5,691	877-518-9161	Y
TIAA-CREF Large-Cap Growth Fund Institutional Class	TILGX	B-	C+	B	Down	3.01	22.28	9.16	69.83	90.47	21.18	5,691	877-518-9161	Y
TIAA-CREF Large-Cap Growth Fund Retail Class	TIRTX	B-	C+	B	Down	2.92	22.09	8.86	68.18	87.45	21.11	5,691	877-518-9161	Y
TIAA-CREF Large-Cap Growth Index Fund Advisor Class	TRIHX	B-	C+	B	Down	4.57	22.50	11.36	65.64	86.35	33.15	7,194	877-518-9161	Y
TIAA-CREF Large-Cap Growth Index Fund Institutional Class	TILIX	B-	C+	B	Down	4.60	22.60	11.51	66.15	87.02	33.19	7,194	877-518-9161	Y
TIAA-CREF Large-Cap Growth Index Fund Retirement Class	TRIRX	B-	C+	B	Down	4.56	22.46	11.22	64.95	84.63	33.42	7,194	877-518-9161	Y
Touchstone Growth Opportunities Fund Class Y	TGVYX	B-	C+	B	Down	5.29	25.91	11.72	64.28	60.94	35.57	132.3	800-543-0407	Y
Touchstone Growth Opportunities Fund Institutional Class	TGVVX	B-	C+	B	Down	5.28	25.97	11.82	64.78	61.68	36.03	132.3	800-543-0407	Y
Touchstone Large Company Growth Fund Class Institutional	DSMLX	B-	C+	B	Down	4.55	24.52	10.73	69.67	84.83	42.95	225.7	800-543-0407	Y
Touchstone Large Company Growth Fund Class Y	TLGYX	B-	C+	B	Down	4.54	24.47	10.66	69.19	84.31	42.82	225.7	800-543-0407	Y
Transamerica Capital Growth Fund Class I	TFOIX	B-	C+	B-	Up	7.39	28.73	14.66	100.63	120.36	31.94	2,036	888-233-4339	Y
Transamerica Capital Growth Fund Class I2		B-	C+	B-	Up	7.89	28.02	14.47	104.00	120.26	15.12	2,036	888-233-4339	Y
Transamerica Concentrated Growth Fund Class A	TORAX	B-	C+	B	Down	2.98	20.82	11.87	49.48	55.28	17.58	176.6	888-233-4339	Y
Transamerica Concentrated Growth Fund Class C	TCCGX	B-	C	B	Down	2.80	20.41	11.14	46.54	50.00	16.87	176.6	888-233-4339	Y
Transamerica Concentrated Growth Fund Class I	TOREX	B-	C+	B	Down	3.06	20.96	12.27	50.96	57.43	17.48	176.6	888-233-4339	Y

Category: US Equity Large Cap Growth (con't)

Fund Name	Ticker Symbol	Overall Rating	Reward Rating	Risk Rating	Recent Up/ Downgrade	3-Month Total Return	6-Month Total Return	1-Year Total Return	3-Year Total Return	5-Year Total Return	NAV	Total Assets (MIL)	Telephone	Open to New Investors
		RATINGS				TOTAL RETURNS & PERFORMANCE					ASSETS		NEW INVESTORS	
Transamerica Concentrated Growth Fund Class I2		B-	C+	B	Down	3.10	20.27	12.40	53.08	57.28	17.74	176.6	888-233-4339	Y
Transamerica US Growth Class A	TADAX	B-	C+	B	Down	5.39	25.00	12.50	63.39	84.54	21.3	1,126	888-233-4339	Y
Transamerica US Growth Class C	TADCX	B-	C+	B	Down	5.12	24.43	11.52	59.40	77.26	19.71	1,126	888-233-4339	Y
Transamerica US Growth Class I	TDEIX	B-	C+	B	Down	5.46	25.15	12.81	64.83	87.45	21.79	1,126	888-233-4339	Y
Transamerica US Growth Class I2		B-	C+	B	Down	5.81	24.69	12.83	67.42	87.73	21.76	1,126	888-233-4339	Y
Transamerica US Growth Class T	TWMTX	B-	C+	B	Down	5.45	25.23	12.85	65.06	87.90	61.84	1,126	888-233-4339	Y
USAA Aggressive Growth Fund	USAUX	B-	C	B	Down	4.75	21.07	9.14	61.42	76.99	44.3	1,659	800-235-8396	Y
USAA Aggressive Growth Fund Institutional Shares	UIAGX	B-	C	B	Down	4.73	21.07	9.15	61.47	77.74	44.93	1,659	800-235-8396	Y
USAA Growth Fund	USAAX	B-	C+	B	Down	5.42	22.99	14.42	60.44	82.65	31.5	2,860	800-235-8396	Y
USAA Growth Fund Institutional Shares	UIGRX	B-	C+	B	Down	5.43	23.01	14.47	60.77	83.26	31.43	2,860	800-235-8396	Y
USAA Nasdaq 100 Index Fund R6 Shares	URNQX	B-	C+	B		4.16	22.49	9.73	79.50	106.40	21.51	2,154	800-235-8396	Y
USAA NASDAQ-100 Index Fund	USNQX	B-	C+	B		4.16	22.49	9.66	79.12	105.96	21.51	2,154	800-235-8396	Y
VALIC Company I Blue Chip Growth Fund	VCBCX	B-	C+	B	Down	3.97	21.78	10.26	80.71	99.04	20.38	828.5		Y
VALIC Company I Growth Fund	VCULX	B-	C+	B		4.29	21.90	8.74	63.37	72.52	17.47	1,157		Y
VALIC Company I Large Capital Growth Fund	VLCGX	B	B	B+		5.67	25.25	18.59	66.05	81.71	16.76	508.4		Y
VALIC Company I Nasdaq-100 Index Fund	VCNIX	B-	C+	B		4.04	22.37	9.46	78.76	105.73	15.16	535.7		Y
Vanguard Growth Index Fund Admiral Shares	VIGAX	B-	C+	B		4.74	23.51	10.44	59.99	76.29	84.14	90,346	877-662-7447	Y
Vanguard Growth Index Fund Institutional Shares	VIGIX	B-	C+	B		4.74	23.53	10.46	60.05	76.39	84.15	90,346	877-662-7447	Y
Vanguard Growth Index Fund Investor Shares	VIGRX	B-	C+	B		4.70	23.42	10.30	59.42	75.16	84.16	90,346	877-662-7447	Y
Vanguard Mega Cap Growth Index Fund Institutional Shares	VMGAX	B-	C+	B		4.47	22.61	9.73	62.46	80.08	257.19	4,447	877-662-7447	Y
Vanguard PRIMECAP Fund Admiral Shares	VPMAX	B-	C	B		2.18	14.23	6.18	64.11	76.57	136.92	64,289	877-662-7447	
Vanguard PRIMECAP Fund Investor Shares	VPMCX	B-	C	B		2.17	14.19	6.11	63.77	75.96	132.09	64,289	877-662-7447	
Vanguard Russell 1000 Growth Index Institutional Shares	VRGWX	B-	C+	B	Down	4.62	22.62	11.49	66.15	86.89	311.83	5,828	877-662-7447	Y
Virtus Zevenbergen Innovative Growth Stock Fund Class A	SAGAX	B-	C+	B-	Up	9.08	38.24	21.78	122.49	105.50	28.45	222.4	800-243-1574	Y
Virtus Zevenbergen Innovative Growth Stock Fund Class I	SCATX	B-	C+	B-	Up	9.15	38.39	22.03	123.85	107.55	30.28	222.4	800-243-1574	Y
Voya Large Cap Growth Portfolio Class A	IEOPX	B-	C+	B	Down	3.62	20.12	10.32	58.79	75.53	19.46	5,704	800-366-0066	Y
Voya Large Cap Growth Portfolio Class I	IEOHX	B-	C+	B	Down	3.81	20.51	11.01	61.72	80.98	21.21	5,704	800-366-0066	Y
Voya Large Cap Growth Portfolio Class R6	VRLCX	B-	C+	B	Down	3.81	20.49	11.06	61.77	80.41	21.22	5,704	800-366-0066	Y
Voya Large Cap Growth Portfolio Class S	IEOSX	B-	C+	B	Down	3.72	20.36	10.78	60.47	78.76	20.63	5,704	800-366-0066	Y
Voya Large Cap Growth Portfolio Class S2	IEOTX	B-	C+	B	Down	3.70	20.22	10.57	59.75	77.36	20.45	5,704	800-366-0066	Y
Voya Large-Cap Growth Fund Class A	NLCAX	B-	C+	B	Down	3.73	20.33	10.85	59.98	77.25	40.54	1,080	800-366-0066	Y
Voya Large-Cap Growth Fund Class C	NLCCX	B-	C+	B	Down	3.53	19.87	9.98	56.37	70.95	33.71	1,080	800-366-0066	Y
Voya Large-Cap Growth Fund Class I	PLCIX	B-	C+	B	Down	3.83	20.51	11.25	61.71	80.44	45.17	1,080	800-366-0066	Y
Voya Large-Cap Growth Fund Class P3	VPLCX	B-	C+	B	Down	4.00	20.86	11.93	62.38	80.94	45.47	1,080	800-366-0066	Y
Voya Large-Cap Growth Fund Class R	VGORX	B-	C+	B	Down	3.68	20.18	10.59	58.82	75.24	44.48	1,080	800-366-0066	Y
Voya Large-Cap Growth Fund Class R6	VGOSX	B-	C+	B	Down	3.86	20.54	11.30	61.96	80.52	45.18	1,080	800-366-0066	Y
Voya Large-Cap Growth Fund Class W	IGOWX	B-	C+	B	Down	3.79	20.48	11.12	61.22	79.64	43.99	1,080	800-366-0066	Y
Voya Russell Large Cap Growth Index Portfolio Class A	IRLAX	B-	C+	B		4.23	20.75	9.88	63.98	86.23	37.64	757.2	800-366-0066	Y
Voya Russell Large Cap Growth Index Portfolio Class I	IRLNX	B-	C+	B		4.32	20.98	10.37	66.25	90.56	37.91	757.2	800-366-0066	Y
Voya Russell Large Cap Growth Index Portfolio Class S	IRLSX	B-	C+	B		4.22	20.81	10.07	65.04	88.21	37.71	757.2	800-366-0066	Y
VY® T. Rowe Price Growth Equity Portfolio Class A	IGEAX	B-	C	B	Down	3.66	21.15	7.77	70.14	84.88	85.16	1,929	800-366-0066	Y
VY® T. Rowe Price Growth Equity Portfolio Class I	ITGIX	B-	C	B	Down	3.79	21.45	8.32	72.71	89.56	93.9	1,929	800-366-0066	Y
VY® T. Rowe Price Growth Equity Portfolio Class S	ITGSX	B-	C	B	Down	3.71	21.30	8.03	71.40	87.20	89.57	1,929	800-366-0066	Y
VY® T. Rowe Price Growth Equity Portfolio Class S2	ITRGX	B-	C	B	Down	3.67	21.21	7.88	70.65	85.81	86.57	1,929	800-366-0066	Y
Weitz Value Fund Institutional Class	WVAIX	B-	C	B		7.61	25.01	14.64	43.18	40.68	44.81	819.2	800-304-9745	Y
Weitz Value Fund Investor Class	WVALX	B-	C	B		7.54	24.83	14.34	42.16	39.16	44.23	819.2	800-304-9745	Y
Wells Fargo Capital Growth Fund - Class A	WFCGX	B	B	B		7.79	28.03	15.16	78.41	86.07	9.27	104.8	800-222-8222	Y
Wells Fargo Capital Growth Fund - Class Admin	WFCDX	B	B	B		7.81	28.09	15.26	79.11	87.43	11.17	104.8	800-222-8222	Y
Wells Fargo Capital Growth Fund - Class C	WFCCX	B	B-	B		7.56	27.49	14.28	74.52	79.29	6.26	104.8	800-222-8222	Y
Wells Fargo Capital Growth Fund - Class Inst	WWCIX	B	B	B		7.87	28.16	15.51	80.38	89.68	12.06	104.8	800-222-8222	Y
Wells Fargo Capital Growth Fund - Class R6	WFCRX	B	B	B		7.80	28.27	15.62	80.54	90.07	12.16	104.8	800-222-8222	Y
Wells Fargo Endeavor Select Fund - Class A	STAEX	B	B	B		7.84	27.71	15.25	80.86	87.39	8.11	128.1	800-222-8222	Y

Category: US Equity Large Cap Growth (con't)

Fund Name	Ticker Symbol	RATINGS: Overall Rating	Reward Rating	Risk Rating	Recent Up/ Downgrade	TOTAL RETURNS & PERFORMANCE: 3-Month Total Return	6-Month Total Return	1-Year Total Return	3-Year Total Return	5-Year Total Return	ASSETS: NAV	Total Assets (MIL)	NEW INVESTORS: Telephone	Open to New Investors
Wells Fargo Endeavor Select Fund - Class Admin	WECDX	B	B	B		7.74	27.87	15.43	82.00	89.48	8.9	128.1	800-222-8222	Y
Wells Fargo Endeavor Select Fund - Class C	WECCX	B	B-	B		7.49	27.15	14.27	76.88	80.47	4.73	128.1	800-222-8222	Y
Wells Fargo Endeavor Select Fund - Class Inst	WFCIX	B	B	B		7.90	27.98	15.71	83.09	91.28	9.42	128.1	800-222-8222	Y
Wells Fargo Growth Fund - Class A	SGRAX	B-	B-	B-	Down	7.24	29.71	13.85	77.03	83.15	34.92	4,621	800-222-8222	
Wells Fargo Growth Fund - Class Admin	SGRKX	B-	B-	B-	Down	7.30	29.83	14.09	78.06	84.98	40.82	4,621	800-222-8222	
Wells Fargo Growth Fund - Class C	WGFCX	B-	B-	B-	Down	7.07	29.23	13.03	73.02	76.35	25.42	4,621	800-222-8222	
Wells Fargo Growth Fund - Class Inst	SGRNX	B-	B-	B-	Down	7.37	29.99	14.34	79.18	86.96	44.86	4,621	800-222-8222	
Wells Fargo Growth Fund - Class R6	SGRHX	B-	B-	B-	Down	7.37	30.02	14.39	79.47	87.34	45	4,621	800-222-8222	Y
Wells Fargo Large Cap Growth Fund - Class A	STAFX	B-	B-	B	Down	5.44	25.07	12.22	70.48	78.06	43.6	1,016	800-222-8222	Y
Wells Fargo Large Cap Growth Fund - Class Admin	STDFX	B-	B-	B	Down	5.46	25.12	12.35	71.09	79.14	44.23	1,016	800-222-8222	Y
Wells Fargo Large Cap Growth Fund - Class C	STOFX	B-	C+	B	Down	5.22	24.58	11.37	66.65	71.46	38.87	1,016	800-222-8222	Y
Wells Fargo Large Cap Growth Fund - Class Inst	STNFX	B-	B-	B	Down	5.51	25.26	12.57	72.07	81.16	45.17	1,016	800-222-8222	Y
Wells Fargo Large Cap Growth Fund - Class R	STMFX	B-	C+	B	Down	5.36	24.88	11.93	69.12	75.79	42.26	1,016	800-222-8222	Y
Wells Fargo Large Cap Growth Fund - Class R4	SLGRX	B-	B-	B	Down	5.50	25.20	12.52	71.87	80.65	45.06	1,016	800-222-8222	Y
Wells Fargo Large Cap Growth Fund - Class R6	STFFX	B-	B-	B	Down	5.53	25.31	12.68	72.63	81.99	45.39	1,016	800-222-8222	Y
Wells Fargo Omega Growth Fund - Class A	EKOAX	B-	B-	B	Down	7.48	28.98	15.14	78.15	77.00	54.15	836.3	800-222-8222	Y
Wells Fargo Omega Growth Fund - Class Admin	EOMYX	B	B-	B		7.52	29.11	15.36	79.13	78.79	59.43	836.3	800-222-8222	Y
Wells Fargo Omega Growth Fund - Class C	EKOCX	B-	B-	B	Down	7.28	28.53	14.30	74.20	70.47	35.18	836.3	800-222-8222	Y
Wells Fargo Omega Growth Fund - Class Inst	EKONX	B	B-	B		7.61	29.28	15.66	80.52	81.04	61.49	836.3	800-222-8222	Y
Wells Fargo Omega Growth Fund - Class R	EKORX	B-	B-	B	Down	7.41	28.83	14.86	76.85	74.78	50.85	836.3	800-222-8222	Y
Wells Fargo Opportunity Fund - Class A	SOPVX	B-	C	B		4.12	20.84	7.95	47.58	47.66	42.37	1,721	800-222-8222	Y
Wells Fargo Opportunity Fund - Class Admin	WOFDX	B-	C	B		4.16	20.96	8.16	48.49	49.20	46.73	1,721	800-222-8222	Y
Wells Fargo Opportunity Fund - Class Inst	WOFNX	B-	C	B		4.21	21.09	8.42	49.58	51.06	47.71	1,721	800-222-8222	Y
Wells Fargo Premier Large Company Growth Fund - Class A	EKJAX	B-	B-	B	Down	6.70	27.71	14.03	74.06	77.96	14.01	2,423	800-222-8222	Y
Wells Fargo Premier Large Company Growth - Cls Admin	WFPDX	B-	B-	B	Down	6.71	27.79	14.06	74.61	79.11	14.3	2,423	800-222-8222	Y
Wells Fargo Premier Large Company Growth Fund - Class C	EKJCX	B-	B-	B-	Down	6.50	27.09	13.08	70.02	71.24	10.32	2,423	800-222-8222	Y
Wells Fargo Premier Large Company Growth Fund - Class Inst	EKJYX	B-	B-	B	Down	6.82	27.96	14.48	76.29	81.76	14.87	2,423	800-222-8222	Y
Wells Fargo Premier Large Company Growth Fund - Class R4	EKJRX	B-	B-	B	Down	6.82	27.91	14.39	75.68	80.79	14.71	2,423	800-222-8222	Y
Wells Fargo Premier Large Company Growth Fund - Class R6	EKJFX	B-	B-	B	Down	6.87	28.04	14.57	76.53	82.25	14.93	2,423	800-222-8222	Y
William Blair Growth Fund Class I	BGFIX	B	B-	B		4.99	23.93	14.42	64.60	74.67	11.34	259.9	800-621-0687	Y
William Blair Growth Fund Class N	WBGSX	B	B-	B		4.87	23.78	14.07	63.18	72.06	9.68	259.9	800-621-0687	Y
William Blair Growth Fund Class R6	BGFRX	B	B-	B		4.86	23.77	14.06	63.17	72.05	11.34	259.9	800-621-0687	Y
William Blair Large Cap Growth Fund Class I	LCGFX	B	B-	B		7.29	25.53	16.32	77.29	101.32	15.73	230.6	800-621-0687	Y
William Blair Large Cap Growth Fund Class N	LCGNX	B	B-	B		7.20	25.35	16.01	75.93	98.80	14.88	230.6	800-621-0687	Y
William Blair Large Cap Growth Fund Class R6	LCGJX	B	B-	B		7.37	25.62	16.40	77.41	101.46	15.73	230.6	800-621-0687	Y

Category: US Equity Large Cap Value

Fund Name	Ticker Symbol	RATINGS: Overall Rating	Reward Rating	Risk Rating	Recent Up/ Downgrade	TOTAL RETURNS & PERFORMANCE: 3-Month Total Return	6-Month Total Return	1-Year Total Return	3-Year Total Return	5-Year Total Return	ASSETS: NAV	Total Assets (MIL)	NEW INVESTORS: Telephone	Open to New Investors
AB Equity Income Fund Advisor Class	AUIYX	B-	C	B+		2.00	15.17	7.99	35.31	38.74	27.34	539.3	212-969-1000	Y
AB Equity Income Fund Class A	AUIAX	B-	C	B		1.92	15.04	7.76	34.34	36.90	27.05	539.3	212-969-1000	Y
AB Equity Income Fund Class B	AUIBX	B-	C	B	Up	1.72	14.61	6.91	31.30	31.80	26.69	539.3	212-969-1000	
AB Equity Income Fund Class C	AUICX	B-	C	B	Up	1.71	14.58	6.92	31.31	31.93	26.65	539.3	212-969-1000	Y
AB Equity Income Fund Class I	AUIIX	B-	C	B		1.98	15.19	7.98	35.21	38.64	26.98	539.3	212-969-1000	Y
AB Equity Income Fund Class K	AUIKX	B-	C	B	Up	1.89	14.94	7.59	33.87	36.34	27.05	539.3	212-969-1000	Y
AB Equity Income Fund Class R	AUIRX	B-	C	B	Up	1.82	14.79	7.29	32.70	34.31	26.9	539.3	212-969-1000	Y
AB Equity Income Fund Class Z	AUIZX	B-	C	B+		1.97	15.21	8.06	35.63	39.27	26.96	539.3	212-969-1000	Y
AB Relative Value Fund Advisor Class	CBBYX	B-	C	B+		3.57	15.30	8.43	43.05	52.09	5.5	1,816	212-969-1000	Y
AB Relative Value Fund Class A	CABDX	B-	C	B+		3.61	15.22	8.15	42.01	50.17	5.45	1,816	212-969-1000	Y
AB Relative Value Fund Class B	CBBDX	B-	C	B		3.39	14.64	7.23	38.82	44.51	5.48	1,816	212-969-1000	
AB Relative Value Fund Class C	CBBCX	B-	C	B		3.42	14.79	7.41	38.74	44.87	5.43	1,816	212-969-1000	Y

Category: US Equity Large Cap Value (con't)

Fund Name	Ticker Symbol	RATINGS: Overall Rating	Reward Rating	Risk Rating	Recent Up/ Downgrade	TOTAL RETURNS & PERFORMANCE: 3-Month Total Return	6-Month Total Return	1-Year Total Return	3-Year Total Return	5-Year Total Return	ASSETS: NAV	Total Assets (MIL)	NEW INVESTORS: Telephone	Open to New Investors
AB Relative Value Fund Class I	CBBIX	B-	C	B+		3.53	15.11	8.30	43.08	52.25	5.56	1,816	212-969-1000	Y
AB Relative Value Fund Class K	CBBKX	B-	C	B+		3.46	15.20	8.07	41.98	50.21	5.38	1,816	212-969-1000	Y
AB Relative Value Fund Class R	CBBRX	B-	C	B		3.48	15.05	7.89	40.81	48.26	5.35	1,816	212-969-1000	Y
AB Relative Value Fund Class Z	CBBZX	B-	C	B+		3.73	15.35	8.44	43.18	52.28	5.56	1,816	212-969-1000	Y
American Beacon The London Company Income Equity A Cls	ABCAX	B-	C	B+		2.43	17.08	13.96	34.44	50.09	18.19	1,114	800-658-5811	Y
American Beacon The London Company Income Equity C Cls	ABECX	B-	C	B		2.25	16.64	13.03	31.40	44.55	18.05	1,114	800-658-5811	Y
American Beacon The London Company Income Equity Inst Cls	ABCIX	B-	C+	B+		2.48	17.23	14.31	35.82	52.77	18.37	1,114	800-658-5811	Y
American Beacon The London Company Income Equity Inv Cls	ABCVX	B-	C	B+		2.41	17.03	13.92	34.51	50.31	18.3	1,114	800-658-5811	Y
American Beacon The London Company Income Equity Y Cls	ABCYX	B-	C	B+		2.48	17.15	14.18	35.51	52.25	18.27	1,114	800-658-5811	Y
American Century Capital Value Fund Class A	ACCVX	B-	C	B	Up	3.87	15.55	6.94	32.17	35.31	8.84	135.8	800-444-4015	Y
American Century Capital Value Fund I Class	ACPIX	B-	C	B	Up	3.97	15.88	7.51	33.96	38.42	8.9	135.8	800-444-4015	Y
American Century Capital Value Fund Investor Class	ACTIX	B-	C	B	Up	3.86	15.79	7.31	33.24	36.96	8.87	135.8	800-444-4015	Y
American Century Equity Income Fund A Class	TWEAX	B	C+	A-		4.46	16.23	11.77	33.94	54.23	9.02	11,975	800-444-4015	Y
American Century Equity Income Fund C Class	AEYIX	B	C+	A-		4.27	15.82	11.07	31.00	48.61	9.02	11,975	800-444-4015	Y
American Century Equity Income Fund I Class	ACIIX	B	C+	A-		4.57	16.60	12.25	35.69	57.83	9.03	11,975	800-444-4015	Y
American Century Equity Income Fund Investor Class	TWEIX	B	C+	A-		4.53	16.36	12.05	34.93	56.16	9.02	11,975	800-444-4015	Y
American Century Equity Income Fund R Class	AEURX	B	C+	A-		4.30	16.03	11.41	32.78	52.36	8.98	11,975	800-444-4015	Y
American Century Equity Income Fund R5 Class	AEIUX	B	C+	A-		4.46	16.47	12.26	35.50	56.82	9.02	11,975	800-444-4015	Y
American Century Equity Income Fund R6 Class	AEUDX	B	C+	A-		4.61	16.66	12.53	36.26	58.94	9.04	11,975	800-444-4015	Y
American Century Equity Income Fund Y Class	AEIYX	B	C+	A-		4.61	16.66	12.53	36.06	57.46	9.04	11,975	800-444-4015	Y
American Century Large Company Value Fund A Class	ALPAX	B-	C	B	Up	4.05	17.09	8.41	33.06	36.30	10.2	868.8	800-444-4015	Y
American Century Large Company Value Fund C Class	ALPCX	B-	C	B	Up	3.86	16.69	7.71	30.11	31.34	10.2	868.8	800-444-4015	Y
American Century Large Company Value Fund I Class	ALVSX	B-	C	B		4.16	17.32	8.89	34.82	39.37	10.21	868.8	800-444-4015	Y
American Century Large Company Value Fund Investor Class	ALVIX	B-	C	B	Up	4.22	17.34	8.78	34.18	38.15	10.21	868.8	800-444-4015	Y
American Century Large Company Value Fund R Class	ALVRX	B-	C	B	Up	3.98	16.94	8.24	32.03	34.71	10.21	868.8	800-444-4015	Y
American Century Large Company Value Fund R5 Class	ALVGX	B-	C	B		4.26	17.43	8.99	34.75	38.74	10.22	868.8	800-444-4015	Y
American Century Large Company Value Fund R6 Class	ALVDX	B-	C	B		4.20	17.53	9.16	35.43	40.43	10.21	868.8	800-444-4015	Y
American Century NT Large Company Value Fund G Class	ACLLX	B-	C	B		4.33	17.78	9.56	36.25	39.33	11.14	1,603	800-444-4015	Y
American Funds American Mutual Fund® Class 529-A	CMLAX	B	C	A-		3.06	13.05	9.38	37.81	51.27	41.62	57,149	800-421-4225	Y
American Funds American Mutual Fund® Class 529-C	CMLCX	B-	C	A-	Down	2.89	12.65	8.58	34.70	45.62	41.42	57,149	800-421-4225	Y
American Funds American Mutual Fund® Class 529-E	CMLEX	B-	C	A-	Down	3.02	12.96	9.15	36.87	49.52	41.45	57,149	800-421-4225	Y
American Funds American Mutual Fund® Class 529-F	CMLFX	B	C	A-		3.12	13.19	9.63	38.76	52.98	41.68	57,149	800-421-4225	Y
American Funds American Mutual Fund® Class A	AMRMX	B	C	A-		3.10	13.12	9.48	38.18	51.95	41.73	57,149	800-421-4225	Y
American Funds American Mutual Fund® Class C	AMFCX	B-	C	A-	Down	2.87	12.67	8.63	34.91	46.01	41.1	57,149	800-421-4225	Y
American Funds American Mutual Fund® Class F-1	AMFFX	B	C	A-		3.07	13.06	9.38	37.79	51.30	41.53	57,149	800-421-4225	Y
American Funds American Mutual Fund® Class F-2	AMRFX	B	C	A-		3.12	13.23	9.68	38.89	53.28	41.71	57,149	800-421-4225	Y
American Funds American Mutual Fund® Class F-3	AFMFX	B	C	A-		3.17	13.28	9.79	39.12	52.99	41.71	57,149	800-421-4225	Y
American Funds American Mutual Fund® Class R-1	RMFAX	B-	C	A-	Down	2.87	12.65	8.55	34.72	45.73	41.26	57,149	800-421-4225	Y
American Funds American Mutual Fund® Class R-2	RMFBX	B-	C	A-	Down	2.89	12.68	8.61	34.86	45.96	41.22	57,149	800-421-4225	Y
American Funds American Mutual Fund® Class R-2E	RMEBX	B-	C	A-	Down	2.94	12.82	8.88	36.00	48.59	41.57	57,149	800-421-4225	Y
American Funds American Mutual Fund® Class R-3	RMFCX	B-	C	A-	Down	2.98	12.89	9.07	36.61	49.16	41.38	57,149	800-421-4225	Y
American Funds American Mutual Fund® Class R-4	RMFEX	B	C	A-		3.07	13.08	9.41	37.86	51.44	41.58	57,149	800-421-4225	Y
American Funds American Mutual Fund® Class R-5	RMFFX	B	C	A-		3.16	13.25	9.73	39.15	53.79	41.73	57,149	800-421-4225	Y
American Funds American Mutual Fund® Class R-5E	RMFHX	B	C	A-		3.13	13.22	9.64	38.70	52.60	41.68	57,149	800-421-4225	Y
American Funds American Mutual Fund® Class R-6	RMFGX	B	C	A-		3.17	13.30	9.79	39.35	54.15	41.74	57,149	800-421-4225	Y
AMG River Road Dividend All Cap Value Fund Class I	ARIDX	B-	C	B		2.69	14.60	6.05	28.41	37.88	11.91	682.8	800-835-3879	
AMG River Road Dividend All Cap Value Fund Class N	ARDEX	B-	C	B		2.53	14.35	5.67	27.30	36.00	11.91	682.8	800-835-3879	
AMG River Road Dividend All Cap Value Fund Class Z	ARZDX	B-	C	B		2.62	14.63	6.10	28.09	36.84	11.91	682.8	800-835-3879	Y
AMG River Road Dividend All Cap Value Fund II Class I	ADIVX	B-	C	B		2.96	15.02	6.66	29.62	39.39	12.91	74.6	800-835-3879	Y
AMG River Road Dividend All Cap Value Fund II Class N	ADVTX	B-	C	B		2.90	14.81	6.37	28.48	37.37	12.88	74.6	800-835-3879	Y
AMG River Road Dividend All Cap Value Fund II Class Z	ADVZX	B-	C	B		2.98	15.06	6.73	29.76	39.54	12.91	74.6	800-835-3879	Y
AMG Yacktman Focused Fund Class I	YAFIX	B	C+	A		3.21	12.74	11.64	47.40	55.80	19.91	3,800	800-835-3879	Y

Category: US Equity Large Cap Value (con't)

Fund Name	Ticker Symbol	RATINGS				TOTAL RETURNS & PERFORMANCE					ASSETS		NEW INVESTORS	
		Overall Rating	Reward Rating	Risk Rating	Recent Up/ Downgrade	3-Month Total Return	6-Month Total Return	1-Year Total Return	3-Year Total Return	5-Year Total Return	NAV	Total Assets (MIL)	Telephone	Open to New Investors
AMG Yacktman Focused Fund Class N	YAFFX	B	C+	A		3.15	12.65	11.42	46.63	54.40	19.94	3,800	800-835-3879	Y
Auxier Focus Fund Class A	AUXAX	B-	C	B+		1.88	12.02	6.80	31.93	35.74	22.7	231.4		Y
Auxier Focus Fund Class Investor	AUXFX	B-	C	B+		1.91	12.17	7.07	32.89	36.95	22.34	231.4		Y
Auxier Focus Fund Institutional	AUXIX	B-	C	B+		1.96	12.24	7.23	33.61	38.16	22.81	231.4		Y
BlackRock Advantage Large Cap Value Fund Class K	MLVKX	B-	C	B	Up	2.81	15.93	6.69	44.33	49.16	27.92	636.7	800-441-7762	Y
BlackRock Advantage Large Cap Value Fund Class R	MRLVX	B-	C	B	Up	2.68	15.62	6.07	41.98	45.07	26.17	636.7	800-441-7762	Y
BlackRock Advantage Large Cap Value Institutional Shares	MALVX	B-	C	B	Up	2.81	15.93	6.64	44.26	49.09	27.91	636.7	800-441-7762	Y
BlackRock Advantage Large Cap Value Fund Investor A Shares	MDLVX	B-	C	B	Up	2.72	15.75	6.34	43.14	46.98	27.3	636.7	800-441-7762	Y
BlackRock Advantage Large Cap Value Fund Investor C Shares	MCLVX	B-	C	B	Up	2.57	15.37	5.58	39.96	41.50	25.23	636.7	800-441-7762	Y
BlackRock Advantage Large Cap Value Fund Service Shares	MSLVX	B-	C	B	Up	2.76	15.78	6.36	43.16	46.98	27.7	636.7	800-441-7762	Y
BlackRock Equity Dividend Fund Institutional Shares	MADVX	B-	C	B	Up	4.66	16.41	7.56	40.75	51.49	21.46	19,552	800-441-7762	Y
BlackRock Equity Dividend Fund Investor A Shares	MDDVX	B-	C	B	Up	4.67	16.34	7.30	39.75	49.58	21.39	19,552	800-441-7762	Y
BlackRock Equity Dividend Fund Investor C Shares	MCDVX	B-	C	B	Up	4.44	15.84	6.50	36.73	44.29	20.5	19,552	800-441-7762	Y
BlackRock Equity Dividend Fund Investor C1 Shares	BEDCX	B-	C	B	Up	4.45	15.90	6.62	37.37	45.50	20.55	19,552	800-441-7762	Y
BlackRock Equity Dividend Fund K Shares	MKDVX	B-	C	B	Up	4.74	16.50	7.70	41.29	52.13	21.46	19,552	800-441-7762	Y
BlackRock Equity Dividend Fund R Shares	MRDVX	B-	C	B	Up	4.54	16.09	6.97	38.43	47.21	21.56	19,552	800-441-7762	Y
BlackRock Equity Dividend Fund Service Shares	MSDVX	B-	C	B	Up	4.62	16.23	7.24	39.70	49.30	21.36	19,552	800-441-7762	Y
BlackRock High Equity Income Fund Institutional Shares	BMCIX	B-	C	B+	Up	2.77	13.00	5.56	34.93	35.66	26.61	432.9	800-441-7762	Y
BlackRock High Equity Income Fund Investor A Shares	BMEAX	B-	C	B+	Up	2.71	12.88	5.32	33.87	33.52	22.49	432.9	800-441-7762	Y
BlackRock High Equity Income Fund Investor C Shares	BMECX	B-	C	B+	Up	2.46	12.41	4.52	30.84	28.57	14.47	432.9	800-441-7762	Y
BlackRock High Equity Income Fund Service Shares	BMCSX	B-	C	B+	Up	2.71	12.84	5.28	33.84	33.46	23.96	432.9	800-441-7762	Y
BMO Dividend Income Fund Class A	BADIX	B-	C	B		0.97	13.37	5.74	46.01	53.00	14.34	236.1	800-236-3863	Y
BMO Dividend Income Fund Class I	MDIVX	B-	C	B	Down	1.03	13.54	5.98	47.08	54.88	14.29	236.1	800-236-3863	Y
BMO Low Volatility Equity Fund Class A	BLVAX	B	B-	A-		4.94	17.98	15.67	36.68	60.47	15.4	182.3	800-236-3863	Y
BMO Low Volatility Equity Fund Class I	MLVEX	B	B-	A-		5.05	18.13	16.05	37.73	62.74	15.46	182.3	800-236-3863	Y
BNY Mellon Equity Income Fund Class A	DQIAX	B-	C	B	Up	1.17	12.24	3.57	35.74	46.87	19.27	1,109		Y
BNY Mellon Equity Income Fund Class C	DQICX	B-	C	B	Up	0.94	11.82	2.81	32.73	41.53	19	1,109		Y
BNY Mellon Equity Income Fund Class I	DQIRX	B-	C	B	Up	1.18	12.37	3.81	36.81	48.73	19.31	1,109		Y
BNY Mellon Equity Income Fund Class Y	DQIYX	B-	C	B	Up	1.23	12.43	4.23	37.70	49.57	19.42	1,109		Y
BNY Mellon Income Stock Fund Class A	BMIAX	B-	C	B	Up	5.08	16.98	6.20	37.00	46.59	8.81	1,011	800-645-6561	Y
BNY Mellon Income Stock Fund Class I	BMIIX	B-	C	B	Up	5.16	17.13	6.47	38.05	47.72	8.81	1,011	800-645-6561	Y
BNY Mellon Income Stock Fund Class M	MPISX	B-	C	B	Up	5.17	17.17	6.50	38.13	47.80	8.81	1,011	800-645-6561	Y
BNY Mellon Income Stock Fund Class Y	BMIYX	B-	C	B	Up	5.18	17.19	6.49	37.96	47.61	8.8	1,011	800-645-6561	Y
BNY Mellon Income Stock Fund Investor shares	MIISX	B-	C	B	Up	5.16	17.08	6.27	37.04	45.77	8.92	1,011	800-645-6561	Y
BrandywineGLOBAL - Diversified US Large Cap Value Cls I	LBWIX	B-	C	B	Up	2.78	15.10	5.85	41.60	45.11	19.58	946.7	877-721-1926	Y
BrandywineGLOBAL - Diversified US Large Cap Value Cls IS	LBISX	B-	C	B	Up	2.77	15.15	5.95	42.01	45.69	19.6	946.7	877-721-1926	Y
Bridge Builder Large Cap Value Fund	BBVLX	B-	C	B	Up	4.58	18.87	8.45	40.72		12.71	8,688		Y
Calamos Dividend Growth Fund Class A	CADVX	B-	C	B		4.25	18.89	9.96	47.24	44.81	12.98	17.1	800-582-6959	Y
Calamos Dividend Growth Fund Class C	CCDVX	B-	C	B		4.09	18.35	9.09	44.05	39.56	12.7	17.1	800-582-6959	Y
Calamos Dividend Growth Fund Class I	CIDVX	B-	C	B		4.32	18.94	10.16	48.36	46.60	12.96	17.1	800-582-6959	Y
Calvert US Large Cap Value Responsible Index Fund Class A	CFJAX	B-	C	B	Up	4.77	18.28	7.95	37.97		23.03	378.8	301-951-4881	Y
Calvert US Large Cap Value Responsible Index Fund Class I	CFJIX	B-	C	B	Up	4.84	18.45	8.26	39.39		23.17	378.8	301-951-4881	Y
Carillon Eagle Growth & Income Fund Class A	HRCVX	B	C+	A-		3.58	15.23	12.94	42.63	48.51	21.29	812.9	800-421-4184	Y
Carillon Eagle Growth & Income Fund Class C	HIGCX	B	C+	B+		3.42	14.79	12.11	39.46	42.95	20.28	812.9	800-421-4184	Y
Carillon Eagle Growth & Income Fund Class I	HIGJX	B	C+	A-		3.71	15.41	13.28	43.91	50.56	21.25	812.9	800-421-4184	Y
Carillon Eagle Growth & Income Fund Class R3	HIGRX	B	C+	A-		3.51	15.03	12.64	41.42	45.98	21.19	812.9	800-421-4184	Y
Carillon Eagle Growth & Income Fund Class R5	HIGSX	B	C+	A-		3.67	15.41	13.15	43.75	49.69	21.27	812.9	800-421-4184	Y
Carillon Eagle Growth & Income Fund Class R6	HIGUX	B	C+	A-		3.73	15.46	13.37	44.23	50.80	21.2	812.9	800-421-4184	Y
Carillon Eagle Growth & Income Fund Class Y	HIGYX	B	C+	A-		3.59	15.18	12.77	42.26	48.12	21.2	812.9	800-421-4184	Y
Castle Focus Fund Class Investor	MOATX	B-	C	B+	Up	4.32	11.98	5.19	20.82	28.21	21.21	115.6	877-743-7820	Y
ClearBridge Large Cap Value Fund Class 1	LCLIX	B-	C	B		5.36	19.40	9.90	37.47	41.51	33.04	1,676	877-721-1926	Y
ClearBridge Large Cap Value Fund Class A	SINAX	B-	C	B	Up	5.31	19.28	9.66	36.62	40.09	33.06	1,676	877-721-1926	Y

Category: US Equity Large Cap Value (con't)

Fund Name	Ticker Symbol	RATINGS: Overall Rating	Reward Rating	Risk Rating	Recent Up/ Downgrade	TOTAL RETURNS & PERFORMANCE: 3-Month Total Return	6-Month Total Return	1-Year Total Return	3-Year Total Return	5-Year Total Return	ASSETS: NAV	Total Assets (MIL)	NEW INVESTORS: Telephone	Open to New Investors
ClearBridge Large Cap Value Fund Class A2	LIVVX	B-	C	B	Up	5.27	19.17	9.51	36.02	38.98	33.03	1,676	877-721-1926	Y
ClearBridge Large Cap Value Fund Class C	SINOX	B-	C	B	Up	5.11	18.86	8.87	33.61	34.90	32.06	1,676	877-721-1926	Y
ClearBridge Large Cap Value Fund Class I	SAIFX	B-	C	B		5.36	19.40	9.96	37.81	42.15	32.98	1,676	877-721-1926	Y
ClearBridge Large Cap Value Fund Class IS	LMLSX	B-	C	B		5.37	19.43	10.01	38.01	42.57	32.99	1,676	877-721-1926	Y
ClearBridge Large Cap Value Fund Class R	LCBVX	B-	C	B	Up	5.19	18.97	9.03	34.96	36.78	33.1	1,676	877-721-1926	Y
Cognios Large Cap Value Fund Institutional Class	COGVX	B-	C	B	Up	4.08	22.30	12.55			9.43	20.5		Y
Cognios Large Cap Value Fund Investor Class	COGLX	B-	C	B	Up	4.07	22.59	12.89			9.44	20.5		Y
Cohen & Steers Alternative Income Fund Class A	DVFAX	B-	C	B		3.87	17.72	9.27	41.28	44.74	11.89	49.9	212-832-3232	Y
Cohen & Steers Alternative Income Fund Class C	DVFCX	B-	C	B	Up	3.69	17.32	8.55	38.51	40.03	11.8	49.9	212-832-3232	Y
Cohen & Steers Alternative Income Fund Class Institutional	DVFIX	B-	C	B		3.96	17.96	9.69	42.81	47.33	11.92	49.9	212-832-3232	Y
Cohen & Steers Alternative Income Fund Class R	DVFRX	B-	C	B	Up	3.83	17.69	9.17	40.69	43.72	11.91	49.9	212-832-3232	Y
Cohen & Steers Alternative Income Fund Class Z	DVFZX	B-	C	B		3.94	17.94	9.68	42.79	47.31	11.92	49.9	212-832-3232	Y
Columbia Dividend Income Fund Advisor Class	CVIRX	B	C+	B+		4.09	17.51	12.95	44.58	62.82	23.09	14,746	800-345-6611	Y
Columbia Dividend Income Fund Class A	LBSAX	B-	C+	B+	Down	4.05	17.38	12.65	43.49	60.81	22.68	14,746	800-345-6611	Y
Columbia Dividend Income Fund Class C	LBSCX	B-	C+	B+	Down	3.84	16.92	11.86	40.34	54.92	21.95	14,746	800-345-6611	Y
Columbia Dividend Income Fund Class R	CDIRX	B-	C+	B+	Down	3.98	17.22	12.42	42.46	58.85	22.7	14,746	800-345-6611	Y
Columbia Dividend Income Fund Class V	GEQAX	B	C+	B+		4.05	17.37	12.65	43.46	60.72	22.69	14,746	800-345-6611	
Columbia Dividend Income Fund Institutional 2 Class	CDDRX	B	C+	B+		4.11	17.57	13.05	44.96	63.72	23.07	14,746	800-345-6611	Y
Columbia Dividend Income Fund Institutional 3 Class	CDDYX	B	C+	B+		4.12	17.58	13.08	45.23	64.16	23.1	14,746	800-345-6611	Y
Columbia Dividend Income Fund Institutional Class	GSFTX	B	C+	B+		4.11	17.50	12.92	44.59	62.84	22.7	14,746	800-345-6611	Y
Columbia Dividend Opportunity Fund Advisor Class	CDORX	B-	C	B+	Down	2.62	16.30	10.09	31.29	41.93	9.47	2,777	800-345-6611	Y
Columbia Dividend Opportunity Fund Class A	INUTX	B-	C	B+	Down	2.50	16.11	9.79	30.25	40.24	9.28	2,777	800-345-6611	Y
Columbia Dividend Opportunity Fund Class C	ACUIX	B-	C	B+		2.25	15.70	8.84	27.21	34.92	9.05	2,777	800-345-6611	Y
Columbia Dividend Opportunity Fund Class R	RSOOX	B-	C	B+		2.55	16.11	9.52	29.30	38.52	9.28	2,777	800-345-6611	Y
Columbia Dividend Opportunity Fund Institutional 2 Class	RSDFX	B-	C	B+	Down	2.67	16.42	10.16	31.51	42.55	9.35	2,777	800-345-6611	Y
Columbia Dividend Opportunity Fund Institutional 3 Class	CDOYX	B-	C	B+	Down	2.53	16.31	10.18	31.63	42.84	9.49	2,777	800-345-6611	Y
Columbia Dividend Opportunity Fund Institutional Class	CDOZX	B-	C	B+	Down	2.66	16.44	10.13	31.35	42.09	9.33	2,777	800-345-6611	Y
Columbia Large Cap Value Fund Advisor Class	RDERX	B-	C	B	Up	4.46	19.05	8.54	38.10	44.00	13.57	1,984	800-345-6611	Y
Columbia Large Cap Value Fund Class A	INDZX	B-	C	B	Up	4.40	18.89	8.26	37.06	42.19	13.58	1,984	800-345-6611	Y
Columbia Large Cap Value Fund Class R	RDEIX	B-	C	B	Up	4.36	18.79	8.04	36.09	40.41	13.49	1,984	800-345-6611	Y
Columbia Large Cap Value Fund Institutional 2 Class	RSEDX	B-	C	B	Up	4.48	19.07	8.61	38.36	44.54	13.58	1,984	800-345-6611	Y
Columbia Large Cap Value Fund Institutional 3 Class	CDEYX	B-	C	B	Up	4.51	19.13	8.68	38.55	44.83	13.74	1,984	800-345-6611	Y
Columbia Large Cap Value Fund Institutional Class	CDVZX	B-	C	B	Up	4.55	19.07	8.62	38.14	43.93	13.56	1,984	800-345-6611	Y
Commerce Value Fund	CFVLX	B-	C	B+	Down	3.16	15.10	12.51	36.96	53.61	30.53	256.6		Y
Copley Fund	COPLX	B	B	A		3.37	13.28	14.41	43.80	70.69	115.32	100.4	877-881-2751	Y
Cullen High Dividend Equity Fund Class C	CHVCX	B-	C	B+		0.56	12.41	8.88	26.99	36.35	16.69	1,603	800-582-6757	Y
Cullen High Dividend Equity Fund Class Institutional	CHDVX	B-	C	B+	Down	0.88	12.95	10.01	30.87	43.35	16.92	1,603	800-582-6757	Y
Cullen High Dividend Equity Fund Class R1	CHDRX	B-	C	B+	Down	0.72	12.57	9.21	28.03	38.12	14.34	1,603	800-582-6757	Y
Cullen High Dividend Equity Fund Class R2	CHDPX	B-	C	B+	Down	0.75	12.73	9.44	28.91	39.85	14.57	1,603	800-582-6757	Y
Cullen High Dividend Equity Fund Retail Class	CHDEX	B-	C	B+	Down	0.76	12.82	9.67	29.90	41.53	16.91	1,603	800-582-6757	Y
Cullen Value Fund Class C	CVLFX	B-	C	B+		3.70	14.42	8.64	36.06	35.72	16.55	40.3	800-582-6757	Y
Cullen Value Fund Class I	CVLVX	B-	C	B+		3.95	14.97	9.73	40.19	42.58	16.55	40.3	800-582-6757	Y
Cullen Value Fund Retail Class	CVLEX	B-	C	B+		3.89	14.82	9.47	39.19	40.97	16.56	40.3	800-582-6757	Y
Cutler Equity Fund	CALEX	B-	C	B+	Down	4.80	15.09	10.36	36.00	46.04	20.67	159.8		Y
Davenport Value & Income Fund	DVIPX	B-	C	B	Up	2.50	14.68	5.34	29.52	42.28	16.68	686.4		Y
Delaware Value® Fund Class A	DDVAX	B-	C	B+		0.49	11.77	5.86	27.88	45.06	21.51	14,534		
Delaware Value® Fund Class C	DDVCX	B-	C	B+		0.35	11.38	5.12	25.05	39.77	21.48	14,534		
Delaware Value® Fund Class R	DDVRX	B-	C	B+		0.47	11.68	5.62	26.95	43.29	21.51	14,534		Y
Delaware Value® Fund Class R6	DDZRX	B-	C	B+		0.63	12.03	6.29	29.29	47.33	21.51	14,534		Y
Delaware Value® Fund Institutional Class	DDVIX	B-	C	B+		0.60	11.91	6.18	28.84	46.87	21.51	14,534		
Diamond Hill Large Cap Fund Class A	DHLAX	B-	C+	B	Up	6.87	21.79	12.25	48.35	54.10	27.66	6,056	888-226-5595	Y
Diamond Hill Large Cap Fund Class C	DHLCX	B-	C	B	Up	6.66	21.34	11.39	45.05	48.41	26.09	6,056	888-226-5595	Y

Category: US Equity Large Cap Value (con't)

Fund Name	Ticker Symbol	Overall Rating	Reward Rating	Risk Rating	Recent Up/ Downgrade	3-Month Total Return	6-Month Total Return	1-Year Total Return	3-Year Total Return	5-Year Total Return	NAV	Total Assets (MIL)	Telephone	Open to New Investors
Diamond Hill Large Cap Fund Class I	DHLRX	B-	C+	B	Up	6.94	21.96	12.57	49.70	56.31	27.87	6,056	888-226-5595	Y
Diamond Hill Large Cap Fund Class Y	DHLYX	B-	C+	B	Up	6.97	22.04	12.68	50.18	57.21	27.9	6,056	888-226-5595	Y
Dodge & Cox Stock Fund	DODGX	B-	C	B	Up	2.59	14.02	4.14	51.77	48.73	187.1	67,165	415-981-1710	Y
Dunham Large Cap Value Fund Class A	DALVX	B-	C	B	Up	4.16	16.62	8.00	32.88	31.93	14.52	82.9	800-442-4358	Y
Dunham Large Cap Value Fund Class C	DCLVX	B-	C	B	Up	3.89	16.17	7.19	29.89	27.06	13.86	82.9	800-442-4358	Y
Dunham Large Cap Value Fund Class N	DNLVX	B-	C	B	Up	4.21	16.81	8.31	33.91	33.66	14.59	82.9	800-442-4358	Y
DWS CROCI Equity Dividend Fund - Class A	KDHAX	B-	C	B+	Down	2.51	16.30	13.01	44.63	51.85	55.16	1,160		Y
DWS CROCI Equity Dividend Fund - Class C	KDHCX	B-	C	B+	Down	2.42	15.92	12.31	41.54	46.38	55.08	1,160		Y
DWS CROCI Equity Dividend Fund - Class Inst	KDHIX	B-	C	B+	Down	2.58	16.45	13.34	45.77	53.82	55.18	1,160		Y
DWS CROCI Equity Dividend Fund - Class R	KDHRX	B-	C	B+	Down	2.47	16.13	12.70	43.46	49.87	55.02	1,160		Y
DWS CROCI Equity Dividend Fund - Class R6	KDHTX	B-	C	B+	Down	2.60	16.50	13.39	46.07	53.85	55.18	1,160		Y
DWS CROCI Equity Dividend Fund - Class S	KDHSX	B-	C	B+	Down	2.57	16.44	13.26	45.65	53.70	55.14	1,160		Y
DWS CROCI Equity Dividend Fund - Class T	KDHUX	B-	C	B+	Down	2.53	16.30	13.06	44.70	51.89	55.16	1,160		Y
Eaton Vance Focused Value Opportunities Fund Class A	EAFVX	B-	C+	B		6.56	20.93	10.93	45.58	49.93	16.23	104.5		Y
Eaton Vance Focused Value Opportunities Fund Class C	ECFVX	B-	C+	B		6.42	20.52	10.17	42.33	44.51	15.91	104.5		Y
Eaton Vance Focused Value Opportunities Fund Class I	EIFVX	B-	C+	B		6.61	21.11	11.23	46.67	51.86	16.29	104.5		Y
Eaton Vance Large-Cap Value Fund Class A	EHSTX	B-	C+	B		5.78	20.20	10.88	39.75	41.88	19.54	1,726		Y
Eaton Vance Large-Cap Value Fund Class I	EILVX	B-	C+	B		5.82	20.39	11.17	40.79	43.60	19.62	1,726		Y
Eaton Vance Large-Cap Value Fund Class R	ERSTX	B-	C	B		5.67	20.04	10.63	38.66	40.02	19.48	1,726		Y
Eaton Vance Large-Cap Value Fund Class R6	ERLVX	B-	C+	B		5.78	20.42	11.24	41.11	44.17	19.63	1,726		Y
Eaton Vance Tax-Managed Value Fund Class A	EATVX	B-	C+	B		3.61	17.90	9.14	40.95	43.02	28.64	620.9		Y
Eaton Vance Tax-Managed Value Fund Class C	ECTVX	B-	C	B		3.42	17.45	8.31	37.81	37.70	27.45	620.9		Y
Eaton Vance Tax-Managed Value Fund Class I	EITVX	B-	C+	B		3.67	18.04	9.39	41.99	44.68	28.52	620.9		Y
Edgar Lomax Value Fund	LOMAX	B-	C	B+		2.64	13.02	10.56	40.46	52.86	13.97	115.3	703-719-0026	Y
EIC Value Fund Class A	EICVX	B-	C	B+	Up	2.20	13.84	4.86	28.93	30.75	13.9	206.0	404-239-0111	Y
EIC Value Fund Class C	EICCX	B-	C	B	Up	2.02	13.48	4.09	25.99	25.98	13.63	206.0	404-239-0111	Y
EIC Value Fund Institutional Class	EICIX	B-	C	B+	Up	2.28	14.03	5.15	29.91	32.43	13.89	206.0	404-239-0111	Y
EQ/Large Cap Value Index Portfolio Class IA		B-	C	B	Up	0.91	4.22	2.49	30.45	39.58		666.2	877-222-2144	Y
EQ/Large Cap Value Index Portfolio Class IB		B-	C	B	Up	0.91	4.23	2.50	30.39	39.54		666.2	877-222-2144	Y
EQ/Large Cap Value Index Portfolio Class K		B-	C	B	Up	1.03	4.40	2.77	31.40	40.95		666.2	877-222-2144	Y
EquityCompass Quality Dividend Fund Class A	QDVAX	B-	C	B		0.81	13.83	9.26	29.43	35.91	12.76	70.0	443-224-1231	Y
EquityCompass Quality Dividend Fund Institutional Class	QDVIX	B-	C	B		0.88	13.95	9.58	30.37	36.90	12.76	70.0	443-224-1231	Y
FBP Equity & Dividend Plus Fund	FBPEX	B-	C	B	Up	0.66	10.15	2.62	33.83	32.00	25.19	28.7		Y
FDP BlackRock Equity Dividend Fund Institutional Shares	MAVVX	B-	C	B	Up	4.58	16.21	7.17	47.60	39.25	12.54	60.7		Y
FDP BlackRock Equity Dividend Fund Investor A Shares	MDVVX	B-	C	B	Up	4.57	16.18	6.87	46.51	37.59	12.35	60.7		Y
FDP BlackRock Equity Dividend Fund Investor C Shares	MCVVX	B-	C	B	Up	4.37	15.71	6.12	43.22	32.49	11.93	60.7		Y
Federated MDT All Cap Core Fund Class A Shares	QAACX	B-	C	B	Down	4.13	21.33	10.16	60.22	57.97	29.69	314.2	800-341-7400	Y
Federated MDT All Cap Core Fund Class C Shares	QCACX	B-	C	B	Down	3.96	20.90	9.35	56.61	52.10	27.82	314.2	800-341-7400	Y
Federated MDT All Cap Core Fund Class R6 Shares	QKACX	B-	C	B	Down	4.23	21.56	10.50	61.41	57.75	29.54	314.2	800-341-7400	Y
Federated MDT All Cap Core Fund Institutional Shares	QIACX	B-	C	B	Down	4.22	21.53	10.49	61.64	60.31	30.08	314.2	800-341-7400	Y
Federated MDT Large Cap Value Fund Class A	FSTRX	B-	C	B	Up	1.98	14.27	5.21	39.13	36.28	27.17	1,161	800-341-7400	Y
Federated MDT Large Cap Value Fund Class B	QBLVX	B-	C	B	Up	2.37	15.11	5.55	34.79	32.54	27.22	1,161	800-341-7400	Y
Federated MDT Large Cap Value Fund Class C	QCLVX	B-	C	B	Up	2.38	15.14	5.59	34.86	32.61	27.21	1,161	800-341-7400	Y
Federated MDT Large Cap Value Fund Class R	QRLVX	B-	C	B	Up	2.48	15.31	5.96	36.09	34.49	27.19	1,161	800-341-7400	Y
Federated MDT Large Cap Value Fund Class R6	FSTLX	B-	C	B		2.61	15.73	6.72	39.16	38.90	27.2	1,161	800-341-7400	Y
Federated MDT Large Cap Value Fund Institutional Shares	FMSTX	B-	C	B	Up	2.63	15.70	6.65	38.99	39.29	27.19	1,161	800-341-7400	Y
Federated MDT Large Cap Value Fund Service Shares	FSTKX	B-	C	B	Up	2.57	15.56	6.41	38.04	37.78	27.21	1,161	800-341-7400	Y
Fidelity Advisor® Equity Value Fund Class A	FAVAX	B-	C	B	Up	2.80	13.61	3.80	31.18	33.12	17.61	233.2	617-563-7000	Y
Fidelity Advisor® Equity Value Fund Class C	FAVCX	B-	C	B	Up	2.56	13.10	3.01	28.13	28.04	17.17	233.2	617-563-7000	Y
Fidelity Advisor® Equity Value Fund Class M	FAVTX	B-	C	B	Up	2.68	13.40	3.51	30.06	31.29	17.6	233.2	617-563-7000	Y
Fidelity Advisor® Equity Value Fund Class Z	FAEVX	B-	C	B	Up	2.92	13.85	4.22	32.72	35.47	17.92	233.2	617-563-7000	Y
Fidelity Advisor® Equity Value Fund I Class	FAIVX	B-	C	B	Up	2.87	13.71	4.08	32.26	35.01	17.91	233.2	617-563-7000	Y

Category: US Equity Large Cap Value (con't)

Fund Name	Ticker Symbol	RATINGS: Overall Rating	Reward Rating	Risk Rating	Recent Up/ Downgrade	TOTAL RETURNS & PERFORMANCE: 3-Month Total Return	6-Month Total Return	1-Year Total Return	3-Year Total Return	5-Year Total Return	ASSETS: NAV	Total Assets (MIL)	NEW INVESTORS: Telephone	Open to New Investors
Fidelity Advisor® Stock Selector Large Cap Value Cls A	FLUAX	B-	C	B	Up	4.03	16.32	6.48	30.05	34.50	20.09	981.9	617-563-7000	Y
Fidelity Advisor® Stock Selector Large Cap Value Cls I	FLUIX	B-	C	B	Up	4.13	16.42	6.76	30.93	36.25	20.13	981.9	617-563-7000	Y
Fidelity Advisor® Stock Selector Large Cap Value Cls M	FLUTX	B-	C	B	Up	3.99	16.11	6.14	28.76	32.37	20.03	981.9	617-563-7000	Y
Fidelity Advisor® Stock Selector Large Cap Value Cls Z	FSCZX	B-	C	B	Up	4.13	16.53	6.93	31.55	36.85	20.16	981.9	617-563-7000	Y
Fidelity® Equity-Income Fund	FEQIX	B-	C	B		3.72	17.20	9.26	36.82	37.93	58.36	6,371	617-563-7000	Y
Fidelity® Equity-Income Fund Class K	FEIKX	B-	C	B		3.75	17.27	9.37	37.25	38.69	58.33	6,371	617-563-7000	Y
Fidelity® Large Cap Value Enhanced Index Fund	FLVEX	B-	C	B	Up	2.60	14.76	6.31	38.37	44.52	12.98	3,738	617-563-7000	Y
Fidelity® Series Large Cap Value Index Fund	FIOOX	B-	C	B		3.86	17.18	8.60	36.03	43.22	12.89	4,259	617-563-7000	Y
Fidelity® Series Stock Selector Large Cap Value Fund	FBLEX	B-	C	B	Up	4.32	16.79	7.60	32.08	38.05	12.31	10,814	617-563-7000	Y
Fidelity® Series Value Discovery Fund	FNKLX	B-	C	B+	Up	2.80	13.72	4.45	30.43	33.92	12.84	8,022	617-563-7000	Y
Fidelity® Stock Selector Large Cap Value Fund	FSLVX	B-	C	B	Up	4.11	16.50	6.79	31.16	36.45	20.26	981.9	617-563-7000	Y
Fidelity® Value Discovery Fund	FVDFX	B-	C	B	Up	2.86	13.73	4.35	32.76	36.09	28.4	2,431	617-563-7000	Y
Fidelity® Value Discovery Fund Class K	FVDKX	B-	C	B	Up	2.86	13.77	4.43	33.22	36.91	28.41	2,431	617-563-7000	Y
First Investors Equity Income Fund Advisor Class	FIUUX	B-	C	B	Up	3.36	14.00	5.09	30.56	36.60	9.59	503.2	800-423-4026	Y
First Investors Equity Income Fund Class A	FIUTX	B-	C	B	Up	3.44	13.96	4.90	29.40	34.43	9.54	503.2	800-423-4026	Y
First Investors Equity Income Fund Institutional Class	FIUVX	B-	C	B	Up	3.51	14.27	5.31	31.03	37.01	9.53	503.2	800-423-4026	Y
Franklin Equity Income Fund Advisor Class	FEIFX	B-	C	B+	Down	3.89	15.83	10.11	39.01	46.49	25.51	2,260	650-312-2000	Y
Franklin Equity Income Fund Class A	FISEX	B-	C	B+	Down	3.83	15.69	9.84	37.96	44.70	25.47	2,260	650-312-2000	Y
Franklin Equity Income Fund Class C	FRETX	B-	C	B+		3.61	15.26	8.98	34.85	39.33	25.27	2,260	650-312-2000	Y
Franklin Equity Income Fund Class R	FREIX	B-	C	B+	Down	3.77	15.58	9.58	37.02	42.96	25.47	2,260	650-312-2000	Y
Franklin Equity Income Fund Class R6	FEIQX	B-	C	B+	Down	3.90	15.86	10.20	39.44	47.35	25.51	2,260	650-312-2000	Y
Goldman Sachs Equity Income Fund Class A	GSGRX	B-	C	B+		3.99	16.29	10.28	32.86	36.29	38.98	366.2	800-526-7384	Y
Goldman Sachs Equity Income Fund Class C	GSGCX	B-	C	B+		3.79	15.81	9.52	29.97	31.34	37.18	366.2	800-526-7384	Y
Goldman Sachs Equity Income Fund Class P	GABPX	B-	C	B+		4.10	16.46	10.70	33.48	36.93	39.64	366.2	800-526-7384	Y
Goldman Sachs Equity Income Fund Class R	GRGRX	B-	C	B+		3.92	16.12	9.98	31.82	34.57	38.77	366.2	800-526-7384	Y
Goldman Sachs Equity Income Fund Class R6	GRGUX	B-	C	B+		4.10	16.50	10.69	34.44	38.45	39.65	366.2	800-526-7384	Y
Goldman Sachs Equity Income Fund Institutional Class	GSIIX	B-	C	B+		4.07	16.46	10.65	34.37	38.96	39.64	366.2	800-526-7384	Y
Goldman Sachs Equity Income Fund Investor Class	GRGTX	B-	C	B+		4.04	16.39	10.52	33.84	37.98	38.9	366.2	800-526-7384	Y
Goldman Sachs Equity Income Fund Service Class	GSGSX	B-	C	B+		3.96	16.16	10.13	32.41	35.56	39.12	366.2	800-526-7384	Y
Goldman Sachs Large Cap Value Fund Class A	GSLAX	B-	C	B	Up	3.59	16.87	8.00	29.09	26.45	14.68	496.0	800-526-7384	Y
Goldman Sachs Large Cap Value Fund Class P	GMYPX	B-	C	B	Up	3.69	17.05	8.28	30.33	28.73	15.17	496.0	800-526-7384	Y
Goldman Sachs Large Cap Value Fund Class R6	GSVUX	B-	C	B	Up	3.62	17.05	8.27	30.61	29.06	15.17	496.0	800-526-7384	Y
Goldman Sachs Large Cap Value Fund Institutional Class	GSLIX	B-	C	B	Up	3.70	17.04	8.32	30.32	28.72	14.83	496.0	800-526-7384	Y
Goldman Sachs Large Cap Value Fund Investor Class	GSVTX	B-	C	B	Up	3.67	16.98	8.20	29.94	28.00	14.67	496.0	800-526-7384	Y
Gotham Large Value Fund Institutional Class	GVALX	B-	C	B	Down	3.07	18.03	9.00	50.70		13.09	57.2	877-974-6852	Y
Great-West T. Rowe Price Equity Income Fund Class L	MXTQX	B-	C	B	Up	3.85	15.64	4.48	38.77	33.10	9.15	742.5		Y
Great-West T. Rowe Price Equity Income Institutional Cls	MXVHX	B-	C	B	Up	4.00	15.91	5.12	41.40	37.18	7.73	742.5		Y
Great-West T. Rowe Price Equity Income Fund Investor Class	MXEQX	B-	C	B	Up	3.92	15.75	4.72	40.02	35.22	20.76	742.5		Y
Hamlin High Dividend Equity Institutional Cls Shares	HHDFX	B-	C	B+	Up	3.59	14.21	6.17	31.47	31.51	22.14	765.8		Y
Hamlin High Dividend Equity Fund Investor Class Shares	HHDVX	B-	C	B+	Up	3.51	13.99	5.83	29.98	28.42	22.18	765.8		Y
Hartford Dividend and Growth HLS Fund Class IA	HIADX	B-	C	B+		3.60	16.44	10.06	45.10	53.36	23.01	3,214	888-843-7824	Y
Hartford Dividend and Growth HLS Fund Class IB	HDGBX	B-	C	B		3.48	16.32	9.79	44.00	51.43	22.87	3,214	888-843-7824	Y
Hartford Quality Value Fund Class A	HVOAX	B-	C	B	Up	3.68	18.31	7.84	36.11	31.46	20.28	207.8	888-843-7824	Y
Hartford Quality Value Fund Class F	HVOFX	B-	C	B	Up	3.79	18.57	8.34	37.41	32.71	19.98	207.8	888-843-7824	Y
Hartford Quality Value Fund Class I	HVOIX	B-	C	B	Up	3.78	18.54	8.26	37.43	33.66	20.01	207.8	888-843-7824	Y
Hartford Quality Value Fund Class R3	HVORX	B-	C	B	Up	3.66	18.22	7.61	34.94	29.58	20.63	207.8	888-843-7824	Y
Hartford Quality Value Fund Class R4	HVOSX	B-	C	B	Up	3.68	18.36	7.94	36.16	31.63	20.82	207.8	888-843-7824	Y
Hartford Quality Value Fund Class R5	HVOTX	B-	C	B	Up	3.80	18.52	8.26	37.43	33.56	20.99	207.8	888-843-7824	Y
Hartford Quality Value Fund Class R6	HVOVX	B-	C	B	Up	3.79	18.60	8.38	36.91	32.22	21.04	207.8	888-843-7824	Y
Hartford Quality Value Fund Class Y	HVOYX	B-	C	B	Up	3.80	18.61	8.31	37.73	34.12	21.03	207.8	888-843-7824	Y
Heartland Select Value Fund Institutional Class	HNSVX	B-	C	B+		3.32	15.26	6.18	43.31	40.52	25.82	216.7	800-432-7856	Y
Heartland Select Value Fund Investor Class	HRSVX	B-	C	B+		3.22	15.11	5.93	42.28	38.77	25.9	216.7	800-432-7856	Y

Category: US Equity Large Cap Value (con't)

Fund Name	Ticker Symbol	RATINGS: Overall Rating	Reward Rating	Risk Rating	Recent Up/ Downgrade	TOTAL RETURNS & PERFORMANCE: 3-Month Total Return	6-Month Total Return	1-Year Total Return	3-Year Total Return	5-Year Total Return	ASSETS: NAV	Total Assets (MIL)	NEW INVESTORS: Telephone	Open to New Investors
Hennessy Cornerstone Large Growth Fund Institutional Class	HILGX	B-	C	B	Up	1.60	13.78	3.88	43.65	38.93	10.15	134.4	800-966-4354	Y
Hennessy Cornerstone Large Growth Fund Investor Class	HFLGX	B-	C	B	Up	1.51	13.55	3.50	42.44	37.34	10.05	134.4	800-966-4354	Y
Hillman Fund No Load Shares	HCMAX	B	B-	B+	Up	4.05	21.94	14.88	55.58	65.26	26.95	44.8		Y
Homestead Funds Value Fund	HOVLX	B-	C	B	Down	3.71	17.24	11.19	45.42	54.39	53.31	938.5		Y
Integrity Dividend Harvest Fund Class A Shares	IDIVX	B-	C+	B	Down	1.55	13.61	12.87	27.30	49.88	14.05	135.1	800-276-1262	Y
Integrity Dividend Harvest Fund Class C	IDHCX	B-	C	B	Down	1.37	13.16	12.03	24.48	44.40	13.96	135.1	800-276-1262	Y
Integrity Dividend Harvest Fund Class I	IDHIX	B-	C+	B	Down	1.69	13.72	13.14	28.21	50.96	14.06	135.1	800-276-1262	Y
Invesco Exchange Fund	ACEHX	B-	C	B+		2.21	16.30	10.66	30.76	28.84	625.69	59.0	800-659-1005	
Invesco Oppenheimer Dividend Opportunity Fund Class A	OSVAX	B-	C	B+	Up	4.10	15.48	5.89	31.14	35.37	23.91	258.4	800-659-1005	Y
Invesco Oppenheimer Dividend Opportunity Fund Class C	OSCVX	B-	C	B+	Up	3.88	15.08	5.11	28.21	30.42	23.03	258.4	800-659-1005	Y
Invesco Oppenheimer Dividend Opportunity Fund Class R	OSVNX	B-	C	B+	Up	4.04	15.33	5.61	30.17	33.68	23.65	258.4	800-659-1005	Y
Invesco Oppenheimer Dividend Opportunity Fund Class R5	DVOPX	B-	C	B+		4.12	15.51	5.92	31.17	35.40	23.9	258.4	800-659-1005	Y
Invesco Oppenheimer Dividend Opportunity Fund Class R6	OSVIX	B-	C	B+	Up	4.22	15.73	6.35	32.82	38.34	23.88	258.4	800-659-1005	Y
Invesco Oppenheimer Dividend Opportunity Fund Class Y	OSVYX	B-	C	B+	Up	4.17	15.63	6.17	32.12	37.11	23.88	258.4	800-659-1005	Y
Invesco Oppenheimer Equity Income Fund Class A	OAEIX	B-	C	B	Up	2.98	15.27	5.09	34.11	21.76	29.95	2,936	800-659-1005	Y
Invesco Oppenheimer Equity Income Fund Class R	ONEIX	B-	C	B	Up	2.90	15.12	4.80	33.06	20.19	28.48	2,936	800-659-1005	Y
Invesco Oppenheimer Equity Income Fund Class R5	ETYIX	B-	C	B		3.02	15.31	5.13	34.16	21.80	29.93	2,936	800-659-1005	Y
Invesco Oppenheimer Equity Income Fund Class R6	OEIIX	B-	C	B	Up	3.11	15.54	5.54	35.75	24.35	29.89	2,936	800-659-1005	Y
Invesco Oppenheimer Equity Income Fund Class Y	OYEIX	B-	C	B	Up	3.05	15.41	5.35	35.10	23.26	29.91	2,936	800-659-1005	Y
Janus Henderson Large Cap Value Fund Class A	JAPAX	B-	C	B	Up	4.34	18.23	7.30	33.43	36.93	13.94	95.0	877-335-2687	Y
Janus Henderson Large Cap Value Fund Class C	JAPCX	B-	C	B	Up	4.27	17.94	6.65	30.84	32.86	13.67	95.0	877-335-2687	Y
Janus Henderson Large Cap Value Fund Class D	JNPLX	B-	C	B	Up	4.47	18.38	7.55	34.26	38.32	13.78	95.0	877-335-2687	
Janus Henderson Large Cap Value Fund Class I	JAPIX	B-	C	B	Up	4.44	18.44	7.61	34.43	38.67	13.87	95.0	877-335-2687	Y
Janus Henderson Large Cap Value Fund Class N	JPLNX	B-	C	B	Up	4.45	18.40	7.66	34.79	39.26	13.83	95.0	877-335-2687	Y
Janus Henderson Large Cap Value Fund Class S	JAPSX	B-	C	B	Up	4.55	18.42	7.39	33.42	36.90	14.01	95.0	877-335-2687	Y
Janus Henderson Large Cap Value Fund Class T	JPLTX	B-	C	B	Up	4.40	18.31	7.42	33.81	37.63	13.76	95.0	877-335-2687	Y
JNL/DoubleLine® Shiller Enhanced CAPE® Fund Class A		B-	B-	B		4.84	22.88	13.29	60.28		15.14	1,770		Y
JNL/DoubleLine® Shiller Enhanced CAPE® Fund Class I		B-	B-	B	Down	4.97	23.07	13.67	61.24		15.2	1,770		Y
JNL/Mellon Capital Dow Index Fund Class A		B-	C	B+	Down	3.03	16.30	11.46	58.43	66.28	30.53	960.3		
JNL/Mellon Capital Dow Index Fund Class I		B-	C	B+	Down	3.12	16.54	11.83	59.41	67.32	30.72	960.3		Y
JNL/S&P 4 Fund Class A		B-	C	B	Up	1.48	15.24	4.04	34.70	40.04	21.85	6,353		Y
JNL/S&P 4 Fund Class I		B-	C	B	Up	1.57	15.44	4.37	35.45	40.80	21.97	6,353		Y
JNL/S&P Dividend Income & Growth Fund Class A		B-	C	B+		4.31	18.10	11.65	31.60	54.42	15.72	5,049		Y
JNL/S&P Dividend Income & Growth Fund Class I		B-	C	B+		4.44	18.28	12.00	32.60	56.16	15.98	5,049		Y
JNL/T. Rowe Price Value Fund Class A		B-	C	B	Up	4.65	18.70	8.83	39.54	42.69	16.18	4,398		Y
JNL/T. Rowe Price Value Fund Class I		B-	C	B	Up	4.75	18.83	9.16	40.53	44.40	16.97	4,398		Y
JNL/Vanguard Equity Income Fund Class A		B-	C	B+		2.89	14.84	8.28	35.21	46.96	11.37	282.4		Y
JNL/Vanguard Equity Income Fund Class I		B-	C	B+		2.97	14.97	8.64	36.55	49.30	11.44	282.4		Y
John Hancock Funds II Equity Income Fund Class 1	JIEMX	B-	C	B	Up	4.24	16.58	5.05	37.91	36.43	18.62	1,796	800-225-5913	Y
John Hancock Funds II Equity Income Fund Class NAV		B-	C	B	Up	4.31	16.63	5.16	38.17	36.85	18.6	1,796	800-225-5913	Y
JPMorgan Equity Income Fund Class A	OIEIX	B-	C	B+	Down	4.20	16.53	11.17	41.87	52.83	17.83	23,652	800-480-4111	Y
JPMorgan Equity Income Fund Class C	OINCX	B-	C	B+		4.06	16.29	10.66	39.76	49.06	17.47	23,652	800-480-4111	Y
JPMorgan Equity Income Fund Class I	HLIEX	B-	C	B+	Down	4.25	16.65	11.44	42.94	54.75	18.14	23,652	800-480-4111	Y
JPMorgan Equity Income Fund Class R2	OIEFX	B-	C	B+	Down	4.10	16.34	10.89	40.76	50.95	17.74	23,652	800-480-4111	Y
JPMorgan Equity Income Fund Class R3	OIEPX	B-	C	B+	Down	4.15	16.49	11.19	41.94	52.90	17.81	23,652	800-480-4111	Y
JPMorgan Equity Income Fund Class R4	OIEQX	B-	C	B+	Down	4.19	16.66	11.45	42.91	54.72	18.13	23,652	800-480-4111	Y
JPMorgan Equity Income Fund Class R5	OIERX	B-	C	B+	Down	4.28	16.79	11.66	43.67	56.29	18.16	23,652	800-480-4111	Y
JPMorgan Equity Income Fund Class R6	OIEJX	B-	C	B+	Down	4.31	16.79	11.72	44.02	56.82	18.14	23,652	800-480-4111	Y
JPMorgan Growth And Income Fund Class A	VGRIX	B-	C	B	Up	3.81	16.22	6.65	41.00	47.69	49.83	652.5	800-480-4111	Y
JPMorgan Growth And Income Fund Class C	VGICX	B-	C	B	Up	3.71	15.94	6.14	38.94	44.06	44.59	652.5	800-480-4111	Y
JPMorgan Growth And Income Fund Class I	VGIIX	B-	C	B	Up	3.88	16.37	6.94	42.09	49.55	52.69	652.5	800-480-4111	Y
JPMorgan Growth And Income Fund Class R2	VGRTX	B-	C	B	Up	3.76	16.07	6.38	39.96	45.86	50	652.5	800-480-4111	Y

Category: US Equity Large Cap Value (con't)

Fund Name	Ticker Symbol	RATINGS: Overall Rating	Reward Rating	Risk Rating	Recent Up/ Downgrade	TOTAL RETURNS & PERFORMANCE: 3-Month Total Return	6-Month Total Return	1-Year Total Return	3-Year Total Return	5-Year Total Return	ASSETS: NAV	Total Assets (MIL)	NEW INVESTORS: Telephone	Open to New Investors
JPMorgan Growth and Income Fund Class R3	JGAVX	B-	C	B	Up	3.82	16.24	6.66	41.05	47.75	52.66	652.5	800-480-4111	Y
JPMorgan Growth and Income Fund Class R4	JGRUX	B-	C	B	Up	3.90	16.39	6.93	41.70	48.43	52.69	652.5	800-480-4111	Y
JPMorgan Growth And Income Fund Class R5	VGIFX	B-	C	B	Up	3.93	16.45	7.08	42.82	49.97	53.06	652.5	800-480-4111	Y
JPMorgan Growth And Income Fund Class R6	VGINX	B-	C	B	Up	3.95	16.50	7.18	43.13	50.36	53.07	652.5	800-480-4111	Y
JPMorgan Value Advantage Fund Class A	JVAAX	B-	C	B	Up	3.77	17.68	6.99	37.76	40.13	35.46	10,840	800-480-4111	Y
JPMorgan Value Advantage Fund Class I	JVASX	B-	C	B	Up	3.84	17.83	7.28	38.80	41.91	35.67	10,840	800-480-4111	Y
JPMorgan Value Advantage Fund Class L	JVAIX	B-	C	B	Up	3.87	17.90	7.44	39.57	43.41	35.69	10,840	800-480-4111	Y
JPMorgan Value Advantage Fund Class R2	JGAQX	B-	C	B	Up	3.70	17.50	6.75	37.06	39.43	35.24	10,840	800-480-4111	Y
JPMorgan Value Advantage Fund Class R3	JVAPX	B-	C	B	Up	3.78	17.67	7.00	37.87	40.96	35.08	10,840	800-480-4111	Y
JPMorgan Value Advantage Fund Class R4	JVAQX	B-	C	B	Up	3.82	17.81	7.27	38.88	42.70	35.52	10,840	800-480-4111	Y
JPMorgan Value Advantage Fund Class R5	JVARX	B-	C	B	Up	3.84	17.90	7.40	39.43	43.27	35.62	10,840	800-480-4111	Y
JPMorgan Value Advantage Fund Class R6	JVAYX	B-	C	B	Up	3.90	17.99	7.56	39.83	43.68	35.67	10,840	800-480-4111	Y
Lord Abbett Affiliated Fund Class A	LAFFX	B-	C	B	Up	3.81	15.70	8.24	38.89	45.93	14.95	6,252	201-827-2000	Y
Lord Abbett Affiliated Fund Class C	LAFCX	B-	C	B	Up	3.67	15.28	7.45	35.84	40.65	15.01	6,252	201-827-2000	Y
Lord Abbett Affiliated Fund Class F	LAAFX	B-	C	B+	Up	3.84	15.78	8.53	39.57	47.14	14.96	6,252	201-827-2000	Y
Lord Abbett Affiliated Fund Class F3	LTFOX	B-	C	B+		3.85	15.80	8.68	39.95	47.05	15.07	6,252	201-827-2000	Y
Lord Abbett Affiliated Fund Class I	LAFYX	B-	C	B+	Up	3.85	15.85	8.53	39.90	47.72	15.02	6,252	201-827-2000	Y
Lord Abbett Affiliated Fund Class P	LAFPX	B-	C	B	Up	3.76	15.53	8.02	38.54	45.64	14.92	6,252	201-827-2000	
Lord Abbett Affiliated Fund Class R2	LAFQX	B-	C	B	Up	3.72	15.49	7.93	37.55	43.52	14.97	6,252	201-827-2000	Y
Lord Abbett Affiliated Fund Class R3	LAFRX	B-	C	B	Up	3.74	15.55	8.10	38.01	44.33	14.95	6,252	201-827-2000	Y
Lord Abbett Affiliated Fund Class R4	LAFSX	B-	C	B	Up	3.81	15.72	8.24	38.93	45.98	14.93	6,252	201-827-2000	Y
Lord Abbett Affiliated Fund Class R5	LAFTX	B-	C	B+	Up	3.85	15.84	8.54	39.99	47.47	15.03	6,252	201-827-2000	Y
Lord Abbett Affiliated Fund Class R6	LAFVX	B-	C	B+		3.85	15.82	8.62	40.25	47.86	15.06	6,252	201-827-2000	Y
Lord Abbett Fundamental Equity Class R4	LAVSX	B-	C	B	Up	2.26	14.43	7.00	32.35	35.80	12.21	2,533	201-827-2000	Y
Lord Abbett Fundamental Equity Class R5	LAVTX	B-	C	B	Up	2.23	14.44	7.19	33.34	37.10	12.36	2,533	201-827-2000	Y
Lord Abbett Fundamental Equity Class R6	LAVVX	B-	C	B	Up	2.30	14.57	7.35	33.69	37.71	12.42	2,533	201-827-2000	Y
Lord Abbett Fundamental Equity Fund Class A	LDFVX	B-	C	B	Up	2.16	14.35	6.94	32.24	36.61	12.27	2,533	201-827-2000	Y
Lord Abbett Fundamental Equity Fund Class C	GILAX	B-	C	B	Up	1.97	13.86	6.14	29.29	31.70	10.84	2,533	201-827-2000	Y
Lord Abbett Fundamental Equity Fund Class F	LAVFX	B-	C	B	Up	2.27	14.42	7.19	32.92	37.76	12.14	2,533	201-827-2000	Y
Lord Abbett Fundamental Equity Fund Class F3	LDFOX	B-	C	B	Up	2.22	14.48	7.35	32.46	34.93	12.41	2,533	201-827-2000	Y
Lord Abbett Fundamental Equity Fund Class I	LAVYX	B-	C	B	Up	2.23	14.55	7.27	33.30	38.43	12.36	2,533	201-827-2000	Y
Lord Abbett Fundamental Equity Fund Class P	LAVPX	B-	C	B	Up	2.12	14.13	6.69	31.42	35.28	12.03	2,533	201-827-2000	
Lord Abbett Fundamental Equity Fund Class R2	LAVQX	B-	C	B	Up	2.12	14.17	6.56	30.87	34.31	12	2,533	201-827-2000	Y
Lord Abbett Fundamental Equity Fund Class R3	LAVRX	B-	C	B	Up	2.12	14.23	6.66	31.25	34.97	12.04	2,533	201-827-2000	Y
LSV U.S. Managed Volatility Fund Institutional Class	LSVMX	B-	C	A-	Down	1.88	13.69	11.71	30.32	51.96	12.95	72.8		Y
LSV U.S. Managed Volatility Fund Investor Class	LVAMX	B-	C	A-	Down	1.80	13.47	11.35	29.59	50.40	12.97	72.8		Y
Macquarie Pooled Trust Large Cap Value Portfolio	DPDEX	B-	C	B+		0.59	11.96	6.44	29.27	47.26	23.86	84.4	215-255-2300	Y
Madison Dividend Income Fund Class Y	BHBFX	B	C+	A-		4.34	17.03	16.68	48.93	60.39	27	177.9	800-767-0300	Y
MainStay Epoch U.S. Equity Yield Fund Class A	EPLPX	B-	C	B+	Down	3.04	15.23	10.52	30.16	48.68	16.47	1,056	800-624-6782	Y
MainStay Epoch U.S. Equity Yield Fund Class B	EPLBX	B-	C	B		2.83	14.61	9.46	26.75	42.61	15.91	1,056	800-624-6782	Y
MainStay Epoch U.S. Equity Yield Fund Class C	EPLKX	B-	C	B		2.83	14.61	9.46	26.54	41.97	15.91	1,056	800-624-6782	Y
MainStay Epoch U.S. Equity Yield Fund Class I	EPLCX	B-	C+	B+	Down	3.14	15.36	10.75	31.15	50.53	16.63	1,056	800-624-6782	Y
MainStay Epoch U.S. Equity Yield Fund Class R1	EPLRX	B-	C	B+	Down	3.05	15.23	10.57	30.79	50.12	16.62	1,056	800-624-6782	Y
MainStay Epoch U.S. Equity Yield Fund Class R2	EPLSX	B-	C	B+	Down	3.02	15.10	10.34	29.82	48.26	16.46	1,056	800-624-6782	Y
MainStay Epoch U.S. Equity Yield Fund Class R3	EPLTX	B-	C	B+	Down	2.89	14.97	10.07	28.92	46.49	16.46	1,056	800-624-6782	Y
MainStay Epoch U.S. Equity Yield Fund Class R6	EPLDX	B-	C+	B+	Down	3.10	15.41	10.85	31.43	50.84	16.63	1,056	800-624-6782	Y
MainStay Epoch U.S. Equity Yield Fund Investor Class	EPLIX	B-	C	B+	Down	3.00	15.03	10.20	29.35	47.29	16.39	1,056	800-624-6782	Y
Manning & Napier Disciplined Value Series Class I	MNDFX	B-	C	B+	Down	1.66	13.45	8.63	46.08	55.84	13.58	311.8	585-325-6880	Y
Manning & Napier Disciplined Value Series Class S	MDFSX	B-	C	B+	Down	1.62	13.38	8.42	44.99	53.97	7.41	311.8	585-325-6880	Y
Manning & Napier Disciplined Value Series Class W	MDVWX	B-	C	B+	Down	1.87	13.68	8.86	46.38	56.16	7.42	311.8	585-325-6880	Y
Manning & Napier Disciplined Value Series Class Z	MDVZX	B-	C	B+	Down	1.68	13.48	8.66	46.12	55.88	13.58	311.8	585-325-6880	Y
Manning & Napier Equity Income Series Class I	MNEIX	B-	C	B		3.86	19.22	9.56	36.56	41.17	12.33	77.2	585-325-6880	Y

Category: US Equity Large Cap Value (con't)

		RATINGS				TOTAL RETURNS & PERFORMANCE					ASSETS		NEW INVESTORS	
Fund Name	Ticker Symbol	Overall Rating	Reward Rating	Risk Rating	Recent Up/ Downgrade	3-Month Total Return	6-Month Total Return	1-Year Total Return	3-Year Total Return	5-Year Total Return	NAV	Total Assets (MIL)	Telephone	Open to New Investors
Manning & Napier Equity Income Series Class S	MNESX	B-	C	B		3.76	18.98	9.30	35.62	39.59	12.33	77.2	585-325-6880	Y
Manning & Napier Equity Income Series Class W	MNEWX	B-	C	B		3.97	19.34	9.67	36.71	41.32	12.32	77.2	585-325-6880	Y
Manning & Napier Equity Income Series Class Z	MNEZX	B-	C	B		3.94	19.32	9.65	36.68	41.29	12.33	77.2	585-325-6880	Y
MassMutual Select Diversified Value Administrative Cls	MDDLX	B-	C	B	Up	3.44	15.82	6.05	40.88	42.68	11.42	354.1		Y
MassMutual Select Diversified Value Fund Class A	MDDAX	B-	C	B	Up	3.38	15.77	5.83	39.94	41.03	11.3	354.1		Y
MassMutual Select Diversified Value Fund Class I	MDDIX	B-	C	B	Up	3.47	16.11	6.40	42.25	44.90	11.31	354.1		Y
MassMutual Select Diversified Value Fund Class R4	MDDRX	B-	C	B	Up	3.43	15.78	5.95	40.38	41.69	11.15	354.1		Y
MassMutual Select Diversified Value Fund Class R5	MDVSX	B-	C	B	Up	3.47	15.96	6.27	41.79	44.14	11.33	354.1		Y
MassMutual Select Diversified Value Fund Service Class	MDVYX	B-	C	B	Up	3.46	15.95	6.19	41.37	43.45	11.34	354.1		Y
MFS Blended Research Value Equity Fund Class A	BRUDX	B-	C	B	Up	1.74	14.33	5.31	34.61		12.84	186.2	877-960-6077	Y
MFS Blended Research Value Equity Fund Class B	BRUEX	B-	C	B	Up	1.66	13.94	4.62	31.72		12.83	186.2	877-960-6077	Y
MFS Blended Research Value Equity Fund Class C	BRUGX	B-	C	B	Up	1.58	13.86	4.58	31.63		12.81	186.2	877-960-6077	Y
MFS Blended Research Value Equity Fund Class I	BRUHX	B-	C	B	Up	1.89	14.45	5.63	35.71		12.91	186.2	877-960-6077	Y
MFS Blended Research Value Equity Fund Class R1	BRUJX	B-	C	B	Up	1.58	13.86	4.54	31.68		12.81	186.2	877-960-6077	Y
MFS Blended Research Value Equity Fund Class R2	BRUKX	B-	C	B	Up	1.73	14.19	5.04	33.72		12.87	186.2	877-960-6077	Y
MFS Blended Research Value Equity Fund Class R3	BRULX	B-	C	B	Up	1.81	14.26	5.34	34.76		12.9	186.2	877-960-6077	Y
MFS Blended Research Value Equity Fund Class R4	BRUMX	B-	C	B	Up	1.89	14.53	5.66	35.73		12.92	186.2	877-960-6077	Y
MFS Blended Research Value Equity Fund Class R6	BRUNX	B-	C	B	Up	1.89	14.52	5.77	36.10		12.93	186.2	877-960-6077	Y
MFS Equity Income Fund Class A	EQNAX	B-	C	B		2.16	15.25	6.19	36.89	39.24	15.39	211.4	877-960-6077	Y
MFS Equity Income Fund Class B	EQNBX	B-	C	B	Up	1.91	14.78	5.34	33.76	34.15	15.38	211.4	877-960-6077	Y
MFS Equity Income Fund Class C	EQNCX	B-	C	B	Up	1.98	14.84	5.38	33.82	34.05	15.39	211.4	877-960-6077	Y
MFS Equity Income Fund Class I	EQNIX	B-	C	B		2.22	15.46	6.46	38.05	41.07	15.4	211.4	877-960-6077	Y
MFS Equity Income Fund Class R1	EQNRX	B-	C	B	Up	1.91	14.78	5.31	33.76	33.99	15.46	211.4	877-960-6077	Y
MFS Equity Income Fund Class R2	EQNSX	B-	C	B		2.05	15.11	5.86	35.73	37.36	15.42	211.4	877-960-6077	Y
MFS Equity Income Fund Class R3	EQNTX	B-	C	B		2.15	15.23	6.19	36.91	39.23	15.42	211.4	877-960-6077	Y
MFS Equity Income Fund Class R4	EQNUX	B-	C	B		2.15	15.37	6.38	37.89	40.92	15.4	211.4	877-960-6077	Y
MFS Equity Income Fund Class R6	EQNVX	B-	C	B		2.22	15.47	6.58	38.36	41.93	15.5	211.4	877-960-6077	Y
MFS Value Fund Class 529A	EAVLX	B-	C	B	Up	5.00	19.30	10.52	35.73	48.70	41	48,073	877-960-6077	Y
MFS Value Fund Class 529B	EBVLX	B-	C	B	Up	4.81	18.99	10.28	34.31	45.40	40.55	48,073	877-960-6077	Y
MFS Value Fund Class 529C	ECVLX	B-	C	B	Up	4.79	18.83	9.66	32.58	42.96	40.35	48,073	877-960-6077	Y
MFS Value Fund Class A	MEIAX	B-	C	B	Up	5.01	19.32	10.55	35.77	48.77	41.35	48,073	877-960-6077	Y
MFS Value Fund Class B	MFEBX	B-	C	B	Up	4.79	18.85	9.71	32.76	43.27	41.17	48,073	877-960-6077	Y
MFS Value Fund Class C	MEICX	B-	C	B	Up	4.80	18.85	9.72	32.74	43.30	40.88	48,073	877-960-6077	Y
MFS Value Fund Class I	MEIIX	B-	C	B	Up	5.07	19.47	10.82	36.82	50.65	41.58	48,073	877-960-6077	Y
MFS Value Fund Class R1	MEIGX	B-	C	B	Up	4.80	18.85	9.71	32.76	43.31	40.55	48,073	877-960-6077	Y
MFS Value Fund Class R2	MVRRX	B-	C	B	Up	4.92	19.15	10.27	34.78	46.93	40.92	48,073	877-960-6077	Y
MFS Value Fund Class R3	MEIHX	B-	C	B	Up	5.01	19.31	10.54	35.79	48.76	41.18	48,073	877-960-6077	Y
MFS Value Fund Class R4	MEIJX	B-	C	B	Up	5.07	19.46	10.83	36.84	50.65	41.34	48,073	877-960-6077	Y
MFS Value Fund Class R6	MEIKX	B-	C	B	Up	5.10	19.52	10.92	37.22	51.40	41.33	48,073	877-960-6077	Y
Multi-Manager Value Strategies Fund Class A	CDEIX	B-	C	B	Up	4.64	17.98	8.65	41.66	45.86	13.84	3,055	800-345-6611	Y
Multi-Manager Value Strategies Fund Institutional Class	CZMVX	B-	C	B	Up	4.67	18.14	8.85	42.33	46.55	13.69	3,055	800-345-6611	Y
Nationwide Ziegler Equity Income Fund Class A	NWGYX	B-	C	B+	Up	3.23	14.82	6.91	35.56	43.08	12.76	37.0	800-848-0920	Y
Nationwide Ziegler Equity Income Fund Class C	NWGZX	B-	C	B	Up	3.03	14.44	6.05	32.47	37.84	12.57	37.0	800-848-0920	Y
Nationwide Ziegler Equity Income Fund Class R6	NWJAX	B-	C	B+	Up	3.22	14.93	7.06	36.72	45.34	12.82	37.0	800-848-0920	Y
Nationwide Ziegler Equity Income Institutional Service Cls	NWJBX	B-	C	B+	Up	3.30	14.99	7.13	36.40	44.69	12.83	37.0	800-848-0920	Y
Neiman Large Cap Value Fund A Shares	NEAMX	B-	C	B+	Up	3.41	15.90	6.91	36.53	42.91	28.54	33.6	858-551-4078	Y
Neiman Large Cap Value Fund No-Load Shares	NEIMX	B-	C	B+	Up	3.41	15.90	6.91	36.53	42.91	28.54	33.6	858-551-4078	Y
Neuberger Berman Equity Income Fund Class A	NBHAX	B	C+	B+	Up	2.95	14.78	5.50	30.37	36.35	13	1,490	212-476-9000	Y
Neuberger Berman Equity Income Fund Class C	NBHCX	B-	C	B+		2.77	14.37	4.73	27.56	31.39	12.92	1,490	212-476-9000	Y
Neuberger Berman Equity Income Fund Class R3	NBHRX	B	C+	B+	Up	2.90	14.68	5.22	29.36	34.56	12.97	1,490	212-476-9000	Y
Neuberger Berman Equity Income Fund Institutional Class	NBHIX	B	C+	A-	Up	3.03	14.94	5.79	31.84	38.88	13.04	1,490	212-476-9000	Y
Neuberger Berman Large Cap Value Fund Advisor Class	NBPBX	B	C+	A-		4.18	15.35	14.26	52.37	48.01	31.1	1,707	212-476-9000	

Category: US Equity
Large Cap Value (con't)

Fund Name	Ticker Symbol	RATINGS: Overall Rating	Reward Rating	Risk Rating	Recent Up/ Downgrade	TOTAL RETURNS & PERFORMANCE: 3-Month Total Return	6-Month Total Return	1-Year Total Return	3-Year Total Return	5-Year Total Return	ASSETS: NAV	Total Assets (MIL)	NEW INVESTORS: Telephone	Open to New Investors
Neuberger Berman Large Cap Value Fund Class A	NPNAX	B	C+	A-		4.18	15.40	14.40	52.86	48.86	31.09	1,707	212-476-9000	Y
Neuberger Berman Large Cap Value Fund Class C	NPNCX	B	C+	A-		4.04	15.02	13.59	49.51	43.51	31.15	1,707	212-476-9000	Y
Neuberger Berman Large Cap Value Fund Class R3	NPNRX	B	C+	A-		4.14	15.25	14.12	51.56	46.82	31.13	1,707	212-476-9000	Y
Neuberger Berman Large Cap Value Fund Class R6	NRLCX	B	C+	A-		4.33	15.66	14.80	54.02	50.65	31.07	1,707	212-476-9000	Y
Neuberger Berman Large Cap Value Fund Institutional Class	NBPIX	B	C+	A-		4.29	15.64	14.86	54.62	51.76	31.05	1,707	212-476-9000	Y
Neuberger Berman Large Cap Value Fund Investor Class	NPRTX	B	C+	A-		4.26	15.54	14.68	53.86	50.50	31.07	1,707	212-476-9000	
Neuberger Berman Large Cap Value Fund Trust Class	NBPTX	B	C+	A-		4.22	15.44	14.45	53.08	49.19	31.09	1,707	212-476-9000	
Neuberger Berman Value Fund Class A	NVAAX	B	C+	A-		4.03	15.33	15.16	53.84	48.73	18.58	28.7	212-476-9000	Y
Neuberger Berman Value Fund Class C	NVACX	B	C+	A-		3.87	14.97	14.42	50.58	43.33	17.97	28.7	212-476-9000	Y
Neuberger Berman Value Fund Institutional Class	NLRLX	B	C+	A		4.13	15.63	15.70	55.70	51.55	18.64	28.7	212-476-9000	Y
Nicholas Equity Income Fund Class I	NSEIX	B-	C	B		5.32	19.15	9.87	36.07	40.91	19.11	394.3	800-544-6547	Y
Northern Large Cap Core Fund	NOLCX	B-	C	B	Up	2.41	15.29	5.90	42.57	49.81	19.74	246.4	800-595-9111	Y
Northern Large Cap Value Fund	NOLVX	B-	C	B		2.80	15.85	6.65	36.46	37.50	16.88	69.0	800-595-9111	Y
Nuance Concentrated Value Fund Institutional Class	NCVLX	B	B-	A	Up	5.10	17.49	14.47	35.93	39.66	14.27	437.7		Y
Nuance Concentrated Value Fund Investor Class	NCAVX	B	C+	A-	Up	5.03	17.27	14.11	34.59	37.56	14.23	437.7		Y
Pacific Funds Large-Cap Value Advisor Class	PFVDX	B-	C	B	Up	4.20	16.46	8.11	34.26		11.39	19.5	800-722-2333	Y
Pacific Funds Large-Cap Value Class A	PFAAX	B-	C	B	Up	4.22	16.29	7.77	33.27		11.35	19.5	800-722-2333	Y
Pacific Funds Large-Cap Value Class C	PFVCX	B-	C	B	Up	3.97	15.84	6.94	30.20		11.26	19.5	800-722-2333	Y
Pacific Funds Large-Cap Value S Class	PFVIX	B-	C	B	Up	4.33	16.59	8.15	34.51		11.31	19.5	800-722-2333	Y
Parametric Dividend Income Fund Institutional Class	EIPDX	B-	C	B		1.90	15.19	4.66	33.01	51.62	13	54.6		Y
Parametric Dividend Income Fund Investor Class	EAPDX	B-	C	B		1.83	14.97	4.40	32.08	49.74	12.98	54.6		Y
Payden Equity Income Fund	PYVLX	B-	C+	B+		4.27	18.94	10.33	35.50	51.91	17.51	1,358	614-470-8006	Y
Payden Equity Income Fund Adviser Class	PYVAX	B-	C+	B		4.22	18.81	10.09	34.48	50.05	17.5	1,358	614-470-8006	Y
Payden Equity Income Fund SI Class	PYVSX	B-	C+	B+		4.29	19.06	10.48	35.98	52.86	17.52	1,358	614-470-8006	Y
PF Large-Cap Value Fund Class P		B-	C	B	Up	5.43	19.65	9.81	36.62	40.39	12.6	172.3	800-722-2333	Y
PGIM Jennison Value Fund- Class R6	PJVQX	B-	C	B	Up	3.82	17.35	6.60	40.31	26.09	19.27	446.9	800-225-1852	Y
PGIM Jennison Value Fund- Class Z	PEIZX	B-	C	B	Up	3.82	17.33	6.49	39.79	25.35	19.29	446.9	800-225-1852	Y
PIMCO RAE Low Volatility PLUS Fund Class A	PXLVX	B-	C+	B+		2.49	15.64	9.81	34.19	53.25	8.8	68.0	866-746-2602	Y
PIMCO RAE Low Volatility PLUS Fund Institutional Class	PILVX	B-	C+	B+		2.74	15.94	10.39	35.98	56.55	8.98	68.0	866-746-2602	Y
Pioneer Equity Income Fund Class A	PEQIX	B-	C	B	Up	1.70	15.16	4.44	34.41	49.20	34.42	2,634	617-742-7825	Y
Pioneer Equity Income Fund Class C	PCEQX	B-	C	B	Up	1.52	14.72	3.66	31.47	43.83	33.88	2,634	617-742-7825	Y
Pioneer Equity Income Fund Class K	PEQKX	B-	C	B	Up	1.82	15.37	4.79	35.85	51.97	34.47	2,634	617-742-7825	Y
Pioneer Equity Income Fund Class R	PQIRX	B-	C	B	Up	1.67	14.98	4.00	32.82	46.35	35.13	2,634	617-742-7825	Y
Pioneer Equity Income Fund Class Y	PYEQX	B-	C	B	Up	1.77	15.30	4.70	35.40	51.16	34.86	2,634	617-742-7825	Y
Praxis Value Index Fund Class A	MVIAX	B-	C	B	Up	4.52	18.19	8.91	39.48	41.62	13.85	224.0		Y
Praxis Value Index Fund Class I	MVIIX	B-	C	B		4.63	18.43	9.37	41.44	44.93	13.77	224.0		Y
Principal Equity Income Fund Class A	PQIAX	B-	C	B+		5.35	17.81	10.96	44.94	51.99	32.07	7,444	800-787-1621	Y
Principal Equity Income Fund Class C	PEUCX	B-	C	B+		5.16	17.38	10.19	41.75	46.48	31.21	7,444	800-787-1621	Y
Principal Equity Income Fund Class J	PEIJX	B-	C	B+		5.34	17.84	10.99	44.99	52.04	32.11	7,444	800-787-1621	Y
Principal Equity Income Fund Institutional Class	PEIIX	B-	C+	B+	Down	5.44	18.00	11.39	46.53	54.92	32.11	7,444	800-787-1621	Y
Principal Equity Income Fund R-1 Class	PIEMX	B-	C	B+		5.22	17.51	10.44	42.76	48.26	31.93	7,444	800-787-1621	Y
Principal Equity Income Fund R-2 Class	PEINX	B-	C	B+		5.25	17.61	10.58	43.38	49.30	32.08	7,444	800-787-1621	Y
Principal Equity Income Fund R-3 Class	PEIOX	B-	C	B+		5.28	17.68	10.77	44.13	50.61	31.97	7,444	800-787-1621	Y
Principal Equity Income Fund R-4 Class	PEIPX	B-	C	B+		5.32	17.80	10.97	44.91	52.08	32.03	7,444	800-787-1621	Y
Principal Equity Income Fund R-5 Class	PEIQX	B-	C	B+		5.38	17.89	11.13	45.49	53.04	32.08	7,444	800-787-1621	Y
Principal LargeCap Value Fund III Class J	PLVJX	B-	C	B		4.41	16.25	8.62	38.82	45.45	16.31	2,138	800-787-1621	Y
Principal LargeCap Value Fund III Institutional Class	PLVIX	B-	C	B		4.47	16.37	8.92	40.09	47.84	16.56	2,138	800-787-1621	Y
Principal LargeCap Value Fund III R-1 Class	PESAX	B-	C	B	Up	4.30	15.88	8.07	36.56	41.50	16.49	2,138	800-787-1621	Y
Principal LargeCap Value Fund III R-2 Class	PPSNX	B-	C	B	Up	4.28	15.96	8.13	36.96	42.35	16.56	2,138	800-787-1621	Y
Principal LargeCap Value Fund III R-3 Class	PPSFX	B-	C	B	Up	4.38	16.10	8.35	37.81	43.71	17.37	2,138	800-787-1621	Y
Principal LargeCap Value Fund III R-4 Class	PPSSX	B-	C	B	Up	4.41	16.22	8.56	38.59	45.10	16.55	2,138	800-787-1621	Y
Principal LargeCap Value Fund III R-5 Class	PPSRX	B-	C	B		4.38	16.23	8.65	39.02	45.87	16.68	2,138	800-787-1621	Y

Category: US Equity Large Cap Value (con't)

Fund Name	Ticker Symbol	RATINGS: Overall Rating	Reward Rating	Risk Rating	Recent Up/ Downgrade	TOTAL RETURNS & PERFORMANCE: 3-Month Total Return	6-Month Total Return	1-Year Total Return	3-Year Total Return	5-Year Total Return	ASSETS: NAV	Total Assets (MIL)	NEW INVESTORS: Telephone	Open to New Investors
Putnam Equity Income Fund Class R5	PEQLX	B-	C	B	Up	4.22	17.45	6.84	42.23	47.06	24.49	12,785	617-292-1000	Y
Putnam Equity Income Fund Class R6	PEQSX	B-	C	B	Up	4.24	17.49	6.92	42.64	47.77	24.48	12,785	617-292-1000	Y
Putnam Equity Income Fund Class Y	PEIYX	B-	C	B	Up	4.21	17.43	6.81	42.14	46.77	24.48	12,785	617-292-1000	Y
Queens Road Value Fund	QRVLX	B-	C	B+	Down	4.00	17.55	12.65	44.31	54.00	24.17	41.7	888-353-0261	Y
Rydex Dow Jones Industrial Average® Fund Class A	RYDAX	B-	C	B	Down	2.77	15.70	10.22	53.75		72.5	42.6	800-820-0888	Y
Rydex Dow Jones Industrial Average® Fund Class C	RYDKX	B-	C	B		2.58	15.30	9.41	50.38		70.52	42.6	800-820-0888	Y
Rydex Dow Jones Industrial Average® Fund Class H	RYDHX	B-	C	B	Down	2.77	15.72	10.21	53.88		72.55	42.6	800-820-0888	Y
Schwab Fundamental US Large Company Index Fund	SFLNX	B-	C	B	Up	3.54	17.24	7.08	39.34	49.38	16.93	5,093	877-824-5615	Y
Segall Bryant & Hamill Workplace Equality Inst Cls	WEQIX	B	C+	B+	Up	5.70	20.77	18.95	44.67	52.68	6.58	17.4	312-474-1222	Y
Segall Bryant & Hamill Workplace Equality Retail Cls	WEQRX	B	C+	B+	Up	5.65	20.87	18.78	43.69	51.01	6.41	17.4	312-474-1222	Y
SEI Inst Investments Trust U.S. Managed Volatility Cls A	SVYAX	B	C+	A-		3.01	15.21	11.53	36.65	60.54	13.71	1,237	800-342-5734	Y
SEI Institutional Managed Trust Large Cap Value Cls F	TRMVX	B-	C	B	Up	1.83	13.81	3.24	38.40	33.18	23.19	1,362	800-342-5734	Y
SEI Institutional Managed Trust Large Cap Value Cls I	SEUIX	B-	C	B	Up	1.76	13.73	3.04	37.52	31.73	23.21	1,362	800-342-5734	Y
SEI Institutional Managed Trust Large Cap Value Cls Y	SVAYX	B-	C	B	Up	1.89	13.99	3.55	39.51	34.41	23.2	1,362	800-342-5734	Y
SEI Inst Managed Trust Tax-Managed Managed Vol Cls Y	STVYX	B	C+	B+		4.12	15.99	12.29	35.35	59.03	17.22	1,075	800-342-5734	Y
SEI Inst Managed Trust Tax-Managed Volatility Cls F	TMMAX	B	C+	B+		3.99	15.77	12.01	34.26	57.37	17.21	1,075	800-342-5734	Y
SEI Inst Managed Trust U.S. Managed Volatility Cls F	SVOAX	B	C+	A-		3.48	15.74	11.54	33.58	54.71	17.4	1,822	800-342-5734	Y
SEI Inst Managed Trust U.S. Managed Volatility Cls I	SEVIX	B	C+	A-		3.35	15.60	11.25	32.58	52.75	17.39	1,822	800-342-5734	Y
SEI Inst Managed Trust U.S. Managed Volatility Cls Y	SUSYX	B	C+	A-		3.54	15.96	11.82	34.65	56.44	17.41	1,822	800-342-5734	Y
Shelton Capital Management Core Value Fund Class K	EQTKX	B-	C	B	Up	3.39	16.13	5.19	26.77	33.60	19.95	154.6	800-955-9988	Y
Shelton Capital Management Core Value Fund Direct Shares	EQTIX	B-	C	B	Up	3.53	16.40	5.72	28.75	36.99	20.25	154.6	800-955-9988	Y
Smead Value Fund Class A	SVFAX	B-	C	B		6.87	16.61	12.02	50.32	56.28	47.58	1,198	206-838-9850	Y
Smead Value Fund Class I1	SVFFX	B-	C	B		6.93	16.75	12.28	51.29	58.28	47.94	1,198	206-838-9850	Y
Smead Value Fund Class R1	SVFDX	B-	C	B		6.77	16.41	11.65	48.89	54.04	46.95	1,198	206-838-9850	Y
Smead Value Fund Class R2	SVFKX	B-	C	B+	Down	6.81	16.50	15.80	53.94	59.63	48.77	1,198	206-838-9850	Y
Smead Value Fund Class Y	SVFYX	B-	C	B+		6.97	16.87	12.44	51.98	59.22	48	1,198	206-838-9850	Y
Smead Value Fund Investor Class	SMVLX	B-	C	B		6.87	16.60	12.04	50.07	56.17	47.9	1,198	206-838-9850	Y
State Street Disciplined U.S. Equity Fund Class I	SSJIX	B-	C	A		-1.90	3.79	5.71				4.0	617-664-7338	Y
Sterling Capital Equity Income Fund Class A	BAEIX	B-	C+	B+	Down	4.11	15.79	13.26	51.53	51.48	20.81	1,774	800-228-1872	Y
Sterling Capital Equity Income Fund Class C	BCEGX	B-	C	B+	Down	3.96	15.34	12.47	48.21	45.90	20.6	1,774	800-228-1872	Y
Sterling Capital Equity Income Fund Class R	BAERX	B-	C+	B+	Down	4.08	15.60	12.98	50.44	49.58	20.64	1,774	800-228-1872	Y
Sterling Capital Equity Income Fund Class R6	STREX	B	C+	B+		4.25	15.98	13.68	52.96	53.61	20.88	1,774	800-228-1872	Y
Sterling Capital Equity Income Fund Institutional Shares	BEGIX	B	C+	B+		4.22	15.92	13.61	52.75	53.40	20.88	1,774	800-228-1872	Y
Strategic Advisers® Value Fund	FVSAX	B-	C	B	Up	3.02	15.54	5.04	40.05	44.73	19.4	9,966	617-563-7000	Y
T. Rowe Price Equity Income Fund	PRFDX	B-	C	B	Up	4.28	16.64	5.50	38.49	37.56	31.25	20,244	410-345-2000	Y
T. Rowe Price Equity Income Fund Advisor Class	PAFDX	B-	C	B	Up	4.26	16.53	5.22	37.32	35.65	31.19	20,244	410-345-2000	Y
T. Rowe Price Equity Income Fund Class R	RRFDX	B-	C	B	Up	4.13	16.29	4.89	36.13	33.78	31.12	20,244	410-345-2000	Y
T. Rowe Price Equity Income Fund I Class	REIPX	B-	C	B	Up	4.35	16.71	5.63	38.91	38.07	31.27	20,244	410-345-2000	Y
T. Rowe Price Institutional Large Cap Value Fund	TILCX	B-	C	B	Up	4.32	16.96	6.22	37.57	44.54	22.89	3,438	410-345-2000	Y
T. Rowe Price Value Fund	TRVLX	B-	C	B	Up	4.65	18.74	8.94	40.07	43.67	35.98	24,947	410-345-2000	Y
T. Rowe Price Value Fund Advisor Class	PAVLX	B-	C	B	Up	4.61	18.63	8.70	39.10	42.03	35.39	24,947	410-345-2000	Y
T. Rowe Price Value Fund I Class	TRPIX	B-	C	B	Up	4.71	18.85	9.10	40.71	44.55	36	24,947	410-345-2000	Y
The Hartford Dividend and Growth Fund Class A	IHGIX	B-	C	B+		3.48	16.04	9.54	43.20	50.06	24.77	8,710	888-843-7824	Y
The Hartford Dividend and Growth Fund Class C	HDGCX	B-	C	B		3.29	15.56	8.66	39.93	44.53	23.85	8,710	888-843-7824	Y
The Hartford Dividend and Growth Fund Class F	HDGFX	B-	C	B+		3.59	16.25	9.94	44.78	52.87	24.62	8,710	888-843-7824	Y
The Hartford Dividend and Growth Fund Class I	HDGIX	B-	C	B+		3.53	16.14	9.84	44.27	51.82	24.63	8,710	888-843-7824	Y
The Hartford Dividend and Growth Fund Class R3	HDGRX	B-	C	B		3.37	15.82	9.12	41.65	47.49	25.14	8,710	888-843-7824	Y
The Hartford Dividend and Growth Fund Class R4	HDGSX	B-	C	B+		3.46	16.02	9.52	42.98	49.80	25.33	8,710	888-843-7824	Y
The Hartford Dividend and Growth Fund Class R5	HDGTX	B-	C	B+		3.54	16.13	9.82	44.27	52.06	25.43	8,710	888-843-7824	Y
The Hartford Dividend and Growth Fund Class R6	HDGVX	B-	C	B+		3.60	16.22	9.96	44.75	52.73	25.44	8,710	888-843-7824	Y
The Hartford Dividend and Growth Fund Class Y	HDGYX	B-	C	B+		3.54	16.20	9.87	44.60	52.68	25.44	8,710	888-843-7824	Y
The Hartford Equity Income Fund Class A	HQIAX	B-	C+	B+		3.98	16.73	9.77	36.44	46.05	19.43	4,020	888-843-7824	Y

Category: US Equity Large Cap Value (con't)

Fund Name	Ticker Symbol	RATINGS: Overall Rating	Reward Rating	Risk Rating	Recent Up/ Downgrade	TOTAL RETURNS & PERFORMANCE: 3-Month Total Return	6-Month Total Return	1-Year Total Return	3-Year Total Return	5-Year Total Return	ASSETS: NAV	Total Assets (MIL)	NEW INVESTORS: Telephone	Open to New Investors
The Hartford Equity Income Fund Class C	HQICX	B-	C	B		3.74	16.32	8.95	33.35	40.69	19.33	4,020	888-843-7824	Y
The Hartford Equity Income Fund Class F	HQIFX	B-	C+	B+		4.09	16.98	10.15	37.85	48.64	19.31	4,020	888-843-7824	Y
The Hartford Equity Income Fund Class I	HQIIX	B-	C+	B+		4.01	16.90	10.02	37.35	47.78	19.31	4,020	888-843-7824	Y
The Hartford Equity Income Fund Class R3	HQIRX	B-	C	B		3.88	16.57	9.34	34.90	43.44	19.46	4,020	888-843-7824	Y
The Hartford Equity Income Fund Class R4	HQISX	B-	C	B+		3.94	16.71	9.71	36.22	45.69	19.49	4,020	888-843-7824	Y
The Hartford Equity Income Fund Class R5	HQITX	B-	C+	B+		4.05	16.91	10.05	37.47	47.88	19.59	4,020	888-843-7824	Y
The Hartford Equity Income Fund Class R6	HQIVX	B-	C+	B+		4.07	17.00	10.15	37.88	48.67	19.64	4,020	888-843-7824	Y
The Hartford Equity Income Fund Class Y	HQIYX	B-	C+	B+		4.06	16.96	10.08	37.72	48.49	19.64	4,020	888-843-7824	Y
TIAA-CREF Large-Cap Value Index Fund Advisor Class	THCVX	B-	C	B	Up	3.79	17.06	8.29	35.22	42.52	19.96	6,476	877-518-9161	Y
TIAA-CREF Large-Cap Value Index Fund Institutional Class	TILVX	B-	C	B	Up	3.84	17.09	8.43	35.67	42.99	20	6,476	877-518-9161	Y
TIAA-CREF Large-Cap Value Index Fund Retirement Class	TRCVX	B-	C	B	Up	3.72	16.90	8.14	34.58	41.13	20.33	6,476	877-518-9161	Y
TIAA-CREF Quant Large-Cap Value Fund Class W	TELWX	B-	C	B	Up	2.84	15.11	5.52	30.96	35.66	10.13	2,655	877-518-9161	Y
TIAA-CREF Quant Large-Cap Value Fund Institutional Class	TEVIX	B-	C	B	Up	2.74	14.88	5.22	30.59	35.27	10.11	2,655	877-518-9161	Y
Torray Fund	TORYX	B-	C	B	Up	4.33	15.79	6.40	26.24	35.48	49.58	411.7	800-443-3036	Y
Touchstone Value Fund Class A	TVLAX	B-	C	B		4.27	15.72	8.53	37.54	41.10	9.41	337.8	800-543-0407	Y
Touchstone Value Fund Class Y	TVLYX	B-	C	B		4.44	15.81	8.81	38.52	42.99	9.45	337.8	800-543-0407	Y
Touchstone Value Fund Institutional	TVLIX	B-	C	B		4.37	15.93	8.96	39.17	43.93	9.42	337.8	800-543-0407	Y
Transamerica Large Value Opportunities Fund Class I3	TLOTX	B-	C	B	Up	1.76	14.25	5.07	38.70	34.22	9.15	563.6	888-233-4339	Y
Transamerica Large Value Opportunities Fund Class R	TLORX	B-	C	B	Up	1.63	14.09	4.60	36.93	31.85	9.16	563.6	888-233-4339	Y
Transamerica Large Value Opportunities Fund Class R4	TLOFX	B-	C	B	Up	1.81	14.23	4.92	38.07	33.61	9.16	563.6	888-233-4339	Y
TS&W Equity Portfolio Institutional Class Shares	TSWEX	B-	C	B+		3.69	13.47	8.55	38.04	38.87	12.27	34.5		Y
USAA Income Stock Fund	USISX	B-	C	B+	Down	3.36	15.64	9.73	35.16	44.93	19.68	2,891	800-235-8396	Y
USAA Income Stock Fund Institutional Shares	UIISX	B-	C	B+	Down	3.32	15.55	9.72	35.19	45.14	19.65	2,891	800-235-8396	Y
USAA Income Stock Fund R6 Shares	URISX	B-	C	B+	Down	3.34	15.65	9.79	35.50	45.30	19.66	2,891	800-235-8396	Y
VALIC Company I Dividend Value Fund	VCIGX	B-	C	B	Up	2.30	13.64	5.40	34.74	47.62	11.55	991.7		Y
Vanguard Equity-Income Fund Admiral Shares	VEIRX	B-	C	B+	Down	3.43	15.80	9.72	39.19	53.85	75.33	35,525	877-662-7447	Y
Vanguard Equity-Income Fund Investor Shares	VEIPX	B-	C	B+	Down	3.41	15.75	9.63	38.80	53.14	35.94	35,525	877-662-7447	Y
Vanguard High Dividend Yield Index Fund Admiral	VHYAX	B-	C	B+		2.74	14.67	8.73	36.30	53.73	26.34	33,225	877-662-7447	Y
Vanguard High Dividend Yield Index Fund Investor Shares	VHDYX	B-	C	B+		2.72	14.60	8.58	35.99	53.19	34.61	33,225	877-662-7447	Y
Vanguard Mega Cap Value Index Fund Institutional Shares	VMVLX	B-	C	B+	Down	4.02	15.55	11.43	44.01	57.38	159.74	2,619	877-662-7447	Y
Vanguard Russell 1000 Value Index Institutional Shares	VRVIX	B-	C	B	Up	3.83	17.13	8.44	35.66	42.72	217.9	3,851	877-662-7447	Y
Vanguard S&P 500 Value Index Fund Institutional Shares	VSPVX	B-	C	B	Up	3.99	17.56	8.59	37.24	45.80	246.58	1,095	877-662-7447	Y
Vanguard Value Index Fund Admiral Shares	VVIAX	B-	C	B+		3.77	15.91	9.87	43.37	55.54	43.3	80,262	877-662-7447	Y
Vanguard Value Index Fund Institutional Shares	VIVIX	B-	C	B+		3.77	15.91	9.91	43.41	55.66	43.3	80,262	877-662-7447	Y
Vanguard Value Index Fund Investor Shares	VIVAX	B-	C	B+		3.76	15.85	9.78	42.86	54.60	43.32	80,262	877-662-7447	Y
Voya Corporate Leaders Trust Fund Series B	LEXCX	B-	C	B	Down	2.28	16.73	10.32	40.62	41.55	40.19	815.8	800-366-0066	Y
Voya Large Cap Value Fund Class A	IEDAX	B-	C	B	Up	4.26	16.51	7.67	34.06	33.96	11.73	775.8	800-366-0066	Y
Voya Large Cap Value Fund Class C	IEDCX	B-	C	B	Up	3.99	16.11	6.85	30.97	28.95	11.7	775.8	800-366-0066	Y
Voya Large Cap Value Fund Class I	IEDIX	B-	C	B	Up	4.32	16.80	8.06	35.46	36.25	12.78	775.8	800-366-0066	Y
Voya Large Cap Value Fund Class O	ILVOX	B-	C	B	Up	4.15	16.53	7.48	33.86	33.80	11.77	775.8	800-366-0066	Y
Voya Large Cap Value Fund Class R	IEDRX	B-	C	B	Up	4.18	16.48	7.40	33.11	32.44	11.74	775.8	800-366-0066	Y
Voya Large Cap Value Fund Class R6	IEDZX	B-	C	B	Up	4.34	16.75	8.01	35.49	36.35	12.76	775.8	800-366-0066	Y
Voya Large Cap Value Fund Class W	IWEDX	B-	C	B	Up	4.29	16.65	8.03	35.16	35.66	12.76	775.8	800-366-0066	Y
Voya Large Cap Value Fund ClassP3	VLVPX	B-	C	B	Up	4.47	17.11	8.81	35.48	35.38	12.87	775.8	800-366-0066	Y
Voya Large Cap Value Portfolio Class A	IPEAX	B-	C	B	Up	4.22	16.45	7.48	33.00	32.49	12.1	1,091	800-366-0066	Y
Voya Large Cap Value Portfolio Class I	IPEIX	B-	C	B	Up	4.38	16.90	8.14	35.50	36.64	12.38	1,091	800-366-0066	Y
Voya Large Cap Value Portfolio Class S	IPESX	B-	C	B	Up	4.27	16.74	7.86	34.49	34.92	12.2	1,091	800-366-0066	Y
Voya Large Cap Value Portfolio Class S2	IPETX	B-	C	B	Up	4.26	16.73	7.79	34.05	34.08	12.21	1,091	800-366-0066	Y
Voya Large Cap Value Portfolio R6	VLCRX	B-	C	B	Up	4.38	16.91	8.24	35.79	36.58	12.37	1,091	800-366-0066	Y
Voya Russell Large Cap Value Index Portfolio Class A	IRVAX	B-	C	B+	Up	3.91	15.81	9.82	34.61	39.66	22	382.7	800-366-0066	Y
Voya Russell Large Cap Value Index Portfolio Class I	IRVIX	B-	C	B+		4.04	16.12	10.44	36.63	43.16	22.2	382.7	800-366-0066	Y
Voya Russell Large Cap Value Index Portfolio Class S	IRVSX	B-	C	B+		3.97	15.98	10.16	35.56	41.36	22.06	382.7	800-366-0066	Y

Category: US Equity Large Cap Value (con't)

Fund Name	Ticker Symbol	RATINGS: Overall Rating	Reward Rating	Risk Rating	Recent Up/ Downgrade	TOTAL RETURNS & PERFORMANCE: 3-Month Total Return	6-Month Total Return	1-Year Total Return	3-Year Total Return	5-Year Total Return	ASSETS: NAV	Total Assets (MIL.)	NEW INVESTORS: Telephone	Open to New Investors
Voya U.S. High Dividend Low Volatility Fund Class A	VHDAX	B-	C	B	Up	4.50	17.57	10.19			12.03	325.7	800-366-0066	Y
Voya U.S. High Dividend Low Volatility Fund Class I	VHDIX	B-	C	B	Up	4.55	17.73	10.50			12.08	325.7	800-366-0066	Y
Voya U.S. High Dividend Low Volatility Fund P3	VHDPX	B-	C	B	Up	4.70	17.98	10.94			12.13	325.7	800-366-0066	Y
VY® T. Rowe Price Equity Income Portfolio Class A	ITEAX	B-	C	B	Up	4.19	16.41	4.93	36.96	34.15	12.41	817.9	800-366-0066	Y
VY® T. Rowe Price Equity Income Portfolio Class I	ITEIX	B-	C	B	Up	4.35	16.71	5.54	39.42	38.31	12.71	817.9	800-366-0066	Y
VY® T. Rowe Price Equity Income Portfolio Class S	IRPSX	B-	C	B	Up	4.17	16.48	5.21	38.37	36.44	12.72	817.9	800-366-0066	Y
VY® T. Rowe Price Equity Income Portfolio Class S2	ITETX	B-	C	B	Up	4.24	16.48	5.13	37.79	35.57	12.51	817.9	800-366-0066	Y
Wells Fargo Large Company Value Fund - Class Inst	WLCIX	B-	C	B	Up	3.63	15.09	4.93	34.55	31.76	13	216.7	800-222-8222	Y
Wells Fargo Large Company Value Fund Class R6	WTLVX	B-	C	B	Up	3.65	15.14	4.98	34.53	31.18	13	216.7	800-222-8222	Y
Zacks Dividend Fund Institutional Class Shares	ZDIIX	B-	C	B+	Down	4.59	16.39	11.57	39.04	47.77	20.72	71.5		Y
Zacks Dividend Fund Investor Class	ZDIVX	B-	C	B+		4.58	16.25	11.32	38.29	46.97	20.73	71.5		Y

Category: US Equity Mid Cap

Fund Name	Ticker Symbol	RATINGS: Overall Rating	Reward Rating	Risk Rating	Recent Up/ Downgrade	TOTAL RETURNS & PERFORMANCE: 3-Month Total Return	6-Month Total Return	1-Year Total Return	3-Year Total Return	5-Year Total Return	ASSETS: NAV	Total Assets (MIL.)	NEW INVESTORS: Telephone	Open to New Investors
Alger SMid Cap Focus Fund Class A	ALMAX	B-	B	C+	Up	3.58	36.81	12.26	89.96	83.13	14.16	557.9	800-992-3863	Y
Alger SMid Cap Focus Fund Class C	ALMCX	B-	B-	C+	Up	3.32	36.26	11.37	85.62	76.12	9.62	557.9	800-992-3863	Y
Alger SMid Cap Focus Fund Class I	ASIMX	B-	B	C+	Up	3.63	36.81	12.34	90.08	83.09	14.53	557.9	800-992-3863	Y
Alger SMid Cap Focus Fund Class Y	ASYMX	B-	B	C+	Up	3.68	37.07	12.74	91.41	84.53	14.64	557.9	800-992-3863	Y
Alger SMid Cap Focus Fund Class Z	ASMZX	B-	B	C+	Up	3.65	37.06	12.61	91.83	86.16	15.05	557.9	800-992-3863	Y
American Beacon Stephens Mid-Cap Growth Fund A Class	SMFAX	B-	C+	B	Down	6.68	27.43	13.86	78.97	74.01	22.34	231.7	800-658-5811	Y
American Beacon Stephens Mid-Cap Growth Fund C Class	SMFCX	B-	C+	B	Down	6.48	26.90	13.04	75.02	67.58	20.85	231.7	800-658-5811	Y
American Beacon Stephens Mid-Cap Growth Fund Class R6	SFMRX	B-	C+	B	Down	6.80	27.71	14.17	79.68	74.71	26.84	231.7	800-658-5811	Y
American Beacon Stephens Mid-Cap Growth Institutional Cls	SFMIX	B-	C+	B	Down	6.76	27.64	14.29	81.05	77.46	26.83	231.7	800-658-5811	Y
American Beacon Stephens Mid-Cap Growth Investor Cls	STMGX	B-	C+	B	Down	6.70	27.41	13.89	79.26	74.29	22.45	231.7	800-658-5811	Y
American Beacon Stephens Mid-Cap Growth Fund Y Class	SMFYX	B-	C+	B	Down	6.73	27.58	14.17	80.49	76.54	26.64	231.7	800-658-5811	Y
American Century Heritage Fund A Class	ATHAX	B-	C+	B		6.88	29.31	15.88	52.62	59.96	19.72	4,738	800-444-4015	Y
American Century Heritage Fund C Class	AHGCX	B-	C+	B	Up	6.69	28.82	15.00	49.20	54.16	14.66	4,738	800-444-4015	Y
American Century Heritage Fund I Class	ATHIX	B-	C+	B		7.02	29.58	16.38	54.68	63.65	23.61	4,738	800-444-4015	Y
American Century Heritage Fund Investor Class	TWHIX	B-	C+	B		6.95	29.38	16.15	53.70	61.96	21.84	4,738	800-444-4015	Y
American Century Heritage Fund R Class	ATHWX	B-	C+	B		6.77	29.09	15.54	51.42	57.94	19.7	4,738	800-444-4015	Y
American Century Heritage Fund R5 Class	ATHGX	B-	C+	B		7.02	29.58	16.38	54.43	62.73	23.61	4,738	800-444-4015	Y
American Century Heritage Fund R6 Class	ATHDX	B-	B-	B		7.07	29.64	16.57	55.39	64.86	23.92	4,738	800-444-4015	Y
American Century Heritage Fund Y Class	ATHYX	B-	B-	B		7.02	29.64	16.57	54.94	63.26	23.92	4,738	800-444-4015	Y
American Century NT Heritage Fund G Class	ACLWX	B-	B-	B		7.27	30.05	17.07	56.70	65.74	12.98	621.3	800-444-4015	Y
AMG River Road Focused Absolute Value Fund Class I	AFAVX	B-	C	B	Up	4.64	21.33	11.84	54.27		12.17	87.9	800-835-3879	Y
AMG River Road Focused Absolute Value Fund Class N	ARRFX	B-	C	B+	Up	4.48	21.22	11.56	53.02		12.11	87.9	800-835-3879	Y
AMG River Road Focused Absolute Value Fund Class Z	ARRZX	B-	C	B	Up	4.64	21.33	11.97	54.38		12.17	87.9	800-835-3879	Y
AMG TimesSquare Mid Cap Growth Fund Class I	TQMIX	B-	B-	B	Down	8.37	27.79	14.28	56.73	62.97	19.54	2,001	800-835-3879	Y
AMG TimesSquare Mid Cap Growth Fund Class N	TMDPX	B-	B-	B	Down	8.35	27.80	14.13	56.02	61.55	18.94	2,001	800-835-3879	
AMG TimesSquare Mid Cap Growth Fund Class Z	TMDIX	B-	B-	B	Down	8.36	27.90	14.38	56.94	63.20	19.57	2,001	800-835-3879	
Artisan Mid Cap Fund Advisor Class	APDMX	B-	B-	B-		10.15	35.61	19.58	59.54	63.50	38.95	5,139	800-344-1770	
Artisan Mid Cap Fund Institutional Class	APHMX	B-	B-	B-		10.18	35.72	19.76	60.09	64.55	43.16	5,139	800-344-1770	
Artisan Mid Cap Fund Investor Class	ARTMX	B-	B-	B-		10.11	35.49	19.44	58.93	62.60	38.63	5,139	800-344-1770	
Baird MidCap Fund Institutional Class	BMDIX	B-	B-	B	Down	6.86	27.95	16.51	64.69	64.43	22.43	2,043	800-792-2473	Y
Baird MidCap Fund Investor Class	BMDSX	B-	B-	B	Down	6.80	27.74	16.18	63.40	62.36	21.18	2,043	800-792-2473	Y
Baron Asset Fund Class R6	BARUX	B	B	B		9.90	33.48	19.69	79.23	87.87	87.74	4,431	800-992-2766	Y
Baron Asset Fund Institutional Class	BARIX	B	B	B		9.91	33.49	19.70	79.27	88.71	87.76	4,431	800-992-2766	Y
Baron Asset Fund Retail Class	BARAX	B	B	B		9.84	33.31	19.39	77.85	86.19	84.35	4,431	800-992-2766	Y
Baron Growth Fund Class R6	BGRUX	B	B	B-	Up	7.02	30.98	14.50	68.80	70.70	82.27	6,942	800-992-2766	Y
Baron Growth Fund Institutional Shares	BGRIX	B	B	B-	Up	7.02	30.98	14.51	68.81	71.41	82.26	6,942	800-992-2766	Y

Category: US Equity Mid Cap (con't)

Fund Name	Ticker Symbol	RATINGS: Overall Rating	Reward Rating	Risk Rating	Recent Up/ Downgrade	TOTAL RETURNS & PERFORMANCE: 3-Month Total Return	6-Month Total Return	1-Year Total Return	3-Year Total Return	5-Year Total Return	ASSETS: NAV	Total Assets (MIL)	NEW INVESTORS: Telephone	Open to New Investors
Baron Growth Fund Retail Shares	BGRFX	B	B	B-	Up	6.95	30.81	14.21	67.51	69.22	79.55	6,942	800-992-2766	Y
BlackRock Mid-Cap Growth Equity Portfolio Class K	BMGKX	B	B+	B		9.34	33.48	19.02	93.35	107.40	29.74	4,326	800-441-7762	Y
BlackRock Mid-Cap Growth Equity Portfolio Class R	BMRRX	B	B+	B		9.20	33.11	18.38	89.75	101.08	25.23	4,326	800-441-7762	Y
BlackRock Mid-Cap Growth Equity Portfolio Inst Shares	CMGIX	B	B+	B		9.32	33.39	18.90	92.77	106.77	29.68	4,326	800-441-7762	Y
BlackRock Mid-Cap Growth Equity Portfolio Inv A Shares	BMGAX	B	B+	B		9.22	33.22	18.59	91.17	103.59	25.66	4,326	800-441-7762	Y
BlackRock Mid-Cap Growth Equity Portfolio Inv C Shares	BMGCX	B	B+	B		9.02	32.77	17.70	87.04	96.31	19.94	4,326	800-441-7762	Y
BlackRock Mid-Cap Growth Equity Portfolio Service Shares	CMGSX	B	B+	B		9.22	33.26	18.63	91.65	103.84	26.85	4,326	800-441-7762	Y
Boston Trust Midcap Fund	BTMFX	B-	C+	B	Down	5.23	20.84	12.99	48.45	65.40	18.9	109.4	617-814-1215	Y
Bridge Builder Small/Mid Cap Growth Fund	BBGSX	B-	C	B	Down	5.24	24.34	11.65	61.73		14.25	4,023		Y
Bright Rock Mid Cap Growth Fund Institutional Class	BQMGX	B-	C+	B		6.51	22.08	9.75	45.76	66.06	19.46	69.6	781-982-6593	Y
Bright Rock Mid Cap Growth Fund Investor Class	BQMIX	B-	C+	B		6.43	21.92	9.42	44.64	64.10	19.85	69.6	781-982-6593	Y
Brown Capital Management Mid Company Institutional Shares	BCMIX	B-	B	B-	Up	8.38	34.54	19.73	62.58	42.16	12.93	26.6		Y
Brown Capital Management Mid Company Fund Investor Shares	BCMSX	B-	B-	B-	Up	8.42	34.34	19.45	61.39	40.43	12.36	26.6		Y
Buffalo Discovery Fund	BUFTX	B-	B-	B		6.32	28.16	13.11	59.79	71.10	26.89	1,797	800-492-8332	Y
Calvert Mid-Cap Fund Class A	CCAFX	B-	C	B		5.35	22.05	9.95	40.64	36.78	34.04	217.9	301-951-4881	Y
Calvert Mid-Cap Fund Class C	CCACX	B-	C	B		5.16	21.59	9.13	37.52	31.63	23.42	217.9	301-951-4881	Y
Calvert Mid-Cap Fund Class I	CCPIX	B-	C+	B		5.39	22.17	10.24	42.09	39.76	40.44	217.9	301-951-4881	Y
Cambiar SMID Fund Institutional Class	CAMUX	B-	C	B+	Down	4.22	22.17	12.78	59.39	40.23	18.51	47.1	866-777-8227	Y
Cambiar SMID Fund Investor Class Shares	CAMMX	B-	C	B+	Down	4.16	22.09	12.71	59.16	40.01	18.51	47.1	866-777-8227	Y
Catalyst IPOx Allocation Fund Class A	OIPAX	B-	B-	B-	Down	4.97	25.89	8.88	66.77		14.34	3.3	866-447-4228	Y
Catalyst IPOx Allocation Fund Class C	OIPCX	B-	C+	B-		4.75	25.40	8.07	62.94		13.87	3.3	866-447-4228	Y
Catalyst IPOx Allocation Fund Class I	OIPIX	B-	B-	B-	Down	5.07	26.13	9.18	67.88		14.48	3.3	866-447-4228	Y
Champlain Mid Cap Fund Advisor Class	CIPMX	B-	C+	B	Down	2.90	21.01	14.22	63.92	81.41	19.81	3,493		Y
Champlain Mid Cap Fund Institutional Class	CIPIX	B-	C+	B	Down	3.00	21.19	14.57	65.16	83.77	20.24	3,493		Y
CIBC Atlas Mid Cap Equity Fund Institutional Class	AWMIX	B-	C+	B		5.15	25.44	13.36	45.56	64.34	16.12	715.6	312-368-7700	Y
Clarkston Partners Fund Founders Class	CFSMX	B-	C	B+	Up	3.18	15.14	2.87	34.38		12.62	919.6	844-680-6562	Y
Clarkston Partners Fund Institutional Class	CISMX	B-	C	B+	Up	3.11	15.10	2.76	33.85		12.57	919.6	844-680-6562	Y
ClearBridge Select Fund Class A	LCLAX	B-	C+	B	Down	4.31	23.55	11.15	107.41	109.90	27.07	603.6	877-721-1926	Y
ClearBridge Select Fund Class A2	LCLTX	B-	C+	B	Down	4.31	23.48	11.21	107.47	110.34	27.08	603.6	877-721-1926	Y
ClearBridge Select Fund Class C	LCLCX	B-	C+	B	Down	4.15	23.07	10.38	102.75	102.03	25.82	603.6	877-721-1926	Y
ClearBridge Select Fund Class FI	LCBSX	B-	C+	B	Down	4.32	23.57	11.16	107.10	109.88	27.05	603.6	877-721-1926	Y
ClearBridge Select Fund Class I	LBFIX	B-	C+	B	Down	4.43	23.73	11.50	109.04	112.99	27.79	603.6	877-721-1926	Y
ClearBridge Select Fund Class IS	LCSSX	B-	C+	B	Down	4.40	23.76	11.56	109.44	113.71	27.76	603.6	877-721-1926	Y
Columbia Mid Cap Growth Fund Advisor Class	CPGRX	B-	B-	B-		6.41	27.17	11.54	54.89	64.08	27.05	1,744	800-345-6611	Y
Columbia Mid Cap Growth Fund Class A	CBSAX	B-	B-	B-		6.38	27.03	11.30	53.76	62.08	24.01	1,744	800-345-6611	Y
Columbia Mid Cap Growth Fund Class C	CMCCX	B-	C+	B-	Up	6.16	26.50	10.42	50.32	56.06	18.95	1,744	800-345-6611	Y
Columbia Mid Cap Growth Fund Class R	CMGRX	B-	C+	B-		6.30	26.86	10.99	52.58	60.02	22.76	1,744	800-345-6611	Y
Columbia Mid Cap Growth Fund Class V	CBSTX	B-	B-	B-		6.36	27.00	11.26	53.77	62.03	23.89	1,744	800-345-6611	
Columbia Mid Cap Growth Fund Institutional 2 Class	CMGVX	B-	B-	B		6.46	27.22	11.62	55.32	64.92	26.36	1,744	800-345-6611	Y
Columbia Mid Cap Growth Fund Institutional 3 Class	CMGYX	B-	B-	B		6.45	27.26	11.69	55.51	65.39	26.37	1,744	800-345-6611	Y
Columbia Mid Cap Growth Fund Institutional Class	CLSPX	B-	B-	B		6.44	27.20	11.54	54.90	64.10	26.09	1,744	800-345-6611	Y
Commerce MidCap Growth Fund	CFAGX	B	B	B		8.46	29.40	17.93	59.15	80.35	43.83	210.1		Y
Conestoga SMid Cap Fund Institutional Class	CCSGX	B-	B	C+		8.67	28.05	11.69	87.69	84.11	17.16	113.5	800-320-7790	Y
Conestoga SMid Cap Fund Investors Class	CCSMX	B-	B	C+		8.64	27.90	11.40	86.33	82.18	16.96	113.5	800-320-7790	Y
Congress Mid Cap Growth Fund Institutional Class	IMIDX	B-	C+	B	Down	4.50	23.91	15.14	45.63	67.98	21.35	1,106	888-688-1299	Y
Congress Mid Cap Growth Fund Retail Class	CMIDX	B-	C	B	Down	4.50	23.81	14.89	44.57	65.86	21.11	1,106	888-688-1299	Y
Davenport Equity Opportunities Fund	DEOPX	B-	B-	B	Up	8.82	30.23	19.01	50.70	53.57	20	448.6		Y
Dean Mid Cap Value Fund	DALCX	B-	C	B	Up	3.98	18.09	7.47	33.14	44.33	20.62	43.7	888-899-8343	Y
DF Dent Midcap Growth Fund Institutional Shares	DFMGX	B	B+	B		10.36	32.85	20.44	78.04	88.16	25.88	101.3		Y
DF Dent Midcap Growth Fund Investor Shares	DFDMX	B	B+	B		10.29	32.73	20.27	77.70	87.81	25.83	101.3		Y
Eaton Vance Atlanta Capital SMID-Cap Fund Class A	EAASX	B-	B-	B		8.91	27.41	13.73	56.78	87.89	33.83	12,862		
Eaton Vance Atlanta Capital SMID-Cap Fund Class C	ECASX	B-	B-	B-		8.75	26.95	12.93	53.35	81.06	30.94	12,862		

Category: US Equity Mid Cap (con't)

Fund Name	Ticker Symbol	RATINGS: Overall Rating	Reward Rating	Risk Rating	Recent Up/ Downgrade	TOTAL RETURNS & PERFORMANCE: 3-Month Total Return	6-Month Total Return	1-Year Total Return	3-Year Total Return	5-Year Total Return	ASSETS: NAV	Total Assets (MIL)	NEW INVESTORS: Telephone	Open to New Investors
Eaton Vance Atlanta Capital SMID-Cap Fund Class I	EISMX	B	B	B	Up	8.99	27.59	14.02	57.98	90.25	37.68	12,862		
Eaton Vance Atlanta Capital SMID-Cap Fund Class R	ERSMX	B-	B-	B-		8.84	27.27	13.46	55.65	85.56	32.85	12,862		
Eaton Vance Atlanta Capital SMID-Cap Fund Class R6	ERASX	B	B	B	Up	9.00	27.66	14.13	58.42	91.19	37.89	12,862		Y
Eaton Vance Special Equities Fund Class A	EVSEX	B-	C+	B		6.55	24.08	9.12	52.01	50.12	24.37	48.8		Y
Eaton Vance Special Equities Fund Class C	ECSEX	B-	C+	B		6.36	23.57	8.28	48.58	44.58	21.23	48.8		Y
Eaton Vance Special Equities Fund Class I	EISEX	B-	C+	B		6.64	24.27	9.42	53.22	52.09	25.03	48.8		Y
EQ/Janus Enterprise Portfolio Class IA		B-	C	B	Down	3.18	14.22	9.34	61.85	47.27		1,035	877-222-2144	Y
EQ/Janus Enterprise Portfolio Class IB		B-	C	B	Down	3.17	14.20	9.31	61.90	47.24		1,035	877-222-2144	Y
EQ/Janus Enterprise Portfolio Class K		B-	C	B	Down	3.27	14.41	9.60	63.10	49.15		1,035	877-222-2144	Y
Eventide Gilead Class A	ETAGX	B	B	B		3.10	33.75	16.35	90.85	80.06	41.57	2,652		Y
Eventide Gilead Class C	ETCGX	B	B	B-		2.89	33.27	15.50	86.63	73.38	38.37	2,652		Y
Eventide Gilead Class I	ETILX	B	B	B		3.17	33.93	16.66	92.29	82.31	42.59	2,652		Y
Eventide Gilead Class N	ETGLX	B	B	B		3.13	33.80	16.43	91.18	80.47	41.76	2,652		Y
FAM Equity-Income Fund Investor Class	FAMEX	B	B-	B+		6.96	24.71	19.64	57.94	72.24	36.61	358.4		Y
FAM Value Fund Institutional Class	FAMWX	B-	C+	B		7.52	21.88	12.62	47.74	61.19	79.99	1,337		
FAM Value Fund Investor Class	FAMVX	B-	C+	B		7.48	21.77	12.43	47.11	60.52	79.8	1,337		Y
Federated Kaufmann Fund Class A Shares	KAUAX	B-	B-	B	Down	5.47	27.71	14.58	77.58	91.09	6.36	6,797	800-341-7400	Y
Federated Kaufmann Fund Class B Shares	KAUBX	B-	C+	B	Down	5.17	27.31	13.71	75.03	86.22	5.08	6,797	800-341-7400	
Federated Kaufmann Fund Class C Shares	KAUCX	B-	C+	B	Down	5.40	27.38	13.96	74.84	86.14	5.07	6,797	800-341-7400	Y
Federated Kaufmann Fund Class R Shares	KAUFX	B-	C+	B	Down	5.46	27.65	14.37	77.40	91.17	6.37	6,797	800-341-7400	Y
Federated Kaufmann Fund Institutional Shares	KAUIX	B-	C+	B	Down	5.54	27.86	15.07	79.77	93.73	6.47	6,797	800-341-7400	Y
Fidelity® Mid-Cap Stock Fund	FMCSX	B-	C	B	Up	4.81	18.39	6.22	44.31	45.83	35.23	7,698	617-563-7000	Y
Fidelity® Mid-Cap Stock Fund Class K	FKMCX	B-	C	B		4.85	18.50	6.34	44.86	46.69	35.25	7,698	617-563-7000	Y
FMI Common Stock Fund	FMIMX	B-	C+	B		4.83	21.62	9.41	44.60	40.42	26.66	999.0	800-811-5311	
FMI Common Stock Fund Institutional Class	FMIUX	B-	C+	B		4.83	21.65	9.53	44.97	40.78	26.68	999.0	800-811-5311	Y
Franklin Small-Mid Cap Growth Fund Advisor Class	FSGAX	B-	C+	B		5.46	28.50	14.59	57.22	56.23	41.48	3,324	650-312-2000	Y
Franklin Small-Mid Cap Growth Fund Class A	FRSGX	B-	C+	B		5.42	28.37	14.38	56.09	54.36	37.51	3,324	650-312-2000	Y
Franklin Small-Mid Cap Growth Fund Class C	FRSIX	B-	C+	B		5.22	27.88	13.65	52.73	48.78	25.18	3,324	650-312-2000	Y
Franklin Small-Mid Cap Growth Fund Class R	FSMRX	B-	C+	B		5.33	28.21	14.12	54.95	52.46	33.95	3,324	650-312-2000	Y
Franklin Small-Mid Cap Growth Fund Class R6	FMGGX	B-	C+	B	Down	5.52	28.62	14.75	58.19	57.94	42.24	3,324	650-312-2000	Y
Frost Mid Cap Equity Fund Class Institutional	FIKSX	B-	C	B	Up	2.94	18.38	5.80	47.31	37.11	7.34	4.8		Y
Frost Mid Cap Equity Fund Investor Class Shares	FAKSX	B-	C	B	Up	3.00	18.64	5.61	47.02	36.10	7.19	4.8		Y
Gabelli Value 25 Fund Class A	GABVX	B-	C	B	Up	4.11	15.90	4.08	26.98	19.90	14.94	372.6	914-921-5135	Y
Gabelli Value 25 Fund Class AAA	GVCAX	B-	C	B	Up	4.12	15.97	4.16	27.00	19.94	14.88	372.6	914-921-5135	Y
Gabelli Value 25 Fund Class I	GVCIX	B-	C	B	Up	4.18	16.18	4.58	28.49	21.92	14.93	372.6	914-921-5135	Y
Goldman Sachs Growth Opportunities Fund Class A	GGOAX	B-	C+	B		6.92	27.61	15.15	52.21	53.64	18.07	1,315	800-526-7384	Y
Goldman Sachs Growth Opportunities Fund Class C	GGOCX	B-	C+	B		6.74	27.10	14.29	48.86	47.98	10.13	1,315	800-526-7384	Y
Goldman Sachs Growth Opportunities Fund Class P	GGQPX	B-	B-	B		7.01	27.83	15.60	53.85	56.49	22.87	1,315	800-526-7384	Y
Goldman Sachs Growth Opportunities Fund Class R	GGORX	B-	C+	B		6.90	27.51	14.89	51.18	51.79	16.87	1,315	800-526-7384	Y
Goldman Sachs Growth Opportunities Fund Class R6	GGOUX	B-	B-	B		7.02	27.85	15.61	53.91	56.54	22.86	1,315	800-526-7384	Y
Goldman Sachs Growth Opportunities Institutional Cls	GGOIX	B-	B-	B		7.02	27.81	15.57	53.81	56.45	22.84	1,315	800-526-7384	Y
Goldman Sachs Growth Opportunities Fund Investor Class	GGOTX	B-	B-	B		7.00	27.81	15.49	53.45	55.62	19.39	1,315	800-526-7384	Y
Goldman Sachs Growth Opportunities Fund Service Class	GGOSX	B-	C+	B		6.85	27.50	14.96	51.53	52.60	16.83	1,315	800-526-7384	Y
Gotham Enhanced Return Fund Institutional Class Shares	GENIX	B-	C	B	Up	2.28	13.89	6.99	41.42	35.98	14.34	554.0	877-974-6852	Y
Government Street Mid-Cap Fund	GVMCX	B-	C	B	Up	3.45	18.82	6.26	41.42	54.69	27.67	47.6		Y
Great-West T. Rowe Price Mid Cap Growth Fund Class L	MXTMX	B-	C+	B	Down	6.48	24.19	14.48	60.05	77.60	6.55	1,864		Y
Great-West T. Rowe Price Mid Cap Growth Institutional Cls	MXYKX	B-	C+	B	Down	6.70	24.51	15.14	63.01	82.72	8.5	1,864		Y
Great-West T. Rowe Price Mid Cap Growth Investor Cls	MXMGX	B-	C+	B	Down	6.54	24.23	14.65	61.27	79.96	29.78	1,864		Y
Guggenheim RBP® Dividend Fund Class A	TVEAX	B-	C	B	Up	2.65	16.79	5.66	35.21	43.63	11.83	22.3	212-518-9290	Y
Guggenheim RBP® Dividend Fund Class I	TVEIX	B-	C	B	Up	2.69	16.87	5.93	36.33	45.87	11.54	22.3	212-518-9290	Y
Guggenheim RBP® Dividend Fund Class P	TVEFX	B-	C	B	Up	2.66	16.71	5.67	35.22	44.02	11.96	22.3	212-518-9290	Y
Harbor Mid Cap Growth Fund Administrative Class	HRMGX	B-	B-	B-	Down	6.09	33.50	15.37	77.86	74.29	10.44	257.7	800-422-1050	Y

Category: US Equity Mid Cap (con't)

		RATINGS				TOTAL RETURNS & PERFORMANCE					ASSETS		NEW INVESTORS	
Fund Name	Ticker Symbol	Overall Rating	Reward Rating	Risk Rating	Recent Up/ Downgrade	3-Month Total Return	6-Month Total Return	1-Year Total Return	3-Year Total Return	5-Year Total Return	NAV	Total Assets (MIL)	Telephone	Open to New Investors
Harbor Mid Cap Growth Fund Institutional Class	HAMGX	B-	B-	B-	Down	6.14	33.57	15.55	79.18	76.48	11.06	257.7	800-422-1050	Y
Harbor Mid Cap Growth Fund Investor Class	HIMGX	B-	B-	B-	Down	6.11	33.42	15.13	77.23	73.24	10.06	257.7	800-422-1050	Y
Harbor Mid Cap Growth Fund Retirement Class	HNMGX	B-	B-	B-	Down	6.12	33.61	15.62	79.56	76.85	11.09	257.7	800-422-1050	Y
Heartland Mid Cap Value Fund Institutional Class	HNMDX	B-	C	B	Up	3.00	17.40	5.19	40.75		11.67	13.1	800-432-7856	Y
Heartland Mid Cap Value Fund Investor Class	HRMDX	B-	C	B	Up	3.00	17.20	4.95	39.68		11.65	13.1	800-432-7856	Y
Hennessy Focus Fund Institutional Class	HFCIX	B-	C+	B	Up	8.30	24.06	10.14	41.90	59.98	82.85	1,794	800-966-4354	Y
Hennessy Focus Fund Investor Class	HFCSX	B-	C+	B	Up	8.21	23.85	9.75	40.31	57.10	80.38	1,794	800-966-4354	Y
Invesco Oppenheimer Discovery Mid Cap Growth Fund A	OEGAX	B-	B-	C+	Up	8.96	31.26	14.69	58.20	77.12	22	1,557	800-659-1005	Y
Invesco Oppenheimer Discovery Mid Cap Growth Fund Class R5	DMCFX	B-	B-	B-		9.04	31.45	14.95	59.35	79.28	22	1,557	800-659-1005	Y
Invesco Oppenheimer Discovery Mid Cap Growth Fund R6	OEGIX	B-	B-	B-		9.04	31.54	15.12	60.10	80.88	25.31	1,557	800-659-1005	Y
Invesco Oppenheimer Discovery Mid Cap Growth Fund Y	OEGYX	B-	B-	C+		9.00	31.41	14.91	59.30	79.23	24.93	1,557	800-659-1005	Y
Ivy Mid Cap Growth Fund Class A	WMGAX	B-	C+	B	Down	4.78	28.32	13.98	69.48	67.00	26.5	4,525		Y
Ivy Mid Cap Growth Fund Class E	IMCEX	B-	C+	B	Down	4.79	28.27	13.88	69.36	66.35	25.77	4,525		Y
Ivy Mid Cap Growth Fund Class I	IYMIX	B-	C+	B	Down	4.90	28.59	14.41	71.09	69.60	28.87	4,525		Y
Ivy Mid Cap Growth Fund Class N	IGRFX	B-	C+	B	Down	4.93	28.66	14.48	71.64	70.72	29.13	4,525		Y
Ivy Mid Cap Growth Fund Class Y	WMGYX	B-	C+	B	Down	4.78	28.34	13.98	69.63	67.36	27.8	4,525		Y
Ivy Mid Cap Income Opportunities Fund Class A	IVOAX	B-	C	B		4.72	17.33	8.42	37.08		14.59	679.3		Y
Ivy Mid Cap Income Opportunities Fund Class C	IVOCX	B-	C	B		4.55	17.01	7.69	34.18		14.53	679.3		Y
Ivy Mid Cap Income Opportunities Fund Class E	IVOEX	B-	C	B		4.77	17.51	8.60	37.71		14.6	679.3		Y
Ivy Mid Cap Income Opportunities Fund Class I	IVOIX	B-	C	B		4.81	17.50	8.75	38.28		14.61	679.3		Y
Ivy Mid Cap Income Opportunities Fund Class N	IVOSX	B-	C	B		4.82	17.62	8.85	38.74		14.62	679.3		Y
Ivy Mid Cap Income Opportunities Fund Class R	IVORX	B-	C	B		4.65	17.19	8.11	35.70		14.57	679.3		Y
Ivy Mid Cap Income Opportunities Fund Class Y	IVOYX	B-	C	B		4.66	17.35	8.44	37.01		14.59	679.3		Y
Jackson Square SMID-Cap Growth Fund Institutional Class	JSMTX	B-	C+	B	Up	2.69	28.75	13.33	69.37	94.81	24.76	970.4		Y
Jackson Square SMID-Cap Growth Fund Investor Class	JSMVX	B-	C+	B	Up	2.63	28.57	12.99	67.91	92.16	24.57	970.4		Y
Jackson Square SMID-Cap Growth Fund IS Class	DCGTX	B-	C+	B	Up	2.73	28.83	13.27	69.53	94.98	24.75	970.4		Y
Janus Henderson Contrarian Fund Class D	JACNX	B-	C+	B	Up	7.50	28.77	13.94	54.39	29.20	21.21	2,574	877-335-2687	
Janus Henderson Contrarian Fund Class I	JCONX	B-	C+	B	Up	7.49	28.74	14.01	54.67	29.63	21.23	2,574	877-335-2687	Y
Janus Henderson Contrarian Fund Class N	JCNNX	B-	C+	B	Up	7.51	28.83	14.07	54.77	29.52	21.18	2,574	877-335-2687	Y
Janus Henderson Contrarian Fund Class T	JSVAX	B-	C+	B	Up	7.45	28.65	13.82	53.98	28.65	21.19	2,574	877-335-2687	Y
Janus Henderson Enterprise Fund Class A	JDMAX	B	B-	B		7.09	27.52	16.37	68.88	92.86	134.72	19,965	877-335-2687	Y
Janus Henderson Enterprise Fund Class C	JGRCX	B	B-	B		6.94	27.16	15.69	65.91	87.02	124.34	19,965	877-335-2687	Y
Janus Henderson Enterprise Fund Class D	JANEX	B	B-	B		7.17	27.72	16.74	70.45	95.82	138.39	19,965	877-335-2687	
Janus Henderson Enterprise Fund Class I	JMGRX	B	B-	B		7.19	27.75	16.80	70.74	96.45	139.11	19,965	877-335-2687	Y
Janus Henderson Enterprise Fund Class N	JDMNX	B	B-	B		7.22	27.81	16.91	71.23	97.37	139.64	19,965	877-335-2687	Y
Janus Henderson Enterprise Fund Class R	JDMRX	B	B-	B		7.01	27.33	16.04	67.41	90.14	130.14	19,965	877-335-2687	Y
Janus Henderson Enterprise Fund Class S	JGRTX	B	B-	B		7.08	27.50	16.33	68.70	92.54	134.02	19,965	877-335-2687	Y
Janus Henderson Enterprise Fund Class T	JAENX	B	B-	B		7.15	27.65	16.62	69.98	94.98	137.46	19,965	877-335-2687	Y
Janus Henderson Select Value Fund Class A	JVSAX	B-	C	B		4.02	17.69	7.46	39.43	48.96	13.17	55.9	877-335-2687	Y
Janus Henderson Select Value Fund Class C	JVSCX	B-	C	B		3.83	17.09	6.52	36.02	43.13	12.74	55.9	877-335-2687	Y
Janus Henderson Select Value Fund Class D	JSVDX	B-	C	B		4.08	17.68	7.56	40.19	50.53	13.24	55.9	877-335-2687	Y
Janus Henderson Select Value Fund Class I	JVSIX	B-	C	B		4.13	17.70	7.65	40.41	50.96	13.36	55.9	877-335-2687	Y
Janus Henderson Select Value Fund Class N	JVSNX	B-	C	B		4.08	17.79	7.72	40.63	51.19	13.24	55.9	877-335-2687	Y
Janus Henderson Select Value Fund Class S	JSVSX	B-	C	B		4.22	17.85	7.51	39.32	49.08	13.07	55.9	877-335-2687	Y
Janus Henderson Select Value Fund Class T	JSVTX	B-	C	B		4.09	17.72	7.51	39.77	49.89	13.22	55.9	877-335-2687	Y
Janus Henderson VIT Enterprise Portfolio Institutional Cls	JAAGX	B	B-	B		7.31	27.98	17.30	73.71	101.11	79.89	1,393	877-335-2687	Y
Janus Henderson VIT Enterprise Portfolio Service Class		B	B-	B		7.25	27.83	17.02	72.44	98.64	74.78	1,384	877-335-2687	Y
Jensen Quality Value Fund Class I	JNVIX	B-	C	B		3.56	20.52	9.05	39.45	39.69	13	38.9	800-992-4144	Y
Jensen Quality Value Fund Class J	JNVSX	B-	C	B		3.57	20.35	8.84	38.64	38.47	13.08	38.9	800-992-4144	Y
JNL/JPMorgan MidCap Growth Fund Class A		B-	B-	B-	Down	6.62	31.06	16.06	67.13	69.67	38.31	2,373		Y
JNL/JPMorgan MidCap Growth Fund Class I		B-	B-	B-	Down	6.69	31.21	16.40	68.42	71.67	39.51	2,373		Y
JNL/T. Rowe Price Mid-Cap Growth Fund Class A		B-	C+	B	Down	6.83	25.65	15.59	59.93	81.60	52.99	6,233		Y

Category: US Equity Mid Cap (con't)

		RATINGS				TOTAL RETURNS & PERFORMANCE					ASSETS		NEW INVESTORS	
Fund Name	Ticker Symbol	Overall Rating	Reward Rating	Risk Rating	Recent Up/ Downgrade	3-Month Total Return	6-Month Total Return	1-Year Total Return	3-Year Total Return	5-Year Total Return	NAV	Total Assets (MIL)	Telephone	Open to New Investors
JNL/T. Rowe Price Mid-Cap Growth Fund Class I		B-	C+	B	Down	6.91	25.82	15.90	61.17	83.70	55.69	6,233		Y
John Hancock Funds II Mid Cap Stock Fund Class 1	JIMSX	B-	B-	B-	Down	5.27	32.18	14.97	73.59	76.54	22.55	1,643	800-225-5913	Y
John Hancock Funds II Mid Cap Stock Fund Class NAV	JHMSX	B-	B-	B-	Down	5.25	32.19	15.05	73.82	76.95	22.83	1,643	800-225-5913	Y
JPMorgan Mid Cap Equity Fund Class A	JCMAX	B-	C+	B		4.70	24.67	9.91	46.03	52.28	50.52	2,791	800-480-4111	
JPMorgan Mid Cap Equity Fund Class I	VSNGX	B-	C+	B		4.75	24.84	10.19	47.33	54.71	51.35	2,791	800-480-4111	
JPMorgan Mid Cap Equity Fund Class R5	JMEEX	B-	C+	B		4.79	24.92	10.36	47.90	55.64	51.37	2,791	800-480-4111	
JPMorgan Mid Cap Equity Fund Class R6	JPPEX	B-	C+	B		4.83	24.99	10.47	48.27	56.15	51.41	2,791	800-480-4111	
JPMorgan Mid Cap Growth Fund Class A	OSGIX	B-	B-	B-		6.46	30.61	15.37	64.93	65.35	32.94	4,565	800-480-4111	Y
JPMorgan Mid Cap Growth Fund Class C	OMGCX	B-	C+	B-		6.33	30.28	14.78	62.43	61.20	25.34	4,565	800-480-4111	Y
JPMorgan Mid Cap Growth Fund Class I	HLGEX	B-	B-	B-	Down	6.55	30.77	15.72	66.45	67.91	38.37	4,565	800-480-4111	Y
JPMorgan Mid Cap Growth Fund Class R2	JMGZX	B-	C+	B-		6.39	30.43	15.09	63.83	63.72	35.91	4,565	800-480-4111	Y
JPMorgan Mid Cap Growth Fund Class R3	JMGPX	B-	B-	B-		6.47	30.61	15.38	64.97	65.59	38.01	4,565	800-480-4111	Y
JPMorgan Mid Cap Growth Fund Class R4	JMGQX	B-	B-	B-	Down	6.53	30.76	15.65	66.17	67.63	38.3	4,565	800-480-4111	Y
JPMorgan Mid Cap Growth Fund Class R5	JMGFX	B-	B-	B-	Down	6.57	30.88	15.88	67.16	69.10	38.9	4,565	800-480-4111	Y
JPMorgan Mid Cap Growth Fund Class R6	JMGMX	B-	B-	B-	Down	6.59	30.94	15.96	67.43	69.54	39.1	4,565	800-480-4111	Y
Kinetics Paradigm Fund Advisor Class A	KNPAX	B-	B	C+	Down	5.60	28.92	7.26	80.55	62.25	51.44	811.6	800-930-3828	Y
Kinetics Paradigm Fund Advisor Class C	KNPCX	B-	B	C+	Down	5.48	28.58	6.73	77.89	58.27	47.68	811.6	800-930-3828	Y
Kinetics Paradigm Fund Class Institutional	KNPYX	B	B	C+		5.71	29.22	7.75	83.00	65.97	53.81	811.6	800-930-3828	Y
Kinetics Paradigm Fund No Load Class	WWNPX	B	B	C+		5.67	29.07	7.52	81.93	64.30	53.27	811.6	800-930-3828	Y
Lord Abbett Growth Opportunities Fund Class A	LMGAX	B-	B-	B		6.38	28.88	18.16	54.76	60.74	23.65	879.5	201-827-2000	Y
Lord Abbett Growth Opportunities Fund Class C	LMGCX	B-	C+	B		6.20	28.45	17.26	51.34	54.89	17.11	879.5	201-827-2000	Y
Lord Abbett Growth Opportunities Fund Class F	LGOFX	B	B-	B	Up	6.42	28.99	18.32	55.41	61.96	24.69	879.5	201-827-2000	Y
Lord Abbett Growth Opportunities Fund Class F3	LOMGX	B	B-	B	Up	6.47	29.13	18.50	55.87	61.90	27.3	879.5	201-827-2000	Y
Lord Abbett Growth Opportunities Fund Class I	LMGYX	B	B-	B	Up	6.43	29.05	18.43	55.87	62.79	27.14	879.5	201-827-2000	Y
Lord Abbett Growth Opportunities Fund Class P	LGOPX	B-	B-	B		6.34	28.75	17.89	53.83	59.16	22.97	879.5	201-827-2000	
Lord Abbett Growth Opportunities Fund Class R2	LGOQX	B-	C+	B		6.27	28.67	17.73	53.14	57.97	22.35	879.5	201-827-2000	Y
Lord Abbett Growth Opportunities Fund Class R3	LGORX	B-	B-	B		6.32	28.78	17.87	53.54	58.80	22.86	879.5	201-827-2000	Y
Lord Abbett Growth Opportunities Fund Class R4	LGOSX	B-	B-	B		6.38	28.88	18.16	54.68	60.74	23.65	879.5	201-827-2000	Y
Lord Abbett Growth Opportunities Fund Class R5	LGOTX	B	B-	B	Up	6.42	29.08	18.41	55.89	62.42	27.16	879.5	201-827-2000	Y
Lord Abbett Growth Opportunities Fund Class R6	LGOVX	B	B-	B	Up	6.47	29.09	18.51	56.32	63.08	27.29	879.5	201-827-2000	Y
Madison Mid Cap Fund Class A	MERAX	B	B	B+	Up	8.23	24.35	16.70	50.79	65.06	10.52	552.8	800-767-0300	Y
Madison Mid Cap Fund Class B	MERBX	B	B-	B+	Up	7.96	23.89	15.84	47.35	58.85	8.4	552.8	800-767-0300	Y
Madison Mid Cap Fund Class R6	MMCRX	B	B	B+	Up	8.20	24.75	17.35	53.53	70.17	11.34	552.8	800-767-0300	Y
Madison Mid Cap Fund Class Y	GTSGX	B	B	B+	Up	8.20	24.63	17.10	52.57	67.95	11.08	552.8	800-767-0300	Y
Marsico 21st Century Fund	MXXIX	B	B	B		7.21	28.08	15.90	71.38	72.20	33.89	283.2	888-860-8686	Y
MassMutual Select Mid Cap Growth Fund Administrative Class	MMELX	B-	C+	B	Down	5.89	25.59	14.76	57.98	76.47	21.54	8,748		Y
MassMutual Select Mid Cap Growth Fund Class A	MEFAX	B-	C+	B	Down	5.84	25.41	14.45	56.80	74.24	19.74	8,748		Y
MassMutual Select Mid Cap Growth Fund Class I	MEFZX	B-	C+	B	Down	6.00	25.81	15.13	59.42	79.11	23.49	8,748		Y
MassMutual Select Mid Cap Growth Fund Class R3	MEFNX	B-	C+	B	Down	5.79	25.38	14.31	56.11	73.01	18.08	8,748		Y
MassMutual Select Mid Cap Growth Fund Class R4	MEFFX	B-	C+	B	Down	5.85	25.48	14.59	57.29	75.26	19.89	8,748		Y
MassMutual Select Mid Cap Growth Fund Class R5	MGRFX	B-	C+	B	Down	5.97	25.68	14.98	58.92	78.19	23.24	8,748		Y
MassMutual Select Mid Cap Growth Fund Service Class	MEFYX	B-	C+	B	Down	5.89	25.66	14.87	58.41	77.28	22.62	8,748		Y
MFS Mid Cap Growth Fund Class 529A	EAMCX	B	B	B		9.06	30.87	17.24	71.58	90.50	19.37	5,405	877-960-6077	Y
MFS Mid Cap Growth Fund Class 529B	EBCGX	B	B	B		8.90	30.32	16.32	67.65	83.29	15.9	5,405	877-960-6077	Y
MFS Mid Cap Growth Fund Class 529C	ECGRX	B	B	B		8.91	30.31	16.34	67.74	83.33	15.39	5,405	877-960-6077	Y
MFS Mid Cap Growth Fund Class A	OTCAX	B	B	B		9.11	30.82	17.23	71.73	90.74	19.99	5,405	877-960-6077	Y
MFS Mid Cap Growth Fund Class B	OTCBX	B	B	B		8.93	30.43	16.40	67.91	83.72	16.33	5,405	877-960-6077	Y
MFS Mid Cap Growth Fund Class C	OTCCX	B	B	B		8.95	30.42	16.42	68.00	83.76	15.82	5,405	877-960-6077	Y
MFS Mid Cap Growth Fund Class I	OTCIX	B	B	B		9.19	31.07	17.57	73.14	93.11	21.26	5,405	877-960-6077	Y
MFS Mid Cap Growth Fund Class R1	OTCGX	B	B	B		8.91	30.41	16.41	67.94	83.68	16.25	5,405	877-960-6077	Y
MFS Mid Cap Growth Fund Class R2	MCPRX	B	B	B		9.00	30.71	16.94	70.44	88.29	18.77	5,405	877-960-6077	Y
MFS Mid Cap Growth Fund Class R3	OTCHX	B	B	B		9.12	30.82	17.23	71.66	90.62	19.86	5,405	877-960-6077	Y

Category: US Equity Mid Cap (con't)

Fund Name	Ticker Symbol	RATINGS: Overall Rating	Reward Rating	Risk Rating	Recent Up/ Downgrade	TOTAL RETURNS & PERFORMANCE: 3-Month Total Return	6-Month Total Return	1-Year Total Return	3-Year Total Return	5-Year Total Return	ASSETS: NAV	Total Assets (MIL.)	NEW INVESTORS: Telephone	Open to New Investors
MFS Mid Cap Growth Fund Class R4	OTCJX	B	B	B		9.20	31.06	17.54	73.03	93.13	20.76	5,405	877-960-6077	Y
MFS Mid Cap Growth Fund Class R6	OTCKX	B	B	B		9.23	31.10	17.68	73.62	94.15	21.41	5,405	877-960-6077	Y
Monongahela All Cap Value Fund	MCMVX	B-	C	B		2.25	16.93	7.66	49.81	52.55	14.06	13.0	855-392-9331	Y
Morgan Stanley Inst Trust Discovery Portfolio Cls A	MACGX	B	B	B-	Up	12.72	45.06	30.36	107.27	82.41	17.8	927.2	855-332-5306	
Morgan Stanley Inst Trust Discovery Portfolio Cls C	MSMFX	B	B	C+	Up	12.52	44.37	29.29	102.22	75.32	17.34	927.2	855-332-5306	Y
Morgan Stanley Inst Trust Discovery Portfolio Cls I	MPEGX	B	B	B-	Up	12.77	45.17	30.68	109.12	84.94	21.98	927.2	855-332-5306	
Morgan Stanley Inst Trust Discovery Portfolio Cls IS	MMCGX	B	B	B-	Up	12.78	45.29	30.84	109.35	85.80	22.23	927.2	855-332-5306	
Morgan Stanley Inst Trust Discovery Portfolio Cls L	MSKLX	B	B	B-	Up	12.53	44.65	29.74	103.69	77.30	15.71	927.2	855-332-5306	
Nationwide Geneva Mid Cap Growth Fund Class A	NWHVX	B-	C+	B-		6.31	24.69	11.07	49.22	65.31	21.71	606.5	800-848-0920	Y
Nationwide Geneva Mid Cap Growth Fund Class R6	NWKAX	B-	B-	B		6.43	24.97	11.50	50.89	68.44	23.17	606.5	800-848-0920	Y
Nationwide Geneva Mid Cap Growth Institutional Service Cls	NWHYX	B-	B-	B		6.42	24.97	11.46	50.36	67.39	22.87	606.5	800-848-0920	Y
Nicholas II Fund Class I	NCTWX	B	B-	B		6.70	25.90	14.12	58.34	68.34	29.11	919.5	800-544-6547	Y
Nicholas II Fund Class N	NNTWX	B	B-	B		6.63	25.66	13.73	56.79	65.49	28.45	919.5	800-544-6547	Y
Nuance Mid Cap Value Fund Institutional Class	NMVLX	B	B-	A-		5.67	19.18	13.32	46.97	56.34	12.93	1,211		Y
Nuance Mid Cap Value Fund Investor Class	NMAVX	B	B-	A-		5.69	19.02	13.13	45.95	54.45	12.93	1,211		Y
Nuance Mid Cap Value Fund Z Class Shares	NMVZX	B	B-	A-		5.76	19.28	13.56	47.54	56.95	12.96	1,211		Y
Papp Small & Mid-Cap Growth Fund	PAPPX	B	B-	B		7.67	28.55	17.18	59.26	67.53	24.83	37.8		Y
Parnassus Mid Cap Fund	PARMX	B	C+	B+		4.95	23.03	12.00	42.84	57.84	35.15	3,771	999-350-5	Y
Parnassus Mid Cap Fund Institutional Shares	PFPMX	B	B-	B+		4.97	23.10	12.22	43.74	59.32	35.22	3,771	999-350-5	Y
PGIM Jennison Mid-Cap Growth Fund- Class A	PEEAX	B-	C+	B		6.88	29.15	13.78	49.69	52.94	28.88	3,442	800-225-1852	
PGIM Jennison Mid-Cap Growth Fund- Class R	JDERX	B-	C+	B	Up	6.82	29.07	13.56	48.85	51.47	27.39	3,442	800-225-1852	
PGIM Jennison Mid-Cap Growth Fund- Class R2	PEGEX	B-	C+	B		6.87	29.17	13.75	49.78	53.18	32.63	3,442	800-225-1852	Y
PGIM Jennison Mid-Cap Growth Fund- Class R4	PEGGX	B-	C+	B		6.98	29.34	14.08	50.94	55.14	32.79	3,442	800-225-1852	Y
PGIM Jennison Mid-Cap Growth Fund- Class R6	PJGQX	B-	C+	B		7.01	29.48	14.33	51.87	56.63	32.94	3,442	800-225-1852	
PGIM Jennison Mid-Cap Growth Fund- Class Z	PEGZX	B-	C+	B		6.98	29.35	14.08	50.95	55.15	32.3	3,442	800-225-1852	
Principal MidCap Fund Class A	PEMGX	B	B	B		9.18	31.36	17.80	62.13	78.43	28.77	16,562	800-787-1621	
Principal MidCap Fund Class C	PMBCX	B	B	B	Up	8.98	30.87	16.94	58.59	72.02	25.6	16,562	800-787-1621	
Principal MidCap Fund Class J	PMBJX	B	B	B		9.20	31.43	17.95	62.92	79.72	27.64	16,562	800-787-1621	
PRINCIPAL MIDCAP FUND Class R-6	PMAQX	B	B	B		9.25	31.62	18.20	63.73	80.76	29.51	16,562	800-787-1621	Y
Principal MidCap Fund Institutional Class	PCBIX	B	B	B		9.28	31.56	18.12	63.58	81.19	29.55	16,562	800-787-1621	
Principal MidCap Fund R-1 Class	PMSBX	B	B	B		9.04	31.06	17.25	59.78	74.13	26.41	16,562	800-787-1621	
Principal MidCap Fund R-2 Class	PMBNX	B	B	B		9.07	31.14	17.37	60.39	75.24	26.91	16,562	800-787-1621	
Principal MidCap Fund R-3 Class	PMBMX	B	B	B		9.14	31.25	17.57	61.22	76.92	28.05	16,562	800-787-1621	
Principal MidCap Fund R-4 Class	PMBSX	B	B	B		9.20	31.39	17.80	62.21	78.55	29.3	16,562	800-787-1621	
Principal MidCap Fund R-5 Class	PMBPX	B	B	B		9.22	31.46	17.92	62.76	79.69	29.12	16,562	800-787-1621	
Principal MidCap Growth Fund III Class J	PPQJX	B-	C+	B-		7.12	27.80	12.88	55.66	58.56	9.47	1,126	800-787-1621	Y
Principal MidCap Growth Fund III Institutional Class	PPIMX	B-	C+	B-		7.32	28.14	13.30	57.57	61.60	12.02	1,126	800-787-1621	Y
Principal MidCap Growth Fund III R-3 Class	PPQMX	B-	C+	B-		7.06	27.71	12.64	54.75	56.88	11.06	1,126	800-787-1621	Y
Principal MidCap Growth Fund III R-4 Class	PPQSX	B-	C+	B-		7.19	27.87	12.90	55.57	58.42	11.47	1,126	800-787-1621	Y
Principal MidCap Growth Fund III R-5 Class	PPQPX	B-	C+	B-		7.19	27.99	13.02	56.35	59.54	12.07	1,126	800-787-1621	Y
Prospector Opportunity Fund	POPFX	B	C+	B+	Up	8.10	20.19	11.32	45.31	60.21	22.02	132.3	877-734-7862	Y
RBC SMID Cap Growth Fund Class I	TMCIX	B-	C+	B-		6.16	28.84	12.33	52.25	66.35	15.32	97.8	800-422-2766	Y
RBC SMID Cap Growth Fund Class R6	RSMRX	B-	C+	B-		6.22	28.88	12.38	52.40	66.52	15.35	97.8	800-422-2766	Y
Riverbridge Eco Leaders® Fund Institutional Class	RIVEX	B-	C+	B	Down	6.89	25.59	18.18	70.62		14.72	7.0		
Riverbridge Eco Leaders® Fund Investor Class	ECOLX	B-	C+	B	Down	6.90	25.53	17.97	69.41		14.55	7.0		
Riverbridge Growth Fund Institutional Class	RIVBX	B-	C+	B	Down	6.22	23.52	16.88	69.85	82.98	21.32	111.3		Y
Riverbridge Growth Fund Investor Class	RIVRX	B-	C+	B	Down	6.12	23.43	16.64	68.68	80.88	20.96	111.3		Y
Seven Canyons Strategic Income Fund Investor Class	WASIX	B-	C	B+	Up	2.83	13.20	3.27	26.99	17.59	12.14	34.5		Y
T. Rowe Price Diversified Mid Cap Growth Fund	PRDMX	B	B-	B		7.10	29.24	17.19	65.74	81.21	34.69	1,347	410-345-2000	Y
T. Rowe Price Diversified Mid Cap Growth Fund I Class	RPTTX	B	B-	B		7.12	29.31	17.33	66.27	81.79	34.72	1,347	410-345-2000	Y
T. Rowe Price Institutional Mid-Cap Equity Growth Fund	PMEGX	B-	C+	B	Down	7.26	26.93	16.65	64.64	89.34	60.56	7,975	410-345-2000	
T. Rowe Price Mid-Cap Growth Fund	RPMGX	B-	C+	B	Down	6.92	25.70	15.93	61.36	83.75	94.91	33,863	410-345-2000	

Category: US Equity Mid Cap (con't)

		RATINGS				TOTAL RETURNS & PERFORMANCE					ASSETS		NEW INVESTORS	
Fund Name	Ticker Symbol	Overall Rating	Reward Rating	Risk Rating	Recent Up/ Downgrade	3-Month Total Return	6-Month Total Return	1-Year Total Return	3-Year Total Return	5-Year Total Return	NAV	Total Assets (MIL)	Telephone	Open to New Investors
T. Rowe Price Mid-Cap Growth Fund Advisor Class	PAMCX	B-	C+	B	Down	6.85	25.57	15.64	60.12	81.40	91.78	33,863	410-345-2000	
T. Rowe Price Mid-Cap Growth Fund I Class	RPTIX	B-	C+	B	Down	6.96	25.76	16.06	61.98	84.63	94.94	33,863	410-345-2000	Y
T. Rowe Price Mid-Cap Growth Fund R Class	RRMGX	B-	C+	B	Down	6.79	25.38	15.31	58.84	79.06	88.77	33,863	410-345-2000	
T. Rowe Price New Horizons Fund	PRNHX	B	B	B		8.02	31.98	18.01	93.51	107.76	62.88	27,636	410-345-2000	
T. Rowe Price New Horizons Fund I Class	PRJIX	B	B	B		8.06	32.05	18.15	94.26	108.79	62.99	27,636	410-345-2000	Y
Touchstone Mid Cap Fund Class A	TMAPX	B-	B-	B		5.83	23.18	12.35	55.23	61.82	36.61	1,350	800-543-0407	Y
Touchstone Mid Cap Fund Class Y	TMCPX	B	B-	B	Up	5.89	23.31	12.62	56.40	63.83	37.02	1,350	800-543-0407	Y
Touchstone Mid Cap Fund Class Z	TMCTX	B	B-	B	Up	5.84	23.19	12.34	55.26	61.77	36.38	1,350	800-543-0407	Y
Touchstone Mid Cap Fund Institutional	TMPIX	B	B-	B	Up	5.94	23.38	12.71	56.73	64.43	37.09	1,350	800-543-0407	Y
Touchstone Mid Cap Growth Fund Class A	TEGAX	B-	B-	B	Down	5.57	29.08	13.73	64.53	71.42	30.89	1,212	800-543-0407	Y
Touchstone Mid Cap Growth Fund Class Y	TEGYX	B-	B-	B	Down	5.63	29.24	14.01	65.81	73.66	32.22	1,212	800-543-0407	Y
Touchstone Mid Cap Growth Fund Institutional Class	TEGIX	B-	B-	B	Down	5.65	29.24	14.05	66.01	74.25	32.53	1,212	800-543-0407	Y
Transamerica Mid Cap Value Opportunities A	MCVAX	B-	C	B	Up	2.78	17.69	6.09	28.31	44.83	11.44	1,708	888-233-4339	Y
Transamerica Mid Cap Value Opportunities C	MCVCX	B-	C	B	Up	2.81	17.42	5.43	25.60	39.79	11.32	1,708	888-233-4339	Y
Transamerica Mid Cap Value Opportunities I	MVTIX	B-	C	B		3.03	18.13	6.46	29.43	46.95	11.53	1,708	888-233-4339	Y
Transamerica Mid Cap Value Opportunities I2		B-	C	B		3.12	18.11	6.60	29.89	47.57	11.54	1,708	888-233-4339	Y
Transamerica Mid Cap Value Opportunities I3	TOTTX	B-	C	B		3.11	18.14	6.49	29.55	45.86	11.59	1,708	888-233-4339	Y
Transamerica Mid Cap Value Opportunities R	TOTRX	B-	C	B	Up	3.02	17.90	6.04	27.70	42.35	11.59	1,708	888-233-4339	Y
Transamerica Mid Cap Value Opportunities R4	TOTFX	B-	C	B	Up	3.02	18.02	6.32	28.73	44.21	11.59	1,708	888-233-4339	Y
Transamerica Mid Cap Value Opportunities R6	MVTRX	B-	C	B		3.10	18.08	6.47	29.70	46.02	11.62	1,708	888-233-4339	Y
VALIC Company I Mid Cap Strategic Growth Fund	VMSGX	B-	B-	B	Down	7.71	30.07	15.44	66.45	68.20	16.61	323.2		Y
Value Line Mid Cap Focused Fund	VLIFX	B+	B	B+	Up	8.63	29.08	26.38	68.39	89.95	24.41	329.8	800-243-2729	Y
Value Line Mid Cap Focused Fund Institutional Class	VLMIX	B+	B	B+	Up	8.73	29.30	26.67	69.20	90.85	24.53	329.8	800-243-2729	Y
Value Line Premier Growth Fund	VALSX	B	B	B		8.15	29.56	23.10	65.21	74.95	39.13	450.9	800-243-2729	Y
Vanguard Mid-Cap Growth Fund Investor Shares	VMGRX	B-	C+	B-		5.73	29.17	13.30	59.32	61.55	28.56	4,765	877-662-7447	Y
Vanguard Mid-Cap Growth Index Fund Admiral Shares	VMGMX	B-	C+	B		4.81	26.54	12.04	52.04	62.31	64.29	14,046	877-662-7447	Y
Vanguard Mid-Cap Growth Index Fund Investor Shares	VMGIX	B-	C+	B		4.78	26.48	11.91	51.49	61.34	58.74	14,046	877-662-7447	Y
Victory RS Investors Fund Class A	RSINX	B-	C+	B	Up	4.83	22.83	9.46	39.96	31.00	13.02	42.1	800-539-3863	Y
Victory RS Investors Fund Class Y	RSIYX	B-	C+	B	Up	4.87	22.92	9.73	41.08	32.82	13.35	42.1	800-539-3863	Y
Victory RS Value Fund Class A	RSVAX	B-	C+	B	Up	4.43	22.98	9.41	40.04	38.84	24.72	391.4	800-539-3863	Y
Victory RS Value Fund Class R	RSVKX	B-	C	B	Up	4.32	22.74	8.95	38.41	36.08	23.42	391.4	800-539-3863	Y
Victory RS Value Fund Class Y	RSVYX	B-	C+	B	Up	4.49	23.12	9.59	40.99	40.38	25.34	391.4	800-539-3863	Y
Virtus Ceredex Mid-Cap Value Equity Fund Class A	SAMVX	B-	C	B		4.33	20.27	6.53	41.73	38.28	12.04	3,123	800-243-1574	Y
Virtus Ceredex Mid-Cap Value Equity Fund Class C	SMVFX	B-	C	B		4.18	19.99	6.10	39.91	35.52	11.7	3,123	800-243-1574	Y
Virtus Ceredex Mid-Cap Value Equity Fund Class I	SMVTX	B-	C	B		4.35	20.49	6.89	43.17	40.48	12.23	3,123	800-243-1574	Y
Virtus Ceredex Mid-Cap Value Equity Fund Class R6	SMVZX	B-	C	B		4.42	20.55	7.07	44.11	42.37	12.26	3,123	800-243-1574	Y
Virtus KAR Mid-Cap Core Fund Class A	VMACX	B-	C+	B	Down	6.11	21.66	9.72	55.30	83.05	34.71	396.5	800-243-1574	Y
Virtus KAR Mid-Cap Core Fund Class C	VMCCX	B-	C	B	Down	5.89	21.23	8.92	51.84	76.31	32.32	396.5	800-243-1574	Y
Virtus KAR Mid-Cap Core Fund Class I	VIMCX	B-	C+	B	Down	6.15	21.77	9.98	56.43	85.27	35.34	396.5	800-243-1574	Y
Virtus KAR Mid-Cap Core Fund Class R6	VRMCX	B-	C+	B	Down	6.18	21.86	10.10	56.70	85.58	35.39	396.5	800-243-1574	Y
Virtus KAR Mid-Cap Growth Fund Class A	PHSKX	B	B+	B		9.48	36.50	19.48	99.81	115.01	39.49	427.4	800-243-1574	Y
Virtus KAR Mid-Cap Growth Fund Class C	PSKCX	B	B	B-		9.27	36.00	18.62	95.41	107.21	31.09	427.4	800-243-1574	Y
Virtus KAR Mid-Cap Growth Fund Class I	PICMX	B	B+	B		9.54	36.67	19.79	101.37	117.76	40.84	427.4	800-243-1574	Y
Virtus KAR Mid-Cap Growth Fund Class R6	VRMGX	B	B+	B		9.60	36.84	20.06	101.20	116.50	40.97	427.4	800-243-1574	Y
Virtus KAR Small-Cap Core Fund Class A	PKSAX	B	B+	B		5.13	28.66	12.56	87.73	110.13	36.85	1,508	800-243-1574	Y
Virtus KAR Small-Cap Core Fund Class C	PKSCX	B	B	B	Up	4.95	28.19	11.77	83.62	102.46	30.74	1,508	800-243-1574	Y
Virtus KAR Small-Cap Core Fund Class I	PKSFX	B	B+	B		5.19	28.82	12.88	89.22	112.80	38.88	1,508	800-243-1574	Y
Virtus KAR Small-Cap Core Fund Class R6	VSCRX	B	B+	B		5.23	28.89	12.97	89.69	113.78	39.03	1,508	800-243-1574	Y
Voya Russell Mid Cap Growth Index Portfolio Class I	IRGJX	B-	C+	B	Down	5.30	27.19	13.45	58.59	66.49	33.56	302.5	800-366-0066	Y
Voya Russell Mid Cap Growth Index Portfolio Class S	IRGUX	B-	C+	B		5.23	27.03	13.16	57.40	64.39	33.5	302.5	800-366-0066	Y
Voya Russell Mid Cap Growth Index Portfolio Class S2	IRGVX	B-	C+	B		5.19	26.92	13.01	56.72	63.20	33.44	302.5	800-366-0066	Y
VY® Baron Growth Portfolio Class A	IBSAX	B-	B	B-		6.54	28.93	12.18	65.42	65.79	31.59	816.9	800-366-0066	Y

Category: US Equity Mid Cap (con't)

Fund Name	Ticker Symbol	RATINGS: Overall Rating	Reward Rating	Risk Rating	Recent Up/ Downgrade	TOTAL RETURNS & PERFORMANCE: 3-Month Total Return	6-Month Total Return	1-Year Total Return	3-Year Total Return	5-Year Total Return	ASSETS: NAV	Total Assets (MIL)	NEW INVESTORS: Telephone	Open to New Investors
VY® Baron Growth Portfolio Class I	IBGIX	B	B	B-	Up	6.69	29.22	12.73	67.90	69.99	35.24	816.9	800-366-0066	Y
VY® Baron Growth Portfolio Class R6	VYRBX	B	B	B-	Up	6.68	29.25	12.72	67.92	70.06	35.26	816.9	800-366-0066	Y
VY® Baron Growth Portfolio Class S	IBSSX	B	B	B-	Up	6.61	29.08	12.48	66.65	67.89	33.51	816.9	800-366-0066	Y
VY® Baron Growth Portfolio Class S2	IBCGX	B-	B	B-		6.57	28.98	12.32	65.89	66.62	31.91	816.9	800-366-0066	Y
VY® T. Rowe Price Diversified Mid Cap Growth Port Cls A	IAXAX	B-	B-	B	Down	7.03	28.69	16.20	62.75	76.38	11.57	1,109	800-366-0066	Y
VY® T. Rowe Price Diversified Mid Cap Growth Port Cls I	IAXIX	B-	B-	B	Down	7.11	29.11	16.81	65.21	80.95	12.95	1,109	800-366-0066	Y
VY® T. Rowe Price Diversified Mid Cap Growth Port Cls R6	VYRIX	B	B-	B		7.11	28.98	16.70	65.19	81.10	12.95	1,109	800-366-0066	Y
VY® T. Rowe Price Diversified Mid Cap Growth Port Cls S	IAXSX	B-	B-	B	Down	7.06	28.97	16.53	63.92	78.71	12.42	1,109	800-366-0066	Y
VY® T. Rowe Price Diversified Mid Cap Growth Port Cls S2	IAXTX	B-	B-	B	Down	6.98	28.76	16.32	63.16	77.31	11.64	1,109	800-366-0066	Y
Walden Midcap Fund	WAMFX	B-	C+	B	Down	4.89	20.80	12.87	47.73	63.95	18.64	54.7	617-814-1215	Y
Wells Fargo Discovery Fund - Class A	WFDAX	B-	B	C+		10.74	38.02	17.44	76.95	76.21	34.74	2,582	800-222-8222	Y
Wells Fargo Discovery Fund - Class Admin	WFDDX	B-	B	C+		10.73	38.04	17.51	77.35	76.97	36.1	2,582	800-222-8222	Y
Wells Fargo Discovery Fund - Class C	WDSCX	B-	B-	C+		10.53	37.48	16.53	73.02	69.66	29.6	2,582	800-222-8222	Y
Wells Fargo Discovery Fund - Class Inst	WFDSX	B-	B	C+		10.81	38.23	17.81	78.72	79.23	38.11	2,582	800-222-8222	Y
Wells Fargo Discovery Fund - Class R6	WFDRX	B-	B	C+		10.86	38.27	17.91	79.22	80.03	38.37	2,582	800-222-8222	Y
Wells Fargo Enterprise Fund - Class A	SENAX	B	B	B-		9.33	35.60	18.39	68.45	68.54	50.84	782.5	800-222-8222	Y
Wells Fargo Enterprise Fund - Class Admin	SEPKX	B	B	B-		9.35	35.66	18.51	68.86	69.47	54.01	782.5	800-222-8222	Y
Wells Fargo Enterprise Fund - Class C	WENCX	B	B	B-	Up	9.12	35.11	17.51	64.67	62.32	43.75	782.5	800-222-8222	Y
Wells Fargo Enterprise Fund - Class Inst	WFEIX	B	B	B-		9.40	35.84	18.77	70.12	71.33	56.88	782.5	800-222-8222	Y
Wells Fargo Enterprise Fund - Class R6	WENRX	B	B	B-		9.43	35.88	18.84	70.36	71.60	57.06	782.5	800-222-8222	Y
William Blair Mid Cap Growth Fund Class I	WCGIX	B	B	B	Up	5.73	29.05	13.04	56.61	62.69	12.17	68.7	800-621-0687	Y
William Blair Mid Cap Growth Fund Class N	WCGNX	B	B	B	Up	5.60	28.84	12.75	55.53	60.69	11.3	68.7	800-621-0687	Y
William Blair Mid Cap Growth Fund Class R6	WCGJX	B	B	B		5.73	29.05	13.04	56.61	62.69	12.17	68.7	800-621-0687	Y
William Blair Small-Mid Cap Growth Fund Class I	WSMDX	B-	C+	B-		6.29	25.88	9.90	68.20	87.17	27.53	2,840	800-621-0687	Y
William Blair Small-Mid Cap Growth Fund Class N	WSMNX	B-	C+	B-		6.23	25.71	9.65	66.90	84.83	26.06	2,840	800-621-0687	Y
William Blair Small-Mid Cap Growth Fund Class R6	WSMRX	B-	C+	B-		6.29	25.87	9.90	68.20	87.17	27.54	2,840	800-621-0687	Y

Category: US Equity Small Cap

Fund Name	Ticker Symbol	RATINGS: Overall Rating	Reward Rating	Risk Rating	Recent Up/ Downgrade	TOTAL RETURNS & PERFORMANCE: 3-Month Total Return	6-Month Total Return	1-Year Total Return	3-Year Total Return	5-Year Total Return	ASSETS: NAV	Total Assets (MIL)	NEW INVESTORS: Telephone	Open to New Investors
AMG River Road Small Cap Value Fund Class I	ARSIX	B-	C+	B		5.91	22.77	9.11	51.68	58.84	13.26	367.3	800-835-3879	Y
AMG River Road Small Cap Value Fund Class N	ARSVX	B-	C+	B		5.79	22.58	8.80	50.50	56.79	12.97	367.3	800-835-3879	Y
AMG River Road Small Cap Value Fund Class Z	ARZMX	B-	C+	B		5.99	22.89	9.26	51.52	57.85	13.26	367.3	800-835-3879	Y
AMG River Road Small-Mid Cap Value Fund Class I	ARIMX	B-	C+	B		5.34	23.28	10.30	56.28	61.71	7.89	103.9	800-835-3879	Y
AMG River Road Small-Mid Cap Value Fund Class N	ARSMX	B-	C+	B		5.33	23.00	10.10	54.99	59.60	7.7	103.9	800-835-3879	Y
AMG River Road Small-Mid Cap Value Fund Class Z	ARSZX	B-	C+	B		5.48	23.28	10.45	55.74	60.37	7.89	103.9	800-835-3879	Y
Boston Trust SMID Cap Fund	BTSMX	B-	C	B		4.31	20.09	8.00	52.90	58.64	17.39	88.7	617-814-1215	Y
Brown Advisory Small-Cap Growth Fund Advisor Shares	BASAX	B-	B-	B-	Down	7.74	32.43	14.07	57.79	77.74	21.15	1,347	800-540-6807	Y
Brown Advisory Small-Cap Growth Fund Institutional Shares	BAFSX	B-	B-	B-	Down	7.84	32.69	14.55	59.71	81.26	44.24	1,347	800-540-6807	Y
Brown Advisory Small-Cap Growth Fund Investor Shares	BIASX	B-	B-	B-	Down	7.79	32.59	14.40	59.02	79.90	22.13	1,347	800-540-6807	Y
Columbia Small Cap Growth Fund I Institutional 3 Class	CSGYX	B-	C+	B-	Down	9.04	35.45	20.05	91.64	102.16	21.7	634.0	800-345-6611	
DF Dent Small Cap Growth Fund Institutional Shares	DFSGX	B-	B-	B-		11.30	31.66	15.20	63.10	72.55	17.13	19.1		Y
DF Dent Small Cap Growth Fund Investor Shares	DFDSX	B-	B-	B-		11.25	31.53	15.00	62.82	72.26	17.1	19.1		Y
Federated Kaufmann Small Cap Fund Class A Shares	FKASX	B	B	B		5.30	30.76	18.44	113.51	118.39	41.91	3,149	800-341-7400	Y
Federated Kaufmann Small Cap Fund Class B Shares	FKBSX	B	B	B		5.10	30.34	17.72	109.61	112.15	35.61	3,149	800-341-7400	
Federated Kaufmann Small Cap Fund Class C Shares	FKCSX	B	B	B		5.13	30.36	17.71	109.72	112.27	35.63	3,149	800-341-7400	Y
Federated Kaufmann Small Cap Fund Class R Shares	FKKSX	B	B	B		5.29	30.76	18.50	113.80	118.85	42.12	3,149	800-341-7400	Y
Federated Kaufmann Small Cap Fund Class R6 Shares	FKALX	B	B	B		5.41	31.06	19.03	115.24	120.16	42.28	3,149	800-341-7400	Y
Federated Kaufmann Small Cap Fund Institutional Shares	FKAIX	B	B	B		5.41	31.06	19.00	116.48	121.92	42.65	3,149	800-341-7400	Y
GuideMark® Small/Mid Cap Core Fund Institutional Shares	GISMX	B-	C	B+	Down	0.00	0.00	1.49	48.11	39.36	18.8801	66.0	603-888-5500	Y

Category: US Equity Small Cap (con't)

Fund Name	Ticker Symbol	RATINGS: Overall Rating	Reward Rating	Risk Rating	Recent Up/ Downgrade	TOTAL RETURNS & PERFORMANCE: 3-Month Total Return	6-Month Total Return	1-Year Total Return	3-Year Total Return	5-Year Total Return	ASSETS: NAV	Total Assets (MIL)	NEW INVESTORS: Telephone	Open to New Investors
Jacob Micro Cap Growth Fund Institutional Class shares	JMIGX	B	B	B-	Up	13.44	37.60	29.81	98.06	56.82	20.42	14.6		Y
Jacob Micro Cap Growth Fund Investor Class shares	JMCGX	B	B	B-	Up	13.34	37.42	29.61	96.73	54.74	18.69	14.6		Y
JNL Multi-Manager Small Cap Growth Fund Class A		B-	B-	C+	Down	7.10	31.17	10.69	83.30	65.04	30.59	2,375		Y
JNL Multi-Manager Small Cap Growth Fund Class I		B-	B-	C+	Down	7.18	31.32	10.99	84.60	66.98	32.24	2,375		Y
Kinetics Small Capital Opportunities Advisor Fund Class A	KSOAX	B-	B-	C+	Down	2.47	22.47	3.80	81.32	49.74	60.87	313.1	800-930-3828	Y
Kinetics Small Capital Opportunities Cls Institutional	KSCYX	B-	B-	C+	Down	2.59	22.74	4.28	83.81	53.18	64.06	313.1	800-930-3828	Y
Kinetics Small Capital Opportunities Fund No Load Class	KSCOX	B-	B-	C+	Down	2.54	22.63	4.08	82.79	51.71	62.9	313.1	800-930-3828	Y
MFS New Discovery Fund Class A	MNDAX	B-	C+	B-	Down	8.94	32.57	13.02	78.26	63.30	28.12	1,451	877-960-6077	Y
MFS New Discovery Fund Class I	MNDIX	B-	C+	B-	Down	9.01	32.73	13.29	79.59	65.32	31.91	1,451	877-960-6077	Y
MFS New Discovery Fund Class R2	MNDRX	B-	C+	B-	Down	8.85	32.39	12.72	76.87	61.23	25.95	1,451	877-960-6077	Y
MFS New Discovery Fund Class R3	MNDHX	B-	C+	B-	Down	8.92	32.59	12.99	78.17	63.21	28.07	1,451	877-960-6077	Y
MFS New Discovery Fund Class R4	MNDJX	B-	C+	B-	Down	9.00	32.75	13.29	79.72	65.48	30.03	1,451	877-960-6077	Y
MFS New Discovery Fund Class R6	MNDKX	B-	C+	B-	Down	9.05	32.85	13.42	80.16	66.34	32.27	1,451	877-960-6077	Y
Needham Small Cap Growth Fund Institutional Class	NESIX	B	B	B	Up	11.06	30.81	17.40	70.71	71.39	16.26	37.4	800-625-7071	Y
Needham Small Cap Growth Fund Retail Class	NESGX	B	B	B	Up	10.88	30.39	16.75	68.39	69.07	16	37.4	800-625-7071	Y
Neuberger Berman Small Cap Growth Fund Advisor Class	NBMVX	B-	B-	B	Down	2.93	33.10	18.06	101.03	87.50	39.24	232.9	212-476-9000	
Neuberger Berman Small Cap Growth Fund Class A	NSNAX	B-	B-	B	Down	2.98	33.25	18.27	102.42	89.72	39.39	232.9	212-476-9000	Y
Neuberger Berman Small Cap Growth Fund Class C	NSNCX	B-	B-	B	Down	2.80	32.74	17.40	97.92	82.81	38.88	232.9	212-476-9000	Y
Neuberger Berman Small Cap Growth Fund Class R3	NSNRX	B-	B-	B	Down	2.88	33.05	17.98	100.87	87.38	39.21	232.9	212-476-9000	Y
Neuberger Berman Small Cap Growth Fund Class R6	NSRSX	B-	B-	B	Down	3.09	33.52	18.68	103.35	90.83	39.67	232.9	212-476-9000	Y
Neuberger Berman Small Cap Growth Fund Institutional Class	NBSMX	B-	B-	B	Down	3.06	33.46	18.69	104.58	93.24	39.64	232.9	212-476-9000	Y
Neuberger Berman Small Cap Growth Fund Investor Class	NBMIX	B-	B-	B	Down	2.97	33.26	18.32	102.73	90.26	39.42	232.9	212-476-9000	
Neuberger Berman Small Cap Growth Fund Trust Class	NBMOX	B-	B-	B	Down	2.95	33.22	18.23	101.91	88.82	39.34	232.9	212-476-9000	
Nicholas Limited Edition Fund Class Institutional	NCLEX	B-	C+	B		5.06	20.51	9.97	57.45	63.35	28.02	448.5	800-544-6547	Y
Nicholas Limited Edition Fund Class N	NNLEX	B-	C+	B		4.95	20.34	9.64	55.92	60.68	26.03	448.5	800-544-6547	Y
Quaker Small/Mid-Cap Impact Value Fund Advisor Class	QUSVX	B-	C	B		-0.22	15.58	3.17	41.06	31.66	17.65	20.0	800-220-8888	Y
Quaker Small/Mid-Cap Impact Value Fund Class Institutional	QSVIX	B-	C	B		-0.10	15.78	3.46	42.23	33.40	19.36	20.0	800-220-8888	Y
T. Rowe Price Institutional Small-Cap Stock Fund	TRSSX	B-	C+	B	Down	5.82	25.73	10.93	61.87	65.59	25.26	5,261	410-345-2000	
T. Rowe Price Small-Cap Stock Fund	OTCFX	B-	C+	B	Down	5.66	25.53	10.63	60.66	63.35	51.28	10,220	410-345-2000	
T. Rowe Price Small-Cap Stock Fund Advisor Class	PASSX	B-	C+	B	Down	5.60	25.35	10.34	59.37	61.17	50.72	10,220	410-345-2000	
T. Rowe Price Small-Cap Stock Fund I Class	OTIIX	B-	C+	B	Down	5.70	25.60	10.77	61.33	64.19	51.31	10,220	410-345-2000	Y
Victory Munder Small Cap Growth Fund Class A	MASCX	B-	C+	B-		8.15	28.87	10.06	80.35		13.39	9.3	800-539-3863	Y
Victory Munder Small Cap Growth Fund Class I	MIGSX	B-	C+	B-		8.21	29.02	10.44	81.76		13.56	9.3	800-539-3863	Y
Victory Munder Small Cap Growth Fund Class Y	MYSGX	B-	C+	B-		8.21	28.73	9.84	80.47		13.44	9.3	800-539-3863	Y
Virtus KAR Small-Cap Growth Fund Class A	PSGAX	B+	B+	B	Up	8.04	32.61	19.06	127.25	167.25	38.26	5,214	800-243-1574	Y
Virtus KAR Small-Cap Growth Fund Class C	PSGCX	B+	B+	B	Up	7.87	32.12	18.21	122.19	157.56	34.26	5,214	800-243-1574	Y
Virtus KAR Small-Cap Growth Fund Class I	PXSGX	B+	B+	B	Up	8.10	32.77	19.37	129.01	170.62	39.09	5,214	800-243-1574	Y
Virtus KAR Small-Cap Growth Fund Class R6	VRSGX	B+	B+	B	Up	8.14	32.84	19.52	129.36	171.03	39.15	5,214	800-243-1574	Y
Walden SMID Cap Fund	WASMX	B-	C	B		4.23	20.05	7.87	51.36	55.99	17.96	56.5	617-814-1215	Y
Wasatch Micro Cap Fund	WMICX	B-	B-	C+		7.16	28.88	9.57	93.38	90.49	7.63	471.5	800-551-1700	Y
Wasatch Small Cap Growth Fund® Institutional Class	WIAEX	B-	B-	B-	Down	8.83	32.50	17.75	81.93	78.59	42.48	1,805	800-551-1700	
Wasatch Small Cap Growth Fund® Investor Class	WAAEX	B-	B-	B-	Down	8.81	32.43	17.60	80.98	77.52	42.1	1,805	800-551-1700	
Wasatch Ultra Growth Fund	WAMCX	B-	C+	B-	Down	5.12	26.18	13.00	103.06	101.73	26.26	623.4	800-551-1700	Y
Wells Fargo Traditional Small Cap Growth Fund - Class A	EGWAX	B-	B-	C+	Down	9.86	35.97	17.04	82.31	71.40	14.59	102.0	800-222-8222	Y
Wells Fargo Traditional Small Cap Growth - Cls Admin	EGWDX	B-	B-	C+	Down	9.84	36.00	17.07	83.30	72.70	16.96	102.0	800-222-8222	Y
Wells Fargo Traditional Small Cap Growth Fund - Class C	EGWCX	B-	B-	C+	Down	9.60	35.50	16.14	78.37	65.13	12.67	102.0	800-222-8222	Y
Wells Fargo Traditional Small Cap Growth Fund - Class Inst	EGRYX	B-	B-	C+	Down	9.97	36.20	17.41	84.29	74.38	17.53	102.0	800-222-8222	Y

Category: US Fixed Income

Fund Name	Ticker Symbol	RATINGS: Overall Rating	Reward Rating	Risk Rating	Recent Up/ Downgrade	TOTAL RETURNS & PERFORMANCE: 3-Month Total Return	6-Month Total Return	1-Year Total Return	3-Year Total Return	5-Year Total Return	ASSETS: NAV	Total Assets (MIL)	NEW INVESTORS: Telephone	Open to New Investors
Cohen & Steers Low Duration Preferred & Income Cls A	LPXAX	B	C+	A-	Up	2.35	6.78	5.25	14.73		10	1,461	212-832-3232	Y
Cohen & Steers Low Duration Preferred & Income Cls C	LPXCX	B-	C	B+	Up	2.17	6.41	4.53	12.37		9.98	1,461	212-832-3232	Y
Cohen & Steers Low Duration Preferred & Income Cls I	LPXIX	B	C+	A-		2.35	6.97	5.51	15.73		9.99	1,461	212-832-3232	Y
Cohen & Steers Low Duration Preferred & Income Cls R	LPXRX	B	C+	A-	Up	2.29	6.75	4.99	13.93		10.01	1,461	212-832-3232	Y
Cohen & Steers Low Duration Preferred & Income Cls Z	LPXZX	B	C+	A-		2.45	6.98	5.51	15.73		9.99	1,461	212-832-3232	Y
Cohen & Steers Preferred Sec & Income Fund, Inc. Cls A	CPXAX	B	B-	B	Up	3.87	11.05	8.11	18.26	30.95	13.77	7,347	212-832-3232	Y
Cohen & Steers Preferred Sec & Income Fund, Inc. Cls C	CPXCX	B-	C+	B	Up	3.72	10.76	7.38	15.94	26.77	13.69	7,347	212-832-3232	Y
Cohen & Steers Preferred Sec & Income Fund, Inc. Cls F	CPXFX	B	B-	B	Up	3.87	11.22	8.40	19.39	33.14	13.79	7,347	212-832-3232	Y
Cohen & Steers Preferred Sec & Income Fund, Inc. Cls I	CPXIX	B	B-	B	Up	3.94	11.27	8.42	19.36	33.11	13.8	7,347	212-832-3232	Y
Cohen & Steers Preferred Sec & Income Fund, Inc. Cls R	CPRRX	B	B-	B	Up	3.75	10.96	7.87	17.63	29.92	13.78	7,347	212-832-3232	Y
Cohen & Steers Preferred Sec & Income Fund, Inc. Cls Z	CPXZX	B	B-	B	Up	3.95	11.30	8.48	19.50	33.27	13.8	7,347	212-832-3232	Y
Destra Flaherty & Crumrine Preferred & Income Cls A	DPIAX	B	B-	B	Up	3.47	11.71	6.88	17.97	32.74	18	231.7	877-855-3434	Y
Destra Flaherty & Crumrine Preferred & Income Cls C	DPICX	B-	B-	B	Up	3.26	11.24	6.06	15.36	27.97	18.08	231.7	877-855-3434	Y
Destra Flaherty & Crumrine Preferred & Income Cls I	DPIIX	B	B-	B	Up	3.54	11.89	7.18	18.93	34.95	17.94	231.7	877-855-3434	Y
First Trust Intermediate Duration Preferred & Income Fund	FPF	B-	B-	C+	Up	4.39	12.82	9.14	28.82	41.43	23.58	1,433	800-621-1675	Y
First Trust Preferred Securities and Income Fund Class A	FPEAX	B	B-	B+	Up	3.36	10.07	7.50	19.88	31.66	21.51	257.4	800-621-1675	Y
First Trust Preferred Securities and Income Fund Class C	FPECX	B	C+	B+	Up	3.21	9.73	6.82	17.48	27.16	21.61	257.4	800-621-1675	Y
First Trust Preferred Securities and Income Fund Class F	FPEFX	B	B-	B+	Up	3.40	10.17	7.62	20.40	32.46	21.75	257.4	800-621-1675	Y
First Trust Preferred Securities and Income Fund Class I	FPEIX	B	B-	B+	Up	3.45	10.24	7.81	21.11	33.63	21.66	257.4	800-621-1675	Y
First Trust Preferred Securities and Income Fund Class R3	FPERX	B	B-	B+	Up	3.31	9.96	7.20	18.96	29.89	21.47	257.4	800-621-1675	Y
Flaherty & Crumrine Preferred Securities Income Fund	FFC	B-	B	C-	Up	5.06	15.94	9.47	29.41	47.35	19.6	868.2	626-795-7300	Y
Nuveen Preferred & Income Opportunities Fund	JPC	B-	B-	C+	Up	3.72	14.05	7.07	22.48	35.45	10.01	1,034	312-917-8146	Y
Nuveen Preferred & Income Securities Fund	JPS	B-	B-	C+	Up	4.66	13.65	8.91	29.78	41.00	9.74	1,985	312-917-8146	Y
Nuveen Preferred Securities & Income Fund Class A	NPSAX	B	B-	B+	Up	3.48	10.56	7.16	18.58	27.43	16.94	3,523	312-917-8146	Y
Nuveen Preferred Securities & Income Fund Class C	NPSCX	B-	C+	B	Up	3.29	10.10	6.31	15.98	22.68	16.95	3,523	312-917-8146	Y
Nuveen Preferred Securities & Income Fund Class I	NPSRX	B	B-	B+	Up	3.60	10.71	7.49	19.59	29.06	16.96	3,523	312-917-8146	Y
Nuveen Preferred Securities & Income Fund Class R3	NPSTX	B	C+	B	Up	3.46	10.38	6.94	17.70	25.82	17.06	3,523	312-917-8146	Y
Nuveen Preferred Securities & Income Fund Class R6	NPSFX	B	B-	B+	Up	3.56	10.66	7.47	19.79	29.28	16.99	3,523	312-917-8146	Y
Orinda Income Opportunities Fund Class A	OIOAX	B-	B-	B-		0.64	14.55	5.15	14.95	15.98	21.43	276.0	855-467-4632	Y
Orinda Income Opportunities Fund Class I	OIOIX	B-	B-	B		0.72	14.74	5.50	16.02	17.81	21.48	276.0	855-467-4632	Y
PIMCO Preferred and Capital Securities Fund Class A	PFANX	B	B-	A-	Up	4.40	11.42	8.29	29.44		10.24	771.6	866-746-2602	Y
PIMCO Preferred and Capital Securities Fund Class I-2	PFPNX	B	B-	A-	Up	4.44	11.62	8.57	30.44		10.26	771.6	866-746-2602	Y
PIMCO Preferred and Capital Securities Fund Class I-3	PFNNX	B	B-	B	Up	4.54	11.61	8.56	30.17		10.25	771.6	866-746-2602	Y
PIMCO Preferred & Capital Securities Institutional Cls	PFINX	B	B-	B	Up	4.55	11.75	8.76	30.84		10.28	771.6	866-746-2602	Y
Principal Capital Securities Fund Class S	PCSFX	B	B-	B+	Up	3.94	10.43	7.79	22.34	30.34	10.04	612.4	800-787-1621	Y
Principal Global Investors Funds Preferred Securities R-6	PPREX	B	B-	B+	Up	3.55	10.45	7.22	17.93	29.22	10.09	5,513	800-787-1621	Y
Principal Preferred Securities Fund Class A	PPSAX	B	B-	B+	Up	3.43	10.30	6.89	16.84	27.31	10.17	5,513	800-787-1621	Y
Principal Preferred Securities Fund Class C	PRFCX	B-	C+	B	Up	3.34	9.89	6.09	14.30	22.59	10.16	5,513	800-787-1621	Y
Principal Preferred Securities Fund Class J	PPSJX	B	B-	B+	Up	3.43	10.26	6.87	16.90	27.27	9.88	5,513	800-787-1621	Y
Principal Preferred Securities Fund Institutional Class	PPSIX	B	B-	B+	Up	3.52	10.40	7.10	17.72	29.00	10.09	5,513	800-787-1621	Y
Principal Preferred Securities Fund R-1 Class	PUSAX	B-	C+	B	Up	3.34	10.04	6.33	14.97	23.97	10.04	5,513	800-787-1621	Y
Principal Preferred Securities Fund R-2 Class	PPRSX	B	C+	B	Up	3.40	10.06	6.50	15.45	24.78	9.98	5,513	800-787-1621	Y
Principal Preferred Securities Fund R-3 Class	PNARX	B	C+	B	Up	3.43	10.23	6.67	16.11	25.88	10.02	5,513	800-787-1621	Y
Principal Preferred Securities Fund R-4 Class	PQARX	B	B-	B	Up	3.49	10.36	6.89	16.71	27.03	10	5,513	800-787-1621	Y
Principal Preferred Securities Fund R-5 Class	PPARX	B	B-	B+	Up	3.50	10.36	6.97	17.18	27.92	10.05	5,513	800-787-1621	Y

Category: Utilities Sector Equity

Fund Name	Ticker Symbol	RATINGS: Overall Rating	Reward Rating	Risk Rating	Recent Up/ Downgrade	TOTAL RETURNS & PERFORMANCE: 3-Month Total Return	6-Month Total Return	1-Year Total Return	3-Year Total Return	5-Year Total Return	ASSETS: NAV	Total Assets (MIL)	NEW INVESTORS: Telephone	Open to New Investors
DNP Select Income Fund	DNP	B	B	C+		4.17	22.44	20.61	30.50	51.20	10.2277	2,921	212-871-2549	Y
Fidelity Advisor® Utilities Fund Class A	FUGAX	B	B	A-	Up	2.83	12.92	12.93	36.79	47.41	31.9	638.2	617-563-7000	Y
Fidelity Advisor® Utilities Fund Class C	FUGCX	B	B	A-	Up	2.60	12.48	12.05	33.69	41.92	31.08	638.2	617-563-7000	Y
Fidelity Advisor® Utilities Fund Class M	FAUFX	B	B	A-	Up	2.76	12.77	12.58	35.58	45.26	31.95	638.2	617-563-7000	Y
Fidelity Advisor® Utilities Fund Class Z	FIKIX	B+	B	A-	Up	2.90	13.14	13.33	38.02	49.62	32.63	638.2	617-563-7000	Y
Fidelity Advisor® Utilities Fund I Class	FUGIX	B+	B	A-	Up	2.90	13.06	13.22	37.88	49.47	32.63	638.2	617-563-7000	Y
Fidelity® Select Utilities Portfolio	FSUTX	B+	B	A-	Up	2.96	13.44	13.63	38.74	50.46	90.62	1,209	617-563-7000	Y
Fidelity® Telecom and Utilities Fund	FIUIX	B	B-	A-	Up	3.23	12.99	12.27	28.45	43.28	27.44	1,054	617-563-7000	Y
Franklin Utilities Fund Advisor Class	FRUAX	B	B	B-		4.01	17.48	20.03	29.84	55.82	21.14	6,287	650-312-2000	Y
Franklin Utilities Fund Class A USD	FKUQX	B	B	B-		3.93	17.25	19.67	28.81	53.82	20.96	6,287	650-312-2000	Y
Franklin Utilities Fund Class A1	FKUTX	B	B	B-		4.00	17.37	19.85	29.26	54.67	20.97	6,287	650-312-2000	Y
Franklin Utilities Fund Class C	FRUSX	B	B	B-		3.85	17.07	19.26	27.31	50.77	20.85	6,287	650-312-2000	Y
Franklin Utilities Fund Class R	FRURX	B	B	B-		3.88	17.12	19.40	27.91	51.98	20.88	6,287	650-312-2000	Y
Franklin Utilities Fund Class R6	FUFRX	B	B	B-		4.03	17.48	20.08	30.23	56.55	21.13	6,287	650-312-2000	Y
Gabelli Utilities Fund Class A	GAUAX	B-	C+	B	Down	2.83	14.43	12.19	22.19	30.47	9.06	2,176	914-921-5135	Y
Gabelli Utilities Fund Class AAA	GABUX	B-	C+	B	Down	2.77	14.30	12.03	22.05	30.31	8.89	2,176	914-921-5135	Y
Gabelli Utilities Fund Class Institutional	GAUIX	B-	C+	B	Down	2.83	14.52	12.35	22.99	31.92	9.4	2,176	914-921-5135	Y
ICON Utilities Fund Class A	ICTVX	B-	B-	B	Down	2.13	14.12	15.44	24.95	55.69	9.54	45.3	303-790-1600	Y
ICON Utilities Fund Class S	ICTUX	B	B-	B		2.26	14.35	15.81	25.87	57.84	9.72	45.3	303-790-1600	Y
JNL/Mellon Utilities Sector Fund Class A		B	B	B		3.20	14.42	17.42	28.04	58.03	15.15	241.9		Y
JNL/Mellon Utilities Sector Fund Class I		B	B	B		3.25	14.69	17.88	28.84	59.01	15.22	241.9		Y
MFS Utilities Fund Class A	MMUFX	B	B	A-		3.18	16.82	14.12	31.31	22.90	22.36	3,322	877-960-6077	Y
MFS Utilities Fund Class B	MMUBX	B	B	B+		2.95	16.35	13.22	28.37	18.31	22.24	3,322	877-960-6077	Y
MFS Utilities Fund Class C	MMUCX	B	B	B+		2.95	16.35	13.22	28.38	18.33	22.24	3,322	877-960-6077	Y
MFS Utilities Fund Class I	MMUIX	B	B	A-		3.23	16.97	14.39	32.31	24.42	22.45	3,322	877-960-6077	Y
MFS Utilities Fund Class R1	MMUGX	B	B	B+		2.96	16.40	13.22	28.36	18.30	22.19	3,322	877-960-6077	Y
MFS Utilities Fund Class R2	MURRX	B	B	B+		3.07	16.65	13.76	30.33	21.29	22.29	3,322	877-960-6077	Y
MFS Utilities Fund Class R3	MMUHX	B	B	A-		3.18	16.82	14.12	31.32	22.90	22.35	3,322	877-960-6077	Y
MFS Utilities Fund Class R4	MMUJX	B	B	A-		3.24	16.97	14.39	32.36	24.38	22.38	3,322	877-960-6077	Y
MFS Utilities Fund Class R6	MMUKX	B+	B	A-		3.20	16.97	14.43	32.67	24.95	22.45	3,322	877-960-6077	Y
PGIM Jennison Utility Fund- Class A	PRUAX	B	B	B		3.09	16.65	16.85	29.80	34.95	14.99	3,277	800-225-1852	Y
PGIM Jennison Utility Fund- Class B	PRUTX	B	B	B		2.87	16.05	15.80	26.61	29.90	14.95	3,277	800-225-1852	
PGIM Jennison Utility Fund- Class C	PCUFX	B	B	B		2.85	16.18	15.98	26.97	30.19	14.92	3,277	800-225-1852	Y
PGIM Jennison Utility Fund- Class R	JDURX	B	B	B		3.03	16.44	16.54	28.87	33.45	14.98	3,277	800-225-1852	Y
PGIM Jennison Utility Fund- Class R6	PRUQX	B	B	B		3.10	16.80	17.20	28.83	32.18	15	3,277	800-225-1852	Y
PGIM Jennison Utility Fund- Class Z	PRUZX	B	B	B		3.16	16.78	17.16	30.89	36.97	15	3,277	800-225-1852	Y
Reaves Utility Income Trust	UTG	B-	B-	C+	Down	3.90	22.60	17.80	30.29	56.75	35.11	1,709	800-644-5571	Y
Rydex Utilities Fund Class A	RYUTX	B	B	B	Up	2.37	13.10	15.19	25.02	47.87	43.51	118.4	800-820-0888	Y
Rydex Utilities Fund Class C	RYCUX	B	B	B	Up	2.16	12.65	14.32	22.26	42.49	36.4	118.4	800-820-0888	Y
Rydex Utilities Fund Class H	RYAUX	B	B	B	Up	2.34	13.06	15.14	24.97	47.50	41.88	118.4	800-820-0888	Y
Rydex Utilities Fund Class Investor	RYUIX	B	B	B	Up	2.40	13.22	15.49	25.94	49.75	47.34	118.4	800-820-0888	Y
Vanguard Utilities Index Fund Admiral Shares	VUIAX	B	B	B		3.32	14.80	18.24	30.52	63.21	66.7	4,967	877-662-7447	Y
Wells Fargo Utility and Telecommunications Fund - Class A	EVUAX	B	B	B		5.44	19.28	22.80	33.04	47.59	25.26	425.3	800-222-8222	Y
Wells Fargo Utility & Telecommunications - Cls Admin	EVUDX	B	B	B		5.52	19.41	23.06	33.85	49.06	25.29	425.3	800-222-8222	Y
Wells Fargo Utility and Telecommunications Fund - Class C	EVUCX	B	B	B		5.28	18.81	21.91	30.10	42.14	25.31	425.3	800-222-8222	Y
Wells Fargo Utility & Telecommunications - Cls Inst	EVUYX	B	B	B		5.53	19.48	23.25	34.51	50.32	25.25	425.3	800-222-8222	Y

Appendix:

Glossary

This section contains an explanation of the fields of data used throughout this guide.

1-Year Total Return
The rate of return on an investment over one year that includes interest, capital gains, dividends and distributions realized.

3-Year Total Return
The rate of return on an investment over three years that includes interest, capital gains, dividends and distributions realized.

3-Month Total Return
The rate of return on an investment over three months that includes interest, capital gains, dividends and distributions realized.

3-Year Beta
A three year measure of volatility, or systematic risk, of a security in comparison to the market as a whole. A beta of less than 1 means that the security will be less volatile than the market, a beta larger than 1 means more volatility. Beta value cannot be calculated if less than 24 months of pricing is available.

3-Year Standard Deviation
A statistical measurement of dispersion about an average, which depicts how widely the returns varied over the past three years. Investors use the standard deviation of historical performance to try to predict the range of returns that are most likely for a given fund. When a fund has a high standard deviation, the predicted range of performance is wide, implying greater volatility. Standard deviation is most appropriate for measuring risk if it is for a fund that is an investor's only holding. The figure cannot be combined for more than one fund because the standard deviation for a portfolio of multiple funds is a function of not only the individual standard deviations, but also of the degree of correlation among the funds' returns. If a fund's returns follow a normal distribution, then approximately 68 percent of the time they will fall within one standard deviation of the mean return for the fund, and 95 percent of the time within two standard deviations.

5-Year Total Return
The rate of return on an investment over five years that includes interest, capital gains, dividends and distributions realized.

6-Month Total Return
The rate of return on an investment over six months that includes interest, capital gains, dividends and distributions realized.

Address
The company's street address.

Asset & Performance History
Indicates the fund's **NAV (Net Asset Value)** and **1-Year Total Return** for the previous 6 years.

Asset Allocation
Indicates the percentage of assets in each category. Used as an investment strategy that attempts to balance risk versus reward by adjusting the percentage of each asset in an investment portfolio according to the investor's risk tolerance, goals and investment time frame. Allocation percentages may not add up to 100%. Negative values reflect short positions. See Cash, Stocks, US Stocks, Bonds, US Bonds, Other)

Back End Fee (%)
A fee that investors pay when withdrawing money from an investment within a specified number of years, usually five to 10 years. The back-end load is designed to discourage withdrawals and typically declines for each year that a shareholder remains in a fund. The fee is a percentage of the value of the share being sold. Fees are displayed as a percent.

Bear Market
A financial market condition in which the prices of securities are falling, investors anticipate losses, and selling of securities increases.

Bonds (%)
The percentage of the fund's assets invested in bonds. A bond is an unsecured debt security issued by companies, municipalities, states and sovereign governments to raise funds. When a company issues a bond it borrows money from the bondholder to boost the business, in exchange the bondholder receives the principal amount back plus the interest on the determined maturity date.

Bull Market
A financial market condition in which prices are rising or are expected to rise. Bull markets are characterized by optimism, investor confidence and expectations that strong results will continue.

BUY-HOLD-SELL Indicator
Funds that are rated in the A or B range are, in our opinion, a potential BUY. Funds in the C range will indicate a HOLD status. Funds in the D or E range will indicate a SELL status.

Cash (%)
The percentage of the fund's assets invested in short-term obligations, usually less than 90 days, that provide a return in the form of interest payments. This type of investment generally offers a low return compared to other investments but has a low risk level.

Category
Identifies funds according to their actual investment styles as measured by their portfolio holdings. This categorization allows investors to spread their money around in a mix of funds with a variety of risk and return characteristics.

Class A
This class of Mutual Fund typically has a front-end sales load and a loaded fee structure. Although the fees for Class A may typically be lower, because they normally charge front end fees, your initial amount invested will be lower and your overall return will be affected. An annual asset based fee may well be levied, although this is typically lower than other classes.

Class B
This class of shares, instead of a front-end or back-end sales load normally charges fees called a contingent deferred sales charge (CDSC). This fee is paid if you sell the shares within a certain period of time and may well decline after each year. An annual asset based fee is likely to be levied. Often a Class B share will convert to Class A within a couple of years of reaching the end of the CDSC expiry at which point Class A fees will be initiated.

Class C
A C-share is a class of mutual fund with a level load. They typically don't have front-end loads, but do sometimes have back-end loads. They are usually around 1% but are sometimes eliminated after the shares are held for over a year. Annual asset based fees are normal for this class of share.

Class I
This class is sold to institutional shareholders. Also called Y-Shares, these have different fees and do not charge traditional loads.

Class R
R share funds, Also known as K shares, are for retirement accounts, and the R share class mutual funds are only available through employer-sponsored retirement plans. R share mutual funds do not have any loads, but they do have annual asset based fees typically of around 0.25% to 0.50%.

Closed End Fund
They are launched through an Initial Public Offering in order to raise money and then trade in the open market just like a stock or an ETF. They only issue a set amount of shares and, although their value is also based on the Net Asset Value (NAV), the actual price of the fund is affected by supply and demand, allowing it to trade at prices above or below its real value.

Dividend Yield (TTM)
Trailing twelve months dividends paid out relative to the share price. Expressed as a percentage and measures how much cash flow an investor is getting for each invested dollar. **Trailing Twelve Months** (TTM) is a representation of a fund's financial performance over the most recent 12 months. TTM uses the latest available financial data from a company's interim, quarterly or annual reports.

Expense Ratio

A measure of what it costs an investment company to operate a mutual fund. An expense ratio is determined through an annual calculation, where a fund's operating expenses are divided by the average dollar value of its assets under management. Operating expenses may include money spent on administration and management of the fund, advertising, etc. An expense ratio of 1 percent per annum means that each year 1 percent of the fund's total assets will be used to cover expenses.

Front End Fee (%)

A commission or sales charge applied at the time of the initial purchase of an investment. The fee percentage is generally based on the amount of the investment. Larger investments, both initial and cumulative, generally receive percentage discounts based on the dollar value invested. Fees are displayed as a percent.

Fund Name

Describes the fund's assets, regions of investments and investment strategies. Many funds have similar names, so you want to make sure the fund you look up is really the one you are interested in evaluating.

Fund Type

Describes the fund's assets, regions of investments and investment strategies. (See **Open End Fund, Closed End Fund**.)

Inception Date

The date on which the fund began its operations. The commencement date indicates when a fund began investing in the market. Many investors prefer funds with longer operating histories. Funds with longer histories have longer track records and can thereby provide investors with a more long-standing picture of their performance.

Institutional Only

This indicates if the fund is offered to institutional clients only (pension funds, mutual funds, money managers, insurance companies, investment banks, commercial trusts, endowment funds, hedge funds, and some hedge fund investors). See **Services Offered**.

Investment Strategy

A set of rules, behaviors or procedures, designed to guide an investor's selection of an investment portfolio. Individuals have different profit objectives, and their individual skills make different tactics and strategies appropriate.

Last Bear Market Total Return

The fund's total return (the rate of return on an investment over a period of time that includes interest, capital gains, dividends and distributions realized) during the last market downturn. A **Bear Market** is a financial market condition in which the prices of securities are falling, investors anticipate losses, and selling of securities increases.

Last Bull Market Total Return
The fund's total return (the rate of return on an investment over a period of time that includes interest, capital gains, dividends and distributions realized) during the last market upswing. A **Bull Market** is a financial market condition in which prices are rising or are expected to rise. Bull markets are characterized by optimism, investor confidence and expectations that strong results will continue.

Manager/Tenure (Years)
The name of the manager and the number of years spent managing the fund.

Minimum Initial Investment
The smallest investment amount a fund will accept to establish a new account. This amount could be $0 or any other number set by the fund.

Minimum Subsequent Investment
The smallest additional investment amount a fund will accept in an existing account.

NAV (Net Asset Value)
A fund's price per share. The value is calculated by dividing the total value of all the securities in the portfolio, less any liabilities, by the number of fund shares outstanding.

Open End Fund
A type of mutual fund that does not have restrictions on the amount of shares the fund will issue. If demand is high enough, the fund will continue to issue shares no matter how many investors there are. Open-end funds also buy back shares when investors wish to sell.

Open to New Investments
Indicates whether the fund accepts investments from those who are not existing investors. A "Y" in this column identifies that the fund accepts new investors. No data in this column indicates that the fund is closed to new investors. The fund may be closed to new investors because the fund's asset base is getting too large to effectively execute its investing style. Although, the fund may be closed, in most cases, existing investors are able to add to their holdings.

Other (%)
The percentage of the fund's assets invested in other financial instruments. See **Asset Allocation**.

Overall Rating
The Weiss rating measured on a scale from A to E based on each fund's risk and performance. See the preceding section, "What Our Ratings Mean," for an explanation of each letter grade rating.

Performance Chart
A graphical representation of the fund's total returns over the past year.

Phone Exchange
This indicates that investors can move money between different funds within the same fund family over the phone. See **Services Offered**.

Phone Number
The company's phone number.

Prospectus Objective
Gives a general idea of a fund's overall investment approach and goals.

Provider
The legal company that issues the fund.

Ratings History
Indicates the fund's Overall, Risk and Reward Ratings for the previous five years. Ratings are listed as of June 30, 2019 (Q2-19), December 31, 2018 (Q4-18), December 31, 2017 (Q4-17), December 31, 2016 (Q4-16), and December 31, 2015 (Q4-15). See **Overall Rating, Risk Rating, Reward Rating.**

Recent Upgrade/Downgrade
An "Up" or "Down" indicates that the Weiss Mutual Fund rating has changed since the publication of the last print edition. If a fund has had a rating change since March 31, 2019, the change is identified with an "Up" or "Down."

Reward Rating
This is based on the total return over a period of up to five years, including net asset value and price growth. The total return figure is stated net of the expenses and fees charged by the fund. Based on proprietary modeling the individual components of the risk and reward ratings are calculated and weighted and the final rating is generated.

Risk Rating
This is includes the risk ratings of component stocks where applicable and also includes the financial stability of the fund, turnover where applicable, together with the level of volatility as measured by the fund's daily returns over a period of up to five years. Funds with greater stability are considered less risky and receive a higher risk rating. Funds with greater volatility are considered riskier, and will receive a lower risk rating. In addition to considering the fund's volatility, the risk rating also considers an assessment of the valuation and quality of a fund's holdings.

Services Offered
Services offered by the fund provider. Such services can include:

Systematic Withdrawal Plan
A plan offered by mutual funds that pays specific amounts to shareholders at predetermined intervals.

Institutional Only
This indicates if the fund is offered to institutional clients only (pension funds, mutual funds, money managers, insurance companies, investment banks, commercial trusts, endowment funds, hedge funds, and some hedge fund investors).

Phone Exchange
This indicates that investors can move money between different funds within the same fund family over the phone.

Wire Redemption
This indicates whether or not investors can redeem electronically.

Qualified Investment
Under a qualified plan, an investor may invest in the variable annuity with pretax dollars through an employee pension plan, such as a 401(k) or 403(b). Money builds up on a tax-deferred basis, and when the qualified investor makes a withdrawal or annuitizes, all contributions received are taxable income.

Stocks (%)
The percentage of the fund's assets invested in stock. See **Asset Allocation**.

Sub-Category
A subdivision of funds, usually with common characteristics as the category.

Systematic Withdrawal Plan
A plan offered by mutual funds that pays specific amounts to shareholders at predetermined intervals. See **Services Offered**.

Ticker Symbol
An arrangement of characters (usually letters) representing a particular security listed on an exchange or otherwise traded publicly. When a company issues securities to the public marketplace, it selects an available ticker symbol for its securities which investors use to place trade orders. Every listed security has a unique ticker symbol, facilitating the vast array of trade orders that flow through the financial markets every day. If a ticker symbol is not assigned to a particular fund, the International Securities Identification Number (ISIN) is displayed.

Top Holdings
The highest amount of publicly traded assets held by a fund. These publicly traded assets may include company stock, mutual funds or other investment vehicles.

Total Returns (%)
See **3-Month Total Return, 6-Month Total Return, 1-Year Total Return, 3-Year Total Return, 5-Year Total Return.**

Traded On (Exchange)
The stock exchange on which the fund is listed. The core function of a stock exchange is to ensure fair and orderly trading, as well as efficient dissemination of price information. Exchanges such as: NYSE (New York Stock Exchange), AMEX (American Stock Exchange), NNM (NASDAQ National Market), and NASQ (NASDAQ Small Cap) give companies, governments and other groups a platform to sell securities to the investing public. NASDAQ CM is abbreviated as NAS in this table.

Turnover Ratio
The percentage of a mutual fund or other investment vehicle's holdings that have been replaced with other holdings in a given year. Generally, low turnover ratio is favorable, because high turnover equates to higher brokerage transaction fees, which reduce fund returns.

US Stocks (%)
The percentage of the fund's assets invested in US stock. See **Asset Allocation.**

US Bonds (%)
The percentage of the fund's assets invested in US bonds. See **Asset Allocation.**

Website
The company's web address.

Wire Redemption
This indicates whether or not investors can redeem electronically. See **Services Offered.**

This section lists all of the Providers in Section I: Index of Stock Mutual Funds. Address, Telephone and Website are provided where available.

1290 Funds
1290 Funds 1290 Avenue of the Americas New York NY 10104 United States
212-554-1234
http://www.1290Funds.com

13D Activist Fund
13D Activist Fund 17605 Wright Street, Suite 2 Omaha NE 68130 United States
877-413-3228
http://www.13DActivistFund.com

1919 Funds
1919 Funds P.O. Box 701 Milwaukee WI 53201-0701 United States
http://www.1919Funds.com

360 Funds
360 Funds 6000 Poplar Avenue Suite 250 Memphis TN 38119 United States
http://www.stringeram.com

361 Funds
361 Funds 4600 South Syracuse Street, Suite 500 Denver CO 80237 United States
866-361-1720
http://www.361capital.com

7Twelve
7Twelve 1720 West End Ave., Suite 540 Nashville TN 37203 United States
http://www.7twelveadvisors.com

AAM
AAM 18925 Base Camp Road Monument CO 80132 United States
800-617-0004
http://www.aamlive.com/publicsite/mutual-funds

AAMA
AAMA P.O. Box 46707 Cincinnati OH 45246-0707 United States
http://www.aamafunds.com

Aasgard
Aasgard P.O. Box 701 United States
http://www.coldstream.com/mutual-fund-home

Abbey Capital
Abbey Capital PO Box 9841 Providence RI 02940-8041 United States
http://www.abbeycapital.com/

Aberdeen
Aberdeen Asset Management 1735 Market Street 32nd Floor Philadelphia PA 19103 United States
866-667-9231
http://www.aberdeen-asset.us

Aberdeen Asset Managers Limited
Via Dante, 16 Milano Italy
http://www.aberdeen-asset.it

ABR
ABR 48 Wall Street Suite 1100 New York NY 10005 United States
http://www.abrdynamicfunds.com/

Absolute Capital
Absolute Capital 101 Pennsylvania Boulevard Pittsburgh PA 15228 United States
http://www.abscap.com

Absolute Strategies
Absolute Strategies 350 Lincoln Street, Suite 216 Portland ME 4101 United States
888-992-2765
http://www.absoluteadvisers.com

AC ONE
AC ONE United States
http://www.AC-ONE-AMC.com

Acadian Funds
Acadian Funds 1 Post Office Square Boston MA 2109 United States
http://www.acadian-asset.com

ACM
ACM United States
http://www.ACM-Funds.com

ACR Alpine Capital Research
8000 Maryland Avenue, Suite 700 Suite 700 Saint Louis MO 63105 United States
314-932-7600
http://www.acr-invest.com

Acuitas Investments
Acuitas Investments 520 Pike Street Seattle WA 98101 United States
http://www.acuitasinvestments.com

Adalta
Adalta United States

Adam Asset Funds
Adam Asset Funds 11111 N. Scottsdale Rd. Ste. 205 Scottsdale AZ 85254 United States
http://www.funddocuments.com

Adams Diversified Equity Fund Inc
500 East Pratt Street Suite 1300 Baltimore MD 21202 United States
410-752-5900
http://www.AdamsFunds.com

Adams Natural Resources Fund Inc
500 East Pratt Street Suite 1300 Baltimore MD 21202 United States
410-752-5900
http://www.AdamsFunds.com

Adirondack Funds
Adirondack Funds 2390 Western Avenue Guilderland NY 12084 United States
518-690-0470
http://www.adirondackfunds.com

Adler
Adler P.O. Box 46707 Cincinnati OH 45246-0707 United States
http://www.adlervaluefund.com

Advantus
Advantus Capital Management, Inc. 400 Robert Street North St. Paul MN 551001-2098 United States
800-665-6005
http://www.advantusfunds.com

AdvisorOne Funds
Advisorone Funds 4020 South 147th Street Omaha NE 68137 United States
http://www.advisoronefunds.com

Advisors Preferred
Advisors Preferred United States
http://www.advisorspreferred.com

Advisory Research
180 N Stetson Ave Ste 5500 Chicago IL 606016737 United States
312-565-1414
http://www.advisoryresearch.com

Aegis
Aegis Value 11100 N. Gleve Road, Suite 1040 Arlington VA 22201 United States
800-528-3780
http://www.aegisfunds.com

AGF Investments
66 Wellington Street West 31st Floor Toronto ON M5K 1E9 Canada
800-268-8583
http://www.agf.com

AIG
AIG Harborside Financial Center, 3200 Plaza 5 Jersey City NJ 07311 United States
800-858-8850
http://https://www.aig.com/getprospectus

Akre
Akre 2 W. Washington Street Middleburg VA 20118 United States
877-862-9556
http://www.akrefund.com

Al Frank
Al Frank Fund c/o US Bancorp Fund Services, LLC, PO BOX 701 Milwaukee WI 53201 United States
888-263-6443
http://www.alfrank.com

Alambic
Alambic 655 Montgomery Street, Suite 1905 San Francisco CA 94111 United States
http://www.alambicfunds.com

Alger
Alger 360 Park Avenue South New York NY 10010 United States
800-992-3863
http://www.alger.com

All Terrain Funds
All Terrain Funds 235 W. Galena Street, Milwaukee, Wisconsin Milwaukee Wisconsin 53201 United States
http://www.allterrainfunds.com

AllianceBernstein
AllianceBernstein 11345 Avenue of the Americas New York NY 10105 United States
212-969-1000
http://www.abglobal.com

Allianz Funds
Allianz Funds 1633 BROADWAY New York NY 10109 United States
800-498-5413
http://us.allianzgi.com

Allianz Global Investors
1633 Broadway New York New York 10019 United States
877-716-9787
http://www.US.allianzGI.com

Allianz Group
1 New York United States

Allied Asset
Allied Asset 7745 McClintock Drive, Suite 314 Burr Ridge IL 60527 United States
http://www.investaaa.com

AlphaCentric Funds
17605 Wright Street Suite 2 United States
http://www.AlphaCentricFunds.com.

AlphaCore
AlphaCore AlphaCore Capital 875 Prospect St. Suite 315 La Jolla CA 92037 United States
http://https://alphacorefunds.com/

AlphaMark
AlphaMark Funds PO Box 46707 Cincinatti OH 45246-0707 United States
866-420-3350
http://www.alphamarkfunds.com

AlphaOne Funds
AlphaOne Funds P.O. Box 219009 Kansas City MI 64121-9009 United States
http://www.alphaonecapital.com

ALPS
ALPS 1290 Broadway, Suite 1100 Denver CO 80203 United States
866-759-5679
http://www.alpsfunds.com

ALPS Advisors Inc
Alps Advisors, Inc. 1290 Broadway, Suite 1100 Denver CO 80203 United States
866-432-2926
http://www.alpsfunds.com

Alta Capital Management LLC
6440 South Wasatch Blvd Suite 260 Salt Lake City UT 84121 United States
801-274-6010
http://www.altacapital.com

Altair
Altair Bellevue Park Corporate Center, 103 Bellevue Parkway Wilmington DE 19809 United States

Altegris
Altegris 1200 Prospect Street, Suite 400 La Jolla CA 92037 United States
858-459-7040
http://www.altegrismutualfunds.com

Altegris Funds
1200 Prospect St. Suite 400 La Jolla CA 92109 United States
888-524-9441
http://altegris.com

Amana
Amana Bellingham WA 98227-0596 United States
888-732-6262
http://www.amanafunds.com

AmericaFirst Funds
630 Fitzwatertown Road Building A, 2nd Floor Willow Grove PA 19090 United States
877-217-8363
http://www.afcm-quant.com

American Beacon
American Beacon 220 East Las Colinas Blvd., Suite 1200 Irving TX 75039 United States
800-658-5811
http://www.americanbeaconfunds.com

American Century Investments
American Century Investments P.O. Box 419200,4500 Main Street Kansas City, MO 64141 United States
800-444-4015
http://www.americancentury.com

American Funds
American Funds 333 South Hope Street Los Angeles CA 90071-1406 United States
800-421-4225
http://www.americanfunds.com

American Growth
American Growth Fund PO Box 8113 Boston MA 02266-8113 United States
800-525-2406
http://www.americangrowthfund.com

American Independence
American Independence 225 West 34th Street 9th Floor New York NY 10122 United States
http://www.americanindependence.com

American Money Management
American Money Management 14249 Ranco Santa Fe Farms Road Ranco Santa Fe CA 92067 United States
http://www.amminvest.com.

American Trust
American Trust 1 Court Street, Suite 350 Lebanon NH 3766 United States
800-385-7003
http://www.amertrust.com

AMF
AMF 2230 W. Monroe Street Chicago IL 60606 United States
800-247-9780
http://www.amffunds.com

AMG Funds
AMG Funds 600 Steamboat Road, Suite 300 Norwalk CT 06830 United States
800-835-3879
http://www.amgfunds.com

AMIDEX
AMIDEX 630-A Fitzwatertown Road, 2nd Floor Willow Grove PA 19090 United States
888-876-3566
http://www.amidex.com

Anchor
Anchor 17605 Wright Street, Suite 2 Omaha NE 68130 United States
http://www.anchorcapitalfunds.com

Ancora
Ancora 2000 Auburn Drive, Suite 430 Cleveland OH 44122 United States
http://www.ancorafunds.com

Appleseed Fund
Appleseed Fund 2960 N. Meridian St., Suite 300 Indianapolis IN 46208 United States
http://www.appleseedfund.com

AQR Funds
AQR Funds Two Greewich Plaza,3rd Floor Greenwich CT 06830 United States
203-742-3600
http://www.aqrfunds.com

Aquila
Aquila 120 West 45th Street, Suite 3600 New York NY 10036 United States
800-437-1020
http://www.aquilafunds.com

Arabesque Asset Management
Arabesque Asset Management P.O. Box 9829 Providence RI 02940-8029 United States
844-567-2134

Arbitrage Fund
c/o DST Systems, Inc. P.O. Box 219842 Kansas City MO 64121-9842 United States
800-285-4485
http://https://arbitragefunds.com

Archer
Archer c/o Unified Fund Services Inc., P.O. Box 6110 Indianapolis IN 46206 United States
http://www.thearcherfunds.com

Argent
Argent 100 S. Brentwood Blvd., Suite 110 St. Louis MO 63105 United States
http://argentcapital.com/

Ariel Investments
200 E. Randolph Suite 2900 Chicago IL 60601 United States
312-726-0140
http://www.arielinvestments.com

Aristotle
Aristotle P.O. Box 2175 Milwaukee WI 53201-2175 United States
http://www.aristotlefunds.com

Arrow Funds
Arrow Funds 6100 Chevy Chase Drive, Suite 100 New York MD 20707 United States
877-277-6933
http://www.arrowfunds.com

Artisan
875 E. Wisconsin Avenue, Suite 800 Milwaukee WI 53202 United States
800-344-1770
http://www.artisanfunds.com

Ashmore
Ashmore United States
866-876-8294
http://www.ashmoregroup.com/

Aspiration Funds
Aspiration Funds 4551 Glencoe Avenue Los Angeles CA 90292 United States
424-279-9351
http://www.aspiration.com.

Aspiriant
c/o UMB Fund Services, Inc. 235 West Galena Street Milwaukee WI 53212 United States
877-997-9971
http://www.aspiriantfunds.com

Astor
Astor 111 S. Wacker Dr. Suite 3950 Chicago, IL 60606 Chicago IL 60606 United States
877-738-0333
http://www.astorimfunds.com

ATAC Fund
ATAC Fund United States
http://www.atacfund.com

Athena Fund
Athena Fund 17605 Wright Street, Suite 2 Omaha NE 68130 United States
888-868-9501
http://www.athenavaluefund.com

Auer
Auer 2960 N. Meridian St., Suite 300 Indianapolis IN 46208 United States
http://www.auergrowthfund.com

Auxier Funds
Auxier Funds 5000 SW Meadows Road, Suite 410 Lake Oswego OR 97035 United States
http://www.auxierasset.com

Ave Maria Mutual Funds
Ave Maria Mutual Funds LLC135 Merchant Street, Suite 230 Cincinnati OH 45246 United States
888-726-9331
http://www.avemariafunds.com

AXA Equitable
AXA Equitable 1290 Avenue of the Americas New York NY 10104 United States
877-222-2144
http://www.axa-equitablefunds.com

Azzad Fund
Azzad Fund United States
http://www.azzadfunds.com.

Baillie Gifford Funds
1 Rutland Court Edinburgh Scotland Uk Eh3 8e4 X0 00000 United States

Baird
Baird 777 E. Wisconsin Avenue, Suite 2100 Milwaukee WI 53202 United States
800-792-2473
http://www.bairdfunds.com

Balter
Balter United States
http://www.balterliquidalts.com

Barings Funds
Barings 1500 Main Street, Ste. 2800 Springfield MA 01115 United States
http://www.barings.com

Baron Capital Group
no United States
800-992-2766
http://www.BaronFunds.com/performance

Barrett
Barrett 90 Park Avenue, 34th Floor New York NY 10016 United States
877-363-6333
http://www.barrettasset.com

Baywood
Baywood Funds P.O. Box 588 Portland MA 04112 United States
http://www.baywoodfunds.com

BBH
140 Broadway New York NY 10005 United States
800-575-1265
http://www.bbhfunds.com

Beacon Investment Advisory
Beacon Investment Advisory 163 Madison Avenue, Suite 600 Morristown NJ 07960 United States
http://www.beacontrust.com/

Beck, Mack & Oliver
Beck, Mack & Oliver P.O. Box 588 Portland ME 4112 United States
http://www.beckmack.com

Becker
Becker 1211 SW 5th Ave, Suite 2185 Portland OR 97204 United States
http://www.beckervaluefunds.com

Beech Hill
Beech Hill 880 Third Ave., 16th Floor United States
http://www.bh-adv.com

BeeHive
BeeHive P.O. Box 588 Portland ME 4112 United States
http://www.TheBeeHiveFund.com

Belmont Capital Group
1875 Century Park East Suite 1780 Los Angeles CA 90067 United States
310-203-2670
http://www.belmontcapgroup.com

Belpointe Asset Management LLC
125 GREENWICH AVE GREENWICH CT 06830 2036293300 United States

Berkshire
Berkshire 3555 Farnam Street, Suite 1440 Omaha NE 68131 United States
877-526-0707
http://www.berkshirefunds.com

Bernzott Capital Advisors
Bernzott Capital Advisors 888 West Ventura Blvd., Suite B Camarillo CA 93010 United States
805-389-9445
http://www.bcafunds.com

Bexil Corp
11 Hanover Sq New York NY 10005 New York NY 10005 United States
212-785-0900

BFS
Bradley, Foster & Sargent, Inc. CityPlace II, 11th Floor United States
860-527-8050
http://www.bfsfunds.com

Biondo Investment Advisor
540 Routes 6 and 209 PO Box 909 Milford PA 18337 United States
570-296-5525
http://www.thebiondogroup.com

BlackRock
BlackRock Funds Providence RI 02940-8019 United States
800-441-7762
http://www.blackrock.com

BlackRock
BlackRock Funds P.O. Box 9819 Providence RI 02940-8019 United States
800-441-7762
http://www.blackrock.com

Blackstone
Blackstone 345 Park Avenue, 31st Floor New York NY 10154 United States
http://www.blackstone.com

Blue Chip Investor Fund
Blue Chip Investor Fund 4480 N. Magnolia Ave., Suite 103 El Cajon CA 92020 United States
http://www.bluechipinvestorfund.com

Blue Current Funds
United States United States
http://www.bluecurrentfunds.com

BLUEROCK
BLUEROCK 16500 North Park Dr., Suite 202 Southfield, MI 48075 Southfield MI 48075 United States
http://bluerockre.com/investments/tif/

BMO Funds
BMO Funds Boston United States
800-236-3863
http://www.bmofunds.com

BMT
c/o U.S. Bancorp Fund Services, LLC P.O. Box 701 Milwaukee WI 53201-0701 United States
http://www.bmtc.com

BNP Paribas AM
BNP Paribas AM United States
844-426-7726
http://www.bnpparibas-am.us

BNY Mellon
BNY Mellon 240 Greenwich Street New York NY 10286 United States
http://www.bnymellonim.com/us

BNY Mellon Funds
BNY Mellon Funds 200 Park Avenue New York NY 10166 United States
800-645-6561
http://www.bnymellon.com

Bogle
Bogle 2310 Washington St., Suite 310 Newton MA 2462 United States
877-264-5346
http://www.boglefunds.com

Boston Common
c/o U.S. Bancorp Fund Services, LLC P.O. Box 701 Milwaukee WI 53201-0701 United States
877-777-6944
http://www.bostoncommonfunds.com

Boston Partners
1 Beacon St, 30th Floor Boston MA 02108 United States
617-832-8200
http://www.boston-partners.com

Boston Trust & Walden Funds
BOSTON TRUST & WALDEN FUNDS 100 SUMMER STREET Boston MA 43229 United States
617-814-1215
http://www.btim.com

Boulder Capital, LLC
2344 Spruce Street Suite A. Boulder CO, 80302 Boulder CO 80302 United States
303-444-5483

Boyar Value Fund
Boyar Value Fund 590 Madison Avenue New York NY 10022 United States
http://www.boyarvalue.com

Brandes
Brandes 11988 El Camino Real, Suite 500 San Diego CA 92130 United States
800-331-2979
http://www.brandesfunds.com/

Bretton Fund
Bretton Fund 8000 Town Centre Drive, Suite 400 Broadview Heights OH 44147 United States
http://www.brettonfund.com

Bridge Builder
Bridge Builder 615 East Michigan Street Milwaukee WI 53202 United States
http://www.bridgebuildermutualfunds.com

Bridges
Bridges 8401 W. Dodge Road, Suite 256 Omaha NE 68114 United States
http://www.bridgesinv.com

Bridgeway
Bridgeway 55615 Kirby Drive, Suite 518 Houston TX 77005 United States
800-661-3550
http://www.bridgeway.com

Bright Rock
Bright Rock 2036 Washington Street Hanover MA 02339 United States
781-982-6593
http://www.brightrockfunds.com

Broadstone Asset Management
N/A United States

Broadview Funds
Broadview Funds 330 East Kilbourn Avenue, Suite 1475 Milwaukee WI 53202 United States
414-918-3900
http://www.bvafunds.com

Brookfield Investment Funds
Brookfield Investment Funds Three World Financial Center, 200 Vesey Street, 10th Floor New York NY 10281-1010 United States
212-549-8400
http://www.brookfieldim.com

Brookfield Public Securities Group LLC
71 South Wacker Drive Suite 3400 Chicago IL 60606-2841 United States
312-377-8300
http://www.brookfield.com

Brown Advisory Funds
Brown Advisory Incorporated 901 S. Bond Street Suite 400 Baltimore MD 21231 United States
800-540-6807
http://www.brownadvisoryfunds.com

Brown Capital Management
Brown Capital Management, LLC 1201 North Calvert Street, Baltimore MD 21202 United States
http://www.browncapital.com/mid-funds-overview.html.

Bruce
Bruce 220 N. Wacker Drive, Suite 2414 Chicago IL 60606 United States
http://www.thebrucefund.com

Buffalo
Buffalo 55420 W. 61st Place Shawnee Mission KS 66205 United States
800-492-8332
http://www.buffalofunds.com

Bulldog Investors, LLC
PARK 80 WEST 250 PEHLE AVE. SUITE 708 201 556-0092 Saddle brook NJ 07663 United States
914-747-5262

Bullfinch
Bullfinch 33909 Rush Mendon Road Mendon NY 14506 United States

Calamos
Calamos 2020 Calamos Court Naperville IL 60563 United States
800-582-6959
http://www.calamos.com

Calamos Asset Management Inc
2020 Calamos Court Naperville IL 60563-2787 Naperville IL 60563-1493 United States
630-245-7234
http://https://www.calamos.com/fundinvestor/contact us

Caldwell & Orkin
Caldwell & Orkin 55185 Peachtree Parkway, Suite 370 Norcross GA 30092 United States
800-237-7073
http://www.caldwellorkin.com

Calvert Research and Management
Calvert Research and Management 4550 Montgomery Avenue, Suite 1000N Bethesda MD 20814 United States
301-951-4881
http://www.calvert.com

Cambiar Funds
Cambiar Funds 200 Columbine Street, Suite 800 Denver CO 80206 United States
866-777-8227
http://www.cambiar.com

Camelot Funds
c/o Gemini Fund Services, LLC 17605 Wright Street, Suite 2 Omaha NE 68130 United States
http://www.CamelotFunds.com

Campbell & Company
Campbell & Company 2850 Quarry Lake Drive Baltimore MD 21209 United States
800-698-7235
http://www.campbell.com

Canterbury Investment Management
23 East Cedar Street Zionsville IN 46077 United States
317-732-2075
http://www.canterburygroup.com

Capital Advisors
Capital Advisors 320 South Boston Suite 825 Tulsa OK 74103 United States
918-599-0045
http://capadvfunds.com/

Capital Group
333 South Hope Street Los Angeles CA 90071 United States
213-486-9200
http://www.capitalgroup.com

Caravan
Caravan P.O. Box 588 Portland MA 04112 United States
844-856-1516

Cardinal Capital
Cardinal Capital P.O. Box 588 Portland ME 04112 United States
http://www.cardcap.com/mutualfunds

Cargile
Cargile 8000 Town Centre Drive, Suite 400 Broadview Heights OH 44147 United States
888-204-1128
http://www.cargilefund.com

Carillon Family of Funds
Carillon Family of Funds P.O. Box 23572 St. Petersburg FL 33742 United States
800-421-4184
http://www.carillontower.com

Castle Investment Management
Castle Investment Management 8000 Town Centre Drive, Suite 400 Broadview Heights OH 44147 United States
877-743-7820
http://www.castleim.com

Catalyst Mutual Funds
Catalyst Mutual Funds 630-A Fitzwatertown Road, 2nd Floor Willow Grove PA 19090 United States
866-447-4228
http://www.catalystmutualfunds.com

Catholic Investor
Knights Of Columbus One Columbus Plaza New Haven CT 06510 United States
203-772-2130
http://www.kofcassetadvisors.org

Causeway
Causeway 1 Freedom Valley Drive Oaks PA 19465 United States
866-947-7000
http://www.causewayfunds.com

Cavalier
Cavalier Funds Post Office Box 4365 Rocky Mount NC 27803 United States
800-773-3863
http://www.cavalierfunds.com

Cavanal Hill funds
Cavanal Hill Funds 3435 Stelzer Road Columbus OH 43219 United States
http://www.cavanalhillfunds.com

CBOE Vest
CBOE Vest 8730 Stony Point Parkway, Suite 205 Richmond VA 23235 United States
855-505-8378
http://www.cboevestfunds.com

CBRE Clarion Securities, LLC
CBRE Clarion Securities, LLC 201 King of Prussia Road, Suite 600 Radnor PA 19087 United States
610-995-2500
http://www.cbreclarion.com

CCA Funds
CCA Funds 190 North Canon Dr., Suite 402, Beverly Hills, CA 90210 Beverly Hills CA 90210 United States
800-595-4866
http://www.ccafunds.com

Centaur
Centaur 145 East 57th Street, 10th Floor New York NY 10022 United States
http://www.centaurmutualfunds.com.

Center Coast Capital Advisors, LP
1100 Louisiana Suite 5025 Houston TX 77002 United States
713-759-1400
http://www.centercoastcap.com

Centerstone Investors
Centerstone Investors 135 5th Avenue New York New York 10010 Luxembourg
212-503-5790
http://www.centerstoneinv.com/

Central Securities
Central Securities United States

Centre Funds
Centre Funds 48 Wall Street New York NY 10005 United States
855-298-4236
http://www.centrefunds.com

CG funds
Capital Guardian 733 Third Avenue, 24th Floor New York NY 10017 United States
http://www.cgfundstrust.com

CGM
CGM One International Place Boston MA 2110 United States
800-343-5678
http://www.cgmfunds.com

Chadwick & D'Amato
Chadwick & D'Amato 224 Main Street, PO Box 1978 New London NH 03257 United States
http://www.chadwick-damato.com

Champlain Funds
Champlain Funds 346 Shelburne Road, 6th Floor Burlington VT 5401 United States
http://www.cipvt.com

Chartwell Investment Partners
Chartwell Investment Partners 1205 Westlakes Drive Suite 100 Berwyn PA 19312 United States
610-296-1400
http://www.chartwellip.com

Chase
Chase 270 Park Avenue Floor 12 New York NY 10017 United States
212-270-6000
http://www.chasegrowthfunds.com

Chesapeake
Chesapeake 1 Rockenfeller Plaza, Suite 1210 New York NY 10020 United States
800-430-3863
http://www.chesapeakefunds.com

Chiron Investment Management
1350 Avenue of the Americas, Suite 700 New York NY NY 10019 United States
http://www.chironfunds.com

Chou America
Chou America 3 Canal Plaza, Suite 600 Portland ME 04101 United States
207-347-2088
http://www.chouamerica.com

Christopher Weil
Christopher Weil United States

CIBC Private Wealth Management
One South Wacker Drive Suite 3500 Chicago IL 60606 United States
312-368-7700

City National Rochdale
City National Rochdale c/o SEI Investments Distribution Co. Oaks PA 19456 United States
http://www.citynationalrochdalefunds.com

Clark Fork Trust
Clark Fork Trust 218 East Front Street, Suite 205 Missoula MT 59802 United States
406-541-0130
http://www.tarkiofund.com

Clarkston Funds
Clarkston Funds P.O. Box 1920 Denver CO 80201 United States
844-680-6562
http://www.clarkstonfunds.com

Clifford Capital
Clifford Capital Partners Fund 8730 Stony Point Parkway, Suite 205 Richmond VA 23235 United States
http://www.cliffordcapfunds.com

Clipper Fund
Clipper Fund 30 Dan Road Canton MA 02021-2809 United States
800-432-2504
http://www.clipperfund.com

Clough
Clough 1290 Broadway, Suite 1100 Denver CO 80203 United States
877-256-8445
http://www.cloughglobal.com

Clough Capital Partners L.P.
Clough Capital Partners L.P. One Post Office Square, 40th Floor Boston United States

CM Advisors
CM Advisors 805 Las Cimas Parkway, Suite 430 Austin TX 78746 United States
888-859-5856
http://www.cmadvisorsfunds.com

CMG
CMG 150 N. Radnor Chester Road, Suite A150 Radnor PA 19087 United States
http://www.cmgmutualfunds.com

Cognios
Cognios 1290 Broadway, Suite 1100, Denver, Colorado Denver CO 80203 United States
303-623-5277
http://www.cogniosfunds.com

Cognios Capital
Cognios Capital P.O. Box 1920 Denver Colorado 80201 United States
http://www.cogniosfunds.com

Cohen & Steers
Cohen & Steers 280 Park Ave New York NY 10017 United States
212-832-3232
http://www.cohenandsteers.com

Coho
Coho Partners, Ltd. 300 Berwyn Park Berwyn PA 19312 United States
http://www.cohofunds.com

Columbia
Liberty Financial Funds P.O. Box 8081 Boston MA 02266-8081 United States
800-345-6611
http://www.columbiathreadneedleus.com

Commerce
Commerce 11000 Walnut Street Kansas City MO 64121 United States
http://www.commercefunds.com

Commonwealth Intl Series Tr
Commonwealth Intl Series Tr 5847 San Felipe Ste 850 Houston TX 77057 United States
888-345-1898
http://www.commonwealthfunds.com

Community Capital Management
1830 Main Street Ste 204 Weston FL 33326 United States
877-272-1977
http://www.ccmfixedincome.com

Concorde
Concorde 11000 Three Lincoln Centre Dallas TX 75240 United States

Conductor
Conductor 17605 Wright Street, Suite 2 Omaha NE 68130 United States
http://www.conductorfund.com

Conestoga Capital Advisors
Conestoga Capital Advisors 259 N. Radnor-Chester Road Radnor PA 19087 United States
800-320-7790
http://www.conestogacapital.com

Congress
Congress 2 Seaport Lane Boston MA 2210 United States
888-688-1299
http://www.congressasset.com/funds

Convergence
Convergence Core Plus Fund c/o U.S. Bancorp Fund Services, LLC PO BOx 701 Milwaukee WI 53201 United States
877-677-9414
http://www.investcip.com

Cook & Bynum
Cook & Bynum United States
http://www.cookandbynum.com/cobyx

Copeland Funds
Copeland Funds United States
888-926-7352
http://www.copelandfunds.com

Copley
Copley 2245 Sunrise Avenue Palm Beach FL 33480 United States
877-881-2751

CornerCap
CornerCap 1355 Peachtree Street, NE, Suite 1700 Atlanta GA 30309 United States
888-813-8637
http://www.cornercap.com

Cornerstone
Cornerstone 74 W. Broad Street, Suite 340 Bethlehem PA 18018 United States
http://www.aicfundholdings.com

Cornerstone Advisors
1075 Hendersonwille Road Suite 250 Asheville North Carolina 28803 United States

Cornerstone Advisors, Inc.
One West Park Square Ste 1650 Asheville NC 28801 United States
828-210-8184

Counterpoint Mutual Funds
Counterpoint Mutual Funds 12707 High Bluff Drive, Suite 200 San Diego CA 92130 United States
http://www.counterpointmutualfunds.com

Cove Street Capital
Cove Street Capital, LLC 2321 Rosecrans Avenue, El Segundo CA 90245 United States
866-497-0097
http://www.covestreetfunds.com

Covered Bridge
Covered Bridge 17605 Wright Street, Suite 2 Omaha NE 68130 United States
http://www. thecoveredbridgefund.com

Crawford
Crawford 2960 North Meridian Street, Suite 300 Indianapolis IN 46208 United States
http://www.crawfordinvestment.com

Credit Suisse (New York, NY)
Credit Suisse Eleven Madison Avenue New York NY United States
877-870-2874
http://www.credit-suisse.com/us/funds

CRM
CRM 520 Madison Avenue, 20th Floor New York NY 10022 United States
800-276-2883
http://www.crmfunds.com

Cross Shore
Cross Shore 111 Great Neck Road, Suite 210, Great Neck New York NY 11021 United States
http://www.crossshorefunds.com/

CrossingBridge
CrossingBridge Funds P.O. Box 701 Milwaukee WI 53201-0701 United States
http://www.crossingbridgefunds.com

Crossmark Steward Funds
Capstone 5847 San Felipe, Suite 4100 Houston TX 77057 United States
800-262-6631
http://www.stewardmutualfunds.com.

Crow Point
Crow Point Partners, LLC 10 New Driftway, Suite 203 Scituate, MA 02066 United States
http://www.cppfunds.com

CS McKee
One Gateway Center, 8th Floor Pittsburgh PA 15222 United States
412-566-1234
http://www.csmckee.com

Cullen Funds Trust
Cullen Funds Trust 645 Fifth Ave New York NY 10022 United States
800-582-6757
http://www.cullenfunds.com

Cushing Asset Management LP
300 Crescent Court Suite 1700 Dallas TX 75201 United States
214-692-6334
http://www.cushingasset.com

Cushing Funds
Cushing Funds P.O. Box 701 Milwaukee WI 53201-0701 United States
888-878-4080
http://www.cushingfunds.com

Cutler
Cutler 306 Main Street, 2nd Floor Worcester MA 1608 United States
http://www.cutler.com

CVR
CVR P.O. Box 588 Portland ME 04112 United States
http://cvrfunds.com

Dana Investment
Dana Investment 15800 W. Bluemound Rd. Ste. 250 Brookfield WI 53005 United States
262-782-3631
http://www.danafunds.com

Davenport
Davenport & Company LLC 901 East Cary Street Richmond VA 23219 United States
http://www.investdavenport.com/davenport-asset-management

Davidson Mutual Funds
Davidson Mutual Funds 615 East Michigan Street Milwaukee WI 53202 United States
http://www.davidsonmutualfunds.com

Davis Dinsmore
Davis Dinsmore 65 Madison Avenue Morristown NJ 07960 United States

Davis Funds
Davis Funds 2949 E. Elvira Rd., Suite 101 Tucson AZ 85706 United States
800-279-0279
http://www.davisfunds.com

Day Hagan
Day Hagan 330 S. Orange Avenue Sarasota FL 34236 United States
http://www.dayhagan.com

Dean Fund
Dean Fund 2200 Kettering Tower Dayton OH 45423 United States
888-899-8343
http://www.deanmutualfunds.com

Dearborn Partners
Dearborn Partners P.O. Box 701 Milwaukee WI 53201-0701 United States
888-983-3380
http://www.dearbornfunds.com

Delaware Funds by Macquarie
Delaware Funds by Macquarie Philadelphia United States

Destinations Funds
Destination Funds 1277 Treat Boulevard,#200 Walnut Creek CA 94597 United States
http://www.destinationfunds.com

Destra
Destra Capital Advisors, LLC 901 Warrenville Road, Suite 15 Lisle IL 60532 United States
877-855-3434
http://destracapital.com

Deutsche Investment Management Inc
222 South Riverside Chicago IL 60606 United States

DF Dent Funds
DF Dent Funds 2 E. Read Street, 6th Floor Baltimore MD 21202 United States
http://www.dfdent.com

DGHM
DGHM 565 Fifth Avenue, Suite 2101 New York NY 10017-2413 United States
212-557-2445
http://www.dghm.com

DGI
The Disciplined Growth Investors Fund PO Box 275 Denver CO 80201 United States
855-344-3863
http://www.dgifund.com/howtoinvest.php

Diamond Hill Funds
Diamond Hill Funds 325 John H. Mcconnell Boulevard,Suite 200 Columbus OH 43215 United States
888-226-5595
http://www.diamond-hill.com

Dimensional Fund Advisors
Dimensional Fund Advisors 1299 Ocean Avenue, 11th Floor Santa Monica CA 90401 United States
512-306-7400
http://www.dimensional.com

Direxion Funds
Direxion Funds 1301 Avenue Of The Americas (6th Avenue) New York NY 10019 United States
646-572-3390
http://www.direxionfunds.com

Dodge & Cox
Dodge and Cox 555 California Street, 40th Floor San Francisco CA 94104 United States
415-981-1710
http://www.dodgeandcox.com

Domini
Domini 5536 Broadway, 77th Floor New York NY 10012 United States
800-582-6757
http://www.domini.com

DoubleLine
DoubleLine 333 South Grand Avenue Los Angeles CA 90071 United States
877-354-6311
http://www.doublelinefunds.com

Driehaus
Driehaus 25 E. Erie Street Chicago IL 60611 United States
877-779-0079
http://www.driehaus.com

Duff & Phelps
55 Park Avenue Plz New York NY 100550002 United States
212-871-2549

DUNDAS
DUNDAS P.O. Box 588 Portland Maine 04112 United States
844-536-7414
http://www.dundasglobal.com

Dunham Funds
Dunham Funds 10251 Vista Sorrento Parkway Suite 200 San Diego CA 92121 United States
800-442-4358
http://www.dunham.com

DuPont
DuPont 1007 Market Street Wilmington DE 19898 United States
888-447-0014
http://www.dupont.com

DWS
DWS 210 West 10th Street Kansas City MO 64105-1614 United States
http://dws.com

Eagle Asset Management, Inc.
Eagle Asset Management, Inc. P.O. Box 10520 St. Petersburg FL 33733-0520 United States
800-235-3903
http://www.eagleasset.com

Eagle MLP
Eagle MLP United States

Eaton Vance
P.O. Boc 43027 Providence RI 02940-3027 United States

Eaton Vance
c/o Boston Management and Research Two International Place Boston MA 02110 United States
800-836-2414
http://www.eatonvance.com

Edgar Lomax
Edgar Lomax 6564 Loisdale Court, Suite 310 Springfield VA 22150 United States
703-719-0026
http://www.edgarlomax.com

Edgewood
Edgewood P.O. Box 219009 Kansas City MO 64121 United States
800-791-4226
http://www.edgewoodfunds.com

EIP Funds
EIP Funds EIP Growth and Income Fund 49 Riverside Avenue Westport, Connecticut 06880 Westport Connecticut 06880 United States

Emerald
Emerald 1703 Oregon Pike Lancaster PA 17605 United States
855-828-9909
http://www.emeraldmutualfunds.com

Empiric Funds
Empiric Funds 6300 Bridgepoint Parkway Building 2, Suite 105 Austin TX 78730 United States
888-839-7424
http://www.empiricfunds.com

Ensemble Fund
8000 Town Centre Drive Suite 400 Broadview Heights Ohio 44147 United States
800-785-8165
http://www.ensemblefund.com

EntrepreneurShares
EntrepreneurShares 175 Federal Street, Suite #875 Boston MA 02110 United States
http://www.ershares.com

Equable Shares
1016 Collier Center Way, Suite 106, Naples, Florida 34110. United States
http://www.equableshares.com

Equinox
Equinox 17605 Wright Street, Suite 2 Omaha NE 68130 United States
http://www.equinoxfunds.com

Equity Investment Corp
1776 Peachtree Street NW Suite 600S Atlanta GA 30309 United States
404-239-0111
http://eicatlanta.com/

EquityCompass
1 South Street, 16th Floor Baltimore Maryland 21202 United States
443-224-1231
http://www.equitycompass.com

Essex Funds
Essex Funds United States
http://www.essexfunds.com

Euro Pacific Asset Management
Euro Pacific Asset Management, LLC 1201 Dove Street, Suite 370 Newport Beach CA 92660 United States
http://www.europacificfunds.com

E-Valuator funds
8730 Stony Point Parkway, Suite 205 Richmond Richmond Virginia 23235 United States
888-507-2798
http://e-valuator.com/

Eventide Funds
Eventide Funds 60 State Street, Suite 700 Boston MA 2109 United States
http://www.eventidefunds.com

Evermore
Evermore 89 Summit Avenue Summit NJ 7901 United States
866-383-7667
http://www.evermoreglobal.com

Fairholme
Fairholme 83 General Warren Blvd., Suite 170 Malvern PA 19355 United States
866-202-2263
http://www.fairholmefunds.com

FAM
FAM 384 N. Grand Street Cobleskill NY 12043 United States
http://www. famfunds.com

FDP Series Funds
FDP Series Funds 1100 Bellevue Parkway Wilmington DE 19809 United States
http://www.blackrock.com/funds

Federated
Federated Investors Funds 4000 Ericsson Drive Warrendale PA 15086-7561 United States
800-341-7400
http://www.federatedinvestors.com

Fidelity Investments
Fidelity Investments 82 Devonshire Street Boston MA 2109 United States
617-563-7000
http://www.institutional.fidelity.com

Fiera Capital
1501 McGill College Avenue, Suite 800 375 Park Avenue, 8th Floor Montreal Quebec H3A 3M8 United States
855-771-7119
http://https://us.fieracapital.com/

FinTrust
FinTrust 4520 Main Street Suite 1425 Kansas City Missouri 64111 United States
877-244-6235

First Eagle
First Eagle 1345 Avenue of the Americas New York NY 10105 United States
800-334-2143
http://www.firsteaglefunds.com

First Investors
First Investors Life Insurance 95 Wall Street New York NY 10005 United States
800-423-4026
http://www.firstinvestors.com

First Pacific
First Pacific 11400 W. Olympic Blvd., Suite 1200 Los Angeles CA 90064 United States

First State
615 East Michigan Street Milwaukee, Wisconsin 53202 United States
http://www.firststatefunds.com

First Trust
First Trust 120 E. Liberty Drive, Suite 400 Wheaton IL 60187 United States
800-621-1675
http://www.ftportfolios.com/

First Trust Advisors L.P.
First Trust Advisors L.P. 120 E. Liberty Wheaton IL 60187 United States
866-848-9727
http://www.ftglobalportfolios.com

Firsthand Funds
Firsthand Funds 150 ALMADEN BLVD, SUITE 1250 SAN JOSE CA 95113 United States
888-884-2675
http://www.firsthandfunds.com

Flaherty & Crumrine
301 E. Colorado Blvd, Suite 720 Pasadena CA 91101 United States
626-795-7300
http://www.flaherty-crumrine.com

Flippin, Bruce & Porter Funds
Flippin, Bruce & Porter Funds P.O. Box 46707 Cincinnati OH 45246-0707 United States
http://www.fbpfunds.com

FMI Funds
FMI Funds 225 East Mason Street Milwaukee WI 53202 United States
800-811-5311
http://www.fmifunds.com.

Foothill Capital Management
Foothill Capital Management P.O. Box 2175 Milwaukee WI 53201 United States
http://www.cannabisgrowthfunds.com

Footprints
Footprints 11422 Miracle Hills Drive, Suite 208 Omaha NE 68154 United States
http://www.footprintsfund.com

Forester
8000 Town Centre Drive Suite 400 Broadview Heights OH 44147 United States
http://www.forestervalue.com

FormulaFolios
FormulaFolios Jenison, MI 49428 Jenison MI 49428 United States
http://formulafolios.com/

Fort Pitt Capital Funds
Fort Pitt Capital Funds 680 Anderson Drive Foster Plaza Ten Pittsburgh PA 15220 United States
http://www.fortpittcapital.com

Foundry
Foundry Partners, LLC Funds 4520 Main Street, Suite 1425 Kansas City MO 64111 United States
http://www.foundrypartnersllc.com

FPA
FPA 111400 W. Olympic Blvd., Suite 1200 Los Angeles CA 90064 United States
800-982-4372
http://www.fpafunds.com

Frank Funds
Frank Funds 6 Stacy CT Parsippany NJ 07054-3347 United States
800-869-1679
http://www.frankfunds.com

Franklin Templeton
500 East Broward Blvd Suite 2100 Ft. Lauderdale FL 33394-3091 United States
954-527-7500
http://www.franklintempleton.com

Franklin Templeton Investments
Franklin Templeton Investments One Franklin Parkway, Building 970, 1st Floor San Mateo CA 94403 United States
650-312-2000
http://www.franklintempleton.com

Friess Associates
3711 Kennett Pike, Suite 100 P.O. Box 4166 Greenville DE 19807 United States
302-656-3017
http://www.friess.com

Frontier Funds
Frontier Funds 130 East Capitol Drive Hartland WI 53029-2136 United States
http://www.frontiermutualfunds.com

Frost Funds
Frost Funds 100 W. Houston Street, 15th Floor San Antonio TX 78205 United States
http://www.frostbank.com

FS Investments
FS 201 Rouse Boulevard Philadelphia PA 19112 United States
877-628-8575
http://www.fsinvestments.com

Fulcrum
NA United States

Fuller & Thaler
c/o Huntington Asset Services, Inc. P.O. Box 6110 United States
http://www.fullerthalerfunds.com

Fund X
c/o US Bancorp Mutual Fund Services, LLC PO Box 701 Milwaukee WI 53201 United States
866-455-3863
http://www.upgraderfunds.com

FundVantage
FundVantage 301 Bellevue Parkway Wilmington DE 19809 United States

Gabelli
Gabelli 1 Corporate Center Rye NY NY United States
914-921-5135
http://www.gabelli.com

Gabelli Funds Inc
Gabelli Funds One Corporate Center Rye NY 10580-1434 United States
http://www.gabelli.com

Gator
Gator United States
http://www.gatorcapital.com

<u>General American Investors Company Inc</u>
450 Lexington Avenue Suite 3300 New York NY 10017
United States
212-916-8400

<u>Gerstein Fisher</u>
Gerstein Fisher 565 Fifth Avenue, 27th Floor New York
NY 10017 United States
800-846-6202
http://www.gersteinfisherfunds.com

<u>Glenmede</u>
Glenmede 11650 Market Street, Suite 1200
Philadelphia PA 19103 United States
800-442-8299
http://www.glenmede.com

<u>GMO</u>
GMO 40 Rowes Wharf Boston MA 02110 United
States
617-330-7500
http://www.gmo.com

<u>Goehring & Rozencwajg</u>
Goehring & Rozencwajg 110 Wall Street New York NY
10005 United States
646-216-9777
http://www.gorozen.com/#

<u>Goldman Sachs</u>
Goldman Sachs 200 West Stree New York NY 10282
United States
800-526-7384
http://www.gsamfunds.com

<u>Goldman Sachs</u>
71 South Wacker Drive, Chicago, Illinois 60606,
Chicago United States
312-362-3000
http://www.gsamfunds.com

<u>Golub</u>
Golub 1850 Gateway Drive, Suite 600 San Mateo CA
94404 United States

<u>Good Harbor</u>
Good Harbor 17605 Wright Street,Omaha, NE Omaha
NE 68130 United States
877-270-2848
http://www.ghf-funds.com

<u>GoodHaven</u>
GoodHaven United States
http://www.goodhavenfunds.com

<u>Gotham</u>
Gotham 535 Madison Avenue, 30th Floor New York RI
10022 United States
877-974-6852
http://www.Gothamfunds.com

<u>GQG Partners</u>
GQG Partners P.O. Box 219009 Kansas City MO
64121-9009 United States
866-362-8333
http://www.gqgpartners.com

<u>Grandeur Peak Funds</u>
Grandeur Peak Funds 1290 Broadway, Suite 1100
Denver CO 80203 United States
855-377-7325
http://www.grandeurpeakglobal.com

<u>Grant Park</u>
Grant Park United States
866-501-4758

<u>Great Lakes Funds</u>
Great Lakes Funds 222 South Riverside Plaza, 28th
Floor, Chicago, Illinois Chicago IL 60606 United States
http://www.glafunds.com

<u>Great-West Funds</u>
Maxim 88525 E. Orchard Road Greenwood Village CO
80111 United States
http://www.greatwestfunds.com

<u>Green Century</u>
Green Century 114 State Street, Suite 200 Boston MA
2109 United States
800-221-5519
http://www.greencentury.com

<u>Green Owl</u>
Green Owl 225 Pictoria Drive, Suite 450 Cincinnati IN
45246 United States
http://www.greenowlfund.com

<u>Greenspring</u>
Greenspring 2330 W. Joppa Road, Suite 110
Lutherville MD 21093 United States
800-366-3863
http://www.greenspringfund.com

<u>Griffin Capital</u>
Griffin Capital Griffin Capital Plaza, 1520 Grand
Avenue El Segundo CA 90245 United States
310-469-6100
http://www.griffincapital.com

<u>Guggenheim Investments</u>
Guggenheim Investments 330 Madison Avenue New
York NY 10017 United States
212-518-9290
http://www.guggenheimpartners.com

<u>Guggenheim Investments Asset Management</u>
135 E. 57th Street New York NY 10022 United States
312-827-0100
http://www.guggenheimpartners.com

Guggenheim Investments Asset Management
227 West Monroe Street Chicago IL 60606 United States
312-827-0100
http://www.guggenheimpartners.com

GuideMark
GuideMark 7A Greenridge Park Nashua NH 003060 United States
603-888-5500
http://www.AssetMark.com

GuidePath
GuidePath 2300 Contra Costa Blvd., Suite 600 Pleasant Hill, CA Pleasant Hill CA 94523 United States
800-664-5345
http://www.AssetMark.com

GuideStone Funds
Guidestone Funds Suite 2200 Dallas TX 75244-6152 United States
214-720-1171
http://www.guidestonefunds.org

Guinness Atkinson
Guinness Atkinson 21550 Oxnard Street, Suite 750 Woodland Hills CA 91367 United States
800-915-6566
http://www.gafunds.com

Hambrecht & Quist

Hamlin Funds
Hamlin Funds United States

Hancock Horizon
Hancock Horizon 2600 Citiplace Drive, Suite 100 Baton Rouge LA 70808 United States
800-990-2434
http://www.hancockhorizonfunds.com

Hanlon
Hanlon 17605 Wright Street, Suite 2 Omaha NE 68130 United States
http://www.HanlonFunds.com

Harbor
Harbor 111 S. Wacker Drive, 34th Floor Chicago IL 60606 United States
800-422-1050
http://www.harborfunds.com

Harding Loevner
Harding Loevner 400 Crossings Blvd Bridgewater NJ 08807 United States
877-435-8105
http://www.hardingloevnerfunds.com

Hartford Mutual Funds
Hartford Mutual Funds United States
888-843-7824
http://www.hartfordfunds.com

Harvest Volatility Management
Harvest Volatility Management 1290 Broadway, Suite 1100 Denver CO 80203 United States
http://www.hvmfunds.com

Haverford
http://www.haverfordfunds.com

HC Capital Trust

Heartland
Heartland 1290 Broadway, Suite 1100 Denver CO 80203 United States
800-432-7856
http://www.heartlandfunds.com/

Hedeker Wealth
Hedeker Wealth One Overlook Point Suite 250 Lincolnshire IL 60069 United States
847-913-5594
http://www.hedekerwealth.com

Heitman
Heitman United States

Hennessy
Hennessy 7250 Redwood Blvd., Suite 200 Novato CA 94945 United States
800-966-4354
http://www.hennessyfunds.com

Herzfeld
Herzfeld PO Box 161465 Miami FL 33116 United States
http://www.herzfeld.com

Highland Capital Management Fund Advisors, L.P.
Highland Funds Asset Management, L.P. 200 Crescent Ct, Ste 700 Dallas TX 75201 United States
877-665-1287
http://www.highlandfunds.com

Highland Funds
Highland Funds 200 Crescent Court, Suite 700 Dallas TX 75201 United States
877-665-1287
http://www.highlandfunds.com

Hillman Capital Management
Hillman Capital Management 7501 Wisconsin Avenue, Suite 1100 E Bethesda MD 20814 United States
http://www.hillmancapital.com

Hodges
Hodges Fund 2905 Maple Ave Dallas TX 75201 United States
http://www.hodgesfund.com

Holland Series Trust
Holland Series Trust 375 Park Avenue New York NY 10152 United States
http://www.thehollandfund.com

Homestead
Homestead 4301 Wilson Blvd., IFS8-305 Arlington VA 22203 United States
http://www.homesteadfunds.com

Hood River Capital Management
Hood River Capital United States

Horizon Investments
13024 Ballantyne Corporate Place Suite 225 Charlotte NC 28277 United States
http://www.horizonmutualfunds.com

Hotchkis & Wiley
Hotchkis & Wiley 725 South Figueroa Suite 400 Los Angeles CA 90017 United States
866-493-8637
http://www.hwcm.com

Howard Capital Management
c/o Gemini Fund Services, LLC 17605 Wright Street, Suite 2 Omaha NE 68130 United States
855-969-8464
http://www.howardcmfunds.com

HSBC
HSBC 452 Fifth Avenue, 17th Floor New York NY 10018 United States
888-936-4722
http://www.investorfunds.us.hsbc.com

Huber Funds
Huber Funds United States
888-482-3726
http://www.hubercap.com

Hundredfold
Hundredfold United States
855-582-8006
http://www.HundredfoldSelect.

Hussman Funds
Hussman Funds PO Box 46707 Cincinnati OH 45246 United States
800-487-7626
http://www.hussmanfunds.com

HVIA Equity Fund
c/o Ultimus Fund Solutions, LLC P.O. Box 46707 Cincinnati Ohio 45246-0707 United States

ICM Series Trust
ICM Series Trust 803 Cathedral Street Baltimore MD 21201 United States
http://www.icomd.com

ICON Funds
ICON Funds 5299 DTC Boulevard, Suite 1200 Greenwood Village CO 80111 United States
303-790-1600
http://www.iconfunds.com

Impulsora Del Fondo Mexico, SC
Impulsora Del Fondo Mexico, SC Mexico City 11560 Mexico
http://www.themexicofund.com

IMS
IMS 8995 SE Otty Road Portland OR 97086 United States
877-244-6235
http://www.imsfunds.com

Independent Franchise Partners
Independent Franchise Partners United States
http://www.franchisepartners.com/funds

Index Funds
Index Funds 1290 Broadway Denver Colorado United States
844-464-6339
http://www.INDEX.Fund

Infinity Q
Infinity Q P.O. Box 701 Milwaukee WI 53201-0701 United States
http://www.infinityqfunds.com

Innealta Capital
13215 Bee Cave Pkwy Building A Suite 240 Austin TX 78738 United States
512-354-7041
http://www.innealtacapital.com/

Innovative
8801 River Crossing Blvd, Suite 100 Indianapolis, Indiana United States

Insignia Macro
P.O. Box 1920 P.O. Box 1920 Denver CO 80201 United States
855-674-4642
http://www.insigniafunds.com

IntegrityVikingFunds
Integrity 1 Main Street Minot ND 58703 United States
800-276-1262
http://www.integrityvikingfunds.com

Intrepid Funds
Intrepid Funds 1400 Marsh Landing Pkwy., Suite 106 Jacksonville Beach FL 32250 United States
http://www.intrepidcapitalfunds.com

Invesco
Invesco 11 Greenway Plaza, Ste. 2500 Houston TX 77046 United States
800-659-1005
http://www.invesco.com/us

Investec Asset Management
Investec Asset Management 666 5th Avenue, 15th Floor New York NY 10103 United States
http://www.investecassetmanagement.com

Investment House Funds
Investment House Funds United States

Ironclad Funds
121 South Orange Avenue, Suite 1500 Orlando, FL 32801 Orlando FL 32801 United States
888-979-4766
http://www.IroncladFunds.com

Issachar Fund
P.O. Box 541150 Omaha United States
http://www.LIONX.net

IVA Funds
IVA Funds P.O. Box 8077 Boston MA 02266-8077 United States
866-941-4482
http://www.ivafunds.com

Ivy Funds
Ivy Funds Inc 6300 Lamar Ave Overland Park KS 66202 United States
http://www.ivyfunds.com

Jackson National
Jackson Natl Life Insurance Co P.O. Box 30389 Lansing MI 48909-7889 United States
http://www.jackson.com

Jackson Square
Jackson Square 101 California St Suite 3750 San Francisco San Francisco 94111 United States
http://www.jspfunds.com

Jacob
Jacob 5507 Paseo De La Playa Redondo Beach CA 90277 United States
http://www.jacobinternet.com

JAG Capital Management
JAG Capital Management 9841 Clayton Road St. Louis MS 63124 United States
http://www.JAGCapitalFunds.com

Jaguar
Jaguar United States
http://www.jaguarlp.com

James Advantage
James Advantage 2960 Meridian St., Suite 300 Indianapolis IN 46208 United States
800-995-2637
http://www.jamesfunds.com

Janus Henderson
Janus 151 Detroit Street Denver CO 80206 United States
877-335-2687
http://janushenderson.com

Jensen
Jensen 5300 Meadows Road, Suite 250 Lake Oswego OR 97035 United States
800-992-4144
http://www.jenseninvestment.com

JF International Management, Inc.
PO Box 3151 Road Town Tortola British Virgin Islands

JOHCM Funds
JOHCM P.O. Box 4766 Chicago Illinois United States
866-260-9549
http://www.johcm.com

John Hancock
601 Congress Street, Boston MA 02210 United States
800-225-5913
http://jhinvestments.com

John Hancock
John Hancock PO Box 55913 Boston MA 02205-5913 United States
800-225-5913
http://jhinvestments.com

Johnson Mutual Funds
Johnson Mutual Funds 3777 West Fork Rd Cincinnati OH 45247 United States
http://www.johnsonmutualfunds.com

JPMorgan
JPMorgan 270 Park Avenue New York NY 10017-2070 United States
800-480-4111
http://www.jpmorganfunds.com

JPMorgan
JPMorgan 4 MetroTech Center Brooklyn NY 11245 United States

JPMorgan
JPMorgan One Beacon Street Boston MA 02108 United States

Kayne Anderson
Kayne Anderson 811 Main Street, 14th Floor Houston TX 77002 United States
877-657-3863
http://www.kaynecapital.com

KBI
KBI P.O. Box 588 Portland ME 04112 United States

KCM
KCM 5075 Westheimer, Suite 1177 Houston TX 77056 United States
http://kcmtx.com/

Keeley
Keeley 401 S. LaSalle Street, Suite 1201 Chicago IL 60605 United States
888-933-5391
http://www.keeleyfunds.com

Kellner
212-350-0200
http://www.kellnerfunds.com

Kempner
Kempner United States

Kinetics
Kinetics 615 E. Michigan Street Milwaukee WI 53202 United States
800-930-3828
http://www.kineticsfunds.com

Kirr Marbach Partners
Kirr Marbach Partners 621 Washington Street Columbus IN 47202 United States
http://www.kmpartnersfunds.com

KKM
KKM 17605 Wright Street, Suite 2 Omaha NE 68130 United States
http://www.KKMarmorfunds.com

Kleinwort Benson Investors Dublin Ltd
Kleinwort Benson Investors Dublin Ltd 3rd Floor,2 Harbourmaster Place Dublin Ireland
http://www.kleinwortbensoninvestors.com

Knowledge Leaders Capital
Knowledge Leaders Capital 370 17th Street, Suite 4930 Denver CO 80202 United States
303-763-1810
http://www.knowledgeleadersfunds.com

Kopernik
Kopernik Global Investors, LLC 302 Knights Run Ave, Suite 1225 Tampa FL 33602 United States
855-887-4544
http://www.kopernikglobal.com

KP Funds
KP Funds One Freedome Valley Drive OAKS PA 19456 United States
http://www.kp-funds.com

Ladenburg Thalmann
c/o Gemini Fund Services, LLC 17605 Wright Street, Suite 2 Omaha NE 68130 United States
877-803-6583
http://www.ladenburgfunds.com

Lateef
Lateef Investment Management United States

Laudus Funds
Laudus Funds PO Box 8032 Boston MA 02266 United States
888-832-4386
http://www.mondrian.com/mutualfunds/

Lawson Kroeker
Lawson Kroeker United States

Lazard
Lazard Asset Management LLC 30 Rockefeller Plaza, New York NY 10112-6300 United States
800-823-6300
http://www.lazardassetmanagement.com

Lazard Freres Asset Management
Lazard Asset Management Securities LLC 30 Rockefeller Plaza NEW YORK NY 10112 United States

Leavell
Leavell P.O. Box 46707 Cincinnati OH 45246 United States
http://www.leavellinvestments.com

Legg Mason
Legg Mason/Western 100 International Drive Baltimore MD 21202 United States
877-721-1926
http://www.leggmason.com

Legg Mason Partners Fund Advisor, LLC
100 International Drive Baltimore Maryland 21202 United States

Leland Funds
Leland Funds 17605 Wright Street, Suite 2 Omaha Nebraska 68130 United States
877-270-2848
http://www.lelandfunds.com

Leuthold
Leuthold 33 Sixth Street, Suite 4600 Minneapolis MN 55402 United States
800-273-6886
http://www.leutholdfunds.com

LGM Capital
LGM Capital United States

Liberty Street
Liberty Street 803 W. Michigan Street Milwaukee WI 53233 United States
800-207-7108
http://www.libertystreetfunds.com

Linde Hansen
25 B Vreeland Road FLORHAM PARK NJ United States
http://www.lindehansen.com

Lisanti Capital Growth, LLC
Lisanti Capital Growth, LLC 475 Park Avenue South, 9th Floor New York New York 10016 United States
212-792-6990
http://www.lisantismallcap.com

Litman Gregory Masters Funds
Litman Gregory Masters Funds United States
800-960-0188
http://www.mastersfunds.com.

LKCM
LKCM 301 Commerce Street, Suite 1600 Fort Worth TX 76102 United States
800-688-5526
http://www.lkcm.com

LMCG Funds
LMCG Funds United States
http://www.lmcgfunds.com

LoCorr Funds
LoCorr Funds United States
855-523-8637
http://www.LoCorrFunds.com

Logan Capital
Logan Capital United States
http://www.logancapital.com

Long Short
Long Short Market Street, Suite 3323 Philadelphia PA 19103 United States
http://www.longshortadvisors.com

Longboard
c/o Gemini Fund Services, LLC 17605 Wright Street, Suite 2 Omaha NE 68130 United States
855-294-7540
http://www.longboardmutualfunds.com

Longleaf Partners
Longleaf Partners 101 Sabin Street Pawtucket RI 2860 United States
800-445-9469
http://www.longleafpartners.com

Loomis Sayles Funds
Loomis Sayles Funds P.O. Box 219594 Kansas City MO 64121-9594 United States
800-633-3330
http://www.loomissayles.com

Lord Abbett
Lord Abbett 90 Hudson Street Jersey City NJ 7302 United States
201-827-2000
http://www.lordabbett.com

LS
LS P.O. Box 2175 Milwaukee WI 53201 United States
http://www.lsthetafund.com

LSV Fund
LSV Fund 1 N. Wacker Drive, Suite 4000 Chicago IL 60606 United States
http://www.lsvasset.com

Lyrical
Lyrical Asset Management LP 405 Park Avenue, Floor 6 New York NY 10022 United States
888-884-8099
http://www.lyricalam.com

Macquarie Group Ltd
Level 3, 25 National Circuit Forrest Act 2603 C3 00000 United States

Macquarie Investment Management
Macquarie Investment Management 2005 Market Street, One Commerce Square Philadelphia PA 19103 United States
215-255-2300
http://macquarie.com/investment-management

Madison Asset Management, LLC
550 Science Drive Madison WI 53711 United States
800-767-0300
http://www.madisonadv.com

Madison Funds
Madison 420 W 7th Street STE 219083 Kansas City MO 53711 United States
800-767-0300
http://www.madisonfunds.com

MAI
MAI 1360 E. Ninth Street, Suite 1100 Cleveland OH 44114 United States
866-624-9584
http://www.divplusfund.com.

Main Management
Main Management 601 California Street, Suite 620 San Francisco California 94108 United States
http://www.mainmgtfunds.com

MainGate Trust
MainGate Trust 6075 POPLAR AVE. SUITE 720 MEMPHIS TN 38119 United States
901-537-1866
http://www.maingatefunds.com

MainStay
MainStay 30 Hudson Street Jersey City NJ 10010 United States
800-624-6782
http://mainstayinvestments.com/

Mairs & Power
Mairs & Power United States
800-304-7404
http://www.mairsandpower.com

Manning & Napier
Manning Napier 290 Woodcliff Drive Fairport NY 14450 United States
585-325-6880
http://www.manning-napier.com

Manor Investment Funds
Manor Investment Funds United States
http://www.morriscapitaladvisors.com

Marathon Funds
PO Box 5536 Hauppauge NY 11788-0132 United States
http://www.spectrumadvisory.com

Marketfield Funds
Marketfield Funds 292 Madison Avenue, 14th Floor NEW YORK NY 10017 United States
http://www.marketfield.com

Marmont Funds
Marmont Funds United States

Marshfield
Marshfield P.O. Box 46707 Cincinnati Ohio 45246-0707 United States
http://www.marshfieldfunds.com

Marsico Investment Fund
Marsico Investment Fund 1200 17th St, Ste 1600 Denver CO 80202 United States
888-860-8686
http://www.marsicofunds.com

MassMutual
MML Investment Advisers, LLC 100 Bright Meadow Blvd., Enfield CT 06082 United States
http://www.massmutual.com/funds

Matrix Advisors Funds Trust
Matrix Advisors Funds Trust 747 Third Avenue, 31st Floor New York New York 10017 United States

Matrix/LMH
Matrix/LMH 747 Third Avenue, 31st Floor NEW YORK NY 10017 United States
866-209-1965
http://www.matrixadvisorsvaluefund.com

Matthew 25
Matthew 25 605 Cloverly Avenue Jenkintown PA 19046 United States
215-884-4458
http://www.matthew25fund.com

Matthews Asia Funds
Matthews Asia Funds Four Embarcadero Center Suite 550 San Francisco CA 94111 United States
800-789-2742
http://www.matthewsasia.com

MD Sass
MD Sass United States
http://www.mdsassfunds.com

Measured Risk Portfolios
Measured Risk Portfolios 5405 Morehouse Drive, Suite 230 San Diego CA 92121 United States
http://www.mrp.fund

Meeder Funds
Meeder Funds 6125 Memorial Dr. PO Box 7177 Dublin OH 43017 United States
http://www.meederfunds.com

Meehan Focus
Meehan Focus 555 E North Ln Ste 6160 Conshohocken PA 19428 United States
http://www.meehanmutualfunds.com.

Mercer Funds

Meridian
Meridian 660 E. Sir Francis Drake Blvd., Suite 306 Larkspur CA 94939 United States
800-446-6662
http://www.meridianfund.com

Meritage Portfolio Management
Suite 1212 7500 College Boulevard Overland Park KS 662104035 United States
913-345-7000
http://www.meritageportfolio.com

Metropolitan West Funds
METROPOLITAN WEST ASSET MANAGEMENT 865 S. FIGUEROA STREET, SUITE 2100 LOS ANGELES CA 90017 United States
800-241-4671
http://www.mwamllc.com

MFS
MFS 111 Huntington Avenue Boston MA 02199-7632 United States
877-960-6077
http://www.mfs.com

MH Elite
MH Elite 220 Russell Avenue Rahway NJ 7065 United States
http://www.mhelite.com

Midas
Midas 11 Hanover Square New York NY 10005 United States
800-400-6432
http://www.midasfunds.com

Midas Management Corporation
Midas Management Corporation 11 Hanover Square New York NY 10005 United States
212-785-0900

Miles Capital
Miles Capital 1415 28th Street, Suite 200 West Des Moines IA 50266 United States
http://www.milescapitalfunds.com

Miller Investment
Miller Investment 2 Deanna Drive Oxford CT 6478 United States
877-441-4434
http://www.millerconvertiblefund.com

Miller Value Funds
Miller Value Funds P.O. Box 701 Milwaukee WI 53201-0701 United States
http://www.millervaluefunds.com

Miller/Howard Funds Trust
Miller/Howard Funds Trust 10 Dixon Avenue Woodstock New York 12498 United States
845-679-9166
http://www.mhinvest.com/

Miller/Howard Investments, Inc.
P O Box 549 10 Dixon Avenue Woodstock NY 12498 United States
845-679-9166
http://www.mhinvest.com

Mirae Asset Global Investments
Mirae Asset Global Investments (USA) LLC 625 Madison Avenue, 3rd Floor New York NY 10022 United States
212-205-8300
http://investments.miraeasset.us

Mission Funds
Mission Funds 2651 North Harwood Street, Suite 525 Dallas TX United States
http://www.themissionfunds.com

MOERUS FUNDS
MOERUS FUNDS 307 West 38th Street, Suite 2003 New York NY 10018 United States
212-461-4088
http://moerusfunds.com/

Moncapfund
Moncapfund P.O. Box 588 Portland ME 04112 United States
855-392-9331
http://www.Moncapfund.com

Mondrian
Mondrian Two Commerce Square, 2001 Market Str., Suite 3810 Philadelphia PA 19103-7039 United States
888-832-4386
http://www.mondrian.com/mutualfunds

Monetta
Monetta 1776-A S. Naperville Road, Suite 100 Wheaton IL 60189 United States
800-684-3416
http://www.monetta.com

Monteagle Funds
Monteagle Funds 8000 Town Centre Drive, Suite 400 OH 44147 United States
http://www.monteaglefunds.com

Morgan Dempsey
Morgan Dempsey P.O. Box 701 Milwaukee WI 53201-0701 United States
http://www.morgandempsey.com

Morgan Stanley
Morgan Stanley 1221 Avenue of the Americas New York NY 10020 United States
855-332-5306
http://www.morganstanley.com

Morningstar
225 North Michigan Ave Suite 400 Chicago IL 60601 United States
312-616-1620
http://www.morningstar.com

Motley Fool
Motley Fool 2000 Duke Street, Suite 175 Alexandria VA 22314 United States
http://www.foolfunds.com

MP 63
The MP 63 Fund 555 Theodore Fremd Ave, Ste B-103 Rye NY 10580 United States
http://www.mp63fund.com

MProved
MProved United States

MT Lucas
MT Lucas United States
http://www.mtlucas.com

Muhlenkamp
Muhlenkamp Fund 3000 Stonewood Dr. Ste 310 Wexford PA 15090-0598 United States
http://www.muhlenkamp.com

Multi-Strategy
Multi-Strategy 450 Wireless Boulevard | Hauppauge, NY 11788 Hauppauge NY 11788 United States
855-601-3841
http://www.growthandincomefund.com/

Mundoval Funds
Mundoval Funds 7855 Ivanhoe Ave., Ste 210 La Jolla CA 92037 United States
http://www.mundoval.com

Mutual of America
Mutual of America 666 Fifth Avenue New York NY 10103 United States
http://www.mutualofamerica.com

Nationwide
Nationwide One Nationwide Plaza Columbus OH 43215 United States
800-848-0920
http://www.nationwide.com/mutualfunds

Natixis Funds
Natixis Funds 399 Boylston Street Boston MA 02116 United States
800-862-4863
http://NGAM.natixis.com

Navigator Funds
Navigator Funds United States
http://www.navigatorfund.com.

Needham
Needham 445 Park Avenue New York NY 10022 United States
800-625-7071
http://www.needhamfunds.com

Neiman Funds
Neiman Funds 6631 Main Street Williamsville NY 14221 United States
858-551-4078
http://www.neimanfunds.com

Neuberger Berman
Neuberger Berman 1290 Avenue of the Americas New York NY 10104 United States
212-476-9000
http://www.nb.com

New Alternatives
New Alternatives 150 Broadhollow Road Melville NY 11747 United States
800-423-8383
http://www.newalternativesfund.com

New Covenant
New Covenant P.O. Box 701 Milwaukee WI 53201 United States
http://www.newcovenantfunds.com

Newfound
Newfound 425 Boylston Street, 3rd Floor Boston MA 02116 United States
http://www.thinknewfound.com

NexPoint
NexPoint 300 Crescent Court Suite 700 Dallas Texas 75201 United States
http://www.nexpointres.com

NexPoint Advisors, L.P.
200 Crescent Court, Suite 700 Dallas, TX 75201 Dallas United States

Nicholas
Nicholas P.O. Box 701 Milwaukee WI 53201 United States
800-544-6547
http://www.nicholasfunds.com

Nicholas Investment Partners
P.O. Box 9267 Rancho Santa Fe CA 92067 United States
858-759-4545
http://www.nicpartners.com

Nomura Asset Management Co Ltd
Chuo-ku, Nihonbashi 1 chome 12-1 Tokyo 103-8260 Japan
813-324-1951
http://www.nomura.com

North Country Funds
Gemini Fund Services, Llc. 450 Wireless Boulevard Hauppauge NY 11788 United States
http://www.arrowfinancial.com

North Square
N/A United States

North Star
North Star 20 N. Wacker Drive Chicago IL 60606 United States
312-580-0
http://www.nsinvestfunds.com

NorthCoast
North Coast Am United States
http://www.northcoastam.com.

Northern Funds
Northern Funds 50 South Lasalle Chicago IL 60603 United States
800-595-9111
http://www.northernfunds.com

NorthPointe Funds
NorthPointe P.O. Box 2085 Milwaukee WI 53201 United States
http://www.northpointefunds.com

Northquest Capital Fund Inc
Northquest Capital Fund Inc 16 Rimwood Lane Colts Neck NJ 7722 United States
http://www.northquestfund.com

NorthStar
NorthStar 5299 DTC Blvd. Ste. 900 Greenwood Village CO 80111 United States
http://www.northstarsecurities.com/

Nottingham
Nottingham 116 South Franklin Street Rocky Mount NC 27804 United States
252-442-4226
http://www.ncfunds.com

Nuance Investments
Nuance Investments 4900 Main Street, Suite 220 Kansas MO 64112 United States
http://www.nuanceinvestments.com

Nuveen
Nuveen Investment Trust John Nuveen & Co. Inc. Chicago IL 60606 United States
312-917-8146
http://www.nuveen.com

Nuveen Asset Management, LLC
Nuveen Asset Management, LLC 333 West Wacker Drive Chicago IL 60606 United States
312-917-7700
http://www.nuveen.com/NuveenAssetManagement/

Nysa
Nysa 5507 Plum Street, Suite 120 Syracuse NY 13204 United States
http://www.nysfunds.com

Oak Associates
Oak Associates P.O. Box 219441 Kansas City MO 64121 United States
888-462-5386
http://www.oakfunds.com

Oakhurst
Oakhurst P.O. Box 701 United States

Oakmark
Oakmark P.O. Box 219558 Kansas City MO 64121 United States
641-219-558
http://www.oakmark.com

Oberweis
Oberweis 3333 Warrenville Road, Suite 500 Lisle IL 60532 United States
http://www.oberweisfunds.com

OCM
OCM 11299 Ocean Avenue, Suite 210 Santa Monica CA 90401 United States
http://www.ocmgoldfund.com

Old Westbury
Old Westbury 630 5Th Ave New York NY 10111 United States
212-708-9100

Olstein
Olstein 44 Manhattanville Road New York NY 10577 United States
800-799-2113
http://www.olsteinfunds.com

Orchard Capital Management
Orchard Small Cap Value Fund 17605 Wright Street, Suite 2 Omaha NE 68130 United States
844--

Orinda Funds
Orinda Funds United States
855-467-4632
http://www.orindafunds.com

O'Shaughnessy Asset Management
O'Shaughnessy Asset Management 6 Suburban Avenue Stamford CT 06901 United States

O'Shaughnessy Mutual Funds
O'Shaughnessy Mutual Funds United States
http://www.osfunds.com

Osterweis
One Maritime Plaza Suite 800 San Francisco CA 94111 United States
866-236-0050
http://www.osterweis.com

Otter Creek
Otter Creek 222 Lakeview Avenue Suite 1100 West Palm Beach FL 33401 United States
561-832-4110
http://www.ottercreekfunds.com

Pacific Advisors Funds
Pacific Advisors Funds 101 N. Brand Flvd., Suite 1950 Glendale CA 91203 United States
http://www.pacificadvisorsfunds.com

Pacific Funds Series Trust
Pacific Funds 700 Newport Center Drive Post Offfice Box 7500 Newport Beach CA 92660 United States
800-722-2333
http://www.pacificlife.com

Palmer Square
Palmer Square 11300 Tomahawk Creek Parkway, Suite 200 Leawood KS 66211 United States
866-933-9033
http://www.palmersquarefunds.com

Papp
Papp 225 Pictoria Drive Suite 450 Cincinnati OH 45246 United States
http://www.pappmutualfunds.com

Paradigm Funds
Paradigm Funds Nine Elk Street Albany NY 12207 United States
800-239-0732
http://www.paradigm-funds.com

Parnassus
Parnassus 1 Market Street, Suite 1600 San Francisco CA 94105 United States
999-350-5
http://www.parnassus.com

Patriot
c/o Gemini Fund Services, LLC 17605 Wright Street, Suite 2 Omaha NE 68130 United States
http://www.patriotfund.com

Pax World
Pax World 30 Penhallow Street, Suite 400 Portsmouth NH 3801 United States
800-767-1729
http://www.paxworld.com

Paydenfunds
Paydenfunds 333 S Grand Ave, 32nd Floor Los Angeles CA 90071 United States
614-470-8006
http://www.payden.com

Payson Funds
Payson Funds 1 Portland Square, 5th Floor Portland ME 4112 United States
http://www.hmpayson.com

Pear Tree Funds
Pear Tree Funds 55 OLD BEDFORD ROAD SUITE 202 LINCOLN NE 01773 United States
800-326-2151
http://www.peartreefunds.com

Penn Capital Management
Penn Capital Management United States
http://www.penncapitalfunds.com

Perkins
Perkins 730 E. Lake Street Wayzata MN 55391 United States
http://www.perkinscapital.com

Permanent Portfolio
Permanent Portfolio 600 Montgomery Street, 27th Floor San Francisco CA 94111 United States
800-531-5142
http://www.permanentportfoliofunds.com

Perritt
Perritt 300 S. Wacker Drive, Suite 2880 Chicago IL 60606 United States
800-332-3133
http://www.perrittmutualfunds.com

Persimmon Capital Management LP
Persimmon Capital Management, LP 1777 Sentry Parkway West Gwynedd Hall, Suite 102 Blue Bell, PA 19422 Blue Bell PA United States
http://www.persimmonfunds.com

Persimmon Funds
Persimmon Funds United States

PFM Asset Management LLC
PFM Asset Management LLC 1 Keystone Plaza, Suite 300 Harrisburg PA 17101-2044 United States

PGIM Funds (Prudential)
PGIM Funds (Prudential) PO Box 9658 Providence RI 02940 United States
800-225-1852
http://www.pgiminvestments.com

Pichardo Asset Management SA De CV
408 Teopanzolco Avenue 3rd Floor Reforma Cuernavaca Morelos 62260 Mexico

PIMCO
PIMCO 840 Newport Center Drive, Suite 100 Newport Beach CA 92660 United States
866-746-2602
http://www.pimco.com

PineBridge
Brazos Mutual Funds 55949 Sherry Lane, Suite 1600 Dallas TX 75225 United States
http://www.PineBridge.com/USMutualFunds

Pinnacle
Pinnacle 8000 Town Centre Drive, Suite 400 Broadview Heights OH 44147 United States
http://www.pinnacledynamicfunds.com

Pinnacle Capital Management
Pinnacle Capital Management 5 Burlington Woods, Suite 102 Burlington MA 01803 United States
617-399-0900
http://www.pcm-advisors.com

Pioneer Investments
Pioneer Investments 60 State Street Boston MA 02109 United States
617-742-7825
http://www.pioneerinvestments.com

Plumb Funds
Plumb Funds 8030 Excelsior Drive, Suite 307 Madison WI 53717 United States
http://www.plumbfunds.com

PMC Funds
PMC Funds 35 E. Wacker Drive, Suite 1600 Chicago IL 60601 United States
http://www.investpmc.com

PNC Funds
PNC Funds 103 Bellevue Parkway Suite 152
Wilmington DE 19809 United States
800-622-3863
http://www.pncfunds.com

Polaris Funds
Polaris Funds P.O. Box 588 Portland ME 4112 United States
http://www.polariscapital.com

Polen Capital
2700 N. Military Trail Suite 230 Boca Raton FL 33431 United States
561-241-2425
http://www.polencapital.com

Poplar Forest Capital
Poplar Forest Capital 615 East Michigan Street
Milwaukee WI 53202 United States
877-522-8860
http://www.poplarforestfunds.com

Port Street Investments
Port Street Investments 24 Corporate Plaza, Suite 150
Newport Beach CA 92660 United States
http://www.portstreetinvest.com

Portfolio Strategies
Portfolio Strategies, Inc. 1724 W Union Avenue
Tacoma WA 98405 United States
http://www.portstrat.com/

Potkul Funds
Potkul Funds 3633 Hill Road, 3rd Floor Parsippany NJ 7054 United States
http://www.breadandbutterfund.com

Powell Capital
Powell Capital United States

Power Mutual Funds
629 Washington Street Norwood, MA 02062 United States
877-779-7462
http://www.powermutualfunds.com/

Praxis Mutual Funds
Praxis Mutual Funds 303 Broadway, Suite 900
Cincinnati OH 45202 United States
http://www.praxismutualfunds.com

PREDEX
#NAME?

Preserver Funds
c/o Ultimus Asset Services, LLC 225 Pictoria Drive,
Suite 450 Cincinnati OH 45246 United States
http://www.preserverfunds.com

Price Asset Management
141 W Jackson Blvd, Suite 1320A Chicago IL 60604 United States
888-430-0043
http://pcscommodityfunds.com

Primary Trend
Primary Trend 3960 Hillside Drive, Suite 204 Delafield WI 53018 United States
http://www.primarytrendfunds.com

PRIMECAP Odyssey Funds
PRIMECAP Odyssey Funds 225 South Lake Avenue,
Suite 400 Pasadena CA 91101 United States
800-729-2307
http://www.odysseyfunds.com

Princeton
Princeton United States
http://www.pfstrategyfund.com

Principal Funds
Principal Funds 430 W 7th St, Ste 219971 Kansas City MO 64105-1407 United States
800-787-1621
http://www.principalfunds.com

Private Capital Management
Private Capital Management 8889 Pelican Bay Blvd # 500 Naples FL 34108 United States
239-254-2500
http://www.private-cap.com

Probabilities Fund
www.probabilitiesfund.com Probabilities Fund San Diego CA 92101 United States
855-224-7204
http://www.probabilitiesfund.com

ProFunds
Profunds 3435 Stelzler Rd Columbus OH 43219 United States
614-470-8626
http://www.profunds.com

Prospector Funds
Prospector Funds 3370 Church Street Guilford CT 6437 United States
877-734-7862
http://www.prospectorfunds.com

Provident
Provident Trust N16 W23217 Stone Ridge Drive, Suite 310 Waukesha WI 53188 United States
855-739-9950
http://www.provfunds.com

PSG Funds
PSG Funds United States
http://www.psgfunds.com

Putnam
Putnam 100 Federal Street Boston MA 02110 United States
617-292-1000
http://www.putnam.com

Pzena
Pzena 120 West 45th Street 20th Floor New York NY 10036 United States
http://www.pzena.com

Quaker
Quaker P.O. Box 701 Milwaukee WI 53201 United States
800-220-8888
http://www.quakerfunds.com

Queens Road Funds
Queens Road Funds 1031 South Caldwell Street, Suite 200 Charlotte NC 28203 United States
888-353-0261
http://www.queensroadfunds.com

Ranger Funds
Ranger Funds United States
http://www.rangerfunds.com

Rareview Capital
United States United States
http://www.rareviewfunds.com/

Rational Funds
Rational Funds 36 North New York Avenue NY Huntington 11743 United States
800-253-0412
http://www.rationalmf.com

RBB Funds
RBB Funds 125 W. 55th Street New York NY 10019 United States
http://www.matsonmoney.com

RBC Global Asset Management.
RBC Global Asset Management 100 South Fifth Street, Suite 2300 Minneapolis MN 55402 United States
800-422-2766
http://www.rbcgam.us

RCM Asia Pacific Limited
852-223-8863

Reaves Asset Management
Reaves Utility Income Fund 1625 Broadway Denver CO 80202 United States
800-644-5571
http://www.reavesassetmanagement.com

Reaves Select Research
Reaves Select Research 10 Exchange Place, 18th Floor Jersey City NJ 7302 United States
http://www.whreaves.com

Redmont
Redmont 1290 Broadway, Suite 1100 Denver CO 80203 United States
855-268-2242
http://www.redmontfunds.com

Redwood
Redwood United States
http://www.redwoodmutualfund.com

Reinhartfunds
Reinhart Partners, Inc. 1500 West Market Street, Mequon, Wisconsin 53092 Mequon WI 53092 United States
855-774-3863
http://www.reinhartfunds.com

REMSGroup
REMSGroup United States
http://www.theworldfundstrust.com

Renn Capital Group Inc
8080 N Central Expressway Ste 210 Lb-59 Dallas TX 75206 United States
214-891-8294
http://www.rencapital.com

Resource Real Estate
Resource Real Estate One Commerce Square 2005 Market Street, 15th Floor Philadelphia PA United States
855-747-9559
http://www.RREDIF.com

RESQ Funds
9383 E. Bahia Drive, Suite 120 United States
http://www.RESQFunds.com

Reynders McVeigh Capital Management, LLC
121 High Street Boston MA 02110 United States
617-226-9999
http://www.reyndersmcveigh.com

Reynolds
45 Broad St The Atrium New York NY 100042516 United States
212-742-1616
http://www.reynoldsfunds.com

Rice Hall James
Rice Hall James 600 W Broadway, Suite 1000 San Diego CA 92101 United States
619-239-9005
http://www.rhjfunds.com

Riverbridge
Riverbridge 801 Nicollet Mall, Midwest Plaza West Minneapolis MN 55402 United States
http://www.riverbridge.com

Rivernorth Capital Management, LLC
325 N LaSalle St Suite 645 325 N. LaSalle Street, Suite 645 Chicago IL 60654 United States
312-832-1440
http://www.rivernorth.com

RiverNorth Funds
RiverNorth Funds 325 N Lasalle St. Suite 645 Chicago IL 60654 United States
312-832-1440
http://www.rivernorthfunds.com

RiverPark Funds
RiverPark Funds 156 West 56th Street, 17th Floor, New York, NY 10011 United States
888-564-4517
http://www.riverparkfunds.com

RMB Capital Management
115 South LaSalle Street Suite 3400 Chicago Illinois 60603 United States
312-993-5800
http://www.rmbcap.com

RMB Funds
RMB Funds United States
http://www.rmbfunds.com

RMR Advisors LLC
RMR Advisors, Inc. 400 Centre Street Newton MA 02458-2076 United States

RNC Genter Capital Management
11601 Wilshire Blvd, Twenty-fifth Floor Los Angeles CA 90025 United States
800-877-7624
http://www.RNCGenter.com

Rockefeller & Co.
Rockefeller & Co. United States
http://www.rockefellerfunds.com

Rondure Global
Rondure Funds 1290 Broadway, Suite 1100 Denver CO 80203 United States
303-623-2577
http://www.rondureglobal.com

Royce
Royce & Associates, LLC 745 Fifth Avenue New York NY 10151 United States
800-221-4268
http://www.roycefunds.com

Royce & Associates, LP
Royce & Associates, LLC 745 Fifth Avenue, New York, NY New York NY 10151 United States
212-486-1445
http://www.roycefunds.com

RQSI
RQSI 1515 Ormsby Station Ct. Louisville KY 40223 United States
http://www.rqsifunds.com

Rrecurrent Advisors
Rrecurrent Advisors United States
http://www.recurrentadvisors.com/

Russell
1301 Second Avenue 18th Floor Seattle 98101 United States
800-426-7969
http://https://russellinvestments.com

RVX
RVX 20900 NE 30th Avenue, Suite 402 Aventura FL 33180 United States
305-675-0394
http://rvx-am.com

RWC
RWC P.O. Box 219009 Kansas City MO 64121-9009 United States
442-072-2760
http://www.rwcpartners.com

Rydex Funds
Rydex Funds 9601 Blackwell Rd, Suite 500 Rockville MD 20850 United States
800-820-0888
http://www.guggenheiminvestments.com

SA Funds
SA Funds 3055 Olin Ave,Suite 2000 San Jose CA 95128 United States
http://www.sa-funds.net

Salient Capital Advisors, LLC
4265 SAN FELIPE 8TH FLOOR HOUSTON TX 77027 Houston TX 77027 United States
713-993-4675

Salient Funds
Salient Funds 4265 San Felipe, Suite 800, Houston, Texas 77027 United States
866-667-9228
http://www.salientfunds.com

Sands Capital
Sands Capital 1101 Wilson Boulevard, Suite 2300 Arlington VA 22209 United States
http://www.sandscapital.com

Saratoga
Saratoga 99 Wall Street, Suite 1200 New York NY 10005 United States
800-807-3863
http://www.saratogacap.com/

Sarofim
2907 Two Houston Center 909 Fannin Street Houston TX 77010 United States
http://www.sarofim.com

Saturna Sustainable Funds
United States United States
http://www.saturnasustainable.com

Savos Investments Trust
1655 Grant Street, 10th Floor Concord, CA 94520 Concord CA 94520 United States
http://www.geassetmanagement.com

Scharf Investments
Scharf Investments 5619 Scotts Valley Drive, Suite 140 Scotts Valley CA 95066 United States
831-429-6513
http://www.scharfinvestments.com/

Schneider Funds
Schneider Funds 460 East Swedesford Road, Suite 2000 Wayne PA 19087 United States
888-520-3277
http://www.schneidercap.com

Schroder
Schroders 875 Third Avenue, 22nd Floor New York NY United States
800-464-3108
http://www.schroderfunds.com/

Schroder Investment Management North America Inc.
875 Third Avenue New York 10022 United States
800-730-2932

Schwab Funds
Schwab Funds 101 Montgomery Street San Francisco CA 94104 United States
877-824-5615
http://www.schwabfunds.com

Schwartz
Schwartz 3707 West Maple Road Bloomfields Hills MI 48301 United States
888-726-0753
http://www.schwartzvaluefund.com

Seafarer Funds
Seafarer United States
http://seafarerfunds.com

Second Nature Investments
Second Nature Investments 8000 Town Centre Road, Suite 400 Broadview Heights OH 44147 United States
http://www.secondnatureinvestments.com

Secure Investment Management
Secure Investment Management 3067 W. Ina Rd., Suite 125 Tucson AZ 85741 United States
888-802-0427
http://www.secureinvestmentmanagement.com/

Segall Bryant & Hamill
Segall Bryant & Hamill 540 West Madison Street, Suite 1900 Chicago IL 60661-2551 United States
312-474-1222
http://sbhic.com

SEI
SEI Asset Allocation Trust 1 Freedom Valley Drive Oaks PA 19456 United States
800-342-5734
http://www.seic.com

Selected Funds
Selected Funds 2949 E. Elvira Rd. Ste 101 Tucson AZ 85706 United States
800-243-1575
http://www.selectedfunds.com

Selective
Selective 828 Main Street, Suite 1703, Lynchburg, VA 24504 Lynchburg VA 24504 United States
http://www.selectivewealthmanagement.com

Sequoia
Sequoia Fund 767 Fifth Avenue New York NY 10153 United States
800-686-6884
http://www.sequoiafund.com

Seven Canyons
Seven Canyons 79 South Main Street,Fourth Floor Salt Lake City UT 84111 United States
http://www.sevencanyonsadvisors.com

Sextant Mutual Funds
Sextant United States
http://www.sextantfunds.com

SharesPost 100
SharesPost 100 1150 Bayhill Drive, Suite 300 San Bruno California 94066 United States
http://www.sharespost100fund.com

Shelton Capital Management
Shelton Capital Management 455 Market Street, Suite 1600 San Francisco CA 94105 United States
800-955-9988
http://www.sheltoncap.com

Silk Invest
Silk Invest United States
http://www.silkinvest.com/

SilverPepper
SilverPepper United States
http://www.silverpepperfunds.com

Sims Capital Management LLC
Sims Capital Management 205 E. Wisconsin Avenue, Suite 120 Milwaukee WI 53202 United States
414-765-1107
http://www.simscapital.com

Sirios
Sirios Capital Management One International Place Boston MA 02110 United States
http://www.sirioslp.com

Sirius Funds
Sirius Funds 11390 Dutchman's Creek Road Lovettsville VA 20180 United States
http://www.SiriusFunds.com

Sit
Sit 101 Sabin Street Pawtucket RI 2860 United States
800-332-5580
http://www.sitfunds.com

SkyBridge
SkyBridge 527 Madison Avenue, 16th Fl. New York NY 10022 United States
http://www.skybridgecapital.com

Smead Funds
Smead Funds 1411 Fourth Avenue, Suite 1550 Seattle WA 98101 United States
206-838-9850
http://www.smeadfunds.com

SMI Funds
Sound Mind P.O. Box 6110, Indianapolis IN 46206 United States
http://www.smifund.com

Smith Group
Smith Group 100 Crescent Court, Ste 1150 Dallas TX 75201 United States
888-572-0968
http://www.smithgroupfunds.com

Snow Capital Funds
Snow Capital Funds 2000 Georgetowne Drive, Suite 200, Sewickley, PA 15143 PA 15143 United States
877-244-6235
http://www.snowfunds.com

Sound Shore
Sound Shore Fund 2 Portland Square Portland ME 04101 United States
800-551-1980
http://www.soundshorefund.com

Soundwatch Capital
485 Madison Avenue 7th Floor New York NY 10022 United States
http://www.soundwatch.com

Sparrow
Sparrow 11330 Olive Blvd Suite 230 Saint Louis MI 63141 United States
http://www.sparrowfunds.com

SPDR State Street Global Advisors
SPDR State Street Global Advisors State Street Financial Center, 1 Lincoln Street Boston MA 02111-2900 United States
617-786-3000
http://www.spdrs.com

Spirit of America
Spirit of America 477 Jericho Turnpike Syosset NY 11791 United States

Sprott Asset Management L.P.
Royal Bank Plaza 200 Bay Street Toronto ON M5J 2J1 Canada
866-299-9906
http://www.sprott.com

Spyglass Capital Management
580 California Street San Francisco United States
415-318-2366
http://www.spyglassfunds.com/

STAAR Investment Trust
STAAR Investment Trust 604 McKnight Park Drive Pittsburgh PA 15237 United States
http://www.staarinvest.com

Stadion Funds
Stadion Funds 1061 Cliff Dawson Road Watkinsville GA 30677 United States
706-353-8737
http://www.stadionfunds.com

State Farm
State Farm Life Insurance Company One State Farm Plaza Bloomington IL 61710-0001 United States
http://www.statefarm.com

State Street Global Advisors
State Street Global Advisors One Iron Street Boston MA 02210 United States
617-664-7338
http://www.ssga.com

Steben & Company
Steben & Company 9711 Washingtonian Blvd., Suite 400 United States
http://www.steben.com

Sterling Capital Funds
434 Fayetteville Street Mall 5th Floor,434 Fayetteville Street Mall Raleigh NC 27601 United States
800-228-1872
http://www.sterlingcapitalfunds.com

Stone Harbor
5015 District Blvd Vernon CA 900582719 United States
323-277-2777
http://www.shiplp.com

STONE RIDGE
STONE RIDGE 405 Lexington Ave., 55th Floor New York, NY 10174 New York NY 10174 United States

Stralem Fund
C/O Ultimus Fund Solutions, LLC 225 Pictoria Drive, Suite 450 Cincinnati OH 45246 United States
http://www.stralemfund.com

Strategic Global Advisors
100 Bayview Circle Suite 650 Newport Beach California 92660 United States
http://www.sgadvisors.com

STRF
STRF P.O. Box 219731 Kansas City MO 219731 United States
888-292-3178
http://www.sierratotalreturnfund.com/

Summit Global Investments
620 South Main St. Bountiful UT 84010 United States
888-251-4847
http://summitglobalinvestments.com

Superfund
Marc Aurel-Str. 10-12 Vienna Austria

Swan
United States United States
http://www.swandefinedriskfunds.com

Symmetry Partners
151 National Drive Glastonbury CT 06033 United States
800-786-3309
http://www.symmetrypartners.com

Symons
Symons Capital Management Inc 650 Washington Road, Suite 800 Pittsburgh PA 15228 United States
http://www.scm-funds.com

T. Rowe Price
T. Rowe Price 100 East Pratt Street Baltimore MD 21202 United States
410-345-2000
http://www.troweprice.com

Tanaka
Tanaka Growth 369 Lexington Avenue 20F New York NY 10017 United States
877-482-6252
http://www.tanaka.com

Taylor Frigon Capital Management
Taylor Frigon Capital Management Santa Rosa Street, Suite 3B San Luis Obispo California 93401 United States
http://www.taylorfrigonfunds.com

TCM Funds
Tygh Capital Management, Inc. C/O U.S. Bancorp Fund Services, P.O. Box 701 Milwaukee WI United States
http://www.tyghcap.com

TCW
TCW 865 South Figueroa Street,Suite 1800 Los Angeles CA 90017 United States
213-244-0000
http://www.tcw.com

Teberg
The Teberg Fund U.S. Bancorp Fund Services, LLC Milwaukee WI 53202 United States
http://www.tebergfund.com

Tekla Capital Management LLC
Hambrecht & Quist Capital Management LLC 30 Rowes Wharf Boston MA 02110 United States
617-772-8500

Teton Westwood Funds
Teton Westwood Funds One Corporate Center Rye NY 10580-1434 United States
http://www.gabelli.com

The Pacific Financial Group
The Pacific Financial Group 777 108th Avenue NE Suite 2100 Bellevue WA 98004 United States
800-735-7199
http://www.TPFG.com

Third Avenue
Third Avenue Funds 622 Third Avenue, 32nd Floor New York NY 10017 United States
800-443-1021
http://www.thirdavenuefunds.com

Thomas White Funds
Thomas White Funds 440 S. LaSalle Street Suite 3900 Chicago IL 60605 United States
800-811-0535
http://www.thomaswhite.com

Thompson IM Funds Inc
Thompson IM Funds Inc 918 Deming Way, 3rd Floor Madison WI 53717 United States
800-999-0887
http://www.thompsonim.com

Thomson Horstmann & Bryant
Thomson Horstmann & Bryant P.O. Box 219009 Kansas City MI 64121-9009 United States
http://www.thbinc.com

Thornburg
Thornburg Investment Management 2300 North Ridgetop Road Santa Fe NM 87506 United States
800-847-0200
http://www.thornburg.com

Thrivent
Thrivent Mutual Funds 625 Fourth Avenue South Minneapolis MN 55415 United States
http://www.thrivent.com

Thrivent Funds
Thrivent Funds 625 Fourth Avenue South Minneapolis MN 55415 United States
http://ThriventFunds.com

TIAA Investments
TIAA-CREF Funds P.O. Box 1259 Charlotte NC 28201 United States
877-518-9161
http://www.tiaa.org

Timothy Plan
Timothy Plan 1055 Maitland Center Commons Maitland FL 32759 United States
800-662-0201
http://www.timothyplan.com

TOBAM Core Investments
12 East 49th Street, Suite 3603, New York,NY 10017, USA 49-53, avenue des Champs-Elysées,75008 Paris – France United States
http://www.tobam.fr/

Tocqueville
Tocqueville Funds 40 West 57th St. 19th FL New York NY 10019 United States
212-698-0800
http://www.tocqueville.com

Toews Funds
Toews Funds P.O. Box 446 Portland ME 04112 United States
http://www.ToewsCorp.com.

TOPS
TOPS Portfolios 4020 South 147th Street, Suite 2 Omaha NE 68137 United States
855-572-5945

Toreador
Toreador Funds 2960 N. Meridian Street, Suite 300 Indianapolis IN 46208 United States
http://www.theworldfundstrust.com

Torray
Torray Funds 7501 Wisconsin Avenue, Suite 750W Bethesda MD 20814 United States
800-443-3036
http://www.torray.com

Torray Resolute
7501 Wisconsin Avenue #750 Bethesda, MD 20814 United States
http://www.torrayresolute.com/

Tortoise Capital Advisors
Tortoise Capital Advisors 11550 Ash Street, Suite 300 Leawood KS 66211 United States
866-362-9331
http://www.tortoiseadvisors.com/

Touchstone
Touchstone 303 Broadway, Suite 1100, PO Box 5354 Cincinnati OH 45201-5354 United States
800-543-0407
http://www.touchstoneinvestments.com

Towle
Towle Fund P.O. Box 2175 Milwaukee WI 53201-2175 United States
888-998-6953
http://www.towlefund.com

Transamerica
Transamerica Funds 1801 California Street, Suite 5200 Denver CO 80202 United States
888-233-4339
http://www.transamericafunds.com

Tributary Funds
Tributary Funds PO Box 219022 Kansas City MO 64121-9022 United States
http://www.tributaryfunds.com

Trillium Mutual Funds
Trillium Funds P.O. Box 701 Milwaukee WI 53201-0701 United States
866-209-1962
http://www.trilliummutualfunds.com

TS&W Funds
TS&W Funds P.O. Box 219009 Kansas City MO 64121 United States
http://www.tswinvest.com

Tweedy, Browne
Tweedy, Browne Company LLC 350 Park Ave 9th Fl New York NY 10022 United States
800-432-4789
http://www.tweedy.com

Two Oaks Investment Management, Inc.
Two Oaks Investment Management, Inc. 7110 North Fresno Street, Suite 450 Fresno CA 93720 United States
888-806-8633
http://www.twooaks.com

U.S. Global Investors
U.S. Global Investors P.O. Box 781234 San Antonio TX 78278-1234 United States
800-873-8637
http://www.usfunds.com

Voya Investments, LLC
Voya Investments, LLC 7337 East Doubletree Ranch Road Scottsdale AZ 85258 United States

Vulcan Value Partners
Vulcan Value Partners Three Protective Center, 2801 Highway 280 South, Suite 300 Birmingham Al 35223 United States
205-803-1582
http://www.vulcanvaluepartners.com

Waddell & Reed
Waddell & Reed Financial Advisors 6300 Lamar Ave Overland Park KS 66202 United States
888-923-3355
http://www.waddell.com

Wall Street
Wall Street Fund 230 Park Avenue Ste 1635 New York NY 10169 United States
http://www.evercorewealthfunds.com

Walthausen Funds
Walthausen Funds 9 Executive Park Drive, Suite B Clifton Park NY 12065 United States
888-925-8428
http://www.walthausenfunds.com

Wanger
Wanger 227 W. Monroe St Ste 3000 Chicago IL 60606 United States
http://www.columbiathreadneedle.com/us

Wasatch
Wasatch Funds Inc P.O. Box 2172 Milwaukee WI United States
800-551-1700
http://www.wasatchfunds.com

Waycross
Waycross Cincinnati, Ohio OH 46707 United States
http://www.waycrossfunds.com

WCM Investment Management
WCM Investment Management 281 Brooks Street Laguna Beach CA 92651 United States
949-380-0200
http://www.wcminvest.com

Wealthfront
203 FOREST AVENUE Palo Alto California 94301 United States

Weiss
Weiss 320 Park Avenue, 20th Floor New York NY 10022 United States
212-415-4500
http://www.gweiss.com

Weitz
Weitz Funds 1125 South 103rd Street, Suite 200 Omaha NE 68124-1071 United States
800-304-9745
http://www.weitzfunds.com

Wellington Shields
Wellington Shields 140 Broadway New York NY 10005 United States
888-626-3863
http://www.wellingtonshields.com/

Wells Fargo
Wells Fargo 420 MONTGOMERY STREET San Francisco NULL NULL United States
877-709-8009
http://www.wellsfargo.com/

Wells Fargo Funds
Wells Fargo Funds 525 Market Street San Francisco CA 94105 United States
800-222-8222
http://https://www.wellsfargofunds.com/

WesMark
WesMark Funds 5800 Corporate Drive Pittsburgh PA United States
800-861-1013
http://www.wesmarkfunds.com

Westchester Capital
WESTCHESTER CAPITAL 100 Summit Lake Drive Valhalla NY 10595 United States
http://www.westchestercapitalfunds.com

Westfield Capital
Westfield Capital United States
http://www.westfieldcapital.com

Westwood
The WHG Funds P.O. Box 219009 Kansas City MO United States
http://www.westwoodfunds.com

Wilbanks Smith & Thomas
Wilbanks Smith & Thomas 150 West Main Street, Suite 1700 Norfolk VA 23510 United States
865-243-8000
http://www.wstamfunds.com

Wildermuth Advisory
Wildermuth Advisory 11525 Park Woods Circle Alpharetta GA 30005 United States
877-562-0856
http://www.wildermuthendowmentfund.com/

William Blair
William Blair 150 North Riverside Plaza Chicago IL 60606 United States
800-621-0687
http://www.williamblair.com

Williamsburg Investment Trust
C/O Ultimus Fund Solutions, LLC 225 Pictoria Drive, Suite 450 Cincinnati OH 45246 United States
866-738-1126
http://www.jamestownfunds.com

Wilmington Funds
Wilmington Funds 100 e. Pratt Street,17th Floor Baltimore MD 21202 United States
800-836-2211
http://www.wilmingtonfunds.com

Wilshire Mutual Funds
Wilshire Mutual Funds 1299 Ocean Avenue, Suite 700 King Of Prussia PA 19406 United States
888-200-6796
http://www.advisor.wilshire.com

Wireless
Wireless Fund 480 N Magnolia Ave, Ste 103 El Cajon CA 92020 United States
800-590-0898
http://www.wireless-fund.com

WOA
c/o Gemini Fund Services, LLC 17605 Wright Street, Suite 2 Omaha NE 68130 United States
855-754-7935

World Funds Trust
World Funds Trust 8730 Stony Point Parkway, Suite 205 Richmond VA 23235 United States
800-673-0550
http://www.theworldfundstrust.com

WP Trust
Wp Trust 129 NW 13th Street, Suite D-26 Boca Raton FL FL 33432 United States
800-950-9112

YCG FUNDS
YCG FUNDS 11701 Bee Cave Road, Suite 207 Austin TX 78738 United States
http://www.ycgfunds.com

Yorktown Funds
Yorktown Funds 2303 Yorktown Ave Lynchburg VA 24501 United States
800-544-6060
http://www.yorktownfunds.com

Zacks Funds
United States United States
http://www.zacksfunds.com

Zevenbergen Capital Investments
Zevenbergen Capital Investments LLC 601 Union Street, Suite 4600 City WA WA 98101 United States
http://www.zci.com

Zweig
Zweig 900 Third Avenue New York NY 10022 United States

Weiss Ratings Investment Series

Weiss Ratings Investment Research Guide to Bond & Money Market Mutual Funds

Weiss Ratings Investment Research Guide to Bond & Money Market Mutual Funds offers readers a one-stop source for important, up-to-date financial data and easy-to-use Weiss Investment Ratings for 8,000 bond and money market mutual funds. Weiss Ratings takes the guesswork out of investment research, providing consumers and investors with understandable information and proven investment ratings.

- Index of Bond & Money Market Mutual Funds – over 8,000 funds
- Analysis of 100 Largest Bond & Money Market Mutual Funds
- Best All-Around Bond & Money Market Mutual Funds
- High Performance Bond & Money Market Mutual Funds
- Low Volatility Bond & Money Market Mutual Funds
- BUY Rated Bond & Money Market Mutual Funds by Category

Annual Subscription of 4 Quarterly Issues: $549 | Single Issue: $279

Weiss Ratings Investment Research Guide to Exchange-Traded Funds

With investing such a complex subject and the growing popularity of exchange-traded funds as a simple way to enter the markets it is no surprise that consumers need assistance. *Weiss Ratings Investment Research Guide to Exchange-Traded Funds* answers this need, by providing accurate, easy-to-understand ratings and financial data on more than 2,200 ETFs.

- Index of Exchange-Traded Funds – over 2,200 funds are included
- Expanded Analysis of All BUY Rated Exchange-Traded Funds
- Expanded Analysis of ETFs with Assets over 50 Million
- Best One-Year Return BUY Rated Exchange-Traded Funds
- Best Low Expense Exchange-Traded Funds
- BUY Rated Exchange-Traded Funds by Category

Annual Subscription of 4 Quarterly Issues: $549 | Single Issue: $279

Weiss Ratings Investment Research Guide to Stocks

Taking into account the thousands of stock options available, it is no surprise that consumers need assistance. It is a complex subject and consumers want unbiased, independent guidance in helping them find a path to investing that is focused on their needs. *Weiss Ratings Investment Research Guide to Stocks* gives investors and consumers independent, unbiased data on which stocks to consider and those that should be avoided.

- Index of Stocks – over 11,000 U.S. traded stocks are listed
- Best Performing Stocks
- High Yield BUYs
- Stocks with High Volatility
- Undervalued Stocks by Sector
- BUY Rated Stocks by Sector
- Expanded Analysis of All A Rated Stocks

Annual Subscription of 4 Quarterly Issues: $549 | Single Issue: $279